Langenscheidts
Compact
German Dictionary

German-English
English-German

by

Heinz Messinger, Gisela Türck
and
Helmut Willmann

Completely revised edition 1993

LANGENSCHEIDT
NEW YORK · BERLIN · MUNICH
VIENNA · ZURICH

*Neither the presence nor the absence of a designation
that any entered word constitutes
a trademark should be regarded as affecting
the legal status of any trademark.*

---

*This dictionary is also available in a larger type size
in the Langenscheidt Standard Dictionary Series.*

Preface

This edition of "Langenscheidt's Compact German Dictionary" has been completely revised for the nineties.

All Langenscheidt dictionaries are regularly revised. After being updated and expanded in the eighties, this dictionary has now undergone a complete revision as well as a formal redesigning by Langenscheidt's editorial staff. The present Compact German Dictionary has been specifically prepared for the English-speaking user; it provides the pronunciation and stress of the German entry, states the genitive and plural of nouns and, in the case of verbs, indicates whether they are conjugated with "haben" or "sein". All irregular forms are also given.

The introduction of new typefaces has made the dictionary even clearer and thus more user-friendly. The headwords now appear in sans serif letters, which makes them easier to find. Phrases – example sentences, idioms, collocations – are emphasized by a new boldface type, which, as it is an italic face, cannot be confused with the boldface of the headwords.

Another feature that adds to the clarity of presentation is the restructuring of the individual entries making more use of Roman and Arabic numerals to separate the main meanings from subsidiary meanings, and more economical use of the tilde to represent the headword.

As part of the updating process, every entry of the previous edition has been carefully examined and any obsolescent vocabulary "rooted out", thus guaranteeing that the present revised edition truly reflects the language of today.

One of the Compact German Dictionary's strengths has always been its large number of new words. Great care has therefore again been taken to ensure that alongside general vocabulary and modern technical terms, a particularly large number of new colloquialisms and young people's jargon should be taken up.

The editors responsible for the present German-English/English-German Compact Dictionary, Helmut Willmann, Heinz Messinger and Gisela Türck, also compiled "Langenscheidts Kleiner Muret-Sanders" (1982, 1985). Thus we have been able to draw on their long experience as lexicographers.

The result is a dictionary ultimately suitable for today's user.

LANGENSCHEIDT

Herausgegeben von der Langenscheidt Redaktion

Table of Contents

First Part

Second Part

First Part

German-English

by

Heinz Messinger
and
Gisela Türck

Completely revised edition 1993

Guide for the User

1. Alphabetical order has been maintained throughout the dictionary. Note that the umlaut forms ä, ö and ü are treated as a, o and u. Thus "Müll" will be found directly after "Mull" and before "Müsli". ß is treated as ss.

2. The **tilde** or **swung dash** (~, ~) is used for economy of space. The boldface tilde (~) stands for the entire headword or, in the case of compounds, for the part of the word preceding the vertical bar (|). In the example phrases and the explanations in *italics*, the tilde (~, ~) stands for the boldfaced word immediately preceding, which itself may have been formed with the aid of the boldfaced tilde.

When the initial letter of a headword changes from a capital to a small letter, or vice versa, this is indicated by a circle placed above the tilde: ⌀ or ⌀, e.g.

Abflug *m* ... takeoff, ... **⌀bereit** *adj* ready for takeoff. **~halle** *f* ...

3. Arrangement of the entries. Entries are generally divided up by means of

a) Roman numerals to distinguish parts of speech (noun, adjective, adverb; transitive, intransitive or reflexive verb, etc.).

b) Arabic numerals (running consecutively within the article and independent of Roman numerals) to differentiate between meanings,

c) small letters for further differentiation of meaning.

Examples:

a) **gehen** ['ge:ən] (ging, gegangen, sn) **I** *v/i* **1.** (**zu Fuß ~**) walk, ... **II** *v/impers* **17.** *fig.* **es geht** a) it works, ... **III** *v/t* **20.** walk (*distance etc*), ...

b) **böse** ['bø:zə] **I** *adj* **1.** bad, evil, ... **II** *adv* **6.** badly ...

c) **machen** ... **13.** do: **laß ihn nur ~!** a) let him (do as he pleases)!, b) just leave it to him!

4. Semantic differences are indicated by symbols and abbreviations preceding the translation (see list on page 8).

5. Untranslatable German words are defined in *italics*:

Assessor ... civil servant (*lawyer, teacher, etc*) who has completed his/her second state examination.

6. Spelling. Differences in British and American spelling are indicated as follows:

colo(u)r
defen/ce (*Am.* -se)
program(me *Br.*)
sulphonamide (*Am.* -f-)

The abbreviations *esp. Am.* and *esp. Br.* indicate that the spelling or translation referred to also occurs in British and American English respectively, though far less frequently.

7. Pronunciation. As a general rule either full or partial pronunciation is given for every simple entry word. The symbols used are those laid down by the International Phonetic Association. All the phonetic symbols used in the dictionary are explained in the Key to Pronunciation on page 10ff.

Every headword that does not consist of words listed and phonetically transcribed elsewhere in the dictionary is followed by its pronunciation in square brackets: **Blüte** ['bly:tə] ...

Compound and derivative entries formed with elements listed and phonetically transcribed elsewhere in the dictionary are provided with a stress mark ['] in front of the stressed syllable: **'Blütenhonig** ...

Derivatives after a simple entry are often only provided with accents and part of the pronunciation. That part of the word which is not transcribed phonetically has, except for differences in stress, a pronunciation identical with that of the corresponding part of the preceding entry:

> **Kondensat** [kɔndɛn'za:t] *n* ... **Kondensation** [-za'tsĭo:n] *f* ... **Kondensator** [-'za:tɔr] *m* ... **kondensieren** [-'zi:rən] ...

A number of the more common initial and final elements occurring in derivatives and compounds have not been transcribed phonetically after every derivative entry. They have been collected, together with their phonetic transcription, in a comprehensive list on page 12.

8. Symbols

~ø }	see Guide for the User, paragraph 2, on page 7 and paragraph 1.4 on page 722	🚂	railway
		✈	aviation
F	familiar, colloquial language	🕾	postal affairs
V	vulgar	♪	musical term
†	obsolete	△	architecture
⊞	technical term	⚡	electrical engineering, electronics
⚘	botany	⚖	legal term
⊙	technology	A	mathematics
⚒	mining	✎	agriculture
✕	military term	🜍	chemistry
⚓	nautical term	✿	medicine
♀	economic term	→	see

9. Abbreviations

a.	also	antiq.	antiquity, Antike
abbr.	abbreviation	art	article
acc	accusative (case)	astr.	astronomy
adj	adjective	attr	attributively
adm.	administrative	bibl.	biblical
adv	adverb	biol.	biology
allg.	allgemein, generally	Br.	in British usage only
Am.	(originally or chiefly) American English	b.s.	bad sense
		coll	collective noun
amer.	American, amerikanisch	comp	comparative
anat.	anatomy		

conj	conjunction		*j-n, j-n*	jemanden, *somebody*
contp.	contemptuously		*j-s, j-s*	jemandes, *of somebody*
cpds.	compound words		*k-e, k-e*	keine
dat	dative (case)		*k-m, k-m*	keinem
d-e, d-e	deine, *your*		*k-n, k-n*	keinen
dem	demonstrative		*k-r, k-r*	keiner
dial.	dialectal		*k-s, k-s*	keines
d-m, d-m	deinem, *to your*		*ling.*	linguistics
d-n, d-n	deinen, *your*		*lit.*	literary
d-r, d-r	deiner, *of your, to your*		*m*	masculine
d-s, d-s	deines, *of your*		*m-e, m-e*	meine, *my*
eccl.	ecclesiastical		*metall.*	metallurgy
e-e, e-e	eine, *a, an*		*meteor.*	meteorology
e-m, e-m	einem, *to a(n)*		*min.*	mineralogy
e-n, e-n	einen, *a, an*		*m-m, m-m*	meinem, *to my*
engS.	in engerem Sinne, *more strictly taken*		*m-n, m-n*	meinen, *my*
			mot.	motoring
e-r, e-r	einer, *of a(n), to a(n)*		*mount.*	mountaineering
e-s, e-s	eines, *of a(n)*		*m-r, m-r*	meiner, *of my, to my*
esp.	especially		*m-s, m-s*	meines, *of my*
et., et.	etwas, *something*		*mst*	mostly
etc	et cetera, *and others, and so forth*		*myth.*	mythology
euphem.	euphemistic		*n*	neuter
f	feminine		*neg*	negative
fenc.	fencing		*nom*	nominative (case)
fig.	figurative		*npr*	proper name
fr.	French		*n.s.*	in the narrower sense
gastr.	gastronomical		*nucl.*	nuclear physics
GB	Great Britain		*obs.*	obsolete
gen	genitive (case)		*od.*	oder, *or*
geogr.	geography		*opt.*	optics
geol.	geology		*orn.*	ornithology
ger	gerund		*o.s.*	oneself
Ggs.	Gegensatz, *antonym*		*paint.*	painting
gym.	gymnastics		*parl.*	parliamentary term
hist.	history		*part*	particle
humor.	humorously		*ped.*	pedagogics
hunt.	hunting		*pers*	personal
ichth.	ichthyology		*pharm.*	pharmacy
imp	imperative (mood)		*philos.*	philosophy
impers	impersonal		*phot.*	photography
ind	indicative (mood)		*phys.*	physics
indef	indefinite		*physiol.*	physiology
inf	infinitive (mood)		*pl*	plural
insep	inseparable		*poet.*	poetry
int	interjection		*pol.*	politics
interrog	interrogative		*pos*	possessive
invar	invariable		*pp*	past participle
ir.	Irish		*pred*	predicative
iro.	ironically		*prep*	preposition
irr.	irregular		*pres*	present
Jh.	Jahrhundert, *century*		*pres p*	present participle
j-d	jemand, *someone*		*pret*	preterite
j-m, j-m	jemandem, *to somebody*		*print.*	printing

10

pron	pronoun	
psych.	psychology	
reflex	reflexive	
rel	relative	
rhet.	rhetoric	
s	substantive	
s-e, s-e	seine, *his, one's*	
schott.	schottisch, *Scottish*	
sep	separable	
sg	singular	
sl.	slang	
s-m, s-m	seinem, *to his, to one's*	
s-n, s-n	seinen, *his, one's*	
s.o., s.o.	someone	
sociol.	sociology	
s-r, s-r	seiner, *of his*	
s-s, s-s	seines, *of his, of one's*	
s.th., s.th.	something	
su	substantive	
subj	subjunctive (*mood*)	
sup	superlative	

surv.	surveying
tel.	telegraphy
teleph.	telephone
textil.	textiles
thea.	theatre
(TM)	Trademark
TV	television
univ.	university
USA	United States
usu.	usually
v/aux	auxiliary verb
vet.	veterinary medicine
v/i	intransitive verb
v/impers	impersonal verb
v/t	transitive verb
w.s./weitS.	more widely taken
z. B.	zum Beispiel, *for instance*
zo.	zoology
zs.-, Zs.-	zusammen, *together*
Zssg(n)	Zusammensetzung(en), *compound word(s)*

10. Key to Pronunciation. The phonetic alphabet used in this German-English dictionary is that of the Association Phonétique Internationale (A.P.I. or I.P.A. = International Phonetic Association). A long vowel is indicated by [:] following the vowel symbol, the stress by ['] preceding the stressed syllable. [̃] placed over a vowel indicates that the vowel in question is nonsyllabic. A glottal stop [ʔ] is the forced stop between one word or syllable and the following one beginning with a stressed vowel, as in "beobachten" [bəˈʔoːbaxtən].

Symbol	Examples	Nearest English Equivalents	Remarks
		A. Vowels	
a	Mann [man]		short a as in French "c**a**rte" or in British English "c**a**st" said quickly
aː	Wagen [ˈvaːgən]	f**a**ther	long a
e	egal [eˈgaːl]	b**e**d	
eː	Weg [veːk]		unlike any English sound, though it has a resemblance to the sound in "d**ay**"
ə	Bitte [ˈbɪtə]	**a**go	a short sound, that of unaccented e
ɛ	Männer [ˈmɛnər] Geld [gɛlt]	f**air**	There is no *-er* sound at the end. It is one pure short vowel-sound.
ɛː	prägen [ˈprɛːgən]		same sound, but long
ɪ	Wind [vɪnt]	**i**t	
iː	hier [hiːr]	m**ee**t	
ɔ	Ort [ɔrt]	l**o**ng	
o	Modell [moˈdɛl]	m**o**lest	
oː	Boot [boːt]		[oː] resembles the English sound in g**o** [gəʊ] but without the [ʊ]

Symbol	Examples	Nearest English Equivalents	Remarks
ø:	schön [ʃøːn]		as in French "**feu**". The sound may be acquired by saying [e] through closely rounded lips.
ø	Ödem [øˈdeːm]		same sound, but short
œ	öffnen [ˈœfnən]		as in French "**neuf**". The sound has a resemblance to the English vowel in "**her**". Lips, however, must be well rounded as for ɔ.
ʊ	Mutter [ˈmʊtər]	b**oo**k	
uː	Uhr [uːr]	b**oo**t	
ʏ	Glück [glʏk]		almost like the French u as in s**ur**. It may be acquired by saying [i] through fairly closely rounded lips.
yː	führen [ˈfyːrən]		same sound, but long

B. Diphthongs

aɪ	Mai [maɪ]	l**i**ke	
aʊ	Maus [maʊs]	m**ou**se	
ɔʏ	Beute [ˈbɔʏtə]	b**oy**	
	Läufer [ˈlɔʏfər]		

C. Consonants

b	besser [ˈbɛsər]	**b**etter	
d	du [duː]	**d**ance	
f	finden [ˈfɪndən] Vater [ˈfaːtər] Photo [ˈfoːto]	**f**ind	
g	Gold [gɔlt] Geld [gɛlt]	**g**old	
ʒ	Genie [ʒeˈniː]	mea**s**ure	
h	Haus [haʊs]	**h**ouse	
ç	Licht [lɪçt] manch [manç] traurig [ˈtraʊrɪç]		An approximation to this sound may be produced by assuming the mouth configuration for [i] and emitting a strong current of breath.
x	Loch [lɔx]	Scotch: lo**ch**	Whereas [ç] is pronounced at the front of the mouth, x is pronounced in the throat.
j	ja [jaː]	**y**ear	
k	keck [kɛk] Tag [taːk] Chronist [kroˈnɪst] Café [kaˈfeː]	**k**ick	
l	lassen [ˈlasən]	**l**ump	pronounced like English initial "clear l"
m	Maus [maʊs]	**m**ouse	

Symbol	Examples	Nearest English Equivalents	Remarks
n	nein [naɪn]	**n**ot	
ŋ	klingen ['klɪŋən] sinken ['zɪŋkən]	si**ng** dri**n**k	
p	Paß [pas] Weib [vaɪp] obgleich [ɔp'glaɪç]	**p**ass	
r	rot [roːt]	**r**ot	There are two pronunciations: the frontal or lingual r and the uvular r (the latter unknown in England).
s	Glas [glaːs] Masse ['masə] Mast [mast] naß [nas]	mi**ss**	unvoiced when final, doubled, or next to a voiceless consonant
z	Sohn [zoːn] Rose ['roːzə]	**z**e- ro	voiced when at the beginning of a word or a syllable
ʃ	Schiff [ʃɪf] Charme [ʃarm] Spiel [ʃpiːl] Stein [ʃtaɪn]	**sh**op	
t	Tee [teː] Thron [troːn] Stadt [ʃtat] Bad [baːt] Findling ['fɪntlɪŋ] Wind [vɪnt]	**t**ea	
v	Vase ['vaːzə] Winter ['vɪntər]	**v**ast	

ã, ɛ̃, ɔ̃ are nasalized vowels. Examples: Engagement [ãgaʒə'mãː], Terrain [tɛ'rɛ̃ː], Feuilleton [fœjə'tɔ̃ː].

11. List of Initial and Final Elements normally given without Phonetic Transcription

Initial elements

be- [bə]	ent- [ɛnt]	miß- [mɪs]	ver- [fɛr]
er- [ɛr]	ge- [gə]	un- [ʊn]	zer- [tsɛr]

Final elements

-bar [baːr]	-fach [fax]	-kunft [kʊnft]	-schaft [ʃaft]
-chen [çən]	-haft [haft]	-lein [laɪn]	-st [st]
-d [t]	-halber [halbər]	-lich [lɪç]	-ste [ʃtə]
-e [ə]	-haltig [haltɪç]	-los [loːs]	-stel [ʃtəl]
-ei [aɪ]	-heit [haɪt]	-n [n]	-t [t]
-el [əl]	-ig [ɪç]	-nis [nɪs]	-te [tə]
-en [ən]	-in [ɪn]	-s [s]	-tät [tɛːt]
-end [ənt]	-isch [ɪʃ]	-sal [zaːl]	-tum [tuːm]
-er [ər]	-keit [kaɪt]	-sam [zaːm]	-ung [ʊŋ]
			-wärts [vɛrts]

12. Grammatical References. Parts of speech (adjective, verb, etc.) have been indicated throughout. Entries have been subdivided by Roman numerals to distinguish the various parts of speech.

Nouns. The inflectional forms (genitive singular/nominative plural) follow immediately after the indication of gender. No forms are given for compounds if the parts appear as separate headwords. The horizontal stroke replaces that part of the word which remains unchanged in the inflexion:

Affe *m* (-n; -n): des Affen, die Affen   **Affäre** *f* (-; -n): der Affäre, die Affären

The sign " indicates that an umlaut appears in the inflected form in question:

Blatt *n* (-[e]s; "er): des Blatt(e)s, die Blätter

Verbs

a) The past participle is generally formed by prefixing ge- and adding -(e)t to the stem of the verb: **bändigen** – gebändigt, **heiraten** – geheiratet.

Verbs ending with -ieren or -eien do not use the prefix ge-: **reagieren** – reagiert, **prophezeien** – prophezeit.

Verbs with the inseparable prefixes be-, em-, ent-, er-, ge-, ver- and zer- simply add -(e)t to the stem: **begrüßen** – begrüßt, **entbehren** – entbehrt, etc.

In all the above cases the entries indicate only whether the perfect tense is formed with "haben" or "sein": **bändigen** ... *v/t* (h) ..., **klettern** ... *v/i* (sn) ...

b) The preterite and past participle of an irregular verb are given under the headword: **gehen** ... (ging, gegangen, sn) **I** *v/i* **1.** ...: the perfect tense of this verb is formed by means of the auxiliary verb "sein": er ging, er ist gegangen.

c) Separable verbs form the past participle by placing -ge- between the prefix and the stem: **hinausgehen** *v/i* (*irr, sep,* -ge-, sn, → **gehen**): The reference *irr* indicates that the compound verb "hinausgehen" is conjugated like the root verb "gehen", the → refers the user to the entry "gehen" for the preterite and past participle. *sep* indicates that the verb is separated: er geht/ging hinaus, er ist hinausgegangen.

d) Homographic verbs like "über'treten", "'übertreten" are differentiated as follows:

'übertreten (*irr, sep,* -ge-, sn, → **treten**): er trat über, er ist übergetreten
über'treten (*irr, insep, no* -ge-, h, → **treten**): er übertrat, er hat übertreten

Prepositions. Prepositions governing a headword are given in both languages. The grammatical construction following a German preposition is indicated only if the preposition governs two different cases. If a German preposition applies to all translations, it is given only with the first, whereas its English equivalents are given after each translation:

schützen ... (**gegen, vor** *dat*) protect (from, against), defend (against), shelter (from) ...

A

A, a [a:] *n* (-; -) A, a (*a. ♪*): *fig. das A und O* the be-all and end-all, the essence; *von A bis Z* from beginning to end; *wer A sagt, muß auch B sagen* in for a penny, in for a pound.

à [a] *prep* ✝ (at) ... each.

Aal [a:l] *m* (-[e]s, -e) eel: *fig. sich winden wie ein ~* wriggle like an eel.

aalen ['a:lən] *sich ~* (h) F laze; *sich in der Sonne ~* bask in the sun.

'aal'glatt *adj fig.* (as) slippery as an eel.

Aas [a:s] *n* (-[e]s) **1.** *no pl* carrion. **2.** V *pl Äser* beast, (*woman*) *a.* bitch: *kein ~* not a blessed soul.

'Aasgeier *m* (-s; -) F *fig.* vulture.

ab [ap] **I** *adv* **1.** off, away, *thea.* exit, *pl* (*beide or alle ~*) exeunt: *links ~* (to the) left; *weit ~* far off; F ~ (*durch die Mitte*)*!* off with you! **2.** F *der Knopf etc ist ~* the button is (*or* has come) off; → *Hut*[1] 1. **3.** from: 🚆 *Berlin ~ 16:30* dep. (= departure from) Berlin 16:30; F *von ... ~* → 6. **4.** ~ *und zu* now and then. **II** *prep* **5.** from: ~ *Seite 17* from page 17; ✝ ~ *Berlin* (*Fabrik*) ex Berlin (factory). **6.** from ... (on): ~ *heute* from (*adm.* as of) today. **7.** ~ *18 Jahren persons* from (the age of) 18 up(wards); ~ *30 DM* shoes *etc* from DM 30 up. **8.** ✝ less, deducting. **III** *adj pred* **9.** F *sie war ganz ~* she was dead beat (*or* bushed).

ab'ändern *v/t* (*sep*, -ge-, h) alter, change, modify, *parl.* amend, ⚖ commute.

Ab'änderung *f* (-; -en) alteration, modification, *parl.* amendment, ⚖ commutation. **Ab'änderungsantrag** *m parl. e-n ~ einbringen* move an amendment.

'abarbeiten: sich ~ (*sep*, -ge-, h) slave (away): → *abgearbeitet*.

Abart ['ap'a:rt] *f* (-; -en) *biol.* variety.

abartig ['ap'a:rtiç] *adj* abnormal, *sexually: a.* perverse.

'Abbau *m* (-[e]s; *no pl*) **1.** ⚙ dismantling. **2.** ⚒ working, exploitation (*of a mine*), mining (*of coal*): ~ *unter Tage* underground working. **3.** 🜂 decomposition, disintegration, *physiol.* breakdown (*of*

blood alcohol *etc*). **4.** *fig.* decline (*of physical or mental powers*). **5.** *fig.* a) reduction, cutback (*of expenditures etc*), b) dismissal (*of employee*), retrenchment (*of personnel*). **6.** *fig.* (gradual) overcoming (*of prejudices etc*).

'abbauen (*sep*, -ge-, h) **I** *v/t* **1.** ⚙ dismantle, take down. **2.** ⚒ work (*a mine*), mine (*coal etc*). **3.** 🜂 (*a. sich ~*) decompose, *a. physiol.* break down: *sich ~* be broken down. **4.** *fig.* reduce, cut back (*expenditures etc*), dismiss (*employee*). **5.** *fig.* (gradually) overcome (*prejudices etc*). **II** *v/i* **6.** → *nachlassen* 2.

'abbeißen *v/t* (*irr, sep*, -ge-, h, → *beißen*) bite off.

'abbeizen *v/t* (*sep*, -ge-, h) remove with corrosives. **'Abbeizmittel** *n* remover.

'abbekommen *v/t* (*irr, sep*, h, → *bekommen*) **1.** get *s.th.* off. **2.** get: *et. ~* a) *a. sein Teil ~* get one's share, b) get hurt, c) be damaged.

'abberufen *v/t* (*irr, sep*, h, → *berufen*) recall (*ambassador etc*): *j-n von e-m Amt ~* relieve s.o. from office.

'abbestellen *v/t* (*sep*, h) cancel (one's order for), discontinue (*newspaper*).

'Abbestellung *f* (-; -en) cancel(l)ation.

'abbetteln *v/t* (*sep*, -ge-, h) *j-m et. ~* wheedle s.th. out of s.o.

'abbiegen (*irr, sep*, -ge-, → *biegen*) **I** *v/i* (sn) turn (off): (*nach*) *links ~* turn off left. **II** *v/t* (h) F *fig.* head off, avoid.

'Abbiegespur *f* (-; -en) turning lane.

'Abbild *n* (-[e]s; -er) **1.** copy. **2.** a) picture, b) image, likeness. **3.** *fig.* reflection. **'abbilden** *v/t* (*sep*, -ge-, h) **1.** copy. **2.** portray, depict: *wie oben abgebildet* as shown above. **'Abbildung** *f* (-; -en) picture, illustration.

'abbinden (*irr, sep*, -ge-, h, → *binden*) **I** *v/t* **1.** untie, undo, take off (*necktie etc*). **2.** tie off, ⚕ ligate. **II** *v/i* **3.** *cement*: set.

'Abbitte *f* (-; -n) apology: *j-m ~ leisten* apologize to s.o. (*wegen* for).

'abbitten v/t (irr, sep, -ge-, h, → **bitten**) **j-m et.** ~ ask s.o.'s pardon for s.th.

'abblasen v/t (irr, sep, -ge-, h, → **blasen**) **1.** ◎ blow off (steam etc). **2.** F fig. call of, cancel (meeting etc).

'abblättern v/i (sep, -ge-, sn) **1.** shed its leaves (or petals). **2.** paint etc: flake off.

'abblenden (sep, -ge-, h) **I** v/t **1.** dim (light etc), mot. dip (Am. dim) (the headlights). **II** v/i **2.** mot. dip (Am. dim) the headlights. **3.** phot. stop down. **'Abblendlicht** n mot. dipped (Am. dimmed) headlights, low beam.

'abblitzen v/i (sep, -ge-, sn) F (bei j-m) ~ meet with a rebuff (from s.o.); **j-n ~ lassen** send s.o. packing.

abblocken ['apblɔkən] v/t (sep, -ge-, h) a. fig. block.

'abbrechen (irr, sep, -ge-, → **brechen**) **I** v/t (h) **1.** break off: F **sich e-n ~** nearly kill o.s. (**bei** doing s.th.). **2.** demolish, pull down (house etc), take down (scaffolding etc), strike (tent): **das Lager ~** break camp. **3.** fig. stop (fight, match, etc), break off (relations), call off (a strike), abandon (studies, test, etc), raise (a siege). **II** v/i **4.** (sn) break off. **5.** (h) fig. break off, stop.

'abbremsen v/t, v/i (sep, -ge-, h) slow down, brake.

'abbrennen (irr, sep, -ge-, → **brennen**) **I** v/t (h) burn down, let off (fireworks). **II** v/i (sn) burn down: → **abgebrannt**.

'abbringen v/t (irr, sep, -ge-, h, → **bringen**) **j-n ~ von** dissuade s.o. from; **j-n davon ~, et. zu tun** stop s.o. doing s.th., talk s.o. out of doing s.th.

'abbröckeln v/i (sep, -ge-, sn) crumble (away), fig. prices etc: crumble.

'Abbruch m (-[e]s; no pl) **1.** demolition. **2.** fig. breaking off (of diplomatic relations etc), esp. sports: break-off, stop(ping). **3.** ~ **tun** (dat) detract from, be detrimental to; **das tut der Sache k-n ~!** that makes no difference!

'abbruchreif adj due for demolition, adm. condemned.

'abbuchen v/t (sep, -ge-, h) **1.** e-e Summe von j-s Konto ~ debit a sum to s.o.'s account. **2.** → **abschreiben** 2.

'Abbuchung f (-; -en) **1.** debit entry. **2.** payment by standing order.

'Abbuchungsauftrag m debit order.

ABC-Waffen [a:be:'tse:-] pl NBC-weapons.

'Abdampf m (-[e]s; ·e) ◎ exhaust steam.

'abdampfen v/i (sep, -ge-, sn) **1.** F clear (or push) off. **2.** ◎ (a. v/t) evaporate.

'abdanken v/i (sep, -ge-, h) hang, ruler: abdicate. **'Abdankung** f (-; -en) resignation, abdication.

'abdecken v/t (sep, -ge-, h) **1.** take off, uncover; untile (roof), unroof (house), clear (the table), turn down (the bed). **2.** cover (up), phot. blank out. **3.** ✝ cover, meet (debts).

'abdichten v/t (sep, -ge-, h) ◎ seal, pack, ca(u)lk, make s.th. watertight.

'abdrängen v/t (sep, -ge-, h) push (or force) s.o., s.th. aside.

'abdrehen (sep, -ge-, h) **I** v/t **1.** ◎ twist off. **2.** turn off (gas, water), ⚡ a. switch off. **3.** finish (shooting) (a film). **II** v/i **4.** a. (sn) ✈, ⚓ turn away, sheer off.

'abdriften v/i (sep, -ge-, sn) drift off.

'Abdruck[1] m (-[e]s; ·e) **1.** (im)print, mark. **2.** in wax etc: impression.

'Abdruck[2] m (-[e]s) **1.** no pl printing. **2.** (pl -e) copy.

'abdrucken v/t (sep, -ge-, h) print.

'abdrücken (sep, -ge-, h) **I** v/t **1.** fire (off) (gun) (**auf** acc at). **2.** make an impression of s.th.: **sich ~** leave an imprint. **3.** F j-n ~ hug s.o., squeeze s.o. **II** v/i **4.** pull the trigger: **auf j-n ~** fire at s.o.

'abdüsen v/i (sep, -ge-, sn) F zoom off.

'abebben v/i (sep, -ge-, sn) ebb away, anger, noise, etc: a. die down, subside.

Abend ['a:bənt] m (-s; -e) evening, night (both a. performance): **am (späten) ~** (late) in the evening, (late) at night; **heute** 2 this evening, tonight; **morgen (gestern)** 2 tomorrow (last) night; **Sonntag** 2 Sunday evening; **guten ~!** good evening!; **zu ~ essen** have supper (or dinner); **es wird ~** it's getting dark; **man soll den Tag nicht vor dem ~ loben** don't count your chickens before they are hatched; **es ist noch nicht aller Tage ~** things may take a turn yet.

'Abend|**andacht** f evening prayer(s). **~blatt** n evening paper. **~dämmerung** f dusk. **~essen** n evening meal, dinner, supper. 2**füllend** adj full-length (film). **~kasse** f box office. **~kleid** n evening dress (Am. gown). **~kurs** m, **~kursus** m evening class(es).

'Abendland n (-[e]s; no pl) the Occident.

abendländisch ['a:bəntlɛndɪʃ] adj occidental, Western.

'abendlich adj of (or in) the evening.

'Abendmahl n (-[e]s; no pl) eccl. the Holy Communion, the Lord's (paint. the Last) Supper: **das ~ nehmen** take Communion.

abends ['a:bənts] adv in the evening(s): **bis ~** till evening; **um 7 Uhr ~** at 7 p.m.

'Abend|schule f night school. **~sonne** f setting sun. **~stern** m evening star. **~vorstellung** f thea. evening performance. **~zeitung** f → **Abendblatt**.

Abenteuer ['a:bəntɔyər] n (-s; -) adventure (a. in cpds film, novel, playground, etc). **'Abenteuerleben** n adventurous life. **'abenteuerlich** adj adventurous, fig. risky, wild (idea, plan, etc), eccentric, odd (getup etc). **'Abenteuerlust** f (-; no pl) love of adventure.

'Abenteurer m (-s; -) adventurer.

'Abenteurerin f (-; -nen) adventuress.

aber ['a:bər] **I** conj but: **~ dennoch** yet, (but) still; **oder ~** otherwise, or else. **II** interj **~, ~!** come, come!; **~ ja!, ~ sicher!** (but) of course!; **~ nein!** oh no!, of course not!; **das ist ~ nett von dir** that's really nice of you. **III** adv **hundert und ~ hundert** hundreds and hundreds.

'Aber n (-s; -) but: **die Sache hat ein ~** there's just one catch to it; → **Wenn**.

'Aberglaube m (-ns; no pl) superstition.

abergläubisch ['a:bərɡlɔybɪʃ] adj superstitious.

aberkennen v/t (irr, sep, h, → **erkennen**) esp. ⚖ j-m et. ~ deprive s.o. of. **'Aberkennung** f (-; -en) deprivation.

abermalig ['a:bərma:lɪç] adj renewed, repeated. **abermals** ['a:bərma:ls] adv again, once more.

'aberwitzig adj crazy, mad.

'abfackeln v/t (h) burn off (gas).

'abfahren (irr, sep, -ge-, → **fahren**) **I** v/i (sn) **1.** (nach) for) leave, depart, start, ⚓ sail: F **j-n ~ lassen** send s.o. packing. **2.** skiing: run (n.s. start) downhill. **3.** F **auf j-n (et.) (voll) ~** be wild about s.o. (s.th.), dig s.o. (s.th.) (the big way). **II** v/t (h) **4.** cart off, remove. **5.** a) cover, travel (a distance), b) patrol. **6.** wear down (a tyre). **7.** start, run (film, tape). **8.** use up (a ticket). **9. ihm wurde ein**

Bein etc **abgefahren** he was run over and lost a leg etc.

'Abfahrt f (-; -en) **1.** (nach) for) start, departure. **2.** exit (of a motorway). **3.** skiing: a) downhill (run), b) slope. **'abfahrtbereit** adj ready to leave. **'Abfahrtslauf** m skiing: downhill (run). **'Abfahrtsläufer(in** f) m downhiller. **'Abfahrtszeit** f time of departure.

'Abfall¹ m (-[e]s; ⸚e) pl a) waste (a. ☢), refuse, rubbish, Am. garbage, b) offal, c) litter.

'Abfall² m (-[e]s; no pl) **1.** decrease (a. ⚡, a. fig.), drop. **2.** pol. defection: **~ von e-r Partei** desertion from a party. **3.** eccl. apostasy.

'Abfallbeseitigung f waste disposal. **'Abfalleimer** m rubbish (or litter) bin, Am. garbage can.

'abfallen v/i (irr, sep, -ge-, sn, → **fallen**) **1.** fall off, drop off: fig. **von j-m ~** fear etc: fall away from s.o., leave s.o. **2.** terrain: fall away, slope: **steil ~** drop steeply. **3.** fig. fall (off), drop, decrease, runner etc: drop back: **~ gegen** compare badly with. **4.** be left (over). **5.** F be gained (bei) by: **was fällt für mich dabei ab?** what's in it for me? **6. von e-r Partei ~** break away (or defect) from a party. **7.** eccl. apostatize (**von** from). **'abfallend** adj sloping (terrain etc): **steil ~** steep, precipitous.

'abfällig adj disparaging (remark), adverse (criticism), unfavo(u)rable (opinion etc): **~ sprechen über** (acc) speak disparagingly of.

'Abfallpro,dukt n **1.** waste product. **2.** spin-off, by-product. **'Abfallverwertung** f waste recovery, recycling.

'abfangen v/t (irr, sep, -ge-, h, → **fangen**) **1.** catch. **2.** intercept (message, letter, etc). **3.** check (attack). **4.** sports: parry (blow), catch up with (a runner). **5.** get a car etc under control, ✈ pull out. **6.** △ prop up. **7.** ☉ absorb, cushion (shocks).

'Abfangjäger m interceptor (plane).

'abfärben v/i (sep, -ge-, h) run: **~ auf** (acc) a) run into, b) fig. rub off on.

'abfassen v/t (sep, -ge-, h) write, draft, esp. adm. draw up, formulate, word. **'Abfassung** f (-; -en) composition, drafting, wording.

'abfaulen v/i (sep, -ge-, sn) rot off.

'**abfedern** v/t (sep, -ge-, h) ⊕ absorb (shocks), cushion (a. fig.), spring.

'**abfeilen** v/t (sep, -ge-, h) ⚙ file off.

'**abfertigen** v/t (sep, -ge-, h) **1.** a) ✈, 🚂 dispatch, clear, b) check in (passengers): **e-n Zug ~** start a train. **2.** attend to, serve, deal with (customers): F **j-n kurz ~** give s.o. short shrift. **3.** F sports: dispose of, beat.

'**Abfertigung** f (-; -en) **1.** dispatch (a. ✈, 🚃), (customs) clearance. **2.** 🚂 attendance (gen to customers, an order). **3.** → '**Abfertigungsschalter** m dispatch counter, ✈ check-in counter.

'**abfeuern** v/t (sep, -ge-, h) fire (off) (gun etc), sports: let go with (a shot).

'**abfinden** (irr, sep, -ge-, h) **I** v/t a) pay (off), satisfy (creditors), buy out (a partner), b) pay s.o. compensation. **II sich ~ mit** come to terms with, resign o.s. to, put up with, accept; **damit kann ich mich nicht ~!** I just can't accept it!

'**Abfindung** f (-; -en) a) satisfaction, paying off, b) of employees: severance pay, c) compensation.

'**abflachen** v/t (sep, -ge-, h) (a. **sich ~**) flatten (out).

'**abflauen** v/i (sep, -ge-, sn) wind etc: drop, a. fig. die down, abate, crisis, traffic, etc: ease off, 🚂 business etc: slacken (off), interest etc: flag.

'**abfliegen** (irr, sep, -ge-, → **fliegen**) **I** v/i (sn) ✈ start, take off, passenger: fly. **II** v/t (h) patrol (by plane).

'**abfließen** v/i (irr, sep, -ge-, sn, → **fließen**) flow off (a. capital).

'**Abflug** m (-[e]s; ⁻e) takeoff, departure. **²bereit** adj ready for takeoff. **~halle** f departure lounge. **~zeit** f (time of) departure.

'**Abfluß** m (-sses; ⁻sse) **1.** flowing off, discharge, outflow (of capital). **2.** ⊕ outlet. '**Abflußrohr** n ⊕ drainpipe.

'**abfordern** v/t (sep, -ge-, h) j-m et. ~ a. fig. demand sth. of s.o.

'**abfragen** v/t (sep, -ge-, h) **1.** j-n (et.) ~ test (Am. quiz) s.o. (on sth.). **2.** computer: interrogate.

'**abfressen** v/t (irr, sep, -ge-, h, → **fressen**) crop, eat bare.

'**abfrieren** v/t (irr, sep, -ge-, sn, → **frieren**) **ihm sind drei Zehen etc abgefroren** he lost three toes etc through frostbite; F **sich e-n ~** be freezing to death.

Abfuhr ['apfu:r] f (-; -en) **1.** removal. **2.** a) fig. rebuff, F brush-off, b) sports: defeat, beating: **sich e-e ~ holen** get a beating, fig. meet with a rebuff.

'**abführen** (sep, -ge-, h) **I** v/t **1.** lead s.o. away, forcibly: march s.o. off, take prisoner into custody: **j-n ~ lassen** have s.o. taken away. **2.** fig. ~ **von** lead away from (a subject). **3.** ~ **an** (acc) pay money, taxes (over) to. **4.** ⊕ drain off (water), carry off (heat). **II** v/i **5.** ⚕ a) act as a laxative, b) move the bowels.

'**abführend** adj, '**Abführmittel** n (-s; -) ⚕ laxative.

'**Abfüllanlage** f bottling plant.

'**abfüllen** v/t (sep, -ge-, h) draw off, fill, rack (off) (wine etc): **in Beutel ~** bag; **in** (or **auf**) **Flaschen ~** bottle.

'**abfüttern** v/t (sep, -ge-, h) a. F fig. feed.

'**Abgabe** f (-; -n) **1.** no pl a) delivery, handing over, b) depositing (luggage), Am. checking (baggage), c) making (an offer, a comment, etc), giving (an opinion etc), d) emission (of heat, steam, etc), release (of energy), ⚽ output, e) 🚂 sale, f) firing (of a shot). **2.** a) tax, duty, b) rate, Am. local tax, c) (social) contribution. **3.** sports: pass.

'**abgabenfrei** adj a) tax-free, b) duty-free. '**abgabenpflichtig** adj person: liable to payment of taxes (etc), goods: dutiable, income: taxable.

'**Abgang** m (-[e]s; ⁻e) **1.** no pl leaving, departure, a. thea. exit, retirement (**aus** from an office): **nach dem ~ von der Schule** after leaving school; fig. **sich e-n guten ~ verschaffen** make a graceful exit. **2.** no pl a) ⚙ dispatch, b) 🚂 etc departure, ⚓ sailing, c) ⚕ discharge (of blood, pus), passage (of stones). **3.** gym. dismount. **4.** 🚂 a) → **Absatz** 3, b) loss, c) banking: items disposed of.

'**Abgangszeugnis** n (school-)leaving certificate, Am. diploma.

'**Abgas** n (-es; -e) waste gas, mot. exhaust fumes. **²arm** adj low-emission. **~entgiftung** f waste gas detoxification. **²frei** adj emission-free. **~test** m mot. fume emission test.

'**abgearbeitet I** pp of **abarbeiten**. **II** adj worn(-)out.

'**abgeben** (irr, sep, -ge-, h, → **geben**) v/t **1.** (**bei**) a) hand in (or over) (to), deliver (to), b) deposit (luggage etc) (at), *Am.* check (*baggage etc*) (at). **2.** (**an** *acc* to) a) give away, b) transfer (*employee*): **j-m et. ~ von** *a.* share s.th. with s.o. **3.** ✝ sell (**an** *acc* to). **4.** *sports:* (**an** *acc* to) pass (*the ball*), lose (*game, set*), concede (*a point*). **5.** make (*a statement*), give (*one's opinion*), cast (*one's vote*). **6.** give off, emit (*heat, steam, etc*), release (*energy*). **7. e-n Schuß ~** fire (*sports: a.* deliver) a shot, shoot. **8.** F be, act as (*referee etc*), provide, serve as (*background etc*): **er würde e-n guten Lehrer** *etc* **~** he would make a good teacher *etc.* **II** *v/i sports:* pass (the ball). **III sich ~ mit** concern o.s. with; F **sich mit j-m ~** have dealings with s.o., associate with s.o.; **damit kann ich mich nicht ~!** I can't be bothered with that!

'abgebrannt I *pp of* **abbrennen. II** *adj* F *fig.* broke.

'abgebrüht *adj* F *fig.* hardened.

'abgedroschen *adj* F trite, hackneyed.

'abgefahren I *pp of* **abfahren. II** *adj* bald (*tyre*).

'abgegriffen *adj* **1.** a) (well-)worn, b) well-thumbed (*book*). **2.** → **abgedroschen.**

'abgehackt I *pp of* **abhacken. II** *adj* chopped (*speech*), disjointed (*sentences*).

'abgehangen I *pp of* **abhängen². II** *adj* hung (*meat*).

'abgehärtet I *pp of* **abhärten. II** *adj* tough, (**gegen**) inured (to), *a. fig.* hardened (against).

'abgehen (*irr, sep, -ge-, sn,* → **gehen**) **I** *v/i* **1.** leave, ✈, ➔ *a.* depart, ⚓ *a.* sail (*all: nach* for), *letter, parcel, etc:* go off, be dispatched: **von der Schule ~** leave school. **2.** *thea., a. fig.* make one's exit: **... geht (gehen) ab** exit (exeunt) ... **3.** *button, paint, etc:* come off. **4.** 🜨 *fetus:* be aborted, *stones etc:* be discharged, pass. **5.** *road etc:* branch off. **6.** → **weggehen. 2.** *amount etc:* be deducted (**von** from): **hiervon gehen 7% ab** 7 per cent is to be deducted (from this amount). **8.** *fig.* **von e-r Regel** *etc* **~** deviate (*totally:* depart) from a rule *etc;* **davon gehe ich nicht ab!** nothing can change my mind about that!; **davon kann ich nicht ~!** I must insist on that! **9.** F *fig.* **was ihm abgeht, ist Mut** what he lacks is courage; **ihm geht jeder**

Humor ab he has no sense of humo(u)r at all; **ihr geht nichts ab** she doesn't go short of anything. **10. gut** (**glatt** *etc*) **~** go well (smoothly *etc*); **schlecht ~** turn out badly; **es kann nicht gut ~** there's sure to be trouble; **es ging nicht ohne Streit ab** there was a quarrel after all. **II** *v/t* **11.** a) go (*or* walk) along, b) patrol.

'abgehend *adj* 🚂, 📞 outgoing.

'abgehetzt I *pp of* **abhetzen. II** *adj* **1.** breathless, *pred* out of breath. **2.** worn(-)out, exhausted.

'abgekämpft *adj* exhausted, spent.

'abgekartet *adj* F **~es Spiel** put-up job.

'abgeklärt I *pp of* **abklären. II** *adj* balanced (*opinion etc*), mellow (*person*).

'abgelagert I *pp of* **ablagern. II** *adj* seasoned (*wood etc*), matured (*wine*).

'abgelegen *adj* remote, secluded.

'abgelten *v/t* (*irr, sep,* -ge-, h, → **gelten**) satisfy (*claims*).

'abgemagert I *pp of* **abmagern. II** *adj* emaciated.

'abgeneigt *adj* **nicht ~ sein, et. zu tun** be quite prepared to do s.th.

'abgenutzt I *pp of* **abnutzen. II** *adj a. fig.* worn(-out).

Abgeordnete ['apgəˈɔrdnətə] *m, f* (-n; -n) a) delegate, representative, b) Member of Parliament, *Am.* Congressman (Congresswoman).

'Abgeordnetenhaus *n* chamber of deputies, *Am.* House of Representatives.

'abgepackt I *pp of* **abpacken. II** *adj* ✝ prepacked, packaged.

'abgerissen I *pp of* **abreißen. II** *adj* **1.** ragged, *person: a.* seedy. **2.** incoherent, disjointed (*sentences etc*).

'abgerundet I *pp of* **abrunden. II** *adj* round(ed) (*sum etc*), *fig.* (well-)rounded. **III** *adv* in round figures.

'Abgesandte *m, f* (-n; -n) envoy, *pol. a.* emissary.

'abgeschieden *adj* secluded.

'Abgeschiedenheit *f* (-; *no pl*) seclusion.

'abgeschlafft *adj* F whacked, dead beat.

'abgeschlossen I *pp of* **abschließen. II** *adj* **1.** completed. **2.** ⊙ self-contained.

'abgeschmackt *adj fig.* a) tasteless, *pred* in bad taste, b) fatuous.

'abgesehen *adv* **~ von** apart (*esp. Am.* aside) from, except for; **vom Wetter ganz ~** to say nothing of the weather.

'abgespannt *adj* worn(-)out, exhausted.

'**Abgespanntheit** f (-; *no pl*) exhaustion.
'**abgestanden** *adj a. fig.* stale.
'**abgestorben I** *pp of* **absterben. II** *adj* dead, numb.
'**abgestumpft I** *pp of* **abstumpfen. II** *adj fig.* deadened, dull(ed), *person:* insensitive (**gegen** to).
'**abgetakelt** *adj* F down(-)at(-)heel.
'**abgetragen I** *pp of* **abtragen. II** *adj* worn, shabby, worn-down (*shoes*).
'**abgewinnen** *v/t* (*irr, sep,* h, → **gewinnen**) *j-m et.* ~ win s.th. from s.o.; *e-r Sache Geschmack* ~ acquire a taste for s.th.
'**abgewirtschaftet** *adj* run(-)down.
'**abgewöhnen** *v/t* (*sep,* h) *j-m et.* ~ cure (*or* break) s.o. of s.th.; *j-m das Rauchen* ~ make s.o. stop smoking; *sich das Rauchen* ~ give up smoking.
'**abgezehrt** *adj* emaciated.
'**abgießen** *v/t* (*irr, sep,* -ge-, h, → **gießen**) **1.** a) pour off, b) strain (*vegetables etc*). **2.** ⊙ cast.
'**Abglanz** m (*fig. schwacher* ~ pale) reflection.
'**abgleichen** *v/t* (*irr, sep,* -ge-, h, → **gleichen**) ⊙ equalize, ✦ align.
'**abgleiten** *v/i* (*irr, sep,* -ge-, sn, → **gleiten**) slip (off): *fig. Kritik etc gleitet von ihm ab* he is deaf to criticism *etc.*
abgöttisch ['apɡœtɪʃ] *adj* idolatrous: ~ *lieben* idolize, adore.
'**abgrasen** *v/t* (*sep,* -ge-, h) **1.** graze. **2.** F *fig.* (*nach* for) scour, comb.
'**abgrenzen** *v/t* (*sep,* -ge-, h) **1.** a. fig. mark off, demarcate (*gegen* from). **2.** *fig.* a) differentiate, b) define.
'**Abgrenzung** f (-; -en) **1.** demarcation. **2.** *fig.* a) differentiation, b) definition.
'**Abgrund** m (-[e]s, ⸚e) abyss (*a. fig.*), chasm, precipice: *fig. die Abgründe der Seele etc* the depths of the soul *etc;* *am Rande des* ~*s* on the brink of ruin (*or* disaster). **abgründig** ['apɡrʏndɪç] *adj* **1.** cryptic. **2.** → '**abgrundtief** *adj* abysmal (*a. fig.*), *fig.* deadly (*hate etc*).
'**abgucken** *v/t* (*sep,* -ge-, h) F *j-m et.* ~ learn (*or* copy) s.th. from s.o.
'**Abguß** m (-sses; ⸚sse) ⊙ cast.
'**abhaben** *v/t* (*irr, sep,* -ge-, h, → **haben**) F *er kann et.* ~ he can have some (of it).
'**abhacken** *v/t* (*sep,* -ge-, h) chop off, cut off: → **abgehackt.**
'**abhaken** *v/t* (*sep,* -ge-, h) **1.** unhook. **2.**

tick (*Am.* check) off: *fig. et.* ~ cross s.th. off one's list.
'**abhalftern** *v/t* (*sep,* -ge-, h) F *fig.* sack.
'**abhalten** *v/t* (*irr, sep,* -ge-, h, → **halten**) **1.** hold *s.th.* away (*von sich* from o.s.). **2.** keep away (*or* off), ward off. **3.** deter, discourage: *j-n* ~ *von* stop (*or* keep, prevent) s.o. from *doing;* *lassen Sie sich (durch mich) nicht* ~! don't let me disturb you! **4.** hold (*conference, exam, election, etc*), give (*lesson, lecture*): *abgehalten werden* be held, take place. **5.** *ein Kind* ~ hold a child over the pot. **6.** ⚓ (*a. v/i*) bear off.
'**abhandeln** *v/t* (*sep,* -ge-, h) **1.** *j-m et.* ~ buy s.th. from s.o.; *j-m 10 Mark vom Preis* ~ beat s.o. down by ten marks. **2.** deal with, treat (*a subject etc*).
abhanden [ap'handn] *adv* ~ *kommen* get lost; *mir ist mein Bleistift* ~ *gekommen* I have lost my pencil.
'**Abhandlung** f (-; -en) (*über acc* on) treatise, paper.
'**Abhang** m (-[e]s; ⸚e) slope, precipice.
'**abhängen**¹ **I** *v/t* (h) **1.** take down, unhook, 🚃 *etc* uncouple. **2.** *fig.* shake off, give *s.o.* the slip. **II** *v/i* teleph. hang up.
'**abhängen**² *v/i* (*irr, sep,* -ge-, h, → **hängen**¹) **1.** hang: → **abgehangen II. 2.** ~ *von* depend on, *financially:* be dependent on; *letztlich* ~ *von* hinge on; *es hängt von ihm ab* it's for him to decide.
abhängig ['aphɛnɪç] *adj* (*von*) dependent (on), 🜛, *psych.* addicted (to): *ling.* ~*e Rede* indirect speech; ~*er Satz* subordinate clause; ~ *sein von* → **abhängen**² 2; ~ *machen von* make *s.th.* conditional on. '**Abhängigkeit** f (-; -en) (*von*) dependence (on), 🜛, *psych.* dependency (on), addiction (to): *gegenseitige* ~ interdependence.
'**abhärmen:** *sich* ~ (*sep,* -ge-, h) pine away; *sich* ~ *um* grieve over.
'**abhärten** *v/t* (*sep,* -ge-, h) (*gegen* to, against) toughen, *a. fig.* harden (*sich* o.s.). '**Abhärtung** f (-; *no pl*) hardening.
'**abhauen** (*irr, sep,* -ge-, → **hauen**) **I** *v/t* (h) cut off, chop off. **II** *v/i* (sn) F beat it: *hau ab!* beat it!, get lost!
'**abheben** (*irr, sep,* -ge-, h, → **heben**) **I** *v/t* **1.** lift off, take off, teleph. pick up. **2.** cut (*cards*). **3.** slip (*meshes*). **4.** withdraw (*money*). **II** *v/i* **5.** ✈ take off. **6.** F *fig.* flip. **7.** answer the (tele)phone. **8.**

cards: cut. **9.** *esp. adm.* ~ **auf** (*acc*) refer to. **III sich** ~ (**gegen, von**) contrast (with), stand out (against).

'**abheften** *v/t* (*sep*, -ge-, h) file (away).

'**abheilen** *v/i* (*sep*, -ge-, sn) heal (up).

'**abhelfen** *v/i* (*irr*, *sep*, -ge-, h, → **helfen**) **e-r Sache** ~ remedy s.th.

'**abhetzen: sich** ~ (*sep*, -ge-, h) rush, *w.s.* wear (or tire) o.s. out.

'**Abhilfe** *f* (-; *no pl*) remedy: ~ **schaffen** remedy things.

'**abhobeln** *v/t* (*sep*, -ge-, h) ⊙ plane off.

'**abholen** *v/t* (*sep*, -ge-, h) call for, come for, pick up, collect: ~ **lassen** send for; **j-n von der Bahn** ~ go to meet s.o. at the station.

'**abholzen** *v/t* (*sep*, -ge-, h) cut down (*trees*), deforest (*area*).

'**Abhöranlage** *f* bugging system.

'**abhorchen** *v/t* (*sep*, -ge-, h) ⚕ sound, auscultate.

'**abhören** *v/t* (*sep*, -ge-, h) **1.** → **abfragen** 1. **2.** → **abhorchen. 3.** intercept (*radio message etc*), listen in on, monitor, F bug (*phone calls*), tap (*telephone*). **4.** play back (*tape recording*).

Abi ['abi] *n* (-s; *no pl*) F → **Abitur.**

'**abirren** *v/i* (*sep*, -ge-, sn) *a. fig.* stray (**von** from).

Abitur [abi'tuːr] *n* (-s; *no pl*) school-leaving (*Am.* final) examination.

Abiturient [abitu'riɛnt] *m* (-en; -en) a) candidate for the school-leaving examination, b) school-leaver with the Abitur.

Abi'turzeugnis *n* Abitur certificate, *Br.* GCE A-levels, *Am.* (Senior High School) graduation diploma.

'**abjagen** *v/t* (*sep*, -ge-, h) **j-m et.** ~ snatch s.th. away from s.o.

'**abkanzeln** *v/t* (*sep*, -ge-, h) F **j-n** ~ give s.o. a dressing-down.

'**abkapseln: sich** ~ (*sep*, -ge-, h) shut (or cut) o.s. off.

'**abkarten** *v/t* (*sep*, -ge-, h) F fix, rig: → **abgekartet.**

'**abkas,sieren** *v/i* (*sep*, -ge-, h) F *fig.* cash in.

'**abkaufen** *v/t* (*sep*, -ge-, h) buy (*dat* from): F *fig.* **das kaufe ich dir** *etc* **nicht ab!** I won't buy that!

Abkehr ['apkeːr] *f* (-; *no pl*) break (**von** with). '**abkehren** *v/t* (*sep*, -ge-, h) (*a.* **sich** ~) turn away (**von** from): *fig.* **sich**

~ **von** a. turn one's back on (*a person*), abandon (*a policy etc*).

'**abklappern** *v/t* (*sep*, -ge-, h) F scour (*shops*) (**nach** for), do (*museums etc*).

'**abklären** *v/t* (*sep*, -ge-, h) clear: → **abgeklärt.**

'**Abklatsch** *m* (-[e]s; -e) *fig.* imitation.

'**abklemmen** *v/t* (*sep*, -ge-, h) pinch off, ⚡ clamp, ⚡ disconnect.

'**abklingen** *v/i* (*irr*, *sep*, -ge-, sn, → **klingen**) *noise etc*: abate, *pain*: ease, *fever, swelling*: go down, *effect*: wear off, *excitement, storm, etc*: subside, die down.

'**abklopfen** (*sep*, -ge-, h) **I** *v/t* **1.** brush off (*dust etc*). **2.** *esp.* ⚕ tap, percuss. **3.** F *fig.* scrutinize (**auf** *acc* for). **II** *v/i* **4.** ♪ stop the orchestra.

'**abknallen** *v/t* (*sep*, -ge-, h) F bump *s.o.* off.

'**abknicken** *v/t* (*sep*, -ge-, h), *v/i* (sn) snap (off): ~**de Vorfahrt** left-hand (*or* right-hand) turn of a main road at a road junction.

'**abknöpfen** *v/t* (*sep*, -ge-, h) **1.** unbutton. **2.** F **j-m et.** ~ wangle s.th. out of s.o.

'**abknutschen** *v/t* (*sep*, -ge-, h) F kiss and cuddle: **sich** ~ snog, smooch.

'**abkochen** *v/t* (*sep*, -ge-, h) boil, scald.

'**abkom,dieren** *v/t* (*sep*, h) a) detail, b) second (*officer*) (**nach, zu** to).

'**abkommen** *v/i* (*irr*, *sep*, -ge-, sn, → **kommen**) **1.** get away (*a. sports*): **vom Kurs** ~ deviate (from one's course); *mot.* **von der Straße** ~ get (or skid) off the road; **vom Thema** ~ stray from the point; **vom Wege** ~ lose one's way, *fig.* go astray. **2.** ~ **von** give up, drop (*idea, plan, etc*); **von e-r Ansicht** ~ change one's views about s.th.

'**Abkommen** *n* (-s; -) *esp. pol.* agreement.

abkömmlich ['apkœmlɪç] *adj* available: **er ist nicht** ~ he cannot get away.

'**Abkömmling** *m* (-s; -e) ⚘ derivative.

'**abkoppeln** *v/t* (*sep*, -ge-, h) uncouple.

'**abkratzen** (*sep*, -ge-) **I** *v/t* (h) scrape off. **II** *v/i* (sn) F kick the bucket.

'**abkühlen** *v/t*, *v/i and* **sich** ~ (*sep*, -ge-, h) *a. fig.* cool off.

'**Abkühlung** *f* (-; *no pl*) cooling.

'**abkürzen** (*sep*, -ge-, h) **I** *v/t* shorten, abridge, abstract (*word*): (**den Weg**) ~ take a short cut. **II** *v/i* take (*road etc*: be) a short cut. '**Abkürzung** *f* (-; -en) **1.** abbreviation, abridg(e)ment. **2.** *a. fig.*

short cut. '**Abkürzungsverzeichnis** *n* list of abbreviations.

'**abküssen** *v/t* (*sep*, -ge-, h) *j-n* ~ smother s.o. with kisses.

'**abladen** *v/t* (*irr*, *sep*, -ge-, h, → **laden**) **1.** a) unload, b) dump. **2.** *fig.* off-load: *s-n Ärger ~ bei* vent one's anger on.

'**Abladeplatz** *m* a) unloading point, b) dump.

'**Ablage** *f* (-; -n) **1.** *no pl* filing. **2.** a) place to put s.th., b) file.

'**ablagern** *v/t* (*sep*, -ge-, h) **1.** (*a. sich ~*) 🐌, *geol.*, 🌱 deposit. **2.** (*a. v/i*) season (*wood etc*), mature (*wine*).

'**Ablagerung** *f* (-; -en) 🐌, *geol.*, 🌱 a) deposition, b) deposit, sediment.

Ablaß ['aplas] *m* (-sses; ⸚sse) *eccl.* indulgence.

'**ablassen** (*irr*, *sep*, -ge-, h, → **lassen**) **I** *v/t* **1.** let s.th. off (*or* out), drain off (*water etc*), drain (*tank etc*), blow off (*steam*): *die Luft ~ aus* deflate. **2.** 🌱 a) sell (*dat* to), b) *et.* (*vom Preis*) ~ knock s.th. off the price. **II** *v/i* **3.** ~ *von* a) stop doing, give s.th. up, b) leave s.o. alone.

Ablativ ['ablati:f; -ap'-] *m* (-s; -e) *ling.* ablative.

'**Ablauf** *m* (-[e]s; ⸚e) **1.** 🌐 a) discharge, b) outlet, drain. **2.** course, run, *of program(me)*: *der ~ der Ereignisse* the course of events. **3.** *no pl* end, 🌀, 🌱 expiration (*of contract etc*), maturity (*of bill of exchange*): *nach ~* upon expiration (*gen* of); *nach ~ von zwei Wochen* after two weeks.

'**ablaufen** (*irr*, *sep*, -ge-, → **laufen**) **I** *v/i* (sn) **1.** (*a. ~ lassen*) *water etc*: run off, drain off: *fig. an ihm läuft alles ab* everything runs off him like water off a duck's back. **2.** *fig.* go: *alles ist gut abgelaufen* everything went off well. **3.** end, run out, expire. **4.** unwind, *film, tape*: run, *watch*: run down: *fig. s-e Uhr ist abgelaufen* his hour is come. **II** *v/t* (h) **5.** walk the length of. **6.** (*nach for*) scour, comb (*shops*). **7.** wear out, wear down (*heels*): → **Rang** 1.

'**Ableben** *n* (-s; *no pl*) death, decease.

'**ablecken** *v/t* (*sep*, -ge-, h) lick off.

'**ablegen** (*irr*, *sep*, -ge-, h) **I** *v/t* **1.** a) take off (*one's coat etc*), b) discard (*old clothes*): *abgelegte Kleider* cast-offs. **2.** put down (*load*). **3.** file (*papers*), discard (*playing cards*). **4.** *zo.* deposit (*eggs*). **5.**

give up, drop (*habit*). **6.** take (*oath etc*): *e-e Prüfung ~* take (*or* pass) an examination; → **Gelübde, Geständnis, Rechenschaft** *etc.* **II** *v/i* **7.** take off one's things (*or* coat, hat, *etc*): *bitte, legen Sie ab!* take off your coat, please! **8.** ⚓ cast off, *space shuttle*: separate.

'**Ableger** *m* (-s; -) 🌿 layer, scion.

'**ablehnen** (*sep*, -ge-, h) **I** *v/t* **1.** refuse, turn down, reject (*a. parl.*), decline, 🎾 challenge (*witness*). **2.** disapprove of, condemn. **II** *v/i* **3.** refuse, decline.

'**ablehnend** *adj* negative, disapproving.

'**Ablehnung** *f* (-; -en) refusal, rejection (*a. parl.*), disapproval (*gen* of).

'**ableisten** *v/t* (*sep*, -ge-, h) serve: → **Wehrdienst.**

'**ableiten** *v/t* (*sep*, -ge-, h) **1.** 🌐 divert, drain off (*water*), carry off (*steam*). **2.** 🐌, 🅰, *ling.*, *a. fig.* derive (*aus* from): *sich ~ a.* be derived; *s-e Herkunft ~ von* trace one's origin back to.

'**Ableitung** *f* (-; -en) **1.** 🌐 diversion, draining off (*etc*, → **ableiten** 1). **2.** 🅰, *ling. etc* a) derivation, b) derivative.

'**ablenken** (*sep*, -ge-, h) **I** *v/t* **1.** a) divert, b) deflect (*ball, light rays, etc*). **2.** *fig.* divert, distract: *den Verdacht von sich ~* divert suspicion from o.s.; *j-n* (*von s-n Sorgen*) ~ take s.o.'s mind off his worries. **II** *v/i* **3.** change the subject. **4.** be a diversion: *das lenkt ab* that takes one's mind off things. '**Ablenkung** *f* (-; -en) **1.** deviation, deflection. **2.** diversion, distraction. '**Ablenkungsma͵növer** *n* diversion, *fig. a.* red herring.

'**ablesen**[1] *v/t* (*irr*, *sep*, -ge-, h, → **lesen**) pick off. '**ablesen**[2] *v/t* (*irr*, *sep*, -ge-, h, → **lesen**) **1.** read a speech (*from notes*). **2.** 🌐 read: *Strom* (*Gas*) ~ read the gas (electricity) meter. **3.** *fig.* see (*an dat* from): *j-m et. vom Gesicht ~* read s.th. in s.o.'s face; *j-m e-n Wunsch von den Augen ~* anticipate s.o.'s wish.

'**Ablesung** *f* (-; -en) 🌐 reading.

'**abliefern** *v/t* (*sep*, -ge-, h) deliver (*bei* to, at).

'**ablösbar** *adj* 🌀 redeemable.

Ablöse ['aplø:zə] *f* (-; -n) F *sports*: transfer fee.

'**ablösen** *v/t* (*sep*, -ge-, h) **1.** remove, detach. **2.** relieve (*guards etc*), take over from, replace (*a colleague*): *j-n ~ a.* relieve s.o. of his duties; *sich* (*or einan-*

der) ~ take turns (**bei** at). **3.** *fig.* follow. **4.** redeem (*mortgage*), pay off (*debt*).

'**Ablösesumme** *f sports*: transfer fee.

'**Ablösung** *f* (-; -en) **1.** removal. **2.** relief. **3.** ✝ redemption, repayment.

'**Abluft** *f* (-; *no pl*) ☉ waste air.

'**ablutschen** *v/t* (*sep*, -ge-, h) lick (off).

'**abmachen** *v/t* (*sep*, -ge-, h) **1.** remove, take off. **2.** arrange, agree on, settle on: **abgemacht!** agreed!, it's a deal!, o.k.!

'**Abmachung** *f* (-; -en) arrangement, agreement.

'**abmagern** *v/i* (*sep*, -ge-, sn) grow thin, lose weight: → **abgemagert.**

'**Abmagerungskur** *f* (-; -en) (**e-e ~ ma-chen** go [*or* be] on a) slimming diet.

'**abmalen** *v/t* (*sep*, -ge-, h) paint, copy.

'**Abmarsch** *m* [-[e]s; -*e*] marching off.

'**abmar,schieren** *v/i* (*sep*, -ge-, sn) march off.

'**abmelden** (*sep*, -ge-, h) **I** *v/t* cancel: **sein Auto ~** take one's car off the road; **sein Telefon ~** have one's telephone disconnected; **j-n ~** a) give notice of s.o.'s change of address (*to the police*), b) cancel s.o.'s membership (*of a club etc*); F **bei mir ist er abgemeldet!** I'm through with him! **II sich ~** a) give notice of one's change of address (*to the police*), b) cancel one's membership (*of a club etc*); **sich bei j-m** (*vom Dienst etc*) ~ report to s.o. that one is leaving.

'**Abmeldung** *f* (-; -en) **1.** cancel(l)ation. **2.** notice of change of address.

'**abmessen** *v/t* (*irr, sep*, -ge-, h, → **mes-sen**) measure. '**Abmessung** *f* (-; -en) measurement: **~en** *a.* dimensions.

'**abmon,tieren** *v/t* (*sep*, -ge-, h) ☉ take off, dismount, remove.

'**abmühen: sich ~** (*sep*, -ge-, h) try hard (**to** do *s.th.*); **sich ~ mit** struggle with.

'**abmurksen** *v/t* (*sep*, -ge-, h) F do *s.o.* in.

'**abmustern** *v/t* (*sep*, -ge-, h) ⚓ pay off.

'**abnabeln** *v/t* (*sep*, -ge-, h) cut *a baby's* umbilical cord; *fig.* **sich ~** cut the cord.

'**abnagen** *v/t* (*sep*, -ge-, h) gnaw off: **e-n Knochen ~** gnaw (*person*: pick) a bone.

'**abnähen** *v/t* (*sep*, -ge-, h) take in, tuck. '**Abnäher** *m* (-s; -) tuck.

'**Abnahme** *f* (-; *no pl*) **1.** taking off (*or* down), removal, ✻ amputation. **2.** ✝ (**bei ~** on) purchase (**von** of). **3.** ☉ a) acceptance, b) inspection (test). **4.** ~ **e-r Parade** review (of the troops). **5.** *fig.*

decrease, decline, drop (*all: gen* in), loss (*gen* in, *of speed, weight*), flagging (*of interest*), waning (*of the moon*).

'**abnehmbar** *adj* detachable.

'**abnehmen** (*irr, sep*, -ge-, h, → **neh-men**) **I** *v/t* **1.** take off, ☉ a. remove, ✻ a. amputate, take down (*picture etc*), shave off (*beard*), gather (*fruit*), pick up (*the receiver*): **j-m Blut ~** take a blood sample from s.o.; **j-m Fingerabdrücke ~** take s.o.'s fingerprints. **2. j-m et. ~** a) relieve s.o. of s.th., save s.o. (*trouble, an errand, etc*), b) take s.th. (away) from s.o., c) charge s.o. s.th.; **j-m zuviel ~** overcharge s.o. **3.** (*dat* from) buy, pur-chase: F *fig.* **das nimmt ihm keiner ab!** nobody will buy that! **4.** ☉ a) accept, b) inspect, test. **5. die Parade ~** review the troops. **6.** hold (*an examination*): → **Beichte, Eid** etc. **7.** decrease (*meshes*). **8.** lose, get rid of (*pounds, weight*). **II** *v/i* **9.** decrease, diminish, drop off, *strength etc*: decline, *vision etc*: fail, *in-terest*: flag, *speed*: slacken (off), slow down, *storm*: abate, *moon*: (be on the) wane, *days*: grow shorter. **10.** a) lose weight, b) be slimming. '**Abnehmer** *m* (-s; -) ✝ a) buyer, b) customer, c) con-sumer: **keine ~ finden** find no market.

'**Abneigung** *f* (-; -en) (**gegen**) dislike (of, for), aversion (to).

abnorm [ap'nɔrm] *adj* abnormal, *w.s.* exceptional, strange.

Abnormität [apnɔrmi'tɛ:t] *f* (-; -en) **1.** abnormality. **2.** monstrosity.

'**abnötigen** *v/t* (*sep*, -ge-, h) **j-m Respekt ~** command s.o.'s respect.

'**abnutzen** *v/t* (*sep*, -ge-, h) (*a.* **sich ~**) wear out. '**Abnutzung** *f* (-; *no pl*) wear and tear. '**Abnutzungserscheinung** *f* sign of wear, ✻ sign of degeneration.

Abonnement [abɔnə'mã:] *n* (-s; -s) sub-scription (**auf** acc to), *thea. a.* season ticket (**bei** for). **Abonnent** [abɔ'nɛnt] *m* (-en; -en) subscriber (*gen* to), *thea.* sea-son-ticket holder.

abonnieren [abɔ'ni:rən] *v/t* (h) sub-scribe to: **abonniert sein auf** (*acc*) have a subscription to, take (*a paper*).

'**abordnen** *v/t* (*sep*, -ge-, h) delegate. '**Abordnung** *f* (-; -en) delegation.

'**abpacken** *v/t* (*sep*, -ge-, h) ✝ pack(age).

'**abpassen** *v/t* (*sep*, -ge-, h) wait for.

'**abpausen** *v/t* (*sep*, -ge-, h) trace.

'**abpfeifen** v/t, v/i (irr, sep, -ge-, h, → *pfeifen*) (*das Spiel*) ~ stop the game.
'**Abpfiff** m (-[e]s; -e) sports: final whistle.
'**abprallen** v/i (sep, -ge-, sn) rebound, bounce off, *bullet*: ricochet: *fig.* **an j-m** ~ make no impression on s.o.
'**Abpraller** m (-s; -) sports: rebound.
'**abputzen** v/t (sep, -ge-, h) clean, wipe: **sich die Schuhe** ~ wipe one's feet.
'**abquälen**: *sich* ~ (sep, -ge-, h) 1. worry (o.s.), fret. 2. slave (away). 3. → *abmühen*.
abquali,fizieren v/t (sep, h) dismiss.
'**abrackern**: *sich* ~ (sep, -ge-, h) F slave (away).
'**abraten** v/i (irr, sep, -ge-, h, → *raten*) *j-m* ~ **von** advise (*or* warn) s.o. against (doing).
'**abräumen** v/t (sep, -ge-, h) clear away, remove: **den Tisch** ~ clear the table.
'**abrea,gieren** (sep, h) I v/t (*an dat* on) abreact, work off. II *sich* ~ get rid of one's aggressions, F let off steam.
'**abrechnen** (sep, -ge-, h) I v/t deduct, account for (*expenses etc*) II v/i settle accounts: **mit j-m** ~ settle up with s.o., *fig. a.* get even with s.o.
'**Abrechnung** f (-; -en) 1. a) settlement (of accounts), b) statement. 2. *fig.* requital: **Tag der** ~ day of reckoning.
'**abreiben** v/t (irr, sep, -ge-, h, → *reiben*) 1. a) rub off, b) rub down (*body*). 2. wipe *s.th.* clean, polish. 3. grate (*lemon etc*). '**Abreibung** f (-; -en) 1. ☞ rub-down, sponge-down. 2. F beating.
'**Abreise** f (-; -n) (*bei m-r etc* ~ on my *etc*) departure (*nach* on).
'**abreisen** v/i (sep, -ge-, sn) (*nach* for) depart, leave.
'**Abreiß...** tear-off (*pad, calendar, etc*).
'**abreißen** (irr, sep, -ge-, → *reißen*) I v/t (h) a) tear (*or* pull, rip) off, b) pull down, demolish (*building*). II v/i (sn) come off, *thread etc*: snap, *fig.* break off: **die Arbeit reißt nicht ab** ~ there's no end of work.
'**abrichten** v/t (sep, -ge-, h) train (*animal*), break in (*horse*).
'**abriegeln** v/t (sep, -ge-, h) 1. bolt, bar. 2. block (off), cordon off, ✕ seal off.
'**abringen** v/t (irr, sep, -ge-, h, → *ringen*) *j-m et.* ~ wrest s.th. from s.o.; **sich ein Lächeln** ~ force a smile.
'**Abriß** m (-sses, -sse) 1. a) summary,

outline, b) survey, c) compendium. 2. demolition.
'**abrollen** (sep, -ge-) I v/t (h) unroll, unwind, unreel. II v/i (sn) *fig.* unfold.
'**abrücken** (sep, -ge-) I v/t (h) move away. II v/i (sn) march off, move off: *fig.* **von j-m** ~ disassociate o.s. from s.o.
'**Abruf** m (-[e]s; *no pl*) 1. recall: **sich auf** ~ **bereithalten** stand by. 2. ✝ **auf** ~ on call. '**abrufbereit** *adj* on call.
'**abrufen** v/t (irr, sep, -ge-, h, → *rufen*) 1. call *s.o.* away, recall. 2. ✝ call (for) (*goods*). 3. *computer*: call in (*data*).
'**abrunden** v/t (sep, -ge-, h) round off: *nach oben* (*unten*) ~ round up (down); → *abgerundet*.
abrupt [ap'rʊpt] *adj* abrupt, sudden.
'**abrüsten** v/i (sep, -ge-, h) disarm.
'**Abrüstung** f (-; *no pl*) disarmament.
'**abrutschen** v/i (sep, -ge-, sn) 1. slip off, slip down, *knife*: slip. 2. *fig.* go down.
'**absacken** v/i (sep, -ge-, sn) F 1. sag, *a.* ⚓ sink, ✈ pancake. 2. *fig.* go down.
'**Absage** f (-; -n) 1. cancel(l)ation. 2. refusal, *fig.* rejection (*an acc* of).
'**absagen** (sep, -ge-, h) I v/t cancel, call off. II v/i beg off, cry off: *j-m* ~ tell s.o. that one can't come.
'**absägen** v/t (sep, -ge-, h) 1. saw off. 2. F *fig.* ax(e), fire.
'**absahnen** v/t (sep, -ge-, h) F cream off.
'**absatteln** v/t (sep, -ge-, h) unsaddle.
'**Absatz** m (-[e]s; ⸚e) 1. heel: **Schuhe mit hohen Absätzen** high-heeled shoes. 2. 🕮, *print.* paragraph: *neuer* ~ new line. 3. ✝ sale(s): **guten (reißenden)** ~ *finden* find a ready market (F sell like hot cakes). 4. (staircase) landing.
'**Absatz|gebiet** n ✝ market(ing area). **~markt** m, **~möglichkeit** f ✝ market, outlet. **~steigerung** f ✝ sales increase. **~stockung** f ✝ stagnation of trade.
'**Absatztrick** m soccer: backheel trick.
'**absaufen** v/i (irr, sep, -ge-, sn, → *saufen*) F ✗, *mot.* be flooded, ⚓ go down, *person*: drown.
'**absaugen** v/t (sep, -ge-, h) 1. suck off, *a.* ☞ aspirate. 2. vacuum (*carpet*).
'**abschaben** v/t (sep, -ge-, h) scrape off.
'**abschaffen** v/t (sep, -ge-, h) 1. abolish. 2. get rid of, give up.
'**Abschaffung** f (-; *no pl*) abolition.
'**abschalten** (sep, -ge-, h) I v/t switch off,

turn off, ✄ cut off, disconnect. **II** *v/i* F *fig.* switch off, relax.

'**abschätzen** *v/t* (*sep*, -ge-, h) estimate, *a. fig.* assess, F *fig.* size *s.o.*, *s.th.* up.

'**abschätzend** *adj* assessing, speculative.

abschätzig ['apʃɛtsɪç] *adj* contemptuous, disparaging.

'**Abschaum** *m* (-[e]s; *no pl*) scum: *fig.* ~ **der Menschheit** scum of the earth.

'**Abscheu** *m* (-s; *no pl*) (**vor** *dat*, **gegen**) disgust (at, for), loathing (for): **e-n** ~ **haben vor** (*dat*) detest, loathe.

'**abscheuern** *v/t* (*sep*, -ge-, h) **1.** scrub (off). **2.** rub off, scrape. **3.** (*a.* **sich** ~) wear thin.

ab'scheulich *adj* dreadful, abominable, heinous, atrocious (*a. crime etc*).

'**abschicken** *v/t* (*sep*, -ge-, h) → **absenden**.

'**abschieben** (*irr*, *sep*, -ge-, → **schieben**) **I** *v/t* (h) **1.** push away (**von** from). **2.** deport. **3.** F get rid of. **II** *v/i* (sn) **4.** F push off. '**Abschiebung** *f* (-; -en) ⚖ deportation. '**Abschiebungshaft** *f* (*j-n* **in** ~ **nehmen** put s.o. on) remand pending deportation.

Abschied ['apʃiːt] *m* (-[e]s; *no pl*) **1.** farewell, parting, departure: ~ **nehmen** (**von**) take leave (of), say goodbye(e) (to); **beim** ~, **zum** ~ on parting. **2.** dismissal, ✗ discharge, resignation.

'**Abschieds...** farewell (*letter*, *visit*, *etc*). **~kuß** *m* goodbye(e) kiss: **j-m e-n** ~ **geben** kiss s.o. goodbye(e). **~schmerz** *m* (-es; *no pl*) wrench. **~stunde** *f* hour of parting. **~worte** *pl* words of farewell.

'**abschießen** *v/t* (*irr*, *sep*, -ge-, h, → **schießen**) **1.** fire (*gun*), shoot (*bullet*, *arrow*, *etc*), launch (*rocket*). **2.** shoot, kill, shoot (or bring) down (*plane*): F *fig.* **j-n** ~ put the skids under s.o.; → **Vogel** 1.

'**abschirmen** *v/t* (*sep*, -ge-, h) (**gegen**) shield (from), protect (against). '**Abschirmung** *f* (-; -en) protection.

'**abschlachten** *v/t* (*sep*, -ge-, h) *a. fig.* slaughter.

'**abschlaffen** *v/i* (*sep*, -ge-, sn) F wilt: → **abgeschlafft**.

'**Abschlag** *m* (-[e]s; ⸚e) **1.** *soccer*: goal kick, *golf*: tee(-off). **2.** ✝ a) drop (in prices), b) reduction, c) part payment: **auf** ~ on account. '**abschlagen** *v/t* (*irr*, *sep*, -ge-, h, → **schlagen**) **1.** knock off

(or down), cut off. **2.** (*a. v/i*) *soccer*: kick off, *golf*: tee off. **3.** beat off (*attack*). **4.** *fig.* refuse, turn down.

'**abschlägig** ['apʃlɛːgɪç] *adj* negative: *adm.* **j-n** (**j-s Bitte**) ~ **bescheiden** reject s.o. (s.o.'s request).

'**Abschlagszahlung** *f* part payment.

'**abschleifen** *v/t* (*irr*, *sep*, -ge-, h, → **schleifen**) ⚙ grind off, *a. fig.* polish: **sich** ~ *a. fig.* wear off.

'**Abschleppdienst** *m* breakdown (*Am.* wrecking) service. '**abschleppen** *v/t* (*sep*, -ge-, h) ⚓, *mot.* tow off.

'**Abschleppwagen** *m* breakdown lorry, *Am.* wrecker (truck).

'**abschließbar** *adj* lockable.

'**abschließen** (*irr*, *sep*, -ge-, h, → **schließen**) **I** *v/t* **1.** lock (up). **2.** shut off, ⚙ *a.* seal (off): → **abgeschlossen** 2. **3.** a) end, close, finish, b) complete; → **abgeschlossen** 1. **4.** ✝ conclude, sign (*contract*), settle (*accounts*), close, balance (*books*), effect (*sale*): **e-n Handel** ~ strike a bargain, close a deal; **e-e Versicherung** ~ take out a policy; → **Wette**. **II** *v/i* **5.** end, close (*a.* ✝), finish: **mit dem Leben abgeschlossen haben** have done with life.

'**abschließend I** *adj* concluding, closing, final. **II** *adv* in conclusion, finally.

'**Abschluß** *m* (-sses; ⸚sse) **1.** *no pl* conclusion, ✝ closing (*of books etc*), settlement (*of accounts*): **zum** ~ **bringen** → **abschließend** II; **et. zum** ~ **bringen** bring s.th. to a close. **2.** ✝ deal, sale. **3.** F *ped.*, *univ.* final examination. **~prüfung** *f* **1.** final examination, finals, *Am.* a. graduation: **s-e** ~ **machen** (**an** *dat*) graduate (at, *Am.* from). **2.** ✝ audit (*of books*). **~zeugnis** *n* (school-)leaving certificate, *Am.* (high-school) diploma.

'**abschmecken** *v/t* (*sep*, -ge-, h) season.

'**abschmieren** *v/t* (*sep*, -ge-, h) ⚙ grease.

'**abschminken** *v/t* (*sep*, -ge-, h) (*a.* **sich** ~) take off (or remove) *s.o.'s* (one's) make-up: F *fig.* **das kannst du dir** ~! forget it!

'**abschnallen** *v/t* (*sep*, -ge-, h) undo, take off: **sich** ~ unfasten one's seat belt.

'**abschneiden** (*irr*, *sep*, -ge-, h, → **schneiden**) **I** *v/t* **1.** cut off (*a. fig. supplies etc*): **j-m den Weg** ~ bar s.o.'s way; **j-m das Wort** ~ cut s.o. short. **II** *v/i* **2.** (**den Weg**) ~ take a short cut. **3.** **gut** (*schlecht*) ~ do (*or* come off) well (badly). **'Abschneiden** *n* (-s) performance.

'Abschnitt *m* (-[e]s; -e) **1.** section, paragraph (*of a book etc*). **2.** *biol.*, ~ segment. **3.** *a.* ✕ sector. **4.** period, phase, stage (*a. of a trip*). **5.** ✝ counterfoil, stub (*of ticket etc*), coupon.

'abschnüren *v/t* (*sep*, -ge-, h) **1.** → *abbinden* 2. **2.** *esp.* ✕ cut off. **3.** *j-m die Luft* ~ choke s.o.

'abschöpfen *v/t* (*sep*, -ge-, h) skim off (*a.* ✝ *profits*), ✝ absorb (*excessive buying power*): *a. fig. den Rahm* ~ take the cream off.

'abschotten: *sich* ~ (*sep*, -ge-, h) *fig.* batten down the hatches, seal o.s. off.

'abschrägen *v/t* (*sep*, -ge-, h) bevel.

'abschrauben *v/t* (*sep*, -ge-, h) screw off.

'abschrecken *v/t* (*sep*, -ge-, h) **1.** deter, put *s.o.* off. **2.** ⊚ quench. **3.** *gastr.* rinse with cold water. **'abschreckend** *adj* deterrent: ~*es Beispiel* warning; ~*e Strafe* exemplary punishment; ~ *wirken* act as a deterrent.

'Abschreckung *f* (-; -en) deterrence: *zur* ~ *dienen* act as a deterrent. **'Abschreckungs|poli,tik** *f* policy of deterrence. **~waffe** *f* deterrent (weapon).

'abschreiben (*irr*, *sep*, -ge-, h, → *schreiben*) **I** *v/t* **1.** copy (out), *ped.* crib. **2.** ✝ depreciate, write down (*equipment*), *totally*: write off (*a.* F *fig. s.o.*, *s.th.*), deduct (*amount*). **II** *v/i* **3.** *ped.* crib. **'Abschreibung** *f* (-; -en) ✝ depreciation, write-off.

'Abschrift *f* (-; -en) copy: → *beglaubigt*.

'abschürfen *v/t* (*sep*, -ge-, h) 🩹 graze.

'Abschürfung *f* (-; -en) 🩹 graze.

'Abschuß *m* (-sses; -ˇsse) **1.** discharge (*of gun*). **2.** launching (*of rocket*).

abschüssig ['apʃʏsɪç] *adj* steep.

'Abschußliste *f* F hit list: *j-n auf die* ~ *setzen* put the skids under s.o.; *auf der* ~ *stehen* be a marked man. **'Abschußrampe** *f* launching pad.

'abschütteln *v/t* (*sep*, -ge-, h) *a. fig.* shake off.

'abschwächen (*sep*, -ge-, h) **I** *v/t* weaken, soften (*a. impact*), tone down (*a. remark etc*). **II** *sich* ~ weaken, *noise*, *storm*, *etc*: subside.

'abschweifen *v/i* (*sep*, -ge-, sn) *fig.* deviate, stray, *thoughts etc*: wander: *vom Thema* ~ digress (from one's subject).

'abschwellen *v/i* (*irr*, *sep*, -ge-, sn, → *schwellen*) **1.** 🩹 go down. **2.** *noise*: die down.

'abschwirren *v/i* (*sep*, -ge-, sn) F buzz off.

'abschwören *v/i* (*irr*, *sep*, -ge-, h, → *schwören*) *s-m Glauben* ~ renounce one's faith.

'absegnen *v/t* (*sep*, -ge-, h) F *humor.* give one's blessing to.

'absehbar *adj in* ~*er Zeit* in the foreseeable future. **'absehen** (*irr*, *sep*, -ge-, h, → *sehen*) **I** *v/t* **1.** foresee: *es ist kein Ende abzusehen* there's no end in sight. **2.** *es abgesehen haben auf* (*acc*) a) be out to get, have an eye on, b) *j-n* have it in for s.o. **3.** → *abgucken*. **II** *v/i* **4.** ~ *von* a) refrain from, b) disregard: → *abgesehen*.

'abseifen *v/t* (*sep*, -ge-, h) soap down.

'abseilen (*sep*, -ge-, h) *v/t* (*a. sich* ~) rope down: F *fig. sich* ~ make off.

'absein *v/i* (*irr*, *sep*, -ge-, sn) → *ab* 2, 9.

abseits ['apzaɪts] **I** *prep* (*gen*) off the road etc. **II** *adv* ~ *stehen* stand aside, *sports*: be offside; ~ *liegen* be out of the way; *fig. sich* ~ *halten* keep aloof.

'Abseits *n* (-; -) *sports*: (*im* ~ *stehen* be) offside; *fig. sich ins* ~ *manövrieren*, *ins* ~ *geraten* get (o.s.) isolated. ~*falle* *f* *sports*: offside trap. ~*tor* *n* *sports*: goal scored from an offside position.

'absenden *v/t* (*irr*, *sep*, -ge-, h, → *senden*) send (off), dispatch, forward, post, *Am.* mail. **'Absender** *m* (-s; -) **1.** sender. **2.** sender's address.

'absetzbar *adj* **1.** ✝ sal(e)able. **2.** (*steuerlich* ~) deductible (for taxation). **3.** *official etc*: removable.

'absetzen (*sep*, -ge-, h) **I** *v/t* **1.** set down (*load*), take off (*hat*, *glasses*, *etc*), lift (*violin bow*). **2.** set down (*passengers*), drop (*a. parachutist*). **3.** remove *official* (from office), depose (*ruler*). **4.** cancel (*meeting etc*), remove (*item on the agenda*), take off (*film etc*). **5.** ✝ a) deduct, b) sell: *steuerlich* ~ deduct from tax. **6.** 🩹 stop taking (*a medicament*), go off (*a drug*), break off (*treatment*). **7.** *print.* set up (in type: *e-e Zeile* ~ begin a new paragraph. **8.** 🩹 *etc* deposit. **II** *v/i* **9.** stop, break off: *ohne abzusetzen* in one go, *drink* in one gulp. **III** *sich* ~ **10.** ✕ retreat, *sports: runner etc*: break away, F *fig.* make off. '**Absetzung** *f* (-; -en) **1.** removal (from office), deposition (*of a ruler*). **2.** cancel(l)ation (*of a meeting etc*), withdrawal (*of a film etc*).

'**absichern** (*sep*, -ge-, h) **I** *v/t* → **sichern**. **II** *sich* ~ cover o.s.

'**Absicht** *f* (-; -en) intention, *a.* ⚖ intent, aim, object: **in der** ~ **zu** *inf* with the intention (*of ger*); **ich habe die** ~ **zu kommen** I intend (*or* I'm planning) to come; **mit e-r bestimmten** ~ for a purpose; **mit** ~ on purpose. '**absichtlich I** *adj* intentional, deliberate, *esp.* ⚖ wil(l)ful. **II** *adv* intentionally *etc*, on purpose. '**Absichtserklärung** *f* (-; -en) declaration of intent.

'**absitzen** (*irr*, *sep*, -ge-, → *sitzen*) **I** *v/i* (sn) rider: dismount. **II** *v/t* (h) F sit out (*time*), serve (*a sentence*).

absolut [apzo'luːt] *adj* absolute, total, complete: ~ **nicht** by no means. **Absolution** [apzolu'tsĭoːn] *f* (-; -en) *eccl.* absolution.

Absolutismus [apzolu'tɪsmʊs] *m* (-; *no pl*) *pol.* absolutism.

Absolvent [apzɔl'vɛnt] *m* (-en; -en), **Absol'ventin** *f* (-; -nen) school-leaver, *Am.* graduate. **absolvieren** [apzɔl'viː-rən] *v/t* (h) **1.** *ped.* finish, *Am.* graduate from. **2.** attend, complete (*a course*). **3.** pass (*an exam*). **4.** F do, get through.

ab'sonderlich *adj* odd, peculiar.

'**absondern** (*sep*, -ge-, h) **I** *v/t* **1.** separate, ☘ isolate. **2.** *biol.* secrete. **II** *sich* ~ *fig.* cut o.s. off (*von* from). '**Absonderung** *f* (-; -en) **1.** separation, ☘ isolation. **2.** *biol.* secretion.

absorbieren [apzɔr'biːrən] *v/t* (h) *a. fig.* absorb.

'**abspalten** *v/t* (*irr*, *sep*, -ge-, h, → *spalten*) (*a. sich* ~) split off.

'**Abspann** *m* (-[e]s, -e) *film*, *TV* end titles (and credits).

'**Abspannung** *f* (-; *no pl*) exhaustion.

'**absparen** *v/t* (*sep*, -ge-, h) **sich et.** (**vom Munde**) ~ pinch and scrape for s.th.

'**abspecken** (*sep*, -ge-, h) F → **abnehmen** 8, 10.

'**abspeisen** *v/t* (*sep*, -ge-, h) F feed: *fig.* **j-n** ~ **mit** fob s.o. off with.

abspenstig ['apʃpɛnstɪç] ~ **machen** lure away (*dat* from); **j-m die Freundin** ~ **machen** steal s.o.'s girl(friend).

'**absperren** *v/t* (*sep*, -ge-, h) **1.** block off

(*road*), *police:* cordon off. **2.** turn (*adm.* cut) off (*gas etc*). **3.** *dial.* lock (up).

'**Absperrhahn** *m* ⚙ stopcock. '**Absperrung** *f* (-; -en) **1.** barrier, cordon. **2.** blocking off (*etc*, → **absperren**).

'**abspielen** (*sep*, -ge-, h) **I** *v/t* **1.** play (*record, tape, etc*). **2.** pass (*the ball*). **II** *sich* ~ a) happen, take place, b) be going on: F **da spielt sich nichts ab!** nothing doing!

'**absplittern** *v/i* (*sep*, -ge-, sn) *and* *v/t* (h) (*a. sich* ~ *fig.* group) splinter off.

'**Absprache** *f* (-; -n) arrangement: **laut** ~ → '**absprachegemäß** *adv* as agreed.

'**absprechen** (*sep*, -ge-, h, → *sprechen*) **I** *v/t* **1.** *j-m et.* ~ dispute (*or* deny) s.o.'s talent *etc*; ⚖ **j-m ein Recht** ~ deprive s.o. of a right. **2.** agree (up)on, arrange. **II** *sich* ~ **mit** *j-m* ~ agree with s.o. (**über** *acc* about).

'**abspringen** *v/i* (*irr*, *sep*, -ge-, sn, → *springen*) **1.** jump off, *sports:* a. take off, ✈ jump, bail out, *varnish etc:* come off, *ball etc:* bounce off. **2.** F *fig.* quit, get (*or* back) out (*von* of).

'**abspritzen** *v/t* (*sep*, -ge-, h) hose down.

'**Absprung** *m* (-[e]s; -e) jump, *sports:* take-off. ~**balken** *m* take-off board.

'**abspulen** *v/t* (*sep*, -ge-, h) unreel.

'**abspülen** *v/t* (*sep*, -ge-, h) rinse (off).

'**abstammen** *v/i* (*sep*, *no pp*) (**von** from) be descended, *ling.* be derived.

'**Abstammung** *f* (-; *no pl*) **1.** descent, origin: **deutscher** ~ of German extraction. **2.** *ling.* derivation. '**Abstammungslehre** *f* theory of evolution.

'**Abstand** *m* (-[e]s; -e) **1.** distance (*a. fig.*), space, *a. time:* interval, *fig.* gap, difference: **mit** ~ a) **besser** far better, b) **gewinnen** win by a wide margin; **in regelmäßigen Abständen** at regular intervals; *fig.* ~ **halten** (*or* **wahren**) keep one's distance; **von et.** ~ **nehmen** refrain from (doing) s.th. **2.** → '**Abstandssumme** *f* indemnity.

abstatten ['apʃtatən] *v/t* (*sep*, -ge-, h) *j-m* **e-n Besuch** ~ pay s.o. a visit; → **Dank**.

'**abstauben** (*sep*, -ge-, h) **I** *v/t* **1.** dust. **2.** F swipe. **II** *v/i* **3.** *soccer:* tap the ball in.

'**abstechen** (*irr*, *sep*, -ge-, h, → *stechen*) **I** *v/t* stick (*pigs*). **II** *v/i* ~ **von** stand out against (*fig.* from).

'**Abstecher** *m* (-s; -) *a. fig.* excursion.

'**abstecken** *v/t* (*sep*, -ge-, h) **1.** fit (*dress*

etc). **2.** mark out (*area, course, etc*), stake out, mark (*borders etc*). **3.** *fig.* define (*positions*).

'**abstehen** *v/i* (*irr, sep,* -ge-, h, → **stehen**) stick out.

Absteige ['apʃtaɪgə] *f* (-; -n) F *contp.* dosshouse, *Am.* flophouse. '**absteigen** *v/i* (*irr, sep,* -ge-, sn, → **steigen**) **1.** climb down, get off (*a bike, horse*). **2.** (*in dat*) stay, put up. **3.** *sports:* go down, be relegated. '**Absteiger** *m* (-s; -) *sports:* relegated team (*or* club).

'**abstellen** *v/t* (*sep,* -ge-, h) **1.** put down. **2.** leave (**bei** with), *mot.* park. **3.** turn (*adm.* cut) off (*gas etc*), stop (*machine*), switch off (*radio, engine, etc*). **4.** *fig.* remedy, stop (*grievances*). **5.** *fig.* (*auf acc*) gear (to), aim (at). **6.** → **abkommandieren.**

'**Abstell|fläche** *f mot.* parking space. **~gleis** *n* siding: *fig. j-n aufs ~ schieben* shelve s.o. '**~raum** *m* storeroom.

'**abstempeln** *v/t* (*sep,* -ge-, h) stamp (*a. fig.*), postmark.

'**absterben** *v/i* (*irr, sep,* -ge-, sn, → **sterben**)**1.** die (*a. fig.*), *toes etc:* go numb. **2.** F *mot.* stall.

Abstieg ['apʃtiːk] *m* (-[e]s; -e) **1.** descent, way down. **2.** *fig.* decline, comedown. **3.** *sports:* relegation.

'**abstillen** *v/t* (*sep,* -ge-, h) wean (*baby*).

'**abstimmen** (*sep,* -ge-, h) **I** *v/i* **1.** vote (*über acc* on): *über et. ~ lassen* put s.th. to the vote. **II** *v/t* **2.** (*auf acc*) tune (to), *a.* match colo(u)rs (with), *fig.* coordinate *interests* (with): *aufeinander ~* synchronize. **3.** ♰ balance (*accounts*). **III** *sich ~* come to an agreement (*mit* with). '**Abstimmung** *f* (-; -en) **1.** voting, vote (*über acc* on), poll: *die ~ ist geheim* voting is by ballot; *e-e ~ vornehmen* take a vote. **2.** tuning (*etc,* → **abstimmen** II).

abstinent [apsti'nɛnt] *adj* abstinent, abstemious. **Abstinenz** [apsti'nɛnts] *f* (-; *no pl*) (total) abstinence. **Absti'nenzler** *m* (-s; -) teetotal(l)er.

'**Abstoß** *m* (-[e]s; ⸚e) *soccer:* goal kick. '**abstoßen** (*irr, sep,* -ge-, h, → **stoßen**) **I** *v/t* **1.** (*a. v/i*) push off (*boat etc*). **2.** knock, batter (*furniture*), scuff (*shoes*). **3.** shed (*skin, antlers*): → **Horn** 1. **4.** ♣ reject (*tissue etc*). **5.** *phys.* repel. **6.** *fig.* get rid of. **7.** ♰ a) sell off, b) get out of

(*debt*). **8.** *fig.* repel, disgust. **II** *v/i* **9.** *soccer:* take a goal kick. '**abstoßend** *adj fig.* repulsive (*a. phys.*), repellent, revolting. '**Abstoßung** *f* (-; *no pl*) **1.** *phys., a. fig.* repulsion. **2.** ♣ rejection.

'**abstottern** *v/t* (*sep,* -ge-, h) F *et. ~* pay for s.th. in instal(l)ments.

abstrahieren [apstra'hiːrən] *v/t, v/i* (h) abstract. **abstrakt** [ap'strakt] *adj* abstract. **Abstraktion** [apstrak'tsɪoːn] *f* (-; -en) abstraction. **Abstraktum** [ap'straktʊm] *n* (-s; -ta) abstract noun.

'**abstreifen** *v/t* (*sep,* -ge-, h) **1.** slip off. **2.** wipe (*shoes*). **3.** search, scour.

'**abstreiten** *v/t* (*irr, sep,* -ge-, h, → **streiten**) **1.** deny. **2.** → **absprechen** 1.

'**Abstrich** *m* (-[e]s; -e) **1.** (*an dat* in) cut, curtailment: *fig. ~e machen müssen* have to lower one's sights. **2.** ♣ (*e-n ~ machen* take a) smear (*from tonsils:* swab). **3.** downstroke, ♪ down-bow.

abstrus [ap'struːs] *adj* abstruse.

'**abstufen** *v/t* (*sep,* -ge-, h) **1.** terrace. **2.** shade off. **3.** *fig.* grade, graduate. '**Abstufung** *f* (-; -en) **1.** shade. **2.** *fig.* gradation.

'**abstumpfen** (*sep,* -ge-) **I** *v/t* (h) *a. fig.* blunt, dull: *j-n ~* make s.o. insensible. **II** *v/i* (sn) become blunt (*fig.* dulled, *person:* insensible); → **abgestumpft.**

'**Absturz** *m* (-[e]s; ⸚e) **1.** plunge, ✈ crash. **2.** *fig.* downfall. '**abstürzen** *v/i* (*sep,* -ge-, sn) plunge (down), ✈ crash.

'**abstützen** *v/t* (*sep,* -ge-, h) △ prop.

'**absuchen** *v/t* (*sep,* -ge-, h) (*nach* for) search all over, scour, comb (*area*), sweep, scan (*horizon, sky*).

absurd [ap'zʊrt] *adj* absurd. **Absurdität** [apzʊrdi'tɛːt] *f* (-; -en) absurdity.

Abszeß [aps'tsɛs] *m* (-sses; -sse) abscess.

Abszisse [aps'tsɪsə] *f* (-; -n) ♉ abscissa.

Abt [apt] *m* (-[e]s; ⸚e) abbot.

'**abtasten** *v/t* (*sep,* -ge-, h) **1.** feel (*nach* for), ♣ palpate: *fig. j-n ~* feel s.o. out, size s.o. up. **2.** ⚡, TV scan.

'**abtauchen** *v/i* (*sep,* -ge-, sn) **1.** dive under. **2.** F *fig.* go to earth.

'**abtauen** (*sep,* -ge-) **I** *v/t* (h) thaw (*ice*), defrost (*refrigerator*). **II** *v/i* (sn) thaw.

Abtei [ap'taɪ] *f* (-; -en) *eccl.* abbey.

Abteil [ap'taɪl] *n* (-[e]s; -e) compartment. '**abteilen** *v/t* (*sep,* -ge-, h) divide, partition off. '**Abteilung** *f* (-; -en) division, partitioning.

Ab'teilung² f (-; -en) **1.** department, ✺ ward. **2.** ✕ detachment. **3.** *sports*: section, squad.

Ab'teilungsleiter(in f) m a) head of a department, b) floor manager(ess).

'abtippen v/t (sep, -ge-, h) F type (out).

Äbtissin [ɛp'tɪsɪn] f (-; -nen) abbess.

'abtöten v/t (sep, -ge-, h) kill, deaden.

'abtragen v/t (irr, sep, -ge-, h, → **tragen**) **1.** clear away, pull down (house), level (hill). **2.** (a. **sich** ~) wear out. **3.** pay off.

abträglich ['aptrɛːklɪç] adj detrimental (dat to).

'abtrai,nieren v/t (sep, h) work off.

'Abtrans,port m (-[e]s, -e) transportation. **'abtranspor,tieren** v/t (sep, h) take away.

'abtreiben (irr, sep, -ge-, → **treiben**) I v/t (h) ✺. **1.** ✺ abort. II v/i **2.** (h) ✺ have an abortion. **3.** (sn) drift off (course).

'Abtreibung f (-; -en) ✺ (**e-e** ~ **vornehmen lassen** have an) abortion.

'abtrennen v/t (sep, -ge-, h) **1.** separate. **2.** detach. **3.** take off (sleeve etc). **4.** sever (limb).

'abtreten (irr, sep, -ge-, → **treten**) I v/t (h) **1.** (dat, an acc to) give up, ♗ cede: **j-m et.** ~ **a.** let s.o. have s.th. **2.** wear (out) (carpet etc), wear down (heels etc). **3.** wipe off (mud, snow): F (**sich**) **die Füße** ~ wipe one's shoes. II v/i (sn) **4.** go off, thea. (make one's) exit (a. F fig.), government etc: resign. **5.** ✕ ⤙ dismiss! **'Abtretung** f (-; -en) (an acc to) ♗ transfer, cession.

'abtrocknen v/t, v/i (sep, -ge-, h) dry: (Geschirr) ~ dry up.

abtrünnig ['aptrʏnɪç] adj unfaithful, disloyal: ~ **werden** (dat) → **abfallen** 6, 7.

Abtrünnige ['aptrʏnɪgə] m, f (-n; -n) deserter, eccl. apostate.

'abtun v/t (irr, sep, -ge-, h, → **tun**) fig. dismiss (**als** as).

'abtupfen v/t (sep, -ge-, h) dab.

'abverlangen v/t (sep, h) → **abfordern**.

'abwägen v/t (irr, sep, -ge-, h, → **wägen**) fig. weigh.

'abwählen v/t (sep, -ge-, h) **1. j-n** ~ vote s.o. out of office. **2.** ped. drop (subject).

'abwälzen v/t (sep, -ge-, h) (**auf** acc on[to]) shuffle off, offload: **die Verantwortung auf j-n** ~ shift the responsibility (F pass the buck) to s.o.

'abwandeln v/t (sep, -ge-, h) modify.

'abwandern v/i (sep, -ge-, sn) **1.** move (away), migrate, sports: leave (the club). **2.** ✝ capital: be drained off.

'Abwanderung f (-; -en) migration, a. ✝ exodus, of scientists: brain drain.

'Abwandlung f (-; -en) modification.

'Abwärme f (-; no pl) waste heat.

'abwarten (sep, -ge-, h) I v/t wait for: **das bleibt abzuwarten** that remains to be seen. II v/i wait (and see): F ~ (**und Tee trinken**)! (let's) wait and see!

abwärts ['apvɛrts] adv down, downward(s). **'abwärtsgehen** v/impers (irr, sep, -ge-, sn, → **gehen**) **es geht abwärts mit** s.o., s.th. is going downhill.

'Abwärtstrend m downward trend.

'Abwasch m (-[e]s; no pl) **1.** washing-up: F **das ist ein** ~! that can be done in one go! **2.** dirty dishes. **'abwaschbar** adj washable. **'abwaschen** (irr, sep, -ge-, h, → **waschen**) I v/t wash off, wash up. II v/i do the dishes, do the washing-up.

'Abwaschwasser n dishwater.

'Abwasser n (-s; ⸚) waste water, sewage.

'Abwasserleitung f sewerage.

'abwechseln v/i (sep, -ge-, h) alternate, persons: (a. **sich** ~) a. take turns (**bei** in), rotate. **'abwechselnd** I adj alternating. II adv alternately, by turns.

'Abwechslung f (-; -en) change, diversion: ~ **brauchen** need a change; ~ **bringen in** (acc) vary, liven up; **zur** ~ for a change. **'abwechslungsreich** adj varied, life: eventful.

'Abweg m (-[e]s; -e) fig. **auf** ~**e geraten** go astray. **abwegig** ['apveːgɪç] adj **1.** wrong. **2.** absurd.

'Abwehr f (-; no pl) **1.** warding off, repulse (of attack etc). **2.** sports: a) defen/ce (Am. -se), b) by goalkeeper: save. **3.** fig. refusal. **4.** (**auf** ~ **stoßen** meet with) resistance. **5.** F ✕ counterintelligence. **'abwehren** (sep, -ge-, h) I v/t **1.** a) beat back, repulse (attack), b) sport: block (shot, punch), c) fig. ward off (danger etc). **2.** fig. refuse (thanks). II v/i **3.** fig. refuse. **4.** sports: block, goalkeeper: save, soccer: clear.

'Abwehr|haltung f psych. defensiveness. **~kräfte** pl ✺ resistance. **~mecha,nismus** m defen/ce (Am. -se) mechanism. **~reakti,on** f defensive reaction (**gegen** to). **~spieler(in** f) m sports: defender, *pl* defen/ce (*Am.* -se). **~stoffe** *pl* ✿ antibodies.

'**abweichen** *v/i* (*irr, sep,* -ge-, sn, → **weichen**) deviate (**vom Kurs** from the course), depart (**von der Regel** from the rule): (**voneinander**) ~ differ, vary; **vom Thema** ~ digress from the subject.

'**abweichend** *adj* divergent: (**voneinander**) ~ differing, varying.

'**Abweichler** *m* (-s; -) *pol.* deviationist.

'**Abweichung** *f* (-; -en) **1.** difference. **2.** (**von** from) deviation, digression, departure.

'**abweiden** *v/t* (*sep,* -ge-, h) crop.

'**abweisen** *v/t* (*irr, sep,* -ge-, h, → **weisen**) **1.** turn *s.o.* away, refuse to see: **schroff** ~ rebuff. **2.** reject, refuse, 🏛 dismiss. **3.** ✕ repulse. '**abweisend** *adj* unfriendly, cool. '**Abweisung** *f* (-; -en) rejection, refusal, 🏛 *etc* dismissal.

'**abwenden** *v/t* (*irr, sep,* -ge-, h, → **wenden**) turn away (*a.* **sich ~**), *a. fig.* avert, ward off: **sich** (**innerlich**) ~ **von** turn one's back on.

'**abwerben** *v/t* (*irr, sep,* -ge-, h, → **werben**) entice away.

'**abwerfen** *v/t* (*irr, sep,* -ge-, h, → **werfen**) **1.** throw off (*coat etc*). **2.** drop (*bombs*). **3.** throw (*rider*). **4.** shed (*skin, leaves, etc*). **5.** discard (*playing card*). **6.** *fig.* yield (*profit*), bear (*interest*).

'**abwerten** *v/t* (*sep,* -ge-, h) ♥ devalue.

'**abwertend** *adj fig.* depreciative.

'**Abwertung** *f* (-; -en) **1.** ♥ devaluation. **2.** *fig.* depreciation.

'**abwesend** *adj* **1.** absent, *pred* away, out, not in. **2.** *fig.* absent-minded, faraway (*look*). '**Abwesende** *m, f* (-n; -n) absentee: **die ~n** those absent.

'**Abwesenheit** *f* (-; *no pl*) **1.** (**durch** ~) **glänzen** be conspicuous by one's absence. **2.** *fig.* absent-mindedness.

'**abwetzen** *v/t* (*sep,* -ge-, h) wear out.

'**abwickeln** *v/t* (*sep,* -ge-, h) **1.** unwind. **2.** ♥ deal with, handle (*orders*), transact, settle (*business*), carry out (*or* through), conduct, 🏛 wind up.

'**Abwicklung** *f* (-; -en) ♥ handling, settlement, 🏛 winding-up, *Am.* wind-up.

'**abwiegen** *v/t* (*irr, sep,* -ge-, h, → **wiegen**) weigh out.

'**abwimmeln** *v/t* (*sep,* -ge-, h) F brush *s.o.* off.

'**abwinkeln** *v/t* (*sep,* -ge-, h) bend.

'**abwinken** (*sep,* -ge-, h) **I** *v/t mot. racing:* flag down. **II** *v/i* give a sign of refusal.

'**abwischen** *v/t* (*sep,* -ge-, h) a) wipe *s.th.* (clean), b) wipe *s.th.* off.

abwracken ['apvrakən] *v/t* (*sep,* -ge-, h) break up, scrap.

'**abwürgen** *v/t* (*sep,* -ge-, h) **1.** stall, kill (*engine*). **2.** *fig.* choke off (*discussion*).

'**abzahlen** *v/t* (*sep,* -ge-, h) a) pay off, b) pay by instal(l)ments.

'**abzählen** *v/t* (*sep,* -ge-, h) a) count, b) count out: F **das kann man sich an den Fingern ~** that's not hard to guess.

'**Abzahlung** *f* (-; -en) a) payment by (*Am.* on) instal(l)ments, b) payment (in full), c) instal(l)ment: **auf ~** on hire purchase, on the instal(l)ment plan.

'**abzapfen** *v/t* (*sep,* -ge-, h) tap, draw.

'**abzäunen** ['aptsɔynən] *v/t* (*sep,* -ge-, h) fence off (*or* in).

'**Abzeichen** *n* (-s; -) badge, ✕ *a.* insignia, ✈ marking.

'**abzeichnen** (*sep,* -ge-, h) **I** *v/t* **1.** (**von** from) copy, draw. **2.** initial, sign. **II** **sich ~ 3.** stand out (**gegen** against), show. **4.** *fig.* be emerging, be in the offing, *danger etc*: loom.

'**abziehen** (*irr, sep,* -ge-, → **ziehen**) **I** *v/t* (h) **1.** take off, pull off (*ring etc*). **2.** strip off (*skin, bedsheets*), strip (*bed*), skin (*rabbit, tomato, etc*). **3.** take out (*key*). **4.** (**von** from) ♈ subtract, ♥ deduct. **5.** make a copy (*or* copies) of, *phot.* print. **6.** whet, sharpen (*knife*), surface (*parquet*). **7.** ✕ withdraw. **8.** draw off, tap. **9.** F give, throw (*a party*): → **Schau** 2. **II** *v/i* (sn) **10.** move off, F a. go off, clear out (*or* off), *esp.* ✕ a. withdraw. **11.** *smoke:* escape. **12.** *storm:* pass.

'**abzielen** *v/i* (*sep,* -ge-, h) ~ **auf** (*acc*) aim at, be aimed at.

'**Abzug** *m* (-[e]s; ⸚e) **1.** *no pl esp.* ✕ withdrawal. **2.** ⊙ outlet, escape. **3.** copy, *phot. print. print.* proof. **4.** ♥ a) deduction, b) discount: **nach ~ aller Kosten** all charges deducted; **vor** (**nach**) ~ **der Steuern** before (after) taxation. **5.** trigger (*of gun*). **abzüglich** ['aptsy:klıç] *prep* (*gen*) less, deducting.

'**abzugsfähig** *adj* deductible.

'**Abzugshaube** *f* cooker hood.

'**Abzugsrohr** *n* ⊙ offlet.

'**Abzweigdose** *f* ⚡ conduit box.

'abzweigen (*sep*, -ge-) **I** *v/i* (sn) branch off. **II** *v/t* (h) set aside.

'Abzweigung *f* (-; -en) turn-off.

Accessoires [aksɛ'sŏa:r(s)] *pl* accessories.

Acetat [atse'ta:t] *n* (-s; -e) 🜊 acetate.

ach [ax] *int* oh!: **~ je!** oh dear!; **~ komm!** come on!; **~ nein?** you don't say so?; **~ so!** oh, I see!; **~ was!**, **~ wo!** of course not!; **~ und weh schreien** wail. **Ach: F mit ~ und Krach** by the skin of one's teeth; **mit ~ und Krach durch e-e Prüfung kommen** scrape through an exam.

Achat [a'xa:t] *m* (-[e]s; -e) *min.* agate.

Achillesferse [a'xɪlɛs-] *f* (-; *no pl*) *fig.* Achilles' heel. **A'chillessehne** *f anat.* Achilles' tendon.

Achse [a'ksə] *f* (-; -n) axis, *pl* axes, ⚙ axle: F **auf (der) ~ sein** be on the move.

Achsel ['aksəl] *f* (-; -n) shoulder: **die ~** (*or* **mit den ~n) zucken** shrug one's shoulders. **~höhle** *f* armpit. **~zucken** *n* (-s) shrug (of one's shoulders).

Achsschenkel *m* (-s; -) *mot.* stub axle, *Am.* steering knuckle.

Achsschenkelbolzen *m mot.* kingpin.

acht [axt] *adj* eight: **in ~ Tagen** in a week('s time); **heute in ~ Tagen** today week; **vor ~ Tagen** a week ago; **alle ~ Tage** every other week.

Acht[1] *f* (-; -en) eight.

Acht[2] *f* (-; *no pl*) *hist.* outlawry.

Acht[3]: **außer ♀ lassen** disregard; **et. in ♀ nehmen** take care of s.th., watch s.th.; **sich in ♀ nehmen vor** (*dat*) beware of.

'achte *adj eighth:* **am ~n Mai** on the eighth of May, on May the eighth.

Achteck *n* (-[e]s; -e) ⯎ octagon.

Achtel ['axtəl] *n* (-s; -) eighth (part). **~note** *f ♪* quaver. **~takt** *m ♪* quaver time.

achten ['axtən] (h) **I** *v/t* **1.** respect. **2.** observe (*laws*). **II** *v/i* **~ auf** (*acc*) a) pay attention to, b) keep an eye on, c) be careful with, d) attach importance to; **~ Sie darauf, daß ...** see to it that ...

ächten ['ɛçtən] *v/t* (h) *hist.* outlaw, *fig.* ostracize.

achtens ['axtəns] *adv* eighthly.

'Achter *m* (-s; -) *rowing:* eight. **~bahn** *f* roller coaster. **~deck** *n ⚓* quarterdeck.

achtfach *adj and adv* eightfold.

'achtgeben *v/i* (*irr, sep*, -ge-, h, → **geben**) **~ auf** (*acc*) → **achten** II a-c; **gib acht!** look out!, be careful!

acht'hundert *adj* eight hundred.

achtjährig ['axtjɛ:rɪç] *adj* **1.** eight-year--old. **2.** *period etc* of eight years.

'achtlos *adj* careless, thoughtless.

'Achtlosigkeit *f* (-; *no pl*) carelessness.

'achtmal *adv* eight times.

'achtsam *adj* attentive, careful.

Acht'stundentag *m* eight-hour day.

'achtstündig [-ʃtʏndɪç] *adj* eight-hour.

'achttägig [-tɛ:gɪç] *adj* lasting a week, a week's *trip etc.*

'Achtung *f* (-; *no pl*) **1.** (**vor** for) respect, esteem: **große ~ genießen** be highly regarded; **in j-s ~ steigen** rise in s.o.'s esteem; **sich ~ verschaffen** make o.s. respected; F **alle ~!** hats off! **2. ~!** look out!, *esp. adm. and* ✕ attention!, *on signboards:* danger!, caution!

'Ächtung *f* (-; -en) *hist.* outlawing, *fig.* ostracism.

'Achtungserfolg *m* succès d'estime.

'achtungsvoll *adj* respectful.

'achtzehn *adj* eighteen.

achtzig ['axtsɪç] *adj* eighty: F **auf ~ sein** be hopping mad. **'Achtzig** *f* (-; *no pl*) eighty: **er ist Mitte (der) ~** he is in his mid-eighties. **achtziger** ['axtsɪgər] *adj* **die ~ Jahre** the eighties. **'Achtziger** *m* (-s; -), **'Achtzigerin** *f* (-; -nen) octogenarian, man (woman) in his (her) eighties. **'achtzigst** *adj* eightieth.

ächzen ['ɛçtsən] *v/i* (h) groan (**vor** with).

Acker ['akər] *m* (-s; ⸚) field, farmland. **~bau** *m* (-[e]s; *no pl*) agriculture, farming. **~land** *n* (-[e]s; *no pl*) farmland.

ackern ['akərn] *v/i* (h) **1.** plough, *Am.* plow. **2.** F slog (away).

Acrylfarbe [a'kry:l-] *f* acrylic paint.

ad absurdum [at ap'zʊrdom] *et.* **~ führen** reduce s.th. to absurdity.

ad acta [at 'akta] *fig. et.* **~ legen** consider s.th. closed.

Adam ['a:dam] *m* (-s; *no pl*) *Bibl. and fig.* Adam: F **seit ~s Zeiten** from the beginning of time. **'Adam 'Riese:** F *humor.* **nach ~** according to Cocker.

'Adamsapfel *m anat.* Adam's apple.

'Adamsko,stüm *n* F *humor.* **im ~** in one's birthday suit.

Adapter [a'daptər] *m* (-s; -) ⚡ adapter.

adäquat [adɛ'kva:t] *adj* adequate.

addieren [a'di:rən] *v/t* (h) add (up).

Ad'dierma,schine *f* adding machine.

Addition [adi'tsĭo:n] *f* (-; -en) addition.

ade [a'de:] *int* good-bye(e) (*a. fig.*).

Adel ['a:dəl] *m* (-s; *no pl*) a) aristocracy, b) title: **von ~ sein** be of noble birth. **ad(e)lig** ['a:d(ə)lɪç] *adj* noble (*a. fig.*), titled. **Ad(e)lige** ['a:d(ə)lɪgə] *m, f* (-n; -n) aristocrat, nobleman (noblewoman): **die ~n** the nobility. **adeln** ['a:dəln] *v/t* (h) make *s.o.* a peer, *a. fig.* ennoble.

'Adelskrone *f* coronet.

'Adelsstand *m* (-[e]s; *no pl*) nobility: **in den ~ erheben** raise to the peerage.

Ader ['a:dər] *f* (-; -n) vein, *fig. a.* bent: **er hat e-e humoristische ~** he has a streak of humo(u)r.

'Aderlaß *m* (-sses; -sse) 💉, *a. fig.* bloodletting, bleeding.

ädern ['ɛ:dərn] *v/t* (h) vein.

Adjektiv ['atjɛkti:f] *n* (-s; -e) adjective. **adjektivisch** ['atjɛkti:vɪʃ] *adj* adjectival.

Adjutant [atju'tant] *m* (-en; -en) ✗ adjutant.

Adler ['a:dlər] *m* (-s; -) eagle. **'Adlerauge** *n* eagle eye: *fig.* **~n haben** be eagle-eyed. **'Adlernase** *f* aquiline nose.

Admiral [atmi'ra:l] *m* (-s; -e) admiral. **Admiralität** [atmirali'tɛ:t] *f* (-; -en) admiralty. **Admi'ralstab** *m* naval staff.

adoptieren [adɔp'ti:rən] *v/t* (h) adopt. **Adoption** [adɔp'tsio:n] *f* (-; -en) adoption. **Adop'tiveltern** *pl* adoptive parents. **Adop'tivkind** *n* adopted child.

Adrenalin [adrena'li:n] *n* (-s; *no pl*) 🐾, 💉 adrenalin(e).

Adreßbuch [a'drɛsbu:x] *n* directory.

Adresse [a'drɛsə] *f* (-; -n) address: ✝ **erste ~** first-class borrower; F *fig.* **bei j-m an die falsche ~ geraten** come to the wrong person. **A'dressenverzeichnis** *n* mailing list.

adressieren [adrɛ'si:rən] *v/t* (h) (**an** *acc* to) address, direct: *falsch ~* misdirect.

adrett [a'drɛt] *adj* neat.

adsorbieren [atzɔr'bi:rən] *v/t* (h) 🐾 adsorb. **Adsorption** [atzɔrp'tsio:n] *f* (-; -en) 🐾 adsorption.

Advent [at'vɛnt] *m* (-[e]s; *no pl*) Advent. **Ad'vents...** Advent (*wreath, season, etc*).

Adverb [at'vɛrp] *n* (-s; -bien [-biən]) adverb. **adverbial** [-'bia:l] *adj* adverbial.

Aerobic [ɛ'ro:bɪk] *n* (-s; *no pl*) aerobics. **aerodynamisch** [aerody'na:mɪʃ] *adj* aerodynamic.

Affäre [a'fɛ:rə] *f* (-; -n) affair: F *sich aus der ~ ziehen* get out of it.

Affe [a'fə] *m* (-n; -n) monkey, ape: F (**blöder**) **~** twit; **eingebildeter ~** conceited ass.

Affekt [a'fɛkt] *m* (-[e]s; -e) emotion: *im ~* in the heat of passion. **~handlung** *f* ⚖ act committed in the heat of passion. **affektiert** [afɛk'ti:rt] *adj* affected.

Affek'tiertheit *f* (-; *no pl*) affectation.

'affenartig *adj* apelike, simian.

'Affen|brotbaum *m* baobab. **~liebe** *f* F doting love. **~schande** *f* F crying shame. **~the,ater** *n* F hell of a fuss. **~zahn** *m* F (**e-n ~ draufhaben** go at) breakneck speed.

affig ['afɪç] *adj* F silly, affected.

Äffin ['ɛfɪn] *f* (-; -nen) she-ape, she-monkey.

Afghane [af'ga:nə] *m* (-n; -n), **Af'ghanin** *f* (-; -nen), **af'ghanisch** *adj* Afghan. **Afghanistan** [af'ga:nɪsta:n] *n* (-s) Afghanistan.

Afrika ['a:frika] *n* (-s) Africa. **Afrikaner** [afri'ka:nər] *m* (-s; -), **Afri'kanerin** *f* (-; -nen), **afri'kanisch** *adj* African.

Afro-Look [a'frolʊk] *m* (-s; *no pl*) (**im ~** with an) Afro hairstyle.

After ['aftər] *m* (-s; -) *anat.* anus.

Agent [a'gɛnt] *m* (-en; -en), **A'gentin** *f* (-; -nen) agent.

Agentur [agɛn'tu:r] *f* (-; -en) agency.

Aggregat [agre'ga:t] *n* (-[e]s; -e) aggregate, ⚙ unit. **Aggre'gatzustand** *m* *phys.* aggregate (state).

Aggression [agrɛ'sio:n] *f* (-; -en) aggression. **aggressiv** [agrɛ'si:f] *adj* aggressive. **Aggressivität** [agrɛsivi'tɛ:t] *f* (-; *no pl*) aggressiveness. **Aggressor** [a'grɛsɔr] *m* (-s; -en [agrɛ'so:rən]) aggressor.

agieren [a'gi:rən] *v/i* (h) act.

Agitation [agita'tsio:n] *f* (-; -en) political agitation. **Agitator** [agi'ta:tɔr] *m* (-s; -en [-'ta'to:rən]) (political) agitator. **agitatorisch** [agita'to:rɪʃ] *adj* rabble-rousing. **agitieren** [agi'ti:rən] *v/i* (h) agitate.

Agonie [ago'ni:] *f* (-; -) death throes.

Agrar... [a'gra:r-] agrarian, agricultural. **~erzeugnisse** *pl* agricultural produce. **~markt** *m* agricultural commodities market. **~poli,tik** *f* agricultural policy.

Ägypten [ɛ'gʏptən] *n* (-s) Egypt.

Ägypter [ɛ'gʏptər] *m* (-s; -), **Ä'gypterin** *f* (-; -nen), **ä'gyptisch** *adj* Egyptian.

ah [a:] *int* oh!, ah! **ah!** **äh** [ɛ:] *int* **1.** ugh! **2.** er!

aha [a'ha:] *int* aha!, I see!

A'ha-Erlebnis *n* aha-experience.

Ahle ['a:lə] *f* (-; -n) awl, pricker.

Ahn [a:n] *m* (-[e]s, -en; -en) ancestor.

ahnden ['a:ndən] *v/t* (h) punish.

ähneln ['ɛ:nəln] *v/i* (h) (*dat*) be (*or* look) like, resemble, take after *one's father*: **sich** (*or* **einander**) ~ be (*or* look) alike.

ahnen ['a:nən] *v/t* (h) **1.** foresee, have a presentiment (*or* foreboding) of. **2.** suspect, guess: **ohne zu** ~, **daß ...** without dreaming that ...; **wie konnte ich** ~, **daß ...** how was I to know that ...; **ich habe es geahnt!** I knew it!

'Ahnentafel *f* genealogical table.

ähnlich ['ɛ:nlɪç] *adj* similar (*dat* to): ~ **sein** → **ähneln;** F **das sieht ihm** ~! that's just like him!; **so et. Ähnliches** s.th. like that. **'Ähnlichkeit** *f* (-; -en) (*mit* to) likeness, resemblance, similarity: ~ **haben mit** → **ähneln.**

'Ahnung *f* (-; -en) presentiment, foreboding, misgiving, suspicion, F hunch: F k-e ~! no idea!; **er hat k-e (blasse)** ~ **davon** he doesn't know the first thing about it, he hasn't got a clue.

'ahnungslos *adj* **1.** unsuspecting. **2.** ignorant.

'ahnungsvoll *adj* full of misgivings.

Ahorn ['a:hɔrn] *m* (-s; -e) maple.

Ähre ['ɛ:rə] *f* (-; -n) ear: ~**n lesen** glean.

A-is ['a:ɪs] *n* (-; -) ♪ A sharp.

Akademie [akade'mi:] *f* (-; -n) academy.

Akademiker [aka'de:mikər] *m* (-s; -), **Aka'demikerin** *f* (-; -nen) university man (woman).

akademisch [aka'de:mɪʃ] *adj* academic: ~**e Bildung** university education.

Akazie [a'ka:tsiə] *f* (-; -n) acacia.

akklimatisieren [aklimati'zi:rən] *v/t* (h) (*a.* **sich** ~) *a. fig.* acclimatize. **Akklimati'sierung** *f* (-; -en) acclimatization.

Akkord [a'kɔrt] *m* (-[e]s; -e) ♪ chord.

Ak'kord² *m* ✝ (**im** ~ **arbeiten** do) piecework. ~**arbeit** *f* → **Akkord².** ~**arbeiter(in** *f*) *m* pieceworker.

Akkordeon [a'kɔrdeɔn] *n* (-s; -s) ♪ accordion.

Ak'kordlohn *m* piece wages.

akkreditieren [akredi'ti:rən] *v/t* (h) **1.** *pol.* accredit (**bei** to). **2.** ✝ open a credit for. **Akkreditiv** [akredi'ti:f] *n* (-s; -e) **1.**

pol. credentials. **2.** ✝ letter of credit (*abbr.* L/C): **j-m ein** ~ **eröffnen** open a credit in favo(u)r of s.o.

Akku ['aku] *m* (-s; -s) F, **Akkumulator** [akumu'la:tɔr] *m* (-s; -en [-a'to:rən]) accumulator.

Akkusativ ['akuzati:f] *m* (-s; -e) accusative (case). ~**ob,jekt** *n* direct object.

Akne ['aknə] *f* (-; -n) ✝ acne.

Akquisiteur [akvizi'tø:r] *m* (-s; -e) ✝ canvasser, agent.

Akribie [akri'bi:] *f* (-; *no pl*) meticulousness.

Akrobat [akro'ba:t] *m* (-en; -en), **Akro'batin** *f* (-; -nen) acrobat.

akro'batisch *adj* acrobatic.

Akt [akt] *m* (-[e]s; -e) **1.** *a. thea.* act. **2.** (sexual) act. **3.** *paint., phot.* nude.

Akte ['aktə] *f* (-; -n) *usu. pl* file, record: **e-e** ~ **anlegen** open a file (**über** *acc* on); **zu den** ~**n legen** file, *fig.* shelve.

'Akten|deckel *m* folder. ~**koffer** *m* attaché case. **&kundig** *adj* on record. ~**mappe** *f* **1.** folder. **2.** → **Aktentasche.** ~**no,tiz** *f* note, memorandum, F memo. ~**ordner** *m* file. ~**schrank** *m* filing cabinet. ~**tasche** *f* briefcase. ~**wolf** *m* (paper) shredder. ~**zeichen** *n* file (*letter: reference*) number.

Akteur [ak'tø:r] *m* (-s; -e) *a. fig.* actor.

'Aktfoto *n* nude (photograph).

Aktie ['aktsiə] *f* (-; -n) share, *Am.* stock: ~**n besitzen** hold shares (*Am.* stock) (*gen* in, of); F **wie stehen die** ~**n?** how are things?

'Aktien|gesellschaft *f* joint-stock company, *Am.* (stock) corporation. ~**kapi,tal** *n* share capital, (joint) stock. ~**mehrheit** *f* majority of stock: **die** ~ **besitzen** hold the controlling interest. ~**pa,ket** *n* block of shares.

Aktion [ak'tsio:n] *f* (-; -en) action, measure(s), ✝ campaign, drive: ~**en** activities; **in** ~ **treten** act.

Aktionär [aktsio'nɛ:r] *m* (-s; -e), **Aktio'närin** *f* (-; -nen) ✝ shareholder, *Am.* stockholder.

Akti'onsradius *m* range (of action).

aktiv [ak'ti:f] *adj* active, ✝ favo(u)rable (*balance*), ✕ regular: ~**es Wahlrecht** right to vote; ~**er Wortschatz** *a.* using vocabulary. **'Aktiv** *n* (-s; *rare* -e) *ling.* active voice. **Aktiva** [ak'ti:va] *pl* ✝ assets: ~ **und Passiva** assets and liabilities. **aktivieren** [akti'vi:rən] v/t (h) a. fig. activate.

Ak'tivposten m ✝, a. fig. asset.

Ak'tivurlaub m sporting holiday.

'Aktmo,dell n nude model.

aktualisieren [aktŭali'zi:rən] v/t (h) make topical. **aktuell** [ak'tŭɛl] adj a) topical, current, present-day, b) modern, up(-)to(-)date: **~es Problem** acute (or immediate) problem; **~e Sendung** current-affairs program(me Br.).

Akupunkteur [akupuŋk'tø:r] m (-s; -e) acupuncturist. **Akupunktur** [akupuŋk'tu:r] f (-; -en) acupuncture.

Akustik [a'kustik] f (-; no pl) acoustics.

a'kustisch adj acoustic.

akut [a'ku:t] adj acute, fig. a. urgent.

Akzent [ak'tsɛnt] m (-[e]s; -e) accent: fig. **besonderen ~ legen auf** (acc) stress. **ak'zentfrei** adj and adv without an accent. **akzentuieren** [aktsɛntu'i:rən] v/t (h) accent, esp. fig. accentuate, stress.

Akzept [ak'tsɛpt] n (-[e]s; -e) acceptance. **akzeptabel** [aktsɛp'ta:bəl] adj acceptable (**für** to). **Akzeptanz** [-'tants] f (-; no pl) fig. acceptance. **akzeptieren** [-'ti:rən] v/t (h) accept (a. ✝), agree to.

Alarm [a'larm] m (-[e]s; -e) (**blinder ~** false) alarm: a. fig. **~ schlagen** sound the alarm. **~anlage** f alarm (system).

A'larmbereitschaft f (**in ~** on the) alert.

alarmieren [alar'mi:rən] v/t (h) alarm (a. fig.), alert, call (police).

A'larm|si,gnal n alarm signal. **~stufe** f alert phase. **~zustand** m (-[e]s; no pl) (**in den ~ versetzen** put on the) alert.

Albanien [al'ba:niən] n (-s) Albania. **Al'banier** m (-s; -), **Al'banierin** f (-; -nen), **al'banisch** adj Albanian.

albern ['albərn] **I** adj silly. **II** v/i (h) fool around. **2.** silly remark. **'Albernheit** f (-; -en) **1.** no pl silliness. **2.** silly remark.

Album ['albʊm] n (-s; Alben) album.

Alchimie [alçi'mi:] f (-; no pl) alchemy.

Alge ['algə] f (-; -n) alga, pl algae.

Algebra ['algəbra] f (-; no pl) algebra.

alge'braisch [-'bra:ɪʃ] adj algebraic(al).

Algerien [al'ge:riən] n (-s) Algeria.

Al'gerier m (-s; -), **Al'gerierin** f (-; -nen) **al'gerisch** adj Algerian.

Alibi ['a:libi] n (-s; -s) alibi.

'Alibifrau f token woman.

'Alibifunkti,on f cover-up function.

Alimente [ali'mɛntə] pl maintenance.

alkalisch [al'ka:lɪʃ] adj ↑ alkaline.

Alkohol ['alkoho:l] m (-[e]s; -e) alcohol, liquor, drink. **~einfluß** m unter ~ under the influence of alcohol. **~frei** adj nonalcoholic, soft drink. **~gehalt** m alcoholic content. **~genuß** m consumption of alcohol.

Alkoholiker [alko'ho:likər] m (-s; -), **Alko'holikerin** f (-; -nen), **alko'holisch** adj alcoholic. **alkoholisieren** [alkoholi'zi:rən] v/t (h) alcoholize: **alkoholisiert** drunk. **Alkoholismus** [alko'holismʊs] m (-; no pl) alcoholism.

'Alkohol|mißbrauch m excessive drinking. **~nachweis** m mot. alcohol test. **~schmuggel** m bootlegging. **~spiegel** m blood alcohol concentration. **2süchtig** adj addicted to alcohol. **~sünder(in** f) m F mot. drunken driver. **~vergiftung** f alcoholic poisoning.

all [al] indef pron a) all, b) every: **~e beide** both (of them); **wir ~e** all of us; **fast ~e** almost everyone; **~(e) und jeder** all and sundry; **~e Welt** all the world; **ohne ~en Zweifel** without any doubt; → **alle, alles, Fall** 2.

All n (-s; no pl) **1.** universe. **2.** (outer) space.

alle ['alə] adj pred F **1.** all gone, finished, money: all spent: **~ machen** finish. **2.** dead beat, bushed.

Allee [a'le:] f (-; -n) avenue.

Allegorie [alego'ri:] f (-; -n) allegory.

allein [a'laın] **I** adj pred and adv a) alone, a. by oneself, on one's own, a. in private, b) only: **ganz ~** all alone; **~ stehen** be unattached, be single; **einzig und ~** (simply and) solely; **du ~ bist schuld!** it's all your fault!; (**schon) ~ der Gedanke** the very (or mere) thought. **II** conj but, however.

Al'lein|erbe m sole heir. **~erbin** f sole heiress. **~erziehende,** m f (-n; -n) single parent (or father, mother). **~gang** m solo: **im ~** sports: solo, fig. a. single-handed. **~herrschaft** f autocracy. **~herrscher(in** f) m autocrat.

al'leinig adj only, sole, exclusive.

Al'lein|inhaber(in f) m sole owner. **2reisend** adj **~e Kinder** unaccompanied minors. **~schuld** f (-; no pl) sole responsibility. **~sein** n (-s; no pl) loneliness: **Angst vor dem ~** fear of being alone. **2stehend** adj single, w.s. unattached.

~stehende m, f (-n; -n) single. ~unterhalter(in f) m thea. solo entertainer. ~verdiener(in f) m sole earner. ~vertretung f (-; no pl) sole agency. ~vertrieb m (-s; no pl) den ~ haben für be the sole distributors of.

'alle|mal adv 1. always, every time: ein für ~ once and for all. 2. F easily.

'allen'falls adv 1. if need be. 2. possibly, perhaps. 3. at (the) most, at best.

'allent'halben adv everywhere.

aller... [alər-] with sup very best, highest, etc, best, highest, etc of all.

'aller'dings [-'dɪŋs] adv 1. but, though, however. 2. F indeed, certainly.

'aller'erst adv zu ~ first of all.

Allergen [alɛr'geːn] n (-s; -e) allergenic.

Allergie [alɛr'giː] f (-; -n) allergy.

al'lergisch [-gɪʃ] allergic (gegen to).

'aller'hand adj F quite a lot, a good deal: das ist ja ~! a) not bad!, b) that's a bit thick!

'Aller'heiligen n (-) All Saints' Day.

'aller'höchstens adv at the very most.

allerlei ['alər'laɪ] adj all kinds of.

'Aller'lei n (-s; no pl) medley.

'aller'letzt adj very latest.

'aller'liebst adj (very) lovely, sweet.

'Aller'seelen n (-) All Souls' Day.

'aller'seits adv F guten Morgen ~! good morning everybody!

'Aller'welts... ordinary, common.

'Aller'werteste m (-n; -n) F posterior.

'alles indef pron 1. all, everything, the lot: ~ in allem (taken) all in all; vor allem above all; er kann ~ he can do anything; auf ~ gefaßt sein be prepared for the worst; j-n über ~ lieben love s.o. more than anything; F um ~ in der Welt! for heaven's sake!; → Mädchen 2. 2. F everybody: ~ aussteigen! get out everybody, please!

'alle'samt adv F all (of them or us etc).

'all'gegenwärtig adj omnipresent.

'allge'mein I adj general: von ~em Interesse of general interest; auf ~en Wunsch by popular request; unter ~er Zustimmung by common consent; ~es Wahlrecht universal suffrage; ~e Wehrpflicht compulsory military service; im ~en → II adv generally, in general, on the whole: es ist ~ bekannt, daß it is a well-known fact that; ~ beliebt popular with everyone; ~ gespro

chen generally speaking; es ist ~ üblich it is common usage.

'Allge'mein|befinden n general state of health. ~bildung f general education.

'allge'meingültig adj universally valid.

'Allge'meinheit f (-; no pl) (general) public.

'Allge'meinmedi‚zin f general medicine: Arzt für ~ general practitioner.

'allge'meinverständlich adj (easily) intelligible.

'Allge'meinwissen n general knowledge. ~wohl n public welfare.

All'heilmittel n a. fig. cure-all.

Allianz [a'liants] f (-; -en) alliance.

Alligator [ali'gaːtor] m (-s; -en [-gaːto:rən]) alligator.

alliiert [ali'iːrt] adj allied: hist. die Alliierten the Allies.

'all'jährlich adj annual(ly adv), yearly, adv a. every year.

'All'macht f (-; no pl) omnipotence.

all'mächtig adj omnipotent, almighty.

allmählich [al'mɛːlɪç] adj gradual(ly adv), adv a. by degrees, slowly.

Allopathie [alopa'tiː] f (-; no pl) ✻ allopathy.

'Allpar'teien... all-party ...

'Allrad... all-wheel (drive etc).

allseitig ['alzaɪtɪç] adj general, universal, allround: zur ~en Zufriedenheit to the satisfaction of everybody.

'allseits adv on (or from) all sides.

'Alltag m (-[e]s; no pl) everyday life: (grauer) ~ daily routine. all'täglich adj everyday, usual, ordinary, banal.

'alltags adv on workdays.

'Alltags... everyday (clothes etc).

Allüren [a'lyːrən] pl contp. affectation, airs (and graces).

'all'wissend adj omniscient.

all'wöchentlich adj and adv weekly.

'allzu adv far too: nicht ~ spät not too late. ~'gut adv too well. ~'sehr adv all too much. ~'viel adv too much: ~ ist ungesund enough is as good as a feast.

'Allzweck... all-purpose ...

Alm [alm] f (-; -en) alpine pasture, alp.

Almosen ['almoːzən] n (-s; -) alms, fig. contp. pittance, Am. handout.

'Almosenempfänger(in f) m pauper.

Alpen ['alpən] pl Alps. ~rose f Alpine rose. ~veilchen n cyclamen. ~vorland n (-[e]s; no pl) foothills of the Alps.

Alphabet [alfa'be:t] *n* (-[e]s; -e) alphabet. **alpha'betisch** *adj* alphabetical: **~ ordnen → alphabetisieren** [-beti'zi:rən] *v/t* (h) arrange in alphabetical order. **alphanu'merisch** *adj* alphanumeric.

alpin [al'pi:n] *adj* Alpine: **→ Kombination 3. Alpinismus** [alpi'nɪsmʊs] *m* (-; *no pl*) alpinism. **Alpinist** [-'nɪst] *m* (-en; -en), **Alpi'nistin** *f* (-; -nen) alpinist.

'Alptraum *m* a. *fig.* nightmare.

als [als] *conj* **1.** a) as, *after comp*: than: **sobald ~ möglich** as soon as possible; **mehr ~ genug** more than enough, b) *negation*: but: **alles andere ~ hübsch** anything but pretty. **2.** as, in one's capacity of: **~ Entschuldigung** as (*or* by way of) excuse; **er starb ~ Bettler** he died (as) a beggar; **~ Mädchen hatte sie k-e Chance** being a girl she had no chance. **3.** ~ **ob** as if, as though. **4.** a) when, as, b) while: **damals**, ~ at the time when; **gerade** ~ just as.

also ['alzo] *conj* **1.** so, therefore. **2.** F then: **~ gut!** very well (then)!; **na ~!** there you are!; **du kommst ~ nicht?** you're not coming then?

alt [alt] *adj* **1.** old, aged: **~ werden → altern; wie ~ bist du?** how old are you?; **er ist zehn Jahre ~** he is ten (years old); **ein zehn Jahre ~er Junge** a ten-year-old boy; **er ist (doppelt) so ~ wie ich** he is (twice) my age; **auf m-e ~en Tage** in my old age; **fig. das ~e Lied** the same old story; *humor.* **hier werde ich nicht ~** I won't be here much longer; **~ älter, Hase.** **2.** old, ancient: **das ~e Rom** ancient Rome; **die ~en Sprachen** the classical languages. **3.** old, long-standing (*friendship etc*). **4.** old, former (*pupil etc*): **in ~en Zeiten** in former times; **es bleibt alles beim ~en** everything remains as it was (before). **5.** old, stale (*bread etc*) used, second-hand: **→ Eisen.**

Alt *m* (-s; -e) ♩ alto.

Altar [al'ta:r] *m* (-[e]s; ̈-e) altar. **~bild** *n*, **~blatt** *n*, **~gemälde** *n* altarpiece.

'altbacken *adj* **1.** stale. **2.** F *fig.* antiquated.

'Altbau *m* (-[e]s; -ten) old building.

'Altbausa,nierung *f* rehabilitation of old housing. **'Altbauwohnung** *f* flat (*Am.* apartment) in an old building.

'altbe'kannt *adj* well-known.

'altbe'währt *adj* well-tried.

'altdeutsch *adj* old German.

Alte[1] ['altə] *m* (-n; -n) old man: **die ~n** old people; F **der ~** a) (*father, husband*) the old man, b) the boss; **er ist wieder ganz der ~** he is quite himself again.

'Alte[2] *f* (-n; -n) **1.** old woman: F **die ~** a) (*mother, wife*) the old lady, b) the boss. **2.** *zo.* mother.

'alt'ehrwürdig *adj* time-hono(u)red.

'alt'eingesessen *adj* old-established.

'Alteisen *n* scrap iron.

'Altenheim *n* old people's home. **'Altenpfleger(in** *f*) *m* geriatric nurse. **'Altenteil** *n* sich aufs **~ zurückziehen** retire.

Alter ['altər] *n* (-s; *no pl*) **1.** a) age, b) (old) age: **im ~ von 20 Jahren** at the age of 20; **er ist in m-m ~** he is my age; **mittleren ~s** middle-aged. **2.** old people.

älter ['ɛltər] *adj* **1.** older, elder: **mein ~er Bruder** my elder brother; **er ist (3 Jahre)** ~ **als ich** he is my senior (by three years); **er sieht (10 Jahre)** ~ **aus als er ist** he looks (10 years) more than his age. **2.** elderly. **3.** ⚖ prior.

altern ['altərn] *v/i* (sn) grow old, age.

alternativ [alterna'ti:f] *adj*, **Alternative** [-'ti:və] *f* (-; -n) alternative.

'Alters|erscheinung *f* sign of old age. **~genosse** *m*, **~genossin** *f* contemporary. **~grenze** *f* age-limit: **flexible** ~ flexible retirement age. **~gründe** *pl* **aus ~n** for reasons of age. **~gruppe** *f* age group. **~heim** *n* old people's home. **~klasse** *f* *esp. sports*: age group. **~pyra,mide** *f* *sociol.* age pyramid. **~rente** *f* old-age pension. ⚖**schwach** *adj* infirm, *a.* F *fig.* decrepit, rickety. **~schwäche** *f* (-; *no pl*) infirmity (of old age): **an ~ sterben** die of old age. **~unterschied** *m* age difference. **~versorgung** *f* old-age pension (scheme).

'Altertum *n* (-[e]s; *no pl*) antiquity.

altertümlich ['altərty:mlıç] *adj* **1.** ancient. **2.** antiquated.

ältest ['ɛltəst] *adj* **1.** oldest. **2.** eldest (*son etc*). **'Älteste** *m*, *f* (-n; -n) eldest, oldest: **mein ~r** my eldest son.

'Altglas *n* ♺ used glass.

'Altgriechisch *n* Old Greek.

'alt'hergebracht *adj* traditional.

'Althochdeutsch *n* Old High German.

Altist [al'tıst] *m* (-en; -en), **Al'tistin** *f* (-; -nen) ♩ alto(-singer).

'**altjüngferlich** adj old-maidish.
'**altklug** adj precocious.
'**Altlasten** pl old neglected deposits of toxic waste.
ältlich ['ɛltlɪç] adj elderly, oldish.
'**Altmateri,al** n ⚙ salvage.
'**Altmeister** m 1. sports: ex-champion. 2. fig. past master.
'**Altme,tall** n scrap metal.
'**altmodisch** adj old-fashioned.
'**Altöl** n ⚙ waste oil, used oil.
'**Altpa,pier** n ⚙ waste (or used) paper.
'**Altphilo,loge** m classical philologist.
altruistisch [altru'ɪstɪʃ] adj altruistic.
'**altsprachlich** adj classical.
'**Altstadt** f old town.
'**Altstimme** f ♪ alto (voice).
'**Altwarenhändler(in** f) m second-hand dealer.
Alt'weibersommer m Indian summer.
Alufolie ['alu:-] f alumin(i)um foil.
Aluminium [alu'mi:niʊm] n (-s; no pl) aluminium, Am. aluminum.
am [am] (= an dem) prep 1. at the, on the, time: a. in the: ~ **Fenster** at the window; ~ **Ufer** on the shore; ~ **1. Mai** (on) May 1st, (on) the first of May; ~ **Anfang** at the beginning; ~ **Himmel** in the sky; ~ **Leben** alive; ~ **Morgen** in the morning; ~ **Wege** by the wayside. 2. before sup er war ~ **tapfersten** he was (the) bravest; ~ **besten** best.
Amalgam [amal'ga:m] n (-s; -e) 🜂 amalgam. **amalgamieren** [amalga'mi:rən] v/t (h) a. fig. amalgamate.
Amateur [ama'tø:r] m (-s; -e) amateur (a. in cpds. boxer, sport, etc).
Amazone [ama'tso:nə] f (-; -n) Amazon.
Ambiente [am'biɛntə] n (-s; no pl) ambience.
Ambition [ambi'tsi̯o:n] f (-; -en) ambition.
ambivalent [ambiva'lɛnt] adj ambivalent.
Amboß ['ambɔs] m (-sses; -sse) anvil.
ambulant [ambu'lant] adj 1. ambulant, (a. ~ **behandelter Patient**) outpatient: ~ **behandelt werden** receive outpatient treatment. 2. itinerant (trade etc).
Ambulanz [ambu'lants] f (-; -en) a) mot. ambulance, b) outpatients' department, c) first-aid room.
Ameise ['a:maɪzə] f (-; -n) ant.
'**Ameisen|bär** m anteater. ~**haufen** m anthill. ~**säure** f 🜂 formic acid.

amen ['a:mɛn] int amen: **zu allem ja und** ~ **sagen** agree (meekly) to everything.
Amerika [a'me:rika] n (-s) America.
Amerikaner [ameri'ka:nər] m (-s; -), **Ameri'kanerin** f (-; -nen), **ameri'kanisch** adj American. **amerikanisieren** [amerikani'zi:rən] v/t (h) Americanize.
Amerikanismus [ameri'kanɪsmʊs] m (-; -men) ling. Americanism.
Amethyst [ame'tʏst] m (-en; -en) min. amethyst.
Ami ['ami] m (-[s]; -[s]) F Yank.
Aminosäure [a'mi:no-] f 🜂 amino acid.
Amme ['amə] f (-; -n) (wet) nurse. '**Ammenmärchen** n contp. old wives' tale.
Ammer ['amər] f (-; -n) zo. bunting.
Ammoniak [amo'ni̯ak] n (-s; no pl) 🜂 ammonia.
Amnesie [amne'zi:] f (-; -n) ♣ amnesia.
Amnestie [amnɛs'ti:] f (-; -n), **amne-'stieren** [-'ti:rən] v/t (h) 🜂🜂 amnesty.
Amöbe [a'mø:bə] f (-; -n) am(o)eba.
Amok ['a:mɔk]: ~ **laufen (fahren)** run (drive) amok. '**Amokfahrer** m mad driver. '**Amokläufer** m person running amok. '**Amokschütze** m mad gunman.
Amor ['a:mɔr] m (-s; no pl) Cupid.
amorph [a'mɔrf] adj amorphous.
Amortisation [amɔrtiza'tsi̯o:n] f (-; -en) ♱ amortization. **amortisieren** [amɔrti'zi:rən] v/t (h) amortize.
Ampel ['ampəl] f (-; -n) 1. hanging lamp. 2. traffic light(s).
Amperemeter [ampɛr'me:tər] n (-s; -) ⚡ ammeter. **Amperestunde** [am'pɛ:r-] f ⚡ ampere-hour.
Amphibien... [am'fi:bi̯ən-] amphibian.
Amphitheater [am'fi:teatər] n (-s; -) amphitheat/re (Am. -er).
Ampulle [am'pʊlə] f (-; -n) ampoule.
Amputation [amputa'tsi̯o:n] f (-; -en) ♣ amputation. **amputieren** [ampu'ti:rən] v/t (h) ♣ amputate.
Ampu'tierte m, f (-n; -n) ♣ amputee.
Amsel ['amzəl] f (-; -n) zo. blackbird.
Amt [amt] n (-[e]s; ⸚er) 1. a) post, office, b) (official) duty, function, c) task: **von** ~**s wegen** ex officio, officially; → **antreten** 1 etc. 2. office, agency, department. 3. teleph. exchange. **amtieren** [am'ti:rən] v/i (h) hold office: ~ **als** act (or officiate) as. **am'tierend** adj a) acting (mayor etc), b) reigning (champion etc). '**amtlich** adj official.

'**Amts|antritt** m bei s-m etc ~ upon his etc assuming office. **~arzt** m public-health officer. **~bereich** m competence. **~blatt** n official gazette. **~eid** m den ~ ablegen take the oath of office, be sworn in. **~enthebung** f removal from office, dismissal. **~führung** f administration (of [an] office). **~geheimnis** n a) official secret, b) official secrecy. **~gericht** n lower district court. **~geschäfte** pl official duties. **~gewalt** f (official) authority. **~handlung** f official act. **~mißbrauch** m abuse of (official) authority. **2müde** adj weary of one's office. **~peri|ode** f term (of office). **~schimmel** m humor. red tape. **~stunden** pl office hours. **~träger(in** f) m office holder. **~vorgänger(in** f) m predecessor (in office). **~vormund** m public guardian. **~zeichen** n teleph. dial(ling) tone. **~zeit** f term (of office).

Amulett [amu'lɛt] n (-[e]s; -e) charm.

amüsant [amy'zant] adj amusing.

amüsieren [amy'zi:rən] **I** v/t amuse, entertain. **II** sich ~ a) amuse o.s., have a good time, b) (über acc) laugh (at), make fun (of).

an [an] **I** prep (dat) **1.** time: on: ~ e-m kalten Tag on a cold day. **2.** place: on, at, by, near, next to: ~ der Themse on the Thames; ~ der Wand on the wall; ~ der Kreuzung at the crossing; alles ist ~ s-m Platz everything is in its place; Tür ~ Tür wohnen live door to door; fig. Kopf ~ Kopf neck and neck; er hat so et. ~ sich there is s.th. about him; es ist ~ ihm zu reden it is up to him to speak; ~ s-r Stelle in his place. **3.** by: j-n ~ der Hand führen lead s.o. by the hand; j-n ~ der Stimme erkennen recognize s.o. from (or by) his voice. **4.** ~ (und für) sich in itself, as such. **II** prep (acc) **5.** to, for: ein Brief ~ mich a letter for me. **6.** at, against: ~ die Tür klopfen knock at the door. **III** adv **7.** von ... ~ from ... (on or onward); von heute ~ from today (on); von nun ~ from now on, henceforth. **8.** F ~ - aus - on - off; das Licht ist ~ the light is on; er hatte noch s-n Mantel ~ he still had his coat on. **9.** F ~ die 100 Mark about 100 marks.

Anabolikum [ana'bo:likʊm] n (-s; -ka) ⚕ anabolic drug.

Anachronismus [anakro'nɪsmʊs] m (-; -men) anachronism.

anal [a'na:l] adj ⚕, psych. anal.

Analgetikum [anal'ge:tikʊm] n ⚕ analgesic.

analog [ana'lo:k] adj analogous (zu to).

Ana'logrechner m analogue computer.

Analpabet [analfa'be:t] m (-en; -en), **Analpha'betin** f (-; -nen) illiterate (person). **Analpha'betentum** n (-s; no pl) illiteracy.

Analyse [ana'ly:zə] f (-; -n) analysis. **analysieren** [analy'zi:rən] v/t (h) analy/se (Am. -ze). **Analysis** [a'na:lyzɪs] f (-; no pl) analysis. **Analytiker** [ana'ly:tikar] m (-s; -), **Ana'lytikerin** f (-; -nen) psych. analyst. **ana'lytisch** adj analytic(al).

Anämie [anɛ'mi:] f (-; -n) ⚕ an(a)emia.

Ananas ['ananas] f (-; -[se]) pineapple.

Anarchie [anar'çi:] f (-; -n) anarchy.

Anarchismus [anar'çɪsmʊs] m (-; no pl) anarchism. **Anarchist** [-'çɪst] m (-en; -en), **Anar'chistin** f (-; -nen) anarchist. **anar'chistisch** adj anarchic(al).

Anästhesie [anɛstɛ'zi:] f (-; -n) ⚕ an(a)esthesia. **anästhesieren** [anɛstɛ'zi:rən] v/t (h) ⚕ an(a)esthetize. **Anästhe'sist** [-'zɪst] m (-en; -en), **Anästhe'sistin** f (-; -nen) ⚕ an(a)esthetist.

Anatomie [anato'mi:] f (-; -n) **1.** anatomy. **2.** institute of anatomy. **anatomisch** [ana'to:mɪʃ] adj anatomical.

'**anbahnen** (sep, -ge-, h) **I** v/t a) pave the way for, b) open, begin (talks etc). **II** sich ~ be developing.

anbändeln ['anbɛndəln] v/i (sep, -ge-, h) F mit j-m ~ a) make up to s.o., b) pick a quarrel with s.o.

'**Anbau¹** m (-[e]s; no pl) ✎ cultivation. '**Anbau²** m (-[e]s; -ten) △ annex, extension. '**anbauen** v/t (sep, -ge-, h) **1.** cultivate, grow. **2.** (an acc) to build, add. '**Anbau|fläche** f (≠) arable land, b) area under cultivation. **~küche** f unit kitchen. **~möbel** pl sectional (or unit) furniture. **~schrank** m cupboard unit. **~wand** f wall unit.

'**anbehalten** v/t (irr, sep, h, → behalten) keep on (coat etc).

an'bei adv ✝ enclosed: ~ schicke ich Ihnen ... I am enclosing ...

'**anbeißen** (irr, sep, -ge-, h, → beißen) **I**

v/t bite into. **II** *v/i* bite, *a. fig.* take the bait.

'anbellen *v/t* (*sep*, -ge-, h) *a. fig.* bark at.

anberaumen ['anbəraʊmən] *v/t* (*sep*, h) fix, appoint.

'anbeten *v/t* (*sep*, -ge-, h, → *bieten*) **I** *v/t* offer. **II** *sich* ~ *person:* offer one's services, *opportunity:* present itself.

'Anbeter *m* (-s; -) ♂ (potential) seller.

'anbinden *v/t* (*irr, sep*, -ge-, h, → *binden*) (*an dat or acc* to) tie (up), bind, ⚓ moor, *fig.* link: → *angebunden*.

'Anblick *m* (-[e]s; -e) sight.

'anblicken *v/t* (*sep*, -ge-, h) look at, glance at: *j-n finster* ~ scowl at s.o.

'anblinken *v/t* (*sep*, -ge-, h) flash one's headlights at.

'anbrechen (*irr, sep*, -ge-, → *brechen*) **I** *v/t* (h) break into (*supplies*), start (on) (*can, pack*), open (*bottle*). **II** *v/i* (sn) begin, *a. fig.* dawn.

'anbrennen *v/i* (*irr, sep*, -ge-, sn, → *brennen*) (*a.* ~ *lassen*) burn: F *fig. er läßt nichts* ~ he doesn't miss a trick.

'anbringen *v/t* (*irr, sep*, -ge-, h, → *bringen*) **1.** a) put up (*curtain, sign, etc*), b) (*an dat* to) fix, fasten. **2.** F bring (along). **3.** make (*a request, improvements, etc*), get in (*a remark etc*), display (*knowledge*), land (*a blow*): *Kritik* ~ criticize; → *angebracht*.

'Anbruch *m* (-[e]s; *no pl*) beginning.

'anbrüllen *v/t* (*sep*, -ge-, h) bawl at.

Andacht ['andaxt] *f* (-; -en) *eccl.* a) devotion, b) prayers, c) (short) service.

andächtig ['andɛçtɪç] *adj* **1.** devout, pious, **2.** a) rapt, attentive, b) solemn: ~ *zuhören* listen with rapt attention.

'andauern *v/i* (*sep*, -ge-, h) continue, last, go on. **'andauernd** *adj* constant, continual, incessant: *er störte uns* ~ he kept interrupting us.

'Andenken *n* (-s; -) **1.** *no pl* memory: *zum* ~ *an* (*acc*) in memory of. **2.** a) keepsake, b) souvenir (*an acc* of).

ander ['andər] **I** *adj* **1.** a) other, b) different: *ein* ~*es Buch* another book; *am* ~*en Tag* (on) the next day; *das* ~*e Geschlecht* the opposite sex; *er ist ein ganz* ~*er Mensch* he is a changed man; → *Ansicht* 1. **II** *indef pron* **2.** *ein* ~*er, e-e* ~*e* someone else; *die* ~*en* the others; *der eine oder* ~*e* someone or other; *kein* ~*er als* a) no one else (*or* none) but, b) no less than. **3.** ~*es, andres* other things; *alles* ~*e* everything else; *alles* ~*e als* anything but, far from; *unter* ~*em* among other things; *eins nach dem* ~*en* one thing after the other; *das ist et. ganz* ~*es* that's a different thing altogether.

'anderen'falls *adv* otherwise.

'anderer'seits *adv* on the other hand.

'andermal *adv ein* ~ some other time.

ändern ['ɛndərn] **I** *v/t* change, alter, vary: *sein Testament* ~ alter one's will; *es läßt sich nicht* ~ it can't be helped; *ich kann es nicht* ~ I cannot help it; *das ändert nichts an der Tatsache, daß ...* that doesn't alter the fact that ... **II** *sich* ~ alter, change; *die Zeiten* ~ *sich* times are changing.

'anders *adv* **1.** differently (*als* from): ~ *werden* change; ~ *als s-e Freunde* unlike his friends; ~ *gesagt* in other words. **2.** *with pron* else: *jemand* ~ somebody (*or* anybody) else; *niemand* ~ *als er* nobody but he; *wer* ~? who else? **'andersartig** *adj* different. **'andersdenkend** *adj* thinking differently, *pol. a.* dissident. **'andersgläubig** *adj* of a different faith, heterodox. **'andersher,um I** *adv* the other way round. **II** *adj* F gay, queer.

'anderswo *adv*, **'anderswo,hin** *adv* F elsewhere, somewhere else.

'andert'halb ['andərt-] *adj* one and a half: ~ *Pfund* a pound and a half.

'Änderung *f* (-; -en) change, alteration.

'Änderungsantrag *m pol.* amendment.

'ander'weitig [-'vaɪtɪç] **I** *adj* **1.** other, further. **II** *adv* **2.** otherwise: → *vergeben* give *s.th.* to s.o. else. **3.** elsewhere.

'andeuten *v/t* (*sep*, -ge-, h) **I** *v/t* **1.** a) hint at, suggest, intimate, b) indicate, mention *s.th.* briefly. **2.** *a. fig.* outline. **II** *sich* ~ be in the offing. **'Andeutung** *f* (-; -en) hint, suggestion, insinuation.

'**andeutungsweise** adv ~ zu verstehen geben → andeuten 1 a.

'**Andrang** m (-[e]s; no pl) a) crush, press, b) rush, ✝ run (auf acc on).

'**andrehen** v/t (sep, -ge-, h) **1.** turn on, switch on (light etc). **2.** F fig. j-m et. ~ fob s.th. off on s.o.

'**androhen** v/t (sep, -ge-, h) j-m et. ~ threaten s.o. with s.th.

'**Androhung** f (-; -en) threat.

'**anecken** v/i (sep, -ge-, sn) F bei j-m ~ give offen/ce (Am. -se) to s.o.

'**aneignen** v/t (sep, -ge-, h) sich ~ **1.** a) appropriate s.th. to o.s., take possession of, b) misappropriate, usurp. **2.** acquire (knowledge), adopt (view etc).

'**Aneignung** f (-; no pl) **1.** appropriation. **2.** acquisition.

anein'ander adv (to of, etc) each other: ~ denken think of each other. ~**geraten** v/i (irr, sep, sn, → geraten) (mit with) a) clash, b) come to blows. ~**grenzen** v/i (sep, -ge-, h) border on each other. ~**reihen** v/t (sep, -ge-, h) line up, fig. string words etc together.

Anekdote [anɛk'do:tə] f (-; -n) anecdote.

'**anekeln** v/t (sep, -ge-, h) disgust, sicken: es ekelt mich an it makes me sick.

Anemone [ane'mo:nə] f (-; -n) anemone.

'**Anerbieten** n (-s; -) offer.

'**anerkannt** adj recognized, accepted.

'**anerkennen** v/t (irr, sep, h, → erkennen) a) acknowledge, recognize, b) appreciate, c) approve: sports: (nicht) ~ (dis)allow; ~**de Worte** appreciative words. '**anerkennenswert** adj commendable. '**Anerkennung** f (-; no pl) a) acknowledgement, recognition (a. pol.), b) appreciation, c) approval, ✝ acceptance (of bill): in ~ (gen) in recognition of; ~ verdienen deserve credit.

'**anerziehen** v/t (irr, sep, h, → erziehen) j-m et. ~ instil(l) s.th. into s.o.

'**anerzogen** adj acquired.

'**anfachen** v/t (sep, -ge-, h) **1.** fan. **2.** fig. kindle, stir up.

'**anfahren** (irr, sep, -ge-, → fahren) **I** v/i (sn) **1.** start (up). **II** v/t (h) **2.** deliver. **3.** ram, run into, hit. **4.** stop (♣ call) at. **5.** ✿ start. **6.** F j-n ~ snap at s.o.

'**Anfahrt** f (-; -en) **1.** journey, ride. **2.** approach, drive(way). **3.** delivery.

'**Anfall** m (-[e]s; ⁻e) **1.** ✚ attack, fit (a. fig.): humor. in e-m ~ von Großzügig-

keit in a fit (or burst) of generosity. **2.** ✝, 🔢 accrual (of a dividend etc).

'**anfallen** (irr, sep, -ge-, → fallen) **I** v/t (h) attack. **II** v/i (sn) result, work etc: come up, costs etc: arise, profit etc: accrue. '**anfällig** adj ~ für a. fig. susceptible (or prone) to. '**Anfälligkeit** f (-; no pl) proneness (für to), w.s. delicacy.

'**Anfang** m (-[e]s; ⁻e) beginning, start: am ~, im ~, zu ~ → anfangs; von ~ an (right) from the beginning (or start); ~ Mai early in May; den ~ machen begin, lead off; ein ~ ist gemacht a start has been made; noch in den Anfängen stecken be still in its infancy.

'**anfangen** (irr, sep, -ge-, h, → fangen) **I** v/t a) begin, start, b) do: ein neues Leben ~ turn over a new leaf; was soll ich bloß ~? what on earth am I to do?; er hat wieder angefangen zu rudern he has taken up rowing again; et. schlau ~ set about s.th. cleverly; mit ihm ist nichts anzufangen he's hopeless. **II** v/i begin, start: mit der Arbeit ~ begin (or start) (to) work; bei e-r Firma ~ start work(ing) with a firm; ich weiß nichts damit anzufangen I don't know what to do with (fig. make of) it; das fängt ja gut an! that's a fine start; du hast angefangen! you started it!; fängst du schon wieder an? are you at it again? '**Anfänger** m (-s; -), '**Anfängerin** f (-; -nen) beginner. '**Anfängerkurs(us)** m beginners' course.

anfänglich ['anfɛŋlɪç] **I** adj initial, original. **II** adv → '**anfangs** adv at first, at (or in) the beginning.

'**Anfangs|buchstabe** m initial letter: großer (kleiner) ~ capital (small) letter. ~**gehalt** n starting (or initial) salary. ~**gründe** pl rudiments. ~**kapital** n opening capital. ~**stadium** n initial stage. ~**zeit** f starting time.

'**anfassen** (sep, -ge-, h) **I** v/t **1.** seize, grab (an dat by), touch: j-n ~ take s.o. by the hand; fig. zum ♀ politician etc of the people, popular. **2.** fig. treat, handle, tackle (problem etc). **II** v/i (mit) ~ lend a hand, help.

'**anfauchen** v/t (sep, -ge-, h) cat: spit at; fig. j-n ~ snap at s.o.

anfechtbar ['anfɛçtba:r] adj a. 🔢 contestable. '**anfechten** v/t (irr, sep, -ge-, h, → fechten) contest (a. 🔢), appeal

from (*sentence*). **'Anfechtung** *f* (-; -en)
1. contesting, ⚖ appeal (*gen* from). **2.**
temptation.

anfeinden ['anfaɪndən] *v/t* (*sep*, -ge-, h)
be hostile to: *angefeindet werden*
meet with hostility. **'Anfeindung** *f* (-;
-en) hostility (*gen* to).

'anfertigen *v/t* (*sep*, -ge-, h) make, do,
✝, ⚙ manufacture, *pharm.* prepare:
ein Gutachten ~ deliver an expert
opinion (*über acc* on). **'Anfertigung** *f*
(-; -en) making *etc*, manufacture.

'anfeuern *v/t* (*sep*, -ge-, h) a) encourage,
b) cheer (on), *Am.* F root for.

'anflehen *v/t* (*sep*, -ge-, h) implore.

'anfliegen (*irr, sep, -ge-, → fliegen*) **I** *v/t*
(h) a) fly to, b) land at. **II** *v/i* (sn)
approach: *angeflogen kommen* come
flying (along). **'Anflug** *m* [-[e]s; ⸚e) **1.** ✈
approach: *im* ~ *sein auf* (*acc*) be approaching. **2.** *fig.* touch, trace, hint.

'Anflugschneise *f* ✈ approach lane.

'anfordern *v/t* (*sep*, -ge-, h) ask for, demand, request. **'Anforderung** *f* (-; -en)
1. (*gen* for) demand, request: *auf* ~ on
request. **2.** *pl* demands, standard: *allen*
~en genügen meet all requirements,
fill the bill; *den ~en nicht genügen* not
to be up to standard; *hohe ~en stellen*
make high demands (*an acc* on), *task*
etc: a. be very exacting.

'Anfrage *f* (-; -n) inquiry, *a. parl.* question. **'anfragen** *v/i* (*sep*, -ge-, h) inquire
(*bei j-m wegen et.* of s.o. about s.th.).

anfreunden ['anfrɔyndən] *sich* ~ (*sep*,
-ge-, h) become friends; *sich mit j-m* ~
make friends with s.o.; *sich mit e-m*
Gedanken etc ~ get to like the idea *etc*.

'anfügen *v/t* (*sep*, -ge-, h) **1.** add. **2.** enclose. **3.** ⚙ join, attach.

'anfühlen *v/t* (*sep*, -ge-, h) (*a. sich* ~) feel.

'anführen *v/t* (*sep*, -ge-, h) **1.** lead, be at
the head of, ✕ command. **2.** state,
mention, specify, give (*facts, reasons*),
produce (*evidence*), quote (*example,*
book): *zur Entschuldigung* ~ plead (as
an excuse). **3.** F dupe. **'Anführer** *m* (-s;
-), **'Anführerin** *f* (-; -nen) leader.

'Anführungs|striche, **~zeichen** *pl* quo-
tation marks, inverted commas.

'Angabe *f* (-; -n) **1.** statement, declaration, specification: *~n* information; *~n*
zur Person personal data; *nähere ~n*
machen give (further) details; *ohne* ~

von Gründen without giving reasons.
2. F showing-off. **3.** *tennis etc*: service.

'angeben (*irr, sep, -ge-, h, → geben*) **I**
v/t **1.** give, state, specify, fix (*deadline*),
name (*witness etc*). **2.** declare (*value*
etc), quote (*prices*). **3.** indicate (*direc-*
tion etc), set (*the pace*). **II** *v/i* **4.** F (*mit*)
show off ([with] *s.o., s.th.*), brag (*about,*
of). **5.** *cards*: deal first. **6.** *tennis etc*:
serve. **'Angeber** *m* (-s; -), **'Angeberin** *f*
(-; -nen) F show-off. **Angebe'rei** *f* (-;
-en) F showing-off. **'angeberisch** *adj* F
bragging.

angeblich ['angə:plɪç] *adj* alleged, *contp.*
would-be: ~ *ist er* ... he is said to be ...

'angeboren *adj* innate, inborn (*both:*
dat in), *psych.* congenital, hereditary.

'Angebot *n* (-[e]s; -e) offer, *auction*: bid,
supply (*of goods*), ✝ tender, *Am.* bid: ~
und Nachfrage supply and demand.

'angebracht **I** *pp* of **anbringen**. **II** *adj* a)
advisable, b) proper, appropriate: *es*
für ~ *halten zu gehen etc* see fit to go
etc; *nicht* ~ inappropriate.

'angebunden **I** *pp* of **anbinden**. **II** *adj*
fig. kurz ~ curt, short.

'angegossen *adj* F *wie* ~ *passen* (or
sitzen) fit like a glove.

'angegriffen **I** *pp* of **angreifen**. **II** *adj*
exhausted, weakened, poor (*health*),
affected (*organ*), strained (*nerves*).

'angehaucht **I** *pp* of **anhauchen**. **II** *adj* F
fig. er ist kommunistisch ~ he has
Communist leanings.

'angeheiratet *adj* (related) by marriage:
~er Vetter cousin by marriage.

'angeheitert *adj* (a bit) tipsy, merry.

'angehen (*irr, sep, -ge-, → gehen*) **I** *v/i*
(sn) **1.** F begin, start. **2.** *light etc*: go on,
fire etc: (begin to) burn. **3.** *plant etc*:
take root. **4.** ~ *gegen* fight against. **II**
v/t **5.** (h) attack, *fig.* tackle (*problem*). **6.**
(sn) *fig.* concern: *das geht dich nichts*
an! that's none of your business!; *was*
geht mich das an? what's that got to
do with me? **7.** (sn) F *j-n um et.* ~ ask
s.o. for s.th. **III** *v/impers* (sn) **8.** *es geht*
an it's passable; *es kann nicht* ~, *daß* ...
it can't be true that ...

'angehend *adj* future, budding.

'angehören *v/i* (*sep*, h) (*dat*) belong (to)
(*a. fig.*), be a member (of).

'Angehörige *m, f* (-n; -n) **1.** relative,

dependant: **die nächsten ~n** the next of kin; **m-e ~n** my family. **2.** member.

Angeklagte ['angəklaːktə] *m, f* (-n; -n) ⚖ defendant.

Angel[1] ['aŋəl] *f* (-; -n) hinge: *a. fig.* **aus den ~n heben** unhinge; **zwischen Tür und ~** a) in passing, b) in a hurry.

'Angel[2] *f* (-; -n) fishing rod.

'Angelegenheit *f* (-; -en) affair, matter: **das ist m-e ~** that's my business; **kümmere dich um d-e ~en!** mind your own business!

angelehnt ['angəleːnt] *adj* ajar.

angelernt I *pp of* **anlernen.** II *adj* semi-skilled (*worker*).

'Angelgerät *n* fishing tackle.

'Angelhaken *m* fish(ing) hook.

angeln ['aŋəln] I *v/i* (h) (**nach** for) fish, angle. II *v/t* (h) (*a.* F *fig.* **sich ~**) hook.

'Angelpunkt *m fig.* pivot, central issue.

'Angelrute *f* fishing rod.

'Angelsachse *m*, **'Angelsächsin** *f*, **'angelsächsisch** *adj* Anglo-Saxon.

'Angelschein *m* fishing permit.

'Angelschnur *f* fishing line.

angemessen *adj* suitable, adequate (*both: dat* to), reasonable, fair (*price*).

angenehm *adj* (*dat* to) pleasant, agreeable: → **verbinden** 2.

angenommen I *pp of* **annehmen.** II *adj* adopted, *a.* assumed (*name*). III *conj* suppose, supposing.

angepaßt I *pp of* **anpassen.** II *adj* *psych.* adjusted.

angeregt I *pp of* **anregen.** II *adj* lively.

angeschlagen I *pp of* **anschlagen.** II *adj* **1.** chipped. **2.** *boxing:* groggy. **3.** shaken, shaky, weakened (*health etc*).

angeschlossen I *pp of* **anschließen.** II *adj* ⚡ linked-up, connected.

angeschmutzt *adj* soiled.

angesehen I *pp of* **ansehen.** II *adj* respected, reputable.

'Angesicht *n* (-[e]s; -er) face: **von ~** by sight; **von ~ zu ~** face to face; **im ~** (*gen*) → **angesichts** 2. **'angesichts** *prep* (*gen*) **1.** at the sight of. **2.** in view of.

angespannt I *pp of* **anspannen.** II *adj* *fig.* tense, strained (*nerves etc*).

Angestellte ['angəʃtɛltə] *m, f* (-n; -n) (salaried) employee: **† die ~n** a. the staff. **'Angestelltenversicherung** *f* employees' insurance.

angestrengt ['angəʃtrɛŋt] I *pp of* **an-**strengen. II *adj* **1.** strained. **2.** close (*attention etc*): **~ nachdenken** think hard.

'angetan I *pp of* **antun.** II *adj* **~ sein von** be taken with.

'angetrunken I *pp of* **antrinken.** II *adj* slightly drunk.

'angewandt I *pp of* **anwenden.** II *adj* applied (*arts etc*).

'angewiesen I *pp of* **anweisen.** II *adj* **~ sein auf** (*acc*) depend on.

'angewöhnen *v/t* (*sep*) **j-m et. ~** get s.o. used to s.th.; **sich et. ~** get into the habit of, take to *smoking etc*.

'Angewohnheit *f* (-; -en) habit.

'angewurzelt *adj* **wie ~ dastehen** stand rooted to the spot.

Angina [aŋˈgiːna] *f* (-; -nen) ⚕ tonsil(l)itis: **~ pectoris** angina (pectoris).

'angleichen *v/t* (*irr, sep*, -ge-, h, → **gleichen**) (*a.* **sich ~**) (*dat, an acc* to) adapt, adjust. **'Angleichung** *f* (-; -en) (*an acc* to) adaptation, adjustment.

Angler ['aŋlər] *m* (-s; -) angler.

'angliedern *v/t* (*sep*, -ge-, h) (*an acc* to) affiliate, *pol.* annex. **'Angliederung** *f* (-; -en) affiliation, *pol.* annexation.

Anglikaner [aŋgliˈkaːnər] *m* (-s; -), **Angliˈkanerin** *f* (-; -nen), **angliˈkanisch** *adj* Anglican.

Anglist [aŋˈglɪst] *m* (-en; -en), **An'glistin** *f* (-; -nen) professor (*or* student) of English. **Anglistik** [aŋˈglɪstɪk] *f* (-; *no pl*) English language and literature, *Am.* English philology. **Anglizismus** [aŋgliˈtsɪsmʊs] *m* (-; -men) Anglicism.

Anglo... [aŋglo-] Anglo-...

'anglotzen *v/t* (*sep*, -ge-, h) F stare at.

Angorawolle [aŋˈgoːra-] *f* angora wool.

'angreifbar *adj* open to attack, *fig. a.* vulnerable. **'angreifen** (*irr, sep*, -ge-, h, → **greifen**) I *v/t* **1.** attack, 🔥 corrode: ⚖ **tätlich ~** assault. **2.** weaken, affect (*eyes etc*), strain (*nerves*): → **angegriffen** II. **3.** break into (*supplies*). **4.** → **anpacken** 2. II *v/i* attack. **'Angreifer** *m* (-s; -) attacker, *pol.* aggressor.

'angrenzen *v/i* (*sep*, -ge-, h) **~ an** (*acc*) border on. **'angrenzend** *adj* adjacent, adjoining, *fig.* related (*subjects etc*).

'Angriff *m* (-[e]s; -e) attack: ⚖ **tätlicher ~** assault (and battery); **zum ~ übergehen** take the offensive; *fig.* **et. in ~ nehmen** tackle s.th.

'**Angriffs|fläche** f fig. point of attack: **e-e ~ bieten** be vulnerable to attack; **j-m e-e ~ bieten** give s.o. a handle. **~krieg** m war of aggression. **2lustig** adj aggressive. **~spiel** n sports: attacking play. **~waffe** f offensive weapon.

'**angrinsen** v/t (sep, -ge-, h) grin at.

Angst [aŋst] f (-; ⁻e) fear, dread, terror (all: **vor** dat of), a. psych. anxiety (**um** about): (**nur**) **k-e ~!** don't be afraid!; **aus ~ lügen** lie out of fear; **aus ~, bestraft zu werden** for fear of being punished; **~ haben** be afraid (**vor** dat of); **um j-n ~ haben** be worried about s.o.; **j-n in ~ (und Schrecken) versetzen** frighten s.o. (to death); **es mit der ~ (zu tun) bekommen** get the wind up; **mir ist ⁹ und bange** I'm scared stiff.

'**Angstgegner** m sports: bogy team.

'**Angsthase** m F scaredy-cat.

ängstigen ['ɛŋstɪɡən] v/t (h) a) frighten, alarm, b) worry: **sich ~ be** afraid (**vor** dat of), be worried (**um** about).

'**Angstkäufe** [-kɔyfə] pl panic buying.

ängstlich ['ɛŋstlɪç] adj timid, nervous, anxious: **~ gehütet** jealously guarded; **~ bemüht** anxious (**zu** to). '**Ängstlichkeit** f (-; no pl) nervousness, anxiety.

'**Angstneu,rose** f anxiety neurosis.

'**Angstschrei** m cry of fear.

'**Angstschweiß** m cold sweat.

'**angstvoll** adj anxious, fearful.

'**angucken** v/t (sep, -ge-, h) F look at.

'**anhaben** v/t (irr, sep, -ge-, h, → haben) **1.** F wear, have on. **2.** **j-m nichts ~ können** be unable to get at s.o.

'**anhaften** v/i (sep, -ge-, h) **1.** (dat to) stick, cling. **2.** fig. be inherent (dat in).

'**anhalten** (irr, sep, -ge-, h, → halten) **I** v/t **1.** stop: **den Atem ~** hold one's breath; **mit angehaltenem Atem** with bated breath. **2.** **j-n zu Fleiß** etc **~** urge s.o. to be diligent etc. **II** v/i **3.** stop, pull up. **4.** last, continue, go on, weather: **hold.** '**anhaltend** adj constant, persistent, sustained. '**Anhalter** m (-s; -), '**Anhalterin** f (-; -nen) F hitchhiker: **per Anhalter fahren** hitchhike.

'**Anhaltspunkt** m clue: **k-e ~e haben** have nothing to go by.

'**Anhang** ['anhaŋ] m (-[e]s; ⁻e) **1.** a) appendix, b) supplement, c) annex. **2.** dependants, family. **3.** followers.

'**anhängen¹** (sep, -ge-, h) **I** v/t **1.** hang

up. **2.** (an acc to) mot., ⚙ couple, fig. add. **3.** F j-m et. ~ → andrehen 2; j-m **e-n Mord** etc ~ pin a murder etc on s.o. **II** **sich ~** (an acc) to hold on, cling; F fig. **sich ~ an** (acc) in a race etc: follow.

'**anhängen²** v/i (irr, sep, -ge-, h, → hängen¹) follow (a fashion etc), believe in (an idea etc): **j-m ~ reputation** etc: cling to s.o. **Anhänger** ['anhɛŋər] m (-s; -) **1.** follower, supporter, disciple, fan. **2.** pendant. **3.** mot. trailer. **4.** tag, label. '**Anhängerin** f (-; -nen) → **Anhänger 1.** '**Anhängerschaft** f (-; no pl) followers, following, fans. **anhängig** ['anhɛŋɪç] adj esp. ⚖ pending: **e-e Klage ~ machen** institute legal proceedings (**gegen** against). **anhänglich** ['anhɛŋlɪç] adj devoted. **2.** affectionate. **Anhängsel** ['anhɛŋzəl] n (-s; -) a. fig. appendage.

'**anhauchen** v/t (sep, -ge-, h) **1.** breathe on. **2.** → **angehaucht** II.

'**anhauen** v/t (sep, -ge-, h) F j-n ~ touch s.o. (**um** for).

'**anhäufen** v/t (sep, -ge-, h) (a. sich ~) accumulate, pile up. '**Anhäufung** f (-; -en) accumulation.

'**anheben** v/t (irr, sep, -ge-, h, → heben) lift (up), a. fig. raise.

'**anheften** v/t (sep, -ge-, h) (an acc to) a) fasten, b) tack, baste, c) pin.

anheimelnd ['anhaiməlnd] adj hom(e)y, cosy, familiar.

anheimstellen [an'haim-] v/t (sep, -ge-, h) **es** j-m ~ leave it to s.o.('s discretion).

'**anheizen** v/t (sep, -ge-, h) **1.** fire. **2.** F fig. fuel (strife), heat up (⚓ boom): **die Stimmung ~** whip up emotions.

'**anheuern** v/t, v/i (sep, -ge-, h) sign on.

'**Anhieb:** F **auf ~** a) at the first go, b) right off, off the cuff.

'**anhimmeln** v/t (sep, -ge-, h) F idolize.

'**Anhöhe** f (-; -n) rise, hill, elevation.

'**anhören** (sep, -ge-, h) **I** v/t listen to (a. **sich ~**), hear (witness etc): **mit ~** overhear; **j-n bis zu Ende ~** hear s.o. out; **das hört man ihm an!** you can tell by the way he talks! **II** **sich ~** sound; F **das hört sich gut an!** that sounds good! '**Anhörung** f (-; -en) ⚖ hearing.

Anilinfarbe [ani'li:n-] f anilin(e) dye.

animalisch [ani'ma:lɪʃ] adj animal.

Animateur [anima'tø:r] m (-s; -e) animator, entertainer.

Animierdame [ani'mi:r-] *f* hostess.
animieren [ani'mi:rən] *v/t* (h) **1.** encourage. **2.** *film*: animate.
Animosität [animozi'tɛ:t] *f* (-; -en) animosity.
Anis [a'ni:s] *m* (-[es]; -e) **1.** ⚘ anise. **2.** aniseed. **3.** aniseed brandy.
'ankämpfen *v/i* (*sep*, -ge-, h) ~ **gegen** fight (*or* struggle) against.
'Ankauf *m* (-[e]s; ⸚e) buying, purchase.
'ankaufen *v/t* (*sep*, -ge-, h) purchase, buy.
Anker ['aŋkər] *m* (-s; -) **1.** ⚓ anchor: *vor* ~ *gehen* drop anchor; *den* ~ *lichten* weigh anchor; *vor* ~ *liegen* ride at anchor. **2.** ⚡ armature. **~kette** *f* cable.
ankern ['aŋkərn] *v/i* (h) a) (cast) anchor, b) ride at anchor.
'Ankerplatz *m* anchorage.
'Ankerwinde *f* windlass.
'anketten *v/t* (*sep*, -ge-, h) chain (*an acc* to).
'Anklage *f* (-; -n) accusation, charge, ⚖ *a.* indictment (*wegen* for): ~ *erheben* bring (*or* prefer) a charge (*wegen* of); *unter* ~ *stehen* (*wegen*) a) be accused (of), b) be on trial (for). **'Anklagebank** *f* (-; ⸚e) ⚖ (*auf der* ~ in the) dock.
'anklagen *v/t* (*sep*, -ge-, h) (*gen or wegen*) accuse (of), charge (with). **'anklagend** *adj* accusing. **'Ankläger** *m* (-s; -) ⚖ accuser: *öffentlicher* ~ Public Prosecutor. **'Anklageschrift** *f* (bill of) indictment. **'Anklagevertreter** *m* counsel for the prosecution.
'anklammern (*sep*, -ge-, h) (*an acc* to) **I** *v/t* peg (on), ⚙ cramp. **II** *sich* ~ cling.
'Anklang *m* (-[e]s; ⸚e) **1.** reminiscence (*an acc* of). **2.** ~ *finden* (*bei*) be well received (by), go down well (with); *k-n* ~ *finden* fall flat.
'ankleben *v/t* (*sep*, -ge-, h) stick on (*an acc* to).
'Ankleideˌkabine *f* cubicle. **'ankleiden** *v/t* (*sep*, -ge-, h) (*a. sich* ~) dress.
'Ankleideraum *m* dressing room.
'anklopfen *v/i* (*sep*, -ge-, h) knock (*an acc or dat* at).
'anknabbern *v/t* (*sep*, -ge-, h) nibble at.
'anknipsen *v/t* (*sep*, -ge-, h) F switch on.
'anknüpfen (*sep*, -ge-, h) **I** *v/t* **1.** (*an acc* to) tie, knot. **2.** *fig.* begin, start (*conversation etc*), establish (*contacts*). **II** *v/i* **3.** *fig.* ~ *an* (*acc or dat*) a) go on from, b)

go back to (*s.o.'s words etc*), c) pick up the thread of (*a story etc*), d) continue (*a tradition*). **'Anknüpfungspunkt** *m fig.* starting point.
'ankommen (*irr, sep*, -ge-, sn, → **kommen**) **I** *v/i* **1.** arrive (*in dat* at, in): ~ *in* (*dat*) *a.* reach; ~ *um train etc*: arrive at, be due at. **2.** F ~ (*bei* with) a) get a job, b) go down well, *a. person*: be a success; *nicht* ~ *a.* be a flop; *damit kommt er bei mir nicht an* that cuts no ice with me. **3.** ~ *gegen* cope (*or* deal) with, *j-n a.* get the better of s.o.; *nicht* ~ *gegen a.* be powerless against. **II** *v/impers* **4.** ~ *auf* (*acc*) depend on; *es kommt* (*ganz*) *darauf an* it (all) depends. **5.** ~ *auf* (*acc*) matter; *worauf es* (*ihm*) *ankommt, ist* ... *zu gewinnen* the important thing (to him) is to win; *darauf kommt es an* that's the point. **6.** *es auf et.* ~ *lassen* risk s.th.; *ich lasse es darauf* ~ I'll risk it, I'll take a chance. **7.** *es kommt mich hart an* I find it hard.
Ankömmling ['ankœmlɪŋ] *m* (-s; -e) arrival.
'ankoppeln *v/t* (*sep*, -ge-, h) (*an acc* couple (to), dock *spacecraft* (with).
'ankotzen *v/t* (*sep*, -ge-, h) V *es kotzt e-n an* it makes you sick.
'ankreiden *v/t* (*sep*, -ge-, h) F *j-m et.* ~ blame s.o. for s.th.
'ankreuzen *v/t* (*sep*, -ge-, h) mark *s.th* with a cross.
'ankündigen (*sep*, -ge-, h) **I** *v/t* announce, bill, advertise, *fig.* herald. **II** *sich* ~ announce one's visit (*fig.* itself).
'Ankündigung *f* (-; -en) announcement (*a. fig.*), advertisement.
Ankunft ['ankʊnft] *f* (-; *no pl*) arrival.
'Ankunfts... arrival (*airport, lounge, etc*)
'Ankunftszeit *f* time of arrival.
'ankurbeln *v/t* (*sep*, -ge-, h) *fig.* step up, boost.
'anlächeln *v/t* (*sep*, -ge-, h) smile at.
'anlachen *v/t* (*sep*, -ge-, h) smile (*or* laugh) at: F *sich j-n* ~ pick s.o. up.
'Anlage *f* (-; -n) **1.** *no pl* a) laying out, b) construction, c) arrangement, layout. **2.** installation, facility, (manufacturing) plant, work(s): *sanitäre* ~*n* sanitary facilities. **3.** a) (public) garden(s) (*or park*), grounds, b) sports facilities. **4.** F (hi-fi) set. **5.** draft, structure, design. **6.** (*zu* for) talent, gift. **7.** (*zu*

(natural) tendency (of), *a*. ✻ disposition (to). **8.** ✝ investment: **~n** assets. **9.** enclosure: **in der** (*or* **als**) **~ sende ich Ihnen** enclosed please find.

'**anlagebedingt** *adj* inherent.

'**Anlage|berater(in** *f*) *m* investment consultant. **~kapi̱tal** *n* invested capital. **~pa̱piere** *pl* investment securities. **~vermögen** *n* fixed assets.

Anlaß ['anlas] *m* (-sses; ⸚sse) **1.** occasion: **aus ~** (*gen*) → **anläßlich. 2.** cause, reason: **~ geben zu** give rise to; **j-m ~ zur Klage geben** give s.o. cause to complain; **beim geringsten ~** at the slightest provocation; **ohne jeden ~** for no reason at all; **ich sehe k-n ~ zu gehen** I see no reason to go; **et. zum ~ nehmen** take occasion (**zu** to).

'**anlassen** (*irr*, *sep*, -ge-, h, → **lassen**) I *v/t* **1.** F → **anbehalten. 2.** leave *the light, radio, etc* on. **3.** start (up) (*engine etc*). II **sich gut ~** shape up well, *business etc*: promise well; **wie läßt er sich an?** how is he making out?

Anlasser ['anlasər] *m* (-s; -) *mot*. starter.

anläßlich ['anlɛslɪç] *prep* (*gen*) on the occasion of.

'**anlasten** *v/t* (*sep*, -ge-, h) **j-m et. ~** blame s.o. for s.th.

Anlauf *m* (-[e]s; ⸚e) **1.** *sports*: run-up, *ski jumping*: approach: **(e-n) ~ nehmen** take a run. **2.** *fig*. (**beim ersten ~** at the first) attempt: **e-n neuen ~ nehmen** have another go. **3.** *a*. ⚙ start.

'**anlaufen** (*irr*, *sep*, -ge-, → **laufen**) I *v/i* (sn) **1.** *sports*: run up (for the jump). **2.** **angelaufen kommen** come running along. **3. ~ gegen** → **anrennen** 1. **4.** (*a*. **~ lassen**) start (up). **5.** *fig*. start, get under way, *film*: be shown. **6.** *costs etc*: mount up, *interest etc*: accrue. **7.** *glass*: fog, *metal*: tarnish: **blau ~** go blue. II *v/t* (h) **8.** call at (*a port etc*).

'**Anlauf|schwierigkeiten** *pl* initial problems. **~stelle** *f* address (*or* office) to turn to. **~zeit** *f* initial period.

Anlaut *m* (-[e]s; -e) *ling*. initial sound.

'**anlauten** *v/i* (*sep*, -ge-, h) *ling*. begin.

Anlegebrücke *f* landing stage.

'**anlegen** (*sep*, -ge-, h) I *v/t* **1.** put on (*jewellery etc*). **2.** (**an** *acc*) put up *a ladder etc* (against), line up *a ruler etc* (against), lay down *a card etc* (next to): **e-n strengen Maßstab ~** apply a strict

standard; → **Hand. 3.** lay out (*garden*), plan, design, construct, set up, instal(l). **4.** start (*a file*). **5.** get in (*supplies*). **6.** invest (*capital*), spend *a sum* (**für** on). **7. e-n Säugling ~** give a baby the breast. **8. die Ohren ~** *dog etc*: set back its ears. **9.** put on (*coals etc*). **10.** apply (*bandage*). **11. es ~ auf** (*acc*) be out for (*or* to *inf*); **darauf angelegt sein zu** *inf* be designed to *inf*. II *v/i* **12.** land: **im Hafen** (*or* **am Kai**) **~** dock. **13.** (take) aim (**auf** *acc* at). III **sich mit j-m ~** tangle with s.o.

Anleger ['anle:gər] *m* (-s; -) ✝ investor.

'**Anlegestelle** *f* ⚓ landing place.

'**anlehnen** (*sep*, -ge-, h) I *v/t* **1.** lean (**an** *acc* against). **2.** leave ajar. II **sich ~ an** (*acc*) **3.** lean against. **4.** *fig*. be model(l)ed on.

'**Anlehnung** *f* (-; -en) dependence (**an** *acc* on): **in ~ an** (*acc*) following.

Anleihe ['anlaɪə] *f* (-; -n) ✝ loan: **e-e ~ bei j-m machen** borrow money from s.o., *fig*. borrow from s.o.

'**anleiten** *v/t* (*sep*, -ge-, h) **1.** guide, instruct. **2.** → **anhalten** 2.

'**Anleitung** *f* (-; -en) **1.** guidance, direction. **2.** directions, instructions.

'**anlernen** *v/t* (*sep*, -ge-, h) teach, train: → **angelernt** II.

Anlernling ['anlɛrnlɪŋ] *m* (-s; -e) trainee.

'**anliegen** *v/i* (*irr*, *sep*, -ge-, h, → **liegen**) **1. eng ~** fit tightly, cling (**an** *dat* to). **2.** F **was liegt an?** what's on the agenda?

'**Anliegen** *n* (-s; -) **1.** request. **2.** matter, concern: **ein nationales ~** a matter of national concern.

'**anliegend** *adj* **1. eng ~** tight(-fitting), clinging. **2.** adjacent. **3.** ✝ enclosed (**senden wir Ihnen** please find).

Anlieger ['anli:gər] *m* (-s; -) *mot*. resident: **~ frei!** residents only! **~staat** *m* neighbo(u)ring (*on waters*: riparian) state. **~verkehr** *m* resident traffic.

'**anlocken** *v/t* (*sep*, -ge-, h) *fig*. attract.

'**anlügen** *v/t* (*irr*, *sep*, -ge-, h, → **lügen**) **j-n ~** lie to s.o.

'**anmachen** *v/t* (*sep*, -ge-, h) F **1.** fasten (**an** *dat* to). **2.** switch on (*light*), light (*fire*). **3.** *gastr*. prepare, dress. **4. j-n ~ a)** give s.o. the come-on, **b)** snap at s.o., **c)** turn s.o. on.

'**anmalen** *v/t* (*sep*, -ge-, h) paint: F **sich ~** paint one's face.

'**Anmarsch** *m* (-[e]s; *no pl*) ✕ *im* ~ *sein* be advancing (**auf** *acc* towards).

anmaßen ['anma:sən] *v/t* (*sep*, -ge-,) **sich et.** ~ arrogate s.th. to o.s.; usurp s.th.; **sich** ~ **zu** *inf* presume to *inf*.

'**anmaßend** *adj* arrogant, overbearing.

'**Anmaßung** *f* (-; -en) arrogance.

'**Anmeldeformu,lar** *n* application form.

'**anmelden** (*sep*, -ge-, h) **I** *v/t* **1.** announce (*visitor etc*). **2.** *j-n in der* **Schule** (**zu e-m Kursus** *etc*) ~ enrol(l) s.o. at school (for a course *etc*); *j-n beim Arzt* ~ make an appointment for s.o. with the doctor; *j-n polizeilich* ~ register s.o. (with the police). **3.** *teleph.* book, *Am.* place: **den Fernseher** (**das Radio**) ~ get a television (radio) licen/ce (*Am.* -se). **4.** put forward (*claims etc*), raise (*doubts etc*): → **Patent** 1. **II sich** ~ **5.** announce o.s. **6.** enrol(l) (**zu** for, **in** *dat* at): **sich beim Arzt** *etc* ~ make an appointment with the doctor *etc*; **sich polizeilich** ~ register (with the police).

'**Anmeldung** *f* (-; -en) **1.** announcement. **2.** enrol(l)ment: (**polizeiliche**) ~ registration (with the police); **nur nach vorheriger** ~ by appointment only. **3.** reception (desk).

'**anmerken** *v/t* (*sep*, -ge-, h) **1.** a) mark, b) make a note of. **2.** remark, observe. **3.** *j-m s-e Verlegenheit etc* ~ notice s.o.'s embarrassment *etc*; **sich nichts** ~ **lassen** not to show one's feelings; **man merkte ihr sofort an, daß ...** you only had to look at her to see that ...; **laß dir nichts** ~**!** don't let on!

'**Anmerkung** *f* (-; -en) (**über** *acc* on) remark, comment, (foot)note, annotation: **mit** ~**en versehen** annotate.

Anmut ['anmu:t] *f* (-; *no pl*) grace(fulness), charm, sweetness.

'**anmuten** *v/t* (*sep*, -ge-, h) *j-n seltsam etc* ~ strike s.o. as (being) odd *etc*.

'**anmutig** *adj* graceful, charming.

'**annageln** *v/t* (*sep*, -ge-, h) nail on (**an** *acc* to).

'**annähen** *v/t* (*sep*, -ge-, h) sew on (**an** *acc* to).

'**annähernd I** *adj* approximate. **II** *adv* (**nicht** ~ not) nearly. '**Annäherung** *f* (-; -en) approximation (*a. fig.*), *pol.* rapprochement. '**Annäherungsversuche** *pl* approaches, (*amorous*) advances.

Annahme ['ana:mə] *f* (-; -n) **1.** accept-ance. **2.** adoption (*of a child, motion, etc*), passing (*of a law*). **3.** (**in der** ~ on the) assumption (**daß** that): **ich habe Grund zu der** ~**, daß ...** I have reasons to believe that ...; **gehe ich recht in der** ~**, daß ...?** am I right in thinking that ...? **4.** → ~**stelle** *f* receiving office. ~**verweigerung** *f* nonacceptance.

Annalen [a'na:lən] *pl* annals.

annehmbar ['ane:mba:r] *adj* a) acceptable (**für** to), *a.* reasonable, fair (*price etc*), b) passable. '**annehmen** (*irr*, *sep*, -ge-, h, → **nehmen**) **I** *v/t* **1.** accept (*gift, letter, etc*). **2.** adopt (*child, name, title*). **3.** *parl.* carry (*a motion*), pass (*a bill*). **4.** admit (*students*). **5.** assume (*shape etc*), take (on) (*colo[u]r, smell, etc*), acquire (*habit etc*). **6.** assume, suppose, guess: **das ist nicht anzunehmen** that's unlikely; **ich nehme es an** I suppose so; **nehmen wir an** (*or* **angenommen**), **er stirbt** suppose he dies. **II sich j-s** (**e-r Sache**) ~ take care of s.o. (s.th.).

'**Annehmlichkeit** *f* (-; -en) amenity: ~**en des Lebens** *a.* comforts of life.

annektieren [anɛk'ti:rən] *v/t pol.* annex.

Annonce [a'nõ:sə] *f* (-; -n) advertisement, F ad. **annoncieren** [anõ'si:rən] *v/t, v/i* (h) advertise.

annullieren [anʊ'li:rən] *v/t* (h) annul, ⊥ cancel (*order*), *sports:* disallow (*goal*).

Anode [a'no:də] *f* (-; -n) ⚡ anode, plate **anöden** ['anøːdən] *v/t* (*sep*, -ge-, h) F *j-n* ~ bore s.o. stiff.

anomal ['anoma:l] *adj* anomalous.

Anomalie [anoma'li:] *f* (-; -n) anomaly

anonym [ano'ny:m] *adj* anonymous.

Anonymität [anonymi'tɛ:t] *f* (-; *no pl*) anonymity.

Anorak ['anorak] *m* (-s; -s) anorak.

'**anordnen** *v/t* (*sep*, -ge-, h) **1.** arrange. **2.** order, direct.

'**Anordnung** *f* (-; -en) **1.** arrangement. **2.** order, direction: **auf** ~ **von** (*or* **gen**) by order of; ~**en treffen** give orders.

Anorexie [anorɛ'ksi:] *f* (-; *no pl*) ⚕ anorexia (nervosa).

'**anor,ganisch** *adj* inorganic.

'**anormal** *adj* abnormal.

'**anpacken** (*sep*, -ge-, h) **I** *v/t* **1.** → **pak ken** 2. **2.** F *fig.* treat, tackle. **II** *v/i* → **anfassen** II.

'**anpassen** (*sep*, -ge-, h) **I** *v/t* **1.** fit (on) **2.** (*dat or* **an** *acc*) adapt (to), *a.* ⊥, ⚙

adjust (to), *in colo[u]r*: match (with). **II sich ~** (*dat* or *an acc* to) adapt (o.s.), adjust (o.s.): → **angepaßt.**

'**Anpassung** *f* (-; -en) (*an acc* to) adaptation, adjustment. '**anpassungsfähig** *adj* adaptable (*an acc* to). '**Anpassungsfähigkeit** *f* (-; *no pl*) adaptability. '**Anpassungsschwierigkeiten** *pl* difficulties in adapting.

'**anpeilen** *v/t* (*sep*, -ge-, h) **1.** ✗, ♨ take a bearing of. **2.** *fig.* aim at.

'**anpfeifen** *v/t* (*irr, sep*, -ge-, h, → **pfeifen**) **1.** *sports*: *ein Spiel ~* give the starting whistle. **2.** F *j-n ~* blow s.o. up.

'**Anpfiff** *m* (-[e]s; -e) **1.** *sports*: (starting) whistle. **2.** F *e-n ~ kriegen* get ticked off.

'**anpflanzen** *v/t* (*sep*, -ge-, h) **1.** plant. **2.** cultivate, grow.

'**anpöbeln** *v/t* (*sep*, -ge-, h) molest, mob.

'**Anprall** *m* (-[e]s; *no pl*) impact (*gegen* [up]on).

anprangern ['anpraŋərn] *v/t* (*sep*, -ge-, h) denounce.

'**anpreisen** *v/t* (*irr, sep*, -ge-, h, → **preisen**) praise, F plug.

'**Anprobe** *f* (-; -n) (*zur ~* for a) fitting.

'**anpro,bieren** *v/t, v/i* (h) try on, fit on.

'**anpumpen** *v/t* (*sep*, -ge-, h) F *j-n ~* touch s.o. (*um* for).

'**Anraten** *n* (-[e]s; -e) (*auf acc* to) right, claim.

'**Anrede** *f* (-; -n) address. '**anreden** *v/t* (*sep*, -ge-, h) *j-n ~* address s.o.

'**anregen** *v/t* (*sep*, -ge-, h) **1.** stimulate (*a. v/i*), whet (*appetite*), *fig. a.* encourage: *j-n zum Nachdenken ~* give s.o. food for thought. **2.** suggest. '**anregend** *adj* stimulating: *~ wirken* have a stimulating effect. '**Anregung** *f* (-; -en) **1.** *no pl* stimulation, *fig. a.* encouragement. **2.** suggestion: *auf ~ von* (or *gen*) at the suggestion of.

'**anreichern** (*sep*, -ge-, h) **I** *v/t* 🐾, 🜚 enrich. **II sich ~** accumulate.

'**Anreise** *f* (-; -n) **1.** journey there (or

here). **2.** arrival. '**anreisen** *v/i* (*sep*, -ge-, sn) **1.** travel. **2.** arrive.

'**anreißen** *v/t* (*irr, sep*, -ge-, h, → **reißen**) **1.** F → **anbrechen** I. **2.** *fig.* raise.

'**Anreiz** *m* (-es; -e) incentive.

'**anrennen** *v/i* (*irr, sep*, -ge-, sn, → **rennen**) **1.** *~ gegen* run against, ✗ attack. **2.** *angerannt kommen* come running (up).

Anrichte ['anrıçtə] *f* (-; -n) sideboard.

'**anrichten** *v/t* (*sep*, -ge-, h) **1.** *gastr.* prepare, dress: *es ist angerichtet!* dinner *etc* is served! **2.** *fig.* cause (*disaster etc*), do (*damage*).

anrüchig ['anrvçıç] *adj* disreputable, dubious, F shady.

'**anrücken** *v/i* (*sep*, -ge-, sn) approach, ✗ advance, F turn up, come.

'**Anruf** *m* (-[e]s; -e) call. **Anrufbeantworter** *m* (telephone) answering machine.

'**anrufen** (*irr, sep*, -ge-, h, → **rufen**) **I** *v/t* *j-n ~* a) call s.o., b) *teleph.* call (or ring) s.o. (up), c) *fig.* appeal to s.o. (*um Hilfe etc* for help *etc*); *ein Gericht ~* appeal to a court. **II** *v/i* make a (phone)call: *bei j-m ~* → I b.

'**anrühren** *v/t* (*sep*, -ge-, h) **1.** touch (*a. fig.*). **2.** mix.

ans = *an das*: → *Herz, Licht etc.*

Ansage ['anza:gə] *f* **1.** *radio, TV* announcement. **2.** *cards*: bid(ding).

'**ansagen** *v/t, v/i* (*sep*, -ge-, h) announce, *cards*: bid: *Trumpf ~* declare trumps; F *Sparen ist angesagt!* saving is the word!; → *Kampf* 1. '**Ansager** *m* (-s; -), '**Ansagerin** *f* (-; -nen) announcer.

'**ansammeln** *v/t* (*sep*, -ge-, h) a) (*a. sich ~*) collect, gather, assemble, b) accumulate, amass. '**Ansammlung** *f* (-; -en) **1.** accumulation. **2.** gathering, crowd.

ansässig ['anzɛsıç] *adj* resident (*in dat* at, in): *~ werden* take up (one's) residence, settle.

'**Ansatz** *m* (-es; ⸗e) **1.** 🜚 deposit, crust. **2.** *anat.* base: → *Haaransatz.* **3.** *fig.* a) first sign(s), b) attempt, c) approach: *im ~ richtig* basically right; *gute* (*gewisse*) *Ansätze zeigen* show (some) promise; *in den Ansätzen stekkenbleiben* get stuck at the beginning. **4.** 🜨 statement. **5.** 🜋 estimate.

'**Ansatzpunkt** *m fig.* point of departure.

'**ansaugen** *v/t* (*sep*, -ge-, h) suck in.

'**anschaffen** *v/t* (*sep*, -ge-, h) buy: F *sich*

Kinder ~ have children. **'Anschaffung** *f* (-; -en) **1.** buying, purchase. **2.** acquisition. **'Anschaffungskosten** *pl* purchase cost.

'anschalten *v/t* (*sep*, -ge-, h) switch on. **'anschauen** *v/t* (*sep*, -ge-, h) → **ansehen. anschaulich** ['anʃaʊlɪç] *adj* clear, vivid, graphic. **'Anschauung** *f* (-; -en) view, opinion, idea.

'Anschauungs|materi,al *n* illustrative material, *n.s.* audiovisual aids. **~unterricht** *m* **1.** object-teaching, visual instruction. **2.** *fig.* object-lesson.

'Anschein *m* (-[e]s; *no pl*) appearance: *allem ~ nach* to all appearances; *den ~ erwecken* give the impression; *sich den ~ geben* pretend, make believe; *es hat den ~, als ob* it looks as if.

'anscheinend *adj* apparent: *er ist ~ krank* he seems to be ill.

'anschicken: *sich* ~ (*sep*, -ge-, h) get ready (*or* going) (*zu* to).

'anschieben *v/t* (*irr*, *sep*, -ge-, h, → **schieben**) *mot.* push-start.

'anschirren *v/t* (*sep*, -ge-, h) harness.

'Anschlag *m* (-[e]s; ⸗e) **1.** a) poster, bill, b) notice. **2.** attack (*auf acc* on): *~ auf j-n (j-s Leben)* attempt on s.o.'s life; *e-m ~ zum Opfer fallen* be assassinated. **3.** a) ♩ touch, b) *on typewriter*: stroke: *sie schreibt 400 Anschläge in der Minute* she types 400 strokes per minute. **4.** ✝ estimate. **5.** ⚙ (limit) stop. **6.** *das Gewehr im ~ halten* point the gun (*auf acc* at). **7.** impact, *swimming*: touch. **'Anschlagbrett** *n* notice (*Am.* bulletin) board.

'anschlagen (*irr*, *sep*, -ge-, → **schlagen**) **I** *v/t* (h) **1.** a) fasten (*an acc* to), b) stick up, put up (*notice etc*). **2.** strike, hit (*key*, *note*), ring (*bell*): *fig.* **e-n anderen Ton ~** change one's tune; *ein schnelleres Tempo ~* quicken one's pace. **3.** a) strike, hit, knock, b) chip. **II** *v/i* **4.** (sn) hit (*waves*: break) (*an acc* against): *mit dem Kopf an die Wand ~* hit one's head against the wall. **5.** (h) (begin to) ring, *dog*: bark. **6.** (h) *swimming*: touch. **7.** (h) (*bei* on) take effect, F *food*: show.

'anschleppen *v/t* (*sep*, -ge-, h) (*a. angeschleppt bringen*) drag along.

'anschließen (*irr*, *sep*, -ge-, h, → **schließen**) **I** *v/t* **1.** (*an acc* to) lock, chain. **2.** (*an acc*) ⚡, ⚙ connect (to, with), link

up (with), ⚡ *a.* plug in: → **angeschlossen. 3.** add (*dat* to). **II** *sich ~* **4.** (*an acc*) adjoin (*s.th.*), border (on). **5.** *fig.* follow: *an den Vortrag schloß sich e-e Diskussion an* the lecture was followed by a discussion. **6.** *sich j-m ~* follow s.o., join s.o., *fig.* take s.o.'s side; *sich j-s Meinung ~* agree with s.o.; *ich schließe mich an* a) I agree, b) I'll join you! **7.** *sich an j-n ~* befriend s.o.; *er schließt sich leicht an* he makes friends easily. **III** *v/i* **8.** fit closely.

'anschließend I *adj* **1.** adjacent, next. **2.** following. **3.** close-fitting. **II** *adv* **4.** afterward(s): *~ an die Vorstellung* following the performance.

'Anschluß *m* (-sses; ⸗sse) **1.** ⚡, ⚙, ⚙ *etc* a) connection, telephone (connection), b) line: *teleph.* **k-n ~ bekommen** not to get through; ⚙ **~ haben** have a connection (*nach* to); *s-n ~ verpassen* miss one's connection; *fig.* **den ~ verpassen** miss the boat; *den ~ finden an* (*acc*) catch up with. **2.** affiliation (*an acc* with *a party etc*), *pol.* union. **3.** *im ~ an* (*acc*) after, following. **4.** F contact, acquaintance: *~ finden* make contact (*or* friends) (*bei* with); *~ suchen* look for company. **~dose** *f* ⚡ wall socket. **~flug** *m* connecting flight. **~schnur** *f* ⚡ flex. **~treffer** *m* goal that leaves one more to level the score. **~zug** *m* connecting train.

'anschmiegen: *sich* ~ (*sep*, -ge-, h) (*an acc*) nestle (against), *dress etc*: cling (to). **'anschmiegsam** *adj* affectionate.

'anschmieren *v/t* (*sep*, -ge-, h) F cheat.

'anschnallen (*sep*, -ge-, h) **I** *v/t* a) buckle on, b) put on (*skis*). **II** *sich ~* ✈, *mot.* fasten one's seat belt.

'Anschnallgurt *m* seat belt.

'anschnauzen *v/t* (*sep*, -ge-, h) F *j-n ~* blow s.o. up.

'anschneiden *v/t* (*irr*, *sep*, -ge-, h, → **schneiden**) **1.** cut into (*bread etc*). **2.** cut (*ball etc*). **3.** *fig.* broach: *ein anderes Thema ~* change the subject.

'Anschnitt *m* (-[e]s; -e) first slice.

'anschreiben (*irr*, *sep*, -ge-, h, → **schreiben**) **I** *v/t* **1.** write down: *j-m et. ~* charge s.o. with s.th.; *et. ~ lassen* buy s.th. on credit; *bei j-m gut (schlecht) angeschrieben sein* be in s.o.'s good (bad) books. **2.** *j-n ~* write to s.o.

ˈ**Anschreiben** n (-s; -) covering letter.
ˈ**anschreien** v/t (irr, sep, -ge-, h, → schreien) shout at, scream at.
ˈ**Anschrift** f (-; -en) address.
Anschuldigung [ˈanʃʊldɪɡʊŋ] f (-; -en) accusation.
ˈ**anschwärzen** v/t (sep, -ge-, h) F a) run s.o. down, b) denounce (bei to).
ˈ**anschwellen** v/i (irr, sep, -ge-, sn, → schwellen) swell, fig. increase, rise.
ˈ**anschwemmen** v/t (sep, -ge-, h) a) wash ashore, b) geol. deposit.
ˈ**ansehen** (irr, sep, -ge-, h, → sehen) v/t look at: sich et. ~ take a look at, examine, watch; sich e-n Film (e-e Fernsehsendung) ~ go and see a film (watch a program[me]); sich et. genau ~ have a close look at s.th.; man sieht es ihr an, daß ... you can tell by her face that ...; man sieht ihm sein Alter nicht an he doesn't look his age; ich sehe es für (or als) m-e Pflicht an zu inf I consider it my duty to inf; et. mit ~ watch (or witness) s.th.; ich kann es nicht länger mit ~! I can't stand it any longer!; F sieh mal einer an! fancy that!; → finster 2, schief 3.
ˈ**Ansehen** n (-s) **1.** reputation, prestige: von hohem ~ of high standing; großes ~ genießen be highly esteemed; an ~ verlieren lose credit. **2.** fig. ohne ~ der Person without respect of persons.
ansehnlich [ˈanseːnlɪç] adj handsome, considerable.
ˈ**anseilen** v/t (sep, -ge-, h) (a. sich ~) rope (up).
ˈ**ansetzen** (sep, -ge-, h) **I** v/t **1.** (an acc) put (on, to), apply drill etc (to), put flute, glass, etc to one's lips. **2.** (an acc to) a) add, join, b) sew on. **3.** fix, set (date etc), assess (costs), quote (price). **4.** ⚗ set up (equation). **5.** develop, ⚗ a. put forth (buds), put on (rust): Fett ~ put on weight. **6.** gastr. prepare (a. 🍷), make, mix. **7.** bring in: j-n ~ auf (acc) put s.o. onto; e-n Hund (auf e-e Spur) ~ set a dog on the trail. **II** v/i **8.** begin, (make a) start: a. fig. zum Endspurt ~ set o.s. for the final spurt; zur Landung ~ come in (to land); zum Sprechen ~ start to speak; zum Sprung ~ get ready for the jump. **9.** fig. criticism, reform, etc: set in. **III** sich ~ accumulate.
Ansicht f (-; -en) **1.** (über acc) opinion

(on), view (of): m-r ~ nach in my opinion, as I see it; der ~ sein (or die ~ vertreten), daß ... take the view that ...; anderer ~ sein take a different view, w.s. disagree; die ~en sind geteilt opinion differs; zu der ~ gelangen (or kommen), daß ... decide that ... **2.** view (a. ⚙). **3.** ✝ zur ~ on approval.
Ansichts(post)karte f picture postcard.
ˈ**Ansichtssache**: das ist ~ that's a matter of opinion.
ˈ**ansiedeln** v/t (sep, -ge-, h) **1.** settle (a. sich ~), ✝ base, site: in London angesiedelt London-based. **2.** fig. place.
ˈ**Ansiedler(in** f) m settler.
ˈ**Ansiedlung** f (-; -en) settlement.
ˈ**Ansinnen** n (-s; -) request, demand.
ˈ**anspannen** v/t (sep, -ge-, h) **1.** harness (an acc to). **2.** tighten, stretch (rope etc). **3.** flex (muscles). **4.** fig. strain: alle Kräfte ~ strain every nerve.
ˈ**Anspannung** f (-; -en) fig. strain.
ˈ**anspielen** (sep, -ge-, h) **I** v/i **1.** cards: (have the) lead. **2.** sports: lead off, soccer: kick off. **3.** fig. ~ auf (acc) allude to, insinuate (s.th.). **II** v/t **4.** lead (card). **5.** sports: j-n ~ pass to s.o.
ˈ**Anspielung** f (-; -en) (auf acc) allusion (to), insinuation (about).
ˈ**anspinnen**: sich ~ (irr, sep, -ge-, h, → spinnen) fig. develop.
ˈ**anspitzen** v/t (sep, -ge-, h) point.
ˈ**Ansporn** m (-[e]s; no pl) incentive (für to). ˈ**anspornen** v/t (sep, -ge-, h) a. fig. spur (on).
ˈ**Ansprache** f (-; -n) **1.** (e-e ~ halten deliver an) address (an acc to). **2.** F k-e ~ haben have no one to talk to.
ansprechbar [ˈanʃprɛçbaːr] adj **1.** 🞂 responsive. **2.** F er war nicht ~ you couldn't talk to him. ˈ**ansprechen** (irr, sep, -ge-, h, → sprechen) **I** v/t **1.** speak to, address, appeal to s.o. (wegen for). **2.** please, appeal to. **3.** touch (up)on (problem etc). **II** v/i **4.** a. 🞂 respond (auf acc to). **5.** appeal (to the public).
ˈ**ansprechend** adj pleasing, attractive.
ˈ**Ansprechpartner** m person to turn to.
ˈ**anspringen** (irr, sep, -ge-, → springen) **I** v/i (sn) start (up). **II** v/t 🞂 jump at.
ˈ**Anspruch** m (-[e]s; ⸚e) (auf acc to) a. 🞐 claim, right, contp. pretension: hohe Ansprüche stellen be very demanding; an j-n make heavy demands on s.o.; ~

haben auf (*acc*) be entitled to; **in ~ nehmen** a) *a.* **~ erheben auf** (*acc*) lay claim to, b) call on (*s.o.*, *s.o.'s help*), take up (*s.o.'s time etc*); **j-n in ~ nehmen** keep s.o. busy; **j-n ganz in ~ nehmen** claim s.o.'s full attention.

'**anspruchslos** *adj* **1.** a) undemanding (*a. fig. book, music, etc*), b) easily satisfied. **2.** plain, simple. '**Anspruchslosigkeit** *f* (-; *no pl*) undemandingness, modesty. '**anspruchsvoll** *adj* demanding (*a. fig.*), particular.

'**anspucken** *v/t* (*sep*, -ge-, h) spit at.

'**anstacheln** *v/t* (*sep*, -ge-, h) goad on.

'**Anstalt** ['anʃtalt] *f* (-; -en) **1.** establishment, institution, *ped.* institute, school. **2.** a) sanatorium, *Am.* sanitarium, b) F mental home: **j-n in e-e ~ einweisen** institutionalize s.o. **3.** **~en treffen zu** make arrangements for; **~en machen zu gehen** *etc* get ready to go *etc*.

'**Anstand** ['anʃtant] *m* (-[e]s; *no pl*) **1.** (sense of) decency. **2.** (good) manners.

'**anständig** ['anʃtɛndiç] *adj* **1.** proper, decent, respectable: **benimm dich ~!** behave yourself! **2.** F fair (*price etc*): **ein ~es Essen** a decent meal; **e-e ~e Arbeit** a good job. '**Anstandsbesuch** *m* formal call. '**Anstandsdame** *f* chaperon. '**anstandshalber** *adv* for decency's sake. '**anstandslos** *adv* **1.** unhesitatingly. **2.** freely.

'**anstarren** *v/t* (*sep*, -ge-, h) stare at.

an'statt I *prep* (*gen*) instead of. II *conj* **~ zu arbeiten** *etc* instead of working *etc*.

'**anstauen** (*sep*, -ge-, h) I *v/t* dam up. II **sich ~** accumulate, *fig.* rage *etc*: build up; **angestaute Wut** pent-up rage.

'**anstechen** *v/t* (*irr*, *sep*, -ge-, h, → **stechen**) prick, tap (*barrel*).

'**anstecken** (*sep*, -ge-, h) I *v/t* **1.** pin on, put on, slip on. **2.** set *house* on fire, light (*cigar, candle*). **3.** ✒, *a. fig.* infect (**mit** with): **er hat mich** (**mit s-m Schnupfen**) **angesteckt** he has given me his cold. II *v/i* **4.** ✒, *a. fig.* be infectious. III **sich ~ 5. ich habe mich bei ihm** (**mit Grippe**) **angesteckt** I have caught the flu from him. '**ansteckend** *adj* ✒, *a. fig.* infectious. **Ansteckung** ['anʃtɛkʊŋ] *f* (-; -en) ✒ infection. '**Ansteckungsgefahr** *f* danger of infection.

'**anstehen** *v/i* (*irr*, *sep*, -ge-, h, → **ste-** **hen**) **1.** queue (*Am.* line) up (**nach** for). **2.** ✝, 🜨 be up (**zur Entscheidung** for decision), be on the agenda.

'**ansteigen** *v/i* (*irr*, *sep*, -ge-, sn, → **steigen**) rise.

an'stelle *prep* **~ von** (*or gen*) instead of.

'**anstellen** (*sep*, -ge-, h) I *v/t* **1.** (**an** *acc* against) put, lean. **2.** start (*machine*), turn on (*heating etc*), switch on (*radio etc*). **3.** employ, *Am.* hire: **angestellt sein bei** work for; F **j-n zu et. ~** have s.o. do s.th. **4.** a) make, carry out, b) F do, manage: **Nachforschungen ~** make inquiries; F **was haben sie mit dir angestellt?** what have they done to you?; **Dummheiten ~, et.** (**Dummes**) **~** get up to mischief; **was hast du** (**da**) **wieder angestellt?** what have you been up to (again)?; **wie hast du das angestellt?** how did you manage that?; → **Überlegung.** II **sich ~ 5.** queue (*Am.* line) up (**nach** for). **6.** F act, make (**als ob** as if): **sich bei et. ungeschickt ~** go about s.th. clumsily; **stell dich nicht so an!** don't make such a fuss!; **stell dich nicht so dumm an!** don't act so stupid!

anstellig ['anʃtɛlɪç] *adj* handy, clever.

'**Anstellung** *f* (-; -en) place, employment, job.

'**ansteuern** *v/t* (*sep*, -ge-, h) head for.

'**Anstieg** ['anʃtiːk] *m* (-[e]s; -e) **1.** ascent. **2.** *fig.* (*gen*) rise (in), increase (of).

'**anstiften** *v/t* (*sep*, -ge-, h) (**zu** to) incite, instigate: **j-n ~ zu** *a.* put s.o. up to. '**Anstifter** *m* (-s; -), '**Anstifterin** *f* (-; -nen) instigator. '**Anstiftung** *f* (-; -en) (**auf** → *gen* at the) instigation (of).

'**anstimmen** *v/t* (*sep*, -ge-, h) ♪ strike up: **ein Lied ~** break into a song.

'**Anstoß** *m* (-es; ⁓e) **1.** *soccer:* kickoff. **2.** impulse: **den ~ geben zu** start off, initiate. **3.** F **bei j-m ~ erregen** scandalize s.o., give offen|ce (*Am.* -se) to s.o.; **~ nehmen an** (*dat*) take exception to.

'**anstoßen** (*irr*, *sep*, -ge-, → **stoßen**) I *v/t* (h) **1.** knock (*or* bump) against: **sich den Kopf ~** bump one's head (**an** *dat* against); **j-n** (**mit dem Ellbogen**) **~** nudge s.o. (with the elbow). II *v/i* **2.** (h) clink glasses: **~ auf** (*acc*) drink to. **3.** (sn) (**an** *dat*) knock (against), bump (into): **mit dem Kopf ~** → **1.** **4.** (h) **mit der Zunge ~** lisp. **5.** (h) *soccer:* kick off.

anstößig ['anʃtøːsɪç] *adj* a) offensive, scandalous, b) indecent.

'anstrahlen *v/t* (*sep*, -ge-, h) illuminate: **mit Scheinwerfern ~** floodlight; F *fig.* **j-n ~** beam at s.o.

'anstreben *v/t* (*sep*, -ge-, h) aim at, strive for.

'anstreichen *v/t* (*irr*, *sep*, -ge-, h, → **streichen**) **1.** paint. **2.** mark (**rot** *etc* in red *etc*). **'Anstreicher** *m* (-s; -) painter.

anstrengen ['anʃtrɛŋən] (*sep*, -ge-, h) **I** *v/t* **1.** strain, be a strain on, exhaust: **angestrengt** 1. **2.** → **Prozeß** 2. **II** *v/i* **3.** be exhausting, be a strain. **III sich ~** make an effort, try (hard), exert o.s.; **streng dich mal an!** you could try a bit harder! **'anstrengend** *adj* strenuous, trying (**für** to). **'Anstrengung** *f* (-; -en) **1.** (**mit äußerster ~** with a supreme) effort. **2.** strain, exertion.

'Anstrich *m* (-[e]s; -e) **1.** a) painting, b) paint, c) coat. **2.** *no pl* air, semblance.

'Ansturm *m* (-[e]s; ⸚e) onrush (*a. fig.*), ✗ assault, *a. sports*: attack; ⭳ (**auf** *acc*) run (on), rush (for). **'anstürmen** *v/i* (*sep*, -ge-, sn) **~ gegen** *a. fig.* attack.

Antagonismus [antago'nɪsmʊs] *m* (-; -men) antagonism.

antarktisch [ant'arktɪʃ] *adj* Antarctic.

'antasten *v/t* (*sep*, -ge-, h) infringe on (*rights etc*), touch (*capital*), break into (*supplies*).

'Anteil *m* (-[e]s; -e) **1.** (**an** *dat*) share (of, in), ⭳ *a.* interest (in), participation (of); *fig.* **er hatte k-n ~ am Erfolg** he had no part in the success. **2.** *no pl* a) interest, b) sympathy: **~ nehmen an** (*dat*) take an interest (in), **j-s Unglück** sympathize with s.o. in his misfortune, **j-s Freude** share in s.o.'s joy. **anteilig** ['antaɪlɪç], **'anteilmäßig** *adj and adv* proportionate(ly). **'Anteilnahme** *f* (-; *no pl*) sympathy (**an** *dat* with).

'Anteilschein *m* (-[e]s; -e) → **Aktie.**

'Anteilseigner(in *f*) *m* → **Aktionär(in).**

Antenne [an'tɛnə] *f* (-; -n) aerial, *Am.* antenna (*a. fig.*).

Anthologie [antolo'giː] *f* (-; -n) anthology.

Anthrazit [antra'tsiːt] *m* (-s; -e) *min.* anthracite.

Anti..., **anti...** [anti-] anti...

Antialko'holiker(in *f*) *m* teetotal(l)er.

Anti'babypille *f* F *the* pill.

Antibiotikum [antibi'oːtikʊm] *n* (-s; -ka), **antibi'otisch** [-tɪʃ] *adj* antibiotic.

Antibloc'kiersy,stem *n mot.* (*abbr.* **ABS**) antilocking system.

Antidepressivum [antidepre'siːvʊm] *n* (-s; -va) antidepressant.

Antifa'schismus *m* antifascism.

Antifa'schist(in *f*) *m*, **antifa'schistisch** *adj* antifascist.

Antigen [anti'geːn] *n* (-s; -e) ✱ antigen.

Anti'haftbeschichtung: mit ~ nonstick.

antik [an'tiːk] *adj* **1.** classical, ancient. **2.** antique, period (*furniture etc*).

An'tike[1] *f* (-; *no pl*) (classical) antiquity.

An'tike[2] *f* (-; -n) *usu. pl* antique.

'Antikörper *m* ✱ antibody.

Antilope [anti'loːpə] *f* (-; -n) antelope.

Antipathie [antipa'tiː] *f* (-; -n) (**gegen** antipathy (to, against), dislike (for).

Antipode [anti'poːdə] *m* (-n; -n) antipode.

Antiqua [an'tiːkva] *f* (-; *no pl*) *print.* Roman (type).

Antiquar [anti'kvaːr] *m* (-s; -e), **Anti'quarin** *f* (-; -nen) **1.** second-hand bookseller. **2.** antique dealer.

Antiquariat [antikvaˈrĭaːt] *n* (-[e]s; -e) second-hand bookshop. **antiquarisch** [-'kvaːrɪʃ] *adj and adv* second-hand.

antiquiert [anti'kviːrt] *adj* antiquated.

Antiquität [antikvi'tɛːt] *f* (-; -en) antique. **Antiqui'täten|händler(in** *f*) *m* antique dealer. **~laden** *m* antique shop.

Antise'mit(in *f*) *m* anti-Semite.

antise'mitisch *adj* anti-Semitic.

Antisemi'tismus *m* anti-Semitism.

anti'septisch *adj* antiseptic.

anti'statisch *adj* antistatic.

Antrag ['antraːk] *m* (-[e]s; ⸚e) **1.** application (**auf** *acc* for), ⚖ petition, *parl.* motion, bill: **e-n ~ stellen auf** (*acc*) apply (⚖ petition, *parl.* move) for; **auf ~ von** (*or gen*) on the application *etc* of. **2.** *er machte ihr e-n ~* he proposed to her. **3.** → **'Antragsformu,lar** *n* application form. **'Antragsteller** [-ˈʃtɛlər] *m* (-s; -), **'Antragstellerin** *f* (-; -nen) applicant, *parl.* mover.

'antreffen *v/t* (*irr*, *sep*, -ge-, h, → **treffen**) find, come across.

'antreiben *v/t* (*irr*, *sep*, -ge-, h, → **treiben**) **1.** *a. fig.* drive (on), urge (on). **2.** ⚙ drive. **3.** *a. v/i* drift ashore.

'antreten (*irr*, *sep*, -ge-, → **treten**) **I** *v/t*

(h) **1.** *ein Amt* ~ take up an office; *die Arbeit* (*den Dienst*) ~ report for work (duty); *e-e Reise* ~ start off on a journey; *e-e Strafe* ~ begin to serve a sentence; → *Erbschaft.* **2.** kick (*bike*). **II** *v/i* (sn) **3.** line up. **4.** report (*bei* to). **5.** *sports*: enter (*bei, zu* for): ~ *gegen* compete against.

'**Antrieb** *m* (-[e]s; -e) **1.** *fig.* a) impulse, urge, b) motive, c) incentive: *aus eigenem* ~ of one's own accord; *neuen* ~ *geben* a) give a fresh impetus to s.th., b) *j-m* give s.o. a new interest. **2.** ⚙ drive.

'**Antriebs|agge,gat** *n* ⚙ drive assembly. ~**kraft** *f* driving power. ~**schwäche** *f* (-; *no pl*) *psych.* lack of drive.

'**antriebsstark** *adj psych.* full of drive.

'**Antriebswelle** *f mot.* axle-drive shaft.

'**antrinken** *v/t* (*irr, sep,* -ge-, h, → *trinken*) F *sich e-n* ~ get drunk; *sich Mut* ~ give o.s. Dutch courage.

'**Antritt** *m* (-[e]s; *no pl*) *bei* ~ a) *s-r Reise* upon setting out on his journey, b) *s-s Amtes* on entering upon his office, c) *der Macht* on coming into power, d) *e-r Erbschaft* upon accession to an inheritance. '**Antrittsbesuch** *m* first call. '**Antrittsrede** *f* inaugural speech, *parl.* maiden speech.

'**antun** *v/t* (*irr, sep,* -ge-, h, → *tun*) **1.** *j-m et.* ~ do s.th. to s.o; *j-m et. Gutes* ~ do s.o. a good turn; *sich et.* ~ lay hands upon o.s. **2.** *es j-m* ~ take s.o.'s fancy; → *angetan.*

Antwort ['antvɔrt] *f* (-; -en) (*auf acc* to) answer, *fig. a.* response. '**antworten** *v/i, v/t* (h) answer, reply, *fig.* respond: *auf e-e Frage* ~ answer a question; *j-m* ~ answer s.o., reply to s.o.

'**Antwortschein** *m* (international) reply coupon.

'**anvertrauen** (*sep,* h) **I** *v/t j-m et.* ~ a) entrust s.o. with s.th., b) confide s.th. to s.o. **II** *sich j-m* ~ a) confide in s.o., b) entrust o.s. to s.o.

'**anwachsen** *v/i* (*irr, sep,* -ge-, sn, → *wachsen¹*) **1.** grow on (*an acc* to), take root. **2.** *fig.* increase (*auf acc* to).

'**Anwachsen** *n* (-s) *fig.* increase, growth.

Anwalt ['anvalt] *m* (-[e]s; ̈e), **Anwältin** ['anvɛltɪn] *f* (-; -nen) **1.** ⚖ a) lawyer, *Am.* attorney(-at-law), b) solicitor, barrister, *Am.* counselor-at-law, counsel (*des Angeklagten* for the defence). **2.** *fig.* advocate.

'**Anwaltschaft** *f* (-; -en) *the* Bar.

'**Anwalts|hono,rar** *n* lawyer's fee. ~**kammer** *f* Bar Council (*Am.* Association). ~**kosten** *pl* lawyer's fees.

'**Anwandlung** *f* (-; -en) (*aus e-r* ~ *heraus* on an) impulse.

'**anwärmen** *v/t* (*sep,* -ge-, h) warm (up).

'**Anwärter(in** *f*) *m* (*auf acc*) candidate (for), aspirant (to).

Anwartschaft ['anvart͜ʃaft] *f* (-; -en) (*auf acc*) candidacy (for), qualification (for), ⚖ expectancy (of).

'**anweisen** *v/t* (*irr, sep,* -ge-, h, → *weisen*) **1.** a) instruct, direct, b) guide, train. **2.** assign (*dat* to): *j-m e-n Platz* ~ show s.o. to his seat. **3.** (*dat* to) remit (*sum*), order the payment of (*fee etc*).

'**Anweisung** *f* (-; -en) **1.** instruction, direction. **2.** assignment. **3.** remittance.

anwendbar ['anvɛntbaːr] *adj* applicable (*auf acc* to). '**anwenden** *v/t* (*irr, sep,* -ge-, h, → *wenden*) use, make use of, *a.* ⚖, ⚕ apply (*auf acc* to): *falsch* ~ misapply; *nutzbringend* ~ make good use of; → *äußerlich, Gewalt* 1.

'**Anwender** *m* (-s; -) *computer*: user.

'**Anwendung** *f* (-; -en) **1.** use, application (*auf acc* to): *unter* ~ *von Zwang* by (using) force. **2.** ⚕ (hydrotherapeutic) treatment.

'**Anwendungs|beispiel** *n* example of use. ~**pro,gramm** *n computer*: application program. ~**vorschrift** *f* directions for use.

'**anwerben** *v/t* (*irr, sep,* -ge-, h, → *werben*) recruit, ⚔ *a.* enlist.

'**Anwerbung** *f* (-; -en) recruitment.

'**Anwesen** *n* (-s; -) property, estate.

anwesend ['anveːzənt] *adj* present (*bei* at): *nicht* ~ *sein* be absent. '**Anwesende** *m, f* (-n; -n) person present: ~ *ausgenommen* present company excepted. '**Anwesenheit** *f* (-; *no pl*) presence (*in* ~ *von* (*or gen*) in the presence of).

'**Anwesenheitsliste** *f* attendance list.

'**anwidern** *v/t* (*sep,* -ge-, h) → *anekeln*

Anwohner ['anvoːnər] *m* (-s; -), '**Anwohnerin** *f* (-; -nen) resident.

'**Anzahl** *f* (-; *no pl*) number.

'**anzahlen** *v/t* (*sep,* -ge-, h) (pay *a sum* as) a) deposit, make a down payment (on).

'**Anzahlung** f (-; -en) deposit, down payment.

'**anzapfen** v/t (sep, -ge-, h) tap (a. F fig.).

'**Anzeichen** n (-s; -) (**für** of) sign, a. ✴ symptom: **alle ~ sprechen dafür, daß ...** there is every indication that ...

Anzeige ['antsaɪɡə] f (-; -n) **1.** announcement, notice, esp. ✝ advice. **2.** advertisement, F ad(vert): **e-e ~ aufgeben** a. advertise. **3.** notification, ⚖ information: (**bei der Polizei**) **~ erstatten →** anzeigen 3. '**anzeigen** v/t (sep, -ge-, h) **1.** j-m et. **~** notify s.o. of s.th. **2.** indicate, ⊙ a. register. **3.** denounce: **j-n** (**bei der Polizei**) **~** report s.o. to the police. **4.** fig. indicate: **es erscheint angezeigt zu** inf it seems advisable to inf.

'**Anzeigen|blatt** n advertising paper. **~teil** m newspaper: advertisements.

'**Anzeiger** m (-s; -) **1.** gazette. **2.** ⊙ indicator.

'**Anzeigetafel** f sports: scoreboard.

'**anzetteln** v/t (sep, -ge-, h) instigate.

'**anziehen** (irr, sep, -ge-, h, → **ziehen**) **I** v/t **1.** put on (clothes): **j-n ~** dress s.o. **2.** phys. attract (a. fig.), absorb (humidity etc). **3.** fig. draw (people). **4.** tighten (screw, rope), apply (brake), draw in (reins). **5.** draw up (legs). **II** v/i **6.** horse etc: pull away. **7.** fig. prices etc: go up. **III** sich **~** dress (o.s.), get dressed.

'**anziehend** adj fig. attractive, charming: **~ wirken auf** (acc) attract.

'**Anziehung** f (-; no pl) a. fig. attraction.

'**Anziehungskraft** f **1.** phys. a. attraction, b) gravitational pull. **2.** no pl (**auf** acc) attraction (for), appeal (to).

'**Anziehungspunkt** m fig. cent/re (Am. -er) of attraction.

'**Anzug** m (-[e]s; ⸚e). **1.** suit. **2.** **im ~ sein** be approaching, storm: be coming up.

anzüglich ['antsy:klɪç] adj personal (remark), suggestive (joke): **~ werden** get personal. '**Anzüglichkeit** f (-; -en) usu. pl personal remark.

'**anzünden** v/t (sep, -ge-, h) light (cigar etc), strike (match), set house on fire.

'**Anzünder** m (-s; -) lighter.

'**anzweifeln** v/t (sep, -ge-, h) question, doubt.

Aorta [a'ɔrta] f (-; -ten) anat. aorta.

apart [a'part] adj striking, unusual.

Apartheid [a'parthaɪt] f (-; no pl) apartheid. **~poli,tik** f apartheid policy.

Apartment [a'partmənt] n (-s; -s) flatlet, Am. apartment. **~haus** n block of flatlets, Am. apartment building.

Apathie [apa'ti:] f (-; -n) apathy.

apathisch [a'pa:tɪʃ] adj apathetic.

Aperitif [aperi'ti:f] m (-s; -s, -s) aperitif.

Apfel ['apfəl] m (-s; ⸚) apple: → **sauer** 1.

'**Apfel|baum** m apple tree. **~kuchen** m **gedeckter ~** apple pie. **~mus** n apple sauce. **~saft** m apple juice.

Apfelsine [apfəl'zi:nə] f (-; -n) orange.

'**Apfelstrudel** m gastr. apfelstrudel.

'**Apfelwein** m cider.

Aphorismus [afo'rɪsmʊs] m (-; -men) aphorism.

Apokalypse [apoka'lʏpsə] f (-; -n) apocalypse.

Apostel [a'pɔstəl] m (-s; -) a. fig. apostle. **A'postelgeschichte** f bibl. the Acts (of the Apostles). **apostolisch** [apɔs'to:lɪʃ] adj apostolic.

Apostroph [apɔs'tro:f] m (-s; -e) apostrophe.

Apotheke [apo'te:kə] f (-; -n) chemist's shop, pharmacy. **apo'thekenpflichtig** adj obtainable in a pharmacy only.

Apotheker [apo'te:kər] m (-s; -), **Apo'thekerin** f (-; -nen) pharmacist, (dispensing) chemist.

Apparat [apa'ra:t] m (-[e]s; -e) **1.** a) apparatus (a. fig.), fig. a. machinery, b) instrument, c) device. **2.** camera. **3.** a) radio, b) (TV) set. **4.** F phone: **am ~!** speaking!; **am ~ bleiben** hold the line.

Apparatur [apara'tu:r] f (-; -en) equipment.

Appartement [apartə'mã:] n (-s; -s) **1.** → **Apartment. 2.** (hotel) suite.

Appell [a'pɛl] m (-s; -e) ✕ roll call: fig. **e-n ~ richten an** (acc) → **appellieren** [apɛ'li:rən] v/i (h) **~ an** (acc) (make an) appeal to.

Appetit [ape'ti:t] m (-[e]s; -e) (**j-m ~ machen** give s.o. an) appetite (**auf** acc for); **ich habe ~ auf ...** I feel like ... **appe'titanregend** adj, **appe'titlich** adj a. fig. appetizing. **Appe'titlosigkeit** f (-; no pl) loss of appetite. **Appe'titzügler** m (-s; -) appetite suppressant.

applaudieren [aplaʊ'di:rən] v/i (h) (dat) applaud, cheer. **Applaus** [a'plaʊs] m (-es; no pl) applause.

apportieren [apɔr'ti:rən] v/t (h) retrieve.

appretieren [aprε'tiːrən] *v/t* (h), **Appretur** [aprε'tuːr] *f* (-; -en) ⊛ finish.

approbiert [apro'biːrt] *adj* qualified.

Aprikose [apri'koːzə] *f* (-; -n) apricot.

April [a'prɪl] *m* (-[s]; -e) April: *j-n in den ~ schicken* make an April fool of s.o.; *~, ~!* April fool! **~scherz** *m* April-fool joke. **~wetter** *n* April weather.

Aquaplaning [akva'plaːnɪŋ] *n* (-[s]; *no pl*) *mot.* aquaplaning.

Aquarell [akva'rεl] *n* (-s; -e), **Aqua'rellfarbe** *f* water colo(u)r. **Aqua'rellmaler(in** *f*) *m* water colo(u)rist.

Aquarium [a'kvaːriʊm] *n* (-s; -rien) aquarium.

Äquator [ε'kvaːtɔr] *m* (-s; *no pl*) equator. **~taufe** *f* crossing-the-line ceremony.

äquivalent [εkviva'lεnt] *adj* equivalent. **Äquiva'lent** *n* (-[e]s; -e) equivalent.

Ära ['εːra] *f* (-; *rare* Ären) era.

Araber ['araːbɐr] *m* (-s; -) Arab (*a. horse*). **'Araberin** *f* (-; -nen) Arab (woman).

Arabien [a'raːbiən] *n* (-s) Arabia.

a'rabisch [-bɪʃ] *adj* Arab *states etc*, Arabian *nights etc*, Arabic *language etc*.

Arbeit ['arbaɪt] *f* (-; -en) **1.** a) work (*a. phys.*), b) hard work, labo(u)r, c) task, job: *Tag der ~* May Day, *Am.* Labor Day; *geistige ~* brainwork; *an (or bei) der ~* at work; *an die ~ gehen* start work; *zur* (F *auf*) *~ gehen* go to work; *et. in ~ haben* be working on s.th. **2.** (*j-m viel*) *~ machen* give s.o. a lot of) trouble. **3.** work, employment, job: *~ suchen* look for a job; *~ haben* be in work, have a job; *k-e ~ haben* be out of work, be without a job. **4.** a) (piece of) work, b) workmanship: *künstlerische ~* work of art. **5.** *ped., univ.* paper: *wissenschaftliche ~* treatise.

'arbeiten [-bɪ] **I** *v/i* work, ⊛ function, run, *a.* ☨ operate: *~ an (dat)* be working on; *~ bei* work for; *(geschäftlich) ~ mit* deal with, do business with; *mit Verlust ~* operate at a loss; *sein Geld ~ lassen* invest one's money. **II** *v/t* make. **III** *sich ~ durch* work one's way through.

'Arbeiter *m* (-s; -) a) worker, workman, b) labo(u)rer: *die ~ → Arbeiterschaft*; *~ und Unternehmer* labo(u)r and management.

'Arbeiter... workers' ..., working-class (*family*, *area*, *etc*). **~gewerkschaft** *f* trade (*Am.* labor) union.

'Arbeiterin *f* (-; -nen) **1.** (female) worker. **2.** *zo.* worker (bee *or* ant).

'Arbeiterklasse *f* working class(es).

'Arbeiterpar,tei *f* workers' party.

'Arbeiterschaft *f* (-; *no pl*) working class(es), *a. pol.* Labo(u)r.

'Arbeitgeber *m* (-s; -) employer. **~anteil** *m* employer's contribution. **~verband** *m* employers' association.

'Arbeitnehmer *m* (-s; -) employee. **~anteil** *m* employee's contribution.

'Arbeitsablauf *m* work routine.

'arbeitsam *adj* industrious, diligent.

'Arbeits|amt *n* employment exchange, *Br.* job centre. **~bedingungen** *pl* working (⊛ operating) conditions. **~be,schaffungspro,gramm** *n* job creation scheme. **~bescheinigung** *f* certificate of employment. **~bogen** *m* *ped.* work folder. **~eifer** *m* zeal. **~einkommen** *n* earned income. **~einstellung** *f* a) stoppage of work, b) shutdown, c) strike. **~erlaubnis** *f* work permit. **~essen** *n* working lunch (*or* dinner). **2fähig** *adj* fit for work: *pol.* **~e Mehrheit** working majority. **~fläche** *f* *in kitchen*: worktop. **~frieden** *m* industrial peace. **~gang** *m* ⊛ working cycle: *in einem ~* in a single pass. **~gebiet** *n* sphere of work. **~gemeinschaft** *f* working pool, *ped. etc* study group. **~gericht** *n* industrial tribunal. **~grundlage** *f* working basis. **2inten,siv** *adj* labo(u)r-intensive. **~kampf** *m* labo(u)r dispute. **~kleidung** *f* work clothes. **~klima** *n* work climate. **~kraft** *f* **1.** capacity for work. **2.** worker, *pl* manpower. **~kräftemangel** *m* manpower shortage. **~leistung** *f* efficiency, ⊛ *a.* output. **~lohn** *m* wages, pay.

'arbeitslos *adj* unemployed, jobless: *~ sein* a. be out of work. **'Arbeitslose** *m*, *f* (-n; -n) unemployed person: *die ~n* the unemployed, the jobless.

'Arbeitslosen|geld *n* unemployment benefit: *~ beziehen* F be on the dole. **~hilfe** *f* unemployment relief. **~zahl** *f* unemployment figures.

'Arbeitslosigkeit *f* (-; *no pl*) unemployment.

'Arbeits|markt *m* labo(u)r (*or* job) market: *die Lage auf dem ~* the job situation. **~mi,nister** *m* employment (*Am.* labor) minister. **~mo,ral** *f* (working)

morale. ~nachweis m employment agency. **~niederlegung** f (-; -en) walkout, strike.

'arbeitsparend adj labo(u)r-saving.
'Arbeitspensum n workload.
'Arbeitsplatz m **1.** job: *freie Arbeitsplätze* vacancies; *Schaffung von Arbeitsplätzen* job creation. **2.** working place. **~beschreibung** f job description. **~sicherung** f job security. **~vernichter** m job killer.
'Arbeitspro,zeß m *j-n wieder in den ~ eingliedern* put s.o. back to work. **~raum** m workroom. **~recht** n industrial law. ♀**reich** adj busy. ♀**scheu** adj work-shy. **~schluß** m end of work: *~ ist um ...* work finishes at ...; *nach ~* after work. **~schutz** m industrial safety. **~speicher** m computer: main memory. **~stunde** f manhour, pl working hours. ♀**süchtig** adj *~ sein* be a workaholic. **~tag** m working day, workday. **~teilung** f division of labo(u)r. **~tier** n F demon for work.
'Arbeitssuche f (-; *no pl*) (*auf ~ sein* be) job-hunting. **'Arbeitssuchende** m, f (-n; -n) job seeker, job hunter.
'arbeitsunfähig adj a) unfit for work, b) permanently disabled.
'Arbeits|unfall m industrial accident. **~vermittlung** f employment agency. **~vertrag** m employment contract. **~vorbereitung** f ⚙ operations scheduling. **~weise** f (working) method, ⚙ a. procedure. **~willige** m, f (-n; -n) person willing to work, *n.s.* nonstriker. **~zeit** f (*gleitende ~* flexible) working hours. **~zeitverkürzung** f reduction in working hours. **~zimmer** n study.
Archäologe [arçεo'lo:gə] m (-n; -n) arch(a)eologist. **Archäologie** [-lo'gi:] f (-; *no pl*) arch(a)eology. **archäologisch** [-'lo:gɪʃ] adj arch(a)eological.
Arche ['arçə] f (-; -n) ark: *die ~ Noah* Noah's ark.
Archipel [arçi'pe:l] m (-s; -e) geogr. archipelago.
Architekt [arçi'tεkt] m (-en; -en), **Archi'tektin** f (-; -nen) architect.
architektonisch [arçitεk'to:nɪʃ] adj architectural. **Architektur** [arçitεk'tu:r] f (-; -en) architecture.
Archiv [ar'çi:f] n (-s; -e) archives.
Ar'chivbild n library picture.

Areal [are'a:l] n (-s; -e) area.
Arena [a're:na] f (-; -nen) arena.
arg [ark] **I** adj bad: *mein ärgster Feind* my worst enemy; *im ~en liegen* be in a bad way. **II** adv badly, F a. awfully.
Argentinien [argεn'ti:niən] n (-s) Argentina, *the* Argentine. **Argen'tinier** m (-s; -), **Argen'tinierin** f (-; -nen), **argen'tinisch** adj Argentine.
Ärger ['εrgər] m (-s; *no pl*) **1.** (*über* acc at, about s.th., with s.o.) annoyance, irritation, anger: *zu m-m ~* to my annoyance. **2.** (*j-m ~ machen* cause s.o.) trouble: *das gibt ~* there will be trouble. **'ärgerlich** adj **1.** (*über* acc at, about s.th., with s.o.) annoyed, angry, F cross. **2.** annoying: *wie ~!* a. what a nuisance! **'ärgern** (h) **I** v/t annoy, make s.o. angry. **II** *sich ~* (*über* acc at, about s.th., with s.o.) be angry, be (*or* get) annoyed: *ärgere dich nicht!* take it easy! **'Ärgernis** n (-ses; -se) annoyance: *~ erregen* give offen/ce (*Am.* -se); ⚖ *öffentliches ~* public nuisance.
'arglistig adj malicious, ⚖ fraudulent: *~e Täuschung* wilful deceit.
'arglos adj a) innocent, b) unsuspecting.
'Arglosigkeit f (-; *no pl*) innocence.
Argument [argu'mεnt] n (-[e]s; -e) argument. **Argumentation** [argumenta-'tsɪo:n] f (-; -en) argumentation.
argumen'tieren v/i (h) argue, reason.
Argwohn ['arkvo:n] m (-[e]s; *no pl*) suspicion (*gegen* of). **argwöhnisch** ['arkvø:nɪʃ] adj suspicious (*gegen* of).
Arie ['a:riə] f (-; -n) ♪ aria.
Arier ['a:riər] m (-s; -), **'Arierin** f (-; -nen), **'arisch** adj Aryan.
Aristokrat [arɪsto'kra:t] m (-en; -en), **Aristo'kratin** f (-; -nen) aristocrat. **Aristokratie** [arɪstokra'ti:] f (-; -n) aristocracy. **aristokratisch** [arɪsto'kra:tɪʃ] adj aristocratic.
Arithmetik [arɪt'me:tɪk] f (-; *no pl*) arithmetic.
Arktis ['arktɪs] f (-; *no pl*) *the* Arctic (regions). **'arktisch** adj a. fig. arctic.
arm [arm] adj poor (*an* dat in).
Arm m (-[e]s; -e) arm: *in die ~e nehmen* embrace, hug; *mein ärgster Feind* pick s.o. up, b) F fig. pull s.o.'s leg; *j-m in die ~e laufen* bump into s.o.; *j-m unter die ~e greifen* (*mit*) help s.o. (out with).

Armatur [arma'tu:r] f (-; -en) armature,
pl fittings.
Arma'turenbrett n dashboard.
'**Armband** n (-[e]s, ⁔er) bracelet.
'**Armbanduhr** f wrist watch.
'**Armbinde** f **1.** armlet. **2.** ⚕ sling.
'**Arme** m, f (-n; -n) poor man (woman):
die ⁓n the poor; **ich ⁓(r)!** poor me!
Armee [ar'me:] f (-; -n) army.
Ar'meekorps n army corps.
Ärmel ['ɛrməl] m (-s; -) sleeve: **ohne ⁓**
sleeveless; F **et. aus dem ⁓ schütteln** a)
pull s.th. out of a hat, b) do s.th. off the
cuff. '**Ärmelaufschlag** m cuff.
'**ärmellos** adj sleeveless.
armieren [ar'mi:rən] v/t (h) **1.** armo(u)r
(cable). **2.** reinforce (concrete).
...armig ...-armed, ...-branched.
'**Armlehne** f arm. '**Armleuchter** m (-s;
-) **1.** chandelier. **2.** F contp. idiot, twerp.
ärmlich ['ɛrmlıç] adj poor, w.s. a.
shabby: **in ⁓en Verhältnissen leben** be
poorly off; **aus ⁓en Verhältnissen
stammen** come from a poor family.
'**Armreif(en)** m bangle.
armselig ['armze:lıç] adj wretched, a.
fig. miserable.
'**Armsessel** m, '**Armstuhl** m armchair.
Armut ['armu:t] f (-; no pl) poverty (a.
fig. **an** dat in, of).
'**Armuts|grenze** f **an (unter) der ⁓ lie-
gen** be on (under) the poverty line.
⁓zeugnis n j-m (sich) **ein ⁓ ausstellen**
show s.o.'s (one's) incompetence.
Aroma [a'ro:ma] n (-s; -men) a) aroma,
b) flavo(u)r. **aromatisch** [aro'ma:tıʃ]
adj aromatic. **aromatisieren** [aroma-
ti'zi:rən] v/t (h) flavo(u)r.
arrangieren [arã'ʒi:rən] (h) **I** v/t arrange. **II sich ⁓** come to an arrangement (or agreement) (**mit** with).
Arrest [a'rɛst] m (-[e]s; -e) detention.
arretieren [are'ti:rən] v/t (h) ✪ arrest,
stop.
arriviert [ari'vi:rt] adj successful.
arrogant [aro'gant] adj arrogant.
Arsch [arʃ] m (-[e]s; ⁔e) V **1.** arse, Am. a.
ass: **leck mich am ⁓!** fuck you!; **er (es)
ist im ⁓** he (it) has had it; **j-m in den ⁓
kriechen** suck up to s.o. **2.** → **Arschloch.** '**Arschkriecher** m V arse licker.
'**Arschloch** n V arsehole, Am. a. ass-
hole, (person) a. (stupid) bastard, shit.
Arsen [ar'ze:n] n (-s; no pl) 🜍 arsenic.

Arsenal [arze'na:l] n (-s; -e) arsenal.
Art [art] f (-; -en) **1.** nature, kind: **sie hat
e-e nette ⁓ mit Kindern** she has a way
with children; **es ist nicht s-e ⁓ zu** inf
he's not the sort to inf; **das entspricht
nicht ihrer ⁓** it's not like her; **Fragen
allgemeiner ⁓** questions of general interest. **2.** a. **⁓ und Weise** way, manner,
method; **auf diese ⁓** in this way; **s-e ⁓
zu sprechen** the way he talks; gastr.
nach ⁓ des Hauses à la maison. **3.** F
behavio(u)r, manners. **4.** kind, sort,
type, biol. species: **... aller ⁓** all sorts of
...; iro. **e-e ⁓ Dichter** a poet of sorts; fig.
aus der ⁓ schlagen go one's own way.
Arterie [ar'te:riə] f (-; -n) artery.
Arteriosklerose [arterioskle'ro:zə] f (-;
-n) ⚕ arteriosclerosis.
'**artfremd** adj biol., 🜍 alien, foreign.
artig ['artıç] adj well-behaved: **sei ⁓!** be
good!, be a good boy (girl)!
Artikel [ar'ti:kəl] m (-s; -) article.
artikulieren [artiku'li:rən] (h) **I** v/t articulate. **II sich ⁓** express o.s.
Artillerie [artılə'ri:] f (-; -n) artillery.
Artischocke [arti'ʃɔkə] f (-; -n) 🜏 artichoke. **Arti'schockenboden** m gastr.
artichoke heart.
Artist [ar'tıst] m (-en; -en), **Ar'tistin** f (-;
-nen) (variety) artist.
ar'tistisch adj artistic, acrobatic.
Arznei [arts'naı] f (-; -en) (**gegen** for)
medicine, medicament, drug.
Arz'neikunde f (-; no pl) pharmaceutics.
Arz'neimittel n → **Arznei.** **⁓abhängig-
keit** f drug dependence. **⁓mißbrauch** m
drug abuse.
Arz'neipflanze f medicinal plant.
Arz'neischrank m medicine cabinet.
Arzt [a:rtst] m (-es; ⁔e) doctor, physician:
zum ⁓ gehen (go to) see the doctor.
'**Arztberuf** m medical profession.
Ärztekammer ['ɛrtstə-] f medical association. '**Ärztemuster** n drug sample.
'**Ärzteschaft** f (-; no pl) medical profession. '**Arzthelferin** f doctor's receptionist (or assistant). **Ärztin** ['ɛrtstın] f
(-; -nen) lady doctor (or physician).
ärztlich ['ɛrtstlıç] adj medical: **⁓es Attest** medical (or doctor's) certificate; **⁓
behandeln** attend; **⁓ verordnet** prescribed by a doctor.
as [as], **As**[1] n (-; -) ♪ A flat.
As[2] [as] n (-ses; -se) ace (a. F person).

Asbest [as'bɛst] m (-[e]s; -e) asbestos.
Asche ['aʃə] f (-; ⊙ -n) ashes (a. fig.), (cigarette etc) ash: **glühende** ~ embers.
'**Aschen|bahn** f sports: cinder (mot. dirt) track. ~**becher** m ashtray. ~**brödel** [-brø:dəl] n (-s; -), ~**puttel** [-pʊtəl] n (-s; -) fig. Cinderella.
Ascher'mittwoch m Ash Wednesday.
'**aschfahl** adj ashen.
'**aschgrau** adj ash-grey, Am. ash-gray.
Ascorbinsäure [askɔr'bi:n-] f ascorbic acid.
äsen ['ɛ:zən] v/i (h) graze, browse.
aseptisch [a'zɛptɪʃ] adj aseptic.
Asiat [a'zĭa:t] m (-en; -en), **Asi'atin** f (-; -nen), **asi'atisch** adj Asian. **Asien** ['a:zĭən] n (-s) Asia.
Askese [as'ke:zə] f (-; no pl) asceticism.
Asket [as'ke:t] m (-en; -en), **As'ketin** f (-; -nen), **as'ketisch** adj ascetic.
asozial ['azotsĭa:l] adj antisocial.
Aspekt [as'pɛkt] m (-[e]s; -e) aspect.
Asphalt [as'falt] m (-s; ⊙ -e), **asphaltieren** [asfal'ti:rən] v/t (h) asphalt.
aß [a:s] pret of **essen**.
Assessor [a'sɛsɔr] m (-s; -en), **Assessorin** [asɛ'so:rɪn] f (-; -nen) civil servant (lawyer, teacher, etc) who has completed his/her second state examination.
Assistent [asɪs'tɛnt] m (-en; -en), **Assi'stentin** f (-; -nen) assistant.
Assi'stenzarzt m assistant doctor.
assistieren [asɪs'ti:rən] v/i (h) assist (bei in).
Assoziation [asotsĭa'tsĭo:n] f (-; -en) association. **assoziieren** [asotsĭ'i:rən] v/t (h) associate.
Ast [ast] m (-[e]s; -[e]s; ~e) branch, in wood: knot: F **auf dem absteigenden** ~ **sein** be going downhill.
Aster ['astər] f (-; -n) ♀ aster.
Ästhet [ɛs'te:t] m (-en; -en), **Äs'thetin** f (-; -nen) (a)esthetical.
äs'thetisch adj (a)esthetical.
Asthma ['astma] n (-s; no pl) ♂ asthma.
Asthmatiker [ast'ma:tɪkər] m (-s; -), **asth'matisch** [-tʃ] adj asthmatic.
Astrologe [astro'lo:gə] m (-n; -n) astrologer. **Astrologie** [-lo'gi:] f (-; no pl) astrology. **Astronaut** [-'naʊt] m (-en; -en) astronaut. **Astronomie** [-no'mi:] f (-; no pl) astronomy. **astronomisch** [-'no:mɪʃ] adj a. F fig. astronomic(al).
Astrophy'sik f astrophysics.

Asyl [a'zy:l] n (-s; no pl) (**um politisches** ~ **bitten** ask for political) asylum.
Asylant [azy'lant] m (-en; -en), **Asy'lantin** f (-; -nen) person seeking (or having been granted) (political) asylum.
A'sylrecht n right of asylum.
'**asymmetrisch** adj asymmetric(al).
'**asynchron** adj asynchronous.
Atelier [ate'lĭe:] n (-s; -s) studio.
Atem ['a:təm] m (-s; no pl) breath: **außer** ~ (**kommen** get) out of breath; ~ **holen** take a breath; fig. **mir stockte der** ~ my heart stood still; **das verschlug mir den** ~ that took my breath away; **j-n in** ~ **halten** keep s.o. on the jump (or in suspense); → **anhalten** 1. '**atemberaubend** adj fig. breathtaking. '**Atembeschwerden** pl difficulty in breathing. '**Atemgerät** n breathing apparatus, ♂ respirator. '**atemlos** adj a. fig. breathless. '**Atempause** f F breather. '**Atemwege** pl respiratory tract. '**Atemzug** m breath: **im gleichen** ~ in one breath.
Atheismus [ate'ɪsmʊs] m (-; no pl) atheism. **Atheist** [ate'ɪst] m (-en; -en) atheist. **athe'istisch** adj atheistic(al).
Äther ['ɛ:tər] m (-s; no pl) ♂ ether.
ätherisch [ɛ'te:rɪʃ] adj ethereal, etheric: ~**es Öl** essential (or volatile) oil.
Äthiopien [ɛ'tĭo:pĭən] n (-s) Ethiopia. **Äthi'opier** m (-s; -), **Äthi'opierin** f (-; -nen), **äthi'opisch** adj Ethiopian.
Athlet [at'le:t] m (-en; -en), **Ath'letin** f (-; -nen) athlete. **ath'letisch** adj athletic.
Äthyl [ɛ'ty:l] n (-s; no pl) ethyl.
Äthylen [ɛty'le:n] n (-s; no pl) ethylene.
atlantisch [at'lantɪʃ] adj Atlantic: **der** ⊙**e Ozean** the Atlantic (Ocean).
Atlas ['atlas] m (-[ses]; -se) atlas.
atmen ['a:tmən] v/i, v/t (h) breathe: **tief** ~ breathe deep. '**Atmen** n (-s) breathing.
Atmosphäre [atmo'sfɛ:rə] f (-; -n) a. fig. atmosphere. **atmo'sphärisch** adj atmospheric: ⚡ ~**e Störungen** statics, atmospherics.
'**Atmung** f (-; no pl) breathing, respiration: **künstliche** ~ artificial respiration.
Atom [a'to:m] n (-s; -e) atom.
atomar [ato'ma:r] adj atomic, nuclear.
A'tom|bombe f atom(ic) (or nuclear) bomb, A-bomb. ~**bunker** m nuclear shelter. ~**ener,gie** f atomic energy. ~**explosi,on** f atomic explosion. ~**forschung** f atomic research. ⊙**getrieben**

adj nuclear-powered. **~gewicht** *n* atomic weight. **~hülle** *f* atomic shell.
atomisieren [atomi'zi:rən] *v/t* (h) *a. fig.* atomize.
A'tom|kern *m* atomic nucleus. **~kraft** *f* (-; *no pl*) nuclear power. **~kraftwerk** *n* nuclear power station. **~krieg** *m* atomic (*or* nuclear) war(fare). **~macht** *f pol.* nuclear power. **~mo,dell** *n* atomic model. **~müll** *m* radioactive waste. **~phy,sik** *f* atomic physics. **~pilz** *m fig.* mushroom cloud. **~re,aktor** *m* atom reactor. **~spaltung** *f* atom splitting. **~sperrvertrag** *m pol.* nonproliferation treaty. **~sprengkopf** *m* nuclear warhead. **~test** *m* nuclear test. **~teststopp(abkommen** *n*) *m* test ban (treaty). **~tod** *m* nuclear death. **~U-Boot** *n* nuclear(-powered) submarine.
A'tomwaffen *pl* atomic (*or* nuclear) weapons. **2frei** *adj* nuclear-free *zone*. **~gegner(in** *f*) *m* anti-nuclear protester.
A'tomzahl *f* atomic number.
A'tomzeitalter *n* atomic age.
atonal ['atona:l] *adj ♩* atonal.
Atrophie [atro'fi:] *f* (-; -n) *♣* atrophy.
ätsch [ɛ:tʃ] *int* there!, serves you right!
Attaché [ata'ʃe:] *m* (-s; -s) attaché.
Attacke [a'takə] *f* (-; -n), **attackieren** [ata'ki:rən] *v/t, v/i* (h) attack.
Attentat [atɛn'ta:t] *n* (-[e]s; -e) a) (**ein ~ auf j-n verüben** make an) attempt on s.o.'s life, b) assassination.
Atten'täter(in *f*) *m* assassin.
Attest [a'tɛst] *n* (-[e]s; -e) certificate.
Attraktion [atrak'tsio:n] *f* (-; -en) attraction. **attraktiv** [-'ti:f] *adj* attractive.
Attrappe [a'trapə] *f* (-; -n) dummy.
Attribut [atri'bu:t] *n* (-[e]s; -e) attribute. **attributiv** [atribu'ti:f] *adj* attributive.
ätzen ['ɛtsən] *v/t* (h) **1. 🔥** corrode, eat into. **2. ♣** cauterize. **3.** *arts:* etch.
'ätzend *adj* corrosive, *a. fig.* caustic.
au [aʊ] *int* **1.** ouch! **2. ~ ja!** oh yes!
Aubergine [obɛr'ʒi:nə] *f* (-; -n) ♧ aubergine, eggplant.
auch [aʊx] *adv* **1.** also, too, as well: **so habe Hunger - ich ~** I am hungry - so am I (F me too); **ich glaube es - ich ~** I believe it - so do I; **ich kann es nicht - ich ~ nicht** I can't do it - nor (*or* neither) can I. **2.** even: **ohne ~ nur zu fragen** without so much as asking. **3. wenn ~** even if, although; **so sehr ich es ~**

bedauere however much I regret it. **4. wann ~ (immer)** whenever; **wer es ~ (immer) sei** whoever it may be; **was er ~ (immer) sagt** whatever he may say; **so schwierig es ~ sein mag** difficult as it may be. **5. wirst du es ~ tun?** are you really going to do it?; **so schlimm ist es ~ wieder nicht!** it's not all that bad!
Audienz [aʊ'diɛnts] *f* (-; -en) audience (**bei** with).
audiovisu'ell [aʊdio-] *adj* audiovisual.
Auditorium [aʊdi'to:riʊm] *n* (-s; -rien) **1.** *univ.* (**~ maximum** main) lecture hall. **2.** audience.
auf [aʊf] *I prep* (*dat*) **1.** *space:* on, in, at: **~ dem Tisch** on the table; **~ der Straße** in (*Am.* on) the street, on the road; **~ See** at sea; **~ der Post** at the post office; **~ der Welt** in the world; **~ dem Land** in the country; **er ist ~ s-m Zimmer** he is in his room. **2.** at, during, on: **~ dem Ball** at the ball; **~ s-r Reise** during (*or* on) his journey; **~ Urlaub** on vacation, *esp. Br.* on holiday. **II** *prep* (*acc*) **3.** *place:* a) (down) on, onto, into, b) up, c) to, toward(s): **er setzte sich ~ e-n Stuhl** he sat down on a chair; **~ die Erde fallen** fall (on)to the ground; **er ging ~ die Straße** he went (out) into the street; **ich ging ~ die Post** I went to the post office; **geh ~ dein Zimmer!** go to your room!; **sie zogen ~ das Land** they moved (in)to the country; *fig.* **~ Besuch kommen** come for a visit; **~ Reisen gehen** go on a journey. **4.** *time:* a) for: **~ ein paar Tage** for a few days; **~ Jahre hinaus** for years to come; **es geht ~ 9** (*Uhr*) it's getting on for nine (o'clock); F **~ e-e Tasse Kaffee** for a cup of coffee, b) after: **Stunde ~ Stunde verging** hour after hour went by, c) until: **~ morgen verschieben** postpone until tomorrow; F **~ bald!** see you soon! **5. ~ diese Weise** (in) this way; **~ deutsch** in German; **~ s-n Befehl** by (*or* at) his order; **~ m-e Bitte** (**hin**) on my request. **6.** *quantities:* **von 80 Tonnen ~ 100 erhöhen** increase from 80 tons to 100; **~ jeden entfallen ...** there is/are ... (for) each; **~ die Sekunde** to the second; **~ 100 m** *see, hear, etc* at (*or* from) a hundred metres, *come etc* as close as 100 metres. **III** *adv* **7.** F a) open: **Augen ~!** watch out!, b) awake,

c) up (and going): **ich war die ganze Nacht ~** I was up all night. **8. ~ und ab gehen** walk up and down (*or* to and fro); F **~ und davon gehen** run away. **IV** *int* **~!** a) (get) up!, b) F a. **~ geht's!** let's go!, c) come on!

Auf: das ~ und Ab des Lebens the ups and downs of life; **das ~ und Ab der Preise** the rise and fall of prices.

'aufarbeiten *v/t* (*sep*, -ge-, h) **1.** work (*or* clear) off, catch up on. **2.** furbish up, do up. **3.** *fig.* a work *s.th.* up, b) digest.

'aufatmen *v/i* (*sep*, -ge-, h) draw a deep breath, *fig.* breathe again (*or* freely).

'aufbahren *v/t* (*sep*, -ge-, h) put *coffin* on the bier, lay *body* out (in state).

'Aufbau *m* (-[e]s; -ten) **1.** *no pl* building, erection, construction, ⚙ assembly; *fig.* **im ~ (begriffen) sein** be in its initial stages. **2.** *no pl fig.* structure. **3.** *mot.* car body. **4.** *no pl computer:* format.

'aufbauen (*sep*, -ge-, h) **I** *v/t* **1.** build, erect, construct: **wieder ~** rebuild, reconstruct. **2.** *fig.* a) build up (*business, attack*, F *politician etc*), b) organize, set up: **sich e-e Existenz ~** build o.s. an existence; **e-e Theorie etc ~ auf** (*dat*) base (*or* found) a theory *etc* on. **3.** ⚙ a) assemble, b) set up, c) arrange. **II** *v/i* **4.** (*a.* **sich ~**) *auf* (*dat*) be based (*or* founded) on: **sich ~ gegen** rebel against.

'aufbäumen: sich ~ (*sep*, -ge-, h) *horse:* rear; *fig.* **sich ~ gegen** rebel against.

'aufbauschen *v/t* (*sep*, -ge-, h) *fig.* exaggerate.

'Aufbauten *pl* of **Aufbau** ⇩ superstructure.

'aufbegehren *v/i* (*sep*, h) rebel.

'aufbehalten *v/t* (*irr, sep*, h, → **behalten**) F **den Hut ~** keep one's hat on.

'aufbekommen *v/t* (*irr, sep*, h, → **bekommen**) F **1.** get *the door* open, get *a knot* undone. **2.** be given *a task* (to do).

'aufbereiten *v/t* (*sep*, h) prepare, process, ⚙ *a.* treat, *computer:* edit, *fig.* work *s.th.* up.

'aufbessern *v/t* (*sep*, -ge-, h) **1.** improve. **2.** raise (*salary*).

'aufbewahren *v/t* (*sep*, h) preserve, keep, store (up). **'Aufbewahrung** *f* (-; *no pl*) (**sichere ~**) safekeeping: **j-m et. zur ~ geben** leave s.th. with s.o.

'aufbieten *v/t* (*irr, sep*, -ge-, h, → **bieten**) **1.** muster, summon (up) (*courage*), use (*one's influence*). **2.** ✕ mobilize.

'Aufbietung *f* (-; *no pl*) **unter ~ aller Kräfte** by (a) supreme effort.

'aufbinden *v/t* (*irr, sep*, -ge-, h, → **binden**) undo, untie: → **Bär.**

'aufblähen (*sep*, -ge-, h) **I** *v/t* **1.** (*a.* **sich ~**) blow out, swell. **2.** ✝, 🟥 inflate. **II sich ~** F *contp.* puff o.s. up.

'aufblasbar *adj* inflatable. **'aufblasen** (*irr, sep*, -ge-, h, → **blasen**) **I** *v/t* blow up, inflate. **II sich ~** F puff o.s. up.

'aufbleiben *v/i* (*irr, sep*, -ge-, sn, → **bleiben**) **1.** sit up, stay up. **2.** remain open.

'aufblenden *v/i* (*sep*, -ge-, h) **1.** *mot.* turn on the headlights full beam. **2.** *phot.* open the diaphragm.

'aufblicken *v/i* (*sep*, -ge-, h) look up: **zu j-m ~** look up at s.o. (*esp. fig.* to s.o.).

'aufblitzen *v/i* (*sep*, -ge-, sn) flash (up).

'aufblühen *v/i* (*sep*, -ge-, sn) **1.** (begin to) bloom. **2.** *fig. girl:* blossom (out), *town, economy, etc:* (begin to) flourish.

'aufbocken *v/t* (*sep*, -ge-, h) jack up.

'aufbohren *v/t* (*sep*, -ge-, h) a) bore open, b) rebore (*engine*), c) drill (*tooth*).

'aufbrauchen *v/t* (*sep*, -ge-, h) use up.

'aufbrausen *v/i* (*sep*, -ge-, sn) flare up.

'aufbrausend *adj fig.* quick-tempered.

'aufbrechen (*irr, sep*, -ge-, → **brechen**) **I** *v/t* (h) **1.** a) break (*or* prize) open, b) break up. **II** *v/i* (sn) **2.** bud, boil, *etc:* (burst) open, *ice:* break up. **3.** (*nach* for) start, set out.

'aufbringen *v/t* (*irr, sep*, -ge-, h, → **bringen**) **1.** → **aufbekommen** 1. **2.** muster, summon (up) (*courage etc*). **3.** raise (*money*). **4.** start (*rumo[u]r, fashion*). **5.** anger: **j-n gegen sich ~** get s.o.'s back up; → **aufgebracht. 6.** ⇩ capture.

'Aufbruch *m* (-[e]s; ⁻e) (**nach, zu** for) departure, start: **das Zeichen zum ~ geben** give the sign to leave.

'aufbrühen *v/t* (*sep*, -ge-, h) make (*coffee, tea*).

'aufbügeln *v/t* (*sep*, -ge-, h) **1.** transfer *pattern* (**auf** *acc* on). **2.** iron, press.

'aufbürden *v/t* (*sep*, -ge-, h) *fig.* **j-m et. ~** saddle s.o. with s.th.

'aufdecken (*sep*, -ge-, h) **I** *v/t* **1.** uncover, *fig. a.* reveal, expose. **2.** **das Bett ~** turn down the bed. **II** *v/i* **3.** lay the table.

'aufdrängen (*sep*, -ge-, h) **I** *v/t* **j-m et. ~**

force s.th. on s.o. **II sich ~** a) (dat on) intrude, impose o.s., b) suggest itself.

'**aufdrehen** (sep, -ge-, h) **I** v/t a) turn on (gas etc). **2.** untwist (rope). **3.** F turn up (radio). **4.** put up one's hair in curlers. **II** v/i **5.** F mot. step on the gas. **6.** F fig. person: get going: → **aufgedreht**.

'**aufdringlich** adj obtrusive, a. importunate, **angewiesen sein** depend pushing (person), a. loud (colo[u]r), noisy (music), overpowering (smell). '**Aufdringlichkeit** f (-; no pl) obtrusiveness.

'**Aufdruck** m (-[e]s; -e) imprint, philat. ɒverprint. '**aufdrucken** v/t (sep, -ge-, h) print (**auf** acc on).

'**aufdrücken** v/t (sep, -ge-, h) **1.** push (or press) open. **2.** F squeeze boil open. **3.** impress stamp etc (dat or **auf** acc on).

aufein'ander adv **1.** one on top of another (or the other). **2.** one another, each other; **~ angewiesen sein** depend on each other; **~ abgestimmte Farben** matching colo(u)rs. **3.** one after the other. **~folgen** v/i (sep, -ge-, sn) succeed (one another). **~folgend** adj successive, consecutive: **an drei ~en Tagen** on three days running. **~prallen** v/i (sep, -ge-, sn), **~stoßen** v/i (irr, sep, -ge-, sn, → **stoßen**) collide, fig. a. clash. **~treffen** v/i (irr, sep, -ge-, sn, → **treffen**) meet (one another).

Aufenthalt ['aʊfɛnthalt] m (-[e]s; -e) **1.** stay. **2.** 🚆 etc (**fünf Minuten** ~ five minutes') stop: **ohne** ~ nonstop; **wir hatten zwei Stunden** ~ **in ...** we stopped in ... for two hours.

'**Aufenthalts|erlaubnis** f residence permit. **~ort** m a) whereabouts, b) residence. **~raum** m a) hotel etc: lounge, b) school etc: common room.

'**auferlegen** v/t (sep, h) impose (dat on): **sich k-n Zwang** ~ be free and easy.

'**auferstehen** v/i (irr, sep, sn, → **erstehen**) eccl. rise (from the dead). '**Auferstehung** f (-; no pl) resurrection.

'**aufessen** v/t (irr, sep, -ge-, h, → **essen**) eat up, finish.

auffädeln ['aʊfɛːdəln] v/t (sep, -ge-, h) thread, string.

'**auffahren** (irr, sep, -ge-, → **fahren**) **I** v/i (sn) **1.** ~ **auf** (acc) mot. crash into, ⚓ run on; mot. **zu dicht** ~ tailgate. **2.** fig. a) (give a) start, b) flare up. **II** v/t (h) **3.** F bring on (food etc). '**Auffahrt** f (-; -en)

1. driving up. **2.** a) approach, b) slip road, c) drive(way Am.).

'**Auffahrunfall** m rear-end collision.

'**auffallen** v/i (irr, sep, -ge-, sn, → **fallen**) be conspicuous, attract attention: **j-m** ~ strike s.o.; **das fällt nicht auf** nobody will notice; **unangenehm** ~ make a bad impression. '**auffallend** adj a) noticeable, b) striking (beauty, resemblance, etc). '**auffällig** adj **1.** → **auffallend**. **2.** a) conspicuous, b) odd, strange, c) loud, F flashy (clothes etc).

'**auffangen** v/t (irr, sep, -ge-, h, → **fangen**) **1.** catch (a. fig. words etc). **2.** pick up, intercept (message). **3.** cushion (fall etc), parry, block (blow), stop (attack), absorb (price increases etc). **4.** collect. **5.** receive (refugees).

'**Auffanglager** n reception camp.

'**auffassen** v/t (sep, -ge-, h) **1.** understand, grasp. **2.** interpret: **et. als Scherz** ~ take s.th. as a joke; **falsch** ~ misunderstand, misinterpret.

'**Auffassung** f (-; -en) **1.** view, opinion: **nach m-r** ~ in my view, as I see it. **2.** interpretation. **3.** no pl → '**Auffassungsgabe** f (-; no pl) intellectual grasp, intelligence.

auffindbar ['aʊffɪntbaːr] adj **nicht** ~ not to be found. '**auffinden** v/t (irr, sep, -ge-, h, → **finden**) find, discover.

'**auffischen** v/t (sep, -ge-, h) F **1.** fish out (of the water). **2.** → **aufgabeln**.

'**aufflackern** v/i (sep, -ge-, sn) flicker up.

'**aufflammen** v/i (sep, -ge-, sn) a. fig. flare up.

'**auffliegen** v/i (irr, sep, -ge-, sn, → **fliegen**) **1.** fly up. **2.** door etc: fly open. **3.** F plan etc: blow up: ~ **lassen** expose (s.o.), bust (gang), break up (meeting).

'**auffordern** v/t (sep, -ge-, h) **1.** **j-n** ~ (, **et. zu tun**) ask (or order, ⚖ summon) s.o. (to do s.th.); **j-n dringend** ~ urge s.o. **2.** invite: **e-e Dame** (**zum Tanz**) ~ ask a lady to dance.

'**Aufforderung** f (-; -en) **1.** request, call. **2.** order, ⚖ summons. **3.** invitation.

'**aufforsten** v/t (sep, -ge-, h) reafforest.

'**auffressen** v/t (irr, sep, -ge-, h, → **fressen**) eat up, devour: F fig. **die Arbeit frißt mich auf** I'm drowning in work.

'**auffrischen** (sep, -ge-, h) **I** v/t **1.** freshen up, refresh (a. fig. memory). **2.** replenish (supplies). **3.** fig. brush up (knowledge), revive (*friendship etc*). **II** *v/i* **4.** *wind*: freshen.

'Auffrischungskurs *m* refresher course.

'aufführen (*sep*, -ge-, h) **I** *v/t* **1.** ♪, *thea. etc* perform, present, *a.* show (*film*). **2.** state, show, list: **namentlich ~** name; **einzeln ~** specify, itemize. **II sich ~** behave: **sich schlecht ~** *a.* misbehave.

'Aufführung *f* (-; -en) *thea. etc* performance, showing, show. **'Aufführungsrechte** *pl* performing rights.

'auffüllen *v/t* (*sep*, -ge-, h) fill up, top up (*glass etc*), replenish (*stocks*).

'Aufgabe *f* (-; -n) **1.** *no pl* posting, *Am.* mailing (*of letter*), sending (*of telegram[me]*). **2.** *no pl* registering, *Am.* checking (*of luggage*). **3.** *no pl* insertion (*of an ad*), giving, placing (*of orders*). **4.** *no pl* giving up (*a. sports*), ♟ closing down (*of business etc*), resignation (*gen* from *an office*). **5.** a) task, assignment, job, b) duty, c) purpose, function: **es ist nicht m-e ~ zu** *inf* it's not my job to *inf*; **es ist zur ~ machen zu** *inf* make it one's business to *inf*. **6.** ♐ *etc* problem, *ped.* homework, lesson, exercise. **7.** *sports*: service.

'aufgabeln *v/t* (*sep*, -ge-, h) F pick up.

'Aufgabenbereich *m* (**nicht in j-s ~ fallen** be outside s.o.'s) scope of duties.

'Aufgang *m* (-[e]s; ⸚e) **1.** *no pl* rising (*of the sun etc*). **2.** stairway.

'aufgeben (*irr*, *sep*, -ge-, h, → **geben**) **I** *v/t* **1.** post, *Am.* mail (*letter*), send (*telegram[me]*). **2.** register, *Am.* check (*luggage*). **3.** insert (*ad*), give, place (*orders*). **4.** give up (*job, business, hope, patient, etc*), retire from (*office etc*), abandon (*plan etc*), stop (*contest*): **das Rauchen ~** give up (*or* stop) smoking; F **gib's auf!** give (it) up! **5.** ask (*riddle*), *ped.* set, give (*task*). **6.** *sports*: serve. **II** *v/i* **7.** give up.

'aufgeblasen **I** *pp of* **aufblasen**. **II** *adj* F *fig.* arrogant, bumptious.

'Aufgebot *n* (-[e]s; -e) **1. das ~ bestellen** give notice of an intended marriage, ask the banns. **2.** *no pl* array, crowd, (*police*) force, *sports*: a) team, b) squad, pool of players: **mit starkem ~ erscheinen** turn out (*or* up) in full force.

'aufgebracht **I** *pp of* **aufbringen**. **II** *adj* (**gegen** with, **über** *acc* at, about) angry, furious.

'aufgedonnert *adj* F dolled-up.

'aufgedreht **I** *pp of* **aufdrehen**. **II** *adj* F *fig.* in high spirits.

'aufgehen *v/i* (*irr*, *sep*, -ge-, sn, → **gehen**) **1.** *sun etc*, *a.* dough: rise, *curtain*: *a.* go up. **2.** *seed etc*: come up. **3.** open, *knot etc*: *a.* come undone, *seam*: come open, *boil etc*: burst. **4.** ♐ come out even: **die Aufgabe geht nicht auf** the sum doesn't work out; → **Rechnung** 1. **5. ~ in** (*dat*) be (all) wrapped up in one's work *etc*. **6. j-m ~** dawn on s.o.: **jetzt geht mir die Bedeutung s-r Worte auf** now I realize what he meant; → **Licht** 2. **7. in Flammen ~** go up in flames.

'aufgehoben **I** *pp of* **aufheben**. **II** *adj* **gut ~ sein** be in good hands (**bei** with).

'aufgeilen *v/t* (*sep*, -ge-, h) V **I** *v/t* turn s.o. on. **II sich ~ an** (*dat*) get turned on by.

'aufgeklärt **I** *pp of* **aufklären**. **II** *adj* enlightened: **~ sein** know the facts of life.

'aufgeknöpft **I** *pp of* **aufknöpfen**. **II** *adj* F *fig.* chatty.

'aufgekratzt **I** *pp of* **aufkratzen**. **II** *adj* F *fig.* chirpy.

'aufgelegt **I** *pp of* **auflegen**. **II** *adj* **zu et. ~ sein** be in the mood for s.th., feel like (doing) s.th.; **gut (schlecht) ~ sein** be in a good (bad) mood.

'aufgelöst **I** *pp of* **auflösen**. **II** *adj fig.* **1.** distraught. **2.** all in.

'aufgeräumt **I** *pp of* **aufräumen**. **II** *adj fig.* cheerful.

'aufgeregt **I** *pp of* **aufregen**. **II** *adj* upset, excited, nervous.

'aufgeschlossen **I** *pp of* **aufschließen**. **II** *adj fig.* open (**für** to), open-minded.

'Aufgeschlossenheit *f* (-; *no pl*) open-mindedness.

'aufgeschmissen *adj* F **~ sein** be stuck.

'aufgeschossen *adj* **hoch ~** lanky.

'aufgesetzt **I** *pp of* **aufsetzen**. **II** *adj fig.* artificial.

'aufgesprungen **I** *pp of* **aufspringen**. **II** *adj* chapped (*lips etc*).

'aufgestaut **I** *pp of* **aufstauen**. **II** *adj* pent-up (*rage etc*).

'aufgeweckt **I** *pp of* **aufwecken**. **II** *adj fig.* bright, clever.

'aufgießen *v/t* (*irr*, *sep*, -ge-, h, → **gießen**) **1.** make (*tea etc*). **2.** add, pour on.

'aufgliedern *v/t* (*sep*, -ge-, h) a) (sub)divide, b) classify, c) break down (**nach** by), d) analyze (*sentence*).

'**aufgraben** v/t (irr, sep, -ge-, h, → **graben**) dig up.

'**aufgreifen** v/t (irr, sep, -ge-, h, → **greifen**) **1.** pick up, seize. **2.** take up (idea).

auf'**grund** → **Grund** 3.

'**Aufguß** m (-sses; ◡sse) **1.** infusion. **2.** fig. rehash.

'**aufhaben** (irr, sep, -ge-, h, → **haben**) F **I** v/t **1.** have a hat etc on. **2.** have door etc open. **3.** ped. have to do: **wir haben heute nichts auf** we have no homework today. **II** v/i **4.** shop etc: be open.

'**aufhacken** v/t (sep, -ge-, h) pick up.

'**aufhaken** v/t (sep, -ge-, h) unhook.

'**aufhalsen** ['aufhalzən] v/t (sep, -ge-, h) F **j-m et.** ~ land s.o. with s.th.

'**aufhalten** (irr, sep, -ge-, h, → **halten**) **I** v/t **1.** keep open. **2.** stop, hold up, check, stay, delay: **ich wurde durch den Regen aufgehalten** I was delayed by the rain; **ich will Sie nicht länger** ~ don't let me keep you. **II sich** ~ **3.** stay (**im Ausland** abroad, **bei Freunden** with friends). **4. sich** ~ **mit** spend (contp. waste) one's time on.

'**aufhängen** (irr, sep, -ge-, h, → **hängen**) **I** v/t **1.** (an dat) hang (up) (on), ⊚ suspend (from): **j-n** ~ hang s.o. **2.** F → **aufbürden.** **II sich** ~ hang o.s.

'**Aufhänger** m (-s; -) **1.** tab. **2.** F fig. ~ (**für e-n Artikel** etc) peg (on which to hang a story etc).

'**Aufhängung** f (-; -en) ⊚ suspension.

'**aufhäufen** v/t (sep, -ge-, h) (a. **sich** ~) pile up, heap up, accumulate.

'**aufheben** v/t (irr, sep, -ge-, h, → **heben**) **1.** pick up, lift (up), raise: **j-n** ~ help s.o. up. **2.** keep (**für später** for later): → **aufgehoben. 3.** close (meeting), raise (siege), call off (boycott etc). **4.** abolish (law), cancel (contract), annul (marriage etc), quash (sentence): **ein Verbot** ~ lift a ban. **5.** compensate, cancel, neutralize: **sich** (or **einander**) ~ cancel each other out (a. ⅋), neutralize each other. '**Aufheben** n (-s; no pl) fuss, ado: **viel** ~(**s**) **machen** make a big fuss (**von** about). '**Aufhebung** f (-; -en) **1.** abolition (**der Todesstrafe** of capital punishment), abrogation (of a law), cancel(l)ation (of contract), annulment (of marriage etc). **2.** a) termination, b) calling-off (of strike etc). **3.** neutralization.

aufheitern ['aufhaitərn] (sep, -ge-, h) **I**
v/t **j-n** ~ cheer s.o. up. **II sich** ~ weather: clear (up), a. fig. brighten (up). '**Aufheiterungen** pl meteor. sunny spells.

aufhellen ['aufhɛlən] (sep, -ge-, h) **I** v/t **1.** lighten (a. phot.). **2.** fig. shed light on. **II sich** ~ → **aufheitern** II.

'**aufhetzen** v/t (sep, -ge-, h) **j-n** ~ incite s.o. (**zu et.** to [do] s.th.); **j-n** ~ **gegen** set s.o. against. '**Aufhetzung** f (-; -en) instigation, pol. agitation.

'**aufheulen** v/i (sep, -ge-, h) (give a) howl, mot. roar.

'**aufholen** (sep, -ge-, h) **I** v/t catch up on: **e-n Rückstand** (or **Zeitverlust**) ~ make up leeway. **II** v/i (**gegenüber**) catch up (with, on), gain (on).

'**aufhorchen** v/i (sep, -ge-, h) prick up one's ears, fig. sit up (and take notice).

'**aufhören** v/i (sep, -ge-, h) stop (a. ~ **mit**), (come to) an end: **sie hörte nicht auf zu reden** she didn't stop talking; **wo haben wir aufgehört?** where did we leave off?; **hör auf** (**damit**)! stop it!; ~ **zu arbeiten** F knock off (work); **ohne aufzuhören** without letup.

'**aufkaufen** v/t (sep, -ge-, h) buy up. '**Aufkäufer** m (-s; -) (wholesale) buyer.

'**aufklappen** (sep, -ge-) v/t (h), v/i (sn) open.

'**aufklaren** v/i (sep, -ge-, h) meteor. clear.

'**aufklären** (sep, -ge-, h) **I** v/t **1.** clear up (mystery etc), solve (crime), correct (mistake). **2.** enlighten, inform (**über** acc of): **j-n** ~ explain the facts of life to s.o. ⅹ reconnoit/re (Am. -er). **II sich** ~ **4.** be cleared up, be solved. **5.** → **aufklaren.** '**Aufklärung** f (-; -en) **1.** clearing up, solution: ~ **verlangen** demand an explanation. **2.** enlightenment, education, information. **3.** no pl (**sexuelle**) ~ sex education. **4.** ⅹ reconnaissance. **5.** no pl philos. hist. Enlightenment.

'**Aufklärungs**|**film** m sex education film. **~flugzeug** n reconnaissance (or scout) plane. **~quote** f clear-up rate.

'**aufkleben** v/t (sep, -ge-, h) stick on (**auf** acc to), phot. mount.

'**Aufkleber** m (-s; -) sticker.

'**aufknöpfen** v/t (sep, -ge-, h) unbutton, undo.

'**aufkochen** v/t (sep, -ge-, h) (a. ~ **lassen**) bring s.th. to the boil.

'**aufkommen** v/i (irr, sep, -ge-, sn, →

kommen) **1.** arise (*a. suspicion etc*): **Zweifel ~ lassen** give rise to doubt; **nicht ~ lassen** suppress. **2.** *wind*: spring up, *fog etc*: come up. **3.** *rumo(u)r etc*: start. **4.** *miniskirts etc*: come into fashion. **5. ~ für** a) answer for, be responsible for, b) pay; **für den Schaden ~** compensate for the damage. **6. ~ gegen** prevail against; **er kommt gegen sie nicht auf** he is no match for her; **niemanden neben sich ~ lassen** suffer no rival. **7. → aufholen** II.

'**Aufkommen** *n* (-s) **1.** rise. **2.** ♥ yield.

'**aufkratzen** *v/t* (*sep*, -ge-, h) scratch open: **sich ~** scratch o.s. sore.

'**aufkreuzen** *v/i* (*sep*, -ge-, sn) F turn up.

'**aufladen** (*irr, sep*, -ge-, h, → **laden**) I *v/t* **1.** load (**auf** *acc* onto): F *fig.* **j-m** (**sich**) **et. ~** saddle s.o. (o.s.) with s.th. **2.** supercharge, boost (*engine*), charge (*battery*). II **sich ~** ⚡ become charged.

'**Auflader** *m* (-s; -) *mot.* supercharger.

'**Auflage** *f* (-; -n) **1.** edition (*of book*), circulation (*of newspaper*). **2.** ([*j-m*] **et. zur ~ machen** make s.th. a) condition (for s.o.). **3.** ⊕ a) rest, support, b) layer, c) coating, lining. '**Auflagenhöhe** *f* a) number of copies, b) circulation.

'**auflassen** *v/t* (*irr, sep*, -ge-, h, → **lassen**) **1.** F leave *door etc* open. **2.** F keep *hat etc* on. **3.** 🏛 convey (*property*).

'**auflauern** *v/i* (*sep*, -ge-, h) **j-m ~** waylay s.o., lie in wait for s.o.

'**Auflauf** *m* (-[e]s; ⸚e) **1.** crowd. **2.** riot. **3.** *gastr.* soufflé. '**auflaufen** *v/i* (*irr, sep*, -ge-, sn, → **laufen**) **1.** ⚓ run aground: **auf e-e Mine ~** hit a mine. **2.** run (*or* bump) (**auf** *acc* into): **j-n ~ lassen** a) *sports*: obstruct s.o. unfairly, b) *fig.* give s.o. what for. **3.** *money etc*: accumulate, run up, *interest*: a. accrue.

'**Auflaufform** *f* ovenproof dish.

'**aufleben** *v/i* (*sep*, -ge-, sn) (**wieder**) **~** *a. fig.* revive; **er lebte förmlich auf** he really livened up.

'**auflegen** (*sep*, -ge-, h) I *v/t* **1.** put on (*coal, disc, make-up, etc*), lay (*tablecloth etc*): **den** (**Telefon**)**Hörer ~ →** 4; → **Gedeck** 1. **2.** publish, print: **wieder ~** reprint. **3.** ♥ issue (*shares*). II *v/i* **1.** *teleph.* replace the receiver, hang up.

'**auflehnen**: **sich ~** (**gegen**) oppose (*s.o., s.th.*), rebel (against). '**Auflehnung** *f* (-; -en) rebellion (**gegen** against).

'**auflesen** *v/t* (*irr, sep*, -ge-, h, → **lesen**) pick up (*a.* F *fig. s.o.*).

'**aufleuchten** *v/i* (*sep*, -ge-, h) light up.

'**aufliegen** (*irr, sep*, -ge-, h, → **liegen**) I *v/i* lie (*or* rest, lean) (**auf** *dat* on). II **sich ~** F 💥 get bedsore(s).

'**auflisten** *v/t* (*sep*, -ge-, h) list, make a list of.

'**auflockern** *v/t* (*sep*, -ge-, h) **1.** loosen (*the soil*). **2.** *fig.* a) liven up, b) relax.

'**auflodern** *v/i* (*sep*, -ge-, sn) flare up.

'**auflösen** (*sep*, -ge-, h) I *v/t* **1.** a) dissolve, b) break off (*engagement*), c) ✕ disband (*unit*): ([**sich**] **in s-e Bestandteile**) **~** disintegrate. **2.** 🜂 resolve (*equation, a. riddle*), remove (*brackets*). **3.** a) cancel, annul, b) ♥ liquidate, wind up. II **sich ~ 1.** dissolve, *meeting etc*: a. break up, ✕ *unit*: disband: **sich in nichts ~** vanish (into thin air), *hope etc*: go up in smoke. '**Auflösung** *f* (-; -en) **1.** disintegration (*a. fig.*), dissolution, *a.* breakup (*of meeting*). **2.** ♥ a) liquidation, b) annulment. **3.** ✕ disbandment. **4.** 🜂, ♪, *phot.* resolution.

'**Auflösungszeichen** *n* ♮ natural.

'**aufmachen** (*sep*, -ge-, h) I *v/t* F **1.** open: **mach d-e Augen auf!** watch out! **2.** make up, get up, design: **et. in der Presse groß ~** splash s.th. out; **e-e Rechnung ~** write out (*fig.* present) a bill. II *v/i* F open, answer the door: **j-m ~** let s.o. in. III **sich ~** set out (**nach** for). '**Aufmacher** *m* (-s; -) F lead, *n.s.* feature story (*or* photo). '**Aufmachung** *f* (-; -en) **1.** presentation, getup, *print.* layout: **et. in großer ~ herausbringen** feature s.th. prominently. **2.** F outfit, getup.

'**Aufmarsch** *m* (-[e]s; ⸚e) marching up, ✕ *a.* deployment. '**aufmar,schieren** *v/i* (sn) *a.* march up.

aufmerksam ['aʊfmɛrkzaːm] *adj* a) attentive, b) watchful, c) obliging: **j-n ~ machen auf** (*acc*) call (*or* draw) s.o.'s attention to; **~ werden auf** (*acc*) notice, become aware of; **~ zuhören** listen attentively; **et. ~ verfolgen** follow s.th. closely. '**Aufmerksamkeit** *f* (-; -en) **1.** *no pl* attention, attentiveness: **~ erregen** attract attention; (*dat*) **~ schenken** pay attention (to). **2.** small gift.

'**aufmöbeln** *v/t* (*sep*, -ge-, h) F jazz up.

aufmuntern *v/t* (*sep*, -ge-, h) **1.** → **er-**

muntern 1. 2. *j-n* ~ cheer (F pep) s.o. up: *~de Worte* pep talk.

'Aufmunterung *f* (-; -en) cheering up.

aufmüpfig ['aʊfmʏpfɪç] *adj* F rebellious.

'aufnähen *v/t* (*sep*, -ge-, h) sew on (*auf acc* to).

Aufnahme ['aʊfnaːmə] *f* (-; -n) **1.** *no pl* a) taking up (*of activity etc*), establishing (*relations*), b) intake (*of food*), c) *fig.* absorption (*of knowledge, a. phys.*), taking in (*impressions*). **2.** *no pl* (*in acc*) a) integration (within), b) inclusion (into), c) admission (in[to]), d) registration: *~ finden* be admitted (*bei* [in]to). **3.** *no pl* (*a. fig.* **e-e kühle** *etc* **~ finden** meet with a cool *etc* reception (*bei* from). **4.** *no pl* a) accommodation, ✚ admission (*in acc* to), b) reception (office). **5.** *no pl* ✝ a) raising (*of funds*), b) assessment (*of damage*). **6.** a) film *etc*: taking, shooting, b) photo(graph), shot, c) (sound) recording, pickup: *e-e ~ machen* (*von* of) take a picture, make a (tape-)recording; *Achtung ~!* Action!, Camera! **'aufnahmefähig** *adj* receptive (*für* to). **'Aufnahmefähigkeit** *f* (-; *no pl*) receptivity.

'Aufnahme|gebühr *f* admission fee. **~leiter** *m* film: production (radio: recording) manager. **~prüfung** *f* entrance examination. **~raum** *m* film *etc*: studio. **~wagen** *m* recording van (*Am.* truck).

'aufnehmen *v/t* (*irr, sep*, -ge-, h, → *nehmen*) **1.** pick up (*load, fig. trail etc*), take up (*meshes*). **2.** receive (*a. fig. news*), accommodate, admit (*in acc* to a club, hospital, *etc*), enter (*in acc* into a list *etc*), include (*in acc* into): *j-n bei sich ~* put s.o. up; *fig. et. übel ~* take s.th. amiss. **3.** hold (*audience, cargo*), seat (*passengers etc*). **4.** take in (*impressions*), (*a. in sich ~*) grasp, absorb (*knowledge*). **5.** a) ✖, *phys.* absorb, b) take in (*food*). **6.** take up (*activity etc*), enter into (*relations etc*), open (*traffic*): *wieder ~* resume; *fig.* **den Kampf mit j-m ~** take s.o. on; *ich kann es mit ihm nicht ~* I'm no match for him; → *Kontakt.* **7.** a) record, draw up, b) make an inventory of, c) assess (*damage*). **8.** record, tape(-record). **9.** take (down) (*dictation etc*), take (*order, picture, telegram[me]*), shoot (*film*): *j-n ~* take s.o.'s

picture. **10.** ✝ borrow (*money*), raise mortgage (*auf acc* on).

'aufopfern *v/t* (*sep*, -ge-, h) sacrifice (*sich* o.s.): *~d* self-sacrificing.

'aufpäppeln *v/t* (*sep*, -ge-, h) F feed *s.o.* up.

'aufpassen *v/i* (*sep*, -ge-, h) **1.** pay attention: *paß(t) auf!* watch out!; F *paß(t) mal auf!* listen! **2.** *~ auf* (*acc*) a) look after, take care of, b) watch (over); F *paß gut auf dich auf!* take care (of yourself)! **'Aufpasser** *m* (-s; -), **'Aufpasserin** *f* (-; -nen) *contp.* watchdog.

'aufpeitschen *v/t* (*sep*, -ge-, h) *a. fig.* whip up: *sich ~* whip o.s. up.

'aufpflanzen *v/t* (*sep*, -ge-, h) plant: *fig. sich ~* plant o.s. (*vor dat* before).

'aufplustern: *sich* ~ (*sep*, -ge-, h) a *bird*: ruffle its feathers, b) F *fig.* puff o.s. up.

'aufpo,lieren *v/t* (*sep*, -ge-, h) polish up.

Aufprall *m* (-[e]s; *no pl*) impact.

'aufprallen *v/i* (*sep*, -ge-, sn) *~ auf* (*acc*) hit, car *etc*: a. crash into.

Aufpreis *m* (-es; -e) ✝ extra charge.

'aufpumpen *v/t* (*sep*, -ge-, h) pump up.

'aufputschen *v/t* (*sep*, -ge-, h) **1.** → *aufhetzen.* **2.** a) *with drugs etc*: F pep up (*sich* o.s.), b) *fig.* hype up, psych up. **'Aufputschmittel** *n* stimulant, F pep pill, *sl.* upper.

'aufraffen (*sep*, -ge-, h) **I** *v/t* snatch up. **II** *sich* ~ *fig.* pull o.s. together; *sich ~, et. zu tun* bring o.s. to do s.th.

'aufragen *v/i* (*sep*, -ge-, h) loom (up).

'aufräumen *v/t, v/i* (*sep*, -ge-, h) tidy (up): *~ mit* do away with (*abuses etc*).

'aufrechnen *v/t* (*sep*, -ge-, h) *et.* ~ set s.th. off (*gegen* against).

'aufrecht *adj* upright (*a. fig.*), erect: *~ sitzen* sit up. **~erhalten** *v/t* (*irr, sep*, h, → *erhalten*) **1.** maintain. **2.** adhere to. **2erhaltung** *f* (-; *no pl*) maintenance.

'aufregen (*sep*, -ge-, h) **I** *v/t* a) excite, b) worry, upset, c) annoy. **II** *sich* ~ (*über acc* about) get excited, be upset. **'aufregend** *adj* a) exciting, b) upsetting. **'Aufregung** *f* (-; -en) excitement: *nur k-e ~!* don't panic!

'aufreiben (*irr, sep*, -ge-, h, → *reiben*) *v/t* **1.** *fig.* wear down. **2.** ✖ wipe out. **II** *sich* ~ *fig.* wear o.s. out. **'aufreibend** *adj* exhausting, trying, stressful.

'aufreihen *v/t* (*sep*, -ge-, h) (*a. sich ~,* line up, put *books etc* in a row.

'**aufreißen** *v/t* (*irr, sep,* -ge-, → *reißen*) **I** *v/t* (h) **1.** tear open (*package etc*), tear up (*road*). **2.** fling *door etc* open, F open *eyes, mouth* wide. **3.** F a) *j-n* ~ pick s.o. up, b) land (*a job etc*). **II** *v/i* (sn) burst, split, break up.

'**aufreizend** *adj* provocative.

'**aufrichten** (*sep,* -ge-, h) **I** *v/t* **1.** → **er-richten. 2.** a) set *s.th.* upright, b) straighten up, c) raise (*s.o. in bed*), d) help *s.o.* up. **3.** *fig.* a) comfort, b) encourage. **II** *sich* ~ **4.** a) straighten o.s. (up), b) sit up (*in bed*). **5.** *fig.* take heart (**an** *dat* from).

'**aufrichtig** *adj* sincere, heartfelt, honest: **es tut mir ~ leid** I really am sorry.

'**Aufrichtigkeit** *f* (-; *no pl*) sincerity.

'**aufriegeln** *v/t* (*sep,* -ge-, h) unbolt.

'**Aufriß** *m* (-sses; -sse) △, ⚙ elevation.

'**aufrollen** *v/t* (*sep,* -ge-, h) **1.** roll up, furl. **2.** unroll, unfurl. **3.** *fig.* (*wieder*) ~ bring *a subject etc* up (again), reopen (*a case etc*).

'**aufrücken** *v/i* (*sep,* -ge-, sn) **1.** move up (**zu** to, with). **2.** be promoted, rise. **3.** ✕ close the ranks.

'**Aufruf** *m* (-[e]s; -e) call, appeal (**an** *acc* to). '**aufrufen** *v/t* (*irr, sep,* -ge-, h, → *rufen*) *j-n* ~ call (out) s.o.'s name; *j-n* ~, **et. zu tun** call (up)on s.o. to do s.th.; **zum Streik** ~ call a strike.

Aufruhr ['aʊfruːr] *m* (-[e]s; -e) a) turmoil (*a. fig.*), b) uprising, revolt, c) riot (*a. ⚖*). '**aufführen** *v/t* (*sep,* -ge-, h) *fig.* **1.** a) rouse (*feelings etc*), b) rake up (*old scandals etc*). **2.** → *aufwühlen* 2.

Aufrührer ['aʊfryːrər] *m* (-s; -), '**Aufrüh-rerin** *f* (-; -nen) rebel, *pol.* agitator.

'**aufrührerisch** *adj* rebellious, seditious.

'**aufrunden** *v/t* (*sep,* -ge-, h) round up (**auf** *acc* to).

'**aufrüsten** *v/t, v/i* (*sep,* -ge-, h) ✕ arm: **wieder** ~ rearm.

'**Aufrüstung** *f* (-; -en) armament.

aufs [aʊfs] = **auf das.**

'**aufsagen** *v/t* (*sep,* -ge-, h) recite.

aufsässig ['aʊfzɛsɪç] *adj* rebellious.

'**Aufsatz** *m* (-es; ⷺe) **1.** essay, *ped. a.* composition, *univ.* paper, (*newspaper*) article. **2.** ⚙ top, cap.

'**aufsaugen** *v/t* (*sep,* -ge-, h) absorb.

'**aufscheuchen** *v/t* (*sep,* -ge-, h) *a. fig.* startle.

'**aufschichten** *v/t* (*sep,* -ge-, h) stack up.

'**aufschieben** *v/t* (*irr, sep,* -ge-, h, → *schieben*) **1.** push open. **2.** *fig.* (**auf** *acc, bis* till) put off, postpone.

'**Aufschlag** *m* (-[e]s; ⷺe) **1.** impact (**auf** *acc or dat* on): **dumpfer** ~ thud. **2.** a) cuff, b) turnup, c) lapel. **3.** ⚙ extra charge. **4.** *tennis:* service: *j-m* **den** ~ **abnehmen** break s.o.'s serve; ~ **haben** serve. **~ball** *m tennis:* service (ball).

'**aufschlagen** (*irr, sep,* -ge-, → *schla-gen*) **I** *v/i* **1.** (sn) hit: **auf den** (or **dem**) **Boden** ~ hit the ground; **dumpf** ~ thud. **2.** (h) *tennis:* serve. **II** *v/t* **3.** break (open), crack (*an egg*). **4.** open (*a book, one's eyes*), turn down (*the bed*): **Seite 10** ~ open at page 10. **5.** roll up (*sleeve*). **6.** *sich das Knie etc* ~ bruise one's knee *etc.* **7.** mount (*scaffold etc*), pitch (*tent*): *s-n* **Wohnsitz in X** ~ take up residence in X. **8.** add *5% etc* (**auf** *acc* to).

'**Aufschläger** *m* (-s; -) *tennis etc:* server.

'**aufschließen** (*irr, sep,* -ge-, h, → *schließen*) **I** *v/t* **1.** unlock, open. **2.** *biol.,* ⚗ break down (*or* up). **3.** develop (*land, resources*). **II** *v/i* **4.** open the door *etc* (*j-m* for s.o.). **5.** ✕ close (the) ranks, *sports:* move up: ~ **zu** catch up with.

'**aufschlitzen** *v/t* (*sep,* -ge-, h) slit open, slash.

'**Aufschluß** *m* (-sses; ⷺsse) ~ **geben** (**über** *acc*) give information (on), explain (*s.th.*), *j-m* inform s.o. (about). '**auf-schlüsseln** *v/t* (*sep,* -ge-, h) allocate, *statistically:* break down. '**aufschluß-reich** *adj* informative, *w.s.* revealing.

'**aufschnallen** *v/t* (*sep,* -ge-, h) **1.** unbuckle. **2.** strap *s.th.* on (**auf** *acc* to).

'**aufschnappen** *v/t* (*sep,* -ge-, h) F *fig.* pick up.

'**aufschneiden** (*irr, sep,* -ge-, h, → *schneiden*) **I** *v/t* cut open, slice (*bread etc*), carve (*meat*), ⚕ open, lance (*boil*). **II** *v/i* F brag, boast, show off.

'**Aufschneider** *m* (-s; -) F show-off.

'**Aufschnitt** *m* (-[e]s; *no pl*) cold cuts.

'**aufschnüren** *v/t* (*sep,* -ge-, h) untie, undo, unlace.

'**aufschrauben** *v/t* (*sep,* -ge-, h) **1.** unscrew. **2.** screw *s.th.* on (**auf** *acc* to).

'**aufschrecken** (*sep,* -ge-) **I** *v/t* (h) startle: *j-n* **aus** rouse s.o. from. **II** *v/i* (sn) (give a) start: **aus dem Schlaf** ~ wake with a start.

'**Aufschrei** *m* (-[e]s; -e) cry, *fig.* outcry.

'**aufschreiben** v/t (irr, sep, -ge-, h, → **schreiben**) write down, take a note of: F **j-n ~** book s.o.

'**aufschreien** v/i (irr, sep, -ge-, h, → **schreien**) cry out (**vor** with).

'**Aufschrift** f (-; -en) inscription.

'**Aufschub** m (-[e]s; ⁓e) postponement, delay, ✝ respite, ⚖️ a. fig. reprieve: **k-n ~ dulden** bear no delay.

'**aufschürfen** v/t (sep, -ge-, h) graze: **sich das Knie ~** bark one's knee.

'**aufschütteln** v/t (sep, -ge-, h) plump up.

'**aufschütten** v/t (sep, -ge-, h) heap up.

'**aufschwatzen** v/t (sep, -ge-, h) F **j-m et. ~** talk s.o. into buying s.th.

'**aufschweißen** v/t (sep, -ge-, h) weld open.

'**aufschwemmen** v/t (sep, -ge-, h) bloat.

'**aufschwingen: sich ~** (irr, sep, -ge-, h, → **schwingen**) soar (up).

'**Aufschwung** m (-[e]s; ⁓e) 1. gym. swing-up. 2. no pl fig. (fresh) impetus, ✝ upswing, recovery, boom,

'**aufsehen** v/i (irr, sep, -ge-, h, → **sehen**) → **aufblicken**. '**Aufsehen** n (-s) ~ **erregen** attract attention, w.s. cause a stir (or sensation); **um ~ zu vermeiden** to avoid notice. '**aufsehenerregend** adj sensational. '**Aufseher** m (-s; -), '**Aufseherin** f (-; -nen) 1. attendant. 2. (prison) warder, Am. guard.

'**aufsein** v/i (irr, sep, -ge-, sn, → **sein**) F 1. door etc: be open. 2. person: be up.

'**aufsetzen** (sep, -ge-, h) I v/t 1. a. fig. put on: **aufgesetzte Tasche** patch pocket. 2. draft (speech etc). 3. a. v/i ✈ land: **weich ~** make a soft landing. II **sich ~** sit up (**im Bett** in bed). '**Aufsetzer** m (-s; -) soccer etc: bounce shot.

'**Aufsicht** f (-; -en) 1. no pl supervision, ⚖️ custody: **die ~ haben** (or **führen**) be in charge (**über** acc of), invigilate (**an** exam); **unter ärztlicher ~** under medical supervision; **ohne ~** unattended (children). 2. supervisor, person in charge. '**aufsichtführend** adj supervisory, teacher etc in charge. '**Aufsichts**|**beamte** m 1. supervisor. 2. (prison) warder, Am. guard. **⁓behörde** f supervisory board. **⁓rat** m ✝ supervisory board.

'**aufsitzen** v/i (irr, sep, -ge-, sn, → **sitzen**) 1. get on, mount (horse etc). 2. fig. be

taken in (dat by). 3. F **j-n ~ lassen** let s.o. down.

'**aufspannen** v/t (sep, -ge-, h) spread out, put up (umbrella etc).

'**aufsparen** v/t (sep, -ge-, h) save (up).

'**aufsperren** v/t (sep, -ge-, h) open wide: F **Mund und Nase ~** gape.

'**aufspielen** (sep, -ge-, h) I v/t, v/i play. II **sich ~** F give o.s. airs; **sich als Held** etc **~** play the hero etc.

'**aufspießen** v/t (sep, -ge-, h) a) spear, impale, b) a. fig. skewer.

'**aufspringen** v/i (irr, sep, -ge-, sn, → **springen**) 1. jump up, leap up, ball: bounce: **~ auf** (acc) jump on to (a train etc). 2. buds, door: burst open. 3. skin: chap, lips: crack.

'**aufspulen** v/t (sep, -ge-, h) wind (up).

'**aufspüren** v/t (sep, -ge-, h) track down.

'**aufstampfen** v/i (sep, -ge-, h) (**mit dem Fuß**) ~ stamp one's foot.

'**Aufstand** m (-[e]s; ⁓e) 1. rebellion, revolt. 2. F fig. (big) fuss. '**Aufständische** m, f (-n; -n) rebel, insurgent.

'**aufstauen** v/t (sep, -ge-, h) dam up.

'**aufstechen** v/t (irr, sep, -ge-, h, → **stechen**) puncture, ✚ lance.

'**aufstecken** v/t (sep, -ge-, h) 1. put up, pin up (one's hair). 2. put on (candles): → **Licht** 3. a. v/i F give up.

'**aufstehen** v/i (irr, sep, -ge-, sn, → **stehen**) 1. rise, get up (**vom Tisch** from the table): **~ dürfen** patient: be allowed (to get) up. 2. fig. rise (in arms), rebel.

'**aufsteigen** v/i (irr, sep, -ge-, sn, → **steigen**) 1. rise, bird: a. soar (up), ✈ take off, mount. go up. 2. fig. be promoted (a. sports). 3. **~ auf** (acc) get on, mount (vehicle, horse). 4. fig. feeling etc: rise, well up: **ein Verdacht stieg in mir auf** I had a suspicion (**daß** that). '**Aufsteiger** m (-s; -) 1. F a) social climber, b) (professional) success, F whiz kid. 2. sports: (newly-)promoted team.

'**aufstellen** (sep, -ge-, h) I v/t 1. a) set up, put up, raise (ladder), pitch (tent), b) arrange, c) line up, place, post (guard etc), d) erect (monument), e) install (machine), f) set (trap): **die Ohren ~** animal: prick its ears. 2. nominate (candidate, player), compose (team), ✗ activate (troops): pol. **sich (als Kandidaten) ~ lassen** stand (Am. run) for election etc. 3. make (up), prepare (list). 4. advance (*theory*), lay down, state (*rules etc*), &. form (*equation*): **e-n Rekord ~** set (up) (*or* establish) a record. **II sich ~** place o.s. (**vor** *dat* before), ✕ form up; **sich hintereinander ~** line up.

'**Aufstellung** *f* (-; -en) **1.** *no pl* setting up (*etc*, → **aufstellen** 1), installation. **2.** *no pl* nomination (*of candidate, player*), line-up (*of team*). **3.** list, table, survey, ♰ statement: **e-r Bilanz** preparation of a balance sheet.

'**aufstemmen** *v/t* (*sep*, -ge-, h) prize open.

Aufstieg ['aʊfʃtiːk] *m* (-[e]s; -e) **1.** ascent (*a.* ✈), way up. **2.** *fig.* rise, promotion (*a. sports*): **im ~ begriffen sein** be on the rise, be rising; *sports*: **den ~ schaffen** be|promoted.

'**Aufstiegs|chancen** *pl* promotion prospects. **~spiel** *n sports*: promotion tie.

'**aufstöbern** *v/t* (*sep*, -ge-, h) track down.

'**aufstocken** *v/t* (*sep*, -ge-, h) **1.** △ raise. **2.** increase (*one's capital*).

'**aufstöhnen** *v/i* (*sep*, -ge-, h) (give a loud) groan.

'**aufstoßen** (*irr, sep*, -ge-, h, → **stoßen**) **I** *v/t* push open. **II** *v/i* burp, belch: **j-m ~** repeat on s.o., *F fig.* strike s.o.

'**aufstrebend** *adj fig.* a) up-and-coming, rising, b) emergent (*nation*).

'**Aufstrich** *m* (-[e]s; -e) spread.

'**aufstützen** (*sep*, -ge-, h) **I** *v/t* prop up (**auf** *dat, acc* on). **II sich ~ auf** (*dat, acc*) lean (up)on.

'**aufsuchen** *v/t* (*sep*, -ge-, h) a) visit, (go and) see (*a doctor etc*), b) go to.

'**auftakeln** (*sep*, -ge-, h) **I** *v/t* ⚓ rig out. **II sich ~** *F* get dolled up.

'**Auftakt** *m* (-[e]s; -e) **1.** ♪ upbeat. **2.** *fig.* (**den ~ bilden** be a) prelude (**zu** to).

'**auftanken** *v/t, v/i* (*sep*, -ge-, h) fill up, refuel.

'**auftauchen** *v/i* (*sep*, -ge-, sn) come up (*a. fig. problem etc*), emerge, *submarine*: surface, *fig.* turn up, *doubts etc*: arise.

'**auftauen** (*sep*, -ge-) **I** *v/t* (h) a) thaw, b) defrost. **II** *v/i* (sn) *a. fig.* thaw.

'**aufteilen** *v/t* (*sep*, -ge-, h) **1.** distribute, share (out). **2.** divide (**in** *acc* into).

'**auftischen** ['aʊftɪʃən] *v/t* (*sep*, -ge-, h) *a. fig.* dish up.

Auftrag ['aʊftraːk] *m* (-[e]s; ⸚e) **1.** ♰ order, commission: **et. in ~ geben** order

(*or* commission) s.th. (**bei j-m** from s.o.); **im ~ und auf Rechnung von** by order and for account of. **2.** order(s) (*a.* ✕), instructions, (*a.* ✕ combat) mission: **im ~ von** (*or gen*) by order of, **handeln** act on behalf of.

'**auftragen** (*irr, sep*, -ge-, h, → **tragen**) **I** *v/t* **1.** serve (up) (*food*). **2.** apply, put on (*make-up, paint, etc*). **3.** **j-m et. ~, j-m ~, et. zu tun** instruct (*or* tell) s.o. to do s.th. **4.** wear out (*clothes*). **II** *v/i* **5.** pullover *etc*: make s.o. look fat(ter); *F fig.* **dick ~** lay it on thick.

'**Auftraggeber(in** *f*) *m* client, customer.

'**Auftrags|bestätigung** *f* ♰ confirmation (*by supplier*): acknowledge[e]ment of (an) order. **~buch** *n* ♰ order book. **~dienst** *m* telephone answering service. **gemäß** *adv* according to instructions, ♰ as per order. **~lage** *f* ♰ orders situation. **~polster** *n* ♰ filled order books. **~werk** *n* commissioned work.

'**auftreffen** *v/i* (*irr, sep*, -ge-, sn, → **treffen**) hit (**auf** *dat, acc* on).

'**auftreiben** *v/t* (*irr, sep*, -ge-, h, → **treiben**) *F* get hold of, find.

'**auftrennen** *v/t* (*sep*, -ge-, h) undo (*a seam*), unravel (*knitting*).

'**auftreten** *v/i* (*irr, sep*, -ge-, sn, → **treten**) **1.** *leise* ~ tread softly; **er kann mit dem verletzten Fuß nicht ~** he can't walk on his injured foot. **2.** *thea.* a) make one's entrance, b) appear (*on stage*) (**als** as), *a. musician*: perform: **Hamlet tritt auf** enter Hamlet; **zum ersten Mal ~** make one's debut. **3.** *a.* appear (**öffentlich** in public, **als Zeuge** as a witness, **vor Gericht** in court), b) present o.s. (**als** as), c) behave: **als Vermittler ~** act as go-between. **4.** *fig.* problem, *doubts, etc*: arise, *epidemic etc*: occur. '**Auftreten** *n* (-s) **1.** appearance, *thea.* performance. **2.** occurrence, arising. **3.** behavio(u)r.

'**Auftrieb** *m* (-[e]s; *no pl*) **1.** *phys.* buoyancy, ✈ *a.* lift. **2.** *fig.* (fresh) impetus, ♰ upswing: **(neuen) ~ verleihen** give a (fresh) impetus (*dat* to).

'**Auftritt** *m* (-[e]s; -e) **1.** *thea.* a) entrance, b) scene. **2.** *fig.* scene, *F* row.

'**auftrumpfen** *v/i* (*sep*, -ge-, h) *fig.* come it strong: **~ gegen** make a strong showing against; **mit e-m Rekord** *etc* **~** come up with a record *etc*.

'**auftun:** sich ~ (irr, sep, -ge-, h, → **tun**) a. fig. open

'**auftürmen** (sep, -ge-, h) v/t pile up.

'**aufwachen** v/i (sep, -ge-, sn) wake up: **aus der Narkose ~** come round.

'**aufwachsen** v/i (irr, sep, -ge-, sn, → **wachsen**) grow up.

'**aufwallen** v/i (sep, -ge-, sn) **1.** boil (up). **2.** fig. surge, well up.

Aufwand ['aʊfvant] m (-[e]s; no pl) **1.** expenditure (**an** dat of), cost, expense: **e-n großen ~ an Energie** etc **erfordern** require a great deal of energy etc; **der ganze ~ war umsonst** it was a waste of time (energy, money, etc). **2.** luxury, extravagance: **e-n großen ~ treiben** be very extravagant. '**Aufwandsentschädigung** f expense allowance.

'**aufwärmen** (sep, -ge-, h) **I** v/t **1.** warm up, heat up. **2.** fig. rehash. **II** sich ~ warm o.s., sports: limber up.

aufwärts ['aʊfvɛrts] adv up, upward(s).

'**Aufwärtsentwicklung** f upward trend.

'**aufwärtsgehen** v/impers (irr, sep, -ge-, sn, → **gehen**) **es geht aufwärts** (**mit ihm**) things are looking up (with him); **mit dem Geschäft geht es aufwärts** business is improving.

'**Aufwärtshaken** m boxing: uppercut.

'**Aufwasch** m (-[e]s; no pl) → **Abwasch**.

'**aufwaschen** v/t (irr, sep, -ge-, h) → **abwaschen**.

'**aufwecken** v/t (sep, -ge-, h) wake (up).

'**aufweichen** (sep, -ge-) **I** v/t (h) **1.** a) soak, b) make soggy. **2.** fig. undermine. **II** v/i (sn) become soggy, a. fig. soften.

'**aufweisen** v/t (irr, sep, -ge-, h, → **weisen**) et. ~, et. **aufzuweisen haben** have (or show) s.th.; **große Mängel ~** have many defects.

'**aufwenden** v/t (irr, sep, -ge-, h, → **wenden**) a) use, apply, b) spend (**für** on): (**viel**) **Mühe ~** take (great) pains.

'**aufwendig** adj **1.** large-scale. **2.** expensive. '**Aufwendungen** pl expenditure.

'**aufwerfen** (irr, sep, -ge-, h, → **werfen**) **I** v/t **1.** throw up (dam etc). **2.** fig. raise (question etc). **II** sich ~ set o.s. up (**zum Richter** etc as judge etc).

'**aufwerten** v/t (sep, -ge-, h) ♀ revalue (upward), a. fig. upvalue.

'**Aufwertung** f (-; -en) ♀ revaluation (upward), fig. upgrading.

'**aufwickeln** v/t (sep, -ge-, h) **1.** (a. sich ~)

roll (or coil) up. **2.** F put one's hair up in curlers. **3.** → **auswickeln**.

aufwiegeln ['aʊfvi:gəln] v/t (sep, -ge-, h) → **aufhetzen**.

'**aufwiegen** v/t (irr, sep, -ge-, h, → **wiegen**) fig. offset, make up for.

'**Aufwind** m (-[e]s; -e) **1.** ✈ upwind. **2.** → **Auftrieb 2**. **3.** ♱ **im ~** on the upswing.

'**aufwirbeln** v/t (sep, -ge-, h) whirl up (a. v/i, sn), raise (dust): fig. (**viel**) **Staub ~** cause quite a stir.

'**aufwischen** v/t (sep, -ge-, h) a) mop up, b) wipe, mop.

'**aufwühlen** v/t (sep, -ge-, h) **1.** turn up (ground), churn up (sea). **2.** fig. j-n ~ stir s.o. deeply; **~d** stirring.

'**aufzählen** v/t (sep, -ge-, h) enumerate. '**Aufzählung** f (-; -en) enumeration.

'**aufzäumen** v/t (sep, -ge-, h) bridle: → **Pferd 1**.

'**aufzehren** v/t (sep, -ge-, h) fig. use up.

'**aufzeichnen** v/t (sep, -ge-, h) **1.** a) record, write down, b) tape(-record), TV (video-)tape. **2.** draw (**auf** acc on), sketch, ⊙ trace. '**Aufzeichnung** f (-; -en) **1.** a. ⊙, TV recording. **2.** pl notes, record, w.s. papers: **sich ~en machen** make notes (**über** acc of).

'**aufzeigen** v/t (sep, -ge-, h) show, demonstrate, point out.

'**aufziehen** (irr, sep, -ge-, → **ziehen**) **I** v/t (h) **1.** wind up: **Spielzeug zum ⚙ Aufziehen** clockwork toys. **2.** draw up, pull up, hoist (flag etc), thea. raise (the curtain). **3.** (pull) open (drawer), open, draw (curtains), undo (knot). **4.** mount (tyre), put on (strings), mount picture (on cardboard): fig. **andere Saiten ~** change one's tune. **5.** raise, bring up, rear. **6.** F organize, mount, set up (business etc). **7.** F j-n ~ tease s.o., pull s.o.'s leg. **8.** ⚕ fill (syringe). **II** v/i (sn) **9.** clouds: gather, storm: a. be brewing (a. fig.). **10.** ✕ march up.

'**Aufzucht** f (-; -en) breeding, raising.

'**Aufzug** m (-[e]s; -ᵉe) **1.** procession, parade. **2.** lift, Am. elevator. **3.** F contp. getup. **4.** thea. act. **5.** gym. pull-up.

'**aufzwingen** v/t (irr, sep, -ge-, h, → **zwingen**) j-m et. ~ force s.th. (up)on s.o., impose one's will on s.o.

'**Augapfel** m anat. eyeball: fig. **et. wie s-n ~ hüten** guard s.th. like gold.

Auge ['aʊgə] n (-s; -n) **1.** anat. eye: **gute**

(*schlechte*) *~n haben* have good (bad) eyesight (*or* eyes); *vor aller ~n* openly, in full view; *unter vier ~n* in private; *nur fürs ~* just for show; *~ um ~!* an eye for an eye!; F *fig. blaues ~* black eye; *mit e-m blauen ~ davonkommen* get off cheaply; *mit bloßem ~* with the naked eye; *vor m-m geistigen ~* in my mind's eye; *a. fig. mit verbundenen ~n* blindfold; *das ~ des Gesetzes* the law; *im ~ behalten* keep an eye on, *fig.* keep *s.th.* in mind; *ins ~ fallen* catch the eye; *ins ~ fallend* a) striking, b) obvious; *ins ~ fassen* consider; *j-m et. vor ~n führen* make *s.th.* clear to *s.o.*; F *das kann leicht ins ~ gehen* that can easily go wrong; *das hätte leicht ins ~ gehen können!* that was close!; *et. im ~ haben* have *s.th.* in mind; *ein ~ haben auf* (*acc*) have an eye on *s.o.*, *s.th.*; *s-e ~n überall haben* see everything; *sich et. vor ~n halten* bear *s.th.* in mind; *nicht aus den ~n lassen* keep one's eyes on; *große ~n machen* gape; F *er wird ~n machen!* he's in for a surprise!; *sie hat (vielleicht) ~n gemacht!* you should have seen her face!; *j-m (schöne) ~n machen* make eyes at *s.o.*; *fig. j-m die ~n öffnen* open *s.o.*'s eyes; *soweit das ~ reicht* as far as the eye can see; F *ein ~ riskieren* risk a glance; *dem Tod etc ins ~ sehen* look death *etc* in the eye, face death *etc*; *j-m in die ~n sehen* look *s.o.* full in the face; *fig. in die ~n springen* leap to the eye, be obvious; *das stach mir ins ~* it caught my fancy; *ich traute m-n ~n kaum* I could hardly believe my eyes; *aus den ~n verlieren* lose sight of; *die ~n verschließen vor* close one's eyes to; F *ein ~ zudrücken* turn a blind eye; *ich habe kein ~ zugetan* I didn't sleep a wink. **2.** *on dice, card:* pip. **3.** ♀ egg. **4.** globule of fat.

äugen ['ɔʏgən] *v/i* (h) *esp. hunt.* look.

'**Augen|arzt** *m* eye specialist, ophthalmologist. **~bank** *f* (-; -en) ♂ eye bank.

'**Augenblick** *m* (-[e]s; -e) moment: *e-n ~ bitte!* just a moment, please!; *im ~* at the moment; *im ersten ~* for a moment; *im letzten ~* at the (very) last moment; *alle ~e* every (*or* any) moment. '**augenblicklich** *I adj* **1.** immediate. **2.** present, current. **3.** momenta-ry. **II** *adv* **4.** immediately. **5.** at the moment, (just) now.

'**Augen|braue** *f* eyebrow. **~brauenstift** *m* eyebrow pencil. **~fältchen** *pl* crow's-feet. **~farbe** *f* colo(u)r of eyes. **~heilkunde** *f* ophthalmology. **~höhe** *f* (*in ~* at) eye level. **~höhle** *f* *anat.* eye socket, orbit. **~innendruck** *m* ♂ intra-ocular pressure. **~klappe** *f* eye patch. **~klinik** *f* eye clinic. **~leiden** *n* eye disease. **~licht** *n* (-[e]s; *no pl*) (eye)sight. **~lid** *n* eyelid. **~maß** *n* (-es; *no pl*) **1.** *ein gutes ~ haben* have a sure eye. **2.** *fig.* (good) *political etc* judg(e)ment.

'**Augenmerk** *n sein ~ richten auf* (*acc*) direct one's attention to.

'**Augen|muskel** *m* eye muscle. **~nerv** *m* optic nerve. **~operati,on** *f* eye operation. **~salbe** *f* eye ointment.

'**Augenschein** *m* (-[e]s; *no pl*) appearance(s): *dem ~ nach* to all appearances; *in ~ nehmen* inspect closely.

'**augenscheinlich** *adj* evident, apparent, obvious.

'**Augen|spiegel** *m* ♂ ophthalmoscope. **~tropfen** *pl* ♂ eyedrops. **~weide** *f* *fig.* feast for the eyes. **~wimper** *f* eyelash. **~wischerei** [-vɪʃəˈraɪ] *f* (-; -en) F eyewash. **~zahn** *m* eyetooth. **~zeuge** *m* eyewitness. **~zeugenbericht** *m* eyewitness report. **~zwinkern** *n* (-s) (*mit e-m ~* with a) wink.

August [aʊˈɡʊst] *m* (-[e]s, -; -e) (*im ~* in) August.

Auktion [aʊkˈtsi̯oːn] *f* (-; -en) ✝ auction (sale), public sale. **Auktionator** [aʊk-tsi̯oˈnaːtɔr] *m* (-s; -en [-naˈtoːrən]) auctioneer. **Aukti'onshaus** *n* auctioneers.

Aula ['aʊla] *f* (-; -s, Aulen) *ped., univ.* assembly hall.

Au-pair-Mädchen [oˈpɛːr-] *n* au pair (girl).

aus [aʊs] **I** *prep* (*dat*) **1.** out of, from: *~ dem Fenster sehen* look out of (*Am.* out) the window; *~ dem Haus gehen* leave the house; ≋ *~ Berlin* from Berlin; *~ unserer Mitte* from among us; *~ der Flasche* drink from the bottle. **2.** (*origin*) from, (*time*) *a.* of: *er ist ~ Berlin* he comes from Berlin; *~ ganz Spanien* from all over Spain; *~ dem 19. Jh.* of the 19th century; *er liest ~ s-m Roman* he reads from his novel; *~ dem Deutschen translated* from (the) German. **3.** (made) of, from: *fig.* **~ ihm wurde ein guter Arzt** he became a good doctor. **4. ~ Mitleid** (*Neugier etc*) out of pity (curiosity *etc*); **~ Liebe** from love; **~ Liebe zu** for the love of; **~ Prinzip** on principle; **~ Spaß** for fun; **~ Versehen** by mistake. **II** *adv* **5. von ... ~** from; **von hier ~** from here; *fig.* **von Natur ~** by nature; **von mir ~ kann er gehen** he may go, for all I care; **F von mir ~!** I don't care!; **von sich ~** of one's own accord. **6.** F a) (*switched*) off, out: **ein - aus** on - off, b) over, out; **die Schule ist ~** school is over; **damit ist es (jetzt) ~!** that's all over now!; **mit ihm ist es ~** he has had it; **~ der Mode** out of fashion. **7. ~ und ein** in and out; *fig.* **bei j-m ein und ~ gehen** be a frequent visitor at s.o.'s house; **ich weiß nicht mehr ein noch ~** I'm at my wits' end.

Aus *n* (-; *no pl*) *sports:* **im** (**ins**) **~**; *a. fig.* **das bedeutete das ~ für ihn** with that he was out (of the game).

'**ausarbeiten** *v/t* (*sep, -ge-, h*) work out, elaborate, develop, draw up.

'**Ausarbeitung** *f* (-; -en) **1.** working out, elaboration, development. **2.** draft.

'**ausarten** *v/i* (*sep, -ge-, sn*) degenerate (**in** *acc,* **zu** into), *game, party, etc:* get out of hand.

'**ausatmen** *v/i, v/t* (*sep, -ge-, h*) breathe out, exhale.

'**ausbaden** *v/t* (*sep, -ge-, h*) F **et. ~ müssen** have to carry the can.

'**ausbaggern** *v/t* (*sep, -ge-, h*) excavate, dredge.

'**ausbalan,cieren** *v/t* (*sep, h*) *a. fig.* balance out.

'**Ausbau** *m* (-[e]s; *no pl*) **1.** ⚙ disassembly, removal. **2.** △ a) extension, b) interior works. **3.** *a. fig.* expansion, development. **4.** *fig.* consolidation.

'**ausbauen** *v/t* (*sep, -ge-, h*) **1.** ⚙ dismantle, remove. **2.** △ extend: **das Dach ~** build rooms into the attic. **3.** *a. fig.* extend, expand, develop; *sports:* **s-n Vorsprung ~** increase one's lead. **4.** strengthen, consolidate. '**ausbaufähig** *adj* capable of development: **~e Stellung** position with good prospects.

'**ausbedingen** *v/t* (*sep, irr, h, → bedingen*) **sich et. ~** reserve (o.s.) s.th.; **sich ~, daß ...** make it a condition that ...

'**ausbessern** *v/t* (*sep, -ge-, h*) mend, re-

pair. '**Ausbesserung** *f* (-; -en) repair(s).

'**ausbeulen** *v/t* (*sep, -ge-, h*) **1.** ⚙ beat out. **2.** make *trousers etc* baggy.

'**Ausbeute** *f* (-; *no pl*) profit, *a.* 🗡, ⚙ yield, output, *fig.* result(s). '**ausbeuten** *v/t* (*sep, -ge-, h*) exploit (*a. b.s.*), 🗡 work. '**Ausbeuter** *m* (-s; -) *b.s.* exploiter. '**ausbeuterisch** *adj b.s.* exploitative. '**Ausbeutung** *f* (-; *no pl*) *a. b.s.* exploitation.

'**ausbilden** (*sep, -ge-, h*) **I** *v/t* **1.** a) train, instruct, educate, b) develop: **j-n zum Sänger ~** train s.o. to be a singer. **2.** *biol.* form, develop. **II** **sich ~** (**lassen**) **zu** train (*or* be trained, study) to be: → **ausgebildet.** '**Ausbilder** *m* (-s; -) *a.* 🗡 instructor. '**Ausbildung** *f* (-; -en) training, *ped., univ.* education: **in der ~ stehen** be undergoing training.

'**Ausbildungs\|beihilfe** *f* grant. **~gang** *m* training. **~platz** *m* training post. **~zeit** *f* period of training.

'**ausbitten** *v/t* (*sep, irr, -ge-, h, → bitten*) **sich et. ~** ask for s.th.

'**ausblasen** *v/t* (*irr, sep, -ge-, h, → blasen*) blow out.

'**ausbleiben** *v/i* (*irr, sep, -ge-, sn, → bleiben*) a) fail to come, b) stay away, c) stop: ⚕ **ihre Periode blieb aus** she missed her period; *fig.* **es konnte nicht ~, daß** it was inevitable that; (**nicht**) **lange ~** (not to) be long in coming.

'**Ausbleiben** *n* (-s) absence.

'**ausbleichen** *v/i* (*sep, -ge-, sn*) bleach (*a. v/t,* h), fade.

'**ausblenden** *v/t* (*sep, -ge-, h*) *film, radio:* fade out.

'**Ausblick** *m* (-[e]s; -e) view (**auf** *acc* of): **Zimmer mit ~ auf den See** room(s) overlooking the lake.

'**ausbomben** *v/t* (*sep, -ge-, h*) bomb out.

'**ausbooten** *v/t* (*sep, -ge-, h*) **1.** ⚓ disembark. **2.** F *fig.* oust, get rid of *s.o.*

'**ausbrechen** (*irr, sep, -ge-, → brechen*) **I** *v/t* **1.** break up (*or* off). **2.** → **erbrechen** 2. **II** *v/i* (sn) **3. ~ aus** (*dat*) break out of, escape from; *fig.* break away from (*a. sports*); F **aus der Gesellschaft ~** drop out of society. **4.** *fire, war, epidemic, etc:* break out, *volcano:* erupt. **5. in Tränen ~** burst into tears; **ihm brach der Schweiß aus** he broke into a sweat; **in Gelächter ~** burst out laughing; **in Beifall ~** break into applause. **6.** *mot.* swerve out of line.

'**Ausbrecher** *m* (-s; -) escaped prisoner.

'**ausbreiten** (*sep*, -ge-, h) **I** *v/t* **1.** spread (out). **2.** *fig.* extend, expand (*power etc*), display (*knowledge*). **II** *sich ~* **3.** fire, epidemic, *etc*: spread. **4.** *terrain*: spread (out), stretch (out), *panorama*: open up (**vor** *j-m* before s.o.). **5.** F spread (o.s.) out. '**Ausbreitung** *f* (-; *no pl*) spread(ing), extension, expansion.

'**ausbrennen** (*irr, sep*, -ge-, → **brennen**) **I** *v/t* (h) burn out, ✄ cauterize: → **ausgebrannt**. **II** *v/i* (sn) burn out.

'**Ausbruch** *m* (-[e]s; ⁼e) **1.** escape: **~ aus dem Gefängnis** jailbreak, breakout. **2.** *fig.* outbreak (*of war, epidemic, etc*), eruption (*of volcano*): **zum ~ kommen** break out. **3.** *fig.* outburst.

'**ausbrüten** *v/t* (*sep*, -ge-, h) *a. fig.* hatch, F be sickening for (*a disease*).

'**ausbuchen** *v/t* (*sep*, -ge-, h) **1.** ✝ cancel. **2.** → **ausgebucht**.

'**ausbuchten**: **sich ~** (*sep*, -ge-, h) bulge (*or curve*) out(wards).

'**ausbuddeln** *v/t* (*sep*, -ge-, h) F dig up.

'**ausbügeln** *v/t* (*sep*, -ge-, h) *a.* F *fig.* iron out.

'**ausbürgern** *v/t* (*sep*, -ge-, h) denaturalize.

'**ausbürsten** *v/t* (*sep*, -ge-, h) brush down.

'**Ausdauer** *f* (-; *no pl*) perseverance, *a.* ⚙ endurance, tenacity, *esp. sports*: staying power, stamina. '**ausdauernd** *adj* **1.** persevering, tireless. **2.** ✿ perennial.

'**ausdehnen** (*sep*, -ge-, h) (*a.* **sich ~**) *a. phys.*, ⚙ stretch, expand, extend (**auf** *acc* to): → **ausgedehnt**. '**Ausdehnung** *f* (-; en) **1.** *no pl* extension (**auf** *acc* to), expansion, spread(ing). **2.** extent, size.

'**ausdenken** *v/t* (*irr, sep*, -ge-, h, → **denken**) **sich et. ~** a) think s.th. up, F come up with, b) imagine c) invent, devise; **nicht auszudenken sein** be inconceivable; **die Folgen sind nicht auszudenken** the consequences could be disastrous.

'**ausdisku,tieren** *v/t* (*sep*, h) thresh out.

'**ausdörren** *v/t* (*sep*, -ge-, h) dry up, parch: → **ausgedörrt**.

'**ausdrehen** *v/t* (*sep*, -ge-, h) F turn off.

'**Ausdruck**[1] *m* (-[e]s; ⁼e) expression (*a.* & *etc*), word, term, phrase: **idiomati-**

scher ~ idiom; **juristischer ~** legal term; **zum ~ bringen** express; **zum ~ kommen** be expressed; F **das ist gar kein ~!** that's putting it mildly!

'**Ausdruck**[2] *m* (-[e]s; -e) *computer*: printout. '**ausdrucken** *v/t* (*sep*, -ge-, h) print s.th. in full, *computer*: print out.

'**ausdrücken** (*sep*, -ge-, h) **I** *v/t* **1.** stub out (*cigarette*). **2.** squeeze (out). **3.** *fig.* a) express, put into words, b) show, reveal: **ich weiß nicht, wie ich es ~ soll** I don't know how to put it; **anders ausgedrückt** in other words. **II** *sich ~* **4.** express o.s. **5.** be revealed.

'**ausdrücklich** **I** *adj* express: **~er Befehl** strict order. **II** *adv* expressly, specially.

'**Ausdruckskraft** *f* (-; *no pl*) expressiveness. '**ausdruckslos** *adj* blank, expressionless. '**ausdrucksvoll** *adj* expressive. '**Ausdrucksweise** *f* style, diction.

'**ausdünsten** *v/t* (*sep*, -ge-, h) give off. '**Ausdünstung** *f* (-; -en) odo(u)r.

ausein'ander *adv* apart, separated, F *marriage*: on the rocks: **~ schreibt man ~** ... is written in two words; **die Kinder sind zwei Jahre ~** the children are two years apart in age. **~brechen** *v/t* (*irr, sep*, -ge-, h, → **brechen**) *and v/i* (sn) break asunder. **~bringen** *v/t* (*irr, sep*, -ge-, h, → **bringen**) separate. **~fallen** *v/i* (*irr, sep*, -ge-, sn, → **fallen**) fall apart, *fig. a.* break up. **~gehen** *v/i* (*irr, sep*, -ge-, sn, → **gehen**) **1.** separate, part, *crowd*: disperse. **2.** *fig. opinions etc*: be divided (**über** *acc* on): **~d** differing, divergent. **3.** F come apart, *fig. relationship etc*: break off, *engagement*: be broken off, *marriage*: go on the rocks. **4.** F grow fat. **~halten** *v/t* (*irr, sep*, -ge-, h, → **halten**) tell apart, distinguish between. **~leben**: **sich ~** (*sep*, -ge-, h) drift apart. **~nehmen** *v/t* (*irr, sep*, -ge-, h, → **nehmen**) **1.** take apart, ⚙ *a.* dismantle. **2.** F *sports*: clobber. **~reißen** *v/t* (*irr, sep*, -ge-, h, → **reißen**) tear apart, *fig. a.* separate.

ausein'andersetzen (*sep*, -ge-, h) **I** *v/t* **j-m et.** ~ explain s.th. to s.o. **II** *sich ~ mit* deal with, tackle (*a problem etc*). **Ausein'andersetzung** *f* (-; -en) **1.** dealing (**mit** with). **2.** argument: *esp. pol.* **kriegerische ~** armed conflict.

'**ausfahren** (*irr, sep*, -ge-, → **fahren**) **I** *v/t* (h) **1.** a) ⚙ extend, b) lower (*landing* *gear).* **2.** *mot.* run *the engine* at top speed, round *(curve).* **3.** take *s.o.* out for a drive. **4.** deliver *(goods).* **5.** wear out, rut: → **ausgefahren** II. **II** *v/i (sn)* **6.** go for a drive. **'Ausfahrt** *f* (-; -en) **1.** drive. **2.** a) gateway, b) exit *(of motorway),* c) mouth *(of port):* *mot.* **~ freihalten!** keep exit clear!

'Ausfall *m* (-[e]s; ⸚e) **1.** ⚙ failure, breakdown. **2.** *no pl* a) loss, b) absence, c) cancel(l)ation *(of lesson etc).* **3.** *sports:* **ein glatter ~** *(player)* F a dead loss. **4.** *fenc.* lunge. **5.** *fig.* attack *(gegen* on).

'ausfallen *v/i (irr, sep, -ge-, sn, → fallen)* **1.** ⚙ fail, break down. **2.** *hair etc:* fall out. **3.** not to take place: **~ lassen** call off, cancel *(lecture etc);* **morgen fällt die Schule aus** there is no school tomorrow. **4.** *person:* be absent, be unavailable. **5.** **gut (schlecht) ~** turn out well (badly); **der Sieg fiel knapp aus** it was a close victory.

'ausfällen *v/t (sep, -ge-, h) ℞* precipitate.

'ausfallend ~ **'ausfällig** *adj* **(er wurde ~** he became) abusive.

'Ausfall|muster *n* ✝ production *(or* proof) sample. **~(s)erscheinung** *f* ✚ deficiency *(in addicts:* withdrawal) symptom. **~straße** *f* arterial road.

'ausfasern *v/i (sep, -ge-, sn)* fray (out).

'ausfechten *v/t (irr, sep, -ge-, h, → fechten)* *fig.* fight out.

'ausfertigen *v/t (sep, -ge-, h)* draw up, execute *(document), adm.* issue *(passport etc).* **'Ausfertigung** *f* (-; -en) **1.** drawing up, ⚖ execution. **2.** (⚖ certified) copy: → **doppelt** II, **dreifach.**

'ausfindig *adv* **~ machen** find, discover.

'ausfliegen *v/i (irr, sep, -ge-, sn, → fliegen)* fly out *(a. v/t ✕,* h), *birds:* leave the nest.

'ausfließen *v/i (irr, sep, -ge-, sn, → fließen)* flow out.

'ausflippen *v/i (sep, -ge-, sn)* F a) freak out, b) flip one's lid.

'Ausflucht *f* (-; ⸚e) *usu. pl* excuse.

'Ausflug *m* (-[e]s; ⸚e) **(e-n ~ machen)** (make an) excursion, (go on a ~) trip, (go for an) outing. **'Ausflügler** [-fly:glər] *m* (-s; -) day tripper, excursionist.

'Ausfluß *m* (-sses; ⸚sse) **1.** ⚙ a) outflow, b) outlet. **2.** ✚ discharge.

'ausfragen *v/t (sep, -ge-, h)* **(über** *acc* about) question, quiz, *contp.* pump.

'ausfransen *v/i (sep, -ge-, h)* fray (out).

'ausfressen *v/t (irr, sep, -ge-, h, → fressen)* F *fig.* **was hat er** *etc* **ausgefressen?** what has he *etc* been up to?

'Ausfuhr *f* (-; -en) **1.** *no pl* export. **2.** exports. **'ausfuhrbar** *adj* **1.** practicable. **2.** ✝ exportable. **'ausführen** *v/t (sep, -ge, h)* **1.** ✝ export. **2.** carry out, execute: **Reparaturen ~** make repairs. **3.** explain, argue. **4.** take *s.o.* out, take *a dog* for a walk.

'Ausführende *m, f* (-n; -n) ♪ performer.

'Ausfuhr|genehmigung *f* ✝ export licen/ce (*Am.* -se). **~handel** *m* export trade. **~land** *n* exporting country.

ausführlich ['aosfy:rlıç] **I** *adj* detailed, full. **II** *adv* in detail: **sehr ~** at great length; **~ beschreiben** give a detailed description *(or* account) of.

'Ausführprämie *f* export bounty.

'Ausfuhrquote *f* export quota.

'Ausfuhrsperre *f* embargo on exports.

'Ausführung *f* (-; -en) **1.** *no pl* carrying out, execution, *w.s.* completion. **2.** a) quality, b) type, model, c) design. **3.** *pl* remarks, comments.

'Ausfuhrzoll *m* export duty.

'ausfüllen *v/t (sep, -ge-, h)* **1.** fill, *fig. a.* occupy: **ihre Arbeit füllt sie nicht aus** she is not satisfied by her work. **2.** fill in, *Am.* fill out, complete *(form).*

'Ausgabe *f* (-; -n) **1.** *no pl* a) handing out, distribution, b) issue *(of order, material, etc,* ✝ *of shares),* emission *(of banknotes).* **2.** a) edition, copy *(of a book),* b) issue, number *(of a periodical).* **3.** *pl* expenditure, expense(s). **4.** *computer:* output. **~kurs** *m* ✝ issue price. **~stelle** *f* issuing office.

'Ausgang *m* (-[e]s; ⸚e) **1.** way out, exit: **am ~ des Dorfes** at the end of the village. **2.** *no pl* a) end, close, b) result, outcome: **Unfall mit tödlichem ~** fatal accident. **3.** *no pl* beginning: **s-n ~ nehmen von** start from. **4.** outing: **~ haben** have the day off, ✕ have a pass.

'Ausgangspunkt *m a. fig.* starting point.

'Ausgangssperre *f* → **Ausgehverbot.**

'Ausgangssprache *f* source language.

'ausgeben *(irr, sep, -ge-, h, → geben)* **I** *v/t* **1.** hand out, distribute, deal *(cards),* ✝ issue *(shares etc),* spend *(money), computer:* output: F **e-n** *(or* **e-e Runde) ~** stand a round of drinks. **2.** **~ für, ~**

'als pass *s.o., s.th.* off as. II *sich* ~ 3. pose (*für, als* sg.). 4. → *verausgaben* 2.

'ausgebeult I *pp of* **ausbeulen.** II *adj* baggy (*pants etc*).

'ausgebildet I *pp of* **ausbilden.** II *adj* trained.

'ausgebombt I *pp of* **ausbomben.** II *adj* bombed(-)out.

'ausgebrannt I *pp of* **ausbrennen.** II *adj* gutted (by fire), *a. fig.* burnt(-)out.

'ausgebucht I *pp of* **ausbuchen.** II *adj* booked(-)up.

'ausgedehnt I *pp of* **ausdehnen.** II *adj* a) *a. fig.* extensive, b) long (*period etc*).

'ausgedient *adj* useless, discarded.

'ausgefahren I *pp of* **ausfahren.** II *adj* worn(-)out, rutty: ~ *Gleis.*

'ausgefallen I *pp of* **ausfallen.** II *adj fig.* unusual, F off-beat.

'ausgebucht I *pp of* **ausfallen.** II *adj fig.* unusual, F off-beat.

'ausgebuht I *adj fig.* polished.

'ausgeglichen I *pp of* **ausgleichen.** II *adj fig.* (well-)balanced.

'ausgehen *v/i* (*irr, sep, -ge-, sn, →* **gehen**) **1.** go out: *er ist ausgegangen a.* he is not in. **2.** end: *gut ~ a.* turn out well; *ling.* **auf e-n Vokal ~** end in a vowel; *sports:* **unentschieden ~** end in a draw. **3.** light, *cigar, etc:* go out. **4.** *fig. money, supplies, etc:* run out: *mir ging das Geld aus* I ran out of money; *ihr ging die Geduld aus* she lost all patience; F *ihm ging die Puste aus* he ran out of steam. **5.** → **ausfallen** 2. **6.** ~ *von fig.* a) idea *etc:* come from, b) proceed from, assume; *wenn wir davon ~, daß* proceeding on the assumption that; *man kann (ruhig) davon ~, daß ...* it is safe to assume that ...; *ich gehe davon aus, daß ...* I would think (that) ... **7.** ~ *auf (acc)* be bent on; *auf Abenteuer ~* seek adventure; *auf Betrug ~* be out to cheat. **8.** *leer ~* come away empty-handed, F be left out in the cold; *(straf)frei ~* get off scot-free.

'ausgehend *adj das ~e Mittelalter* the late Middle Ages; *im ~en 19. Jh.* toward(s) the end of the 19th century.

'ausgehungert I *pp of* **aushungern.** II *adj* starved (*fig. nach* for).

'Ausgehverbot *n* curfew: ✗ ~ *bekommen* (*haben*) be confined to barracks.

'ausgeklügelt [-kly:gəlt] *adj* ingenious.

'ausgekocht I *pp of* **auskochen.** II *adj* F *fig.* shrewd, crafty.

'ausgelassen I *pp of* **auslassen.** II *adj* gay, exuberant, boisterous: ~ *sein a.* be in high spirits.

'ausgelastet I *pp of* **auslasten.** II *adj a.* **voll ~** ✝, ⚙ working to capacity, *person:* fully stretched.

'ausgelaugt *adj* F ~ *sein* be washed out.

'ausgemacht I *pp of* **ausmachen.** II *adj* **1.** settled: *e-e ~e Sache* a foregone conclusion. **2.** utter, perfect (*fool etc*).

'ausgemergelt [-mɛrgəlt] *adj* emaciated.

'ausgenommen I *pp of* **ausnehmen.** II *conj* (a. ~, *wenn*) unless *it rains etc:* ~, *daß* except that. III *prep* except(ing), with the exception of: → **Anwesende.**

'ausgeprägt *adj* marked, pronounced: ~*es Pflichtgefühl* strongly developed sense of duty.

'ausgepumpt I *pp of* **auspumpen.** II *adj* F *fig.* bushed, *Am.* pooped.

'ausgerechnet I *pp of* **ausrechnen.** II *adv* F *fig.* ~ *er* he of all people; ~ *Bananen* bananas of all things; ~ *heute* today of all days; ~ *jetzt* just now.

'ausgereift *adj* a) mature(d) (*a. fig.*), b) perfected (*design etc*).

'ausgeschlossen I *pp of* **ausschließen.** II *adj* **1.** *sich* ~ *fühlen* feel left out of things. **2.** impossible: *das ist ~!* that's out of the question!; *jeder Zweifel ist* ~ there is no doubt about it.

'ausgeschnitten I *pp of* **ausschneiden.** II *adj* (*tief*) ~ low-necked.

'ausgesprochen I *pp of* **aussprechen.** II *adj fig.* pronounced, marked: *das war ~es Pech* that really was bad luck; *es ist* ~ *falsch* it is positively wrong.

'ausgestorben I *pp of* **aussterben.** II *adj* extinct: *wie* ~ completely deserted.

'ausgesucht I *pp of* **aussuchen.** II *adj fig.* select, exquisite: ~*e Qualität* choice quality.

'ausgewachsen I *pp of* **auswachsen.** II *adj* **1.** full(y)-grown. **2.** F *fig.* full-blown (*scandal etc*).

'Ausgewiesene ['aʊsgəvi:zənə] *m, f* (*-n; -n*) expellee.

'ausgewogen I *pp of* **auswiegen.** II *adj fig.* (well-)balanced.

'ausgezeichnet I *pp of* **auszeichnen.** II *adj* excellent: *das paßt mir* ~ that suits me fine.

'ausgiebig [-gi:bɪç] I *adj* ~*en Gebrauch*

machen von make full use of. **II** *adv* ~ *duschen* have a good long shower.

'ausgießen *v/t* (*irr, sep*, -ge-, h, → *gießen*) pour out, empty.

'Ausgleich *m* (-[e]s; -e) **1.** a) balance (*für* to), b) settlement (*of account, bill*), c) compensation: *als* ~ *für* by way of compensation for; *zum* ~ (*gen*) in settlement of. **2.** *sports*: equalizer: *den* ~ *erzielen* → *ausgleichen* **3.** **'ausgleichen** (*irr, sep*, -ge-, h, → *gleichen*) **I** *v/t* **1.** compensate (for), offset: ~*de Gerechtigkeit* poetic justice. **2.** ✝ a) balance, settle (*accounts etc*), b) cover (*loss etc*). **II** *v/i* **3.** *sports*: equalize.

'Ausgleichs|getriebe *n mot.* differential (gear). **~sport** *m ich jogge als* ~ **I** do jogging to keep fit. **~tor** *n*, **~treffer** *m* equalizer.

'ausgleiten *v/i* (*irr, sep*, -ge-, sn, → *gleiten*) a. *fig.* slip.

'ausgraben *v/t* (*irr, sep*, -ge-, h, → *graben*) a. *fig.* dig up. **'Ausgrabung** *f* (-; -en) excavation, *F* dig.

'ausgrenzen *v/t* (*sep*, -ge-, h) exclude.

'Ausguck *m* (-[e]s; -e) ⚓, ✗ lookout.

'Ausguß *m* (-sses; ⸚sse) sink, ⚙ outlet.

'aushaken (*sep*, -ge-, h) **I** *v/t* unhook. **II** *v/impers* *F* **es hakte bei ihm aus** a) he lost the thread, b) he lost his cool, c) he flipped; *da hakt's bei mir aus!* I just don't get it!

'aushalten (*irr, sep*, -ge-, h, → *halten*) **I** *v/t* **1.** a) bear, stand (*pain etc*), b) sustain: *es ist nicht auszuhalten* (*or zum* ⚇) it is unbearable. **2.** *F* keep (*a woman*). **3.** ♪ hold. **II** *v/i* **4.** hold out: *er hält* (*es*) *nirgends lange aus* he never lasts long in any place (*or job*).

'aushandeln *v/t* (*sep*, -ge-, h) negotiate.

aushändigen ['aʊshɛndɪgən] *v/t* (*sep*, -ge-, h) hand over.

'Aushang *m* (-[e]s; ⸚e) notice, bulletin.

'aushängen *v/t* (*sep*, -ge-, h) **1.** take *door etc* off its hinges. **2.** put up (*notice etc*), show (*paintings*). **'Aushängeschild** *n* **1.** sign. **2.** *fig.* figurehead.

'ausharren *v/i* (*sep*, -ge-, h) hold out.

'ausheben *v/t* (*irr, sep*, -ge-, h, → *heben*) **1.** dig. **2.** → *aushängen* 1. **3.** *fig.* round up (*gang*).

'aushecken *v/t* (*sep*, -ge-, h) *F* cook up.

'ausheilen *v/i* (*sep*, -ge-, sn) be (completely) cured, *wound*: heal up.

'aushelfen *v/i* (*irr, sep*, -ge-, h, → *helfen*) *j-m* ~ help s.o. out (*mit* with).

'Aushilfe *f* (-; -n) **1.** temporary help: *zur* ~ *bei j-m arbeiten* help s.o. out. **2.** → **'Aushilfskraft** *f* temporary worker.

'aushilfsweise *adv* temporarily.

'aushöhlen *v/t* (*sep*, -ge-, h) hollow out, *geol., a. fig.* erode, undermine.

'ausholen *v/i* (*sep*, -ge-, h) (*weit* ~ a) swing back (*to strike*), b) *fig.* narrator: go far back; *mit der Axt* (*zum Schlag*) ~ raise the axe (to strike).

'aushorchen *v/t* (*sep*, -ge-, h) *j-n* ~ sound s.o. out (*über acc* on).

'aushungern *v/t* (*sep*, -ge-, h) starve (out): → *ausgehungert*.

'auskennen: sich ~ (*irr, sep*, -ge-, h, → *kennen*) **1.** *sich* ~ *in* (*dat*) know (one's way around) *a place*. **2.** *fig.* *sich* ~ *in* (*dat*), *sich* ~ *mit* know all about *s.th.*

'ausklammern *v/t* (*sep*, -ge-, h) *fig.* leave *s.th.* out of consideration, ignore.

'Ausklang *m* (-[e]s; *no pl*) *a. fig.* finale.

'auskleiden *v/t* (*sep*, -ge-, h) ⚙ line.

'ausklingen *v/i* (*irr, sep*, -ge-, sn, → *klingen*) *fig.* end (*in dat* with).

'ausklinken *v/t* (*sep*, -ge-, h) ⚙ release.

'ausknipsen *v/t* (*sep*, -ge-, h) *F* switch off.

'ausknobeln *v/t* (*sep*, -ge-, h) *F fig.* *et.* ~ figure s.th. out.

'auskochen *v/t* (*sep*, -ge-, h) boil, ⚕ sterilize (by boiling); → *ausgekocht* II.

'auskommen *v/i* (*irr, sep*, -ge-, sn, → *kommen*) **1.** ~ *mit* make do (*or* manage) with; *mit s-m Geld* ~ make both ends meet; ~ *ohne* manage (*or* do) without. **2.** *mit j-m* ~ get on (*or* along) with s.o. **'Auskommen** *n* (-s) **1.** livelihood: *sein* ~ *haben* make a (decent) living. **2.** *mit ihr ist kein* ~ you can't get on with her.

'auskosten *v/t* (*sep*, -ge-, h) *fig.* enjoy to the full.

'auskratzen *v/t* (*sep*, -ge-, h) **1.** scrape out. **2.** ⚕ curette.

'auskühlen (*sep*, -ge-) **I** *v/t* (h) chill *body* through. **II** *v/i* (sn) cool (off).

'auskundschaften *v/t* (*sep*, -ge-, h) spy out.

Auskunft ['aʊskʊnft] *f* (-; ⸚e) **1.** information (*über acc* on, about): *nähere* ~ further particulars; *Auskünfte einholen* make inquiries. **2.** information office (*or* desk), *a. teleph.* Inquiries.

Auskunftei [aʊskʊnfˈtaɪ] *f* (-; -en) ⚕ inquiry office.

Auskunftsbeamte *m* inquiry clerk.

Auskunftsbü‚ro *n* inquiry office.

auskuppeln *v/i* (*sep*, -ge-, h) *mot.* declutch.

auslachen *v/t* (*sep*, -ge-, h) laugh at.

ausladen *v/t* (*irr*, *sep*, -ge-, h, → *laden*) **1.** unload, ⚓ disembark. **2.** F disinvite: *j-n ~* ask s.o. not to come.

ausladend *adj* **1.** projecting, jutting out. **2.** *fig.* sweeping (*gesture*).

Auslage *f* (-; -n) **1.** a) (window) display, b) shop-window. **2.** *pl* (*j-m s-e ~n ersetzen* refund s.o.'s) expenses.

Ausland *n* (-[e]s; *no pl*) foreign countries: *im* (*ins*) *~* abroad; *aus dem ~* from abroad; *die Reaktion des ~s* reactions abroad. **Ausländer** ['aʊslɛn-dər] *m* (-s; -), **'Ausländerin** *f* (-; -nen) foreigner. **'ausländerfeindlich** *adj* hostile to foreigners. **'Ausländer-feindlichkeit** *f* anti-alien feeling.

'ausländisch *adj* foreign: *~e Besucher* a. visitors from abroad.

'Auslands... foreign (*department etc*). **~aufenthalt** *m* stay abroad. **~flug** *m* international flight. **~gespräch** *n* *teleph.* international call. **~reise** *f* journey (*or* trip) abroad. **~schutzbrief** *m* *mot.* (certificate of) international travel cover. **~tour‚nee** *f* tour abroad. **~verschuldung** *f* ⚕ foreign debts.

'auslassen (*irr*, *sep*, -ge-, h, → *lassen*) **I** *v/t* **1.** leave out, omit (*word etc*), skip (*page etc*), miss (*opportunity*). **2.** vent one's anger etc (*an dat* on): *s-n Ärger an j-m ~* take it out on s.o. **3.** melt (*butter etc*). **4.** let out (*seam*). **II** *sich ~* talk (at length) (*über acc* about).

'Auslassung *f* (-; -en) omission.

'auslasten *v/t* (*sep*, -ge-, h) ⚙ use to capacity: → *ausgelastet.*

'Auslauf *m* (-[e]s; ⸚e) **1.** *sports:* run-out. **2.** (chicken etc) run: *die Kinder haben k-n ~* the children have nowhere to play. **'auslaufen** *v/i* (*irr*, *sep*, -ge-, sn, → *laufen*) **1.** liquid, *tank etc:* run out. **2.** ⚓ sail. **3.** end, *contract etc:* run out: ⚕ *~ lassen* phase out, discontinue (*model*). **4.** *colo(u)r:* run, bleed.

'Ausläufer *pl* **1.** foothills. **2.** outskirts.

'Auslaufmo‚dell *n* ⚕ phase-out model.

'Auslaut *m* (-[e]s; -e) *ling.* final sound.

'ausleben: *sich ~* (*sep*, -ge-, h) live it up.

'auslecken *v/t* (*sep*, -ge-, h) lick out.

'auslegen *v/t* (*sep*, -ge-, h) **1.** lay out, display (*goods*). **2.** a) cover, b) inlay: *mit Teppich ~* a. carpet; *mit Papier ~* line with paper. **3.** advance (*sum*). **4.** interpret: *falsch ~* misinterpret. **5.** ⚙ design (*auf acc* for).

'Ausleger *m* (-s; -) **1.** jib, boom. **2.** a. **'Auslegerboot** *n* outrigger.

'Auslegeware *f* (-; *no pl*) floor coverings, a. wall-to-wall carpeting.

'Auslegung *f* (-; -en) interpretation.

'ausleiern *v/t* (*sep*, -ge-, h) (a. *sich ~*) wear out.

'ausleihen *v/t* (*irr*, *sep*, -ge-, h, → *leihen*) **1.** lend (out), loan. **2.** *sich et. ~ von* borrow s.th. from.

'auslernen *v/i* (*sep*, -ge-, h) complete one's training: *man lernt nie aus* (we) live and learn.

'Auslese *f* (-; -n) **1.** choice, selection: *biol. natürliche ~* natural selection. **2.** *fig.* élite, flower. **3.** wine made from selected grapes.

'auslesen[1] *v/t* (*irr*, *sep*, -ge-, h, → *lesen*) select, ⚙ sort. **'auslesen**[2] *v/t* (*irr*, *sep*, -ge-, h, → *lesen*) finish (reading).

'ausleuchten *v/t* (*sep*, -ge-, h) a. *fig.* illuminate.

'ausliefern *v/t* (*sep*, -ge-, h) **1.** hand over (*dat* to), ⚕ deliver: *fig. j-m ausgeliefert sein* be at s.o.'s mercy. **2.** *pol.* extradite. **'Auslieferung** *f* (-; -en) **1.** ⚕ delivery. **2.** *pol.* extradition. **'Auslieferungs-vertrag** *m* ⚕⚖, *pol.* extradition treaty.

'ausliegen *v/i* (*irr*, *sep*, -ge-, h, → *liegen*) be on display, *newspapers:* be available.

'auslöffeln *v/t* (*sep*, -ge-, h) spoon up: → *Suppe.*

'auslöschen *v/t* (*sep*, -ge-, h) **1.** → *löschen* 1. **2.** *fig.* wipe out.

'auslosen *v/t* (*sep*, -ge-, h) draw (lots) for.

'auslösen *v/t* (*sep*, -ge-, h) **1.** *phot.*, ⚙ release, a. *fig.* trigger (off). **2.** *fig.* produce (*effect*), cause (*panic etc*), arouse (*enthusiasm etc*). **3.** redeem (*pawned object*). **'Auslöser** *m* (-s; -) release, a. *fig.* trigger. **'Auslösung** *f* (-; -en) **1.** releasing, triggering (*etc*, → *auslösen*). **2.** ⚕ compensation.

'Auslosung *f* (-; -en) draw.

'ausloten v/t (sep, -ge-, h) a. fig. sound.

'ausmachen v/t (sep, -ge-, h) **1.** F → a) **löschen** 1, b) **ausschalten** 1. **2.** make out, spot, locate. **3.** → **abmachen** 1. **2.** amount to. **5.** fig. make up, form (part of): **das macht den Reiz s-r Bilder aus** this is what makes his pictures so attractive. **6. das macht nichts (viel) aus** that doesn't matter (it matters a great deal); **wenn es Ihnen nichts ausmacht** if you don't mind; **macht es Ihnen et. aus, wenn ich rauche?** do you mind my smoking?; **die Kälte macht mir nichts aus** I don't mind the cold.

'ausmalen v/t (sep, -ge-, h) **1.** a) paint, b) colo(u)r (picture). **2.** fig. depict (dat to): **sich et. ~** picture s.th. (to o.s.).

'Ausmaß n (-es; -e) dimensions, a. fig. extent: **das ~ des Schadens** the extent of the damage; **gewaltige ~e annehmen** assume horrendous proportions.

'ausmerzen v/t (sep, -ge-, h) eliminate.

'ausmessen v/t (irr, sep, -ge-, h, → **messen**) measure.

'ausmisten v/t (sep, -ge-, h) muck out.

'ausmustern v/t (sep, -ge-, h) **1.** sort out, discard. **2.** ✗ reject (as unfit).

Ausnahme ['aʊsnaːmə] f (-; -n) exception: **mit ~ von** (or gen) with the exception of, except (for); **e-e ~ bilden** a. be exceptional; **bei j-m e-e ~ machen** make an exception in s.o.'s case.

'Ausnahme... exceptional (athlete, case, etc). **'Ausnahmezustand** m (**den ~ verhängen** declare a) state of emergency (**über** acc in).

'ausnahmslos adv and adj without exception. **'ausnahmsweise** adv a) by way of exception, b) for once.

'ausnehmen v/t (irr, sep, -ge-, h, → **nehmen**) **1.** gut (fish etc), draw (goose etc). **2.** F j-n ~ fleece s.o. **3.** exclude, except.

'ausnüchtern v/i (sep, -ge-, h) sober up.

'ausnutzen v/t (sep, -ge-, h) a. b.s. use, exploit, b.s. take advantage of. **'Ausnutzung** f (-; no pl) a. b.s. exploitation.

'auspacken (sep, -ge-, h) **I** v/t unpack, unwrap. **II** v/i F fig. spill the beans.

'auspfeifen v/t (irr, sep, -ge-, h, → **pfeifen**) boo.

'ausplaudern v/t (sep, -ge-, h) blab out.

'auspo,saunen v/t (sep, -ge-, h) F broadcast.

'auspressen v/t (sep, -ge-, h) squeeze (out).

'auspro,bieren v/t (sep, h) try (out).

'Auspuff m (-[e]s; -e) mot. exhaust.

'Auspufftopf m silencer, Am. muffler.

'auspumpen v/t (sep, -ge-, h) pump out.

'ausquar,tieren v/t (sep, h) lodge s.o. elsewhere.

'ausquetschen v/t (sep, -ge-, h) F fig. **j-n ~** grill s.o.

'ausra,dieren v/t (sep, h) **1.** erase. **2.** fig. wipe out, wipe town etc off the map.

'ausran,gieren v/t (sep, h) throw out.

'ausrasten v/i (sep, -ge-, sn) **1.** ⊙ be released. **2.** F fig. flip.

'ausrauben v/t (sep, -ge-, h) rob.

'ausräuchern v/t (sep, -ge-, h) fumigate, hunt., a. fig. smoke out.

'ausräumen v/t (sep, -ge-, h) **1.** clear (room etc), remove furniture (**aus** dat from). **2.** fig. clear up (misunderstanding etc), dispel (doubts).

'ausrechnen v/t (sep, -ge-, h) (fig. sich) et. ~ work s.th. out (for o.s.); F **er ist leicht auszurechnen** he is quite predictable; → **ausgerechnet**.

'Ausrede f (-; -n) desperate (**faule** lame) excuse.

'ausreden (sep, -ge-, h) **I** v/i finish (speaking): **j-n ~ lassen** hear s.o. out; **j-n nicht ~ lassen** cut s.o. short. **II** v/t **j-m et. ~** talk s.o. out of s.th.

'ausreichen v/i (sep, -ge-, h) be enough: **~ für** last (a week etc). **'ausreichend** adj **1.** sufficient, enough. **2.** ped. D.

'Ausreise f (-; -n) departure: **bei der ~** on leaving the country; **j-m die ~ verweigern** refuse s.o. permission to leave the country. **~visum** n exit visa.

'ausreißen (irr, sep, -ge-, → **reißen**) **I** v/t (h) pull out, tear out. **II** v/i (sn) F run away (**vor** j-m before s.o., **von zu Hause** from home). **'Ausreißer** m (-s; -), **'Ausreißerin** f (-; -nen) F runaway.

'ausreiten v/i (irr, sep, -ge-, sn, → **reiten**) ride out.

'ausrenken v/t (sep, -ge-, h) **sich den Arm** etc ~ dislocate one's arm etc.

'ausrichten v/t (sep, -ge-, h) **1.** a) straighten, b) align, c) adjust (a. fig., **nach** to): **sich ~** line up; fig. **sich (or sein Verhalten) ~ nach** orientate o.s. to; **ausgerichtet auf** (acc) aimed at. **2.** achieve: **er wird (bei ihr) nichts ~ (können)** he won't get anywhere (with her). **3.** tell: **kann ich et. ~?** can I take a message?; **bitte richten Sie ihm Grüße**

von mir aus please give him my (kind) regards. **4.** organize, arrange.

'**Ausrichter** *m* (-s; -) organizer.

'**ausrollen** (*sep*, -ge-, h) **I** *v/t* roll (out) (*dough*). **II** *v/i mot.* coast (✓ *taxi*) to a standstill.

'**ausrotten** *v/t* (*sep*, -ge-, h) exterminate.

'**Ausrottung** *f* (-; -en) extermination.

'**ausrücken** (*sep*, -ge-) **I** *v/i* (sn) **1.** *fire brigade etc*: turn out, ✕ march out. **2.** F → **ausreißen** II. **II** *v/t* (h) **3.** *print.* move out.

'**Ausruf** *m* (-[e]s; -e) cry, exclamation.

'**ausrufen** *v/t* (*irr, sep*, -ge-, h, → **rufen**) **1.** call out (*name etc*): **j-n ~ lassen** page s.o. **2.** call (*strike*), *pol.* proclaim: **j-n zum König ~** proclaim s.o. king. '**Ausrufungszeichen** *n* exclamation mark.

'**ausruhen** *v/i* (*sep*, -ge-, h) (*a.* **sich ~**) rest.

'**ausrüsten** *v/t* (*sep*, -ge-, h) *a. fig.* equip (**mit** with). '**Ausrüstung** *f* (-; -en) **1.** equipment, gear. **2.** accessories.

'**ausrutschen** *v/i* (*sep*, -ge-, sn) slip (**auf** *dat* on). '**Ausrutscher** *m* (-s; -) F *fig.* slip, gaffe.

'**Aussaat** *f* (-; -en) a) sowing, b) seed.

'**Aussage** *f* (-; -n) statement, *a. author's etc* message, ⚖ *a.* testimony: **nach Ihrer ~** according to what you said; ⚖ **die ~ verweigern** refuse to give evidence; **hier steht ~ gegen ~** it's his word against hers *etc*. '**aussagen** (*sep*, -ge-, h) **I** *v/i* ⚖ testify, give evidence. **II** *v/t* state, say, *esp. fig.* express.

'**Aussagesatz** *m* clause of statement.

'**Aussatz** *m* (-es; *no pl*) ⚕ leprosy.

'**Aussätzige** *m, f* (-n; -n) *a. fig.* leper.

'**aussaugen** *v/t* (*sep*, -ge-, h) suck: *fig.* **j-n (bis aufs Blut) ~** bleed s.o. (white).

'**ausschaben** *v/t* (*sep*, -ge-, h) ⚕ curette. '**Ausschabung** *f* (-; -en) ⚕ curettage.

'**ausschachten** *v/t* (*sep*, -ge-, h) dig.

'**ausschalten** *v/t* (*sep*, -ge-, h) **1.** switch off (*light, radio, etc*), cut out (*current*), stop, cut (*engine*). **2.** *fig.* eliminate, *esp. sports*: neutralize.

'**Ausschaltung** *f* (-; -en) *fig.* elimination.

'**Ausschau**: **~ halten** → '**ausschauen** *v/i* (*sep*, -ge-, h) look out (**nach** for).

'**ausscheiden** (*irr, sep*, -ge-, → **scheiden**) **I** *v/t* (h) **1.** eliminate, exclude, sort out, remove. **2.** *physiol.* excrete. **II** *v/i* (sn) **3.** be ruled out, *person*: be not

eligible. **4. ~ aus** (*dat*) a) retire from (*an office*), leave (*a firm*), b) *sports*: be eliminated from (*contest*), drop out of (*a race*). '**Ausscheidung** *f* (-; -en) **1.** elimination. **2.** *physiol.* excretion, excrements. **3.** → '**Ausscheidungskampf** *m sports*: qualifying contest.

'**ausschenken** *v/t* (*sep*, -ge-, h) **1.** pour (out). **2.** sell.

'**ausscheren** *v/i* (*sep*, -ge-, sn) **1.** *mot.* swing out. **2.** *fig.* deviate (**aus** from).

'**ausschiffen** *v/t* (*sep*, -ge-, h) (*a.* **sich ~**) disembark.

'**ausschlachten** *v/t* (*sep*, -ge-, h) **1.** cut up. **2.** F *fig.* a) cannibalize (*car etc*), b) *contp.* exploit, capitalize on.

'**ausschlafen** (*irr, sep*, -ge-, h, → **schlafen**) **I** *v/t* sleep off. **II** *v/i* (*a.* **sich ~**) a) get a good night's sleep, b) sleep late.

'**Ausschlag** *m* (-[e]s; ⸚e) **1.** ⚕ (**e-n ~ bekommen** break out into) a rash. **2.** *fig.* **den ~ geben für** be decisive of; **das gab den ~** that decided (*or* settled) it. **3.** *phys.* a) swing (*of pendulum*), deflection (*of pointer*), b) amplitude. '**ausschlagen** (*irr, sep*, -ge-, h, → **schlagen**) **I** *v/i* **1.** *horse*: kick out. **2.** *pendulum etc*: swing, *pointer etc*: deflect. **3.** ⚘ sprout, *tree*: come into leaf. **II** *v/t* **4.** knock out (*tooth*): → **Faß. 5.** line. **6.** refuse, turn *s.th.* down. '**ausschlaggebend** *adj* (*a.* **von ⸚er Bedeutung**) decisive (**für** of).

'**ausschließen** (*irr, sep*, -ge-, h, → **schließen**) **I** *v/t* **1.** → **aussperren. 2.** (**aus** from) exclude, expel (*from the party etc*), bar, *sports*: disqualify: **zeitweilig ~** suspend; ⚖ **die Öffentlichkeit ~** exclude the public. **3.** a) rule out (*mistake etc*), b) exclude, → **ausgeschlossen. II sich ~** exclude o.s. (**von** from).

'**ausschließlich** *adj* exclusive.

'**Ausschluß** *m* (-sses; ⸚sse) (**aus** from) a) exclusion, expulsion, b) *sports*: disqualification: **zeitweiliger ~** suspension; ⚖ **unter ~ der Öffentlichkeit** in closed session.

'**ausschmücken** *v/t* (*sep*, -ge-, h) **1.** decorate. **2.** *fig.* embroider (*story etc*).

'**ausschneiden** *v/t* (*irr, sep*, -ge-, h, → **schneiden**) **1.** cut out: → **ausgeschnitten. 2.** ✗ prune (*trees etc*).

'**Ausschnitt** *m* (-[e]s; -e) **1.** neck(line): **mit tiefem ~** décolleté, low-necked. **2.** (*newspaper*) cutting, *Am.* clipping. **3.**

phot. etc detail, *sports, TV* scene. **4.** *fig.* (*aus*) part (of), extract (from).
'**ausschöpfen** *v/t* (*sep*, -ge-, h) **1.** bail out. **2.** *fig.* exhaust (*subject*).
'**ausschreiben** *v/t* (*irr, sep*, -ge-, h, → **schreiben**) **1.** a) write out, b) write figure out (in words). **2.** → **ausstellen** 2. **3.** a) announce, b) advertise (*post*), c) ✝ invite tenders (for): *e-n Wettbewerb* ~ invite entries (✝ tenders) for a competition; *Wahlen* ~ go to the country.
'**Ausschreibung** *f* (-; -en) ✝ invitation to bid (*sports*: to a competition).
'**Ausschreitung** *f* (-; -en) *usu. pl* riot.
'**Ausschuß** *m* (-sses; ⸚sse) **1.** (*in e-m* ~ *sein* be or sit on a) committee. **2.** ✝ rejects, ⊚ waste, scrap. '**Ausschußmitglied** *n* committee member. '**Ausschußsitzung** *f* committee meeting.
'**ausschütteln** *v/t* (*sep*, -ge-, h) shake out.
'**ausschütten** (*sep*, -ge-, h) **I** *v/t* **1.** a) pour out, empty (*bucket etc*), b) spill: *fig. j-m sein Herz* ~ unburden o.s. to s.o. **2.** ✝ pay (*dividend*). **II** *sich* (*vor Lachen*) ~ split one's sides laughing.
'**ausschweifend** *adj* unbridled (*imagination*), dissolute (*life*).
'**Ausschweifungen** *pl* excesses.
'**ausschweigen: sich** ~ (*irr, sep*, -ge-, h, → **schweigen**) remain silent (*über acc* about).
'**ausschwitzen** *v/t* (*sep*, -ge-, h) exude.
'**aussehen** (*irr, sep*, -ge-, h, → **sehen**) **I** *v/i* look: *gut* ~ a) be good-looking, b) look well; *schlecht* ~ look bad (*or* ill); *wie sieht er aus?* what does he look like?; F *sie sah vielleicht aus!* she did look a sight!; *so siehst du aus!* nothing doing! **II** *v/impers* F *es sieht nach Regen aus* it looks like rain; *damit es nach et. aussieht* to make it look impressive.
'**Aussehen** *n* (-s) looks, appearance.
'**aussein** *v/i* (*irr, sep*, -sn, → *sein*) F **1.** be over: *fig. mit ihm ist es aus* he is finished. **2.** *light, radio, etc*: be off, *fire etc*: be out. **3.** *wir waren gestern abend aus* we were out last night. **4.** *sports*: be out. **5.** ~ *auf* (*acc*) be out for (*or* to get); *sie ist auf sein Geld aus* she is after his money.
außen ['aʊsən] *adv* outside: *von* ~ from (the) outside; *nach* ~ outward(s), *fig.*

outwardly (*calm etc*); F *er bleibt* ~ *vor* he's (left) out of it.
'**Außen|aufnahmen** *pl* film: location shooting. **~bezirke** *pl* outskirts.
'**Außenbordmotor** *m* outboard motor.
'**aussenden** *v/t* (*irr, sep*, -ge-, h, → **senden**) send out.
'**Außendienst** *m* field work: *im* ~ in the field. **~mitarbeiter(in** *f*) *m* field worker, ✝ *a.* sales representative.
'**Außen|handel** *m* foreign trade. **~kante** *f* outer edge. **~mi‚nister** *m* Foreign Minister (*Br.* Secretary), *Am.* Secretary of State. **~mini‚sterium** *n* Foreign Ministry (*Br.* Office), *Am.* State Department. **~poli‚tik** *f* foreign politics (*or* policy). ⊙**po‚litisch** *adj* foreign: **~e De‚batte** on foreign affairs.
'**Außenseite** *f* outside. **Außenseiter** ['aʊsənzaɪtər] *m* (-s; -) outsider.
'**Außenspiegel** *m* mot. outside rear-view mirror.
Außenstände ['aʊsənʃtɛndə] *pl* ✝ outstanding debts.
'**Außen|stelle** *f* branch (office). **~stürmer** *m* sports: winger, outside. **~wand** *f* outer wall. **~welt** *f* outside world.
außer ['aʊsər] **I** *prep* (*dat*) **1.** out of: → *Atem, Betrieb* 2, *Dienst* 2, *Reichweite*; *fig.* ~ *sich sein* be beside o.s. (*vor* with); ~ *sich geraten* lose control of o.s. **2.** apart from, except (for): *alle* ~ *dir* all except (*or* but) me. **3.** besides, in addition to. **II** *conj* **4.** ~ (*wenn*) unless; ~ *daß* except that.
'**außerberuflich** *adj* private.
'**außerbetrieblich** *adj* external.
'**außerdem** *adv* besides.
äußere ['ɔysərə] *adj* outer, outside, external, ✝, *pol.* foreign: *k-e* ~*n Verletzungen* no external injuries; *pol.* ~ *Angelegenheiten* foreign affairs.
'**Äußere** *n* (-n) outside, (outward) appearance, *s.o.'s* looks: *von angenehmem* ~*n* personable; *auf sein* ~ *achten* be particular about one's appearance.
'**außerehelich** *adj* illegitimate (*child*), extramarital (*relationship*).
'**außergerichtlich** *adj* extrajudicial: **~er Vergleich** settlement out of court.
'**außergewöhnlich** *adj* exceptional, uncommon, ✝ extraordinary.
'**außerhalb** **I** *prep* (*gen*) out of: ~ *des*

Hauses outdoors, outside. **II** *adv* a) outside, b) out of town.

'**außerirdisch** *adj* (*a.* ~es *Wesen*) extraterrestrial.

äußerlich ['ɔysərlıç] *adj a. fig.* a) outward, external, b) superficial: *nur zur* ~*en Anwendung* for external use only; ~ *betrachtet* on the face of it.

'**Äußerlichkeit** *f* (-; -en) *fig.* superficiality: *bloße* ~ mere formalities.

äußern ['ɔysərn] (h) **I** *v/t* a) utter, express, b) voice (*criticism etc*). **II** *sich* ~ a) (*über acc* on) express o.s., give one's opinion, b) (*in dat* in) be shown, *disease etc*: manifest itself.

'**außerordentlich** *I adj* extraordinary, unusual, remarkable, outstanding: ~*er Professor* senior lecturer, *Am.* associate professor. **II** *adv* extremely.

'**außerparlamen̦tarisch** *adj* extraparliamentary. '**außerplanmäßig** *adj* a) extraordinary, b) supernumerary (*official*). '**außersinnlich** *adj* ~*e Wahrnehmung* extrasensory perception.

äußerst ['ɔysərst] **I** *adj* **1.** outermost, remotest: *pol.* **die** ~*e Linke* the extreme left. **2.** latest, final: ~*er Termin* a. deadline. **3.** *fig.* extreme, utmost: *von* ~*er Wichtigkeit* of utmost importance; *im* ~*en Fall* at worst; *mit* ~*er Kraft* by a supreme effort. **II** *adv* **4.** extremely.

'**Äußerste** *n* (-n) *fig.* a) the limit, the most, b) the worst: *sein* ~*s tun* do one's utmost; *zum* ~*n entschlossen sein* be desperate; *bis zum* ~*n gehen* go to the last extreme; *auf das* ~ *gefaßt sein* be prepared for the worst.

'**außerstande** *adj* ~ *sein* be unable.

Äußerung ['ɔysərʊŋ] *f* (-; -en) **1.** statement, remark. **2.** expression, sign.

'**aussetzen** (*sep*, -ge-, h) **I** *v/t* **1.** expose (*dat* to, *a. fig.* to danger, *criticism etc*), abandon (*child*), release (*pet*). **2.** ⚓ lower (*boat*), disembark, *b.s.* maroon (*passengers*). **3.** offer *award etc* (*dat* to): *e-n Preis auf j-s Kopf* ~ put a price on s.o.'s head. **4.** interrupt, ✝, ⚖ suspend: → *Bewährung* **5.** *et.* ~ (*or auszusetzen haben*) *an* (*dat*) object to, criticize; *was ist daran auszusetzen?* what's wrong with it?; *er hat an allem et. auszusetzen* he finds fault with everything. **II** *v/i* **6.** fail, *mot.* misfire, *heart*: miss a beat. **7.** a) stop, break off, b)

take a rest, c) *in a game*: sit out: ~ *mit* interrupt (*treatment etc*); *ohne auszusetzen* without interruption; *at games*: (*e-e Runde*) ~ miss a turn.

'**Aussicht** *f* (-; -en) (*auf acc* of) **1.** *no pl* view: *ein Zimmer mit* ~ *auf das Meer* a room overlooking the sea. **2.** chance, prospect, *pl a.* outlook: *er hat* ~*en zu gewinnen* he stands a chance to win; *gute* ~*en auf Erfolg haben* stand a good chance of success. '**aussichtslos** *adj* hopeless: ~*e Sache* lost cause; *e-n* ~*en Kampf führen* fight a losing battle. '**Aussichtslosigkeit** *f* (-; *no pl*) hopelessness.

'**aussichtsreich** *adj* promising.

'**Aussichtsturm** *m* observation tower.

'**aussiedeln** *v/t* (*sep*, -ge-, h) resettle. '**Aussiedler(in** *f*) *m* → *Umsiedler(in*).

aussöhnen ['aʊszø:nən] *v/t* (*sep*, -ge-, h) reconcile (*sich* o.s.) (*mit*, with, to). '**Aussöhnung** *f* (-; -en) reconciliation.

'**aussondern** *v/t* (*sep*, -ge-, h), '**aussor̦tieren** *v/t* (*sep*, h) sort out.

'**ausspannen** (*sep*, -ge-, h) *I v/t* **1.** unharness: F *fig.* **j-m die Freundin** ~ steal s.o.'s girl. **2.** spread out, stretch out. **II** *v/i* **3.** relax, (take a) rest.

'**aussparen** *v/t* (*sep*, -ge-, h) **1.** ⚙ leave open. **2.** leave out, avoid (*subject etc*).

'**aussperren** *v/t* (*sep*, -ge-, h) **j-n** ~ a. ✝ lock s.o. out (*aus* of). '**Aussperrung** *f* (-; -en) ✝ lockout.

'**ausspielen** (*sep*, -ge-, h) **I** *v/t* play (*card*), *fig.* bring *one's skill etc* to bear: *j-n gegen j-n* ~ play s.o. off against s.o. **II** *v/i cards*: lead: *fig.* **er hat ausgespielt** he's finished.

'**ausspinnen** *v/t* (*irr*, *sep*, -ge-, h, → *spinnen*) *fig.* spin out.

'**ausspio̦nieren** *v/t* (*sep*, h) spy out, spy on s.o.

'**Aussprache** *f* (-; -n) **1.** *no pl* pronunciation. **2.** discussion, *a. parl.* debate.

'**aussprechen** (*irr*, *sep*, -ge-, h, → *sprechen*) **I** *v/t* **1.** pronounce: → *ausgesprochen*. **2.** express (*one's sympathy*, *views*, *etc*): → *Vertrauen*. **3.** grant (*divorce*). **II** *v/i* **4.** → *ausreden* I. **III** *sich* ~ **5.** express one's views (*über acc* on, about), speak (*für* for, *gegen* against). **6.** a) *bei j-m* unburden o.s. to s.o., b) *mit j-m* F have it out with s.o.

'**Ausspruch** *m* (-[e]s, ~e) remark, saying.

'**ausspucken** v/t, v/i (sep, -ge-, h) spit out. '**ausspülen** v/t (sep, -ge-, h) rinse.
'**ausstaf,fieren** v/t (sep, h) F rig out.
'**Ausstand** m (-[e]s; ⸚e) strike, F walkout: *in den ~ treten* go on strike, walk out.
ausstatten ['aʊsʃtatən] v/t (sep, -ge-, h) (*mit* with) 1. fit out, equip, a. furnish (*flat*), get up (*book*). 2. ⸖ endow (*with capital, a. fig. with talent etc*), ⚖ vest (*with power etc*). '**Ausstattung** f (-; -en) a) outfit, equipment, b) furnishing, décor, c) *thea. etc* sets and costumes, d) design, e) get-up. '**Ausstattungsstück** n *thea.* spectacular (show).
'**ausstechen** v/t (irr, sep, -ge-, h, → **stechen**) 1. *gastr.* cut out. 2. *fig.* outdo (*s.o.*), cut out (*rival*).
'**ausstehen** (irr, sep, -ge-, h, → **stehen**) **I** v/t stand, bear, suffer: *es ist noch nicht ausgestanden* it's not over yet; F *ich kann ihn nicht ~* I can't stand him. **II** v/i *decision:* be pending, *payment:* be outstanding: *s-e Antwort steht noch aus ~* he hasn't answered yet.
'**aussteigen** v/i (irr, sep, -ge-, sn, → **steigen**) (*aus*) get out (of, *a. fig. an enterprise etc*), get off (*a train, bus, etc*), ⚓ disembark, F ✓ bail out (of), *fig.* opt out (of *business venture, nuclear power, etc*), drop out (of *society etc*).
'**Aussteiger** m (-s; -) F dropout.
'**ausstellen** (sep, -ge-, h) **I** v/t **1.** display, show, exhibit. **2.** make *bill, cheque, etc* out (*auf j-s Namen* in s.o.'s name), issue (*passport*), draw bill of exchange (*auf acc* on). **II** v/i **3.** exhibit.
Aussteller ['aʊsʃtɛlər] m (-s; -) **1.** exhibitor. **2.** ⸖ drawer.
'**Ausstellfenster** n *mot.* ventipane.
'**Ausstellung** f (-; -en) **1.** exhibition, show, fair. **2.** issue (*of document etc*).
'**Ausstellungs|datum** n date of issue. **~gelände** n exhibition grounds. **~halle** f exhibition hall. **~raum** m show-room. **~stück** n exhibit.
'**ausstempeln** v/t (sep, -ge-, h) clock out.
'**aussterben** v/i (irr, sep, -ge-, sn, → **sterben**) die out: → **ausgestorben**.
'**Aussteuer** f (-; -n) trousseau.
'**aussteuern** v/t (sep, -ge-, h) modulate.
'**Ausstieg** m (-[e]s; -e) **1.** exit (door). **2.** (*aus*) exit (from), getting out (of), *fig. a.* opting out (of *nuclear energy, a business, etc*). **~luke** f (escape) hatch.

'**ausstopfen** v/t (sep, -ge-, h) stuff.
'**Ausstoß** m (-es; *rare* ⸚e) ⸖ output, production. '**ausstoßen** v/t (irr, sep, -ge-, h, → **stoßen**) **1.** ⚙ eject, blow off, exhaust. **2.** ⸖ turn out, produce. **3.** utter (*words*), give (*yell etc*), heave (*a sigh*). **4.** *j-n* ~ expel s.o. (*aus* from); *j-n aus der Gesellschaft* ~ ostracize s.o.
'**ausstrahlen** v/t (sep, -ge-, h) **1.** *a. fig.* radiate. **2.** broadcast, *TV a.* televise. '**Ausstrahlung** f (-; -en) **1.** *of person:* radiation, charisma. **2.** broadcast(ing).
'**ausstrecken** v/t (sep, -ge-, h) (*a. sich ~*) stretch out: *die Hand ~ nach* reach (out) for; → **Fühler** 1.
'**ausstreichen** v/t (irr, sep, -ge-, h, → **streichen**) cross out.
'**ausströmen** (sep, -ge-) **I** v/i (sn) (*aus* from), *a. fig.* radiate, *smell:* emanate, *gas etc:* escape. **II** v/t (h) radiate (*a. fig.*), give off (*smell*).
'**aussuchen** v/t (sep, -ge-, h) choose, select: → **ausgesucht**.
'**Austausch** m (-[e]s; *no pl*) (*im* ~ in) exchange (*für* for). '**Austausch...** *ped., univ.* exchange (*teacher, student, etc*). '**austauschbar** *adj* interchangeable. '**austauschen** v/t (sep, -ge-, h) (*gegen*) a) exchange (for), b) replace (by). '**Austauschmotor** m replacement engine.
'**austeilen** v/t (sep, -ge-, h) distribute (*an acc* to, *unter acc* among), deal (out) (*cards, blows*).
Auster ['aʊstər] f (-; -n) oyster.
'**Austernbank** f (-; ⸚e) oyster bed.
'**austoben:** *sich* ~ (sep, -ge-, h) have one's fling, *children:* have a good romp.
'**austragen** (irr, sep, -ge-, h, → **tragen**) v/t **1.** deliver (*letters etc*). **2.** ⚕ carry *baby* to (full) term, *w.s.* have. **3.** settle (*dispute*): *die Sache ~* F have it out. **4.** hold (*tournament etc*), play (*match*). **5.** cancel (*data etc*). **II** *sich* ~ sign out.
'**Austragungsort** m *sports:* venue.
Australien [aʊsˈtraːliən] n (-s) Australia. **Auˈstralier** m (-s; -), **Auˈstralierin** f (-; -nen), **auˈstralisch** *adj* Australian.
'**austreiben** (irr, sep, -ge-, h, → **treiben**) **I** v/t exorcize: *fig. j-m et.* ~ cure s.o. of s.th. **II** v/i ⚘ sprout.
'**austreten** (sep, -ge-, → **treten**) **I** v/t (h) **1.** stamp out (*fire etc*). **2.** tread (*path*). **3.** wear out (*shoes*), wear down (*steps*). **II** v/i (sn) **4.** (*aus*) come out (of),

gas etc: escape (from). **5. ~ aus** leave (*club etc*). **6.** F (go and) spend a penny.

'**austricksen** *v/t* (*sep*, -ge-, h) F trick.

'**austrinken** *v/t*, *v/i* (*irr*, *sep*, -ge-, h, → *trinken*) drink up, finish (one's drink).

'**Austritt** *m* (-[e]s; -e) (*aus dat*) leaving (*a club etc*).

'**austrocknen** *v/t* (*sep*, -ge-, h) *and v/i* (sn) dry up.

'**austüfteln** *v/t* (*sep*, -ge-, h) F work out.

'**ausüben** *v/t* (*sep*, -ge-, h) **1.** carry on (*trade etc*), practise (*profession etc*), perform (*function*), hold (*office*). **2.** exercise (*power, right, etc*). **3.** (**auf** *acc* on) exert (*influence etc*), have (*effect*), use (*coercion*): → **Druck**[1]. '**Ausübung** *f* (-; *no pl*) carrying on (*etc*), exercise: **in ~ s-r Pflicht** in the execution of his duty.

'**ausufern** *v/i* (*sep*, -ge-, sn) get out of hand.

'**Ausverkauf** *m* (-[e]s; ⸚e) a) selling off, b) (**im ~ kaufen** buy at) a) sale, c) *fig*. sellout. '**ausverkaufen** *v/t* (*sep*, h) sell off: **ausverkauft** sold out, *thea. etc a*. full (*house etc*).

'**auswachsen** (*irr*, *sep*, -ge-, → **wachsen**) **I** *v/t* (h) grow out of. **II** *v/i* (sn) ⚘ go to seed: F **es ist zum** ⚡! a) it's enough to drive you crazy, b) it's dreadfully boring. **III sich ~** (h) *fig*. develop (**zu** into): → **ausgewachsen**.

'**Auswahl** *f* (-; *no pl*) **1.** selection, ⚘ *a*. choice, range: **... in großer ~** a large assortment of ...; **... zur ~ ...** to choose from; **e-e ~ treffen** select (**aus** from). **2.** → **Auswahlmannschaft**. '**auswählen** *v/t* (*sep*, -ge-, h) choose, select.

'**Auswahlmannschaft** *f* representative team.

'**Auswanderer** *m* (-s; -) emigrant.

'**auswandern** *v/i* (*sep*, -ge-, sn) emigrate.

'**Auswanderung** *f* (-; -en) emigration.

auswärtig ['aʊsvɛrtɪç] *adj* **1.** nonlocal, *a*. ⚘ out-of-town. **2.** *pol*. foreign (*affairs, office, etc*).

auswärts ['aʊsvɛrts] *adv* **1.** out, away (from home), out of town: **~ essen** eat out; *sports*: **~ spielen** play away from home; **~ wohnen** live out of town. **2.** outward(s). ⚘**spiel** *n* away match.

'**auswaschen** *v/t* (*irr*, *sep*, -ge-, h, → **waschen**) wash out.

auswechselbar ['aʊsvɛksəlbaːr] *adj* (**gegen**) exchangeable (for), replace-

able (by). '**auswechseln** *v/t* (*sep*, -ge-, h) (**gegen**) exchange (for), replace (by), change (*tyre*), substitute (*player*).

'**Auswechselspieler(in** *f*) *m* substitute.

'**Auswechs(e)lung** *f* (-; -en) exchange, replacement, *sports*: substitution.

'**Ausweg** *m* (-[e]s; -e) *fig*. way out (**aus** of): **als letzter ~** as a last resort.

'**ausweglos** *adj* hopeless. '**Ausweglosigkeit** *f* (-; *no pl*) hopelessness.

'**ausweichen** *v/i* (*irr*, *sep*, -ge-, sn, → **weichen**) **1.** (*dat*) make way (for), get out of the way (of), dodge: **j-s Blicken ~** avoid s.o.'s eyes; **e-r Frage ~** evade a question. **2.** be evasive. **3. ~ auf** (*acc*) switch to. '**ausweichend** *adj* evasive. '**Ausweich|manöver** *n fig*. evasive action. **~möglichkeit** *f* alternative.

'**ausweinen: sich ~** (*sep*, -ge-, h) have a good cry (**bei j-m** on s.o.'s shoulder).

'**Ausweis** *m* (-es; -e) identity (*abbr*. ID) card, (*membership*) card, pass.

'**ausweisen** (*irr*, *sep*, -ge-, h, → **weisen**) **I** *v/t* **1.** (**aus** from) a) expel, b) deport (*alien*). **2.** *fig*. **j-n als** show s.o. to be (*an expert etc*). **II sich ~** prove one's identity: **sich als Experte** *etc* **~** prove o.s. an expert *etc*.

'**Ausweis|kon|trolle** *f* ID check. **~papiere** *pl* (identification *or* ID) papers.

'**Ausweisung** *f* (-; -en) (**aus** from) a) expulsion, b) deportation (*of aliens*).

'**ausweiten** *v/t* (*sep*, -ge-, h) (*a*. **sich ~**) expand (*a. fig*. **zu** into).

'**Ausweitung** *f* (-; -en) expansion.

'**auswendig** *adv* by heart: ♪ **~ spielen** play from memory; **et. in- und ~ kennen** know s.th. inside out.

'**auswerfen** *v/t* (*irr*, *sep*, -ge-, h, → **werfen**) cast (*anchor etc*).

'**auswerten** *v/t* (*sep*, -ge-, h) **1.** evaluate. **2.** utilize, ⚘ *a*. exploit. '**Auswertung** *f* (-; -en) **1.** evaluation. **2.** utilization.

'**auswickeln** *v/t* (*sep*, -ge-, h) unwrap.

'**auswirken: sich ~** (*sep*, -ge-, h) a) have consequences, b) **auf** (*acc*) affect, c) **in** (*dat*) result in; **sich positiv** (*negativ*) **~** have a favo(u)rable (negative) effect.

'**Auswirkung** *f* (-; -en) **1.** effect (**auf** *acc* on). **2.** → **Rückwirkung**.

'**auswischen** *v/t* (*sep*, -ge-, h) wipe out: F **j-m eins ~** play a nasty trick on s.o.

'**auswringen** *v/t* (*irr*, *sep*, -ge-, h, → **wringen**).

'**Auswuchs** m (-es; ⸚e) **1.** ⚘ outgrowth. **2.** fig. a) pl excesses, b) product (of the imagination).

'**Auswurf** m (-[e]s; no pl) **1.** ⚘ sputum. **2.** → **Abschaum.**

'**auszahlen** (sep, -ge-, h) **I** v/t pay (out) (sum), pay s.o. off, buy out (partner). **II** sich ~ fig. pay.

'**auszählen** v/t (sep, -ge-, h) count out.

'**Auszahlung** f (-; -en) payment.

'**auszeichnen** (sep, -ge-, h) **I** v/t **1.** distinguish, hono(u)r: **mit e-m Preis** ~ award a prize to; (**mit e-m Orden**) ~ decorate. **2.** ✝ price (goods). **II** sich ~ distinguish o.s. '**Auszeichnung** f (-; -en) **1.** a) (mark of) distinction, b) decoration, c) award: **mit** ~ **bestehen** pass an exam with distinction. **2.** ✝ pricing.

'**ausziehbar** adj pull-out, telescopic. '**ausziehen** (irr, sep, -ge-, h) **I** v/t (h) **1.** take off (clothes): **j-n** ~ undress s.o. **2.** pull out (table etc). **3.** 🜍, ⚗ extract. **II** v/i (sn) **4.** set out. **5.** (**aus e-r Wohnung**) ~ move out (of a flat). **III** sich ~ (h) undress.

'**Auszieh|feder** f drawing pen. ~**platte** f (table) leaf. ~**tisch** m pull-out table. ~**tusche** f drawing ink.

'**Auszubildende** m, f (-n; -n) trainee.

'**Auszug** m (-[e]s; ⸚e) **1.** departure, demonstrative: walkout: ~ (**aus e-r Wohnung**) move (from a flat). **2.** a) 🜍 extraction, b) a. fig. extract (**aus** from), c) ♩ arrangement. **3.** ✝ statement (of account). '**auszugsweise** adv in parts: **et.** ~ **vorlesen** read extracts from s.th.

'**auszupfen** v/t (sep, -ge-, h) pluck out.

autark [aʊˈtark] adj ✝ autarkic.

Autarkie [aʊtarˈkiː] f (-; -n) autarky.

authentisch [aʊˈtɛntɪʃ] adj authentic.

Auto [ˈaʊto] n (-s; -s) (motor)car, esp. Am. auto(mobile): ~ **fahren** drive (a car); **mit dem** ~ **fahren** go by car; **können Sie** ~ **fahren?, fahren Sie** ~? do you drive?; → **mitnehmen** 1.

'**Autoapo|theke** f (driver's) first-aid kit.

'**Autoatlas** m road atlas.

'**Autobahn** f (-; -en) motorway, Am. expressway, freeway. ~**auffahrt** f motorway etc approach, slip road. ~**ausfahrt** f exit. ~**gebühr** f toll. ~**kreuz** n motorway etc intersection.

'**Autobahnmeisterei** [-maɪstəraɪ] f (-; -en) motorway maintenance area.

'**Autobahn|raststätte** f motorway service area. ~**zubringer** m slip road.

Autobiographie [aʊtobiograˈfiː] f (-; -n) autobiography.

'**Autobus** m bus, Br. a. coach.

Autodidakt [aʊtodiˈdakt] m (-en; -en), **Autodi'daktin** f (-; -nen) autodidact.

'**Auto|dieb** m car thief. ~**diebstahl** m car theft. ~**fähre** f car ferry. ~**fahrer(in** f) m motorist, (car) driver. ~**fahrt** f drive.

'**autofrei** adj traffic-free.

'**Autofriedhof** m F fig. car dump.

autogen [aʊtoˈgeːn] adj 🜍, ⚙ autogenous: ~**es Training** autogenic training.

Autogramm [aʊtoˈgram] n (-[e]s; -e) autograph. **Auto'grammjäger(in** f) m F autograph hunter. **Auto'grammstunde** f autograph(ing) session.

'**Auto|händler** m car dealer. ~**indu,strie** f car industry. ~**kino** n drive-in (cinema). ~**knacker** m (-s; -) F car burglar. ~**ko,lonne** f line of cars, convoy.

Automat [aʊtoˈmaːt] m (-en; -en) **1.** a) vending machine, b) slot machine, c) juke box, d) ⚙ automatic machine. **2.** fig. (person) robot.

Auto'matenrestau,rant n automat.

Automatik [aʊtoˈmaːtɪk] f (-; ⚙ -en) automatism, ⚙ automatic system, mot. automatic transmission. **Auto'matikgurt** m reel seat belt. **Automation** [aʊtomaˈtsʲoːn] f (-; no pl) automation. **automatisch** [aʊtoˈmaːtɪʃ] adj automatic. **automatisieren** [aʊtomatiˈtsiːrən] v/t (h) automate.

'**Autome,chaniker** m car mechanic.

Automobil [aʊtomoˈbiːl] n (-s; -e) automobile. ~**ausstellung** f motor show. ~**klub** m automobile association.

autonom [aʊtoˈnoːm] adj autonomous. **Autonomie** [aʊtonoˈmiː] f (-; -n) autonomy.

'**Autonummer** f (car) number.

'**Autopi,lot** m (-en; -en) ✈ autopilot.

Autopsie [aʊtoˈpsiː] f (-; -n) 🜍 autopsy, post-mortem.

Autor [ˈaʊtɔr] m (-s; -en), **Autorin** [aʊˈtoːrɪn] f (-; -nen) author, writer.

'**Auto|radio** n car radio. ~**reifen** m tyre, Am. tire. ~**reisezug** m motorail train. ~**rennen** n car (or motor) race. ~**rennsport** m motor racing.

autorisieren [aʊtoriˈziːrən] v/t (h) authorize.

autoritär [aʊtori'tɛ:r] *adj* authoritarian.
Autorität [aʊtori'tɛ:t] *f* (-; -en) **1.** *no pl* authority. **2.** (*auf dem Gebiet gen*) authority (on), expert (of).
'**Auto|schalter** *m* of a bank: drive-up counter. **~schlosser** *m* car mechanic. **~schlüssel** *m* car key. **~skooter** [-sku:tər] *m* (-s; -) dodgem. **~stop(p)** *m* ~ **machen** hitchhike. **~straße** *f* motor road, *Am.* highway.
Autosuggesti'on *f* autosuggestion.
'**Auto|tele,fon** *n* car telephone. **~unfall** *m* car accident: *er kam bei e-m ~ ums Leben* he died in a car crash. **~verleih** *m* car hire service, *esp. Am.* rent-a-car

(service). **~waschanlage** *f* carwash. **~werkstatt** *f* garage, repair shop.
Avantgarde [avã'gardə] *f* (-; -n), **avant-gardistisch** [-'dɪstɪʃ] *adj* avant-garde.
Aversion [avɛr'zǐo:n] *f* (-; -en) aversion (*gegen* to).
Avitaminose [avitami'no:zə] *f* (-; -n) 𝔐 avitaminosis.
Avocato [avo'ka:to] *f* (-; -s) 𝕈 avocado.
Axt [akst] *f* (-; ⸚e) axe, *Am.* ax.
Azalee [atsa'le:ə] *f* (-; -n) 𝕈 azalea.
Azteke [ats'te:kə] *m* (-n; -n) *hist.* Aztec.
Azubi [a'tsu:bi] *m* (-s; -s), *f* (-; -s) F → *Auszubildende.*
azurblau [a'tsu:r-] *adj* azure (blue).

B

B, b [be:] *n* (-; -) B, b, ♪ B flat.
babbeln ['babəln] *v/t, v/i* (h) F babble.
Baby ['be:bi] *n* (-s; -s) baby. **~ausstattung** *f* layette. **~nahrung** *f* baby food. **~sitter** *m* (-s; -) babysitter. **~speck** *m* F puppy fat. **~sprache** *f* babytalk. **~tragetasche** *f* carrycot.
Bach [bax] *m* (-[e]s; ⸚e) stream, brook.
Bache ['baxə] *f* (-; -n) *zo.* (wild) sow.
'**Bachfo,relle** *f* river trout.
'**Bachstelze** *f zo.* (water) wagtail.
'**Backblech** ['bak-] *n* baking tray.
'**backbord** *adv* ⚓ to port.
'**Backbord** *n, m* (-s; *no pl*) ⚓ port (side).
Backe ['bakə] *f* (-; -n) **1.** cheek. **2.** ⦿ a) jaw, the. **3.** *on ski:* toe piece.
backen ['bakən] (backte, † buk, gebak-ken, h) **I** *v/t, a. v/i a*) bake, b) *dial.* fry. **II** *v/i snow etc:* cake, stick.
'**Backen|bart** *m* sideburns. **~knochen** *m* cheekbone. **~zahn** *m* molar.
Bäcker ['bɛkər] *m* (-s; -) baker: *beim ~* at the baker's. **Bäckerei** [bɛkə'raɪ] *f* (-; -en) **1.** baker's (shop). **2.** *no pl* a) baking, b) baker's trade. '**Bäckerladen** *m* → *Bäckerei* 1. '**Bäckermeister** *m* master baker.
'**Back|fett** *n gastr.* shortening. **~form** *f* baking tin. **~hefe** *f* baker's yeast. **~obst** *n* dried fruit. **~ofen** *m* oven. **~pflaume** *f*

prune. **~pulver** *n* baking powder. **~röhre** *f* oven. **~stein** *m* brick. **~waren** *pl* bread, cakes and pastries.
Bad [ba:t] *n* (-[e]s; ⸚er) **1.** a) bath (*a.* ♨ *and* 𝔐), b) swim: *ein ~ nehmen* → *baden* 1. **2.** → a) *Badeanstalt,* b) *Badeort,* c) *Badezimmer.*
'**Bade|anstalt** *f* swimming pool, public baths. **~anzug** *m* swimsuit. **~gast** *m* **1.** bather. **2.** → *Kurgast.* **~hose** *f* swimming trunks. **~kappe** *f* bathing cap. **~mantel** *m* bathrobe. **~matte** *f* bath mat. **~meister** *m* **1.** pool attendant. **2.** *at beaches:* lifeguard.
baden ['ba:dən] (h) **I** *v/i* **1.** have (*or* take) a bath. **2.** swim: *~ gehen* a) go swimming, b) F *fig.* come a cropper, *thing:* go phut. **II** *v/t* **3.** bath, *Am.* bathe. **III** *sich ~* **4.** → 1. **5.** *fig.* bask (*in dat* in).
'**Bade|ofen** *m* bathroom boiler. **~ort** *m* **1.** seaside resort. **2.** health resort, spa. **~salz** *n* bath salts. **~schuhe** *pl* beach shoes. **~strand** *m* beach. **~tuch** *n* (-[e]s; ⸚er) bath towel. **~wanne** *f* bath(tub). **~zeug** *n* swimming things. **~zimmer** *n* bathroom.
baff [baf] *adj* F *~ sein* be flabbergasted.
Bagage [ba'ga:ʒə] *f* (-; *no pl*) *contp.* bunch, lot.
Bagatelle [baga'tɛlə] *f* (-; -n) trifle.

bagatellisieren [bagatɛli'zi:rən] v/t (h) play down.

Baga'tellschaden m petty damage(s).

Bagger ['bagər] m (-s; -) ⚙ excavator. **baggern** ['bagərn] v/i, v/t (h) excavate, dredge. **'Baggersee** m flooded quarry.

Bahn [ba:n] f (-; -en) **1.** path, course: fig. **sich ~ brechen** forge ahead; **auf die schiefe ~ geraten** go astray; **~ frei!** make way! **2.** a) road, b) lane, c) (racing) track, d) skiing: course, piste. **3.** a) trajectory, b) astr. course, c) orbit. **4.** a) (skating) rink, b) (bowling) alley. **5.** a) railway, Am. railroad, b) train, c) tram, Am. streetcar: **mit der ~** by train, by rail; **j-n zur ~ bringen** see s.o. off (at the station). **6.** web (of paper), width (of cloth). **Bahn...** railway (Am. railroad) (official etc). **'bahnbrechend** adj pioneer(ing), revolutionary. **'Bahndamm** m railway embankment. **bahnen** ['ba:nən] v/t (h) clear (path): **sich e-n Weg ~** force one's way (**durch** through).

'Bahnfahrt f train journey. **~fracht** f ⚒ rail carriage (Am. freight). ⚒**frei** adj and adv ⚒ free on rail (or board) (abbr. f.o.r., f.o.b.). **~hof** m railway (Am. railroad) station: **auf dem ~** at the station; F fig. **großer ~** red-carpet treatment.

'Bahnhofs|halle f concourse. **~restaurant** n station restaurant. **~vorsteher** m stationmaster.

'Bahn|körper m permanent way. ⚒**lagernd** adv ⚒ to be called for at the station. **~linie** f railway line. **~poli,zei** f railway police. **~reise** f train journey. **~steig** [-ʃtaık] m (-[e]s; -e) platform. **~strecke** f line, Am. track. **~übergang** m level (Am. grade) crossing. **~wärter** m level crossing attendant.

Bahre ['ba:rə] f (-; -n) **1.** stretcher. **2.** bier.

Baiser [bɛ'ze:] n (-s; -s) gastr. meringue.

Baisse ['bɛ:sə] f (-; -n) ⚒ slump.

Baissier [bɛ'sie:] m (-s; -s) ⚒ bear.

Bajonett [bajo'nɛt] n (-[e]s; -e) bayonet. **Bajo'nettverschluß** m ⚙ bayonet joint (phot. mount).

Bake ['ba:kə] f (-; -n) beacon.

Bakterie [bak'te:riə] f (-; -n) bacterium, germ. **bakteriell** [bakte'riɛl] adj bacterial. **Bakteriologe** [bakterio'lo:gə] m (-n; -n) bacteriologist.

Balance [ba'laŋsə] f (-; -n) balance. **Ba'lanceakt** m balancing act. **balancie-**

ren [balaŋ'si:rən] v/t, v/i (h) balance.

bald [balt] adv **1.** soon: **~ darauf** shortly afterwards; **so ~ als möglich** as soon as possible; **bis ~!** see you soon! **2.** F almost, nearly.

Baldachin ['baldaxi:n] m (-s; -e) canopy.

baldig ['baldıç] adj speedy, early.

Baldrian ['baldria:n] m (-s; -e) valerian.

Balg¹ [balk] m (-[e]s; ⸚e) **1.** skin. **2.** (organ) bellows.

Balg² m, n (-[e]s; ⸚er) F brat.

balgen ['balgən] sich ~ (h), **Balgerei** [-'rai] f (-; -en) (**um** for) scuffle, tussle.

Balken ['balkən] m (-s; -) **1.** beam: F **lügen, daß sich die ~ biegen** lie in one's teeth. **2.** crossbar. **3.** → **Schwebebalken. ~decke** f timbered ceiling. **~überschrift** f banner headline.

Balkon [bal'kɔŋ] m (-s; -s) balcony, thea. a. dress circle. **~tür** f French window(s).

Ball¹ [bal] m (-[e]s; ⸚e) ball: F fig. **am ~ bleiben** keep at it. **Ball²** m (-[e]s; ⸚e) (**auf e-m ~** at a) ball (or dance).

Ballade [ba'la:də] f (-; -n) ballad.

Ballast [ba'last] m (-[e]s; -e) a. fig. ballast. **Bal'laststoffe** pl ⚒ roughage.

ballen ['balən] (h) **I** v/t **1.** make into a ball. **2.** **die Faust ~** clench one's fist. **II** **sich ~** form into a ball, clouds: gather.

Ballen m (-s; -) **1.** anat. ball (of one's foot or hand). **2.** ⚒ bale.

Ballerina [balə'ri:na] f (-; -rinen) ballerina, ballet dancer.

Ballermann ['balərman] m (-s; ⸚er) F shooter, Am. sl. rod.

ballern ['balərn] v/i (h) F bang (away).

Ballett [ba'lɛt] n (-[e]s; -e) a) ballet, b) ballet company.

Bal'lettänzer(in f) m ballet dancer.

Bal'lettschule f ballet school.

Ballistik [ba'lıstık] f (-; no pl) ballistics. **ballistisch** [ba'lıstıʃ] adj ballistic.

'Balljunge m ball boy.

'Ballkleid n ball dress.

Ballon [ba'lɔŋ] m (-s; -s) **1.** balloon. **2.** a) carboy, b) demijohn.

Bal'lonreifen m balloon tyre (Am. tire).

'Ballsaal m ballroom.

'Ballspiel n ball game.

'Ballung f (-; -en) concentration.

'Ballungs|gebiet n, **~raum** m, **~zentrum** n conurbation, ⚒ area of industrial concentration.

'Ballwechsel m tennis: exchange.

Balsam ['balza:m] *m* (-s; -e) *a. fig.* balm.
balsamieren [balza'mi:rən] *v/t* (h) embalm.
baltisch ['baltɪʃ] *adj* Baltic.
Balz [balts] *f* (-; -en) *zo.* a) courting, b) mating season.
'balzen *v/i* (h) *zo.* a) court, b) mate.
Bambus ['bambus] *m* (-ses; -se) bamboo. **~sprossen** *pl* bamboo sprouts.
Bammel ['baməl] *m* (-s; *no pl*) F **~ haben (vor** *dat*) be in a blue funk (of).
banal [ba'na:l] *adj* trite, banal.
Banalität [banali'tɛ:t] *f* (-; -en) banality.
Banane [ba'na:nə] *f* (-; -n) banana.
Ba'nanenstecker *m ⚡* banana plug.
Banause [ba'nauzə] *m* (-n; -n) *contp.* Philistine, lowbrow.
band [bant] *pret of* **binden**.
Band¹ *m* (-[e]s; **~e**) volume: *fig. das spricht Bände* that speaks volumes.
Band² *n* (-[e]s; **~er**) **1.** a) ribbon, b) (apron) string, c) (hat) band. **2.** ⚙, *video etc, a. sports:* tape: *auf ~ aufnehmen* tape(-record). **3.** ⚙ a) (conveyor) belt, b) assembly line: *fig. am laufenden ~* one after the other, *w.s.* nonstop. **4.** *anat.* ligament. **5.** *radio:* wave band. **6.** (*pl* -e) *fig.* bond (*of love etc*).
Band³ [bɛnt] *f* (-; -s) ♪ band, group.
Bandage [ban'da:ʒə] *f* (-; -n) bandage: *fig. mit harten ~n* with the gloves off.
bandagieren [banda'ʒi:rən] *v/t* (h) bandage.
'Bandaufnahme *f* tape recording.
'Bandbreite *f* **1.** ⚙ band width. **2.** *statistics etc:* spread. **3.** *fig.* spectrum.
Bande¹ ['bandə] *f* (-; -n) gang, F *contp. a.* bunch: *die ganze ~* the whole lot.
'Bande² *f* billiard, bowling: cushion, *ice hockey etc:* boards.
Bänderriß ['bɛndər-] *m ⚕* torn ligament.
'Bänderzerrung *f ⚕* pulled ligament.
'Bandfilter *n, m radio:* band(-pass) filter.
'Bandförderer *m ⚙* belt conveyor.
bändigen ['bɛndɪgən] *v/t* (h) tame, *fig. a.* subdue, restrain, control.
'Bändigung *f* (-; *no pl*) taming (*etc*).
Bandit [ban'di:t] *m* (-en; -en) bandit.
'Bandmaß *n* measuring tape.
'Bandnudeln *pl* ribbon noodles.
'Bandscheibe *f anat.* (intervertebral) disc. **'Bandscheibenschaden** *m ⚕* **1.** damaged disc. **2.** → **'Bandscheibenvorfall** *m* slipped disc.

'Bandwurm *m* tapeworm. **'Bandwurmsatz** *m humor.* endless sentence.
bange ['baŋə] *adj* (*um* about) anxious, worried: *j-m* (*or j-n*) **~ machen** frighten s.o. **'Bange** *f* (*nur*) *k-e ~!* don't worry!
bangen ['baŋən] *v/i* (h) be worried (*um* about): *um j-s Leben ~* fear for s.o.'s life; *es bangt ihr vor* she is afraid of.
Bank¹ [baŋk] *f* (-; **~e**) a) bench, b) *ped.* desk, c) *eccl.* pew: *fig. et. auf die lange ~ schieben* put s.th. off; F *durch die ~* without exception, down the line.
Bank² *f* (-; -en) **1.** ♱ bank: *Geld auf der ~ haben* have money in the bank. **2.** bank: *die ~ halten* (*sprengen*) hold (break) the bank. **~angestellte** *m, f* bank clerk. **~anweisung** *f* banker's order. **~ausweis** *m* bank return (*Am.* statement). **~beamte** *m* bank clerk. **~di, rektor** *m* bank manager. **~dis, kont** *m* bank discount. **~einlage** *f* deposit.
Bankett [baŋ'kɛt] *n* (-[e]s; -e) **1.** banquet. **2.** ⚙ shoulder (*of road*).
'Bank|fach *n* (-[e]s; **~er**) **1.** *no pl* banking. **2.** safe(-deposit) box. **⟨fähig** *adj* bankable. **~geheimnis** *n* banker's secrecy. **~geschäft** *n* **1.** banking transaction. **2.** banking (business). **~guthaben** *n* **1.** bank balance. **2.** bank account. **~halter** *m* (-s; -) banker.
Bankier [baŋ'kie:] *m* (-s; -s) banker.
'Bank|kaufmann *m* bank clerk. **~konto** *n* bank account. **~leitzahl** *f* bank code (number). **~note** *f* (bank)note, *Am.* bill. **~raub** *m* bank robbery. **~räuber** *m* bank robber.
bankrott [baŋ'krɔt] *adj a. fig.* bankrupt.
Bank'rott *m* (-[e]s; -e) (*a. fig. den ~ erklären* declare) bankruptcy; **~ machen** go bankrupt. **Bank'rotterklärung** *f a. fig.* declaration of bankruptcy.
'Bank|überfall *m* bank holdup. **~überweisung** *f* bank transfer. **~verbindung** *f* **1.** bank account. **2.** correspondent. **~wesen** *n* (-s; *no pl*) banking.
Bann [ban] *m* (-[e]s; *no pl*) **1.** ban, *eccl.* excommunication: *in den ~ tun* outlaw, *eccl.* excommunicate. **2.** spell: *in s-n ~ schlagen* (*or ziehen*) → **bannen** 3; *unter dem ~ stehen von* (*or gen*) be under the spell of. **'bannen** *v/t* (h) **1.** exorcize. **2.** ward off (*danger*). **3.** a) transfix, b) captivate, spellbind: → *gebannt.* **4.** *fig. et. ~ auf* (*acc*) capture

s.th. on *paper etc.* '**Banner** *n* (-s; -) banner (*a. fig.*), standard.

'**Bannkreis** *m fig.* sphere (of influence).

'**Bannmeile** *f* neutral zone.

Bantamgewicht ['bantam-] *n* (-[e]s; *no pl*) *sports*: bantamweight.

bar [ba:r] *adj* **1.** ~es Geld (ready) cash; (in) ~ bezahlen pay cash; gegen ~ for cash; ~ ohne Abzug net cash. **2.** pure (*gold etc*), *contp. a.* downright: ~er Unsinn sheer nonsense; → Münze 1. **3.** ~ jeglicher Vernunft devoid of any sense.

Bar *f* (-; -s) bar, nightclub: an der ~ at the bar.

Bär [bɛːr] *m* (-en; -en) bear (*a. ♉*): *astr.* der Große (Kleine) ~ the Great (Little) Bear; F *fig.* j-m e-n ~en aufbinden tell s.o. a whopping lie.

Baracke [ba'rakə] *f* (-; -n) hut, *contp.* shack.

'**Barauszahlung** *f* cash payment.

Barbar [bar'ba:r] *m* (-en; -en) barbarian. **Barbarei** [barba'raɪ] *f* (-; -en) a) barbarism, b) barbarity. **barbarisch** [bar'ba:rɪʃ] *adj* barbarian, barbarous (*a. fig. contp.*), atrocious, F awful.

bärbeißig [bɛːr'baɪsɪç] *adj* gruff.

'**Barbestand** *m* cash in hand, *of bank*: cash reserve.

'**Bardame** *f* barmaid.

'**Bareinnahmen** *pl* cash receipts.

'**Bärendienst** *m* j-m e-n ~ erweisen do s.o. a disservice. '**Bärenhunger** *m* F e-n ~ haben be ravenous.

Barett [ba'rɛt] *n* (-[e]s; -e) beret.

'**barfuß, barfüßig** ['ba:rfy:sɪç] *adj and adv* barefoot(ed).

barg [bark] *pret of* **bergen**.

'**Bargeld** *n* cash.

'**bargeldlos** *adj and adv* cashless.

'**barhäuptig** [-hɔyptɪç] *adj* bareheaded.

'**Barhocker** *m* barstool.

Bärin ['bɛːrɪn] *f* (-; -nen) she-bear.

Bariton ['ba:riton] *m* (-s; -e) baritone.

Barkasse [bar'kasə] *f* (-; -n) (motor) launch.

'**Barkauf** *m* cash purchase.

'**Barkeeper** *m* (-s; -) barman.

'**Barkre**,**dit** *m* cash loan.

barmherzig [barm'hɛrtsɪç] *adj* (gegen to) a) merciful, b) charitable: → Samariter. **Barm'herzigkeit** *f* (-; *no pl*) a) mercy, b) charity.

'**Barmittel** *pl* cash.

'**Barmixer** *m* (-s; -) barman, bartender.

barock [ba'rɔk] *adj* baroque, *fig. a.* bizarre. **Ba'rock** *n*, *m* (-s; *no pl*) a) baroque period, b) baroque style.

Barometer [baro'me:tər] *n* (-s; -) *a. fig.* barometer.

Baron [ba'ro:n] *m* (-s; -e) baron. **Ba'ronin** *f* (-; -nen) baroness.

Barren ['barən] *m* (-s; -) **1.** bullion, ingot. **2.** *gym.* parallel bars.

Barriere [ba'riɛ:rə] *f* (-; -n) barrier.

Barrikade [bari'ka:də] *f* (-; -n) barricade: auf die ~n gehen mount the barricades (für for).

barsch [barʃ] *adj* gruff, brusque.

Barsch *m* (-[e]s; -e) *zo.* perch.

'**Barschaft** *f* (-; *no pl*) (ready) money, F cash.

'**Barscheck** *m* uncrossed cheque (*Am.* check).

barst [barst] *pret of* **bersten**.

Bart [ba:rt] *m* (-[e]s; ⸚e) **1.** beard: sich e-n ~ wachsen lassen (or stehenlassen) grow a beard; F so ein ~! that's an old one! **2.** bit (*of key*). **bärtig** ['bɛːrtɪç] *adj* bearded. '**Bartstoppeln** *pl* stubble.

'**Barvermögen** *n* liquid funds.

'**Barzahlung** *f* cash payment: gegen ~ cash down.

Basar [ba'za:r] *m* (-s; -e) bazaar.

Base[1] ['ba:zə] *f* (-; -n) female cousin.

Base[2] *f* (-; -n) 🜔 base.

basieren [ba'zi:rən] *v/i* (h) ~ auf (*dat*) be based on.

Basilika [ba'zi:lika] *f* (-; -ken) basilica.

Basilikum [ba'zi:likum] *n* (-s; *no pl*) 🜲 basil.

Basis ['ba:zɪs] *f* (-; Basen) **1.** △, ⅍, ✕ *etc* base. **2.** *fig.* foundation: *pol.* (an der) ~ (at the) grassroots.

basisch ['ba:zɪʃ] *adj* 🜔 basic.

'**Basisdemokra**,**tie** *f* grassroots democracy. '**Basislager** *n mount.* base camp.

Baskenmütze ['baskən-] *f* beret.

Baß [bas] *m* (-sses; ⸚sse) bass. ~**geige** *f* (double) bass. ~**gi**,**tarre** *f* bass guitar.

Bassin [ba'sɛ̃:] *n* (-s; -s) tank, basin.

Bassist [ba'sɪst] *m* (-en; -en) ♪ **1.** bass (singer). **2.** bass player.

'**Baßregler** *m radio etc*: bass control.

'**Baßschlüssel** *m* ♪ bass clef.

'**Baßstimme** *f* bass (voice, ♪ *a.* part).

Bast [bast] *m* (-[e]s; -e) bast, raffia.

basta ['basta] *int* F (**und damit**) ~*!* and that's that!

Bastard ['bastart] *m* (-[e]s; -e) 💎, *zo.* hybrid, cross(breed), (*dog*) mongrel.

'**Bastelarbeit** *f* 1. handicraft (work). 2. → **Basteln. basteln** ['bastəln] (h) I *v/t* make, rig up, build. II *v/i* do handicrafts: ~ **an** (*dat*) *a. fig.* tinker at.

'**Basteln** *n* (-s) handicrafts, home mechanics, *a. fig.* tinkering.

Bastion [bas'tĭo:n] *f* (-; -en) bastion.

'**Bastler** *m* (-s; -) home mechanic, hobbyist.

bat [ba:t] *pret of* **bitten**.

Bataillon [batal'jo:n] *n* (-s; -e) ✗ battalion.

Batik ['ba:tɪk] *f* (-; -en) batik.

batiken ['ba:tɪkən] *v/t, v/i* (h) batik.

Batist [ba'tɪst] *m* (-[e]s; -e) batiste, cambric.

Batterie [batə'ri:] *f* (-; -n) ⚡, ✗, ⊙, *a. fig.* battery. 2**betrieben** *adj* battery-operated. ~**ladegerät** *n* battery charger.

Bau [bau] *m* (-[e]s; Bauten) 1. *no pl* construction: **im** ~ under construction, being built. 2. building: → **Bauten**. 3. *no pl* ⊙ design, structure. 4. *no pl* building trade: F *fig.* **er ist vom** ~ he is an expert. 5. (*pl* Baue) earth (*of fox*), burrow (*of rabbits*). 6. *no pl* F ✗ detention: **3 Tage** ~ 3 days in the guardhouse.

'**Bau|amt** *n* Building Authorities. ~**arbeiten** *pl* construction work, roadworks. ~**arbeiter** *m* construction worker. ~**art** *f* a) style, ⊙ design, b) model, type. ~**aufsichtsbehörde** *f* building supervisory board.

Bauch [baux] *m* (-[e]s; ~e) belly (*a. fig.*), stomach, *anat.* abdomen, *contp.* paunch: **sich den** ~ **halten vor Lachen** split one's sides laughing; *fig.* **aus dem** ~ from the guts, guts (*reaction etc*).

'**Bauch|ansatz** *m* beginnings of a paunch. ~**fell** *n anat.* peritoneum. ~**entzündung** *f* ✚ peritonitis.

bauchig ['bauxɪç] *adj* bulbous.

'**Bauch|klatscher** *m* (-s; -) F belly flop. ~**landung** *f* ✈ belly landing: **e-e** ~ **machen** bellyland. ~**muskel** *m* stomach muscle. ~**nabel** *m* navel, F belly button. 2**reden** *v/i* (*only inf*) ventriloquize. ~**redner** *m* ventriloquist. ~**schmerzen** *pl* stomach-ache. ~**speicheldrüse** *f*

pancreas. ~**tanz** *m* belly dance. ~**tänzerin** *f* belly dancer.

'**Bauchweh** *n* (-s; *no pl*) F stomach-ache.

'**Baudenkmal** *n* historical monument.

bauen ['bauən] (h) I *v/t* 1. build, construct, ⊙ *a.* make. 2. ✔ cultivate, grow. 3. F *fig.* a) make, b) take, pass (*exam*), c) cause: **e-n Unfall** ~ have an accident. II *v/i* 4. build (a house). 5. *fig.* ~ **auf** (*acc*) rely on, count on.

Bauer[1] ['bauər] *m* (-s; -) (bird)cage.

'**Bauer**[2] *m* (-n; -n) 1. farmer, *fig. contp.* peasant, boor. 2. *chess*: pawn, *cards*: jack. **Bäuerin** ['bɔyərɪn] *f* (-; -nen) farmer's wife. '**bäuerlich** *adj* rustic.

'**Bauernbrot** *n* (coarse) brown bread.

'**Bauernfänger** *m* con man. **Bauernfängerei** [-fɛŋə'rai] *f* (-; *no pl*) con game.

'**Bauern|haus** *n* farmhouse. ~**hof** *m* farm. ~**möbel** *pl* rustic furniture. ~**regel** *f* F peasants' weather maxim.

'**bauernschlau** *adj* crafty.

'**Bauerwartungsland** *n* development area. '**Baufach** *n* (-[e]s; *no pl*) 1. architecture. 2. building trade.

'**baufällig** *adj* dilapidated.

'**Bau|firma** *f* builders and contractors. ~**gelände** *n* 1. building area. 2. → **Baustelle** 1. ~**genehmigung** *f* planning (and building) permission. ~**genossenschaft** *f* cooperative building association. ~**gerüst** *n* scaffolding. ~**gewerbe** *n* building trade. ~**grund(stück** *n*) *m* (building) site. ~**handwerker** *m* workman in the building trade. ~**herr** *m* client, building owner. ~**ingenieur** *m* civic engineer. ~**jahr** *n* construction year: *mot.* ~ **1991** (a) 1991 model. ~**kasten** *m* 1. box of bricks. 2. construction set. ~**kastensy,stem** *n* ⊙ unit construction system. ~**klotz** *m* building block: F **da staunt man Bauklötze!** it's mind-boggling! ~**kunst** *f* (-; *no pl*) architecture. ~**land** *n* (-[e]s; *no pl*) building land. ~**leiter** *m* site manager.

'**baulich** *adj* architectural, structural: **in gutem** ~**en Zustand** in good repair.

Baum [baum] *m* (-[e]s; ~e) tree.

'**Bauma,schinen** *pl* construction (or building) machines.

'**Baumblüte** *f* **während der** ~ while the trees are in blossom.

'**Baumeister** *m* master builder, *w.s.* architect.

baumeln ['baʊməln] v/i (h) **1.** (*an dat* from) dangle, swing: *mit den Beinen ~* dangle one's legs. **2.** F swing.

'**Baum|grenze** f timberline. **~krone** f tree-top. **~kuchen** m pyramid cake.

'**baumlos** *adj* treeless.

'**Baum|schere** f pruning shears. **~schule** f (tree) nursery. **~stamm** m a) trunk, b) log. **~stark** *adj fig.* (as) strong as an ox. **~sterben** n (-s) death of trees.

'**Baumwolle** f, '**baumwollen** *adj* cotton.

'**Bau|plan** m architect's plan, ⊚ blueprint. **~platz** m (building) site. **~projekt** n building project.

'**baureif** *adj* a. ⊚ developed.

Bausch [baʊʃ] m (-[e]s; ⸚e) wad (*a.* 🐾): *fig.* **in ~ und Bogen** lock, stock and barrel. '**bauschen** (h) **I** v/t (*a.* **sich ~**) billow. **II** v/t puff out.

'**bauschig** *adj* puffed out.

'**Bau|schlosser** m building fitter. **~sparkasse** f building society. **~sparvertrag** m building savings agreement. **~stahl** m structural steel. **~stein** m **1.** brick, stone (for building). **2.** *fig.* element, component, contribution. **3.** ⚡ module. **~stelle** f **1.** building site. **2.** roadworks. **~stil** m (architectural) style. **~stoff** m building material. **~stopp** m **e-n ~ verhängen** impose a halt on building. **~sub,stanz** f fabric (of a building). **~techniker** m constructional engineer. **~teil** n structural member, component part.

Bauten ['baʊtən] pl **1.** buildings, structures. **2.** *thea. etc* setting.

'**Bau|träger** m **1.** builder. **2.** institution *etc* responsible for the building project. **~unternehmer** m building contractor. **~vorhaben** n building project. **~weise** f (method of) construction, style (of architecture). **~werk** n building. **~zeichnung** f construction drawing.

Bayer ['baɪər] m (-n; -n), '**Bayerin** f (-; -nen), '**bay(e)risch** *adj* Bavarian.

Bazillenträger(in) f) m [ba'tsilən-] germ carrier. **Bazillus** [ba'tsilʊs] m (-; -len) bacillus (pl -cilli), germ, F bug.

beabsichtigen [bə'ʔapzɪçtɪɡən] v/t (h) intend (*zu tun* to do, doing): *das war beabsichtigt* that was intentional.

be'achten v/t (h) a) pay attention to, note, b) take into account, consider, c) notice, d) observe (*rules etc*): *bitte*

zu ~ please note; *nicht ~* ignore, disregard.

be'achtenswert *adj* noteworthy.

be'achtlich *adj* considerable.

Be'achtung f (-; *no pl*) (*gen*) a) attention (to), b) observing (of), c) consideration (of): *~ schenken* (*dat*) → *beachten*.

Beamte [bə'ʔamtə] m (-n; -n) (government) official, *Br.* civil (*Am.* public) servant, (*police or customs*) officer.

Be'amtenlaufbahn f civil service career.

Be'amtin f (-; -nen) → *Beamte*.

be'ängstigend *adj* worrying, alarming.

be'anspruchen v/t (h) **1.** claim (*a right etc*). **2.** a) demand, require, b) take up (*room, time*): *j-n ganz ~* keep s.o. busy. **3.** avail o.s. of (*s.o.'s help etc*). **4.** ⊚ stress. **Be'anspruchung** f (-; -en) (*gen* on) **1.** claim. **2.** demand (*on s.o.'s time etc*). **3.** *a.* ⊚ strain, stress.

beanstanden [bə'ʔan∫tandən] v/t (h) object to, criticize, *a.* ✝ complain about, reject (*goods*).

Be'anstandung f (-; -en) (*gen*) objection (to), complaint (about).

beantragen [bə'ʔantra:ɡən] v/t (h) **1.** apply for (*bei j-m* to s.o.). **2.** propose, 🏛 *parl.* move (for).

be'arbeiten v/t (h) **1.** work, 🌱 *a.* cultivate, till, ⊚ *a.* machine, process, treat. **2.** *fig.* a) work on, deal with, *adm. a.* process, b) be in charge of. **3.** edit, revise (*book*), adapt (*a play etc for the stage etc*). **4.** ♪ arrange. **5.** *j-n ~* a) work on s.o., b) F give s.o. a working over.

Be'arbeitung f (-; -en) **1.** working (*etc*, → *bearbeiten*), treatment, 🌱 cultivation, *adm.* processing. **2.** a) revision, b) revised edition, *thea. etc* adaptation. **3.** ♪ arrangement.

Be'atmung f (-; *no pl*) (*künstliche*) ~ artificial respiration.

beaufsichtigen [bə'ʔaʊfzɪçtɪɡən] v/t (h) supervise, look after. **Be'aufsichtigung** f (-; -en) supervision.

be'auftragen v/t (h) a) instruct, b) commission (*artist etc*), c) appoint: *j-n mit e-m Fall ~* put s.o. in charge of a case. **Be'auftragte** m, f (-n; -n) representative, *adm.* commissioner.

be'bauen v/t (h) **1.** build on. **2.** 🌱 cultivate. **Be'bauung** f (-; -en) **1.** development. **2.** 🌱 cultivation.

beben ['be:bən] v/i (h) shake, tremble (*a.*

fig. **vor** *dat* with). **'Beben** *n* (-s; -) trembling, *geol.* tremor, earthquake.
bebildern [bə'bɪldərn] *v/t* (h) illustrate.
bebrillt [bə'brɪlt] *adj* spectacular.
Becher ['bɛçər] *m* (-s; -) **1.** tumbler, mug, beaker. **2.** tub (*of ice cream etc*) **3.** ☕ cup, calix. **'bechern** *v/i* (h) F booze.
Becken ['bɛkən] *n* (-s; -) **1.** bowl, basin (*a.* ☉), (*kitchen*) sink. **2.** (*swimming*) pool. **3.** *anat.* pelvis. **4.** ♩ cymbal.
'Becken... pelvic (*bone etc*).
'Beckenbruch *m* ♩ fractured pelvis.
Becquerel [bɛkə'rɛl] *n* (-s; -) Becquerel.
bedacht [bə'daxt] **I** *pp of* **bedenken.** **II** *adj* ~ **sein auf** (*acc*) be intent on; **darauf** ~ **sein zu** *inf* be anxious to *inf*.
be'dachte *pret of* **bedenken.**
bedächtig [bə'dɛçtɪç] *adj* a) careful, b) circumspect, c) slow.
be'danken: sich ~ (h) say thank you, express one's thanks (*bei j-m* to s.o.); **ich bedanke mich!** thank you!; *iro.* **dafür bedanke ich mich!** no, thank you very much!
Bedarf [bə'darf] *m* (-[e]s; *no pl*) (*an dat*) need (of), *esp.* ♀ a) demand (for), b) consumption (of), c) requirements (of): **bei** (*nach*) ~ if (as) required; ~ **haben an** (*dat*) need; *den* ~ **decken** meet the demand; *s-n* ~ **decken** get everything one needs.
Be'darfs|ar,tikel *m* commodity, *pl* a. consumer goods. **~fall** *m im* ~ in case of need, if required. **~güter** *pl* consumer goods. **~haltestelle** *f* request stop.
bedauerlich [bə'daʊərlɪç] *adj* regrettable, unfortunate. **be'dauerlicherweise** *adv* unfortunately. **be'dauern** *v/t* (h) regret (*s.th.*), feel sorry for (*s.o.*): **ich bedaure sehr, daß ...** I am very sorry that ...; **bedaure!** sorry! **Be'dauern** *n* (-s) regret (*über acc* for): **zu m-m** ~ to my regret. **be'dauernswert** *adj* **1.** pitiable. **2.** → **bedauerlich.**
be'decken (h) **I** *v/t* cover (up). **II sich** ~ cover o.s., *sky:* cloud over. **be'deckt** *adj* **1.** overcast (*sky*). **2.** *fig. sich* ~ **halten** keep a low profile. **Be'deckung** *f* (-; -en) **1.** covering. **2.** escort, convoy.
be'denken *v/t* (bedachte, bedacht, h) **1.** a) consider, think *s.th.* over, b) bear *s.th.* in mind. **2** *j-n mit et.* ~ give s.o. s.th.; *j-n in s-m Testament* ~ remember s.o. in one's will. **be'denken** *n* (-s; -)

usu. pl a) objection, b) doubt: *k-e* ~ **haben** have no reservations (*wegen* about). **be'denkenlos I** *adj* unscrupulous. **II** *adv* without hesitation (*or scruple*). **be'denklich** *adj* **1.** dubious. **2.** alarming, critical, serious, dangerous. **3.** worried, sceptical. **Be'denkzeit** *f* time to think it over: *ich gebe dir bis morgen* ~ I'll give you till tomorrow.
be'deuten *v/t* (h) **1.** mean, *symbol, word, etc: a.* stand for: *was soll das* (*denn*) ~? what's the meaning of this?, *picture etc:* what's that supposed to be?, *contp.* what's the idea?; *das hat nichts zu* ~ a) it doesn't mean a thing, b) it doesn't matter; *das bedeutet nichts Gutes* that's a bad thing; *das bedeutet mir viel* that's very important to me. **2.** *j-m et.* ~ point s.th. out to s.o.; *j-m* ~, *daß* ... give s.o. to understand that ... **be'deutend I** *adj* important, considerable, great, outstanding. **II** *adv* considerably, a great deal *better etc*.
be'deutsam → **bedeutungsvoll.**
Be'deutung *f* (-; -en) **1.** meaning. **2.** *no pl* importance, *w.s.* import: *von* ~ important, significant, relevant (*für* to); *nichts von* ~ nothing important; → **beimessen** b. **be'deutungslos** *adj* **1.** important, significant. **2.** meaningful.
be'dienen (h) **I** *v/t* **1.** serve: *iro.* **ich bin bedient!** I've had enough! **2.** operate. **3.** F *sports:* pass (the ball) to. **II sich** ~ **4.** help o.s.; ~ *Sie sich!* help yourself! **5.** *sich e-r Sache* ~ use s.th. **III** *v/i* **6.** serve, wait at (*Am.* on) table.
Be'dienung *f* (-; -en) **1.** *no pl* a) service, b) operation. **2.** waiter, waitress.
Be'dienungs|anleitung *f* instructions for use, operating instructions. **~knopf** *m* control knob. **~kom,fort** *m* easy operation.
bedingen [bə'dɪŋən] *v/t* (h) **1.** require. **2.** imply. **3.** entail. **4.** stipulate. **5.** cause.
be'dingt I *adj* **1.** ~ *durch,* ~ *von* conditional on, dependent on; ~ *sein durch a.* be determined by. **2.** qualified (*approval, success, etc*). **II** *adv* **3.** conditionally. **4.** up to a point, partly.
Be'dingung *f* (-; -en) condition: ~*en* a) terms, b) conditions; ~*en stellen* make stipulations; (*es*) *zur* ~ *machen, daß* ... make it a condition that ...; *unter der* ~, *daß* ... provided (that) ...; *unter diesen*

~en under these circumstances; *unter k-r ~* on no account; *↑ zu günstigen ~en* on easy terms. **be'dingungslos** *adj* **1.** unconditional. **2.** unquestioning. **Be'dingungssatz** *m* conditional clause.

be'drängen *v/t* (h) **1.** press *s.o.* hard: (*schwer*) *bedrängt sein* be in (bad) trouble, be hard-pressed. **2.** pester (*mit Fragen etc* with questions etc): *bedrängt von* beset by *doubts etc*:

be'drohen *v/t* (h) threaten: *zo. bedrohte Arten* endangered species. **be'drohlich** *adj* a) threatening, menacing, b) alarming, c) ominous. **Be'drohung** *f* (-; -en) (*gen* or) a. *fig.* threat, menace.

be'drucken *v/t* (h) print.

be'drücken *v/t* (h) **1.** oppress. **2.** depress. **be'drückend** *adj* depressing. **Be'drückung** *f* (-; -en) **1.** oppression. **2.** depression.

be'dürfen *v/i* (bedurfte, bedurft, h) (*gen*) need, require, take: *es bedarf k-r weiteren Beweise* no further evidence is required. **Be'dürfnis** [bə'dʏrfnɪs] *n* (-sses; -sse) a) need (*nach* for), requirement, b) urge. **Be'dürfnisanstalt** *f* public convenience. **be'dürfnislos** *adj* *er ist ~* he doesn't need much.

be'dürftig *adj* needy, poor. **Be'dürftigkeit** *f* (-; *no pl*) neediness, poverty.

Beefsteak ['bi:fste:k] *n* (-s; -s) steak: *deutsches ~* beefburger.

be'ehren *v/t* (h) hono(u)r.

beeid(ig)en [bə'ʔaɪd(ɪg)ən] *v/t* (h) swear to. **be'eidigt** *adj* *ɪ̣ɪ̣* sworn. **Be'eidigung** *f* (-; -en) confirmation by oath.

be'eilen: *sich ~* (h) hurry; *beeil dich!* hurry up!, F get a move on!

beeindrucken [bə'ʔaɪndrʊkən] *v/t* (h) impress.

beeinflussen [bə'ʔaɪnflʊsən] *v/t* (h) influence. **Be'einflussung** *f* (-; -en) influence (*gen* on).

beeinträchtigen [bə'ʔaɪntrɛçtɪgən] *v/t* a) impair, affect, b) detract from (*beauty etc*), c) impede, d) reduce. **Be'einträchtigung** *f* (-; -en) (*gen*) a) impairment (of), b) detraction (from), c) impeding (of), d) reduction (in).

beend(ig)en [bə'ʔɛnd(ɪg)ən] *v/t* (h) (bring *s.th.* to an) end, conclude, close. **Be'endigung** *f* (-; *no pl*) conclusion.

beengen [bə'ʔɛŋən] *v/t* (h) cramp.

be'erben *v/t* (h) *j-n ~* be s.o.'s heir.

beerdigen [bə'ʔe:rdɪgən] *v/t* (h) bury. **Be'erdigung** *f* (-; -en) burial, funeral. **Be'erdigungsinsti,tut** *n* undertaker's, funeral directors.

Beere ['be:rə] *f* (-; -n) a) berry, b) grape. **'Beerenauslese** *f* quality wine made from selected grapes.

Beet [be:t] *n* (-[e]s; -e) bed.

Beete → Bete.

befähigen [bə'fɛ:ɪgən] *v/t* (h) enable, qualify (*für, zu* for): *j-n* (*dazu*) ~, *et. zu tun* enable s.o. to do s.th. **be'fähigt** *adj* (*zu*) **1.** capable (of). **2.** qualified (for). **Be'fähigung** *f* (-; -en) **1.** qualification (*zu* for). **2.** ability, competence. **Be'fähigungsnachweis** *m* certificate of qualification.

befahl [bə'fa:l] *pret of* **befehlen.**

be'fahrbar *adj* passable, ♣ navigable. **be'fahren¹** *v/t* (befuhr, befahren, h) drive on, use (*a road*), cover (*distance*). **be'fahren²** II *pp of* **befahren¹.** II *adj* *sehr* (*or stark*) ~*e Straße* busy road.

be'fallen *v/t* (befiel, befallen, h) attack (*a. ♣*), *fig.* seize: ~ *werden von* a) be infested by (*insects etc*), b) be seized by (*fear etc*).

be'fand *pret of* **befinden.**

be'fangen *adj* **1.** inhibited, shy, self-conscious. **2.** *a.* *ɪ̣ɪ̣* bias(s)ed: *in e-m Irrtum ~ sein* be labo(u)ring under a delusion. **Be'fangenheit** *f* (-; *no pl*) **1.** shyness, self-consciousness. **2.** *ɪ̣ɪ̣* *etc* bias.

be'fassen: *sich ~ mit* (h) concern o.s. with, deal with (*a problem etc*).

Befehl [bə'fe:l] *m* (-[e]s; -e) order, command: *auf ~ von* (or *gen*) by order of; (*den*) ~ *haben zu inf* be under orders to *inf*; *den ~ haben* (*übernehmen*) be in (take) command (*über acc* of).

be'fehlen (befahl, befohlen, h) I *v/t j-m et.* ~ order s.o. to do s.th. II *v/i* give the orders. **befehligen** [bə'fe:lɪgən] *v/t* (h) be in command of.

Be'fehlsbereich *m* ✕ (area of) command. **Be'fehlsform** *f ling.* imperative. **Befehlshaber** [bə'fe:lsha:bər] *m* (-s; -) commander. **Be'fehlsverweigerung** *f* refusal to obey an order.

be'festigen *v/t* (h) **1.** (*an dat*) to fasten fix. **2.** pave. **3.** ✕ fortify. **Be'festigung** *f* (-; -en) **1.** fastening, fixing. **2.** ✕ fortification.

befeuchten [bə'fɔʏçtən] *v/t* (h) moisten

be'finden (befand, befunden, h) I v/t et. für gut etc ~ think s.th. is good etc. II sich ~ a) be, house etc: a. be located, b) be, feel. III v/i decide.

Be'finden n (-s) (state) of health.

befindlich [bə'fıntlıç] adj alle im Haus ~en Möbel all furniture in the house.

befingern [bə'fıŋərn] v/t (h) finger.

be'flaggen v/t (h) flag.

be'flecken v/t (h) stain, soil, fig. sully.

be'fliegen v/t (beflog, beflogen, h) fly.

beflügeln [bə'fly:gəln] v/t (h) inspire, spur s.o. on, fire (s.o.'s imagination).

befohlen [bə'fo:lən] pp of befehlen.

be'folgen v/t (h) a) follow, take (advice), b) observe (rule). Be'folgung f (-; no pl) following (etc), observance (gen of).

be'fördern v/t (h) 1. convey, transport, ✝ forward, ship. 2. promote: er wurde zum Major befördert he was promoted (to the rank of) major. Be'förderung f (-; -en) 1. no pl conveyance, transport(ation), ✝ forwarding, shipment. 2. promotion. Be'förderungsmittel n (means of) transport(ation).

befrachten [bə'fraxtən] v/t (h) load, ⚓, a. fig. freight.

be'fragen v/t (h) (nach, über acc about) 1. question, ask. 2. poll, interview. 3. consult. Be'fragung f (-; -en) 1. interview. 2. (public opinion) poll.

befreien [bə'fraıən] (h) (von from) I v/t 1. a) free, liberate, b) rescue. 2. excuse, exempt (from taxes etc), release (from obligations), relieve (from burden, pain, etc). II sich ~ free o.s., liberate o.s.: sich von et. ~ get rid of s.th. Be'freier m (-s; -) liberator. Be'freiung f (-; no pl) (von from) 1. a) freeing, liberation, b) rescue. 2. exemption, release.

Be'freiungs|bewegung f liberation movement. ~kampf m fight for independence. ~krieg m war of liberation.

befremden [bə'frɛmdən] v/t (h) j-n ~ take s.o. aback. Be'fremden n (-s) astonishment (über acc at).

befreunden [bə'frɔyndən] sich ~ (h) become friends; sich ~ mit make friends with, fig. get used to s.th.

be'freundet adj friendly (a. pol.): ~ sein be friends (mit with).

be'frieden v/t (h) pol. pacify.

befriedigen [bə'fri:dıgən] v/t (h) satisfy (s.o., s.o.'s curiosity etc), please (s.o.),

meet (demand etc), come up to (expectations): schwer zu ~ hard to please. be'friedigend adj satisfactory (a. ped. mark). be'friedigt adj and adv satisfied, pleased. Be'friedigung f (-; no pl) satisfaction (über acc at).

be'fristen v/t (h) et. (auf e-n Monat) ~ set a time limit (of one month) on s.th. be'fristet adj limited (in time) (auf acc to). Be'fristung f (-; -en) 1. setting of a time limit. 2. time limit.

be'fruchten v/t (h) biol. fertilize (a. fig.), ⚘ pollinate, fig. stimulate: (künstlich) ~ inseminate (artificially).

Be'fruchtung f (-; -en) biol. fertilization (a. fig.), ⚘ pollination: künstliche ~ artificial insemination.

Befugnis [bə'fu:knıs] f (-; -se) a. pl authority, power(s): j-m (die) ~ erteilen (zu inf) authorize s.o. (to inf).

befugt [bə'fu:kt] adj authorized.

be'fühlen v/t (h) feel, touch.

befuhr [bə'fu:r] pret of befahren[1].

Be'fund m (-[e]s; -e) findings: ✗ ohne ~ negative. be'funden pp of befinden.

be'fürchten v/t (h) fear: es ist zu ~, daß ... it is feared that ...; wir müssen das Schlimmste ~ we must be prepared for the worst. Be'fürchtung f (-; -en) fear, pl a. misgivings.

befürworten [bə'fy:rvɔrtən] v/t (h) 1. advocate, recommend. 2. support. Be'fürworter m (-s; -) supporter, advocate. Be'fürwortung f (-; -en) recommendation, support.

begab [bə'ga:p] pret of begeben.

begabt [bə'ga:pt] adj gifted, talented.

Begabung [bə'ga:bʊŋ] f (-; -en) gift, (a. person) talent.

begangen [bə'ganən] pp of begehen.

begann [bə'gan] pret of beginnen.

begatten [bə'gatən] v/t (h) copulate with, zo. mate with. Be'gattung f (-; -en) copulation, zo. mating.

be'geben (begab, begeben, h) I sich ~ 1. happen, occur. 2. sich ~ nach (or zu) go to; sich in ärztliche Behandlung ~ have medical treatment; sich an die Arbeit ~ set to work; sich auf die Reise ~ set out (on one's journey); → Gefahr. II v/t 3. ✝ negotiate (bill). Be'geben-heit f (-; -en) occurrence, incident.

begegnen [bə'ge:gnən] v/i (sn) (dat) 1. meet, F bump into, come across: sich ~

meet. **2.** meet with (*difficulties*), face (*s.o., situation, etc*), obviate (*danger etc*). **3.** be found (**bei**) in. **4.** *j-m freundlich etc* ~ treat s.o. kindly *etc*.

Be'gegnung *f* (-; -en) **1.** meeting, encounter. **2.** *sports*: bout, match.

begehbar [bə'ge:ba:r] *adj* passable.

Be'gehen *v/t* (beging, begangen, h) **1.** walk on. **2.** inspect. **3.** make (*mistake*), commit (*crime*). **4.** celebrate (*birthday etc*), observe (*holiday*).

begehren [bə'ge:rən] *v/t* (h) desire, crave for, demand: (**sehr**) **begehrt** (much) sought after, (very) much in demand. **Be'gehren** *n* (-s) desire (*nach* for). **be'gehrenswert** *adj* desirable. **be'gehrlich** *adj* covetous, greedy.

Be'gehung *f* (-; -en) **1.** inspection. **2.** commission (*of crime*). **3.** celebration.

begeistern [bə'gaistərn] **I** *v/t* (h) fill *s.o.* with enthusiasm (*für* about), inspire. **II** *sich ~ für* be (*or* get) enthusiastic about. **III** *v/i* arouse enthusiasm (**durch** by). **be'geisternd** *adj* rousing, inspiring, marvel(l)ous. **be'geistert I** *adj* (*von*) enthusiastic (about), keen (on): *~er Anhänger* (*gen or von*) fan (of); *...begeistert* ...-minded, F ...-mad. **II** *adv* enthusiastic(ally): ~ *sprechen von a.* rave about. **Be'geisterung** *f* (-; *no pl*) enthusiasm (*für* for, about): *mit ~ a.* enthusiastically.

Begierde [bə'gi:rdə] *f* (-; -n) (*nach* for) a) appetite, b) desire, lust. **be-'gierig** *adj* eager (*nach, auf acc* for): *ich bin ~ zu erfahren* I am anxious to know.

be'gießen *v/t* (begoß, begossen, h) **1.** pour water *etc* over (*or* on), water. **2.** F *fig.* celebrate (with a drink): *das müssen wir ~!* that calls for a drink!

beging [bə'gɪŋ] *pret of* **begehen**.

Beginn [bə'gɪn] *m* (-[e]s; *no pl*) (*zu ~* at) the beginning. **be'ginnen** *v/t*, *v/i* (begann, begonnen, h) begin, start.

beglaubigen [bə'glaʊbɪgən] *v/t* (h) **1.** certify (*document*). **2.** accredit *diplomat* (**bei** to). **be'glaubigt** *adj* (**öffentlich**) ~ certified (by a notary public); *~e Abschrift* certified copy, *as a note:* a true copy. **Be'glaubigung** *f* (-; -en) **1.** certification. **2.** accreditation. **Be'glaubigungsschreiben** *n* credentials.

be'gleichen *v/t* (beglich, beglichen, h) ✝

pay, settle. **Be'gleichung** *f* (-; *no pl*) settlement, payment.

be'gleiten *v/t* (h) accompany (a. ♪ *or fig.*), a. ♌, ✕, *mot.* escort.

Be'gleiter *m* (-s; -) **1.** companion. **2.** attendant. **3.** ♪ accompanist. **4.** escort.

Be'gleiterin *f* (-; -nen) → **Begleiter** 1-3

Be'gleit|erscheinung *f* concomitant, ♌ attendant symptom. *~flugzeug n* escort plane. *~mu,sik f* incidental music *fig.* accompaniment. *~per,son f* escort *~schein m* ✝ **1.** waybill. **2.** (custom's permit. *~schiff n* escort vessel *~schreiben n* covering letter. *~umstände pl* attendant circumstances.

Be'gleitung *f* (-; -en) **1.** a) company, a ♌, ✕, escort, b) entourage: *ohne* unaccompanied; *in ~ von* (*or gen*) accompanied by. **2.** ♪ accompaniment.

beglich [bə'glɪç] *pret of* **begleichen**.

be'glichen *pp of* **begleichen**.

be'glücken *v/t* (h) *j-n* ~ make s.o. happy

be'glückwünschen *v/t* (h) *j-n* (*zu et.*) congratulate s.o. (on s.th.).

begnadet [bə'gna:dət] *adj* inspired highly gifted: ~ *mit* blessed with.

begnadigen [bə'gna:dɪgən] *v/t* (h) **Be'gnadigung** *f* (-; -en) pardon, *pol* amnesty.

begnügen [bə'gny:gən] *sich ~* (h) (*m* with) be content, make do.

Begonie [be'go:niə] *f* (-; -n) ❀ begonia

begonnen [bə'gɔnən] *pp of* **beginnen**.

begoß [bə'gɔs] *pret of* **begießen**.

be'gossen *pp of* **begießen**.

be'graben *v/t* (begrub, begraben, h) a *fig.* bury. **Begräbnis** [bə'grɛ:pnɪs] (-ses; -se) burial, funeral.

begradigen [bə'gra:dɪgən] *v/t* (h straighten.

be'greifen *v/t* (begriff, begriffen, h) understand (*a. v/i*), grasp: *das begreif ich nicht!* that's beyond me!; *schnell ~* F catch on quickly, be quick on the uptake. **be'greiflich** *adj* understandable: *j-m et. ~ machen* make s.th. clea to s.o. **be'greiflicherweise** *adv* understandably (enough).

be'grenzen *v/t* (h) **1.** mark off. **2.** form the boundary of. **3.** *fig.* (*auf acc* to limit, restrict. **Be'grenztheit** *f* (-; *no pl* limitations. **Be'grenzung** *f* (-; -en) (*auf acc* to) limiting, restriction. **2** bounds, limit.

Be'grenzungslicht n mot. sidelight.
begriff [bə'grɪf] pret of **begreifen**.
Be'griff m (-[e]s; -e) 1. a) idea, notion, philos. concept, b) term: **sich e-n ~ machen von** get an idea of, imagine; **du machst dir k-n ~!** you have no idea!; **ist dir das ein ~?** does that mean anything to you?; **nach m-n ~en** as I see it. 2. F **schwer von ~** slow (in the uptake). 3. **im ~ sein, et. zu tun** be about to do s.th.
be'griffen I pp of **begreifen**. **II** adj **im Aufbruch ~ sein** be about to leave.
be'grifflich adj conceptual, abstract.
Be'griffsbestimmung f definition.
be'griffsstutzig adj dense, slow.
begrub [bə'gru:p] pret of **begraben**.
be'gründen v/t (h) 1. give reasons for, explain, justify. 2. found, establish, set up, fig. lay the foundations of.
be'gründet adj well-founded, justified: **~er Verdacht** reasonable suspicion.
Be'gründung f (-; -en) 1. reason(s), argument(s), explanation: **mit der ~, daß ...** on the grounds that ...; **ohne jede ~** without giving any reasons. 2. establishment, foundation, setting up.
be'grüßen v/t (h) greet, welcome: **es ist zu ~, daß** we welcome the fact that.
be'grüßenswert adj welcome.
Be'grüßung f (-; -en) greeting, welcome.
Be'grüßungs|ansprache f welcoming speech. **~worte** pl words of welcome.
begünstigen [bə'gʏnstɪgən] v/t (h) a) favo(u)r, b) promote. **Be'günstigte** m, f (-n; -n) ✝, ⚖ beneficiary. **Be'günstigung** f (-; -en) 1. a) favo(u)ring, b) promotion. 2. preferential treatment. 3. (financial) benefit. 4. ⚖ acting as accessory after the fact.
be'gutachten v/t (h) 1. give an (expert's) opinion on: **et. ~ lassen** obtain an expert's opinion on s.th. 2. examine.
begütert [bə'gy:tərt] adj rich, wealthy, well-off, well-to-do.
begütigen [bə'gy:tɪgən] v/t (h) appease.
behaart [bə'ha:rt] adj hairy, hirsute.
behäbig [bə'hɛ:bɪç] adj 1. sedate. 2. portly.
behaftet [bə'haftət] adj **~ mit** full of (mistakes), afflicted with (disease), tainted with (flaw).
behagen [bə'ha:gən] v/i (h) **j-m ~** a) suit s.o., b) please s.o.; **das behagt mir (ganz und gar) nicht** I don't like that

(at all). **Be'hagen** n (-s) a) ease, comfort, b) pleasure. **be'haglich** adj comfortable, cosy. **Be'haglichkeit** f (-; no pl) comfort, cosiness.
be'halten v/t (behielt, behalten, h) 1. keep: **recht ~** be right (in the end); **für sich ~** keep secret to o.s.; **behalte das für dich!** keep it under your hat! 2. remember.
Behälter [bə'hɛltər] m (-s; -) container, tank.
be'handeln v/t (h) treat (a. ✶, ⚙), fig. a. deal with, handle. **Be'handlung** f (-; -en) treatment, handling: **in (ärztlicher) ~** under medical treatment.
be'hängen v/t (h) hang, drape, decorate: F contp. **mit Schmuck behängt** decked (out) with jewels.
be'harren v/i (h) **(auf dat)** persist (in), F stick (to): **darauf ~, daß ...** insist that ...
be'harrlich adj persistent, steadfast, stubborn. **Be'harrlichkeit** f (-; no pl) perseverance, stubbornness.
be'hauen v/t (h) hew.
behaupten [bə'hauptən] (h) **I** v/t 1. maintain, claim, say (daß that): F **steif und fest ~, daß ...** insist that ... 2. maintain, assert. **II sich ~** 3. hold one's own. 4. ✝ prices etc: remain firm. **Be'hauptung** f (-; -en) 1. claim, assertion. 2. no pl maintenance, assertion.
Behausung [bə'hauzʊŋ] f (-; -en) dwelling.
be'heben v/t (behob, behoben, h) remove, repair (damage), remedy (grievance). **Be'hebung** f (-; no pl) removal.
beheimatet [bə'haima:tət] adj **~ in** (dat) resident in, living in, coming from.
be'heizbar adj heatable.
be'heizen v/t (h) heat.
Behelf [bə'hɛlf] m (-[e]s; -e) makeshift.
be'helfen: sich ~ (behalf, beholfen, h) **(mit** with) make do, manage.
Be'helfs..., be'helfsmäßig adj makeshift, temporary.
behelligen [bə'hɛlɪgən] v/t (h) bother.
beherbergen [bə'hɛrbɛrgən] v/t (h) put up, accommodate, a. fig. house.
be'herrschen (h) **I** v/t 1. rule (over), govern. 2. fig. control (situation, market, one's feelings, etc): **j-n ~** dominate s.o. 3. have a good command of, speak (German etc), know: **sein Handwerk ~** know one's trade. **II sich ~** control o.s.

be'herrschend *adj* dominating.
Be'herrscher *m* ruler (*gen* over, of).
Be'herrschung *f* (-; *no pl*) **1.** rule, domination. **2.** *fig.* (*gen* of) a) control, b) mastery, command. **3.** self-control.
beherzigen [bə'hɛrtsɪgən] *v/t* (h) *et.* ~ bear s.th. in mind.
beherzt [bə'hɛrtst] *adj* courageous.
behielt [bə'hi:lt] *pret of* **behalten.**
behilflich [bə'hɪlflɪç] *adj j-m* ~ *sein* help (*or* assist) s.o. (*bei* in).
be'hindern *v/t* (h) (*bei* in) hinder, hamper, *a. sports:* obstruct.
be'hindert *adj* (*körperlich or geistig*) ~ (physically *or* mentally) handicapped.
Be'hinderte *m*, *f* (-n; -n) handicapped person. **Be'hinderung** *f* (-; -en) **1.** hindrance, impediment, *a. sports:* obstruction. **2.** ✱ handicap.
behob [bə'ho:p] *pret of* **beheben.**
behoben [bə'ho:bən] *pp of* **beheben.**
beholfen [bə'hɔlfən] *pp of* **behelfen.**
Behörde [bə'hø:rdə] *f* (-; -n) (public) authority: *die* ~*n* the authorities.
behördlich [bə'hø:rtlɪç] *adj* official.
be'hüten *v/t* (h) protect (*vor dat* from).
behutsam [bə'hu:tza:m] *adj* cautious, careful, gentle. **Be'hutsamkeit** *f* (-; *no pl*) caution, gentleness.
bei [baɪ] *prep* (*dat*) **1.** ~ *Berlin* near Berlin; *die Schlacht* ~ *Waterloo* the Battle of Waterloo; ~*m Bäcker* at the baker's; ~ *Familie Braun,* ~ *Brauns* at Braun's; ~ *Braun* c/o (= care of) Braun; ~ *Hofe* at court; ~ *j-m sitzen* sit with s.o.; *arbeiten* ~ work for; *e-e Stellung* ~ a job with; ~*m Heer* (~ *der Marine*) in the army (navy); ~ *uns* a) with us, b) (*zu Hause*) at home, c) (*in Deutschland*) in Germany, at home; *ich habe kein Geld* ~ *mir* I have no money one me; *er hatte s-n Hund* ~ *sich* he had his dog with him. **2.** ~ *s-r Geburt* (*Hochzeit*) at his birth (wedding); ~ *Tag* (*Nacht*) by night (day), during the night (day); ~ *Licht* by light; ~ *70 Grad* at 70 degrees; ~ *schönem Wetter* when the weather is fine; ~*m Arbeiten* while working; ~ *offenem Fenster* with the window open; ~ *Regen* (*Gefahr*) in case of rain (danger); F *er ist nicht ganz* ~ *sich* he's not all there. **3.** ~ *so vielen Problemen* with (*or* considering) all the problems; ~ *solcher Hitze* in such heat; ~ *all s-n Be-*

mühungen for all his efforts; → *a. corresponding headwords.*
'beibehalten *v/t* (*irr, sep,* h, → *behalten*) retain, maintain, keep.
'Beiblatt *n* supplement (*gen* to).
'Beiboot *n* dinghy.
'beibringen *v/t* (*irr, sep,* -ge-, h, → *bringen*) *j-m et.* ~ a) teach s.o. s.th., b) get s.th. across to s.o.; *j-m et. schonend* ~ break s.th. gently to s.o.
Beichte ['baɪçtə] *f* (-; -n) confession: *j-m die* ~ *abnehmen* confess s.o.
beichten ['baɪçtən] *v/t, v/i* (h) confess.
'Beicht|geheimnis *n* confessional secret. ~*kind* *n* penitent. ~*stuhl* *m* confessional. ~*vater* *m* (father) confessor.
beide ['baɪdə] *adj* a) both, b) the two, c) either: *m-e* ~ *Brüder* both my brothers, my two brothers; *wir* ~ both of us, we two; *alle* ~ both of them; *in* ~*n Fällen* in either case; *kein(e)s von* ~*n* neither (of the two).
'beidemal *adv* both times.
beiderlei ['baɪdərlaɪ] *adj* (of) both kinds: ~ *Geschlechts* of either sex. **'beiderseitig** [-zaɪtɪç] *adj and adv* a) on both sides, b) mutual(ly *adv*). **'beiderseits** [-zaɪts] **I** *adv* on both sides, *fig. a.* mutually. **II** *prep* (*gen*) on both sides (of).
beidhändig ['baɪthɛndɪç] *adj* ambidextrous, *sports:* two-handed.
'beidrehen *v/i* (*sep,* -ge-, h) ⚓ heave to.
beiein'ander *adv* together: (*dicht*) ~ next to each other. ~*haben* *v/t* (*irr, sep,* -ge-, h, → *haben*) F have got *s.th.* together: *du hast wohl nicht alle beieinander!* you must be out of your mind. ~*halten* *v/t* (*irr, sep,* -ge-, h, → *halten*) F keep *s.th.* together. ~*sein* *v/i* (*irr, sep,* -ge-, sn, → *sein*) F *gut* ~ be in good shape; *er ist nicht ganz beieinander* he's not all there.
'Beifahrer *m* in car: front passenger, *in truck:* driver's mate, *in races:* co-driver.
'Beifahrersitz *m* front-passenger seat.
'Beifall *m* (-[e]s; *no pl*) applause, (loud) cheers, *fig.* approval: ~ *ernten,* ~ *finden* draw applause, *fig.* meet with approval, be acclaimed; ~ *klatschen,* ~ *spenden* applaud (*j-m* s.o.).
'beifällig *adj* approving.
'Beifallsruf *m* cheer(s).
'Beifallssturm *m* thunderous applause.
'Beifilm *m* supporting film.

'**beifügen** v/t (sep, -ge-, h) (dat) a) add
(to), b) enclose (with a letter).

'**Beifügung** f (-; -en) ling. apposition.

'**Beigabe** f (-; -n) **1.** addition, extra: **als ~**
a. into the bargain. **2.** → **Beilage** 2.

beige [be:ʃ] adj, **Beige** n (-; no pl) beige.

'**beigeben** (irr, sep, -ge-, h, → **geben**) **I**
v/t add (dat to). **II** v/i **F klein ~** knuckle
under, climb down.

'**Beigeordnete** m, f (-n; -n) assistant,
pol. town council(l)or.

'**Beigeschmack** m (-[e]s; no pl) (unpleasant) taste, fig. smack (**von** of).

'**Beihilfe** f **1.** a) aid, b) grant, c) subsidy.
2. ⚖ aiding and abetting: **(j-m) ~ lei-**
sten aid and abet (s.o.).

'**beikommen** v/i (irr, sep, -ge-, sn, →
kommen) (dat) get at (s.o.), cope with.

Beil [baɪl] n (-[e]s; -e) a) ax(e), hatchet, b)
(meat) chopper.

'**Beilage** f (-; -n) **1.** supplement, insertion, inset. **2.** gastr. side dish: **Fleisch**
mit ~ a. meat and vegetables.

'**beiläufig** **I** adj casual. **II** adv casually,
by the way: **et. ~ erwähnen** mention
s.th. in passing.

'**beilegen** v/t (sep, -ge-, h) **1.** (dat) add
(to), enclose (with). **2.** give (a name). **3.**
settle (quarrel).

beileibe [baɪ'laɪbə] adv **~ nicht**(!) certainly not(!), by no means(!).

'**Beileid** n (-[e]s; no pl) (**j-m sein ~ aus-**
sprechen offer s.o. one's condolences: (**mein**) **herzliches ~!** a. iro. my
heartfelt sympathy!

'**Beileidsbesuch** m visit of condolence.

'**Beileidsbrief** m letter of condolence.

'**Beileidskarte** f condolence card.

'**beiliegen** v/i (irr, sep, -ge-, h, → **liegen**)
be enclosed (dat with). '**beiliegend** adj
and adv enclosed: **~ übersenden wir**
Ihnen ... enclosed please find ...

beim [baɪm] = **bei dem**.

'**beimessen** v/t (irr, sep, -ge-, h, → **mes-**
sen) (dat) a) **Glauben ~** give credence
to, b) **Bedeutung** etc **~** attach importance etc to.

'**beimischen** v/t (sep, -ge-, h) (dat) **et. ~**
mix s.th. with, add s.th. to.

'**Beimischung** f (-; -en) admixture.

Bein [baɪn] n (-[e]s; -e) leg (a. of pants,
table, etc): (**früh**) **auf den ~en sein** be
up and about (early); **dauernd auf den**
~en sein be always on the go; **wieder**

auf den ~en sein be back on one's feet
(again); F **j-m ~e machen** make s.o. get
a move on; **ich muß mich auf die ~e**
machen! I must be off!; F **die ~e in die**
Hand nehmen take to one's heels, run;
fig. **auf eigenen ~en stehen** stand on
one's own two feet; fig. **j-n** (et.) **auf die**
~e stellen set s.o. (s.th.) up; **j-m ein ~**
stellen a. fig. trip s.o. up; **sich die ~e**
vertreten stretch one's legs; → **Grab.**

beinah(e) ['baɪna:(ə)] adv almost, nearly: **~ et. tun** come near doing s.th.

'**Beinahezusammenstoß** m near miss.

'**Beiname** m epithet.

'**Bein|arbeit** f boxing: footwork, swim-
ming: legwork. **~bruch** m 🎿 fractured
leg: F fig. **das ist kein ~!** that's no
tragedy! **~freiheit** f mot. legroom.

beinhalten [bə'ʔɪnhaltən] v/t (h) contain, say, imply.

'**Beinprothese** f artificial leg.

'**beiordnen** v/t (sep, -ge-, h) **1.** **j-m j-n ~**
assign s.o. to s.o. **2.** ling. coordinate.

'**Beipackzettel** m instructions.

'**beipflichten** ['baɪpflɪçtən] v/i (sep, -ge-,
h) agree (dat to).

'**Beipro,gramm** n film: supporting pro-
gram(me Br.).

'**Beirat** m (-[e]s; ⸚e) advisory board.

beirren [bə'ʔɪrən] v/t (h) disconcert: **er**
läßt sich nicht ~ he stands firm.

beisammen [baɪ'zamən] adv together.

Bei'sammensein n (-s) being together:
geselliges ~ get-together.

'**Beischlaf** m ⚖ sexual intercourse.

'**Beisein:** im **~ von** (or gen) in the presence of.

bei'seite adv aside; **~ lassen** disregard;
~ legen set aside; **~ schaffen** remove,
get rid of; **~ schieben** push (argument;
brush) aside; **~ treten** step aside.

'**beisetzen** v/t (sep, -ge-, h) bury.

'**Beisetzung** f (-; -en) burial, funeral.

'**Beispiel** n (-[e]s; -e) a) example, b) model: (**wie**) **zum ~** for instance, for example (abbr. e.g.); **ein ~ geben, mit gutem**
~ vorangehen set an example; **sich ein**
~ an j-m (et.) **nehmen** take s.o. (s.th.)
as an example. '**beispielhaft** adj exemplary, model. '**beispiellos** adj unprecedented, unheard-of. '**beispielsweise**
adv for example, (as) for instance.

beißen ['baɪsən] v/t, v/i (biß, gebissen) h)
bite (**auf** acc, **in** acc s.th.), smoke, pep-

per, etc: a. burn: **nach j-m ~** snap at s.o.; F **die Farben ~ sich** the colo(u)rs clash; F **er wird dich schon nicht ~!** he won't eat you! **'beißend** adj biting (wind, a. criticism etc), acrid (smell).

'Beißring m teething ring.

'Beistand m (-[e]s; ⸚e) **1.** no pl help, aid, support: **j-m ~ leisten** → **beistehen. 2.** → **Rechtsbeistand. 'Beistandspakt** m pol. mutual assistance pact.

'beistehen v/i (irr, sep, -ge-, h, → **stehen**) **j-m ~** help (or assist, stand by) s.o., come to s.o.'s aid, ⚖ attend s.o.

'beisteuern v/t, v/i (sep, -ge-, h) contribute (**zu** to).

'Beistrich m comma.

Beitrag ['baitraːk] m (-[e]s; ⸚e) a) contribution (a. fig.), b) subscription (fee), fee: **e-n ~ leisten** make a contribution (**zu** to). **'beitragen** v/t, v/i (irr, sep, -ge-, h, → **tragen**) contribute (**zu** to).

'beitragsfrei adj noncontributary.

'beitragspflichtig adj liable to contributions.

'beitreiben v/t (irr, sep, -ge-, h, → **treiben**) collect (taxes etc), recover (debts).

'beitreten v/i (irr, sep, -ge-, sn, → **treten**) (dat) join (club etc), accede to (treaty).

'Beitritt m (-[e]s; -e) (**zu**) joining (a club etc). **'Beitrittserklärung** f application for membership.

'Beiwagen m mot. sidecar. **~ma͜schine** f (motorcycle) combination.

'beiwohnen v/i (sep, -ge-, h) (dat) **1.** a) be present at, attend, b) witness. **2.** ⚖ have sexual intercourse with s.o.

'Beiwort n (-[e]s; ⸚er) epithet.

Beize¹ ['baitsə] f (-; -n) **1.** corrosive, for wood: stain, for dies: mordant, metall. pickle. **2.** (tobacco) sauce. **3.** gastr. marinade. **'Beize²** f (-; -n) hawking.

beizeiten [bai'tsaitən] adv in good time.

beizen ['baitsən] v/t (h) **1.** corrode, stain (wood), bate (hides), metall. pickle. **2.** sauce (tobacco). **3.** gastr. marinade.

bejahen [bə'jaːən] v/t (h) answer in the affirmative (a. v/i), a. fig. say yes to.

be'jahend adj affirmative.

Be'jahung f (-; -en) affirmation, fig. positive attitude (**gen** towards).

bejahrt [bə'jaːrt] adj advanced in years.

be'jammern v/t (h) lament.

bekam [bə'kaːm] pret of **bekommen**.

be'kämpfen v/t (h) fight (against), combat. **Be'kämpfung** f (-; no pl) fight (**gen** against).

bekannt [bə'kant] **I** pp of **bekennen**. **II** adj (well-)known (**wegen** for): **~ mit** acquainted with; **j-n ~ machen mit** introduce s.o. to; **sich ~ mit et. ~ machen** familiarize o.s. with s.th.; **das ist mir ~** I know (that); **dafür ~ sein, daß ...** have a reputation for ger. **be'kannte** pret of **bekennen. Be'kannte** m, f (-n; -n) friend, acquaintance.

Be'kanntenkreis m (circle of) friends.

Be'kanntgabe f (-; no pl) announcement. **be'kanntgeben** v/t (irr, sep, -ge-, h, → **geben**) announce.

Be'kanntheitsgrad m (-[e]s; no pl) name recognition (rating).

be'kanntlich adv as everybody knows.

be'kanntmachen v/t (sep, -ge-, h) announce, make s.th. known.

Be'kanntmachung f (-; -en) announcement, publication, bulletin.

Be'kanntschaft f (-; -en) **1.** no pl (**bei näherer ~** on closer) acquaintance: **j-s ~ machen** become acquainted with s.o. **2.** (circle of) friends.

be'kanntwerden v/i (irr, sep, -ge-, sn, → **werden**) become known, come out.

be'kehren v/t (h) a. fig. convert (**zu** to): **sich ~ (zu** to) become a convert, fig. a. come round.

Be'kehrte m, f (-n; -n) convert.

Be'kehrung f (-; -en) conversion.

be'kennen (bekannte, bekannt, h) **I** v/t confess (**zu** to). **II sich ~ zu** a) confess (deed), b) profess (faith etc); **sich zu j-m ~** stand by s.o., stand up for s.o.; → **Farbe 1, schuldig 1.**

Be'kenntnis n (-ses; -se) **1.** confession. **2.** eccl. a) creed, b) denomination. **~schule** f denominational school.

be'klagen (h) **I** v/t lament, deplore **II sich ~** complain (**über** acc of). **be'klagenswert** adj deplorable, sorry, per son: pitiable. **Beklagte** [bə'klaːktə] m, (-n; -n) ⚖ defendant.

be'klauen v/t (h) F **j-n ~** steal from s.o.

be'kleben v/t (h) **1.** paste s.th. over. **2** et. **~ mit** stick (or paste) s.th. on s.th.

be'kleckern v/t **1** v/t stain, mess up. **sich ~ mit ...** spill ... over o.s.

be'kleiden v/t (h) **1.** dress: fig. **~ mi** (in)vest with. **2.** hold (an office).

Be'kleidung f (-; -en) clothing, clothes.

Be'kleidungsindu,strie f clothing industry.

be'klemmen v/t (h) oppress. **be'klemmend** adj oppressive, fig. a. eerie. **Beklemmung** f (-; -en) oppression, fig. a. anxiety. **beklommen** [bə'klɔmən] adj uneasy, anxious. **Be'klommenheit** f (-; no pl) uneasiness, anxiety.

bekloppt [bə'klɔpt], **beknackt** [-'knakt] adj F nutty, batty, crazy, pred nuts.

be'kommen (bekam, bekommen) **I** v/t (h) get, a. ✠ a. catch (a. F bus etc), have (child, young): **Hunger** (**Durst**) ~ get hungry (thirsty); **sie bekommt ein Kind** she's going to have a baby; **Zähne** ~ cut one's teeth; **et. geschenkt** ~ be given s.th. (as a present); **wieviel ~ Sie** (**von mir**)? how much do I owe you? **II** v/i (sn) **j-m** (**gut**) ~ agree with s.o.; **j-m nicht** (**or schlecht**) ~ disagree with s.o.; **wohl bekomm's!** cheers!; fig. **es wird ihm schlecht** ~ he will regret it.

bekömmlich [bə'kœmlɪç] adj wholesome, a. easily digestible, light (food), salubrious (air, climate).

beköstigen [bə'kœstɪgən] v/t (h) feed: **sich selbst** ~ cook for o.s. **Beköstigung** f (-; no pl) feeding, b) food.

be'kräftigen v/t (h) confirm. **Be'kräftigung** f (-; -en) confirmation.

be'kreuzigen: sich ~ (h) cross o.s.

be'kriegen v/t (h) make war on: **sich** ~ be at war with one another.

be'kritteln v/t (h) contp. criticize.

be'kritzeln v/t (h) scribble on.

be'kümmern v/t (h) grieve, worry.

bekunden [bə'kʊndən] v/t (h) **1.** show, demonstrate. **2.** state, ✠✠ a. testify.

be'lächeln v/t (h) smile (condescendingly) at.

be'laden v/t (belud, beladen, h) load, fig. a. burden.

Belag [bə'laːk] m (-[e]s; ⁓e) **1.** a) covering, ✪ a. coating, b) surface (of road), c) (brake) lining. **2.** (sandwich) filling. **3.** ✗ a) coating (of tongue), b) plaque.

be'lagern v/t (h) a. fig. besiege. **Be'lagerung** f (-; -en) siege.

Belang [bə'laŋ] m (-[e]s; -e) **1.** no pl **von** ~ of importance (**für** to); **ohne** ~ a) unimportant, b) irrelevant. **2.** pl interests. **be'langen** v/t (h) ✠✠ a) sue, b) prosecute. **be'langlos** adj a) unimportant, b) irrelevant (**für** to), c) negligible. **Be'langlo-**

sigkeit f (-; -en) **1.** no pl a) insignificance, b) irrelevance. **2.** pl trivialities.

be'lassen v/t (beließ, belassen, h) **et. an s-m Platz** ~ leave s.th. in its place; **es dabei** ~ leave it at that; **alles beim alten** ~ leave things as they are.

belastbar [bə'lastba:r] adj **1.** ✪ having a load capacity (**bis zu** of). **2.** fig. strong, resilient. **Be'lastbarkeit** f (-; no pl) **1.** ✪ load(ing) capacity. **2.** ability to cope with pressure (or strain): **bis zur Grenze der** ~ to breaking point. **be'lasten** v/t (h) **1.** ⚡, ✪ load. **2.** fig. burden (**mit** with, **sich** o.s.), put (or be) a strain on, weigh on, worry: **das belastet mich sehr** that's a great burden (or worry) to me; **damit kann ich mich jetzt nicht** ~ I can't be bothered with that now; → **erblich. 3.** ✝ a) charge, b) encumber (house etc): **j-n** (**or j-s Konto**) (**mit e-m Betrag**) ~ charge a sum to s.o.'s account. **4.** ✠✠, pol. incriminate.

belästigen [bə'lɛstɪgən] v/t (h) a) molest, b) (**mit** with) pester, bother. **Be'lästigung** f (-; -en) **1.** molestation, pestering: **sexuelle** ~ sexual harassment. **2.** nuisance.

Be'lastung f (-; -en) **1.** loading (etc, → **belasten**). **2.** ⚡, ✪ load: **zulässige** ~ safe load. **3.** fig. (gen or für) a) (financial etc) burden (to, on), b) worry (to), c) trouble (to), d) (mental) strain (on), stress (on): **er ist zu e-r ~ geworden** he has become a liability. **4.** ✝ (gen) a) charge (to an account), b) encumbrance (of property). **5.** ✠✠, pol. incrimination. **Be'lastungs|materi,al** n ✠✠ incriminating evidence. **~probe** f **1.** ✪ load test. **2.** fig. (severe) test. **~zeuge** m, **~zeugin** f witness for the prosecution.

belaubt [bə'laʊpt] adj leafy, in leaf.

be'laufen: sich ~ (belief, belaufen, h) (**auf** acc) amount (to), run up (to), total.

be'lauschen v/t (h) eavesdrop on.

be'leben (h) **I** v/t a) liven up, stimulate, drink etc: a. revive, b) brighten (room): **neu** ~ put new life into. **II sich** ~ street etc: come to life. **be'lebt** adj animated, lively, busy (street etc).

Beleg [bə'le:k] m (-[e]s; -e) **1.** esp. ✝ a) record, b) proof, c) voucher, d) receipt. **2.** ling. a) example, b) reference.

be'legen v/t (h) **1.** a) cover, b) line (a.

brakes): **mit Teppichboden ~** carpet; **mit Schinken** etc ~ put ham etc on; → **belegt 4. 2.** a) occupy (*room* etc), b) reserve (*seat* etc). **3.** *univ.* enrol(l) for (*a subject*). **4.** *sports:* **den ersten (zweiten** etc) **Platz ~** be placed (*or* come in) first (second etc). **5. mit e-r Strafe (Steuer** etc) ~ impose a penalty (tax etc) on. **6.** a) supply evidence for, verify, b) give a reference for (*text, word*); → **belegt 5.**

Be'legexem,plar *n* author's copy.

Be'legschaft *f* (-; -en) personnel, staff, employees, workers, work force.

Be'legschein *m* (-[e]s; -e) voucher.

be'legt *adj* **1.** a) taken, occupied, b) full (up). **2.** 🎵 husky (*voice*), coated (*tongue*). **3.** *teleph.* engaged, *Am.* busy. **4.** *gastr.* **~es Brot** sandwich; **~es Brötchen** filled roll. **5.** documented: **das ist nirgends ~** there is no evidence for that.

be'lehren *v/t* (h) a) instruct, b) inform (**über** *acc* of): **er ist nicht zu ~** he won't listen to reason; **j-n e-s Besseren ~** set s.o. right, *w.s.* open s.o.'s eyes. **be'lehrend** *adj* instructive. **Be'lehrung** *f* (-; -en) a) instruction, b) advice.

beleibt [bə'laɪpt] *adj* corpulent, stout.

beleidigen [bə'laɪdɪɡən] *v/t* (h) offend (*a. fig.*), insult: **ich wollte Sie nicht ~ !** no offen/ce (*Am.* -se) meant! **be'leidigend** *adj* insulting. **Be'leidigung** *f* (-; -en) insult, ⚖ a) slander, b) libel.

be'lesen *adj* well-read.

Be'lesenheit *f* (-; *no pl*) wide reading.

be'leuchten *v/t* (h) light (up), illuminate, *fig.* throw light on.

Be'leuchter *m* (-s; -) *thea.* etc lighting technician.

Be'leuchtung *f* (-; -en) lighting, illumination (*a. fig.*), light(s). **Be'leuchtungskörper** *m* lighting fixture, lamp.

Belgien ['bɛlɡiən] *n* (-s) Belgium.

'Belgier *m* (-s; -), **'Belgierin** *f* (-; -nen), **'belgisch** *adj* Belgian.

belichten [bə'lɪçtən] *v/t* (h) *phot.* expose.

Be'lichtung *f* (-; -en) *phot.* exposure.

Be'lichtungs|auto,matik *f* automatic exposure. **~messer** *m* light meter. **~zeit** *f* exposure (time).

be'lieben (h) **I** *v/t esp. iro.* deign. **II** *v/i* please: **wie es Ihnen beliebt** as you wish. **Be'lieben** *n* (-s) **nach ~** at will; **ganz nach ~** as you like. **be'liebig I** *adj* any ... (you like): **jeder ~e** anyone; **in**

~er Reihenfolge in any order (*you* etc like). **II** *adv* at will: **~ viele** as many as you etc like. **be'liebt** *adj* popular (**bei** with), 🏵 very much in demand: **sich ~ machen bei** ingratiate o.s. with.

Be'liebtheit *f* (-; *no pl*) popularity (**bei** with). **Be'liebtheitsgrad** *m* (-[e]s; *no pl*) popularity (rating).

belief [bə'li:f] *pret of* **belaufen**.

be'liefern *v/t* (h) supply (**mit** with).

Be'lieferung *f* (-; -en) supply.

belieβ [bə'li:s] *pret of* **belassen**.

bellen ['bɛlən] *v/i, v/t* (h) bark.

Belletristik [bɛlə'trɪstɪk] *f* (-; *no pl*) fiction. **belle'tristisch** *adj* belletristic.

belobigen [bə'lo:bɪɡən] *v/t* (h) praise.

Be'lobigung *f* (-; -en) praise.

belog [bə'lo:k] *pret of* **belügen**.

belogen [bə'lo:ɡən] *pp of* **belügen**.

be'lohnen *v/t* (h) reward (**für** for).

Be'lohnung *f* (-; -en) (**zur ~** as a) reward.

belud [bə'lu:t] *pret of* **beladen**.

be'lüften *v/t* (h) ventilate.

Be'lüftung *f* (-; *no pl*) ventilation.

Be'lüftungsanlage *f* ventilation system.

be'lügen *v/t* (belog, belogen, h) **j-n ~** lie to s.o.; **sich selbst ~** deceive o.s.

belustigen [bə'lʊstɪɡən] *v/t* (h) amuse.

Be'lustigung *f* (-; -en) amusement.

bemächtigen [bə'mɛçtɪɡən] **sich j-s (e-r Sache) ~** seize s.o. (s.th.).

be'malen *v/t* (h) paint.

bemängeln [bə'mɛŋəln] *v/t* (h) criticize, fault: **daran ist nichts zu ~** it can't be faulted.

bemannen [bə'manən] *v/t* (h) man: **bemannter Raumflug** manned space flight.

bemänteln [bə'mɛntəln] *v/t* (h) **1.** cover up. **2.** palliate.

bemaß [bə'ma:s] *pret of* **bemessen**.

bemerkbar [bə'mɛrkba:r] *adj* noticeable: **sich ~ machen** draw attention to o.s., show, make itself felt. **be'merken** *v/t* **1.** notice. **2.** remark. **be'merkenswert** *adj* remarkable (**wegen** for).

Be'merkung *f* (-; -en) a) remark, comment, b) note, annotation.

be'messen (bemaß, bemessen, h) **I** *v/t* **1.** (**nach**) a) proportion (to), b) *fig.* measure (by). **2.** a) calculate, b) time. **3.** 🎛 a) dimension, b) rate (*performance*) **4.** fix (*penalty* etc). **II sich ~** be proportioned (etc, → I). **III** *adj* (**knapp**) **~**

beraten

limited; *ihre Zeit ist knapp ~* she is pressed for time.

›emitleiden [bə'mɪtlaɪdən] *v/t* (h) pity.

›e'mitleidenswert *adj* pitiable.

›e'mogeln *v/t* (h) F cheat.

›e'mühen (h) **I** *v/t* trouble (*mit* with, *um* for), call in (*doctor etc*). **II** *sich ~* take trouble (*or* pains) (*mit* over), make an effort, try (hard); *sich ~ um* a) try to get (*a job etc*), apply for (*a post etc*), b) try to help s.o.; *sich um j-n* (*or j-s Gunst*) *~* court s.o.'s favo(u)r; *bemüht sein zu inf* endeavo(u)r to *inf*, be anxious to *inf*; *~ Sie sich nicht!* don't trouble (*or* bother)! **Be'mühung** *f* (-; -en) effort(s), endeavo(u)r(s), trouble.

›emüßigt [bə'my:sɪçt] *adj* *sich ~ fühlen zu inf* feel bound (*or* obliged) to *inf*.

›emuttern [bə'mʊtərn] *v/t* (h) mother.

›e'nachbart *adj* neighbo(u)ring.

›enachrichtigen [bə'na:xrɪçtɪgən] *v/t* (h) (*von* of) inform, notify, ✝ advise.

Be'nachrichtigung *f* (-; -en) notification, ✝ advice.

›enachteiligen [bə'na:xtaɪlɪgən] *v/t* (h) a) put s.o. at a disadvantage, b) discriminate against; (*sozial*) *benachteiligt* underprivileged. **Be'nachteiligung** *f* (-; -en) 1. discrimination (*gen* against). 2. disadvantage, handicap.

›enannt [bə'nant] *pp of* benennen.

›e'nannte *pret of* benennen.

›enebelt [bə'ne:bəlt] *adj* F fig. fuddled.

›enefiz... [bene'fi:ts-] charity (*concert, match, etc*).

›e'nehmen: sich ~ (benahm, benommen, h) behave (*gegenüber* towards): *sich gut ~* behave well, behave o.s.; *sich schlecht ~* behave badly, misbehave; *benimm dich!* behave yourself!

›e'nehmen *n* (-s) 1. behavio(u)r, conduct, manners. 2. *adm. im ~ mit* in agreement with; *sich mit j-m ins ~ setzen* get in touch with s.o.

›e'neiden *v/t* (h) *j-n* (*um et.*) *~* envy s.o. (s.th.). **be'neidenswert** *adj* enviable.

›e'nennen *v/t* (benannte, benannt, h) 1. name, call. 2. fix (*date etc*), nominate (*candidate*): *j-n als Zeugen ~* call s.o. as a witness. **Be'nennung** *f* (-; -en) a) naming, b) name.

›e'netzen *v/t* (h) moisten, sprinkle.

›engel ['bɛŋəl] *m* (-s; -) rascal.

›enommen [bə'nɔmən] *adj* dazed.

Be'nommenheit *f* (-; *no pl*) daze.

benoten [bə'no:tən] *v/t* (h) *ped.* mark, *Am.* grade.

benötigen [bə'nø:tɪgən] *v/t* (h) need: *dringend ~* be in urgent need of.

Be'notung *f* (-; -en) a) marking, *Am.* grading, b) marks, *Am.* grades.

be'nutzen *v/t* (h) a) use, make use of, b) profit by. **Be'nutzer** *m* (-s; -) user.

be'nutzerfreundlich *adj* user-friendly.

Be'nutzung *f* (-; *no pl*) use.

Be'nutzungsgebühr *f* fee, charge.

Benzin [bɛn'tsi:n] *n* (-s; -e) 1. *mot.* petrol, *Am.* gasoline, F gas. 2. 🔧 benzine. **~feuerzeug** *n* fuel lighter. **~fresser** *m* F *mot.* fuel guzzler. **~gutschein** *m* petrol (*Am.* gas) coupon. **~hahn** *m* fuel cock. **~ka‚nister** *m* petrol can, F jerry can. **~leitung** *f* fuel line. **~motor** *m* petrol (*Am.* gasoline) engine. **~pumpe** *f* fuel pump. **~tank** *m* fuel tank. **~uhr** *f* fuel ga(u)ge. **~verbrauch** *m* petrol (*Am.* gasoline) consumption.

Benzol [bɛn'tso:l] *n* (-s; -e) 🔧, 🔧 benzene, benzol.

beobachten [bə'ʔo:baxtən] *v/t* (h) 1. watch, observe. 2. notice. 3. observe (*rule etc*). **Be'obachter** *m* (-s; -) a) observer (*a.* ✗, *pol. etc*), b) onlooker.

Be'obachtung *f* (-; -en) 1. observation. 2. observance (*gen* of).

Be'obachtungsgabe *f* powers of observation. **Be'obachtungsstati‚on** *f* observation station (🔧 ward).

beordern [bə'ʔɔrdərn] *v/t* (h) a) order (*nach* [to go] to), b) summon.

be'packen *v/t* (h) load (*mit* with).

be'pflanzen *v/t* (h) plant (*mit* with).

be'quatschen *v/t* (h) F 1. thrash s.th. out. 2. *j-n ~ zu* talk s.o. into doing s.th.

bequem [bə'kve:m] **I** *adj* 1. comfortable, easy (*a.* ✝ terms *etc*), convenient: *es sich ~ machen* make o.s. comfortable (*or* at home), *fig.* take the easy way out. 2. a) comfort-loving, b) lazy. **II** *adv* 3. easily. **be'quemen: sich ~** (h) deign (*or* bring o.s.) (*et. zu tun* to do s.th.); *sich zu e-r Antwort etc ~* deign to give an answer *etc*. **Be'quemlichkeit** *f* (-; -en) 1. *no pl* comfort, ease. 2. *no pl* indolence. 3. convenience, *pl a.* amenities.

berappen [bə'rapən] *v/t, v/i* (h) F pay.

be'raten (beriet, beraten, h) **I** *v/t* 1. a) advise s.o. (*bei* on), b) discuss: *sich ~*

lassen von consult; **gut (schlecht) ~ sein** be well-(ill-)advised. **II sich mit j-m über et. ~** discuss s.th. with s.o.

be'ratend *adj* advisory. **Be'rater** *m* (-s; -), **Be'raterin** *f* (-; -nen) adviser: **fachmännischer (or fachärztlicher) Berater** consultant. **Be'ratung** *f* (-; -en) **1.** a) discussion (**über** *acc* of) b) consultation. **2.** → **Be'ratungsstelle** *f* information cent/re (*Am.* -er).

be'rauben *v/t* (h) (*gen* of) rob, *fig. a.* deprive.

be'rauschen *v/t* (h) intoxicate: *fig.* **sich ~** get intoxicated (**an** *dat* with).

be'rauschend *adj a. fig.* intoxicating: *iro.* **nicht gerade ~** not so hot.

berechenbar [bə'rɛçənbɑːr] *adj* calculable, *fig.* predictable. **be'rechnen** *v/t* (h) a) calculate (*a. fig.*), b) estimate (**auf** *acc* at), c) † charge (*j-m et.* s.o. s.th.).

be'rechnend *adj fig.* calculating.

Be'rechnung *f* (-; -en) calculation: *fig.* **mit ~** with deliberation.

berechtigen [bə'rɛçtɪgən] (h) **I** *v/t j-n* (**zu e-r Sache**) **~** entitle s.o. (to [do] s.th.), authorize s.o. (to do s.th.). **II** *v/i zu e-r Sache* **~** entitle to s.th.: **zu der Annahme (Hoffnung) ~, daß ...** warrant the assumption (hope) that ... **be'rechtigt** *adj* (**zu** to) a) entitled, authorized, b) justified, c) legitimate (*claim* etc).

Be'rechtigung *f* (-; *no pl*) right (**zu** to), authorization, authority, legitimacy.

be'reden *v/t* (h) **1.** discuss. **2.** → **überreden**. **Beredsamkeit** [bə'reːtzaːmkaɪt] *f* (-; *no pl*) eloquence. **beredt** [bə'reːt] *adj a. fig.* eloquent.

Be'reich *m* (-[e]s; -e) **1.** area. **2.** *fig.* field, sphere, sector: **im ~ des Möglichen liegen** be possible, be within the bounds of possibility; **im sozialen ~** in the social sector, socially; **im persönlichen ~** on the personal side, personally.

bereichern [bə'raɪçərn] *v/t* (h) *a. fig.* enrich (**sich** o.s.). **Be'reicherung** *f* (-; -en) *a. fig.* enrichment.

bereifen [bə'raɪfən] *v/t* (h) put tyres (*Am.* tires) on. **Be'reifung** *f* (-; -en) tyres, *Am.* tires.

be'reinigen *v/t* (h) settle (*quarrel*, † *account*), iron out (*mistake* etc), *statistics*: adjust. **Be'reinigung** *f* (-; *no pl*) settlement, adjustment.

be'reisen *v/t* (h) travel around, tour.

bereit [bə'raɪt] *adj pred* ready, prepared, willing: **sich ~ erklären (or finden) zu** *inf* agree (*or* volunteer) to *inf*; **bist du ~?** (are you) ready?

be'reiten *v/t* (h) **1.** prepare, make (*tea* etc). **2.** cause (*trouble* etc): **j-m Vergnügen ~** give s.o. pleasure.

be'reithalten (*irr, sep,* -ge-, h, → **halten**) **I** *v/t et.* **~** have s.th. ready. **II sich ~** be ready (**für** for).

be'reitliegen *v/i* (*irr, sep,* -ge-, h, → **liegen**) be ready.

be'reitmachen *v/t* (*sep,* -ge-, h) (*a.* **sich ~**) (**zu** for) get ready, prepare (o.s.).

bereits [bə'raɪts] *adv* already.

Be'reitschaft *f* (-; -en) **1.** *no pl* readiness: **in ~ sein → bereitstehen; (sich) in ~ halten → bereithalten. 2.** (police) squad.

Be'reitschafts|arzt *m* duty doctor. **~dienst** *m* standby duty. **~poli,zei** *f* riot police. **~tasche** *f* carrying (*phot.* camera) case.

be'reitstehen *v/i* (*irr, sep,* -ge-, h, → **stehen**) **1.** be ready, ✕ stand by. **2.** be available.

be'reitstellen *v/t* (*sep,* -ge-, h) provide, make *s.th.* available.

Be'reitstellung *f* (-; *no pl*) provision.

be'reitwillig *adj* willing, eager.

Be'reitwilligkeit *f* (-; *no pl*) willingness.

bereuen [bə'rɔɪən] *v/t* (h) regret.

Berg [bɛrk] *m* (-[e]s; -e) mountain (*a. fig.*), hill: *fig.* **~e von** piles of; **~e versetzen** move mountains; **j-m goldene ~e versprechen** promise s.o. the moon; **über den ~ sein** be over the worst; **über alle ~e** off and away; **die Haare standen ihm zu ~e** his hair stood on end; **er hielt damit nicht hinterm ~** he made no bones about it.

berg'ab *adv a. fig.* downhill.

'Bergarbeiter *m* miner.

berg'auf *adv* uphill: *fig.* **es geht wieder ~** things are looking up.

'Berg|bahn *f* mountain railway. **~bau** *m* (-[e]s; *no pl*) mining (industry).

bergen ['bɛrgən] *v/t* (barg, geborgen, h) **1.** a) rescue, b) recover, salvage, c) ✦ take in (*sails*). **2.** contain, hold, *a.* involve (*danger*).

'Bergführer *m* mountain guide.

bergig ['bɛrgɪç] *adj* mountainous.

'Berg|kette *f* mountain range. **~kri,sta...**

m crystallized quartz. **~land** *n* mountainous country. **~mas|siv** *n* massif. **~predigt** *f bibl.* Sermon on the Mount. **~rücken** *m* (mountain) ridge. **~schuh** *m* mountaineering boot. **~spitze** *f* mountain peak. **~steigen** *n* (-s) mountaineering. **~steiger** *m* (-s; -) mountaineer. **~straße** *f* mountain road. **~tour** *f* mountain tour.

Berg-und-'Tal-Bahn *f* switchback (railway), *Am.* roller coaster.

Bergung *f* (-; -en) a) rescue, b) recovery, salvage.

Bergungs|arbeiten *pl* rescue work, salvage operations. **~dienst** *m* recovery (*or* salvage) service. **~fahrzeug** *n* recovery (✈ crash) vehicle. **~mannschaft** *f* rescue party, ⚓ salvage crew.

Berg|wacht *f* (-; *no pl*) mountain rescue service. **~wanderung** *f* mountain hike. **~werk** *n* (-[e]s; -e) mine.

Bericht [bə'rɪçt] *m* (-[e]s; -e) (*über acc*) report (on), account (of): **(j-m) ~ erstatten** report (to s.o.). **be'richten** *v/t, v/i* (h) report (*über acc* on, *j-n* to s.o.), relate: **j-m et. ~** inform s.o. of s.th.

Be'richterstatter *m* (-s; -) reporter, *abroad:* correspondent, *radio, TV a.* commentator.

Be'richterstattung *f* (-; -en) a) reporting, *a.* coverage (*by the press*), b) report, *radio, TV a.* commentary.

berichtigen [bə'rɪçtɪgən] *v/t* (h) correct (*sich* o.s.), rectify (*s.th.*), ⊙ *a.* adjust.

Be'richtigung *f* (-; -en) correction, ⊙ *a.* adjustment.

Be'richtsjahr *n* ✝ year under review.

be'riechen *v/t* (beroch, berochen, h) sniff at.

berief [bə'riːf] *pret of* **berufen.**

be'rieseln *v/t* (h) irrigate, sprinkle.

Be'rieselung *f* (-; *no pl*) **1.** irrigation, sprinkling. **2.** F *fig.* constant exposure (**mit Musik** *etc* to music *etc*).

beriet [bə'riːt] *pret of* **beraten.**

beritten [bə'rɪtən] *adj* mounted.

Berliner[1] [bɛr'liːnər] I *m* (-s; -) Berliner. II *adj* (of) Berlin.

Ber'liner[2] *m* (-s; -) *gastr.* doughnut.

Bernhardiner [bɛrnhar'diːnər] *m* (-s; -) St. Bernard (dog).

Bernstein ['bɛrn-] *m* (-[e]s; *no pl*) amber.

beroch [bə'rɔx] *pret of* **beriechen.**

berochen [bə'rɔxən] *pp of* **beriechen.**

bersten ['bɛrstən] *v/i* (barst, geborsten, sn) burst (*fig.* **vor** *dat* with).

berüchtigt [bə'rʏçtɪçt] *adj* notorious (**wegen** for).

berücksichtigen [bə'rʏksɪçtɪgən] *v/t* (h) consider, take *s.th.* into consideration, bear *s.th.* in mind, allow for. **Be'rücksichtigung** *f* (-; *no pl*) consideration: **unter ~ s-s Alters** considering his age.

Beruf [bə'ruːf] *m* (-[e]s; -e) a) occupation, F job, b) profession, c) trade, d) business, e) line: **von ~** by profession, by trade. **be'rufen** (berief, berufen, h) **I** *v/t j-n ~* appoint s.o. (**zu e-m Amt** to a office, **zum Vorsitzenden** chairman). **II sich ~ auf** (*acc*) cite; **sich auf ~** a) rely on, ~ plead (*ignorance etc*); **sich darauf ~, daß ...** plead that ...; **darf ich mich auf Sie ~?** may I mention your name? **III** *adj* qualified: **sich ~ fühlen zu** inf feel called upon to inf; **aus ~em Munde** from a competent authority.

be'ruflich *adj* professional, vocational.

Be'rufs|ausbildung *f* vocational training. **~aussichten** *pl* career prospects. **~berater(in** *f)* *m* vocational adviser. **~beratung** *f* vocational guidance. **~bild** *n* job description. **~erfahrung** *f* (vocational) experience. **~fachschule** *f* vocational college. **~geheimnis** *n* professional secret (*as duty:* secrecy). **~krankheit** *f* occupational disease. **~leben** *n* professional (*or* active) life. **~risiko** *n* occupational hazard. **~schule** *f* vocational school. **~sol|dat** *m* regular (soldier). **~spieler** *m sports:* professional (player). **~sportler(in** *f)* *m* professional. **~stand** *m* profession. **⏚tätig** *adj* a) working, b) employed. **~tätige** *m, f* (-n; -n) working person. **~verbot** *n* disqualification from a profession. **~verkehr** *m* rush-hour traffic.

Be'rufung *f* (-; -en) **1.** calling. **2.** appointment (**zu** to). **3. unter ~ auf** (*acc*) with reference to. **4.** ⚖️ (**~ einlegen** file an) appeal (**bei** with, **gegen** from).

Be'rufungsgericht *n*, **Be'rufungsin,stanz** *f* ⚖️ court of appeal.

Be'rufungsverfahren *n* ⚖️ **1.** appeal proceedings. **2.** appellate procedure.

be'ruhen *v/i* (h) **1. ~ auf** (*dat*) a) rest on, be based on, b) be due to. **2. et. auf sich ~ lassen** let s.th. rest; **lassen wir die Sache auf sich ~!** let's leave it at that!

beruhigen [bə'ru:ɪgən] **I** v/t (h) a) reassure, b) calm (down): **~ Sie sich doch!** calm down!; **seien Sie beruhigt, ich werde ...** rest assured I'll ...; **wenn Sie das beruhigt** if that puts your mind at rest. **II sich ~** calm down, *situation:* quieten down. **be'ruhigend** *adj* **1.** reassuring. **2.** ⚕ sedative.

Be'ruhigung f (-; -en) **1.** no pl calming (down), of *situation: a.* stabilization: **sie braucht et. zur ~** she needs s.th. to calm her down. **2.** reassurance: **zu d-r ~** to put your mind at rest.

Be'ruhigungs|mittel n, **~pille** f ⚕ sedative, *fig.* soporific. **~spritze** f sedative injection.

berühmt [bə'ry:mt] *adj* famous (**wegen** for): F *fig.* **das ist nicht gerade ~!** that's nothing to write home about!

Be'rühmtheit f (-; -en) **1.** no pl fame: **~ erlangen** become famous. **2.** celebrity.

be'rühren (h) **I** v/t **1.** touch, *fig. a.* affect: **j-n (un)angenehm ~** (dis)please s.o.; **~ peinlich 3. 2.** *fig.* touch (up)on (*subject*), concern (*s.o.'s interests*). **II sich ~** touch, *fig. a.* meet. **Be'rührung** f (-; -en) **1.** touch. **2.** contact: **in ~ kommen mit** come into contact with.

Be'rührungspunkt m point of contact.

be'sagen v/t (h) say, mean: **das besagt (noch) gar nichts!** that doesn't mean anything! **be'sagt** adj adm. aforesaid.

besah [bə'za:] pret of **besehen**.

besamen [bə'za:mən] v/t (h) inseminate, ⚕ pollinate.

Besan [be'za:n] m (-s; -e) ⚓ miz(z)en.

besänftigen [bə'zɛnftɪgən] v/t (h) (*a. sich ~*) calm down: **j-n ~** placate s.o.

besang [bə'zaŋ] pret of **besingen**.

besann [bə'zan] pret of **besinnen**.

besaß [bə'za:s] pret of **besitzen**.

besät [bə'zɛ:t] adj fig. covered (**mit** with).

Besatz [bə'zats] m (-es; ⸚e) trimming(s).

Be'satzung f (-; -en) **1.** ⚔ a) occupying forces, b) garrison. **2.** ✈, ⚓ crew.

Be'satzungs|macht f occupying power. **~streitkräfte** pl occupying forces.

be'saufen: sich ~ (besoff, besoffen, h) F get sloshed. **Be'säufnis** [bə'zɔyfnɪs] n (-ses; -se) F booze-up.

be'schädigen v/t (h) damage. **Be'schädigung** f (-; -en) **1.** damaging. **2.** a. pl damage (**gen** to).

be'schaffen v/t (h) j-m et. ~ get (or procure) s.o. s.th.; (*sich*) et. ~ get s.th.

Be'schaffenheit f (-; no pl) condition state, quality, nature.

Be'schaffung f (-; no pl) procurement

beschäftigen [bə'ʃɛftɪgən] (h) **I** v/t **1.** j-n ~ occupy s.o., keep s.o. busy. **2.** employ. **3.** occupy, *problem:* preoccupy, be on *s.o.'s* mind. **II sich ~** (**mit**) b busy (with), work (at); **sich mit e-m Problem** etc ~ deal with a problem etc **be'schäftigt** adj **1.** busy. **2.** employee (**bei** with). **Be'schäftigte** m, f (-; -n; employee. **Be'schäftigung** f (-; -en) **1.** occupation, work, activity: **sie muß haben** she must have s.th. to do. **2.** employment, job: **ohne ~** unemployed out of work. **Be'schäftigungsthera ,pie** f occupational therapy.

be'schälen v/t (h) cover (*mare*).

be'schämen v/t (h) j-n ~ a) shame s.o. b) put s.o. to shame. **be'schämend** ad shameful. **be'schämt** adj ashamed (*über acc* of). **Be'schämung** f (-; no pl shame: **zu m-r ~** to my shame.

be'schatten v/t (h) fig. shadow.

be'schauen v/t (h) (a. sich et. ~) (have a look at. **be'schaulich** adj contemplative, tranquil.

Bescheid [bə'ʃaɪt] m (-[e]s; -e) answer adm. notice, information (**über** ac about): **~ bekommen** be informed; **j-n ~ geben** let s.o. know (**über** acc about) F **j-m ~ stoßen**, **j-m gehörig ~ sage** give s.o. a piece of one's mind; **~ wis sen** a) be informed (**über** acc of), b **mit, in** (dat) know all about, c) be in the know, iro. know the score.

bescheiden[1] [bə'ʃaɪdən] (beschied, be schieden, h) **I** v/t **1.** adm. notify: **~ abschlägig. 2. es war ihm nich beschieden zu** inf it was not granted to him to inf. **II sich ~** be conten (**mit** with).

be'scheiden[2] adj a. fig. modest.

Be'scheidenheit f (-; no pl) modesty.

be'scheinen v/t (beschien, beschienen h) shine on.

bescheinigen [bə'ʃaɪnɪgən] v/t (h) certi fy: **j-m et. ~** a. iro. attest s.o. s.th.; **de Empfang ~** (gen or von) a) acknowl edge receipt of, b) give a receipt for **hiermit wird bescheinigt, daß ...** this i to certify that ...

Be'scheinigung f (-; -en) **1.** no pl attestation, certification. **2.** certificate.
be'scheißen v/t (beschiß, beschissen, h) V **j-n ~** cheat (or do) s.o. (**um** out of).
be'schenken· v/t (h) **j-n ~** give s.o. a present; **j-n mit et. ~** give s.o. s.th.
be'scheren v/t (h) **j-m et. ~** give (fig. bring) s.o. s.th. **Be'scherung** f (-; -en) distribution of (Christmas) presents; fig. **e-e schöne ~!** a fine mess!; **da haben wir die ~!** there you are!; F **die ganze ~** the whole bag of tricks.
bescheuert [bə'ʃɔʏərt] → **bekloppt.**
be'schichten v/t (h) ⚙ coat.
be'schicken v/t (h) **1.** exhibit at (a fair). **2.** send delegates to. **3.** ⚙ charge.
beschied [bə'ʃiːt] pret, beschieden [bə'ʃiːdən] pp of **bescheiden¹.**
beschien [bə'ʃiːn] pret, be'schienen pp of **bescheinen.**
be'schießen v/t (beschoß, beschossen, h) a) fire at, b) bombard (a. phys.).
be'schildern v/t (h) signpost.
Be'schilderung f (-; -en) **1.** signposting. **2.** signposts.
be'schimpfen v/t (h) call s.o. names.
Be'schimpfung f (-; -en) abuse.
beschiß [bə'ʃɪs] V pret of **bescheißen.**
Be'schiß m (-sses; no pl) V **1.** swindle, rip-off. **2.** frost. **be'schissen** V I pp of **bescheißen.** II adj lousy, rotten.
Be'schlag m (-[e]s; ⸚e) **1.** usu. pl metal fitting(s). **2.** a) condensation, b) film. **3.** **in ~ nehmen, mit ~ belegen** F grab, monopolize. **be'schlagen** (beschlug, beschlagen, h) I v/t **1.** put metal fittings on. **2.** shoe (a horse). **3.** steam up. II **sich ~** a) mirror etc: steam up, b) metal: oxidize, c) go mo(u)ldy. III adj **gut ~ sein in** (dat) be well up in.
Be'schlagenheit f (-; no pl) sound knowledge (**in** dat of).
Beschlagnahme [bə'ʃlaːknaːmə] f (-; -n) seizure, confiscation.
be'schlagnahmen v/t (h) **1.** seize, confiscate. **2.** → **Beschlag** 3.
be'schleunigen [bə'ʃlɔʏnɪgən] v/t, v/i (h) (a. **sich ~**) accelerate (a. mot., phys.), speed up: **s-e Schritte ~** quicken one's steps; **das Tempo ~** speed up.
Be'schleuniger m (-s; -) ⚙, phys. accelerator. **Be'schleunigung** f (-; -en) acceleration (a. mot., phys.), speeding up.
Be'schleunigungs|spur f mot. acceleration lane. **~vermögen** n (-s; no pl) mot. acceleration.
be'schließen v/t (beschloß, beschlossen, h) **1.** (**zu** inf to inf) decide, make up one's mind. **2.** close, end, settle.
be'schlossen adj agreed, settled.
beschlug [bə'ʃluːk] pret of **beschlagen.**
Be'schluß m (-sses; ⸚sse) decision, resolution: **e-n ~ fassen** parl. pass a resolution. **be'schlußfähig** adj **~ sein** constitute a quorum; **die Versammlung** etc **ist** (**nicht**) **~** there is a (no) quorum.
be'schmieren v/t (h) smear.
be'schmutzen v/t (h) dirty, soil, fig. sully; → **Nest** 1.
be'schneiden v/t (beschnitt, beschnitten, h) **1.** trim, prune, cut. **2.** ⚕ circumcise. **3.** fig. cut (down), curtail.
Be'schneidung f (-; -en) **1.** trimming (etc). **2.** ⚕ circumcision. **3.** fig. curtailment, cut, reduction.
be'schnüffeln v/t (h), be'schnuppern v/t (h) sniff at: F fig. **sich** (**gegenseitig**) **~** take stock of each other.
beschönigen [bə'ʃøːnɪgən] v/t (h) palliate, gloss over: **~d** palliative.
Be'schönigung f (-; -en) palliation.
beschoß [bə'ʃɔs] pret, be'schossen pp of **beschießen.**
beschränken [bə'ʃrɛŋkən] (h) I v/t (**auf** acc to) limit, restrict. II **sich ~ auf** (acc) confine o.s. to, be: be confined to.
be'schränkt adj **1.** limited, restricted. **2.** contp. a) dense, b) narrow-minded.
Be'schränktheit f (-; no pl) **1.** limitedness. **2.** contp. stupidity, narrow-mindedness. **Be'schränkung** f (-; -en) (**auf** acc) limitation, restriction.
be'schreiben v/t (beschrieb, beschrieben, h) **1.** write on. **2.** describe (a. ⎇): **nicht zu ~** indescribable.
Be'schreibung f (-; -en) **1.** (**das spottet jeder ~** that beggars) description. **2.** ⚙ specification.
be'schreiten v/t (beschritt, beschritten, h) walk on: fig. **neue Wege ~** tread new paths.
beschrieb [bə'ʃriːp] pret, beschrieben [bə'ʃriːbən] pp of **beschreiben.**
beschriften [bə'ʃrɪftən] v/t (h) a) inscribe, b) mark (boxes), label (goods).
Be'schriftung f (-; -en) inscription.
beschritt [bə'ʃrɪt] pret, be'schritten pp of **beschreiten.**

beschuldigen [bə'ʃʊldɪɡən] v/t (h) **j-n ~** accuse s.o. (gen of). **Be'schuldigte** m, f (-n; -n) accused. **Be'schuldigung** f (-; -en) accusation, charge.

be'schummeln v/t (h) F **j-n** (**um et.**) **~** cheat s.o. (out of s.th.).

Be'schuß m (-sses; no pl) fire, bombardment (a. phys.): **unter ~ geraten** a. fig. come under fire; **unter ~ nehmen** a) → **beschießen**, b) fig. attack.

be'schützen v/t (h) protect (**vor** dat, **gegen** from). **Be'schützer** m (-s; -) protector. **Be'schützerin** f (-; -nen) protectress.

be'schwatzen v/t (h) **j-n ~, et. zu tun** coax s.o. to do (or into doing) s.th.

Beschwerde [bə'ʃveːrdə] f (-; -n) **1.** trouble, ✄ usu. pl complaint: **sein Herz macht ihm ~n** his heart is giving him trouble. **2.** complaint (**über** acc about). ⚖ appeal (**gegen** from). **~buch** n complaints book. **2frei** adj ✄ free of pain. **~führer(in** f) m ⚖ complainant.

beschweren [bə'ʃveːrən] **I** v/t **1.** weight. **2.** fig. weigh down. **II sich ~** complain (**über** acc about, of, **bei** to).

be'schwerlich adj onerous, tiring.

beschwichtigen [bə'ʃvɪçtɪɡən] v/t (h) appease (a. pol.), calm down, placate. **Be'schwichtigungspoli,tik** f policy of appeasement.

be'schwindeln v/t (h) **j-n ~** lie to s.o.

beschwingt [bə'ʃvɪŋt] adj elated, buoyant, lively, lilting (melody).

be'schwipst adj F tipsy, merry.

be'schwören v/t (beschwor, beschworen, h) **1.** esp. ⚖ swear to. **2.** a) conjure up (ghosts, a. fig.), b) exorcize. **3.** implore s.o. **Be'schwörung** f (-; -en) **1.** entreaty. **2.** a) invocation, b) exorcism.

beseelt [bə'zeːlt] adj (**von** with) inspired, filled.

be'sehen v/t (besah, besehen, h) (a. **sich et. ~**) have a look at, examine.

beseitigen [bə'zaɪtɪɡən] v/t (h) remove, dispose of, fig. a. eliminate: **j-n ~** do away with s.o. **Be'seitigung** f (-; no pl) removal, disposal, fig. a. elimination.

Besen ['beːzən] m (-s; -) **1.** broom, brush; fig. **neue ~ kehren gut** a new broom sweeps clean; F **ich fresse e-n ~, wenn ...** I'll eat my hat if ... **2.** contp. (old) hag. **'Besenstiel** m broomstick.

besessen [bə'zɛsən] **I** pp of **besitzen. II**

adj **1.** (**von**) possessed (by), fig. a. obsessed (with). **2.** frantic: **wie ~** like mad. **Be'sessenheit** f (-; no pl) fig. obsession.

be'setzen v/t (h) **1.** take (a seat), occupy (country, house, etc). **2.** fill (a post): **wir wollen diesen Posten mit e-r Frau ~** we want to put a woman in this position. **3.** thea. cast: **neu ~** recast. **4.** trim (dress (**mit** with). **be'setzt** adj **1.** occupied (a. ✕, pol.), seat: a. taken, bus etc: full (up). **2.** thea. **das Stück ist gut besetzt** the play is well cast. **3.** teleph. engaged, Am. busy. **4.** ⚖ **~ mit** court etc composed of. **Be'setztzeichen** n teleph. engaged (Am. busy) signal.

Be'setzung f (-; -en) **1.** occupation. **2.** a) filling (of post), b) staff, c) composition (of court, team), d) entrants. **3.** thea. a) casting, b) cast.

besichtigen [bə'zɪçtɪɡən] v/t (h) view, inspect, visit, see: **zu ~ sein** be on view. **Be'sichtigung** f (-; -en) inspection (a. ✕), visit (gen to): **~ von Sehenswürdigkeiten** sight-seeing.

be'siedeln v/t (h) settle, colonize: **dicht (dünn) besiedelt** densely (sparsely) populated. **Be'sied(e)lung** f (-; -en) settlement, colonization.

be'siegeln v/t (h) a. fig. seal.

be'siegen v/t (h) defeat, beat, fig. overcome, conquer. **Be'siegte** m, f (-n; -n) the defeated, loser.

be'singen v/t (besang, besungen, h) **1.** sing (of). **2.** e-e Platte etc ~ make a record etc.

be'sinnen: sich ~ (besann, besonnen, h) **1.** reflect, think: **ohne sich zu ~** without thinking twice; **sich anders ~** change one's mind; **sich e-s Besseren ~** think better of it. **2.** **sich auf j-n** (et.) **~** remember s.o. (s.th.).

be'sinnlich adj contemplative.

Be'sinnung f (-; no pl) **1.** (**die ~ verlieren** lose) consciousness; **wieder zur ~ kommen** regain consciousness, fig come to one's senses; **fig. j-n zur ~ bringen** bring s.o. to his senses. **2.** (**auf** acc) contemplation (of), reflection (on).

be'sinnungslos adj unconscious.

Be'sinnungslosigkeit f (-; no pl) unconsciousness.

Besitz [bə'zɪts] m (-es; no pl) **1.** possession (gen, **an** dat, **von** of): **~ ergreifen von** a) **. in ~ nehmen** take possession

Bestand

of, b) *fig.* take hold of *s.o.*; **im ~ sein von** (*or gen*) be in possession of; → **gelangen** 1. **2.** possession(s), property, estate. **be'sitzanzeigend** *adj* **~es Fürwort** possessive pronoun. **besitzen** *v/t* (besaß, besessen, h) possess, own, have. **Be'sitzer** *m* (-s; -), **Be'sitzerin** *f* (-; -nen) possessor, owner, holder (*of passport etc*): **den Besitzer wechseln** change hands. **Be'sitzergreifung** *f* (-; *no pl*) **(von** *of*) taking possession, seizure. **be'sitzlos** *adj* unpropertied. **Be'sitztum** *n* (-s; ⸚er), **Be'sitzung** *f* (-; -en) possession(s), property, estate.

besoff [bə'zɔf] *pret of* **besaufen**.
be'soffen I *pp of* **besaufen**. **II** *adj* F sloshed, plastered.
besohlen [bə'zo:lən] *v/t* (h) sole.
besolden [bə'zɔldən] *v/t* (h) pay.
be'soldet *adj* salaried.
Be'soldung *f* (-; -en) pay, salary.
besonder [bə'zɔndər] *adj* **1.** a) special, particular, specific, b) exceptional, great (*joy, hono[u]r*): **nichts Besonderes** nothing unusual; **in diesem ~en Fall** in this particular case. **2.** separate. **Be'sonderheit** *f* (-; -en) special quality (*or* feature). **be'sonders** *adv* **1.** especially, particularly, above all. **2.** exceptionally. **3.** very much.
besonnen [bə'zɔnən] *pp of* **besinnen**. **II** *adj* sensible, level-headed, calm. **Be'sonnenheit** *f* (-; *no pl*) level-headedness, prudence.
be'sorgen *v/t* (h) **1.** *j-m et.* ~ get s.o. s.th., provide s.o. s.th.; **sich et. ~** get (*or* buy) s.th.; F **dem werde ich's ~!** I'll give him what for! **2.** see to, deal with, manage (*household*): F **wird besorgt!** will do! **Besorgnis** [bə'zɔrknɪs] *f* (-; -se) anxiety. **be'sorgniserregend** *adj* alarming, worrying. **be'sorgt I** *pp of* **besorgen**. **II** *adj* (**um** about) worried, concerned. **Be'sorgtheit** *f* (-; *no pl*) **1.** anxiety. **2.** (**um** for) solicitude, concern. **Be'sorgung** *f* (-; -en) **1.** *no pl* procurement. **2.** a) purchase, b) errand: **~en machen** go shopping. **3.** *no pl* (*gen*) dealing (with), management (of).
be'spannen *v/t* (h) **1.** cover (*with silk etc*). **2.** string (*violin etc*). **Be'spannung** *f* (-; -en) **1.** cover. **2.** strings.
be'spielen *v/t* (h) **ein Tonband** *etc* (**mit et.**) ~ record (*s.th.*) on tape *etc*.

be'spielt *adj* prerecorded (*cassette etc*).
be'spitzeln *v/t* (h) *j-n* ~ spy on s.o.
be'sprechen *v/t* (besprach, besprochen, h) **1.** discuss, talk *s.th.* over: **sich mit j-m** ~ discuss the matter (*or* talk things over) with s.o. **2.** review. **3.** record *s.th.* on *tape etc*. **4.** ⚕ cure by magic formulas. **Be'sprechung** *f* (-; -en) **1.** discussion. **2.** meeting, conference: **er ist in e-r** ~ he is in conference. **3.** review.
Be'sprechungsexem,plar *n* review copy.
be'sprengen *v/t* (h) sprinkle, spray.
be'spritzen *v/t* (h) spatter, splash.
besprochen [bə'ʃprɔxən] *pp of* **besprechen**.
be'spucken *v/t* (h) spit at, spit on.
besser ['bɛsər] *adj and adv* better (**als** than): *contp.* **e-e ~e Scheune** a glorified barn; **immer ~** better and better; **um so ~** so much the better; (**oder**) ~ **gesagt** or rather; ~ **ist ~** let's keep on the safe side; ~ **werden** improve, get better; **es geht ihm heute ~** he is better today; **es geht** (**wirtschaftlich**) ~ things are looking up; **er ist ~ dran als ich** he is better off than me; **ich weiß es ~** I know better; **er täte ~** (**daran**) **zu gehen** he had better go; **Besseres zu tun haben** have more important things to do; **j-n e-s Besseren belehren** set s.o. right, *w.s.* open s.o.'s eyes; → **besinnen** 1, **Hälfte**.
'bessergestellt *adj* better-off.
'bessern (h) **I** *v/t* **1.** improve. **2.** reform (*s.o.*). **II sich** ~ **3.** improve. **4.** mend one's ways.
'Besserung *f* (-; *no pl*) improvement: ⚕ **auf dem Wege der** ~ on the way to recovery; **gute ~!** hope you feel better soon!
'Besserwisser *m* (-s; -) know-(it-)all.
bestach [bə'ʃtax] *pret of* **bestechen**.
bestahl [bə'ʃta:l] *pret of* **bestehlen**.
Bestallung [bə'ʃtalʊŋ] *f* (-; -en) appointment.
bestand [bə'ʃtant] *pret of* **bestehen**.
Be'stand *m* (-[e]s; ⸚e) **1.** *no pl* a) (continued) existence, b) duration: **von ~ sein**, ~ **haben** be lasting, last; **k-n** ~ **haben** be short-lived, ⚖ not to be valid (in law). **2.** (**an** *dat*) stock, supplies, ⚘, *zo.* population; → **eisern**. **3.** ⚕ a) assets, b) (stock) holdings, c) cash in hand, d)

stock on hand, e) inventory. **4.** rolling stock, fleet. **5.** ✕ (effective) strength.

bestanden [bə'ʃtandən] *pp of* **bestehen.**

be'ständig *adj* **1.** constant, lasting. **2.** steady (*a.* ✝ *demand etc*), stable, settled (*weather*). **3.** resistant (*gegen* to).

Be'ständigkeit *f* (-; *no pl*) **1.** constancy, lastingness. **2.** steadiness, stability. **3.** resistance (*gegen* to).

Be'standsaufnahme *f* (-; -n) ✝ stock-taking, *Am.* inventory: **e-e ~ machen** *a. fig.* take stock.

Be'standteil *m* (-[e]s; -e) a) part, component, constituent (part), b) element, c) ingredient: → **auflösen** 1.

be'stärken *v/t* (h) (*in dat* in) a) confirm, strengthen, b) encourage.

bestätigen [bə'ʃtɛːtɪgən] (h) **I** *v/t* a) confirm (*a.* ✝ *an order*), b) acknowledge (receipt of), c) certify. **II sich ~** be confirmed, prove true.

Be'stätigung *f* (-; -en) **1.** confirmation, acknowledgement. **2.** a) letter of confirmation, b) certificate.

bestatten [bə'ʃtatən] *v/t* (h) bury.

Be'stattung *f* (-; -en) funeral, burial.

Be'stattungsinsti,tut *n* undertakers, *Am.* funeral home.

be'stäuben *v/t* (h) **1.** dust, spray. **2.** ❀ pollinate. **Be'stäubung** *f* (-; -en) **1.** spraying, dusting. **2.** ❀ pollination.

be'staunen *v/t* (h) marvel at.

beste ['bɛstə] *adj and adv* best: **mein ~r Freund** my best friend; **der (die) erste ~** the first comer; **das erste ~** the first thing; **am ~n wissen** *etc* know *etc* best; **am ~n, wir besuchen ihn** the best thing to do would be to call on him; **im ~n Fall** at best; **im ~n Alter, in den ~n Jahren** in the prime of life; **in ~m Zustand** in perfect condition; **mit ~m Dank** with many thanks; **(von) ~r Qualität** of first-class quality; **e-e Geschichte (ein Lied) zum ~n geben** tell a story (oblige with a song); **j-n zum ~n haben** pull s.o.'s leg; **sein Bestes tun** (*or* **geben**) do one's best; **das Beste daraus machen** make the best of it; **... sind nicht die ~n** ... are not of the best; → **bestens, Kraft** 1.

be'stechen *v/t* (h) (*bestach, bestochen, h*) **1.** bribe: **sich ~ lassen** take bribes. **2.** *fig. a. v/i* impress (*durch* by). **be'stechend** *adj fig.* impressive, brilliant.

be'stechlich *adj* corrupt(ible).

Be'stechlichkeit *f* (-; *no pl*) corruptibility. **Be'stechung** *f* (-; -en) bribery: **passive ~** taking of bribes.

Be'stechungsgeld *n* bribe money. **~versuch** *m* attempted bribery.

Be'stechungs|af,färe *f* corruption scandal. **~geld** *n* bribe money. **~versuch** *m* attempted bribery.

Besteck *n* (-[e]s; -e) **1.** knife, fork and spoon, *coll. or* **~e** cutlery. **2.** ✚ (set of) instruments.

be'stehen (bestand, bestanden, h) **I** *v/t* **1.** go (*or* come) through, win (*fight*), pass (*exam*): **nicht ~** fail; *fig.* **die Probe ~** stand the test. **II** *v/i* **2.** a) exist, be, b) continue, last, c) remain, survive, have survived. **3. ~ aus** be made of, consist of (*a. fig.*). **4. ~ auf** (*dat*) insist on; **ich bestehe darauf(, daß du kommst) I** insist (on your coming). **5.** pass.

Be'stehen *n* (-s) **1.** existence: **seit ~ der Firma** ever since the firm was founded; **das 50jährige ~ feiern** celebrate the fiftieth anniversary. **2.** passing. **3.** insistence (*auf dat* on).

be'stehenbleiben *v/i* (*irr, sep,* -ge-, *sn,* → **bleiben**) continue (to exist), survive.

be'stehend *adj* existing, present.

be'stehlen *v/t* (*bestahl, bestohlen, h*) rob, steal from.

be'steigen *v/t* (*bestieg, bestiegen, h*) climb (up), ascend (*mountain etc*), mount (*horse etc*), board (*train etc*).

Be'steigung *f* (-; -en) ascent.

Bestellbuch [bə'ʃtɛl-] *n* ✝ order book.

be'stellen *v/t* (h) **1.** order (*a.* ✝), book (*room*), call (*taxi*). **2. j-n (zu sich)** ~ ask s.o. to come, send (*or* send) s.o. **3. j-m e-e Nachricht** *etc* ~ give (*or* send) s.o. a message *etc*; **kann ich et. ~?** can I take a message? **4.** ✔ cultivate. **5.** → **ernennen. 6. es ist schlecht um ihn etc bestellt** things are looking bad for him *etc*. **7.** F *fig.* **er hat nicht viel zu ~** he doesn't rate high (*bei* with).

Be'steller *m* (-s; -) ✝ orderer, buyer.

Be'stell|karte *f*, **~schein** *m* order form.

Be'stellung *f* (-; -en) **1.** order: **auf ~ gemacht** made to order, *Am.* custom-made. **2.** message. **3.** ✔ cultivation. **4.** → **Ernennung.**

'besten'falls *adv* at best.

'bestens *adv* extremely well: **(ich) danke ~!** thank you very much!; F **ist ja ~!** that's just great!

be'steuern v/t (h) tax.

Be'steuerung f (-; -en) taxation.

bestialisch [bɛsˈtiːalɪʃ] adj atrocious, F fig. a. awful.

Bestie [ˈbɛstiə] f (-; -n) beast, fig. brute.

bestieg [bəˈʃtiːk] pret, **bestiegen** [bəˈʃtiːɡən] pp of **besteigen**.

be'stimmen (h) **I** v/t **1.** a) determine, b) decide, c) fix (date, price, etc). **2.** order, decide: **er hat (dabei) nichts zu ~** he has no say (in this matter). **3.** contract, law: provide. **4.** determine (a policy etc): **bestimmt werden durch** (or **von**) be determined by, depend on. **5.** intend (**für, zu** for): **j-n zu s-m Nachfolger ~** name s.o. as one's successor; → **bestimmt** 3. **6.** a) phys. etc: determine, b) define. **II** v/i **7.** give orders: **hier bestimme ich!** F I'm the boss here! **8.** ~ **über** (acc) dispose over.

be'stimmend adj determinant (factor etc), ling. determinative.

be'stimmt I pp of **bestimmen**. **II** adj **1.** a) certain (day, number, etc), b) special (plan etc), c) definite: **et. Bestimmtes** something (or anything) special (or definite). **2.** determined, firm. **3.** ~ **sein a**) **für** be meant for, b) **zu et.** be destined for (or to be). **4.** (**nach** for) 🕆 destined, ✈, ⚓ bound. **II** adv **5.** certainly, for certain: (**ganz**) ~ definitely; ~ **wissen, daß** know for sure that; **er kommt ~** he is sure to come; **ich kann es nicht ~ sagen** I can't tell with certainty. **6.** firmly, categorically.

Be'stimmtheit f (-; no pl) a) certainty, b) firmness: **mit ~** → **bestimmt** II.

Be'stimmung f (-; -en) **1.** no pl (gen) decision (on), fixing (of date etc). **2.** regulation, rule, provision. **3.** a) phys., etc: determination, b) definition. **4.** no pl intended purpose: **et. s-r ~ übergeben** inaugurate s.th., open s.th. to the public. **5.** ling. qualification: **adverbiale ~** adverbial element. **6.** no pl fate, destiny.

Be'stimmungs|bahnhof m station of destination. **2gemäß** adj and adv as directed. **~flughafen** m airport of destination. **~ort** m (place of) destination.

Bestleistung f sports: best performance: **persönliche ~** personal best.

Bestmarke f sports: record.

best'möglich adj best possible.

---

bestochen [bəˈʃtɔxən] pp of **bestechen**.

bestohlen [bəˈʃtoːlən] pp of **bestehlen**.

be'strafen v/t (h) punish (**wegen, für** for), a. sports: penalize, ⚖ a. sentence (**mit** to). **Be'strafung** f (-; -en) punishment, a. sports: penalty.

be'strahlen v/t (h) **1.** shine on, illuminate. **2.** phys. irradiate, ⚕ a. give s.o. ray treatment. **Be'strahlung** f (-; -en) phys. irradiation, ⚕ a. ray treatment.

bestrebt [bəˈʃtreːpt] adj ~ **sein zu** inf endeavo(u)r (or strive, be anxious) to inf. **Be'strebung** f (-; -en) effort, endeavo(u)r.

be'streichen v/t (bestrich, bestrichen, h) ~ **mit** spread s.th. on; **mit Butter ~** butter.

be'streiken v/t (h) go out (or be) on strike against. **be'streikt I** pp of **bestreiken**. **II** adj strike-bound.

be'streiten v/t (bestritt, bestritten, h) **1.** a) dispute, contest, b) deny. **2.** bear, meet, pay (for) (expenses etc). **3.** fill (program[me]): **sie bestritt die Unterhaltung allein** she did all the talking.

be'streuen v/t (h) strew: **mit Salz etc ~** sprinkle with salt etc.

bestrich [bəˈʃtrɪç] pret, **be'strichen** pp of **bestreichen**.

be'stritt [bəˈʃtrɪt] pret, **be'stritten** pp of **bestreiten**.

'Bestseller m (-s; -) best seller.

be'stücken [bəˈʃtʏkən] v/t (h) ⚓, ✕ arm (with guns), w.s. equip (**mit** with).

Be'stuhlung f (-; -en) seating.

be'stürmen v/t (h) **1.** storm. **2.** fig. a) urge, b) implore, c) bombard (**mit** with questions etc).

be'stürzen v/t (h) dismay. **be'stürzend** adj dismaying. **be'stürzt** adj dismayed (**über** acc at). **Be'stürzung** f (-; no pl) (**zu** s-r etc ~ to his etc) dismay.

Besuch [bəˈzuːx] m (-[e]s; -e) **1.** a) visit (gen, bei, in dat to), call (**bei** j-m on s.o., at s.o.'s house etc), b) stay (**bei** at): **auf ~, zu ~** on a visit; **bei** j-m **zu ~ sein** be staying with s.o.; **e-n ~ machen bei** → **besuchen** 1. **2.** (gen) attendance (at school etc). **3.** visitor(s), guest(s), company. **be'suchen** v/t (h) **1.** go and see, visit, pay a visit to, call on. **2.** a) visit (place), go to, a. frequent (restaurant etc), b) go to, attend (school, meeting, etc): **gut besucht** well attended.

Be'sucher m (-s; -), **Be'sucherin** f (-; -nen) a) visitor (gen to), caller, b) guest, c) spectator.

Be'suchszeit f visiting hours.

be'sudeln v/t (h) soil, fig. sully.

besungen [bə'zʊŋən] pp of **besingen**.

Betablocker ['be:tablɔkər] m (-s; -) 🛠 beta blocker.

betagt [bə'ta:kt] adj aged, old.

be'tasten v/t (h) feel, touch.

betätigen [bə'tɛːtɪgən] (h) **I** v/t ⚙ operate (machine), actuate (button, lever, etc), apply (brake). **II sich ~** (in dat in) be active, work, busy o.s.; **sich ~ als** act (or work) as; **sich politisch (sportlich) ~** be active in politics (do sports).

Be'tätigung f (-; -en) **1.** activity, work, job: **körperliche ~** (physical) exercise. **2.** ⚙ actuation, operation.

Be'tätigungsfeld n field (of activity), w.s. outlet.

betäuben [bə'tɔʏbən] (h) **I** v/t a. fig. stun, daze, b) make s.o. unconscious, F knock s.o. out, c) deafen, d) intoxicate, e) 🛠 an(a)esthetize, deaden: fig. **wie betäubt** stunned. **II sich ~** fig. seek consolation (**mit, durch** in). **Be'täubung** f (-; -en) **1.** stunning (etc). **2.** daze. **3.** 🛠 a) an(a)esthetization, b) (**örtliche**) ~ (local) an(a)esthesia. **Be'täubungsmittel** n narcotic, 🛠 a. an(a)esthetic.

Bete ['be:tə] f (-; -n) 🌶 beet: **rote ~** beetroot.

beteiligen [bə'taɪlɪgən] (h) **I** v/t **j-n ~** (**an** dat in) a) a. 🌶 give s.o. a share, b) let s.o. take part; **beteiligt sein** (**an** dat) participate (in), 🌶 have a share (in), share (in the profit), be involved (in an accident etc), 🏛 be a party (to). **II sich ~** (**an** dat) a) participate (in), b) contribute (to), help (in); **sich an den Kosten ~** share (in) the expenses.

Be'teiligte m, f (-n, -n) person concerned (or involved). **Be'teiligung** f (-; -en) **1.** participation. **2.** (**an** dat) interest, share. **3.** 🌶 a) investment, b) holding(s), c) partnership. **4.** (**an** dat) attendance, turnout (at election etc).

beten ['be:tən] v/i (h) pray (**um** for), say a prayer.

beteuern [bə'tɔʏərn] v/t (h) protest (**s-e Unschuld** one's innocence), swear to, a. 🏛 affirm (solemnly).

Be'teuerung f (-; -en) protestation, a. 🏛 solemn affirmation.

betiteln [bə'ti:təln] v/t (h) **1.** entitle (book etc). **2.** F contp. **j-n ... ~** call s.o. ...

Beton [be'tɔŋ] m (-s; -s, -e) concrete.

betonen [be'to:nən] v/t (h) a. fig. stress emphasize.

betonieren [beto'ni:rən] v/t (h) concrete. **Be'tonklotz** m **1.** concrete block **2.** contp. concrete pile. **Be'tonmisch ma,schine** f cement mixer.

be'tont pp of **betonen**. **II** adj fig. emphatic, marked: **mit ~er Gleichgültig keit** with studied (or marked) indifference. **III** adv markedly. **Be'tonung** (-; -en) a. fig. stress, emphasis.

betören [bə'tøːrən] v/t (h) bewitch, turr s.o.'s head.

Betracht [bə'traxt] **in ~ ziehen** take into consideration; **außer ~ lassen** disregard; (**nicht**) **in ~ kommen** be a possibility (be out of the question).

be'trachten v/t (h) look at, fig. a. view: **j-n als Freund ~** look upon s.o. as (o consider s.o.) a friend; **genau betrach tet** strictly speaking. **Be'trachter** m (-s -), **Be'trachterin** f (-; -nen) viewer, observer. **beträchtlich** [bə'trɛçtlɪç] aa considerable. **Be'trachtung** f (-; -en) **1** no pl view (gen of). **2.** reflection: **~el anstellen über** (acc) reflect on; **be näherer ~** on closer inspection.

betraf [bə'tra:f] pret of **betreffen**.

Betrag [bə'tra:k] m (-[e]s; ~e) amount sum: **im ~e von** to the amount of.

be'tragen (betrug, betragen, h) **I** v/ amount to, total. **II sich ~** behave.

Be'tragen n (-s) behavio(u)r, conduct

betrank [bə'traŋk] pret of **betrinken**.

betrat [bə'tra:t] pret of **betreten²**.

be'trauen v/t (h) entrust (**mit** with).

be'trauern v/t (h) mourn.

Betreff [bə'trɛf] m (-[e]s; -e) 🌶 reference in letters: (abbr. Betr.) re: ... **be'treffen** v/t (betraf, betroffen, h) **1.** a) concern b) refer to: **was mich betrifft** as for me as far as I am concerned; **was das betrifft** as to that. **2.** affect: → **betroffen 2. be'treffend** adj **1.** concerning. **2** concerned: **die ~e Person** the person concerned (or in question); **das ~ Buch** the book referred to.

be'treiben v/t (betrieb, betrieben, h) **1** pursue, manage, run (enterprise etc)

go in for, do (*sports*). **2.** ☼ operate, run.
Be'treiben *n* (-s) **auf ~ von** (*or gen*) at
the instigation of. **Be'treiber** *m* (-s; -)
person (*pl* body) running an enterprise.
be'treten¹ *adj* embarrassed, awkward.
be'treten² *v/t* (betrat, betreten, h) **1.** step
on (to). **2.** enter. **Be'treten** *n* (-s) **~**
verboten! keep off!, no entrance!
betreuen [bə'trɔʏən] *v/t* (h) look after,
attend to, *sports:* coach, ✝ serve (*area*).
Be'treuer *m* (-s; -), **Be'treuerin** *f* (-;
-nen) s.o. who looks after s.o. (*or* s.th.),
sports: coach. **Be'treuung** *f* (-; *no pl*)
care (**von** *or gen* of, for).
betrieb [bə'tri:p] *pret of* **betreiben**.
Be'trieb *m* (-[e]s; -e) **1.** enterprise, company, business, firm, factory, works,
plant: **öffentliche ~e** public utilities. **2.**
no pl a) management, running, b) ☼
operation: **in ~** working, in operation;
außer ~ a) not working, b) out of order; **in ~ setzen** put into operation,
start; **außer ~ setzen** put out of action.
3. *no pl* F a) activity, bustle, b) (heavy)
traffic: **wir hatten heute viel ~** we were
very busy today.
betrieben [bə'tri:bən] *pp of* **betreiben**.
be'trieblich *adj* internal, company.
be'triebsam *adj* active, busy. **Be'trieb-**
samkeit *f* (-; *no pl*) activity, bustle.
Be'triebs|angehörige *m, f* employee.
~anleitung *f* operating instructions.
~ausflug *m* (annual) work outing.
⊇blind *adj* routine-blinded. **⊇eigen** *adj*
company(-owned). **⊇fähig** *adj* in
(good) working condition. **~ferien** *pl*
works holidays. **~fest** *n* company fête.
⊇fremd *adj* outside ...: **~e Person** outsider. **~geheimnis** *n* trade secret.
⊇in,tern *adj* internal. **~kapi,tal** *n* working capital. **~klima** *n* work climate.
~kosten *pl* running costs. **~leiter** *m*
works (*or* production) manager. **~ob-**
mann *m* works steward. **~rat** *m* (member of the) works council. **⊇sicher** *adj*
fail-safe, reliable (in service). **~sicher-**
heit *f* safety (in operation), reliability.
~stillegung *f* closure, shutdown. **~stö-**
rung *f* ☼ stoppage, breakdown. **~sy,stem**
n computer: operating sys-
tem. **~unfall** *m* industrial accident.
~verfassung *f* industrial-relations
scheme. **~versammlung** *f* works meeting. **~wirt** *m* graduate in business man-

agement. **~wirtschaft** *f* (-; *no pl*) business management. **~zugehörigkeit** *f*
(period of) employment: **nach zehn-**
jähriger ~ after ten years(' employment) with the company.
be'trinken: sich ~ (betrank, betrunken,
h) get drunk.
betroffen [bə'trɔfən] **I** *pp of* **betreffen**. **II**
adj **1.** shocked, dismayed, *pred* taken
aback. **2.** affected (**von** by): **die ~en**
Personen the persons concerned.
Be'troffenheit *f* (-; *no pl*) (**über** *acc* at)
dismay, shock.
betrog [bə'tro:k] *pret*, **betrogen** [bə-
'tro:gən] *pp of* **betrügen**.
be'trüben *v/t* (h) sadden.
betrüblich [bə'try:plɪç] *adj* sad.
be'trübt *adj* sad (**über** *acc* at, about).
betrug [bə'tru:k] *pret of* **betragen**.
Be'trug *m* (-[e]s; *no pl*) cheat, swindle, ⚖
fraud, deception. **be'trügen** *v/t*, *v/i*
(betrog, betrogen, h) cheat, swindle, ⚖
defraud, deceive (*wife etc*): **j-n um et.~**
cheat (*or* do) s.o. out of s.th.; **sich**
(**selbst**) **~** deceive o.s. **Be'trüger** *m* (-s;
-), **Be'trügerin** *f* (-; -nen) swindler,
fraud. **Betrüge'rei** *f* (-; -en) **1.** cheating. **2.** deceit, *a.* ⚖ fraud. **be'trüge-**
risch *adj* deceitful, fraudulent.
betrunken [bə'trʊŋkən] **I** *pp of* **betrin-**
ken. II *adj* drunken, *pred* drunk.
Be'trunkene *m, f* (-n; -n) drunk.
Be'trunkenheit *f* (-; *no pl*) drunkenness.
Bett [bɛt] *n* (-[e]s; -en) bed (*a.* geol., ☼):
im ~ in bed; **j-n zu ~ bringen** put s.o. to
bed; **ins ~ gehen** go to bed (F **mit j-m**
with s.o.), F turn in; **das ~ hüten (müs-**
sen) be laid up (**wegen** with).
'Bettbezug *m* duvet cover. **'Bettcouch** *f*
bed settee. **'Bettdecke** *f* a) blanket, b)
quilt, c) bedspread.
Bettel ['bɛtəl] *m* (-s; *no pl*) **der ganze ~**
the whole (wretched) business.
bettel'arm *adj* desperately poor. **'Bet-**
telbrief *m* begging letter. **betteln**
['bɛtəln] *v/i* (h) beg (**um** for): **~ gehen**
go begging. **'Bettelstab** *m* **j-n an den ~**
bringen reduce s.o. to poverty.
betten ['bɛtən] *v/t* (h) bed (*a.* ☼): **wie**
man sich bettet, so liegt man as you
make your bed, so you must lie on it.
'Bettjacke *f* bed jacket. **bettlägerig**
['bɛtlɛːgərɪç] *adj* laid up. **'Bettlaken** *n*
sheet. **'Bettlek,türe** *f* bedtime reading.

Bettler ['bɛtlər] m (-s; -), **'Bettlerin** f (-; -nen) beggar.

Bettnässer ['bɛtnɛsər] m (-s, -), **'Bettnässerin** f (-; -nen) bed-wetter.

'Bettruhe f (period of) bed rest: **j-m ~ verordnen** order s.o. to stay in bed.

'Bettung f (-; -en) ❂ bed(ding).

'Bettvorleger m bedside rug.

'Bettwäsche f, **'Bettzeug** n bed linen.

betucht [bə'tu:xt] adj F well-heeled.

be'tupfen v/t (h) dab, ✚ swab.

beugen ['bɔʏɡən] (h) **I** v/t **1.** bend (a. fig. the law), bow: **vom Alter gebeugt** bowed with age. **2.** ling. inflect, decline (noun), conjugate (verb). **II** sich ~ **3.** bend. **4.** fig. (dat to) bow, submit.

Beule ['bɔʏlə] f (-; -n) **1.** bump, swelling. **2.** dent.

beunruhigen [bə'ʔʊnru:ɪɡən] (h) **I** v/t worry, alarm. **II** sich ~ be worried (über, wegen about). **Be'unruhigung** f (-; -en) anxiety, worry.

beurkunden [bə'ʔu:rkʊndən] v/t (h) a) record, b) certify, c) register (birth etc). **Be'urkundung** f (-; -en) a) recording, b) certification, c) registration.

beurlauben [bə'ʔu:rlaʊbən] v/t (h) give s.o. leave (or time off), w.s. suspend s.o. (from office): **beurlaubt** a) on leave, b) temporarily suspended.

Be'urlaubung f (-; -en) (granting of a) leave, w.s. suspension (from office).

be'urteilen v/t (h) judge (nach by): **das kann ich nicht ~!** I am no judge of (this)!; **falsch ~** misjudge. **Be'urteilung** f (-; -en) judg(e)ment, assessment, in personal file: confidential report.

Beute ['bɔʏtə] f (-; no pl) **1.** booty, loot. **2.** zo. prey (a. fig. gen to), hunt. bag: (dat) **zur ~ fallen** a. fig. fall a prey to.

Beutel ['bɔʏtəl] m (-s; -) bag, F purse, zo. pouch, sac. **'beuteln** v/t (h) F fig. shake (up). **'Beuteltier** n marsupial.

bevölkern [bə'fœlkərn] v/t (h) **1.** populate. **2.** inhabit.

Be'völkerung f (-; -en) population.

Be'völkerungs|dichte f population density. **~explosi,on** f population explosion. **~poli,tik** f population policy. **~rückgang** m decline in population. **~schicht** f social stratum (or class).

bevollmächtigen [bə'fɔlmɛçtɪɡən] v/t (h) **j-n ~** authorize s.o. (et. zu tun to do s.th.), ⚖ give s.o. power of attorney.

Be'vollmächtigte m, f (-n; -n) authorized person (✝, ⚖ representative), pol. plenipotentiary. **Be'vollmächtigung** f (-; -en) **1.** authorization. **2.** authority, power, ⚖ power of attorney.

be'vor adv before: **nicht ~** not until.

bevormunden [bə'fo:rmʊndən] v/t (h) **j-n ~** keep s.o. in leading strings.

bevorrechtigt [bə'fo:rrɛçtɪçt] adj privileged.

be'vorstehen v/i (irr, sep, -ge-, h, → **stehen**) be approaching, problems etc: lie ahead, crisis etc: be imminent: **j-m ~** be in store for s.o., await s.o. **be'vorstehend** adj approaching, forthcoming, pleasures etc to come, imminent.

bevorzugen [bə'fo:rtsu:ɡən] v/t (h) (vor dat) prefer (to), favo(u)r (above), give s.o. preferential treatment. **be'vorzugt** adj **1.** privileged: **~e Behandlung** preferential treatment. **2.** favo(u)rite. **3.** (most) popular. **Be'vorzugung** f (-; -en) preference (gen given to).

be'wachen v/t (h) guard, watch, sports: mark. **Be'wacher** m (-s; -) guard, sports: marker.

be'wachsen adj **~ mit** overgrown with.

Be'wachung f (-; -en) **1.** no pl guarding (etc). **2.** guard(s).

bewaffnen [bə'vafnən] v/t (h) arm (sich o.s., a. fig.). **be'waffnet** adj armed (mit with). **Be'waffnung** f (-; -en) **1.** no pl arming. **2.** arms, weapons.

be'wahren v/t (h) **1.** keep: **die Fassung ~** keep one's head, keep cool. **2.** (vor dat from) keep, preserve; → **Gott.**

bewähren [bə'vɛ:rən] sich ~ (h) **1.** prove one's (or its) worth, stand the test, principle: hold good; **sich ~ als ...** prove to be ...; **sich nicht ~** prove a failure.

bewahrheiten [bə'va:rhaɪtən] sich ~ (h) **1.** prove (to be) true. **2.** come true.

bewährt [bə'vɛ:rt] adj **1.** well-tried, reliable. **2.** experienced.

Be'wahrung f (-; no pl) (vor dat from) preservation, keeping.

Be'währung f (-; -en) **1.** trial, (crucial) test. **2.** ⚖ (release on) probation: **drei Monate Gefängnis auf ~** a suspended sentence of three months; **die Strafe wurde zur ~ ausgesetzt** the defendant was placed on probation.

Be'währungs|frist f ⚖ (period of

probation. **~helfer(in** f) m probation officer. **~probe** f fig. (acid) test.

bewaldet [bə'valdət] adj wooded.

bewältigen [bə'vɛltɪgən] v/t (h) cope with, master, manage. **Be'wältigung** f (-; no pl) coping (gen with), mastering.

bewandert [bə'vandərt] adj (**gut**) **~ in** (dat) well versed (or well up) in.

Bewandtnis [bə'vantnɪs] f (-; -se) **damit hat es folgende ~** the case is this; **das hat s-e eigene ~** thereby hangs a tale.

bewarb [bə'varp] pret of **bewerben.**

bewarf [bə'varf] pret of **bewerfen.**

be'wässern v/t (h) irrigate. **Be'wässerung** f (-; -en) irrigation.

bewegen[1] [bə've:gən] (h) **I** v/t **1.** move, ⚙ a. work, set s.th. going: fig. **et. ~** move s.th., get things moving. **2.** fig. move, touch: **sage mir, was dich bewegt!** tell me what's on your mind! **II sich ~** a. fig. move; **sich nicht von der Stelle ~** (**lassen**) not to budge; **~ sich zwischen ... und ...** prices etc range between ... and ...

be'wegen[2] v/t (bewog, bewogen, h) **j-n ~ zu** inf prompt (or get) s.o. to inf; **was hat ihn** (**nur**) **dazu bewogen?** what(ever) made him do it?

be'wegend adj fig. moving.

Be'weggrund m (tieferer ~ real) motive.

beweglich [bə've:klɪç] adj **1.** movable (a. holiday), mobile, ⚙ a. fig. flexible: **~ Teile** (**~es Ziel**) moving parts (target); 🜨 **~e Sachen** movables. **2.** agile. **Be'weglichkeit** f (-; no pl) **1.** mobility, flexibility. **2.** agility.

be'wegt adj **1.** rough. **2.** fig. turbulent. **3.** fig. moved, touched. **Be'wegung** f (-; -en) **1.** a) movement, motion (a. phys.), b) move: **k-e ~!** don't move!; **in ~** ⚙ in motion, fig. astir; **in ~ setzen** a. fig. start; **sich in ~ setzen** start to move; fig. **in e-e Sache ~ bringen** get s.th. moving. **2.** (physical) exercise. **3.** pol. etc movement. **4.** emotion.

Be'wegungsfreiheit f (-; no pl) freedom of movement (⚙ motion, fig. action), fig. elbowroom.

be'wegungslos adj and adv motionless. **Be'wegungs|studie** f motion study. **~thera,pie** f therapeutic exercises. ⚗**unfähig** adj unable to move.

be'weinen v/t (h) mourn, lament.

Beweis [bə'vaɪs] m (-es; -e) (**für** of)

proof, 🜨 a. pl evidence: **zum ~** (gen) in proof of, to prove s.th.; **bis zum ~ des Gegenteils** pending proof to the contrary; **den ~ erbringen** (or **liefern**) **für et., et. unter ~ stellen** prove s.th.; **als ~ s-r Zuneigung** as a token of his affection. **Be'weisaufnahme** f (-; no pl) 🜨 hearing of evidence. **be'weisbar** adj provable: **ist es ~?** can it be proved?

be'weisen v/t (bewies, bewiesen, h) **1.** prove (**j-m et.** s.th. to s.o.). **2.** show.

Be'weis|führung f (-; no pl) argumentation, 🜨 presentation of (the) evidence. **~kraft** f (-; no pl) conclusiveness. ⚗**kräftig** adj conclusive. **~lage** f nach der ~ on the evidence. **~last** f **die ~ obliegt dem Kläger** the onus (of proof) is on the plaintiff. **~materi,al** n evidence. **~mittel** n (piece of) evidence: **die ~** the evidence (**für** of). **~stück** n (piece of) evidence, in court: exhibit.

be'wenden v/i **es dabei ~ lassen** leave it at that.

be'werben: sich ~ (bewarb, beworben, h) (**um** for) a) apply (**bei** to), b) pol. stand, Am. a. run, c) compete. **Be'werber** m (-s; -), **Be'werberin** f (-; -nen) **1.** applicant, candidate. **2.** competitor, sports: a. entrant.

Be'werbung f (-; -en) application (**um** for). **Be'werbungsschreiben** n (letter of) application.

be'werfen v/t (bewarf, beworfen, h) **j-n ~ mit** pelt s.o. with.

bewerkstelligen [bə'vɛrkʃtɛlɪgən] v/t (h) manage.

be'werten v/t (h) **1.** assess, judge, rate: **wird mit 7 Punkten bewertet** the jump etc rates (or scores) 7 points. **2.** ✝ (**mit** at) value, assess: **zu hoch** (**niedrig**) **~** overrate (underrate).

Be'wertung f (-; -en) assessment, ✝ a. valuation, ped. mark(s), Am. grade(s), sports: point(s), score(s).

bewies [bə'vi:s] pret, **bewiesen** [bə'vi:zən] pp of **beweisen.**

bewilligen [bə'vɪlɪgən] v/t (h) **1.** allow (**j-m et.** s.o. s.th.). **2.** grant (funds etc), parl. appropriate. **Be'willigung** f (-; -en) **1.** grant(ing), parl. appropriation. **2.** permission.

be'wirken v/t (h) cause, bring s.th. about, give rise to, result in: **das Gegenteil ~** produce the opposite effect.

bewirten [bə'vɪrtən] v/t (h) entertain.

be'wirtschaften v/t (h) **1.** run (*estate etc*): *bewirtschaftet hotel etc:* open (to the public). **2.** ✍ cultivate. **3.** ⚜ ration.

Be'wirtschaftung f (-; -en) **1.** running. **2.** ✍ cultivation. **3.** ⚜ rationing.

Bewirtung [bə'vɪrtʊŋ] f (-; -en) **1.** entertainment. **2.** food and service.

bewog [bə'vo:k] pret, **bewogen** [bə'vo:-gən] pp of **bewegen**.

bewohnbar [bə'vo:nba:r] adj (in)habitable. **be'wohnen** v/t (h) inhabit, live in. **Be'wohner** m (-s; -), **Be'wohnerin** f (-; -nen) a) occupant, b) tenant, c) inhabitant.

bewölken [bə'vœlkən] sich ~ (h) cloud over, get cloudy. **be'wölkt** adj cloudy. **Be'wölkung** f (-; no pl) **1.** clouding over. **2.** clouds. **Be'wölkungsauflockerung** f cloud dispersal. **Be'wölkungszunahme** f increasing cloudiness.

beworben [bə'vɔrbən] pp of **bewerben**.

beworfen [bə'vɔrfən] pp of **bewerfen**.

Bewunderer [bə'vʊndərər] m (-s; -), **Be'wunderin** f (-; -nen) admirer.

be'wundern v/t (h) admire (**wegen** for).

be'wundernswert, **be'wundernswürdig** adj admirable.

Be'wunderung f (-; no pl) admiration.

bewußt [bə'vʊst] adj **1.** conscious (gen of): *sich e-r Sache ~ sein (werden)* be aware of (realize) s.th. **2.** deliberate. **3.** said. **be'wußtlos** adj unconscious: ~ *werden* lose consciousness. **Be'wußtlosigkeit** f (-; no pl) unconsciousness. **Be'wußtsein** n (-s) consciousness, fig. a. awareness: *bei (vollem) ~* (fully) conscious; *das ~ verlieren* lose consciousness; *j-n zum ~ bringen* bring s.o. round; *j-m et. zum ~ bringen* bring s.th. home to s.o.; *wieder zu(m) ~ kommen* come round, regain consciousness; *j-m zum ~ kommen* dawn on s.o.; *im ~ zu inf (or daß)* conscious of ger. **be'wußtseinserweiternd** adj mind-expanding (drug).

be'zahlen v/t, v/i (h) pay (for): fig. et. *teuer ~* pay dearly for s.th.; *sich bezahlt machen* pay (off). **Be'zahlung** f (-; no pl) (**gegen ~** for) payment, pay.

be'zähmen v/t (h) restrain (sich o.s.).

be'zaubern v/t (h) bewitch, enchant, fig. a. charm: **~d** charming, delightful.

be'zeichnen v/t (h) **1.** mark. **2.** a) de-

scribe (als as), call, b) indicate, c) stand for. **be'zeichnend** adj (für of) typical, characteristic. **be'zeichnenderweise** adv typically (enough). **Be'zeichnung** f (-; -en) **1.** no pl marking. **2.** designation, name, term.

be'zeugen v/t (h) ⚖, a. fig. testify (to).

bezichtigen [bə'tsɪçtɪgən] v/t (h) accuse (gen of).

beziehbar [bə'tsi:ba:r] adj **1.** ready for occupation. **2.** ⚜ obtainable.

be'ziehen (bezog, bezogen, h) **I** v/t **1.** put clean sheets on (bed), (neu ~ re-)cover (settee etc). **2.** move into (a flat etc). **3. Posten ~** take up one's post. **4.** a) get, obtain, b) draw (salary etc), c) take (newspaper). **5. et. ~ auf** (acc) relate (or apply) s.th. to; *er bezog es auf sich* he took it personally. **II** sich ~ **6.** sky: cloud over. **7. sich ~ auf** (acc) refer to, matter: relate to; *sich auf j-n ~* use s.o.'s name (as a reference). **Be'zieher** m (-s; -) **1.** ⚜ buyer, customer. **2.** subscriber (gen to a newspaper).

Be'ziehung f (-; -en) (zu) relation (to), relationship (with), connection (with): *diplomatische ~en* diplomatic relations; *gute ~en haben* a) have good connections, b) zu *j-m* be on good terms with s.o.; *in dieser (jeder) ~* in this (every) respect; *in gewisser ~* in a way; *in politischer ~* politically.

Be'ziehungskiste f F fig. relationship.

Be'ziehungssatz m ling. relative clause.

be'ziehungsvoll adj suggestive.

be'ziehungsweise conj **1.** or rather. **2.** or ... respectively: *mit dem Auto ~ mit der Bahn* by car or train respectively.

Be'ziehungswort n ling. antecedent.

beziffern [bə'tsɪfərn] v/t (h) **1.** number. **2.** estimate (auf acc at): *sich ~ auf* (acc) amount to.

Bezirk [bə'tsɪrk] m (-[e]s; -e) district.

bezog [bə'tso:k] pret, **bezogen** [bə'tso:gən] pp of **beziehen**.

Bezug [bə'tsu:k] m (-[e]s; ~e) **1.** cover (pillow) slip. **2.** no pl moving in(to (a flat etc). **3.** no pl a) purchase, b) subscription (gen to): *bei ~ von ...* on orders of 10 pieces. **4.** fig. reference (auf acc to): *in ½ auf* (acc) → *bezüglich* II; *~ nehmen auf* (acc) refer to. **5.** pl income, salary. **bezüglich** [bə'tsy:klɪç] **I** adj: *auf* (acc) relating to; *ling. ~es Fürwor*

relative pronoun. **II** prep (gen) concerning, with reference to.
Be'zugnahme f adm. **unter ~ auf** (acc)
with reference to.
Be'zugs|bedingungen pl terms of sale.
~per,son f j-s **~** person to whom s.o.
relates most closely, parent person.
~preis m purchase (or subscription)
price. **~punkt** m reference point. **~quel-**
le f source (of supply).
bezwang [bə'tsvaŋ] pret of **bezwingen**.
bezwecken [bə'tsvɛkən] v/t (h) **et. ~** be
aiming at s.th.
be'zweifeln v/t (h) doubt, question.
be'zwingen v/t (bezwang, bezwungen,
h) overcome, conquer, a. sports: defeat: **sich ~** restrain o.s. **Be'zwinger** m
(-s; -) conqueror, sports: winner (gen
over). **Be'zwingung** f (-; no pl) overcoming, defeat(ing), conquest.
Bibel ['bi:bəl] f (-; -n) Bible. '**bibelfest**
adj well versed in the Scriptures.
'**Bibelspruch** m verse from the Bible.
Biber ['bi:bər] m (-s; -) zo. beaver.
Bibliographie [bibliogra'fi:] f (-; -n)
bibliography. **Bibliothek** [biblio'te:k] f
(-; -en) library. **Bibliothekar** [biblio-
te'ka:r] m (-s; -e), **Bibliothe'karin** f (-;
-nen) librarian. **Biblio'thekswissen-**
schaft f library science.
bieder ['bi:dər] adj honest, flexible,
iro. simple.
biegen ['bi:gən] (bog, gebogen) **I** v/t (h)
bend. **II sich ~** (h) bend; → **Lachen**. **III**
v/i (sn) **nach links** (**rechts**) **~** turn left
(right); **um e-e Ecke ~** turn (round) a
corner. '**Biegen** (-s) bending: **auf ~**
oder Brechen by hook or by crook.
biegsam ['bi:kza:m] adj pliable, flexible,
supple. '**Biegsamkeit** f (-; no pl) plia-
bility, flexibility, suppleness.
'**Biegung** f (-; -en) bend.
Biene ['bi:nə] f (-; -n) **1.** zo. bee. **2.** F
chick.
'**Bienen|fleiß** m assiduity. **~haus** n bee-
house, apiary. **~königin** f queen bee.
~korb m beehive. **~schwarm** m swarm
of bees. **~staat** m colony of bees. **~stich**
m bee-sting. **~stock** m beehive. **~wabe**
f honeycomb. **~wachs** n beeswax.
~zucht f beekeeping. **~züchter** m
beekeeper.
Bier [bi:r] n (-[e]s; -e) beer: **helles ~**
lager, Am. light beer; **dunkles ~** etwa
brown ale, Am. dark beer; **~ vom Faß**

beer on draught; F **das ist dein ~!** that's
your problem!
'**Bier|brauerei** f brewery. **~deckel** m
beer mat. **~dose** f beer can. **~faß** n beer
barrel. **~flasche** f beer bottle. **~garten**
m beer garden. **~glas** n beer glass.
~hefe f brewer's yeast. **~keller** m beer
tavern. **~krug** m beer mug, Am. stein.
~stube f beer tavern. **~zelt** n beer tent.
Biest [bi:st] n (-[e]s; -er) a. F fig. beast.
bieten ['bi:tən] (bot, geboten, h) **I** v/t **1.**
offer (**j-m et.** s.o. s.th.), present (sight,
difficulties, etc): **das läßt sie sich nicht**
~ she won't stand for that; → **Stirn**. **2.**
† bid. **II sich ~** present itself. '**Bieter** m
(-s; -), '**Bieterin** f (-; -nen) † bidder.
Bigamie [biga'mi:] f (-; -n) bigamy.
bigott [bi'gɔt] adj contp. bigoted.
Bikini [bi'ki:ni] m (-s; -s) bikini.
Bilanz [bi'lants] f (-; -en) a) balance, b)
balance sheet: **die ~ ziehen** (gen of)
strike the balance, fig. a. take stock;
fig. **negative ~** negative record.
Bi'lanzjahr n financial year.
Bi'lanzposten m balance-sheet item.
Bild [bɪlt] n (-[e]s; -er) a) picture (a. TV or
fig.), photo, illustration, image (a. opt.,
TV), painting, portrait, b) fig. sight, c)
fig. idea, rhet. image, metaphor: **~ der**
Zerstörung etc scene of destruction
etc; **im ~e sein** be in the picture, **über**
(acc) know about; **sich ein ~ machen**
von get an idea of, visualize; **du machst**
dir kein ~! you have no idea!; **j-n ins ~**
setzen inform s.o., put s.o. in the picture; **ein falsches ~ bekommen** get a
wrong impression.
'**Bildar,chiv** n photographic archives.
'**Bildausfall** m TV picture loss, blackout. '**Bildband** m (-[e]s; ⁀e) illustrated
book. '**Bildbericht** m photo-report.
'**bilden** (h) **I** v/t **1.** form, shape (a. fig.),
make up (sentence). **2.** create, establish,
set up (committee etc), form (government). **3.** form, develop (buds). **4.** fig.
form, be; → **Ausnahme**. **5.** educate,
cultivate; → **gebildet**. **II** v/i **6.** broaden
the mind. **III sich ~ 7.** form, develop. **8.**
educate o.s., improve one's mind.
'**bildend** adj educational, informative:
~e Künste fine arts.
'**Bilder|buch** n picture book. **~buch...** F
fig. storybook (career, landing, etc).
~gale,rie f picture gallery. **~rätsel** n

picture puzzle. **2reich** *adj* richly illustrated (*book*), *fig.* language rich in images. **~schrift** *f* pictographic script. **~sprache** *f* imagery.

'**Bildfläche** *f* TV image area: F *fig.* **auf der ~ erscheinen** turn up; **von der ~ verschwinden** disappear.

'**Bildfunk** *m* radio picture transmission. '**bildhaft** *adj fig.* graphic. '**Bildhauer** *m* (-s; -) sculptor. '**Bildhaue'rei** *f* (-; *no pl*) sculpture. '**Bildhauerin** *f* (-; -nen) sculptress. '**bildhauern** [-haʊərn] *v/i, v/t* (h) F sculpt. '**bild'hübsch** *adj* (very) lovely. '**bildlich** *adj* **1.** pictorial, graphic. **2.** *ling.* figurative (*expression etc*).

'**Bildnis** *n* (-ses; -se) portrait. '**Bild|platte** *f* video disc. **~plattenspieler** *m* video disc player. **~quali,tät** *f* *phot.*, TV picture quality. **~redak,teur** *m* picture editor. **~re,gie** *f* camerawork. **~röhre** *f* picture tube. **~schärfe** *f* definition, sharpness.

'**Bildschirm** *m* screen. **~gerät** *n* visual display unit. **~text** *m* view data. **bild'schön** *adj* (very) beautiful. '**Bildstörung** *f* TV image interference. '**Bildtele,fon** *n* videophone. '**Bildtonkamera** *f* sound-film camera. '**Bildung** *f* (-; -en) **1.** a) forming, formation, b) development, c) creation, d) establishment, setting-up *p* (*of committee etc*): **~ des Perfekts** forming (of) the perfect. **2.** *no pl* a) education, culture, b) *ped.*, *univ.* formal education: **et. für s-e ~ tun** improve one's mind. **3.** *no pl* (good) breeding.

'**Bildungs...** educational (*reform etc*). **2fähig** *adj* educable. **~gang** *m* (course of) education. **~grad** *m* educational level. **~lücke** *f* gap in one's education. **2po,litisch** *adj* politico-educational. **~urlaub** *m* educational leave. **~weg** *m* education: **der zweite ~** evening classes (*with a view to obtaining university qualification*); **auf dem zweiten ~** through evening classes. **~wesen** *n* (-s; *no pl*) education.

'**Billard** ['bɪljart] *n* (-s; -e) billiards. **~kugel** *f* billiard ball. **~stock** *m* cue. '**Billiarde** [bɪl'Iardə] *f* (-; -n) trillion, *Am.* quadrillion.

'**billig** ['bɪlɪç] *adj* **1.** a) cheap, inexpensive, b) low (*price*). **2.** *fig.* cheap, poor (*ad-*

vice etc), lame (*excuse etc*). **3.** fair. '**Billig...** cut-price, *Am.* cut-rate. '**billigen** ['bɪlɪgən] *v/t* (h) approve of, sanction, *adm.* approve. '**Billigkeit** *f* (-; *no pl*) cheapness. '**Billigung** *f* (-; *no pl*) (*gen* of) approval, sanction.

'**Billion** [bɪ'lio:n] *f* (-; -en) billion, *Am.* trillion.

'**bimmeln** ['bɪməln] *v/i* (h) ring, tinkle. '**Bimsstein** ['bɪms-] *m* pumice (stone). '**binär** [bi'nɛːr] *adj*, **Bi'när...** binary. '**Binde** ['bɪndə] *f* (-; -n) **1.** a) armband, bandage, b) sling, c) blindfold, d) F sanitary towel (*Am.* napkin). **2.** F *fig.* **e-n hinter die ~ gießen** hoist one. '**Binde|gewebe** *n* *anat.* connective tissue. **~glied** *n* (connecting) link. **~haut** *f* *anat.* conjunctiva. **~hautentzündung** *f* 🔹 conjunctivitis. **~mittel** *n* **1.** ⚙ bonding agent. **2.** *gastr.* thickening.

'**binden** (band, gebunden, h) **I** *v/t* **1.** tie (*an acc* to), tie (up), make (*bouquet*), tie (*knot etc*). **2.** bind (*book*). **3.** *gastr.* bind, thicken. **4.** ♪ a) tie, b) slur. **5.** ⚓ tie up (*funds*), tie (*prices*). **6.** *fenc.*, *a.* ✗ bind. **7.** *fig.* bind, commit (*s.o.*); → **gebunden** 4. **II** *v/i* **8.** bind. **9.** *gastr.* bind, thicken. **10.** ⚙ cement *etc*: harden, set, *plastic*: bond. **III sich ~** *fig.* commit o.s., tie o.s. down. '**bindend** *adj fig.* binding (**für** upon).

'**Bindestrich** *m* hyphen: **mit ~ schreiben** hyphen(ate).

'**Bindewort** *n* (-[e]s; ⁻er) conjunction. '**Bindfaden** *m* string.

'**Bindung** *f* (-; -en) **1.** a) (*an acc*) ties (to, with), bond (with), attachment (to), b) (lasting) relationship. **2.** *ski:* binding. **3.** 🔹, *phys.* bond. **4.** ♪ ligature.

'**binnen** *prep* (*dat or gen*) within: **~ kurzem** before long.

'**Binnen|gewässer** *n* inland water. **~hafen** *m* inland port. **~handel** *m* domestic trade. **~land** *n* interior. '**binnenländisch** [-lɛndɪʃ] *adj* inland. '**Binnen|markt** *m* home (*EC:* single) market. **~meer** *n* inland sea. **~schiffahrt** *f* inland navigation. **~verkehr** *m* inland traffic.

'**Binse** ['bɪnzə] *f* (-; -n) 🌿 rush: F **in die ~n gehen** go to pot.

'**Binsenweisheit** *f* truism. '**Biochemie** [bioçe'mi:] *f* biochemistry.

Bio'chemiker(in f) m biochemist.
bio'chemisch adj biochemical.
'Biogas n biogas.
Bioge'netik f biogenetics.
Biograph [bio'graːf] m (-en; -en),
Bio'graphin f (-; -nen) biographer.
Biographie [biogra'fiː] f (-; -n) biography. bio'graphisch adj biographical.
'Bioladen m F whole food shop.
Biologe [bio'loːgə] m (-n; -n), Bio'login
f (-; -nen) biologist. Biologie [biolo'giː]
f (-; no pl) biology. bio'logisch adj biological.
'Biomasse f (-; no pl) biomass.
Biophy'sik f biophysics.
Biopsie [biɔp'siː] f (-; -n) ✗ biopsy.
'Biorhythmus m biorhythm.
'Biotechnik f bioengineering.
Biotop [bio'toːp] n (-s; -e) biotope.
Birke ['bɪrkə] f (-; -n) birch(-tree).
'Birnbaum m pear-tree. Birne ['bɪrnə] f
1. ❧ pear. 2. ⚡ bulb. 3. F noodle.
'birnenförmig adj pear-shaped.
bis [bɪs] I prep 1. a) till, until, b) by: ~
heute so far, to date; ~ jetzt up to now;
~ jetzt (noch) nicht not as yet; ~ auf
weiteres for the present, until further
notice; ~ in die Nacht into the night; ~
vor einigen Jahren until a few years
ago; ~ zum Ende (right) to the end; (in
der Zeit) vom ... ~ between ... and; F ~
dann (morgen)! see you later (tomorrow)! 2. (up) to, as far as: ~ hierher up
to here; ~ wohin? how far?; (von hier)
~ London (from here) to London. 3. 7 ~
10 Tage from 7 to 10 days, between 7
and 10 days; ~ zu 10 Meter hoch as
high as ten metres; ~ zu 100 Personen
as many as 100 persons; ~ drei zählen
count up to three. 4. ~ auf das letzte
Stück down to the last bit. 5. ~ auf (acc)
except, but. II prep till, until, until.
Bisam ['biːzam] m (-s; -e) 1. zo. musk. 2.
musquash. 'Bisamratte f zo. muskrat.
Bischof ['bɪʃɔf] m (-s; ⁓e) bishop.
bischöflich ['bɪʃøːflɪç] adj episcopal.
'Bischofssitz m episcopal see.
bisexuell [bizɛ'ksŭɛl] adj bisexual.
bis'her adv up to now, so far: ~ (noch)
nicht not (as) yet; wie ~ as before; die ~
beste Leistung the best performance
so far. bisherig [bɪs'heːrɪç] adj a) past,
previous, b) present: die ⁓en Ergebnisse results so far.

Biskuit [bɪs'kviːt] m (-[s]; -s, -e) gastr.
sponge. Bis'kuitrolle f Swiss roll.
bis'lang → bisher.
biß [bɪs] pret of beißen.
Biß m (Bisses; Bisse) bite.
'bißchen adj and adv ein (kleines) ~ a
(little) bit, a little; kein ~ not a bit.
'Bissen m (-s; -) 1. bite, morsel, mouthful. 2. bite, snack.
'bissig adj 1. vicious: ein ⁓er Hund a. a
dog that bites. 2. fig. cutting (remark),
snappish (person). c) Bißwunde f bite.
Bistum ['bɪstuːm] n (-s; ⁓er) bishopric.
Bit [bɪt] n (-[s]; -[s]) computer: bit.
bitte ['bɪtə] adv 1. please: ~, gib mir die
Zeitung! hand me the paper, please!; ~
nicht! please don't!; (aber) ~! certainly!, go ahead! 2. ~ (sehr or schön)! a)
after "danke": that's all right!, esp. Am.
(you are) welcome!, b) after excuses:
it's all right!, c) when offering s.th.:
there you are!, d) come in, please! 3.
wie ~? (I beg you?) pardon?, sorry? 4.
(na) ~! there!, I told you so!
'Bitte f (-; -n) a) request, b) entreaty: auf
j-s ~ at s.o.'s request; ich habe e-e ~ an
Sie I have a favo(u)r to ask of you.
bitten ['bɪtən] v/t, v/i (bat, gebeten, h) a)
ask (j-n um et. s.o. for s.th.), request,
beg, b) implore: um j-s Namen (Erlaubnis) ~ ask s.o.'s name (permission); j-n zu sich ~ ask s.o. to come; für
j-n ~ intercede for s.o.; es wird gebeten, daß ... it is requested that ...; darf
ich ~? a) come in, please!, b) may I have
this dance?, c) dinner is served!
bitter ['bɪtər] adj and adv bitter: fig. es ist
mein ⁓er Ernst I mean it!; er hat es ~
nötig he badly needs it; das ist ~! that's
hard! bitter'böse adj a) wicked, b) furious. 'Bitterkeit f (-; no pl) a. fig. bitterness. 'bitterlich adv ~ weinen weep
bitterly. 'bittersüß adj bitter-sweet.
'Bittgesuch n, 'Bittschrift f petition.
Bittsteller ['bɪtʃtɛlər] m (-s; -), 'Bittstellerin f (-; -nen) petitioner.
Biwak ['biːvak] n (-s; -s, -e), biwakieren
[biva'kiːrən] v/i bivouac.
bizarr [bi'tsar] adj bizarre.
Bizeps ['biːtsɛps] m (-[es]; -e) biceps.
blähen ['blɛːən] (h) I v/i cause flatulence,
give you wind. II v/t (a. sich ~) fill out.
'Blähungen pl wind, flatulence.
blamabel [bla'maːbəl] adj embarrass-

ing, disgraceful. **Blamage** [bla'ma:ʒə] *f* (-; -n) disgrace, fiasco.

blamieren [bla'mi:rən] (h) **I** *v/t j-n* ~ make s.o. look like a fool, *w.s.* compromise s.o. **II** *sich* ~ make a fool of o.s., *w.s.* compromise o.s.

blank [blaŋk] *adj* **1.** shining, polished, shiny. **2.** naked, bare (*a.* ⊛). **3.** F broke. **4.** F *~er Unsinn etc* sheer nonsense *etc.*

blanko ['blaŋko] *adj* ✝ (*adv* in) blank. **'Blankoscheck** *m* blank cheque (*Am.* check). **'Blankovollmacht** *f* full discretionary power, *fig.* carte blanche.

Bläschen ['blɛ:sçən] *n* (-s; -) **1.** small bubble. **2.** ⊛ *a)* small blister, *b)* pustule.

Blase ['bla:zə] *f* (-; -n) **1.** (air) bubble, *in glass etc:* flaw. **2.** *comics:* balloon. **3.** *a)* *anat.* bladder, *b)* ✿ blister. **4.** F *contp.* bunch, lot. **'Blasebalg** *m* bellows.

blasen ['bla:zən] *v/t, v/i* (blies, geblasen, h) blow, ♪ *a.* play.

'Blasen|entzündung *f*, **~ka,tarrh** *m* cystitis. **~leiden** *n* bladder trouble.

Bläser ['blɛ:zər] *m* (-s; -) ♪ wind player: *die* ~ the wind (section).

blasiert [bla'zi:rt] *adj* conceited.

'Blasinstru,ment *n* ♪ wind instrument.

'Blaska,pelle *f* brass band.

'Blasmu,sik *f* **1.** music for brass instruments. **2.** (playing of a) brass band.

Blasphemie [blasfe'mi:] *f* (-; -n) blasphemy.

blaß [blas] *adj* pale (*vor* with), *fig.* colo(u)rless: ~ *werden* (turn) pale; ~ *vor Neid* green with envy; → *Ahnung.* **Blässe** ['blɛsə] *f* (-; *no pl*) paleness, pallor.

Blatt [blat] *n* (-[e]s; ✽er) **1.** ✿ leaf: *fig. kein* ~ *vor den Mund nehmen* not to mince matters. **2.** *a)* leaf, sheet, *b)* page: ♪ *vom* ~ *spielen* sight-read; *fig. das steht auf e-m anderen* ~ that's a different matter altogether; *das* ~ *hat sich gewendet* the tide has turned. **3.** (news)paper. **4.** *art:* *a)* print, *b)* drawing, *c)* engraving. **5.** (playing) card, *w.s. a good etc* hand. **6.** blade (*of saw etc*).

Blättchen ['blɛtçən] *n* (-s; -) **1.** small leaf (*etc*, → *Blatt*). **2.** *anat.*, ✿, ✿ lamella, ⊛ membrane. **3.** slip (of paper). **4.** local paper.

Blatter ['blatər] *f* (-; -n) ✽ pock.

'Blattern *pl* ✽ smallpox.

blättern ['blɛtərn] *v/i* (h) *in e-m Buch etc* ~ leaf through a book *etc.*

'Blätterteig *m* flaky pastry.

'Blatt|feder *f* ⊛ leaf spring. **~gold** *n* gold leaf. **~grün** *n* (-s; *no pl*) chlorophyll. **~laus** *f* greenfly. **~pflanze** *f* green plant. **~sa,lat** *m* green salad.

blau [blau] *adj* **1.** blue: *~er Fleck* bruise; F *~er Brief* *a)* (letter of) dismissal, *b) ped.* letter of warning; → *Auge, Blut.* **2.** F tight, sloshed. **Blau** *n* (-s; -) blue.

'blauäugig [-ɔʏgɪç] *adj a. fig.* blue-eyed.

'Blaubeere *f* ✿ bilberry, *Am.* blueberry.

'blaublütig [-bly:tɪç] *adj* blue-blooded.

'Blaue *n Fahrt ins* ~ mystery tour.

Bläue ['blɔʏə] *f* (-; *no pl*) blue(ness).

bläuen ['blɔʏən] *v/t* (h) dye blue.

'Blaufuchs *m zo.* arctic (✝ silver) fox.

'blaugrau *adj* bluish grey (*Am.* gray).

'Blaukraut *n gastr.* red cabbage.

bläulich ['blɔʏlɪç] *adj* bluish.

'Blaulicht *n* flashing light(s): *mit* ~ *ambulance etc* with its lights flashing.

'blaumachen *v/i* (*sep*, -ge-, h) F stay away (from work), *sl.* scive.

'Blaumeise *f zo.* blue tit. **'Blaupause** *f* blueprint. **'Blausäure** *f* ✿ prussic acid. **'Blaustrumpf** *m* bluestocking.

Blech [blɛç] *n* (-[e]s; -e) **1.** *a)* sheet metal, *b)* metal sheet. **2.** baking tray. **3.** F rubbish. **'Blechbüchse** *f*, **'Blechdose** *f* tin, (tin) can.

blechen ['blɛçən] *v/t, v/i* (h) F cough up.

'blechern *adj* **1.** (of) tin. **2.** tinny (*sound*).

'Blech|instru,ment *n* ♪ brass instrument. **~schaden** *m mot.* bodywork damage. **~schere** *f* plate shears.

blecken ['blɛkən] *v/t* (h) *die Zähne* ~ *animal:* bare its fangs.

Blei [blaɪ] *n* (-[e]s; *no pl*) **1.** lead: *aus* ~ (made of) lead; *fig.* (*schwer*) *wie* ~ leaden. **2.** *hunt.* shot.

Bleibe ['blaɪbə] *f* (-; -n) F place to stay.

bleiben ['blaɪbən] *v/i* (blieb, geblieben, sn) **1.** stay (*im Bett* in bed, *zu Hause* at home, *zum Essen* for dinner); *wo bleibt er denn nur?* what has taken him?; F *fig. und wo bleibe ich?* and where do I come in?; → *Ball*[1]. **2.** ~ *bei* stick to (*der Wahrheit* the truth); → *Sache* 2. **3.** remain, keep: *geschlossen* (*gesund etc*) ~ stay closed (healthy *etc*); *für sich* ~ keep to o.s.; *das bleibt unter uns!* F keep it under your hat!; ~

Sie (doch) sitzen! don't get up!; *es bleibt dabei!* that's final!; *und dabei bleibt es!* and that's that! **4.** be left (*dat* to), remain. **'bleibend** *adj* lasting, permanent. **'bleibenlassen** *v/t* (*irr, sep, no* -ge-, h, → *lassen*) **et. ~** a) not to do s.th., b) stop (doing) s.th.; *laß das bleiben!* stop it!; *das werde ich schön ~!* I'll do nothing of the kind!

bleich [blaiç] *adj* pale (*vor* with): **~ werden** (turn) pale.

bleichen ['blaiçən] *v/t, v/i* (h) bleach.

'Bleichgesicht *n* paleface.

'Bleichmittel *n* bleach(ing agent).

bleiern ['blaiərn] *adj a. fig.* leaden.

'Bleifarbe *f* lead paint. **'bleifrei** *adj* unleaded. **'bleihaltig** [-haltiç] *adj* containing, leaded (*petrol*). **'Bleikri,stall** *n* lead crystal. **'Bleistift** *m* (lead) pencil. **'Bleistiftspitzer** *m* pencil sharpener. **'Bleivergiftung** *f* lead poisoning.

Blendauto,matik ['blɛnt-] *f phot.* automatic aperture control.

'Blende ['blɛndə] *f* (-; -n) **1.** screen. **2.** *phot.* a) diaphragm, b) aperture, c) f-stop: (*bei*) **~ 8** at f-8. **3.** facing.

'blenden (h) **I** *v/t* **1.** *a. fig.* dazzle. **2.** blind. **II** *v/i* **3.** dazzle, be dazzling (*a. fig.*). **4.** *fig.* deceive. **'Blenden** *n* (-s) *mot.* glare. **'blendend** *adj* dazzling, *fig. a.* brilliant: **~ aussehen** look great; *sich ~ amüsieren* have a great time. **'Blenden|einstellung** *f phot.* aperture setting. **~skala** *f* aperture ring. **~zahl** *f phot.* f-stop.

'Blender *m* (-s; -) *fig.* fake.

'blendfrei *adj* antiglare.

'Blendschutz|scheibe *f mot.* antiglare screen. **~zaun** *m mot.* antiglare barrier.

'Blendung *f* (-; -en) **1.** blinding, *mot. etc* dazzle, glare. **2.** *fig.* deception.

'Blick [blik] *m* (-[e]s; -e) **1.** (*auf acc* at) look, glance: *auf den ersten ~* at first sight; *mit einem ~* at a glance; *e-n ~ werfen auf* (*acc*) have a look at. **2.** view (*auf acc* of): *mit ~ auf* (*acc*) with a view of, overlooking *the lake etc.*

'blicken *v/i* (h) look (*auf acc* at): *um sich ~* look around; *sich ~ lassen* show o.s.; *das liegt tief ~!* that's very revealing!

'Blick|fang *m* eyecatcher. **~feld** *n a. fig.* field of vision. **~kon,takt** *m* eye contact. **~punkt** *m* **1.** *opt.* visual focus: *fig. im ~ stehen* be in the centre of interest. **2.**

fig. point of view. **~richtung** *f* **1.** line of vision. **2.** *fig.* direction. **~winkel** *m* **1.** angle of view. **2.** *fig.* point of view.

blieb [bli:p] *pret of* **bleiben**.

blies [bli:s] *pret of* **blasen**.

blind [blint] **I** *adj* **1.** blind (*a.* △, ⊙, *a. fig.* **gegen, für** to, **vor** *dat* with): *auf einem Auge ~* blind in one eye; *j-n ~ machen gegen* blind s.o. to; → *Passagier*. **2.** cloudy (*mirror*), tarnished (*metal*). **II** *adv fly etc* blind, *fig. trust etc* blindly.

'Blinddarm *m* appendix. **~entzündung** *f* appendicitis. **~operati,on** *f* appendectomy.

'Blinde *m, f* (-n; -n) blind man (woman): *die ~n* the blind; *das sieht doch ein ~r!* you can see that with half an eye!

'Blinden|heim *n* home for the blind. **~hund** *m* guide dog, *Am.* seeing-eye dog. **~schrift** *f* braille. **~stock** *m* white stick, (blind person's) cane.

'Blindflug *m* instrument flying.

Blindgänger ['blintgɛŋər] *m* (-s; -) **1.** ✗ dud. **2.** *F fig.* dud, washout.

'Blindheit *f* (-; *no pl*) blindness.

blindlings ['blintlɪŋs] *adv* blindly.

'Blindschleiche *f zo.* blindworm.

'blindschreiben *v/i* (*irr, sep,* -ge-, h, → *schreiben*) touch-type.

blinken ['blɪŋkən] *v/i* (h) **1.** sparkle. **2.** *a. v/t* (flash a) signal, flash. **'Blinker** *m* (-s; -) **1.** *mot.* indicator. **2.** spoon bait. **'Blinklicht** *n* (-[e]s; -er) *mot.* a) flashing light, b) → *Blinker* 1. **'Blinkzeichen** *n* flashing (*mot.* indicator) signal.

blinzeln ['blɪntsəln] *v/i* (h) blink.

Blitz [blɪts] *m* (-es; -e) **1.** a) lightning, b) flash (of lightning): *vom ~ getroffen* struck by lightning; *fig.* ~ **aus heiterem Himmel** a bolt from the blue; *wie vom ~ getroffen* thunderstruck; *wie der ~, → blitzschnell* **II. 2.** *phot.* flash. **'Blitzableiter** *m* lightning conductor. **'blitzartig → blitzschnell.**

'Blitzaufnahme *f phot.* flash shot.

'Blitzbesuch *m* lightning visit.

'Blitzbirne *f phot.* flashbulb.

'blitzblank *adj and adv* sparkling clean.

blitzen ['blɪtsən] **I** *v/i* (h) **1.** *es hat geblitzt* there was (a flash of) lightning. **2.** flash, *a.* sparkle. **II** *v/t* **3.** *phot.* F flash. **'Blitzgerät** *n* (electronic) flash (gun). **'Blitzlampe** *f phot.* flashbulb. **'Blitzlicht** *n phot.* flashlight: *mit ~ foto-*

grafieren (use a) flash. '**blitzsauber** *adj* F (as) clean as a whistle. '**Blitz-schlag** *m* lightning. '**blitzschnell** I *adj* lightning ... II *adv* with lightning speed, like a flash. '**Blitzstart** *m* lightning start. '**Blitzwürfel** *m phot.* flashcube.

Block [blɔk] *m* (-[e]s; ⁔e) 1. block (*a. of stamps, houses, etc*), (writing) pad, book (of tickets). 2. boulder. 3. ✝, *parl., pol.* bloc.

Blockade [blɔ'ka:də] *f* (-; -n) 1. blockade. 2. ✿ block(ing).

'**Blockbuchstabe** *m* block letter.

'**Blockflöte** *f* recorder.

'**blockfrei** *adj pol.* nonaligned.

'**Blockhaus** *n* log cabin.

blockieren [blɔ'ki:rən] *v/t* (h) block, (*a. v/i wheels*) lock, ✿ jam.

'**Blockschoko,lade** *f* cooking chocolate.

'**Blockschrift** *f* block letters.

'**Blockstaat** *m pol.* aligned state.

blöd [blø:t] *adj* 1. ✿ imbecile. 2. F stupid, silly. **Blödel...** ['blø:dəl] slapstick (*show etc*). '**blödeln** *v/i* (h) fool around. '**Blödheit** *f* (-; -en) 1. *no pl* ✿ imbecility. 2. F stupidity, silliness. '**Blödmann** *m* (-[e]s; ⁔er) F idiot, silly ass. '**Blödsinn** *m* (-; *no pl*) 1. ✿ imbecility. 2. F nonsense, rubbish. '**blödsinnig** *adj* idiotic.

blöken ['blø:kən] *v/i* (h) *sheep:* bleat, *cow:* low.

blond [blɔnt] *adj* blond(e), fair(-haired). **blondieren** [blɔn'di:rən] *v/t* (h) dye *one's hair* blond. **Blon'dine** *f* (-; -n) blonde.

bloß [blo:s] I *adj* 1. bare, naked: *mit ⁔en Füßen* barefoot(ed); *mit ⁔en Händen* with one's bare hands; *mit dem ⁔en Auge* with the naked eye. 2. mere: *der ⁔e Gedanke* the mere thought. II *adv* 3. only, simply, merely: *komm ⁔ nicht rein!* don't you dare come in!

Blöße ['blø:sə] *f* (-; -n) 1. bareness, nakedness. 2. *sports or fig.* opening: *sich e-e ⁔ geben* leave o.s. wide open.

'**bloßlegen** *v/t* (*sep*, -ge-, h) lay bare, expose (*a. fig.*). '**bloßstellen** *v/t* (*sep*, -ge-, h) expose, show *s.o.* up.

'**Bloßstellung** *f* (-; -en) exposure.

Blouson [blu'zõ:] *m, n* (-s; -s) blouson.

Bluff [blɔf] *m* (-s; -s), '**bluffen** *v/i, v/t* (h) *contp.* bluff.

blühen ['bly:ən] *v/i* (h) blossom (*a. fig.*), be in bloom, *fig.* thrive: F *wer weiß, was uns noch blüht!* who knows

what's in store for us!

'**blühend** *adj* 1. flowering, blooming. 2. *fig.* flourishing, glowing (*health*), lively (*imagination*): *⁔ aussehen* look the picture of health.

Blume ['blu:mə] *f* (-; -n) 1. flower: *j-m et. durch die ⁔ sagen* hint to s.o. that. 2. bouquet (*of wine*), head, froth (*on beer*).

'**Blumen|beet** *n* flower bed. **⁔erde** *f* garden mo(u)ld. **⁔händler(in** *f*) *m* florist. **⁔kohl** *m* cauliflower. **⁔laden** *m* flower shop. **⁔muster** *n* floral design. **⁔strauß** *m* bunch of flowers, bouquet. **⁔topf** *m* flowerpot. **⁔zwiebel** *f* flower bulb.

blumig *adj* 1. *fig.* flowery. 2. *wine:* with a fine bouquet.

Bluse ['blu:zə] *f* (-; -n) blouse.

Blut [blu:t] *n* (-[e]s; *no pl*) blood: *sie kann kein ⁔ sehen* she can't stand the sight of blood; *⁔ spenden* donate (*or* give) blood; *fig.* **blaues (junges) ⁔** blue (young) blood; *ruhig ⁔!* take it easy!; *j-n bis aufs ⁔ reizen* drive s.o. wild; F *⁔ (und Wasser) schwitzen* sweat blood; *⁔ vergießen* shed blood; *böses ⁔ machen* breed bad blood; *die Musik liegt ihm im ⁔* music is in his blood.

'**Blut|alko,hol(gehalt)** *m* blood alcohol. **⁔arm** *adj* an(a)emic. **⁔armut** *f* an(a)emia. **⁔bad** *n fig.* massacre. **⁔bank** *f* (-; -en) ✿ blood bank. **⁔bild** *n* ✿ blood count. **⁔blase** *f* blood blister.

'**Blutdruck** *m* (-[e]s; *no pl*) blood pressure: *j-s ⁔ messen* take s.o.'s blood pressure.

'**blutdrucksenkend** *adj* hypotensive.

'**blutdürstig** [-dyrstiç] *adj* bloodthirsty.

Blüte ['bly:tə] *f* (-; -n) 1. blossom, flower. 2. *no pl* flowering time, blossom: *in voller ⁔* in (full) bloom. 3. *no pl fig.* heyday, ✝ time of prosperity: *in höchster ⁔ stehen* be flourishing; *in der ⁔s-r Jahre* in his prime. 4. *fig.* flower, élite. 5. F *dud,* counterfeit money.

'**Blutegel** *m zo.* leech.

bluten ['blu:tən] *v/i* (h) bleed (*aus* from): F *fig.* **schwer ⁔ müssen** have to pay through the nose.

'**Blüten|honig** *m* honey made from blossoms and flowers. **⁔knospe** *f* (flower) bud. **⁔lese** *f fig.* anthology. **⁔staub** *m* pollen. **⁔weiß** *adj* snow-white.

'**Bluter** *m* (-s; -) ✿ h(a)emophiliac.

'**Blut|erguß** *m* ✿ h(a)ematoma, bruise.

~farbstoff m h(a)emoglobin. **~fleck** m bloodstain. **~gefäß** n 🗲 blood vessel. **~gerinnsel** n 🗲 blood clot. **~gruppe** f blood group. **~hochdruck** m 🗲 high blood pressure. **~hund** m bloodhound.
blutig adj **1.** a) bloody (a. fig.), b) blood-stained: fig. **~er Anfänger** rank beginner. **2.** gastr. rare (steak).
blutjung adj very young.
Blut|kon,serve f unit of stored blood. **~körperchen** n blood corpuscle. **~kreislauf** m blood circulation. **~lache** f pool of blood. 🗨**leer** adj a. fig. bloodless. **~o,range** f blood orange. **~plasma** n blood plasma. **~probe** f **1.** blood (🗲 alcohol) test. **2.** 🗲 blood sample. **~rache** f vendetta.
blutrot adj (dark) crimson.
blutrünstig ['blu:trynstɪç] adj fig. gory: **~er Film** etc blood-curdling film etc.
Blutsauger m a. fig. bloodsucker.
Blutschande f incest. **blutschänderisch** ['blu:tʃɛndərɪʃ] adj incestuous.
Blutsenkung f 🗲 blood sedimentation.
Blutspender(in f) m blood donor.
blutstillend adj (a. **~es Mittel**) styptic.
Blutstropfen m drop of blood.
Blutsturz m 🗲 h(a)emorrhage.
blutsverwandt adj related by blood (**mit** to). **Blutsverwandte** m, f (-n; -n) blood relation. **Blutsverwandtschaft** f consanguinity.
Bluttransfusi,on f blood transfusion.
bluttriefend adj dripping with blood.
blutüberströmt adj covered with blood.
Blutübertragung f blood transfusion.
Blutung f (-; -en) bleeding, h(a)emorrhage.
blutunterlaufen adj bloodshot.
Blut|vergießen n (-s; no pl) bloodshed. **~vergiftung** f blood poisoning. **~verlust** m loss of blood. **~wäsche** f 🗲 (h[a]emo)dialysis. **~wurst** f gastr. black pudding. **~zucker(spiegel)** m 🗲 blood sugar (level). **~zufuhr** f blood supply.
Bö [bø:] f (-; -en) gust, squall.
Bob [bɔp] m (-s; -s) sports: bob(sleigh).
Bobbahn f bob(sleigh) run.
Bock [bɔk] m (-[e]s; ⸚e) **1.** zo. a) buck, b) ram, c) he-goat: fig. **e-n ~ schießen** make a blunder; **den ~ zum Gärtner machen** set the fox to keep the geese; → **null. 2.** ⊙ a) stand, b) jack. **3.** gym. buck. **4.** bock (beer).

bockbeinig [-baɪnɪç] adj F stubborn.
Bockbier n bock (beer).
bocken v/i (h) **1.** a. mot. buck. **2.** be stubborn, sulk. **bockig** adj stubborn.
Bockshorn n j-n **ins ~ jagen** scare s.o.
Bockspringen n (-s) leapfrog.
Boden ['bo:dən] m (-s; ⸚) **1.** ground, 🗲 soil, bottom (of a vessel, the sea), floor: **am ~, auf dem ~** on the ground (or floor); sports: **am ~ sein** be down; **zu ~ fallen** fall to the ground; F fig. **er war (völlig) am ~ zerstört** he was absolutely shattered; **auf britischem ~** on British soil; **den ~ unter den Füßen verlieren** a. fig. get out of one's depth; **(an) ~ gewinnen (verlieren)** gain (lose) ground; **aus dem ~ schießen** mushroom (up); **et. aus dem ~ stampfen** conjure s.th. up. **2.** attic.
Boden|abstand m mot. ground clearance. **~belag** m floor covering. **~fläche** f **1.** 🗲 acreage. **2.** △ floor space. **~frost** m ground frost. **~haftung** f mot. road holding.
bodenlos adj **1.** bottomless. **2.** F fig. incredible, shocking.
Boden|nebel m ground fog. **~perso,nal** n 🗲 ground crew. **~radar** n ground-based radar. **~re,form** f land reform. **~satz** m **1.** sediment. **2.** fig. contp. dregs. **~schätze** pl mineral resources.
bodenständig adj native, local.
Boden|stati,on f earth (or tracking) station. **~stewardeß** f ground hostess. **~streitkräfte** pl ground forces. **~turnen** n floor exercises.
bog [bo:k] pret of **biegen**.
Bogen ['bo:gən] m (-s; -) **1.** bow: fig. **den ~ überspannen** overdo it. **2.** curve, bend: fig. **e-n großen ~ machen um j-n** give s.o. a wide berth. **3.** 🗲, ⊼ arc, △ arch, vault, ⊙ bend. **4.** skating: curve, skiing: turn. **5.** sheet (of paper).
Bogenfenster n arched window.
bogenförmig adj arched.
Bogen|gang m arcade. **~lampe** f arc lamp. **~schießen** n archery. **~schütze** m archer.
Bohemien [boe'mĩɛ:] m (-s; -s) bohemian.
Bohle ['bo:lə] f (-; -n) plank.
Böhme ['bø:mə] m (-n; -n), **Böhmin** f (-; -nen) Bohemian. **böhmisch** adj Bohe-

mian: *das sind für mich* ~*e Dörfer* that's (all) Greek to me.

Bohne ['boːnə] *f* (-; -n) **&** a) bean, b) broad bean: *grüne* ~*n* French (*or* string) beans; *weiße* ~*n* haricot beans; F *nicht die* ~*!* not a bit!

'**Bohnenkaffee** *m* (F real) coffee.

'**Bohnenstange** *f* beanpole (*a.* F *person*).

'**Bohnenstroh** *n* F *dumm wie* ~ as thick as two short planks.

Bohner ['boːnər] *m* (-s; -) floor polisher.

'**bohnern** *v/t* (h) polish.

'**Bohnerwachs** *n* floor polish.

bohren ['boːrən] (h) **I** *v/t* **1. ⚙** a) drill, b) bore. **II** *v/i* **2.** drill (*nach* for), bore: → *Nase.* **3.** *fig.* pain *etc*: gnaw (*in dat* at). **4.** *fig.* a) probe, b) keep at it (*bis* until). **III** *sich* ~ *in* (*acc*) bore into.

'**bohrend** *adj* **1.** gnawing (*pain etc*), piercing (*look*), probing (*questions*).

'**Bohrer** *m* (-s; -) drill.

'**Bohrinsel** *f* oil rig. '**Bohrloch** *n* drill hole. '**Bohrma,schine** *f* drill(ing machine). '**Bohrmeißel** *m,* '**Bohrstahl** *m* boring tool. '**Bohrturm** *m* derrick.

'**Bohrung** *f* (-; -en) **1.** drilling. **2.** (drill) hole. **3.** *mot.* bore.

'**Bohrversuch** *m* trial drilling.

böig ['bøːɪç] *adj* gusty, ✈ bumpy.

Boiler ['bɔylər] *m* (-s; -) water heater, ⚙ boiler.

Boje ['boːjə] *f* (-; -n) buoy.

Bollwerk *n* ['bɔlvɛrk] *n a. fig.* bulwark.

Bolschewismus [bɔlʃə'vɪsmʊs] *m* (-; *no pl*) Bolshevism. **Bolschewist** [-'vɪst] *m* (-en; -en), **Bolsche'wistin** *f* (-; -nen), **bolsche'wistisch** *adj* Bolshevist.

Bolzen ['bɔltsən] *m* (-s; -) ⚙ bolt.

bombardieren [bɔmbar'diːrən] *v/t* (h) bomb, *a. phys. or fig.* bombard.

bombastisch [bɔm'bastɪʃ] *adj* bombastic.

Bombe ['bɔmbə] *f* (-; -n) **1.** bomb: → *einschlagen* 6. **2.** F soccer: rocket.

'**Bomben|a,larm** *m* bomb alert. ~**an**-**griff** *m* bomb attack. ~**anschlag** *m* **1.** bomb attack. **2.** → ~**atten,tat** *n* bomb attempt (*auf j-n* on s.o.'s life). ~**beset-zung** *f* F *thea. etc* star cast. ~**drohung** *f* bomb threat. ~**erfolg** *m* F huge success, smash hit. &**fest** *adj* bombproof: F ~ **überzeugt** dead sure. ~**gehalt** *n* F fantastic salary. ~**geschäft** *n* F roaring business. ~**sache** *f* F knockout. &**si-**

cher *adj* **1.** bombproof. **2.** F sure-fire: *es ist e-e* ~*e Sache* it's a dead cert. ~**stimmung** *f* F *es herrschte e-e* ~ everybody was in roaring high spirits.

'**Bomber** *m* (-s; -) bomber (*a.* F *fig.* soccer). '**bombig** *adj* F great, terrific.

Bon [bɔŋ] *m* (-s; -s) **1.** voucher. **2.** receipt.

Bonbon [bɔŋ'bɔŋ] *m, n* (-s; -s) **1.** sweet, *Am.* candy. **2.** F *fig.* bonbon.

Bonmot [bõ'moː] *n* (-s; -s) bon mot.

Bonus ['boːnʊs] *m* (-[ses]; -se) **1.** bonus, premium. **2.** special dividend.

Bonze ['bɔntsə] *m* (-n; -n) *contp.* bigwig.

Boot [boːt] *n* (-[e]s; -e) boat: ~ *fahren* go boating; *fig.* *wir sitzen alle im gleichen* ~ we are all in the same boat.

'**Bootsfahrt** *f* boat trip. '**Bootshaus** *n* boathouse. '**Bootsmann** *m* (-[e]s; -leu-te) **⚓** boatswain, ✕ petty officer. '**Bootsverleih** *m* boat hire.

Bord¹ [bɔrt] *n* (-[e]s; -e) shelf.

Bord² *m* (-[e]s; -e) **1.** ✈, **⚓** *an* ~ on board, aboard; *an* ~ *gehen* go aboard, ✈ board the plane; *an* ~ *nehmen* take aboard; *über* ~ *gehen a. fig.* go by the board; *über* ~ *werfen a. fig.* throw overboard. **2.** edge. '**Bordbuch** *n* **⚓** logbook. '**Bordcom,puter** *m* on-board (*mot. a.* dashboard) computer.

Bordell [bɔr'dɛl] *n* (-s; -e) brothel.

'**Bord|funk** *m* a) ship's radio, b) aircraft radio (equipment). ~**karte** *f* ✈ board-ing pass. ~**me,chaniker** *m* ✈ flight me-chanic. ~**radar** *n* airborne radar. ~**stein** *m* kerb(stone), *Am.* curb(stone). ~**verpflegung** *f* in-flight meals.

Borg [bɔrk] *m auf* ~ on credit. **borgen** ['bɔrgən] *v/t* (h) **1.** borrow: *sich et.* ~ borrow s.th. **2.** lend, *Am.* loan.

Borke ['bɔrkə] *f* (-; -n) bark, *a.* 🌿 crust.

borniert [bɔr'niːrt] *adj* narrow-minded.

Börse ['bœrzə] *f* (-; -n) **1.** purse. **2.** † (*an* [*auf*] *der* ~ on the) stock exchange: *an die* ~ *gehen firm:* go public.

'**Börsen|bericht** *m* market report. ~**blatt** *n* financial (news)paper. &**fähig** *adj* marketable, listed: ~*e Wertpapiere* listed securities. ~**geschäft** *n* stock-market transaction. ~**krach** *m* F (stock-exchange) crash. ~**kurs** *m* market price, quotation. ~**makler** *m* stock-broker. ~**no,tierung** *f* quotation. ~**speku,lant** *m* stock-exchange specu-lator. ~**zettel** *m* stock list.

Borste ['bɔrstə] f (-; -n) bristle.
'borstig adj 1. bristly. 2. F fig. gruff.
Borte ['bɔrtə] f (-; -n) border, braid.
bösartig ['bøːz-] adj 1. vicious. 2. ✻ malignant. **'Bösartigkeit** f (-; no pl) 1. viciousness. 2. ✻ malignancy.
Böschung ['bœʃʊŋ] f (-; -en) slope, embankment.
böse ['bøːzə] I adj 1. bad, evil, wicked: *e-e ~ Sache* a bad business. 2. vicious, nasty. 3. naughty, bad. 4. angry: *j-m (or auf j-n) ~ sein* be angry (F mad) at s.o., be cross with s.o.; *~ werden* get angry; *bist du mir ~, wenn ...?* would you mind terribly if ...? 5. F ✻ bad, sore: *~ Erkältung* bad cold; *~r Finger* sore finger. II adv 6. badly (*etc*): *es sieht ~ aus* things look bad; *ich habe es nicht ~ gemeint* I meant no harm.
'Böse I m, f (-n; -n) bad person. II n (-n) evil, harm: *~s im Sinn haben* be up to no good.
'Bösewicht m (-[e]s; -er) a. iro. villain.
boshaft ['bɔːshaft] adj malicious.
'Bosheit f (-; -en) 1. no pl malice: *aus ~ out of spite. 2. snide remark. 3. nasty trick.
Boß [bɔs] m (Bosses; Bosse) F boss.
'böswillig adj malicious, ⚖ a. wilful.
'Böswilligkeit f (-; no pl) malevolence, ⚖ wilfulness.
bot [boːt] pret of **bieten**.
Botanik [bo'taːnɪk] f (-; no pl) botany.
Bo'taniker m (-s; -) botanist.
bo'tanisch adj botanic(al).
Bote ['boːtə] m (-n; -n) messenger.
'Botengang m (*e-n ~ machen* run an) errand.
Botschaft ['boːtʃaft] f (-; -en) 1. message (*a. fig.*), news. 2. pol. embassy.
'Botschafter m (-s; -) ambassador.
'Botschafterin f (-; -nen) ambassadress.
Böttcher ['bœtçər] m (-s; -) cooper.
Bottich ['bɔtɪç] m (-s; -e) vat, tub.
Bouillon [bʊl'jɔŋ] f (-; -s) clear soup.
Boulevard [bulə'vaːr] m (-s; -s) boulevard. **~presse** f (-; no pl) gutter press. **~zeitung** f tabloid.
Boutique [bu'tiːk] f (-; -n) boutique.
Bowle ['boːlə] f (-; -n) 1. punch bowl. 2. gastr. (cold) punch.
Box [bɔks] f (-; -en) 1. box (*for horses*). 2. motor racing: pit. 3. parking space. 4. box camera. 5. → **Lautsprecherbox**.

'boxen v/i (h) box, fight. **'Boxen** n (-s) boxing. **'Boxer** m (-s; -) boxer (*a. dog*).
'Boxhandschuh m boxing glove. **'Boxkampf** m fight, boxing match. **'Boxring** m ring. **'Boxsport** m boxing.
Boykott [bɔy'kɔt] m (-[e]s; -s, -e), **boykottieren** [-'tiːrən] v/t (h) boycott.
brach [braːx] pret of **brechen**.
Brachialgewalt [braˈxiaːl-] f (*mit ~ by*) brute force.
Brachland ['braːx-] n fallow (land).
'brachliegen v/i (*irr, sep, -ge-, h, → liegen*) 1. lie fallow. 2. fig. go to waste.
brachte ['braxtə] pret of **bringen**.
Brahmane [braˈmaːnə] m (-n; -n), **brah'manisch** adj Brahman.
Branche ['brãːʃə] f (-; -n) 1. industrial sector, trade. 2. line (of business).
'Branchen|kenntnis f knowledge of the trade. **♀üblich** adj usual in the trade. **~verzeichnis** n classified directory.
Brand [brant] m (-[e]s; ⁓e) 1. (*in ~ on*) fire: *in ~ geraten* catch fire; *in ~ stecken* set fire to; F *e-n ~ haben* be dying of thirst. 2. ♀ blight, mildew. 3. ✻ gangrene. **~blase** f blister. **~bombe** f incendiary bomb.
branden ['brandən] v/i (sn) a. fig. surge.
'Brand|gefahr f fire hazard. **~geruch** m burnt smell. **~herd** m 1. source of (the) fire. 2. fig. trouble spot. **~kata,strophe** f fire disaster. **~mal** n (-[e]s; -e) 1. brand. 2. fig. stigma.
brandmarken ['brantmarkən] v/t (*insep, ge-, h*) a. fig. brand.
'Brand|mauer f fire wall. **~schaden** m fire damage. **~sohle** f insole. **~stelle** f scene of the fire. **~stifter(in** f) m incendiary. **~stiftung** f arson.
'Brandung f (-; no pl) surf, breakers.
'Brand|ursache f cause of the fire. **~wunde** f burn. **~zeichen** n brand.
brannte ['brantə] pret of **brennen**.
'Branntwein m spirits.
Brasilianer [braziˈliaːnər] m (-s; -), **Brasili'anerin** f (-; -nen), **brasili'anisch** adj Brazilian. **Brasilien** [braˈziːliən] n (-s) Brazil.
brassen ['brasən] v/t ⚓ brace.
'Bratapfel m baked apple.
braten ['braːtən] v/t, v/i (briet, gebraten, h) roast, fry: *auf dem Rost ~ grill, broil; am Spieß ~ barbecue; F (in der Sonne) ~ roast (in the sun).

'**Braten** m (-s; -) roast, joint: F fig. **den ~ riechen** smell a rat; **fetter ~** fine catch.
'**Bratenfett** n dripping. '**Bratensoße** f gravy. '**bratfertig** adj oven-ready.
'**Bratfett** n cooking fat. '**Bratfisch** m fried fish. '**Brathering** m grilled (and pickled) herring. '**Brathuhn** n roaster, broiler. '**Bratkar,toffeln** pl fried potatoes. '**Bratofen** m oven. '**Bratpfanne** f frying-pan. '**Bratröhre** f oven.
Bratsche ['braːtʃə] f (-; -n) ♪ viola.
'**Bratscher** m (-s; -), '**Bratscherin** f (-; -nen) viola player.
'**Bratspieß** m spit.
'**Bratwurst** f fried (or grilled) sausage.
Brauch [braʊx] m (-[e]s; ⁻e) custom, tradition, practice, † usage. '**brauchbar** adj useful, serviceable. '**Brauchbarkeit** f (-; no pl) usefulness. '**brauchen** (h) I v/t 1. need, require, take: **wie lange wird er ~?** how long will it take him? 2. → a) **gebrauchen**, b) **verbrauchen**. II v/aux need, have to: **du brauchst es nicht zu tun** you needn't (or you don't have to) do it; **du brauchst es nur zu sagen!** just say so! '**Brauchtum** n (-s; no pl) custom(s), tradition.
Braue ['braʊə] f (-; -n) (eye)brow.
'**brauen** v/t (h) brew. '**Brauer** m (-s; -) brewer. **Braue'rei** f (-; -en) brewery.
braun [braʊn] adj brown, a. (sun)tanned: **~ werden** tan, get a tan.
Bräune ['brɔynə] f (-; no pl) 1. brownness. 2. (sun)tan. '**bräunen** (h) I v/t 1. brown. 2. tan (skin, person). II v/i (a. **sich ~**) a) get brown, b) tan, get a tan.
'**braungebrannt** adj tanned.
'**Braunkohle** f brown coal, lignite.
bräunlich ['brɔynlɪç] adj brownish.
'**Bräunungs|creme** f liquid tan (make-up). **~studio** n solarium.
Brause ['braʊzə] f (-; -n) 1. sprinkler, rose. 2. → **Dusche**. 3. F pop. '**Brausebad** n shower. '**Brause|limo,nade** f (fizzy) lemonade, Am. lemon soda.
'**brausen** v/i 1. (h) wind etc: roar, organ etc: surge. 2. (sn) F zoom. 3. (h) (have a) shower.
'**Brausepulver** n sherbet powder.
Braut [braʊt] f (-; ⁻e) a) bride, b) fiancée, c) F (my etc) girl. **Bräutigam** ['brɔytɪɡam] m (-s; -e) a) (bride)groom, b) fiancé. '**Brautjungfer** f bridesmaid.
'**Brautkleid** n wedding dress. '**Braut-**

paar n a) engaged couple, b) bride and bridegroom. '**Brautschleier** m bridal veil.
brav [braːf] adj 1. good, well-behaved: **sei ~!** be good!; **sei (schön) ~ und geh zu Bett!** go to bed like a good boy (or girl)! 2. honest, good, a. iro. worthy.
bravo ['braːvo] int well done!, bravo!
'**Bravo** n (-s; -s), **~ruf** m bravo, pl cheers.
Bravour [bra'vuːr] f (-; no pl) 1. dash: **mit ~** brilliantly. 2. bravery.
bravourös [bravu'røːs] adj brilliant.
Bra'vourstück n 1. brilliant feat. 2. ♪ bravura.
'**Brech|durchfall** m ⚕ diarrh(o)ea with vomiting. **~eisen** n ◎ crowbar.
brechen ['brɛçən] (brach, gebrochen) I v/t (h) 1. break (a. fig. oath, record, resistance, etc), fig. a. violate (contract, law): **(sich) den Arm ~** break one's arm; **die Ehe ~** commit adultery. 2. phys. break, refract (rays). 3. F ⚕ vomit. II v/i 4. (sn) break (a. fig. voice etc). 5. (sn) **~ aus** (dat) burst out of. 6. (h) fig. **~ mit** (dat) break with (s.o., a habit, etc). 7. (h) F ⚕ be sick, vomit. III **sich ~** (h) 8. waves: break, phys. light etc: be refracted. '**Brecher** m (-s; -) breaker.
'**Brech|mittel** n 1. ⚕ emetic. 2. F fig. **er (es) ist ein ~** sl. he (it's) enough to make you want to puke. **~reiz** m ⚕ nausea. **~stange** f ◎ crowbar.
'**Brechung** f (-; -en) phys. refraction.
Brei [braɪ] m (-[e]s; -e) a) mush (a. fig.), b) porridge, c) mash, d) ◎ pulp: F **j-n zu ~ schlagen** beat s.o. to a pulp; → **Katze, Koch**. '**breiig** adj mushy.
breit [braɪt] adj broad (a. fig. accent etc), a. ◎ wide, fig. widespread: **die ~e Öffentlichkeit** the public at large; **ein ~es Publikum** a wide public; → **Masse** 4.
'**Breitband...** radio: wide-band ...
'**breitbeinig** [-baɪnɪç] adj and adv with legs apart.
Breite f (-; -n) width, breadth (a. fig.), astr., geogr. latitude: F **in die ~ gehen** put on weight.
'**Breiten|grad** m (degree of) latitude: **der 30. ~** the 30th parallel. **~kreis** m parallel. **~sport** m mass sport(s).
'**breitgefächert** adj wide-ranging.
'**breitmachen: sich ~** (sep, -ge-, h) F a) spread o.s. out, b) fig. fear etc: spread.
'**breitschlagen** v/t (irr, sep, -ge-, h, →

schlagen F *j-n* ~ talk s.o. round, *zu et.* talk s.o. into (doing) s.th.; *sich ~ lassen* give in.

breitschult(e)rig ['braɪtʃʊlt(ə)rɪç] *adj* broad-shouldered.

'**Breitseite** *f* 1. long side (*of table etc*). 2. ♣, ✗, *a. fig.* broadside.

'**breitspurig** *adj* 🚂 broad-ga(u)ge.

'**breittreten** *v/t* (*irr, sep, -ge-*, h, → **treten**) F *fig.* enlarge (up)on (*a subject*): *et. überall* ~ talk about s.th. too much.

'**Breitwandfilm** *m* wide-screen film.

Bremsbelag ['brɛms-] *m* brake lining.

Bremse[1] ['brɛmzə] *f* (-; -n) *mot.* brake.

Bremse[2] *f* (-; -n) *zo.* horsefly.

bremsen (h) I *v/t* 1. brake. 2. cushion (*fall*). 3. F *fig.* check, slow down. II *v/i* 4. brake, apply the brakes. III *sich* ~ F restrain o.s., *mit et.* cut down on s.th.

'**Brems|flüssigkeit** *f* brake fluid. ~**kraftverstärker** *m* brake booster. ~**leuchte** *f*, ~**licht** *n* stop light. ~**pe,dal** *n* brake pedal. ~**scheibe** *f* brake disc. ~**spur** *f* skid mark(s). ~**trommel** *f* brake drum.

'**Bremsung** *f* (-; -en) 1. braking. 2. *nucl.* retardation.

'**Bremsvorrichtung** *f* brake mechanism.

'**Bremsweg** *m* braking distance.

brennbar ['brɛnba:r] *adj* combustible.

brennen ['brɛnən] (brannte, gebrannt, h) I *v/t* 1. burn. 2. distil(l) (*spirits*), roast (*coffee*). 3. have *the light etc* on. II *v/i* 4. burn, *house etc*: *a.* be on fire: *es brennt!* fire!; F *fig. wo brennt's denn?* what's wrong?; *vor Ungeduld* ~ be burning with impatience; F *darauf* ~ *zu inf* be dying to *inf.* 5. *wound, nettle*: sting, *pepper etc*: be hot, *light, lamp*: be on. '**brennend** *adj* burning (*a. fig. question etc*): *es interessiert mich* ~ a) I'm terribly interested in it, b) *ob* I'm dying to know if.

'**Brenner** *m* (-s; -) 1. distiller. 2. ⊚ burner. **Brenne'rei** *f* (-; -en) distillery.

'**Brennessel** *f* ♣ (stinging) nettle.

'**Brenn|holz** *n* firewood. ~**materi,al** *n* fuel. ~**ofen** *m* kiln, *metall.* furnace. ~**punkt** *m a. fig.* focal point, focus: *fig. in den* ~ *rücken* focus attention on; *im* ~ *des Interesses stehen* be in the focus of attention. ~**spiegel** *m* burning mirror. ~**spiritus** *m* methylated spirit. ~**stab** *m nucl.* fuel rod. ~**stoff** *m* fuel. ~**weite** *f opt.* focal distance.

brenzlig ['brɛntslɪç] *adj* F *fig.* ticklish.

Bresche ['brɛʃə] *f* (-; -n) breach: *e-e* ~ *schlagen a. fig.* clear the way (*für* for); *in die* ~ *springen* step into the breach.

Brett [brɛt] *n* (-[e]s; -er) a) board, b) shelf, c) tray, d) *sports*: springboard: *Schwarzes* ~ notice (*Am.* bulletin) board; F ~**er** skis; F *fig. ein* ~ *vor dem Kopf haben* be very dense.

'**Brettspiel** *n* board game.

Brevier [bre'vi:r] *n* (-s; -e) breviary.

Brezel ['bre:tsəl] *f* (-; -n) pretzel.

Brief [bri:f] *m* (-[e]s; -e) letter (*an acc* to). ~**beschwerer** *m* paperweight. ~**bogen** *m* sheet of writing paper. ~**bombe** *f* letter bomb. ~**freund(in** *f*) *m* penfriend. ~**geheimnis** *n* privacy of correspondence. ~**kasten** *m* 1. letterbox, *Am.* mailbox: *toter* ~ letter drop. 2. suggestion box, *newspaper*: Question and Answer Column. ~**kastenfirma** *f* letter-box company. ~**kopf** *m* letterhead.

'**brieflich** *adj and adv* in writing, by letter(s).

'**Briefmarke** *f* (postage) stamp.

'**Briefmarken|album** *n* stamp album. ~**auto,mat** *m* stamp machine. ~**sammler(in** *f*) *m* stamp collector, philatelist. ~**sammlung** *f* stamp collection.

'**Brief|öffner** *m* letter opener. ~**pa,pier** *n* notepaper. ~**post** *f* mail, post, *Am.* first-class mail. ~**tasche** *f* wallet, *Am. a.* billfold. ~**taube** *f zo.* carrier pigeon. ~**tele,gramm** *n* letter telegram, *Am.* lettergram. ~**träger(in** *f*) *m* postman (postwoman). ~**umschlag** *m* envelope. ~**waage** *f* letter balance. ~**wahl** *f* postal vote, absentee voting. ~**wechsel** *m* correspondence.

Bries [bri:s] *n* (-es; -e) *gastr.* sweetbread.

briet [bri:t] *pret of* **braten**.

Brigade [bri'ga:də] *f* (-; -n) brigade.

Brikett [bri'kɛt] *n* (-s; -s) briquette.

brillant [bril'jant] *adj* brilliant.

Bril'lant *m* (-en; -en) diamond.

Brille ['brɪlə] *f* (-; -n) 1. (*e-e* ~ a pair of) glasses (*or* spectacles), F specs. 2. goggles. 3. toilet seat.

'**Brillen|e,tui** *n* spectacle case. ~**fassung** *f*, ~**gestell** *n* spectacle frame. ~**glas** *n* lens, glass. ~**schlange** *f* 1. *zo.* spectacled cobra. 2. F foureyes. ~**träger(in** *f*) *m* ~ *sein* wear glasses.

bringen ['brɪŋən] *v/t* (brachte, gebracht,

h) **1.** bring, get, fetch (*all:* **j-m et. s.o. s.th.**). **2.** take ([**zu**] **j-m** to s.o.): **j-n ins Krankenhaus** ~ take s.o. to the hospital; **j-n nach Hause** ~ take (*or* see) s.o. home. **3.** cause, bring (*luck, relief, etc*), bear (*interest*). **4.** **j-n dazu** ~**, daß er es tut** make s.o. do s.th. **5.** show, present (*film etc*), *thea. a.* bring, ♪ play, sing, newspaper etc: bring, have, carry (*an article etc*). **6.** do, manage: **es zu et.** ~ make one's mark (in life); F **das bringt's!** that's the stuff!; **das bringt's (auch) nicht!** that's no use!; **er bringt es nicht!** a) he just can't do it!, b) he's no good!; → **Leistung** 1, **weit** 6. **7.** *with prep* **an sich** ~ get hold of; **er brachte es auf 7 Punkte** he managed seven points; **es bis zum Major** *etc* ~ make it to major *etc*; **mit sich** ~ a) involve, b) require, make it necessary; **ich kann es nicht über mich** (*or* **übers Herz**) ~**, das zu tun** I can't bring myself to do it; **j-n um et.** ~ rob s.o. of s.th.; **j-n wieder zu sich** ~ bring s.o. round (*or* to); **j-n zum Lachen** *etc* ~ make s.o. laugh *etc*; → **hinter** I.

brisant [bri'zant] *adj* high-explosive, *fig.* explosive. **Brisanz** [bri'zants] *f* (-; *no pl*) explosive effect, *fig.* explosiveness.

Brise ['bri:zə] *f* (-; -n) breeze.

Brite ['bri:tə] *m* (-n; -n) British man, Briton, F Brit: **die** ~**n** the British. '**Britin** *f* (-; -nen) British woman. '**britisch** *adj* British: **die** ℒ**en Inseln** the British Isles.

bröck(e)lig ['brœk(ə)lıç] *adj* crumbly.

bröckeln ['brœkəln] *v/t, v/i* (h) crumble.

Brocken ['brɔkən] *m* (-s; -) **1.** piece, hunk, lump: F **ein** ~ (**von Mann**) a hulk of a man; *fig.* **ein harter** ~ a toughie. **2.** *pl* scraps (*of German slang etc*), snatches (*of conversation*).

brodeln ['bro:dəln] *v/i* (h) bubble, simmer, *fig.* seethe (**vor** *dat* with).

Brokat [bro'ka:t] *m* (-[e]s; -e) brocade.

Brom [bro:m] *n* (-s; *no pl*) bromine.

Brombeere ['brɔmbe:rə] *f* blackberry.

Bromid [bro'mi:t] *n* (-[e]s; -e) bromide.

'**Bromsilber** *n* bromide of silver.

Bronchial... [brɔn'çia:l-] bronchial (*asthma etc*). **Bronchien** ['brɔnçiən] *pl* bronchi. **Bronchitis** [brɔn'çi:tıs] *f* (-; -tiden [-çi'ti:dən]) bronchitis.

Bronze ['brõ:sə] *f* (-s; -n) bronze.

'**Bronzeme,daille** *f* bronze medal.

'**Bronzezeit** *f archeol.* Bronze Age.

Brosame ['bro:za:mə] (-; -n) *fig.* crumb.

Brosche ['brɔʃə] *f* (-; -n) brooch.

broschiert [brɔ'ʃi:rt] *adj* paperback.

Broschüre [brɔ'ʃy:rə] *f* (-; -n) pamphlet.

Brot [bro:t] *n* (-[e]s; -e) bread, loaf: (**belegtes**) ~ sandwich; *fig.* **das tägliche** ~ one's daily bread; **sein** ~ **verdienen** earn a living. '**Brotaufstrich** *m* spread.

'**Brötchen** ['brø:tçən] *n* (-s; -) roll.

'**Brötchengeber(in** *f*) *m* F boss.

'**Brot|getreide** *n* breadgrain. **~kasten** *m* bread bin, *Am.* breadbox. **~korb** *m* bread basket: **j-m den** ~ **höher hängen** put s.o. on short commons. **~krume** *f*, **~krümel** *m* (bread)crumb.

'**brotlos** *adj* **1.** jobless. **2.** unprofitable: **das ist e-e** ~**e Kunst!** there is no money in it!

'**Brot|messer** *n* bread knife. **~neid** *m* professional jealousy. **~röster** *m* (-s; -) toaster. **~schneidema,schine** *f* bread slicer. **~zeit** *f* (-; -en) *dial.* snack.

brr [br] *int* **1.** whoa! **2.** ugh!

Bruch [brʊx] *m* (-[e]s; ᵂe) **1.** a) breaking, b) breakage: **zu** ~ **gehen** break, be smashed; ~ **machen** crash; **zu** ~ **fahren** smash up (*a car*). **2.** *fig.* breaking-off, rupture, breach (*of oath, peace*), violation (*of a law*): ~ **mit der Vergangenheit** (clean) break with the past; **in die Brüche gehen** break up, *marriage:* a. go on the rocks. **3.** ☀ a) fracture, b) rupture, hernia: **sich e-n** ~ **heben** rupture o.s. **4.** F *contp.* junk. **5.** ₳ fraction.

'**Bruchband** *n* (-[e]s; ᵂer) ☀ truss.

'**Bruchbude** *f* F *contp.* hovel, dump (*sl.*).

brüchig ['brʊçıç] *adj* **1.** fragile, brittle. **2.** *fig.* cracked (*voice*), shaky (*marriage*).

'**Bruch|landung** *f* crash landing. **~rechnung** *f* fractions. **~schaden** *m* breakage. ℒ**sicher** *adj* breakproof. **~stelle** *f* crack, ₳ point of fracture.

'**Bruchstrich** *m* ₳ fraction stroke.

'**Bruchstück** *n* fragment (*a. fig.*), *pl fig.* *a.* snatches. '**bruchstückhaft I** *adj* fragmentary. **II** *adv* in fragments.

'**Bruch|teil** *m* fraction: **im** ~ **e-r Sekunde** in a split second. **~zahl** *f* fraction.

Brücke ['brʏkə] *f* (-; -n) **1.** bridge (*a.* ☀, ⚓, ⚔, *gym.*): **e-e** ~ **bauen** (*or* **schlagen**) **über** (*acc*) build a bridge across; *fig.* **alle** ~**n hinter sich abbrechen** burn one's boats. **2.** rug.

'Brückenkopf *m* bridgehead.
'Brückenpfeiler *m* bridge pier.
Bruder ['bru:dər] *m* (-s; ·) brother (*a. eccl.*, *pl* brethren), *eccl.* monk, F guy: **unter Brüdern** among friends.
'Bruderkrieg *m* fratricidal war. **brüderlich** ['bry:dərlıç] *adj* brotherly. **Brüderlichkeit** *f* (-; *no pl*) brotherliness.
'Brudermord *m*, **'Brudermörder(in** *f*) *m* fratricide. **'Bruderschaft** *f* (-; -en) 1. brotherhood. 2. (*mit j-m*) **~ trinken** drink the pledge of close friendship.
Brühe ['bry:ə] *f* (-; -n) 1. *gastr.* stock, broth. 2. F *contp.* a) dirty water, b) slop, swill, dishwater. 3. F sweat.
brühen ['bry:ən] *v/t* (h) scald.
'brüh|**heiß** *adj* scalding (hot). **~warm** *adj* hot (*news etc*): **j-m et. ~ wiedererzählen** tell s.th. straightaway to s.o.
'Brühwürfel *m* stock cube.
brüllen ['brylən] *v/i*, *v/t* (h) roar (*a. fig. gun*, *engine*, *etc*), cow: bellow, low, *children*: shout, bawl: **vor Lachen ~** roar with laughter *etc*; F **er (es) ist zum ♀!** he's (it's) a scream!
Brummbär ['brʊm-] *m fig.* grumbler.
brummen ['brʊmən] *v/i*, *v/t* (h) 1. *bear etc*: growl. 2. *a.* ♫ hum: **mir brummt der Kopf** my head is throbbing. 3. *fig.* (*über dat* about) growl, grumble. 4. F *in prison*: do time. **'Brummer** *m* (-s; -) 1. a) bluebottle, b) bumblebee. 2. F (*dicker ~*) **'Brummi** *m* (-s; -s) F juggernaut. **'brummig** *adj* grumpy.
'Brummkreisel *m* humming top.
'Brummschädel *m* F 1. headache. 2. hangover.
brünett [bry'nɛt] *adj*, **Brü'nette** *f* (-n; -n) brunette.
Brunft [brʊnft] *f* (-; ⁓e), **'brunften** *v/i* (h) *hunt.* rut. **'Brunftzeit** *f* rutting season.
Brunnen ['brʊnən] *m* (-s; -) well, spring, fountain (*a. fig.*), ♣ (mineral) waters.
'Brunnenkresse *f* ♣ watercress.
'Brunnenkur *f* mineral-water cure.
'Brunnenvergiftung *f fig.* calumny.
Brunst [brʊnst] *f* (-; ⁓e) *zo.* a) rut, b) heat, c) rutting season. **brünstig** ['brʏnstıç] *adj zo.* a) rutting, b) in heat.
brüsk [brysk] *adj* brusque.
brüskieren [brys'ki:rən] *v/t* (h) snub.
Brust [brʊst] *f* (-; ⁓e) 1. *no pl* breast, chest: *swimming:* **100 m ~** 100 metres breaststroke; F *fig.* **e-n zur ~ nehmen**

have a quick one; **sich j-n zur ~ nehmen** give s.o. hell. 2. bosom, breasts: (*dat*) **die ~ geben** breastfeed. 3. → **Bruststück. ~bein** *n* 1. *anat.* breastbone. 2. wishbone. **~beutel** *m* money bag. **~bild** *n* head-and-shoulder portrait. **~drüse** *f anat.* mammary gland.
brüsten ['brystən] **sich ~** (h) boast (*mit* about).
'Brust|**fell** *n anat.* pleura. **~fellentzündung** *f* ♣ pleurisy. **~kasten** *m*, **~korb** *m* rib cage, chest. **~krebs** *m* ♣ breast cancer. **~schwimmen** *n* breaststroke. **~stimme** *f* ♩ chest voice. **~stück** *n gastr.* a) brisket, b) breast. **~tasche** *f* breast pocket. **~ton** *m fig.* **im ~ der Überzeugung** with deep conviction.
'Brüstung *f* (-; -en) 1. parapet. 2. balustrade.
'Brustwarze *f* nipple.
Brustweite *f* chest measurement, bust.
Brut [bru:t] *f* (-; -en) 1. *no pl* brooding. 2. a) brood, b) spawn. 3. *no pl* F *fig.* a) (*children*) brood, b) scum.
brutal [bru'ta:l] *adj* brutal. **Brutalität** [brutali'tɛ:t] *f* (-; -en) brutality.
'Brutapparat *m* incubator.
brüten ['bry:tən] (h) **I** *v/i* brood (*fig. über dat* over), hatch, *hen:* sit: **~de Hitze** sweltering heat. **II** *v/t* → **Rache.**
'Brüter *m* (-s; -) → **Brutreaktor:** *phys.* **schneller ~** fast breeder (reactor).
'Bruthenne *f* sitting hen. **'Brutkasten** *m* incubator. **'Brutplatz** *m zo.* breeding ground. **'Brutreaktor** *m phys.* breeder reactor. **'Brutstätte** *f fig.* hotbed.
brutto ['bruto] *adj*, **'Brutto...** gross (*income*, *weight*, *register ton*, *etc*).
'Bruttosozi,alpro,dukt *n* gross national product.
Bub [bu:p] *m* (-en; -en) *dial.* boy. **Bube** ['bu:bə] *m* (-n; -n) *cards:* jack. **Bubi** ['bu:bi] *m* (-s; -s) F *contp.* pipsqueak.
Buch [bu:x] *n* (-[e]s; ⁓er) 1. book (*a.* ♀): **~ führen** keep accounts, *a.* the bookkeeping; **~ führen über** (*acc*) keep a record of; *fig.* **wie er (es) im ~ steht** typical. 2. *film:* script. **'Buchbesprechung** *f* book review. **'Buchbinder** *m* (-s; -) bookbinder. **'Buchdruck** *m* (-[e]s; *no pl*) printing. **'Buchdrucker** *m* printer. **'Buchdruckerei** *f* (-; -en) 1. printing plant, press. 2. *no pl* printing.
Buche ['bu:xə] *f* (-; -n) beech (tree).

buchen ['buːxən] v/t (h) **1.** book, reserve (*room*, *flight*, *etc*). **2.** ♣ book: *fig. et. als Erfolg* ~ put s.th. down as a success.

Bücherei [byːçəˈraɪ] f (-; -en) library. '**Bücher|freund(in** f) m book lover. **~gutschein** m book token. **~narr** m bibliomaniac. **~re**‚**gal** n bookshelf. **~revisi**‚**on** f ♣ audit. **~schrank** m bookcase. **~ständer** m bookstand. **~stütze** f bookend. **~wand** f wall of bookshelves. **~weisheit** f book knowledge. **~wurm** m humor. bookworm.

'**Buchfink** m zo. chaffinch.

'**Buchforderungen** pl ♣ book claims.

'**Buchführung** f (-; no pl) ♣ bookkeeping, accountancy: *doppelte* ~ double-entry bookkeeping. '**Buchgemeinschaft** f book club. '**Buchhaltung** f (-; -en) **1.** accounts department. **2.** no pl → *Buchführung.* '**Buchhandel** m book trade. '**Buchhändler(in** f) m bookseller. '**Buchhandlung** f bookshop, *Am.* bookstore. '**Buchhülle** f jacket, wrapper. '**Buchmacher** m (-s; -) bookmaker. '**buchmäßig** adj and adv ♣ according to the books. '**Buchmesse** f book fair. '**Buchprüfer** m auditor, accountant. '**Buchprüfung** f audit.

Buchsbaum ['buksbaʊm] m (-s; no pl) ♣ box (tree).

Buchse ['buksə] f (-; -n) ⊛ bush(ing), liner, ⚡ socket.

Büchse ['byksə] f (-; -n) **1.** tin, can, box. **2.** gun, rifle.

'**Büchsen|bier** n canned beer. **~fleisch** n tinned (*or* canned) meat. **~milch** f tinned (*or* canned) milk. **~öffner** m (-s; -) tin (*or* can) opener.

Buchstabe ['buːxʃtaːbə] m (-n; -n) letter: *großer* (*kleiner*) ~ capital (small) letter. '**buchstabengetreu** adj literal. **buchstabieren** [buːxʃtaˈbiːrən] v/t (h) a) spell, b) spell out: *falsch* ~ misspell. '**Buchsta**‚**bieren** n (-s) spelling. **buchstäblich** ['buːxʃtɛːplɪç] adj literal.

Bucht [buxt] f (-; -en) bay, inlet.

'**Buchumschlag** m dustjacket.

'**Buchung** f (-; -en) **1.** booking, reservation. **2.** ♣ a) booking, b) entry.

'**Buchweizen** m ♣ buckwheat.

Buckel ['bukəl] m (-s; -) **1.** a) hump (a. fig.), hunchback, b) stoop: *e-n* ~ *machen* stoop, *cat:* arch its back. **2.** F back. **3.** F hillock. '**buck(e)lig** adj

hunchbacked. '**Buck(e)lige** m, f (-n; -n) hunchback.

bücken ['bykən] sich ~ (h) bend (down) (*nach et.* to pick up s.th.).

Bückling ['byklɪŋ] m (-s; -e) **1.** gastr. smoked herring. **2.** F bow.

buddeln ['budəln] v/i, v/t (h) F dig.

Buddhismus [buˈdɪsmʊs] m (-; no pl) Buddhism. **Buddhist** [buˈdɪst] m (-en; -en), **bud**'**dhistisch** adj Buddhist.

Bude ['buːdə] f (-; -n) **1.** kiosk, stall. **2.** F a) contp. hovel, dump, b) place, digs, *Am.* pad, c) contp. joint (*sl.*): *Leben in die* ~ *bringen* liven things up.

Budget [byˈdʒeː] n (-s; -s) budget: *et. im* ~ *vorsehen* budget for s.th.

Büfett [byˈfeː] n (-s; -s) **1.** sideboard. **2.** counter, bar. **3.** gastr. buffet.

Büffel ['byfəl] m (-s; -) zo. buffalo.

büffeln ['byfəln] v/t, v/i (h) F swot, cram.

Büffler ['byflər] m (-s; -), '**Büfflerin** f (-; -nen) F swot.

Bug [buːk] m (-[e]s; -e) **1.** ♣ bow, ✈ nose: *fig. Schuß vor den* ~ warning shot. **2.** zo. shoulder (a. gastr.).

Bügel ['byːgəl] m (-s; -) **1.** hanger. **2.** stirrup. **3.** ear piece (*of spectacles*). **4.** ⊛ bow, shackle. **~brett** n ironing board. **~eisen** n iron. **~falte** f crease.

bügelfrei adj noniron, drip-dry.

bügeln ['byːgəln] v/t, v/i (h) iron, press.

'**Bügelpresse** f (laundry) press.

Buggy ['bagi] m (-s; -s) (*car:* beach) buggy.

Bügler ['byːglər] m (-s; -), '**Büglerin** f (-; -nen) ironer, presser.

bugsieren [buˈksiːrən] v/t **1.** ♣ tow. **2.** F fig. steer.

buh [buː] int boo! **Buh** n (-s; -s) F boo.

buhen ['buːən] v/i (h) F boo.

buhlen ['buːlən] v/i (h) ~ *um* strive after; *um j-s Gunst* ~ court s.o.'s favo(u)r.

'**Buhmann** m (-[e]s; ⸚er) fig. bogey man.

Buhne ['buːnə] f (-; -n) ♣ groyne.

Bühne ['byːnə] f (-; -n) **1.** thea. scene, w.s. theat/re (*Am.* -er): *hinter der* ~ a. fig. backstage; F fig. *et. über die* ~ *bringen* bring s.th. off; *glatt über die* ~ *gehen* go off smoothly; *von der politischen etc* ~ *abtreten* quit the political etc scene. **2.** a. ⊛ platform.

'**Bühnen|anweisung** f stage direction. **~arbeiter** m stage hand. **~bearbeitung** f stage adaptation. **~beleuchtung** *f* stage lighting. **~bild** *n* (stage) set. **~bildner(in** *f*) *m* stage designer. **~fassung** *f* stage version. **~künstler(in** *f*) *m* stage artist. **~laufbahn** *f* stage career. **~meister** *m* stage manager. **~rechte** *pl* stage rights. **2reif** *adj* ready for the stage. **~stück** *n* (stage) play. **~werk** *n* drama. **2wirksam** *adj* stageworthy.

'**Buhrufe** *pl* boos.

Bukett [bu'kɛt] *n* (-s; -s, -e) bouquet.

Bulette [bu'lɛtə] *f* (-; -n) *gastr.* meatball.

Bulgare [bʊl'ga:rə] *m* (-n; -n) Bulgarian.

Bulgarien [bʊl'ga:riən] *n* (-s) Bulgaria.

Bul'garin *f* (-; -nen), **bul'garisch** *adj* Bulgarian.

'**Bullauge** *n* ♪ porthole.

'**Bulldogge** *f zo.* bulldog.

Bulle¹ ['bʊlə] *m* (-n; -n) **1.** *zo.* bull (*a.* F *contp. man*). **2.** F *contp.* cop, bull: *die ~n a.* the fuzz.

'**Bulle²** *f* (-; -n) *eccl.* (papal) bull.

'**Bullenhitze** *f* F scorching heat.

Bulletin [bʏl'tɛ̃:] *n* (-s; -s) bulletin.

'**bullig** *adj* **1.** bull-like, hefty. **2.** F scorching (*heat*).

'**Bully** ['bʊli] *n* (-s; -s) **1.** *hockey*: bully. **2.** *icehockey*: face-off.

'**bum** [bʊm] *int* bang!

Bumerang ['bu:məraŋ] *m* (-s; -e, -s) boomerang.

'**Bummel** ['bʊməl] *m* (-s; -) F stroll. **Bummelant** [bʊmə'lant] *m* (-en; -en), **Bumme'lantin** *f* (-; -nen) → **Bummler(in)** 2. **Bumme'lei** *f* (-; -en) F a) dawdling, b) loafing. '**bumm(e)lig** *adj* F dawdling, slow. '**bummeln** *v/i* (h) F **1.** (go for a) stroll: **~ gehen** go for a stroll, *w.s.* go on a binge. **2.** a) dawdle, b) loaf. '**Bummelstreik** *m* go-slow. '**Bummelzug** *m* F slow train. '**Bummler** *m* (-s; -), '**Bummlerin** *f* (-; -nen) F **1.** stroller. **2.** a) dawdler, b) loafer.

'**bums** [bʊms] *int* bang! **Bums** *m* (-es; -e) bang, crash. **bumsen** ['bʊmzən] *v/i* (h) **1.** bang, crash. **2.** V *mit j-m* (*v/t j-n*) **~** bang s.o., screw s.o., have it off with s.o. '**Bumsio,kal** *n* F low dive.

Bund¹ [bʊnt] *n* (-[e]s; -e) bundle, bunch. **Bund²** *m* (-[e]s; *-e*) **1.** union, bond: **~ der Ehe** union, bond of marriage. **2.** pact: *im ~e mit* together with, *b.s.* in league with. **3.** *pol.* alliance, *n.s.* federation: *der ~* a) the Federal Government, b) →

Bundesrepublik, c) F → *Bundeswehr*. **4.** association, union.

Bund³ *m* (-[e]s; *-e*) waistband.

Bündel ['bʏndəl] *n* (-s; -) bundle.

'**bündeln** *v/t* (h) bundle up, bunch, *phys.* focus.

'**bündelweise** *adv* in bundles.

'**Bundes...** *pol.* (German) Federal ... **~bahn** *f* Federal Railway(s). **~bank** *f* (-; *no pl*) German Central Bank. **~behörde** *f* federal authority. **~bürger(in** *f*) *m* German citizen. **2deutsch** *adj* (German) Federal. **~ebene** *f auf ~* on a national level. **~gebiet** *n* Federal territory. **~genosse** *m* ally. **~gerichtshof** *m* Federal Supreme Court. **~kabi,nett** *n* (German) federal cabinet. **~kanzler** *m* German (*or* Federal) Chancellor. **~kar,tellamt** *n* Federal Cartel Office. **~krimi,nalamt** *n* Federal Bureau of Criminal Investigation. **~land** *n* (federal) state, land, Land: *die neuen Bundesländer* the newly-formed German states. **~liga** *f sports*: **erste** (**zweite**) **~** First (Second) Division. **~mi,nister(in** *f*) *m* minister (*für* of). **~post** *f* Federal Post Office. **~präsi,dent** *m* German (*or* Federal) President. **~presseamt** *n* Federal Information Agency. **~rat** *m* Bundesrat, Upper House (of the Federal parliament). **~re,gierung** *f* Federal Government. **~repu,blik** *f* **~ Deutschland** Federal Republic of Germany. **~staat** *m* a) federal state, b) (con)federation. **~straße** *f* major road. **~tag** *m* Bundestag, Lower House (of the German parliament). **~tagspräsi,dent(in** *f*) *m* speaker of the Bundestag. **~tagswahl** *f* parliamentary elections. **~trainer(in** *f*) *m* coach of the national team. **~verfassungsgericht** *n* Federal Constitutional Court. **~wehr** *f* (-; *no pl*) (German) armed forces.

'**bundesweit** *adj* and *adv* nation-wide.

bündig ['bʏndɪç] *adj* a) concise, b) precise, c) curt: → *kurz* 4.

Bündnis ['bʏntnɪs] *n* (-ses; -se) alliance.

'**Bündnisfrei** *adj pol.* nonaligned.

'**Bündnispartner** *m* ally.

'**Bundweite** *f* waist (size).

Bungalow ['bʊŋgalo] *m* (-s; -s) bungalow.

Bunker ['bʊŋkər] *m* (-s; -) ✕ a) bunker (*a. for coal, a. golf*), b) air-raid shelter.

Bunsenbrenner ['bʊnzən-] *m* 🜊 Bunsen burner.

bunt [bʊnt] *adj* **1.** colo(u)rful (*a. fig.*), (multi)colo(u)red, stained (*glass*); → **Hund. 2.** *fig.* chequered, *Am.* checkered, motley, mixed, varied: **~er Abend** variety show; F **er treibt es zu ~** he goes too far.

'**Buntdruck** *m* (-[e]s; -e) **1.** colo(u)r printing. **2.** colo(u)r print. '**Buntstift** *m* crayon. '**Buntwäsche** *f* colo(u)reds.

Bürde ['byrdə] *f* (-; -n) *a. fig.* burden.

Burg [bʊrk] *f* (-; -en) castle.

Bürge ['byrgə] *m* (-n; -n) **1.** 🜚 guarantor (*a. fig.*), surety. **2.** reference.

'**bürgen** *v/i* (h) **~ für** 🜚 stand surety for, *w.s.* guarantee, vouch for.

Bürger *m* (-s; -), '**Bürgerin** *f* (-; -nen) a) citizen, b) inhabitant, resident.

'**Bürgerinitia,tive** *f* civic action group. '**Bürgerkrieg** *m* civil war.

'**bürgerlich** *adj* **1.** middle-class, *contp.* bourgeois; **~e Küche** home cooking. **2.** untitled. **3.** civil, civic: **~es Gesetzbuch** Civil Code; **~es Recht** civil law; **~rechtlich** civil-law, under civil law.

'**Bürgerliche** *m, f* (-n; -n) commoner.

'**Bürgermeister** *m* mayor. '**bürgernah** *adj* people-oriented, grassroots (*politician, politics, etc*). '**Bürgerpflicht** *f* civic duty. '**Bürgerrecht** *n usu. pl* civil rights. '**Bürgerrechtler** [-rɛçtlər] *m* (-s; -), '**Bürgerrechtlerin** *f* (-; -nen) civil rights activist. '**Bürgerrechtsbewegung** *f* civil rights movement. '**Bürgerschaft** *f* (-; -en) citizens. '**Bürgersteig** *m* pavement, *Am.* sidewalk. '**Bürgertum** *n* (-s; *no pl*) *the* middle classes.

'**Burgfriede** *m fig.* truce. '**Burggraben** *m* moat. '**Burggraf** *m* burgrave.

'**Bürgschaft** *f* (-; -en) 🜚 surety, guarantee (*a. fig.*), bail: **~ leisten, die ~ übernehmen** a) stand surety, b) go (*or* give) bail, c) **für e-n Wechsel** *etc* guarantee a bill *etc*.

Burgunder [bʊr'gʊndər] *m* (-s; -), **Bur'gunderwein** *m* burgundy.

burlesk [bʊr'lɛsk] *adj* burlesque, farcical. **Bur'leske** *f* (-; -n) burlesque, farce.

Büro [by'roː] *n* (-s; -s) (**im ~** at the) office. **~angestellte** *m, f* office employee (*or* worker, clerk). **~arbeit** *f* office work.

~bedarf *m* office supplies. **~chef** *m* head clerk. **~gebäude** *n* office building. **~klammer** *f* paper clip.

Bürokrat [byro'kraːt] *m* (-en; -en) bureaucrat. **Bürokratie** [byrokra'tiː] *f* (-; -n) **1.** bureaucracy. **2.** → **Bürokratismus. büro'kratisch** *adj* bureaucratic. **Bürokratismus** [byrokra'tɪsmʊs] *m* (-; *no pl*) red tape.

Bü'ro|ma,schine *f* office machine. **~möbel** *pl* office furniture. **~perso,nal** *n* office staff. **~schluß** *m* (-sses; *no pl*) (office) closing time: **nach ~** after hours. **~stunden** *pl* office hours.

Bursche ['bʊrʃə] *m* (-n; -n) **1.** boy, lad. **2.** fellow, F guy: **ein übler ~** a bad egg. '**Burschenschaft** *f* (-; -en) (students') fraternity.

burschikos [bʊrʃi'koːs] *adj* pert.

Bürste ['byrstə] *f* (-; -n) brush (*a. ⚡, ⚙*).

'**bürsten** *v/t* (h) brush.

'**Bürstenschnitt** *m* crew cut.

Bürzel ['byrtsəl] *m* (-s; -) **1.** *zo.* rump. **2.** *hunt.* tail. **3.** F *gastr.* parson's nose.

Bus [bʊs] *m* (-ses; -se) F bus, coach: **mit dem ~ fahren** go by bus.

'**Busbahnhof** *m* bus terminal.

Busch [bʊʃ] *m* (-es; -e) **1.** a) bush (*a. primeval forest*), shrub, b) copse, thicket: F **bei j-m auf den ~ klopfen** sound s.o.; **hinterm ~ halten mit** be quiet about; **et. ist im ~!** there's s.th. going on! **2.** bunch.

Büschel ['byʃəl] *n* (-s; -) **1.** bunch. **2.** tuft, wisp (*of hair etc*). **3.** cluster (*of flowers etc*). **4.** *phys.* pencil, brush.

'**Buschhemd** *n* jacket shirt.

'**buschig** *adj* bushy.

'**Buschwindröschen** *n* wood anemone.

Busen ['buːzən] *m* (-s; -) breast(s), bust, bosom (*a. fig.*).

'**Busenfreund(in** *f*) *m* bosom friend.

'**Busfahrer(in** *f*) *m* bus driver.

'**Busfahrt** *f* bus ride, *w.s.* coach tour.

'**Bushaltestelle** *f* bus stop. '**Buslinie** *f* bus route: **die ~ 8** (bus) number 8.

Bussard ['bʊsart] *m* (-s; -e) *zo.* buzzard.

Buße ['buːsə] *f* (-; -n) **1.** 🜚 penalty, fine. **2.** penance, atonement: **~ tun → büßen** ['byːsən] *v/t, v/i* (h) do penance: **~ für** atone for, *fig.* pay (*or* suffer) for; **das sollst du mir ~!** I'll pay for that!

'**Büßer** *m* (-s; -), '**Büßerin** *f* (-; -nen) penitent. '**bußfertig** *adj* penitent.

charakteristisch

'**Bußgeld** *n* fine. **~bescheid** *m* notice of fine due. **~kata,log** *m* list of fines.
'**Buß-** und '**Bettag** *m* Day of Prayer and Repentance.
Büste ['by:stə] *f* (-; -n) bust.
'**Büstenhalter** *m* brassière, F bra.
Butan [bu'ta:n] *n* (-s; *no pl*) 🔥 butane.
Butt [bʊt] *m* (-[e]s; -e) flounder.
Bütte ['bʏtə] *f* (-; -n) tub, vat.
'**Büttenpa,pier** *n* handmade paper.
'**Büttenrede** *f* carnival speech.
Butter ['bʊtər] *f* (-; *no pl*) butter: F *alles in ~!* everything's okay! **~berg** *m* F *fig.* butter mountain. **~blume** *f* buttercup.
~brot *n* (slice of) bread and butter: F *für ein ~* a) *get s.th.* for a song, b) *work* for peanuts. **~brotpa,pier** *n* greaseproof paper. **~creme** *f gastr.* butter cream. **~dose** *f* butter dish. **~messer** *n* butter knife. **~milch** *f* buttermilk.
buttern ['bʊtərn] (h) **I** *v/t* **1.** (spread with) butter. **2.** F *Geld in et.* ~ sink money into s.th. **II** *v/i* **3.** make butter.
'**butterweich** *adj a.* F *fig.* very soft.
Butzenscheibe ['bʊtsən-] *f* bull's-eye (pane).
Byte [baɪt] *n* (-[s]; -[s]) *computer:* byte.

C

C, c [tse:] *n* (-; -) *a.* ♪ C, c.
Café [ka'fe:] *n* (-s; -s) café. **Cafeteria** [kafete'ri:a] *f* (-; -s) cafeteria.
campen ['kɛmpən] *v/i* (h) camp.
'**Camper** *m* (-s; -) camper (*a. mot.*).
Camping|ausrüstung ['kɛmpɪŋ-] *f* camping gear. **~bus** *m* camper. **~führer** *m* camping guide. **~platz** *m* camping site, campsite. **~tisch** *m* folding table.
Cape [ke:p] *n* (-s; -s) cape.
Caravan ['ka(:)ravan] *m* (-s; -s) a) estate car, *Am.* station wagon, b) caravan, *Am.* trailer.
Cäsium ['tsɛ:ziʊm] *n* (-s; *no pl*) 🔥 c(a)esium.
Catcher ['kɛtʃər] *m* (-s; -) all-in wrestler.
CB-Funk [tse:'be:-] *m* CB (= citizens' band) radio.
C-Dur ['tse:-] *n* (-; *no pl*) ♪ C major.
Cellist [tʃɛ'lɪst] *m* (-en; -en), **Cel'listin** *f* (-; -nen) cellist.
Cello ['tʃɛlo] *n* (-s; -s) cello.
Cellophan [tsɛlo'fa:n] *n* (-s; *no pl*) (TM) cellophane.
Celsius ['tsɛlziʊs] *n undeclined* celsius: *20 Grad ~ a.* 20 degrees centigrade.
Cembalist [tʃɛmba'lɪst] *m* (-en; -en), **Cemba'listin** *f* (-; -nen) harpsichordist. **Cembalo** ['tʃɛmbalo] *n* (-s; -s, -li) harpsichord.
Ces [tsɛs] *n* (-; -) ♪ C flat.

Chalet [ʃa'le:] *n* (-s; -s) chalet.
Chamäleon [ka'mɛ:leɔn] *n* (-s; -s) *zo. or fig.* chameleon.
Champagner [ʃam'panjər] *m* (-s; -) champagne.
Champignon ['ʃampɪnjɔŋ] *m* (-s; -s) (button) mushroom.
Chance ['ʃã:sə] *f* (-; -n) chance, *pl a.* prospects: *k-e ~, nicht die geringste ~* not a chance; *bei j-m ~n haben* stand a chance with s.o. '**Chancengleichheit** *f* equal opportunities.
Chanson [ʃã'sõ:] *n* (-s; -s) chanson.
Chaos ['ka:ɔs] *n* (-; *no pl*) chaos.
Chaote [ka'o:tə] *m* (-n; -n) F chaotic person, *pol.* violent anarchist, *w.s.* yob.
cha'otisch *adj* chaotic.
Charakter [ka'raktər] *m* (-s; -e [-'te:rə]) character, nature: *vertraulichen ~s talks etc* of a confidential nature.
Cha'rakter|darsteller(in *f) m* character actor (actress). **~eigenschaft** *f* trait. **~fehler** *m* weakness, flaw.
cha'rakterfest *adj* of strong character.
charakterisieren [karakteri'zi:rən] *v/t* (h) **1.** characterize, mark. **2.** describe (*als* as). **Charakteri'sierung** *f* (-; -en) **1.** characterization. **2.** description.
Charakteristik [karakte'rɪstɪk] *f* (-; -en) **1.** characterization. **2.** 🄰, ⚙ characteristic. **charakte'ristisch** *adj* (*für* of)

characteristic, typical. **cha'rakterlich**
I *adj* of (one's) character, moral. **II** *adv*
in character.

cha'rakterlos *adj* **1.** unprincipled, weak.
2. colo(u)rless. **Cha'rakterlosigkeit** *f*
(-; *no pl*) lack of character.

Cha'rakter|rolle *f* thea. character part.
~schwäche *f* weakness (of character).
~stärke *f* strength (of character). **~voll**
adj full of character. **~zug** *m* trait.

Charge ['ʃarʒə] *f* (-; -n) **1.** thea. supporting part. **2.** metall. charge.

Charisma ['ça:rɪsma] *n* (-s; -men, -mata)
charisma. **charismatisch** [çarɪs'ma:-
tɪʃ] *adj* charismatic.

charmant [ʃar'mant] *adj* charming.

Charme [ʃarm] *m* (-s; *no pl*) (**s-n ~ spielen lassen** turn on the old) charm.

Charta ['karta] *f* (-; -s) pol. charter.

Charter ['(t)ʃartər] *m* (-s; -s) charter.
'**Charterflug** *m* charter flight.
'**Charterma,schine** *f* charter plane.
chartern ['(t)ʃartərn] *v/t* (h) charter.

Chassis [ʃa'si:] *n* (-; -) chassis.

Chauffeur [ʃo'fø:r] *m* (-s; -e) driver,
chauffeur.

Chauvi ['ʃo:vi] *m* (-s; -s) F male chauvinist (pig). **Chauvinismus** [ʃovi'nɪs-
mʊs] *m* (-; *no pl*) (**männlicher ~** male)
chauvinism. **Chauvi'nist** *m* (-en; -en)
1. chauvinist. **2.** → *Chauvi*. **chauvi'ni-**
stisch *adj* chauvinistic.

checken ['tʃɛkən] *v/t* (h) check.
'**Checkliste** *f* check list.

Chef [ʃɛf] *m* (-s; -s) **1.** chief, head, F boss.
2. gastr. chef. '**Chefarzt** *m* medical su-
perintendent. '**Chefe,tage** *f* executive
floor. '**Chefideo,loge** *m* chief ideo-
logue. '**Chefin** *f* (-; -nen) **1.** → *Chef*. **2.**
F the boss's wife. '**Chefkonstruk,teur**
m chief designer. '**Chefpi,lot** *m* chief
pilot. '**Chefredak,teur(in** *f*) *m* editor in
chief. '**Chefsekre,tär(in** *f*) *m* executive
(or personal) assistant, Am. executive
(or private) secretary.

Chemie [çe'mi:] *f* (-; *no pl*) chemistry.
Che'miefaser *f* synthetic fibre (Am.
fiber). **Che'mieindu,strie** *f* chemicals
industry. **Chemikalien** [çemi'ka:lĭən]
pl chemicals. **Chemiker** [çe'mi:kər] (-s;
-), '**Chemikerin** *f* (-; -nen) (analytical)
chemist. **chemisch** ['çe:mɪʃ] *adj* chemical: **~e Reinigung** dry cleaning; **et. ~**
reinigen lassen have s.th. dry-cleaned.

Chemo'techniker(in *f*) *m* [çe:mo-]
laboratory technician.

Chicorée ['ʃɪkore] *m* (-s; *no pl*) chicory.

Chiffre ['ʃɪfrə] *f* (-; -n) **1.** cipher, code. **2.**
box number. '**Chiffreanzeige** *f* box-
-number advertisement.

chiffrieren [ʃɪ'fri:rən] *v/t* (h) (en)code.

Chile ['tʃi:le] *n* (-s) Chile. **Chilene**
[tʃi'le:nə] *m* (-n; -n), **Chi'lenin** *f* (-;
-nen), **chi'lenisch** *adj* Chilean.

China ['çi:na] (-s) China. **Chinese**
[çi'ne:zə] *m* (-n; -n), **Chi'nesin** *f* (-;
-nen), **chi'nesisch** *adj* Chinese.

Chinin [çi'ni:n] *n* (-s; *no pl*) quinine.

Chip [tʃɪp] *m* (-s; -s) **1.** computer: chip.
2. *pl* gastr. (potato) crisps (Am. chips).

Chirurg [çi'rʊrk] *m* (-en; -en) surgeon.
Chirurgie [çirʊr'gi:] *f* (-; *no pl*) surgery.
Chir'urgin *f* (-; -nen) surgeon.
chir'urgisch [-gɪʃ] *adj* surgical.

Chlor [klo:r] *n* (-s; *no pl*) 🔔 chlorine.
'**Chlorgas** *n* 🔔 chloric gas.

Chlorid [klo:'ri:t] *n* (-s; -e) 🔔 chloride.
chlorieren [klo:'ri:rən] *v/t* (h) chlorinate.

Chlorophyll [kloro'fʏl] *n* (-s; *no pl*) 🌿
chlorophyll.

Cholera ['ko:lera] *f* (-; *no pl*) 🐛 cholera.

cholerisch [ko'le:rɪʃ] *adj* choleric.

Cholesterin [çoleste'ri:n] *n* (-s; *no pl*) 🐛
cholesterol. **Choleste'rinspiegel** *m*
cholesterol level.

Chor [ko:r] *m* (-s; -̈e) choir (a. △),
chorus (a. thea.): fig. **im ~** in chorus.

Choral [ko'ra:l] *m* (-s; Choräle) hymn,
chorale.

Choreograph [koreo'gra:f] *m* (-en; -en),
Choreo'graphin *f* (-; -nen) choreogra-
pher. **Choreographie** [koreogra'fi:] *f*
(-; -n) choreography.

'**Chor|gesang** *m* choral singing (or mu-
sic). **~gestühl** *n* (choir) stalls. **~knabe**
m choirboy. **~sänger(in** *f*) *m* chorister.

Christ... [krɪst-] → *Weihnachts...*

Christ *m* (-en; -en), '**Christin** *f* (-; -nen)
Christian. '**Christenheit** *f* (-; *no pl*)
Christendom. '**Christentum** *n* (-s; *no*
pl) Christianity. '**Christkind** *n* (-[e]s; *no*
pl) **1.** infant Jesus. **2.** F Father Christmas, Santa Claus. '**christlich** *adj* (adv
like a) Christian.

Chrom [kro:m] *n* (-s; *no pl*) chromium.
chromatisch [kro'ma:tɪʃ] *adj* ♪ chromatic.

Chromosom [kromo'zo:m] *n* (-s; -en)
chromosome.

Chronik ['kro:nɪk] f (-; -en) chronicle.
chronisch ['kro:nɪʃ] adj ♂ chronic.
Chronist ['kro:nɪst] m (-en; -en), **Chro'ni-stin** f (-; -nen) chronicler.
Chronologie [kronolo'gi:] f (-; -n) chronology. **chronologisch** [krono'lo:gɪʃ] adj chronological.
circa ['tsɪrka] adv about, approximately.
Cis [tsɪs] n (-; -) ♩ C sharp.
City ['sɪti] f (-; -s) (town) centre, Am. downtown.
Clique ['klɪkə] f (-; -n) clique, F crowd.
Clou [klu:] m (-s; -s) **1.** high spot, climax. **2.** point.
Cockpit ['kɔkpɪt] n ✈, ♣, mot. cockpit.
Code [ko:t] m (-s; -s) code.
codieren [ko'di:rən] v/t (h) (en)code.
Co'dierung f (-; -en) (en)coding.
Collage [kɔ'la:ʒə] f (-; -n) collage.
Computer [kɔm'pju:tər] m (-s; -) computer. **com'putergesteuert** adj computer-controlled. **com'putergestützt** adj computer-aided. **computerisieren** [kɔmpju:təri'zi:rən] v/t (h) computerize. **Com'puterspiel** n computer game.
Conférencier [kõferã'sĭe:] m (-s; -s) compère, Am. emcee.

Container [kɔn'te:nər] m (-s; -) container. **~schiff** n container ship.
Contergankind [kɔntər'ga:n-] n F thalidomide child.
Couch [kautʃ] f (-; -es) couch.
'Couchgarni,tur f three-piece suite.
'Couchtisch m coffee table.
Coup [ku:] m (-s; -s) coup.
Coupé [ku'pe:] n (-s; -s) **1.** railway compartment. **2.** coupé (a. mot.).
Coupon [ku'põ:] m (-s; -s) coupon, counterfoil.
Courage [ku'ra:ʒə] f (-; no pl) F courage, pluck. **couragiert** [kura'ʒi:rt] adj F courageous, plucky.
Cousin [ku'zɛ̃:] m (-s; -s) (male) cousin.
Cousine [ku'zi:nə] f (-; -n) (female) cousin; → a. **Kusine**.
Creme [kre:m] f (-; -s) **1.** cream. **2.** gastr. crème. **'cremefarben** adj cream-colo(u)red. **'Cremetorte** f cream gateau. **'cremig** adj creamy.
Cup [kap] m (-s; -s) sports: Cup.
'Cupfi,nale n sports: Cup Final.
Curry ['kœri] 'kari] n (-s; -s) **1.** curry. **2.** curry powder.
Cutter ['katər] m (-s; -), **'Cutterin** f (-; -nen) film etc: cutter.

D

D, d [de:] n (-; -) D, d, ♩ D.
da [da:] **I** adv **1.** a) there, b) here; der (die, das) ... ~ that ... (there); ~ und dort here and there; er ist ~ he's here, he has arrived; ~ kommt sie here she comes; ~ liegt die Schwierigkeit that's the difficulty; ~ (hast du)! there you are!; sieh ~! look at that!; ~ haben wir's! there (you are)!; nichts ~! nothing doing!; → dasein. **2.** then, at that time: ~ erst only then; hier und ~ now and then. **3.** (in that case) there, here: ~ bin ich Ihrer Meinung I do agree with you there; was kann man ~ machen? what's to be done?; was gibt's denn ~ zu lachen? what's so funny about it?; und ~ zögerst du noch? and you still

hesitate? **II** conj as, since, because.
dabei [da'baɪ] adv **1.** near, near by, close by: ein Brief war nicht ~ there was no letter (with it). **2.** ~ sein, et. zu tun be about to do, be on the point of doing. **3.** at the same time: sie strickte und hörte Radio ~ while knitting she listened to the radio. **4.** as well, into the bargain. **5.** yet, nevertheless. **6.** on the occasion, as a result: ~ gab es Streit this led to a quarrel; alle ~ entstehenden Kosten all costs incurred; es kommt nichts ~ heraus nothing will come of it. **7.** present, there: → bleiben 3, dabeisein. **8.** ich dachte mir nichts ~ a) I meant no harm, b) I paid no particular attention to it; es ist nichts ~! a)

there's nothing to it!, b) there's no harm in it!; **was ist schon ~?** what of it?; **lassen wir es ~!** let's leave it at that! **II** conj but, (and) yet.

da'beibleiben v/i (irr, sep, -ge-, sn, → **bleiben**) stay (or remain) with it, them etc; → a. **bleiben** 3.

da'beihaben v/t (irr, sep, -ge-, h, → **haben**) F have s.o., s.th. there: **kein Geld ~** have no money on one.

da'beisein v/i (irr, sep, -ge-, sn, → **sein**) a) be present, be there, take part, b) be a witness: **ich bin dabei!** count me in!

da'beistehen v/i (irr, sep, -ge-, h, → **stehen**) stand by (or there).

'dableiben v/i (irr, sep, -ge-, sn, → **bleiben**) remain, stay.

Dach [dax] n (-[e]s, ⸚er) roof, mot. a. top, fig. a. shelter: **unter ~ und Fach bringen** a) shelter, b) fig. complete; F fig. **eins aufs ~ kriegen** get it in the neck.

'Dach|an,tenne f roof (mot. over-car) aerial (Am. antenna). **~balken** m rooftree. **~boden** m loft. **~decker** [-dɛkər] m (-s; -) roofer. **~fenster** n dormer (window). **~first** m ridge (of a roof). **~garten** m roof garden. **~gepäckhalter** m mot. roof rack. **~geschoß** n attic stor(e)y, loft. **~gesellschaft** f ✝ holding company. **~kammer** f attic, garret. **~luke** f skylight. **~pappe** f roofing (felt). **~rinne** f gutter, eaves.

Dachs [daks] m (-es; -e) zo. badger.

'Dachstuhl m roof truss, timbering.

dachte [ˈdaxtə] pret of **denken**.

'Dach|ter,rasse f roof terrace. **~verband** m ✝ umbrella organization. **~wohnung** f attic flat. **~ziegel** m (roofing) tile.

Dackel [ˈdakəl] m (-s; -) zo. dachshund.

dadurch [daˈdʊrç] **I** adv **1.** through it (or there), that way. **2.** a) by it, b) because of that: **alle ~ verursachten Schäden** all damages caused thereby; **sie verschlief und kam ~ zu spät** she overslept, and so she was late. **II** conj **3.**, **daß es regnete** because of the rain. **4.**, **daß er weniger ißt** by eating less.

dafür [daˈfyːr] **I** adv **1.** for it (them, this, etc). **2.** in return (for it), instead (of it). **3.** ~ **sein** be for it, be in favo(u)r of it; **ich bin ~ zu bleiben** I'm for staying; **ich bin sehr ~!** I'm all for it!; parl. **die**

Mehrheit ist ~ the ayes have it; → **sprechen** I. **4.** ~ **wirst du ja bezahlt** that's what you are paid for. **II** conj **5. er wurde ~ bestraft, daß er gelogen hatte** he was punished for lying. **6.** ~ **sorgen, daß** see to it that. **7.** but (then): **sie arbeiten langsam, ~ aber sorgfältig** they are slow but diligent.

Da'fürhalten n (-s) **nach m-m etc ~** in my etc opinion, as I etc see it.

da'fürkönnen v/t (irr, sep, -ge-, h, → **können**) F **ich kann nicht dafür** it's not my fault, I cannot help it.

dagegen [daˈgeːgən] **I** adv **1.** against it (or that): **~ hilft Wärme** warmth is good for it; **~ hilft nichts** there is no remedy (for it), w.s. it can't be helped; **~ sein** be against it; **ich bin ~, daß du allein gehst** I'm against you(r) going alone; **haben Sie et. ~, wenn ich rauche?** do you mind if I smoke?; **ich habe nichts ~** I don't mind. **2.** by (or in) comparison, compared with. **3.** in exchange (for it). **II** conj a) but, however, on the other hand, b) whereas, while.

da'gegenhalten v/i (irr, sep, -ge-, h, → **halten**) argue (against it). **da'gegensprechen** v/i (irr, sep, -ge-, h, → **sprechen**) speak against it. **da'gegenstellen: sich ~** (sep, -ge-, h) fig. oppose it.

daheim [daˈhaɪm] adv dial. a) at home, b) back home. **Da'heim** n (-s) home.

daher [daˈheːr] **I** adv **1.** from there. **2.** a. **von ~** therefore; **~ kommt es, daß** that's why (or how); **~ ihr Mißtrauen** hence her suspicion. **II** conj a. **von ~** that's why, (and) so.

da'hergelaufen adj F contp. jeder **~e Kerl** any guy who happens along.

dahin [daˈhɪn] **I** adv **1.** there: **auf dem Weg ~** on the way there; **ist es noch weit bis ~?** is it much farther? **2. bis ~** a) until then, till then, b) by then; **bis ~ bin ich fertig** I'll be finished by then. **3.** to the effect: **sich ~ (gehend) einigen, daß** agree that. **4. es ~ bringen, daß** bring matters to the stage where; **j-n ~ bringen, daß** bring s.o. to the point of ger. **II** adj gone, lost.

da'hingestellt adj **et. ~ sein lassen** leave it open as to whether; **das bleibt ~,** that remains to be seen.

da'hinreden, da'hinsagen v/t (sep, -ge-, h) say s.th. without thinking.

da'hinschleppen: *sich* ~ (*sep*, -ge-, h) **1.** drag o.s. along. **2.** *fig.* drag on.
da'hinsiechen *v/i* (*sep*, -ge-, sn) waste away.
dahinten [da'hɪntən] *adv* back there.
dahinter [da'hɪntər] *adv* behind it *etc*, at the back (of him *etc*): *fig.* **es ist nichts ~** there's nothing behind it.
da'hinterklemmen: *sich* ~ (*sep*, -ge-, h) F buckle down (to it).
da'hinterkommen *v/i* (*irr, sep*, -ge-, sn, → **kommen**) F find out (about it).
da'hinterstecken *v/i* (*sep*, -ge-, h) *fig.* be behind it, be at the bottom of it: *es steckt mehr dahinter* there's more to it than meets the eye.
da'hinvege,tieren *v/i* (*sep*, h) vegetate.
da'hinziehen *v/i* (*sep*, -ge-, h, → **ziehen**) move (*clouds*: drift) along.
Dahlie ['da:liə] *f* (-; -n) ❀ dahlia.
'dalassen *v/t* (*irr, sep*, -ge-, h, → **lassen**) F leave.
'daliegen *v/i* (*irr, sep*, -ge-, h, → **liegen**) lie (there).
dalli ['dali] *adv* F ~, *~!, ein bißchen ~!, mach ~!* get a move on!
damalig ['da:ma:lɪç] *adj* then, at that time: *in der ~en Zeit* → **damals** ['da:ma:ls] *adv* then, in those days.
Damast [da'mast] *m* (-[e]s; -e) damask.
Dame ['da:mə] *f* (-; -n) **1.** a) lady, b) (dancing) partner: ~ *des Hauses* hostess; *m-e ~n und Herren!* ladies and gentlemen! **2.** a) draughts, *Am.* checkers, b) king, c) *chess etc*: queen. **~brett** *n* draughtboard, *Am.* checkerboard.
'Damen|binde *f* sanitary towel (*Am.* napkin). **~doppel** *n* *tennis*: the women's doubles. **~einzel** *n* *tennis*: the women's singles. **~fahrrad** *n* lady's bicycle. **~fri,seur** *m* ladies' hairdresser.
'damenhaft *adj* ladylike.
'Damen|konfekti,on *f* ladies' ready-made (*Am.* ready-to-wear) clothing. **~mannschaft** *f* women's team. **~schneider(in** *f)* *m* dressmaker. **~toi,lette** *f* ladies' toilet (*Am.* restroom). **~unterwäsche** *f* ladies' underwear, lingerie. **~wahl** *f* ladies' choice.
'Damespiel *n* → **Dame** 2 a.
damit [da'mɪt] **I** *adv* with it (or them, *emphatic*: that, those), by it: *ich bin ~ fertig* I've finished with it; *was willst du ~?* what do you want it for?; *was soll ich ~?* what am I supposed to do

with it?; *was willst du ~ sagen?* what are you trying to say?; ~ *ist der Fall erledigt* so much for that. **II** *conj* so that: ~ *nichts passiert* lest anything should happen.
dämlich ['dɛ:mlɪç] *adj* F stupid, silly.
Damm [dam] *m* (-[e]s; ⁻e) **1.** a) bank, b) dike, c) dam, d) embankment, e) roadway: F *fig.* **ich fühle mich nicht auf dem** ~ I don't feel well; *sie ist wieder auf dem* ~ she's fit again. **2.** *anat.* perineum.
'Dammbruch *m* bursting of a dam.
dämm(e)rig ['dɛm(ə)rɪç] *adj* **1.** *es ist* ~ → **dämmern** I a. **2.** faint, dim (*light*).
'Dämmerlicht *n* (-[e]s; *no pl*) twilight.
dämmern ['dɛmərn] (h) **I** *v/impers es dämmert* a) it is getting light (*or* dark), b) F *fig.* (*bei*) *j-m* it's beginning to dawn on s.o. **II** *v/i vor sich hin* ~ doze, be half asleep. **'Dämmerung** *f* (-; -en) a) dawn, b) dusk, twilight: *in der* ~ at dawn, at dusk, at nightfall.
Dämmung ['dɛmʊŋ] *f* (-; -en) insulation.
Dämon ['dɛ:mɔn] *m* (-s; -en) demon.
dämonisch [dɛ'mo:nɪʃ] *adj* demoniac(al).
Dampf [dampf] *m* (-[e]s; ⁻e) a) steam, b) vapo(u)r, fume: F *fig.* ~ *ablassen* let off steam; ~ *dahinter machen* put on steam; *j-m* ~ *machen* make s.o. get a move on. **'Dampfbad** *n* steam bath.
'Dampfbügeleisen *n* steam iron.
dampfen ['dampfən] *v/i* (h *or* sn) steam.
dämpfen ['dɛmpfən] *v/t* (h) **1.** *gastr.*, ⊙ steam. **2.** deaden, silence, muffle (*sounds*), lower (*one's voice*), mute (*trumpet etc*). **3.** cushion, absorb (*shock*). **4.** soften (*colo[u]r, light*): → *gedämpft*. **5.** *fig.* restrain, subdue (*feelings*), put a damper on (*mood*).
Dampfer ['dampfər] *m* (-s; -) steamer.
Dämpfer ['dɛmpfər] *m* (-s;) damper, ♪ *a.* mute: F *fig.* **e-n** ~ *bekommen* be damp(en)ed; (*dat*) **e-n** ~ *aufsetzen* put a damper on.
'Dampf|heizung *f* steam heating. **~kessel** *m* steam boiler. **~kochtopf** *m* pressure cooker. **~ma,schine** *f* steam engine. **~schiff** *n* steamship. **~walze** *f* a. *fig.* steamroller.
Damwild ['dam-] *n* *zo.* fallow deer.
danach [da'na:x] *adv* **1.** a) after (that), afterward(s), b) later on: *bald* ~ soon after. **2.** then, next, behind (*or* after)

him *etc.* **3.** according to it, accordingly:
F *aber es war auch ~* the meal etc was
cheap but I tasted like it, too; *mir ist
nicht ~* I don't feel like it. **4.** *~ fragen*
ask for it; *sich ~ sehnen zu inf* long to
inf; *sich ~ erkundigen* inquire about it.

Däne ['dɛːnə] *m* (-n; -n) Dane.

daneben [da'neːbən] *adv* **1.** beside (*or*
next to) it (*or* them): *im Haus ~* next
door. **2.** *a. conj* a) besides, b) at the
same time. **3.** beside it (*or* them *etc*), in
comparison. **4.** off the mark: *~!* missed!
*~benehmen: sich ~ (irr, sep, h, → be-
nehmen)* F behave badly. *~gehen v/i*
(irr, sep, -ge-, sn, → gehen) **1.** shot etc:
miss. **2.** F misfire, go wrong. *~greifen*
v/i (irr, sep, -ge-, h, → greifen) **1.** ♪
strike a wrong (*fig.* false) note. **2.** miss.
3. F *fig.* be wide of the mark. *~schie-
ßen v/i (irr, sep, -ge-, h, → schießen)* **1.**
miss. **2.** F *fig.* be wide of the mark.

Dänemark ['dɛːnəmark] *n* (-s) Denmark. **Dänin** ['dɛːnɪn] *f* (-; -nen) Dane.
'dänisch *adj* Danish.

dank [daŋk] *prep (gen, dat) a. iro.* thanks
to. **Dank** *m* (-[e]s; *no pl*) thanks, gratitude, reward: *vielen (or herzlichen,
besten, schönen) ~!* many thanks!,
thank you very much!; *als ~, zum ~* by
way of thanks; *j-m s-n ~ abstatten* express one's thanks to s.o.; *j-m ~ schulden* owe s.o. a debt of gratitude; *das ist
der (ganze) ~!* that's gratitude for
you!; → *Gott.* **'dankbar** *adj* **1.** grateful
(*j-m für et.* to s.o. for s.th.), appreciative: *ich wäre Ihnen ~, wenn Sie kämen* I'd be much obliged if you came.
2. rewarding (*task etc*). **3.** F hard-wearing (*material etc*). **'Dankbarkeit** *f* (-; *no
pl*) (*aus ~* out of) gratitude (*für* for).

danken ['daŋkən] (h) **I** *v/i* **1.** thank (*j-m
für et.* s.o. for s.th.): *danke (schön)!*
(many) thanks!, thank you (very
much)!; *(nein) danke!* no, thank you!,
no, thanks!; *nichts zu ~* you are welcome; *wie kann ich Ihnen nur ~?* how
can I begin to thank you?; F *na, ich
danke!* thank you for nothing! **2.** decline. **II** *v/t* **3.** *j-m et. ~* reward s.o. for
s.th. **4.** → *verdanken.*

'dankenswerter'weise *adv* **1.** kindly. **2.**
fig. commendably.

'Dankesbrief *m* thank-you letter.

'Dankeschön *n* (-s; *no pl*) thank-you.

'Dankesschuld *f* debt of gratitude.

'Dankesworte *pl* words of thanks.

'Dankgebet *n* thanksgiving (prayer).

'Dankschreiben *n* letter of thanks.

dann [dan] **I** *adv* **1.** then, after that: *~ und
wann* every now and then; *was pas-
sierte ~?* what happened next?; F *bis ~!*
see you (later)! **2.** then, in that case. **II**
conj F (well) then, so: *~ eben nicht!* all
right, forget it!

daran [da'ran] *adv* **1.** at (*or* on, in, to) it
(*or* that): *halt dich ~ fest!* hold on to it!;
nahe ~ close to it; → *nahe* II. **2.** *~
anschließend, im Anschluß ~* after-
ward(s). **3.** *es ist er. (nichts)* ~ there's
s.th. (nothing) in it; *~ ist kein wahres
Wort* there's not a word of truth in it; *~
stirbt man nicht* you don't die of it; *du
tust gut ~ zu gehen* you are wise to go;
das Schönste ~ war the best thing
about it was; → *denken* 3, *liegen* 4 *etc.*

dar'angehen *v/i (irr, sep, -ge-, sn, →
gehen)* get down to it: *~, et. zu tun* get
down to doing s.th. **dar'anmachen:
sich ~ (sep, -ge-, h)** F → *darangehen.*
dar'ansetzen *v/t (sep, -ge-, h)* *alles ~,
um zu inf* spare no effort to *inf.*

darauf [da'raʊf] *adv* **1.** on it *etc*, on top
of it. **2.** after (that), then: *bald ~* soon
after; *e-e Woche ~* a week later. **3.** *fig.*
ich freue mich ~ I'm looking forward
to it; *~ wollen wir trinken!* let's drink to
that!; *sie ging direkt ~ zu* she went
straight for it; *~ steht Gefängnis* there
is a prison penalty for that; *~ bin ich
stolz* I'm proud of it; *wie kommt er nur
~?* whatever makes him think of that?;
ich komme nicht ~ (F *drauf*) I can't
think of it!

daraufhin [daraʊf'hɪn] *adv* **1.** as a result,
consequently. **2.** after that. **3.** *et. ~
prüfen, ob* examine s.th. to see if.

daraus [da'raʊs] *adv* **1.** from it *etc*: *~
lernen (vorlesen)* learn (read) from it.
2. of it *etc*: *was ist ~ geworden?* what
has become of it?; *~ wird nichts!* F
nothing doing! **3.** for it *etc*: *ich mache
mir nichts ~* a) I don't care for it, b)
that doesn't worry me (a bit)!

darben ['darbən] *v/i (h)* suffer want.

darbieten ['daːr-] *v/t (irr, sep, -ge-, h, →
bieten)* **1.** present (*sich* itself). **2.** perform. **'Darbietung** *f* (-; -en) **1.** presentation. **2.** *thea. etc* performance.

darbringen *v/t* (*irr, sep,* -ge-, h, → **bringen**) (*dat* to) present, give.

darin [da'rɪn] *adv* **1.** in it *etc*: **was ist ~?** what's in it (*or* inside)? **2.** there, in this (respect): **~ irren Sie sich!** there you are mistaken!; **~ liegt der Unterschied** that's the difference. **3.** at it, at that: **~ ist er sehr gut** he is very good at that.

darlegen *v/t* (*sep,* -ge-, h) show, state: **j-m et. ~** explain s.th. to s.o.

Darlegung *f* (-; -en) **1.** explanation. **2.** statement.

Darlehen ['da:rle:ən] *n* (-s; -) loan: **ein ~ aufnehmen** raise (*or* take up) a loan.

Darlehens... loan (*bank, contract, etc*).

Darm [darm] *m* (-[e]s; ⁓e) **1.** *anat.* intestine(s), bowel(s), gut(s): **den ~ entleeren** evacuate the bowels, defecate. **2.** (sausage) skin.

Darm|entleerung *f* defecation. **~flora** *f* intestinal flora. **~geschwür** *n* intestinal ulcer. **~grippe** *f* gastroenteric influenza. **~krebs** *m* 🖉 cancer of the intestine. **~saite** *f* ♪ catgut (string). **~spiegelung** *f* enteroscopy. **~trägheit** *f* constipation. **~verschluß** *m* 🖉 ileus.

Darre ['darə] *f* ⚙ drying kiln.

darstellen *v/t* (*sep,* -ge-, h) **1.** represent, describe (*a.* ⚗), portray, show, express, constitute, mean: **falsch ~** misrepresent; **was soll das ~?** what's that supposed to be?; **e-e Belastung ~** be a burden. **2.** *thea. etc* act, play, *w.s.* interpret. **3.** 🎭 prepare. **4.** *computer:* display. **'darstellend** *adj* **1.** **~e Geometrie** descriptive geometry. **2.** → **Kunst** 1.

Darsteller *m* (-s; -) player, actor: **der ~ des Faust** the actor playing Faust.

Darstellerin *f* (-; -nen) actress, player.

darstellerisch *adj* acting: **s-e ~e Leistung** his performance, his acting.

Darstellung *f* (-; -en) **1.** representation, description, account: **graphische ~** graph, diagram. **2.** *thea. etc* acting, performance, *w.s.* interpretation. **3.** 🎭 preparation. **4.** *computer:* display.

darüber [da'ry:bər] *adv* **1.** over it (*or* that) (*a. time*), above it *etc*: **das Zimmer ~** the room above; **ich bin ~ eingeschlafen** I fell asleep over it. **2.** more. **3.** **~ hinaus** a) beyond it *etc*, b) *fig.* over and above that, moreover; **er ist ~ hinaus** he is past (all) that. **4.** *fig.* about (*or* that), (*on a subject*) on that, on it:

ich freue mich ~ I'm glad about it; **~ vergißt er alle s-e Sorgen** that takes his mind off his problems; **~ kam sie nicht hinweg** she didn't get over it.

dar'überstehen *v/i* (*irr, sep,* -ge-, h, → **stehen**) *fig.* be above it.

darum [da'rʊm] *adv* **1.** (a)round it *etc*. **2.** **ich bat ihn ~** I asked him: a) for it, b) to do it; **~ geht es nicht!** that's not the point! **3.** → **deshalb**.

darunter [da'rʊntər] *adv* **1.** under it *etc*, underneath: **das Zimmer ~** the room below; **~ trug sie ...** underneath she was wearing ... **2.** less, under: F **~ tut er es nicht** he won't do it for less. **3.** a) among them, b) including. **4.** **~ leiden, daß** suffer from *ger*; **was versteht man ~?** what do you understand by it?; **~ kann ich mir nichts vorstellen** that doesn't mean anything to me.

dar'unterfallen *v/i* (*irr, sep,* -ge-, sn, → **fallen**) *fig.* come under (*a law etc*).

dar'unterliegen *v/i* (*irr, sep,* -ge-, h, → **liegen**) *fig.* be below (standard).

dar'untersetzen *v/t* (*sep,* -ge-, h) put *signature etc* to it.

Darwinismus [darvi'nɪsmʊs] *m* (-; *no pl*) Darwinism.

das [das] **I** *def art* the: **~ Buch des Monats** the book of the month. **II** *dem pron* this (one), that (one): **~ war sie!** that was her!; **~ sind s-e Bücher** those are his books; **~ ist es ja (gerade)!** that's the point!; **nur ~ nicht!** anything but that! **III** *rel pron* which: **~ Geschäft, ~ ich meine** the shop (which) I'm talking of. **IV** *pers pron* F for **es**.

'dasein *v/i* (*irr, sep,* -ge-, → **sein**) **1.** a) be there, be present, b) exist: **bist du noch da?** are you still here?; **ist noch Brot da?** is there any bread left?; **ich bin gleich wieder da!** I'll be right back!; **ist j-d dagewesen?** has anyone been?; *fig.* **noch nie dagewesen** unprecedented, unheard-of. **2.** F (**voll**) a) be all there, b) be in great shape, c) conscious.

'Dasein *n* (-s; *no pl*) existence.

'dasitzen *v/i* (*irr, sep,* -ge-, h, → **sitzen**) sit there: *fig.* **~ ohne** be left without.

daß [das] *conj* that: **so ~** so that; **es sei denn, ~** unless; **ohne ~** without *ger*; **ich weiß, ~ ich recht habe** I know I'm right; **er entschuldigte sich, ~ er zu**

spät kam he apologized for being late; **nicht, ~ ich wüßte** not that I know of; **es ist lange her, ~ ich sie gesehen habe** it's a long time since I saw her; F **~ du ja hingehst!** be sure to go!

'**dastehen** v/i (irr, sep, -ge-, h, → **stehen**) stand there: fig. **gut ~** be in a good position, firm: be flourishing; **mittellos ~** be penniless; F **wie stehe ich jetzt da!** what a fool I look now!

Datei [da'tai] f (-; -en) data file.

Daten ['da:tən] pl data, facts, particulars. **~ausgabe** f data output. **~austausch** m data exchange. **~bank** f (-; -en) data bank. **~eingabe** f data input. **~erfassung** f data collection. **~mißbrauch** m data abuse. **~netz** n data network. **~schutz** m data protection. **~schutzbeauftragte** m, f data protection commissioner. **~sichtgerät** n (visual) display unit, (video) terminal. **~speicher** m data memory. **~speicherung** f data storage. **~technik** f data systems engineering. **~träger** m data medium. **~typist** [-ty‚pɪst] m (-en: -en), **~ty‚pistin** f (-; -nen) data typist. **~übermittlung** f, **~übertragung** f data transfer (or communication). **~umsetzung** f data conversion. **~verarbeitend** adj data-processing. **~verarbeitung** f data processing. **~verarbeitungsanlage** f data-processing equipment.

datieren [da'ti:rən] v/t, v/i (h) date.

Dativ ['da:ti:f] m (-s; -e) dative (case). **~ob‚jekt** n dative (or indirect) object.

Dattel ['datəl] f (-; -n) ♣ date.

Datum ['da:tʊm] n (-s; Daten) date: **ohne ~** undated; **welches ~ haben wir heute?** what's the date today?; **neueren ~s** of recent date. '**Datumsgrenze** f geogr. date line. '**Datumsstempel** m a) date stamp, b) dater.

Dauer ['dauər] f (-; no pl) duration (a. ling., ♪), period (of time), esp. ⚖ term, length: **von ~** lasting; **von kurzer** (or **nicht von**) **~ sein** be short-lived, not to last long; **auf die ~** in the long run; **der Lärm ist auf die ~ unerträglich** you can't stand the noise for long; **das kann auf die ~ nicht so weitergehen** that can't go on indefinitely; **für die ~ von** (or gen) for the duration (or a period) of.

'**Dauer|arbeitslosigkeit** f chronic un-

employment. **~auftrag** m ✝ periodical payment order. **~belastung** f 1. ⚙ continuous load. 2. fig. permanent stress. **~brenner** m F long-running success (or hit). **~gast** m permanent guest.

'**dauerhaft** adj permanent, lasting, durable, hard-wearing (goods): **~ sein** a wear well. '**Dauerhaftigkeit** f (-; no pl) durability, permanence.

'**Dauer|karte** f season ticket. **~lauf** m jogging: **im ~** at a jog (trot). **~lutscher** m (-s; -) F lollipop.

dauern ['dauərn] v/i (h) last, go on, take: **zwei Stunden ~** take two hours; **wie lange dauert es denn noch?** how much longer will it take?; **es wird lange ~** it will be a long time before you; **das dauert mir zu lange!** that's too long for me! '**dauernd I** adj constant: **~er Wohnsitz** permanent residence. **II** adv constantly; → et. tun keep doing; **er kommt ~ zu spät** he is always late; **das passiert ~** that happens all the time.

'**Dauer|parker** m long-term parker. **~regen** m continuous rain. **~stellung** f permanent post. **~welle** f (**~n haben** F have a) perm. **~zustand** m zum ~ werden become permanent (b.s. chronic).

Daumen ['daumən] m (-s; -) thumb: **~lutschen** suck one's thumb; F **j-m die ~ drücken** keep one's fingers crossed fo s.o.; **(die) ~ drehen** twiddle one' thumbs; **über den ~ gepeilt** at a rough estimate. **~nagel** m thumbnail.

Daunen ['daunən] pl down.

'**Daunendecke** f eiderdown.

davon [da'fɔn] adv 1. **das Dorf liegt nicht weit ~** (entfernt) the village is no far away (or from it); **~ zweigt ein Weg ab** a path branches off it. 2. **ich wachte ~ auf** I was awakened by it; **~ wird mar dick** that makes you fat; F **das komm ~!** that'll teach you!; **was habe ich ~** what do I get out of it? 3. **hast du schon ~ gehört?** have you heard abou it yet?; **genug ~!** enough of that! 4. **au und ~** up and away.

da'vonfliegen v/i (irr, sep, -ge-, sn, → **fliegen**) fly off, fly away. **da'vonjager** v/t (sep, -ge-, h) chase away.

da'vonkommen v/i (irr, sep, -ge-, sn, → **kommen**) get away, get off, escape: **mi dem Leben ~** survive; → **Schreck**.

da'vonlaufen v/i (irr, sep, -ge-, →

laufen) run away. **da'vonmachen:**
sich ~ (*sep*, -ge-, h) F make off, beat it.
da'vonstehlen: *sich ~* (*irr*, *sep*, -ge-, h,
→ *stehlen*) steal away. **da'vontragen**
v/t (*irr*, *sep*, -ge-, h, → *tragen*) **1.** *a. fig.*
carry off. **2.** sustain (*injury*), get, catch
(*disease*). **da'vonziehen** *v/i* (*irr*, *sep*,
-ge-, sn, → *ziehen*) move away (*or* off):
sports: j-m ~ pull away from s.o.
davor [da'foːr] *adv* **1.** before (*or* in front
of) it *etc*: *mit e-m Garten ~* with a
garden in front. **2.** *time*: before that. **3.**
~ habe ich Angst I'm afraid of that; *ich*
habe ihn ~ gewarnt I warned him of it.
dazu [da'tsuː] *adv* **1.** in addition to it,
besides: *sie sang und spielte ~ Gitarre*
she sang and accompanied herself on
the guitar; *möchten Sie Reis ~?* would
you like rice with it?; *und sie ist noch ~*
hübsch and she is pretty into the bargain. **2.** for it, for that purpose: *~ ist er*
ja da! that's what he is there for! **3.** *wie*
ist es ~ gekommen? how did that
come about?; *~ darf es nicht kommen*
that must not happen; *ich kam nie ~* I
never got (a)round to it; F *wie komme*
ich ~? why on earth should I?
da'zugehören *v/i* (*sep*, -ge-, h) belong to
it *etc*; → *a. gehören*. **da'zugehörig** *adj*
belonging to it (*or* them).
da'zukommen *v/i* (*irr*, *sep*, -ge-, sn, →
kommen) **1.** (*gerade ~*) happen to
come along (*als* when). **2.** a) join s.o.,
b) be added. **da'zulernen** *v/t*, *v/i* (*sep*,
-ge-, h) learn (s.th. new). **da'zutun** *v/t*
(*irr*, *sep*, -ge-, h, → *tun*) F add: *ohne*
sein etc ⌀ without his *etc* help.
dazwischen [da'tsvɪʃən] *adv* between
(them), in between (*a. time*), among
them. **~fahren** *v/i* (*irr*, *sep*, -ge-, sn, →
fahren) a) step in, interfere, b) interrupt. **~kommen** *v/i* (*irr*, *sep*, -ge-, sn, →
kommen) intervene: *wenn nichts da-*
zwischenkommt if all goes well.
~liegen *v/i* (*irr*, *sep*, -ge-, h, → *liegen*)
intervene. **~reden** *v/i* (*sep*, -ge-, h) *j-m ~*
interrupt s.o. **~treten** *v/i* (*irr*, *sep*, -ge-,
sn, → *treten*) intervene.
Dealer ['diːlər] *m* (-s; -) dealer.
Debakel [de'baːkəl] *n* (-s; -) débâcle.
Debatte [de'batə] *f* (-; -n) *a. parl.* debate:
zur ~ stehen be under discussion; *das*
steht nicht zur ~ that's not the issue.
debattieren [deba'tiːrən] *v/t*, *v/i* (h)

(*über e-e Sache* s.th.) debate, discuss.
Debet ['deːbɛt] *n* (-s; -s) ✝ debit. **~saldo**
m debit balance. **~seite** *f* debit side.
debil [de'biːl] *adj* ♬ feebleminded.
Debüt [de'byː] *n* (-s; -s) debut: *sein ~*
geben → **debütieren** [deby'tiːrən] *v/i*
(h) make one's debut.
dechiffrieren [deʃɪ'friːrən] *v/t* (h) decipher, decode.
Deck [dɛk] *n* (-[e]s; -s) ⚓ deck: *an* (*or*
auf) *~* on deck.
'**Deck|adresse** *f* cover (address).
'**Deckanstrich** *m* top (*or* finishing) coat.
'**Deckbett** *n* feather quilt.
'**Deckblatt** *n* wrapper (*of cigar*).
Deckchen ['dɛkçən] *n* (-s; -) doily.
Decke ['dɛkə] *f* (-; -n) **1.** a) blanket, b)
(bed)cover, c) (table)cloth: F *mit j-m*
unter einer ~ stecken be in league with
s.o.; *fig. sich nach der ~ strecken* cut
one's coat according to one's cloth. **2.**
ceiling: F *fig.* (*vor Freude*) *an die ~*
springen jump with joy; (*vor Wut*) *an*
die ~ gehen go through the roof; *mir*
fiel die ~ auf den Kopf I felt shut in. **3.**
⚙ *civ.eng.* surface, sur-
facing. **5.** tyre cover (*of car, bicycle*).
Deckel ['dɛkəl] *m* (-s; -) lid (*a. humor.*
hat), cover, (screw) cap: F *j-m eins auf*
den ~ geben tick s.o. off (properly).
decken ['dɛkən] (h) **I** *v/t* **1.** *~ über* (*acc*)
cover *s.th.* with. **2.** *roof: mit Stroh* (*Zie-*
geln, Schiefer) *~* thatch (tile, slate) *a*
roof. **3.** *den Tisch ~* lay (*or* set) the table
(*für drei Personen* for three). **4.** *a. fig.*
or contp. shield, protect; *j-n ~* cover up
for s.o., *sports*: mark s.o.; *den Rück-*
zug ~ cover the retreat. **5.** cover (*costs*),
meet (*demand*). **6.** *zo.* cover, serve. **II** *v/i*
7. *paint etc*: cover (*well etc*). **8.** *sports*:
cover, mark, *boxer*: cover (up). **III** *v/refl*
*~ **9.** cover o.s., *boxer*: cover up. **10.** (*mit*
with) ⚈ coincide, *fig. a.* tally.
'**Decken|balken** *m* ceiling beam. **~be-**
leuchtung *f* ceiling lighting. **~gemäl-**
de *n* ceiling fresco. **~leuchte** *f* ceiling
lamp, *mot.* dome lamp.
'**Deck|farbe** *f* ⚙ body colo(u)r. **~fe-**
der *f* deck feather. **~mantel** *m* *fig.*
cloak. **~name** *m* pseudonym, ✕ code
name.
'**Deckung** *f* (-; *no pl*) **1.** (*in ~ gehen* take)
cover. **2.** ✝ a) cover, security, b) supply: *k-e ~* no funds. **3.** *sports*: covering,

marking, *boxing etc*: guard. **4.** ♣ *or fig.* coincidence.

'**deckungsgleich** *adj* ♣ congruent.

'**Deckweiß** *n* opaque white.

Defätismus [defɛ'tɪsmʊs] *m* (-; *no pl*) defeatism. **defä'tistisch** *adj* defeatist.

defekt [de'fɛkt] *adj* defective, faulty.

De'fekt *m* (-[e]s; -e) defect (**an** *dat* in).

defensiv [defɛn'ziːf] *adj* defensive.

Defensive [defɛn'ziːvə] *f* (-; -n) (**in der ~** on the) defensive.

defilieren [defi'liːrən] *v/i* (sn) march past.

defi'nierbar *adj* definable: *schwer ~* difficult to define. **definieren** [defi'niːrən] *v/t* (h) define. **Definition** [defini'tsi̯oːn] *f* (-; -en) definition. **definitiv** [-'tiːf] *adj* definite (*answer*), positive (*offer*): *es steht ~ fest, daß ...* it is definite that ...

Defizit ['deːfitsit] *n* (-s; -e) *a. fig.* deficit.

Deflation [defla'tsi̯oːn] *f* (-; -en) *fig.* deflation. **deflationär** [-tsi̯o'nɛːr], **deflatorisch** [-'toːrɪʃ] *adj* ♣ deflationary.

deflorieren [deflo'riːrən] *v/t* (h) deflower.

deformieren [defɔr'miːrən] *v/t* (h) deform, ✿ *a.* distort.

deftig ['dɛftɪç] *adj* F solid (*meal*), earthy (*joke*), steep (*prices*), sound (*blow etc*).

Degen ['deːgən] *m* (-s; -) sword, *fenc.* épée.

Degeneration [degenera'tsi̯oːn] *f* (-; -en) degeneration. **degenerativ** [degenera'tiːf] *adj* degenerative.

degenerieren [degene'riːrən] *v/i* (sn), **degene'riert** *adj* degenerate.

'**Degenfechten** *n sports*: épée fencing.

degradieren [degra'diːrən] *v/t* (h) ✗ demote, *esp. fig.* degrade.

'**dehnbar** *adj a. fig.* elastic. '**Dehnbarkeit** *f* (-; *no pl*) elasticity. **dehnen** ['deːnən] (h) **I** *v/t* stretch (*a. fig.*). **2.** lengthen (*vowels*); drawl (*words*). **II** *sich ~* stretch (o.s.). '**Dehnung** *f* (-; -en) **1.** stretch(ing). **2.** *ling.* lengthening.

dehydrieren [dehy'driːrən] *v/t* (h) ✿ dehydrate.

Deich [daɪç] *m* (-[e]s; -e) dike, dam, *of river*: embankment, *Am.* levee.

Deichsel ['daɪksəl] *f* (-; -n) a) pole, b) shaft. '**deichseln** *v/t* F (h) wangle.

dein [daɪn] *adj* **1.** your: *eccl. ~ Wille geschehe* Thy will be done. **2.** *pred ~er, ~e, ~(e)s, der (die, das) ~e* yours;

e-r ~er Freunde a friend of yours. **3.** *der (die, das) ~(ig)e* your own, yours; *die* ⚥*(ig)en* your family, your people.

'**deiner** *pers pron* (of) you: *wir werden ~ gedenken* we shall remember you.

'**deinerseits** *adv* on your part.

'**deines'gleichen** *indef pron* people like you, *contp.* the likes of you.

deinetwegen ['daɪnətveːgən] *adv* a) for your sake, b) because of you.

deinig ['daɪnɪç] → *dein* 3.

Dekade [de'kaːdə] *f* (-; -n) decade.

dekadent [deka'dɛnt] *adj* decadent.

Dekadenz [deka'dɛnts] *f* (-; *no pl*) decadence.

Dekan [de'kaːn] *m* (-s; -e) dean. **Dekanat** [deka'naːt] *n* (-s; -e) dean's office.

deklamieren [dekla'miːrən] *v/t, v/i* (h) declaim.

deklarieren [dekla'riːrən] *v/t* (h) ✝ declare.

deklassieren [dekla'siːrən] *v/t* (h) declass, *sports*: outclass.

Deklination [deklina'tsi̯oːn] *f* (-; -en) **1.** *ling.* declension. **2.** *phys.* declination.

dekli'nierbar *adj* declinable.

deklinieren [dekli'niːrən] *v/t* (h) decline.

Dékolleté [dekɔl'teː] *n* (-s; -s) (*tiefes ~* plunging) neckline.

dékolletiert [dekɔl'tiːrt] *adj* décolleté.

dekontaminieren [dekɔntami'niːrən] *v/t* (h) decontaminate.

Dekor [de'koːr] *m, n* (-s; -s) **1.** a) decoration, b) décor, c) pattern. **2.** *thea.* décor, set(s). **Dekorateur** [dekora'tøːr] *m* (-s; -e), **Dekora'teurin** *f* (-; -nen) **1.** window-dresser. **2.** interior designer. **3.** *thea. etc* scene painter. **Dekoration** [dekora'tsi̯oːn] *f* (-; -en) decoration, *a.* window display, furnishings, *thea. etc* set(s). **dekorativ** [-'tiːf] *adj* decorative.

dekorieren [deko'riːrən] *v/t* (h) decorate (*a. with an order*), dress (*shop window*).

Dekret [de'kreːt] *n* (-[e]s; -e) decree.

Delegation [delega'tsi̯oːn] *f* (-; -en) delegation. **delegieren** [dele'giːrən] *v/t* (h) delegate.

Dele'gierte *m, f* (-n; -n) delegate.

delikat [deli'kaːt] *adj* delicious, *a. fig.* delicate. **Delikatesse** [delika'tɛsə] *f* (-; -n) delicacy, *fig. a.* discretion.

Delika'teßgeschäft *n* delicatessen.

Delikt [de'lɪkt] *n* (-[e]s; -e) ⚖ offen/ce

(*Am.* -se). **Delinquent** [delɪŋ'kvɛnt] *m* (-en; -en) offender.

Delirium [de'li:rĭʊm] *n a. fig.* delirium.

Delle ['dɛlə] *f* (-; -n) F dent.

Delphin [dɛl'fi:n] *m* (-s; -e) *zo.* dolphin.

Del'phin(schwimmen) *n* (-s) butterfly.

Delta ['dɛlta] *n* (-s; -s) *geogr.* delta.

'**Deltamuskel** *m* deltoid (muscle).

dem [de:m] **I** *def art* **gib es ~ Jungen** give it to the boy. **II** *dem pron* **wie ~ auch sei** however that may be; **nach ~, was ich gehört habe** from what I've heard. **III** *rel pron* **der, ~ ich es gab** the one (*or* the person) I gave it to.

Demagoge [dema'go:gə] *m* (-n; -n) demagogue. **Demagogie** [demago'gi:] *f* (-; -n) demagogy. **demagogisch** [dema'go:gɪʃ] *adj* demagogic.

Demarkationslinie [demarka'tsĭo:ns-] *f* demarcation line.

demaskieren [demas'ki:rən] *v/t* (h) *a. fig.* unmask.

Dementi [de'mɛnti] *n* (-s; -s) *pol.* (official) denial. **dementieren** [demɛn-'ti:rən] *v/t* (h) deny (officially).

'**dementsprechend** *adv* accordingly.

'**demgegen'über** *adv* in contrast to this.

'**demge'mäß** *adv* accordingly.

'**demnach** *adv* **1.** therefore. **2.** → *demgemäß.*

dem'nächst *adv* shortly, soon: **~ er- scheinend** *etc* forthcoming.

Demo [de'mo:] *f* (-; -s) F demo.

Demograph [demo'gra:f] *m* (-en; -en) demographer. **Demographie** [demogra'fi:] *f* (-; -n) demography. **demographisch** [-'gra:fɪʃ] *adj* demographic.

Demokas,sette *f* F demo (tape).

Demokrat [demo'kra:t] *m* (-en; -en), **Demo'kratin** *f* (-; -nen) *pol.* democrat. **Demokratie** [demokra'ti:] *f* (-; -n) democracy. **demokratisch** [-'kra:tɪʃ] *adj* democratic. **demokratisieren** [demokrati'zi:rən] *v/t* (h) democratize.

demolieren [demo'li:rən] *v/t* (h) demolish, wreck.

Demo'lierung *f* (-; -en) demolition.

Demonstrant [demɔn'strant] *m* (-en; -en), **Demon'strantin** *f* (-; -nen) demonstrator, protester. **Demonstration** [-stra'tsĭo:n] *f* (-; -en) (*pol.* e-e ~ veran- stalten hold a) demonstration; *fig.* e-e ~ der Macht a show of force.

onstrate. **~verbot** *n* ban on demonstra- tions. **~zug** *m* protest march.

demonstrativ [demɔnstra'ti:f] *adj* de- monstrative. **Demonstra'tivpro,no- men** *n* demonstrative (pronoun).

demonstrieren [demɔn'stri:rən] *v/t, v/i* (h) demonstrate.

Demontage [demɔn'ta:ʒə] *f* (-; -n) ⊙ *or fig.* dismantling.

demontieren [demɔn'ti:rən] *v/t* (h) dis- mantle (*a. fig.*), take down, take apart.

demoralisieren [demorali'zi:rən] *v/t* (h) demoralize.

Demoskopie [demosko'pi:] *f* (-; -n) (public) opinion research. **demosko- pisch** [demo'sko:pɪʃ] *adj* ~**e Umfrage** (public) opinion poll.

Demut ['de:mu:t] *f* (-; *no pl*) humility.

demütig ['de:my:tɪç] *adj* humble.

demütigen ['de:my:tɪgən] *v/t* (h) humil- iate: **sich ~** humble o.s.

'**Demütigung** *f* (-; -en) humiliation.

denaturieren [denatu'ri:rən] *v/t* (h) 🔬, *phys.* denature.

'**Denkanstoß** *m* impulse: **j-m e-n ~ ge- ben**, (**bei j-m**) **als ~ wirken** set s.o. thinking. '**Denkart** *f* way of thinking.

'**Denkaufgabe** *f* problem, brain teaser.

'**denkbar** *adj* thinkable, conceivable: **es ist durchaus ~, daß** it's quite possible that; **die ~ beste Methode** the best method imaginable.

denken ['dɛŋkən] *v/t, v/i* (dachte, ge- dacht, h) **1.** think, *a.* imagine, suppose, *Am.* F guess: **das gibt e-m zu ~** that makes you think; **ich denke schon I** (should) think so; **das habe ich mir gedacht** I thought as much; **das hät- test du dir ~ können!** you should have known that!; **ich dachte mir nichts dabei** I thought nothing of it; **solange ich ~ kann** as long as I remember; F **denkste!** that's what you think! **2.** think of, consider: **er denkt daran zu kommen** he thinks of coming; **ich den- ke nicht daran!** I wouldn't dream of it! **3. ~ an** (*acc*) a) think of (*or* about), b) remember; **daran ist nicht zu ~** it's out of the question; **an Schlaf war nicht zu ~** sleep was out of the question; **wenn ich nur daran denke!** the mere thought of it! **4. ~ über** (*acc*) think about (*or* of).

'**Denken** *n* (-s) thinking, thought.

'**Denker** *m* (-s; -) thinker. '**Denkfa,brik** *f*

F think-tank. **'denkfähig** *adj* intelligent. **'denkfaul** *adj* mentally lazy. **'Denkfehler** *m* flaw in one's reasoning. **'Denkmal** *n* -[e]s; ⁻er) monument: *j-m ein ~ setzen* put up a monument to s.o. **'Denkmalpflege** *f* preservation of historic buildings and monuments. **'Denkmalschutz** *m unter ~ stehen* be listed (as a historic monument). **'Denk|muster** *n* thought pattern. **~pause** *f* pause for reflection. **~pro,zeß** *m* thought process. **~schrift** *f* memorandum. **~vermögen** *n* (-s; *no pl*) intellectual capacity, intelligence. **~weise** *f* way of thinking. **2würdig** *adj* memorable. **~zettel** *m* (*j-m e-n ~ verpassen* teach s.o. a) lesson.

denn [dɛn] **I** *conj* **1.** because, since. **2.** than: *mehr ~ je* more than ever. **3.** *es sei ~* unless. **II** *adv* **4.** then: *war es ~ so schlimm?* was it really that bad?; *was ist ~?* what is it now?; *wieso ~?* (but) why?; *wo warst du ~ nur?* where on earth have you been?

dennoch ['dɛnɔx] *conj* (but) still, yet.

Dental [dɛn'ta:l] *m* (-[e]s; -e) *ling.* dental. **Denunziant** [denʊn'tsi̯ant] *m* (-en; -en), **Denunzi'antin** *f* (-; -nen) informer.

denunzieren [denʊn'tsi:rən] *v/t* (h) *j-n ~* denounce s.o. (*bei* to).

Deodorant [de⁹odo'rant] *n* (-s; -e, -s) deodorant.

deplaziert [depla'tsi:rt] *adj* out of place, *a.* misplaced (*remark etc*).

Deponie [depo'ni:] *f* (-; -n) dump, tip. **deponieren** [depo'ni:rən] *v/t* (h) (*bei* with) deposit, leave.

Deportation [deporta'tsi̯o:n] *f* (-; -en) deportation. **deportieren** [depor'ti:rən] *v/t* (h) deport. **Depor'tierte** *m, f* (-n; -n) deportee.

Depot [de'po:] *n* (-s; -s) depot, ✝ *ca. account* deposit. **De'potwirkung** *f* ✝ controlled sustained release.

Depression [deprɛ'si̯o:n] *f* (-; -en) depression. **depressiv** [-'si:f] *adj psych.* depressive. **deprimieren** [depri'mi:rən] *v/t* (h) depress; **~d** depressing.

der [de:r] **I** *art* the: *~ arme Peter* poor Peter. **II** *dem pron* that (one), this (one): *~ mit ~ Brille* the one with the glasses; *contp. ~ und sein Wort halten?* him keep his word? **III** *rel pron* who, which. **IV** *pers pron* F *for* **er.**

derart ['de:r'⁹a:rt] *adv* so, in such a way. **'der'artig I** *adj* such: *nichts Derartiges* nothing of the kind. **II** *adv → derart.*

derb [dɛrp] *adj* **1.** strong, sturdy, coarse (*food etc*). **2.** *fig.* coarse, crude (*joke etc*). **'Derbheit** *f* (-; -en) **1.** *no pl* coarseness. **2.** *pl* crude jokes (*or* remarks).

derentwegen ['de:rəntve:gən] **I** *adv* because of her (*or* that *etc*). **II** *rel pron* because of whom (*or* which).

'der'gleichen *dem pron* **1.** such. **2.** such a thing, the like: *nichts ~* no such thing; *und ~ mehr* and so on, and the like.

Derivat [deri'va:t] *n* (-[e]s; -e) 🜍, *ling* derivative.

derjenige ['de:rje:nigə] *dem pron* that: *~, der* he (*or* the one) who.

dermaßen ['de:rma:sən] *adv → derart.*

Dermatologe [dɛrmato'lo:gə] *m* (-n; -n)] 💉 dermatologist. **Dermatose** [-'to:zə], (-; -n) dermatosis, skin disease.

derselbe [de:r'zɛlbə] *dem pron* the same. **'der'zeit** *adv* at present. **'der'zeitig** *adj* **1.** present. **2.** then, (of *or* that) the time.

Des [dɛs] *n* (-; -) ♪ D flat.

desensibilisieren [dezɛnzibili'zi:rən] *v/t* (h) 💉, *phot.* desensitize.

Deserteur [dezɛr'tø:r] *m* (-s; -e) deserter. **desertieren** [-'ti:rən] *v/i* (sn) desert. **'des'gleichen** *adv and conj* likewise.

'deshalb *adv and conj* therefore, that's why: *gerade ~!* that's just why!; *sie is ~ nicht glücklicher* she isn't any happier for it.

designiert [dezɪ'gni:rt] *adj der ~e Präsident* the president designate.

desillusionieren [dɛs⁹ɪluzi̯o'ni:rən] *v/* (h) disillusion.

Desinfektion [dɛs⁹ɪnfɛk'tsi̯o:n] *f* (-; -en) disinfection. **Desinfekti'onsmittel** *n* disinfectant, 💉 *a.* antiseptic. **desinfizieren** [-fi'tsi:rən] *v/t* (h) disinfect.

Desinformati'on *f* (-; -en) disinformation.

'Desinter,esse *n* (-s; *no pl*) lack of interest, indifference (*an dat* to). **'desinteres,siert** *adj* uninterested, indifferent.

desolat [dezo'la:t] *adj* desolate.

Desorganisati'on *f* disorganization.

desorien'tiert *adj psych.* confused.

Despot [dɛs'po:t] *m* (-en; -en) despot. **des'potisch** *adj* despotic(al).

Despotismus [dɛspo'tɪsmʊs] *m* (-; *no pl*) despotism.

dessen ['dɛsən] **I** rel pron whose, of which. **II** dem pron **sich ~ bewußt sein, daß ...** be aware (of the fact) that ...; **~ bin ich sicher** I'm quite sure of that. **III** poss pron **mein Bruder und ~ Frau** my brother and his wife.

dessenunge'achtet adv nevertheless.

Dessert [dɛ'sɛːr] n (-s; -s) gastr. dessert.

Destillat [dɛstɪ'laːt] n (-[e]s; -e) distillate.

destillieren [-'liːrən] v/t, v/i (h) distil(l).

desto ['dɛsto] **I** adv (all) the: **~ besser!** all (or so much) the better!; **~ schlimmer** so much the worse. **II** conj the ...: **je mehr (eher** etc), **~ besser** the more (sooner etc) the better.

destruktiv [destrʊk'tiːf] adj destructive.

deswegen ['dɛs'veːgən] → **deshalb.**

Detail [de'taɪ] n (-s; -s) detail.

detaillieren [detaˈjiːrən] v/t (h) specify.

detail'liert **I** adj detailed. **II** adv in detail.

Detektiv [detɛkˈtiːf] m (-s; -e) detective.

Detek'tivbü,**ro** n detective agency.

Detek'tivro,**man** m detective story.

Detonation [detonaˈtsɪoːn] f (-; -en) detonation, blast. **detonieren** [detoˈniːrən] v/i (sn) detonate.

deuten ['dɔʏtən] (h) **I** v/t interpret, read: **falsch ~** misinterpret, fig. misconstrue. **II** v/i **~ auf** (acc) point at (esp. fig. to); **alles deutet darauf hin, daß** there is every indication that.

deutlich ['dɔʏtlɪç] adj clear, distinct, legible, plain: **~er Wink** broad hint; **~er Fortschritt** visible progress; F fig. **~ werden** speak in very plain terms; **muß ich noch ~er werden?** do I have to spell it out (to you)?

Deutlichkeit f (-; no pl) clarity, clearness: **in aller ~** in plain terms.

deutsch [dɔʏtʃ] adj (auf ~, in ~ in) German: **~ reden** talk (in) German; F fig. **mit j-m ~ reden** speak plainly with s.o.

Deutsch, das ~e German: **er kann gut ~** he speaks German well.

Deutsch|ameri,kaner(in f) m, **2ame-ri,kanisch** adj German-American.

deutsch-'deutsch adj pol. hist. inter-German, German-German.

Deutsche m, f (-n; -n) German.

deutsch-'englisch adj pol. Anglo-German, ling. German-English.

deutschfeindlich adj anti-German.

deutsch-fran'zösisch adj pol. Franco-German, ling. German-French.

deutschfreundlich adj pro-German.

Deutschland n (-s) Germany.

Deutschlehrer m German teacher.

deutschsprachig [-ˈʃpraːxɪç] adj German-language (text), German-speaking (area).

Deutschunterricht m German lessons.

Deutung f (-; -en) interpretation.

Devise [deˈviːzə] f (-; -n) **1.** motto. **2.** pl ✝ foreign exchange (or currency).

De'visen|abkommen n foreign exchange agreement. **~bestimmungen** pl currency regulations. **~börse** f foreign exchange market. **~geschäft** n foreign exchange transaction. **~händler** m foreign exchange dealer. **~knappheit** f (foreign) currency stringency. **~vergehen** n currency offen/ce (Am. -se).

devot [deˈvoːt] adj contr. servile.

Devotionalien [devotsɪoˈnaːlɪən] pl eccl. devotional objects.

Dezember [deˈtsɛmbər] m (-[s]; -) (im ~ in) December.

dezent [deˈtsɛnt] adj discreet, unobtrusive, soft (colo[u]r, music, etc).

dezentralisieren [detsɛntraliˈziːrən] v/t (h) decentralize.

Dezernat [detsɛrˈnaːt] n (-[e]s; -e) department. **Dezernent** [detsɛrˈnɛnt] m (-en; -en) head of (a department.

Dezibel ['deːtsibɛl] n (-s; -) decibel.

Dezimal|bruch [detsiˈmaːl-] m & decimal (fraction). **~stelle** f decimal (place). **~sy**,**stem** n decimal system. **~zahl** f decimal.

Dezimeter ['deːtsimeːtər] m, n (-s; -) decimet/re (Am. -er). **dezimieren** [detsiˈmiːrən] v/t (h) decimate.

Dia ['diːa] n (-s; -s) F slide.

Diabetes [diaˈbeːtɛs] m (-; no pl) diabetes. **Diabetiker** [diaˈbeːtikər] m (-s; -), **Dia'betikerin** f (-; -nen) diabetic.

Diabetrachter m slide viewer.

diabolisch [diaˈboːlɪʃ] adj diabolic(al).

Diafilm m dia film.

Diagnose [diaˈgnoːzə] f (-; -n) (e-e ~ stellen make a) diagnosis.

diagnostizieren [diagnɔstiˈtsiːrən] v/t, v/i (h) diagnose.

diagonal [diagoˈnaːl] adj, **Diago'nale** f (-; -n) diagonal. **Diago'nalreifen** m mot. cross-ply tyre (Am. tire).

Diagramm [diaˈgram] n (-s; -e) diagram, graph.

Diakon [dia'ko:n] *m* (-s, -en; -e[n]) *eccl.* deacon. **Diakonisse** [diako'nisə] *f* (-; -n) Protestant (nursing) sister.

Dialekt [dia'lɛkt] *m* (-[e]s; -e) dialect.
Dialektik [dia'lɛktɪk] *f* (-; *no pl*) dialectics.

Dialog [dia'lo:k] *m* (-[e]s; -e) (**e-n ~ füh-ren** carry on a) dialog(ue *Br.*).

Dialyse [dia'ly:zə] *f* (-; -n) 🟦 dialysis.

Diamant [dia'mant] *m* (-en; -en), **dia'manten** *adj* diamond.

dia'metral [dia'metra:l] *adj* diametric(al): **~ entgegengesetzt** diametrically opposed (*dat* to).

Diapositiv ['di:apoziti:f] *n* (-s; -e) slide.
'Diapro,jektor *m* slide projector.
'Diarahmen *m* slide frame.

Diät [di'ɛ:t] *f* (-; -en) (special) diet: **~ halten, ♀ leben** (keep to a) diet; **j-n auf ~ setzen** put s.o. on a diet.
Di'ätassi,stent(in *f*) *m* dietician.
Di'äten *pl parl.* attendance allowance.
Di'ätfahrplan *m* F dietary schedule.
Di'ätkost *f* dietary food.
Di'ätvorschrift *f* dietary.

dich [dɪç] **I** *pers pron* you. **II** *reflex pron* yourself: **schau ~ an!** look at yourself!

dicht [dɪçt] **I** *adj* **1.** dense (*wood, crowd, fog, etc*), *a.* heavy (*traffic*), thick (*hair, hedge*), close(ly-woven) (*fabric*). **2.** watertight, leakproof: F *fig.* **er ist nicht ganz ~** he's got a screw loose. **3.** compact, *fig.* tight (*plot*). **II** *adv* **4.** densely, thickly: **~ schließen** shut tightly, **~ ge-drängt stehen** stand closely packed. **5.** **~ an** (*dat*), **~ bei** close to; **~ aufeinan-derfolgen** follow closely (*or* in rapid succession); **~ hinter j-m** close (*or* hard) on s.o.'s heels.

'dichtbehaart *adj* (very) hairy.
'dichtbevölkert *adj* densely populated.
'Dichte *f* (-; *no pl*) density (*a. phys.*), denseness, thickness, tightness.
dichten¹ ['dɪçtən] *v/t* (h) 🟦 seal, pack.
'dichten² (h) **I** *v/t* write. **II** *v/i* write poetry (*or* plays *etc*).
'Dichter *m* (-s; -) poet, *w.s.* author, writer. **'Dichterin** *f* (-; -nen) poetess, *w.s.* authoress, writer.
'dichterisch *adj* poetic(al); → **Freiheit.**
'dichthalten *v/i* (*irr, sep,* -ge-, h, → **hal-ten**) F keep one's mouth shut.
'Dichtkunst *f* (-; *no pl*) poetry.
'dichtmachen (*sep,* -ge-, h) F **I** *v/t* shut

(up). **II** *v/i* (**den Laden**) **~** shut up shop.
'Dichtung¹ *f* (-; -en) 🟦 seal, packing.
'Dichtung² *f* (-; -en) a) literature, b) poetry, c) poem, d) (literary *or* poetic) work(s): *fig.* **~ und Wahrheit** fact and fiction.
'Dichtungs|masse *f* 🟦 sealing compound. **~ring** *m*, **~scheibe** *f* washer.

dick [dɪk] **I** *adj* **1.** thick, *w.s. a.* a) dense, b) big, large, c) stout, fat: F **~er Ver-kehr** heavy traffic; **~ machen** be fattening; **~ werden** grow fat; **durch ~ und dünn** through thick and thin. **2.** F a) close, intimate, b) big: **sie sind ~e Freunde** they are (as) thick as thieves, **~es Lob ernten** reap lavish praise; **~er Auftrag** fat order; → **Ende** 1, **Luft** 1. **II** *adv* **3.** thick(ly). **4.** F very: **~ befreundet sein** be great pals (**mit j-m** with s.o.); **ich habe ihn** (**es**) **~** I'm sick of him (it), → **auftragen** 5.
'dickbäuchig [-bɔʏçɪç] *adj* fat-bellied.
'Dickdarm *m anat.* colon.
'Dicke¹ *f* (-; *no pl*) thickness, 🟦 *a.* diameter, *w.s. a.* a) denseness, b) bigness, c) stoutness, fatness.
'Dicke² *m*, *f* (-n; -n) F fat person.
'Dickerchen *n* (-s; -) F fatso.
'dickfellig [-fɛlɪç] *adj* F thick-skinned.
'Dickfelligkeit *f* (-; *no pl*) F callousness.
'dickflüssig *adj* thick(-flowing).
Dickhäuter ['dɪkhɔʏtər] *m* (-s; -) *zo.* pachyderm.
Dickicht ['dɪkɪçt] *n* (-s; -e) **1.** thicket. **2.** *fig.* labyrinth.
'Dickkopf *m* F *fig.* pigheaded fellow: **e-n ~ haben** → **'dickköpfig** [-kœpfɪç] *adj* **~ sein** be pigheaded. **'Dickköpfigkeit** *f* (-; *no pl*) pigheadedness, stubbornness.
'dicklich *adj* **1.** plump. **2.** → **dickflüssig.**
'Dickmilch *f* soured milk.
'dickschalig [-ʃa:lɪç] *adj* thick-skinned.
'Dickwanst *m* F fatso.

Didaktik [di'daktɪk] *f* (-; *no pl*) didactics.
di'daktisch *adj* didactic.

die [di:] **I** *def art* the. **II** *dem pron* this (one), that (one): **~ nicht!** not she! **III** *rel pron* who, which. **IV** *pers pron* F *for* **sie** 1.

Dieb [di:p] *m* (-[e]s; -e) thief.
'Diebes|bande ['di:bas-] *f* gang o thieves. **~beute** *f*, **~gut** *n* stolen goods
Diebin [di'bɪn] *f* (-; -nen) thief.
diebisch [di'bɪʃ] *adj* **1.** thievish. **2.** mali

cious (*joy*): **sich ~ freuen (über** *acc*) F be tickled pink (at), gloat (at, over).

▌iebstahl ['di:pʃta:l] *m* (-[e]s; ~e) theft, ⚖⚖ larceny: **einfacher (schwerer) ~** petty (grand) larceny; **geistiger ~** plagiarism. **2sicher** *adj* theftproof. **~sicherung** *f mot*. theft protection. **~versicherung** *f* insurance against theft.

▌iele ['di:lə] *f* (-; -n) **1.** floorboard. **2.** (entrance) hall, *Am.* hallway.

▌ienen ['di:nən] *v/i* (h) serve ([**bei**] *j-m* s.o., ✕ **bei** in, **zu** for, **als** as): **dazu ~ zu** *inf* serve to *inf*; **womit kann ich ~?** what can I do for you?; **damit ist mir nicht gedient** that's of no use to me; **wozu soll das ~?** what's the use of that?

▌iener *m* (-s; -) *a. fig.* servant. **'Dienerin** *f* (-; -nen) maid(servant), *fig.* handmaid. **'Dienerschaft** *f* (-; *no pl*) servants. **'dienlich** *adj* useful (*dat* to), expedient: **~ sein** a) *j-m* be of help (*or* use) to s.o., b) **e-r Sache** further s.th.

▌ienst [di:nst] *m* (-es; -e) **1.** service (**an** *dat* to), ✕ *a.* duty: **öffentlicher ~** civil service; **im (außer) ~** on (off) duty; **~ haben** be on duty, *pharmacy:* be open; **j-m e-n guten (schlechten) ~ erweisen** do s.o. a good (bad) turn; **j-m gute ~e leisten** serve s.o. well; **in ~ stellen** put *ship etc* into service; **(j-m) den ~ versagen** fail (s.o.); **~ nach Vorschrift** work-to-rule (campaign). **2.** post, employment, work: **im ~e** (*gen*) **stehen** be employed by, work for, *contp.* be on s.o.'s payroll; **außer ~** retired; **den ~ quittieren** resign; → **antreten** 1.

▌ienstag ['di:nsta:k] *m* (-[e]s; -e) (**am ~** on) Tuesday. **'dienstags** *adv* on Tuesdays: **~ abends** (on) Tuesday evenings. **Dienst│alter** *n* (*nach dem ~* by) seniority. **~älteste** *m, f* (-n; -n) senior. **~antritt** *m* (**bei ~** on) taking up duty (*or* one's job). **~auffassung** *f* work ethic. **dienstbar** *adj* subservient (*dat* to): **sich et. ~ machen** utilize (*or* exploit) s.th. **dienstbereit** *adj* **1.** a) on duty, b) open. **2.** helpful.

▌ienst│eid *m* oath of office. **~eifer** *m* zeal, *b.s.* officiousness. **2eifrig** *adj* zealous, *b.s.* officious. **2frei** *adj* **~er Tag** day off; **~ haben** be off duty. **~gebrauch** *m* **nur für den ~** for official use only. **~geheimnis** *n* official secret (*or* secrecy). **~gespräch** *n teleph.* official

call. **~grad** *m* ✕ rank, *Am.* grade, ♪ rating. **2habend** *adj* on duty. **~herr** *m* employer. **~jahre** *pl* years of service. **~leistung** *f* service (rendered): **~en** services.

'Dienstleistungs│betrieb *m* (**öffentlicher ~** public) services enterprise. **~gewerbe** *n* service industries.

'dienstlich *adj* official: **~ verhindert** prevented by official duties.

'Dienst│mädchen *n* maid(servant), help. **~marke** *f* identity disc. **~pi‚stole** *f* service pistol. **~plan** *m* duty roster. **~reise** *f* official trip. **~schluß** *m* **nach ~** after (office) hours. **~stelle** *f* office, department. **~stunden** *pl* office hours. **2tauglich** *adj* fit for (✕ active) service. **2untauglich** *adj* unfit for (military) service. **~verhältnis** *n* (contract of) employment. **~vorschrift** *f* regulations. **~wagen** *m* official car. **~weg** *m* (**auf dem ~** through) official channels. **~wohnung** *f* company, army *etc* flat (*or* house). **~zeit** *f* **1.** office (*or* working) hours. **2.** (period of) service.

diesbezüglich ['di:s-] *adj and adv* concerning this, in this connection.

Dieselmotor ['di:zəl-] *m* Diesel engine.

dieser ['di:zər] *, diese, dieses, a. dies* [di:s], *pl* **diese** *dem pron* **I** this, *pl* these: **dieser Tage** a) the other day, b) one of these days. **II** a) this one, *pl* these, b) he, she, it, *pl* they: **dieses und jenes, dies und das** this and that, various things.

diesig ['di:zɪç] *adj* hazy.

diesjährig ['di:sjɛ:rɪç] *adj* this year's.

'diesmal *adv* this time.

diesseitig ['di:szaɪtɪç] *adj* near, on this side. **diesseits** ['di:szaɪts] *adv* on this side (*gen* of).

Dietrich ['di:trɪç] *m* (-s; -e) a) picklock, b) skeleton key.

diffamieren [dɪfa'mi:rən] *v/t* (h) slander, defame.

Differential│getriebe [dɪfərɛn'tsIa:l-] *n mot.* differential (gear). **~rechnung** *f* ♣ differential calculus.

Differenz [dɪfə'rɛnts] *f* (-; -en) difference. **differenzieren** [dɪfərɛn'tsi:rən] *v/t, v/i* (h) differentiate. **differieren** [dɪfə'ri:rən] *v/i* (h) differ (**um** by).

diffus [dɪ'fu:s] *adj* **1.** *phys.* diffuse(d). **2.** *fig.* vague.

digital [digi'ta:l] *adj* digital.

Digi'talanzeige f digital display.
digitalisieren [digitali'zi:rən] v/t (h) digitize.
Digi'talrechner m digital computer.
Digi'taluhr f digital watch (or clock).
Diktat [dɪk'ta:t] n (-[e]s; -e) **1.** (ped. ~ **schreiben** write or do) dictation; **das ~ aufnehmen** take the dictation. **2.** fig. dictate. **Diktator** [dɪk'ta:tɔr] m (-s; -en [-ta'to:rən]) dictator. **diktatorisch** [dɪkta'to:rɪʃ] adj dictatorial. **Diktatur** [dɪkta'tu:r] f (-; -en) dictatorship.
diktieren [dɪk'ti:rən] v/t, v/i (h) a. fig. dictate (**j-m** to s.o.).
Dik'tiergerät n dictating machine.
Dilemma [di'lɛma] n (-s; -s, -ta) dilemma, f fix.
Dilettant [dile'tant] m (-en; -en), **dilet-'tantisch** adj dilettante.
Dill [dɪl] m (-[e]s; -e) ♀ dill.
Dimension [dimɛn'zi̯o:n] f (-; -en) **1.** A, phys. dimension. **2.** pl dimensions, fig. a. extent.
Ding [dɪŋ] n (-[e]s; -e, F -er) **1.** thing, a. object: **vor allen ~en** above all; F **die armen ~er!** the poor (little) things!; fig. **guter ~e sein** be cheerful. **2.** pl things, matters: **der Stand der ~e** the state of affairs; **(so,) wie die ~e liegen** as matters stand; **das geht nicht mit rechten ~en zu** F there's s.th. fishy about it. **3.** F **ein tolles ~** a wow; **ein ~ drehen** pull a job; → **verpassen** 2.
'dingfest adj **j-n ~ machen** arrest s.o.
Dings [dɪŋs] m, f, n (-; no pl), **'Dings-bums** m, f, n (-; no pl), **'Dingsda** m, f, n (-; no pl) F what's-his(-her, -its)-name, thingumajig.
Dinosaurier [dino'zaʊri̯ɐr] m (-s; -) dinosaur.
Diode [di'o:də] f (-; -n) ⚡ diode.
Dioxyd ['di:'ʔɔksy:t] n (-s; -e) 🜍 dioxide.
Diözese [diø'tse:zə] f (-; -n) diocese.
Diphtherie [dɪfte'ri:] f (-; -n) diphtheria.
Diphthong [dɪf'tɔŋ] m (-s; -e) diphthong.
Diplom [di'plo:m] n (-[e]s; -e) diploma.
Di'plom... diplomaed, graduate (engineer etc), qualified (interpreter etc).
Di'plomarbeit f dissertation.
Diplomat [diplo'ma:t] m (-en; -en) diplomat. **Diplo'matenkoffer** m attaché case. **Diplomatie** [diploma'ti:] f (-; no pl) a. fig. diplomacy. **Diplo'matin** f (-;

-nen) diplomat. **diplo'matisch** adj a. fig. diplomatic.
dir [di:r] **I** pers pron you, to you. **II** refle pron yourself: **wasch ~ die Hände** wash your hands!
direkt [di'rɛkt] **I** adj **1.** a) direct (a. ling., b) immediate, c) plain: **~e Informatio nen** a. firsthand information. **II** adv **2** direct, a. fig. straight. **3.** directly, immediately: **~ vor dir** right in front c you. **4.** directly, exactly: **~ nach Süde liegen** face due south. **5.** F **das ist lächerlich** etc that's downright ridicu lous etc. **6.** radio, TV live.
Di'rektflug m direct flight.
Direktion [dirɛk'tsi̯o:n] f (-; -en) **1.** man agement. **2.** manager's office. **3.** direc tion. **Direkti'onsassi,stent(in** f) junior executive, assistant manager.
Direktive [dirɛk'ti:və] f (-; -n) instruc tion(s).
Direktor [di'rɛktɔr] m (-s; -en [-'to:rən] **1.** ✝ director, manager. **2.** ped. heac master, principal. **Direktorat** [dirɛkto 'ra:t] n (-[e]s; -e) **1.** directorship. **2** headmaster's office. **Direktorin** [dirɛk 'to:rɪn] f (-; -nen) **1.** directress, manag eress. **2.** ped. headmistress, principa **Direktorium** [dirɛk'to:ri̯ʊm] n (- -rien) board of directors. **Direktrice** [dirɛk'tri:sə] f (-; -n) textı directress.
Di'rektsendung f live broadcast.
Di'rektwahl f teleph. direct dial(l)ing.
Dirigent [diri'gɛnt] m (-en; -en) ♩ con ductor. **Diri'gentin** f (-; -nen) condu tress. **dirigieren** [diri'gi:rən] v/t, v/i (h direct, ✝ a. control, ♩ conduct.
Dirigismus [diri'gɪsmʊs] m (-; no pl) planned economy.
Dirndl ['dɪrndəl] n (-s; -), **~kleid** n dirnd **Dirne** ['dɪrnə] f (-; -n) prostitute, whor **Dis** [dɪs] n (-; -) ♩ D sharp.
Disharmonie f (-; -n) a. fig. discord.
dishar'monisch adj a. fig. discordant
Diskant [dɪs'kant] m (-s; -e) ♩ treble.
Diskette [dɪs'kɛtə] f computer: disk(ette
Diskjockey ['dɪsk-] m disc jockey.
Disko ['dɪsko] f (-s; -s) F disco.
Diskont [dɪs'kɔnt] m (-s; -e) discoun **diskontieren** [-'ti:rən] v/t (h) ✝ di count. **Dis'kontsatz** m discount rate
Diskothek [dɪsko'te:k] f (-; -en) disc theque.

Diskrepanz [dɪskre'pants] f (-; -en) discrepancy.

diskret [dɪs'kre:t] adj discreet.

Diskretion [dɪskre'tsi̯oːn] f (-; no pl) discretion.

diskriminieren [dɪskrimi'niːrən] v/t (h) discriminate against.

Diskrimi'nierung f (-; -en) discrimination (gen against).

Diskus ['dɪskʊs] m (-[ses]; -se, Disken) sports: discus.

Diskussion [dɪskʊ'si̯oːn] f (-; -en) discussion (über acc on).

Diskussi'ons|leiter m (panel) chairman. **~teilnehmer(in** f) m panel(l)ist. **~veranstaltung** f forum.

Diskuswerfen n (-s) discus throwing. **Diskuswerfer(in** f) m discus thrower.

diskutabel [dɪsku'taːbəl] adj debatable.

diskutieren [dɪsku'tiːrən] v/t, v/i (h) discuss, debate.

dispensieren [dɪspɛn'ziːrən] v/t (h) j-n ~ exempt s.o. (von from [doing]).

disponieren [dɪspo'niːrən] v/i (h) make (one's) arrangements, plan ahead: ~ über (acc) dispose of. **dispo'niert** adj gut etc ~ sein be in good etc form. **Disposition** [dɪspozi'tsi̯oːn] f (-; -en) 1. a. ✠ disposition. 2. (s-e ~en treffen make one's) arrangements. **Disposi-ti'onskre‚dit** m ✠ overdraft facilities.

Disqualifikation [dɪskvalifika'tsi̯oːn] f (-; -en) disqualification (wegen for).

disqualifizieren [dɪskvalifi'tsiːrən] v/t (h) a. fig. disqualify (wegen for).

Dissertation [dɪsɛrta'tsi̯oːn] f (-; -en) dissertation, thesis.

Dissident [dɪsi'dɛnt] m (-en; -en), **Dis-si'dentin** f (-; -nen) pol. dissident.

Dissonanz [dɪso'nants] f (-; -en) ♪ dissonance, fig. a. pl discord.

Distanz [dɪs'tants] f (-; no pl) distance, fig. a. detachment: ~ wahren keep one's distance (gegenüber from).

distanzieren [dɪstan'tsiːrən] sich ~ (h) keep one's distance; **sich ~ von** dis(as)sociate o.s. from. **distan'ziert** adj fig. distanced, reserved.

Distel ['dɪstəl] f (-; -n) ♀ thistle.

Distelfink m zo. goldfinch.

Distrikt [dɪs'trɪkt] m (-[e]s; -e) district.

Disziplin [dɪstsi'pliːn] f (-; -en) 1. no pl discipline. 2. branch, discipline. 3. sports: event. **disziplinarisch** [dɪstsi-pliˈnaːrɪʃ] adj disciplinary. **Diszi-pli'narstrafe** f disciplinary punishment. **Diszipli'narverfahren** n disciplinary proceedings. **diszipli'niert** adj disciplined. **diszi'plinlos** adj undisciplined, unruly. **Diszi'plinlosigkeit** f (-; no pl) lack of discipline.

Diva ['diːva] f (-; -s, Diven) star.

divergieren [dɪvɛr'giːrən] v/i (h) a. fig. diverge.

divers [di'vɛrs] adj various, sundry.

diversifizieren [dɪvɛrzifi'tsiːrən] v/t, v/i (h) ✠ diversify.

Dividend [divi'dɛnt] m (-en; -en) ✠ dividend. **Dividende** [divi'dɛndə] f (-; -n) ✠ dividend. **dividieren** [divi'diːrən] v/t, v/i ✠ divide (durch by). **Division** [divi'zi̯oːn] f (-; -en) ✠, ✗ division. **Divisor** [di'viːzɔr] m (-s; -en [divi'zoːrən]) ✠ divisor.

doch [dɔx] **I** conj **1.** but. **II** adv **2.** yet, however, nevertheless: höflich, ~ bestimmt polite yet firm; also ~! I knew it!; er hat also ~ recht! so he's right after all! **3.** du kommst nicht mit? - ~! you won't come along? - Oh yes, I will!; er kommt ~? he will come, won't he?; ja ~! of course!; nicht ~! a) don't!, b) certainly not!; setzen Sie sich ~! do sit down, please!; frag ihn ~! just ask him!; sei(d) ~ mal still! be quiet, will you!; das ist ~ Peter! but that's Peter!

Docht [dɔxt] m (-[e]s; -e) wick.

Dock [dɔk] n (-s; -s) dock. **Dockarbeiter** m docker. **'docken** v/i (h) dock.

Dogge ['dɔgə] f (-; -n) zo. deutsche ~ Great Dane; englische ~ mastiff.

Dogma ['dɔgma] n (-s; -men) dogma.

dogmatisch [dɔg'maːtɪʃ] adj dogmatic.

Dohle ['doːlə] f (-; -n) zo. (jack)daw.

Doktor ['dɔktɔr] m (-s; -en [-'toːrən]) doctor (a. F ✚): s-n ~ machen take (or work for) one's doctor's degree.

Doktorand [dɔkto'rant] m (-en; -en) doctoral candidate.

'Doktor|arbeit f (doctoral) thesis. **~vater** m supervisor. **~würde** f doctorate.

Doktrin [dɔk'triːn] f (-; -en) doctrine.

Dokument [doku'mɛnt] n (-[e]s; -e) document (a. fig.), ✠ a deed: ✚ ~ gegen Zahlung documents against payment.

Dokumentar... [dokumɛn'taːr-] documentary (report, play, etc). **Doku-men'tarfilm** m documentary (film).

dokumen'tarisch adj documentary.
Dokumentation [dokumɛnta'tsĭo:n] f (-; -en) documentation.
dokumentieren [dokumɛn'ti:rən] v/t (h) document, fig. a. demonstrate, show.
Dolch [dɔlç] m (-[e]s; -e) dagger. **.stoß** m dagger thrust, fig. stab in the back.
Dolde ['dɔldə] f (-; -n) ⚕ umbel.
Dollar ['dɔlar] m (-[s]; -s) dollar.
Dolle ['dɔlə] f (-; -n) ⚓ thole(pin).
dolmetschen ['dɔlmɛtʃən] v/i (h) interpret (a. v/t), act as interpreter.
'Dolmetscher m (-s; -), **'Dolmetscherin** f (-; -nen) interpreter.
'Dolmetscherinsti,tut n school (univ. institute) for interpreters.
Dom [do:m] m (-[e]s; -e) cathedral.
Domäne [do'mɛ:nə] f (-; -n) domain.
domestizieren [domɛsti'tsi:rən] v/t (h) domesticate.
dominant [domi'nant] adj dominant.
Domi'nante f (-; -n) ♪, biol. dominant.
dominieren [domi'ni:rən] v/t, v/i (h) dominate. **.d** dominant, dominating.
Dominikaner [domini'ka:nər] m (-s; -), **Domini'kanerin** f (-; -nen), **domini'kanisch** adj Dominican.
Domini'kaner(mönch) m Dominican.
Domino ['do:mino] n (-s; -s), **.spiel** n (game of) dominoes. **.stein** m domino.
Domizil [domi'tsi:l] n (-s; -e) domicile.
Dompteur [dɔmp'tø:r] m (-s; -e), **Dompteuse** [-'tø:zə] f (-; -n) animal trainer.
Donner ['dɔnar] m (-s; -) thunder, fig. a. roar: **wie vom ~ gerührt** thunderstruck. **'donnern** I v/impers (h) **1. es donnert** it is thundering. **II** v/i (sn) fig. **2.** thunder, roar. **3.** F **~ gegen** crash against (or into). **III** v/t (h) fig. **4.** roar (commands etc). **5.** F slam. **'donnernd** adj fig. thunderous (applause etc).
'Donnerschlag m a. fig. thunderclap.
'Donnerstag m (am ~ on) Thursday.
'donnerstags adv (on) Thursdays.
'Donnerwetter F **I** n (-s; -) row. **II** int ~! wow!; **warum (wo** etc) **zum ~?** why (where etc) the hell?
doof [do:f] adj F dopey, dumb.
dopen ['dɔpən, 'do:pən] v/t (h) dope: **sich ~** take dope. **Doping** ['dɔpiŋ, 'do:pɪŋ] n (-s; -s) doping.
'Dopingkon,trolle f dope test.
Doppel ['dɔpəl] n (-s; -) **1.** duplicate. **2.**

tennis: doubles. **.a,gent(in** f) m double agent. **.bett** n double bed.
Doppeldecker ['dɔpəldɛkər] m (-s; -) **1.** biplane. **2.** F (bus) double-decker.
'Doppelfehler m tennis: double fault.
'Doppelfenster n double window.
Doppelgänger ['dɔpəlɡɛŋər] m (-s; -), **'Doppelgängerin** f (-; -nen) double.
'Doppel|haushälfte f semi-detached (house). **.kinn** n double chin. **.name** m hyphenated name. **.punkt** m colon **.rolle** f a. fig. double role.
'doppelseitig [-zaitɪç] **I** adj reversible (cloth). **II** adv on both sides.
'Doppelsieg m sports: double win.
'Doppelsinn m double meaning, ambiguity.
'doppelsinnig adj ambiguous.
'Doppelspiel n **1.** contp. (ein ~ treiben play a) double game. **2.** → Doppel 2.
'Doppelstecker m ⚡ two-way adapter.
'doppelt I adj double, esp. ⚙ dual, twin, esp. ⚡ duplex: **den ~en Preis** (or das 2e) **zahlen** pay double the price; **in ~er Ausfertigung** in duplicate. **II** adv doubly (painful etc), double, twice: **~ so groß (viel)** twice as big (much).
'Doppel|tür f double doors. **.verdiener** pl dual-income family. **.vierer** m (-s; -) rowing: sculling four.
'doppelwandig [-vandɪç] adj double-walled.
'Doppel|zentner m quintal. **.zimmer** n double room. **.zweier** m (-s; -) rowing: double sculls.
Dorf [dɔrf] n (-[e]s; ⁓er) village.
'Dorfbewohner(in f) m villager.
'dörflich ['dœrflɪç] adj village (life etc).
Dorn [dɔrn] m (-[e]s; -en) **1.** ⚕ thorn, spine (a. zo.): **j-m ein ~ im Auge sein** be a thorn in s.o.'s side. **2.** ⚙ spike.
'Dornenkrone f crown of thorns.
'dornenlos adj thornless.
'dornenreich adj fig. thorny.
'Dornenstrauch m bramble.
Dorn'röschen n (-s) Sleeping Beauty.
dörren ['dœrən] v/t (h) dry.
'Dörrobst n dried fruit.
Dorsch [dɔrʃ] m (-es; -e) zo. cod.
dort [dɔrt] adv there: **~ drüben** over there; **von ~** → **'dorther** adv from there. **'dorthin** adv there.
Dose ['do:zə] f (-; -n) **1.** box. **2.** tin, can. **3.** ⚡ outlet.

dösen ['dø:zən] *v/i* (h) F **1.** doze. **2.** day-dream.

Dosen... → *Büchsen...*

dosieren [do'zi:rən] *v/t* (h) dose, *fig.* give *s.th.* in small *etc* doses.

Do'sierung *f* (-; -en) *a. fig.* dosage.

Dosis ['do:zɪs] *f* (-; Dosen) *a. fig.* dose: **zu geringe ~** underdose.

dotieren [do'ti:rən] *v/t* (h) endow (**mit** with): **ein mit 100 000 DM dotiertes Turnier** a tournament carrying a 100,000 mark prize; **e-e gut dotierte Stellung** a well-paid position.

Do'tierung *f* (-; -en) **1.** endowment. **2.** payment, remuneration.

Dotter ['dɔtər] *n* (-s; -) yolk.

doubeln ['du:bəln] *v/t*, *v/i* (h) *film etc:* double. **Double** ['du:bəl] *n* (-s; -s) double, stand-in.

Dozent [do'tsɛnt] *m* (-en; -en), **Do'zentin** *f* (-; -nen) (university) lecturer, *Am.* assistant professor. **dozieren** [do'tsi:rən] *v/t*, *v/i* (h) lecture (**über** *acc* on).

Drache ['draxə] *m* (-n; -n) dragon.

Drachen ['draxən] *m* (-s; -) **1.** (**e-n ~ steigen lassen** fly a) kite. **2.** *sports:* hang glider. **3.** F *contp.* battle-ax(e).

Drachen|fliegen *n* (-s) hang gliding. **~flieger(in** *f* *m*) hang glider (pilot).

Dragée [dra'ʒe:] *n* (-s; -s) dragée, coated tablet.

Draht [dra:t] *m* (-[e]s; ⁻e) wire: *pol.* **heißer ~** hot line; F **auf ~ sein** a) be in good form, b) be on the ball. **~bürste** *f* wire brush. **~esel** *m* *humor.* bike. **~funk** *m* wired radio. **~glas** *n* wire(d) glass.

Drahthaar... *zo.* wirehaired (*terrier etc*).

drahtig *adj* *fig.* person: wiry.

drahtlos *adj* wireless, radio-...

Drahtsaite *f* ♩ wire.

Drahtseil *n* wire rope, *circus:* tightrope. **'Drahtseilakt** *m* tightrope act (*fig.* walk). **'Drahtseilbahn** *f* cable railway.

Drahtzaun *m* wire fence.

Drahtzieher *m* (-s; -) *fig.* wirepuller.

drakonisch [dra'ko:nɪʃ] *adj* Draconian.

drall [dral] *adj* buxom, strapping.

Drall *m* (-[e]s; -e) ♳ twist, *a. sports:* spin.

Drama ['dra:ma] *n* (-s; -men) drama.

Dramatik [dra'ma:tɪk] *f* (-; *no pl*) drama. **Dramatiker** [dra'ma:tɪkər] *m* (-s; -) dramatist. **dra'matisch** *adj* dramatic. **dramatisieren** [dramati'zi:rən] *v/t* (h) dramatize.

Dramaturg [drama'tʊrk] *m* (-en; -en), **Drama'turgin** [-gɪn] *f* (-; -nen) dramaturge. **Dramaturgie** [dramatʊr'gi:] *f* (-; -n) dramaturgy.

dran [dran] *adv* F **1.** → *daran.* **2. ich bin ~** it's my turn; **jetzt ist er ~!** now he's (in) for it! **3. du bist gut ~!** you are lucky!; **er ist übel ~** he's in a bad way; **spät ~ sein** be late; **an der Sache ist was ~** there is s.th. in it; **man weiß nie, wie man mit ihr ~ ist** you never know what to make of her; **jetzt weiß ich, wie ich ~ bin** now I know where I stand; → **drauf** 2, **Drum, glauben** II.

'dranbleiben *v/i* (*irr, sep, -ge-, sn, → bleiben*) F *fig.* **~ an** (*dat*) stick to; **bleib dran!** a) keep at it!, b) hold the line!

drang [draŋ] *pret of* dringen.

Drang *m* (-[e]s; *no pl*) a) urge, impulse, b) desire (**nach** for).

Drängelei [drɛŋə'laɪ] *f* (-; -en) F pushing and shoving.

drängeln ['drɛŋəln] *v/t*, *v/i* (h) F **1.** push, shove. **2.** *fig.* pester. **3.** *mot.* tailgate.

drängen ['drɛŋən] (h) **I** *v/t* **1.** push: *fig.* **j-n ~, et. zu tun** urge s.o. to do s.th., pressure s.o. into doing s.th.; **ich lasse mich nicht ~!** I won't be rushed. **II** *v/i* **2.** push, throng. **3.** *fig.* be urgent, be pressing: **die Zeit drängt** time is running short. **4. auf Zahlung ~** press for payment; **auf e-e Entscheidung ~** urge a decision. **III** *sich* **~** crowd (**um** round); **sich nach vorne** (**zur Tür** *etc*) **~** force one's way to the front (towards the door *etc*); *fig.* **sich nach et. ~** be keen on (doing) s.th. **'Drängen** *n* (-s) **auf sein** *etc* **~** hin at his *etc* insistence. **'drängend** *adj* urgent.

'Drängler *m* (-s; -) F **1.** pusher. **2.** *mot.* tailgater.

drangsalieren [draŋza'li:rən] *v/t* (h) torment.

'dranhalten: sich ~ (*irr, sep, -ge-, h, → halten*) F a) hurry up, b) keep at it.

'drankommen *v/i* (*irr, sep, -ge-, sn, → kommen*) F **1. jetzt komme ich dran** now it's my turn; **als nächster ~** be next. **2.** *ped.* be asked (a question).

'drankriegen *v/t* (*sep, -ge-, h*) F get.

'drannehmen *v/t* (*irr, sep, -ge-, h, → nehmen*) F take (*patient*), ask (*pupil*).

drapieren [dra'pi:rən] *v/t* (h) drape.

drastisch ['drastɪʃ] *adj* drastic.

drauf [drauf] F *adv* **1.** → **darauf. 2. ~ und dran sein, et. zu tun** be on the point of doing s.th.; **gut ~ sein** a) be in great form, b) *a.* (**schwer**) **was ~ haben** be (just) great (**in** *dat* at); **er hatte 150 Sachen ~** he was doing 100 miles.

Draufgänger ['draufgɛŋər] *m* (-s; -) a) daredevil, b) go-getter, c) casanova, wolf. **'draufgängerisch** *adj* reckless.

'draufgehen *v/i* (*irr, sep*, -ge-, sn, → **gehen**) F **1.** be killed. **2.** a) be lost, *money:* go down the drain, b) go to pot.

'draufkommen *v/i* (*irr, sep*, -ge-, sn, → **kommen**) F **j-m ~** find s.o. out.

'draufkriegen *v/t* (*sep*, -ge-, h) F **eins ~** a) get it in the neck, b) *sports:* get a thrashing.

'drauflegen *v/t* (*sep*, -ge-, h) F pay an extra *100 marks etc.*

drauf|los F **I** *adv* straight ahead. **II** *int* (**feste**) **~!** come on! **drauf'losgehen** *v/i* (*irr, sep*, -ge-, sn, → **gehen**) F make straight for it. **drauf'losreden** *v/i* (*sep*, -ge-, h) F start rattling away.

'draufmachen *v/t* (*sep*, -ge-, h) F **e-n ~** have a ball (*or* a booze-up), go to town.

'draufstoßen *v/t* (*irr, sep*, -ge-, h, → **stoßen**) F *fig.* **j-n ~** spell it out to s.o.

'draufzahlen *v/t* (*sep*, -ge-, h) F **I** *v/t* pay an extra *100 marks etc.* **II** *v/i* lose money.

draus [draus] F *for* **daraus.**

draußen ['drausən] *adv* outside, in the open (air), ⚓ at sea: **im Garten** out in the garden; **bleib(t) ~!** keep out!

drechseln ['drɛksəln] *v/t* (h) turn: **~ gedrechselt.** **Drechsler** ['drɛkslər] *m* (-s; -) wood turner.

Dreck [drɛk] *m* (-[e]s; *no pl*) **1.** dirt, filth, mud: *fig.* **im ~ sitzen** be in a mess; **j-n** (**et.**) **in den ~ ziehen** drag s.o.'s name (s.th.) in the mud; **j-n wie** (**den letzten**) **~ behandeln** treat s.o. like dirt; **er hat** (**viel**) **~ am Stecken** he has a lot to answer for. **2.** *fig.* rubbish, crap: **er kümmert sich e-n ~ darum** he doesn't care a damn; **das geht dich e-n ~ an!** that's none of your business!

'Dreckding *n* (-[e]s; -er) F damn thing.

'dreckig *adj* F dirty, filthy, *fig. a.* nasty, mean: **~e Witze** dirty jokes; **es geht ihm ~** he's having a bad time.

'Drecknest *n* F *contp.* dump, hole.

'Drecksau *f*, **'Dreckschwein** *n* V **1.** (dirty) pig. **2.** swine.

'Dreckskerl *m* F swine, bastard.

'Dreckwetter *n* F filthy weather.

Dreh [dre:] *m* (-[e]s; -e) F trick: **den richtigen ~ heraushaben** have got the hang of it.

'Dreharbeiten *pl film:* shooting.

'Drehbank *f* ☉ lathe.

'drehbar *adj* rotatable.

'Drehbleistift *m* propelling pencil.

'Drehbuch *n* script, *a. fig.* scenario.

'Drehbuchautor(**in** *f*) *m* scriptwriter.

'Drehbühne *f* revolving stage.

drehen ['dre:ən] (h) **I** *v/t* **1.** a) turn, b) twist (*a. fig.*): *fig.* **man kann es ~ und wenden** (**wie man will**) whichever way you look at it. **2.** roll (*cigarette etc.*). **3.** shoot (*film*). **4.** F *fig.* wangle: → **Ding 3. 5.** ☉ turn. **II** *v/i* **6.** turn (round): **~ an** (*dat*) turn, *a. fig.* fiddle with; F **daran ist nichts zu ~ und zu deuteln** that's a fact. **III sich ~** turn, go (*or* spin) round: **die Erde dreht sich um die Sonne** the earth revolves around the sun; **mir dreht sich alles** my head is spinning; *fig.* **sich ~ um** revolve round, *talk:* be about; **es dreht sich darum, ob** it's a question of whether.

'Dreher *m* (-s; -) ☉ lathe operator.

'Dreh|kraft *f* rotatory force. **~kran** *m* slewing crane. **~kreuz** *n* turnstile. **~mo,ment** *n* ☉ torque. **~orgel** *f* barrel organ. **~pause** *f film:* shooting break. **~punkt** *m* ☉ *or fig.* pivot. **~schalter** *m* rotary switch. **~scheibe** *f* 🖥 turntable.

'Drehstrom *m* ⚡ threephase current. **~motor** *m* threephase A.C. motor.

'Drehstuhl *m* swivel chair.

'Drehtür *f* revolving door.

'Drehung *f* (-; -en) turn(ing), rotation: **schnelle ~** spin.

'Drehzahl *f* revolutions per minute (*abbr.* r.p.m.). **~messer** *m* revolution counter. **~regelung** *f* speed control.

drei [drai] *adj* three: **sie kann nicht bis ~ zählen** she is pretty dim(witted).

Drei *f* (-; -en) a) (number) three, b) *pea* satisfactory.

'dreibeinig [-bainiç] *adj* three-legged.

'dreidimensio,nal *adj* three-dimensional.

'Dreieck *n* (-[e]s; -e) triangle.

'dreieckig *adj* triangular.

'Dreiecksverhältnis *n* (love) triangle.

'Drei'einigkeit *f* (-; *no pl*) *eccl.* Trinity.

'**dreifach** *adj* threefold, triple: *die ~e Menge* three times the amount; *in ~er Ausfertigung* in triplicate; *das Dreifache* three times as much, triple.
'**dreifarbig** *adj* tricolo(u)r.
'**Dreiganggetriebe** *n* three-speed gear.
'**dreihundert** *adj* three hundred.
'**dreijährig** [-jɛːrɪç] *adj* **1.** three-year-old. **2.** lasting (*or* of) three years.
'**Dreijährige** [-jɛːrɪgə] *m, f* (-n; -n) three- -year-old (child).
'**Dreiklang** *m* ♪ triad.
Drei'könige *pl eccl.* (**zu** ~ on) Epiphany.
'**dreimal** *adv* three times.
Drei'meilenzone *f* three-mile limit.
'**Dreimeterbrett** *n* three-metre (diving) board.
dreinblicken ['draɪn-] *v/i* (*sep, -ge-*, h) F look *sad etc.*
'**dreinschlagen** *v/i* (*irr, sep, -ge-*, h, → *schlagen*) F lay about one.
'**Dreirad** *n* tricycle.
'**Dreisatz** *m* (-es; *no pl*) ♣ rule of three.
'**dreisilbig** [-zɪlbɪç] *adj* trisyllabic.
'**Dreisprung** *m sports*: triple jump.
'**dreispurig** [-ʃpuːrɪç] *adj* three-lane(d).
dreißig ['draɪsɪç] *adj* thirty. '**Dreißig** *f* (-) thirty: *sie ist Ende (der)* ~ she is in her late thirties. **dreißiger** ['draɪsɪgər] *adj* **die ~ Jahre** the thirties (*of a century*). '**Dreißiger** *m* (-s; -), '**Dreißigerin** *f* (-; -nen) man (woman) of thirty (*or* in his [her] thirties). '**dreißigst** *adj* thirtieth.
dreist [draɪst] *adj* impudent, impertinent, F cheeky, brazen (*lie etc*).
'**dreistellig** [-ʃtelɪç] *adj* ♣ three-digit.
'**Dreistigkeit** *f* (-; *no pl*) impudence, impertinence, F cheek.
'**dreistufig** [-ʃtuːfɪç] *adj* ❂ three-stage.
'**dreitägig** [-tɛːgɪç] *adj* three-day.
'**dreiteilig** [-taɪlɪç] *adj* three-piece.
'**dreiviertel** *adj* three-quarter: *es war ~ zwei* it was a quarter to two; *~ voll* three-quarters full.
'**dreiwertig** [-veːrtɪç] *adj* ♠ trivalent.
'**dreiwöchig** [-vœçɪç] *adj* three-week.
'**Dreizack** *m* (-s; -e) trident.
'**dreizehn** *adj* thirteen: F *jetzt schlägt's aber ~!* that's the limit!
'**dreizehnt** *adj* thirteenth.
'**Dresche** ['drɛʃə] *f* (-; *no pl*) F hiding.
'**dreschen** *v/t, v/i* (drosch, gedroschen, h) ✗ thresh: → *Phrase*.
Dreschma,schine *f* threshing machine.

Dresseur [drɛˈsøːr] *m* (-s; -e) animal trainer. **dressieren** [drɛˈsiːrən] *v/t* (h) train (*animal*), drill (*child*).
Dressman ['drɛsmən] *m* (-s; -men) male model.
Dressur [drɛˈsuːr] *f* (-; -en) **1.** (animal) training. **2.** → **Dres'surreiten** *n* dressage.
Drift [drɪft] *f* (-; -en) ♣ drift (current).
driften ['drɪftən] *v/i* (sn) ♣ *or fig.* drift.
Drill [drɪl] *m* (-[e]s; *no pl*) ✗ *or fig.* drill.
drillen ['drɪlən] *v/t* (h) *a. fig.* drill.
Drilling ['drɪlɪŋ] *m* (-s; -e) triplet.
drin [drɪn] *adv* F **1.** → *darin: er ist ~* he's inside. **2.** *es ist noch nicht alles ~* anything is still possible; *das ist (bei mir) nicht ~!* that's not on!, that's out!; *mehr war nicht ~* that was the best I *etc* could do.
dringen ['drɪŋən] (drang, gedrungen) *v/i* **1.** (sn) *~ durch* force one's way through, *light etc*: penetrate, *water etc*: seep through. **2.** (sn) *~ aus* (dat) sounds *etc*: come from. **3.** (sn) *~ in* (acc) penetrate (into), *water*: *a.* seep into, *a. fig.* invade; *in die Öffentlichkeit ~* leak out. **4.** (sn) *~ bis zu* reach, get as far as. **5.** (h) *~ auf* (acc) insist on, press for. **6.** (sn) (*mit Fragen etc*) *in j-n ~* press s.o. (with questions *etc*). '**dringend** *adj* urgent, pressing, strong (*suspicion etc*), compelling (*reasons*): *~ brauchen* need urgently (*or* badly); *~ empfehlen* recommend strongly; *~ notwendig* imperative; *~ verdächtig* highly suspect.
'**dringlich** *adj* pressing.
'**Dringlichkeit** *f* (-; *no pl*) urgency: *von größter ~* of top (*or* first) priority.
'**Dringlichkeitsantrag** *m parl.* emergency motion. '**Dringlichkeitsstufe** *f* priority (class): *höchste ~* top priority.
drinnen ['drɪnən] *adv* inside, indoors.
'**drinstecken** *v/i* (*sep, -ge-*, h) F *da steckt viel Arbeit drin* a lot of work has gone into it.
dritt [drɪt] *adj* third: *~er Klasse* third- -class; *wir gingen zu ~ hin* three of us went; *pol. die ② e Welt* the Third World.
'**Dritte** *m, f* (-n; -n) third, ⚎ third party: *~(r) werden sports*: finish third.
Drittel ['drɪtəl] *n* (-s; -) third.
'**drittens** ['drɪtəns] *adv* third(ly).
'**drittklassig** [-klasɪç] *adj fig.* third-rate.
'**drittletzt** *adj* last but two.
Droge ['droːgə] *f* (-; -n) drug.

'**drogenabhängig** *adj* addicted to drugs. '**Drogenabhängige** *m, f* (-n; -n) drug addict. '**Drogenabhängigkeit** *f* (-; *no pl*) drug addiction.

'**Drogen|handel** *m* drug trafficking. **~händler** *m* drug dealer. **~kon|sum** *m* use of drugs. **~mißbrauch** *m* drug abuse. **~rausch** *m* F (**im ~** on a) trip. **~sucht** *f* drug addiction. 2**süchtig** *adj* addicted to drugs. **~süchtige** *m, f* (-n; -n) drug addict. **~szene** *f* drug scene.

Drogerie [drogə'ri:] *f* (-; -n) chemist's (shop), *Am.* drugstore, pharmacy.

Drogist [dro'gist] *m* (-en; -en), **Dro'gistin** *f* (-; -nen) chemist, *Am.* druggist.

'**Drohbrief** *m* threatening letter.

drohen ['dro:ən] *v/i* (h) threaten (*j-m* s.o.): *j-m ~ a*) *mit der Faust* shake one's fist at s.o., b) *fig.* be in store for s.o.; *mit der Polizei ~* threaten to call the police; *er drohte zu ertrinken* he was in danger of drowning.

'**drohend** *adj* threatening, *fig. a.* imminent: **~e Gefahr** threat, menace.

Drohne ['dro:nə] *f* (-; -n) *a. fig.* drone.

dröhnen ['drø:nən] *v/i* (h) a) boom, roar, b) resound (**von** with): *fig. mein Kopf dröhnt* my head is ringing.

'**Drohung** *f* (-; -en) threat, menace.

drollig ['drɔlɪç] *adj* droll, funny.

Dromedar [drome'da:r] *n* (-s; -e) *zo.* dromedary.

Drops [drɔps] *m, n* (-; -) fruit drop.

drosch [drɔʃ] *pret of* **dreschen.**

Drossel[1] ['drɔsəl] *f* (-; -n) *zo.* thrush.

Drossel[2] *f* (-; -n) ⊕ choke.

'**Drosselklappe** *f mot.* throttle (valve).

drosseln ['drɔsəln] *v/t* (h) ⊕ throttle (*a. fig.*), turn down (*heating*).

drüben ['dry:bən] *adv* (**da**) **~** over there.

Druck[1] *m* (-[e]s; no pl) pressure, *fig. a.* stress, ✽ sensation of pressure: *auf j-n ~ ausüben, j-n unter ~ setzen* put s.o. under pressure; F *im ~ sein* be pressed for time.

Druck[2] *m* (-[e]s; -e) **1.** *no pl* printing: *in ~ gehen* go to press; *im ~ sein* be printing. **2.** *paint., print., textil.* print.

'**Druck|abfall** *m* drop in pressure. **~anstieg** *m* increase in pressure. **~ausgleich** *m* pressure compensation.

'**Druckbuchstabe** *m* block letter: *in ~n schreiben a.* print.

Drückeberger ['drykəbɛrgər] *m* (-s; -) F shirker.

'**druckempfindlich** *adj* sensitive to pressure, *fruit*: easily bruised.

drucken ['drukən] *v/t* (h) print.

drücken ['drykən] (h) **I** *v/t* **1.** press, squeeze, push (*button, key*): *j-m die Hand ~* shake hands with s.o.; *j-m et. in die Hand ~* put (*or* slip) s.th. into s.o.'s hand; *j-n* (*an sich*) *~* hug s.o.; → *Daumen.* **2.** *j-n ~ shoe:* pinch s.o., *fig.* worries *etc:* weigh heavily on s.o. **3.** bring (*or* force) down (*performance, prices*), better *a record* (*um* by). **4.** *sl.* shoot up (*drug*). **II** *v/i* **5.** press, *shoe:* pinch, *backpack etc:* a. hurt, *fig. heat etc:* be oppressive: *~ auf* (*acc*) press on, press, push (*button etc*); *auf die Stimmung ~* cast a gloom (on everything). **III** *sich ~ vor* (*dat*) F shirk.

'**drückend** *adj fig.* heavy (*debts*), oppressive (*heat etc*).

'**Drucker** *m* (-s; -) *a. computer:* printer

'**Drücker** *m* (-s; -) a) latch, b) *on gun:* trigger: F *auf den letzten ~* at the last minute; *am ~ sitzen* be at the controls

Drucke'rei *f* (-; -en) printing office.

'**Druckerzeugnis** *n* publication.

'**Druckfehler** *m* misprint.

'**Druckfehlerverzeichnis** *n* errata.

'**druckfertig** *adj* ready for (the) press: *~es Manuskript* fair copy.

'**Druck|ka|bine** *f* ✈ pressurized cabin **~knopf** *m* press-stud, F popper, *Am.* snap fastener, ⊕ push button. **~luft** *f* compressed air. **~luftbremse** *f* air brake. **~ma|schine** *f* printing machine **~messer** *m* ⊕ pressure ga(u)ge. **~mittel** *n fig.* lever. **~posten** *m* F cushy job 2**reif** → *druckfertig.* **~sache** *f* **1.** ✽ printed (*Am. a.* second-class) matter. **2.** *parl.* Document. **~schrift** *f* **1.** block letters: *in ~ schreiben a.* print. **2.** printing type. **3.** publication. **~stelle** *f* tender spot, *on fruit:* bruise. **~verband** *m* ✽ compression bandage. **~welle** *f* blast shock wave. **~zeile** *f* printline.

drum [drum] *adv* F → *darum.*

Drum: *das ganze ~ und Dran* everything that goes with it; *mit allem ~ und Dran* with all the trimmings.

drunter ['druntər] *adv* F **1.** → *darunter.* **2.** *es ging alles ~ und drüber* it was absolutely chaotic.

Drüse ['dry:zə] f (-; -n) gland.

Dschungel ['dʒʊŋəl] m (-s; -) jungle.

Dschunke ['dʒʊŋkə] f (-; -n) junk.

du [du:] *pers pron* you: **bist ~ es?** is that you?; **~ Glückliche(r)!** lucky you!; **mit j-m per ~ sein** → **duzen** b.

Dübel ['dy:bəl] m (-s; -), **'dübeln** v/t (h) dowel, peg.

Dublee... [du'ble:-] gold-plated.

ducken ['dʊkən] (h) **I** v/t **den Kopf ~** duck one's head. **II** *sich ~* a) crouch (down), b) duck, c) *fig.* cringe (**vor** before). **Duckmäuser** ['dʊkmɔyzər] m (-s; -) F *contp.* 1. cringer. 2. hypocrite.

dudeln ['du:dəln] v/t, v/i (h) F tootle. **'Dudelsack** m bagpipe(s).

Duell [du'ɛl] n (-s; -e) duel (**auf Pistolen** with pistols), *fig. a.* fight. **duellieren** [duɛ'li:rən] *sich ~* (h) fight a duel.

Duett [du'ɛt] n (-[e]s; -e) ♪ duet.

Duft [dʊft] m (-[e]s; ⁀e) smell, scent, fragrance, aroma. **'duften** v/i (h) smell (**nach** of): **süß ~** smell sweet. **'duftend** *adj* fragrant.

duftig ['dʊftiç] *adj* gossamer, filmy.

'Duftnote f special scent.

'Duftstoff m scent, aroma.

dulden ['dʊldən] v/t (h) 1. tolerate: **ich dulde es nicht** I won't have it (**daß** that); → **Aufschub**. 2. endure, suffer. **'Dulder** m (-s; -), **'Dulderin** f (-; -nen) (patient) sufferer. **'Duldermiene** f *iro.* **mit ~** with a martyred expression.

'duldsam *adj* (**gegen**) tolerant (of), patient (with). **'Duldsamkeit** f (-; *no pl*) tolerance (**gegen** of), forbearance. **'Duldung** f (-; *no pl*) toleration.

dumm [dʊm] *adj* stupid, F dumb, *a.* silly, *fig. a.* awkward: **zu ~!**, **so et. ₂es!** how stupid!, what a nuisance!; F **~es Zeug** rubbish; **sich ~ stellen** act the fool; **ich lasse mich nicht für ~ verkaufen** I'm not that stupid; **die Sache wird mir zu ~** I'm sick and tired of it; **j-m ~ kommen** get fresh with s.o. **'Dumme** m, f (-n; -n) fool: **der ~ sein** be left holding the baby. **'dummerweise** *adv* F 1. **~ habe ich es vergessen** like a fool I forgot it. 2. unfortunately. **'Dummheit** f (-; -en) 1. *no pl* stupidity. 2. stupid thing: **was für e-e ~!** what a stupid thing to do!; **(mach) k-e ~en!** don't do anything stupid!, none of your tricks! **'Dummkopf** m fool, idiot.

dumpf [dʊmpf] *adj* 1. dull, muffled: **~er Aufprall** thud. 2. stuffy, musty. 3. *fig.* dark (*feeling etc*), dull (*pain*), gloomy (*silence etc*).

Düne ['dy:nə] f (-; -n) dune.

Dung [dʊŋ] m (-[e]s; *no pl*) manure, dung. **'Düngemittel** n → **Dünger**.

düngen ['dʏŋən] v/t, v/i (h) fertilize. **'Dünger** m (-s; -) a) fertilizer, b) manure, dung. **'Dunggrube** f manure pit.

dunkel ['dʊŋkəl] *adj* 1. dark, *a. fig.* gloomy: **es wird ~** it is getting dark. 2. deep (*voice etc*). 3. *fig.* dark, vague, dim, mysterious, *b.s.* shady, dubious: **j-n im ~n lassen** keep s.o. in the dark (**über** *acc* about); F **im ~n tappen** grope in the dark; **sich ~ erinnern** remember dimly. **'Dunkel** n (-s) the dark.

Dünkel ['dʏŋkəl] m (-s; *no pl*) conceit.

'dunkelblau *adj* dark blue. **'dunkelblond** *adj* dark blond. **'dunkelhaarig** *adj* dark(-haired). **'dunkelhäutig** [-hɔytɪç] *adj* dark(-skinned), swarthy. **'Dunkelheit** f (-; *no pl*) darkness, *fig. a.* obscurity: → **Einbruch** 2.

'Dunkelkammer f *phot.* darkroom.

'dunkelrot *adj* dark red.

'Dunkelziffer f estimated number of unknown cases.

dünn [dʏn] *adj* 1. thin, *a.* flimsy (*dress etc*), *phys.* rare (*air*), weak (*tea etc*). 2. *fig.* poor. **'dünnbesiedelt** *adj* sparsely populated. **'Dünndarm** m *anat.* small intestine. **'Dünndruck(ausgabe** f) m India-paper edition. **'dünnemachen: sich ~** (*sep*, -ge-, h) F make o.s. scarce. **'dünnflüssig** *adj* thin, liquid, thin-bodied (*oil*). **'dünngesät** *adj* F *fig.* scarce, rare. **'dünnhäutig** [-hɔytɪç] *adj a. fig.* thin-skinned. **'Dünnheit** f (-; *no pl*) thinness, weakness.

Dunst [dʊnst] m (-[e]s; ⁀e) a) haze, mist, b) vapo(u)r, fumes, steam: F *fig.* **er hat k-n (blassen) ~ davon** he hasn't the foggiest (idea) about it.

dünsten ['dʏnstən] v/t, v/i (h) stew.

'Dunstglocke f blanket of smog.

'dunstig *adj* hazy, misty.

'Dunstschleier m (veil of) haze.

Dünung ['dy:nʊŋ] f (-; -en) ⚓ swell.

Duo ['du:o] n (-s; -s) ♪ duo.

Duplikat [dupli'ka:t] n (-[e]s; -e) duplicate, copy.

Dur [du:r] n (-; *no pl*) ♪ (**in ~** in) major.

durch [dʊrç] **I** *prep* **1.** through: *quer ~* across; *~ ganz Amerika* travel etc all over America. **2.** by, by means of, through: *~ Zufall* by chance. **3.** A *10 ~ 2* 10 divided by 2. **4.** due to, through. **II** *adv* **5.** during, through(out): *das ganze Jahr ~* throughout the year; *die ganze Nacht ~* all night long; F *es ist 5 Uhr ~* it is past five. **6.** F *~ und ~* through and through, completely.

'**durchackern** *v/t* (*sep*, -ge-, h) F *fig.* plough (*Am.* plow) through.

'**durcharbeiten** (*sep*, -ge-, h) **I** *v/t* work (*or* go) through. **II** *v/i* work through (without a break). **III** *sich ~ a. fig.* work one's way through.

'**durchatmen** *v/i* (*sep*, -ge-, h) (*tief ~*) breathe deeply.

durch'aus *adv* **1.** thoroughly, quite: *~!* absolutely!; *~ möglich!* quite possible!; *wenn er ~ kommen will* if he insists on coming. **2.** *~ nicht* by no means; *~ nicht!* absolutely not!; *er wollte ~ nicht gehen* he absolutely refused to go.

'**durchbeißen** (*irr*, *sep*, -ge-, h, → *beißen*) **I** *v/t* bite through. **II** *sich ~* F *fig.* struggle through.

'**durchbiegen: sich ~** (*irr*, *sep*, -ge-, h, → *biegen*) sag.

'**durchblättern** *v/t* (*sep*, -ge-, h) leaf through.

'**Durchblick** *m* **1.** view (*auf acc* of). **2.** F *fig.* grasp: *~ haben* → *durchblicken* 3; *sich den (nötigen) ~ verschaffen* find out what's what. '**durchblicken** *v/i* (*sep*, -ge-, h) **1.** look through. **2.** *fig. ~ lassen* intimate (*daß* that). **3.** F a) get it, b) know the score: *da blicke ich nicht durch!* I don't get it!

durch'bluten *v/t* (h) supply with blood. **Durch'blutung** *f* (*; no pl*) (blood) circulation. **durch'blutungsfördernd** *adj* stimulating (blood) circulation. **Durch'blutungsstörung** *f* circulatory disturbance.

durch'bohren *v/t* (*insep*, *no* -ge-, h) stab, pierce: *j-n mit Blicken ~* look daggers at s.o.; *~der Blick* piercing look.

'**durchbrechen¹** (*irr*, *sep*, -ge-, → *brechen*) **I** *v/t* (h) **1.** break *s.th.* in two. **II** *v/i* (sn) **2.** break (in two), break through (*a.* X *or* sports). **3.** burst, *teeth:* erupt. **4.** *fig.* reveal itself.

durch'brechen² *v/t* (*irr*, *insep*, *no* -ge-, h,

→ *brechen*) **1.** break through *s.th.* **2.** break (*rule etc*).

durch'brennen *v/i* (*irr*, *sep*, -ge-, sn, → *brennen*) **1.** fuse: blow, *bulb:* burn out. **2.** F *fig.* run away, make off.

'**durchbringen** (*irr*, *sep*, -ge-, h, → *bringen*) **I** *v/t* **1.** get *s.o., s.th.* through, pull *a patient* through, support (*family etc*). **2.** squander, blue. **II** *sich ~* get by.

'**Durchbruch** *m* (-[e]s, ⁓e) **1.** breakthrough (*a. fig.*), *fig.* perforation, of *teeth:* eruption: *fig. zum ~ kommen* show, become manifest. **2.** opening.

durchdacht [-'daxt] *adj* reasoned.

durch'denken *v/t* (*irr*, *insep*, *no* -ge-, h, → *denken*) reason *s.th.* (out).

'**durchdrängen: sich ~** (*sep*, -ge-, h) force one's way through.

'**durchdrehen** (*sep*, -ge-, h) **I** *v/t* **1.** *gastr.* mince. **II** *v/i* **2.** *wheels:* spin. **3.** (*a.* sn) F *fig.* a) flip, b) panic.

durch'dringen¹ *v/t* (*irr*, *insep*, *no* -ge-, h, → *dringen*) **1.** go through, penetrate. **2.** *fig.* fill, pervade. '**durchdringen²** *v/i* (*irr*, *sep*, -ge-, sn, → *dringen*) **1.** penetrate, get through, *voice etc:* be heard: *fig. bis zu j-m ~* reach s.o. **2.** *fig. ~ mit* succeed with, get *s.th.* accepted.

durch'dringend *adj* penetrating, piercing, loud, shrill (*voice etc*), pungent (*smell*), biting (*cold etc*).

'**durchdrücken** *v/t* (*sep*, -ge-, h) **1.** straighten. **2.** F → *durchsetzen¹*.

durch'drungen *II pp of durchdringen¹* **II** *adj fig.* filled (*von* with).

durchein'ander *adv* *~ sein* be at sixes and sevens, be in a mess; *ganz ~ sein person:* a) be all mixed up, b) be in a flap. **Durchein'ander** *n* (-s) *a. fig.* confusion, mess.

durchein'ander|bringen *v/t* (*irr*, *sep* -ge-, h, → *bringen*) jumble up, *a. fig.* mix up (*notions etc*), confuse, get *s.o.* all flustered: *alles ~* get everything mixed up. *~geraten* *v/i* (*irr*, *sep*, -ge-, sn, → *geraten*) get mixed up. *~reden* *v/i* (*sep* -ge-, h) talk all at once.

'**durchfahren¹** *v/i* (*irr*, *sep*, -ge-, sn, → *fahren*) pass (*or* go, drive) through, *a.* go nonstop (*bis* to): *die Nacht ~* travel all night. **durch'fahren²** *v/t* (*irr insep*, *no* -ge-, h, → *fahren*) pass (*or* go drive, *fig.* flash) through.

'**Durchfahrt** f a) passage, b) gate(way): ~ **verboten!** no thoroughfare!

'**Durchfahrtsstraße** f through road.

'**Durchfall** m 1. ✻ diarrh(o)ea. 2. F thea. flop. '**durchfallen** v/i (irr, sep, -ge-, sn, → **fallen**) 1. fall through. 2. F a) ped., univ. (a. ~ **lassen**) fail, Am. flunk, b) in elections: be defeated, c) proposal etc: be turned down, d) thea. etc be a flop.

'**Durchfallquote** f ped. etc failure rate.

'**durchfeiern** v/i (sep, -ge-, h) F make a night of it.

'**durchfinden** v/i (irr, sep, -ge-, h, → **finden**) (a. **sich** ~) find one's way through: fig. (**sich**) **nicht mehr** ~ be lost.

'**durchfliegen¹** v/i (irr, sep, -ge-, sn, → **fliegen**) 1. fly through, a. fly nonstop. 2. → **durchfallen** 2 a. **durch'fliegen²** v/t (irr, insep, no -ge-, h, → **fliegen**) 1. a) fly through, b) fly, cover (distance). 2. fig. skim (or glance) through.

'**durchfließen** v/t (irr, sep, -ge-, sn, → **fließen**) flow (or run) through.

'**durchfragen: sich** ~ (sep, -ge-, h) ask one's way (**zu** to).

durchfroren ['-'fro:rən] adj frozen stiff.

Durchfuhr [-fu:r] f (-; -en) ✝ transit.

'**durchführbar** adj practicable, feasible: **schwer** ~ difficult to carry out.

'**durchführen** (sep, -ge-, h) I v/t 1. lead (or take) s.o., s.th. through. 2. carry out (or through) (work, plan, etc), realize (project), organize (event). 3. enforce (a law). II v/i 3. → **durch** lead through. '**Durchführung** f (-; -en) carrying out, realization, ⚖ enforcement.

'**Durchfuhrzoll** m ✝ transit duty.

'**durchfüttern** v/t (sep, -ge-, h) F feed.

'**Durchgang** m (-[e]s, ⸚e) 1. passage, alley: ~ **verboten!**, **kein** ~! no thoroughfare!; **den** ~ **versperren** block the passage. 2. astr., ✝ transit. 3. stage, of vote, a. sports: round, of race: heat.

'**durchgängig** adj general.

'**Durchgangs|lager** n transit camp. ~**straße** f through road. ~**verkehr** m 1. through traffic. 2. ✝ transit.

'**durchgeben** v/t (irr, sep, -ge-, h, → **geben**) pass on: telefonisch ~ phone; (**im Radio**) ~ announce (on the radio).

'**durchgebraten** adj gastr. well done.

'**durchgefroren** → **durchfroren**.

'**durchgehen** (irr, sep, -ge-, sn, → **gehen**) I v/i 1. go through, motion, bill, etc: a. be passed: **et.** ~ **lassen** let s.th. pass, tolerate s.th.; F **j-m et.** ~ **lassen** let s.o. get away with s.th. 2. F run away, make off, horse: bolt: fig. **mit j-m** ~ imagination etc: run away with s.o.; **ihm gingen die Nerven durch** he lost his head. II v/t 3. go over, go through.

'**durchgehend** I adj through (train etc), continuous (operation etc, a. ⚙). II adv throughout: ~ **geöffnet** open all day.

durch'geistigt adj spiritual.

'**durchgreifen** v/i (irr, sep, -ge-, h, → **greifen**) (**gegen**) take steps (against), F crack down (on). '**Durchgreifen** n (-s) (**hartes** etc) (**gegen**) (rigorous etc) action (against), F crackdown (on).

'**durchgreifend** adj drastic (measures), radical, sweeping (changes etc).

'**durchhalten** (irr, sep, -ge-, h, → **halten**) I v/i hold out (to the end), F stick it out. II v/t keep s.th. up, stand (the pace).

'**Durchhaltevermögen** n (-s; no pl) staying power, stamina.

'**durchhängen** v/i (irr, sep, -ge-, h, → **hängen**) 1. sag. 2. F fig. a) feel low, b) show etc: be dull. '**Durchhänger** m (-s; -) F **e-n** ~ **haben** feel low.

'**durchhecheln** v/t (sep, -ge-, h) F fig. gossip about, run s.o., s.th. down.

'**durchkämmen¹** v/t (sep, -ge-, h) 1. comb out (hair). 2. → **durch'kämmen²** v/t (insep, no -ge-, h) comb (**nach** for).

'**durchkämpfen** (sep, -ge-, h) I **sich** ~ a. fig. fight one's way through. II v/t fight s.th. through.

'**durchkauen** v/t (sep, -ge-, h) chew s.th. well: F fig. **et.** ~ go over s.th. again and again.

'**durchkommen** v/i (irr, sep, -ge-, sn, → **kommen**) 1. come through, patient: a. pull through, teleph. get through, ped. pass. 2. (**mit**) manage, get by: **mit dieser Ausrede kommt er nicht durch** he won't get away with this excuse.

durch'kreuzen v/t (insep, no -ge-, h) fig. thwart.

'**durchkriechen** v/i (irr, sep, -ge-, sn, → **kriechen**) creep (or crawl) through.

Durchlaß ['dʊrçlas] m (-sses; ⸚sse) passage. '**durchlassen** v/t (irr, sep, -ge-, h, → **lassen**) let s.o., s.th. through (or pass), transmit (light): **Wasser** ~ leak; F fig. **et.** ~ let s.th. pass, overlook s.th.

'**durchlässig** adj pervious (**für** to).

'Durchlauf m (-[e]s; ⸚e) **1.** ⚙, computer: pass. **2.** sports: heat. **'durchlaufen¹** (irr, sep, -ge-, → **laufen**) **I** v/i (sn) run through, computer: (a. ~ **lassen**) pass (through). **II** v/t (h) wear s.th. through. **durch'laufen²** v/t (irr, insep, no -ge-, h, → **laufen**) run (fig. a. pass) through, cover (distance). **'durchlaufend** adj a. ⚙ continuous. **'Durchlauferhitzer** m instantaneous water heater.

durch'leben v/t (insep, no -ge-, h) go (or live) through: (**im Geiste**) **noch einmal** ~ relive.

'durchlesen v/t (irr, sep, -ge-, h, → **lesen**) read s.th. through, peruse.

durch'leuchten¹ v/t (insep, no -ge-, h) **1.** ☢ screen, x-ray. **2.** investigate, probe into s.o.'s past etc. **'durchleuchten²** v/i (sep, -ge-, h) shine through.

Durch'leuchtung f (-; -en) x-ray examination, screening.

durch'löchern v/t (insep, no -ge-, h) **1.** make holes in, perforate: **von Kugeln durchlöchert** riddled with bullets. **2.** F fig. shoot holes in (argument etc).

'durchmachen (sep, -ge-, h) **I** v/t go through, undergo: **er hat viel durchgemacht** he has been through a lot. **II** v/i F (**die Nacht**) ~ make a night of it.

'Durchmesser m (-s; -) diameter.

'durchmogeln: sich ~ F wangle one's way through.

durch'nässen v/t (insep, no -ge-, h) soak, drench.

'durchnehmen v/t (irr, sep, -ge-, h, → **nehmen**) ped. do, go through.

'durchpausen v/t (sep, -ge-, h) trace.

'durchpeitschen v/t (sep, -ge-, h) parl. rush s.th. through, F railroad.

durch'queren v/t (insep, no -ge-, h) cross, traverse.

'durchrasen v/i (sep, -ge-, sn) race (or tear) through.

'durchrechnen v/t (sep, -ge-, h) check.

'Durchreiche f (-; -n) (service) hatch.

'Durchreise f (**auf der** ~ on one's way through. ~**visum** n transit visa.

'durchringen: sich ~ (irr, sep, -ge-, h, → **ringen**) make up one's mind: **sich ~, et. zu tun** finally bring o.s. to do s.th.

'durchrosten v/i (sep, -ge-, sn) rust through.

'durchrutschen v/i (sep, -ge-, sn) F slip through (a. fig.).

'durchrütteln v/t (sep, -ge-, h) shake (up), jolt.

'durchsacken v/i (sep, -ge-, sn) ✈ pancake.

'Durchsage f (-; -n) announcement.

'durchsagen v/t (sep, -ge-, h) pass on, radio: announce.

'durchsägen v/t (sep, -ge-, h) saw through.

durch'schaubar adj obvious, transparent (motives etc): **schwer** ~ puzzling.

durch'schauen v/t (insep, no -ge-, h) see through: **du bist durchschaut!** F I've got your number!

'durchscheinen v/i (irr, sep, -ge-, h, → **scheinen**) shine through: ~**d** transparent, translucent.

'durchscheuern v/t (sep, -ge-, h) wear through.

'durchschlafen v/i (irr, sep, -ge-, h, → **schlafen**) sleep through.

'Durchschlag m (-[e]s; ⸚e) **1.** strainer. **2.** (carbon) copy, F carbon. **3.** ⚡ blowout.

'durchschlagen¹ (irr, sep, -ge-, → **schlagen**) **I** v/t (h) **1.** cut in two. **2.** gastr. pass s.th. through a strainer. **II** v/i **3.** (sn) wetness: come through, colo(u)r: show through. **4.** (sn) ⚡ fuse: blow. **5.** (h) law etc: have its effect: ~ **auf** (acc) affect. **III sich** ~ (h) fight one's way through: **sich mühsam** ~ scrape through; **sich allein** ~ fend for o.s. **durch'schlagen²** v/t (irr, insep, no -ge-, h, → **schlagen**) penetrate.

durch'schlagend adj fig. sweeping (success), conclusive (evidence): **mit** ~**em Erfolg** very successful.

'Durchschlagpapier n copy paper.

'Durchschlagskraft f (-; no pl) penetration, fig. force (of an argument etc).

'durchschlängeln: sich ~ (sep, -ge-, h) thread one's way through (fig. wriggle) through.

'durchschleusen v/t (sep, -ge-, h) **1.** ⚓ lock. **2.** fig. get s.o., s.th. through.

'durchschlüpfen v/i (sep, -ge-, sn) slip through.

'durchschmoren v/i (sep, -ge-, sn) F ⚡ char, scorch.

'durchschneiden¹ v/t (irr, sep, -ge-, h → **schneiden**) cut (in two).

durch'schneiden² v/t (irr, insep, no -ge-, h, → **schneiden**) **1.** cut. **2.** intersect, cut through (road), cleave (air, waves).

dürfen

'**Durchschnitt** m (-[e]s; -e) average: **im ~
→ durchschnittlich** II; **über** (**unter**) **~**
above (below) (the) average; (**guter**) **~
sein** be a (good) average.

'**durchschnittlich** I adj a) average, b)
ordinary, c) contp. mediocre. II adv on
(an or the) average: **~ verdienen** etc a.
average.

'**Durchschnitts...** average (age, income,
speed, temperature, etc).

'**Durchschreibeblock** m carbon-copy
pad. '**durchschreiben** v/t (irr, sep,
-ge-, h, → **schreiben**) make a (carbon)
copy of. '**Durchschrift** f (carbon) copy.

durch'schwimmen v/t (insep, no
-ge-, h, → **schwimmen**) swim (through
or across).

'**durchschwitzen** v/t (sep, -ge-, h) soak
with sweat.

'**durchsehen** (irr, sep, -ge-, h, → **sehen**)
I v/i see (or look) through. II V/t look
s.th. over, go through, check.

'**durchsetzen**[1] (sep, -ge-, h) I v/t et. **~** get
s.th. through (or accepted); **~, daß et.
geschieht** succeed in getting s.th.
done; **~ im Kopf** (or **Willen**) **~** have one's
way. II **sich ~** a) assert o.s., have one's
way, b) idea etc: be accepted, catch on,
party, candidate: be successful; **sich ~
gegen** prevail against, F win out over
(a. sports); **er kann sich nicht ~** he has
no authority. **durch'setzen**[2] v/t (insep,
no -ge-, h) intersperse (**mit** with).

'**Durchsetzungsvermögen** n (-s; no pl)
self-assertion, authority: **~ haben** a. be
able to assert o.s.

'**Durchsicht** f (-; no pl) examination, inspection: **bei ~ der Akten** on looking
through (or on checking) the papers.

durchsichtig ['dʊrçsɪçtɪç] adj transparent, fig. a. obvious. '**Durchsichtigkeit** f
(-; no pl) a. fig. transparency.

'**durchsickern** v/i (sep, -ge-, sn) seep out,
fig. a. leak out.

'**durchspielen** v/t (sep, -ge-, h) **1.** thea.
etc play s.th. right through. **2.** fig. rehearse, go through.

'**durchsprechen** v/t (irr, sep, -ge-, h, →
sprechen) talk s.th. over, discuss.

'**durchstarten** v/i (sep, -ge-, sn) ✈ climb
and reaccelerate, F go round again.

durchstecken v/t (sep, -ge-, h) put (or
pass) s.th. through.

durchstehen v/t (irr, sep, -ge-, h, →

stehen) **1.** fig. get through. **2.** →
durchhalten II.

'**durchstellen** v/t (sep, -ge-, h) teleph. **ein
Gespräch ~** put a call through.

'**durchstoßen**[1] v/i (irr, sep, -ge-, sn, →
stoßen) break (or push) through.

durch'stoßen[2] v/t (irr, insep, no -ge-, h,
→ **stoßen**) pierce, break through.

'**durchstreichen** v/t (irr, sep, -ge-, h, →
streichen) cross out, cancel.

durch'strömen v/t (insep, no -ge-, h) a.
fig. flow through.

durch'suchen v/t (insep, no -ge-, h) a)
search, b) comb. **Durch'suchung** f (-;
-en) search. **Durch'suchungsbefehl** m
search warrant.

'**durchtrai,niert** adj top fit.

'**durchtreten** v/t (irr, sep, -ge-, h, →
treten) mot. step on, Am. floor (pedal),
kick (starter).

durchtrieben [dʊrç'tri:bən] adj sly.

durch'wachsen adj **1.** streaky (bacon).
2. pred F fig. so-so, mixed.

'**Durchwahl** f (-; no pl) direct dial(l)ing.
'**durchwählen** v/i (sep, -ge-, h) **~ nach**
dial through to, dial ... direct.

durchweg ['dʊrçvɛk] adv all of it (or
them), without exception.

durch'weicht adj drenched, soaked.

durch'wühlen v/t (insep, no -ge-, h) rummage through.

'**durchwursteln: sich ~** (sep, -ge-, h) F
muddle through.

'**durchzählen** v/t (sep, -ge-, h) count off.

'**durchziehen**[1] (irr, sep, -ge-, → **ziehen**)
I v/t (h) **1.** pull s.th. through. **2.** F push
(or see) project etc through. II v/i (sn) **3.**
pass (or march) through. **4.** gastr. **gut ~
lassen** soak well. III **sich ~** (h) motif
etc: run through.

durch'ziehen[2] v/t (irr, insep, no -ge-, h,
→ **ziehen**) pass through, river etc, a.
motif etc: run through, smell: fill, pain
etc: shoot through.

'**durchzucken** v/t (insep, no -ge-, h) a.
fig. flash through.

'**Durchzug** m (-[e]s; ⁓e) **1.** passage,
march through. **2.** no pl draught, Am.
draft: **~ machen** air room thoroughly.

dürfen ['dʏrfən] F/aux (durfte, dürfte,
h) et. tun **~** be allowed to do s.th.; **darf
ich es behalten?** may I keep it?; **ja, Sie
~** yes, you may; **nein, Sie ~ es nicht** no,
you can't; **wir ~ stolz auf ihn sein** we

can be proud of him; *was darf es sein?* *shop assistant*: what can I do for you?, *hostess*: what would you like?; *das dürfte genügen* that should be enough. II *v/i* (durfte, gedurft, h) *er darf (es)* he is allowed to; *wenn ich nur dürfte* if only I were allowed to.

dürftig ['dʏrftiç] *adj* poor, meag/re (*Am.* -er), scanty: **.e Kenntnisse** scanty knowledge. '**Dürftigkeit** *f* (-; *no pl*) poorness, meag/reness (*Am.* -er.).

dürr [dʏr] *adj* **1.** a) dry, b) barren (*soil*). **2.** thin, skinny, scrawny (*neck*), spindly (*legs*): *fig.* **in .en Worten** in plain terms. '**Dürre** *f* (-; -n) drought. '**Dürre-kata,strophe** *f* disastrous drought. '**Dürreschäden** *pl* drought damage.

Durst [dʊrst] *m* (-es; *no pl*) thirst (*fig.* **nach** for): **. haben** (*bekommen*) be (get) thirsty; F *er hat e-n über den .* *getrunken* he has had one too many. **dürsten** ['dʏrstən] *v/i* (h) thirst (*nach* for). '**durstig** *adj* thirsty (*fig.* **nach** for). '**durstlöschend** *adj* thirst-quenching. '**Durststrecke** *f* hard slog, hard times.

'**Duschbad** *n* shower bath. **Dusche** ['dʊʃə; 'du:ʃə] *f* (-; -n) shower, douche (*a.* 🏥): *wie e-e kalte . auf j-n wirken* bring s.o. down to earth with a bump. '**duschen** *v/i* (h) (*a.* **sich .**) (have a) shower. '**Duschgel** *n* shower foam. '**Duschka,bine** *f* shower cubicle. '**Duschraum** *m* shower room. '**Duschvorhang** *m* shower curtain. **Düse** ['dy:zə] *f* (-; -n) nozzle.

Dusel ['du:zəl] *m* (-s; *no pl*) F fluke, luck: **. haben** be lucky; *mit .* by a fluke. **düsen** ['dy:zən] *v/i* (sn) F zoom. '**Düsen|antrieb** *m* jet propulsion: *mit .* jet-propelled. **.flugzeug** *n* jet plane. **.jäger** *m* ✕ jet fighter. **.pi,lot** *m* jet pilot. **.triebwerk** *n* jet engine. **.ver-kehrsflugzeug** *n* jetliner.

Dussel ['dʊsəl] *m* (-s; -) F dope. **düster** ['dy:stər] *adj* *a.* *fig.* dark, gloomy, dismal: **.e Aussichten** bleak prospects; **.e Stimmung** black mood.

Dutzend ['dʊtsənt] *n* (-s; -e) dozen: **.e von Leuten** dozens of people; *zu .en* in dozens.

'**dutzendmal** *adv* dozens of times. '**dutzendweise** *adv* in dozens.

duzen ['du:tsən] *v/t* (h) *j-n .* a) address s.o. with "du", b) *a.* *sich mit j-m .* be on first-name terms with s.o.

'**Duzfreund(in** *f*) *m* intimate friend.

Dynamik [dy'na:mɪk] *f* (-; *no pl*) dynamics, *fig.* *a.* dynamism. **dy'namisch** *adj* *a.* *fig.* dynamic: **.e Rente** index-linked pension. **dynamisieren** [dynami'zi:-rən] *v/t* (h) **1.** speed *s.th.* up. **2.** index-link (*pensions etc*).

Dynamit [dyna'mi:t] *n* (-s; *no pl*) dynamite.

Dynamo [dy'na:mo] *m* (-s; -s) dynamo.

Dynastie [dynas'ti:] *f* (-; -n) dynasty. **Dystonie** [dysto'ni:] *f* (-; -n) 🏥 dystonia: *vegetative .* neurodystonia.

'**D-Zug** *m* fast train.

E

E, e [e:] *n* (-; -) E, e (*a.* ♪).

Ebbe ['ɛbə] *f* (-; -n) low tide: *es ist .* the tide is out.

eben ['e:bən] I *adj* **1.** even, level, flat, smooth. II *adv* **2.** just (now): **. erst** only just; *ich wollte . gehen* I was just going to leave. **3.** just, exactly: (*das ist es ja*) **.!** that's it!; **. nicht!** on the contrary! **4.** **. noch** only just. **5.** just: *es taugt . nichts* it's just no good; *er ist .*

der Bessere he's better, that's all; *so ist es .!* that's the way it is!; *dann . nicht!* all right, forget it!

'**Ebenbild** *n* image: *das . s-s Vaters* the spit and image of his father.

ebenbürtig ['e:bənbʏrtiç] *adj* equal: *j-m . sein* be s.o.'s equal, match s.o.

'**ebender('selbe),** '**ebendie('selbe),** '**ebendas('selbe)** I *dem pron* the very same. II *adj* that very *man*, *woman*.

thing. '**eben'deswegen** *adv* for that very reason.

Ebene ['e:bənə] *f* (-; -n) **1.** *geogr.* plain. **2.** *A* plane. **3.** *fig.* level: *auf staatlicher (höchster)* ~ at government (top) level.

'**ebenerdig** *adj* at ground level.

'**ebenfalls** *adv* likewise, too, as well: *er hat ~ kein Geld* he has no money either.

'**Ebenheit** *f* (-; *no pl*) evenness, flatness.

'**Ebenholz** *n* ebony.

'**Ebenmaß** *n* (-es; *no pl*) harmony, symmetry. '**ebenmäßig** *adj* well-proportioned, regular (*face, features*).

'**ebenso** *adv* **1.** just as *good etc.* **2.** (in) the same way. **3.** likewise. '**ebensogut** *adv* (just) as well. '**ebensoviel** *indef pron* just as much (*or* many).

Eber ['e:bər] *m* (-s; -) *zo.* boar.

'**Eberesche** *f* **♀** mountain ash.

'**ebnen** ['e:bnən] *v/t* (h) level: → *Weg*.

Echo ['ɛço] *n* (-s; -s) echo: *fig. ein lebhaftes* ~ *finden* meet with a lively response. '**Echolot** *n* echo sounder.

echt [ɛçt] **I** *adj* genuine (*a. fig.*), authentic (*document*), fast (*colo[u]r*), natural (*hair*), pure, real (*gold, leather, etc*): ~*er Engländer (Freund)* true Englishman (friend). **II** *adv* really: F ~ *gut!* real good!; *das ist* ~ *Paul!* that's Paul all over! '**Echtheit** *f* (-; *no pl*) genuineness (*etc*), authenticity.

'**Eckball** *m* sports: corner.

Ecke ['ɛkə] *f* (-; -n) **1.** corner (*a. sports*): *an der* ~ at (*house*: on) the corner; *fig. an allen* ~*n und Enden* everywhere; *es fehlte an allen* ~*n und Enden* we were short on everything; F *j-n um die* ~ *bringen* bump s.o. off. **2.** F a) piece, b) stretch, c) corner, region.

'**Eckfahne** *f* sports: corner flag.

'**Eckhaus** *n* corner house.

eckig ['ɛkɪç] *adj* square, angular, *fig.* awkward. **...eckig** ..-cornered.

'**Ecklohn** *m* basic wage. '**Eckpfeiler** *m* **1.** △ corner pillar. **2.** *fig.* cornerstone. '**Eckplatz** *m* corner seat. '**Eckstoß** *m* sports: corner kick. '**Eckzahn** *m* eyetooth. '**Eckzins** *m* basic interest rate.

edel ['e:dəl] *adj* **1.** *a. fig.* noble. **2.** exquisite (*wine etc*), precious (*stone, metal*). '**Edelgas** *n* inert gas. ~**holz** *n* rare wood. ~**kitsch** *m* glorified trash. ~**mann** *m* (-[e]s; -leute) nobleman. ~**me,tall** *n* precious metal. ~**pilzkäse** *m* blue cheese.

~**stahl** *m* high-grade steel. ~**stein** *m* precious stone, gem. ~**tanne** *f* silver fir. '**Edelweiß** *n* -[e]s; -e) **♀** edelweiss.

EDV-Anlage [e:de:'vau-] *f* electronic data-processing equipment.

Efeu ['e:fɔʏ] *m* (-s; *no pl*) **♀** ivy.

Eff-eff [ɛf''ɛf] *n* F *et. aus dem* ~ *können* be a real wizard at s.th.

Effekten [ɛ'fɛktən] *pl* **♥** a) securities, b) stocks and bonds. ~**börse** *f* stock exchange. ~**händler** *m* stock dealer. ~**makler** *m* stockbroker.

Ef'fekthascherei [-haʃəraɪ] *f* (-; *no pl*) sensationalism, (cheap) showmanship.

effektiv [ɛfɛk'ti:f] *adj* actual.

ef'fektvoll *adj* effective, striking.

Effet [ɛ'fe:] *m* sports: spin.

Effizienz [ɛfi'tsiɛnts] *f* (-; -en) efficiency.

egal [e'ga:l] *adj pred* **1.** F *das ist (ganz)* ~ it doesn't matter; *das ist mir (ganz)* ~ I don't care; *das ist mir nicht* ~ I do care; *ganz* ~, *wer (warum etc)* no matter who (why *etc*). **2.** the same.

Egel ['e:gəl] *m* (-s; -) *zo.* leech.

Egge ['ɛgə] *f* (-; -n) harrow. '**eggen** ['ɛgən] *v/t* (h) harrow.

Egoismus [ego'ɪsmʊs] *m* (-; *no pl*) egoism. **Egoist** [ego'ɪst] *m* (-en; -en), **Ego'istin** *f* (-; -nen) ego(t)ist. **ego'istisch** *adj* egotistic(al), selfish.

ego'zentrisch *adj* self-centred.

eh [e:] *adv* **1.** dial. → *ohnehin*. **2.** *seit* ~ *und je* always; *wie* ~ *und je* as ever.

ehe ['e:ə] *conj* before: *nicht* ~ not until; → *eher, ehest*.

'**Ehe** *f* (-; -n) marriage: *sie hat e-e Tochter aus erster* ~ she has a daughter by her first marriage; *die* ~ *brechen* commit adultery; *sie führen e-e glückliche* ~ they are happily married.

'**Eheberater(in** *f m*) *m* marriage guidance counsel(l)or. '**Eheberatung(sstelle)** *f* marriage guidance (bureau). '**Ehebett** *n* marriage bed. '**Ehebrecher(in** *f m*) *m* adulterer(-ess). '**ehebrecherisch** *adj* adulterous. '**Ehebruch** *m* adultery. '**Ehefrau** *f* wife, *w.s.* married woman. '**Eheleben** *n* married life. '**Eheleute** *pl* husband and wife. '**ehelich** *adj* **1.** marital. **2.** ⚖ legitimate (*child*).

ehelichen ['e:əlıçən] *v/t* (h) marry.

'**Ehelichkeit** *f* (-; *no pl*) ⚖ legitimacy.

'**Ehelosigkeit** *f* (-; *no pl*) unmarried state, *eccl.* celibacy.

ehemalig ['e:əma:lıç] *adj* **1.** former, ex-... **2.** late.

ehemals ['e:əma:ls] *adv* formerly.

'**Ehemann** *m* (-[e]s; ⁺er) husband, *w.s.* married man. '**ehemündig** *adj* ꜰꜰ marriageable. '**Ehepaar** *n* married couple: *das ~ Brown* Mr. and Mrs. Brown. '**Ehepartner(in** *f*) *m* (marriage) partner.

eher ['e:ər] *adv* **1.** earlier, sooner: *je ~, desto besser* the sooner the better. **2.** a) rather, b) more easily, c) more, d) more likely.

'**Eherecht** *n* (-[e]s; *no pl*) matrimonial law. '**Ehering** *m* wedding ring.

ehern ['e:ərn] *adj* **1.** (of) brass. **2.** *fig.* iron (*law, rule, will*).

'**Ehescheidung** *f* divorce.

'**Eheschließung** *f* marriage.

ehest ['e:əst] **I** *adj* earliest. **II** *adv* **am ~en** a) (the) earliest, (the) first, b) best; *er kann uns am ~en helfen* if anyone can help us, it's him.

'**Ehestand** *m* (-[e]s; *no pl*) matrimony.

'**Ehestreit** *m* marital row. '**Ehevermittlungsinsti,tut** *n* marriage bureau.

'**ehrbar** *adj* hono(u)rable, respectable.

Ehre ['e:rə] *f* (-; -n) hono(u)r: *zu ~n* (*gen or von*) in hono(u)r of; *ihm zu ~n* in his hono(u)r; *j-m die letzte ~ erweisen* pay one's last respects to s.o.; *j-m (k-e) ~ machen* be a (be no) credit to s.o.; *in ~n halten* hold in hono(u)r.

'**ehren** *v/t* (h) a) hono(u)r, b) respect: *das ehrt ihn* that does him credit.

'**Ehren|amt** *n* honorary post. **ꜱamtlich I** *adj* honorary. **II** *adv* in an honorary capacity. **~bürger(in** *f*) *m* honorary citizen. **~doktor** *m* honorary doctor. **~gast** *m* guest of hono(u)r. **~gericht** *n* disciplinary court.

'**ehrenhaft** *adj* hono(u)rable, upright.

'**ehrenhalber** [-halbər] *adv* for hono(u)r's sake: *Doktor ~* doctor honoris causa.

'**Ehren|kodex** *m* code of hono(u)r. **~legi,on** *f* Legion of Hono(u)r. **~mann** *m* (-[e]s; ⁺er) man of hono(u)r. **~mitglied** *n* honorary member. **~platz** *m* place of hono(u)r. **~rechte** *pl* ꜰꜰ **bürgerliche ~** civil rights. **~runde** *f* sports: (*e-e ~ laufen or drehen* do a) lap of hono(u)r. **~sache** *f* matter of hono(u)r. **~tag** *m* great day. **~titel** *m* hono-

rary title. **~treffer** *m* sports: consolation goal. **~tri,büne** *f* VIP lounge. **ꝰvoll** *adj* hono(u)rable. **ꝰwert** *adj* respectable. **~wort** *n* word of hono(u)r: *sein ~ geben* give one's word; *~!* I promise (you)! **~zeichen** *n* decoration.

ehrerbietig ['e:r'ɛrbi:tıç] *adj* (*gegen* towards) respectful, deferential.

'**Ehrfurcht** *f* (-; *no pl*) respect (for), awe (of). '**ehrfurchtgebietend** *adj* awe-inspiring. **ehrfürchtig** ['e:rfʏrçtıç] *adj* respectful, reverential.

'**Ehrgefühl** *n* (-[e]s; *no pl*) sense of hono(u)r.

'**Ehrgeiz** *m* (-es; *no pl*) ambition.

'**ehrgeizig** *adj* ambitious.

'**ehrlich I** *adj* honest, sincere, frank: *~ währt am längsten* honesty is the best policy; *seien wir (doch) ~!* let's face it! **II** *adv* honestly (*etc*): *~ gesagt* truth to tell; F *~?* really?

'**Ehrlichkeit** *f* (-; *no pl*) honesty.

'**ehrlos** *adj* disgraceful.

'**Ehrung** *f* (-; -en) hono(u)r (*gen* conferred on).

'**Ehrwürden** *eccl. Seine ~* the Reverend.

'**ehrwürdig** *adj* venerable, *eccl.* Reverend.

ei [aı] *int* oh.

Ei *n* (-[e]s; -er) **1.** egg, *physiol.* ovum: *fig. wie ein ~ dem anderen gleichen* be as like as two peas; F *wie aus dem ~ gepellt* spick and span; *j-n wie ein rohes ~ behandeln* handle s.o. with kid gloves. **2.** *pl* F quid, *Am.* bucks. **3.** *pl* V (*testicles*) balls.

Eibe ['aıbə] *f* (-; -n) ꝗ yew (tree).

Eiche ['aıçə] *f* (-; -n) a) oak (tree), b) oak.

Eichel ['aıçəl] *f* (-; -n) **1.** ꝗ acorn. **2.** *anat.* glans.

'**eichen** *v/t* (h) ⚙ adjust, calibrate.

Eichhörnchen *n* (-s; -) *zo.* squirrel.

Eid [aıt] *m* (-[e]s; -e) oath: *e-n ~ ablegen* (*or leisten, schwören*) take an oath, swear (*auf die Bibel* on the Bible); *j-m e-n ~ abnehmen* administer an oath to s.o.; *unter ~ aussagen* testify on oath; ꜰꜰ *an ~es Statt → eidesstattlich.*

Eidechse ['aıdɛksə] *f* (-; -n) *zo.* lizard.

'**eidesstattlich** *adj and adv* in lieu of (an) oath: *~e Erklärung* affidavit.

'**Eidgenosse** *m* Swiss (citizen). **eidgenössisch** ['aıtɡənœsıʃ] *adj* Swiss.

'**eidlich I** *adj* *~e Aussage, ~e Erklärung*

a) sworn statement, b) affidavit. **II** *adv* on (*or* under) oath.
'**Eidotter** *n* (egg) yolk.

'**Eier**|**becher** *m* eggcup. **~kocher** *m* egg boiler. **~kopf** *m* F egghead. **~kuchen** *m* pancake. **~löffel** *m* egg spoon. **~schale** *f* eggshell. **~speise** *f* egg dish. **~stock** *m* *anat.* ovary. **~wärmer** *m* egg cosy.

Eifer ['aɪfər] *m* (-s; *no pl*) zeal, eagerness, enthusiasm, fervo(u)r: *blinder ~* rashness; *blinder ~ schadet nur* haste is waste; *im ~ des Gefechts* in the heat of the moment. '**Eiferer** *m* (-s; -) fanatic.
'**eifern** *v/i* (h) **1.** *~ nach* strive for. **2.** *~ gegen* rail against. **3.** → **wetteifern**.
'**Eifersucht** *f* (-; *no pl*) jealousy (*auf acc* of).

'**eifersüchtig** *adj* jealous (*auf acc* of).
'**eifrig** ['aɪfrɪç] *adj* a) keen, ardent, b) busy: *~ bemüht zu inf* anxious to *inf*.
eigen ['aɪgən] *adj* **1.** own, of one's own: *sich zu ~ machen* make *s.th.* one's own, adopt; *ein ~es Zimmer* a room of one's own. **2.** own, personal, private: *für den ~en Gebrauch* for one's own use; *~e Ansichten* personal views. **3.** characteristic, typical: *mit dem ihr ~en Charme* with her characteristic charm. **4.** particular, fussy.
'**...eigen** ...-owned: *staats~* state-owned.
'**Eigenart** *f* (-; -en) peculiarity.
'**eigenartig** *adj* peculiar. '**eigenartigerweise** *adv* strangely enough.
'**Eigenbedarf** *m* a) one's personal needs, b) domestic requirements.
Eigenbrötler ['aɪgənbrøːtlər] *m* (-s; -) **1.** eccentric. **2.** solitary (person).
'**Eigenfinan**|**zierung** *f* self-financing.
'**Eigengewicht** *n* dead (⊛ net) weight.
'**eigenhändig** [-hɛndɪç] **I** *adj* personal: *~e Unterschrift* one's own signature. **II** *adv* personally, oneself.
'**Eigenheim** *n* house of one's own.
'**Eigenheit** *f* (-; -en) peculiarity.
'**Eigen**|**initia**,**tive** *f* one's own initiative. **~kapi**,**tal** *n* capital resources. **~leben** *n* (-s; *no pl*) one's own (*or* private) life: *ein ~ entwickeln* take on a life of its own. **~liebe** *f* self-love, narcissism. **~lob** *n* self-praise. ²**mächtig** *adj* **1.** high-handed. **2.** unauthorized. **~mächtigkeit** *f* (-; -en) **1.** *no pl* high-handedness. **2.** arbitrary act. **~name** *m* proper name (*or* noun).

'**Eigennutz** *m* (-es; *no pl*) self-interest.
'**eigennützig** [-nʏtsɪç] *adj* selfish.
eigens ['aɪgəns] *adv* (e)specially.
'**Eigenschaft** *f* (-; -en) quality, characteristic, feature, ♠, *phys.*, ⊛ property: *in s-r ~ als* in his capacity of (*or* as). '**Eigenschaftswort** *n* (-[e]s; ¨er) *ling.* adjective.
'**Eigensinn** *m* (-[e]s; *no pl*) stubbornness.
'**eigensinnig** *adj* stubborn.
'**eigenständig** *adj* independent.
eigentlich ['aɪgəntlɪç] **I** *adj* real, actual: *im ~en Sinne* in the true sense of the word. **II** *adv* a) actually, really, b) by rights.
'**Eigentor** *n* a. *fig.* own goal.
'**Eigentum** *n* (-s; *no pl*) property, ownership. **Eigentümer** ['aɪgəntyːmər] *m* (-s; -), '**Eigentümerin** *f* (-; -nen) owner, proprietor (proprietress).
'**eigentümlich** [-tyːmlɪç] *adj* **1.** characteristic (*dat* of). **2.** peculiar, strange.
'**Eigentümlichkeit** *f* (-; -en) peculiarity.
'**Eigentums**|**recht** *n* (right of) ownership, title (*an dat* of). **~wohnung** *f* freehold flat, *Am.* condominium.
'**Eigenwille** *m* self-will. '**eigenwillig** *adj* **1.** self-willed, headstrong. **2.** *fig.* very individual. '**Eigenwilligkeit** *f* (-; *no pl*) *fig.* (strong) individualism.
eignen ['aɪgnən] *sich ~* (h) (*als* as, *zu* as, for) be suitable, *person:* be suited; *sich als* (*or zum*) *Lehrer ~* a. make a good teacher. '**Eigner** *m* (-s; -) owner.
'**Eignung** *f* (-; *no pl*) (*zu, für*) suitability (for), *of a person:* a. qualification (for, to be). '**Eignungstest** *m* aptitude test.
'**Eilauftrag** *m* ♥ rush order. '**Eilbote** *m* *durch ~n* express, *Am.* (by) special delivery. '**Eilbrief** *m* express letter, *Am.* special delivery (letter).
Eile ['aɪlə] *f* (-; *no pl*) hurry, rush: *in ~* in a hurry; *es hat k-e ~* there's no hurry.
'**Eileiter** *m* *anat.* Fallopian tube.
eilen ['aɪlən] *v/i* **1.** (sn) hurry. **2.** (h) be urgent: *Eilt!* urgent!; *es eilt nicht* there's no hurry. **eilends** ['aɪlənts] *adv* in a hurry, hurriedly, hastily.
'**Eilfracht** *f* express goods, *Am.* fast freight.
'**eilig** ['aɪlɪç] *adj* a) hurried, b) urgent: *es ~ haben* be in a hurry.
'**eiligst** *adv* in a hurry, hurriedly.
'**Eiltempo** *n* *im ~* in double quick time.

'**Eilzug** *m* fast train.

'**Eilzustellung** *f* 🐝 special delivery.

Eimer ['aımər] *m* (-s; -) bucket (*a.* ⚙), pail: F *die Uhr ist im* ~ the watch has had it. '**eimerweise** *adv* in bucketfuls.

ein¹ [aın] **I** *adj* one: ~ *für allemal* once and for all; ~ *und derselbe* (*Mann*) one and the same person. **II** *indef art* a, an: ~ (*gewisser*) *Herr Brown* a (or one) Mr. Brown; ~*es Tages* one day. **III** *indef pron* a) one (*Mr. X etc*), b) one thing: ~*er von beiden* one of them.

ein² *adv* **1.** *switch*: on: ~ - *aus* on - off. **2.** ~ *und aus gehen* come and go (*bei j-m* at s.o.'s place); *ich weiß nicht mehr* ~ *noch aus* I'm at my wits' end.

Einakter ['aın,aktər] *m* (-s; -) *thea.* one-act play.

einander [aı'nandər] *adv* each other, one another.

'**einarbeiten** (*sep*, -ge-, h) **I** *v/t* **1.** *j-n* ~ acquaint s.o. with his (new) work, F break s.o. in. **2.** *et.* ~ *in* (*acc*) work s.th. into. **II** *sich* ~ get into the (new) job (or subject *etc*).

einarmig ['aın'armıç] *adj* one-armed.

einäschern ['aın'ɛʃərn] *v/t* (*sep*, -ge-, h) **1.** burn to ashes. **2.** cremate. '**Einäscherung** *f* (-; -en) cremation.

'**einatmen** *v/t, v/i* (*sep*, -ge-, h) breathe in, inhale: *tief* ~ take a deep breath.

einäugig ['aın'ɔygıç] *adj* one-eyed.

'**Einbahn...** one-way (*street, traffic*).

'**einbalsa,mieren** *v/t* (*sep*, h) embalm.

'**Einband** *m* (-[e]s; ~e) binding, cover.

'**einbändig** [-bɛndıç] *adj* in one volume.

'**Einbau** *m* (-[e]s; -ten) installation, fitting. '**Einbau...** built-in, fitted (*kitchen, cupboard, etc*). '**einbauen** *v/t* (*sep*, -ge-, h) build in, install, fit: *fig. ein Zitat etc* ~ work in a quotation *etc.*

'**einbegriffen** *adj* (*mit*) ~ included.

'**einbehalten** *v/t* (*irr, sep*, h, → *behalten*) keep back, withhold, deduct.

'**einberufen** *v/t* (*irr, sep*, h, → *berufen*) **1.** call (*assembly*), *parl.* convoke. **2.** ✕ (*zu*) call up (for), *Am.* draft (to). '**Einberufung** *f* (-; -en) **1.** calling, *parl.* convocation. **2.** ✕ conscription, *Am.* draft. '**Einberufungsbescheid** *m* ✕ call-up order, *Am.* draft papers.

'**einbetten** *v/t* (*sep*, -ge-, h) embed.

'**Einbettka,bine** *f* ⚓ single-berth cabin.

'**Einbettzimmer** *n* single room.

'**einbeziehen** *v/t* (*irr, sep*, h, → *beziehen*) include (*in acc* in).

'**einbiegen** *v/i* (*irr, sep*, -ge-, sn, → *biegen*) (*in acc* into *a street etc*): *links* ~ turn left.

'**einbilden**: *sich* ~ (*sep*, -ge-, h) **1.** imagine, think: *bilde dir ja nicht ein, daß ...* don't think that ...; *das bildest du dir nur ein* you're imagining things; *was bildest du dir eigentlich ein?* who do you think you are? **2.** *sich et.* ~ (*auf acc*) be (very) conceited (about). '**Einbildung** *f* (-; *no pl*) **1.** illusion: *das ist reine* ~ you're (he is *etc*) imagining things. **2.** conceit. '**Einbildungskraft** *f* (-; *no pl*) imagination.

'**einbinden** *v/t* (*irr, sep*, -ge-, h, → *binden*) **1.** bind (*book*). **2.** *fig.* integrate.

'**einblenden** (*sep*, -ge-, h) **I** *v/t film, radio, TV* fade in. **II** *sich* ~ (*acc*) tune in to. '**Einblendung** *f* (-; -en) fade-in.

einbleuen ['aınblɔyən] *v/t* (*sep*, -ge-, h) *j-m et.* ~ drum s.th. into s.o.'s head.

'**Einblick** *m* (-[e]s; -e) *fig.* insight (*in acc* into): ~ *nehmen in* (*acc*) inspect.

'**einbrechen** (*irr, sep*, -ge-, → *brechen*) **I** *v/i* (sn) **1.** *in ein Haus etc* ~ break into a house *etc*; *bei ihm wurde eingebrochen* his house was burgled. **2.** ~ *in* (*acc*) invade (*a country etc*). **3.** collapse, *fig.* break down, *sports*: a. wilt. **4.** (*ins Eis*) ~ break through the ice. **5.** *frost etc*: set in, *night*: fall. **6.** ✝ suffer heavy losses, *prices*: slump. **II** *v/t* (h) **7.** break down (*door etc*).

'**Einbrecher** *m* (-s; -) burglar.

'**einbringen** *v/t* (*irr, sep*, -ge-, h, → *bringen*) **1.** bring in (*harvest etc*). **2.** invest (*capital*), *a. fig.* contribute (*in acc* to). **3.** bring (in), yield (*profit etc*): *es bringt mir ... ein* it gets me ...; *das bringt nichts ein!* it doesn't pay! **4.** make up (for *time etc*). **5.** *e-e Gesetzesvorlage* ~ introduce a bill. **6.** ⚖ bring in, file (*action*). **7.** *print.* take in (*line*).

'**einbrocken** *v/t* (*sep*, -ge-, h) F *sich et.* ~ let o.s. in for s.th.; *das hat er sich selbst eingebrockt!* it's his own fault!

'**Einbruch** *m* (-[e]s; ~e) **1.** break-in, burglary. **2.** *bei* ~ *der Dunkelheit* at nightfall; *bei* ~ *der Kälte* when the cold (weather) sets in; ~ *von Kaltluft* influx of cold air. **3.** invasion (*in acc* of a country). **4.** collapse, *fig.* setback. **5.** ✝

slump. **'Einbruchdiebstahl** m burglary. **'einbruchsicher** adj burglar-proof.

einbürgern ['aɪnbʏrgərn] v/t (sep, -ge-, h) ♘, ♆, zo. naturalize; fig. **sich** ~ **word:** be adopted; **es hat sich (bei uns) so eingebürgert** it has become a custom (with us).

'Einbürgerung f (-; -en) naturalization.

'Einbuße f (-; -n) loss (**an** dat of).

'einbüßen (sep, -ge-, h) **I** v/t lose. **II** v/i ~ **an** (dat) lose some of.

'einchecken v/t, v/i (sep, -ge-, h) ✈ check in.

'eincremen v/t (sep, -ge-, h) cream.

'eindämmen v/t (sep, -ge-, h) dam up, fig. a. check, get fire etc under control, pol. contain. **'Eindämmungspoli,tik** f policy of containment.

'eindecken (sep, -ge-, h) **I** v/t j-n ~ **mit** supply s.o. with; **gut eingedeckt** well stocked; F **mit Arbeit eingedeckt sein** be swamped with work. **II sich** ~ stock up (**mit** on).

eindeutig ['aɪndɔʏtɪç] adj clear, plain.

'Eindeutigkeit f (-; no pl) clearness.

eindeutschen ['aɪndɔʏtʃən] v/t (sep, -ge-, h) Germanize.

'eindimensio,nal adj one-dimensional.

'eindrängen: sich ~ (sep, -ge-, h) (**in** acc) a) push one's way in(to), b) intrude (into).

'eindringen v/i (irr, sep, -ge-, sn, → **dringen**) (**in** acc) get in(to), force one's way in(to), bullet etc: penetrate (s.th.), ✗ a. invade (a country): **auf j-n** ~ a) attack s.o., press s.o. (**mit** questions etc). **'eindringlich** adj urgent (warning etc), forceful (speech etc).

'Eindringlichkeit f (-; no pl) urgency.

'Eindruck m (-[e]s; ⸚e) **1.** impression: ~ **machen** be impressive; **auf j-n** ~ **machen** impress s.o.; **e-n schlechten** ~ **machen** make a bad impression (**auf** acc on); **den** ~ **erwecken, daß** ... give the impression that ...; **ich habe den** ~, **daß** ... I have a feeling that ...; → **schinden** 2. **2.** imprint.

'eindrücken v/t (sep, -ge-, h) break (window), force (door), dent (car body).

'eindrucksvoll adj impressive.

'einebnen v/t (sep, -ge-, h) flatten, level (out fig.).

'Einehe f monogamy.

eineiig ['aɪnʔaɪç] adj ~**e Zwillinge** identical twins.

'einengen v/t (sep, -ge-, h) narrow down, restrict: **sich eingeengt fühlen** feel cramped.

'einer pron someone, somebody; → a. **ein'** III. **'Einer** m (-s; -) **1.** ⌀ digit. **2.** ⚓ single (sculler). **'einerlei** adj pred all the same, all one: **das ist mir** ~! I don't care!; ~ **wer** (**wo** etc) no matter who (where etc). **'Einerlei** n (-s; no pl) monotony: (**ewiges**) ~ routine.

'einerseits adv on the one hand.

einfach ['aɪnfax] **I** adj **1.** simple, a. easy (task), a. plain (food). **2.** single: ~**e Fahrkarte** single (ticket), Am. one-way ticket. **II** adv **3.** simply, just: **ich mußte** ~ **lachen** I couldn't help laughing.

'Einfachheit f (-; no pl) simplicity, plainness: **der** ~ **halber** to simplify matters.

'einfädeln (sep, -ge-, h) **I** v/t **1.** thread. **2.** fig. arrange, contrive. **II sich** ~ mot. filter (**in** acc into): **sich links** ~ filter to the left.

'einfahren (irr, sep, -ge-, → **fahren**) **I** v/i (sn) **1.** come in, arrive. **2.** ⚒ descend into a mine. **II** v/t (h) **3.** bring in (harvest). **4.** run in (car). **5.** retract (landing gear etc). **6.** crash into.

'Einfahrt f (-; -en) **1.** drive(way), entrance, to motorway: approach: ~ **freihalten!** keep clear of the gate(s)! **2.** no pl entry (**in** acc into): **der Zug aus** ... **hat** ~ **auf Gleis 1** the train from ... is now coming in on track 1; **Vorsicht bei der** ~! please stand back! **3.** ⚒ descent.

'Einfall m (-[e]s; ⸚e) **1.** idea. **2.** ✗ invasion (**in** acc of). **3.** no pl phys. incidence (of light).

'einfallen v/i (irr, sep, -ge-, sn, → **fallen**) **1.** j-m ~ occur to s.o.; **mir fällt eben ein, daß** ... a. I've just remembered that...; **es fällt mir (jetzt) nicht ein** I can't think of it now; **was fällt dir ein?** a) how dare you!, b) you must be joking!; **sich et.** ~ **lassen** come up with s.th.; **das fällt mir nicht im Traum ein!** I wouldn't dream of (doing) it! **2.** ✗ **in ein Land** ~ invade a country; F fig. **bei j-m** ~ descend on s.o. **3.** light: enter. **4.** ♪ enter, join in.

'einfallslos adj unimaginative, dull.

'Einfallslosigkeit f (-; no pl) lack of

ideas. '**einfallsreich** *adj* imaginative, inventive. '**Einfallsreichtum** *m* (-s; *no pl*) wealth of ideas.

'**Einfallswinkel** *m* angle of incidence.

einfältig ['aɪnfɛltɪç] *adj* naive, simple.

'**Einfa‚milienhaus** *n* detached house.

'**einfangen** *v/t* (*irr, sep*, -ge-, h, → *fangen*) *a.* *fig.* catch, capture.

'**einfarbig** *adj* unicolo(u)r(ed), plain.

'**einfassen** *v/t* (*sep*, -ge-, h) **1.** a) surround, b) edge, border (*dress etc*). **2.** set (*diamond etc*), frame (*lens etc*).

'**Einfassung** *f* (-; -en) **1.** a) enclosure, b) border, edge. **2.** setting.

'**einfetten** *v/t* (*sep*, -ge-, h) grease.

'**einfinden**: sich ~ (*irr, sep*, -ge-, h, → *finden*) assemble, arrive, F turn up.

'**einflechten** *v/t* (*irr, sep*, -ge-, h, → *flechten*) *fig. et.* ~ mention s.th. in passing; *et.* ~ *in* (*acc*) work s.th. into.

'**einfliegen** (*irr, sep*, -ge-, → *fliegen*) **I** *v/t* (h) fly in, test-(fly). **II** *v/i* (sn) approach: ~ *in* (*acc*) fly into, enter.

'**einfließen** *v/i* (*irr, sep*, -ge-, sn, → *fließen*) flow in(to *in acc*); *fig. et.* ~ *lassen* slip s.th. in, give s.th. to understand.

'**einflößen** *v/t* (*sep*, -ge-, h) *j-m et.* ~ a) give s.o. s.th. (to drink), b) fill (*or* inspire) s.o. with *admiration, courage*, *etc*; *j-m Angst* ~ fill s.o. with fear.

'**Einflugschneise** *f* approach corridor.

'**Einfluß** *m* (-sses; ⸚sse) influence (*auf acc* on): ~ *haben auf* (*acc*) a) have an influence on, influence, b) have an effect on, affect; → *geltend*. '**Einflußbereich** *m* sphere of influence. '**Einflußnahme** *f* (-; *no pl*) intervention (*auf acc* on).

'**einflußreich** *adj* influential.

einförmig ['aɪnfœrmɪç] *adj* uniform, monotonous. **Einförmigkeit** *f* (-; *no pl*) uniformity, monotony.

'**einfrieren** (*irr, sep*, -ge-, → *frieren*) **I** *v/i* (sn) **1.** *water*: freeze over, *pipe etc*: freeze (up), *ship*: become icebound. **2.** *fig.* freeze. **II** *v/t* (h) **3.** (deep-)freeze (*food*). **4.** *fig.* freeze (*wages, assets etc*).

'**einfügen** (*sep*, -ge-, h) **I** *v/t* (*in acc*) fit in(to), insert (into). **II** sich ~ (*in acc*) *fig.* fit in (with), *person*: adjust (to).

'**Einfügung** *f* (-; -en) insertion, addition.

'**einfühlen**: sich ~ (*sep*, -ge-, h) empathize (*in acc* with). '**einfühlsam** *adj* sensitive. '**Einfühlungsvermögen** *n* (-s; *no pl*) empathy.

Einfuhr ['aɪnfuːr] *f* (-; -en) ✝ **1.** *no pl* import. **2.** imports. ~**ar‚tikel** *m* imported article, *pl* imports. ~**bestimmungen** *pl* import regulations.

'**einführen** *v/t* (*sep*, -ge-, h) **1.** introduce, *a.* adopt (*method etc*). **2.** *j-n* ~ introduce s.o. (*in acc* into, *bei* to); *j-n* (*in ein Amt*) ~ inaugurate s.o. **3.** (*in acc* into) insert, introduce. **4.** ✝ import.

'**Einfuhr‚genehmigung** *f* import licence (*Am.* license). ~**hafen** *m* port of entry. ~**handel** *m* import trade. ~**land** *n* importing country. ~**stopp** *m* import ban.

'**Einführung** *f* (-; -en) (*in acc*) introduction (to), inauguration (into).

'**Einführungs...** introductory (*course, price, offer, etc*).

'**Einfuhrverbot** *n* import ban (*für* on).

'**Einfuhrzoll** *m* import duty.

'**einfüllen** *v/t* (*sep*, -ge-, h) pour in(to *in acc*).

'**Eingabe** *f* (-; -n) **1.** application (*bei* to, *um, für* for). **2.** *computer*: input. '**Eingabedaten** *pl computer*: input data.

'**Eingang** *m* (-[e]s; ⸚e) **1.** entrance, way in, entry. **2.** (*zu* to) access, entry, admission. **3.** *no pl* arrival (*of goods*), receipt (*of mail*): *bei* ~, *nach* ~ on receipt. **4.** *pl* ✝ a) arrivals, b) incoming mail, c) receipts. **5.** *no pl* (*zu* ~ at the) beginning (*gen* of). **6.** ⚡ input.

'**eingängig** *adj* catchy (*tune, slogan*).

'**eingangs** ['aɪŋaŋs] **I** *adv* at the beginning. **II** *prep* (*gen*) at the beginning of.

'**Eingangs‚datum** *n* date of receipt. ~**halle** *f* entrance hall. ~**stempel** *m* date stamp. ~**worte** *pl* opening words.

'**eingebaut** *adj* built-in, ⊙ *a.* integrated.

'**eingeben** *v/t* (*irr, sep*, -ge-, h, → *geben*) (*dat*) **1.** (to) give, administer (*drug*): *fig. j-m e-n Gedanken* ~ give s.o. an idea. **2.** feed data (into).

'**eingebildet** *adj* **1.** imaginary. **2.** conceited (*auf acc* about), arrogant.

'**Eingeborene** *m, f* (-n; -n) native.

'**Eingebung** *f* (-; -en) inspiration.

eingedenk ['aɪŋədɛŋk] *adj pred* mindful (*gen* of).

'**eingefallen** *adj fig.* hollow (*cheeks*).

eingefleischt ['aɪŋəflaɪʃt] *adj* inveterate, confirmed (*bachelor etc*).

'**eingehen** (*irr, sep*, -ge-, sn, → *gehen*) *v/i* **1.** *goods, mail, etc*: come in, arrive ~**d** incoming. **2.** ~ *in* (*acc*) enter (*a lan-*

guage etc): → **Geschichte** 2. **3. bei j-m ein- und ausgehen** be a frequent visitor at s.o.'s place. **4. ~ auf** (acc) a) accept, agree to, b) deal with (details etc), go into (a question etc), go along with (a joke): **auf j-n ~** listen (or respond) to s.o., humo(u)r s.o. **5.** animal, plant: die (a. F person: **vor** dat with), F athlete etc: go under, business etc: fold up. **6.** fabric: shrink. **7.** F **das geht ihm nicht ein** he can't grasp it. II v/t enter into (contract, marriage, etc); → **Risiko, Wette.**

'**eingehend** I adj fig. thorough, detailed. II adv thoroughly, in detail.

'**eingeklemmt** I pp of **einklemmen.** II adj ✚ strangulated (hernia), trapped (nerve).

'**eingemacht** I pp of **einmachen.** II adj preserved (fruit), pickled (gherkins etc).

eingemeinden ['aɪŋgəmaɪndən] v/t (sep, -ge-, h) incorporate (in acc into).

'**eingenommen** I pp of **einnehmen.** II adj **~ sein von** be taken with; contp. **von sich ~ sein** be full of o.s.

'**eingerostet** adj a. fig. rusty.

'**eingeschnappt** I pp of **einschnappen.** II adj F cross: **~ sein** be in a huff.

'**eingespielt** I pp of **einspielen.** II adj (**gut**) **aufeinander ~ sein** a. fig. make a good team.

'**Eingeständnis** n (-ses; -se) admission.

'**eingestehen** v/t (irr, sep, h, → **gestehen**) admit.

'**eingestellt** I pp of **einstellen.** II adj **1. ~ gegen** opposed to. **2. ~ auf** (acc) geared to, prepared for. **3. sozial** etc **~** socially etc minded.

'**eingetragen** I pp of **eintragen.** II adj ✞ registered.

Eingeweide ['aɪŋgəvaɪdə] pl a) insides, F innards, b) intestines, guts.

'**Eingeweihte** m, f (-n; -n) initiate, insider.

'**eingewöhnen: sich ~** (sep, h) (in dat) get accustomed (to), settle (into).

'**eingießen** v/t (irr, sep, -ge-, h, → **gießen**) pour (out).

'**eingipsen** v/t (sep, -ge-, h) ✚ put in plaster.

eingleisig ['aɪŋglaɪzɪç] adj single-track.

'**eingliedern** (sep, -ge-, h) I v/t (in acc into) integrate, incorporate: **j-n wieder**

~ rehabilitate s.o. II **sich ~** (in acc) fit in (with), person: adjust (to).

'**Eingliederung** f (-; -en) integration.

'**eingraben** (irr, sep, -ge-, h, → **graben**) I v/t **1.** bury, dig in. **2.** engrave (in acc on). II **sich ~** dig (o.s.) in, entrench o.s., zo. burrow itself (in or out).

'**eingravieren** v/t (sep, h) engrave (in acc on).

'**eingreifen** v/i (irr, sep, -ge-, h, → **greifen**) **1.** step in, intervene, a. ⚙ interfere (in acc with rights), ✗ go into action: **in ein Gespräch ~** cut in on a conversation; **in die Debatte ~** interfere in the debate; **in j-s Leben ~** affect s.o.'s life. **2.** ⚙ mesh (in acc with). '**Eingreifen** n (-s) intervention, interference, action. '**eingreifend** adj fig. drastic, far-reaching. '**Eingriff** m (-[e]s; -e) **1.** ✚ operation. **2.** (in acc in) intervention, interference (a. with).

'**einhacken** v/i (sep, -ge-, h) **~ auf** (acc) hack at; fig. **auf j-n ~** keep on at s.o.

'**einhaken** (sep, -ge-, h) I v/t hook s.th. in. II **sich ~** link arms (**bei j-m** with s.o.). III v/i fig. cut in (**bei** on): **bei e-r Sache ~** take s.th. up.

'**Einhalt:** (dat) **~ gebieten** put a stop to.

'**einhalten** v/t (irr, sep, -ge-, h, → **halten**) keep (promise), keep to, observe (contract, deadline, rule, etc), meet (obligation). '**Einhaltung** f (-; no pl) (gen) adherence (to), observance (of).

'**einhämmern → einbleuen.**

'**Einhand...** ⚓ single-handed.

'**einhandeln** v/t (sep, -ge-, h) et. **für** (or **gegen**) et. **~** exchange s.th. for s.th.; F fig. **sich et. ~** land o.s. with s.th.

einhändig ['aɪnhɛndɪç] adj and adv single-handed.

'**einhängen** (sep, -ge-, h) I v/t **1.** put door on its hinges. **2. den Hörer ~** hang up, replace the receiver. II **sich bei j-m ~** take s.o.'s arm. III v/i → 2.

'**einheimisch** adj local, native, a. ✿, zo. indigenous, ✞ domestic: **~e Mannschaft** home team. '**Einheimische** m, f (-n; -n) a) native, b) resident, local.

einheimsen ['aɪnhaɪmzən] v/t (sep, -ge-, h) F rake in (money), win (praise).

'**einheiraten** v/i (sep, -ge-, h) **~ in** (acc) marry into.

Einheit ['aɪnhaɪt] f (-; -en) **1.** unit: **e-e**

geschlossene ~ **bilden** form an integrated whole. **2.** *a. pol.* unity.
'**einheitlich** *adj* a) uniform, homogeneous, b) standard(ized), c) united.
'**Einheitlichkeit** *f* (-; *no pl*) **1.** uniformity. **2.** unity.
'**Einheits|front** *f pol.* united front. ~**liste** *f pol.* single list (*Am.* ticket). ~**preis** *m* a) standard price, b) flat-rate price. ~**staat** *m* centralized state. ~**wert** *m taxation*: rateable value.
'**einheizen** *v/i* (*sep*, -ge-, h) F *fig. j-m* ~ give s.o. hell.
einhellig ['anhɛlıç] *adj* unanimous.
ein'her... *walk etc* along.
'**einholen** (*sep*, -ge-, h) **I** *v/t* **1.** catch up with (*a. fig.*), make up for (*lost time etc*). **2.** get, obtain: **Auskünfte** ~ make inquiries (**über** *acc* about); **Rat** ~ seek advice (**bei** from). **3.** ⚓ strike (*sails*), tow in (*ship*). **II** *v/i* **4.** F ~ **gehen** go shopping.
'**Einhorn** *n* (-[e]s; ⸗er) unicorn.
'**einhüllen** *v/t* (*sep*, -ge-, h) (*in acc*) wrap up (in), cover (with): *fig.* **eingehüllt in Nebel** *etc* enveloped in fog *etc*.
'**einhundert** *adj* a (or one) hundred.
einig ['aınıç] *adj* **1.** united. **2.** in agreement (**mit** with): (**sich**) ~ **werden** come to an agreement (**über** *acc* about); **sich** ~ **sein, daß** ... be agreed that ...; **sich nicht** ~ **sein** (**über** *acc*) disagree (on).
'**einige** ['aınıgə] *indef pron* **I** *adjectival* **1.** a few, some, several. **2.** a) quite a (bit of), b) some, c) quite a few: **es besteht** ~ **Hoffnung, daß** ... there is some hope that ...; ~**s Aufsehen erregen** cause quite a stir. **3.** some *hundred marks etc.* **II** *substantival* **4.** *pl* a few, some, several. **5.** → **einiges**.
'**einigemal** *adv* several times.
'**einigen** (h) **I** *v/t* unite. **II sich** ~ (**über** *acc*, **auf** *acc*) agree (on), reach an agreement (about).
einiger'maßen *adv* a) to some extent, somewhat, b) quite, fairly, c) fairly well, F so-so.
'**einiges** *indef pron* a) something, some things, b) quite a bit: ~ **davon** some of it; **er hat** ~ **gelernt** he has learned a thing or two; **sein Plan hat** ~ **für sich** there is s.th. to be said for his plan.
'**Einigkeit** *f* (-; *no pl*) **1.** unity, harmony. **2.** agreement, consensus: **es herrschte**

~ **darüber, daß** ... we (*or* they) all agreed that ...
'**Einigung** *f* (-; -en) **1.** unification. **2.** agreement: **es wurde k-e** ~ **erzielt** no agreement was reached (**über** *acc* on).
'**einimpfen** *v/t* (*sep*, -ge-, h) *fig. j-m et.* ~ a) indoctrinate s.o. with s.th., b) → **einbleuen**.
'**einjagen** *v/t* (*sep*, -ge-, h) *j-m e-n Schreck* ~ give s.o. a fright.
einjährig ['aınjɛ:rıç] *adj* **1.** one-year-old. **2.** one-year (*course etc*). **3.** ⚘ annual.
'**einkalku,lieren** *v/t* (*sep*, -ge-, h) take *s.th.* into account, allow for.
'**Einkauf** *m* (-[e]s; ⸗e) **1.** purchase: *Einkäufe machen* → *einkaufen* II. **2.** purchasing, buying. **3.** *no pl* ✝ purchasing department. '**einkaufen** (*sep*, -ge-, h) **I** *v/t* buy, purchase. **II** *v/i* ~ (*gehen*) go (*or* do one's) shopping. '**Einkäufer(in** *f*) *m* ✝ buyer.
'**Einkaufs|bummel** *m e-n* ~ **machen** go on a shopping spree. ~**liste** *f* shopping list. ~**preis** *m* (*zum* ~ at the) purchase price. ~**tasche** *f* shopping bag. ~**zentrum** *n* shopping cent/re (*Am.* -er).
'**einkehren** *v/i* (*sep*, -ge-, h) stop off (*in dat* at).
'**einkeilen** *v/t* (*sep*, -ge-, h) wedge in.
'**einkellern** *v/t* (*sep*, -ge-, h) put down.
'**einkerben** *v/t* (*sep*, -ge-, h), '**Einkerbung** *f* (-; -en) notch.
'**einklagen** *v/t* (*sep*, -ge-, h) *et.* (**gegen** *j-n*) ~ sue (s.o.) for s.th.
'**einklammern** *v/t* (*sep*, -ge-, h) put *s.th.* in brackets.
'**Einklang** *m* (-[e]s; *no pl*) ♪ unison, *fig. a.* harmony: *fig.* **in** ~ **bringen** reconcile (**mit** with); **nicht im** ~ **stehen** be at variance (**mit** with).
'**einkleben** *v/t* (*sep*, -ge-, h) stick *s.th.* in(to *in acc*).
'**einkleiden** (*sep*, -ge-, h) **I** *v/t j-n* ~ *a.* ✕ fit s.o. out. **II sich** (*neu*) ~ fit o.s. out with a new set of clothes.
'**einklemmen** *v/t* (*sep*, -ge-, h) (**sich**) **den Finger** ~ get one's finger caught (*in dat* in); → **eingeklemmt**.
'**einkochen** *v/t* (*sep*, -ge-, h) **1.** boil down. **2.** preserve.
'**Einkommen** *n* (-s; -) **1.** income, earnings. **2.** revenue. '**Einkommensgruppe** *f* income bracket. '**einkommensschwach** *adj* low-income.

'**Einkommenssteuer** f income tax. **~erklärung** f income-tax return.
'**einköpfen** v/t (sep, -ge-, h) soccer: head in.
'**einkreisen** v/t (sep, -ge-, h) **1.** surround, encircle. **2.** narrow down (problem etc).
Einkünfte ['aınkʏnftə] pl **1.** income, earnings. **2.** revenue.
'**einkuppeln** v/i (sep, -ge-, h) mot. let in the clutch.
'**einladen** (irr, sep, -ge-, h, → **laden**) I v/t **1.** load (in). **2.** j-n ~ invite s.o. (**zum Essen** to lunch etc), ask s.o. (round); **ich lade dich (dazu) ein!** that's my treat!, this is on me! II v/i **3.** a. fig. invite. '**einladend** adj fig. a) inviting, b) tempting, c) delicious(-looking).
'**Einladung** f (-; -en) invitation: **auf ~ von** (or gen) at the invitation of.
'**Einlage** f (-; -n) **1.** in letter: enclosure, in newspaper etc: insert. **2.** a) (arch) support, b) insole. **3.** in panties etc: liner. **4.** padding. **5.** in tooth: temporary filling. **6.** in soups: garnish. **7.** ✝ a) in bank: deposit, b) (capital) contribution. **8.** thea. etc interlude, extra.
Einlaß ['aınlas] m (-sses; no pl) admittance (**zu** to): **sich ~ verschaffen** get in; **~ ab 18 Uhr** opening at 18:00 hours.
'**einlassen** (irr, sep, -ge-, h, → **lassen**) I v/t **1.** let s.o., s.th. in, admit: **Wasser in die Wanne** ~ run a bath. **2.** (in acc in) set (diamond etc), ⚙ embed. II **sich ~ auf** (acc) a) get involved in, b.s. let o.s. in for, b) agree to (a proposal), c) go into (a question); **laß dich nicht darauf ein!** leave it alone!; **sich mit j-m ~** get involved with s.o. (a. amorously); **sich mit j-m auf e-n Kampf (ein Wortgefecht) ~** F tangle with s.o.
'**Einlauf** m (-[e]s; ⸚e) **1.** ✝ (e-n ~ machen give s.o. an) enema. **2.** sports: finish.
'**einlaufen** (irr, sep, -ge-, → **laufen**) I v/i (sn) **1.** come in (a. sports), ⚓ put in. **2.** water: run in: **Badewasser ~ lassen** run a bath. **3.** fabric: shrink: **nicht ~d** nonshrink. II v/t (h) break in (shoes). III **sich ~** (h) sports: warm up.
'**einläuten** v/t (sep, -ge-, h) ring in.
'**einleben**: → **eingewöhnen**.
'**Einlegearbeit** f inlaid work.
'**einlegen** v/t (sep, -ge-, h) **1.** put in, insert (film etc): **et.. ~ in** (acc) a. enclose s.th. in (or with); fig. **e-e Pause ~** have

a break; **e-n Spurt ~** put in a spurt; → **Wort** 2. **2.** deposit (money in bank). **3.** gastr. (**in Essig**) ~ pickle. **4.** ⚙ inlay (**mit** with). **5.** lodge, file (appeal etc): → **Berufung** 4, **Protest**, **Veto**. **6.** j-m (**sich**) **die Haare ~** set s.o.'s (one's) hair.
'**Einleger** m (-s; -) ✝ depositor.
'**Einlegesohle** f insole.
'**einleiten** v/t (sep, -ge-, h) **1.** start, begin, a. open (negotiations), initiate (reforms etc), introduce (a. ling. clause). **2.** ✗ induce (birth). ⚖ institute: **e-n Prozeß ~ gegen** bring an action against. '**einleitend** I adj introductory, opening, preliminary. II adv by way of introduction. '**Einleitung** f (-; -en) **1.** opening, start, introduction (a. ling.). **2.** preface. **3.** ✗ induction. **4.** ⚖ institution.
'**einlenken** v/i (sep, -ge-, h) fig. relent.
'**einlesen** v/t (irr, sep, -ge-, h, → **lesen**) computer: read in.
'**einleuchten** v/i (sep, -ge-, h) make sense (**j-m** to s.o.). '**einleuchtend** adj clear, convincing.
'**einliefern** v/t (sep, -ge-, h) **1.** j-n **ins Krankenhaus (Gefängnis) ~** take s.o. to (the) hospital (to prison). **2.** post, mail. '**Einlieferung** f (-; -en) **1.** (in acc) admission (to hospital), committal (to prison etc). **2.** posting, mailing.
'**Einlieferungsschein** m postal receipt.
'**einlochen** v/t (sep, -ge-, h) **1.** golf: put(t). **2.** F j-n ~ put s.o. in clink.
'**einlösen** v/t (sep, -ge-, h) **1.** redeem (pawn, securities), cash (cheque). **2.** fig. keep (promise etc).
'**einlullen** v/t (sep, -ge-, h) F fig. lull.
'**einmachen** v/t (sep, -ge-, h) preserve.
'**einmal** adv **1.** once: ~ **im Jahr** once a year; ~ **und nie wieder** never again; **noch ~** once more; **erst ~** first; **auf ~** a) at one go, b) at the same time, c) suddenly. **2.** once, before: **das war ~** that's all in the past; **es war ~** once upon a time there was; **ich war schon ~ da** a) I've been there before, b) I was there once; **haben Sie schon ~ ...?** have you ever ...? **3.** one day, some day (or other), later on: **wenn du ~ groß bist** when you grow up. **4.** **nicht ~** not even, not so much as. **5.** **ich bin ~ so!** I can't help it!; **es ist nun ~ so** that's the way it is; **laßt ihn doch ~ reden!** let him talk, will you!; **stell dir ~ vor!** just imagine!

Einmal'eins n (-; no pl) **1.** (multiplication) table. **2.** fig. basics.

'**einmalig** adj **1.** single, nonrecurring: **~e Abfindung** single payment. **2.** unique, singular, unparallel(l)ed, F fantastic: **e-e ~e Chance** the chance of a lifetime; **~ schön** absolutely beautiful.

'**Einmannbetrieb** m one-man business.

'**Einmarsch** m marching in, a. invasion.

'**einmar,schieren** v/i (sep, sn) march in: **in ein Land ~** invade a country.

'**einmieten: sich ~** (sep, -ge-, h) take a room (or rooms) (**in** dat at, **bei** with).

'**einmischen: sich ~** (**in** acc in, with) meddle, interfere; **sich in ein Gespräch ~** join in (or F butt in on) a conversation; **misch dich da nicht ein!** just keep out of it!

'**Einmischung** f (-; -en) interference.

'**einmo,torig** adj single-engined.

einmotten ['aınmɔtən] v/t (sep, -ge-, h) put s.th. in mothballs, fig. a. mothball.

'**einmünden** v/i (sep, -ge-, sn) a) flow into, b) road: lead into, c) fig. lead to.

'**Einmündung** f (-; -en) a) estuary, mouth, b) (road) junction.

einmütig ['aınmy:tıç] adj unanimous.

'**Einmütigkeit** f (-; no pl) unanimity.

Einnahme ['aınna:mə] f (-; -n) **1.** taking, ✕ a. capture, occupation. **2.** pl a) receipts, b) proceeds, c) income, earnings, d) revenue.

'**Einnahmequelle** f source of income.

'**einnehmen** v/t (irr, sep, -ge-, h, → **nehmen**) **1.** have (lunch etc), take (medicament). **2.** take in, earn (money). **3.** ✕ capture, occupy. **4.** take up (space): **s-n Platz ~** take one's seat. **5.** hold (position etc). **6.** fig. **j-n (für sich) ~** win s.o. over, charm s.o.; **j-n gegen sich ~** set s.o. against o.s. '**einnehmend** adj fig. winning, engaging.

'**einnicken** v/i (sep, -ge-, sn) F nod off.

'**einnisten: sich ~** (sep, -ge-, h) nest, fig. person: install o.s.

'**Einöde** f (-; -n) wilderness.

'**einölen** v/t (sep, -ge-, h) a) oil, b) rub oil into.

'**einordnen** (sep, -ge-, h) **I** v/t **1.** arrange (**nach** according to), file. **2.** a) classify, b) integrate (**in** acc into a system etc), c) place, date (work of art), d) class (**unter** acc with). **II sich ~ 3.** → **einfügen** II. **4.**

mot. get in lane: **sich links ~** get into the left lane, Br. filter to the left.

'**einpacken** (sep, -ge-, h) **I** v/t pack (up), wrap up, do up. **II** v/i pack: F fig. **da können wir ~!** we might as well pack up and leave!

'**einparken** v/t, v/i (sep, -ge-, h) park (between two cars).

'**einpendeln: sich ~** (sep, -ge-, h) fig. find its (own) level.

'**einpferchen** v/t (sep, -ge-, h) coop up.

'**einpflanzen** v/t **1.** 🌱 plant. **2.** 🗲 implant (organ).

Ein'phasen..., **einphasig** ['aınfa:zıç] adj ⚡ single-phase.

'**einplanen** v/t (sep, -ge-, h) **1.** include (in the plan), plan. **2.** allow for.

einpolig ['aınpo:lıç] adj ⚡ single-pole.

'**einprägen** (sep, -ge-, h) **I** v/t imprint (**in** acc on): **j-m et. ~** impress s.th. on s.o.; **sich** et. **~** a) remember, b) memorize. **II sich j-m ~** stick in s.o.'s mind.

'**einprägsam** adj easily remembered, catchy (tune).

'**einquar,tieren** (sep, h) **I** v/t ✕ billet (**bei** on). **II sich ~ bei** move in with.

'**Einquar,tierung** f (-; -en) ✕ billeting.

'**einrahmen** v/t (sep, -ge-, h) frame.

'**einrammen** v/t (sep, -ge-, h) ram s.th. in(**to in** acc).

'**einrasten** v/i (sep, -ge-, sn) **1.** ⚙ click into place, engage. **2.** F go into a huff.

'**einräumen** v/t (sep, -ge-, h) **1.** a) put away, b) put the furniture in a room: **e-n Schrank ~** put (the) things into a cupboard. **2.** fig. **j-m et. ~** grant s.th. to s.o. '**einräumend** adj ling. concessive.

'**Einrede** f (-; -n) ⚖ plea, demurrer.

'**einreden** (sep, -ge-, h) **I** v/t **j-m (sich) et. ~** talk s.o. (o.s.) into (believing) s.th.; **j-m (sich) ~, daß ...** persuade s.o. (o.s.) that ...; **das redest du dir (doch) nur ein!** you're imagining it! **II** v/i **auf j-n ~** a) talk insistently to s.o., b) urge s.o.

'**einregnen** (sep, -ge-) **I** v/i (sn) **einge-regnet sein** be caught by the rain; fig. **auf j-n ~** rain on s.o. **II** v/impers (h) **es regnet sich ein** the rain is settling in.

'**einreiben** v/t (irr, sep, -ge-, h, → **reiben**) rub s.th. in: **~ mit** rub with.

'**Einreibemittel** n liniment.

'**einreichen** v/t (sep, -ge-, h) (**bei** to) send in, hand in, submit: ⚖ **e-e Klage ~** file (or bring) an action.

'**einreihen** (sep, -ge-, h) **I** sich ~ (in acc) take one's place (in), join (s.th.). **II** v/t class (in class with): **j-n ~ unter** (acc) rank s.o. with.

'**Einreiher** m (-s; -) single-breasted suit.
'**Einreise** f (-; -n) entry. **~genehmigung** f entry permit. **~visum** n entry visa.
'**einreißen** (irr, sep, -ge-, → **reißen**) **I** v/t (h) **1.** tear. **2.** demolish, pull house etc down. **II** v/i (sn) **3.** tear. **4.** F nuisance etc: spread.

einrenken ['aınrɛŋkən] (sep, -ge-, h) **I** v/t **1.** ✻ set. **2.** F fig. straighten s.th. out. **II** sich ~ **5.** fig. sort itself out.
'**einrichten** (sep, -ge-, h) **I** v/t **1.** furnish (room etc), fit kitchen, shop, etc out, equip, install. **2.** set up, mount, establish. **3.** arrange: **es ~, daß ...** a. see (to it) that ...; **wenn du es ~ kannst** if you can (manage to). **4.** ✻ set (broken bone). **II** sich ~ **5.** sich (neu) ~ (re)furnish one's flat (or house); → **häuslich**. **6.** make ends meet. **7.** sich ~ auf (acc) prepare for; **auf so et. sind wir nicht eingerichtet** we're not prepared for that sort of thing.
'**Einrichtung** f (-; -en) **1.** furniture, fittings, equipment. **2.** installation: **die sanitären ~** a. sanitation. **3.** ✻ fig. setting up, foundation. **4.** (**öffentliche ~** public) institution, w.s. facility: **zu e-r ständigen ~ werden** become a permanent institution. **5.** → **Vorrichtung**.
'**Einrichtungsgegenstände** pl equipment, fixtures.

'**einrosten** v/i (sep, -ge-, sn) get rusty.
'**einrücken** (sep, -ge-) **I** v/t (h) **1.** indent (line). **2.** put an advertisement in a newspaper etc. **II** v/i **3.** ✗ a) be called up, b) march in: ~ **in** (acc) march into.
eins [aıns] **I** adj **1.** one: **um ~** at one (o'clock); sports: ~ **zu zwei** one two; F fig. ~ **zu null für dich!** score one for you! **2.** **es ist mir alles ~** I couldn't care less; **das ist doch alles ~** it all amounts to the same thing. **II** indef pron one thing: ~ **nach dem andern!** one thing at a time!; **noch ~!** another thing!
Eins f (-; -en) (number) one, ped. A: **e-e ~ schreiben** get an A; F **wie e-e ~** just super.
'**einsacken** (sep, -ge-, h) **I** v/t (h) bag, F fig. a. pocket. **II** v/i (sn) sag.
einsam ['aınza:m] adj lonely, isolated,

secluded. '**Einsamkeit** f (-; no pl) loneliness, seclusion, isolation.
'**einsammeln** v/t (sep, -ge-, h) gather, collect.
'**Einsatz** m (-es; ⸚e) **1.** insert, on dress: inset, (filter) element. **2.** stake (a. fig.): **den ~ verdoppeln** double the stake(s). **3.** risk: **unter ~ s-s Lebens** at the risk of one's life. **4.** ♪ entry: **den ~ geben** give the cue. **5.** effort(s), hard work, zeal, dedication: **harter ~** sports: hard tackling; **mit vollem ~** all out. **6.** use, employment, ✗ deployment: **im ~ ◎** in operation. **7.** ✗, police etc: action, (combat) mission: **im ~ stehen** be on duty, ✗ be in action; **zum ~ kommen** be brought in(to action).
'**Einsatz|befehl** m ✗ combat order. **⚹bereit** adj ready for duty (✗ action, ◎ use): sich ~ **halten** stand by; et. ~ **halten** have s.th. ready. **~besprechung** f before a mission: briefing, after a mission: debriefing. **⚹fähig** adj a) available, usable, ✗ operational, b) fit to work (or play etc). **⚹freudig** adj keen, zealous. **~gruppe** f, **~kom'mando** n task force. **~wagen** m police car (or van).
'**einsaugen** v/t (sep, -ge-, h) suck in.
'**einschalten** (sep, -ge-, h) **I** v/t **1.** switch on, turn on, ◎ a. connect: **e-n Sender ~** tune in to; **den Motor ~** start the engine; **den dritten Gang ~** shift into third gear. **2.** fig. put in, insert: **e-e Pause ~** have a break. **3.** fig. call in: **in e-n** (or **bei e-n**) **Fall Sachverständige ~** call (or bring) in experts on a case. **II** sich ~ **4.** fig. step in, intervene: sich in **ein Gespräch ~** join in a conversation. **5.** TV tune in (in acc to). **6.** ◎ switch itself on (automatically).
'**Einschaltquote** f radio, TV viewing figures, ratings.
'**einschärfen** v/t (sep, -ge-, h) **j-m ~ zu** inf urge (or warn) s.o. to inf.
'**einschätzen** v/t (sep, -ge-, h) **1.** judge, assess: **falsch ~** misjudge; **zu hoch (niedrig) ~** overrate (underrate). **2.** assess, estimate. '**Einschätzung** f (-; -en) **1.** assessment. **2.** estimation, judg(e)ment: **nach m-r ~** in my estimation.
'**einschenken** v/t (sep, -ge-, h) pour (out).
'**einschicken** v/t (sep, -ge-, h) send in.
'**einschieben** v/t (irr, sep, -ge-, h, →

schieben) **1.** put in, insert. **2.** *fig.* fit in.

Einschiebung *f* (-; -en) insertion.

einschießen: sich ~ (*irr, sep,* -ge-, h, → **schießen**) *a. fig.* zero in (**auf** *acc* on).

einschiffen: sich ~ (*sep,* -ge-, h) embark (**nach** for), board a (*or* the) ship.

einschlafen *v/i* (*irr, sep,* -ge-, sn, → **schlafen**) **1.** fall asleep, *a. leg etc:* go to sleep. **2.** *fig.* correspondence *etc:* peter out. **3.** *fig.* die peacefully, pass away.

einschläfern *v/t* (*sep,* -ge-, h) **1.** a) lull (**#** put) *s.o.* to sleep, b) make *s.o.* drowsy; *fig.* **j-n** ~ lull s.o. (into a false sense of security). **2.** put down (*dog etc*). **einschläfernd** *adj* soporific.

Einschlag *m* (-[e]s, ∺e) **1.** impact (*of bomb etc*), striking (*of lightning*). **2.** *fig.* touch: **ein südländischer** ~ an element of the Mediterranean. **3.** *mot.* lock.

einschlagen (*irr, sep,* -ge-, h, → **schlagen**) **I** *v/t* **1.** drive *nail* in(to **in** *acc*). **2.** break, smash (in): **j-m den Schädel** ~ F bash s.o.'s head in; **sich die Zähne** ~ knock one's teeth out. **3.** wrap up. **4.** take (*direction, road*). **5.** *fig.* enter (*a career*), adopt (*a policy etc*): **e-n anderen Weg** ~ adopt a different method. **II** *v/i* **6.** (**in** *acc*) bomb *etc:* hit (*lightning:* strike) (*the house etc*); *fig.* **wie e-e Bombe** ~ fall like a bombshell, cause a sensation. **7.** *fig.* (**gut**) ~ be a (great) success, be a (big) hit. **8.** ~ **auf** (*acc*) beat. **III sich** ~ (h) *tennis:* warm up.

einschlägig ['aɪnʃlɛːgɪç] *adj* relevant: **ein ~er Fall** a case in point; ~ **vorbestraft** previously convicted for the same offence.

einschleichen: sich ~ (*irr, sep,* -ge-, h, → **schleichen**) creep in(to **in** *acc*); **sich in j-s Vertrauen** ~ worm one's way into s.o.'s confidence.

einschleppen *v/t* (*sep,* -ge-, h) bring *a disease etc* in(to **in** *acc*).

einschleusen *v/t* (*sep,* -ge-, h) (**in** *acc*) infiltrate *s.o.* (into), smuggle *s.o., s.th.* in(to).

einschließen *v/t* (*irr, sep,* -ge-, h, → **schließen**) **1.** lock (*or* shut) *s.o., s.th.* (**sich** o.s.) up (**in** *acc*). **2.** enclose, *a.* ✕ surround, encircle. **3.** *fig.* include (**in** *acc* in). **einschließlich I** *prep* (*gen*) including, inclusive of: ~ **Porto** postage included. **II** *adv* **bis Seite 7** ~ up to and

including page 7; **von Montag bis** ~ **Freitag** from Monday to Friday inclusive, *Am.* Monday through Friday.

einschmeicheln: sich ~ (*sep,* -ge-, h) ingratiate o.s. (**bei j-m** with s.o.).

einschmeichelnd *adj* ingratiating.

einschmelzen *v/t* (*irr, sep,* -ge-, h, → **schmelzen**) melt *s.th.* (down).

einschnappen *v/i* (*sep,* -ge-, sn) **1.** catch, click. **2.** F *fig.* go into a huff: → **eingeschnappt**.

einschneiden (*irr, sep,* -ge-, h, → **schneiden**) **I** *v/t* (**in** *acc* into) cut, carve. **II** *v/i* cut into. **einschneidend** *adj fig.* incisive, drastic, crucial, decisive.

einschneien *v/t* (*sep,* -ge-, sn) **eingeschneit sein** be snowed in (*or* up).

Einschnitt *m* **1.** cut, incision, notch. **2.** *fig.* a) crucial event, b) turning point.

einschränken [-ʃrɛŋkən] (*sep,* -ge-, h) **I** *v/t* **1.** (**auf** *acc* to) restrict, reduce (*production etc*), cut down (*expenditure*): **das Rauchen** ~ cut down on smoking. **2.** qualify (*statement etc*). **II sich** ~ economize (**in** *dat* in), cut down expenses. **einschränkend** *adj* restrictive (*a. ling.*), qualifying (*remark*).

Einschränkung *f* (-; -en) **1.** restriction, reduction, cut. **2.** qualification: **ohne** ~ without reservation.

einschrauben *v/t* (*sep,* -ge-, h) screw in(to **in** *acc*).

Einschreibe|brief *m* registered letter. **~gebühr** *f* registration fee.

einschreiben (*irr, sep,* -ge-, h, → **schreiben**) **I** *v/t* **1.** **e-n Brief** ~ **lassen** have a letter registered; **2! registered! 2.** enter, *as a member:* enrol(l): **sich ~ lassen** → **II sich** ~ sign up, *univ.* register, enrol(l). **Einschreibung** *f* (-; -en) signing up, *univ.* enrol(l)ment.

einschreiten *v/i* (*irr, sep,* -ge-, sn, → **schreiten**) intervene, step in: ~ **gegen** take action against.

Einschub *m* (-[e]s; ∺e) insertion, ◎ insert, ∮ slide-in module.

einschüchtern *v/t* (*sep,* -ge-, h) intimidate. **Einschüchterung** *f* (-; -en) intimidation.

einschulen *v/t* (*sep,* -ge-, h) **ein Kind** ~ put a child to school.

Einschuß *m* (-sses; ∺sse) bullet hole, ∮ entry wound.

'einschweißen v/t (sep, -ge-, h) shrink-wrap.

'einschwenken v/i (sep, -ge-, sn) turn (**in** acc into): **nach links** ~ turn (to the) left; fig. ~ (**auf** acc) come round (to).

'Einsegnung f (-; -en) eccl. **1.** consecration. **2.** confirmation.

'einsehen v/t (irr, sep, -ge-, h, → **sehen**) **1.** have a look at, inspect. **2.** see, ✕ observe (terrain). **3.** fig. understand, see, realize: **ich sehe nicht ein, weshalb** I don't see why. **'Einsehen** n (-s) **ein ~ haben** a) show some consideration (**mit** for), b) be reasonable.

'einseifen v/t (sep, -ge-, h) **1.** lather, soap. **2.** F fig. **j-n ~** take s.o. in.

'einseitig ['aınzaıtıç] adj **1.** one-sided (a. fig.), pol. unilateral, ♚ on one side: **~e Ernährung** unbalanced diet; **~ beschrieben** written on one side (only). **2.** bias(s)ed: **et. sehr ~ darstellen** give a one-sided description of s.th. **'Einseitigkeit** f (-; no pl) one-sidedness, fig. a. bias, partiality.

'einsenden v/t (irr, sep, -ge-, h, → **senden**) send in. **'Einsender(in** f) m (-s; -) **1.** sender. **2.** contributor. **'Einsendeschluß** m closing date (for entries). **'Einsendung** f (-; -en) a) sending in, b) at competition: entry.

Einser ['aınzər] m (-s; -) F → **Eins**.

'einsetzen (sep, -ge-, h) **I** v/t **1.** put in, insert. **2.** set up (committee). **3.** use, employ, apply, bring **influence** etc into play. **4.** put into action, call in (the police), employ (work force etc): **j-n ~ in** (dat) (or **bei**) assign s.o. to; **j-n als Erben** ~ appoint s.o. one's heir. **5.** stake, bet: fig. **sein Leben ~** risk one's life. **II 6.** sich ~ exert o.s.; **sich voll ~** go all out; **sich ~ für** support, speak up for, champion; **sich bei j-m für j-n ~** intercede with s.o. for s.o. **III** v/i **7.** start (off), rain etc: set in. **8.** ♪ come in. **'Einsetzung** f (-; -en) **1.** insertion. **2.** appointment.

'Einsicht f (-; -en) **1.** no pl examination (**in Akten** of records): **~ nehmen in** (acc) examine. **2.** insight, understanding: **zur ~ kommen** listen to reason. **'einsichtig** adj reasonable.

'Einsichtnahme f (-; no pl) inspection.

'einsickern v/i (sep, -ge-, sn) seep in: **~ in** (acc) seep into, a. fig. infiltrate into.

'Einsiedler m (-s; -) hermit.

'einsilbig ['aınzılbıç] adj monosyllabic, fig. a. taciturn. **'Einsilbigkeit** f (-; no pl) fig. taciturnity.

'einsinken v/i (irr, sep, -ge-, sn, → **sinken**) a) sink in(to acc), b) cave in.

'einsitzen v/i (irr, sep, -ge-, h, → **sitzen**) ⚖ serve a sentence.

'Einsitzer ['aınzıtsər] m (-s; -) ✈, mot. single-seater.

'einsortieren v/t (sep, h) sort in(to **in** acc).

'einspannen v/t (sep, -ge-, h) **1.** harness. **2.** ⚙ clamp, fix: **e-n Bogen** (**in die Schreibmaschine**) ~ insert a sheet of paper into the typewriter. **3.** F fig. **j-n ~** rope s.o. in.

'einsparen v/t (sep, -ge-, h) **1.** save. **2.** eliminate (jobs). **'Einsparung** f (-; -en) **1.** saving. **2.** (job) elimination.

'einspeichern v/t (sep, -ge-, h) computer: read in.

'einspeisen v/t (sep, -ge-, h) ⚙ feed (**in** acc into).

'einsperren v/t (sep, -ge-, h) lock up.

'einspielen (sep, -ge-, h) **I** v/t **1.** bring in (money). **2.** TV a) show, b) fade in. **3.** ♪ play in. **4.** record. **II** sich ~ get into practice, sports: warm up, fig. get going (properly): **sich aufeinander ~** get used to one another; → **eingespielt**.

'Einspielergebnisse pl box-office returns.

einsprachig ['aınʃpra:xıç] adj monolingual.

'einspringen v/i (irr, sep, -ge-, sn, → **springen**) fig. help out, step in(to the breach): **für j-n ~** fill in for s.o.

Einspritz... mot. (fuel) injection (engine, pump, etc). **'einspritzen** v/t (sep, -ge-, h) inject (**in** acc into): **j-m et. ~** inject s.o. with, give s.o. an injection of.

'Einspruch m (-[e]s; ⁻e) (**gegen**) objection (to) (a. ⚖), protest (against), esp. pol. veto (against), ⚖ appeal (against): **~ erheben** (**gegen**) object (to), ⚖ (file an) appeal (against), pol. veto (s.th.). **'Einspruchsfrist** f appeal period. **'Einspruchsrecht** n **1.** ⚖ right to appeal. **2.** pol. (power of) veto.

einspurig ['aınʃpu:rıç] adj a) single-track, b) single-lane.

einst [aınst] adv **1.** once. **2.** one day.

'einstampfen v/t (sep, -ge-, h) pulp.

'**Einstand** m (-[e]s; no pl) **1.** (s-n ~ **geben** celebrate the) start of one's new job. **2.** fig. debut. **3.** tennis: deuce.

'**einstecken** v/t (sep, -ge-, h) **1.** put in. **2.** put s.th. in one's pocket (or bag etc), take. **3.** F fig. pocket (profit etc), swallow (reprimand etc), take (a blow): **er kann viel ~** he can take a lot.

'**einstehen** v/i (irr, sep, -ge-, h, → **stehen**) ~ **für** a) answer for, take reponsibility for, b) vouch for.

'**einsteigen** v/i (irr, sep, -ge-, sn, → **steigen**) get in(to in acc): **alle(s)** ~**!** all aboard!; ~ **in** (acc) a) get on (a bus, train, plane), b) F fig. get in on (a project etc), start on (or in); **er ist in die Politik eingestiegen** he went into politics; **hart** ~ sports: play rough.

'**einstellbar** adj adjustable.

'**einstellen** (sep, -ge-, h) **I** v/t **1.** put s.th. in(to in acc), store (furniture), put car in the garage. **2.** take on (workers etc). **3.** (**auf** acc) ✪ set (to), adjust (to) (a. fig.), tune (radio etc in (to), opt. focus (on). **4.** stop, discontinue (**vorübergehend**) ~ suspend; ⚖ **die Klage** ~ drop the action; **das Verfahren** ~ dismiss the case; **die Arbeit** ~ a) stop work, b) (go on) strike, walk out; **den Betrieb** ~ shut down; ✕ **das Feuer** ~ cease fire. **5.** tie, equal (a record). **II sich** ~ **6.** appear, turn up, fig. fever etc: set in, problems etc: arise. **7. sich** ~ **auf** (acc) a) adjust (to), b) prepare (o.s.) for; **sich ganz auf j-n** ~ give s.o. one's undivided attention.

einstellig ['aɪnʃtɛlɪç] adj ℞ one-digit.

'**Einstellknopf** m control knob.

'**Einstellung** f (-; -en) **1.** employment (of personnel). **2.** ✪ adjustment, setting, opt., phot. focus(s)ing, focus. **3.** film: a) (camera) angle, b) take. **4.** discontinuance, cessation (a. ✕ of hostilities), stoppage (of work, operation), suspension (of payments): ⚖ **des Verfahrens** dismissal of a case; ~ **e-r Klage** withdrawal of an action. **5.** fig. adjustment (**auf** acc to). **6.** (zu) attitude (towards), opinion (of): **s-e politische** ~ his political views, F his ideology.

Einstieg ['aɪnʃtiːk] m (-[e]s; -e) **1.** way in, entrance. **2.** fig. (**in** acc) entry (into), start (in or on), getting in (on): ~ **in die Kernenergie** opting for nuclear ener-

gy. '**Einstiegluke** f (access) hatch.

'**Einstiegsdroge** f gateway drug.

einstig ['aɪnstɪç] adj former.

'**einstimmen** (sep, -ge-, h) **I** v/i **1. in ein Lied** (**das Gelächter**) ~ join in a song (the laughter). **II** v/t **2.** ♪ tune (up). **3.** fig. **j-n** (**sich**) ~ (**auf** acc) get s.o. (o.s.) in the proper mood (for).

einstimmig ['aɪnʃtɪmɪç] adj **1.** ♪ for one voice. **2.** unanimous (decision etc). '**Einstimmigkeit** f (-; no pl) unanimity, consensus.

einstöckig ['aɪnʃtœkɪç] adj one-stor(e)y.

'**einstöpseln** v/t (sep, -ge-, h) plug in.

'**einstreuen** v/t (sep, -ge-, h) fig. insert: **Zitate** etc **in s-e Rede** ~ intersperse one's speech with quotations etc.

'**einströmen** v/i (sep, -ge-, sn) flow in(to **in** acc).

'**einstu,dieren** v/t (sep, -ge-, h) learn s.th. (by heart), thea. rehearse. '**Einstu,dierung** f (-; -en) thea. production.

'**einstufen** v/t (sep, -ge-, h) class, grade, rate: **hoch** ~ rate high. '**einstufig** adj single-stage. '**Einstufung** f (-; -en) classification, rating.

einstündig ['aɪnʃtʏndɪç] adj one-hour.

'**einstürmen** v/i (sep, -ge-, sn) ~ **auf** (acc) rush at, ✕ attack; fig. **auf j-n** ~ assail s.o. (**mit Fragen** with questions).

Einsturz m (-es; ⸚e) collapse. '**einstürzen** v/i (sep, -ge-, sn) collapse, cave in.

einst'weilen adv **1.** meanwhile, in the meantime. **2.** for the time being.

einst'weilig adj temporary: ⚖ ~**e Verfügung** a) interim order, b) injunction.

eintägig ['aɪntɛːgɪç] adj one-day.

'**Eintagsfliege** f **1.** zo. day fly, ephemera. **2.** fig. nine days' wonder.

'**eintasten** v/t (sep, -ge-, h) computer: key in.

'**eintauchen** (sep, -ge-, h) **I** v/t dip in(to **in** acc). **II** v/i dive in(to **in** acc).

'**eintauschen** v/t (sep, -ge-, h) (**gegen** for) **1.** exchange. **2.** trade s.th. in.

'**einteilen** v/t (sep, -ge-, h) **1.** a) divide (up) (**in** acc into), b) rate (**nach** according to). **2.** organize (one's time), budget (money), use material etc sparingly. **3. j-n** ~ **zu** assign s.o. to, ✕ detail s.o. for.

'**Einteiler** m (-s; -), **einteilig** ['aɪntaɪlɪç] adj one-piece. '**Einteilung** f (-; -en) **1.** (**in** acc into) a) division, b) classification. **2.** planning, organization (*of work, time, etc*), budgeting (*of money*).

'**eintippen** *v/t* (*sep*, -ge-, h) type in(to *in acc*), *computer:* key in.

'**eintönig** *adj* monotonous.

'**Eintönigkeit** *f* (-; *no pl*) monotony.

'**Eintopf** *m* -[e]s; ⸚e) *gastr.* stew.

'**Eintracht** *f* (-; *no pl*) harmony.

'**einträchtig** *adj* harmonious, peaceful.

Eintrag *f* (⸚a:ntra:k] *m* (-[e]s; ⸚e) entry.

'**eintragen** (*irr, sep*, -ge-, h, → **tragen**) **I** *v/t* **1.** enter (*a.* †), *adm.* register, enrol(l) (**als Mitglied** as a member): *sich* ~ *lassen* (*bei*) register (with), enrol(l) (in); → *eingetragen*. **2.** *j-m et.* ~ earn s.o. *praise, sympathy, etc*. **II** *sich* ~ a) register, b) put one's name down: *sich in e-e Anwesenheitsliste* ~ sign in.

einträglich [⸚a:ntrɛ:klɪç] *adj* profitable.

'**Eintragung** *f* (-; -en) **1.** registration, enrol(l)ment. **2.** → *Eintrag*.

'**eintreffen** *v/i* (*irr, sep*, -ge-, sn, → **treffen**) **1.** arrive (*in dat, auf dat* at). **2.** *fig.* a) happen, b) prove (*or* come) true.

'**Eintreffen** *n* (-s) arrival.

'**eintreiben** *v/t* (*irr, sep*, -ge-, h, → **treiben**) collect.

'**eintreten** (*irr, sep*, -ge-, → **treten**) **I** *v/i* **1.** (sn) go in, come in: *er trat ins Haus ein* he went into (*or* entered) the house; *bitte, treten Sie ein!* do come in, please! **2.** (sn) ~ *in* (*acc*) join, enter (*club, firm, etc*); *in den Krieg* ~ enter the war; *in Verhandlungen* ~ enter into negotiations. **3.** (sn) take place, happen, *a. death:* occur, *case etc:* arise: *es trat Stille ein* silence fell; *es ist e-e Besserung eingetreten* there has been an improvement. **4.** (sn) ~ *für* stand up for *s.o.*, support *s.th*. **5.** (h) ~ *auf* (*acc*) kick. **II** *v/t* (h) **6.** kick in (*or* down). **7.** break in (*shoes*). **8.** *ich habe mir e-n Dorn (in den Fuß) eingetreten* I've run a thorn into my foot.

'**eintrichtern** → *einbleuen*.

'**Eintritt** *m* (-[e]s; -e) **1.** (*in acc* into) entry, entrance: *bei s-m* ~ *in den Klub* on his joining the club. **2.** beginning, onset (*of winter etc*): *nach* ~ *der Dunkelheit* after dark. **3.** occurrence. **4.** admission: ~ *frei!* admission free!; ~ *verboten!* no entry! **5.** → '*Eintrittsgebühr f*, '*Eintrittsgeld n* admission (fee).

'**Eintrittskarte** *f* (admission) ticket.

'**eintrocknen** *v/i* (*sep*, -ge-, sn) dry up.

'**eintrudeln** *v/i* (*sep*, -ge-, sn) F turn up.

'**einüben** *v/t* (*sep*, -ge-, h) practi/se (*Am.* -ce), learn.

einverleiben ['ainfɛrlaibən] *v/t* (*sep*, *no* -ge-, h) **1.** (*dat, in acc* to) add, annex (*territory*). **2.** F *sich et.* ~ put away (*food, drink*).

'**Einvernehmen** *n* (-s; *no pl*) agreement, (good) understanding: *in gutem* ~ on good terms; *im* ~ *mit* in agreement with.

'**einverstanden** *adj* ~ *sein* agree; *mit et.* ~ *sein* agree to (*or* approve of) s.th.; ~*!* all right!, okay! '**Einverständnis** *n* (-ses; *no pl*) **1.** (*zu*) approval (of), consent (to): ~ *sein* ~ *erklären* (give one's) consent. **2.** → *Einvernehmen*.

'**einwachsen** *v/i* (*irr, sep*, -ge-, sn, → *wachsen*) grow in(to *in acc*).

Einwand ['ainvant] *m* (-[e]s; ⸚e) objection (*gegen* to).

'**Einwanderer** *m* (-s; -), '**Einwanderin** *f* (-; -nen) immigrant. '**einwandern** *v/i* (*sep*, -ge-, sn) immigrate (*in acc* to). '**Einwanderung** *f* (-; -en) immigration. '**Einwanderungs...** immigration (*quota, country, etc*).

'**einwandfrei** *adj* impeccable, flawless, perfect: ~ *der Beste* undoubtedly the best; *es steht* ~ *fest* it is beyond question.

einwärts ['ainvɛrts] *adv* inward(s).

'**einwechseln** *v/t* (*sep*, -ge-, h) **1.** change money (*in acc, gegen* into). **2.** *sports:* *j-n* ~ send s.o. on the field.

'**einwecken** → *einmachen*.

'**Einwegflasche** *f* nonreturnable bottle.

'**Einwegspritze** *f* ⚕ disposable syringe.

'**einweichen** *v/t* (*sep*, -ge-, h) soak.

'**einweihen** *v/t* (*sep*, -ge-, h) **1.** open, inaugurate, *eccl.* consecrate. **2.** F *fig.* christen (*a. dress etc*). **3.** *j-n* ~ *in* (*acc*) initiate s.o. into; *j-n in ein Geheimnis* ~ let s.o. into a secret; *eingeweiht sein* be in the know; → *Eingeweihte*.

'**Einweihung** *f* (-; -en) (formal) opening, *eccl.* consecration.

'**Einweihungsfeier** *f* opening ceremony.

'**einweisen** *v/t* (*irr, sep*, -ge-, h, → *weisen*) **1.** *j-n* ~ *in* (*acc*) send s.o. to, 🏛 commit s.o. to (*a mental institution*); *j-n in ein Krankenhaus* ~ hospitalize s.o. **2.** *j-n* ~ *in* (*acc*) brief s.o. in, introduce s.o. to (*a task etc*), inaugurate s.o. into (*an office*). **3.** direct *car, driver* (**in** *acc* into). **'Einweisung** *f* (-; -en) **1.** 🏛 committal (*in acc to an institution*); **~ ins Krankenhaus** hospitalization. **2.** (*in acc*) briefing (in), introduction (to).

'einwenden *v/t* (*irr, sep,* -ge-, h, → **wenden**) *et.* **~** (**gegen**) object (to); **~, daß ...** argue that ...; **ich habe nichts dagegen einzuwenden** I have no objections; **es läßt sich nichts dagegen ~** there is nothing to be said against it.

'Einwendung *f* (-; -en) → **Einwand.**

'einwerfen *v/t* (*irr, sep,* -ge-, h, → **werfen**) **1.** throw in (*a. fig. remark*). **2.** smash (*window etc*). **3.** post, *Am.* mail (*letter etc*). **4.** insert, put in (*coin*).

einwertig ['aɪnveːrtɪç] *adj* monovalent.

'einwickeln *v/t* (*sep,* -ge-, h) **1.** wrap up. **2.** F *j-n* **~** a) take s.o. in, b) softsoap s.o.

einwilligen ['aɪnvɪlɪɡən] *v/i* (*sep,* -ge-, h) (**in** *acc* to) agree, consent. **'Einwilligung** *f* (-; -en) approval, consent.

'einwirken *v/i* (*sep,* -ge-, h) **~ auf** (*acc* a) have an effect on, b) affect (*a.* 🜨), c) influence; **auf j-n ~** work on s.o.; **et. ~ lassen** let s.th. take effect.

'Einwirkung *f* (-; -en) (**auf** *acc* on) a) effect, b) influence.

Einwohner ['aɪnvoːnər] *m* (-s; -), **'Einwohnerin** *f* (-; -nen) inhabitant, resident. **'Einwohnermeldeamt** *n* residents' registration office. **'Einwohnerschaft** *f* (-; *no pl*) inhabitants, population.

'Einwurf *m* **1.** *sports*: throw-in. **2.** a) insertion (*of coins*), b) *for letters etc*: slit, opening, *for coins*: slot. **3.** *fig.* remark.

Einzahl *f* (-; *no pl*) *ling.* singular.

'einzahlen *v/t* (*sep,* -ge-, h) pay in: **Geld bei der Bank ~** deposit money at the bank; **Geld** (**auf ein Konto**) **~** pay money into an account. **'Einzahlung** *f* (-; -en) payment, *at bank*: deposit.

'Einzahlungsschein *m* paying-in (*or* deposit) slip.

einzäunen ['aɪntsɔʏnən] *v/t* (*sep,* -ge-, h) fence in. **'Einzäunung** *f* (-; -en) fence.

'einzeichnen *v/t* (*sep,* -ge-, h) a) sketch in, b) mark (**in, auf** *dat* on): **... ist nicht eingezeichnet** ... isn't on the map.

Einzel ['aɪntsəl] (-s; -) *n tennis*: singles.

'Einzel|anfertigung *f* special design: **es ist e-e ~** it was custom-built. **~antrieb**

m ⚙ separate drive. **~aufstellung** *f* 🟇 itemized list. **~beispiel** *n* isolated case. **~betrag** *m* (single) item. **~bett** *n* single bed. **~diszi,plin** *f* *sports*: individual event. **~exem,plar** *n* unique specimen (*book*: copy). **~fall** *m* isolated case.

Einzelgänger ['aɪntsəlɡɛŋər] *m* (-s; -) **'Einzelgängerin** *f* (-; -nen) loner.

'Einzel|haft *f* solitary confinement. **~handel** *m* retail trade. **~handelspreis** *m* retail price. **~händler(in** *f*) *m* retailer. **~haus** *n* detached house.

'Einzelheit *f* (-; -en) detail: **bis in alle ~en** down to the last detail; **auf ~er eingehen** go into detail.

'Einzelkind *n* only child.

einzellig ['aɪntsɛlɪç] *adj* monocellular.

'einzeln I *adj* **1.** a) single, individual, b) separate, isolated: **ein ~er Schuh** an odd shoe. **2. ~e** several, some, a few *meteor.* **~e Schauer** scattered showers. **II** *adv* **3.** a) singly, individually, b) separately: **~ eintreten** enter one by one (*or* one at a time); **~ aufführen** specify, itemize. **'einzelne I** *m*, *f* (-n; -n) individual: **~** *pl* some, a few; **jeder ~** (*von uns*) every (single) one (of us). **II das ~** (-n; *no pl*) the detail(s): **im ~n** a) in detail, b) in particular; **ins ~ gehen** go into detail; **~s gefällt mir nicht** I don' like some things (*or* points).

'Einzel|spiel *n tennis*: singles (match). **~stück** *n* **1.** odd piece. **2.** unique specimen. **~teil** *n* ⚙ (component) part. **~unterricht** *m* private lessons. **~wesen** *n* individual (being). **~zelle** *f* 🟇 solitar cell. **~zimmer** *n* single room.

'einziehbar *adj* **1.** ⚙ retractable. **2.** 🟇 collectible. **'einziehen** (*irr, sep,* -ge-, **~ziehen**) **I** *v/t* (h) **1.** draw *s.th.* in, ⚙ retract, haul *flag* down: **den Kopf ~** duck; **die Segel ~** take in sail; **die Riemen ~** ship the oars. **2.** draw in, inhale breathe. **3.** put in. **4.** ✕ call up, draft. **5** 🟇 seize, confiscate, withdraw *bank notes* (from circulation). **6.** collec (*taxes etc*). **7.** → **Erkundigung. II** *v/* (sn) **8.** enter, march in (**in** *acc*) *lodger*: move in(to **in** *acc*, **bei** with): **e zog ins Parlament ein** he took his sea in Parliament. **9.** *liquid*: soak in.

einzig ['aɪntsɪç] **I** *adj* **1.** only, single, sole **kein ~es Auto** not a single car; **sein ~e Halt** his sole support; **nicht ein ~es Ma**

not once. **2.** *der* (*die*) ~e the only one; *nicht ein* ~er not (a single) one; *das* ~e the only thing. **3.** → *einzigartig* I. **II** *adv* **4.** only, (*a.* ~ *und allein*) solely, entirely: *das ist das* ~ *Richtige* that's the only thing to do.

'**einzigartig** *adj* unique, singular, unequal(l)ed, fantastic, marvel(l)ous.

Ein'zimmerwohnung *f* one-room flat (*Am.* apartment).

'**Einzug** *m* (-[e]s; ⁓e) **1.** a) entry, b) moving in(to *in a house etc*), c) *fig.* coming. **2.** *print.* indent.

'**Einzugsermächtigung** *f* standing order for a direct debit.

'**Einzugsgebiet** *n geol.* catchment area.

'**Eipulver** *n* dried egg.

E-is ['eːɪs] *n* (-; -) ♪ E sharp.

Eis [aɪs] *n* (-es; *no pl*) a) ice, b) ice cream: F *fig. et. auf* ~ *legen* put s.th. on ice; *das* ~ *brechen* break the ice. ~**bahn** *f* (ice-)skating rink. ~**bär** *m* polar bear. ~**becher** *m gastr.* sundae. ~**bein** *n gastr.* pickled knuckle of pork. ~**berg** *m* iceberg: → *Spitze*[1]. ~**beutel** *m* ❋ ice bag. ~**blumen** *pl* frostwork. ~**bombe** *f gastr.* bombe glacée.

'**Eischnee** *m gastr.* beaten egg white.

'**Eisdiele** *f* ice-cream parlo(u)r.

Eisen ['aɪzən] *n* (-s; *no pl*) iron: *fig. ein heißes* ~ *anfassen* tackle a hot issue; *j-n zum alten* ~ *werfen* throw s.o. on the scrap heap, shelve s.o.; *er gehört zum alten* ~ he's past it; *zwei* ~ *im Feuer haben* have more than one string to one's bow; (*man muß*) *das* ~ *schmieden, solange es heiß ist* strike while the iron is hot.

'**Eisenbahn** *f* a) railway, *Am.* railroad, b) train: *mit der* ~ by rail, by train.

Eisenbahner ['aɪznbaːnər] *m* (-s; -) F railwayman, *Am.* railroadman.

'**Eisenbahn|knotenpunkt** *m* (railway, *Am.* railroad) junction. ~**netz** *n* railway (*Am.* railroad) network. ~**schaffner** *m* guard, conductor, *Am.* railroad car. ~**wagen** *m* railway carriage, coach, *Am.* railroad car.

'**Eisen|erz** *n* iron ore. ~**gehalt** *m* iron content. ~**gießerei** *f* iron foundry. ~**guß** *m* (-sses; *no pl*) **1.** iron casting. **2.** cast iron.

'**eisenhaltig** *adj* **1.** ~ *sein* contain iron. **2.** *min.* ferruginous.

'**Eisen|hut** *m* (-[e]s; *no pl*) ❋ monkshood.

~**hütte** *f*, ~**hüttenwerk** *n* ironworks. ~**mangel** *m* ❋ iron deficiency. ~**o,xyd** *n* ❋ ferric oxide.

'**Eisenwaren** *pl* ironware, hardware. ~**geschäft** *n* hardware store.

'**Eisenzeit** *f* (-; *no pl*) *hist.* the Iron Age.

eisern ['aɪzɔrn] *adj* a) *a. fig.* iron, of iron, *nerves* of steel, b) adamant, firm: ~**e** *Sparsamkeit* rigorous economy; ~**e** *Gesundheit* cast-iron constitution; ~**er** *Bestand* permanent stock; ~**e** *Regel* hard and fast rule; *s-e* ~**e** *Ruhe* his imperturbability; ~ *festhalten an* (*dat*) adhere rigidly to; ~ *sparen* save rigorously; → *Lunge* 1.

'**Eiseskälte** *f* icy cold.

'**eisfrei** *adj* free of ice. '**eisgekühlt** *adj* chilled. '**Eisglätte** *f* icy roads.

'**Eishockey** *n* ice hockey. ~**schläger** *m* ice-hockey stick. ~**spieler** *m* ice-hockey player.

eisig ['aɪzɪç] *adj a. fig.* icy.

'**Eiskaffee** *m gastr.* iced coffee.

'**eiskalt** *adj* **1.** ice-cold. **2.** *gastr.* chilled. **3.** *fig.* a) icy (*look etc*), b) cold (*as ice*), c) cool, d) brazen.

'**Eiskübel** *m* ice bucket.

'**Eiskunstlauf** *m* (-[e]s; *no pl*) figure skating. '**Eiskunstläufer(in** *f*) *m* figure skater. '**Eislauf** *m* (-[e]s; *no pl*) ice-skating. '**eislaufen** *v/i* (*sep,* -ge-, *sn*) ice-skate. '**Eisläufer(in** *f*) *m* ice-skater.

'**Eismeer** *n polar sea*: *Nördliches* (*Südliches*) ~ Arctic (Antarctic) Ocean.

'**Eispickel** *m* ice pick.

'**Eisprung** *m physiol.* ovulation.

'**Eis|re,vue** *f* ice show. ~**sa,lat** *m* iceberg lettuce. ~**schießen** *n* curling. ~**schnelllauf** *m* (-[e]s; *no pl*) speed skating. ~**schnelläufer(in** *f*) *m* speed skater. ~**scholle** *f* ice floe. ~**schrank** *m* refrigerator, F fridge, *Am.* icebox. ~**stadion** *n* ice stadium. ~**tanz** *m* ice dancing. ~**torte** *f* ice-cream gateau. ~**waffel** *f* ice-cream wafer. ~**wasser** *n* ice water. ~**würfel** *m* ice cube. ~**zapfen** *m* icicle.

'**Eiszeit** *f* (-; *no pl*) ice age, glacial period. '**Eiszeitmensch** *m* glacial man.

eitel ['aɪtəl] *adj* **1.** vain, conceited. **2.** vain, futile: *eitle Hoffnung* idle hope. '**Eitelkeit** *f* (-; *no pl*) vanity, *a.* futility.

Eiter ['aɪtər] *m* (-s; *no pl*) ❋ pus. '**Eiterbeule** *f* abscess, boil, *fig.* festering sore. '**Eiterbläschen** *n* pustule. '**eit(e)rig**

adj suppurative, festering. **'eitern** *v/i* (h) fester, suppurate. **'Eiterpfropf** *m* core. **'Eiterung** *f* (-; -en) suppuration.

'Eiweiß *n* (-es; -e) white of egg, (egg) white, *biol.* albumen, protein. **2arm** *adj* low in protein, low-protein (*diet*). **~be-darf** *m* protein requirement. **~mangel** *m* protein deficiency. **2reich** *adj* rich in protein, high-protein (*diet*).

Eizelle *f biol.* egg cell, ovum.

Ejakulation [ejakula'tsĭo:n] *f* (-; -en) *physiol.* ejaculation.

Ekel¹ ['e:kəl] *m* (-s; *no pl*) (**vor** *dat*) disgust (at), revulsion (against): **~ empfin-den → ekeln; ~ ... ist (sind) mir ein ~** I can't stand ... I loathe ...

'Ekel² *n* (-s; -) F nasty person, beast.

'ekelerregend *adj* repulsive. **'Ekelge-fühl** *n* revulsion. **'ekelhaft**, **'ek(e)lig** *adj* revolting, disgusting. **'ekeln: sich ~** (h) **ich ekle mich davor (vor ihm)** it (he) makes me sick.

Eklat [e'kla:] *m* (-s; -s) a) stir, sensation, b) scandal, c) row.

eklatant [ekla'tant] *adj* a) striking, b) *contp.* flagrant, blatant.

Eklipse [e'klipsə] *f* (-; -n) *astr.* eclipse.

Ekstase [ɛk'sta:zə] *f* (-; -n) ecstasy: **in ~ geraten** go into ecstasies (**über** *acc* over). **ekstatisch** [-tɪʃ] *adj* ecstatic.

Ekzem [ɛk'tse:m] *n* (-s; -e) *✗* eczema.

Elan [e'la:n] *m* (-s; *no pl*) verve, zest.

Elastik [e'lastɪk] *n* (-s; -s) elastic.

elastisch [e'lastɪʃ] *adj* elastic (*a. fig.*), springy, *mot.*, ⚙ flexible (*a. fig.*).

Elastizität [elastitsi'tɛ:t] *f* (-; *no pl*) *a. fig.* elasticity, flexibility.

Elch [ɛlç] *m* (-[e]s; -e) *zo.* elk, moose.

Elefant [ele'fant] *m* (-en; -en) elephant: **wie ein ~ im Porzellanladen** like a bull in a china shop.

Ele'fanten|bulle *m zo.* bull elephant. **~hochzeit** *f ✝* giant merger. **~kuh** *f zo.* cow elephant. **~rüssel** *m* trunk.

elegant [ele'gant] *adj* elegant (*a. fig.*), smart: **e-e ~e Lösung** a neat (*or* clever) solution. **Eleganz** [ele'gants] *f* (-; *no pl*) *a. fig.* elegance.

Elegie [ele'gi:] *f* (-; -n) elegy. **elegisch** [e'le:gɪʃ] *adj* elegiac, *fig. a.* melancholy.

elektrifizieren [elɛktrifi'tsi:rən] *v/t* (h) electrify. **Elektrifi'zierung** *f* (-; -en) electrification. **Elektrik** [e'lɛktrɪk] *f* (-; *no pl*) **1.** electricity. **2.** electrical system.

Elektriker [e'lɛktrɪkər] *m* (-s; -) electrician. **elektrisch** [e'lɛktrɪʃ] **I** *adj* electric(al): **~er Schlag (Strom, Stuhl)** electric shock (current, chair). **II** *adv* electrically, by electricity. **elektrisieren** [elɛktri'zi:rən] *v/t* (h) *a. fig.* electrify. **Elektrizität** [elɛktritsi'tɛ:t] *f* (-; *no pl*) electricity, (electric) current.

Elektrizi'tätsversorgung *f* electricity (*or* power) supply. **Elektrizi'tätswerk** *n* (electric) power station.

Elektroauto [e'lɛktro-] *n* electric car.

E'lektrobohrer *m* electric drill.

E'lektroche,mie *f* electrochemistry.

Elektrode [elɛk'tro:də] *f* (-; -n) electrode: **negative ~** cathode; **positive ~** anode.

E'lektro|enzephalo,gramm *n ✗* (*abbr.* EEG) electroencephalogram. **~fahr-zeug** *n* electric vehicle. **~gerät** *n* electrical appliance. **~geschäft** *n* electrical shop. **~herd** *m* electric cooker. **~inge-ni,eur** *m* electrical engineer. **~kardio-,gramm** *n ✗* (*abbr.* EKG) electrocardiogram.

Elektrolyse [elɛktro'ly:zə] *f* (-; -n) electrolysis.

E'lektromotor *m* (electric) motor.

Elektron ['e:lɛktrɔn] *n* (-s; -en [elɛk-'tro:nən]) *phys.* electron.

Elek'tronen|blitz(gerät *n*) *m phot.* electronic flash (gun). **~gehirn** *n* electronic brain. **~mikro,skop** *n* electron microscope. **~rechner** *m* computer. **~röhre** *f* electronic valve (*Am.* tube).

Elektronik [elɛk'tro:nɪk] *f* (-; *no pl*) **1.** electronics. **2.** electronic system.

elek'tronisch [-nɪʃ] *adj* electronic.

E'lektro|ofen *m* electric stove. **~ra,sie-rer** *m* electric razor. **~schock** *m ✗* electroshock.

Elektro|'technik *f* electrical engineering. **~'techniker** *m* electrical engineer. **2'technisch** *adj* electrotechnical, electrical (*component, industry, etc*).

Elektrothera'pie *f ✗* electrotherapy.

Element [ele'mɛnt] *n* (-[e]s; -e) element **⚡** a. battery, cell: *fig.* **in s-m ~ sein** be in one's element; *contp.* **asoziale ~e** antisocial elements.

elementar [elemɛn'ta:r] *adj* **1.** elemental. **2.** elementary (*duty, mistake, etc*).

Elemen'tar|begriff *m* fundamental idea. **~gewalt** *f* elemental force. **~teil**

chen *n phys.* elementary particle. **~unterricht** *m* elementary instruction.

elend ['e:lɛnt] **I** *adj* **1.** *a. fig. contp.* miserable, wretched: **~ aussehen** look ill; **sich ~ fühlen** feel wretched (*or* terrible). **2.** poverty-stricken, pitiable. **3.** F *fig.* terrible, awful. **II** *adv* **4.** miserably. **5.** F *fig.* terribly, awfully. **'Elend** *n* (-s; *no pl*) misery, poverty: → **stürzen** 3.

'Elendsquar,tier *n* hovel.

'Elendsviertel *n* slum(s).

elf [ɛlf] *adj* eleven. **Elf¹** *f* (-; -en) **1.** (number) eleven. **2.** *soccer:* team.

Elf² *m* (-en; -en), **Elfe** ['ɛlfə] *f* (-; -n) elf. **'Elfenbein** *n* (-[e]s; *no pl*) ivory. **'elfenbeinern** *adj*, **'elfenbeinfarbig** *adj* ivory. **'Elfenbeinturm** *m fig.* ivory tower.

elft [ɛlft] *adj*, **Elfte** ['ɛlftə] *m, f* (-n; -n) eleventh. **elftens** ['ɛlftəns] *adv* in the eleventh place.

eliminieren [elimi'ni:rən] *v/t* (h) eliminate.

elitär [eli'tɛ:r] *adj* elitist. **Elite** [e'li:tə] *f* (-; -n) élite. **E'litedenken** *n* elitism.

Elixier [eli'ksi:r] *n* (-s; -e) elixir.

'Ellbogen *m* (-s; -) elbow. **~freiheit** *f* elbow room. **~gelenk** *n* elbow joint. **~gesellschaft** *f* dog-eat-dog society. **~mensch** *m* ruthless go-getter.

ellenlang ['ɛlən-] *adj* F *fig.* endless.

Ellipse [ɛ'lɪpsə] *f* (-; -n) ♈ ellipse.

elliptisch [ɛ'lɪptɪʃ] *adj* ♈ elliptic(al).

Elsässer ['ɛlzɛsər] *m* (-s; -), **Elsässerin** *f* (-; -nen), **'elsässisch** *adj* Alsatian.

Elster ['ɛlstər] *f* (-; -n) *zo.* magpie.

elterlich ['ɛltərlɪç] *adj* parental (*duty, love, etc*), parents' (*bedroom etc*).

Eltern ['ɛltərn] *pl* parents: F *fig.* **nicht von schlechten ~** terrific.

'Elternabend *m* parent-teacher meeting. **'Elternbeirat** *m ped.* parents' council. **'Elternhaus** *n* (one's parents') home. **'elternlos** *adj* orphan(ed).

'Elternschaft *f* (-; *no pl*) **1.** parenthood. **2.** parents. **'Elternsprechtag** *m ped.* open day. **'Elternteil** *m* parent.

Email ['e:maɪ(l)] *n* (-s; -s), **Emaille** [e'maljə] *f* (-; -n), **emaillieren** [ema(l)'ji:rən] *v/t* (h) enamel.

Emanze [e'mantsə] *f* (-; -n) F *contp.* women's libber. **Emanzipation** [emantsipa'tsio:n] *f* (-; -en) emancipation: **die**

~ der Frau *a.* women's liberation. **emanzipatorisch** [emantsipa'to:rɪʃ] *adj* emancipatory. **emanzipieren** [emantsi'pi:rən] (h) **I** *v/t* emancipate. **II sich ~** become emancipated.

Embargo [ɛm'bargo] *n* (-s; -s) embargo.

Emblem [ɛm'ble:m] *n* (-s; -e) emblem.

Embolie [ɛmbo'li:] *f* (-; -n) ♠ embolism.

Embryo ['ɛmbryo] *m* (-s; -s, -nen [ɛmbryo'o:nən]) embryo. **embryonal** [ɛmbryo'na:l] *adj* embryonic, embryo.

emeritieren [emeri'ti:rən] *v/t* (h) retire.

Emigrant [emi'grant] *m* (-en; -en), **Emi'grantin** *f* (-; -nen) emigrant.

Emigration [emigra'tsio:n] *f* (-; -en) emigration: **in der (die) ~** in(to) exile.

emigrieren [emi'gri:rən] *v/i* (sn) emigrate.

Emission [emi'sio:n] *f* (-; -en) **1.** *phys.* emission. **2.** ♈ issue.

Emotion [emo'tsio:n] *f* (-; -en) emotion. **emotional** [emotsio'na:l] *adj* emotional. **emotionalisieren** [emotsio̯nali'zi:rən] *v/t* emotionalize.

emotionell [emotsio'nɛl] *adj* emotional.

empfahl [ɛm'pfa:l] *pret of* **empfehlen.**

empfand [ɛm'pfant] *pret of* **empfinden.**

Empfang [ɛm'pfaŋ] *m* (-[e]s; ⸚e) **1.** *no pl* receipt: **nach ~, bei ~** on receipt; **in ~ nehmen** a) receive, b) meet (*s.o.*). **2.** *no pl* reception (*a. radio etc*), welcome: **j-m e-n begeisterten ~ bereiten** give s.o. an enthusiastic reception. **3.** *hotel etc:* reception (desk). **4.** reception.

emp'fangen (empfing, empfangen, h) **I** *v/t* receive (*a. radio etc*), welcome: **sie empfängt niemanden** she refuses to see anybody; **wir wurden sehr freundlich ~** we met with a friendly reception. **II** *v/i biol.* conceive.

Empfänger [ɛm'pfɛŋər] *m* (-s; -) receiver (*a. radio etc*), recipient, ✉ addressee. **empfänglich** [ɛm'pfɛŋlɪç] *adj* (**für** to) receptive, susceptible (*a. ♠*), ♠ prone. **Emp'fänglichkeit** *f* (-; *no pl*) (**für** to) receptivity, *a. ♠* susceptibility.

Empfängnis [ɛm'pfɛŋnɪs] *f* (-; *no pl*) *biol.* conception. **♀verhütend** *adj* (*a. ~es Mittel*) contraceptive. **~verhütung** *f* contraception.

Emp'fangs|an,tenne *f* reception aerial (*Am.* antenna). **~bereich** *m radio etc:* **1.** range of reception. **2.** frequency range. **~bescheinigung** *f* receipt. **~be-**

stätigung f acknowledg(e)ment of receipt. **~chef(in** f) m reception (*Am.* room) clerk. **~dame** f receptionist.

empfehlen [ɛm'pfeːlən] (empfahl, empfohlen, h) **I** v/t **1.** recommend (*j-m et.* s.th. to s.o.): **nicht zu ~** not to be recommended; **es empfiehlt sich zu** inf it is advisable to inf. **II** sich ~ **2.** recommend itself. **3.** take one's leave.

emp'fehlenswert adj a) recommendable, b) advisable. **Emp'fehlung** f (-; -en) (*auf ~* on) recommendation: **gute ~en haben** have good references.

Emp'fehlungsschreiben n letter of recommendation.

empfinden [ɛm'pfɪndən] v/t (empfand, empfunden, h) feel (*a.* v/i): **et. als lästig ~** find s.th. a nuisance. **Emp'finden** n (-s) a) feeling, b) opinion, c) sense: **nach m-m ~** the way I see it.

empfindlich [ɛm'pfɪntlɪç] adj **1.** sensitive (**gegen** to) (*a.* ✵, phot., ◎), delicate: fig. **~e Stelle** tender spot. **2.** touchy, irritable (*a.* stomach): **~ reagieren** overreact. **3.** severe (cold, penalty, etc), bad (loss): **~ kalt** bitterly cold; fig. **er war ~ getroffen** he was badly hit.

Emp'findlichkeit f (-; no pl) **1.** a) sensitivity (**gegen** to), phot. a. speed, b) delicacy. **2.** touchiness, irritability.

emp'findsam adj **1.** sensitive. **2.** sentimental. **Emp'findsamkeit** f (-; no pl) sensitivity, sentimentality.

Emp'findung f (-; -en) a) sensation, perception, b) feeling, emotion.

emp'findungslos adj insensitive (**für, gegen** to), numb (limb).

empfing [ɛm'pfɪŋ] pret of **empfangen**.

empfohlen [ɛm'pfoːlən] **I** pp of **empfehlen**. **II** adj recommended.

empfunden [ɛm'pfʊndən] pp of **empfinden**.

empirisch [ɛm'piːrɪʃ] adj empirical.

empor [ɛm'poːr] adv lit. up, upward(s).

Empore [ɛm'poːrə] f (-; -n) △ gallery.

empören [ɛm'pøːrən] (h) **I** v/t **1.** shock, outrage. **II** sich ~ **2.** be outraged (**über** acc at). **3.** rebel (**gegen** against).

em'pörend adj outrageous, shocking.

Emporkömmling [ɛm'poːrkœmlɪŋ] m (-s; -e) upstart, parvenu.

em'pört I pp of **empören**. **II** adj indignant (**über** acc at).

Em'pörung f (-; -en) **1.** no pl indignation

(**über** acc at). **2.** revolt, rebellion.

emsig ['ɛmzɪç] adj busy, industrious, hard-working. **'Emsigkeit** f (-; no pl) **1.** bustle. **2.** industry, zeal.

Emulsion [emɔl'zi̯oːn] f (-; -en) emulsion.

'E-Mu‚sik f (-; no pl) serious music.

'Endabrechnung f final account.

'Endbahnhof m terminus.

'Endbetrag m (sum) total.

Ende ['ɛndə] n (-s; -n) **1.** no pl end, a. ending (of film etc): **~ (der Durchsage)!** end of the message!, radio: over (and out)!; **~ Mai** at the end of May; **~ der dreißiger Jahre** in the late thirties; **am ~** a) in the end, after all, b) eventually, c) maybe; **letzten ~s** when all is said and done; **ich bin am ~** I'm finished; **bis zum bitteren ~** to the bitter end; **e-r Sache ein ~ machen** (or **bereiten**) put an end to s.th.; **et. zu ~ führen** finish s.th., see s.th. through; **zu ~ gehen** a) → **enden,** b) run short; **zu ~ sein** be over, time: be up; **ein böses ~ nehmen** come to a bad end; **~ gut, alles gut** all's well that ends well; F **das dicke ~ kommt nach** there will be hell to pay; **die Arbeit geht ihrem ~ entgegen** the work is nearing completion; **es geht mit ihm zu ~** he's going fast; → **Latein, Lied, Weisheit. 2.** F a) (small) piece, b) no pl (long) distance (or way).

'Endef‚fekt ['ɛnt-] m final result: **im ~** in the final analysis, in the end.

endemisch [ɛn'deːmɪʃ] adj ✵ endemic.

enden ['ɛndən] v/i (h) (come to an) end, draw to a close, finish, stop, contract etc: expire: **mit e-r Prügelei ~** end in a brawl; ling: **~ auf** (acc) end with; **nicht ~ wollend** unending; **das Stück endet tragisch** the play has a tragic ending.

'Endergebnis n final result.

'Endgeschwindigkeit f final velocity.

'endgültig I adj final: **e-e ~e Antwort** a definite answer. **II** adv a) finally, b) for good: **das steht ~ fest** that's final.

'Endgültigkeit f (-; no pl) finality.

Endivie [ɛn'diːvi̯ə] f (-; -n) ⚘ endive.

'Endkampf m sports: (**in den ~ kommen** reach the) final(s). **'Endlagerung** f ultimate disposal (of nuclear waste).

endlich ['ɛntlɪç] **I** adj final, ultimate, A, philos. finite. **II** adv finally, at last.

'endlos adj endless.

'**Endlosigkeit** f (-; no pl) endlessness.
'**Endlösung** f pol. hist. Final Solution.
endogen [ɛndo'geːn] adj endogenous.
Endoskop [ɛndo'skoːp] n (-s; -e) ♟ endoscope.
'**End|phase** f final stage. **~preis** m retail price. **~pro,dukt** n end product. **~reim** m end rhyme. **~resul,tat** n final result. **~runde** f sports: final(s). **~silbe** f final syllable. **~spiel** n sports: final(s): **ins ~ einziehen** go to the finals. **~spurt** m a. fig. final sprint, finish. **~stati,on** f 1. terminus. 2. fig. end of the road. **~summe** f (sum) total.
'**Endung** f (-; -en) ling. ending.
'**End|verbraucher** m end user. **~verstärker** m ⚡ output amplifier. **~ziel** n final objective, ultimate goal. **~ziffer** f last number. **~zweck** m final purpose.

Energie [enɛr'giː] f (-; -n) energy (a. fig.), ⚡ a. power. **Ener'giebedarf** m energy demand. **ener'giegeladen** adj fig. bursting with energy. **Ener'giekrise** f energy crisis. **ener'gielos** adj lacking in energy, weak. **Ener'gielosigkeit** f (-; no pl) lack of energy. **Ener'gie|poli,tik** f energy policy. **~quelle** f source of energy. **⚡sparend** adj energy-saving. **~verbrauch** m energy consumption. **~verschwendung** f waste of energy (fig. of effort). **~versorgung** f power supply. **~wirtschaft** f (-; no pl) energy industry.
energisch [e'nɛrgɪʃ] adj energetic, firm (words etc), strong (protest etc): **~ werden** put one's foot down.
eng [ɛŋ] adj 1. narrow (a. fig.), crowded, cramped, tight (skirt etc): **~er werden** narrow; **ein Kleid ~er machen** take a dress in; **auf ~em Raum zs.-leben** live crowded together; fig. **in ~en Grenzen** within narrow bounds; F **das wird zeitlich sehr ~ für mich** I've got a tight schedule already; F **das darf man nicht so ~ sehen!** let's be (more) broadminded!; → **Sinn** 5, **Wahl** 2. 2. fig. close (cooperation etc): **~ befreundet sein** be close friends; → **Kreis** 1.
Engagement [ãgaʒə'mãː] n (-s; -s) 1. thea. etc engagement. 2. pol. or fig. commitment. **engagieren** [ãga'ʒiːrən] (h) I v/t engage, employ, take s.o. on. II **sich ~** pol. or fig. get (or be) involved (in

dat in). **enga'giert** adj fig. dedicated, pol. committed.
'**enganliegend** adj tight(-fitting).
Enge ['ɛŋə] f (-; -n) 1. no pl narrowness (a. fig.), tightness: **in großer ~ leben** live in very cramped conditions; fig. **j-n in die ~ treiben** drive s.o. into a corner. 2. narrow passage, (of sea) strait.
Engel ['ɛŋəl] m (-s; -) angel: F **die ~ im Himmel singen hören** see stars.
'**engelhaft** adj angelic.
'**Engelsgeduld** f endless patience.
'**engherzig** adj small-minded. '**Engherzigkeit** f (-; no pl) small-mindedness.
Engländer ['ɛŋlɛndər] m (-s; -) 1. Englishman: **er ist ~** he is English; **die ~** the English. 2. ⊕ monkey wrench.
'**Engländerin** f (-; -nen) Englishwoman.
englisch ['ɛŋlɪʃ] adj English: **die ~e Staatskirche** the Anglican Church; (**gut**) **~ sprechen** speak English (well); **~ geschrieben** (written) in English.
'**Englisch** n (-[s]) English, the English language: **aus dem ~en übersetzt** translated from (the) English; **im ~en** in English; **er spricht gut(es) ~** he speaks good English.
'**englisch-'deutsch** adj 1. pol. Anglo--German. 2. ling. English-German.
'**Englischhorn** n ♪ cor anglais.
'**englischsprachig** adj English-language. '**englischsprechend** adj English-speaking. '**Englischunterricht** m English lesson(s).
'**engmaschig** [-maʃɪç] adj fine-meshed, fig. close-meshed.
'**Engpaß** m (-sses; ~sse) fig. a) bottleneck, b) supply shortfall. ↑
en gros [ã'gro] adv ♥ wholesale.
engstirnig ['ɛŋʃtɪrnɪç] adj narrow-minded. '**Engstirnigkeit** f (-; no pl) narrow-mindedness.
Enkel ['ɛŋkəl] m (-s; -) a) grandchild, b) grandson.
'**Enkelin** f (-; -nen) granddaughter.
Enklave [ɛn'klaːvə] f (-; -n) enclave.
enorm [e'nɔrm] adj enormous, huge, F terrific: **~ schnell** incredibly fast.
en passant [ãpa'sãː] adv in passing.
Ensemble [ã'sãːbl] n (-s; -s) 1. ♪, fashion: ensemble. 2. thea. a) company, b) cast.
entarten [ɛnt'ʔartən] v/i (sn) degenerate.

ent'artet I *pp of* **entarten. II** *adj* degenerate, *fig. a.* decadent.

Ent'artung *f* (-; -en) degeneration.

entband [ɛnt'bant] *pret of* **entbinden.**

entbehren [ɛnt'be:rən] *v/t* (h) **1.** do without: **kannst du ... ~?** can you spare ...? **2.** miss. **ent'behrlich** *adj* dispensable, expendable.

Ent'behrung *f* (-; -en) privation, want.

entbinden (entband, entbunden, h) **I** *v/t* **1.** ℳ deliver *woman* (**von** of): **entbunden werden von ...** give birth to ... **2.** *fig.* (**von** from) release, excuse. **II** *v/i* **3.** ℳ give birth to a child.

Ent'bindung *f* (-; -en) **1.** ℳ delivery. **2.** *fig.* release (**von** from).

Ent'bindungsklinik *f* maternity clinic.

Ent'bindungsstati|on *f* maternity ward.

ent'blättern (h) **I** *v/t* **1.** strip *s.th.* of leaves. **II** *sich ~* **2.** shed (its) leaves. **3.** *humor.* shed one's clothes, strip.

entblöden [ɛnt'blø:dən] (h) *sich nicht ~ zu inf* have the nerve to *inf.*

entblößen [ɛnt'blø:sən] *v/t* (h) bare.

ent'blößt I *pp of* **entblößen. II** *adj* bare.

ent'brennen *v/i* (entbrannte, entbrannt, sn) *fight etc:* break out, *a.* rage *etc:* flare up.

ent'decken *v/t* (h) a) discover, find out, b) see, spot: *zufällig ~* stumble (up)on.

Ent'decker *m* (-s; -) discoverer.

Ent'deckung *f* (-; -en) discovery.

Ent'deckungsreise *f a. fig.* expedition.

Ente ['ɛntə] *f* (-; -n) **1.** *zo.* duck: *junge ~* duckling; F *fig.* **lahme ~** lame duck. **2.** *gastr.* a) roast duck, b) *kalte ~* white wine cup with champagne. **3.** canard, hoax. **4.** ℳ (bed) urinal.

ent'ehren *v/t* (h) dishono(u)r, disgrace, degrade. **Ent'ehrung** *f* (-; -en) dishono(u)r(ing), degradation.

ent'eignen *v/t* (h) expropriate.

Ent'eignung *f* (-; -en) expropriation.

ent'eisen *v/t* (h) clear of ice, ⚙ defrost, de-ice. **Ent'eisung** *f* (-; *no pl*) ⚙ defrosting, de-icing.

'Enten|braten *m* roast duck. **~ei** *n* duck's egg. **~jagd** *f* duck shooting.

ent'erben *v/t* (h) disinherit.

Enterich ['ɛntərɪç] *m* (-s; -e) *zo.* drake.

entern ['ɛntərn] *v/t* (h) board.

entfachen [ɛnt'faxən] *v/t* (h) **1.** kindle (*fire*). **2.** *fig.* a) rouse, b) provoke.

ent'fallen *v/i* (entfiel, entfallen, sn) **1.** *es*

ist mir ~ it has slipped my memory; *der Name ist mir ~* the name escapes me. **2.** be cancel(l)ed: **entfällt** not applicable. **3.** *auf j-n ~* fall to s.o.

ent'falten (h) **I** *v/t* **1.** unfold (*a. fig.*), open, spread out. **2.** *fig.* develop (*talents etc*), launch into (*activity etc*), display (*pomp etc*). **II** *sich ~* **3.** *blossom etc:* open, unfold. **4.** *fig.* develop (**zu** into). **Ent'faltung** *f* (-; -en) **1.** unfolding. **2.** *fig.* a) development, b) display.

ent'färben *v/t* (h) remove the colo(u)r from, ⚗, ⚙ decolo(u)rize, bleach.

entfernen [ɛnt'fɛrnən] (h) **I** *v/t* remove: *j-n von der Schule ~* expel s.o. from school. **II** *sich ~* leave, go away.

ent'fernt *adj a. fig.* remote, distant, *a.* faint (*similarity etc*): *e-e Meile ~ von* a mile away from; *zwei Meilen voneinander ~* two miles apart; *(weit) ~* far away; *fig.* **weit davon ~ zu** *inf* far from *ger*; *~ verwandt* distantly related; *nicht im ~esten* not in the least.

Ent'fernung *f* (-; -en) **1.** a) distance, b) range: *in e-r ~ von* at a distance of; *aus der (einiger) ~* from the (a) distance; *aus kurzer ~* at close range. **2.** removal.

Ent'fernungs|messer *m phot.* range finder. **~skala** *f phot.* focus(s)ing scale.

ent'fesseln *v/t* (h) unleash, provoke: *e-n Krieg ~* start a war.

ent'fesselt *adj* raging (*elements etc*).

ent'fetten *v/t* (h) remove the grease (*or* fat) from, ⚙ degrease.

entfiel [ɛnt'fi:l] *pret of* **entfallen.**

ent'flammbar *adj* inflammable.

ent'flammen I *v/t* (h) **1.** ⚙ ignite. **2.** *fig.* inflame, rouse, kindle. **II** *v/i* (sn) → **1.**

ent'flechten *v/t* (entflocht, entflochten, h) ✞ decartelize.

ent'fliegen *v/i* (entflog, entflogen, sn) fly away (*dat* from).

entfliehen *v/i* (entfloh, entflohen, sn) (*aus* *dat* from) flee, escape.

entfremden [ɛnt'frɛmdən] (h) **I** *v/t* alienate (*dat* from). **II** *sich (j-m) ~* become estranged (from s.o.).

Ent'fremdung *f* (-; -en) estrangement, *a. sociol.* alienation.

ent'frosten *v/t* (h) ⚙ defrost.

Ent'froster *m* (-s; -) ⚙ defroster.

ent'führen *v/t* (h) kidnap, abduct, ✈ hijack. **Ent'führer** *m* (-s; -) kidnap-

(p)er, ✈ hijacker. **Ent'führung** f (-; -en) kidnap(p)ing, ✈ hijacking.

entgalt [ɛnt'galt] pret of **entgelten**.

entgangen [ɛnt'gaŋən] pp of **entgehen**.

ent'gegen I prep (dat) contrary to, against: ~ *allen Erwartungen* contrary to all expectations. II adv towards.

ent'gegenbringen v/t (irr, sep, -ge-, h, → *bringen*) *j-m Vertrauen (Zuneigung)* ~ show trust in (affection for) s.o.; *e-r Sache Interesse* ~ show an interest in s.th.

ent'gegengehen v/i (irr, sep, -ge-, sn, → *gehen*) (dat) 1. walk towards, go to meet. 2. fig. face (danger, the future, etc), be heading for (disaster etc): *dem Ende* ~ be drawing to a close.

ent'gegengesetzt adj 1. opposite. 2. fig. contrary, opposed (dat to), opposing.

ent'gegenhalten v/t (irr, sep, -ge-, h, → *halten*) fig. object (dat to): *dem ist nichts entgegenzuhalten* there is no objection to that.

ent'gegenkommen v/i (irr, sep, -ge-, sn, → *kommen*) *j-m* ~ come towards s.o., fig. oblige s.o., make s.o. concessions; *j-m auf halbem Wege* ~ esp. fig. meet s.o. halfways; *j-s Wünschen* ~ comply with s.o.'s wishes. **Ent'gegenkommen** n (-s) obligingness: ~ *zeigen* be willing to make concessions. **ent'gegenkommend** adj oncoming, fig. obliging.

ent'gegenlaufen v/i (irr, sep, -ge-, sn, → *laufen*) *j-m* ~ run towards s.o.

Ent'gegennahme [-na:mə] f (-; no pl) acceptance.

ent'gegennehmen v/t (irr, sep, -ge-, h, → *nehmen*) accept, take.

ent'gegensehen v/i (irr, sep, -ge-, h, → *sehen*) (dat) a) await, b) look forward (to), c) face.

ent'gegensetzen v/t (sep, -ge-, h) *Widerstand* ~ offer resistance (dat to).

ent'gegenstehen v/i (irr, sep, -ge-, h, → *stehen*) fig. stand in the way (dat of): *dem steht nichts entgegen* there's nothing to be said against that.

ent'gegenstellen: sich ~ (sep, -ge-, h) fig. (dat) resist, oppose.

ent'gegentreten v/i (irr, sep, -ge-, sn, → *treten*) 1. *j-m* ~ step (or walk) up to s.o., fig. oppose s.o. 2. take steps against (abuses etc), contradict (rumo[u]r).

ent'gegenwirken v/i (sep, -ge-, h) (dat)

work against, counteract, fight.

entgegnen [ɛnt'ge:gnən] v/i (h) a) reply (auf acc to), b) retort.

ent'gehen v/i (entging, entgangen, sn) escape (a. death etc): fig. *j-m* ~ escape s.o.('s notice); *sich et.* ~ *lassen* let s.th. slip; *er ließ sich die Gelegenheit nicht* ~ he seized the opportunity.

entgeistert [ɛnt'gaɪstərt] adj and adv dum(b)founded, aghast.

Entgelt [ɛnt'gɛlt] n (-[e]s; -e) a) remuneration, payment, b) pay, c) fee, ⚖ consideration, d) reward: *gegen* ~ against payment; *als* ~ *für* in consideration of.

ent'gelten v/t (entgalt, entgolten, h) *j-m et.* ~ pay s.o. for s.th.

entgiften [ɛnt'gɪftən] v/t (h) a) detoxicate, b) decontaminate (toxic waste etc), c) fig. clear (the atmosphere).

entging [ɛnt'gɪŋ] pret of **entgehen**.

entgleisen [ɛnt'glaɪzən] v/i (sn) 1. 🚂 run off the rails, be derailed. 2. fig. go too far, make a faux pas. **Ent'gleisung** f (-; -en) 1. 🚂 derailment. 2. fig. faux pas, gaffe.

ent'gleiten v/i (entglitt, entglitten, sn) *j-m* ~ slip out of s.o.'s hand(s), fig. slip away from s.o.

entgolten [ɛnt'gɔltən] pp of **entgelten**.

entgräten [ɛnt'grɛ:tən] v/t (h) bone.

ent'haaren v/t (h) depilate. **Ent'haarungscreme** f depilatory cream.

ent'halten (enthielt, enthalten, h) I v/t a) contain, hold, b) comprise: *mit* ~ *sein* be included (in dat in). II *sich* ~ abstain (gen from); *sich der Stimme* ~ abstain.

ent'haltsam adj abstinent, abstemious, sexually: continent.

Ent'haltsamkeit f (-; no pl) abstinence.

Ent'haltung f (-; parl. -en) abstention.

ent'härten v/t (h) soften (water).

enthaupten [ɛnt'haʊptən] v/t (h) behead, decapitate. **Ent'hauptung** f (-; -en) beheading, decapitation.

ent'häuten v/t (h) skin.

ent'heben v/t (enthob, enthoben, h) (gen) relieve (of), release (or exempt) (from), remove (from office).

enthielt [ɛnt'hi:lt] pret of **enthalten**.

enthüllen [ɛnt'hylən] (h) I v/t 1. unveil, bare, show. 2. fig. reveal, bring s.th. to light, expose. II *sich* ~ fig. reveal o.s., matter: be revealed (dat to). **Ent'hüllung** f (-; -en) 1. unveiling. 2. fig. disclosure, exposure. **Ent'hüllungsjourna,lismus** *m* investigative journalism.

Enthusiasmus [ɛntu'ziasmʊs] *m* (-; *no pl*) enthusiasm. **Enthusiast** [ɛntu'ziast] *m* (-en; -en), **Enthusi'astin** *f* (-; -nen) enthusiast, F fan. **enthusi'astisch** *adj* enthusiastic.

entjungfern [ɛnt'jʊŋfərn] *v/t* (h) deflower.

ent'kalken *v/t* (h) descale.

ent'kernen *v/t* (h) stone, core.

ent'kleiden *v/t* (h) **1.** (*a.* **sich ~**) undress. **2.** *fig.* (*gen* of) divest, strip.

ent'kommen *v/i* (entkam, entkommen, sn) ([*aus*] *dat* from) get away, escape. **Ent'kommen** *n* (-s) escape, F getaway.

ent'korken *v/t* (h) uncork.

entkräften [ɛnt'krɛftən] *v/t* (h) **1.** weaken, exhaust. **2.** *fig.* invalidate (*a.* ⚖️), refute. **Ent'kräftung** *f* (-; -en) **1.** a) weakening, b) weakness, exhaustion. **2.** *fig.* invalidation (*a.* ⚖️), refutation.

ent'laden (entlud, entladen, h) **I** *v/t* **1.** unload, *a.* ⚡ discharge. **2.** *fig.* give vent to, vent (*one's rage*). **II sich ~ 3.** *storm:* break. **4.** ⚡ discharge. **5.** *rifle etc:* go off. **6.** *fig. suspense:* be released, *rage:* erupt. **Ent'ladung** *f* (-; -en) **1.** unloading, *a.* ⚡ discharge. **2.** ⚡ explosion.

ent'lang *adv and prep* along: **die Straße ~** along (*or* down) the street; **hier ~, bitte!** this way, please! **ent'langgehen** *v/t* (*irr, sep,* -ge-, sn, → **gehen**) (*v/i* **an** *dat*) go (*or* walk) along.

entlarven [ɛn'larfən] *v/t* (h) unmask, expose. **Ent'larvung** *f* (-; -en) unmasking, exposure.

ent'lassen (entließ, entlassen, h) *v/t* **1.** a) dismiss, b) pension off: **j-n fristlos ~** dismiss s.o. without notice. **2.** (*aus dat* from) discharge (*patient etc*), release (*prisoner*). **Ent'lassung** *f* (-; -en) **1.** dismissal. **2.** (*aus dat* from) discharge, release. **Ent'lassungspa,piere** *pl* discharge papers.

ent'lasten *v/t* (h) relieve (*fig.* **von** of), ⚖️ exonerate, clear *s.o.* of a charge, ✝ give *s.o.* a release. **ent'lastend** *adj* ⚖️ exonerating. **Ent'lastung** *f* (-; -en) relief, ⚖️ exoneration, ✝ release. **Ent'lastungs|materi,al** *n* ⚖️ exonerating evidence. **~straße** *f* bypass. **~zeuge** *m* ⚖️ witness for the defen/ce (*Am.* -se). **~zug** *m* 🚂 relief train.

entlaubt [ɛnt'laʊpt] *adj* leafless, bare.

ent'laufen *v/i* (entlief, entlaufen, sn) run away (*dat* from).

entlausen [ɛnt'laʊzən] *v/t* (h) delouse.

entledigen [ɛnt'le:dɪgən] **sich ~** (h) (*gen*) **1.** get rid of, take off (*clothing*). **2.** carry out, discharge (*a task*), fulfil(l), meet (*an obligation*).

ent'leeren *v/t* (h) empty: **den Darm ~** evacuate (the bowels).

ent'legen *adj* remote, out-of-the-way.

ent'lehnen *v/t* (h) borrow *word etc* (*dat, aus, von* from).

ent'leihen *v/t* (h) (entlieh, entliehen, h) borrow (*aus, von* from).

entlief [ɛnt'li:f] *pret of* **entlaufen.**

entließ [ɛnt'li:s] *pret of* **entlassen.**

ent'loben: sich ~ (h) break off one's engagement.

ent'locken *v/t* (h) (*dat* from) elicit, draw.

ent'lohnen *v/t* (h) pay. **Ent'lohnung** *f* (-; -en) pay, payment, remuneration.

entlud [ɛnt'lu:t] *pret of* **entladen.**

ent'lüften *v/t* (h) deaerate, bleed (*brake*). **Ent'lüfter** *m* (-s; -) deaerator. **Ent'lüftung** *f* (-; -en) aeration, airing. **Ent'lüftungsschraube** *f* vent screw.

entmachten [ɛnt'maxtən] *v/t* (h) **j-n (et.) ~** deprive s.o. (s.th.) of his (its) power.

entmenscht [ɛnt'mɛnʃt] *adj* inhuman, brutish.

entmilitarisieren [ɛntmilitari'zi:rən] *v/t* (h) demilitarize. **Entmilitari'sierung** *f* (-; -en) demilitarization.

entmündigen [ɛnt'mʏndɪgən] *v/t* (h) (legally) incapacitate. **Ent'mündigung** *f* (-; -en) (legal) incapacitation.

entmutigen [ɛnt'mu:tɪgən] *v/t* (h) discourage, dishearten. **Ent'mutigung** *f* (-; -en) discouragement, disheartening.

entnahm [ɛnt'na:m] *pret of* **entnehmen.**

Ent'nahme *f* (-; -n) taking (*of samples*), withdrawal (*of money*).

entnazifizieren [ɛntnatsifi'tsi:rən] *v/t* (h) *hist.* denazify. **Entnazifi'zierung** *f* (-; -en) denazification.

ent'nehmen *v/t* (entnahm, entnommen, h) (*dat*) take (from, out of), borrow (from *a book etc*), quote (from): *fig.* **et. ~ aus** (*or* dat) learn (*or* gather) s.th. from.

ent'nerven *v/t* (h) enervate.

ent'ölen *v/t* (h) remove the oil from.

entper'sönlichen *v/t* (h) depersonaliz

entpoliti'sieren *v/t* (h) depoliticize.

entprivati'sieren *v/t* (h) deprivatize.

entpuppen [ɛnt'pʊpən] (h) *sich ~ als fig.* turn out to be.

ent'rahmen *v/t* (h) skim (*milk*).

entrann [ɛnt'ran] *pret of* **entrinnen**.

ent'rätseln *v/t* (h a) solve, unravel, b) decipher.

entrechten [ɛnt'rɛçtən] *v/t* (h) *j-n ~* deprive s.o. of his rights.

ent'reißen *v/t* (entriß, entrissen, h) *j-m et. ~ a. fig.* snatch s.th. from s.o.

ent'richten *v/t* (h) pay.

entriegeln [ɛnt'ri:gəln] *v/t* (h) unlock.

ent'rinnen *v/i* (entrann, entronnen, sn) (*dat* from) escape, get away.

Ent'rinnen *n* (-s) escape.

entriß [ɛnt'rɪs] *pret,* **ent'rissen** *pp of* **entreißen**.

ent'rollen *v/t* (h) unroll, unfurl.

ent'rosten *v/t* (h) remove the rust from.

ent'rücken *v/t* (h) (*dat* from) carry away. **ent'rückt** *adj* enraptured.

entrümpeln [ɛnt'rʏmpəln] *v/t* (h) clear out.

ent'rüsten (h) **I** *v/t* fill *s.o.* with indignation, shock, scandalize. **II** *sich ~* (*über acc*) get indignant (at *s.th.*, with *s.o.*), be shocked (at). **ent'rüstet** *adj* indignant, shocked. **Ent'rüstung** *f* (-; -en) indignation: *Schrei der ~* outcry.

entsaften [ɛnt'zaftən] *v/t* (h) extract the juice from. **Ent'safter** *m* (-s; -) juice extractor, juicer.

ent'sagen *v/i* (h) *e-r Sache ~* renounce s.th. **Ent'sagung** *f* (-; -en) renunciation. **ent'sagungsreich** *adj ein ~es Leben* a life full of privations.

entsann [ɛnt'zan] *pret of* **entsinnen**.

ent'schädigen *v/t* (h) (*für* for) compensate (*a. fig.*), reimburse: *die Aussicht entschädigte uns für den langen Aufstieg* the view made up for the long climb. **Ent'schädigung** *f* (-; -en) compensation (*a. fig.*), reimbursement.

ent'schärfen *v/t* (h) defuse (*a. fig. crisis etc*), deactivate (*ammunition*), *fig.* take the edge off (*a speech etc*).

Ent'scheid [ɛnt'ʃaɪt] *m* (-[e]s; -e) decree, decision. **ent'scheiden** (entschied, entschieden, h) **I** *v/t* decide, settle, 𝄐 rule (*über acc* on): *damit war die Sache entschieden* that settled it; *das mußt du ~* that's up to you. **II** *v/i* (*über*

acc) a) decide (on), b) be decisive (for). **III** *sich ~* be decided, *person:* decide, make up one's mind; *sich ~ für* decide on, settle on; *er entschied sich dagegen* he decided against it. **ent'scheidend** *adj* a) decisive, b) crucial (*moment etc*): *~e Stimme* casting vote.

Ent'scheidung *f* (-; -en) (*über acc* on) decision, 𝄐 *a.* ruling: *e-e ~ treffen* (*or fällen*) make (*or* come to) a decision.

Ent'scheidungs|bedarf *m* es besteht *~* this calls for a decision. **~freiheit** *f* freedom of choice. **~kampf** *m* **1.** ✕ decisive battle. **2.** *fig.* showdown. **~spiel** *n* *sports:* a) deciding match, decider, b) final. **~träger** *m* decision-maker.

entschied [ɛnt'ʃi:t] *pret of* **entscheiden**.

entschieden [ɛnt'ʃi:dən] **I** *pp of* **entscheiden**. **II** *adj* **1.** a) determined, firm, b) sta(u)nch (*supporter*), declared, decided (*enemy etc*). **2.** decided, definite. **II** *adv* **3.** firmly, decidedly, definitely: *ich bin* (*ganz*) *~ dafür* I'm strongly in favo(u)r of it, I'm all for it. **Ent'schiedenheit** *f* (-; *no pl*) determination, firmness: *mit* (*aller*) *~* categorically.

entschlacken [ɛnt'ʃlakən] *v/t* (h) **1.** ✪ remove the slag from. **2.** ✚ a) purify, b) purge. **Ent'schlackung** *f* (-; -en) ✚ a) purification, b) purge.

ent'schlafen *v/i* (sn) *fig.* pass away.

ent'schließen: sich ~ (entschloß, entschlossen, h) (*zu, für* on, *zu tun* to do) decide, make up one's mind; *sich anders ~* change one's mind. **Ent'schließung** *f* (-; -en) *pol.* resolution.

entschloß [ɛnt'ʃlɔs] *pret of* **entschließen**. **entschlossen** **I** *pp of* **entschließen**. **II** *adj* determined, firm, resolute: *zu allem ~ sein* be ready for anything; *kurz ~* without a moment's hesitation. **Ent'schlossenheit** *f* (-; *no pl*) determination, resolution, firmness.

Ent'schluß *m* (-sses; ⸰sse) decision: *e-n ~ fassen, zu e-m ~ kommen* make (*or* reach) a decision, make up one's mind.

entschlüsseln [ɛnt'ʃlʏsəln] *v/t* (h) decipher, decode.

entschuldbar [ɛnt'ʃʊltba:r] *adj* excusable. **entschuldigen** [ɛnt'ʃʊldɪgən] (h) **I** *v/t* excuse: *das ist nicht zu ~* that is impardonable; *bitte, ~ Sie mich* (*für heute abend*) I beg to be excused (for tonight). **II** *v/i ~ Sie!* a) excuse me!, b) sorry! III **sich ~** a) apologize (**bei j-m für et.** to s.o. for s.th.), b) excuse o.s. **ent'schuldigend** *adj* apologetic. **Ent'schuldigung** f (-; -en) a) excuse, b) apology: **j-n um ~ bitten** apologize to s.o. (**wegen** for); **als ~, zur ~** as an excuse (**für** for); **~!** → **entschuldigen** II. **Ent'schuldigungsgrund** m (**et. als ~ anführen** offer s.th. as an) excuse.

Entschwefelungsanlage [ɛnt'ʃveːfə-lʊŋs-] f ☼ desulphurization plant.

ent'setzen (h) I *v/t* horrify, shock, appal(l). II **sich ~** (**über** *acc* at) be horrified, be shocked. **Ent'setzen** n (-s) horror, terror. **entsetzlich** [ɛnt'zɛtslɪç] I *adj* horrible, terrible, atrocious. II *adv* terribly, F *a.* awfully (**cold, boring**, *etc*). **Ent'setzlichkeit** f (-; -en) a) terribleness, horribleness, b) atrocity.

entseuchen [ɛnt'zɔʏçən] *v/t* (h) decontaminate. **Ent'seuchung** f (-; -en) decontamination.

ent'sichern *v/t* (h) release the safety catch of (*a gun*), cock.

ent'sinnen: sich ~ (entsann, entsonnen, h) (*gen*) recall, recollect; **wenn ich mich recht entsinne** if I remember rightly.

ent'sorgen *v/t* (h) dispose of the nuclear (*or toxic etc*) waste (of a plant *etc*). **Ent'sorgung** f (-; -en) disposal of nuclear (*or toxic etc*) waste.

entspann [ɛnt'ʃpan] *pret of* **entspinnen**. **ent'spannen** (h) I **sich ~** relax, *person: a.* take it easy, *fig. situation etc:* ease off. II *v/t* relax. III *v/i* be relaxing. **Ent'spannung** f (-; -en) relaxation (*a. fig.*), *pol.* détente, ✚ easing. **Ent'spannungs|poli,tik** f policy of détente. **~übung** f relaxation exercise.

ent'spiegelt *adj* opt. antireflection.

ent'spinnen: sich ~ (entspann, entsponnen, h) (**aus** from) arise, develop.

ent'sprechen *v/i* (entsprach, entsprochen, h) (*dat*) **1.** a) correspond (to, with), agree (with), b) be equivalent (to): **er entspricht nicht der Beschreibung** he doesn't answer the description. **2.** a) meet, come up (to *expectations etc*), b) comply (with *a request*): **den Anforderungen nicht ~** fail to meet the requirements. **ent'sprechend** I *adj* (*dat* to) a) corresponding, b) appropriate, c) adequate, d) equivalent, e) respective. II *adv* correspondingly,

accordingly. III *prep* (*dat*) according to: **den Umständen ~** as can be expected under the circumstances.

ent'springen *v/i* (entsprang, entsprungen, sn) **1.** have its source (**in** *dat* in). **2.** (*dat*, **aus** from) spring, arise, come.

entstaatlichen [ɛnt'ʃtaːtlɪçən] *v/t* (h) denationalize. **Ent'staatlichung** f (-; -en denationalization.

ent'stammen *v/i* (sn) (*dat* from) descend, *fig.* come, derive.

ent'stehen *v/i* (entstand, entstanden, sn **1.** come into being, develop (**aus** from) **2.** arise, come about, *costs, problems etc:* (**aus, durch**) arise (*or* result (from), be caused (by). **3.** be created (*o* built, produced, written, composed painted). **Ent'stehen** n (-s) → **Entstehung: im ~ begriffen** in the making. **Ent'stehung** f (-; -en) a) coming into being, development, emergence, b) origin, beginning, c) creation.

Ent'stehungsgeschichte f genesis.

ent'steigen *v/i* (entstieg, entstiegen, sn (*dat*) get out of.

entsteinen [ɛnt'ʃtaɪnən] *v/t* (h) stone.

ent'stellen *v/t* (h) disfigure, *fig.* distort (*facts*), garble (*report*). **Ent'stellung** (-; -en) disfigurement, *fig.* distortion.

ent'stören *v/t* (h) ☄ radioshield, screen **Ent'störung** f (-; -en) screening, *radic* interference suppression.

ent'tarnen *v/t* (h) unmask, expose (*spy*)

ent'täuschen (h) I *v/t* disappoint, let s.c down. II *v/i* be disappointing. **Ent'täu schung** f (-; -en) disappointment.

ent'thronen *v/t* (h) *a. fig.* dethrone.

entvölkert [-'fœlkɛrt] *adj* depopulated.

ent'wachsen *v/i* (entwuchs, entwach sen, sn) **e-r Sache ~** grow out of s.th outgrow s.th.

entwaffnen [ɛnt'vafnən] *v/t* (h) disarm *fig.* **~des Lächeln** disarming smile.

entwand [ɛnt'vant] *pret of* **entwinden**.

entwarf [ɛnt'varf] *pret of* **entwerfen**.

ent'warnen *v/i* (h) give the all-clear.

Ent'warnung f (-; -en) all-clear (signal)

ent'wässern *v/t* (h) **1.** drain. **2.** 🜀 dehy drate. **Ent'wässerung** f (-; -en) ¹ draining. **2.** 🜀 dehydration. **Ent'wäs serungsanlage** f drainage system.

entweder ['ɛntveːdər] *conj* **~ ... ode** either ... or; **~ oder!** take it or leave it **'Entweder-'Oder** n **hier gibt es nu**

ein ~ you've got to decide one way or the other.

ent'weichen *v/i* (entwich, entwichen, sn) escape (*dat, aus* from).

ent'weihen *v/t* (h) desecrate.

Ent'weihung *f* (-; -en) desecration.

ent'wenden *v/t* (h) *j-m et.* ~ steal (*or* purloin) s.th. from s.o.

ent'werfen *v/t* (entwarf, entworfen, h) **1.** sketch, outline (*a. fig. a plan etc*), design. **2.** plan (*program[me] etc*), work out, devise (*plan*). **3.** draw up, draft (*contract*). **Ent'werfer(in** *f) m* designer.

ent'werten *v/t* (h) **1.** cancel (*ticket, stamp, etc*). **2.** ✝ a) demonetize, b) → *abwerten*. **3.** *fig.* devalue: (*völlig*) ~ invalidate. **Ent'wertung** *f* (-; -en) **1.** cancel(l)ation. **2.** *fig.* devaluation.

entwich [ɛnt'vɪç] *pret*, **ent'wichen** *pp of* **entweichen.**

ent'wickeln (h) **I** *v/t* **1.** develop (*a. phot.,* ⊙), *phys. a.* generate, evolve, work out (*plan, method, etc*): *er entwickelte mir s-e Theorie* he expounded his theory to me. **2.** display, show (*energy, an interest, etc*). **II** *sich* ~ (*aus, zu*) develop (from, into), grow (out of, into); *sich gut* ~ be shaping well.

Ent'wickler *m* (-s; -) *phot.* developer.

Ent'wicklung *f* (-; -en) development (*a. fig.*), *a.* trend, *a. biol.* evolution.

Ent'wicklungs|abteilung *f* planning department, Development. **~alter** *n* formative years, *n.s.* age of puberty. **≈fähig** *adj* capable of development, progressive (*post etc*). **~geschichte** *f* history, *biol.* genesis. **~helfer(in** *f) m* development aid worker, *Br.* member of the Voluntary Service Overseas, *Am.* Peace Corps Worker. **~hilfe** *f* development aid. **~jahre** *pl* → *Entwicklungsalter.* **~land** *n* developing country. **~poli,tik** *f* third world policy. **~pro,zeß** *m* (process of) development. **~stufe** *f* stage of development, phase. **~zeit** *f* **1.** period of development. **2.** → *Entwicklungsalter.* **3.** *phot.* developing time.

ent'winden *v/t* (entwand, entwunden, h) *j-m et.* ~ wrest s.th. from s.o.

ent'wirren *v/t* (h) disentangle, unravel.

ent'wischen *v/i* (sn) F (*dat* from) escape, slip away: *j-m* ~ *a.* give s.o. the slip.

entwöhnen [ɛnt'vøːnən] *v/t* (h) **1.** wean (*a baby*). **2.** *j-n* ~ cure s.o. (*gen of an*

addiction etc). **Ent'wöhnung** *f* (-; -en) **1.** weaning. **2.** curing, cure.

entworfen [ɛnt'vɔrfən] *pp of* **entwerfen.**

ent'würdigen *v/t* (h) degrade (*sich* o.s.).

ent'würdigend *adj* degrading.

Ent'würdigung *f* (-; -en) degradation.

Ent'wurf *m* (-[e]s; ⸗e) **1.** a) (first) draft, sketch, b) plan, blueprint, c) design, d) model. **2.** ✝, ⚖ draft, *parl.* bill.

Ent'wurfsstadium *n* planning stage.

ent'wurzeln *v/t* (h) *a. fig.* uproot.

ent'ziehen (entzog, entzogen, h) **I** *v/t* **1.** *j-m et.* ~ withdraw s.th. from s.o. (*a.* ⚗), withhold s.th. from s.o., deprive (*or* strip) s.o. of rights etc; *j-m den Führerschein (die Lizenz etc)* ~ revoke s.o.'s licen/ce (*Am.* -se); *et. j-s Zugriff (Einfluß)* ~ remove s.th. from s.o.'s reach (influence); *parl. etc j-m das Wort* ~ rule s.o. out of order. **2.** ⚗ extract (*dat* from). **II** *sich* ~ (*dat*) evade, avoid; → *Kenntnis.* **Ent'ziehung** *f* (-; -en) withdrawal (*a.* ⚗), deprivation.

Ent'ziehungs|anstalt *f* drying-out cent/re (*Am.* -er). **~erscheinung** *f* ⚕ withdrawal symptom. **~kur** *f* withdrawal treatment.

entziffern [ɛnt'tsɪfərn] *v/t* (h) **1.** decipher, *w.s.* make out. **2.** decode.

Ent'zifferung *f* (-; -en) **1.** deciphering. **2.** decoding.

entzücken [ɛnt'tsʏkən] *v/t* (h) charm, delight. **Ent'zücken** *n* (-s) delight (*über acc* at). **ent'zückend** *adj* charming, delightful, lovely, F sweet. **ent'zückt** *adj* delighted (*über acc* at, *von* with).

Ent'zug *m* (-[e]s; *no pl*) → *Entziehung.*

entzündbar [ɛnt'tsʏndbaːr] *adj* inflammable. **ent'zünden** (h) **I** *v/t* **1.** light. **II** *sich* ~ **2.** catch fire (*an dat* from). **3.** ⚕, ⊙ ignite. **4.** ⚗ become inflamed. **5.** *fig.* (*an dat* by) *passion etc*: be roused, *argument*: be sparked off. **ent'zündet** *adj* ⚕ inflamed, red (*eyes*). **ent'zündlich** *adj* ⚕ inflammatory. **Ent'zündung** *f* (-; -en) ⚕ inflammation. **ent'zündungshemmend** *adj* ⚕ antiphlogistic.

ent'zwei *adj pred* **1.** in two, in half. **2.** in pieces, broken. **ent'zweibrechen** (*irr, sep,* -ge-, → *brechen*) *v/t* (h), *v/i* (sn) break in two. **entzweien** [ɛnt'tsvaɪən] (h) **I** *v/t* divide: *Freunde* ~ turn friends against each other. **II** *sich* ~ fall out (*mit* with). **ent'zweigehen** *v/i* (*irr, sep,*

-ge-, sn, → **gehen**) break, go to pieces.
Ent'zweiung f (-; -en) split, rupture.
Enzephalitis [ɛntsefa'liːtɪs] f (-; -litiden
[-li'tiːdən] $\mathscr{F}$ encephalitis.
Enzian ['ɛntsiaːn] m (-s; -e) $\mathscr{Q}$ gentian.
Enzyklopädie [ɛntsyklopɛ'diː] f encyc-
clop(a)edia. **enzyklopädisch** [ɛntsy-
klo'pɛːdɪʃ] adj encyclop(a)edic.
Enzym [ɛn'tsyːm] n (-s; -e) biol. enzyme.
Epen ['eːpən] pl of **Epos.**
ephemer [efe'meːr] adj ephemeral.
Epidemie [epide'miː] f (-; -n) epidemic.
epidemisch [epi'deːmɪʃ] adj epidemic.
Epidermis [epi'dɛrmɪs] f (-; -men) $\mathscr{F}$ epi-
dermis.
Epigone [epi'goːnə] m (-n; -n) epigone.
Epigramm [epi'gram] n (-s; -e) epigram.
Epik ['eːpɪk] f (-; no pl) **1.** epic poetry. **2.**
narrative literature. **Epiker** m (-s; -) **1.**
epic poet. **2.** narrative author.
Epilepsie [epilɛp'siː] f (-; -n) $\mathscr{F}$ epilepsy.
Epileptiker [epi'lɛptɪkər] m (-s; -),
Epi'leptikerin f (-; -nen), **epileptisch**
[epi'lɛptɪʃ] adj epileptic.
Epilog [epi'loːk] m (-s; -e) epilog(ue Br.).
episch ['eːpɪʃ] adj epic.
Episode [epi'zoːdə] f (-; -n) episode.
epi'sodenhaft adj episodic.
Epoche [e'pɔxə] f (-; -n) epoch.
e'pochemachend adj epoch-making.
Epos ['eːpɔs] n (-; Epen) epic (poem).
er [eːr] pers pron he, it. **es ist es!** it's him!
Er m (-; -s) F **es ist ein** ~ it's a he.
Er'achten [ɛr-] n **m-s** ~**s** in my opinion.
er'arbeiten v/t (h) **1.** (a. **sich** ~) work
(hard) for, acquire. **2.** a) compile, b)
develop.
Erbadel ['ɛrp-] m hereditary nobility.
'Erbanlage f genetic make-up, $\mathscr{F}$ hereditary disposition.
'Erbanspruch m hereditary title.
erbarmen [ɛr'barmən] (h) **I** v/t **j-n** ~
move s.o. to pity. **II sich** ~ (gen) take
pity (on). **Er'barmen** n (-s) pity, com-
passion: **kein** ~ **kennen** be merciless.
erbärmlich [ɛr'bɛrmlɪç] **I** adj **1.** pitiful,
a. miserable, wretched, a. paltry. **2.**
mean, vile. **3.** F terrible, awful. **II** adv **4.**
pitifully (etc). **5.** F awfully: ~ **wenig**
precious little. **Er'bärmlichkeit** f (-; no
pl) pitifulness, miserableness (etc).
er'barmungslos adj merciless.
er'bauen (h) **I** v/t **1.** build, erect. **2.** fig.
edify: F **er ist nicht besonders erbaut**

davon he's not exactly enthusiasti
about it. **II sich** ~ (an dat by) be de
lighted, be edified. **Er'bauer** m (-s; ~
a) builder, b) founder. **er'baulich** ac
edifying (a. iro.), eccl. devotional.
Er'bauung f (-; no pl) **1.** building, con
struction, erection. **2.** fig. edification.
Erbe[1] ['ɛrbə] m (-n; -n) heir, successo
(j-s of or to s.o., a. fig.): ~ **e-s Vermö**
gens heir (or successor) to an estate
j-n zum ~**n einsetzen** make s.o. one'
heir. **'Erbe**[2] n (-s; no pl) inheritance, fig
heritage. **'erben** v/t (h) inherit (a. fig.)
a. come into (money). **'Erbengemein**
schaft f $\mathfrak{z\bar{z}}$ community of heirs.
er'betteln v/t (h) (**sich** et.) ~ get s.th. b
begging, b.s. scrounge s.th. (**von** off)
erbeuten [ɛr'bɔytən] v/t (h) χ capture
'Erbfaktor m gene. **'Erbfehler** m hered
tary defect. **'Erbfeind** m sworn enemy
'Erbfolge f (**gesetzliche** ~ intestate
succession. **'Erbgut** n biol. genotype.
Erbin ['ɛrbɪn] f (-; -nen) heiress.
erbittern [ɛr'bɪtərn] v/t (h) anger. **er'bi**
tert adj **1.** fierce (enemy, fight, etc). **2**
embittered (**über** acc at, by). **Er'bitte**
rung f (-; no pl) **1.** bitterness. **2.** anger
'Erbkrankheit f hereditary disease.
'Erblasser ['ɛrplasər] m (-s; -), **'Erb**
lasserin f (-; -nen) $\mathfrak{z\bar{z}}$ a) the deceased
b) testator (testatrix). **'Erblast** f fig
(evil) legacy. **erblich** ['ɛrplɪç] adj hered
itary, inheritable (title etc): ~ **belaste**
$\mathscr{F}$ subject to a(n) hereditary taint.
er'blicken v/t (h) see, catch sight of.
erblinden [ɛr'blɪndən] v/i (sn) go blind
Er'blindung f (-; -en) going blind, loss c
(one's) sight.
er'blühen v/i (sn) blossom (fig. **zu** into
'Erbmasse f **1.** $\mathfrak{z\bar{z}}$ estate. **2.** biol. geneti
make-up. **'Erbonkel** m F rich uncle.
er'brechen (erbrach, erbrochen, h)
v/t **1.** break open, force (door), ope
(letter). **2.** $\mathscr{F}$ vomit, bring up. **II** v/i (
sich ~) $\mathscr{F}$ vomit, be sick. **Er'brechen**
(-s) $\mathscr{F}$ vomiting: fig. **bis zum** ~ ad nau
seam.
'Erbrecht n $\mathfrak{z\bar{z}}$ **1.** law of succession. **2**
hereditary title.
'Erbschaft f (-; -en) inheritance: **e-e**
machen inherit; **e-e** ~ **antreten** suc
ceed to an estate.
'Erbschaftssteuer f death duties.
'Erbschein m certificate of heirship.

Erbschleicher ['ɛrpʃlaɪçər] *m* (-s; -) *contp.* legacy-hunter.
Erbse ['ɛrpsə] *f* (-; -n) pea.
'Erbsensuppe *f* pea soup.
'Erbstück *n* heirloom. **'Erbsünde** *f* *eccl.* original sin. **'Erbtante** *f* F rich aunt. **'Erbteil** *n* share of the inheritance.
Erd|achse ['e:rt-] *f* earth's axis. **~anziehungskraft** *f* gravity. **~arbeiten** *pl* excavations. **~atmo,sphäre** *f* (earth's) atmosphere. **~bahn** *f* earth's orbit. **~ball** *m* (-[e]s; *no pl*) globe, *w.s.* earth.
~beben *n* (-s; -) earthquake. **~gebiet** *n* **1.** earthquake area. **2.** area hit by an earthquake. **~herd** *m* seismic focus.
'Erdbeere *f* (-; -n) strawberry.
'Erd|bevölkerung *f* population of the earth. **~bewohner** *m* inhabitant of the earth. **~boden** *m* ground, earth: *dem ~ gleichmachen* raze *s.th.* to the ground; *es (er) war wie vom ~ verschluckt* he (it) had vanished (into thin air).
Erde ['e:rdə] *f* (-; -n) **1.** earth, soil, ground: *über der ~* above ground. **2.** *no pl* (planet) earth: *auf ~n* on earth; *auf der ganzen ~* all over the world. **3.** ⚡ (*a.* **an ~ legen**) earth, Am. ground.
'erden *v/t* (h) ⚡ earth, Am. ground.
erdenklich [ɛr'dɛŋklɪç] *adj* imaginable, conceivable: *sich alle ~e Mühe geben* do one's utmost.
Erdgas *n* natural gas.
Erdgeschichte *f* history of the earth.
Erdgeschoß *n* ground (Am. first) floor.
er'dichten *v/t* (h) make up, invent.
erdig ['e:rdɪç] *adj* earthy.
Erdinnere *n* interior of the earth.
Erdkabel *n* underground cable.
Erdkruste *f* crust of the earth.
Erdkugel *f* globe, *w.s.* earth.
Erdkunde *f* (-; *no pl*) geography.
erdkundlich *adj* geographic(al).
Erdnuß(butter) *f* peanut (butter).
Erdoberfläche *f* surface of the earth.
Erdöl *n* (mineral) oil, petroleum.
erdolchen [ɛr'dɔlçən] *v/t* (h) *j-n ~* stab s.o. to death.
erdreich *n* (-[e]s; *no pl*) earth, soil.
erdreisten [ɛr'draɪstən] *sich ~* (h) dare (or have the cheek) (*zu inf* to *inf*).
erdrosseln [ɛr'drɔsəln] *v/t* (h) strangle.
er'drücken *v/t* (h) crush *s.o.* (to death), *fig.* crush, overwhelm: *von Arbeit erdrückt werden* be swamped with work.

er'drückend *adj* *fig.* overwhelming (*majority etc*), damning (*evidence*).
'Erdrutsch *m* *a. pol.* landslide.
'Erdschicht *f* layer of the earth, stratum.
'Erdstoß *m* seismic shock.
'Erdteil *m* continent.
er'dulden *v/t* (h) endure, suffer.
'Erdumdrehung *f* rotation of the earth.
'Erdumkreisung *f* orbit around the earth.
'Erdung *f* (-; -en) ⚡ earth(ing), Am. ground(ing).
'Erdwärme *f* geothermal energy.
er'eifern: sich ~ (h) get excited (*or* worked up) (*über acc* about).
ereignen [ɛr'ʔaɪɡnən] *sich ~* (h) happen, occur, take place. **Ereignis** [ɛr'ʔaɪɡnɪs] *n* (-ses; -se) a) event, b) incident, c) great event, sensation. **er'eignislos** *adj* uneventful. **er'eignisreich** *adj* very eventful, exciting.
er'eilen *v/t* (h) *j-n ~* catch up with s.o.
Erektion [ɛrɛk'tsi̯o:n] *f* (-; -en) erection.
Eremit [ere'mi:t] *m* (-en; -en) hermit.
er'erbt *adj* inherited, *biol. a.* hereditary.
er'fahren (erfuhr, erfahren, h) **I** *v/t* **1.** hear, be told, find out. **2.** a) experience, b) suffer, c) receive. **II** *v/i* **3.** *~ von* get to know about, hear about (*or* that). **III** *adj* **4.** experienced, seasoned: *~ sein in* (*dat*) be well versed in, be an old hand at. **Er'fahrenheit** *f* (-; *no pl*) experience.
Er'fahrung *f* (-; -en) experience: *technische ~* a. know-how; *aus (eigener) ~* from experience; *durch ~ klug werden* learn the hard way; *in ~ bringen* learn, find out; *die ~ machen, daß ...* find that ...; *die ~ hat gezeigt, daß ...* past experience has shown that ...
Er'fahrungs|austausch *m* exchange of experience. **2gemäß** *adv* as experience shows, we know from experience.
erfand [ɛr'fant] *pret of* **erfinden.**
er'fassen *v/t* (h) **1.** seize, grasp, take: *er wurde vom Auto erfaßt* he was hit by the car; *Furcht erfaßte sie* she was seized with fear. **2.** grasp, understand: *er hat's erfaßt!* he's got it! **3.** a) register, record, b) include, cover: *zahlenmäßig ~* count; *steuerlich ~* tax.
Er'fassung *f* (-; -en) a) registration, b) inclusion, coverage.
er'finden *v/t* (erfand, erfunden, h) a) invent, b) make *s.th.* up. **Er'finder** *m*

inventor. **Er'findergeist** m (-[e]s; no pl) inventiveness. **er'finderisch** adj inventive, imaginative, resourceful: → **Not** 2. **Er'findung** f (-; -en) invention, fig. contp. a. fabrication. **Er'findungsgabe** f inventive talent, imagination.

Erfolg [ɛr'fɔlk] m (-[e]s; -e) a) success, achievement, b) result, outcome, effect: **guter** ~ good result; **es war ein großer** ~ it was a great success; ~ **haben** succeed, be successful; **k-n** ~ **haben** be unsuccessful, fail; **es zu e-m** ~ **gestalten** make a success of it; **mit dem** ~, **daß** ... with the result that ...

er'folgen v/i (sn) 1. follow. 2. take place, happen, payment: be made.

er'folglos adj unsuccessful, fruitless.

Er'folglosigkeit f (-; no pl) failure.

er'folgreich adj successful.

Er'folgs|aussichten pl chances of success. **~autor** m best-selling author. **~beteiligung** f profit-sharing. **~chance** f chance (of success). **~erlebnis** n 1. success experience. 2. → **~gefühl** n sense of achievement. **~kurs** m auf ~ on the road to success (or victory). **~mensch** m go-getter. **~quote** f success rate. **~ro₁man** m best-selling novel. **~typ** m born winner, achiever. **~zwang** m unter ~ stehen be under pressure to succeed (or do well).

er'folgversprechend adj promising.

erforderlich [ɛr'fɔrdərlıç] adj necessary, required: **unbedingt** ~ essential.

er'fordern v/t (h) require, call for, a. take (time, courage, etc).

Erfordernis [ɛr'fɔrdərnıs] n (-ses; -se) requirement, demand, prerequisite.

er'forschen v/t (h) investigate, study, research, explore. **Er'forscher** m explorer. **Er'forschung** f (-; -en) (gen) investigation (of, into), research (into), exploration (of).

er'fragen v/t (h) ask (for).

er'freuen (h) **I** v/t please. **II sich** ~ **an** (dat), **sich** ~ (gen) enjoy. **erfreulich** [ɛr'frɔylıç] adj a) pleasant, pleasing, welcome (news etc), b) encouraging.

er'freulicherweise adv fortunately.

er'frieren (erfror, erfroren) **I** v/i (sn) freeze to death, plants: be killed by frost: **ihm sind zwei Finger erfroren** he lost two fingers through frostbite. **II**

v/t (h) **sich die Ohren erfroren habe** have frostbitten ears.

Er'frierung f (-; -en) 🦶 frostbite.

erfrischen [ɛr'frıʃən] v/t (h) refresh (**sic** o.s.). **er'frischend** adj refreshing.

Er'frischung f (-; -en) refreshment.

Er'frischungs|getränk n 1. soft drink 2. cool drink. **~raum** m refreshmen room. **~tuch** n moistened tissue.

erfuhr [ɛr'fuːr] pret of **erfahren**.

er'füllen (h) **I** v/t 1. a. fig. fill (**mit** with **ein erfülltes Leben** a full life; **s-e Ar beit erfüllt ihn** he finds his work ver satisfying. 2. fulfil(l) (duty, contrac etc), grant (a wish), meet (condition expectations, etc), keep (promise): **s- Zweck** ~ serve its purpose. **II sich** ~ come true. **Er'füllung** f (-; -en) fu fil(l)ment: **in** ~ **gehen** come true.

Er'füllungsort m ✝, ⚖ place of fu fil(l)ment.

erfunden I pp of **erfinden**. **II** adj imag nary, contp. fictitious, (all) made up

ergaben [ɛr'gaːbən] pp of **ergeben**.

ergänzen [ɛr'gɛntsən] v/t (h) 1. comple ment (**sich** or **einander** one another 2. a) complete, b) supplement, add: **e laufend** ~ keep s.th. up to date. 3. r plenish (supplies etc). **er'gänzend I** a a) complementary, b) supplementar c) additional. **II** adv in addition.

Er'gänzung f (-; -en) 1. a) completio b) supplementation, c) addition. complement (a. ling., Ⓐ), supplemen addition, parl. amendment. **Er'gä zungsband** m (-[e]s; ⸚e) supplement

ergattern [ɛr'gatərn] v/t (h) F (manag to) get hold of.

er'geben (ergab, ergeben, h) **I** v/t 1. result in, b) come to, c) yield. 2. sho prove. **II sich** ~ 3. a) (dat to) esp. surrender, capitulate, b) (in acc) resi o.s. (to), c) (dat) take to (drink[ing] et 4. problems etc: arise, discussion et ensue: **sich** ~ **aus** result (or arise) fron **daraus ergibt sich, daß** ... it follov that ...; **es hat sich so** ~ it just hap pened that way. **III** adj 5. (dat to) loyal, devoted, b) resigned, c) addicte

Er'gebenheit f (-; no pl) a) devotio loyalty, b) resignation.

Ergebnis [ɛr'geːpnıs] n (-ses; -se) resu outcome, a. findings (of investigation sports: a. score.

er'gebnislos adj without result: ~ **bleiben** (or **verlaufen**) come to nothing.

Er'gebung f (-; no pl) **1.** esp. ✕ surrender. **2.** resignation (in acc to).

er'gehen (erging, ergangen) **I** v/i (sn) **1.** (an acc to) order etc: be issued, invitation etc: be sent. **2.** ⚖ law: come out, decision, judg(e)ment: be passed. **3.** et. über sich ~ lassen endure s.th. **II** ~ (h) a) hold forth (über acc on a subject), b) indulge (in dat in conjectures etc). **III** v/impers **es ist ihm schlecht ergangen** he had a bad time of it; **wie ist es dir ergangen?** how did you fare?; **mir ist es genauso ergangen** it was the same with me.

ergiebig [ɛrˈgiːbɪç] adj **1.** productive (a. fig.), rich (deposits etc), lucrative (business etc), fruitful (subject etc). **2.** economical.

er'gießen: sich ~ (ergoß, ergossen, h) (in, über acc) pour (into, over).

ergötzen [ɛrˈgœtsən] **sich ~** (h) (an dat) a) be amused (by), b) gloat (over).

er'grauen v/i (sn) (turn) grey (Am. gray): **im Dienst ergraut** grown old in service.

er'greifen v/t (ergriff, ergriffen, h) **1.** seize, a. arrest (criminal). **2.** take (measures etc): → **Besitz** 1, **Flucht**[1], **Wort** 2. **3.** a) overcome, seize, b) move: **Angst ergriff sie** she was seized with fear. **er'greifend** adj moving.

ergriffen [ɛrˈgrɪfən] **I** pp of **ergreifen**. **II** adj moved.

Er'griffenheit f (-; no pl) emotion.

er'gründen v/t (h) get to the bottom of.

Er'guß m (-sses; ·sse) **1.** ✸ a) effusion (of blood), b) ejaculation. **2.** fig. effusion, a. iro. outpouring.

Er'gußgestein n geol. effusive rock.

er'haben adj **1.** ⊚ raised, embossed. **2.** fig. lofty, sublime, grand. **3.** fig. ~ **über** (acc) above, beyond (reproach etc).

Er'habenheit f (-; no pl) grandeur.

er'halten (erhielt, erhalten, h) **I** v/t **1.** get, receive, obtain: **e-n Preis ~** be awarded (or given) a prize. **2.** keep, maintain, preserve: **j-n am Leben ~** keep s.o. alive; **das erhält jung** that keeps you young; **j-m das Augenlicht ~** save s.o.'s eyesight. **3.** keep, support (family etc). **II sich ~** a) survive, b) subsist (von on). **III** adj **gut ~ sein** be in

good condition; ~ **bleiben** survive; **noch ~ sein** remain, be left.

erhältlich [ɛrˈhɛltlɪç] adj obtainable, available: **schwer ~** hard to get hold of.

Er'haltung f (-; no pl) preservation, maintenance, upkeep.

er'hängen v/t (h) hang (**sich** o.s.).

er'härten v/t (h) corroborate, confirm.

er'haschen v/t (h) catch.

er'heben (erhob, erhoben, h) **I** v/t **1.** raise (a. fig. one's voice, objections, etc), lift (up): **j-n in den Adelsstand ~** raise s.o. to the peerage; → **Anklage**, **Anspruch**. **2.** levy, impose (duties, taxes), charge (a fee). **II sich ~ 3.** rise (to one's feet), get up. **4.** hill, house, etc: rise (über dat above). **5.** wind, fig. doubts, shouting, etc: arise. **6.** rise (in arms), revolt. **er'hebend** adj edifying.

erheblich [ɛrˈheːplɪç] **I** adj a) considerable, b) important. **II** adv considerably: ~ **besser** much better.

Er'hebung f (-; -en) **1.** elevation, rise (in the ground). **2.** elevation (in den Adelsstand to a peerage). **3.** levy (of duties, taxes), charge (of fees). **4.** statistics: survey: **~en anstellen** (über acc) make investigations (about), investigate (into). **5.** uprising, revolt.

erheitern [ɛrˈhaɪtərn] v/t (h) amuse.

Er'heiterung f (-; no pl) amusement.

erhellen [ɛrˈhɛlən] (h) **I** v/t light up, illuminate, fig. shed light (up)on. **II sich ~** brighten.

erhielt [ɛrˈhiːlt] pret of **erhalten**.

erhitzen [ɛrˈhɪtsən] (h) **I** v/t heat (up): **die Gemüter ~** make feelings run high. **II sich ~** get hot, fig. get heated (person: excited). **er'hitzt** adj hot, person: a. flushed, fig. heated (debate etc).

erhob [ɛrˈhoːp] pret of **erheben**.

erhoben [ɛrˈhoːbən] pp of **erheben**.

er'hoffen v/t (h) (a. **sich ~**) hope for.

er'hofft adj hoped-for.

erhöhen [ɛrˈhøːən] (h) **I** v/t raise (a. fig. **auf** acc to, **um** by), fig. a. increase, intensify, enhance, heighten. **II sich ~** increase, price etc: rise, go up.

Er'höhung f (-; -en) **1.** raising. **2.** rise, increase (gen in), fig. a. intensification, enhancement, heightening; → **Gehalts-**, **Lohnerhöhung**.

er'holen: sich ~ (h) a) recover (**von** from, a. ✝), b) take a rest, relax: **du**

siehst sehr erholt aus you look very rested (or fit). **er'holsam** adj restful, relaxing. **Er'holung** f (-; no pl) **1.** a) recovery (**von** from, a. ✝), b) rest, relaxation. **2.** holiday, Am. vacation.

Er'holungs|aufenthalt m holiday, Am. vacation. 2**bedürftig** adj in need of a rest (or holiday). **~gebiet** n recreation area. **~heim** n rest home. **~ort** m (health or holiday) resort. **~pause** f rest, breather. **~reise** f holiday (Am. vacation) trip. **~urlaub** m holiday, Am. vacation, ✕ convalescent leave. **~wert** m recreational value. **~zentrum** n recreation park.

er'hören v/t (h) hear, answer (prayer).

erigieren [eri'gi:rən] (sn) become erect.

Erika ['e:rika] f (-; -s, -ken) ⚘ heather.

erinnern [ɛr'ʔɪnərn] (h) **I** v/t **j-n** ~ remind s.o. (**an** acc of); **j-n daran** ~, **daß** remind s.o. that. **II** sich ~ (**an** acc) remember, recall; **wenn ich mich recht erinnere** if I remember rightly; **soviel ich mich** ~ **kann** as far as I remember. **III** v/i ~ **an** (acc) remind one of, fig. a. be suggestive of. **Er'innerung** f (-; -en) a) memory, recollection, reminiscence (all: **an** acc of), b) memento, souvenir, keepsake, c) reminder: **~en** reminiscences, memoirs; **zur** ~ **an** (acc) in memory of; **in guter** ~ **behalten** have fond memories of.

Er'innerungstafel f memorial tablet.

Er'innerungsvermögen n memory.

Er'innerungswert m sentimental value.

erkalten [ɛr'kaltən] v/i (sn) **1.** get cold. **2.** fig. cool (off).

erkälten [ɛr'kɛltən] sich ~ (h) catch a cold; (**stark**) **erkältet sein** have a (bad) cold. **Er'kältung** f (-; -en) cold.

er'kämpfen v/t (h) gain (or win) (after a hard struggle): **sich et. hart** ~ **müssen** have to struggle hard for s.th.

er'kaufen v/t (h) buy: **et. teuer** ~ **müssen** (have to) pay a high price for s.th.; **j-s Schweigen** ~ bribe s.o. into silence.

er'kennbar adj **1.** recognizable. **2.** discernible, to be seen.

er'kennen (erkannte, erkannt, h) **I** v/t **1.** a) recognize (**an** dat by), b) make out, see, c) detect, ✕ spot, d) identify, ✄ diagnose: ~ **an** (dat) a. know by; ~ **lassen** show, reveal; **zu** ~ **geben** indicate, give to understand; **sich zu** ~ **geben**

disclose one's identity; ⚖ **j-n für schu dig** ~ find s.o. guilty. **2.** realize, see. v/i **3.** ⚖ ~ **über** (acc) decide on; ~ **a** (acc) pass a sentence of.

er'kenntlich adj **sich** (**j-m**) ~ **zeige** show (s.o.) one's gratitude.

Er'kenntnis f (-; -se) a) knowledge, realization, c) idea, d) discovery: **neu ste** the latest findings; **zu der gelangen, daß** (come to) realize tha

Er'kennung f (-; no pl) a) recognition, identification.

Er'kennungs|dienst m criminal iden fication department. **~marke** f identi disc, Am. identification tag. **~melo,d** f signature tune. **~wort** n passwor **~zeichen** n **1.** sign to be recognized **2.** ✔ identification sign.

Erker ['ɛrkər] m (-s; -) △ oriel.

'Erkerfenster n bay window.

erklärbar [ɛr'klɛ:rba:r] adj explainabl

er'klären (h) **I** v/t **1.** explain (**j-m et.** s. to s.o.): **kannst du mir ~, warum?** c you tell me why?; **ich kann es mir nic** ~ I don't understand it. **2.** a) interpr b) illustrate (**an e-m Beispiel** by example). **3.** declare, pronounce: ~ **für gesund** ~ pronounce s.o. health ⚖ **er wurde für tot erklärt** he was cl clared dead; → **Einverständnis Rücktritt** 1. **II** sich ~ a) declare o. explain o.s., b) be explained; **sich** ~ **f (gegen)** declare for (against); **sich e verstanden** ~ consent (**mit** to); **si solidarisch** ~ declare one's solidar (**mit** with). **er'klärend** adj explanator

er'klärlich adj **1.** explainable. **2.** und standable. **er'klärlicherweise** adv u derstandably (enough).

er'klärt adj declared (enemy etc).

Er'klärung f (-; -en) **1.** (**zur** ~ by way explanation (**für** of). **2.** a. pol. declara tion, statement: **e-e** ~ **abgeben** mak statement (**zu** on).

er'klettern v/i (h) climb (up).

er'klingen v/i (erklang, erklungen, s be heard, sound, ring out.

er'kranken v/i (sn) fall ill (or sick) (**an** dat with), organ: be diseased: ~ **an** (d a. get, come down with; **erkrankt se an** (dat) a. have. **Er'krankung** f (-; -e illness, sickness, disease (of an orga

erkunden [ɛr'kʊndən] v/t (h) explore, reconnoit/re (Am. -er), find out,

erkundigen [ɛr'kʊndɪgən] *sich ~* (h) (*über acc* about) ask, inquire, make inquiries; *sich nach dem Weg ~* ask the way; *sich nach j-m* (*or j-s Befinden*) *~* inquire after s.o. **Er'kundigung** *f* (-; -en) inquiry: *~en einziehen* make inquiries (*über acc* about).

Er'kundung *f* (-; -en) ⚔ reconnaissance.

erlag [ɛr'laːk] *pret of* **erliegen**.

er'lahmen *v/i* (sn) **1.** grow weary, tire. **2.** *fig.* interest, zeal, *etc*: flag, wane.

er'langen *v/t* (h) a) get, obtain, b) attain, reach, c) gain, acquire.

Erlaß [ɛr'las] *m* (-sses; -sse) **1.** (*gen*) release (from *debts etc*), remission (of *penalty etc*). **2.** a) issuing, enactment (of *a law*), b) decree.

er'lassen *v/t* (erließ, erlassen, h) **1.** issue, publish (*ordinance*), enact (*a law*). **2.** remit (*penalty*), waive (*fees*): *j-m et. ~* release s.o. from s.th.

erlauben [ɛr'laʊbən] *v/t* (h) allow, permit (*j-m et.* s.o. to do s.th.): *j-m ~, et. zu tun a.* give s.o. permission to do s.th.; *~ Sie, daß ich rauche?* may I smoke?; *wenn Sie ~* if you don't mind; *sich ~ zu inf* take the liberty of *ger, b.s. a.* dare (to) *inf*; *~ Sie mal!, was ~ Sie sich?* who do you think you are?; *er kann sich das ~ w.s.* he can get away with it.

Erlaubnis [ɛr'laʊpnɪs] *f* (-; *no pl*) permission: *j-n um ~ bitten* ask s.o.'s (*or* s.o. for) permission (*et. zu tun* to do s.th.); *die ~ erhalten* be given permission.

er'läutern *v/t* (h) explain, comment (up)on: *durch Beispiele ~* illustrate. **er'läuternd** *adj* explanatory, illustrative. **Er'läuterung** *f* (-; -en) a) explanation, b) illustration, c) note.

Erle ['ɛrlə] *f* (-; -n) ⚘ alder.

er'leben *v/t* (h) a) experience, live (*adventures etc*), c) go through (*bad times etc*), d) live to see, e) see: *ich habe (es) selbst erlebt, was es heißt, arm zu sein* I know from experience what it means to be poor; *ich habe es oft erlebt(, daß)* I've often seen it happen (that); *wir werden es ja ~!* we'll see!

Erlebnis [ɛr'leːpnɪs] *n* (-ses; -se) a) experience, b) event, c) adventure. **er'lebnisreich** *adj* eventful.

erledigen [ɛr'leːdɪgən] (h) **I** *v/t* **1.** a) finish (off), b) deal with, take care of, c) settle (*problem, deal, etc*), d) carry out

(*order, task*): *würden Sie das für mich ~?* would you do that for me? **2.** dismiss. **3.** F *j-n ~* finish s.o. (*a. sports*), a. do s.o. in. **II** *sich selbst ~* take care of itself, F sort itself out. **er'ledigt** *adj* **1.** settled, finished: *das wäre ~!* that's that!; *das ist für mich ~* the matter's closed as far as I'm concerned; F *du bist für mich ~!* I'm through with you! **2.** F *person*: a) finished, b) done in, whacked: *der ist ~!* he's done for!

Er'ledigung *f* (-; -en) **1.** *no pl* settlement: *zur umgehenden ~* for immediate attention. **2.** *pl* errands, shopping.

er'legen I *pp of* **erliegen. II** *v/t* (h) hunt. shoot, kill.

erleichtern [ɛr'laɪçtərn] *v/t* (h) a) make *a task* easier, facilitate, b) lighten (*a burden*), c) relieve (*need, pain, etc*), ease (*one's conscience*): *sich das Herz ~* unburden one's heart; *das erleichterte mich sehr* that was a great relief to me; F *j-n ~ um ...* relieve s.o. of *wallet etc*.

er'leichtert *adj* relieved: *ich war ~, als ...* it was a relief to me when ...; *~ aufatmen* breathe a sigh of relief.

Er'leichterung *f* (-; -en) **1.** facilitation, lightening, easing. **2.** *no pl* relief (*über acc* at): *zu m-r ~* to my relief. **3.** *pl* ✝, *pol.* relief, facilities.

er'leiden *v/t* (erlitt, erlitten, h) a) suffer, go through, b) sustain: *den Tod ~* die. **erlernbar** [ɛr'lɛrnbaːr] *adj* learnable.

er'lernen *v/t* (h) learn.

er'lesen *adj* select, choice, exquisite.

er'leuchten *v/t* (h) **1.** light (up), illuminate. **2.** *fig.* enlighten. **Er'leuchtung** *f* (-; -en) **1.** illumination. **2.** *fig.* a) enlightenment, b) idea, inspiration.

er'liegen *v/i* (erlag, erlegen, sn) (*dat*) succumb (to *temptation etc*), be the victim (of *a mistake etc*). **Er'liegen** *n* (-s) *zum ~ kommen* break down; *et. zum ~ bringen* bring s.th. to a standstill.

erließ [ɛr'liːs] *pret of* **erlassen.**

erlitt [ɛr'lɪt] *pret of* **erleiden.**

erlogen [ɛr'loːgən] *adj* made(-)up: *das ist ~* that's a lie.

Erlös [ɛr'løːs] *m* (-es; -e) proceeds.

erloschen [ɛr'lɔʃən] **I** *pp of* **erlöschen. II** *adj* **1.** extinct. **2.** *fig.* dead. **3.** *contract etc*: expired.

er'löschen *v/i* (erlosch, erloschen, sn)

go out, *a. fig. life:* be extinguished, *contract etc:* expire.

Er'löschen *n* (-s) a) extinction, b) expiry.

er'lösen *v/t* (h) (**von** from) a) release, free, b) rescue: *j-n ~ iro.* put s.o. out of his (her) misery, *eccl.* save (*or* redeem) s.o.; *er ist erlöst* his sufferings are over. **er'lösend** *adj das ~e Wort sprechen* break the tension; *ein ~es Gefühl* a great relief. **Er'lösung** *f* (-; -en) **1.** release. **2.** *eccl.* salvation. **3.** relief.

ermächtigen [ɛr'mɛçtigən] *v/t* (h) authorize (*j-n zu et.* s.o. to do s.th.).

Er'mächtigung *f* (-; -en) **1.** authorization. **2.** authority.

er'mahnen *v/t* (h) admonish (*j-n zur Vorsicht etc* s.o. to be careful *etc*), caution, warn (*a. sports*).

Er'mahnung *f* (-; -en) admonition, warning, *esp. sports:* (first) caution.

Er'mangelung: *in ~* (*gen*) for want of.

er'mäßigen (h) **I** *v/t* reduce, cut: *zu ermäßigten Preisen* at reduced prices. **II** *sich ~* be reduced (*auf acc* to).

er'messen *v/t* (ermaß, ermessen, h) a) estimate, assess, b) judge, c) appreciate, realize. **Er'messen** *n* (-s) judg(e)ment, discretion: *ich stelle es in Ihr ~* I leave it to you(r discretion); *das liegt ganz in Ihrem ~ a.* it's entirely up to you. **Er'messensfrage** *f* matter of opinion. **Er'messensspielraum** *m* latitude.

ermitteln [ɛr'mɪtəln] (h) **I** *v/t* a) find out, establish, locate (*place etc*), b) determine. **II** *v/i police:* investigate, carry out investigations (*gegen* concerning). **Er'mittlung** *f* (-; -en) **1.** a) finding out *s.th.*, b) determination. **2.** investigation, inquiry: *~en anstellen* a) make inquiries (*über acc* about), b) → *ermitteln* II. **3.** *pl* findings. **Er'mittlungs|ausschuß** *m* fact-finding committee. **~beamte** *m* investigating officer. **~verfahren** *n* 🏛 preliminary proceedings.

ermöglichen [ɛr'mø:klɪçən] *v/t* (h) a) make *s.th.* possible, b) allow: *j-m ~, et. zu tun* make it possible for (*or* enable) s.o. to do s.th.

er'morden *v/t* (h) murder. **Er'mordete** *m, f* (-n; -n) (murder) victim. **Er'mordung** *f* (-; -en) murder.

ermüden [ɛr'my:dən] *v/t* (h), *v/i* (sn) tire. **er'müdend** *adj* tiring. **er'müdet** *adj*

tired. **Er'müdung** *f* (-; *no pl*) tiredness *a.* 🔧 fatigue. **Er'müdungserschei-nung** *f a.* 🔧 sign of fatigue.

ermuntern [ɛr'montərn] *v/t* (h) **1.** encourage *s.o.* (*zu et., et. zu tun* to do s.th.). **2.** stimulate. **er'munternd** *adj* encouraging. **Er'munterung** *f* (-; -en) **1.** encouragement. **2.** stimulation.

ermutigen [ɛr'mu:tɪgən] *v/t* (h) encourage *s.o.* (*zu et., et. zu tun* to do s.th.). **er'mutigend** *adj* encouraging, reassuring. **Er'mutigung** *f* (-; -en) (*zur ~ as an*) encouragement.

er'nähren (h) **I** *v/t* a) feed, nourish, b) support: *schlecht ernährt* malnourished. **II** *sich ~* (*von*) live (on), *fig.* make a living (by). **Er'nährer** *m* (-s; -) **Er'nährerin** *f* (-; -en) supporter, breadwinner. **Er'nährung** *f* (-; *no pl*) **1.** a) feeding, 🌱 nutrition, b) food: *schlechte ~* malnutrition. **2.** support. **Er'nährungs|weise** *f* eating habits. **~wissenschaft** *f* (-; *no pl*) dietetics. **~wissenschaftler(in** *f) m* dietician.

er'nennen *v/t* (ernannte, ernannt, h) appoint (*j-n zu et.* s.o. to s.th.). **Er'nennung** *f* (-; -en) appointment (*zum ~* as *or* to the post of).

erneuern [ɛr'nɔyərn] (h) **I** *v/t* renew (*contract, offer, etc*), **b)** replace, *fig. a.* revive. **II** *sich ~* be renewed, revive. **Er'neuerung** *f* (-; -en) renewal, 🔧 *a.* replacement, *fig. a.* revival.

erneut [ɛr'nɔyt] **I** *adj* renewed, new, repeated, fresh. **II** *adv* again, once more.

erniedrigen [ɛr'ni:drɪgən] (h) **I** *v/t* **1.** a) degrade, b) humiliate. **2.** → *herabsetzen* 2. **II** *sich ~* degrade o.s.: *sich* (*so weit*) *~, et. zu tun* lower o.s. to do s.th. **er'niedrigend** *adj* degrading, humiliating. **Er'niedrigung** *f* (-; -en) a) degradation, b) humiliation.

ernst [ɛrnst] **I** *adj* serious, a. earnest, b) a. grave, solemn, c) *a.* severe, d) *a.* weighty: *~e Musik* serious music. **II** *adv* seriously (*etc*), in earnest: *ich meine es ~* I'm serious about it, I mean it; **b)** (*et.*) *~ nehmen* take s.o. (s.th.) seriously; *das war nicht ~ gemeint!* I (*etc*) didn't mean it!

Ernst *m* (-es; *no pl*) seriousness, *a.* earnestness, gravity, severity: *allen ~es* in all seriousness; *~ machen mit* go ahead with; *ich meine es im ~, es ist mein voller ~* I'm dead serious.

'**Ernstfall** *m* emergency: *im ~* a) in case of emergency, b) if things come to the worst, c) ✕ in the event of a war.

'**ernstgemeint** *adj* serious, sincere.

'**ernsthaft** *adj* serious: *sich ~e Sorgen machen um* be seriously worried about.

'**Ernsthaftigkeit** *f* (-; *no pl*) seriousness.

'**ernstlich** I *adj* serious. II *adv ~ krank* seriously ill; *~ böse* really angry.

'**ernstzunehmend** *adj* serious.

Ernte ['ɛrntə] *f* (-; -n) **1.** *a. fig.* harvest. **2.** crop. '**Ernteausfall** *m* crop failure. '**Erntedankfest** *n* harvest festival. **ernten** ['ɛrntən] *v/t, v/i* (h) harvest, reap (*a. fig.*). '**Ernteschäden** *pl* crop damage. '**Erntezeit** *f* harvest time.

er'nüchtern (h) sober: *fig.: j-n ~ a.* bring s.o. down to earth again.

Er'nüchterung *f* (-; -en) **1.** sobering-up. **2.** *fig.* disillusionment.

Er'oberer *m* (-s; -) conqueror. **erobern** [ɛr'ʔoːbərn] *v/t* (h) *a. fig.* conquer: → **Sturm** 2. **Er'oberung** *f* (-; -en) (*fig. e-e ~ machen* make) a conquest.

er'öffnen (h) I *v/t* **1.** open, inaugurate: ✕ *das Feuer ~* open fire. **2.** *fig.* open (up), offer (*prospects etc*). **3.** *j-m et. ~* disclose s.th. to s.o., inform s.o. of s.th. II *v/i* open (*a. at chess*). III *sich ~ opportunity etc*: present itself.

Er'öffnung *f* (-; -en) **1.** opening (*a. at chess*), inauguration. **2.** disclosure. **Er'öffnungs|ansprache** *f* inaugural address. **~beschluß** *m* ⚖ **1.** order to proceed. **2.** bankruptcy order. **~feier** *f* opening ceremony. **~kurs** *m* ✝ opening quotation.

erogen [ero'geːn] *adj* erogenous.

erörtern [ɛr'ʔœrtərn] *v/t* (h) discuss. **Er'örterung** *f* (-; -en) discussion (*gen* of).

Erosion [ero'zi̯oːn] *f* (-; -en) erosion.

Erotik [e'roːtɪk] *f* (-; *no pl*) eroticism.

erotisch [e'roːtɪʃ] *adj* erotic.

erpicht [ɛr'pɪçt] *adj ~ sein auf* (*acc*) be very (F dead) keen on, be bent on.

er'preßbar *adj* open to blackmail.

er'pressen *v/t* (h) *j-n ~* blackmail s.o. (*et. zu tun* into doing s.th.); *et. ~* extort s.th. (*von* from). **Er'presser** *m* (-s; -), **Er'presserin** *f* (-; -nen) blackmailer. **Er'presserbrief** *m* blackmail letter.

Er'pressung *f* (-; -en) blackmail. **Er'pressungsversuch** *m* blackmail attempt.

er'proben *v/t* (h) try (out), test. **er'probt** *adj* **1.** well-tried. **2.** experienced.

Er'probung *f* (-; -en) trial, test.

errang [ɛr'raŋ] *pret of* **erringen**.

er'raten *v/t* (erriet, erraten, h) guess.

er'rechnen *v/t* (h) work out, calculate: *sich ~ aus* be calculated from.

erregbar [ɛr're:kbaːr] *adj* a) excitable, b) irritable. **Er'regbarkeit** *f* (-; *no pl*) a) excitability, b) irritability. **er'regen** (h) I *v/t* **1.** excite (*a. ⚥, a. sexually*), *b.s.* irritate, infuriate. **2.** *fig.* cause: *j-s Zorn ~* provoke s.o.'s anger; *Bewunderung ~* excite admiration; → **Ärgernis, Aufsehen**. II *sich ~* (*über acc* about) a) get excited, get all worked up, b) get angry.

er'regend *adj* exciting. **Er'reger** *m* (-s; -) **1.** *a. ⚥* exciter. **2.** 💊 pathogen, germ. **er'regt** *adj* excited (*a. sexually*), heated (*debate etc*). **Er'regung** *f* (-; -en) **1.** creation, excitation (*a. ⚥*), causing. **2.** excitement, *sexually: a.* (state of) arousal. **3.** anger.

erreichbar [ɛr'raɪçbaːr] *adj* a) within reach, *fig.* attainable, b) available: *leicht ~* within easy reach; *zu Fuß (mit dem Wagen) leicht ~* within easy walking (driving) distance; *er ist nie ~* you just can't get hold of him. **er'reichen** *v/t* (h) **1.** a) reach, catch (*bus, train, etc*), b) catch up with: *j-n telefonisch ~* get s.o. on the phone; *ein hohes Alter ~* live to an old age; *leicht zu ~* within easy reach. **2.** *fig.* a) achieve, b) obtain, get: *et. ~* get somewhere; *(es) ~, daß ...* succeed in *ger*; *haben Sie (bei ihm) et. erreicht?* did you get anywhere (with him)? **Er'reichung** *f* (-; *no pl*) attainment: *nach ~ der Altersgrenze* on reaching the retirement age.

er'richten *v/t* (h) **1.** build, erect, put up. **2.** *fig.* found, *esp.* ✝ set up. **Er'richtung** *f* (-; *no pl*) **1.** building, erection. **2.** *fig.* foundation.

erriet [ɛr'riːt] *pret of* **erraten**.

er'ringen *v/t* (errang, errungen, h) gain, *a.* win (*prize*), *a.* achieve (*success*).

er'röten *v/i* (sn) blush (*vor* with, *über acc* at).

Errungenschaft [ɛr'rʊŋənʃaft] *f* (-; -en) **1.** acquisition. **2.** *fig.* achievement.

ersah [ɛr'za:] *pret of* **ersehen.**

Ersatz [ɛr'zats] *m* (-es; *no pl*) **1.** substitute, replacement(s ✕): **als ~ für j-n** to replace s.o.; **er (das) ist kein ~ für ...** he (that) can't replace ... **2.** ✝, ⚔ a) compensation, b) damages: **als ~ für** by way of compensation, in exchange (*or* return) for. **~anspruch** *m* claim for compensation. **~bank** *f sports*: substitutes' bench. **~batterie** *f* spare battery. **~befriedigung** *f psych.* compensation. **~handlung** *f psych.* displacement activity, *w.s.* compensation. **~kasse** *f* health insurance society. **~leistung** *f* compensation. **~mann** *m* substitute (*a. sports*), replacement (*a.* ✕). **~mine** *f* refill. **~mittel** *n* substitute, ersatz. **~mutter** *f* mother-substitute.

er'satzpflichtig *adj* liable for damages.
Er'satzreifen *m* spare tyre (*Am.* tire).
Er'satzspieler(in *f*) *m sports*: substitute.
Er'satzteil *m, n* ⚙ replacement part, spare (part). **~chirurgie** *f* spare parts surgery. **~lager** *n* spare parts store.
er'satzweise *adv* alternatively.
ersaufen *v/i* (ersoff, ersoffen, sn) F drown.
ersäufen [ɛr'zɔyfən] *v/t* (h) drown.
er'schaffen *v/t* (erschuf, erschaffen, h) create, make.
Er'schaffung *f* (-; *no pl*) creation.
er'scheinen *v/i* (erschien, erschienen, sn) **1.** appear (*a.* ghost: *j-m* to s.o.), come, F turn up: **vor Gericht ~** appear in court. **2.** appear, come out, be published: **soeben erschienen** just published. **3.** (*j-m* to s.o.) seem, appear: **es erscheint ratsam** it would seem advisable. **Er'scheinen** *n* (-s) **1.** appearance, *a.* publication. **2.** attendance (**bei** at).
Er'scheinung *f* (-; -en) **1.** a) appearance, b) apparition, c) vision: **in ~ treten** appear, *fig. a.* make itself felt; **stark (kaum) in ~ treten** be very (not) much in evidence; **er tritt kaum in ~** he keeps very much in the background. **2.** *fig.* sign, symptom (*a.* ✚). **3.** a) (outward) appearance, b) figure. **Er'scheinungsjahr** *n* year of publication.
er'schießen (erschoß, erschossen, h) **I** *v/t* shoot (dead): **j-n ~ lassen** have s.o. shot. **II sich ~** shoot o.s.
Er'schießung *f* (-; -en) shooting, ✕ execution (by a firing squad).

erschlaffen [ɛr'ʃlafən] *v/i* (sn) *muscles etc*: grow tired, *skin*: (begin to) sag.
er'schlagen (erschlug, erschlagen, h) **I** *v/t* kill. **II** *adj* **F wie ~** a) dum(b)founded, b) dead-beat, whacked.
er'schleichen *v/t* (erschlich, erschlichen, h) **sich ~** obtain s.th. by trickery; **sich j-s Vertrauen ~** worm o.s. into s.o.'s confidence.
er'schließen (erschloß, erschlossen, h) **I** *v/t* open (up) (*a.* market etc), develop (*area, building estates*). **II sich j-m ~** *mystery etc*: be revealed to s.o., *opportunities etc*: open up before s.o.
Er'schließung *f* (-; -en) opening (up) development.
er'schöpfen (h) **I** *v/t a. fig.* exhaust. **II sich ~** exhaust o.s., *fig.* be exhausted **sich ~ in** (*dat*) *activity etc*: be limited to **er'schöpfend** *adj* **1.** exhausting. **2.** exhaustive. **er'schöpft** *adj* a) exhausted (**von** by), b) spent. **Er'schöpfung** *f* (-; *no pl*) exhaustion: **bis zur ~** to the point of) exhaustion. **Er'schöpfungszustand** *m* (stat of) exhaustion.
erschoß [ɛr'ʃɔs] *pret*, **er'schossen** *pp c* **erschießen.**
er'schrecken[1] *v/t* (h) frighten, scare startle: **→ Tod. er'schrecken**[2] *v/i* (er schrak, erschrocken, sn) be frightene (**über** *acc* at). **Er'schrecken** *n* (-s fright. **er'schreckend** *adj* frightening appalling: **~ wenige** alarmingly few.
erschrocken [ɛr'ʃrɔkən] **I** *pp of* e **schrecken**[2]. **II** *adj and adv* frightened
erschuf [ɛr'ʃu:f] *pret of* **erschaffen.**
erschüttern [ɛr'ʃʏtərn] *v/t* (h) **1.** *a. fi* shake. **2.** *fig.* a) shock, b) move s. deeply. **er'schütternd** *adj* a) shockin b) deeply moving. **Er'schütterung** *f* -en) a) shock (*a. fig.*), b) *fig.* emotio
erschweren [ɛr'ʃve:rən] *v/t* (h) a) mak s.th. (more) difficult, complicate, in pede, b) *a.* ⚔ aggravate.
er'schwerend *adj* ⚔ aggravating.
er'schwindeln *v/t* (h) **sich et. von j-m** cheat s.th. out of s.o.
erschwinglich [ɛr'ʃvɪŋlɪç] *adj* with s.o.'s means: **zu ~en Preisen** at reaso able prices.
er'sehen *v/t* (ersah, ersehen, h) (a from) see, gather.
er'sehnen *v/t* (h) long for.
ersetzbar [ɛr'zɛtsba:r] *adj* replaceab

(*a.* ⊗), reparable (*damage*), recoverable (*loss*). **er'setzen** *v/t* (h) a) replace (*durch* by), *a.* take the place of *s.o.*, b) compensate for, make up for: **j-m den Schaden (die Auslagen)** ~ compensate s.o. for the damage (reimburse s.o. for expenses). **Er'setzung** *f* (-; -en) a) replacement, b) compensation, reimbursement (*of expenses*).

er'sichtlich *adj* apparent, evident, clear: **ohne** ~**en Grund** for no apparent reason; **daraus wird** ~ hence it appears.

ersoff [ɛr'zɔf] *pret of* **ersaufen**.

ersoffen [ɛr'zɔfən] *pp of* **ersaufen**.

er'spähen *v/t* (h) F spot.

er'sparen *v/t* (h) **1.** (*a.* sich ~) save. **2.** *fig.* sich et. ~ spare o.s. s.th.; **j-m Arbeit (Kosten etc)** ~ save s.o. work (money etc); **ihr bleibt nichts erspart** she gets all the bad news.

Er'sparnis [ɛr'ʃpaːrnɪs] *f* (-; -se) **1.** saving (**an** *dat* in). **2.** *pl* savings.

ersprießlich [ɛr'ʃpriːslɪç] *adj* fruitful, profitable.

erst [ɛrst] *adv* a) (at) first, b) first, c) only, just, d) only, not till, no until: (**eben**) ~ just (now); ~ **als** (**dann, jetzt**) only when (then, now); ~ **nächste Woche** not before next week; ~ **nach** only (*or* not until) after; **es ist** ~ **fünf Uhr** it's only five o'clock; **ich muß** ~ **telefonieren** I've got to make a phone call first.

erstach [ɛr'ʃtaːx] *pret of* **erstechen**.

erstand [ɛr'ʃtant] *pret of* **erstehen**.

erstanden [ɛr'ʃtandən] *pp of* **erstehen**.

er'starken [ɛr'ʃtarkən] *v/i* (sn) grow strong(er).

er'starren *v/i* (sn) a) grow stiff, stiffen, go numb (*with cold*), b) 🔥 *etc* solidify, *blood*: coagulate, c) freeze (*a. fig.* **vor** *dat* with), *fig.* run cold: **vor Schreck** ~ *a.* be paralysed with fear. **er'starrt** *adj* stiff, numb, *fig.* paralysed. **Er'starrung** *f* (-; *no pl*) a) stiffness, numbness, b) 🔥 solidification, c) *fig.* paralysis, rigidity.

erstatten [ɛr'ʃtatən] *v/t* (h) **1.** refund (*j-m* to s.o.). **2.** **Anzeige** ~ **gegen** report s.o. to the police; → **Bericht.**

Er'stattung *f* (-; -en) refund(ing).

Erstaufführung *f thea. etc* première, *film:* a. first run.

er'staunen I *v/t* (h) astonish, amaze. II *v/i* → **staunen** I. **Er'staunen** *n* (-s) astonishment, amazement: **in** ~ **setzen**

astonish, amaze; (**sehr**) **zu m-m** ~ (much) to my surprise. **er'staunlich** *adj* astonishing, amazing. **er'staunlicherweise** *adv* astonishingly, to my *etc* surprise (*or* amazement). **er'staunt** *adj* (**über** *acc* at) astonished, amazed.

'Erstausgabe *f* first edition.

'erst'beste I *adj* the first, F any (old). II **der** (**die**) ~ the first person one happens to see, just anyone; **das** ~ the next best (F any old) thing *etc*.

erste ['eːrstə] *adj* first: **Karl der** ⅔ (**Karl I.**) Charles the First (Charles I); ~ **Qualität** prime quality; **der** ⅔ **des Monats** the first (day) of the month; ~ **beste** → **erstbeste; als** ~(**r**), **als** ~ first; **er war der** ~ he was first; **er war der** ~**, der ...** he was the first to *inf*; **fürs** ~ for the moment; → **Blick** 1, **Geige, Hand, Hilfe** 1 *etc.*

er'stechen *v/t* (erstach, erstochen, h) stab *s.o.* (to death).

er'stehen (erstand, erstanden) I *v/i* (sn) rise, be built. II *v/t* (h) buy, get.

er'steigen *v/t* (erstieg, erstiegen, h) climb (up to), ascend.

er'steigern *v/t* (h) buy at an auction.

Er'steigung *f* (-; -en) ascent, climbing.

er'stellen *v/t* (h) **1.** erect, build. **2.** prepare, draw up (*report etc*).

erstemal ['eːrstəmaːl] *adv* **das** ~ the first time; **beim erstenmal** the first time; **zum erstenmal** for the first time.

erstens ['eːrstəns] *adv* first(ly), first of all.

'erster → **erste.**

erstere ['eːrstərə] *adj* the former.

'erstgeboren *adj* first-born.

'Erstgeburtsrecht *n* birthright.

'erstgenannt *adj* first-mentioned.

ersticken [ɛr'ʃtɪkən] I *v/t* (h) suffocate, choke, *a. fig.* smother, stifle: → **Keim** 1. II *v/i* (sn) suffocate (**durch, an** *dat* from): **an e-r Gräte** ~ choke (to death) on a bone; *fig. in* **Arbeit** ~ be swamped with work. **Er'sticken** *n* (-s) suffocation: **zum** ~ (**heiß**) stifling(ly) hot. **er'stickend** *adj a. fig.* stifling. **Er'stickung** *f* (-; *no pl*) suffocation. **Er'stickungs|anfall** *m* choking fit. ~**tod** *m* death from suffocation.

erstieg [ɛr'ʃtiːk] *pret of* **ersteigen.**

erstiegen [ɛr'ʃtiːgən] *pp of* **ersteigen.**

'erstklassig *adj* first-class, first-rate, top-quality (*goods etc*).

Erstling ['e:rstlɪŋ] *m* (-s; -e) **1.** first-born child. **2.** *fig.* first work.
erstmalig ['e:rstma:lɪç] **I** *adj* first. **II** *adv, a.* **'erstmals** for the first time.
'Erstmeldung *f* exclusive report, F scoop.
erstochen [ɛr'ʃtɔxən] *pp of* **erstechen.**
er'strahlen *v/i* (sn) shine.
erstrangig [ɛr'ʃtraŋɪç] *adj* first-rate.
er'streben *v/t* strive after, aim for.
er'strebenswert *adj* desirable.
er'strecken: sich ~ a) (*bis zu*) to extend, stretch, b) *fig.* (*über acc*) cover (*area etc*), c) *fig.* (*auf acc*) concern, apply to.
'Erstschlag *m* ✗ first strike.
er'stürmen *v/t* (h) (take by) storm.
Er'stürmung *f* (-; -en) storming.
'Erstwähler (*in f*) *m* first-time voter.
er'suchen *v/t* (h) *j-n ~ zu inf* ask (*or* request) s.o. to *inf*; *j-n um et. ~* request s.th. from s.o. **Er'suchen** *n* (-s; -) (*auf sein ~ hin* at his) request.
er'tappen *v/t* (h) catch (*bei* at): *j-n beim Stehlen ~* catch s.o. stealing.
er'teilen *v/t* **1.** give (*lessons, advice, etc*): ✝ *j-m e-n Auftrag ~* place an order with s.o.; *j-m das Wort ~* ask s.o. to speak. **2.** (*dat*) grant (*s.o. a patent etc*), confer (*a right etc* on *s.o.*).
Ertrag [ɛr'tra:k] *m* (-[e]s; ⁓e) **1.** yield, ✗ *etc* output. **2.** (*aus* from) proceeds, returns.
er'tragen *v/t* (ertrug, ertragen, h) a) endure, bear, stand, b) put up with: *das ist kaum noch zu ~* that is hardly bearable; *ich kann die Gedanken nicht ~, daß ...* I can't bear to think that ...
er'tragfähig *adj* **1.** ✓ productive. **2.** ✝ profit-yielding.
erträglich [ɛr'trɛ:klɪç] **I** *adj* bearable, tolerable. **II** *adv* tolerably well.
er'tragreich *adj* productive, profitable.
Er'tragslage *f* ✝ profit situation.
er'tränken *v/t* (h) drown (*sich* o.s.).
er'träumen *v/t* (h) *sich et. ~* dream of.
er'trinken *v/i* (ertrank, ertrunken, sn) drown, be drowned.
ertrug [ɛr'tru:k] *pret of* **ertragen.**
Ertüchtigung [ɛr'tʏçtɪgʊŋ] *f* (-; -en) physical training.
erübrigen [ɛr'ʔy:brɪgən] (h) **I** *v/t* save (*money*), spare (*time*). **II** *sich ~* be unnecessary, be superfluous.
eruieren [eru'i:rən] *v/t* (h) find out.

Eruption [erʊp'tsĭo:n] *f* (-; -en) eruptio⟨
er'wachen *v/i* (sn) wake up (*a. fig.* awake, *fig.* feelings *etc*: be awaken⟨ *suspicion etc*: be aroused. **Er'wachen** (-s) (*fig. unsanftes ~* rude) awakenin⟨
er'wachsen[1] *v/i* (erwuchs, erwachse⟨ sn) arise (*aus* from).
er'wachsen[2] *adj*, **Er'wachsene** *m*, (-n; -n) grown-up, adult. **Er'wachse⟨ nenbildung** *f* adult education.
erwägen [ɛr've:gən] *v/t* (erwog, erw⟨ gen, h) consider, think *s.th.* over: *de⟨ Kauf e-s Autos ~* consider buying a ca⟨ **Er'wägung** *f* (-; -en) (*et. in ~ ziehen* ta⟨ *s.th.* into) consideration.
er'wähnen *v/t* (h) mention.
er'wähnenswert *adj* worth mentionir⟨
Er'wähnung *f* (-; -en) mention.
erwarb [ɛr'varp] *pret of* **erwerben.**
er'wärmen (h) **I** *v/t* warm (up): *fig. j⟨ für et. ~* get s.o. interested in s.th. **sich ~** get warm(er); *fig. sich für et.⟨* warm to s.th.
er'warten *v/t* (h) a) expect, b) wait fc⟨ *fig. j-n ~ surprise etc*: be in store for s.c⟨ *ein Kind ~* be expecting (a baby); i⟨ *kann es kaum ~* (*zu inf*) I can hard⟨ wait (to *inf*); *das war zu ~* that was ⟨ be expected. **Er'warten** *n* (-s) *üb⟨ alles ~* beyond all expectation; *wider ⟨* contrary to all expectations.
Er'wartung *f* (-; -en) a) expectation, expectancy, anticipation: *in ~* (*ge⟨* awaiting; *den (j-s) ~en entspreche⟨* come up to (s.o.'s) expectations; *hint⟨ den (j-s) ~en zurückbleiben* fall sho⟨ of (s.o.'s) expectations.
er'wartungsgemäß *adv* as expected.
Er'wartungs|haltung *f* expectancy, e⟨ pectations. **~hori,zont** *m* (-[e]s; *no ⟨* horizon of expectations.
er'wartungsvoll *adj* expectant.
er'wecken *v/t* **1.** *a. fig. wieder zu⟨ Leben ~* revive. **2.** *fig.* arouse (*intere⟨ suspicion, etc*), bring back (*memorie⟨* raise (*hopes*), inspire (*trust*): → *A⟨ schein, Eindruck* 1 *etc.*
er'wehren: sich ~ (h) (*gen*) ward c⟨ resist; *sich nicht ~ können* (*gen*) helpless against; *man konnte sich d⟨ Eindrucks nicht ~, daß ...* you could⟨ help feeling that ...
er'weichen *v/t* (h) soften, *fig. a.* mo⟨ **sich ~ lassen** give in.

er'weisen (erwies, erwiesen, h) I v/t 1. prove, show. 2. do (a good turn etc), grant (a favo[u]r), show (respect): → Ehre. II sich ~ als prove (or turn out) to be; sich (j-m gegenüber) dankbar ~ show one's gratitude (towards s.o.).

erweitern [ɛr'vaɪtərn] (h) I v/t widen (road etc), extend (building, business, etc, a. fig. powers etc), enlarge (book), broaden (knowledge), ✿ dilate. II sich ~ a) fig. widen, expand, b) ✿ dilate. Er'weiterung f (-; -en) widening (etc), extension, enlargement, ✿ dilatation.

Erwerb [ɛr'vɛrp] m (-[e]s; -e) acquisition, purchase. er'werben v/t (erwarb, erworben, h) a) acquire (a. fig. rights, knowledge, etc), purchase, b) earn, fig. gain, win (fame, wealth, etc): sich Verdienste ~ um render great service(s) to.

er'werbsfähig adj fit for work: im ~en Alter of employable age. Er'werbsfähigkeit f (-; no pl) ability to work.

er'werbsleben n working life.

er'werbslos → arbeitslos. Er'werbsminderung f (-; no pl) reduction in earning capacity. Er'werbsquelle f source of income. er'werbstätig adj (gainfully) employed. Er'werbstätige m, f (-n; -n) employed person. Er'werbstätigkeit f gainful employment. er'werbsunfähig adj unfit for work. Er'werbsunfähigkeit f incapacity to work. Er'werbszweig m a) branch of industry, b) line (of business).

Er'werbung f (-; -en) acquisition.

erwidern [ɛr'vi:dərn] v/t (h) 1. (auf acc to) reply, answer: auf m-e Frage erwiderte er ... in reply to my question he said ... 2. return (greeting, visit, etc, ✗ fire). Er'widerung f (-; -en) 1. (auf acc to) reply, answer. 2. fig. return.

erwies [ɛr'vi:s] pret, erwiesen [ɛr'vi:zən] pp of erweisen. er'wiesenermaßen adv as has been proved.

er'wirken v/t (h) obtain, secure.

er'wirtschaften v/t (h) make.

er'wischen v/t (h) catch (a. fig.): sich ~ lassen get caught; F ihn hat's bös erwischt! he's got it bad!

erwog [ɛr'vo:k] pret of erwägen.

erwogen [ɛr'vo:gən] pp of erwägen.

erworben [ɛr'vɔrbən] pp of erwerben.

erwuchs [ɛr'vu:ks] pret of erwachsen¹.

erwünscht [ɛr'vʏnʃt] adj a) desired, b) welcome, c) desirable.

er'würgen v/t (h) strangle.

Erz [ɛːrts] n (-es; -e) ore.

er'zählen (h) I v/t tell, narrate: man hat mir erzählt I've been told; man erzählt sich they say; F das kannst du mir nicht ~! pull another one! II v/i tell a story (or stories): ~ von, ~ über (acc) tell (s.o.) of (or about); erzähl mal! do tell! er'zählenswert adj worth telling. Er'zähler m (-s; -), Er'zählerin f (-; -nen) 1. narrator, storyteller. 2. narrative writer. Er'zählung f (-; -en) a) narration, story, tale, b) account, c) literature: (short) story.

Erzbischof ['ɛrts-] m archbishop. 'erzbischöflich adj archiepiscopal. 'Erzbistum n, 'Erzdiö‚zese f archbishopric. 'Erzengel m archangel.

er'zeugen v/t (h) produce, ⊕ a. make, ✔ a. grow, 🍷 phys. generate, fig. a. cause, create. Er'zeuger m (-s; -) 1. father. 2. producer, a. ⊕ manufacturer, ✔ a. grower. Er'zeugerland n country of origin. Er'zeugnis n (-ses; -se) product (a. fig.), ✔ usu. pl produce, (novel etc) production: eigenes ~ my etc own make. Er'zeugung f (-; no pl) production, ⊕ a. manufacture, 🍷, phys. generation, fig. creation. Er'zeugungskosten pl production costs.

'Erzfeind m archenemy. 'Erzfeindschaft f archrivalry, deadly feud. 'Erzherzog m archduke. 'Erzherzogin f archduchess. 'Erzhütte f smelting works.

er'ziehbar adj educable: schwer ~es Kind problem child. er'ziehen v/t (erzog, erzogen, h) a) bring s.o. up, raise, b) educate: j-n zu et. ~ train (or teach) s.o. to be (or do) s.th.; → erzogen. Er'zieher m (-s; -) a) educator, b) teacher, c) tutor. Er'zieherin f (-; -nen) a) (lady) teacher, b) nursery-school teacher, c) governess. er'zieherisch adj educational. Er'ziehung f (-; no pl) 1. a) upbringing, b) education, c) training. 2. a) breeding, b) manners. Er'ziehungs‚anstalt f approved (Am. reform) school. ~berater(in f) m educational adviser. ~beratung f child guidance. ~berechtigte m, f (-n; -n) a) parent, b) (legal) guardian. ~wis-

senschaft f (-; no pl) educational science.

er'zielen v/t (h) a) obtain, get, achieve (success etc), b) reach (an agreement etc), c) make (a profit), fetch (a prize), d) sports: score (goals, points).

er'zittern v/i (sn) tremble.

'erzkonserva,tiv adj ultra-conservative.

erzog [ɛr'tso:k] pret of **erziehen**.

erzogen [ɛr'tso:gən] I pp of **erziehen**. II adj **gut ~** well-bred; **schlecht ~** ill-bred.

er'zürnen (h) I v/t anger, infuriate. II **sich ~** get angry (**über** acc at).

er'zürnt adj angry, furious.

erzwungen [ɛr'tsvʊŋən] pp of **erzwingen**.

es [ɛs] pers pron a) it, b) he, she: **ich bin ~!** it's me!; **bist du ~?** is it you?; **~ gibt** there is, there are; **ich hoffe ~** I hope so; **ich weiß ~** (**nicht**) I (don't) know; **er kann nicht schwimmen, aber ich kann ~** he can't swim, but I can; **du bist müde, ich bin ~ auch** you are tired, so am I; **ich will ~** I want to; **ich will ~ versuchen** I'll try; **~ wurde getanzt** there was dancing, we (they) danced.

Es n (-; -) ♪ E flat.

Esche ['ɛʃə] f (-; -n) ♀ ash (tree).

Esel ['e:zəl] m (-s; -) **1.** donkey, jackass. **2.** F fig. (silly) ass: **alter ~** old fool.

'Eselin f (-; -nen) she-ass.

'Eselsbrücke f F mnemonic (aid): **j-m e-e ~ bauen** give s.o. a hint.

Eskalation [ɛskala'tsĭo:n] f (-; -en) escalation. **eskalieren** [ɛska'li:rən] v/i, v/t (h) escalate.

Eskapade [ɛska'pa:də] f (-; -n) escapade.

Eskimo ['ɛskimo] m (-s; -s) Eskimo.

Eskorte [ɛs'kɔrtə] f (-; -n) escort. **eskortieren** [ɛskɔr'ti:rən] v/t (h) escort.

Espe ['ɛspə] f (-; -n) ♀ asp. **'Espenlaub** n **zittern wie ~** tremble like an aspen leaf.

Espresso [ɛs'prɛso] m (-[s]; -s) espresso.

Esprit [ɛs'pri:] m (-s; no pl) wit.

Essay ['ɛse] m (-s; -s) essay (**über** acc on). **Essayist** [ɛse'ɪst] m (-en; -en), **Essay'istin** f (-; -nen) essayist.

'eßbar adj a) eatable, b) edible: **~er Pilz** (edible) mushroom.

'Eßbesteck n cutlery (set).

Esse ['ɛsə] f (-; -n) **1.** chimney. **2.** forge.

essen ['ɛsən] v/t, v/i (aß, gegessen, h) eat: et. **gern ~** like; **man ißt dort ganz**

gut the food is quite good there; → **Abend, Mittag** etc.

'Essen n (-s; -) **1.** no pl eating. **2.** a) food, b) dish, c) meal, d) dinner (party): **~ und Trinken** food and drink. **~marke** f meal ticket, Br. a. luncheon voucher.

'Essenszeit f mealtime, n.s. lunchtime, dinnertime.

Essenz [ɛ'sɛnts] f (-; -en) a. fig. essence.

'Esser m (-s; -) eater: → **stark** 1.

'Eßgeschirr n crockery, dinner service.

'Eßgewohnheiten pl eating habits.

Essig ['ɛsɪç] m (-s; -e) vinegar: F **damit ist es ~!** it's all off! **Essiggurke** f gherkin. **'Essigsäure** f acetic acid.

'Essig- und 'Ölständer m cruet stand.

'Eßka,stanie f (sweet) chestnut. **'Eßlöffel** m tablespoon: **zwei ~** two tablespoonfuls. **'Eßlo,kal** n restaurant. **'Eßstäbchen** pl chopsticks. **'Eßtisch** m dining table. **'Eßwaren** pl food. **'Eßzimmer** n dining room.

Estragon ['ɛstragɔn] m (-s; no pl) ♀ tarragon.

etablieren [eta'bli:rən] **sich ~** (h) a. fig. establish o.s., become established, b) set (o.s.) up (**als** as), start a business.

Etablissement [etablɪs(ə)'mã:] n (-s; -s) establishment.

Etage [e'ta:ʒə] f (-; -n) floor, stor(e)y. **E'tagen|bett** n bunk bed. **~heizung** f single-stor(e)y heating (system). **~wohnung** f flat, Am. apartment.

Etappe [e'tapə] f (-; -n) a. sports: stage, leg: **in ~n** in stages.

Etat [e'ta:] m (-s; -s) budget. **E'tatansatz** m budgetary estimate. **E'tatentwurf** m draft budget. **E'tatjahr** n fiscal year.

e'tatmäßig adj a) budgetary (expenditure), b) permanent (civil servant).

etepetete [e:təpe'te:tə] adj F **1.** la-di-da. **2.** fussy, finicky.

Ethik ['e:tɪk] f (-; -en) ethics.

ethisch ['e:tɪʃ] adj ethical.

ethnisch ['ɛtnɪʃ] adj ethnic.

Ethnographie [ɛtnografi:] f (-; -n) ethnography. **ethnographisch** [ɛtno'gra:fɪʃ] adj ethnographic.

Ethnologe [ɛtno'lo:gə] m (-n; -n) ethnologist. **Ethnologie** [ɛtnolo'gi:] f (-; -n) ethnology.

Ethos ['e:tɔs] n (-; no pl) ethos, w.s. ethics.

Etikett [eti'kɛt] n (-[e]s; -e) **1.** label. **2**

price tag. **Etikette** [eti'kɛtə] *f* (-; -n) (*Verstoß gegen die* ~ breach of) etiquette. **etikettieren** [etikɛ'ti:rən] *v/t* (h) put a label on, *fig.* label.

tliche ['ɛtlɪçə] *indef pron pl* several: ~s a number of things.

etlichemal *adv* several times.

tmal ['ɛtma:l] *n* (-[e]s; -e) ♣ run.

.tüde [e'ty:də] *f* (-; -n) ♪ étude.

tui [ɛt'vi:] *n* (-s; -s) case.

twa ['ɛtva] *adv* **1.** *a.* in ~ about, approximately, F around; *in ~ dasselbe* more or less the same; *wann* ~? approximately when?, *a.* F around what time? **2.** a) by any chance, b) for instance, (let's) say: *nicht* ~, *daß* ... not that *it mattered etc*; *ist das* ~ *besser?* is that any better?; *du glaubst doch nicht* ~ ...? surely you don't think ...?

twaig ['ɛtva:ɪç] *adj* any.

twas ['ɛtvas] **I** *indef pron* something, anything: ~ *anderes* something (anything) else. **II** *adj* some, any, a little: *ich brauche* ~ *Geld* I need some money. **III** *adv* a little: *es erscheint* ~ *merkwürdig* it seems a bit funny.

Etwas *n* (-; -) something: F *das gewisse* ~ the certain something.

tymologie [etymolo'gi:] *f* (-; -n) etymology. **etymologisch** [etymo'lo:gɪʃ] *adj* etymological.

uch [ɔyç] *pers pron* (to) you, *reflexive*: yourselves, *after prep*: you: *setzt* ~*!* sit down!

ucharistie [ɔyçarɪs'ti:] *f* (-; -n) *the* Eucharist.

uer ['ɔyər] **I** *adj* **1.** your: *eu(e)re Mutter* your mother; *unser und* ~ *Haus* our house and yours. **2.** *der* (*die, das*) *eu(e)re* yours. **II** *pers pron* (*gen of ihr*) of you.

ugenik [ɔy'ge:nɪk] *f* (-; *no pl*) eugenics.

ule ['ɔylə] *f* (-; -n) owl: *fig.* ~*n nach Athen tragen* carry coals to Newcastle.

unuch [ɔy'nu:x] *m* (-en; -en) eunuch.

uphemismus [ɔyfe'mɪsmʊs] *m* (-; -men) euphemism. **euphemistisch** [ɔyfe'mɪstɪʃ] *adj* euphemistic.

uphorie [ɔyfo'ri:] *f* (-; -n) euphoria.

ure ['ɔyrə] → *euer*. '**eurerseits** *adv* for (*or* on) your part. '**eures'gleichen** *pron* people like yourselves, *contp.* the likes of you. '**eurethalben**, '**euretwe-**

gen, (*um*) '**euretwillen** *adv* a) because of you, b) for your sake.

Eurhythmie [ɔyryt'mi:] *f* (-; *no pl*) eurhythmics.

eurig ['ɔyrɪç] → *euer* 2.

Europa [ɔy'ro:pa] *n* (-s) Europe. **Europäer** [ɔyro'pɛ:ər] *m* (-s; -), **Euro'päerin** *f* (-; -nen) European. **euro'päisch** *adj* European: *Europäische Gemeinschaft* (*abbr.* **EG**) European (Economic) Community (*abbr.* E[E]C).

Eu'ropa|meister(in *f*) *m sports*: European champion. ~**meisterschaft** *f* European championships. ~**po͵kal** *m* European cup. ~**poli͵tik** *f* Euro-politics. ~**rat** *m* (-[e]s; *no pl*) Council of Europe.

Euroscheck ['ɔyro-] *m* Eurocheque.

Eurovisi'on *f TV* Eurovision.

Euter ['ɔytər] *n* (-s; -) udder.

Euthanasie [ɔytana'zi:] *f* (-; *no pl*) euthanasia.

evakuieren [evaku'i:rən] *v/t* (h) *a.* ✕ *and phys.* evacuate.

Evaku'ierung *f* (-; -en) evacuation.

evangelisch [evaŋ'ge:lɪʃ] *adj* Protestant. **Evangelist** [evaŋge'lɪst] *m* (-en; -en) evangelist. **Evangelium** [evaŋ'ge:liʊm] *n* (-s; -lien) gospel (*a. fig.*): *das* ~ *des Matthäus* the Gospel according to St. Matthew.

'**Evasko͵stüm** ['efa:s-] *n* F *im* ~ in the nude.

Eventualität [evɛntuali'tɛ:t] *f* (-; -en) eventuality. **eventuell** [evɛn'tŏɛl] **I** *adj* possible. **II** *adv* a) possibly, b) if necessary, c) should the occasion arise.

evident [evi'dɛnt] *adj* obvious.

Evolution [evolu'tsĭo:n] *f* (-; -en) evolution.

ewig ['e:vɪç] **I** *adj* **1.** eternal, everlasting: ~*er Schnee* perpetual snow; *die* ̴e *Stadt* (*Rome*) the Eternal City; *seit* ~*en Zeiten* from time immemorial, F for ages. **2.** F eternal, constant, endless. **II** *adv* **3.** eternally, forever: *auf immer und* ~ for ever and ever; F *es ist* ~ *schade* it's just too bad; ~ (*lange*) for ages; *es dauert* ~ it's taking ages.

'**Ewigkeit** *f* (-; -en) eternity: *bis in alle* ~ to the end of time; F *es ist e-e* ~*, seit* ... it's ages since ...; *ich habe e-e* ~ *gewartet* I've waited for ages.

Ex... [ɛks...] ex-...

exakt [ɛˈksakt] *adj* precise, exact: **~e Wissenschaften** exact sciences.

Ex'aktheit *f* (-; *no pl*) precision.

Examen [ɛˈksaːmən] *n* (-s; -) examination, F exam: **(s)ein ~ machen** take one's exams.

exekutieren [ɛksekuˈtiːrən] *v/t* (h) execute. **Exekution** [ɛksefuˈtsĭoːn] *f* (-; -en) execution.

exekutiv [ɛkseˈkuˈtiːf] *adj*, **Exekutive** [ɛkseˈkuˈtiːvə] *f* (-; -n) executive. **Exeku'tivgewalt** *f* executive power.

Exempel [ɛˈksɛmpəl] *n* (-s; -) **ein ~ statuieren** set a warning example.

Exemplar [ɛksɛmˈplaːr] *n* (-s; -e) **1.** specimen, sample. **2.** a) copy (*of book*), b) number, issue (*of magazine etc*). **exem'plarisch I** *adj* exemplary. **II** *adv* **j-n ~ bestrafen** make an example of s.o.

exerzieren [ɛksɛrˈtsiːrən] *v/t, v/i* (h) ✗ drill.

Exhibitionismus [ɛkshibitsĭoˈnɪsmʊs] *m* (-; *no pl*) exhibitionism, ⚥ indecent exposure. **Exhibitionist** [-ˈnɪst] *m* (-en; -en) exhibitionist.

exhumieren [ɛkshuˈmiːrən] *v/t* (h) exhume.

Exil [ɛˈksiːl] *n* (-s; -e) (**im ~** in) exile: **ins ~ gehen** go into exile.

E'xilre,gierung *f* government in exile.

Existentialismus [ɛksɪstɛntsĭaˈlɪsmʊs] *m* (-; *no pl*) existentialism. **Existentialist** [-ˈlɪst] *m* (-en; -en), **existentialistisch** [-ˈlɪstɪʃ] *adj* existentialist.

existentiell [ɛksɪstɛnˈtsĭɛl] *adj* **1.** existential. **2.** *von* **~er Bedeutung** vitally important.

Existenz [ɛksɪsˈtɛnts] *f* (-; -en) **1.** a) existence, b) livelihood: **gesicherte ~** secure position. character: → **verkracht 2. ~angst** *f psych.* existential anxiety, *w.s.* economic fears. **~berechtigung** *f* **1.** right to exist. **2.** raison d'être. **~kampf** *m* struggle for existence. **~minimum** *n* subsistence level.

existieren [ɛksɪsˈtiːrən] *v/i* (h) **1.** exist, be: **nur wenige ~ noch** there are only a few left. **2.** (*von* on) exist, live.

Exitus [ˈɛksitʊs] *m* (-; *no pl*) ⚕ exitus, death.

exklusiv [ɛkskluˈziːf] *adj* exclusive.

Exklu'sivbericht *m* exclusive (story).

Exklu'sivrechte *pl* exclusive rights.

exkommunizieren [ɛkskɔmuniˈtsiːrən] *v/t* (h) excommunicate.

Exkrement [ɛkskreˈmɛnt] *n* (-[e]s; -) excrement.

Exkursion [ɛkskʊrˈzĭoːn] *f* (-; -en) excursion, field trip.

exmatrikulieren [ɛksmatrikuˈliːrən] *v/* (h) **j-n** (**sich**) **~** take s.o.'s (one's) name off the (university) register.

Exodus [ˈɛksodʊs] *m* (-; *no pl*) exodus

Exot [ɛˈksoːt] *m* (-en; -en), **E'xotin** *f* (- -nen) exotic. **e'xotisch** *adj* exotic.

Expander [ɛksˈpandər] *m* (-s; -) *sports* expander.

Expansion [ɛkspanˈzĭoːn] *f* (-; -en) expansion.

Expansi'onspoli,tik *f* expansionism.

expedieren [ɛkspeˈdiːrən] *v/t* (h) dispatch. **Expedition** [ɛkspediˈtsĭoːn] *f* (- -en) **1.** expedition. **2.** ✝ forwarding (department).

Experiment [ɛksperiˈmɛnt] *n* (-[e]s; -e) experiment. **Experimental...** [ɛksperimɛnˈtaːl-], **experimentell** [-ˈtɛl] *adj* experimental. **experimentieren** [-ˈtiːrən] *v/i* (h) experiment (**an** *dat* on, **mit** with)

Experte [ɛksˈpɛrtə] *m* (-n; -n) expert.

Expertise [ɛksperˈtiːzə] *f* (-; -n) **1.** expertise. **2.** expert's opinion.

explodieren [ɛksploˈdiːrən] *v/i* (sn) explode. **Explosion** [ɛksploˈzĭoːn] *f* (- -en) explosion, blast.

explosi'onsartig *adj a. fig.* explosive.

Explosi'onsgefahr *f* danger of explosion. **~kraft** *f* explosive force.

explosiv [ɛksploˈziːf] *adj* explosive.

Exponat [ɛkspoˈnaːt] *n* (-[e]s; -e) exhibit

Exponent [ɛkspoˈnɛnt] *m* (-en; -en) Å, *c fig.* exponent.

exponieren [ɛkspoˈniːrən] *v/t* (h) expose (**sich** o.s.). **expo'niert** *adj* exposed.

Export [ɛksˈpɔrt] *m* (-[e]s; -e) **1.** *no p* exportation, exporting. **2.** exports.

Ex'port|abteilung *f* export department **~ar,tikel** *m* export article (*or* item), *pl c* exports. **~ausführung** *f* export model

Exporteur [ɛkspɔrˈtøːr] *m* (-s; -e) exporter. **Ex'portgeschäft** *n*, **Ex'porthandel** *m* export trade. **exportieren** [ɛkspɔrˈtiːrən] *v/t* (h) export (**nach** to).

Ex'portland *n* exporting country.

Ex'portleiter *m* export manager.

Exposé [ɛkspoˈzeː] *n* (-s; -s) exposé.

expreß [ɛks'prɛs] *adv* ~ **schicken** send express (*Am.* by special delivery).
Expressionismus [ɛksprɛsĭo'nɪsmʊs] *m* (-; *no pl*) expressionism. **Expressionist** [-'nɪst] *m* (-en; -en), **expressionistisch** [-'nɪstɪʃ] *adj* expressionist.
extern [ɛks'tɛrn] *adj* external.
extra ['ɛkstra] **I** *adj* extra. **II** *adv* a) extra, *a.* separately, b) specially, c) F on purpose: ~ **für dich** just for you.
'**Extra** *n* (-s; -s) extra. ~**blatt** *n* extra.
extrahieren [ɛkstra'hiːrən] *v/t* (h), **Extrakt** [ɛks'trakt] *m* (-[e]s; -e) extract.
extravagant [ɛkstrava'gant] *adj* flamboyant.

extravertiert [ɛkstraver'tiːrt] *adj* (*a.* ~**er Mensch**) extrovert.
extrem [ɛks'treːm] *adj* extreme.
Ex'trem *n* (-s; -e) extreme. **Extremismus** [ɛkstre'mɪsmʊs] *m* (-; *no pl*) extremism. **Extremist** [-'mɪst] *m* (-en; -en), **extre'mistisch** *adj* extremist.
Extremitäten [ɛkstremi'tɛːtən] *pl* extremities.
extrover'tiert [ɛkstro-] → **extravertiert**.
Exzellenz [ɛktse'lɛnts] *f* (-; -en) (*Eure, Seine* ~ your, his) Excellency.
Exzentriker [ɛks'tsɛntrikər] *m* (-s; -), **Ex'zentrikerin** *f* (-; -nen) eccentric.
ex'zentrisch [-trɪʃ] *adj a.* ⚓, ⚙ eccentric.
Exzeß [ɛks'tsɛs] *m* (-sses; -sse) excess.

F

F, f [ɛf] *n* (-; -) F, f (*a.* ♪).
Fabel ['faːbəl] *f* (-; -n) a) fable, *fig. a.* story, b) plot (*of drama etc*).
'**fabelhaft** *adj* fantastic.
Fabrik [fa'briːk] *f* (-; -en) factory, works, mill. **Fa'brikanlage** *f* (manufacturing) plant. **Fabrikant** [fabri'kant] *m* (-en; -en) **1.** factory owner. **2.** manufacturer. **Fa'brikarbeit** *f* **1.** factory work. **2.** → **Fabrikware**. **Fa'brikarbeiter(in** *f*) *m* factory worker. **Fabrikat** [fabri'kaːt] *n* (-[e]s; -e) product, make. **Fabrikation** [fabrika'tsĭoːn] *f* (-; -en) production.
Fabrikati'ons|nummer *f* serial number. ~**pro,gramm** *n* production schedule.
Fa'brik|besitzer(in *f*) *m* factory owner. ~**gebäude** *n* factory building. ~**gelände** *n* factory site. ⚙**neu** *adj* brand-new. ~**schiff** *n* factory ship. ~**ware** *f* manufactured product(s).
fabrizieren [fabri'tsiːrən] *v/t* (h) **1.** manufacture, make, *fig.* concoct. **2.** *fig.* get up to.
Facette [fa'sɛtə] *f* (-; -n) facet.
Fa'cettenauge *n zo.* compound eye.
Fach [fax] *n* (-[e]s; ~er) **1.** a) compartment, partition, b) shelf. **2.** field, line: *er ist vom* ~ he is an expert; *das*

schlägt nicht in mein ~ that's not in my line. **3.** *ped., univ.* subject.
...fach *in cpds.* ...fold, times.
'**Fach|arbeit** *f* skilled work. ~**arbeiter(in** *f*) *m* skilled worker, *pl* skilled labo(u)r. ~**arzt** *m*, ~**ärztin** *f* specialist (*für* in). ⚖**ärztlich** *adj* (*adv* by a) specialist. ~**ausbildung** *f* special(ized) training. ~**ausdruck** *m* technical term. ~**bereich** *m* **1.** → **Fachgebiet**. **2.** *univ.* department. ~**buch** *n* specialist book.
Fächer ['fɛçər] *m* (-s; -) **1.** fan. **2.** *fig.* range, spectrum. '**fächerförmig** *adj* fan-like: *sich* ~ *ausbreiten* fan out. '**fächern** *v/t* (h) (*a. sich* ~) fan out.
'**Fach|frau** *f* (woman) expert. ~**gebiet** *n* (special) field. ⚖**gerecht** *adj* expert, professional. ~**geschäft** *n* specialist shop (*Am.* store). ~**handel** *m* specialized trade (*or* dealers). ~**hochschule** *f* college. ~**idi,ot** *m* F *contp.* specialist borné. ~**jar,gon** *m* technical jargon. ~**kenntnis(se** *pl*) *f* specialized knowledge, know-how. ~**kräfte** *pl* qualified personnel. ~**kreis** *m in* ~**en** among the experts. ⚖**kundig** *adj* competent, expert. ~**lehrer(in** *f*) *m* subject teacher. ~**leute** *pl* experts.
'**fachlich** *adj* technical, professional.

'**Fachlitera,tur** f specialized literature.

'**Fachmann** m (-[e]s; -leute) (**in** dat in, at, **für** on) expert, specialist.

fachmännisch ['faxmɛnɪʃ] adj expert, specialist, professional (work): **~es Urteil** expert opinion.

'**Fach|perso,nal** n qualified personnel. **~presse** f trade press. **~richtung** f field. **~schule** f technical college.

Fachsimpelei [faxzɪmpəˈlaɪ] f (-; -en) F shoptalk. '**fachsimpeln** v/i (insep, pp gefachsimpelt, h) talk shop.

'**Fach|sprache** f technical language (or terminology). **~studium** n special(ized) studies. **~übersetzer(in** f) m technical translator. **~verband** m professional (or trade) association. **~werk** n (-[e]s; no pl) half-timbering. **~werkhaus** n half-timbered house. **~wissen** n → **Fachkenntnis(se)**. **~wörterbuch** n specialized dictionary. **~zeitschrift** f (professional or trade) journal.

Fackel ['fakəl] f (-; -n) a. fig. torch.

'**fackeln** v/i (h) F **nicht lange ~** waste no time.

fade ['faːdə] adj **1.** tasteless, stale, flat (beer). **2.** fig. boring, dull.

Faden ['faːdən] m (-s; ") thread (a. fig.), ♪, ⚙ filament, ✿ stitch, string (of puppets etc): ✿ **die Fäden ziehen** remove the stitches; **der rote ~** the thread (running through the story etc); **den ~ verlieren** lose the thread (of one's speech etc); **es hing an e-m ~** it hang by a thread; **er hält alle Fäden in der Hand** he pulls the strings. '**Fadenkreuz** n opt. reticule. '**Fadennudeln** pl vermicelli.

fadenscheinig ['faːdənʃaɪnɪç] adj threadbare, fig. a. flimsy (excuse etc).

Fagott [faˈɡɔt] n (-[e]s; -e) ♪ bassoon.

Fagottist [faɡɔˈtɪst] m (-en; -en), **Fagot'tistin** f (-; -nen) bassoonist.

fähig ['fɛːɪç] adj a) able, capable, b) gifted, talented, c) qualified: **~ sein zu** be capable of; b.s. **zu allem** ~ capable of anything, desperate; (dazu) **~ sein, et. zu tun** be capable of doing s.th., be able (or qualified) to do s.th.

'**Fähigkeit** f (-; -en) a) ability, capability, b) talent.

fahl [faːl] adj pale, ashen (face).

Fähnchen ['fɛːnçən] n (-s; -) **1.** pennant, sports: marker. **2.** F cheap, flimsy dress.

fahnden ['faːndən] v/i (h) **~ nach** search

for. '**Fahnder** m (-s; -) investigator.

'**Fahndung** f (-; -en) search.

'**Fahndungs|akti,on** f (police) search. **~dienst** m tracing and search department. **~liste** f wanted list.

Fahne ['faːnə] f (-; -n) **1.** flag, fig. banner, ♣, ✗ colo(u)rs: fig. **mit fliegenden ~n** with flying colo(u)rs. **2.** F **e-e ~ haben** reek of the bottle. **3.** print. galley (proof).

'**Fahneneid** m ✗ oath of allegiance.

'**Fahnenflucht** f (-; no pl) desertion.

'**fahnenflüchtig** adj **~ sein** be a deserter; **~ werden** desert.

'**Fahnen|mast** m, **~stange** f flagpole.

Fähnrich ['fɛːnrɪç] m (-s; -e) ✗ cadet: ♣ **zur See** midshipman.

'**Fahrausweis** m ticket. '**Fahrbahn** f road, carriageway, lane. '**fahrbar** adj mobile. '**Fahrbereitschaft** f car pool.

Fähre ['fɛːrə] f (-; -n) ferry.

'**Fahreigenschaften** pl mot. road performance.

fahren ['faːrən] (fuhr, gefahren) **I** v/i (sn) **1.** a) go (**mit** by bus, train, etc), ride (on bicycle, etc), mot. drive, ♣ sail, b) run, c) leave, depart, go, d) be moving: **der Zug fährt zweimal am Tag** the train runs (or goes) twice a day; **über e-e Brücke ~** cross a bridge; **rechts ~!** keep to the right!; **mit Diesel ~** run on diesel, be diesel-driven; fig. **mit der Hand ~ über** (acc) run one's hand over; **in et. ~** bullet, knife, etc: go into; **gut (schlecht) ~ bei** fare well (ill) with, do well (badly) by; **es (der Gedanke) fuhr mir durch den Kopf** it flashed through my mind; **was ist in ihn gefahren?** what has got into him?; F **e-n ~ lassen** fart, let go; ~ **Haut. II** v/t **2.** (h) a) drive, b) take (s.o. or s.th. somewhere), transport, ♣ sail. **3.** (sn) drive, cover (distance etc), do: **das Auto fährt 150 km/h** the car does 150 km/h. **4.** (h or sn) sports: make, clock (ten minutes etc): **ein Rennen ~** participate in a race. **5.** (h) ⊙ a) work (a shift), b) run (a line), operate (plant unit). **6.** (h) TV run.

'**fahrend** adj travel(l)ing, itinerant.

'**Fahrer** m (-s; -), '**Fahrerin** f (-; -nen) a) driver, b) chauffeur (chauffeuse).

'**Fahrerflucht** f **~ begehen** commit a hit-and-run offen/ce (Am. -se).

'**Fahrersitz** m driver's seat.

'**Fahr|gast** *m* passenger, *of taxi*: fare. **~geld** *n* fare. **~gelegenheit** *f* (means of) transport(ation). **~gemeinschaft** *f* car pool. **~gestell** *n* **1.** *mot.* chassis, ✈ undercarriage. **2.** F (*legs*) pins.

fahrig ['fa:rɪç] *adj* a) nervous, jumpy, b) inattentive.

'**Fahrkarte** *f* ticket (*nach* to).

'**Fahrkarten|auto,mat** *m* ticket machine. **~kon,trolle** *f* ticket inspection. **~kontrol,leur** *m* ticket inspector. **~schalter** *m* ticket office.

'**Fahrkom,fort** *m mot.* driving comfort.

'**fahrlässig** *adj* careless, *a.* ⚖ negligent: **~e Tötung** manslaughter (*Am.* in the second degree). '**Fahrlässigkeit** *f* (-; -en) carelessness, *a.* ⚖ negligence.

'**Fahrlehrer(in** *f*) *m* driving instructor.

'**Fährmann** *m* ferryman.

'**Fahrplan** *m* timetable (*a. fig.*), schedule. **~änderung** *f* change in the timetable.

'**fahrplanmäßig I** *adj* scheduled. **II** *adv* according to schedule, on time.

'**Fahr|praxis** *f* driving experience. **~preis** *m* fare. **~prüfung** *f* driving test. **~rad** *n* bicycle, F bike. **~rinne** *f* ⚓ lane. **~schein** *m* ticket. **~schule** *f* driving school. **~schüler(in** *f*) *m mot.* learner (driver). **~spur** *f* lane. **~stuhl** *m* lift, *Am.* elevator. **~stunde** *f* driving lesson.

Fahrt [fa:rt] *f* (-; -en) **1.** a) drive, ride, b) journey, trip, ⚓ *a.* voyage, cruise: **auf ~ gehen** go on a trip; **auf der ~ nach X** on the way to X; **gute ~!** have a good trip! **2.** speed (*a.* ⚓): **in voller ~** at full speed; **in ~ kommen** a) get under way, b) F *fig.* get going; F **j-n in ~ bringen** a) get s.o. going, b) make s.o. wild; F **in ~ sein** *person*: a) be going it strong, b) be wild.

'**Fahrtdauer** *f* length of the trip: **die ~ beträgt 3 Stunden** it will take 3 hours (to get there).

'**Fährte** ['fɛ:rtə] *f* (-; -n) *a. fig.* trail, track: *fig.* **auf der falschen ~ sein** be on the wrong track.

'**Fahrtenbuch** *n mot.* logbook.

'**Fahrtenschreiber** *m mot.* tachograph.

'**Fahrtrichtungsanzeiger** *m mot.* direction indicator.

'**fahrtüchtig** *adj car*: roadworthy, *driver*: fit to drive.

'**Fahrtunterbrechung** *f* stop.

'**Fahrtwind** *m* airstream.

'**Fahr|verbot** *n* **j-n mit ~ belegen** suspend s.o.'s driving licence (*Am.* driver's license). **~verhalten** *n mot.* road behavio(u)r. **~wasser** *n* (-s; *no pl*) **1.** → **Fahrrinne. 2.** F *fig.* track: **im richtigen ~ sein** be in one's element. **~weise** *f* (way of) driving. **~werk** *n mot.* chassis, ✈ undercarriage. **~zeit** *f* → **Fahrtdauer.**

'**Fahrzeug** *n* (-[e]s; -e) vehicle, ⚓ vessel. **~brief** *m mot.* (vehicle) registration document. **~halter(in** *f*) *m* car owner. **~pa,piere** *pl* documents.

Faible ['fɛ:bəl] *n* (-s; -s) → **Schwäche** 3.

fair [fɛ:r] *adj* fair.

Fairneß ['fɛ:rnɛs] *f* (-; *no pl*) fairness.

Fäkalien [fɛ'ka:liən] *pl* f(a)eces.

Fakir ['fa:kɪr] *m* (-s; -e) fakir.

Faksimile [fak'zi:mile] *n* (-s; -s) facsimile.

faktisch ['faktɪʃ] *adj* actual(ly *adv*), *adv a.* in fact. **Faktor** ['faktor] *m* (-s; -ren [-'to:rən]) *a. biol.,* ⚗ factor. '**Faktum** *n* (-s; -ten) a) fact, b) *pl* facts, data.

fakturieren [faktu'ri:rən] *v/t* (h) invoice.

Fakultät [fakʊl'tɛ:t] *f* (-; -en) *univ.* faculty, *esp. Am.* department.

fakultativ [fakʊlta'ti:f] *adj* optional.

Falke ['falkə] *m* (-n; -n) *zo.* falcon, *hunt. and pol. a.* hawk.

Fall [fal] *m* (-[e]s; ⸚e) **1.** fall (*a.* ⚔), ⚓ *a.* drop, *fig.* downfall: **zu ~ bringen** a) **j-n** cause s.o. to fall, *in a fight or fig.* bring s.o. down, trip s.o. up, b) thwart (*plans etc*), defeat (*bill, motion, etc*); *fig.* **zu ~ kommen** fall, be ruined. **2.** case (*a.* ⚖, *ling.,* 🝆), matter, affair: **auf alle Fälle** a) in any case, b) definitely, c) *a.* **für alle Fälle** just in case, to be on the safe side; **für den** (*or im*) **~, daß er kommt** in case he should come; **im ~e** (*gen*) in the event of; **gesetzt den ~** suppose, supposing; **in diesem ~** in that case; F **klarer ~!** sure (thing)!; **das ist** (**nicht**) **ganz mein ~** that's right up my street (not my cup of tea); **das ist auch bei ihr der ~** it's the same with her.

Falle ['falə] *f* (-; -n) trap (*a. fig.*), snare: *fig.* **j-m in die ~ gehen** walk into the trap set by s.o.; **j-m e-e ~ stellen** set a trap for s.o.

fallen ['falən] *v/i* (fiel, gefallen, sn) **1.** fall (**von** from, off), fall down, drop: **~ lassen** *a. fig.* let fall, drop; **von der Leiter ~** fall off a ladder; **ich bin gefallen** I had a fall; *er ließ sich in e-n Sessel ~* he dropped into a chair. **2.** ✕ fall, *soldier: a.* be killed (in action). **3.** *temperature, prices, etc:* fall, drop, go down. **4.** *name, remark, etc:* fall, *decision etc: a.* be made: *sein Name fiel auch* his name was mentioned too; *es fielen harte Worte* there were harsh words; *die Entscheidung ist noch nicht gefallen* the matter is still undecided. **5.** *sports: goal etc:* be scored: *die Entscheidung fiel in der letzten Minute* the decider came in the last minute. **6.** *Schüsse fielen* shots were fired. **7.** *obstacle etc:* be removed, go. **8.** *an j-n ~ inheritance etc:* fall (*or* go) to s.o. **9.** *~ auf (acc) a. fig.* fall on; *die Wahl fiel auf sie* she was chosen. **10.** *~ unter* come under. **11.** *~ in (acc)* fall into; *in Schlaf ~* fall asleep; *fig. j-m in den Arm ~* restrain s.o.; → *Ohnmacht* 2.

fällen ['fɛlən] *v/t* (h) **1.** cut down (*tree etc*). **2.** ⚖ *ein Urteil ~* (*über acc* on) pass sentence, *a. fig.* pass judg(e)ment; → *Entscheidung.*

'**fallenlassen** *v/t* (*irr, sep,* h, → *lassen*) drop (*plan, friend, hint, etc*).

'**Fallgeschwindigkeit** *f phys.* rate of fall.

'**Fallgrube** *f* pit, *a. fig.* trap.

fällig ['fɛlıç] *adj* ✝ due, payable: *längst ~* (long) overdue; *~ werden* a) become due (*or* payable), b) expire.

'**Fälligkeit** *f* (*-; no pl*) (*bei ~* at) maturity.

'**Fallobst** *n* windfall.

Fallout ['fɔ:laʊt] *m* (*-s; -s*) *nucl.* fallout.

'**Fallrückzieher** *m* soccer: falling overhead kick.

falls [fals] *conj* if, in case: *~ nicht* unless.

'**Fallschirm** *m* parachute. *~***absprung** *m* parachute jump (*or* descent). *~***abwurf** *m* airdrop. *~***jäger** *m* ✕ paratrooper. *~***springen** *n* parachute jumping, *sports:* skydiving. *~***springer(in** *f*) *m* parachutist, *sports:* skydiver.

'**Fallstrick** *m fig.* trap. '**Fallstudie** *f* case study. '**Falltreppe** *f* foldaway stairs. '**Falltür** *f* trapdoor.

falsch [falʃ] **I** *adj* **1.** a) wrong, b) untrue, *pred* not true: *~e Darstellung* misrepresentation. **2.** a) false, artificial, b) forged, fake(d), counterfeit: *~er Name* fictitious name. **3.** false, insincere. **II** *adv* **4.** wrongly, falsely (*etc*): *~ aussprechen* mispronounce; *~ gehen watch:*

be wrong; *~ geraten!* wrong guess!; *~ schreiben* misspell; *~ singen* sing ou(t) of tune; *~ spielen* cheat; *~ verbunden* sorry, wrong number!; *~ verstehen* misunderstand.

'**Falschaussage** *f* ⚖ false testimony.
'**Falscheid** *m* ⚖ false oath.

fälschen ['fɛlʃən] *v/t* (h) fake, forge, counterfeit, ✝ tamper with (*books etc*).
'**Fälscher** *m* (*-s; -*) forger, counterfeiter.
'**Falschgeld** *n* counterfeit money.
'**Falschheit** *f* (*-; no pl*) falseness.
fälschlich ['fɛlʃlıç] **I** *adj* wrong, false. **II** *adv* → '**fälschlicherweise** *adv* a) wrongly, falsely, b) by mistake.
'**Falschmeldung** *f* false report, hoax.
'**Falschmünzer** [-myntsər] *m* (*-s; -*) counterfeiter.
'**Falschspieler** *m* cardsharper, cheat.
'**Fälschung** *f* (*-; -en*) **1.** forging, counterfeiting. **2.** fake, forgery.
'**Faltbett** *n* folding bed. '**Faltblatt** *n* leaf let. '**Faltboot** *n* folding canoe.
Fältchen ['fɛltçən] *n* (*-s; -*) wrinkle, *pl* crow's-feet.
Falte ['faltə] *f* (*-; -n*) a) fold, b) crease, c) pleat (*in skirt etc*), d) wrinkle, line (*in face*): *~n werfen* pucker.
fälteln ['fɛltəln] *v/t* (h) pleat.
falten ['faltən] *v/t* (h) a) fold, b) pleat.
'**Faltenrock** *m* pleated skirt.
Falter ['faltər] *m* (*-s; -*) *zo.* butterfly.
faltig ['faltıç] *adj* creased, *a.* wrinkled (*skin*), *a.* lined (*face*).
'**Faltkarte** *f* folding (*or* pull-out) map.
'**Faltkar,ton** *m* collapsible cardboar(d) box. '**Falttür** *f* folding door.
Falz [falts] *m* (*-es; -e*), '**falzen** *v/t* (h) **1.** fold. **2.** ⚙ rabbet.
familiär [famiˈlɛːɐ] *adj* **1.** family (*affair etc*). **2.** a) familiar, b) informal. **3.** *ling.* familiar, colloquial.
Familie [faˈmiːljə] *f* (*-; -n*) family: (*die*) *Miller* the Miller family; *e-e ~ gründen* start a family; *~ haben* have children: *es liegt in der ~* it runs in the family.
Fa'milien|angehörige *m*, *f* member of the family. *~***angelegenheit** *f* family affair. *~***anschluß** *m* ~ *haben* liv(e) (there) as one of the family. *~***betrieb** *m* family business (*or* farm). *~***fest** *n* family celebration. *~***gericht** *n* ⚖ family court. *~***kreis** *m* family circle: *im eng(sten) ~ celebrate etc* with the immediat(e)

family. **~leben** n family life. **~mitglied** n member of the family. **~name** m surname, last name. **~oberhaupt** n head of the family. **~packung** f family pack. **~planung** f family planning. **~ro‚man** m roman fleuve. **~sinn** m (-[e]s; no pl) sense of family. **~stand** m marital status. **~unterhalt** m upkeep of the family. **~vater** m **1.** head of the family. **2.** family man. **~verhältnisse** pl family background. **~zuwachs** m addition to the family.

Fan [fɛn] m (-s; -s) fan.

Fanatiker [fa'na:tikər] m (-s; -), **Fa'natikerin** f (-; -nen) fanatic. **fanatisch** [fa'na:tɪʃ] adj fanatic(al). **Fanatismus** [fana'tɪsmʊs] m (-; no pl) fanaticism.

fand [fant] pret of **finden**.

Fanfare [fan'fa:rə] f (-; -n) **1.** fanfare. **2.** mot. multitone horn.

Fang [faŋ] m (-[e]s; ⁀e) **1.** a. fig. catch, haul. **2.** zo. usu. pl a) claw, b) fang, tusk (of boar). **'Fangarm** m zo. tentacle.

fangen ['faŋən] (fing, gefangen, h) **I** v/t **1.** catch, fig. a. trap: **sich ~ lassen** get caught; → **Feuer** 1. **II sich ~ 2.** be caught. **3.** catch o.s. stumbling etc. **4.** fig. **sich** (**wieder**) **~** rally (a. sports), recover, w.s. get a grip on o.s. (again).

'Fangen n (-s) catch, Am. tag.

Fänger ['fɛŋər] m (-s; -) catcher.

'Fangfrage f trick question.

Fangopackung ['faŋgo-]f 🟊 mud pack.

'Fangzahn m zo. fang.

'Fanklub m fan club.

'Farbabzug m phot. colo(u)r print.

'Farbaufnahme f colo(u)r photo.

Farbband n typewriter ribbon.

Farbe ['farbə] f (-; -n) **1.** a) colo(u)r, b) shade, c) paint, d) dye: **in ~ TV** in colo(u)r; → **leuchtend. 2.** complexion, colo(u)r. **3.** cards: suit: **~ bekennen** follow suit, fig. show one's true colo(u)rs. **4.** pl colo(u)rs (of club etc).

farbecht adj colo(u)rfast, nonfading.

Färbemittel n dye.

färben ['fɛrbən] (h) **I** v/t **1.** a) dye (hair, cloth), stain (glass, paper), b) tint, colo(u)r (a. fig.): **gefärbter Bericht** colo(u)red report. **2.** lose colo(u)r, stain. **II sich ~** (leaves: change) colo(u)r: **sich rot** etc **~** turn red etc.

farbenblind adj colo(u)r-blind.

farben|freudig, ~froh adj colo(u)rful.

'Farben(kunst)druck m colo(u)r plate.

'Farbenlehre f theory of colo(u)rs.

'farbenprächtig adj colo(u)rful.

'Farbenskala f colo(u)r chart.

'Farbenspiel n play of colo(u)rs.

Färber ['fɛrbər] m (-s; -) dyer.

Färberei [fɛrbə'raɪ] f (-; -en) dyeworks.

'Farb|fernsehen n colo(u)r television (or TV). **~fernseher** m, **~fernsehgerät** n colo(u)r television (or TV) set. **~film** m colo(u)r film. **~filter** n, m phot. colo(u)r filter. **~foto** n colo(u)r photo. **~fotogra‚fie** f **1.** colo(u)r photography. **2.** colo(u)r photo.

farbig ['farbɪç] adj colo(u)red (a. race), fig. colo(u)rful. **'Farbige** m, f (-n; -n) colo(u)red person (or man, woman), nonwhite: **die ~n** the colo(u)reds, the colo(u)red people, the nonwhites.

'Farbko‚pierer m colo(u)r copier.

'farblich adj colo(u)r, a. adv in colo(u)r.

'farblos adj a. fig. colo(u)rless.

'Farb|skala f colo(u)r chart. **~stift** m colo(u)red pencil, crayon. **~stoff** m 🟊 dye, in foods: colo(u)ring. **~ton** m hue, tint, shade, paint., phot. tone.

'Färbung f (-; -en) colo(u)ring, hue.

'Farbwiedergabe f colo(u)r fidelity.

'Farbzusammenstellung f colo(u)r scheme.

Farce ['farsə] f (-; -n) thea. burlesque, a. fig. farce.

Farm [farm] f (-; -en) farm.

'Farmer m (-s; -) farmer.

Farn [farn] m (-[e]s; -e), **~kraut** n 🌿 fern.

Färse ['fɛrzə] f (-; -n) zo. heifer.

Fasan [fa'za:n] m (-[e]s; -e) zo. pheasant.

Fasching ['faʃɪŋ] m (-s; -e, -s) carnival.

'Faschings... carnival ...

Faschismus [fa'ʃɪsmʊs] m (-; no pl) fascism. **Faschist** [fa'ʃɪst] m (-en; -en), **Fa'schistin** f(-; -nen), **faschistisch** adj [fa'ʃɪstɪʃ] fascist.

faseln ['fa:zəln] v/i (h) F drivel.

Faser ['fa:zər] f (-; -n) fibre, Am. fiber.

'faserig adj fibrous, stringy (meat etc).

fasern ['fa:zərn] v/i (h) fray.

'Faserplatte f fib/reboard (Am. -er-).

Faß [fas] n (Fasses; Fässer) a) barrel, b) vat, tub: **Bier vom ~** → **Faßbier;** (frisch) vom ~ beer on tap (or draught), wine from the wood; fig. **das ist ein ~ ohne Boden** there is no end to it; **das**

schlägt dem ~ den Boden aus! that's the last straw!

Fassade [fa'sa:də] *f* (-; -n) façade, front.

Fas'sadenkletterer *m* cat burglar.

Fas'sadenreiniger *m* exterior cleaner.

'**faßbar** *adj* comprehensible: *schwer ~* difficult (to understand).

'**Faßbier** *n* draught beer.

Fäßchen ['fɛsçən] *n* (-s; -) keg.

fassen ['fasən] (h) **I** *v/t* **1.** take hold of, grasp, seize, *a.* ⊙ grip: F *zu ~ kriegen* get hold of; *j-n an (or bei) der Hand ~* take s.o. by the hand. **2.** apprehend, catch (*criminal etc*). **3.** mount (*in silver etc*), set (*jewel*). **4.** a) *room etc*: hold, *a.* accommodate, seat (*persons*), b) contain. **5.** *fig.* a) grasp, understand, b) believe: *nicht zu ~* unbelievable, incredible. **6.** put, formulate: *et. in Worte ~* put s.th. into words. **7.** *e-n Gedanken ~* form an idea; → *Beschluß, Entschluß, Fuß* 1, *Plan* 1. **II** *v/i* **8.** *~ an* (*acc*) touch; *~ nach* grasp at. **III** *sich ~* **9.** regain one's composure, compose o.s.: → *gefaßt* 1. **10.** *sich kurz ~* be brief; *fasse dich kurz!* make it brief!; → *Geduld*.

'**faßlich** *adj* comprehensible: *leicht (schwer) ~* easy (hard) to understand.

Fasson [fa'sõ:] *f* (-; -s) **1.** a) shape, b) cut: *fig. nach s-r (eigenen) ~* after one's own fashion. **2.** → **Fas'sonschnitt** a) trim, short back and sides.

'**Fassung** *f* (-; -en) **1.** frame (*of spectacles*), socket (*of lamp*), setting (*of diamond etc*). **2.** a) formulation, b) text, wording, c) version (*of book, film, etc*). **3.** *no pl* composure: *j-n aus der ~ bringen* put s.o. out; *die ~ bewahren* keep one's head; *die ~ verlieren* lose one's composure (*or temper*); *s-e ~ wiedergewinnen (or fassen* 9); *er war ganz außer ~* he was completely beside himself; → *ringen* I.

'**Fassungskraft** *f* (-; *no pl*) (powers of) comprehension, mental capacity.

'**fassungslos** *adj* stunned, speechless: *~ vor Glück etc* beside o.s. with joy *etc*.

'**Fassungslosigkeit** *f* (-; *no pl*) shock.

'**Fassungsvermögen** *n* **1.** capacity. **2.** → *Fassungskraft.*

fast [fast] *adv* a) almost, nearly, b) hardly: *~ nie* hardly ever.

fasten ['fastən] *v/i* (h) fast. '**Fasten** *n* (-s)

fast(ing). '**Fastenkur** *f* starvation cure.

'**Fastentag** *m* day of fasting.

'**Fastenzeit** *f* Lent.

'**Fastnacht** *f* (-; *no pl*) **1.** Shrove Tuesday, Mardi gras. **2.** → *Fasching(s...)*

Faszination [fastsina'tsĭo:n] *f* (-; *no pl*) fascination. **faszinieren** [fastsi'ni:rən] *v/t* (h) fascinate.

fatal [fa'ta:l] *adj* **1.** fatal, disastrous. **2.** (very) awkward.

Fatalismus [fata'lɪsmʊs] *m* (-; *no pl*) fatalism. **Fatalist** [fata'lɪst] *m* (-en; -en) fatalist. **fata'listisch** *adj* fatalistic(ally).

fauchen ['fauxən] *v/i* (h) snarl, *cat:* hiss

faul [faul] *adj* **1.** a) rotten (*egg, tooth, etc*), b) putrid: F *fig. ~er Kompromiß* hollow compromise; *~er Kunde* shady customer; *~e Sache* fishy business; *~er Witz* bad joke; *an der Sache ist et. ~* there is s.th. fishy about it; → *Ausrede.* **2.** lazy, idle.

Fäule ['fɔylə] *f* (-; *no pl*) **1.** 🌱 rot. **2.** → *Fäulnis.* '**faulen** *v/i* (sn, h) go bad, rot

faulenzen ['faulɛntsən] *v/i* (h) loaf, laze around, *contp. a.* be lazy.

'**Faulenzer** *m* (-s; -) idler, lazybones.

'**Faulheit** *f* (-; *no pl*) laziness.

faulig ['faulɪç] *adj* a) rotten, b) mo(u)ldy, c) rotting. **Fäulnis** ['fɔylnɪs] *f* (-; *no pl*) a) rottenness, decay (*a.* 🐟), b) putrefaction: *in ~ übergehen* (begin to) rot.

'**Faulpelz** *m* (-es; -e) F *contp.* lazybones.

'**Faultier** *n* **1.** *zo.* sloth. **2.** → *Faulpelz*

Faun [faun] *m* (-[e]s; -e) faun.

Fauna ['fauna] *f* (-; *Faunen*) fauna.

Faust [faust] *f* (-; *~e*) fist: *fig. auf eigene ~* F off one's own bat; *mit eiserner ~* with an iron hand; *mit der ~ auf den Tisch schlagen* put one's foot down; *das paßt wie die ~ aufs Auge* a) it goes together like chalk and cheese, b) *iro.* it fits (perfectly); → *ballen* 2.

Fäustchen ['fɔystçən] *n* (-s; -) *fig. sich ins ~ lachen* laugh up one's sleeve.

'**faust'dick** *adj* as big as your fist: F *fig. ~e Lüge* whopping great lie; *er hat es hinter den Ohren* he's a sly one.

'**fausten** *v/t* (*v/i*) (h) *sports:* fist (the ball).

'**faustgroß** *adj* as big as your fist.

'**Faust|handschuh** *m* mitt(en). *~regel* rule of thumb, general rule. *~schlag* *m* punch. *~skizze* *f* rough sketch.

favorisieren [favori'zi:rən] *v/t* (h

favo(u)r. **Favorit** [favoˈriːt] *m* (-en; -en), **Favoˈritin** *f* (-; -nen) favo(u)rite.

Fax [faks] *n* (-; -[e]). **faxen** *v/t* (h) fax.

Faxen [ˈfaksən] *pl* nonsense: ~ **machen** a) pull faces, b) clown about.

Fazit [ˈfaːtsɪt] *n* (-s; -s) a) result, upshot, b) conclusion: **das ~ ziehen aus** sum *s.th.* up, draw one's conclusion from.

Februar [ˈfeːbruar] *m* (-[s]; *rare* -e) (**im ~** in) February.

Fecht... fencing (*glove, mask, etc*).

fechten [ˈfɛçtən] *v/i* (focht, gefochten, h) **1.** fence, *a. fig.* fight. **2.** F *beg:* ~ **gehen** go begging. **Fechten** *n* (-s) fencing.

Fechter *m* (-s; -), **Fechterin** *f* (-; -nen) fencer. **Fechtsport** *m* fencing.

Feder [ˈfeːdər] *f* (-; -n) **1.** a) feather, b) plume: **sich mit fremden ~n schmücken** adorn o.s. with borrowed plumes; F **noch in den ~n liegen** be still in bed; **~n lassen müssen** not to escape unscathed. **2.** a) nib, b) pen. **3.** ⚙ spring. **Federball** *m* (-[e]s; ˀe) **1.** shuttlecock. **2.** *no pl* badminton.

Federbett *n* duvet, featherbed.

federführend *adj* responsible.

Federgewicht *n sports:* featherweight.

Federhalter *m* fountain pen.

federleicht *adj* (as) light as a feather.

Federlesen *n* **nicht viel ~s machen mit** make short work of.

federn [ˈfeːdərn] (h) **I** *v/i* **1.** be springy, be elastic, bounce. **2.** *gym.* flex. **II** *v/t* **3.** *a.* ⚙ spring, cushion: **gut gefedert sein** be well sprung.

federnd *adj* springy, elastic, resilient.

Federschmuck *m zo.* plumage.

Federstrich *m* stroke of the pen.

Federung *f* (-; -en) springs, *mot.* suspension.

Federwolke *f* cirrus (cloud).

Federzeichnung *f* pen-and-ink drawing.

Fee [feː] *f* (-; -n) fairy.

Fegefeuer *n* (-s; *no pl*) purgatory.

fegen [ˈfeːgən] **I** *v/t* (h) sweep: **Schnee ~** clear away the snow; → **Platz** 5. **II** *v/i* (sn) *fig.* sweep, F *a.* flit, rush.

Feh [feː] *n* (-[e]s; -e) *zo.* squirrel.

Fehde [ˈfeːdə] *f* (-; -n) feud.

fehl [feːl] *adv* → **Platz** 2.

Fehlanzeige *f* ✗, ⚙ nil return: F ~! negative!

fehlbar *adj* fallible.

Fehlbarkeit *f* (-; *no pl*) fallibility.

Fehlbesetzung *f* **1.** *thea.* miscast. **2.** *sports etc:* wrong choice.

Fehlbetrag *m* deficit.

Fehlbezeichnung *f* misnomer.

Fehldiagnose *f* 🝿 wrong diagnosis.

Fehleinschätzung *f* misjudg(e)ment.

fehlen [ˈfeːlən] *v/i* (h) **1.** be absent (**in der Schule, bei e-r Sitzung** *etc* from school, a meeting, *etc*). **2.** be missing: **ihm ~ zwei Zähne** he has two teeth missing; **du hast uns sehr gefehlt!** we really missed you! **3.** be lacking: **ihm fehlt (es an) Mut** he is lacking (in) courage; **uns fehlt es am nötigen Geld** we haven't got the money; **es ~ uns immer noch einige Helfer** we still need some helpers; **es fehlt uns an nichts** we have got everything we want; **es fehlte an jeder Zs.-arbeit** there was no cooperation whatsoever; **das fehlte gerade noch!** that's all we needed!; **wo fehlt's denn?** what's the trouble?; **fehlt Ihnen etwas?** is anything wrong with you?; **es fehlte nicht viel und er ...** he very nearly ... **4.** *weit gefehlt!* far from it!

Fehlen *n* (-s) **1.** a) absence (**bei, in** *dat* from), b) absenteeism. **2.** lack, absence.

fehlend *adj* **1.** absent. **2.** missing. **3.** outstanding.

Fehlentscheidung *f* wrong decision.

Fehlentwicklung *f* undesirable development.

Fehler [ˈfeːlər] *m* (-s; -) **1.** mistake, error, *sports:* fault: **grober ~** blunder; **e-n ~ machen** make a mistake; **dein (eigener) ~!** (that's) your (own) fault! **2.** fault, defect, flaw.

fehlerfrei *adj* faultless, perfect, flawless.

fehlerhaft *adj* faulty (*a.* ⚙), incorrect, full of mistakes: ⚙ **~e Stelle** flaw.

fehlerlos → **fehlerfrei**.

Fehlerquelle *f* source of error (⚙ trouble). **~quote** *f* error rate. **~verzeichnis** *n* errata.

Fehlgeburt *f* 🝿 miscarriage.

fehlgeleitet *adj fig.* misguided.

Fehlgriff *m* mistake, *a.* wrong choice.

Fehlinvestition *f* bad investment.

Fehlkalkulation *f* miscalculation.

Fehlkonstruktion *f* **e-e ~ sein** be badly designed.

Fehlleistung *f* (**Freudsche ~** Freudian) slip.

'Fehlpaß m *sports*: bad pass.
'Fehlplanung f bad planning.
'Fehlschlag m *fig.* failure, F washout.
'fehlschlagen v/i (*irr, sep,* -ge-, sn, →
  schlagen) fail, go wrong.
'Fehlschluß m fallacy.
'Fehlstart m false start: **e-n ~ verursa-
chen** *sports*: jump the gun.
'Fehlurteil n misjudg(e)ment.
'Fehlverhalten n lapse.
'Fehlversuch m unsuccessful attempt.
'Fehlzeit f time debit.
'Fehlzündung f *mot.* misfire, backfire.
Feier ['faiər] f (-; -n) a) celebration, par-
ty, fête, b) ceremony: **zur ~ des Tages**
to mark the occasion.
'Feierabend m **~ machen** finish (work),
F knock off, *shop*: close; **nach ~** after
work.
'feierlich *adj* a) solemn, b) ceremon-
ious.
'Feierlichkeit f (-; -en) **1.** *no pl* solem-
nity, ceremoniousness. **2.** ceremony.
feiern ['faiərn] (h) **I** v/t celebrate, *a.*
keep, observe (*holiday*), *a.* commemorate (*anniversary*). **II** v/i celebrate, have
a party.
'Feiertag m (**gesetzlicher ~** public) holiday; **kirchlicher ~** religious holiday.
feige ['faigə] *adj* cowardly.
'Feige f (-; -n) 🌿 fig.
'Feigenbaum m fig tree.
'Feigenblatt n *a. fig.* fig leaf.
'Feigheit f (-; *no pl*) cowardice.
'Feigling m (-s; -e) coward.
Feile ['failə] f (-; -n) file. **'feilen** v/t, v/i
(h) file: *fig.* **~ an** (*dat*) polish.
feilschen ['failʃən] v/i (h) haggle (**um**
about).
fein [fain] **I** *adj* **1.** fine, *a.* delicate: **~es
Gebäck** fancy cakes; **~er Regen** (light)
drizzle. **2.** a) fine, *a.* choice, excellent
(*quality*), b) elegant, c) refined: **~e Art,
~er Ton** good form; **nur vom Feinsten**
only of the best. **3.** keen, sharp (*ear
etc*), fine, sensitive: **~er Humor** subtle
humo(u)r; **~er Unterschied** subtle (*or*
fine) distinction. **4.** *a. iro.* nice, fine: **~!**
fine!, good! **II** *adv* **5.** finely (*etc*): **er ist ~
heraus** he's sitting pretty.
'Feinabstimmung f 🎵, ⚙ fine tuning.
'Feinarbeit f precision work.
Feind [faint] m (-[e]s; -e) enemy, adversary: **Feund und ~** friend and foe; **sich ~e**

machen make enemies; **sich j-n zum ~
machen** antagonize s.o.
Feindin ['faindin] f (-; -nen) enemy.
'feindlich *adj* ✗ enemy (*troops etc*), *a.*
hostile (*attitude etc* **gegen** to[wards]).
'Feindlichkeit f (-; -en) hostility.
'Feindschaft f (-; -en) enmity, hostility.
'feindselig *adj* hostile (**gegen** to).
'Feindseligkeit f (-; -en) **1.** *no pl* hostility
(**gegen** to). **2.** *pl* ✗ hostilities.
'Feindstaat m enemy state.
'feinfühlig [-fy:liç] *adj* sensitive, delicate,
tactful. **'Feingefühl** n (-[e]s; *no pl*) sensitiveness, *a.* tact.
'Feingehalt m standard.
'Feingold n fine gold.
'Feinheit f (-; -en) **1.** *no pl* a) fineness, *a.*
delicacy, *a.* exquisiteness, b) refine-
ment, c) elegance. **2.** subtlety: **die ~en**
the finer points, the niceties; **die letzten ~en** the finishing touches.
'Feinkostladen m delicatessen (shop).
'feinmachen: sich ~ (*sep,* -ge-, h) F dress
up.
'feinmaschig *adj* fine-meshed.
'Feinme,chanik f precision mechanics.
'Feinschmecker m (-s; -) gourmet
  ~lo,kal n gourmet restaurant.
'Feinschnitt m (-[e]s; *no pl*) fine cut.
'feinsinnig *adj* sensitive, subtle.
'Feinwäsche f delicate fabrics.
'Feinwaschmittel n washing powder for
  delicate fabrics.
feist [faist] *adj* fat, stout.
feixen ['faiksən] v/i (h) F smirk.
Feld [felt] n (-[e]s; -er) field (*a. fig.*), △ *a.*
panel, *chess*: square: **auf dem ~** in th
field; **das ~ anführen** *sports*: lead th
field; **das ~ behaupten** stand one'
ground; **das ~ räumen** beat a retrea
zu ~e ziehen gegen fight against.
'Feld|arbeit f **1.** 🌾 work in the fields. **2**
research etc: fieldwork. **~bett** n camp
bed. **~flasche** f ✗ water bottle. **~for
schung** f field research, fieldwork
~küche f field kitchen. **~lager** n
bivouac, camp. **~laza,rett** n casualt
clearing station, *Am.* evacuation hosp
tal. **~marschall** m field marsha
~sa,lat m 🌿 lamb's lettuce. **~spieler**(i
f) m *sports*: outfield player.
'Feldstecher m (-s; -) field glasses.
Feld-Wald-und-'Wiesen... F commo
  -or-garden..., run-of-the-mill ...

'**Feldwebel** [-ve:bəl] *m* (-s; -) sergeant.
'**Feldweg** *m* country lane.
'**Feldzug** *m* ✗ campaign.
Felge ['fɛlgə] *f* (-; -n) **1.** ⚙ rim. **2.** *gym.* circle. '**Felgenbremse** *f* rim brake.
Fell [fɛl] *n* (-[e]s; -e) **1.** *zo.* coat. **2.** a) hide, skin, b) pelt, c) fur: *das ~ abziehen* (*dat*) skin; *fig.* *ein dickes ~ haben* have a thick skin; F *j-m das ~ über die Ohren ziehen* fleece s.o.; *s-e ~e davonschwimmen sehen* see one's hopes dashed.
Fels [fɛls] *m* (-en; -en) rock.
'**Felsblock** *m* boulder.
'**Felsen** ['fɛlzən] *m* (-s; -) rock, cliff.
'**felsenfest** *adj* unshakable: *~ davon überzeugt* absolutely convinced of it.
'**Felsenküste** *f* rocky coast.
felsig ['fɛlzɪç] *adj* rocky.
'**Felsklettern** *n* (-s) rock climbing.
'**Felsspalte** *f* crevice. '**Felswand** *f* wall of rock, rock face. '**Felszacke** *f* crag.
feminin [femi'ni:n] *adj* feminine (*a. ling.*), *contp.* effeminate. **Feminismus** [femi'nɪsmus] *m* (-; *no pl*) feminism. **Femi'nist** *m* (-en; -en), **Femi'nistin** *f* (-; -nen), **femi'nistisch** *adj* feminist.
Fenchel ['fɛnçəl] *m* (-s; *no pl*) ♣ fennel.
Fenster ['fɛnstər] *n* (-s; -) window: *das Geld zum ~ hinauswerfen* throw one's money away; F *er ist weg vom ~* he has had his chips. '**Fenster|bank** *f* (-; ⁼e), **~brett** *n* windowsill. **~briefumschlag** *m* window envelope. **~glas** *n* window glass. **~laden** *m* shutter. **~leder** *n* chamois (leather). **~platz** *m* window seat. **~rahmen** *m* window frame. **~scheibe** *f* windowpane. **~tür** *f* French window.
Ferien ['fe:riən] *pl* holidays, 🎓 *univ.* or *Am.* vacation, *parl.* recess: *die großen ~* the long vacation; *~ machen* go on holiday (*Am.* vacation).
'**Ferien...** holiday (*camp, flat, etc*). **~ort** *m* holiday resort. **~reise** *f* holiday (*Am.* vacation) trip. **~reisende** *m, f* (-n; -n) holidaymaker. **~zeit** *f* holiday period.
Ferkel ['fɛrkəl] *n* (-s; -) *zo.* young pig, piglet; *fig. contp. du ~!* you (dirty) pig! **Ferke'lei** *f* (-; -en) F *contp.* obscenity, dirty joke. '**ferkeln** *v/i* (h) *zo.* farrow.
'**Fermate** [fɛr'ma:tə] *f* (-; -n) ♪ pause, fermata.

Ferment [fɛr'mɛnt] *n* (-s; -e) enzyme, ferment.
fern [fɛrn] **I** *adj* a) far (*a. adv*), b) far-off, *a. fig.* distant, remote: *der ‚e Osten* the Far East; *von ~* from (*or* at) a distance, from afar; *in nicht allzu ~er Zukunft* in the not too distant future; *nichts liegt mir ~er* (*als*) nothing is further from my mind (than). **II** *prep* (*dat*) far (away) from. **fern'ab** *adv* far away.
'**Fernauslöser** *m phot.* cable release.
'**Fernbedienung** *f* remote control.
'**fernbleiben** *v/i* (*irr, sep,* -ge-, sn, → *bleiben*) (*dat* from) stay away, be absent. '**Fernbleiben** *n* (-s) a) absence, b) absenteeism.
'**Fernbrille** *f* distance glasses.
Ferne ['fɛrnə] *f* (-; *no pl*) distance: *aus der ~* from (*or* at) a distance, from afar; *in der ~* far away, far off; *fig.* (*noch*) *in weiter ~* (still) a long way off.
ferner ['fɛrnər] **I** *adj* further: → *a.* **fernliegen**. **II** *adv* further(more), besides: F *fig. er erschien unter ~ liefen* he was among the also rans.
'**fernerhin** *adv* for the (*or* in) future: *auch ~ tun* continue to do.
'**Fern|fahrer** *m mot.* long-distance lorry driver, *Am.* long-haul truck driver, F trucker. **~fahrt** *f* long-distance trip. **~flug** *m* long-distance flight. **‚gelenkt** *adj* remote-controlled, ✗ guided (*missile etc*). **~gespräch** *n* long-distance call. **~glas** *n* binoculars.
'**fernhalten** *v/i* (*irr, sep,* -ge-, h, → *halten*) keep away (*a. sich ~, von* from): *j-n von sich ~* keep s.o. at a distance; *et. von j-m ~* keep s.th. from s.o.
'**Fernheizung** *f* district heating.
fern'her *adv* (*von*) *~* from afar.
'**Fern|ko‚pierer** *m* telecopier. **~kursus** *m* correspondence course. **~laster** [-lastər] *m* (-s; -) F, **~lastwagen** *m* long-distance lorry, *Am.* long-haul truck. **~leitung** *f teleph.* long-distance line, ⚡ transmission line, ⚙ pipeline. **~lenkung** *f* remote control. **~lenkwaffe** *f* guided weapon (*or* missile). **~licht** *n mot.* full (*or* high) beam.
'**fernliegen** *v/i* (*irr, sep,* -ge-, h, → *liegen*) *es liegt mir fern zu inf* far be it from me to *inf*; *nichts lag mir ferner* nothing was farther from my mind.
'**Fernmelde|amt** *n* telephone exchange.

~satel¦lit m (tele)communication satellite. **~technik** f (-; no pl) (tele)communications. **~turm** m radio and TV tower. **~wesen** n (-s; no pl) (tele)communications.

'**fernmündlich** → *telefonisch*.

'**Fern¦ost...**, '**fern¦östlich** adj Far Eastern.

'**Fernrohr** n (-[e]s; -e) telescope.

'**Fernschreiben** n (-s; -) (per ~ by) telex.

'**Fernschreiber** m telex machine.

'**Fernseh...** television (or TV) (aerial, camera, interview, studio, network, etc).

'**Fernseh¦ansager(in** f) m television (or TV) announcer. **~ansprache** f television (or televised) address. **~anstalt** f television company. **~appa¦rat** m → *Fernsehgerät*. **~diskussi¦on** f (TV) panel discussion. **~empfänger** m → *Fernsehgerät*.

'**fernsehen** v/i (irr, sep, -ge-, h, → **sehen**) watch television. '**Fernsehen** n (-s) (im ~ on) television (or TV): im ~ bringen (or übertragen) telecast, televise. '**Fernseher** m (-s; -) F 1. → *Fernsehgerät*. 2. → *Fernsehzuschauer*.

'**Fernseh¦fassung** f television (or TV) adaptation. **~gerät** n television (set), TV (set). **~pro¦gramm** n 1. television (or TV) program(me Br.). 2. TV guide. **~publikum** n television audience. **~röhre** f television tube. **~satel¦lit** m TV (or television) satellite. **~schirm** m (television) screen. **~sender** m 1. television transmitter. 2. television (broadcasting) station. 3. television channel. **~sendung** f (television or TV) program(me Br.), telecast. **~spiel** n television (or TV) play. **~teilnehmer** m 1. TV licen¦ce (Am. -se) holder. 2. → *Fernsehzuschauer*. **~turm** m television (or TV) tower. **~übertragung** f television (or TV) broadcast. **~zeitschrift** f TV guide. **~zuschauer** m a) (television or TV) viewer, b) pl → *Fernsehpublikum*.

'**Fernsicht** f view.

'**Fernsprech¦amt** n telephone exchange. **~auftragsdienst** m answering service. **~auto¦mat** m pay phone. **~buch** n telephone directory, F phone book.

'**Fernsprecher** m (-s; -) (öffentlicher ~ public) telephone, F phone.

'**Fernsprech¦gebühren** pl telephone

charges. **~teilnehmer** m telephone subscriber.

'**fernstehen** v/i (irr, sep, -ge-, h, → **stehen**) j-m ~ have no contact with s.o.

'**fernsteuern** v/t (sep, -ge-, h) operate s.th. by remote control.

'**Fern¦steuerung** f remote control. **~straße** f 1. major road. 2. motorway, Am. freeway. **~trans¦port** m long-distance (Am. long-haul) transport. **~unterricht** m correspondence course. **~verkehr** m long-distance traffic. **~wärmenetz** n long-distance heating system. **~ziel** n long-term objective. **~zug** m long-distance train.

Ferse ['fɛrzə] f (-; -n) heel: j-m auf den ~n a) sein be hard on s.o.'s heels, b) folgen dog s.o.'s footsteps.

fertig ['fɛrtɪç] adj 1. ready: (Achtung,) ~, los! ready, steady, go! 2. finished, completed: ~ sein mit have finished (with); fig. ~ werden mit a) cope (or deal) with, b) get over (grief etc); (gut) ohne ... ~ werden manage (or get along) (quite well) without ... 3. a) ❂ finished, prefabricated, b) ready-to-eat, precooked, instant (food), c) ready-made (clothes). 4. fig. accomplished, mature. 5. F fig. a) a. fix und ~ bushed, b) done for, c) flabbergasted: der ist ~! he has had it! → *fertigmachen*.

'**Fertigbauweise** f ❂ prefabricated construction.

'**fertigbringen** v/t (irr, sep, -ge-, h, → **bringen**) et. ~ get s.th. done, manage s.th., bring s.th. off; es ~ zu inf manage to inf; ich brachte es nicht fertig I couldn't (w.s. bring myself to) do it.

fertigen ['fɛrtɪɡən] v/t (h) produce, make.

'**Fertig¦erzeugnis** n finished product. **~gericht** n gastr. instant meal. **~haus** n prefabricated house, F prefab.

'**Fertigkeit** f (-; -en) a) skill, b) talent, c) proficiency (in dat in).

'**fertigmachen** v/t (sep, -ge-, h) 1. get s.o., a th. ready. 2. finish. 3. F j-n ~ a) finish s.o. (off), b) get s.o. down, c) slam s.o., d) sl. clobber s.o. (a. sports).

'**Fertigmon¦tage** f final assembly.

'**Fertigpro¦dukt** n finished product.

'**fertigstellen** v/t (sep, -ge-, h) finish complete.

'**Fertigstellung** f (-; no pl) completion.

'**Fertigteil** *n* prefabricated part, *pl* assembly units.

'**Fertigung** *f* (-; *no pl*) manufacture, production.

'**Fertigungsstraße** *f* ⚙ production line.

'**Fertigwaren** *pl* finished products.

Fes [fɛs] *m* (-[es]; -[e]) fez.

fesch [fɛʃ] *adj* F smart, chic.

'**Fessel**[1] ['fɛsəl] *f* (-; -n) *a. fig.* shackle, fetter: *j-m ~n anlegen* → *fesseln* 1.

'**Fessel**[2] *f* (-; -n) **1.** ankle. **2.** *zo.* pastern.

'**fesseln** ['fɛsəln] *v/t* (h) **1.** *j-n ~* tie s.o. up (*an acc* to): *fig. ans Bett gefesselt* confined to one's bed, bedridden. **2.** *fig.* a) fascinate, captivate, b) catch (*s.o.'s eye, attention, etc*). '**fesselnd** *adj fig.* fascinating, riveting, gripping.

fest [fɛst] *adj* **1.** a) firm (*a. fig.* decision, prices, *etc*), solid (*a. phys.*), ⚙ *a.* tight, (firmly) fixed, b) strong, sturdy: *~ werden* harden, solidify, *cement etc*: set. **2.** *fig.* fixed (*costs, date, income, prices, etc*), *a.* binding (*agreement etc*), regular (*customer*), permanent (*domicile, position, etc*), F steady (*girlfriend etc*): *~er Wohnsitz* 🏛️ a fixed abode; *~er Schlaf* sound sleep; *~e Freundschaft* lasting friendship. **II** *adv* **3.** firmly (*etc*): *~ schlafen* sleep soundly; *et. ~ abmachen* settle s.th. definitely; *Kapital ~ anlegen* tie up capital; *j-n ~ anstellen* employ s.o. on a permanent basis; *ich bin ~ davon überzeugt, daß ...* I'm absolutely convinced that ...; *das habe ich ihr ~ versprochen* I gave her my word for it. **4.** F *a. ~e* properly; *immer ~e!* go at it!

Fest *n* (-[e]s; -e) **1.** a) celebration, festivities, b) party, fête: *ein ~ feiern* celebrate. **2.** holiday, *eccl.* feast.

'**Festakt** *m* ceremony.

'**festangelegt** *adj* tied-up (*funds*). '**festangestellt** *adj* permanently employed.

'**Festaufführung** *f* gala performance.

'**festbinden** *v/t* (*irr, sep, -ge-, h, → binden*) tie (*an dat* to), tie s.o., s.th. up.

'**festbleiben** *v/i* (*irr, sep, -ge-, sn, → bleiben*) remain firm.

'**Festessen** *n* dinner, banquet.

'**festfahren: sich ~** (*irr, sep, -ge-, h, → fahren*) *a. fig.* get stuck, *talks*: reach a deadlock.

'**festfressen: sich ~** (*irr, sep, -ge-, h, → fressen*) ⚙ seize, jam.

'**Festgeldkonto** *n* fixed-term deposit account.

'**festgelegt**, '**festgesetzt** *adj* fixed.

'**festhalten** (*irr, sep, -ge-, h, → halten*) **I** *v/t* **1.** hold on to, grip. **2.** hold, keep, *a.* detain. **3.** *fig.* a) record, b) photograph, film, capture: *e-n Gedanken ~* make a (mental) note of an idea; *et. schriftlich ~* put s.th. down in writing. **II** *v/i* (*an* ~ a) hold tight, b) *a. fig.* hold on (*an dat* to).

'**festigen** ['fɛstɪɡən] (h) **I** *v/t* strengthen, consolidate, *a.* stabilize (*currency*). **II** *sich ~* strengthen, grow stronger, *currency etc*: *a.* stabilize, *knowledge*: improve.

'**Festiger** *m* (-s; -) setting lotion.

'**Festigkeit** *f* (-; *no pl*) firmness, strength, steadiness, stability.

'**Festigung** *f* (-; -en) strengthening, consolidation, stabilization.

'**festklammern: sich ~** (*sep, -ge-, h*) cling (*an dat* to).

'**festkleben** *v/t, v/i* (*sep, -ge-, h*) stick (*an dat* to).

'**festklemmen** (*sep, -ge-, h*) **I** *v/t* clamp (fast), wedge. **II** *v/i* stick (fast), get stuck, jam, be jammed.

'**Festkon,zert** *n* gala concert.

'**Festkörper** *m phys.* solid.

'**Festkurs** *m* ✝ fixed rate.

'**Festland** *n* a) mainland, b) land, c) continent. '**Festland(s)...** continental.

'**festlegen** (*sep, -ge-, h*) **I** *v/t* **1.** → *festsetzen* 1. **2.** lay down, define (*principles etc*). **3.** ♣ plot (*course*). **4.** ✝ tie up (*capital*). **5.** *j-n auf e-e Sache ~* pin s.o. down to s.th. **II** *sich ~ auf* (*acc*) a) commit o.s. to, b) decide on.

'**festlich I** *adj* festive, splendid. **II** *adv* festively (*etc*): *~ begehen* celebrate; *~ gestimmt* in a festive mood.

'**Festlichkeit** *f* (-; -en) **1.** festivity. **2.** *no pl* festive atmosphere.

'**festliegen** *v/i* (*irr, sep, -ge-, h, → liegen*) **1.** be fixed, *capital*: be tied up. **2.** *mot.* be stuck, ♣ be grounded.

'**festmachen** (*sep, -ge-, h*) **I** *v/t* **1.** (*an dat* to) fix, fasten, ♣ moor. **2.** *fig.* fix, settle, *a.* clinch (*a deal*): *et. ~ an* (*dat*) fix s.th. on. **II** *v/i* **3.** ♣ moor.

'**Festmeter** *m, n* cubic met/re (*Am.* -er).

'**festnageln** *v/t* (*sep, -ge-, h*) nail down (*a. fig. auf acc* to).

Festnahme ['fɛstnaːmə] *f* (-; -n) arrest.

'festnehmen *v/t (irr, sep,* -ge-, h, → **nehmen**) arrest.

'Festplatte *f computer:* hard disc.

'Festpreis *m* fixed price.

'Festrede *f* (ceremonial) address.

'Festredner(in *f) m* official speaker.

'Festsaal *m* (banqueting) hall.

'Festschrift *f* commemorative publication.

'festsetzen *(sep,* -ge-, h) **I** *v/t* **1.** a) *(auf acc* for) fix, arrange *(place, time, etc),* b) *(auf acc* at) fix *(price, penalty, salary, etc),* c) assess *(damage, tax),* d) lay down, agree on *(conditions).* **2.** arrest. **II** *v/refl* ~ **sich** settle *(in dat* in).

'festsitzen *v/i (irr, sep,* -ge-, h, → **sitzen**) *mot.* be stuck *(a.* F *fig.),* ♟ be stranded.

'Festspeicher *m computer:* read-only memory *(abbr.* ROM).

'Festspiel *n* festival performance: ~**e** *pl* → **Festspielwoche** *f* festival.

'feststehen *v/i (irr, sep,* -ge-, h, → **stehen**) a) be fixed, b) be certain, be a fact.

'feststehend *adj* **1.** ☯ stationary. **2.** *fig.* established *(fact etc).*

'feststellbar *adj* **1.** ascertainable. **2.** noticeable. **3.** ☯ lock-type.

'Feststellbremse *f* parking brake.

'feststellen *v/t (sep,* -ge-, h) **1.** a) find out, discover, establish, b) locate *(fault, place, etc),* c) ☯ diagnose. **2.** realize, see, notice. **3.** state, say. **4.** ☯ lock.

'Feststellung *f* (-; -en) **1.** establishing *(etc,* → **feststellen**), discovery. **2.** observation: **er machte die ~, daß ...** he found *(or* realized) that ... **3.** a) remark, b) statement.

'Feststoff,rakete *f* solid-fuel rocket.

'Festtag *m (eccl.* religious) holiday.

'festtäglich *adj* festive.

'Festung *f* (-; -en) fortress, fort.

'festverzinslich *adj* ☯ fixed interest (bearing): ~**e Anlagepapiere** investment bonds.

'Festwoche *f, a. pl* festival.

'Festzelt *n* marquee.

'festziehen *v/t (irr, sep,* -ge-, h, → **ziehen**) tighten.

'Festzug *m* procession.

Fetisch ['fe:tɪʃ] *m* (-(e)s; -e) fetish.

Fetischismus [feti'ʃɪsmʊs] *m* (-; *no pl)* fetishism.

Fetischist [-'ʃɪst] *m* (-en; -en) fetishist.

fett [fɛt] *adj* **1.** fat, *a.* obese *(person),* fatty

(food): ~ **machen** fatten; ~ **essen** eat fatty food. **2.** F *fig.* fat, rich, big: ~**e Beute** big haul. **3.** *print.* bold.

Fett *n* (-(e)s; -e) **1.** fat: F **sein ~ weghaben** have caught it. **2.** *of body:* fat, F flab: ~ **ansetzen** put on (a lot of) weight. **3.** ☯ grease.

'fettarm *adj* low-fat ..., *pred* low in fat.

'Fettauge *n* blob of fat.

'Fettcreme *f* rich oil-based cream.

'Fettdruck *m print.* bold(-faced) type.

fetten ['fɛtən] (h) **I** *v/t* grease. **II** *v/i* be greasy.

'Fettfleck *m* grease spot.

'fettgedruckt *adj* in bold type.

'Fettgehalt *m* (-(e)s; -e) fat content.

'Fettgewebe *n* fatty tissue.

'fetthaltig *adj* containing fat, fatty, oil-based *(lotion).*

fettig ['fɛtɪç] *adj* fat, fatty, oily, greasy *(hair, skin, etc).*

'Fettleber *f* 🩺 fatty liver.

fettleibig ['fɛtlaɪbɪç] *adj* obese.

'Fettleibigkeit *f* (-; *no pl)* obesity.

'Fettnäpfchen *n* F **(bei j-m) ins** ~ **treten** put one's foot in it. **'Fettsack** *m* F *contp.* fatso. **'Fettsalbe** *f* greasy ointment. **'Fettschicht** *f* layer of fat. **'Fettsucht** *f* (-; *no pl)* 🩺 obesity. **'Fettwanst** *m* F *contp.* **1.** paunch. **2.** fatso.

Fetus ['fe:tʊs] *m* (-; -[ses] -se) f(o)etus.

Fetzen ['fɛtsən] *m* (-s; -) **1.** rag *(a. humor. dress),* scrap *(of paper),* shred *(of cloth):* **in** ~ in shreds and tatters; F **daß die** ~ **fliegen** like crazy. **2.** *pl* F *fig.* snatches *(of conversation etc).*

fetzig ['fɛtsɪç] *adj* F wild.

feucht [fɔʏçt] *adj* damp, moist *(a. eyes, lips, skin, etc),* wet *(climate),* humid *(air):* ~**e Hände** sweaty palms.

'feucht'fröhlich *adj* F (very) merry.

'Feuchtigkeit *f* (-; *no pl)* damp(ness), moisture, humidity: **vor** ~ **schützen!** keep in a dry place!

'Feuchtigkeits|creme *f* moisturizing cream, moisturizer. ~**gehalt** *m* moisture content, *of air:* a. humidity.

feudal [fɔʏ'da:l] *adj* **1.** *hist.* feudal. **2.** *fig.* a) sumptuous, b) posh.

Feudalismus [fɔʏda'lɪsmʊs] *m* (-; *no pl)* *hist.* feudalism.

Feuer ['fɔʏɐ] *n* (-s; -) **1.** fire: ✗ ~**!** fire!; **haben Sie** ~**?** have you got a light?; ~ **fangen** catch fire; **j-m** ~ **geben** give s.o.

a light; *das Olympische* ~ the Olympic flame; *fig. durchs* ~ *gehen für* go through fire and water for; *mit dem* ~ *spielen* play with fire; *zwischen zwei* ~ *geraten* be caught between the devil and the deep blue sea; → **eröffnen** 1. **2.** ⚓ beacon. **3.** *fig.* fire, *a.* fervo(u)r, spirit: ~ *und Flamme sein* be all for it.

'Feuer|a,larm *m* fire alarm. **~anzünder** *m* fire lighter. **~bestattung** *f* cremation. **~eifer** *m* zeal. **~einstellung** *f* ✕ cessation of fire. **2fest** *adj* **1.** fireproof. **2.** incombustible. **~gefahr** *f* danger of fire. **2gefährlich** *adj* flammable. **~gefecht** *n* ✕ gun battle. **~haken** *m* poker. **~kraft** *f* (*; no pl*) ✕ fire power. **~leiter** *f* **1.** fire ladder. **2.** fire escape. **~löscher** *m* fire extinguisher. **~melder** *m* (*-s; -*) fire alarm.

feuern ['fɔʏərn] *v/t* (h) **1.** fire (*stove,* ✕ *salute*), *a.* burn (*wood, coal*). **2.** F hurl, *sports:* slam (*the ball*): *j-m e-e* ~ land s.o. one. **3.** F fire, sack.

'Feuer|probe *f fig.* acid test. **2rot** *adj* fiery (red), flaming red. **~schaden** *m* damage caused by fire. **~schiff** *n* lightship. **~schlucker** *m* fire-eater. **~schutz** *m* **1.** fire prevention. **2.** ✕ covering fire. **~stein** *m* flint. **~stelle** *f* fireplace, hearth. **~taufe** *f fig.* baptism of fire. **~teufel** *m* F fire bug. **~treppe** *f* fire escape.

'Feuerung *f* (*-; -en*) **1.** heating. **2.** *no pl* fuel.

'Feuer|versicherung *f* fire insurance. **~wache** *f* fire station. **~waffe** *f* firearm. **'Feuerwehr** *f* (*-; -en*) fire brigade: F *wie die* ~ like a flash. **~mann** *m* fireman. **'Feuerwerk** *n* (*-s; -e*) fireworks (*a. fig.*). **'Feuerwerkskörper** *m* firework. **'Feuerzangenbowle** *f* burnt punch. **'Feuerzeug** *n* (*-[e]s; -e*) (cigarette) lighter. **'Feuerzeugben,zin** *n* lighter fluid. **Feuilleton** [fœjə'tõ:] *n* (*-s; -s*) feature pages. **Feuilletonist** [fœjətoˈnɪst] *m* (*-en; -en*) feature writer.

feurig ['fɔʏrɪç] *adj fig.* **1.** fiery, ardent, passionate. **2.** rich, heady (*wine*).

Fiasko ['fiasko] *n* (*-s; -s*) fiasco.

Fibel ['fiːbəl] *f* (*-; -n*) *ped.* primer.

Fiber ['fiːbər] *f* (*-; -n*) fibre, *Am.* fiber.

'Fiberglas *n* fibre (*Am.* fiber) glass.

Fichte ['fɪçtə] *f* (*-; -n*) ⚘ spruce, F pine (tree). **'Fichtenholz** *n* deal.

ficken ['fɪkən] *v/t, v/i* (h) V fuck.

fidel [fi'deːl] *adj* cheerful.

Fieber ['fiːbər] *n* (*-s; no pl*) fever (*a. fig.*), (high) temperature: ~ *haben* → **fiebern** 1; *j-m* (*or j-s*) ~ *messen* take s.o.'s temperature.

'Fieberanfall *m* attack of fever.

'fieberfrei *adj sie ist* ~ her temperature is back to normal again.

'fieberhaft *adj fig.* feverish.

'Fieberkranke *m, f* (*-n; -n*) fever case.

'Fieberkurve *f* temperature curve.

'Fiebermittel *n* antipyretic.

fiebern ['fiːbərn] *v/i* (h) **1. a)** have (*or* be running) a temperature, **b)** be delirious. **2.** *fig.* be feverish (*vor* with): ~ *nach* yearn for.

'Fieber|ta,belle *f* temperature chart. **~thermo,meter** *n* (clinical) thermometer. **~traum** *m* feverish dream.

fiebrig ['fiːbrɪç] → **fieberhaft.**

Fiedel ['fiːdəl] *f* (*-; -n*) fiddle.

fiedeln ['fiːdəln] *v/t, v/i* (h) F fiddle.

fiel [fiːl] *pret of* **fallen.**

fies [fiːs] *adj* F nasty, mean.

Fiesling ['fiːslɪŋ] *m* (*-s; -e*) F meanie.

Figur [fiˈɡuːr] *f* (*-; -en*) **1.** figure (*a. ♟, ♪*), *a.* build: *fig. e-e gute* (*schlechte*) ~ *machen* cut a fine (poor) figure. **2.** *in film, novel, etc:* figure, character: *komische* ~ **a)** figure of fun, **b)** strange character. **3.** *chess:* piece, *pl a.* chessmen. **4.** *arts:* **a)** figure, statue, **b)** figurine.

figurativ [figuraˈtiːf] *adj ling.* figurative.

figurieren [figuˈriːrən] *v/i* (h) figure (*als* as). **figürlich** [fiˈɡyːrlɪç] *adj* **1.** *paint. etc* figured. **2.** *ling.* figurative.

Fiktion [fɪkˈtsjoːn] *f* (*-; -en*) fiction.

fiktiv [fɪkˈtiːf] *adj* fictitious.

Filet [fiˈleː] *n* (*-s; -s*) *gastr.* fillet. **~steak** *n* fillet steak. **~stück** *n* piece of sirloin.

Filiale [fiˈliaːlə] *f* (*-; -n*) **1.** branch (office), subsidiary. **2.** chain store.

Fili'alleiter(in *f*) *m* branch manager.

Filigran [filiˈɡraːn] *n* (*-s; -e*), **Fili'gran-arbeit** *f* filigree.

Film [fɪlm] *m* (*-s; -e*) **1.** *phot.* film. **2.** film, *esp. Am. a.* movie: *e-n* ~ *drehen* (*über acc*) shoot (*or* make) a film (of), film *s.th.*; F *fig. mir ist der* ~ *gerissen* I had a blackout. **3.** the cinema, *esp. Am.* the movies: *beim* ~ *sein* **a)** be in the film (*esp. Am. a.* movie) business, **b)** be a film (*esp. Am. a.* movie) actor (*or* actress). **4.** film, coat(ing). **~ar‚chiv** n film library. **~ateli‚er** n film studio. **~aufnahme** f **1.** shooting (of a film). **2.** shot, take. **~bericht** m film report.

'Filmemacher(in f) m film (esp. Am. a. movie) maker.

filmen ['fɪlmən] (h) **I** v/t film, shoot. **II** v/i be filming, make a film, a. be on location.

'Film‚festspiele pl film festival. **~gelände** n studio lot. **~gesellschaft** f film (Am. motion-picture) company. **~indu‚strie** f film (Am. motion-picture) industry.

filmisch ['fɪlmɪʃ] adj cinematic.

'Film‚kamera f **1.** film (or movie) camera. **2.** cinecamera. **~kri‚tik** f film review. **~kritiker(in** f) m film critic. **~kunst** f (-; no pl) cinematography. **~materi‚al** n footage. **~mu‚sik** f **1.** film music. **2.** the music to the film. **~pack** m film pack. **~preis** m film (esp. Am. a. movie) award. **~produ‚zent(in** f) m (film) producer. **~pro‚jektor** m film (esp. Am. a. movie) projector. **~regis‚seur(in** f) m film (esp. Am. a. movie) director. **~re‚klame** f screen advertising. **~schauspieler(in** f) m film (or screen, esp. Am. a. movie) actor (actress). **~star** m film (esp. Am. a. movie) star. **~streifen** m reel, w.s. strip. **~studio** n film studio. **~the‚ater** n cinema, Am. movie theater. **~verleih** m **1.** film distribution. **2.** film distributors. **~vorführer** m projectionist. **~vorführung** f film (esp. Am. a. movie) show. **~vorschau** f a) preview, b) trailer, c) in newspaper: forthcoming films. **~welt** f film world, Am. a. movieland.

Filter ['fɪltər] m, n (-s; -) filter. **~anlage** f filtration plant. **~einsatz** m filter element. **~kaffee** m filtered coffee.

filtern ['fɪltərn] v/t (h) filter, a. percolate.

'Filter‚pa‚pier n filter paper. **~ziga‚rette** f filter(-tipped) cigarette.

Filtrat [fɪl'traːt] n (-[e]s; -e) filtrate.

filtrieren [fɪl'triːrən] v/t (h) filter.

Filz [fɪlts] m (-es; -e) **1.** felt. **2.** F felt hat. **3.** F contp. a) skinflint, b) pol. corruption. **filzen** ['fɪltsən] (h) **I** v/t F fig. frisk. **II** v/i wool.: felt. **'Filzhut** m felt hat.

filzig ['fɪltsɪç] adj **1.** a) felted, b) matted (hair). **2.** F fig. mean, stingy.

'Filzlaus f zo. crab louse.

'Filzpan‚toffel m felt slipper.

'Filzstift m felt(-tipped) pen.

Fimmel ['fɪməl] m (-s; -) F craze: **e-n ~ haben für** be mad about.

Finale [fi'naːlə] n (-s; -) **1.** finale. **2.** sports: final (round), finals.

Finalist [fina'lɪst] m (-en; -en), **Fina'listin** f (-; -nen) sports: finalist.

Fi'nalsatz m ling. final clause.

Finanz... [fi'nants-] financial (adviser, paper, etc). **~amt** n inland (Am. internal) revenue (office), fig. contp. the Tax Man. **~ausschuß** m finance committee. **~beamte** m revenue officer.

Fi'nanzen pl finances.

Fi'nanzgericht n tax tribunal. **Fi'nanzgeschäft** n financial transaction.

finanziell [finan'tsiɛl] adj financial.

finanzieren [finan'tsiːrən] v/t (h) finance: → **frei** 12. **Finan'zierung** f (-; -en) financing. **Finan'zierungsgesellschaft** f finance company.

Fi'nanz‚jahr n fiscal (or financial) year. **2kräftig** adj financially strong, potent. **~lage** f financial situation. **~mann** m financier. **~mi‚nister** m minister of finance, Br. Chancellor of the Exchequer, Am. Secretary of the Treasury. **~mini‚sterium** n ministry of finance, Br. Treasury, Am. Treasury Department. **~poli‚tik** f financial (or fiscal) policy. **2schwach** adj financially weak. **~spritze** f F shot in the arm. **~welt** f financial world. **~wesen** n (-s; no pl) (public) finance.

finden ['fɪndən] (fand, gefunden, h) **I** v/t find, fig. a. think: **nirgends zu ~** nowhere to be found; fig. **ein Ende ~** come to an end; **ich fand k-e Worte** I was at a loss for words; **ich finde es gut** (, daß ...) I think it's good (that ...); **wie ~ Sie das Buch?** how do you like (or what do you think of) the book?; **~ Sie (nicht)?** do (don't) you think so?; **ich weiß nicht, was sie an ihm findet** I don't know what she sees in him. **II sich ~** a) be found, b) find o.s.; **das wird sich ~** we'll see. **III** v/i nach Hause ~ find one's way home; **zu sich selbst ~** sort o.s out.

'Finder m (-s; -), **'Finderin** f (-; -nen) finder. **'Finderlohn** m finder's reward.

Findling ['fɪntlɪŋ] m (-s; -e) geol. erratic block.

Fistel

Finesse [fiˈnɛsə] *f* (-; -n) finesse, *pl* tricks: **mit allen ~n** car etc with all the refinements.

fing [fɪŋ] *pret of* **fangen**.

Finger [ˈfɪŋər] *m* (-s; -) finger: **sich die ~ verbrennen** *a. fig.* burn one's fingers; **sich in den ~ schneiden** a) cut one's finger, b) *fig.* make a big mistake; **j-m auf die ~ klopfen** *a. fig.* rap s.o.'s knuckles; **laß die ~ davon!** a) hands off!, b) *fig.* leave well alone!; *fig.* **sich et. aus den ~n saugen** make s.th. up; **j-m auf die ~ sehen** keep a sharp eye on s.o.; **j-n um den kleinen ~ wickeln** twist s.o. round one's little finger; **k-n ~ rühren** not to lift a finger; **er hat überall s-e ~ im Spiel** he's got a finger in every pie; → **abzählen**.

'Finger|abdruck *m* fingerprint: → **abnehmen.** **~alpha,bet** *n* finger alphabet.

'fingerfertig *adj* nimble-fingered.

'Fingerfertigkeit *f* (-; *no pl*) dexterity.

'Fingerhut *m* **1.** ❀ foxglove. **2.** thimble.

fingern [ˈfɪŋərn] (h) **I** *v/i* **~ an** (*dat*) finger. **II** *v/t* F wangle.

'Finger|nagel *m* fingernail. **~ring** *m* ring. **~schale** *f* finger bowl. **~spitze** *f* fingertip. **~spitzengefühl** *n* a) sure instinct, b) tact. **~sprache** *f* finger language. **~übung** *f* finger exercise.

'Fingerzeig *m* (-[e]s; -e) hint, pointer.

fingieren [fɪŋˈgiːrən] *v/t* (h) **1.** fake: **fingiert** fake(d), fictitious. **2.** fabricate.

Finish [ˈfɪnɪʃ] *n* (-s; -s) *sports*, ◉ finish.

Fink [fɪŋk] *m* (-en; -en) *zo.* finch.

Finne¹ [ˈfɪnə] *f* (-; -n) fin.

'Finne² *m* (-n; -n), **'Finnin** *f* (-; -nen) Finn. **finnisch** [ˈfɪnɪʃ] *adj* Finnish.

'Finnland *n* (-s) Finland.

finster [ˈfɪnstər] *adj* **1.** *a. fig.* dark, black, gloomy. **2.** a) grim, b) evil, sinister: **~er Blick** black look; **j-n ~ ansehen** glower at s.o. **3.** F *fig.* a) shady, b) bad: **es sieht ~ aus!** things are looking bad!

'Finsternis *f* (-; -se) *a. fig.* darkness, gloom(iness).

Finte [ˈfɪntə] *f sports* feint, *fig. a.* trick.

Firlefanz [ˈfɪrləfants] *m* (-es; *no pl*) F *contp.* a) frippery, junk, b) nonsense.

Firma [ˈfɪrma] *f* (-; -men) firm, company: **die ~ Bosch** (the) Bosch (Company).

Firmament [fɪrmaˈmɛnt] *n* (-[e]s; -e) firmament, sky.

'firmen [ˈfɪrmən] *v/t* (h) *eccl.* confirm.

'Firmen|inhaber(in *f*) *m* owner of a (*or* the) firm. **~name** *m* company name. **~schild** *n* company name, facia, *on machine etc:* nameplate. **~sitz** *m* (company) headquarters. **~stempel** *m* firm('s) stamp. **~verzeichnis** *n* trade directory. **~wagen** *m* company car. **~wert** *m* (-[e]s; *no pl*) goodwill. **~zeichen** *n* F logo.

firmieren [fɪrˈmiːrən] *v/i* (h) **~ als** have the company name of.

'Firmling *m* (-s; -e) *eccl.* confirmand.

'Firmung *f* (-; -en) *eccl.* confirmation.

Firn [fɪrn] *m* (-[e]s; -e) corn snow.

Firnis [ˈfɪrnɪs] *m* (-ses; -se) varnish.

firnissen [ˈfɪrnɪsən] *v/t* (h) varnish.

First [fɪrst] *m* (-[e]s; -e) ridge.

Fis [fɪs] *n* (-; -) ♪ F sharp.

Fisch [fɪʃ] *m* (-[e]s; -e) **1.** fish: F *fig.* **ein großer** (*or* **dicker**) **~** a big fish; **kleine ~e** peanuts, small beer. **2.** *pl astr.* Pisces. **'Fischauge** *n phot.* fish-eye (lens).

fischen [ˈfɪʃən] *v/t, v/i* (h) fish (**nach** for): → **trübe 1.** **'Fischen** *n* (-s) fishing.

'Fischer *m* (-s; -) fisherman. **~boot** *n* fishing boat. **~dorf** *n* fishing village. **Fische'rei** *f* (-; *no pl*) **1.** fishing. **2.** fishing industry. **~flotte** *f* fishing fleet. **~grenze** *f* fishing limit. **~hafen** *m* fishing port. **~recht** *n* fishing right(s).

'Fisch|fang *m* fishing. **~fi,let** *n gastr.* fish fillet. **~gabel** *f* fish fork. **~gericht** *n gastr.* fish dish. **~geruch** *m* fishy smell. **~geschäft** *n* fishmonger('s). **~gräten-muster** *n* herringbone (pattern). **~gründe** *pl* fishing grounds, fishery. **~händler(in** *f*) *m* fishmonger, *Am.* fish dealer. **~indu,strie** *f* fish-processing industry. **~kon,serven** *pl* tinned (*or* canned) fish. **~kunde** *f* (-; *no pl*) ichthyology. **~kutter** *m* (fishing) trawler. **~laich** *m* (fish) spawn. **~markt** *m* fish market. **~mehl** *n* fishmeal. **~messer** *n* fish knife. **~otter** *m zo.* otter. **~reiher** *m zo.* heron. **~restau,rant** *n* fish (*or* seafood) restaurant. **~schuppe** *f* scale. **~stäbchen** *n gastr.* fish finger, *Am.* fish stick. **~sterben** *n* fish kill. **~vergiftung** *f* fish poisoning. **~zucht** *f* fish farming. **~zug** *m* catch, *fig. a.* haul.

Fiskus [ˈfɪskʊs] *m* (-; *no pl*) **1.** Treasury. **2.** government.

Fistel [ˈfɪstəl] *f* (-; -n) ✇ fistula.

'**Fistelstimme** f **1.** ♩ falsetto. **2.** contp. squeaky voice.

fit [fɪt] adj (**sich ~ halten** keep) fit.

Fitneß ['fɪtnɛs] f (-; no pl) fitness.

'**Fitneßcenter** n health club, gym.

'**Fitneßraum** m exercise room.

Fittich ['fɪtɪç] m (fig. **j-n unter s-e ~e nehmen** take s.o. under one's) wing.

fix [fɪks] **I** adj **1.** fixed (salary, costs, etc): **~e Idee** fixed idea, obsession. **2.** F a) quick (**in** dat at), b) smart, sharp. **3.** ~ **und fertig** a) all ready, b) → **fertig** 5 a. **II** adv **4.** F quickly, in a flash.

fixen ['fɪksən] v/i (h) sl. fix, shoot, main-line. **Fixer** ['fɪksər] m (-s; -), '**Fixerin** f (-; -nen) sl. junkie.

Fi'xierbad n phot. fixer.

fixieren [fɪ'ksiːrən] v/t (h) **1.** a. phot, ⚕ fix, fig. a. determine: **schriftlich ~** formulate, record. **2.** psych. **fixiert sein auf** (acc) be fixated on. **3.** stare at.

Fi'xiermittel n phot. fixative.

Fi'xierung f (-; -en) **1.** fixing (a. phot. etc). **2.** psych. fixation.

'**Fixstern** m fixed star.

Fixum ['fɪksʊm] n (-s; Fixa) ✝ fixed sum (or salary).

Fjord [fjɔrt] m (-[e]s; -e) fjord, fiord.

FKK [ɛfka:'ka:] → **Freikörperkultur.**
FK'K-Strand m nudist beach.

flach [flax] adj **1.** flat, a. level, even: ~ **machen** (**klopfen** etc) flatten; ~ **werden** flatten (out); **mit der ~en Hand** with the flat of one's hand. **2.** a. fig. shallow: **~er Teller** shallow (w.s. dinner) plate. **3.** low (a. sports: shot).

'**Flachboot** n flat-bottomed boat.

'**Flachdach** n flat roof.

Fläche ['flɛçə] f (-; -n) a) surface (a. ⟨), b) area, space: (**weite**) ~ expanse.

'**Flächen|ausdehnung** f area. **~brand** m extensive fire. **♀deckend** adj overall, global. **~inhalt** m ⟨ area. **~maß** n ⟨ surface measurement.

'**flachfallen** v/i (irr, sep, -ge-, sn, → **fallen**) F fall through.

'**Flachheit** f (-; no pl) flatness, fig. shallowness.

'**Flachmann** m (-[e]s; ⸚er) F hip flask. '**Flachland** n flat country. '**Flachpaß** m soccer: low pass. '**Flachreli,ef** n bas-relief. '**Flachrennen** n flat race.

Flachs [flaks] m (-es; no pl) **1.** ♀ flax. **2.** F kidding: **ohne ~!** no kidding!

'**Flachschuß** m soccer: low ball.

flachsen ['flaksən] v/i (h) F kid.

flackern ['flakərn] v/i (h) flicker.

Fladen ['flaːdən] m (-s; -) flat cake.

'**Fladenbrot** n round flat loaf.

Flagge ['flagə] f (-; -n) flag: fig. **unter falscher ~ segeln** sail under false colo(u)rs; ~ **zeigen** make a stand.

flaggen ['flagən] (h) **I** v/i fly (or hoist) a flag (or flags). **II** v/t flag, signal.

'**Flaggschiff** n a. fig. flagship.

Flair [flɛːr] n (-s; no pl) **1.** aura. **2.** flair.

Flak [flak] f (-; -, -s) **1.** → **Flakgeschütz 2.** → '**Flakartille,rie** f antiaircraft artillery. '**Flakfeuer** n antiaircraft fire, ♀ flak. '**Flakgeschütz** n antiaircraft gun.

Flakon [fla'kõː] n, m (-s; -s) small bottle.

flambieren [flam'biːrən] v/t (h) flame.

Flamingo [fla'mɪŋgo] m (-s; -s) zo. flamingo.

flämisch ['flɛːmɪʃ] adj Flemish.

Flamme ['flamə] f (-; -n) a. fig. flame: **in (hellen) ~n stehen** be ablaze; **auf kleiner ~ cook** on a low heat. '**flammend** adj fig. fiery, stirring (speech etc).

'**Flammenmeer** n sea of flames.

Flanell [fla'nɛl] m (-s; -e) flannel.

Flanke ['flaŋkə] f (-; -n) **1.** flank, side. **2.** a) soccer: cent/re (Am. -er), b) gym (flank) vault.

'**flanken** v/i (h) soccer: cent/re (Am. -er)

flankieren [flaŋ'kiːrən] v/t (h) flank: fig. **~de Maßnahme** supporting measure.

Flansch [flanʃ] m (-[e]s; -e) ⊙ flange.

flapsig ['flapsɪç] adj loutish.

Fläschchen ['flɛʃçən] n (-s; -) **1.** small bottle, pharm. phial. **2.** (baby) bottle

Flasche ['flaʃə] f (-; -n) **1.** bottle: **e-e ~ Wein** a bottle of wine; **e-m Baby die ~ geben** give a baby its bottle; **m der ~ aufziehen** bottle-feed. **2.** F dud flop.

'**Flaschen|bier** n bottled beer. **~gas** bottled gas. **♀grün** adj bottle-green **~kind** n bottle-fed baby. **~milch** f bot tled milk. **~öffner** m bottle opener **~pfand** n deposit (on a bottle). **~post** bottle post. **~wein** m bottled wine.

'**flaschenweise** adv by the bottle.

'**Flaschenzug** m ⊙ block and pulley.

'**flatterhaft** adj flighty, fickle.

flattern ['flatərn] v/i **1.** (sn) flutter. **2.** (h flutter (a. ♠, ⊙), flap, wheels: wobble

flau [flaʊ] adj **1.** a) queasy, b) faint, c

listless. **2.** stale (*taste*). **3.** *phot.* flat, fuzzy, weak. **4.** ✝ slack.

Flaum [flaʊm] *m* (-[e]s; *no pl*) down. '**flaumig** *adj* downy.

Flausch [flaʊʃ] *m* (-es; -e) *textil.* coating. '**flauschig** *adj* fluffy.

Flausen ['flaʊzən] *pl* F silly ideas.

Flaute ['flaʊtə] *f* (-; -n) **1.** ♻ lull. **2.** ✝ slack period.

Flechte ['flɛçtə] *f* (-; -n) **1.** ♣ lichen. **2.** 🕱 eczema. **3.** braid.

'**flechten** *v/t* (flocht, geflochten, h) plait (*hair*), bind (*wreath*), weave (*basket*).

Fleck [flɛk] *m* (-[e]s; -e) **1.** spot, stain: *blauer ~* bruise. **2.** *fig.* blemish. **3.** F a) spot, place, b) patch: *am falschen ~ a.* *fig.* in the wrong place; *fig.* **nicht vom ~ kommen** not to make any headway; *sich nicht vom ~ rühren* not to budge.

'**Fleckchen** *m* (-s; -) **1.** speck. **2.** *fig.* (*ein schönes ~* [*Erde*] a lovely spot.

flecken *v/i* (h) stain.

'**Flecken** *m* (-s; -) → *Fleck.*

'**Fleckenentferner** *m* stain remover.

'**fleckenlos** *adj* a. *fig.* spotless.

'**fleckig** *adj* a) spotted, b) stained.

'**Flecktyphus** *m* 🕱 (epidemic) typhus.

Fledermaus ['fle:dər-] *f zo.* bat.

Flegel ['fle:gəl] *m* (-s; -) lout. **Flege'lei** *f* (-; -en) loutish behavio(u)r. '**flegelhaft** *adj* loutish. '**Flegeljahre** *pl* (*in den ~n sein* be at an) awkward age.

flehen ['fle:ən] *v/i* (h) ~ *um* beg for, implore. '**Flehen** *n* (-s) entreaty.

'**flehend**, '**flehentlich** *adj* imploring, urgent (*request*): ~ *bitten um* → **flehen.**

Fleisch [flaɪʃ] *n* (-es; *no pl*) **1.** a. *fig.* flesh: *das eigene ~ und Blut* one's own flesh and blood; *j-m in ~ und Blut übergehen* become second nature to s.o.; F *sich ins eigene ~ schneiden* cut off one's nose to spite one's face; *vom ~ fallen* grow thin. **2.** *gastr.* a) meat, b) flesh (*of fruit*). **~brühe** *f* a) consommé, beef tea, b) (beef) stock.

'**Fleischer** *m* (-s; -) butcher.

Fleische'rei *f* (-; -en), '**Fleischerladen** *m* butcher's shop.

'**fleischfarben** *adj* flesh-colo(u)red.

'**fleischfressend** *adj* ♣, *zo.* carnivorous.

'**Fleischfresser** *m zo.* carnivore.

'**Fleischgericht** *n* meat dish.

'**fleischig** *adj* fleshy. meaty.

'**Fleisch|kloß** *m* **1.** *gastr.* meatball. **2.** F

fig. mound of flesh. **~kon,serven** *pl* tinned (*or* canned) meat.

'**fleischlich** *adj* carnal.

'**fleischlos** *adj* meatless (*diet*).

'**Fleisch|to,mate** *f* beef tomato. **~vergiftung** *f* 🕱 meat poisoning. **~waren** *pl* meat products. **~wolf** *m* mincer, *Am.* meat grinder. **~wunde** *f* 🕱 flesh wound. **~wurst** *f* pork sausage.

Fleiß [flaɪs] *m* (-es; *no pl*) diligence, industry, hard work: *viel ~ verwenden auf* (*acc*) take great pains over; *ohne ~ kein Preis* no sweet without sweat.

'**fleißig I** *adj* diligent, hard-working, busy. **II** *adv* diligently, F a lot.

flektieren [flɛk'ti:rən] *v/t* (h) *ling.* inflect.

fletschen ['flɛtʃən] *v/t* (h) *die Zähne ~* snarl.

flexibel [flɛ'ksi:bəl] *adj* a. *fig.* flexible.

Flexibilität [flɛksibili'tɛ:t] *f* (-; *no pl*) a. *fig.* flexibility.

Flexion [flɛ'ksio:n] *f* (-; -en) inflection.

flicken ['flɪkən] *v/t* (h) a) mend, b) a. F *fig.* patch up. '**Flicken** *m* (-s; -) patch.

'**Flickwerk** *n* (-[e]s; *no pl*) *fig.* patch-up job(s). '**Flickzeug** *n* **1.** sewing kit. **2.** *mot. etc* repair kit.

Flieder ['fli:dər] *m* (-s; -) ♣ lilac.

Fliege ['fli:gə] *f* (-; -n) **1.** *zo.* fly: *er tut k-r ~ was zuleide* he wouldn't hurt a fly; *sterben wie die ~n* die like flies; *zwei ~n mit einer Klappe schlagen* kill two birds with one stone. **2.** bow tie.

fliegen ['fli:gən] (flog, geflogen) **I** *v/i* (sn) **1.** fly, a. go by air: ~ *lassen* fly; ~ *Luft* **3.** **2.** *fig.* fly, rush. **3.** F *fig.* be fired, get the sack: *aus der Schule etc* ~ be kicked out of school *etc.* **4.** F *fig.* ~ *auf* (*acc*) really go for; *auf j-n* ~ a. fall for s.o. **II** *v/t* (h) **5.** fly (*persons, plane, etc*).

'**Fliegen** *n* (-s) a) flying, b) aviation.

'**fliegend** *adj* flying (a. *sports*): **~er Händler** hawker.

'**Fliegen|fänger** *m* flypaper. **~gewicht** *n* (-s; *no pl*) *sports*: flyweight. **~klatsche** *f* fly swatter. **~pilz** *m* toadstool.

'**Flieger** *m* (-s; -) **1.** *zo.*, *horse racing*: flier, flyer. **2.** airman (*a.* ✈), pilot. **3.** ✈ *Br.* aircraftman 2nd class, *Am.* airman basic. **4.** F plane. **5.** *cycling*: sprinter. **~a,larm** *m* air-raid warning. **~angriff** *m* air raid. **~horst** *m* air base.

'**Fliegerin** *f* (-; -nen) airwoman, woman pilot. '**fliegerisch** *adj* flying.

'Fliegerjacke f bomber jacket.
fliehen ['fliːən] (floh, geflohen) **I** v/i (sn) (**vor** dat from, **nach, zu** to) flee, run away, escape. **II** v/t (h) avoid, shun.
'fliehend adj fig. receding (chin etc).
'Fliehkraft f phys. centrifugal force.
Fliese ['fliːzə] f (-; -n) tile.
'Fliesenboden m tiled floor.
'Fliesenleger m (-s; -) tiler.
'Fließarbeit f (-; no pl) assembly-line work.
'Fließband n (-[e]s; ⸚er) **1.** assembly line. **2.** conveyor belt. **⸚arbeiter** m assembly-line worker. **⸚fertigung** f assembly-line production.
fließen ['fliːsən] v/i (floß, geflossen, sn) flow (a. fig.), river, water, etc: a. run.
'fließend adj **1.** flowing: **⸚es Wasser** running water. **2.** fast-moving (traffic). **3.** fig. fluid, fluent: **er spricht ⸚ Englisch** he speaks fluent English.
'Fließ|heck n mot. fastback. **⸚komma** n computer: floating decimal point.
flimmern ['flɪmərn] v/i (h) shimmer, TV flicker.
flink [flɪŋk] adj quick, nimble.
Flinte ['flɪntə] f (-; -n) gun: F fig. **die ⸚ ins Korn werfen** throw in the towel.
Flipper ['flɪpər] m (-s; -) pinball machine.
flippern ['flɪpərn] v/i (h) F play pinball.
Flirt [flœrt] m (-s; -s) **1.** flirtation. **2.** flirt.
flirten ['flœrtən] v/i (h) flirt.
Flittchen ['flɪtçən] n (-s; -) F hussie.
Flitter ['flɪtər] m (-s; no pl) **1.** coll. sequins. **2.** fig. a) a. **'Flitterglanz** m glitter, b) a. **'Flitterkram** m tinsel.
'Flitterwochen pl honeymoon.
flitzen ['flɪtsən] v/i (sn) F **1.** flit. **2.** streak.
Flitzer ['flɪtsər] m (-s; -) F **1.** nippy little car. **2.** streaker.
floaten ['floʊtən] v/t, v/i (h) † float.
flocht [flɔxt] pret of **flechten**.
Flocke ['flɔkə] f (-; -n) **1.** flake. **2.** fluff.
flocken ['flɔkən] v/i (h) flake. **'flockig** adj **1.** flaky. **2.** fluffy. **3.** 🍄 flocculent.
flog [floːk] pret of **fliegen**.
floh [floː] pret of **fliehen**.
Floh m (-[e]s; ⸚e) zo. flea: F fig. **j-m e-n ⸚ ins Ohr setzen** put ideas into s.o.'s head. **'Flohmarkt** m flea market.
Flor¹ [floːr] m (-s; no pl) **1.** bloom. **2.** mass of flowers (or blossoms).
Flor² m (-s; -e) textil. **1.** gauze. **2.** pile.
Flora ['floːra] f (-; Floren) flora.

floral [floˈraːl] adj floral.
Florett [floˈrɛt] n (-[e]s; -e) foil.
Flo'rettfechten n foil fencing.
florieren [floˈriːrən] v/i (h) flourish.
Floskel ['flɔskəl] f (-; -n) empty phrase.
'floskelhaft adj meaningless, empty.
Floß [floːs] n (-es; ⸚e) raft.
Flosse ['flɔsə] f (-; -n) **1.** zo. a) fin, b) flipper (a. sports). **2.** ✈ stabilizer fin. **3.** F a) paw, mitt, b) trotter.
flößen ['fløːsən] v/t, v/i (h) float.
Flöte ['fløːtə] f (-; -n) **1.** ♪ flute. **2.** flute glass. **3.** cards: flush. **'flöten** v/t, v/i ♪ play the flute, a. fig. flute, bird: sing.
'flötengehen v/i (irr, sep, -ge-, sn, → **gehen**) F go down the drain.
Flötist [fløˈtɪst] m (-en; -en), **Flö'tistin** f (-; -nen) flautist, flute-player.
flott [flɔt] adj **1.** brisk, lively, zippy. **2.** F a) smart, snazzy, b) dashing, c) gay: **ein ⸚es Leben führen** live it up. **3.** ⚓ **⸚ sein** be afloat; → **flottmachen** 1.
Flotte ['flɔtə] f (-; -n) ✓, ⚓ fleet.
'Flottenstützpunkt m ⚓ naval base.
Flottille [flɔˈtɪl(j)ə] f (-; -n) ⚓ flotilla.
'flottmachen v/t (sep, -ge-, h) **1.** ⚓ float, set s.th. afloat. **2.** get car going again.
Flöz [fløːts] n (-es; -e) 🜨, geol. seam.
Fluch [fluːx] m (-[e]s; ⸚e) **1.** curse. **2.** curse, oath, swearword.
fluchen ['fluːxən] v/i (h) curse, swear: **auf** (or **über**) **j-n** (et.) **⸚** curse s.o. (s.th.).
Flucht¹ [flʊxt] f (-; -en) a) flight (**vor** dat from, a. fig.), b) escape: **auf der ⸚ erschossen** etc shot etc while fleeing (or attempting to escape); **auf der ⸚ sein** be on the run (**vor** dat from); **die ⸚ ergreifen** → **flüchten** 1; in **die ⸚ schlagen** put s.o. to flight; fig. **die ⸚ nach vorn antreten** seek refuge in attack.
Flucht² f (-; -en) 🜨, ⊙ alignment, row.
'fluchtartig I adj hasty. **II** adv hastily, in a hurry.
flüchten ['flʏçtən] v/i (sn) **1.** flee (**nach, zu** to), run away, prisoner: escape (**aus** from), ⚖ abscond (**vor** dat from). **2.** (a. **sich ⸚**) take shelter (or refuge) (**in** acc in): fig. **sich in Ausreden ⸚** resort to excuses.
'Fluchthelfer(in f) m escape agent.
'flüchtig I adj **1.** a) hasty, b) brief, flying, c) cursory, superficial, d) careless, slapdash: **⸚e Bekanntschaft** passing acquaintance. **2.** fleeting (glance etc). **3.**

fugitive, escaped, ⚖ absconding: **~er Fahrer** hit-and-run driver. **4.** 🦌 volatile. **II** adv **5.** hastily (etc): **~ durchlesen** skim over; **~ kennen** know s.o., s.th. vaguely; **~ sehen** catch a glimpse of.

'**Flüchtige** m, f (-n; -n) fugitive.

'**Flüchtigkeitsfehler** m slip.

Flüchtling ['flʏçtlɪŋ] m (-s; -e) fugitive, pol. refugee.

'**Flüchtlingslager** n refugee camp.

'**Fluchtversuch** m attempt to escape.

'**Fluchtwagen** m getaway car.

'**Fluchtweg** m escape route.

Flug [fluːk] m (-[e]s; ⸚e) flight: fig. (wie) **im ~(e)** very quickly. **~bahn** f trajectory, ✈ flight path. **~ball** m tennis: volley. **~begleiter(in** f) m flight attendant. **⸚bereit** adj ready for take-off. **~betrieb** m (-[e]s; no pl) air traffic. **~blatt** n leaflet. **~boot** n flying boat, seaplane.

Flügel ['flyːɡəl] m (-s; -) **1.** wing (a. pol. or sports), ✕ a. flank, blade (of propeller etc), panel (of altar etc): fig. **j-m die ~ stutzen** clip s.o.'s wings; (dat) **~ verleihen** lend wings to; → **link. 2.** ♪ grand (piano): **am ~ ...** accompanied by ...

'**Flügelfenster** n casement (window).

'**flügellos** adj wingless.

'**Flügel|mutter** f ⚙ wing nut. **~schlag** m flapping of wings. **~schraube** f ⚙ thumbscrew. **~stürmer(in** f) m sports: wing, winger. **~tür** f folding door(s).

'**flugfähig** adj airworthy.

'**Fluggast** m (air) passenger.

'**Fluggastabfertigung** f **1.** passenger clearance. **2.** check-in desk.

flügge ['flʏɡə] adj fully fledged: **~ werden** a) fledge, b) fig. begin to stand on one's own two feet.

'**Flug|geschwindigkeit** f flying speed. **~gesellschaft** f airline. **~hafen** m airport. **~höhe** f (flying) altitude. **~kapi,tän** m (flight) captain. **~karte** f **1.** (air) ticket. **2.** aeronautical map. **~körper** m flying object, ✕ missile. **~lehrer(in** f) m flying instructor. **~leitung** f air traffic control. **~linie** f **1.** (air) route. **2.** ✈ airline (company). **~lotse** m air traffic controller. **~nummer** f flight number. **~ob,jekt** n unbekanntes ~ unidentified flying object. **~passa,gier** m (air) passenger. **~perso,nal** n aircrew, coll. flying personnel. **~plan** m timetable. **~platz** m a) airfield, b) airport. **~preis**

m (air) fare. **~reise** f journey by air. **~schalter** m flight desk. **~schein** m **1.** (air) ticket. **2.** pilot's licen/ce (Am. -se). **~schneise** f approach corridor. **~schreiber** m flight recorder, black box. **~sicherung** f air traffic control. **~steig** m gate. **~strecke** f **1.** (air) route. **2.** distance flown. **3.** leg. **~stunde** f **1.** flying hour. **2.** nach zwei **~n** after a two-hour flight; **sechs ~n entfernt** six flight-hours away. **⸚tauglich** adj fit to fly, airworthy. **~ticket** n (air) ticket. **~überwachung** f air traffic control. **~verbindung** f air connection. **~verkehr** m **1.** air traffic. **2.** air services. **~wetter** n flying weather. **~zeit** f flying time.

'**Flugzeug** n (-[e]s; -e) (aero)plane, Am. (air)plane, aircraft: **mit dem ~** by air, by plane. **~absturz** m air (or plane) crash. **~bau** m (-[e]s; no pl) aircraft construction. **~besatzung** f aircrew. **~entführer(in** f) m hijacker, skyjacker. **~entführung** f hijacking, skyjacking. **~fa,brik** f aircraft factory. **~führer** m pilot. **~halle** f hangar. **~indu,strie** f aircraft industry. **~konstruk,teur** m aircraft designer. **~träger** m ⚓, ✕ aircraft carrier. **~unglück** n air disaster, air (or plane) crash.

'**Flugziel** n destination.

Fluidum ['fluːidom] n (-s; -da) aura, air, atmosphere.

fluktuieren [flʊktuˈiːrən] v/i (h) fluctuate.

Flunder ['flʊndər] f (-; -n) zo. flounder.

flunkern ['flʊŋkərn] v/i (h) fib.

Fluor ['fluːɔr] n (-s; no pl) fluorine: **mit ~ anreichern** fluoridate.

fluoreszieren [fluores'tsiːrən] v/i (h) fluoresce: **~d** fluorescent.

Flur¹ [fluːr] m (-[e]s; -e) **1.** hall. **2.** corridor.

Flur² f (-; -en) open fields: fig. **allein auf weiter ~** all alone. **~bereinigung** f consolidation (of farmland). **~schaden** m crop damage.

Fluse ['fluːzə] f (-; -n) fluff, Am. lint.

Fluß [flʊs] m (-sses; ⸚sse) **1.** river. **2.** no pl flow(ing): **in ~ kommen** get going.

fluß'ab(wärts) adv down the river, downstream.

'**Flußarm** m arm of a river.

fluß'auf(wärts) adv up the river, upstream.

'**Flußbett** n riverbed.
Flüßchen ['flʏsçən] n (-s; -) small river.
'**Flußdia,gramm** n flowchart.
flüssig ['flʏsɪç] **I** adj **1.** a) liquid, b) molten: ~ **werden** liquefy, melt. **2.** fig. flowing, fluent: → a. **fließend** 3. **3.** † liquid, available. **II** adv **4.** in liquid form. **5.** write, speak fluently, traffic etc go smoothly. '**Flüssiggas** n liquid gas.
'**Flüssigkeit** f (-; -en) **1.** no pl liquidity (a. †), a. fig. fluidity. **2.** liquid, fluid.
'**Flüssigkeits|bremse** f mot. hydraulic brake. ~**getriebe** n mot. fluid drive. ~**maß** n liquid measure.
'**Flüssigkri,stall-Sichtanzeige** f computer: liquid crystal display (LCD).
'**flüssigmachen** v/t (sep, -ge-, h) † realize, convert into cash.
'**Fluß|krebs** m zo. freshwater crayfish. ~**lauf** m course of a river. ~**mündung** f mouth (of a river), estuary. ~**pferd** n hippopotamus, F hippo. ~**ufer** n riverbank, riverside.
flüstern ['flʏstərn] v/t, v/i (h) (speak in a) whisper: F **dem werde ich was ~!** I'll tell him a thing or two! '**Flüstern** n (-s) whisper(ing). '**Flüsterpropa,ganda** f whispering campaign. '**Flüsterton** m **im ~** in a whisper.
Flut [flu:t] f (-; -en) **1.** high tide: **es ist ~** the tide is in. **2.** often pl waters, waves. **3.** fig. flood (of tears, letters, etc), a. torrent (of words etc).
fluten ['flu:tən] **I** v/i (sn) a. fig. flood, stream, pour. **II** v/t (h) flood.
'**Flut|kata,strophe** f flood disaster. ~**licht** n (-[e]s; no pl) floodlights: **bei ~** under floodlight. ~**welle** f tidal wave.
focht [fɔxt] pret of **fechten**.
Fock [fɔk] f (-; -en) ⚓ **1.** foremast. **2.** a. **Focksegel** n foresail.
Föderalismus [fœdera'lɪsmʊs] m (-; no pl) federalism. **föderalistisch** [fœdera'lɪstɪʃ] adj a) federal, b) federalistic (efforts etc). **Föderation** [fœdera-'tsi̯oːn] f (-; -en) (con)federation.
fohlen ['foːlən] v/i (h) zo. foal.
'**Fohlen** n (-s; -) a) foal, b) colt, c) filly.
Föhn ['føːn] m (-[e]s; -e), ~**wind** m föhn.
Föhre ['føːrə] f (-; -n) ♀ pine (tree).
Fokus ['foːkʊs] m (-; -se) focus.
fokussieren [foku'siːrən] v/t (h) focus.
Folge ['fɔlɡə] f (-; -n) **1.** succession, sequence: **in der ~** subsequently; **dreimal**

etc **in ~** three times etc running (or in a row); **in rascher ~** in rapid succession. **2.** a) instal(l)ment, TV part, sequel, serial, b) number, issue. **3.** a) consequence, b) aftermath, aftereffect: **als ~ davon** as a consequence; **zur ~ haben** result in, lead to; (**üble**) **~n haben** have (dire) consequences; **die ~n tragen** bear the consequences; **die ~n sten → folgen** 2.
'**Folgeerscheinung** f → **Folge** 3.
'**Folgekosten** pl follow-up costs.
folgen ['fɔlɡən] v/i (sn) **1.** (dat) follow (s.o., s.th.): ~ **auf** (acc) a. succeed (s.o.), a. come after (s.o., s.th.); **Brief folgt!** letter will follow!; **wie folgt** as follows; **daraus folgt, daß** (from this) it follows that; **j-s Beispiel ~** follow s.o.'s example; **können Sie mir ~?** do you follow me?; **ich kann Ihnen da(rin) nicht ~** I can't agree with you there. **2.** (dat) obey (an order), comply with a request etc, accept (an invitation). **3.** F obey (j-m s.o.). '**folgend** adj following, next, subsequent: **am ~en Tage** the following (or next) day; **im ~en** in the following; **es handelt sich um ~es** the matter is as follows.
'**folgendermaßen** adv as follows.
'**folgenschwer** adj momentous, grave.
'**folgerichtig** adj logical, consistent.
folgern ['fɔlɡərn] v/t (h) (**aus** from) conclude, deduce. '**Folgerung** f (-; -en) (**e-e ~ ziehen** draw a) conclusion.
'**Folgesatz** m **1.** ling. consecutive clause. **2.** ♀, philos. corollary. '**Folgeschäden** pl ♂ secondary (⚖ consequential) damage. '**Folgezeit** f (**in der ~** in the period following.
'**folglich** ['fɔlklɪç] conj a) thus, b) consequently, therefore.
folgsam ['fɔlkzaːm] adj obedient, good
Folie ['foːli̯ə] f (-; -n) foil (a. fig.), film.
'**Folienkar,toffeln** pl baked potatoes.
Folklore [fɔlk'loːrə] f (-; no pl) folklore.
folkloristisch [fɔlklo'rɪstɪʃ] adj folkloristic.
Follikel [fɔ'liːkəl] m (-s; -) follicle.
Fol'likelsprung m physiol. ovulation.
Folter ['fɔltər] f (-; -n) torture, fig. a. torment: **j-n auf die ~ spannen** keep s.o. on tenterhooks. '**foltern** v/t (h) torture. '**Folterung** f (-; -en) torture.
Fön [føːn] m (-[e]s; -e) TM hair drier.

Fond [fõ:] *m* (-s; -s) **1.** background. **2.** *mot.* back (of the car).

Fonds [fõ:] *m* (-; - [fõ:s]) ✝ **1.** fund. **2.** funds. **3.** government stocks.

Fondue [fõ'dy:] *n* (-s; -s) *gastr.* fondue.

fönen ['fø:nən] *v/t* (h) (blow-)dry.

Fontäne [fɔn'tɛ:nə] *f* (-; -n) **1.** fountain. **2.** jet of water.

forcieren [fɔr'si:rən] *v/t* (h) force.

'Förderanlage *f* conveyor (system).

'Förderband *n* conveyor belt.

'Förderer *m* (-s; -), **'Förderin** *f* (-; -nen) a) promoter, supporter, b) patron(ess), sponsor. **'förderlich** *adj* (*dat* to) conducive, useful, beneficial.

'Fördermenge *f* ⚒ output.

fordern ['fɔrdərn] *v/t* (h) **1.** demand (*von j-m* of s.o.), a. call for, ✝ *a.* claim, ask (for *a price*): **zuviel ~** a) ask (*or* expect) too much, b) overcharge (*von j-m* s.o.). **2.** challenge, *sports:* a. push s.o. to the limit: *er war voll gefordert* he was fully stretched; *nun ist der Minister gefordert* now it's for the minister to act. **3.** claim (*human lives etc*).

fördern ['fœrdərn] *v/t* (h) **1.** a) promote, support, b) patronize, sponsor, c) encourage, d) help, be good for: **~des Mitglied** supporting member. **2.** ⚒ produce; → *zutage*.

Förderpreis *m* (literary *etc*) award.

'Förderung *f* (-; -en) **1.** demand (*nach* for, *an acc* on), ⚖ claim: *~en stellen* make demands, enter claims. **2.** ✝ a) call, b) charge.

'Förderung *f* (-; -en) **1.** a) promotion, b) patronage, sponsorship, c) encouragement. **2.** production, output (*of oil etc*).

Forelle [fo'rɛlə] *f* (-; -n) *zo.* trout.

Forke ['fɔrkə] *f* (-; -n) ✄ pitchfork.

Form [fɔrm] *f* (-; -en) **1.** form (*a. ling., phys., a. fig.*), shape (*a. fig.*): *ling.* **aktive** (**passive**) **~** active (passive) voice; *in aller ~* formally; *in ~ von* (*or gen*) in the form of; *in höflicher* (*netter*) **~** politely (in a nice way); *der ~ halber* a) pro forma, b) to keep up appearances; *die ~ wahren* observe the proprieties; *fig.* (**greifbare**) **~(en)** *annehmen* take shape. **2.** ⚙ a) model, b) mo(u)ld, c) die. **3.** a) cake tin, b) pastry cutter. **4.** *esp. sports:* form, condition: *in* (**guter**) **~** in good form (*or* shape); *in bester* **~**, *groß in* **~** in top form; *nicht in* **~** off

form; *in ~ bleiben, sich in ~ halten* keep in trim, keep fit; *in ~ kommen* a) get into shape, b) *fig.* get going.

formal [fɔr'ma:l] *adj* formal.

Formaldehyd ['fɔrm°aldəhy:t] *m* (-s; *no pl*) 🜊 formaldehyde.

Formalien [fɔr'ma:liən] *pl* formalities.

Formalität [fɔrmali'tɛ:t] *f* (-; -en) formality.

Format [fɔr'ma:t] *n* (-[e]s; -e) **1.** format, size. **2.** *fig.* stature, calib/re (*Am.* -er).

Formation [fɔrma'tsio:n] *f* (-; -en) formation. **Formati'ons...** formation (*flying, dancing, etc*).

'formbar *adj metall.* malleable.

'Formblatt *n* form.

Formel ['fɔrməl] *f* (-; -n) **1.** 🜊, ⚖, *a. fig.* formula. **2.** a) (set) formula, b) (set) phrase. **Formel-I-Rennen** *n mot.* formula-one race.

formell [fɔr'mɛl] *adj* formal.

'Formelwagen *m mot.* formula car.

formen ['fɔrmən] *v/t* (h) form, shape (*both a.* **sich ~**), ⚙ mo(u)ld (*a. fig. s.o.*).

'Formenlehre *f* **1.** *ling.* morphology. **2.** ♪ theory of musical forms.

'Formfehler *m* a) irregularity, ⚖ formal defect, b) faux pas.

'Formgebung *f* (-; -en), **'Formgestaltung** *f* ⚙ styling, design.

formieren [fɔr'mi:rən] *v/t* (*a.* **sich ~**) form up.

'Formkrise *f sports:* *in e-r ~ stecken* be off form.

förmlich ['fœrmlɪç] **I** *adj* **1.** formal, ceremonious. **2.** F regular. **II** *adv* **3.** F literally. **'Förmlichkeit** *f* (-; -en) formality.

'formlos *adj* **1.** shapeless. **2.** informal.

'Formsache *f* matter of form, (**reine ~**) mere) formality.

'formschön *adj* ⚙ very stylish.

Formular [fɔrmu'la:r] *n* (-s; -e) form.

formulieren [fɔrmu'li:rən] *v/t* (h) formulate, phrase, word: *wie soll ich es ~?* how shall I put it?

Formu'lierung *f* (-; -en) **1.** formulation, wording, phrasing. **2.** phrase.

'Formung *f* (-; -en) forming, shaping.

'formvollendet *adj* a) perfect (*manners etc*), b) perfectly shaped, finished.

forsch [fɔrʃ] *adj* spirited, brisk, F peppy.

forschen ['fɔrʃən] *v/i* (h) **1.** do research (work). **2.** *~ nach* search for.

'forschend *adj* inquiring, searching.

'**Forscher** m (-s; -) **1.** researcher, a. (research) scientist. **2.** explorer. **~drang** m, **~geist** m inquiring mind.
'**Forscherin** f (-; -nen) → **Forscher**.
'**Forschheit** f (-; no pl) spirit(edness), dash, F pep.
'**Forschung** f (-; -en) research (**auf dem Gebiet** gen on).
'**Forschungs...** research (work, institute, etc). **~auftrag** m research assignment. **~reise** f **1.** expedition. **2.** research trip. **~reisende** m, f (-n; -n) explorer.
Forst [fɔrst] m (-[e]s; -e[n]) forest.
Förster ['fœrstər] m (-s; -) forester.
'**Forsthaus** n forester's house.
'**Forstre,vier** n forest district.
'**Forstwirtschaft** f (-; no pl) forestry.
fort [fɔrt] adv **1.** away, off, gone: **sie sind schon ~** they have already gone (or left); **ich muß ~** I must be going. **2.** gone, lost. **3. und so ~** and so on.
Fort [fɔːr] n (-s; -s) ✕ fort.
Fort..., fort... → a. **Weg..., weg..., Weiter..., weiter...**.
'**Fortbestand** m (-[e]s; no pl) continued existence. '**fortbestehen** v/i (irr, sep, h, → **bestehen**) continue (to exist).
'**fortbewegen** (sep, h) **I** v/t move. **II sich ~** move, walk. '**Fortbewegung** f movement, (loco)motion.
'**fortbilden: sich ~** (sep, h) a) continue one's education (or training), b) do a course, c) improve one's knowledge. '**Fortbildung** f further education (or training). '**Fortbildungskurs** m (continuation) course.
'**fortbleiben** v/i (irr, sep, -ge-, sn, → **bleiben**) stay away.
'**fortdauern** v/i (sep, -ge-, h) continue, last: **~d** continuous, lasting.
forte ['fɔrtə] adv, '**Forte** n (-s; -s) ♪ forte.
'**fortfahren** v/i (irr, sep, -ge-, sn, → **fahren**) **1.** leave, mot. a. drive away. **2.** a. (h) continue: **~ zu reden** continue (or go on) talking; **~ mit** continue (with) (one's story etc); **fahren Sie fort!** go on!
'**fortfliegen** v/i (irr, sep, -ge-, sn, → **fliegen**) fly away, fly off.
'**fortführen** v/t (sep, -ge-, h) **1.** lead s.o. away. **2.** continue, carry on.
'**Fortführung** f (-; no pl) continuation.
'**Fortgang** m (-[e]s; no pl) **1.** departure. **2.** progress. '**fortgehen** v/i (irr, sep, -ge-,

sn, → **gehen**) **1.** go (away), leave. **2.** go on, continue.
'**fortgeschritten** adj advanced: **Kurs für Fortgeschrittene** advanced course.
'**fortgesetzt I** adj continued, constant. **II** adv continually, constantly.
'**fortlaufen** v/i (irr, sep, -ge-, sn, → **laufen**) **1.** run away ([**vor**] j-m from s.o.). **2.** continue. '**fortlaufend** adj a) continuous, b) consecutive (numbers): **~ numeriert** numbered consecutively.
'**fortpflanzen** (sep, -ge-, h) **I** v/t propagate, biol. a. reproduce, phys. a. transmit, fig. a. spread. **II sich ~** biol. reproduce, phys. be propagated, travel, fig. spread. '**Fortpflanzung** f (-; no pl) propagation, biol. a. reproduction, phys. a. transmission, fig. a. spread(ing). '**Fortpflanzungsor,gan** n reproductive organ.
'**Fortsatz** m anat. process, appendix.
'**fortschreiben** v/t (irr, sep, -ge-, h, → **schreiben**) **1.** update (statistics etc), reassess (value). **2.** fig. perpetuate.
'**fortschreiten** v/i (irr, sep, -ge-, sn, → **schreiten**) fig. advance, progress.
'**fortschreitend** adj progressive.
'**Fortschritt** m progress, improvement: **~e machen** make progress (or headway); **große ~e machen** make great strides. '**fortschrittlich** adj progressive, advanced, (very) modern, up-to-date.
'**Fortschrittsglaube** m belief in progress.
'**fortsetzen** v/t (sep, -ge-, h) continue (a. **sich ~**), resume. '**Fortsetzung** f (-; -en) continuation, sequel: **~ folgt** to be continued; **~ auf (von) Seite 2** continued on (from) page 2.
'**Fortsetzungsro,man** m serial.
Fortuna [fɔr'tuːna] f (-; no pl) fortune.
'**fortwährend** → **ständig**.
'**Fortzahlung** f continued payment.
Forum ['fɔːrʊm] n (-s; Foren, Fora) forum, fig. a. platform.
fossil [fɔ'siːl] adj fossil.
Fossil [fɔ'siːl] n (-s; -ien [-liən]) fossil.
Foto ['foːto] n (-s; -s) F photo. **~album** n photo album. **~appa,rat** m camera. **~ausrüstung** f photographic equipment. **~finish** n sports: photo finish.
fotogen [foto'geːn] adj photogenic.
Fotograf [foto'graːf] m (-en; -en) photographer. **Fotografie** [fotogra'fiː] f (-; -n)

1. *no pl* photography. **2.** photograph, picture. **fotografieren** [fotografiː'riːrən] *v/i, v/t* (h) photograph, take a picture (*or* pictures) (of). **Foto'grafin** *f* (-; -nen) photographer. **fotografisch** [foto'graːfiʃ] *adj* photographic.

Foto|ko'pie *f*, **~ko'pieren** *v/t* (h) photocopy. **~ko'piergerät** *n* photocopier. **~la,bor** *n* photographic laboratory. **~mo,dell** *n* (photographer's) model. **~mon,tage** *f* photomontage. **~repor,tage** *f* photographic reportage. **~satz** *m print.* photocomposition: *im ~ herstellen* photocompose.

Fotothek [foto'teːk] *f* (-; -en) photographic library.

'Fotozelle *f* ⚡ photocell.

Fötus ['føːtʊs] *m* (-ses; -se) f(o)etus.

Foul [faʊl] *n* (-s; -s) *sports:* foul.

foulen ['faʊlən] *v/i, v/t* (h) *sports:* foul.

Foxtrott ['fɔkstrɔt] *m* (-s; -e, -s) (*a.* **~ tanzen**) foxtrot.

Foyer [fŏa'jeː] *n* (-s; -s) foyer, lounge, *Am.* lobby.

Fracht [fraxt] *f* (-; -en) **1.** load, freight, cargo. **2.** carriage, *Am.* freight(age), ⚓ freightage. **'Frachtbrief** *m* consignment note, *Am.* waybill.

Frachter *m* (-s; -) freighter, cargo ship.

'Fracht|flugzeug *n* (air) freighter. **⚡frei** *adj* carriage paid, *Am.* freight prepaid. **~führer** *m* carrier. **~gebühr** *f*, **~geld** *n* → **Fracht** 2. **~gut** *n* freight, cargo: *als ~* by goods (*Am.* freight) train. **~kosten** *pl* freight charges (*or* costs). **~raum** *m* **1.** cargo hold. **2.** freight capacity. **~sätze** *pl* freight rates. **~schiff** *n* cargo ship, freighter. **~verkehr** *m* freight traffic.

Frack [frak] *m* (-[e]s; ⁓e) tailcoat, tails: *im ~* in evening dress, in tails. **'Frackhemd** *n* dress shirt.

'Frage ['fraːgə] *f* (-; -n) **1.** a) question, b) query, c) inquiry: *e-e ~ an j-n haben* have a question to ask s.o.; (*j-m*) *e-e ~ stellen* ask (s.o.) a question; *die ~ stellt sich nicht* the question does not arise; *ohne ~* undoubtedly; *das ist eben die ~* that's just the point; *in ~ stellen* a) question, doubt, b) jeopardize; F *k-e ~!* of course! **2.** matter, question: *e-e ~ der Zeit* a matter of time; *das ist e-e andere ~* that's a different matter. **3.** *in ~ kommen* be a possibility, *person:*

a. be eligible; *das kommt gar nicht in ~* that's out of the question.

'Frage|bogen *m* form, questionnaire. **~form** *f ling.* interrogative form. **~für~ wort** *n ling.* interrogative (pronoun).

fragen ['fraːgən] *v/t, v/i* (h) ask, question: *nach et.* (*j-m*) *~* inquire about s.th. (after s.o.); (*j-n*) *et. ~* ask (s.o.) a question; (*j-n*) *~ nach* ask (s.o.) for; *j-n nach s-m Namen* (*dem Weg*) *~* ask s.o. his name (the way); *es fragt sich, ob ...* it's a question of whether ...; *ich frage mich, warum* I (just) wonder why; *niemand fragte danach* nobody bothered about it; ✝ (*sehr*) *gefragt* in (great) demand; *da fragst du mich zuviel* I'm afraid I can't tell you that. **'Fragen** *n* (-s) *~ kostet nichts* there's no harm in asking. **'fragend** *adj* questioning, inquiring, *ling.* interrogative.

Frager ['fraːgər] *m* (-s; -), **'Fragerin** *f* (-; -nen) questioner.

'Frage|satz *m ling.* interrogative clause (*or* sentence). **~stellung** *f a. fig.* question. **~stunde** *f parl.* question time.

'Frage-und-'Antwort-Spiel *n* quiz, *a. fig.* question and answer game.

'Frage|wort *n ling.* interrogative. **~zei~ chen** *n* question mark, *a. fig.* query.

fraglich ['fraːklɪç] *adj* **1.** doubtful. **2.** in question. **'fraglos** *adv* undoubtedly.

Fragment [fra'gmɛnt] *n* (-[e]s; -e) fragment. **fragmentarisch** [fragmɛn'taːrɪʃ] **I** *adj* fragmentary. **II** *adv* fragmentarily, in fragmentary form.

fragwürdig ['fraːkvʏrdɪç] *adj* questionable, dubious, F shady.

Fraktion [frak'tsĭoːn] *f* (-; -en) **1.** *parl.* a) parliamentary party, b) faction. **2.** 🔬 fraction. **frakti'onslos** *adj* independent. **Frakti'onsvorsitzende** *m, f* (-n; -n) party (*Am.* floor) leader. **Frakti'onszwang** *m* obligation to vote according to party policy.

Fraktur [frak'tuːr] *f* (-; -en) 🔬 fracture.

Franke ['fraŋkə] *m* (-n; -n) Franconian.

'Franken *m* (-s; -) (Swiss) franc.

frankieren [fraŋ'kiːrən] *v/t* (h) 🖂 prepay, stamp, frank. **fran'kiert** *adj* prepaid, post paid: *der Brief ist nicht ausreichend ~* they didn't put enough stamps on this letter.

franko ['fraŋko] *adv* prepaid.

Franse ['franzə] *f* (-; -n) fringe.

'**fransen** (h) I *v/i* fray. II *v/t* fringe.

'**fransig** *adj* 1. fringed. 2. frayed.

Franziskaner [frantsıs'ka:nər] *m* (-s; -) Franciscan (friar).

Franzose [fran'tso:zə] *m* (-n; -n) Frenchman: *die ~n* the French; *er ist ~* he is a Frenchman, he is French.

Französin [fran'tsø:zın] *f* (-; -nen) Frenchwoman: *sie ist ~* she is French.

fran'zösisch I *adj* French: *~es Bett* (double) divan. II *2 n ling.* French: *aus dem 2en* (*ins 2e*) from (into) French.

frappieren [fra'pi:rən] *v/t* (h) amaze: *~d* striking, amazing, remarkable.

Fräse ['frɛ:zə] *f* (-; -n) 1. ✏ rotary hoe. 2. ⚙ milling machine. '**fräsen** *v/t*, *v/i* ⊙ mill.

fraß [fra:s] *pret of* **fressen.**

Fraß *m* (-es; *no pl*) 1. F *contp.* muck. 2. feed (*for animals*). 3. 🔧 corrosion.

Fratze ['fratsə] *f* (-; -n) 1. grimace: *~n schneiden* pull faces. 2. F mug (*sl.*).

Frau [frau] *f* (-; -en) 1. a) woman, *adm.* female, b) Mrs, Ms *Brown etc*: *die ~ von heute* modern woman. 2. wife: *wie geht es Ihrer ~?* how is Mrs X? 3. lady: *gnädige ~!* madam!

Frauen|arzt *m*, **~ärztin** *f* gyn(a)ecologist. **~beauftragte** *f* women's representative. **~beruf** *m* female profession. **~bewegung** *f* (-; *no pl*) women's movement. **2feindlich** *adj* anti-women. **~frage** *f* question of women's rights. **~fußball** *m* women's soccer. **~haus** *n* women's refuge (*Am.* shelter). **~heilkunde** *f* gyn(a)ecology. **~held** *m* ladykiller. **~leiden** *n* gyn(a)ecological disorder. **~rechte** *pl* women's rights.

Frauenrechtler ['frauənrɛçtlər] *m* (-s; -), '**Frauenrechtlerin** *f* (-; -nen) feminist.

'**Frauen|sport** *m* women's sport(s). **~stimmrecht** *n* votes for women. **~zeitschrift** *f* women's magazine.

'**fraulich** *adj* womanly, feminine.

'**Fraulichkeit** *f* (-; *no pl*) womanliness.

frech [frɛç] *adj* 1. F impudent, F cheeky, saucy, *Am.* fresh, b) bold, brazen.

'**Frechheit** *f* (-; -en) impudence, F cheek: *so e-e ~!* what (a) cheek!

Fregatte [fre'gatə] *f* (-; -n) frigate.

'**frei** [frai] I *adj* 1. free (*von* from, of), *a.* clear (*road etc*): *ist dieser Platz noch*

~? is this seat taken?; *Zimmer ~!* room(s) to let (*Am.* rent)!; *ein ~er Tag* a) a free day, b) a day off; *den Oberkörper ~ machen* strip to the waist; *~e Fahrt mot.* clear road, 🚂 green light; *~e Fahrt haben a. fig.* have the green light; → *Fuß* 1, *Hand, Stück* 1. 2. a) free, independent, unattached, b) free and easy, c) liberal: *~er Beruf* independent profession; *~e Künste* liberal arts; *die ~e Wirtschaft* free enterprise; *ein ~er Mensch* a free agent. 3. free, frank, open. 4. blank: *e-n ~en Platz lassen* leave a blank. 5. open, vacant: *~e Stelle* vacancy. 6. open: *in der ~en Natur, im 2en* in the open (country); → *Himmel.* 7. a) free (of charge), b) prepaid: *Eintritt ~* admission free. 8. freelance (*journalist etc*). 9. *phys.* free, 🔧 *a.* uncombined: *Wärme wird ~* heat is released. 10. *teleph.* vacant, *Am.* not busy. 11. *sports*: unmarked. II *adv* 12. freely (*etc*): *~ sprechen* a) speak openly, b) speak without notes; *~ erfunden* entirely fictitious, made(-)up; 🚢 *an Bord* free on board (f.o.b.); *Lieferung ~ Haus* no delivery charge; *~ finanziert* privately financed.

'**Freiaktie** *f* bonus share.

'**Freibad** *n* open-air swimming pool.

'**freibekommen** *v/t* (*irr, sep*, h, → *bekommen*) 1. F *e-n Tag etc ~* get a day etc off. 2. *j-n ~* get s.o. released; *et. ~* free s.th.

'**Freiberufler** *m* (-s; -), '**Freiberuflerin** *f* (-; -nen) freelance. '**freiberuflich** *adj* self-employed, freelance, *lawyer, doctor, etc* in private practice: *~ tätig sein a.* work (as a) freelance.

'**Freibetrag** *m* tax allowance.

'**Freibier** *n* (-[e]s; *no pl*) free beer.

'**freibleibend** *adj and adv* 🚢 without engagement.

'**Freibrief** *m fig.* excuse (*für* for).

'**Freidenker(in** *f*) *m* freethinker.

Freier ['fraiər] *m* (-s; -) 1. suitor. 2. customer (*of a prostitute*).

'**Freiexem,plar** *n* free copy.

'**Freifahrschein** *m* free ticket.

'**Freiflug** *m* 'free flight.

'**Freifrau** *f*, '**Freifräulein** *n* baroness.

'**Freigabe** *f* (-; *no pl*) release, 🚢 floating (*of exchange rate*), ✈ clearance.

'**freigeben** *v/t* (*irr, sep*, -ge-, h, → *ge-*

ben) 1. *j-m e-n Tag etc* ~ give s.o. a day *etc* off. **2.** release, ✝ float (*exchange rate*), ✔ *etc* clear: *et. für den Verkehr* ~ open s.th. to traffic; *et. zur Veröffentlichung* ~ release s.th. for publication.

freigebig ['fraɪgeːbɪç] *adj* generous.

'**Freigebigkeit** *f* (-; *no pl*) generosity.

'**Freigehege** *n* open-air enclosure.

'**Freigepäck** *n* baggage allowance.

'**Freigrenze** *f* tax exemption limit.

'**freihaben** *v/i* (*irr*, *sep*, -ge-, h) F have the day off: *Freitag habe ich frei* Friday is my day off.

'**Freihafen** *m* free port.

'**freihalten** *v/t* (*irr*, *sep*, -ge-, h, → *halten*) **1.** keep (*seat*). **2.** keep *entrance etc* clear. **3.** keep *a post etc* open. **4.** *j-n* ~ treat s.o., pay for s.o.

'**Freihandel** *m* free trade.

'**Freihandelszone** *f* free trade area.

freihändig ['fraɪhɛndɪç] *adj and adv shooting* without support, *cycling etc* with no hands. '**Freihandzeichnung** *f* freehand drawing.

'**Freiheit** *f* (-; -en) freedom, liberty: *dichterische* ~ poetic licen|ce (*Am.* -se); *in* ~ *sein* be free; *sich die* ~ *nehmen zu inf* take the liberty of *ger*; *sich* ~ *en erlauben* take liberties (*gegenüber* with).

'**freiheitlich** *adj* free, liberal.

'**Freiheits|beraubung** *f* deprivation of liberty, ⚖ illegal detention. ~**bewegung** *f pol.* freedom movement. ~**entzug** *m* imprisonment. ~**kampf** *m* struggle for freedom, revolt. ~**kämpfer(in** *f*) *m* freedom fighter. ~**krieg** *m* war of liberation. ~**liebe** *f* love of freedom. ~**strafe** *f* ⚖ prison sentence: *zu e-r* ~ *von 5 Jahren verurteilt werden* be sentenced to 5 years' imprisonment.

freiher'aus *adv* frankly, point-blank.

'**Freiherr** *m* baron.

'**Freikarte** *f* free ticket.

'**freikaufen** (*sep*, -ge-, h) **I** *v/t* pay for *s.o.'s* release. **II** *sich* ~ pay to be set free, *fig.* buy a clear conscience.

'**freikommen** *v/i* (*irr*, *sep*, -ge-, sn, → *kommen*) **1.** get free, get away. **2.** ⚖ a) be released, b) be acquitted.

'**Freikörperkul,tur** *f* (-; *no pl*) nudism: *Anhänger(in) der* ~ nudist.

'**Freilandgemüse** *n* outdoor vegetables.

'**freilassen** *v/t* (*irr*, *sep*, -ge-, h, → *lassen*), '**Freilassung** *f* (-; -en) release.

'**Freilauf** *m* (*a. im* ~ *fahren*) freewheel.

'**freilaufend** *adj* ~*e Hühner* free-running chicken.

'**freilegen** *v/t* (*sep*, -ge-, h) lay open, expose, uncover.

'**freilich** *adv* of course.

'**Freilicht|bühne** *f*, ~**the,ater** *n* open-air theat|re (*Am.* -er). ~**kino** → **Autokino.**

'**freiliegen** *v/i* (*irr*, *sep*, -ge-, h, → *liegen*) lie exposed, lie open.

'**Freilos** *n* **1.** free (lottery) ticket. **2.** *sports:* (*ein* ~ *ziehen* draw a) bye.

'**Freiluft...** open-air ..., outdoor ...

'**freimachen** (*sep*, -ge-, h) **I** *v/t* 🖃 stamp, prepay. **II** *sich* ~ free o.s. (*von* from), F arrange to be free.

'**Freimaurer** *m* freemason. ~**loge** *f* freemason's (*or* Masonic) lodge.

'**Freimut** *m* cando(u)r, openness.

freimütig ['fraɪmyːtɪç] *adj* candid, open.

'**freinehmen** *v/t* (*irr*, *sep*, -ge-, h, → *nehmen*) (*sich*) *e-n Tag* ~ take a day off.

'**Freiplastik** *f* free-standing sculpture.

'**freischaffend** *adj* freelance.

'**freischwimmen: sich** ~ (*irr*, *sep*, -ge-, h, → *schwimmen*) a) pass one's 15-minute swimming test, b) *fig.* learn to stand on one's own two feet.

'**freisetzen** *v/t* (*sep*, -ge-, h) 🐾, *phys.* release (*a. fig.*): *j-n* ~ make s.o. redundant; *freigesetzte Arbeitskräfte* redundant workers. '**Freisetzung** *f* (-; -en) a) release (*a. fig.*), b) redundancy.

'**freispielen: sich** ~ (*sep*, -ge-, h) *sports:* break clear.

'**freisprechen** *v/t* (*irr*, *sep*, -ge-, h, → *sprechen*) **1.** (*von*) ⚖ acquit (of), exonerate (from), clear (of *a suspicion*), *eccl.* absolve (from). **2.** release *apprentice* from his (*or* her) articles.

'**Freispruch** *m* (-[e]s; ⁻e) ⚖ acquittal.

'**Freistaat** *m* free state, republic.

'**Freistatt** *f*, '**Freistätte** *f* sanctuary.

'**freistehen** *v/i* (*irr*, *sep*, -ge-, h, → *stehen*) **1.** *sports:* be unmarked. **2.** *j-m* ~ be up to s.o.: *es steht Ihnen frei zu inf* you are at liberty (*or* free) to *inf*.

'**freistellen** *v/t* (*sep*, -ge-, h) **1.** *j-n* ~ a. ✗ exempt s.o. (*von* from). **2.** *j-m et.* ~ leave s.th. (up) to s.o. '**Freistellung** *f* (-; -en) exemption (*von* from).

'**Freistil** *m* (-[e]s; *no pl*), '**Freistil...** *sports:* freestyle.

'**Freistoß** *m* *soccer:* free kick.

'**Freistunde** f ped. free period.
'**Freitag** m (-[e]s; -e) (**am ~** on) Friday.
'**freitags** adv on Friday(s).
'**freitragend** adj △, ⚙ cantilever, self-supporting.
'**Freitreppe** f (outdoor) steps.
'**Freiübungen** pl exercises.
'**Freiumschlag** m stamped addressed envelope.
'**Freiverkehr** m ✝ **im ~** in the open market, Am. over the counter.
'**Freiverkehrsbörse** f ✝ kerb market.
frei'weg adv F straight out.
'**Freiwild** n fig. fair game.
'**freiwillig** I adj a) voluntary, b) spontaneous. II adv voluntarily, of one's own free will: **sich ~ melden** volunteer (**zu** for).
'**Freiwillige** m, f (-n; -n) volunteer.
'**Freiwilligkeit** f (-; no pl) voluntariness.
'**Freiwurf** m sports: free throw.
'**Freizeichen** n teleph. dial(l)ing tone.
'**Freizeit** f (-; -en) **1.** no pl free (or leisure, spare) time. **2.** ped. holiday (or week-end) course.
'**Freizeit|beschäftigung** f leisure-time activity (or activities), n.s. hobby. **~gestaltung** f leisure-time activities. **~kleidung** f casual (or leisure) wear. **~zentrum** n leisure cent/re (Am. -er).
'**Freizone** f free zone.
'**freizügig** adj **1.** ✝ unrestricted. **2.** generous, liberal. **3.** permissive, free.
'**Freizügigkeit** f (-; no pl) **1.** ✝ free(dom of) movement. **2.** generosity. **3.** permissiveness.
fremd [frɛmt] adj **1.** strange, a. a) unfamiliar, unknown, b) odd: **~e Leute** strangers; **~e Hilfe** outside help; **~es Eigentum** other people's property; **ich bin hier ~** I'm a stranger here. **2.** a. fig. foreign, alien.
'**Fremdarbeiter(in** f) m foreign worker.
'**fremdartig** adj a. fig. foreign, strange, exotic.
'**Fremdartigkeit** f (-; no pl) strangeness.
'**Fremde**[1] m, f (-n; -n) a) stranger, b) foreigner, c) tourist.
'**Fremde**[2] f (-; no pl) foreign parts: **in die** (**der**) **~** away from home, abroad.
'**Fremden|führer(in** f) m (tourist) guide. **~haß** m xenophobia. **~heim** n guesthouse. **~indu,strie** f tourist industry. **~legi,on** f Foreign Legion. **~verkehr**

m tourism. **~verkehrsbü,ro** n tourist office. **~zimmer** n room (to let).
'**fremdgehen** v/i (irr, sep, -ge-, sn, → **gehen**) be unfaithful (to one's husband or wife).
'**Fremd|herrschaft** f foreign rule. **~kapi,tal** n loan capital. **~körper** m **1.** ✹ foreign body. **2.** fig. alien element.
'**fremdländisch** [-lɛndɪʃ] adj foreign, exotic.
'**Fremdling** m (-s; -e) stranger.
'**Fremdsprache** f foreign language.
'**Fremdsprachen|korrespon,dent(in** f) m foreign correspondence clerk. **~sekre,tär(in** f) m linguist-secretary. **~unterricht** m foreign-language teaching (or lessons).
'**fremdsprachig** adj **1.** speaking a foreign language. **2.** → '**fremdsprachlich** adj foreign-language.
'**Fremdwort** n (-[e]s; ⸚er) foreign word.
frequentieren [frekvɛn'tiːrən] v/t (h) frequent. **Frequenz** [fre'kvɛnts] f (-; -en) **1.** ⚡, phys. frequency. **2.** ✹ (pulse) rate. **3.** number of visitors. **4.** density of traffic. **Fre'quenzbereich** m ⚡ frequency range.
Fresko ['frɛsko] n (-s; -ken) fresco.
Fressalien [frɛ'saːliən] pl ⋀ grub.
Fresse ['frɛsə] f (-; -n) V mug, kisser.
fressen ['frɛsən] (fraß, gefressen, h) I v/t **1.** eat, a. a) devour, F person: a. stuff o.s. with, b) feed on: **e-m Tier** (...) **zu ~ geben** feed an animal (on ...); F **er wird dich schon nicht ~** he won't eat you; → **Besen** 1, **Narr.** 2. F fig. gobble up (money), guzzle (fuel etc). II v/i **3.** eat, F person: guzzle, eat like a pig. **4.** fig. **~ an** (dat) eat away, corrode. III sich ~ in (acc) fig. eat into.
'**Fressen** n (-s) food, feed, F grub: F fig. **das war ein gefundenes ~ für ihn** that was just what he was waiting for.
'**Fresser** m (-s; -) F guzzler, glutton.
'**Freßgier** f voraciousness.
'**Freßsack** m F glutton.
Frettchen ['frɛtçən] n (-s; -) zo. ferret.
Freude ['frɔydə] f (-; -n) joy (**über** acc at), pleasure, delight: **~ haben** (or **finden**) **an** (dat) enjoy; **j-m ~ bereiten** make s.o. happy; **ich hoffe, es macht dir ~!** I hope it will give you pleasure; **es macht mir k-e ~** I don't enjoy it; **zu m-r großen ~** much to my delight.

'Freuden|fest n celebration. **~feuer** n bonfire. **~geschrei** n cheers, cheering. **~schrei** m cry of joy. **~tag** m red-letter day. **~taumel** m **in e-n ~ geraten** go into ecstasies. **~tränen** pl tears of joy.

'freudestrahlend adj radiant (with joy).

'freudig adj joyful, cheerful, happy (event): **j-n begrüßen** be happy to see s.o.; **~ überrascht** pleasantly surprised.

freudlos ['frɔytloːs] adj cheerless, bleak.

Freudsch ['frɔytʃ] adj → **Fehlleistung**.

freuen ['frɔyən] (h) **I** sich **~** be glad (or happy, pleased) (über acc about); sich **~ an** (dat) enjoy; sich **~ auf** (acc) be looking forward to. **II** v/t please: **das freut mich sehr** I'm glad to hear that; **ich hoffe, es freut dich** I hope it will give you pleasure. **III** v/impers **es freut mich, Sie zu sehen** nice to see you; **es würde mich ~, wenn ...** I'd be very pleased if ...

Freund [frɔynt] m (-[e]s; -e) friend (a. fig.), boyfriend: **~ und Feind** friend and foe; fig. **ein ~ sein von** be fond of; **ein ~ der Musik** a music lover; → **dick** 2.

'Freundchen n (-s; -) iro. laddie, Am. buddy.

'Freundeskreis m (circle of) friends.

'Freundin ['frɔyndɪn] f (-; -nen) friend (a. fig.), girlfriend.

'freundlich adj **1.** friendly (gegen to), kind, nice: **~e Grüße** kind regards (an acc to); **bitte seien Sie so ~ und ...** (will) you be so kind as to ...; **sehr ~!** very kind of you! **2.** fig. mild, pleasant (climate etc), cheerful (room etc).

'freundlicherweise adv kindly.

'Freundlichkeit f (-; no pl) friendliness, kindness.

'Freundschaft f (-; -en) friendship: **~ schließen mit** make friends with; **aus ~** because we etc are friends.

'freundschaftlich adj amicable, friendly: **~ verbunden** on friendly terms.

'Freundschafts|besuch m pol. goodwill visit. **~dienst** m (**j-m e-n ~ erweisen** do s.o. a) good turn. **~spiel** n sports: friendly (game).

'Frevel ['freːfəl] m (-s; -) **1.** sacrilege. **2.** (an dat, gegen against) crime, outrage.

'frevelhaft adj sacrilegious, w.s. outrageous. **'Freveltat** f outrage, crime.

Frevler ['freːflər] m (-s; -), **'Frevlerin** f (-; -nen) offender, esp. eccl. sinner.

Frieden ['friːdən] m (-s; no pl) a) peace, b) tranquil(l)ity: **innerer ~** peace of mind; **im ~** in peacetime; **~ machen** make peace, **mit j-m** make it up with s.o.; **laß mich in ~!** leave me alone!

'Friedens|bedingungen pl peace terms. **~bewegung** f pol. peace movement. **~bruch** m ⚖ breach (pol. violation) of the peace. **~forschung** f peace research. **~gespräche** pl peace talks. **~initia,tive** f peace initiative. **~konfe,renz** f peace conference. **~kundgebung** f peace rally. **~no,belpreis** m Nobel Peace Prize. **~poli,tik** f policy of peace. **~schluß** m conclusion of the peace treaty. **~taube** f fig. dove of peace. **~truppe** f peacekeeping force. **~verhandlungen** pl peace negotiations. **~vertrag** m peace treaty. **~zeit** f often pl peacetime, time of peace.

friedfertig ['friːt-] adj peaceable.

Friedhof ['friːthoːf] m cemetery.

friedlich ['friːtlɪç] adj peaceful.

'Friedlichkeit f (-; no pl) peacefulness.

friedliebend ['friːt-] adj peace-loving.

frieren ['friːrən] v/i and v/impers (fror, gefroren, h) freeze: **ich friere, mich friert, es friert mich** I am cold; **es friert** it is freezing.

frigide [fri'giːdə] adj frigid. **Frigidität** [frigidi'tɛːt] f (-; no pl) frigidity.

Frikadelle [frika'dɛlə] f (-; -n) meat-ball.

Frikassee [frika'seː] n (-s; -s) fricassee.

Friktion [frɪk'tsiʊːn] f (-; -en) friction.

frisch [frɪʃ] **I** adj **1.** fresh, a. freshly-laid (egg), a. new (bread): **~e Farbe** fresh (or wet) paint; **~e Luft schöpfen** get some fresh air; **noch in ~er Erinnerung** fresh in my etc mind. **2.** a) clean (linen etc), b) fresh, new (page etc): **sich ~ machen** freshen up; fig. **mit ~en Kräften** with renewed strength. **3.** fresh, cool, chilly. **4.** fresh, brisk, lively: **~ und munter** F alive and kicking. **5.** fresh (complexion etc), bright (colo[u]r). **II** adv freshly (etc): **~ gestrichen!** wet paint!; **~ gebacken** fresh from the oven.

'Frische f (-; no pl) **1.** freshness, fig. a. vigo(u)r, briskness, liveliness: fig. **in alter ~** as alive and well as ever. **2.** coolness, chilliness.

'Frischei n fresh(ly laid) egg.

'Frischfleisch n fresh meat.

'**Frischhalte|beutel** *m* polythene bag. **~packung** *f* keep-fresh package.
'**Frischmilch** *f* fresh milk.
'**Frischzellenthera,pie** *f* 🕮 living-cell therapy.
Friseur [fri'zø:r] *m* (-s; -e) hairdresser: *beim ~* at the hairdresser's. **Fri'seursa,lon** *m* hairdresser's shop.
Friseuse [fri'zø:zə] *f* (-; -n) hairdresser.
frisieren [fri'zi:rən] (h) **I** *v/t* **1.** *j-n ~* do s.o.'s hair. **2.** F doctor (*accounts etc*), soup up (*engine*): *er hat sich die Haare ~ lassen* he has had his hair done. **Fri'siersa,lon** *m* hairdresser's salon. **Fri'siertisch** *m* dresser.
Frist [frɪst] *f* (-; -en) a) (fixed) period of time, time limit, b) deadline, c) ✝ respite: *e-e ~ setzen* (*einhalten*) fix (meet) a deadline; *innerhalb e-r ~ von 10 Tagen* within a ten-day period; *in kürzester ~* at very short notice.
fristen ['frɪstən] *v/t* (h) *sein Leben* (*or Dasein*) *~* scrape a (bare) living.
'**fristgemäß**, '**fristgerecht** *adj and adv* in time, within the prescribed time limit.
'**fristlos** *adj and adv* without notice.
'**Fristverlängerung** *f* extension (of the deadline).
Frisur [fri'zu:r] *f* (-; -en) a) hairstyle, b) haircut.
Friteuse [fri'tø:zə] *f* (-; -n) deep fryer.
fritieren [fri'ti:rən] *v/t* (h) deep-fry.
frivol [fri'vo:l] *adj* **1.** frivolous. **2.** risqué.
Frivolität [frivoli'tɛ:t] *f* (-; -en) **1.** *no pl* frivolity. **2.** frivolous remark.
froh [fro:] *adj* glad (*über acc* of, about), cheerful: *sei ~, daß du nicht dabei warst* be thankful you weren't there.
fröhlich ['frø:lɪç] *adj* cheerful, merry.
'**Fröhlichkeit** *f* (-; *no pl*) cheerfulness.
froh'locken *v/i* (h) (*über acc*) a) rejoice (in, at), b) gloat (over). **Froh'locken** *n* (-s) a) jubilation, b) gloating.
'**Frohna,tur** *f* (-; -en) cheerful person.
'**Frohsinn** *m* (-[e]s; *no pl*) cheerfulness.
fromm [frɔm] *adj* **1.** pious, devout: *fig. ~er Betrug* pious fraud; *~e Lüge* white lie; *~er Wunsch* wishful thinking. **2.** gentle, steady (*horse*). **Frömmelei** [frœmə'laɪ] *f* (-; -en) sanctimoniousness. **Frömmigkeit** ['frœmɪçkaɪt] *f* (-; *no pl*) piety.
Fron [fro:n] *f* (-; -en) *fig.* drudgery.
frönen ['frø:nən] *v/i* (h) (*dat*) indulge in.
Fron'leichnam *m* (-[e]s) Corpus Christi.

Front [frɔnt] *f* (-; -en) front, ✕ *a.* front line: *an der ~* at the front; *hinter der ~* behind the lines; *fig. ~ machen gegen* turn against, resist; *sports: in ~ gehen* (*liegen*) take (be in) the lead.
Frontal... [frɔn'ta:l-] head-on, frontal. **~angriff** *m* frontal attack. **~zusammenstoß** *m* head-on collision.
'**Frontantrieb** *m mot.* front-wheel drive.
'**Frontkämpfer** *m* **1.** front-line soldier. **2.** ex-serviceman, *Am.* veteran.
'**Frontlader** *m* (-s; -) a) ⚙ loading shovel, b) ✓ front loader.
'**Frontwechsel** *m fig.* about-face.
fror [fro:r] *pret of* **frieren**.
Frosch [frɔʃ] *m* (-[e]s; ⸚e) **1.** *zo.* frog: F *sei kein ~!* don't be a spoilsport! **2.** squib. **~laich** *m* frog spawn. **~mann** *m* (-[e]s; ⸚er) frogman. **~perspek,tive** *f* (*aus der ~ sehen* have a) worm's-eye view. **~schenkel** *m gastr.* frog's leg.
Frost [frɔst] *m* (-[e]s; ⸚e) frost.
'**frostbeständig** *adj* frost-resistant.
'**Frostbeule** *f* chilblain.
'**Frosteinbruch** *m* sudden frost.
frösteln ['frœstəln] *v/i* (h) shiver (with cold): *mich fröstelt* I feel shivery. '**Frösteln** *n* (-s) shivering.
'**frosten** ['frɔstən] *v/t* (h) freeze.
'**frostfrei** *adj* free of frost, frost-free.
'**Frostgrenze** *f* frost line.
frostig ['frɔstɪç] *adj* frosty, *fig. a.* icy.
'**Frostsalbe** *f* chilblain ointment.
'**Frostschaden** *m* frost damage.
'**Frostschutz** *m* frost protection. **~mittel** *n* antifreeze. **~scheibe** *f mot.* defrosting screen.
'**Frostwetter** *n* frosty weather.
Frottee [frɔ'te:] *m, n* (-[s]; -s) towel(l)ing, terry(cloth).
frottieren [frɔ'ti:rən] *v/t* (h) rub down.
Frot'tier(hand)tuch *n* terry towel.
Frucht [fruxt] *f* (-; ⸚e) **1.** 🌶 fruit: *Früchte tragen a. fig.* bear fruit. **2.** *pl fig.* fruit(s). '**fruchtbar** *adj a. fig.* fertile, fruitful, prolific: *auf ~en Boden fallen* fall on fertile ground. '**Fruchtbarkeit** *f* (-; *no pl*) *a. fig.* fertility, fruitfulness.
'**Fruchtbon,bon** *m, n* fruit drop.
'**Fruchteis** *n* fruit-flavo(u)red ice cream.
fruchten ['fruxtən] *v/i* (h) be of use, have an effect: *nichts ~* be no use, be in vain.
'**Fruchtfleisch** *n* (fruit) flesh.
'**fruchtlos** *adj* fruitless, *fig. a.* futile.

'**Frucht|presse** f juicer. **~saft** m fruit juice. **~wasser** n physiol. amniotic fluid. **~zucker** m fructose.

frugal [fru'ga:l] adj frugal.

früh [fry:] I adj early: **ein ~er van Gogh** an early (work by van Gogh; → **früher, frühest, frühestens.** II adv early: **heute ~** this morning; **(schon) ~** early on; **~ genug** soon enough; **von ~ bis spät** from morning till night; **zu ~ kommen** be early.

'**Frühaufsteher** m (-s; -), '**Frühaufsteherin** f (-; -nen) early riser (F bird).

'**Frühe** f (-; no pl) (early) morning: **in aller ~** early in the morning.

'**früher** I adj a) earlier, b) former, c) past: **der ~e Besitzer** the previous owner. II adv a) earlier, a. sooner, b) in the past: **~ oder später** sooner or later; **~ habe ich geraucht** I used to smoke; **ich kenne sie von ~** I know her from way back.

'**Früherkennung** f ✱ early diagnosis.

'**frühest** adj earliest: **in ~er Kindheit** at a very early age.

'**frühestens** adv at the earliest.

'**Früh|geburt** f premature birth. **~geschichte** f (-; no pl) early history.

'**Frühjahr** n (-s; -e) (**im ~** in [the]) spring.

'**Frühjahrs|mode** f spring fashions. **~müdigkeit** f spring tiredness.

'**Frühkar,toffeln** pl new potatoes.

Frühling ['fry:lɪŋ] m (-s; -e) a. fig. spring(time): **im ~** in (the) spring.

'**frühlingshaft** adj springlike, spring.

'**Frühlingsrolle** f gastr. spring roll.

'**Frühmesse** f eccl. matins.

früh'morgens adv early in the morning.

'**Früh|nebel** m early morning fog. **Qreif** adj a. fig. precocious. **~reife** f precociousness, fig. a. precocity. **~schicht** f early shift. **~schoppen** m pre-lunch drink(s). **~sommer** m early summer. **~sport** m early morning exercises. **~stadium** n early stage.

'**Frühstück** n (-s; -e) breakfast: **zweites ~** mid-morning snack, Br. elevenses.

'**frühstücken** (h) I v/i (have) breakfast. II v/t have s.th. for breakfast.

'**Frühstückspause** f morning break.

'**Früh|warnsy,stem** n early warning system. **~zeit** f 1. early period. 2. prehistoric times. **Qzeitig** I adj a) early, b) untimely, premature. II adv early, in good time. **~zug** m early train. **~zün-**

dung f mot. advanced ignition.

Frust [frʊst] m (-[e]s; no pl) F, **Frustration** [frʊstra'tsĭo:n] f (-; -en) psych. frustration. **frustrieren** [frʊs'tri:rən] v/t (h) frustrate.

Fuchs [fʊks] m (-es; ⁓e) **1.** zo. a) fox, b) sorrel. **2.** → **Fuchspelz. 3.** fig. **alter ~** cunning old devil; **schlauer ~** sly fox.

'**Fuchsbau** m (-[e]s; -e) fox's den.

Fuchsie ['fʊksiə] f (-; -n) ♀ fuchsia.

Füchsin ['fʏksɪn] f (-; -nen) zo. vixen.

'**Fuchs|jagd** f fox hunt(ing). **~pelz** m fox (fur). **Qrot** adj ginger. **~schwanz** m **1.** zo. foxtail. **2.** ✺ pad saw.

'**fuchs'teufels'wild** adj F hopping mad.

Fuchtel ['fʊxtəl] f (-; no pl) F **unter j-s ~ stehen** be under s.o.'s thumb.

fuchteln ['fʊxtəln] v/i (h) **~ mit** wave s.th. around, brandish; **mit den Händen ~** gesticulate wildly.

Fug [fu:k] **mit ~ und Recht** rightly.

Fuge[1] ['fu:gə] f (-; -n) ♪ fugue.

'**Fuge**[2] f (-; -n) ✺ a) joint, b) seam, c) groove: **aus den ~n gehen** fall apart, fig. be thrown out of joint.

fugen ['fu:gən] v/t (h) joint.

fügen ['fy:gən] (h) I v/t ✺ joint. II **sich ~** (dat or in acc to) a) submit, give in, b) resign o.s.; **sich e-m Befehl ~** comply with an order; **~ unabänderlich.** III v/impers **es fügt sich, daß ...** it so happens that ... **fügsam** ['fy:kza:m] adj obedient. '**Fügung** f (-; -en) (act of) providence, (stroke of) fate: **durch e-e glückliche ~** by a lucky coincidence.

'**fühlbar** adj fig. noticeable, considerable: **sich ~ machen** make itself felt.

fühlen ['fy:lən] (h) I v/t feel, sense. II v/i feel: **~ nach** feel for; **mit j-m ~** feel with s.o. III **sich glücklich etc ~** feel happy etc; **sich ~ als** see o.s. as.

'**Fühler** m (-s; -) **1.** zo. feeler, antenna, tentacle: fig. **die ~ ausstrecken** put out one's feelers. **2.** ✺ sensor.

'**Fühlung** f (-; no pl) contact: **~ haben mit** be in touch with; **~ nehmen mit** contact, get in touch with; **die ~ verlieren** lose touch (**mit** with). '**Fühlungnahme** [-na:mə] f (-; -n) contact.

fuhr [fu:r] pret of **fahren.**

Fuhre ['fu:rə] f (-; -n) a) loaded cart, b) (cart)load.

führen ['fy:rən] (h) I v/t **1.** lead (**nach, zu** to), take, guide: **j-n in ein Zimmer**

(*durchs Haus*) ~ show s.o. into a room (over the house); → **Leine.** **2.** a) lead, head, ✗ a. command, b) be in charge of, manage, run, c) hold (*an office*), d) keep (*books etc*), e) conduct (*business, lawsuit, etc*), carry on (*negotiations etc*): → **Gespräch, Klage** 2. **3.** bear (*a name*), go by (*the name of*), hold (*a title*), have (*coat of arms*): → **Schild**[1] 1. **4.** ✞ a) carry (in stock), b) sell, deal in. **5.** use, wield (*brush etc*). **6.** have s.th. with (*or* on) one, carry (*weapon etc*): ⚡ **Strom** ~ a) be live, b) conduct current. **7.** **e-n Schlag** ~ strike a blow. **8.** ~ **durch** (*um etc*) pass *line, tool, etc* through (around *etc*). **II** *v/i* lead, *sports: a.* be in the lead: ~ **nach**, *a. fig.* ~ **zu** lead to; **das führt zu nichts** that won't get us anywhere; *sports:* **mit zwei Toren** ~ be two goals ahead. **III** *sich gut etc* ~ conduct o.s. well *etc*.

'führend *adj* leading, prominent: ~ **sein** lead, rank in first place.

'Führer *m* (-s; -) **1.** leader, head. **2.** guide. **3.** *mot.* driver, ✈ pilot, ⚙ operator. **4.** guide(book). **'Führerin** *f* (-; -nen) → **Führer** 1-3. **'führerlos** *adj* **1.** without a leader (*or* guide *etc*). **2.** *mot.* driverless, ✈ pilotless.

'Führerna¦tur *f* born leader.

'Führerschaft *f* (-; *no pl*) **1.** leadership. **2.** *coll. the* leaders.

'Führerschein *m* mot. driving licence, *Am.* driver's license: **s-n ~ machen** take one's driving test. **~entzug** *m* revocation of s.o.'s driving licence (*etc*).

'Fuhrpark *m* car pool, fleet (of vehicles).

'Führung (-; -en) *f* **1.** *no pl* guidance, *ped. etc* leadership, ✗ command, ✞ management, *coll. the* leaders: **unter der ~ von** headed by; **die ~ übernehmen** take charge (→ *a.* 5). **2.** (guided) tour. **3.** *no pl* conduct (*of negotiations etc*). **4.** *no pl* conduct, behavio(u)r. **5.** *no pl sports:* lead: **in ~ gehen, die ~ übernehmen** take the lead; **in ~ liegen** be in the lead. **6.** *tech* ↑ use (of title).

'Führungs¦aufgabe *f* executive function. **~e¦tage** *f* executive floor. **~gremium** *n* executive committee. **~kraft** ✞ executive, *pl* executive personnel, *pol.* leaders. **~schicht** *f* ruling class(es). **~schwäche** *f* weak leadership. **~spitze** *f* top echelons. **~stil** *m* style of leader-

ship. **~tor** *n*, **~treffer** *m* goal that puts a team into the lead. **~zeugnis** *n* certificate of (good) conduct.

'Fuhrunternehmen *n* haulage company. **'Fuhrunternehmer** *m* haulage contractor. **'Fuhrwerk** *n* wag(g)on.

Fülle ['fʏlə] *f* (-; *no pl*) **1.** fullness, *fig. a.* richness: → **Hülle** 4. **2.** wealth, abundance. **3.** corpulence.

füllen ['fʏlən] *v/t* (h) **1.** (*a. sich* ~) fill: **in Flaschen** ~ bottle; **der Aufsatz füllte drei Seiten** the essay took up three pages. **2.** *gastr.* stuff.

Füller ['fʏlər] *m* (-s; -) F, **Füll¦(feder)halter** *m* fountain pen.

füllig ['fʏlɪç] *adj* full, plump.

Füllsel ['fʏlzəl] *n* (-s; -) filler.

'Füllung *f* (-; -en) **1.** filling (*a. of tooth*), *gastr. a.* stuffing, cent¦re (*Am.* -er) (*of chocolates*). **2.** padding.

'Füllwort *n* (-[e]s; ⸚er) filler.

fummeln ['fʊməln] *v/i* (h) F **1.** fiddle around (*an dat* with). **2.** pet.

Fund [fʊnt] *m* (-[e]s; -e) a) discovery, finding, b) (**e-n ~ machen** make a) find.

Fundament [fʊnda'mɛnt] *n* (-[e]s; -e) △ foundations. **fundamental** [fʊnda-mɛn'taːl] *adj* fundamental, basic.

Fundamentalismus [fʊndamɛnta'lɪs-mʊs] *m* (-; *no pl*) fundamentalism.

'Fundbü¦ro *n* lost property office.

'Fundgrube *f fig.* (gold)mine.

fundieren [fʊn'diːrən] *v/t* (h) **1.** substantiate. **2.** ✞ fund. **fun'diert** *adj* **1.** sound (*knowledge etc*). **2.** ✞ founded.

fündig ['fʏndɪç] *adj* ~ **werden** *a. fig.* strike gold.

'Fundort *m* (-[e]s; -e) site (of discovery).

'Fundsache *f* lost article, *pl a.* lost property.

Fundus ['fʊndʊs] *m* (-; -) **1.** *thea.* general equipment. **2.** store (**von, an** *dat* of).

fünf [fʏnf] *adj* five: *fig.* (**alle**) **~e gerade sein lassen** stretch a point.

Fünf *f* (-; -en) five, *ped.* poor, *Br.* E, *Am.* F. **'Fünfeck** *n* (-[e]s; -e) pentagon.

'fünfeckig *adj* pentagonal.

'Fünfer *m* (-s; -) **1.** five-pfennig (*or* five -mark) piece. **2.** → **Fünf.**

'fünffach *adj and adv* fivefold.

'fünfhundert *adj* five hundred.

fünfjährig ['fʏnfjɛːrɪç] *adj* **1.** five-year -old: **ein ~es Kind** *a.* a child of five. **2.** five-year, *period etc* of five years.

'**Fünfkampf** m sports: pentathlon.
'**Fünfkämpfer**(in f) m pentathlete.
'**Fünflinge** pl quintuplets, F quins.
'**fünfmal** adv five times.
Fünfpro'zentklausel f parl. five per cent hurdle.
fünfstellig ['fʏnfʃtɛlɪç] adj five-digit.
Fünf'tagewoche f five-day working week.
fünfte ['fʏnftə] adj fifth: → **Kolonne**, **Rad** 1. '**Fünftel** n (-s; -) fifth.
'**fünfzehn** adj fifteen.
fünfzig ['fʏnftsɪç] adj fifty. '**Fünfzig** f (-; no pl) fifty: **sie ist Mitte** (**der**) ~ she is in her mid-fifties. '**fünfziger** adj **die** ~ **Jahre** the fifties (of a century).
'**Fünfziger** m (-s; -) **1.** man of fifty: **er ist in den** ~ he is in his fifties. **2.** F a) fifty-pfennig piece, b) fifty-mark note (Am. bill). '**Fünfzigerin** f (-; -nen) woman of fifty (**in** ~ in her fifties).
fungieren [fʊŋ'giːrən] v/i (h) ~ **als** act (thing: serve) as.
Funk [fʊŋk] m (-s; no pl) radio; → **Rundfunk**, **Radio**. ~**ama,teur** m radio ham. ~**ausstellung** f radio and TV exhibition. ~**bild** n photo-radiogram.
Fünkchen ['fʏŋkçən] n (-s; -) → **Funke** ['fʊŋkə] m (-n; -n) a. fig. spark: **ein** ~ (**von**) **Verstand** a modicum of sense; **kein** ~ **Hoffnung** not a flicker of hope.
funkeln ['fʊŋkəln] v/i (h) sparkle (a. fig.).
'**funkel'nagel'neu** adj F brand-new.
funken ['fʊŋkən] v/t (h) radio (a. v/i), send out: F **zwischen uns hat es sofort gefunkt** we clicked the moment we met.
'**Funken** m (-s; -) → **Funke**.
'**funkentstört** adj radio-screened.
Funker ['fʊŋkər] m (-s; -) radio operator.
'**Funk|gerät** n transmitter. ~**haus** n broadcasting cent/re (Am. -er). ~**meldung** f radio message. ~**peilgerät** n radio direction finder. ~**rufempfänger** m bleep(er). ~**si,gnal** n radio signal.
'**Funksprech|gerät** n walkie-talkie. ~**verkehr** m radio telephony.
'**Funk|spruch** m radio message. ~**sta-ti,on** f, ~**stelle** f radio station. ~**stille** f radio silence. ~**streife** f 1. radio patrol. **2.** → ~**streifenwagen** m radio patrol car. ~**taxi** n radio cab. ~**technik** f radio engineering. ~**tele,gramm** n radiotelegram, radiogram.

Funktion [fʊŋk'tsɪoːn] f (-; -en) function, a. position: **in** ~ **treten** go into action.
Funktionär [fʊŋktsɪo'nɛːr] m (-s; -e), **Funktio'närin** f (-; -nen) official.
funktionell [fʊŋktsɪo'nɛl] adj functional.
funktionieren [fʊŋktsɪo'niːrən] v/i (h) function, work (a. F fig.).
funkti'onsfähig adj functioning.
Funkti'onsstörung f ⚕ malfunction.
'**Funk|turm** m radio tower. ~**verbindung** f radio contact. ~**verkehr** m radio communication(s). ~**wagen** m **1.** radio van. **2.** → **Funkstreifenwagen**.
für [fyːr] prep for, a. a) in exchange (or return) for, b) in favo(u)r of, c) instead of: **Jahr** ~ **Jahr** year after year; ~ **mich** for me, to me, in my opinion; **ich** ~ **m-e Person** I myself; ~ **s erste** for the moment; ~ **sich leben** live by o.s.; **an und** ~ **sich** actually; **e-e Sache** ~ **sich** another matter entirely; **das hat viel** ~ **sich** there's a lot to be said for it; **was** ~ (**ein**) **...?** what (kind of) ...?
Für n **das** ~ **und Wider** the pros and cons.
'**Fürbitte** f a. eccl. intercession.
Furche ['fʊrçə] f (-; -n) **1.** ✧, anat. furrow, geol., ☯ a. groove. **2.** rut.
Furcht [fʊrçt] f (-; no pl) (**vor** dat of) fear, dread: **aus** ~ **vor** for fear of; **j-m** ~ **einflößen** (or **einjagen**) frighten s.o.
'**furchtbar I** adj terrible, dreadful. **II** adv terribly, F a. awfully.
'**furchteinflößend** adj frightening.
fürchten ['fʏrçtən] (h) **I** v/t be afraid of, dread: **ich fürchte, wir schaffen es nicht** I fear we're not going to make it. **II** v/i **für** j-n ~ fear for s.o. **III sich** ~ (**vor** dat of) be afraid, be scared, be frightened; **sich** ~ **vor** (dat) a. dread; **sich** (**davor**) ~ **zu** inf be afraid of ger.
fürchterlich ['fʏrçtərlɪç] → **furchtbar**.
'**furchterregend** adj frightening.
'**furchtlos** adj fearless, intrepid.
'**Furchtlosigkeit** f (-; no pl) fearlessness.
'**furchtsam** adj timorous.
'**Furchtsamkeit** f (-; no pl) timorousness.
fürein'ander adv for each other, for one another.
Furie ['fuːrɪə] f (-; -n) fig. hellcat, virago.
Furnier [fʊr'niːr] n (-s; -e) veneer.
furnieren [fʊr'niːrən] v/t (h) veneer.
Furore [fu'roːrə] ~ **machen** cause a sensation.
'**Fürsorge** f (-; no pl) **1.** a) care (**für** for),

b) solicitude: *ärztliche* ~ medical care.
2. *öffentliche* ~ public welfare.
'fürsorglich *adj* considerate, solicitous.
'Fürsprache *f* (-; *no pl*) **1.** intercession
(*für* for, *bei* with). **2.** recommendation.

'Fürsprecher(in *f*) *m* a) intercessor, b) advocate.

Fürst [fyrst] *m* (-en; -en) a) prince, b)
ruler: *F leben wie ein* ~ live like a king.
'Fürstenhaus *n* dynasty. **'Fürstentum** *n*
(-s; ¨er) principality. **'Fürstin** *f* (-; -nen)
princess. **'fürstlich** *adj* princely (*a. fig.*),
prince's, *fig.* sumptuous, generous (*tip
etc*): *j-n ~lich bewirten* (**belohnen**) entertain (reward) s.o. royally.

Furt [furt] *f* (-; -en) fjord.
Furunkel [fu'ruŋkəl] *m* (-s; -) 🩹 boil.
'Fürwort *n* (-[e]s; ¨er) *ling.* pronoun.
Furz [furts] *m* (-es; ¨e) V fart.
furzen ['furtsən] *v/i* (h) V fart.
Fusel ['fu:zəl] *m* (-s; -) F rotgut.
Fusion [fu'zïo:n] *f* (-; -en) **1.** 🍄 fusion. **2.**
🪙 merger. **fusionieren** [fuzïo'ni:rən]
v/t, *v/i* (h) 🪙 merge.

Fuß [fu:s] *m* (-es; ¨e) **1.** foot: *zu* ~ on foot;
zu ~ *gehen* walk; *zu* ~ *erreichbar* within walking distance; *gut zu* ~ *sein* be a
good walker; *fig.* (*festen*) ~ *fassen* gain
a foothold; (*dat*) *auf dem* ~*e folgen*
follow on the heels of; *fig. auf die Füße
fallen* fall on one's feet; *auf freiem* ~ at
large; *j-n auf freien* ~ *setzen* release
s.o.; *auf eigenen Füßen stehen* stand
on one's own two feet; *auf großem* ~*e
leben* live in grand style; *auf gutem* ~*e
stehen mit* be on good terms with; *auf
schwachen Füßen stehen* be shaky;
mit beiden Füßen auf der Erde stehen
have both feet firmly on the ground;
kalte Füße bekommen F *fig.* get cold
feet; → **link**. **2.** foot, bottom (*of list,
page, etc*), leg (*of chair etc*), stem (*of
wineglass etc*), stand (*of lamp*): *am* ~*e
des Berges* at the foot of the mountain. **3.** foot (= 30,48 cm): *10* ~ ten feet.
'Fußabdruck *m* footprint.
'Fußangel *f* mantrap, *fig.* trap.
'Fußbad *n* footbath.
'Fußball *m* (-[e]s; ¨e) **1.** football, *Am.*
soccer ball. **2.** *no pl* football, *esp. Am.*
soccer. **'Fußball...** football (*club etc*).
'Fußballen *m* anat. ball of the foot.
'Fußballer [-balər] *m* (-s; -) F footballer.

'Fußballländerspiel *n* (*getr.* -ll,l-) international (football) match.
'Fußballplatz *m* football pitch. ~**spieler** *m* football player. ~**toto** *m*, *n* football pools, F the pools. ~**verband** *m*
football association. ~**weltmeister** *m*
World Cup holders. ~**weltmeisterschaft** *f* World Cup.
'Fußbank *f* footstool.
'Fußboden *m* **1.** floor. **2.** → ~**belag** *m*
floor covering, flooring. ~**heizung** *f*
underfloor heating.
'Fußbreit *m* k-n ~ *weichen* not to budge
an inch.
'Fußbremse *f* mot. footbrake.
Fussel ['fusəl] *f* (-; -n) F fluff, *Am.* lint.
'fusselig *adj* F covered in fluff: *fig. sich
den Mund* ~ *reden* talk one's head off.
fußen ['fu:sən] *v/i* (h) ~ *auf* (*dat*) be based
(up)on.
'Fußende *n* (*am* ~ at the) foot.
Fußgänger ['fu:sgɛŋər] *m* (-s; -) pedestrian. ~**brücke** *f* footbridge.
'Fußgängerin *f* (-; -nen) pedestrian.
'Fußgänger|übergang *m*, ~**überweg** *m*
pedestrian crossing. ~**unterführung** *f*
(pedestrian) underpass, *Br. a.* subway.
~**zone** *f* pedestrian precinct.
'Fuß|gelenk *n* anat. ankle. ⚹**hoch** *adj*
ankle-deep. ~**matte** *f* doormat, mot.
floor mat. ~**note** *f* footnote. ~**pfad** *m*
footpath. ~**pflege** *f* pedicure. ~**pfleger(in** *f*) *m* pedicurist, chiropodist.
~**pilz** *m* 🩹 athlete's foot. ~**puder** *m* foot
powder. ~**sohle** *f* sole (of the foot).
~**spur** *f* footprint. ~**stapfe** *f* (-; -n) footstep: *fig. in j-s* ~*n treten* follow s.o.'s
footsteps. ~**tritt** *m* **1.** footstep. **2.** footprint. **3.** kick: *j-m e-n* ~ *geben* a. kick
s.o. ~**volk** *n* fig. rank and file. ~**weg** *m*
1. footpath. **2.** *e-e Stunde etc* ~ an
hour's *etc* walk.
futsch [futʃ] *adj pred* F a) gone, b) broken, *sl.* bust: *es ist* ~ *a.* it has had it.
Futter[1] ['futər] *n* (-s; *no pl*) **1.** 🌾 fodder,
feed, food. **2.** F grub (*sl.*), chow (*sl.*).
Futter[2] *n* (-s; -) lining, 🔩 casing.
Futteral [futə'ra:l] *n* (-s; -e) case, cover.
'Futtermittel *n* feed, fodder.
futtern ['futərn] *v/i* (h) F tuck in(*to*)
v/t).
füttern[1] ['fytərn] *v/t* (h) feed.
'füttern[2] *v/t* (h) line.
'Futternapf *m* feeding bowl.

'**Futterneid** *m fig.* envy, jealousy.
'**Futterstoff** *m* lining (material).
'**Fütterung** *f* (-; -en) feeding.
Futur [fu'tu:r] *n* (-s; *no pl*) *ling.* (*a.* **erstes** ~) future (tense); **zweites** ~ future perfect (tense).

Futurismus [futu'rɪsmʊs] *m* (-; *no pl*) futurism. **Futurist** [futu'rɪst] *m* (-en; -en), **futu'ristisch** *adj* futurist.
Futurologe [futuro'lo:gə] *m* (-n; -n) futurologist. **Futurologie** [futurolo-'gi:] *f* (-; *no pl*) futurology.

G

G, g [ge:] *n* (-; -) *a.* ♪ G, g.
gab [ga:p] *pret of* **geben**.
Gabardine ['gabardi:n] *m* (-s; *no pl*), *a. f* (-; *no pl*) gabardine.
Gabe ['ga:bə] *f* (-; -n) **1.** (*an acc* to) a) gift, present, b) contribution: **milde** ~ charity. **2.** gift, talent.
Gabel ['ga:bəl] *f* (-; -n) **1.** a fork (*a. on bike*), b) ✍ (pitch)fork. **2.** *teleph.* rest, cradle. **3.** *zo.* spire. **gabeln** ['ga:bəln] (h) **I sich** ~ fork (off *or* out). **II** *v/t* fork.
'**Gabelstapler** *m* (-s; -) forklift (truck).
'**Gabelung** *f* (-; -en) fork.
'**Gabentisch** *m* table with (the) presents.
gackern ['gakərn] *v/i* (h) cluck.
gaffen ['gafən] *v/i* (h) gape, stare.
Gag [gɛk] *m* (-s; -s) gag.
Gage ['ga:ʒə] *f* (-; -n) fee.
gähnen ['gɛ:nən] *v/i* (h) *a. fig.* yawn: ~**d leer** completely empty.
'**Gähnen** *n* (-s) yawn(ing).
Gala ['ga:la] *f* (-; *no pl*) gala dress.
'**Gala...** gala (*concert, performance, etc*).
galant [ga'lant] *adj* gallant. **Galanterie** [galantə'ri:] *f* (-; -n) gallantry.
Galeere [ga'le:rə] *f* (-; -n) galley.
Galerie [galə'ri:] *f* (-; -n) gallery.
Galerist [galə'rɪst] *m* (-en; -en), **Gale'ristin** *f* (-; -nen) gallery owner.
Galgen ['galgən] *m* (-s; -) gallows.
'**Galgenhu,mor** *m* gallows humo(u)r.
'**Galionsfi,gur** [ga'lǐo:ns-] *f* figurehead.
gälisch ['gɛ:lɪʃ] *adj* Gaelic.
'**Gallapfel** *m* oakapple.
Galle ['galə] *f* (-; -n) **1.** *anat.* gall bladder. **2.** *physiol., a. fig.* bile, *a.* ⚕, *zo.* gall: **mir kam die** ~ **hoch** my blood was up.
Gallen|blase *f* *anat.* gall bladder. ~**gang** *m* bile (*or* gall) duct. ~**kolik** *f*

bilious attack. ~**leiden** *n* bilious complaint. ~**stein** *m* ⚕ gallstone.
Gallert ['galərt] *n* (-[e]s; -e) jelly.
'**gallertartig** *adj* jelly-like, gelatinous.
Gallier ['galǐər] *m* (-s; -) *hist.* Gaul.
gallig ['galɪç] *adj a. fig.* bilious.
Galopp [ga'lɔp] *m* (-s; -s, -e) gallop: **im** ~ at a gallop, *fig. a.* in a hurry.
galoppieren [galɔ'pi:rən] *v/i* (sn) gallop.
galt [galt] *pret of* **gelten**.
galvanisch [gal'va:nɪʃ] *adj* galvanic.
galvanisieren [galvani'zi:rən] *v/t* (h) galvanize (*a.* ✦), ⚙ *a.* electroplate.
Galvanotechnik [gal'va:no-] *f* electroplating.
Gamasche [ga'maʃə] *f* (-; -n) a) gaiter, b) puttee.
Gamet [ga'me:t] *m* (-en; -en) gamete.
Gammaglobulin [gamaglobu'li:n] *n* (-s; *no pl*) ✦ gamma globulin.
'**Gammastrahl** *m* *phys.* gamma ray.
'**Gammastrahlung** *f* gamma radiation.
Gamme'lei *f* (-; *no pl*) F loafing around.
'**gammelig** *adj* F **1.** old (*meat etc*), rotten (*fruit etc*). **2.** scruffy. **gammeln** ['gaməln] *v/i* (h) F loaf (*or* bum) around.
Gammler ['gamlər] *m* (-s; -), '**Gammlerin** *f* (-; -nen) F layabout, loafer, bum.
gang [gaŋ] *adj* ~ **und gäbe sein** be quite common (*or* usual).
Gang *m* (-[e]s; ⸚e) **1.** → **Gangart. 2.** a) walk, b) errand, c) way, d) visit. **3.** course: **s-n** ~ **gehen** take its course. **4.** ⚙ a) running, working, action, b) operation: **in** ~ **setzen** (*or* **bringen**) get going, *fig.* start, get *s.th.* going; **in** ~ **kommen** *a. fig.* get going (*or* started); **im** ~(**e**) **sein** ⚙ be running, be working, *fig.* be under way, be in progress; **es ist et. im** ~**e**

s.th. is going on; *in vollem ~e sein* be in full swing. **5.** *mot.* gear, *a.* ⚙ speed: *erster ~* first (*or* bottom) gear; *in den dritten ~ schalten* change (*Am.* shift) into third (gear); *den ~herausnehmen* put the car in neutral. **6.** a) corridor (*a.* 🚂), hall(way), b) passage(way), c) aisle, d) walkway, e) tunnel. **7.** *anat.* duct. **8.** *gastr.* course: *ein Essen mit fünf Gängen* a five-course meal.

'**Gangart** *f* gait, walk, pace (*of horse*).
'**gangbar** *adj* passable (*road etc*), practicable (*a. fig.*).
gängeln ['gɛŋəln] *v/t* (h) *F j-n* ~ keep s.o. in leading strings.
gängig ['gɛŋɪç] *adj* **1.** current (*expression*), (very) common (*method etc*). **2.** 🛒 saleable, fast-selling.
'**Gangschaltung** *f mot.* gear change, *Am.* gearshift.
Gangster ['gɛŋstər] *m* (-s; -) gangster.
'**Gangsterbande** *f* gang of criminals.
'**Gangsterbraut** *f* moll.
'**Gangstertum** *n* (-s; *no pl*) gangsterism.
Gangway ['gæŋweɪ] *f* (-; -s) **1.** ✈ steps. **2.** ⚓ gangway.
Ganove [ga'noːvə] *m* (-n; -n) F crook.
Gans [gans] *f* (-; ⸚e) goose: *junge ~* gosling; *dumme ~es* stupid thing (*or* girl).
'**Gänschen** ['gɛnsçən] *n* (-s; -) gosling.
Gänse|blümchen ['gɛnzə-] *n* daisy.
~braten *m* roast goose. **~füßchen** *pl F* quotation marks, inverted commas.
~haut *f* gooseflesh, goose pimples: *ich kriege e-e ~* it gives me the creeps.
~leberpa,stete *f* pâté de foie gras.
~marsch *m im ~* in single file.
Gänserich ['gɛnzərɪç] *m* (-s; -e) gander.
'**Gänseschmalz** *n* goose dripping.
ganz [gants] **I** *adj* **1.** whole, complete: ~ *Deutschland* all (*or* the whole of) Germany; *die ~e Stadt* the whole town; *in der ~en Welt* all over the world; *~e Länge* total (*or* overall) length; *~e Zahl* whole number; *~e zwei Stunden* a) for two solid hours, b) for just two hours; *von ~em Herzen* with all my *etc* heart; *den ~en Tag* all day; *die ~e Nacht* (*hindurch*) all night long; *die ~e Zeit* all the time; *F ihr ~es Geld* all her money. **2.** F intact, in one piece: ~ *machen* mend. **II** *adv* **3.** (*a.* ~ *und gar*) completely, totally: ~ *aus Holz* all wood *etc*; *das ist et.* ~ *anderes* that's a

different matter altogether; *nicht* ~ not quite; *nicht* ~ *zehn Minuten* just under ten minutes; ~ *und gar nicht* not at all; ~ *gewiß* certainly; ~ *naß* wet through; ~ *wie du willst* just as you like; (*ich bin*) ~ *Ihrer Meinung* I quite agree; *er ist* ~ *der Vater* he's just like his father; → *Ohr.* **4.** a) quite, F pretty, b) very, really: ~ *gut* quite good, not bad; ~ *wenig* a tiny bit; ~ *besonders, weil* (e)specially since. **5.** *im* ~*en* altogether, in all, 🛒 wholesale: → *groß* 6, 7.
Ganze ['gantsə] *n* (-n; *no pl*) whole: *einheitliches ~s* integral whole; *als ~s* as a whole, in its entirety; *das ~* the whole thing; *aufs ~ gehen* go all out; *jetzt geht es ums ~* it's all *or* nothing now.
'**Ganzheit** *f* (-; *no pl*) (*in s-r ~*) as a) whole.
'**Ganzheitsme,thode** *f ped.* **1.** whole-word method. **2.** *a.* '**Ganzheitsunterricht** *m* integrated curriculum.
ganzjährig ['gantsjɛːrɪç] *adj* all-year: ~ *geöffnet* open all year round.
gänzlich ['gɛntslɪç] *adj and adv* total(ly), complete(ly), entire(ly).
'**Ganzme,tall...** ⚙ all-metal.
ganzseitig ['gantszaɪtɪç] *adj* full-page.
ganztägig ['gantstɛːgɪç] *adj* all-day: ~ *geöffnet* open all day.
'**Ganztags|beschäftigung** *f* full-time job. **~schule** *f* all-day school(ing).
gar¹ [gaːr] *adj gastr.* done, cooked.
gar² *adv* **1.** ~ *nicht* not at all; ~ *nichts* not a thing, nothing at all, absolutely nothing; ~ *nicht so schlecht* (*viel*) not all that bad (much); ~ *keiner* nobody at all; *es besteht* ~ *kein Zweifel* there's no doubt whatsoever. **2.** a) perhaps, b) even; *oder* ~ *...* let alone ...
Garage [ga'raːʒə] *f* (-; -n) garage.
Garant [ga'rant] *m* (-en; -en) guarantor.
Garantie [garan'tiː] *f* (-; -n) guarantee: *die Uhr hat ein Jahr ~* the watch has got a year's guarantee; *die Reparatur geht noch auf ~* the repair is covered by the guarantee; *dafür kann ich k-e ~ übernehmen* I can't guarantee that; *F er fällt unter ~ durch* he's bound to fail.
garantieren [garan'tiːrən] *v/t* (h) (*v/i ~ für*) guarantee (*a. fig.*).
Garan'tieschein *m* guarantee.
Garan'tiezeit *f* guarantee.
Garbe ['garbə] *f* (-; -n) ✧ sheaf.

Garde ['gardə] f ✕ *the* Guards: *fig.* **die alte ~** the Old Guard.

Garderobe [gardə'ro:bə] f (-; -n) **1.** cloakroom, *Am.* checkroom. **2.** *thea.* dressing room. **3.** coat rack. **4.** *no pl* a) coat (and hat), b) clothes, wardrobe.

Garde'roben|frau f cloakroom (*Am.* checkroom) attendant. **~marke** f cloakroom ticket, *Am.* check. **~ständer** m coat rack.

Garderobier [gardəro'biɛ:] m (-s; -s), **Garderobiere** [gardəro'biɛ:rə] f (-; -n) *thea.* dresser.

Gardine [gar'di:nə] f (-; -n) curtain.

gären ['gɛ:rən] v/i (gärte, *or* gor, gegoren, h) **1.** (*a.* **~ lassen**) ferment. **2.** seethe: *im Volk gärte es* there was unrest among the people.

Garn [garn] n (-[e]s; -e) thread; cotton; *fig.* **j-m ins ~ gehen** fall into the (*or* s.o.'s) trap; *ein ~ spinnen* spin a yarn.

Garnele [gar'ne:lə] f (-; -n) shrimp, prawn.

garnieren [gar'ni:rən] v/t (h) decorate, *a.* trim (*hat etc*), *gastr. a.* garnish.

Garnison [garni'zo:n] f (-; -en) garrison.

Garnitur [garni'tu:r] f (-; -en) **1.** set. **2.** trimmings. **3.** *fig.* **zur ersten** (**zweiten**) **~ gehören** be first-rate (second-rate).

Garten ['gartən] m (-s; ¨) garden: *botanischer ~* botanical gardens. **~arbeit** f gardening. **~archi,tekt(in** f) m landscape gardener. **~bau** m (-[e]s; *no pl*) horticulture. **~bau...** horticultural (*show etc*). **~fest** n garden party. **~geräte** pl gardening tools. **~haus** n summerhouse. **~lo,kal** n beer garden. **~möbel** pl garden furniture. **~schere** f pruning shears, *esp. Br.* secateurs. **~stadt** f garden city. **~zaun** m garden fence. **~zwerg** m **1.** (garden) gnome. **2.** F *fig.* little squirt.

Gärtner ['gɛrtnər] m (-s; -), **Gärtnerin** f (-; -nen) gardener.

Gärtne'rei f (-; -en) **1.** *no pl* F gardening. **2.** market (*Am.* truck) garden.

Gärung f (-; -en) **1.** fermentation. **2.** *fig.* (state of) unrest. **Gärungspro,zeß** m (process of) fermentation.

Gas [ga:s] n (-es; -e) gas: *mot.* **~ geben** step on the gas (*a.* F *fig.*); **~ wegnehmen** throttle back (*or* down); *mit ~ vergiften* gas. **'Gasableser** m (-s; -) gasman. **'Gasanzünder** m gaslighter.

'**Gasbehälter** m gasholder, gas tank. '**gasbeheizt** *adj* gas-fired. '**Gasflasche** f gas cylinder. '**gasförmig** *adj* gaseous. '**Gashahn** m gas tap. '**Gasheizung** f gas heating. '**Gasherd** m gas stove. '**Gaskammer** f gas chamber. '**Gasleitung** f gas mains. '**Gasmaske** f gas mask. '**Gaspe,dal** n *mot.* accelerator, *Am.* gas pedal.

Gasse ['gasə] f (-; -n) alley, *a. fig.* lane.

Gast [gast] m (-[e]s; ¨e) **1.** a) guest, b) customer, c) visitor: *Gäste haben a.* have company. **2.** *thea.* guest (artist *or* performer). **~arbeiter(in** f) m foreign worker. **~diri,gent** m guest conductor. **~do,zent(in** f) m guest lecturer.

Gästebuch ['gɛstə-] n visitors' book. '**Gästehaus** n guesthouse. '**Gästezimmer** n guestroom. '**gastfreundlich** *adj* hospitable. '**Gastfreundschaft** f (-; *no pl*) hospitality. '**Gast|geber** m **1.** host. **2.** *pl sports*: home team. **~geberin** f hostess. **~haus** n, **~hof** m restaurant, inn. **~hörer(in** f) m *univ.* guest student, *Am.* auditor.

gastieren [gas'ti:rən] v/i (h) *thea.* give a guest performance, *esp. Am.* guest. '**Gastland** n host country. '**gastlich** *adj* hospitable. '**Gastlichkeit** f (-; *no pl*) hospitality. '**Gast|mannschaft** f visiting team. **~pro,fessor** m visiting professor. **~recht** n (**~ genießen** enjoy) hospitality.

Gastritis [gas'tri:tɪs] f (-; -tiden [-tri'ti:dən]) ⚕ gastritis.

'**Gastrolle** f *thea.* guest part.

Gastronom [gastro'no:m] m (-en; -en) restaurant proprietor (*cook:* chef). **Gastronomie** [gastrono'mi:] f (-; *no pl*) **1.** catering trade. **2.** gastronomy. **gastronomisch** [gastro'no:mɪʃ] *adj* **1.** catering. **2.** gastronomic(al).

'**Gastspiel** n *thea.* guest performance. '**Gaststätte** f restaurant. '**Gaststättengewerbe** n catering trade. '**Gaststube** f lounge, taproom. '**Gastur,bine** f gas turbine. '**Gastvorlesung** f, '**Gastvortrag** m guest lecture. '**Gastvorstellung** f *thea.* guest performance. '**Gastwirt** m landlord, proprietor. '**Gastwirtin** f landlady, proprietress. '**Gastwirtschaft** f restaurant. '**Gasvergiftung** f gas poisoning.

'**Gaswerk** n gasworks.
'**Gaszähler** m gasmeter.
Gatte ['gatə] m (-n; -n) husband, ⚭ spouse.
Gatter ['gatər] n **1.** gate. **2.** fence.
'**Gattersäge** f ⚙ gate (or frame) saw.
Gattin ['gatɪn] f (-; -nen) wife, ⚭ spouse.
Gattung ['gatʊŋ] f (-; -en) **1.** biol. genus. **2.** species, kind, type. **3.** a) (art) form, b) literature: genre.
'**Gattungsbegriff** m generic term.
'**Gattungsname** m **1.** biol. generic name. **2.** ling. collective (or common) noun.
gaukeln ['gaʊkəln] v/i (sn) flutter around. **Gaukler** ['gaʊklər] m (-s; -) **1.** tumbler. **2.** clown.
Gaul [gaʊl] m (-[e]s; ⸚e) horse, contp. nag: alter ~ (old) jade; fig. e-m geschenkten ~ sieht man nicht ins Maul never look a gift horse in the mouth.
Gaumen ['gaʊmən] m (-s; -) palate.
'**Gaumenlaut** m ling. palatal.
'**Gaumenzäpfchen** n anat. uvula.
Gauner ['gaʊnər] m (-s; -) **1.** swindler, crook, sl. con man. **2.** rascal.
'**Gaunersprache** f thieves' Latin.
'**Gaunerstück** n swindle.
Gaze ['ga:zə] f (-; -n) gauze (a. ⚕).
Gazelle [ga'tsɛlə] f (-; -n) zo. gazelle.
geachtet [gə'ʔaxtət] adj esteemed.
Geächtete [gə'ʔɛçtətə] m, f (-n; -n) outlaw.
Geäder [gə'ʔɛ:dər] n (-s; -) veins.
geädert [gə'ʔɛ:dərt] adj veined.
geartet [gə'ʔartət] adj disposed: er ist so ~, daß ... he is the kind of person that ...; anders ~ sein be different.
Gebäck [gə'bɛk] n (-[e]s; -e) a) (fancy) cakes, b) biscuits, Am. cookies.
ge'backen pp of **backen.**
Gebälk [gə'bɛlk] n (-[e]s; -e) beams.
geballt [gə'balt] adj **1.** clenched. **2.** fig. concentrated.
gebannt [gə'bant] adj and adv spellbound.
gebar [gə'ba:r] pret of **gebären.**
Gebärde [gə'bɛ:rdə] f (-; -n) gesture.
ge'bärden: sich ~ (h) behave, act.
Ge'bärden|spiel n gestures, gesticulation, pantomime (a. fig.). **~sprache** f **1.** sign language. **2.** thea. mimicry.
Gebaren [gə'ba:rən] n (-s; no pl) behavio(u)r, ⚕ conduct.
gebären [gə'bɛ:rən] (gebar, geboren, h)

I v/t give birth to: **geboren werden** be born; → **geboren.** II v/i give birth.
Ge'bärmutter f (-; ⸚) anat. womb.
Ge'bärmutter|krebs m ⚕ cancer of the womb. **~vorfall** m (uterine) prolapse.
Gebäude [gə'bɔydə] n (-s; -) building, edifice (a. fig.), fig. structure. **~komplex** m complex (of buildings).
'**gebefreudig** adj open-handed.
Gebein [gə'baɪn] n (-[e]s; -e) **1.** bones. **2.** pl (mortal) remains.
Gebell [gə'bɛl] n (-[e]s; no pl) barking.
geben ['ge:bən] (gab, gegeben, h) I v/t (j-m et. s.o. s.th., s.th. to s.o.) give, a. (hand), b) grant: laß dir e-e Quittung ~! ask for a receipt!; ~ Sie mir bitte Frau X teleph. can I speak to Mrs X, please; F fig. es j-m ~ let s.o. have it; → Anlaß 2, Bescheid, gegeben. **2.** give (lessons etc), teach. **3.** give (a concert etc), a. have (a party etc), perform (play etc), show (a film): was wird heute abend gegeben? what's on tonight? **4.** yield, produce: Milch ~ give milk; zweimal fünf gibt zehn two times five makes ten; das gibt e-e gute Suppe that will make a good soup; Flecken ~ make (or leave) stains; das gibt k-n Sinn that doesn't make sense; ein Wort gab das andere one word led to another. **5.** von sich ~ a) 🍃 give off, emit, b) make (remark etc), give, let out (shout etc), c) bring up, vomit; sie gab k-n Ton von sich she didn't utter a sound. **6.** viel ~ auf (acc) set great store by s.th., think highly (or a lot) of s.o.; ich gebe nicht viel auf (acc) I don't think much of. II v/i **7.** give (mit vollen Händen freely). **8.** cards: deal: wer gibt? whose deal is it? **9.** tennis: serve. III sich ~ **10.** act, behave: sich gelassen ~ pretend to be calm; er gibt sich gern als Experte he likes to act the expert. **11.** a) pass, F blow over, b) come right: das wird sich alles ~ everything will be all right. IV v/impers es gibt there is, there are; der beste Spieler, den es je gab the best player of all time; es gab viel zu tun there was a lot to do; F was gibt's? what's up?; was gibt's Neues? what's new?; was gibt es zum Mittagessen? what's for lunch?; was gibt's heute abend im Fernsehen? what's on in television tonight?; das gibt es (be-

mir) nicht! that's out!; *das gibt's doch nicht!* you're joking!; *heute wird's noch was ~* I think we're in for s.th.; *er hat recht, da gibt's nichts!* he's right, and no mistake about it!

'Geben *n* (-s) **1.** giving: *~ ist seliger denn Nehmen* it is more blessed to give than to receive. **2.** *cards:* **am *~* sein** be dealing; *er ist am ~* it's his deal. **Geber** ['ge:bər] *m* (-s; -) **1.** giver, *cards:* dealer. **2.** *tel.* transmitter. **'Geberin** *f* (-; -nen) → **Geber** 1. **'Geberlaune** *f in ~ sein* be in a generous mood.

Gebet [gə'be:t] *n* (-[e]s; -e) prayer: F *fig. j-n ins ~ nehmen* give s.o. a good talking-to. **Ge'betbuch** *n* prayerbook.

ge'beten *pp of* **bitten.**

Gebiet [gə'bi:t] *n* (-[e]s; -e) **1.** a) region, area, b) district, zone, c) territory. **2.** *fig.* field, *a.* sphere: *er ist Fachmann auf dem ~* he is an authority on.

ge'bieten (gebot, geboten, h) **I** *v/t* **1.** *j-m ~ et. zu tun* order s.o. to do s.th. **2.** command (*respect etc*). **3.** require, call for: *die Vernunft gebietet uns zu inf* reason demands of us to *inf.* **II** *v/i* **4.** *~ über* (*acc*) control, rule over, b) have at one's disposal; → **geboten.**

Ge'bieter *m* (-s; -) **1.** master, lord. **2.** ruler. **Ge'bieterin** *f* (-; -nen) mistress. **ge'bieterisch** *adj* domineering, peremptory (*tone*).

Ge'biets|anspruch *m* territorial claim. **~hoheit** *f* (-; *no pl*) territorial sovereignty. **~leiter** *m* ✝ regional manager.

Gebilde [gə'bildə] *n* (-s; -) a) thing, object, b) work, creation, c) structure.

gebildet [gə'bildət] *adj* a) educated, (well-)informed, b) cultured, refined.

Gebinde [gə'bində] *n* (-s; -) arrangement.

Gebirge [gə'birgə] *n* (-s; -) mountains.

gebirgig [gə'birgiç] *adj* mountainous. **Ge'birgskette** *f* mountain range.

Gebiß [gə'bis] *n* (-sses; -sse) **1.** a) (set of) teeth, b) dentures. **2.** bit.

Ge'bißabdruck *m* (dental) impression.

gebissen [gə'bisən] *pp of* **beißen.**

Gebläse [gə'blɛ:zə] *n* (-s; -) ⚙ a) fan, b) blower. **Ge'bläsemotor** *m mot.* supercharger engine.

ge'blasen *pp of* **blasen.**

geblieben [gə'bli:bən] *pp of* **bleiben.**

geblümt [gə'bly:mt] *adj* floral, flowered.

Geblüt [gə'bly:t] *n* (-[e]s; *no pl*) blood.

gebogen [gə'bo:gən] *pp of* **biegen.**

gebongt [gə'bɔŋt] *adj* F *ist ~!* will do!

geboren [gə'bo:rən] **I** *pp of* **gebären. II** *adj* born: *~er Deutscher* (*Berliner*) *sein* be German (a Berliner) by birth; *Frau X, ~e Braun* Mrs X, née Braun; *sie ist e-e ~e Braun* her maiden name is Braun; *fig. ~ sein zu* be born to be (*or* to do), be cut out for (*a job*); *er ist der ~e Geschäftsmann* he is a born businessman; → *a.* **gebären.**

geborgen [gə'bɔrgən] **I** *pp of* **bergen. II** *adj* safe, secure. **Ge'borgenheit** *f* (-; *no pl*) safety, security.

geborsten [gə'bɔrstən] *pp of* **bersten.**

gebot [gə'bo:t] *pret of* **gebieten.**

Ge'bot *n* (-[e]s; -e) **1.** *bibl.* commandment. **2.** rule. **3.** requirement, necessity: *das ~ der Vernunft* (*des Herzens, der Stunde*) the dictates of reason (of one's heart, of the moment). **4.** ✝ bid. **5.** *j-m zu ~e stehen* be at s.o.'s disposal.

ge'boten I *pp of* **bieten** *and* **gebieten. II** *adj* a) necessary, b) imperative, c) due.

Ge'botsschild *n* mandatory sign.

gebracht [gə'braxt] *pp of* **bringen.**

gebrannt [gə'brant] **I** *pp of* **brennen. II** *adj* burnt, roasted, fired: → **Kind.**

ge'braten *pp of* **braten.**

Gebräu [gə'brɔy] *n* (-[e]s; -e) *contp.* brew, *fig. a.* concoction.

Ge'brauch *m* (-[e]s; ⁻e) **1.** *no pl* use, ✎ *a.* application, *ling.* usage: *~ machen von* use, make use of; *guten ~ machen von* put *s.th.* to good use; *außer ~ kommen* pass out of use; *im ~ sein* be in use, be used; *et. in ~ nehmen* put s.th. into use; *der ~ s-s linken Arms* the use of his left arm; *zum persönlichen ~* for personal use; *vor ~ schütteln!* shake before use! **2.** *usu. pl* practice, custom.

ge'brauchen *v/t* (h) **1.** use: *kannst du das ~?* can you make use of that?; *das kann ich gut ~* I can make good use of that; F *er ist zu nichts zu ~* he is hopeless. **2.** F use, do with (*a drink etc*).

gebräuchlich [gə'brɔyçliç] *adj* common (*a. ling.*), normal: *allgemein ~* in common use; *nicht mehr ~* no longer used.

Ge'brauchs|anleitung *f*, **~anweisung** *f* directions for use, instructions (for use). **~artikel** *m* article of daily use. **⁀fähig** *adj* usable. **~fahrzeug** *n* utility vehicle. 2**fertig** *adj* ready for use. **~gra-phik** *f* commercial art. **~güter** *pl* (consumer) durables. **~muster** *n* registered design. **~wert** *m* practical value.

ge'braucht I *pp of* **brauchen.** II *adj* used, ✝ *a.* second-hand.

Ge'brauchtwagen *m* used (*or* second--hand) car. **~händler** *m* used car dealer.

gebräunt [gə'brɔynt] *adj* tanned.

Ge'brechen *n* (-s; -) disability, (physical) handicap, infirmity. **gebrechlich** [gə'brɛçlɪç] *adj* frail, infirm. **Ge'brech-lichkeit** *f* (-; *no pl*) frailty, infirmity.

gebrochen [gə'brɔxən] I *pp of* **brechen.** II *adj* broken (*a.* ling.), fig. *a.* broken--hearted: **sie spricht nur ~ Englisch** she speaks only broken English.

Gebrüder [gə'bry:dər] *pl* ~ (*abbr.* **Gebr.**) **Wolf** Wolf Brothers (*abbr.* Bros.).

Gebrüll [gə'brʏl] *n* (-[e]s; *no pl*) roar(ing), bellow(ing) (*a. zo.*).

gebückt [gə'bʏkt] *adj* stooping.

Gebühr [gə'by:r] *f* (-; -en) **1.** a) charge, fee, b) rate, c) postage, d) *mot.* toll: **ermäßigte ~** reduced rate. **2.** **nach ~** duly; **über ~** unduly, excessively.

ge'bühren *v/i* (h) *j-m ~* be due to s.o. **ge'bührend** *adj* due (*dat* to), proper. II *adv* duly, properly.

Ge'bühren|einheit *f* unit. **~erlaß** *m* remission of fees. 2**frei** *adj* free of charge. **~ordnung** *f* scale of fees (*or* charges).

ge'bührenpflichtig *adj* subject to charges: **~e Straße** toll road; **~e Verwarnung** summary fine.

gebündelt [gə'bʏndəlt] *adj* bundled.

gebunden [gə'bʊndən] I *pp of* **binden.** II *adj* **1.** *print.* bound. **2.** ♞ bound (*a. phys.*), fixed: **~e Wärme** latent heat. ♪ legato. **4.** *fig.* bound, tied, engaged: **vertraglich ~** bound by contract; **sich ~ fühlen an** (*acc*) feel committed to. **5.** tied (up) (*capital*). **6.** *gastr.* thickened.

Geburt [gə'bu:rt] *f* (-; -en) **1.** birth (*a. fig.*), descent: **er ist von ~ Deutscher** he is German by birth. **2.** ♂ a) (child-)birth, b) delivery: **von ~ an** from birth; F *fig.* **e-e schwere ~** a tough job.

Ge'burten|kon|trolle *f*, **~regelung** *f* birth control. **~rückgang** *m* decline in the birthrate. 2**schwach** *adj* low-birth-rate (*year etc*). 2**stark** *adj* high-birth-rate (*year etc*). **~überschuß** *m* excess of births. **~ziffer** *f* birthrate.

gebürtig [gə'bʏrtɪç] *adj* **er ist ~er Eng-länder** he was born in England.

Ge'burts|anzeige *f* birth announcement. **~datum** *n* date of birth. **~haus** *n* **mein** *etc* **~** the house where I *etc* was born. **~helfer** *m* obstetrician. **~helfe-rin** *f* midwife. **~hilfe** *f* a) obstetrics, b) midwifery. **~jahr** *n* year of birth. **~jahr-gang** *m* cohort. **~land** *n* native country. **~ort** *m* birthplace: **~ und Geburts-tag** place and date of birth. **~stadt** *f* native town. **~stunde** *f* **1.** hour of birth **2.** *fig.* birth.

Ge'burtstag *m* birthday, *adm.* date of birth: **sie hat heute ~** it's her birthday today; **(ich) gratuliere zum ~** many happy returns of the day.

Ge'burtstags... birthday (*present etc*).

Ge'burtstagskind *n* birthday boy (girl).

Ge'burtsurkunde *f* birth certificate.

Gebüsch [gə'bʏʃ] *n* (-[e]s; -e) bushes shrubbery.

gedacht [gə'daxt] I *pp of* **denken** *and* **gedenken.** II *adj* assumed: **~ als** intended as (*or* to be).

ge'dachte *pret of* **gedenken.**

Gedächtnis [gə'dɛçtnɪs] *n* (-ses; -se) **1** memory: **aus dem ~** a) from memory b) by heart; **sich et. ins ~ zurückrufen** recall s.th. **2.** *no pl* commemoration **zum ~ an** (*acc*) a. in memory of. **~hilfe** *f* mnemonic (aid). **~lücke** *f* lapse of memory. **~schwund** *m* amnesia, loss of memory. **~störung** *f* partial amnesia **~training** *n* memory training.

gedämpft [gə'dɛmpft] *adj* **1.** muffled (*sound*), subdued (*colo[u]r, light, voice etc, fig.* mood *etc*): **~er Optimismus** guarded optimism. **2.** *gastr.* steamed.

Gedanke [gə'daŋkə] *m* (-n; -n) thought (**an** *acc* of, **über** *acc* on), idea: **kei schlechter ~!** not a bad idea!; **in ~** absent-mindedly; **in ~n versunken** los in thought; **s-e ~n beisammen halte** keep one's wits about one; **j-n auf an dere ~n bringen** get s.o.'s mind on to other things; **j-n auf den ~n bringen zu** *inf* give s.o. the idea of *ger*; **j-n auf dumme ~n bringen** give s.o. silly ideas **j-s ~n lesen** read s.o.'s mind; **sich ~ machen über** (*acc*) a) think about, b be worried about; **wie kommst du au den ~n?** what makes you think o that?; → **spielen** 1, **tragen** 9.

Ge'danken|austausch m exchange of ideas. **~blitz** m sudden inspiration, F brainwave. **~freiheit** f (-; no pl) freedom of thought. **~gang** m train of thought. **~leser(in** f) m mind-reader.
ge'dankenlos adj a) thoughtless, inconsiderate, b) careless. **Ge'dankenlosigkeit** f (-; no pl) thoughtlessness.
Ge'dankenreich adj full of ideas.
Ge'danken|sprung m jump (from one idea to the other). **~strich** m dash. **~übertragung** f telepathy.
ge'dankenvoll adj pensive.
ge'danklich adj intellectual.
Gedärm [gə'dɛrm] n (-[e]s, -e) usu. pl intestines, zo. entrails.
Gedeck [gə'dɛk] n (-[e]s; -e) **1.** cover: **ein ~ mehr auflegen** set another place. **3.** cover charge.
Gedeih [gə'daɪ]: **auf ~ und Verderb** come what may. **ge'deihen** v/i (gedieh, gediehen, sn) thrive, prosper, develop well, fig. a. progress: **so weit gediehen sein, daß** have reached a point where.
Ge'deihen n (-s) thriving, prosperity.
ge'denken v/i (gedachte, gedacht, h) **I** v/i (gen) a) think of, remember, b) mention, c) commemorate. **II** v/t **zu tun ~** think of doing, intend to do.
Ge'denken n (-s) (**zum ~ an** acc in) memory (of); → **a. Andenken.**
Ge'denk|feier f commemoration (ceremony). **~gottesdienst** m memorial service. **~mi,nute** f a minute's silence (**für** in memory of). **~münze** f commemorative coin. **~rede** f commemorative address. **~stätte** f memorial (place). **~stein** m memorial (stone). **~stunde** f hour of remembrance. **~tafel** f commemorative plaque. **~tag** m day of remembrance.
Gedicht [gə'dɪçt] n (-[e]s; -e) poem: **das Kleid ist ein ~** the dress is a (perfect) dream. **Ge'dichtsammlung** f a) collection of poems, b) anthology.
|ediegen [gə'di:gən] adj **1.** metall. solid (a. fig. character etc), pure. **2.** ♣ a) good-quality, b) tasteful.
:e'diegenheit f (-; no pl) solidity.
|edieh [gə'di:] pret of **gedeihen.**
|e'diehen pp of **gedeihen.**
|edränge [gə'drɛŋə] n (-s; no pl) **1.** crowd, F crush: F fig. **damit wir nicht ins ~ kommen** so that we don't get

pushed for time. **2.** rush (**nach, um** for). **3.** rugby: scrummage.
Ge'drängel n (-s; no pl) F pushing.
ge'drängt adj **1.** (a. **~voll**) crowded, F (jam-)packed. **2.** concise (style etc).
gedrechselt [gə'drɛksəlt] adj fig. stilted.
gedroschen [gə'drɔʃən] pp of **dreschen.**
gedruckt [gə'drʊkt] adj printed: F **lügen wie ~** lie through one's teeth.
gedrückt [gə'drʏkt] adj a. ♣ depressed: **~er Stimmung sein** a. be in low spirits; **die Stimmung war ~** spirits were low.
gedrungen [gə'drʊŋən] **I** pp of **dringen. II** adj stocky.
Geduld [gə'dʊlt] f (-; no pl) patience: **~ haben mit** be patient with; **jetzt reißt mir aber die ~!** that's done it!; **sich in ~ fassen** have patience.
gedulden [gə'dʊldən] **sich ~** (h) have patience, be patient; **~ Sie sich bitte e-n Augenblick!** wait a minute, please!
geduldig [gə'dʊldɪç] adj patient.
Ge'dulds|probe f **e-e ~ für j-n sein** be a test of s.o.'s patience. **~spiel** n puzzle.
gedungen [gə'dʊŋən] adj hired (killer).
gedunsen [gə'dʊnzən] adj bloated.
gedurft [gə'dʊrft] pp of **dürfen.**
geehrt [gə'e:rt] adj hono(u)red: in letter: **Sehr ~er Herr X!** Dear Mr X; **Sehr ~e Herren!** Dear Sirs, Gentlemen.
geeignet [gə'aɪgnət] adj (**für**) suited, suitable, right, qualified: **er ist nicht dafür ~** he's not the right man for it; **im ~en Augenblick** at the right moment; **~e Maßnahmen** appropriate measures.
Gefahr [gə'fa:r] f (-; -en) danger, threat (both: **für**, to, for), risk: **auf eigene ~** at one's own risk; **außer ~** out of danger; **auf die ~ hin zu** inf at the risk of ger; **sich e-r ~ aussetzen, sich in ~ begeben** expose o.s. to danger, take risks; **laufen zu** inf run the risk of ger; **in ~ bringen** → **gefährden; es besteht k-e ~** it's perfectly safe; → **schweben** 1.
gefährden [gə'fɛ:rdən] v/t (h) endanger, threaten, (put at) risk, jeopardize.
ge'fährdet adj endangered: **~ sein** a. be in danger, be at risk. **Ge'fährdung** f (-; -en) **1.** endangering (etc, → **gefährden**). **2.** (gen to) danger, threat.
ge'fahren pp of **fahren.**
Ge'fahren|herd m (constant) source of danger, pol. trouble spot. **~stelle** f

danger spot. **~zone** f danger zone. **~zu-
lage** f danger money.

gefährlich [gə'fɛːrlıç] *adj* dangerous
(*dat*, **für** to), risky, grave, critical: **~e
Krankheit** serious illness.

Ge'fährlichkeit f (-; *no pl*) danger(ous-
ness), risk, gravity, seriousness.

ge'fahrlos *adj* not dangerous, safe.

Gefährte [gə'fɛːrtə] *m* (-n; -n), **Ge'fähr-
tin** f (-; -nen) companion.

ge'fahrvoll *adj* dangerous, risky.

Gefälle [gə'fɛlə] *n* (-s; -) **1.** fall, slope,
incline, gradient, *esp. Am.* grade. **2.** ⚡,
🔊, *phys.* gradient. **3.** a) difference(s), b)
(*wage etc*) differential.

ge'fallen¹ *v/i* (gefiel, gefallen, h) **1.**
please: *es gefällt mir (nicht)* I (don't)
like it; F *er gefällt mir nicht* he doesn't
look too well; *solche Filme ~ der Masse* films like that appeal to the masses;
hat dir das Konzert ~? did you enjoy
the concert? *wie gefällt es Ihnen in
Berlin?* how do you like Berlin? **2.** *sich
et. ~ lassen* put up with s.th.; *das lasse ich mir nicht ~!* I'm not going to put
up with it!; *sie läßt sich von ihm nichts
~* she won't stand any nonsense from
him; *das lasse ich mir ~!* now you're
talking! **3.** *sich ~ in* (*dat*) indulge in;
sich in der Rolle des Fachmanns ~
fancy o.s. as an expert.

ge'fallen² I *pp of fallen and gefallen*¹. II
adj fallen, ✗ *a.* killed in action: *die
Gefallenen* the dead.

Ge'fallen¹ *m* (-s; -) (*j-m e-n ~ tun* do s.o.
a) favo(u)r: *j-n um e-n ~ bitten* ask a
favo(u)r of s.o.

Ge'fallen² *n* (-s; *no pl*) pleasure: *~ finden
an* a) enjoy, take pleasure in (*s.th.*), b)
like, take a (fancy) to (*s.o.*).

Ge'fallenendenkmal *n* war memorial.

ge'fällig *adj* **1.** agreeable, pleasant. **2.**
obliging, kind: *j-m ~ sein* oblige s.o.,
help s.o.; F *et. zu trinken ~?* would you
like s.th. to drink?; → *gefälligst*.

Ge'fälligkeit f (-; -en) **1.** *no pl* obligingness: *et. aus ~ tun* do s.th. out of sheer
kindness. **2.** → *Gefallen*¹.

ge'fälligst *adv iro.* if you don't mind: *sei
~ still!* be quiet, will you!

ge'fangen I *pp of fangen.* II *adj* a)
caught, ✗ captive, b) imprisoned, in
prison, c) *fig.* captivated. **Ge'fangene**
m, f (-n; -n) prisoner, convict.

Ge'fangenenlager *n* prison camp, ✗
prisoner-of-war camp.

ge'fangenhalten *v/t* (*irr, sep,* -ge-, h, →
halten) *j-n ~* keep (*or* hold) s.o. prisoner, *fig.* have s.o. spellbound.

Ge'fangennahme f (-; *no pl*) arrest, ✗
capture. **ge'fangennehmen** *v/t* (*irr,
sep,* -ge-, h, → *nehmen*) arrest, ✗ capture, take *s.o.* prisoner, *fig.* captivate.

Ge'fangenschaft f (-; *no pl*) (*in ~* in)
captivity (*a. zo.*), imprisonment: *in ~
geraten* be taken prisoner.

Gefängnis [gə'fɛŋnıs] *n* (-ses; -se) prison, jail, *Br. a.* gaol: *ins ~* be
sent (*or* go) to prison. **~di,rektor** *m*
governor, *Am.* warden. **~strafe** f →
Freiheitsstrafe. **~zelle** f prison cell.

Gefasel [gə'faːzəl] *n* (-s; *no pl*) F drivel.

Gefäß [gə'fɛːs] *n* (-es; -e) a) vessel (*a.
anat., biol.*), receptacle, b) bowl, c) jar.

ge'fäßerweiternd *adj* 🦠 vasodilating.

Ge'fäßkrankheit f vascular disease.

gefaßt [gə'fast] *adj* **1.** calm, composed.
2. *~ sein auf* (*acc*) be prepared for; *sich
~ machen auf* (*acc*) prepare for; F *er
kann sich auf et. ~ machen* he's in for
it now. **Ge'faßtheit** f (-; *no pl*) calmness, composure.

Gefecht *n* (-[e]s; -e) **1.** fight, battle: *außer ~ setzen* a. *fig.* put *s.o., s.th.* out of
action; → *Eifer, Hitze.* **2.** fencing bout.
Ge'fechtskopf *m* ✗ warhead.

ge'feit [gə'faıt] *adj* immune (*gegen* to).

Gefieder [gə'fiːdər] *n* (-s; -) plumage,
feathers. **ge'fiedert** *adj* feathered.

gefiel [gə'fiːl] *pret of gefallen.*

Geflecht [gə'flɛçt] *n* (-[e]s; -e) **1.** *a. fig.*
network, mesh. **2.** *anat.* plexus.

gefleckt [gə'flɛkt] *adj* spotted.

geflochten [gə'flɔxtən] *pp of flechten.*

geflogen [gə'floːgən] *pp of fliegen*

geflohen [gə'floːən] *pp of fliehen.*

geflossen [gə'flɔsən] *pp of fließen.*

Ge'flügel *n* (-s; *no pl*) poultry (*a. in cpds
disease, farm, farming, etc*).

Ge'flügelhändler(in f) *m* poulterer.

Ge'flügelsa,lat *m gastr.* chicken salad.

Ge'flügelschere f poultry shears.

ge'flügelt *adj* winged: **~es Wort** saying.

Geflunker [gə'flʊŋkər] *n* (-s; *no pl*) fib-
bing, fibs.

Geflüster [gə'flʏstər] *n* (-s; *no pl*) whispering, whispers.

gefochten [gə'fɔxtən] *pp of fechten.*

Gefolge [gə'fɔlgə] n (-s; -) **1.** entourage, attendants. **2.** cortège, mourners. **3.** fig. **im ~ von** (or gen) in the wake of.

Ge'folgschaft f (-; -en) followers, adherents. **Ge'folgsmann** m **1.** hist. vassal. **2.** esp. pol. follower, supporter.

gefräßig [gə'frɛːsɪç] adj greedy, zo. voracious. **Ge'fräßigkeit** f (-; no pl) greediness, zo. voracity.

Gefreite [gə'fraɪtə] m (-n; -n) ✕ lance corporal, Am. private first class, ✈ aircraftman first class, Am. airman third class.

ge'fressen pp of **fressen**.

Ge'frieranlage f refrigeration plant.

Ge'frierbeutel m freezer bag.

ge'frieren v/i (gefror, gefroren, sn) freeze.

Ge'frier|fach n freezer, freezing compartment. **~punkt** m (**auf dem ~** at) freezing point. **~schrank** m freezer. **~schutzmittel** n ⊛ antifreeze.

Ge'friertrocknen v/t (h) freeze-dry.

Ge'friertruhe f deep freeze, freezer.

gefror [gə'froːr] pret of **gefrieren**.

ge'froren pp of **frieren** and **gefrieren**.

Gefüge [gə'fyːgə] n (-s; -) structure.

gefügig [gə'fyːgɪç] adj docile, compliant: **j-n ~ machen** bring s.o. to heel.

Gefühl [gə'fyːl] n (-[e]s; -e) **1.** feeling, sentiment: **für mein ~, m-m ~ nach** my feeling is that, I think that; **ich habe das ~, daß ...** I have a feeling that ...; **mit ~ → gefühlvoll** II. **2.** no pl sensation, touch, feel: **ein ~ der Kälte** a cold sensation. **3.** no pl (**für**) a) sense (of), b) flair (for languages etc): **sich auf sein ~ verlassen** rely on one's instinct. **4.** usu. pl feeling, emotion: **j-s ~e verletzen** hurt s.o.'s feelings.

ge'fühllos adj **1.** numb. **2.** fig. insensitive (**gegen** to), unfeeling, heartless. **Ge'fühllosigkeit** f (-; no pl) **1.** numbness. **2.** fig. heartlessness, cruelty.

ge'fühlsarm adj (emotionally) cold.

Ge'fühlsausbruch m outburst.

ge'fühlsbetont adj emotional.

Ge'fühlsduse'lei f (-; -en) F sentimentality.

Ge'fühlsleben n emotional life.

ge'fühlsmäßig adj emotional, w.s. intuitive, instinctive.

ge'fühlvoll I adj full of feeling, emotion-

al, a. contp. sentimental. II adv feelingly (etc), **sing** etc with feeling.

ge'füllt adj filled, gastr. a. stuffed.

gefunden [gə'fʊndən] pp of **finden**.

gegangen [gə'gaŋən] pp of **gehen**.

ge'geben I pp of **geben**. II adj given: **als ~ voraussetzen** take s.th. for granted; **unter den ~en Umständen** under the circumstances; **zu ~er Zeit** a) when the occasion arises, b) at some future time.

ge'gebenenfalls adv **1.** should the occasion arise. **2.** if necessary.

Ge'gebenheit f (-; -en) given fact: **~en** a) circumstances, b) reality.

gegen [geːgən] I prep **1.** toward(s), time: a. at about: **~ Osten** toward(s) the east, eastward(s); **~ zehn (Uhr)** (at) about ten o'clock. **2.** against (a. fig.): **die Wand lehnen** lean against the wall; **ein Mittel ~ a** remedy for; **~ die Vernunft** contrary to reason. **3.** toward(s), to: **freundlich ~** kind to. **4.** compared with. **5.** in return for: **✝ ~ Bezahlung** against payment; **~ bar** for cash. **6.** ⚖ sports: versus. II adv **7.** about, around.

'Gegen|angebot n counteroffer. **~angriff** m a. fig. counterattack. **~argument** n counterargument. **~beispiel** n counterexample. **~besuch** m return visit: **j-m e-n ~ machen** return s.o.'s visit. **~bewegung** f esp. fig. countermovement. **~beweis** m (**den ~ antreten** furnish) proof to the contrary.

Gegend ['geːgənt] f (-; -en) a) region (a. anat.), area, b) countryside, c) neighbo(u)rhood: **in der ~ von** (or gen) near, around, in the Munich etc area; **in unserer ~** where we live.

'Gegendarstellung f correction, reply.

'Gegendemonstrati,on f counterdemonstration.

gegenein'ander adv **1.** against (or toward[s]) each other (or one another). **2.** mutually.

'Gegen|einladung f return invitation. **~erklärung** f counterstatement. **~fahrbahn** f opposite lane. **~frage** f counterquestion. **~gerade** f sports: back straight, Am. backstretch. **~gewicht** n counterweight: fig. **das ~ bilden zu** counterbalance. **~gift** n antidote. **~kandi,dat(in** f) m rival (candidate). **~klage** f ⚖ cross action. **~leistung** f return (service): **als ~** in return (**für** for).

'**Gegenlicht** n back light(ing): *bei ~* against the light. **~aufnahme** f contre-jour shot. **~blende** f lens hood.

'**Gegen|liebe** f *er stieß mit s-m Vorschlag auf wenig ~* his suggestion didn't go down particularly well. **~maßnahme** f countermeasure: *~n ergreifen* take steps (*gegen* against). **~mittel** n a. fig. antidote. **~offen,sive** f counteroffensive. **~par,tei** f opposite (*or* other) side, pol. opposition, sports: opponents. **~pol** m fig. counterpart. **~probe** f (*a. die ~ machen*) crosscheck. **~revoluti,on** f counterrevolution. **~richtung** f the opposite direction: *aus der ~* oncoming (traffic etc).

'**Gegensatz** m (-es; ⁀e) **1.** contrast: *im ~ zu* in contrast to (*or* with), as opposed to, unlike the British etc; *im ~ dazu* by way of contrast. **2.** the opposite. **3.** pl differences. '**gegensätzlich** [-zɛtslɪç] adj contrary, opposite, different.

'**Gegenschlag** m a. fig. counterblow: *zum ~ ausholen* get ready to hit back.

'**Gegenseite** f opposite (*or* other) side. '**gegenseitig** [-zaɪtɪç] adj mutual, reciprocal: *~e Abhängigkeit* interdependence; *~es Interesse* mutual interest; *sich ~ helfen* help one another (*or* each other). '**Gegenseitigkeit** f (-; *no pl*) reciprocity, mutuality: *auf ~ beruhen* be mutual; iro. *das beruht auf ~!* the feeling is mutual!

'**Gegen|sinn** m *im ~* in the opposite direction. **~spieler** m antagonist, a. sports: opponent, a. pol. opposite number. **~spio,nage** f counterespionage. **~sprechanlage** f intercom (system). '**Gegenstand** m (-[e]s; ⁀e) **1.** object (*a.* fig.), thing, esp. ✝ item, article: *~ des Mitleids* object of pity; *~ des Spottes* figure of fun. **2.** a) subject, b) subject-matter, c) matter, affair, d) issue: *zum ~ haben* deal with. '**gegenständlich** [-ʃtɛntlɪç] adj **1.** a. ling. concrete. **2.** graphic. **3.** paint. etc: representational. '**gegenstandslos** adj **1.** abstract, paint. etc: a. nonrepresentational. **2.** fig. a) invalid, b) unfounded.

'**Gegen|stimme** f **1.** parl. vote against. **2.** fig. objection. **~strömung** f **1.** countercurrent. **2.** fig. countermovement. **~stück** n (*zu*) counterpart (of), paint. etc pendant (to). **~teil** n opposite (*von*

of): (*ganz*) *im ~* on the contrary.

'**gegenteilig** adj contrary, opposite: *~er Meinung sein* disagree; ⚖ *~ entscheiden* come to a different decision.

Gegen|tor n, **~treffer** m goal against.

gegen|über I adv **1.** opposite, across the way (*or* street), person: a. face to face: *sie saßen einander ~* they sat facing one another. II prep (*dat*) **2.** opposite, facing. **3.** fig. to, toward(s): *er war mir ~ sehr höflich* he was very polite to me. **4.** compared with, as against. **5.** in contrast to. **6.** in view of, in the face of.

Gegen|über n (-s; -) **1.** person opposite, vis-à-vis, sports: opponent, pol. etc opposite number. **2.** house opposite.

gegen|überliegen v/i (irr, sep, -ge-, h, → liegen) (*dat*) be opposite, face.

gegen|übersehen: sich ~ (irr, sep, -ge-, h, → sehen) (*dat*) be confronted with.

gegen|überstehen v/i (irr, sep, -ge-, h, → stehen) **1.** *j-m ~* face s.o.; *sich* (*or einander*) *~* be facing each other, feindlich be enemies. **2.** (*dat*) be faced (*or* confronted) with, F be up against.

gegen|überstellen v/t (sep, -ge-, h) fig. (*dat* with) confront (s.o.), compare (s.th.). **Gegen|überstellung** f (-; -en) **1.** a. ⚖ confrontation. **2.** comparison.

gegen|übertreten v/i (irr, sep, -ge-, sn, → treten) *j-m ~* face s.o.

'**Gegenverkehr** m oncoming traffic.

'**Gegenvorschlag** m counterproposal.

Gegenwart ['geːɡənvart] f (-; *no pl*) **1.** the present (time): *... der ~* present-day, contemporary. **2.** (*in ihrer* etc *~ in her* etc) presence. **3.** ling. present (tense).

gegenwärtig ['geːɡənvɛrtɪç] I adj present, current, present-day, contemporary, today's. II adv a) at the moment, a) present, b) nowadays, these days.

'**Gegenwarts|litera,tur** f contemporary literature. **⚘nah(e)** adj topical. **~pro,bleme** pl present-day problems.

'**Gegenwehr** f (-; *no pl*) resistance.

'**Gegenwert** m equivalent (value).

'**Gegenwind** m headwind.

'**Gegenwirkung** f countereffect.

'**gegenzeichnen** v/i, v/t (sep, -ge-, h) countersign.

'**Gegenzug** m **1.** chess: countermove, fig. *im ~ zu* as a countermove. **2.** train coming from the other direction.

gegessen [ɡəˈɡɛsən] pp of **essen**.

geglichen [gə'glɪçən] *pp of* **gleichen**.
ge'gliedert *adj* **1.** jointed. **2.** *fig.* a) organized, structured, b) subdivided.
geglitten [gə'glɪtən] *pp of* **gleiten**.
Gegner ['ge:gnər] *m* (-s; -) **1.** opponent (*a. sports*), adversary, enemy, rival: **ein ~ sein von** be against. **2.** ⚖ opposing party. '**Gegnerin** *f* (-; -nen) → **Gegner**. '**gegnerisch** *adj* opposing (*a.* ⚖ *or sports*), antagonistic, *a.* ✕ enemy, hostile: **die ~e Partei** *a.* the other side.
Gegnerschaft *f* (-; -en) **1.** opposition, opponents. **2.** *no pl* opposition (**gegen** to).
gegolten [gə'gɔltən] *pp of* **gelten**.
gegoren [gə'go:rən] *pp of* **gären**.
gegossen [gə'gɔsən] *pp of* **gießen**.
ge'graben *pp of* **graben**.
gegriffen [gə'grɪfən] *pp of* **greifen**.
Ge'habe *n* (-s; *no pl*) affectation, airs.
gehabt [gə'ha:pt] *pp of* **haben**.
Ge'hackte *n* (-n; *no pl*) → **Hackfleisch**.
Ge'halt¹ *m* (-[e]s; -e) **1.** *fig.* a) content, b) substance. **2.** (**an** *dat* of) content, 🜛 *a.* concentration: **~ an Öl** oil content.
Gehalt² *n* (-[e]s; ⁻er) salary, pay: **mit vollem ~** on full pay.
ge'halten *pp of* **halten**.
ge'haltlos *adj* **1.** unsubstantial (*food*). **2.** *fig.* empty, lacking substance.
Ge'halts|abzug *m* deduction from salary. **~ansprüche** *pl* salary expectations. **~empfänger** *m* salaried employee. **~erhöhung** *f* salary increase, (pay) rise, *esp. Am.* raise. **~forderung** *f* salary claim. **~gruppe** *f*, **~klasse** *f* salary bracket. **~kürzung** *f* salary cut. **~liste** *f* payroll. **~streifen** *m* pay slip. **~stufe** *f* salary bracket. **~zahlung** *f* payment of salary. **~zulage** *f* **1.** bonus. **2.** → **Gehaltserhöhung**.
ge'haltvoll *adj* **1.** substantial (*food*). **2.** *fig.* rich in content, profound.
gehangen [gə'haŋən] *pp of* **hängen¹**.
ge'harnischt *adj fig.* sharp, withering.
gehässig [gə'hɛsɪç] *adj* spiteful, venomous. **Ge'hässigkeit** *f* (-; -en) **1.** *no pl* spite(fulness), venom, venomousness. **2.** spiteful words (*or* act).
ge'hauen *pp of* **hauen**.
Gehäuse [gə'hɔyzə] *n* (-s; -) **1.** ⚙ case, casing, cabinet, *phot.* body. **2.** *zo.* shell.
gehbehindert *adj* **sie ist ~** she can't walk properly.

Gehege [gə'he:gə] *n* (-s; -) enclosure, pen, *hunt.* preserve: *fig.* **j-m ins ~ kommen** get in s.o.'s way, cross s.o.
geheim [gə'haɪm] *adj* **1.** secret, *a.* a) confidential, b) hidden: **im ~en** secretly; **in ~er Wahl** by closed ballot; **streng ~!** top-secret! **2.** occult.
Ge'heim... a) secret (*agent, agreement, order, etc*), b) occult. **~akte** *f* classified document, *pl* secret files. **~dienst** *m* secret service. **~fach** *n* secret drawer.
ge'heimhalten *v/t* (*irr, sep, -ge-, h,* → **halten**) keep *s.th.* secret (**vor** *dat* from).
Ge'heimhaltung *f* (-; *no pl*) secrecy.
Ge'heimkonto *n* secret account.
Ge'heimnis *n* (-ses; -se) secret (**vor** *dat* from), *a.* mystery: **kein ~ machen aus** make no secret out of. **Ge'heimniskrämer** [-krɛ:mər] *m* (-s; -) mystery-monger. **Ge'heimnisträger** *m* bearer of official secrets. **ge'heimnisumwittert** *adj* shrouded in mystery, mysterious. **Ge'heimnisverrat** *m* betrayal of a state (*or* trade) secret. **ge'heimnisvoll** *adj* mysterious.
Ge'heim|nummer *f* secret (*teleph.* ex-directory) number. **~poli,zei** *f* secret police. **~poli,zist** *m* member of the secret police. **~sache** *f* secret (✕, *pol.* security) matter. **~tip** *m* F hot tip.
ge'heißen *pp of* **heißen**.
ge'hemmt *adj* inhibited.
gehen ['ge:ən] (ging, gegangen, sn) **I** *v/i* **1.** (*zu Fuß ~*) walk, go (on foot): **schwimmen ~** go swimming; **auf die** (*or zur*) **Bank** (**Post**) ~ go to the bank (post office); **auf die Straße ~** a) go out into the street, b) *fig.* take to the streets; **über die Brücke ~** cross the bridge; *fig.* **an die Arbeit ~** get down to work; **das geht zu weit** that is going too far; **wie ich ging und stand** a) as I was, b) at once. **2.** go, leave, *adm. a.* resign: **er ist gegangen** he's gone, he has left; **j-n ~ lassen** let s.o. go. **3.** 🚂 *etc* (*nach, bis* to, *as far as*) go, run: **über München ~** go via Munich. **4.** (*nach* to) go, lead: **~ um** go round. **5.** ⚙ go, work, *machine: a.* run, *bell:* go, ring, *radio etc:* be on: *fig.* **das Gedicht geht so ...** the poem goes like this ... **6.** 🜛 (*gut*) ~ sell (well); **wie ~ die Geschäfte?** how's business? **7.** *dough:* rise. **8.** *wind:* blow. **9.** ~ **an** (*acc*) *fig.* a) go as far as, reach to, b)

inheritance etc: fall to, go to. **10. das Fenster geht auf die Straße** the window looks out on(to) the street. **11. das geht gegen dich** this is meant for you. **12. in die Industrie (Politik** etc) **~** go into industry (politics etc); **in den Saal ~ 100 Personen** the hall holds (or seats) 100 persons; **der Schaden geht in die Millionen** the damage runs into millions; **wie oft geht 2 in 10?** how many times goes 2 into 10?; **in sich ~** do a bit of soul-searching. **13.** F **~ mit** go out with (a boy or girl); **fest ~** go steady. **14. die Fenster ~ nach Westen** the windows face (or look) west; **nach s-n Worten zu ~** to go by his words; **wenn es nach ihr ginge** if she had her way. **15. ~ über** (acc) go beyond; **es geht nichts über ...** there's nothing like ...; **ihre Familie geht ihr über alles** her family means everything to her. **16. vor sich ~** happen; **wie geht das vor sich?** how does it go (or work)? **II** v/impers **17.** fig. **es geht** a) it works, b) I can manage; **es geht nicht** a) it doesn't work, b) it can't be done, it's impossible; **es wird schon ~** it'll be all right; **es geht (eben) nicht anders** it can't be helped. **18.** be, feel: **wie geht es Ihnen?,** F **wie geht's?** a) how are you?, b) how are you feeling?; **es geht mir gut** a) I'm fine, b) ✝ I'm doing fine; **es geht mir schlecht** a) I'm not feeling too good, b) ✝ things aren't going too well; **mir geht es genauso** F same here; **ihm ist es genauso gegangen** it was the same with him; **so geht es, wenn man lügt** that's what comes of lying; **es sich gut ~ lassen** have a good time, enjoy o.s. **19. es geht auf 10 (Uhr)** it is getting on for ten. **20. es geht über m-e Kraft** it's too much for me. **21. es geht um den Frieden (sein Leben)** peace (his life) is at stake; **ihr geht es nur ums Geld** she's just interested in the money; **worum geht es?** what's it all about?, what's the problem?; **es geht darum zu** inf it's a question of ger; **darum geht es (ja)!** that's the (whole) point!; **darum geht es hier gar nicht** that's not the point. **III** v/t **22.** walk (distance etc), go (on foot): humor. **er ist gegangen worden** he was sacked.

'Gehen n (-s) walking: **50 km ~** sports: 5ʔ kilomet/res (Am. -ers) walk.

'gehenlassen: sich ~ (irr, sep, no -ge-, h → **lassen) 1.** let o.s. go, lose one' temper. **2.** relax.

Geher ['geːɐr] m (-s; -) sports: walker

geheuer [gəˈhɔʏər] adj nicht (ganz) **~** a creepy, b) fishy, c) a bit risky; **er (di~ Sache) ist mir nicht ~** I've got a funn feeling about him (it).

Geheul [gəˈhɔʏl] n (-[e]s; no pl) F howl ing, howls.

Gehilfe [gəˈhɪlfə] m (-n; -n), **Ge'hilfin** (-; -nen) **1.** helper, assistant. **2.** clerk. 3 🕱 accessory before the fact.

Gehirn [gəˈhɪrn] n (-[e]s; -e) **1.** a. fig brain. **2.** F brain(s), mind. **~ab**cerebral; **~blutung** f cerebra h(a)emorrhage. **~chirur,gie** f brai surgery. **~erschütterung** f concussior **~hautentzündung** f meningitis. **~tu mor** m cerebral tumo(u)r. **~wäsche** pol. brainwashing; **j-n e-r ~ unterzie hen** brainwash s.o.

gehoben [gəˈhoːbən] **I** pp of heben. **I** adj high, senior, elevated, ✝ up-marke (article, shop, etc): **~ Ansprüche** ex pensive tastes; **in ~er Stimmung** in hig spirits.

Gehöft [gəˈhœft] n (-[e]s; -e) farm(stead

geholfen [gəˈhɔlfən] pp of **helfen.**

Gehölz [gəˈhœlts] n (-es; -e) copse, cop pice, small wood.

Gehör [gəˈhøːr] n (-[e]s; no pl) **1.** (sens of) hearing, ear(s): **feines ~** sensitiv ear; ♪ **absolutes ~** perfect pitch; nac **dem ~ by** ear. **2.** (**~ finden** get a) hea ing: **e-r Bitte kein ~ schenken** turn deaf ear to a request; **sich ~ verscha fen** make o.s. heard.

ge'horchen v/i (h) j-m (m-em Befehl etc **(nicht) ~** (dis)obey s.o. (an order etc

gehören [gəˈhøːrən] (h) **I** v/i **1.** belon (dat to): **wem gehört das Buch?** whos book is this?; **gehört es dir?** is it yours?; **es gehört mir** it belongs to m it is mine; fig. **das gehört nicht hierhe** that's beside the point; **der Raumfah gehört die Zukunft** the future belong to space travel. **2. ~ zu** a) belong to, k part of, b) rank (or be) among; **er ge hört zu den besten Spielern** he is on of the best players; **es gehört zu s Arbeit** it is part of his job; **dazu gehör**

a) **Geld** you need money for that, b) **Zeit** that kind of thing takes time, c) (**viel**) **Mut** it takes (a lot of) courage; **dazu gehört schon einiges!** that takes a lot of doing!; **es gehört nicht viel dazu!** there's nothing to it! **3.** ~ **unter** (acc) come under. **4.** ~ **in** (acc) be in; **du gehörst ins Bett!** you should be in bed! **II sich** ~ be proper; **wie es sich gehört** properly; **er weiß, was sich gehört** he knows how to behave; **das gehört sich nicht!** it's not done!

Ge'hörfehler m hearing defect.

Ge'hörgang m auditory canal.

gehörig [gə'hø:rɪç] **I** adj **1.** ~ **in** belonging to; (**nicht**) **zur Sache** ~ (ir)relevant. **2.** right, due, proper. **3.** F good, sound: **j-m e-n** ~**en Schrecken einjagen** put the fear of God into s.o. **II** adv **4.** duly, properly: → **Meinung.**

ge'hörlos adj deaf. **Ge'hörlosenschule** f school for the deaf.

Ge'hörnerv m auditory nerve.

gehörnt [gə'hœrnt] adj horned: ~**er Ehemann** cuckolded husband.

gehorsam [gə'ho:rza:m] adj obedient (**gegen** to). **Gehorsam** m (-s; no pl) obedience (**gegen**[**über**] to): **j-m den** ~ **verweigern** disobey s.o.

Ge'hörsinn m (-[e]s; no pl) → **Gehör.**

Gehsteig m pavement, Am. sidewalk.

Ge'hupe n (-s; no pl) F blaring horns.

Gehversuch m attempt to walk.

Geier ['gaiɐr] m (-s; -) a. fig. vulture.

Geifer ['gaifɐr] m (-s; no pl) **1.** slaver, foam. **2.** fig. venom. **'geifern** v/i (h) **1.** dribble, slaver. **2.** fig. ~ **gegen** rail at.

Geige ['gaigə] f (-; -n) violin: (**auf der**) ~ **spielen** play (on) the violin; (**die**) **erste** (**zweite**) ~ **spielen** play first (second) violin (fig. fiddle).

geigen ['gaigən] v/i (h) play the violin. **'Geigen|bauer** m (-s; -) violin-maker. ~**harz** n resin. ~**kasten** m violin case. ~**strich** m stroke of the bow.

Geiger ['gaigɐr] m (-s; -), **'Geigerin** f (-; -nen) violinist.

Geigerzähler m Geiger counter.

geil [gail] adj **1.** F contp. a) randy, V horny, b) lecherous: fig. ~ **sein auf** (acc) be hot for, be dead keen on. **2.** rank (plant). **3.** F (**echt**) ~ hot, terrific.

Geisel ['gaizəl] f (-; -n) (**j-n als** ~ **nehmen** take s.o.) hostage. **'Geiseldrama**

n hostage drama. **'Geiselnahme** f (-; -n) taking of hostages. **'Geiselnehmer** m (-s; -) hostage-taker.

Geiß [gais] f (-; -en) zo. **1.** (nanny) goat. **2.** doe.

Geißel ['gaisəl] f (-; -n) **1.** whip. **2.** biol. flagellum. **3.** fig. scourge. **'geißeln** v/t (h) whip, eccl. flagellate, fig. castigate. **'Geißeltierchen** n flagellate.

'Geißelung f (-; -en) **1.** flagellation. **2.** fig. castigation.

Geist [gaist] m (-[e]s; -er) **1.** no pl a) mind, intellect, b) spirit, c) wit: ~ **und Körper** mind and body; **ein Mann von** ~ a (man of) wit; **im** ~**e** a) see s.th. in one's mind's eye, b) be with s.o. in one's thoughts; humor. **den** ~ **aufgeben** give up the ghost, engine etc: a. conk out; F **j-m auf den** ~ **gehen** get on s.o.'s nerves; → **scheiden** III. **2.** no pl spirit, morale: **der** ~ **der Zeit** the spirit of the times; **wes** ~**es Kind er ist** what sort of person he is. **3.** spirit, ghost: **böser** ~ evil spirit, demon; **der Heilige** ~ the Holy Ghost. **4.** mind: **ein großer** ~ a great mind (or thinker).

'Geister|bahn f ghost train. ~**beschwörung** f exorcism. ~**bild** n TV double image. ~**erscheinung** f apparition. ~**fahrer** m wrong-way driver, Am. ghost driver.

'geisterhaft adj ghostly.

'Geisterhand f **wie von** ~ as if by magic.

'Geisterstadt f ghost town.

'Geisterstunde f witching hour.

'geistesabwesend adj absent-minded.

'Geistesabwesenheit f (-; no pl) absent-mindedness.

'Geistes|arbeit f brainwork. ~**blitz** m (flash of) inspiration, brainwave.

'Geistesgegenwart f presence of mind.

'geistesgegenwärtig adv ~ **sprang er zur Seite** he had the presence of mind to jump aside.

'Geistesgeschichte f (-; no pl) history of thought (or ideas): **die deutsche** ~ the history of German thought.

'geistesgestört adj mentally disturbed.

'geisteskrank adj mentally ill, a. contp. insane. **'Geisteskranke** m, f (-n; -n) insane person, mental case (or patient), pl the mentally ill. **'Geisteskrankheit** f insanity, mental disease (or illness).

'Geistes|leben n (-s; no pl) intellectual

life. **2schwach** adj feeble-minded.
~schwäche f (-; no pl) feeble-minded-
ness. **~störung** f mental disorder.
~verfassung f frame of mind. **2ver-
wandt** adj congenial. **~verwirrung** f
confused state of mind. **2wissenschaft**
f arts subject, pl the arts, the humani-
ties. **~wissenschaftler** m 1. scholar. 2.
arts student. **2wissenschaftlich** adj
arts ... **~zerrüttung** f mental derangement, dementia. **~zustand** m (-[e]s; no
pl) mental state.

'**geistig**¹ adj a) mental (a. psych.), b)
intellectual, c) spiritual: **~es Eigentum**
intellectual property; **~ anspruchsvoll**
demanding, highbrow; **~ behindert**
mentally handicapped; → **Diebstahl.**

'**geistig**² adj **~e Getränke** spirits, alcoholic drinks.

'**geistlich** adj 1. religious, spiritual,
sacred (music etc): **~er Orden** religious
order. 2. clerical, ecclesiastical: **der ~e
Stand** the clergy; **~es Amt** ministry.

'**Geistliche** m (-n; -n) clergyman, (Protestant) minister, (Catholic) priest, ✕
chaplain, padre.

'**Geistlichkeit** f (-; no pl) the clergy.

'**geistlos** adj trivial, dull, insipid, stupid.

'**Geistlosigkeit** f (-; -en) 1. no pl lack of
wit, dullness, insipidity. 2. platitude.

'**geistreich** adj witty, clever, brilliant.

'**geisttötend** adj soul-destroying.

'**geistvoll** adj 1. witty. 2. profound.

Geiz [gaɪts] m (-es; no pl) stinginess,
meanness. '**geizen** v/i (h) be stingy (**mit**
with); **mit Lob ~** be sparing with one's
praise. '**Geizhals** m miser, F meanie.
'**geizig** adj miserly, stingy, mean.

Ge'jammer n (-s; no pl) F contp. moaning, (endless) lamentation.

Gejohle [gə'joːlə] n (-s; no pl) F howling.

gekannt [gə'kant] pp of **kennen.**

Gekicher [gə'kiçər] n (-s; no pl) F contp.
giggling, giggle, titter.

Gekläff [gə'klɛf] n (-[e]s; no pl) F contp.
yapping.

Ge'klapper n (-s; no pl) F rattling.

Geklimper [gə'klimpər] n (-s; no pl) F
contp. tinkling.

geklungen [gə'kluŋən] pp of **klingen.**

geknickt [gə'knikt] adj F fig. crestfallen.

gekniffen [gə'knifən] pp of **kneifen.**

Geknister [gə'knistər] n (-s; no pl) F
contp. rustling.

ge'kommen pp of **kommen.**

gekonnt [gə'kɔnt] **I** pp of **können. II** adj
competent, masterly.

gekränkt [gə'krɛŋkt] adj offended, hurt

Gekreisch [gə'kraɪʃ] n (-[e]s; no pl
screaming, shrieking.

Gekritzel [gə'kritsəl] n (-s; no pl) contp
scrawl(ing), scribbling, scribble.

gekrochen [gə'krɔxən] pp of **kriechen**

gekünstelt [gə'kynstəlt] adj affected.

gekürzt [gə'kyrtst] adj abridged.

Gel [ge:l] n (-s; -e) 🜨, cosmetics: gel.

Gelächter [gə'lɛçtər] n (-s; -) laughter

ge'laden I pp of **laden**¹ and **laden**². **II**
adj **1.** loaded, ✕ a. charged. **2.** F **auf j-**
~ sein be furious (or mad) at s.o.

Ge'lage n (-s; -) feast, banquet.

ge'lagert adj fig. **anders ~** different; **i**
besonders ~en Fällen in special cases

Gelände [gə'lɛndə] n (-s; -) country
ground, terrain, site. **Ge'lände.**
cross-country (car, race, etc).

ge'ländegängig adj mot. all-terrain.

Geländer [gə'lɛndər] n (-s; -) a) railing
b) banisters, c) balustrade.

gelang [gə'laŋ] pret of **gelingen.**

ge'langen v/i (sn) **1. ~ an** (acc) (or nach
zu, auf acc) reach, arrive at, get (c
come) to; **ans Ziel ~** a) reach one'
destination, b) fig. achieve one's end,
make it; **in den Besitz ~ von** (acc) get
hold of, acquire; **in j-s Hände ~** g
into (or reach) s.o.'s hands. **2. zu et.**
win (or gain, achieve) s.th.; **zu Reich**
tum ~ become rich; → **Ansicht** 1, **E**
kenntnis, Macht 1. **3.** zur **Aufführung**
be performed.

ge'langweilt adj and adv bored.

ge'lassen I pp of **lassen. II** adj calm
composed. **Ge'lassenheit** f (-; no p
calmness, composure: **mit ~** calmly.

Gelatine [ʒela'tiːnə] f (-; -n) gelatine.

ge'laufen pp of **laufen.**

ge'läufig adj **1.** a) common, current (e.
pression etc), b) familiar: **das ist mir**
I'm familiar with that. **2.** fluent.

Ge'läufigkeit f (-; no pl) **1.** familiarity.
fluency.

gelaunt [gə'laʊnt] adj **gut** (**schlecht**)
sein be in a good (bad) mood.

Geläut [gə'lɔyt] n (-[e]s; no pl) ringing

gelb [gɛlp] adj, **Gelb** n (-s; -, F -s) yellow
traffic lights: amber: **bei Gelb** at an
ber; **Gelbe Seiten** Yellow Pages.

Gelbe ['gɛlbə] *n* (-n; *no pl*) yolk: F **auch nicht das ~ vom Ei!** not all that good!

Gelbfilter *n, m phot.* yellow filter.

gelblich *adj* yellowish.

Gelbsucht *f* (-; *no pl*) *✵* jaundice.

Geld [gɛlt] *n* (-[e]s; -er) money: **~er** funds, money; **bares ~** cash; **großes ~** notes, *Am.* bills; **kleines ~** change; F **das große ~ machen** make big money, make a packet; **et. zu ~ machen** turn s.th. into cash, sell s.th. off; **um ~ spielen** play for money; F **im ~ schwimmen** be rolling in money; **das geht ins ~** that costs a packet; **~ spielt k-e Rolle** money is no object; → **Heu.**

Geld|**abwertung** *f* (currency) devaluation. **~angelegenheiten** *pl* money (*or* financial) matters. **~anlage** *f* investment. **~anweisung** *f* money order, remittance. **~aufwertung** *f* (currency) revaluation. **~ausgabe** *f* (financial) expenditure. **~auto,mat** *m* cash dispenser. **~betrag** *m* amount (*or* sum) of money. **~beutel** *m* purse. **~buße** *f* fine. **~einwurf** *m* **1.** insertion of coins. **2.** (coin) slot. **~entwertung** *f* currency depreciation, inflation. **~geber** *m* financial backer, investor. **~geschäfte** *pl* money transactions. **~geschenk** *n* gift of money. **~gier** *f* greed for money, avarice. **2gierig** *adj* greedy for money, avaricious. **~knappheit** *f* lack of money, (financial) stringency.

geldlich *adj* financial, pecuniary.

Geld|**mangel** *m* lack of money. **~mann** *m* (-[e]s; -leute) financier. **~markt** *m* money market. **~mittel** *pl* funds. **~prämie** *f* a) bonus, b) reward, c) award, (cash) prize. **~quelle** *f* source of money (*or* income). **~schein** *m* (bank)note, *Am.* bill. **~schrank** *m* safe. **~sendung** *f* (cash) remittance. **~sorgen** *f pl* financial worries. **~spende** *f* donation, contribution. **~strafe** *f* (*a. j-n mit e-r ~ belegen*) fine. **~stück** *n* coin. **~umtausch** *m* exchange of money, conversion. **~verdienen** *n* (-s) moneymaking. **~verdiener(in** *f*) *m* moneymaker, breadwinner. **~verlegenheit** *f* financial embarrassment: *in ~ sein* be short of money, F be hard up. **~verschwendung** *f* waste of money. **~wäsche** *f* money laundering. **~wechsel** *m* **1.** → **Geldumtausch. 2.** (*office*) Change. **~wechsler** *m* change machine. **~wert** *m* cash (*or* currency) value.

Gelee [ʒe'le:] *n* (-s; -s) jelly.

ge'legen I *pp of* **liegen. II** *adj* **1.** situated, located. **2.** convenient, suitable: **es kommt mir sehr ~** it suits me fine.

Ge'legenheit *f* (-; -en) **1.** opportunity, chance: **die ~ nutzen** (*or* **beim Schopf packen**) seize the opportunity; **die ~ verpassen** miss the chance; **bei der ersten besten ~** at the first opportunity; → **passend 2. 2.** occasion: **bei ~** sometime; **bei dieser ~** on this occasion. **3.** ✝ bargain.

Ge'legenheits|**arbeit** *f* casual work (*or* job). **~arbeiter** *m* casual labo(u)rer.

gelegentlich [gə'le:gəntlɪç] **I** *adj* occasional. **II** *adv* a) occasionally, *a.* sometimes, b) sometime.

gelehrig [gə'le:rɪç] *adj* clever, quick to learn. **gelehrt** [gə'le:rt] *adj* learned. **Ge'lehrte** *m, f* (-n; -n) learned man (woman), scholar, scientist.

Geleit [gə'laɪt] *n* (-[e]s; -e) *a.* ✕ escort, ⚓ *a.* convoy: **freies ~** 🚸 safe-conduct.

ge'leiten *v/t* (h) escort (*a.* ⚓, ✕).

Ge'leit|**schiff** *n* escort ship. **~schutz** *m* escort, ⚓ *a.* convoy. **~zug** *m* ⚓ convoy.

Gelenk [gə'lɛŋk] *n* (-[e]s; -e) joint, ❂ *a.* link. **Ge'lenk...** ❂ articulated.

Ge'lenkentzündung *f* *✵* arthritis.

ge'lenkig *adj* flexible (*a.* ❂), supple, lithe. **Ge'lenkigkeit** *f* (-; *no pl*) flexibility, suppleness, litheness.

Ge'lenkrheuma,tismus *m* *✵* articular rheumatism.

gelernt [gə'lɛrnt] *adj* trained.

ge'lesen *pp of* **lesen.**

geliebt [gə'li:pt] *adj* dear, beloved. **Ge'liebte[1]** *m* (-n; -n) lover. **Ge'liebte[2]** *f* (-n; -n) a) love(r), sweetheart, b) mistress.

geliehen [gə'li:ən] *pp of* **leihen.**

gelieren [ʒe'li:rən] *v/i* (h) jell.

gelinde [gə'lɪndə] *adv* **~ gesagt** to put it mildly.

gelingen [gə'lɪŋən] *v/i and v/impers* (gelang, gelungen, sn) succeed, be successful, be a success, turn out well: **nicht ~** not to succeed (*etc*), fail; **im gelang die Flucht, es gelang ihm zu fliehen** he succeeded in escaping, he managed to escape; **es gelang ihm nicht(, das zu tun)** he failed (to bring it off); *endlich ist es mir gelungen* at last I managed (*or* made) it.

Ge'lingen *n* (-s) success: *gutes ~!* good luck!; *auf gutes ~!* to success!

gelitten [gə'lɪtən] *pp of* **leiden**.

gellend ['gɛlənt] *adj* piercing, shrill: *~er Schrei* scream; *~ aufschreien* shriek (*vor dat* with).

ge'loben *v/t* (h) promise, vow, swear.

Ge'löbnis [gə'lø:pnɪs] *n* (-ses; -se) vow.

gelobt [gə'lo:pt] *adj das Gelobte Land Bibl.* the Land of Promise.

gelogen [gə'lo:gən] *pp of* **lügen**.

gelöst [gə'lø:st] *adj fig.* relaxed.

gelten ['gɛltən] (galt, gegolten, h) **I** *v/t* **1.** be worth (*10 dollars etc*): *fig. wenig ~* count for little (*bei* with); *was er sagt, gilt* what he says goes; *→ Wette.* **II** *v/i* **2.** be valid, be good, *contract etc:* be effective: (*weiterhin*) *~ hold* (good); *~ für* apply to; *das gilt für alle* that applies to (F goes for) all of you; *~ lassen* allow (*a. sports*), (*als*) accept (as), let *s.o., s.th.* pass (for); *das lasse ich ~!* I'll agree to that!; *es gilt!* done!, it's a deal!; *das gilt nicht!* a) that's not allowed (*or* fair), b) *sports etc:* that doesn't count!; *mein Angebot gilt noch!* my offer still stands! **3.** *~* als be regarded as, be considered to be. **4.** *j-m ~ remark etc:* be meant for (*or* aimed at) s.o. **III** *v/impers* **es gilt zu** *inf* it is necessary (for us *etc*) to *inf*; *es gilt als sicher, daß ...* it seems certain that ...

'**geltend** *adj* a) current(ly valid), *a.* effective (*law etc*), b) accepted, prevailing: *~ machen* assert, enforce (*claims, rights*), plead (*illness etc*); *~ machen, daß ...* maintain that ...; (*bei j-m*) *s-n Einfluß ~ machen* bring one's influence to bear (on s.o.).

'**Geltung** *f* (-; *no pl*) **1.** validity: *~ haben → gelten* 2. **2.** a) value, b) prestige: *an ~ verlieren* lose prestige. **3.** weight, influence (*of person*): *a.* authority; (*dat*) *~ verschaffen* enforce; *sich ~ verschaffen* make o.s. respected; *et. zur ~ brin-gen* show s.th. (off) to advantage; *zur ~ kommen* show to advantage.

'**Geltungsbedürfnis** *n,* '**geltungsbe-dürftig** *adj* craving for admiration.

Gelübde [gə'lʏpdə] *n* (-s; -) vow: *ein ~ ablegen* take (*or* make) a) vow.

gelungen [gə'lʊŋən] **I** *pp of* **gelingen**. **II**

adj successful: *die Party war ~* the party was a success.

Gelüst [gə'lʏst] *n* (-[e]s; -e) craving (*nach* for). **ge'lüsten** *v/impers* (h) *es gelüstet mich nach* I am craving for, I feel like.

gemächlich [gə'mɛːçlɪç] *adj* leisurely, unhurried.

gemacht [gə'maxt] *adj ein ~er Mann* a made man; *sie waren ~e Leute* they had got it made.

ge'mahlen *pp of* **mahlen**.

Gemälde [gə'mɛːldə] *n* (-s; -) painting, picture. *~ausstellung f* exhibition of paintings. *~gale,rie f* picture gallery.

gemäß [gə'mɛːs] **I** *adj* appropriate (to). **II** *prep* according to, in accordance with, pursuant to, under (*a law*).

gemäßigt [gə'mɛːsɪçt] *adj* **1.** moderate (*a. pol.*). **2.** *geogr.* temperate.

Gemecker [gə'mɛkɐ] *n* (-s) F *contp.* grouch, *sl.* bellyaching.

ge'mein *adj* **1.** *contp.* a) low, mean, nasty, F awful (*job etc*), b) vulgar, dirty, filthy (*joke etc*): *~er Trick* dirty trick. **2.** *et. ~ haben* have s.th. in common (*mit* with). **3.** common (*a. ♀, ♪, zo.*), general: *das ~e Volk* the common people.

Gemeinde [gə'maɪndə] *f* (-; -n) **1.** *pol.* a) municipality, b) local government (*or* authority), c) community. **2.** *eccl.* a) parish, b) parishioners, c) congregation. **3.** *fig.* following, audience.

Ge'meinde|amt *n* **1.** local authority. **2.** municipal office. *~bezirk m* district. *~haus n* **1.** parish hall. **2.** *→ Gemeinde-zentrum.* *~rat m* municipal council (*person:* council[l]or). *~schwester f* district nurse. *~steuern pl* (local) rates, *Am.* local taxes. *~verwaltung f → Ge-meinde* 1 b. *~vorstand m* local board. *~wahl f* local election. *~zentrum n* community cent/re (*Am.* -er).

ge'meingefährlich *adj* dangerous: *~ sein a.* be a public danger.

Ge'meingut *n* (-[e]s; *no pl*) *a. fig.* common property.

Ge'meinheit *f* (-; -en) **1.** *no pl* meanness, nastiness. **2.** mean thing (to do *or* say) so e-e *~!* a) what a dirty trick!, b) what rotten luck!

ge'meinhin *adv* generally.

Ge'meinkosten *pl* overhead (cost).

gemeinnützig [gə'maɪnnʏtsɪç] *adj* for

the public benefit, public welfare ..., nonprofit(-making) (*organization etc*).

Ge'meinplatz *m* commonplace.

ge'meinsam I *adj* common (*a.* Ⓐ), joint (*account, ownership, etc*), mutual: **~e Sache machen** make common cause (**mit** with); *vieles* ~ *haben* have a great deal in common; → **Nenner. II** *adv* jointly, together: *et.* ~ *tun* do s.th. together; ~ *vorgehen* take joint action.

Ge'meinsamkeit *f* (-; -en) **1.** common ground: ~*en entdecken* discover things in common. **2.** *no pl* a) mutuality, b) solidarity.

Ge'meinschaft *f* (-; -en) a) community (*a. pol.*), b) team, c) association: *eheliche* ~ ⚖ matrimony; *in enger* ~ *leben* live close together (**mit** with).

ge'meinschaftlich → **gemeinsam.**

Ge'meinschafts|anschluß *m teleph.* party line. **~an¡tenne** *f* communal aerial (*Am.* antenna). **~arbeit** *f* teamwork. **~erziehung** *f* **1.** *ped.* coeducation. **2.** social education. **~geist** *m* community spirit. **~produkti¡on** *f* coproduction. **~raum** *m* communal room. **~sendung** *f* simultaneous broadcast, hookup.

Ge'mein|schuldner *m* bankrupt. **~sinn** *m* (-[e]s; *no pl*) public spirit. Ⓢ**verständlich** *adj* intelligible to all, popular. **~wesen** *n* **1.** community. **2.** polity.

ge'messen I *pp of* **messen. II** *adj fig.* **1.** measured. **2.** formal. **3.** solemn, grave.

Gemetzel [gə'mɛtsəl] *n* (-s; -) slaughter.

gemieden [gə'miːdən] *pp of* **meiden.**

Gemisch [gə'mɪʃ] *n* (-[e]s; -e) mixture.

ge'mischt *adj a. fig.* mixed. **ge'mischt-wirtschaftlich** *adj* ✝ mixed-type.

Gemme ['gɛmə] *f* (-; -n) gem.

gemocht [gə'mɔxt] *pp of* **mögen.**

gemolken [gə'mɔlkən] *pp of* **melken.**

'**Gemsbock** *m zo.* chamois buck.

'**Gemse** ['gɛmzə] *f* (-; -n) *zo.* chamois.

Gemüse [gə'myːzə] *n* (-s; -) vegetable, *coll.* vegetables, greens. **~(an)bau** *m* (-[e]s; *no pl*) vegetable gardening, *Am.* truck farming. **~garten** *m* kitchen garden. **~händler** *m* greengrocer. **~kon¡serven** *f/pl* tinned (*or* canned) vegetables. **~laden** *m* greengrocer's shop.

gemußt [gə'mʊst] *pp of* **müssen** II.

ge'mustert *adj* (*a. in sich* ~) patterned.

'**Gemüt** [gə'myːt] *n* (-[e]s; -er) **1.** *no pl* mind, soul, heart, feeling, disposition,

nature: F *sich e-e Flasche Wein zu* ~*e führen* get outside a bottle of wine. **2.** soul: *die* ~*er bewegen* cause quite a stir; → **erhitzen I.**

ge'mütlich *adj* **1.** comfortable, snug, cosy, pleasant: *mach es dir* ~*!* a) make yourself at home!, b) *a. sei* ~*!* relax! **2.** good-natured, pleasant (*person*). **3.** leisurely, unhurried. **Ge'mütlichkeit** *f* (-; *no pl*) **1.** cosiness (*etc*). **2.** cosy (*or* relaxed) atmosphere. **3.** leisure(liness).

Ge'müts|art *f* disposition, nature. **~be¡wegung** *f* emotion. Ⓢ**krank** *adj* emotionally disturbed. **~krankheit** *f* emotional disturbance, mental disorder. **~mensch** *m* F a) warm-hearted person, b) *iro.* callous beast. **~ruhe** *f* peace of mind: F *in aller* ~ calmly, *iro.* as you please. **~verfassung** *f*, **~zustand** *m* frame of mind, (mental) state.

ge'mütvoll *adj* a) soulful, sentimental, b) warm(-hearted) (*person*).

Gen [geːn] *n* (-s; -e) *biol.* gene.

genannt [gə'nant] *pp of* **nennen.**

genas [gə'naːs] *pret of* **genesen.**

genau [gə'naʊ] *I adj* a) exact, accurate, precise, b) detailed (*report etc*), c) careful, d) strict: *Genaueres* particulars, further details; *man weiß nichts Genaues* we don't know anything definite. **II** *adv* exactly (*etc*): ~ *das Gegenteil* exactly (*or* just) the opposite; ~ *das, was ich brauche* just what I need; ~ *in der Mitte* right in the middle; ~ (*um*) *10 Uhr* (at) ten o'clock sharp; ~ *zuhören* listen sharp; *ich weiß es* ~ I know it for sure; *sich* ~ *an die Regeln halten* keep strictly to the rules; *es nicht sehr* ~ *nehmen* not to be particular (*mit* about); (*stimmt*) ~*!* exactly!

ge'naugenommen *adv* strictly speaking, to be exact.

Ge'nauigkeit *f* (-; *no pl*) exactness, accuracy, precision, thoroughness.

ge'nau → **ebenso.**

ge'nausogut → **ebensogut.**

Genealogie [genealo'giː] *f* (-; *no pl*) genealogy.

genehm [gə'neːm] *adj j-m* ~ *sein* suit s.o.

genehmigen [gə'neːmɪgən] *v/t* (h) approve (*a. adm.*, ⚖), permit, *adm.* authorize: F *sich e-n* ~ have a drink.

Ge'nehmigung *f* (-; -en) **1.** approval, permission, authorization. **2.** permit.

geneigt [gə'naıkt] *adj* inclined (**zu** to).
General [gene'ra:l] *m* (-s; -e, ⸗e) general.
Gene'ral... general (*agency, amnesty, etc*). **⸗baß** *m* ♩ basso continuo. **⸗bevollmächtigte** *m, f* (-n; -n) **1.** *pol.* plenipotentiary. **2.** ♁ general representative. **⸗di,rektor** *m* general manager. **⸗konsul** *m* consul general. **⸗konsu,lat** *n* consulate general. **⸗leutnant** *m* lieutenant general. **⸗ma,jor** *m* major general. **⸗probe** *f a. fig.* dress rehearsal. **⸗sekre,tär(in** *f) m* secretary-general. **⸗staatsanwalt** *m* Chief State Prosecutor. **⸗stab** *m* ✕ General Staff. **⸗stabskarte** *f* (*1:100 000*) ordnance survey map, *Am.* strategic map. **⸗streik** *m* general strike. **⸗überholung** *f* ⚙ complete overhaul. **⸗versammlung** *f* **1.** ♁ general meeting. **2.** *pol.* General Assembly (of the UN). **⸗vertreter** *m* general agent. **⸗vollmacht** *f* general power of attorney.
Generation [genera'tsio:n] *f* (-; -en) generation. **Generati'onskon,flikt** *m* generation gap.
Generator [gene'ra:tor] *m* (-s; -en [-ra'to:rən]) ⚡ generator.
generell [gene'rɛl] *adj* general.
genesen [gə'ne:zən] *v/i* (genas, genesen, sn) recover (**von** from), get well.
Ge'nesung *f* (-; *no pl*) a) convalescence, b) recovery. **Ge'nesungs...** convalescent (*home, leave, etc*).
Genetik [ge'ne:tık] *f* (-; *no pl*) genetics. **Genetiker** [ge'ne:tikər] *m* (-s; -) genetic scientist. **ge'netisch** *adj* genetic.
genial [ge'nia:l] *adj* of genius, inspired, brilliant, ingenious: **e-e ⸗e Idee** *a.* a brilliant idea. **Genialität** [geniali'tɛ:t] *f* (-; *no pl*) genius, brilliancy, ingenuity.
Genick [gə'nık] *n* (-[e]s; -e) (back of the) neck: (**sich**) **das ⸗ brechen** break one's neck; *fig.* **das brach ihm das ⸗** that was his undoing.
Ge'nickschuß *m* shot in the neck.
Genie [ʒe'ni:] *n* (-s; -s) genius.
genieren [ʒe'ni:rən] (h) **I** *v/t* **j-n ⸗** a) embarrass s.o., b) bother s.o. **II sich ⸗** be embarrassed, be shy; **⸗ Sie sich nicht!** don't be shy!
ge'nießbar *adj* edible, eatable, drinkable. **genießen** [gə'ni:sən] *v/t* (genoß, genossen, h) **1.** enjoy. **2.** have, eat, drink. **3.** *fig.* enjoy, have (reputation

etc), receive, get (*education etc*): **j-s Vertrauen ⸗** be in s.o.'s confidence.
Ge'nießer *m* (-s; -) bon vivant.
Genitalien [geni'ta:liən] *pl* genitals.
Genitiv ['ge:niti:f] *m* (-s; -e) *ling.* genitive (case), possessive (case).
Genius ['ge:niʊs] *m* (-; *no pl*) genius.
genommen [gə'nɔmən] *pp of* **nehmen.**
genormt [gə'nɔrmt] *adj* standardized.
genoß [gə'nɔs] *pret of* **genießen.**
Genosse [gə'nɔsə] *m* (-n; -n), **Ge'nossin** *f* (-; -nen) **1.** *pol.* comrade. **2.** F pal.
genossen [gə'nɔsən] *pp of* **genießen.**
Ge'nossenschaft *f* (-; -en), **ge'nossenschaftlich** *adj* ♁ cooperative.
Genre [ʒã:r] *n* (-s; -s) genre.
'Gentechnolo,gie *f* genetic engineering.
genug [gə'nu:k] *adj and adv* enough, sufficient(ly): **mehr als ⸗** more than enough; **ich habe nicht ⸗ Zeit** I haven't enough time (*or* time enough) *to do it;* ⸗ (**davon**)*!* enough (of that)*!*; **ich habe ⸗ davon!** I've had enough of that!
Genüge [gə'ny:gə] **1.** **zur ⸗** a) enough, sufficiently, b) only too well, c) often enough. **2. ⸗ tun** (*dat*) → **genügen** 2.
ge'nügen *v/i* (h) **1.** be enough, be sufficient: **das genügt (mir)***!* that's enough (for me)*!*, that'll do (for me)*!, fig. a* that's good enough (for me)*!* **2.** satisfy, meet (*requirements etc*). **ge'nügend** *adj* **1.** *a. adv* → **genug** 2. satisfactory.
genügsam [gə'ny:kza:m] *adj* content with little, modest, frugal. **Ge'nügsamkeit** *f* (-; *no pl*) modesty, frugality.
Ge'nugtuung *f* (-; *no pl*) (**über** *acc* at) satisfaction, gratification: **mit ⸗ hören, daß ...** be gratified to hear that ...
Genuß [gə'nʊs] *m* (-sses; ⸗sse) **1.** *no pl* a) consumption, eating, drinking, b) taking (*of drugs*). **2.** pleasure: **mit ⸗** with relish; **ein wahrer ⸗** a real treat. **3.** *a.* ♁♂ enjoyment: **in den ⸗ e-r Sache kommen** get (the benefit of) s.th.
Ge'nußmittel *n* **1.** semiluxury food, drink, and tobacco. **2.** stimulant.
Ge'nußsucht *f* (-; *no pl*) hedonism.
ge'nußsüchtig *adj* hedonistic.
Geodäsie [geodɛ'zi:] *f* (-; *no pl*) geodesy.
Geograph [geo'gra:f] *m* (-en; -en) geographer. **Geographie** [geogra'fi:] *f* (-; *no pl*) geography. **geographisch** [geo'gra:fıʃ] *adj* geographic(al).
Geologe [geo'lo:gə] *m* (-n; -n) geologist

Geologie [geolo'giː] f (-; no pl) geology.
geologisch [geo'loːgiʃ] adj geological.
Geometer [geo'meːtər] m (-s; -) surveyor. **Geometrie** [geome'triː] f (-; -n) geometry. **geometrisch** [geo'meːtriʃ] adj geometric(al).
Geophy'sik f geophysics.
Geopoli'tik f geopolitics.
geopo'litisch adj geopolitical.
Gepäck [gə'pɛk] n (-[e]s; no pl) luggage, esp. Am. baggage. **~abfertigung** f 1. 🚉 luggage (esp. Am. baggage) processing, ✈ checking-in of luggage (esp. Am. baggage). **2.** luggage (esp. Am. baggage) office, ✈ check-in counter. **~ablage** f luggage (esp. Am. baggage) rack. **~aufbewahrung** f left-luggage office, Am. baggage room. **~kon'trolle** f luggage (esp. Am. baggage) check. **~schein** m luggage ticket, Am. baggage check. **~stück** n piece of luggage (esp. Am. baggage). **~träger** m 1. porter. 2. on bike: carrier, roof rack. **~wagen** m 🚉 luggage van, Am. baggage car.
ge'panzert adj armo(u)red.
Gepard ['geːpart] m (-s; -e) zo. cheetah.
ge'pfeffert adj steep (prices etc), tough (test etc), sharp (letter etc), juicy (joke).
gepfiffen [gə'pfifən] pp of pfeifen.
ge'pflegt adj 1. well-groomed. 2. select, excellent (wine). 3. cultured, refined.
Gepflogenheit [gə'floːgənhaɪt] f (-; -en) habit, custom, ✝ etc practice.
Geplänkel [gə'plɛŋkəl] n (-s; -) a. fig. skirmish.
Ge'plapper n (-s; no pl) F babbling, contp. a. chatter(ing).
Ge'plauder n (-s; no pl) chatting, chat.
Ge'polter n (-s; no pl) rumbling.
Gepräge [gə'prɛːgə] n (-s; no pl) fig. stamp, character.
gepriesen [gə'priːzən] pp of preisen.
ge'quält adj pained, forced (smile).
Ge'quassel n (-s; no pl), **Ge'quatsche** n (-s; no pl) F blather.
gequollen [gə'kvɔlən] pp of quellen.
gerade [gə'raːdə] I adj 1. a) straight, b) upright, erect, c) even (a. number). 2. fig. straight, sincere, upright. II adv 3. just: **~ erst** only just; **nicht ~ schön** etc not exactly beautiful etc; **er wollte ~ gehen** he was just about to leave; **ich war ~ dort als ...** I happened to be there

when ...; **nun ~!** now more than ever!; **~ du!** especially you!; **warum ~ ich?** why me of all people?; **~ an diesem Tag** on that very day.
Ge'rade f (-n; -n) 1. 📐 straight line. 2. sports: straight: **linke (rechte) ~** boxing: straight left (right).
gerade'aus adv straight ahead (or on).
ge'radebiegen v/t (irr, sep, -ge-, h, → biegen) F fig. straighten out.
geradeher'aus adv openly, bluntly.
gerädert [gə'rɛːdərt] adj F fig. **(wie) ~** whacked.
ge'radeso etc → ebenso etc.
ge'radestehen v/i (irr, sep, -ge-, h, → stehen) fig. answer (**für** for).
ge'radewegs adv a) straight, directly, b) straightaway.
ge'radezu¹ adv almost, next to, really.
gerade'zu² adv straight.
Geradheit [gə'raːthaɪt] f (-; no pl) straightness, fig. a. uprightness.
geradlinig [gə'raːtliːnɪç] adj 1. straight (a. adv), lineal, direct (descent etc), linear (motion). 2. fig. straight(forward).
gerammelt [gə'raməlt] adj F **~voll (von)** chock-full (of), jam-packed (with).
Gerangel [gə'raŋəl] n (-s; no pl) (**um** over) F tussle, fig. a. wrangling.
gerann [gə'ran] pret of gerinnen.
gerannt [gə'rant] pp of rennen.
Gerät [gə'rɛːt] n (-[e]s; -e) 1. ⚙ device, instrument, appliance, apparatus (a. gym.), F gadget. 2. (radio or TV) set. 3. coll. a) equipment, gear, b) tools, c) utensils. 4. (motorbike etc) machine.
ge'raten¹ v/i (irr, geraten, sn) 1. turn out (**zu kurz** too short etc). 2. **~ an** (acc) come across s.o., come by (or get) s.th.; **an e-n Betrüger ~** fall into the hands of a swindler; **in Schwierigkeiten ~** get into difficulties; **in e-n Sturm ~** be caught in a storm; → **Abweg, Adresse, außer 1, Bahn 1, Brand 1** etc. 3. **~ nach** take after (one's father etc).
ge'raten² I pp of raten and geraten¹. II adj advisable.
Ge'räteschuppen m toolshed.
Ge'räteturnen n apparatus gymnastics.
Gerate'wohl n F **aufs ~** at random.
Ge'rätschaften pl → Gerät 3.
Ge'ratter n (-s; no pl) rattling, rattle.
geräumig [gə'rɔʏmɪç] adj roomy, spa-

cious. **Ge'räumigkeit** f (-; no pl) roominess, spaciousness.

Geräusch [gə'rɔʏʃ] n (-[e]s; -e) sound, a. ☢ noise. **Ge'räuscharm** adj noiseless, silent. **Ge'räuschdämpfung** f (-; -en) silencing. **Ge'räuschku,lisse** f background noise. **ge'räuschlos** adj a. ☢ noiseless, silent, quiet. **Ge'räuschlosigkeit** f (-; no pl) noiselessness. **Ge'räuschpegel** m decibel (or noise) level. **ge'räuschvoll** adj noisy, loud.

gerben ['gɛrbən] v/t (h) tan. **'Gerber** m (-s; -) tanner. **Gerbe'rei** f (-; -en) tannery. **Gerbsäure** ['gɛrp-] f tannic acid.

ge'recht adj 1. just, fair. 2. (dat) ~ **werden** do justice to (s.o., s.th.), meet, fulfil(l) (requirements etc), come up to (expectations). **ge'rechterweise** adv 1. justly. 2. to be fair.

ge'rechtfertigt adj justified.

Ge'rechtigkeit f (-; no pl) justice, fairness: → widerfahren.

Ge'rechtigkeitssinn m sense of justice.

Ge'rede n (-s; no pl) F 1. (leeres ~ idle) talk. 2. gossip: ins ~ kommen get o.s. talked about, set tongues wagging.

ge'regelt adj regular.

ge'reizt adj irritable, irritated (a. ✷).

Ge'reiztheit f (-; no pl) irritation.

Geriatrie [geria'tri:] f (-; no pl) geriatrics.

Gericht¹ [gə'rɪçt] n (-[e]s; -e) gastr. 1. dish. 2. course.

Ge'richt² n (-[e]s; -e) a) (law) court, fig. tribunal, b) the court, c) courthouse: das Jüngste ~ eccl. the Last Judgement; vor ~ bringen take s.o., s.th. to court; vor ~ gehen go to court; vor ~ aussagen testify in court; j-n vor ~ stellen bring s.o. to trial; fig. mit j-m ins ~ gehen take s.o. to task; zu ~ sitzen über (acc) sit in judg(e)ment on.

ge'richtlich adj judicial, legal.

Ge'richtsbarkeit f (-; no pl) jurisdiction.

Ge'richts|beschluß m court order: durch ~ by order of the court. ~gebäude n law court, courthouse. ~hof m court of justice, law court. ~kosten pl costs (of an action). ~medi,zin f forensic medicine. ~medi,ziner m medical expert (Am. examiner). ~referen,dar(in f) m junior lawyer (who has passed his/her first State Examination). ~saal m courtroom. ~stand m venue,

legal domicile, place of jurisdiction. ~urteil n a) sentence, b) judg(e)ment. ~verfahren n 1. a) (legal) proceedings, lawsuit, b) trial. 2. court procedure. ~verhandlung f a) (judicial) hearing, b) trial. ~vollzieher m bailiff, Am. marshal. ~weg m auf dem ~ by legal proceedings; den ~ einschlagen take legal action.

gerieben [gə'ri:bən] pp of reiben.

geriet [gə'ri:t] pret of geraten¹.

gering [gə'rɪŋ] adj a) little, small, slight, b) low (price etc), a. poor (opinion etc), slim (chance, hope, etc), minor (importance etc): in ~erem Maße to a less degree; kein ℒerer als no less a person than; nicht im ~sten not in the least; das soll m-e ~ste Sorge sein! that's the least of my worries!; → Chance.

ge'ringachten v/t (sep, -ge-, h) 1. think little of. 2. disregard (danger etc).

ge'ringfügig [-fy:gɪç] adj insignificant, negligible, slight, minor, small, petty.

Ge'ringfügigkeit f (-; no pl) insignificance, slightness, smallness.

ge'ringschätzig [-ʃɛtsɪç] adj contemptuous, disparaging.

Ge'ringschätzung f (-; no pl) (für, gen) disdain (of), low regard (for).

ge'rinnen v/i (gerann, geronnen, sn) coagulate, clot, milk: curdle.

Ge'rinnsel [gə'rɪnzəl] n (-s; -) ✷ clot.

Ge'rinnung f (-; no pl) coagulation, clotting, curdling.

Gerippe [gə'rɪpə] n (-s; -) a. fig. skeleton.

ge'rippt adj ribbed.

gerissen [gə'rɪsən] I pp of reißen. II adj F fig. cunning, crafty.

geritten [gə'rɪtən] pp of reiten.

Germane [gɛr'ma:nə] m (-n; -n). **Ger'manin** f (-; -nen) Teuton.

ger'manisch adj Germanic (a. ling.). Teutonic. **Germanist** [gɛrma'nɪst] m (-en; -en), **Germa'nistin** f (-; -nen) Germanist, a. student of German.

Germanistik [gɛrma'nɪstɪk] f (-; no pl) German (studies or philology).

gern [gɛrn], **'gerne** adv gladly, with pleasure: (ja,) ~! a) yes, certainly!, b) I'd love to!; (aber) ~! of course!, gladly!; herzlich (or liebend) ~! with great pleasure!; ~ geschehen! not at all!, (you're) welcome!; ~ haben like, be fond of; (sehr) ~ tun like (love) to do (*or doing*), b) tend to do; **~ essen** (**trinken**) like; **~ lesen** like reading; *ich hätte ~ e-e Tasse Tee* I'd like a cup of tea; *ich möchte ~ wissen, ob ...* a) I'd like to know if ..., b) I wonder if ...; *er kann ~ kommen!* a) he's welcome!, b) I don't mind if he comes!; *das kannst du ~ haben!* you're welcome to it!; *er sieht es nicht ~* he doesn't like it; F *du kannst mich ~ haben!* go to blazes!

'**Gernegroß** *m* (-; -e) F show-off.

gerochen [gə'rɔxən] *pp of* **riechen**.

Geröll [gə'rœl] *n* (-[e]s; -e) scree, rubble.

geronnen [gə'rɔnən] *pp of* **gerinnen and rinnen**.

Gerste ['gɛrstə] *f* (-; -n) ⚕ barley.

'**Gerstenkorn** *n* 1. barleycorn. 2. 🌿 sty.

Gerte ['gɛrtə] *f* (-; -n) switch, twig.

'**gertenschlank** *adj* (slim and) willowy.

Geruch [gə'rʊx] *m* (-[e]s; -̈e) smell, scent, *b.s.* odo(u)r (*a. fig.*).

ge'ruchlos *adj* odo(u)rless.

Ge'ruchs|nerv *m* olfactory nerve. **~sinn** *m* (-[e]s; *no pl*) (sense of) smell.

Gerücht [gə'rʏçt] *n* (-[e]s; -e) rumo(u)r: *es geht das ~* it is rumo(u)red.

gerufen [gə'ruːfən] *pp of* **rufen**.

ge'ruhen *v/t* (h) ~, *et. zu tun* deign to do s.th.

ge'rührt *adj fig.* touched, moved.

Gerümpel [gə'rʏmpəl] *n* (-s; *no pl*) junk.

Gerundium [gə'rʊndiʊm] *n* (-s; -dien) *ling.* gerund.

gerungen [gə'rʊŋən] *pp of* **ringen**.

Gerüst [gə'rʏst] *n* (-[e]s; -e) 1. a) scaffold(ing), b) stage, c) frame. 2. *fig.* frame(work).

ge'rütteln *adj fig.* **ein ~ Maß an** (*dat*) a fair amount of.

ges, Ges [gɛs] *n* (-; -) ♪ G flat.

ge'salzen I *pp of* **salzen**. **II** *adj* 1. salted. 2. → **gepfeffert**.

ge'sammelt *adj* 1. **~e Werke** collected works. 2. *fig.* concentrated.

gesamt [gə'zamt] *adj* 1. whole, entire, all. 2. total (*amount etc*).

Ge'samt|ansicht *f* general view. **~auflage** *f* a) total circulation, b) total number of copies published. **~ausgabe** *f* 1. complete edition. 2. *pl* ✝ total expenditure. **~betrag** *m* total (amount). **~bevölkerung** *f* total population. **~bild** *n* overall picture. ₴**deutsch** *adj* all-German. **~eindruck** *m* general impression.

Ge'samtheit *f* (-; *no pl*) totality, *the* whole: *die ~ der Arbeiter* all the workers; *in s-r ~* in its entirety, as a whole.

Ge'samt|hochschule *f* comprehensive university. **~kosten** *pl* overall (*or* total) cost. **~länge** *f* overall length. **~note** *f ped.* aggregate mark. **~schule** *f* comprehensive school. **~sieger(in** *f*) *m* overall winner. **~summe** *f* (sum) total, total amount. **~werk** *n* complete works. **~zahl** *f* total (number).

gesandt [gə'zant] *pp of* **senden²**.

Gesandte [gə'zantə] *m, f* (-n; -n) envoy.

Ge'sandtschaft *f* (-; -en) legation.

Gesang [gə'zaŋ] *m* (-[e]s; -̈e) 1. *no pl* singing: **~ studieren** study voice. 2. song. **Ge'sangbuch** *n eccl.* hymnbook. **Ge'sanglehrer(in** *f*) *m* singing teacher. **ge'sanglich** *adj* vocal. **Ge'sangunterricht** *m* singing lessons. **Ge'sangverein** *m* choral society.

Gesäß [gə'zɛːs] *n* (-es; -e) buttocks, F bottom. **Ge'säßtasche** *f* back pocket.

ge'schaffen *pp of* **schaffen**.

Geschäft [gə'ʃɛft] *n* (-[e]s; -e) 1. a) business, b) trade, c) (business) deal, transaction: *ein gutes* (*schlechtes*) **~** a good (bad) deal; *ein gutes ~ machen* make a good profit (F a packet) (*mit* out of); **~e machen mit** deal in, *w.s.* make money out of; *mit j-m ~e machen, mit j-m ins ~ kommen* do business with s.o.; *gut im ~ sein* be doing well; **~ ist ~!** business is business!; *er versteht sein ~!* he knows his business (*or* stuff!) 2. a) enterprise, firm, b) office, c) shop, store. 3. *fig.* business, affair.

ge'schäftehalber *adv* on business.

Ge'schäftemacher *m contp.* profiteer.

ge'schäftig *adj* busy, active.

Ge'schäftigkeit *f* (-; *no pl*) activity.

ge'schäftlich *adj* business, commercial: **~ verreist** away on business; **~ zu tun haben** have (some) business (*mit* with); **~ verhindert** prevented by business.

Ge'schäfts|abschluß *m* (business) transaction (*or* deal). **~bedingungen** *pl* terms of business. **~bereich** *m* sphere of activity, scope, *pol.* portfolio, ⚖ jurisdiction. **~bericht** *m* (business) report. **~beziehungen** *pl* business connections. **~brief** *m* business letter. ₴**fähig** *adj* competent, having legal capacity. **~fähigkeit** *f* (-; *no pl*) legal capacity.

~frau f businesswoman. **~freund** m business friend. **⚲führend** adj managing, executive, acting. **~führer(in** f) m manager(ess), secretary (of a club etc). **~führung** f management. **~gebaren** n business methods. **~geheimnis** n business secret. **~haus** n **1.** office building. **2.** commercial firm, company. **~inhaber(in** f) m owner (of a business), proprietor (proprietress). **~jahr** n financial year. **~kosten** pl business expenses: **auf ~** on expense account. **~lage** f business situation. **~leben** n (**im ~** in) business (life). **~leitung** f management. **~mann** m (-[e]s; **-leute)** businessman.

ge'schäftsmäßig adj businesslike.

Ge'schäfts|ordnung f rules of procedure, parl. standing orders: **zur ~** on a point of order. **~partner(in** f) m (business) partner. **~räume** pl business premises, offices. **~reise** f (**auf ~** on a) business trip. **⚲schädigend** adj damaging to business. **~schädigung** f 🗲 injurious malpractice, w.s. trade libel (gen on). **~schluß** m closing time: **nach ~** a. after business hours. **~sinn** m (-[e]s; no pl) business sense. **~sitz** m place of business. **~stelle** f office(s). **~straße** f shopping street. **~träger** m pol. chargé d'affaires. **⚲tüchtig** adj smart, efficient (in business). **~tüchtigkeit** f (-; no pl) business efficiency, smartness. **⚲unfähig** adj 🗲 legally incapacitated. **~unfähigkeit** f (-; no pl) 🗲 legal incapacity. **~verbindung** f business connection. **~verkehr** m business (dealings). **~viertel** n commercial district, Am. a. downtown. **~wert** m goodwill. **~zweig** m branch (of business).

geschehen [gə'ʃeːən] v/i (geschah, sn) happen, occur, take place: **ihm wird nichts ~** nothing will happen to him; **was soll damit ~?** what's to be done with it?; **es muß et. ~!** s.th. must be done!; **da war es um ihn ~** he was done for; → **recht** 5.

Ge'schehen n (-s) happenings, events.

gescheit [gə'ʃaɪt] adj **1.** clever, intelligent, bright. **2.** wise, sensible.

Geschenk [gə'ʃɛŋk] n (-[e]s; -e) present, gift: **j-m et. zum ~ machen** give s.o. s.th. (as a present); **als ~ verpacken** gift-wrap. **~ar,tikel** m gift. **~packung** f gift box.

Geschichte [gə'ʃɪçtə] f (-; -n) **1.** story, a. narrative. **2.** no pl history: **die ~ der Neuzeit** modern history; **~ machen** make history; **in die ~ eingehen** go down in history. **3.** F business, thing: **die ganze** (iro. **e-e schöne) ~** the whole (a nice) business.

ge'schichtlich adj historical, historic.

Ge'schichts|buch n history book. **~forscher(in** f) m historian. **~forschung** f historical research. **~lehrer(in** f) m history teacher. **~unterricht** m history lesson.

Geschick¹ [gə'ʃɪk] n (-[e]s; -e) fate, lot.

Ge'schick² n (-[e]s; no pl) skill.

Ge'schicklichkeit f (-; no pl) **1.** skill, dexterity. **2.** cleverness.

ge'schickt adj skil(l)ful (**zu** at, **in** dat in), a. clever.

geschieden [gə'ʃiːdən] **I** pp of **scheiden. II** adj/person: divorced, marriage: dissolved: **m-e ~e Frau** my ex-wife.

Ge'schiedene¹ m (-n; -n) divorcé, divorced man. **Ge'schiedene²** f (-n; -n) divorcée, divorced woman.

geschienen [gə'ʃiːnən] pp of **scheinen.**

Geschirr [gə'ʃɪr] n (-[e]s; -e) **1.** no pl a. dishes, tableware, b) kitchenware, pots and pans: **das ~ abräumen** clear the table; **~ spülen** do the dishes, wash up. **2.** china. **3.** harness.

Ge'schirr|schrank m (china) cupboard. **~spüler** m (-s; -) F, **~spülma,schine** f dishwasher. **~tuch** n tea towel.

geschissen [gə'ʃɪsən] pp of **scheißen.**

ge'schlafen pp of **schlafen.**

ge'schlagen I pp of **schlagen. II** adj **1.** beaten, defeated: **sich ~ geben** admit defeat. **2.** F full: **zwei ~e Stunden** (**lang** for) two solid hours.

Geschlecht [gə'ʃlɛçt] n (-[e]s; -er) **1.** biol. sex: **beiderlei ~s** of both sexes; **das andere** (**schwache, schöne) ~** the opposite (weaker, fair) sex. **2.** ling. gender. **3.** a) race, b) lineage, c) family: **das menschliche ~** the human race.

ge'schlechtlich adj sexual.

Ge'schlechts|akt m sexual act. **~hor,mon** n sex hormone. **⚲krank** adj suffering from a venereal disease, having VD. **~krankheit** f venereal disease (abbr. V.D.). **~leben** n sex life.

ge'schlechtslos adj sexless, asexual.

Ge'schlechts|merkmal n sex characteristic. **~or,gan** n sex(ual) organ. **~reife** f

geschwommen

sexual maturity. **~teile** pl genitals. **~trieb** m sexual urge. **~umwandlung** f sex change. **~verkehr** m sexual intercourse. **~wort** n ling. article.

geschlichen [gə'ʃlɪçən] pp of **schleichen**.

geschliffen [gə'ʃlɪfən] **I** pp of **schleifen**[1]. **II** adj **1.** cut (glass). **2.** fig. polished.

geschlossen [gə'ʃlɔsən] **I** pp of **schließen**. **II** adj **1.** closed, ling., ✗ close: (**in sich**) **~** a. ☉ self-contained, fig. compact; **~e Gesellschaft** a) closed society, b) private party; **~e Veranstaltung** private meeting; **~e Ortschaft** built-up area. **2.** united: **~ stimmen für** vote unanimously for, be solid for; **~ hinter j-m stehen** be solidly behind s.o.

geschlungen [gə'ʃlʊŋən] pp of **schlingen**.

Geschmack [gə'ʃmak] m (-[e]s; ⁻e, F ⁻er) taste (a. fig. **an** dat for), flavo(u)r: **~ finden an** (dat) develop a taste for; **e-n guten ~ haben** a) taste good, b) fig. have good taste; **für m-n ~** for my taste; **das ist nicht nach m-m ~** that's not to my taste; **über ~ läßt sich nicht streiten** there's no accounting for tastes.

ge'schmacklich adj in taste.

ge'schmacklos adj tasteless: **~ sein** fig. a. be in bad taste. **Ge'schmacklosigkeit** f (-; no pl) a. fig. tastelessness: **das war e-e ~** that was in bad taste.

Ge'schmacks|richtung f taste. **~sache** f (**es ist ~** it's a) matter of taste. **~sinn** m (-[e]s; no pl) (sense of) taste. **~verirrung** f lapse of taste.

ge'schmackvoll adj tasteful: **~ sein** fig. a. be in good taste.

Geschmeide [gə'ʃmaɪdə] n (-s; -) jewels, jewel(le)ry.

geschmeidig [gə'ʃmaɪdɪç] adj **1.** supple, pliant, sleek, soft. **2.** fig. flexible.

geschmissen [gə'ʃmɪsən] pp of **schmeißen**.

geschmolzen [gə'ʃmɔltsən] pp of **schmelzen**.

Geschmuse [gə'ʃmuːzə] n (-s; no pl) F smooching.

Ge'schnatter n (-s; no pl) **1.** cackling. **2.** F fig. chatter(ing).

geschnitten [gə'ʃnɪtən] pp of **schneiden**.

geschoben [gə'ʃoːbən] pp of **schieben**.

gescholten [gə'ʃɔltən] pp of **schelten**.

Geschöpf [gə'ʃœpf] n (-[e]s; -e) **1.** creature. **2.** fig. creation.

geschoren [gə'ʃoːrən] pp of **scheren**.

Geschoß[1] [gə'ʃɔs] n (-sses; -sse) projectile, bullet, missile.

Ge'schoß[2] n (-sses; -sse) stor(e)y, floor.

geschossen [gə'ʃɔsən] pp of **schießen**.

geschraubt [gə'ʃraʊpt] adj fig. stilted.

Ge'schrei n (-[e]s; no pl) **1.** a) shouting, yelling, bawling, b) shouts, screams. **2.** F fig. (**um** about) fuss, noise.

geschrieben [gə'ʃriːbən] pp of **schreiben**.

geschrie(e)n [gə'ʃriː(ə)n] pp of **schreien**.

geschritten [gə'ʃrɪtən] pp of **schreiten**.

ge'schult adj trained (a. eye).

geschunden [gə'ʃʊndən] pp of **schinden**.

Geschütz [gə'ʃʏts] n (-es; -e) gun: fig. **schweres ~ auffahren** bring up one's heavy guns. **~feuer** n gunfire, shelling.

ge'schützt adj protected.

Ge'schützturm m turret.

Geschwader [gə'ʃvaːdər] n (-s; -) ⚓ squadron, ✈ group, Am. wing.

Ge'schwafel n (-s; no pl) F contp. waffle.

Geschwätz [gə'ʃvɛts] n (-es; no pl) F contp. **1.** twaddle. **2.** gossip.

ge'schwätzig adj contp. **1.** talkative, F gabby. **2.** gossipy. **Ge'schwätzigkeit** f (-; no pl) contp. talkativeness.

ge'schweige conj (**~ denn**) not to mention, let alone, much less.

geschwiegen [gə'ʃviːgən] pp of **schweigen**.

Geschwindigkeit [gə'ʃvɪndɪçkaɪt] f (-; -en) speed, pace, rate, phys. velocity: **mit e-r ~ von** at a speed (or rate) of.

Ge'schwindigkeits|beschränkung f speed limit. **~messer** m tachometer, mot. a. speedometer. **~re,kord** m speed record. **~überschreitung** f speeding.

Geschwister [gə'ʃvɪstər] pl brother(s) and sister(s), siblings.

ge'schwisterlich adj a) brotherly, b) sisterly.

Ge'schwisterpaar n a) brother and sister, b) two brothers (or sisters).

geschwollen [gə'ʃvɔlən] **I** pp of **schwellen**. **II** adj **1.** swollen. **2.** fig. pompous, bombastic.

geschwommen [gə'ʃvɔmən] pp of **schwimmen**.

geschworen [gə'ʃvoːrən] **II** *pp of*
schwören. **II** *adj* sworn (*enemy*).

Ge'schworene *m, f* (-n; -n) juror: *die*
~n the (members of the) jury.

Ge'schworenenbank *f* **1.** jury box. **2.**
the jury.

Ge'schwulst *f* (-; ⁓e) 🩺 tumo(u)r.

geschwunden [gə'ʃvʊndən] *pp of*
schwinden.

geschwungen [gə'ʃvʊŋən] **I** *pp of*
schwingen. **II** *adj* curved.

Geschwür [gə'ʃvyːr] *n* (-[e]s; -e) 🩺 ulcer,
abscess, boil.

ge'sehen *pp of* **sehen.**

Geselle [gə'zɛlə] *m* (-n; -n) journeyman.

ge'sellen (h) *sich zu j-m* ~ join s.o.

ge'sellig *adj* social, gregarious (*a. fig.*),
sociable (*person*): *~es Leben* social life.

Ge'selligkeit *f* (-; *no pl*) **1.** sociability. **2.**
social life: *die* ~ *lieben* be fond of com-
pany.

Gesellschaft [gə'zɛlʃaft] *f* (-; -en) **1.** *no pl*
society: *die vornehme* ~ high society;
Dame der ~ society lady. **2.** *no pl* company: *in s-r* ~ in his company; *j-m* ~
leisten a) keep s.o. company, b) join
s.o. (*bei* in). **3.** a) party, b) guests: *e-e*
~ *geben* give a party. **4.** society, 🕇 company; → *Haftung*². **5.** *no pl* F hunch.

Ge'sellschafter *m* (-s; -), **Ge'sellschaf-
terin** *f* (-; -nen) **1.** companion. **2.** 🕇
partner. **ge'sellschaftlich** *adj* social.

Ge'sellschafts|anzug *m* formal dress.
⁓fähig *adj* **1.** socially acceptable. **2.**
presentable. **⁓kri,tik** *f* social criticism.
⁓kritisch *adj* socio-critical. **⁓ordnung** *f*
social order. **⁓recht** *n* (-[e]s; *no pl*) company law. **⁓reise** *f* package (*or* conducted) tour. **⁓schicht** *f* (social) class,
social stratum. **⁓spiel** *n* parlo(u)r
game. **⁓sy,stem** *n* social system. **⁓tanz**
m ballroom dance. **⁓wissenschaft** *f* **1.**
sociology. **2.** *pl* social sciences.

Gesenk [gə'zɛŋk] *n* (-[e]s; -e) ⚙ swage.

gesessen [gə'zɛsən] *pp of* **sitzen.**

Gesetz [gə'zɛts] *n* (-es; -e) law, *parl.* act:
nach dem ~ under the law (*über* acc
on); *vor dem* ~ in the eyes of the law.

Ge'setz|blatt *n* law gazette. **⁓buch** *n*
code (of law). **⁓entwurf** *m* (draft) bill.

Ge'setzeskraft *f* legal force: ~ *erhalten*
pass into law; (*dat*) ~ *verleihen* enact.

Ge'setzeslücke *f* loophole in the law.

Ge'setzesvorlage *f* (draft) bill.

ge'setzgebend *adj* legislative.

Ge'setzgeber *m* (-s; -) legislator.

Ge'setzgebung *f* (-; *no pl*) legislation.

ge'setzlich *adj* legal, statutory, lawful,
legitimate: ~ *geschützt* protected (by
law), patented (*invention etc*), registered (*trademark etc*), copyright (*book
etc*). **Ge'setzlichkeit** *f* (-; *no pl*) legality, lawfulness.

Ge'setzlosigkeit *f* (-; *no pl*) lawlessness.

ge'setzmäßig *adj* **1.** 🛠 legal, lawful,
legitimate. **2.** regular. **Ge'setzmäßig-
keit** *f* (-; *no pl*) **1.** 🛠 legality, lawfulness,
legitimacy. **2.** regularity.

ge'setzt **I** *adj* **1.** sedate: *~en Alters, ~
em Alter* of mature age. **2.** *sports:*
~er Spieler seeded. **II** *conj* → *Fall* 2.
Ge'setztheit *f* (-; *no pl*) sedate-
ness.

ge'setzwidrig *adj* unlawful, illegal.

Ge'setzwidrigkeit *f* (-; -en) **1.** *no pl* un-
lawfulness, illegality. **2.** offen/ce (*Am.*
-se), illegal act.

Gesicht [gə'zɪçt] *n* (-[e]s; -er) **1.** face, *a.*
look: *ein trauriges* ~ *machen* look
sad; *ein langes* ~ *machen* pull a long
face; *das* ~ *verziehen* make a face; *j-m
et. ins* ~ *sagen* tell s.o. s.th. to his (her)
face; *j-m wie aus dem* ~ *geschnitten
sein* be the spit and image of s.o.; *fig.
sein wahres* ~ *zeigen* show one's true
face; *das* ~ *verlieren* (*wahren*) lose
(save one's) face; *das gibt der Sache
ein ganz anderes* ~ that puts a different complexion on the matter. **2.** (eye)-
sight: *das zweite* ~ second sight; *zu* ~
bekommen catch sight of, see; *aus
dem* ~ *verlieren* lose sight of.

Ge'sichts|ausdruck *m* (facial) expres-
sion, face. **⁓creme** *f* face cream. **⁓far-
be** *f* complexion. **⁓feld** *n* opt. field of
vision. **⁓kreis** *m* horizon.

ge'sichtslos *adj* *fig.* featureless.

Ge'sichts|maske *f* face mask.
⁓mas,sage *f* facial massage, F facial.
⁓muskel *m* facial muscle. **⁓packung** *f*
face pack. **⁓pflege** *f* care of one's face.
⁓punkt *m* **1.** point of view, viewpoint,
angle: *von diesem* ~ *aus* (*gesehen*)
(looked at) from this point of view. **2.**
point, aspect. **⁓wasser** *n* face lotion.
⁓winkel *m* opt. visual angle. **⁓züge** *pl*
features.

Gesindel [gə'zɪndəl] *n* (-s; *no pl*) riffraff.

Ge'triebeschaden *m* mot. gearbox trouble.

getroffen [gə'trɔfən] *pp of* treffen.

getrogen [gə'tro:gən] *pp of* trügen.

ge'trost *adj* confidently, safely.

getrunken [gə'trʊŋkən] *pp of* trinken.

Getto ['gɛto] *n* (-s; -s) ghetto.

Getue [gə'tu:ə] *n* (-s; *no pl*) F fuss (*um* about).

Getümmel [gə'tʏml] *n* (-s; -) turmoil.

geübt [gə'y:pt] *adj* practised, trained (*eye etc*), experienced.

Gewächs [gə'vɛks] *n* (-es; -e) **1.** plant. **2.** ♥ produce, growth. **3.** a) wine, b) vintage. **4.** ♂ growth.

ge'wachsen I *pp of* wachsen¹. II *adj j-m ~ sein* be a match for s.o.; *e-r Sache ~ sein* be up (*or* equal) to s.th.; *sich der Lage ~ zeigen* rise to the occasion.

Ge'wächshaus *n* greenhouse, hothouse.

gewagt [gə'va:kt] *adj* a) daring (*a. fig.*), risky, b) risqué (*joke etc*).

gewählt [gə'vɛ:lt] *adj fig.* refined.

Gewähr [gə'vɛ:r] *f* (-; *no pl*) guarantee: *ohne ~* a) without guarantee, b) subject to change; *für et. ~ bieten* (*or* leisten) guarantee s.th. ge'währen *v/t* (h) a) grant (*j-m e-e Bitte* s.o. a request), b) give, afford (*an insight, protection, etc*): *j-n ~ lassen* let s.o. have his way. Ge'währleisten *v/t* (h) guarantee.

Ge'wahrsam *m* (-s; *no pl*) *in ~ nehmen* a) take *s.th.* in safe keeping, b) take *s.o.* into custody.

Ge'währsmann *m* informant, source.

Gewalt [gə'valt] *f* (-; -en) **1.** *no pl* force, violence: *mit ~* by force; *mit aller ~* a) with all one's might, b) *fig.* at all costs; *~ anwenden* use force; → roh 3. **2.** a) power, *adm.*, ‡‡ authority, b) control (*über acc* of): *höhere ~* act of God; *die gesetzgebende ~* the legislature; *et. in s-e ~ bringen* gain control of s.th.; *et.* (*sich*) *in der ~ haben* have s.th. (o.s.) under control; *in j-s ~ sein* be in s.o.'s power (*or* hands); *die ~ verlieren über* (*acc*) lose control over.

Ge'waltakt *m* act of violence.

Ge'waltanwendung *f* (use of) force.

Ge'waltenteilung *f pol.* separation of powers.

Ge'waltherrschaft *f* tyranny. Ge'waltherrscher(in *f*) *m* despot, tyrant.

ge'waltig *adj* **1.** powerful, mighty. **2.** enormous, huge.

ge'waltlos I *adj* nonviolent. II *adv* without violence. Ge'waltlosigkeit *f* (-; *no pl*) nonviolence.

Ge'waltmaßnahme *f* drastic measure.

ge'waltsam I *adj* forcible, violent: *~er Tod* violent death. II *adv* forcibly, by force: *et. ~ öffnen* force s.th. (open).

Ge'waltsamkeit *f* (-; *no pl*) violence.

Ge'walttat *f* act of violence, outrage.

ge'walttätig *adj* violent, brutal.

Ge'walttätigkeit *f* (-; -en) **1.** *no pl* violence, brutality. **2.** act of violence.

Ge'waltverbrechen *n* crime of violence.

Ge'waltverbrecher *m* violent criminal.

Ge'waltverzichtsabkommen *n pol.* nonaggression treaty.

Gewand [gə'vant] *n* (-[e]s; ⁻er) robe.

gewandt [gə'vant] I *pp of* wenden². II *adj* a) agile, nimble, b) elegant, c) clever. Ge'wandtheit *f* (-; *no pl*) a) agility, nimbleness, b) elegance, c) cleverness.

gewann [gə'van] *pret of* gewinnen.

gewappnet [gə'vapnət] *adj fig.* prepared (*für* for).

gewärtig [gə'vɛrtɪç] *adj ~ sein* (*gen*) → ge'wärtigen [-tɪgən] *v/t* (h) expect, reckon with: *zu ~ haben* be in for *s.th.*

Gewäsch [gə'vɛʃ] *n* (-[e]s; *no pl*) F *contp.* blather.

ge'waschen *pp of* waschen.

Gewässer [gə'vɛsər] *n* (-s; -) (stretch of) water, *pl* waters, rivers and lakes.

Ge'wässerschutz *m* prevention of water pollution.

Gewebe [gə've:bə] *n* (-s; -) a) (woven) fabric, b) tissue (*a. anat. or fig.*), c) weave. *~probe f ♂* tissue sample.

Gewehr [gə've:r] *n* (-[e]s; -e) gun, rifle. *~kolben m* (rifle) butt. *~kugel f* (rifle) bullet. *~lauf m* (rifle) barrel.

Geweih [gə'vai] *n* (-[e]s; -e) antlers, horns.

Gewerbe [gə'vɛrbə] *n* (-s; -) trade, business, occupation: *Handel und ~* trade and industry. *~freiheit f* freedom of trade. *~lehrer(in f) m* teacher at a trade school. *~ordnung f* industrial code. *~schein m* trade licen/ce (*Am.* -se). *~schule f* trade school. *~steuer f* trade tax. *≗treibend adj* carrying on a trade, industrial. *~treibende m, f* (-n; -n) person carrying on a trade, trader. *~zweig m* (branch of) trade (*or* industry).

gewerblich [gə'vɛrplɪç] *adj* commercial, industrial, trade. **ge'werbsmäßig** *adj* professional, gainful, *adv* a. for gain.

Gewerkschaft [gə'vɛrkʃaft] *f* (-; -en) trade (*Am.* labor) union.

Ge'werkschaftler *m* (-s; -) (trade, *Am.* labor) unionist. **ge'werkschaftlich** *adj* trade (*Am.* labor) union: ~ **organisiert** unionized, organized.

Ge'werkschafts... (trade, *Am.* labor) union (*boss, member, etc*). ~**bund** *m* federation of trade (*Am.* labor) unions.

ge'wesen *pp* of **sein¹**.

gewichen [gə'vɪçən] *pp* of **weichen**.

Gewicht [gə'vɪçt] *n* (-[e]s; -e) a. *fig.* weight: **ein ~ von ... haben** weigh ...; **nach ~ verkaufen** sell by weight; *fig.* ~ **haben** carry weight (**bei** with); (**nicht**) **ins ~ fallen** be of (no) importance; (**dat**) ~ **legen auf** (*acc*) stress, emphasize; (*dat*) ~ **beimessen** attach importance to; (*dat*) ~ **verleihen** lend weight to; → **spezifisch**. **ge'wichten** *v/t* (h) *statistics*: weigh; *fig.* (**neu**) ~ (re)assess.

Ge'wichtheben *n* (-s) weight lifting.

Ge'wichtheber *m* (-s; -) weight lifter.

gewichtig [gə'vɪçtɪç] *adj* a. *fig.* weighty.

Ge'wichts|klasse *f sports*: weight (class). ~**verlust** *m* loss of weight. ~**zunahme** *f* increase in weight.

gewiesen [gə'vi:zən] *pp* of **weisen**.

gewillt [gə'vɪlt] *adj* ~ **sein**, **et. zu tun** be willing (*or* ready) to do s.th.

Gewimmel [gə'vɪməl] *n* (-s; *no pl*) a) swarm(ing), swarming mass (*of insects etc*), b) milling crowd.

Gewinde [gə'vɪndə] *n* (-s; -) ⊕ thread.

Ge'windebohrer *m* (screw) tap.

Gewinn [gə'vɪn] *m* (-[e]s; -e) 1. ✝ profit, gain(s): **mit ~** at a profit; ~ **ziehen aus** profit by. 2. *fig.* a) profit, gain, advantage, b) asset (**für** for et.). 3. a) prize, b) winnings. 4. → **Gewinnlos**. ~**anteil** *m* share in (the) profits, dividend. ~**beteiligung** *f* profit sharing. ~**bringend** *adj* profitable. ~**chance** *f* chance of winning).

gewinnen [gə'vɪnən] (gewann, gewonnen, h) **I** *v/t* 1. win, *fig.* a. get, gain: **Höhe ~** ✈ gain height; **j-n für sich ~** win s.o. over; **j-n für et. ~** win s.o. to s.th.; → **Spiel** 2. 2. produce, ⚒ mine, win, recover (**aus** from *scrap etc*). **II** *v/i* 3. (**bei, in** *dat* at) win, be the winner,

number, ticket, etc: come up a winner. 4. gain: *fig.* **an Bedeutung ~** gain in importance; **sie hat sehr gewonnen** she has greatly improved.

ge'winnend *adj* a. *fig.* winning, engaging. **Ge'winner** *m* (-s; -), **Ge'winnerin** *f* (-; -nen) winner.

Ge'winn|los *n* winning ticket, winner. ~**maxi,mierung** *f* ✝ maximization of profits. ~**spanne** *f* profit margin. ~**sucht** *f* (-; *no pl*) (**aus ~** from) greed.

Ge'winn-und-Ver'lust-Rechnung *f* profit and loss account.

Ge'winnung *f* (-; *no pl*) winning, production.

Ge'winnzahl *f* winning number.

Gewinsel [gə'vɪnzəl] *n* (-s; *no pl*) *contp.* whining.

Gewirr [gə'vɪr] *n* (-[e]s; -e) tangle (a. *fig.*).

gewiß [gə'vɪs] **I** *adj* certain: **in gewissem Sinne** in a sense; **ich bin mir m-r Sache ~** I am sure of my ground; → **Etwas**. **II** *adv* certainly, for certain: ~**!** certainly!, sure!; **aber ~!** but of course!

Ge'wissen *n* (-s; -) conscience: **j-m ins ~ reden** reason with s.o.

ge'wissenhaft *adj* conscientious.

Ge'wissenhaftigkeit *f* (-; *no pl*) conscientiousness.

ge'wissenlos *adj* unscrupulous.

Ge'wissenlosigkeit *f* (-; *no pl*) unscrupulousness.

Ge'wissens|bisse *pl* twinges of remorse. ~**frage** *f* matter of conscience. ~**freiheit** *f* (-; *no pl*) freedom of conscience. ~**gründe** *pl* **aus ~n** for reasons of conscience. ~**kon,flikt** *m*, ~**not** *f* moral dilemma.

gewissermaßen [gə'vɪsər'ma:sən] *adv* in a way, so to speak.

Ge'wißheit *f* (-; *no pl*) certainty: **mit ~** for certain; **sich ~ verschaffen** make sure (**über** *acc* of); (**zur**) ~ **werden** become a certainty.

Gewitter [gə'vɪtər] *n* (-s; -) thunderstorm, *fig.* storm. **ge'wittern** *v/impers* (h) **es gewittert** there is a thunderstorm. **Ge'witterwolke** *f* thundercloud. **ge'wittrig** [-trɪç] *adj* thundery.

gewitzt [gə'vɪtst] *adj* F smart, clever.

gewogen [gə'vo:gən] **I** *pp* of **wiegen²**. **II** *adj fig.* **j-m ~ sein** be well disposed to (*or* toward[s]) s.o.

gewöhnen [gə'vø:nən] *v/t*, a. **sich ~** (h)

get used (**an** *acc* to); **man gewöhnt sich an alles** you get used to anything.

Gewohnheit [gə'vo:naɪt] *f* (-; -en) (**aus** ~ from) habit: **die ~ haben, et. zu tun** be in the habit of doing s.th.; **sich et. zur ~ machen** make a habit of s.th.

Ge'wohnheits... habitual (*drinker etc*). **ge'wohnheitsmäßig** *adj and adv* habitual(ly), *adv a.* out of habit. **Ge'wohnheitssache** *f* matter of habit. **Ge'wohnheitstäter** *m* F creature of habit.

gewöhnlich [gə'vø:nlɪç] **I** *adj* **1.** a) common, ordinary, b) usual. **2.** common, vulgar. **II** *adv* **3.** commonly (*etc*): (**für**) ~ usually, normally; **wie** ~ as usual.

gewohnt [gə'vo:nt] *adj* usual: **et.** (**zu tun**) ~ **sein** to be used to (doing) s.th.

Ge'wöhnung *f* (-; *no pl*) (**an** *acc* to) **1.** habituation. **2.** addiction.

Gewölbe [gə'vœlbə] *n* (-s; -) vault.

gewölbt [gə'vœlpt] *adj* **1.** △ arched, vaulted. **2.** domed.

gewollt [gə'vɔlt] *pp of* **wollen**².

gewonnen [gə'vɔnən] *pp of* **gewinnen**.

geworben [gə'vɔrbən] *pp of* **werben**.

geworden [gə'vɔrdən] *pp of* **werden**.

geworfen [gə'vɔrfən] *pp of* **werfen**.

gewrungen [gə'vrʊŋən] *pp of* **wringen**.

Gewühl [gə'vy:l] *n* (-[e]s; *no pl*) milling crowd.

gewunden [gə'vʊndən] **I** *pp of* **winden**. **II** *adj* winding, *a. fig.* tortuous.

Gewürz [gə'vʏrts] *n* (-es; -e) spice, condiment, seasoning.

Ge'würz|gurke *f* pickled gherkin. **~mischung** *f* mixed herbs (*or* spices). **~nelke** *f* clove. **~ständer** *m* spice rack.

gewußt [gə'vʊst] *pp of* **wissen**.

ge'zahnt, ge'zähnt *adj* toothed, serrated (*a.* ⚙), perforated (*stamp*).

Ge'zeiten *pl* tide(s).

Ge'zeiten... tidal (*power plant etc*). **~wechsel** *m* turn of the tide.

Ge'zeter *n* (-s; *no pl*) *contp.* nagging.

ge'zielt *adj fig.* specific (*measure etc*), calculated (*indiscretion etc*).

ge'ziert *adj* affected.

gezogen [gə'tso:gən] *pp of* **ziehen**.

Ge'zwitscher *n* (-s; *no pl*) chirping, twitter(ing).

gezwungen [gə'tsvʊŋən] **I** *pp of* **zwingen**. **II** *adj fig.* forced (*smile etc*), stiff, constrained (*manner etc*): **~ lachen** force a laugh.

ge'zwungenermaßen *adv* of necessity: **~ et. tun** be forced to do s.th.

Gicht [gɪçt] *f* (-; *no pl*) ⚕ gout. **'Gichtknoten** *m* gouty node. **'Gichtkranke** *m, f* (-n; -n) gout case, gouty person.

Giebel [gi:bəl] *m* (-s; -) gable. **'Giebelseite** *f*, **'Giebelwand** *f* gable end.

Gier [gi:r] *f* (-; *no pl*) greed(iness) (**nach** for). **'gierig** *adj* greedy (**nach** for).

gießen [gi:sən] (goß, gegossen, h) **I** *v/t* **1.** pour. **2.** water. **3.** ⚙ found, *art:* cast. **II** *v/i* **4.** pour: **es gießt** (**in Strömen**) it is pouring (with rain). **'Gießer** *m* (-s; -) ⚙ founder. **Gießerei** [gi:sə'raɪ] *f* (-; -en) ⚙ **1.** *no pl* casting. **2.** foundry.

'Gießkanne *f* watering can.

Gift [gɪft] *n* (-[e]s; -e) *a. fig.* poison, *zo.* venom: F **darauf kannst du ~ nehmen!** you bet your life on it. **'Giftgas** *n* poison gas. **'giftig** *adj* a) poisonous, *fig. a.* venomous, ⚕, toxic, b) poisoned. **'Giftmischer** *m* (-s; -), **'Giftmischerin** *f* (-; -nen) F poisoner. **'Giftmüll** *m* toxic waste. **'Giftpilz** *m* poisonous mushroom, toadstool. **'Giftschlange** *f* venomous (*or* poisonous) snake, *fig.* snake. **'Giftstoff** *m* poisonous (*or* toxic) substance. **'Giftzahn** *m* (poison) fang.

Gigant [gi'gant] *m* (-en; -en) *fig.* giant. **gi'gantisch** *adj* gigantic.

Gilde [gɪldə] *f* (-; -n) guild.

ging [gɪŋ] *pret of* **gehen**.

Ginster [gɪnstər] *m* (-s; -) ⚘ broom.

Gipfel [gɪpfəl] *m* (-s; -) summit (*a. fig. pol.*), top, peak: *fig.* **auf dem ~ der Macht** at the height (*or* peak) of power; F **das ist** (**doch**) **der ~!** that's the limit. **~konferenz** *f pol.* summit conference.

'gipfeln *v/i* (h) ~ **in** (*dat*) culminate in.

'Gipfeltreffen *n pol.* summit (meeting).

Gips [gɪps] *m* (-es; -e) ⚙ plaster, *art,* ⚕ plaster of Paris, ⚘ gypsum. **~abdruck** *m* plaster cast. **~bein** *n* F leg in plaster.

'gipsen *v/t* (h) (⚕ put in) plaster.

'Gipsverband *m* ⚕ plaster cast.

Giraffe [gi'rafə] *f* (-; -n) *zo.* giraffe.

girieren [ʒi'ri:rən] *v/t* (h) ✝ endorse.

Girlande [gɪr'landə] *f* (-; -n) garland.

Giro|bank ['ʒi:ro-] *f* (-; -en) ✝ clearing bank. **~konto** *n* current (*Am.* checking) account. **~zentrale** *f* clearing house.

Gis, gis [gɪs] *n* (-; -) ♪ G sharp.

Gischt [gɪʃt] *m* (-[e]s; *no pl*) (sea) spray.

Gitarre [gi'tarə] *f* (-; -n) guitar.

Gitarrist [gita'rɪst] *m* (-en; -en), **Gitar'ristin** *f* (-; -nen) guitarist.

Gitter ['gɪtər] *n* (-s; -) **1.** a) lattice, grille, b) bars, c) (wire) screen, d) grate: *hinter* **~n** behind bars. **2.** *opt.* grating. **3.** ⚡, *a. maps*: grid. **~bett** *n* cot, *Am.* crib. **~fenster** *n* lattice (*or* barred) window. **~mast** *m* ⚡ pylon. **~netz** *n* maps: grid.

Glacéhandschuhe [gla'se:-] *pl* (*fig. j-n mit ~n anfassen* handle s.o. with) kid gloves.

Gladiole [gla'dĭo:lə] *f* (-; -n) ♣ gladiolus.

Glanz [glants] *m* (-es; *no pl*) **1.** lust/re (*Am.* -er) (*a. fig.*), shine, gloss, glitter, brilliance (*a. fig.*). **2.** *fig.* glamo(u)r, splendo(u)r.

glänzen ['glɛntsən] *v/i* (h) shine (*a. fig.*), gleam, *fabric, nose, etc*: be shiny.

'glänzend *adj* **1.** lustrous, glossy, shining, shiny. **2.** *fig.* brilliant, splendid: *sich ~ amüsieren* have a great time.

'Glanzleistung *f* brilliant performance (*or* feat). **'glanzlos** *adj* dull. **'Glanznummer** *f* star turn. **'Glanzpa,pier** *n* glazed paper. **'Glanzpunkt** *m* highlight, high spot. **'Glanzstück** *n* pièce de résistance. **'glanzvoll** *adj* splendid, magnificent. **'Glanzzeit** *f* heyday.

Glas [gla:s] *n* (-es; ⁓er) **1.** *no pl* glass. **2.** a) glass, b) jar: *drei ~ Wein* three glasses of wine. **3.** *opt.* a) lens, glass, b) glasses.

'Glasbläser *m* glass blower.

Glaser ['gla:zər] *m* (-s; -) glazier.

Glase'rei *f* (-; -en) glazier's (work)shop.

gläsern ['glɛːzərn] *adj* **1.** (of) glass. **2.** *fig.* glassy.

'Glas|faser *f*, **~fiber** *f* glass fib/re (*Am.* -er). **~haus** *n wer im ~ sitzt, soll nicht mit Steinen werfen* people who live in glass houses should not throw stones. **~hütte** *f* ⚙ glassworks.

glasieren [gla'zi:rən] *v/t* (h) **1.** ⚙ glaze. **2.** *gastr.* ice, *Am.* frost.

glasig ['gla:zɪç] *adj* glassy (*a. fig.*), vitreous.

'Glas|kasten *m* glass case. ②*klar adj a. fig.* crystal-clear. **~körper** *m anat.* vitreous body. **~malerei** *f* glass painting. **~scheibe** *f* (glass) pane. **~scherben** *pl* (pieces of) broken glass. **~schneider** *m* glass cutter. **~schrank** *m* glass-fronted cupboard.

Glasur [gla'zu:r] *f* (-; -en) **1.** ⚙ glaze, enamel. **2.** *gastr.* icing, *Am.* frosting.

'Glaswaren *pl* glassware.

'glasweise *adv* by the glass.

'Glaswolle *f* glass wool.

glatt [glat] **I** *adj* **1.** a) smooth (*a. fig.*), b) even, c) polished: **~es Haar** straight hair. **2.** slippery. **3.** F *fig.* plain, clear: **~e Absage** flat refusal; **~e Lüge** downright (*or* outright) lie; *das ist ~er Wahnsinn* that's sheer madness. **II** *adv* **4.** a) smoothly (*etc*), b) clean: *~* (*anliegend*) ⊙ flush; *~ durchschneiden* cut clean through; *~ gestrickt* plainly knit; *fig. ~ gewinnen* win clearly, win hands down. **5.** F *fig.* **~ ablehnen** (*leugnen*) refuse (deny) flatly; *das bringt er ~ fertig* I wouldn't put it past him; *et. ~ vergessen* clean forget (about) s.th.

Glätte ['glɛtə] *f* (-; *no pl*) **a)** smoothness, b) slipperiness (*a. contp.*).

'Glatteis *n* a) (black, *Am.* glare) ice, b) icy ground, icy roads: *fig. j-n aufs ~ führen* trip s.o. up.

glätten ['glɛtən] (h) **I** *v/t* a) smooth, b) polish (*a. fig.*). **II** *sich ~* smooth down.

'glattgehen *v/i* (*irr, sep*, -ge-, sn, → *gehen*) go smoothly.

'glattra,siert *adj* clean-shaven.

'glattstellen *v/t* (*sep*, -ge-, h) ✝ square, even up.

'glattweg *adv* F → *glatt* 5.

Glatze ['glatsə] *f* (-; -n) bald head: *e-e ~ haben* (*bekommen*) be (go) bald.

'Glatzkopf *m* **1.** → *Glatze*. **2.** F bald-head, baldy. **glatzköpfig** ['glatskœpfɪç] *adj* bald(headed).

Glaube ['glaʊbə] *m* (-ns; *no pl*) (*an acc* in) belief, faith: *~n schenken* (*dat*) believe, give credence to; *in gutem ~n* in good faith; *den ~n verlieren* lose faith.

'glauben (h) **I** *v/t* believe, *a.* think, suppose: *das glaube ich dir nicht!* I don't believe you!; *es ist nicht zu ~!* it's incredible! **II** *v/i* believe (*an acc* in): *an j-n ~ a.* have faith in s.o., trust s.o.; *ich glaube, ja!* I think so!; F *er* (*es*) *hat dran ~ müssen* he (it) has had it; *er wird dran ~ müssen* he's for it.

'Glaubens|bekenntnis *n* creed (*a. fig.*), confession. **~freiheit** *f* (-; *no pl*) religious freedom. **~gemeinschaft** *f* denomination, church. **~genosse** *m* fellow believer. **~krieg** *m* religious war. **~lehre** *f*, **~satz** *m* dogma.

glaubhaft ['glaʊphaft] *adj* a) credible,

plausible, b) convincing: *et. ~ machen* a. ⚖ substantiate s.th.

'**gläubig** ['glɔʏbıç] *adj* believing, *eccl. a.* religious, devout. **Gläubige** ['glɔʏbıgə] *m, f* (-n; -n) believer: *die ~n* the faithful. **Gläubiger** ['glɔʏbıgər] *m* (-s; -) creditor.

'**glaublich** ['glaʊblıç] *adj das ist kaum ~* that's hard to believe.

'**glaubwürdig** ['glaʊbvʏrdıç] *adj* credible, reliable. '**Glaubwürdigkeit** *f* (-; *no pl*) credibility, reliability.

gleich [glaıç] **I** *adj* **1.** same, equal (*a.* ⅋), identical: *3 mal 3 ist ~ 9* three times three equals (*or* is) nine; *in ~er Höhe mit* level with; *auf ~e Weise* (in) the same way; *zur ~en Zeit* at the same time; *das ist mir ~!* it's all the same to me!, *contp.* I don't care!; *ganz ~, wann* (*wer etc*) no matter when (who *etc*); *das* ⅋e the same (thing). **II** *adv* **2.** equally, alike: *~ alt* (*groß*) of the same age (size); *~ schnell* just as fast; *~ aussehen* look alike; *alle ~ behandeln* treat everybody the same way. **3.** at once, right away, in a moment: *~ darauf* immediately afterwards; *~ nach ...* right after ...; *es ist ~ 11* (*Uhr*) it's almost eleven (o'clock); *ich komme ~!* (I'm) coming!, just a minute!; *ich bin ~ wieder da!* I'll be right back!; F *bis ~!* see you soon (*or* later)! **4.** immediately, directly; *~ neben ...* right next to ...; *~ gegenüber* just (*or* directly) opposite.

'**gleichaltrig** [-ʔaltrıç] *adj* (of) the same age. '**gleichartig** *adj* **1.** of the same kind, homogeneous. **2.** like, similar. '**gleichbedeutend** *adj* (*mit*) synonymous (with) (*a. ling.*), equivalent (to). '**Gleichbehandlung** *f* equal treatment. '**gleichberechtigt** *adj* having equal rights. '**Gleichberechtigung** *f* (-; *no pl*) equal rights, equality. '**gleichbleiben** *v/i* (*irr, sep,* -ge-, sn, → **bleiben**) (*a.* alike ~) stay the same (*or* unchanged): F *das bleibt sich gleich!* that makes no difference!

gleichen ['glaıçən] *v/i* (glich, geglichen, h) (*dat*) be (*or* look) like: *sich* (*or* einander) ~ be (*or* look) alike, be similar; *j-m ~ an* (*dat*) equal s.o. in.

'**gleicher**|'**maßen** *adv* **1.** equally. **2.** → ~'**weise** *adv* in like manner, likewise.

'**gleichfalls** *adv* also, likewise: *danke, ~!* (thanks,) the same to you!

'**gleichförmig** *adj* **1.** uniform, monotonous. **2.** regular. '**Gleichförmigkeit** *f* (-; *no pl*) **1.** uniformity, monotony. **2.** regularity. '**gleichgesinnt** *adj* like-minded. '**Gleichgewicht** *n* (-[e]s *no pl*) *a. fig.* balance, equilibrium: *das ~ verlieren* (*halten*) lose (keep) one's balance; *j-n aus dem ~ bringen* *a. fig.* throw s.o. off balance; *seelisches ~* (mental) equilibrium; *das ~ der Kräfte* *pol.* the balance of power.

'**gleichgültig** *adj* **1.** indifferent (*gegen* to): *er ist mir ~* I don't care for him. **2.** unimportant, trivial: *es ist mir ~* I don't care; *es ist ~, ob ...* it doesn't matter whether ...; *~, wann* no matter when. '**Gleichgültigkeit** *f* (-; *no pl*) **1.** indifference (*gegen* to). **2.** apathy. '**Gleichheit** *f* (-; *no pl*) **1.** equality, identity. **2.** uniformity. '**Gleichheitszeichen** *n* ⅋ equality sign. '**gleichkommen** *v/i* (*irr, sep,* -ge-, sn, → **kommen**) (*dat*) **1.** equal (*an dat* in). **2.** amount to.

'**gleichlautend** *adj* identical: *~es Wort* homonym.

gleichmachen *v/t* (*sep,* -ge-, h) make equal (*dat* to): → **Erdboden. Gleichmache'rei** *f* (-; *no pl*) egalitarianism. '**gleichmäßig** *adj* a) regular, even, b) constant: *et. ~ verteilen* distribute s.th. evenly. '**Gleichmäßigkeit** *f* (-; *no pl*) a) regularity, evenness, b) constancy. '**Gleichmut** *m* (-[e]s; *no pl*) equanimity, calmness. '**gleichmütig** ['glaıçmy:tıç] *adj* calm, imperturbable.

gleichnamig ['glaıçna:mıç] *adj* **1.** of the same name. **2.** ⅋ with a common denominator.

'**Gleichnis** *n* (-ses; -se) parable.

gleichrangig ['glaıçraŋıç] *adj* **1.** of the same rank. **2.** *fig.* of equal importance. '**Gleichrichter** *m* (-s; -) ⚡ rectifier. '**gleichschalten** *v/t* (*sep,* -ge-, h) *fig.* coordinate, *pol.* bring into line. '**gleichseitig** *adj* equilateral. '**gleichsetzen** *v/t* (*sep,* -ge-, h) **1.** equate (*dat, mit* with). **2.** → **gleichstellen** 2. '**Gleichstand** *m* (-[e]s; *no pl*) level score. '**gleichstellen** *v/t* (*sep,* -ge-, h) **1.** → **gleichsetzen** 1. **2.** *j-n ~* put s.o. on an equal footing (*dat* with). '**Gleichstellung** *f* (-; *no pl*) equalization.

'**Gleichstrom** m ⚡ direct current (DC).

'**gleichtun** v/t (irr, sep, -ge-, h, → **tun**) **es j-m ~** equal s.o. (**an** or **in** dat in).

'**Gleichung** f (-; -en) equation.

'**gleichwertig** adj **1.** of the same value, equivalent. **2.** equally good: **~e Gegner** evenly matched opponents.

'**gleichzeitig** adj and adv simultaneous(ly), adv a. at the same time.

'**gleichziehen** v/i (irr, sep, -ge-, h, → **ziehen**) a) a. fig. (**mit** with) catch up, draw level, b) equalize, level the score.

Gleis [glaɪs] n (-es; -e) rail(s), track(s), line: fig. **auf ein totes ~ schieben** put s.o., s.th. on ice; **das ausgefahrene ~** a) the beaten track, b) a. **das alte ~** the same old rut.

'**Gleiskörper** m permanent way.

'**Gleitboot** n hydroglider, hydroplane.

gleiten ['glaɪtən] v/i (glitt, geglitten, sn) **1.** glide, slide, slip, hand etc: pass. **2.** fig. employee: make use of flex(i)time.

'**gleitend** adj fig. sliding (scale): **~e Arbeitszeit** → **Gleitzeit**.

'**Gleit|fläche** f sliding surface. **~flug** m glide. **~flugzeug** n glider. **~klausel** f ✝ escalator clause. **~komma** n floating point. **~mittel** n lubricant. **~schirm** m paraglider. **~schutz** m mot. antiskid device. **~sichtgläser** pl multifocal lenses. **~wachs** n skiing: gliding wax.

'**Gleitzeit** f (-; no pl) flexible working hours, flex(i)time. **~karte** f time card.

'**Gletscher** ['glɛtʃər] m (-s; -) glacier.

'**Gletscherbrand** m glacial sunburn.

'**Gletscherspalte** f crevasse.

glich [glɪç] pret of **gleichen**.

Glied [gli:t] n (-[e]s; -er) **1.** limb, member (a. fig.): **der Schreck fuhr ihr in die ~er** she had a bad shock. **2.** penis, (male) member. **3.** a. fig. link. **4.** ✕ rank.

gliedern ['gli:dərn] (h) **I** v/t a) arrange, organize, b) (sub)divide (**in** acc into). **II sich ~ in** (acc) be (sub)divided into.

'**Glieder|puppe** f jointed doll, art: lay figure. **~schmerz** m rheumatism.

Gliederung ['gli:dərʊŋ] f (-; -en) a) arrangement, organization, structure, b) (sub)division.

'**Gliedmaßen** pl limbs.

'**Glimmer** m (-s; -) min. mica.

'**Glimmstengel** m F fag.

glimpflich ['glɪmpflɪç] adj mild, light: **~ mit j-m verfahren** be lenient with s.o.;

~ davonkommen get off lightly.

glitschig ['glɪtʃɪç] adj F slippery.

glitt [glɪt] pret of **gleiten**.

glitzern ['glɪtsərn] v/i (h) glitter.

global [glo'ba:l] adj global.

Globus ['glo:bʊs] m (-[ses]; -ben) globe.

'**Glöckchen** ['glœkçən] n (-s; -) little bell.

Glocke ['glɔkə] f (-; -n) **1.** bell: **F et. an die große ~ hängen** shout s.th. from the housetops. **2.** (cheese etc) cover.

'**Glocken|blume** f bellflower. **~geläut** n bell ringing. **~gießer** m bell founder. **~rock** m flared skirt. **~schlag** m stroke (of the clock). **~spiel** n chime(s), carillon. **~stuhl** m, **~turm** m belfry.

Glorie ['glo:riə] f (-; -n) **1.** glory. **2.** → '**Glorienschein** m fig. halo.

glorreich ['glo:raɪç] adj glorious.

Glossar [glɔ'sa:r] n (-s; -e) glossary.

Glosse ['glɔsə] f (-; -n) **1.** gloss. **2.** commentary. **3.** pl snide remarks: **s-e ~n machen über** (acc) remark on, jeer at.

'**Glotzaugen** pl F goggle-eyes.

Glotze ['glɔtsə] f (-; -n) F gogglebox, Am. tube. '**glotzen** v/i (h) F goggle, gawp.

Glück n **1.** fortune, (good) luck: **auf gut ~** a) on the off-chance, b) at random; **zum ~** fortunately; **zu m-m ~** luckily for me; **~ haben** be lucky; **er hatte kein ~** he had no luck; **das ~ haben zu** inf have the good fortune to inf; **~ gehabt!** that was lucky!; **nochmal ~ gehabt!** that was close!; **viel ~!** good luck!; **j-m ~ wünschen** a) wish s.o. luck, b) congratulate s.o. (**zu et.** on s.th.), **zum Geburtstag** wish s.o. (on s.th.) a happy birthday; **(es ist) ein ~, daß ...** (it's a) good thing that ...; **er kann von ~ sagen, daß ...** he may thank his lucky stars that ... **2.** happiness, bliss.

'**glückbringend** adj lucky.

Glucke ['glʊkə] f (-; -n) **1.** zo. sitting hen. **2.** fig. (mother-)hen.

'**glucken** v/i (h) a) sit, b) cluck.

'**glücken** v/i, v/impers (sn) → **gelingen** I.

'**gluckern** ['glʊkərn] v/i (h) glug, gurgle.

'**glücklich I** adj a) happy, b) lucky, fortunate: **sich ~ preisen** (or **schätzen**) count o.s. lucky; **ein ~er Einfall** a happy thought. **II** adv a) happily, b) luckily, c) safely, d) F finally, at (long) last.

'**glücklicherweise** adv luckily, fortunately, as luck would have it.

'**Glücksache** f es ist ~ it is a matter of luck.

'**Glücksbringer** m mascot, lucky charm.

glück'selig adj blissful, very happy.

Glück'seligkeit f (-; no pl) bliss.

glucksen ['glʊksən] v/i (h) 1. gurgle. 2. chuckle.

'**Glücks|fall** m lucky chance (F break), stroke of luck. **~göttin** f Fortune. **~kind** n child of Fortune. **~klee** m four-leaf clover. **~pfennig** m lucky penny. **~pilz** m F fig. lucky dog. **~ritter** m soldier of fortune. **~spiel** n 1. game of chance, coll. gambling. 2. fig. gamble. **~spieler(in** f) m gambler. **~stern** m lucky star. **~strähne** f streak of luck. **~tag** m lucky (or happy) day.

'**glückstrahlend** adj radiant (with happiness).

'**Glückstreffer** m 1. sports: fluke (hit or shot). 2. fig. stroke of luck.

'**Glückwunsch** m congratulations (**zu** on), good wishes (**für** for): **m-n** (or **herzlichen**) ~! congratulations!, **zum Geburtstag** happy birthday!

'**Glückwunsch|karte** f greetings card. **~tele|gramm** n greetings telegram.

'**Glühbirne** f (incandescent) bulb.

glühen ['gly:ən] (h) **I** v/i (**vor** dat with) glow, fig. a. burn. **II** v/t ⊕ anneal.

'**glühend** adj 1. glowing (a. fig.), red-hot (metal), live (coals): ~ **heiß** scorching. 2. fig. burning, ardent.

'**Glühkerze** f mot. heater plug.

'**Glühlampe** f incandescent lamp.

'**Glühwein** m mulled claret.

'**Glühwürmchen** n (-s; -) glow-worm.

Glut [glu:t] f (-; -en) 1. (blazing) heat. 2. (glowing) fire. 3. a) embers, pl live coals. 4. fig. ardo(u)r, glow.

Glutaminsäure [gluta'mi:n-] f glutamic acid.

Glyzerin [glytse'ri:n] n (-s; no pl) glycerin(e).

Gnade ['gna:də] f (-; no pl) 1. mercy: **j-m auf ~ und Ungnade ausgeliefert sein** be at s.o.'s mercy; **~ vor Recht ergehen lassen** show mercy. 2. favo(u)r. 3. eccl. grace. '**gnaden** v/i dann gnade dir Gott! (then) God help you!

'**Gnaden|akt** m ☠ act of grace. **~frist** f reprieve: **e-e ~ von drei Tagen** three days' grace. **~gesuch** n ☠ petition for mercy.

'**gnadenlos** adj merciless.

'**Gnadenstoß** m coup de grâce.

gnädig ['gnɛ:dɪç] adj a) gracious, b) merciful: **~e Frau** madam.

Gnom [gno:m] m (-en; -en) gnome.

Gobelin [gobə'lɛ̃:] m (-s; -s) Gobelin (tapestry).

Gold [gɔlt] n (-[e]s; no pl) gold: **~ waschen** pan for gold; **~ gewinnen** sports: win gold; **treu wie ~** good as gold; **das ist nicht mit ~ aufzuwiegen** that is priceless; **es ist nicht alles ~, was glänzt** all that glitters is not gold.

'**Goldader** f vein of gold.

'**Goldbarren** m ingot of gold.

golden ['gɔldən] adj 1. a) (of) gold, b) gilt. 2. fig. golden (wedding, disc, etc).

'**Gold|fisch** m goldfish. **⅋gelb** adj golden(-yellow). **~gräber** [-grɛbər] m gold digger. **~grube** f F fig. goldmine. **~hamster** m zo. golden hamster.

goldig ['gɔldɪç] adj F sweet, Am. a. cute.

'**Gold|krone** f ✚ gold cap. **~me,daille** f gold medal. **~me,daillengewinner(in** f) m gold medal(l)ist. **~mine** f ⚒ goldmine. **~münze** f gold coin. **~plombe** f gold filling. **~rahmen** m gilt frame. ⅋'**richtig** adj and adv F dead right: **er ist ~** he is okay. **~schmied** m goldsmith. **~schnitt** m gilt edge(s): **Buch mit ~** gilt-edged book. **~stück** n 1. gold coin. 2. F fig. jewel. **~waage** f jedes Wort auf die ~ legen weigh every word. **~währung** f gold standard. **~waren** pl gold articles.

Golf¹ [gɔlf] m (-[e]s; -e) geogr. gulf.

Golf² n (-s; no pl) sports: golf.

'**Golfplatz** m golf course, (golf) links.

'**Golfschläger** m golf club.

'**Golfspiel** n 1. golf. 2. game of golf.

'**Golfspieler(in** f) m golfer.

'**Golfstrom** m geogr. Gulf Stream.

Gondel ['gɔndəl] f (-; -n) gondola.

Gong [gɔŋ] m (-s; -e) gong.

gönnen ['gœnən] v/t (h) 1. **j-m et. ~** not to (be)grudge s.o. s.th.; **j-m et. nicht ~** → **mißgönnen**. 2. **j-m (sich) et. ~** allow s.o. (o.s.) s.th.

'**Gönner** m (-s; -) patron.

'**gönnerhaft** adj patronizing.

'**Gönnerin** f (-; -nen) patroness.

Gonokokken [gono'kɔkən] pl ✚ gonococci.

gor [go:r] pret of **gären.**

Gör [gøːr] n (-[e]s; -en) F contp. brat.

Gorilla [goˈrɪla] m (-s; -s) gorilla (a. sl. bodyguard).

goß [gɔs] pret of **gießen**.

Gosse [ˈgɔsə] f (-; -n) a. fig. gutter.

Gotik [ˈgoːtɪk] f a) Gothic (style), b) Gothic period. **'gotisch** adj Gothic.

Gott [gɔt] m (-es; ꙮer) a) no pl God, b) god, deity: **der liebe ꙮ** the good Lord; **ꙮ sei Dank!** thank God!; **leider ꙮes** unfortunately; **ꙮ bewahre!**, **ꙮ behüte!** God forbid!; **weiß ꙮ(, was** etc) God knows (what etc); **um ꙮes Willen!** for God's sake!; **großer ꙮ!**, **lieber ꙮ!** good Lord!; → **gnaden, wahr**.

'gottähnlich adj godlike.

'gottbegnadet adj god-gifted, inspired.

Götterbild [ˈgœtər-] n idol.

'Götterspeise f gastr. jelly.

Gottesdienst [ˈgɔtəs-] m (divine) service.

'gottesfürchtig [-fʏrçtɪç] adj godfearing.

'Gottes|haus n house of God, church. **ꙮlästerer** m (-s; -) blasphemer. **ꙮlästerung** f (-; -en) blasphemy. **ꙮmutter** f (-; no pl) Mother of God. **ꙮsohn** m (-[e]s; no pl) Son of God.

Gottheit f (-; -en) deity, God, goddess.

Göttin [ˈgœtɪn] f (-; -nen) goddess.

'göttlich adj divine, godlike.

'gottlos adj godless, ungodly, wicked.

'gottser'bärmlich adj F awful.

'gottverdammt adj V (god)damned.

'gottverlassen adj F godforsaken.

'Gottvertrauen n trust in God.

'gottvoll adj F fig. capital, very funny.

Götze [ˈgœtsə] m (-n; -n) idol.

Gouverneur [guvɛrˈnøːr] m (-s; -e) governor.

Grab [graːp] n (-[e]s; ꙮer) grave, tomb: **mit einem Bein im ꙮe stehen** have one foot in the grave; **sich im ꙮe umdrehen** turn in one's grave; **verschwiegen wie das ꙮ** (as) silent as the grave.

graben [ˈgraːbən] (grub, gegraben, h) I v/t dig, burrow (hole etc), sink (shaft etc). II v/i dig (nach for). III sich ꙮ (in acc into) dig, zo. burrow itself, fig. bury itself; **sich in j-s Gedächtnis ꙮ** engrave itself on s.o.'s memory.

'Graben m (-s; ꙮ) ditch, ✕ trench, hist. moat, geol. graben, rift.

Grabesstille [ˈgraːbəs-] f deathly silence. **'Grabesstimme** f (mit ꙮ in a) sepulchral voice.

'Grab|fund m grave find. **ꙮgewölbe** n (burial) vault, tomb. **ꙮinschrift** f epitaph. **ꙮkammer** f burial chamber. **ꙮmal** n (-[e]s; ꙮer) a) tomb, b) monument. **ꙮrede** f funeral oration. **ꙮstätte** f burial place, tomb. **ꙮstein** m tombstone, gravestone.

Grad [graːt] m (-[e]s; -e) degree (a. univ. or fig.), ✕ etc rank, grade: **10 ꙮ Wärme (Kälte)** ten degrees above (below) zero (or freezing point); **Verbrennungen dritten ꙮes** third-degree burns; **Verwandte(r) zweiten (dritten) ꙮes** relative once (twice) removed; **bis zu e-m gewissen ꙮ** to a certain degree, up to a point; **im höchsten ꙮe** in the highest degree, extremely.

'Gradeinteilung f graduation.

gradieren [graˈdiːrən] v/t (h) graduate.

'Gradmesser m fig. ga(u)ge, barometer.

'Gradnetz n (map) grid.

graduell [graˈdŭɛl] adj gradual.

graduieren [graduˈiːrən] (h) I v/t **1.** ꙮ graduate. **2.** univ. confer a degree upon. II v/i **3.** univ. graduate.

Gradu'ierte, m, f (-n; -n) graduate.

Graf [graːf] m (-en; -en) count, Br. earl.

Graffito [graˈfiːto] m, n (-[s]; -ti) graffito.

Gräfin [ˈgrɛːfɪn] f (-; -nen) countess.

'Grafschaft f (-; -en) county.

gram [graːm] adj **j-m ꙮ sein** bear s.o. a grudge (**wegen** gen because of s.th.).

Gram m (-[e]s; no pl) grief, sorrow.

grämen [ˈgrɛːmən] (h) I v/t grieve. II **sich ꙮ** (**über** acc, **wegen**) a) grieve (over), b) worry (about).

Gramm [gram] n (-s; -e) gram, Br. a. gramme: **100 ꙮ** 100 grams.

Grammatik [graˈmatɪk] f (-; -en) **1.** no pl grammar. **2.** grammar book. **grammatikalisch** [gramatiˈkaːlɪʃ], **grammatisch** [graˈmatɪʃ] adj grammatical.

Grammophon [gramoˈfoːn] n (-s; -e) TM gramophone, Am. phonograph.

Granat [graˈnaːt] m (-[e]s; -e) min. garnet. **Gra'natapfel** m ⚘ pomegranate.

Granate [graˈnaːtə] f (-; -n) **1.** ✕ a) shell, b) grenade. **2.** F sports: cannonball.

Gra'nat|feuer n shellfire. **ꙮsplitter** m shell splinter. **ꙮwerfer** m mortar.

grandios [granˈdiːos] adj grandiose, F terrific.

Granit [graˈniːt] m (-s; -e) granite.

Granne ['granə] f (-; -n) **1.** ✒ beard, awn. **2.** zo. beak.

Graphik ['gra:fɪk] f (-; -en) **1.** no pl a) graphic arts, b) art(work). **2.** a) graphic (a. computer), print, b) ⊚ graph, diagram, c) illustration(s). **~dia,gramm** n computer: graphic drawing.

Graphiker ['gra:fikər] m (-s; -), **'Graphikerin** f (-; -nen) **1.** (graphic) artist. **2.** commercial artist, (graphic) designer.

'graphisch adj **1.** graphic, art ... **2.** ⊚ graphic, diagrammatic: **~e Darstellung → Graphik 2.**

Graphit [gra'fi:t] m (-s; -e) graphite.

Graphologe [grafo'lo:gə] m (-n; -n), graphologist. **Graphologie** [grafolo'gi:] f (-; no pl) graphology. **graphologisch** [grafo'lo:gɪʃ] adj graphological.

Gras [gra:s] n (-es; ⸚er ['grɛ:zər]) grass: F **ins ~ beißen** bite the dust; **das ~ wachsen hören** hear the grass grow; **über et. ~ wachsen lassen** let the grass grow over s.th. **'grasbedeckt** adj grassy.

'grasen ['gra:zən] v/i (h) graze.

'grasfressend adj zo. graminivorous. **'grasgrün** adj grass-green. **'Grashalm** m blade of grass. **'Grashüpfer** m zo. grasshopper. **'Grasnarbe** f turf.

grassieren [gra'si:rən] v/i (h) be rife, disease: a. rage: **es ~ Gerüchte, daß ...** there are rumo(u)rs that ...

gräßlich ['grɛslɪç] adj horrible, ghastly, dreadful, monstrous, atrocious.

Grat [gra:t] m (-[e]s; -e) **1.** ⊚ bur(r). **2.** ridge.

Gräte ['grɛ:tə] f (-; -n) (fish)bone.

Gratifikation [gratifika'tsɪo:n] f (-; -en) gratuity, bonus.

gratis ['gra:tɪs] adv free (of charge).

'Gratisaktie f bonus share, pl scrip issues. **'Gratisprobe** f free sample.

Grätsche ['grɛ:tʃə] f (-; -n) gym. a) straddle, b) straddle vault.

'grätschen v/t, v/i (h) gym. straddle.

Gratulant [gratu'lant] m (-en; -en) congratulator, well-wisher. **Gratulation** [gratula'tsɪo:n] f (-; -en) congratulations (**zu** on). **gratulieren** [gratu'li:rən] v/i (h) congratulate (**j-m zu et.** s.o. on s.th.): **j-m zum Geburtstag ~** wish s.o. many happy returns (of the day); (**ich**) **gratuliere!** congratulations!

'Gratwanderung f fig. tightrope walk.

grau [graʊ] adj grey, Am. gray, fig. a.

bleak: **der ~e Alltag** the drab monotony of everyday life; → **Haar, Vorzeit.**

'Graubrot n rye bread.

grauen ['graʊən] v/i, v/impers (h) **mir graut** (or **es graut mir**) **vor** (dat) I dread the thought of, I am terrified of. **'Grauen** n (-s; -) horror (**vor** dat of).

'grauenhaft, 'grauenvoll adj horrible.

'grauhaarig adj grey-(Am. gray-)haired.

graulen ['graʊlən] (h) F **I sich ~** be afraid (**vor** dat of). **II** v/t **j-n aus dem Haus ~** freeze s.o. out.

gräulich ['grɔʏlɪç] adj greyish, Am. grayish.

'graume,liert adj greying, Am. graying.

Graupe ['graʊpə] f (-; -n) pearl barley.

Graupel ['graʊpəl] f (-; -n) soft hail.

'graupeln v/impers (h) **es graupelt** a soft hail is falling.

'grausam adj **1.** cruel. **2.** F fig. awful. **'Grausamkeit** f (-; -en) cruelty.

grausen ['graʊzən] → **grauen.**

'Grausen n (-s; no pl) horror.

grausig ['graʊzɪç] → **grauenhaft.**

'Grauzone f fig. grey (Am. gray) area.

Graveur [gra'vø:r] m (-s; -e) engraver.

gravieren [gra'vi:rən] v/t (h) engrave.

gra'vierend adj fig. serious.

Gra'vierung f (-; -en) engraving.

Gravitation [gravita'tsɪo:n] f (-; no pl) phys. gravitation. **gravitieren** [gravi'ti:rən] v/i (h) a. fig. (**zu, auf** acc towards) gravitate, tend.

Grazie ['gra:tsɪə] f (-; no pl) grace.

graziös [gra'tsɪø:s] adj graceful.

'greifbar adj **1.** handy, available: **in ~er Nähe, ~ nahe** a. fig. within reach, near at hand. **2.** fig. tangible, concrete: **~e Formen annehmen** be taking shape.

greifen ['graɪfən] (griff, gegriffen, h) **I** v/t **1.** seize, take hold of, grab: **zum ⸚ nah** within reach; fig. **zu hoch gegriffen** figure etc: too high. **2.** ♩ stop (string), strike (note etc). **II** v/i **1.** nach (acc) touch; **~ nach** reach for, grasp at, grab for; **~ in** (acc) reach into; **~ zu** reach for, fig. resort to; fig. **um sich ~** spread; → **Arm, Tasche 2. 4.** ⊚ grip, grab. **5.** fig. be effective, F bite.

'Greifer m (-s; -) ⊚ grab, gripper.

'Greifvogel m bird of prey.

'Greifzange f gripping tongs.

'Greifzirkel m cal(l)ipers.

greis [graɪs] adj (very) old. **Greis** m (-es;

-e) (very) old man. '**Greisenalter** n old age. '**greisenhaft** adj senile. '**Greisenhaftigkeit** f (-; no pl) senility. **Greisin** ['graɪzɪn] f (-; -nen) (very) old woman.

grell [grɛl] adj glaring (a. fig.), a. loud (colo[u]r), shrill, strident (sound).

Gremium ['greːmiʊm] n (-s; -mien) body (of experts etc), group.

Grenzbereich m 1. border area. 2. fig. borderland. '**Grenzbewohner(in** f) m inhabitant of the border area.

Grenze ['grɛntsə] f (-; -n) 1. border, frontier, boundary (a. fig.): **an der ~** on the border, at the frontier; fig. **die ~ ziehen bei** draw the line at. 2. fig. a) borderline, b) limit (gen to), bounds (gen of): **in ~n** within limits, up to a point; **ohne ~ → grenzenlos; sich in ~n halten** keep within (reasonable) limits, iro. success etc: be rather limited; **~n setzen** set limits (dat to); **alles hat s-e ~n** there is a limit to everything.

'**grenzen** v/i (h) border (**an** acc on).

'**grenzenlos** adj boundless, immense, infinite (misery, patience, etc), unlimited (power): **~ dumm** incredibly stupid.

'**Grenzfall** m fig. borderline case.

Grenzgänger ['grɛntsgɛŋər] m (-s; -) frontier commuter.

'**Grenz|gebiet** n 1. border area. 2. fig. borderland. **~kon,flikt** m border dispute. **~kon,trolle** f border control. **~kosten** pl ✝ marginal cost. **~linie** f boundary (line), borderline (a. fig.), pol. demarcation line, sports: line. **~pfahl** m boundary post. **~posten** m border guard. **~schutz** m 1. frontier protection. 2. border police. **~stadt** f frontier town. **~stein** m boundary stone. **~übergang** m checkpoint, border crossing(-point). 2**überschreitend** adj border-crossing, across the border(s). **~verkehr** m (**kleiner ~** local) border traffic. **~wert** m limit(ing value), threshold value. **~zwischenfall** m border incident.

Greuel ['grɔʏəl] m (-s; -) 1. horror: **er (es) ist mir ein ~** I loathe him (it). 2. atrocity. '**Greuelmärchen** n atrocity story. '**Greueltat** f atrocity.

greulich ['grɔʏlɪç] → **gräßlich**.

Grieben ['griːbən] pl gastr. greaves.

Grieche ['griːçə] m (-n; -n) Greek.

'**Griechenland** n (-s) Greece.

'**Griechin** f (-; -nen) Greek (woman).

'**griechisch** adj Greek, art: a. Grecian: **~-römisch** Gr(a)eco-Roman; **~-orthodox** Greek (Orthodox).

'**Griechisch** n (-[s]) ling. Greek.

griesgrämig ['griːsgrɛːmɪç] adj F sullen, grumpy, grouchy.

Grieß [griːs] m (-es; -e) 1. gastr. semolina. 2. ⊙ grit. 3. ⊛ gravel. '**Grießbrei** m semolina pudding.

griff [grɪf] pret of **greifen**.

Griff m (-[e]s; -e) 1. no pl (nach) grasp (at), grab (for), reaching (for): **~ nach der Macht** bid for power; **e-n guten ~ tun** make a good choice (mit with); **im ~ haben (in den ~ bekommen)** have (get) s.th. under control, have (get) a (good) grip on; **mit sicherem ~** right away, fig. with a sure touch. 2. grip (a. gym.), wrestling etc: hold, ♪ stop. 3. a) handle, b) grip, c) in bus etc: strap. 4. textil. feel.

'**griffbereit** adj (ready) to hand, handy.

'**Griffbrett** n ♪ fingerboard.

Griffel ['grɪfəl] m (-s; -) style.

griffig ['grɪfɪç] adj 1. handy. 2. road: having a good grip, handling (wheels).

Grill [grɪl] m (-s; -s) gastr. grill.

Grille ['grɪlə] f (-; -n) 1. zo. cricket. 2. F fig. silly idea, whim.

grillen ['grɪlən] v/t (h) grill, barbecue.

'**Grillparty** f barbecue.

Grimasse [grɪ'masə] f (-; -n) grimace: **~n schneiden** pull faces, grimace.

grimmig ['grɪmɪç] adj a. fig. grim, fierce.

Grind [grɪnt] m (-[e]s; -e) ✱ scab.

grinsen ['grɪnzən] v/i (h), **Grinsen** n (-s) (**über** acc at) a) grin, b) sneer.

grippal [grɪ'paːl] adj **~er Infekt** influenza(l) infection. **Grippe** ['grɪpə] f (-; -n) influenza, F 'flu. '**Grippe...** influenza (epidemic, virus, etc). '**grippekrank** adj down with influenza, F having the 'flu. '**Grippewelle** f wave of influenza.

grob [groːp] adj 1. coarse (a. ⊙), rough (a. fig. sketch, work, etc): **~ behauen** rough-hewn; **in ~en Zügen** roughly; **wir sind aus dem Gröbsten heraus** we are over the worst; **→ schätzen** 1. 2. fig. gross (lie, mistake, etc). 3. fig. rude, coarse: **~ werden gegen** be rude to.

'**grobgemahlen** adj coarse-ground.

'**Grobheit** f (-; -en) 1. no pl coarseness, roughness, fig. a. rudeness. 2. pl rude words: **j-m ~en an den Kopf werfen** be rude to s.o., insult s.o.

Grobian ['gro:bĭa:n] *m* (-s; -e) rude fellow.

'**grobkörnig** *adj* coarse-grained.

'**grobmaschig** *adj* wide-meshed.

'**Grobschnitt** *m* (*tobacco*) coarse cut.

grölen ['grø:lən] *v/i, v/t* (h) bawl, roar.

Groll [grɔl] *m* (-[e]s; *no pl*) ranco(u)r, resentment, anger. '**grollen** *v/i* (h) **1.** be angry: **j-m ~** have a grudge against s.o. (**wegen** because of). **2.** *fig.* rumble.

Gros [gro:] *n* (- [gro:(s)]; - [gro:s]) main body.

Groschen ['grɔʃən] *m* (-s; -) ten-pfennig piece, *fig.* penny, *Am.* cent: F **der ~ ist gefallen!** the penny has dropped!

'**Groschenro,man** *m* F penny dreadful, *Am.* dime novel.

groß [gro:s] **I** *adj* **1.** big, large, *a.* capital (*letter*): **wie ~ ist es?** what size is it? **2.** tall, high: **wie ~ sind Sie?** what is your height?; **sie sind gleich ~** they are of equal height. **3.** great (*distance*), long (*trip etc*). **4.** a) elder, F big (*brother, sister*), big (*event*): **die Großen** the grown-ups. **5.** *fig.* great, big, bad (*mistake etc*), severe (*loss etc*): **Friedrich der Große** Frederick the Great; **e-e größere Sache** a major affair; **~e Worte** big words; **Großes leisten** achieve great things; → **Ferien, Geld, Los** 1, **Rede** 1, **Welt.** **6.** great, grand: F **ganz ~** super, terrific; **in et. ~ sein** be great at (doing) s.th.; **er ist kein ~er Tänzer** he's no great dancer. **7.** **im ~en** on a large scale, ✝ wholesale, in bulk; **im ~en (und) ganzen** on the whole, by and large. **II** *adv* **8.** **~ schreiben** capitalize; F **et. ~ feiern** celebrate s.th. in great style; **~ in Mode sein** be all the rage; **~ ankommen** be a big success (**bei** with); **er kümmert sich nicht ~ darum** he doesn't bother much about it; → **herausbringen, herauskommen** 1.

'**Großabnehmer** *m* ✝ bulk purchaser.

'**Großaktio,när** *m* major shareholder.

'**großangelegt** *adj* large-scale.

'**Großangriff** *m* ✗ large-scale attack.

'**großartig** *adj* grand, great, marvel-(l)ous, fantastic.

'**Großaufnahme** *f* *film*: close-up.

'**Großauftrag** *m* ✝ large (*or* big) order.

'**Großbank** *f* (-; -en) big (*or* major) bank.

'**Großbetrieb** *m* large-scale enterprise.

'**Großbuchstabe** *m* capital (letter).

Größe ['grø:sə] *f* (-; -n) **1.** a) size, b) height, c) dimensions, area: **welche ~ haben Sie?** what size do you take? **2.** ⚛, *phys.* quantity, *astr.* magnitude. **3.** *no pl fig.* a) extent, b) greatness. **4.** F *fig.* great figure, celebrity, *film, sports, etc*: star: **e-e ~ auf dem Gebiet** (*gen*) an authority on.

'**Großeinkauf** *m* ✝ bulk purchase.

'**Großeinsatz** *m* large-scale operation.

'**Großeltern** *pl* grandparents.

'**Großenkel** *m etc* → **Urenkel** *etc.*

'**Größenordnung** *f* **1.** *astr. etc* order (of magnitude). **2.** *fig.* scale: **dieser ~ of** this order.

'**großenteils** *adv* mostly, largely.

'**Größenverhältnisse** *pl* proportions.

'**Größenwahn** *m* megalomania.

'**größenwahnsinnig** *adj* megalomaniac.

'**Großfahndung** *f* dragnet operation.

'**Großfa,milie** *f* extended family.

'**Großfeuer** *n* big blaze, four-alarm fire.

'**Großflughafen** *m* major airport.

'**Großfor,mat** *n* large size.

'**Großgrundbesitz** *m* large land holdings, large estates. '**Großgrundbesitzer(in** *f*) *m* big landowner.

'**Großhandel** *m* ✝ wholesale trade: **im ~** wholesale. '**Großhandels...** wholesale.

'**Großhändler(in** *f*) *m* wholesaler.

'**Großhandlung** *f* wholesale firm.

'**Großherzog(in** *f*) *m* grand duke (duchess).

'**Großhirn** *n* *anat.* cerebrum.

'**Großindu,strie** *f* big industry.

'**Großindustri,elle** *m* big industrialist.

Grossist [grɔ'sɪst] *m* (-en; -en) wholesaler.

'**großjährig** → **volljährig.**

'**Großkapi,tal** *n* big business.

'**Großkaufmann** *m* big merchant.

'**Großkon,zern** *m* big concern.

großkotzig ['gro:skɔtsɪç] *adj* F a) flash, b) show-off(ish), arrogant.

'**Großkraftwerk** *n* super power station.

'**Großküche** *f* canteen kitchen.

'**Großkundgebung** *f* mass rally.

'**Großmacht** *f* super power.

'**Großmama** *f* F grandma.

'**Großmaul** *n* F bigmouth.

'**Großmut** *f* (-; *no pl*) magnanimity, generosity. **großmütig** ['gro:smy:tɪç] *adj* magnanimous, generous.

'Großmutter f grandmother.

'Großneffe m grandnephew.

'Großnichte f grandniece.

'Großonkel m great-uncle.

'Großpapa m F grandpa.

'Großpro,jekt n large-scale project.

'Großraum m der ~ München Greater Munich. **~bü,ro** n open-plan office.

'Großrechner m large(-scale) computer.

'Großschreibung f capitalization.

'großsprecherisch adj boastful.

großspurig ['gro:sʃpu:rɪç] adj arrogant.

'Großstadt f big city.

'Großstädter(in f) m city-dweller.

'großstädtisch adj of a big city, urban.

'Großtante f great-aunt.

'Großtat f great feat.

'Großteil m large part. **'größtenteils** adv for the most part, mostly.

'großtun v/i (irr, sep, -ge-, h, → **tun**) talk big: ~ **mit** brag about, show off with.

'Großunternehmen n ✝ large-scale (or big) enterprise.

'Großvater m grandfather.

'Großveranstaltung f big event.

'Großverdiener(in f) m big earner.

'Großwildjagd f big game hunt(ing).

'großziehen v/t (irr, sep, -ge-, h, → **ziehen**) raise, rear, bring up (child).

'großzügig adj 1. generous. 2. broad-minded. 3. spacious. 4. large-scale.

'Großzügigkeit f (-; no pl) 1. generosity. 2. broad-mindedness. 3. large scale.

grotesk [gro'tɛsk] adj grotesque.

Grotte ['grɔtə] f (-; -en) grotto.

grub [gru:p] pret of **graben**.

Grübchen ['gry:pçən] n (-s; -) dimple.

Grube ['gru:bə] f (-; -n) pit, ⚒ a. mine.

Grübelei [gry:bə'laɪ] f (-; -en) brooding.

grübeln ['gry:bəln] v/i (h) (**über** acc over, on) brood, muse.

'Grubenarbeiter m miner.

'Grubenunglück n mine disaster.

Grübler ['gry:blər] m (-s; -) brooder.

Gruft [gruft] f (-; ⸚e) tomb, vault, crypt.

grün [gry:n] adj green (a. fig.): **~er He-** ring fresh herring; **~er Salat** lettuce; F **~er Junge** greenhorn; **die Grünen** pol. the Green (Party); fig. **~es Licht geben** (**bekommen**) give s.o. (get) the green light (**für** for); **e-e Entscheidung vom ~en Tisch** an armchair decision; ~ **vor Neid** green with envy; **j-n ~ und blau schlagen** beat s.o. black and blue; **auf**

k-n ~en Zweig kommen get nowhere; F **er ist dir nicht ~** he has it in for you.

Grün n (-s; -) green (a. golf): **bei ~, auf ~** mot. at green; F **das ist dasselbe in ~** it's practically the same thing.

Grund [grunt] m (-[e]s; ⸚e) 1. no pl a) ground, b) bottom (a. fig.): **am ~, auf dem ~** at the bottom; **auf ~ laufen** ⚓ run aground; **e-r Sache auf den ~ gehen** (**kommen**) go (get) to the bottom of s.th. 2. no pl (**und Boden**) land, property; **sich in ~ und Boden schä-men** be terribly ashamed; **in ~ und Bo-den verdammen** condemn s.o., s.th. outright. 3. no pl fig. basis, founda-tion(s): **auf ~ von** (or gen) a) on the basis (or strength) of, b) because of; **von ~ auf** change etc entirely (or rad-ically); **im ~e** (**genommen**) actually, basically. 4. reason, cause: **aus diesem ~ for this reason; aus persönlichen Gründen** for personal reasons; **aus gu-tem ~** for good reason, justly; **allen ~ haben zu** inf have every reason to inf; **ich frage aus e-m bestimmten ~** I ask for a reason; **(k-n ~) zur Klage haben** have (no) cause for complaint.

'Grund|anstrich m priming coat. **~aus-bildung** f ✗ basic training. **~bedeu-tung** f primary meaning. **~bedingung** f basic condition, prerequisite. **~begriff** m basic concept, pl fundamentals.

'Grund|besitz m landed property, real estate. **~besitzer(in** f) m landowner.

'Grundbestandteil m basic component.

'Grundbuch n land register. **~amt** n land registry. **~auszug** m extract from the land register.

'grund|ehrlich adj thoroughly honest.

gründen ['gryndən] I v/t found, establish, set up: fig. **et. ~ auf** (acc) base (or found) s.th. on. II **sich ~ auf** (acc) fig. be based on. III v/i ~ **auf** (dat) a) rest (or be based) on, b) be due to.

Gründer ['gryndər] m (-s; -), **'Gründe-rin** f (-; -nen) founder.

'grundfalsch adj absolutely wrong.

'Grund|farbe f phys. primary colo(u)r. **~fläche** f area, ⏚ base, △ floor space. **~gebühr** f basic rate. **~gedanke** m basic idea. **~gehalt** n (-[e]s; ⸚er) basic salary. **~gesetz** n basic (constitutional) law.

grundieren [grun'di:rən] v/t (h) ground,

❀ prime. **Grun'dierfarbe** f primer.
Grun'dierung f (-; -en) priming coat.
'**Grund|kapi,tal** n initial capital, stock.
~**kenntnisse** pl basic knowledge. ~**lage** f foundation, fig. a. basis: *jeder* ~ *entbehren* be completely unfounded.
~**lagenforschung** f basic research.

'**grundlegend** adj basic, fundamental, definitive (book etc).

gründlich ['grʏntlɪç] adj thorough, careful: F *sich* ~ *irren* be jolly well mistaken.

'**Gründlichkeit** f (-; no pl) thoroughness.
'**Grundlinie** f A, sports: base line.
'**Grundlohn** m basic wage(s).
'**grundlos I** adj fig. groundless, unfounded. **II** adv for no reason (at all).
'**Grund|mauer** f foundation wall. ~**nahrungsmittel** pl basic food(stuff).
Grün'donnerstag m Maundy Thursday.
'**Grund|pfeiler** m 1. △ supporting pillar. 2. fig. cornerstone. ~**prin,zip** n basic principle. ~**rechnungsart** f *die vier* ~**en** the four fundamental operations of arithmetics. ~**rechte** pl pol. basic rights. ~**regel** f ground rule. ~**riß** m 1. △ ground plan. 2. fig. outline(s).
'**Grundsatz** m principle: *es sich zum* ~ *machen zu* inf make it a rule to inf.
'**grundsätzlich** [-zɛtslɪç] **I** adj fundamental. **II** adv in principle: *ich bin* ~ *dagegen* I am absolutely against it.
'**Grund|schule** f primary (Am. a. grade) school. ~**schüler(in** f) m primary pupil. ~**stein** m △ foundation stone: fig. *den* ~ *legen zu* lay the foundations of. ~**steinlegung** f (-; -en) laying (of) the foundation stone. ~**stock** m (-[e]s; no pl) basis. ~**stoff** m 1. 🜛 element. 2. raw material. ~**stoffindu,strie** f basic industry. ~**stück** n 1. plot (of land), ⚘, 🜛 property, real estate. 2. (building) site.
'**Grundstücks|makler(in** f) m (real) estate agent, Am. realtor. ~**markt** m property market. ~**preis** m land price.
'**Grund|studium** n basic study. ~**stufe** f ped. elementary classes. ~**ton** m 1. ♩ keynote. 2. paint. ground shade. ~**umsatz** m ♥ basal metabolic rate.

'**Gründung** f (-; -en) foundation.
'**grund|ver'kehrt** adj utterly wrong.
~**ver'schieden** adj entirely different.
'**Grundwasser** n (-s; no pl) ground water. ~**spiegel** m ground-water level.
'**Grund|wehrdienst** m basic military service. ~**wortschatz** m basic vocabulary. ~**zahl** f cardinal number. ~**zug** m characteristic (feature), pl outline(s), basics: *in s-n Grundzügen schildern* outline.

'**Grün|fläche** f a) green space, lawn, b) park area. ~**futter** n ⚘ green fodder. ~**gürtel** m green belt. ~**kohl** m kale.
'**grünlich** adj greenish.
'**Grünschnabel** m F whippersnapper.
'**Grünspan** m (-[e]s; no pl) verdigris.
'**Grünspecht** m zo. green woodpecker.
'**Grünstreifen** m → *Mittelstreifen*.
grunzen ['grʊntsən] v/i, v/t (h) grunt.
'**Grünzeug** n F a) greens, b) herbs.
Gruppe ['grʊpə] f (-; -n) **1.** group (a. ✝). **2.** team. **3.** 🗶 squad.
'**Gruppen|arbeit** f teamwork. ~**dy,namik** f group dynamics. ~**reise** f group travel. ~**sex** m group sex. ~**thera,pie** f group therapy.
'**gruppenweise** adv in groups.
gruppieren [grʊ'piːrən] (h) **I** v/t group: *neu* ~ regroup. **II** *sich* ~ form a group (or groups) (*um* [a]round).
Grup'pierung f (-; -en) **1.** grouping, formation. **2.** group(s).
Grusel- ['gruːzəl...] horror (film, story, etc). '**gruselig** adj creepy, spooky.
'**gruseln** v/t, v/i, v/impers *es gruselt mir* (or *mich*), *mich graust* it gives me the creeps; *es war zum Gruseln* it was enough to give you the creeps.
Gruß [gruːs] m (-es; ⁓e) greeting(s) (*aus* from), 🗶 salute: *viele Grüße* (or *e-n schönen* ~) *an ...* give my regards (or my love) to ...; *in letter*: *mit besten* (or *freundlichen*) *Grüßen* Yours sincerely; *herzliche Grüße* love, best wishes.
grüßen ['gryːsən] (h) **I** v/t greet, esp. 🗶 salute, F say hello: F *grüß dich!* hello (there)!, hi!; ~ *Sie ihn von mir!* give my regards (or my love) to him! **II** v/i say good morning (etc), say hello, esp. 🗶 salute.
'**Grußwort** n (-[e]s; -e) greeting.
gucken ['gʊkən] v/i (h) look, peep.
'**Guckloch** n peephole.
Guerillakrieg [ge'rɪlja-] m guer(r)illa war(fare).
Gulasch ['gʊlaʃ] n (-[e]s; -e, -s) goulash.
'**Gulaschsuppe** f goulash soup.

Gulden ['gʊldən] *m* (-s; -) guilder.

gültig ['gʏltɪç] *adj* valid (*a. fig.*), good (*a. sports*), effective (**ab, vom** as from), in force, legal: **~ werden** become valid, *contract etc*: become effective.

'**Gültigkeit** *f* (-; *no pl*) validity, ⚖, *pol.* legal force.

'**Gültigkeitsdauer** *f* (period of) validity, *a.* term (*of contract*).

Gummi ['gʊmi] **1.** *m, n* (-s; -[s]) ⚙ a) rubber, b) gum. **2.** *m* (-s; -s) F rubber. **3.** *n* (-s; -s) → **Gummiband. 4.** *m* (-s; -s) → **Radiergummi.**

'**gummiartig** *adj* rubbery.

'**Gummi|band** *n* rubber band, elastic. **~bärchen** *n gastr.* jelly baby. **~baum** *m* **1.** rubber tree. **2.** rubber plant.

gummieren [gʊ'miːrən] *v/t* (h) gum, ⚙ rubberize.

'**Gummi|handschuh** *m* rubber glove. **~linse** *f phot.* zoom lens. **~para,graph** *m* F elastic clause. **~stiefel** *m* wellington (boot), *Am.* rubber boot. **~strumpf** *m* elastic stocking. **~waren** *pl* rubber goods. **~zug** *m* elastic.

Gunst [gʊnst] *f* (-; *no pl*) favo(u)r.

günstig ['gʏnstɪç] *adj* **1.** favo(u)rable (**für** to): **~e Gelegenheit** opportunity; **im ~sten Fall** at best; **zu ~en Bedingungen** on easy terms; **~es Angebot, ~er Kauf** bargain. **2.** convenient.

Günstling ['gʏnstlɪŋ] *m* (-s; -e) favo(u)rite. '**Günstlingswirtschaft** *f* (-; *no pl*) favo(u)ritism.

Gurgel ['gʊrgəl] *f* (-; -n) a) throat, b) gullet. '**Gurgelmittel** *n* gargle.

'**gurgeln** *v/i* (h) **1.** gargle. **2.** gurgle.

Gurke ['gʊrkə] *f* (-; -n) **1.** a) cucumber, b) gherkin. **2.** F *contp.* lemon.

'**Gurkenhobel** *m* cucumber slicer. '**Gurkensa,lat** *m* cucumber salad.

gurren ['gʊrən] *v/i* (h) coo.

Gurt [gʊrt] *m* (-[e]s; -e) **1.** belt, ✈, *mot.* seat belt. **2.** strap.

'**Gurtband** *n* (-[e]s; ⸚er) waistband.

Gürtel ['gʏrtəl] *m* (-s; -) belt: **den ~ enger schnallen** *a. fig.* tighten one's belt. **~linie** *f* waist(line): **unter der** (*or* **die**) **~** *a. fig.* below the belt. **~reifen** *m* radial(-ply) tyre (*Am.* tire). **~rose** *f* (-; *no pl*) ⚕ shingles. **~schnalle** *f* belt buckle. **~tier** *n* armadillo.

Guß [gʊs] *m* (-sses; ⸚sse) **1.** ⚙ a) casting, founding, b) cast iron: *fig.* (**wie) aus**

einem ~ of a piece. **2.** a) gush, jet, b) downpour. **3.** *gastr.* icing.

'**Gußeisen** *n* cast iron. '**gußeisern** *adj* cast-iron. '**Gußform** *f* casting mo(u)ld. '**Gußstahl** *m* cast steel. '**Gußstück** *n* casting.

gut [guːt] **I** *adj* good, fine: **ganz ~** quite good, not bad; **also ~!** all right (then)!; **schon ~!** never mind!; **(es ist) ~, daß ..., nur ~, daß ...** (it's a) good thing that ...; **auch ~!, es ist ganz ~ so!** it's just as well!; **(wieder) ~ werden** come right (again), be all right; **sei (bitte) so ~ und ...** would you be good enough to ...; **~ sein in** (*dat*) be good at (doing *s.th.*); **das ist ~ gegen** (*or* **für**) **Erkältungen** that's good for colds; **mir ist nicht ~!** I don't feel (so) well!; **wozu soll das ~ sein?** what's that in aid of?; **laß (mal** *or* **es) ~ sein!** that'll do!; **Gut und Böse** good and evil; **im ~en** in a friendly way, amicably. **II** *adv* well, *look, taste, etc* good: **er spricht ~ Englisch** he speaks good English; **es ~ haben** have it good, have a good time; **du hast es ~!** you are lucky!; **es ist ~ möglich, es kann ~ sein** it may well be; **es gefällt mir ~** I (do) like it; **~ gemacht!** well done!; **so ~ wie gewonnen** as good as won; **so ~ wie nichts** hardly anything; **so ~ wie unmöglich** practically impossible; **~ zwei Stunden** a good two hours; **~ (und gern)** easily; **ich kann ihn doch nicht ~ fragen** I can't very well ask him; F **mach's ~!** a) good luck, b) so long!, take care (of yourself)!; → **Gute, gutgehen** *etc, Reise.*

Gut *n* (-[e]s; Güter) **1.** good(s), property, possession(s): *fig.* **das höchste ~** the greatest good. **2.** *usu. pl* ✝ goods, b) 🚂 goods, *Am.* freight. **3.** estate. **4.** ⚙ material, stock.

'**Gutachten** *n* (-s; -) (expert) opinion. '**Gutachter** *m* (-s; -), '**Gutachterin** *f* (-; -nen) expert, ⚖ expert witness.

'**gutartig** *adj* **1.** good-natured. **2.** ⚕ benign. '**Gutartigkeit** *f* (-; *no pl*) **1.** good nature. **2.** ⚕ benignity.

'**gutaussehend** *adj* good-looking. '**gutbezahlt** *adj* well-paid.

'**gut|bürgerlich** *adj* solid middle-class: **~e Küche** good plain cooking.

Gutdünken ['guːtdʏŋkən] *n* (-s; *no pl*)

discretion: **handle nach (eigenem)** ~ use your own discretion.

'**Gute** *n* (-n) the good: **das** ~ **an der Sache** the good thing about it; ~**s tun** do good; **des** ~**n zuviel tun** overdo it; **das ist des** ~**n zuviel** that's too much of a good thing; **alles** ~**!** all the best!

Güte ['gy:tə] *f* (-; *no pl*) **1.** goodness, kindness; **würden Sie die** ~ **haben zu** *inf* would you be so kind as to *inf*; F (**du**) **m-e** ~**!** good gracious! **2.** quality: **erster** ~ a) first-class, b) *iro.* of the first water. '**Güteklasse** *f* ✝ grade, quality.

Gute'**nachtgeschichte** *f* bedtime story.

Gute'**nachtkuß** *m* goodnight kiss.

Güter|bahnhof ['gy:tər-] *m* goods station, *Am.* freight depot. ~**gemeinschaft** *f* ⚖ community of property. ~**trennung** *f* ⚖ separation of property. ~**verkehr** *m* goods (*Am.* freight) traffic. ~**wagen** *m* 🚂 (goods) waggon, *Am.* freight car. ~**zug** *m* goods (*Am.* freight) train.

'**Gütezeichen** *n* mark of quality.

'**gutgebaut** *adj* well-built.

'**gutgehen** *v/i* (*irr, sep, -ge-, sn,* → **gehen**) **1.** go (off) well, work out well: **das kann nicht** ~**!** that's bound to go wrong!; **wenn alles gutgeht** if nothing goes wrong. **2. mir geht es gut** a) I'm fine, b) I'm doing fine.

'**gutgelaunt** *adj* in a good mood.

'**gutgemeint** *adj* well-meant.

'**gutgläubig** *adj* **1.** credulous. **2.** acting (*or* done) in good faith, bona fide.

'**Gutgläubigkeit** *f* (-; *no pl*) credulity, gullibility.

'**Guthaben** *n* (-s; -) **1.** credit (balance). **2.** account.

'**gutheißen** *v/t* (*irr, sep, -ge-, h,* → **heißen**) **et.** ~ approve (of) s.th.

'**gutherzig** *adj* kind(-hearted).

gütig ['gy:tɪç] *adj* kind (**zu** to).

gütlich ['gy:tlɪç] **I** *adj* **1.** amicable. **II** *adv* **2.** amicably. **3. sich** ~ **tun an** (*dat*) help o.s. to, take (*or* eat, drink) one's fill of.

'**gutmachen** *v/t* (*sep, -ge-, h*) make good, make up for.

'**gutmütig** [-my:tɪç] *adj* good-natured.

'**Gutmütigkeit** *f* (-; *no pl*) good nature.

'**Gutschein** *m* coupon, voucher.

'**gutschreiben** *v/t* (*irr, sep, -ge-, h,* → **schreiben**) **j-m et.** ~ credit s.o. with s.th., pass s.th. to s.o.'s credit.

'**Gutschrift** *f* **1.** credit (entry). **2.** credit voucher. ~**anzeige** *f* credit note.

'**Gutshaus** *n* manor (house).

'**Gutsherr(in** *f*) *m* lord (lady) of the manor. '**Gutshof** *m* estate.

'**gutsitu,iert** *adj* well-to-do, well-off.

'**guttun** *v/i* (*irr, sep, -ge-, h,* → **tun**) **j-m** ~ do s.o. good.

guttural [gʊtu'ra:l] *adj* guttural.

'**gutunterrichtet** *adj* well-informed.

'**gutwillig** *adj* willing (to oblige).

'**Gutwilligkeit** *f* (-; *no pl*) willingness.

Gymnasialbildung [gʏmna'zĭa:l-] *f* secondary school education. **Gymnasiast** [gʏmna'ziast] *m* (-en; -en) grammar-school (*Am.* high-school) student.

Gymnasium [gʏm'na:zĭʊm] *n* (-s; -ien) (**humanistisches** ~ classical) secondary school, *Br. a.* grammar school.

Gymnastik [gʏm'nastɪk] *f* (-; *no pl*) gymnastics, (physical) exercises, callisthenics. **Gym'nastikanzug** *m* leotard.

gym'nastisch *adj* gymnastic.

Gynäkologe [gʏnɛko'lo:gə] *m* (-n; -n) gyn(a)ecologist. **Gynäkologie** [gʏnɛkolo'gi:] *f* (-; *no pl*) gyn(a)ecology. **gynäko'logisch** *adj* gyn(a)ecological.

H

H, h [ha:] *n* (-; -) **1.** H, h. **2.** ♪ B.

ha [ha(:)] *int* ha, ah.

Haar [ha:r] *n* (-[e]s; -e) hair: **sich die** ~**e kämmen** (F **machen**) comb (do) one's hair; **sich die** ~**e schneiden lassen** get a haircut; **sich die** ~**e raufen** tear one's hair; *fig.* **aufs** ~ to a T; **sich aufs** ~ **gleichen** be absolutely identical; **um ein** ~ by a hair's breadth; **um ein** ~ **wäre er überfahren worden** he just missed being run over, he had a narrow escape; **er (es) ist um kein ~ besser** he (it) is not a bit better; **~e spalten** split hairs; **ein ~ in der Suppe finden** find a fly in the ointment; **sich in die ~e geraten** quarrel, clash; **sich in den ~en liegen** be at loggerheads, be quarrel(l)ing; **sie hat ~e auf den Zähnen** she's a tough customer; **das ist bei den ~en herbeigezogen** that's (pretty) far-fetched; **ihr wurde kein ~ gekrümmt** they did not touch a hair on her head; **~e lassen müssen** not to escape unscathed; **kein gutes ~ an j-m lassen** pull s.o. to pieces; **ihm standen die ~e zu Berge, ihm sträubten sich die ~e** it made his hair stand on end; **laß dir deshalb k-e graue ~e wachsen!** don't lose any sleep over it!

'Haar|ansatz m hairline. **~ausfall** m loss of hair. **~bürste** f hairbrush.

'haaren v/i (h) **1.** a. **sich ~** zo. lose its hair. **2.** fur etc: shed (hairs).

'Haarentferner m (-s; -) hair remover.

'Haaresbreite f entging **um ~ e-m Unfall** he escaped an accident by a hair's breadth; **sie ging nicht um ~ von ihrer Meinung ab** she didn't budge from her opinion one little bit.

'Haar|farbe f hair colo(u)r. **~färbemittel** n hair dye. **~festiger** m setting lotion. **~gefäß** n anat. capillary (vessel).

'haarge'nau adj F precise: **(stimmt) ~!** dead right!

haarig ['haːrɪç] adj hairy (a. F fig.).

...haarig ...haired.

'haar'klein adj (down) to the last detail.

'Haarklemme f hair clip.

'haarlos adj **1.** hairless. **2.** bald.

'Haar|mittel n hair restorer. **~nadel** f hairpin. **~nadelkurve** f mot. hairpin bend. **~netz** n **1.** hairnet. **2.** hair lacquer. **~öl** n hair oil. **~pflege** f hair care. **~riß** m hairline crack. **²scharf I** adj very precise, exact. **II** adv by a hair's breadth. **~schleife** f (hair) ribbon, bow. **~schnitt** m a) haircut, b) hairstyle. **~schuppen** pl dandruff.

Haarspalte'rei f (-; -en) **(das ist ~** that's just) splitting hairs.

'Haar|spange f (hair) slide, Am. barrette. **~spitzen** pl hair tips. **~spray** m, n hairspray. **~strähne** f strand of hair.

'haarsträubend adj hair-raising.

'Haar|teil n hairpiece. **~trockner** m hair-drier. **~wäsche** f shampoo. **~waschmittel** n shampoo. **~wasser** n hair tonic. **~wuchs** m **1.** growth of (the) hair. **2.** hair. **~wuchsmittel** n hair restorer. **~wurzeln** pl roots of one's hair.

Hab [haːp] **(all sein) ~ und Gut** all one's possessions.

Habe ['haːbə] f (-; no pl) possessions.

haben ['haːbən] (hatte, gehabt, h) **I** v/t have (got), own, possess: **et. ~ wollen** want (to have) s.th.; **er will es so ~** that's the way he wants it; **(noch) zu ~ sein** be (still) available; F **sie ist noch zu ~** she's still to be had; **was hast du?** what's wrong?; F **er hat es im Hals** he has a bad throat; **wir ~ schönes Wetter** the weather is fine (here); **wir ~ Winter!** it's winter!; dial. **es hat viel Schnee** there's a lot of snow; **welche Farbe hat das Kleid?** what colo(u)r is the dress?; **da hast du's!** there you are!, fig. a. I told you so!; **das hätten wir!** well, that's that!; F **er hat's ja!** he can (well) afford it!; **woher hast du das?** a) where did you get that from?, b) who told you?; **was hast du gegen ihn?** what have you got against him?; **was habe ich davon?** a) what do I get out of it?, b) **wenn ...?** what's the good if ...?; **ich habe nicht viel davon gehabt** I didn't get much out of it; **das hast du nun davon!** there (you are)!; F **ich hab's!** (I've) got it!; **das werden wir gleich ~!** (that's) no problem!; **wie gehabt** as had, same as ever; F **sie ~ et. miteinander** they are lovers; **die Prüfung hatte es in sich** the exam was pretty tough; **er hat et. Überspanntes** there's s.th. eccentric about him; **das hat er so an sich** that's the way he is; **ich habe viel zu erzählen** I have a lot to tell ; **dafür bin ich nicht zu ~!** count me out!; **hab dich nicht so!** a) don't make a fuss!, b) don't take on so! **II** v/aux have: **hast du ihn gesehen?** have you seen him?; **du hättest es mir sagen sollen!** you should (or might) have told me!; **er hätte es tun können** he could have done it.

'Haben n (-s; -) ✝ credit: → **Soll**.

'Habenichts m (-[e]s; -e) have-not.

'Habenseite f ✝ credit side.

Habgier ['haːpgiːr] f (-; no pl) greed.

'**habgierig** *adj* greedy.
habhaft ['ha:phaft] *adj* ~ **werden** (*gen*) get hold of, *a.* catch (*criminal etc*).
Habicht ['ha:bɪçt] *m* -(e)s; -e) *zo.* hawk.
Habilitation [habilitaˈtsɪoːn] *f* (-; -en) university lecturing qualification.
habilitieren [habiliˈtiːrən] *sich* ~ (h) qualify to give lectures at a university.
Habitat [habiˈtaːt] *n* (-s; -e) *zo.* habitat.
Habseligkeiten ['ha:p-] *pl* belongings.
Habsucht ['ha:p-] *f* (-; *no pl*) greed.
'**habsüchtig** *adj* greedy.
Hachse ['haksə] *f* (-; -n) **1.** *zo.* hock. **2.** *gastr.* knuckles. **3.** F leg, *pl* pins.
'**Hackbeil** *n* chopper. '**Hackbraten** *m* meat loaf. '**Hackbrett** *n* **1.** chopping board. **2.** ♪ dulcimer.
Hacke¹ ['hakə] *f* (-; -n) **1.** ✗ hoe. **2.** pickax(e). '**Hacke²** *f* (-; -n) *dial.* heel.
'**hacken** (h) **I** *v/t* **1.** hack, ✗ *a.* hoe. **2.** chop. **II** *v/i* **3.** (*nach* at) pick, peck.
'**Hackepeter** *m* (-s; *no pl*) *raw minced meat mixed with onions and spices.*
'**Hacker** *m* (-s; -) F *computer:* hacker.
'**Hackfleisch** *n* minced (*Am.* ground) meat: F *aus dir mache ich* ~*!* I'll make mincemeat of you!
'**Hackmesser** *n* chopper.
'**Hackordnung** *f a. fig.* pecking order.
'**Häcksel** ['hɛksəl] *m, n* (-s; *no pl*) ✗ chaff.
'**Hacksteak** *n gastr.* beefburger.
Hader ['ha:dər] *m* (-s; *no pl*) quarrel.
'**hadern** *v/i* (h) quarrel (*mit* with).
Hafen *m* **1.** a) harbo(u)r, b) port, c) dock(s): *in den* ~ *einlaufen* put into port. **2.** *fig.* (*ruhiger*) ~ haven.
'**Hafen|anlagen** *pl* docks. ~**arbeiter** *m* docker. ~**becken** *n* harbo(u)r basin, (wet) dock. ~**einfahrt** *f* harbo(u)r entrance. ~**gebühren** *pl* harbo(u)r dues. ~**meister** *m* harbo(u)r master. ~**rundfahrt** *f* boat tour of a harbo(u)r. ~**stadt** *f* (sea)port. ~**viertel** *n* dockland(s).
Hafer ['ha:fər] *m* (-s; -) oats: F *ihn sticht der* ~ he's getting cocky. '**Haferbrei** *m* porridge. '**Haferflocken** *pl* rolled oats. '**Hafergrütze** *f* groats. '**Hafermehl** *n* oatmeal. '**Haferschleim** *m* gruel.
Haff [haf] *n* (-[e]s; -s) lagoon.
Haft [haft] *f* (-; *no pl*) **1.** custody: *in* ~ under arrest, in custody; *j-n in* ~ *nehmen* take s.o. into custody. **2.** imprisonment. '**Haftanstalt** *f* prison.
'**haftbar** *adj* (*für* for) responsible, ⅊⅊

liable: *j-n* ~ *machen* make s.o. liable.
'**Haftbefehl** *m* arrest warrant: ~ *gegen j-n* warrant for s.o.'s arrest.
'**haften¹** *v/i* (h) (*an dat* to) cling, stick: *im Gedächtnis* ~ stick (in one's mind).
'**haften²** *v/i* (h) (*für* for) be (held) responsible, ⅊⅊ be liable: ~ *für* guarantee.
'**Haftfähigkeit** *f* (-; *no pl*) **1.** → *Haftvermögen*. **2.** ⅊⅊ fitness to undergo detention.
'**Häftling** ['hɛftlɪŋ] *m* (-s; -e) prisoner.
'**Haftpflicht** *f* (legal) liability.
'**haftpflichtig** *adj* liable (*für* for).
'**Haftpflichtversicherung** *f* third party (liability) insurance.
'**Haftrichter(in** *f*) *m* magistrate.
'**Haftschale** *f opt.* contact lens.
'**Haftstrafe** *f* imprisonment.
'**Haftung¹** *f* (-; *no pl*) ⊙ adhesion.
'**Haftung²** *f* (-; -en) a) (legal) liability, b) guarantee: *beschränkte* ~ limited liability; *Gesellschaft mit beschränkter* ~ private limited (liability) company; ~ *übernehmen* accept liability (*für* for).
'**Haftvermögen** *n* (-s; *no pl*) adhesive power(s).
Hagebutte ['ha:gəbʊtə] *f* (-; -n) rose hip.
Hagel ['ha:gəl] *m* (-s; *no pl*) **1.** hail. **2.** *fig.* hail, shower (*of blows etc*), torrent (*of invective etc*). '**Hagelkorn** *n* hailstone.
hager ['ha:gər] *adj* gaunt.
haha [ha'ha(:)] *int* ha ha.
Häher ['hɛːər] *m* (-s; -) *zo.* jay.
Hahn [ha:n] *m* (-[e]s; ⁓e) **1.** *zo.* cock, rooster: F ~ *im Korbe sein* be cock of the walk; *es kräht kein* ~ *danach* nobody cares (two hoots) about it. **2.** ⊙ a) tap, *Am.* faucet, b) spigot. **3.** *of gun:* hammer.
Hähnchen ['hɛːnçən] *n* (-s; -) chicken.
'**Hahnenkamm** *m a.* ✿ cockscomb.
'**Hahnenkampf** *m* cockfight.
Hahnrei ['ha:nraɪ] *m* (-[e]s; -e) cuckold.
Hai [haɪ] *m* (-[e]s; -e), '**Haifisch** *m* shark.
'**Haifischflosse** *f* shark fin.
Häkchen ['hɛːkçən] *n* (-s; -) **1.** small hook. **2.** *on list etc:* tick, *Am.* check. **3.** *ling.* apostrophe.
'**Häkelarbeit** *f*, **Häke'lei** *f* (-; -en) crochet work. **häkeln** ['hɛːkəln] *v/t, v/i* (h) crochet. '**Häkelnadel** *f* crochet needle.
haken ['ha:kən] *v/t* (h) hook (*an acc* onto).
'**Haken** *m* (-s; -) **1.** hook, peg: ~ *und Öse*

hook and eye; *boxing*: *rechter (linker)* ~ right (left) hook. **2.** → *Häkchen* 2. **3.** F *fig*. *der* ~ *an der Sache* the snag; *die Sache hat e-n* ~ there is a catch to it.

'**Hakenkreuz** *n* swastika.

'**Hakennase** *f* hooked nose.

Halali [hala'li:] *n* (-s; -[s]) *hunt*. mort.

halb [halp] **I** *adj* half: *e-e* ~*e Stunde* half an hour; ~ *drei* half past two; ~ *Europa* half of Europe; ~*e Note* ♪ half note; ~*er Ton* ♪ semitone; *auf* ~*er Höhe* halfway (up); *die* ~*e Summe* half the sum; *zum* ~*en Preis* for half the price, (at) half-price; *nur die* ~*e Wahrheit* only half the truth; *fig*. *e-e* ~*e Sache* a half-measure; *er macht k-e* ~*en Sachen* he doesn't do things by halves; *nichts Halbes und nichts Ganzes* neither one thing nor the other; *j-m auf* ~*em Wege entgegenkommen* meet s.o. halfway; *sich auf* ~*em Wege einigen* split the difference. **II** *adv* half: ~ *soviel* half as much; ~ *und* ~ a) half and half, b) partly; F *(mit j-m) halbe-halbe machen* go halves (or fifty-fifty) (with s.o.); *es ist* ~ *so schlimm* it's not as bad as all that; *das ist ja* ~ *geschenkt* that's a giveaway; *damit war die Sache* ~ *gewonnen* that was half the battle.

'**halbamtlich** *adj* semiofficial.

'**Halbärmel** *m* half-sleeve.

'**halbauto**,**matisch** *adj* semiautomatic.

'**Halbbildung** *f* superficial knowledge.

'**halbbitter** *adj* plain (*chocolate*).

'**Halbblut** *n* **1.** half-caste. **2.** half-breed.

'**Halbblut...**, '**Halbblüter** [-bly:tər] *m* (-s; -), '**halbblütig** *adj zo*. half-breed.

'**Halbbruder** *m* half brother.

'**halbdunkel** *adj* dusky, dimly-lit (*room*).

'**Halbdunkel** *n* semidarkness, twilight.

Halbe ['halbə] *m*, *f*, *n* (-n; -n) pint (of beer).

'**Halbedelstein** *m* semiprecious stone.

'**...halben**, '**...halber** *in cpds*. a) on account of, due to, b) for the sake of, c) for.

'**Halbfabri**,**kat** *n* semifinished product.

'**halbfertig** *adj* half-finished, ✝ semifinished.

'**halbfett** *adj* **1.** semibold. **2.** medium-fat.

'**Halbfi**,**nale** *n sports*: semifinal.

'**halbgar** *adj gastr*. underdone, rare.

'**halbgebildet** *adj* semiliterate.

'**Halbgott** *m* (~**göttin** *f*) demigod(dess).

'**Halbheit** *f* (-; -en) half measure.

'**halbherzig** *adj* half-hearted.

'**halbhoch** *adj* medium-high, *sports etc*: shoulder-high.

halbieren [hal'bi:rən] *v/t* (h) halve, cut (*or* divide) in half, ✝ bisect. **Hal'bierung** *f* (-; -en) halving, ✝ bisection.

'**Halbinsel** *f* peninsula.

'**Halbjahr** *n* half-year, (period of) six months. '**Halbjahr(e)s...** half-yearly, six-month ... '**halbjährig** [-jɛ:rɪç] *adj* a) half-yearly, six-month ..., of six months, b) six-month-old. '**halbjährlich** *adj and adv* half-yearly, semiannual(ly), *adv* a. every six months.

'**Halbkreis** *m* semicircle.

'**Halbkugel** *f a*. *geogr*. hemisphere.

'**halblang** *adj* a) medium-length, b) knee-length (*skirt etc*), c) *ling*. half-long (*vowel*): F *mach mal* ~*!* draw it mild!

'**halblaut** **I** *adj* low. **II** *adv* in an undertone.

'**Halbleder** *n print*. half-leather: *in* ~ *gebunden* half-bound.

'**Halbleinen** *n* half-linen (cloth): *in* ~ *gebunden print*. half-cloth.

'**Halbleiter** *m* ⚡ semiconductor.

Halb'linke *m*, *f* (-n; -n), **halb'links** *adv sports*: inside left.

'**halbmast** *adv* (*auf* ~ at) half-mast.

'**Halbmesser** *m* (-s; -) radius.

'**Halbmittelgewicht** *n sports*: light middleweight.

'**Halbmond** *m* half moon, crescent: *wir haben* ~ there's a half moon.

'**halbmondförmig** *adj* crescent-shaped.

'**halbnackt** *adj* half-naked.

'**halboffen** *adj a*. *ling*. half-open.

'**halboffizi**,**ell** *adj* semiofficial.

'**halbpart** [-part] *adv* F (*mit j-m*) ~ *machen* go halves (or fifty-fifty) with s.o.

'**Halbpensi**,**on** *f* half-board.

'**Halbpro**,**fil** *n* semiprofile.

Halb'rechte *m*, *f* (-n; -n), **halb'rechts** *adv sports*: inside right.

'**Halbreli**,**ef** *n* half relief, mezzo-relievo.

'**halbrund** *adj* semicircular.

'**Halbrund** *n* (-[e]s; *no pl*) semicircle.

'**Halbschlaf** *m* doze: *im* ~ half asleep.

'**Halbschuh** *m* (low) shoe.

'**Halbschwergewicht** *n sports*: light heavyweight.

'**Halbschwester** *f* half sister.

'**halbseiden** *adj* **1.** half-silk. **2.** *contp.* (*a.* *~es Milieu*) demimonde.

'**halbseitig** *adj* **1.** *print.* half-page. **2.** *☞* unilateral: *~e Lähmung* hemiplegia.

'**Halbstarke** *m*, *f* (-*n*; -*n*) F yob(bo).

'**Halbstiefel** *m* ankle boot.

'**halbstündig** [-ʃtyndɪç] *adj* half-hour.

'**halbstündlich** *adj and adv* half-hourly, *adv a.* every half-hour.

'**halbtägig** [-tɛːgɪç] *adj* half a day's, half-day. '**halbtags** *adv* ~ **arbeiten** work part-time. '**Halbtags...** half-day, part-time (*job etc*). '**Halbtagskraft** *f* part-time worker.

'**Halbton** *m* **1.** ♪ semitone. **2.** *phot.*, *print.* half-tone.

'**halbtot** *adj* half-dead.

'**halbverhungert** *adj* starving.

'**Halbvo,kal** *m* *ling.* semivowel.

'**halbvoll** *adj* half-full.

'**halbwach** *adj* half-awake, dozing.

'**Halbwahrheit** *f* (-; -en) half-truth.

'**Halbwaise** *f* half-orphan.

'**Halbwelt** *f* (-; *no pl*) demimonde.

'**Halbwertszeit** *f* *nucl.* half-life.

'**Halbwissen** *n* superficial knowledge.

Halbwüchsige ['halpvyːksɪgə] *m*, *f* (-*n*; -*n*) adolescent, teenager.

'**Halbzeit** *f* **1.** half(-time): *erste* (*zweite*) ~ first (second) half. **2.** → *~pause* *f* half-time. *~stand* *m* half-time score.

Halde ['haldə] *f* (-; -*n*) **1.** a) dump, b) slag heap, c) coal stocks. **2.** *↑* (surplus) stocks: *auf ~ legen* stockpile; *auf ~ liegen* be (excessively) stockpiled.

half [half] *pret of* **helfen**.

Hälfte ['hɛlftə] *f* (-; -*n*) half: *die ~ der Leute* (*Zeit*) half the people (time); *um die ~ teurer sein* cost half as much again; *Kinder zahlen die ~* children pay half(-price); *zur ~* half (of it *or* them); F *m-e bessere ~* my better half.

Halfter ['halftər] *n* (-*s*; -) **1.** *a. m* halter. **2.** *a. f* (-; -*n*) (pistol) holster.

Halle ['halə] *f* (-; -*n*) **1.** a) hall, b) foyer, lounge, c) entrance hall. **2.** *☉* shop, *✈* hangar. **3.** a) gymnasium, F gym, b) covered court(s), c) indoor (swimming) pool: *in der ~* indoors. **4.** *🏛* concourse.

Halleluja [hale'luːja] *n* (-*s*; -*s*) hallelujah.

hallen ['halən] *v/i* (h) (*von* with) reverberate, echo.

'**Hallen...** indoor (*handball, tennis, etc*).

'**Hallenfußball** *m* five-a-side football.

'**Hallen(schwimm)bad** *n* indoor (swimming) pool.

hallo ['halo] *int* a) hello, F hi, b) hey: *~ (, Sie)!* excuse me!, F hey, you! **Hallo** [ha'loː] *n* (-*s*; -*s*) *fig.* hullabaloo. **Hallodri** [ha'loːdri] *m* (-*s*; -[*s*]) F scallywag.

Halluzination [halutsinaˈtsĭoːn] *f* (-; -*en*) hallucination. **halluzinatorisch** [-'toːrɪʃ] *adj* hallucinatory. **halluzinieren** [-'niːrən] *v/i* (h) hallucinate. **Halluzinogen** [-noˈgeːn] *n* (-*s*; -*e*) hallucinogenic.

Halm [halm] *m* (-[*e*]*s*; -*e*) blade, stalk.

Halogenscheinwerfer [haloˈgeːn-] *m* *mot.* halogen headlight.

Hals [hals] *m* (-*es*; *~e*) a) neck, b) throat: *☞ steifer ~* stiff neck; *aus vollem ~(e)* a) *yell etc* at the top of one's voice, b) *lachen* roar with laughter; *~ über Kopf* headlong, helter-skelter; *sich ~ über Kopf verlieben* fall in love head over heels; *bis an den ~* up to one's neck (*fig. a.* ears); F *auf dem* (*or am*) *~ haben* have *s.o.*, *s.th.* on one's back; *j-m die Polizei etc auf den ~ hetzen* get the police *etc* onto s.o.; *sich j-n* (*et.*) *vom ~(e) schaffen* get rid of s.o. (s.th.); *j-m um den ~ fallen* fling one's arms round s.o.'s neck; *sich j-m an den ~ werfen* throw o.s. at s.o.; *sich den ~ brechen* break one's neck; *fig. das bricht ihm den ~* that'll be his undoing; F *e-r Flasche den ~ brechen* crack a bottle; F *er hat es in den falschen ~ bekommen* he took it the wrong way; F *es hängt mir zum ~(e) heraus!* I'm fed up (to the teeth) with it!; *bleib mir damit vom ~(e)!* don't bother me with that!; → *umdrehen, Wasser.* '**Halsabschneider** *m* (-*s*; -) F *fig.* cutthroat. '**Halsband** *n* (-[*e*]*s*; *~er*) **1.** necklace. **2.** (dog) collar.

'**halsbrecherisch** *adj* breakneck.

'**Halsentzündung** *f* *☞* sore throat.

'**Halskette** *f* necklace.

'**Hals-'Nasen-'Ohren-Arzt** *m*, *~-Ärztin* *f* ear, nose and throat specialist.

'**Halsschlagader** *f* carotid (artery).

'**Halsschmerzen** *pl* *~ haben* have a sore throat.

halsstarrig ['halsʃtarɪç] *adj* stubborn.

'**Halstuch** *n* a) neckerchief, b) scarf.

'**Hals- und 'Beinbruch!** F break a leg!

'**Halsweite** *f* collar size.

'**Halswirbel** *m* *anat.* cervical vertebra.

halt¹ [halt] *int* a) stop, *esp.* ✗ halt, b) wait (a minute), c) that'll do.

halt² *adv dial.* → **eben** 5.

Halt *m* (-[e]s; -e, -s) **1.** *no pl* hold, *a.* foothold, *a. fig.* support, *fig.* (moral) stability. **2.** stop: **ohne ~** nonstop; *fig.* **~ gebieten** (*dat*) call a halt to, stop; → **haltmachen**.

'haltbar *adj* **1.** durable, hard-wearing, ☺ *a.* wear-resistant. **2.** not perishable: **begrenzt ~** perishable; **~ sein** keep (well); **~ machen** preserve; **~ bis ...** best before ... **3.** *fig.* tenable. **'Haltbarkeit** *f* (-; *no pl*) **1.** durability, ☺ *a.* (long *etc*) service life, ♥ shelf life. **2.** keeping quality: **von geringer ~** perishable. **3.** *fig.* tenability. **'Haltbarkeitsdatum** *n* best-by (*or* best--before, *Am.* pull) date.

'Haltebucht *f mot.* lay-by, *Am.* rest stop.

'Haltegriff *m* strap.

'Haltelinie *f mot.* stop line.

halten ['haltən] (hielt, gehalten, h) **I** *v/t* **1.** a) hold, b) hold (up), support: **er hielt ihr den Mantel** he held her coat for her; **et. gegen das Licht ~** hold s.th. to the light; → **Stellung 2. 2.** hold back, stop, keep: **er war nicht zu ~** there was no holding him; **mich hält hier nichts mehr** there is nothing holding me here any more; **haltet den Dieb!** stop thief! **3.** a) keep (**sauber, trocken** *etc* clean, dry, *etc*), keep (up) maintain, hold: **der Raum war ganz in Weiß gehalten** everything in the room was done in white; **der Film hielt nicht, was er versprach** the film did not live up to its promise; → **Diät, Ordnung, Schritt** 1, **Takt** 1, **Wort** 3. **4.** *sports:* a) stop, block, save, b) hold (a record): **s-n Vorsprung ~** stay in the lead. **5.** hold, contain. **6.** make, deliver (speech *etc*), give (lecture): → **Predigt, Rede** 1, **Vorlesung. 7. sich ~** keep (car, dog, personnel, *etc*), take (newspaper). **8.** treat: **er hielt s-e Kinder sehr streng** he was very strict with his children. **9. ~ für** (mis)take *s.o., s.th.* for, consider *s.o., s.th.* (to be): **ich halte es für ratsam** I think it advisable; **man sollte es nicht für möglich ~, aber ...** you wouldn't believe it but ...; **wofür ~ Sie mich (eigentlich)?** who do you think I am?; **für wie alt hältst du ihn?** how old do you think he is? **10. viel ~ von** think highly (*or* the world) of; **nicht viel ~ von** not to think much of; **er hält nichts vom Sparen** he doesn't believe in saving; **was ~ Sie von ...?** a) what do you think of ...?, b) **e-r Tasse Tee** *etc?* how about a cup of tea *etc?* **11.** do, handle: **wie hältst du es mit ...?** what do you usually do about ...?; **das kannst du ~, wie du willst!** please yourself! **12. et. auf sich ~** → 19. **II** *v/i* **13.** hold (*a. fig. weather*), last, **flowers, food,** *etc:* keep. **14.** stop, *mot. a.* draw up, pull up. **15.** *sports:* save. **16. an sich ~** restrain o.s., control o.s. **17. ~ auf** (*acc*) a) pay attention to, b) set great store by, c) insist on. **18. ~ auf** (*acc*) a) ♣ *a.* **~ nach** head for, b) aim at; **nach Süden ~** be heading south; **mehr nach links ~** keep (aim) more to the left. **19. auf sich ~** a) be particular about one's appearance, b) be self-respecting. **20. zu j-m ~** a) stand by s.o., F stick to s.o., b) side with s.o. **III sich ~ 21.** hold on (**an** *dat* to): *fig.* **sich ~ an** (*acc*) keep to, F stick to (**facts, rules,** *etc*); **sich an j-n ~** a) rely on s.o., b) hold s.o. liable. **22.** wear well, last long, **food, flowers,** *etc:* keep, **weather:** hold: **F sie hat sich gut gehalten** she is well-preserved. **23. sich ~ für** think (*or* consider) o.s. (to be); **sie hält sich für et. Besonderes** she thinks she's s.th. special. **24. sich aufrecht ~** hold (*or* carry) o.s. upright; **ich kann mich kaum noch auf den Beinen ~** I'm ready to drop. **25.** keep, stay: **sich warm ~** keep warm; **halte dich mehr links** keep more to the left; **er hat sich bei der Firma nicht lange gehalten** he didn't last long with the firm.

'Halten *n* (-s) **1.** *mot.* **zum ~ bringen** stop, bring *s.th.* to a standstill; *fig.* **da gab es kein ~ mehr** there was no holding them (*etc*). **2.** → **Haltung** 4.

'Haltepunkt *m* stop.

'Halter *m* (-s; -) **1.** ☺ a) holder, b) handle, c) rest. **2.** ♣♣ owner.

'Halterung *f* (-; -en) ☺ holding device.

'Halteschild *n* stop sign. **'Haltesi,gnal** *n* stop signal. **'Haltestelle** *f* stop. **'Halteverbot** *n* no stopping (zone). **'Halteverbotsschild** *n* no stopping sign.

'haltlos *adj* **1.** unstable, weak. **2.** untenable, unfounded. **'Haltlosigkeit** *f* (-; *no* *pl*) **1.** weakness, instability. **2.** untenableness, unfoundedness.

'haltmachen *v/i* (*sep*, -ge-, h) (make a) stop: *fig. vor nichts* ~ stop at nothing.

'Haltung *f* (-; -en) **1.** a) posture, b) *a. sports*: position, c) pose: ~ *annehmen* ✗ stand to attention. **2.** *no pl* a) deportment, behavio(u)r, b) attitude (*gegenüber* towards): *politische* ~ political outlook (*or* views). **3.** *no pl* composure: ~ *bewahren* a) control o.s., b) *a.* ~ *zeigen* bear up well. **4.** *no pl* keeping (*animals etc*).

Halunke [ha'luŋkə] *m* (-n; -n) scoundrel.

Hamburger ['hambʊrgər] **I** *m* (-s; -) **1.** *a.* **'Hamburgerin** *f* (-; -nen) Hamburgian. **2.** *gastr.* hamburger. **II** *adj* **3.** (of) Hamburg.

Häme ['hɛ:mə] *f* (-; *no pl*) F sneers, snide remarks: *voller* ~ sneeringly.

'hämisch *adj* malicious, sneering.

Hammel ['haməl] *m* (-s; -) **1.** *zo.* wether. **2.** *gastr.* mutton. **3.** F *fig.* idiot.

Hammelbraten *m* roast mutton.

'Hammelfleisch *n* mutton.

'Hammelkeule *f* leg of mutton.

Hammelsprung *m parl.* division.

Hammer ['hamər] *m* (-s; ⁀) **1.** hammer (*a.* ♪, *sports or at auctions*), mallet, *parl. etc*: gavel: *unter den* ~ *und Sichel* hammer and sickle: *unter den* ~ *kommen* come under the hammer. **2.** F *fig.* whammy: *das ist ein* ~*!* that beats everything!

'Hammerkla,vier *n* piano(forte).

'hämmern ['hɛmərn] (h) **I** *v/i* **1.** hammer, *fig. heart etc*: *a.* pound. **2.** ~ *auf* (*acc*), ~ *gegen* hammer away at, pound (at). **II** *v/t* **3.** ☉ *a.* hammer, beat, b) forge.

Hammer|werfen *n* (-s) *sports*: hammer throwing. **~werfer** *m* hammer thrower.

Hämoglobin [hɛmoglo'bi:n] *n* (-s; *no pl*) h(a)emoglobin.

Hämophile [hɛmo'fi:lə] *m* (-n; -n) ♂ h(a)emophiliac.

Hämorrhoiden [hɛmoro'i:dən] *pl* ♂ h(a)emorrhoids, F piles.

Hampelmann ['hampəlman] *m* (-[e]s; ⁀er) **1.** jumping Jack. **2.** F *contp.* clown.

Hamster ['hamstər] *m* (-s; -) *zo.* hamster.

Hamsterer *m* (-s; -) hoarder.

Hamsterkäufe *pl* panic buying.

'hamstern ['hamstərn] *v/t*, *v/i* (h) hoard.

Hand [hant] *f* (-; ⁀e) hand (*a.* cards): *j-m die* ~ *geben* (*or* **reichen**, **schütteln**)

shake hands with s.o.; ~ *in* ~ *gehen* walk (*fig.* go) hand in hand (*mit* with); *Hände hoch* (*weg*)*!* hands up (off)!; ~*!* soccer: hands!; *fig. die öffentliche* ~ the public authorities, the State; *j-s rechte* ~ s.o.'s right-hand man; *an* ~ *von* (*or gen*) by means of, on the basis of; *aus erster* (*zweiter*) ~ *buy*, *know*, *etc* first-hand (secondhand); *bei der* ~, *zur* ~ at hand, handy; *mit der* ~, *von* ~ *make etc* by hand; *unter der* ~ on the quiet; *zu Händen* c/o (= care of), *adm.* Attention Mr Smith *etc*; *mit leeren Händen abziehen* go away empty-handed; (*mit*) ~ *anlegen* lend a hand; *et. in die Hände bekommen* get hold of s.th.; *j-m in die Hände fallen* fall into s.o.'s hands; *j-m et. an die* ~ *geben* furnish s.o. with s.th.; *aus der* ~ *geben* part with; *j-n in der* ~ *haben* have s.o. in one's grip (F over a barrel); ~ *und Fuß haben* make sense; *j-m freie* ~ *lassen* give s.o. a free hand; *von der* ~ *in den Mund leben* live from hand to mouth; *letzte* ~ *an et. legen* put the finishing touches to s.th.; *fig. die Hände in den Schoß legen* twiddle one's thumbs; *aus der* ~ *legen* lay aside; *s-e* ~ *ins Feuer legen für* put one's hand into the fire for; *es liegt in s-r* ~ it's up to him; *es liegt klar auf der* ~ it's obvious; *fig. et. in die* ~ *nehmen* take charge of s.th.; *j-m* (*et.*) *in die Hände spielen* play (s.th.) into s.o.'s hands; *alle Hände voll zu tun haben* have one's hands full; *in andere Hände übergehen* change hands; *das war von langer* ~ *vorbereitet* that was carefully planned long beforehand; *e-e* ~ *wäscht die andere* you scratch my back and I'll scratch yours; *sich mit Händen und Füßen* (*gegen et.*) *wehren* fight (s.th.) tooth and nail; *von der* ~ *weisen* dismiss; *es läßt sich nicht von der* ~ *weisen, daß …* it can't be denied that …; *mit beiden Händen zugreifen* jump at the chance; → *Spiel* **2.**

'Handarbeit *f* **1.** *no pl* manual work. **2.** a) *no pl* handiwork, handicraft, b) handmade article: *diese Vase ist* ~ this vase is handmade. **3.** needlework.

'Handarbeiter(**in** *f*) *m* manual worker.

'Handaufheben *n* (-s) *parl. durch* ~ by a show of hands.

'**Handball** m (-[e]s; no pl) handball.
'**Handballen** m anat. ball of the thumb.
'**Handballer** [-balɐ] m (-s; -), '**Handballerin** f (-; -nen) F, '**Handballspieler(in** f) m handball player.
'**handbetätigt** adj ✪ hand-operated, manual.
'**Handbetrieb** m (-[e]s; no pl) manual operation: mit ~ → handbetätigt.
'**Handbewegung** f gesture.
'**Handbiblio‚thek** f reference library.
'**Handbohrma‚schine** f hand drill.
'**handbreit** adj a few inches wide.
'**Handbreit** f (-; -) hand's breadth.
'**Handbremse** f handbrake.
'**Handbuch** n manual, handbook, guide.
Händchen ['hɛntçən] n (-s; -) little hand: F ~ halten hold hands.
'**Handcreme** f hand cream.
Hände|druck ['hɛndə-] m handshake.
~**klatschen** n (-s) clapping, applause.
Handel ['handəl] m (-s; no pl) **1.** commerce, business, trade (mit in s.th., with s.o.), a. contp. traffic: ~ und Gewerbe trade and industry; ~ mit Waffen (Drogen etc) trade (or traffic) in arms (drugs etc); im ~ on the market; nicht mehr im ~ off the market; in den ~ bringen (kommen) put (be) on the market; ~ treiben mit a) et. deal in s.th., b) j-m trade (or do business) with s.o. **2.** (business) transaction, F deal, fig. a. bargain.
Händel ['hɛndəl] pl quarrel, fight.
handeln ['handəln] (h) **I** v/i **1.** act, take action. **2.** ✝ trade, do business (mit j-m with s.o.): ~ mit trade (or deal, contp. traffic) in. **3.** (um) bargain (for), haggle (over): er läßt mit sich ~ he is open to an offer (w.s. a suggestion). **4.** ~ von book, film, etc: be about, deal with. **II** v/t gehandelt werden a) ✝ be sold, on the stock exchange: be traded, be listed, b) name etc: be mentioned. **III** v/impers es handelt sich um it concerns, it is a question of, it is about; worum handelt es sich? what is it (all) about?, what's the problem?; es handelt sich darum, ob (wer etc) the question is whether (who etc); darum handelt es sich (nicht)! that's just (not) the point!; bei dem Opfer handelt es sich um e-n Ausländer the victim is a foreigner.
'**Handeln** n (-s) acting (etc): gemeinsa-

mes (rasches) ~ joint (quick) action.
'**Handels|abkommen** n trade agreement. ~**atta‚ché** m commercial attaché. ~**bank** f (-; -en) merchant bank. ~**beschränkungen** pl trade restrictions. ~**betrieb** m commercial enterprise. ~**bezeichnung** f trade name. ~**beziehungen** pl trade relations. ~**bi‚lanz** f (aktive ~ surplus, passive ~ adverse) balance of trade. ~**defizit** n trading deficit. ²**einig** adj ~ werden come to terms (mit with). ~**em‚bargo** n (trade) embargo. ~**flotte** f merchant fleet. ~**genossenschaft** f traders' cooperative. ~**gericht** n commercial court. ~**gesellschaft** f (trading) company, Am. (business) corporation: offene ~ general partnership. ~**gesetzbuch** n Commercial Code. ~**hafen** m trading port. ~**kammer** f Chamber of Commerce. ~**klasse** f Äpfel der ~ A grade one apples. ~**korrespon‚denz** f commercial correspondence. ~**lehrer** m teacher at a commercial school. ~**macht** f (great) trading nation. ~**ma‚rine** f merchant navy. ~**marke** f brand. ~**mi‚nister** m minister of commerce, Br. Secretary of State for Trade and Industry, Am. Secretary of Commerce. ~**mini‚sterium** n ministry of commerce, Br. Board of Trade, Am. Department of Commerce. ~**name** n trade name. ~**nati‚on** f trading nation. ~**niederlassung** f **1.** business establishment. **2.** registered seat. **3.** branch. ~**partner** m trading partner. ~**platz** n trading cent/re (Am. -er). ~**poli‚tik** f trade policy. ~**recht** n (-[e]s; no pl) commercial law. ~**re‚gister** n trade register: ins ~ eintragen (lassen) register, Am. incorporate. ~**reisende** m, f (-n; -n) commercial travel(l)er. ~**schiff** n trading vessel. ~**schiffahrt** f merchant shipping. ~**schranke** f trade barrier. ~**schule** f commercial school. ~**spanne** f trade margin. ²**üblich** adj usual in the trade: ~e Qualität commercial quality. ~**verkehr** m trade trading. ~**vertrag** m trade agreement. ~**vertreter(in** f) m commercial representative. ~**vertretung** f commercial agency, pol. trade mission. ~**vo‚lumen** n volume of trade. ~**ware** f commodity: ~n merchandise. ~**weg** m trade

route. ~**wert** m market value. ~**zweig** m line of business.

'**handeltreibend** adj trading.

'**händeringend** adv a) imploringly, b) despairingly.

'**Händeschütteln** n (-s) shaking of hands, handshake.

'**Handfertigkeit** f manual skill.

'**handfest** adj **1.** sturdy, strong. **2.** fig. huge (scandal etc), solid (proof etc), whopping (lie).

'**Hand|feuerlöscher** m fire extinguisher. ~**feuerwaffe** f hand gun, pl small arms. ~**fläche** f palm. ⸂**gearbeitet**, ⸂**gefertigt** pf handmade. ~**gelenk** n wrist: F *aus dem* ~ off the cuff, just like that. ⸂**gemalt** adj handpainted. ~**gemenge** n (-s; -) fray, brawl. ~**gepäck** n hand luggage (Am. baggage). ⸂**geschrieben** adj handwritten. ⸂**gestrickt** adj **1.** handknitted. **2.** F contp. home-made. ⸂**gewebt** adj handwoven. ~**gra**,**nate** f hand grenade.

handgreiflich ['hantgraɪflɪç] adj **1. er wurde** ~ a) he got violent, b) he started to paw. **2.** fig. obvious, plain.

'**Handgreiflichkeiten** pl violence.

'**Handgriff** m **1.** handle, grip. **2.** fig. a) movement of the hand, b) manipulation: *mit wenigen* ~**en** do s.th. in no time (or deftly).

'**Handhabe** f (-; -n) a) proof, b) lever: *er hat keinerlei* ~ he hasn't got a leg to stand on. '**handhaben** v/t (handhabte, gehandhabt, h) **1.** use, handle, operate. **2.** fig. a) handle, deal with, b) apply. '**Handhabung** f (-; -en) handling (a. fig.), use, operation.

Handicap ['hɛndɪkæp] n (-s; -s) a. fig. handicap (*für* to).

'**Hand|kante** f side of the hand: *Schlag mit der* ~ → ~**kantenschlag** m (karate) chop. ~**karren** m handcart. ~**koffer** m small suitcase. ~**kuß** m *j-m e-n* ~ *geben* kiss s.o.'s hand; F fig. *mit* ~ gladly.

'**Handlanger** m (-s; -) odd-job man, contp. dogsbody, pol. etc henchman.

Händler ['hɛndlər] m (-s; -), '**Händlerin** f (-; -nen) trader, merchant, dealer.

'**Handlesekunst** f (-; no pl) palmistry.

'**handlich** adj handy.

'**Handlichkeit** f (-; no pl) handiness.

'**Handlung** f (-; -en) **1.** act, action. **2.** of film etc: action, story, plot: *Ort der* ~ scene (of action). **3.** ✝ shop.

'**Handlungs|bedarf** m *es besteht (kein)* ~ this calls (there is no need) for action. ~**bevollmächtigte** m, f (authorized) agent, proxy. ~**fähig** adj **1.** ⚖ having disposing capacity. **2.** functioning, working (government etc). ~**fähigkeit** f (-; no pl) **1.** ⚖ legal capacity. **2.** capacity to act. ~**freiheit** f freedom of action: *j-m* ~ *geben* give s.o. a free hand. ~**gehilfe** m, ~**gehilfin** f **1.** (commercial) clerk. **2.** shop assistant. ⸂**reich** adj full of action, action-packed. ~**reisende** m, f commercial travel(l)er. ~**spielraum** m room for manoeuvre (Am. maneuver). ~**vollmacht** f limited authority to act and sign. ~**weise** f **1.** way of acting, conduct. **2.** procedure.

Hand|pflege f manicure. ~**puppe** f glove puppet. ~**rücken** m back of the hand. ~**schelle** f handcuff: *j-m* ~**n** *anlegen* handcuff s.o. ~**schlag** m (-[e]s; no pl) handshake: *durch* ~ *bekräftigen* shake hands on; F *er tut k-n* ~ he doesn't lift a finger. ~**schrift** f **1.** handwriting, hand. **2.** manuscript. ⸂**schriftlich I** adj handwritten. **II** adv in writing, correct etc by hand. ~**schuh** m glove. ~**schuhfach** n mot. glove compartment. ~**spiegel** m hand mirror. ~**spiel** n soccer: hands. ~**stand** m gym. handstand. ~**standüberschlag** m handspring. ~**steuerung** f manual control. ~**streich** m coup (de main). ~**tasche** f handbag, Am. purse.

'**Handtuch** n (*das* ~ *werfen* a. F fig. throw in the towel. ~**auto**,**mat** m towel dispenser. ~**halter** m towel rack.

'**Handumdrehen** n *im* ~ in no time.

'**handverlesen** adj a. fig. handpicked.

'**Handvoll** f (-; -) a. fig. handful.

'**handwarm** adj lukewarm.

'**Handwaschbecken** n hand basin.

'**Handwerk** n (-[e]s; -e) trade, craft: *das* ~ the trade; *ein* ~ *lernen* learn a trade; fig. *j-m das* ~ *legen* put a stop to s.o.('s game); *j-m ins* ~ *pfuschen* botch at s.o.'s trade; *er versteht sein* ~ he knows his stuff. '**Handwerker** m (-s; -) (skilled) workman, craftsman.

'**handwerklich** adj craftsman's, craft: ~**er Beruf** skilled trade; ~**es Können** craftsmanship, craft skills.

'Handwerks|kammer *f* chamber of handicrafts. **~meister** *m* master craftsman. **~zeug** *n* tools (*a. fig.*).
'Hand|wörterbuch *n* concise dictionary. **~wurzel** *f anat.* wrist, carpus. **~zeichen** *n* **1.** sign. **2.** *parl.* show of hands. **~zettel** *m* leaflet.
Hanf [hanf] *m* (-[e]s; *no pl*) hemp.
Hang [haŋ] *m* (-[e]s; ⁓e) **1.** slope. **2.** *gym.* hang. **3.** *fig.* (**zu**) a) bent (for), tendency (to), b) proneness (to).
Hangar [haŋar] *m* (-s; -s) hangar.
'Hängebacken *pl* flabby cheeks.
'Hängebrücke *f* suspension bridge.
'Hängebusen *m* sagging breasts.
'Hängelampe *f* hanging lamp.
hangeln ['haŋəln] *v/i* (h) *gym.* climb (or travel) hand over hand.
'Hängematte *f* hammock.
'Hangen: mit ~ und Bangen in anxious anticipation.
hängen[1] ['hɛŋən] *v/i* (hing, gehangen, h) **1.** hang (**an** *dat* from *or* on): **voller Äpfel** *etc* ⁓ be full of apples *etc*; **über** *j-m* ⁓ *a. fig.* hang over s.o.; *fig.* **die ganze Arbeit hängt an mir** I am stuck with all the work; → *Tropf.* **2.** (**an** *dat* to) *mud etc*: cling; stick. **3.** be stuck, be caught: F *fig.* **woran hängt's?** what's the problem?; **er hängt in Latein** he's bad at Latin. **4.** ~ **an** (*dat*) love (*life, money, etc*), cling to (*a custom etc*); **an** *j-m* ~ be fond of (*or* devoted to) s.o. **5.** be lopsided.
'hängen[2] (h) **I** *v/t* **1.** *j-n* ~ hang s.o.; **gehängt werden** be hanged. **2.** *et.* ~ **an** (*acc*) hang s.th. from (*or* on); *fig.* **sein Herz** ~ **an** (*acc*) set one's heart on. **II** **sich** ~ **an** (*acc*) hang on to; F **sich ans Telefon** ~ get on the phone; **sich an** *j-n* ~ a) cling to s.o., b) trail s.o., c) *runner:* drop in behind s.o.
'Hängen *n* (-s) F **mit** ~ **und Würgen** only just, barely.
'hängenbleiben *v/i* (*irr, sep,* -ge-, sn, → **bleiben**) F **1.** (**an** *dat*) get (*or* be) caught (by), catch (on, in), get (*or* be) stuck (in): *fig.* **im Gedächtnis** ~ stick in one's mind. **2.** *fig.* be held up, *sports:* be stopped (**an** *dat* by).
'hängenlassen (*irr, sep, no* -ge-, h, → **lassen**) **I** *v/t* **1.** let *s.th.* hang, (let *s.th.*) dangle. **2.** F *j-n* ~ leave s.o. in the lurch. **II** **sich** ~ let o.s. go.

'Hängeohren *pl* floppy ears.
'Hängepar,tie *f chess:* adjourned game.
'Hängepflanze *f* hanging plant.
'Hänger *m* (-s; -) loose dress (*or* coat).
'Hängeschrank *m* wall cabinet.
Hans'dampf *m* (-[e]s; -e) F ~ **in allen Gassen** jack-of-all-trades.
hanseatisch [hanze'a:tɪʃ] *adj* Hanseatic.
Hänse'lei *f* (-; -en) teasing, F kidding.
hänseln ['hɛnzəln] *v/t* (h) tease, F kid.
Hansestadt ['hanzə-] *f* Hanse town.
'Hanswurst *m* (-[e]s; -e) *a. contp.* clown.
Hantel ['hantəl] *f* (-; -n) dumbbell.
hantieren [han'ti:rən] *v/i* (h) **1.** potter around. **2.** ~ **mit** work with, handle; ~ **an** (*dat*) work on, *contp.* fiddle with.
hapern ['ha:pərn] *v/impers* (h) F **es hapert mit** (*or* **bei**) there are problems with; **es hapert an** (*dat*) there isn't (*or* aren't) enough; **im Englischen hapert es bei ihm** English is his weak point.
Häppchen ['hɛpçən] *n* (-s; -) a) morsel, b) titbit, c) canapé.
Happen ['hapən] *m* (-s; -) **1.** bite (to eat): **e-n** ~ **essen** have a bite. **2.** *fig.* (**ein fetter** ~) a fine) catch.
happig ['hapɪç] *adj* F steep (*prices etc*).
Härchen ['hɛ:rçən] *n* (-s; -) little hair.
Harem ['ha:rɛm] *m* (-s; -s) harem.
Harfe ['harfə] *f* (-; -n) ♪ harp. **Harfenist** [harfə'nɪst] *m* (-en; -en), **Harfe'nistin** *f* (-; -nen) harpist.
Harke ['harkə] *f* (-; -n) rake: F *j-m* **zeigen, was e-e** ~ **ist** show (*or* tell) s.o. what's what.
harmlos ['harmlo:s] *adj* harmless.
'Harmlosigkeit *f* (-; *no pl*) harmlessness.
Harmonie [harmo'ni:] *f* (-; -n) harmony.
Harmo'nielehre *f* (-; *no pl*) ♪ harmony.
harmonieren [harmo'ni:rən] *v/i* (h) harmonize (**mit** with). **harmonisch** [har'mo:nɪʃ] *adj* ♪, ♪ harmonic(al), *a. fig.* harmonious. **harmonisieren** [harmoni'zi:rən] *v/t* (h) *a. fig.* harmonize.
Harn [harn] *m* (-[e]s; -e) ⚕ urine.
'Harnblase *f anat.* bladder.
'harnen *v/i* (h) pass water, urinate.
'Harnflasche *f* urinal.
'Harngrieß *m* ⚕ gravel.
Harnisch ['harnɪʃ] *m* (-s; -e) a) (suit of) armo(u)r, b) cuirass: F *j-n* **in** ~ **bringen** get s.o.'s back up; **in** ~ **geraten** get (really) furious; **in** ~ **sein** be up in arms.
'Harn|leiter *m anat.* ureter. **~probe** *f* ⚕

urine sample. **~röhre** f anat. urethra.
~säure f ⚕ uric acid. **⚕treibend** adj
diuretic. **~untersuchung** f urinalysis.
~wege pl anat. urinary tract.

Harpune [har'puːnə] f (-; -n) harpoon.
harren ['harən] v/i (h) (gen or auf acc)
wait (for), await (s.o., s.th.).
Harsch [harʃ] m (-es; no pl) crusted
snow. **'harschig** adj crusted.
hart [hart] **I** adj 1. hard: **~ werden** harden (a. fig.); **~es Ei** hard-boiled egg;
fig. **~e Währung (Droge)** hard currency
(drug). **2.** fig. a) hard, b) hardened,
tough, sports: rough: **er ist ~ im Nehmen** he can take a lot of punishment;
er blieb ~ he stood firm. **3.** fig. hard
(work, life, winter, etc), severe (criticism, punishment, etc), harsh (words
etc), heavy (blow, loss, etc), tough (policy etc): **~e Tatsachen** hard facts; **das
war ~** that was tough!; **das war ~ für
ihn** that was hard on him; → **Nuß,
Schule. II** adv **4.** hard, severely: **~ arbeiten** work hard; **es ging ~ auf ~** it
was either do or die; **wenn es ~ auf ~
geht** when it comes to the crunch. **5. ~
an** (dat) close to; **⚓ ~ am Wind** close-
hauled.
Härte ['hɛrtə] f (-; -n) **1.** hardness. **2.** fig.
toughness, sports: roughness, rough
play. **3.** fig. hardness, harshness, severity: **⚖ (unbillige ~** undue) hardship. **4.**
phot. contrast. **~fall** m hardship case.
härten ['hɛrtən] (h) **I** v/t a) harden, b)
temper (steel). **II** v/i harden, grow hard.
'Hartfaserplatte f hardboard, Am.
fiberboard.
'hartgefroren adj frozen hard.
'hartgekocht adj hard-boiled.
'Hartgeld n (-es; no pl) coins.
'hartgesotten [-gəzɔtən] adj fig. hard-
-boiled.
'Hartgummi n, m hard rubber.
'hartherzig adj hard-hearted.
'Hartkäse m hard cheese.
'hartnäckig [-nɛkɪç] adj stubborn, persistent, ✚ refractory. **'Hartnäckigkeit** f
(-; no pl) stubbornness, persistence.
'Hartplatz m hard pitch (tennis: court).
'Härtung f (-; -en) hardening, tempering.
'Hartwurst f hard sausage.
Harz [harts] n (-es; -e) resin, rosin.
'harzig adj resinous.
Hasardspiel [ha'zart-] n fig. gamble.

Hasch [haʃ] n (-s; no pl) F hash.
Haschee [ha'ʃeː] n (-s; -s) gastr. hash.
haschen[1] ['haʃən] (h) **I** v/t (sich ~ play)
catch. **II** v/i ~ **nach** snatch at, fig. seek;
nach Komplimenten ~ fish for compliments.
'haschen[2] v/i (h) F smoke hash.
Häschen ['hɛːsçən] n (-s; -) **1.** young
hare. **2.** F bunny.
Hascherl ['haʃərl] n (-s; -[n]) dial. (ar-
mes) ~ poor little thing, poor creature.
Haschisch ['haʃɪʃ] n (-; no pl) hashish.
Hase ['haːzə] m (-n; -n) hare: fig. alter ~
old hand; **sehen, wie der ~ läuft** see
how things develop; **da liegt der ~ im
Pfeffer** that's the real problem; **mein
Name ist ~(, ich weiß von nichts)!**
search me!
Haselnuß ['haːzəl-] f **1.** hazelnut. **2.** →
'Haselnußstrauch m hazelnut (tree).
'Hasenbraten m roast hare.
'Hasenfuß m F coward.
'Hasenpfeffer m gastr. jugged hare.
'Hasenscharte f ✚ hare lip.
Häsin ['hɛːzɪn] f (-; -nen) female hare,
doe.
Haspel ['haspəl] f (-; -n) ⚙ hasp, reel.
haspeln ['haspəln] v/t (h) **1.** ⚙ reel,
wind. **2.** a. v/i splutter.
Haß [has] m (-sses; no pl) (auf acc, gegen
of, for) hatred, hate: **aus ~** out of hatred; **e-n ~ haben auf** (acc) → **hassen**
['hasən] v/t (h) hate: → **Pest.**
'hassenswert adj hateful. **'haßerfüllt**
adj full of hate, venomous (look etc).
häßlich ['hɛslɪç] adj ugly, fig. a. nasty.
'Haßliebe f love-hate relationship.
Hast [hast] f (-; no pl) hurry, rush.
hasten ['hastən] v/i (sn) hurry.
'hastig **I** adj **1.** hasty, hurried: **nicht so ~!**
just a minute! **2.** slapdash. **3.** nervous.
II adv **4.** hastily, in a hurry.
hätscheln ['hɛːtʃəln] v/t (h) **1.** cuddle. **2.**
fig. pamper.
hatte ['hatə] pret of **haben.**
Haube ['haʊbə] f (-; -n) **1.** a) bonnet, b)
hood (a. ⚙), c) cap, d) eccl. cornet: fig.
unter die ~ bringen find a husband for.
2. (hair-)drier. **3.** zo. crest. **4.** mot. bonnet, Am. hood.
Hauch [haʊx] m (-[e]s; no pl) **1.** a) breath,
b) breath (of wind), c) whiff. **2.** ling.
aspiration. **3.** fig. touch. **'hauch'dünn**
adj **1.** a) wafer-thin, b) flimsy. **2.** fig.

very slim (*chance etc*), bare (*majority etc*): **~er Sieg** knife-edge victory.

hauchen ['haʊxən] *v/i*, *v/t* (h) breathe, *ling.* aspirate.

'**Hauchlaut** *m ling.* aspirate.

'**Haudegen** *m* (-s; -) **alter ~** F warhorse.

Haue[1] ['haʊə] *f* (-; -n) *dial.* hoe.

'**Haue**[2] *f* (-; *no pl*) F (**~ kriegen** get a) spanking.

hauen ['haʊən] (haute *or* hieb, gehauen, h) **I** *v/t* **1.** F hit, slap, thrash, spank: *sich* **~** fight, scrap; → **Ohr, Pauke. 2.** F bang, slam. **3.** *dial.* a) hew, cut, b) chop (*wood*), c) chop down (*tree*). **II** *v/i* **4.** hit (out) (*nach* at). '**Hauer** *m* (-s; -) **1.** *zo.* tusk. **2.** ⚒ face worker.

Häufchen ['hɔʏfçən] *n* (-s; -) small heap (*or* pile): **wie ein ~ Unglück** (looking) the picture of misery.

Haufen ['haʊfən] *m* (-s; -) **1.** heap, pile: F **über den ~ rennen** knock s.o. over, **über den ~ fahren** (*or run*), *s.th.* down; *j-n* **über den ~ schießen** shoot s.o. down; *über den ~ werfen* a) upset (*plan etc*), b) explode (*theory etc*). **2.** F loads of, a lot (*or* lots) of (*friends, money, etc*): *e-n ~ Geld kosten* (*verdienen*) cost (make) a packet. **3.** F crowd, bunch, ⚔ outfit. **4.** ⚒ turd.

häufen ['hɔʏfən] (h) **I** *v/t* heap up, *fig. a.* accumulate: *sich* **~ gehäuft.** **II** *sich* **~** *fig. a.* accumulate, pile up, *debts: a.* mount, b) increase (in number).

'**haufenweise** *adv* F a) in piles, b) in crowds, a lot of, lots of, loads of.

'**Haufenwolke** *f* cumulus (cloud).

häufig ['hɔʏfɪç] **I** *adj* frequent, *a.* widespread. **II** *adv* frequently, often: **~ besuchen** *a.* frequent, (high) incidence. '**Häufigkeit** *f* (-; *no pl*) frequency, (high) incidence. '**Häufung** *f* (-; -en) accumulation, increase, spreading, frequent occurrence.

Haupt [haʊpt] *n* (-[e]s; ⸚er) *a. fig.* head: *et. an* **~ *und Gliedern reformieren*** reform s.th. root and branch.

'**Haupt...** main, chief, principal. **~abteilungsleiter** *m* senior head of department. **~aktio,när** *m* principal shareholder (*Am.* stockholder). **~ak,zent** *m ling.* primary stress. **~al,tar** *m* high altar. ⸚**amtlich** *adj and adv* full-time. **~angeklagte** *m, f* principal defendant. **~anschluß** *m teleph.* main line. **~anteil** *m* principal (*fig.* lion's) share. **~attrakti,on** *f* main attraction, highlight. **~auf-** **gabe** *f* main duty (*or* work). **~augenmerk** *n* **sein ~ richten auf** (*acc*) give one's special attention to. **~bahnhof** *m* main station. ⸚**beruflich** *adj and adv* full-time, *adv a.* as one's main job. **~beschäftigung** *f* main job. **~bestandteil** *m* main constituent. ⸚**betrieb** *m* ✝ a) head office, b) central works. **~buch** *n* ✝ main ledger. **~darsteller(in)** *f m* leading actor (actress), lead. **~einfahrt** *f*, **~eingang** *m* main entrance. **~erbe** *m* chief (*or* principal) heir. **~fach** *n ped.*, *univ.* main subject, *Am.* major: *als* (*or im*) **~ studieren** study s.th. as a main subject, *Am.* major in. **~feldwebel** *m* ⚔ sergeant major, *Am.* first sergeant. **~fi,gur** *f* central figure, *thea. etc* main character. **~film** *m* feature film. **~gang** *m gastr.* main course. **~gebäude** *n* main building. **~gericht** *n gastr.* main course. **~geschäft** *n* **1.** main business. **2.** → **geschäftsstelle** *f* a) head office, b) main store. **~geschäftszeit** *f* peak business hours. **~gewicht** *n fig.* main emphasis. **~gewinn** *m* first prize. **~grund** *m* main reason. **~hahn** *m* ⊙ main tap. **~kasse** *f* main cash desk, *thea.* box office. **~last** *f* main burden: *die* **~ tragen** bear the brunt (*gen* of).

Häuptling ['hɔʏptlɪŋ] *m* (-s; -e) **1.** chieftain. **2.** F boss.

'**Haupt|mahlzeit** *f* main meal. **~mangel** *m* main fault (*or* weakness). **~mann** *m* (-[e]s; -leute) ⚔ captain. **~merkmal** *n* chief characteristic. **~nahrung** *f* staple (food). **~nenner** *m* ⅍ common denominator. **~niederlassung** *f* ✝ head office, headquarters. **~per,son** *f* most important person, central figure (*thea. a.* character). **~postamt** *n* main post office. **~probe** *f thea.* dress (✝ general) rehearsal. **~quar,tier** *n* headquarters. **~reisezeit** *f* peak tourist season. **~rolle** *f thea. etc* leading role, main part, lead: *fig. die* **~ spielen** a) be all-important, b) be the central figure. **~sache** *f* (-; *no pl*) main (*or* most important) thing: **~, du bist da!** (the) main thing (is), you're here! ⸚**sächlich** *adj and adv* main(ly), chief(ly), *adv a.* above all. **~sai,son** *f* peak season. **~satz** *m ling.* main clause. **~schalter** *m* ⚡ master switch. **~schlagader** *f anat.* aorta. **~schlüssel** *m* master key. **~schuld** *f* **er trägt die ~ daran** it's mainly his fault. **~schuldige** *m, f* chief culprit, ⚖ principal. **~schule** *f* secondary modern school. **~sendezeit** *f TV* prime time. **~sitz** *m* head office, headquarters. **~sorge** *f* main concern. **~speicher** *m computer:* main memory. **~stadt** *f* capital (city). **~straße** *f* main street. **~stütze** *f fig.* mainstay. **~täter** *m* ⚖ principal (in the first degree). **~teil** *m* main part, most of it. **~thema** *n* main subject. **~ton** *m* 1. *ling.* main stress. 2. ♪ keynote. **~tor** *n* main gate. **~treffer** *m* first prize, F jackpot. **~tri,büne** *f* grandstand. **~unterschied** *m* main difference. **~verfahren** *n,* **~verhandlung** *f* ⚖ trial. **~verkehrsstraße** *f* main road. **~verkehrszeit** *f* rush hour. **~versammlung** *f* general meeting. **~vertreter** *m* general agent. **~verwaltung** *f* head office. **~wort** *n* (-[e]s; ⸚er) noun. **~zeuge** *m,* **~zeugin** *f* chief witness. **~ziel** *n* main objective. **~zweck** *m* main object, chief purpose.

hau ruck ['hau 'rʊk] *int* heave-ho.

Haus [haus] *n* (-es; ⸚er) a) house (*a. astr.*, ♈, *thea.*), building, b) family, c) dynasty: *parl.* **das (Hohe) ~** the House; *aus gutem ~(e) sein* come from a good family; *außer ~* out, not in; *im ~* inside, ♈ on the premises; *ins ~* in(doors); *fig. ins ~ stehen* be forthcoming; *das steht uns noch ins ~* we are yet in for that; *j-n nach ~(e) bringen* take (*or* see) s.o. home; *nach ~(e) kommen* come (*or* get) home; *zu ~(e) a. sports:* at home; *er ist nicht zu ~e a.* he is not in; *bei uns zu ~(e)* where I come from, at home; *fig. in e-r Sache zu ~e sein* be at home in s.th.; *sich wie zu ~(e) fühlen* feel at home; *fühl dich (ganz) wie zu ~e!* make yourself at home!; *frgb. von ~(e) aus* originally, actually; *thea. vor vollem ~(e) spielen* play to a full house.

Haus|al,tar *m* family altar. **~angestellte** *f* domestic (servant). **~an,tenne** *f* roof aerial (*Am.* antenna). **~apo,theke** *f* medicine cabinet. **~arbeit** *f* 1. housework. 2. *a. pl ped.* homework. **~ar,rest** *m* (*j-n unter ~ stellen* place s.o. under) house arrest. **~arzt** *m,* **~ärztin** *f* family doctor, *at spa etc:* resident doctor. **~aufgabe(n** *pl) f* (*s-e ~ machen a. fig.* do one's) homework. **~aufsatz** *m ped.* essay to be written at home. **~ball** *m*

private dance, house party. **~bar** *f* a) cocktail cabinet, b) bar. **~bau** *m* (-[e]s; *no pl*) house building. **~besetzer** *m* squatter. **~besetzung** *f* (-; -en) squatting. **~besitzer(in** *f) m* 1. house owner. 2. landlord (landlady). **~besuch** *m* home visit. **~bewohner** *m* a) occupant, b) tenant. **~boot** *n* houseboat. **~brand** *m* (-[e]s; *no pl*) domestic fuel.

Häuschen ['hɔysçən] *n* (-s; -) 1. small house, cottage: F (*ganz*) *aus dem ~ geraten* get into a flap (*wegen* about, *vor dat* with); *ganz aus dem ~ sein* F be wild (*vor* with). 2. F loo, *Am.* john.

'Hausdetek,tiv(in *f) m* store detective.

hausen ['hauzən] *v/i* (h) F 1. live. 2. (*übel*) *~* wreak havoc (*unter dat* among).

Häuserblock ['hɔyzərblɔk] *m* block (of houses).

'Haus|flur *m* hall(way). **~frau** *f* housewife. **~freund** *m iro.* (secret) lover. **~friedensbruch** *m* ⚖ illegal entry of *s.o.*'s house, *w.s.* violation of *s.o.*'s privacy. **~gebrauch** *m für den ~* for use in the home; F *fig. für den ~ reichen* be enough to get by on. ②**gemacht** *adj a. fig.* home-made. **~gemeinschaft** *f* 1. house community. 2. household.

'Haushalt *m* (-[e]s; -e) 1. household: (*j-m*) *den ~ führen* run the household (for s.o.); *im ~ helfen* help in the house. 2. *pol.* budget. 3. *biol.* balance. **'haushalten** *v/i* (*irr, sep,* -ge-, h, → **halten**) economize: *~ mit* be economical with; *mit s-n Kräften ~* husband one's energies. **'Haushälterin** [-hɛltərɪn] *f* (-; -nen) housekeeper. **'haushälterisch** *adj* economical.

'Haushalts... a) household (*article etc*), b) ♈, *pol.* budget (*committee, debate, etc*), budgetary (*deficit, policy, etc*). **~führung** *f* (-; *no pl*) housekeeping. **~geld** *n* housekeeping money. **~gerät** *n* household appliance. **~jahr** *n* fiscal year. **~mittel** *pl* budgetary means: (*gebilligte*) *~* appropriations. **~packung** *f* economy pack. **~plan** *m parl.* budget: *im ~ vorsehen* budget for.

'Hausherr *m* 1. head of (the) household. 2. landlord. 3. host.

'Hausherrin *f* 1. lady of the house. 2. landlady. 3. hostess.

'haushoch *adj* huge: *haushoher Sieg*

smashing victory; **haushohe Niederlage** crushing defeat; **~ gewinnen** win hands down; **~ schlagen** trounce; **~ verlieren** get an awful drubbing; **j-m überlegen sein** be streets ahead of s.o.

hausieren [haʊˈziːrən] *v/i* (h) **mit et. ~** (**gehen**) hawk s.th., *a. fig.* peddle s.th.

Hausierer *m* (-s; -) hawker, peddler.

'Hauslehrer(in *f)* *m* private tutor(ess).

häuslich [ˈhɔʏslɪç] *adj* a) household, domestic, b) family, c) homekeeping, domesticated: ✚ **~e Gemeinschaft** joint household; **im ~en Kreis** in the family circle; **er ist sehr ~** he's a real housebody; **sich ~ einrichten** (*or* **niederlassen**) settle down, *iro.* **bei j-m** come to stay with s.o.

'Häuslichkeit *f* (-; *no pl*) domesticity.

'Hausmacherart *f gastr.* **nach ~** home-made, traditional-style ...

'Haus|mädchen *n* maid. **~mann** *m* (-[e]s; ⸚er) house husband. **~mannskost** *f* good plain cooking. **~marke** *f* a) own brand, b) house wine, c) **F** s-e favo(u)rite brand. **~meister** *m* caretaker. **~mittel** *n* household remedy. **~müll** *m* household waste. **~mu‚sik** *f* music-making in the home. **~nummer** *f* house number. **~ordnung** *f* house rules. **~pflege** *f* home nursing (*or* care).

'Hausrat *m* (-[e]s; *no pl*) household effects. **'Hausratversicherung** *f* household contents insurance.

'Haus|sammlung *f* door-to-door collection. **~schlüssel** *m* front-door key. **~schuh** *m* slipper.

Hausse [ˈhoːs(ə)] *f* (-; -n) bull market, boom: **auf ~ spekulieren** bull the market. **'Haussespeku‚lant** *m* bull.

'Haussuchung *f* (-; -en) house search.

'Haus|tele‚fon *n* intercom. **~tier** *n* domestic animal, pet. **~tür** *f* front door. **~verwalter** *m* **1.** → **Hausmeister. 2.** property manager. **~verwaltung** *f* property management. **~wirt** *m* landlord. **~wirtin** *f* landlady. **~wirtschaft** *f* (-; *no pl*) **1.** housekeeping. **2.** → **~wirtschaftslehre** *f* domestic science, *Am.* home economics. **~zelt** *n* frame tent.

Haut [haʊt] *f* (-; ⸚e) skin (*a. fig.*), *a.* hide, *anat.*, ⚕ *a.* membrane, ♣ *a.* peel, *on milk etc*: *a.* film: **bis auf die ~ durchnäßt** soaked to the skin; **F mit ~ und Haar** completely; **F auf der faulen ~ liegen**, **sich auf die faule ~ legen** loaf; **e-e dicke ~ haben** *a. fig.* have a thick skin; **mit heiler ~ davonkommen** come out of it unscathed; **F aus der ~ fahren** go through the roof; **s-e (eigene) ~ retten** save one's skin; **sich s-r ~ wehren** defend o.s.; **ich möchte nicht in s-r ~ stecken** I wouldn't like to be in his shoes; **er ist nur noch ~ und Knochen** he's just skin and bones; **es kann eben k-r aus s-r ~** a leopard can't change his spots; **das geht e-m unter die ~** it gets under your skin.

'Hautabschürfung *f* abrasion, graze.

'Hautarzt *m* dermatologist.

'Hautausschlag *m* (skin) rash: **e-n ~ bekommen** come out in a rash.

Häutchen [ˈhɔʏtçən] *n* (-s; -) *anat.*, ⚕ membrane, cuticle, *on milk etc*: skin.

'Hautcreme *f* skin cream.

haute [ˈhaʊtə] *pret of* **hauen.**

häuten [ˈhɔʏtən] (h) **I** *v/t* skin, flay. **II** **sich ~** *zo.* shed its skin, slough off.

'hauteng *adj* skin-tight.

Hautevolee [(h)oːtvoˈleː] *f* (-; *no pl*) *a.* *iro.* upper crust (F).

'Hautfarbe *f* colo(u)r (of one's skin) complexion. **'hautfarben** *adj* flesh-colo(u)red, skin-colo(u)red.

'Hautkrankheit *f* skin disease.

'Hautkrebs *m* ⚕ skin cancer.

'hautnah *adj* **1.** *a. sports*: (very) close. **2.** **F** *fig.* vivid, realistic.

'Hautpflege *f* skin care.

'Hautpflegemittel *n* skin-care product.

'Hautpilz *m* ⚕ fungal infection.

'Hautschere *f* cuticle scissors.

'Hauttransplanta‚tion *f* skin graft(ing).

'Häutung *f* (-; -en) *zo.* sloughing.

'Hautunreinheit *f* (skin) blemish.

'Hautwunde *f* (skin) lesion.

Havarie [havaˈriː] *f* (-; -n) a) accident, b) damage: ⚓ **(große) ~** (general) average; **(kleine) ~** (petty) average.

he [heː] *int* **F** hey.

Hebamme [ˈheːpˀamə] *f* (-; -n) midwife.

'Hebebaum *m* ⚙ heaver. **'Hebebühne** ⚙ lifting platform, *mot.* car lift.

Hebel [ˈheːbəl] *m* (-s; -) lever: **den ~ ansetzen** apply the lever, *fig.* tackle it, *fig.* **alle ~ in Bewegung setzen** move heaven and earth; **am längeren ~ sitzen** be in the stronger position; **an den ~n der Macht sitzen** be at the controls

~arm m lever arm. **~griff** m lever hold. **~kraft** f, **~mo‚ment** n phys. leverage.

heben ['he:bən] (hob, gehoben, h) I v/t **1.** lift, raise, ⊙ a. hoist: **ein Wrack (e-n Schatz)** ~ raise a wreck (treasure); F fig. **e-n** ~ have a drink, hoist one. **2.** fig. raise (eyes, voice, morale, etc), improve, enhance. **3.** dial. hold. II **sich** ~ **4.** curtain etc: rise, go up, fog: lift: **sich ~ und senken** rise and fall. **5.** fig. rise.

'**Heben** n (-s) lifting (etc). '**Heber** m (-s; -) **1.** ‚ siphon. **2.** → **Gewichtheber**.

'**Hebezeug** n (-[e]s; -e) ⊙ hoist.

hebräisch [he'brɛːɪʃ] adj Hebrew.

Hebung f (-; -en) **1.** lifting, a. raising (of treasure, wreck). **2.** no pl fig. improvement, rise, promotion. **3.** metr. stress(ed syllable).

hecheln ['hɛçəln] v/i (h) pant.

Hecht [hɛçt] m (-[e]s; -e) **1.** zo. pike: F fig. **toller** ~ gay dog; **er ist (wie) der ~ im Karpfenteich** he really stirs things up. **2.** F fug. '**hechten** v/i (h) do a pike-dive, gym. do a long-fly, soccer etc: dive full-length.

'**Hechtsprung** m pike-dive, gym. long-fly, soccer etc: (flying) dive.

Heck [hɛk] n (-[e]s; -e, -s) ♆ stern, mot. rear, back, ✈ tail. '**Heckantrieb** m mot. rear-wheel drive.

Hecke ['hɛkə] f (-; -n) hedge.

'**Hecken|rose** f dogrose. **~schere** f hedge clippers. **~schütze** m sniper. '**Heckfenster** n mot. rear window. '**Heckklappe** f mot. tailgate. '**Hecklastig** adj ✈, mot. tailheavy. '**Hecklicht** n ✈, mot. taillight. '**Heckmotor** m rear engine. '**Heckscheibe** f mot. rear window. '**Heckscheibenheizung** f rear-window defroster. '**Heckscheibenwischer** m rear wiper. **Heckspoiler** m mot. back spoiler.

'**heda** ['he:da] int hey (there).

Hedonismus [hedo'nɪsmʊs] m (-; no pl) hedonism. **Hedonist** [hedo'nɪst] m (-en; -en) hedonist. **hedo'nistisch** adj hedonistic.

'**Heer** [he:r] n (-[e]s; -e) army, fig. host. **Heeres...** army (command, group, etc). **Heerschar** f fig. host.

'**Hefe** ['he:fə] f (-; -n) **1.** yeast. **2.** fig. dregs. '**Hefeteig** m yeast dough.

'**Heft¹** [hɛft] n (-[e]s; -e) **1.** ped. exercise book. **2.** number, issue. **3.** booklet.

Heft² n (-[e]s; -e) handle, of dagger etc: hilt: fig. **das ~ in der Hand haben (behalten)** hold the rein (stay in control). **Heftchen** ['hɛftçən] n (-s; -) book.

heften ['hɛftən] (h) I v/t **1.** (an acc to) fix, pin. **2.** baste, tack. **3.** print. stitch: **geheftet** in sheets. II **sich an j-s Fersen** ~ stick hard on s.o.'s heels; **sich ~ auf** (acc) eyes etc: be fixed (or riveted) on. **Hefter** ['hɛftər] m (-s; -) file.

'**Heft|faden** m, **~garn** n tacking thread.

heftig ['hɛftɪç] adj **1.** violent, severe, fierce (argument), heavy (rain), acute (pain), splitting (headache), heated (debate etc): **et. ~ verteidigen** defend s.th. vehemently. **2.** irascible, vehement: **er wird schnell ~** he flares up quickly. '**Heftigkeit** f (-; no pl) **1.** violence, fierceness, vehemence. **2.** hot temper. '**Heft|klammer** f paper clip, ⊙ staple. **~ma‚schine** f ⊙ stapler. **~pflaster** n ✚ (sticking) plaster. **~zwecke** f drawing pin, Am. thumbtack.

Hegemonie [hegemo'niː] f (-; -n) hegemony.

hegen ['he:gən] v/t (h) **1.** preserve (wildlife etc), tend (plants), protect: **~ und pflegen** a. take loving care of. **2.** fig. have (doubts, a suspicion, etc), cherish (hope, love, etc).

Hehl [he:l] **kein(en)** ~ **machen aus** make no secret of.

Hehler ['he:lər] m (-s; -) ⚖ receiver, sl. fence. **Hehle'rei** f (-; -en) ⚖ receiving, sl. fencing.

hehr [he:r] adj sublime, noble.

Heide¹ ['haɪdə] m (-n; -n) heathen, pagan.

'**Heide²** f (-; -n) **1.** heath(land). **2.** → '**Heidekraut** n (-[e]s; no pl) ✿ heather. **Heidelbeere** ['haɪdəlbeːrə] ✿ bilberry, Am. blueberry.

'**Heiden...** F → **Mords...** '**Heidengeld** n F **ein** ~ a fortune, a packet.

'**Heidentum** n (-s; no pl) heathenism, paganism.

Heidin ['haɪdɪn] f (-; -nen) → **Heide¹**.

heidnisch ['haɪdnɪʃ] adj heathen, pagan.

Heidschnucke ['haɪtʃnʊkə] f (-; -n) zo. moorland sheep.

heikel ['haɪkəl] adj **1.** delicate, tricky: **ein heikler Punkt** a sore point. **2.** dial. a) fussy, b) squeamish.

heil [haɪl] adj person: unharmed, safe

and sound, *thing*: undamaged, whole, intact: **wieder ~** a) healed(-up), mended, b) repaired; *fig.* **e-e ~e Welt** an intact world. **Heil** *n* (-s; *no pl*) well-being, good, *eccl.* salvation: **sein ~ versuchen** try one's luck; **sein ~ in der Flucht suchen** take flight, run for it.

Heiland ['haɪlant] *m* (-[e]s; *no pl*) *eccl.* Savio(u)r.

'Heilanstalt *f* **1.** sanatorium. **2.** (mental) home.

'heilbar *adj* curable.

'Heilbarkeit *f* (-; *no pl*) curability.

Heilbutt ['haɪlbʊt] *m* (-[e]s; -e) halibut.

heilen ['haɪlən] **I** *v/t* (h) cure, heal: **j-n ~ von** *a. fig.* cure s.o. of. **II** *v/i* (sn) heal (up). **'heilend** *adj* healing, curative.

'Heilerde *f* healing earth.

'heilfroh *adj* F **~ sein** be really glad.

heilig ['haɪlɪç] *adj* a) holy, b) sacred (*a. fig.*), c) sacrosanct, d) saintly, pious: **der ~e** (*abbr.* **hl.**) **Paulus** Saint (*abbr.* St.) Paul; **der 2e Abend** Christmas Eve; **die 2e Jungfrau** the Blessed Virgin; **die 2e Nacht** Holy Night; **der 2e Vater** the Holy Father; **das 2e Land** the Holy Land; *fig.* **~e Kuh** sacred cow; **ihm ist nichts ~** nothing is sacred to him; → **Geist 3**, **Schrift 2**, **Stuhl 1**.

'Heilige *m*, *f* (-n; -n) *a. fig.* saint.

'heiligen ['haɪlɪgən] *v/t* (h) **1.** hallow, sanctify; → **Zweck. 2.** → **heilighalten.**

'Heiligenschein *m* halo, gloriole.

'heilighalten *v/t* (*irr, sep,* -ge-, h, → **halten**) a) hold s.th. sacred, b) keep s.th. (holy), observe (*Sunday etc.*)

'Heiligkeit *f* (-; *no pl*) a) holiness, *a. fig.* sacredness, sanctity, b) saintliness: **Seine ~** (the *Pope*) His Holiness.

'heiligsprechen *v/t* (*irr, sep,* -ge-, h, → **sprechen**) canonize. **'Heiligsprechung** *f* (-; -en) canonization.

'Heiligtum *n* (-s; -⁻er) **1.** shrine. **2.** (sacred) relic, F s.th. sacred: **das ist sein ~!** that's sacred to him!

'Heilung *f* (-; *no pl*) **1.** *a. fig.* sanctification. **2.** observance (*of Sunday etc*).

'Heilklima *n* healthy climate.

'Heilkraft *f* healing power(s).

'heilkräftig *adj* curative.

'Heilkunde *f* (-; *no pl*) medicine.

'heillos *adj* F hopeless, unholy (*mess etc*), *a.* frightful (*scare etc*).

'Heil|me,thode *f* cure, treatment. **~mit-**

tel *n* (**gegen** for) *a. fig.* cure, remedy, b) medicine. **~päda,gogik** *f* therapeutic pedagogy. **~pflanze** *f* medicinal herb. **~praktiker(in** *f*) *m* nonmedical practitioner. **~quelle** *f* mineral spring.

'heilsam *adj a. fig.* salutary, healthy: **~ sein (für)** *a.* be good (for).

'Heilsar,mee *f* Salvation Army.

'Heilschlaf *m* 🧿 hypnotherapy.

'Heilserum *n* 🧿 antiserum.

'Heilung *f* (-; -en) a) (**von** of) curing, cure (*a. fig.*), b) healing, c) recovery.

'Heilungs|aussichten *pl* chances of recovery. **~pro,zeß** *m* healing process.

'Heilverfahren *n* treatment, therapy.

'Heilwirkung *f* therapeutic effect.

heim [haɪm] *adv* home.

Heim *n* (-[e]s; -e) **1.** home. **2.** home, hostel. **'Heimarbeit** *f* homework. **'Heimarbeiter(in** *f*) *m* homeworker.

Heimat ['haɪmaːt] *f* (-; *no pl*) home (*a. fig.*), 🧿, *zo.* habitat: **zweite ~** second home, F home from home; **in der ~** at home; **in m-r ~** a. where I come from. **~dichtung** *f* regional literature. **~film** *m* (sentimental) film with a regional background. **~hafen** *m* ⚓ home port. **~kunde** *f* (-; *no pl*) *ped.* local studies. **~land** *n* home country.

'heimatlich *adj* a) home, native, b) homelike, *pred* like home, *Am.* hom(e)y. **'heimatlos** *adj* homeless.

'Heimat|mu,seum *n* museum of local history. **~ort** *m* home town (*or* village). **~stadt** *f* home town. **~vertriebene** *m, f* (-n; -n) expellee.

'heimbegleiten *v/t* (*sep,* h) **j-n ~** see s.o. home.

Heimchen ['haɪmçən] *n* (-s; -) *zo.* (house) cricket.

'Heimcom,puter *m* home computer.

heimelig ['haɪməlɪç] *adj* cosy, F hom(e)y.

'heimfahren *v/i* (*irr, sep,* -ge-, sn, → **fahren**) go home, (*a. v/t*) drive home.

'Heimfahrt *f* journey home.

'heimfinden *v/i* (*irr, sep,* -ge-, h, → **finden**) find one's way home.

'heimgehen *v/i* (*irr, sep,* -ge-, sn, → **gehen**) **1.** go home. **2.** pass away, die.

'Heimindu,strie *f* cottage industry.

'heimisch *adj* a) domestic, home, b) 🧿, *zo.* native, indigenous, c) inland: **~ Gewässer** home waters; **~ sein in** (*dat* *a. fig.* be at home in; **~ werden** settle (down), become acclimatized (*in dat* to); **sich ~ fühlen** feel at home.

Heimkehr ['haɪmkeːr] *f* (-; *no pl*) return (home). **'heimkehren** *v/i* (*sep*, -ge-, sn) return home, come back. **'Heimkehrer** *m* (-s; -) homecomer, *pol.* repatriate.

'Heimkind *n* institution child.

'Heimkino *n* home movies.

'heimkommen *v/i* (*irr, sep*, -ge-, sn, → **kommen**) return (*or* come, get) home. **'Heimleiter(in** *f*) *m* head of a home (*or* hostel).

'heimleuchten *v/t* (*sep*, -ge-, h) F *j-m ~* send s.o. packing.

heimlich I *adj* a) secret, b) clandestine, c) furtive. **II** *adv* secretly (*etc*), in secret, (*a.* **~, still und leise**) F on the quiet. **'Heimlichkeit** *f* (-; -en) **1.** *no pl* secrecy, furtiveness. **2.** *pl* secrets.

Heimlichtue'rei *f* (-; *no pl*) secretiveness.

'heimlichtun *v/i* (*irr, sep*, -ge-, h, → **tun**) be secretive (*mit* about).

'Heimmannschaft *f sports*: home team.

'Heimniederlage *f sports*: home defeat.

Heimorgel *f* ♪ electric organ.

'Heimreise *f* journey home: **auf der ~** on the way home. **'heimreisen** *v/i* (*sep*, -ge-, sn) go (*or* travel) home.

'Heimsieg *m sports*: home victory.

'Heimspiel *n sports*: home game.

'Heimstärke *f sports*: home strength.

'Heimstätte *f a. fig.* home.

'heimsuchen *v/t* (*sep*, -ge-, h) **1.** strike, visit (*a. bibl.*), plague, afflict, *premonitions etc, a. ghost*: haunt: **heimgesucht von** struck (*etc*) by; **von Dürre (Krieg) heimgesucht** drought-ridden (war-torn). **2.** F descend on. **'Heimsuchung** *f* (-; -en) visitation, affliction, trial.

'Heimtrainer *m* home exerciser.

'Heimtücke *f* (-; *no pl*) perfidy, treachery. **'heimtückisch** *adj* insidious (*a.* ♪), treacherous.

'Heimvorteil *m sports*: home advantage.

heimwärts ['haɪmvɛrts] *adv* homeward(s), home.

'Heimweg *m* way home.

'Heimweh *n* (-[e]s; *no pl*) homesickness: **~ haben** be homesick (*nach* for).

Heimwerker ['haɪmvɛrkər] *m* (-s; -) do-it-yourselfer, home mechanic.

Heimwerker... do-it-yourself (*kit etc*).

'heimzahlen *v/t* (*sep*, -ge-, h) *j-m et. ~* repay s.o. for s.th.

'heimzu *adv* F on the way home.

Heini ['haɪni] *m* (-s; -s) F *contp.* twerp.

Heinzelmännchen ['haɪntsəlmɛnçən] *n* (-s; -) brownie.

Heirat ['haɪraːt] *f* (-; -en) marriage.

heiraten ['haɪraːtən] *v/t, v/i* (h) (*j-n*) *~* marry (s.o.), get married (*to* s.o.).

'Heirats|an‚nonce *f* marriage ad. **~antrag** *m* (marriage) proposal: **e-n ~ machen** propose (*dat* to). **~anzeige** *f* **1.** marriage announcement. **2.** marriage ad. **⸗fähig** *adj* marriageable: **im ~en Alter** of marriageable age. **~markt** *m* marriage market. **~schwindler** *m* marriage impostor. **~urkunde** *f* marriage certificate. **~vermittlung** *f* **1.** marriage brokerage. **2.** marriage bureau.

heiser ['haɪzər] *adj* hoarse.

'Heiserkeit *f* (-; *no pl*) hoarseness.

heiß [haɪs] **I** *adj* **1.** hot, *fig. a.* a) ardent, passionate, b) fierce (*battle etc*), heated (*discussion etc*): **~e Zone** torrid zone; **et. ~ machen** heat s.th. up; **mir ist (wird) ~** I'm (getting) hot; → **Draht, Eisen, Hölle, Ofen** 2. **2.** F fig. hot: **~e Ware** hot goods; **~er Tip** hot tip. **II** *adv* **3.** hotly (*etc*): **et. ~ ersehnen** long for s.th. (fervently); **sich ~ und innig lieben** adore each other; → **hergehen**.

'heißblütig [-bly:tɪç] *adj* hot-blooded, passionate.

heißen ['haɪsən] (hieß, geheißen, h) **I** *v/i* **1.** be called (*nach* after): **wie ~ Sie?** what's your name?; **wie heißt das?** a) what's that called?, b) **auf Englisch?** what's that (mean) in English. **2.** *text*: read, be. **3.** *mean*: **was heißt das?**, **was soll das ~?** a) what does it mean?, b) what do you mean (by this)?, c) what's the (big) idea?; **das hieße, das würde —** that would mean; **das will (et)was ~!** that's saying something!; **das will nichts ~!** that doesn't mean a thing!; **soll das ~, daß ...?** do you mean to say that ...?; **das soll nicht ~, daß** that doesn't mean that; **das heißt** that is (*abbr.* i.e.). **II** *v/impers* **4.** **es heißt, daß** they say that; **in dem Brief heißt es, daß** the letter says that. **5.** **jetzt heißt es handeln!** now it's time to act! **III** *v/t* **6.** call. **7.** *j-n et. tun ~* tell s.o. to do s.th.; → **willkommen**.

'**heißersehnt** *adj* longed-for.
'**heißgeliebt** *adj* dearly loved.
'**Heißhunger** *m* ♣ b(o)ulimia, *a. fig.* (sudden) craving (*nach* for).
'**heißlaufen** *v/i* (*irr, sep,* -ge-, sn, → *laufen*) (*a. sich ~* [h]) ⊙ overheat, F *telephone lines*: be buzzing.
'**Heißluft...** hot-air ...
'**heißumkämpft** *adj* fiercely embattled.
'**heißumstritten** *adj* **1.** highly controversial. **2.** hotly debated.

heiter ['haɪtər] *adj* **1.** a) cheerful, gay, b) serene, c) funny, amusing: F *iro. (das) kann ja ~ werden!* nice prospects! **2.** bright, sunny: → *Himmel*. **3.** ♪ scherzando. '**Heiterkeit** *f* (-; *no pl*) **1.** a) cheerfulness, b) serenity: *~ erregen* cause amusement. **2.** brightness.
'**Heizanlage** *f* heating system.
'**heizbar** *adj* heatable, with heating.
'**Heizdecke** *f* electric blanket.
'**Heizele,ment** *n* heating element.
heizen ['haɪtsən] (h) **I** *v/t* heat (*room etc*), fire (*stove*). **II** *v/i* put (*or* have) the heating on.
Heizer *m* (-s; -) boilerman, ♣, 🚂 stoker.
'**Heizgas** *n* fuel gas. '**Heizgerät** *n* heater.
'**Heizkessel** *m* boiler. '**Heizkissen** *n* electric pad. '**Heizkörper** *m* radiator, ♨ heater. '**Heizkosten** *pl* heating costs.
'**Heizlüfter** *m* fan heater. '**Heizmateri,al** *n* fuel. '**Heizöl** *n* (-s; *no pl*) fuel oil.
'**Heizung** *f* (-; -en) **1.** (central) heating. **2.** → *Heizkörper*.
'**Heizungsanlage** *f* heating system.
'**Heizungsmon,teur** *m* heating engineer.
Hektar ['hɛkta:r] *n, m* (-s; -e) hectare.
Hektik ['hɛktɪk] *f* (-; *no pl*) a) hectic atmosphere, mad rush, b) nervy state: F *nur k-e ~!* take it easy!
'**hektisch** *adj* hectic.
Hektoliter ['hɛktoli:tər] *m, n* hectolit/re (*Am.* -er).
Held [hɛlt] *m* (-en; -en) hero.
heldenhaft ['hɛldən-] *adj* heroic.
'**Heldensage** *f* saga. '**Heldentat** *f* heroic deed. '**Heldente,nor** *m* ♪ heroic tenor.
'**Heldentum** *n* (-s; *no pl*) heroism.
'**Heldenverehrung** *f* hero worship.
Heldin ['hɛldɪn] *f* (-; -nen) heroine.
helfen ['hɛlfən] *v/i* (half, geholfen, h) **1.** (*dat*) help, assist, aid, lend *s.o.* a hand: *j-m bei et. ~* help s.o. with s.th.; *j-m aus dem* (*in den*) *Mantel ~* help s.o. off (on)

with his *etc* coat; *fig. j-m aus e-r Verlegenheit ~* help s.o. out of a difficulty; *ihm ist nicht zu ~* there is no help for him, *iro.* he's hopeless; *er weiß sich zu ~* a) he can look after himself, b) he is resourceful; *sich nicht mehr zu ~ wissen* be at one's wits' end; *ich kann mir nicht ~* a) I can't help it, b) ..., *ich muß einfach lachen* I can't help laughing. **2.** help: *das half* that worked; *das hilft gegen Schnupfen* that's good for colds; *das hilft mir wenig!* that's not much help!, F a fat lot it helps!; *es hilft nichts* it's no use; *da hilft kein Jammern!* it's no use complaining!; *da hilft nur eines* there's only one thing for it.
'**Helfer** *m* (-s; -), '**Helferin** *f* (-; -nen) helper, assistant: *ein Helfer in der Not* a friend in need.
'**Helfershelfer(in** *f*) *m* accomplice.
Helium ['he:liʊm] *n* (-s; *no pl*) 🔬 helium.
hell [hɛl] *adj* **1.** light, bright (*sunshine etc*), fair (*hair, complexion, etc*), light-colo(u)red (*clothes*), clear (*voice etc*): *~es Bier* lager; *~es Blau* light blue; *fig. ~es Gelächter* loud laughter; *es wird schon ~* it is getting light already. **2.** *fig.* bright, intelligent. **3.** F great, utter (*nonsense etc*), pure (*envy etc*): *~er Wahnsinn* sheer madness; *~ begeistert* (absolutely) enthusiastic.
'**hellblond** *adj* very fair.
helle ['hɛlə] *adj pred* F bright, intelligent.
'**Helle¹** *f, n* (-; *no pl*) brightness, (bright) light. '**Helle²** *n* (-n; -n) F (glass of) beer (*Br.* lager): *zwei ~!* two beers!
Heller ['hɛlər] *m* (-s; -) F *k-n* (*roten*) *~ wert* not worth a cent; *auf ~ und Pfennig* to the last penny.
'**hellgrün** *adj* light-green.
'**hellhörig** *adj* **1.** *fig. das machte ihn ~* that made him prick up his ears. **2.** poorly soundproofed.
hellicht ['hɛlɪçt] *adj am ~en Tage* in broad daylight.
Helligkeit ['hɛlɪçkaɪt] *f* (-; *no pl*) brightness (*a. TV*), light, *phys.* luminosity.
Helling ['hɛlɪŋ] *f* (-; -en) ♣ slip(way) (building) cradle.
'**hellrot** *adj* light-red.
'**hellsehen** *v/i* (*only inf*) have second sight, be clairvoyant. '**Hellsehen** *n* (-s; ...) clairvoyance. '**Hellseher(in** *f*) *m* ... '**hellseherisch** *adj* clairvoyant.

'hell'wach adj a. fig. wide-awake.
Helm [hɛlm] m (-[e]s; -e) helmet.
Hemd [hɛmt] n (-[e]s; -en) a) shirt, b) vest, Am. undershirt: fig. **j-n bis aufs ~ ausziehen** fleece s.o.
Hemdbluse f shirt.
Hemdblusenkleid n shirtwaister.
Hemdsärmel m shirtsleeve: **in ~n** in (one's) shirtsleeves. **'hemdsärm(e)lig** [-ɛrm(ə)lıç] adj a. fig. shirtsleeve.
Hemisphäre [hemi'sfɛːrə] f (-; -n) hemisphere.
hemmen ['hɛmən] v/t (h) **1.** a. fig. a) stop, check, b) hinder, impede. **2.** psych. inhibit: → **gehemmt**.
Hemmnis ['hɛmnıs] n (-ses; -se) obstacle.
Hemmschuh m fig. drag (**für** on).
Hemmung f (-; -en) **1.** hindrance, check. **2.** psych. inhibition, w.s. scruple: **~en haben** be inhibited; **nur k-e ~en!** don't be shy! **3.** ☼ stop, escapement (of watch). **'hemmungslos** adj **1.** unrestrained, uncontrollable (weeping etc). **2.** unscrupulous. **'Hemmungslosigkeit** f (-; no pl) **1.** lack of restraint, recklessness. **2.** unscrupulousness.
Hengst [hɛŋst] m (-[e]s; -e) a) stallion, b) stud. **'Hengstfohlen** n colt.
Henkel ['hɛŋkəl] m (-s; -) handle.
henken ['hɛŋkən] v/t (h) hang.
Henker m (-s; -) executioner: F **wer** (**wo** etc) **zum ~?** who (where etc) the hell?
Henna ['hɛna] n (-; no pl) henna.
Henne ['hɛnə] f (-; -n) zo. hen.
Hepatitis [hepa'tiːtıs] f (-; -titiden [-ti'tiːdən]) ❋ hepatitis.
her [heːr] adv **1.** ago: **wie lange ist es ~?** how long ago was it?; **das ist lange ~** that was a long time ago; **es ist ein Jahr ~, daß ...** it's a year since ... **2.** von ... ~ from; **von oben ~** from above; **von weit ~** from afar; **um mich ~** around me; **~ damit!** give (it to me)!; → **herhaben** etc, **hinter** I. **3.** fig. **von ... ~** from the point of view of; **vom Technischen ~** from a technical point of view, technically (speaking).
herab [hɛ'rap] adv down: fig. **von oben ~** condescendingly.
her'ab... down; → a. **herunter..**
her'abfallen, her'abhängen, her'abkommen → **heruntergehen** etc.
her'ablassen (irr, sep, -ge-, h, → **lassen**) **I** v/t let down, lower. **II** fig. **sich ~**

zu antworten etc deign to answer etc.
her'ablassend adj condescending (**zu** towards). **Her'ablassung** f (-; no pl) condescension.
her'absehen v/i (irr, sep, -ge-, h, → **sehen**) **~ auf** (acc) a. fig. look down on.
her'absetzen v/t (sep, -ge-, h) **1.** reduce, lower, cut (back): (**im Preis**) **~** reduce (in price); **zu herabgesetzten Preisen** at reduced prices, cut-price ... **2.** fig. disparage, belittle.
her'absetzend adj fig. disparaging.
Her'absetzung f (-; -en) **1.** reduction, cut. **2.** fig. disparagement.
her'absteigen v/i (irr, sep, -ge-, sn, → **steigen**) **1.** descend, climb (or come) down. **2.** dismount.
her'abwürdigen v/t (h) degrade (**sich** o.s.).
Heraldik [he'raldık] f (-; no pl) heraldry.
heran [hɛ'ran] adv near, close: **~ an** (acc) up to; **nur ~!** come closer!
her'anbilden v/t (sep, -ge-, h) (a. **sich ~**) train (**zu** to be).
her'anbringen v/t (irr, sep, -ge-, h, → **bringen**) bring up (**an** acc to).
her'anführen v/t (sep, -ge-, h) lead (or bring) up (**an** acc to): fig. **j-n an et. ~** introduce s.o. to s.th.
her'angehen v/i (irr, sep, -ge-, sn, → **gehen**) **~ an** (acc) a) go up to, b) fig. approach, tackle (a task etc).
her'anholen v/t (sep, -ge-, h) **1.** fetch, get. **2.** phot. zoom in on.
her'ankämpfen: sich ~ (sep, -ge-, h) (**an** acc) sports: close in (on), pull up (to).
her'ankommen v/i (irr, sep, -ge-, sn, → **kommen**) **1.** draw near, approach. **2. ~ an** (acc) a) come up to (a. fig.), approach, come near (a standard etc), b) get at, get hold of; **er (es) kommt nicht an ... heran** a. he (it) can't touch ...; fig. **an j-n ~** get through to s.o.; **die Sache** (or **es**) **an sich ~ lassen** wait and see.
her'anmachen: sich ~ (sep, -ge-, h) (**an** acc) F a) set to work (on s.th.), b) sidle up (to s.o.): fig. **sich an j-n ~** a) approach s.o., b) make up to s.o., c) start working on s.o.
her'anreichen v/i (sep, -ge-, h) **~ an** (acc) come up to, fig. a. touch.
her'anreifen v/i (sep, -ge-, sn) (**zu** into) ripen, fig. plan etc: a. mature, person: a. grow up.

her'anrücken v/i (sep, -ge-, sn) **1.** come close(r) (**an** acc to): **an j-n** ~ move up (close) to s.o. **2.** draw near, approach.

her'antreten v/i (irr, sep, -ge-, sn, → **treten**) **an j-n** ~ go up to s.o., a. fig. approach s.o., fig. confront s.o.

her'anwachsen v/i (irr, sep, -ge-, sn, → **wachsen**) grow up: ~ **zu** grow into.

Her'anwachsende m, f (-n; -n) young person, adolescent.

her'anwagen: sich ~ (sep, -ge-, h) (**an** acc) venture near, dare to approach (s.o.), fig. dare to tackle (a task etc).

her'anziehen (irr, sep, -ge-, → **ziehen**) I v/t (h) **1.** pull s.th. up (**an** acc to). **2.** a) raise, b) train. **3.** **j-n** ~ (**zu**) call on s.o. (to do s.th.), enlist s.o.('s services) (for s.th.): **e-n Fachmann** ~ call in an expert. **4.** cite, invoke. II v/i (sn) **5.** draw near, approach.

herauf [hɛ'raʊf] adv up, upwards: (**hier**) ~ up here; **den Berg** ~ up the hill, uphill; **den Fluß** ~ up the river, upstream; **die Treppe** ~ up the stairs, upstairs; **in** cpds. → a. **empor...**

her'aufbeschwören v/t (irr, sep, h, → **beschwören**) **1.** conjure up (memories etc). **2.** bring on (disaster etc).

her'aufkommen v/i (irr, sep, -ge-, sn, → **kommen**) come up (**zu** to).

her'aufsetzen v/t (sep, -ge-, h) raise.

her'aufsteigen v/t (irr, sep, -ge-, sn, → **steigen**) climb, mount (stairs etc).

her'aufziehen (irr, sep, -ge-, → **ziehen**) I v/t (h) pull s.o., s.th. up. II v/i (sn) draw near, approach.

heraus [hɛ'raʊs] adv out (**aus** of): **zum Fenster** ~ out of the window; fig. **aus e-m Gefühl der Verlassenheit** etc ~ from (or out of) a sense of loneliness etc; ~ **damit!** out with it!; ~ **mit der Sprache!** F spit it out!; F **jetzt ist es** ~! now the secret's out!

her'ausarbeiten (sep, -ge-, h) I v/t a. fig. work out. II **sich** ~ **aus** work one's way out of, fig. a. manage to get out of.

her'ausbekommen v/t (irr, sep, h, → **bekommen**) **1.** get stain etc out (**aus** of). **2.** fig. a) F work out, solve, figure out, get, b) find s.th. out: **wie bekomme ich j-n** ~ get s.th. out of s.o. **3.** **Sie bekommen noch 10 Mark heraus** you get ten marks change.

her'ausbringen v/t (irr, sep, -ge-, h, →

bringen). **1.** bring out (a. fig.), print. a. publish, thea. produce: **sie brachte kein Wort heraus** she couldn't say a word; **j-n (et.) groß** ~ give s.o. (s.th.) a big buildup.

her'ausfahren (irr, sep, -ge-, → **fahren**) I v/i (sn) **1.** come (or drive) out (**aus** of). **2.** remark etc: slip out. II v/t (h) **3.** drive out (**aus** of): sports: **er hat e-e gute Zeit (den Sieg) herausgefahren** he made good time (won the race).

her'ausfallen v/i (irr, sep, -ge-, sn, → **fallen**) (**aus** of) fall out, drop out.

her'ausfiltern v/t (sep, -ge-, h) a. fig. filter out.

her'ausfinden (irr, sep, -ge-, h, → **finden**) I v/t a) find, b) find out, discover. II v/i find one's way out (**aus** of).

Her'ausforderer m (-s; -) challenger, pol. rival (candidate). **her'ausfordern** (sep, -ge-, h) I v/t challenge, defy, provoke: **das Schicksal** ~ court disaster, F ask for it; **Kritik (Protest)** ~ → II. II v/i **zur Kritik (zum Protest)** ~ invite (or provoke) criticism (protest). **her'ausfordernd** adj challenging, defiant, provocative. **Her'ausforderung** (-; -en) challenge (a. fig.), provocation.

Her'ausgabe f (-; no pl) **1.** surrender, delivery. **2.** print. edition, publication. **her'ausgeben** (irr, sep, -ge-, h, → **geben**) I v/t **1.** (dat to) hand s.th. over, give s.th. back, return. **2.** a) publish, b) edit, c) issue (stamps, a. rules etc). **3.** **j-m zehn Mark** ~ give s.o. ten marks change. II v/i **4.** (j-m) ~ give (s.o. change (**auf** acc for). **Her'ausgeber(in** f) m a) publisher, b) editor.

her'ausgehen v/i (irr, sep, -ge-, sn, → **gehen**) **1.** → **hinausgehen** 1; fig. **aus sich** ~ come out of one's shell. **2.** stain etc: come out (**aus** of).

her'ausgreifen v/t (irr, sep, -ge-, h, → **greifen**) a) pick out, b) cite (examples).

her'aushaben v/t (irr, sep, -ge-, → **haben**) F fig. have found s.th. out, have got, have solved (problem etc): **er hat es heraus** he has got the hang of it.

her'aushalten v/t (irr, sep, -ge-, → **halten**) F **j-n (sich) aus der Sache** ~ keep s.o. (o.s.) out of it.

her'ausheben v/t (irr, sep, -ge-, → **heben**) **1.** lift (or take) s.o., s.th. out (**aus** of). **2.** → **hervorheben**.

her'aushelfen v/i (irr, sep, -ge-, h, → **helfen**) j-m ~ help s.o. out (**aus** of).

her'ausholen v/t (sep, -ge-, h) a. fig. get s.o., s.th. out (**aus** of): *das Letzte aus sich* ~ make a supreme effort.

her'aushören v/t (sep, -ge-, h) hear, fig. detect (**aus** in s.o.'s words etc).

her'auskehren v/t (sep, -ge-, h) fig. act, play *the expert etc*, show, display.

her'auskommen v/i (irr, sep, -ge-, sn, → **kommen**) 1. (**aus**) emerge (from), come out (of), a. fig. come out (of): *er kam aus dem Lachen nicht heraus* he couldn't stop laughing; F *groß* ~ be a great success. 2. fig. come out, *book*: a. be published, appear, *stamps etc*: be issued: ☞ *mit e-m neuen Modell* ~ come out with a new model; F ~ *mit* come out with, admit. 3. (**aus** of) a) ℞ be the result, b) fig. come out: *es kommt nichts dabei heraus* it doesn't pay; *es kommt auf eins (or dasselbe) heraus* it boils down to the same thing; → a. herausspringen 2.

her'auskristalli,sieren v/t (sep, h) (a. *sich* ~) a. fig. crystallize (**aus** out of).

her'auslassen v/t (irr, sep, -ge-, h, → **lassen**) let out (**aus** of).

her'auslaufen (irr, sep, -ge-, → **laufen**) I v/i (sn) run out (**aus** of). II v/t (h) *sports:* gain (lead, victory, etc).

her'auslocken v/t (sep, -ge-, h) 1. j-n ~ lure s.o. out (**aus** of). 2. et. aus j-m ~ draw (or worm) s.th. out of s.o.

her'ausmachen: *sich* ~ (sep, -ge-, h) fig. be coming on well.

her'ausnehmen v/t (irr, sep, -ge-, h, → **nehmen**) (**aus**) take s.o., s.th. out (of), remove (from): fig. *sich Freiheiten* ~ take liberties (**gegenüber** with).

her'ausplatzen v/i (sep, -ge-, sn) F 1. burst out laughing. 2. ~ *mit* blurt out.

her'ausputzen v/t (sep, -ge-, h) (*sich* ~) dress (o.s.) up, F spruce (o.s.) up.

her'ausragen v/i (sep, -ge-, h) (**aus** from) a) jut out, b) fig. stand out.

her'ausragend adj fig. outstanding.

her'ausreden: *sich* ~ (sep, -ge-, h) talk one's way out (**aus** of).

her'ausreißen v/t (irr, sep, -ge-, h, → **reißen**) 1. pull (or tear) s.th. out. 2. fig. j-n ~ *aus* tear s.o. away from (surroundings etc), rouse s.o. from (sleep etc),

interrupt s.o. in (one's work etc); F *j-n* ~ *performance etc:* save s.o.

her'ausrücken (sep, -ge-) F I v/t (h) → II b. II v/i (sn) ~ *mit* a) come out with, b) fork out, cough up (money); *mit der Sprache* ~ talk, come out with it.

her'ausrutschen v/i (sep, -ge-, sn) F fig. slip out: *das ist mir einfach so herausgerutscht* it just slipped out.

her'ausschinden v/t (irr, sep, -ge-, h, → **schinden**) manage to get (**aus** out of).

her'ausschlagen v/t (irr, sep, -ge-, h, → **schlagen**) (**aus** of) 1. knock s.th. out. 2. F get s.th. out: *Geld* ~ *aus* make money out of; *möglichst viel* ~ make the most of it.

her'ausschneiden v/t (irr, sep, -ge-, h, → **schneiden**) cut s.th. out (**aus** of).

her'aussehen v/i (irr, sep, -ge-, h, → **sehen**) look out (**aus** of).

her'ausspringen v/i (irr, sep, -ge-, sn, → **springen**) 1. jump out (**aus** of). 2. F fig. be gained (**bei** by): *was springt für Sie dabei heraus?* what's in it for you?

her'ausstellen (sep, -ge-, h) I v/t 1. put s.th. out(side). 2. fig. a) point out, b) emphasize, underline: *groß* ~highlight, feature (a. thea.). 3. → hinausstellen 2. II *sich* ~ turn out (**als** to be), come to light: *es stellte sich heraus, daß sie recht hatte* she turned out to be right.

her'ausstrecken v/t (sep, -ge-, h) stick out (**aus** of): → Zunge.

her'ausstreichen v/t (irr, sep, -ge-, h, → **streichen**) 1. cross out (**aus** of). 2. fig. praise s.o., s.th. (to the skies).

her'aussuchen v/t (sep, -ge-, h) (**aus**) choose (from), pick out (of).

her'auswinden: *sich* ~ (irr, sep, -ge-, h, → **winden**) fig. wriggle out (**aus** of).

herb [hɛrp] adj 1. sour, tart, dry (wine), tangy (smell). 2. fig. harsh (words, criticism, etc), bitter (disappointment, loss, etc), austere (beauty, style, etc).

herbei [hɛr'baɪ] adv here, up, over; → a. **her...**, **heran...** **her'beieilen** v/i (sep, -ge-, sn) come running (up).

her'beiführen v/t (sep, -ge-, h) fig. bring about, cause, lead to, esp. ☞ induce.

her'beilassen: *sich* ~ (irr, sep, -ge-, h, → **lassen**) condescend (**zu** to).

her'beischaffen v/t (sep, -ge-, h) bring (up), fetch, get.

her'beisehnen v/t (sep, -ge-, h) long for.

'herbemühen (*sep*, h) **I** *v/t* **j-n ~** ask s.o. to come (here). **II sich ~** take the trouble to come.

Herberge ['hɛrbɛrgə] *f* (-; -n) youth hostel. **'Herbergsmutter** *f*, **'Herbergsvater** *m* (hostel) warden.

'herbeten *v/t* (*sep*, -ge-, h) rattle off.

'Herbheit *f* (-; *no pl*) **1.** sourness, *of wine:* dryness. **2.** *fig.* austerity.

'herbitten *v/t* (*irr, sep*, -ge-, h, → **bitten**) **j-n ~** ask s.o. to come.

'herbringen *v/t* (*irr, sep*, -ge-, h, → **bringen**) bring s.o., s.th. (along).

Herbst [hɛrpst] *m* (-[e]s; -e) autumn, *Am. a.* fall. **'Herbstfärbung** *f* autumnal tints. **'Herbstferien** *pl* autumn break. **'herbstlich** *adj* autumn(al). **'Herbstzeitlose** *f* (-; -n) 🌸 meadow saffron.

Herd [hɛrt] *m* (-[e]s; -e) **1.** a) (kitchen) stove, cooker, b) oven. **2.** *fig.* hearth. **3.** *fig.* cent/re (*Am.* -er), seat, focus (*a.* 🐾).

Herde ['hɛrdə] *f* (-; -n) **1.** herd, flock. **2.** *fig. contp. the* (common) herd.

'Herdentier *n zo.* gregarious animal: *fig. contp.* **ein ~ sein** follow the herd.

'Herdentrieb *m a. fig.* herd instinct.

'Herdplatte *f* hotplate.

herein [hɛ'raɪn] *adv* in: **von draußen ~** from outside; **~!** come in!; → *a.* **ein..., hinein..., F rein...**

her'einbekommen *v/t* (*irr, sep*, h, → **bekommen**) F 🕯 get s.th. in.

her'einbitten *v/t* (*irr, sep*, -ge-, h, → **bitten**) **j-n ~** ask s.o. (to come) in.

her'einbrechen *v/i* (*irr, sep*, -ge-, sn, → **brechen**) *night:* fall, *storm:* break, *winter:* set in: **~ über** (*acc*) *misfortune etc:* befall.

her'einbringen *v/t* (*irr, sep*, h, → **bringen**) bring in, get in.

her'einfallen *v/i* (*irr, sep*, -ge-, sn, → **fallen**) F *fig.* **~ auf** (*acc*) be taken in by (or fall for) s.o., s.th.; **~ mit** make a (bad) mistake with.

her'einführen *v/t* (*sep*, -ge-, h) **j-n ~** show s.o. in(to **in** *acc*).

her'einholen *v/t* (*sep*, -ge-, h) **1.** bring s.o., s.th. in. **2.** 🕯 get (in *orders*).

her'einkommen *v/i* (*irr, sep*, -ge-, sn, → **kommen**) a) come in (*a.* 🕯 *orders*), b) get in: **~ in** (*acc*) come into (or inside).

her'einlassen *v/t* (*irr, sep*, -ge-, h, → **lassen**) let s.o., s.th. in.

her'einlegen *v/t* (*sep*, -ge-, h) F *fig.* **j-n ~**

take s.o. for a ride, take s.o. in; **man hat uns hereingelegt** we have been had.

her'einplatzen *v/i* (*sep*, -ge-, sn) F burst in(to **in** *acc*).

her'einschauen *v/i* (*sep*, -ge-, h) F (**bei j-m**) ~ drop by (at s.o.'s place).

her'einschneien *v/i* (*sep*, -ge-, sn) F *fig.* (**bei j-m**) ~ blow in (at s.o.'s place).

her'fahren (*irr, sep*, -ge-, → **fahren**) **I** *v/i* (sn) travel (or come, drive) here: **hinter j-m ~** drive behind s.o., follow s.o.'s car. **II** *v/t* (h) **j-n ~** drive s.o. here.

'Herfahrt *f* (**auf der ~** on the) journey (or way) here.

'herfallen *v/i* (*irr, sep*, -ge-, sn, → **fallen**) **~ über** (*acc*) fall upon, attack.

'herfinden *v/i* (*irr, sep*, -ge-, h, → **finden**) find one's way.

'herführen *v/t* (*sep*, -ge-, h) **j-n ~** bring s.o. here; **was führt Sie her?** what brings you here?

'Hergang *m* (-[e]s; *no pl*) course (of events), the way s.th. happened, the circumstances: **schildern Sie (mir) den ~!** tell me what (or how it) happened!

'hergeben *v/t* (*irr, sep*, -ge-, h, → **geben**) *et.* ~ hand s.th. over, give s.th. away; *et.* **wieder ~** give s.th. back; **gib (es) her!** give (it to me)!; give F or **s-n Namen ~** lend one's name (**zu, für** to).

'hergehen *v/impers* (*irr, sep*, -ge-, sn, → **gehen**) **es ging hoch (heiß) her** things were pretty lively (the sparks flew).

'herhaben *v/t* (*irr, sep*, -ge-, h, → **haben**) F **wo hast du das her?** a) where did you get that (from)?, b) *fig.* who told you that?

'herhalten *v/i* (*irr, sep*, -ge-, h, → **halten**) F **~ müssen** a) have to suffer (for it), b) have to serve (**als** as).

'herholen *v/t* (*sep*, -ge-, h) fetch: *fig.* **weit hergeholt** far-fetched.

Hering ['heːrɪŋ] *m* (-s; -e) **1.** *zo.* herring humor. **wie die ~e** packed like sardines **2.** tent peg.

'herkommen *v/i* (*irr, sep*, -ge-, sn, → **kommen**) come (here): **komm her** come here!; *fig.* **~ von** come from; **wo kommen Sie her?** where do you come from?

herkömmlich ['heːrkœmlɪç] *adj* conventional, customary, traditional.

Herkunft ['heːrkʊnft] *f* (-; *no pl*) origin *of person: a.* birth, descent, *w.s.* origins background: **er ist deutscher ~** he is of German extraction.

Herkunftsland n country of origin.

'herlaufen v/i (irr, sep, -ge-, sn, → **laufen**) run here: **hinter j-m ~** a. fig. run after s.o.

'herleiten v/t (sep, -ge-, h) (a. **sich**) **~ von** derive from.

'hermachen: sich ~ (sep, -ge-, h) F (**über** acc) set about, tackle (task etc), attack (food, fig. s.o.).

Hermelin [hɛrmə'li:n] (-s; -e) **1.** n zo. ermine. **2.** m ermine (fur).

hermetisch [hɛr'me:tɪʃ] adj hermetic.

'hernehmen v/t (irr, sep, -ge-, h, → **nehmen**) (**von** from) take, get.

hernieder(...) [hɛr'ni:dər] → **herab(...)**, **herunter(...)**.

Heroin [hero'i:n] n (-s; no pl) heroin.

hero'insüchtig adj heroin-addicted.

Hero'insüchtige m, f heroin addict.

heroisch [he'ro:ɪʃ] adj heroic.

Heroismus [hero'ɪsmʊs] m (-; no pl) heroism. **Heros** [ˈheːrɔs] m (-; Heroen [he'ro:ən]) hero.

Herr [hɛr] m (-n; -en) a) gentleman, b) master, c) ruler (**über** acc over, of): **mein ~!** Sir!; **m-e ~en!** gentlemen!; **~ Miller** Mr Miller; **~ Doktor** (**Professor** etc) Doctor (Professor etc); **Ihr ~ Vater** your father; sports: **~en** men; (**Gott**) **der ~** the Lord (God); **der ~ Jesus** Our Lord Jesus; **sein eigener ~ sein** be one's own boss; **~ werden** (gen) master, (get s.th. under) control; **~ der Lage sein** have the situation well in hand; → **Land** 3.

Herrchen n (-s; -) master (of a dog).

Herren|ausstatter [ˈhɛrən-] m (-s; -) men's outfitter, Am. haberdasher. **~bekleidung** f men's wear. **~doppel** n tennis: men's doubles. **~einzel** n tennis: men's singles. **~fahrrad** n man's bicycle. **~fri.seur** m barber, men's hairdresser. **~haus** n mansion. **~konfekti,on** f men's ready-to-wear clothes.

herrenlos adj ownerless, stray (dog).

Herren|mode f men's fashion. **~schneider** m men's tailor. **~toi,lette** f men's toilet (Am. restroom).

Herrgott m (-s; no pl) the Lord (God), God; V **~** (**noch mal**)! for God's sake!

Herrgottsfrühe f **in aller ~** at an unearthly hour.

'herrichten v/t (sep, -ge-, h) **1.** get s.th. ready. **2.** do up. **3.** tidy (room).

Herrin [ˈhɛrɪn] f (-; -nen) **1.** mistress, lady. **2.** ruler. **'herrisch** adj **1.** imperious. **2.** peremptory.

herrlich [ˈhɛrlɪç] adj marvel(l)ous, wonderful, magnificent, F fantastic.

'Herrschaft f (-; -en) **1.** no pl (**über** acc over) a) power, control, b) rule, reign: fig. **die ~ verlieren über** (acc) lose control of. **2.** m-e ~**en!** ladies and gentlemen!, F folks! **'herrschaftlich** adj a) nobleman's, hist. manorial, b) stately.

herrschen [ˈhɛrʃən] v/i (h) **1.** rule (**über** acc over): **über e-n Staat etc ~** rule a state etc. **2.** fig. prevail, reign: **es herrschte Frieden** a. there was peace; **es herrschte Stille** silence reigned. **'herrschend** adj **1.** ruling (class etc). **2.** fig. prevailing, current (opinion etc). **Herrscher** [ˈhɛrʃər] m (-s; -) ruler, sovereign, monarch. **'Herrscherhaus** n a) dynasty, b) ruling house. **'Herrscherin** f (-; -nen) → **Herrscher**.

'Herrschsucht f (-; no pl) domineering (F bossy) nature. **'herrschsüchtig** adj domineering, F bossy.

'herrühren v/i (sep, -ge-, h) **~ von** come (or date) from, be due to.

'hersehen v/i (irr, sep, -ge-, h, → **sehen**) look (here).

'herstellen v/t (sep, -ge-, h) **1.** ✝, ⚙ produce (a. film), manufacture, make. **2.** fig. establish (order, contact, etc)

Hersteller [ˈheːrʃtɛlər] m (-s; -) maker, manufacturer, producer (a. film).

'Herstellerfirma f manufacturers.

'Herstellerin f (-; -nen) → **Hersteller**.

'Herstellung f (-; no pl) **1.** a) manufacture, production (a. print. and film), b) Production (Department). **2.** fig. establishment, making (of contacts etc).

'Herstellungs|kosten pl production cost(s). **~land** n producer country. **~verfahren** n manufacturing process.

Hertz [hɛrts] n (-; -) phys. hertz.

herüber [hɛˈry:bər] adv **1.** over (here), across: **hier ~!** over here!, this way! **2.** F → **hinüber**. **her'überkommen** v/i (irr, sep, -ge-, sn, → **kommen**) come over (a. on a visit), come across.

'Herübersetzung f translation from the foreign language.

herum [hɛˈrʊm] adv **1.** around: **immer**

um et. ~ round and round s.th. **2.** about, (a)round (*the room, town, etc*). **3.** around, near(by): **(irgendwo) hier** ~ somewhere around here, hereabouts. **4. um die Ecke** ~ (a)round the corner; **rechts** ~ (to the) right; **anders (falsch, so)** ~ the other (the wrong, this) way round. **5.** F **um ...** ~ around, about (*two o'clock, ten dollars, etc*); **um Ostern** ~ around Easter. **6.** *time etc*: over, up.

her'um... *dance, move, travel, walk, etc* (a)round, about.

her'umärgern: sich ~ (*sep*, -ge-, h) be plagued (**mit** with).

her'umdrehen (*sep*, -ge-, h) **I** *v/t* a) (*a. sich* ~) turn round, b) F turn over. **II** *v/i* F ~ **an** (*dat*) fiddle with.

her'umdrücken: sich ~ (*sep*, -ge-, h) F **1.** hang around. **2.** *um et.* dodge s.th.

her'umfahren (*irr, sep, -ge-, → fahren*) **I** *v/i* (sn) **1.** drive (*or* go, travel) around: *um et.* ~ drive round s.th. **2.** spin round. **II** *v/t* (h) **3.** drive (*or* take) *s.o., s.th.* around.

her'umfragen *v/i* (*sep*, -ge-, h) ask around.

her'umführen (*sep*, -ge-, h) **I** *v/t j-n* ~ lead s.o. around; *j-n im Haus etc* ~ show s.o. around the house *etc*; ~ **Nase. II** *v/i um et.* ~ *road, fence, etc*: run (a)round s.th.

her'umfuhrwerken *v/i* (*sep*, -ge-, h) F bustle around.

her'umgehen *v/i* (*irr, sep, -ge-, sn, → gehen*) **1.** walk (*or* go) around (**im Park** *etc* the park *etc*): *j-m im Kopf* ~ go round and round in s.o.'s head. *2.* **um et.** ~ *a.* F *belt etc*: go round s.th. **3.** be passed around. **4.** *rumo[u]r etc*: make the round. **5.** *time, day, etc*: pass.

her'umhängen *v/i* (*irr, sep, -ge-, h, → hängen*) F *fig.* hang around (**mit** with).

her'umkomman,dieren *v/t* (*sep*, h) *j-n* ~ order s.o. around.

her'umkommen *v/i* (*irr, sep, -ge-, sn, → kommen*) **1.** *um et.* ~ come (*fig.* get) round s.th., *fig. a.* avoid s.th.; *um die-se Tatsache kommen wir nicht herum* we can't get away from that (fact). **2.** get around: *er ist weit herumgekommen* he has seen a lot of the world.

her'umkriegen *v/t* (*sep*, -ge-, h) F **1.** *j-n* ~ get s.o. round; *j-n dazu* ~, *daß er et. tut*

talk s.o. into doing s.th. **2.** get through (*time, day, etc*).

her'umlaufen *v/i* (*irr, sep, -ge-, sn, → laufen*) (*um et.*) ~ run (*or* go) around (s.th.); *frei* ~ *criminal etc*: be at large *dog etc*: run free.

her'umliegen *v/i* (*irr, sep, -ge-, h, → liegen*) F lie around, lie about.

her'umlungern *v/i* (*sep*, -ge-, h) loiter (*or* hang, loaf) around.

her'umpfuschen *v/i* (*sep*, -ge-, h) ~ **an** (*dat*) monkey (about) with.

her'umreichen (*sep*, -ge-, h) **I** *v/t* hand (*or* pass) *s.th.* (a)round: F *j-n* ~ intro- duce s.o. to (all) one's friends. **II** *v/i* (*um et.*) ~ *belt etc*: go (a)round (s.th.).

her'umreiten *v/i* (*irr, sep, -ge-, sn, → reiten*) (*um et.*) ~ ride (a)round s.th.: F *fig.* ~ *auf* (*dat*) keep harping on.

her'umschlagen: sich ~ (*irr, sep, -ge-, h, → schlagen*) a) **mit** *j-m* fight with s.o., b) **mit e-r Sache** struggle with s.th.

her'umschnüffeln *v/i* (*sep*, -ge-, h) F *fig.* snoop around.

her'umsein *v/i* (*irr, sep, -ge-, sn, → sein*) *time etc*: be over.

her'umstehen *v/i* (*irr, sep, -ge-, h, → stehen*) ~ **um** stand (a)round.

her'umstoßen *v/t* (*irr, sep, -ge-, h, → stoßen*) F *fig. j-n* ~ push s.o. around.

her'umtragen *v/t* (*irr, sep, -ge-, h, → tragen*) **1.** carry *s.o., s.th.* around (**mit** sich with one). **2.** *fig.* spread (*news etc*).

her'umtrampeln *v/i* (*sep*, -ge-, h) tram- ple (**auf** *dat* on): *fig.* **auf** *j-m* ~ treat s.o. like a doormat.

her'umtreiben: sich ~ (*irr, sep, -ge-, h, → treiben*) F **1.** knock around. **2.** → **herumlungern. Her'umtreiber** *m* (-s -) **1.** loiterer, loafer. **2.** tramp.

her'umzeigen *v/t* (*sep*, -ge-, h) **et.** ~ show (*or* pass) s.th. round.

herunter [hɛ'rʊntər] *adv* **1.** a) down, b) off: ~ **damit!** down (*or* off) with it!; **die Treppe** ~ down the stairs, downstairs → **heruntersein. 2.** F → **hinunter.**

herunter... [hɛ'rʊntər] down; → *a.* **her ab..., hinab..., hinunter....**

her'unterbekommen *v/t* (*irr, sep, h, → bekommen*) F get *s.th.* down (*or* off).

her'unterfallen *v/i* (*irr, sep, -ge-, sn, → fallen*) fall down (*or* off).

her'untergehen *v/i* (*irr, sep, -ge-, sn, → gehen*) go down (*a.* ✈), *fig. a.* fall

drop: **mit der Geschwindigkeit (den Preisen)** ~ slow down (reduce prices).
her'untergekommen I *pp of* **herunterkommen. II** *adj* F a) seedy, shabby, down-at-heel, b) run-down, *pred* in bad shape, c) dissolute, d) dilapidated.
her'unterhandeln *v/t* (*sep*, -ge-, h) beat *price etc* down (**um** by).
her'unterholen *v/t* (*sep*, -ge-, h) **1.** get *s.o.*, *s.th.* down. **2.** F shoot *s.th.* down.
her'unterklappen *v/t* (*sep*, -ge-, h) turn *s.th.* down.
her'unterkommen *v/i* (*irr*, *sep*, -ge-, sn, → **kommen**) **1.** come (*or* get) down. **2.** F a) go to seed, b) get into bad shape, c) go downhill, d) go to rack and ruin, d) sink low; → **heruntergekommen. 3.** ~ **von** F get over, *sl.* kick (*drugs etc*).
her'untermachen *v/t* (*sep*, -ge-, h) F **1.** knock, pull *s.o.*, *s.th.* to pieces. **2.** → **her'unterputzen** *v/t* (*sep*, -ge-, h) F *j-n* ~ blow s.o. up.
her'unterrasseln *v/t* (*sep*, -ge-, h) F rattle off.
her'unterschalten *v/i* (*sep*, -ge-, h) *mot.* (**in den ersten Gang**) ~ change (*or* shift) down (into first [gear]).
her'unterschrauben *v/t* (*sep*, -ge-, h) *fig.* lower.
her'untersein *v/i* (*irr*, *sep*, -ge-, sn, → **sein**) F *fig.* be run down, be in bad shape: **er ist mit den Nerven ganz herunter** he is a nervous wreck.
her'unterspielen *v/t* (*sep*, -ge-, h) F *fig.* **et.** ~ play s.th. down.
her'unterwirtschaften *v/t* (*sep*, -ge-, h) F **et.** ~ run s.th. down, mismanage s.th.
hervor [hɛr'foːr] *adv* out of, (out) from, forth: **hinter ... ~** from behind *a tree etc*; **unter ... ~** from under *the bed etc*.
her'vorbringen *v/t* (*irr*, *sep*, -ge-, h, → **bringen**) produce.
her'vorgehen *v/i* (*irr*, *sep*, -ge-, sn, → **gehen**) **1.** (**aus** from) follow, result: **daraus geht hervor, daß** from this follows that; **aus dem Brief geht nicht hervor, ob** the letter doesn't say whether; **als Sieger** ~ emerge victorious; **aus der Ehe gingen drei Kinder hervor** there were three children of this marriage.
her'vorheben *v/t* (*irr*, *sep*, -ge-, h, → **heben**) **1.** *paint.*, *print.* set *s.th.* off. **2.** *fig.* a) emphasize, stress, b) point out.

her'vorholen *v/t* (*sep*, -ge-, h) **et.** ~ (**aus**) get s.th. out (of), produce s.th. (from).
her'vorragen *v/i* (*sep*, -ge-, h) **1.** project, stick out. **2.** *fig.* stand out (**unter dat** among). **her'vorragend I** *adj* **1.** projecting. **2.** *fig.* outstanding, excellent, superior, prominent. **II** *adv* **3.** excellently, outstandingly (well).
her'vorrufen *v/t* (*irr*, *sep*, -ge-, h, → **rufen**) **1.** *thea.* call for. **2.** *fig.* cause, give rise to, provoke.
her'vorstechen *v/i* (*irr*, *sep*, -ge-, h, → **stechen**) stand out (**aus** from).
her'vorstechend *adj* **1.** → **hervorragend** 2. striking.
her'vortreten *v/i* (*irr*, *sep*, -ge-, sn, → **treten**) **1.** step forth, (**aus** *dat*) step out (of), emerge (from). **2.** a) stand out, b) *fig.* emerge, become evident: **et.** ~ **lassen** set s.th. off, *fig.* bring s.th. out, show s.th. **3.** *veins*, *eyes*: protrude. **4.** → **her'vortun: sich** ~ (*irr*, *sep*, -ge-, h, → **tun**) distinguish o.s. (**als** as, **durch** by).
'herwagen: sich ~ (*sep*, -ge-, h) dare to come (here).
'Herweg *m* (**auf dem** ~ on the) way here.
Herz [hɛrts] *n* (-en; -en) heart (a. *fig.*), *cards*: hearts: **im Grunde s-s ~ens** at heart; **leichten ~ens** with a light heart; **schweren ~ens** with a heavy heart, very reluctantly; **von ~en gern** with (the greatest) pleasure, gladly; **j-m von (ganzem) ~en danken** thank s.o. with all one's heart; **von ~en kommend** heartfelt; **auf ~ und Nieren prüfen** put *s.th.* to the acid test, F vet *s.o.*, *s.th.* (thoroughly); **j-m das ~ brechen** break s.o.'s heart; **sich ein ~ fassen** take heart, pluck up courage; **j-m zu ~en gehen** move s.o. deeply; **er ist mir sehr ans ~ gewachsen** I have grown very fond of him; **was haben Sie auf dem ~en?** a) what's on your mind?, b) what can I do for you?; **j-m et. ans ~ legen** enjoin s.th. on s.o.; **das liegt mir sehr am ~en** that's very important to me; **s-m ~en Luft machen** give vent to one's feelings; **j-n ins ~ schließen** take s.o. to one's heart; **sie sind ein ~ und eine Seele** they are very close, F they are as thick as thieves; → **ausschütten** 1, **bringen** 7, **Stoß** 1, **tief** I.
'Herzanfall *m* heart attack.
'Herzas *n* *cards*: ace of hearts.

'**Herzasthma** n 🩺 cardiac asthma.
'**Herzbeschwerden** pl heart trouble.
'**Herzbeutel** m anat. pericardium.
'**Herzchen** ['hɛrtsçən] n (-s; -) darling.
'**Herzchir,urg** m heart surgeon.
'**Herzdame** f cards: queen of hearts.
'**herzeigen** v/t (sep, -ge-, h) F show: **zeig (mal) her!** let me see!
herzen ['hɛrtsən] v/t (h) hug, cuddle.
'**Herzens|brecher** m (-s; -) F ladykiller.
~**lust** f **nach** ~ to one's heart's content.
~**wunsch** m dearest wish.
'**herzerfrischend** adj (very) refreshing.
'**herzergreifend** adj (deeply) moving.
'**Herzfehler** m 🩺 cardiac defect.
'**Herzflimmern** n (-s) 🩺 heart flutter.
'**herzförmig** [-fœrmɪç] adj heart-shaped.
'**herzhaft** adj 1. hearty. 2. → **beherzt**.
'**herziehen** (irr, sep, -ge-, → **ziehen**) I v/t (h) 1. **hinter sich** ~ drag s.o., s.th. along (behind one). II v/i (sn) 2. move here. 3. F ~ **über** (acc) run s.o., s.th. down.
herzig ['hɛrtsɪç] adj sweet, lovely.
'**Herz|in,farkt** m 🩺 cardiac infarction, F heart attack, coronary. ~**kammer** f anat. ventricle. ~**ka,theter** m 🩺 cardiac catheter. ~**klappe** f anat. cardiac valve. ~**klappenfehler** m 🩺 valvular (heart) defect. ~**klopfen** n (-s) beating (• palpitation) of the heart: **er hatte** ~ his heart was thumping (**vor** dat with). ⅋**krank** adj suffering from a heart condition, cardiac. ~**kranke** m, f cardiac. ~**kranzgefäß** n anat. coronary vessel. ~**leiden** n heart disease (or condition).
'**herzlich** I adj a) cordial, warm, friendly, b) sincere, heartfelt: ~**e Grüße, mit** ~**en Grüßen** kind regards (**an** acc to), (with) love; → **Beileid, Dank, Gruß.**
'**Herzlichkeit** f (-; no pl) a) warmth, cordiality, b) sincerity.
'**herzlos** adj heartless.
'**Herzlosigkeit** f (-; no pl) heartlessness.
'**Herz-'Lungen-Ma'schine** f 🩺 heart-lung machine.
'**Herzmas,sage** f 🩺 heart massage.
Herzog ['hɛrtso:k] m (-s; ⁃e) duke. **Herzogin** ['hɛrtso:gɪn] f (-en; -en) duchess. '**herzoglich** adj ducal.
'**Herzogtum** n (-s; ⁃er) dukedom, duchy.
'**Herz|operati,on** f heart operation. ~**rhythmusstörung** f arrhythmia. ~**schlag** m 1. heartbeat. 2. heart attack

(or failure). ~**schrittmacher** m cardiac pacemaker. ~**schwäche** f cardiac insufficiency. ~**spezia,list** m heart specialist. ⅋**stärkend** adj cardiotonic. ~**stillstand** m cardiac arrest. ~**stück** n fig. core. ~**tod** m death by heart failure.
herzu(...) [hɛr'tsu:] → **heran(...), herbei(...), hinzu(...).**
'**Herzversagen** n 🩺 heart failure.
'**Herzverpflanzung** f heart transplant.
'**herzzerbrechend** adj heartbreaking.
'**herzzerreißend** adj heartrending.
Hesse ['hɛsə] m (-n; -n), '**Hessin** f (-; -nen), '**hessisch** adj Hessian.
heterogen [hetero'ge:n] adj heterogeneous.
heterosexu'ell adj, **Heterosexu'elle** m, f (-n; -n) heterosexual.
Hetze ['hɛtsə] f (-; -n) 1. (**gegen** against) agitation, smear campaign. 2. F (mad) rush. 3. → **Hetzjagd** 1, 2.
'**hetzen** I v/t (h) 1. a. fig. hunt, hound. 2. **e-n Hund** etc ~ **auf** (acc) set a dog etc on. 3. (a. **sich** ~) rush. II v/i 4. (h) (**gegen** against) agitate, stir up hatred. 5. (sn) F rush, hurry.
'**Hetzer** m (-s; -) agitator.
Hetze'rei f (-; no pl) → **Hetze** 1, 2.
'**hetzerisch** adj inflammatory.
'**Hetzjagd** f 1. hunt(ing) (with hounds). 2. fig. chase. 3. → **Hetze** 1, 2.
'**Hetzrede** f inflammatory speech.
Heu [hɔy] n (-[e]s; no pl) hay: F **er hat Geld wie** ~ he's rolling in money.
'**Heuboden** m hayloft.
Heuche'lei f (-; -en) 1. no pl hypocrisy, dissimulation. 2. cant. **heucheln** ['hɔyçəln] (h) I v/t simulate, feign. II v/i a) play the hypocrite, b) dissemble, c) cant. '**Heuchler** m (-s; -), '**Heuchlerin** f (-; -nen) hypocrite. '**heuchlerisch** adj hypocritical.
heuen ['hɔyən] v/i (h) make hay.
Heuer ['hɔyər] f (-; -n) 🚢 pay.
heuern ['hɔyərn] v/t (h) 🚢 hire.
'**Heuernte** f hay harvest.
'**Heugabel** f hayfork, pitchfork.
heulen ['hɔylən] v/i (h) 1. zo. howl. 2. F bawl, a. fig. siren: wail: fig. **es ist zum** ⅋ it's a (great) shame.
'**Heuler** m (-s; -) 1. F **das ist (ja) der letzte** ~**!** a) would you believe it, b) it's absolutely super. 2. zo. baby seal.
'**Heulsuse** f (-; -n) F crybaby.

Heurige ['hɔyrɪgə] m (-n; no pl) Austrian new wine.

'Heuschnupfen m hay fever.

'Heuschober m haystack.

Heuschrecke ['hɔyʃrɛkə] f (-; -n) zo. grasshopper, locust.

heute ['hɔytə] **I** adv today, this day: ~ **abend** this evening, tonight; ~ **in acht Tagen** a week from now, Br. a. today week; ~ **vor acht Tagen** a week ago (today); **von** ~ → **heutig**; **von** ~ **an** from today; fig. **von** ~ **auf morgen** overnight; fig. ~ **auf morgen** overnight. **II** **das Heute** the present, today.

heutig ['hɔytɪç] adj today's, of today, a. present(-day), modern: **bis auf den** ~**en Tag** to this day.

'heutzutage adv nowadays, today.

Hexe ['hɛksə] f (-; -n) witch (a. fig.), sorceress, fig. hellcat: (**alte**) ~ (old) hag.

hexen ['hɛksən] v/i (h) practise witchcraft: F **ich kann doch nicht** ~! I can't work miracles!

'Hexen|jagd f fig. witch-hunt. ~**kessel** m fig. inferno. ~**meister** m sorcerer. ~**schuß** m (-sses; no pl) ♂ F lumbago.

Hexe'rei f (-; -en) witchcraft, magic (a. fig.): **das ist k-e** ~! there's nothing to it!

hieb [hi:p] pret of **hauen**.

Hieb m (-[e]s; -e) **1.** stroke, blow, punch: F ~**e bekommen** get a thrashing; **auf einen** ~ at one go. **2.** fig. dig (**auf** acc at). '**hieb- und 'stichfest** adj watertight (argument), cast-iron (proof etc).

hielt [hi:lt] pret of **halten**.

hier [hi:r] adv here (a. fig. in this case), a. present: ~ **drinnen** (**draußen, oben**) in (out, up) here; ~ **und da** a) here and there, b) now and then; ~ **und heute** here and now; **von** ~ **an** (or **ab**) from here (on); ~, **bitte!** here you are!

hieran ['hi:'ran] adv **1.** ~ **kann man sehen, daß** you can see from this that; ~ **ist kein wahres Wort** there is not a word of truth in this. **2.** ~ **schließt sich** ... **an** is followed by ...

Hierarchie [hierar'çi:] f (-; -n) hierarchy.

hieraus ['hi:'raʊs] adv from it (or this).

'**hier'bei** adv a) here, b) on this occasion, c) in this connection.

'**hierbleiben** v/i (irr, sep, -ge-, sn, → **bleiben**) stay here.

'**hier'durch** adv by this, hereby.

'**hier'für** adv for this, for it.

'**hier'her** adv here, this way, over here:

bis ~ up to here, a. time: so far; **bis** ~ **und nicht weiter** this far and no further; (**komm**) ~! come here!

hier'hergehören v/i (sep, h) belong here: fig. **das gehört so nicht hierher** that's irrelevant.

hierherum ['hi:rhɛ'rʊm] adv **1.** this way (a)round. **2.** F hereabout(s).

'**hier'hin** adv this way. '**hierhin'auf** adv up here. '**hierhin'ein** adv in here.

hierin ['hi:'rɪn] adv a. fig. in this, here.

'**hier'mit** adv with this, herewith.

'**hier'nach** adv **1.** after this (or it). **2.** according to this.

Hieroglyphe [hiero'gly:fə] f (-; -n) hieroglyph.

'**hiersein** v/i (irr, sep, -ge-, sn, → **sein**) be here, be present: **während s-s Hierseins** during his stay (here).

hierüber ['hi:'ry:bər] adv fig. about this.

hierum ['hi:'rʊm] adv **1.** (a)round this. **2.** → **hierherum 2. 3.** fig. about this (or it): ~ **geht es nicht** that's not the point.

hierunter ['hi:'rʊntər] adv **1.** under this, among these. **2.** fig. understand etc: by this, by that: ~ **fällt** ... this includes ...

'**hier'von** adv of (or from) this.

'**hier'zu** adv **1.** for this. **2.** to this (or these): **im Gegensatz** ~ in contrast to this.

'**hierzu'lande** adv in this country, here.

hiesig ['hi:zɪç] adj local, here, of this place (or country).

hieß [hi:s] pret of **heißen**.

hieven ['hi:fən] v/t (h) a. fig. heave.

Hi-Fi ['haɪfi] abbr. of **High Fidelity**.

'**Hi-Fi-'Anlage** f hi-fi set.

Hilfe ['hɪlfə] f (-; -n) **1.** help, aid, assistance, relief: **ärztliche** ~ medical assistance; **Erste** ~ first aid; **j-m** ~ **leisten** help s.o., aid s.o.; **j-m zu** ~ **kommen** come to s.o.'s aid; **zu** ~ **nehmen** make use of, use; **um** ~ **rufen** call for help; **mit** ~ **von** (or gen) with the help of, fig. a. by means of; **ohne** ~ unaided, without help; (**zu**) ~! help! **2.** (person) help.

'**hilfeflehend** adj imploring.

'**Hilfeleistung** f aid, assistance, help.

'**Hilferuf** m a. fig. cry for help.

'**Hilfestellung** f (-; no pl) a. fig. support.

'**hilfesuchend** adj seeking (for) help.

'**hilflos** adj helpless.

'**Hilflosigkeit** f (-; no pl) helplessness.

'**hilfreich** adj a. fig. helpful.

'**Hilfs|akti,on** f relief (or rescue) action. **~arbeiter(in** f) m unskilled worker. **2bedürftig** adj a) in need (of help), b) needy. **~bedürftigkeit** f (-; no pl) neediness, need. 2**bereit** adj ready to help, helpful. **~bereitschaft** f (-; no pl) readiness to help. **~fonds** m relief fund. **~kraft** f **1.** assistant, help. **2.** temporary worker. **~mittel** n aid. **~motor** m auxiliary engine (✈ motor). **~organisati,on** f relief organization. **~quelle** f source of help, pl resources. **~verb** n auxiliary verb. **~werk** n relief organization. **~wissenschaft** f auxiliary science.

Himbeere ['hɪmbeːrə] f (-; -n) raspberry.
'**Himbeersaft** m raspberry juice.
'**Himbeerstrauch** m raspberry bush.

Himmel ['hɪməl] m (-s; -) sky, eccl. or fig. heaven; **der ~ auf Erden** heaven on earth; **am ~** in the sky; fig. (**wie**) **aus heiterem ~** out of the blue; **unter freiem ~** in the open air; **zum ~ (empor)** skyward(s), heavenward(s); **im ~ sein** be in heaven; **in den ~ heben** praise s.o., s.th. to the skies; F **weiß der ~(, wo)!** God knows (where)!; **das schreit zum ~** it's a crying shame; F **das stinkt zum ~** that stinks to high heaven; **um ~s willen!** a) (**ach,**) **du lieber ~!** good heavens!, b) a. (**noch mal**)! for Heaven's sake!

'**himmel|angst** adj **mir war** (or **wurde**) **~** I was scared to death.
'**Himmelbett** n four-poster.
'**himmelblau** adj sky-blue.
'**Himmelfahrt** f (-; no pl) **Christi ~** a) the Ascension of Christ, b) Ascension Day; **Mariä ~** a) the Assumption of the Virgin Mary, b) Assumption Day.
'**Himmelfahrtstag** m (**am ~** on) Ascension Day.
'**Himmelreich** n kingdom of heaven.
'**Himmelschlüssel** m ♣ primrose.
'**himmelschreiend** adj outrageous, terrible: **~e Schande** crying shame.
'**Himmelskarte** f star map.
'**Himmelskörper** m celestial body.
'**Himmelsrichtung** f direction.
'**himmelweit** adj fig. vast: **es ist ein ~er Unterschied zwischen ...** there is a world of difference between ...; **~ verschieden sein** differ enormously.
himmlisch ['hɪmlɪʃ] adj heavenly, divine.
hin [hɪn] I adv **1.** there: **nichts wie ~!** let's

go!; **~ zu** to, towards; **bis ~ zu** a) as far as, b) fig. (even) including, c) till; **über** (acc) **~** over; **~ und her** to and fro, back and forth; **~ und zurück** a) there and back, b) return (Am. round-trip) (ticket); **~ und her gerissen sein** a) **zwischen** be torn between, b) F **von** be gone over. **2.** **auf e-e Sache ~** a) as a result of, b) on the basis of, c) because of, d) in reply to, on; **auf s-e Bitte ~** at his request; **auf s-n Rat ~** at his advice. **3.** **~ und wieder** now and then. **4.** F **~ oder her** a) more or less, give or take (**ten dollars, years, etc**), b) a. **... ~, ... her** I don't care; **Anstand ~, Anstand her** fairness or no. II adj pred → **hinsein.**

Hin n → **Hin und Her.**
hinab(...) [hɪ'nap] → **hinunter(...), herab(...), herunter(...).**
'**hinarbeiten** v/i (sep, -ge-, h) **~ auf** (acc) work towards, aim at.
hinauf [hɪ'naʊf] adv up: **da ~** up there; **bis ~ zu** up to; **den Berg ~** up the hill, uphill; (**die Treppe**) **~** upstairs.
hin'auf... climb, drive, look, etc up, → a. **empor..., hoch...**
hin'aufgehen (irr, sep, -ge-, sn, → **gehen**) I v/i go up (a. fig.): **mit dem Preis ~** raise the price. II v/t go up: **die Treppe ~** a. go upstairs.
hinaus [hɪ'naʊs] adv up, out, outside: **~ aus** out of; **da ~!** this way (out)!; **zum Fenster ~** out of the window; **nach vorn (hinten) ~ wohnen** live at the front (back); **~ (mit dir** or **euch)!** out (with you)!, get out!; **~ damit!** out with it! **2. über** (acc) **~** a. fig. a) beyond, b) above, over; **auf Jahre ~** for years (to come); → **darüber 3, hinaussein.**
hin'ausbegleiten v/t (sep, h) **j-n ~** see s.o. out (**aus** of).
hin'ausekeln v/t (sep, -ge-, h) F **j-n ~** freeze s.o. out (**aus** of).
hin'ausfliegen v/i (irr, sep, -ge-, sn, → **fliegen**) **1.** fly out. **2.** F fig. get kicked out, a. get the sack.
hin'ausgehen v/i (irr, sep, -ge-, sn, → **gehen**) **1.** go out (**aus** of). **2.** fig. **~ auf** (acc) window etc: open on(to). **3.** fig. **~ über** (acc) go beyond, a. exceed.
hin'auslaufen v/i (irr, sep, -ge-, sn, → **laufen**) **1.** run out (**aus** of). **2.** fig. **~ auf** (acc) come to, amount to, lead to; **es**

Hingabe

läuft auf dasselbe hinaus it comes (or amounts) to the same thing.

hin'ausschieben v/t (irr, sep, -ge-, h, → **schieben**) fig. put s.th. off, postpone.

hin'aussein v/i (irr, sep, -ge-, sn, → **sein**) ~ **über** (acc) be beyond, be past; **über das Alter** (or **darüber**) **ist er hinaus** he is past that age.

hin'ausstellen v/t (sep, -ge-, h) **1.** put s.th. out(side). **2.** sports: **j-n** ~ send (or order) s.o. off the field.

hin'auswachsen v/i (irr, sep, -ge-, sn, → **wachsen**) fig. ~ **über** (acc) surpass.

hin'auswagen: sich ~ (sep, -ge-, h) venture (or go) out (**aus** of).

hin'auswerfen v/t (irr, sep, -ge-, h, → **werfen**) **1.** throw s.th. out (**aus** of): → **Fenster. 2.** F throw (or kick) s.o. out (**aus** of), a. sack, fire.

hin'auswollen v/i (irr, sep, -ge-, h, → **wollen**) **1.** want to go (or get) out (**aus** of). **2.** fig. **worauf will er hinaus?** what is he driving at?; **hoch** ~ be aiming high.

hin'ausziehen (irr, sep, -ge-, → **ziehen**) **I** v/t (h) **1.** pull s.o., s.th. out (**aus** of). **2.** fig. et. ~ drag s.th. out. **II** v/i (sn) go out, march out. **III sich** ~ (h) a) drag on, b) take longer than expected.

hin'auszögern v/t (sep, -ge-, h) delay: **sich** ~ be delayed.

'hinbiegen v/t (irr, sep, -ge-, h, → **biegen**) F fig. et. ~ wangle s.th.

'Hinblick m im ~ **auf** (acc) with regard to.

'hinbringen v/t (irr, sep, -ge-, h, → **bringen**) **1.** take s.o., s.th. there. **2.** pass, spend (time). **3.** → **fertigbringen**.

hinderlich ['hɪndərlɪç] adj troublesome: ~ **sein** (dat) hamper, impede, be a handicap to. **hindern** ['hɪndərn] v/t (h) a) hamper, impede, b) interfere (**bei** with): **j-n am Arbeiten** ~ prevent (or keep) s.o. from working.

'Hindernis n (-ses; -se) obstacle (**für** to): **j-m** ~**se in den Weg legen** put obstacles in s.o.'s way; **auf** ~**se stoßen** run into difficulties. ~**lauf** m sports: obstacle race. ~**rennen** n steeplechase.

'hindeuten v/i (sep, -ge-, h) ~ **auf** (acc) point at, fig. point to, indicate.

Hindu ['hɪndʊ] m (-[s]; -[s]) Hindu.

Hinduismus [hɪndʊ'ɪsmʊs] m (-; no pl) Hinduism.

hin'durch adv **1.** through. **2.** through(out): **die Nacht** ~ all night (long); **das ganze Jahr** ~ throughout the year.

hinein [hɪ'naɪn] adv in, inside, a. into (May etc): **da** ~ in there; **bis tief in die Nacht** ~ far into the night; F ~! let's go!

hin'einbekommen v/t (irr, sep, h, → **bekommen**) get s.o., s.th. in(to **in** acc).

hin'eindenken: sich ~ (irr, sep, -ge-, h, → **denken**) **in** (acc) go into; **sich in j-n** ~ put o.s. into s.o.'s position.

hin'eingehen v/i (irr, sep, -ge-, sn, → **gehen**) **1.** (**in** acc) go in(to), enter (the house etc). **2.** hold (two litres etc), seat, accommodate (500 persons etc).

hin'einknien: sich ~ (sep, -ge-, h) F fig. buckle down (**in** acc to).

hin'einkommen v/i (irr, sep, -ge-, sn, → **kommen**) come (or get) in(to **in** acc).

hin'einleben v/i (sep, -ge-, h) **in den Tag** ~ take it easy.

hin'einlegen v/t (sep, -ge-, h) **1.** put s.th. in(to **in** acc). **2.** → **hereinlegen**.

hin'einpassen v/i (sep, -ge-, h) **1.** fit in(to **in** acc). **2.** → **hineingehen** 2.

hin'einreden v/i (sep, -ge-, h) **1.** ~ interrupt s.o.; **j-m** (**in s-e Angelegenheiten**) ~ interfere with s.o.'s affairs.

hin'einstecken v/t (sep, -ge-, h) F a. fig. put s.th. in(to **in** acc): → **Nase**.

hin'einsteigern: sich ~ (sep, -ge-, h) get worked up (**in** acc over); **sich in s-e Wut** ~ work o.s. up into a rage.

hin'einziehen (irr, sep, -ge-, → **ziehen**) **I** v/t (h) pull s.o., s.th. in(to **in** acc): **j-n in e-e Sache** ~ involve s.o. in s.th. **II** v/i (sn) march (or move) in(to **in** acc).

'hinfahren v/t (irr, sep, -ge-, → **fahren**) **I** v/t (h) take (or drive) s.o., s.th. there. **II** v/i (sn) go (mot. a. drive) there.

'Hinfahrt f journey there: **auf der** ~ on the (or our etc) way there.

'hinfallen v/i (irr, sep, -ge-, sn, → **fallen**) fall (down). **'hinfällig** adj **1.** frail. **2.** fig. invalid: **et.** ~ **machen** invalidate s.th.

'hinfinden v/i (irr, sep, -ge-, h, → **finden**) (a. **sich** ~) find one's way there.

'Hinflug m outward flight: **auf dem** ~ a. on the flight there.

'hinführen (sep, -ge-, h) **I** v/t **j-n** ~ lead (or take) s.o. there (or **zu** to). **II** v/i lead (or go) there: fig. **wo soll das** (**noch**) ~? where is this leading to?

hing [hɪŋ] pret of **hängen'**.

'Hingabe f (-; no pl) **1.** (**an** acc to) devotion, dedication: **mit** ~ a. lovingly. **2.**

sacrifice. '**hingeben** (*irr*, *sep*, -ge-, h, →
geben) **I** *v/t* give away, sacrifice, give
up. **II** *sich* ~ (*dat*) devote (*or* dedicate)
o.s. to *a task etc*, abandon o.s. to *despair etc*; **sich j-m** ~ give o.s. to s.o.; **sich
Hoffnungen** (**Illusionen**) ~ have hopes
(illusions).

'**hingebungsvoll** *adj and adv* devot-
ed(ly), *adv a.* with dedication.

hin'gegen *conj* however, on the other
hand.

'**hingehen** *v/i* (*irr*, *sep*, -ge-, sn, →
gehen) **1.** go (there): **wo gehst du hin**?
where are you going? **2.** pass, go by. **3.**
fig. pass, do: **et.** ~ **lassen** let s.th. pass.

'**hingehören** *v/i* (*sep*, h) belong: **wo gehört das hin**? *a.* where does this go?

'**hingeraten** *v/i* (*irr*, *sep*, sn, → **geraten**)
get (**irgendwo** somewhere): **wo ist es
~**? what has become of it?

'**hingerissen I** *adj* (*von*) enraptured
(by), ecstatic (*pred* in raptures, F gone)
(over). **II** *adv* in raptures, ecstatically.

'**hinhalten** *v/t* (*irr*, *sep*, -ge-, h, → **halten**)
1. **j-m et.** ~ hold s.th. out to s.o.; →
Kopf 1. **2.** *fig.* **j-n** ~ put s.o. off, keep s.o.
on a string.

'**Hinhaltetaktik** *f* delaying tactics.

'**hinhauen** (*irr*, *sep*, -ge-, h, → **hauen**) F **I**
v/t **1.** slam *s.th.* down. **2.** *fig.* knock off
(*essay, sketch, etc*). **II** *v/i* *fig.* a) work,
b) be okay, c) be right, d) do. **III** *sich* ~
a) hit the ground, b) hit the sack.

'**hinhören** *v/i* (*sep*, -ge-, h) listen.

hinken ['hɪŋkən] *v/i* (h) (walk with a)
limp: **der Vergleich hinkt** that's a lame
comparison.

'**hinkommen** *v/i* (*irr*, *sep*, -ge-, sn, →
kommen) **1.** come (*or* get) there: **wo
kämen wir denn hin, wenn ...** where
would we be if ... ? **2.** F go, belong: **wo
kommt das hin**? where does that go? **3.**
F manage (**mit** with). **4.** F be right:
wieder ~ come right.

'**hinkriegen** *v/t* (*sep*, -ge-, h) F manage:
das hat er prima hingekriegt he's
made a first-rate job of it; **j-n wieder** ~
put s.o. right again.

'**hinlangen** *v/i* (*sep*, -ge-, h) F (**kräftig**) ~
a) let go with a wallop, b) *fig.* (really)
go to town (**bei** on).

'**hinlänglich** *adj* sufficient.

'**hinlegen** (*sep*, -ge-, h) **I** *v/t* **1.** put (*or*
lay) down. **2.** F fork out (*money*). **3.** F

do *s.th.* brilliantly: **sie haben ein tolles
Spiel hingelegt** they played a fantastic
game. **II** *sich* ~ lie down.

'**hinmachen** (*sep*, -ge-, h) F **I** *v/t* **1.** fix. **2.**
a) kill, b) wreck, break. **II** *v/i* **3.** *dial.*
hurry up: **mach(t) hin!** get a move on!

'**hinnehmen** *v/t* (*irr*, *sep*, -ge-, h, → **nehmen**) **1.** accept, *fig. a.* take, put up
with. **2.** F **mit** ~ take *s.o.*, *s.th.* along.

'**hinreichend** *adj* sufficient.

'**Hinreise** *f* journey there (*or* out), ⚓
voyage out: **auf der** ~ on the way there.

'**hinreißen** *v/t* (*irr*, *sep*, -ge-, h, → **reißen**) **1.** enrapture, thrill: → **hingerissen. 2.** *sich* ~ **lassen** (let o.s.) be carried away (**von** by, **zu** into doing).

'**hinreißend** *adj* breathtaking, fantastic.

'**hinrichten** *v/t* (*sep*, -ge-, h) execute.

'**Hinrichtung** *f* (-; -en) execution.

'**hinsehen** *v/i* (*irr*, *sep*, -ge-, h, → **sehen**)
look: **ohne hinzusehen** without look-
ing; **bei näherem** ♀ at a closer look.

'**hinsein** *v/i* (*irr*, *sep*, -ge-, sn, → **sein**) F
1. a) be wrecked, *a. fig.* be ruined, b) be
gone, c) be dead(-beat), d) be done for:
es (**er**) **ist hin** *a.* it (he) has had it; **hin
ist hin!** gone is gone! **2.** (**ganz**) ~ (**von**)
→ **hingerissen I**.

'**hinsetzen** (*sep*, -ge-, h) **I** *v/t* a) set (*or*
put) *s.th.* down, b) seat (*a. child*), sit *child*
down. **II** *sich* ~ sit down, take a seat.

'**Hinsicht** *f* **in dieser** (**in jeder**) ~ in this
(in every) respect; **in mancher** (**vieler**)
~ in some (many) respects (*or* ways); **in
politischer** ~ politically. '**hinsichtlich**
prep (*gen*) with regard to, concerning.

'**Hinspiel** *n* sports: first leg.

'**hinstellen** (*sep*, -ge-, h) **I** *v/t* **1.** a) put,
place, b) put down. **2.** F put up (*a house
etc*). **3.** *fig.* **j-n** (**et.**) ~ **als** make s.o.
(s.th.) out to be. **II** *sich* ~ **4.** stand (**vor
j-n** in front of s.o.). **5.** *fig.* **sich** ~ **als**
claim (*or* pretend) to be.

hintansetzen [hɪnt'?an-], **hint'anstellen** *v/t* (*sep*, -ge-, h) *fig.* a) put *s.th.* last,
b) neglect.

hinten ['hɪntən] *adv* a) at the back (*or*
rear), b) in the background: ~ **im Garten** at the back of the garden; ~ **am
Auto** at the rear of the car; ~ **im Buch** at
the end of the book; **nach** ~ a) to the
back, b) back, c) backwards; **von** ~
from the back, from behind; F **das
reicht** ~ **und vorn nicht** that's not

nearly enough; *das stimmt ~ und vorn nicht* that's all wrong.

'**hinten'herum** *adv* F **1.** (a)round the back. **2.** *fig.* on the quiet.

'**hinten'über** *adv* backwards.

hinter ['hɪntər] **I** *prep* F (*dat or acc*) behind: *~ dem Haus* behind (*or* at the back of) the house; *et. ~ sich bringen* a) get s.th. over (with), b) (*distance*); *~ et. kommen* a) find out about s.th., b) get (the hang of) s.th.; *j-n* (*et.*) *~ sich lassen* leave s.o. (s.th.) behind; *et. ~ sich haben* have s.th. behind one; *er hat schon viel ~ sich* he has been through a lot; *fig. ~ j-m stehen* be behind s.o., *a. sich ~ j-n stellen* back s.o. (up); *~ j-m* (*et.*) *her sein* be after s.o. (s.th.). **II** *adj* → *hintere*.

'**Hinterachse** *f mot.* rear axle.

'**Hinterausgang** *m* rear exit.

'**Hinterbacke** *f* F buttock.

Hinterbänkler ['hɪntərbɛŋklər] *m* (-s; -) *parl.* backbencher.

'**Hinterbein** *n* hind leg: F *fig. sich auf die ~e stellen* put up a fight.

Hinterbliebene [hɪntər'bliːbənə] *m, f* (-n; -n) surviving dependant: *die ~n* the bereaved.

hinter'bringen *v/t* (*irr, insep, no* -ge-, h, → *bringen*) *j-m et.* ~ inform s.o. of s.th.

'**Hinterdeck** *n* ⚓ afterdeck.

'**hintere** *adj* back, rear: *die ~n Reihen* the back rows, the rows at the back; *am ~n Ende* at the far end.

hinterein'ander *adv* a) one behind the other, b) one after the other: *drei Tage* (*dreimal*) ~ three days (times) running (*or* in a row). **2.** → *nacheinander.*
~gehen *v/i* (*irr, sep,* -ge-, sn, → *gehen*) walk one behind the other. *~schalten* *v/t* (*sep,* -ge-, h) *⚡* connect in series.

'**Hintereingang** *m* back entrance.

hinter'fragen *v/t* (*insep, no* -ge-, h) scrutinize (closely).

'**Hinterfuß** *m* hind foot.

'**Hintergedanke** *m* ulterior motive.

hinter'gehen *v/t* (*irr, insep, no* -ge-, h, → *gehen*) deceive, cheat.

'**Hintergrund** *m* (*fig. vor dem ~* against the) background (*gen* of); *in den ~ drängen* push *s.o., s.th.* into the background; *sich im ~ halten* keep a low profile; *die Hintergründe* the background (*of a deed* etc). '**Hinter-**

grund... background (*information, music,* etc).

'**hintergründig** [-grʏndɪç] *adj* a) enigmatic, cryptic, b) profound, c) subtle (*humo[u]r* etc).

'**Hinterhalt** *m* (-[e]s; -e) **1.** (*a. aus dem ~ angreifen*) ambush. **2.** *fig. et. im ~ haben* have s.th. in reserve.

'**hinterhältig** [-hɛltɪç] → *hinterlistig*.

'**Hinterhand** *f* (-; *no pl*) **1.** *zo.* hindquarters. **2.** *fig.* (*noch*) *et. in der ~ haben* have s.th. up one's sleeve.

'**Hinterhaus** *n* back building.

hinter'her *adv* **1.** behind, after. **2.** afterwards, after the event.

hinter'hersein *v/i* (*irr, sep,* -ge-, sn, → *sein*) F **1.** *j-m* ~ be after s.o. **2.** ~, *daß* see (to it) that, make sure that.

'**Hinterhof** *m* backyard. '**Hinterkopf** *m* back of one's head: F *et. im ~ haben* have s.th. at the back of one's mind.

'**Hinterland** *n* (-[e]s; *no pl*) hinterland.

hinter'lassen (*irr, insep, no* -ge-, h, → *lassen*) **I** *v/t* leave (behind), *testator*: *a.* bequeath (*dat* to). **II** *adj* posthumous (*works*). **Hinter'lassenschaft** *f* (-; -en) *⚖* estate, *fig.* legacy.

Hinter'lassung *f unter ~ von* (*or gen*) leaving *s.th.* behind.

hinter'legen *v/t* (*insep, no* -ge-, h) deposit (*bei* with). **Hinter'legung** *f gegen ~ von* (*or gen*) on depositing *s.th.*

'**Hinterlist** *f* (-; *no pl*) **1.** a) cunning, b) underhandedness. **2.** underhand(ed) trick. '**hinterlistig** *adj* a) crafty, cunning, b) underhand(ed).

'**Hintermann** *m* (-[e]s; ̈er) **1.** *mein etc* ~ the man (*or* car) behind me *etc.* **2.** *fig. usu. pl* the man behind it.

'**Hintermannschaft** *f* defen/ce (*Am.* -se).

'**Hintern** *m* (-s; -) F bottom, backside, behind: *j-m in den ~ kriechen* suck up to s.o.

'**Hinterrad** *n* rear wheel. '**Hinterradantrieb** *m mot.* rear-wheel drive.

hinterrücks ['hɪntərrʏks] *adv* **1.** from behind. **2.** *fig.* behind *s.o.'s* back.

'**Hinterseite** *f* back.

'**Hintersitz** *m* back seat.

'**hinterste** *adj* (very) last, hindmost: *am ~n Ende* at the very end.

'**Hinterteil** *n* → *Hintern*.

'**Hintertreffen** *n ins ~ geraten* a) fall behind, b) be losing out.

hinter'treiben v/t (irr, insep, no -ge-, h, → *treiben*) prevent, foil.

'**Hintertreppe** f back stairs.

'**Hintertür** f 1. back door. 2. a. '**Hintertürchen** n fig. loophole.

'**Hinterwäldler** [-vɛltlər] m (-s; -) back-woodsman, Am. a. hick.

hinter'ziehen v/t (irr, insep, no -ge-, h, → *ziehen*) Steuern ~ evade taxes.

'**Hinterzimmer** n back room.

'**hintun** v/t (irr, sep, -ge-, h, → *tun*) F put: fig. *ich weiß nicht, wo ich ihn ~ soll* I can't place him.

hinüber [hɪˈnyːbər] adv over, across: *da ~!* over there! **~fahren** (irr, sep, -ge-, → *fahren*) **I** v/t (h) take (or drive) s.o., s.th. over (or across) (*über acc a bridge etc*). **II** v/i (sn) go (or travel, drive) across (or over) (*nach, zu* to). **~sein** v/i (irr, sep, -ge-, sn, → *sein*) F a) be dead, be gone, b) be dead to the world, c) be ruined, have had it, d) *food:* have gone bad.

'**Hinübersetzung** f translation into the foreign language.

Hin und Her: *das ~* the coming and going, a. fig. the to-and-fro; *nach langem ~* after endless discussions.

'**Hin- und 'Rück|fahrkarte** f return (*Am.* round-trip) ticket. **~fahrt** f return journey, *Am.* round trip. **~flug** m return (*Am.* round-trip) flight.

hinunter [hɪˈnʊntər] adv down: *die Treppe ~* down the stairs, downstairs; *die Straße ~* down the street.

hin'unter... *fall, look, walk, etc* down; → *a. herunter...*

hin'unterspülen v/t (sep, -ge-, h) a. fig. wash down.

hin'unterstürzen (sep, -ge-) **I** v/t 1. (h) throw s.o., s.th. down. 2. (sn) rush down (*the stairs etc*). 3. (h) gulp down. **II** v/i 4. (sn) crash down.

'**hinwagen**: *sich ~* (sep, -ge-, h) venture there.

hinweg [hɪnˈvɛk] adv 1. away, off. 2. ~ *über* (acc) over, across; *fig. über j-n* (or *j-s Kopf*) ~ over s.o.'s head; *darüber ist er ~* he has got over that.

'**Hinweg** m (*auf dem ~* on the) way there.

hin'weggehen v/i (irr, sep, -ge-, sn, → *gehen*) *fig. ~ über* (acc) pass over, ignore; *lachend* (*achselzuckend*) *über et. ~* laugh (shrug) s.th. off.

hin'weghelfen v/i (irr, sep, -ge-, h, → *helfen*) *j-m über et. ~* a. fig. help s.o. to get over s.th.

hin'wegkommen v/i (irr, sep, -ge-, sn, → *kommen*) *über et. ~* a. fig. get over s.th.

hin'wegsehen v/i (irr, sep, -ge-, h, → *sehen*) *über et. ~* a) see (or look) over s.th., b) fig. ignore s.th., overlook s.th.

hin'wegsetzen (sep, -ge-) **I** v/i (h, sn) ~ *über* (acc) jump over. **II** *sich ~* (h) → *hinweggehen*.

Hinweis [ˈhɪnvaɪs] m (-es; -e) (*auf acc*) 1. a) tip, hint (as to), b) a. *pl* information (on, about), c) indication (of), clue (as to), d) note (about), comment (on): *sachdienliche ~* relevant information; *~e zur Benutzung* directions for use. 2. reference (to). 3. allusion (to).

'**hinweisen** (irr, sep, -ge-, h, → *weisen*) **I** v/t *j-n auf et. ~* point s.th. out to s.o. **II** v/i ~ *auf* (acc) a) point to, fig. a. indicate, b) refer to; *darauf* ~, *daß* point out that. '**hinweisend** adj *~es Fürwort* demonstrative pronoun.

'**Hinweis|schild** n, **~tafel** f sign.

'**hinwerfen** v/t (irr, sep, -ge-, h, → *werfen*) 1. throw s.th. down, F drop (a. fig. *remark etc*): *sich ~* throw o.s. down; *j-m et. ~* throw s.th. to s.o. 2. F chuck (*job*). 3. F dash off (*letter etc*).

'**hinwirken** v/i (sep, -ge-, h) ~ *auf* (acc) work towards.

'**hinwollen** v/i (irr, sep, -ge-, h, → *wollen*) F want to go: *wo willst du hin?* where are you going?

'**hinziehen** (irr, sep, -ge-, → *ziehen*) **I** v/t (h) 1. draw s.th. (*zu* to, towards): *fig. sich hingezogen fühlen zu* feel drawn towards. 2. fig. drag s.th. out. **II** v/i (sn) 3. a) move (*über acc* across, *zu* towards), b) move there. **III** *sich ~* (h) 4. drag on (*über Wochen etc* for weeks etc). 5. stretch (*bis zu* to, as far as).

hinzu [hɪnˈtsuː] adv in addition, besides.

hin'zufügen v/t (sep, -ge-, h) add, append.

Hin'zufügung f (-; *no pl*) addition: *unter ~ von* (or *gen*) (by) adding.

hin'zukommen v/i (irr, sep, -ge-, sn, → *kommen*) 1. come (along): ~ *zu* join (s.o., s.th.). 2. a) be added, b) follow: *hinzu kommt, daß ...* add to this ..., besides ...; *es kommt noch hinzu, daß er ...* what is more he ...

hin'zuziehen v/t (irr, sep, -ge-, h, → *ziehen*) *j-n ~* call s.o. in, consult s.o.

Hiobsbotschaft ['hi:ɔps-] f bad news.
Hirn [hɪrn] n (-[e]s; -e) **1.** anat. brain. **2.** gastr. brains. **3.** fig. brain(s), head, mind: **sich das ~ zermartern** rack one's brains.
'Hirngespinst n (**ein reines ~** a mere) fantasy, w.s. pipe dream.
'Hirnhaut f anat. meninges. **'Hirnhautentzündung** f ⚕ meningitis.
'hirnlos adj a. F fig. brainless.
'Hirnrinde f anat. cerebral cortex.
'hirnrissig, 'hirnverbrannt adj F mad.
Hirsch [hɪrʃ] m (-es; -e) stag. **~braten** m roast venison. **~fänger** m hunting knife. **~kalb** n fawn. **~keule** f gastr. haunch of venison. **~kuh** f hind. **~leder** n, **2ledern** adj buckskin.
Hirse ['hɪrzə] f (-; -n) ⚕ millet.
Hirte ['hɪrtə] m (-n; -n) herdsman, shepherd (a. eccl.). **'Hirtenbrief** m eccl. pastoral letter. **'Hirtenvolk** n pastoral tribe. **'Hirtin** f (-; -nen) shepherdess.
his, His [hɪs] n (-; -) ♪ B sharp.
hissen ['hɪsən] v/t (h) hoist.
Historiker [hɪs'to:rikər] m (-s; -) historian. **historisch** [hɪs'to:rɪʃ] adj a) historical, b) historic (figure, moment, etc).
Hit [hɪt] m (-[s]; -s) ♪ or F fig. hit.
'Hitliste f ♪ the top ten etc (of the week etc). **'Hitparade** f ♪ hit parade.
Hitze ['hɪtsə] f (-; no pl) (**bei dieser ~** in this) heat: ⚕ **fliegende ~** hot flushes; **in der ~ des Gefechts** in the heat of the moment. **2beständig** adj heat-resistant. **2empfindlich** adj sensitive to heat. **2frei** adj **~ haben** have time off from school because of very hot weather. **~grad** m degree of heat. **~schild** m heat shield. **~welle** f heat wave.
'Hitzkopf m hothead.
'hitzköpfig [-kœpfɪç] adj hotheaded.
'Hitzschlag m heat stroke.
H-Milch ['ha:mɪlç] f long-life milk.
hob [ho:p] pret of **heben**.
Hobby ['hɔbi] n (-s; -s) hobby.
Hobel ['ho:bəl] m (-s; -) plane.
hobeln ['ho:bəln] v/t, v/i (h) plane.
hoch [ho:x] **I** adj **1.** high (a. fig. costs, income, etc), a. tall (tree etc), deep (snow, water), a. great (speed etc, a. hono[u]r, value, etc), heavy (penalty), high(-pitched) (sound, voice): **ein hohes Alter erreichen** live to a ripe old age; **hohe Niederlage** sports: crushing

defeat; ♪ **das hohe C** top C; parl. **das Hohe Haus** the House; **der hohe Norden** the far North; fig. **das ist mir zu ~!** that's above me!; → **Maß**[1] 3, **Roß**, **Tier** etc. **II** adv **2.** high, fig. highly: **~ oben** high up, on high; **~ gewinnen** win high; **~ verlieren** sports: get trounced; **~ spielen** play (a. fig. gamble) high; **sie kamen drei Mann ~** there were three of them; **j-m et. ~ und heilig versprechen** promise s.o. s.th. solemnly; **wenn es ~ kommt** at (the) most; **mit vorzüglicher ~** → **Hände ~!** hands up!; **~ lebe ...!** long live ...!; **~ soll er leben!** three cheers for him!; → **hinauswollen** 2. **3.** → a) **hinauf**, b) **herauf**. **4.** A **fünf ~ zwei** five (raised) to the second power; **sechs ~ drei** six cubed.
Hoch n (-s; -s) **1.** meteor. high(-pressure area). **2.** cheers. **3.** fig. high.
'Hochachtung f deep respect: **alle ~!** my compliment!; **mit vorzüglicher ~ →** **'hochachtungsvoll** adv Yours faithfully, Sincerely yours.
'Hochadel m high nobility.
'hochaktu,ell adj highly topical.
'hochal,pin adj (high) alpine.
'Hochal,tar m high altar.
'hochangesehen adj highly esteemed.
'Hochan,tenne f overhead aerial (Am. antenna).
'hocharbeiten: sich ~ (sep, -ge-, h) work one's way up.
'Hochbahn f elevated railway (Am. railroad).
'Hochbau m (-[e]s; -ten) structural engineering.
'hochbegabt adj highly gifted.
'hochbetagt adj very old, aged.
'Hochbetrieb m (-[e]s; no pl) intense activity, rush: **es herrschte ~** they (or we) were extremely busy.
'hochbezahlt adj highly paid.
'hochbringen v/t (irr, sep, -ge-, h, → **bringen**) **1.** bring s.o., s.th. up. **2.** F get s.th. up. **3.** make a firm a going concern: **e-e Firma wieder ~** put a firm back on its feet.
'Hochburg f fig. stronghold.
'hochdeutsch adj, **'Hochdeutsch** n standard (or High) German.
'hochdo,tiert adj a) highly paid, b) tournament etc carrying a high prize.
'Hochdruck m (-[e]s; no pl) **1.** meteor., phys. high pressure: fig. **mit ~ arbeiten**

work (at) full blast. **2.** ☞ high blood pressure. **'Hochdruckgebiet** n meteor. high-pressure area.

'Hochebene f plateau.

'hochempfindlich adj highly sensitive, phot. high-speed (film).

'hochentwickelt adj highly developed, ✪ sophisticated.

'hocherfreut adj (most) delighted (**über** acc at).

'Hochfi‚nanz f (-; no pl) high finance.

'hochfliegen (irr, sep, -ge-, sn, → **fliegen**) fly up, soar. **'hochfliegend** adj fig. ambitious, high-flown (plans).

'Hochform f (-; no pl) (**in** ~ in) top form.

'Hochfor‚mat n upright format.

'Hochfre‚quenz f high frequency.

'Hochga‚rage f multistor(e)y car park.

'Hochgebirge n high mountain region.

'Hochgebirgs... alpine, mountain.

'hochgehen (irr, sep, -ge-, sn, → **gehen**) **I** v/i **1.** go up, curtain, prices: a. rise. **2.** F bomb etc: explode, blow up, fig. person: a. hit the ceiling: **et. ~ lassen** blow s.th. up. **3.** F criminal etc: be caught: ~ **lassen** a) expose, b) nab, c) round up, sl. bust (gang). **II** v/t → **hinaufgehen** II.

'Hochgenuß m (real) treat.

'hochgeschlossen adj high-necked.

'Hochgeschwindigkeits... high-speed.

'hochgespannt adj high (expectations etc), ambitious (plans).

'hochgestellt adj fig. high-ranking.

'hochgestochen adj F **1.** stuck-up. **2.** jumped-up, very highbrow.

'hochgewachsen adj tall.

'Hochglanz m high polish (or gloss).

'Hochglanzpa‚pier n high-gloss paper.

'hochgradig [-gra:dɪç] adj **1.** extreme, ✪ high-grade. **2.** F utter (nonsense etc).

'hochhackig [-hakɪç] adj high-heeled.

'hochhalten v/t (irr, sep, -ge-, h, → **halten**) **1.** hold s.o., s.th. up. **2.** fig. uphold, hono(u)r (s.o.'s memory).

'Hochhaus n tower block, high rise.

'hochheben v/t (irr, sep, -ge-, h, → **heben**) lift (up), raise.

'hochinteres‚sant adj most interesting.

'hochjubeln v/t (sep, -ge-, h) F glorify.

'hochkant adv on end: ~ **stellen** up-end.

'hochka‚rätig adj **1.** high-carat. **2.** fig. 24-carat, top-flight.

'hochklappen v/t (sep, -ge-, h) turn up (collar etc).

'hochkommen v/i (irr, sep, -ge-, sn, → **kommen**) **1.** come up: (**wieder**) ~ get up (again), fig. get back on one's feet. **2.** fig. get ahead, F make it. **3. wenn es hochkommt** at the most, at best.

'Hochkonjunk‚tur f ✪ boom.

'hochkrempeln v/t (sep, -ge-, h) roll up.

'Hochland n highland(s).

'hochleben v/i (sep, -ge-, h) ~ **lassen** a) give three cheers for, b) toast; **er lebe hoch!** three cheers for him!

'Hochleistung f high performance.

'Hochleistungs... ✪ high-power(ed), high-speed ..., heavy-duty ... **~sport** m high-performance sport(s). **~sport-ler(in** f) m top athlete.

'hochmo‚dern adj ultramodern.

'Hochmut m arrogance: ~ **kommt vor dem Fall** pride goes before a fall.

hochmütig ['ho:xmy:tɪç] adj arrogant.

hochnäsig ['ho:xnɛ:zɪç] adj stuck-up.

'hochnehmen v/t (irr, sep, -ge-, h, → **nehmen**) **1.** pick s.o., s.th. up. **2.** F fig. j-n ~ a) pull s.o.'s leg, b) fleece s.o., take s.o. for a ride, c) nab s.o.

'Hochofen m ✪ (blast) furnace.

'hochpro‚zentig adj **1.** 🔬 highly concentrated. **2.** high-proof (spirits).

'hochqualifi‚ziert adj highly qualified.

'hochrechnen v/t (sep, -ge-, h) project.

'Hochrechnung f projection, a. (computer) forecast.

'Hochruf m cheer.

'Hochsai‚son f peak season.

'hochschätzen v/t (sep, -ge-, h) **j-n** ~ esteem s.o. highly.

'hochschaukeln v/t (sep, -ge-, h) F fig. play up: **sich (gegenseitig)** ~ get each other all worked up.

'hochschnellen v/i (sep, -ge-, sn) **1.** bounce up. **2.** fig. prices: rocket.

'hochschrauben v/t (sep, -ge-, h) force up (prices), raise (expectations etc).

'Hochschul|absol‚vent m (university or college) graduate. **~ausbildung** f university (or college) education.

'Hochschule f a) university, b) college; → **technisch**. **'Hochschüler(in** f) m university (or college) student.

'Hochschul|lehrer(in f) m university (or college) teacher (or lecturer). **~reife** f university entrance qualification(s).

'hochschwanger adj far advanced in pregnancy.

'**Hochsee** f (-; no pl) high sea(s).
'**Hochseefische,rei** f deep-sea fishing.
'**Hochseejacht** f ocean-going yacht.
'**Hochseilakt** m tight-rope act.
'**Hochsitz** m hunt. (raised) hide.
'**Hochsommer** m (im ~ in) midsummer.
'**Hochspannung** f (-; -en) **1.** ⚡ high ten-sion (or voltage). **2.** no pl fig. a) high tension, b) great suspense: **politische** ~ high political tension. '**Hochspan-nungskabel** n high-voltage cable.
'**hochspielen** v/t (sep, -ge-, h) fig. **et.** ~ play s.th. up.
'**Hochsprache** f standard language: **die deutsche** ~ Standard German.
'**hochsprachlich** adj standard: **nicht** ~ substandard.
'**Hochspringer(in** f) m high jumper.
'**Hochsprung** m (-[e]s; no pl) high jump.
höchst [høːçst] adv highly, extremely, most: → **höchste.**
'**Höchstalter** n maximum age.
Hochstape'lei f (-; -en) **1.** a. fig. impos-ture. **2.** (gross) overstatement.
'**hochstapeln** v/i (sep, -ge-, h) **1.** be an impostor. **2.** exaggerate.
'**Hochstapler** m (-s; -), '**Hochstaplerin** f (-; -nen) impostor, fig. fraud.
'**Höchstbelastung** f ⚙ maximum load.
'**Höchstbetrag** m maximum (amount).
höchste ['høːçstə] adj highest, ⚓, ⚙ a. maximum, top, a. tallest, a. uppermost, a. extreme, utmost: **am** ~**n** highest; → **Instanz, Zeit.**
'**höchstens** adv **1.** at (the) most, at best: adm. **von** ~ not exceeding. **2.** except.
'**Höchstfall** m **im** ~ → **höchstens 1.**
'**Höchstform** f sports: top form.
'**Höchstgeschwindigkeit** f maximum (or top) speed: **mit** ~ at top speed; **zu-lässige** ~ speed limit.
'**Höchstgrenze** f upper limit.
'**Höchstleistung** f top performance, sports: a. record, ⚙ a. maximum output, research etc: supreme achievement.
'**Höchstmaß** n **ein** ~ **an Sicherheit** etc a maximum of safety etc.
'**Höchstpreis** m maximum price: **zum** ~ at the highest price.
'**Höchststand** m highest level: **e-n** ~ **er-reichen** peak.
'**Höchststrafe** f maximum penalty.
'**höchstwahr'scheinlich** adv in all probability.

'**Höchstwert** m maximum value.
'**höchstzulässig** adj maximum (permis-sible).
'**Hochtouren** pl **auf** ~ **bringen** a) rev en-gine up to full speed, b) fig. get s.o., s.th. really going; **auf** ~ **laufen** run at full speed, a. fig. go at full blast.
'**hochtrabend** adj pompous.
'**Hoch- und 'Tiefbau** m (-[e]s; no pl) structural and civil engineering.
'**hochverdient** adj a) well-deserved (suc-cess etc), b) person of great merit.
'**hochverehrt** adj a) highly esteemed, b) Dear Mr Brown etc.
'**Hochverrat** m high treason.
'**hochverräterisch** adj treasonable.
'**hochverzinslich** adj high-interest--bearing.
'**Hochwald** m timber forest.
'**Hochwasser** n (-s; -) **1.** high tide (or water). **2.** flood: **der Fluß führt** ~ the river is in flood. ~**gefahr** f danger of flooding. ~**kata,strophe** f flood disas-ter. ~**stand** m high-water level.
'**hochwerfen** v/t (irr, sep, -ge-, h, → **werfen**) throw s.o., s.th. up.
'**hochwertig** adj a) high-grade, high--quality, b) highly nutritious.
'**Hochwild** n big game.
Hochzeit ['hɔxtsaɪt] f (-; -en) wedding, marriage: ~ **haben,** ~ **feiern** get mar-ried; **zur** ~ **schenken** (**bekommen**) give (get) as a wedding present.
'**Hochzeits...** wedding (present, dress, etc). ~**nacht** f wedding night. ~**reise** f honeymoon (trip): **auf** ~ honeymoon-ing. ~**tag** m a) wedding day, b) wedding anniversary.
'**hochziehen** v/t (irr, sep, -ge-, h, → **ziehen**) draw up, pull up (a. ✈), hoist (flag, sail): **sich** ~ **an** (dat) a) pull o.s. up by, b) F fig. get an ego-boost out of.
Hocke ['hɔkə] f (-; -n) **1.** squat, crouch: **in der** ~ in a crouch; **in die** ~ **gehen** squat down. **2.** diving: tuck (position).
hocken ['hɔkən] v/i (h) **1.** squat, crouch. **2.** dial. sit, bird: perch: **über s-n Bü-chern** ~ pore over one's books.
'**Hocker** m (-s; -) stool.
Höcker ['hœkər] m (-s; -) zo. hump.
Hockey ['hɔkɛ] n (-s; no pl) hockey.
'**Hockeyschläger** m hockey stick.
'**Hockeyspieler(in** f) m hockey player.

'**Hocksprung** *m* a) *gym.* squat jump, squat vault, b) *diving:* tuck(ed) jump.
Hode ['ho:də] *f* (-; -n), **Hoden** *m* (-s; -) *anat.* testicle. '**Hodensack** *m* scrotum.
Hof [ho:f] *m* (-[e]s; ⸚e) **1.** a) yard, b) court(yard), c) backyard, d) schoolyard. **2.** farm. **3.** court: **am** ⸚, **bei** ⸚e at court; *j-m den* ⸚ **machen** court s.o. **4.** *astr.*, *⚕*, *opt.* halo.
'**Hofdame** *f* lady-in-waiting.
hoffen ['hɔfən] *v/i* (h) (**auf** *acc*) a) hope (for), b) trust (in): *ich hoffe* I hope so; *ich hoffe nicht* I hope not; *ich hoffe es* I hope so; *das will ich nicht* ⸚ I hope not; *wir das Beste!* let's hope for the best! *verzweifelt* ⸚ hope against hope.
hoffentlich ['hɔfəntlɪç] *adv* I (*or* we) hope so, let's hope so, F hopefully: ⸚ *nicht!* I hope not!
Hoffnung ['hɔfnʊŋ] *f* (-; -en) hope (**auf** *acc of*): **die** ⸚ **aufgeben** abandon hope; *j-m* ⸚*en machen* raise s.o.'s hopes; *er machte mir k-e* ⸚*en* he didn't hold out any hopes for me; *sich* ⸚*en machen* have hopes (**auf** *acc of ger*): *mach dir k-e (falschen)* ⸚*en!* don't be too hopeful!; *s-e* ⸚ *setzen auf* (*acc*) pin one's hopes on; *j-n in s-n* ⸚*en enttäuschen* dash s.o.'s hopes; (*neue*) ⸚ *schöpfen* have new hopes; *es besteht k-e* ⸚ there is no hope; *in der* ⸚ *zu inf* hoping to *inf*; *er ist m-e einzige* ⸚ he is my only hope; *pol., sports etc* **die große** ⸚ the great white hope.
'**Hoffnungslauf** *m* *sports:* repechage.
'**hoffnungslos** *adj* hopeless, *pred a.* past (all) hope: *fig.* **er ist ein** ⸚*er Fall* he's hopeless. '**Hoffnungslosigkeit** *f* (-; *no pl*) hopelessness, despair.
'**Hoffnungsschimmer** *m* glimmer of hope. '**Hoffnungsträger** *m* *pol., sports etc:* the great white hope.
'**hoffnungsvoll** *adj* hopeful, *pred* full of hope (*a. adv*), promising (*talent etc*).
höfisch ['hø:fɪʃ] *adj* courtly.
höflich ['hø:flɪç] *adj* (*zu* to) polite, courteous. '**Höflichkeit** *f* (-; -en) **1.** *no pl* (*aus* ⸚ *out of*) politeness: *in aller* ⸚ very politely. **2.** *usu. pl* compliment.
'**Höflichkeitsbesuch** *m* courtesy visit.
'**Hofnarr** *m* *hist.* or *iro.* court jester.
hohe ['ho:ə] → **hoch** I.
Höhe ['hø:ə] *f* (-; -n) **1.** height, *astr.*, *✈*, *geogr.* altitude, level: *in e-r* ⸚ *von ...* at a

height (*or* an altitude) of ...; *in die* ⸚ up (→ *a. cpds. with hoch...*); *an* ⸚ *verlieren* lose height; *auf der* ⸚ *von* a) *geogr.* in the latitude of *London etc*, b) *⚓* off *Dover etc*; *auf gleicher* ⸚ (*fig.* on a) level (*mit* with); *fig. auf der* ⸚ *s-s Ruhms* (*s-r Macht*) at the height of his fame (power); F *auf der* ⸚ *sein* be in good form; *auf der* ⸚ (*der Zeit*) *sein* be up to date; *ich bin nicht ganz auf der* ⸚ I'm not feeling up to the mark; F *das ist doch die* ⸚*!* that's the limit!; → *treiben* 1. **2.** amount: *e-e Summe in* ⸚ *von* a sum (to the amount) of; *bis zu e-r* ⸚ *von* up to, not exceeding. **3.** → **Anhöhe**.
Hoheit ['ho:hait] *f* (-; -en) **1.** *no pl pol.* sovereignty. **2.** (*Seine, Ihre*) ⸚ (His, Her) Highness. **3.** *no pl fig.* grandeur, majesty. '**hoheitlich** *adj* sovereign.
'**Hoheits**|**abzeichen** *n* national emblem. ⸚**gebiet** *n* territory. ⸚**gewässer** *pl* territorial waters.
'**Höhen**|**flosse** *f* *✈* tail plane. ⸚**flug** *m* **1.** high-altitude flight. **2.** *fig.* (*intellectual etc*) flight. ⸚**krankheit** *f* altitude sickness. ⸚**kurort** *m* mountain (health) resort. ⸚**lage** *f* altitude. ⸚**leitwerk** *n* elevator unit. ⸚**sonne** *f* **1.** mountain sun. **2.** *⚕* sunray lamp, sunlamp. ⸚**unterschied** *m* difference in altitude. ⸚**zug** *m* range of hills, mountain range.
'**Höhepunkt** *m* peak, height, climax (*a. orgasm*), highlight (*of event etc*): *auf dem* ⸚ (*gen*) at the height of ([one's] power, fame, etc).
höher ['hø:ər] *adj and adv* higher (*a. fig.*), *a.* senior: ⸚*er Dienst* senior service; ⸚*e Bildung* higher education; ⸚*e Schule* secondary school; *in* ⸚*em Maße* to a greater extent, more; *nach Höherem streben* strive for higher things.
hohl [ho:l] *adj a. fig.* hollow: *in der* ⸚*en Hand* in the hollow of one's hand.
'**hohläugig** [-ɔʏɡɪç] *adj* hollow-eyed.
'**Hohlblock(stein)** *m* cavity block.
Höhle ['hø:lə] *f* (-; -n) **1.** cave. **2.** *zo.* hole: *fig. sich in die* ⸚ *des Löwen wagen* beard the lion in his den. **3.** *anat.* cavity, (*eye*) socket. **4.** F hole, hovel.
'**Höhlen**|**forscher** *m* spel(a)eologist, potholer. ⸚**forschung** *f* spel(a)eology. ⸚**mensch** *m* cave man.
'**Hohlheit** *f* (-; *no pl*) *a. fig.* hollowness.

'Hohl|kehle f ⊙ groove. **~kopf** m F numskull. **~körper** m Ⓐ hollow body. **~kreuz** n ⚕ hollow back. **~kugel** f hollow sphere. **~maß** n measure of capacity, dry measure. **~raum** m cavity, hollow. **~saum** m hemstitch. **~schliff** m hollow grinding: **mit ~** hollow-ground. **~spiegel** m concave mirror.

'Höhlung f (-; -en) hollow, cavity.

'Hohl|weg m ravine. **~ziegel** m a) cavity brick, b) hollow tile.

Hohn [ho:n] m (-[e]s; no pl) a) scorn, derision: **nur ~ und Spott ernten** earn but scorn and derision; **der rein(st)e** (or **blanke**) **~** sheer mockery. **höhnen** ['hø:nən] v/i (h) (**über** acc at) sneer, jeer. **'Hohngelächter** n derisive laughter. **'höhnisch** adj sneering: **~e Bemerkung, ~es Lächeln** sneer.

'hohnlächeln v/i (sep or insep, -ge-, h), **'Hohnlächeln** n (-s) sneer.

'hohnsprechen v/i (irr, sep, -ge-, h, → **sprechen**) make a mockery (dat of).

Hokuspokus [ho:kʊs'po:kʊs] m (-; no pl) hocus-pocus, contp. a. mumbo jumbo: **~! hey presto!**

hold [hɔlt] adj **1.** lovely, sweet. **2.** das Glück war ihm ~ he was lucky.

Holdinggesellschaft ['ho:ldɪŋ-] f ✝ holding company.

holen ['ho:lən] v/t (h) **1.** get, fetch: **j-n et. ~** get s.th. for s.o.; **et. aus der Tasche ~** take (or draw) s.th. out of one's pocket; F **da ist nichts zu ~!** there's nothing in it (for us)!; **bei ihm ist nichts zu ~!** you won't get anything out of him!; → **Atem, Luft 2. 2.** call: **j-n ~ lassen** send for s.o. **3.** come for, pick s.o., s.th. up. **4.** sich et. ~ a) get s.o., s.th., b) F catch, get (a cold etc); **du wirst dir noch et. ~!** you'll catch s.th. yet!; **sich bei j-m e-n Rat ~** ask s.o.'s advice; F **sich e-n Preis ~** win (or get) a prize; → **Abfuhr 2.**

Holland ['hɔlant] n (-s) Holland, the Netherlands. **Holländer** ['hɔlɛndər] m (-s; -) Dutchman: **die ~** the Dutch. **'Holländerin** f (-; -nen) Dutchwoman. **'holländisch** [-dɪʃ] adj, Ⓢ n (-[s]) Dutch.

Hölle ['hœlə] f (-; -n) hell: **in der ~** in hell; **die ~ auf Erden** hell on earth; F **j-m die ~ heiß machen** give s.o. hell; **j-m das Leben zur ~ machen** make life a perfect hell for s.o.; **zur ~ damit!** to hell with it!; **die ~ ist los!** all hell has broken loose!

'Höllen|angst f F **e-e ~ haben** be scared stiff (**vor** dat of). **~lärm** m infernal noise: **e-n ~ machen** make a hell of a noise. **~qual** f F agony: **~en ausstehen** suffer hell. **~tempo** n F (**mit e-m ~** at) breakneck speed.

höllisch ['hœlɪʃ] adj infernal, F hellish: **~ aufpassen** watch out like a hawk, be damn careful; **~ weh tun** hurt like hell.

Holm [hɔlm] m (-[e]s; -e) beam, gym. bar, ✈ spar.

Hologramm [holo'gram] n (-s; -e) opt. holograph.

holp(e)rig ['hɔlp(ə)rɪç] adj **1.** bumpy. **2.** fig. clumsy. **holpern** ['hɔlpərn] v/i **1.** (sn) bump, jolt. **2.** (h) fig. stumble.

Holunder [ho'lʊndər] m (-s; -) ⚘ elder. **Ho'lunderbeere** f elderberry. **Ho'lundertee** m elderflower tea.

Holz [hɔlts] n (-es; ⸚er) **1.** a) no pl wood, b) timber: **aus ~** wooden, (made of) wood; fig. **klopf auf ~!** touch wood!; **aus e-m anderen ~ geschnitzt** of a different stamp; **aus härterem ~ geschnitzt** made of sterner stuff; F **sie hat ~ vor der Hütte** she's well stacked. **2.** (nine)pin: **Gut ~!** good bowling! **3.** no pl ♪ the woodwind. **~bauweise** f timber construction. **~bearbeitung** f woodworking. **~bläser** m ♪ woodwind player, pl the woodwind (section).

holzen ['hɔltsən] v/i (h) F soccer: clog, play rough.

hölzern ['hœltsərn] adj wooden, fig. a. clumsy.

'Holzfäller [-fɛlər] m (-s; -) woodcutter, Am. lumberjack.

'Holzfaser f wood fibre (Am. fiber). **~platte** f wood fibreboard (Am. fiberboard). **~stoff** m a) wood cellulose, b) wood pulp.

'holzfrei adj wood-free (paper).

'Holz|hacken n (-s) wood chopping. **~hammer** m mallet: F fig. **mit dem ~** with a sledgehammer. **~handel** m timber (Am. lumber) trade. **~haus** n wooden house.

holzig ['hɔltsɪç] adj a) woody, b) stringy.

'Holz|kitt m plastic wood. **~kohle** f charcoal. **~scheit** n log. **~schnitt** m wood engraving. **~stoß** m stack of wood. **~täfelung** f wood(en) panel(l)ing. Ⓢverarbeitend *adj*, **~verarbeitung** *f* wood processing. **~weg** m **F** *auf dem ~ sein* a) be on the wrong track, b) be very much mistaken. **~wolle** *f* wood wool, excelsior. **~wurm** m woodworm.

Homo ['ho:mo] m (-s; -s) **F** homo, queer, gay.

homogen [homo'ge:n] *adj* homogeneous.

Homonym [homo'ny:m] n (-s; -e) *ling.* homonym.

Homöopath [homøo'pa:t] m (-en; -en) **☞** hom(o)eopath. **Homöopathie** [-pa'ti:] *f* (-; *no pl*) hom(o)eopathy. **homöopathisch** [-'pa:tɪʃ] *adj* hom(o)eopathic.

Homosexuali'tät *f* homosexuality. **homosexu'ell** *adj*, **Homosexu'elle** m, *f* (-n; -n) homosexual, **F** gay.

Honig ['ho:nɪç] m (-s; -e) honey: **F** *j-m ~ ums Maul schmieren* soft-soap s.o. **~kuchen** m gingerbread. **~lecken** n **F** *das war kein ~!* that was no picnic! **~me₁lone** *f* honeydew melon. **☾süß** *adj* (as) sweet as honey, *fig.* honeyed.

Honorar [hono'ra:r] n (-s; -e) fee, *of author:* royalty.

Honoratioren [honora'tsîo:rən] *pl* notabilities, local dignitaries.

honorieren [hono'ri:rən] *v/t* (h) **1.** *j-n* ~ pay (a fee to) s.o. **2.** *et.* ~ pay for s.th. **3.** **☞** hono(u)r, *fig. a.* reward.

honoris causa [ho'no:rɪs 'kaʊza] *Professor etc* ~ honorary professor *etc.*

Hopfen ['hɔpfən] m (-s; *no pl*) **☘** hop: **F** *an ihm ist ~ und Malz verloren* he's hopeless, he's a dead loss.

hopp [hɔp] *int* a) hop!, b) quick!

hoppeln ['hɔpəln] *v/i* (sn) hop.

hoppla ['hɔpla] *int* a) (wh)oops!, b) hey!

hops [hɔps] *int* jump! **Hops** m (-es; -e) hop. **hopsa** ['hɔpsa] *int* (wh)oops!

hopsen ['hɔpsən] *v/i* (sn) hop.

Hopser ['hɔpsər] m (-s; -) **F** hop.

'**hopsgehen** *v/i* (*irr, sep, -ge-, sn*, → *gehen*) **F** a) get broken, b) go down the drain, c) get nabbed, d) kick the bucket. '**hopsnehmen** *v/t* (*irr, sep, -ge-, h*, → *nehmen*) **F** *j-n* ~ nab s.o.

'**hörbar** *adj* audible. '**Hörbehinderte** m, *f* hearing-impaired person. '**Hörbild** n radio feature. '**Hörbrille** *f* earglasses. '**Hörbuch** n talking book.

horchen ['hɔrçən] *v/i* (h) listen (*auf acc* to), *a.* eavesdrop: *horch!* listen!

'**Horcher** m (-s; -) eavesdropper.

Horde ['hɔrdə] *f* (-; -n) *a. fig.* horde, *contp. a.* mob, gang.

hören ['hø:rən] (h) **I** *v/i* **1.** a) hear, b) listen (*auf acc* to): *univ.* ~ *bei* attend the lectures of; **F** *mir verging ♫ und Sehen* I was stunned; ~ *Sie mal!* listen!, look here!; *na, ~ Sie mal!* well, really!; *das läßt sich eher* ~ that sounds more like it; *ich lasse von mir* ~ I'll be in touch; *man hörte nie wieder von ihm* he was never heard of again; → *schwer* 4. **2.** obey, listen. **II** *v/t* **3.** a) hear, b) listen to (*concert etc*): *et.* ~ *von* hear s.th. about (*or* of); *er ließ nichts von sich* ~ he sent no news; *er wollte nichts davon* ~ he would not hear of it; *wie ich höre, will er kommen* I understand he wants to come; *soviel man hört* from all accounts; → *Radio.* **4.** *univ.* attend (*lectures*), take (*subject*).

'**Hörensagen** n (-s) (*vom* ~ by) hearsay. '**Hörer** m (-s; -) **1.** listener, *univ.* student. **2.** *teleph.* receiver: *den* ~ *auflegen* hang up. '**Hörerin** *f* (-; -nen) → *Hörer* 1. '**Hörerschaft** *f* (-; -en) **1.** *the* listeners, audience. **2.** (number of) students. '**Hörfolge** *f* radio series (*or* serial). '**Hörfunk** m radio. '**Hörgerät** n, '**Hörhilfe** *f* hearing aid. **hörig** ['hø:rɪç] *adj j-m* ~ *sein* be enslaved to s.o. '**Hörigkeit** *f* (-; *no pl*) bondage.

Horizont [hori'tsɔnt] m (-[e]s; -e) (*am* ~ on the) horizon (*a. fig.*): *s-n* ~ *erweitern* broaden one's mind; **F** *das geht über m-n* ~ that's beyond me.

horizontal [horitsɔn'ta:l] *adj* horizontal. **Horizon'tale** *f* (-; -n) horizontal.

Hormon [hɔr'mo:n] n (-s; -e) hormone. **Hor'mon..., hormonal** [hɔrmo'na:l] *adj* hormonal.

'**Hörmuschel** *f* *teleph.* earpiece.

Horn [hɔrn] n (-[e]s; ⸚er) **1.** *zo.* horn, *a.* feeler (*of snail*): *aus* ~ (made of) horn; *fig. sich die Hörner abstoßen* sow one's wild oats; **F** *j-m Hörner aufsetzen* cuckold s.o.; → *Stier* 1. **2.** **♪** horn, **✕** bugle: **F** *ins gleiche* ~ *stoßen* chime in with s.o.

'**Hornbläser(in** *f*) m **♪** horn player. '**Hornbrille** *f* horn-rimmed spectacles. '**Hörnerv** m auditory nerve. '**Hornhaut** *f* **1.** callus. **2.** *of eye:* cornea. **Hornisse** [hɔr'nɪsə] *f* (-; -n) *zo.* hornet.

Hornist [hɔr'nɪst] m (-en; -en) ♪ hornist.

'**Hornvieh** n (-s; no pl) horned cattle.

Horoskop [horo'sko:p] n (-s; -e) (j-m das ~ stellen cast s.o.'s) horoscope.

Horror ['hɔrɔr] m (-s; no pl) horror (vor dat of). '**Horrorfilm** m horror film.

'**Hörsaal** m lecture hall.

'**Hörspiel** n radio play.

Horst [hɔrst] m (-es; -e) nest, eyrie.

'**Hörsturz** m ✿ aural attack.

Hort [hɔrt] m (-[e]s; -e) 1. hoard, treasure. 2. (safe) refuge. 3. fig. stronghold. 4. day nursery. '**horten** v/t (h) hoard.

Hortensie [hɔr'tɛnziə] f (-; -n) ⚘ hydrangea.

'**Hörtest** m hearing test: e-n ~ machen lassen have one's hearing tested.

'**Hörvermögen** n (-s; no pl) hearing.

'**Hörweite** f (-; no pl) hearing range: in (außer) ~ within (out of) earshot.

Höschen [hœsçən] n (-s; -) panties.

Hose ['ho:zə] f (-; -n) (a. ein Paar ~n) (a pair of) trousers (Am. pants): kurze ~(n) shorts; zwei ~n two pairs of trousers (etc); (sich) in die ~(n) machen make a mess in one's pants, F fig. be scared stiff; F die ~n anhaben wear the trousers (Am. pants); das ging in die ~ that was a complete flop; e-e tote ~ sein be a complete washout.

'**Hosen|anzug** m trouser suit, Am. pantsuit. ~bein n trouser leg. ~boden m (trouser) seat: F sich auf den ~ setzen buckle down to work. ~bügel m trouser hanger. ~bund m waistband. ~klammer f trouser clip. ~rock m culottes. ~schlitz m fly. ~tasche f trouser(s) pocket. ~träger pl (pair of) braces (Am. suspenders).

hospitieren [hɔspi'ti:rən] v/i (h) sit in on classes (or lectures) (bei with).

Hospiz [hɔs'pi:ts] n (-es; -e) hospice.

Hostess [hɔs'tɛs] f (-; -en) hostess.

Hostie ['hɔstiə] f (-; -n) eccl. host.

Hotel [ho'tɛl] n (-s; -s) hotel: ~ garni bed and breakfast hotel.

Ho'telfach n (-[e]s; no pl) hotel business.

Ho'telgewerbe n hotel industry.

Hotelier [hotə'lie:] m (-s; -s) hotelier.

Ho'telverzeichnis n list of hotels.

Ho'telzimmer n hotel room.

Hub [hu:p] m (-[e]s; -e) mot., ✿ stroke.

hüben ['hy:bən] adv over here, on this side: ~ wie drüben on both sides.

'**Hubraum** m mot. cubic capacity.

hübsch [hypʃ] adj a) pretty, good-looking, b) nice, F fig. a. fine: ein ~es Sümmchen a tidy sum; das wirst du ~ bleiben lassen! you're not going to do anything of the sort!

'**Hubschrauber** m (-s; -) helicopter.

'**Hubschrauberlandeplatz** m heliport.

'**Hubstapler** [-ʃta:plər] m (-s; -) stacker truck.

huch [hux] int ooh!

'**huckepack** adv F pick-a-back. '**Huckepackverkehr** m pick-a-back traffic.

hudeln ['hu:dəln] v/i (h) F work sloppily.

Huf [hu:f] m (-[e]s; -e) hoof.

'**Hufeisen** n horseshoe. '**Hufeisenform** f (in ~ arranged in a) horseshoe.

'**hufeisenförmig** [-fœrmɪç] adj horseshoe-shaped.

'**Huflattich** m ⚘ coltsfoot.

'**Hüftbein** n hipbone. **Hüfte** ['hyftə] f (-; -n) hip. '**Hüftgelenk** n hip joint. '**Hüftgürtel** m, '**Hüfthalter** m suspender (Am. garter) belt. '**hüfthoch** adj and adv waist-high, water: waist-deep. '**Hüftweite** f hip measurement.

Hügel ['hy:gəl] m (-s; -) hill, a. hillock, b) mound. '**hüg(e)lig** adj hilly.

Huhn [hu:n] n (-[e]s; -er) fowl, chicken (a. gastr.), hen: mit den Hühnern aufstehen (zu Bett gehen) get up with the lark (go to bed early); F da lachen ja die Hühner! that's a laugh!; dummes ~ silly goose; verrücktes ~ crazy thing.

Hühnchen ['hy:nçən] n (-s; -) 1. (young) chicken: F mit j-m ein ~ zu rupfen haben have a score to settle with s.o. 2. gastr. (roast) chicken.

Hühnerauge ['hy:nər-] n corn: F fig. j-m auf die ~n treten tread on s.o.'s corns.

'**Hühneraugenpflaster** n corn plaster.

'**Hühner|brühe** f chicken broth. ~brust f 1. gastr. chicken breast. 2. ✿ pigeon breast. ~ei n hen's egg. ~farm f chicken farm. ~futter n chickenfeed. ~hof m chicken yard. ~leiter f chicken ladder. ~pest f vet. fowl pest. ~stall m henhouse. ~zucht f chicken farming.

huldigen ['huldigən] v/i (h) j-m ~ pay homage to s.o. '**Huldigung** f (-; -en) homage (an acc to).

Hülle ['hylə] f (-; -n) 1. wrap(ping), cover, (record) sleeve, Am. jacket (a. of book), envelope: die sterbliche ~ the mortal remains. **2.** F clothes. **3.** *fig.* veil, cloak. **4.** *in ~ und Fülle* in abundance, plenty of, *whisky etc* galore.

hüllen ['hʏlən] *v/t* (h) (*in acc*) wrap *s.o.*, *s.th.* (up) (in), cover (with): *sich in Schweigen ~* remain silent (*über acc* about); *in Dunkel* (*Nebel*) *gehüllt* shrouded in darkness (fog).

'**hüllenlos** *adj* naked.

Hülse ['hʏlzə] *f* (-; -n) **1.** ♣ a) hull, husk, b) pod. **2.** ⊙ a) sleeve, socket, b) case.

'**Hülsenfrucht** *f* legume(n), *pl* pulse.

human [hu'ma:n] *adj* humane, F *a.* decent, ⚕ human. **Hu'mange,netik** *f* human genetics.

Humanismus [huma'nɪsmʊs] *m* (-; *no pl*) humanism: *hist. der ~* Humanism. **Humanist** [-'nɪst] *m* (-en; -en) humanist, *ped., univ.* classicist, *hist.* Humanist. **huma'nistisch** *adj* humanist(ic), *ped., univ.* classical: → *Gymnasium.*

humanitär [humani'tɛ:r] *adj* humanitarian. **Humanität** [humani'tɛ:t] *f* (-; *no pl*) humaneness, humanity.

Hu'manmedi,zin *f* human medicine.

Humbug ['hʊmbʊk] *m* (-s; *no pl*) humbug.

Hummel ['hʊməl] *f* (-; -n) bumblebee.

Hummer ['hʊmər] *m* (-s; -) lobster.

Humor [hu'mo:r] *m* (-s; *no pl*) humo(u)r: *k-n Sinn für ~ haben* have no sense of humo(u)r; *den ~ behalten* keep one's sense of humo(u)r; *et. mit ~ nehmen* take s.th. in good humo(u)r; *du hast* (*vielleicht*) *~!* you've got a nerve!

Humoreske [humo'rɛskə] *f* (-; -n) humoresque, humorous sketch (*or* story).

Humorist [humo'rɪst] *m* (-en; -en) humorist. **humo'ristisch** *adj* humorous.

hu'morlos *adj* humo(u)rless: *er ist völlig ~ a.* he has absolutely no sense of humo(u)r. **hu'morvoll** *adj* humorous.

humpeln ['hʊmpəln] *v/i* (h *or* sn) limp.

Humpen ['hʊmpən] *m* (-s; -) tankard.

Humus ['hu:mʊs] *m* (-; *no pl*) humus.

'**Humusschicht** *f* humus layer, topsoil.

Hund [hʊnt] *m* (-[e]s; -e) dog, *hunt.* hound: *junger ~* puppy; *fig. schlauer* (*feiger*) *~* sly (yellow) dog; F (*gemeiner*) *~* bastard; *der arme ~!* (the) poor sod!; *das ist ja ein dicker ~!* that takes the cake!; *auf den ~ kommen* go to the dogs; (*ganz*) *auf dem ~ sein* be down and out, *a.* be a wreck; *vor die ~e*

gehen a) go to the dogs, b) kick the bucket; *wie ~ und Katze leben* lead a cat-and-dog life; *er ist bekannt wie ein bunter ~* he's known all over the place; *da liegt der ~ begraben!* that's it (*or* why)!; *damit kann man k-n ~ hinterm Ofen hervorlocken!* that won't tempt anybody!; *~e, die bellen, beißen nicht* barking dogs seldom bite.

'**Hundeausstellung** *f* dog show.

'**hunde'elend** *adj* F *mir ist ~* I feel lousy.

'**Hunde|futter** *n* dog food. **~halsband** *n* dog collar. **~hütte** *f* (dog) kennel.

'**hunde'kalt** *adj* F freezing cold.

'**Hunde|kuchen** *m* dog biscuit. **~leben** *n* F dog's life. **~leine** *f* dog lead, dog leash. **~marke** *f* dog licence disc, *Am.* dog tag.

'**hunde'müde** *adj* F dog-tired.

hundert ['hʊndərt] *adj* a (*or* one) hundred: *einige* (*or* *ein paar*) *~ Leute* a few hundred people. '**Hundert**[1] *n* (-s; -e) hundred: *zu ~en* in hundreds; *zehn von ~* ten in a hundred, ten per cent. '**Hundert**[2] *f* (-; -en) hundred.

Hunderter ['hʊndərtər] *m* (-s; -) **1.** ♣ a) (the) hundred, b) three-figure number. **2.** F one-hundred-mark *etc* note (*Am.* bill). '**hunderter'lei** *adj* a hundred kinds of. '**hundertundein** *adj* a hundred and one. '**hundertfach I** *adj* hundredfold. **II** *adv* a hundred times.

Hundert'jahrfeier *f* centenary, *Am.* centennial. '**hundertjährig** [-jɛ:rɪç] *adj* **1.** one-hundred-year-old. **2.** of a hundred years, hundred years' ...

'**hundertmal** *adv* a hundred times.

Hundert'markschein *m* one-hundred-mark note (*Am.* bill). **Hundert'meterlauf** *m* the 100-metres (*Am.* meters).

'**hundertpro,zentig** *adj* a hundred percent (*a. fig.*), pure (*alcohol, wool, etc*), *fig.* out-and-out (*conservative etc*): F *das weiß ich ~* I'm dead sure.

'**hundertst** *adj* hundredth. '**hundertstel** *adj*, '**Hundertstel** *n* (-s; -) hundredth.

'**hundert'tausend** *adj* a (*or* one) hundred thousand.

'**Hundesa,lon** *m* dog parlo(u)r.

'**Hundezucht** *f* **1.** dog breeding. **2.** (breeding) kennel(s).

'**Hundezüchter**(**in** *f*) *m* dog breeder.

Hündin ['hʏndɪn] *f* (-; -nen) bitch.

hündisch ['hʏndɪʃ] *adj fig.* cringing.

'**hundsge**'**mein** *adj* F a) dirty, low-down, nasty, b) hellish (*job etc*).
'**hundsmise**,**rabel** *adj* F lousy.
'**Hundstage** *pl* dog days.
Hüne ['hy:nə] *m* (-n; -n) giant.
'**Hünengrab** *n* megalithic grave.
'**hünenhaft** *adj* gigantic.
Hunger ['hʊŋər] *m* (-s; *no pl*) **1.** hunger (*a. fig. nach* for): **~ haben** (*bekommen*) be (get) hungry; **~ leiden** go hungry; **vor ~ sterben** starve to death; F **ich sterbe vor ~** I'm starving; **~ ist der beste Koch** hunger is the best sauce. **2.** → **Hungersnot.**
'**Hungerleider** [-laɪdər] *m* (-s; -) starveling.
'**Hungerlohn** *m* starvation wages.
hungern ['hʊŋərn] (h) **I** *v/i* a) go hungry, starve, *fig.* hunger (*nach* for), b) starve o.s., go without food. **II sich vor Tode ~** starve o.s. to death.
'**hungernd** *adj* hungry, starving.
'**Hungerö,dem** *n* 🔬 famine (o)edema.
'**Hungersnot** *f* famine.
'**Hungerstreik** *m* (**in den ~ treten** go on a) hunger strike. **Hungertod** *m* (-[e]s; *no pl*) death from starvation. '**Hungertuch** *n* F *fig.* **am ~ nagen** be starving.
hungrig ['hʊŋrɪç] *adj* a. *fig.* hungry (*nach* for): **~ sein** be (*or* feel) hungry; **das macht ~** that makes you hungry.
Hunne ['hʊnə] *m* (-n; -n) *hist.* Hun.
Hupe ['hu:pə] *f* (-; -n) horn: **auf die ~ drücken** → **hupen** ['hu:pən] *v/i* (h) hoot, honk, sound the horn.
hüpfen ['hypfən] *v/i* (sn) hop, skip, *ball*: bounce.
'**Hupsi,gnal** *n* honk, hoot.
Hürde ['hʏrdə] *f* (-; -n) **1.** (*a. fig.* **e-e ~ nehmen** take a) hurdle. **2.** fold.
'**Hürdenlauf** *m* sports: hurdles.
'**Hürdenläufer**(**in** *f*) *m* sports: hurdler.
Hure ['hu:rə] *f* (-; -n) whore.
hurra [hʊ'ra:] *int* hurray!, hurrah!
Hurrikan ['hʊrɪka:n] *m* (-s; -e) hurricane.
husch [hʊʃ] *int* a) whoosh!, b) shoo!
huschen ['hʊʃən] *v/i* (sn) flit.
hüsteln ['hy:stəln] *v/i* (h) cough slightly.
husten ['hu:stən] (h) **I** *v/i* cough (*a. F engine*): **stark ~** have a bad cough; F **auf** (*acc*) **~** not to give a damn for. **II** *v/t* cough up: F **dem werde ich was ~!** to hell with him!

'**Husten** *m* (-s; -) cough. **~anfall** *m* coughing fit. **~bon,bon** *m, n* cough drop. **~reiz** *m* tickle in one's throat. **~saft** *m* cough syrup. **~tee** *m* bronchial tea. **~tropfen** *pl* cough drops.
Hut¹ *m* (-[e]s; ⸚e) **1.** hat: F *fig.* **ein alter ~** old hat; **den ~ abnehmen** (*or ziehen*) take off one's hat (*fig. vor j-m* to s.o.); **~ ab** (*vor dir*)! I'll take my hat off to you!; **alles unter einen ~ bringen** reconcile things; F **damit habe ich nichts am ~** I can't be bothered with that; **ihm ging der ~ hoch** he blew his top; F *fig.* **den ~ nehmen müssen** have to go (*or* resign); **das kannst du dir an den ~ stecken!** (you can) keep it! **2.** ♀ cap.
Hut² *f* (-; *no pl*) **1. in j-s ~** in s.o.'s care; **in guter** (*or sicherer*) **~ sein** be safe (*bei* with). **2. auf der ~ sein** be on one's guard (*vor dat* against).
'**Hutablage** *f* hat rack.
hüten ['hy:tən] (h) **I** *v/t* look after, mind (*children etc*), guard (*a. secret etc*): → **Bett. II sich ~** (*vor dat*) be on one's guard (against), watch out (for); **sich ~**, **et. zu tun** take care not to do s.th.; **ich werde mich ~!** I'll do nothing of the sort!; **hüte dich vor ...!** beware of ...!
'**Hüter** *m* (-s; -), '**Hüterin** *f* (-; -nen) guardian, keeper: *humor.* **der Hüter des Gesetzes** (the arm of) the Law.
'**Hutgeschäft** *n* hat shop. '**Hutgröße** *f* hat size. '**Hutkrempe** *f* (hat) brim.
'**Hutmacher** *m* (-s; -) hatter.
'**Hutmacherin** *f* (-; -nen) milliner.
'**Hutschnur** *f* hat string: F *fig.* **das geht mir über die ~!** that's going too far!
Hütte ['hʏtə] *f* (-; -n) **1.** a) hut, cabin, b) *contr.* shack, shanty, c) refuge. **2.** → **Hüttenwerk.**
'**Hüttenindu,strie** *f* iron and steel industry. '**Hüttenwerk** *n* metallurgical plant.
Hyäne [hy'ɛ:nə] *f* (-; -n) *zo.* hyena.
Hyazinthe [hya'tsɪntə] *f* (-; -n) hyacinth.
Hybride [hy'bri:də] *f* (-; -n) hybrid.
Hydrant [hy'drant] *m* (-en; -en) hydrant.
Hydrat [hy'dra:t] *n* (-[e]s; -e) 🔬 hydrate.
Hydraulik [hy'draʊlɪk] *f* (-; *no pl*) hydraulics. **hy**'**draulisch** *adj* hydraulic.
hydrieren [hy'dri:rən] *v/t* (h) hydrogenate.
Hy'**drierwerk** *n* hydrogenation plant.
Hydrody'**namik** [hydro-] *f* hydrodynamics.

Hydrokul,tur ['hy:dro-] *f* hydroponics.
Hydrolyse [hydro'ly:zə] *f* (-; -n) 🜂
hydrolysis.
Hygiene [hy'gĭe:nə] *f* (-; *no pl*) hygiene.
hygi'enisch *adj* hygienic.
Hygrometer [hygro'me:tər] *n* (-s; -)
hygrometer.
Hymne ['hymnə] *f* (-; -n) hymn (**an** *acc*
to).
Hyperbel [hy'pɛrbəl] *f* (-; -n) **1.** 🜨 hyper-
bola. **2.** *ling.* hyperbole.
hypermo'dern [hypər-] *adj* ultramodern.
Hypertonie [hypərto'ni:] *f* (-; -n) 🜊
hypertension.
Hypnose [hyp'no:zə] *f* (-; -n) (**in** ~ under)
hypnosis. **hyp'notisch** [-tɪʃ] *adj* hyp-
notic. **Hypnotiseur** [hypnoti'zø:r] *m*
(-s; -e) hypnotist. **hypnotisieren** [hyp-
noti'zi:rən] *v/t* (h) hypnotize.
Hypochonder [hypo'xɔndər] *m* (-s; -),

hypo'chondrisch *adj* hypochondriac.
Hypotenuse [hypote'nu:zə] *f* (-; -n) 🜨
hypotenuse.
Hypothek [hypo'te:k] *f* (-; -en) 🜊 mortgage: **e-e** ~ **aufnehmen** raise a mortgage (**auf** *acc* on); **mit e-r** ~ **belasten**
(encumber *s.th.* with a) mortgage.
hypothekarisch [hypote'ka:rɪʃ] *adj and
adv by* (or on) mortgage.
Hypo'theken|bank *f* mortgage bank.
~**brief** *m* mortgage deed. ②**frei** *adj* un-
mortgaged. ~**gläubiger(in** *f*) *m* mort-
gagee. ~**pfandbrief** *m* mortgage bond.
~**schuldner(in** *f*) *m* mortgagor.
Hypothese [hypo'te:zə] *f* (-; -n) hypothesis. **hypo'thetisch** *adj* hypothetical.
Hypotonie [hypoto'ni:] *f* (-; -n) 🜊 hypo-
tension.
Hysterie [hyste'ri:] *f* (-; *no pl*) 🜊 hysteria.
hysterisch [hys'te:rɪʃ] *adj* hysterical: ~**er
Anfall** hysterics.

I

I, i [i:] *n* (-; -) I, i: *i wo!* not a bit of it!
iberisch [i'be:rɪʃ] *adj geogr.* Iberian.
ich [ɪç] *pers pron* I: ~ **bin's!** it is I!, F it's
me!; ~ **selbst** (I) myself; ~ *Idiot!* what a
fool I am!
Ich *n* (-[s]; -[s]) self, *psych.* ego: *mein
besseres* ~ my better self; *zweites* ~
alter ego. '**ichbezogen** *adj* egocentric.
'**Ichform** *f* (-; *no pl*) (**in der** ~ **geschrieben** written in the) first person.
ideal [ide'a:l] *adj*, **Ide'al** *n* (-s; -e) ideal.
Ide'alfall *m* ideal case: *im* ~ ideally.
idealisieren [ideali'zi:rən] *v/t* (h) idealize. **Idealismus** [idea'lɪsmʊs] *m* (-; *no
pl*) idealism. **Idealist** [idea'lɪst] *m* (-en;
-en), **Idea'listin** *f* (-; -nen) idealist.
idea'listisch *adj* idealistic.
Idee [i'de:] *f* (-; -n) **1.** idea, *a.* thought,
concept: *gute* ~*!* good idea!; *ich kam
auf die* ~ *zu inf* it occurred to me to *inf*;
wie kamst du auf die ~*?* what gave you
the idea?; *wie kamst du auf die* ~ *ihn
einzuladen?* what made you invite
him? **2.** F *e-e* ~ (just) a bit.

ideell [ide'ɛl] *adj* a) ideal (*a.* 🜨), b) idealistic: ~**er Wert** sentimental value.
i'deenarm, i'deenlos *adj* lacking in
ideas, unimaginative. **i'deenreich** *adj*
full of ideas, imaginative. **I'deenreich-
tum** *m* (-s; *no pl*) wealth of ideas.
identifi'zierbar *adj* identifiable.
identifizieren [idɛntifi'tsi:rən] *v/t* (h)
identify: *sich* ~ *mit* identify (o.s.) with.
Identifi'zierung *f* (-; -en) identification.
identisch [i'dɛntɪʃ] *adj* identical.
Identität [idɛnti'tɛ:t] *f* (-; *no pl*) identity.
Identi'täts|krise *f* identity crisis. ~**nach-
weis** *m* proof of (one's) identity.
Ideologe [ideo'lo:gə] *m* (-n; -n) ideo-
logue. **Ideologie** [ideolo'gi:] *f* (-; -n)
ideology. **ideo'logisch** *adj* ideological.
Idiom [i'dĭo:m] *n* (-s; -e) **1.** idiom. **2.**
language.
Idiomatik [idĭo'ma:tɪk] *f* (-; *no pl*) **1.**
phraseology. **2.** idioms (and phrases).
idiomatisch [idĭo'ma:tɪʃ] *adj* idiomatic.
Idiot [i'dĭo:t] *m* (-en; -en) idiot.
Idi'otenhügel *m* F nursery slope.

idi'otensicher *adj* F foolproof.
Idiotie [idiˈoːtiː] *f* (-; -n) **1.** *F* imbecility, idiocy. **2.** F *pure ~* sheer lunacy.
idiotisch [iˈdjoːtɪʃ] *adj* idiotic.
Idol [iˈdoːl] *n* (-s; -e) idol.
Idyll [iˈdʏl] *n* (-s; -e) idyll. **Idylle** [iˈdʏlə] *f* (-; -n) **1.** idyll. **2.** pastoral poem (*paint.* scene). **idyllisch** [iˈdʏlɪʃ] *adj* idyllic.
Igel [ˈiːɡəl] *m* (-s; -) *zo.* hedgehog.
ignorant [ɪɡnoˈrant] *adj* ignorant.
Igno'rant *m* (-en; -en) ignorant person.
Igno'ranz [ɪɡnoˈrants] *f* (-; *no pl*) ignorance.
ignorieren [ɪɡnoˈriːrən] *v/t* (h) ignore.
ihm [iːm] *pers pron* (*dat of er and es*) (to) him, (to) it: *ich glaube (es) ~* I believe him; *ein Freund von ~* a friend of his.
ihn [iːn] *pers pron* (*acc of er*) him, *of things*: it.
ihnen [ˈiːnən] **I** *pers pron* (*dat pl of er, sie, es*) (to) them: *ich habe es ~ gesagt* I've told them; *ein Freund von ~* a friend of theirs. **II Ihnen** (*dat of Sie*) (to) you: *ist er ein Freund von Ihnen?* is he a friend of yours?
ihr [iːr] **I** *pers pron* **1.** (*dat of sie sg*) (to) her, *of things*: (to) it: *e-e Tante von ~* an aunt of hers; → *a.* **ihm. 2.** (*nom pl of du, in letters*: **Ihr**) you. **II** *adj* **3.** *sg* her, *of things*: its, *pl* their: *e-r ~er Brüder* one of her (*or* their) brothers, a brother of hers (*or* theirs). **4.** *Ihr address*: your. **III** *pos pron* **5.** *der* (*die, das*) *ihr(ig)e* hers (*pl* theirs, *address*: **Ihr(ig)e** yours).
'ihrer'seits [-ˈzaɪts] *adv* as far as she's (*pl* they're, *address*: **Ihrerseits** you're) concerned.
'ihres'gleichen *indef pron* **1.** the likes of her (*pl* them), her (*pl* their) equals. **2.** *Ihresgleichen* the likes of you, your equals.
'ihret'wegen *adv* **1.** for her (*pl* their) sake. **2. 'Ihret'wegen** for your sake.
'ihrig → **ihr** III.
Ikone [iˈkoːnə] *f* (-; -n) icon.
illegal [ˈɪleɡaːl] *adj* illegal.
illegitim [ˈɪleɡitiːm] *adj* illegitimate.
Illusion [ɪluˈzjoːn] *f* (-; -en) illusion: *sich ~n hingeben* delude o.s.; *darüber mache ich mir k-e ~en* I have no illusions about that. **illusi'onslos** *adj and adv* without (any) illusions.
illusorisch [ɪluˈzoːrɪʃ] *adj* illusory.
Illustration [ɪlʊstraˈtsjoːn] *f* (-; -en) illus-

tration, picture. **illustrieren** [ɪlʊsˈtriːrən] *v/t* illustrate, *fig. a.* demonstrate.
Illu'strierte *f* (-; -n) magazine, F mag.
im [ɪm] = *in dem* → **in**[1].
Image [ˈɪmɪtʃ] *n* (-[s]; -s) image. **'Image-pflege** *f* (-; *no pl*) image cultivation.
imaginär [ɪmaɡiˈnɛːr] *adj* imaginary.
Imbiß [ˈɪmbɪs] *m* (-sses; -sse) snack.
'Imbiß|halle *f*, **~stube** *f* snack bar.
Imitation [ɪmitaˈtsjoːn] *f* (-; -en) imitation, copy.
imitieren [ɪmiˈtiːrən] *v/t* (h) imitate.
Imker [ˈɪmkər] *m* (-s; -) beekeeper.
immanent [ɪmaˈnɛnt] *adj* inherent (*dat* in).
Immatrikulation [ɪmatrikulaˈtsjoːn] *f* (-; -en) *univ.* enrolment.
immatrikulieren [ɪmatrikuˈliːrən] *v/t* (*a. sich ~ lassen*) enrol (*an dat* at).
immens [ɪˈmɛns] *adj* immense.
immer [ˈɪmər] *adv* **1.** always, constantly, all the time, *a.* every time: *noch ~* still; *noch ~ nicht* not yet; *~ wenn* whenever; *~ wieder* over and over again, time and again; *~ wieder tun* keep doing; *sie redete ~ weiter* F she went on and on. **2.** *before comp*: *~ besser* better and better; *~ schlimmer* worse and worse; *~ größer werdend* ever increasing. **3.** F *~ zwei* two at a time. **4.** *wann (auch) ~* whenever; *was (auch) ~* whatever; *wer (auch) ~* whoever; *wie (auch) ~* however; *wo (auch) ~* wherever.
'immergrün *adj* evergreen.
'immer'hin *adv* **1.** still, after all: *~!* not too bad! **2.** at least.
'immer'während *adj* everlasting.
Immigrant [ɪmiˈɡrant] *m* (-en; -en), **Immi'grantin** *f* (-; -nen) immigrant.
Immigration [ɪmiɡraˈtsjoːn] *f* (-; -en) immigration. **immigrieren** [ɪmiˈɡriːrən] *v/i* (sn) immigrate.
Immobilien [ɪmoˈbiːljən] *pl* real estate, (real) property. **~händler(in** *f*) *m*, **~makler(in** *f*) *m* estate agent, *Am.* realtor. **~markt** *m* property market.
immun [ɪˈmuːn] *adj* immune (*gegen* to): *~ machen* → **immunisieren** [ɪmuniˈziːrən] *v/t* immunize (*gegen* against).
Immunität [ɪmuniˈtɛːt] *f* (-; *no pl*) immunity (*gegen* to, against, from).
Im'munkörper *m* antibody.
Immunologe [ɪmunoˈloːɡə] *m* (-n; -n)

immunologist. **Immunologie** [ımuno-
lo'gi:] f (-; no pl) immunology.
Im'mun∣schwäche f ⚕ immunodefi-
ciency. **~sy₁stem** n immune system.
Impedanz [impe'dants] f (-; -en) ⚡
impedance.
Imperativ ['imperati:f] m (-s; -e) ling.
imperative.
Imperfekt ['imperfɛkt] n (-s; -e) ling.
imperfect (tense).
Imperialismus [imperĭa'lısmʊs] m (-; no
pl) imperialism.
imperia'listisch adj imperialist(ic).
Imperium [im'pe:rĭʊm] n (-s; -rien) a.
fig. empire.
'Impf∣akti₁on f ⚕ vaccination pro-
gram(me Br.). **~arzt** m vaccinator.
impfen ['impfən] v/t (h) vaccinate, inoc-
ulate: **sich ~ lassen (gegen** against) be
vaccinated, get a vaccination.
'Impf∣paß m vaccination card. **~pi₁stole**
f vaccination gun. **~schein** m vaccination certificate. **~stoff** m vaccine.
'Impfung f (-; -en) vaccination, inocula-
tion.
Implantat [implan'ta:t] n (-[e]s; -e), **implantieren** [-'ti:rən] v/t (h) ⚕ implant.
implizieren [impli'tsi:rən] v/t (h) imply.
implodieren [implo'di:rən] v/i (sn) im-
plode. **Implosion** [implo'zĭo:n] f (-;
-en) implosion.
imponieren [impo'ni:rən] v/i (h) **j-m ~** a)
impress s.o., b) command s.o.'s re-
spect. **impo'nierend** adj impressive.
Impo'niergehabe n 1. zo. display be-
havio(u)r. 2. fig. attempt to impress.
Import [im'pɔrt] m (-[e]s; -e) 1. no pl
importing. 2. imports. **Im'port...** import (agency, trade, etc). **Importeur**
[impɔr'tø:r] m (-s; -e) importer.
Im'portgeschäft n 1. import trade. 2.
import company. **importieren** [impɔr-
'ti:rən] v/t (h) import.
imposant [impo'zant] adj imposing, impressive.
impotent ['impotɛnt] adj impotent.
'Impotenz [-tɛnts] f (-; no pl) impotence.
'inakzep₁tabel adj unacceptable.
imprägnieren [imprɛ'gni:rən] v/t (h)
impregnate, a. waterproof.
Imprä'gnierung f (-; -en) impregnation,
waterproofing.
Impression [imprɛ'sĭo:n] f (-; -en) impression. **Impressionismus** [imprɛsĭo-
'nısmʊs] m (-; no pl) impressionism.

Impressionist [-'nıst] m (-en; -en) impressionist. **impressio'nistisch** adj
impressionist(ic).
Impressum [im'prɛsʊm] n (-s; -sen) imprint, of newspaper: a. masthead.
Improvisation [improviza'tsĭo:n] f (-;
-en) improvisation. **improvisieren**
[improvi'zi:rən] v/t, v/i (h) improvise,
speaker etc: a. extemporize, F ad-lib.
Impuls [im'pʊls] m (-es; -e) impulse: **e-m
~ folgend** on (an) impulse; fig. **neue ~e
geben** give a fresh impetus (dat to).
impulsiv [impʊl'zi:f] adj impulsive: **~
handeln** act on impulse.
Im'pulskauf m ↑ impulsive buying.

im'stande adj pred **zu et. ~ sein** be capable of (doing) s.th.; **(nicht) ~ sein, et.
zu tun** be (un)able to do s.th.; **dazu ist
er glatt ~** iro. I wouldn't put it past him.
in¹ [ın] prep **1.** a) in, at, b) within, c) into,
in: **~ England** in England; **waren Sie
schon einmal ~ England?** have you
ever been to England?; **im Haus**
in(side) the house, indoors; **~ der (die)
Schule** at (to) school; **er ist Kassierer
~ e-r Bank** he is a cashier in (or at) a
bank. **2.** a) in, b) during, c) within: **im
Mai** in May; **~ diesem Jahr** this year; **~
diesem Alter** at this age. **3. ~ größter
Eile** in a great rush; **im Kreis** in a circle;
~ Behandlung sein be having treatment; **ein Mann ~ s-r Stellung** a man in
his position; **gut ~ Chemie** good at
chemistry.
in² adj **~ sein** F be in.
'inaktiv adj inactive, 🜛 a. inert.
Inaktivi'tät f (-; no pl) inactivity.
In'angriffnahme [-na:mə] f (-; -n) adm.
(gen) starting (on), tackling (of).
In'anspruchnahme [-na:mə] f (-; -n)
(gen, von) **1.** use (of). **2.** demands (on).
'Inbegriff m (-[e]s; -e) epitome.
'inbegriffen adj **~ sein** be included.
Inbe'sitznahme [-na:mə] f (-; -n) (gen
of) taking possession, occupation.
Inbe'triebnahme [-na:mə] f (-; -n) (gen
of) opening, starting: **bei ~ der Anlage**
when the plant is put into operation.
'Inbrunst f (-; no pl) ardo(u)r, fervo(u)r.
'inbrünstig adj ardent, fervent.
in'dem conj **1.** by: **er entkam, ~ er aus
dem Fenster sprang** he escaped by
jumping out of the window. **2.** while.

Inder ['ındər] m (-s; -), **'Inderin** f (-; -nen) Indian.

in'dessen I adv **1.** meanwhile. **2.** however. **II** conj → **wohingegen**.

Index ['ındeks] m (-es; -e, -dizes [-ditses]) index. **~lohn** m index-linked wages.

Indianer [ın'dĭa:nər] m (-s; -), **Indi'anerin** f (-; -nen), **indi'anisch** adj (Red) Indian.

Indien ['ındĭən] n (-s) India.

Indikation [ındika'tsĭo:n] f (-; -en) ✱ indication: **soziale ~** social grounds for termination of pregnancy.

Indikativ ['ındikati:f] m (-s; -e) ling. indicative (mood).

'indirekt adj indirect: **~e Rede** ling. indirect (or reported) speech.

indisch ['ındıʃ] adj Indian.

'indiskret adj indiscreet.

Indiskreti'on f (-; -en) indiscretion.

indiskutabel ['ındıskuta:bəl] adj impossible: **~ sein** a. be out of the question.

'indisponiert adj indisposed.

individualisieren [ındividŭali'zi:rən] v/t (h) individualize. **Individualismus** [-'lısmʊs] m (-; no pl) individualism. **Individualist** [-'lıst] m (-en; -en) individualist. **individua'listisch** adj individualist(ic). **Individualität** [-'tɛ:t] f (-; no pl) individuality. **individuell** [ındivi'dŭɛl] adj individual: **~ gestalten** individualize; **das ist ~ verschieden** that varies from person to person.

Individuum [ındi'vi:dŭɔm] n (-s; -duen [-dŭən]) individual.

Indiz [ın'di:ts] n (-es; -zien [-tsĭən]) **1.** indication, sign. **2.** usu. pl → **In'dizienbeweis(e** pl) m ✚ circumstantial evidence.

indoeuro'päisch [ındo-], **indoger'manisch** adj Indo-European.

indoktrinieren [ındɔktri'ni:rən] v/t (h) indoctrinate.

Indonesien [ındo'ne:zĭən] n (-s) Indonesia. **Indonesier** [ındo'ne:zĭər] m (-s; -), **Indo'nesierin** f (-; -nen), **indo'nesisch** [-zıʃ] adj Indonesian.

Indossament [ındɔsa'mɛnt] n (-s; -e) ✚ endorsement. **Indossant** [ındɔ'sant] m (-en; -en) endorser. **Indossat** [ındɔ'sa:t] m (-en; -en) endorsee. **indossieren** [ındɔ'si:rən] v/t (h) endorse.

Induktion [ındʊk'tsĭo:n] f (-; -en) induc-

tion. **Induktivität** [ındʊktivi'tɛ:t] f (-; no pl) inductivity.

industrialisieren [ındʊstrĭali'zi:rən] v/t (h) industrialize. **Industriali'sierung** f (-; no pl) industrialization.

Industrie [ındʊs'tri:] f (-; -n) a) industry, b) → **Industriezweig**.

Indu'strie... industrial (nation, diamond, product, etc). **~anlage** f industrial plant. **~arbeiter(in** f) m industrial worker. **~betrieb** m industrial company (or plant). **~gebiet** n industrial area. **~gelände** n industrial estate. **~gesellschaft** f industrial society. **~gewerkschaft** f industry-wide union: **~ Metall** metalworkers' union. **~kaufmann** m officer (or clerk) in an industrial company.

industriell [ındʊstri'ɛl] adj industrial.

Industri'elle m, f (-n; -n) industrialist.

Indu'strie|macht f industrial power. **~messe** f industrial fair. **~müll** m industrial waste. **~park** m industrial park. **~spio͜nage** f industrial espionage. **~stadt** f industrial town. **~ und Handelskammer** f chamber of industry and commerce. **~verband** m federation of industries. **~zweig** m (branch of) industry.

induzieren [ındu'tsi:rən] v/t (h) induce.

inein'ander adv in(to) one another (or each other), in cpds. a. inter...: **~ verliebt** in love (with each other).

inein'anderfließen v/i (irr, sep, -ge-, sn, → **fließen**) merge into one another, colo(u)rs: a. run.

inein'andergreifen v/i (irr, sep, -ge-, h, → **greifen**) **1.** ⚙ interlock, gears etc: mesh. **2.** fig. interlink.

inein'anderschieben v/t (irr, sep, -ge-, h, → **schieben**) (a. sich ~ lassen) telescope.

infam [ın'fa:m] adj infamous, disgraceful. **Infamie** [ınfa'mi:] f (-; -n) infamy.

Infanterie [ınfantə'ri:] f (-; -n) infantry. **Infanterist** [ınfantə'rıst] m (-en; -en) infantryman.

infantil [ınfan'ti:l] adj infantile.

Infarkt [ın'farkt] m (-[e]s; -e) ✱ infarct.

Infekt [ın'fɛkt] m (-[e]s; -e), **Infektion** [ınfɛk'tsĭo:n] f (-; -en) infection.

Infekti'ons|gefahr f risk of infection. **~herd** m focus of infection. **~krankheit** f infectious disease.

infektiös [ɪnfɛk'tsiø:s] *adj* infectious, contagious.

Inferno [ɪn'fɛrno] *n* (-s; *no pl*) inferno.

infiltrieren [ɪnfɪl'tri:rən] *v/t* (h), *v/i* (sn) infiltrate.

Infinitesimalrechnung [ɪnfinitezi'ma:l-] *f* infinitesimal calculus.

Infinitiv ['ɪnfiniti:f] *m* (-s; -e) infinitive.

infizieren [ɪnfi'tsi:rən] (h) **I** *v/t* infect. **II** *sich* ~ catch an infection, become infected: *er hat sich bei ihr infiziert* he caught the disease from her.

in flagranti [ɪn fla'granti] *adv* ~ *ertappen* catch *s.o.* in the act (*or* red-handed).

Inflation [ɪnfla'tsio:n] *f* (-; -en) inflation.

inflationär [ɪnflatsio'nɛ:r], **inflationistisch** [-'nɪstɪʃ] *adj* inflationary.

Inflati'onspoli,tik *f* inflationary policy.

Inflati'onsrate *f* inflation rate.

Info ['ɪnfo] *n* (-s; -s) F → *Informationsblatt.*

in'folge *prep* (*gen*) as a result of, owing to. **infolge'dessen** *adv* as a result (of this), consequently.

Informant [ɪnfɔr'mant] *m* (-en; -en), **Infor'mantin** *f* (-; -nen) informant.

Informatik [ɪnfɔr'ma:tɪk] *f* (-; *no pl*) computer science, informatics. **Infor'matiker** [-tikər] *m* (-s; -) computer specialist.

Information [ɪnfɔrma'tsio:n] *f* (-; -en) (*zu Ihrer* ~ for your) information.

Informati'ons|blatt *n* newssheet. **~bü,ro** *n* information office. **~fluß** *m* (-sses; *no pl*) flow of information. **~materi,al** *n* information(al material). **~schalter** *m*, **~stand** *m* information desk.

informativ [ɪnfɔrma'ti:f] *adj* informative.

informieren [ɪnfɔr'mi:rən] (h) **I** *v/t* (*über* *acc*) inform (of, about), *a.* notify (of), let *s.o.* know (about), *a.* instruct (as to), brief (on): *falsch* ~ misinform. **II** *sich* ~ (*über* *acc* about) inform o.s., find out.

infor'miert *adj* informed: *~e Kreise* well-informed circles.

'Infostand *m* F → *Informationsstand.*

infrarot ['ɪnfra-] *adj*, **'Infrarot...** infrared.

'Infraschall *m* infrasound.

'Infraschall... infrasound...

'Infrastruk,tur *f* infrastructure.

Infusion [ɪnfu'zio:n] *f* (-; -en) infusion.

Infusorien [ɪnfu'zo:riən] *pl zo.* infusoria.

Inge'brauchnahme [-na:mə] *f* (-; *no pl*)

adm. **vor** ~ (*gen*) before using *s.th.*

Ingenieur [ɪnʒe'niø:r] *m* (-s; -e) engineer.

Ingeni'eurbü,ro *n* **1.** (firm of) consulting engineers. **2.** engineering office.

Ingwer ['ɪŋvər] *m* (-s; *no pl*) ginger.

Inhaber ['ɪnha:bər] *m* (-s; -), **'Inhaberin** *f* (-; -nen) a) owner, proprietor (-tress), b) occupant (*of flat*), c) holder (*of title, office, patent, record, etc*), ✝ *a.* bearer.

'Inhaber|aktie *f* bearer share. **~scheck** *m* cheque (*Am.* check) to bearer.

inhaftieren [ɪnhaf'ti:rən] *v/t* (h) arrest, take *s.o.* into custody. **Inhaf'tierung** *f* (-; -en) **1.** arrest(ing). **2.** detention.

Inhalation [ɪnhala'tsio:n] *f* (-; -en) inhalation. **Inhalati'onsappa,rat** *m* inhaler. **inhalieren** [-'li:rən] *v/t* (h) inhale.

Inhalt ['ɪnhalt] *m* (-[e]s; -e) **1.** a) contents, b) capacity, volume. **2.** *fig.* a) content(s), subject matter, b) meaning: *des ~s, daß* to the effect that; *wesentlicher* ~ essence; *mein Leben hat k-n* ~ my life is meaningless (*or* empty).

'inhaltlich *adv* in content.

'Inhaltsangabe *f* summary, synopsis.

'Inhaltserklärung *f* ✝ list of contents.

'inhaltslos *adj* empty, meaningless, lacking in substance. **'inhaltsreich** *adj* rich in substance, full, rich (*life*).

'Inhaltsverzeichnis *n* list (*book:* table) of contents.

'inhuman *adj* inhuman.

Initiale [ini'tsia:lə] *f* (-; -n) initial.

Initiative [initsia'ti:və] *f* (-; -n) **1.** (*die* ~ *ergreifen* take the) initiative: *auf s-e* ~ *hin* on his initiative; *aus eigener* ~ on one's own initiative. **2.** action group.

Initiator [ini'tsia:tor] *m* (-s; -en [-tsia'to:rən]), **Initia'torin** *f* (-; -nen) initiator.

Injektion [ɪnjɛk'tsio:n] *f* (-; -en) injection, F shot. **Injekti'onsnadel** *f* hypodermic needle. **Injekti'onsspritze** *f* (hypodermic) syringe.

injizieren [ɪnji'tsi:rən] *v/t* (h) inject.

Inkasso [ɪn'kaso] *n* (-s; -s) ✝ collection.

In'kasso... collection (*agency, business, etc*). **~vollmacht** *f* authority to collect.

inklusive [ɪnklu'zi:və] **I** *prep* (*nom, gen*) including, inclusive of: ~ *Verpackung* packing included. **II** *adv* **bis zum 4. Mai** ~ up to and including May 4th.

inkognito [ɪn'kɔgnito] *adv* incognito.

In'kognito *n* (-s; -s) incognito.

'inkompetent *adj* incompetent.

'inkonsequent *adj* inconsistent.

'Inkonsequenz *f* (-; -en) inconsistency.

In'krafttreten *n* (-s) coming into force: **bei** ~ upon taking effect; **Tag des** ~**s** effective date.

inkriminieren [ɪnkrimiˈniːrən] *v/t* (h) incriminate.

Inkubationszeit [ɪnkubaˈtsi̯oːns-] *f* 🐝 incubation period.

Inkubator [ɪnkuˈbaːtɔr] *m* (-s; -en [-baˈtoːrən]) 🐝 incubator.

'Inland *n* (-[e]s; *no pl*) **1.** home: **im Inund Ausland** at home and abroad. **2.** inland, interior. **'Inland...** → **inländisch. Inländer** [ˈɪnlɛndər] *m* (-s; -), **'Inländerin** *f* (-; -nen) native. **'inländisch** *adj* home, domestic, internal.

'Inlands|absatz *m* ↑ domestic sales. ~**flug** *m* domestic (*or* internal) flight. ~**markt** *m* home (*or* domestic) market. ~**post** *f* inland (*Am.* domestic) mail.

Inlett [ˈɪnlɛt] *n* (-[e]s; -e) ticking.

in'mitten *prep* (*gen*) in the middle of.

innehaben [ˈɪnə-] *v/t* (*irr, sep,* -ge-, h, → **haben**) hold.

'innehalten *v/i* (*irr, sep,* -ge-, h, → **halten**) stop, pause.

innen [ˈɪnən] *adv* inside, *a.* indoors: ~ **und außen** inside and out(side); **nach** ~ (**zu**) inwards; **von** ~ from (the) inside.

'Innen|ansicht *f* interior view. ~**archi,tekt(in** *f*) *m* interior designer. ~**architek,tur** *f* interior design. ~**aufnahme** *f* *phot.* indoor (*film:* studio) shot. ~**ausstattung** *f* a) interior decoration, b) décor, furnishings, *mot.* trim. ~**bahn** *f* *sports:* inside lane. ~**dienst** *m* office work: **im** ~**tätig sein** work in the office. ~**durchmesser** *m* inside diameter. ~**einrichtung** *f* interior decoration. ~**hof** *m* (inner) courtyard. ~**leben** *n* (-s; *no pl*) inner life. ~**leuchte** *f* *mot.* interior light. ~**mi,nister** *m* minister of the interior, *Br.* Home Secretary, *Am.* Secretary of the Interior. ~**mini,sterium** *n* ministry of the interior, *Br.* Home Office, *Am.* Department of the Interior. ~**poli,tik** *f* domestic politics (*or* policy), home affairs. ⚲**po,litisch** *adj* domestic, internal: ~ (**gesehen**) concerning domestic policy. ~**raum** *m* interior. ~**seite** *f* inside. ~**spiegel** *m* *mot.* inside mirror. ~**stadt** *f* inner city, (town) cent/re (*Am.* -er), *Am. a.* downtown: **in der** ~

von Chicago in downtown Chicago. ~**tasche** *f* inside pocket. ~**tempera,tur** *f* internal (*or* indoor) temperature. ~**wand** *f* inside wall.

inner [ˈɪnər] *adj* a) inside, ✝, *pol.* domestic, *a.* 🐝 internal, b) *fig.* inner, mental: ~**er Halt** moral backbone; ~**e Ruhe** peace of mind; **ein** ~**er Widerspruch** an inner contradiction.

'innerbetrieblich *adj* ↑ internal.

'innerdeutsch *adj* **1.** German, (German) domestic, internal. **2.** *hist.* German-German (*relations, traffic, etc*).

Innere [ˈɪnərə] *n* (-n; *no pl*) **1.** interior (*a. geogr.*), inside, heart, cent/re (*Am.* -er): **im** ~**n** inside, *geogr.* in the interior. **2.** *fig.* heart, soul, mind, core: **in ihrem tiefsten** ~**n** deep down; → *a.* **Innerste.**

Innereien [ɪnəˈraɪən] *pl* innards, guts.

'innerhalb I *prep* (*gen*) **1.** inside, within: ~ **der Familie** within the family. **2.** a) in, within, b) during: ~ **der Arbeitszeit** during working hours; ~ **weniger Tage** within a few days. **II** *adv* ~ **von** within.

'innerlich I *adj* **1.** inner, *a.* 🐝 internal. **2.** *fig.* a) inward(-looking), b) emotional, c) thoughtful. **3.** internally: ~ (**anzuwenden**) *pharm.* for internal use (only). **4.** *fig.* inwardly, *a.* secretly.

'Innerlichkeit *f* (-; *no pl*) a) inwardness, b) sensitivity, depth of feeling.

'innerpar,teilich *adj* inner-party ..., internal.

'innerparteilich *v/i* (*sep,* -ge-, h) be inherent (*dat* in).

'innerst [ˈɪnərst] *adj* innermost, inmost.

'innerstaatlich *adj* internal.

'innerstädtisch *adj* urban.

'Innerste *n* (-n; *no pl*) the innermost part, *a.* heart, midst.

'innewohnen *v/i* (*sep,* -ge-, h) be inherent (*dat* in).

innig [ˈɪnɪç] *adj* a) tender, b) ardent, fervent, *a.* devout, c) heartfelt, sincere, d) close, intimate: **j-n** ~ **lieben** love s.o. dearly, be devoted to s.o.

'Innigkeit *f* (-; *no pl*) a) tenderness, b) ardo(u)r, c) sincerity.

Innovation [ɪnovaˈtsi̯oːn] *f* (-; -en) innovation. **innovati'onsfreudig, innovativ** [ɪnovaˈtiːf] *adj* innovative.

Innung [ˈɪnʊŋ] *f* (-; -en) guild.

'inoffizi,ell *adj* **1.** unofficial. **2.** informal.

in petto [ɪn ˈpɛto] *adv et.* ~ **haben** have s.th. up one's sleeve.

in puncto [ɪn ˈpʊŋkto] *prep* as regards

Insasse ['ɪnzasə] m (-n; -n), **'Insassin** f (-; -nen) **1.** passenger. **2.** inmate.

'Insassenversicherung f mot. passenger insurance (cover).

'Inschrift f (-; -en) inscription.

Insekt [ɪn'zɛkt] n (-[e]s; -en) insect, bug. **In'sekten|bekämpfungsmittel** n insecticide. **~fresser** m zo. insectivore. **~kunde** f (-; no pl) entomology. **~stich** m insect bite.

Insektizid [ɪnzɛkti'tsiːt] n (-s; -e) insecticide.

Insel ['ɪnzəl] f island (a. fig.), poet. or before proper names: isle: **die ~ Wight** the Isle of Wight; **die Britischen ~n** the British Isles. **~bewohner** m islander. **~gruppe** f archipelago. **~staat** m island state. **~volk** n islanders. **~welt** f islands.

Inserat [ɪnze'raːt] n (-[e]s; -e) advertisement, F ad. **Inserent** [ɪnze'rɛnt] m (-en; -en), **Inse'rentin** f (-; -nen) advertiser. **inserieren** [ɪnze'riːrən] (h) **I** v/t advertise. **II** v/i **~ in** (dat) advertise in, put an advertisement (F ad) into.

insge'heim adv secretly.

insge'samt adv a) altogether, in all, b) as a whole: **~ betragen** total.

in'sofern[1] adv as far as that goes.

inso'fern[2] conj **~ (als)** in so far as.

Insolvenz ['ɪnzɔlvɛnts] f (-; -en) † insolvency.

Inspekteur [ɪnspɛk'tøːr] m (-s; -e) inspector. **Inspektion** [ɪnspɛk'tsioːn] f (-; -en) **1.** inspection. **2.** (**das Auto zur ~ bringen** put the car in for a) service. **Inspektor** [ɪn'spɛktɔr] m (-s; -en [-'toːrən]), **Inspektorin** [ɪnspɛk'toːrɪn] f (-; -nen) inspector.

Inspiration [ɪnspira'tsioːn] f (-; -en) inspiration. **inspirieren** [ɪnspi'riːrən] v/t (h) **j-n zu et. ~** inspire s.o. to (do) s.th.; **sich ~ lassen** be inspired (**von** by).

Inspizient [ɪnspi'tsiɛnt] m (-en; -en) thea. etc stage manager. **inspizieren** [ɪnspi'tsiːrən] v/t (h) inspect, examine.

instand [ɪn'ʃtant] adv **~ halten** keep s.th. in good order, maintain, service; **~ setzen** a) repair, b) renovate. **In'standhaltung** f (-; -en) maintenance.

in'ständig adj urgent: **j-n ~ um et. bitten** implore s.o. for s.th.

In'standsetzung f (-; -en) a) repair, b) renovation. **In'standsetzungsarbeit** f repair work, repairs.

Instanz [ɪn'stants] f (-; -en) authority, ⚖ instance: **höhere ~en** higher authorities (⚖ courts); **in erster ~** ⚖ at first instance; **Gericht erster ~** court of first instance; **in letzter ~** a. fig. in the last instance. **In'stanzenweg** m ⚖ (successive) stages of appeal; **auf dem ~** through the prescribed channels.

Instinkt [ɪn'stɪŋkt] m (-[e]s; -e) instinct, w.s. feeling: **aus ~** from (or by) instinct, instinctively. **instinktiv** [ɪnstɪŋk'tiːf] adj instinctive. **in'stinktlos** adj fig. showing a sad lack of flair.

Institut [ɪnsti'tuːt] n (-s; -e) institute. **Institution** [ɪnstitu'tsioːn] f (-; -en) a. fig. institution. **institutionalisieren** [ɪnstitutsionali'ziːrən] v/t (h) institutionalize. **institutionell** [ɪnstitutsio'nɛl] adj institutional.

instruieren [ɪnstru'iːrən] v/t (h) a) give s.o. instructions, a. ✕ brief, b) inform. **Instruktion** [ɪnstrɔk'tsioːn] f (-; -en) instruction.

instruktiv [ɪnstrɔk'tiːf] adj instructive.

Instrument [ɪnstru'mɛnt] n (-[e]s; -e) instrument.

Instrumentalmu,sik [ɪnstrumɛn'taːl-] f instrumental music.

Instrumentarium [ɪnstrumɛn'taːriom] n (-s; -rien) instruments.

Instru'menten|bau m (-[e]s; no pl) ♪ instrument making. **~brett** n instrument panel, mot. a. dashboard. **~flug** m instrument flying.

instrumentieren [ɪnstrumɛn'tiːrən] v/t (h) ♪ orchestrate.

Insuffizienz ['ɪnzʊfitsiɛnts] f (-; -en) a. ✿ insufficiency.

Insulaner [ɪnzu'laːnər] m (-s; -) islander.

Insulin [ɪnzu'liːn] n (-s; no pl) insulin.

inszenieren [ɪntse'niːrən] v/t (h) thea. a) stage (a. fig.), a. film, TV produce, b) direct. **Insze'nierung** f (-; -en) production: **in der ~ von X** produced by X.

intakt [ɪn'takt] adj intact.

Intarsien [ɪn'tarzion] pl inlaid work.

integer [ɪn'teːgər] adj man of integrity.

integral [ɪnte'graːl] adj integral.

Inte'gral n (-s; -e) Å integral.

Inte'gralrechnung f integral calculus.
Integration [ɪntegra'tsi̯oːn] f (-; -en) integration. **integrieren** [ɪnte'griːrən] v/t (h) (a. **sich ~**) integrate (**in** acc into, within). **inte'griert** adj integrated.
Integrität [ɪntegri'tɛːt] f (-; no pl) integrity.
Intellekt [ɪntɛ'lɛkt] m (-[e]s; no pl) intellect. **intellektuell** [ɪntɛlɛk'tu̯ɛl] adj, **Intellektu'elle** m, f (-n; -n) intellectual, F highbrow.
intelligent [ɪntɛli'gɛnt] adj intelligent.
Intelligenz [ɪntɛli'gɛnts] f (-; no pl) **1.** intelligence. **2.** intelligentsia.
Intelli'genz,quoti,ent m intelligence quotient, I.Q. **~test** m intelligence test.
Intendant [ɪntɛn'dant] m (-en; -en) thea. etc director.
Intensität [ɪntɛnzi'tɛːt] f (-; no pl) intensity. **intensiv** [ɪntɛn'ziːf] adj **1.** intensive. **2.** intense, strong. **intensivieren** [ɪntɛnzivi'rən] v/t (h) intensify. **Intensi'vierung** f (-; no pl) intensification.
Inten'sivkurs m crash course.
Inten'sivstati,on f 🕊 intensive-care unit: **auf der ~ liegen** be in intensive care.
Intercity-Zug [ɪntər'sɪti-] m inter-city train.
interessant [ɪntərɛ'sant] adj interesting.
Interesse [ɪntə'rɛsə] n (-s; -n) interest (**an** dat, **für** in): **~ haben an** (or **für**) → **interessieren** II; **~ zeigen** show an interest (**an** dat, **für** in); **im öffentlichen ~** in the public interest; **ich tat es in d-m ~** I did it for your sake; **es liegt in d-m eigenen ~** it's in your own interest; **j-s ~n vertreten** (or **wahrnehmen**) look after (or represent) s.o.'s interests; **es besteht kein ~ an** (dat) nobody is interested in, 🕊 there is no demand for.
inter'essehalber [-halbər] adv out of interest. **inter'esselos** adj uninterested, indifferent. **Inter'esselosigkeit** f (-; no pl) indifference.
Inter'essen,gebiet n field (or area) of interest. **~gemeinschaft** f community of interests, 🕊 combine, pool. **~kolli,si,on** f clash of interests. **~sphäre** f sphere of influence.
Interessent [ɪntərɛ'sɛnt] m (-en; -en) person interested, interested party, 🕊 prospective buyer: **~en werden gebeten** those interested are requested.
interessieren [ɪntərɛ'siːrən] (h) **I** v/t interest (**für** in): **das Buch interessiert mich nicht** the book doesn't interest me, I'm not interested in the book; **das interessiert mich (überhaupt) nicht!** a) I'm not a (bit) interested!, b) I couldn't care less!; **es wird dich ~ (zu hören), daß** you'll be interested to know that; **wen interessiert das schon?** who cares? **II sich ~ für** be interested in, take (or show) an interest in. **III** v/i be of interest: **das interessiert hier nicht!** that's irrelevant!
interes'siert I adj interested (**an** dat in).
II adv with interest, interestedly.
Interimsre,gierung ['ɪntərɪms-] f interim government.
interkonfessio'nell [ɪntərkɔnfesi̯o'nɛl] adj interdenominational.
Interkontinentalflug [ɪntərkɔntinen-'taːl-] m intercontinental flight.
Interkontinen'talra,kete f intercontinental ballistic missile.
Intermezzo [ɪntər'mɛtso] n (-s; -s or -zi) ♪ intermezzo, interlude (a. fig.).
intern [ɪn'tɛrn] adj internal.
Internat [ɪntər'naːt] n (-[e]s; -e) boarding school.
international [ɪntərnatsi̯o'naːl] adj international. **internationalisieren** [-nali'ziːrən] v/t (h) internationalize.
Inter'natsschüler(in f) m boarder.
internieren [ɪntər'niːrən] v/t (h) intern.
Inter'nierte m, f (-n; -n) internee.
Inter'nierung f (-; -en) internment.
Inter'nierungslager n internment camp.
Internist [ɪntər'nɪst] m (-en; -en), **Inter'nistin** f (-; -nen) 🕊 internist.
interparlamen'tarisch adj interparliamentary.
Interpret [ɪntər'preːt] m (-en; -en), **Inter'pretin** f (-; -nen) interpreter, ♪ a. performer, singer. **Interpretation** [ɪntərpreta'tsi̯oːn] f (-; -en) interpretation. **interpretieren** [ɪntərpre'tiːrən] v/t (h) interpret, a. read, 🕊 construe.
Interpunktion [ɪntərpuŋk'tsi̯oːn] f (-; no pl) punctuation. **Interpunkti'onszeichen** n punctuation mark.
Interrogativ... [ɪntəroga'tiːf] interrogative (pronoun, sentence, etc).
Intervall [ɪntər'val] n (-s; -e) interval. **~training** n sports: interval training.
intervenieren [ɪntərve'niːrən] v/i (h) in-

tervene. **Intervention** [ɪntərvɛn'tsĭoːn] *f* (-; -en) intervention.

Interview [ɪntər'vjuː] *n* (-s; -s) interview. **interviewen** [-'vjuːən] *v/t* (h) interview.

Inter'viewer *m* (-s; -) interviewer.

intim [ɪn'tiːm] *adj* intimate, *a.* cosy (*room etc*): **mit j-m ~e Beziehungen haben** (*or* ~ **sein**) have intimate relations with s.o.; **ein ~er Kenner sein von** (*or gen*) have an intimate knowledge of.

In'tim|bereich *m* 1. *anat.* genitals. 2. → Intimsphäre. **~feind** *m* archenemy.

Intimität [ɪntimi'tɛːt] *f* (-; -en) intimacy: **es kam zu ~en zwischen ihnen** they became intimate.

In'timsphäre *f* (-; *no pl*) (**in j-s ~ eindringen** violate s.o.'s) privacy.

In'timspray *m* vaginal spray.

'intolerant *adj* intolerant.

'Intoleranz *f* intolerance.

Intonation [ɪntona'tsĭoːn] *f* (-; -en) *ling.*, ♪ intonation.

intonieren [ɪnto'niːrən] *v/t* (h) intonate.

'intransitiv *adj ling.* intransitive.

intrave'nös [ɪntra-] *adj* 🎗 intravenous.

Intrigant [ɪntri'gant] *m* (-en; -en), **Intri'gantin** *f* (-; -nen) schemer.

Intrige [ɪn'triːgə] *f* (-; -n) plot, intrigue, scheme. **intrigieren** [ɪntri'giːrən] *v/i* (h) (plot and) scheme.

introvertiert [ɪntrovɛr'tiːrt] *adj* introverted: **~er Mensch** introvert.

intuitiv [ɪntui'tiːf] *adj* intuitive.

Intuition [ɪntui'tsĭoːn] *f* (-; -en) intuition.

Invalide [ɪnva'liːdə] *m* (-n; -n) invalid.

Inva'lidenversicherung *f* disability insurance.

Invalidität [ɪnvalidi'tɛːt] *f* (-; *no pl*) disablement, disability.

Invasion [ɪnva'zĭoːn] *f* (-; -en) invasion.

Inventar [ɪnvɛn'taːr] *n* (-s; -e) *a* inventory, b) stock: **festes ~** fixture(s); **totes ~** dead stock; **lebendes ~** livestock; **ein ~ aufnehmen** → **inventarisieren** [ɪnvɛntari'ziːrən] (h) **I** *v/i* take inventory (*or* stock). **II** *v/t* take an inventory of.

Inventur [ɪnvɛn'tuːr] *f* (-; -en) inventory, stocktaking: **~ machen** take inventory (*or* stock).

Inversion [ɪnvɛr'zĭoːn] *f* (-; -en) inversion.

investieren [ɪnvɛs'tiːrən] *v/t*, *v/i* (h) invest (**in** *acc or dat* in).

Inve'stierung *f* (-; -en) investment.

Investition [ɪnvɛsti'tsĭoːn] *f* (-; -en) 1. investment. 2. capital expenditure.

Investiti'ons... investment (*bank, loan, etc*). **~anreiz** *m* investment incentive. **~güter** *pl* capital goods. **~pro,gramm** *n* capital expenditure program(me *Br.*).

In'vestment|fonds *m* investment fund. **~gesellschaft** *f* investment company.

Investor [ɪn'vɛstor] *m* (-s; -en [-'toːrən]) 🕇 investor.

'inwendig *adj* inwardly: F **in- und auswendig kennen** know *s.th.* inside out.

inwie'fern *conj* in what way, how.

inwie'weit *conj* to what extent.

In'zahlungnahme [-naːmə] *f* (-; -en) part exchange, trade-in.

Inzest [ɪn'tsɛst] *m* (-[e]s; -e) incest.

inzestuös [ɪntsɛstu'øːs] *adj* incestuous.

'Inzucht *f* (-; *no pl*) intermarriage, *a. zo.* inbreeding.

in'zwischen *adv* meanwhile.

Ion [i'oːn] *n* (-s; -en) *phys.* ion.

ionisieren [ioni'ziːrən] *v/t* (h) ionize.

Iono'sphäre [iono-] *f* (-; *no pl*) ionosphere.

'I-Punkt *m* dot over the i: **bis auf den ~** *fig.* down to the last detail.

Irak [i'raːk] *m* (-s) Iraq, Irak. **I'raker** *m* (-s; -), **I'rakerin** *f* (-; -nen), **i'rakisch** *adj* Iraqi, Iraki.

Iran [i'raːn] *m* (-s) Iran. **I'raner** *m* (-s; -), **I'ranerin** *f* (-; -nen), **i'ranisch** *adj* Iranian.

irdisch ['ɪrdɪʃ] *adj* a) earthly, b) worldly, c) mortal.

Ire ['iːrə] *m* (-n; -n) Irishman: **die ~n** the Irish.

irgend ['ɪrgənt] *adv* 1. **~ jemand** someone, anyone, somebody, anybody. 2. **~ etwas** something, anything; **wir müssen ~ etwas tun** we've got to do something; F **~ so ein ...** some sort of ... 3. **wann** (**wo**) **es ~ geht** whenever (wherever) it might be possible; **wenn ich ~ kann** if I possibly can; **so rasch wie ~ möglich** as soon as at all possible.

'irgend'ein *indef pron* some, any: **auf ~e Weise** somehow; **besteht noch ~e Hoffnung?** is there any hope at all?

'irgend'einer → **irgend** 1.

'irgend'wann *adv* 1. some time (or other). 2. any time.

'irgend'was F → **irgend** 2.

'irgend'welche *indef pron* any: *ohne ~ Kosten* without any expense at all.
'irgend'wie *adv* somehow, some way (or other).
'irgend'wo *adv* somewhere, anywhere: *~ anders* somewhere else. **~wo'her** *adv* from somewhere, from anywhere. **~wo'hin** *adv* somewhere, anywhere.
Irin ['iːrɪn] *f* (-; -nen) Irishwoman: *sie ist ~* she is Irish.
Iris ['iːrɪs] *f* (-; -) *anat.*, ⚘ iris.
irisch ['iːrɪʃ] *adj* Irish: **2e Republik** Irish Republic, Eire. **'Irisch** *n ling.* Irish.
Irland ['ɪrlant] *n* (-s) Ireland.
Irländer ['ɪrlɛndər] *m* (-s; -) Irishman.
Irländerin *f* (-; -nen) Irishwoman.
Ironie [iro'niː] *f* (-; -n) irony.
ironisch [i'roːnɪʃ] *adj* ironic.
ironisieren [ironi'ziːrən] *v/t* (h) *et. ~* treat s.th. with irony.
irrational ['ɪratsi̯onaːl] *adj* irrational.
irre ['ɪrə] **I** *adj* **1.** mad, insane, crazy: *~s Zeug reden* be raving. **2.** F *fig.* mind-blowing, crazy, mad: *~ (gut)* fantastic, super, wild; *ein ~r Typ* a super guy; *es war e-e ~e Hitze* it was awfully hot; *wie ~ work etc* like crazy. **II** *adv* **3.** F a) awfully (*big*, *hot*, *etc*), b) *work etc* like crazy: *~ viel(e)* an awful lot of.
'Irre¹ *m*, *f* (-n; -n) madman (madwoman), lunatic, F *fig.* nutcase: F *wie ein ~r work*, *drive*, *etc* like crazy.
'Irre² *f j-n in die ~ führen* → **irreführen**.
'irreal *adj* **1.** unreal. **2.** unrealistic.
'irreführen *v/t* (*sep*, -ge-, h) *fig.* mislead, *a.* deceive: *sich ~ lassen* be deceived (*von* by). **'irreführend** *adj* misleading.
'irregeleitet *adj fig.* misguided.
'irregulär *adj* irregular.
'irrelevant *adj* irrelevant.
irren ['ɪrən] **I** *sich ~* (h) **1.** (*in dat* about *s.o.*, in *s.th.*) be wrong, be mistaken: *ich habe mich im Datum geirrt* I got the date wrong; *er hat sich in der Tür geirrt* he went to the wrong door; *ich kann mich (auch) ~* (of course,) I may be wrong; *da irrst du dich aber (gewaltig)!* you're very much mistaken there!; *wenn ich mich nicht irre* if I'm not mistaken. **II** *v/i* **2.** (sn) *a. fig.* wander, err, stray. **3.** (h) be wrong, be mistaken: *Irren ist menschlich* we all make mistakes.
'Irrenanstalt *m* mental home.

'Irrenhaus *n* F *fig.* madhouse.
'irreparabel *adj* irreparable.
'Irrfahrt *f* odyssey. **'Irrgarten** *m* mace, labyrinth. **'Irrglaube** *m* **1.** heresy. **2.** erroneous belief.
'irrig(er)'weise (*adv*) *adj* wrong(ly).
irritieren [ɪri'tiːrən] *v/t* (h) irritate, *a.* annoy, *a.* confuse.
'Irrläufer *m* stray letter *etc*.
'Irrlehre *f* false doctrine, heresy.
'Irrlicht *n* (-[e]s, -er) will-o'-the-wisp.
'Irrsinn *m* (-[e]s; *no pl*) *a. fig.* madness.
irrsinnig ['ɪrzɪnɪç] → **irre**. **Irrsinnige** ['ɪrzɪnɪgə] *m*, *f* (-n; -n) → **Irre¹**.
'Irrtum *m* (-s; Ꞌer) a) mistake, error (*a.* ⚖️), b) misunderstanding: *im ~ sein* be mistaken, be wrong; *da muß ein ~ vorliegen!* there must be some mistake!; F *~! you're wrong there!*
'irrtümlich [ˈɪrtyːmlɪç] *adj* wrong(ly *adv*).
'irrtümlicher'weise *adv* by mistake.
Ischias ['ɪʃi̯as] *m*, *n*, ⚕ *f* (-; *no pl*) sciatica.
'Ischiasnerv *m* sciatic nerve.
Islam [ɪs'laːm; 'ɪslam] *m* (-s; *no pl*) Islam.
islamisch [ɪs'laːmɪʃ] *adj* Islamic.
Island ['iːslant] *n* (-s) Iceland. **Isländer** ['iːslɛndər] *m* (-s; -), **'Isländerin** *f* (-; -nen) Icelander. **'isländisch** [-dɪʃ] *adj* Icelandic.
Isobare [izo'baːrə] *f* (-; -) isobar.
Isolation [izola'tsi̯oːn] *f* (-; -en) **1.** isolation. **2.** ⚡, ⚙ insulation.
Iso'lierband *n* (-[e]s; Ꞌer) insulating tape.
isolieren [izo'liːrən] (h) **I** *v/t* **1.** isolate. **2.** ⚡, ⚙ insulate (*gegen* against). **II** *sich ~* isolate o.s., cut o.s. off.
Iso'lier|materi̱al *n* insulating material, insulant. **~schicht** *f* insulating layer. **~stati̱on** *f* ⚕ isolation ward.
Iso'lierung *f* (-; -en) **1.** isolation. **2.** ⚡, ⚙ insulation.
Isotop [izo'toːp] *n* (-s; -e) isotope.
Israel ['ɪsraɛl] *n* (-s) Israel. **Israeli** [ɪsra'eːli] *m* (-[s]; -[s]), *f* (-; -[s]) Israeli. **isra'elisch** [-lɪʃ] *adj* Israeli.
Israelit [ɪsrae'liːt] *m* (-en; -en), **Israe'litin** *f* (-; -nen) Israelite. **israe'litisch** *adj* Israelite.
'Ist-Bestand *m* ✝ a) actual amount , b) actual stock.
Italien [i'taːli̯ən] *n* (-s) Italy. **Italiener** [ita'li̯eːnər] *m* (-s; -), **Itali'enerin** *f* (-; -nen) Italian. **itali'enisch** *adj* Italian. **Itali'enisch** *n ling.* Italian.

J

J, j [jɔt] *n* (-; -) J, j.

ja [ja] *adv* **1.** yes, *parl.* aye, *Am.* yea, *at wedding:* I do: **~?** a) really?, b) right?, c) *teleph.* hello; **nun ~** well (yes); **~ doch!, aber ~!** yes, of course!, sure!; **~ sagen (zu** to) say yes, *fig. a.* agree; **ich glaube ~!** I think so! **2.** after all: **du kennst ihn ~** you know what he's like. **3. da bist du ~!** there you are!; **ich hab's dir ~ gesagt** didn't I tell you?; **das ist ~ schrecklich!** but that's just terrible!; **es regnet ~!** oh dear, it's raining! **4. sei ~ vorsichtig!** do be careful!; **bring es ~ mit!** make sure you bring it!; **sag's ihm ~ nicht!** don't tell him! **5. ~, weißt (or wußtest) du denn (das) nicht?** do you mean to say you didn't know? **6. ich würde es ~ gern tun, aber ...** I'd really like to do it, but ...

Ja *n* (-[s]; -[s]) yes, *parl.* aye, *Am.* yea: **mit ~ oder Nein antworten** answer yes or no.

Jacht [jaxt] *f* (-; -en) yacht.

'Jachtklub *m* yacht club.

Jacke ['jakə] *f* (-; -n) jacket, coat, *a.* cardigan: F **das ist ~ wie Hose** it's much of a muchness.

'Jackenkleid *n* two-piece dress.

Jacketkrone ['dʒɛkɪt-] *f* jacket crown.

Jackett [ʒa'kɛt] *n* (-s; -s) jacket, coat.

Jade ['jaːdə] *m* (-[s]; *no pl*) *min.* jade.

Jagd [jaːkt] *f* (-; -en) **1.** hunt(ing), shoot(ing): **auf (die) ~ gehen** go hunting. **2.** *fig.* (**nach**) chase (after), pursuit (of): **~ machen auf** (*acc*) chase (after), pursue; **wilde ~ nach** mad rush for.

'Jagd|beute *f* bag. **~bomber** *m* fighter bomber. **~flieger** *m* fighter pilot. **~flugzeug** *n* fighter (plane). **~hund** *m* **1.** hound. **2.** short-haired pointer. **~hütte** *f* (hunting) lodge. **~rennen** *n* steeplechase. **~re,vier** *n* hunting ground. **~schein** *m* hunting licen/ce (*Am.* -se). **~zeit** *f* hunting season.

jagen ['jaːgən] **I** *v/t* (h) **1.** hunt, shoot. **2.** *fig.* a) chase (after), hunt (for): **ein Ereignis jagte das andere** things happened really fast; F **damit kannst du mich ~!** I just hate that! **3.** F *j-m* (**sich**) **e-e Kugel durch den Kopf ~** blow s.o.'s (one's) brains out; **den Ball ins Netz ~** slam the ball home; **et. in die Luft ~** blow s.th. up. **II** *v/i* **4.** (h) go hunting, go shooting, hunt. **5.** (sn) *fig.* race. **6.** (h) **~ nach** *fig.* chase after, hunt for.

'Jagen *n* (-s) hunt(ing), shoot(ing).

Jäger ['jɛːgər] *m* (-s; -) **1.** huntsman, hunter. **2.** → **Jagdflieger, -flugzeug.**

Jaguar ['jaːgŭaːr] *m* (-s; -e) *zo.* jaguar.

jäh [jɛː] **I** *adj* **1.** sudden, abrupt: *fig.* **ein ~es Erwachen** a rude awakening. **2.** steep: **~er Abhang** precipice. **II** *adv* **3.** all of a sudden, abruptly. **4.** **~abfallend** precipitous.

Jahr [jaːr] *n* (-[e]s; -e) year: **ein halbes ~** half a year, six months; **das Kind ist zwei ~e (alt)** the child is two (years) old; **mit 20 ~en** at the age of twenty; **alle ~e** every year; **~ für ~** year after year; **im ~ 1989** in (the year of) 1989; **in diesem (im nächsten) ~** this (next) year; **heute vor einem ~** a year ago today; **von ~ zu ~** from year to year; **auf ~e hinaus** for years to come; **seit ~en (nicht)** (not) for years; **im Lauf der ~e** through (or over) the years; **in die ~e kommen** be getting on; **in den besten ~en** in the prime of life; → **jünger** 1.

jahr'aus *adv* **~, jahrein** year in, year out.

'Jahrbuch *n* yearbook, almanac.

'jahrelang I *adj* longstanding, lasting for years: **~e Erfahrung** years of experience. **II** *adv* for years.

jähren ['jɛːrən] **heute jährt sich ...** it's a year today since (*or* that) ...

'Jahres... annual (*balance sheet, report, ring, etc.*), yearly. **~abrechnung** *f*, **~abschluß** *m* † annual accounts. **~beginn** *m* (**zum ~** at the) beginning of the year. **~bestleistung** *f sports:* record of the year. **~einkommen** *n* yearly income. **~ende** *n* (**zum ~, am ~** at the) end of the year. **~gehalt** *n* (-[e]s; **~er**) annual salary. **~hälfte** *f* **erste (zweite) ~** first (second) half of the year. **~hauptversammlung** *f* annual general meeting. **~tag** *m* anniversary. **~zahl** *f* year. **~zeit** *f* season: **in dieser ~** at this time of year. **2zeitlich** *adj* seasonal.

'Jahrgang *m* **1.** age group, *ped.* year: **sie**

ist ~ 1900 she was born in 1900; **er ist mein ~** we were born in the same year; **die Jahrgänge 1970-80** the 1970-80 age group. **2.** *gastr.* vintage, year. **3.** volume *(of magazine etc)*.

Jahr'hundert *n* (-s; -e) century.

jahr'hunderte|alt *adj* centuries old. **~lang** *adj* lasting for centuries.

Jahr'hundert|feier *f* centenary, centennial. **~wende** *f* turn of the century.

...jährig [-jɛːrɪç] *in cpds.* ...-year-old.

jährlich ['jɛːrlɪç] **I** *adj* yearly, annual. **II** *adv* a) yearly, every year, once a year, b) *1000 marks* a year (*or* per annum).

'Jahrmarkt *m* (*auf dem* ~ at the) fair.

Jahr'tausend *n* (-s; -e) millennium.

Jahr'tausendfeier *f* millenary.

Jahr'zehnt *n* (-[e]s; -e) decade, ten years.

jahr'zehntelang I *adj* lasting for decades: **~e Forschungsarbeit** decades of research. **II** *adv* for decades.

'Jähzorn *m* (*im* ~ in a fit of) violent temper. **'jähzornig** *adj* irascible: **er ist ~ a.** he has a violent temper.

Jalousie [ʒaluˈziː] *f* (-; -n) (Venetian) blind(s).

Jammer ['jamər] *m* (-s; *no pl*) **1.** misery: F **es ist ein ~, daß** it's such a shame (*or* too bad) that. **2.** lamentation, wailing.

jämmerlich ['jɛmərlɪç] **I** *adj* **1.** miserable, wretched, pitiful, *fig. contp. a.* deplorable: **mir war ~ zumute** I felt (just) miserable. **2.** heart-rending, piteous. **II** *adv* **3.** miserably (*etc*): **~ weinen** cry piteously; **~ (schlecht)** sing *etc* terribly; **~ versagen** fail miserably.

jammern ['jamərn] *v/i* (h) moan, wail: **~ nach** cry for; **~ über** (*acc*) a) moan (about), b) complain (of).

'Jammern *n* (-s) moaning, wailing.

'jammerschade *adj* (**es ist**) ~, **daß ...** it's such a shame (*or* too bad) that ...

Januar ['janŭaːr] *m* (-[s]; -e) (*im* ~ in) January.

Japan ['jaːpan] *n* (-s) Japan. **Japaner** [jaˈpaːnər] *m* (-s; -), **Ja'panerin** *f* (-; -nen) Japanese. **ja'panisch** *adj*, **Ja'panisch** *n ling.* Japanese.

Jargon [ʒarˈgõː] *m* (-s; -s) jargon.

'Jasager *m* (-s; -) *contp.* yes-man.

Jasmin [jasˈmiːn] *m* (-s; -e) ❀ jasmin.

'Ja-Stimme *f* aye, *Am.* yea.

jäten ['jɛːtən] *v/t, v/i* (h) weed.

Jauche ['jaʊxə] *f* (-; -n) liquid manure.

'Jauchegrube *f* cesspool.

jauchzen ['jaʊxtsən] *v/i* (h) shout for joy.

jaulen ['jaʊlən] *v/i* (h) *a. fig.* howl.

ja'wohl *adv* a) yes, ✕ yes, Sir, b) that's right.

Jazz [dʒɛs] *m* (-; *no pl*) jazz.

'Jazzband *f*, **'Jazzka,pelle** *f* jazz band.

'Jazzmu,sik *f* jazz (music).

'Jazzsänger(in *f*) *m* jazz singer.

je [jeː] **I** *adv* **1.** ever: **ohne ihn ~ gesehen zu haben** without ever having seen him. **2.** → **eh 2, jeher. 3. sie kosten ~ e-n Dollar** they cost a dollar each; **für ~ 10 Personen** for every ten persons; **es gibt sie in Schachteln mit ~ 10 Stück** they come in boxes of ten. **4. ~ nach** according to; **~ nachdem** it (all) depends (→ 6). **II** *conj* **5. ~ eher, desto besser** the sooner the better; **~ länger, ~ lieber** the longer the better. **6. ~ nachdem** according to *what* he says, depending on *how* you do it (→ 4).

Jeansanzug ['dʒiːns-] *m* denim suit.

'Jeansjacke *f* denim jacket.

jede ['jeːdə], **'jeder**, **'jedes** *indef pron* **1.** a) each, b) any, c) either, d) every: **ich hörte ~s (einzelne) Wort** I heard every (single) word; **~s zweite Auto** every other car; **ohne ~n Zweifel** without any doubt; **(zu) ~r Zeit** any time; **bei ~m Wetter** in any weather. **2.** each (*or* every) one, everyone: **~(r) von ihnen** each (*or* all) of them.

'jeden'falls *adv* **1.** in any case, at any rate, anyway. **2.** be that as it may. **3.** at least.

'jedermann *indef pron* everyone, everybody: **das ist nicht ~s Sache** it's not everyone's cup of tea.

'jeder'zeit *adv* any time, always.

'jedes'mal *adv* a) every time, b) always.

je'doch *adv* however, still.

je'her *adv* **von ~** always.

jein [jaɪn] *adv* F yes and no.

jemals ['jeːmaːls] *adv* ever.

jemand ['jeːmant] *indef pron* a) somebody, someone, b) anybody, anyone: **es kommt ~** somebody's coming; **ist ~ hier?** is anybody here?; **~ anders** someone (*or* anyone) else; **sonst noch ~?** anyone else?

jene ['jeːnə], **'jener**, **'jenes** *dem pron* **1.** that, *pl* those: **seit ~m Tag** from that day on. **2.** that one, *pl* those.

jenseitig ['je:nzaıtıç] *adj* on the other side: *das ~e Ufer* the opposite bank.

jenseits ['je:nzaıts] **I** *prep* (gen) on the other side of, beyond, across. **II** *adv* on the other side: *~ von* beyond. **'Jenseits** *n* (-; *no pl*) *the* hereafter: F *j-n ins ~ befördern* send s.o. to kingdom come.

Jesus ['je:zʊs] *m* (Jesu; *no pl*) Jesus: *~ Christus* Jesus Christ.

'Jesuskind *n the* infant Jesus.

Jet [dʒɛt] *m* (-[s]; -s) ✈ jet. **'Jet-set** *m* (-s; -s) jet set. **'jetten** *v/i* (sn) F jet.

jetzig ['jɛtsıç] *adj* a) present(-day), current, b) existing.

jetzt [jɛtst] *adv* now, a. nowadays: *erst ~* only now; *noch ~* even now; *bis ~* so far, *negative: a.* (as) yet. **Jetzt** *n* (-; *no pl*) *the* present (time).

jeweilig ['je:vaılıç] **I** *adj* a) respective, b) prevailing: *der ~e Präsident* the president then in office; *der ~en Mode entsprechend* according to the fashion (at the time). **II** *adv* → **jeweils** 4.

jeweils ['je:vaıls] *adv* **1.** *~ zwei* two at a time. **2.** always: *sie kommt ~ am Montag* she comes every Monday; *er trainiert ~ zwei Stunden* he does two hours of training a time. **3.** each: *mit ~ 20 Fragen* exercises etc with 20 questions each. **4.** in each case.

jiddisch ['jıdıʃ] *adj* Yiddish. **'Jiddisch** *n ling.* Yiddish.

Job [dʒɔp] *m* (-s; -s) F job. **jobben** ['dʒɔbən] *v/i* (h) F job.

Joch [jɔx] *n* (-[e]s; -e) yoke. **'Jochbein** *n anat.* cheekbone.

Jockei, Jockey ['dʒɔke] *m* (-s; -s) jockey.

Jod [jo:t] *n* (-[e]s; *no pl*) ⚗ iodine. **jodeln** ['jo:dəln] *v/t, v/i* (h) yodel. **'jodhaltig** *adj* containing iodine.

jodieren [jo'di:rən] *v/t* (h) **1.** ⚗ iodinate. **2.** ✻, *phot.* iodize. **'Jodsalbe** *f* iodine ointment. **'Jodsalz** *n* iodized salt. **'Jodta_blette** *f* iodine tablet. **'Jodtink_tur** *f* tincture of iodine.

Joga → **Yoga.**

joggen ['dʒɔgən] *v/i* (h) jog, go jogging. **Jogger** ['dʒɔgər] *m* (-s; -), **'Joggerin** *f* (-; -nen) jogger. **Jogging** ['dʒɔgıŋ] *n* (-s) jogging.

Joghurt ['jo:gʊrt] *m, n* (-[s]; *no pl*) yog(h)urt.

Johannisbeere [jo'hanıs-] *f rote ~* redcurrant; *schwarze ~* blackcurrant.

johlen ['jo:lən] *v/i* (h) bawl, yell.

Jolle ['jɔlə] *f* (-; -n) ⛵ dinghy.

Jongleur [ʒõˈglø:r] *m* (-s; -e) juggler. **jonglieren** [ʒõˈgli:rən] *v/t, v/i* (h) *a. fig.* juggle (*mit* [with] *s.th.*).

Jordanien [jɔrˈda:niən] *n* (-s) Jordan. **Jor'danier** [-niər] *m* (-s; -), **Jor'danierin** *f* (-; -nen), **jor'danisch** *adj* Jordanian.

Jota ['jo:ta] *n* (-[s]; -s) iota.

Joule [dʒu:l] *n* (-[s]; -) *phys.* joule.

Journalismus [ʒʊrnaˈlısmʊs] *m* (-; *no pl*) journalism. **Journalist** [ʒʊrnaˈlıst] *m* (-en; -en), **Journa'listin** *f* (-; -nen) journalist. **journalistisch** [ʒʊrnaˈlıstıʃ] *adj* journalistic.

jovial [joˈviaːl] *adj* affable.

Jubel ['ju:bəl] *m* (-s; *no pl*) jubilation, cheers. **'Jubeljahr** *n eccl.* jubilee: F *alle ~e einmal* once in a blue moon. **jubeln** ['ju:bəln] *v/i* (h) cheer: (*vor Freude*) *~* shout for joy, rejoice.

Jubilar [jubiˈla:r] *m* (-s; -e), **Jubi'larin** *f* (-; -nen) person celebrating his (her) jubilee. **Jubiläum** [jubiˈlɛ:ʊm] *n* (-s; -läen) jubilee, anniversary. **Jubi'läumsausgabe** *f* jubilee edition.

jucken ['jʊkən] *v/t, v/i, v/impers* (h) itch: *mich juckt's* I'm itching; *sich ~* scratch o.s.; *es juckt mich am Arm, mein Arm juckt* my arm's itchy; *der Pullover juckt* the pullover's scratchy; F *fig.* *es juckt mich zu inf* I'm itching to *inf*; *das juckt mich nicht!* what do I care. **'Jucken** *n* (-s) itch, itching. **'Juckreiz** *m* itch, itching.

Jude ['ju:də] *m* (-n; -n) Jew. **'Judenhaß** *m* anti-Semitism. **'Judentum** *n* (-s; *no pl*) **1.** Judaism. **2.** *the* Jews, Jewry. **3.** Jewishness. **'Judenverfolgung** *f* persecution of (the) Jews. **Jüdin** ['jy:dın] *f* (-; -nen) Jewess. **'jüdisch** *adj* Jewish.

Judo ['ju:do] *n* (-[s]; *no pl*) judo. **Judoka** [ju'do:ka] *m* (-s; -s) judoka.

Jugend ['ju:gənt] *f* (-; *no pl*) **1.** youth: *von ~ an* from childhood, from a child; *in m-r ~* when I was young. **2.** youth, youthfulness. **3.** youth, young people: *die ~ von heute* the young people of today; *die deutsche ~* the young Germans (of today). **4.** → **Jugendklasse, Jugendmannschaft.**

'Jugend|amt *n* youth welfare department. **~arbeitslosigkeit** *f* youth unemployment. **~ar,rest** m ⚖ short-term detention for young offenders. **~buch** n book for young people. **2frei** adj film: U-certificate, Am. G-rated; **nicht ~** for adults only. **~freund(in** f) m friend from one's youth. **2gefährdend** adj harmful to young persons. **~gericht** n juvenile court. **~herberge** f youth hostel. **~klasse** f sports: youth class. **~kriminali,tät** f juvenile delinquency. **~lager** n youth camp.

'**jugendlich** adj youthful (a. clothes, look), young, ⚖ juvenile.

'**Jugendliche** m, f (-n; -n) young person, m a. youth, ⚖ a. juvenile.

'**Jugendlichkeit** f (-; no pl) youthfulness.

'**Jugend|liebe** f a) puppy love, b) old flame. **~mannschaft** f sports: youth team. **~meister(in** f) m sports: youth champion. **~richter(in** f) m judge of a juvenile court. **~schutz** m legal protection for children and young persons. **~stil** m (-s; no pl) Jugendstil, art nouveau. **~strafanstalt** f remand home. **~zeit** f (-; no pl) youth.

Jugoslawe [jugo'sla:və] m (-n; -n) Yugoslav. **Jugoslawien** [jugo'sla:vĭən] n (-s) Yugoslavia. **Jugo'slawin** f (-; -nen), **jugo'slawisch** adj Yugoslav.

Juli ['ju:li] m (-[s]; -s) (im ~ in) July.

jung [jʊŋ] adj a) young, b) youthful: **ziemlich ~** youngish; **~es Unternehmen** new company; **~er Wein** new wine; **von ~ auf** from childhood; **~ und alt** young and old; **~ heiraten (sterben)** marry (die) young; → **jünger, jüngst** 1, **Gemüse, Hund.**

'**Junge¹** m (-n; -n) boy: **dummer ~** silly boy; F **schwerer ~** (criminal) heavy; **~, ~!** boy, oh boy!

'**Junge²** n (-n; -n) zo. young (one), a. puppy, a. kitten, a. cub, of elephant, seal etc: calf: **die ~n** the young; **~ werfen (or bekommen)** → **jungen** ['jʊŋən] v/i (h) zo. have young (or puppies or kittens).

'**jungenhaft** adj boyish.

'**jünger** ['jʏŋər] adj **1.** younger: **sie sieht ~ aus als sie ist** she doesn't look her age; **das macht sie um Jahre ~** that takes years off her age. **2.** more recent, later: **ein Foto ~en Datums** a more recent photograph.

'**Jünger** m (-s; -) disciple, fig. a. follower.

Jungfer ['jʊŋfər] f (-; -n) alte ~ old maid.

'**Jungfern|fahrt** f maiden voyage. **~flug** m maiden flight. **~häutchen** n anat. hymen. **~rede** f maiden speech.

'**Jungfrau** f **1.** virgin: **die Heilige ~, die ~ Maria** the Holy Virgin, the Virgin Mary. **2.** astr. **(er ist ~** he is [a]) Virgo.

jungfräulich ['jʊŋfrɔʏlɪç] adj virginal, fig. virgin.

'**Jungfräulichkeit** f (-; no pl) virginity.

'**Junggeselle** m (-n; -n) bachelor.

'**Junggesellin** f (-; -nen) bachelor girl.

Jüngling ['jʏŋlɪŋ] m (-s; -e) youth.

jüngst [jʏŋst] adj **1.** youngest. **2.** latest (events etc): **der Jüngste Tag** the Day of Judg(e)ment; **der ~en Vergangenheit** of the recent past.

'**Jüngste** m, f, n (-n; -n) the youngest: **unser ~r, unsere ~** our youngest (child); **sie ist auch nicht mehr die ~** she is no spring chicken any more.

'**Jungsteinzeit** f (-; no pl) Neolithic age.

'**jungverheiratet** adj newly-wed.

'**Jungvieh** n young stock.

Juni ['ju:ni] m (-[s]; -s) (im ~ in) June.

junior ['ju:nĭor] adj **1. Herr X ~** (abbr. **jun., jr.**) Mr X, Junior (abbr. jr.).

'**Junior** m (-s; -en [ju'nĭo:rən]) **1.** F and sports: junior. **2.** ♣ a) son of the owner, b) a. '**Juniorchef** m junior partner.

Juni'oren... sports: junior (team etc).

Junktim ['jʊŋktɪm] n (-s; -s) pol. package deal.

Junta ['xʊnta] f (-; -ten) pol. junta.

Jura¹ ['ju:ra] m (-; no pl) geol. Jurassic (period).

Jura²: **~ studieren** study (Br. a. read) law. '**Jurastu,dent(in** f) m law student. '**Jurastudium** n law studies.

Jurist [ju'rɪst] m (-en; -en) **1.** lawyer. **2.** law student. **Ju'ristensprache** f legalese. **Ju'ristin** f (-; -nen) → **Jurist.** **ju'ristisch** adj legal: **~e Fakultät** faculty of law, Am. a. law school; **~e Person** legal entity, juristic person.

Jury [ʒy'ri:] f (-; -s) **1.** a) jury, (panel of) judges, b) selection committee. **2.** ⚖ jury.

ju'stierbar adj adjustable.

justieren [jʊs'ti:rən] v/t (h) adjust.

Ju'stierung f (-; -en) adjustment.

Justitiar [jʊsti'tsĭa:r] m (-s; -e), **Justiti'arin** f (-; -nen) legal adviser.

Justiz [jʊs'ti:ts] f (-; no pl) justice, the

law. **~beamte** *m*, **~beamtin** *f* judicial officer. **~behörde** *f* judicial authority. **~gewalt** *f* judiciary (power). **~irrtum** *m* judicial error, miscarriage of justice. **~mi̦nister** *m* minister of justice, *Br.* Lord Chancellor, *Am.* Attorney General. **~mini̦sterium** *n* ministry of justice, *Am.* Department of Justice. **~mord** *m* judicial murder. **~verwal-**

tung *f* a) administration of justice, b) legal administrative body.
Jute ['ju:tə] *f* (-; *no pl*) jute.
Juwel [ju've:l] *n* (-s; -en) *a. fig.* jewel: **~en** jewel(le)ry, precious stones.
Juwelier [juvə'li:r] *m* (-s; -e) jewel(l)er.
Juwe'liergeschäft *n* jewel(l)er's shop.
Jux [jʊks] *m* (-es; -e) F (practical) joke.

K

K, k [ka:] *n* (-; -) K, k.
Kabarett [kaba'rɛt] *n* (-s; -s, -e) cabaret (show), (satirical) revue.
Kabarettist [kabarɛ'tɪst] *m* (-en; -en), **Kabaret'tistin** *f* (-; -nen) cabaret artist.
kabbelig ['kabəlıç] *adj* choppy (*sea*).
Kabel ['ka:bəl] *n* (-s; -) cable. '**Kabelfernsehen** *n* cable television (*or* TV).
Kabeljau ['ka:bəljaʊ] *m* (-s; -e, -s) cod(fish).
Kabine [ka'bi:nə] *f* (-; -n) **1.** ✈, ⚓ cabin. **2.** a) cage (*of lift*), b) cable car. **3.** cubicle, *sports:* a. locker room.
Kabinett [kabi'nɛt] *n* (-s; -e) *pol.* cabinet. **Kabi'netts|beschluß** *m* decision of the cabinet. **~bildung** *f* formation of a (*or* the) cabinet. **~krise** *f* cabinet crisis. **~liste** *f* list of cabinet members. **~sitzung** *f* cabinet meeting. **~umbildung** *f* cabinet reshuffle.
Kabrio ['ka:brio] *n* (-s; -s), **Kabriolett** [ka:brio'lɛt] *n* (-s; -s) *mot.* convertible.
Kachel ['kaxəl] *f* (-; -n) tile. '**kacheln** *v/t* (h) tile. '**Kachelofen** *m* tiled stove.
Kacke ['kakə] *f* (-; *no pl*), '**kacken** *v/t, v/i* (h) V crap, shit. '**Kacker** *m* (-s; -) V shit.
Kadaver [ka'da:vər] *m* (-s; -) carcass. **~gehorsam** *m contp.* blind obedience.
Kadenz [ka'dɛnts] *f* (-; -en) ♪ cadence, cadenza.
Kader ['ka:dər] *m* (-s; -) ✗, *pol.* cadre, *sports:* a. pool.
Kadett [ka'dɛt] *m* (-en; -en) ⚓, ✗ cadet.
Kadi ['ka:di] *m* (-s; -s) F (**j-n vor den ~ schleppen** haul s.o. before the) judge.
Kadmium *n* (-s; *no pl*) 🜛 cadmium.

Käfer ['kɛ:fər] *m* (-s; -) **1.** *zo.* beetle (*a. mot.* F *VW*). **2.** F *fig.* chick, girlie.
Kaff [kaf] (-s; -s, -e) *n* F *contp.* dump, awful hole.
Kaffee ['kafe:, ka'fe:] *m* (-s; -s) coffee: **~ kochen** (*or machen*) make coffee; **zwei ~, bitte!** two coffees, please!; **~ mit Milch** white coffee; F *fig.* **das ist doch kalter ~!** that's old hat!
'**Kaffee|auto̦mat** *m* coffee machine. **~bohne** *f* coffee (bean). **~haus** *n* café, coffee house. **~kanne** *f* coffee pot. **~klatsch** *m* F coffee (*or* hen) party, *Am.* coffee klatsch. **~löffel** *m* coffee spoon. **~ma̦schine** *f* coffeemaker, percolator, coffee urn. **~mühle** *f* coffee grinder. **~pause** *f* coffee break. **~satz** *m* coffee grounds. **~ser̦vice** *n* coffee set. **~strauch** *m* coffee shrub. **~tasse** *f* coffee cup. **~weißer** *m* coffee whitener (*Am.* creamer).
Käfig ['kɛ:fıç] *m* (-s; -e) cage.
kahl [ka:l] *adj* **1.** (**~ werden** go *or* grow) bald. **2.** *fig.* bare, a. leafless (*tree*), a. barren, bleak (*region etc*).
'**kahlgeschoren** *adj* shaven.
'**Kahlheit** *f* (-; *no pl*) **1.** baldness. **2.** *fig.* bareness (*etc*, → **kahl** 2).
'**Kahlkopf** *m* F baldhead(ed person).
'**kahlköpfig** [-kœpfıç] *adj* bald(headed).
'**Kahlschlag** *m* **1.** a) deforestation, b) clearing. **2.** *fig.* demolition. **~sa̦nierung** *f* wholesale redevelopment.
Kahn [ka:n] *m* (-[e]s; ⸚e) **1.** (rowing *or* fishing) boat: **~ fahren** go boating. **2.** barge. **3.** F tub. '**Kahnfahrt** *f* boat trip.

Kai [kaɪ] *m* (-s; -s) quay, wharf.
'Kaimauer *f* quay wall.
'Kaiser ['kaɪzər] *m* (-s; -) emperor.
'Kaiserin *f* (-; -nen) empress.
'Kaiserkrone *f* imperial crown.
'kaiserlich *adj* imperial.
'Kaiserreich *n* empire.
'Kaiserschnitt *m* ✻ C(a)esarean section.
Kajak ['ka:jak] *m*(-s; -s) *a. sports:* kayak.
Ka'jütboot *n* cabin boat.
Kajüte [ka'jy:tə] *f* (-; -n) cabin.
Kakadu ['kakadu] *m* (-s; -s) cockatoo.
Kakao [ka'kaʊ, ka'ka:o] *m*(-s; -s) cocoa: F *fig.* **durch den ~ ziehen** make fun of, roast. **Ka'kaobaum** *m* cacao (tree).
Kaktee [kak'te:] *f* (-; -n), **Kaktus** ['kaktʊs] *m* (-; -teen) ⚘ cactus.
Kalauer ['ka:laʊər] *m* (-s; -) dreadful pun, corny joke.
Kalb [kalp] *n* (-[e]s; ⁻er) calf. **kalben** ['kalbən] *v/i* (h) calve. **'Kalbfell** *n* calfskin. **'Kalbfleisch** *n* veal.
'Kalbs|braten *m* roast veal. **~haxe** *f* knuckle of veal. **~keule** *f* leg of veal. **~kopf** *m* calf's head. **~leder** *n* calf(-skin). **~schnitzel** *n* escalope of veal.
Kaleidoskop [kalaɪdo'sko:p] *n* (-s; -e) *a. fig.* kaleidoscope.
Kalender [ka'lɛndər] *m* (-s; -) calendar. **Ka'lenderjahr** *n* calendar year.
Kali ['ka:li] *n* (-s; -s) ⚘ potash.
Kaliber [ka'li:bər] *n* (-s; -) calib/re (*Am.* -er), F *fig. a.* sort, type.
Kalium ['ka:liʊm] *n* (-s; *no pl*) ⚘ potassium.
Kalk [kalk] *m* (-[e]s; -e) **1.** ⚘ a) lime, b) quicklime. **2.** ✻ calcium. **3.** *min.* limestone. **4.** → **~dünger** *m* lime fertilizer.
'kalken *v/t* (h) **1.** whitewash. **2.** ✓ lime.
'kalkig *adj* limy.
'Kalkmangel *m* (-s; *no pl*) ✻ calcium deficiency. **'Kalkstein** *m* limestone.
Kalkül [kal'ky:l] *n* (-s; -e) calculation: *et. ins ~ ziehen* take s.th. into consideration.
Kalkulation [kalkula'tsïo:n] *f* (-; -en) *a. fig.* calculation.
kalkulieren [kalku'li:rən] *v/t, v/i* (h) *a. fig.* calculate: *falsch ~* miscalculate.
Kalorie [kalo'ri:] *f* (-; -n) calorie.
kalo'rienarm *adj* low-calorie: **~ sein** be low in calories. **Kalo'rienbedarf** *m* calorie requirement. **Kalo'riengehalt** *m* calorie content. **kalo'rienreich** *adj*

high-calorie: **~ sein** be rich in calories.
kalt [kalt] **I** *adj* cold, *fig. a.* frigid: *mir ist ~* I'm cold; *es* (*mir*) *wird ~* it's (I'm) getting cold; **~er Krieg** Cold War; *gastr.* **~e Platte** cold meats; F *j-m die ~e Schulter zeigen* give s.o. the cold shoulder. **II** *adv* coldly: *et. ~ stellen* put s.th. to cool; **~ essen** have a cold meal; *es überlief mich ~* a cold shiver ran down my spine.
'kaltbleiben *v/i* (*irr, sep,* -ge-, sn, → **bleiben**) F *fig.* keep cool, keep one's head.
'Kaltblüter [-bly:tər] *m* (-s; -) cold--blooded animal. **'kaltblütig** [-bly:tɪç] **I** *adj* cold-blooded, *fig. a.* cool. **II** *adv* a) coolly, b) *kill etc* in cold blood. **'Kaltblütigkeit** *f* (-; *no pl*) a) coolness, sangfroid, b) cold-bloodedness.
Kälte ['kɛltə] *f* (-; *no pl*) cold, *a. fig.* coldness, frigidity: *es sind 10 Grad ~* the temperature is ten degrees below zero; *bei dieser ~* in this cold.
'kältebeständig *adj* cold-resistant.
'Kälte|einbruch *m* (-[e]s) cold spell. **~grad** *m* degree of frost. **~peri.ode** *f* cold spell. **~pol** *m* cold pole. **~welle** *f* cold wave.
'kaltlächelnd *adv* F (as) cool as you please, without turning a hair.
'kaltlassen *v/t* (*irr, sep,* -ge-, h, → **lassen**) F *das läßt mich kalt* that leaves me cold.
'Kaltluft *f* (-; *no pl*) cold air: *polare ~* polar air.
'kaltmachen *v/t* (*sep,* -ge-, h) F *j-n ~* bump s.o. off, do s.o. in.
'Kaltmiete *f* rent exclusive of heating charges.
'kaltschnäuzig [-ʃnɔʏtsɪç] *adj* F cool.
'Kaltstart *m mot.* cold start.
'kaltstellen *v/t* (*sep,* -ge-, h) F neutralize.
Kalzium ['kaltsïʊm] *n* (-s; *no pl*) calcium.
kam [ka:m] *pret of* **kommen**.
Kamel [ka'me:l] *n* (-[e]s; -e) **1.** *zo.* camel. **2.** F idiot, blockhead.
Ka'melhaar... camel-hair...
Kamelie [ka'me:liə] *f* (-; -n) ⚘ camellia.
Kamera ['kaməra] *f* (-; -s) camera.
Kamerad [kamə'ra:t] *m* (-en; -en) comrade, companion, fellow, mate, F pal, buddy. **Kame'radschaft** *f* (-; *no pl*) comradeship, fellowship. **kame'radschaftlich** *adj and adv* comradely.
'Kameraführung *f film:* camerawork.
'Kameramann *m* cameraman.

'**Kameratasche** f camera case.
Kamille [ka'mɪlə] f (-; -n) camomile.
Kamin [ka'miːn] m (-s; -e) 1. chimney (a. mount.). 2. (offener) ~ fireside, fireplace; am ~ by the fireside.
Kamm [kam] m (-[e]s; ⸚e) 1. comb: fig. alle über einen ~ scheren lump them all together. 2. zo. comb, crest. 3. crest (of wave). 4. (mountain) ridge.
kämmen ['kɛmən] (h) I v/t comb (a. ⊙): j-n ~, j-m die Haare ~ comb s.o.'s hair; sich die Haare ~ → II sich ~ comb (or do) one's hair.
Kammer ['kamər] f (-; -n) 1. chamber (a. anat., ⊙), small room, closet. 2. parl. chamber, house. 3. association.
'**Kammer|diener** m valet. **~mu‚sik** f chamber music. **~or‚chester** n chamber orchestra. **~ton** m ♪ concert pitch.
'**Kammgarn** n, '**Kammgarn...** worsted.
Kampagne [kam'panjə] f (-; -n) campaign.
Kampf [kampf] m (-[e]s; ⸚e) 1. a) fig. fight, battle, struggle (gegen against, um for), b) conflict, controversy: den ~ ansagen declare war (dat on); j-m den ~ ansagen challenge s.o.; ~ dem Hunger! war on hunger!; sich zum ~ stellen give battle; innere Kämpfe inner conflicts; → Dasein. 2. ✕ combat, fight. 3. sports: contest, fight, bout, match. **~abstimmung** f 1. parl. crucial vote. 2. strike ballot. **~ansage** f challenge (an acc to). **2bereit** adj fig. ready for battle (sports: to fight).
kämpfen ['kɛmpfən] (h) I v/i (für, um for) a. fig. fight, battle, struggle: mit Schwierigkeiten zu ~ haben have (to struggle against) difficulties; mit j-m sports: fight (with) s.o.; ich habe lange mit mir gekämpft I had a long battle with myself; sie kämpfte mit den Tränen she was fighting back her tears. II v/t fight. III sich ~ struggle (or fight one's way) (durch through, nach oben a. fig. up). '**kämpfend** adj fighting: **~e Truppen** combatant troops.
Kampfer ['kampfər] m (-s; no pl) 🜍 camphor.
Kämpfer ['kɛmpfər] m (-s; -) fighter, ✕ a. combatant. '**kämpferisch** adj fighting, fig. a. aggressive.
Kampf|flugzeug n tactical (or combat) aircraft. **~geist** m (-[e]s; no pl) fighting

spirit: ~ zeigen show fight. **~gericht** n sports: the judges. **~handlung** f ✕ fighting, action. **~hubschrauber** m (helicopter) gunship.
'**kampflos** adj and adv without a fight: ~ gewinnen sports: win by default.
'**kampflustig** adj belligerent.
'**Kampf|maßnahme** f militant action. **~platz** m battlefield, sports: arena (a. fig.). **~richter(in** f) m judge, tennis etc: umpire. **~schwimmer** m ✕ frogman. **~sport** m combative sports, (carate etc) martial arts. **~stoff** m ✕ agent, chemical etc weapon. **~truppe** f ✕ combat troops. **2unfähig** adj disabled, out of action: j-n ~ machen put s.o. out of action. **~verband** m ✕ combat unit.
kampieren [kam'piːrən] v/i (h) camp.
Kanada ['kanada] n (-s) Canada.
Kanadier¹ [ka'naːdiər] m (-s; -) Canadian (canoe).
Ka'nadier² m (-s; -), **Ka'nadierin** f (-; -nen), **ka'nadisch** adj Canadian.
Kanal [ka'naːl] m (-s; ⸚e) 1. a) channel, b) canal, duct, c) conduit: fig. dunkle Kanäle secret channels; F den ~ voll haben a) be sloshed, b) be fed up to here. 2. anat. duct. 3. radio, TV: channel.
Kanalisation [kanaliza'tsi̯oːn] f (-; -en) 1. canalization. 2. drains (in house), sewage system (of town). **kanalisieren** [kanali'ziːrən] v/t (h) 1. canalize. 2. provide with sewers. 3. fig. channel.
Ka'nalküste f the Channel coast.
Ka'nalwähler m radio, TV tuner.
Kanarienvogel [ka'naːriən-] m canary.
kanarisch [ka'naːrɪʃ] adj die 2en Inseln the Canaries, the Canary Islands.
Kandare [kan'daːrə] f (-; -n) curb (bit): j-n an die ~ nehmen take s.o. in hand.
Kandelaber [kandə'laːbər] m (-s; -) candelabrum.
Kandidat [kandi'daːt] m (-en; -en), **Kandi'datin** f (-; -nen) a. fig. candidate.
Kandi'datenliste f list of candidates pol. Am. a. ticket. **Kandidatur** [kandi-da'tuːr] f (-; -en) candidacy.
kandidieren [kandi'diːrən] v/i (h) be a candidate, stand, run: für das Amt de. Präsidenten ~ run for president.
kandiert [kan'diːrt] adj candied (fruit).
Kandiszucker ['kandɪs-] m candy.
Känguruh ['kɛŋguru] n (-s; -s) kangaroo.

Kaninchen [ka'ni:nçən] n (-s; -) rabbit.
Ka'ninchenstall m rabbit hutch.
Kanister [ka'nıstər] m (-s; -) can(ister).
Kännchen ['kɛnçən] n (-s; -) jug: *ein ~ Kaffee gastr.* a pot of coffee.
Kanne ['kanə] f (-; -n) a) can, b) pot.
Kannibale [kani'ba:lə] m (-n; -n) cannibal. **kanni'balisch** adj cannibal.
kannte ['kantə] pret of *kennen.*
Kanon ['ka:nɔn] m (-s; -s) canon.
Kanone [ka'no:nə] f (-; -n) **1.** ⚔ cannon, gun: *unter aller ~* just lousy. **2.** F gun, shooter. **3.** F (*in dat* at) wizard, ace.
Kanonier [kano'ni:r] m (-s; -e) gunner.
kanonisch [ka'no:nɪʃ] adj eccl. canonical: *~es Recht* canon law.
Kantate [kan'ta:tə] f (-; -n) ♪ cantata.
Kante ['kantə] f (-; -n) **1.** edge, a. border: F *et. auf die hohe ~ legen* save some money; *et. auf der hohen ~ haben* have saved some money. **2.** selvage.
kanten ['kantən] v/t (h) **1.** cant, tilt, carve (*ski*). **2.** ⊙ edge.
'Kanten m (-s; -) crust (*of bread*).
Kanter ['kantər] m (-s; -) canter.
kantig ['kantɪç] adj squared, angular.
Kantine [kan'ti:nə] f (-; -n) canteen.
Kanton [kan'to:n] m (-s; -e) canton.
Kanu ['ka:nu, ka'nu:] n (-s; -s) canoe.
Kanüle [ka'ny:lə] f (-; -n) 🎗 cannula, (drain) tube.
Kanute [ka'nu:tə] m (-n; -n) canoeist.
Kanzel ['kantsəl] f (-; -n) **1.** (*auf der ~* in the) pulpit. **2.** ✈ cockpit. **3.** ⚔ turret.
Kanzlei [kants'lai] f (-; -en) office.
Kanzler ['kantslər] m (-s; -) **1.** pol. chancellor. **2.** univ. vice-chancellor. *~amt* n **1.** chancellor's office. **2.** chancellorship. *~kandi,dat* m candidate for the chancellorship.
Kap [kap] n (-s; -s) geogr. cape.
Kapazität [kapatsi'tɛ:t] f (-; -en) **1.** no pl capacity (a. fig.), ⚡ capacitance. **2.** fig. (leading) authority (*auf dem Gebiet gen* on the subject of).
Kapelle [ka'pɛlə] f (-; -n) **1.** eccl. chapel. **2.** ♪ band. **Ka'pellmeister** m a) director of music, b) conductor, c) bandmaster (a. ⚔), bandleader.
Kaper ['ka:pər] f (-; -n) 🌿 caper.
kapern ['ka:pərn] v/t (h) ⚓ capture, seize, F fig. nab.
kapieren [ka'pi:rən] (h) **I** v/t get. **II** v/i

get it, catch on to: *kapiert?* (have you) got it?
Kapillargefäß [kapɪ'la:r-] n anat. capillary (vessel).
kapital [kapi'ta:l] adj F capital (*error*).
Kapi'tal n (-s; -e, -ien) a) capital, b) capital stock: *~ und Zinsen* principal and interest; *~ schlagen aus* capitalize on.
Kapi'tal|abwanderung f capital outflow. *~anlage* f investment. *~anlagegesellschaft* f investment trust. *~anleger(in* f) m investor. *~bildung* f accumulation of capital. *~einkommen* n investment income. *~erhöhung* f increase of capital. *~ertragssteuer* f capital yields tax. *~flucht* f flight of capital. *~geber(in* f) m financier. *~gesellschaft* f joint-stock company, Am. (stock) corporation.
kapitalisieren [kapitali'zi:rən] v/t (h) capitalize. **Kapitalismus** ['-lɪsmʊs] m (-; no pl) capitalism. **Kapitalist** ['-lɪst] m (-en; -en) capitalist. **kapita'listisch** adj capitalist(ic).
kapi'talkräftig adj (financially) powerful, potent.
Kapi'talmarkt m capital market.
Kapi'talverbrechen n capital crime.
Kapitän [kapi'tɛ:n] m (-s; -e) captain.
Kapi'tänspa,tent n master's certificate.
Kapitel [ka'pɪtəl] n (-s; -) chapter (a. eccl.): fig. *ein ~ für sich* another story.
Kapitell [kapi'tɛl] n (-s; -e) △ capital.
Kapitulation [kapitula'tsio:n] f (-; -en) a. fig. capitulation, surrender.
kapitulieren [kapitu'li:rən] v/i (h) (*vor dat* to) a. fig. capitulate, surrender.
Kaplan [ka'pla:n] m (-s; Kapläne) chaplain.
Kappe ['kapə] f (-; -n) **1.** cap: F *et. auf s-e ~ nehmen* take the responsibility for s.th. **2.** ⊙ top, cap. **3.** (toe) cap.
kappen ['kapən] v/t (h) **1.** cut (*rope etc*). **2.** lop (*tree etc*).
Käppi ['kɛpi] n (-s; -s) cap, ⚔ a. kepi.
Kapriole [kapri'o:lə] f (-; -n) caper.
kaprizieren [kapri'tsi:rən] *sich ~* (h) *auf* (*acc*) set one's heart on, insist on.
kapriziös [kapri'tsiø:s] adj capricious.
Kapsel ['kapsəl] f (-; -n) **1.** case, container. **2.** anat., 🌿, pharm. etc: capsule.
kaputt [ka'pʊt] adj F *~ sein* **1.** be broken, be bust, be torn, ⊙ be out of order, 🎗 *heart etc*: be ruined, be bad, *nerves*: be

shattered, *fig. marriage etc*: be broken; **mein Auto ist ~** my car has broken down (*or* has had it). **2.** *person*: a) be ruined, be finished, b) be worn out, be all in: **~er Typ** complete wreck.

ka'puttfahren *v/t* (*irr, sep*, -ge-, h, → **fahren**) F smash up, wreck.

ka'puttgehen *v/i* (*irr, sep*, -ge-, sn, → **gehen**) F **1.** break, tear, *car etc*: break down, *fig. marriage etc*: break up. **2.** *person*: crack (up), go to pieces.

ka'puttlachen: sich ~ (*sep*, -ge-, h) F kill o.s. laughing.

ka'puttmachen (*sep*, -ge-, h) F **I** *v/t* **1.** break, smash, *fig*. ruin, bust. **2.** *j-n ~* a) ruin s.o., b) get s.o. down, wear s.o. out, c) kill s.o. **II sich ~** wear o.s. out, kill o.s. (*mit* over, doing *s.th*.).

Kapuze [ka'pu:tsə] *f* (-; -n) **1.** hood. **2.** cowl.

Karabiner [kara'bi:nər] *m* (-s; -) **1.** ⚔ carbine. **2.** → **~haken** *m* spring hook.

Karaffe [ka'rafə] *f* carafe, *a*. decanter.

Karambolage [karambo'la:ʒə] *f* (-; -n) **1.** *billiards*: cannon, *Am*. carom. **2.** F crash, collision.

Karamel [kara'mɛl] *n* (-s; *no pl*) caramel.

Karat [ka'ra:t] *n* (-[e]s; -e) carat.

Karate [ka'ra:tə] *n* (-[e]s; *no pl*) karate.

Ka'ratekämpfer *m* karateka.

Ka'rateschlag *m* karate chop.

...karätig [karɛtɪç] ...-carat.

Karawane [kara'va:nə] *f* (-; -n) caravan.

Kardangelenk [kar'da:n-] *n* ⚙ cardan (*or* universal) joint.

Kar'danwelle *f* ⚙ cardan shaft.

Kardinal [kardi'na:l] *m* (-s; -e) cardinal.

Kardi'nal... cardinal (*fault, question, etc*). **~zahl** *f* cardinal (number).

Kardiologe [kardio'lo:gə] *m* (-n; -n) ⚕ cardiologist.

Karenzzeit [ka'rɛnts-] *f insurance*: waiting period, ✝ period of restriction.

Kar'freitag [ka:r-] *m* eccl. Good Friday.

karg [kark] *adj* **1.** meagre, *Am*. meager, scanty, poor, frugal (*meal, life*), barren (*soil*). **2.** austere. **3.** sparing: **~ bemessen** (very) meagre, *fig*. (very) limited.

kargen ['kargən] *v/i* (h) **~ mit** be stingy with *money*.

'**Kargheit** *f* (-; *no pl*) meag/reness (*Am*. -er-), poorness.

kärglich ['kɛrklɪç] *adj* → **karg** 1.

kariert [ka'ri:rt] *adj* checked, chequered, *Am*. checkered.

Karies ['ka:riɛs] *f* (-; *no pl*) ⚕ tooth decay, dental caries.

Karikatur [karika'tu:r] *f* (-; -en) cartoon, caricature (*a. fig*.). **Karikaturist** [karikatu'rɪst] *m* (-en; -en) cartoonist, caricaturist. **karikieren** [kari'ki:rən] *v/t* (h) cartoon, caricature.

kariös [ka'riø:s] *adj* ⚕ carious, decayed.

karitativ [karita'ti:f] *adj* charitable.

Karmin [kar'mi:n] *n* (-s; *no pl*) carmine.

kar'minrot *adj* crimson.

Karneval ['karnəval] *m* (-s; -e) carnival.

Karo ['ka:ro] *n* (-s; -s) **1.** check, square. **2.** *cards*: diamonds.

Karosserie [karəsə'ri:] *f* (-; -n) *mot*. (car) body.

Karotin [karo'ti:n] *n* (-s; *no pl*) carotene.

Karotte [ka'rɔtə] *f* (-; -n) carrot.

Karpfen ['karpfən] *m* (-s; -) carp.

Karre ['karə] *f* (-; -n) **1.** F (**alte**) **~** bus, crate, banger. **2.** → **Karren.**

Karren ['karən] *m* (-s; -) cart, (wheel)barrow: F *fig. j-m an den ~ fahren* step on s.o.'s toes; **den ~ in den Dreck fahren** mess things up; **den ~ wieder aus dem Dreck ziehen** clear up the mess; *j-n vor s-n ~ spannen* rope s.o. in.

Karriere [ka'riɛ:rə] *f* (-; -n) career: **machen** make a career for o.s.

Karri'erefrau *f* career woman (*or* girl).

Karri'eremacher *m contp.* careerist.

Karte ['kartə] *f* (-; -n) a) card, b) map, ⚔ chart, c) 🚋, *thea. etc*: ticket, d) menu, wine list: **nach der ~ speisen** dine à la carte; **die gelbe (rote) ~** *soccer*: the yellow (red) card; **~n spielen** play cards; **gute ~n haben** have a good hand; *s-e ~n auf den Tisch legen a. fig.* show one's hand, put one's cards on the table; **alles auf eine ~ setzen** put all one's eggs in one basket; → **legen** 6.

Kartei [kar'tai] *f* (-; -en) (**~ führen** keep) a) card index (*über acc* on).

Kar'teikarte *f* file (*or* index) card.

Kar'teikasten *m* card-index box.

Kartell [kar'tɛl] *n* (-s; -e) cartel, ✝ combine, trust.

'**Karten|haus** *n* **1.** ⚓ chartroom. **2.** house of cards. **~kunststück** *n* card trick. **~leger** *m* (-s; -), **~legerin** *f* (-; -nen) fortune-teller. **~spiel** *n* **1.** a) card playing, b) card game. **2.** pack (*Am*. ...

deck) of cards. **~verkauf** m sale of tickets. **~vorverkauf** m advance booking. **~zeichen** n conventional sign.

Kartoffel [kar'tɔfəl] f (-; -n) potato. **Kar'toffel|brei** m mashed potatoes. **~chips** pl potato crisps (Am. chips). **~käfer** m potato beetle (Am. bug). **~puffer** m potato fritter. **~sa‚lat** m potato salad. **~schäler** m potato peeler.

Kartograph [karto'gra:f] m (-en; -en) cartographer. **Kartographie** [kartogra'fi:] f (-; no pl) cartography.

Karton [kar'tɔŋ, kar'to:n] m (-s; -s) **1.** cardboard. **2.** cardboard box, carton.

kartoniert [karto'ni:rt] adj print. paperback(ed).

Karussell [karʊ'sɛl] n (-s; -s, -e) roundabout, merry-go-round, whirligig.

'Karwoche f eccl. Holy Week.

karzinogen [kartsino'ge:n] adj ☢ carcinogenic. **Karzinom** [kartsi'no:m] n (-s; -e) ☢ carcinoma, cancer.

kaschieren [ka'ʃi:rən] v/t (h) conceal. **Kaschmir** [ˈkaʃmɪr] m (-s; -e) cashmere.

Käse [ˈkɛːzə] m (-s; -) **1.** cheese. **2.** F a) rubbish, b) stupid business.

'Käse|blatt n F rag. **~gebäck** n cheese biscuits. **~glocke** f cheese cover. **~kuchen** m cheesecake. **~platte** f gastr. cheese platter. **~rinde** f cheese rind.

Kaserne [ka'zɛrnə] f (-; -n) barracks. **Ka'sernenhof** m barrack square.

kasernieren [kazɛr'ni:rən] v/t (h) quarter in barracks.

'Käsestange f cheese straw.

käsig [ˈkɛːzɪç] adj **1.** caseous, cheesy. **2.** F pale, pasty (face).

Kasino [ka'zi:no] n (-s; -s) **1.** casino, club. **2.** a) (officers') mess, b) cafeteria, canteen.

Kaskoversicherung [ˈkasko-] f mot. insurance against damage to one's own vehicle; → **Teilkaskoversicherung, Vollkaskoversicherung.**

Kasper [ˈkaspər] m (-s; -) **1.** Punch. **2.** fig. clown. **'Kasperlethe‚ather** n Punch and Judy (show).

Kassageschäft [ˈkasa-] n ✝ cash transaction. **'Kassara‚batt** m cash discount.

Kasse [ˈkasə] f (-; -n) **1.** a) cashbox, b) till, c) cash register: **der Film hat volle ~n gebracht** the film was a box-office success. **2.** in shop, bank, etc: cash desk, in supermarket: checkout (counter), in

cinema etc: ticket window, thea. etc a. box office: **zahlen Sie bitte an der ~!** pay at the desk, please!; fig. **j-n zur ~ bitten** make s.o. pay up. **3.** ✝ cash (payment): **gegen ~** for cash; **netto ~** net cash. **4.** cash: **~ machen** a) cash up, b) F count one's cash, c) F fig. cash in heavily, make a packet; F **gut bei ~ sein** be flush; **knapp bei ~ sein** be (a bit) hard up; **gemeinsame ~ machen** split the expenses; **getrennte ~ machen** go Dutch. **5.** F (**er ist in k-r ~** he has no) health insurance. **6.** F (savings) bank.

'Kassen|abschluß m balancing of the (cash) accounts. **~anweisung** f cash order. **~arzt** m health-plan doctor. **~bestand** m cash balance. **~bon** m sales check f. (-; receipt. **~buch** n cashbook. **~erfolg** m thea. etc box-office hit. **~ma‚gnet** m F crowd-puller. **~pati‚ent(in** f) m health-plan patient. **~prüfung** f cash audit: **e-e ~ vornehmen** audit the cash. **~schlager** m F **1.** crowd-puller. **2.** moneymaker. **~sturz** m **~ machen** count one's cash. **~wart** m (-[e]s; -e) treasurer. **~zettel** m sales check (Am. slip), receipt.

Kasserolle [kasə'rɔlə] f (-; -n) casserole.

Kassette [ka'sɛtə] f (-; -n) **1.** a) box, b) casket, c) cashbox. **2.** slipcase (for books), box set (for records). **3.** phot., TV etc cassette, cartridge. **4.** △ coffer.

Kas'setten|deck n cassette deck. **~re‚corder** m cassette recorder.

kassieren [ka'si:rən] (h) **I** v/t **1.** collect (rent etc). **2.** F a) collect, take (fees etc), b) seize (property), c) nab, catch (criminal), d) suffer (loss etc), take, get (beating, etc). **3.** ⚖ quash (sentence). **II** v/i **4.** collect (the money): F fig. **kräftig ~ cash** in (heavily) (**bei** on); **darf ich bei Ihnen ~?** would you mind paying now?

Kassierer [ka'si:rər] m (-s; -), **Kas'siererin** f (-; -nen) cashier, esp. Am. teller.

Kastagnette [kastan'jɛtə] f (-; -n) castanet.

Kastanie [kas'ta:niə] f (-; -n) chestnut: fig. **für j-n die ~n aus dem Feuer holen** pull the chestnuts out of the fire for s.o.

Ka'stanienbaum m chestnut (tree). **ka'stanienbraun** adj chestnut.

Kästchen [ˈkɛstçən] n (-s; -) **1.** small box (or case), casket. **2.** print. square, box.

Kaste [ˈkastə] f (-; -n) caste.

kasteien [kas'taɪən] *sich* ~ (h) **1.** *eccl.* mortify the flesh. **2.** *fig.* deny o.s.

Kasten ['kastən] *m* (-s; ») **1.** box (*a. print.*), case, chest, (*beer etc*) crate: F *er hat was auf dem* ~ he's brainy, he's on the ball. **2.** F (*goal, house, TV set*) box, (*car, plane*) bus, crate, (*ship*) tub.

'**Kastengeist** *m* (-[e]s; *no pl*) caste spirit.

'**Kastenwesen** *n* (-s; *no pl*) caste system.

Kastration [kastra'tsĭo:n] *f* (-; -en) castration.

kastrieren [kas'tri:rən] *v/t* (h) castrate.

Kasus ['ka:zʊs] *m* (-; -) *ling.* case.

Kat [kat] *m* (-s; -s) → *Katalysator* 2.

Katakomben [kata'kɔmbən] *pl* catacombs.

Katalog [kata'lo:k] *m* (-[e]s; -e) catalog(ue *Br.*).

katalogisieren [katalogi'zi:rən] *v/t* (h) catalog(ue *Br.*).

Katalysator [kataly'za:tɔr] *m* (-s; -en [-za'to:rən]) **1.** 🖈 *or fig.* catalyst. **2.** *mot.* catalytic converter.

Katapult [kata'pʊlt] *n, m* (-[e]s; -e), **katapultieren** [-'ti:rən] *v/t* (h) catapult. **Kata'pultstart** *m* ✈ catapult takeoff.

Katarrh [ka'tar] *m* (-s; -e) 🖈 catarrh.

Kataster [ka'tastər] *m, n* (-s; -) land register.

katastrophal [kastastro'fa:l] *adj* catastrophic, *a.* F *fig.* disastrous.

Katastrophe [kata'stro:fə] *f* (-; -n) *a.* F *fig.* catastrophe, disaster.

Kata'strophen|a,larm *m* red alert. **~einsatz** *m* (*im* ~ on) duty in a disaster area. **~fall** *m* (*im* ~ in an) emergency. **~film** *m* disaster film. **~gebiet** *n* disaster area. **~hilfe** *f* disaster relief. **~schutz** *m* disaster control (*or* prevention).

Katechismus [kate'çɪsmʊs] *m* (-; -men) *eccl.* catechism.

Kategorie [katego'ri:] *f* (-; -n) category.

kategorisch [kate'go:rɪʃ] *adj* categorical: ~ *ablehnen a.* refuse flatly.

Kater ['ka:tər] *m* (-s; -) **1.** *zo.* tom(cat). **2.** F hangover: *e-n* ~ *haben a.* be hung over.

Katheder [ka'te:dər] *n, a. m* (-s; -) (teacher's *or* lecturer's) desk.

Kathedrale [kate'dra:lə] *f* (-; -n) cathedral.

Katheter [ka'te:tər] *m* (-s; -) 🖈 catheter.

Kathode [ka'to:də] *f* (-; -n) cathode.

Katholik [kato'li:k] *m* (-en; -en), **Katho'likin** *f* (-; -nen), **katholisch** [ka'to:lɪʃ] *adj* (Roman) Catholic.

Katholizismus [katoli'tsɪsmʊs] *m* (-; *no pl*) Catholicism.

Kätzchen ['kɛtsçən] *n* (-s; -) **1.** *zo.* kitten. **2.** 🌿 catkin.

Katze ['katsə] *f* (-; -n) cat: F *fig. das ist für die Katz* that's all for nothing; *Katze und Maus spielen mit* play cat and mouse with; *die* ~ *im Sack kaufen* buy a pig in a poke; *die* ~ *aus dem Sack lassen* let the cat out of the bag; *wi die* ~ *um den heißen Brei gehen* beat about the bush.

'**Katzenauge** *n* **1.** cat's eye (*a. min.*). **2.** rear reflector.

'**katzenhaft** *adj* catlike, feline.

'**Katzen|jammer** *m* F hangover: (*mora lischen*) ~ *haben a.* have the blues. **~klo** *n* cat tray. **~sprung** *m fig. ein* ~ *von hier* a stone's throw from here. **~streu** *f* cat litter. **~wäsche** *f* F *fig.* (*machen* have a) cat's lick.

Kauderwelsch ['kaʊdərvɛlʃ] *n* (-[s]; *no pl*) double Dutch, lingo.

kauen ['kaʊən] *v/t, v/i* (h) chew: *an den Nägeln* ~ bite one's nails; *fig. an e-Sache* ~ chew s.th. over.

kauern ['kaʊərn] *v/i* (*a. sich* ~) (h crouch (*or* squat) down.

Kauf [kaʊf] *m* (-[e]s; »e) **1.** buying, purchase: *zum* ~ for sale; *beim* ~ whe buying; *et. in* ~ *nehmen* put up wit s.th.; *leichten* ~*es davonkommen* g off cheaply. **2.** purchase, F buy: *ei guter* ~ a good bargain (*or* buy).

'**kaufen** *v/t, v/i* (h) buy (*a.* F *fig.*), purchase: ~ *bei* go to, buy at; *sich ein Aut* ~ buy (o.s.) a car; F *dafür kann ich m nichts* ~! that's no use to me!; *de kaufe ich mir!* I'll tell him what's wha

Käufer ['kɔʏfər] *m* (-s; -), '**Käuferin** *f* (-nen) buyer, purchaser.

'**Kauf|frau** *f* businesswoman. **~halle** small department store. **~haus** *n* de partment store. **~kraft** *f* (-; *no pl*) pu chasing power (*of money*), spendin power (*of consumers*). 🔟**kräftig** *adj* well-to-do, b) hard (*currency*).

käuflich ['kɔʏflɪç] *adj* **1.** purchasable *(nicht)* ~ *sein* (not to) be for sale; ~ *Liebe* prostitution; ~ *erwerben* purchase. **2.** *fig.* venal, corrupt.

'**Käuflichkeit** *f* (-; *no pl*) *fig.* venality.

'**Kaufmann** *m* (-[e]s; -leute) **1.** busines

man, merchant, trader, dealer. **2.** shopkeeper, *Am. a.* storekeeper, *n.s.* grocer.
kaufmännisch ['kaʊfmɛnɪʃ] *adj* commercial, business: **~e(r) Angestellte(r)** (commercial) clerk.
'Kaufpreis *m* (purchase) price.
'Kaufvertrag *m* contract of sale.
'Kaufzwang *m* obligation (to buy).
'Kaugummi *m, a. n* (-s; -s) chewing gum.
Kaulquappe ['kaʊlkvapə] *f* (-; -n) *zo.* tadpole.
kaum [kaʊm] *adv* a) hardly, scarcely, b) barely, only just: **~ zu glauben** hard to believe; **~ möglich** hardly possible; **wohl ~!**(!) hardly(!); **ich glaube ~, daß** I hardly think that; **~ war sie gegangen, als ...** no sooner had she gone than ...
'Kaumuskel *m* masticatory muscle.
kausal [kaʊ'za:l] *adj* causal. **Kausalität** [kaʊzali'tɛ:t] *f* (-; -en) causality.
Kau'sal|satz *m ling.* causal clause. **~zu-sammenhang** *m* causal connection.
Kaution [kaʊ'tsĭo:n] *f* (-; -en) ✝ security, ⚖ bail: **~ stellen** ✝ furnish security, ⚖ stand bail; **gegen ~** ⚖ on bail.
Kautschuk ['kaʊtʃʊk] *m* (-s; -e) caoutchouc, India rubber.
'Kauwerkzeuge *pl* masticatory organs.
Kauz [kaʊts] *m* (-es; ~e) **1.** *zo.* screech-owl. **2.** F *(komischer)* ~ odd (*or* queer) fellow, *Am.* oddball.
kauzig ['kaʊtsɪç] *adj* F queer, odd.
Kavalier [kava'li:r] *m* (-s; -e) gentleman.
Kava'liersde,likt *n* peccadillo.
Kavallerie [kavalə'ri:] *f* (-; -n) cavalry.
Kavallerist [kavalə'rɪst] *m* (-en; -en) cavalryman, trooper.
Kaviar ['ka:vĭar] *m* (-s; -e) caviar(e).
keck [kɛk] *adj* pert, saucy.
Kegel ['ke:gəl] *m* (-s; -) **1.** Å, ⚙ cone. **2.** ninepin, skittle(pin): → **Kind.**
'Kegelbahn *f* skittle (*or* bowling) alley.
'kegelförmig [-fœrmɪç] *adj* conical.
'Kegelklub *m* skittles (*or* bowling) club.
'Kegelkugel *f* skittle (*or* bowling) ball.
kegeln ['ke:gəln] *v/i* (h) play (at) skittles (*or* ninepins), bowl, go bowling.
'Kegelsport *m* skittles, bowling.
'Kegelstumpf *m* Å truncated cone.
Kegler ['ke:glər] *m* (-s; -), **'Keglerin** *f* (-; -nen) skittles player, bowler.
Kehle ['ke:lə] *f* (-; -n) **1.** *anat.* throat: **j-m die ~ durchschneiden** cut s.o.'s throat; *fig.* **et. in die falsche ~ bekommen** take

s.th. the wrong way. **2.** ⚙ flute.
'Kehlkopf *m anat.* larynx. **~entzündung** *f* 🩺 laryngitis. **~krebs** *m* 🩺 cancer of the larynx, F throat cancer.
'Kehllaut *m* guttural (sound).
Kehre ['ke:rə] *f* (-; -n) **1.** (sharp) bend. **2.** *skating etc:* turn, *gym.* rear vault.
kehren¹ ['ke:rən] (h) **I** *v/t* **1.** *et. nach oben* **(unten, außen** *etc)* **~** turn s.th. upwards (down, outside, *etc*); **den Rücken ~** *a. fig.* turn one's back (*dat* on); *in sich gekehrt* withdrawn, *psych.* introvert(ed); → **oberst.** **II** *sich* **~ 2.** → **wenden** 4. **3.** *sich nicht* **~** *an* (*dat*) ignore. **III** *v/i* **4. kehrt!** ✗ about turn!
'kehren² *v/t, v/i* (h) sweep.
Kehricht ['ke:rɪçt] *m, n* (-s; *no pl*) **1.** sweepings. **2.** rubbish, *Am.* garbage.
'Kehr,schine *f* road sweeper.
'Kehrreim *m* burden, refrain.
'Kehrseite *f* **1.** reverse. **2.** *humor.* back. **3.** *fig.* a) *the* other side, b) drawback.
kehrtmachen ['ke:rt-] *v/i* (*sep*, -ge-, h) **1.** turn round, ✗ face about. **2.** turn back.
'Kehrtwendung *f a. fig.* about-face.
keifen ['kaɪfən] *v/i* (h) nag, bicker.
Keil [kaɪl] *m* (-[e]s; -e) **1.** wedge. **2.** gore, gusset. **'Keilabsatz** *m* wedge heel.
keilen ['kaɪlən] (h) **I** *v/t j-n* **~** rope s.o. in (*für* for). **II** *sich* **~** fight.
Keiler ['kaɪlər] *m* (-s; -) *zo.* wild boar.
'keilförmig [-fœrmɪç] *adj* wedge-shaped.
'Keilriemen *m* ⚙ V-belt.
'Keilschrift *f* cuneiform (script).
Keim [kaɪm] *m* (-[e]s; -e) **1.** *biol.* germ, embryo (*both a. fig.*), 🌱 *a.* bud, 🌱 *a.* seed(s): *im* **~** in embryo; *im* **~ ersticken** nip *s.th.* in the bud. **2.** 🦠 germ, bacillus. **~blatt** *n* 🌱 cotyledon. **2.** *biol.* germ layer. **~drüse** *f physiol.* gonad.
keimen ['kaɪmən] *v/i* (h) **1.** *biol.* germinate. **2.** *fig.* grow, stir.
'keimfähig *adj* germinable.
'keimfrei *adj* sterile: **~ machen** sterilize.
'Keimling *m* (-s; -e) *biol.* embryo.
'keimtötend *adj* germicidal, antiseptic: **~es Mittel** germicide.
'Keimträger *m* 🩺 (germ) carrier.
'Keimzelle *f* **1.** germ cell. **2.** *fig.* nucleus.
kein [kaɪn] *indef pron* no, not any, not a: *ich habe* **~ Geld** I haven't (got) any money; *du bist* **~ Kind mehr** you are not a child any more; **~ Wort mehr!** not another word!; **~ anderer als X** none

keine

333

other than X; **es kostet ~e 100 Mark** it costs less than 100 marks.

'keine, 'keiner, 'keines (*or* **keins**) *indef pron* **1.** no one, nobody, not one, none: **~(r) von uns** a) neither of us, b) none of us. **2.** not any, none, not one: **keins von beiden** neither (of the two).

'keinerlei *adj* no ... what(so)ever, no ... at all.

'keines'falls *adv* on no account, under no circumstances. **'keines'wegs** *adv* by no means, not at all, not in the least. **'keinmal** *adv* not once, never.

Keks [ke:ks] *m* (-[es]; -e) biscuit, *Am.* cookie.

Kelch [kɛlç] *m* (-[e]s; -e) **1.** goblet, *eccl.* chalice, cup (*a. fig.*). **2.** ♀ calyx, cup. **~blatt** *n* ♀ sepal. **~hülle** *f* ♀ calycle.

Kelle ['kɛlə] *f* (-; -n) **1.** *gastr.* ladle. **2.** △ trowel. **3.** 🚋 *etc* signal(l)ing disc.

Keller ['kɛlər] *m* (-s; -) cellar.

Kellerei [kɛlə'raɪ] *f* (-; -en) wine cellars.

'Kellergeschoß *n* basement.

'Kellermeister *m* cellarman.

Kellner ['kɛlnər] *m* (-s; -) waiter.

'Kellnerin *f* (-; -nen) waitress.

Kelte ['kɛltə] *m* (-n; -n) Celt.

Kelter ['kɛltər] *f* (-; -n) (wine)press.

keltern ['kɛltərn] *v/t* (h) press.

Keltin *f* (-; -nen) Celt.

keltisch ['kɛltɪʃ] *adj* Celtic.

kennen ['kɛnən] *v/t* (kannte, gekannt, h) know, a. be acquainted (*or* familiar) with, *a.* recognize (**an** *dat* by): **wir ~ uns** we know each other, **schon** a. we have already met; **ich kenne sie von der Schule** we were at school together; **kennst du mich noch?** do you remember me?; **das ~ wir!** we know all about that!; **er kennt nichts als s-e Arbeit** he lives only for his work; **sie kennt k-e Müdigkeit** she never gets tired; **kein Erbarmen ~** know no mercy.

'kennenlernen *v/t* (*sep*, -ge-, h) become acquainted with, get (*or* come) to know: **j-n ~** meet s.o.; **j-n näher ~** (get to) know s.o. better; **wir haben uns in B. kennengelernt** we first met in B.

Kenner ['kɛnər] *m* (-s; -), **'Kennerin** *f* (-; -nen) **1.** connoisseur. **2.** (*gen*) expert (at, in, of), authority (on).

'Kennerblick *m* (**mit ~** with an) expert's eye. **'Kennermiene** *f* (**e-e ~ aufsetzen**) assume (an) air of an expert.

'Kennmelo,die *f* signature tune.

kenntlich ['kɛntlıç] *adj* recognizable (**a** *dat* by): **~ machen** ~.

Kenntnis ['kɛntnıs] *f* (-; -se) knowledge: **gute ~se haben in** (*dat*) have a goo knowledge of, be well grounded in; **da entzieht sich m-r ~** I don't know any thing about it; **von et. ~ haben** know (about) s.th., be aware of s.th.; **et. zur ~ nehmen** take note of (*or* note) s.th.; **j-n in ~ setzen von** inform s.o. of.

'Kenntnisnahme [-na:mə] *f* **zu Ihrer et ~** for your *etc* attention.

'Kennwort *n* code word, ✕ *a.* passwor (*a. computer*).

'Kennzeichen *n* **1.** a) (distinguishing mark, characteristic, b) sign, sympton (*a.* 🐾): **besondere ~** distinguishin marks. **2.** *fig.* hallmark. **3.** (**polizeil ches**) **~** *mot.* registration (*Am.* license number. **4.** *computer:* flag.

'Kennzeichen|leuchte *f* *mot.* num ber-plate (*Am.* license-plate) light **~schild** *n* number (*Am.* license) plate **'kennzeichnen** *v/t* (h) **1.** mark. **2.** *fig* characterize, (go to) show. **'kenn zeichnend** *adj* characteristic (**für** of)

'Kennziffer *f* code number, ✝ referenc number, *of ad:* box number.

kentern ['kɛntərn] *v/i* (sn) capsize.

Keramik [ke'ra:mık] *f* (-; -en) **1.** *no p* ceramics, pottery. **2.** ceramic (article piece of pottery. **Ke'ramiker** *m* (-s; - **Ke'ramikerin** *f* (-; -nen) ceramist.

Kerbe ['kɛrbə] *f* (-; -n) notch.

Kerbel ['kɛrbəl] *m* (-s; *no pl*) ♀ chervil

kerben ['kɛrbən] *v/t* (h) notch.

Kerbholz ['kɛrp-] *n* F **et. auf dem ~ ha ben** have done s.th. wrong; **er hat ein ges auf dem ~** he has quite a record.

Kerl [kɛrl] *m* (-s; -e) F fellow, blok chap, *Am.* guy, *contp.* type: **er ist ei anständiger ~** he is a decent sort; **ei feiner ~** a splendid fellow, *Am.* a grea guy; **ein lieber** (*or* **netter**) **~** a dear; **ei** (**ganzer**) **~** a real man; **ein übler ~** nasty customer.

Kern [kɛrn] *m* (-[e]s; -e) **1.** ♀ pip, b stone, *Am.* pit, c) kernel: *fig.* **sie hat e-guten ~** she is good at heart. **2.** *fig.* cor (*a.* ⚡, *phys.*, ⚙), nucleus (*a. phys.*), es sence: **der ~ der Sache** the heart of th matter; *pol.* **harter ~** hard cor **~brennstoff** *m* nuclear fuel. **~ener,g**

f nuclear energy. **~explosi͵on** *f* nuclear explosion. **~fach** *n ped., univ.* basic subject. **~fa͵milie** *f sociol.* nuclear family. **~forschung** *f* nuclear research. **~frage** *f* crucial question. **~fusi͵on** *f* nuclear fusion. **~gehäuse** *n* & core.

'**kerngesund** *adj* thoroughly healthy, F (as) sound as a bell.

'**kernig** *adj fig.* a) robust, b) pithy, c) earthy, d) F super, terrific.

'**Kernkraft** *f* nuclear power. **~gegner(in** *f) m* antinuclear campaigner. **~werk** *n* nuclear power station.

'**kernlos** *adj* & seedless.

'**Kern|obst** *n* pome. **~phy͵sik** *f* nuclear physics. **~physiker** *m* nuclear physicist. **~punkt** *m* central point (*or* issue). **~re͵aktor** *m* nuclear reactor. **~schmelze** *f* (-; *no pl*) (nuclear core) meltdown. **~seife** *f* curd soap. **~spaltung** *f* nuclear fission. **~stück** *n fig.* essential part, main item. **~waffe** *f* nuclear weapon. **~waffenverbot** *n* ban on nuclear weapons. **~waffenversuch** *m* nuclear weapons test. **~zeit** *f* core time. **~zerfall** *m* nuclear disintegration.

Kerosin [kero'zi:n] *n* (-s; *no pl*) kerosene.

Kerze ['kɛrtsə] *f* (-; -n) **1.** candle (*a.* &, *phys.*). **2.** *mot.* spark(ing) plug.

'**kerzengerade** *adv* bolt upright.

'**Kerzenhalter** *m* candlestick.

'**Kerzenlicht** *n* (*bei* ~ by) candlelight.

'**Kerzenschlüssel** *m mot.* plug wrench.

keß [kɛs] *adj* F pert, saucy.

Kessel ['kɛsəl] *m* (-s; -) **1.** kettle, cauldron, ⊙ vat, boiler. **2.** *geol.* basin, hollow. **3.** ✕ pocket.

'**Kesselstein** *m* (-[e]s; *no pl*) scale, fur.

'**Kesseltreiben** *n* (-s) *fig.* (*gegen*) hunt (for), *pol.* witch hunt (against).

Kette ['kɛtə] *f* (-; -n) **1.** chain (*a.* 🐾, 🜋, 🜊), *a.* necklace: *j-n an die* ~ *legen* put s.o. on a short leash. **2.** *fig.* a) chain, series (*of accidents, events, etc*), b) string, line: *e-e* ~ *bilden* form a cordon (*or* line). **3.** *hunt.* covey. **4.** *mot.* track. **5.** *textil.* warp: ~ *und Schuß* warp and weft.

'**ketten** ['kɛtən] *v/t* (h) chain (*an acc* to).

'**Ketten|brief** *m* chain letter. **~fahrzeug** *n* tracked vehicle. **~glied** *n* chain link. **~karus͵sell** *n* chairoplane. **~laden** *m* chain store. **~raucher(in** *f) m* chain-smoker. **~reakti͵on** *f* chain reaction.

Ketzer ['kɛtsər] *m* (-s; -) heretic.

Ketzerei [kɛtsə'raɪ] *f* (-; -en) heresy.

'**Ketzerin** *f* (-; -nen) heretic.

'**ketzerisch** *adj* heretical.

keuchen ['kɔyçən] *v/i* (h) pant, puff (*a.* 🜋), *a. v/t* gasp.

'**Keuchhusten** *m* 🜋 whooping cough.

Keule ['kɔylə] *f* (-; -n) **1.** club. **2.** *chemische* ~ Mace (*TM*). **3.** *gastr.* leg.

'**Keulenschlag** *m* **1.** blow with a club. **2.** *fig.* crushing blow.

keusch [kɔyʃ] *adj* chaste.

'**Keuschheit** *f* (-; *no pl*) chastity.

Kibbuz [kɪ'bu:ts] *m* (-; -e) kibbutz.

kichern ['kɪçərn] *v/i* (h) (*über acc* at) giggle, snigger.

kicken ['kɪkən] *v/t, v/i* (h) kick.

Kiebitz ['ki:bɪts] *m* (-es; -e) **1.** *zo.* peewit, lapwing. **2.** F *fig.* kibitzer.

Kiefer¹ ['ki:fər] *f* (-; -n) & pine.

Kiefer² *m* (-s; -) *anat.* jaw.

'**Kieferhöhle** *f anat.* maxillary sinus.

'**Kiefernzapfen** *m* & pine cone.

'**Kieferortho͵päde** *m* & orthodontist.

Kiel [ki:l] *m* (-[e]s; -e) ⚓ keel. **kiel'oben** *adv* ⚓ bottom up. '**Kielraum** *m* ⚓ bilge. '**Kielwasser** *n* (-s; -) (*fig. in j-s* ~ *segeln* sail in s.o.'s) wake.

Kieme ['ki:mə] *f* (-; -n) gill.

Kies [ki:s] *m* (-es; -e). (*a. mit* ~ *bestreuen*) gravel. **2.** F *fig.* lolly, *Am.* bread.

Kiesel ['ki:zəl] *m* (-s; -) flint, pebble.

'**Kieselerde** *f* 🜋 silica, siliceous earth.

'**Kieselsäure** *f* 🜋 silicic acid.

'**Kieselstein** *m* → **Kiesel**.

'**Kies|grube** *f* gravel pit. **~strand** *m* shingle (beach). **~weg** *m* gravel path.

Kiez [ki:ts] *m* (-es; -e) F district, area.

kiffen ['kɪfən] *v/i* (h) F smoke pot (*or* hash).

killen ['kɪlən] *v/t* (h) F kill.

Killer ['kɪlər] *m* (-s; -) F killer.

Kilo ['ki:lo] *n* (-s; -[s]), **Kilogramm** [kilo'gram] *n* kilogram(me Br.).

Kilo'hertz [kilo-] *n* ⚡, *phys.* kilohertz.

Kilo'joule *n phys.* kilojoule.

Kilo'meter *m* kilomet/re (*Am.* -er). **~geld** *n* mileage allowance. **~pau͵schale** *f* flat mileage allowance. **~stand** *m* mileage (reading). **~stein** *m* milestone. **Ωweit** *adv* for miles (and miles). **~zähler** *m* mileage indicator.

Kilo'volt *n* kilovolt.

Kilo'watt(stunde *f) n* kilowatt (hour).

Kimm [kɪm] f (-; no pl) ⚓ visual horizon.
Kimme ['kɪmə] f (-; -n) ✕ notch.
Kind [kɪnt] n (-[e]s; -er) child (a. fig.), F kid, a. baby: **ein ~ erwarten (bekommen)** be expecting (going to have) a baby; **von ~ auf** from childhood; F **mit ~ und Kegel** (with) bag and baggage; fig. **das ~ mit dem Bade ausschütten** throw the baby out with the bathwater; **das ~ beim rechten Namen nennen** call a spade a spade; **(ein) gebranntes ~ scheut das Feuer** once bitten, twice shy; → **Geist** 2, **lieb.**
'**Kindbettfieber** n ♣ puerperal fever.
'**Kinder**|**arbeit** f child labo(u)r. **~arzt** m, **~ärztin** f p(a)ediatrician. **~bett(chen)** n cot, Am. crib. **~buch** n children's book. **~dorf** n children's village. **~ermäßigung** f reduction for children. **~erziehung** f bringing up children. **~fahrrad** n child's bicycle. **2feindlich** adj hostile to children, antichildren. **2freundlich** adj 1. fond of children. 2. suitable for children. **~garten** m kindergarten. **~gärtner(in** f) m kindergarten teacher. **~geld** n children's allowance. **~heim** n children's home. **~hort** m day nursery. **~kleidung** f children's wear. **~krankheit** f children's disease, fig. teething troubles. **~krippe** f crèche, day nursery. **~lähmung** f ♣ (**spinale**) **~** polio(myelitis). **2leicht** adj dead easy. **2lieb** adj very fond of children. **~lied** n children's song.
'**kinderlos** adj childless.
'**Kinder**|**mädchen** n nurse(maid), nanny. **~pflege** f child care. **~psychologie** f child psychology. **2reich** adj with many children: **~e Familie** large family. **~schuhe** pl children's shoes: fig. **noch in den ~n stecken** be still in its infancy. **~sendung** f children's program(me Br.). **2sicher** adj childproof. **~sicherung** f mot. childproof lock. **~spiel** n fig. **das ist ein ~ (für ihn)** that's child's play (for him). **~spielplatz** m children's playground. **~stube** f fig. upbringing. **~tagesstätte** f day nursery, day-care cent/re (Am. -er). **~wagen** m pram, Am. baby carriage. **~zimmer** n children's room, nursery. **~zulage** f children's allowance.
'**Kindes**|**alter** n a) infancy, b) childhood. **~liebe** f filial love. **~mißhandlung** f

child abuse. **~tötung** f ♣♣ infanticide.
'**Kindheit** f (-; no pl) childhood: **von ~ an** from a child.
'**kindisch** adj childish.
'**kindlich** adj 1. childlike, childish. 2. filial (love etc).
'**Kindlichkeit** f (-; no pl) childishness.
'**Kindskopf** m F fig. (big) child, silly.
'**Kindtaufe** f christening.
Kinetik [ki'ne:tɪk] f (-; no pl) kinetics.
ki'netisch adj kinetic.
Kinkerlitzchen ['kɪŋkərlɪtsçən] pl F 1. gimcrackery, frills. 2. trivia.
Kinn [kɪn] n (-[e]s; -e) chin.
'**Kinnlade** [-la:də] f (-; -n) jaw(bone).
'**Kinnhaken** m boxing: hook to the chin.
Kino ['ki:no] n (-s; -s) 1. cinema, Am. motion-picture (F movie) theater. 2. cinema, esp. Am. the movies: **ins ~ gehen** go to the picture (or movies).
'**Kinogänger** [-gɛŋər] m (-s; -) cinemagoer, esp. Am. moviegoer.
Kiosk [kiɔsk] m (-[e]s; -e) kiosk.
Kippe¹ ['kɪpə] f (-; -n) F stub, fag end, butt.
Kippe² f (-; -n) 1. ✕ tip, (a. rubbish) dump. 2. gym. upstart, Am. kip. 3. F fig. **es (er) steht auf der ~** it is touch and go (with him).
kippen ['kɪpən] I v/t (h) 1. a) tilt, tip over, b) tip out: F **e-n ~** have a quick one. 2. F fig. overturn (government, project, etc), drop (program[me]), sack (s.o.), sports: turn (the match). II v/i (sn) 3. a) tip (over), b) overturn, capsize.
'**Kipper** m (-s; -) mot. tipper, Am. dump truck.
'**Kippfenster** n tilting window.
'**Kippfre,quenz** f ⚡ sweep frequency.
'**Kippschalter** m ⚡ toggle switch.
'**kippsicher** adj stable.
Kirche ['kɪrçə] f (-; -n) (**in der ~** at) church: **zur ~ gehen** go to church; F **wir wollen doch die ~ im Dorf lassen!** let's not exaggerate things!
'**Kirchen**|**buch** n parish register. **~chor** m church choir. **~diener** m sexton. **~gemeinde** f parish. **~geschichte** f church history. **~jahr** n ecclesiastical year. **~lied** n hymn. **~mu,sik** f sacred music. **~rat** m (member of the) consistory. **~recht** n (-[e]s; no pl) canon law. **~schiff** n △ nave. **~steuer** f church tax. **~stuhl** m pew. **~tag** m Church congress

'**Kirchgang** *m* churchgoing. '**Kirchgänger** [-gɛŋər] *m* (-s; -) churchgoer.
'**Kirchhof** *m* churchyard, graveyard.
'**kirchlich** *adj* church ..., ecclesiastical: *sich ~ trauen lassen, ~ heiraten* have a church wedding; *~ bestattet werden* be given a Christian burial.
'**Kirchturm** *m* church tower, steeple.
'**Kirschbaum** *m* cherry tree.
'**Kirschblüte** *f* a) cherry blossom, b) (*zur Zeit der ~* at) cherry-blossom time.
Kirsche ['kɪrʃə] *f* (-; -n) cherry: *fig. mit ihm ist nicht gut ~n essen* it's best not to tangle with him.
'**Kirsch|kern** *m* cherry stone. *~kuchen* *m* cherry cake. *~li,kör* *m* cherry brandy. **&rot** *adj.* cherry(-red). *~saft* *m* cherry juice. *~torte* *f* cherry gateau. *~wasser* *n* (-s; -) kirsch.
Kissen ['kɪsən] *n* (-s; -) a) cushion, b) pillow. '**Kissenbezug** *m* a) cushion slip, b) pillowcase.
Kiste ['kɪstə] *f* (-; -n) **1.** box, *✝* case, chest, crate. **2.** → *Kasten* 2.
Kitsch [kɪtʃ] *m* (-es; *no pl*) kitsch, trash.
'**kitschig** *adj* kitschy, trashy.
Kitt [kɪt] *m* (-[e]s; -e) **1.** cement. **2.** putty.
Kittchen ['kɪtçən] *n* (-s; -) → *Knast.*
Kittel ['kɪtəl] *m* (-s; -) a) smock, b) overall, c) (*doctor's*) (white) coat.
kitten ['kɪtən] *v/t* (h) cement, putty, *fig.* patch up (*marriage etc*).
Kitz [kɪts] *n* (-es; -e) *zo.* a) kid, b) fawn.
Kitzel ['kɪtsəl] *m* (-s; *no pl*) **1.** tickle, itch. **2.** *fig.* thrill, kick. '**kitzeln** *v/t, v/i* (h) tickle. **Kitzler** ['kɪtslər] *m* (-s; -) *anat.* clitoris, *F* clit. '**kitzlig** *adj* a. *fig.* ticklish.
Kiwi¹ ['kiːvi] *m* (-s; -s) *zo.* kiwi.
'**Kiwi²** *f* (-; -s) **✿** kiwi.
Klacks [klaks] *m* (-es; -e) *F* dollop, blob; *fig. das ist ein ~* that's nothing.
Kladde ['kladə] *f* (-; -n) **1.** scribbling pad. **2.** *✝* waste book. **3.** rough copy.
klaffen ['klafən] *v/i* (h) gape, *fig. a.* yawn: *~de Wunde* gaping wound.
'**kläffen** ['klɛfən] *v/i* (h) a. *fig.* yap.
Klage ['klaːgə] *f* (-; -n) **1.** lament(ation) (*um, über* acc for, over). **2.** complaint (*über* acc about): *~ führen über* (*acc* for), lawsuit, *fig.* b) statement of claim: *~ erheben* institute proceedings (*ge-*

gen against, *wegen* for) (→ *a. klagen* 3); *e-e ~ abweisen* dismiss an action.
'**Klagegrund** *m* ⚖ cause of action.
'**Klagelied** *n* lamentation.
klagen ['klaːgən] (h) *I v/i* **1.** lament (*um, über* acc over, about). **2.** *~ über* (*acc*) complain of (*a. ✿*) (*or* about); *ohne zu ~* without complaining; *ich kann nicht ~* I have no cause for complaint. **3.** ⚖ go to s.o.: *gegen j-n ~* (*wegen* for) sue s.o., bring an action against s.o. **II** *v/t → Leid* 1.
Kläger ['klɛːgər] *m* (-s; -), '**Klägerin** *f* (-; -nen) ⚖ plaintiff.
'**Klageschrift** *f* ⚖ statement of claim.
'**Klageweg** *m* ⚖ *auf dem* (*or im*) *~* by entering legal action.
'**klaglos** *adv* without complaining.
Klamauk [kla'maʊk] *m* (-s; *no pl*) *F* **1.** racket. **2.** to-do. **3.** *thea. etc* slapstick.
klamm [klam] *adj* **1.** clammy. **2.** numb (with cold). **3.** *F fig. ~ sein* be hard up.
Klamm *f* (-; -en) *geol.* narrow gorge.
Klammer ['klamər] *f* (-; -n) **1.** a) clip, ☉ a. clamp, cramp, b) clothes peg, *Am.* clothespin. **2.** ✞ brace(s). **3.** Ⓐ, *print.* parenthesis, bracket, brace: *in ~n setzen* put *s.th.* in parentheses, bracket; *~ auf* (*zu*) open (close) brackets; *die ~(n) auflösen* Ⓐ remove the brackets.
klammern ['klamərn] (h) *I v/t* (*an* acc to) a) clip, ☉ a. clamp, b) peg, pin. **II** *sich ~ an* (*acc*) a. *fig.* cling to.
'**klamm'heimlich** *adv* *F* on the quiet.
Klamotte [kla'mɔtə] *f* (-; -n) *F* **1.** (*alte*) *~* (*film etc*) oldie. **2.** *pl* a) rags, togs, b) things, junk.
klang [klaŋ] *pret of klingen.*
Klang *m* (-[e]s; ⁻e) a) sound, ring, b) tone, c) timbre: *unter den Klängen von* (*or gen*) to the strains of.
'**Klangfarbe** *f* timbre.
'**Klangfülle** *f* sonority.
'**klanglich** *adj* tonal.
'**klanglos** *adj* toneless.
'**Klangregler** *m* radio etc: tone control.
'**klangrein** *adj ~ sein* have a pure sound.
'**Klangtreue** *f* fidelity.
'**klangvoll** *adj* **1.** sonorous, melodious. **2.** *fig.* illustrious (*name etc*).
'**Klangwiedergabe** *f* sound reproduction.
'**klappbar** *adj* **1.** collapsible, folding. **2.**

hinged. **'Klappbett** n folding bed. **'Klappdeckel** m snap lid.

Klappe ['klapə] f (-; -n) **1.** flap (a. ⊚), leaf (of table). **2.** anat. valve. **3.** (eye) patch. **4.** ♪ key. **5.** F fig. mouth, trap: **e-e große ~ haben** have a big mouth; **halt die ~!** shut up!

klappen ['klapən] (h) **I** v/t **1.** nach oben ~ → **hochklappen**; nach unten ~ → **herunterklappen**; **der Sitz läßt sich nach hinten ~** the seat folds back. **II** v/i **2.** a) clack, bang, b) click shut. **3.** F fig. work, go off well: **~ wie am Schnürchen** go like clockwork; **es klappt nicht** it won't work; **nichts klappte** nothing worked; **wenn alles klappt** if all goes well; **es wird schon ~!** it'll work out all right!; **hat es mit dem Job geklappt?** did you get the job all right?

'Klappentext m blurb.

'Klappenven,til n ⊚ flap valve.

Klapper ['klapər] f (-; -n) rattle. **~kasten** m, **~kiste** f F rattletrap, old banger.

klappern ['klapərn] v/i (h) **1.** clatter, rattle, knitting needles: clack: **mit dem Geschirr ~** rattle the dishes; **auf der Schreibmaschine ~** clatter away on the typewriter. **2.** shiver: **er klapperte vor Kälte (Angst) mit den Zähnen** his teeth are chattering with cold (fear).

'Klappern n (-s) clatter(ing) (etc.).

'Klapperschlange f zo. rattlesnake.

'Klapp(fahr)rad n folding bicycle.

'Klappfenster n top-hung window.

'Klappmesser n jackknife.

klapprig ['klapriç] adj F **1.** rattly, rickety. **2.** fig. shaky, doddering.

'Klappsitz m folding (or jump) seat.

'Klappstuhl m folding (or camp) chair.

'Klapptisch m folding table.

'Klappverdeck n mot. folding hood (Am. top).

Klaps [klaps] m (-es; -e) **1.** (a. j-m e-n ~ geben) slap, smack. **2.** F e-n ~ haben be nuts, have a screw loose.

'Klapsmühle f F funny farm, nut-house.

klar [kla:r] adj clear (a. fig.), a. distinct, fig. a. clear-cut (aim, decision, etc), a. lucid (moments etc), a. plain, obvious: **~er Sieg** clear victory; **~ zum Start** ready for takeoff; **e-n ~en Kopf behalten** keep one's wits about one; **sich in ~es Bild machen von** get a clear idea of; **~e Verhältnisse schaffen** get things

straight; **es ist ~, daß** it is clear (or evident) that; **es ist mir ~** (or **ich bin mir darüber im ~en**), **daß** I realize (or I'm aware) that; **ist das ~?** is that clear?; **das ist mir (nicht ganz) ~** I (don't quite) understand; **(na) ~!** of course!, sure!; **alles ~?** a) everything o.k.?, b) got it?; **~ und deutlich** clearly, distinctly, b) fig. straight; **et. ~ zum Ausdruck bringen** make s.th. plain; → a. **klargehen**, **klarkommen** etc.

'Kläranlage f sewage (purification) plant. **'Klärbecken** n settling basin.

'klären ['klɛ:rən] (h) **I** v/t **1.** purify, clear. **2.** fig. clear up, clarify, sort s.th. out. **II** sich ~ **3.** weather: clear (up). **4.** fig. issue: be settled, problem: be solved.

'klargehen v/i (irr, sep, -ge-, sn, → gehen) F be all right.

'Klarheit f (-; no pl) a. fig. clearness, clarity: **sich ~ verschaffen über** (acc) find out about.

Klarinette [klari'nɛtə] f (-; -n) clarinet.

'klarkommen v/i (irr, sep, -ge-, sn, → kommen) F manage: **mit j-m ~** get along (fine) with s.o.; **kommst du damit klar?** can you manage?

'klarmachen v/t (sep, -ge-, h) **1.** F j-m et. ~ make s.th. clear (or explain s.th.) to s.o.; **sich ~, daß** realize that. **2.** ♣ clear, get s.th. ready. **3.** F **alles ~** settle it.

'Klärschlamm m sewage sludge.

'Klarschrift f computer: (a. in ~) clear. **~leser** m (optical) character reader.

'klarsehen v/i (irr, sep, -ge-, h, → sehen) F fig. see (the light).

'Klarsicht|folie f cling film, transparent sheet. **~packung** f transparent packing. **~scheibe** f mot. antimist panel.

'klarstellen v/t (sep, -ge-, h) **et. ~** a) get s.th. straight, b) state s.th. clearly.

'Klartext m clear text: **im ~** a) in clear, b) fig. in plain language.

'Klärung f (-; -en) **1.** purification. **2.** fig. clarification, clearing up.

'klarwerden v/i (irr, sep, -ge-, sn, → werden) become clear (dat to): **sich ~ über** (acc) a) get s.th. clear in one's mind, b) make up one's mind about; **es wurde mir klar, daß** I realized that.

Klasse ['klasə] f (-; -n) **1.** class, ped. a. form, Am. grade. **2.** ✝ class, quality grade, (tax, age) bracket: **erster ~** a. fig. first-class; **nach ~n ordnen** class classify; F ~*!* super!, great!; **große** (*or* **einsame**) ~ *sein* be super (*or* fantastic).

'**Klassen|arbeit** *f ped.* (class) test. ~**bewußtsein** *n* class consciousness. ~**buch** *n* (class) register, *Am.* classbook. ~**gesellschaft** *f* class society. ~**kame ,rad(in** *f)* *m* classmate. ~**kampf** *m pol.* class struggle. ~**lehrer(in** *f)* *m* class (*Am. a.* homeroom) teacher.

'**klassenlos** *adj* classless.

'**Klassen|lotte,rie** *f* class lottery. ~**sprecher(in** *f)* *m ped.* class representative, *Br.* form captain. ~**unterschied** *m* class difference. ~**zimmer** *n* classroom.

klassifizieren [klasifi'tsi:rən] *v/t* (h) classify. **Klassifi'zierung** *f* (-; -en) classification.

Klassik ['klasɪk] *f* (-; *no pl*) **1.** classical period. **2.** classical music. **Klassiker** ['klasɪkər] *m* (-s; -) **1.** classic(al author). **2.** a) great artist (*etc*), b) (*work*) classic. '**klassisch** *adj* **1.** classical. **2.** *fig.* classic. **Klassizismus** [klasi'tsɪsmʊs] *m* (-; *no pl*) classicism. **klassizistisch** [klasi'tsɪstɪʃ] *adj* classicistic.

Klatsch [klatʃ] *m* (-es; -e) **1.** splash. **2.** smack, slap. **3.** *no pl* F gossip.

'**Klatschbase** *f* F gossip(monger).

Klatsche ['klatʃə] *f* (-; -n) **1.** (fly)swatter. **2.** F *ped.* crib. **3.** F gossip(monger).

klatschen ['klatʃən] (h) **I** *v/i* **1.** applaud, clap: *in die Hände* ~ clap one's hands. **2.** (*an acc* against) *rain etc*: splash, *waves*: crash. **3.** F gossip (*über acc* about). **II** *v/t* **4. et.** ~ *auf* (*acc*) *or* *gegen, an acc*) slap (*or* bang) s.th. on (*or* against). **5.** *Beifall* ~ applaud, clap.

Klatsche'rei *f* (-; -en) F gossip(ing).

'**Klatsch|kolum,nist(in** *f)* *m* F gossip columnist. ~**maul** *n* F real gossip.

'**klatschnaß** *adj* F dripping wet.

'**Klatschspalte** *f* F gossip column.

Klaue ['klaʊə] *f* (-; -n) **1.** *zo.* claw (*a.* ⚙), *a.* talon: *fig.* **in j-s** ~ *geraten* fall into s.o.'s clutches. **2.** F *fig.* scrawl.

klauen ['klaʊən] *v/t, v/i* (h) F swipe, pinch, *fig.* steal, borrow (*ideas etc*).

Klause ['klaʊzə] *f* (-; -n) hermitage.

Klausel ['klaʊzəl] *f* (-; -n) ⚖ a) clause, stipulation, b) proviso.

Klaustrophobie [klaʊstrofo'bi:] *f* (-; *no pl*) claustrophobia.

Klausur [klaʊ'zu:r] *f* (-; -en) **1.** *no pl* seclusion. **2.** *ped., univ.* test, paper.

Klau'surarbeit *f* → *Klausur* 2.
Klau'surtagung *f* closed meeting.
Klaviatur [klavia'tu:r] *f* (-; -en) ♩ keyboard.

Klavier [kla'vi:r] *n* (-s; -e) piano(forte): *auf dem* (*am*) ~ on (at) the piano; ~ *spielen* (*können*) play the piano.

Kla'vier|abend *m* piano recital. ~**auszug** *m* piano score. ~**begleitung** *f* piano accompaniment. ~**kon,zert** *n* **1.** piano concert. **2.** → *Klavierabend*. ~**lehrer(in** *f)* *m* piano teacher. ~**schemel** *m* piano stool. ~**schule** *f* (*book*) piano tutor. ~**so,nate** *f* piano sonata. ~**spieler(in** *f)* *m* pianist. ~**stimmer** *m* (piano) tuner. ~**stunde** *f* piano lesson. ~**unterricht** *m* piano lessons.

'**Klebeband** *n* adhesive (*or* sticky) tape.
'**Klebefolie** *f* adhesive film.
kleben ['kle:bən] (h) **I** *v/t* **1.** (*an acc* to) glue, paste. **2.** F *j-m e-e* ~ paste s.o. one. **II** *v/i* **3.** be sticky. **4.** (*an dat* to) adhere, stick: *fig.* *an j-m* ~ remain glued to s.o.; *an s-m Posten* ~ hang on to one's job.

'**klebenbleiben** *v/i* (*irr, sep, -ge-, sn,* → *bleiben*) **1.** stick (*an dat* to). **2.** F *fig.* get stuck (*in dat* in, at).

'**Klebepresse** *f film:* splicer.
'**Kleber** *m* (-s; -) **1.** gluten. **2.** F adhesive, glue.

'**Klebe|stelle** *f film:* splice. ~**stift** *m* glue stick. ~**streifen** *m* adhesive (*or* sticky) tape. ~**zettel** *m* gummed label.

klebrig ['kle:brɪç] *adj* sticky.
'**Klebrigkeit** *f* (-; *no pl*) stickiness.
Klebstoff ['kle:p-] *m* adhesive, glue.

kleckern ['klekərn] (h) F **I** *v/i* **1.** make a mess. **2.** drip. **II** *v/t* **3. et.** ~ *auf* (*acc*) spill s.th. on.

'**kleckerweise** *adv* F in dribs and drabs.

Klecks [klɛks] *m* (-es; -e) F **1.** stain, blot. **2.** blob. '**klecksen** *v/i* (h) F **1.** make blots (*or* stains), make a mess. **2.** daub.

Klee [kle:] *m* (-s; *no pl*) ♣ clover: *fig.* **über den grünen** ~ *loben* praise s.o., s.th. to the skies. '**Kleeblatt** *n* **1.** cloverleaf: *vierblättriges* ~ four-leaf(ed) clover. **2.** *mot.* cloverleaf (intersection).

Kleiber ['klaɪbər] *m* (-s; -) *zo.* nut hatch.
Kleid [klaɪt] *n* (-es; -er) **1.** dress (*a. fig.*), frock, gown. **2.** *pl* clothes, clothing: ~*er machen Leute* fine feathers make fine birds. **3.** *hunt.* a) fur, coat, b) plumage.
kleiden ['klaɪdən] (h) **I** *v/t* **1.** clothe,

dress: *fig. et. in Worte* ~ couch s.th. in words. **2. j-n** (*gut*) ~ suit (*or* become) s.o., look well on s.o. **II sich** ~ dress; *sich* ~ **in** (*acc*) wear.

Kleider|bügel ['klaɪdər-] *m* coat hanger. **~bürste** *f* clothes brush. **~haken** *m* coat hook. **~puppe** *f* dummy, mannequin. **~schrank** *m* wardrobe. **~ständer** *m* clothes tree (*or* rack). **~stoff** *m* dress material.

'**kleidsam** *adj* becoming.

Kleidung ['klaɪdʊŋ] *f* (-; *no pl*) clothing, clothes, garments. '**Kleidungsstück** *n* article of clothing, garment.

Kleie ['klaɪə] *f* (-; -) bran.

klein [klaɪn] **I** *adj* **1.** small, little (*finger, toe, house, etc*): *sehr* ~, *winzig* ~ very small, tiny, F teeny; *ziemlich* ~ rather small, smallish; *von* ~ *auf* from a child; *im ~en* in miniature; *mein ~er Bruder* my little (*or* young) brother; *die Welt ist* (*doch*) ~*!* it's a small world! **2.** *fig.* small, little, *a.* ♫ minor, petty: *aus ~en Verhältnissen kommen* have a humble background; *~e Geister* small minds; *der ~e Mann* the man in (*Am.* on) the street; *das ~ere Übel* the lesser evil; *bis ins ~ste* (down) to the last detail; *das ist m-e ~ste Sorge* that's the least of my worries. **II** *adv* small: *ein Wort* ~ *schreiben* write a word with a small (initial) letter; F *ein* (*ganz*) ~ *wenig* a little (*or* tiny) bit; *~ anfangen* start in a small way; → *beigeben* II.

'**Klein|aktie** *f* baby share (*Am.* stock). **~aktio,när(in** *f*) *m* small shareholder (*Am.* stockholder). **~anzeige** *f* classified advertisement (F ad). **~arbeit** *f a. mühevolle* ~ painstaking and detailed work. **~auto** *n* small car. **~bauer** *m* small farmer. **~betrieb** *m* small enterprise. **~bildkamera** *f* 35 mm camera. **~buchstabe** *m* small letter. **~bürger(in** *f*) *m*, **≈bürgerlich** *adj* petty bourgeois. **~bus** *m* minibus.

'**Kleine¹** *m*, *f* (-n; -n) little one.

'**Kleine²** *f* (-n; -n) F baby.

'**Klein|fa,milie** *f sociol.* nuclear family. **~for,mat** *n* small size: *im* ~ small-format. **~garten** *m* allotment (garden). **~gärtner(in** *f*) *m* allotment gardener.

'**Kleingedruckte** *n das* ~ *lesen* read the small print.

'**Kleingeld** *n* (small) change: *fig. das nö-*

tige ~ *haben* have the wherewithal.

'**kleingläubig** *adj* of little faith.

'**Kleinhandel** *m* → *Einzelhandel.*

'**Kleinheit** *f* (-; *no pl*) smallness (*a. fig.*).

'**Kleinhirn** *n anat.* cerebellum.

'**Kleinholz** *n* (-es; *no pl*) firewood: F *fig.* ~ *machen aus* a) *j-m* make mincemeat of s.o., b) *e-r Sache* smash s.th. to pieces.

'**Kleinigkeit** *f* (-; -en) a) trifle, small thing, b) (*gift*) little something, c) minor detail: *e-e* ~ *essen* have a bite; *das war e-e* (*k-e*) ~ that was (not) easy.

'**Kleinindu,strie** *f* small industry.

'**kleinka,riert** *adj* **1.** small-check(ed). **2.** F *fig.* small-minded.

'**Klein|kind** *n* infant. **~kram** *m* trifles. **~kre,dit** *m* small(-scale) credit. **~krieg** *m* guer(r)illa warfare: *fig.* **e-n** ~ *führen mit* keep up a running battle with.

'**kleinkriegen** *v/t* (*sep*) (*man*age to) break: *fig. j-n* ~ a) wear s.o. out, b) get s.o. down; *nicht kleinzukriegen a. person:* indestructible.

'**kleinlich** *adj* **1.** pedantic. **2.** narrow-minded. **3.** mean.

'**Kleinlichkeit** *f* (-; *no pl*) **1.** pedantry. **2.** narrow-mindedness. **3.** meanness.

Kleinod ['klaɪnoːt] *n* (-[e]s; -e) jewel.

'**Kleinrentner(in** *f*) *m* person receiving a small pension.

'**kleinschneiden** *v/t* (*irr, sep*, -ge-, h, → *schneiden*) cut up, chop (up).

'**kleinschreiben** *v/t* (*irr, sep*, -ge-, h, → *schreiben*) F *Ordnung etc wird bei ihm kleingeschrieben* he isn't a great one for order *etc.*

'**Kleinstaat** *m* minor state.

'**Klein|stadt** *f* small town. **~städter(in** *f*) *m*, **≈städtisch** *adj* provincial.

'**Kleinst|bildkamera** *f* subminiature camera. **~lebewesen** *n biol.* microorganism. **≈möglich** *adj* smallest possible. **~wagen** *m* minicar, midget car.

'**Klein|tier** *n* small (domestic) animal. **~vieh** *n* small domestic animals: F *fig. ~ macht auch Mist* many a little makes a mickle. **~wagen** *m* small car.

kleinwüchsig ['klaɪnvyːksɪç] *adj* small, short.

Kleister ['klaɪstər] *m* (-s; -) paste.

'**kleistern** *v/t* (h) paste (*an, auf acc* on).

Klematis [kle'maːtɪs] *f* (-; -) ♀ clematis.

Klemme ['klɛmə] *f* (-; -n) **1.** clamp (*a.* ⊕), clip, ⚡ terminal. **2.** F *fig. in der* ~

sein (*or* *sitzen*) be in a fix (*or* tight spot); *j-m aus der ~ helfen* help s.o. out of a fix.

klemmen ['klɛmən] (h) **I** *v/t* **1.** a) jam (*a.* ☺), b) squeeze, pinch, c) stick: *ich habe mir den Finger geklemmt* → 3. **II** *v/i* **2.** be jammed, be stuck: F *wo klemmt's?* what's wrong?, where's the snag? **III** *sich ~* 3. jam one's finger (*etc*), get one's finger (*etc*) caught. **4.** squeeze o.s. (*in acc* into, *hinter acc* behind): F *sich ~ hinter* a) e-e *Sache* get down to s.th., b) *j-n* get to work on s.o.

Klempner ['klɛmpnər] *m* (-s; -) **1.** tinsmith. **2.** plumber. **Klempnerei** [klɛmpnə'raɪ] *f* (-; -en) tinsmith's (*or* plumber's) workshop. '**Klempnermeister** *m* master tinsmith (*or* plumber).

Kleptomane [klɛpto'ma:nə] *m* (-n; -n) kleptomaniac. **Kleptomanie** [-ma'ni:] *f* (-; *no pl*) kleptomania. **Klepto'manin** *f* (-; -nen) kleptomaniac.

klerikal [kleri'ka:l] *adj* clerical.

Kleriker ['kle:rikər] *m* (-s; -) cleric.

Klerus ['kle:rʊs] *m* (-; *no pl*) clergy.

Klette ['klɛtə] *f* (-; -n) ❀ bur(r) (*a.* *fig.*): *sich wie e-e ~ an j-n hängen* cling to s.o. like a leech.

'**Kletterer** *m* (-s; -) climber.

'**Klettergerüst** *n* climbing frame.

klettern ['klɛtərn] *v/i* (sn) climb, ❀ *a.* creep, *fig. a.* go up (*auf acc* to): *auf e-n Baum ~* climb a tree.

'**Kletter|pflanze** *f* climber. **~rose** *f* rambler. **~stange** *f* climbing pole.

'**Klettverschluß** *m* Velcro (*TM*).

klicken ['klɪkən] *v/i* (h) click.

Klient [kli'ɛnt] *m* (-en; -en) ⚖ client.

Kliff [klɪf] *n* (-[e]s; -e) *geol.* cliff.

Klima ['kli:ma] *n* (-s; -s) climate, *fig. a.* atmosphere: *soziales ~* social climate.

'**Klimaanlage** *f* air-conditioning: *mit e-r ~ ausrüsten* air-condition.

Klimakterium [klimak'te:riʊm] *n* (-s; *no pl*) menopause, climacteric.

klimatisch [kli'ma:tɪʃ] *adj* climatic.

klimatisieren [klimati'zi:rən] *v/t* (h) air-condition.

Klimatologie [klimatolo'gi:] *f* (-; *no pl*) climatology.

'**Klimaveränderung** *f*, '**Klimawechsel** *m* change in climate.

Klimmzug ['klɪm-] *m gym.* chin-up: *e-n ~ machen* do a chin-up, chin o.s. up.

klimpern ['klɪmpərn] *v/i* (h) **1.** (*a. ~ mit*) jingle. **2.** *~ auf* (*dat*) strum on *the guitar*, tinkle on *the piano*.

Klinge ['klɪŋə] *f* (-; -n) blade.

Klingel ['klɪŋəl] *f* (-; -n) bell.

'**Klingelknopf** *m* bell push, call button.

klingeln ['klɪŋəln] (h) **I** *v/i* **1.** ring ([*nach*] *j-m* for s.o., *bei j-m* s.o.'s doorbell): *es klingelt* a) the doorbell is ringing, b) there's the bell. **2.** *engine*: ping. **II** *v/t* **3.** *j-n aus dem Bett ~* get s.o. out of bed.

'**Klingelzeichen** *n* ring, bell signal (signal).

klingen ['klɪŋən] *v/i* (klang, geklungen, h) sound (*a. fig.*), ring, *glasses*: clink, *metal*: clash: *fig. das klingt schon besser* that sounds better; *das klingt nach Neid* that sounds like envy.

'**klingend** *adj* melodious.

Klinik ['kli:nɪk] *f* (-; -en) clinic, nursing home. **Klinikum** ['kli:nikʊm] *n* (-s; -ka, -ken) clinical cent/re (*Am.* -er).

klinisch ['kli:nɪʃ] *adj* clinical: *~ tot* clinically dead.

Klinke ['klɪŋkə] *f* (-; -n) (door) handle.

Klinker ['klɪŋkər] *m* (-s; -) 🏛 clinker.

klipp [klɪp] *adv* *~ und klar* clearly, plainly; *ich habe ihm ~ und klar gesagt, daß ...* I told him straight out that ...

Klippe ['klɪpə] *f* (-; -n) *geol.* reef, rock: *fig. e-e ~ umschiffen* clear an obstacle.

klirren ['klɪrən] *v/i* (h) **1.** a) rattle, clatter, b) clink, chink, jingle: *~ mit* rattle (*one's chains, keys, etc*). **2.** *radio*: produce harmonic distortion.

'**Klirrfaktor** *m radio*: distortion factor.

Klischee [klɪ'ʃe:] *n* (-s; -s) *fig.* cliché. **~vorstellung** *f* stereotyped idea.

Klistier [klɪs'ti:r] *n* (-s; -e) ✚ enema. **Kli'stierspritze** *f* enema syringe.

Klitoris ['kli:torɪs] *f* (-; -) *anat.* clitoris.

klitschig ['klɪtʃɪç] *adj* doughy (*bread etc*).

klitzeklein ['klɪtsə-] *adj* F teeny(-weeny).

Klo [klo:] *n* (-s; -s) F loo, *Am.* john.

Kloake [klo'a:kə] *f* (-; -n) sewer.

Kloben ['klo:bən] *m* (-s; -) **1.** ☺ block. **2.** log.

'**klobig** *adj* bulky, *a. fig.* clumsy.

klönen ['klø:nən] *v/i* (h) F have a natter.

'**Klopa,pier** *n* F toilet (*Br. a.* loo) paper.

klopfen ['klɔpfən] (h) **I** *v/i* **1.** (*an acc* at, on) knock, tap: *es klopft* there's somebody (knocking) at the door; → *Busch* 1, *Finger, Schulter*. **2.** *heart etc*: beat, throb: *fig. mit ~dem Herzen* with (a) beating heart. **3.** *engine*: knock. **II** *v/t* **4.** beat (*carpet etc*): **den Takt ~** beat time.

'Klopfer *m* (-s; -) **1.** doorknocker. **2.** carpet-beater.

'klopffest *adj meist.* knockproof.

Klöppel ['klœpəl] *m* (-s; -) **1.** clapper (*of bell*). **2.** *textil.* (lace) bobbin. **'Klöppelkissen** *n* lace pillow. **'klöppeln** *v/i* (h) make lace. **'Klöppelspitze** *f* bone lace.

Klosett [klo'zɛt] *n* (-s; -s) lavatory, toilet. **~deckel** *m* toilet lid. **~pa,pier** *n* toilet paper. **~sitz** *m* toilet seat.

Kloß [klo:s] *m* (-es; ⸚e) dumpling: *fig.* **ich hatte e-n ~ im Hals** I had a lump in my throat.

Kloster ['klo:stər] *n* (-s; ⸚) a) monastery, b) convent, nunnery: **ins ~ gehen** enter a monastery (*etc*), become a monk (*or* nun). **~bruder** *m* friar. **~frau** *f* nun. **~leben** *n* monastic life.

klösterlich ['klø:stərlıç] *adj* monastic.

Klotz [klɔts] *m* (-es; ⸚e) **1.** block (*of wood*), log: F **er ist mir nur ein ~ am Bein** he is just a millstone round my neck. **2.** F *contp.* oaf, *Am. sl.* klutz.

'klotzig *adj* bulky, heavy.

Kluft¹ [kluft] *f* (-; ⸚e) *fig.* gap.

Kluft² *f* (-; -en) F togs, gear.

klug [klu:k] **I** *adj* **1.** a) intelligent, clever, smart, bright, shrewd, b) sensible, wise, judicious, c) prudent: **ein ~er Rat** a sound advice; **so ~ wie zuvor** none the wiser; **der Klügere gibt nach** the wiser head gives in. **2.** F **ich werde aus ihr** (**der Sache**) **nicht ~** I can't make her (it) out; **wirst du daraus ~?** ·does it make sense to you? **II** *adv* intelligently (*etc*): **du hättest klüger daran getan zu** *inf* you would have been wise to *inf*.

klugerweise ['klu:gər-] *adv* wisely, sensibly: **~hat sie geschwiegen** *a.* she had the good sense to keep quiet.

'Klugheit *f* (-; *no pl*) a) intelligence, brightness, b) good sense, c) prudence.

'Klugscheißer *m* F smart aleck, smarty.

klumpen ['klumpən] *v/i* (h) clot, become lumpy. **Klumpen** *m* (-s; -) lump, clot, clod. **'Klumpfuß** *m* clubfoot. **klumpig** ['klumpıç] *adj* lumpy, clotted.

Klüngel ['klyŋəl] *m* (-s; -) *contp.* clique.

Klunkern ['klʊŋkərn] *pl* F rocks, ice.

Klüver ['kly:vər] *m* (-s; -) ⚓ jib.

knabbern ['knabərn] *v/i, v/t* (h) (**an** *dat* at) nibble, gnaw: F *fig.* **ich hatte lange**

daran zu ~ a) I didn't get over it easily, b) it took me some time to figure it out.

Knabe ['kna:bə] *m* (-n; -n) boy, lad.

'Knabenalter *n* boyhood. **'Knabenchor** *m* boys' choir. **'knabenhaft** *adj* boyish.

Knäckebrot ['knɛkə-] *n* crispbread.

knacken ['knakən] (h) **I** *v/t a. fig.* crack: F **ein Auto ~** break into a car. **II** *v/i* a) crack, b) snap. **'Knacker** *m* (-s; -) F **alter ~** old fog(e)y. **Knacki** ['knaki] *m* (-s; -s) F jailbird. **'knackig** *adj* **1.** crisp crunchy. **2.** F *fig.* dishy.

'Knacklaut *m ling.* glottal stop.

'Knackpunkt *m* F *fig.* crunch (point).

Knacks [knaks] *m* (-es; -e) **1.** crack. **2.** F *fig.* defect: **er hat e-n ~** (**weg**) a) his health is shaken, b) his nerves are all shot, c) he is badly hit, d) he's slightly cracked; **ihre Ehe hat e-n ~** their marriage is cracking up.

Knall [knal] *m* (-[e]s; -e) **1.** bang, pop (*o, a cork*). **2.** *fig.* quarrel, row. **3.** F **e-n ~ haben** be nuts. **4.** F **~ und Fall** (all) of a sudden; **j-n ~ und Fall entlassen** dismiss s.o. on the spot.

'Knallbon,bon *m, n* (party) cracker.

'Knallef,fekt *m* F clou, sensation.

knallen ['knalən] (h) **I** *v/i* **1.** (*a. ~ mit*) *door etc*: bang, slam, *whip*: crack, *cork:* pop: **es knallte zweimal** there were two loud bangs. **2.** F bang, fire. **3.** F crash (**gegen** into): **mit dem Kopf an die Windschutzscheibe ~** hit one's head on the windscreen; F **sonst knallt's!** or else! **4.** F *sun:* beat down. **II** *v/t* **5.** bang, slam: **den Ball ins Tor ~** slam the ball home; F **j-m e-e ~** paste s.o. one.

'Knaller *m* (-s; -) F **1.** → **Knallkörper. 2.** → **Knüller.**

'Knallerbse *f* (toy) torpedo.

'Knallfrosch *m* jumping cracker.

'Knallgas *n* 🔬 oxyhydrogen (gas).

'knall'hart *adj* F **1.** smashing, powerful (*blow etc*). **2.** *fig.* tough, brutal: **~ fragen** *etc* ask *etc* with brutal frankness.

'knallig F **I** *adj* **1.** loud, glaring (*colo[u]r*). **2.** skintight. **II** *adv* **~ bunt** gaudy; **~ heiß** scorching.

'Knallkopf *m* F idiot.

'Knallkörper *m* banger.

'knall'rot *adj* bright red, crimson.

'knall'voll *adj* F **1.** jam-packed. **2.** dead drunk, paralytic.

knapp [knap] **I** *adj* **1.** scanty, meag/re

(*Am.* -er): **~ sein** be scarce, be in short supply; **~ werden** run short; → **Kasse** 4. **2.** *fig.* narrow: **~e Mehrheit** bare majority. **3.** *fig.* concise, terse (*style etc*), brief, short (*answer etc*): **in ~en Worten** in a few words. **4. ~(e) zwei Stunden** just under two hours; **in e-m ~en Jahr** just under a year; **~ 10 Minuten** barely (*or* just) ten minutes. **5.** tight (*skirt etc*). **II** *adv* **6.** only just: **~ gewinnen** win by a narrow margin; **e-e Prüfung ~ bestehen** scrape through an examination; F **(aber) nicht zu ~!** a) you bet!, b) plenty of it!, c) and how! **7. ~ sitzen** fit tightly; *fig.* **m-e Zeit ist ~ bemessen** I'm pushed for time.

'**knapphalten** *v/t* (*irr, sep,* -ge-, h, → **halten**) F *j-n* ~ keep s.o. short.

'**Knappheit** *f* (-; *no pl*) **1.** a) scantiness, b) scarcity, shortage. **2.** *fig.* narrowness. **3.** *fig.* terseness, conciseness, shortness. **4.** tightness.

'**Knappschaft** *f* (-; -en) miners' association.

Knarre ['knarə] *f* (-; -n) F gun.

knarren ['knarən] *v/i* (h) creak.

Knast [knast] *m* (-[e]s; -e, ⸚e) F (*im ~* in) clink: **~ schieben** do time.

'**Knastbruder** *m* F jailbird.

knattern ['knatərn] *v/i* (h) rattle, *motorbike etc*: roar, *flag, sail*: flap.

Knäuel ['knɔʏəl] *m, n* (-s; -) **1.** ball (*of wool*). **2.** tangle. **3.** cluster (*of people*).

Knauf [knaʊf] *m* (-[e]s; ⸚e) **1.** knob. **2.** △ capital. **3.** pommel.

Knauser ['knaʊzər] *m* (-s; -) F miser.

Knause'rei *f* (-; -en) F stinginess.

'**knauserig** *adj* F stingy.

knausern ['knaʊzərn] *v/i* (h) F be stingy.

knautschen ['knaʊtʃən] *v/i* (h) F crease, crumple.

'**Knautschzone** *f mot.* crumple zone.

Knebel ['kne:bəl] *m* (-s; -) gag.

knebeln ['kne:bəln] *v/t* a. *fig.* gag.

Knecht [knɛçt] *m* (-[e]s; -e) **1.** farmhand. **2.** *fig.* slave. **knechten** ['knɛçtən] *v/t* enslave. '**Knechtschaft** *f* (-; *no pl*) slavery. '**Knechtung** *f* (-; -en) enslavement.

kneifen ['knaɪfən] (kniff, gekniffen, h) **I** *v/t* **1.** pinch: *j-n* (*or j-m*) **in den Arm ~** pinch s.o.'s arm. **II** *v/i* **2.** pinch. **3.** F (**vor** *dat*) dodge (*s.th.*), back out (of), chicken out (of, on).

'**Kneifzange** *f* (e-e ~ a pair of) pincers.

Kneipe ['knaɪpə] *f* (-; -n) F pub, *Am.* bar. '**Kneipenbummel** *m* (*a.* **e-n ~ machen**) pub-crawl.

Kneippkur ['knaɪp-] *f* ⚕ Kneipp('s) cure.

Knete ['kne:tə] *f* (-; *no pl*) F **1.** → **Knetmasse**. **2.** lolly, *Am.* bread. '**kneten** *v/t* (h) a) knead, *a.* massage, b) mo(u)ld. '**Knetmasse** *f* plasticine.

Knick [knɪk] *m* (-[e]s; -e) **1.** (sharp) bend: **die Straße macht e-n ~** *a.* the road bends sharply. **2.** a) crease, fold, b) kink. **3.** *fig.* (sharp) drop, falling off.

knicken ['knɪkən] *v/t* (h) **1.** (*a. v/i*) break, snap: → **geknickt**. **2.** crease, fold: *nicht ~!* do not bend! **3.** (*a. v/i*) buckle, bend.

knickerig ['knɪkərɪç] *adj* F stingy, mean.

Knicks [knɪks] *m* (-es; -e) curtsy: **e-n ~ machen** → **knicksen** ['knɪksən] *v/i* (h) (drop a) curtsy (*vor j-m* to s.o.).

Knie [kni:] *n* (-s; - ['kni:(ə)]) **1.** knee: **bis an die ~** up to one's knees, knee-deep; *j-n auf den ~n bitten* beg s.o. on bended knees; **in die ~ brechen** collapse; **in die ~ gehen** a) sag at the knees, b) *fig.* go to the wall; *j-n in die ~ zwingen* a. *fig.* force s.o. on his knees; *fig. et. übers ~ brechen* rush s.th.; F **weiche ~ bekommen** go weak at the knees, become scared; *j-n übers ~ legen* give s.o. a spanking. **2.** ⊙ elbow, bend.

'**Kniebeuge** *f gym.* knee bend. '**Kniefall** *m eccl.* genuflection. '**kniefrei** *adj* above-the-knee. '**Kniegelenk** *n a.* ⊙ knee joint. '**Kniekehle** *f anat.* hollow of the knee. '**knielang** *adj* knee-length.

knien [kni:n, 'kni:ən] (h) **I** *v/i* (**vor** *dat* before) kneel, be on one's knees. **II** *sich ~* kneel down; F *fig.* **sich ~ in** (*acc*) get down to.

'**Kniescheibe** *f anat.* kneecap. '**Knieschützer** *m sports:* kneepad. '**Kniestrumpf** *m* knee-length sock. '**knietief** *adj* knee-deep.

kniff [knɪf] *pret of* **kneifen.**

Kniff *m* (-[e]s; -e) **1.** crease, fold. **2.** *fig.* trick. **kniffelig** ['knɪfəlɪç] *adj* tricky.

kniffen ['knɪfən] *v/t* (h) fold, crease.

knipsen ['knɪpsən] (h) **I** *v/t* **1.** punch (*ticket*). **2.** *j-n* ~ take s.o.'s picture, snap s.o. **II** *v/i* **3.** F take photos, snap.

Knirps [knɪrps] *m* (-es; -e) little chap (*Am.* guy), *contp.* squirt.

knirschen ['knɪrʃən] *v/i* (h) grate, *snow,*

sand, etc: crunch: *mit den Zähnen ~* grind (*or* gnash) one's teeth.

knistern ['knɪstərn] *v/i* (h) crackle, *silk, paper, etc*: rustle: *fig. der Saal knisterte vor Spannung* the atmosphere in the hall was electric.

'**Knitterfalte** *f* crease. '**knitterfrei** *adj* creaseproof, noncrease. **knittern** ['knɪtərn] *v/i, v/t* (h) crease, wrinkle.

knobeln ['kno:bəln] *v/i* (h) **1.** (*um* for) throw dice, toss. **2.** F puzzle (*an dat* over).

Knoblauch ['kno:p-] *m* ♣ garlic. **~kapsel** *f* garlic pill. **~zehe** *f* clove of garlic.

Knöchel ['knœçəl] *m* (-s; -) a) knuckle, b) ankle. '**Knöchelbruch** *m* ✚ ankle fracture. '**knöchellang** *adj* ankle-length.

Knochen ['knɔxən] *m* (-s; -) bone: *Fleisch mit (ohne) ~* meat on (off) the bone; *bis auf die ~* a) *abgemagert* just skin and bones, b) *naß* soaked to the skin; F *der Schreck fuhr mir in die ~* I was shaken to the core; *das ist ihm in die ~ gefahren* it really got to him; *sich bis auf die ~ blamieren* make an absolute fool of o.s.

'**Knochen|arbeit** *f* hard slog, gruel(l)ing work. **~bau** *m* (-[e]s; *no pl*) bone structure. **~bruch** *m* ✚ fracture. **~gerüst** *n* skeleton. **♣hart** *adj* F (as) hard as stone. **~haut** *f* periosteum. **~krebs** *m* ✚ bone cancer. **~mark** *n* (bone) marrow. **~mehl** *n* ♣ bone meal. **~mühle** *f* F sweatshop. **~splitter** *m* bone splinter.

'**knochentrocken** *adj* F bone-dry.

knöchern ['knœçərn] *adj* bone ..., bony.

knochig ['knɔxɪç] *adj* bony.

Knödel ['knø:dəl] *m* (-s; -) dumpling.

Knolle ['knɔlə] *f* (-; -n) ♣ tuber, bulb.

Knollen ['knɔlən] *m* (-s; -) lump.

'**Knollenblätterpilz** *m* death cup.

'**Knollennase** *f* F bulbous nose.

knollig ['knɔlɪç] *adj* ♣ tuberous, bulbous.

Knopf [knɔpf] *m* (-[e]s; ꞏe) button: ⊙ *auf e-n ~ drücken* push a button. **2.** → *Knauf* 1, 3. '**Knopfdruck** *m auf (or per) ~* at the touch of a button.

knöpfen ['knœpfən] *v/t* (h) button: *zum ⊙ buttoned*.

'**Knopfloch** *n* buttonhole.

Knorpel ['knɔrpəl] *m* (-s; -) **1.** *anat.* cartilage. **2.** *gastr.* gristle. '**knorpelig** *adj* **1.** *anat.* cartilaginous. **2.** *gastr.* gristly.

Knorren ['knɔrən] *m* (-s; -) knot, snag.

'**knorrig** *adj* **1.** gnarled, knotty. **2.** *fig.* gruff.

Knospe ['knɔspə] *f* (-; -n) bud.

knospen ['knɔspən] *v/i* (h) bud.

knospig ['knɔspɪç] *adj* full of buds.

knoten ['kno:tən] *v/t* (h) knot, tie a knot.

'**Knoten** *m* (-s; -) **1.** knot: *e-n ~ machen* tie a knot (*in acc* into); F *bei ihm ist endlich der ~ geplatzt* he has caught on at last. **2.** bun, knot. **3.** ⚓ knot: *10 ~ machen* do ten knots. **4.** ♣, ✚ knot, a. *astr., phys.* node. '**Knotenpunkt** *m* **1.** 🚆 *etc* junction. **2.** *fig.* cent/re (*Am.* -er).

knotig ['kno:tɪç] *adj a. fig.* knotty.

Knuff [knʊf] *m* (-[e]s; ꞏe) F poke, nudge: *j-m e-n ~ geben* → **knuffen** ['knʊfən] *v/t* (h) *j-n ~* punch (*or* nudge) s.o.

Knülch [knʏlç] *m* (-[e]s; -e) F bloke, *Am.* guy, *sl.* creep.

knüllen ['knʏlən] *v/t, v/i* (h) crumple.

Knüller ['knʏlər] *m* (-s; -) F sensation, (big) hit, scoop.

knüpfen ['knʏpfən] (h) **I** *v/t* tie, make, knot (*carpet*): *~ an* (*acc*) fasten (*fig.* attach *conditions, hopes, etc*) to. **II** *sich ~ an* (*acc*) *fig.* condition *etc*: be attached to, *memories etc*: be connected with.

Knüppel ['knʏpəl] *m* (-s; -) **1.** a) (heavy) stick, club, b) truncheon, *Am.* billy: *fig. j-m e-n ~ zwischen die Beine werfen* put a spoke in s.o.'s wheels. **2.** ✈ stick. '**Knüppeldamm** *m* corduroy road.

knüppeln ['knʏpəln] *v/t* (h) beat, club.

'**Knüppelschaltung** *f mot.* floor shift, floor-mounted gear change

knurren ['knʊrən] *v/i* (h) **1.** (*a. v/t*) growl, snarl. **2.** *fig.* grumble (*über acc* at). **3.** *stomach*: rumble: *mir knurrt der Magen* I'm famished.

knurrig ['knʊrɪç] *adj* F *fig.* grumpy.

knusp(e)rig ['knʊsp(ə)rɪç] *adj* crisp.

Knute ['knu:tə] *f* (-; -n) knout: *fig. unter j-s ~ stehen* be under s.o.'s thumb.

knutschen ['knu:tʃən] *v/i* (h) F (*a. sich ~*) neck, smooch, snog.

'**Knutschfleck** *m* F love bite.

k.o. [ka:'ʔo:] *adj* *pred boxing*: knocked out: *j-n ~ schlagen* knock s.o. out; F *fig. ich bin ~* I'm all in, I'm bushed.

K.'o. *m* (-; -) *boxing*: knockout.

Koalition [koʔali'tsio:n] *f* (-; -en) *pol.* coalition.

Kobalt ['ko:balt] *m* (-[e]s; *no pl*) cobalt. '**Kobaltblau** *n* cobalt blue.

Kobold ['koːbɔlt] m (-[e]s; -e) goblin.

Koch [kɔx] m (-[e]s; ⁓e) cook: **viele Köche verderben den Brei** too many cooks spoil the broth.

'**Kochbuch** n cookery book, cookbook.

'**kochecht** adj (boil)fast.

kochen ['kɔxən] (h) I v/t **1.** a) cook, b) boil, c) make (tea etc). II v/i **2.** cook, do the cooking: **sie kocht gut** she is a good cook. **3.** food: be cooking, water: be boiling: **leicht ⁓, auf kleiner Flamme ⁓** simmer; fig. **er kochte innerlich** (or **vor Wut**) he was seething with rage.

'**Kochen** n (-s) cooking: **et. zum ⁓ bringen** bring s.th. to the boil; fig. **j-n zum ⁓ bringen** make s.o.'s blood boil.

'**kochendheiß** adj boiling hot, scalding.

Kocher ['kɔxər] m (-s; -) cooker.

Köcher ['kœçər] m (-s; -) **1.** quiver. **2.** phot. lens case.

'**kochfertig** adj ready-to-cook, instant.

'**Kochgelegenheit** f cooking facilities.

'**Kochgeschirr** n ⚔ mess tin (Am. kit).

Köchin ['kœçɪn] f (-; -nen) cook.

'**Koch|kunst** f **1.** no pl gastronomy. **2.** **ihre Kochkünste** her cooking (ability). **⁓kurs(us)** m cookery course. **⁓löffel** m spoon. **⁓nische** f kitchenette. **⁓platte** f hot plate. **⁓re,zept** n recipe.

'**Kochsalz** n **1.** table salt. **2.** ⚗ sodium chloride. **⁓lösung** f ⚕ saline (solution).

'**Kochtopf** m cooking pot, saucepan.

'**Kochwäsche** f boil wash.

Köder ['køːdər] m (-s; -) bait.

ködern ['køːdərn] v/t (h) a. fig. bait: **er läßt sich mit Geld nicht ⁓** he is not tempted by money.

Koeffizient [koʔɛfiˈtsiɛnt] m (-en; -en) ⅍ coefficient.

Koexistenz ['koːʔɛksɪstɛnts] f (-; no pl) coexistence.

Koffein [kɔfeˈiːn] n (-s; no pl) caffeine.

koffe'infrei adj decaffeinated.

Koffer ['kɔfər] m (-s; -) a) bag, case, suitcase, b) trunk: **⁓ packen** pack one's bags; F fig. **die ⁓ packen** leave; **aus dem ⁓ leben** live out of a suitcase. **⁓anhänger** m luggage tag. **⁓gerät** n, **⁓radio** n portable. **⁓raum** m mot. boot, Am. trunk: **viel ⁓ haben** have much luggage space.

Kognak ['kɔnjak] m (-s; -s) cognac, brandy.

Kohl [koːl] m (-[e]s; -e) **1.** ⚘ cabbage. **2.** F fig. (**red k-n ⁓** don't talk) rubbish.

'**Kohldampf** m F **⁓ haben** be starving.

Kohle ['koːlə] f (-; -n) **1.** a) coal, b) charcoal (a. paint.): **ausgeglühte ⁓** cinders; **glühende ⁓** ember; fig. **weiße ⁓** white coal, waterpower; **ich saß** (**wie**) **auf** (**glühenden**) **⁓n** I was on tenterhooks. **2.** F fig. lolly, Am. bread: **Hauptsache, die ⁓n stimmen!** it's all right as long as the money is right!

'**kohlehaltig** adj carboniferous.

'**Kohlehy,drat** n carbohydrate.

'**Kohlekraftwerk** n coal power plant.

'**Kohlenbergbau** m coal mining.

'**Kohlenbergwerk** n coal mine.

Kohlen'dio,xyd n ⚗ carbon dioxide.

'**Kohlen|eimer** m coal scuttle. **⁓flöz** n coal seam. **⁓grube** f coal mine. **⁓händler(in** f) m coal merchant.

Kohlen'mono,xyd n ⚗ carbon monoxide.

'**Kohlen|re,vier** n coalfield. **⁓säure** f ⚗ carbonic acid. **⁓staub** m coal dust. **⁓stoff** m ⚗ carbon. **⁓wasserstoff** m ⚗ hydrocarbon.

'**Kohle|pa,pier** n carbon (paper). **⁓stift** m charcoal. **⁓ta,blette** f charcoal tablet. **⁓vorkommen** n coal deposit(s). **⁓zeichnung** f charcoal (drawing).

'**Kohlkopf** m ⚘ cabbage.

'**Kohlmeise** f zo. great titmouse.

'**kohl'raben'schwarz** adj coal-black.

Kohlrabi [koːlˈraːbi] m (-[s]; -[s]) ⚘ kohlrabi.

'**Kohlrübe** f ⚘ swede.

Kohlweißling ['koːlvaɪslɪŋ] m (-s; -e) zo. cabbage butterfly.

Koitus ['koːitʊs] m (-; -) coitus, coition.

Koje ['koːjə] f (-; -n) ⚓ berth, bunk.

Kokain [kokaˈiːn] n (-s; no pl) cocaine.

Kokarde [koˈkardə] f (-; -n) ✕ cockade.

kokett [koˈkɛt] adj coquettish, flirtatious. **Koketterie** [kokɛtəˈriː] f (-; -n) coquetry. **kokettieren** [kokɛˈtiːrən] v/i (h) a. fig. flirt (**mit** with).

Kokken ['kɔkən] pl ⚕ cocci.

Kokolores [kokoˈloːrəs] m (-; no pl) F rubbish.

Kokon [koˈkõː] m (-s; -s) cocoon.

'**Kokos|faser** ['koːkɔs-] f coconut fibre (Am. fiber), coir. **⁓fett** n coconut fat. **⁓milch** f coconut milk. **⁓nuß** f coconut. **⁓palme** f coconut palm.

Koks¹ [kɔks] m (-es; -e) **1.** ⊙ coke. **2.** F fig. lolly, Am. bread.

Koks² m (-es; no pl) sl. coke.

koksen ['kɔksən] v/i (h) sl. take coke.

Kolben ['kɔlbən] m (-s; -) **1.** ⊙ a) piston, b) plunger (a. ✿). **2.** ♨ flask. **3.** (rifle) butt. **4.** ♀ spike. **5.** F conk.

'Kolben|fresser m mot. F jamming of the piston. **~hub** m piston stroke. **~ring** m piston ring. **~stange** f piston rod.

Kolchos ['kɔlçɔs] m (-; -e [kɔl'çoːzə]), **Kolchose** [kɔl'çoːzə] f (-; -n) kolkhoz, collective farm.

Kolibakterie ['koːli-] f ✿ colibacillus.

Kolibri ['koːlibri] m (-s; -s) zo. humming-bird.

Kolik ['koːlɪk] f (-; -en) ✿ colic.

Kollaborateur [kɔlabora'tøːr] m (-s; -e) pol. collaborator.

Kollaps ['kɔlaps] m (-es; -e) ✿ (a. **e-n ~ erleiden**) collapse.

Kolleg [kɔ'leːk] n (-s; -s, -ien [-giːən]) univ. a) (single) lecture, b) course of lectures, c) → **Kollegstufe: ein ~ halten über** (acc) lecture on.

Kollege [kɔ'leːgə] m (-n; -n) colleague.

kollegial [kɔle'giaːl] adj cooperative, helpful: **sich ~ verhalten** be loyal (**gegenüber** to[wards]).

Kollegin [kɔ'leːgɪn] f (-; -nen).

Kollegium [kɔ'leːgiʊm] n (-s; -ien) ped. (teaching) staff, Am. a. faculty.

Kol'legmappe f (underarm) briefcase.

Kol'legstufe f ped. sixth-form college.

Kollekte [kɔ'lɛktə] f (-; -n) collection.

Kollektion [kɔlɛk'tsioːn] f (-; -en) a) collection, ✚ a. range, b) samples, c) selection.

kollektiv [kɔlɛk'tiːf] adj, **Kollek'tiv** n (-s; -e) collective. **kollektivieren** [kɔlɛkti-'viːrən] v/t (h) collectivize.

Kollek'tivschuld f collective guilt.

Kollektivum [kɔlɛk'tiːvʊm] n ling. (-s; -va) collective (noun).

Kollektor [kɔ'lɛktor] m (-s; -en [-'toːrən]) ⚡ commutator, collector.

Koller [kɔ'lər] m (-s; -) F (**e-n ~ kriegen** fly into a) tantrum.

kollern ['kɔlərn] v/i **1.** (sn) roll. **2.** (h) turkey: gobble.

kollidieren [kɔli'diːrən] v/i **1.** (sn) collide. **2.** (h) fig. collide, clash.

Kollier [kɔ'lieː] n (-s; -s) necklace.

Kollision [kɔli'zioːn] f (-; -en) collision,

fig. a. clash, conflict. **Kollisi'onskurs** m a. fig. (**auf ~ on** a) collision course.

Kolloquium [kɔ'loːkviʊm] n (-s; -ien) colloquium.

Kölner ['kœlnər] I m (-s; -) inhabitant of Cologne. II adj (of) Cologne: **der ~ Dom** Cologne Cathedral.

'Kölnerin f (-; -nen) → **Kölner** I.

Kölnischwasser ['kœlnɪʃ-] n (-s; no pl) eau-de-Cologne.

Kolonial... [kolo'nia:l] colonial (empire, power, etc). **Kolonialismus** [kolonia-'lɪsmʊs] m (-; no pl) colonialism.

Kolonie [kolo'ni:] f (-; -n) colony.

Kolonisation [koloniza'tsio:n] f (-; -en) colonization. **kolonisieren** [koloni-'zi:rən] v/t (h) colonize. **Kolonist** [kolo'nɪst] m (-en; -en) colonist, settler.

Kolonnade [kɔlɔ'na:də] f (-; -n) △ colonnade.

Kolonne [ko'lɔnə] f (-; -n) column (a. ℞, print.), a. mot. line, ✕ convoy: **~ fahren** drive in line (or convoy); pol. **die Fünfte ~** the Fifth Column.

Ko'lonnenspringer m mot. F queue jumper.

Kolophonium [kolo'fo:niʊm] n (-s; no pl) colophony, rosin.

Koloratur [kolora'tu:r] f (-; -en) coloratura. **~so,pran** m coloratura soprano.

kolorieren [kolo'ri:rən] v/t (h) colo(u)r.

Kolorit [kolo'ri:t, -'rɪt] n (-[e]s; -e) **1.** ♪ colo(u)r. **2.** paint. colo(u)ring. **3.** fig. (local) colo(u)r, atmosphere.

Koloß [ko'lɔs] m (-sses; -sse) colossus.

kolossal [kolo'sa:l] adj colossal, huge, gigantic, F fig. a. enormous: **~ viel** an enormous amount (of).

Kolportage [kɔlpɔr'ta:ʒə] f (-; -n) **1.** sensationalism. **2.** → **Kolpor'tageliteratur** f trashy (or sensational) literature. **kolportieren** [kɔlpɔr'ti:rən] v/t (h) spread.

Kolumne [ko'lʊmnə] f (-; -n) print. column. **Ko'lumnentitel** m (**lebender ~** running) head(line). **Kolumnist** [kolʊm'nɪst] m (-en; -en) columnist.

Kombi ['kɔmbi] m (-[s]; -s) → **Kombiwagen**. **'Kombikarte** f combi-ticket.

Kombinat [kɔmbi'na:t] n (-[e]s; -e) ✚ combined collective.

Kombination [kɔmbina'tsio:n] f (-; -en) **1.** combination (a. chess, of lock etc) soccer etc: (combined) move. **2.** fig. a)

deduction, b) conjecture. **3.** *fashion*: set, ensemble. **4.** a) overalls, b) flying suit. **5.** *skiing*: **Alpine (Nordische) ~** Alpine (Nordic) Combined.
Kombinati'ons|gabe *f* power(s) of deduction. **~schloß** *n* combination lock.
kombinieren [kɔmbi'ni:rən] (h) **I** *v/t* **1.** combine (*mit* with). **II** *v/i* **2.** *sports*: combine: **gut ~** show excellent teamwork. **3.** *fig.* a) deduct, b) conjecture.
'**Kombiwagen** *m* estate car, *Am.* station wagon.
Kombüse [kɔm'by:zə] *f* (-; -) ♣ galley.
Komet [ko'me:t] *m* (-en; -en) comet.
ko'metenhaft *adj* comet-like, meteoric.
Komfort [kɔm'fo:r] *m* (-s; *no pl*) a) comfort, b) luxury, c) conveniences: **mit allem ~** flat etc with all modern conveniences, *car etc* with all the extras.
komfortabel [kɔmfɔr'ta:bəl] *adj* a) comfortable, b) luxurious.
Kom'fortwohnung *f* luxury flat.
Komik ['ko:mɪk] *f* (-; *no pl*) a) the comic, b) comic effect (*or* touch): **e-r gewissen ~ nicht entbehren** have a comic side. '**Komiker** *m* (-s; -) comedian (*a.* F *fig.*), comic actor. '**Komikerin** *f* (-; -nen) comedienne, comic actress.
komisch ['ko:mɪʃ] *adj* **1.** comic(al), funny: **~e Oper** comic opera; **was ist daran so ~?** what's so funny about it? **2.** F *fig.* funny, queer: **ich habe so ein ~es Gefühl** I feel funny; **das kam mir sehr ~ vor** I found that very strange; **das Komische daran ist** the funny thing about it is; **~, daß ...** (it's) funny that ...
'**komischerweise** *adv* funnily enough.
Komitee [komi'te:] *n* (-s; -s) committee.
Komma ['kɔma] *n* (-s; -s, -ta) a) comma, b) ♣ (decimal) point: **vier ~ fünf** (4,5) four point five; **null ~ drei** point three.
Kommandant [kɔman'dant] *m* (-en; -en) commander. **Kommandantur** [kɔmandan'tu:r] *f* (-; -en) (garrison, *Am.* post) headquarters. **Kommandeur** [kɔman-'dø:r] *m* (-s; -e) commanding officer.
kommandieren [kɔman'di:rən] (h) *v/t* **1.** command, be in command of: **j-n ~ zu** detail (*or* detail) s.o. to. **II** *v/i* **2.** (*be in*) command: **~der General** commanding general. **3.** F give the orders.
Kommanditgesellschaft [kɔman'di:t-] *f* ♣ limited partnership.

Kommanditist [kɔmandi'tɪst] *m* (-en; -en) ♣ limited partner.
Kommando [kɔ'mando] *n* (-s; -s) a) command, order, b) commando (unit), c) detachment: (*wie*) **auf ~** (as if) by command. **~brücke** *f* ♣ bridge. **~kapsel** *f* command module. **~raum** *m* control room. **~sprache** *f* computer: command language. **~zen,trale** *f* control cent/re (*Am.* -er).
kommen ['kɔmən] (kam, gekommen, sn) **I** *v/i* **1.** come (*a.* F *orgasmically*), *a.* arrive, *a.* approach, *a.* get (*bis* to): **angelaufen ~** come running; **j-n ~ sehen** see s.o. coming (*or* come); **ich habe es ~ sehen** I saw it coming; **~ lassen** a) send for, call (*s.o.*), b) order (*s.th.*); **weit ~** *a. fig.* get far; **er wird bald ~** he won't be long; **wann kommt der nächste Zug?** when is the next train due (to arrive)?; **zur Schule ~** start school; **komme, was wolle** come what may; **mir kam der Gedanke** it occurred to me; **ihr kamen die Tränen** her eyes filled with tears; **später kamen mir Zweifel** afterwards I started to have doubts; **(na,) komm schon!** come on!; **ich komme (schon)!** (I'm) coming!; F **~ Sie mir nicht so!** don't (you) try that on me!; → **Gefängnis, spät II. 2. ~ auf** (*acc*) a) hit on, b) think of, c) amount to, come to; **ich komme nicht darauf!** I just can't think of it!; **darauf komme ich gleich** (*zu sprechen*)! I'll be coming to that!; **wie kommst du darauf?** what makes you think (*or* say) that?; **auf jeden von uns ~ zwei Äpfel** each of us will get two apples; **er kommt auf 3000 Mark im Monat** he makes 3,000 marks a month; → **Schliche, Sprache** 2 *etc.* **3.** *hinter et.* ~ find out. **4.** F **er kommt nach s-r Mutter** he takes after his mother. **5. was ist über dich gekommen?** what has come over (*or* got into) you? **6. ~ um** (*acc*) a) lose, b) miss. **7. ~ von** come from, *fig. a.* be due to. **8. ~ zu** come by, get; **zu Geld ~** come into money; (*wieder*) **zu sich ~** come round (*or* to), *w.s.* recover; **sie ist nicht dazu gekommen, den Brief zu schreiben** she didn't get round to writing the letter; **wie ~ Sie dazu?** how dare you? **II** *v/impers* **9. es kommt j-d** s.o. is coming. **10.** happen, come (about): **so mußte**

es ja ~! it was bound to happen that way!; **wie kommt es, daß ...?** why is it that ...?, F how come ...?; **daher kommt es, daß ...** that's why ...; **es kam zum Krieg** there was a war; **es ist so weit gekommen, daß ...** things have got to a stage where ...

'**Kommen** n (-s) a) coming, b) arrival: fig. **... sind wieder im ~** ... are coming (or are on the way in) again.

'**kommend** adj coming, a. future: **~e Woche** next week; **in den ~en Jahren** in the years to come; **die ~e Generation** the rising generation; **er ist der ~e Mann** he is the coming man.

Kommentar [komɛn'taːr] m (-s; -e) (**zu** on) a) commentary, b) (**kein ~!** no) comment(!). **kommen'tarlos** adv without comment. **Kommentator** ['-'taːtor] m (-s; -en [-taː'toːrən]) commentator. **kommentieren** [komɛn'tiːrən] v/t (h) comment (on).

kommerzialisieren [komɛrtsǐali'ziːrən] v/t (h) commercialize. **kommerziell** [komɛr'tsǐɛl] adj commercial.

Kommilitone [komili'toːnə] m (-n; -n), **Kommili'tonin** f (-; -nen) univ. fellow student.

Kommiß [ko'mɪs] m (-sses; no pl) F (**beim ~** in the) army.

Kommissar [komi'saːr] m (-s; -e) 1. commissioner. 2. → **Kriminalkommissar.**

kommissarisch [komi'saːrɪʃ] adj 1. temporary. 2. deputy.

Kommission [komi'sǐoːn] f (-; -en) (a. ✝ **in ~** on) commission, committee.

Kommissionär [komisǐo'nɛːr] m (-s; -e) ✝ commission agent.

Kommissi'onsbuchhändler(in f) m wholesale bookseller.

Kommode [ko'moːdə] f (-; -n) chest of drawers.

Kommodore [komo'doːrə] m (-s; -n, -s) ♣ commodore.

kommunal [komu'naːl] adj local, municipal.

Kommu'nal|abgaben pl local rates (Am. taxes). **~beamte** m municipal officer. **~poli,tik** f local politics. **~verwaltung** f local government. **~wahlen** pl local elections.

Kommune [ko'muːnə] f (-; -n) 1. community. 2. commune.

Kommunikation [komunika'tsǐoːn] f (-; -en) communication.

Kommunikati'ons|mittel n means of communication, pl a. (mass) media. **~schwierigkeiten** pl **~ haben** have difficulty communicating. **~technik** f communications technology. **~wissenschaft** f communication(s) science.

kommunikativ [komunika'tiːf] adj communicative.

Kommunion [komu'nǐoːn] f (-; -en) eccl. (Holy) Communion.

Kommuniqué [komyni'keː] n (-s; -s) communiqué.

Kommunismus [komu'nɪsmʊs] m (-; no pl) communism.

Kommunist [komu'nɪst] m (-en; -en), **Kommu'nistin** f (-; -nen) communist. **kommu'nistisch** adj communist(ic).

kommunizieren [komuni'tsiːrən] v/i (h) communicate.

kommutieren [komu'tiːrən] v/t (h) ⚡ commutate.

Komödiant [komø'dǐant] m (-en; -en), **Komödi'antin** f (-; -nen) actor (actress), fig. contp. play-actor. **Komödie** [ko'møːdǐə] f (-; -n) comedy, fig. farce.

Kompagnon [kompan'jõː] m (-s; -s) ✝ partner.

kompakt [kom'pakt] adj compact.

Kompanie [kompa'niː] f (-; -n) ✕ company. **~chef** m company commander.

Komparativ ['komparatiːf] m (-s; -e) ling. comparative (degree).

Komparse [kom'parzə] m (-n; -n), **Kom'parsin** f (-; -nen) film etc: extra.

Kompaß ['kompas] m (-sses; -sse) compass. **~haus** n ♣ binnacle. **~nadel** f compass needle. **~rose** f compass card.

kompatibel [kompa'tiːbəl] adj compatible.

Kompensation [kompɛnza'tsǐoːn] f (-; -en) compensation.

kompensieren [kompɛn'ziːrən] v/t (h) compensate (for) (a. psych.).

kompetent [kompe'tɛnt] adj competent, a. responsible (**für** for), a. authorized.

Kompetenz [kompe'tɛnts] f (-; -en) competence, a. responsibility (**für** for), a. authority: **s-e ~en überschreiten** exceed one's authority. **~bereich** m sphere of authority. **~streit** m, **~streitigkeit** f usu. pl demarcation dispute.

kompilieren [kɔmpi'li:rən] *v/t* (h) compile.

Komplementärfarbe [kɔmplɛmɛn'tɛ:r-] *f* complementary colo(u)r.

komplett [kɔm'plɛt] *adj* complete.

komplex [kɔm'plɛks] *adj* complex.

Kom'plex *m* (-es; -e) *psych.* (*wegen* about) complex, F hangup.

Komplikation [kɔmplika'tsio:n] *f* (-; -en) complication.

Kompliment [kɔmpli'mɛnt] *n* (-[e]s; -e) (*j-m ein ~ machen* pay s.o. a) compliment; *~!* congratulations!

Komplize [kɔm'pli:tsə] *m* (-n; -n), **Kom'plizin** *f* (-; -nen) accomplice.

komplizieren [kɔmpli'tsi:rən] *v/t* (h) complicate. **kompli'ziert** *adj* complicated, complex (*character etc*), intricate (*problem etc*): *⚕ ~er Bruch* compound fracture. **Kompli'ziertheit** *f* (-; *no pl*) complexity.

Komplott [kɔm'plɔt] *n* (-[e]s; -e) (*a. ein ~ schmieden*) plot (*gegen* against).

Komponente [kɔmpo'nɛntə] *f* (-; -en) component.

komponieren [kɔmpo'ni:rən] *v/t, v/i* (h) *a. fig.* compose. **Komponist** [-'nɪst] *m* (-en; -en) composer. **Komposition** [kɔmpozi'tsio:n] *f* (-; -en) composition.

Kompositum [kɔm'po:zitum] *n* (-s; -ta) *ling.* compound (word).

Kompost [kɔm'pɔst] *m* (-[e]s; -e), **kompostieren** [-'ti:rən] *v/t* (h) compost.

Kompott [kɔm'pɔt] *n* (-[e]s; -e) stewed fruit.

Kompresse [kɔm'prɛsə] *f* (-; -n) *⚕* compress. **Kompressor** [kɔm'prɛsɔr] *m* (-s; -en [-'so:rən]) ⚙ compressor, *mot.* supercharger. **komprimieren** [kɔmpri'mi:rən] *v/t* (h) compress.

Kompromiß [kɔmpro'mɪs] *m* (-sses; -sse) compromise: *e-n ~ schließen* (make a) compromise (*über acc* on). **~bereitschaft** *f* willingness to compromise.

kompro'mißlos *adj* uncompromising.

Kompro'miß|lösung *f* compromise solution. **~vorschlag** *m* compromise proposal: *e-n ~ machen* suggest a compromise.

kompromittieren [kɔmprɔmɪ'ti:rən] *v/t* (h) compromise (*sich* o.s.).

Kondensat [kɔndɛn'za:t] *n* (-[e]s; -e) condensate. **Kondensation** [-za'tsio:n] *f* (-; -en) condensation. **Kondensator**

[-'za:tɔr] *m* (-s; -en [-za'to:rən]) **1.** ⚙ condenser. **2.** *⚡* capacitor. **kondensieren** [-'zi:rən] *v/t, v/i* (h) condense.

Kondens|milch [kɔn'dɛns-] *f* evaporated milk. **~streifen** *m* ✈ condensation trail. **~wasser** *n* condensation water.

Kondition [kɔndi'tsio:n] *f* (-; -en) **1.** *no pl sports:* condition, trim, shape: *e-e ausgezeichnete ~ haben* be very fit. **2.** *usu. pl* ✝ condition.

Konditional [kɔnditsio'na:l] *m* (-s; -e) *ling.* conditional (mood).

Konditio'nalsatz *m* conditional clause.

Konditi'ons|schwäche *f sports:* lack of stamina, poor shape. **2stark** *adj* very fit. **~training** *n* fitness training.

Konditor [kɔn'di:tɔr] *m* (-s; -en [-di'to:rən]) pastry cook. **Konditorei** [kɔndito'raɪ] *f* (-; -en) a) cake shop, b) café.

Kondolenz(...) [kɔndo'lɛnts-] → *Beileid(s...)*. **kondolieren** [kɔndo'li:rən] *v/i* (h) *j-m ~* express one's condolences to s.o. (*zu* on).

Kondom [kɔn'do:m] *n, m* (-s; -e) condom, *Am. a.* prophylactic.

Konfekt [kɔn'fɛkt] *n* (-[e]s; -e) a) sweets, *Am.* (soft) candy, b) chocolates.

Konfektion [kɔnfɛk'tsio:n] *f* (-; -en) (manufacture of) ready-to-wear (*or* ready-made) clothing (*or* clothes).

Konfekti'ons... ready-to-wear (*clothes, suit, etc*). **~größe** *f* size.

Konferenz [kɔnfe'rɛnts] *f* (-; -en) meeting, conference. **Konfe'renzschaltung** *f radio etc:* conference system.

konferieren [kɔnfe'ri:rən] *v/i* (h) **1.** confer (*über acc* on). **2.** *a. v/t* compère.

Konfession [kɔnfɛ'sio:n] *f* (-; -en) (*welcher ~ gehören Sie an?* what is your [religious] denomination(?). **konfessionell** [kɔnfɛsio'nɛl] *adj* denominational. **konfessi'onslos** *adj* nondenominational. **Konfessi'onsschule** *f* denominational school.

Konfetti [kɔn'fɛti] *n* (-[s]; *no pl*) confetti.

Konfirmand [kɔnfir'mant] *m* (-en; -en), **Konfir'mandin** [-dɪn] *f* (-; -nen) confirmand. **Konfirmation** [kɔnfirma'tsio:n] *f* (-; -en) confirmation. **konfirmieren** [kɔnfir'mi:rən] *v/t* (h) confirm.

konfiszieren [kɔnfɪs'tsi:rən] *v/t* (h) confiscate, seize.

Konfitüre [kɔnfi'ty:rə] *f* (-; -n) jam.

Konflikt [kɔn'flɪkt] *m* (-[e]s; -e) (*in ~ ge-raten* come into) conflict (*mit* with).
Kon'fliktstoff *m* matter for conflict.
Konföderation [kɔnfødera'tsi̯oːn] *f* (-; -en) confederation.
konform [kɔn'fɔrm] *adj* conforming, ⅋ conformal: *mit j-m ~ gehen* agree with s.o. (*in dat* about).
Konformist [kɔnfɔr'mɪst] *m* (-en; -en), **komfor'mistisch** *adj* conformist.
Konfrontation [kɔnfrɔnta'tsi̯oːn] *f* (-; -en) confrontation. **konfrontieren** [-'tiːrən] *v/t* (h) confront (*mit* with).
konfus [kɔn'fuːs] *adj* confused: *ich bin ganz ~ a.* I'm in a muddle. **Konfusion** [kɔnfu'zi̯oːn] *f* (-; -en) confusion.
Konglomerat [kɔnglome'raːt] *n* (-[e]s; -e) *a. fig.* conglomerate.
Kongreß [kɔn'grɛs] *m* (-sses; -sse) congress, convention: *pol. Am. der ~ Am.* Congress. **Kon'greßmitglied** *n pol. Am.* Congressman (Congresswoman).
kongruent [kɔngru'ɛnt] *adj* ⅋ congruent (*a. fig.*). **Kongruenz** [-'ɛnts] *f* (-; -en) ⅋ congruence (*a. fig.*). **kongruieren** [-'iːrən] *v/i* (h) ⅋ be congruent (*a. fig.*).
Konifere [koni'feːrə] *f* (-; -n) ⅋ conifer.
König ['køːnɪç] *m* (-s; -e) king.
Königin ['køːnɪgɪn] *f* (-; -nen) *a. zo.* queen. **'Königinmutter** *f* queen mother. **'Königinwitwe** *f* queen dowager.
königlich ['køːnɪklɪç] *adj* royal, *a.* regal (*insignia, power, etc*), *fig. a.* kingly: F *sich ~ amüsieren* have great fun.
Königreich ['køːnɪk-] *n* kingdom.
'Königs|haus *n* royal house (*or* dynasty). **~krone** *f* royal crown. **~sohn** *m* king's son, prince. **~tiger** *m zo.* Bengal tiger. **~tochter** *f* king's daughter, princess. **⅋treu** *adj* a) loyal (to the king), b) royalist.
'Königtum *n* (-s; *no pl*) monarchy.
konisch ['koːnɪʃ] *adj* conic(al).
Konjugation [kɔnjuga'tsi̯oːn] *f* (-; -en) *ling.* conjugation. **konjugieren** [kɔnju-'giːrən] *v/t* (h) *ling.* conjugate.
Konjunktion [kɔnjʊnk'tsi̯oːn] *f* (-; -en) *ling.* conjunction.
Konjunktiv ['kɔnjʊŋktiːf] *m* (-s; -e) *ling.* subjunctive (mood).
'Konjunktivsatz *m* subjunctive clause.
Konjunktur [kɔnjʊŋk'tuːr] *f* (-; -en) ⅋ a) business (cycle, b) boom, c) economic trend (*or* situation). **~abschwächung** *f*

downswing. **~aufschwung** *m* upswing.
⅋bedingt *adj* cyclic(al). **~bericht** *m* economic report. **⅋dämpfend** *adj* countercyclical.
konjunkturell [kɔnjʊŋktu'rɛl] *adj* cyclical, economic, business (*trend etc*).
Konjunk'tur|poli,tik *f* trade-cycle policy. **~schwankungen** *pl* cyclical fluctuations. **~spritze** *f* F shot in the arm. **~verlauf** *m* economic trend.
konkav [kɔn'kaːf] *adj* concave.
Konkordat [kɔnkɔr'daːt] *n* (-[e]s; -e) concordat.
konkret [kɔn'kreːt] *adj* concrete, *a.* definite, specific, precise.
konkretisieren [kɔnkreti'ziːrən] *v/t* (h) put *s.th.* in concrete form (*or* terms).
Konkurrent [kɔnkʊ'rɛnt] *m* (-en; -en) competitor, (⚕ *a.* business) rival.
Konkurrenz [kɔnkʊ'rɛnts] *f* (-; -en) **1.** *no pl* competition, rivalry: *j-m ~ machen* compete with s.o. **2.** *no pl* competitor(s), rival(s), *coll. a.* competition: *die ~ ausschalten* eliminate one's competitors. **3.** competition, contest, *sports: a.* event: *außer ~* hors concours.
Konkur'renz|erzeugnis *n* rival product. **⅋fähig** *adj* competitive. **~firma** *f*, **~geschäft** *n* rival firm. **~kampf** *m* (*mörderischer ~* cutthroat) competition; *endloser ~* F rat race. **~klausel** *f* restraint clause.
konkur'renzlos *adj* unrival(l)ed.
konkurrieren [kɔnkʊ'riːrən] *v/i* (h) *mit j-m ~* compete with s.o. (*um* for).
Konkurs [kɔn'kʊrs] *m* (-es; -e) bankruptcy: *in ~ gehen, ~ machen* go bankrupt. **~antrag** *m* petition in bankruptcy. **~er-klärung** *f* declaration of insolvency. **~masse** *f* bankrupt's estate. **~verfah-ren** *n* (*das ~ eröffnen* institute) bankruptcy proceedings. **~verwalter** *m* a) trustee in bankruptcy, b) ⅗⅔ receiver.
können ['kœnən] *v/aux, v/i, v/t* (konnte, gekonnt, h) **1.** be able to: *kannst du es?* can you do it?; *er hätte es tun ~* he could have done it; *ich habe nicht ar-beiten ~* I was unable to work; *ich kann nicht mehr!* a) I can't go on!, b) I've had it!, b) I can't take any more!, c) I can't manage (*or* eat) any more!; F *da kann man nichts machen!* there's nothing to be done!; *du kannst mich mal!* go to hell! **2.** know: *~ Sie tanzen?*

do you (know how to) dance?, can you dance?; **sie kann kein Spanisch** she doesn't know (*or* speak) Spanish; F **er kann etwas** (*gar nichts*) he is a capable fellow (he's absolutely incapable). **3.** be allowed to: **kann ich jetzt gehen?** can I go now?; **Sie ~** (*es*) *mir glauben!* (you may) believe me!; F **das kann doch nicht wahr sein!** but that's impossible! **4. es kann sein, daß er noch kommt** he may (*or* might) come yet; **ich kann mich irren** I may be mistaken; **wann könnte das gewesen sein?** when might that have been?; **du könntest recht haben** you may (*or* could) be right; F **kann sein!** maybe! **5. ich kann nichts für ...** I'm not responsible for ...; **ich konnte doch nichts dafür!** it wasn't my fault! **6.** F **mit j-m** (*gut*) **~** get on with s.o. (like a house on fire).

'**Können** n (-s) skill, ability.

Könner ['kœnər] m (-s; -), '**Könnerin** f (-; -nen) expert, *sports*: ace.

Konsekutivsatz [konzeku'ti:f-] m ling. consecutive clause.

konsequent [konze'kvɛnt] adj a) consistent, logical, b) firm, resolute, c) uncompromising: **~ bleiben** remain firm.

Konsequenz [konze'kvɛnts] f (-; -en) **1.** consequence: **die ~en ziehen** draw the conclusions (*aus* from), act accordingly. **2.** consistency.

konservativ [konzɛrva'ti:f] adj, **Konservative** [konzɛrva'ti:və] m, f (-n; -n) conservative, *pol. Br. a.* Tory.

Konservator [konzɛr'va:tɔr] m (-s; -en [-va'to:rən]) curator.

Konservatorium [konzɛrva'to:riʊm] n (-s; -rien) conservatory.

Konserve [kon'zɛrvə] f (-; -n) **1.** a) preserve(d food), b) tin, can: **~n** tinned (*or* canned) food; **von ~n leben** live out of tins (*or* cans); F fig. **Musik aus der ~** canned music. **2.** → **Blutkonserve**.

Kon'serven|büchse f, **~dose** f tin, can. **~fa,brik** f canning factory, cannery.

konservieren [konzɛr'vi:rən] v/t (h) preserve. **Konser'vierung** f (-; -en) preservation. **Konser'vierungsmittel** n preservative.

Konsistenz [konzis'tɛnts] f (-; -en) consistency.

Konsole [kon'zo:lə] f (-; -n) console.

konsolidieren [konzoli'di:rən] v/t (*a.* **sich ~**) (h) consolidate.

Konsonant [konzo'nant] m (-en; -en) consonant. **konso'nantisch** adj consonant(al).

Konsortium [kon'zɔrtsiʊm] n (-s; -tien) ✝ syndicate.

Konspiration [konspira'tsio:n] f (-; -en) conspiracy, plot. **konspirativ** [-'ti:f] adj conspiratorial. **konspirieren** [konspi'ri:rən] v/i (h) conspire, plot.

konstant [kon'stant] adj constant.

Kon'stante f (-; -n) a. fig. constant.

Konstellation [konstɛla'tsio:n] f (-; -en) constellation.

konstituieren [konstitu'i:rən] v/t (h) constitute: *parl.* **sich ~** resolve itself into ...; **konstituierende Versammlung** constituent assembly.

Konstitution [konstitu'tsio:n] f (-; -en) ✼, *pol.* constitution. **konstitutionell** [konstitutsio'nɛl] adj constitutional.

konstruieren [konstru'i:rən] v/t (h) construct (*a. ling.*, ✿), ⊕ a. design, build, fig. contp. fabricate. **Konstrukteur** [konstruk'tø:r] m (-s; -e) design engineer. **Konstruktion** [konstruk'tsio:n] f (-; -en) a) construction (*a. ling.*, ✿), b) design, c) structure. **Konstrukti'onsfehler** m constructional fault, faulty design. **konstruktiv** [konstruk'ti:f] adj **1.** fig. constructive. **2.** ⊕ constructional, structural, design.

Konsul ['konzʊl] m (-s; -n) consul. **Konsular...** [konzu'la:r-] consular.

Konsulat [-'la:t] n (-[e]s; -e) consulate.

Konsultation [konzʊlta'tsio:n] f (-; -en) consultation. **konsultieren** [konzʊl-'ti:rən] v/t (h) consult.

Konsum¹ ['konzu:m] m (-s; -s) cooperative (store), F co-op.

Konsum² [kon'zu:m] m (-s; *no pl*) a. fig. consumption. **Kon'sumdenken** n (-s) consumerism. **Konsument** [konzu-'mɛnt] m (-en; -en) a. fig. consumer. **Kon'sumgesellschaft** f consumer society. **Kon'sumgüter** pl consumer goods. **konsumieren** [konzu'mi:rən] v/t (h) a. fig. consume. **Kon'sumterror** m F pressure to buy.

Kontakt [kon'takt] m (-[e]s; -e) contact: **mit j-m in ~ stehen** be in contact (*or* touch) with s.o.; **mit j-m ~ aufnehmen** get in touch with s.o., contact s.o. **~ab-**

zug *m phot.* contact print. **2arm** *adj* unsociable: **er ist ~ a.** F he is a bad mixer. **2freudig** *adj* sociable: **er ist ~ a.** F he is a good mixer. **~gespräche** *pl* initial talks. **~gift** *n* contact poison. **~linse** *f opt.* contact lens. **~mann** *m* contact. **~per,son** *f a. ⚓ contact. **~schalter** *m* touch sensitive switch.

Kontamination [kɔntamina'tsɪo:n] *f* (-; -en) contamination. **kontaminieren** [kɔntami'ni:rən] *v/t* (h) contaminate.

Konteradmi,ral ['kɔntər-] *m* ⚓ rear admiral.

kontern ['kɔntərn] *v/i, v/t* (h) counter.

'**Konterrevoluti,on** *f* counterrevolution.

Kontext ['kɔntɛkst] *m* (-[e]s; -e) context.

Kontinent [kɔnti'nɛnt] *m* (-[e]s; -e) continent. **kontinental** [kɔntinɛn'ta:l] *adj* continental.

Kontingent [kɔntɪŋ'gɛnt] *n* (-[e]s; -e) contingent (*a.* ✕), ⚔ *a.* quota.

kontingentieren [kɔntɪŋgɛn'ti:rən] *v/t* (h) 1. fix a quota for. 2. ration.

kontinuierlich [kɔntinu'i:rlɪç] *adj* continuous. **Kontinuität** [kɔntinui'tɛ:t] *f* (-; *no pl*) continuity.

Konto ['kɔnto] *n* (-s; -ten) account: **ein ~ haben bei** have (*or* keep) an account with (*or* at); F *fig.* **das geht auf sein ~** that's his doing. **~auszug** *m* bank statement. **~führungsgebühr** *f* service charge. **~inhaber(in** *f*) *m* account holder. **~nummer** *f* account number.

Kontorist [kɔnto'rɪst] *m* (-en; -en), **Konto'ristin** *f* (-; -nen) (office) clerk.

'**Kontostand** *m* balance: **wie ist der ~?** how does the account stand?; **Ihr ~ beläuft sich auf ...** you have ... to your credit.

kontra ['kɔntra] **I** *prep* contra, ⚖ *or fig.* versus (*abbr.* vs.). **II** *adv* **sie ist immer ~ (eingestellt)** she's against everything.

'**Kontra** *n* (-s; -s) *fig.* objection: **~ geben** cards: double; F **j-m ~ geben** hit back at s.o.; → **Pro.**

'**Kontrabaß** *m* ♪ double bass.

Kontrahent [kɔntra'hɛnt] *m* (-en; -en) ⚖ contracting party, *fig.* opponent, *a.* *sports:* rival.

'**Kontraindikati,on** *f* contraindication.

Kontraktion [kɔntrak'tsɪo:n] *f* (-; -en) contraction.

'**kontraproduk,tiv** *adj* counterproductive.

'**Kontrapunkt** *m* (-[e]s; *no pl*) ♪ counterpoint.

konträr [kɔn'trɛ:r] *adj* contrary.

Kontrast [kɔn'trast] *m* (-[e]s; -e) contrast: **e-n ~ bilden (zu) → kontrastieren.** **kon'trastarm** *adj phot.* flat. **kontrastieren** [-'ti:rən] *v/i* (h) (**mit**) contrast (with), form a contrast (to).

Kon'trast|mittel *n* ⚕ radiopaque material. **2reich** *adj phot., TV* contrasty.

Kon'trollabschnitt *m* stub.

Kon'trollbehörde *f* control authority.

Kontrolle [kɔn'trɔlə] *f* (-; -n) a) control (**über** *acc* of), *a.* ⚙ inspection, check, b) supervision: **unter (außer) ~** under (out of) control; **unter ärztlicher ~** under medical supervision; **er verlor die ~ über s-n Wagen** he lost control of his car; **... steht unter ständiger ~** a constant check is kept on ...

Kon'trolleuchte *f* pilot lamp.

Kontrolleur [kɔntrɔ'lø:r] *m* (-s; -e) inspector, supervisor.

Kon'troll|funkti,on *f* controlling function. **~gang** *m* round.

kontrollieren [kɔntrɔ'li:rən] *v/t* (h) a) control, check, b) supervise.

Kon'trolliste *f* checklist.

Kon'troll|punkt *m* checkpoint. **~turm** *m* ✈ control tower. **~uhr** *f* time clock.

Kontroverse [kɔntro'vɛrzə] *f* (-; -n) controversy, argument.

Kontur [kɔn'tu:r] *f* (-; -en) contour, outline.

Konus ['ko:nʊs] *m* (-; -se) ⚙ cone.

Konvention [kɔnvɛn'tsɪo:n] *f* (-; -en) convention.

Konventionalstrafe [kɔnvɛntsɪo'na:l-] *f* (contractual) penalty.

konventionell [kɔnvɛntsɪo'nɛl] *adj* conventional.

konvergieren [kɔnvɛr'gi:rən] *v/i* (h) ⚗ converge.

Konversation [kɔnvɛrza'tsɪo:n] *f* (-; -en) conversation. **Konversati'onslexikon** *n* encyclop(a)edia.

konver'tierbar *adj* convertible.

konvertieren [kɔnvɛr'ti:rən] *v/t* (h), *v/i* (sn) convert (**~ in** *acc* into, *eccl.* **zu** to): **er ist (or hat) konvertiert** *a.* he was converted, he turned Catholic.

Konvertit [kɔnvɛr'ti:t] *m* (-en; -en), **Konver'titin** *f* (-; -nen) *eccl.* convert.

konvex [kɔn'vɛks] *adj* ⚗ convex.

Konvoi ['kɔnvɔɪ] m (-s; -s) convoy.
Konzentrat [kɔntsɛn'traːt] n (-[e]s; -e) 🜍 concentrate. **Konzentration** [kɔntsɛntra'tsi̯oːn] f (-; -en) a. 🜍 concentration. **Konzentrati'ons|fähigkeit** f power(s) of concentration. **~lager** n pol. concentration camp. **~schwäche** f lack of concentration.
konzentrieren [kɔntsɛn'triːrən] v/t (a. **sich ~**) (h) concentrate (**auf** acc on). **konzen'triert** adj concentrated: **in ~er Form** a. in tabloid form; **~ arbeiten** etc a. work etc with concentration.
konzentrisch [kɔn'tsɛntrɪʃ] adj concentric.
Konzept [kɔn'tsɛpt] n (-[e]s; -e) a) rough draft (or copy), a. notes, b) plan(s): fig. **j-n aus dem ~ bringen** put s.o. off his stroke, F rattle s.o.; **aus dem ~ kommen** lose the thread; **F j-m das ~ verderben** thwart s.o.'s plans; **das paßte ihr nicht ins ~** that didn't suit her at all.
Konzeption [kɔntsɛp'tsi̯oːn] f (-; -en) conception.
Konzern [kɔn'tsɛrn] m (-s; -e) 🜍 group, combine.
Konzert [kɔn'tsɛrt] n (-[e]s; -e) **1.** a) concert, b) recital: **ins ~ gehen** go to a concert. **2.** ♪ concerto. **~agen,tur** f concert agency. **~besucher** m concert-goer. **~flügel** m concert grand. **~führer** m concert guide.
konzer'tiert [kɔntsɛr'tiːrt] adj 🜍, pol. **~e Aktion** concerted action.
Kon'zert|meister m leader, Am. concertmaster. **~saal** m concert hall.
Konzession [kɔntsɛ'si̯oːn] f (-; -en) **1.** concession (**an** acc to). **2.** licen/ce (Am. -se). **Konzessivsatz** [kɔntsɛ'siːf-] m concessive clause.
Konzil [kɔn'tsiːl] n (-s; -e) council.
konzipieren [kɔntsi'piːrən] v/t (h) a) conceive, b) draft: **konzipiert für** a. 🜍 designed for.
Kooperation [ko'ʔopera'tsi̯oːn] f (-; no pl) cooperation. **kooperativ** [ko'ʔopera'tiːf] adj cooperative. **kooperieren** [ko'ʔope'riːrən] v/i (h) cooperate.
Koordinate [ko'ʔordi'naːtə] f (-; -n) ⅄ coordinate. **Koordination** [-na'tsi̯oːn] f (-; -en) coordination. **koordinieren** [ko'ʔordi'niːrən] v/t (h) coordinate.
Kopf [kɔpf] m (-[e]s; ⸚e) **1.** a) head (a. ⚘,

♪, ⚙), b) (letter)head, c) (pipe) bowl, d) top: **~ hoch!** cheer up!, chin up!; **~ an ~** in race, election: neck to neck; **von ~ bis Fuß** from head to foot, from top to toe; **mit bloßem ~** bare-headed; **über j-s ~ hinweg** a. fig. over s.o.'s head; fig. pro **~** per person, a head; **sie ist nicht auf den ~ gefallen** she is no fool; **ich war wie vor den ~ geschlagen** I was thunderstruck; **den ~ hängen lassen** a. fig. hang one's head; F **sein Geld auf den ~ hauen** blow one's money; **den ~ hinhalten** take the blame (**für** for); **~ und Kragen riskieren** risk one's neck; **ich weiß nicht, wo mir der ~ steht** I don't know whether I'm coming or going; **j-m zu ~e steigen** go to s.o.'s head; **auf den ~ stellen** turn s.th. upside down; F **und wenn du dich auf den ~ stellst!** and if it kills you!; **j-n vor den ~ stoßen** offend s.o.; **j-m über den ~ wachsen** a) outgrow s.o., b) fig. be too much for s.o.; **j-m den ~ waschen** a) wash s.o.'s hair, b) fig. tell s.o. off; **sie will immer mit dem ~ durch die Wand** she always wants to have her own way regardless; **j-m et. auf den ~ zusagen** tell s.o. straight out; → **Nagel, schütteln. 2.** fig. head, a. mind, brains, a. leader, brain: **er war der ~ des Unternehmens** he was the head (or brain) of the enterprise; **aus dem ~** by heart; **et. im ~ rechnen** work s.th. out in one's head; F **das hältst du ja im ~ nicht aus!** it's incredible!; **e-n kühlen (klaren) ~ bewahren** keep a cool (clear) head; **sich et. durch den ~ gehen lassen** think s.th. over; **ich habe die Zahlen nicht im ~** I can't give you the figures off the cuff; **er hat andere Dinge im ~** he has other things on his mind; **er hat nur Fußball im ~** he thinks of nothing but football; **schlag dir das aus dem ~!** forget it!; **sich et. in den ~ setzen** take s.th. into one's head; **j-m den ~ verdrehen** turn s.o.'s head; **den ~ verlieren** lose one's head; **sich den ~ zerbrechen** rack one's brains (**über** acc over); → **herumgehen 1, richtig** 1.
'**Kopf|-an-Kopf-Rennen** n sports: neck-and-neck race. **~arbeit** f brainwork. **~arbeiter(in** f) m brainworker. **~bahnhof** m terminal. **~ball** m header.

Köpfchen ['kœpfçən] n (-s; -) **1.** small head. **2.** F ~ **haben** have brains.

köpfen ['kœpfən] v/t (h) **1.** behead. **2.** head (ball).

'**Kopf|ende** n head. **~haar** n hair (on the head). **~haut** f scalp. **~hörer** m headphone, pl a. headset. **~kissen** n pillow.

'**kopflastig** [-lastıç] adj top-heavy.

'**kopflos** adj **1.** headless. **2.** fig. panicky: ~ **werden** lose one's head, panic.

'**Kopf|nicken** n nod. **~rechnen** n mental arithmetic. **~sa‚lat** m lettuce. **♀scheu** adj ~ **machen** confuse, intimidate; ~ **werden** become confused. **~schmerzen** pl (~ **haben** have a) headache. **~schuß** m shot in the head. **♀schüttelnd** adv with a shake of the head. **~sprung** m header. **~stand** m headstand.

'**kopfstehen** v/i (irr, sep, -ge-, h, → **stehen**) F fig. be in a flap.

'**Kopf|steinpflaster** n cobblestone pavement. **~steuer** f poll tax. **~stimme** f ♩ head voice, falsetto. **~stütze** f headrest. **~tuch** n (head)scarf.

kopf'über adv head first, headlong.

'**Kopf|verletzung** f head injury. **~zerbrechen** n j-m ~ **machen** puzzle s.o.

Kopie [ko'pi:] f (-; -n) copy, phot. a. print, a. duplicate. **kopieren** [ko'pi:rən] v/t (h) copy (a. fig.), a. ⊙ duplicate, phot. a. print, fig. a. imitate.

Ko'pier|gerät n copier. **~pa‚pier** n copying paper. **~stift** m indelible pencil.

Kopi‚lot ['ko:-] m copilot.

Koppel¹ ['kɔpəl] f (-; -n) **1.** a) enclosure, b) paddock. **2.** e-e ~ a leash (of dogs), a string (of horses).

Koppel² n (-s; -) ✕ belt.

koppeln ['kɔpəln] v/t (h) (an acc to) link, couple: **Raumschiffe** ~ dock spaceships; fig. **et. ~ mit** couple (or combine) s.th. with.

Kopplung f (-; -en) coupling (a. fig.), docking (of spaceships).

Koralle [ko'ralə] f (-; -n) coral.

Ko'rallenbank f coral reef.

Koran [ko'ra:n] m (-s; no pl) Koran.

Korb [kɔrp] m (-[e]s; -e ['kœrbə]) **1.** basket (a. sports): **ein ~ (voll) Äpfel** a basketful of apples; → **Hahn** 1. **2.** F fig. j-m e-n ~ **geben** turn s.o. down; e-n ~ **bekommen** be turned down.

'**Korbball** m (-[e]s; no pl) netball.

'**Korbblüter** [-bly:tər] m (-s; -) ♣ composite.

'**Körbchen** ['kœrpçən] n (-s; -) **1.** basket. **2.** cup (of bra).

'**Korbmöbel** pl wicker furniture.

'**Korbwaren** pl wickerwork.

Kord [kɔrt] m (-[e]s; -e) corduroy.

Kordel ['kɔrdəl] f (-; -n) cord.

'**Kordhose** f cords, corduroys.

Kordon [kɔr'dõ:] m (-s; -s) cordon.

'**Kordsamt** m corduroy, cord velvet.

Korea [ko're:a] n (-s) Korea. **Koreaner** [kore'a:nər] m (-s; -), **Kore'anerin** f (-; -nen), **kore'anisch** adj Korean.

Korinthe [ko'rıntə] f (-; -n) currant.

Kork [kɔrk] m (-[e]s; -e) m cork.

Korken ['kɔrkən] m (-s; -) cork.

'**Korkenzieher** m (-s; -) corkscrew.

Korn¹ [kɔrn] n (-[e]s; -er) **1.** no pl grain, cereals: → **Flinte**. **2.** grain.

Korn² n (-[e]s; no pl) **1.** ✕ front sight: F fig. **aufs ~ nehmen** attack, go for. **2.** phot., ⊙ grain.

Korn³ m (-[e]s; -) F grain whisky.

'**Kornblume** f cornflower.

Körnchen ['kœrnçən] n (-s; -) granule: fig. **ein ~ Wahrheit** a grain of truth.

'**Kornfeld** n cornfield, Am. grainfield.

körnig ['kœrnıç] adj grainy, granular, rice etc: al dente, in cpds. ...-grained.

'**Kornkammer** f a. fig. granary.

Koronar... [koro'na:r-] anat., ⚕ coronary (artery, vessel, sclerosis).

Körper ['kœrpər] m (-s; -) body (a. of wine), ⚕, phys. a. solid: ~ **und Geist** body and mind; **am ganzen ~** all over one's body; **am ganzen ~ zittern** tremble all over. **~bau** m (-[e]s; no pl) build, physique. **~behinderte** f (-n; -n) physically disabled (or handicapped) person: **die ~n** a. the handicapped. **~behinderung** f physical handicap.

'**Körperchen** n (-s; -) corpuscle, particle.

'**körpereigen** adj biol. endogenous.

'**Körper|geruch** m body odo(u)r. **~haltung** f posture. **~kon‚takt** m physical contact. **~kraft** f physical strength.

'**körperlich** adj a) physical, bodily, b) corporeal (a. ♐): **~e Arbeit** manual work; → **Züchtigung**.

'**Körperpflege** f care of the body, personal hygiene. **~mittel** n cosmetic.

'**Körperschaft** f (-; -en) corporation, (corporate) body: **gesetzgebende ~**

legislative (body). '**Körperschafts-steuer** f corporation tax.

'**Körpersprache** f body language. **~teil** m part (or member) of the body. **~verletzung** f (schwere ~ grievous) bodily harm. **~wärme** f body heat.

Korps [ko:r] n (-s; -) corps.

korpulent [kɔrpu'lɛnt] adj corpulent, stout. **Korpulenz** [kɔrpu'lɛnts] f (-; no pl) corpulence, stoutness.

korrekt [kɔ'rɛkt] adj correct. **Kor'rektheit** f (-; no pl) correctness.

Korrektor [kɔ'rɛktɔr] m (-s; -en [-'to:rən]) (proof)reader.

Korrektur [kɔrɛk'tu:r] f (-; -en) a) correction, b) print. proofreading: ~ **lesen** proofread. **~bogen** m, **~fahne** f proof. **~zeichen** n proofreader's mark.

Korrespondent [kɔrɛspɔn'dɛnt] m (-en; -en) **1.** correspondent. **2.** ✝ correspondence clerk. **Korrespondenz** [-'dɛnts] f (-; -en) correspondence. **korrespondieren** [-'di:rən] v/i (h) correspond.

Korridor ['kɔrido:r] m (-s; -e) corridor.

korrigieren [kɔri'gi:rən] v/t (h) correct, ped. a. mark, a. change, alter.

korrodieren [kɔro'di:rən] v/t (h), v/i (sn) corrode. **Korrosion** [kɔro'zio:n] f (-; -en) corrosion. **korrosi'onsbeständig** adj corrosion-resistant. **Korrosi'onsschutz** m corrosion prevention, in cpds. anticorrosive (agent, paint, etc).

korrumpieren [kɔrʊm'pi:rən] v/t (h) corrupt. **korrupt** [kɔ'rʊpt] adj corrupt. **Korruption** [kɔrʊp'tsio:n] f (-; -en) corruption.

Korse ['kɔrzə] m (-n; -n) Corsican.

Korsett [kɔr'zɛt] n (-[e]s; -e) corset.

Korsika ['kɔrzika] n (-s) Corsica.

Korsin ['kɔrzɪn] f (-; -nen), '**korsisch** adj Corsican.

Kortison [kɔrti'zo:n] n (-s; no pl) cortisone.

Koryphäe [kory'fɛ:ə] f (-; -n) (eminent) authority.

koscher ['ko:ʃər] adj a. F fig. kosher.

Kosename ['ko:zə-] m pet name.

Kosinus ['ko:zɪnʊs] m (-; -, -se) ✝ cosine.

Kosmetik [kɔs'me:tɪk] f (-; no pl) **1.** beauty care. **2.** fig. cosmetics.

Kosmetikerin [kɔs'me:tikərɪn] f (-; -nen) cosmetician, beautician.

Kos'metik|koffer m vanity box (or case). **~sa,lon** m beauty parlo(u)r.

Kosmetikum [kɔs'me:tikʊm] n (-s; -ka) cosmetic. **kos'metisch** adj cosmetic.

kosmisch ['kɔsmɪʃ] adj cosmic.

Kosmonaut [kɔsmo'naʊt] m (-en; -en), **Kosmo'nautin** f (-; -nen) cosmonaut.

Kosmopolit [kɔsmopo'li:t] m (-en; -en), **kosmopo'litisch** adj cosmopolitan.

Kosmos ['kɔsmɔs] m (-; no pl) cosmos.

Kost [kɔst] f (-; no pl) a) food, fare (a. fig.), diet, b) cooking, c) board: **fleischlose** ~ meatless diet; **(freie)** ~ **und Logis** (free) board and lodging.

'**kostbar** adj precious, valuable (a. fig. time etc), a. expensive: **jede Minute ist** ~ every minute counts.

'**Kostbarkeit** f (-; -en) **1.** no pl preciousness, valuableness. **2.** precious object, treasure, pl a. valuables.

kosten¹ ['kɔstən] v/t (v/i ~ **von**) (h) taste (a. fig.), try.

'**kosten²** v/t (h) cost, fig. a. take (time etc): **was kostet das?** how much is that?; F **er hat es sich et.** ~ **lassen** he spent a lot of money on it; **es hat mich viel Mühe gekostet** it gave me a lot of trouble; **es kostete ihn das Leben** it cost him his life; **koste es, was es wolle** at all costs; F **das kostet Nerven!** that's hard on the nerves.

'**Kosten** pl cost(s), expenses, expenditure: **die** ~ **tragen** bear (or meet) the cost(s); **auf** ~ **von** (or gen) a. fig. at the expense of; **auf m-e** ~ at my expense; **k-e** ~ **scheuen** spare no expense; ⚖ **j-n zu den** ~ **verurteilen** award costs against s.o.; fig. **auf s-e** ~ **kommen** get one's money's worth. **~anstieg** m increase in costs. **~aufwand** m expenditure, cost: **mit e-m** ~ **von ...** at a cost of ... **~beteiligung** f cost sharing. ⚖**dämpfend** adj cost-cutting. **~dämpfung** f curbing (of) costs. ⚖**deckend** adj cost-covering. **~explosi,on** f runaway costs. **~faktor** m cost factor. **~frage** f **es ist e-e** ~ it is a question of cost (or of what it costs). ⚖**günstig** adj cost-effective. ⚖**inten,siv** adj cost-intensive. **~la,wine** f escalating costs.

kostenlos adj and adv free, gratis.

'**Kosten-'Nutzen-Ana'lyse** f cost-benefit analysis.

'**kostenpflichtig** adj a) liable to pay the costs, b) tow away etc at the owner's expense: **e-e Klage ~ abweisen** dismiss a case with costs.

'**Kosten|punkt** m F costs: **~?** how much? **~rechnung** f ♱ cost accounting. **2senkend** adj cost-cutting. **~senkung** f reduction in costs. **2sparend** adj cost-saving. **~steigerung** f cost increase. **~voranschlag** m estimate, quotation.

'**Kostgeld** n board (allowance).

köstlich ['kœstlıç] adj a) delicious (food etc), b) fig. delightful (humo[u]r etc): **sich ~ amüsieren** have great fun.

'**Köstlichkeit** f (-; -en) **1.** no pl deliciousness. **2.** gastr. titbit, delicacy.

'**Kostprobe** f a. fig. sample, taste.

kostspielig ['kɔstʃpiːlıç] adj expensive.

Kostüm [kɔs'tyːm] n (-s; -e) **1.** (woman's) suit. **2.** costume (a. thea.), dress.

Ko'stümball m fancy-dress ball.

kostümieren [kɔsty'miːrən] v/t (h) dress s.o. up: **sich ~** dress up (als as).

Ko'stümprobe f thea. dress rehearsal.

Ko'stümverleih m costume rental.

Kot [koːt] m (-[e]s; no pl) excrement, f(a)eces.

Kotelett [kɔt'lɛt] n (-s; -s) gastr. chop, cutlet. **Kote'letten** pl sideboards, Am. sideburns.

Köter ['køːtər] m (-s; -) contp. cur.

'**Kotflügel** m mudguard, Am. fender.

kotzen ['kɔtsən] v/i (h) V throw up, sl. puke: **ich finde ihn zum Kotzen!** he makes me sick!; **das ist ja zum Kotzen!** that's enough to make one puke!

Krabbe ['krabə] f (-; -n) shrimp, prawn.

krabbeln ['krabəln] I v/i (sn) crawl. II v/t (h) tickle.

Krach [krax] m (-[e]s; ⁀e) **1.** crash, bang. **2.** no pl (loud) noise, din, F row, racket: **~ machen** make a racket, be noisy. **3.** F row, quarrel: **mit j-m ~ haben** have a row with s.o.; **~ schlagen** raise hell.

krachen ['kraxən] I v/i **1.** (h) crash, crack. **2.** (sn) slam, bang: **~ gegen** (or **in** acc) crash into. II **sich ~** (h) F have a row.

krächzen ['krɛçtsən] v/t, v/i (h) croak.

kraft [kraft] prep (gen) ♱ by virtue of.

Kraft f (-; ⁀e) **1.** a. fig. strength, a. phys. force, energy, ⚡, phys., ⚙ power: **mit aller ~** with all one's might; **mit frischer (letzter) ~** with renewed (one's last ounce of) strength; ⚓ **volle ~ voraus** full speed ahead; **Kräfte sammeln**

build up one's strength; **m-e Kräfte lassen nach** my strength fails; **das geht über m-e ~** that's too much for me; **ich bin am Ende m-r Kräfte** I can't take any more; **nach (besten) Kräften** to the best of one's ability; **~ schöpfen** gain strength (aus from); **er tat, was in s-n Kräften stand** he did everything within his power; → **vereinen. 2.** pol. etc: force. **3.** ♱♱ **in ~ sein (setzen)** be in (put into) force; **in ~ treten** come into force, become effective; **außer ~ setzen** a) annul, invalidate, repeal (law), cancel (contract), b) suspend; **außer ~ treten** expire. **4.** worker, employee, pl a. personnel, staff.

'**Kraft|akt** m stunt. **~anstrengung** f, **~aufwand** m (strenuous) effort. **~ausdruck** m swearword. **~brühe** f beef tea.

'**Kräfteverfall** m loss of strength.

'**Kräfteverschleiß** m waste of energy.

'**Kraftfahrer(in** f) m driver, motorist.

'**Kraftfahrzeug** n motor vehicle. **~brief** m vehicle registration document. **~me,chaniker** m car mechanic. **~schein** m vehicle registration document. **~steuer** f road (Am. automobile) tax.

'**Kraftfeld** n phys. field of force.

'**Kraftfutter** n ⚜ concentrated feed.

kräftig ['krɛftıç] I adj **1.** a) a. ⚙ strong, robust, sturdy, b) powerful (a. blow etc): F **er nahm e-n ~en Schluck** he took a good swig; fig. **~e Farbe** deep (or rich) colo(u)r; ♱ **~er Aufschwung** sharp upswing. **2.** substantial, nourishing. II adv **3.** strongly (etc), F soundly, heartily: **er ist ~ gebaut** he is powerfully built; **~ zuschlagen** hit hard.

kräftigen ['krɛftıgən] v/t (h) strengthen.

'**Kräftigungsmittel** n ⚕ tonic.

'**kraftlos** adj weak, feeble.

'**Kraft|probe** f trial of strength. **~protz** m F muscleman. **~rad** n motorcycle.

'**Kraftstoff** m fuel. **~anzeiger** m fuel ga(u)ge. **~leitung** f fuel pipe (or line). **~-'Luft-Gemisch** n fuel(-air) mixture. **~pumpe** f fuel pump. **~verbrauch** m fuel consumption.

'**kraftstrotzend** adj bursting with strength, vigorous, powerful.

'**Kraft|übertragung** f power transmission. **~verkehr** m motor traffic. **~verschwendung** f waste of energy.

'**kraftvoll** adj powerful, vigorous, strong.

'**Kraftwagen** *m* motor vehicle.
'**Kraftwerk** *n* power station.
'**Kragen** ['kra:gən] *m* (-s; ») collar: F *ihm platzte der ~* he blew his top; *jetzt geht es ihm an den ~* he is in for it now.
'**Kragenweite** *f* collar size: *welche ~ haben Sie?* what size collar do you take?; F *sie (das) ist genau m-e ~!* she's (it's) just my cup of tea!
Krähe ['krɛ:ə] *f* (-; -n) *zo.* crow: *fig. e-e ~ hackt der anderen kein Auge aus* dog does not eat dog.
krähen ['krɛ:ən] *v/i* (h) crow.
'**Krähenfüße** *pl fig.* crow's-feet.
Krake ['kra:kə] *m* (-n; -n) *zo.* octopus.
Krakeel [kra:ke:l] *m* (-s; *no pl*) F row.
kra'keelen *v/i* (h) F make a row.
Kra'keeler *m* (-s; -) F roisterer.
Krakel ['kra:kəl] *m* (-s; -) F scrawl.
'**krak(e)lig** *adj* F scrawly.
krakeln ['kra:kəln] *v/t, v/i* (h) F scrawl.
Kral [kra:l] *m* (-s; -e) kraal.
Kralle ['kralə] *f* (-; -n) claw: *fig. j-m die ~n zeigen* show s.o. one's claws.
krallen ['kralən] (h) **I** *v/t s-e Finger ~ in* (*acc*) dig one's fingers into. **II** *sich ~* a) *an* (*acc*) cling to, b) *in* (*acc*) dig one's claws (*person*: nails) into.
Kram [kra:m] *m* (-[e]s; *no pl*) F **1.** a) things, stuff, b) junk, rubbish. **2.** *fig.* business: *den ganzen ~ hinschmeißen* chuck the whole thing; *j-m nicht in den ~ passen* not to suit s.o.'s plans.
kramen ['kra:mən] (h) F **I** *v/i* rummage (about) (*nach* for): *in Erinnerungen ~* take a trip down memory lane. **II** *v/t et. ~ aus* fish s.th. out of *one's* bag etc.
Krampe ['krampə] *f* (-; -n) © cramp.
Krampf [krampf] *m* (-[e]s; »e) **1.** ⚕ a) cramp, b) spasm, convulsion: *e-n ~ bekommen* get a cramp. **2.** *no pl* F *fig.* (*das ist doch alles ~* that's just a lot of) rubbish. '**Krampfader** *f* varicose vein.
'**krampfartig** *adj* convulsive.
krampfen ['krampfən] *v/t* (a. *sich ~*) (h) clench (*hand* etc).
'**krampfhaft** *adj* **1.** ⚕ convulsive, spasmodic. **2.** *fig.* desperate, frantic, forced (*laughter*): *sich ~ festhalten an* (*dat*) cling desperately to.
'**krampflösend** *adj* spasmolytic.
Kran [kra:n] *m* (-[e]s; »e) © crane.
'**Kranführer** *m* crane driver.
Kranich ['kra:niç] *m* (-s; -e) *zo.* crane.

krank [kraŋk] *adj* a) sick (*a. fig.*), *pred* ill, diseased (*organ*), bad (*tooth*), b) invalid, suffering, ailing (*a. fig.*): *~ werden* fall ill (*or* sick), be taken ill; *sich ~ fühlen* feel ill; *sich ~ melden* report sick; *j-n ~ schreiben* write s.o. off sick, ✗ put s.o. on the sick list; *er macht mich ganz ~!* he's driving me crazy!
'**Kranke** *m, f* (-n; -n) sick person, patient.
kränkeln ['krɛŋkəln] *v/i* (h) be in poor health, be sickly, be ailing (*a. fig.*).
kranken ['kraŋkən] *v/i* (h) *a. fig. ~ an* (*dat*) suffer from.
kränken ['krɛŋkən] *v/t* (h) hurt, wound, offend: *j-n ~* hurt s.o.'s (feelings).
'**Kranken|anstalt** *f* hospital. **~auto** *n* ambulance. **~besuch** *m* visit (to a sick person, *of doctor*: sick call: **~e machen** *a.* visit patients. **~bett** *n* sickbed. **~blatt** *n* medical record. **~geld** *n* sick pay. **~geschichte** *f* case (*or* medical) history. **~gym,nast(in** *f*) *m* physiotherapist. **~gym,nastik** *f* remedial gymnastics.
'**Krankenhaus** *n* hospital. **~aufenthalt** *m* stay in (*or* to) hospital. **~einweisung** *f* hospitalization. **~kosten** *pl* hospital expenses. **~tagegeld** *n sum paid by a private sickness insurance fund for each day in hospital.*
'**Kranken|kasse** *f* a) health insurance scheme, b) health insurance company. **~lager** *n* sickbed: *nach langem ~* after a long illness. **~pflege** *f* nursing. **~pfleger** *m* male nurse. **~pflegerin** *f* nurse. **~schein** *m* health insurance certificate. **~schwester** *f* nurse. **~stand** *m* number of sick persons. **~träger** *m* stretcher-bearer. **~versicherung** *f* health insurance. **~wagen** *m* ambulance. **~zimmer** *n* sickroom.
'**krankfeiern** *v/i* (*sep*, -ge-, h) F go sick, malinger, *Br.* skive off.
'**krankhaft** *adj* **1.** ⚕ pathological. **2.** *fig.* morbid, abnormal.
'**Krankheit** *f* (-; -en) illness, sickness, disease: *nach langer ~* after a long illness.
'**Krankheits|bild** *n* clinical picture. **~erscheinung** *f* symptom.
'**krankheitshalber** [-halbər] *adv* owing to illness.
'**Krankheits|herd** *m* focus of a disease. **~keim** *m* germ. **~überträger** *m* carrier.
'**kranklachen:** *sich ~* (*sep*, -ge-, h) F nearly die with laughter.

kränklich ['krɛŋklɪç] *adj* sickly.

'**Krankmeldung** *f* notification of illness (to one's employer): *zehn ~en* ten persons reported sick.

'**Kränkung** *f* (-; -en) insult.

Kranz [krants] *m* (-es; ⁓e) **1.** garland, (*e-n ~ niederlegen* lay a) wreath. **2.** *fig.* circle, ring. **3.** *gastr.* ring. **4.** *astr.* corona. **Kränzchen** ['krɛntsçən] *n* (-s; -) *fig.* (ladies') circle, coffee (F hen) party.

'**Kranzgefäß** *n anat.* coronary artery.

Krapfen ['krapfən] *m* (-s; -) doughnut.

kraß [kras] *adj* crass, gross: *krasser Egoist (Außenseiter)* crass egotist (rank outsider); *krasser Widerspruch (Unterschied)* flagrant contradiction (huge difference); *krasse Lüge* blatant lie; *sich ~ ausdrücken* be very blunt.

Krater ['kra:tər] *m* (-s; -) crater.

Krätze ['krɛtsə] *f* (-; *no pl*) ⚕ scabies.

kratzen ['kratsən] *v/t, v/i* (h) a) scratch, b) scrape: *sich ~* scratch o.s.; *sich am Ohr ~* scratch one's ear; *den Rest aus dem Topf ~* scrape the last bit from the pot; *der Pullover kratzt (mich am Hals)* the pullover scratches (my neck); *fig. mein Hals kratzt* I've got a sore throat; F *das kratzt mich nicht!* that doesn't worry me!; → *Kurve.* **Kratzer** *m* (-s; -) F scratch. '**kratzfest** *adj* scratch-resistant. '**kratzig** *adj* scratchy.

'**Kratzwunde** *f* scratch.

Kraul [kraʊl] *n* (-s; *no pl*) crawl.

kraulen¹ ['kraʊlən] *v/t, v/i* (h, sn) crawl.

kraulen² *v/t* (h) ruffle (*fur etc*).

'**Kraulschwimmen** *n* crawl.

'**Kraulschwimmer(in** *f*) *m* crawler.

kraus [kraʊs] *adj* **1.** frizzy, curly (*hair*), wrinkled (*brow*): *~ ziehen → krausen.* **2.** *fig.* confused, muddled (*ideas*).

Krause ['kraʊzə] *f* (-; -n) frill, ruffle.

kräuseln ['krɔʏzəln] (h) **I** *v/t* **1.** gather (*cloth*). **2.** friz(z), crimp (*hair*). **3.** ruffle, ripple (*water*). **4.** *die Lippen ~* curl one's lips; → *a.* **krausen. II** *sich ~* **5.** → 2. **6.** *smoke etc*: curl up.

krausen ['kraʊzən] *v/t* (h) wrinkle, pucker: *die Nase ~* wrinkle one's nose.

'**kraushaarig** *adj* curly-haired.

Kraut [kraʊt] *n* (-[e]s; ⁓er) **1.** *no pl* (stem and) leaves, tops: *ins ~ schießen* run to leaf, *fig.* run wild; F *wie ~ und Rüben (durcheinander)* in a jumble (*or* mess). **2.** herb: *fig. gegen ... ist kein ~ ge-*

wachsen there is no remedy for ... **3.** *no pl dial.* a) cabbage, b) sauerkraut. **4.** F weed, tobacco.

Kräuter|butter ['krɔʏtər-] *f* herb butter. ⁓**essig** *m* aromatic vinegar. ⁓**käse** *m* green cheese. ⁓**li|kör** *m* herb-flavo(u)red liqueur. ⁓**tee** *m* herb tea.

Krawall [kra'val] *m* (-s; -e) **1.** riot. **2.** F (*~ machen or schlagen* kick up a) row.

Kra'wallmacher *m* rioter, rowdy.

Krawatte [kra'vatə] *f* (-; -n) tie, *Am.* necktie.

Kra'watten|muffel *m* (-s; -) *er ist ein ~* he's no tie man. ⁓**nadel** *f* tiepin.

kraxeln ['kraksəln] *v/i* (h) F *dial.* climb.

Kreation [krea'tsjo:n] *f* (-; -en) creation.

kreativ [krea'ti:f] *adj* creative. **Kreativität** [krea'ti'tɛ:t] *f* (-; *no pl*) creativity.

Kreatur [krea'tu:r] *f* (-; -en) creature.

Krebs [kre:ps] *m* (-es; -e) **1.** a) crayfish, *Am.* crawfish, b) crab. **2.** *astrol.* (*ich bin [ein]* ~ I am [a]) Cancer. **3.** ⚕ cancer. '**krebsartig** *adj* ⚕ cancerous.

krebserregend, krebserzeugend *adj* carcinogenic: *~ wirken* cause cancer.

'**Krebs|forschung** *f* ⚕ cancer research. ⁓**früherkennung** *f* early cancer diagnosis. ⁓**geschwulst** *f* carcinoma, cancerous tumo(u)r. ⁓**geschwür** *n* **1.** cancerous ulcer. **2.** *fig.* canker. ⁓**knoten** *m* cancerous lump. ⁓**kranke** *m, f* (-n; -n) person suffering from cancer, cancer patient. ⁓**krankheit** *f*, ⁓**leiden** *n* cancer. ⁓**tiere** *pl* crustaceans.

'**Krebsvorsorge** *f* ⚕ cancer prevention. ⁓**untersuchung** *f* cancer screening.

'**Krebszelle** *f* ⚕ cancer(ous) cell.

Kredit¹ ['kre:dit] *n* (-s; -s) ♥ credit (side).

Kredit² [kre'di:t] *m* (-[e]s; -e) ♥ credit, *a.* loan: *e-n ~ aufnehmen (überziehen)* raise (overdraw) a credit; *ich habe bei der Bank ~* my credit with the bank is good; *auf ~ kaufen* buy on credit.

Kre'dit|aufnahme *f* borrowing. ⁓**brief** *m* letter of credit. ⁓**geber** *m* lender. ⁓**hai** *m* F *contp.* loan shark.

kreditieren [kredi'ti:rən] *v/t* (h) *j-m et. ~* credit s.o.('s account) with s.th.

Kre'dit|insti|tut *n* credit bank. ⁓**karte** *f* credit card. ⁓**kauf** *m* purchase on credit. ⁓**markt** *m* credit market. ⁓**nehmer** *m* borrower. ⁓**spritze** *f* credit injection.

kre'ditwürdig *adj* creditworthy.

kregel ['kre:gəl] *adj* F chirpy, chipper.

Kreide ['kraɪdə] f (-; -n) chalk, paint. a. crayon: F *bei j-m in der ~ stehen* owe s.o. money. ♀'**bleich**, ♀'**weiß** adj (as) white as a sheet. ~**zeichnung** f chalk drawing. ~**zeit** f (-; no pl) the Cretaceous period.

kreieren [kre'i:rən] v/t (h) create.

Kreis [kraɪs] m (-es; -e) **1.** a) circle (a. fig. of lines etc), b) cycle, c) ⚡ circuit, d) fig. sphere, field: *sich im ~e drehen* a. fig. move in a circle; *der Skandal zog weite ~e* the scandal involved more and more persons; *hier schließt sich der ~* we've come full circle; *im engsten ~e feiern* celebrate within the family circle (or with one's close friends); *im ~e der Familie* in the family (circle); *weite ~e der Bevölkerung* wide sections of the population; *aus gutunterrichteten ~en* from well-informed quarters. **2.** pol. district, Am. county.

'**Kreis|abschnitt** m 🜂 segment. ~**ausschnitt** m 🜂 sector. ~**bahn** f orbit. ~**bogen** m 🜂 arc of a circle.

kreischen ['kraɪʃən] v/i (h) shriek.

'**Kreischen** n (-s) shrieking, shrieks pl.

Kreisel ['kraɪzəl] m (-s; -) **1.** (peg)top. **2.** phys. gyro(scope).

'**Kreiselkompaß** m gyrocompass.

kreisen ['kraɪzən] **I** v/i (sn) (move in a) circle, esp. ◉ rotate, revolve (a. fig. thoughts etc), money: circulate, ✈ orbit: *et. ~ lassen* pass s.th. round; *die Erde kreist um die Sonne* the earth revolves (a)round the sun. **II** v/t (h) gym. *die Arme etc ~* swing one's arms etc around.

'**Kreisfläche** f 🜂 area of a circle.

'**kreisförmig** adj circular.

'**Kreislauf** m cycle (a. ◉), of blood, money: circulation, ⚡ ◉ a. circuit, astr. revolution. ~**störung** f ✚ circulatory disturbance, pl bad circulation. ~**versagen** n ✚ circulatory collapse.

'**kreisrund** adj circular.

'**Kreissäge** f circular saw.

Kreißsaal ['kraɪs-] m ✚ delivery room.

'**Kreisstadt** f district town, Am. county seat.

'**Kreisverkehr** m roundabout, Am. rotary (traffic).

Krem [kre:m] f (-; -s) → **Creme** etc.

Krematorium [krema'to:riʊm] n (-s; -rien) crematorium, Am. crematory.

Kreml ['kre:məl; 'krɛməl] m (-s; no pl) the Kremlin.

Krempe ['krɛmpə] f (-; -n) brim.

krepieren [kre'pi:rən] v/i (sn) **1.** F die, perish. **2.** bomb etc: burst, explode.

Krepp [krɛp] m (-s; -s) crepe.

'**Kreppa,pier** n crepe paper.

Kresse ['krɛsə] f (-; -n) 🍃 cress.

Kreta ['kre:ta] n (-s) Crete. **Kreter** ['kre:tər] m (-s; -), '**Kreterin** f (-; -nen), '**kretisch** adj Cretan.

kreuz [krɔʏts] adv ~ **und quer**, a. ~ **und quer durchziehen** crisscross.

Kreuz n (-es; -e) **1.** cross (a. fig.), print. dagger, obelisk: astr. *das ~ des Südens* the Southern Cross; *über ~* crosswise; *ein ~ schlagen* make the sign of the cross; *es ist ein ~ mit ihm* he is a real problem; F *zu ~e kriechen* knuckle under (*vor j-m* to s.o.). **2.** (small of the) back: *mir tut das ~ weh* my back aches; F *j-n aufs ~ legen* take s.o. for a ride. **3.** ♪ sharp. **4.** cards: club(s).

'**Kreuz|band** n (-[e]s; ⸚er) anat. crucial ligament. ~**bein** n anat. sacrum.

kreuzen ['krɔʏtsən] (h) **I** v/t **1.** cross, ◉ a. intersect, biol. a. crossbreed. **II** v/i ⚓ cruise. **III** sich ~ **3.** → 1. **4.** fig. cross, interests etc: clash: *ihre Blicke kreuzten sich* their eyes met.

'**Kreuzer** m (-s; -) ⚓ **1.** ✕ cruiser. **2.** sports: (cabin) cruiser.

'**Kreuzfahrer** m hist. crusader.

'**Kreuzfahrt** f **1.** hist. crusade. **2.** ⚓ (e-e ~ machen) go on a cruise.

'**Kreuzfeuer** n a. fig. crossfire: *ins ~ der öffentlichen Meinung (or der Kritik) geraten* come under fire from all sides.

'**Kreuzgang** m 🜂 cloister.

kreuzigen ['krɔʏtsɪɡən] v/t (h) crucify.

'**Kreuzigung** f (-; -en) crucifixion.

'**Kreuzotter** f zo. common viper.

'**Kreuzritter** m hist. Knight of the Cross.

'**Kreuzstich** m cross-stitch.

'**Kreuzung** f (-; -en) **1.** crossing, biol. a. crossbreeding, (race) crossbreed. **2.** crossing, intersection, junction.

'**Kreuzverhör** n cross-examination, F grilling: *j-n ins ~ nehmen* cross-examine (F grill) s.o.

'**Kreuzweg** m eccl. Way of the Cross.

'**kreuzweise** adv crosswise.

'**Kreuzworträtsel** n crossword (puzzle).

'Kreuzzug m hist. or fig. (a. **e-n ~ unternehmen**) crusade (**gegen** against).

kribbelig ['krɪbəlɪç] adj F a) nervous, jittery, b) edgy: **sie macht mich ganz ~** she gets terribly on my nerves.

kribbeln ['krɪbəln] v/i **1.** (h) itch, tickle, tingle: F **es kribbelte mir in den Fingern, et. zu tun** I was itching to do s.th. **2.** (sn) crawl, swarm.

Kricket ['krɪkət] n (-s; no pl) cricket.

'Kricketspieler m cricketer.

kriechen ['kriːçən] v/i (kroch, gekrochen, sn) creep, crawl: fig. contp. **vor j-m ~** toady to s.o. **'Kriecher** m (-s; -) contp. crawler, toady. **'kriecherisch** adj contp. crawling, toadying.

'Kriechspur f **1.** trail. **2.** mot. slow (or creeper) lane. **'Kriechstrom** m ⚡ leak current. **'Kriechtier** n reptile.

Krieg [kriːk] m (-[e]s; -e) a) war, b) warfare: **kalter ~** cold war; **im ~ mit** at war with; (dat) **den ~ erklären** a. fig. declare war on; **~ führen gegen** be at war against; **in den ~ ziehen** go to war.

kriegen ['kriːɡən] v/t (h) F get, a. catch; → a. **bekommen I**; **es mit j-m zu tun ~** get into trouble with s.o.

Krieger ['kriːɡər] m (-s; -) warrior. **'Kriegerdenkmal** n war memorial. **'kriegerisch** adj warlike, martial, a. fig. belligerent: **~e Auseinandersetzung** armed conflict.

'Kriegerwitwe f war widow.

'kriegführend adj belligerent.

'Kriegführung f (-; no pl) warfare.

'Kriegs|ausbruch m outbreak of (the) war: **bei ~** when the war broke out. **~berichterstatter** m war correspondent. **~beschädigte** m, f (-n; -n) war-disabled person. **~dienst** m military service. **~dienstverweigerer** m conscientious objector. **~ende** n end of (the) war: **bei ~** a. when the war ended. **~entschädigungen** pl reparations. **~erklärung** f declaration of war. **~fall** m **im ~** in case of war. **~film** m war film. **~flotte** f navy, fleet. **~freiwillige** m (war) volunteer. **~fuß** m **auf ~ stehen mit** a) **j-m** be at daggers drawn with s.o., b) **e-r Sache** have (great) trouble with s.th. **~gebiet** n war zone. **~gefahr** f threat of war. **~gefangene** m prisoner of war, P.O.W. **~gefangenenlager** n prisoner-of-war (or P.O.W.) camp. **~gefan-**

genschaft f captivity: **in ~ geraten** be taken prisoner. **~gegner** m **1.** pacifist. **2.** the enemy. **~gericht** n (a. **vor ein ~ stellen**) court-martial.

'Kriegsgewinnler [-ɡəvɪnlər] m (-s; -) war profiteer.

'Kriegs|gräberfürsorge f War Graves Commission. **~hafen** m naval port. **~held** m war hero. **~hetzer** m warmonger. **~hinterbliebenen** pl war widows and orphans. **~kamerad** m fellow soldier. **~marine** f navy. **~material** n matériel. **~opfer** n war victim. **~pfad** m **auf dem ~ sein** a. F fig. be on the warpath. **~recht** n (-[e]s; no pl) martial law. **~schauplatz** n theat/re (Am. -er) of war. **~schiff** n warship. **~schulden** pl war debts. **~schuld(frage)** f (question of) war guilt. **~spielzeug** n war toys. **~tanz** m war dance. **~teilnehmer** m **1.** combatant. **2.** ex-serviceman, Am. (war) veteran. **~trauung** f wartime wedding. **~treiber** m warmonger. **~verbrechen** n war crime.

'Kriegsverbrecher m war criminal. **~prozeß** m war crimes trial.

'Kriegs|waise f war orphan. ⚤**wichtig** adj essential to the war effort: **~e Ziele** strategic targets. **~zeit** f wartime: **in ~en** in time(s) of war. **~zustand** m (state of) war: **im ~** at war.

Krimi ['kriːmi; 'krɪmi] m (-[s]; -[s]) F thriller (a. fig.), whodun(n)it.

Kriminal|beamte [krimi'naːl-] m detective, C.I.D. officer. **~fall** m criminal case. **~film** m crime film (or thriller).

kriminalisieren [kriminali'ziːrən] v/t (h) criminalize.

Kriminalist [krimina'lɪst] m (-en; -en) **1.** criminologist. **2.** detective. **Kriminalität** [kriminali'tɛːt] f (-; no pl) **1.** criminality. **2.** crime: **ansteigende ~** increasing crime rate.

Krimi'nal|kommis,sar m detective superintendent, Am. captain of police. **~poli,zei** f criminal investigation department (C.I.D.), plain-clothes police. **~poli,zist** m → **Kriminalbeamte**. **~ro,man** m detective (or crime) novel. **kriminell** [krimi'nɛl] adj criminal. **Krimi'nelle** m, f (-n; -n) criminal.

Krippe ['krɪpə] f (-; -n) **1.** ✝ manger, crib. **2.** (Christmas) crib, Am. crèche. **3.** crèche, day nursery.

'**Krippenspiel** n Nativity play.
Krise ['kri:zə] f (-; -n) crisis: **in e-e ~ geraten** enter a state of crisis.
kriseln ['kri:zəln] v/impers (h) **es kriselt** a) there is trouble brewing, b) **in ihrer Ehe** they seem to be going through a crisis, c) **in der Regierung** a government crisis is looming.
'**krisenanfällig** adj crisis-prone.
'**krisenfest** adj stable.
'**Krisengebiet** n crisis area.
'**krisengeschüttelt** adj crisis-ridden.
'**Krisen|herd** m trouble spot. **~management** n crisis management. **~situati,on** f crisis (situation). **~sitzung** f crisis meeting. **~zeit** f time of crisis.
Kristall¹ [krɪs'tal] m (-[e]s; -e) crystal.
Kri'stall² n (-[e]s; no pl) **1.** crystal (glass), cut glass. **2.** crystal (goods).
kri'stallen adj crystalline, a. fig. crystal.
kristallinisch [krɪsta'li:nɪʃ] adj crystalline. **Kristallisation** [krɪstaliza'tsi̯o:n] f (-; -en) crystallization. **kristallisieren** [krɪstali'zi:rən] v/i (h) crystallize.
kri'stallklar adj crystal-clear.
Kristallographie [krɪstalogra'fi:] f (-; no pl) crystallography.
Kriterium [kri'te:ri̯ʊm] n (-s; -rien) **1.** criterion (**für** of). **2.** sports: circuit race.
Kritik [kri'ti:k] f (-; -en) a) criticism (**an** dat of), b) review, c) the critics: **~ hervorrufen** give rise to criticism; **~ üben an** (dat) criticize; **e-e ~ schreiben über** (acc) a. review; **gute ~en haben** get (or have) good reviews, have a good press; F **unter aller ~ sein** be beneath contempt. **Kritiker** ['kri:tikər] m (-s; -), '**Kritikerin** f (-; -nen) a) critic, b) reviewer. **Kri'tikfähigkeit** f critical faculties. **kri'tiklos** adj uncritical. **kritisch** ['kri:tɪʃ] adj a. phys., ⊚ critical (**gegenüber** of), fig. a. crucial. **kritisieren** [kriti'zi:rən] v/t, v/i (h) criticize.
kritteln ['krɪtəln] v/i (h) carp (**an** dat at).
Kritzelei [krɪtsə'laɪ] f (-; -en) scribble.
kritzeln ['krɪtsəln] v/t, v/i (h) scribble.
kroch [krɔx] pret of **kriechen.**
Krocket ['krɔkət] n (-s; no pl) croquet.
Krokant [kro'kant] m (-[e]s; no pl) brittle.
Krokette [kro'kɛtə] f (-; -en) croquette.
Kroko ['kro:ko] n (-[s]; -s) † → **Krokodilleder. Krokodil** [kroko'di:l] n (-s; -e) crocodile. **Kroko'dilleder** n crocodile

(skin or leather). **Kroko'dilstränen** pl F (**~ vergießen** shed) crocodile tears.
Krokus ['kro:kʊs] m (-; -[se]) ⚘ crocus.
Krone ['kro:nə] f **1.** crown (a. fig.), coronet: **die ~ der Schöpfung** the pride of creation; F **das setzt allem die ~ auf!** that beats everything!; **e-n in der ~ haben** be tight. **2.** ⚙ a) cap, top, b) crown, crest. **3.** crown (of tooth). **4.** (Swedish coin) krona, (Danish or Norwegian coin) krone. **5.** chandelier.
krönen ['krø:nən] v/t (h) crown (**j-n zum König** s.o. king), fig. a. climax: **von Erfolg gekrönt** crowned with success.
'**Kronenkorken** m crown cork.
'**Kronju,welen** pl crown jewels.
'**Kronleuchter** m chandelier.
'**Kronprinz** m crown prince (a. fig.), Br. Prince of Wales. '**Kronprin,zessin** f crown princess, Br. Princess Royal.
'**Krönung** f (-; -en) **1.** coronation. **2.** fig. crowning (event): **die ~ s-r Laufbahn** the climax of his career; **die ~ des Abends** the highlight (F high spot) of the evening.
'**Kronzeuge** m, '**Kronzeugin** f chief witness: **~ werden** turn Queen's (King's, Am. State's) evidence.
Kropf [krɔpf] m (-[e]s; ⁔e) **1.** zo. crop. **2.** ✿ goitre, Am. goiter.
kroß [krɔs] adj crisp.
Kröte ['krø:tə] f (-; -n) **1.** zo. toad. **2.** pl F dough, pennies.
Krücke ['krykə] f (-; -n) **1.** crutch: **an ~n gehen** walk on crutches. **2.** crook (of walking stick etc). **3.** F contp. a) washout, b) **alte ~** rattletrap.
Krug [kru:k] m (-[e]s; ⁔e) **1.** jug, pitcher. **2.** → **Maßkrug. 3.** dial. pub, inn.
Krume ['kru:mə] f (-; -n) **1.** ✶ topsoil. **2.** → **Krümel** ['kry:məl] m (-s; -) crumb.
krümelig ['kry:məlɪç] adj crumbly.
krümeln ['kry:məln] v/t, v/i (h) crumble.
krumm [krʊm] I adj crooked (a. F fig. dishonest), hooked, a. bent: **~e Haltung** stoop; **~er Schnabel** curved beak; **~ biegen** bend; **ganz ~ und schief** awry, lopsided; F **sich ~ und schief lachen** laugh one's head off; **~e Sache, ~e Tour** crooked business; ein **Ding drehen** pull a fast one; **et. auf die ~e Tour versuchen** try to wangle s.th. II adv **~ gewachsen** crooked; **sich ~ halten, ~ gehen** stoop.

'**krummbeinig** [-baınıç] *adj* bow-legged.
krümmen ['krymən] (h) **I** *v/t* bend,
crook. **II** *sich* ~ bend, *road*: *a.* curve,
worm etc: squirm: *sich ~ vor* (*dat*)
writhe with *pain etc*, squirm with *embarrassment*; *sich vor Lachen* ~ →
krummlachen.
Krümmer ['krymər] *m* (-s; -) **1.** *mot.*
manifold. **2.** ⊗ bend, elbow.
'**krummlachen**: *sich* ~ (*sep*, -ge-, h) F
laugh one's head off. '**krummlegen**:
sich ~ (*sep*, -ge-, h) F pinch and scrape.
'**krummnehmen** *v/t* (*irr*, *sep*, -ge-, h, →
nehmen) F *et.* ~ take s.th. amiss.
'**Krümmung** *f* (-; -en) bend, curve, turn,
⚓, ⚡, *phys.*, ⊗ curvature.
Kruppe ['krupə] *f* (-; -n) croup (*of horse*).
Krüppel ['krypəl] *m* (-s; -) (*a. zum* ~
machen) cripple: *zum* ~ *werden* be
crippled. '**krüpp(e)lig** *adj* crippled.
Kruste ['krustə] *f* (-; -n) crust, *gastr. a.*
crackling. '**Krustentier** *n* crustacean.
krustig ['krustıç] *adj* crusty.
Kruzifix ['kru:tsıfıks] *n* (-es; -e) crucifix.
Krypta ['krypta] *f* (-; -ten) ⌂ crypt.
Kuba ['ku:ba] *n* (-s) Cuba. **Kubaner**
[ku'ba:nər] *m* (-s; -), **Ku'banerin** *f* (-;
-nen), **ku'banisch** *adj* Cuban.
Kübel ['ky:bəl] *m* (-s; -) a) bucket (*a.* ⊗),
pail, b) tub: F *es gießt wie aus* ~*n* it's
coming down in buckets.
Kubik|inhalt [ku'bi:k-] *m* cubic content.
~**maß** *n* cubic measure. ~**meter** *m*, *n*
cubic metre (*Am.* meter). ~**wurzel** *f* ⚓
cube root. ~**zahl** *f* cube.
kubisch [ku'bi:ʃ] *adj* cubic(al).
Kubismus [ku'bısmus] *m* (-; *no pl*)
cubism. **Ku'bist** *m* (-en; -en) cubist.
ku'bistisch *adj* cubist(ic).
Kubus ['ku:bus] *m* (-; Kuben) ⚓ cube.
Küche ['kyçə] *f* (-; -n) **1.** kitchen, kitch-
enette; → *Teufel.* **2.** a) cooking, cookery, cuisine, b) meals, food: *kalte* (*warme*) ~ cold (hot) meals; *die chinesische* ~ Chinese cooking; → *gutbürger-
lich.* **3.** F → *Küchenpersonal.*
Kuchen ['ku:xən] *m* (-s; -) cake.
'**Küchenbenutzung** *f mit* ~ with use of
kitchen.
'**Kuchenblech** *n* baking sheet (*or* tin).
'**Küchenchef** *m* chef (de cuisine).
'**Kücheneinrichtung** *f* kitchen furniture
and fittings.
'**Kuchenform** *f* cake tin.

'**Kuchengabel** *f* pastry fork.
'**Küchen|gerät** *n* kitchen utensil (*or* ap-
pliance). ~**geschirr** *n* kitchenware.
~**herd** *m* kitchen range. ~**hilfe** *f* kitch-
enmaid. ~**kraut** *n* potherb. ~**messer** *n*
kitchen knife. ~**perso,nal** *n* kitchen
staff. ~**schrank** *m* (kitchen) cupboard.
'**Kuchenteig** *m* cake mixture.
'**Kuchenteller** *m* dessert plate.
'**Küchen|tisch** *m* kitchen table. ~**waage**
f kitchen scales. ~**wecker** *m* (kitchen)
timer. ~**zettel** *m* menu.
Kuckuck ['kukuk] *m* (-s; -e) **1.** cuckoo: F
wo (*wer etc*) *zum* ~*!* where (who *etc*)
the devil! **2.** *humor.* bailiff's seal.
'**Kuckucks|ei** *n* F *fig. ein* ~ a cuckoo in
the nest. ~**uhr** *f* cuckoo clock.
Kufe ['ku:fə] *f* (-; -n) runner, ✓ skid.
Küfer ['ky:fər] *m* (-s; -) cooper.
Kugel ['ku:gəl] *f* (-; -n) **1.** ball (*a.* ⊗),
globe, *astr.*, ⚓ sphere: *die Erde ist e-e*
~ the earth is a sphere. **2.** bullet; →
jagen 3. **3.** *sports*: a) shot, b) bowl: *er
stieß die* ~ *auf 22 m* he put the shot at
22 metres; F *fig. e-e ruhige* ~ *schieben*
have a cushy job.
'**Kugelabschnitt** *m* ⚓ spherical segment.
'**Kugelfang** *m* butt.
'**kugelförmig** *adj* globular, spherical.
'**Kugelgelenk** *n* (ball-and-)socket joint.
'**Kugelhagel** *m* hail of bullets.
'**Kugelkopf**(**schreibma,schine** *f*) *m*
golfball (typewriter).
'**Kugellager** *n* ⊗ ball bearing.
kugeln ['ku:gəln] F **I** *v/t, v/i* roll. **II**
sich ~ roll about (*im Schnee* in the
snow).
'**kugel'rund** *adj* (as) round as a ball.
'**Kugelschreiber** *m* ballpoint (pen), *Br.
a.* Biro (*TM*). ~**mine** *f* refill.
'**kugelsicher** *adj* bulletproof.
'**Kugelstoßen** *n* shot put. '**Kugelstoßer**
m (-s; -), '**Kugelstoßerin** *f* (-; -nen)
shot-putter.
Kuh [ku:] *f* (-; ~e) cow: *fig. heilige* ~
sacred cow; F *contp. dumme* ~*!* silly
cow! ~**fladen** *m* cowpat. ~**glocke** *f*
cowbell. ~**handel** *m* F *fig.* horse trading. ~**haut** *f* cowhide: F *fig. das geht
auf k-e* ~*!* it's just incredible!
kühl [ky:l] *adj a. fig.* cool, chilly: *es* (*mir*)
wird ~ it's getting (I feel) chilly; (*j-m
gegenüber*) ~ *bleiben* remain cool
(toward[s] s.o.); *et.* ~ *lagern* store s.th.

cool; **j-n ~ empfangen** give s.o. a cool reception; → **Kopf** 2.

'**Kühl|anlage** f cooling plant (*mot. system*). **~appa,rat** m cooling apparatus. **~con,tainer** m (-s; -) cooltainer.

'**Kühle** f (-; *no pl*) coolness (*a. fig.*), cool.

'**kühlen** (h) **I** *v/t* cool (*a.* ⚙), chill. **II** *v/i* have a cooling effect.

'**Kühler** m (-s; -) **1.** ⚙ cooler. **2.** *mot.* radiator. **~block** m *mot.* radiator core. **~fi,gur** f *mot.* radiator mascot.

'**Kühl|haus** n cold-storage house. **~mittel** n coolant. **~raum** m cold-storage chamber, ♻ refrigerating hold. **~schiff** n refrigerator ship. **~schlange** f cooling coil. **~schrank** m refrigerator, F fridge. **~tasche** f cool box (*or* bag). **~truhe** f (chest) freezer, deep-freeze. **~turm** m cooling tower.

'**Kühlung** f (-; -en) **1.** *a.* ⚙ cooling. **2.** ⚙ cooling system. **3.** *no pl* coolness.

'**Kühlwagen** m 🚃 refrigerator wagon (*Am.* car), *mot.* refrigerator truck.

'**Kühlwasser** n cooling water.

'**Kuhmilch** f cow's milk.

kühn [ky:n] *adj a. fig.* bold, daring: *das übertrifft m-e* **~sten Träume** that goes beyond my wildest dreams.

'**Kühnheit** f (-; *no pl*) boldness.

'**Kuhpocken** pl 🐛 cowpox.

'**Kuhstall** m cowshed.

Küken ['ky:kən] n (-s; -) *a. fig.* chick.

kulant [ku'lant] *adj* ✝ accommodating, fair (*price*).

Kuli ['ku:li] m (-s; -s) coolie.

kulinarisch [kuli'na:rɪʃ] *adj* culinary.

Kulisse [ku'lɪsə] f (-; -n) *usu. pl thea. etc* scenery, set, wing, *a. fig.* background: **hinter den ~n** *a. fig.* behind the scenes, backstage.

kulminieren [kʊlmi'ni:rən] *v/i* (h) *astr.* culminate (*fig.* **in** *dat*).

Kult [kʊlt] m (-[e]s; -e) cult: **e-n ~ treiben** make a cult (**mit** out of). '**Kultfi,gur** f cult figure. '**Kulthandlung** f ritual act.

'**kultisch** *adj* ritual, cultic.

kultivieren [kʊlti'vi:rən] *v/t* (h) cultivate. **kulti'viert** *adj* cultured, cultivated, *a.* civilized (*person*), refined (*taste*).

Kultur [kʊl'tu:r] f (-; -en) **1.** *no pl* a) culture, *a.* refinement, b) civilization: *die abendländische* **~** the Western civilization; *er hat (k-e)* **~** he is (un)cultured; F *in* **~ machen** be into culture. **2.**

no pl 🌱 cultivation. **3.** 🌱, 🌿 culture.

Kul'tur|abkommen n *pol.* cultural agreement. **~austausch** m cultural exchange. **~ba,nause** m F philistine. **~betrieb** m (-[e]s *no pl*) F cultural activities. **~beutel** m toilet bag. **~denkmal** n cultural monument.

kulturell [kʊltu'rɛl] *adj* cultural.

Kul'tur|erbe n cultural heritage. **~film** m documentary. **~geschichte** f **1.** history of civilization (*a. book*). **2.** *no pl* a) cultural history of France *etc*, b) history of culture. ⚲**geschichtlich** *adj* cultural-historical. **~gut** n cultural asset(s). **~landschaft** f **1.** land developed and cultivated by man. **2.** *fig.* cultural scene. **~leben** n cultural life.

kul'turlos *adj* uncultured, uncivilized.

Kul'tur|mensch m civilized man. **~pessi,mismus** m cultural pessimism. **~pflanze** f cultivated plant. **~poli,tik** f cultural and educational policy. ⚲**po,litisch** *adj* politico-cultural. **~revoluti,on** f cultural revolution. **~schock** m cultural shock. **~sprache** f cultural (*or* civilized) language. **~stätte** f place of cultural interest. **~stufe** f stage (*or* level) of civilization. **~szene** f (-; *no pl*) cultural scene. **~volk** n civilized people (*or* nation, race).

Kultusmi,nister ['kʊltus-] m Minister of Culture, Education, and Church Affairs.

Kümmel ['kʏml] m (-s; -) **1.** 🌿 caraway: **Echter ~** cumin. **2.** *gastr.* kümmel.

Kummer ['kʊmər] m (-s; *no pl*) a) grief, sorrow, b) trouble, worry, worries, problems: **~ haben** have problems; **j-m viel ~ machen** cause s.o. a lot of worry (*or* trouble); F *ich bin ~ gewöhnt!* I'm used to this sort of thing!

kümmerlich ['kʏmərlɪç] *adj* miserable, *a.* poor, meagre, *Am.* meager, sparse (*vegetation etc*): *sich ~ durchschlagen* (*mit Stundengeben etc*) eke out a bare existence (by giving lessons *etc*).

kümmern ['kʏmərn] (h) **I** *sich ~ um* a) look after, take care of, b) care about, c) pay attention to, d) see to; *ich muß mich um das Mittagessen ~* I have to see to our lunch; *kümmere dich um d-e eigenen Angelegenheiten!* mind your own business!; *sich nicht ~ um* a) not to bother about, ignore, b) neglect. **II**

v/t was kümmert mich ... what do I care about ...; *was kümmert's mich?* that's not my problem!; *was kümmert dich das?* what concern is that of yours? **III** *v/i* develop poorly.

'kummervoll *adj* woebegone, sad.

Kumpan [kʊm'paːn] *m* (-s; -e) F a) companion, fellow, b) *b.s.* accomplice.

Kumpel ['kʊmpəl] *m* (-s; -) **1.** ⚒ pitman, miner. **2.** F mate, pal, chum, *Am.* buddy. **'kumpelhaft** *adj* chummy.

kündbar ['kʏntbaːr] *adj* terminable (*contract*), *capital* at call, redeemable (*loan*), *lease, position, etc* subject to notice: *er ist jederzeit ~* he can be given notice at any time.

Kunde ['kʊndə] *m* (-n; -n) customer, client: *fester ~* regular customer.

'Kunden|beratung *f* (customer) advisory service (*or* office). **~dienst** *m* a) service (to the customer), b) after-sales service, c) service department. **~fang** *m* (-[e]s; *no pl*) *contp.* (*auf ~ ausgehen* be) touting. **~kar,tei** *f* list of customers. **~kreis** *m* customers, clientele. **~nummer** *f* client code. **~stamm** *m* regular customers (*or* clientele). **~werbung** *f* canvassing (of customers).

Kundgebung ['kʊntgeːbʊŋ] *f* (-; -en) *pol.* meeting, rally.

kundig ['kʊndɪç] *adj* experienced, expert, *a.* conversant.

kündigen ['kʏndɪɡən] (h) **I** *v/t* terminate (*contract etc*), cancel (*subscription etc*), call in (*capital*): *s-e Stellung ~* quit one's job; *die Wohnung ~* give notice of one's intention to leave, *j-m* give s.o. notice to quit; F *j-n ~* dismiss s.o., sack s.o. **II** *v/i j-m (zum 1. Mai) ~* give s.o. notice (*landlord:* to quit) (for May 1st), dismiss s.o. (as of May 1st); *(j-m) drei Monate im voraus ~* give (s.o.) three months' notice; *bei e-r Firma ~* hand in one's notice to a firm; *mir ist (zum 1. Mai) gekündigt worden* I'm under notice to leave (on May 1st).

'Kündigung *f* (-; -en) a) notice, notice of withdrawal (*of loan etc*), termination (*of contract*), cancel(l)ation (*of subscription etc*), b) dismissal: *~ (e-r Wohnung) by landlord:* notice to quit, *by tenant:* notice of one's intention to leave; *vierteljährliche ~ vereinbaren* agree on three months' notice.

'Kündigungs|frist *f* period of notice: *mit halbjähriger ~* at six months' notice. **~grund** *m* grounds for giving notice (*or* for dismissal). **~schreiben** *n* a) (written) notice, b) letter of dismissal. **~schutz** *m* protection against unlawful dismissal (*or* unwarrranted eviction).

Kundin ['kʊndɪn] *f* (-; -nen) (female) customer (*etc*); → **Kunde.**

Kundschaft ['kʊntʃaft] *f* (-; *no pl*) a) customers, clientele, b) F customer, c) patronage.

'Kundschafter *m* (-s; -) scout, spy.

künftig ['kʏnftɪç] **I** *adj* future, coming: *~e Generationen a.* generations to come. **II** *adv* in future, from now on.

Kunst [kʊnst] *f* (-; ⁓e) **1.** *die schönen Künste* the fine arts; *die bildende ~* graphic art; *die darstellenden Künste* a) the performing arts, b) the pictorial arts; *die ~ der Gegenwart* contemporary art; F *was macht die ~?* how are things?; *~ schön* 1. **2.** a) skill, art, b) trick: *die ~ des Schreibens* the art of writing; *ärztliche ~* medical skill; F *das ist k-e ~!* that's easy!; *das ist e-e brotlose ~* there's no money in it; *die ganze ~ besteht darin zu inf* the whole trick is to *inf*; *sie ließ alle ihre Künste spielen* she used all her wiles.

'Kunst|akade,mie *f* academy of arts. **~auge** *n* artificial eye. **~ausstellung** *f* art exhibition. **~band** *m* (-[e]s; ⁓e) art book. **~betrieb** *m* (-[e]s; *no pl*) *contp.* cultural activities. **~denkmal** *n* monument of art. **~druck** *m* (-[e]s; -e) **1.** *no pl* art printing. **2.** art print. **~dünger** *m* artificial fertilizer. **~eisbahn** *f* artificial ice rink. **~erzieher(in** *f*) *m* art teacher. **~erziehung** *f* art (education). **~faser** *f* synthetic fibre (*Am.* fiber). **~fehler** *m* 🕱 professional blunder.

'kunstfertig *adj* skil(l)ful, skilled.

'Kunst|flieger *m* stunt flyer. **~flug** *m* aerobatics, stunt flying. **~flug...** aerobatic (*figure, team, etc*). **~freund(in** *f*) *m* art lover. **~gale,rie** *f* art gallery. **~gegenstand** *m* objet d'art.

'kunstgerecht *adj* skil(l)ful, expert.

'Kunst|geschichte *f* (-; *no pl*) art history. **~gewerbe** *n* (-s; *no pl*) arts and crafts, applied art(s). **~glied** *n* artificial limb. **~griff** *m* trick. **~handel** *m* art trade. **~händler** *m* art dealer. **~hand-**

365

kurieren

lung f art dealer('s shop). **~handwerk** n → **Kunstgewerbe.** **~handwerker(in** f) m artisan. **~herz** n ♂ artificial heart. **~hi,storiker** m art historian. **~hochschule** f art college. **~honig** m artificial honey. **~kritiker** m art critic. **~leder** n imitation leather.

Künstler ['kʏnstlər] m (-s; -), **'Künstlerin** f (-; -nen) artist, ♪, thea. performer, (circus etc) artiste. **'künstlerisch** adj artistic: **~er Leiter** art director; **ein ~ wertvoller Film** of artistic merit; **~ begabt sein** have an artistic talent.

'Künstlername m thea. etc stage name. **'Künstlertum** n (-s; no pl) artistry, coll. the artistic world.

'Künstlerviertel n artists' quarter.

künstlich ['kʏnstlɪç] adj artificial (a. fig.), a. false (teeth etc), man-made, synthetic (fibres): **~e Niere** kidney machine; **~ ernähren** feed s.o. artificially.

'Kunstlicht n phot. artificial light.

'Kunstliebhaber(in f) m art lover.

'kunstlos adj simple, plain.

'Kunstmaler(in f) m artist, painter. **~pause** f iro. e-e **~ machen** pause for effect. **~reiter(in** f) m trick rider. **~sammler(in** f) m art collector. **~sammlung** f art collection. **~schätze** pl art treasures. **~schule** f art school. **~schwimmen** n water ballet. **~seide** f artificial silk, rayon. **~seiden** adj (of) rayon. **~sprache** f artificial language. **~springen** n (fancy) diving. **~springer(in** f) m (fancy) diver.

'Kunststoff m synthetic material, plastic (material): **~e** plastics; **aus ~** (of) plastic. **~beschichtet** adj plastic-laminated. **~indu,strie** f plastics industry. **~rasen** m artificial lawn.

'Kunst|stopfen n (-s) invisible mending. **~stück** n a (real) trick, a. stunt, fig. a. (great) feat: iro. **~!** small wonder!, big deal!; **das ist doch kein ~!** anyone can do that! **~stu,dent(in** f) m art student. **~tischler** m cabinetmaker. **~turnen** n gymnastics. **~turner(in** f) m gymnast. **2verständig** adj 1. artistic. 2. expert. **~verständnis** n appreciation (or expert knowledge) of art.

'kunstvoll adj a) (highly) artistic, b) elaborate, c) ingenious.

'Kunst|werk n work of art. **~wort** n coinage. **~zeitschrift** f art magazine.

kunterbunt ['kʊntər-] adv **~ durcheinander** higgledy-piggledy, in a jumble.

Kupfer ['kʊpfər] n (-s; no pl) copper. **'Kupferblech** n sheet copper. **'Kupferdraht** m copper wire. **'kupferhaltig** adj containing copper. **kupfern** ['kʊpfərn] adj (of) copper. **'Kupferstecher** m (-s; -) copperplate engraver. **'Kupferstich** m (-[e]s; -e) copperplate (engraving).

kupieren [ku'piːrən] v/t (h) dock.

Kupon [ku'põː] m (-s; -s) coupon.

Kuppe ['kʊpə] f (-; -n) 1. (hill)top. 2. (finger)tip.

Kuppel ['kʊpəl] f (-; -n) dome. **'kuppelförmig** adj dome-shaped.

Kuppelei [kʊpə'laɪ] f (-; -en) ⚖ procuration. **kuppeln** ['kʊpəln] (h) I v/t 1. ⚙ (an acc) couple (with), connect (to). II v/i 2. mot. a) (let in the) clutch, b) declutch. 3. matchmake. **'Kuppler** m (-s; -), **'Kupplerin** f (-; -nen) a) ⚖ procurer (procuress), b) matchmaker.

'Kupplung f (-; -en) 1. 🛒, ⚙ coupling. 2. mot. clutch: **die ~ treten (loslassen)** → **kuppeln** 2.

'Kupplungs|belag m mot. clutch facing. **~pe,dal** n clutch pedal. **~scheibe** f clutch disc. **~stecker** m ⚡ coupler plug.

Kur [kuːr] f (-; -en) cure, (course of) treatment: **e-e ~ machen** take a cure (or a course of treatment); **zur ~ fahren** go to a health resort (or spa).

Kür [kyːr] f (-; -en) a) gym. free (or voluntary) exercise(s), b) free skating (etc).

Kurator [ku'raːtor] m (-s; -en [kura-'toːrən]) trustee. **Kuratorium** [kura-'toːriʊm] n (-s; -rien) board of trustees.

'Kuraufenthalt m stay at a health resort.

Kurbel ['kʊrbəl] f (-; -n) crank, handle. **kurbeln** ['kʊrbəln] (h) I v/i crank, F mot. turn the steering wheel. II v/t et. **in die Höhe ~** wind s.th. up.

'Kurbelwelle f mot. crankshaft.

Kürbis ['kʏrbɪs] m (-ses; -se) 1. 🌿 pumpkin. 2. F nut.

Kurde ['kʊrdə] m (-n; -n), **'Kurdin** f (-; -nen) **'kurdisch** adj Kurd.

Kurfürst(in f) m elector (electress).

'Kurgast m visitor (to a health resort).

'Kurhaus n kurhaus, casino.

'Kurho,tel n health-resort hotel.

Kurie ['kuːriə] f (-; -n) eccl. Curia.

Kurier [ku'riːr] m (-s; -e) courier.

kurieren [ku'riːrən] v/t (h) cure (**von** of).

Ku'riergepäck n diplomatic bag.
kurios [ku'riːos] adj curious, odd. **Kuriosität** [kuriozi'tɛːt] f (-; -en) **1.** curiosity. **2.** curio. **Kuriosum** [ku'riːozʊm] n (-s; -sa) odd thing, odd fact.
'**Kurort** m spa, health resort.
'**Kurpfuscher(in** f) m quack. **Kurpfusche'rei** f (-; no pl) quackery.
Kurs [kurs] m (-es; -e) **1.** ✝ a) rate (of exchange), exchange rate, b) price, quotation: **zum ~ von** at a rate of; **au-ßer ~ setzen** withdraw from circulation; **die ~e geben nach** (**ziehen an**) prices are softening (hardening); **hoch im ~ stehen** a) be high, b) fig. be popular (**bei** with). **2.** ✈, ⚓ course, fig. a. line: **~ nehmen auf** (acc) set course for, a. fig. head for; **e-n falschen ~ ein-schlagen** take the wrong course (fig. a wrong line); pol. **harter** (**weicher**) **~** hard (soft) line; → **abweichen. 3.** class, course: **e-n ~ für Englisch besuchen** attend a course in English.
'**Kursänderung** f **1.** ✈, ⚓ change of course (a. fig.). **2.** ✝ change in the ex-change rate. '**Kursanstieg** m ✝ rise (in rates or prices). '**Kursbericht** m ✝ (stock) market report. '**Kursbuch** n (railway, Am. railroad) timetable.
Kürschner ['kʏrʃnər] m (-s; -) furrier. **Kürschnerei** [kʏrʃnə'raɪ] f (-; -en) **1.** no pl furrier's trade. **2.** furrier's shop.
'**Kurseinbruch** m ✝ fall in prices, slump.
'**Kursgewinn** m ✝ a) (price) gains, b) exchange profits.
kursieren [kʊr'ziːrən] v/i (h) circulate, fig. rumo(u)r etc; a. go round.
'**Kursindex** m ✝ share price index.
kursiv [kʊr'ziːf] adj italic: **et. ~ drucken** print s.th. in italics.
'**Kurskorrek,tur** f course correction: **e-e ~ vornehmen** correct the course.
'**Kursleiter** m instructor, teacher.
'**Kursno,tierung** f ✝ quotation.
'**Kursrückgang** m ✝ decline in prices.
'**Kursschwankung** f ✝ a) exchange rate fluctuation, b) price fluctuation.
Kursus ['kʊrzʊs] m (-; Kurse) → **Kurs** 3.
'**Kursverlust** m ✝ a) exchange loss, b) (stock price) loss.
'**Kurswechsel** m pol. change of policy.
'**Kurswert** m ✝ market value.
'**Kurszettel** m ✝ price list, stock list.
'**Kurtaxe** f health resort tax.

'**Kürübung** f sports: free exercise.
Kurve ['kʊrvə] f (-; -n) curve, ⚹ a. graph, a. bend, turn (of road etc), pl F curves (of woman): **die Straße macht e-e ~** the road bends; **unübersichtliche ~** blind bend; mot. **die ~ schneiden** cut the curve; **e-e ~ fliegen** bank; F fig. **die ~ kratzen** beat it, push off; **der kriegt die ~ nie!** he'll never make it!
kurven ['kʊrvən] v/i (sn) curve, ⚹ bank.
'**Kurven|bild** n diagram, graph. **~festig-keit** f, **~lage** f mot. cornering stability. **~line,al** n (French) curve. **ℤreich** adj **1.** road: full of bends, winding. **2.** F fig. curvaceous. **~technik** f mot. cornering technique. **~vorgabe** f sports: stagger.
kurz [kurts] **I** adj **1.** short (a. fig.), brief: **kürzer werden** (**machen**) get (make) shorter, shorten; **5 m zu ~ sein** be five metres short; **den kürzeren ziehen** come off worst, lose out; F **et. ~ und klein schlagen** smash s.th. to bits; **~es Gedächtnis** short memory; **mit ein paar ~en Worten** in a few words, briefly; **in kürzester Zeit** in no time; **binnen ~em** shortly; **seit ~em** for some little time (now); **bis vor ~em** until quite recently; F **mach's ~!** be brief! **2.** short, curt (**gegen j-n** with s.o.). **II** adv **3.** short: **~ vor ...** just before ... ; **~ hinter dem Bahnhof** just after the station; **zu ~ werfen** throw (too) short; **er wird ~ Tom genannt** he is called Tom for short; **zu ~ kommen** get a bad deal, matter: be neglected. **4.** a) briefly, b) for a while, c) for a moment; **~ vor ...**, **~ zuvor** shortly before (...); **~ nach ...**, **~ darauf** shortly after (...); **über ~ oder lang** sooner or later; **j-n ~ abweisen** be short with s.o.; **sich ~ ausruhen** take a short rest; **~ entschlossen** without the slightest hesitation; **~** (**gesagt**), **um es ~ zu machen** to cut a long story short; **~ und gut** in short; **fasse dich ~!** please be brief!; **~ und bündig** brief(ly), concise(ly); **~ angebunden** short, curt (**gegen** with).
'**Kurzarbeit** f short time, short-time working. '**kurzarbeiten** v/i (sep, -ge-, h) be on (or work) short time. '**Kurzarbeiter(in** f) m short-time worker.
'**kurzärm(e)lig** [-ɛrm(ə)lıç] adj short-sleeved.

'**kurzatmig** [-a:tmɪç] *adj* short-winded.

'**kurzbeinig** [-baɪnɪç] *adj* short-legged.

'**Kurzbericht** *m* brief report, summary.

'**Kurzbiogra,phie** *f* profile.

Kürze ['kʏrtsə] *f* (-; *no pl*) shortness (*a. fig.*), *a.* briefness, brevity, *fig.* conciseness: **in ~** shortly, before long; **in aller ~** very briefly. **Kürzel** ['kʏrtsəl] *n* (-s; -) shorthand symbol. '**kürzen** *v/t* (h) shorten (**um** by), *a.* abridge (*book etc*), cut (*wages etc*), ₳ reduce (*fraction*): **drastisch ~** F slash; *j-s Lohn um 50 Mark ~* dock 50 marks off s.o.'s wages.

'**kurzerhand** *adv* without further ado: **~ ablehnen** refuse flatly.

'**kürzertreten** *v/i* (*irr, sep*, -ge-, h, → **treten**) F a) tighten one's belt, b) take things easy, go slow.

'**Kurzfassung** *f* abridged version.

'**Kurzfilm** *m* short (film).

'**Kurzform** *f* short(ened) form.

'**kurzfristig** [-frɪstɪç] **I** *adj* **1.** ✝ short-term. **2.** *fig.* a) short-range (*plans etc*), b) sudden, c) immediate. **II** *adv* **3.** a) at short notice, b) for a short period.

'**Kurzgeschichte** *f* short story.

'**kurzgeschnitten** *adj* cropped.

'**Kurzhaar...** *esp. zo.*, '**kurzhaarig** *adj* short-haired.

'**kurzhalten** *v/t* (*irr, sep*, -ge-, h, → **halten**) F *j-n ~* keep s.o. very short (*mit Geld* of money).

'**kurzlebig** [-le-bɪç] *adj* short-lived.

'**Kurzlehrgang** *m* short (*or* crash) course.

kürzlich ['kʏrtslɪç] *adv* recently, not long ago: (**erst**) ~ (just) the other day.

'**Kurzmeldung** *f* news flash.

'**Kurznachrichten** *pl* news bulletin.

'**kurzschließen** *v/t* (*irr, sep*, -ge-, h, → **schließen**) ⚡ short(-circuit).

'**Kurzschluß** *m* **1.** ⚡ short circuit: *e-n ~ verursachen in* (*dat*) short-circuit. **2.** → **~handlung** ⚡ panic action: *e-e ~ begehen* a) do s.th. rash, b) panic.

'**Kurzschrift** *f* (**in** ~ in) shorthand.

'**kurzsichtig** *adj* shortsighted (*a. fig.*), nearsighted. '**Kurzsichtige** *m, f* (-n; -n) shortsighted (*or* nearsighted) person. '**Kurzsichtigkeit** *f* (-; *no pl*) shortsightedness (*a. fig.*), nearsightedness.

'**Kurzstrecke** *f* short distance.

'**Kurzstrecken...** short-distance, short-range. **~läufer(in** *f*) *m* sprinter. **~ra,kete** *f* short-range missile.

'**kurztreten** → **kürzertreten.**

kurz'um *adv* in short.

Kürzung *f* (-; -en) shortening, *a.* abridg(e)ment (*of book etc*), cut (*gen in expenses etc*), ₳ reduction (*of fraction*).

'**Kurzurlaub** *m* short holiday.

'**Kurzwaren** *pl* haberdashery, *Am.* dry goods, notions.

'**Kurzwelle** *f* **1.** *radio*: short wave. **2.** 🎯 radiothermy.

'**Kurzwellen...** short-wave (*transmitter, range, etc.*). **~thera,pie** *f* radiothermy.

'**kurzwellig** *adj* short-wave.

'**Kurzwort** *n* (-[e]s; ⁺er) contraction.

'**Kurzzeitgedächtnis** *n* short-term memory. '**kurzzeitig** *adj* brief, short.

kuschelig ['kuʃəlɪç] *adj* F a) (soft and) cuddly, b) cosy.

kuscheln ['kuʃəln] **sich ~** (h) snuggle (*an acc* up to *s.o.*, **in** *acc* down in *bed etc*).

'**Kuscheltier** *n* cuddly toy.

kuschen ['kuʃən] *v/i* (h) **1.** *dog*: lie down. **2.** F (*vor j-m*) **~** knuckle under (to s.o.).

Kusine [ku'zi:nə] *f* (-; -n) (female) cousin.

Kuß [kus] *m* (Kusses; Küsse) kiss: *flüchtiger ~* peck; *sich mit e-m ~* (*von j-m*) *verabschieden* kiss s.o. goodbye.

'**kußecht** *adj* kissproof.

küssen ['kʏsən] *v/t, v/i* (h) kiss: *sie küßten sich* (*zum Abschied*) they kissed (goodbye); *j-m die Hand ~* kiss s.o.'s hand.

'**Kußhand** *f j-m e-e ~ zuwerfen* blow s.o. a kiss; F *fig. mit ~* gladly.

Küste ['kʏstə] *f* (-; -n) coast, shore: *an der ~ leben* live at the seaside.

'**Küsten|bewohner(in** *f*) *m* coastal inhabitant. **~fischerei** *f* inshore fishing. **~gebiet** *n* coastal area. **~gewässer** *pl* coastal waters. **~linie** *f* coast line. **~schiffahrt** *f* coastal shipping. **~schutz** *m* shore protection. **~straße** *f* coast(al) road. **~streifen** *m*, **~strich** *m* coastal strip. **~wache** *f* coast guard (station).

Küster ['kʏstər] *m* (-s; -) *eccl.* sexton.

Kutsche ['kutʃə] *f* (-; -n) carriage, coach: *humor.* *alte ~* (old) rattletrap.

'**Kutscher** *m* (-s; -) coachman, driver.

Kutte ['kutə] *f* (-; -n) cowl.

Kutter ['kʊtər] *m* (-s; -) ⚓ cutter.
Kuwait [ku'vaɪt] *n* (-s) Kuwait. **Ku'waiter** *m* (-s; -), **Ku'waiterin** *f* (-; -nen), **ku'waitisch** *adj* Kuwaiti.
Kybernetik [kybɛr'ne:tɪk] *f* (-; *no pl*) cybernetics.

Kyber'netiker *m* (-s; -) cyberneticist.
kyber'netisch *adj* cybernetic.
kyrillisch [ky'rɪlɪʃ] *adj* Cyrillic.
KZ [ka:'tsɛt] *n* (-[s]; -[s]) concentration camp. **K'Z-Häftling** *m* concentration camp prisoner.

L

L, l [ɛl] *n* (-; -) L, l.
labberig ['labərɪç] *adj* F *a. fig.* **1.** a) sloppy, b) insipid, c) stale. **2.** limp.
Labial [la'bĭa:l] *m* (-s; -e) labial (sound).
labil [la'bi:l] *adj* unstable, labile.
Labilität [labili'tɛ:t] *f* (-; *no pl*) instability, lability.
Labor [la'bo:r] *n* (-s; -s, -e) F lab: *im ~ untersuchen* lab-examine.
Laborant [labo'rant] *m* (-en; -en), **Labo'rantin** *f* (-; -nen) laboratory assistant. **Laboratorium** [labora'to:riʊm] *n* (-s; -rien) laboratory.
La'borbefund *m* test result(s).
laborieren [labo'ri:rən] *v/i* (h) F 🎗 suffer (*an dat* from).
La'betechniker(in *f*) *m* laboratory technician.
Labyrinth [laby'rɪnt] *n* (-[e]s; -e) *a. fig.* labyrinth, maze.
¹Lachanfall *m* laughing fit.
Lache¹ ['laxə] *f* (-; -n) pool, puddle.
Lache² *f* (-; -n) F laugh.
lächeln ['lɛçəln] *v/i* (h) (*über acc* at) smile, grin: *sie lächelte freundlich* she gave a friendly smile; *immer nur ~!* keep smiling! **¹Lächeln** *n* (-s) smile.
lachen ['laxən] *v/i* (h) laugh (*über acc* at): *er lachte schallend* he roared with laughter; *sie lachte verlegen* she gave an embarrassed laugh; F *daß ich nicht lache!* don't make me laugh!; *sie hat nichts zu ~* her life is no bed of roses; *du hast gut ~!* you can laugh!; *da kann ich nur ~!* excuse me while I laugh!; *es wäre ja gelacht, wenn ...* it would be ridiculous if ...; *wer zuletzt lacht, lacht am besten* he who laughs last laughs loudest; → *Fäustchen.*

¹Lachen *n* (-s) laughing, laugh(ter): *j-n zum ~ bringen* make s.o. laugh; *sich vor ~ biegen* nearly die laughing; *~ ist gesund* laughter is the best medicine; F *das ist nicht zum ~* that's no joke; → *zumute.*
¹lachend *adj* laughing: *~e Erben* joyful heirs; *der ~e Dritte* the real winner.
¹Lacher *m* (-s; -) **1.** laugher: *er hatte die ~ auf s-r Seite* he had the laugh on his side. **2.** F laugh.
¹Lacherfolg *m* **e-n ~ ernten** (*or haben*) raise a laugh.
lächerlich ['lɛçərlɪç] *adj* **1.** ridiculous, absurd, funny: *~ machen* make fun of, ridicule; *sich ~ machen* make a fool of o.s.; *das ²e daran* the ridiculous thing about it; *et. ins ²e ziehen* turn s.th. into a joke; *sich ~ vorkommen* feel ridiculous. **2.** *fig.* trifling, petty: *für e-e ~e Summe* for a ridiculously low sum.
¹Lächerlichkeit *f* (-; -en) **1.** *no pl* ridiculousness. **2.** *usu. pl* trifles.
¹Lachfältchen *pl* laughter lines.
¹Lachgas *n* 🎗 laughing gas.
¹lachhaft *adj* laughable, ridiculous.
Lachs [laks] *m* (-es; -e) salmon.
¹Lachsalve *f* burst of laughter.
¹Lachsfang *m* salmon fishing.
¹lachs\farben, ~rosa *adj* salmon-pink.
¹Lachsschinken *m* smoked, rolled fillet of ham.
Lack [lak] *m* (-[e]s; -e) a) varnish, b) lacquer, c) enamel, d) *mot.* paint(work): F *fig. der ~ ist ab!* all the glamo(u)r is gone! **~farbe** *f* varnish (paint).
lackieren [la'ki:rən] *v/t* (h) **1.** varnish, lacquer, *mot.* paint: *sich die Fingernä-*

'**gel** ~ paint one's nails. **2.** F *fig.* dupe: *er war der Lackierte* he was the dupe.

'**Lac'kierer** *m* (-s; -) ⊕ varnisher, painter.

'**Lac'kierung** *f* (-; -en) → *Lack.*

'**Lackleder** *n* patent leather.

'**Lackmuspa,pier** ['lakmʊs-] *n* 🜨 litmus paper.

'**Lackschaden** *m* *mot.* damage to the paintwork.

'**Lackschuhe** *pl* patent-leather shoes.

'**Lackstift** *m* *mot.* touch-up applicator.

'**Lade|baum** *m* ⚓ beam. **~fläche** *f* loading area. **~gerät** *n* ⚡ battery charger. **~hemmung** *f* ✕ (*a.* ~ **haben**) jam. **~klappe** *f* *mot.* tailboard. **~kon,trollleuchte** *f* *mot.* charge control lamp.

laden¹ ['la:dən] *v/t* (lud, geladen, h) **1.** load. **2.** ⚡, *phys.* charge. **3.** *fig. et. auf sich* ~ burden (*or* saddle) o.s. with.

'**laden²** *v/t* (lud, geladen, h) **1.** invite. **2.** 🜨 summon, cite.

'**Laden** *m* (-s; ~) **1.** shop, *Am.* store: → *dichtmachen* **II. 2.** F *fig.* shop, outfit: → *schmeißen* 3. **3.** shutter.

'**Laden|dieb(in** *f*) *m* shoplifter. **~dieb-stahl** *m* shoplifting. **~hüter** *m* shelf warmer, drug in (*Am.* on) the market. **~inhaber** *m* shopkeeper, *Am.* store-keeper. **~kasse** *f* till. **~kette** *f* chain (*of* shops). **~mädchen** *n* F shopgirl. **~preis** *m* retail price. **~schild** *n* shop sign. **~schluß** *m* closing time. **~straße** *f* shopping street. **~tisch** *m* (*fig. unter dem* ~ under the) counter.

'**Laderampe** *f* loading ramp.

'**Laderaum** *m* loading space, (ship's) hold, ✈ cargo bay.

lädieren [lɛ'di:rən] *v/t* (h) a) damage, b) injure, c) *a. fig.* batter, *fig.* dent.

'**Ladung¹** *f* (-; -en) **1.** ✈ a) load, freight, ✈, ⚓ cargo, b) shipment: F *e-e* ~ *Sand* a load of sand. **2.** ⚡, ✕, *phys.* charge.

'**Ladung²** *f* (-; -en) 🜨 summons.

lag [la:k] *pret of liegen.*

Lage ['la:gə] *f* (-; -n) **1.** a) *a. fig.* position, situation, b) site, location: *in zentraler* ~ centrally situated; *die politische* ~ the political situation; *die rechtliche* ~ the legal position; *die rechtliche* ~ predicament; *nach* ~ *der Dinge* as matters stand; *in der* ~ *sein, et. zu tun* be in a position to do s.th.; → *Herr, peilen* I, *versetzen* 5, 9. **2.** layer, *geol. a.* stratum, ✕ bed, ⊕ ply. **3.** ♪ register. **4.** F

e-e ~ *Bier ausgeben* buy a round of beer.

'**Lagenstaffel** *f* swimming: medley relay.

'**Lageplan** *m* site plan.

Lager ['la:gər] *n* (-s; -, ✕ *a.* ~) **1.** bed, *hunt.* lair. **2.** *a. fig.* camp: *ein* ~ *aufschlagen* pitch camp; *ins gegnerische* ~ *überwechseln* change sides. **3.** ✈ a) stock, store(s), b) storehouse, warehouse: *et. auf* ~ *haben* have s.th. in store (*or* stock, F *fig. a.* up one's sleeve). **4.** ✕ bed, deposit. **5.** ⊕ a) support, b) bearing.

'**Lagerarbeiter** *m* warehouseman.

'**Lagerbier** *n* lager.

'**lagerfähig** *adj* storable.

'**Lagerfähigkeit** *f* (-; *no pl*) shelf life.

'**Lagerfeuer** *n* campfire.

'**Lagergebühr** *f* storage (fee).

'**Lagerhaltung** *f* (-; *no pl*) storekeeping.

'**Lagerhaus** *n* warehouse.

Lagerist [la:gə'rɪst] *m* (-en; -en), **Lage'ristin** *f* (-; -nen) storekeeper.

'**Lagerleben** *n* camp life.

'**Lagerleiter(in** *f*) *m* camp leader.

lagern ['la:gərn] (h) **I** *v/i* **1.** rest, lie down (*both a. sich* ~), ✕ camp. **2.** ✈ be stored. **3.** mature. **II** *v/t* **4.** ✈ store, keep. **5.** lay, rest: *✈ das Bein hoch* ~ put the leg up; → *gelagert.* **6.** ⊕ rest.

'**Lager|raum** *m* storeroom. **~stätte** *f* **1.** bed, *hunt.* lair. **2.** ✕, *geol.* deposit.

'**Lagerung** *f* (-; *no pl*) **1.** storage, warehousing. **2.** seasoning. **3.** ⊕ bearing application.

'**Lagerverwalter(in** *f*) *m* storekeeper.

'**Lageskizze** *f* sketch map.

Lagune [la'gu:nə] *f* (-; -n) lagoon.

lahm [la:m] *adj* **1.** lame. **2.** F stiff, tired, limp. **3.** F *fig.* lame (*excuse etc*), tame, dull (*film etc*): → *Ente* **1.** '**Lahmarsch** *m* V drip. '**lahmarschig** *adj* V slow, lame, listless. '**lahmen** *v/i* (h) limp.

lähmen ['lɛ:mən] *v/t* (h) paralyze: *wie gelähmt vor ...* paralyzed with *fear etc.*

'**Lahmheit** *f* (-; *no pl*) lameness, F *fig. a.* dullness, slowness.

'**lahmlegen** *v/t* (*sep*, -ge-, h) paralyze, *a.* bring *traffic etc* to a standstill, knock out (*machine etc*).

'**Lähmung** *f* (-; -en) **1.** 🜨 paralysis. **2.** *fig.* paralyzing.

Laib [laɪp] *m* (-[e]s; -e) loaf.

Laich [laɪç] *m* (-[e]s; -e) spawn.

laichen ['laiçən] v/i (h) spawn.
Laie ['laiə] m (-n; -n) layman: *da bin ich absoluter ~* I don't know the first thing about it. **'Laien... 1.** lay (*priest etc*). **2.** amateur (*actor etc*).
'laienhaft adj amateurish.
Lakai [la'kai] m (-en; -en) a. fig. contp. lackey.
Lake ['la:kə] f (-; -n) gastr. brine.
Laken ['la:kən] n (-s; -) sheet.
lakonisch [la'ko:niʃ] adj laconic.
Lakritze [la'kritsə] f (-; -n) liquorice.
lallen ['lalən] v/t, v/i (h) speak thickly.
Lama¹ ['la:ma] m (-[s]; -s) eccl. Lama.
Lama² n (-s; -s) zo. llama.
Lamelle [la'mɛlə] f (-; -n) **1.** ♀, ⚙ lamella. **2.** mot. a) rib, b) disc.
lamentieren [lamɛn'ti:rən] v/i (h) F (*über acc* about) complain, moan.
Lametta [la'mɛta] n (-s; no pl) tinsel.
Lamm [lam] n (-[e]s; ꞏer) lamb.
'Lammbraten m roast lamb.
Lämmchen ['lɛmçən] n (-s; -) lambkin.
lammen ['lamən] v/i (h) lamb.
'Lamm|fell n lambskin. **~fleisch** n lamb. **~keule** f gastr. leg of lamb.
Lampe ['lampə] f (-; -n) **1.** lamp, light. **2.** bulb.
'Lampenfieber n stagefright.
'Lampenschirm m lampshade.
Lampion [lam'pioŋ] m (-s; -s) Chinese lantern.
lancieren [lã'si:rən] v/t (h) fig. launch.
Land [lant] n (-es; ꞏer) **1.** land: *zu ~e* by land; *ans ~* ashore; F *e-n Job an ~ ziehen* land a job; *wieder ~ sehen* see daylight again. **2.** a) country, b) soil, c) land: *auf dem ~e* in the country; *aufs ~ (in)*to the country. **3.** pol. a) country, territory, c) FRG: (Federal Land, d) Austria: Province: *außer ~es gehen* go abroad; *aus aller Herren Länder* from all four corners of the earth.
'Landarbeiter(in f) m farm hand.
'Landarzt m country doctor.
'Landbesitz m landed property.
'Landbevölkerung f rural population.
'Lande|anflug m ✈ landing approach. **~bahn** f runway. **~brücke** f ⚓ landing stage. **~deck** n ⚓ flight deck. **~erlaubnis** f landing clearance, permission to land. **~fähre** f landing module.
land'einwärts adv (further) inland.
'Landeklappe f ✈ landing flap.

landen ['landən] v/i (sn), v/t (h) land (*a. fig. blow, success, etc*), ⚓ *a.* disembark, F *fig. a.* end up (*in dat* in): *weich ~* make a soft landing; *sports: auf dem 4. Platz ~* come in fourth; F *damit kannst du bei ihr nicht ~* with that you won't get anywhere with her.
'Landenge f geogr. isthmus.
'Lande|piste f landing strip. **~platz** m **1.** ✈ airstrip. **2.** ⚓ quay, wharf.
Ländereien [lɛndə'raiən] pl lands, estates.
'Länderkampf m sports: **1.** international competition. **2.** → **'Länderspiel** n international match.
'Landes... a) national, b) regional, FRG: (of the) Land, in Austria: Provincial. **~farben** pl national colo(u)rs. **~innere** n interior. **~meister(in** f) m sports: national champion. **~sprache** f national language. **~tracht** f national costume. **~verrat** m treason. **~verteidigung** f national defen/ce (Am. -se). **~währung** f national currency.
'landesweit adj and adv nationwide.
'Landeverbot n ✈ *~ erhalten* be refused permission to land.
'Land|fahrzeug n land vehicle. **~flucht** f rural exodus. **~friedensbruch** m breach of the public peace. **~gemeinde** f rural community. **~gericht** n ⚖ district (or superior) court.
'landgestützt adj ✕ land-based missile.
'Land|gewinnung f land reclamation. **~haus** n country house. **~karte** f map. **~kreis** m (administrative) district.
'landläufig adj common, general.
'Landleben n country life.
ländlich ['lɛntlɪç] adj a) rural, b) rustic.
'Landluft f country air.
'Landma,schine f agricultural machine.
'Landmesser m (-s; -) surveyor.
'Landpfarrer m country parson.
'Landrat m district administrator.
'Landratsamt n district administration (office).
'Landregen m persistent rain.
'Landschaft f (-; -en) **1.** landscape (a. paint.), scenery, countryside: *die politische ~* the political scene. **2.** region, country. **'landschaftlich** adj **1.** geogr. regional. **2.** scenic (beauty etc): *~ schöne Strecke* scenic road.
'Landschafts|gärtner(in f) m landscape

gardener. **~maler(in** *f*) *m* landscape painter. **~pflege** *f*, **~schutz** *m* conservation. **~schutzgebiet** *n* (natural) preserve.

'Landsitz *m* country seat.

'Landsmann *m* (-[e]s; -leute) (fellow) countryman, compatriot.

'Landsmannschaft *f* (-; -en) *FRG*: expellee organization.

'Landstraße *f* country road.

'Landstreicher(in *f*) *m* tramp.

Landstreiche'rei *f* (-; *no pl*) vagrancy.

'Landstreitkräfte *pl* land forces.

'Landtag *m* *FRG*: Landtag, parliament of a Land.

'Landung *f* (-; -en) landing, *✈ a.* touchdown, *⚓ a.* disembarkation: *✈ zur ~ ansetzen* come in to land.

'Landungsbrücke *f* landing stage, jetty.

'Landurlaub *m* *⚓* shore leave.

'Landvermessung *f* (land) surveying.

'Landweg *m* **1.** country road. **2.** overland route: *auf dem ~* by land.

'Landwirt *m* farmer.

'Landwirtschaft *f* (-; -en) **1.** *no pl* agriculture, farming. **2.** farm.

'landwirtschaftlich *adj* agricultural.

'Landwirtschafts... agricultural (*show, school, etc*). **~mi,nister** *m* Minister of Agriculture. **~mini,sterium** *n* Ministry of Agriculture.

'Landzunge *f* *geogr.* promontory.

lang [laŋ] **I** *adj* **1.** long, *a.* lengthy, F tall: *über kurz oder ~* sooner or later; *seit ~em* for a long time; → *Bank*[1] 1, *Gesicht* 1, *Hand*, *Sicht* 1 *etc.* **II** *adv* **2.** long: *4 Fuß ~* 4 feet long; *~ entbehrt* long missed; *länger werden* lengthen; *die Zeit wird mir ~* time hangs heavy on my hands; F *~ und breit* at great length; *e-e Woche ~* for a week; *die ganze Woche ~* all week, the whole week long; *mein ganzes Leben ~* all my life. **3.** along: *fig.* *wissen, wo's ~ geht* know the score; *j-m zeigen, wo's ~ geht* tell s.o. what's what. → *lange*.

'langärm(e)lig [-ɛrm(ə)lıç] *adj* long-sleeved. **'langatmig** [-a:tmıç] *adj* fig. lengthy, long-winded. **'langbeinig** [-baımıç] *adj* long-legged, F leggy.

lange ['laŋə] *adv* long, a long time: *das ist (schon) ~ her* that was a long time ago (→ *a. her* 1); *das ist noch ~ hin* that's still a long way off; *wie ~ noch?*

how much longer?; *wie ~ lernen Sie schon Englisch?* how long have you been learning English?; *noch ~ nicht* not for a long time (yet); *noch ~ nicht fertig (gut genug etc)* not nearly ready (good enough *etc*); *bis ~ nach Mltternacht* until well past midnight; *ich bleibe nicht ~ (weg)* I won't be long.

Länge ['lɛŋə] *f* (-; -n) **1.** *no pl* length: *von 10 Metern ~* ten metres long (or in length); *der ~ nach* lengthwise; *in die ~ ziehen* stretch, *fig.* drag *s.th.* out; *fig. sich in die ~ ziehen* drag on. **2.** *sports:* *er gewann mit zwei ~n Vorsprung* he won by two lengths. **3.** *fig.*, *usu. pl* dull passage, longueur. **4.** *geogr.* longitude. **5.** *ling.*, *metr.* long.

'längelang *adv* (at) full length.

langen ['laŋən] (h) F **I** *v/t* **1.** *j-m et. ~* hand s.o. s.th.; *j-m e-e ~* land s.o. one. **II** *v/i* **2.** *~ nach* reach for; *~ in* (*acc*) reach into. **3.** reach (*bis* to or as far as). **4.** a) be enough (*für* for), b) manage (*mit* with, on): *langt das?* will that do?; *das langt mir* that will do for me; *fig. mir langt's!, jetzt langt's mir!* I've had enough!, I'm sick of it!; → *a. reichen* 3.

'Längen|grad *m* *geogr.* degree of longitude. **~kreis** *m* *geogr.* meridian. **~maß** *n* linear (or long) measure.

'längerfristig [-frıstıç] *adj and adv* covering (or for) a prolonged period.

'langersehnt *adj* long-awaited.

'Langeweile *f* (-; *no pl*) boredom: *~ haben* be (or feel) bored; F *ich sterbe vor ~* I'm bored to death.

'langfristig [-frıstıç] **I** *adj* long-term. **II** *adv* on a long-term basis: *~ (gesehen)* in the long term.

'Langhaar..., **'langhaarig** *adj* long-haired.

'langjährig [-jɛ:rıç] *adj* of many years, long-standing (*friendship etc*), long: *~e Erfahrung* many years of experience.

'Langlauf *m* (-[e]s; *no pl*) cross-country skiing.

'Langläufer(in *f*) *m* cross-country skier.

'langlebig [-le:bıç] *adj* long-lived, *☢* durable, *nucl.* long-life. **'Langlebigkeit** *f* (-; *no pl*) longevity, *☢* durability.

länglich ['lɛŋlıç] *adj* long(ish), oblong.

'langmütig [-my:tıç] *adj* forbearing.

längs [lɛŋs] **I** *prep* along: *~ der Küste* alongshore. **II** *adv* lengthwise.

'**Längsachse** f longitudinal axis.
'**langsam** I adj a. fig. slow: ~er werden (fahren etc) slow down; F fig. ~ treten slow down, a. take it easy. II adv slowly: (immer schön) ~! not so fast!; er wird ~ alt he's getting old; F es wurde ~ Zeit! it was about time!; ~ reicht's mir! I'm getting fed up with this!
'**Langsamkeit** f (-; no pl) slowness.
'**Langschläfer(in** f) m late riser.
'**Langspielplatte** f long-playing record.
'**Längsschnitt** m longitudinal section.
'**längsseits** adv alongside.
längst [lɛŋst] adv long ago, long since: am ~en longest; ~ nicht so gut not nearly as good; das ist ~ vorbei (vergessen) that's long past (forgotten); ich weiß es ~ I've known it for a long time; er sollte ~ dasein he should have been here long ago; → fällig.
längstens ['lɛŋstəns] adv **1.** at the longest (or most). **2.** at the latest.
'**langstielig** [-ʃtiːlɪç] adj long-stemmed.
'**Langstrecke** f long range, sports: (long) distance.
'**Langstrecken...** long-range (flight, missile, etc), sports: long-distance. ~**lauf** m (long-)distance run (or race). ~**läufer(in** f) m (long-)distance runner.
langweilen ['laŋvaɪlən] v/t (h) bore: sich ~ be (or get) bored; sich zu Tode ~ F be bored stiff. '**Langweiler** m (-s; -) F bore. '**langweilig** adj boring, dull: ~ sein a. be a bore.
'**Langwelle** f radio: long wave.
'**Langwellen|bereich** m long-wave band. ~**sender** m long-wave radio station (or transmitter).
langwierig ['laŋviːrɪç] adj lengthy, protracted (a. 🐾).
'**Langwierigkeit** f (-; no pl) lengthiness.
'**Langzeit...** long-term (memory, effect).
Lanze ['lantsə] f (-; -n) lance.
lapidar [lapi'daːr] adj terse, succinct.
Lappalie [la'paːli̯ə] f (-; -n) (mere) trifle.
Lappe ['lapə] m (-n; -n) Lapp.
Lappen ['lapən] m (-s; -) **1.** (piece of) cloth, rag: F j-m durch die ~ gehen a) slip through s.o.'s fingers, b) person: give s.o. the slip. **2.** anat., 🐾 lobe. **3.** F (bank)note, Am. bill. **4.** F (dress) rag.
läppern ['lɛpərn] v/impers (h) F es läppert sich it all adds up.
lappig ['lapɪç] adj F limp, flabby.

Lappin ['lapɪn] f (-; -nen) Lapp.
läppisch ['lɛpɪʃ] adj F silly, childish.
Lapsus ['lapsʊs] m (-; -) slip, lapse.
Lärche ['lɛrçə] f (-; -n) 🐾 larch.
Lärm [lɛrm] m (-[e]s; no pl) **1.** noise, din, racket, roar (of engine etc): ~ machen make much noise, be noisy; F ~ schlagen raise a hue and cry (gegen against). **2.** fig. fuss (um about).
'**Lärmbekämpfung** f noise abatement.
'**Lärmbelästigung** f noise pollution.
'**lärmempfindlich** adj sensitive to noise.
lärmen ['lɛrmən] v/i (h) make much noise, be noisy. '**lärmend** adj noisy.
'**Lärmpegel** m noise (or decibel) level.
'**Lärmschutzwand** f noise barrier.
Larve ['larfə] f (-; -n) zo. larva.
las [laːs] pret of lesen[1] and lesen[2].
lasch [laʃ] adj F **1.** limp (handshake). **2.** fig. lax, slack (discipline etc). **3.** insipid.
Lasche ['laʃə] f (-; -n) flap, on shoe: tongue, 🖙 fishplate, flat link.
Laser ['leːzər] m (-s; -) phys. laser.
'**Laserchirur,gie** f laser surgery.
'**Laserstrahl** m laser beam.
'**Lasertechnik** f laser technology.
lassen ['lasən] (ließ, gelassen, h) I v/aux **1.** let: laß mich sehen let me see; das Licht brennen ~ leave the light(s) on; j-n warten ~ keep s.o. waiting; er läßt sich nicht zwingen he won't be forced. **2.** j-n et. tun ~ have (or make) s.o. do s.th.; den Arzt kommen ~ send for the doctor. **3.** machen ~ have s.th. made (or done); sich die Haare schneiden ~ have one's hair cut; ich ließ es mir zuschicken I had it sent to me. **4.** ich habe mir sagen ~ I have been told; der Wein läßt sich trinken the wine is drinkable; dies Wort läßt sich nicht übersetzen this word is untranslatable; das läßt sich nicht mehr ändern it's too late now to do anything about it; das läßt sich nicht beweisen it can't be proved; die Tür ließ sich leicht öffnen the door opened easily; → machen 13, sagen etc. II v/t **5.** leave: laß alles, wie es ist! leave everything as it is!; wo soll ich mein Gepäck ~? where shall I leave (or put) my luggage? **6.** j-m et. ~ leave s.o. s.th., let s.o. have s.th.; laß mir das Buch noch e-e Weile! let me keep the book a while longer!; F fig. das muß man ihm ~! you've got to

hand it to him! **7.** stop: *laß das!* don't!, stop that!; *~ wir das!* enough of that!; *du solltest das Rauchen ~!* you ought to stop smoking! **III** *v/i* **8. von j-m (e-r Sache)** ~ part from s.o. (with s.th.).

lässig ['lɛsɪç] **I** *adj* a) casual, nonchalant, F cool, b) careless. **II** *adv* F easily: *er gewann ~* he won hands down.

'**Lässigkeit** *f* (-; *no pl*) nonchalance.

'**Lasso** ['laso] *n*, *m* (-s; -s) lasso.

Last [last] *f* (-; -en) **1.** *a. fig.* a) load, burden, b) weight: ⚖ *~ der Beweise* weight of the evidence; *j-m zur ~ fallen* be a burden to s.o.; *j-m et. zur ~ legen* charge s.o. with s.th. **2.** ♱ burden, charge: *öffentliche ~en* public charges; *soziale ~en* social burdens; *zu ~en von ...* to the debit of ... **3.** ⚡ load.

'**Lastauto** *n* lorry, *Am.* truck.

lasten ['lastən] *v/i* (h) ~ *auf* (*dat*) *a. fig.* weigh (heavily) on, rest on.

'**Lasten|aufzug** *m* goods lift, *Am.* freight elevator. **~ausgleich** *m* equalization of burdens.

'**lastend** *adj fig.* oppressive.

'**Laster**[1] ['lastər] *m* (-s; -) F *mot.* lorry, *Am.* truck.

'**Laster**[2] *n* (-s; -) vice. '**lasterhaft** *adj* depraved, corrupt, wicked, dissolute.

'**Lasterhöhle** *f* F *contp.* den of iniquity.

'**Lasterleben** *n* dissolute life.

'**lästerlich** ['lɛstərlıç] *adj* a) abusive, b) blasphemous.

'**lästern** ['lɛstərn] *v/i* (h) ~ *über* (*acc*) run s.o., s.th. down; *Gott* ~ blaspheme.

'**lästig** ['lɛstɪç] *adj* troublesome, annoying: *j-m ~ fallen* (*or sein*) be a nuisance to s.o., get on s.o.'s nerves.

'**Lastkahn** *m* barge.

'**Lastkraftwagen** *m* lorry, *Am.* truck.

'**Lastschrift** *f* ♱ **1.** debit entry. **2.** → '**Lastschriftanzeige** *f* debit note.

'**Lasttier** *n* pack animal.

'**Lastwagen** *m* lorry, *Am.* truck. **~fahrer** *m* lorry (*Am.* truck) driver.

'**Lastzug** *m mot.* truck trailer.

Lasur [la'zu:r] *f* (-; -en) glaze.

Latein [la'taɪn] *n* (-s; *no pl*) Latin: *fig. ich bin mit m-m ~ am Ende!* I give up!

La'teinameri,kaner(in *f*) *m*, **la'teinameri,kanisch** *adj* Latin-American.

la'teinisch *adj* Latin: *auf ⚥ in* Latin.

latent [la'tɛnt] *adj* latent.

Latenzzeit [la'tɛnts-] *f biol.*, ⚡ latency

period, *nucl. etc* latency time.

Laterne [la'tɛrnə] *f* (-; -n) lantern, lamp.

La'ternenpfahl *m* lamppost.

Latinum [la'ti:nʊm] *n* (-s; *no pl*) *ped. hist.* **großes (kleines)** ~ Latin proficiency (intermediate Latin) certificate.

Latrine [la'tri:nə] *f* (-; -n) latrine.

Latsche ['latʃə] *f* (-; -n) ❀ dwarf pine.

latschen ['la:tʃən] F **I** *v/i* (sn) slouch (along), trudge: *~ auf* (*acc*) step on. **II** *v/t* (h) *j-m e-e* ~ paste s.o. one.

'**Latschen** *m* (-s; -) F a) slipper, b) (old) shoe: *aus den ~ kippen* keel over.

Latte ['latə] *f* (-; -n) **1.** lath, slat, picket. **2.** *sports:* (cross-)bar: *die* ~ *überqueren* clear the bar. **3.** F *fig.* e-e ganze ~ von a whole string of; *j-n auf der ~ haben* have it in for s.o.

'**Lattenkiste** *f* crate.

'**Lattenzaun** *m* paling, picket fence.

Latz [lats] *m* (-es; ⁺e) bib: F *fig. j-m e-e vor den ~ knallen* zap s.o.

Lätzchen ['lɛtsçən] *n* (-s; -) bib.

'**Latzhose** *f* (pair of) dungarees.

lau [laʊ] *adj* lukewarm (*a. fig.*), tepid, mild (*air, weather*).

Laub [laʊp] *n* (-[e]s; *no pl*) foliage, leaves.

'**Laubbaum** *m* deciduous tree.

Laube ['laʊbə] *f* (-; -n) a) arbo(u)r, b) summerhouse.

'**Laubengang** *m* arcade.

'**Laubenkolo,nie** *f* allotment gardens.

'**Laubfrosch** *m* tree frog.

'**Laubsäge** *f* fretsaw. **~arbeit** *f* fretwork.

'**Laubwald** *m* deciduous forest.

'**Laubwerk** *n* (-[e]s; *no pl*) foliage.

Lauch [laʊx] *m* (-[e]s; -e) ❀ leek.

Lauer ['laʊər] *f auf der ~ liegen* be lying in wait.

lauern ['laʊərn] *v/i* (h) lurk: ~ *auf* (*acc*) a) be lying in wait for, b) be watching out for *an opportunity etc*.

'**lauernd** *adj* **1.** lurking. **2.** watchful.

Lauf [laʊf] *m* (-[e]s; ⁺e) **1.** *no pl* run(ning): *sie ließ ihren Tränen freien ~* she let her tears flow freely; *s-n Gefühlen freien ~ lassen* give vent to one's feelings. **2.** *sports:* run, race: *100-Meter-~* 100 metre run (*or* dash). **3.** *no pl* course: *im ~ der Zeit (des Gesprächs)* in the course of time (of the conversation); *im ~e der letzten Jahre* during the last few years; *den Dingen ihren ~ lassen* let things ride. **4.** *no pl* ⊚ movement, run, action, working, operation. **5.** barrel (of rifle etc). **6.** hunt. leg. **7.** ♪ run, passage. **'Laufdiszi‚plin** f sports: running event.

laufen ['laʊfən] (lief, gelaufen) **I** v/i (sn) **1.** a) run (a. fig.), b) walk, go, c) run, flow: **er ließ Wasser in die Wanne ~** he ran water into the tub; F **m-e Nase läuft** my nose is running; **mir lief ein Schauer über den Rücken** a shudder ran down my spine. **2.** ۞ work, engine etc: run: **Kamera läuft!** camera on! **3.** film, play, etc: run, show, be on: **läuft der Hauptfilm schon?** has the main film started yet? **4.** fig. go: F **wie ist es denn gelaufen?** how did it go?; **die Sache ist gelaufen** a) it's all over, b) it's in the bag; **da läuft nichts!** nothing doing!; **so läuft das!** that's the name of the game!; **was da in Berlin so läuft** what's going on in Berlin. **5.** a) trial etc: be in progress, b) application etc: be under consideration. **6.** ♱, 🜨🜨 run, be valid: **der Mietvertrag läuft 5 Jahre** the lease runs for five years; **auf j-s Namen ~** be (made out) in s.o.'s name; **unter dem Namen X ~** go by the name of X. **7.** leak. **II** v/t **8.** (sn) walk. **9.** (h or sn) sports: run, do: **e-n neuen Rekord ~** run a new record; **e-e Zeit von 20 Sekunden ~** clock a time of 20 seconds. **10.** (h) **sich Blasen ~** get blisters (from walking). **III** v/impers (h) **hier läuft es sich schlecht** walking etc is bad here. **IV sich warm ~** (h) warm up.

'laufend I adj **1.** current: **im ~en Monat** this month; **~e Berichterstattung** running commentary; **~e Kosten** overheads; **♱ ~er Meter** running metre; **~e Nummern** serial numbers; **~e Kontrolle** regular inspection. **2.** **auf dem ~en sein** be up to date, a. be fully informed; **j-n (sich) auf dem ~en halten** keep s.o. (o.s.) informed. **3.** **mit ~em Motor** with the engine running. **II** adv **4.** constantly, continually.

'laufenlassen v/t (irr, sep, no -ge-, h, → **lassen**) F **j-n ~** let s.o. go (or off); **die Dinge ~** let things ride.

Läufer ['lɔyfɐ] m (-s; -) **1.** a) runner, b) skater, c) skier. **2.** chess: bishop. **3.** runner, rug. **4.** ۞ slide, cursor, ⚡ rotor.

Lauferei [laʊfə'raɪ] f (-; -en) F running around, fig. a. trouble.

'Läuferin f (-; -nen) → **Läufer** 1.

'Lauf|feuer n (**sich verbreiten wie ein ~** spread like) wildfire. **~gitter** n playpen.

läufig ['lɔyfɪç] adj zo. in heat, on heat.

'Lauf|junge m errand boy. **~kran** m ۞ travel(l)ing crane. **~kundschaft** f casual customers. **~masche** f ladder, Am run. **~paß** m F **j-m den ~ geben** send s.o. packing, ditch s.o. **~planke** f ⚓ gangway. **~schritt** m **im ~** at the double. **~schuhe** pl running (or track) shoes. **~sport** m running. **~steg** m catwalk, ⚓ gangway. **~zeit** f **1.** life, term (of contract etc). **2.** run (of film etc). **3.** ۞, a. of tape etc: running time. **~zette**l m inter-office slip, tracer.

Lauge ['laʊgə] f (-; -n) **1.** lye. **2.** suds.

'Lauheit f (-; no pl) a. fig. lukewarmness.

Laune ['laʊnə] f (-; -n) **1.** mood, temper: **schlechte ~ haben, schlechter ~ sein** be in a bad mood (or temper); **bester ~ sein** be in a great mood; **j-n bei (guter) ~ halten** a. iro. keep s.o. happy; **~ haben** be moody. **2.** whim, caprice.

'launenhaft adj moody, fig. capricious, fickle, weather: changeable.

launig ['laʊnɪç] adj humorous.

launisch ['laʊnɪʃ] adj **1.** → **launenhaft 2.** ill-tempered, peevish.

Laus [laʊs] f (-; ~e) louse (pl lice).

lauschen ['laʊʃən] v/i (h) listen (dat, au acc to): (**heimlich**) **~** eavesdrop (da on). **'Lauscher** m (-s; -), **'Lauscherin** f (-; -nen) listener, eavesdropper.

'lauschig adj snug, cosy.

lausen ['laʊzən] v/t (h) louse: F **mich laust der Affe!** did you ever!

lausig ['laʊzɪç] adj F **1.** lousy, bad. **2.** dreadful, awful (cold etc): **~ wehtu** hurt awfully; **~ kalt** beastly cold.

laut¹ [laʊt] **I** adj loud (a. fig.), noisy: **~ werden** a) become audible, b) fig. become known, wishes etc: be expressed c) person: begin to shout; **es wurde das Gerücht ~, daß ...** it was rumo(u)re that ... **II** adv loud(ly): **et. ~ sagen** say s.th. out loud; **~ (vor)lesen** read aloud; **~ und deutlich** loud and clear.

laut² prep according to, ♱ as per.

Laut m (-[e]s; -e) sound (a. ling.), noise hunt. **~ geben** give tongue; **sie gab k-~ von sich** she didn't utter a sound.

Laute ['laʊtə] *f* (-; -n) ♪ lute.

lauten ['laʊtən] *v/i* (h) **1.** run, read, go: *der Text lautet wie folgt* the text reads as follows. **2.** ~ *auf* (acc) ⚖ *sentence etc*: be; *auf (den Namen) X ~ passport etc*: be (made out) in the name of X.

läuten ['lɔytən] *v/i, v/t* (h) ring, toll: *es läutet* there is a ring at the door, *ped.* the bell is ringing; **F** *ich habe davon ~ hören* I've heard s.th. to that effect.

lauter ['laʊtər] **I** *adj* **1.** pure (*gold etc*). **2.** *fig.* sincere, hono(u)rable. **II** *adv* **3.** nothing but: *aus ~ Bosheit* from sheer spite; *vor ~ Lärm* for all the noise; *das sind ~ Lügen* it's all lies.

'Lauterkeit *f* (-; *no pl*) *fig.* integrity.

'läutern ['lɔytərn] (h) **I** *v/t* purify, *fig. a.* chasten. **II** *sich ~ fig.* reform.

'Läuterung *f* (-; -en) *fig.* reformation.

'lauthals *adv* at the top of one's voice: ~ *lachen* roar with laughter.

'Lautheit *f* (-; *no pl*) loudness, noisiness.

'Lautlehre *f* phonetics.

'lautlos *adj* soundless, noiseless, silent: ~*e Stille* hushed silence.

'Lautschrift *f* phonetic transcription.

'Lautsprecher *m* ⚡ (loud)speaker. ~**anlage** *f* public-address system. ~**box** *f* loudspeaker (cabinet). ~**wagen** *m* loudspeaker van, *Am.* sound truck.

'lautstark *adj a. fig.* loud: ~*e Minderheit* vocal minority.

'Lautstärke *f* loudness, ⚡ *a.* (sound) volume: *mit voller ~* (at) full blast.

'Lautstärkeregler *m* volume control.

'Lautverschiebung *f ling.* sound shift.

'Lautzeichen *n* phonetic symbol.

'lauwarm *adj* lukewarm (*a. fig.*), tepid.

Lava ['laːva] *f* (-; Laven) lava.

Lavendel [la'vɛndəl] *m* (-s; -) 🌿 lavender.

lavieren [la'viːrən] *v/i* (h) *fig.* manoeuvre, *Am.* maneuver.

Lawine [la'viːnə] *f* (-; -n) avalanche.

La'winenartig *adj* and *adv* avalanche-like: ~ *anwachsen* snowball.

La'winen|gefahr *f* danger of avalanches. ⚡**sicher** *adj* avalanche-proof. ~**(such)hund** *m* avalanche search dog. ~**warnung** *f* avalanche warning.

lax [laks] *adj* lax, loose.

Layout [leɪˈaʊt] *n* (-s; -s) layout.

Lay'outer *m* (-s; -) layout man.

Lazarett [latsaˈrɛt] *n* (-[e]s; -e) (military) hospital. ~**schiff** *n* hospital ship.

leasen ['liːzən] *v/t* (h) lease.

Leasing ['liːzɪŋ] *n* (-s; -s) leasing.

'Lebemann *m* (-[e]s; ⸗er) playboy.

leben ['leːbən] (h) **I** *v/i* **1.** live, *a.* be alive, exist: *hier lebt es sich gut* it's not a bad life; *lebt er noch?* is he still alive?; *bescheiden ~* lead a modest life; *~ von* live on; *er lebt vom Stundengeben* he makes a living by teaching; *~ für* live for, devote one's life to; *~ und ~ lassen* live and let live; *es lebe ...!* long live ...! **2.** live, reside: *sie lebt bei ihrer Mutter* she lives with her mother. **II** *v/t* **3.** live.

'Leben¹ *n* (-s) living (*etc*): *zum ~ zuwenig, zum Sterben zuviel* barely enough to keep body and soul together.

'Leben² *n* (-s; -) **1.** life: *das ~ in Kanada* life in Canada; *ein Kampf auf ~ und Tod* a life-and-death struggle; *aus dem ~ gegriffen* taken from life; *am ~ sein* live, be alive; *am ~ bleiben (erhalten)* stay (keep) alive; *sich das ~ nehmen* kill o.s., commit suicide; *ums ~ kommen* lose one's life, be killed; *mit dem ~ davonkommen* escape (alive); *ein neues ~ beginnen* turn over a new leaf; *ins ~ rufen* call into being, launch; *im öffentlichen ~ stehen* be a public figure; *mein ~ lang* all my life; *ich tanze für mein ~ gern* I just love to dance; *ich würde für mein ~ gern ...* I would give anything to *inf*; *F nie im ~, im ~ nicht!* not on your life!; *so ist das ~ (eben)!* such is life!; → *Hölle, schwermachen*. **2.** a) life, activity, b) liveliness, vitality: *~ bringen in* (acc) liven up; → *Bude* 2.

'lebend *adj* living, *ling. a.* modern (*language*), alive, *biol.* live: ~*es Inventar* livestock; *die Lebenden* the living; *die noch Lebenden* those still alive.

'lebendgebärend *adj biol.* viviparous.

'Lebendgewicht *n* live weight.

lebendig [leˈbɛndɪç] *adj* **1.** living, *pred* alive: *bei ~em Leibe* alive; *wieder ~ werden memories etc*: come back. **2.** lively, alert. **3.** vivid. **Le'bendigkeit** *f* (-; *no pl*) **1.** liveliness. **2.** vividness.

'Lebens|abend *m* old age. ~**abschnitt** *m* period of (one's) life. ~**ader** *f fig.* lifeline. ~**alter** *n* age. ~**angst** *f* existential dread. ~**anschauung** *f* view of life, approach to life. ~**arbeitszeit** *f* working life. ~**art** *f* **1.** way of life. **2.** manners. ~**auffassung** *f* philosophy (of life).

~aufgabe f life task: **sich et. zur ~ machen** devote one's life to s.th. **~bedingungen** pl (living) conditions.

'**lebensbedrohlich** adj life-threatening.

'**Lebens|bedürfnisse** pl necessaries of life. **~bejahung** f positive approach to life. **~bereich** m sphere of life. **~beschreibung** f life, biography. **~dauer** f duration of life, lifespan, ☉ life. **~ende** n **bis an mein** etc **~** to the end of my etc days. **~erfahrung** f experience of life. **~erhaltungssy,stem** n ☉, ☉ life-support system. **~erinnerungen** pl memoirs. **~erwartung** f life expectancy.

'**lebensfähig** adj a. fig. viable.

'**Lebens|form** f 1. way of life. 2. biol. form of life. **~frage** f vital question. **~freude** f joy of life, zest (for life).

'**Lebensgefahr** f danger to life: **~!** danger!; **in ~ schweben** be in danger of one's life, ☉ be in a critical condition; **außer ~ sein** be out of danger, ☉ be off the critical list; **unter ~** at the risk of one's life. '**lebensgefährlich** adj extremely dangerous, perilous, very serious (disease, injury).

'**Lebens|gefährte** m, **~gefährtin** f (life) companion, partner in life. **~gemeinschaft** f life partnership. **~geschichte** f life story.

'**lebensgroß** adj life-size(d).

'**Lebensgröße** f **in ~** a) life-size(d), in its actual size, b) F fig. large as life.

'**Lebenshaltung** f (-; no pl) standard of living. '**Lebenshaltungskosten(index** m) pl cost of living (index).

'**Lebens|inter,essen** pl vital interests. **~jahr** n year of one's life: **im 20. ~** at the age of 20. **~kampf** m struggle for survival. **~kraft** f vigo(u)r, vitality.

'**lebenslang** I adj lifelong. II adv all one's life.

'**lebenslänglich** adj ☆☆ (for) life: **~e Freiheitsstrafe** life imprisonment; F **er hat ~ bekommen** he got a life term.

'**Lebenslauf** m 1. (course of) life, career. 2. personal record, curriculum vitae.

'**lebenslustig** adj fond of life, merry.

'**Lebensmittel** pl food(stuffs), groceries, provisions. **~ab,teilung** f food department. **~geschäft** n grocery, food shop (Am. store). **~händler(in** f) m grocer. **~indu,strie** f food industry. **~vergiftung** f food poisoning.

'**lebensmüde** adj weary of life.

'**lebensnotwendig** adj vital, essential.

'**Lebens|quali,tät** f quality of life. **~raum** m living space. **~retter(in** f) m life-saver, rescuer. **~rhythmus** m rhythm (of life). **~standard** m standard of living. **~stellung** f permanent position. **~stil** m life style.

'**lebensunfähig** adj nonviable.

'**Lebens|unterhalt** m (s-n **~ verdienen** earn one's) living (or livelihood) (**mit** out of). **~versicherung** f life insurance. **~wandel** m life, conduct. **~weise** f 1. way of life: **gesunde ~** a) healthy living, b) regimen. 2. habits. **~weisheit** f 1. worldly wisdom. 2. maxim. **~werk** n lifework.

'**lebenswert** adj worth living.

'**lebenswichtig** adj vital, essential.

'**Lebens|wille** m will to live. **~zeichen** n sign of life. **~zeit** f lifetime: **auf ~** for life. **~ziel** n, **~zweck** m aim in life.

Leber ['le:bər] f (-; -n) liver: **frisch** (or **frei**) **von der ~ weg** frankly. '**Leber|fleck** m mole. **~knödel** m gastr. liver dumpling. **~krankheit** f liver disease. **~krebs** m ☆ cancer of the liver. **~pa,stete** f gastr. liver pâté. **~tran** m cod-liver oil. **~wurst** f liver sausage, Am. liverwurst. **~zir,rhose** f ☆ cirrhosis of the liver.

'**Lebewesen** n (-s; -) living being, creature, biol. organism.

lebhaft ['le:phaft] adj lively, fig. a. vivid (imagination etc), a. keen (interest), busy (traffic etc), a. gay (colours), animated (discussion etc), ☂ brisk: **et. ~ bedauern** regret s.th. very much; **das kann ich mir ~ vorstellen** I can just imagine. '**Lebhaftigkeit** f (-; no pl) liveliness, fig. a. vividness.

'**Lebkuchen** m gingerbread (cake).

'**leblos** adj lifeless (a. fig.), inanimate.

'**Lebzeiten** pl zu **s-n ~** a) in his (life)time, b) when he was still alive.

leck [lɛk] adj leaky: **~ sein → lecken**[1]; **~ werden** spring a leak. **Leck** n (-[e]s; -s) leak. **lecken**[1] ['lɛkən] v/i (h) leak, ☂ have sprung a leak.

'**lecken²** v/t (h) a) lick, b) lap (up); → **Arsch** 1.

lecker ['lɛkər] adj delicious, tasty, F yummy. '**Leckerbissen** m a. fig. titbit,

Am. tidbit. **Leckerei** [lɛkəˈraɪ] *f* (-; -en) dainty, sweet.

Leder [ˈleːdər] *n* (-s; -) leather: F **vom ~ ziehen** let go (**gegen** against).

'Leder... leather (*coat, glove, etc*). **~fett** *n* ⊙ dubbing. **2gebunden** *adj* leather-bound. **~hose** *f* leather trousers.

ledern¹ [ˈleːdərn] *adj* **1.** leather. **2.** *fig.* leathery. **3.** *fig.* dull.

'ledern² *v/t* (h) polish with a chamois.

'Lederwaren *pl* leather goods.

ledig [ˈleːdɪç] *adj* single, unmarried: **~e Mutter** unmarried mother.

lediglich [ˈleːdɪklɪç] *adv* only, merely.

Lee [leː] *f* (-; *no pl*) ⚓ lee: **nach ~** leeward.

leer [leːr] *adj* empty (*a. fig.*), *a.* vacant (*house, post, etc*), blank (*cassette, page*): **die Batterie ist ~** the battery has run out (*mot.* is dead); **~es Gerede** idle talk, F hot air; **~ laufen (lassen)** ⊙ idle; **~ stehen** house *etc*: be empty, be unoccupied; **ins Leere gehen** blow *etc*: miss; **ins Leere starren** stare into space; **ins Leere gehen** blow *etc*: miss; → **ausgehen** 8, **Hand, Magen.**

Leere [ˈleːrə] *f* (-; *no pl*) *fig.* emptiness, void. **'leeren** *v/t* (h) empty (*a. sich ~*), *a.* drain (*glass*).

'Leer|gewicht *n* dead weight. **~gut** *n* ✝ empties. **~kas,sette** *f* blank cassette.

'Leerlauf *m* (-[e]s; *no pl*) **1.** a) ⊙ idle running, b) *mot.* neutral (gear): **im ~ fahren** coast. **2.** *fig.* a) wastage (of energy), b) running on the spot.

'leerlaufen *v/i* (*irr, sep, -ge-, sn,* → **laufen**) **1.** (*a. ~ lassen*) drain, run dry. **2.** *sports*: **j-n ~ lassen** sell s.o. a dummy.

'Leerpackung *f* ✝ dummy.

'leerstehend *adj* unoccupied, vacant.

'Leertaste *f* typewriter: space bar.

'Leerung *f* (-; -en) emptying (*etc*): ✉ **nächste ~** next collection.

Lefzen [ˈlɛftsən] *pl* flews.

legal [leˈgaːl] *adj* legal, lawful: **auf ~em Wege** by legal means, lawfully.

legalisieren [legaliˈziːrən] *v/t* (h) legalize.

Legali'sierung *f* (-; -en) legalization.

Legalität [legaliˈtɛːt] *f* (-; *no pl*) legality, lawfulness: **außerhalb der ~** outside the law.

Legasthenie [legasteˈniː] *f* (-; *no pl*) dyslexia. **Legastheniker** [legasˈteːnikər] *m* (-s; -) dyslexic.

Legat¹ [leˈgaːt] *m* (-en; -en) legate.

Le'gat² *n* (-[e]s; -e) ⚖ legacy.

legen [ˈleːgən] (h) **I** *v/t* **1.** a) put, place, b) lay *s.o., s.th.* down: **ein Kind ins Bett ~** put a child to bed; **er legte die Entscheidung in m-e Hände** he placed the decision in my hands. **2.** lay (*carpet, cable, mines, etc*), plant (*bomb*). **3.** fold. **4.** set (*hair*): **bitte, waschen und ~** shampoo and set, please. **5.** *zo.* lay (*eggs*). **6. Karten ~** tell fortunes by the cards. **7.** *sports*: **j-n ~** bring s.o. down. **II** *sich ~ 8.* lie down: **sich ins Bett ~** go to bed. **9.** *wind, rage, noise, etc*: die down, blow over, *pain, enthusiasm, etc*: wear off, *tension*: ease off. **10.** *fig.* **sich ~ auf** (*acc*) take up, go in for (*activity etc*). **11. sich j-m aufs Gemüt ~** (begin to) depress s.o. **III** *v/t* **12.** *zo.* lay (*eggs*).

legendär [legɛnˈdɛːr] *adj* legendary.

Legende [leˈgɛndə] *f* (-; -n) legend.

leger [leˈʒɛːr] *adj* casual, informal.

legieren [leˈgiːrən] *v/t* (h) **1.** ⊙ alloy. **2.** *gastr.* thicken.

Le'gierung *f* (-; -en) ⊙ alloy.

Legion [leˈgi̯oːn] *f* (-; -en) legion. **Legionär** [legi̯oˈnɛːr] *m* (-s; -e) legionnaire.

Legislative [legislaˈtiːvə] *f* (-; -n) **1.** legislative body, legislature. **2.** legislative power.

Legisla'turperi,ode *f* legislative period.

legitim [legiˈtiːm] *adj* legitimate.

Legitimation [legitimaˈtsi̯oːn] *f* (-; -en) **1.** legitimation, proof of identity, credentials. **2.** authority.

legitimieren [legitiˈmiːrən] (h) **I** *v/t* **1.** legitimate. **2.** authorize. **II sich ~** prove one's identity.

Legitimität [legitimiˈtɛːt] *f* (-; *no pl*) legitimacy.

Leguan [leˈgu̯aːn] *m* (-s; -e) *zo.* iguana.

Lehen [ˈleːən] *n* (-s; -) *hist.* fief.

Lehm [leːm] *m* (-[e]s; -e) a) loam, b) clay, c) F mud. **'Lehmboden** *m* loamy soil. **'lehmig** *adj* a) loamy, b) F muddy.

Lehne [ˈleːnə] *f* (-; -n) a) back(rest), b) arm(rest). **'lehnen** *v/t, v/i* (*a. sich ~*) (h) lean (*an acc, gegen* against): **sich aus dem Fenster ~** lean out of the window.

'Lehnsherr *m hist.* feudal lord.

'Lehnsmann *m hist.* vassal.

'Lehnwort *n* (-[e]s; ⸚er) loan (word).

'Lehramt *n* a) teaching (profession), b) teaching post. **'Lehranstalt** *f* educational establishment, school. **'Lehrauf-**

trag *m* *univ.* teaching assignment, lectureship. '**Lehrbeauftragte** *m, f* (-n; -n) *univ.* assistant (*Am.* associate) lecturer. '**Lehrberuf** *m* **1.** *ped.* teaching profession. **2.** ✝ skilled trade. '**Lehrbrief** *m* a) certificate of apprenticeship, b) indentures. '**Lehrbuch** *n* textbook.

Lehre¹ ['le:rə] *f* (-; -n) **1.** teaching(s), doctrine: *die ∼ Hegels* the teachings of Hegel; *die christliche ∼* the Christian doctrine. **2.** theory, science: *die ∼ vom Schall* acoustics. **3.** a) lesson, b) (piece of) advice, c) moral (*of a tale etc*): *e-e ∼ ziehen aus* draw a lesson from. **4.** (e-e ∼ machen) serve one's apprenticeship (*bei* with).

'**Lehre²** *f* (-; -n) ⚙ **1.** ga(u)ge. **2.** model.

lehren ['le:rən] *v/t, v/i* (h) teach: *j-n lesen ∼* teach s.o. (how) to read; *er lehrt Recht univ. a.* he lectures on law; *fig. das wird die Zukunft ∼* time will show. '**Lehrer** *m* (-s; -) a) teacher, *Br. a.* master, b) instructor. **∼ausbildung** *f* teacher training. **∼beruf** *m* teaching profession. **∼fortbildung** *f* in-service training for teachers.

Lehrerin ['le:rərɪn] *f* (-; -nen) (lady) teacher, *Br. a.* mistress.

'**Lehrer|kol,legium** *n* (teaching) staff, *Am. a.* faculty. **∼konfe,renz** *f* staff (*Am. a.* faculty) meeting. **∼mangel** *m* teacher shortage. **∼zimmer** *n* staff room, *Am. a.* teacher's room.

'**Lehrfach** *n* **1.** subject. **2.** → *Lehramt a*. '**Lehrfilm** *m* educational film. '**Lehrgang** *m* course (*für* in). '**Lehrgeld** *n* **∼ zahlen müssen** learn it the hard way. '**Lehrherr** *m* master. '**Lehrjahre** *pl* (years of) apprenticeship. '**Lehrkörper** *m* teaching (*univ.* academic) staff, *Am. a.* faculty. '**Lehrkraft** *f* teacher.

Lehrling ['le:rlɪŋ] *m* (-s; -e) apprentice, trainee.

'**Lehrmeister** *m* master. '**Lehrme,thode** *f* teaching method. '**Lehrmittel** *pl* teaching aids. '**Lehrplan** *m* syllabus, curriculum. '**lehrreich** *adj* instructive, informative. '**Lehrsatz** *m* ℞ theorem, *eccl.* dogma. '**Lehrstelle** *f* apprenticeship: *offene ∼* vacancy for an apprentice. '**Lehrstoff** *m* **1.** a) subject, b) subject matter. **2.** → *Lehrplan*. '**Lehrstuhl** *m* chair (*für* of *law etc*), professorship. '**Lehrveranstaltung** *f* lecture, sem-

inar. '**Lehrvertrag** *m* articles of apprenticeship. '**Lehrwerkstatt** *f* training workshop. '**Lehrzeit** *f* apprenticeship.

Leib [laɪp] *m* (-[e]s; -er) a) body, b) abdomen, c) womb: *am ganzen ∼e zittern* tremble all over; *et. am eigenen ∼ erfahren* experience s.th. for o.s.; *F zu ∼e rücken* a) *j-m* press s.o. hard, attack s.o., b) *e-m Problem* tackle a problem; *sich j-n vom ∼e halten* keep s.o. at arm's length; *und Leben riskieren* risk life and limb; *die Rolle war ihr auf den ∼ geschrieben* she was made for the part; *mit ∼ und Seele* heart and soul; → *lebendig* 1.

'**Leibeigene** *m, f* (-n; -n) serf.

'**Leibes|erben** *pl* ⚖ issue. **∼frucht** *f* ⚖ ♂ f(o)etus. **∼kräfte:** *pl aus ∼n* a) with all one's might, b) *yell etc* at the top of one's voice. **∼übungen** *pl* physical exercise (*ped.* education). **∼visitati,on** *f* body search.

'**Leibgarde** *f* bodyguard.

'**Leibgericht** *n* favo(u)rite dish.

leib'haftig I *adj* real, true: *∼es Ebenbild* living image; *der ∼e Teufel* the devil incarnate. **II** *adv* in person, in the flesh

'**leiblich** *adj* **1.** bodily, physical: *das ∼e Wohl* a) physical well-being, b) creature comforts. **2.** natural (*parents etc*) full, own: *∼er Bruder* blood brother.

'**Leibrente** *f* life annuity.

'**Leibschmerzen** *pl* stomach-ache.

'**Leib|wache** *f,* **∼wächter** *m* bodyguard.

Leiche ['laɪçə] *f* (-; -n) corpse, (dead) body: *über ∼n gehen* stop at nothing F *nur über m-e ∼!* over my dead body

'**Leichen|beschauer** *m* doctor testifying a death. **∼bestatter** *m* undertaker, *Am.* mortician. 2'**blaß** *adj* deathly pale. **∼gift** *n* ptomaine. **∼halle** *f* mortuary. **∼rede** *f* funeral oration **∼schauhaus** *n* morgue. **∼starre** *f* ℞ rigor mortis. **∼tuch** *n* a. *fig.* shroud **∼verbrennung** *f* cremation. **∼wagen** *m* hearse. **∼zug** *m* funeral procession.

Leichnam ['laɪçna:m] *m* (-s; -e) (dead) body, corpse.

leicht [laɪçt] **I** *adj* **1.** light (*a. fig. food music, rain, reading, wine, work, etc*), ⊙ *a.* lightweight: *∼e Erkältung* slight cold; *e-e ∼e Bronchitis* a mild case (*F* touch) of bronchitis; *∼e Steigung* gentle slope; *F ∼es Mädchen* hussy *mit ~er Hand* effortlessly; *et. auf die ~e Schulter nehmen* make light of s.th. **2.** easy, simple: *~er Sieg* walkover; *das ist ~* that's easy; *nichts ~er als das!* no problem at all!; *sie hat es nicht ~ (mit ihm)* she is having a rough time (with him); *es war ihm ein ~es* it was easy for him. **3.** slight, minor (*a.* 🏛), mild (*penalty*): *~er Fehler* slight (*or* minor) mistake; *~e Verletzung* minor injury. **II** *adv* **4.** lightly (*etc*): *~ berühren* touch s.th. gently (*or* lightly). **5.** easily: *sie lernt ~* she is a good learner; *es ist ~ möglich* it is well possible; *das ist ~ gesagt* it's not as easy as that; *~er gesagt als getan* easier said than done; *nimm's ~!* take it easy! **6.** slightly: *ich bin ~ erkältet* I've (got) a slight cold.

'**Leichtath,let(in** *f*) *m* (track-and-field) athlete. '**Leichtath,letik** *f* (track-and-field) athletics.

'**Leichtbauweise** *f* lightweight construction.

'**leichtbekleidet** *adj* lightly (*or* scantily) dressed.

'**Leichtben,zin** *n* light petrol (*Am.* gasoline).

'**leichtblütig** [-bly:tɪç] *adj* lighthearted.

'**leichtentzündlich** *adj* inflammable.

'**Leichter** ['laɪçtər] *m* (-s; -) ⚓ lighter.

'**leichtfallen** *v/i* (*irr, sep, -ge-, sn, → fallen*) *so et. fällt ihm leicht* he finds that sort of thing easy; *es fällt ihm nicht leicht* it isn't easy for him.

'**leichtfertig** *adj* **1.** light, frivolous. **2.** a) careless, b) irresponsible.

'**Leichtfertigkeit** *f* (-; *no pl*) **1.** frivolity. **2.** carelessness.

'**leichtfüßig** [-fy:sɪç] *adj* light-footed.

'**Leichtgewicht** *n* (-[e]s; *no pl*) *sports:* lightweight.

'**leichtgläubig** *adj* gullible.

'**Leichtgläubigkeit** *f* (-; *no pl*) gullibility.

'**leicht'hin** *adv* airily, casually.

'**Leichtigkeit** *f* (-; *no pl*) lightness, *fig. a.* easiness, ease: *mit ~* easily.

'**leichtlebig** [-le:bɪç] *adj* easy-going.

'**Leichtlohngruppe** *f* low-wage unskilled labo(u)r.

'**leichtmachen** *v/t* (*sep, -ge-, h*) *j-m et. ~* make s.th. easy for s.o.; *sich das Leben ~* take it easy; *du machst es dir zu leicht!* it's not as easy as that!

'**Leichtma,trose** *m* ordinary seaman.

'**Leichtme,tall** *n* light metal.

'**Leichtsinn** *m* (-[e]s; *no pl*) **1.** carelessness, recklessness: *sträflicher ~* criminal negligence. **2.** frivolity, flightiness.

'**leichtsinnig** *adj* **1.** careless, reckless, rash. **2.** frivolous, flighty. '**leichtsinnigerweise** *adv* carelessly (enough).

'**leichttun:** *sich ~* (*irr, sep, -ge-, h, → tun*) *F sich mit e-r Sache ~* find s.th. easy.

'**leicht|verdaulich** *adj* easily digestible, light. *~verderblich* *adj* perishable: *~e Waren* perishables. *~verletzt* *adj* slightly injured. *~verständlich* *adj* easy to understand.

leid [laɪt] *adj pred* (*es*) *tut mir ~!* (I'm) sorry!; *es tut mir ~* a) *um* I feel sorry for, b) *daß ...* I am (so) sorry that ...; *das tut mir aber ~!* I'm sorry to hear that!; *es tut mir (ja) ~, aber ich kann nicht kommen etc* I'm afraid I can't come *etc*; *sie tut mir ~* I feel sorry for her; *das wird dir noch ~ tun!* you'll regret it!; *ich bin es ~* a) I'm tired of it, b) *et. zu tun* I'm tired of doing s.th.

Leid *n* (-[e]s; *no pl*) **1.** a) grief, sorrow, b) misfortune: *j-m sein ~ klagen* pour out one's heart to s.o. **2.** a) harm, b) wrong: *j-m ein ~ zufügen* harm s.o.

leiden ['laɪdən] (*litt, gelitten, h*) **I** *v/t* **1.** suffer, bear, endure: *Hunger ~ a.* starve; *→ Not* **1.** **2.** (*nicht*) *~ können* (dis)like; *ich kann ihn nicht ~ a.* I can't stand him. **II** *v/i* **3.** a) suffer (*an or unter dat* from), b) be suffering, be in pain: *s-e Gesundheit hat darunter gelitten* it told on his health.

'**Leiden** *n* (-s; -) **1.** suffering. **2.** 🩺 illness, disease, complaint.

'**leidend** *adj* a) suffering, b) ailing, sickly: *~ aussehen* look ill.

'**Leidenschaft** *f* (-; -en) passion.

'**leidenschaftlich** *adj* passionate, ardent: *ich esse ~ gern Pizza* I just love pizza. '**Leidenschaftlichkeit** *f* (-; *no pl*) passionateness, ardo(u)r.

'**leidenschaftslos** *adj* dispassionate.

'**Leidensgenosse** *m* fellow sufferer.

'**Leidensgeschichte** *f* **1.** *no pl die ~* (*Christi*) Christ's Passion. **2.** *fig.* sad story, *iro.* tale of woe.

'**Leidensmiene** *f iro.* doleful expression.

'**Leidensweg** *m ihr Leben war ein einziger ~* hers was a life of suffering.

leider ['laɪdər] *adv* unfortunately: *~! a.*

alas!; **ich muß ~ gehen** (I am) sorry, but I must be going; I am afraid I have to go; **ja, ~!** I'm afraid so; **~ nein, ~ nicht** unfortunately not, I'm afraid not.

'**leidgeprüft** *adj* sorely tried.

leidig ['laɪdɪç] *adj* tiresome, unpleasant.

'**leidlich** *adj* tolerable, passable: **mir geht es ~** I'm not too bad.

'**Leidtragende** *m, f* (-n; -n) **1.** mourner: **die ~n** the bereaved. **2. er ist** (**immer**) **der ~** he is (always) the one to suffer.

'**Leidwesen** *n* **zu m-m ~** to my regret.

Leier ['laɪər] *f* (-; -n) ♪ *hist.* lyre: F **die alte ~** the same old story.

'**Leierkasten** *m* barrel-organ.

leiern ['laɪərn] *v/t, v/i* (h) drone.

'**Leihbiblio,thek** *f*, '**Leihbüche,rei** *f* lending library.

leihen ['laɪən] *v/t* (lieh, geliehen, h) **1. j-m et. ~** lend (*Am.* loan) s.o. s.th. **2. sich et. ~** borrow s.th. (**bei, von** from).

'**Leihgabe** *f art:* loan. '**Leihgebühr** *f* hire charge, *for books:* lending fee. '**Leihhaus** *n* pawnshop. '**Leihmutter** *f* surrogate mother. '**Leihwagen** *m* hire car. '**leihweise** *adv* on loan.

Leim [laɪm] *m* (-[e]s; -e) glue: F **aus dem ~ gehen** a) come apart, b) grow fat; **j-m auf den ~ gehen** be taken in by s.o.

leimen ['laɪmən] *v/t* (h) **1.** glue. **2.** F **j-n ~** take s.o. for a ride.

'**Leimfarbe** *f* glue colo(u)r.

Lein [laɪn] *m* (-[e]s; -e) ♣ flax.

Leine ['laɪnə] *f* (-; -n) a) string, cord, b) clothesline, c) leash, lead, d) (fishing) line: **den Hund an die ~ nehmen** (**an der ~ führen**) put (keep) the dog on the lead; **j-n an der ~ halten** keep s.o. on a short lead; F **~ ziehen** push off, scram.

leinen ['laɪnən] *adj* linen.

'**Leinen** *n* (-s; -) a) linen, b) canvas, c) *print.* cloth: **in ~ gebunden** clothbound. **~kleid** *n* linen dress. **~pa‚pier** *n* linen paper. **~schuh** *m* canvas shoe.

'**Leinöl** *n* linseed oil.

'**Leinsamen** *m* ♣ linseed.

'**Leinwand** *f* **1.** *a.* paint. canvas. **2.** *film etc:* screen.

leise ['laɪzə] *adj* quiet, low, soft (*voice etc*): **sei(d) ~!** be quiet!, don't make such a noise!; **das Radio ~(r) stellen** turn the radio down; **auf ~n Sohlen** treading softly; **ich habe nicht die leiseste Ahnung** I haven't the faintest

idea; (**sprich**) **~(r)!** not so loud!

'**Leisetreter** *m* (-s; -) F pussyfoot(er).

Leiste ['laɪstə] *f* (-; -n) **1.** *anat.* groin. **2.** lath, strip of wood. **3.** △ fillet.

leisten ['laɪstən] *v/t* (h) **1.** a) do, manage, b) achieve, accomplish, c) *a.* 🏭 perform: **gute Arbeit ~** do a good job; **Erstaunliches ~** achieve amazing things. **2.** render: **für geleistete Dienste** for services rendered; **Ersatz ~** provide a replacement; **Zahlungen ~** make payments; → **Beitrag, Eid** *etc*. **3.** F **sich ~** a) afford, b) treat o.s. to, c) *fig.* get up to (do); **ich kann mir kein Auto ~** can't afford a car; *fig.* **ich kann mir das nicht ~** I can't afford to do that; **er darf sich k-n Fehler mehr ~** he can't afford another mistake; **was hat er sich da wieder geleistet?** what has he been up to again?

'**Leisten** *m* (-s; -) last: F *fig.* **alles über einen ~ schlagen** measure everything by the same yardstick.

'**Leistenbruch** *m* ♣ inguinal hernia.

'**Leistung** *f* (-; -en) **1.** a) a. ♣, *ped.*, *sports*, ◎ *etc* performance, b) achievement, feat, c) work, d) output, e) result(s), ⚡, *phys.*, ◎ *a.* power, ⚡ wattage, output, input: **schulische ~en** achievements at school; **nach ~ bezahlt werden** be paid by results; **e-e gute ~ bringen** make a good showing; F **e-e reife ~!** (*iro.* jolly) good show!; **schwache ~** poor show! **2.** ♣ a) service(s) rendered, b) contribution, c) benefit, d) payment.

'**leistungs|berechtigt** *adj* ♣ entitled to claim. **~bezogen** *adj* performance-oriented.

'**Leistungs|bi‚lanz** *f* balance of current transactions. **~denken** *n* performance-oriented outlook. **~druck** *m* (-[e]s; *no pl*) pressure (to perform).

'**leistungsfähig** *adj* a) efficient, ◎ *etc* powerful, b) ✝ productive, c) fit.

'**Leistungsfähigkeit** *f* (-; *no pl*) a) efficiency, ◎ *a.* power, capacity, b) ✝ productivity, c) *ped. etc* ability, d) fitness.

'**leistungsgerecht** *adj* and *adv* according to performance.

'**Leistungs|gesellschaft** *f* achievement-oriented society. **~knick** *m* sudden drop in performance. **~kon‚trolle** *f ped.* achievement control. **~kurs** *m ped.* course: **ich bin im ~ Geschichte** I am taking history ry as a) special subject. **~lohn** m ✝ achievement wage(s). **~ni̱veau** n standard (of performance), *ped. a.* achievement level. **~priṉzip** n performance principle. **~prüfung** f performance (*ped.* achievement) test.

Ieistungsschwach *adj* inefficient, low-performance (*both a.* ☉), weak.

Ieistungssport m competitive sport(s). **~sportler(in** f) m competitive athlete. **~stand** m performance level.

Ieistungsstark *adj* (highly) efficient, *a.* ☉ high-performance, powerful.

Ieistungssteigernd *adj* performance-enhancing. **'Leistungssteigerung** f increase in performance (*or* efficiency).

Leistungs|träger(in f) m top performer. **~wettbewerb** m ✝ efficiency contest. **~wille** m will to achieve. **~zentrum** n *sports:* training cent/re (*Am.* -er). **~zuschlag** m efficiency bonus.

Leitar,tikel m editorial, *esp. Br.* leader.

Leitbild n model, example.

Ieiten ['laɪtən] *v/t* (h) **1.** a) lead, *a.* guide (*s.o.*), b) head, run, be in charge of, manage, c) direct, route *traffic* (*über acc* over): *e-e Sitzung (Diskussion* ~) chair a meeting (discussion); *sports:* **das Spiel ~** (be the) referee; *ein Orchester ~* conduct an orchestra; *wer leitet die Delegation?* who is the head of the delegation? **2.** pass on (*an an acc* to). **3.** (*a. v/i) phys.* conduct.

Ieitend *adj* **1.** a) leading, guiding, b) ✝ managing, executive: **~e(r) Angestellte(r)** executive; **~e Stellung** managerial (*Am.* executive) post. **2.** *phys.* (*nicht*) ~ (non)conductive.

Leiter¹ ['laɪtər] f (-; -n) ladder.

Leiter² m (-s; -) **1.** a) leader, b) ✝ head, managing director, manager, c) *ped.* headmaster, *Am.* principal, d) ♪ conductor. **2.** *phys.* conductor.

Leiterin f (-; -nen) a) leader, b) ✝ head, manageress, c) *ped.* headmistress, *Am.* principal, d) ♪ conductress.

Leiterwagen m (hand)cart.

Leitfaden m textbook, manual, guide.

Ieitfähig *adj phys.* conductive.

Leitfähigkeit f (-; no pl) conductivity.

Leit|gedanke m central theme. **~hammel** m *a. fig. contp.* bellwether. **~linie** f **1.** *mot.* white line. **2.** *pl fig.* guidelines. **~planke** f *mot.* crash barrier. **~satz** m

guiding principle. **~stelle** f central office. **~strahl** m ✈ guide beam. **~studie** f pilot study. **~tier** n leader.

'Leitung f (-; -en) **1.** *no pl* a) leadership, b) ✝ management, (*a. artistic*) direction, c) organization, d) administration, e) supervision, control: *die ~ haben von* (*or gen*) be in charge of, be the head of, head; *unter s-r ~* under his direction; *♪ unter der ~ von X* conducted by X. **2.** *the* leaders, management. **3.** a) *no pl phys.* conduction, ✈ transmission, b) ⚡ ⚙ line, c) (*gas, water, etc*) main(s), d) ⚡ lead. **4.** *teleph.* line: *die ~ ist besetzt* the line is busy (*or* engaged); F *e-e lange ~ haben* be slow in the uptake.

'Leitungs|mast m pole, pylon. **~netz** n a) supply network, b) mains system. **~schnur** f ⚡ cord, *Br.* flex. **~wasser** n tap water.

'Leitwährung f ✝ key currency.

'Leitwerk n ✈ tail unit.

'Leitzins m central bank discount rate.

Lektion [lɛkˈtsi̯oːn] f (-; -en) *ped.* unit: F *j-m e-e ~ erteilen* teach s.o. a lesson.

Lektor ['lɛktɔr] m (-s; -en [-ˈtoːrən]), **Lektorin** [lɛkˈtoːrɪn] f (-; -nen) **1.** *univ.* lecturer. **2.** (*publisher's*) reader.

Lektüre [lɛkˈtyːrə] f (-; -n) **1.** *no pl* reading. **2.** reading matter.

Lende ['lɛndə] f (-; -n) *anat., gastr.* loin.

'Lenden|gegend f *anat.* lumbar region. **~schurz** m loincloth. **~stück** n *gastr.* sirloin. **~wirbel** m lumbar vertebra.

Leninist [leniˈnɪst] m (-en; -en) Leninist.

leni̱nistisch *adj* Leninist.

'lenkbar *adj* **1.** ☉ manoeuvrable, *Am.* maneuverable, guided (*missile*). **2.** tractable (*child*).

lenken ['lɛŋkən] *v/t* (h) **1.** steer, *mot. a.* drive. **2.** *fig.* direct, guide, govern, control. **3.** *j-s Aufmerksamkeit ~ auf* (*acc*) direct (*or* draw) s.o.'s attention to; *die Unterhaltung ~ auf* (*acc*) steer the conversation round to; *den Verdacht ~ auf* (*acc*) throw suspicion on.

Lenker ['lɛŋkər] m (-s; -) **1.** driver. **2.** a) steering wheel, b) handlebar.

'Lenkflugkörper m ✕ guided missile.

'Lenkrad n *mot.* steering wheel. **~schaltung** f (steering-)column gear change (*Am.* shift). **~schloß** n steering-column (*or* steering-wheel) lock.

'Lenksäule f mot. steering column.
'Lenkstange f handlebar.
'Lenkung f (-; -en) **1.** no pl a) steering (etc., → **lenken**), b) ⊙ guidance, control (a. ✝). **2.** mot. steering mechanism.
lenzen ['lɛntsən] (h) ♣ **I** v/t pump out. **II** v/i scud.
Leopard [leo'part] m (-en; -en) leopard.
Lepra ['le:pra] f (-; no pl) ✹ leprosy.
'Leprakranke m, f (-n; -n) leper.
Lerche ['lɛrçə] f (-; -n) zo. lark.
'lernbar adj learnable.
'lernbegierig adj eager to learn, keen.
'lernbehindert adj learning-disabled.
'Lerneifer m eagerness to learn.
lernen ['lɛrnən] v/t, v/i (h) learn (**aus, bei, von** from), study: **kochen** ~ learn (how) to cook; **er lernt gut** (**schlecht**) he is a good (slow) learner; F **er lernt Autoschlosser** he's training as a car mechanic (**bei** at); **aus s-n Fehlern** ~ learn from one's mistakes; **j-n** (et.) **schätzen** ~ come to appreciate s.o. (s.th.); **das will gelernt sein!** that's not so easy!; F **manche** ~'**s nie!** some people never learn!; **man lernt nie aus!** live and learn!; → **gelernt.**
'Lernende m, f (-n; -n) learner.
'lernfähig adj able to learn.
'Lern|hilfe f learning aid. **~mittelfreiheit** f (-; no pl) free learning aids. **~pro,gramm** n computer: educational program(me Br.). **~pro,zeß** m learning process. **~schwester** f ✹ student nurse. **~spiel** n educational game. **~stoff** m subject matter. **~ziel** n educational objective.
'Lesart f reading, version (a. fig.).
'lesbar adj a) legible, b) readable.
Lesbe ['lɛsbə] f (-; -n) F dike (sl.).
Lesbierin ['lɛsbiərɪn] f (-; -nen) lesbian.
lesbisch ['lɛsbɪʃ] adj lesbian.
Lese ['le:zə] f (-; -n) ✐ **1.** gathering. **2.** vintage.
'Lesebrille f reading glasses.
'Lesebuch n reading book, reader.
'Lesekopf m computer: reading head.
'Leselampe f reading lamp.
lesen[1] ['le:zən] (las, gelesen, h) **I** v/t **1.** read: **falsch** ~ misread; **flüchtig** ~ skim (through); **s-e Schrift ist kaum zu** ~ his handwriting is hard to decipher; **das Buch liest sich gut** the book reads well; **da war** (or **stand**) **zu** ~, **daß ...** it said

there that ...; **et. in j-s Gesicht** ~ s... s.th. in s.o.'s face; → **Messe**[1]. **2.** uni... lecture on. **II** v/i **3.** read (**in** dat in, au... from). **4.** univ. lecture (**über** acc on)
lesen[2] v/t (las, gelesen, h) a) gather, ... glean, c) vintage.
'lesenswert adj worth reading.
Leser ['le:zər] m (-s; -) reader.
'Leseratte f F bookworm.
'Leserbrief m a) reader's letter, b) lett... to the editor.
Leserin f (-; -nen) reader.
'Leserkreis m readers: **e-n großen haben** be widely read.
'leserlich adj legible.
'Leserlichkeit f (-; no pl) legibility.
'Lesesaal m reading room.
'Lesestift m computer: scanner.
'Lesestoff m reading (matter).
'Lesestück n ped. reading (selection).
'Lesezeichen n bookmark.
'Lesung f (-; -en) reading: parl. **in zwe... ter** ~ on second reading.
letal [le'ta:l] adj ✹ lethal.
Lethargie [letar'gi:] f (-; no pl) letha... gy.
Lette ['lɛtə] m (-n; -n), **'Lettin** f (-; -nen... **'lettisch** adj Latvian. **'Lettland** n (-... Latvia.
letzt [lɛtst] adj **1.** last, a. final, a. latter, ... former: **~e Nachrichten** late(st) new... **m-e ~en Ersparnisse** the last of m... savings; (**am**) **~en Sonntag** last Su... day; **in ~er Zeit** lately, recently; **~e... Endes** after all; **~e(r) sein** be last; **a... ~e(r) gehen** go last, be the last to go; **... wäre der Letzte, dem ich vertraue... würde** he is the last person I woul... trust; **das wäre das Letzte, was ic... tun würde** that's the last thing I wou... do; F **das** (**er**) **ist doch das Letzte!** th... (he) is the absolute end!; → **Auge... blick, Hand, Mal**[2]**, Schrei** etc. **2.** la... extreme: **bis ins ~e** down to the la... detail; **bis aufs ~e** completely, totall... → **Ehre, herausholen, Kraft** 1, **Ölur... ** 2. **3.** F poorest, worst: **der ~e Mis... ** absolute rubbish!; → **Dreck** 1.
Letzt: **zu guter ~** in the end.
'letztemal adj **das ~** the last time.
'letztens adv lately.
'letztere adj **der** (**die, das**) ~ the latte...
'letztgenannt adj **the** last-mentioned.
'letzthin adv lately.

'letztjährig [-jɛ:rɪç] *adj das ~e Festival etc* last year's festival *etc.*

'letztlich *adj* **1.** ultimately, in the end. **2.** after all.

'letztmals *adv* for the last time.

'letztwillig *adj* 𝕫 testamentary, *a. adv* by will: *~e Verfügung* last will (and testament).

'Leuchtbombe *f* flare (bomb).

Leuchte ['lɔʏçtə] *f* (-; -n) **1.** lamp, light. **2.** F luminary: *k-e ~ sein* be no genius.

leuchten ['lɔʏçtən] *v/i* (h) a) shine, b) flash, *fig. eyes:* light (up), c) gleam, sparkle: *mit e-r Lampe ~* shine a light; *j-m ~* light the way (*or* shine the torch) for s.o.; *j-m ins Gesicht ~* shine the (*or* a) lamp (*or* torch) in s.o.'s face.

'leuchtend *adj* shining (*eyes etc*), luminous, bright (*colour etc*): *~es Beispiel* shining example; *in ~en Farben schildern* paint *s.th.* in glowing colo(u)rs.

'Leuchter *m* (-s; -) candlestick, b) sconce, *or* chandelier.

'Leucht|farbe *f* luminous paint. **~feuer** *n* beacon. **~gas** *n* → *Stadtgas.* **~kraft** *f* (-; *no pl*) luminosity. **~kugel** *f* (signal) flare. **~pi,stole** *f* flare pistol. **~re,klame** *f* luminous advertising, neon lights. **~röhre** *f* neon tube (*or* lamp). **~schirm** *m* fluorescent screen. **~spurgeschoß** *n* tracer bullet. **~stofflampe** *f*, **~stoffröhre** *f* fluorescent lamp (*or* tube). **~turm** *m* lighthouse. **~zeiger** *m* luminous hand. **~zifferblatt** *n* luminous dial.

leugnen ['lɔʏgnən] (h) **I** *v/t* deny (*et. getan zu haben* having done s.th.): *es läßt sich nicht ~, es ist nicht zu ~* it cannot be denied, it is undeniable. **II** *v/i* deny everything, 𝕫 deny the charge.

Leukämie [lɔʏkɛ'mi:] *f* (-; -n) ⚕ leuk(a)emia.

Leumund *m* ['lɔʏmʊnt] *m* (-[e]s; *no pl*) reputation. **'Leumundszeugnis** *n* certificate of good character.

Leute ['lɔʏtə] *pl* people, ✗ *etc* men: *die ~* people; *m-e ~* my people, F my folks; F *hallo, ~!* hi, folks!; *es waren etwa 20 ~ da* there were about 20 persons present; *et. unter die ~ bringen* make s.th. public, spread s.th.

Leutnant ['lɔʏtnant] *m* (-s; -s) ✗ second lieutenant (*a.* ✈ *Am.*), ✈ pilot officer: *~ zur See* acting sublieutenant, *Am.* ensign.

'leutselig *adj* affable.

'Leutseligkeit *f* (-; *no pl*) affability.

Leviten [le'vi:tən] *pl j-m die ~ lesen* read s.o. the riot act.

Levkoje [lɛf'ko:jə] *f* (-; -n) ⚘ stock.

lexikalisch [lɛksi'ka:lɪʃ] *adj* lexical.

Lexikograph [lɛksiko'gra:f] *m* (-en; -en) lexicographer. **Lexikographie** [lɛksikogra'fi:] *f* (-; *no pl*) lexicography.

lexiko'graphisch *adj* lexicographical.

Lexikon ['lɛksikɔn] *n* (-s; -ka) **1.** encyclop(a)edia. **2.** → *Wörterbuch.*

Libanese [liba'ne:zə] *m* (-n; -n), **Liba'nesin** *f* (-; -nen), **liba'nesisch** *adj* Lebanese. **Libanon** ['li:banɔn] *m* (-s) *der ~* the Lebanon.

Libelle [li'bɛlə] *f* (-; -n) **1.** *zo.* dragonfly. **2.** ⊕ water level, bubble level.

liberal [libe'ra:l] *adj*, **Libe'rale** *m, f* (-n; -n) liberal, *pol.* Liberal. **liberalisieren** [liberali'zi:rən] *v/t* liberalize.

Liberalismus [libera'lɪsmʊs] *m* (-; *no pl*) liberalism. **liberalistisch** [libera'lɪstɪʃ] *adj* liberalistic. **Liberalität** [liberali'tɛ:t] *f* (-; *no pl*) liberality.

Libero ['li:bero] *m* (-s; -s) *soccer:* libero.

Libido ['li:bido] *f* (-; *no pl*) *psych.* libido.

Libretto [li'brɛto] *n* (-s; -s, -tti) libretto.

Libyen ['li:byən] *n* (-s) Libya. **'Libyer** ['li:byər] *m* (-s; -), **'Libyerin** *f* (-; -nen), **libysch** ['li:bɪʃ] *adj* Libyan.

licht [lɪçt] *adj* **1.** bright: *~er Augenblick* lucid interval. **2.** thin, open (*woods*), *a.* thinning (*hair*). **3.** ⊕ *~e Höhe* clear height, overhead clearance; *~e Weite* inside width.

Licht *n* (-[e]s; -er) **1.** *no pl* a) light, b) daylight: *fig. bei ~(e) besehen* a) on closer inspection, b) strictly speaking; *ans ~ bringen (kommen)* bring (come) to light; *~ bringen in* (*acc*) throw light on; *das ~ der Welt erblicken* see the light of day, be born; *et. in e-m anderen ~ erscheinen lassen* reveal s.th. in a different light; F *j-n hinters ~ führen* deceive (*or* dupe) s.o.; *et. ins rechte ~ rücken* put s.th. in its true light; *das ~ scheuen* shun the light; *ein schlechtes* (*or schiefes*) *~ werfen auf* (*acc*) show s.o., s.th. in a bad light. **2.** a) light, b) lamp, c) candle: *~ machen, das ~ anmachen* turn on the light(s); *bei ~ arbeiten* work by lamplight; *die ~er der Großstadt* the lights of the city; F *er ist* *kein großes* ~ he is no genius; *mir geht ein* ~ *auf* I see (daylight); *j-m ein* ~ *aufstecken* open s.o.'s eyes; → **grün, Scheffel. 3.** *paint.* (high)light. **4.** *pl hunt.* eyes.

'**Licht|anlage** *f* lighting system. ~**bild** *n* a) photo(graph), b) slide. ~**bildervortrag** *m* slide lecture. ~**blick** *m fig.* a) ray of hope, b) comfort: *der einzige* ~ (*in m-m Leben*) the only bright spot in my life). ~**bogen** *m ⚡* arc. ⅊**brechend** *adj opt.* refractive. ~**druck** *m* (-[e]s; *no pl*) phototype. ⅊**durchlässig** *adj* permeable to light. ⅊**echt** *adj* lightproof, nonfading. ⅊**empfindlich** *adj* sensitive to light, *opt., phot.* (photo)sensitive: ~**machen** *phot.* sensitize. ~**empfindlichkeit** *f* sensitivity to light, *phot.* speed.

'**lichten¹** ['lɪçtən] (h) **I** *v/t* **1.** thin (out) (*trees etc*). **II** *sich* ~ **2.** *fog etc:* clear, lift. **3.** *trees, ranks, hair, etc:* be thinning (out), *supplies etc:* dwindle.

'**lichten²** *v/t* (h) *den Anker* ~ weigh anchor.

lichterloh ['lɪçtərloː] *adv* ~ *brennen* be ablaze.

'**Licht|filter** *n, m phot.* light filter. ~**geschwindigkeit** *f* (*mit* ~ at) speed of light. ~**griffel** *m computer:* light pen. ~**hof** *m* **1.** △ atrium. **2.** *astr., phot., TV* halo. ~**hupe** *f mot.* (headlamp) flasher: *die* ~ *betätigen* flash one's lights. ~**jahr** *n* light year. ~**kegel** *m* cone of light. ~**leitung** *f ⚡* light circuit (*or* mains). ~**ma̱schine** *f mot.* dynamo. ~**orgel** *f* colo(u)r organ. ~**quelle** *f* source of light. ~**schacht** *m* △ light well. ~**schalter** *m ⚡* light switch.

'**lichtscheu** *adj* **1.** shunning the light. **2.** *fig.* shady.

'**Lichtschranke** *f* photoelectric barrier.
'**Lichtschutzfaktor** *m* protection factor.
'**lichtstark** *adj* fast (*lens*). '**Lichtstärke** *f* luminous intensity, *phot.* speed.
'**Lichtstift** *m computer:* light pen.
'**Lichtstrahl** *m* ray (*or* beam) of light.
'**lichtundurchlässig** *adj* opaque.
'**Lichtung** *f* (-; -en) clearing.
Lid [liːt] *n* (-[e]s; -er) (eye)lid.
'**Lidschatten** *m* eye-shadow.
lieb [liːp] *adj* a) dear, b) sweet, nice, kind, c) good: *Lieber Herr X* in letters: Dear Mr. X; *sei* ~*!* be good!; *sei so* ~*!* be a dear!, do you mind?; *sei so* ~ *und ...* do

me a favo(u)r and ...; *es ist mir* ~, *daß ...* I am glad that ...; *es ist mir nicht* ~, *daß ...* I don't like it that ...; *mehr als mir* ~ *war* more than I really wanted; *das* ~*e Geld* always the money; *sich bei j-m* ~ *Kind machen* ingratiate o.s. with s.o.; → **Gott, lieber, liebst.**

liebäugeln ['liːpˀɔʏɡəln] *v/i* (*insep,* ge-, h) ~ *mit* have one's eye on.

'**Liebchen** *n* (-s; -) love, sweetheart.

Liebe¹ ['liːbə] *f* (-; -n) **1.** *no pl* (*zu*) love (of, for), affection (for): *die* ~ *des Lebens* the love of one's life; *aus* ~ *zu* out of love for; *aus* ~ *heiraten* marry for love; *mit* ~ *decorate etc* with loving care; ~ *macht blind* love is blind; *die* ~ *geht durch den Magen* the way to a man's heart is through his stomach. **2.** *no pl* (*körperliche*) ~ love(making), sex. **3.** F sweetheart, love, flame.

'**Liebe²** *m, f* (-n; -n) dear (person): *m-e* ~*!* my dear (girl)!; *mein* ~*r!* my dear man!; *m-e* ~*n!* my dears!

'**liebebedürftig** *adj* ~ *sein* need a lot of affection.

Liebelei [liːbəˈlaɪ] *f* (-; -en) flirtation.

lieben ['liːbən] (h) **I** *v/t* **1.** love, *a.* like: *j-n* ~ a) love s.o., b) make love to s.o.; *sich* ~ a) love each other, b) make love; *er liebt es nicht, wenn ...* he doesn't like it if ...; *liebend gern!* gladly!; *ich würde liebend gern ...* I'd love to ... **II** *v/i* **2.** (be in) love. **3.** make love.

'**Liebende** *m, f* (-n; -n) lover.
'**liebenswert** *adj* lovable, amiable.
'**liebenswürdig** *adj* kind, obliging: *sehr* ~ *von Ihnen!* very kind of you!
'**liebenswürdiger'weise** *adv* kindly.
'**Liebenswürdigkeit** *f* (-; -en) **1.** *no pl* kindness. **2.** *pl* a) compliments, b) *iro.* insults.

lieber ['liːbər] *adv* rather, sooner, better: ~ *haben* (*als*) prefer (to), like *s.o., sth.* better (than); *du solltest* ~ *gehen* you had better go; *ich wüßte nicht, was ich* ~ *täte!, nichts* ~ *als das!* there's nothing I'd like better; (*ich möchte*) ~ *nicht!* I would (*or* I'd) rather not!

'**Liebes|abenteuer** *n,* ~**af̱̱färe** *f* love affair. ~**brief** *m* love letter. ~**entzug** *m psych.* deprivation. ~**erklärung** *f* declaration of love: (*j-m*) *e-e* ~ *machen* declare one's love (to s.o.). ~**erlebnis** *n* **1.** experience of love. **2.** love (affair)

~gabe f (charitable) gift. **~gedicht** n love poem. **~geschichte** f love story. **~heirat** f love match. **~kummer** m lovesickness: **~ haben** be lovesick. **~leben** n love life. **~lied** n love song. **~mühe** f (all) **vergebene ~!** that's a waste of time! **~paar** n (pair of) lovers, courting couple. **~ro‚man** m romance. **~spiel** n loveplay. **~szene** f love scene.

'**liebevoll** adj loving, affectionate: **~ pflegen** take loving care of.
'**liebgewinnen** v/t (irr, sep, -ge-, h, → **gewinnen**) grow (very) fond of.
'**liebhaben** v/t (irr, sep, -ge-, h, → **haben**) love, be fond of.
Liebhaber ['li:pha:bər] m (-s; -) **1.** lover. **2.** a) (art etc) lover, enthusiast, fan, b) collector, c) at auctions etc: taker. **3.** thea. **jugendlicher ~** juvenile lead.
'**Liebhaber...** collector's (value etc).
Liebhabe'rei f (-; -en) hobby.
'**Liebhaberin** f (-; -nen) **1.** → **Liebhaber 2.** thea. **jugendliche ~** jeune première.
liebkosen [li:p'ko:zən] v/t (insep, ge-, h), **Lieb'kosung** f (-; -en) caress.
'**lieblich** adj **1.** a) lovely, charming, sweet, b) delightful, pleasant. **2.** mellow (wine), sweet (bouquet).
'**Lieblichkeit** f (-; no pl) loveliness, charm, sweetness.
Liebling m darling, favo(u)rite, pet: **~!** (my) love!, darling!
'**Lieblings...** favo(u)rite. **~schüler(in** f) m teacher's pet. **~thema** n pet subject.
'**lieblos** adj loveless, unkind (words etc), uncaring (parents): **~ zubereitet** prepared carelessly (F any old how).
'**Lieblosigkeit** f (-; no pl) unkindness, coldness.
'**Liebschaft** f (-; -en) (love) affair.
liebst I adj a) dearest, b) favo(u)rite: **m-e ~e Sendung** etc a. the program(me) etc I like best. **II** adv **am ~en** best (or most) of all; **am ~en spiele ich Tennis** I like tennis best; **es wäre mir am ~en, wenn ...** it would suit me best if ...
'**Liebste** m, f (-n; -n) (**mein ~r, m-e ~** my) darling (or love, sweetheart).
Lied [li:t] n (-[e]s; -er) song, air, tune, lied: **geistliches ~** hymn; **es ist immer das alte ~** it's the same old story every time; **das Ende vom ~** the upshot; **ich**

kann ein ~ davon singen I can tell you a thing or two about it.
Liederabend ['li:dər-] m lieder recital.
'**Liederbuch** n songbook.
liederlich ['li:dərlıç] adj **1.** slovenly, sloppy. **2.** dissolute (life etc).
'**Liederlichkeit** f (-; no pl) **1.** slovenliness. **2.** dissoluteness.
'**Liedermacher** m singer-songwriter.
Lieferant [lifə'rant] m (-en; -en) a) supplier, b) contractor: **~ für Speisen und Getränke** caterer.
'**lieferbar** adj available: **die Ware ist sofort ~** the article can be supplied (or delivered) at once.
liefern ['li:fərn] (h) **I** v/t **1.** a. fig. **j-m et.~** supply s.o. with s.th. **2.** deliver (dat to). **3.** yield, give, a. fig. provide: **e-n harten Kampf ~** put up a good fight; **ein gutes Spiel ~** play well, make a good showing. **4.** F **er ist geliefert!** he's done for!, he's had it! **II** v/i **5.** supply, deliver.
'**Lieferschein** m delivery note.
'**Liefertermin** m date of delivery.
'**Lieferung** f (-; -en) a) supply, b) delivery: **zahlbar bei ~** cash on delivery (abbr. C.O.D.). **2.** consignment, Am. shipment. **3.** print. install(l)ment.
'**Liefervertrag** m supply contract. **~wagen** m delivery van (Am. truck), pickup. **~werk** n supplier's plant, suppliers. **~zeit** f delivery time.
Liege ['li:gə] f (-; -n) **1.** couch. **2.** campbed. **3.** sunbed.
'**Liegegeld** n ⚓ demurrage.
liegen ['li:gən] v/i (lag, gelegen, h) **1.** lie, be: **laß das Buch ~!** leave the book alone!; **liegst du bequem?** are you comfortable?; (krank) **im Bett ~** be (ill) in bed; F fig. **damit liegst du richtig!** (there) you are on the right track!; **an der Kette ~** be chained up; **es lag Schnee** there was snow; **das Geld liegt auf der Bank** the money is in the bank; sports: **er lag auf dem dritten Platz ~** he was (lying) in third place; **wie die Dinge ~** as matters stand; **die Sache liegt so ...** the matter is as follows ...; **die Preise ~ bei ...** prices are at (or around) ...; **wo ~ s-e Schwächen?** what are his weak points?; **da liegt der Fehler!** that's where the trouble lies! **2.** (an dat) lie (on), be (situated) (at, near): **das Hotel liegt zentral** the hotel is cen-

trally situated; *nach Süden* ~ face south; → *fern* I. **3.** *fig. j-m* ~ a) suit s.o., b) appeal to s.o.; *die Rolle liegt ihr* the part suits her; *er (es) liegt mir nicht* he (it) isn't my cup of tea. **4.** *fig.* *woran liegt es?* what's the reason (for it)?; *woran liegt es, daß er nie gewinnt?* why is it (that) he never wins?; *daran liegt es* that's the reason why; *es liegt daran, daß ...* the reason is that ...; *was liegt daran?* who cares?; *mir liegt viel (wenig) daran* it means a lot (it doesn't mean much) to me; *es liegt nicht an ihr (wenn)* it's not her fault (if); *an mir soll's nicht ~!* a) it's all right by me!, b) I'll do my best!; *es liegt bei (or an) dir (zu entscheiden)* it is up to you (to decide).

'**liegenbleiben** *v/i (irr, sep, -ge-, sn,* → *bleiben*) **1.** remain lying: *(im Bett)* ~ *bleiben!* don't get up! **2.** *car etc:* break down, *driver etc:* be (*or* get) stranded. **3.** *snow:* settle. **4.** *work etc:* be left unfinished: *das kann ~!* that can wait! **5.** *goods:* be left unsold. **6.** be left behind.

'**liegenlassen** *v/t (irr, sep, -ge-, h,* → *lassen*) **1.** leave *s.th.* behind. **2.** leave *task etc* unfinished. **3.** leave *things* lying around; *alles stehen- und* ~ drop everything; → *links* 1.

'**Liegenschaften** *pl* real estate.

'**Liege|platz** *m* ⚓ berth. **~sitz** *m mot.* reclining seat. **~stuhl** *m* deckchair. **~stütz** [-ʃtʏts] *m (-es; -e) gym. (e-n ~ machen* do a) press-up. **~wagen** *m* 🚆 couchette. **~wiese** *f* lawn.

lieh [liː] *pret of* **leihen**.

ließ [liːs] *pret of* **lassen**.

Lift [lɪft] *m (-[e]s; -e, -s)* lift, *Am.* elevator. '**liften** *v/t (h)* 🩺 lift: *sich (das Gesicht)* ~ *lassen* have a facelift.

Liga ['liːga] *f (-; Ligen)* league, *sports: a.* division.

liieren [li'iːrən] *sich* ~ *(h)* team up *(mit* with); *mit j-m liiert sein* have an affair with s.o.

Likör [li'køːr] *m (-s; -e)* liqueur.

lila ['liːla] *adj,* '**Lila** *n (-s; -)* lilac, mauve.

Lilie ['liːliə] *f (-; -n)* 🌼 lily.

Liliputaner [lilipu'taːnər] *m (-s; -),* **Liliputanerin** *f (-; -nen)* Lilliputian.

Limonade [limo'naːdə] *f (-; -n)* fizzy drink, *Am.* soda pop.

Limousine [limu'ziːnə] *f (-; -n) mot.* limousine, saloon (car), *Am.* sedan.

Linde ['lɪndə] *f (-; -n)* 🌳 lime (tree).

'**Lindenblütentee** *m* lime-blossom tea.

lindern ['lɪndərn] *v/t (h)* relieve, alleviate, ease. '**Linderung** *f (-; no pl)* relief, alleviation, easing: *(j-m)* ~ *verschaffen* bring (s.o.) relief.

Lineal [line'aːl] *m (-s; -e)* ruler.

linear [line'aːr] *adj* ⚕, ⚚ linear.

Linguist [lɪŋ'ɡʊɪst] *m (-en; -en)* linguist. **Linguistik** [lɪŋ'ɡʊɪstɪk] *f (-; no pl)* linguistics.

Linie ['liːniə] *f (-; -n)* line *(a. fig.)*, ~ route, *pol. etc* course, policy: *auf die (schlanke)* ~ *achten* watch one's figure; *mit der* ~ *2 fahren* take the number two; *fig. auf der ganzen* ~ all along (*or* down) the line; *auf gleicher* ~ *mit* on a level with; *in erster* ~ in the first place. '**Linien|bus** *m* regular bus. **~dienst** *m* regular service. **~flug** *m* scheduled flight. **~flugzeug** *n,* **~ma|schine** *f* scheduled plane. **~netz** *n* (rail *etc*) network: *das* ~ *der U-Bahn* the underground (system). **~pa|pier** *n* ruled paper. **~richter** *m sports:* linesman. ⚽ **~treu** *adj pol.* loyal (to the line): ~ *sein* follow the party line. **~treue** *m, f (-n; -n)* party liner. **~verkehr** *m* regular service (*o* traffic).

linieren [li'niːrən], **lin, ieren** [lini'iːrən] *v/t (h)* rule, line.

link [lɪŋk] *adj* left: *die* ~*e Seite* of cloth the reverse (side); *auf der* ~*en Seite* ~*er Hand* on your left side; ~*er Hand sehen Sie ...* on your left you see ...; *pol. sports:* ~*er Flügel* left wing; *pol.* ~*en Flügel angehören* be left-wing *fig. er ist wohl mit dem* ~*en Fuß zuers aufgestanden!* he must have got out o bed on the wrong side; ~*e Masche a* purl (stitch), b) *a.* ~*e Tour* F dirty trick F *ein ganz* ~*er Typ* a real bastard.

'**Linke**[1] *f (-n; -n)* **1.** left hand, *boxing* left. **2.** *pol. the* Left. **3.** left (side): *z* *ihrer* ~*n* on her left.

'**Linke**[2] *m, f (-n; -n) pol.* leftist.

'**linken** *v/t (h)* F con, take *s.o.* for a ride

'**linkisch** *adj* awkward, clumsy.

links *adv* **1.** on (*or* to) the left; *nach* ~ *(t* the) left; *von* ~ from the left; ~ *von (* *or* to the) left of; ~ *von mir* on (*or* to my left; ~ *abbiegen* turn left; *sich* ~

halten keep (to the) left; *fig.* ~ **liegen-lassen** ignore; ~ **sein** a) be left-handed, b) a. ~ **stehen** *pol.* be left-wing; ~ **stricken** purl; F *fig.* **das mache ich mit** ~ that's kid's stuff (for me). **2.** on the wrong side, inside out.

'**Linksabbieger** m (-s; -) *mot.* vehicle (*pl* traffic) turning left.

'**Linksaußen** m *sports:* outside left.

'**Linksextre,mist(in** f) m *pol.* left-wing extremist. '**linksextre,mistisch** *adj pol.* (of the) extreme left.

'**linksgerichtet** *adj pol.* left-wing.

'**Linkshänder** [-hɛndər] m (-s; -) left-hander. ~ **sein** be left-handed.

'**linksherum** *adv* **1.** ⊙ anticlockwise. **2.** inside out.

'**Linkskurve** f left turn.

'**linksradi,kal** *adj pol.* (of the) extreme left: *die* **Linksradikalen** the left-wing radicals.

'**linksrheinisch** *adj and adv* on the left bank of the Rhine.

'**Linksruck** m *pol.* swing to the left.

'**Linkssteuerung** f *mot.* left-hand drive.

'**Linksverkehr** m *in* **Großbritannien ist** ~ in Great Britain they drive on the left.

Linoleum [li'no:leʊm] n (-s; *no pl*) linoleum, F lino.

Linse ['lɪnzə] f (-; -n) **1.** ♀ lentil. **2.** *opt.* lens.

Lippe ['lɪpə] f (-; -n) lip: *von den* ~*n* **ablesen** lip-read; *ich bringe es nicht über die* ~*n* I can't bring myself to say it; *sich auf die* ~*n* **beißen** bite one's lip.

'**Lippenbekenntnis** n (*ein* ~ *ablegen* pay) lip service (*zu* to).

'**Lippenblütler** [-bly:tlər] m (-s; -) ♀ labiate.

'**Lippenlaut** m *ling.* labial (sound).

'**Lippenstift** m lipstick.

liquid [li'kvi:t] *adj* ♀ liquid, solvent.

Liquidation [likvida'tsɪo:n] f (-; -en) **1.** ♀ liquidation (*a. pol. murder*), winding up. **2.** fee, charge, bill.

liquidieren [likvi'di:rən] *v/t* (h) **1.** ♀ liquidate (*a. pol. kill*), wind up. **2.** charge.

Liquidität [likvidi'tɛ:t] f (-; *no pl*) ♀ liquidity, solvency.

'**lispeln** ['lɪspəln] *v/t, v/i* (h) lisp.

List [lɪst] f (-; -en) ruse, trick, cunning: *zu* **e-r** ~ **greifen** resort to a ruse.

Liste ['lɪstə] f (-; -n) list: *j-n auf die* ~ **setzen** put s.o.'s name on the list; F

schwarze ~ black list; *j-n auf die* **schwarze** ~ **setzen** blacklist s.o.

'**Listenpreis** m ♥ list price.

'**listig** *adj* cunning, sly, crafty.

Litanei [lita'naɪ] f (-; -en) litany.

Liter ['li:tər] n, m (-s; -) litre, *Am.* liter.

literarisch [lɪtə'ra:rɪʃ] *adj* literary.

Literat [lɪtə'ra:t] m (-en; -en) man of letters, literary man. **Literatur** [lɪtəra'tu:r] f (-; *no pl*) literature.

Litera'tur... literary. ~**angaben** *pl* bibliography. ~**gattung** f literary genre. ~**geschichte** f history of literature. ~**kritiker(in** f) m literary critic. ~**preis** m literary award. ~**wissenschaft** f literature, literary studies.

'**literweise** *adv fig.* by the gallon.

Litfaßsäule ['lɪtfas-] f advertising pillar.

Lithographie [litogra'fi:] f (-; -n) lithography.

litt [lɪt] *pret of* **leiden**.

Liturgie [litʊr'gi:] f (-; -n) liturgy.

Litze ['lɪtsə] f (-; -n) **1.** braid, lace. **2.** ⚡ cord, flex, stranded conductor.

live [laɪf] *adj and adv* live.

'**Live-Sendung** f live broadcast.

Livree [li'vre:] f (-; -n) livery: *in* ~ → **livriert** [li'vri:rt] *adj* liveried.

Lizenz [li'tsɛnts] f (-; -en) licen/ce (*Am.* -se): *in* ~ *produce etc* under licence.

Li'zenz|ausgabe f *print.* edition printed under licence. ~**geber** m (-s; -) licenser, licensor. ~**gebühr** f royalty. ~**inhaber** m, ~**nehmer** m (-s; -) licensee. ~**vertrag** m licensing agreement.

LKW-Fahrer ['ɛlkave-] m lorry driver, *Am.* truck driver.

Lob [lo:p] n (-[e]s; *no pl*) (*über jedes* ~ *erhaben* beyond) praise: *j-s* ~ *singen* sing s.o.'s praises.

Lobby ['lɔbi] f (-; -bys, -bies) lobby.

Lobbyist [lɔbi'ɪst] m (-en; -en) lobbyist.

loben ['lo:bən] *v/t, v/i* (h) (*wegen gen, dat* for) praise, commend: *das lobe ich mir!* that's what I like!; *da lobe ich mir ...* give me ... any time; *j-n* ~*d hervorheben* single s.o. out for praise.

'**lobenswert** *adj* laudable.

Lobhudelei [lo:phudə'laɪ] f (-; -en) base flattery.

löblich ['lø:plɪç] *adj esp. iro.* laudable.

'**Loblied** n *fig.* *ein* ~ *auf j-n singen* sing s.o.'s praises.

'**Lobrede** f eulogy.

Loch [lɔx] n (-[e]s; ⸚er) **1.** hole, in tooth: a. cavity, in tyre: puncture, in fence etc: gap: fig. **ein ~ reißen in** (acc) make a hole in; **ein ~ im Haushalt stopfen** stop a gap in the budget; F **er pfeift auf dem letzten ~** he's on his last legs. **2.** F fig. a) hole, dump, b) jug (sl.).

lochen ['lɔxən] v/t (h) a) punch, b) stamp, c) perforate.

'Locher m (-s; -) ☉ punch, perforator.

löcherig ['lœçərıç] adj a. fig. full of holes.

löchern ['lœçərn] v/t (h) F pester.

Lochstreifen m punched tape.

Lochung f (-; -en) perforation.

'Lochzange f punch pliers, 🎫 ticket punch.

Locke ['lɔkə] f (-; -n) curl: **~n haben** have curly hair.

locken¹ ['lɔkən] v/t (h) (a. **sich ~**) curl.

locken² v/t (h) **1.** lure, bait, call (animal). **2.** fig. lure, tempt: **es lockt mich sehr zu** inf I'm very much tempted to inf; **~des Angebot** tempting offer.

Lockenkopf m curly-head.

Lockenwickler m curler.

locker ['lɔkər] adj **1.** a) loose (a. fig. morals etc), a. slack, b) light (soil, dough, etc): → **Schraube** 1. **2.** fig. easy, relaxed, person: a. cool: F **es geht sehr ~ zu** it's all very relaxed; **das schafft er ~** he can do that easily. **'Lockerheit** f (-; no pl) **1.** a) looseness, slackness, b) lightness. **2.** fig. easy manner.

'lockerlassen v/i (irr, sep, -ge-, h, → **lassen**) F **nicht ~** not to let up, keep (on) trying.

'lockermachen v/t (sep, -ge-, h) F (**bei j-m**) **Geld ~** (make s.o.) fork out (or come across with) money.

lockern ['lɔkərn] (h) **I** v/t loosen, slacken (rope etc), relax (grip, fig. discipline etc): **s-e Muskeln ~** loosen up one's muscles. **II sich ~** become loose (a. fig. morals etc), slacken, sports: limber up, fig. mood etc: relax. **'Lockerung** f (-; no pl) loosening, slackening, fig. relaxation. **'Lockerungsübung** f sports: limbering-up exercise.

lockig ['lɔkıç] adj curly.

'Lockmittel n a. fig. bait. **'Lockruf** m zo. (mating) call. **'Lockspitzel** m pol. stool pigeon, agent provocateur.

'Lockung f (-; -en) lure, temptation.

'Lockvogel m a. fig. decoy. **~werbung** f

🎯 loss-leader selling.

Lodenmantel ['lo:dən-] m loden (coat).

lodern ['lo:dərn] v/i (h) a. fig. blaze.

Löffel ['lœfəl] m (-s; -) **1.** a) spoon, b) spoonful: **zwei ~ (voll) Zucker** two spoonfuls of sugar; F fig. **den ~ weglegen** peg out. **2.** hunt. or F ear: **schreib dir das hinter die ~!** get that into your thick head once and for all!

'Löffelbagger m (power) shovel.

'Löffelbis,kuit m spongefinger.

löffeln ['lœfəln] v/t (h) spoon.

'Löffelstiel m spoon handle.

'löffelweise adv by the spoonful.

log [lo:k] pret of **lügen**.

Loga'rithmentafel f ⅄ log table.

Logarithmus [loga'rıtmʊs] m (-; -men) ⅄ logarithm.

Logbuch ['lo:k-] n ⚓ log(book).

Loge ['lo:ʒə] f (-; -n) **1.** thea. box. **2.** (freemason's) lodge.

Logik ['lo:gık] f (-; no pl) logic.

logisch ['lo:gıʃ] adj logical: F (**das ist doch**) **~!** naturally!, of course!

'logischerweise adv logically.

Logistik [lo'gıstık] f (-; no pl) logistics.

logo ['lo:go] adj pred F sure (thing).

'Logo m, n (-s; -s) 🎯 logo.

Logopäde [logo'pɛ:də] m (-n; -n), **Logo'pädin** f (-; -nen) speech therapist. **Logopädie** [logope'di:] f (-; no pl) logop(a)edics, speech therapy.

Lohn [lo:n] m (-[e]s; ⸚e) **1.** wages, pay. **2.** fig. (**zum ~ in**) reward (**für** for): **s-n wohlverdienten ~ erhalten** a. iro. get one's just deserts. **~abschluß** m wage agreement. **~anteil** m wages. **~ausfall** m loss of wages. **~ausgleich m bei vollem ~** without cuts in pay. **~buchhalter(in** f) m wages clerk. **~bü,ro** n pay office. **~empfänger(in** f) m wage earner.

lohnen ['lo:nən] (h) **I sich ~ 1.** be worthwhile), pay; **die Mühe lohnt sich** it's worth the trouble; **es lohnt sich zu** inf it's worth ger, it pays to inf; **der Film lohnt sich** the film is worth seeing; **Verbrechen lohnt sich nicht** crime doesn't pay. **II** v/t **2.** reward: **j-m etw schlecht ~** ill repay s.o. **3.** die Mühe (**e-n Besuch**) ~ be worth the trouble (a visit). **'lohnend** adj **1.** paying, profitable. **2.** worthwhile, rewarding, a worth seeing (etc).

'**Lohn|erhöhung** f wage increase, (pay) rise, Am. raise. **~forderung** f wage claim. **~fortzahlung** f continued pay (to sick workers). **~gefälle** n wage differential. **~gruppe** f pay bracket.

'**lohninten,siv** adj wage-intensive.

'**Lohn|kampf** m wage dispute. **~kosten** pl wage costs: **sehr hohe ~ haben** have a huge payroll. **~kürzung** f wage cut. **~runde** f round of wage negotiations.

Lohnsteuer f wage(s) tax. **~jahresausgleich** m annual adjustment of income tax. **~karte** f wage(s) tax card.

'**Lohn|stopp** m pay freeze. **~streifen** m pay slip. **~ta,rif** m wage rate.

Löhnung ['løːnʊŋ] f (-; -en) ✕ pay.

Loipe ['lɔʏpə] f (-; -n) cross-country (skiing) trail.

Lok [lɔk] f (-; -s) 🚂 F engine.

lokal [lo'kaːl] adj local.

Lo'kal n (-s; -e) a) restaurant, b) pub, Am. saloon. **Lo'kal...** local (newspaper, reporter, press, etc).

Lokalanästhe,sie f local an(a)esthesia.

lokalisieren [lokali'ziːrən] v/t (h) locate, a. 🩺 localize (**auf** acc to).

Lo'kal|kolo,rit n local colo(u)r. **~ter,min** m 🏛 visit to the scene (of the crime).

Lokomotive [lokomo'tiːvə] f (-; -n) engine. **Lokomo'tivführer** m engine driver, Am. engineer.

Lokus ['loːkʊs] m (-[-es]; -[se]) F loo, Am. john.

Lombardkre,dit ['lɔmbart-] m 🏦 collateral loan. '**Lombardsatz** m rate for (central bank) loans on securities.

Londoner ['lɔndənər] I m (-s; -) Londoner. II adj (of) London.

Lorbeer ['lɔrbeːr] m (-s; -en) 1. ⚘ laurel (tree), bay (tree). 2. gastr. bay leaf. 3. pl fig. laurels: **sich auf s-n ~en ausruhen** rest on one's laurels / **damit kannst du (bei ihr) k-e ~en ernten** that won't get you anywhere (with her).

Lore ['loːrə] f (-; -n) 🚂 tipper.

los¹ [loːs] adj pred 1. off: **der Knopf ist ~** the button is off; **der Hund ist ~** the dog is loose. 2. F **~ sein** be rid of s.o., s.th.; **den wären wir ~!** good riddance!; **mein Geld bin ich ~** my money is gone; → a. **losgehen, loslegen** etc. 3. F **was ist ~** a) (**mit dir**)? what's the matter (with you)?, b) (**hier**)? what's going on (here)?, c) **in Berlin** events etc: what's

on in Berlin?, politically etc: what's going on in Berlin?; **da war (schwer) was ~** a) things were really happening, b) the sparks were flying; **hier ist nichts** (or **nie was**) **~!** nothing doing (or no action) around here!; **wo ist hier was ~?** where can you go around here?; **mit ihm ist nicht viel ~** he isn't up to much. 4. F **er hat (schwer) was ~** he's very good (**in** dat at), he's on the ball.

los² int a) let's go!, b) go!: fig. **schieß ~!** fire away!; sports: **Achtung, fertig, ~!** ready, steady, go!; **nun aber ~!** let's get going (or cracking)!; **nun mal ~!** here goes!; **~, sag schon!** come on, tell me!

Los n (-es; -e) **1.** a) lot, b) ticket, number: **ein ~ ziehen** draw a lot (or ticket); **das große ~ ziehen** win the first prize (s.th.); hit the jackpot; **mit j-m** (et.) **das große ~ ziehen** strike it lucky with s.o. (s.th.); **et. durch das ~ entscheiden** decide s.th. by drawing lots (or by a toss-up); **das ~ fiel auf ihn zu** inf it fell upon him to inf. **2.** fig. lot, fate: **ein schweres ~** a hard lot. **3.** ⚓ lot.

'**lösbar** adj soluble (a. 🧪), solvable.

'**losbinden** v/t (irr, sep, -ge-, h, → **binden**) untie.

'**losbrechen** (irr, sep, -ge-, → **brechen**) I v/t (h) break off. II v/i (sn) storm etc: break, laughter etc: break out.

löschen¹ ['lœʃən] v/t (h) **1.** extinguish, put out (fire, light, etc); **den Durst ~** quench one's thirst. **2.** ⚙ quench, slake (lime). **3.** blot (ink). **4.** strike off, cancel (a. mortgage), a. computer: delete, erase (a. tape recording etc), settle (debt), close (account). **5.** fig. efface.

'**löschen²** v/t (h) ⚓ unload.

'**Lösch|fahrzeug** n fire engine. **~gerät** n fire extinguisher, coll. fire-fighting equipment. **~kopf** m erasing head. **~mannschaft** f fire brigade. **~pa,pier** n blotting paper. **~taste** f erase button, computer: cancel key.

lose ['loːzə] adj a. fig. loose.

'**Lösegeld** n ransom.

'**loseisen: sich** (v/t j-n) (sep, -ge-, h) F get (s.o.) away (**von** from).

losen ['loːzən] v/i (h) draw lots (or toss up) (**um** for).

lösen ['løːzən] (h) I v/t **1.** remove, detach. **2.** a) undo (hair, tie, etc), b) a. 🩺 loosen, relax, c) release (brake etc). **3.**

fig. solve (a. ⚓), answer (*question*), re-solve, settle (*conflict etc*). **4.** fig. dis-solve (*marriage etc*), break off (*engagement*), sever (*relations etc*), terminate (*contract*). **5.** buy, get (*ticket*). **6.** 🜊 dissolve. **II sich ~ 7.** a) come loos (*or undone*), b) come off, c) loosen (*a. ♣*). **8. sich ~ (von** from) free o.s., a. sports: break away. **9.** problem etc: solve itself, *conflict etc*: resolve itself. **10.** *tension etc*: ease; → **gelöst. 11.** 🜊 dissolve.

'losfahren v/i (*irr, sep,* -ge-, sn, → **fahren**) a) leave, b) drive off.

'losgehen v/i (*irr, sep,* -ge-, sn, → **gehen**) **1.** leave, a. rifle, shot, etc: go off. **2.** F start, begin: **gleich geht's los!** it's just about to begin!; **jetzt geht's los!** here goes!, here we go!; **es kann ~!** we're (*or* I'm etc) ready!; **jetzt geht's schon wieder los!** here we go again! **3.** F come off. **4. ~ auf** (acc) head (*or* make) for; **mit dem Messer auf j-n ~** go for s.o. with a knife.

'losheulen v/i (*sep,* -ge-, h) F burst into tears.

'losketten v/t (*sep,* -ge-, h) unchain.

'loskommen v/i (*irr, sep,* -ge-, sn, → **kommen**) a. fig. get away (**von** from).

'loslassen (*irr, sep,* -ge-, h, → **lassen**) **I** v/t **1.** let go of, let *s.o.* go, release: F **j-n auf die Menschheit ~** let s.o. loose on humanity; **das Buch läßt e-n nicht mehr los** the book is quite unputdown-able; **der Gedanke läßt mich nicht (mehr) los** I can't get it out of my mind. **2.** let go with *a blow etc*, let off *fire-works*, launch (*protest etc*), let fly with *a letter etc*, crack (*joke etc*). **II** v/i **3.** let go: **nicht ~!** a. hang on!

'loslegen v/i (*sep,* -ge-, h) F **1.** get cracking. **2.** let fly (**gegen** at): **dann legte er los** then he really got going; **leg schon los!** fire away!

'löslich adj 🜊 soluble.

'losmachen (*sep,* -ge-, h) **I** v/t **1.** untie, undo. **2.** ♣ cast off. **II sich ~** a. fig. free o.s. (**von** from).

'losrasen v/i (*sep,* -ge-, sn) zoom off.

'losreißen: sich ~ (*irr, sep,* -ge-, h, → **reißen**) (**von** from) break away, fig. tear o.s. away.

'losrennen v/i (*irr, sep,* -ge-, sn, → **rennen**) dash off, run off.

'lossagen: sich ~ von (*sep,* -ge-, h) break with.

'losschlagen v/i (*irr, sep,* -ge-, h, → **schlagen**) ✕ strike.

'losschnallen v/t (*sep,* -ge-, h) unbuckle **✈**, mot. **sich ~** undo one's seat belt.

'lossteuern v/i (*sep,* -ge-, sn) **~ auf** (acc a. fig. make (*or* head) for.

Losung¹ ['lo:zʊŋ] f (-; -en) ✕ password fig. watchword, pol. a. slogan.

Losung² f (-; no pl) hunt. droppings.

Lösung f (-; -en) ↗ or fig. solution.

'Lösungsmittel n 🜊 solvent.

'Lösungswort n answer.

'loswerden v/t (*irr, sep,* -ge-, sn, → **werden**) **1.** get rid of: **ich werde da Gefühl nicht los, daß ...** I can't hel feeling that ...; **das mußte ich mal ~!** had to get that off my chest! **2.** F a lose, b) spend.

'losziehen v/i (*irr, sep,* -ge-, sn, → **ziehen**) **1.** set out, march off. **2.** fig. **gegen** lay into, let fly at.

Lot [lo:t] n (-[e]s; -e) **1.** ⚓ (**ein ~ fälle** drop a) perpendicular: **aus dem ~** ou of plumb; fig. **im ~ sein** be in goo order; **et. wieder ins ~ bringen** set s.th right again. **2.** ⚙ plumb (bob). **3.** ⚙ solder.

loten ['lo:tən] v/t, v/i (h) plumb, sound

löten ['lø:tən] v/t (h) ⚙ solder.

Lotion [lo'tsĭo:n] f (-; -en) lotion.

'Lötkolben m soldering iron. **'Lötlampe** f soldering lamp, Am. blowtorch

'Lötnaht f soldered joint.

'lotrecht adj perpendicular, vertical.

Lotse ['lo:tsə] m (-n; -n) ♣ pilot.

lotsen ['lo:tsən] v/t (h) **1.** ♣ pilot. **2.** F j-~ a) guide s.o. (**durch** through), b) dra; s.o. off (**in** acc to).

'Lotsendienst m mot. driver-guid service. **'Lotsengebühr** f ♣ pilotage

Lotterie [lɔtə'ri:] f (-; -en) lottery **~gewinn** m (lottery) prize. **~los** (lottery) ticket. **~spiel** n lottery, fig gamble.

Lotto ['lɔto] n (-s; -s) **1.** lotto, bingo. **2** Lotto, (West German numbers pool lottery: **im ~ spielen** do Lotto.

'Lottoannahme(stelle) f Lotto ticke agency. **'Lottoschein** m Lotto ticket.

Löwe ['lø:və] m (-n; -n) **1.** zo. lion. **2** astr. Leo: **er ist (ein) ~** he's (a) Leo.

'Löwen|anteil m fig. lion's shar

⁓mähne f fig. (thick) mane. **⁓maul** n (-[e]s; no pl) ❀ snapdragon. **⁓zahn** m (-[e]s; no pl) ❀ dandelion.
Löwin ['løːvɪn] f (-; -nen) zo. lioness.
loyal [løˈaˈjaːl] adj loyal.
Loyalität [løajaliˈtɛːt] f (-; no pl) loyalty.
Luchs [lʊks] m (-es; -e) zo. lynx: fig. Augen haben (aufpassen) wie ein ⁓ have eyes (watch) like a hawk.
Lücke ['lʏkə] f (-; -n) gap, fig. a. loophole: fig. e-e ⁓ schließen fill a gap.
'Lückenbüßer(in f) m stopgap.
'lückenhaft adj 1. full of gaps, gappy. 2. fig. incomplete: ⁓es Wissen a. sketchy knowledge.
'lückenlos adj 1. without gaps. 2. fig. complete, full, unbroken (line etc).
lud [luːt] pret of laden¹ and laden².
Luder ['luːdər] n (-s; -) F 1. (gemeines) ⁓ beast, bitch; (ordinäres) ⁓ hussy. 2. armes ⁓ poor creature; dummes ⁓ silly fool. 3. (kleines) ⁓ brat, (little) devil.
Luft [lʊft] f (-; ⁓e) 1. no pl air: die ⁓ ablassen aus deflate; fig. da war die ⁓ raus when the steam was gone; an die (frische) ⁓ gehen, F ⁓ schnappen get some (fresh) air; F fig. j-n an die (frische) ⁓ setzen chuck s.o. out, a. fire s.o.; fig. sich in ⁓ auflösen a) vanish into thin air, b) plan etc: go up in smoke; j-n wie ⁓ behandeln cut s.o. dead; (völlig) aus der ⁓ gegriffen sein be (totally) unfounded; es liegt et. in der ⁓ there is s.th. in the wind; die ⁓ ist rein the coast is clear; F es ist dicke ⁓ there is trouble brewing. 2. no pl breath: die ⁓ anhalten hold one's breath; F halt (mal) die ⁓ an! a) pipe down!, b) come off it!; tief ⁓ holen take a deep breath, fig. swallow hard; nach ⁓ ringen gasp for air; F mir blieb die ⁓ weg I was dumbfounded, vor Schreck I was breathless with shock. 3. sky, air: in die ⁓ jagen, in die ⁓ fliegen blow up; F fig. in die ⁓ gehen blow one's top, hit the roof; das hängt (alles) noch in der ⁓ it's all (still) up in the air. 4. breeze. 5. no pl F space, room: ich muß erst et. ⁓ schaffen I must make some room first; fig. sich in (or s-m Herzen, Zorn etc) ⁓ machen let off steam.
'Luft|abwehr f air defen/ce (Am. -se). **⁓angriff** m air raid. **⁓bal, lon** m balloon. **⁓bild** n aerial view. **⁓bildkarte** f aerial map. **⁓blase** f air bubble.
'Luft-'Boden-... ✕ air-to-ground ...
'Luftbrücke f airlift.
'luftdicht adj (a. ⁓ machen) airproof: ⁓ verschließen airseal.
'Luftdruck m (-[e]s; no pl) meteor. atmospheric pressure, ☉ air pressure.
'Luftdruck... ☉ air-pressure.
'luftdurchlässig adj permeable to air.
lüften ['lʏftən] v/t (h) 1. (a. v/i) air, ventilate: s-e Kleidung ⁓ give one's clothes an airing. 2. lift, raise. 3. fig. ein Geheimnis ⁓ reveal (or disclose) a secret.
Lüfter ['lʏftər] m (-s; -) ☉ a) ventilator, b) exhaustor, c) blower.
'Luft|fahrt f (-; no pl) aviation. **⁓fahrtgesellschaft** f airline. **⁓fahrtindu,strie** f aircraft industry. **⁓fahrzeug** n aircraft. **⁓feuchtigkeit** f (atmospheric) humidity. **⁓filter** n, m air filter. **⁓flotte** f air fleet. **⁓fracht** f airfreight. **⁓frachtbrief** m air waybill. **⁂gekühlt** adj air-cooled. **⁂getrocknet** adj air-dried. **⁓gewehr** n air gun. **⁓herrschaft** f (-; no pl) air supremacy. **⁓hoheit** f (-; no pl) air sovereignty. **⁓hülle** f atmosphere.
'luftig adj 1. airy, breezy: in ⁓er Höhe high up. 2. fig. flimsy, light (clothes).
'Luft|kammer f biol., ☉ air chamber. **⁓kampf** m air combat. **⁓kissenfahrzeug** n air-cushion vehicle, hovercraft. **⁓korridor** m air corridor. **⁂krank** adj airsick. **⁓kühlung** f air cooling. **⁓kurort** m climatic health resort. **⁓landetruppen** pl airborne troops. **⁂leer** adj air-void: ⁓ machen evacuate; ⁓er Raum vacuum. **⁓linie** f 100 km ⁓ 100 km as the crow flies. **⁓loch** n airhole, ✈ a. air pocket. **⁓mangel** m (-s; no pl) 🎇 want of air. **⁓ma,tratze** f air mattress, air bed. **⁓pi,rat** m hijacker, skyjacker. **⁓pi,stole** f air pistol.
'Luftpost f (mit or per ⁓ by) airmail. **⁓brief** m air letter. **⁓pa,ket** n air parcel.
'Luft|pumpe f air pump. **⁓raum** m air space. **⁓reinhaltung** f air-pollution control. **⁓rettungsdienst** m air rescue service. **⁓röhre** f anat. windpipe. **⁓sack** m ✈ windsock, mot. airbag. **⁓schiff** n airship, dirigible. **⁓schlauch** m air tube, mot. etc inner tube. **⁓schlösser** pl castles in the air. **⁓schraube** f ✈ airscrew.
'Luftschutz m air-raid precautions.

~keller *m*, **~raum** *m* air-raid shelter. **~übung** *f* air-raid drill.
Luft|spiegelung *f* mirage. **~sprung** *m* **vor Freude e-n ~ machen** jump for joy. **~streitkräfte** *pl* air force. **~strom** *m* **~strömung** *f* air current. **~stützpunkt** *m* ✕ air base. **~taxi** *n* air taxi. **~trans,port** *m* air transport, airlift.
'Lüftung *f* (-; -en) ventilation.
Luftverkehr *m* air traffic.
'Luftverkehrs|gesellschaft *f* airline (company). **~linie** *f* airline, airway.
'Luft|verschmutzung *f* air pollution. **~verteidigung** *f* air defen|ce (*Am.* -se). **~waffe** *f* ✕ air force. **~weg** *m* **1.** air route: **auf dem ~e** by air. **2.** *pl anat.* respiratory tracts. **~widerstand** *m* air resistance, ✈, ⊙ *a.* drag. **~zufuhr** *f* air supply. **~zug** *m* draught, *Am.* draft.
Lüge ['ly:gə] *f* (-; -n) lie: **~n strafen** belie.
lügen ['ly:gən] *v/i* (log, gelogen, h) lie, tell a lie (*or* lies): **das ist gelogen!** that's a lie!
'Lügen|de,tektor *m* lie detector. **~geschichte** *f* cock-and-bull story.
Lügner ['ly:gnər] *m* (-s; -) liar.
'lügnerisch *adj* a) lying, b) untrue, false.
Luke ['lu:kə] *f* (-; -n) **1.** hatch. **2.** skylight.
lukrativ [lukra'ti:f] *adj* lucrative.
lukullisch [lu'kʊlɪʃ] *adj* sumptuous.
Lümmel ['lyməl] *m* (-s; -) lout.
'lümmelhaft *adj* loutish.
lümmeln ['lyməln] **sich ~** (h) F sprawl.
Lump [lʊmp] *m* (-en; -en) scoundrel.
lumpen ['lʊmpən] *v/t* (h) F **sich nicht ~ lassen** come down handsomely.
'Lumpen *m* (-s; -) **1.** rag. **2.** *pl* rags.
'lumpig *adj* F *fig.* **1.** shabby. **2.** paltry, measly (**ten dollars etc**).
Lunchpa,ket ['lanʃ-] *n* packed lunch.
Lunge ['lʊŋə] *f* (-; -n) **1.** *anat.* lungs: 🗲 **eiserne ~** iron lung; **die grünen ~n e-r Stadt** the lungs of a city. **2.** *gastr.* lights.
'Lungen... pulmonary (**artery, embolism, etc**). **~entzündung** *f* pneumonia. **~flügel** *m anat.* lung. **~heilstätte** *f* sanatorium, *Am.* sanitarium.
'lungenkrank *adj* (**'Lungenkranke** *m*, *f* person) suffering from (a) lung disease.
'Lungen|krankheit *f* lung disease. **~krebs** *m* 🗲 lung cancer. **~tuberku,lose** *f* pulmonary tuberculosis. **~zug** *m* **e-n ~ machen** inhale.

Lunte ['lʊntə] *f* (-; -n) fuse: F *fig.* **~ riechen** smell a rat.
Lupe ['lu:pə] *f* (-; -n) magnifying glass: F *fig.* **unter die ~ nehmen** scrutinize *s.o.*, *s.th.* closely.
'lupenrein *adj* **1.** flawless (**diamond**). **2.** F clean, perfectly honest.
Lupine [lu'pi:nə] *f* (-; -n) 🌺 lupine.
Lust [lʊst] *f* (-; ⸚e) **1.** *no pl* a) inclination, b) desire, c) interest: **hätten Sie ~ zu kommen?** would you like to come?; **ich hätte große ~ zu kommen** I'd love to come; **ich habe ~ zu tanzen** I feel like dancing; F **ich hätte ~ auf ein Bier** I feel like a beer; **ich hätte nicht übel ~ zu** *inf*, I have half a mind to *inf*; **ich habe k-e ~ (dazu** *or* **darauf)** I don't feel like it, I'm not in the mood (for it); **die (or alle) ~ verlieren (an** *dat*) lose all interest (in) **2.** *psych.* a) pleasure, b) (sexual) desire (**or** appetite), *contp.* lust.
'lustbetont *adj psych.* hedonistic.
lüstern ['lystərn] *adj* **1.** greedy (**nach** for). **2.** lecherous, lewd.
'Lüsternheit *f* (-; *no pl*) **1.** greediness. **2.** lecherousness, lewdness.
'Lustgefühl *n* pleasurable sensation.
'Lustgewinn *m psych.* pleasure gain.
'lustig *adj* a) merry, cheerful, jolly, b) funny, amusing: **er (es) ist sehr ~** he (it) is great fun; **sich ~ machen über (acc)** make fun of; *iro.* **das kann ja ~ werden!** nice prospects!; F **sie unterhielten sich ~ weiter** they blithely went on talking (regardless).
'Lustigkeit *f* (-; *no pl*) **1.** gaiety, cheerfulness. **2.** funniness, fun.
Lüstling ['lystlɪŋ] *m* (-s; -e) lecher.
'lustlos *adj* listless, ✦ *a.* slack.
'Lust|molch *m* F (old) lecher. **~mord** *m* sex murder. **~mörder** *m* sex killer. **~ob,jekt** *n* sex object. **~schloß** *n* summer residence. **~spiel** *n thea.* comedy.
lutschen ['lʊtʃən] *v/t*, *v/i* (h) suck (**an** *a. s.th.*): **→ Daumen.** **'Lutscher** *m* (-s; -) **1.** lollipop. **2.** F dummy, *Am.* pacifier.
Luv [lu:f] *n* (-s; *no pl*), **'Luvseite** *f*, **'luv wärts** *adv* ⚓ windward.
luxuriös [lʊksu'riø:s] *adj* luxurious.
Luxus ['lʊksʊs] *m* (-; *no pl*) *a. fig.* luxury.
'Luxus... luxury, de luxe. **~ar,tikel** *m* luxury (article), *pl a.* luxury goods. **~ausführung** *f* de luxe model. **~leben** *n* life of luxury. **~restau,rant** *n* first

-class restaurant. **~wagen** *m mot.* luxury car.

'**Lymphdrüse** *f anat.* lymph gland.

Lymphe ['lʏmfə] *f* (-; -n) **1.** *physiol.* lymph. **2.** ✻ vaccine.

'**Lymphgefäß** *n anat.* lymphatic (vessel).

'**Lymphknoten** *m anat.* lymph node.

lynchen ['lʏnçən] *v/t* (h) lynch.

'**Lynchju͵stiz** *f* (**~ üben** resort to) lynch law. '**Lynchmord** *m* lynching.

Lyrik ['ly:rɪk] *f* (-; *no pl*) **1.** poetry. **2.** lyricism. '**Lyriker** *m* (-s; -), '**Lyrikerin** *f* (-; -nen) (lyric) poet(ess), lyricist.

'**lyrisch** *adj* lyric, *a. fig.* lyrical.

M

M, m [ɛm] *n* (-; -) M, m.

Maat [ma:t] *m* (-[e]s; -e[n]) (ship's) mate.

'**Machart** *f* make, style, type.

'**machbar** *adj* practicable, possible.

Mache ['maxə] *f* (-; *no pl*) F **1.** make-believe, show. **2.** *j-n in die ~ nehmen* work s.o. over.

machen ['maxən] (h) **I** *v/t* **1.** make, *a.* prepare (*dinner etc*), *a.* do (*one's homework etc*), take (*snapshot, examination, etc*): *et. ~ aus* (*dat*) make s.th. of (*or* from); *aus dem Keller e-e Werkstatt ~* turn the cellar into a workshop; *aus j-m e-n Star ~* make a star of s.o.; *j-n zum Abteilungsleiter ~* make s.o. head of the department; *→ gemacht.* **2.** put in order, *a.* fix, repair, make (*bed*), do, tidy up (*room*). **3.** do: *was macht er?* a) what is he doing?, b) what does he do for a living?, c) how is he (getting on)?; *was machst du morgen?* what are you doing tomorrow?; *wird gemacht!* okay, I'll do it!, *sl.* will do!; *gut gemacht!* well done!; *mach's gut!* take care (of yourself)!; *das läßt sich ~* that can be done (*or* arranged); *so et. macht man nicht!* that isn't done!; *da ist nichts zu ~* nothing doing; *da(gegen) kann man nichts ~* it can't be helped; F *er wird es nicht mehr lange ~* he (*the engine etc*): it) won't last much longer; *der Wagen macht 160 km/h* the car does 100 mph. **4.** give (*appetite, pleasure, etc*): *das macht Durst* that makes you thirsty. **5.** *j-n gesund ~* cure s.o.; *j-n glücklich ~* make s.o. happy. **6.** matter: *das macht nichts!* that doesn't matter!, never mind!; *das macht mir*

nichts I don't mind (*contp.* care). **7.** *sich et.* (*nichts*) *~ aus* (*dat*) (not to) care about (*gastr.* for); *mach dir nichts daraus!* don't worry (about it)!; *ich mache mir nichts aus ihm* I don't care (much) for him. **8.** F be: *4 mal 5 macht 20* four times five is twenty; *was* (*or wieviel*) *macht das?* how much is that?; *das macht 10 Mark* that will be ten marks. **9.** F be, act as: *den Schiedsrichter ~* be (the) referee. **II** *sich ~* **10.** F come along (well), be getting on (well): *wie macht sich der Neue?* how is the new man coming along?; *die Sache macht sich* things are shaping up well; *das Bild macht sich gut dort* the picture looks nice there. **11.** *sich an e-e Sache ~* get down to (doing) s.th.; *sich an die Arbeit ~* get down to work. **III** *v/i* **12.** F *mach, daß du fortkommst!* off with you!, get lost!; *mach schnell!*, *mach schon!* hurry up!, get a move on! **13.** do: *laß ihn nur ~!* a) let him (do as he pleases)!, b) just leave it to him!; *das läßt sich ~* that can be done. **14.** F *er macht in Radios* he deals in (*or* sells) radios; *sie macht jetzt in moderner Kunst* she's into modern art now.

'**Machenschaften** *pl* machinations.

Macher ['maxər] *m* (-s; -) *fig.* doer.

Macho ['matʃo] *m* (-s; -s) F macho.

Macht [maxt] *f* (-; ⸚e) **1.** *no pl* power (*über acc* of), *a.* might, force: *mit aller ~* with all one's might; *die ~ der Gewohnheit* the force of habit; *die ~ ergreifen* seize power, take over; *an die ~ kommen* (*or gelangen*) come into power; *an der ~ sein* be in power; *es* *steht nicht in m-r ~* it is not within my power. **2.** *pol. etc* power.

'Machtbefugnis *f* power, authority.

'Machtbereich *m* sphere of influence.

'Machtergreifung *f* seizure of power.

'machtgierig *adj* power-hungry.

'Machthaber [-ha:bər] *m* (-s; -) ruler.

mächtig ['mɛçtɪç] **I** *adj* powerful, mighty (*both a.* blow, voice, *etc*), *a.* enormous. **II** *adv* F tremendously, awfully: *~ gewachsen sein* have grown a lot.

'Machtkampf *m* power struggle.

'machtlos *adj* powerless, helpless.

'Machtpoli,tik *f* power politics.

'Machtübernahme *f* assumption of power, takeover. **'machtvoll** *adj a. fig.* powerful. **'Machtwechsel** *m* transition of power. **'Machtwort** *n ein ~ sprechen* put one's foot down.

'Machwerk *n* concoction, F lousy job.

Macke ['makə] *f* (-; -n) F kink: *e-e ~ haben* a) be nuts, b) ⚙ be acting up.

Mädchen ['mɛ:tçən] *n* (-s; -) **1.** girl. **2.** maid: *fig. ~ für alles* dogsbody. **'mädchenhaft** *adj* girlish. **'Mädchenname** *m* **1.** girl's name. **2.** maiden name.

Made ['ma:də] *f* (-; -n) maggot, worm: F *wie die ~ im Speck leben* be in clover.

Mädel ['mɛ:dəl] *n* (-s; -s) F girl(ie).

madig ['ma:dɪç] *adj* maggoty, worm-eaten: F *~ machen* knock (*s.o., s.th.*); *j-m et. ~ machen* spoil s.th. for s.o.

Madonna [ma'dɔna] *f* (-; -en) Madonna.

Maf(f)ia ['mafia] *f* (-; -s) *a.* F *fig.* mafia.

Mafioso [ma'fio:zo] *m* (-[s]; -si) mafioso.

Magazin [maga'tsi:n] *n* (-s; -e) **1.** depot (*a.* ✗), warehouse. **2.** *phot.,* ⚙ magazine (*a.* of gun *etc*). **3.** *print.* magazine.

Magd [ma:kt] *f* (-; ⁔e) maid.

Magen ['ma:gən] *m* (-s; ⁔) stomach: *auf nüchternen (or leeren) ~* on an empty stomach; *j-m schwer im ~ liegen* lie heavily on s.o.'s stomach, F *fig.* worry s.o. terribly; *sich den ~ verderben* upset one's stomach. **~beschwerden** *pl* stomach trouble. **~bitter** *m gastr.* bitters. **~geschwür** *n* (stomach) ulcer. **~grube** *f* pit of the stomach. ⚨**krank** *adj* ~ *sein* suffer from a stomach complaint. **~krebs** *m* ⚕ stomach cancer. **~leiden** *n* gastric complaint. **~säure** *f* ⚕ gastric acid.

'Magenschleimhaut *f* stomach lining. **~entzündung** *f* gastritis.

'Magenschmerzen *pl* stomach-ache.

'Magenverstimmung *f* indigestion.

mager ['ma:gər] *adj* **1.** lean (*a. fig.*), *a.* thin, *a.* low-fat: **~e** *Kost a. fig.* slender fare. **2.** *fig.* meag/re (*Am.* -er), poor. **3.** *print.* light-faced.

'Magermilch *f* skimmed milk.

'Magerquark *m* low-fat curd cheese.

'Magersucht *f* (-; *no pl*) ⚕ anorexia.

Magie [ma'gi:] *f* (-; *no pl*) magic.

Magier ['ma:giər] *m* (-s; -) magician.

magisch ['ma:gɪʃ] *adj* magic(al).

Magister [ma'gɪstər] *m* (-s; -) *univ.* Master (*Artium* of Arts, *abbr.* M.A.).

Magistrat [magɪs'tra:t] *m* (-[e]s; -e) town council.

Magnat [ma'gna:t] *m* (-en; -en) magnate, tycoon.

Magnesium [ma'gne:ziʊm] *n* (-s; *no pl*) 🜨 magnesium.

Magnet [ma'gne:t] *m* (-en; -e) magnet. **Ma'gnet...** magnetic (*field, needle, etc*). **ma'gnetisch** *adj* magnetic: *fig. j-n ~ anziehen* have a magnetic effect on s.o.

magnetisieren [magneti'zi:rən] *v/t* (h) magnetize. **Magnetismus** [magne'tɪsmʊs] *m* (-; *no pl*) magnetism.

Ma'gnetkarte *f* magnetic card.

Ma'gnetzündung *f* magneto ignition.

Mahagoni [maha'go:ni] *n* (-s; *no pl*), **Maha'goniholz** *n* mahogany.

mähen[1] ['mɛ:ən] *v/t, v/i* (h) mow, cut.

'mähen[2] *v/i* (h) sheep: bleat.

mahlen ['ma:lən] *v/t, v/i* (h) grind.

Mahlzeit ['ma:ltsaɪt] *f* (-; -en) meal: F (*na dann*) *prost ~!* good night!

'Mähma,schine *f* reaper.

'Mahnbescheid *m* (court) order to pay.

Mähne ['mɛ:nə] *f* (-; -n) mane.

mahnen ['ma:nən] *v/t* (h) **1.** admonish, urge (*j-n zur Vorsicht etc* s.o. to be careful *etc*). **2.** a) *a. fig.* remind (*an acc, wegen* of), b) ✝ send *s.o.* a reminder.

'Mahnmal *n* memorial.

'Mahnschreiben *n* (-s; -) ✝ reminder.

'Mahnung *f* (-; -en) **1.** admonition, warning. **2.** ✝ reminder.

'Mahnwache *f pol.* protest vigil.

Mai [maɪ] *m* (-[e]s; *no pl*) (*im ~* in) May: *der Erste ~* May Day.

'Mai|baum *m* maypole. **~feier** *f* May Day celebrations. **~glöckchen** *n* ❀ lily of the valley. **~käfer** *m* cockchafer.

Mais [maɪs] *m* (-es; -e) maize, *Am.* corn.

Mais|flocken pl cornflakes. **~kolben** m (corn)cob, gastr. corn on the cob. **~mehl** n Indian (Am. corn) meal.

Maison(n)ette [mɛzɔ'nɛt] f (-; -s) maison(n)ette, Am. duplex.

Majestät [majɛs'tɛ:t] f (-; no pl) a. fig. majesty: **Seine ~** His Majesty.

maje'stätisch adj majestic.

Major [ma'jo:r] m (-s; -e) ✕ major.

Majoran ['ma:jora:n] m (-s; -e) ♀ marjoram.

makaber [ma'ka:bər] adj macab/re (Am. -er).

Makel ['ma:kəl] m (-s; -) a. fig. flaw.

'makellos adj immaculate, perfect.

mäkeln ['mɛːkəln] v/i (h) carp (**an** dat at).

Makkaroni [maka'ro:ni] pl macaroni.

Makler ['ma:klər] m (-s; -) **1.** (stock)broker. **2.** (Am. real estate agent.

Makrele [ma'kre:lə] f (-; -n) mackerel.

Makro... ['ma:kro-], **'makro...** macro...

Makrone [ma'kro:nə] f (-; -n) macaroon.

mal [ma:l] adv **1.** & times, multiplied by: **der Raum ist 6 ~ 4 Meter** the room is six metres by four. **2.** F → **einmal.**

Mal[1] n (-[e]s; -e) **1.** a) mark, sign, b) spot; → **Muttermal** etc. **2.** baseball etc: base, rugby: in-goal.

Mal[2] n (-[e]s; -e) time: **dieses ~** this time; **dieses eine ~** this once; **ein anderes ~** some other time; **das erste ~, beim ersten ~** the first time; **zum letzten ~** for the last time; **das nächste ~** the next time; **mit einem ~** all of a sudden; **ein für alle ~** once and for all; **von ~ zu ~ besser** better every time.

Malaria [ma'la:ria] f (-; no pl) ♣ malaria.

malen ['ma:lən] (h) **I** v/t paint (a. fig.), portray: **et. zu schwarz ~** paint too black a picture of s.th. **II sich ~** fig. be reflected (in s.o.'s face etc).

'Maler m (-s; -) painter, artist. **Male'rei** f (-; -en) painting. **'Malerin** f (-; -nen) (woman) painter, artist. **'malerisch** adj **1.** picturesque. **2.** artistic (talent).

maliziös [mali'tsjø:s] adj malicious.

'malnehmen v/t (irr, sep, -ge-, h, → **nehmen**) & multiply (**mit** by).

Malve ['malvə] f (-; -n) ♀ mallow.

Malz [malts] n (-es; no pl) malt.

'Malzbier n malt beer.

'Malzeichen n & multiplication sign.

Malzkaf,fee m malt coffee.

Mama ['mama] f (-; -s) F mummy, mum, Am. mom.

Mammographie [mamogra'fi:] f (-; -n) ♣ mammography.

Mammon ['mamɔn] m (-s; no pl) contp. mammon: **schnöder ~** filthy lucre.

Mammut ['mamʊt] n (-s; -s) mammoth.

man [man] indef pron **1.** one, you, we: **~ kann nie wissen** you never can tell; **~ muß es tun** it must be done; **~ nehme** take. **2.** they, people: **~ hat mir gesagt** I have been told; **~ sagt** people say; **~ holte ihn** he was fetched.

managen ['mɛnidʒən] v/t (h) F manage.

'Manager m (-s; -) manager.

'Managerkrankheit f stress disease.

manch [manç] indef pron many a: **~ eine(r)** many (people); **in ~em hat er recht** he's right about some things; **so ~er (~es)** a good many people (things).

'manche pl some, quite a few.

'mancherlei adj a) various, many, a number of, b) a number of things.

'manchmal adv sometimes.

Mandant [man'dant] m (-en; -en), **Man'dantin** f (-; -nen) ⚖ client.

Mandarine [manda'ri:nə] f (-; -n) ♀ tangerine.

Mandat [man'da:t] n (-[e]s; -e) ⚖, parl., pol. mandate, of lawyer: brief: parl. **sein ~ niederlegen** resign one's seat.

Mandel ['mandəl] f (-; -n) **1.** ♀ almond. **2.** anat. tonsil. **~baum** m almond (tree). **~entzündung** f ♣ tonsillitis.

Mandoline [mando'li:nə] f (-; -n) ♪ mandolin(e).

Manege [ma'ne:ʒə] f (-; -n) (circus) ring.

Mangan [maŋ'ga:n] n (-s; no pl) 🜍 manganese.

Mangel[1] ['maŋəl] f (-; -n) mangle: F **in die ~ nehmen** put s.o. through the mill.

'Mangel[2] m (-s; ⸚) **1.** a) defect, fault, flaw, b) drawback. **2.** (an dat) shortage, lack, scarcity (all: of), deficiency (in): **aus ~ an ~ mangels.** **~beruf** m understaffed occupation. **~erscheinung** f ♣ deficiency symptom.

'mangelhaft adj a) faulty, defective, b) insufficient, inadequate, deficient, unsatisfactory (a. ped.), poor.

Mängelhaftung ['mɛŋəl-] f ✝ responsibility for defects.

mangeln[1] ['maŋəln] v/t (h) press.

'mangeln[2] v/i, v/impers (h) be wanting,

be lacking: **es mangelt an** (*dat*) there is a lack (*or* want, shortage) of; **es mangelt mir an Geld** *etc* I am short of money *etc*; **es mangelt ihm an** (*or der*) **Mut** he lacks courage; **ihr ~des Selbstvertrauen** her lack of self-confidence.

'**Mängelrüge** f ✝ notice of defects.

'**mangels** prep (gen) for lack (*or* want) of: **~ Beweisen** for lack of evidence.

'**Mangelware** f scarce commodity: **~ sein** a. F fig. be in short supply.

Manie [ma'niː] f (-; -n) mania.

Manier [ma'niːr] f (-; -en) **1.** no pl manner, way (of doing *s.th.*), *art*: style. **2.** pl manners. **ma'nierlich** adj a) well-mannered, b) good, well-behaved: **sich ~ benehmen** behave o.s., be good.

Manifest [mani'fɛst] n (-[e]s; -e) pol. manifesto. **manifestieren** [manifɛs-'tiːrən] v/t (h) manifest.

Maniküre [mani'kyːrə] f (-; -n) **1.** no pl manicure. **2.** manicurist.

mani'küren v/t, v/i (h) manicure.

Manipulation [manipula'tsi̯oːn] f (-; -en) manipulation. **manipulieren** [manipu'liːrən] v/t (h) manipulate.

manisch ['maːnɪʃ] adj psych. manic. **~depres'siv** adj manic-depressive.

Manko ['maŋko] n (-s; -s) **1.** ✝ a) deficiency, b) deficit. **2.** (-[e]s; -e) fig. shortcoming.

Mann [man] m (-[e]s; ⸚er) a) man, b) husband: **100 ~** a hundred men; **der kleine ~** the man in the street; **ein ~ von Welt** a man of the world; **ein Gespräch von ~ zu ~** a man-to-man talk; **wie ein ~ as one man; bis auf den letzten ~** to a man; **ein Kampf ~ gegen ~** a hand-to-hand fight; **s-n ~ stehen** stand one's ground; **⚓ alle ~ an Deck!** all hands on deck!; **mit ~ und Maus sinken** go down with all hands (on board); F **an den ~ bringen** get rid of (*goods, a joke, etc*); **den starken ~ markieren** throw one's weight about; **ein ~, ein Wort!** a promise is a promise; F **10 Mark pro ~** 10 marks per head; **wir gingen als ~ (hoch)** hin all of us went; F (**mein lieber) ~!** (oh) boy!, wow!

Männchen ['mɛnçən] n (-s; -) **1.** little man, manikin: **~ malen** doodle. **2.** zo. male, cock: F **~ machen** sit up and beg.

Mannequin ['manəkɛ̃] n (-s; -s) mannequin, model.

Männer ['mɛnər] pl of **Mann**: **~ on WC:**

Men, Gentlemen. '**Männer...** man's, men's ... '**Männerchor** m male(-voice) choir. '**männerfeindlich** adj hostile towards men.

'**Mannesalter** n manhood: **im besten ~** in the prime of life.

'**mannhaft** adj manly, a. brave.

mannigfach ['manɪçfax], '**mannigfaltig** adj diverse, manifold.

männlich ['mɛnlɪç] adj **1.** biol., ⚥, ⊚ male. **2.** manly, masculine (a. ling.), mannish. '**Männlichkeit** f (-; no pl) masculinity, manliness, virility.

'**Mannsbild** n F man, fellow.

'**Mannschaft** f (-; -en) sports: team, ✈, ⚓, ✗ crew, ✗ detail, (*rescue etc*) party: ✗ **die ~en** the ranks.

'**Mannschafts|aufstellung** f sports: line-up. **~führer(in** f) m sports: (team) captain. **~geist** m (-[e]s; no pl) team spirit. **~kapi,tän** m sports: (team) captain. **~sport** m team sport. **~wagen** m a) ✗ personnel carrier, b) police van. **~wertung** f sports: team classification. **~wettbewerb** m team event.

'**mannshoch** adj and adv head-high.

'**mannstoll** adj F contp. man-crazy.

'**Mannweib** n contp. mannish woman.

Manometer [mano'meːtər] n (-s; -) ⊚ pressure ga(u)ge.

Manöver [ma'nøːvər] n (-s; -) **1.** a. fig. manoeuvre, Am. maneuver. **2.** ✗ manoeuvres, Am. maneuvers, exercise.

Ma'növerkri,tik f fig. post-mortem.

manövrieren [manø'vriːrən] v/i (h) a. fig. manoeuvre, Am. maneuver.

manö'vrierunfähig adj disabled.

Mansarde [man'zardə] f (-; -n) attic room.

Mansch [manʃ] m (-es; no pl) F **1.** slush. **2.** contp. mush. **manschen** ['manʃən] v/i (h) F mess about.

Manschette [man'ʃɛtə] f (-; -n) **1.** cuff: F **~n bekommen** get the wind up; **~n haben vor** be scared stiff of. **2.** ⊚ sleeve.

Man'schettenknopf m cuff-link.

Mantel ['mantəl] m (-s; ⸚) **1.** coat, cloak: fig. **den ~ nach dem Wind hängen** trim one's sails to the wind. **2.** ⊚ casing.

'**Mantelta,rif(vertrag)** m collective agreement (on working conditions).

manuell [ma'nu̯ɛl] adj manual.

Manuskript [manu'skrɪpt] n (-[e]s; -e) manuscript, film: script, print. copy.

Mappe ['mapə] *f* (-; -n) a) briefcase, b) schoolbag, c) folder, file, d) portfolio.

Marathon ['ma:raton] *m* (-s; -s), **'Marathonlauf** *m* marathon (race).

Märchen ['mε:rçən] *n* (-s; -) fairytale, *fig.* (tall) story, yarn.

'Märchenbuch *n* book of fairytales.

'märchenhaft *adj* magical, fairytale ..., F *fig.* fantastic.

'Märchen|land *n*, **~welt** *f* fairyland.

Marder ['mardər] *m* (-s; -) *zo.* marten.

Margarine [marga'ri:nə] *f* (-; -n) margarine.

Marienbild [ma'ri:ən-] *n* Madonna.

Ma'rienkäfer *m* *zo.* ladybird.

Marihuana [mari'hŭa:na] *n* (-s; *no pl*) marijuana, *sl.* pot.

Marinade [mari'na:də] *f* (-; -n) *gastr.* marinade.

Marine [ma'ri:nə] *f* (-; -n) a) merchant navy, b) navy.

Ma'rine|blau *n*, **₂blau** *adj* navy blue. **~offi,zier** *m* naval officer. **~sol,dat** *m* marine. **~stützpunkt** *m* naval base.

marinieren [mari'ni:rən] *v/t* (h) *gastr.* marinade.

Marionette [mariŏ'nεtə] *f* (-; -n) *a. fig.* marionette, puppet.

Mario'netten|re,gierung *f* *fig.* puppet government. **~spiel** *n* puppet show. **~the,ater** *n* puppet theat/re (*Am.* -er).

Mark[1] [mark] *n* (-[e]s; *no pl*) marrow, *fig. a.* core: *j-m durch* **~** *und Bein gehen* set s.o.'s teeth on edge; *j-n bis ins* **~** *treffen* cut s.o. to the quick.

Mark[2] *f* (-; -) mark: *zehn* **~** ten marks; F *jede* **~** *umdrehen* count every penny.

Mark[3] *f* (-; -en) *hist.* march.

markant [mar'kant] *adj* striking, prominent: **~e Persönlichkeit** outstanding personality.

Marke ['markə] *f* (-; -n) **1.** ₮ make, type, brand. **2.** mark, sign, *computer*: flag, label. **3.** a) voucher, b) coupon, c) stamp; → **Dienstmarke, Essenmarke, Spielmarke** *etc.* **4.** F character.

'Marken|ar,tikel *m* ₮ proprietary article. **~ben,zin** *n* brand name petrol (*Am.* gasoline). **~butter** *f* best quality butter. **~fabri,kat** *n* proprietary make. **~name** *m* trade (*or* brand) name. **~zeichen** *n* trademark.

'markerschütternd *adj* bloodcurdling.

markieren [mar'ki:rən] *v/t* (h) **1.** a)

mark (*a. fig.*), b) accentuate, underline. **2.** act, play: → **Mann. 3.** *sports*: mark (*player*), score (*goal*).

Mar'kierung *f* (-; -en) mark(ing).

'markig *adj* *fig.* pithy.

Markise [mar'ki:zə] *f* (-; -n) sunblind, awning.

'Markstein *m* *fig.* milestone.

Markt [markt] *m* (-[e]s; ≈e) **1.** market: *auf dem* **~** in (*or* on) the market; *et. auf den* **~** *bringen* market s.th. **2.** marketplace. **~ana,lyse** *f* market analysis. **~anteil** *m* share of the market. **~bericht** *m* market report. **~entwicklung** *f* market trend. **~forscher** *m* market researcher. **~forschung** *f* market research. **~führer** *m* market leader. ₂**gängig** *adj* a) marketable, b) current (*price*). **~halle** *f* covered market. **~lücke** *f* opening: *in e-e* **~** *stoßen* fill a gap in the market. **~platz** *m* marketplace.

'marktschreierisch *adj* *fig.* loud.

'Markt|stand *m* (market) stall. **~studie** *f* market analysis. **~wert** *m* market value. **~wirtschaft** *f* market economy: *freie* **~** free enterprise; *soziale* **~** social market economy.

Marmelade [marmə'la:də] *f* (-; -n) jam.

Marme'ladenglas *n* jam jar.

Marmor ['marmɔr] *m* (-s; -e), **marmorieren** [marmo'ri:rən] *v/t* (h) marble.

Marokkaner [marɔ'ka:nər] *m* (-s; -), **Marok'kanerin** *f* (-; -nen), **marok'kanisch** *adj* Moroccan. **Marokko** [ma'rɔ-kɔ] *n* (-s) Morocco.

Marone [ma'ro:nə] *f* (-; -n) ❦ (sweet) chestnut.

Marotte [ma'rɔtə] *f* (-; -n) quirk.

Mars [mars] *m* (-; *no pl*) Mars.

'Marsmensch *m* Martian.

marsch [marʃ] *int* **1.** ✕ (*vorwärts* **~!** forward) march! **2.** F **~!** get a move on!

Marsch[1] *m* (-[e]s; ≈e) walk, ✕ march (*a.* ♪): *sich in* **~** *setzen* move off.

Marsch[2] *f* (-; -en) *geol.* marsh.

'Marschbefehl *m* ✕ marching orders.

'Marschflugkörper *m* ✕ cruise missile.

'Marschgepäck *n* ✕ field kit.

marschieren [mar'ʃi:rən] *v/i* (sn) (*a.* **~** *lassen*) march.

'Marsch|mu,sik *f* military marches. **~ordnung** *f* ✕ march formation. **~route** *f* **1.** ✕ route. **2.** *fig.* strategy. **~verpflegung** *f* ✕ marching rations.

Marstall ['mar-] *m* royal stables.
Marter ['martər] *f* (-; -n) torture, *fig. a.* ordeal. '**martern** *v/t* (h) torture, *fig. a.* torment. '**Marterpfahl** *m* stake.
Martinshorn ['marti:ns-] *n* F (police, ambulance or fire-engine) siren.
Märtyrer ['mɛrtyrər] *m* (-s; -) martyr: *iro. sich zum ~ machen* make a martyr of s.o. **Martyrium** [mar'ty:riʊm] *n* (-s; -rien) martyrdom.
Marxismus [mar'ksɪsmʊs] *m* (-; *no pl*) Marxism. **Marxist** [mar'ksɪst] *m* (-en; -en), **mar'xistisch** *adj* Marxist.
März [mɛrts] *m* (-[es]; *no pl*) (*im ~ in*) March.
Marzipan [martsi'pa:n] *n* (-s; -e) marzipan.
Masche ['maʃə] *f* (-; -n) **1.** a) stitch, b) mesh: *durch die ~n des Gesetzes schlüpfen* find a loophole in the law. **2.** F a) trick, ploy, b) fad, craze.
'**Maschendraht** *m* wire netting.
Maschine [ma'ʃi:nə] *f* (-; -n) **1.** a) machine, b) F engine. **2.** plane, jetliner. **3.** F motorcycle. **4.** typewriter: *mit der ~ schreiben* type. **5.** sewing machine. **6.** washing machine.
maschinell [maʃi'nɛl] **I** *adj* machine ..., mechanical. **II** *adv* machine-..., by machine: *~ bearbeiten* machine; *~ hergestellt* machine-made.
Ma'schinen|bau *m* (-[e]s; *no pl*) mechanical engineering. **~bauer** *m* (-s; -), **~bauingeni,eur** *m* mechanical engineer. **~befehl** *m* computer: machine-code instruction. **~fa,brik** *f* engineering works. **2geschrieben** *adj* typewritten, typed. **~gewehr** *n* machine-gun. **~park** *m* machinery. **~pi,stole** *f* submachine-gun. **~raum** *m* engine-room. **~schaden** *m* mechanical breakdown, ⚓, *mot.* engine trouble. **~schlosser** *m* engine fitter. **~schreiben** *n* (-s) typewriting, typing. **~schrift** *f* typescript. **2waschbar** *adj* machine-washable.
Maschinerie [maʃinə'ri:] *f* (-; -n) a) machinery, b) mechanism.
ma'schineschreiben *v/i* (*schrieb Maschine, hat maschinegeschrieben*) type.
Maschinist [maʃi'nɪst] *m* (-en; -en) machinist, machine operator, 🚂 engine driver, *Am.* engineer.
Maser ['ma:zər] *f* (-; -n) *wood etc*: vein.

Masern ['ma:zərn] *pl* 🕮 measles.
'**Maserung** *f* (-; -en) *of wood*: grain.
Maske ['maskə] *f* (-; -n) mask (*a.* 🕮, computer, phot., *a.* person), *thea.* make-up, *fig. a.* guise: *in der ~* (*gen*) under the guise of; *fig. die ~ fallen lassen* show one's true face.
'**Maskenball** *m* fancy-dress ball.
'**Maskenbildner** *m* (-s; -) make-up artist.
'**maskenhaft** *adj* mask-like.
'**Maskenko,stüm** *n* fancy dress.
Maskerade [maskə'ra:də] *f* (-; -n) *a. fig.* masquerade.
maskieren [mas'ki:rən] (h) **I** *v/t* **1.** *j-n* a) mask s.o., b) dress s.o. up. **2.** *a.* ⚙ conceal. **II** *sich ~* a) dress in disguise, disguise o.s., b) put on a mask. **mas'kiert** *adj* masked. **Mas'kierung** *f* (-; -en) a) disguise, b) mask.
Maskottchen [mas'kɔtçən] *n* (-s; -) mascot.
maskulin [masku'li:n] *adj*, **Maskulinum** [-'li:nʊm] *n* (-s; -na) *ling.* masculine.
Masochismus [mazo'xɪsmʊs] *m* (-; *no pl*) masochism. **Masochist** [-'xɪst] *m* (-en; -en) masochist. **maso'chistisch** *adj* masochistic.
maß [ma:s] *pret of* **messen**.
Maß[1] *n* (-es; -e) **1.** measure: *~e und Gewichte* weights and measures; *mit zweierlei ~ messen* apply double standards; *das ~ überschreiten* overshoot the mark. **2.** *pl* measurements, *of room etc*: *a.* dimensions: *bei j-m ~ nehmen* take s.o.'s measurements; *nach ~ (angefertigt)* made-to-measure (→ *a. maßgeschneidert*). **3.** *fig.* degree, extent: *ein gewisses (hohes) ~ an (dat)* a certain degree (a high measure) of; *in hohem ~e* to a high degree, highly; *in höchstem ~e* extremely; *in gleichem ~e* to the same extent, equally; *in zunehmendem ~e* increasingly; *in dem ~e, wie ...* as ... (accordingly); *über alle ~en* exceedingly. **4.** moderation: *in ~en* a) *a. mit ~ und Ziel* in moderation, b) to some extent; *ohne ~ und Ziel* immoderately; → *maßhalten.*
Maß[2] *f* (-; -e) a) litre (*Am.* liter) of beer, b) → **Maßkrug.**
Massage [ma'sa:ʒə] *f* (-; -n) massage.
Massaker [ma'sa:kər] *n* (-s; -), **massa-**

krieren [masa'kri:rən] *v/t* (h) massacre, slaughter.

'**Maßanzug** *m* tailor-made (*Am.* custom-made) suit.

'**Maßarbeit** *f fig.* precision work.

'**Maßband** *n* (-[e]s; ⸚er) tape measure.

Masse ['masə] *f* (-; -n) **1.** mass (*a. phys.*), *a.* substance, *gastr.* mixture, ⚒ compound. **2.** F **e-e ~ (von), ~n von** masses (*or* lots, loads) of; **e-e ~ Geld** loads of money. **3.** bulk, majority. **4.** crowd: **die (breite) ~** the masses. **5.** ⚖ estate, assets. **6.** ⚡ (*a.* **an ~ legen**) earth, *Am.* ground.

'**Maßeinheit** *f* unit of measure(ment).

'**Massen...** mass (*demonstration, production, tourism, etc*). **~abfertigung** *f a. contp.* mass processing. **~andrang** *m* huge crowd, F terrible crush. **~arbeitslosigkeit** *f* mass unemployment. **~artikel** *m* ⚒ mass-produced article. **~entlassungen** *pl* mass dismissals. **~erzeugung** *f*, **~fabrikati̯on** *f*, **~fertigung** *f* mass production. **~flucht** *f* mass exodus, stampede. **~grab** *n* mass grave. **~güter** *pl* bulk goods.

'**massenhaft** *adv* F masses (*or* lots, heaps) of: **sich ~ vermehren** multiply in huge numbers.

'**Massen̩karambo̩lage** *f mot.* (multiple) pile-up. **~medium** *n* mass medium (*pl* media). **~mensch** *m* mass man. **~mord** *m* mass murder. **~mörder** *m* mass murderer. **~psy̩chose** *f* mass hysteria. **~quar̩tier** *n* mass accommodation. **~schläge̩rei** *f* F free-for-all. **~sport** *m* popular sport. **~sterben** *n* widespread deaths (*zo.* dying-off). **~veranstaltung** *f* mass meeting.

Masseur [ma'sø:r] *m* (-s; -e) masseur.

Mas'seurin *f* (-; -nen) masseuse.

Masseuse [ma'sø:zə] *f* (-; -n) *esp. sex*: masseuse.

'**Maßgabe** *f nach ~* (*gen*) in accordance with; *mit der ~, daß ...* provided that ...

'**maßgebend** *adj* **1.** decisive, authoritative (*opinion etc*), leading, prominent (*personality etc*): *das ist (für mich) nicht ~* that's no criterion (for me); *s-e Meinung ist nicht ~* his opinion does not count (here). **2.** a) competent, b) standard, definitive (*book etc*).

maßgeblich ['ma:sge:plɪç] *adj* decisive: **~en Anteil haben** (*or* **~ beteiligt sein**)

an (*dat*) play a decisive role in, be instrumental in; **~e Kreise** influential circles.

'**maßgerecht** *adj* true-to-size.

'**maßgeschneidert** *adj* tailor-made (*a. fig.*), made-to-measure, *Am.* custom-made.

'**maßhalten** *v/i* (*irr, sep*, -ge-, h, → **halten**) be moderate.

massieren¹ [ma'si:rən] *v/t* (h) massage.

mas'sieren² *v/t* (*a.* **sich ~**) (h) mass, concentrate.

massig ['masɪç] *adj* massive, bulky.

mäßig ['mɛ:sɪç] **I** *adj* **1.** moderate, *a.* temperate. **2.** mediocre, (rather) poor, F (fair to) middling. **II** *adv* **3.** moderately, in moderation. **mäßigen** ['mɛ:sɪgən] (h) **I** *v/t* moderate, *a.* curb, control (*one's rage etc*); → **gemäßigt. II sich ~** restrain (*or* control) o.s.; *sich beim Trinken etc* ~ cut down on drinks *etc.*

'**Mäßigung** *f* (-; *no pl*) moderation.

massiv [ma'si:f] *adj* **1.** solid (*gold, wood, etc*). **2.** *fig.* massive (*threat, attack, etc*): F ~ **werden** cut up rough.

Mas'siv *n* (-s, -e) *geol.* massif. **~bau(weise** *f*) *m* △ massive construction.

'**Maßkrug** *m* beer mug, stein.

'**maßlos I** *adj* immoderate, excessive (*demands etc*). **II** *adv* immoderately (*etc*): ~ **übertrieben** grossly exaggerated; ~ **eifersüchtig** extremely jealous.

'**Maßlosigkeit** *f* (-; *no pl*) immoderateness, lack of restraint, excess.

'**Maßnahme** [-na:mə] *f* (-; -n) measure.

'**maßregeln** *v/t* (*insep*, ge-, h) (*wegen* for) a) reprimand, b) punish, discipline, *sports*: penalize.

'**Maßregelung** *f* (-; -en) a) reprimand, b) disciplinary action, *sports*: penalty.

'**Maßschneider** *m* bespoke (*Am.* custom) tailor.

'**Maßstab** *m* **1.** scale: *im ~ 1:10* on a scale of 1:10; *im verkleinerten (vergrößerten)* ~ on a reduced (an enlarged) scale; *in großem ~ a. fig.* large-scale. **2.** *fig.* standard, yardstick: *hohe Maßstäbe anlegen* apply strict standards (*an acc* to); *das ist kein ~* that's no criterion.

'**maßstabgerecht** *adj* (true) to scale.

'**maßvoll** *adj*) a) moderate, reasonable, b) restrained.

Mast¹ [mast] *m* (-[e]s; -e[n]) a) ⚓ mast, b) ⚡ pylon, c) pole.

Mast² f (-; -en) ✗ **1.** fattening. **2.** mast.
'**Mastdarm** m anat. rectum.
mästen ['mɛstən] (h) I v/t fatten. II sich
~ gorge o.s. (**an** dat on).
Masturbation [mastʊrba'tsio:n] f (-;
-en) masturbation. **masturbieren**
[mastʊr'bi:rən] v/i (h) masturbate.
'**Mastvieh** n fat stock.
Match [mɛtʃ] n, a. -t -[e]s; -s, -e) match,
game. **~ball** m tennis: match point.
Material [mate'ria:l] n (-s; -ien) material
(a. fig.), ☉ coll. materials.
Materi'alfehler m material defect.
Materialismus [materia'lismʊs] m (-; no
pl) materialism. **Materialist** [materia-
'list] m (-en; -en) materialist.
materia'listisch adj materialist(ic).
Materi'alkosten pl cost of materials.
Materi'alprüfung f material test(ing).
Materie [ma'te:riə] f (-; -n) **1.** no pl a.
phys. matter. **2.** fig. subject (matter).
materiell [mate'riɛl] adj **1.** material. **2.**
→ **materialistisch**. **3.** financial.
Mathe ['matə] f (-; no pl) F maths, Am.
math. **Mathematik** [matema'ti:k] f (-;
no pl) mathematics. **Mathematiker**
[mate'ma:tikər] m (-s; -) mathemati-
cian. **mathematisch** [mate'ma:tɪʃ] adj
mathematical.
Matinee [mati'ne:] f (-; -n) thea. morning performance.
Matjeshering ['matjəs-] m gastr. young
salted herring.
Matratze [ma'tratsə] f (-; -n) mattress.
Mätresse [mɛ'trɛsə] f (-; -n) mistress.
Matriarchat [matriar'ça:t] n (-[e]s; -e)
matriarchate.
Matrize [ma'tri:tsə] f (-; -n) **1.** (a. **auf ~
schreiben**) stencil. **2.** print. matrix. **3.**
☉ a) die, b) stencil.
Matrose [ma'tro:zə] m (-n; -n) sailor,
seaman.
Matsch [matʃ] m (-[e]s; no pl) F a) mush,
b) mud, c) slush. '**matschig** adj F **1.**
muddy, slushy. **2.** fruit etc: mushy.
matt [mat] adj **1.** dull (shine, colour, eyes,
etc), a. phot. mat(t), frosted (glass),
opal (bulb), dim (light). **2.** faint, weak,
feeble (a. fig. voice, applause, etc), exhausted. **3.** ✝ slack. **4.** (check)mate.
Matte ['matə] f (-; -n) mat.
'**Mattglas** n frosted glass.
mattieren [ma'ti:rən] v/t (h) a) mat(t), b)
frost (glass).

Mattigkeit ['matɪç-] f (-; no pl) fatigue.
'**Mattscheibe** f **1.** phot. focus(s)ing
screen. **2.** a) TV screen, b) F telly, Am.
tube. **3.** F ~ **haben** have a blackout.
Mätzchen ['mɛtsçən] pl F **1.** nonsense. **2.**
tricks: **k-e ~!** none of your tricks!
Mauer ['mauər] f (-; -n) wall: hist. **die
(Berliner)** ~ the (Berlin) Wall.
'**Mauerblümchen** n F fig. wallflower.
mauern ['mauərn] (h) I v/i **1.** build a
wall etc, lay bricks. **2.** F cards: stone-
wall, sports: shut up shop. II v/t build.
'**Mauer|stein** m (building) brick. **~werk**
n (-[e]s; no pl) masonry, brickwork.
Maul [maul] n (-[e]s; ⁙er) **1.** zo. mouth,
jaws. **2.** V trap (sl.): **das ~ aufreißen**
brag; **halt's ~!** shut up!
maulen ['maulən] v/i (h) F grumble.
'**Maulesel** m mule. '**Maulheld** m F braggart. '**Maulkorb** m (a. dat e-n ~ **anlegen**) muzzle (a. fig.). '**Maultier** n mule.
'**Maul- und 'Klauenseuche** f vet.
foot-and-mouth disease.
'**Maulwurf** m (-[e]s; ⁙e) zo. mole.
'**Maulwurfshügel** m molehill.
Maurer ['maurər] m (-s; -) bricklayer.
'**Maurerkelle** f trowel.
'**Maurermeister** m master mason.
maurisch ['maurɪʃ] adj Moorish.
Maus [maus] f (-; ⁙e) mouse: humor.
weiße ~ traffic policeman; F **graue
~** nondescript person; → **Katze, Mäuse.**
mäuschenstill ['mɔysçən-] adj a) (as)
quiet as a mouse, b) stockstill: **es war ~**
not a sound was to be heard.
Mäuse ['mɔyzə] pl **1.** mice: F **weiße ~
sehen** see pink elephants. **2.** F lolly,
Am. bread.
'**Mausefalle** f **1.** mousetrap. **2.** fig.
deathtrap. '**Mauseloch** n mousehole.
mausern ['mauzərn] v/i (a. **sich ~**) (h)
moult: F fig. **sich ~ zu** develop into.
'**mause'tot** adj F stone-dead.
Mausoleum [mauzo'le:ʊm] n (-s; -leen)
mausoleum.
Maut [maut] f (-; -en) toll. '**Mautstraße** f
toll road, Am. turnpike (road). '**Maut-
stelle** f tollhouse, Am. turnpike.
maximal [maksi'ma:l] I adj maximum.
II adv maximally, at (the) most.
Maxime [ma'ksi:mə] f (-; -n) maxim.
Maximum ['maksimʊm] n (-s; -xima)
maximum.

mehrfach

Mayonnaise [majɔ'nɛ:zə] f (-; -n) *gastr.* mayonnaise.

Mäzen [mɛ'tse:n] m (-s; -e) patron, sponsor.

Mechanik [me'ça:nɪk] f (-; -en) **1.** *no pl* mechanics. **2.** mechanism. **Mechaniker** [me'ça:nikər] m (-s; -) mechanic. **mechanisch** [me'ça:nɪʃ] *adj* mechanical, *fig. a.* automatic. **mechanisieren** [meçani'zi:rən] v/t (h) mechanize. **Mechanisierung** f (-; -en) mechanization. **Mechanismus** [meça'nɪsmʊs] m (-; -men) mechanism.

Meckerer ['mɛkərər] m (-s; -) F grumbler. **meckern** ['mɛkərn] v/i (h) **1.** *zo.* bleat. **2.** F grumble (*über acc* about).

Medaille [me'daljə] f (-; -n) medal: → **Kehrseite**.

Me'daillengewinner(in f) m *sports:* medal(l)ist.

Medaillon [medal'jõ:] n (-s; -s) **1.** *art, gastr.* medallion. **2.** locket.

Medien ['me:diən] *pl* media.

'Medienforschung f media research.

'Medienverbund m multimedia system.

Medikament [medika'mɛnt] n (-[e]s; -e) drug, medicament.

Mediothek [medio'te:k] f (-; -en) media library.

Meditation [medita'tsio:n] f (-; -en) meditation.

meditieren [medi'ti:rən] v/i (h) meditate (*über acc* on).

Medium ['me:diʊm] n (-s; -ien) medium.

Medizin [medi'tsi:n] f (-; -en) **1.** *no pl* medicine: **Doktor der ~** doctor of medicine (*abbr.* M.D.). **2.** medicine, medicament.

Medi'ziner m (-s; -) **1.** medical student, F medic. **2.** physician, doctor.

medi'zinisch *adj* a) medical, b) medicinal. **~technische Assi'stentin** (*abbr.* MTA) medical laboratory assistant.

Medi'zinmann m (-[e]s; ⸚er) medicine man.

Meer [me:r] n (-[e]s; -e) sea (*a. fig.*), ocean: **das offene ~** the high seas; **am ~** by the sea, *a. holidays etc* at the seaside.

Meer|busen m gulf. **~enge** f strait(s).

'Meeres|arm m arm of the sea, inlet. **~biolo,gie** f marine biology. **~boden** m → **Meeresgrund. ~früchte** *pl* seafood. **~grund** m seafloor, bottom of the sea. **~kunde** f (-; *no pl*) oceanography.

~spiegel m (**über dem ~** above) sea level.

'Meerrettich m (-s; -e) ♀ horseradish.

'Meersalz n sea salt.

'Meerschweinchen n *zo.* guinea pig.

'Meerwasser n sea water.

Mega... [mega-] mega (*ton, volt, etc*). **Mega'hertz** n megahertz, megacycle.

Megaphon [mega'fo:n] n (-s; -e) megaphone.

Mehl [me:l] n (-[e]s; -e) flour. **'mehlig** *adj* mealy. **'Mehlspeise** f **1.** farinaceous food. **2.** *Austrian* sweet dish.

mehr [me:r] **I** *indef pron* more: **~ als 50 Autos** more than (*or* over) 50 cars; **und dergleichen ~** and the like; (*immer*) **~ und ~** more and more; **was willst du noch ~?** what more do you want? **II** *adj* more: **~ und ~** (*or* **immer ~**) **Leute** more and more people. **III** *adv* more: **um so ~, nur noch ~** all the more; **um so ~ (als)** all the more (as); **nicht ~** a) no more, b) no longer, not any longer; **nie ~** never again; **ich habe keins** (*or* **keine**) **~** I haven't got any more; **ich habe nichts ~** I've got nothing left; **kein Wort ~ (davon)!** not another word (about it)!; **ich kann nicht ~!** a) I'm finished!, b) I couldn't eat another thing!; **er ist ~ praktisch veranlagt** he is more of a practical man.

Mehr n (-[s]; *no pl*) **ein ~ an Zeit (Erfahrung** *etc*) more time (experience *etc*).

'Mehrarbeit f (-; *no pl*) **1.** extra work. **2.** overtime. **'Mehraufwand** m extra (*or* additional) cost(s), time, *etc.* **'Mehrausgaben** *pl* additional expenditure.

'mehrbändig [-bɛndɪç] *adj* in several volumes.

'Mehrbedarf m extra (*or* increased) demand. **'Mehrbelastung** f additional load (*fig.* burden). **'Mehrbetrag** m **1.** surplus. **2.** extra charge.

'mehrdeutig [-dɔytɪç] *adj* ambiguous.

'Mehreinkommen n additional revenue.

mehren ['me:rən] v/t (*a.* **sich ~**) (h) increase.

mehrere ['me:rərə] *adj or indef pron* several.

'mehrfach I *adj* a) several, b) repeated, c) *esp.* ⊛ *etc* multiple: **~e Verletzungen** multiple injuries; **in ~er Hinsicht** in several respects; **~er deutscher Mei-**

ster several times German champion.
II *adv* a) several times, b) repeatedly:
ein Mehrfaches der Summe several
times the amount; *er ist ~ vorbestraft*
he has several previous convictions.

'Mehrfachstecker *m* multiple plug.

'Mehrfa,milienhaus *n* multiple dwelling. **'Mehrgepäck** *n* excess luggage.
'Mehrgewicht *n* excess weight.

'Mehrheit *f* (-; -en) majority: *mit absoluter (einfacher, knapper, großer) ~*
by an absolute (a simple, a narrow, a
large) majority; *mit zehn Stimmen ~*
by a majority of ten; → *schweigend.*

'mehrheitlich *adj and adv* (by the) majority.

'Mehrheits|beschluß *m* majority decision. **~beteiligung** *f* ✝ controlling interest. **~wahlrecht** *n* majority vote system.

'mehrjährig [-jɛːrɪç] *adj* of (or lasting)
several years, several years' ...

'Mehrkosten *pl* a) additional (or extra)
cost(s), b) extra charge.

'mehrmalig [-maːlɪç] *adj* repeated.
'mehrmals *adv* several times.

'Mehrpar,teiensy,stem *n* multiparty
system.

'mehrseitig [-zaɪtɪç] *adj* **1.** ✠ polygonal.
2. *pol.* multilateral.

'mehrsilbig [-zɪlbɪç] *adj* polysyllabic.

'mehrsprachig [-ʃpraːxɪç] *adj* polyglot,
multilingual.

'mehrstellig [-ʃtɛlɪç] *adj* multidigit.

'mehrstimmig [-ʃtɪmɪç] *adj* polyphonic,
for several voices: *~er Gesang* part
singing.

'mehrstöckig [-ʃtœkɪç] *adj* multistor(e)y.

'mehrstündig [-ʃtʏndɪç] *adj* of (or lasting) several hours.

'mehrtägig [-tɛːgɪç] *adj* of (or lasting)
several days.

'mehrteilig [-taɪlɪç] *adj* consisting of several parts, (*film* etc) in several parts.

'Mehrverbrauch *m* increased consumption. **'Mehrwertsteuer** *f* value-added
tax (*abbr.* VAT). **'Mehrzahl** *f* (-; *no pl*)
1. majority. **2.** *ling.* plural.

'Mehrzweck... multipurpose ...

meiden ['maɪdən] *v/t* (mied, gemieden,
h) avoid.

Meile ['maɪlə] *f* (-; -n) mile.

'Meilenstein *m* a. fig. milestone.

'meilenweit *adv* for miles (and miles): *~
entfernt von a. fig.* miles (away) from.

mein [maɪn] *pos pron* my: *~er, ~e, ~(e)s,
der (die, das) mein(ig)e* mine; *die
Mein(ig)en* my family, F my people,
my folks; *ich habe das Mein(ig)e getan* I've done my share (or bit).

'Meineid *m* (e-n *~ leisten* commit) perjury. **'meineidig** *adj* perjured: *~ werden* perjure o.s., commit perjury.

meinen ['maɪnən] *v/i* (h) **1.** think, believe: *was ~ Sie dazu?* what do you
think?; *~ Sie (wirklich)?* do you (really)
think so? **2.** mean: *wie ~ Sie das?* a)
how do you mean?, b) what do you
mean by that?; *~ Sie das ernst?* do you
really mean it?; *so war es nicht gemeint* I (he *etc*) didn't mean it (like
that); *sie meint es gut* she means well
(*mit dir* by you); *es war gut gemeint* it
was well-meant; *er hat es nicht böse
gemeint* he meant no harm. **3.** refer to,
mean: *~ Sie ihn?* do you mean him? **4.**
mean, signify. **5.** *wenn du meinst* if
you say so; *wie Sie ~* as you wish; *ich
meine ja nur!* it was just a thought!

meiner ['maɪnər] *pers pron* (*gen of ich*)
(of) me: *erinnern Sie sich ~?* do you
remember me? **'meinerseits** [-zaɪts]
adv for my part: *ganz ~!* for one; *ganz ~*
a) the pleasure is (or has been) mine, b)
humor. same here!

'meines'gleichen *indef pron* people like
me, F the likes of me.

meinet'wegen ['maɪnət-] *adv* **1.** a) on
my account, because of me, b) for my
sake. **2.** *~ kann er gehen* I don't mind if
he goes, *iro.* he can go for all I care. **3.**
let's say.

meinige ['maɪnɪgə] → *mein.*

'Meinung *f* (-; -en) opinion (*über acc* of,
about, on): *e-e schlechte ~ haben von*
have a low opinion of; *m-r ~ nach* in
my opinion; *der ~ sein* think, believe,
be of the opinion; *derselben (anderer)
~ sein* (dis)agree; *ganz m-r ~!* I quite
agree!; F *j-m gehörig die ~ sagen* give
s.o. a piece of one's mind; → *geteilt.*

'Meinungs|äußerung *f* expression of
one's opinion, statement. **~austausch**
m exchange of views (*über acc* on).
♀bildend *adj* opinion-forming. **~bildung** *f* forming of an opinion: *öffentliche ~* forming of public opinion. **~for-**

scher *m* pollster. **~forschung** *f* opinion research. **~freiheit** *f* (-; *no pl*) freedom of opinion (*or* speech). **~führer** *m* opinion-leader. **~umfrage** *f* (public) opinion poll. **~umschwung** *m* swing of opinion. **~verschiedenheit** *f* **1.** difference of opinion. **2.** disagreement, argument (**über** *acc* about).

Meise ['maɪzə] *f* (-; -n) **1.** tit(mouse). **2.** F **du hast wohl 'ne ~?** you must be nuts!

Meißel ['maɪsəl] *m* (-s; -) chisel.

meißeln ['maɪsəln] *v/t, v/i* (h) chisel.

Meißner ['maɪsnər] **~ Porzellan** Dresden china.

meist [maɪst] **I** *adj* **1.** most, most of: **die ~en Leute** most people; **die ~e Zeit** most of the time. **II** *indef pron* **2.** **das ~e (davon)** most of it; **die ~en** a) most (of them), b) most people. **III** *adv* **3.** → **meistens. 4. am ~en** most.

'**meistbietend** *adj* **~er Interessent** highest bidder: **~ verkaufen** sell to the highest bidder.

meistens ['maɪstəns], '**meistenteils** *adv* mostly, usually, most of the time.

Meister ['maɪstər] *m* (-s; -) **1.** master (craftsman): **s-n ~ machen** take one's master craftsman's diploma. **2.** foreman. **3.** *a. fig. or iro.* master: → **Übung** 1. **4.** *sports:* champion(s). '**Meisterbrief** *m* master craftsman's diploma.

'**meisterhaft** **I** *adj* masterly. **II** *adv* brilliantly: *iro.* **~ es ~ verstehen zu lügen** *etc* be an expert liar *etc*.

'**Meisterin** *f* (-; -nen) **1.** master craftswoman. **2.** forewoman. **3.** master's wife. **4.** → **Meister** 3, 4.

'**Meisterleistung** *f* masterly performance, great feat.

meistern ['maɪstərn] *v/t* (h) master.

'**Meisterprüfung** *f* examination for the master craftsman's diploma.

'**Meisterschaft** *f* (-; -en) **1.** *no pl* mastery. **2.** *sports:* championship, *a.* title.

'**Meisterstück** *n fig.* masterstroke.

'**Meisterwerk** *n* masterpiece.

Melancholie [melaŋkoˈliː] *f* (-; -n) melancholy. **melancholisch** [melaŋˈkoːlɪʃ] *adj* melancholy.

Melanom [melaˈnoːm] *n* (-s; -e) *🞋* melanoma.

melden ['mɛldən] (h) **I** *v/t* **1.** a) report, register (*birth etc*), b) announce: **j-m et. ~** notify s.o. of s.th.; F **er hat nichts zu ~** he has no say (in the matter), *w.s.* he has no chance (**gegen j-n** against s.o.). **2.** *sports:* enter. **II sich ~ 3.** report (**bei** to, **zur Arbeit** for work): **sich polizeilich ~** register with the police; → **krank.** **4.** get in touch (**bei** with): **sich freiwillig ~** volunteer (**zu** for); **ich werde mich (wieder) ~** I'll be in touch; **wenn du et. brauchst, melde dich!** if you need anything, let me know!; **sich auf ein Inserat ~** answer an advertisement. **5.** answer (the phone): **es meldet sich niemand** there is no reply. **6.** *ped.* put up one's hand. **7.** *sports:* enter (one's name) (**für** for). **8.** *fig.* make itself felt.

'**Meldepflicht** *f* obligatory registration, *🞏* duty of notification.

'**meldepflichtig** *adj* subject to registration, *🞏* notifiable.

'**Meldung** *f* (-; -en) **1.** report, *a.* news (item), announcement, notification, (*radio etc*) message. **2.** registration (**bei** with). **3.** (**zu** for) application, *for exam etc, a. sports:* entry.

melken ['mɛlkən] *v/t, v/i* (melkte/molk, gemelkt/gemolken, h) *a. fig.* milk.

'**Melkma,schine** *f* milking machine.

Melodie [meloˈdiː] *f* (-; -n) melody, tune.

melodiös [meloˈdiøːs], **melodisch** [meˈloːdɪʃ] *adj* melodic.

Melodrama [meloˈdraːma] *n* (-s; -en) *a.* F *fig.* melodrama. **melodra'matisch** *adj a.* F *fig.* melodramatic.

Melone [meˈloːnə] *f* (-; -n) *🞋* melon.

Membran [mɛmˈbraːn] *f* (-; -en) *anat.* membrane, *a.* ⚙ diaphragm.

Memoiren [meˈmŏaːrən] *pl* memoirs.

Memorandum [memoˈrandʊm] *n* (-s; -den, -da) memorandum.

Menge ['mɛŋə] *f* (-; -n) **1.** quantity, amount, ↊ set: **e-e (große) ~ von** a lot of, F lots of; **e-e ~ Bücher** *a.* a great many books; F **jede ~ Geld, Geld in rauhen ~n** heaps of money. **2.** crowd.

mengen ['mɛŋən] (h) **I** *v/t* mix (**in** *acc* into). **II sich ~** → **mischen** II.

'**Mengenangabe** *f* (indication of) quantity. '**Mengenlehre** *f* (-; *no pl*) ↊ set theory. '**mengenmäßig** *adj* quantitative. '**Mengen,batt** *m* ⚖ bulk (*or* quantity) discount.

Meniskus [meˈnɪskʊs] *m* (-; -ken) *anat.* meniscus.

Mensa ['mɛnza] f (-; -s, Mensen) (university) canteen.

Mensch [mɛnʃ] m (-en; -en) **1.** human being: *der ~* man; *ich bin auch nur ein ~!* I'm only human! **2.** → *Menschheit.* **3.** person, man (woman): *kein ~* not a soul, nobody; *(die) ~en* people; *gern unter ~en sein* enjoy human company; *F ~!* → *Menschenkind.*

Mensch, ärgere dich nicht! n ludo.

'Menschen|affe m ape. **~alter** n **1.** generation. **2.** lifetime. **~feind** m misanthropist. **~fresser** m **1.** cannibal. **2.** zo. man-eater. **~freund** m philanthropist. **~gedenken** n *seit ~* within living memory. **~gestalt** f *in ~* in human form; *ein Teufel in ~* a devil incarnate. **~hand** f *von ~ geschaffen* man-made. **~handel** m slave trade. **~haß** m misanthropy. **~kenner** m good judge of character. **~kenntnis** f (-; no pl) knowledge of human nature. **~leben** n **1.** (human) life: *~ sind nicht zu beklagen* there were no fatalities. **2.** lifetime. **2leer** adj deserted. **~menge** f crowd (of people). **2möglich** adj *das ~e* everything that is humanly possible. **~raub** m kidnapping. **~rechte** pl human rights. **2scheu** adj shy, unsociable. **~schlag** m (-[e]s; no pl) breed (of people). **~seele** f **1.** human soul. **2.** *k-e ~* not a living soul.

'Menschenskind int a) good heavens!, b) for heaven's sake.

'menschenunwürdig adj a) degrading, b) *dwelling etc*: unfit for human beings.

'Menschenverstand m *gesunder ~* common sense.

'Menschenwürde f *the* dignity of man.

'Menschheit *die ~* (-; no pl) mankind.

'menschlich adj **1.** human: *die ~e Natur* human nature; *nach ~em Ermessen* as far as one can possibly judge. **2.** humane. **3.** F tolerable.

'Menschlichkeit f (-; no pl) humaneness, humanity: *Verbrechen gegen die ~* crime against humanity.

Menstruation [mɛnstrua'tsi̯oːn] f (-; -en) 🌸 menstruation. **menstruieren** [mɛnstru'iːrən] v/i (h) 🌸 menstruate.

Mentalität [mɛntali'tɛːt] f (-; -en) mentality.

Menthol [mɛn'toːl] n (-s; no pl) 🌿 menthol: *mit ~* mentholated.

Menü [me'nyː] n (-s; -s) **1.** *gastr.* set meal,

set lunch. **2.** *computer*: menu.

Menuett [me'nu̯ɛt] n (-[e]s; -e) ♪ minuet.

Meridian [meri'di̯aːn] m (-s; -e) *astr., geogr.* meridian.

'Merkblatt n leaflet.

merken ['mɛrkən] v/t (h) **1.** a) notice, b) feel, sense, c) realize, see, d) discover: *et. ~ a.* become aware of s.th.; *man merkte an s-r Stimme, daß* you could tell by his voice that. **2.** *~ lassen* show, let on. **3.** *sich ~* a) remember, b) make a mental note of; *merk dir das!* remember that!

'merklich I adj a) noticeable, b) marked, c) considerable. **II** adv noticeably (*etc*).

'Merkmal n (-[e]s; -e) characteristic: *besondere ~e* distinguishing marks.

Merkur [mɛr'kuːr] m (-s; no pl) *astr.* Mercury.

'merkwürdig adj strange, odd. **'merkwürdigerweise** adv oddly enough.

'Meßband n (-[e]s; ⁀er) tape measure.

'meßbar adj measurable.

'Meßbecher m measuring cup.

'Meßdiener m *eccl.* server.

Messe¹ ['mɛsə] f (-; -n) *eccl.* mass: *(die) ~ lesen* say Mass.

'Messe² f (-; -n) ✕ mess.

'Messe³ f (-; -n) (trade) fair.

'Messe|besucher(in f) m visitor to a (or the) fair. **~gelände** n exhibition cent/re (*Am.* -er). **~halle** f exhibition hall.

messen ['mɛsən] (maß, gemessen, h) **I** v/t measure, ⊙ *a.* ga(u)ge: *die Zeit ~* time; *j-n mit Blicken ~* size s.o. up. **II** *sich mit j-m ~* match o.s. against s.o., *sports*: compete with s.o.; *sich nicht ~ können mit* a) *j-m* be no match for s.o., b) *e-r Sache* not to stand comparison with s.th. **III** v/i measure, be ... long (or high, wide, *etc*), *person*: be ... (tall).

Messer ['mɛsər] n (-s; -) knife, 🔪 *a.* scalpel, ⊙ *a.* blade: *Kampf bis aufs ~* fight to the death; *auf (des) ~s Schneide stehen* be on a razor's edge; *F j-n ans ~ liefern* betray s.o.

'messerscharf adj *a.* fig. razor-sharp.

'Messerspitze f knife point: *e-e ~ Salz* a pinch of salt.

'Messerstecherei f knifing.

'Messerstich m **1.** stab. **2.** stab wound.

'Messestand m exhibition stand.

'Meßgerät n measuring instrument.

'Meßglas n graduated measuring glass.

Messias [mɛˈsiːas] *m* (-; *no pl*) Messiah.

Messing [ˈmɛsɪŋ] *n* (-s; *no pl*) brass.

'Meßinstru,ment *n* → **Meßgerät**.

'Meßuhr *f* meter, dial ga(u)ge.

'Meßtischblatt *n* ordnance map.

'Messung *f* (-; -en) measurement.

Metall [meˈtal] *n* (-s; -e) metal.

Me'tallarbeiter *m* metalworker. **~in.du,strie** *f* metalworking industry.

me'tallisch *adj* metal, *a. fig.* metallic.

Metallurgie [metalʊrˈgiː] *f* (-; *no pl*) metallurgy. **metallurgisch** [metaˈlʊr.gɪʃ] *adj* metallurgic(al).

Me'tall|verarbeitung *f* metal processing. **~waren** *pl* metal goods, hardware.

Metamorphose [metamɔrˈfoːzə] *f* (-; -n) metamorphosis.

Metapher [meˈtafər] *f* (-; -n) metaphor.

Metaphy'sik [meta-] *f* metaphysics.

meta'physisch *adj* metaphysical.

Metastase [metaˈstaːzə] *f* (-; -n) *✻* metastasis.

Meteor [meteˈoːr] *m* (-s; -e) meteor.

Meteorit [meteoˈriːt] *m* (-s; -e) meteorite. **Meteorologe** [meteoroˈloːgə] *m* (-n; -n) meteorologist. **Meteorologie** [meteorolo'giː] *f* (-; *no pl*) meteorology. **meteoro'logisch** *adj* meteorological.

Meter [ˈmeːtər] *n, m* (-s; -) metre, *Am.* meter. **'meterlang** *adj* very long.

'Meterware *f* yard goods.

Methode [meˈtoːdə] *f* (-; -n) method.

Methodik [meˈtoːdɪk] *f* (-; -en) **1.** *no pl* methodology. **2.** method(s).

me'thodisch *adj* methodical.

Methylalkohol [meˈtyːl-] *m* (-s; *no pl*) methyl alcohol.

Metier [meˈtĩeː] *n* (-s; -s) profession, job.

Metrik [ˈmeːtrɪk] *f* (-; -en) **1.** metre, *Am.* meter. **metrisch** [ˈmeːtrɪʃ] *adj* **1.** metric. **2.** *♪ etc* metrical.

Metropole [metroˈpoːlə] *f* (-; -) metropolis.

Metzger [ˈmɛtsgər] *m* (-s; -) butcher. **Metzge'rei** *f* (-; -en) butcher's shop.

Meute [ˈmɔʏtə] *f* (-; -n) **1.** *hunt.* pack (of hounds). **2.** F mob.

Meute'rei *f* (-; -en) mutiny. **'Meuterer** *m* (-s; -) mutineer. **meutern** [ˈmɔʏtərn] *v/i* (h) a) mutiny, b) F rebel. **'meuternd** *adj* mutinous.

Mexikaner [mɛksiˈkaːnər] *m* (-s; -), **Mexi'kanerin** *f* (-; -nen), **mexi'ka-**

nisch [-nɪʃ] *adj* Mexican. **Mexiko** [ˈmɛksiko] *n* (-s) Mexico.

miau [miˈaʊ] *int*, **mi'auen** *v/i* (h) miaow.

mich [mɪç] **I** *pers pron* me. **II** *reflex pron* myself.

mick(e)rig [ˈmɪk(ə)rɪç] *adj* F **1.** measly (*pay etc*). **2.** puny, sickly.

mied [miːt] *pret of* **meiden.**

Mieder [ˈmiːdər] *n* (-s; -) bodice.

'Miederhöschen *n* panty girdle.

'Miederwaren *pl* foundation garments.

Mief [miːf] *m* (-[e]s; *no pl*) F fug, pong.

Miene [ˈmiːnə] *f* (-; -n) expression, face: *überlegene* ~ superior air; *e-e ernste* ~ *aufsetzen* look serious; *gute* ~ *zum bösen Spiel machen* put on a brave face, grin and bear it; *~ machen, et. zu tun* make as if to do s.th.; *ohne e-e* ~ *zu verziehen* without batting an eyelid.

'Mienenspiel *n* facial expressions.

mies [miːs] F **I** *adj* bad, lousy: *~e Laune haben* be in a foul mood; *j-n (et.)* ~ *machen* run s.o. (s.th.) down; *~er Kerl* bastard; *~e Sache* dirty business. **II** *adv sich ~ fühlen* feel lousy; *es geht ihm* ~ he's in a bad way.

Miesepeter [ˈmiːzəpeːtər] *m* (-s; -) F sourpuss.

Miesmuschel [ˈmiːs-] *f zo.* mussel.

Miete [ˈmiːtə] *f* (-; -n) rent: *zur* ~ *wohnen* live in a rented flat.

'Mieteinnahme *f* rental income.

mieten [ˈmiːtən] *v/t* (h) rent, a. hire (*car*).

Mieter [ˈmiːtər] *m* (-s; -), **'Mieterin** *f* (-; -nen) tenant. **'Mieterschutz** *m* (legal) protection of tenants.

'mietfrei *adj* rent-free.

'Miet|gebühr *f* rental (charge). **~kauf** *m* hire purchase. **~preis** *m* rent.

'Mietshaus *n* block of flats, *Am.* apartment house.

'Miet|verhältnis *n* tenancy. **~vertrag** *m* a) lease, b) hire contract. **~wagen** *m* hire(d) car. **~wohnung** *f* (rented) flat, *Am.* apartment.

Migräne [miˈgrɛːnə] *f* (-; -n) *✻* migraine.

Mikro [ˈmiːkro] *n* (-s; -s) F mike.

Mikrobe [miˈkroːbə] *f* (-; -n) microbe.

Mikroche'mie [mikro-] *f* microchemistry. **Mikrochirur'gie** *f* microsurgery.

Mikrocom,puter [ˈmiːkro-] *m* microcomputer. **'Mikroelek,tronik** *f* microelectronics. **'Mikrofilm** *m* microfilm.

Mikro'kosmos *m* microcosm.

Mikroorga'nismus *m* microorganism.
Mikrophon [mikro'fo:n] *n* (-s; -e) microphone.
'**Mikropro,zessor** *m* microprocessor.
Mikroskop [mikro'sko:p] *n* (-s; -e) microscope. **mikro'skopisch** *adj* (a. ~ **klein**) microscopic(al).
'**Mikrowelle** *f* microwave.
'**Mikrowellenherd** *m* microwave oven.
Milbe ['mɪlbə] *f* (-; -n) *zo.* mite.
Milch [mɪlç] *f* (-; *no pl*) **1.** (**dicke** *or* **saure** ~ curdled) milk. **2.** *zo.* (soft) roe.
'**Milch|bar** *f* milk bar. **~brei** *m* milk pudding. **~flasche** *f* milk bottle. **~geschäft** *n* dairy. **~glas** *n* ✲ frosted glass.
'**milchig** *adj* milky.
'**Milch|kaf,fee** *m* white coffee. **~kännchen** *n* milk jug. **~kanne** *f* milk can. **~kuh** *f* milcher. **~mädchenrechnung** *F* naive reasoning. **~mixgetränk** *n* milk shake. **~pro,dukte** *pl* dairy products. **~pulver** *n* powdered milk. **~reis** *m* rice pudding. **~schorf** *m* 🌸 milk crust. **~straße** *f* Milky Way. **~wirtschaft** *f* dairy farming. **~zahn** *m* milk tooth.
mild [mɪlt] *adj* mild, *a.* gentle (*climate, reproof, etc*), *a.* lenient (*judge, penalty, etc*), *a.* light (*food*), soft (*light*): **~e gesagt** to put it mildly; **et. ~e beurteilen** take a lenient view of s.th.
Milde ['mɪldə] *f* (-; *no pl*) **1.** mildness (*etc,* → *mild*). **2.** leniency.
mildern ['mɪldərn] (h) **I** *v/t* soften (*blow, contrast, etc*), ease (*pain etc*), soothe, alleviate (*a.* grief *etc*), moderate (*one's views etc*), mitigate (*sentence etc*), reduce (*effect*): ⚖ **~de Umstände** extenuating circumstances. **II sich ~** grow milder, *pain:* ease, *views etc:* soften.
'**Milderung** *f* (-; *no pl*) alleviation, mitigation, moderation. '**Milderungsgrund** *m* ⚖ extenuating circumstance.
Milieu [mi'liø:] *n* (-s; -s) environment (*a. biol.,* 🐾), *a.* (social) background.
mili'eubedingt *adj* due to environmental factors.
mili'eugeschädigt *adj* deprived.
militant [mili'tant] *adj* militant.
Militär [mili'tɛ:r] *n* (-s; *no pl*) **1.** (**beim** ~ in the) armed forces (*or* army). **2.** military personnel, soldiers. **~arzt** *m* medical officer. **~atta,ché** *m* military attaché. **~dikta,tur** *f* military dictatorship.
mili'tärisch *adj* **1.** military. **2.** martial.

Militarismus [milita'rɪsmʊs] *m* (-; *no pl*) militarism. **Militarist** [milita'rɪst] *m* (-en; -en) militarist. **milita'ristisch** *adj* militaristic.
Mili'tär|ka,pelle *f* military band. **~mission** *f* military mission. **~poli,zei** *f* military police. **~putsch** *m* military putsch. **~re,gierung** *f* military government.
Military ['mɪlɪtəri] *f* (-; -s) three-day event. **~reiter** *m* three-day eventer.
Mili'tärzeit *f* time of (military) service.
Miliz [mi'li:ts] *f* (-; -en) militia.
Milliardär [mɪliar'dɛ:r] *m* (-s; -e) multimillionaire.
Milliarde [mɪ'liardə] *f* (-; -n) billion.
Milli|meter [mɪli-] *n, m* millimet/re (*Am.* -er). **~arbeit** *f* F **das war ~** that was a precision job. **~pa,pier** *n* graph paper.
Million [mɪ'lio:n] *f* (-; -en) million: **5 ~en Dollar** five million dollars. **Millionär** [mɪlio'nɛ:r] *m* (-s; -e) millionaire.
Milli'onengeschäft *n* multimillion dollar *etc* deal. **Milli'onenstadt** *f* city of over a million inhabitants.
milli'onstel *adj* millionth.
Milz [mɪlts] *f* (-; -en) *anat.* spleen.
Mime ['mi:mə] *m* (-n; -n) actor. '**mimen** *v/t* (h) act, play. **Mimik** ['mi:mɪk] *f* (-; *no pl*) mimic art. '**mimisch** *adj* mimic.
Mimose [mi'mo:zə] *f* (-; -n) **1.** 🌸 mimosa. **2.** *fig.* oversensitive person.
Minarett [mina'rɛt] *n* (-s; -e) minaret.
minder ['mɪndər] **I** *adv* less: **nicht ~** no less. **II** *adj* a) less(er), b) minor, c) inferior (*quality*). '**minderbegabt** *adj* less gifted. '**minderbemittelt** *adj* less well-off: F **geistig ~** not very bright.
'**Minderheit** *f* (-; -en) minority; → *a.* **Minderzahl.** '**Minderheitsre,gierung** *f* minority(-party) government.
'**minderjährig** [-jɛ:rɪç] *adj* ⚖ minor, under age. '**Minderjährige** [-jɛ:rɪgə] *m, f* (-n; -n) minor.
'**Minderjährigkeit** *f* (-; *no pl*) minority.
mindern ['mɪndərn] (h) **I** *v/t* a) lessen, reduce, lower, b) detract from. **II sich ~** diminish, decrease.
'**Minderung** *f* (-; -en) a) (*gen*) decrease (in), reduction (in, of), b) depreciation.
'**minderwertig** *adj* inferior, ✝ *a.* of inferior quality. '**Minderwertigkeit** *f* (-; *no pl*) inferiority, ✝ inferior quality.

'Minderwertigkeitskom,plex *m* inferiority complex.

'Minderzahl *f* (-; *no pl*) **in der ~ sein** a) be in the minority, b) be outnumbered.

mindest ['mındəst] *adj* least, slightest: **nicht im ~en** not in the least, not at all; **zum ~en** at least; **das ~e** the least.

'Mindest... minimum (*age, price, wage, etc*). **~betrag** *m* minimum (amount).

mindestens ['mındəstəns] *adv* at least.

'Mindestmaß *n* (**auf das ~ beschränken**) keep *s.th.* down to a minimum.

Mine ['mi:nə] *f* (-; -n) **1.** ☊, ✕ mine. **2.** *of pencil*: lead, *of ball pen*: refill.

'Minen|feld *n* ✕ minefield. **~leger** *m* (-s; -) ⚓, ✕ minelayer. **~räumboot** *n*, **~suchboot** *n* ✕ minesweeper.

Mineral [minə'ra:l] *n* (-s; -e, -ien) mineral. **Mineralogie** [minəralo'gi:] *f* (-; *no pl*) mineralogy.

Mine'ral|öl *n* mineral oil. **~quelle** *f* mineral spring. **~wasser** *n* mineral water.

Miniatur [minia'tu:r] *f* (-; -en) miniature.

miniaturisieren [miniaturi'zi:rən] *v/t* (h) ⊛ miniaturize.

Minigolf ['mi:ni-] *n* miniature golf.

Minikleid *n* minidress.

minimal [mini'ma:l] *adj* minimal, minimum, *fig.* negligible. **Minimum** ['mi:nimɔm] *n* (-s; -ma) minimum.

Minirock *m* miniskirt.

Minister [mi'nıstər] *m* (-s; -) minister, *Br.* Secretary of State, *Am.* Secretary.

Ministerialbeamte [ministe'riʾa:l-] *m* ministry official.

Ministerium [minis'te:riʾom] *n* (-s; -rien) ministry, *Am.* department.

Mi'nisterpräsi,dent *m* Prime Minister.

Mi'nisterrat *m* **1.** cabinet (council). **2.** *EC:* Council of Ministers.

Ministrant [minis'trant] *m* (-en; -en) *eccl.* ministrant, server.

Minnesänger ['mınə-] *m* minnesinger.

minus ['mi:nʊs] **I** *prep* minus. **II** *adv* **~ 10 Grad** ten degrees below zero.

'Minus *n* (-; *no pl*) **1.** deficit. **2.** *fig.* disadvantage. **'Minuspunkt** *m* **1.** *sports:* penalty point. **2.** *fig.* minus, drawback. **'Minuszeichen** *n* ⅍ minus sign.

Minute [mi'nu:tə] *f* (-; -n) minute (*a. astr., ⅍*): **auf die ~ pünktlich** on the dot; **in letzter ~** at the last moment; **es klappte auf die ~** it was perfectly timed.

mi'nutenlang I *adj* lasting several min-

utes, several minutes of ... **II** *adv* for (several) minutes.

Mi'nutenzeiger *m* minute-hand.

minuziös [minu'tsiø:s] *adj* detailed, meticulous.

Minze ['mıntsə] *f* (-; -n) ❀ mint.

mir [mi:r] *pers pron* a) me, to me, b) (to) myself: **gib es ~!** give it to me!; **ich wusch ~ die Hände** I washed my hands; **ein Freund von ~** a friend of mine; **von ~ aus** → *meinetwegen*; F **~ nichts, dir nichts** just like that; **wie du ~, so ich dir** tit for tat.

Mirabelle [mira'bɛlə] *f* (-; -n) ❀ yellow plum.

'Mischehe *f* mixed marriage.

mischen ['mıʃən] (h) **I** *v/t* mix (*a. radio, film, etc*), blend (*tea, tobacco, etc*), shuffle (*cards*), *computer:* merge. **II sich ~ unter** (*acc*) mix (*or* mingle) with; **sich ~ in** (*acc*) interfere (*or* meddle) in; **sich in ein Gespräch ~** join in (*or* butt in on) the conversation. **III** *v/i* shuffle.

'Mischer *m* (-s; -) *a. TV* mixer.

'Mischling *m* (-s; -e) **1.** *biol.* hybrid. **2.** half-caste, half-breed.

'Mischmasch ['mıʃmaʃ] *m* (-[e]s; -e) F hotchpotch.

'Mischpult *n* radio, TV mixer.

'Mischrasse *f* mixed race.

'Mischung *f* (-; -en) mixture (*a. fig.*), blend (*of tea etc*), assortment (*of chocolates etc*).

'Mischwald *m* mixed forest.

'Mischwort *n* (-[e]s; -wer) hybrid (word).

miserabel [mizeʾra:bəl] *adj* F lousy.

Misere [mi'ze:rə] *f* (-; -n) calamity.

miß'achten [mıs-] *v/t* (*insep, no -ge-*, h) **1.** ignore. **2.** disdain, despise.

'Mißachtung *f* **1.** disregard. **2.** disdain: **~ des Gerichts** contempt of court.

'Mißbehagen *n* feeling of uneasiness.

'Mißbildung *f* (-; -en) deformity.

miß'billigen *v/t* (*insep, no -ge-*, h) disapprove (of).

'Mißbilligung *f* (-; *no pl*) disapproval.

'Mißbrauch *m* abuse, misuse. **miß'brauchen** *v/t* (*insep, no -ge-*, h) abuse.

miß'deuten *v/t* (*insep, no -ge-*, h) misinterpret.

'Mißdeutung *f* misinterpretation.

'Mißerfolg *m* failure, F flop.

'Mißernte *f* crop failure.

miß'fallen *v/i* (*irr, insep, no -ge-*, h, →

Mißfallen 408

fallen) **er (es) mißfällt mir** I don't like him (it). **'Mißfallen** *n* (-s) disapproval: *j-s ~ erregen* incur s.o.'s displeasure. **'Mißfallensäußerung** *f* expression of disapproval.

'**mißgebildet** *adj* deformed.

'**Mißgeburt** *f* freak.

'**Mißgeschick** *n* (-[e]s; -e) a) bad luck, misfortune, b) mishap.

miß'gönnen *v/t* (*insep, no* -ge-, h) *j-m et. ~* begrudge s.o. s.th.

'**Mißgriff** *m* mistake.

'**Mißgunst** *f* resentment.

'**mißgünstig** *adj* resentful.

miß'handeln *v/t* (*insep, no* -ge-, h) maltreat. **Miß'handlung** *f* maltreatment, ⚖ assault and battery.

Mission [mɪˈsǐoːn] *f* (-; -en) mission.

Missionar [mɪsǐoˈnaːr] *m* (-s; -e), **mis-sio'narisch** *adj* missionary.

missionieren [mɪsǐoˈniːrən] (h) **I** *v/i* do missionary work. **II** *v/t* convert.

'**Mißklang** *m a. fig.* dissonance.

'**Mißkre,dit** *m in ~ bringen* (*geraten*) bring discredit upon (get a bad name).

'**mißlich** *adj* awkward, difficult.

mißlingen [mɪsˈlɪŋən] (mißlang, mißlungen, sn) *v/i* fail, be unsuccessful.

'**mißmutig** *adj* disgruntled, morose.

miß'raten I *v/i* (mißriet, mißraten, sn) fail, turn out a failure: *das ist mir ~* I've bungled it. **II** *adj* wayward (*child*).

'**Mißstand** *m* deplorable state of affairs: *Mißstände abschaffen* remedy abuses.

miß'trauen *v/i* (*insep, no* -ge-, h) (*dat*) distrust, mistrust. '**Mißtrauen** *n* (-s) (*gegen* of) distrust, mistrust: *j-s ~ er-regen* arouse s.o.'s suspicion.

'**Mißtrauensantrag** *m parl.* motion of no confidence. '**Mißtrauensvotum** *n parl.* vote of no confidence.

'**mißtrauisch** [-trauɪʃ] *adj* (*gegen* of) a) distrustful, b) suspicious, c) doubtful: *j-n ~ machen* arouse s.o.'s suspicion.

'**Mißverhältnis** *n* disproportion: *in e-m ~ stehen* be out of proportion (*zu* to).

'**mißverständlich** *adj* misleading.

'**Mißverständnis** *n* (-ses; -se) misunder-standing. '**mißverstehen** *v/t* (mißver-stand, mißverstanden, h) misunder-stand, mistake.

'**Mißwahl** *f* beauty contest.

'**Mißwirtschaft** *f* mismanagement.

Mist [mɪst] *m* (-[e]s; *no pl*) **1.** a) dung, manure, b) droppings. **2.** F rubbish, crap: *~ machen* mess it up; *~ verzap-fen* talk rot; *(so ein) ~!* damn it!

Mistel [ˈmɪstəl] *f* (-; -n) ⚘ mistletoe.

'**Mistelzweig** *m* sprig of mistletoe.

'**Mistgabel** *f* pitchfork. '**Misthaufen** *m* manure heap. '**Mistkäfer** *m* dungbee-tle. '**Mistkerl** *m* V bastard. '**Miststück** *n* V a) bastard, b) bitch.

mit [mɪt] **I** *prep* **1.** with: *ein Haus ~ Gar-ten* a house with a garden; *Zimmer ~ Frühstück* bed and breakfast; *ein Korb ~ Obst* a basket of fruit. **2.** by, with: *~ der Bahn etc* by train etc; *~ Bleistift* in pencil; *~ Gewalt* by force. **3.** *~ Absicht* intentionally; *~ lauter Stimme* in a loud voice; *~ Verlust* at a loss; *~ einem Wort* in a word; *~ 8 zu 11 Stimmen* by 8 votes to 11; *was ist ~ ihm?* what's the matter with him?; *wie steht's ~ dir?* how about you? **4.** *~ 20 Jahren* at (the age of) twenty; *~ dem 3. Mai* as of May 3rd; *~ Zeit* 1. **II** *adv* **5.** also, too: *~ dabeisein* be there too; *das gehört ~ dazu* that's part (and parcel) of it; *er war ~ der beste* he was one of the best.

'**Mitangeklagte** *m, f* co-defendant.

'**Mitarbeit** *f* (-; *no pl*) cooperation, col-laboration, *a.* assistance (*bei* in): *unter ~ von* (*or gen*) in collaboration with.

'**mitarbeiten** *v/i* (*sep,* -ge-, h) a) (*an dat, bei*) a) cooperate (in), collaborate (on), b) contribute (to *a paper etc*), c) *ped.* take an active part in the lessons.

'**Mitarbeiter(in** *f*) *m* **1.** a) employee, *pl* staff, b) collaborator (*bei* on), c) con-tributor (*bei* to *a paper etc*): *freier Mit-arbeiter* freelance(r). **2.** colleague.

'**Mitarbeiterstab** *m* staff.

'**mitbekommen** *v/t* (*irr, sep,* h, → *be-kommen*) **1.** get. **2.** F a) catch, get (*joke etc*), b) pick up: *hast du das mitbe-kommen?* did you get that?

'**mitbenutzen** *v/t* (*sep,* h) share.

'**mitbestimmen** *v/i* (*sep,* h) (*bei e-r Sa-che*) *~* have a say in the matter.

'**Mitbestimmung** *f* (-; *no pl*) codetermi-nation, *a.* worker participation.

'**Mitbewerber(in** *f*) *m* competitor.

'**Mitbewohner(in** *f*) *m* fellow occupant.

'**mitbringen** *v/t* (*irr, sep,* -ge-, h, → *brin-gen*) **1.** bring *s.o., s.th.* along (with one). **2.** *fig.* have, possess (*talents etc*).

Mitbringsel ['mɪtbrɪŋzəl] *n* (-s; -) little present.

Mitbürger(in *f*) *m* fellow citizen.

Miteigentümer(in *f*) *m* joint owner.

mitein'ander *adv* a) with each other, b) together: **alle ～** one and all.

Mitein'ander *n* (-[s]; *no pl*) togetherness.

Mit|erbe *m* co-heir. **～erbin** *f* co-heiress.

miterleben *v/t* (*sep*, h) witness.

Mitesser *m* (-s; -) ✵ blackhead.

mitfahren *v/i* (*irr*, *sep*, -ge-, sn, → **fahren**) **mit j-m ～** ride (*or* go) with s.o.

Mitfahrgelegenheit *f* **biete ～ nach Köln** lift offered to Cologne.

mitfühlen *v/i* (*sep*, -ge-, h) **mit j-m ～** sympathize with s.o.; **～d** sympathetic.

mitführen *v/t* (*sep*, -ge-, h) carry with one.

mitgeben *v/t* (*irr*, *sep*, -ge-, h, → **geben**) **j-m et. ～** give s.o. s.th. (to take with him).

Mitgefangene *m*, *f* fellow-prisoner.

Mitgefühl *n* (-[e]s; *no pl*) sympathy: **j-m sein ～ ausdrücken** offer one's sympathies (*or* condolences) to s.o.

mitgehen *v/i* (*irr*, *sep*, -ge-, sn, → **gehen**) **1.** go along (**mit j-m** with s.o.): F **et. ～ lassen** pinch (*or* lift) s.th. **2.** *fig.* audience: respond (**mit** to).

mitgenommen I *pp* of **mitnehmen. II** *adj* worn out, exhausted: **～ aussehen** look the worse for wear.

Mitgift *f* (-; -en) dowry.

Mitglied *n* (-[e]s; -er) member.

Mitglieder|versammlung *f* general meeting. **～zahl** *f* membership.

Mitgliedsausweis *m* membership card.

Mitgliedsbeitrag *m* (membership) fee (*Am.* dues).

Mitgliedschaft *f* (-; -en) membership.

Mitgliedstaat *m* member state.

mithalten *v/i* (*irr*, *sep*, -ge-, h, → **halten**) **1.** *a. fig.* keep up (**mit** with). **2.** *cards:* stay in the bidding.

Mitherausgeber(in *f*) *m* co-editor.

Mithilfe *f* (-; *no pl*) aid, help, assistance.

mithören (*sep*, -ge-, h) **I** *v/t* a) listen (in) to, b) overhear, c) eavesdrop on, d) monitor, e) intercept. **II** *v/i* listen.

Mitinhaber(in *f*) *m* joint owner, copartner.

mitkommen *v/i* (*irr*, *sep*, -ge-, sn, → **kommen**) **1.** come along. **2.** *ped.* keep up (with the class): **gut ～** get on well;

nicht ～ do badly; F **da komme ich** (**einfach**) **nicht mit!** that's beyond me!

mitlaufen *v/i* (*irr*, *sep*, -ge-, sn, → **laufen**) run (along) with, *sports:* run (in the race). **Mitläufer(in** *f*) *m pol. contp.* **1.** hanger-on. **2.** fellow-travel(l)er.

Mitlaut *m ling.* consonant.

Mitleid *n* (-[e]s; *no pl*) (**aus ～** out of) pity (**für** for); **mit j-m ～ haben** have pity on s.o., be sorry for s.o.

Mitleidenschaft *f* **in ～ gezogen werden** be (adversely) affected (**durch** by).

mitleiderregend *adj* pitiful, pitiable.

mitleidig [-laɪdɪç] *adj* compassionate, sympathetic: **ein ～es Lächeln** a contemptuous smile.

mitleid(s)los *adj* pitiless.

mitmachen (*sep*, -ge-, h) **I** *v/i* **1.** a) take part in, join in, b) cooperate: F **da mache ich nicht mit!** count me out on that! **II** *v/t* **2.** take part in, *a.* attend (*course etc*), go with (*the fashion*), join in (*game etc*). **3.** F **j-s Arbeit ～** do s.o.'s job as well. **4.** F live (*or* go) through, suffer: **das mache ich nicht mehr lange mit!** I won't take that much longer!

Mitmensch *m* fellow (man, being).

mitmischen *v/i* (*sep*, -ge-, h) F be in on the action: **bei et. ～** take part in s.th.

mitnehmen *v/t* (*irr*, *sep*, -ge-, h, → **nehmen**) **1.** a) take along, take with one, b) borrow: **j-n im Auto ～** give s.o. a lift. **2.** take away. **3.** F take, buy. **4.** F take in (*sights etc*). **5.** *fig.* profit (**aus** from). **6.** F *fig.* **j-n** (**sehr**) **～** take it out of s.o.; → **mitgenommen II**.

mitreden *v/t* (*sep*, -ge-, h) **et. mitzureden haben** have a say (**bei** in).

Mitreisende *m*, *f* fellow-passenger.

mitreißen *v/t* (*irr*, *sep*, -ge-, h, → **reißen**) carry along, *fig.* carry away.

mitreißend *adj fig.* thrilling, rousing.

mit'samt *prep* (*dat*) together with.

mitschleppen *v/t* (*sep*, -ge-, h) drag along (with one).

mitschneiden *v/t* (*irr*, *sep*, -ge-, h, → **schneiden**) tape(-record).

mitschreiben (*irr*, *sep*, -ge-, h, → **schreiben**) **I** *v/t* write down. **II** *v/i* take notes.

Mitschuld *f* (-; *no pl*) joint guilt, complicity (**an** *dat* in). **mitschuldig** *adj* **an e-r Sache ～ sein** be implicated in s.th.

Mitschuldige *m*, *f* accessory (**an** *dat* to).

'**Mitschüler(in** f) m classmate.
'**mitschwingen** v/i (irr, sep, -ge-, h, → **schwingen**) **1.** phys. resonate. **2.** fig. have overtones of.
'**mitsingen** v/t, v/i (irr, sep, -ge-, h, → **singen**) join in the singing (of).
'**mitspielen** v/i (sep, -ge-, h) **1.** join in, sports: play, be on the team, thea. appear. F fig. (**bei**) person: play a part (in): **ich spiele nicht mehr mit!** count me out! **3.** F **j-m übel ~** a) treat s.o. badly, b) play a nasty trick on s.o.
'**Mitspieler(in** f) m player, partner, thea. etc member of the cast.
'**Mitspracherecht** n (-[e]s; no pl) right to a say: **ein ~ haben** have a say (**bei** in).
'**Mitstreiter(in** f) m comrade-in-arms.
Mittag ['mɪta:k] m (-[e]s; -e) midday, noon: **heute 2** at noon today; **zu ~ essen** have lunch. '**Mittagessen** n (**beim** [**zum**] **~** at [for]) lunch.
'**mittags** adv a) at noon, b) at lunchtime.
'**Mittags|pause** f lunch break. **~schlaf** m, **~schläfchen** n siesta, afternoon nap. **~zeit** f (-; no pl) lunchtime.
'**Mittäter(in** f) m 🏛 accomplice.
Mitte ['mɪtə] f (-; -n) middle, cent/re (Am. -er): **die goldene ~** the golden mean; pol. die ~ the centre; **in unserer ~** in our midst; **in der ~ zwischen** halfway between; **~ Juli** in the middle of July, in mid-July; **~ der 18. Jhs.** in the mid-18th-century; **~ Dreißig sein** be in one's mid-thirties; F **ab durch die ~!** a) off you go!, b) let's go!
'**mitteilen** (sep, -ge-, h) I v/t **j-m et. ~** a) inform (or notify) s.o. of s.th., tell s.o. s.th., b) impart knowledge to s.o. II **sich j-m ~** a) confide in s.o., b) fig. joy etc: communicate itself to s.o.
'**mitteilsam** adj communicative.
'**Mitteilung** f (-; -en) information, communication, report, notification, message, news.
mittel ['mɪtəl] I adj → **mittler**. II adv F middling, so-so.
'**Mittel** n (-s; -) **1.** a) means, b) method, way, c) expedient: **~ und Wege finden** find ways and means; **~ zum Zweck sein** be a means to an end; **als letztes ~** as a last resort; **ihm ist jedes ~ recht** he stops at nothing. **2.** 💊 remedy (**gegen** for). **3.** pl a) resources, b) funds, means:

aus öffentlichen ~n from the public purse. **4.** (**im ~** on an) average.
'**Mittelalter** n (-s; no pl) Middle Ages.
'**mittelalterlich** adj medi(a)eval.
'**mittelbar** adj indirect.
'**Mittelding** n cross, s.th. in between.
'**mitteleuro|päisch** adj **~e Zeit** (abbr. MEZ) Central European Time.
'**Mittelfeld** n (-[e]s; no pl) soccer: midfield. **~spieler** m midfield player.
'**Mittelfinger** m middle finger.
'**mittelfristig** adj 💰 medium-term.
'**Mittelgebirge** n highlands.
'**Mittelgewicht** n (-[e]s; no pl) sports: middleweight.
'**mittelgroß** adj medium-sized, person: of medium height.
'**Mittelklasse** f **1.** 💰 medium price range. **2.** → **Mittelstand** 1. **~wagen** m medium-range car.
'**Mittellinie** f **1.** a. sports: cent/re (Am. -er) line, tennis: cent/re (Am. -er) service line. **2.** ⅍ median line.
'**mittellos** adj destitute, poor, penniless.
'**Mittelmaß** n (-es; no pl) average, contp. mediocrity.
'**mittelmäßig** adj average, mediocre.
'**Mittelmäßigkeit** f (-; no pl) mediocrity.
'**Mittelmeer** n Mediterranean.
'**Mittelohrentzündung** f inflammation of the middle ear.
'**Mittelpunkt** m cent/re (Am. -er), fig. a. heart, hub: **im ~ des Interesses stehen** be the focus of interest.
'**mittels** prep by (means of), through.
'**Mittelschiff** n ⌂ nave.
'**Mittelstand** m (-[e]s; no pl) **1.** middle classes: **gehobener ~** upper middle class. **2.** 💰 medium-sized and small enterprises. '**mittelständisch** [-ʃtɛndɪʃ] adj, '**Mittelstands...** middle-class: 💰 **mittelständische Betriebe** → **Mittelstand** 2.
'**Mittelstrecken|flugzeug** n medium-range plane. **~läufer(in** f) m sports: middle-distance runner. **~ra¸kete** f ✖ medium-range missile.
'**Mittel|streifen** m central reservation, Am. median strip. **~stück** n middle. **~stufe** f ped. middle school, Am. junior high. **~stürmer** m sports: cent/re (Am. -er) forward. **~weg** m (e-n **~ einschlagen** steer) a) middle course: **der goldene ~** the golden mean. **~welle** f ∮ medi-

um wave. **~wert** m ♥, Ꞵ mean (value). **~wort** n (-[e]s; ⸚er) ling. participle.

mitten ['mɪtən] adv: **~ in (an, auf, unter** dat) in the middle of; **~ in** a. in the thick of; **~ unter uns** in our midst; **~ durch** clean through; **~ hinein** right into it; **~ ins Herz** right into the heart.

mitten'drin adv F right in the middle (of it). **mitten'durch** adv right through (or across), a. cut etc clean through.

Mitternacht ['mɪtər-] f (-; no pl) midnight.

mittler ['mɪtlər] adj a) middle, central, b) average, medium, c) middling, d) phys., ⚙ mean: **~en Alters** middle-aged; **~er Beamter** lower-grade civil servant; **~es Management** middle management; **der ~e Osten** the Middle East; **von ~er Qualität** of medium quality; → **Reife** 2.

'Mittler m (-s; -) mediator.

'mittler'weile adv meanwhile, (in the) meantime, since, by now.

'Mittsommer m midsummer.

Mittwoch ['mɪtvɔx] m (-[e]s; -e) (**am ~ on**) Wednesday.

'mittwochs adv on Wednesday(s).

mit'unter adv now and then.

'mitverantwortlich adj jointly responsible. **'Mitverantwortung** f joint responsibility.

'mitverdienen v/i (sep, h) be earning as well.

'Mitverfasser(in f) m coauthor.

'Mitverschulden n (-s) ⚖ contributory negligence.

'mitwirken v/i (sep, -ge-, h) (**bei**) a) co-operate (in), a. thea. take part (in), ♪ perform, b) matter: contribute (to).

'Mitwirkende m, f (-n; -n) mus. actor, player (a. ♪), pl cast: **~ sind ...** the cast includes ... **'Mitwirkung** f (-; no pl) a) cooperation, b) participation: **unter ~ von** (or gen) assisted by, thea. starring.

'Mitwisser m (-s; -) person who is in on the secret, ⚖ accessory.

'Mixbecher m shaker. **mixen** ['mɪksən] v/t (h) mix. **'Mixer** m (-s; -) **1.** barman, Am. bartender. **2.** TV etc: mixer. **3.** → **'Mixgerät** n mixer, liquidizer.

'Mixgetränk n mixed drink.

Mixtur [mɪks'tuːr] f (-; -en) mixture.

Mob [mɔp] m (-s; no pl) mob.

Möbel ['møːbəl] n (-s; -) a) → **Möbelstück,** b) pl furniture.

'Möbel|geschäft n furniture shop. **~händler** m furniture dealer. **~poli,tur** f furniture polish. **~spediti,on** f removal firm. **~stoff** m furniture fabric. **~stück** n piece of furniture. **~tischler** m cabinet-maker. **~wagen** m furniture van, Am. moving truck.

mobil [mo'biːl] adj **1.** mobile: ✕ **~ machen** mobilize. **2.** F active.

Mobile ['moːbilə] n (-s; -s) mobile.

Mobiliar [mobi'liaːr] n (-s; no pl) furniture.

mobilisieren [mobili'ziːrən] v/t (h) mobilize. **Mobili'sierung** f (-; -en) mobilization. **Mo'bilmachung** f (-; -en) ✕ mobilization.

möblieren [mø'bliːrən] v/t (h) furnish: **neu ~** refurnish; **möbliertes Zimmer** furnished room, bed-sitter; F **möbliert wohnen** live in lodgings.

mochte ['mɔxtə] pret of **mögen.**

Möchtegern... ['mœçtə-] iro. would-be.

modal [mo'daːl] adj modal. **Modalität** [modali'tɛːt] f (-; -en) modality.

Mode ['moːdə] f (-; -n) fashion: contp. **neue ~n** new-fangled ideas; **(die) große ~ sein** be (all) the fashion (or rage); **in (aus der) ~ kommen** come into (go out of) fashion; **mit der ~ gehen** follow the latest fashion.

'Modear,tikel m novelty.

'modebewußt adj fashion-conscious.

'Mode|farbe f fashionable colo(u)r. **~geschäft** n fashion shop. **~haus** n **1.** fashion house. **2.** fashion shop.

Modell [mo'dɛl] n (-s; -e) a) model, b) design, type, c) F mock-up: **j-m ~ stehen** sit (or pose) for s.o.

Mo'dell|ath,let(in f) m model athlete. **~bauer** m (-s; -) ⚙ model(l)er, model builder. **~eisenbahn** f model railway. **~flugzeug** n model airplane.

modellieren [modɛ'liːrən] v/t (h) model.

Mo'dellkleid n model (dress).

Modem ['moːdɛm] m (-s; -s) ⚡ modem.

'Modenschau f fashion show.

Moder ['moːdər] m (-s; no pl) mo(u)ld.

Moderation [modera'tsi̯oːn] f (-; no pl) TV presentation, Am. moderation.

Moderator [mode'raːtɔr] m (-s; -en [-ra'toːrən]), **Moderatorin** [modera-'toːrɪn] f (-; -nen) TV presenter, Am. moderator. **moderieren** [mode'riːrən] v/t (h) TV present, Am. moderate.

'mod(e)rig adj mo(u)ldy, a. musty.
modern¹ ['mo:dɛrn] v/i (h) mo(u)lder.
modern² [mo'dɛrn] adj a) modern, up-to-date, b) fashionable.
Mo'derne f (-; no pl) **1.** modern age. **2. Kunst** etc **der ~** modernist art etc.
modernisieren [modɛrni'zi:rən] v/t (h) modernize. **Moderni'sierung** f (-; -en) modernization.
'Modesa,lon m fashion house.
'Modeschmuck m costume jewel(le)ry.
'Modeschöpfer m couturier.
'Modeschöpferin f couturière.
'Modewort n vogue word.
'Modezeichner m fashion designer.
'Modezeitschrift f fashion magazine.
modifizieren [modifi'tsi:rən] v/t (h) modify, a. qualify (expression). **Modifi'zierung** f (-; -en) modification, qualification.
'modisch adj fashionable, stylish.
Modul ['mo:dul] n (-s; -n) ☯ module.
modulieren [modu'li:rən] v/t (h) modulate.
'Modultechnik f modular technique.
Modus ['mo:dus] m (-; Modi) **1.** way, method, a. ♪ mode. **2.** ling. mood.
Mofa ['mo:fa] n (-s; -s) → **Motorfahrrad.**
mogeln ['mo:gəln] v/i (h) F cheat.
'Mogelpackung f deception package.
mögen ['mø:gən] (mochte, gemocht, h) **I** v/t like, be fond of: **nicht ~** dislike; **ich möchte gern ein Bier** I'd like to (have) a beer; **ich mag k-n Kaffee** I don't like (or care for) coffee; **lieber ~** like better, prefer; **ich möchte lieber ...** I would rather ...; **ich mochte noch nicht nach Hause** I didn't want to go home yet. **II** v/aux (pp mögen) **ich mag nicht essen** I don't want to eat; **ich möchte ihn sehen** I want (or would like) to see him; **ich möchte wissen** I should like to know, I wonder; **mag er sagen, was er will** let him say what he wants; **das mag (wohl) sein** that may be so; **mag sein, daß** perhaps; **wie dem auch sein mag** be that as it may; **wo er auch sein mag** wherever he may be; **was mag das bedeuten?** I wonder what it could mean?
Mogler ['mo:glər] m (-s; -) F cheat.
möglich ['mø:klɪç] adj possible, a. practicable: **~er Käufer** potential buyer; **alle ~en** all sorts of; **alles ~e** all sorts of

things; **sein möglichstes tun** do one's utmost; **es ~ machen →** **ermöglichen;** **nicht ~!** impossible!, F no kidding!; **das ist eher ~!** that's more likely!; **es ist ~, daß er kommt** he may come; **so bald wie ~** as soon as possible.
'möglicherweise adv possibly, perhaps.
'Möglichkeit f (-; -en) possibility, a. opportunity, a. chance: **nach ~** if possible, as far as possible; **es besteht die ~, daß** it is possible that; **ich sehe k-e ~ zu** inf I cannot see any chance of ger; **ist das die ~!** that's not possible!
'möglichst adv **~ bald** etc as soon etc as possible; **~ klein** as small as possible, attr the smallest possible.
Mohammedaner [mohame'da:nər] m (-s; -), **Mohamme'danerin** f (-; -nen), **mohamme'danisch** adj Moslem.
Mohn [mo:n] m (-[e]s; -e) **1.** ❀ poppy. **2. → 'Mohnsamen** m poppy-seed.
Möhre ['mø:rə] f (-; -n), **Mohrrübe** ['mo:r-] f ❀ carrot.
Mokka ['mɔka] m (-s; -s) mocha.
Molch [mɔlç] m (-[e]s; -e) zo. newt.
Mole ['mo:lə] f (-; -n) ⚓ mole, jetty.
Molekül [mole'ky:l] n (-s; -e) molecule.
molekular adj, **Molekular...** [moleku'la:r-] molecular.
molk [mɔlk] pret of **melken.**
Molke ['mɔlkə] f (-; no pl) whey.
Molkerei [mɔlkə'rai] f (-; -en) dairy.
Moll [mɔl] n (-; no pl) ♪ minor (key).
mollig ['mɔlɪç] adj F **1.** cosy. **2.** plump.
Molotowcocktail ['mɔlotɔf-] m (-s; -s) Molotov cocktail, petrol bomb.
Moment¹ [mo'mɛnt] m (-[e]s; -e) (**im ~** at the) moment.
Mo'ment² n (-[e]s; -e) **1.** factor, element, aspect. **2.** phys. momentum.
momentan [momɛn'ta:n] **I** adj **1.** momentary. **2.** present. **II** adv **3.** momentarily. **4.** at the moment.
Monarch [mo'narç] m (-en; -en), **Mon'archin** f (-; -nen) monarch, sovereign. **Monarchie** [monar'çi:] f (-; -n) monarchy. **Monarchist** [monar'çɪst] m (-en; -en), **Monar'chistin** f (-; -nen), **monar'chistisch** adj monarchist.
Monat ['mo:nat] m (-[e]s; -e) month: **im ~ Mai** in the (month of) May; **im ~, pro ~** a month, monthly; F **sie ist im dritten ~** she is three months gone. **'monatelang** **I** adj months of. **II** adv for months.

'**monatlich** adj monthly, adv a. a month.
'**Monats|gehalt** n monthly salary (or pay). **~karte** f monthly season ticket, Am. monthly ticket. **~rate** f monthly instal(l)ment. **~schrift** f monthly.

Mönch [mœnç] m (-[e]s; -e) monk.

'**Mönchskloster** n monastery.

'**Mönchsorden** m monastic order.

Mond [mo:nt] m (-[e]s; -e) moon, a. satellite: F **auf** (or **hinter**) **dem ~ leben** be behind the times.

mondän [mon'dɛ:n] adj fashionable.

'**Mond|aufgang** m moonrise. **~finsternis** f lunar eclipse. **~gestein** n moon rocks. **~landefähre** f lunar module. **~landschaft** f a. fig. moonscape. **~landung** f moon landing. **~nacht** f moonlit night. **~schein** m (-[e]s; no pl) moonlight. **~sichel** f crescent (of the moon). **~stein** m min. moonstone.

Moneten [mo'ne:tən] pl F dough.

Mongole [mɔŋ'go:lə] m (-n; -n), **Mon'golin** f (-; -nen), **mon'golisch** adj Mongol(ian). **Mongolismus** [mɔŋgo-'lɪsmʊs] m (-; no pl) ☞ Down's syndrome. **mongoloid** [mɔŋgolo'i:t] adj ☞ mongoloid.

Monitor ['mo:nitɔr] m (-s; -en [moni-'to:rən]) TV monitor.

mono ['mo:no] adj F (a. ~ **abspielbar**) mono.

monogam [mono'ga:m] adj monogamous.

Monogramm [mono'gram] n (-s; -e) monogram.

Monographie [monogra'fi:] f (-; -n) monograph.

Monolog [mono'lo:k] m (-s; -e) monolog(ue Br.).

Monopol [mono'po:l] n (-s; -e) monopoly (auf acc on). **monopolisieren** [monopoli'zi:rən] v/t (h) monopolize.

monoton [mono'to:n] adj monotonous.

Monotonie [monoto'ni:] f (-; -n) monotony.

Monster ['mɔnstər] m (-s; -) monster.

'**Monster...** F mammoth (enterprise, film, trial, etc).

Monstranz [mɔn'strants] f (-; -en) eccl. monstrance.

monströs [mɔn'strø:s] adj monstrous.

Monstrum ['mɔnstrʊm] n (-s; Monstren) monster.

Monsun [mɔn'zu:n] m (-s; -e) monsoon.

Montag ['mo:nta:k] m (-[e]s; -e) (am ~ on) Monday.

Montage [mɔn'ta:ʒə] f (-; -n) 1. ⚙ a) mounting, fitting, installation, b) assembly: **auf ~ sein** be away on a construction job. 2. phot. etc montage.

Mon'tageband n assembly line.

Mon'tagehalle f assembly shop.

'**montags** adv on Monday(s).

Montanindu,strie [mɔn'ta:n-] f coal, iron, and steel industries.

Monteur [mɔn'tø:r] m (-s; -e) ⚙ fitter, ✈, mot. mechanic. **montieren** [mɔn-'ti:rən] v/t (h) ⚙ a) mount (a. phot. etc), fit, install(l), b) assemble.

Montur [mɔn'tu:r] f (-; -en) F get-up.

Monument [monu'mɛnt] n (-[e]s; -e) monument (für to). **monumental** [monumen'ta:l] adj monumental.

Moor [mo:r] n (-[e]s; -e) fen, bog, moor.

Moos [mo:s] n (-es; -e) 1. 🌿 moss. 2. F dough, sl. lolly.

Moped ['mo:pɛt] n (-s; -s) moped.

Mops [mɔps] m (-es; Möpse) zo. pug.

Moral [mo'ra:l] f (-; no pl) a) morals, b) ethics, c) (working etc) morale: **doppelte ~** double standards; **die ~ heben** raise the morale; **~ predigen** moralize.

moralisch [mo'ra:lɪʃ] adj moral.

Moralist [mora'lɪst] m (-en; -en) moralist.

Morast [mo'rast] m (-[e]s; -e) morass.

morbid [mɔr'bi:t] adj morbid.

Morchel ['mɔrçəl] f (-; -n) 🌿 morel.

Mord [mɔrt] m (-[e]s; -e) murder (an dat of): **e-n ~ begehen** commit murder; F **es gibt ~ und Totschlag** there will be a hell of a row.

'**Mordanklage** f murder charge: **unter ~ stehen** be charged with murder.

'**Mordanschlag** m attempted murder: **e-n ~ auf j-n verüben** make an attempt on s.o.'s life.

morden ['mɔrdən] (h) I v/i commit murder, kill. II v/t murder, kill.

Mörder ['mœrdər] m (-s; -) murderer.

'**Mörderin** f (-; -nen) murderess.

'**mörderisch** adj murderous, a. deadly (fight etc), a. terrible (heat etc), a. gruel(l)ing (job etc), a. breakneck (pace etc), cutthroat (competition etc).

'**Mordfall** m murder case.

'**Mordkommissi,on** f murder (Am. homicide) squad.

'**Mords...** F a) great, terrific, fantastic, b) terrible. **~angst** f e-e ~ haben be in a flat panic, be scared stiff. **~ding** n whopper, humdinger. **~glück** n fantastic stroke of luck. **~kerl** m great guy. **~krach** m F terrific noise, awful racket: e-n ~ **schlagen** raise hell.

'**mordsmäßig** F **I** adj terrific. **II** adv terribly, awfully.

'**Mordverdacht** m suspicion of murder.

'**Mordversuch** m attempted murder.

'**Mordwaffe** f murder weapon.

morgen ['mɔrgən] adv tomorrow: ~ früh tomorrow morning; ~ mittag at noon tomorrow; heute ~ this morning; ~ in 14 Tagen a fortnight tomorrow; ~ in e-r Woche a week from tomorrow; ~ um diese Zeit this time tomorrow.

'**Morgen**[1] m (-s; -) morning: am (frühen) ~ (early) in the morning.

'**Morgen**[2] m (-s; -) acre.

'**Morgen**|**andacht** f morning prayer. **~dämmerung** f dawn, daybreak. **~grauen** n beim ~ at dawn. **~gym,nastik** f s-e ~ machen do one's daily dozen. **~luft** f morning air: fig. ~ wittern see a chance. **~muffel** m F ein ~ sein be grumpy in the morning. **~rock** m dressing gown. **~rot** n (-s; no pl) **1.** red sky. **2.** fig. dawn.

'**morgens** adv in the morning(s): ~ um 4 (Uhr) at four (o'clock) in the morning; von ~ bis abends from morning till midnight.

'**Morgen**|**sonne** f (~ haben get the) morning sun. **~stunde** f morning hour: in den frühen ~n in the small hours.

morgig ['mɔrgɪç] adj tomorrow's: der ~e Tag tomorrow.

Mormone [mɔr'mo:nə] m (-n; -n), **Mor'monin** f (-; -nen), **mor'monisch** adj Mormon.

Morphium ['mɔrfiʊm] n (-s; no pl) morphine.

morsch [mɔrʃ] adj rotten, fig. a. shaky.

Morsealpha,bet ['mɔrzə-] n (-[e]s; no pl) Morse (code).

morsen ['mɔrzən] v/t, v/i (h) morse.

Mörser ['mœrzər] m (-s; -) mortar.

'**Morsezeichen** n Morse signal.

Mörtel ['mœrtəl] m (-s; -) mortar.

Mosaik [moza'i:k] n (-s; -en) mosaic.

Mosa'ikfußboden m tessellated floor.

Moschee [mɔ'ʃe:] f (-; -n) mosque.

Moschus ['mɔʃʊs] m (-; no pl) musk.

Mosel ['mo:zəl] m (-s; -) Moselle.

Moskito [mɔs'ki:to] m (-s; -s) (tropical) mosquito. **~netz** n mosquito net.

Moslem ['mɔslɛm] m (-s; -s) Moslem, Muslim.

Most [mɔst] m (-[e]s; -e) must.

Mostrich ['mɔstrɪç] m (-s; no pl) gastr. mustard.

Motel ['mo:tɛl] n (-s; -s) motel.

Motiv [mo'ti:f] n (-s; -e) **1.** motive (zu for). **2.** art: motif, film etc: a. theme, phot. subject. **Motivation** [motiva-'tsio:n] f (-; -en) motivation.

motivieren [moti'vi:rən] v/t (h) **1.** motivate. **2.** explain, give reasons for.

Motor ['mo:tɔr] m (-s; -en [mo'to:rən]) engine, ⚡ motor (a. fig.). **~boot** n motorboat. **~fahrrad** n motorized bicycle. **~haube** f a) mot. bonnet, Am. hood, b) ✈ (engine) cowling.

motorisch [mo'to:rɪʃ] adj ⚕ motor.

motorisieren [motori'zi:rən] v/t (h) motorize, esp. ✕ mechanize.

'**Motorpumpe** f motor pump.

'**Motorrad** n (~fahren ride a) motorcycle (F motorbike): ~ mit Beiwagen combination. **~fahrer(in** f) m motorcyclist.

'**Motor**|**roller** m (motor) scooter. **~säge** f power saw. **~schaden** m engine trouble. **~schlitten** m snowmobile. **~sport** m motor sport.

Motte ['mɔtə] f (-; -n) zo. moth.

'**Mottenkugel** f mothball.

'**mottenzerfressen** adj motheaten.

Motto ['mɔto] n (-s; -s) motto.

motzen ['mɔtsən] v/i (h) F beef.

Möwe ['mø:və] f (-; -n) zo. (sea)gull.

Mücke ['mʏkə] f (-; -n) zo. mosquito, midge: aus e-r ~ e-n Elefanten machen make a mountain out of a molehill. '**Mückenstich** m mosquito bite.

Mucks [mʊks] m (-es; -e) F (k-n ~ sagen not to a utter a) sound. '**mucksen** v/i (a. sich ~) (h) stir, make a sound.

'**mucksmäuschen'still** adj F person: as quiet as a mouse: es war ~ you could have heard a pin drop.

müde ['my:də] adj (~ werden) get tired: zum Umfallen ~ ready to drop; fig. nicht ~ werden zu inf not to tire of ger.

'**Müdigkeit** f (-; no pl) tiredness.

Muff [mʊf] m (-[e]s; -e) muff.

Muffe ['mʊfə] f (-; -n) ⚙ sleeve, socket.

Muffel ['mʊfəl] *m* (-s; -) F sourpuss.
...muffel *m* → *Krawatten-, Partymuffel.*
muffig ['mʊfɪç] *adj* 1. musty (*air etc*). 2. *fig.* a) stuffy, b) grumpy.
Mühe ['my:ə] *f* (-; -n) a) trouble, pains, b) effort, c) difficulties (*mit* with, in doing): **vergebliche ~** waste of time (*or* energy); **mit ~ und Not** barely, with (great) difficulty; (*nicht*) **der ~ wert** (not) worth the trouble; **sich (große) ~ geben** take (great) trouble (*or* pains) (*mit* over), try hard; **sich die ~ machen zu** *inf* go to the trouble of *ger*; **k-e ~ scheuen** spare no effort (*or* pains); **gib dir k-e ~!, spar dir die ~!** save yourself the trouble!, don't bother!
'mühelos *adj* effortless, easy.
'mühevoll *adj* hard, difficult, laborious.
Mühle ['my:lə] *f* (-; -n) 1. mill: → *Wasser.* 2. F *contp.* ✈, *mot.* crate, bus. 3. *a.* **'Mühlespiel** *n* (nine men's) morris.
'Mühlrad *n* millwheel.
'Mühlstein *m* millstone.
Mühsal ['my:za:l] *f* (-; *no pl*) a) toil, trouble(s), b) strain.
'mühsam I *adj* a) troublesome, b) hard, c) tiring. II *adv* with difficulty: **sich et. ~ verdienen** work hard for s.th.; **sich ~ erheben** struggle to one's feet.
Mulatte [mu'latə] *m* (-n; -n), **Mu'lattin** *f* (-; -nen) mulatto.
Mulde ['mʊldə] *f* (-; -n) hollow.
Mull [mʊl] *m* (-[e]s; -e) muslin, ✚ gauze.
Müll [myl] *m* (-s; *no pl*) rubbish, refuse, *Am.* garbage. **'Müllabfuhr** *f* refuse (*Am.* garbage) collection.
'Mullbinde *f* ✚ gauze bandage.
'Mülleimer *m* rubbish bin, *Am.* garbage can.
Müller ['mylər] *m* (-s; -) miller.
'Müll|fahrer *m* dustman, *Am.* garbage man. **~platz** *m* dump. **~schlucker** *m* rubbish chute. **~tonne** *f* dustbin, *Am.* garbage can. **~verbrennungsanlage** *f* incinerating plant. **~verwertungsanlage** *f* waste utilization plant. **~wagen** *m* dustcart, *Am.* garbage truck.
mulmig ['mʊlmɪç] *adj* F 1. ticklish. 2. **mir ist ganz ~ zumute** a) I feel queasy (*or* funny), b) I've got an uneasy feeling, c) I am scared.
Multi ['mʊlti] *m* (-s; -s) F multinational (concern).
'Multimillio,när *m* multimillionaire.

Multiplikation [mʊltiplika'tsjo:n] *f* (-; -en) ⅄ multiplication. **Multiplikator** [mʊltipli'ka:tor] *m* (-s; -en [-ka'to:rən]) multiplier. **multiplizieren** [mʊltipli-'tsi:rən] *v/t* (h) multiply (*mit* by).
Mumie ['mu:miə] *f* (-; -n) mummy.
Mumm [mʊm] *m* (-s; *no pl*) F spunk, guts.
Mumps [mʊmps] *m* (-; *no pl*) ✚ mumps.
Mund [mʊnt] *m* (-[e]s; ⸚er) mouth: **wie aus einem ~e** as one man; **~ und Nase aufsperren** be dum(b)founded; **den ~ halten** keep one's mouth shut; **halt den ~!** shut up!; F **den ~ voll nehmen** talk big; **du nimmst mir das Wort aus dem ~e** you are taking the very words out of my mouth; F **j-m über den ~ fahren** cut s.o. short; **in aller ~e sein** be the talk of the town; **nicht auf den ~ gefallen sein** have a ready (*or* glib) tongue; → *absparen, Blatt* 1, *stopfen* 3, *verbrennen* 1, *wässerig etc.*
'Mundart *f* dialect.
'Munddusche *f* oral spray.
Mündel ['myndəl] *n* (-s; -) ⚖ ward.
'mündelsicher *adj* ♱ **~e Papiere** gilt-edged securities.
münden ['myndən] *v/i* (sn) **~ in** (*acc*) a) *river*: flow into, b) (*a.* **auf** *acc*) *road etc*: lead into, c) *fig.* lead to, end in.
'Mundgeruch *m* ✚ bad breath, halitosis.
'Mundhar,monika *f* mouth organ.
mündig ['myndɪç] *adj* 1. ⚖ (**~ werden** come) of age. 2. *fig.* responsible.
mündlich ['myntlɪç] *adj* verbal (*statement etc*), oral (*exam*): **~e Überlieferung** oral tradition; **alles weitere ~** I'll tell you the rest when I see you.
'Mund|pflege *f* oral hygiene. **~schutz** *m* ✚ mask, *boxing:* gumshield. **~stück** *n* 1. ♪, ⚙ mouthpiece. 2. (cigarette) tip.
'mundtot *adj* **~ machen** (reduce to) silence, *pol.* gag, muzzle.
'Mündung *f* (-; -en) 1. *river:* a) mouth, b) estuary. 2. *anat.*, ⚙ mouth, ✕ muzzle.
'Mund|wasser *n* (-s; ⸚) mouthwash. **~werbung** *f* word-of-mouth advertising. **~werk** *n* (-[e]s; *no pl*) F **ein loses (gutes) ~ haben** have a loose tongue (the gift of the gab). **~winkel** *m* corner of one's mouth.
'Mund-zu-'Mund-Beatmung *f* mouth--to-mouth resuscitation, F kiss of life.

Munition [muni'tsĭo:n] f (-; *no pl*) ammunition.

Muniti'onslager n ammunition dump.

munkeln ['mʊŋkəln] v/i, v/t (h) whisper: **man munkelt, daß ...** it is rumo(u)red that ...

Münster ['mynstər] n (-s; -) minster, cathedral.

munter ['mʊntər] adj **1.** a) awake, b) up (and about). **2.** a) lively, b) cheerful, chirpy, c) vigorous; → **frisch** 4, **gesund.** '**Munterkeit** f (-; *no pl*) liveliness. '**Muntermacher** m (-s; -) F pick-me-up.

'**Münzauto,mat** m slot machine.

Münze ['myntsə] f (-; -n) **1.** coin: *fig. et. für bare ~ nehmen* take s.th. at face value. **2.** medal. **3.** mint.

'**Münzeinwurf** m coin slot.

münzen ['myntsən] v/t, v/i (h) coin, mint: *fig. gemünzt sein auf* (acc) be meant for.

'**Münzfernsprecher** m pay phone. **~sammlung** f coin collection. **~tank-(auto,mat)** m coin-operated petrol (*Am.* gas) pump. **~wechsler** m (-s; -) change machine.

mürbe ['myrbə] adj **1.** a) crumbly (*pastry etc*), mellow, very ripe (*fruit*), tender (*meat*), b) rotten (*wood*). **2.** *fig.* worn out: *j-n ~ machen* wear s.o. down; *~ werden* give in, wilt.

'**Mürbekuchen** m shortcake.

'**Mürbeteig** m short pastry.

Murks [mʊrks] m (-es; *no pl*) F botch-up: *~ machen* → '**murksen** v/i (h) F make a hash of things.

Murmel ['mʊrməl] f (-; -n) marble.

murmeln ['mʊrməln] v/i, v/t (h) murmur, mutter.

'**Murmeltier** n marmot: *fig. schlafen wie ein ~* sleep like a top (*or* log).

murren ['mʊrən] v/i (h) grumble (*über* acc about).

mürrisch ['myrɪʃ] adj surly, grumpy.

Mus [mu:s] n (-es; -e) puree, mash.

Muschel ['mʊʃəl] f (-; -n) **1.** *zo.* a) mussel, b) shell. **2.** *teleph.* a) earpiece, b) mouthpiece.

'**muschelförmig** adj shell-shaped.

Muse ['mu:zə] f (-; -n) *fig.* muse.

Museum [mu'ze:ʊm] n (-s; Museen) museum.

Musik [mu'zi:k] f (-; *no pl*) **1.** music. **2.** F band. **musikalisch** [muzi'ka:lɪʃ] adj

musical: **~e Untermalung** incidental music. **Musikalität** [muzikali'tɛ:t] f (-; *no pl*) musicality.

Mu'sikbegleitung f (musical) accompaniment. **Mu'sikbox** f jukebox.

Musiker ['mu:zikər] m (-s; -), '**Musikerin** f (-; -nen) musician.

Mu'sikfestspiele pl music festival. **~hochschule** f conservatory. **~instru,ment** n musical instrument. **~ka,pelle** f band. **~lehrer(in** f) m music teacher. **~stück** n piece of music. **~stunde** f music lesson. **~unterricht** m music lessons. **~wissenschaft** f (-; *no pl*) musicology.

musisch ['mu:zɪʃ] adj artistic (*talent etc*): *ped.* **~e Fächer** fine arts (subjects).

musizieren [muzi'tsi:rən] (h) **I** v/i make music. **II** v/t play.

Muskat [mʊs'ka:t] m (-[e]s; -e) nutmeg. **~blüte** f mace. **~nuß** f nutmeg apple.

Muskel ['mʊskəl] m (-s; -n) muscle: *die* **~n spielen lassen** flex one's muscles. **~faser** f muscular fib/re (*Am.* -er). **~kater** m (-s; *no pl*) F sore muscles: *~ haben* feel stiff and aching. **~pa,ket** n, **~protz** m F muscleman. **~riß** m torn muscle. **~zerrung** f pulled muscle.

Muskulatur [mʊskula'tu:r] f (-; -en) muscular system.

muskulös [mʊsku'lø:s] adj muscular.

Müsli ['my:sli] n (-s; -) muesli.

Muß [mʊs] *es ist ein ~* it is a must.

Muße ['mu:sə] f (-; *no pl*) leisure.

'**Mußehe** f shotgun wedding.

müssen ['mysən] (mußte, müssen, h) **I** v/aux have to: *du mußt nicht hingehen* you needn't (*or* don't have to) go; *sie ~ bald kommen* they are bound to come soon; *der Zug müßte längst hier sein* the train is (long) overdue; *ich mußte (einfach) lachen* I couldn't help laughing; *muß das sein?* is that really necessary?, do you have to?; *wenn es unbedingt sein muß* if it can't be helped. **II** v/i (*pp* gemußt) *ich muß* I must, I have (got) to; *ich mußte* I had to; *ich müßte (eigentlich)* I ought to.

'**Mußestunde** f leisure hour.

müßig ['my:sɪç] adj **1.** idle. **2.** pointless. '**Müßiggang** m (-[e]s; *no pl*) idleness. '**Müßiggänger** [-gɛŋər] m (-s; -) idler.

mußte ['mʊstə] *pret of* **müssen.**

Muster ['mʊstər] n (-s; -) **1.** pattern, model: *sie ist das ~ e-r guten Haus-*

frau she's a model housewife. **2.** sample, specimen. **3.** *textil.* pattern, design.

'**Muster|beispiel** *n* classic example (*für* of). **~betrieb** *m* model plant. **~exem,plar** *n* **1.** ✝ sample specimen. **2.** *print.* specimen copy. **3.** *a. iro.* perfect example. **~gatte** *m iro.* model husband.

'**mustergültig, 'musterhaft** *adj* exemplary, model: *sich ~ benehmen* behave perfectly.

'**Muster|haus** *n* show house. **~knabe** *m iro.* paragon, *contp.* ciss. *fig.* **~koffer** *m* sample case. **~kollekti,on** *f* ✝ sample collection.

mustern ['mʊstərn] *v/t* (h) **1.** a) study, scrutinize, b) eye, look *s.o.* up and down, c) size *s.o.* up. **2.** ✕ inspect (*troops*), examine (*conscripts*): *gemustert werden* F have one's medical. **3.** pattern: → *gemustert.*

'**Musterpro,zeß** *m* ⚖ test case.

'**Musterung** *f* (-; -en) **1.** scrutiny. **2.** ✕ a) review (*of troops*), b) medical examination (for military service).

Mut [muːt] *m* (-[e]s; *no pl*) courage, F pluck: *~ fassen* pluck up courage; *j-m den ~ nehmen* discourage *s.o.*; *den ~ sinken lassen* (*or verlieren*) lose heart, despair; *nur ~!* cheer up!

Mutation [muta'tsɪoːn] *f* (-; -en) **1.** *biol.* mutation. **2.** → *Stimmbruch.*

mutieren [mu'tiːrən] *v/i* (h) mutate.

'**mutig** *adj* courageous, brave.

'**mutlos** *adj* discouraged, disheartened, despondent. '**Mutlosigkeit** *f* (-; *no pl*) discouragement, despondency.

mutmaßlich ['muːtmaːslɪç] *adj* probable, ⚖ putative.

'**Mutmaßung** *f* (-; -en) (*über acc* about) conjecture, speculation.

'**Mutprobe** *f* test of courage.

Mutter[1] ['mʊtər] *f* (-; ⸚) mother: *werdende ~* expectant mother; *e-e ~ von vier Kindern* a mother of four.

'**Mutter**[2] *f* (-; -n) ⚙ nut.

'**Mütterberatungsstelle** *f* child welfare centre, *Am.* maternity center.

'**Mutter|bindung** *f psych.* mother tie. **~boden** *m*, **~erde** *f* 🌱 topsoil. **~gesell-**

schaft *f* ✝ parent company.

Mutter'gottes *f* (-; *no pl*) (Virgin) Mary.

'**Mutter|haus** *n eccl.* mother house. **~herz** *n* mother's heart. **~in,stinkt** *m* maternal instinct. **~kom,plex** *m* mother fixation. **~kuchen** *m* 🩻 placenta. **~leib** *m* (-[e]s; *no pl*) womb.

mütterlich ['mʏtərlɪç] *adj* motherly, maternal. '**mütterlicherseits** *adv* on one's mother's side: *Onkel ~* maternal uncle.

'**Mütterlichkeit** *f* (-; *no pl*) motherliness.

'**Mutter|liebe** *f* motherly love. **~mal** *n* 🩻 birthmark. **~milch** *f* mother's milk: *mit ~ genährt* breast-fed. **~mund** *m* (-[e]s; *no pl*) *anat.* uterine orifice.

'**Mutterschaft** *f* (-; *no pl*) motherhood, maternity.

'**Mutterschafts|hilfe** *f* maternity benefits. **~urlaub** *m* maternity leave.

'**Mutterschutz** *m* legal (job-)protection for expectant and nursing mothers.

'**mutter'seelenal'lein** *adj pred* all alone.

'**Muttersöhnchen** [-zøːnçən] *n* (-s; -) F mummy's darling.

'**Muttersprache** *f* mother tongue.

'**Muttersprachler** [-ʃpraːxlər] *m* (-s; -) native speaker.

'**Muttertag** *m* (-[e]s; *no pl*) Mother's Day.

'**Muttertier** *n* mother, dam.

'**Mutterwitz** *m* (-es; *no pl*) **1.** common sense. **2.** natural wit.

Mutti ['mʊti] *f* (-; -s) F mum(my), *Am.* mom.

'**mutwillig** *adj* wilful, wanton.

Mütze ['mʏtsə] *f* (-; -n) cap.

Myrrhe ['mʏrə] *f* (-; -n) myrrh.

mysteriös [mysteˈriøːs] *adj* mysterious.

Mystik ['mʏstɪk] *f* (-; *no pl*) mysticism.

Mystiker ['mʏstɪkər] *m* (-s; -) mystic.

mystisch ['mʏstɪʃ] *adj* **1.** a) mystic, b) mystical. **2.** mysterious.

Mythe ['myːtə] *f* (-; -n) myth.

'**mythisch** *adj* mythical.

Mythologie [mytoloˈgiː] *f* (-; -n) mythology. **mythologisch** [mytoˈloːgɪʃ] *adj* mythological. **mythologisieren** [mytologiˈziːrən] *v/t* (h) mythologize.

Mythos ['myːtɔs] *m* (-; Mythen) myth.

N

N, n [εn] *n* (-; -) N, n.

na [na] *int* F a) well, b) hey: **~, ~!** come on (now)!; **~ also!** there you are!; **~ schön!** all right then!; **~, so (et)was!** just fancy that!; → **warten**, **und.**

Nabe ['na:bə] *f* (-; -n) ⚙ hub.

Nabel ['na:bəl] *m* (-s; -) navel.

Nabelschnur *f* umbilical cord.

nach [na:x] **I** *prep* (*dat*) **1.** to, toward(s), for: **~ England gehen** (**abreisen**) go to (leave) for England; **der Zug ~ Paris** the train for Paris; **das Schiff fährt ~ Singapur** the ship is bound for Singapore. **2.** after: **e-r ~ dem anderen** one after the other, one by one. **3.** a) after, b) within, in (*three days etc*): **zehn Minuten ~ drei** ten minutes past three. **4.** according to, by, from: **~ deutschem Recht** under German law; **~ e-m Roman von Balzac** after a novel by Balzac; **wenn es ~ mir ginge** if I had my way; → **Ansicht** 1, **Natur**, **Uhr** *etc.* **5.** for: **~ Gold graben** dig for gold; **~ j-m fragen** ask for s.o. **II** *adv* **6.** after: **mir ~!** after me!, follow me! **7. ~ und ~** little by little, gradually; **~ wie vor** (now) as ever.

nachäffen [-εfən] *v/t* (*sep*, -ge-, h) F ape.

nachahmen [-a:mən] *v/t* (*sep*, -ge-, h) a) imitate, copy, b) take off, parody.

nachahmenswert *adj* exemplary.

Nachahmung *f* (-; -en) imitation.

Nachbar ['naxba:r] *m* (-n; -n) neighbo(u)r: **die ~n** *a.* the neighbo(u)rhood.

Nachbar... neighbo(u)ring (*district*, *house*, *country*, *etc*).

Nachbarin *f* (-; -nen) neighbo(u)r.

nachbarlich *adj* **1.** *a.* **gut ~** neighbo(u)rly. **2.** next-door (*garden etc*).

Nachbarschaft *f* (-; *no pl*) neighbo(u)rhood, *a.* the neighbo(u)rs.

nachbauen *v/t* (*sep*, -ge-, h) ⚙ copy.

Nachbehandlung *f* ⚙ subsequent treatment, *a.* ⚕ after-treatment.

nachbessern *v/t* (*sep*, -ge-, h) touch up.

nachbestellen *v/t* (*sep*, h) order some more, † place a repeat order for.

Nachbestellung *f* † repeat order (*gen* for).

nachbeten *v/t* (*sep*, -ge-, h) F parrot.

nachbilden *v/t* (*sep*, -ge-, h) copy, reproduce.

Nachbildung *f* (-; -en) copy, replica.

nachdatieren *v/t* (*sep*, h) postdate.

nachdem *conj* **1.** after, when. **2.** → **je** 4. **3.** since.

nachdenken *v/i* (*irr*, *sep*, -ge-, h, → **denken**) think (*über acc* about): **denk mal nach!** think a little!; **Zeit zum ⚥ brauchen** need time to think (it over).

nachdenklich *adj* thoughtful, pensive: **j-n ~ machen** set s.o. thinking.

Nachdruck¹ *m* (-[e]s; *no pl*) stress, emphasis: **mit ~** a) emphatically, b) energetically; **~ legen auf** (*acc*), (*dat*) **~ verleihen** stress, emphasize.

Nachdruck² *m* (-[e]s; -e) reprint: **~ verboten!** all rights reserved!

nachdrucken *v/t* (*sep*, -ge-, h) reprint: **unerlaubt ~** pirate.

nachdrücklich [-drykliç] *adj* emphatic (*warning etc*), forceful (*claim etc*): **et. ~ empfehlen** recommend s.th. strongly; **~ verlangen** insist on.

Nachdrucksrecht *n* right of reproduction.

nacheifern *v/i* (*sep*, -ge-, h) **j-m ~** emulate s.o.

nacheinander *adv* **1.** one after another, *a.* in succession. **2.** by turns.

Nacherzählung *f* ped. summary.

nachfahren *v/i* (*irr*, *sep*, -ge-, sn, → **fahren**) **j-m ~** follow s.o.

Nachfaßschreiben *n* follow-up letter. **~werbung** *f* follow-up advertising.

Nachfolge *f* (-; *no pl*) succession: **j-s ~ antreten** → **nachfolgen** *v/i* (*sep*, -ge-, sn) **j-m** (**im Amt**) **~** succeed s.o. (in office). **nachfolgend** *adj* following.

Nachfolger *m* (-s; -) successor.

Nachforderung *f* additional claim.

nachforschen *v/i* (*sep*, -ge-, h) (*dat*) investigate. **Nachforschung** *f* (-; -en) investigation: **~en anstellen** (**über** *acc*) investigate (*s.th.*).

Nachfrage *f* (-; -n) **1.** † demand (*nach* for). **2.** inquiry. **nachfragen** *v/i* (*sep*, -ge-, h) inquire, ask.

nachfühlen *v/i* (*sep*, -ge-, h) **j-m et. ~**

'**nachfüllen** v/t (sep, -ge-, h) **1.** fill up, refill, top up. **2.** add (water etc).

'**nachgeben** v/i (irr, sep, -ge-, h, → **geben**) **1.** ground etc: give (way). **2.** prices etc: drop. **3.** (dat) to give in, yield.

'**Nachgebühr** f ✝ surcharge.

'**Nachgeburt** f ✱ afterbirth.

'**nachgehen** v/i (irr, sep, -ge-, sn, → **gehen**) (dat) **1.** follow. **2.** fig. look into (a matter), follow, check up on (rumour, tip, etc), attend to (business etc), pursue (one's studies): **s-r Arbeit** ~ go about one's work. **3.** indulge in, seek, pursue (pleasure etc). **4.** be slow, lose: **m-e Uhr geht (e-e Minute) nach** my watch loses (a minute). **5.** fig. **j-m** ~ haunt s.o.

'**nachgemacht I** pp of **nachmachen**. **II** adj a) counterfeit, b) imitation.

'**nachgerade** adv **1.** really. **2.** by now.

'**Nachgeschmack** m a. fig. aftertaste.

'**nachgiebig** [-gi:biç] adj **1.** compliant, soft. **2.** ⚙ flexible, pliant. '**Nachgiebigkeit** f (-; no pl) compliance, softness.

'**nachhaken** v/i (sep, -ge-, h) F follow (it) up: **bei j-m in e-m Punkt** ~ press s.o. on a point.

'**nachhaltig** adj a) lasting (effect etc), sustained (efforts etc), b) strong, effective: ~ **wirken** have a lasting effect; ~ **beeinflussen** influence strongly.

'**nachhelfen** v/i (irr, sep, -ge-, h, → **helfen**) help: **e-r Sache** ~ help s.th. along.

nach'her adv a) afterward(s), b) later (on): **bis** ~! see you later!, so long!

'**Nachhilfe** f private lessons. ~**lehrer(in** f) m (private) tutor. ~**stunde** f **1.** private lesson. **2.** pl → ~**unterricht** m private lessons.

'**nachhinein** adv im ~ after the event.

'**nachhinken** v/i (sep, -ge-, sn) fig. lag behind.

'**Nachholbedarf** m **1.** ✝ backlog demand. **2.** fig. deficit.

'**nachholen** v/t (sep, -ge-, h) **1.** make up for lost time etc, catch up on work, sleep, etc. **2.** fetch s.o., s.th. later.

'**Nachhut** f (-; -en) ✗ rearguard: **die** ~ **bilden** a. fig. bring up the rear.

'**nachjagen** v/i (sep, -ge-, sn) (dat) chase after, a. fig. pursue.

'**Nachklang** m fig. echo, reminiscence.

'**Nachkomme** m (-n; -n) descendant, off-

spring: **ohne** ~**n** 🏛 without issue.

'**nachkommen** v/i (irr, sep, -ge-, sn, → **kommen**) **1.** come later, follow. **2.** a. fig. keep up (**mit** with). **3.** (dat) comply with order, wish, etc, meet (obligation), keep (promise).

'**Nachkommenschaft** f descendants, 🏛 issue. '**Nachkömmling** [-kœmlɪŋ] m (-s; -e) late arrival.

'**Nachkriegs...** post-war ...

'**Nachlaß** [-las] m (-sses; -lässe) **1.** estate: **literarischer** ~ unpublished works. **2.** ✝ reduction: **e-n** ~ **gewähren** allow a discount (**auf** acc on).

'**nachlassen** (irr, sep, -ge-, h, → **lassen**) **I** v/i **1.** decrease, weaken, wind: drop, rain, storm etc: let up, noise etc: subside, pain: ease, effect, strength, etc: wear off, performance, demand, etc: drop (off), interest etc: flag, slacken. **2.** a) deteriorate, grow weaker, fail, b) go off, be slowing down, runner etc: wilt, c) mentally: lose one's grip; **nicht** ~! hang on! **II** v/t **3.** leave (behind): **nachgelassene Werke** unpublished works. **4.** et. **vom Preis** ~ allow a discount.

'**Nachlaßgericht** n 🏛 probate court.

'**nachlässig** adj careless, negligent, sloppy. '**Nachlässigkeit** f (-; no pl) carelessness, negligence, sloppiness.

'**nachlaufen** v/i (irr, sep, -ge-, sn, → **laufen**) **j-m** ~ run after s.o.; **den Mädchen** ~ chase (after) the girls.

'**nachlesen** v/t (irr, sep, -ge-, h, → **lesen**) read up, look s.th. up.

'**nachliefern** v/t (sep, -ge-, h) supply s.th. later (or in addition).

'**nachlösen** v/i, v/t (sep, -ge-, h) (**e-e Fahrkarte**) ~ buy a ticket on the train.

'**nachmachen** v/t (sep, -ge-, h) a) copy, imitate, b) forge: **j-m et.** ~ copy s.th. s.o. does; **das soll ihm erst mal e-r** ~! I'd like to see anyone do better!

'**nachmessen** v/t (irr, sep, -ge-, h, → **messen**) check.

'**Nachmittag** m (**am** ~ in the) afternoon; **heute** ~ this afternoon. '**nachmittags** adv in the afternoon. '**Nachmittagsvorstellung** f thea. etc matinée.

'**Nachnahme** [-na:ma] f (-; -n) **et. als** (or **per**) ~ **schicken** send s.th. cash (Am. collect) on delivery (abbr. C.O.D.).

'**Nachnahmesendung** f C.O.D. parcel.

'**Nachname** m surname, last name.

'**nachplappern** v/t (sep, -ge-, h) F parrot.

'**Nachporto** n surcharge.

'**nachprüfbar** adj verifiable.

'**nachprüfen** v/t (sep, -ge-, h) **1.** check. **2.** a) re-examine, b) examine at a later date. '**Nachprüfung** f (-; -en) **1.** check(ing). **2.** examination at a later date.

'**nachrechnen** v/t (sep, -ge-, h) check.

'**Nachrede** f üble ~ defamation.

Nachricht ['naːxrɪçt] f (-; -en) a) (**e-e ~** a piece of) news, b) message, c) news (item): **~en** radio, TV news; **~ erhalten von** hear from; **j-m ~ geben** let s.o. know; **e-e ~ hinterlassen** leave a message.

'**Nachrichten|agen,tur** f, **~bü,ro** n press agency. **~dienst** m **1.** radio, TV news service. **2.** ✕ intelligence service. **~sa,tel,lit** m communications satellite. **~sendung** f radio, TV newscast, news broadcast. **~sperre** f pol. news blackout. **~sprecher(in** f) m news reader, newscaster. **~technik** f (tele)communication(s) (engineering). **~wesen** n (-s; no pl) communications.

'**nachrücken** v/i (sep, -ge-, sn) **1.** a. fig. move up. **2.** ✕ follow on.

'**Nachruf** m [-[e]s; -e) obituary.

'**nachrüsten** v/i (sep, -ge-, h) **1.** pol. close the armament gap. **2.** a. v/t ⊙ retrofit.

'**Nachrüstsatz** m ⊙ retrofit kit.

'**nachsagen** v/t (sep, -ge-, h) **1.** repeat. **2.** j-m et. ~ say s.th. of s.o.

'**Nachsai,son** f off season.

'**Nachsatz** m **1.** postscript. **2.** ling. final clause.

'**nachschenken** v/t, v/i (sep, -ge-, h) j-m (et.) ~ top s.o. up (with s.th.).

'**nachschlagen** (irr, sep, -ge-, h, → **schlagen**) **I** v/t **1.** look s.th. up. **II** v/i **2.** **im Lexikon** ~ consult a dictionary. **3.** F j-m ~ take after s.o.

'**Nachschlagewerk** n reference book.

'**Nachschlüssel** m duplicate key.

'**Nachschrift** f postscript.

'**Nachschub** m (-[e]s; no pl) (**an** dat of) supply (a. fig.), coll. supplies.

'**Nachschuß** m soccer: follow-up shot.

'**nachsehen** (irr, sep, -ge-, h, → **sehen**) **I** v/i **1.** gaze after. **2.** have a look: **~ ob ...** (go and) see whether ... **II** v/t **3.** inspect, check, ped. correct. **4.** → **nachschlagen** 1. **5.** j-m et. ~ forgive s.o. s.th.

'**Nachsehen:** das ~ haben be the loser.

'**nachsenden** v/t (irr, sep, -ge-, h, → **senden²**) forward.

'**Nachsicht** f a) forbearance, b) leniency: ~ **üben** be lenient; **mit j-m ~ haben** be lenient towards s.o.

'**nachsichtig** adj lenient, forbearing.

'**Nachsilbe** f ling. suffix.

'**nachsitzen** (irr, sep, -ge-, h, → **sitzen**) ~ **müssen** be kept in.

'**Nachsommer** m late (or Indian) summer. '**Nachsorge** f (-; no pl) 🎗 aftercare. '**Nachspeise** f dessert.

'**Nachspiel** n **1.** ♩ postlude. **2.** thea. epilog(ue Br.). **3.** sex: afterplay. **4.** fig. sequel: **die Sache wird ein ~ haben** there are bound to be consequences.

'**nachspielen** v/i (sep, -ge-, h) sports: play (~ **lassen** allow) extra time.

nächst [nɛːçst] **I** sup of **nahe. II** adj **1.** nearest (a. fig. relatives etc), a. shortest: **die ~e Umgebung** the immediate vicinity; **aus ~er Entfernung** at close range. **2.** next: **am ~en Tage** the next day; **in den ~en Tagen** in the next few days; **Mittwoch ~er Woche** Wednesday week; **in ~er Zeit** in the near future; **bei ~er Gelegenheit** at the first opportunity; **im ~en Augenblick** the next moment. **III** adv **3. am ~en** (dat to) next, nearest, closest; fig. j-m **am ~en stehen** be closest to s.o.; (dat) **am ~en kommen** come closest to. **4. fürs ~e** for the time being. **IV** prep **5.** (dat) next to.

'**nächst'best** adj **1.** first (comer etc). **2.** second-best, next-best.

'**Nächstbeste 1.** m, f the next best, the first person. **2.** n the next best (thing).

'**Nächste 1.** m, f (-n; -n) a) neighbo(u)r, one's fellow, b) the next (one): **jeder ist sich selbst der ~** charity begins at home; **der ~, bitte!** next (one) please! **2.** n (-n; -n) the next (or first) thing.

'**nachstehen** v/i (irr, sep, -ge-, h, → **stehen**) j-m ~ **in** (or **an** dat) be inferior to s.o. in; j-m **in nichts ~** be in no way inferior to s.o. '**nachstehend I** adj following. **II** adv in the following.

'**nachstellen** (sep, -ge-, h) **I** v/t **1.** put back (clock etc). **2.** ⊙ (re)adjust. **II** v/i (dat) a) be after, b) persecute.

'**Nachstellung** f (-; -en) fig. persecution.

'**Nächstenliebe** f (-; no pl) charity.

nächstens ['nɛːçstəns] adv (very) soon.

'**nächstliegend** *adj* nearest: *fig. das Nächstliegende* the obvious thing.

Nacht [naxt] *f* (-; ⁻e) (*bei* ~ at) night: *gute ~ l a. iro.* good night!; *heute* ~ tonight; *die* ~ *zum Tage machen* turn night into day; *es wird* ~ it is getting dark; *zu* ~ *essen* have supper; *bis spät* (*or tief*) *in die* ~ till late in the night; *über* ~ *a. fig.* overnight; *die ganze* ~ (*hindurch or lang*) all night (long); *im Schutze* (*or Dunkel*) *der* ~, *bei* ~ *und Nebel* under the cover of night, *w.s.* secretly.

'**Nacht**|**arbeit** *f* nightwork. 2**blind** *adj* night-blind. ~**creme** *f* night cream. ~**dienst** *m* night duty: ~ *haben* be on night duty, *chemist's shop etc*: be open all night.

'**Nachteil** *m* (-[e]s; -e) disadvantage, *a.* drawback, *sports, a. fig.* handicap: *zum* ~ *von* to the disadvantage of; *im* ~ *sein* be at a disadvantage.

'**nachteilig** *adj* disadvantageous, detrimental (*für* to): *nichts Nachteiliges* nothing unfavo(u)rable; ~ *beeinflussen* affect adversely.

'**nächtelang** ['nɛçtə-] **I** *adj* ~**e Diskussionen** *etc* night after night of discussions *etc.* **II** *adv* night after night.

'**Nacht**|**essen** *n* supper. ~**frost** *m* night frost. ~**hemd** *n a*) nightshirt, *b*) nightdress, F nightie.

Nachtigall ['naxtɪgal] *f* (-; -en) *zo.* nightingale.

'**Nachtisch** *m* (-[e]s; -e) dessert, sweet, F afters.

'**Nachtklub** *m* nightclub.

'**Nachtleben** *n* nightlife.

nächtlich ['nɛçtlɪç] *adj* nocturnal, nightly: *der* ~**e Park** the park at night.

'**Nacht**|**lo**,**kal** *n* nightclub. ~**porti**,**er** *m* night porter. ~**quar**,**tier** *n* place for the night, ✕ night quarters.

'**Nachtrag** [-tra:k] *m* (-[e]s; ⁻e [-trɛ:gə]) supplement. '**nachtragen** *v/t* (*irr, sep, -ge-, h,* → *tragen*) **1.** *j-m et.* ~ *fig.* bear s.o. a grudge for s.th. **2.** add (*in writing*). '**nachtragend** *adj* unforgiving.

'**nachträglich** [-trɛ:klɪç] **I** *adj a*) additional, *b*) belated, *c*) later. **II** *adv* subsequently, later: ~ *herzlichen Glückwunsch!* belated best wishes!

'**Nachtragshaushalt** *m* supplementary budget.

'**nachtrauern** *v/i* (*sep, -ge-, h*) *j-m* (*e-r*

Sache) ~ mourn s.o. (s.th.).

'**Nachtruhe** *f* sleep.

'**nachts** *adv* at (*or* during the) night.

'**Nacht**|**schicht** *f* night shift. ~**schwärmer** *m* night owl. ~**schwester** *f* night nurse. ~**speicherofen** *m* night storage heater. ~**strom** *m* off-peak electricity. ~**tisch** *m* bedside table. ~**topf** *m* chamber pot. ~**tre**,**sor** *m* night safe. ~**und**-'**Nebel-Akti**,**on** *f* undercover operation. ~**wache** *f* night watch. ~**wächter** *m* **1.** night watchman. **2.** F *contp.* dope. ~**zug** *m* night train.

'**Nachuntersuchung** *f* checkup.

'**nachvollziehen** *v/t* (*irr, sep, h,* → *vollziehen*) understand, duplicate.

'**nachwachsen** *v/i* (*irr, sep, -ge-, sn,* → *wachsen*) grow again.

'**Nachwahl** *f parl.* by-election, *Am.* special election.

'**Nachwehen** *pl fig.* aftermath.

'**nachweinen** (*sep, -ge-, h*) **I** *v/i* → *nachtrauern.* **II** *v/t* → *Träne.*

Nachweis ['na:xvaɪs] *m* (-es; -e) **1.** a) proof, evidence, *b*) certificate: *den* ~ *führen* (*or* *erbringen*) prove, show. **2.** detection. '**nachweisbar** *adj* demonstrable, detectable: *... sind* ~ *a.* ... can be proved. '**nachweisen** *v/t* (*irr, sep, -ge-, h,* → *weisen*) prove, establish: *man konnte ihm nichts* ~ nothing could be proved against him; *j-m e-n Fehler* ~ show that s.o. has made a mistake. '**nachweislich** **I** *adj* demonstrable. **II** *adv* demonstrably: *er war* ~ *da* there is evidence that he was there.

'**Nachwelt** *f* (-; *no pl*) posterity.

'**nachwirken** *v/i* (*sep, -ge-, h*) have a lasting effect. '**Nachwirkung** *f* after-effect: ~**en** *fig. a.* aftermath.

'**Nachwort** *n* (-[e]s; -e) epilog(ue *Br.*).

'**Nachwuchs** *m* (-es; *no pl*) **1.** a) the young generation, *b*) young talent (*a. sports*), F new blood, ⚘ junior staff, trainees, ✕ *etc* recruits: *der ärztliche* ~ the new generation of doctors. **2.** F a) offspring, *b*) addition to the family.

'**Nachwuchs...** a) talented, young, up-and-coming (*author, actor, etc*), *b*) ⚘ junior, trainee (*salesman etc*).

'**Nachwuchssorgen** *pl* ~ *haben* have difficulty (in) finding young talent.

'**nachzahlen** *v/t, v/i* (*sep, -ge-, h*) pay extra, pay later.

'nachzählen v/t (sep, -ge-, h) check.
'Nachzahlung f additional payment.
'nachziehen (irr, sep, -ge-, → ziehen) I v/t (h) **1.** drag (or pull) behind one, drag (foot etc). **2.** trace (line etc), pencil (eyebrows): **die Lippen ~** touch up one's lips. **3.** ⚙ tighten (screw etc). II v/i **4.** (sn) follow. **5.** (h) F fig. follow suit.
'Nachzügler [-tsy:glər] m (-s; -) **1.** straggler, latecomer. **2.** F late arrival.
Nacken ['nakən] m (-s; -) (nape of the) neck: **j-m im ~ sitzen** be hard on s.o.'s heels, a. fig. be breathing down s.o.'s neck; fig. **den ~ steifhalten** keep a stiff upper lip; → **steifen.**
'Nackenschlag m fig. blow.
'Nackenwirbel m cervical vertebra.
nackt [nakt] adj naked, bare (a. fig.), esp. art: nude: **völlig ~ stark** naked; **~ baden (malen)** swim (paint) in the nude; **sich ~ ausziehen** strip; **~e Tatsachen** hard facts; **die ~e Wahrheit** the plain truth; **das ~e Leben retten** escape with one's bare life.
'Nacktbadestrand m nudist beach.
'Nacktheit f (-; no pl) nakedness, fig. a. bareness.
'Nacktkul.tur f (-; no pl) nudism.
Nadel ['na:dəl] f (-; -n) a) needle, b) of record player: stylus, c) pin. **~baum** m conifer(ous tree). **~öhr** n **1.** eye of a needle. **2.** fig. bottleneck. **~stich** m (fig. pin)prick. **~streifen** m Anzug etc mit **~** pinstripe(d) suit etc. **~wald** m coniferous forest.
Nagel ['na:gəl] m (-s; ~) nail: fig. **et. an den ~ hängen** give s.th. up; **Nägel mit Köpfen machen** do things properly; **den ~ auf den Kopf treffen** hit the nail on the head; **er ist ein ~ zu m-m Sarg** he is a nail in my coffin. **~bett** n anat. nail bed. **~bürste** f nail brush. **~feile** f nail file. **~häutchen** n cuticle.
'Nagellack m nail varnish (or polish, Am. enamel). **~entferner** m nail-varnish (or nail-polish) remover.
nageln ['na:gəln] v/t (h) nail (an acc to).
'nagel'neu adj F brand-new.
'Nagelschere f (pair of) nail scissors.
nagen ['na:gən] v/t, v/i (h) a. fig. gnaw: **~ an** (dat) a. fig. gnaw at. **~nagend** adj fig. gnawing, nagging (doubt etc).
'Nager m (-s; -), **'Nagetier** n rodent.
'Nahaufnahme f film etc: close-up.

nahe ['na:ə] I adj a) near, close (both a. fig.), nearby, b) approaching, imminent (death etc): **der Nahe Osten** the Middle East; **in ~r Zukunft** in the near future; **den Tränen ~** on the verge of tears. II adv near, close, nearby: **~ bei** near (to), close to; **~ beieinander** close together; **~ verwandt** closely related; **von nah und fern** from far and near; **von ~m** up close, at close range; **j-m zu ~ treten** offend s.o.; **ich war ~ daran, ihn zu ohrfeigen** I very nearly slapped his face. III prep (dat) near, close to.
Nähe ['nɛ:ə] f (-; no pl) a) nearness (a. fig.), b) vicinity, neighbo(u)rhood: **aus der ~** at close range; **ganz in der ~** quite near; **in der ~ bleiben** stay around; **in d-r ~** near you; **in greifbare ~ gerückt** near at hand.
'nahe'bei adv nearby.
'nahebringen v/t (irr, sep, -ge-, h, → bringen) fig. **j-m et. ~** make s.o. appreciate s.th.
'nahegehen v/i (irr, sep, -ge-, sn, → gehen) fig. **j-m ~** affect s.o. deeply.
'nahegelegen I pp of **naheliegen.** II adj nearby.
'nahekommen v/i (irr, sep, -ge-, sn, → kommen) fig. come close (dat to): **sich (or einander) ~** become close.
'nahelegen v/t (sep, -ge-, h) fig. **j-m et. ~** suggest s.th. to s.o.; **j-m ~, et. zu tun** urge s.o. to do s.th.
'naheliegen v/i (irr, sep, -ge-, h, → liegen) fig. a) seem (very) likely, b) be the obvious thing: **die Vermutung liegt nahe, daß ...** it is fair to assume that ...
'naheliegend adj obvious.
nähen ['nɛ:ən] (h) I v/t sew, a. ❀ stitch: **sich ein Kleid ~** make a dress for o.s. II v/i sew.
näher ['nɛ:ər] I comp of **nahe.** II adj **1.** nearer, closer: **die ~e Umgebung** the (immediate) vicinity. **2.** further (data etc), more detailed: **bei ~er Betrachtung** on closer inspection. III adv **3.** (an dat, bei to) nearer, closer: **~ kommen** come (or draw) nearer. **4.** more closely: **ich kenne ihn ~** I know him quite well; **sich mit e-r Sache ~ befassen** go into a matter (more closely); **et. ~ erläutern** explain s.th. at greater detail.
'näherbringen v/t (irr, sep, -ge-, h, → bringen) fig. **j-m et. ~** make s.th. acces-

sible to s.o.; **Menschen einander ~** bring people closer together.

'**Nähere** n (-n; no pl) the details, (further) particulars: **ich weiß nichts ~s** I don't know any details.

Näherei [nɛːəˈraɪ] f (-; -en) sewing.

'**Naherholungsgebiet** n recreation area in the immediate vicinity of a big city.

'**näherkommen** v/i (irr, sep, -ge-, sn, → **kommen**) get (or be) nearer (dat to): fig. **j-m ~** become closer to s.o.; **jetzt kommen wir der Sache schon näher!** now we're getting somewhere!

'**näherliegen** v/i (irr, sep, -ge-, h, → **liegen**) fig. be more obvious.

nähern [ˈnɛːərn] **sich ~** (h) approach, a. draw near; **sich j-m ~** approach s.o.

'**Näherungs...** ⟨ approximate (calculation, value, etc).

'**nahestehen** v/i (irr, sep, -ge-, h, → **stehen**) fig. **j-m ~** be close to s.o.

'**nahezu** adv almost, nearly, next to.

'**Nähgarn** n sewing thread.

'**Nahkampf** m 1. ✕ close combat. 2. boxing: infighting.

nahm [naːm] pret of **nehmen**.

'**Nähma,schine** f sewing machine.

'**Nährboden** m 1. culture medium (for bacteria). 2. fig. breeding ground.

'**Nährcreme** f nutrient cream.

nähren [ˈnɛːrən] (h) **I** v/t feed, fig. nourish (hope etc), a. harbo(u)r (hatred etc): **sich ~ von** live on. **II** v/i be nourishing.

'**nahrhaft** adj nutritious, nourishing.

'**Nährmittel** pl cereal products.

'**Nährstoff** m nutrient.

Nahrung [ˈnaːrʊŋ] f (-; no pl) food, diet: **geistige ~** food for the mind.

'**Nahrungsaufnahme** f food intake.

'**Nahrungskette** f biol. food chain.

'**Nahrungsmangel** m lack of food.

'**Nahrungsmittel** n food(stuff), pl foodstuffs. **~chemiker** m food chemist.

'**Nährwert** m nutritional value.

'**Nähseide** f sewing silk.

Naht [naːt] f (-; ⁓e) seam, ⊙ a. joint: F **aus den (or allen) Nähten platzen** a. fig. be bursting at the seams.

'**nahtlos** adj 1. seamless. 2. fig. smooth.

'**Nahverkehr** m local traffic.

'**Nahverkehrszug** m commuter train.

'**Nähzeug** n (-[e]s; no pl) sewing kit.

'**Nahziel** n immediate objective.

naiv [naˈiːf] adj naive: **~er Maler** primitive.

Naivität [naiviˈtɛːt] f (-; no pl) naivety.

Name [ˈnaːmə] m (-n; -n) name, a. reputation: **wie ist Ihr ~?** what is your name?; **im ~n** (gen), **in j-s ~n** → **namens** II; **(nur) dem ~n nach** by name (only); **sich e-n ~n machen** make a name for o.s.; **das Kind beim rechten ~n nennen** call a spade a spade.

'**Namenliste** f list of names.

'**namenlos** adj 1. nameless, a. anonymous. 2. fig. unspeakable.

'**namens I** adv by the name of, called. **II** prep (gen) in the name of, on behalf of.

'**Namens|aktie** f registered share (Am. stock). **~schild** n name plate. **~tag** m name day. **~vetter** m namesake. **~zug** m signature.

namentlich [ˈnaːməntlɪç] **I** adj 1. by name: **~e Abstimmung** roll-call vote. **II** adv 2. by name. 3. fig. (e)specially.

'**namhaft** adj 1. considerable (sum etc). 2. well-known (artist etc). 3. **~ machen** name.

nämlich [ˈnɛːmlɪç] adv 1. namely, that is (to say). 2. for, you see, you know.

nannte [ˈnantə] pret of **nennen**.

nanu [naˈnuː] int hey.

Napalm [ˈnaːpalm] n (-s; no pl) napalm.

Napf [napf] m (-[e]s; ⁓e) bowl.

'**Napfkuchen** m deep-dish cake.

Nappa [ˈnapa] n (-[s]; -s), '**Nappaleder** n nap(p)a (leather).

Narbe [ˈnarbə] f (-; -n) 1. ✿ scar: fig. **~n hinterlassen** leave a scar. 2. ♀ stigma.

'**narbig** adj scarred.

Narkose [narˈkoːzə] f (-; -n) (in ~ under) an(a)esthesia: **aus der ~ aufwachen** come round. **Nar'kosefacharzt** m an(a)esthetist. **Narkotikum** [narˈkoːti-kʊm] n (-s; -ka), **narkotisch** [narˈkoː-tɪʃ] adj narcotic. **narkotisieren** [narko-tiˈziːrən] v/t (h) an(a)esthetize.

Narr [nar] m (-en; -en) fool: F **e-n ~en gefressen haben an** (dat) be crazy about; **j-n zum ~en halten** → '**narren** v/t **j-n ~** make a fool of s.o., fool s.o.

'**Narrenfreiheit** f fool's licen/ce (Am. -se). '**narrensicher** adj F foolproof.

Närrin [ˈnɛrɪn] f (-; -nen) fool.

'**närrisch** adj a) foolish, b) mad, c) odd.

Narzisse [narˈtsɪsə] f (-; -n) ♀ narcissus: **Gelbe ~** daffodil.

Narzißmus [nar'tsɪsmʊs] *m* (-; *no pl*) *psych.* narcissism. **nar'zißtisch** [-tɪʃ] *adj* narcissistic.

nasal [na'za:l] *adj* nasal.

nasalieren [naza'li:rən] *v/t* (h) nasalize. **Na'sallaut** *m* nasal (sound).

naschen ['naʃən] *v/i, v/t* (h) nibble (*an dat, von* at): **gern** ~ have a sweet tooth. **Nasche'rei** *f* (-; -en) sweets, F goodies. **'naschhaft** *adj* sweet-toothed.

Nase ['na:zə] *f* (-; -n) nose: F *pro* ~ *e-n Dollar* one dollar each; *fig.* **e-e gute** (*or feine*) ~ **haben für** have a good nose for; *in der* ~ **bohren** pick one's nose; F *fig. auf die* ~ **fallen** come a cropper; *j-m et. auf die* ~ **binden** tell (s.th. to) s.o.; *j-n an der* ~ **herumführen** lead s.o. up the garden path; *j-m auf der* ~ **herumtanzen** do what one likes with s.o.; *auf der* ~ **liegen** be laid up; *man sieht es dir an der* ~ an it's written all over your face; *es j-m unter die* ~ **reiben** rub it in; *s-e* ~ *in alles* (*hinein*)*stecken* poke one's nose into everything; *die* ~ **voll haben** be fed up (*von* with); *die* ~ **vorn haben** be one step ahead (of one's competitors); *j-m et. vor der* ~ **wegschnappen** take s.th. away from under s.o.'s nose; *der Zug fuhr mir vor der* ~ **weg** I missed the train by an inch; → *zuhalten* 2.

näseln ['nɛ:zəln] *v/i* (h) speak through one's nose. **'Näseln** *n* (-s) (nasal) twang. **'näselnd** *adj* nasal.

'Nasen|bein *n* nasal bone. **~bluten** *n* nosebleed. **~flügel** *m* nostril. **~länge** *f* um *e-e* ~ **gewinnen** win by a whisker. **~loch** *n* nostril. **~rücken** *m* bridge of the nose. **~scheidewand** *f* nasal septum. **~schleimhaut** *f* nasal mucous membrane. **~spitze** *f* tip of the nose. **~spray** *m, n* nose spray. **~tropfen** *pl* nose drops. **~wurzel** *f* root of the nose.

Nashorn ['na:s-] *n* rhinoceros, F rhino.

naß [nas] *adj* wet: ~ **machen** wet (*sich o.s.*); ~ **werden** get wet; *durch und durch* ~, ~ *bis auf die Haut* wet through, wet to the skin; → *triefen*.

Nassauer ['nasaʊər] *m* (-s; -) F sponge. **'nassauern** *v/i* (h) F sponge (*bei* on).

Nässe ['nɛsə] *f* (-; *no pl*) wet, wetness: „*vor* ~ *schützen!*" "keep dry!"

'nässen (h) **I** *v/t* wet. **II** *v/i* *wound*: weep.

'naßkalt *adj* damp and cold, clammy.

'Naßra,sur *f* wet shave.

'Naßzelle *f* (prefab) bathroom unit.

Nation [na'tsi̯o:n] *f* (-; -en) nation.

national [natsi̯o'na:l] *adj* national.

Natio'nalfeiertag *m* national holiday.

Natio'nalflagge *f* national flag.

Natio'nalheld *m* national hero.

Natio'nalhymne *f* national anthem.

nationalisieren [natsi̯onali'zi:rən] *v/t* (h) nationalize. **Nationali'sierung** *f* (-; -en) nationalization.

Nationalismus [natsi̯ona'lɪsmʊs] *m* (-; *no pl*) nationalism. **Nationalist** [-'lɪst] *m* (-en; -en) nationalist.

nationa'listisch *adj* nationalist(ic).

Nationalität [natsi̯onali'tɛ:t] *f* (-; -en) nationality.

Natio'nal|mannschaft *f sports*: national team. **~park** *m* national park. **~sozia,lismus** *m pol. hist.* National Socialism, *contp.* Nazism. **~sozia,list** *m*, **♀sozia,listisch** *adj pol. hist.* National Socialist, *contp.* Nazi. **~spieler(in** *f*) *m sports*: international. **~stolz** *m* national pride.

Natrium ['na:tri̯ʊm] *n* (-s; *no pl*) sodium.

Natron ['na:trɔn] *n* (-s; *no pl*) bicarbonate of soda.

Natter ['natər] *f* (-; -n) *zo.* adder.

Natur [na'tu:r] *f* (-; -en) **1.** *no pl* nature: *in der freien* ~ in the open country; *nach der* ~ *zeichnen* draw from nature (*or* life); *von* ~ (*aus*) by nature; *Fragen grundsätzlicher* ~ fundamental questions; *die Sache ist ernster* ~ it's a serious matter; *er hat e-e gesunde* ~ he has a healthy constitution. **2.** character, person.

Naturalien [natu'ra:li̯ən] *pl* natural produce: *in* ~ *zahlen* pay in kind.

naturalisieren [naturali'zi:rən] *v/t* (h) naturalize.

Naturalismus [natura'lɪsmʊs] *m* (-; *pl*) naturalism.

natura'listisch *adj* naturalist(ic).

Na'turdenkmal *n* natural monument.

Naturell [natu'rɛl] *n* (-s; -e) disposition, temperament.

Na'tur|ereignis *n*, **~erscheinung** *f* natural phenomenon. **~forscher** *m* naturalist. **~forschung** *f* natural science. **~freund(in** *f*) *m* nature lover. **♀gemäß** *adj* natural. **~geschichte** *f* natural history. **~gesetz** *n* law of nature. **♀getreu**

adj true to nature, lifelike. **~gewalt** *f* force of nature. **~heilkunde** *f* naturopathy. **~kata,strophe** *f* natural disaster. **~kunde** *f* (-; *no pl*) natural history. **~lehrpfad** *m* nature trail.

natürlich [na'ty:rlɪç] **I** *adj* natural: **~e Größe** actual size. **II** *adv* naturally, *int* *a.* of course.

Na'türlichkeit *f* (-; *no pl*) naturalness.

Na'tur|park *m* wildlife park. **~pro,dukt** *n* natural product. **~schutz** *m* conservation: **unter ~ stehen** be protected. **~schützer** *m* (-s; -) conservationist. **~schutzgebiet** *n* nature reserve. **~ta,lent** *n* **ein ~ sein** be a natural. ♀**verbunden** *adj* nature-loving. **~volk** *n* primitive race. **~wissenschaft** *f* (natural) science. **~wissenschaftler** *m* (natural) scientist. ♀**wissenschaftlich** *adj* scientific. **~wunder** *n* natural wonder. **~zustand** *m* (-[e]s; *no pl*) natural state, (*im ~* in a) state of nature.

nautisch ['nautɪʃ] *adj* nautical.

Navigation [naviga'tsio:n] *f* (-; *no pl*) navigation. **Navigator** [-'ga:tɔr] *m* (-s; -en [-ga'to:rən]) navigator. **navigieren** [-'gi:rən] *v/t*, *v/i* (h) navigate.

Nazi ['na:tsi] *m* (-s; -s) *pol. hist. contp.* Nazi. **Nazismus** [na'tsɪsmus] *m* (-; *no pl*) *pol. hist. contp.* Nazism. **na'zistisch** [-tɪʃ] *adj pol. hist. contp.* Nazi.

Nebel ['ne:bəl] *m* (-s; -) **1.** fog (*a. fig.*), mist. **2.** *astr.* nebula.

'nebelhaft *adj fig.* nebulous, hazy.

'Nebelscheinwerfer *m mot.* fog lamp.

'Nebelschlußleuchte *f* rear fog lamp.

neben ['ne:bən] *prep* (*dat*) **1.** (*a. acc*) a) beside, by (*or* at) the side of, by, b) close to, near, next to: **setzen Sie sich ~ mich** sit beside (*or* next to) me. **2.** apart from, besides: **~ anderen Dingen** among other things. **3.** compared with (*or* to). **4.** simultaneously with.

'Neben|absicht *f* secondary objective. **~ak,zent** *m ling.* secondary stress.

'nebenamtlich *adj* part-time (*job etc*).

neben'an *adv* a) next door, b) in the next room.

'Neben|anschluß *m teleph.* extension. **~arbeit** *f* **1.** extra work. **2.** minor job. **~ausgaben** *pl* incidental expenses, extras. **~ausgang** *m* side exit. **~bedeutung** *f ling.* connotation.

neben'bei *adv* **1.** besides, in addition. **2.**

in passing: **~ bemerkt** incidentally.

'Nebenberuf *m* sideline: **im ~** → **nebenberuflich** II. **'nebenberuflich** **I** *adj* sideline. **II** *adv* as a sideline.

'Nebenbeschäftigung *f* sideline.

'Nebenbuhler [-bu:lər] *m* (-s; -) rival.

nebenein'ander *adv* side by side: **~ bestehen** coexist. **Nebenein'ander** *n* (-s; *no pl*) coexistence.

nebenein'anderstellen *v/t* (*sep*, -ge-, h) **1.** put (*or* place) side by side (*or* next to each other). **2.** compare.

'Neben|eingang *m* side entrance. **~einkommen** *n*, **~einkünfte** *pl*, **~einnahmen** *pl* incidental earnings, extra income. **~erscheinung** *f* side effect (♣ symptom). **~fach** *n ped.* subsidiary subject, *Am.* minor (subject). **~fluß** *m* tributary. **~gebäude** *n* **1.** adjoining building. **2.** annex(e). **~handlung** *f* subplot.

neben'her *adv* **1.** → **nebenbei** 1. **2.** by his (*or* her) side, beside.

'Neben|höhle *f anat.* sinus. **~kosten** *pl* extras. **~linie** *f* **1.** ♣ branch line. **2.** *descent:* collateral line. **~mann** *m mein etc* → the person next to me *etc.* **~pro,dukt** *n* (*gen*) by-product (of), spin-off (from). **~rolle** *f thea.* minor part, *fig.* minor role. **~sache** *f* minor matter: **das ist ~!** that's quite unimportant (here)! ♀**sächlich** *adj* a) minor, unimportant, b) irrelevant. **~satz** *m ling.* subordinate clause. **~sai,son** *f* low season. ♀**stehend** *adj* in the margin: **~** (*abgebildet*) opposite. **~stelle** *f* a) branch (office), b) *teleph.* extension. **~straße** *f* side street, byroad. **~tisch** *m* (*am ~* at the) next table. **~wirkung** *f* side effect. **~zimmer** *n* next (*or* adjoining) room.

neblig ['ne:blɪç] *adj* foggy, misty.

Necessaire [nesɛ'sɛ:r] *n* (-s; -s) **1.** toilet bag. **2.** manicure set.

necken ['nɛkən] *v/t* (h) tease.

'neckisch *adj* playful.

Neffe ['nɛfə] *m* (-n; -n) nephew.

Negation [nega'tsio:n] *f* (-; -en) negation. **negativ** *adj*, **Negativ** ['ne:gati:f] *n* (-s; -e) Ŗ, *phot., phys.* negative.

Neger ['ne:gər] *m* (-s; -) negro. **2.** F *fig.* a) ghostwriter, b) *TV* idiot board.

'Negerin *f* (-; -nen) negress.

negieren [ne'gi:rən] *v/t* (h) negate, deny.

Negligé [negli'ʒe:] *n* (-s; -s) négligé.

nehmen ['ne:mən] v/t (nahm, genommen, h) **1.** take (a. **an sich ~**, a. bus, curve, obstacle, etc), at table: help o.s. to, a. accept, a. buy, a. engage, hire (s.o.): **et. zu sich ~** eat s.th.; **ich nehme Wein** I'll have wine; (**sich**) **e-n Anwalt ~** retain counsel; **er versteht es, die Kunden zu ~** he has a way with the customers; **wie man's nimmt!** that depends!; F **er ist hart im Nehmen** he can take a lot (of punishment); → **Angriff, Anspruch, Beispiel, ernst** II, **Hürde** I etc. **2.** **j-m et. ~** take s.th. away from s.o., free s.o. of (pain, inhibitions, etc), deprive s.o. of (hope, rights, etc); **es sich nicht ~ lassen zu** inf insist on ger. **3.** fig. **auf sich ~** take upon o.s., assume (office, task, etc). **4.** take, charge (**für** for).

Nehrung ['ne:ruŋ] f (-; -en) geogr. spit.

Neid [naɪt] m (-[e]s; no pl) envy (**auf** acc of), jealousy (**aus** out of envy; **blaß** (or **gelb, grün) vor ~** green with envy; F **das muß ihm der ~ lassen** you have to hand it to him.

neiden ['naɪdən] v/t (h) **j-m et. ~** envy s.o. s.th.

'Neider m (-s; -) **viele ~ haben** be envied by many people.

'neidisch I adj (**auf** acc of) envious, jealous. II adv enviously, with envy.

'neidlos adj and adv without envy.

Neige ['naɪgə] f (-; -n) rest, dregs: fig. **bis zur bitteren ~** to the bitter end.

neigen ['naɪgən] (h) I v/t a) incline, b) bend, bow, c) tilt. II **sich ~** a) incline, terrain: slope, b) bend, bow (**vor** dat to). III v/i **~ zu** have a tendency to, be inclined to, esp. ✠ be prone to; **ich neige zu der Ansicht, daß ...** I am inclined to think that ...

'Neigung f (-; -en) **1.** inclination, slope, gradient. **2.** fig. (**zu**) a) inclination, tendency (to, towards), trend (to), esp. ✠ proneness (to), b) liking (for, of), penchant, predilection (for), c) affection (for), love (of).

'Neigungswinkel m angle of inclination.

nein [naɪn] adv no: **~, so was!** well, I never!; **aber ~!** of course (or certainly) not!; fig. **er kann nicht ~ sagen** he can't refuse anything.

Nein n (-[s]; -[s]) no: **mit (e-m) ~ antwor-**

ten answer in the negative, say no.

'Neinstimme f no (pl noes), Am. nay.

Nektar ['nɛktar] m (-s; -e) nectar.

Nektarine [nɛkta'ri:nə] f (-; -n) ✿ nectarine.

Nelke ['nɛlkə] f (-; -n) **1.** ✿ carnation. **2.** gastr. clove.

nennen ['nɛnən] (nannte, genannt, h) I v/t **1.** call, name: **das nenne ich ...** that's what I call ... **2.** name, mention, give (example, one's name, etc), nominate (candidate), sports: enter (**für** for). II **sich ~** call o.s. (a. iro.), be called: **und das nennt sich Fachmann!** and he is supposed to be an expert!

'nennenswert adj worth mentioning.

'Nenner m (-s; -) & (a. fig. **et. auf e-n gemeinsamen ~ bringen** reduce s.th. to a common) denominator; fig. **e-n gemeinsamen ~ finden** reach an agreement (on the matter).

'Nennleistung f ✪ rated output (⚡ power). **'Nennspannung** f ⚡ rated voltage.

'Nennung f (-; -en) naming, mention, pol. nomination, sports etc: entry.

'Nennwert m ✝ nominal (or face) value: **zum ~** at par; **unter dem ~** below par.

Neofa'schismus [neo-] m neo-fascism.

Neofa'schist m (-en; -en), **neofa'schistisch** adj neo-fascist.

Neon ['ne:ɔn] n (-s; no pl) neon.

'Neonleuchte f neon light.

Nepp [nɛp] m (-s; no pl) F rip-off.

'neppen v/t (h) F fleece, rip s.o. off.

'Nepplo,kal n clip joint.

Nerv [nɛrf] m (-s; -en) nerve, & a. vein: **er hat ~en wie Drahtseile** he's got nerves of steel; **die ~en behalten (verlieren)** keep (lose) one's head; F **j-m auf die ~en gehen** get on s.o.'s nerves; **sie ist mit den ~en am Ende (F völlig fertig)** she's a nervous wreck; **~en zeigen** get nervy; F **du hast vielleicht ~en!** you've got a nerve!

nerven ['nɛrfən] v/t (h) F **j-n ~** get on s.o.'s nerves.

'Nerven|arzt m neurologist. **⚄aufreibend** adj nerve-racking. **~belastung** f (nervous) strain. **~bündel** n F **sie ist ein ~** she is a bundle of nerves. **~entzündung** f neuritis. **~gas** n ✗ nerve gas. **~kitzel** m fig. thrill. **~klinik** f mental hospital, psychiatric clinic. **⚄krank** adj mentally ill. **~krankheit** f nervous

disease. **~krieg** *m fig.* war of nerves.
~probe *f fig.* ordeal. **~sache** *f F das ist reine ~!* that's just a question of nerves!
~säge *f* F pain in the neck. **~schmerz** *m* neuralgia. **²stark** *adj* strong-nerved.
~stärke *f* strong nerves: **~ beweisen** remain cool. **~sy‚stem** *n* nervous system. **~zentrum** *n* nerve cent/re (*Am.* -er). **~zusammenbruch** *m* nervous breakdown.

ˈnervlich *adj* nervous.
nervös [nɛrˈvøːs] *adj* nervous: **~ werden** get nervous; **j-n ~ machen** a) make s.o. nervous, b) get on s.o.'s nerves.
Nervosität [nɛrvoziˈtɛːt] *f* (-; *no pl*) nervousness.
ˈnervtötend *adj* F nerve-racking (*noise etc*), soul-destroying (*work etc*).
Nerz [nɛrts] *m* (-es; -e) **1.** *zo.* mink. **2.** → **ˈNerzmantel** *m* mink (coat).
Nessel [ˈnɛsəl] *f* (-; -n) & nettle: F *sich in die ~n setzen* get o.s. into trouble.
ˈNesselfieber *n* ✿ nettle rash.
Nest [nɛst] *n* (-[e]s; -er) **1.** nest: *fig. das eigene ~ beschmutzen* foul one's own nest; F *das ~ war leer* the bird(s) had flown. **2.** F small place, dump.
ˈNesthäkchen *n* pet of the family.
ˈNestwärme *f fig.* warmth and security.
nett [nɛt] *adj* nice (*a. iro.*): *sei so ~ und hilf mir* be so kind as to help me; F *ein ~es Sümmchen* a nice (*or* tidy) sum.
netto [ˈnɛto] *adv* ✝ net, clear.
ˈNetto|einkommen *n* net income.
~gewicht *n* net weight. **~lohn** *m* take-home pay. **~preis** *m* net price.
Netz [nɛts] *n* (-es; -e) **1.** net: *fig. j-m ins ~ gehen* walk into s.o.'s net. **2.** *fig.* network, system, ⚡ mains: *ans ~ gehen* power station: go into operation.
ˈNetz|anschluß *m* ⚡ mains connection.
~ausfall *m* ⚡ power failure. **~ball** *m* *tennis:* net (ball). **~haut** *f anat.* retina.
~hemd *n* string vest. **~kabel** *n* ⚡ mains cable. **~karte** *f* runaround ticket. **~plan** *m* network. **~plantechnik** *f* network analysis. **~schalter** *m* ⚡ power switch.
~stecker *m* ⚡ mains plug. **~strumpf** *m* net (*or* mesh) stocking. **~teil** *n* ⚡ power supply unit. **~werk** *n* network.
neu [nɔy] **I** *adj* a) new, *a.* fresh (*a. fig.*), *a.* novel, b) recent, modern, c) renewed: *ganz ~* brand-new; *wie ~* as good as new; **~er Anfang** fresh start; *neueren*

Datums of recent date; *~e Schwierigkeiten* more problems; *neuere Sprachen* modern languages; *neueste Nachrichten* latest news; *das ist mir ~!* that's new to me! **II** *adv* a) newly, b) recently, c) anew, afresh: **~ anfangen** start anew; **~ beleben** revive; **~ eröffnen** reopen; **~ gestalten** reorganize, ☉ remodel; **~ schreiben** rewrite.
ˈNeuankömmling *m* newcomer.
ˈNeuanschaffung *f* new acquisition.
ˈneuartig *adj* novel, new (type of).
ˈNeuauflage *f* **1.** *print.* a) new edition, b) reprint. **2.** *fig.* repeat (performance).
ˈNeuausgabe *f* new edition.
ˈNeubau *m* (-[e]s; -ten) new building.
ˈNeubaugebiet *n* new housing estate.
ˈNeubearbeitung *f* **1.** a) revised edition, b) revision. **2.** *thea. etc* adaptation.
ˈNeubildung *f* **1.** (new) formation, reorganization. **2.** a) *physiol.* regeneration, b) ✿ tumo(u)r. **3.** *ling.* neologism.
ˈNeudruck *m* reprint.
ˈNeue¹ *n* (-n) **1.** s.th. new: *das ~ daran* what's new about it; *das Neueste* the latest thing; *was gibt's Neues?* what's new?; *das ist mir nichts Neues* that's no news to me. **2.** *aufs neue, von neuem* afresh, anew; *seit neuem* of late.
ˈNeue² *m, f* (-n; -n) new man (woman).
ˈNeueinstellung *f* **1.** taking on (new) labo(u)r. **2.** new employee.
ˈNeuentdeckung *f* **1.** recent discovery. **2.** rediscovery.
ˈneuerdings *adv* recently, lately, of late.
ˈNeuerer [ˈnɔyərər] *m* (-s; -) innovator.
ˈNeuerscheinung *f* new publication.
ˈNeuerung *f* (-; -en) innovation.
ˈneuestens *adv* quite recently, lately.
ˈNeufassung *f* **1.** revision. **2.** revised version.
ˈneugebacken *adj* F *fig.* newly-fledged.
ˈneugeboren *adj* newborn: *fig. ich fühle mich wie ~* I feel a different person.
ˈNeugeborene *n* (-n; -n) newborn (child).
ˈNeugestaltung *f* reshaping, reorganization, ☉ remodel(l)ing.
ˈNeugier *f* (-; *no pl*) curiosity.
ˈneugierig *adj* (*auf acc*) curious (about, of), inquisitive (after, about): *ich bin ~, ob ...* I wonder if ...
ˈNeugliederung *f* reorganization.
ˈneugotisch *adj* neo-Gothic.

'Neugründung *f* (new) foundation.
'Neuheit *f* (-; -en) **1.** *no pl* newness, novelty. **2.** novelty, ⚙ *a.* innovation.
'Neuigkeit *f* (-; -en) (piece of) news.
'Neuinsze,nierung *f* new production.
'Neujahr *n* New Year('s Day): ***Prosit ~!*** Happy New Year!
'Neujahrstag *m* New Year's Day.
'Neuland *n* (-[e]s; *no pl*) *fig.* ***~ erschließen*** break new ground; ***das ist ~ für mich*** that is new territory to me.
'neulich *adv* the other day, recently.
'Neuling *m* (-s; -e) (***in*** *dat*, ***auf e-m Gebiet***) newcomer (to), novice (at).
'neumodisch *adj contp.* newfangled.
'Neumond *m* new moon.
neun [nɔʏn] *adj* nine: ***alle ~e!*** strike!
Neun *f* (-; -en) (number) nine.
'neunhundert *adj* nine hundred.
'neunjährig [-jɛ:rɪç] *adj* **1.** nine-year-old. **2.** nine-year, of nine years.
'neunmalklug *adj iro.* smart-alecky.
neunt *adj* **1.** ninth. **2. *zu ~*** (the) nine of us (*or* them *etc*). **'Neunte** *m, f* (-n; -n) ninth. **'neuntens** *adv* ninth(ly).
'neunzehn *adj* nineteen.
'neunzehnt *adv* nineteenth.
neunzig ['nɔʏntsɪç] *adj* **1.** ninety.
'Neunzig *f* (-; -en) (number) ninety: ***er ist Anfang ~*** he is in his early nineties.
neunziger ['nɔʏntsɪgər] *adj* ***die ~ Jahre*** the nineties. **'Neunziger** *m* (-s; -), **'Neunzigerin** *f* (-; -nen) man (woman) of ninety, nonagenarian.
'Neuordnung *f* reorganization.
'Neuorien,tierung *f* reorientation.
'Neuphilo,loge *m* teacher (*or* student) of modern languages.
'Neuphilolo,gie *f* modern languages.
Neuralgie [nɔʏral'gi:] *f* (-; -n) ⚕ neuralgia. **neuralgisch** [nɔʏ'ralgɪʃ] *adj* ⚕ neuralgic: *fig.* ***~er Punkt*** critical point, *pol.* trouble spot.
'Neuregelung *f* revision.
'Neureiche *m, f* (-n; -n) parvenue: ***die ~n*** the nouveau riches.
Neurochir'urg *m* neurosurgeon.
Neurologe [nɔʏro'lo:gə] *m* (-n; -n) neurologist.
Neurose [nɔʏ'ro:zə] *f* (-; -n) ⚕ neurosis.
Neurotiker [nɔʏ'ro:tikər] *m* (-s; -), **neu'rotisch** [-tɪʃ] *adj* neurotic.
'Neuschnee *m* fresh-fallen snow.
Neu'seeland *n* (-s) New Zealand.
Neu'seeländer *m* (-s; -), **Neu'seeländerin** *f* (-; -nen) New Zealander.
neu'seeländisch *adj* New Zealand.
'neusprachlich *adj* modern-language.
neutral [nɔʏ'tra:l] *adj* neutral.
neutralisieren [nɔʏtrali'zi:rən] *v/t* (h) neutralize. **Neutralität** [nɔʏtrali'tɛ:t] *f* (-; *no pl*) neutrality.
Neutron ['nɔʏtrɔn] *n* (-s; -en [nɔʏ'tro:nən]) neutron. **Neu'tronenbombe** *f* neutron bomb.
Neutrum ['nɔʏtrʊm] *n* (-s; -tra) neuter.
'Neuverfilmung *f* remake.
'Neuwahl *f* new election.
'neuwertig *adj* practically new.
'Neuwort *n* (-[e]s; ⁼er) neologism.
'Neuzeit *f* (-; *no pl*) modern times.
'neuzeitlich *adj* modern.
nicht [nɪçt] *adv* not: ***~ besser*** no better; ***~ (ein)mal*** not even; ***~ mehr*** no longer; (***bitte***) ***~!*** (please) don't!; ***~, daß ich wüßte!*** not that I know of!; ***er ist krank, ~ wahr?*** he is ill, isn't he?; ***du tust es doch, ~ wahr?*** you will do it, won't you?; → ***auch*** 1, ***gar***² 1, ***nur.***
'Nicht|achtung *f* disregard. **~angriffspakt** *m* nonaggression treaty. **~beachtung** *f* (*gen* of) a) disregard, b) nonobservance (*of rules etc*).
Nichte ['nɪçtə] *f* (-; -n) niece.
'Nicht|einhaltung *f* noncompliance (*gen* with). **~einmischung** *f pol.* noninterference, nonintervention. **~erfüllung** *f* ⚖ nonperformance. **~erscheinen** *n* nonappearance, ⚖ *a.* default.
'nichtexi,stent *adj* nonexisting.
'nichtig *adj* **1.** trivial, vain: ***~er Vorwand*** flimsy excuse. **2.** ⚖ (***null und***) ***~*** (null and) void.
'Nichtigkeit *f* (-; -en) **1.** *no pl* a) triviality, vanity, b) ⚖ nullity. **2.** *pl* trifles.
'Nichtmitglied *n* nonmember.
'Nichtraucher(in *f*) *m* nonsmoker.
'nichtrostend *adj* rustproof, stainless.
nichts *indef pron* nothing, not ... anything: ***~ als Ärger*** nothing but trouble; ***~ weniger als das*** anything but that; ***~ da!*** nothing doing!; ***so gut wie ~*** next to nothing; ***das ist ~ für mich!*** that's not my thing!; ***mir ~, dir ~*** just like that, quite coolly; ***weiter ~?*** is that all?; F ***wie ~*** in a flash; F ***~ wie hin!*** let's go (there fast)!; → ***dergleichen*** 2, ***gar***² 1, ***Nähere*** *etc.*

niedrig

Nichts n (-; no pl) **1.** nothing(ness), void: *aus dem ~* appear etc from nowhere, *make etc* out of nothing; *vor dem ~ stehen* be left with nothing. **2.** *ein ~* a) a trifle, nothing, b) *contp.* a nobody.

nichtsahnend adj unsuspecting.

Nichtschwimmer(in f)m nonswimmer.

nichtsdesto|'trotz adv F, **~'weniger** adv nevertheless, none the less.

Nichtskönner m (-s; -) incompetent person, F washout.

nichtssagend adj empty (words etc), meaningless, vague (answer).

Nichtstuer m (-s; -) idler, loafer.

Nichtstun n idling, loafing, inactivity.

Nichtswisser m (-s; -) ignoramus.

Nichtvorhandensein n nonexistence.

Nichtzahlung f ♱ *bei ~* in default of payment.

Nichtzutreffende n *~s streichen!* delete where inapplicable!

Nickel ['nɪkəl] n (-s; no pl) nickel.

Nickelbrille f steel-rimmed spectacles.

nicken ['nɪkən] v/i (h) nod (one's head).

Nickerchen ['nɪkərçən] n (-s; -) F nap.

nie [niː] adv never: *fast ~* hardly ever; *noch ~* never (before); *~ wieder* never again; *~ und nimmer* never ever.

nieder ['niːdər] **I** adj low (a. fig.), inferior (rank, value), lower (echelon etc). **II** adv low, down: *~ mit ...!* down with ...!

niederbrennen v/t, v/i (irr, sep, -ge-, h, → **brennen**) burn down.

niederbrüllen v/t (sep, -ge-, h) *j-n ~* shout s.o. down.

niederdeutsch adj Low German.

niederdrücken v/t (sep, -ge-, h) **1.** press s.th. down. **2.** fig. depress (s.o.).

Niederfre,quenz f ⚡ low frequency.

Niedergang m (-[e]s; no pl) decline.

niedergehen v/i (irr, sep, -ge-, sn, → **gehen**) come down (a. ✈), rain: fall, storm: burst.

niedergeschlagen I pp of **niederschlagen. II** adj fig. depressed, dejected. **'Niedergeschlagenheit** f (-; no pl) depression, dejection.

niederknien v/i (sep,-ge-,sn) kneel down.

Niederlage f (-; -n) **1.** defeat: *e-e ~ erleiden* be defeated. **2.** ♱ a) depot, warehouse, b) → **Niederlassung** 2.

Niederlande pl the Netherlands.

Niederländer m (-s; -) Dutchman, Netherlander: *die ~* the Dutch.

'Niederländerin f (-; -nen) Dutch woman, Netherlander.

'niederländisch adj Dutch.

niederlassen (irr, sep, -ge-, h, → **lassen**) **I** v/t **1.** lower, let s.th. down. **II** sich ~ **2.** sit down. **3.** settle (in dat in, at). **4.** set up in business (or as a doctor, lawyer, etc), establish o.s. (als as).

'Niederlassung f (-; -en) **1.** establishment, settling. **2.** ♱ a) place of business, b) branch (office).

'niederlegen (sep, -ge-, h) **I** v/t lay down (one's arms etc): *ein Amt ~* resign an office; *die Arbeit ~* (go on) strike, walk out; *et. schriftlich ~* put s.th. down in writing. **II** sich ~ lie down.

'Niederlegung f (-; no pl) (gen) **1.** laying down (of). **2.** resignation (from).

'niedermachen v/t (sep, -ge-, h) **1.** massacre, slaughter. **2.** → **fertigmachen** 3.

'niederreißen (sep, -ge-, h, → **reißen**) pull down (a. fig.), demolish.

'Niederschlag m **1.** meteor. precipitation, rain(fall). **2.** 🜍 a) precipitate, b) sediment: *radioaktiver ~* (nuclear) fallout; fig. *s-n ~ finden in* (dat) be reflected in. **3.** boxing: a) knockdown, b) knockout. **'niederschlagen** (irr, sep, -ge-, h, → **schlagen**) **I** v/t **1.** *j-n ~* knock s.o. down, boxing: knock s.o. out. **2.** cast down (one's eyes). **3.** fig. suppress, put down (revolt etc). **4.** 🜍 quash (proceedings). **II** sich ~ **5.** 🜍 precipitate. **6.** fig. be reflected (in dat in).

'niederschlagsreich adj rainy, wet.

'niederschmettern v/t (sep, -ge-, h) *j-n ~* knock s.o. down, fig. shatter s.o.

'niederschmetternd adj fig. shattering.

'Niederschrift f (-; -en) **1.** writing down. **2.** notes, record, minutes.

'Niederspannung f ⚡ low tension.

'niederstrecken v/t (sep, -ge-, h) fell.

'Niedertracht f (-; no pl) **1.** baseness. **2.** perfidy, F dirty trick.

'niederträchtig adj low, perfidious.

'Niederung f (-; -en) lowland(s).

'niederwerfen: sich ~ (irr, sep, -ge-, h, → **werfen**) throw o.s. down; *sich vor j-m ~* throw o.s. at s.o.'s feet.

niedlich ['niːtlɪç] adj sweet, cute.

niedrig ['niːdrɪç] adj low, inferior (quality etc), a. lowly, humble (origin etc), b.s. a. base: *~ fliegen* fly low; *~ halten* keep prices etc down.

'**Niedrigkeit** f (-; no pl) lowness.
'**niemals** → **nie**.
niemand ['ni:mant] indef pron nobody, no one: **ich habe ~(en) gesehen** I didn't see anybody; **~ anders** nobody else; **~ anders als** none other than; **es ist sonst ~ da** nobody else is present.
'**Niemand** m (-s; no pl) contp. nobody.
'**Niemandsland** n a. fig. no man's land.
Niere ['ni:rə] f (-; -n) kidney: **künstliche ~** kidney machine; F **das geht mir an die ~n** that really gets me down.
'**Nierenbeckenentzündung** f pyelitis.
'**nierenförmig** adj kidney-shaped.
'**Nieren|leiden** n kidney disease. **~spender(in** f) m kidney donor. **~stein** m ♕ kidney stone. **~verpflanzung** f kidney transplant.
nieseln ['ni:zəln] v/i (h) drizzle.
'**Nieselregen** m drizzle.
niesen ['ni:zən] v/i (h) sneeze.
Nießbrauch ['ni:s-] m (-[e]s; no pl) ⚖ usufruct.
Niet [ni:t] m (-[e]s; -e) stud, ⚙ rivet.
Niete ['ni:tə] f (-; -n) **1. (e-e ~ ziehen** draw a) blank. **2.** F flop, washout.
nieten ['ni:tən] v/t, v/i (h) ⚙ rivet.
'**Nietenhose** f jeans (with studs).
Nihilismus [nihi'lısmʊs] m (-; no pl) nihilism. **Nihilist** [nihi'lıst] m (-en; -en) nihilist. **nihi'listisch** [-tıʃ] adj nihilist(ic).
Nikolaustag ['ni:kolaʊs-] m St. Nicholas' Day.
Nikotin [niko'ti:n] n (-s; no pl) nicotine.
niko'tinarm adj low-nicotine.
niko'tinfrei adj nicotine-free.
Niko'tinvergiftung f nicotine poisoning.
Nilpferd ['ni:l-] n zo. hippopotamus.
Nimbus ['nımbʊs] m (-; -se) nimbus, halo, fig. mst pl a. aura.
'**Nimmerwiedersehen** n auf ~ for good.
Nippel ['nıpəl] m (-s; -) ⚙ nipple.
nippen ['nıpən] v/t, v/i (h) sip (**an dat** at).
Nippsachen ['nıp-] pl knick-knacks.
nirgends ['nırgənts] adv nowhere.
'**nirgendwo**,   '**nirgendwohin**   adv nowhere, not ... anywhere.
Nische ['ni:ʃə] f (-; -n) niche, recess.
nisten ['nıstən] v/i (h) nest.
'**Nistplatz** m nesting place.
Nitrat [ni'tra:t] n (-[e]s; -e) 🜛 nitrate.
Nitroglyze'rin [nitro-] n nitroglycerine.
Niveau [ni'vo:] n (-s; -s) level, a. standard: **~ haben** have class; **ein hohes ~**

haben have high standards; **das ist unter m-m ~** that's beneath me; **geistiges ~** level of intelligence (or education).
nivellieren [nive'li:rən] v/t (h) level.
Nixe ['nıksə] f (-; -n) water-nymph.
nobel ['no:bəl] adj **1.** noble(-minded). **2.** F generous. **3.** high-class, F posh, ritzy.
'**Nobelherberge** f F posh hotel.
Nobelpreis [no'bɛl-] m Nobel prize. **~träger(in** f) m Nobel prize winner.
noch [nɔx] **I** adv **1.** still: **immer ~** still; **~ nicht** not yet; **~ nie** never before; **~ gestern** only yesterday; **~ heute** even today; **~ lange nicht** not by a long chalk; **~ im 18. Jahrhundert** as late as the 18th century; **wie heißt sie ~?** what's her name again?; F **~ und ~** a) oodles, piles of, b) awfully. **2.** more: **~ einer** one more, another; **~ einmal** once more; **~ einmal so viel** as much again; **~ etwas!** and another thing!; **~ etwas?** anything else?; **~ besser** even better; **nur ~ 5 Minuten** only five minutes more. **3. sei es ~ so klein** no matter how small (it is). **II** conj → **weder**.
'**nochmalig** adj repeated, second, new.
nochmals ['nɔxma:ls] adv once more.
Nocke ['nɔkə] f (-; -n) ⚙ cam.
'**Nockenwelle** f mot. camshaft.
Nomade [no'ma:də] m (-n; -n) nomad. **No'maden...**, **no'madisch** adj nomadic.
Nominativ ['no:minati:f] m (-s; -e) ling. nominative (case).
nominell [nomi'nɛl] adj nominal.
nominieren [nomi'ni:rən] v/t (h) nominate, name.
Nonne ['nɔnə] f (-; -n) nun.
'**Nonnenkloster** n nunnery, convent.
Nonsens ['nɔnzɛns] m (-[es]; no pl) nonsense.
Nonstop... [nɔn'stɔp-] nonstop.
Noppe ['nɔpə] f (-; -n) nap.
Nord [nɔrt] inv North.
'**Nord'afrika** n (-s) North Africa. **Nordafri'kaner(in** f) m, '**nordafri'kanisch** adj North African.
'**Norda'merika** n (-s) North America. '**Nordameri'kaner(in** f) m, '**nordameri'kanisch** adj North American.
'**norddeutsch** adj, '**Norddeutsche** m, f (-n; -n) North German.
Norden ['nɔrdən] m (-s; no pl) north, North: **nach ~** to(wards) the north; **im ~ von** (or gen) north of.

nordisch ['nɔrdɪʃ] *adj* a) northern, b) Nordic; → **Kombination** 5.

nördlich ['nœrtlıç] **I** *adj* a) northern (*hemisphere etc*), b) northerly (*direction etc*), c) arctic (*ocean*). **II** *adv* ~ **von** (*or gen*) (to the) north of.

'**Nordlicht** *n* northern lights.

Nord'ost(en) *m*, **nord'östlich** *adj and adv* northeast.

'**Nordpol** *m* North Pole.

'**Nordsee** *f* North Sea.

'**nordwärts** *adv* north(wards).

Nord'west(en) *m*, **nord'westlich** *adj and adv* northwest.

'**Nordwind** *m* north wind.

Nörge'lei *f* (-; -en) grumbling, niggling. **nörgeln** ['nœrgəln] *v/i* (h) (**an** *dat* about) grumble, niggle. **Nörgler** ['nœrglər] *m* (-s; -) grumbler, niggler.

Norm [nɔrm] *f* (-; -en) norm, standard.

normal [nɔr'maːl] *adj* normal, ⚙ standard. **Nor'malben,zin** *n* normal (grade) petrol (*Am.* gasoline).

nor'malerweise *adv* normally.

Nor'malfall *m* **im** ~ normally.

normalisieren [nɔrmali'ziːrən] (h) **I** *v/t* normalize. **II sich** ~ return to normal.

Nor'malverbraucher *m* average consumer: F *Otto* ~ Mr. Average.

Nor'malzustand *m* normal state.

normen ['nɔrmən], **normieren** [nɔr'miː-rən] *v/t* (h) standardize.

'**Normung** *f* (-; -en) standardization.

Norwegen ['nɔrveːgən] *n* (-s) Norway. '**Norweger** *m* (-s; -), '**Norwegerin** *f* (-; -nen), '**norwegisch** [-gɪʃ] *adj* Norwegian.

Nostalgie [nɔstal'giː] *f* (-; *no pl*) nostalgia. **nost'algisch** [-gɪʃ] *adj* nostalgic.

Not [noːt] *f* (-; ⸚e) **1.** *no pl* need, misery: ~ **leiden** suffer want; **in** ~ **geraten** become destitute (→ 3). **2.** *no pl* necessity: ~ **macht erfinderisch** necessity is the mother of invention; **zur** ~, F **wenn** ~ **am Mann ist** if need be; **es tut not, daß** it is necessary that. **3.** distress (*a.* ⚓), difficulty, trouble: **in** ~ (*or* **Nöten**) **sein** be in trouble; **in** ~ **geraten** run into difficulties (→ 1); F **s-e** (*liebe*) ~ **haben mit** really have problems with.

'**Notar** [no'taːr] *m* (-s; -e), **No'tarin** *f* (-; -nen) notary. **Notariat** [nota'rĭaːt] *n* (-[e]s; -e) notary's office. **notariell**

[nota'rĭɛl] *adj* notarial: ~ **beglaubigt** attested by a notary.

'**Not|arzt** *m* doctor on call. **~arztwagen** *m* emergency ambulance. **~aufnahmelager** *n* transit camp. **~ausgang** *m* emergency exit. **~behelf** *m* makeshift. **~beleuchtung** *f* emergency lighting. **~bremse** *f* emergency brake. **~dienst** *m* (~ **haben** be on) emergency duty.

'**notdürftig** *adj* **1.** scanty: ~ **bekleidet** scantily dressed. **2.** makeshift: *et.* ~ **reparieren** patch s.th. up.

Note ['noːta] *f* (-; -n) **1.** *ped.* mark, *Am.* grade. **2.** ♩ note: **ganze** ~ semibreve, *Am.* whole note; **halbe** ~ minim, *Am.* half note; **nach** ~n **singen** *etc* sing *etc* from music. **3.** *pol.* note, memorandum. **4.** *no pl fig.* touch: **e-r Sache e-e besondere** ~ **verleihen** add a special touch to s.th. **5.** → **Banknote**.

'**Noten|bank** *f* (-; -en) bank of issue. **~blatt** *n* sheet of music. **~heft** *n* music book. **~pult** *n* music stand. **~sy,stem** *n* *ped.* marking (*Am.* grading) system.

'**Notfall** *m* emergency: **für den** ~ (just) in case; **im** ~ → '**notfalls** *adv* if necessary, if need be, in an emergency.

'**notgedrungen** *adv* of necessity.

'**Notgroschen** *m* nest egg.

notieren [no'tiːrən] (h) **I** *v/t* **1.** make a note of. **2.** ✝ quote (**zu** at). **II** *v/i* **3.** ✝ be quoted (**mit** at, with).

No'tierung *f* (-; -en) ✝ quotation.

nötig ['nøːtıç] *adj* necessary: *et.* (*dringend*) ~ **haben** need s.th. (badly); *iro.* **du hast es** (*gerade*) ~*!* you of all people!; **mit dem** ~**en Respekt** with due respect; (*nur*) **das Nötigste** (just) what is absolutely necessary.

nötigen ['nøːtıgən] *v/t* (h) force, compel, urge, press (*guest*): **lassen Sie sich nicht** ~*!* help yourself!; **er ließ sich nicht lange** ~ he needed no coaxing.

'**Nötigung** *f* (-; -en) coercion.

Notiz [no'tiːts] *f* (-; -en) **1.** note: **sich** ~**en machen** take notes. **2.** (news) item. **3.** (*k-e*) ~ **nehmen von** take (no) notice of.

No'tizblock *m* notepad, *Am.* memo pad.

No'tizbuch *n* notebook.

'**Notlage** *f* predicament, plight.

'**Notlager** *n* shakedown.

'**notlanden** *v/i* (*insep*, -ge-, sn) make a forced landing.

'**Notlandung** *f* forced landing.

notleidend 432

'**notleidend** adj needy.
'**Notlösung** f temporary solution.
'**Notlüge** f white lie.
'**Notmaßnahme** f emergency measure.
notorisch [noˈtoːrɪʃ] adj notorious.
'**Notruf** m teleph. emergency call.
'**Notrufsäule** f emergency telephone.
'**Notschrei** m a. fig. cry for help.
'**Notsi,gnal** n distress signal.
'**Notsitz** m jump seat.
'**Notstand** m 1. → **Notlage**. 2. pol. state of emergency: **den nationalen ~ ausrufen** declare a state of national emergency. '**Notstandsgebiet** n 1. ✝ depressed area. 2. disaster area.
'**Notstromaggre,gat** n emergency generator.
'**Notunterkunft** f provisional accommodation.
'**Notverband** m ✳ emergency dressing.
'**Notwehr** f (-; no pl) (**aus ~, in ~** in) self-defen/ce (Am. -se).
'**notwendig** adj necessary (**für** to, for): **unbedingt ~** imperative.
'**notwendiger'weise** adv of necessity.
'**Notwendigkeit** f (-; -en) necessity.
'**Notzucht** f (-; no pl) ⚖ rape.
Nougat ['nuːɡat] m, n (-s; -s) nougat.
Novelle [noˈvɛlə] f (-; -n) 1. novella. 2. parl. amendment.
November [noˈvɛmbər] m (-s; -) (**im ~** in) November.
Novize [noˈviːtsə] m (-n; -n) novice.
Novum ['noːvʊm] n (-s; -va) s.th. new.
Nu [nuː] f: **im ~** in no time, in a jiffy.
Nuance [ny'ãːsə] f (-; -n) nuance, shade.
nüchtern ['nʏçtərn] adj 1. with an empty stomach: → **Magen**. 2. sober: **wieder ~ werden** sober up. 3. bland (food). 4. fig. a) sober, matter-of-fact, a. unemotional, b) austere, functional (building etc). '**Nüchternheit** f (-; no pl) sobriety, fig. a. austerity.
Nudel ['nuːdəl] f (-; -n) 1. noodle. 2. F **sie ist e-e ulkige ~** she is a funny bird.
nuklear [nukleˈaːr] adj nuclear.
Nukle'ar... nuclear (medicine etc).
null [nʊl] adj nought, esp. Am. or phys., ⊙ etc zero, teleph. 0, Am. zero, sports: nil, Am. zero: **~ Grad** zero degrees; **~ Komma drei** (nought) point three; **~ Fehler** no (Am. zero) mistakes; **zwei zu ~** two-nil, Am. two-zero; tennis: **15:0** fifteen love; **das Spiel endete 0:0** the

match was a scoreless draw; F **er hat ~ Ahnung** (**davon**) he doesn't know a thing about it; **ich habe ~ Bock darauf** I'm not a bit keen on that; → **nichtig** 2.
Null f (-; -en) nought, esp. Am. or phys., ⊙ etc zero: F **er ist e-e ~** he's a cipher (or nobody); **in ~ Komma nichts** in a jiffy; **gleich ~ sein** be nil.
nullacht'fünfzehn adj F run-of-the-mill.
'**Nulldi,ät** f no-calorie (or crash) diet.
'**Nullmenge** f A null set.
'**Nullösung** f zero option.
'**Nullpunkt** m zero, ✹, ⊙ neutral point: **auf dem ~** a. fig. at zero.
'**Nulltarif** m a) free transport, b) free admission: **zum ~** free.
'**Nullwachstum** n ✝ zero growth.
numerieren [numeˈriːrən] v/t (h) number. **Nume'rierung** f (-; -en) numbering. **Nummer** ['nʊmər] f (-; -n) 1. a) number, a. issue, copy (of newspaper etc), b) size (of shoes etc): F **auf ~ Sicher gehen** play it safe. 2. thea. etc act. 3. V fuck, trick, screw.
'**Nummernkonto** n numbered account.
'**Nummernschild** n nr. number plate.
nun [nuːn] I adv 1. a) now, b) then: **von ~ an** from now on, from that time (onward). 2. well: **~ ja** well(, you see); **~ gut!** all right!; **was ~?** what now (or next)?; **es geht ~ mal nicht!** it's just not on! II conj 3. **~ (da)** now that, since.
nur [nuːr] adv a) only, just, simply, b) nothing but, c) except: **~ einmal** just once; **~ noch** only; **~ daß** except (that); **~ weil** just because; **wenn ~** if only; **nicht ~ ..., sondern auch ...** not only ..., but also ...; **~ zu!** go on!; **warum hat er das ~ gesagt?** F why on earth did he say that?; **was meint er ~?** whatever does he mean?; **~ das nicht!** anything but that!; **du weißt ~ zu gut, daß you** know very well that; **soviel ich ~ kann** as much as I possibly can; **ohne auch ~ zu lächeln** without so much as a smile.
nuscheln ['nʊʃəln] v/i (h) mumble.
Nuß [nʊs] f (-; Nüsse) nut: fig. **e-e harte ~** a hard nut to crack.
'**Nußbaum** m 1. walnut tree. 2. no pl → '**Nußbaumholz** n walnut.
'**nußbraun** adj hazel.
'**Nußknacker** m nutcracker.
'**Nußschale** f nutshell.
Nüster ['nʏstər] f (-; -n) zo. nostril.

Nut [nu:t] f (-; -en) ⚙ groove.
Nutte ['nʊtə] f (-; -n) F tart, Am. hooker.
'Nutzanwendung f practical use.
'nutzbar adj useful: ~ **machen** utilize, 🖉 cultivate.
'Nutzbarkeit f (-; no pl) usefulness.
'Nutzbarmachung f (-; no pl) utilization, ⚒ etc exploitation, 🖉 cultivation.
'nutzbringend adj profitable, useful: ~ **anwenden** turn s.th. to good account.
nütze ['nʏtsə] adj **zu et. (nichts)** ~ **sein** be useful, be of use (be [of] no use).
'Nutzef‚fekt m ⚙ etc efficiency.
nutzen ['nʊtsən], **nützen** ['nʏtsən] (h) **I** v/i a) be of use, be useful (**zu** for, **j-m** to s.o.), b) **j-m** be of advantage to s.o., benefit s.o.: **was nützt das?** what good is that?; **das nützt nichts!** that's no use! **II** v/t use, make use of. **'Nutzen** m (-s; no pl) a) use, b) profit, c) advantage, a.

⚒ benefit: ~ **ziehen aus** profit (or benefit) from; **von** ~ **sein** → **nutzen** I.
'Nutz|fahrzeug n utility vehicle. **~fläche** f **1.** usable area. **2.** floor space. **~holz** n timber. **~last** f payload. **~leistung** f effective output (or power).
nützlich ['nʏtslɪç] adj useful, helpful.
'Nützlichkeit f (-; no pl) usefulness.
'nutzlos adj useless.
'Nutzlosigkeit f (-; no pl) uselessness.
Nutznießer ['nʊtsni:sər] m (-s; -), **'Nutznießerin** f (-; -nen) beneficiary.
'Nutzpflanze f useful plant.
'Nutzung f (-; -en) use, utilization.
'Nutzungsrecht n usufruct, right to use.
Nylon ['naɪlɔn] TM n (-s; no pl) nylon.
'Nylonstrümpfe pl nylons.
Nymphe ['nʏmfə] f (-; -n) nymph.
Nymphomanin [nʏmfo'ma:nɪn] f (-; -nen) 🚑, psych. nymphomaniac.

Nutzer ['nʊtsər] m (-s; -) adm. user.

O

O, o [o:] n (-; -) O, o.
o int oh: **o ja!** oh yes!
Oase [o'a:zə] f (-; -n) oasis.
ob [ɔp] conj whether, if: **als** ~ as if; **so tun als** ~ make as if; F (**na**) **und** ~**!** you bet!; ~ **er wohl geht?** I wonder if he will go.
Obacht ['o:baxt] f dial. ~ **geben auf** (acc) pay attention to; ~**!** look out!
Obdach n (-[e]s; no pl) shelter.
'obdachlos adj (~ **werden** be left) homeless. **'Obdachlose** m, f (-n; -n) homeless person. **'Obdachlosena‚syl** n shelter for the homeless.
Obduktion [ɔpdʊk'tsi̯o:n] f (-; -en) postmortem (examination), autopsy.
obduzieren [ɔpdu'tsi:rən] v/t (h) **j-n** ~ carry out an autopsy on s.o.
'O-Beine pl F bow legs, bandy legs.
'O-beinig [-baɪnɪç] adj F bow-legged.
oben ['o:bən] adv a) at the top, b) upstairs, c) (~ **schwimmen** float) on the surface; **ganz** ~ a. fig. right at the top; **hier** ~ up here; **hoch** ~ high up; **nach** ~ up(wards), a. upstairs; **von** ~ a. fig.

from above; **von** ~ **bis unten** from top to bottom; fig. **von** ~ **herab** condescendingly; F ~ **ohne** topless.
oben'an adv at the top (or head).
oben'auf adv on top: F fig. ~ **sein** be fit and well, be on top of the world.
obendrein [-'draɪn] adv on top of it (all).
'obenerwähnt adj above(-mentioned).
oben'hin adv superficially, casually.
'Oben-'ohne-... topless (bar etc).
ober ['o:bər] adj upper; → **oberst.**
'Ober m (-s; -) waiter.
'Ober|arm m upper arm. **~arzt** m, **~ärztin** f assistant medical director. **~befehl** m supreme command (**über** acc of). **~befehlshaber** m ✕ commander-in-chief. **~begriff** m generic term. **~bekleidung** f outer garments. **~bürgermeister** m (Br. Lord) Mayor. **~deck** n ⚓ upper deck. **~feldwebel** m staff sergeant, Am. sergeant 1st class.
'Oberfläche f surface: **an** (or **auf**) **der** ~ on the surface; **an die** ~ **kommen** (come to the) surface.

'**oberflächlich** [-flɛçlɪç] *adj* superficial, *fig. a.* shallow: **~e Bekanntschaft** casual acquaintance; **~ (betrachtet)** on the face of it. '**Oberflächlichkeit** *f* (-; *no pl*) superficiality.

'**Ober|gefreite** *m* lance corporal, *Am.* private 1st class. **~geschoß** *n* upper floor. **~grenze** *f* upper limit, ceiling.

'**oberhalb** *prep* (*gen*) above.

'**Oberhand** *f* **die ~ gewinnen** get the upper hand (**über** *acc* of).

'**Ober|haupt** *n* head, chief. **~haus** *n parl.* upper house, *Br.* House of Lords. **~haut** *f* epidermis. **~hemd** *n* shirt. **~herrschaft** *f* supremacy.

Oberin ['o:bərɪn] *f* (-; -nen) **1.** *eccl.* Mother Superior. **2.** ✚ matron.

'**oberirdisch** *adj and adv* overground, ⚡ overhead.

'**Ober|kellner** *m* head waiter. **~kiefer** *m* upper jaw. **~körper** *m* upper part of the body: **den ~ freimachen** strip to the waist. **~landesgericht** *n* regional court of appeal. **~lauf** *m* upper course (*or* reaches). **~leder** *n* upper. **~leitung** *f* **1.** overall control. **2.** ⚡ overhead cable. **~leutnant** *m* (*Am.* first) lieutenant. **~licht** *n* skylight. **~liga** *f sports*: third division. **~lippe** *f* upper lip. **~priester** *m* high priest. **~schenkel** *m* thigh. **~schicht** *f sociol.* upper class(es). **~schwester** *f* senior nursing officer. **~seite** *f* upper side, top (side).

oberst ['o:bərst] *adj* uppermost, top(most), *a.* highest, *fig. a.* supreme, chief: **das Oberste zuunterst kehren** turn everything upside down.

'**Oberst** *m* (-en; -en) colonel.

'**Oberstaatsanwalt** *m* senior public prosecutor.

'**Oberstimme** *f* ♪ upper part.

'**Oberstleutnant** *m* lieutenant colonel.

Ober'studien|di,rektor *m* headmaster, *Am.* principal. **~di,rek,torin** *f* headmistress, *Am.* principal. **~rat** *m* senior assistant master. **~rätin** [-rɛ:tɪn] *f* (-; -nen) senior assistant mistress.

'**Oberstufe** *f* (-; *no pl*) *ped.* upper school (*Am.* grades).

'**Oberteil** *m, n* top.

'**Oberwasser** *n fig.* (**wieder**) **~ bekommen** (*or* **haben**) be on top (again).

ob'gleich *conj* (al)though, even though.

Obhut ['ɔphu:t] *f* (-; *no pl*) care: **in s-e ~**

nehmen take care (*or* charge) of.

obig ['o:bɪç] *adj* above.

Objekt [ɔp'jɛkt] *n* (-[e]s; -e) object (*a. ling. or art*), ✚ *a.* property.

objektiv [ɔpjɛk'ti:f] *adj* objective, *a.* impartial. **Objek'tiv** *n* (-s; -e) *opt.* (object) lens. **objektivieren** [ɔpjɛkti'vi:rən] *v/t* (h) objectify. **Objektivität** [ɔpjɛktivi'tɛ:t] *f* (-; *no pl*) objectiveness.

Oblate [o'bla:tə] *f* (-; -n) wafer.

obligat [obli'ga:t] *adj iro.* inevitable.

Obligation [obliga'tsi̯o:n] *f* (-; -en) ✚ bond, debenture.

obligatorisch [obliga'to:rɪʃ] *adj* (**für**) obligatory (on), compulsory (for).

'**Obmann** *m* **1.** chief. **2.** *arbitration*: umpire, *of jury*: foreman.

Oboe [o'bo:ə] *f* (-; -n) oboe.

Oboist [obo'ɪst] *m* (-en; -en) oboist.

Observatorium [ɔpzɛrva'to:ri̯ʊm] *n* (-s; -rien) observatory. **observieren** [-'vi:rən] *v/t* (h) put under surveillance.

obskur [ɔps'ku:r] *adj* **1.** obscure. **2.** dubious, F shady.

Obst [o:pst] *n* (-[e]s; *no pl*) fruit. **~bau** *m* (-[e]s; *no pl*) fruit-growing. **~baum** *m* fruit tree. **~ernte** *f* a) fruit-gathering, b) fruit crop. **~garten** *m* orchard. **~händler(in** *f*) *m* fruiterer, *Am.* fruit seller. **~kon,serven** *pl* tinned (*or* canned) fruit. **~kuchen** *m* fruit tart. **~messer** *n* fruit knife.

Obstruktion [ɔpstrʊk'tsi̯o:n] *f* (-; *no pl*) *pol.* obstruction.

'**Obst|saft** *m* (fruit) juice. **~sa,lat** *m* fruit salad. **~wasser** *n* fruit brandy.

obszön [ɔps'tsø:n] *adj* obscene, filthy.

Obszönität [ɔpstsøni'tɛ:t] *f* (-; -en) obscenity.

Obus ['o:bʊs] *m* (-ses; -se) trolley bus.

ob'wohl *conj* (al)though, even though.

Ochse ['ɔksə] *m* (-n; -n) **1.** ox, bullock. **2.** F ass. '**ochsen** *v/t, v/i* (h) F cram, swot.

'**Ochsenschwanzsuppe** *f* oxtail soup.

Ocker ['ɔkər] *m* (-s; -) ochre, *Am.* ocher.

Ode ['o:də] *f* (-; -n) ode.

öde ['ø:də] *adj* **1.** a) deserted, desolate, b) barren, waste. **2.** *fig.* dreary, dull.

'**Öde** *f* (-; -n) **1.** desert, waste(land). **2.** *no pl fig.* dreariness, tedium, emptiness.

Ödem [ø'de:m] *n* (-s; -e) ✚ (o)edema.

oder ['o:dər] *conj* or: **~ (aber)** (or) else, otherwise; **~ ...!** or else!; F **du kommst**

doch, ~? you are coming, aren't you? → **entweder, nicht.**

Odyssee [ody'se:] *f* (-; -n) *fig.* odyssey.

Ofen ['o:fən] *m* (-s; ⁓) **1.** a) stove, b) oven, c) furnace, d) kiln: F *jetzt ist der ~ aus!* it's curtains (for us *etc*)! **2.** F *heißer ~* a) hot rod, b) (big motor)bike. **~heizung** *f* stove heating. **~rohr** *n* stovepipe.

offen ['ɔfən] *adj* open (*a. fig.*), *a.* frank, outspoken; **~e Rechnung** outstanding account; **~e Stelle** vacant post, vacancy; **~er Wein** wine served by the glass; *die ~e See* the open (sea); *mit ~en Augen* with one's eyes open; *zu j-m ~ sein* be open with s.o.; *für Vorschläge ~ sein* be open to suggestions; *s-e Meinung ~ sagen* speak one's mind freely; **~ gestanden, ~ gesagt** frankly (speaking); → **Handelsgesellschaft, Straße 1, Tür.**

'offenbar I *adj* → **offensichtlich. II** *adv* evidently, it seems ...

offenbaren [ɔfən'ba:rən] *v/t* (offenbarte, offenbart, h) reveal.

Offen'barung *f* (-; -en) revelation.

Offen'barungseid *m* ⚖ *or fig.* declaration of bankruptcy.

'offenbleiben *v/i* (*irr, sep,* -ge-, sn, → **bleiben**) *a. fig.* remain open.

'offenhalten *v/t* (*irr, sep,* -ge-, h, → **halten**) *a. fig.* keep s.th. open.

'Offenheit *f* (-; *no pl*) openness, frankness.

'offenherzig *adj* **1.** open-hearted, candid, frank. **2.** *fig.* revealing (*dress etc*).

'offenkundig *adj* obvious.

'offenlassen *v/t* (*irr, sep,* -ge-, h, → **lassen**) *a. fig.* leave s.th. open.

'offensichtlich *adj* evident, obvious.

offensiv [ɔfən'zi:f] *adj* offensive.

Offensive [ɔfən'zi:və] *f* (-; -n) (*die ~ ergreifen* take the) offensive.

'offenstehen *v/i* (*irr, sep,* -ge-, h, → **stehen**) *a.* be open (*fig. j-m* to s.o.): *es steht ihm offen zu gehen* he is free to go. **2.** *accounts:* be outstanding.

öffentlich ['œfəntlıç] *adj* public: **~er Dienst** a) public sector, b) civil service; **~e Mittel** public funds; **~e Schulen** state (*Am.* public) schools; ⚖ *in ~er Sitzung* in open court; **~ auftreten** appear in public; **~ bekanntmachen** make public, publicize; → **Ärgernis, beglaubigt, Persönlichkeit** *etc.*

'Öffentlichkeit *f* (-; *no pl*) a) *the* (general) public, b) *a.* ⚖ publicity: *an die ~ treten* appear before the public; *et. an die ~ bringen* bring s.th. before the public; *an* (*or in*) *die ~ dringen* leak out; *in die ~ flüchten* resort to publicity; → **Ausschluß. 'Öffentlichkeitsarbeit** *f* (-; *no pl*) public relations.

'öffentlich-'rechtlich *adj* under public law, public.

Offerte [ɔ'fɛrtə] *f* (-; -n) ✝ offer.

offiziell [ɔfi'tsɪɛl] *adj* official.

Offizier [ɔfi'tsi:r] *m* (-s; -e) ✗ officer.

Offi'ziersanwärter *m* officer cadet.

offizinell [ɔfitsi'nɛl] *adj pharm.* officinal.

offiziös [ɔfi'tsɪø:s] *adj* semiofficial.

öffnen ['œfnən] *v/t* (*a. sich ~*) (h) open.

'Öffner *m* (-s; -) opener. **'Öffnung** *f* (-; -en) opening, *a.* gap, *a.* aperture.

'Öffnungszeiten *pl* opening hours.

Offsetdruck ['ɔfsɛt-] *m* offset (printing).

oft [ɔft] *adv* often, frequently.

öfter ['œftər] *adv a. des öfteren* often.

oh [o:] *int* oh.

Ohm [o:m] *n* (-[s]; -) ⚡ ohm.

ohmsch [o:mʃ] *adj* ⚡ ohmic: *Ohmsches Gesetz* Ohm's law.

ohne ['o:nə] **I** *prep* (*acc*) without: *~ s-e Verletzung hätte er gewonnen* but for his injury he would have won; F *~ mich!* count me out!; *nicht ~* not half bad; → **Frage** 1 *etc.* **II** *conj* without.

ohne'gleichen *adj* unparallel(l)ed: *e-e Frechheit ~* (an) incredible impudence.

ohne'hin *adv* anyhow, anyway.

'Ohnmacht *f* (-; -en) **1.** *no pl fig.* powerlessness. **2.** ⚕ unconsciousness, faint: *in ~ fallen* faint.

'ohnmächtig *adj* **1.** powerless, helpless. **2.** ⚕ unconscious: *~ werden* faint.

Ohr [o:r] *n* (-[e]s; -en) ear: *ganz ~ sein* be all ears; *nur mit halbem ~ zuhören* listen only with half an ear; F *j-m in den ~en liegen* pester s.o. (*mit* for, with); *viel um die ~en haben* have a lot on one's plate; *sich aufs ~ legen* get some shut-eye; *schreib dir das hinter die ~en!* now don't forget that!; *ich traute m-n ~en nicht!* I couldn't believe my ears!; *j-n übers ~ hauen* cheat s.o.; *j-m zu ~en kommen* come to s.o.'s ears; *halt die ~en steif!* keep a stiff upper lip!; *bis über die ~en in Arbeit* (*Schulden*) *stecken* be up to one's (*or* the) ears in work (debt); → **faustdick, spitzen, taub** 1.

Öhr [øːr] n (-[e]s; -e) eye.

'**Ohren**|**arzt** m, **~ärztin** f ear specialist. **2betäubend** adj deafening. **~leiden** n ear complaint. **~sausen** n buzzing in one's ears. **~schmalz** n ♣ earwax. **~schmerzen** pl earache. **~schützer** pl earmuffs. **~sessel** m wing chair. **~zeuge** m earwitness.

'**Ohrfeige** f (-; -n) slap in the face: **j-m e-e ~ geben → 'ohrfeigen** v/t (h) **j-n ~** slap s.o.('s face).

'**Ohrläppchen** [-lɛpçən] n (-s; -) earlobe. '**Ohrmuschel** f anat. external (or outer) ear, auricle. '**Ohrring** n earring. '**Ohrstecker** m (ear) stud. '**Ohrwurm** m 1. zo. earwig. 2. F catchy tune.

okkult [ɔˈkʊlt] adj occult. **Okkultismus** [ɔkʊlˈtɪsmʊs] m (-; no pl) occultism.

Ökologe [økoˈloːgə] m (-n; -n) ecologist. **Ökologie** [økoloˈgiː] f (-; no pl) ecology. **ökologisch** [økoˈloːgɪʃ] adj ecological. **Ökonomie** [økonoˈmiː] f (-; -n) 1. economy. 2. economics. **ökonomisch** [økoˈnoːmɪʃ] adj economical.

Ökosy|stem ['øːko-] n ecosystem.

Oktaeder [ɔktaˈ'º eːdər] m (-s; -) ᴀ octahedron.

Oktan [ɔkˈtaːn] n (-s; no pl) 🔥 octane.

Ok'tanzahl f octane number.

Oktave [ɔkˈtaːvə] f (-; -n) ♪ octave.

Oktober [ɔkˈtoːbər] m (-[s]; -) (**im ~** in) October.

okulieren [okuˈliːrən] v/t (h) 🌿 graft.

Ökumene [økuˈmeːnə] f (-; no pl) eccl. ecumenical movement. **öku'menisch** [-nɪʃ] adj eccl. ecumenical.

Öl [øːl] n (-[e]s; -e) oil: **nach ~ bohren** drill for oil; **auf ~ stoßen** strike oil; **in ~ malen** paint in oils; **~ ins Feuer gießen** add fuel to the flames; **~ auf die Wogen gießen** pour oil on troubled waters.

'**Ölbaum** m olive tree. '**Ölberg** m bibl. Mount of Olives. '**Ölbild** n oil painting. '**Ölbohrung** f oil drilling. '**Öldruck** m 1. paint. oleograph. 2. 🔧 oil pressure.

Oldtimer ['ɔoldtaɪmɐ] m (-s; -) 1. veteran car (or plane etc). 2. F old-timer.

Oleander [oleˈandər] m (-s; -) oleander.

ölen ['øːlən] v/t (h) oil, 🔧 a. lubricate.

'**Ölfarbe** f oil paint: **mit ~n malen** paint in oils. '**Ölfeld** n oilfield. '**Ölfilter** m, n oil filter. '**Ölförderland** n oil-produc-

ing country. '**Ölgemälde** n oil painting. '**Ölgesellschaft** f petroleum (or oil) company. '**Ölgewinnung** f 1. oil production. 2. oil extraction. '**Ölgötze** m F **wie ein ~** like a stuffed dummy. '**Ölhafen** m oil tanker terminal. '**Ölhaltig** adj containing oil, ♣ oleiferous. '**Ölhaut** f oilskin. '**Ölheizung** f oil heating.

'**ölig** adj oily, fig. a. unctuous.

oliv [oˈliːf] adj olive(-colo[u]red).

Olive [oˈliːvə] f (-; -n) olive. **O'livenbaum** m olive tree. **O'livenöl** n olive oil. **o'livgrün** adj olive-green.

'**Ölkanne** f oil can. '**Ölkrise** f oil crisis. '**Ölkuchen** m ♣ ⊙ oil cake. '**Öllampe** f oil lamp. '**Ölleitung** f a) mot. oil pipe (oil line, b) ♣ pipeline. '**Ölmale'rei** f oil painting. '**Ölmeßstab** m mot. (oil) dipstick. '**Ölofen** m oil furnace. '**Ölpest** f oil pollution. '**Ölprodu,zent** m oil producer. '**Ölquelle** f oil well, gusher. '**Ölsar,dine** f sardine. '**Ölschiefer** m oil shale. '**Ölstandsanzeiger** m oil-leve(u)ge. '**Öltank** m oil tank. '**Öltanker** m oil tanker, oiler. '**Ölteppich** m oil slick.

'**Ölung** f (-; no pl) 1. oiling, ⊙ a. lubrication. 2. eccl. **letzte ~** Extreme Unction. '**Ölvorkommen** n oil deposit (coll. reserves). '**Ölwanne** f mot. oil sump. '**Ölwechsel** m oil change. '**Ölzeug** n oilskins. '**Ölzweig** m olive branch.

Olymp [oˈlʏmp] m (-s; no pl) Olympus. **Olympia...** [oˈlʏmpiaː]- sports: Olympic. **Olympiade** [olʏmˈpiaːdə] f (-; -n) sports: Olympic Games, Olympics.

olympisch [oˈlʏmpɪʃ] adj 1. Olympian. 2. sports: Olympic.

Oma ['oːma] f (-; -s) F grandma, granny.

Omelett [ɔməˈlɛt] n (-[e]s; -e, -s) **Ome'lette** f (-; -n) omelet(te).

Omen ['oːmən] n (-s; -) omen. **ominös** [omiˈnøːs] adj 1. ominous. 2. F shady.

Omnibus(...) ['ɔmnibʊs-] → **Bus(...)**.

Onanie [onaˈniː] f (-; no pl) masturbation. **ona'nieren** v/i (h) masturbate.

ondulieren [ɔnduˈliːrən] v/t (h) wave.

Onkel ['ɔŋkəl] m (-s; -) uncle.

Onyx ['oːnʏks] m (-[es]; -e) min. onyx.

Opa ['oːpa] m (-s; -s) F grandpa.

Opal [oˈpaːl] m (-s; -e) min. opal.

Oper ['oːpər] f (-; -n) opera.

operabel [opeˈraːbəl] adj 🩺 operable.

Operateur [opera'tøːr] *m* (-s; -e) (operating) surgeon. **Operation** [opera'tsi̯oːn] *f* (-; -en) operation.
Operati'ons|basis *f* ⚔ base of operations. **~narbe** *f* postoperative scar. **~saal** *m* operating theatre (*Am.* room). **~schwester** *f* theatre (*Am.* operating-room) nurse. **~tisch** *m* operating table.
operativ [opera'tiːf] *adj* **1.** 🏥 surgical, operative: **~er Eingriff** operation; **et. ~ entfernen** remove s.th. surgically (*or* by surgery). **2.** ⚔ operational.
Operette [ope'rɛtə] *f* (-; -n) operetta.
operieren [ope'riːrən] *v/t, v/i* (h) operate: **j-n ~** operate on s.o. (**wegen** for); **sich ~ lassen** have an operation; **ich muß am Magen operiert werden** I have to have a stomach operation.
'Opern|arie *f* operatic aria. **~ball** *m* opera ball. **~führer** *m* opera guide-book. **~glas** *n* opera glass(es). **~haus** *n* opera house. **~kompo̱nist** *m* opera composer. **~mu̱sik** *f* operatic music. **~sänger(in** *f*) *m* opera singer.
Opfer ['ɔpfər] *n* (-s; -) **1.** a) sacrifice (*a. fig.*), b) offering: **~ bringen** make sacrifices. **2.** victim: (*dat*) **zum ~ fallen** fall victim to. **'opferbereit** *adj* ready to make sacrifices. **'Opferbereitschaft** *f* readiness to make sacrifices. **'Opfergabe** *f* offering. **'opfern** *v/t, v/i* (h) sacrifice (*a. fig.*), give. **'Opferstock** *m eccl.* offertory. **'Opfertier** *n* sacrificial animal. **'Opferung** *f* (-; -en) sacrifice.
Opiat [o'pi̯aːt] *n* (-[e]s; -e) *pharm.* opiate.
Opium ['oːpi̯ʊm] *n* (-s; *no pl*) opium.
Opossum [o'pɔsʊm] *n* (-s; -s) opossum.
Opponent [ɔpo'nɛnt] *m* (-en; -en), **Oppo'nentin** *f* (-; -nen) opponent.
opponieren [ɔpo'niːrən] *v/i* (h) (**gegen** *j-n or* **et.**) **~** oppose (s.o. *or* s.th.).
Opportunist [ɔpɔrtu'nɪst] *m* (-en; -en), **opportu'nistisch** [-tɪʃ] *adj* opportunist.
Opposition [ɔpozi'tsi̯oːn] *f* (-; -en) opposition (**gegen** to).
Oppositi'ons|führer *m pol.* opposition leader. **~paṟtei** *f* opposition (party).
Optativ ['ɔptatiːf] *m* (-s; -e) *ling.* optative (mood).
Optik ['ɔptɪk] *f* (-; -en) **1.** *no pl* optics: *fig.* **nur der ~ wegen** for (optical) effect only. **2.** *phot.* lens system. **'Optiker** *m* (-s; -), **'Optikerin** *f* (-; -nen) optician.
optimal [ɔpti'maːl] *adj* optimal: **~e Be-**

dingungen optimum conditions.
optimieren [ɔpti'miːrən] *v/t* (h) optimize.
Optimismus [ɔpti'mɪsmʊs] *m* (-; *no pl*) optimism. **Optimist** [ɔpti'mɪst] *m* (-en; -en), **Opti'mistin** *f* (-; -nen) optimist. **opti'mistisch** [-tɪʃ] *adj* optimistic.
Optimum ['ɔptimʊm] *n* (-s; -ma) optimum.
Option [ɔp'tsi̯oːn] *f* (-; -en) option.
optisch ['ɔptɪʃ] *adj* optical.
Opus ['oːpʊs] *n* (-; Opera) work: ♪ **~ 12** opus 12.
Orakel [o'raːkəl] *n* (-s; -) oracle.
oral [o'raːl] *adj* oral.
orange [o'rã:ʒə] *adj* orange(-colo[u]red).
O'range *f* (-; -n) orange.
Orangeat [orã'ʒaːt] *n* (-s; -e) candied orange peel.
O'rangen|baum *m* orange tree. **~marme̱lade** *f* marmalade. **~saft** *m* orange juice. **~schale** *f* orange peel.
Orang-Utan ['oːraŋ'ʔuːtan] *m* (-s; -s) *zo.* orang-outang.
Oratorium [ora'toːri̯ʊm] *n* (-s; -rien) ♪ oratorio.
Orbital... [ɔrbi'taːl-] orbital (*rocket etc*).
Orchester [ɔr'kɛstər] *n* (-s; -) orchestra, *a.* band. **~graben** *m* (orchestra) pit. **~mu̱sik** *f* orchestral music.
orchestrieren [ɔrkɛs'triːrən] *v/t* (h) orchestrate.
Orchidee [ɔrçi'deː(ə)] *f* (-; -n) ⚘ orchid.
Orden ['ɔrdən] *m* (-s; -) **1.** *eccl.* order. **2.** order, decoration, medal.
'Ordens|band *n* (-[e]s; ~er) (medal) ribbon. **~bruder** *m eccl.* monk. **~schwester** *f eccl.* sister, nun.
ordentlich ['ɔrdəntlɪç] **I** *adj* **1.** tidy, orderly, neat. **2.** decent, good, respectable. **3.** F a) regular, proper, b) decent: **~e Ausbildung** proper training; **~e Leistung** good job; **ein ~es Frühstück** a decent breakfast. **4.** full (*member, professor*). **II** *adv* **5.** tidily, properly (*etc*): **s-e Sache ~ machen** do a good job. **6.** F properly: **j-m ~ die Meinung sagen** give s.o. a good piece of one's mind; **ich hab's ihm mal ~ gegeben** I really let him have it.
'Ordentlichkeit *f* (-; *no pl*) orderliness.
ordern ['ɔrdərn] *v/t* (h) ✝ order.
Ordinalzahl [ɔrdi'naːl-] *f* ✚ ordinal (number).

ordinär [ɔrdiˈnɛːr] *adj* vulgar, common.
Ordinariat [ɔrdinaˈrǐaːt] *n* -[e]s; -e) **1.** *univ.* (full) professorship. **2.** *eccl.* diocesan authorities.
Ordinarius [ɔrdiˈnaːriʊs] *m* (-; -rien) *univ.* (full) professor.
Ordination [ɔrdinaˈtsǐoːn] *f* (-; -en) **1.** *eccl.* ordination. **2.** *Austrian ⚕* surgery.
ordnen [ˈɔrdnən] *v/t* (h) **1.** a) put *s.th.* in order, b) file (*documents*), c) sort (out), d) arrange: *nach Klassen* ~ classify; *s-e Gedanken* ~ marshal one's thoughts; → *alphabetisch.* **2.** settle.
'Ordner *m* (-s; -) **1.** steward. **2.** file.
'Ordnung *f* (-; -en) order (*a. biol.*, *⚛*), *a.* orderliness: *in alphabetischer* ~ in alphabetical order; *Straße erster* ~ primary road; F *fig.* **erster** ~ of the first order; F (*das ist*) *in* ~*!* all right!, okay!, o.k.!; *es* (*er*) *ist in* ~ it's (he's) all right; *nicht in* ~ *sein* a) be out of order, *fig. a.* be wrong, b) *person:* be out of sorts; *et. ist nicht in* ~ (*damit*) s.th. is wrong (with it); *in* ~ *bringen* a) put *s.th.* right, *fig. a.* straighten *s.th.* out, b) tidy up (*room etc*), c) repair, F fix; ~ *halten* keep order; *et. in* ~ *halten* keep s.th. in order; ~ *schaffen* establish order; *parl.* *j-n zur* ~ *rufen* call s.o. to order.
'ordnungsgemäß I *adj* regular, orderly. **II** *adv* duly.
'ordnungshalber [-halbər] *adv* (only) as a matter of form.
'ordnungsliebend *adj* orderly.
'Ordnungsruf *m parl.* call to order.
'Ordnungsstrafe *f* fine.
'ordnungswidrig *adj* irregular.
'Ordnungszahl *f* ordinal (number).
Organ [ɔrˈgaːn] *n* (-s; -e) **1.** *anat.* organ: *fig.* **kein** ~ **haben für** have no feeling for. **2.** *fig.* organ, publication. **3.** *fig.* organ, authority: **ausführendes** ~ executive body. **4.** F voice. **~bank** *f* (-; -en) *⚕* organ bank. **~empfänger(in** *f)* *m ⚕* organ recipient. **~erkrankung** *f* organic disease. **~handel** *m* sale of (transplant) organs.
Organisation [ɔrganizaˈtsǐoːn] *f* (-; -en) organization.
Organisati'onsta,lent *n er hat* (*or er ist ein*) ~ he has organizing ability.
Organisator [ɔrganiˈzaːtɔr] *m* (-s; -en [-zaˈtoːrən]) organizer. **organisatorisch** [-izaˈtoːrɪʃ] *adj* organizational;

~e Fähigkeit(en) organizing ability.
organisch [ɔrˈgaːnɪʃ] *adj* organic.
organisieren [ɔrganiˈziːrən] *v/t* (h) **1.** organize: **(nicht) organisierter Arbeiter** (non)unionist. **2.** F rustle up.
Organismus [ɔrgaˈnɪsmʊs] *m* (-; -men) organism.
Organist [ɔrgaˈnɪst] *m* (-en; -en), **Orga'nistin** *f* (-; -nen) organist.
Or'gan\spende *f* donation of an organ. **~spender(in** *f)* *m* organ donor. **~verpflanzung** *f* organ transplant(ation).
Orgasmus [ɔrˈgasmʊs] *m* (-; -men) orgasm, climax.
Orgel [ˈɔrgəl] *f* (-; -n) organ. **~bauer** *m* (-s; -) organ builder. **~kon,zert** *n* organ recital. **~pfeife** *f* organ pipe: F *fig.* **wie die** ~**n** in order of size. **~re,gister** *n* organ stop.
Orgie [ˈɔrgǐə] *f* (-; -n) orgy: ~**n feiern** have orgies.
Orient [ˈoːrǐɛnt] *m* (-s) Orient, East: *der* **Vordere** ~ the Near East.
Orientale [orǐɛnˈtaːlə] *m* (-n; -n), **Orien'talin** *f* (-; -nen) Oriental.
orien'talisch [-lɪʃ] *adj* oriental.
orientieren [orǐɛnˈtiːrən] (h) **I** *v/t* **1.** orient(ate) (*nach* according to). **2.** inform (*über acc* about, of): **gut orientiert** well informed. **II** *sich* ~ **3.** (*an dat* by) orient(ate) o.s., be guided. **4.** inform o.s. (*über acc* of, about). **Orien'tierung** *f* (-; *no pl*) **1.** orientation: *die* ~ *verlieren* lose one's bearings. **2.** information: *zu Ihrer* ~ for your guidance.
Orien'tierungs\punkt *m* point of reference. **~sinn** *m* sense of direction. **~stufe** *f ped.* orienteering term.
original [origiˈnaːl] *adj* original: ~ **französisch** genuine French; *et.* ~ **übertragen** broadcast *s.th.* live.
Origi'nal *n* (-s; -e) original, F (*person*) *a.* character: *im* ~ *read* in the original. **~fassung** *f* original version: *in der deutschen* ~ in the original German version. **2getreu** *adj* faithful.
Originalität [originaliˈtɛːt] *f* (-; *no pl*) *a.* *fig.* originality.
Origi'nal\ko,pie *f film etc:* master copy. **~übertragung** *f* live broadcast. **~verpackung** *f* original packing.
originell [origiˈnɛl] *adj* **1.** original, novel. **2.** F funny, quaint.
Orkan [ɔrˈkaːn] *m* (-[e]s; -e) hurricane.

or'kanartig *adj* of hurricane force.

Ornament [ɔrnaˈmɛnt] *n* (-[e]s; -e) ornament.

Ornat [ɔrˈnaːt] *m* (-[e]s; -e) 🕊 robe(s),
eccl. vestments.

Ornithologe [ɔrnitoˈloːgə] *m* (-n; -n)
ornithologist.

Ort[1] [ɔrt] *m* (-[e]s; -e) place (→ *a.* ***Ortschaft***), spot, locality, scene: (*hier*) *am*
~ (here) in this place; ~ *und Zeit* place
and time; ~ *der Handlung* scene (of
action); *an* ~ *und Stelle* on the spot;
höheren ~(*e*)*s* at high quarters.

Ort[2] *n* (-[e]s; Örter) *vor* ~ 🔨 at the pit
face, *fig.* on the scene (of action); *Besichtigung vor* ~ on-site inspection.

orten [ˈɔrtən] *v/t* (h) 🔨 *etc* locate.

orthodox [ɔrtoˈdɔks] *adj* orthodox.

Orthographie [ɔrtograˈfiː] *f* (-; -n) or-
thography, spelling. **orthographisch**
[ɔrtoˈgraˈfiʃ] *adj* orthographic(al): ~
richtig schreiben spell correctly.

Orthopäde [ɔrtoˈpɛːdə] *m* (-n; -n) or-
thop(a)edist. **Orthopädie** [-pɛˈdiː] *f* (-;
no pl) orthop(a)edics. **ortho'pädisch**
[-dɪʃ] *adj* orthop(a)edic.

örtlich [ˈœrtlɪç] *adj a.* 💊 local: ~ *begrenzen* localize (*auf acc* to); ~ *verschieden sein* vary from place to place.

Örtlichkeit *f* (-; -en) locality.

Ortsangabe *f* statement of place.

ortsansässig *adj*, **'Ortsansässige** *m*, *f*
(-n; -n) resident, local.

Ortschaft *f* (-; -en) place, village, (small)
town: *geschlossene* ~ built-up area.

ortsfest *adj* stationary.

Ortsgespräch *n teleph.* local call.

Ortskenntnis *f* knowledge of a place: ~
besitzen → **'ortskundig** *adj* ~ *sein*
know (one's way around) the place.

Orts|name *m* place name. **~netz** *n*
teleph. local exchange. **~schild** *n* place-
name sign. **~sinn** *m* sense of direction.
~teil *m* district. **♀üblich** *adj* customary,
local. **~wechsel** *m* change (of place).
~zeit *f* (-; *no pl*) local time. **~zuschlag**
m 📮 weighting (allowance).

Ortung *f* (-; -en) ⚓ *etc* location.

Öse [ˈøːzə] *f* (-; -n) eye.

Osmose [ɔsˈmoːzə] *f* (-; -n) osmosis.

Ost [ɔst] *invar geogr.* east, *pol.* East.

Ostblock *m pol.* Eastern bloc.

ostdeutsch *adj*, **'Ostdeutsche** *m*, *f* (-n;
-n) East German.

Osten [ˈɔstən] *m* (-s; *no pl*) east, *of town*:
East End, *geogr.*, *pol. the* East: *der
Ferne (Nahe)* ~ the Far (Middle) East;
im ~ in the east; *nach* ~ (to the) east,
eastward(s); *von* ~, *aus* ~ from the east,
easterly (*wind*).

ostentativ [ɔstɛntaˈtiːf] *adj* pointed: **~er
Beifall** demonstrative applause.

Osteoporose [ɔsteopoˈroːzə] *f* (-; -n) 💊
osteoporosis.

Osterei [ˈoːstərˈʔai] *n* Easter egg.

'Osterfest *n* → **Ostern.**

'Osterglocke *f* 🌷 (yellow) daffodil.

'Osterhase *m* Easter bunny.

österlich [ˈøːstərlɪç] *adj* (of) Easter.

Oster'montag *m* Easter Monday.

Ostern [ˈoːstərn] *n* (-; -) (*zu* ~ at) Easter.

Österreich [ˈøːstəraiç] *n* (-s) Austria.
'Österreicher *m* (-s; -), **'Österreiche-
rin** *f* (-; -nen), **'österreichisch** *adj* Austrian.

Oster'sonntag *m* Easter Sunday.

'Osteu,ropa *n* Eastern Europe.

östlich [ˈœstlɪç] **I** *adj* eastern, easterly. **II**
adv ~ *von* (to the) east of.

Östrogen [œstroˈgeːn] *n* (-s; -e) *biol.*
(o)estrogen.

'Ostsee *f* Baltic (Sea).

ostwärts [ˈɔstvɛrts] *adv* east(wards).

'Ostwind *m* east wind.

Oszillograph [ɔstsıloˈgraːf] *m* (-en; -en)
oscilloscope, oscillograph.

Otter[1] [ˈɔtər] *m* (-s; -) *zo.* otter.

'Otter[2] *f* (-; -n) *zo.* viper.

Ouvertüre [uvɛrˈtyːrə] *f* (-; -n) overture.

oval [oˈvaːl] *adj*, **O'val** *n* (-s; -e) oval.

Ovation [ovaˈtsio̯n] *f* (-; -en) ovation.

Ovulation [ovulaˈtsio̯n] *f* (-; -en) *biol.*
ovulation.

Oxyd [ɔˈksyːt] *n* (-[e]s; -e) 🧪 oxide.

Oxydation [ɔksydaˈtsio̯n] *f* (-; -en) oxi-
dation. **oxydieren** [ɔksyˈdiːrən] *v/i* (h,
sn) oxidize.

Ozean [ˈoːtsea:n] *m* (-s; -e) ocean.

'Ozeandampfer *m* ocean liner.

ozeanisch [otseˈaːnɪʃ] *adj* oceanic.

Ozeanographie [otseanograˈfiː] *f* (-; *no
pl*) oceanography.

Ozelot [ˈoːtselɔt] *m* (-s; -e) *zo.* ocelot.

Ozon [oˈtsoːn] *n* (-s; *no pl*) ozone.

o'zonhaltig *adj* ozoniferous.

O'zon|loch *n* hole in the ozone layer.
~schicht *f* ozone layer, ozonosphere.
~werte *pl* ozone levels.

P

P, p [pe:] *n* (-; -) P, p.

paar [pa:r] *indef pron* **ein ~** a few, some, F a couple of. **Paar** *n* (-[e]s; -e) pair, couple: **ein ~ (neue) Schuhe** a (new) pair of shoes. **'paaren** *v/t* (h) **1.** (*a. sich ~*) *zo.* pair, couple, mate. **2.** *sports:* match. **3.** *fig.* (*a. sich ~*) combine.

'Paarlaufen *n* pair skating.

'paarmal *adv* **ein ~** several (*or* a few, F a couple of) times.

'Paarung *f* (-; -en) **1.** *zo.* pairing, mating. **2.** *sports:* a) matching, b) match.

'Paarungszeit *f zo.* mating season.

'paarweise *adv* in pairs, two by two.

Pacht [paxt] *f* (-; -en) a) lease, b) rent. **'pachten** *v/t* (h) (take on) lease: F *fig.* **er meint, er habe es (für sich) gepachtet** he thinks he has got a monopoly on that. **Pächter** ['pɛçtər] *m* (-s; -) lessee, leaseholder, tenant. **'Pachtung** *f* (-; -en) leasing. **'Pachtvertrag** *m* lease.

Pack¹ [pak] *m* (-[e]s; -e, ⁻e) a) pack, pile, b) bundle: → *Sack.*

Pack² *n* (-[e]s; *no pl*) F *contp.* riffraff.

Päckchen ['pɛkçən] *n* (-s; -) small parcel (*a.* ❀), packet, *esp. Am.* pack (*a. of cigarettes*).

'Packeis *n* pack ice.

packen ['pakən] (h) **I** *v/t* **1.** pack (*one's clothes, suitcase, etc*), make up (*parcel etc*): F **pack dich!** beat it! **2.** (*an dat* by) grab, seize. **3.** *fig. j-n ~* a) *fear etc:* seize s.o., b) *novel etc:* grip s.o., thrill s.o.; F **es hat ihn gepackt** he's got it bad. **4.** F *fig.* lick (*problem etc*): **es ~** a) make it, manage, b) get it. **II** *v/i* **5.** pack (up). **'Packen** *m* (-s; -) pack, pile (*a. fig.*). **'packend** *adj fig.* gripping, thrilling. **'Packer** *m* (-s; -), **'Packerin** *f* (-; -en) packer.

'Packesel *m* pack-mule, *fig.* pack-horse. **'Packpa,pier** *n* wrapping paper.

'Packung *f* (-; -en) **1.** pack, *esp. Am.* pack (*a. of cigarettes*). **2.** ⚕ pack. **3.** ⚙ packing, gasket. **4.** F *sports:* **e-e ~ bekommen** take a hammering.

Pädagoge [pɛda'go:gə] *m* (-n; -n), **Päda'gogin** *f* (-; -nen) a) teacher, b) education(al)ist, educator. **Pädagogik** [-'go:gɪk] *f* (-; *no pl*) pedagogy, education. **päda'gogisch** [-gɪʃ] *adj* pedagogical, educational.

Paddel ['padəl] *n* (-s; -) paddle.

'Paddelboot *n* canoe.

paddeln ['padəln] *v/i, v/t* (h) paddle.

paffen ['pafən] *v/i, v/t* (h) F puff (away) (*at one's pipe etc*), smoke.

Page ['pa:ʒə] *m* (-n; -n) **1.** *hist.* page. **2** page, *Am.* bellboy, bellhop.

Pagode [pa'go:də] *f* (-; -n) pagoda.

pah [pa:] *int* bah, pshaw.

Paket [pa'ke:t] *n* (-[e]s; -e) package (*a. fig. pol. etc*), packet, ❀ parcel: **ein ◆ Aktien** a parcel (*or* block) of shares.

Pa'ket|karte *f* (parcel) mailing form **~post** *f* parcel post. **~schalter** *m* par cels counter. **~zustellung** *f* parcel de livery.

Pakistan ['pa:kɪsta:n] *n* (-s) Pakistan **Pakistaner** [pakɪs'ta:nər] *m* (-s; -) **Paki'stanerin** *f* (-; -nen), **paki'sta nisch** *adj* Pakistani.

Pakt [pakt] *m* (-[e]s; -e) pact, agreement. **paktieren** [pak'ti:rən] *v/i* (h) make a dea (*mit* with).

Palast [pa'last] *m* (-[e]s; -läste) palace.

Palästina [palɛ'sti:na] *n* (-s) Palestine **Palästinenser** [palɛsti'nɛnzər] *m* (-s -), **Palästi'nenserin** *f* (-; -nen), **palä sti'nensisch** [-zɪʃ] *adj* Palestinian.

Palatschinke [pala'tʃɪŋkə] *f* (-; -n *Austrian gastr.* pancake.

Palaver [pa'la:vər] *n* (-s; -) F palaver. **Palette** [pa'lɛtə] *f* (-; -n) **1.** *paint.* palette **2.** *fig.* range. **3.** ◉ pallet.

Palisade [pali'za:də] *f* (-; -n) palisade. **Palme** ['palmə] *f* (-; -n) palm (tree): F **j-** **auf die ~ bringen** drive s.o. up the wall **Palm'sonntag** *m eccl.* Palm Sunday. **'Palm|wedel** *m*, **~zweig** *m* palm branch **Pampe** ['pampə] *f* (-; *no pl*) F mush. **Pampelmuse** [pampəl'mu:zə] *f* (-; -n) grapefruit. **Pamphlet** [pam'fle:t] *n* (-[e]s; -e) pam phlet, lampoon. **'pampig** *adj* F **1.** mushy. **2.** stroppy. **panieren** [pa'ni:rən] *v/t* (h) bread. **Pa'niermehl** *n* breadcrumbs. **Panik** ['pa:nɪk] *f* (-; -en) panic: **in ~** pan ic-stricken, F panicky; **in ~ geraten**

(*versetzen*) panic; F *nur k-e ~!* don't panic! '**Panikmache** f (-; *no pl*) scaremongering. '**panisch** *adj* panic: *von ~er Angst erfaßt* panic-stricken; *e-e ~e Angst haben vor* be terrified of.

Panne ['panə] f (-; -n) 1. a) breakdown, b) puncture: *ich hatte e-e ~* my car broke down, I had a puncture. 2. *fig.* a) mishap, b) F slip-up: *böse ~* foul-up.

'**Pannendienst** m breakdown service.

Panorama [pano'ra:ma] n (-s; -men) panorama. ~**fenster** n picture window.

panschen ['panʃən] (h) **I** v/i F splash (about). **II** v/t water down, adulterate.

Pansen ['panzən] m (-s; -) zo. rumen.

Panther ['pantər] m (-s; -) panther.

Pantoffel [pan'tɔfəl] m (-s; -n) slipper: F *unter dem ~ stehen* be henpecked.

Pan'toffelheld m F henpecked husband.

Pan'toffelkino n F telly, *Am. the* tube.

Pantomime¹ [panto'mi:mə] f (-; -n) (panto)mime, dumb show.

Panto'mime² m (-n; -n) mime.

panto'mimisch *adj* pantomimic: *~ darstellen* mime.

Panzer ['pantsər] m (-s; -) 1. *hist.* armo(u)r. 2. ✕ tank. 3. zo. shell. ~**abwehr...** ✕ antitank (*rocket, gun, etc*). ~**divisi,on** f ✕ armo(u)red division. ~**faust** f antitank grenade launcher. ~**glas** n bulletproof glass. ~**kreuzer** m ⚓ ✕ armo(u)red cruiser.

panzern ['pantsərn] v/t (h) armo(u)r: *fig. sich ~* arm o.s.; → **gepanzert.**

'**Panzer|schrank** m safe. ~**sperre** f ✕ antitank obstacle. ~**truppe** f ✕ tank force. ~**tür** f armo(u)red door. ~**wagen** m ✕ armo(u)red car.

Papa ['papa] m (-s; -s) F daddy, dad, pa.

Papagei [papa'gaɪ] m (-en; -e[n]) parrot.

Papa'geienkrankheit f psittacosis.

Papier [pa'pi:r] n (-s; -e) paper: ~**e** a) (identity) papers, b) ✝ securities, papers; (*nur*) *auf dem ~* on paper (only); *zu ~ bringen* commit to paper; *s-e ~e bekommen* get one's cards, be sacked.

pa'pieren *adj* 1. (of) paper. 2. *fig.* prosy.

Pa'pier|fa,brik f paper mill. ~**geld** n paper money. ~**korb** m waste-paper basket. ~**krieg** m F red tape, paper warfare. ~**schlange** f paper streamer. ~**schnipsel** m scrap of paper. ~**ser-vi,ette** f paper napkin. ~**taschentuch** n tissue. ~**tiger** m iro. paper tiger.

Pa'pierwaren pl stationery. ~**geschäft** n stationer's (shop *or* store).

'**Pappband** m 1. pasteboard (binding). 2. paperback. '**Pappbecher** m paper cup. '**Pappdeckel** m pasteboard.

Pappe ['papə] f (-; -n) cardboard, pasteboard: F *nicht von ~* quite something, *person:* quite formidable.

Pappel ['papəl] f (-; -n) ♀ poplar.

'**Pappenstiel** m F *für e-n ~* buy etc s.th. for a song; *k-n ~ wert* not worth a bean.

'**Pappkar,ton** m cardboard box.

Pappmaché [papma'ʃe:] n (-s; -s) papier mâché.

'**Pappteller** m paper plate.

Paprika ['paprika] m (-s; -[s]) 1. *no pl* paprika. 2. ~ = '**Paprikaschote** f green (*or* sweet) pepper.

Papst [pa:pst] m (-[e]s; ⁓e) pope.

päpstlich ['pɛ:pstlɪç] *adj* papal.

'**Papsttum** n (-s; *no pl*) papacy.

Parabel [pa'ra:bəl] f (-; -n) 1. parable. 2. ⅋ parabola.

Parabol,antenne [para'bo:l-] f TV parabolic aerial (*Am.* antenna), F dish.

Parade [pa'ra:də] f (-; -n) 1. ✕ parade, review: F *j-m in die ~ fahren* cut s.o. short. 2. *boxing, fenc.* parry, *soccer:* save. ~**beispiel** n classic example.

Paradeiser [para'daɪzər] m (-s; -) *Austrian* tomato.

Paradies [para'di:s] n (-es; -e) (*im ~* in) paradise. **paradiesisch** [para'di:zɪʃ] *adj* paradisiac(al), *fig.* heavenly.

paradox [para'dɔks] *adj* 1. paradoxical. 2. F strange, absurd.

para'doxerweise *adv* 1. paradoxically. 2. F strangely enough.

Paraffin [para'fi:n] n (-s; -e) 🜊 paraffin.

Paragraph [para'gra:f] m (-en; -en) 1. section, article. 2. paragraph. 3. (*symbol §*) section mark.

parallel [para'le:l] *adj and adv* parallel (*mit, zu* to). **Paral'lele** f (-; -n) parallel (line): *fig. e-e ~ ziehen* draw a parallel (*zu* to). **Parallelogramm** [paralelo-'gram] n (-s; -e) ⅋ parallelogram.

paramili,tärisch ['pa:ra-] *adj* paramilitary.

Paranoia [para'nɔya] f (-; *no pl*) ⚕ paranoia. **Paranoiker** [para'no:ikər] m (-s; -), **paranoisch** [-'no:ɪʃ] *adj* paranoiac.

Paranuß ['pa:ra-] f Brazil nut.

paraphieren [para'fi:rən] v/t (h) initial.

Parapsycholo'gie f parapsychology.
Parasit [para'zi:t] m (-en; -en) parasite.
para'sitisch [-tɪʃ] adj parasitic(al).
parat [pa'ra:t] adj pred ready.
Pärchen ['pɛ:rçən] n (-s; -) (courting) couple, twosome.
pardon [par'dõ:] int sorry.
Parenthese [parɛn'te:zə] f (-; -n) ling. parenthesis.
Parfüm [par'fy:m] n (-s; -e, -s) perfume, scent. **Parfümerie** [parfymə'ri:] f (-; -n) perfumery.
Par'fümfläschchen n scent bottle.
parfümieren [parfy'mi:rən] (h) I v/t perfume, scent. II **sich ~** put on perfume.
parieren [pa'ri:rən] (h) I v/t 1. sports or fig. parry. 2. pull up (horse). II v/i 3. parry. 4. F obey.
Pariser [pa'ri:zər] m (-s; -), **Pa'riserin** f (-; -nen) Parisian.
Parität [pari'tɛ:t] f (-; no pl) parity.
pari'tätisch adj proportional, pro rata.
Park [park] m (-s; -s) park. **~anlage** f park. **~bank** f (-; ⁓e) park bench. **~bucht** f mot. lay-by. **~deck** n mot. parking level.
parken ['parkən] v/t, v/i (h) park: **~de Autos** parked cars; **Parken verboten!** no parking!; **schräg ~** angle-park; **in zweiter Reihe ~** double-park.
Parkett [par'kɛt] n (-[e]s; -e) 1. parquet. 2. (dance) floor. 3. thea. stalls, Am. parquet. **~(fuß)boden** m parquet floor.
'Park|gebühr f parking fee. **~hochhaus** n multistor(e)y car park, Am. parking garage. **~licht** n parking light. **~lücke** f parking space. **~platz** m a) car park, Am. parking lot, b) parking space. **~scheibe** f parking disc. **~sünder(in** f) m F parking offender. **~uhr** f parking meter. **~verbot** n **hier ist ~** there's no parking here; **im ~ stehen** be parked in a towaway zone. **~wächter** m 1. park keeper. 2. mot. car park attendant.
Parlament [parla'mɛnt] n (-[e]s; -e) (**im ~ sitzen** be or sit in) parliament.
Parlamentarier [parlamɛn'ta:rïər] m (-s; -) parliamentarian.
parlamen'tarisch adj parliamentary.
Parlamentarismus [parlamɛnta'rɪs-mʊs] m (-; no pl) parliamentarianism.
Parla'ments|ausschuß m parliamentary committee. **~ferien** pl recess. **~mitglied** n member of parliament.

~sitzung f sitting (of parliament).
~wahlen pl parliamentary elections.
Parmesan [parme'za:n] m (-s; no pl) Parmesan.
Parodie [paro'di:] f (-; -n) parody, F take-off. **parodieren** [paro'di:rən] v/t (h) parody, F take s.o. off. **Parodist** [paro'dɪst] m (-en; -en) parodist.
Parodontose [parodɔn'to:zə] f (-; -n) 🦷 paradontosis.
Parole [pa'ro:lə] f (-; -n) ✕ password, fig. watchword, pol. a. slogan.
Partei [par'taɪ] f (-; -en) a) a. pol. or ⚖ party, b) sports: side, c) tenant: **j-s ~ ergreifen, für j-n ~ nehmen** side with s.o.; **gegen j-n ~ ergreifen** take sides against s.o.; **~ sein** be biassed; **die ~ wechseln** change sides (pol. parties). **~appa‚rat** m party machine. **~basis** f rank and file (of a party). **~buch** n party membership book. **~freund** m fellow-member (of a party). **~führer** m party leader. **~führung** f 1. party leadership. 2. coll. party leaders. **~gänger** [-gɛŋər] m (-s; -) partisan, party man. **~genosse** m party member.
par'teiisch, par'teilich adj partial.
Par'teilinie f party line.
par'teilos adj independent.
Par'teilose m, f (-n; -n) independent.
Par'teimitglied n party member.
Par'teinahme f (-; -n) partisanship.
Par'tei|poli‚tik f party politics. **⚲po‚li-tisch** adj party-political. **~pro‚gramm** n (party) platform. **~spende** f party donation. **~tag** m party conference (Am. convention). **~versammlung** f party meeting. **~vorsitzende** m party leader. **~vorstand** m executive committee (of a party). **~zugehörigkeit** f party membership.
Parterre [par'tɛrə] n (-s; -s) ground (Am. first) floor.
Partie [par'ti:] f (-; -n) 1. part. 2. 🌿 lot. 3. ♪ etc part. 4. game, sports: a. match. 5. F **ich bin mit von der ~!** count me in! 6. F **e-e gute ~ sein** be a good match (or catch); **e-e gute ~ machen** marry a fortune.
partiell [par'tsïɛl] adj partial.
Partikel [par'ti:kəl] f (-; -n) particle.
Partisan [parti'za:n] m (-s, -en; -en) partisan, guerilla.
Partitur [parti'tu:r] f (-; -en) ♪ score.

Partizip [parti'tsi:p] *n* (-s; -ien) *ling.* participle.

Partner ['partnər] *m* (-s; -), **'Partnerin** *f* (-; -nen) partner. **'Partnerschaft** *f* (-; -en) partnership. **'partnerschaftlich** *adj and adv* as (equal) partners, joint(ly). **'Partnerstadt** *f* twin town.

Party ['pa:rti] *f* (-; -s, -ties) *(auf e-e ~ gehen* go to a) party. **~muffel** *m* F party pooper. **~raum** *m* party room.

Parzelle [par'tsɛlə] *f* (-; -n) plot, lot. **parzellieren** [partse'li:rən] *v/t* (h) parcel out.

Pascha ['paʃa] *m* (-s; *no pl*) *hist.* pasha.

Paß [pas] *m* (Passes; Pässe) **1.** (mountain) pass. **2.** passport. **3.** *sports:* pass.

passabel [pa'sa:bəl] *adj* passable.

Passage [pa'sa:ʒə] *f* (-; -n) **1.** passage (*a.* ♩, *in book etc*). **2.** (shopping) arcade.

Passagier [pasa'ʒi:r] *m* (-s; -e) passenger: *blinder ~* ♨ stowaway. **~liste** *f* passenger list. **~schiff** *n* passenger ship.

Passant [pa'sant] *m* (-en; -en), **Pas'santin** *f* (-; -nen) passer-by.

Passat [pa'sa:t] *m* (-[e]s; -e) trade wind.

'Paßbild *n* passport photo(graph).

Passe ['pasə] *f* (-; -n) *dress:* yoke.

passen ['pasən] (h) **I** *v/i* **1.** *a. fig.* fit *(j-m, auf j-n* s.o., *für or zu et.* s.th.): *~ zu in colo(u)r etc:* go well with, match; *fig. sie ~ (gut) zueinander* they are well suited to each other; *das paßt (nicht) zu ihm!* that's just like him (not like him!). **2.** *j-m ~* suit s.o.: *paßt es dir morgen?* would tomorrow suit you (or be all right [with you])?; *das paßt mir gut* that suits me fine; *das (er) paßt mir gar nicht!* I don't like it (him) at all!; F *das könnte dir so ~!* nothing doing! **3.** *cards, a. sports:* pass: *ich passe!* pass!; *fig. da muß ich ~!* you've got me there! **II** *v/t* **4. den Ball ~ zu** pass (the ball) to.

'passend *adj* **1.** fitting (*a. fig.*), in colo(u)r *etc:* matching: *e-e dazu ~e Krawatte* a (neck)tie to match. **2.** suitable, right: *die ~en Worte* the right words; *bei ~er Gelegenheit* at the right moment. **3.** F *haben Sie es ~?* have you got the right money?

Passepartout [paspar'tu:] *n* (-s; -s) mount.

'Paßform *f* (-; *no pl*) fit.

pas'sierbar *adj* passable, practicable.

passieren [pa'si:rən] **I** *v/i* (sn) **1.** take

place, happen: *j-m ~* happen to s.o.; *was ist passiert?* what's happened?; *mir ist nichts passiert* I'm all right. **II** *v/t* (h) **2.** pass (by *or* through). **3.** *gastr.* pass (through a sieve *etc*), strain.

Pas'sierschein *m* pass, permit.

Pas'sierschlag *m tennis:* passing shot.

Passion [pa'sio:n] *f* (-; -en) **1.** passion. **2.** *eccl.*, ♩ *etc* Passion. **passioniert** [pasio'ni:rt] *adj* enthusiastic, keen.

Passi'onsspiel *n* Passion play.

passiv ['pasi:f] *adj* passive: *~es Mitglied* nonactive member; *~er Wortschatz* recognition vocabulary; → *Bestechung.*

'Passiv *n* (-s; -e) *ling.* passive (voice).

Passiva [pa'si:va] *pl* ✝ liabilities.

Passivität [pasivi'tɛ:t] *f* (-; *no pl*) passivity, passiveness, inaction.

'Passivposten *m* ✝ debit item.

'Passivseite *f* ✝ liability side.

'Paßkon,trolle *f* passport control.

'Paßstelle *f* passport office.

'Paßstraße *f* (mountain) pass.

'Paßstück *n* ⚙ fitting piece, adapter.

Passus ['pasʊs] *m* (-; -) passage.

'Paßwort *n a. computer:* password.

Paste ['pastə] *f* (-; -n) paste.

Pastell [pas'tɛl] *n* (-[e]s; -e) pastel. **~farben** *pl* pastel shades. **~stift** *m* crayon.

Pastete [pas'te:tə] *f* (-; -n) pie, pâté.

pasteurisieren [pastøri'zi:rən] *v/t* (h) pasteurize.

Pastille [pas'tɪlə] *f* (-; -n) lozenge.

Pastor ['pasto:r] *m* (-s; -en) pastor.

Pate ['pa:tə] *m* (-n; -n) a) godfather, b) → *Patin,* c) → *Patenkind:* ~ *stehen bei* be godfather (*or* godmother) to, *fig.* sponsor, *w.s.* be behind.

'Patenkind *n* godchild, godson, goddaughter. **'Patenonkel** *m* godfather.

Patenschaft *f* (-; -en) sponsorship; *fig. die ~ übernehmen für* sponsor.

patent [pa'tɛnt] *adj* F ingenious, clever. **Pa'tent** *n* (-[e]s; -e) **1.** patent (*auf acc* for): *ein ~ anmelden* apply for a patent; *(zum) ~ angemeldet* patent pending. **2.** ⚔ commission. **~amt** *n* Patent Office. **~anmeldung** *f* patent application. **~anspruch** *m* patent claim. **~anwalt** *m* patent attorney. **~beschreibung** *f* patent specification.

patentieren [patɛn'ti:rən] *v/t* (h) patent: *et. ~ lassen* take out a patent for s.th.

Pa'tent|inhaber m patentee. **~lösung** f F fig. ready-made solution. **~recht** n a) patent law, b) patent right. **2rechtlich** adj and adv under patent law: **~ geschützt** patented. **~schrift** f patent specification. **~schutz** m protection by patent.

Pater ['pa:tər] m (-s; -, Patres) father.

pathetisch [pa'te:tɪʃ] adj lofty, emotional, contp. pompous.

Pathologe [pato'lo:gə] m (-n; -n) pathologist. **Pathologie** [patolo'gi:] f (-; no pl) pathology. **pathologisch** [pato'lo:gɪʃ] adj pathological.

Pathos ['pa:tɔs] n (-; no pl) emotion(al style or tone).

Patience [pa'sĩã:s] f (-; -n) (**e-e ~ legen** play a) patience (Am. solitaire).

Patient [pa'tsĩɛnt] m (-en; -en), **Patientin** f (-; -nen) patient.

Patin ['pa:tɪn] f (-; -nen) godmother.

Patina ['pa:tina] f (-; no pl) (**~ ansetzen** a. fig.) develop a) patina.

Patriarch [patri'arç] m (-en; -en) patriarch. **patriarchalisch** [patriar'ça:lɪʃ] adj patriarchal.

Patriot [patri'o:t] m (-en; -en), **Patriotin** f (-; -nen) patriot. **patri'otisch** [-tɪʃ] adj patriotic. **Patriotismus** [patrio'tɪsmʊs] m (-; no pl) patriotism.

Patron [pa'tro:n] m (-s; -e) **1.** eccl. patron saint. **2.** F fellow: contp. **übler ~** nasty customer.

Patrone [pa'tro:nə] f (-; -n) cartridge.

Pa'tronenhülse f cartridge case.

Pa'tronin f (-; -nen) eccl. patron saint.

Patrouille [pa'trʊljə] f (-; -n), **patrouillieren** [patrʊl'ji:rən] v/i (h) ✕ patrol.

patsch [patʃ] int splat!, smack!

Patsche ['patʃə] f F **in der ~ sitzen** be in a scrape; **j-m aus der ~ helfen** help s.o. out of a (tight) spot.

'patschen v/i (h, sn) a) splash, b) smack.

Patt [pat] n chess: stalemate (a. fig. pol.).

patzen ['patsən] v/i (h), **Patzer** ['patsər] m (-s; -) F blunder, boob.

patzig ['patsɪç] adj F snotty, stroppy.

Pauke ['paʊkə] f (-; -n) a) bass drum, b) kettledrum: F fig. **auf die ~ hauen** paint the town red; **mit ~n und Trompeten durchfallen** iro. fail gloriously.

'pauken v/i (h) **1.** play the kettledrum(s). **2.** F ped. (a. v/t) cram, swot.

'Paukenschlag m drumbeat: fig. **wie ein ~** like a bombshell.

Pauker ['paʊkər] m (-s; -) **1.** ♪ drummer. **2.** F teacher.

pausbäckig ['paʊsbɛkɪç] adj chubby.

pauschal [paʊ'ʃa:l] **I** adj **1.** all-in(clusive) (price etc). **2.** fig. sweeping. **II** adv **3.** in a lump sum. **4.** fig. wholesale.

Pau'schale f (-; -n) lump sum.

Pau'schal|gebühr f flat rate. **~reise** f package tour. **~urteil** n fig. sweeping judg(e)ment.

Pause[1] ['paʊzə] f (-; -n) pause, rest (a. ♪), ped. break, Am. recess, thea. etc interval, Am. intermission: **e-e ~ machen** a) take a break (or rest), b) pause.

'Pause[2] f (-; -n) ⊕ tracing, copy, blueprint. **'pausen** v/t (h) trace.

'pausenlos adj uninterrupted, nonstop.

'Pausenzeichen n radio, TV interval signal.

pausieren [paʊ'zi:rən] v/i (h) a) pause, b) take a break (or rest).

'Pauspa,pier n tracing paper.

Pavian ['pa:viã:n] m (-s; -e) zo. baboon.

Pavillon ['pavɪljõ:] m (-s; -s) pavilion.

Pazifismus [patsi'fɪsmʊs] m (-; no pl) pacifism. **Pazifist** [patsi'fɪst] m (-en; -en), **pazi'fistisch** [-tɪʃ] adj pacifist.

Pech [pɛç] n (-s; -e) **1.** pitch: fig. **wie ~ und Schwefel zs.-halten** be as thick as thieves. **2.** no pl F bad luck: **~ gehabt!** tough luck!; **~ haben** be unlucky (**bei** with). **'pechschwarz** adj F jet-black (hair etc), pitch-dark (night).

'Pechsträhne f run of bad luck.

'Pechvogel m F unlucky fellow (or girl).

Pedal [pe'da:l] n (-s; -e) pedal.

Pedant [pe'dant] m (-en; -en) pedant. **Pedanterie** [-tə'ri:] f (-; no pl) pedantry. **pe'dantisch** [-tɪʃ] adj pedantic.

Pediküre [pedi'ky:rə] f (-; -n) pedicure.

Pegel [pe'ge:l] m (-s; -) a. fig. level.

'Pegelstand m water level.

peilen ['paɪlən] (h) **I** v/t take the bearings of: fig. **die Lage ~** see how the land lies; **→ Daumen. II** v/i take the bearings.

'Peilfunk m directional radio.

'Peilgerät n radio direction finder.

'Peilung f (-; -en) a) locating, b) bearing.

Pein [paɪn] f (-; no pl) pain, agony.

peinigen ['paɪnigən] v/t (h) torment. **'Peiniger** m (-s; -) tormentor.

peinlich I adj **1.** embarrassing, a. awkward (*silence, situation, etc*): **es ist mir sehr ~** I feel awful about it. **2.** meticulous, scrupulous. **II** *adv* **3.** *j-n ~ berühren* pain s.o.; **~ berührt** embarrassed, pained. **4. ~ (genau)** meticulously; **~ sauber** scrupulously clean; **et. ~st vermeiden** take great care to avoid s.th.

'**Peinlichkeit** *f* (-; -en) **1.** *no pl* awkwardness. **2.** awkward situation (*or* remark).

Peitsche ['paɪtʃə] *f* (-; -n) whip.

'**peitschen** *v/i, v/t* (h) whip, *a. fig.* lash.

'**Peitschenhieb** *m* (whip)lash.

Pekinese [peki'ne:zə] *m* (-n; -n) *zo.* Pekin(g)ese.

Pelargonie [pelar'go:nɪə] *f* (-; -n) 💐 pelargonium.

Pelikan ['pe:lika:n] *m* (-s; -e) *zo.* pelican.

Pelle ['pɛlə] *f* (-; -n) *dial.* skin, peel.

'**pellen** *v/t* (h) skin, peel; → *Ei* 1.

'**Pellkartoffeln** *pl* potatoes (boiled) in their skins, jacket potatoes.

Pelz [pɛlts] *m* (-es; -e) a) fur, b) skin, hide: *j-m auf den ~ rücken* press s.o. hard. ♀**gefüttert** *adj* fur-lined. **~handel** *m* fur trade. **~händler** *m* furrier.

pelzig ['pɛltsɪç] *adj* **1.** furry. **2.** 🖋 furred, coated (*tongue etc*).

'**Pelz|jacke** *f* fur jacket. **~kragen** *m* fur collar. **~mantel** *m* fur coat. **~mütze** *f* fur hat.

'**Pelztier** *n* fur-bearing animal. **~farm** *f* fur farm. **~jäger** *m* trapper. **~zucht** *f* fur farming.

Pendel ['pɛndəl] *n* (-s; -) pendulum.

'**pendeln** *v/i* **1.** (h) swing, oscillate. **2.** (sn) 🚆 *etc* shuttle, *person:* commute.

'**Pendel|tür** *f* swing door. **~uhr** *f* pendulum clock. **~verkehr** *m* **1.** 🚆 shuttle service. **2.** commuter traffic.

Pendler ['pɛndlər] *m* (-s; -) commuter.

penetrant [pene'trant] *adj* **1.** penetrating (*smell etc*). **2.** *contp.* pushy (*person*).

peng [pɛŋ] *int* bang!

penibel [pe'ni:bəl] *adj* fussy.

Penis ['pe:nɪs] *m* (-; -se) *anat.* penis.

Penizillin [penitsɪ'li:n] *n* (-s; -e) penicillin.

Penne ['pɛnə] *f* (-; -n) F **1.** school. **2.** *contp. sl.* dosshouse, *Am.* flophouse.

'**pennen** *v/i* (h) F *contp.* a) *sl.* (have a) kip, b) *fig.* sleep. '**Penner** *m* (-s; -) F *contp.* **1.** *sl.* tramp, bum. **2.** sleepyhead.

Pension [pã'zĭo:n] *f* (-; -en) **1.** (old-age) pension: *in ~ gehen* retire; *in ~ sein* be

retired. **2.** boarding-house, private hotel. **3.** board. **Pensionär** [pãzĭo'nɛ:r] *m* (-s; -e) pensioner. **pensionieren** [-'ni:rən] *v/t* (h) pension (off): *sich ~ lassen* retire. **pensio'niert** *adj* retired. **Pensio'nierung** *f* (-; -en) retirement. **Pensi'onsalter** *n* retirement age.

pensi'ons|berechtigt *adj* eligible for a pension. **~reif** *adj* F due for retirement.

Pensum ['pɛnzʊm] *n* (-s; Pensen) (allotted) task, *w.s.* workload.

Peperoni [pepe'ro:ni] *pl* red peppers.

Pepsin [pɛ'psi:n] *n* (-s; -e) 🖐, 🖋 pepsin.

per [pɛr] *prep* per, by: **~ Adresse** care of (*abbr.* c/o); **~ Bahn** by train; → *du.*

Perestroika [pere'strɔyka] *f* (-; *no pl*) *pol.* perestroika.

perfekt [pɛr'fɛkt] *adj* **1.** perfect. **2.** F settled: *et. ~ machen* clinch s.th.

'**Perfekt** *n* (-s; -e) *ling.* perfect (tense).

Perfektion [pɛrfɛk'tsĭo:n] *f* (-; *no pl*) perfection. **perfektionieren** [-tsĭo'ni:rən] *v/t* (h) (make) perfect. **Perfektionist** [-tsĭo'nɪst] *m* (-en; -en) perfectionist.

perforieren [pɛrfo'ri:rən] *v/t* (h) perforate.

Pergament [pɛrga'mɛnt] *n* (-[e]s; -e) parchment. **Perga'mentpa‚pier** *n* greaseproof paper.

Periode [pe'rĭo:də] *f* (-; -n) period (*a. physiol.*), ✒ cycle. **peri'odisch** [-dɪʃ] *adj* periodic(al), ♭ recurring (*decimal*).

Peripherie [perife'ri:] *f* (-; -n) periphery, *a.* outskirts (*of a town*).

Periskop [peri'sko:p] *n* (-s; -e) periscope.

Perle ['pɛrlə] *f* (-; -n) **1.** a) pearl, b) bead: F **~n vor die Säue werfen** cast (one's) pearls before swine. **2.** bead, drop. **3.** *fig.* jewel, gem.

'**perlen** *v/i* (h) **1.** *drink:* sparkle. **2.** (sn) *sweat, water:* trickle (down).

'**Perlen|kette** *f* pearl (*or* bead) necklace. **~schnur** *f* string of pearls (*or* beads).

'**Perlhuhn** *n* *zo.* guinea fowl.

'**Perlmuschel** *f* pearl oyster.

'**Perlmutt** [-mʊt] *n* (-s; *no pl*), '**Perlmutter** *f* (-; *no pl*) mother-of-pearl.

perplex [pɛr'plɛks] *adj* F bewildered.

Persenning [pɛr'zɛnɪŋ] *f* (-; -e[n]) ⚓ tarpaulin.

Perser ['pɛrzər] *m* (-s; -), **~teppich** *m* Persian carpet.

Persianer [pɛr'zĭa:nər] *m* (-s; -) **1.** Per-

Persianermantel

sian lamb(skin). **2.** → **Persi'anerman-tel** *m* Persian lamb coat.

persisch ['pɛrzɪʃ] *adj* Persian.

Person [pɛr'zo:n] *f* (-; -en) person, *thea.* character: *ling.* **erste** ~ first person; **in eigener** ~ personally; **ich für m-e** ~ I for my part; **pro** ~ each; **ein Tisch für sechs** ~**en** a table for six; **sie ist die Güte in** ~ she is kindness personified; → **juristisch.**

Personal [pɛrzo'na:l] *n* (-s; *no pl*) personnel, staff; ~ **ist unterbesetzt** is understaffed. ~**abbau** *m* personnel reduction. ~**ab,teilung** *f* personnel department. ~**akte** *f* personal file. ~**ausweis** *m* identity card. ~**chef** *m* personnel manager. ~**com,puter** *m* personal computer.

Personalien [pɛrzo'na:liən] *pl* particulars, personal data.

Perso'nal|poli,tik *f* personnel policy. ~**pro,nomen** *n ling.* personal pronoun.

personell [pɛrzo'nɛl] *adj* **1.** personal. **2.** personnel.

Per'sonen|beförderung *f* passenger transport. ~**beschreibung** *f* personal description. ~**gesellschaft** *f* ✝ partnership. ~**kraftwagen** *m* (*abbr.* PKW) motor car, *Am. a.* auto(mobile). ~**kreis** *m* circle. ~**kult** *m* personality cult. ~**schaden** *m* personal injury. ~**stand** *m* marital status. ~**wagen** *m* **1.** ⚭ passenger coach (*Am.* car). **2.** → **Personenkraftwagen.** ~**zug** *m* slow train.

personifizieren [pɛrzonifi'tsi:rən] *v/t* (h) personify.

persönlich [pɛr'zø:nlɪç] **I** *adj* personal. **II** *adv* personally, *a.* in person.

Per'sönlichkeit *f* (-; -en) personality: **e-e** ~ **des öffentlichen Lebens** a public figure.

Perspektive [pɛrspɛk'ti:və] *f* (-; -n) perspective, *fig. a.* a) prospect, b) point of view: **das eröffnet neue** ~ that opens up new vistas. **perspek'tivisch** [-vɪʃ] *adj* perspective, *drawing* in perspective.

Peru [pe'ru:] *n* (-s) Peru. **Peruaner** [pe'rüa:nər] *m* (-s; -), **Peru'anerin** *f* (-; -nen), **peru'anisch** *adj* Peruvian.

Perücke [pe'rykə] *f* (-; -n) wig.

pervers [pɛr'vɛrs] *adj* perverse.

Perversität [pɛrvɛrzi'tɛ:t] *f* (-; -en) perversity. **pervertieren** [pɛrvɛr'ti:rən] *v/t* (h) pervert.

Peseta [pe'ze:ta] *f* (-; Peseten) peseta.

Pessar [pe'sa:r] *n* (-s; -e) ⚕ pessary.

Pessimismus [pɛsi'mɪsmʊs] *m* (-; *no pl*) pessimism. **Pessimist** [-'mɪst] *m* (-en; -en), **Pessi'mistin** *f* (-; -nen) pessimist. **pessi'mistisch** *adj* pessimistic.

Pest [pɛst] *f* (-; *no pl*) plague: **j-n hassen wie die** ~ hate s.o.'s guts; F **stinken wie die** ~ stink to high heaven.

Petersilie [pe:tər'zi:liə] *f* (-; -n) parsley.

Petition [peti'tsio:n] *f* (-; -en) petition.

Petroche'mie [petro-] *f* petrochemistry.

petro'chemisch *adj* (*a.* ~**es Produkt**) petrochemical.

Petroleum [pe'tro:leʊm] *n* (-s; *no pl*) **1.** → **Erdöl. 2.** paraffin, *Am.* kerosene.

petto ['pɛto] **et. in** ~ **haben** have s.th. up one's sleeve.

Petze ['pɛtsə] *f* (-; -n) F *ped.* telltale, sneak. **'petzen** *v/i* (h) F *ped.* sneak.

Pfad [pfa:t] *m* (-[e]s; -e) path.

'Pfadfinder *m* boy scout. **'Pfadfinderin** *f* girl guide, *Am.* girl scout.

Pfaffe ['pfafə] *m* (-n; -n) F *contp.* cleric, Holy Joe.

Pfahl [pfa:l] *m* (-[e]s; ~e) a) stake, b) post, △ pile, c) pole. **'Pfahlbau** *m* (-[e]s; -ten) pile dwelling. **'Pfahlwurzel** *f* tap root.

Pfand [pfant] *n* (-[e]s; ~er ['pfɛndər]) a) security, b) pledge, *in games:* forfeit, c) deposit: **als** ~ **geben** *a. fig.* pledge; ~ **zahlen** pay a deposit (*for*).

pfändbar ['pfɛntba:r] *adj* distrainable.

'Pfandbrief *m* ✝ bond.

pfänden ['pfɛndən] *v/t* (h) distrain (up)on, seize, attach (*claim etc*).

'Pfänderspiel *n* (game of) forfeits.

'Pfandflasche *f* returnable bottle.

'Pfandhaus *n*, **'Pfandleihe** *f* (-; -n) pawnshop. **'Pfandleiher** *m* (-s; -e), **'Pfandleiherin** *f* (-; -nen) pawnbroker.

'Pfandschein *m* pawn ticket.

'Pfändung *f* (-; -en) (*gen*) seizure (of), distraint (upon).

'Pfändungsbefehl *m* distress warrant.

Pfanne ['pfanə] *f* (-; -n) **1.** pan: F **j-n in die** ~ **hauen** a) clobber s.o., b) give s.o. a roasting. **2.** *anat.* socket. **3.** pantile.

'Pfannkuchen *m* pancake: **Berliner** ~ doughnut.

'Pfarramt *n* rectory. **'Pfarrbezirk** *m* parish. **Pfarrei** [pfa'raɪ] *f* (-; -en) rectory, vicarage. **Pfarrer** ['pfarər] *m* (-s; -) a)

pastor, minister, b) (parish) priest.
'Pfarrerin f (-; -nen) woman pastor.
'Pfarr|gemeinde f parish. **~haus** n rectory, vicarage. **~kirche** f parish church.

Pfau [pfau] m (-[e]s; -e) zo. peacock.
'Pfauenauge n zo. peacock (butterfly).

Pfeffer ['pfɛfər] m (-s; -) **1.** pepper: → Hase. **2.** F pep: **~gurke** f gastr. gherkin. **~kuchen** m gingerbread.

'Pfefferminz n (-es; -e) peppermint (drop). **'Pfefferminze** f ♀ peppermint.

'Pfeffermühle f pepper mill.

pfeffern ['pfɛfərn] v/t h. **1.** a. fig. pepper: → **gepfeffert. 2.** F chuck.

'Pfefferstreuer m pepper caster.

Pfeife ['pfaifə] f (-; -n) **1.** a) whistle, b) (organ) pipe: fig. **nach j-s ~ tanzen** dance to s.o.'s tune. **2.** pipe: **~ rauchen** a) smoke a pipe, b) be a pipe smoker. **3.** F idiot, dope.

pfeifen ['pfaifən] (pfiff, gepfiffen, h) **I** v/i **1.** whistle (**j-m** to s.o.), referee etc: blow the whistle, spectator: boo: **ich pfeife auf das Geld** I don't give a damn about the money. **II** v/t **2.** whistle: F **ich werd' dir was ~!** to hell with you! **3.** sports: **ein Spiel ~** referee a match.

'Pfeifen|kopf m bowl. **~raucher** m pipe smoker. **~reiniger** m pipe cleaner. **~stiel** m pipe stem. **~stopfer** m tamper.

'Pfeifkon,zert n (hail of) catcalls.

Pfeil [pfail] m (-[e]s; -e) a) arrow, b) dart: **mit ~ und Bogen** with bow and arrow.

Pfeiler ['pfailər] m (-s; -) pillar (a. fig.), pier.

'pfeilförmig [-fœrmiç] adj V-shaped.

'pfeilge,rade I adj (as) straight as an arrow. **II** adv straight. **'pfeilschnell** adj and adv (as) quick as lightning.

'Pfeilspitze f arrowhead.

Pfennig ['pfɛniç] m (-s; -e) pfennig, fig. penny, Am. cent: F **jeden ~ umdrehen** count every penny; **k-n ~ wert** not worth a thing. **~absatz** m stiletto heel.

Pferch [pfɛrç] m (-[e]s; -e) pen, fold.
'pferchen v/t pen, cram (**in** acc into).

Pferd [pfe:rt] n (-[e]s; -e) **1.** horse: **zu ~e** on horseback; F fig. **das beste ~ im Stall** the number one; **aufs falsche ~ setzen** back the wrong horse; **das ~ beim Schwanze aufzäumen** put the cart before the horse; **mit ihr kann man ~e stehlen** she's a good sport. **2.** gym. (vaulting-)horse. **3.** chess: knight.

Pferde|äpfel ['pfe:rdə-] pl horse droppings. **~fleisch** n horse-meat. **~fuß** m fig. snag. **~koppel** f paddock. **~länge** f sports: **um zwei ~n** by two lengths. **~rennbahn** f racecourse, racetrack. **~rennen** n a) horse racing, b) horse race. **~schwanz** m **1.** zo. horse's tail. **2.** ponytail. **~stall** m stable. **~stärke** f (abbr. PS) horsepower (abbr. HP). **~wagen** m horse-drawn vehicle. **~zucht** f **1.** horse breeding. **2.** stud farm.

pfiff [pfif] pret of **pfeifen.**

Pfiff [pfif] m (-[e]s; -e) **1.** whistle. **2.** F pep: **mit ~ film etc** with a difference; **der Mantel hat ~** the coat's got real style; **der richtige ~** that extra something.

Pfifferling ['pfifərliŋ] m (-s; -e) chanterelle: **k-n ~ wert** not worth a damn.

'pfiffig adj smart. **'Pfiffigkeit** f (-; no pl) smartness. **Pfiffikus** ['pfifikʊs] m (-[ses]; -se) F smart fellow.

Pfingsten ['pfiŋstən] n (-; -) Whitsun.

'Pfingst|fest n → **Pfingsten.** **~montag** m Whit Monday. **~rose** f ♀ peony. **~sonntag** m Whitsunday.

Pfirsich ['pfirziç] m (-s; -e) peach.

Pflanze ['pflantsə] f (-; -n) **1.** plant. **2.** F type, character. **pflanzen** v/t (h) plant.

'Pflanzen|faser f plant fibre (Am. fiber). **~fett** n vegetable fat. **~fresser** m zo. herbivore. **~kost** f vegetable foodstuffs. **~kunde** f botany. **~öl** n vegetable oil. **~reich** n (-[e]s; no pl) vegetable kingdom, flora. **~schutzmittel** n pesticide. **~welt** f (-; no pl) flora.

'pflanzlich adj plant, vegetable.

'Pflanzung f (-; -en) plantation.

Pflaster ['pflastər] n (-s; -) **1.** pavement: fig. **ein heißes (teures) ~** a dangerous (an expensive) place. **2.** ♣ (sticking) plaster, Am. band-aid.

'Pflastermaler(in f) m pavement artist.

'pflastern v/t (h) **1.** pave. **2.** ♣ plaster.

'Pflasterstein m paving stone.

Pflaume ['pflaumə] f (-; -n) **1.** a) plum, b) prune. **2.** F contp. dope, twit.

'Pflaumen|baum m plum (tree). **~kuchen** m plum tart. **~mus** n plum jam.

Pflege ['pfle:gə] f (-; no pl) care, ♣ nursing, ⚙ maintenance, servicing, fig. cultivation (of the arts etc): **in ~ geben** put into care; **in ~ nehmen** a) look after, take into care, b) foster (child).

Ꞷbedürftig *adj* in need of care. **~eltern** *pl* foster parents. **~fall** *m* nursing case. **~heim** *n* nursing home. **~kind** *n* foster child. **Ꞷleicht** *adj* easy-care. **~mutter** *f* foster mother.

pflegen ['pfle:gən] (h) **I** *v/t a)* look after, care for, **~** *a.* nurse, *b) fig.* cultivate (*the arts, a friendship, etc*), *c)* keep *s.th.* in good condition, **☉** *a.* service, groom: → *gepflegt.* **II** *v/i (et.) zu tun* ~ be in the habit of doing (s.th.), usually do (s.th.); *sie pflegte zu sagen* she used to say, she would say. **III** *sich* ~ *a)* take care of one's appearance, *b)* look after o.s.

'Pflegeperso‚nal *n* nursing staff.

Pfleger ['pfle:gər] *m* (-s; -) **1.** **~** (male) nurse. **2.** ⚖ curator.

Pflegerin *f* (-; -nen) ⚖ nurse.

'Pflege|sohn *m* foster son. **~stelle** *f* foster home. **~tochter** *f* foster daughter. **~vater** *m* foster father.

pfleglich ['pfle:klɪç] *adj* careful: *et.* ~ *behandeln* take good care of s.th.

'Pflegschaft *f* (-; -en) ⚖ curatorship.

Pflicht [pflɪçt] *f* (-; -en) duty: *die* ~ *ruft!* duty calls! **2.** → *Pflichtübung.*

'pflichtbewußt *adj* conscientious, dutiful. **'Pflichtbewußtsein** *n* conscientiousness, sense of duty.

'Pflicht|eifer *m* zeal. **~fach** *n ped.* compulsory subject. **~gefühl** *n* sense of duty. **Ꞷgemäß** *I adj* dutiful, due. **II** *adv* duly. **Ꞷgetreu** *adj* dutiful. **~lek‚türe** *f* required reading, set books. **~teil** *m, n* ⚖ legal portion. **~übung** *f sports:* compulsory (*or* set) exercise: *fig. e-e reine* ~ purely a matter of duty. **Ꞷvergessen** *adj* derelict of duty. **~versäumnis** *n* dereliction of duty. **~versicherung** *f* compulsory insurance. **~verteidiger** *m* ⚖ assigned counsel.

Pflock [pflɔk] *m* (-[e]s; ⸚e) **1.** peg. **2.** stake.

pflücken ['pflʏkən] *v/t* (h) pick.

Pflug [pflu:k] *m* (-[e]s; ⸚e), **pflügen** ['pfly:gən] *v/t, v/i* (h) plough, *Am.* plow.

Pforte ['pfɔrtə] *f* (-; -n) gate, door, *fig.* gateway.

Pförtner ['pfœrtnər] *m* (-s; -) gatekeeper, porter, *Am.* doorman. **~haus** *n* lodge. **~loge** *f* porter's office (*or* lodge).

Pfosten ['pfɔstən] *m* (-s; -) **1.** post. **2.** jamb.

Pfote ['pfo:tə] *zo.* paw, F (*hand*) *a. sl.* mitt.

Pfropf [pfrɔpf] *m* (-[e]s; -e) ✛ clot.

pfropfen ['pfrɔpfən] *v/t* (h) **1.** stopper. **2.** F cram. **3.** ✗ graft.

'Pfropfen *m* (-s; -) stopper, cork, plug.

'Pfropf|messer *n* grafter. **~reis** *n* graft.

Pfründe ['pfrʏndə] *f* (-; -n) *a) eccl.* living, *b) fig.* sinecure.

Pfuhl [pfu:l] *m* (-[e]s; -e) murky pool.

pfui [pfʊi] *int a)* (for) shame!, *sports etc:* boo!, *b)* ugh!, *to child or dog:* no!: ~ *Teufel!* ugh!, how disgusting!

Pfund [pfʊnt] *n* (-[e]s; -e) **1.** pound (*abbr.* lb.): **3** ~ *Mehl* three pounds of flour. **2.** ~ (*Sterling*) pound (sterling) (*abbr.* L).

'pfundweise *adj and adv* by the pound.

Pfusch [pfʊʃ] *m* (-[e]s; *no pl*), **'Pfuscharbeit** *f* F bad job, botch-up.

pfuschen ['pfʊʃən] *v/i, v/t* (h) F bungle: → *Handwerk.*

'Pfuscher *m* (-s; -) F bungler.

Pfusche‚rei *f* (-; -en) F bungling.

Pfütze ['pfʏtsə] *f* (-; -n) puddle.

Phallus ['falʊs] *m* (-; Phalli) phallus.

'Phallussym‚bol *n* phallic symbol.

Phänomen [fɛno'me:n] *n* (-s; -e) phenomenon. **phänomenal** [fɛnome'na:l] *adj* phenomenal.

Phantasie [fanta'zi:] *f* (-; -n) **1.** *a)* imagination, b) mind: *schmutzige* ~ dirty mind; *nur in s-r* ~ only in his mind; *ohne* ~ → *phantasielos.* **2.** *usu. pl* fantasy. **3.** ♩ fantasia. **phantasieren** [fanta'zi:rən] *v/i* (h) **1.** fantasize, dream. **2.** ✛ be delirious, *a. fig.* rave (*von* about). **3.** ♩ improvise. **phantasievoll** *adj* imaginative.

Phantast [fan'tast] *m* (-en; -en) dreamer, visionary. **Phantasterei** [fantastə'rai] *f* (-; -en) fantasy. **phan'tastisch** [-tɪʃ] *adj* fantastic, F *a.* terrific, incredible.

Phantom [fan'to:m] *n* (-s; -e) phantom. **Phan'tombild** *n* identikit (*or* photofit) picture (*TM*).

'Pharmaindu‚strie ['farma-] *f* pharmaceutical industry.

Pharmakologe [farmako'lo:gə] *m* (-n; -n) pharmacologist. **Pharmakologie** [-lo'gi:] *f* (-; *no pl*) pharmacology.

'Pharmakon‚zern *m* pharmaceutical company.

Pharmazeut [farma'tsɔyt] *m* (-en; -en),

Pharma'zeutin f (-; -nen) pharmacist. **pharma'zeutisch** adj pharmaceutical.
Pharmazie [farma'tsi:] f (-; no pl) pharmacy.
Phase ['fa:zə] f (-; -n) a. ⚡ phase.
Philanthrop [filan'tro:p] m (-en; -en) philanthropist. **Philanthropie** [filantro'pi:] f (-; no pl) philanthropism. **philan'thropisch** adj philanthropic.
Philatelie [filate'li:] f (-; no pl) philately. **Philatelist** [-'lɪst] m (-en; -en) philatelist.
Philharmonie [filharmo'ni:] f (-; -n) philharmonic orchestra (or society).
Philologe [filo'lo:gə] m (-n; -n) teacher (or scholar) of language and literature, Am. philologist. **Philologie** [-lo'gi:] f (-; -n) study of language and literature, Am. philology. **philo'logisch** [-gɪʃ] adj language and literature ..., Am. philological.
Philosoph [filo'zo:f] m (-en; -en) philosopher. **Philosophie** [-zo'fi:] f (-; -n) philosophy. **philosophieren** [-zo'fi:rən] v/i (h) philosophize. **philo'sophisch** [-fɪʃ] adj philosophic(al).
Phlegma ['flɛgma] n (-s; no pl) phlegm. **Phlegmatiker** [flɛ'gma:tikər] m (-s; -) phlegmatic person. **phleg'matisch** [-tɪʃ] adj phlegmatic.
Phobie [fo'bi:] f (-; -n) psych. phobia.
Phon [fo:n] n (-s; -s) phys. phon: **50 ~** 50 phons.
Phonem [fo'ne:m] n (-s; -e) phoneme.
Phonetik [fo'ne:tɪk] f (-; no pl) phonetics. **Pho'netiker** [-tikər] m (-s; -) phonetician. **pho'netisch** [-tɪʃ] adj phonetic.
Phonotypistin [fonoty'pɪstɪn] f (-; -nen) audio typist.
Phosphat [fɔs'fa:t] n (-[e]s; -e) 🜨 phosphate.
Phosphor ['fɔsfɔr] m (-s; no pl) 🜨 phosphorus.
phosphoreszieren [fɔsfores'tsi:rən] v/i (h) phosphoresce. **~d** phosphorescent.
Photo(...) → **Foto(...)**.
Photoche'mie [foto-] f photochemistry.
Photosyn'these f photosynthesis.
Phrase ['fra:zə] f (-; -n) phrase (a. ♪), contp. a. cliché, pol. catchphrase: F **~n dreschen** talk in platitudes.
'Phrasendrescher m F phrasemonger.
'phrasenhaft adj empty, meaningless.
Physik [fy'zi:k] f (-; no pl) physics.
physikalisch [fyzi'ka:lɪʃ] adj physical.

Physiker ['fy:zikər] m (-s; -) physicist.
Physikum ['fy:zikʊm] n (-s; -ka) preliminary (medical) examination.
Physiognomie [fyziogno'mi:] f (-; -n) physiognomy.
Physiologie [fyzio'lo:gi:] f (-; no pl) physiology. **physiologisch** [fyzio'lo:gɪʃ] adj physiological.
Physiothera'peut(in f) m [fyzio-] 🜨 physiotherapist.
Physiothera'pie f physiotherapy.
physisch ['fy:zɪʃ] adj physical.
Pianist [pia'nɪst] m (-en; -en), **Pia'nistin** f (-; -nen) pianist.
Pickel¹ ['pɪkəl] m (-s; -) a) ⊙ pick(axe), b) ice-pick.
Pickel² m (-s; -) pimple, spot.
pick(e)lig ['pɪk(ə)lɪç] adj pimply, spotty.
picken ['pɪkən] v/t, v/i (h) peck (**nach** at).
Picknick ['pɪknɪk] n (-s; -s) picnic.
'picknicken v/i (h) (have a) picnic.
pieken ['pi:kən] v/t, v/i (h) F prick.
'piek'fein adj F posh, very smart.
piepen ['pi:pən] v/i (h) bird: cheep, chirp, mouse: squeak, ⚡ bleep: F **bei dir piept's wohl?** are you off your rocker?
piepsen ['pi:psən] → **piepen**.
Pier [pi:r] f (-; -s) ⚓ jetty, pier.
Pietät [pie'tɛ:t] f (-; no pl) reverence: **aus ~** out of respect (**gegenüber** of).
pie'tätlos adj irreverent.
pie'tätvoll adj reverent.
Pigment [pɪg'mɛnt] n (-[e]s; -e) pigment.
Pik¹ [pi:k] m F **e-n ~ auf j-n haben** have it in for s.o.
Pik² n (-s; -s) cards: spade(s).
pikant [pi'kant] adj a. fig. piquant, spicy.
Pike ['pi:kə] f F **et. von der ~ auf lernen** learn s.th. from the bottom up.
pikiert [pi'ki:rt] adj fig. piqued (**über** acc about).
Pikkolo ['pɪkolo] m (-s; -s) **1.** apprentice waiter. **2.** F champagne miniature.
'Pikkoloflöte f ♪ piccolo.
Pilger ['pɪlgər] (-s; -) pilgrim. **'Pilgerfahrt** f pilgrimage. **'pilgern** v/i (sn) **1.** go on a pilgrimage. **2.** F wander.
Pille ['pɪlə] f (-; -n) pill: F **die ~ nehmen** be on the pill; fig. **e-e bittere ~** a bitter pill (to swallow).
'Pillenknick m F sudden drop in birthrates. **'Pillenschachtel** f pillbox.
Pilot [pi'lo:t] m (-en; -en) **1.** ✈ pilot. **2.** (racing) driver. **~film** m pilot (film).

~pro,jekt n pilot project. ~sendung f pilot broadcast.

Pilz [pɪlts] m (-es; -e) a) fungus (a. ♣), b) mushroom, c) toadstool: ~e suchen (gehen) go mushrooming; wie ~e aus dem Boden schießen mushroom (up).
'Pilzvergiftung f mushroom poisoning.

pingelig ['pɪŋəlɪç] adj, 'Pingeligkeit f (-; no pl) F nitpicking.

Pinguin ['pɪŋgui̯n] m (-s; -e) penguin.

Pinie ['piːni̯ə] f (-; -n) ♣ (stone) pine.

Pinkel ['pɪŋkəl] m (-s; -) F feiner ~ toff.

'pinkeln v/i (h) F (~ gehen go for a) pee.

Pinne ['pɪnə] f (-; -n) ⚓ helm.

'Pinnwand f pinboard.

Pinscher ['pɪnʃər] m (-s; -) zo. pinscher.

Pinsel ['pɪnzəl] m (-s; -) brush.

'pinseln v/i (h) 1. paint (a. ♣).

'Pinselstrich m stroke of the brush.

Pinzette [pɪn'tsetə] f (-; -n) tweezers.

Pionier [pi̯o'niːr] m (-s; -e) 1. ✕ engineer. 2. fig. pioneer. ~arbeit f (-; no pl) pioneering work: ~ leisten für a. pioneer s.th. ~geist m pioneering spirit.

Pipette [pi'petə] f (-; -n) 🜂 pipette.

Pipi [pi'piː] n (-s; no pl) F ~ machen wee.

Pirat [pi'raːt] m (-en; -en) pirate.

Pi'ratensender m radio: pirate station.

Pirouette [pi'rŭetə] f (-; -n) pirouette.

Pirsch [pɪrʃ] f (-; no pl) stalk, still hunt: auf die ~ gehen go (deer-)stalking.

'pirschen v/i (h) ~ auf (acc) stalk.

Pisse ['pɪsə] f (-; no pl) V piss.

'pissen v/i (h) V piss.

Pistazie [pɪs'taːtsi̯ə] f (-; -n) pistachio.

Piste ['pɪstə] f (-; -n) 1. a) (racing) track, course, b) piste, ski-run. 2. ✈ runway.

'Pistenrowdy m terror of the slopes.

Pistole [pɪs'toːlə] f (-; -n) pistol: mit vorgehaltener ~ at pistol-point; fig. j-m die ~ auf die Brust setzen hold a pistol to s.o.'s head; wie aus der ~ geschossen like a shot.

Pi'stolentasche f holster.

Pizza ['pɪtsa] f (-; -s) gastr. pizza.

Pizzeria [pɪtse'riːa] f (-; -s) pizzeria.

Plackerei [plakə'rai̯] f (-; -en) F grind.

plädieren [plɛ'diːrən] v/i (h) ⚖ plead (für, auf acc for). Plädoyer [plɛdŏa'jeː] n (-s; -s) final speech, fig. plea.

Plage ['plaːgə] f (-; -n) a) trouble, bother, b) nuisance, a. bibl. plague.

plagen ['plaːgən] (h) I v/t a) trouble, worry, b) torment, harass, F plague,

pester (mit with requests etc): geplagt von troubled by. II sich ~ toil away, take pains (mit with).

Plagiat [pla'gi̯aːt] n (-[e]s; -e) plagiarism.

plagiieren [plagi'iːrən] v/i, v/t (h) plagiarize.

Plakat [pla'kaːt] n (-[e]s; -e) a) poster, b) placard. plakatieren [plaka'tiːrən] (h) placard. plakativ [plaka'tiːf] adj fig. slogan-like, graphic.

Plakette [pla'kɛtə] f (-; -n) badge.

plan [plaːn] adj plane, level.

Plan m (-[e]s; ~e) 1. plan, a. schedule, a. project, scheme (a. b.s.): e-n ~ fassen make a plan; Pläne schmieden make plans; was steht heute auf dem ~? what's on today? 2. a) plan, a. design, b) diagram. 3. map.

Plane ['plaːnə] f (-; -n) tarpaulin.

planen ['plaːnən] v/t (h) plan, a. schedule, a. design. 'Planer m (-s; -) planner.

Planet [pla'neːt] m (-en; -en) planet.

planetarisch [plane'taːrɪʃ] adj planetary. Planetarium [plane'taːri̯ŏm] n (-s; -rien) planetarium.

planieren [pla'niːrən] v/t (h) level, grade. Pla'nierraupe f ⚙ bulldozer.

Planke ['plaŋkə] f (-; -n) plank, board.

Plankton ['plaŋktɔn] n (-s; no pl) plankton.

'planlos adj without plan, aimless, unsystematic. 'Planlosigkeit f (-; no pl) aimlessness, lack of system.

'planmäßig I adj 1. planned, systematic. 2. scheduled (arrival, flight, etc). II adv as planned, according to plan (or schedule), arrive etc on schedule.

'Planschbecken n paddle pond.

planschen ['planʃən] v/i (h) splash (about).

'Planstelle f permanent post.

Plantage [plan'taːʒə] f (-; -n) plantation.

'Planung f (-; -en) 1. → Plan 2. 2. planning: in der ~ → 'Planungsstadium n im ~ in the planning stage.

'planvoll adj methodical, systematic.

'Planwirtschaft f planned economy.

'Plappermaul n F chatterbox.

plappern ['plapərn] v/t, v/i (h) F chatter.

plärren ['plɛrən] v/i (h) a) blubber, cry, b) bawl, c) radio etc: blare.

Plasma ['plasma] n (-s; -men) plasma.

Plastik[1] ['plastɪk] f (-; -en) 1. sculpture. 2. ♣ plastic surgery.

plombieren

'**Plastik²** n (-s; no pl) plastic.

'**Plastik|bombe** f plastic bomb. ~**folie** f polythene sheet. ~**geld** n F plastic money. ~**tüte** f plastic bag.

plastisch ['plastɪʃ] adj **1.** plastic. **2.** fig. vivid, graphic. **3.** ~**e Chirurgie** plastic surgery; **Facharzt für** ~**e Chirurgie** plastic surgeon.

Platane [pla'ta:nə] f (-; -n) plane (tree).

Plateau [pla'to:] n (-s; -s) plateau.

Platin ['pla:ti:n] n (-s; no pl) platinum.

platonisch [pla'to:nɪʃ] adj a) Platonic, b) platonic.

platsch int, **platschen** ['platʃən] v/i (h, sn) F splash.

plätschern ['plɛtʃərn] v/i (h) ripple, brook etc: murmur, waves: lap.

platt [plat] adj **1.** a) flat, b) level: ~ **drük-ken** flatten; F ~**e-n Platten haben** have a flat tyre (Am. tire). **2.** fig. trite, banal. **3.** F ~ **sein** be flabbergasted.

Platt n (-[e]s; no pl) Low German.

'**plattdeutsch** adj, '**Plattdeutsch(e)** n Low German.

Platte ['platə] f (-; -n) **1.** a) (stone) slab, b) flag(stone), c) board, d) panel, e) tile, f) sheet (of glass, metal). **2.** (rock) ledge. **3.** (table) top. **4.** hotplate. **5.** dish: **kalte** ~ cold cuts. **6.** record, disc, Am. disk: F fig. **die** ~ **kenn' ich!** I know that line! **7.** (dental) plate. **8.** F bald pate.

'**Platten|album** n record album. ~**hülle** f record sleeve. ~**laufwerk** n computer: disk drive. ~**spieler** m record player. ~**teller** m turntable. ~**wechsler** m record changer.

'**Plattform** f a. pol. platform.

'**Plattfuß** m **1.** flatfoot. **2.** F mot. flat.

'**plattfüßig** [-fy:sɪç] adj flat-footed.

'**Plattheit** f (-; -en) **1.** no pl a) flatness, b) fig. triteness. **2.** platitude.

plattieren [pla'ti:rən] v/t (h) ⚙ plate.

Platz [plats] m (-es; ⸚e) **1.** no pl room, space: ~ **machen** (**für** for) a) make room, b) make way (a. fig.); ~ **sparen** save space; fig. ~ **greifen** spread, arise. **2.** place, spot, position, (camp, building, etc) site: fig. **fehl am** ~ **e sein** be out of place. **3.** (public) square. **4.** seat: ~ **nehmen** take a seat, sit down. **5.** (sports) field, (tennis) court, (golf) course: F **j-n vom** ~ **fegen** play s.o. into the ground; **j-n vom** ~ **verweisen** send s.o. off; **auf eigenem** (**gegnerischem**)

~ **spielen** play at home (out of town). **6.** sports: place: **auf** ~ **drei** in third place; → **belegen** 4.

'**Platzangst** f **1.** psych. agoraphobia. **2.** F claustrophobia.

'**Platzanweiser** m (-s; -) usher. '**Platz-anweiserin** f (-; -nen) usherette.

Plätzchen ['plɛtsçən] n (-s; -) **1.** little place, spot. **2.** F biscuit, Am. cookie.

platzen ['platsən] v/i (sn) **1.** burst, bomb etc: a. explode: fig. **vor Wut** ~ explode (with rage), blow up; **vor Neid** ~ be bursting with envy; F **ins Zimmer** ~ burst into the room; → **Kragen, Naht.** **2.** F fig. come to nothing, sl. bust, go phut, plan etc: fall through, engagement: be broken off, ⸸ cheque etc: bounce: ~ **lassen** bust up (gang etc).

'**Platz|karte** f reservation card. ~**man-gel** m lack of space. ~**pa,trone** f blank cartridge. ⸿**raubend** adj space-consuming. ~**regen** m cloudburst. ⸿**spa-rend** adj space-saving. ~**verweis** m sports: **e-n** ~ **erhalten** be sent off. ~**wunde** f laceration.

Plauderei [plaʊdə'raɪ] f (-; -en) chat.

'**Plauderer** m (-s; -) conversationalist.

plaudern ['plaʊdərn] v/i (h) a) (have a) chat, b) blab; → **Schule.**

plausibel [plaʊ'zi:bəl] adj plausible: **j-m et.** ~ **machen** make s.th. clear to s.o.

plazieren [pla'tsi:rən] v/t (h) place: **sich** ~ position o.s.; sports: **sich als Dritter** ~ be placed third.

Pla'zierung f (-; -en) sports: place.

Plebiszit [plebɪs'tsi:t] n (-[e]s; -e) plebis-cite.

pleite ['plaɪtə] adj F ~ **sein** be broke. '**Pleite** f (-; -n) F **1.** bankruptcy: ~ **ma-chen** go bust. **2.** fig. flop: **so 'ne** ~**!** what a frost!

Plenarsaal [ple'na:r-] m parl. (plenary) assembly room.

Ple'narsitzung f plenary session.

Plenum ['ple:nʊm] n (-s; no pl) plenum.

Pleuelstange ['plɔʏəl-] f ⚙ connecting rod.

Plissee [plɪ'se:] n (-s; -s) pleats.

Plis'seerock m pleated skirt.

plissieren [plɪ'si:rən] v/t (h) pleat.

Plombe ['plɔmbə] f (-; -n) **1.** ⚙ (lead) seal. **2.** ⚕ filling.

plombieren [plɔm'bi:rən] v/t (h) **1.** seal (with lead). **2.** fill (tooth).

plötzlich ['plœtslɪç] **I** *adj* sudden. **II** *adv*
suddenly: *ganz* ~ all of a sudden.

plump [plʊmp] *adj* **1.** a) plump, b) clumsy. **2.** *fig.* clumsy, tactless, gross (*lie etc*), crude (*joke etc*): *plump-vertraulich* chummy.

'**Plumpheit** *f* (-; *no pl*) **1.** plumpness. **2.** *fig.* clumsiness, grossness, *etc*.

plumps [plʊmps] *int*, **Plumps** *m* (-es; -e) F thud. '**plumpsen** *v/i* (sn) F thud.

Plunder ['plʊndər] *m* (-s; *no pl*) F junk, rubbish.

'**Plünderer** *m* (-s; -) looter.

plündern ['plʏndərn] *v/t, v/i* (h) plunder, loot, pillage, F raid (*fridge etc*).

'**Plünderung** *f* (-; -en) plundering, looting, pillage.

Plural ['pluːraːl] *m* (-s; *no pl*) *ling.* plural (number). **Pluralismus** [plura'lɪsmʊs] *m* (-; *no pl*) pluralism. **pluralistisch** [-tɪʃ] *adj* pluralistic.

plus [plʊs] *prep* plus.

Plus *n* (-; -) **1.** & plus sign. **2.** a) surplus, b) profit. **3.** *fig.* plus, asset, advantage.

Plüsch [plyːʃ] *m* (-[e]s; -e) plush.

'**Plüschtier** *n* cuddly toy.

'**Pluspunkt** *m* **1.** credit point. **2.** *fig.* plus, asset, advantage.

Plusquamperfekt ['plʊskvamperfɛkt] *n* (-s; -e) pluperfect (tense), past perfect.

'**Pluszeichen** *n* & plus sign.

pneumatisch [pnɔʏ'maːtɪʃ] *adj* pneumatic.

Po [poː] *m* (-s; -s) F bottom, bum.

Pöbel ['pøːbəl] *m* (-s; *no pl*) rabble.

'**pöbelhaft** *adj* vulgar.

pochen ['pɔxən] *v/i* (h) **1.** (*an dat* at) knock, rap. **2.** *blood etc:* throb, *heart: a.* beat. **3.** *fig.* ~ *auf* (*acc*) insist on.

pochieren [pɔ'ʃiːrən] *v/t* (h) poach.

Pocke ['pɔkə] *f* (-; -n) & **1.** pock. **2.** *pl* smallpox.

'**Pockenimpfung** *f* & (smallpox) vaccination. '**Pockennarbe** *f* pockmark.

'**pockennarbig** *adj* pockmarked, pitted.

Podest [po'dɛst] *n, m* (-[e]s; -e) platform, *fig.* pedestal.

Podium ['poːdiʊm] *n* (-s; -dien) rostrum, platform.

'**Podiumsdiskussi,on** *f*, '**Podiumsgespräch** *n* panel discussion.

Poesie [poe'ziː] *f* (-; *no pl*) poetry.

Poet [po'eːt] *m* (-en; -en) poet.

Poetin [po'eːtɪn] *f* (-; -nen) poetess.

poetisch [po'eːtɪʃ] *adj* poetic(al).

Pogrom [po'groːm] *n* (-s; -e) pogrom.

Pointe ['pŏɛ̃ːtə] *f* (-; -n) point, *a.* punch line. **pointiert** [pŏɛ̃'tiːrt] *adj* pointed.

Pokal [po'kaːl] *m* (-s; -e) cup (*a. sports*), goblet. ~**endspiel** *n* cup final. ~**sieger** *m* cup winner. ~**spiel** *n* cup tie.

Pökelfleisch ['pøːkəl-] *n* salt meat.

pökeln ['pøːkəln] *v/t* (h) salt.

pokern ['poːkərn] *v/i* (h) play poker.

'**Pokerspiel** *n* game of poker.

Pol [poːl] *m* (-s; -e) pole, & *a.* terminal: *fig. ruhender* ~ stabilizing element.

polar [po'laːr] *adj*, **Po'lar...** polar.

polarisieren [polari'ziːrən] *v/t* (*a. sich* ~) (h) polarize.

Polarität [polari'tɛːt] *f* (-; -en) polarity.

Po'larkreis *m* nördlicher (südlicher) ~ Arctic (Antarctic) Circle.

Po'larlicht *n* nördliches (südliches) ~ northern (southern) lights.

Po'larstern *m* Pole Star.

Pole ['poːlə] *m* (-n; -n) Pole.

Polemik [po'leːmɪk] *f* (-; -en) polemic(s). **polemisch** [po'leːmɪʃ] *adj* polemic. **polemisieren** [polemi'ziːrən] *v/i* (h) polemize.

polen ['poːlən] *v/t* (h) & pole.

'**Polen** *n* (-s) Poland.

Police [po'liːsə] *f* (-; -n) policy.

Polier [po'liːr] *m* (-s; -e) foreman.

polieren [po'liːrən] *v/t* (h) polish.

Poliklinik ['poːli-] *f* outpatients' clinic.

Polin [po'liːn] *f* (-; -nen) Pole, Polish woman.

Po'litbü,ro [po'liːt-] *n* politburo.

Politesse [poli'tɛsə] *f* (-; -n) (woman) traffic warden, F meter maid.

Politik [poli'tiːk] *f* (-; -en) **1.** politics: *in der* ~ in politics; *in die* ~ *gehen* go into politics; *über* ~ *reden* talk politics. **2.** policy. **Politiker** [po'liːtikər] *m* (-s; -), **Po'litikerin** *f* (-; -nen) politician.

Politikum [po'liːtikʊm] *n* (-s; -ka) political issue.

politisch [po'liːtɪʃ] *adj* **1.** political: ~*er Berater* policy adviser; *er ist* ~ *tätig* he is in politics; ~ *interessiert sein* be politically minded. **2.** police.

politisieren [politi'ziːrən] *v/i* (h) **I** *v/i* talk politics. **II** *v/t* politicize. **Politi'sierung** *f* (-; *no pl*) politicization.

Politologe [polito'loːgə] *m* (-n; -n) political scientist. **Politologie** [politolo'gi:] *f* (-; *no pl*) political science.

Politur [poli'tu:r] *f* (-; -en) polish.

Polizei [poli'tsaɪ] *f* (-; -en) police: **die ~ rufen** call the police; F **er ist bei der ~** he is in the police force. **~aufgebot** *n* police detachment. **~aufsicht** *f* police supervision. **~beamte** *m* police officer. **~behörde** *f* police (authorities). **~dienststelle** *f* police station. **~einsatz** *m* police operation. **~es̗korte** *f* police motorcade. **~funk** *m* police radio. **~hund** *m* police dog. **~knüppel** *m* truncheon, *Am.* billy. **~kommis̗sar** *m* police inspector. **~kon̗trolle** *f* police check.

poli'zeilich *adj and adv* a) (of the) police, b) by the police.

Poli'zei|präsi̗dent *m* chief of police, *Br.* chief constable. **~prä̗sidium** *n* police headquarters. **~re̗vier** *n* **1.** (police) district, *Am.* precinct. **2.** police station, *Am.* station house. **~schüler** *m* police cadet. **~schutz** *m* police protection. **~staat** *m* police state. **~streife** *f* a) police patrol, b) patrolman. **~stunde** *f* closing time. **~wache** *f* police station, *Am.* station house.

Polizist [poli'tsɪst] *m* (-en; -en) policeman, constable.

Poli'zistin *f* (-; -nen) policewoman.

Pollen ['pɔlən] *m* (-s; -) ♀ pollen.

polnisch ['pɔlnɪʃ] *adj* Polish.

Polo ['po:lo] *n* (-s; -s) *sports*: polo.

'Polohemd *n* polo (shirt).

Polster ['pɔlstər] *n* (-s; -) **1.** a) upholstery, b) cushion. **2.** pad(ding). **3.** F flab, layer of fat. **4.** *fig.* bolster, reserves.

'Polsterer *m* (-s; -) upholsterer.

'Polster|garni̗tur *f* three-piece suite. **~möbel** *pl* upholstered furniture.

polstern ['pɔlstərn] *v/t* (h) a) upholster, b) pad: F **gut gepolstert** well padded.

'Polsterpflanze *f* cushion plant.

'Polstersessel *m* easy chair, armchair.

'Polsterstuhl *m* upholstered chair.

'Polsterung *f* (-; -en) **1.** upholstery. **2.** padding.

'Polterabend *m* eve-of-the-wedding party. **poltern** ['pɔltərn] *v/i* (h) **1.** make a racket, crash about. **2.** bluster.

Polyamid [poly'a'mi:t] *n* (-[e]s; -e) polyamide.

Polyäthy'len *n* polythene.

polygam [poly'ga:m] *adj* polygamous.

polyglott [poly'glɔt] *adj* polyglott.

Polyp [po'ly:p] *m* (-en; -en) **1.** *zo.* polyp. **2.** ✻ polypus, *pl* adenoids. **3.** F cop (*sl.*).

polyphon [poly'fo:n] *adj* ♪ polyphonic.

Polytechnikum [poly'tɛçnikʊm] *n* (-s; -ka) polytechnic.

Pomade [po'ma:də] *f* (-; -n) pomade.

Pommes frites [pɔm'frit] *pl* chips, *Am.* French fries.

Pomp [pɔmp] *m* (-[e]s; *no pl*) pomp.

pompös [pɔm'pø:s] *adj* pompous.

Pontifikat [pɔntifi'ka:t] *n* (-[e]s; -e) pontificate.

Pontius ['pɔntsɪʊs] **von ~ zu Pilatus laufen** F run from pillar to post.

Ponton [põ'tõ:] *m* (-s; -s) pontoon.

Pony¹ ['pɔni] *n* (-s; -s) *zo.* pony.

'Pony² *m* (-s; -s) fringe, *Am.* bangs.

Popel ['po:pəl] *m* (-s; -) F bogey.

'popelig *adj* F piffling, miserable.

Popelin [popə'li:n] *m* (-s; -e) poplin.

popeln ['po:pəln] *v/i* (h) F pick one's nose.

Popgruppe ['pɔp-] *f* pop group.

'Popmu̗sik *f* pop music.

Popo ['po:po] *m* (-s; -s) F bottom, bum.

populär [popu'lɛ:r] *adj* popular.

popularisieren [populari'zi:rən] *v/t* (h) popularize. **Popularität** [populari'tɛ:t] *f* (-; *no pl*) popularity.

Pore ['po:rə] *f* (-; -n) pore.

Porno ['pɔrno] *m* (-s; -s), **'Pornofilm** *m* porn (or blue) movie.

Pornographie [pɔrnogra'fi:] *f* (-; *no pl*) pornography. **pornographisch** [pɔrno'gra:fɪʃ] *adj* pornographic.

'Pornoheft *n* porn (or girlie) magazine.

Porree ['pɔre] *m* (-s; -s) ♀ leek.

Portal [pɔr'ta:l] *n* (-s; -e) portal.

Portemonnaie [pɔrtmɔ'nɛ:] *n* (-s; -s) purse.

Portier [pɔr'tie:] *m* (-s; -s) **1.** porter. **2.** → *Pförtner*.

Portion [pɔr'tsɪo:n] *f* (-; -en) a) portion, b) helping, c) pot *of tea etc*: F *fig.* **halbe ~** shrimp; **e-e gehörige ~ Frechheit** a good deal of impudence.

Porto ['pɔrto] *n* (-s; -s, Porti) postage.

'portofrei *adj* postage paid.

'Portokasse *f* ✝ petty cash.

Porträt [pɔr'trɛ:] *n* (-s; -s) portrait.

porträtieren [pɔrtrɛ'ti:rən] *v/t* (h) **j-n ~** paint s.o.'s portrait, *fig.* portray s.o.

Por'trätmaler(in f) m portraitist.

Portugal ['portugal] n (-s) Portugal.

Portugiese [portu'giːzə] m (-n; -n), **Por-tu'giesin** f (-; -nen), **portu'giesisch** adj Portuguese.

Portwein ['port-] m port.

Porzellan [portsɛ'laːn] n (-s; -e) porcelain, china: F fig. ~ **zerschlagen** do a lot of damage. ~**laden** m china shop: → **Elefant.** ~**waren** pl chinaware.

Posaune [po'zaʊnə] f (-; -n) **1.** (~ **blasen** play the) trombone. **2.** fig. trumpet.

Posaunist [pozaʊ'nɪst] m (-en; -en) trombonist.

Pose ['poːzə] f (-; -n) pose, fig. a. air, act.

posieren [po'ziːrən] v/i (h) pose (**als** as).

Position [pozi'tsjoːn] f (-; -en) **1.** position, sports: a. place: fig. ~ **beziehen** take one's stand. **2.** ✝ item.

positiv ['poːzitiːf] **I** adj positive, a. affirmative. **II** adv F for certain.

Positur [pozi'tuːr] f (-; -en) posture: **sich in ~ setzen** strike an attitude.

Posse ['posə] f (-; -n) farce, burlesque.

possessiv ['posɛsiːf] adj ling. possessive. **Posses'sivpro,nomen** n possessive pronoun.

possierlich [po'siːrlɪç] adj droll, funny.

Post [post] f (-; no pl) a) post, mail, b) postal service, c) post office: **mit der ~** by post, by mail; **mit gleicher** (or **getrennter**) **~** under separate cover; **mit der ~ schicken** post, Am. mail; **ist ~ für mich da?** are there any letters for me?

postalisch [pos'taːlɪʃ] adj postal.

'**Post|amt** n post office. ~**anschrift** f postal (or mailing) address. ~**anweisung** f postal (or money) order. ~**auto** n post-office van, mail van. ~**barscheck** m postal cheque (Am. check). ~**beamte** m post-office (Am. postal) clerk. ~**bote** m postman, Am. mailman. ~**botin** f postwoman. ~**bus** m post bus.

Posten ['postən] m (-s; -) **1.** ✗ post: fig. **auf dem ~ sein** a) be on one's toes, be in good shape; **nicht (ganz) auf dem ~ sein** be a bit under the weather; → **beziehen** 3, **verloren** II. **2.** ✗ guard, sentry: ~ **stehen** be on guard, stand sentry. **3.** post, position, job. **4.** ✝ a) lot, b) item, c) entry.

'**Post|fach** n post-office box, PO box. ~**flugzeug** n mail plane. ~**gebühr** f postage, pl a. postal charges. ~**geheim-**

nis n secrecy of the mails. ~**giroamt** n postal giro office. ~**girokonto** n (post-office) giro account, Br. national giro account.

posthum [pos'tuːm] adj posthumous.

postieren [pos'tiːrən] v/t (h) place.

'**Post|karte** f postcard, Am. postal card. ②**lagernd** adj and adv poste restante, Am. (in care of) general delivery. ~**leitzahl** f postcode, Am. zip code. ~**mi,nister** m postmaster general. ~**scheck** m (post-office) giro cheque (Am. check). ~**sparbuch** n post-office savings book. ~**sparkasse** f post-office savings bank. ~**stempel** m postmark. ~**versandhaus** n mail-order house. ~**wagen** m 🚃 mail van, Am. postal car. ②**wendend** adv by return (of post), by return mail, F fig. right away. ~**wertzeichen** n (postage) stamp. ~**wurfsendung** f direct mail. ~**zug** m mail train. ~**zustellung** f postal delivery.

potent [po'tɛnt] adj potent.

Potential [poten'tsjaːl] n (-s; -e), **potentiell** [poten'tsiɛl] adj potential.

Potenz [po'tɛnts] f (-; -en) **1.** no pl potency. **2.** A power: **zweite ~** square; **dritte ~** cube. **3.** fig. power, strength.

potenzieren [poten'tsiːrən] v/t (h) **1.** A raise to a higher power. **2.** fig. magnify.

Potpourri ['potpuri] n (-s; -s) ♪ potpourri, medley.

Pracht [praxt] f (-; no pl) splendo(u)r: F **es war e-e wahre ~** it was just great.

'**Prachtexem,plar** n F splendid specimen, a. beauty.

prächtig ['prɛçtɪç] adj **1.** a) splendid, magnificent, b) glorious (weather). **2.** F fig. great, super.

'**Prachtkerl** m F great guy.

'**Prachtstraße** f boulevard.

'**prachtvoll** → **prächtig.**

prädestinieren [predɛsti'niːrən] v/t (h) predestine.

Prädikat [predi'kaːt] n (-[e]s; -e) **1.** ling. predicate. **2.** title. **3.** rating, attribute, ped. mark, grade.

Prädi'kats|nomen n ling. predicate complement. ~**wein** m quality-tested wine (with special attributes).

Präfix [prɛ'fiːks] n (-es; -e) ling. prefix.

prägen ['prɛːgən] v/t (h) **1.** a) stamp, b)

mint (*coin*), c) emboss (*leather, metal, etc*). **2.** *fig.* a) coin (*word etc*), b) form, shape, determine, characterize.
Pragmatiker [pra'gma:tikər] *m* (-s; -) pragmatist. **prag'matisch** [-tɪʃ] *adj* pragmatic(al). **Pragmatismus** [pragma'tɪsmʊs] *m* (-; *no pl*) pragmatism.
prägnant [prɛ'gnant] *adj* terse, pithy.
'Prägung [-] *f* (-; -en) **1.** stamping, coining. **2.** *fig.* a) stamp, character, b) forming.
prähi'storisch [-] *adj* prehistoric.
prahlen ['pra:lən] *v/i* (h) talk big: **mit et. ~** brag about s.th., show off (with) s.th.
'Prahler *m* (-s; -) braggart, F show-off.
Prahlerei [pra:lə'raɪ] *f* (-; -en) a) showing-off, boasting, b) boast(s).
Praktik ['praktɪk] *f* (-; -en) practice, method, *pl b.s.* (sharp) practices.
Praktikant [prakti'kant] *m* (-en; -en), **Prakti'kantin** *f* (-; -nen) trainee.
'Praktiker *m* (-s; -) practical man.
Praktikum ['praktikʊm] *n* (-s; -ka) (period of) practical training.
praktisch ['praktɪʃ] **I** *adj* practical, *a.* handy: **~er Arzt** general practitioner; **~e Ausbildung** on-the-job training; **~es Beispiel** concrete example; **~er Versuch** field test. **II** *adv* a) practically, as good as (*done etc*), b) in practice.
praktizieren [prakti'tsi:rən] *v/t, v/i* (h) practise.
Prälat [prɛ'la:t] *m* (-en; -en) *eccl.* prelate.
Praline [pra'li:nə] *f* (-; -n), **Praliné** [prali'ne:] *n* (-s; -s) chocolate.
prall [pral] *adj* **1.** bulging (*bag etc*), hard (*ball etc*), full (*sails*), firm, taut (*muscles*). **2.** blazing (*sun*).
prallen ['pralən] *v/i* (sn) **1.** bounce (**auf** *acc* against), crash (**an** *acc*, **gegen** into). **2.** *sun:* blaze down (**auf** *acc* on).
'prallvoll *adj* F (full to) bursting.
Präludium [prɛ'lu:diʊm] *n* (-s; -dien) prelude.
Prämie ['prɛ:miə] *f* (-; -n) **1.** a) award, prize, b) reward, c) bonus. **2.** premium.
'prämienbegünstigt *adj* bonus-linked: **~es Sparen →** **'Prämiensparen** *n* saving under the (Federal) bonus system.
prämieren [prɛ'mi:rən], **prämiieren** [prɛmi'i:rən] *v/t* (h) **1.** award a prize to. **2.** give a bonus for.
Pranger ['praŋər] *m* (-s; -) *hist.* stocks: *a. fig.* **an den ~ stellen** pillory.
Pranke ['praŋkə] *f* (-; -n) *zo.* paw.

Präparat [prɛpa'ra:t] *n* (-[e]s; -e) **1.** preparation. **2.** *biol.*, ⚗ specimen.
präparieren [prɛpa'ri:rən] *v/t* (h) **1.** prepare (*j-m et.* s.o. with s.th.). **2.** dissect. **3.** preserve.
Präposition [prɛpozi'tsio:n] *f* (-; -en) *ling.* preposition.
Prärie [prɛ'ri:] *f* (-; -n) prairie.
Präsens ['prɛ:zɛns] *n* (-; Präsentia [prɛ'zɛntsia] *ling.* present (tense).
präsentieren [prɛzɛn'ti:rən] (h) **I** *v/t* present (*j-m et.* s.o. with s.th.) **II** *v/i* ✕ present arms. **III** *sich ~* present o.s.
Präsenz [prɛ'zɛnts] *f* (-; *no pl*) presence. **~biblio,thek** *f* reference library.
Präserva'tiv [prɛzɛrva'ti:f] *n* (-s; -e) condom, sheath, *Am. a.* prophylactic.
Präsident [prɛzi'dɛnt] *m* (-en; -en) president, chairman, *parl.* Speaker, 🏛 presiding judge. **Präsi'dentenwahl** *f* presidential election. **Präsi'dentschaft** *f* (-; -en) presidency. **Präsi'dentschaftskandi,dat** *m* presidential candidate.
präsidieren [-'di:rən] *v/i* (h) preside (over). **Präsidium** [prɛ'zi:diʊm] *n* (-s; -dien) **1.** presidency. **2.** (presiding) committee. **3.** → **Polizeipräsidium.**
prasseln ['prasəln] *v/i* (h) *rain, hail:* patter, *fire:* crackle.
prassen ['prasən] *v/i* (h) feast.
Präteritum [prɛ'te:ritʊm] *n* (-s; -ta) *ling.* preterite, past tense.
präventiv [prɛvɛn'ti:f] *adj,* **Präven'tiv...** preventive, ⚕ prophylactic.
Praxis ['praksis] *f* (-; Praxen) **1.** *no pl* practice, experience: **in der ~** in practice; **et. in die ~ umsetzen** put s.th. into practice. **2.** 🏛, ⚕ practice.
Präzedenzfall [prɛtse'dɛnts-] *m* (**e-n ~ schaffen** set a) precedent.
präzis [prɛ'tsi:s] *adj* precise, exact.
präzisieren [prɛtsi'zi:rən] *v/t* (h) specify. **Präzision** [prɛtsi'zio:n] *f* (-; *no pl*) precision.
predigen ['pre:dɪgən] *v/t, v/i* (h) preach.
Prediger ['pre:dɪgər] *m* (-s; -) preacher.
Predigt ['pre:dɪçt] *f* (-; -en) sermon: **e-e ~ halten** preach (a sermon); F *fig.* **j-m e-e ~ halten** lecture s.o.
Preis [praɪs] *m* (-es; -e) **1.** a) price, b) fare: **zum ~e von** at a price of; **im ~ steigen** (**fallen**) go up (drop); *fig.* **um jeden ~** at all costs; **um k-n ~** not at any price. **2.** prize, award: **e-n ~ erringen**

win a prize. **3.** prize, reward. **4.** praise.
~absprache f price agreement. **~änderung** f change in price: **~en vorbehalten** subject to change. **~angabe** f quotation (of prices): **ohne ~** not priced, not marked. **~anstieg** m rise in prices. **~aufschlag** m extra charge. **~ausschreiben** n competition. **2bewußt** adj price-conscious. **~bindung** f price maintenance.

Preiselbeere ['praɪzəl-] f ♀ cranberry.

preisen ['praɪzən] v/t (pries, gepriesen, h) praise; → **glücklich** I.

'**Preis|entwicklung** f price trend. **~erhöhung** f price increase. **~ermäßigung** f price reduction. **~frage** f prize question. **2gekrönt** adj prize-winning. **~gericht** n jury. **~gestaltung** f price formation. **~grenze** f price limit. **2günstig** → **preiswert**. **~klasse** f price range. **~lage** f price range: **in mittlerer (jeder) ~** medium-priced (in all prices).

'**preislich** adj and adv in price.

'**Preis|liste** f price list. **~nachlaß** m discount. **~poli,tik** f price policy. **~rätsel** n competition. **~richter(in** f) m judge. **~schild** n price tag. **~schwankung** f price fluctuation. **~senkung** f price reduction. **~steigerung** f rise in prices. **~stopp** m price freeze. **~sturz** m sudden drop in price(s). **~träger(in** f) m prize winner.

Preistreibe'rei f forcing up of prices.
'**Preis|vergleich** m price comparison. **~verleihung** f presentation (of prizes).

'**preiswert** adj cheap, low-priced: **~ sein** a. be good value, be a bargain.

prekär [prɛ'kɛːr] adj precarious.

'**Prellbock** m ❤ buffer stop, fig. buffer.

prellen ['prɛlən] v/t (h) **1.** ❤ bruise. **2.** fig. cheat (**um** of).

'**Prellung** f (-; -en) ❤ contusion, bruise.

Premiere [prə'mĭɛːrə] f (-; -n) thea. etc first night.

Premiermi,nister [prə'mĭɛ:-] m prime minister.

Presse[^1] ['prɛsə] f (-; -n) ❂ press.

'**Presse**[^2] f (-; no pl) the press: **er hatte e-e gute ~** he got (or had) a good press. **~agen,tur** f press agency. **~amt** n press office. **~ausweis** m press card. **~bericht** m press report. **~bü,ro** n press agency. **~chef** m chief press officer. **~dienst** m news service. **~empfang** m

press reception. **~erklärung** f press release. **~feldzug** m press campaign. **~foto,graf** m press photographer. **~freiheit** f freedom of the press. **~konfe,renz** f press conference. **~meldung** f a) press report, b) news item.

pressen ['prɛsən] v/t (h) a) press (a. v/i), b) squeeze.

'**Presse|refe,rent** m press officer. **~schau** f press review. **~sprecher** m press spokesman. **~stelle** f public relations department. **~stimmen** pl press commentaries. **~tri,büne** f press box (parl. gallery). **~vertreter** m reporter. **~zen,sur** f censorship of the press. **~zentrum** n press cent/re (Am. -er).

'**Preßluft** f compressed air. **~bohrer** m pneumatic drill. **~hammer** m pneumatic hammer.

'**Preßwehen** pl ❀ bearing-down pains.

Prestige [prɛs'tiːʒə] n (-s; no pl) prestige.

Pre'stigeverlust m loss of prestige.

Preuße ['prɔʏsə] m (-n; -n), '**Preußin** f (-; -nen), '**preußisch** adj Prussian.

prickeln ['prɪkəln] v/i (h) **1.** tingle, prickle. **2.** champagne: sparkle. '**prickelnd** adj **1.** tingling, prickly. **2.** fig. thrilling: **~er Reiz** thrill.

pries [priːs] pret of **preisen**.

Priester ['priːstər] m (-s; -) priest.

'**Priesteramt** n priesthood.

'**Priesterin** f (-; -nen) priestess.

'**Priesterschaft** f (-; no pl), '**Priestertum** n (-s; no pl) priesthood.

'**Priesterweihe** f ordination.

prima ['priːma] adj **1.** ❋ prime, first-rate. **2.** F (a. int) great, super.

primär [pri'mɛːr] adj primary.

Primaten [pri'maːtən] pl zoo. primates.

Primel ['priːməl] f (-; -n) ♀ primrose.

primitiv [primi'tiːf] adj primitive.

Primitivität [primitivi'tɛːt] f (-; no pl) primitiveness.

Primzahl ['priːm-] f ❦ prime number.

Prinz [prɪnts] m (-en; -en) prince.

Prinzessin [prɪn'tsɛsɪn] f (-; -nen) princess.

'**Prinzgemahl** m prince consort.

Prinzip [prɪn'tsiːp] n (-s; -ien) (**aus ~** on, **im ~** in) principle. **prinzipiell** [prɪntsi'pĭɛl] adj and adv on principle.

Prior ['priːɔr] m (-s; -en [pri'oːrən]) eccl. prior. **Pri'orin** f (-; -nen) prioress.

Priorität [priori'tɛːt] f (-; -en) priority

(*über, vor* dat over): **~en setzen** establish priorities.

Prise ['pri:zə] f (-; -n) **1.** *e-e ~ Salz* a pinch of salt. **2.** ⚓ prize.

Prisma ['prɪsma] n (-s; -men) prism.

prismatisch [prɪs'ma:tɪʃ] adj prismatic. **'Prismensucher** m phot. prismatic viewfinder.

Pritsche ['prɪtʃə] f (-; -n) **1.** plank bed. **2.** mot. platform. **3.** slapstick.

privat [pri'va:t] **I** adj private, a. personal. **II** adv privately, in private.

Pri'vat|a,dresse f home address. **~besitz** m private (or personal) property: *in ~* privately owned. **~do,zent** m (unsalaried) lecturer, Am. associate professor. **~gespräch** n teleph. private call. **~initia,tive** f private venture.

privatisieren [privati'zi:rən] (h) **I** v/t ~ privatize. **II** v/i live on one's private income.

Pri'vat|klinik f private clinic. **~leben** n private (or personal) life. **~pati,ent(in** f) m private patient. **~recht** n [-(e)s; no pl] private (or civil) law. **~sache** f private matter (or affair): *das ist m-e ~!* that's my (own) business! **~schule** f private school. **~sekre,tär(in** f) m private secretary. **~stunden** pl, **~unterricht** m private lessons. **~wirtschaft** f (-; no pl) private enterprise.

Privileg [privi'le:k] n (-[e]s; -ien [-'gi̯ən]) privilege. **privilegieren** [privile'gi:rən] v/t (h) privilege.

pro [pro:] prep per: *~ Jahr* per annum, a year; *~ Kopf* per head, each; *~ Stück* a piece; *~ Stunde* per hour.

Pro das ... und Kontra the pros and cons.

Probe ['pro:bə] f (-; -n) **1.** ✝, ⚒ etc sample, a. ⚙ specimen, iro. a. taste: *e-e ~ ablegen* (gen) give a sample (iro. taste) of *one's courage etc.* **2.** a) test, try-out, b) check: *auf ~ →* **probeweise**; *j-n auf die ~ stellen* put s.o. to the test, test s.o.; *et. auf e-e harte ~ stellen* put s.th. to a severe test. **3.** thea. rehearsal. **~abzug** m print. proof. **~a,larm** m practice alarm. **~aufnahme** f **1.** film: screen test: *~n machen von* screen-test s.o. **2.** ♫ test recording. **~auftrag** m trial order. **~bohrung** f trial drill. **~exem,plar** n specimen copy. **♀fahren** v/t (only inf and pp probegefahren, h) test-drive. **~fahrt** f test (or trial) run.

~flug m test (or trial) flight. **~jahr** n year of probation. **~lauf** m ⚙ test run.

proben ['pro:bən] v/t, v/i (h) rehearse.

'Probenummer f specimen copy.

'probeweise adv on a trial basis.

'Probezeit f trial period: *nach e-r ~ von 3 Monaten* at the end of three months' probation.

probieren [pro'bi:rən] v/t (h) **1.** try, a. taste, a. test: *es ~ mit* try; *F es bei j-m ~* try it on with s.o. **2.** → **anprobieren.**

Problem [pro'ble:m] n (-s; -e) (*vor e-m ~ stehen* be faced with a) problem.

Problematik [proble'ma:tɪk] f (-; no pl) problematic nature, problems.

proble'matisch adj problematic(al).

Pro'blemkind n problem child.

Pro'blemkreis m complex of problems.

pro'blemlos adj unproblematic(ally adv), adv a. without (any) difficulties.

Pro'blemstellung f **1.** formulation of a problem. **2.** problem.

Pro'blemstück n thea. thesis play.

Produkt [pro'dʊkt] n (-[e]s; -e) a) a. ⚮ product, b) produce. **Pro'duktenwerbung** f ✝ product advertising.

Produktion [prodʊk'tsi̯o:n] f (-; -en) (*in ~ gehen* go into) production.

Produkti'ons|anlage f production plant(s). **~ausfall** m loss of production. **~güter** pl producer goods. **~kapazi,tät** f production capacity. **~kosten** pl production costs. **~leiter** m production manager. **~mittel** pl means of production. **~rückgang** m fall in production. **~steigerung** f increase in production. **~ziel** n production target. **~zweig** m line of production.

produktiv [prodʊk'ti:f] adj productive.

Produktivität [prodʊktivi'tɛ:t] f (-; no pl) productivity.

Produzent [produ'tsɛnt] m (-en; -en) producer, a. grower.

produzieren [produ'tsi:rən] (h) **I** v/t produce, a. grow. **II** sich ~ F show off.

profan [pro'fa:n] adj **1.** profane, secular. **2.** mundane, trivial.

professionell [profesi̯o'nɛl] adj professional.

Professor [pro'fɛsɔr] m (-s; -en [-'so:rən]) professor. **Professorin** [profɛ'so:rɪn] f (-; -nen) (woman) professor.

Professur [profe'su:r] f (-; -en) professorship, chair.

Profi 458

Profi ['pro:fi] *m* (-s; -s) F pro.
'Profi... professional (*football etc*).
Profil [pro'fi:l] *n* (-s; -e) profile (*a. fig.*),
⚙ *a.* section, *mot.* (tyre) tread: **im ~** in
profile; *fig.* ~ **haben** have personality;
an ~ gewinnen improve one's image.
profilieren [profi'li:rən] (h) **I** *v/t* **1.** ⚙
profile, contour. **2.** *fig.* present in clear
outline. **II sich ~** distinguish o.s.
profi'liert *adj fig.* distinguished.
Pro'fil|neu,rose *f* obsession with one's
image. **~sohle** *f* profiled sole. **~stahl** *m*
⚙ section steel.
Profit [pro'fi:t] *m* (-[e]s; -e) profit: ~
schlagen aus profit from (or by).
profitabel [profi'ta:bəl] *adj* profitable.
profitieren [profi'ti:rən] *v/i, v/t* (h) profit
(**von** by, from).
Pro'fitjäger *m contp.* profiteer.
pro forma [pro: 'fɔrma] *adv* as a matter
of form.
profund [pro'funt] *adj* profound.
Prognose [pro'gno:zə] *f* (-; -n) forecast,
esp. 🟥 prognosis.
Programm [pro'gram] *n* (-s; -e) **1.** pro-
gram(me Br.), *pol. a.* platform, *thea. a.*
bill, *TV a.* channel: **was steht heute
auf dem ~?** what's the program(me)
for today?; F **das paßt mir gar nicht
ins ~!** that doesn't suit me at all! **2.**
computer: program. **3.** ⚙ cycle. **~ände-
rung** *f* change of program(me Br.).
programmatisch [progra'ma:tɪʃ] *adj*
programmatic.
pro'grammgemäß *adv* according to
plan.
Pro'gramm|gestaltung *f* program(me
Br.) planning, program(m)ing. **~ge-
steuert** *adj computer:* program-
controlled. **~heft** *n* program(me Br.). **~hin-
weis** *m* program(me Br.) note.
program'mierbar *adj* program(m)able.
programmieren [progra'mi:rən] *v/t* (h)
program(me Br.): *fig.* **programmiert
sein auf** (*acc*) be conditioned to (*do*)
s.th. **Program'mierer** *m* (-s; -) pro-
gram(m)er. **Program'miersprache** *f*
program(m)ing language. **Program-
'mierung** *f* (-; -en) program(m)ing.
Pro'gramm|punkt *m* item, *pol.* plank.
~steuerung *f computer:* program control. **~taste** *f* program key. **~vorschau**
f program(me Br.) roundup, *film:*
trailer(s). **~wahl** *f* **1.** *TV* channel selec-

tion. **2.** ⚙ cycle selection. **~zeitschrift** *f*
program(me Br.) guide.
Progression [progrɛ'sĭo:n] *f* (-; -en)
progression. **progressiv** [-'si:f] *adj*
progressive. **Progressive** [-'si:və] *m, f*
(-n; -n) progressive.
Projekt [pro'jɛkt] *n* (-[e]s; -e) project.
Pro'jektgruppe *f* task force.
Projektion [projɛk'tsĭo:n] *f* (-; -en)
projection. **Projekti'onsappa,rat** *m*,
Projektor [pro'jɛktɔr] *m* (-s; -en
[-'to:rən]) projector. **projizieren**
[proji'tsi:rən] *v/t* (h) project.
Proklamation [proklama'tsĭo:n] *f* (-;
-en) proclamation. **proklamieren**
[prokla'mi:rən] *v/t* (h) proclaim.
Pro-'Kopf-Einkommen *n* per capita
income.
Prokura [pro'ku:ra] *f* (-; -ren) ✝ (power
of) procuration. **Prokurist** [proku'rɪst]
m (-en; -en), **Proku'ristin** *f* (-; -nen)
authorized representative.
Prolet [pro'le:t] *m* (-en; -en) *contp.* prole.
Proletariat [proleta'rĭa:t] *n* (-[e]s; -e)
proletariat(e). **Proletarier** [prole'ta:-
rĭər] *m* (-s; -), **prole'tarisch** [-rɪʃ] *adj*
proletarian.
Prolog [pro'lo:k] *m* (-[e]s; -e) prolog(ue).
prolongieren [prolɔŋ'gi:rən] *v/t* (h) ✝
renew.
Promenade [prome'na:də] *f* (-; -n)
promenade.
Promille [pro'mɪlə] *n* (-[s]; -) per mil, F
mot. blood alcohol. **Pro'millegrenze** *f*
mot. (blood) alcohol limit.
prominent [promi'nɛnt] *adj* prominent.
Promi'nente *m, f* (-n; -n) public figure,
celebrity. **Prominenz** [promi'nɛnts] *f*
(-; -en) public figures, celebrities.
Promotion [promo'tsĭo:n] *f* (-; -en) *univ.*
doctorate. **promovieren** [promo'vi:-
rən] (h) **I** *v/t* confer a doctorate on. **II**
v/i take one's (*doctor's*) degree.
prompt [prɔmpt] *adj* prompt, quick.
Pronomen [pro'no:mən] *n* (-s; -, -mina)
ling. pronoun.
Propaganda [propa'ganda] *f* (-; *no pl*) **1.**
pol. propaganda. **2.** ✝ publicity.
Propagandist [propagan'dɪst] *m* (-en;
-en), **Propagan'distin** *f* (-; -nen),
propagan'distisch *adj* propagandist.
propagieren [propa'gi:rən] *v/t* (h)
propagate.
Propan [pro'pa:n] *n* (-s; *no pl*) propane.

Propeller [pro'pɛlər] *m* (-s; -) propeller.
Prophet [pro'fe:t] *m* (-en; -en) prophet.
pro'phetisch [-tɪʃ] *adj* prophetic.
prophezeien [profe'tsaɪən] *v/t* (h) prophesy, predict. **Prophe'zeiung** *f* (-; -en) prophecy, prediction.
prophylaktisch [profy'laktɪʃ] *adj* 🌶 prophylactic. **Prophylaxe** [profy'laksə] *f* (-; -n) prophylaxis.
Proportion [propɔr'tsĭo:n] *f* (-; -en) proportion. **proportional** [propɔrtsĭo-'na:l] *adj* proportional (**zu** to).
Proporz [pro'pɔrts] *m* (-es; -e) proportional representation.
'**Prorektor** *m univ.* vice-chancellor.
Prosa ['pro:za] *f* (-; *no pl*) prose.
'**Prosadichtung** *f* prose writing.
Prosaiker [pro'za:ikər] *m* (-s; -) **1.** prose writer, prosaist. **2.** *fig.* prosaic person.
prosaisch [pro'za:ɪʃ] *adj fig.* prosaic, matter-of-fact, dull.
prosit ['pro:zɪt] *int* your health!, cheers!
Prospekt [pro'spɛkt] *m* (-[e]s; -e) **1.** a) brochure, b) leaflet. **2.** *thea.* backdrop.
prost [pro:st] → *prosit.*
Prostata ['prɔstata] *f* (-; *no pl*) prostate (gland).
prostituieren [prostitu'i:rən] **sich ~** (h) prostitute o.s. **Prostitu'ierte** *f* (-n; -n) prostitute. **Prostitution** [prostitu-'tsĭo:n] *f* (-; *no pl*) prostitution.
protegieren [prote'ʒi:rən] *v/t* (h) patronize, sponsor: *von j-m protegiert werden* be s.o.'s protégé.
Protein [prote'i:n] *n* (-s; -e) protein.
Protektion [protɛk'tsĭo:n] *f* (-; -en) patronage. **Protektionismus** [protɛk-tsĭo'nɪsmʊs] *m* (-; *no pl*) 🌶 protectionism. **protektio'nistisch** [-tɪʃ] *adj* 🌶 protectionist.
Protektorat [protɛkto'ra:t] *n* (-[e]s; -e) **1.** *pol.* protectorate. **2.** *fig.* patronage.
Protest [pro'tɛst] *m* (-[e]s; -e) protest (*a.* 🌶): *aus ~* in protest; *~ einlegen* enter a protest (*gegen* against).
Protestant [protɛs'tant] *m* (-en; -en), **Prote'stantin** *f* (-; -nen), **prote'stantisch** *adj* Protestant.
Protestantismus [protɛstan'tɪsmʊs] *m* (-; *no pl*) Protestantism.
protestieren [protɛs'ti:rən] *v/i* (h) protest (*gegen et.* against s.th., *Am.* s.th.).
Pro'testkundgebung *f* protest rally.
Pro'testmarsch *m* protest march.

Prothese [pro'te:zə] *f* (-; -n) **1.** artificial limb. **2.** denture(s).
Protokoll [proto'kɔl] *n* (-s; -e) **1.** record, minutes: *~ führen* take the minutes; *zu ~ geben* 🌶🌶 depose, state (in evidence); *zu ~ nehmen* take down. **2.** protocol.
protokollarisch [protoko'la:rɪʃ] *adj* **1.** on record, minuted: *~ festhalten* → *protokollieren.* **2.** (of) protocol.
Proto'koll|chef *m* chief of protocol. **~führer(in** *f*) *m* keeper of the minutes, recording clerk, 🌶🌶 clerk of the court.
protokollieren [protoko'li:rən] *v/t* (h) record, enter in the minutes, take *s.th.* down.
Proton ['pro:tɔn] *n* (-s; -en [-'to:nən]) *phys.* proton.
Proto'plasma [proto-] *n* protoplasm.
Prototyp ['pro:to-] *m* prototype.
protzen ['prɔtsən] *v/i* (h) F show off (*mit* [with] *s.o., s.th.*). '**protzig** *adj* F showy.
Proviant [pro'vĭant] *m* (-s; -e) provisions.
Provinz [pro'vɪnts] *f* (-; -en) **1.** province. **2.** *the* provinces, *fig. contp.* backwater: *finsterste ~ sein* be utterly provincial.
provinziell [provɪn'tsĭɛl] *adj* provincial.
Pro'vinzler *m* (-s; -) *contp.* provincial.
Provision [provi'zĭo:n] *f* (-; -en) 🌶 (*auf ~* on) commission.
provisorisch [provi'zo:rɪʃ] *adj* provisional, temporary. **Provisorium** [provi'zo:rĭʊm] *n* (-s; -rĭen) **1.** provisional agreement. **2.** makeshift.
Provokation [provoka'tsĭo:n] *f* (-; -en) provocation. **provozieren** [provo'tsi:-rən] *v/t* (h) provoke: *~d* provocative.
Prozedur [protse'du:r] *f* (-; -en) procedure, *iro.* ritual.
Prozent [pro'tsɛnt] *n* (-[e]s; -e) **1.** per cent, percent: *zu 5 ~* at five per cent (*or* percent); *zu wieviel ~?* at what percentage? **2.** *pl* F a) percentage, b) discount. *...pro,zentig in cpds.* per cent, percent. **Pro'zentsatz** *m* percentage.
prozentual [protsɛn'tŭa:l] *adj* proportional: *~er Anteil* percentage; *~ am Gewinn beteiligt sein* receive a percentage of the profit.
Prozeß [pro'tsɛs] *m* (-sses; -sse) **1.** process. **2.** 🌶🌶 a) lawsuit, b) trial: *e-n ~ anstrengen gegen* bring an action against; *gegen j-n e-n ~ führen* be engaged in a lawsuit with s.o.; *e-n ~ ver-*

lieren lose a case; *j-m den ~ machen* put s.o. on trial; *fig. kurzen ~ machen* make short work (*mit* of).

prozessieren [protsɛ'si:rən] *v/i* (h) go to court, litigate: *gegen j-n ~* bring an action against s.o.

Prozession [protsɛ'sĭo:n] *f* (-; -en) procession.

Pro'zeßkosten *pl* (legal) costs.

Pro'zeßkostenhilfe *f* (-; *no pl*) legal aid.

Prozessor [pro'tsɛsɔr] *m* (-s; -en [-'so:rən]) *computer:* processor.

Pro'zeßordnung *f* code of procedure.

Pro'zeßsteuerung *f* ⊗ process control.

prüde ['pry:də] *adj* prudish: (*nicht*) ~ *sein* be a (no) prude.

Prüderie [prydə'ri:] *f* (-; -n) prudery.

prüfen ['pry:fən] *v/t* (h) **1.** a) examine, *a.* ⊗ inspect, test, check, ✝ audit, ⚏ review, b) investigate, look into *a matter etc*, c) consider (*proposal etc*): *~der Blick* searching glance. **2.** *ped., univ.* examine, test: → *geprüft.* **3.** afflict.

'Prüfer *m* (-s; -) *ped., univ.* examiner, ⊗ tester, ✝ auditor.

'Prüfling *m* (-s; -e) examinee, candidate.

'Prüf|stand *m* ⊗ test bed: *fig. auf dem ~ being tested.* *~stein m fig.* touchstone.

'Prüfung *f* (-; -en) **1.** *ped.* examination, test, F exam: → *ablegen* 6. **2.** a) examination, inspection, check(ing), ⊗ test, trial, ✝ audit, ⚏ review, b) investigation, c) consideration. **3.** trial, affliction. **4.** *sports:* event.

'Prüfungs|angst *f* F exam nerves. *~arbeit f, ~aufgabe f* examination (*or* test) paper. *~ausschuß m, ~kommissi,on f* board of examiners. *~ordnung f* examination regulations.

'Prüfverfahren *n* method of testing.

Prügel ['pry:gəl] *m* (-s; -) **1.** cudgel. **2.** *pl* F *~ beziehen* get a (sound) thrashing, *a. sports:* get clobbered.

Prüge'lei *f* (-; -en) fight, brawl.

'Prügelknabe *m* scapegoat.

prügeln ['pry:gəln] *v/t* (h) thrash, clobber: *sich ~* (have a) fight.

'Prügelstrafe *f* corporal punishment.

Prunk [prʊŋk] *m* (-[e]s; *no pl*) splendo(u)r, *contp.* pomp. **'Prunkgemach** *n* stateroom. **'Prunkstück** *n* F showpiece.

'prunkvoll *adj* splendid, magnificent.

prusten ['pru:stən] *v/i* (h) snort.

Psalm [psalm] *m* (-s; -e) psalm.

Pseudonym [psɔʏdo'ny:m] *n* (-s; -e) pseudonym, *a.* pen name.

pst [pst] *int* a) shh!, b) psst!

Psyche ['psy:çə] *f* (-; -n) psyche.

Psychiater [psy'çĭa:tər] *m* (-s; -) psychiatrist, F shrink. **Psychiatrie** [psyçĭa'tri:] *f* (-; *no pl*) **1.** psychiatry. **2.** psychiatric ward. **psychi'atrisch** [-trɪʃ] *adj* psychiatric.

psychisch ['psy:çɪʃ] *adj* a) psychic(al), b) psychological, mental: *~e Erkrankung* mental illness.

Psycho|ana'lyse [psyço-] *f* psychoanalysis. *~ana'lytiker m* psychoanalyst.

Psychogramm [psyço'gram] *n* (-s; -e) psychograph, *fig. a.* profile.

Psychologe [psyço'lo:gə] *m* (-n; -n) psychologist. **Psychologie** [psyçolo'gi:] *f* (-; *no pl*) psychology. **psycho'logisch** [-gɪʃ] *adj* psychological.

Psychopath [psyço'pa:t] *m* (-en; -en) psychopath. **psycho'pathisch** [-tɪʃ] *adj* psychopathic.

Psychopharmakon [psyço'farmakɔn] *n* (-s; -ka) psychochemical.

Psychose [psy'ço:zə] *f* (-; -n) psychosis.

psycho'somatisch *adj* psychosomatic.

Pychothera'peut *m* psychotherapist. **psychothera'peutisch** *adj* psychotherapeutic. **Psychothera'pie** *f* psychotherapy.

Pubertät [pubɛr'tɛ:t] *f* (-; *no pl*) puberty.

pubertieren [pubɛr'ti:rən] *v/i* (h) go through puberty.

publik [pu'bli:k] *adj ~ sein* (*werden*) be (become) common knowledge; *et. ~ machen* make s.th. public.

Publikation [publika'tsĭo:n] *f* (-; -en) publication.

Publikum ['pu:blikʊm] *n* (-s; *no pl*) a) the public, audience, *TV a.* viewers, *radio:* *a.* listeners, b) *sports:* spectators, c) customers, visitors.

'Publikums|erfolg *m* great (popular) success. *~geschmack m* public taste. *~liebling m* darling of the public.

publizieren [publi'tsi:rən] *v/t* (h) publish. **Publizist** [publi'tsɪst] *m* (-en; -en) publicist, journalist. **Publizistik** [publi'tsɪstɪk] *f* (-; *no pl*) journalism.

Pudding ['pʊdɪŋ] *m* (-s; -e) pudding, blancmange.

Pudel ['pu:dəl] *m zo.* poodle: F *daste-*

hen wie ein begossener ~ look crestfallen. **'Pudelmütze** f bobble hat.
'pudelnaß adj F soaking wet. **'pudelwohl** adj F **sich ~ fühlen** feel great.
Puder ['pu:dər] m, F a. n (-s; -) powder.
'Puderdose f powder compact.
pudern ['pu:dərn] v/t (h) powder.
'Puderquaste f puff.
'Puderzucker m icing (Am. confectioner's) sugar.
Puff¹ [pʊf] m (-[e]s; ⁻e) **1.** a) thump, b) poke, dig, nudge: F fig. **er (es) kann schon e-n ~ vertragen** he (it) can stand a knock. **2.** pop, bang.
Puff² m, a. n (-s; -s) brothel.
'Puffärmel m puffed sleeve.
puffen ['pʊfən] v/t (h) thump, nudge.
Puffer ['pʊfər] m (-s; -) **1.** buffer. **2.** potato fritter. **'Pufferstaat** m buffer state.
'Puffmais m popcorn.
Pulle ['pʊlə] f (-; -n) F bottle: fig. **volle ~** full blast.
Pulli ['pʊli] m (-s; -s) (light) sweater.
Pullover [pʊ'lo:vər] m (-s; -) sweater, pullover.
Puls [pʊls] m (-es; -e) pulse: **j-m den ~ fühlen** feel s.o.'s pulse, fig. sound s.o. out. **'Pulsader** f artery. **pulsieren** [pʊl'zi:rən] v/i (h) pulsate. **'Pulsschlag** m pulse beat. **'Pulszahl** f pulse rate.
Pult [pʊlt] n (-[e]s; -e) a) desk, b) lectern: ♩ **am ~ XY** XY conducting.
Pulver ['pʊlvər] n (-s; -) a) powder, b) gunpowder: F **er hat das ~ nicht erfunden** he is no great light; → **Schuß** 1.
'Pulverfaß n powder keg: **wie auf e-m ~ sitzen** be sitting on top of a volcano.
pulverisieren [pʊlveri'zi:rən] v/t (h) pulverize.
'Pulverkaffee m instant coffee.
'Pulverschnee m powdery snow.
Puma ['pu:ma] m (-s; -s) zo. puma.
pummelig ['pʊməlɪç] adj F plump.
Pump [pʊmp] m F **auf ~** on tick.
Pumpe ['pʊmpə] f (-; -n) **1.** pump. **2.** F ticker. **'pumpen** v/t, v/i (h) **1.** pump. **2.** F lend, Am. loan: **sich et. ~** borrow s.th. **(bei j-m** from s.o.).
Pumps [pœmps] m (-; -) court shoe.
Punker ['paŋkər] m (-s; -) punk.
Punkt [pʊŋkt] m (-[e]s; -e) **1.** point (a. ♣, sports etc), dot, ling., print. full stop, Am. period: **nach ~en siegen** win on points; **~ 10 Uhr** at ten o'clock sharp. **2.**

spot: fig. **bis zu e-m gewissen ~** up to a point; → **tot, wund. 3.** fig. a) point, item, b) subject: **in vielen ~en** in many respects; F **der springende ~** the crux (of the matter), the whole point; **die Sache auf den ~ bringen** put it in a nutshell; → **strittig.**
punkten ['pʊŋktən] (h) **I** v/t dot. **II** v/i sports: score (points).
punktieren [pʊŋk'ti:rən] v/t (h) ♣ puncture.
pünktlich ['pʏŋktlɪç] **I** adj punctual: **sei ~!** be on time! **II** adv punctually, on time: **~ um 10 Uhr** at ten o'clock sharp.
'Pünktlichkeit f (-; no pl) punctuality.
'Punkt|richter(in f) m sports: judge.
~sieg m win on points. **~sieger(in** f) m winner on points. **~spiel** n league match. **~streik** m strike at selective sites. **~sy,stem** n points system.
punktuell [pʊŋk'tŭɛl] adj selective(ly adv), adv a. at certain points.
Punsch [pʊnʃ] m (-[e]s; -e) gastr. punch.
Pupille [pu'pɪlə] f (-; -n) pupil.
Püppchen ['pʏpçən] n (-s; -) dolly.
Puppe ['pʊpə] f (-; -n) **1.** doll (a. F girl), b) a. fig. puppet, c) dummy: F **bis in die ~n schlafen** sleep till all hours. **2.** zo. a) chrysalis, pupa, b) cocoon.
'Puppen| n puppet show. **~spieler(in** f) m puppeteer. **~stube** f doll's house. **~the,ater** n puppet theat/re (Am. -er). **~wagen** m doll's pram.
pur [pu:r] adj pure, a. sheer, whisky: neat, Am. straight.
Püree [py're:] n (-s; -s) purée, mash.
puritanisch [puri'ta:nɪʃ] adj a) hist. Puritan, b) contp. puritanical.
purpurrot ['pʊrpur-] adj purple.
Purzelbaum ['pʊrtsəl-] m forward roll.
purzeln ['pʊrtsəln] v/i (sn) tumble.
Puste ['pu:stə] f (-; no pl) F breath: **außer ~ sein** be puffed.
Pustel ['pʊstəl] f (-; -n) ♣ pustule.
pusten ['pu:stən] v/i, v/t (h) puff: F mot. **er mußte ~** he was breathalyzed.
Pute ['pu:tə] f (-; -n) zo. turkey (hen): F **dumme ~** silly goose.
Puter ['pu:tər] m (-s; -) zo. turkey (cock).
'puterrot adj (~ **werden** turn) scarlet.
Putsch [pʊtʃ] m (-[e]s; -e) pol. putsch, coup (d'état), revolt. **'putschen** v/i (h) pol. stage a putsch (or coup), revolt.
Putte ['pʊtə] f (-; -n) putto.

Putz [pʊts] *m* (-es; *no pl*) **1.** △ plaster: *unter ~* buried, concealed; F *auf den ~ hauen* a) paint the town red, b) show off. **2.** F row: *~ machen* raise hell.
putzen ['pʊtsən] (h) **I** *v/t* clean, polish, *Am.* shine (*shoes*), preen (*one's feathers*): *sich die Nase ~* blow one's nose; *sich die Zähne ~* brush one's teeth. **II** *v/i* clean: *~ (gehen)* work as a cleaner. **III** *sich ~ a. fig.* preen o.s.
'**Putzfrau** *f* cleaning lady.
'**putzig** *adj* F funny.

'**Putzlappen** *m* cloth.
'**Putzmacherin** *f* (-; -nen) milliner.
'**Putzmittel** *n* cleaning agent.
'**Putzwaren** *pl* millinery.
'**Putzzeug** *n* cleaning things.
puzzeln ['pazəln] *v/i* (h) do a puzzle.
Puzzle ['pazəl] *n* (-s; -) (jigsaw) puzzle.
Pygmäe [pʏ'gmɛːə] *m* (-n; -n) pygmy.
Pyjama [py'dʒaːma] *m* (-s; -s) (pair of) pyjamas (*Am.* pajamas).
Pyramide [pyra'miːdə] *f* (-; -n) pyramid.
pyra'midenförmig *adj* pyramidal.

Q

Q, q [kuː] *n* (-; -) Q, q.
Quacksalber ['kvak-] *m* (-s; -) quack.
Quadrat [kva'draːt] *n* (-[e]s; -e) square: **2 Fuß im ~** 2 feet square; *zum ~ erheben* square; *3 zum* (*or im*) *~* three squared.
Qua'drat... square (*metre*, *root*, *etc*).
qua'dratisch *adj* square, Ⓐ quadratic.
Quadratur [kvadra'tuːr] *f* (-; -en) quadrature: *die ~ des Kreises* the squaring of the circle.
quadrieren [kva'driːrən] *v/t* (h) square.
quadrophon [kvadro'foːn] *adj* quadrophonic.
quaken ['kvaːkən] *v/i* (h) quack, croak.
quäken ['kvɛːkən] *v/i* (h) squawk.
Qual [kvaːl] *f* (-; -en) a) *a. pl* agony, (mental) anguish, b) ordeal: *unter ~en* in (great) pain, *fig.* with great difficulty; *es war e-e ~* it was hell.
quälen ['kvɛːlən] (h) **I** *v/t* a) torment, torture, *fig. a.* haunt, b) pester; *→ gequält.* **II** *sich ~* (*mit*) a) torment o.s. (with), b) struggle hard (with), c) suffer (badly) (from). '**quälend** → **qualvoll.**
Quäle'rei *f* (-; -en) **1.** tormenting (*etc*, *→ quälen* I). **2.** torment, torture.
'**Quälgeist** *m* (-es; -er) pest, tormentor.
Qualifikation [kvalifika'tsɪoːn] *f* (-; -en) qualification. **Qualifikati'onsrunde** *f* *sports*: qualifying round.
qualifizieren [kvalifi'tsiːrən] *v/t* (a. *sich ~*) (h) qualify (*für* for).
Qualität [kvali'tɛːt] *f* (-; -en) quality.

qualitativ [kvalita'tiːf] *adj* qualitative.
Quali'täts|kon,trolle *f* quality control. **~ware** *f* high-quality article, *coll.* quality goods. **~wein** *m* quality-tested wine.
Qualle ['kvalə] *f* (-; -n) *zo.* jellyfish.
Qualm [kvalm] *m* (-[e]s; *no pl*) smoke.
qualmen ['kvalmən] *v/i*, *v/t* (h) smoke.
'**qualmig** *adj* smoky, full of smoke.
'**qualvoll** *adj* agonizing, very painful, excruciating (*pains*).
Quantenphy,sik ['kvantən-] *f* quantum physics.
Quantität [kvanti'tɛːt] *f* (-; -en) quantity.
quantitativ [kvantita'tiːf] *adj* quantitative.
Quantum ['kvantʊm] *n* (-s; Quanten) **1.** quantum, amount. **2.** share, quota.
Quarantäne [karan'tɛːnə] *f* (-; -n) (*unter ~ stellen* put in) quarantine.
Quark [kvark] *m* (-s; *no pl*) **1.** *gastr.* curd cheese. **2.** → **Quatsch.**
Quartal [kvar'taːl] *n* (-s; -e) quarter (year).
Quartett [kvar'tɛt] *n* (-[e]s; -e) **1.** ♪ quartet(te). **2.** *fig.* foursome. **3.** (*game*) happy families.
Quartier [kvar'tiːr] *n* (-s; -e) accommodation, *esp.* ✕ quarters.
Quarz [kvaːrts] *m* (-es; -e) quartz.
quasi ['kvaːzi] *adv* as it were.
quasseln ['kvasəln] *v/i* (h) blather.
Quaste ['kvastə] *f* (-; -n) tassel.
Quatsch [kvatʃ] *m* (-es; *no pl*) F rubbish,

rot: ~ *machen* a) fool around, b) do s.th. stupid; *red k-n ~!* a) don't talk rubbish!, b) you're kidding!

quatschen ['kvatʃən] *v/i* (h) F **1.** talk rubbish. **2.** gossip. **3.** chat, waffle. **4.** blab. '**Quatschkopf** *m* F silly ass.

Quecke ['kvɛkə] *f* (-; -n) ⚲ couch grass.

Quecksilber ['kvɛk-] *n* quicksilver, mercury. ~**säule** *f* mercury column. ~**vergiftung** *f* mercury poisoning.

Quelle ['kvɛlə] *f* (-; -n) a) spring, b) source (*of river etc, a. fig.*), c) well: *et. aus sicherer ~ wissen* have s.th. on good authority. '**quellen** *v/i* (quoll, gequollen, sn) **1.** (*aus* from) pour (*a. fig.*), *blood, water*: well, gush. **2.** swell: ~ *lassen* soak (*peas etc*).

'**Quellen|angabe** *f* reference, *pl* bibliography. ~**materi̱al** *n* source material. ~**steuer** *f* withholding tax. ~**studium** *n* basic research.

'**Quellgebiet** *n* headwaters.

'**Quellwasser** *n* spring water.

quengelig ['kvɛŋəlɪç] *adj* whining.

quengeln ['kvɛŋəln] *v/i* (h) whine.

quer [kveːr] *adv* a) crosswise, across, b) diagonally, c) at right angles (*zu* to): ~ *über* (*acc*) across.

'**Querbalken** *m* crossbeam.

Quere ['kveːrə] *f j-m in die ~ kommen* get in s.o.'s way.

querfeld'ein *adv* across country. **Querfeld'einlauf** *m* cross-country race.

'**Querflöte** *f* transverse flute.

'**Querfoṟmat** *n* horizontal format.

'**quergestreift** *adj* horizontally striped.

'**Querkopf** *m* F pigheaded fellow.

'**querlegen:** *sich* ~ (*sep*, -ge-, h) F *fig.* make trouble.

'**Querpaß** *m sports:* cross pass.

'**querschießen** *v/i* (*irr, sep*, -ge-, h, → *schießen*) F *fig.* make trouble.

'**Querschiff** *n* △ transept.

'**Querschläger** *m* ✕ ricochet.

'**Querschnitt** *m* cross-section (*a. fig. durch* of).

'**querschnitt(s)gelähmt** *adj*, '**Querschnitt(s)gelähmte** *m, f* ✚ paraplegic.

'**Querschnittzeichnung** *f* sectional drawing.

'**Querstraße** *f* intersecting road: *zweite ~ rechts* second turning on the right.

'**Querstrich** *m* horizontal line, dash.

'**Quersumme** *f* & sum of the digits.

'**Quertreiber** *m* (-s; -) F obstructionist.

Querulant [kveru'lant] *m* (-en; -en) troublemaker.

'**Querverbindung** *f* cross connection.

'**Querverweis** *m* cross reference.

quetschen ['kvɛtʃən] *v/t* (h) a) squeeze (*a. fig. sich* o.s.), b) bruise, crush. '**Quetschung** *f* (-; -en) ✚ bruise.

quickle'bendig ['kvɪk-] *adj* F very lively, active.

quieken ['kviːkən] *v/i* (h) squeak.

quietschen ['kviːtʃən] *v/i* (h) squeal, squeak.

'**quietschvergnügt** *adj* F chirpy.

Quinte ['kvɪntə] *f* (-; -n) ♪ fifth.

'**Quintes̱senz** *f* (-; -en) essence.

Quintett [kvɪn'tɛt] *n* (-[e]s; -e) quintet(te).

Quirl [kvɪrl] *m* (-[e]s; -e) **1.** *gastr.* beater. **2.** ⚲ whorl. **3.** *fig.* live wire.

'**quirlen** *v/t* whisk, beat.

'**quirlig** *adj fig.* lively.

quitt [kvɪt] *adj mit j-m ~ sein* (*werden*) be (get) quits with s.o.

Quitte ['kvɪtə] *f* (-; -n) ⚲ quince.

quittieren [kvɪ'tiːrən] *v/t* (h) give a receipt for: *et. mit e-m Lächeln ~* meet s.th. with a smile.

Quittung ['kvɪtʊŋ] *f* (-; -en) (*gegen* ~ on) receipt: *das ist die ~ für d-n Leichtsinn* that's what you get for being so careless. '**Quittungsblock** *m* receipt book.

Quiz [kvɪz] *n* (-; -) quiz.

'**Quizmaster** *m* (-s; -) quizmaster.

'**Quizsendung** *f* quiz program(me *Br.*).

quoll [kvɔl] *pret of* **quellen.**

Quote ['kvoːtə] *f* (-; -n) quota, share.

Quotient [kvo'tsiɛnt] *m* (-en; -en) & quotient.

R

R, r [ɛr] n (-; -) R, r.

Rabatt [ra'bat] m (-[e]s; -e) discount.

Rabbi ['rabi] m (-[s]; -nen [ra'bi:nən]), **Rabbiner** [ra'bi:nər] m (-s; -) rabbi.

Rabe ['ra:bə] m (-n; -n) raven.

'**Rabenmutter** f uncaring mother.

'**raben**'**schwarz** adj jet-black.

'**Rabenvater** m uncaring father.

rabiat [ra'bĭa:t] adj a) furious, b) rough, brutal, c) ruthless.

Rache ['raxə] f (-; no pl) revenge, vengeance: **aus ~** in revenge (**für** for); **~ schwören** vow vengeance; **~ nehmen** (or **üben**) → **rächen** II.

'**Rache**,**akt** m act of revenge.

Rachen ['raxən] m (-s; -) **1.** anat. throat. **2.** zo., a. fig. jaws, maw: F **j-m et. in den ~ schmeißen** cast s.th. into s.o.'s hungry maw; **er kann den ~ nicht voll kriegen** he can't get enough.

rächen ['rɛçən] (h) **I** v/t (**an** dat on, upon) avenge, revenge. **II sich ~** take revenge, get one's own back; **sich an j-m ~** revenge o.s. (or take revenge) on s.o.; **es rächte sich (bitter), daß er ...** he had to pay dearly for ger.

'**Rachenka,tarrh** m ✵ pharyngitis.

Rächer ['rɛçər] m (-s; -) avenger.

Rachitis [ra'xi:tɪs] f (-; no pl) rickets.

ra'chitisch [-tɪʃ] adj ✵ rickety.

'**Rachsucht** f (-; no pl) vindictiveness.

'**rachsüchtig** adj vindictive, revengeful.

rackern ['rakərn] v/i (h) F slave away.

Rad [ra:t] n (-[e]s; ⁓er ['rɛ:dər]) **1.** wheel: **ein ~ schlagen** a) peacock: spread the tail, b) → **radschlagen**; **das fünfte ~ am Wagen sein** be the fifth wheel; F **unter die Räder kommen** go to the dogs. **2.** bicycle, F bike.

Radar [ra'da:r] m, n (-s; no pl) radar. ⁓**falle** f mot. F radar (speed) trap. ⁓**gerät** n radar (set). ⁓**kon,trolle** f radar control. ⁓**schirm** m radar screen.

Radau [ra'daʊ] m (-s; no pl) F row.

'**Raddampfer** m paddle steamer.

radeln ['ra:dəln] v/i (sn) F cycle, pedal.

Rädelsführer ['rɛ:dəls-] m ringleader.

'**Räderwerk** n a) wheels, b) clockwork, c) gear(ing), d) fig. machinery.

'**radfahren** v/i (irr, sep, -ge-, sn, → **fah**ren) **1.** cycle, (ride a) bicycle, F bike. **2.** F contp. toady. '**Radfahrer(in** f) m **1.** cyclist. **2.** F contp. toady.

'**Radfahrweg** m cycle track.

radieren [ra'di:rən] v/t, v/i (h) **1.** erase, rub s.th. out. **2.** art: etch.

Ra'diergummi m eraser, Br. a. rubber.

Ra'dierung f (-; -en) art: etching.

Radieschen [ra'di:sçən] n (-s; -) radish.

radikal [radi'ka:l] adj, **Radi'kale** m, f (-n; -n) radical. **radikalisieren** [-kali'zi:rən] v/t (h) radicalize. **Radikalismus** [-ka'lɪsmʊs] m (-; no pl) radicalism. **Radi'kalkur** f drastic cure.

Radio ['ra:dĭo] n (-s; -s) radio, Br. a. wireless: **im ~** on the radio; **~ hören** listen to the radio, listen in.

radioak'tiv adj radioactive: ⁓**er Niederschlag** fallout.

Radioaktivi'tät f (-; no pl) radioactivity.

'**Radioappa,rat** m radio (set).

Radiologe [radĭo'lo:gə] m (-n; -n) ✵ radiologist.

'**Radiore,corder** m radio cassette recorder. '**Radiowecker** m clock radio.

Radium ['ra:dĭʊm] n (-s; no pl) radium.

Radius ['ra:dĭʊs] m (-; Radien) radius.

'**Radkappe** f hub cap. '**Radrennbahn** f cycling track. '**Radrennen** n cycle race. '**radschlagen** v/i (irr, sep, -ge-, h, → **schlagen**) turn cartwheels. '**Radsport** m cycling. '**Radtour** f cycle tour. '**Radweg** m cycle track.

raffen ['rafən] v/t **1.** snatch up, gather up (skirt etc). **2.** fig. condense, tighten.

Raffinade [rafi'na:də] f (-; -n) refined sugar. **Raffinerie** [rafinə'ri:] f (-; -n) ✪ refinery. **Raffinesse** [rafi'nɛsə] f (-; -n) cleverness, subtlety, sophistication, a. refinement (of taste etc). **raffinieren** [rafi'ni:rən] v/t (h) ✪ refine. **raffi'niert** fig. clever, ingenious (plan etc), subtle, sophisticated (taste etc).

Rage ['ra:ʒə] f (-; no pl) rage, fury: **j-n in ~ bringen** make s.o. furious.

ragen ['ra:gən] v/i **1.** rise (high), tower: **~ aus** (dat) rise (or project) from.

Raglanärmel ['ragla(:)n-] pl raglan sleeves.

Ragout [ra'gu:] n (-s; -s) gastr. ragout.

Rahe ['ra:ə] *f* (-; -n) ⚓ yard.
Rahm [ra:m] *m* (-[e]s; *no pl*) cream; → **abschöpfen**.
rahmen ['ra:mən] *v/t* (h) frame (*picture etc*), mount (*slides*).
¹**Rahmen** *m* (-s; -) frame (*a. mot.*, ⚙), *fig. a.* framework, scope, limits, setting: *im ~ von* (*or gen*) within the scope of; *im ~ des Festes* in the course of the festival; *im ~ der Ausstellung finden ... statt* the exhibition will include ...; *im ~ des Möglichen* within the bounds of possibility; *in großem ~* on a large scale; *aus dem ~ fallen* a) be unusual, be off-beat, b) F get out of line, misbehave; *den ~ sprengen* go beyond the scope (*gen* of). **~abkommen** *n* skeleton agreement. **~bedingungen** *pl* general conditions. **~erzählung** *f* framework story. **~gesetz** *n* skeleton law. **~handlung** *f* frame (story). **~kampf** *m* boxing: supporting fight. **~pro,gramm** *n* fringe events.
rahmig ['ra:mɪç] *adj* creamy.
¹**Rahmkäse** *m* cream cheese.
¹**Rahsegel** *n* square sail.
Rakete [ra'ke:tə] *f* (-; -n) rocket, ✗ *a.* missile.
Ra'keten|abschußbasis *f* rocket launching site, ✗ missile base. **~antrieb** *m* rocket propulsion: *mit ~* rocket-propelled. **~start** *m* rocket-assisted takeoff. **~stützpunkt** *m* ✗ missile base.
Rallye ['rali] *f* (-; -s) (motor) rally.
Ramme ['ramə] *f* (-; -n) pile-driver.
rammen ['ramən] *v/t* (h) ram.
Rampe ['rampə] *f* (-; -n) **1.** ramp. **2.** *thea.* apron.
¹**Rampenlicht** *n thea.* footlights: *fig. im ~ stehen* be in the limelight.
ramponieren [rampo'ni:rən] *v/t* (h) F *a. fig.* batter.
Ramsch [ramʃ] *m* (-es; -e) a) ✝ rejects, b) F *contp.* junk, trash.
ran [ran] F let's go!; *in cpds.* → **heran...**
Rand [rant] *m* (-[e]s; ˇer) **1.** edge, rim (*of plate etc*), brim (*of hat, glass, etc*), margin (*of page etc*), lip (*of wound*), brink (*of abyss, fig. of ruin etc*): *bis zum ~ voll* brimful; *e-n ~ lassen* leave a margin; *am ˇe des Waldes* (*der Stadt*) on the edge of the wood (on the outskirts of the town); *am ˇe* a) *note etc* in the margin, b) *mention etc* in passing; (*nur*

am ~e (only) marginally; *am ~e bemerkt* by the way. **2.** mark, *a.* tidemark. **3.** F *außer ~ und Band* a) completely out of hand, b) quite beside o.s. (*vor* with *joy etc*). **4.** F *er kommt* (*damit*) *nicht zu ~* he can't cope (with it).
randalieren [randa'li:rən] *v/i* (h) raise hell, riot. **Randa'lierer** *m* (-s; -) hooligan, rioter.
¹**Rand|bemerkung** *f* a) marginal note, b) passing remark. **~erscheinung** *f* side issue. **~gebiet** *n* borderland (*a. fig.*), outskirts (*of town*). **~gruppe** *f* fringe group.
¹**randlos** *adj* rimless (*glasses*).
¹**Randpro,blem** *n* side issue.
¹**Randstreifen** *m mot.* shoulder.
rang [raŋ] *pret of* **ringen**.
Rang *m* (-[e]s; ˇe) **1.** a) rank (*a.* ✗), status, position, b) quality: *fig. ersten ~es* first-class, first-rate; *j-m den ~ ablaufen* outstrip s.o.; *j-m den ~ streitig machen* compete with s.o.; *alles, was ~ und Namen hat* all the notables (F VIPs). **2.** *thea. erster ~* dress circle, *Am.* first balcony; *zweiter ~* upper circle, *Am.* second balcony; *dritter ~* gallery; *sports: die Ränge* the terraces. **3.** *lottery etc:* (dividend) class.
¹**Rangabzeichen** *pl* insignia.
¹**rangehen** *v/i* (*irr, sep, -ge-, sn,* → **gehen**) F go in.
rangeln ['raŋəln] *v/i* (h) F scuffle: *fig. um et. ~* wrangle for s.th.
¹**Rangfolge** *f* order of precedence.
rangieren [rãˈʒiːrən] (h) **I** *v/t* 🚂 shunt, *Am.* switch. **II** *v/i fig.* rank (*vor* before).
Ran'giergleis *n* siding.
¹**Rangliste** *f sports:* ranking list, table.
¹**Rangordnung** *f* order of precedence.
¹**ranhalten:** *sich ~* (*irr, sep, -ge-, h,* → **halten**) F a) get on with it, b) dig in.
rank [raŋk] *adj a.* **~ und schlank** slim.
Ranke ['raŋkə] *f* (-; -n) tendril. ¹**ranken** *v/i* (*a. sich ~*) (h) climb, creep.
¹**ranlassen** *v/t* (*irr, sep, -ge-, h,* → **lassen**) F *j-n ~ an* (*acc*) let s.o. (have a go) at; *laß mich mal ran!* let me have a go!
rann [ran] *pret of* **rinnen**.
¹**rannehmen** *v/t* (*irr, sep, -ge-, h,* → **nehmen**) F *j-n ~* ride s.o. hard.
rannte ['rantə] *pret of* **rennen**.
Ranzen ['rantsən] *m* (-s; -) a) knapsack, b) satchel.

ranzig ['rantsıç] *adj* rancid.
rapide [ra'pi:də] *adj* rapid.
Rappe ['rapə] *m* (-n; -n) black horse.
Rappel ['rapəl] *m* (-s; -) F cazy mood:
e-n ~ kriegen flip (one's lid).
Raps [raps] *m* (-es; -e) ♀ rape(-seed).
rar [ra:r] *adj* rare (*a. fig.*), scarce: F **sich ~
machen** make o.s. scarce. **Rarität**
[rari'tɛ:t] *f* (-; -en) rarity, *a.* curiosity.
rasant [ra'zant] *adj* **1.** flat (*trajectory*). **2.**
F a) fast (*car etc*), b) rapid (*development
etc*), c) terrific, d) snazzy.
rasch [raʃ] *adj* quick, swift, speedy, fast:
mach ~! be quick!
rascheln ['raʃəln] *v/i* (h) rustle.
rasen ['ra:zən] *v/i* **1.** (h) rage: *fig.* (*vor
Begeisterung*) ~ be wild with enthu-
siasm. **2.** (sn) F race, tear.
Rasen ['ra:zən] *m* a) grass, b) lawn.
'rasend I *adj* **1.** raging (*fury etc*), agonizing (*pains*): **~e Kopfschmerzen** a splitting headache; **~e Wut** towering rage; **~
werden (machen)** go (drive *s.o.*) mad.
2. breakneck. II *adv* **3.** F madly (*in love
etc*): *et. ~ gern tun* just love to do s.th.
'Rasenmäher *m* lawn mower.
'Rasensprenger *m* sprinkler.
Raser ['ra:zər] *m* (-s; -) F speeder.
Rase'rei [-'raɪ] *f* (-; -en) **1.** F mot. speeding. **2.**
no pl a) fury, b) frenzy: *j-n zur ~ brin-
gen* drive s.o. mad.
Ra'sierappa,rat *m* (safety) razor: *elektrischer ~* electric shaver (*or* razor).
Ra'siercreme *f* shaving cream.
rasieren [ra'zi:rən] (h) I *v/t* (*sich ~ lassen* get a) shave. II *sich ~* (have a)
shave: *sich elektrisch ~* use an electric
shaver.
Ra'sier|klinge *f* razor blade. **~messer** *n*
razor. **~pinsel** *m* shaving brush. **~seife**
f shaving soap. **~wasser** *n* aftershave
(lotion). **~zeug** *n* shaving things.
raspeln ['raspəln] *v/t* (h) grate.
Rasse ['rasə] *f* (-; -n) race, zo. breed.
'Rassehund *m* pedigree dog.
Rassel ['rasəl] *f* (-; -n) rattle.
'rasseln ['rasəln] *v/i* (sn) rattle: F *durch e-e Prüfung ~* fail (*Am.* flunk) (an exam).
'Rassen... racial (*discrimination, problem, policy, etc*). **~kra,wall** *m* race riot.
~mischung *f* mixture of races, zo.
crossbreed. **~schranke** *f* colo(u)r bar.
~trennung *f* segregation, South Africa:
apartheid. **~unruhen** *pl* race riots.

'Rassepferd *n* thoroughbred (horse).
'rasserein *adj* purebred, thoroughbred.
rassig ['rasıç] *adj* thoroughbred.
Rassismus [ra'sısmʊs] *m* (-; *no pl*) racism. **Rassist** [ra'sıst] *m* (-en; -en),
ras'sistisch *adj* racist.
Rast [rast] *f* (-; *no pl*) rest, *a.* break: (*e-e*)
~ machen → **rasten.**
Raste ['rastə] *f* (-; -n) ⚙ catch.
rasten ['rastən] *v/i* (h) (take a) rest.
Raster ['rastər] *m* (-s; -) phot., print.
screen, *TV a.* raster, ✍ grid.
'Rasthaus *n* motorway restaurant.
'rastlos *adj* restless.
'Rastlosigkeit *f* (-; *no pl*) restlessness.
'Rastplatz *m* resting place, mot. layby,
Am. rest stop.
'Raststätte *f* mot. service area.
Rasur [ra'zu:r] *f* (-; -en) shave.
Rat [ra:t] *m* (-[e]s; ∗e) **1.** *no pl* (piece of)
advice, suggestion, recommendation:
auf s-n ~ hin on his advice; *j-n um ~
fragen (j-s ~ folgen)* ask (take) s.o.'s
advice; **~ schaffen** find a way out; *~
suchen* seek advice; *zu ~e ziehen* consult; *~ wissen* know what to do; *k-n ~
mehr wissen* be at a loss. **2.** a) council,
board, b) council(l)or.
Rate ['ra:tə] *f* (-; -n) **1.** instal(l)ment: *in
~n zahlen* pay by (*or* in) instal(l)ments.
2. (*birth, growth, etc*) rate.
raten ['ra:tən] *v/t, v/i* (riet, geraten, h) **1.**
j-m (zu et.) ~ advise s.o. (to do s.th.); *~
et. zu tun* recommend doing s.th.; *zur
Vorsicht ~* recommend caution; *wozu
~ Sie mir?* what do you advise me to
do?, what would you recommend? **2.**
guess, *a.* solve (*puzzle*): F *rate mal!* just
guess!; *falsch geraten!* wrong guess!
'Ratenzahlung *f* payment by in-
stal(l)ments.
'Ratespiel *n* guessing (*TV* panel) game.
'Ratgeber *m* (-s; -) **1.** adviser. **2.** reference book.
'Rathaus *n* townhall, *Am.* city hall.
Ratifikation [ratifika'tsïo:n] *f* (-; -en),
Ratifi'zierung *f* (-; -en) ratification.
ratifizieren [ratifi'tsi:rən] *v/t* (h) ratify.
Ration [ra'tsïo:n] *f* (-; -en) ration.
rational [ratsïo'na:l] *adj* rational.
rationalisieren [ratsïonali'zi:rən] *v/t* (h)
rationalize. **Rationali'sierung** *f* (-;
-en) rationalization. **Rationali'sie-
rungsfachmann** *m* efficiency expert.

Rationalismus [ratsĭona'lɪsmŏs] *m* (-; *no pl*) rationalism.

rationell [ratsĭo'nɛl] *adj* a) rational, b) efficient.

rationieren [ratsĭo'ni:rən] *v/t* (h) ration. **Ratio'nierung** *f* (-; -en) rationing.

'**ratlos** *adj* helpless: ~ **sein** *a.* be at a loss.

'**Ratlosigkeit** *f* (-; *no pl*) helplessness.

'**ratsam** *adj* advisable, wise.

'**Ratschlag** *m* (piece of) advice: *einige gute Ratschläge* some good advice.

Rätsel ['rɛ:tsəl] *n* (-s; -) riddle, puzzle, *fig. a.* mystery: *es ist mir ein (völliges) ~* it's a (complete) mystery to me, F it beats me; *er ist mir ein ~* I can't make him out; *vor e-m ~ stehen* be baffled.

'**rätselhaft** *adj* a) baffling, puzzling, b) mysterious.

'**Rätselraten** *n* (-s) *fig.* speculation.

'**Ratsherr** *m hist.* council(l)or.

Ratte ['ratə] *f* (-; -n) *zo.* rat.

'**Rattenfänger** *m* ratcatcher, *fig.* Pied Piper. **'Rattengift** *n* rat poison.

rattern ['ratərn] *v/i* (h *and* sn), '**Rattern** *n* (-s) rattle, clatter.

Raub [raʊp] *m* (-[e]s; *no pl*) **1.** a) (armed) robbery, b) kidnap(p)ing. **2.** a) loot, b) prey: *ein ~ der Flammen werden* be destroyed by fire.

'**Raubbau** *m* (-[e]s; *no pl*) ruinous exploitation: *~ treiben mit* a) exploit ruthlessly, b) *s-r Gesundheit* ruin one's health.

'**Raubdruck** *m* (-[e]s; -e) pirate edition.

rauben ['raʊbən] *v/t* (h) a) rob, b) kidnap: *j-m et. ~ a. fig.* rob s.o. of s.th.

Räuber ['rɔʏbər] *m* (-s; -) robber, highwayman. **~bande** *f* gang of robbers, holdup gang. **~geschichte** *f* F cock-and-bull story.

'**räuberisch** *adj* rapacious, predatory: *~er Überfall* (armed) robbery, holdup.

'**Raub|fisch** *m* predatory fish. **~gier** *f* rapacity. **Ⴒgierig** *adj* rapacious. **~mord** *m* murder with robbery. **~mörder** *m* murderer and robber. **~ritter** *m hist.* robber baron. **~tier** *n* beast of prey. **~überfall** *m* (armed) robbery, holdup. **~vogel** *m* bird of prey. **~zug** *m* raid.

Rauch [raʊx] *m* (-[e]s; *no pl*) (*fig. sich in ~ auflösen* go up in) smoke.

rauchen ['raʊxən] *v/i, v/t* (h) smoke, 🍷 fume: F *e-e ~* have a smoke; *Rauchen verboten!* No smoking!; → *Pfeife* 2.

Raucher ['raʊxər] *m* (-s; -) **1.** (*starker ~* heavy) smoker. **2.** → *Raucherabteil.*

Räucher... ['rɔʏçər-] *gastr.* smoked.

'**Raucher|ab,teil** *n* smoking compartment. **~husten** *m* 🍷 smoker's cough.

'**Raucherin** *f* (-; -nen) → *Raucher* 1.

räuchern ['rɔʏçərn] *v/t* (h) smoke(-dry).

'**Räucherstäbchen** *n* joss stick.

'**Rauchfahne** *f* trail of smoke.

'**rauchig** *adj* smoky (*a. fig.* voice).

'**Rauch|pilz** *m* mushroom cloud. **~säule** *f* column of smoke. **~verbot** *n* ban on smoking: *~!* No smoking! **~vergiftung** *f* smoke poisoning. **~waren** *pl* **1.** furs. **2.** tobacco products. **~wolke** *f* cloud of smoke. **~zeichen** *n* smoke signal.

Räude ['rɔʏdə] *f* (-; -n) *vet.* mange.

'**räudig** *adj* mangy.

rauf(...) [raʊf] F → *herauf(...), hinauf(...).*

'**Raufbold** [-bɔlt] *m* (-[e]s; -e) brawler.

raufen ['raʊfən] (h) **I** *v/t sich die Haare ~* tear one's hair. **II** *v/i* (*a. sich ~*) brawl, fight (*um* for).

Raufe'rei *f* (-; -en) brawl, fight.

rauh [raʊ] *adj* rough, *a.* harsh (*climate, treatment, voice, etc*), *a.* raw (*air etc*), sore (*throat*), wild, bleak (*region etc*), coarse (*cloth etc*): *~e Hände* chapped hands; *~e See* stormy sea; *~e Stimme* hoarse (*or* husky) voice; *~e Sitten* rough practices; *~, aber herzlich* pretty rough; *die ~e Wirklichkeit* (the) harsh reality; F *in ~en Mengen* lots of.

'**Rauheit** *f* (-; *no pl*) roughness (*etc*).

'**Rauhfaserta,pete** *f* woodchip paper.

'**Rauhhaar...** *zo.* wirehaired.

'**Rauhreif** *m* hoarfrost.

Raum [raʊm] *m* (-[e]s; ~e) **1.** room. **2.** *no pl* room, space (*a. philos., phys.*), *fig. a.* scope: *auf engstem ~ leben* live in cramped surroundings; *fig. im ~ stehen problem etc*: be there; → *luftleer.* **3.** area, region: *im ~ (von) München* in the Munich area. **4.** *phys.* (outer) space. **~anzug** *m* space suit. **~ausstatter** *m* (-s; -) interior decorator. **~deckung** *f sports:* zone defen/ce (*Am.* -se).

räumen ['rɔʏmən] *v/t* (h) **1.** leave, *a.* ✕ evacuate, quit, vacate (*house etc*), clear (*hall, street, etc, a.* ✝ *stores*); → *Feld.* **2.** remove: *Minen ~* sweep mines; → *Weg.*

'**Raumfähre** *f* space shuttle.

'**Raumfahrt** *f* (-; *no pl*) space travel (*or*

flight), astronautics. **'Raumfahrt...** space (*medicine, programme, etc*).

'Räumfahrzeug n **1.** bulldozer. **2.** snow clearer.

'Raumflug m space flight.

'Rauminhalt m volume, capacity.

'Raumkapsel f space capsule.

räumlich ['rɔʏmlɪç] adj a) (of) space, spatial, three-dimensional, b) stereophonic, c) opt. stereoscopic: **~ (sehr) beengt** cramped (for space).

'Räumlichkeit f (-; -en) **1.** room, pl premises. **2.** no pl three-dimensionality.

'Raummaß n solid measure. **'Raummeter** n, a. m cubic metre (Am. meter).

'Raumpflegerin f cleaning lady.

'Raumschiff n spacecraft, spaceship.

'Raumsonde f space probe.

'raumsparend adj space-saving.

'Raumstati,on f space station.

'Räumung f (-; -en) clearing, a. ⚓ clearance, a. ⚔ evacuation, ⚖ eviction.

'Räumungs|befehl m ⚖ eviction order. **~klage** f ⚖ action for eviction. **~verkauf** m ⚓ clearance sale.

raunen ['raʊnən] v/i, v/t (h) whisper.

Raupe ['raʊpə] f (-; -n) zo. caterpillar.

'Raupen|fahrzeug n crawler (truck). **~kette** f crawler. **~schlepper** m tracklaying (or crawler) tractor.

raus [raʊs] int F get out!

raus(...) F → **heraus(...), hinaus(...).**

Rausch [raʊʃ] m (-[e]s, ⇌e) intoxication (a. fig.), drunkenness, F high, fig. ecstasy: **e-n ~ haben** be drunk; **s-n ~ ausschlafen** sleep it off.

'rauscharm adj low-noise.

'rauschen ['raʊʃən] v/i **1.** (h) leaves, silk: rustle, water, stream, etc: rush, surge etc: roar. **2.** (sn) sweep. **'Rauschen** (-s) rustling (etc). **'rauschend** adj **1.** rustling (etc). **2.** fig. glittering (parties), thunderous (applause).

'Rauschgift n drug(s pl coll). **~bekämpfung** f fight against drugs. **~handel** m drug traffic. **~händler** m drug trafficker, F pusher, sl. dealer. **~sucht** f drug addiction. **⚷süchtig** adj drug-addicted: **~ sein** a. be a drug addict, be on drugs. **~süchtige** m, f (-n; -n) drug addict.

'rausfliegen F → **hinausfliegen** 2.

'rausgeben F → **herausgeben.**

räuspern ['rɔʏspərn] sich ~ (h) clear one's throat.

'rausreißen F → **herausreißen.**

'rausschmeißen v/t (irr, sep, -ge-, h, → **schmeißen**) F kick s.o. out, a. fire.

'Rausschmeißer m (-s; -) F **1.** bouncer. **2.** get-out dance.

Raute ['raʊtə] f (-; -n) **1.** lozenge, esp. A rhomb. **2.** ♀ rue.

Razzia ['ratsɪa] f (-; -ien) (police) raid.

Reagenzglas [re'ʔa'gɛnts-] n test tube.

reagieren [re'ʔa'gi:rən] v/i (h) (**auf** acc to) react, fig. a. respond.

Reaktion [re'ʔak'tsɪo:n] f (-; -en) (**auf** acc to) reaction, fig. a. response.

reaktio'när [re'ʔaktsɪo'nɛ:r] adj, **Reaktio'när** m (-s; -e) reactionary.

Reakti'ons|fähigkeit f (-; no pl) reactions. **⚷schnell** adj **~ sein** have fast reactions. **~zeit** f reaction time.

Reaktor [re'ʔaktɔr] m (-s; -en [-'to:rən]) phys. reactor.

real [re'a:l] adj **1.** real. **2.** realistic.

Re'aleinkommen n real income.

realisieren [reali'zi:rən] v/t (h) realize.

Realismus [rea'lɪsmʊs] m (-; no pl) realism. **Realist** [-'lɪst] m (-en; -en) realist. **rea'listisch** [-tɪʃ] adj realistic.

Realität [reali'tɛ:t] f (-; -en) reality.

Re'allohn m real wages.

Re'alschule f secondary school (leading to O-levels), Am. junior high school.

Rebe ['re:bə] f (-; -n) a) vine, b) tendril.

Rebell [re'bɛl] m (-en; -en) rebel.

rebellieren [rebɛ'li:rən] v/i (h) rebel.

Rebellion [rebɛ'lɪo:n] f (-; -en) rebellion. **re'bellisch** [lɪʃ] adj rebellious.

Rebhuhn ['re:p-] n zo. partridge.

Rebstock m ♀ vine.

Rechen ['rɛçən] m (-s; -) rake.

'Rechen|anlage f computer. **~aufgabe** f (arithmetical) problem, sum. **~buch** n arithmetic book. **~fehler** m miscalculation, mistake. **~ma,schine** f calculator: **elektronische ~** computer.

'Rechenschaft f **~ ablegen über** (acc) answer for; **j-n zur ~ ziehen** call s.o. to account (**wegen** for); **j-m ~ schuldig sein** be answerable to s.o. (**für** acc for). **'Rechenschaftsbericht** m **1.** report. **2.** statement (of accounts).

'Rechen|schieber m slide rule. **~zentrum** n computer cent/re (Am. -er).

Recherche [re'ʃɛrʃə] f (-; -n) investigation. **recherchieren** [reʃɛr'ʃi:rən] v/i (h) investigate.

rechnen ['rɛçnən] (h) **I** *v/t* **1.** A calculate, work out. **2.** a) estimate, b) count, allow for: *die Kinder nicht gerechnet* not counting the children. **3.** *j-n* ~ *zu* count s.o. among. **II** *v/i* **4.** calculate, *esp. ped.* do sums: *falsch* ~ miscalculate; *gut* ~ *können* be good at figures. **5.** *fig.* ~ *zu* count among; ~ *mit*, ~ *auf (acc)* a) count on, b) expect, reckon with; *mit mir kannst du nicht* ~*!* count me out! **6.** economize. **'Rechnen** *n* (-s) calculation, *ped.* arithmetic.

'Rechner *m* (-s; -) **1.** calculator: *er ist ein guter* ~ he is good at figures. **2.** ⊙ a) calculator, b) computer. **'rechner-gesteuert** *adj* computer-controlled.

'Rechnung *f* (-; -en) **1.** a) calculation, problem, sum: *die* ~ *ging nicht auf* a. *fig.* it didn't work out; → *Strich* 1. **2.** † account, bill, invoice, *in restaurant*: bill, *Am.* check: *die,* ~ *bitte!* can I have the bill, please!; *auf* ~ on account; *auf* ~ *kaufen* buy on credit; *das geht auf m-e* ~ that's on me!; *fig. das geht auf s-e* ~ that's his doing; *F auf s-e* ~ *kommen* get one's money's worth; *laut* ~ as per invoice; *e-r Sache* ~ *tragen* take s.th. into account; *j-m et. in* ~ *stellen* charge s.th. to s.o.'s account.

'Rechnungs|betrag *m* invoice total. **~führung** *f* accountancy. **~hof** *m* audit division. **~jahr** *n* financial year. **~prüfer** *m* auditor. **~prüfung** *f* audit. **~wesen** *n* (-s; *no pl*) accountancy.

recht [rɛçt] **I** *adj* **1.** right, right-hand, *pol.* right(-wing), rightist; *~er Hand* on the right; *~er Hand sehen Sie ...* on your right you see ...; *im ~en Winkel (zu)* at right angles (to); → *Hand* 1. **2.** right, *a.* correct, *a.* suitable, *a.* just, fair: *das ist nur* ~ *und billig* that's only fair; *so ist's* ~*!* that's it!; *ganz* ~*!* quite right!, exactly!; *zur* ~*en Zeit* at the right moment; *mir ist's* ~ that's all right with me, I don't mind; *mir ist alles* ~ I don't care; *ist es Ihnen* ~, *wenn ...?* would you mind if ...?; *schon* ~*!* it's all right!; → *Ding* 2, *Mittel* 1. **3.** real, true, regular: *er hat k-n* ~*en Erfolg* he is not much of a success. **4.** ~ *haben* be right; → *behalten* be right in the end; *j-m* ~ *geben* agree with s.o. **II** *adv* **5.** a) right(ly), well, correctly, b) properly, c) very, d) rather, quite: ~ *gut* not bad; *es gefällt*

mir ~ *gut* I rather like it; *erst* ~ all the more; *(nun) erst* ~ *nicht* (now) less than ever; *wenn ich es* ~ *überlege* (when I) come to think of it; *ich weiß nicht* ~ I wonder; ~ *daran tun zu* *inf* do right to *inf*; *es geschieht ihm* ~ it serves him right; *das kommt mir gerade* ~ that comes in handy; *man kann es nicht allen* ~ *machen* you can't please everybody; *verstehen Sie mich* ~ don't get me wrong.

Recht *n* (-[e]s; -e) **1.** *no pl* law, justice: ~ *und Ordnung* law and order; *nach deutschem* ~ under German law; *von* ~*s wegen* by law, *fig.* by rights; *gleiches* ~ *für alle* equal rights for all; ~ *sprechen* administer justice; *im* ~ *sein* be in the right; → *a.* **recht** 4. **2.** a) right, *a.* claim, title (*all:* **auf** *acc* to), b) privilege, c) power, authority: *mit* ~, *zu* ~ justly, rightly; *das* ~ *haben zu* *inf* have the right (*or* be entitled) to *inf*; *zu s-m* ~ *kommen* come into one's own; *er hat es mit vollem* ~ *getan* he had every right to do so; *alle* ~*e vorbehalten* all rights reserved.

'Rechte¹ *f* (-n; -n) **1.** right (hand *or* side): *zur* ~*n* on the right (hand); *zu s-r* ~*n* (*or* to) his right. **2.** *boxing:* right. **3.** *pol.* the Right.

'Rechte² *n* (-n) the right thing: *nicht das* ~, *nichts* ~*s* not the real thing; *nach dem* ~*n sehen* look after things.

'Rechteck *n* (-[e]s; -e) rectangle.

'rechteckig *adj* rectangular.

'rechtfertigen *v/t* (h) justify (*sich* o.s.).

'Rechtfertigung *f* (-; -en) justification: *zu m-r* ~ in my defen/ce (*Am.* -se).

'rechtgläubig *adj* orthodox.

'rechthaberisch [-ha:bərɪʃ] *adj* dogmatic, opinionated, pigheaded.

'rechtlich I *adj* legal, *a.* lawful. **II** *adv* legally: ~ *verpflichtet* bound by law.

'rechtlos *adj* without rights.

'rechtmäßig *adj* lawful, legitimate (*heir, claim, etc*), legal: *das steht ihm* ~ *zu* he is (legally) entitled to it.

'Rechtmäßigkeit *f* (-; *no pl*) lawfulness, legitimacy, legality.

rechts [rɛçts] *adv* on the right (hand side): *nach* ~ to the right; ~ *von ihm* on his right; ~ *abbiegen* turn off right; *sich* ~ *halten* keep to the right; *pol.* ~ *stehen* belong to the Right.

'**Rechtsabbieger** m mot. vehicle (pl traffic) turning right.

'**Rechts|anspruch** m legal claim (**auf** acc to). **~anwalt** m, **~anwältin** f lawyer, Br. a. solicitor, in court: counsel, barrister, Am. attorney(-at-law).

'**Rechtsaußen** m (-; -) outside right.

'**Rechts|behelf** m legal remedy. **~beistand** m legal adviser, in court: counsel. **~beratungsstelle** f legal aid office. **~beugung** f perversion of justice. **~bruch** m breach of law.

'**rechtschaffen** adj honest, upright.

'**Rechtschreibfehler** m spelling mistake. '**Rechtschreibung** f spelling.

'**Rechtsextre mist(in** f) m right-wing extremist.

'**rechtsfähig** adj having legal capacity.

'**Rechts|fall** m (law) case. **~frage** f question of law. **~geschäft** n legal transaction. 2**gültig** adj legal(ly valid): **~ machen** validate. **~gutachten** n legal opinion.

'**Rechtshänder** [-hɛndər] m (-s; -) right-hander: **~ sein** be right-handed.

'**rechtsherum** adv to the right.

'**Rechtskraft** f legal force, validity: **~ erlangen** become effective.

'**rechtskräftig** adj legal(ly binding), final (judg[e]ment), effective (law).

'**Rechtskurve** f right-hand bend.

'**Rechts|lage** f legal position. **~mittel** n legal remedy: **ein ~ einlegen** lodge an appeal. **~nachfolger(in** f) m successor in interest. **~norm** f legal norm.

'**rechtsorien tiert** adj pol. right-wing.

'**Rechtspar tei** f right-wing party.

'**Rechtspflege** f (-; no pl) administration of justice. '**Rechtsprechung** f (-; -en) jurisdiction, administration of justice.

'**Rechts|radi kale** m, f right-wing extremist. **~ruck** m pol. swing to the right.

'**Rechtsschutz** m legal protection. **~versicherung** f legal costs insurance.

'**Rechts|spruch** m legal decision, in civil matters: judg(e)ment, in criminal cases: sentence. **~staat** m constitutional state. 2**staatlich** adj constitutional. **~staatlichkeit** f (-; no pl) rule of law.

'**Rechtssteuerung** f right-hand drive.

'**Rechts|streit** m lawsuit, action. **~titel** m legal title. 2**unfähig** adj (legally) disabled. 2**unwirksam** adj ineffective. 2**verbindlich** adj (legally) binding (**für**

on). **~verfahren** n **1.** legal procedure. **2.** (legal) proceedings.

'**Rechtsverkehr** m right-hand traffic: **in ... ist ~** in ... they drive on the right.

'**Rechts|verletzung** f infringement. **~vertreter** m legal representative, (authorized) agent. **~weg** m course of law: **auf dem ~** by legal action; **den ~ beschreiten** go to law. 2**widrig** adj illegal. **~widrigkeit** f (-; -en) **1.** no pl illegality. **2.** unlawful act. **~wissenschaft** f (-; no pl) jurisprudence, law.

'**rechtwink(e)lig** adj right-angled, rectangular.

'**rechtzeitig I** adj punctual. **II** adv a) in time (**zu** for), b) on time: **gerade** (or **genau**) **~** in the nick of time.

Reck [rɛk] n (-[e]s; -e) horizontal bar.

recken ['rɛkən] v/t (h) stretch: **den Hals ~** crane one's neck.

'**Reckturnen** n bar exercises.

Redakteur [redak'tøːr] m (-s; -e) editor. **Redak teurin** f (-; -nen) (woman) editor. **Redaktion** [-'tsĭoːn] f (-; -en) **1.** no pl editing. **2.** a) editorial staff, b) editorial office. **redaktionell** [-tsĭo'nɛl] adj editorial: **~ bearbeiten** edit.

Rede ['reːdə] f (-; -en) **1.** speech, address: **e-e ~ halten** make a speech; F **große ~n schwingen** talk big. **2.** a) talk(ing), speech (a. ling.), b) conversation, talk, c) words, language: **direkte** (**indirekte**) **~** direct (reported or indirect) speech; **es geht die ~, daß** it is rumo(u)red (that); **die ~ kam auf** (acc) the conversation (or talk) turned to; (**j-m**) **~** (**und Antwort**) **stehen** account (to s.o.) (**über** acc for); **j-n zur ~ stellen** take s.o. to task (**wegen** gen for); **davon kann k-e ~ sein!** that's out of the question!; (**aber**) **k-e ~!** by no means!; **es ist nicht der ~ wert** a) it is not worth mentioning, b) don't mention it!, c) never mind!; **der langen ~ kurzer Sinn** to cut a long story short; → **verschlagen¹** 4.

'**Rede|freiheit** f (-; no pl) freedom of speech. **~gabe** f (-; no pl) eloquence.

'**redegewandt** adj eloquent.

'**Redekunst** f rhetoric.

reden ['reːdən] (h) **I** v/t, v/i (**mit** to, **über** acc about, of) speak, talk: **über Politik ~** talk politics; **von sich ~ machen** cause a stir; **j-m ins Gewissen ~** appeal to s.o.'s conscience; **ich habe mit dir zu**

~ I'd like a word with you; *laß uns vernünftig darüber ~!* let's talk sense!; *sie läßt nicht mit sich ~* she won't listen to reason; *nicht zu ~ von ...* not to mention ...; *~ wir von et. anderem!* let's change the subject!; *du hast gut ~!* you can talk!; *darüber läßt sich ~!* that's a possibility! II *sich heiser (in Wut)* ~ talk o.s. hoarse (into a rage).
'**Reden** *n* (-s) talking: *j-n zum ~ bringen* make s.o. talk.
'**Redensart** *f* a) phrase, b) saying, c) *pl* empty talk: *das ist nur so e-e ~* it's just a way of speaking.
'**Rede|schwall** *m* flood of words. **~verbot** *n* ban on speaking: *j-m ~ erteilen* ban s.o. from speaking. **~weise** *f s-e etc* ~ the way he *etc* talks. **~wendung** *f* figure of speech, idiom.
redigieren [redi'gi:rən] *v/t* (h) edit.
redlich ['re:tlɪç] *adj* honest, upright: *sich ~(e) Mühe geben* do one's best.
'**Redlichkeit** *f* (-; *no pl*) honesty, probity.
Redner ['re:dnər] *m* (-s; -) speaker. **~bühne** *f* rostrum, (speaker's) platform. **~pult** *n* lectern.
'**redselig** *adj* talkative.
'**Redseligkeit** *f* (-; *no pl*) talkativeness.
reduzieren [redu'tsi:rən] *v/t* (h) reduce (*auf acc* to): *sich ~* be reduced.
Reede ['re:də] *f* (-; -n) ⚓ roadstead, road(s): *das Schiff liegt auf der ~* the ship is (lying) in the roads. **Reeder** ['re:dər] *m* (-s; -) shipowner. **Reede'rei** *f* (-; -en) shipping company.
reell [re'ɛl] *adj* 1. real (*chance etc*). 2. honest, decent, ✝ good, fair (*price etc*).
Reep [re:p] *n* (-[e]s; -e) ⚓ rope.
Reetdach ['re:t-] *n* thatched roof.
Referat [refe'ra:t] *n* (-[e]s; -e) 1. report, *a.* lecture, *ped., univ.* (seminar) paper: *ein ~ halten → referieren.* 2. department.
Referendar [referɛn'da:r] *m* (-s; -e), **Referen'darin** *f* (-; -nen) → *Gerichts-, Studienreferendar(in).*
Referendum [refe'rɛndʊm] *n* (-s; -den, -da) referendum.
Referent [refe'rɛnt] *m* (-en; -en) 1. official in charge: *er ist persönlicher Referent* he is personal assistant (*gen* to). 2. speaker, ⚖, *parl.* referee.
Referenz [refe'rɛnts] *f* (-; -en) reference.
referieren [refe'ri:rən] *v/t, v/i* (h) (*über*

acc on) a) report, b) (give a) lecture, *univ.* give a paper.
reffen ['rɛfən] *v/t* (h) ⚓ reef.
reflektieren [reflɛk'ti:rən] (h) I *v/t phys.* reflect. II *v/i* F ~ *auf* (*acc*) have one's eye on. **Reflektor** [re'flɛktər] *m* (-s; -en [-'to:rən]) reflector.
Reflex [re'flɛks] *m* (-es; -e) reflex.
Re'flexbewegung *f* reflex action.
Reflexion [reflɛ'ksi̯o:n] *f* (-; -en) reflection.
reflexiv [reflɛ'ksi:f] *adj ling.* reflexive.
Refle'xivpro,nomen *n* reflexive pronoun.
Reform [re'fɔrm] *f* (-; -en) reform.
Reformation [refɔrma'tsi̯o:n] *f* (-; -en) reformation. **Reformator** [refɔr'ma:-tər] *m* (-s; -en [-ma'to:rən]) reformer.
re'formbedürftig *adj* in need of reform.
Re'formhaus *n* health food shop.
reformieren [refɔr'mi:rən] *v/t* (h) reform. **Refor'mierte** *m, f* (-n; -n) member of the Reformed Church.
Re'formkost *f* health food(s).
Refrain [rə'frɛ̃:] *m* (-s; -s) refrain.
Regal [re'ga:l] *n* (-s; -e) shelves. **Re'galwand** *f* wall lined with shelve units.
Regatta [re'gata] *f* (-; -ten) regatta.
rege ['re:gə] *adj* lively, *a.* active, vivid (*imagination*), busy (*traffic etc*): *~n Anteil nehmen an* (*dat*) show an active interest in; *~ Nachfrage* keen demand.
Regel ['re:gəl] *f* (-; -n) 1. rule: *in der ~* as a rule; *zur ~ werden* become a rule (*or* habit); *es sich zur ~ machen zu inf* make it a rule to *inf*; *nach allen ~n der Kunst* in superior style. 2. ⚕ period.
'**regelbar** *adj* adjustable.
'**Regelblutung** *f* ⚕ menstruation.
'**Regelfall** *m im ~* as a rule.
'**regellos** *adj* 1. irregular. 2. disorderly.
'**Regellosigkeit** *f* (-; *no pl*) irregularity.
'**regelmäßig** *adj* a) regular, *a.* periodical, b) regulated, orderly.
'**Regelmäßigkeit** *f* (-; *no pl*) regularity.
regeln ['re:gəln] *v/t* (h) regulate, ⚙ *a.* adjust, *a.* direct (*traffic*), settle (*matter etc*): *das wird sich (schon) alles ~* that will sort itself out.
'**regelrecht I** *adj* 1. proper. 2. F regular, real. II *adv* 3. properly. 4. F downright.
'**Regelstudienzeit** *f* time limit for a course of study.
'**Regelung** *f* (-; -en) 1. regulation, ⚙ *a.*

adjustment, settlement. **2.** provision, rule. **'Regelungstechnik** f control engineering.

'Regelverstoß m sports: foul.

'regelwidrig adj irregular, sports: against the rules, foul. **'Regelwidrigkeit** f (-; -en) irregularity, sports: foul.

regen ['re:gən] v/t (a. **sich ~**) (h) move, stir; fig. ~ feelings etc: stir, arise.

'Regen m (-s; -) rain, fig. a. shower: **saurer ~** acid rain; **ich bin in den ~ gekommen** I was caught in the rain; F **vom ~ in die Traufe kommen** jump out of the frying-pan into the fire; F fig. **ein warmer ~** a windfall.

'regenarm adj with low rainfall.

'Regenbogen m rainbow. **~farben** pl colo(u)rs of the rainbow. **~haut** f anat. iris. **~presse** f rainbow press.

Regeneration [regenera'tsio:n] f (-; -en) regeneration. **Regenerati'onsfähigkeit** f regenerative power.

regenerieren [regene'ri:rən] v/i (a. **sich ~**) (h) regenerate.

'Regen|fälle pl rain(fall). **~guß** m downpour. **~haut** f plastic mac. **~mantel** m raincoat. **2reich** adj rainy. **~rinne** f gutter, mot. roof rail. **~schauer** m shower. **~schirm** m umbrella.

Regent [re'gɛnt] m (-en; -en) regent.

'Regen|tag m rainy day. **~tonne** f water butt. **~tropfen** m raindrop. **~wald** m rain forest. **~wasser** n rainwater. **~wetter** n rainy weather. **~wolke** f raincloud. **~wurm** m earthworm. **~zeit** f rainy season, the rains.

Regie [re'ʒi:] f (-; no pl) **1.** thea. etc direction: **unter der ~ von** a. directed by; **~ führen (bei)** direct (s.th.). **2.** a) management, b) administration: fig. **in eigener ~** on one's own. **~anweisung** f stage direction. **~assi,stent** m assistant director. **~fehler** m humor. slip-up. **~raum** m TV central control room.

regieren [re'gi:rən] (h) **I** v/t a) govern (a. ling.), rule, b) manage, control. **II** v/i rule, monarch: a. reign (a. fig.).

Re'gierung f (-; -en) **1.** reign: **unter der ~ von** (or gen) under the reign of (or der ~ sein be in power; **an die ~ kommen** take over, come into power. **2.** government.

Re'gierungs|beamte m government official. **~bezirk** m administration dis-

trict. **~bildung** f formation of the government. **~chef** m head of government. **~erklärung** f policy statement. **2fähig** adj in a position to govern the country: **~e Mehrheit** etc working majority etc. **~par,tei** f ruling party. **~sitz** m seat of government. **~sprecher** m government spokesman. **~umbildung** f (government) reshuffle. **~vorlage** f government bill. **~wechsel** m change of government. **~zeit** f a) reign, b) term of office.

Regime [re'ʒi:m] n (-s; - [-mə]) regime.

Re'gimekritiker m pol. dissident.

Regiment [regi'mɛnt] n (-[e]s) **1.** (-e) (a. **das ~ führen**) rule. **2.** (-er) ✕ regiment.

Region [re'gio:n] f (-; -en) region.

regional [regio'na:l] adj, **Regio'nal...** regional.

Regisseur [reʒɪ'sø:r] m (-s; -e), **Regis'seurin** f (-; -nen) thea., film: director, TV producer.

Register [re'gɪstər] n (-s; -) register (a. ♪), in book: index: F **alle ~ ziehen** pull all the stops.

Registratur [regɪstra'tu:r] f (-; -en) registry. **registrieren** [regɪs'tri:rən] v/t (h) register (a. fig.), record (a. ⊕), fig. note.

Regi'strierkasse f cash register.

Reglement [reglə'mã:] n (-s; -s) regulation(s).

Regler ['re:glər] m (-s; -) ⊕ controller.

'reglos adj motionless.

regnen ['re:gnən] v/impers (h) rain: **es regnete in Strömen** it was pouring (with rain); fig. **es regnete Anfragen** there was a flood of inquiries.

'regnerisch adj rainy.

Regreß [re'grɛs] m (-sses; -sse) ✝, ⚖ recourse.

re'greßpflichtig adj liable to recourse.

'regsam adj active.

'Regsamkeit f (-; no pl) activity.

regulär [regu'lɛ:r] adj regular.

regu'lierbar adj ⊕ adjustable.

regulieren [regu'li:rən] v/t (h) **1.** a) regulate, b) adjust. **2.** settle (account etc).

Regung ['re:gʊŋ] f (-; -en) a) movement, b) emotion, c) impulse.

'regungslos adj motionless.

Reh [re:] n (-[e]s; -e) **1.** zo. (roe) deer. **2.** gastr. venison.

Rehabilitation [rehabilita'tsio:n] f (-; -en) rehabilitation.

Rehabilitati'onszentrum n ✚ rehabilitation cent/re (*Am.* -er).
rehabilitieren [rehabili'tiːrən] v/t (h) rehabilitate. **Rehabili'tierung** f (-; -en) rehabilitation.
'Reh|bock m roebuck. **~braten** m roast venison. **~geiß** f doe. **~keule** f gastr. leg of venison. **~kitz** n fawn. **~rücken** m gastr. saddle of venison.
Reibach ['raibax] m (-s; *no pl*) F **e-n ~ machen** make one's pile.
'Reibe f (-; -n), **'Reibeisen** n grater.
reiben ['raibən] (rieb, gerieben, h) I v/t **1.** rub: **sich die Hände ~** rub one's hands; → **Nase. 2.** grate. II v/i **3.** chafe.
Reibe'reien pl (constant) friction.
'Reibfläche f striking surface.
'Reibung f (-; -en) a. fig. friction.
'reibungslos adj a. fig. smooth.
'Reibungspunkt m fig. cause of friction.
'Reibungsverlust m ☼ friction(al) loss.
'Reibungswärme f ☼ frictional heat.
reich [raiç] I adj rich (**an** dat in), a. wealthy, a. abundant, copious, a. sumptuous: **e-e ~e Auswahl** a wide selection (**an** dat, **von** of). II adv richly, copiously: **~ beschenkt** loaded with gifts.
Reich n (-[e]s; -e) empire, kingdom (a. eccl. or fig.), rhet. or fig. realm: hist. **das Dritte ~** the Third Reich; **das ~ der Tiere** animal kingdom.
'reichen ['raiçən] (h) I v/t **1.** j-m **et. ~** hand (or pass) s.o. s.th.: **sich die Hände ~** shake hands. **2.** offer, serve. II v/i **3.** → **bis** (or **an** acc) reach to, extend to, come up (or go down) to; **soweit das Auge reicht** as far as the eye can see. **4.** last (out), do, be enough: **das reicht!** that will do!; **das Brot reicht nicht** there isn't enough bread; **damit ~ wir bis Mai** it will last us till May; **es reicht für alle** there is enough to go round; F **mir reicht's!** I've had enough!
'reichhaltig adj extensive, large: **~e Auswahl** wide selection; **~es Programm** varied program(me Br.).
'reichlich I adj ample, abundant, plentiful, plenty of (*time, food*, etc), generous (*pay* etc). II adv F rather, pretty: **~ versehen mit** have plenty of.
'Reichtum m (-s; **~er**) (**an** dat of) riches, a. fig. wealth, abundance.
'Reichweite f reach, ✈, ✗ range: **in** (**außer**) **~** within (out of) reach.

reif [raif] adj ripe, a. fig. mature: **~ werden** → **reifen**.
Reif¹ m (-[e]s; *no pl*) hoarfrost.
Reif² m (-[e]s; -e) ring, bracelet, circlet.
Reife ['raifə] f (-; *no pl*) **1.** ripeness, esp. fig. maturity. **2. mittlere ~** intermediate high school certificate, GCE O-levels.
reifen ['raifən] v/i (sn) ripen, mature (a. fig.): → **lassen** mature.
'Reifen m (-s; -) **1.** mot. etc tyre, Am. tire: **die ~ wechseln** change tyres. **2.** hoop. **~panne** f puncture, blowout, Am. flat. **~pro,fil** n tyre (Am. tire) engraving. **~wechsel** m tyre (Am. tire) change.
'Reifeprüfung f → **Abitur.**
'Reifglätte f mot. slippery frost.
'reiflich I adj **nach ~er Überlegung** after careful consideration. II adv **et. ~ überlegen** consider s.th. carefully.
Reigen ['raigən] m (-s; -) round dance: **den ~ eröffnen** a. fig. lead off.
Reihe ['raiə] f (-; -n) a) row, b) line, c) row (of seats), d) series, number, e) succession: **geometrische ~** geometric progression; **sich in e-r ~ aufstellen** line up; F **e-e ganze ~ von** a whole string of; **aus den ~n** (gen) from among; **Kritiker aus den eigenen ~n** critics from among the own ranks; (**immer**) **der ~ nach** in turn, one after the other; **außer der ~** out of turn; **ich bin an der ~** it's my turn; **warten, bis man an die ~ kommt** wait one's turn; F fig. **aus der ~ sein** be out of sorts; **aus der ~ tanzen** step out of line; **wieder in die ~ bringen** straighten s.o., s.th. out.
'Reihen|folge f order, sequence: **in zeitlicher ~** in chronological order. **~haus** n terrace (Am. row) house. **~untersuchung** f ✚ mass screening.
'reihenweise adv **1.** in rows. **2.** F fig. by the dozen.
Reiher ['raiər] m (-s; -) zo. heron.
Reim [raim] m (-[e]s; -e) rhyme.
reimen ['raimən] v/t, v/i (a. **sich ~**) (h) rhyme (**auf** acc with).
rein [rain] I adj **1.** pure (a. biol., ♪, a. fig.), clean, clear (a. skin, conscience, etc), net, clear (profit), fig. mere, sheer: **~e Wolle** pure wool; **e-e ~e Formalität** a mere formality; **~er Wahnsinn** sheer madness; **die ~e Wahrheit** the (plain) truth; **durch ~en Zufall** by pure accident; **et. ins ~e bringen** sort s.th. out;

mit j-m ins ~e kommen get things straightened out with s.o.; *ins ~e schreiben* make a fair copy of; → *Luft* 1, *Tisch, Wein* 2 etc. **II** adv **2.** purely: *aus ~ persönlichen Gründen* for purely personal reasons; → *zufällig*. **3.** F absolutely.

rein(...) F → **herein(...), hinein(...)**.

Reineclaude [rɛːnəˈkloːdə] f (-; -n) ⚹ greengage.

'**Reinertrag** m net proceeds.

'**Reinfall** m F a) flop, b) letdown, frost.

'**reinfallen** F → **hereinfallen** 2.

'**Reingewicht** n net weight.

'**Reingewinn** m net (or clear) profit.

'**reinhängen** (sep, -ge-, h) F fig. **I** v/t *j-n ~* set s.o. up, frame s.o. **II** sich (voll) ~ go flat out.

'**reinhauen** v/i (irr, sep, -ge-, h, → hauen) F dig in, tuck in.

Reinheit f (-; no pl) purity (a. fig.), cleanness.

reinigen [ˈraɪnɪɡən] v/t (h) clean, dry-clean (clothes), a. ⚹ cleanse (von of), purify (a. fig.), metall. refine.

Reinigung f (-; -en) **1.** cleaning (etc). **2.** dry cleaners: *et. in die ~ geben* send s.th. to the cleaners.

'**Reinigungs|milch** f cosmetics: cleansing milk. **~mittel** n detergent.

'**Reinkul,tur** f F *Kitsch in ~* pure unadulterated trash.

'**reinlegen** F → **hereinlegen**.

'**reinlich** adj clean, person: cleanly, a. neat, tidy. '**Reinlichkeit** f (-; no pl) cleanliness, neatness, tidiness.

'**reinrassig** adj pedigree (dog etc), thoroughbred (horse).

'**Reinschrift** f fair copy.

'**reinseiden** adj (of) pure silk.

'**reinwaschen** v/t (irr, sep, -ge-, h, → waschen) fig. clear (von of).

Reis¹ [raɪs] n (-es; -er) ⚹ **1.** twig. **2.** scion.

Reis² m (-es; no pl) rice.

'**Reisauflauf** m rice pudding.

Reise [ˈraɪzə] f (-; -n) journey, travel, trip, a. tour, ✈, ⚓ voyage: *gute ~!* have a nice trip!, bon voyage!; *e-e ~ mit dem Auto* a journey by car; *ich plane e-e ~ durch Amerika* I'm planning to travel through America; *auf ~n sein* be travel(l)ing; → *antreten* 1.

'**Reise|andenken** n souvenir. **~apo,theke** f first-aid kit. **~bekanntschaft** f travel(l)ing acquaintance. **~bericht** m travelog(ue Br.). **~beschreibung** f book of travels. **~bü,ro** n travel agency. **~bus** m coach. **~diploma,tie** f pol. shuttle-diplomacy. **⚹fertig** adj ready to start. **~führer** m **1.** guide. **2.** guide(-book). **~gefährte** m travel companion. **~geschwindigkeit** f cruising speed. **~gesellschaft** f **1.** tourist party. **2.** → *Reiseveranstalter*.

'**Reisekosten** pl travel(l)ing expenses. **~zuschuß** m travel(l)ing allowance.

'**Reiseland** n tourist country.

'**Reiseleiter(in** f) m courier.

'**reiselustig** adj fond of travel(l)ing.

'**Reisemo,bil** n (-[e]s; -e) camper, Am. mobile home.

reisen [ˈraɪzən] v/i (sn) (nach to) travel, go, make a trip: *zu s-n Verwandten ~* go to visit one's relatives; *er ist weit gereist* he has travel(l)ed a lot; *ins Ausland ~* go abroad; F fig. *~ auf* (acc) coast on. '**Reisen** n (-s) travel, travel(l)ing. '**Reisende** m, f (-n; -n) **1.** a) travel(l)er, b) tourist, c) passenger. **2.** → *Handlungsreisende*.

'**Reise|neces,saire** n sponge bag. **~paß** m passport. **~pro,spekt** m travel brochure. **~provi,ant** m provisions for the journey. **~route** f route, itinerary. **~scheck** m traveller's cheque, Am. traveler's check. **~schreibma,schine** f portable typewriter. **~tasche** f travel(l)ing (or overnight) bag, holdall. **~unterlagen** pl travel documents. **~veranstalter** m tour operator. **~verkehr** m holiday traffic. **~wecker** m travel(l)ing (alarm) clock. **~zeit** f holiday season. **~ziel** n destination.

'**Reißaus:** *~ nehmen* take to one's heels

'**Reißbrett** n drawing-board.

reißen [ˈraɪsən] (riß, gerissen) **I** v/t (h) **1.** tear (in Stücke to pieces), a. snatch (off), pull (off, out, etc): *mit sich ~* drag, flood: sweep; *an sich ~* snatch; *die Macht an sich ~* seize power; *sich ~* tear o.s. (an dat on); F fig. sich ~ um fight over; F *ich reiße mich nicht darum* I can do without; → *Witz* 1. **2.** sports: a) knock down (the bar), b) snatch (the weight). **3.** zo. kill. **II** v/i **4.** (sn) tear, burst, split, ⚹ rupture, rope etc: break, snap; → *Geduld*. **5.** (h) ~ an (dat) tear at. **6.** (h) sports: knock down the bar. '**Reißen** n (-s) F ✷ rheumatism. '**reißend** adj **1.** rapid, torrential (river etc): → **Absatz** 3. **2.** rapacious (animal). **3.** searing (pain).

'**Reißer** m (-s; -) F **1.** thriller. **2.** hit. '**reißerisch** adj sensational, loud: ~e **Werbung** a. F ballyhoo.

'**Reiß|feder** f drawing-pen. ~**leine** f rip cord. ~**nagel** m drawing-pin, Am. thumbtack. ~**verschluß** m zip(per): **den ~ e-r Jacke zumachen (aufmachen)** zip up (unzip) a jacket. ~**zahn** m zo. fang, canine tooth. ~**zwecke** f drawing-pin, Am. thumbtack.

reiten ['raɪtən] v/i (ritt, geritten, sn) ride (a. v/t), go on horseback. '**Reiten** n (-s) riding. '**Reiter** m (-s; -) **1.** rider, horseman. **2.** Reite'rei f (-; -en) cavalry.

'**Reiterin** f (-; -nen) rider, horsewoman.

'**Reit|gerte** f riding crop. ~**hose** f (riding) breeches. ~**peitsche** f riding crop. ~**pferd** n saddle horse. ~**schule** f riding school. ~**sport** m riding. ~**stiefel** pl riding boots. ~**tur,nier** n horse show. ~**weg** m bridle path.

Reiz [raɪts] m (-es; -e) **1.** physiol., psych. or fig. stimulus, ✷ irritation. **2.** a) charm, b) appeal, attraction, c) lure, d) thrill: **der ~ des Neuen** the novelty; **s-n ~ (für j-n) verlieren** pall (on s.o.); ~**e spielen lassen** display one's charms; **das hat k-n ~ für mich** that does not appeal to me.

'**reizbar** adj irritable, touchy. '**Reizbarkeit** f (-; no pl) irritability.

reizen ['raɪtsən] (h) **I** v/t **1.** irritate (a. ✷), a. annoy, provoke. **2.** a) stimulate, b) (a)rouse (curiosity etc). **3.** a) tempt, b) appeal to: **es reizte ihn zu** inf he was tempted to inf; **es würde mich ~ zu** inf I wouldn't mind ger; **das reizt mich gar nicht** that doesn't appeal to me at all. **4.** cards: bid. '**reizend** adj charming, delightful, a. lovely, sweet.

'**Reizhusten** m ✷ dry cough.

'**reizlos** adj **1.** a) unattractive, a. plain, b) boring. **2.** ✷ bland (food).

'**Reizschwelle** f stimulus threshold.

'**Reizüberflutung** f stimulus satiation.

'**Reizung** f (-; -en) a. ✷ irritation, stimulation.

'**reizvoll** adj charming, attractive, fascinating, challenging (task etc).

'**Reizwäsche** f sexy underwear.

'**Reizwort** n emotive word.

rekapitulieren [rekapitu'li:rən] v/t (h) recapitulate.

rekeln ['rɛ:kəln] **sich ~** (h) loll (about).

Reklamation [reklama'tsi̯o:n] f (-; -en) complaint.

Reklame [re'kla:mə] f (-; -n) a) advertising, b) advertisement, F ad: **für et. ~ machen** advertise (F plug) s.th. ~**rummel** m F contp. ballyhoo. ~**tafel** f hoarding, esp. Am. billboard.

reklamieren [rekla'mi:rən] (h) **I** v/i complain (**wegen** about), esp. sports: protest (**gegen** against). **II** v/t complain about.

rekonstruieren [rekonstru'i:rən] v/t (h) reconstruct.

Rekonvaleszent [rekɔnvalɛs'tsɛnt] m (-en; -en) convalescent.

Rekonvaleszenz [rekɔnvalɛs'tsɛnts] f (-; no pl) convalescence.

Rekord [re'kɔrt] m (-[e]s; -e) (**e-n ~ aufstellen** set up a) record. ~**besuch** m record attendance. ~**ernte** f bumper crop. ~**halter(in** f) m, ~**inhaber(in** f) m record holder. ~**versuch** m attempt on the record. ~**zeit** f record time.

Rekrut [re'kru:t] m (-en; -en), **rekrutieren** [rekru'ti:rən] v/t (h) recruit.

rektal [rɛk'ta:l] adj ✷ rectal.

Rektion [rɛk'tsi̯o:n] f (-; -en) ling. government: **die ~ e-s Verbs** the case governed by a verb.

Rektor ['rɛktɔr] m (-s; -en [-'to:rən]) **1.** ped. headmaster, principal. **2.** univ. rector. **Rektorat** [rɛkto'ra:t] n (-[e]s; -e) **1.** rectorship, rectorate. **2.** headmaster's (or principal's, univ. rector's) office.

Rektorin [rɛk'to:rɪn] f (-; -nen) ped. headmistress, principal.

Relais [rə'lɛ:] n (-; - [rə'lɛ:s]) ⚡ relay.

Relation [rela'tsi̯o:n] f (-; -en) relation(ship): **in k-r ~ stehen zu** be out of all proportion to.

relativ [rela'ti:f] adj relative(ly adv), adv a. comparatively. **Relativität** [relativi'tɛ:t] f (-; no pl) relativity. **Relativi-'tätstheo,rie** f theory of relativity.

Rela'tivsatz m ling. relative clause.

relevant [rele'vant] adj relevant (**für** to).

Relief [re'li̯ɛf] n (-s; -s, -e) relief.

Religion [reli'gi̯o:n] f (-; -en) **1.** religion. **2.** no pl ped. religious instruction.

Religi'ons... → **Glaubens... ~freiheit** f

freedom of worship. **~gemeinschaft** f a) confession, b) religious community.
religi'onslos adj irreligious.
Religi'ons|unterricht m → **Religion** 2. **~zugehörigkeit** f religious affiliation.
religiös [reli'giø:s] adj religious.
Relikt [re'lıkt] n (-[e]s; -e) **1.** relic. **2.** biol. relict.
Reling ['re:lıŋ] f (-; -s) ⚓ rail.
Reliquie [re'li:kviə] f (-; -n) relic.
Re'liquienschrein m reliquary.
Remis [rə'mi:] n (-; - [rə'mi:s]) draw.
Remittenden [remi'tɛndən] pl returns.
Remoulade [remu'la:də] f (-; -n) gastr. tartar sauce.
rempeln ['rɛmpəln] v/t (h) F jostle, push.
Ren [rɛn, re:n] n (-s; -s) zo. reindeer.
Renaissance [rənɛ'sã:s] f (-; -n) a) no pl hist. Renaissance, b) fig. renaissance.
Rendezvous [rãde'vu:] n (-; - [-'vu:s]) rendezvous (a. space travel), date.
Rendite [rɛn'di:tə] f (-; -n) 💲 (net) yield.
'Rennbahn f a) racecourse, racetrack (a. mot.), b) (cycling) track.
'Rennboot n speedboat.
rennen ['rɛnən] (rannte, gerannt) **I** v/i (sn) a) run, rush, dash, b) race: **~ gegen** run into; **schneller ~ als** outrun; **sie rannten um die Wette** they raced each other; → **Verderben**. **II** v/t (h) F **j-m ein Messer** etc **in die Brust ~** run a knife etc into s.o.'s chest; **j-n über den Haufen ~** knock s.o. down. **'Rennen** n (-s; -) a) running (etc), b) race, c) heat: **totes ~** dead heat; **das ~ machen** come in first, win, fig. come out on top.
'Renner m (-s; -) F fig. (great) hit.
'Renn|fahrer m a) racing driver, b) racing cyclist. **~läufer** m ski racer. **~pferd** n racehorse. **~rad** n racing cycle. **~schi** m racing ski. **~schuhe** pl spikes. **~sport** m racing. **~stall** m **1.** (racing) stable. **2.** F mot. racing team. **~strecke** f mot. racing course. **~wagen** m racing car.
renommiert [reno'mi:rt] adj (wegen for) famous, noted.
renovieren [reno'vi:rən] v/t (h) a) renovate (building), b) redecorate (room).
Reno'vierung f (-; -en) a) renovation, b) redecoration.
rentabel [rɛn'ta:bəl] adj profitable.
Rentabilität [rɛntabili'tɛ:t] f (-; no pl) profitability.
Rente ['rɛntə] f (-; -n) **1.** pension: F **auf**

(or in) ~ gehen retire; **auf (or in) ~ sein** be retired; → **dynamisch. 2.** annuity.
'Renten|alter n retirement age. **~anpassung** f index-linked adjustment of pensions. **~empfänger(in** f) m → **Rentner(in). ~markt** m 💲 bond market **~pa,piere** pl fixed interest bonds. **~versicherung** f pension scheme.
rentieren [rɛn'ti:rən] **sich ~** (h) be profitable, a. pay, be worthwhile.
Rentner ['rɛntnər] m (-s; -), **'Rentnerin** (-; -nen) pensioner.
reorgani'sieren v/t (h) reorganize.
reparabel [repa'ra:bəl] adj repairable.
Reparation [repara'tsio:n] f (-; -en) reparation.
Reparatur [repara'tu:r] f (-; -en) repair(s): **in ~** being repaired; **zur ~ geben** have s.th. repaired. **2bedürftig** ad, in need of repair. **~kosten** pl cost o repairs. **~werkstatt** f mot. garage.
reparieren [repa'ri:rən] v/t (h) repair, F fix: **nicht mehr zu ~** beyond repair.
repatriieren [repatri'i:rən] v/t (h) repatriate.
Repertoire [repɛr'tŏa:r] n (-s; -s) a. fig repertoire.
Reportage [repɔr'ta:ʒə] f (-; -n) report commentary: **s-e ~ über** (acc) a. his coverage of. **Reporter** [re'pɔrtər] m (-s-), **Re'porterin** f (-; -nen) reporter.
Repräsentant [reprɛzɛn'tant] m (-en -en) representative.
Repräsen'tantenhaus n parl. Am House of Representatives.
Repräsentation [reprɛzɛnta'tsio:n] f (-no pl) representation: **der ~ dienen** be a status symbol. **repräsentativ** [reprɛ zɛnta'ti:f] adj **1.** representative (**für** of) **2.** impressive. **repräsentieren** [reprɛ zɛn'ti:rən] v/t (h) represent.
Repressalie [reprɛ'sa:liə] f (-; -n reprisal.
repressiv [reprɛ'si:f] adj repressive.
reprivati'sieren v/t (h) 💲 denationalize
Reproduktion [reprodʊk'tsio:n] f (-en) reproduction, a. print. reprodu zieren [-du'tsi:rən] v/t (h) reproduce.
Reptil [rɛp'ti:l] n (-[e]s; -ien) reptile.
Republik [repu'bli:k] f (-; -en) republic.
Republikaner [republi'ka:nər] m (-s; - republi'kanisch** [-nɪʃ] adj republican pol. Am. Republican.
Requiem ['re:kviɛm] n (-s; -s) requiem

requirieren [rekvi'ri:rən] v/t (h) ✗ requisition.

Requisiten [rekvi'zi:tən] pl thea. etc properties, F props.

Reservat [rezɛr'va:t] n (-[e]s; -e) **1.** (nature) reserve. **2.** reservation.

Reserve [re'zɛrvə] f (-; -n) **1.** reserve (a. ✗ or fig.): ↑ stille ~n hidden reserves; F j-n aus der ~ (heraus)locken bring s.o. out of his shell. **2.** sports: reserve team. ~bank f (-; ~e) sports: (substitutes') bench. ~ka,nister m spare can. ~rad n mot. spare wheel. ~spieler(in f) m sports: substitute.

reservieren [rezɛr'vi:rən] v/t (h) (a. ~ lassen) reserve, a. book. **reser'viert** adj a. fig. reserved: **sich ~ verhalten** keep one's distance.

Reservist [rezɛr'vɪst] m (-en; -en) ✗ reservist.

Reservoir [rezɛr'vŏa:r] n (-s; -e) a. fig. reservoir.

Residenz [rezi'dɛnts] f (-; -en) residence.

residieren [rezi'di:rən] v/i (h) reside.

Resignation [rezɪgna'tsĭo:n] f (-; no pl) resignation.

resignieren [rezɪ'gni:rən] v/i (h) resign, give up. **resi'gniert** adj resigned.

resistent [rezɪs'tɛnt] adj biol., ✿ resistent (gegen) to.

resolut [rezo'lu:t] adj resolute, determined, forceful.

Resolution [rezolu'tsĭo:n] f (-; -en) resolution.

Resonanz [rezo'nants] f (-; -en) a. fig. resonance.

resorbieren [rezɔr'bi:rən] v/t (h) resorb.

Resorption [rezɔrp'tsĭo:n] f (-; -en) resorption.

resoziali,sieren v/t (h) rehabilitate.

Resoziali'sierung f (-; -en) rehabilitation.

Respekt [re'spɛkt] m (-[e]s; no pl) respect (vor for): **sich ~ verschaffen** make o.s. respected; **bei allem ~** with all due respect. **respektabel** [respɛk'ta:bəl] adj respectable. **respektieren** [respɛk'ti:rən] v/t (h) respect. **re'spektlos** adj irreverent. **re'spektvoll** adj respectful.

Ressentiment [resãti'mã:] n (-s; -s) resentment.

Ressort [re'so:r] n (-s; -s) (das fällt nicht in mein ~ that is not my) department.

Rest [rɛst] m (-[e]s; -e) rest, a. ✿ remain-

der, a. textil. remnant, 🐾, ⚗, ⊙ residue, gastr. leftovers, ↑ balance, fig. vestige, pl remains: **der letzte ~** the last bit(s); **sterbliche ~e** mortal remains; F **das gab ihm den ~** that finished him (off). **~alkohol** m residual alcohol.

Restaurant [rɛsto'rã:] n (-s; -s) restaurant.

Restaurator [rɛstaʊ'ra:tɔr] m (-s; -en [-ra'to:rən] restorer. **restaurieren** [-'ri:rən] v/t (h) restore.

'**Restbestand** m ↑ remaining stock.

'**Restbetrag** m ↑ balance.

'**restlich** adj remaining, a. 🐾, ⚗, ⅋ residual: **die ~e Zeit** a. the rest of his etc time. '**restlos I** adj complete, total. **II** adv completely, perfectly.

'**Restrisiko** n residual risk.

Resultat [rezʊl'ta:t] n (-[e]s; -e) result, sports: score, results. **resultieren** [rezʊl'ti:rən] v/i (h) result (aus from).

Resümee [rezy'me:] n (-s; -s) summary.

Retorte [re'tɔrtə] f (-; -n) retort.

Re'tortenbaby n test-tube baby.

Retrospektive [retrospɛk'ti:və] f (-; -n) retrospective.

retten ['rɛtən] (h) **I** v/t (aus, vor dat from) save, rescue, a. deliver, a. recover, salvage (a. fig.): **j-m das Leben ~** save s.o.'s life; **sich ~** escape; **sich nicht mehr ~ können vor** (dat) be swamped with; F **der Abend war gerettet** the evening was saved. **II** v/i sports: save.

'**Retter** m (-s; -), '**Retterin** f (-; -nen) rescuer.

Rettich ['rɛtɪç] m (-s; -e) ✿ radish.

'**Rettung** f (-; -en) a) rescue, b) escape, c) recovery, esp. ⚓ salvage, d) eccl. salvation: **das war s-e ~** that saved him; **es gab k-e ~ für ihn** he was past help; **du bist m-e einzige** (or **letzte**) **~** you are my last hope.

'**Rettungsjakti,on** f a. fig. rescue operation. ~anker m sheet anchor. ~boje f life-buoy. ~boot n lifeboat. ~dienst m rescue service. ~gerät n life-saving equipment. ~hubschrauber m rescue helicopter.

'**rettungslos** adj hopeless: **~ verloren sein** be beyond all hope.

'**Rettungsjmannschaft** f rescue party. ~ring m lifebelt. ~schwimmer m lifeguard. ~wagen m ambulance.

retuschieren [retu'ʃiːrən] v/t (h) touch up.

Reue ['rɔʏə] f (-; no pl) (**über** acc for) remorse, esp. eccl. repentance. **'reuen** (h) **I** v/t **s-e Tat** (**das Geld**) **reute ihn** he regretted what he had done (the money). **II** v/impers **es reut mich, daß** I regret that. **'reuevoll, 'reuig, 'reumütig** [-myːtɪç] adj repentant, remorseful.

Revanche [re'vãːʃə] f (-; -n) revenge.
Re'vanchespiel n sports: return match.

revanchieren [revã'ʃiːrən] **sich ~** (h) **1.** take one's revenge (**an** dat on), F get one's own back. **2.** return the favo(u)r.

Revanchismus [revã'ʃɪsmʊs] m (-; no pl) pol. revanchism.

Revers [re'veːr] m, n (-; - [-'veːrs]) lapel.

revidieren [revi'diːrən] v/t (h) **1.** revise. **2.** check, audit.

Revier [re'viːr] n (-s; -e) a) district, b) police station, c) (policeman's) beat, (postman's) round, d) a. fig. territory.

Revision [revi'zioːn] f (-; -en) **1.** check(ing), ✝ audit(ing), (custom's) examination. **2.** revision. **3.** ⚖ (**~ einlegen** lodge an) appeal (**bei** with). **4.** print. final proofreading.

Revolte [re'vɔltə] f (-; -n) revolt.

revoltieren [revɔl'tiːrən] v/i (h) revolt.

Revolution [revɔlu'tsioːn] f (-; -en) revolution. **revolutionär** [revɔlutsio'nɛːr] adj, **Revolutio'när** m (-s; -e) revolutionary. **revolutionieren** [revɔlutsio'niːrən] v/t (h) revolutionize.

Revolver [re'vɔlvər] m (-s; -) revolver.
Re'volverblatt n contp. sensational rag.
Re'volverheld m contp. gunslinger.

Revue [rə'vyː] f (-; -n) **1.** thea. revue. **2.** (publication) review.

Rezensent [retsɛn'zɛnt] m (-en; -en), **Rezen'sentin** f (-; -nen) critic, reviewer. **rezensieren** [retsɛn'ziːrən] v/t (h), **Rezension** [-'zioːn] f (-; -en) review.

Rezept [re'tsɛpt] n (-[e]s; -e) a) ✿ prescription, b) gastr. or fig. recipe.

Rezeption [retsɛp'tsioːn] f (-; -en) hotel: reception, Am. check-in desk.

re'zeptpflichtig adj available only on prescription, prescription(-only) ...

Rezession [retsɛ'sioːn] f (-; -en) ✝ recession.

Rezitativ [retsita'tiːf] n (-s; -e) recitative.
rezitieren [retsi'tiːrən] v/t, v/i (h) recite.
'R-Gespräch n teleph. reversed-charge call, Am. collect call.

Rhabarber [ra'barbər] m (-s; no pl) ⚘ rhubarb.

Rhapsodie [rapso'diː] f (-; -n) rhapsody.

Rheinwein ['raɪn-] m Rhine wine, hock.

Rhesus|affe ['reːzʊs-] m rhesus (monkey). **~faktor** m (-s; no pl) rhesus factor.

Rhetorik [re'toːrɪk] f (-; no pl) rhetoric.
rhetorisch [re'toːrɪʃ] adj rhetorical.

Rheuma ['rɔʏma] n (-s; no pl) F ⚕ rheumatism. **rheumatisch** [rɔʏ'maːtɪʃ] adj ⚕ rheumatic. **Rheumatismus** [rɔʏma'tɪsmʊs] m (-; -men) ⚕ rheumatism.

Rhinozeros [ri'noːtseros] n (-[ses]; -se) zo. rhinoceros.

Rhombus ['rɔmbʊs] m (-; -ben) ⅄ rhomb(us).

rhythmisch ['rʏtmɪʃ] adj rhythmical.
Rhythmus ['rʏtmʊs] m (-; -men) rhythm.

'Richtan,tenne f directional aerial (Am. antenna).

richten¹ ['rɪçtən] (h) **I** v/t **1.** direct (**auf** acc to, **gegen** against): **~ auf** (acc) a. point (or level, aim) weapon, camera at, a. turn one's eyes on, a. concentrate attention, efforts, etc on; **~ an** (acc) address letter etc to, put question to. **2.** a) fix, get s.th. ready, prepare, b) bring s.th. in order, tidy s.th. (up), a. do (one's hair, room, etc), c) repair, mend, fix, d) align, adjust, trim (sails), straighten (out fig.): **sich ~ die Zähne ~ lassen** have one's teeth done. **II sich ~ an** (acc) address o.s. to; **sich ~ auf** (acc) attention etc: focus on; **sich ~ gegen** be directed against, remark etc: be aimed at; **sich ~ nach** a) orient(ate) o.s. by, comply with s.o.'s wishes, a. keep to rules, go by s.o.'s judgment, follow the fashion, follow s.o.'s example, b) matter: be model(l)ed on, depend on, be determined by, a. ling. agree with; **ich richte mich nach dir** I leave it to you.

richten² v/t, v/i (h) judge.

'Richter m (-s; -) judge. **'Richteramt** n judicial office. **'Richterin** f (-; -nen) judge. **'richterlich** adj judicial.

'Richtfest n topping-out ceremony.
'Richtfunk m directional radio.
'Richtgeschwindigkeit f mot. recommended speed.

richtig ['rɪçtɪç] **I** adj **1.** right, correct, true, accurate: (**sehr**) **~!** (quite) right!, exactly!; F **er ist nicht ganz ~ im Kopf**

he is not quite right in the head. **2.** a) right, suitable, appropriate, proper, b) fair, just: **es war ~, daß du ihnen geholfen hast** you did right to help them; **so ist's ~!** that's it! **3.** real, true: **ein ~er Engländer** a true Englishman; **s-e ~e Mutter** his real mother; **ein ~er Feigling** a regular coward. **II** *adv* **4.** a) right(ly), correctly (*etc*), b) F thoroughly, properly: **et. ~ machen** do s.th. right; **~ böse** really (F real) angry; **geht d-e Uhr ~?** is your watch right?

'Richtige[1] **m,** f (-n; -n) the right man (woman), F Mr. (Mrs.) Right: *iro.* **sie ist mir die ~n!** a fine lot you are!; F **sechs ~ haben** *Lotto:* have six right.

'Richtige[2] **n** (-n; -n) the right thing: **er hat nichts ~s gelernt** he hasn't really learnt anything; **das ist für sie genau das ~** that's just right for her.

'richtiggehend *adj* real, regular.

'Richtigkeit f (-; *no pl*) correctness, rightness: **das hat schon s-e ~** it's all right.

'richtigstellen *v/t* (*sep*, -ge-, h) put *s.th.* right, correct.

'Richtlinien *pl* guidelines.

'Richtpreis *m* ✝ recommended price.

'Richtschnur f *fig.* guiding principle.

'Richtung f (-; -en) **1.** direction, course (*a.* ✈, ⚓), *fig. a.* line, trend: **in ~ auf** (*acc*) in the direction of; **aus allen ~en** from all directions; *fig.* **et. in dieser ~** s.th. along these lines. **2.** a) line (of thought), views, b) movement, school.

'richtungweisend *adj* trendsetting.

'Richtwert *m*, **'Richtzahl** f index.

'Ricke ['rɪkə] f (-; -n) *zo.* doe.

rieb [ri:p] *pret of* **reiben**.

riechen ['ri:çən] (roch, gerochen, h) **I** *v/i* smell (**nach** of, **an** *dat* at): **es riecht** (bad); **es riecht nach Gas** I can smell gas. **II** *v/t* smell: F **ich kann ihn nicht ~!** I can't stand him!; **er hat es gerochen** he got wind of it; **das konnte ich doch nicht ~!** how was I to know?; → **Braten, Lunte.**

'Riecher *m* (-s; -) F nose: *fig.* **e-n guten ~ haben für** have a good nose for.

Ried [ri:t] *n* (-[e]s; -e) **1.** reed. **2.** marsh.

rief [ri:f] *pret of* **rufen**.

Riege ['ri:gə] f (-; -n) *gym.* squad.

Riegel ['ri:gəl] *m* (-s; -) **1.** a) bolt, bar, b) latch: **e-r Sache e-n ~ vorschieben** put

a stop to s.th. **2.** bar (*of soap*), row, *Am.* strip (*of chocolate*).

Riemen[1] ['ri:mən] *m* (-s; -) strap, sling (*of rifle*), ⊜ belt: **sich am ~ reißen** pull o.s. together.

'Riemen[2] *m* (-s; -) oar.

Riese ['ri:zə] *m* (-n; -n) **1.** giant. **2.** F thousand-mark *etc* note, *sl.* grand.

rieseln ['ri:zəln] *v/i* (sn) *water, sand, etc:* trickle, run, *rain:* drizzle, *snow:* fall softly: **es rieselte mir kalt über den Rücken** a shiver ran down my spine.

'Riesen... giant, gigantic, enormous. **~erfolg** *m* huge success, *a. film etc:* smash hit. **~flege** f *gym.* giant swing.

'riesengroß, 'riesenhaft → **riesig** 1.

'Riesen|rad *n* Ferris wheel. **~schlange** f boa constrictor. **~schritt** *m* giant stride. **~slalom** *m* *skiing:* giant slalom.

riesig ['ri:zɪç] **I** *adj* **1.** a. *fig.* gigantic, colossal, enormous, huge. **2.** F a) tremendous, b) terrific, super. **II** *adv* **3.** F tremendously, terribly, enormously.

Riesin ['ri:zɪn] f (-; -nen) giantess.

riet [ri:t] *pret of* **raten**.

Riff [rɪf] *n* (-[e]s; -e) reef.

rigoros [rigo'ro:s] *adj* rigorous.

Rigorosum [rigo'ro:zʊm] *n* (-s; -sa) *univ.* viva (voce).

Rille ['rɪlə] f (-; -n) groove.

Rind [rɪnt] *n* (-[e]s; -er) **1.** a) cow, b) bull, c) *pl:* **~er** cattle. **2.** *gastr.* beef.

Rinde ['rɪndə] f (-; -n) **1.** bark. **2.** (*bread*) crust, (*cheese*) rind.

Rinder|braten ['rɪndər-] *m* roast beef. **~fi‚let** *n* fillet of beef. **~lende** f beef tenderloin. **~zucht** f cattle farming. **~zunge** f *gastr.* ox tongue.

'Rindfleisch *n* beef.

'Rind(s)leder *n* cowhide.

'Rindvieh *n* **1.** cattle. **2.** F *contp.* idiot.

Ring [rɪŋ] *m* (-[e]s; -e) ring, circle (*a. fig.*).

'Ringbuch *n* ring (*or* loose-leaf) binder. **~einlage** f loose-leaf pages.

ringeln ['rɪŋəln] **I** *v/t* (h) a) curl, b) coil (**um** around). **II** *sich ~* a) curl, coil, b) wind, meander.

'Ringelnatter f *zo.* grass snake.

ringen ['rɪŋən] (rang, gerungen, h) **I** *v/i* wrestle (**mit** with), *fig. a.* struggle (**um, nach** for): **nach Atem ~** gasp for breath; **nach Fassung ~** try to regain one's composure; **nach Worten ~** struggle for words. **II** *v/t* wring.

'**Ringen** n (-s) wrestling, *fig.* struggle.
'**Ringer** m (-s; -) *sports:* wrestler.
'**Ringfinger** m ring finger.
'**ringförmig** adj ring-shaped, annular.
'**Ringkampf** m wrestling (match).
'**Ringrichter** m *boxing:* referee.
rings [rɪŋs], '**ringsher'um**, '**rings'um**
adv all around.
'**Rinne** [rɪnə] f (-; -n) a) groove (a. anat.,
🦵), b) gutter, c) conduit, channel.
rinnen [rɪnən] (rann, geronnen, sn) v/i **1.**
a) run, flow, b) drip, trickle: *das Geld
rinnt ihr durch die Finger* money just
slips through her fingers. **2.** leak.
'**Rinnstein** m gutter.
'**Rippchen** [rɪpçən] n (-s; -) rib (of pork).
'**Rippe** [rɪpə] f (-; -n) **1.** anat. rib. **2.** 🔩 rib,
fin. **3.** row, *Am.* strip (of chocolate).
rippen [rɪpən] v/t (h) rib.
'**Rippenfell** n anat. pleura.
'**Rippenfellentzündung** f 🔬 pleurisy.
'**Rippenstoß** m dig in the ribs.
'**Rips** [rɪps] m (-es; -e) *textil.* rep.
'**Risiko** [riːziko] n (-s; -s, -ken) risk: *auf
eigenes ~* at one's own risk; *mit vollem ~* at all risks; *ein ~ eingehen* take a
risk. '**risikofrei** adj safe. '**risikofreudig**
adj risk-taking, prepared to take a risk
(or risks). '**Risikogruppe** f high-risk
group. '**risikoreich** adj risky.
riskant [rɪsˈkant] adj risky.
riskieren [rɪsˈkiːrən] v/t (h) risk.
'**Rispe** [rɪspə] f (-; -n) 🌾 panicle.
riß [rɪs] pret of **reißen.**
'**Riß** m (Risses; Risse) **1.** a) tear, rent, *in
dry skin:* chap, b) cleft, crevice, *fig.* rift,
split; *e-n ~ bekommen friendship etc:*
begin to break up. **2.** △, 🔩 draft.
rissig [rɪsɪç] adj cracked, fissured, chap-
py, chapped (*skin etc*): *~ werden* crack,
skin: chap; *~e Hände* chapped hands.
'**Rißwunde** f laceration.
Rist [rɪst] m (-es; -e) **1.** instep. **2.** back of
the hand.
ritt [rɪt] pret of **reiten.**
'**Ritt** m (-[e]s; -e) ride.
'**Ritter** [rɪtər] m (-s; -) (a. *zum ~ schlagen*) knight. '**Rittergut** n manor.
'**ritterlich** adj knightly, *fig.* chivalrous.
'**Ritterorden** m order (of knights).
'**Rittersporn** m (-[e]s; -e) 🌾 larkspur.
'**rittlings** [rɪtlɪŋs] adv astride: *~ auf e-m
Stuhl sitzen* sit astride a chair.
Ritual [riˈtuaːl] n (-s; -e, -lien) ritual.

rituell [riˈtuɛl] adj ritual.
Ritus [riːtʊs] m (-; Riten) rite.
Ritz [rɪts] m (-es; -e) scratch.
'**Ritze** [rɪtsə] f (-; -n) crack, gap, chink.
'**Ritzel** [rɪtsəl] n (-s; -) ⚙ pinion.
ritzen [rɪtsən] v/t (h) **1.** scratch. **2.** carve.
Rivale [riˈvaːlə] m (-n; -n), **Ri'valin** f (-;
-nen) rival.
rivalisieren [rivaliˈziːrən] v/i (h) rival.
Rivalität [rivaliˈtɛːt] f (-; -en) rivalry.
Rizinusöl [riːtsinʊs-] n castor oil.
Robbe [rɔbə] f (-; -n) zo. seal.
Robe [roːbə] f (-; -n) gown, robe.
Roboter [rɔbɔtər] m (-s; -) robot.
'**Robotertechnik** f robotics.
robust [roˈbʊst] adj a. *fig.* robust.
roch [rɔx] pret of **riechen.**
röcheln [rœçəln] v/i (h) breathe sterto-
rously, rattle.
Rochen [rɔxən] m (-s; -) zo. ray.
Rock[1] [rɔk] m (-[e]s; ₑe) **1.** skirt. **2.** jacket,
coat.
Rock[2] m (-[s]; no pl) rock (music).
Rocker [rɔkər] m (-s; -) F rocker.
'**Rockmu,sik** f rock (music).
'**Rodelbahn** f toboggan run.
rodeln [roːdəln] v/i (h or sn) toboggan.
roden [roːdən] v/t (h) **1.** root out. **2.**
clear, stub (*land, woods*).
Rodler [roːdlər] m (-s; -) tobogganist.
'**Rodung** f (-; -en) clearing.
Rogen [roːgən] m (-s; -) roe.
Roggen [rɔgən] m (-s; -) rye.
'**Roggenbrot** n rye-bread.
roh [roː] adj **1.** raw, a. crude, a. rough
(*diamond, draft, etc*). **2.** 🍴 gross. **3.** *fig.*
crude, rough, a. brutal: *mit ~er Gewalt*
with brute force.
'**Rohbau** m shell. '**Rohbi,lanz** f 🍴 trial
balance. '**Rohdia,mant** m rough diamond. '**Roheisen** n pig iron.
'**Roheit** f (-; -en) **1.** *no pl* roughness, a.
brutality. **2.** brutal act.
'**Roherz** n crude ore. '**Rohfaser** f crude
fibre (*Am.* fiber). '**Rohfassung** f rough
draft. '**Rohgewinn** m 🍴 gross profit.
'**Rohkost** f raw vegetables and fruit.
'**Rohköstler** [-kœstlər] m (-s; -) vegetarian. '**Rohleder** n rawhide.
Rohling [roːlɪŋ] m (-s; -e) **1.** brute. **2.** ⚙
blank.
'**Rohmateri,al** n raw material. '**Rohöl** n
crude oil. '**Rohpro,dukt** n raw product
Rohr [roːr] n (-[e]s; -e) **1.** 🌾 a) reed, b)

cane. **2.** ⚙ a) tube, pipe, b) duct. **3.** (gun) barrel: F *fig. volles ~* flat out.

'**Rohrbruch** *m* burst pipe.

'**Röhrchen** ['rø:rçən] *n* (small) tube: *j-n ins ~ blasen lassen* breathalyze s.o.

'**Röhre** ['rø:rə] *f* (-; -n) **1.** a) tube, b) pipe. **2.** ⚡, *radio, TV* valve, *Am.* tube: F *in die ~ gucken* a) *TV* sit in front of the box, b) *fig.* be left out in the cold. **3.** oven. **4.** *hunt.* gallery.

'**röhren** ['rø:rən] *v/i* (h) *stag:* bell.

'**Röhrenknochen** *m* long bone.

'**Rohr|kolben** *m* ♣ reed mace. **~leitung** *f* a) conduit, b) plumbing, c) pipeline. **~netz** *n* (water *etc*) mains. **~post** *f* pneumatic post. **~spatz** *m* F *schimpfen wie ein~* rant and rave. **~stock** *m* cane. **~zange** *f* ⚙ pipe wrench. **~zucker** *m* cane sugar.

'**Rohseide** *f* raw silk. '**Rohstahl** *m* crude steel. '**Rohstoff** *m* raw material. '**Rohzucker** *m* unrefined sugar.

'**Rohzustand** *m* (*im~* in the) crude state.

'**Rolladen** *m* shutters.

'**Rollbahn** *f* ✈ runway.

'**Rolle¹** ['rɔlə] *f* (-; -n) a) roll (*a.* ✈, *gym.*), ⚙ a. roller, a. pulley, b) castor, c) reel, coil: *e-e ~ Garn* a reel of cotton.

'**Rolle²** *f* (-; -n) *thea.* part, role (*a. psych.*): *e-e ~ spielen* play a part (*a. fig. bei, in dat* in), *fig. a.* figure (in); *das spielt k-e ~* that doesn't make any difference; *Geld spielt k-e ~* money is no object; *aus der ~ fallen* forget o.s.; *fig. die ~(n) (ver)tauschen* reverse roles.

'**rollen** ['rɔlən] *v/i* (sn), *v/t* (h) roll, wheel, ✈ taxi: *~des Material* 🚂 rolling stock; *fig. ins Rollen kommen* get under way.

'**Rollen|besetzung** *f thea.* casting. **~lager** *n* ⚙ roller bearing. **~spiel** *n psych.* role-playing. **~tausch** *m fig.* reversal of roles. **~verteilung** *f* **1.** *thea.* casting. **2.** *fig.* respective roles.

'**Roller** *m* (-s; -) **1.** *mot. etc* scooter. **2.** *soccer:* daisy cutter.

'**Roll|feld** *n* ✈ taxiway, runway. **~film** *m* roll film. **~kom,mando** *n sl.* heavies. **~kragen(pull,over)** *m* polo neck.

'**Rollschuh** *m* roller skate: *~ laufen* roller-skate. **~bahn** *f* roller-skating rink. **~läufer** *m* roller skater.

'**Roll|stuhl** *m* wheelchair. **~treppe** *f* escalator. **~verdeck** *n* roller roof.

'**Roman** [ro'ma:n] *m* (-[e]s; -e) novel.

~held(in *f*) *m* hero(ine) (of the novel).

Romanik [ro'ma:nɪk] *f* (-; *no pl*) Romanesque (style *or* period). **ro'manisch** *adj* **1.** *ling.* Romance. **2.** Romanesque.

Romanist [roma'nɪst] *m* (-en; -en) student of (*or* lecturer in) Romance languages and literature.

Ro'manlitera,tur *f* fiction.

Ro'manschriftsteller(in *f*) *m* novelist.

Romantik [ro'mantɪk] *f* (-; *no pl*) romanticism, *art:* Romanticism. **Ro'mantiker** *m* (-s; -) Romantic, *fig.* romantic. **ro'mantisch** *adj* romantic, *art etc:* Romantic. **romantisieren** [-ti'zi:rən] *v/t* (h) romanticize.

Romanze [ro'mantsə] *f* (-; -n) romance.

Römer ['rø:mər] *m* (-s; -) **1.** Roman. **2.** rummer. **römisch** ['rø:mɪʃ] *adj* Roman: *~katholisch* Roman Catholic.

Rommé [rɔ'me:] *n* (-s; -s) rummy.

röntgen ['rœntgən] *v/t* (h) ☢ x-ray.

'**Röntgen|appa,rat** *m* x-ray unit. **~arzt** *m* radiologist. **~aufnahme** *f* x-ray (picture). **~behandlung** *f*, **~bestrahlung** *f* x-ray treatment, radiotherapy.

Röntgenologe [rœntgeno'lo:gə] *m* (-n; -n) radiologist.

'**Röntgen|schirm** *m* (fluorescent) screen. **~strahlen** *pl* x-rays. **~untersuchung** *f* x-ray examination.

rosa ['ro:za] *adj* pink.

'**rosarot** *adj a. fig.* rose-colo(u)red.

Rose ['ro:zə] *f* (-; -n) **1.** ♣ rose. **2.** ⚕ erysipelas.

Rosé [ro'ze:] *m* (-s; -s) rosé (wine).

'**Rosenkohl** *m* Brussels sprouts.

'**Rosenkranz** *m eccl.* (*den ~ beten* say the) rosary.

Rosen'montag *m* Monday before Lent.

'**Rosenstock** *m* rose-tree.

'**Rosenstrauß** *m* bunch of roses.

rosig ['ro:zɪç] *adj a. fig.* rosy.

Rosine [ro'zi:nə] *f* (-; -n) raisin: F (*große*) *~n im Kopf haben* have big ideas.

Rosmarin ['ro:smari:n] *m* (-s; *no pl*) ♣ rosemary.

Roß [rɔs] *n* (Rosses; Rösser ['rœsər]) horse: *fig. sich aufs hohe ~ setzen* give o.s. airs. **~äpfel** *pl* horse droppings.

'**Roßhaar** *n* horsehair.

Rost¹ [rɔst] *m* (-[e]s; *no pl*) *a. fig.* rust.

Rost² *m* (-[e]s; -e) **1.** grate. **2.** grill.

'**Röstbrot** *n* toast.

rosten ['rɔstən] v/i (sn or h) rust: **nicht ~d** → **rostfrei**.

rösten ['rœstən] v/t (h) roast (*coffee*), toast (*bread*), fry (*potatoes*).

'rostfrei adj rustproof, stainless.

rostig ['rɔstɪç] adj a. fig. rusty.

'Röstkar,toffeln pl fried potatoes.

'Rostschutzmittel n antirust agent.

'Roststelle f patch of rust.

rot [ro:t] adj red, pol. Red: **das Rote Kreuz** the Red Cross; **~ werden** a) go red, flush, b) blush; **♥ in den ~en Zahlen stehen** be in the red; → **rotsehen**, **Faden, Tuch.**

Rot n (-s; - red: **bei ~** at red; **die Ampel steht auf ~** the lights are at red.

Rotation [rota'tsĭo:n] f (-; -en) rotation.

Rotati'onsdruck m rotary printing.

'rotblond adj sandy-haired, sandy (*hair*).

'rotbraun adj reddish brown.

'Rotbuche f copper beech.

'Rotdorn m (-[e]s; -e) pink hawthorn.

Rote ['ro:tə] m, f (-n; -n) pol. Red.

Röte ['rø:tə] f (-; -) a) redness, b) blush.

Rötel ['rø:təl] m (-s; no pl) red chalk.

'Röteln pl ✿ German measles.

röten ['rø:tən] v/t (h) redden: **sich ~** a. go red, flush.

'rotglühend adj red-hot.

'rothaarig adj red-haired.

'Rothaarige m, f (-n; -n) redhead.

rotieren [ro'ti:rən] v/i (h) a) rotate, b) F fig. flap: **am Rotieren sein** be in a flap.

Rotkäppchen ['ro:tkɛpçən] n (Little) Red Riding Hood.

'Rotkehlchen n zo. robin (redbreast).

'Rotkohl m, **'Rotkraut** n red cabbage.

rötlich ['rø:tlɪç] adj reddish.

'rotsehen v/i (irr, sep, -ge-, h, → **sehen**) F fig. see red.

'Rotstift m red pencil: fig. **den ~ ansetzen** make cuts (**bei** in).

Rotte ['rɔtə] f (-; -n) gang, horde.

'Rötung f (-; -en) reddening.

'Rotwein m red wine.

'Rotwild n red deer.

Rotz [rɔts] m (-es; no pl) V snot. **'Rotzfahne** f V snotrag. **'rotzfrech** adj F snotty.

Rouge [ru:ʒ] n (-s; -s [ru:ʒ]) rouge.

Roulade [ru'la:də] f (-; -n) roulade, roll.

Rouleau [ru'lo:] n (-s; -s) roller blind.

Roulett [ru'lɛt] n (-[e]s; -e) roulette.

Route ['ru:tə] f (-; -n) route, itinerary.

Routine [ru'ti:nə] f (-; no pl) routine, a. practice, experience.

rou'tinemäßig adj routine.

routiniert [ruti'ni:rt] adj experienced.

Rowdy ['raʊdi] m (-s; -s) hooligan.

'Rowdytum n (-s; no pl) hooliganism.

Rübe ['ry:bə] f (-; -n) 1. **weiße ~** turnip: **rote ~** beetroot; **gelbe ~** carrot. 2. F nut.

Rubel ['ru:bəl] m (-s; -) rouble.

rüber(...) ['ry:bər-] F → **herüber(...)**, **hinüber(...)**. **'rüberkommen** v/i (irr, sep, -ge-, sn, → **kommen**) F 1. come over. 2. thea. etc come across. 3. **~ mit** come across with *money etc.*

Rubin [ru'bi:n] m (-s; -e) min. ruby.

Rubrik [ru'bri:k] f (-; -en) 1. heading. 2. column. 3. category.

ruchbar ['ru:x-] adj **~ werden** become known.

Ruck [rʊk] m (-[e]s; -e) jerk, start, jolt (a. fig.), F pol. swing: **in einem ~** at one go; **sich e-n ~ geben** pull o.s. together.

'Rückansicht f back view.

'ruckartig I adj jerky. **II** adv a) with a jerk, b) abruptly.

'rückbezüglich adj ling. reflexive.

'Rückblende f film: flashback (**auf acc** to).

'Rückblick m review (**auf** acc of): **im ~** in retrospect, **auf** (acc) looking back on.

'rückda,tieren v/t (h) backdate.

rücken ['rʏkən] **I** v/t (h) move, a. shift, a. push (away). **II** v/i (sn) a) move, b) move over: **näher ~** draw near, approach; **an j-s Stelle ~** take s.o.'s place.

'Rücken m (-s; -) a) back, b) (*mountain*) ridge, c) bridge (of nose), d) *geart.* saddle: **hinter j-s ~** behind s.o.'s back; **j-m in den ~ fallen** fig. stab s.o. in the back.

'Rücken|deckung f fig. backing, support. **~lehne** f back(-rest). **~mark** n anat. spinal cord. **~muskula,tur** f back muscles. **~schmerzen** pl backache. **~schwimmen** n backstroke. **~wind** m following wind. **~wirbel** m anat. dorsal vertebra.

'Rückeroberung f reconquest.

'rückerstatten v/t (only inf and rücker stattet, h) return, a. refund.

'Rückfahrkarte f return (ticket), Am round-trip ticket.

'Rückfahrt f return journey (or trip): **auf der ~** a. on the way back.

'**Rückfall** m relapse (a. fig.), ⚖ a. recidivism. '**rückfällig** adj relapsing, ⚖ a. recidivist: ~ **werden** (have a) relapse.

'**Rückfenster** n rear window.

'**Rückflug** m return flight.

'**Rückfrage** f checkback.

'**rückfragen** v/i (only inf and pp rückgefragt, h) check (**bei** with).

'**Rückführung** f repatriation.

'**Rückgabe** f return, sports: pass back.

'**Rückgang** m (gen in) decline, drop, fall.

'**rückgängig** adj 1. → **rückläufig**. 2. ~ **machen** a) undo, b) cancel (order etc).

'**Rückgewinnung** f recovery.

'**Rückgrat** n spine, backbone (a. fig.).

'**rückgratlos** adj fig. spineless.

'**Rückhalt** m support. '**rückhaltlos I** adj unreserved, a. frank. **II** adv without reserve: **j-m ~ vertrauen** have complete confidence in s.o.

'**Rückhand** f (-; no pl) tennis: backhand.

'**Rückkampf** m sports: return match.

'**Rückkaufsrecht** n right of repurchase (or redemption).

'**Rückkehr** f (-; no pl) return.

'**Rückkopplung** f ⚡ feedback (a. fig.).

'**Rücklagen** pl reserve(s), savings.

'**rückläufig** adj dropping, declining: ~**e Tendenz** downward tendency.

'**Rücklicht** n (-[e]s; -er) mot. rear light, taillight.

rücklings ['rʏklɪŋs] adv a) backwards, b) from behind.

'**Rückmarsch** m march back. '**Rückpaß** m sports: back pass. '**Rückporto** n return postage. '**Rückprall** m rebound. '**Rückreise** f → **Rückfahrt**. '**Rückruf** m 1. ✝ recall. 2. teleph. ring back.

'**Rucksack** m rucksack, Am. backpack. ~**tou,rismus** m backpacking. ~**tou,rist** m backpacker.

'**Rückschlag** m fig. setback.

'**Rückschluß** m conclusion.

'**Rückschritt** m step back(ward).

'**rückschrittlich** adj pol. reactionary.

'**Rückseite** f back, rear, reverse (of coin etc), B-side, F flip side (of record): **siehe ~!** see overleaf!

'**Rücksendung** f return.

'**Rücksicht** f (-; no pl) consideration: **mit ~ auf** (acc) out of consideration for; **ohne ~ auf** (acc) regardless of; **(k-e) ~ nehmen auf** (acc) show (no) consideration for, make (no) allowances for.

'**Rücksichtnahme** [-na:mə] f (-; no pl) consideration (**auf** acc for).

'**rücksichtslos** adj inconsiderate (**gegen** of), thoughtless, reckless (driving etc), a. ruthless. '**Rücksichtslosigkeit** f (-; no pl) lack of consideration, recklessness. '**rücksichtsvoll** adj considerate (**gegen** of).

'**Rücksitz** m a) backseat, b) pillion.

'**Rückspiegel** m mot. rearview mirror.

'**Rückspiel** n sports: return match.

'**Rücksprache** f (-; -n) consultation: **mit j-m ~ nehmen** consult (with) s.o.

'**Rückstand** m (-[e]s; ⁺e) 1. 🔬 residue. 2. ✝ arrears, a. backlog (of work): **im ~ sein mit** be behind with one's payments etc, sports: be down one goal etc.

'**rückständig** adj 1. backward, a. underdeveloped. 2. ~**e Miete** arrears of rent.

'**Rückständigkeit** f (-; no pl) backwardness.

'**Rückstau** m mot. tailback.

'**Rückstoß** m recoil (of gun).

'**Rückstrahler** m rear reflector.

'**Rücktaste** f of typewriter: back spacer, of tape recorder etc: rewind key.

'**Rücktritt** m 1. (**von**) resignation (from office), withdrawal (from contract): **s-n ~ erklären** announce (or tender) one's resignation. 2. F → '**Rücktrittbremse** f backpedal brake.

'**Rücktritts,gesuch** n (letter of) resignation. ~**recht** n right of rescission.

'**rückübersetzen** v/t (only inf and pp rückübersetzt, h) translate back (**in** acc into English etc).

'**Rückübersetzung** f retranslation.

'**rückvergüten** v/t (only inf and pp rückvergütet, h), '**Rückvergütung** f refund.

'**rückversichern** v/t (only inf and pp rückversichert, h) reinsure (**sich** o.s.): fig. **sich ~** play safe.

'**Rückversicherung** f reinsurance.

'**Rückwand** f back, back wall.

rückwärtig ['rʏkvɛrtɪç] adj back, rear.

rückwärts ['rʏkvɛrts] adv backwards: ~ **fahren** in (acc) (or **aus** dat) back into (or out of). '**Rückwärtsgang** m mot. (**im ~** in) reverse (gear).

'**Rückweg** m way back, return: **den ~ antreten** head for home.

'**ruckweise I** adj jerky. **II** adv jerkily, in jerks.

'**rückwirkend** adj ⚖ retroactive: ~ **ab**

backdated to. '**Rückwirkung** f (**auf** acc upon) reaction, repercussion.

'**rückzahlbar** adj repayable.

'**Rückzahlung** f repayment, refund.

'**Rückzieher** m (-s;-) **1.** soccer: overhead kick. **2.** F **e-n ~ machen** back down.

'**Rückzug** m retreat. '**Rückzugsgefecht** n a. fig. rearguard action.

rüde ['ry:də] adj rude, coarse.

'**Rüde** m (-n;-n) male dog (or wolf, fox).

Rudel ['ru:dəl] n (-s;-) pack (of wolves etc), herd (of deer etc), fig. swarm.

Ruder ['ru:dər] n (-s;-) a) oar, b) rudder (a. ⚓), helm: **am ~** at the helm (a. fig.); fig. **ans ~ kommen** come into power.

'**Ruderboot** n rowing boat.

'**Ruderer** m (-s;-) rower, oarsman.

'**Ruderin** f (-;-nen) oarswoman.

'**Ruderklub** m rowing club.

rudern ['ru:dərn] v/t (h), v/i (h, sn) row.

'**Rudern** n (-s) rowing.

'**Ruderregatta** f boat race, regatta.

'**Rudersport** m rowing.

Ruf [ru:f] m (-[e]s;-e) **1.** call (a. teleph. or fig.), cry, shout: **e-n ~ erhalten nach** be offered an appointment (univ. a chair) at. **2.** no pl reputation: **von ~** artist or of high repute, noted artist etc.

rufen ['ru:fən] (rief, gerufen, h) **I** v/i a) call, b) cry, shout: **~ nach** call for (a. fig.); **um Hilfe ~** cry for help. **II** v/t call, a. summon: **~ lassen** send for; **du kommst mir wie gerufen** you're just the person I need. '**Rufen** n (-s) calling, b) calls. '**Rufer** m (-s;-) caller.

Rüffel ['ryfəl] m (-s;-) F dressing-down.

'**Rufmord** m character assassination. **~name** m name by which one is called. **~nummer** f telephone number. **~weite** f **in ~** within calling distance.

Rüge ['ry:gə] f (-;-[e]s;-e) reprimand, rebuke.

'**rügen** v/t (h) (**wegen** for) reprimand, rebuke (s.o.), criticize, censure (s.th.).

Ruhe ['ru:ə] f (-; no pl) a) rest (a. phys.), b) quiet, silence, c) peace, d) calm(ness), composure: **~ und Ordnung** law and order; **die ~ vor dem Sturm** the calm before the storm; **in aller ~** very calmly, leisurely; **überlege es dir in aller ~** take your time about it; **~ bewahren** keep quiet, keep cool; **sich zur ~ setzen** retire; **zur ~ bringen** quieten down; **~, bitte!** quiet, please!; **laß mich in ~!** leave me alone!; **laß mich damit in**

~! I don't want to hear about it!; **er möchte s-e ~ haben** he wants to be left in peace; F **er hat die ~ weg!** he's (as) cool as a cucumber; **immer mit der ~!** take it easy!

'**ruhebedürftig** adj in need of (a) rest.

'**Ruhegehalt** n pension.

'**ruhelos** adj restless.

'**Ruhelosigkeit** f (-; no pl) restlessness.

ruhen ['ru:ən] v/i (h) rest, work, traffic, etc: be at a standstill, negotiations etc: be suspended: **~ auf** (dat) fig. rest on; **er ruhte nicht, bis** he didn't rest until; **hier ruht** here lies; **laß die Vergangenheit ~!** let bygones be bygones!

'**Ruhe|pause** f break, rest. **~stand** m (-[e]s; no pl) (**vorzeitiger ~** early) retirement: **im ~** retired; **in den ~ treten** (**versetzen**) retire. **~stätte** f resting place. **~stellung** f ⊙ neutral position. **~störer** m disturber of the peace. **~störung** f öffentliche **~** disturbance of the peace. **~tag** m a) day of rest, b) day off, c) closing day: **Montag ~!** closed on Mondays!

ruhig ['ru:iç] **I** adj **1.** a) quiet (a. fig.), a. silent, b) still, c) peaceful, restful, d) calm (sea, a. voice), steady (hand), smooth (a. ⊙), e) leisurely: (**sei**) **~!** (be) quiet!; **sei ganz ~!** don't worry!; **~ bleiben** keep calm; **k-e ~e Minute haben** not to have a moment's peace. **II** adv **2.** quietly (etc): **das Haus liegt ~** the house is in a quiet area; **~ verlaufen** be uneventful. **3.** F easily, very well: **tu das ~!** go right ahead!; **du kannst ~ dableiben!** (you can) stay if you want!

Ruhm [ru:m] m (-[e]s; no pl) fame, glory.

rühmen ['ry:mən] v/t (h) praise (**wegen** for): **sich ~** (gen) pride o.s. (on), boast (s.th.). **rühmenswert → rühmlich.**

'**Ruhmesblatt** n **das ist kein ~ für ihn** that's not exactly to his credit.

'**rühmlich** adj laudable, praiseworthy: **~e Ausnahme** noteworthy exception.

'**ruhmlos** adj inglorious.

'**ruhmreich, ruhmvoll** adj glorious.

Ruhr [ru:r] f (-; no pl) ✿ dysentery.

'**Rührbesen** m gastr. whisk.

'**Rühreier** pl scrambled eggs.

rühren ['ry:rən] (h) **I** v/t **1.** stir, a. move: **er hat k-n Finger gerührt** he did not lift a finger; → **Donner, Trommel. 2.** fig. touch, move (**zu Tränen** to tears): **das**

rührt mich wenig that leaves me cold. **II** *v/i* **3.** stir. **4. ~ an** (*acc*) a) touch, b) touch (up)on *a subject etc.* **III sich ~ 5.** stir, move: ✕ **rührt euch!** (stand) at ease!; **sich nicht (von der Stelle) ~** not to budge (an inch) **6.** F *fig.* do (*or* say) s.th. **'rührend** *adj* **1.** touching, moving. **2.** very kind.

'rührig *adj* active, busy, enterprising. **'Rührigkeit** *f* (-; *no pl*) activity.

'rührselig *adj* sentimental, mawkish: **~e Geschichte** F sob story.

'Rührung *f* (-; *no pl*) emotion: **er brachte vor ~ kein Wort heraus** he was choked with emotion.

Ruin [ru'i:n] *m* (-s; *no pl*) (**vor dem ~ stehen** be on the brink of) ruin.

Ruine [ru'i:nə] *f* (-; -n) ruin(s).

ruinieren [rui'ni:rən] *v/t* (h) ruin.

ruinös [rui'nø:s] *adj* ruinous.

rülpsen ['rylpsən] *v/i* (h) F belch.

Rum [rʊm] *m* (-s; -s) rum.

rum(...) F → **herum(...)**.

Rumäne [ru'mɛ:nə] *m* (-n; -n) Romanian. **Ru'mänien** [-niən] *n* (-s) Romania. **Ru'mänin** *f* (-; -nen), **ru'mänisch** *adj* Romanian.

Rummel ['rʊməl] *m* (-s; *no pl*) F **1.** (hustle and) bustle. **2.** fuss, to-do: **großen ~ machen um** make a big fuss about. **3.** a) fun fair, b) → **'Rummelplatz** *m* fairground, amusement park.

rumoren [ru'mo:rən] *v/i* (h) F bang around.

'Rumpelkammer *f* lumber room.

rumpeln ['rʊmpəln] *v/i* (h, sn) F rumble.

Rumpf [rʊmpf] *m* (-es; ⸚e) **1.** *anat.* trunk. **2.** ♣ hull, ✈ fuselage.

rümpfen ['rympfən] *v/t* (h) **die Nase ~** turn up one's nose (**über** *acc* at).

rund [rʊnt] **I** *adj* **1.** round (*a. fig.*): **Gespräche am ~en Tisch** round-table talks; **~e 1000 Mark** 1,000 marks or so; **e-e ~e Leistung** a perfect performance. **II** *adv* **2.** about, roughly: **~ gerechnet** in round figures. **3. ~ um** (a)round.

'Rundbau *m* (-[e]s; -ten) rotunda.

'Rundblick *m* panorama.

'Runde ['rʊndə] *f* (-; -n) **1.** circle. **2.** round: **s-e ~ machen** make one's rounds, *policeman*: be on one's beat; **F die ~ machen** story *etc*: go the round. **3.** *boxing, golf, etc*: round (*a. fig. of negotiations*), *racing*: lap: F *fig.* **gerade**

so über die ~n kommen just about make it, scrape by, *a. financially*: get by. **4.** round (*of beer etc*). **'runden: sich ~** (h) grow round, *fig.* take shape.

'runderneuern *v/t* (*only inf and pp* runderneuert, h) retread (*tyres*).

'Rundfahrt *f* tour (**durch** of).

'Rundflug *m* circuit.

'Rundfunk *m* (-s; *no pl*) **1.** broadcasting, radio: **im ~** on the radio; **~ hören** listen to the radio; **im ~ übertragen** (*or* **senden, bringen**) broadcast; **beim ~ sein** work in broadcasting. **2.** → **~anstalt** *f* broadcasting company, *Am.* radio corporation. **~gebühren** *pl* radio licen/ce (*Am.* -se) fees. **~gerät** *n* radio (set). **~hörer(in** *f*) *m* listener. **~pro,gramm** *n* radio program(me *Br.*). **~sender** *m* → **Rundfunkstation. ~sendung** *f* broadcast, radio program(me *Br.*). **~sprecher** *m* (radio) announcer. **~stati,on** *f* radio station. **~zeitung** *f* radio journal.

'Rundgang *m* round, tour (**durch** of).

'rundher'aus *adv* flatly, straight out.

'rundher'um *adv* all (a)round.

'rundlich *adj* plump, chubby.

'Rundreise *f* tour (**durch** of).

'Rundschreiben *n* circular (letter).

'Rundstrecke *f* circuit.

rund'um *adv* all (a)round.

'Rundung *f* (-; -en) curve.

'rund'weg *adv* flatly.

Rune ['ru:nə] *f* (-; -n) rune.

runter(...) ['rʊntər-] F → **herunter(...)**, **hinunter(...)**. **'runterhauen** *v/t* (*sep*, -ge-, h) F **j-m e-e ~** slap s.o.('s face).

Runzel ['rʊntsəl] *f* (-; -n) wrinkle, line. **'runz(e)lig** *adj* wrinkled, lined. **'runzeln** *v/t* (h) wrinkle: **die Stirn ~** frown.

Rüpel ['ry:pəl] *m* (-s; -) lout. **'rüpelhaft** *adj* rude, loutish, uncouth.

rupfen ['rʊpfən] *v/t* (h) pluck (*chicken etc*): F **j-n ~** fleece s.o.; → **Hühnchen** 1.

ruppig ['rʊpɪç] *adj* **1.** shaggy. **2.** gruff.

Rüsche ['ry:ʃə] *f* (-; -n) frill.

Ruß [ru:s] *m* (-es; *no pl*) soot.

Russe ['rʊsə] *m* (-n; -n) Russian.

Rüssel ['rʏsəl] *m* (-s; -) proboscis, *a.* (elephant's) trunk, (pig's) snout.

rußen ['ru:sən] *v/i* (h) smoke.

'rußig *adj* sooty.

'Russin *f* (-; -nen), **'russisch** *adj* Russian. **Rußland** ['rʊs-] *n* (-s) Russia.

rüsten ['rystən] (h) (**für, zu** for) **I** *v/i* ✕

arm: *fig.* **gerüstet** armed, ready. **II** *sich* ~ prepare, get ready.

Rüster ['ry:stər] *f* (-; -n) **𝕯** elm.

rüstig ['rystıç] *adj* vigorous, sprightly.

rustikal [rosti'ka:l] *adj* rustic.

'**Rüstung**¹ *f* (-; -en) (knight's) armo(u)r.

'**Rüstung**² *f* (-; -en) ✕ armament.

'**Rüstungs|ausgaben** *pl* defen|ce (*Am.* -se) expenditure. ~**begrenzung** *f* arms limitation. ~**indu,strie** *f* defen|ce (*Am.* -se) industry. ~**kon,trolle** *f* arms control. ~**stopp** *m* arms freeze. ~**wettlauf** *m* arms race.

'**Rüstzeug** *n fig.* equipment.

Rute ['ru:tə] *f* (-; -n) **1.** a) switch, b) rod. **2.** fishing rod. **3.** *hunt.* a) penis, b) tail, (fox's) brush.

'**Rutengänger** [-gɛŋər] *m* (-s; -) diviner.

Rutsch [rotʃ] *m* (-[e]s; -e) **1.** slide, *a.* landslide: F **in einem** ~ in one go; **guten** ~ (**ins Neue Jahr**)! Happy New Year! **2.** F (short) trip, jaunt.

'**Rutschbahn** *f* slide.

'**Rutsche** *f* (-; -n) slide, **☉** *a.* chute.

'**rutschen** *v/i* (sn) slide, glide, slip, *mot. etc* skid. '**rutschig** *adj* slippery.

'**rutschsicher** *adj* nonslip, *mot.* nonskid.

rütteln ['rytəln] (h) **I** *v/t* shake, **☉** vibrate. **II** *v/i mot.* shake, jolt, **☉** vibrate: ~ **an** (*dat*) a) rattle (at) *the door*, b) *fig.* shake, *a.* question; **daran ist nicht zu ~**! that's a fact!

S

S, s [s] *n* (-; -) S, s.

Saal [za:l] *m* (-[e]s; ⸚e) hall.

Saat [za:t] *f* (-; -en) *no pl* sowing. **2.** seed (*a. fig.*), a. crop(s). ~**gut** *n* (-[e]s; *no pl*) seed(s). ~**kar,toffel** *f* seed potato.

Sabbat ['zabat] *m* (-s; -e) Sabbath.

sabbern ['zabərn] *v/i* (h) slaver, drool.

Säbel ['zɛ:bəl] *m* (-s; -) sab|re (*Am.* -er).

Sabotage [zabo'ta:ʒə] *f* (-; -n) sabotage.

Sabo'tageakt *m* act of sabotage.

Saboteur [zabo'tø:r] *m* (-s; -e) saboteur.

sabotieren [-'ti:rən] *v/t* (h) sabotage.

'**Sach|bearbeiter(in** *f*) *m* official (**✝** clerk) in charge (**für** of). ~**beschädigung** *f* damage to property. **2bezogen** *adj* pertinent. ~**buch** *n* nonfiction book, *pl coll.* nonfiction.

'**sachdienlich** *adj* relevant, pertinent.

Sache ['zaxə] *f* (-; -n) **1.** a) thing, object, b) F *pl* things (*a. food etc*), *a.* belongings; F *mot.* **mit 100** ~ at 60 (miles per hour). **2.** a) affair, matter, business, b) problem, c) subject, d) case, **⚖** *or fig.* cause: **e-e** ~ **für sich** a matter apart; **in** ~**n Umwelt** concerning the environment; **in eigener** ~ on one's own behalf; **bei der** ~ **bleiben** stick to the point; **er war nicht bei der** ~ he was inattentive; **für e-e gute** ~ **kämpfen** fight for a good cause; **s-e** ~ **gut machen** do a good job; (**sich**) **s-r** ~ **sicher sein** be sure of one's ground; **zur** ~ **kommen** get to the point, *w.s.* get down to business; **das ist s-e** ~! that's his problem (*or* affair)!; **es ist s-e** ~ **zu** *inf* it's his business to *inf*; **es ist** ~ **des Vertrauens** it's a matter of trust; **das tut nichts zur** ~ that makes no difference; **die** ~ **ist die, daß** the point is that F *j-m sagen,* **was** ~ **ist** tell s.o. what's what; → **gemeinsam** I.

'**Sach|frage** *f* factual issue. **2fremd** *adj* irrelevant. ~**gebiet** *n* subject, field **2gemäß, 2gerecht** *adj* proper, appropriate. ~**kenner** *m* expert. ~**kenntnis** *f* expertise, know-how. ~**kunde** *f* (-; *no pl*) *ped.* general knowledge. **2kundig** *adj* expert: **sich** ~ **machen** inform o.s. ~**lage** *f* (-; *no pl*) state of affairs. ~**leistung** *f* payment in kind.

'**sachlich** *adj* **1.** factual, *a.* technical, *a.* △, **☉** functional: **aus** ~**en Gründen** for technical (*or* practical) reasons; ~ **richtig** factually correct. **2.** a) matter-of-fact, realistic, unemotional, b) objective, c) practical(-minded).

sächlich ['zɛçlɪç] adj ling. neuter.
'**Sachlichkeit** f (-; no pl) matter-of-factness, objectivity, △, ☼ functionalism.
'**Sachre,gister** n (subject) index.
'**Sachschaden** m material damage.
Sachse ['zaksə] m (-n; -n), **Sächsin** ['zɛksɪn] f (-; -nen), **sächsisch** ['zɛksɪʃ] adj Saxon.
'**Sachspende** f donation in kind.
sacht [zaxt] **I** adj soft, gentle. **II** adv a. ~e a) softly, gently, b) cautiously, c) slowly: F (immer) ~e! take it easy!
'**Sachverhalt** m the facts (of the case).
'**Sachvermögen** n tangible property.
'**Sachverstand** m expertise, know-how.
'**sachverständig** adj expert, competent.
'**Sachverständige** m, f (-n; -n) expert, ⚖ expert witness. '**Sachverständigengutachten** n expert opinion.
'**Sachwalter** [-valtər] m (-s; -) **1.** ⚖ trustee. **2.** fig. advocate, champion.
'**Sachwert** m (-[e]s) **1.** no pl real value. **2.** pl material assets.
Sack [zak] m (-[e]s; ~e) **1.** sack, bag, anat., zo. sac: **mit ~ und Pack** with bag and baggage. **2.** V balls.
sacken ['zakən] v/i (sn) sink, give way, sag, person: slump.
'**Sack,gasse** f **1.** cul-de-sac. **2.** fig. dead end, impasse. ~**hüpfen** n sack race.
Sadismus [za'dɪsmʊs] m (-; no pl) sadism. **Sadist** [za'dɪst] m (-en; -en) sadist. **sa'distisch** [-tɪʃ] adj sadistic.
säen ['zɛːən] v/t, v/i (h) sow: fig. **dünn gesät** scarce, few and far between.
Safari [za'faːri] f (-; -s) safari.
Sa'faripark m wildlife reserve.
Safe [seɪf] m, n (-s; -s) safe.
Safran ['zafran] m (-s; -e) saffron.
Saft [zaft] m (-[e]s; ~e) juice (a. F ⚡), ⚕ sap: fig. **ohne ~ und Kraft** → saftlos 2; → schmoren.
'**saftig** adj **1.** juicy, ⚕ lush. **2.** F fig. juicy, spicy (joke etc), resounding (slap), stiff, steep (prices), crushing (defeat etc).
'**saftlos** adj **1.** juiceless, dry. **2.** fig. a. saft- u. kraftlos lame, wishy-washy.
'**Saftpresse** f squeezer, juice extractor.
Sage ['zaːɡə] f (-; -n) **1.** legend. **2.** fig. rumo(u)r.
Säge ['zɛːɡə] f (-; -n) saw. ~**blatt** n saw blade. ~**bock** m sawhorse. ~**fisch** m sawfish. ~**mehl** n sawdust.
sagen ['zaːɡən] v/t, v/i (h) say: j-m et. ~

say s.th. to s.o., tell s.o. s.th.; **ich habe mir ~ lassen, daß** I've been told that; **et. (nichts) zu ~ haben** have a (no) say (bei in); **das hat nichts zu ~** that doesn't matter; ~ **Sie ihm, er soll kommen** tell him to come; **was sagst du zu ...?** a) what do you say to ...?, b) how about ...?; **was willst du damit ~?** what do you mean (by that)?; **das Buch sagt mir nichts** the book doesn't mean a thing to me; **wie sagt man ... auf Englisch?** what is the English for ...?; **ich hab's dir ja gleich gesagt!** I told you so!; **laß dir das gesagt sein!** put that in your pipe and smoke it!; **man sagt, er sei krank** he is said to be ill; **was Sie nicht ~!** you don't say!; F **wem ~ Sie das!** you're telling me!; **(das) sagst du!** F says you!; **sage und schreibe** no less than; **es (or damit) ist nicht gesagt, daß** that doesn't necessarily mean that; **unter uns gesagt** between you and me; **gesagt, getan** no sooner said than done; → **Meinung** etc, **schwer** II.
'**Sagen** n (-s) F **das ~ haben** be the boss, **bei** (or in dat) have the (final) say in.
sägen ['zɛːɡən] v/t, v/i (h) saw.
'**sagenhaft** adj **1.** legendary, mythical. **2.** F fig. fantastic, terrific, incredible.
'**Sägespäne** pl wood shavings.
'**Sägewerk** n sawmill.
sah [zaː] pret of **sehen**.
Sahne ['zaːnə] f (-; no pl) cream.
'**Sahnebon,bon** m, n toffee, Am. taffy.
'**Sahnetorte** f cream gateau.
sahnig ['zaːnɪç] adj creamy.
Saison [zɛ'zõ:] f (-; -s) season. ⚓**abhängig** adj seasonal. ~**arbeiter** m seasonal worker. ~**schlußverkauf** m ✞ seasonal sale.
Saite ['zaɪtə] f (-; -n) ♪ string, chord: → **aufziehen** 4. '**Saiteninstru,ment** n stringed instrument.
Sakko ['zako] m, n (-s; -s) jacket.
sakral [za'kraːl] adj eccl. sacred.
Sakrament [zakra'mɛnt] n (-[e]s) -e) eccl. sacrament.
Sakrileg [zakri'leːk] n (-s; -e) sacrilege.
Sakristei [zakrɪs'taɪ] f (-; -en) vestry.
Salamander [zala'mandər] m (-s; -) zo. salamander.
Salami [za'laːmi] f (-; -[s]) salami.
Salat [za'laːt] m (-[e]s; -e) **1.** gastr. salad: F **da haben wir den ~!** there you are! **2.**

no pl ♣ lettuce. **~besteck** *n* salad servers. **~kopf** *m* (head of) lettuce. **~öl** *n* salad oil. **~soße** *f* salad dressing.

Salbe ['zalbə] *f* (-; -n) ointment.

Salbei ['zalbaɪ] *m* (-s; *no pl*) ♣ sage.

salben ['zalbən] *v/t* (h) anoint.

'**Salbung** *f* (-; -en) anointing, *a. fig.* unction. '**salbungsvoll** *adj* unctuous.

Saldo ['zaldo] *m* (-s; Salden) ♥ balance.

Saline [za'li:nə] *f* (-; -n) saltworks.

Salmiak [zal'mĭak] *m* (-s; *no pl*) 🜍 ammonium chloride.

Salmonellen [zalmo'nɛlən] *pl* salmonellae. **~erkrankung** *f* salmonellosis.

Salon [za'lõː] *m* (-s; -s) drawing-room, salon (*a.* ✿), *Am.* parlor, ⚓ saloon.

sa'lonfähig *adj* a) presentable, b) respectable: *nicht* ~ risqué (*joke*).

salopp [za'lɔp] *adj* casual, off-hand.

Salpeter [zal'pe:tər] *m* (-s; *no pl*) 🜍 saltpet/re (*Am.* -er). **~säure** *f* nitric acid.

Salto ['zalto] *m* (-s; -s, -ti) somersault.

Salut [za'lu:t] *m* (-[e]s; -e) salute.

salutieren [zalu'ti:rən] *v/t, v/i* (h) salute.

Salve ['zalvə] *f* (-; -n) ✕ volley, salvo.

Salz [zalts] *n* (-es; -e) salt.

'**salzarm** *adj* ✎ *Kost* low-salt diet.

'**Salzbergwerk** *n* salt mine.

salzen ['zaltsən] *v/t* (salzte, gesalzen, h) salt, *fig. a.* season; → *gesalzen.*

'**Salzfäßchen** *n* salt cellar.

'**Salzgurke** *f* pickled gherkin.

'**salzhaltig** *adj* saline.

'**Salzhering** *m* salted herring.

'**salzig** ['zaltsıç] *adj* salty.

'**Salzkartoffeln** *pl* boiled potatoes.

'**salzlos** *adj* salt-free.

'**Salzsäure** *f* 🜍 hydrochloric acid.

'**Salzstange** *f* saltstick. '**Salzstreuer** *m* salt shaker. '**Salzwasser** *n* salt water.

Samariter [zama'ri:tər] *m* (-s; -) (*barmherziger* ~ good) Samaritan.

Samen ['za:mən] *m* (-s; -) 1. ♣ *or fig.* seed. 2. *physiol.* sperm, semen. **~bank** *f* (-; -en) 🝐, *vet.* sperm bank. **~erguß** *m* ejaculation. **~faden** *m* spermatozoon. **~flüssigkeit** *f* semen. **~kapsel** *f* ♣ seed capsule. **~leiter** *m* *anat.* vas deferens. **~spender** *m* (sperm) donor. **~strang** *m* *anat.* spermatic cord.

'**Sammel|akti|on** *f* 1. fund-raising campaign. 2. (salvage) collection. **~band** *m* (-[e]s; ⸚e) anthology. **~becken** *n* reservoir (*a. fig.*), *geogr.* catchment area.

~begriff *m* generic term. **~bestellung** *f* collective order. **~büchse** *f* collecting box. **~fahrschein** *m* group ticket. **~lager** *n* assembly camp. **~mappe** *f* file.

sammeln ['zaməln] (h) **I** *v/t* 1. collect (*money, stamps, etc*), gather (*wood etc, fig. experience*); → *gesammelt* 1. 2. assemble, gather: (*wieder*) ~ rally. 3. *opt.* focus. **II** *v/i* 4. (*für* for) collect money, pass the hat (around). **III** *sich* ~ 5. gather, accumulate. 6. assemble, meet, rally. 7. *fig.* a) *a.* **s-e Gedanken** ~ collect one's thoughts, b) compose o.s.; → *gesammelt* 2. 8. *opt.* focus.

'**Sammel|name** *m* collective (noun). **~platz** *m*, **~punkt** *m* 1. assembly point. 2. *a.* **~stelle** *f* collecting point.

Sammelsurium [zaməl'zu:rĭom] *n* (-s; -rien) omnium gatherum.

'**Sammelvisum** *o* group visa.

Sammler[1] ['zamlər] *m* (-s; -) ⚡ accumulator. '**Sammler**[2] *m* (-s; -), '**Sammlerin** *f* (-; -nen) collector.

'**Sammlerwert** *m* collector's value.

'**Sammlung** *f* (-; -en) 1. collection. 2. anthology. 3. museum. 4. *fig.* a) concentration, b) composure.

Samstag ['zams-]*m* (*am* ~ on) Saturday.

'**samstags** *adv* on Saturdays.

samt [zamt] **I** *adv* **und sonders** all of them, F the whole lot. **II** *prep* together with, along with.

Samt *m* (-[e]s; -e) a) velvet, b) velveteen.

'**samtartig** *adj* velvety.

'**Samthandschuh** *m* *fig. j-n mit* **~en anfassen** handle s.o. with kid gloves.

sämtlich ['zɛmtlıç] **I** *adj* all: **~e** *Werke* the complete works. **II** *adv* all of them.

Sanatorium [zana'to:rĭom] *n* (-s; -rien) sanatorium, *Am.* sanitarium.

Sand [zant] *m* (-[e]s; ⸚e) sand: **F** *wie* **~ am Meer** any number of; *im* **~e** *verlaufen* come to nothing; *j-m* **~ in die Augen streuen** throw dust in s.o.'s eyes; F *in den* **~ setzen** waste (*a project etc*).

Sandale [zan'da:lə] *f* (-; -n) sandal.

Sandalette [zanda'lɛtə] *f* (-; -n) high-heeled sandal.

'**Sand|bahn** *f mot.* dirt track. **~bank** *f* (-; ⸚e) sandbank. **~boden** *m* sandy soil.

'**Sanddorn** *m* (-[e]s; -e) ♣ sea buckthorn.

sandig ['zandıç] *adj* sandy.

'**Sand|kasten** *m* sandpit, ✕ sandtable. **~männchen** *n* sandman. **~pa|pier** *n* sandpaper. **~sack** m sandbag. **~stein** m sandstone. **~strand** m sandy beach. **~sturm** m sandstorm.

sandte ['zantə] pret of **senden²**.

'**Sanduhr** f hourglass.

sanft [zanft] adj soft, gentle, peaceful, easy (death etc). '**Sanftheit** f (-; no pl) softness, gentleness.

'**sanftmütig** ['-my:tɪç] adj gentle, meek.

sang [zaŋ] pret of **singen**.

Sänger ['zɛŋər] m (-s; -) **1.** singer. **2.** zo. songbird. **~fest** n choral festival.

'**Sängerin** f (-; -nen) singer.

'**sang- und 'klanglos** adv F quietly.

sanieren [za'ni:rən] (h) **I** v/t redevelop, a. ⚕ rehabilitate. **II** sich ~ a) ⚕ get back on one's feet again, b) F line one's own pockets. **Sa'nierung** f (-; -en) redevelopment, a. ⚕ rehabilitation.

Sa'nierungsgebiet n redevelopment area.

sanitär [zani'tɛ:r] adj sanitary.

Sanitäter [zani'tɛ:tər] m (-s; -) **1.** ambulance (or first-aid) man. **2.** ✕ medical orderly.

Sani'täts|dienst m medical service. **~korps** n ✕ medical corps. **~wache** f first-aid post. **~wagen** m ambulance. **~zelt** n hospital tent.

sank [zaŋk] pret of **sinken**.

Sankt [zaŋkt] (abbr. St.) Saint (abbr. St.).

Sanktion [zaŋktsi̯o:n] f (-; -en) sanction.

sanktionieren [zaŋktsi̯o'ni:rən] v/t sanction.

sann [zan] pret of **sinnen**.

Saphir ['za:fir] m (-s; -e) **1.** sapphire. **2.** a. '**Saphirnadel** f sapphire (needle).

Sardelle [zar'dɛlə] f (-; -n) anchovy.

Sardine [zar'di:nə] f (-; -n) sardine.

Sarg [zark] m (-[e]s; ⁀e) coffin, Am. a. casket.

Sarkasmus [zar'kasmʊs] m (-; no pl) sarcasm.

sarkastisch [zar'kastɪʃ] adj sarcastic.

saß [za:s] pret of **sitzen**.

Satan ['za:tan] m (-s; -e) Satan.

satanisch [za'ta:nɪʃ] adj satanic.

Satellit [zatɛ'li:t] m (-en; -en) satellite.

Satel'liten|bild n, **~foto** n satellite picture. **~staat** m pol. satellite (state). **~stadt** f satellite town. **~übertragung** f TV satellite transmission.

Satin [za'tɛ̃:] m (-s; -s) a) satin, b) sateen.

Satire [za'ti:rə] f (-; -n) satire (**auf** acc

on). **Satiriker** [za'ti:rikər] m (-s; -) satirist. **satirisch** [za'ti:rɪʃ] adj satirical.

satt [zat] adj **1.** satisfied, F full up: ich bin ~ I've had enough; **sich ~ essen** eat one's fill; **das macht ~** that's very filling; ~ **zu essen haben** have enough to eat; F et. (j-n) (gründlich) ~ haben be sick and tired of (or be fed up with) s.th. (s.o.). **2.** full (sound), deep, rich (colour). **3.** fig. complacent. **4.** F stiff, steep (price etc), powerful (blow).

Sattel ['zatəl] m saddle: fig. j-n aus dem ~ heben oust s.o.; fest im ~ sitzen be firmly in the saddle. '**sattelfest** adj well up (in dat in). '**satteln** v/t (h) saddle.

'**Sattel|schlepper** m mot. **1.** road tractor. **2.** articulated lorry, Am. semitrailer (truck). **~tasche** f saddle-bag. **~zeug** n saddle and harness.

sättigen ['zɛtɪɡən] (h) **I** v/t **1.** satisfy, fill. **2.** 🜍, a. ⚗ saturate. **II** v/i **3.** be filling. '**Sättigung** f (-; no pl) a) satiation, b) satiety, a. 🜍 or fig. saturation.

Sattler ['zatlər] m (-s; -) saddler.

Sattlerei [zatlə'rai] f (-; -en) saddlery.

saturieren [zatu'ri:rən] v/t (h) saturate.

Satyr ['za:tyr] m (-s, -n; -n) satyr.

Satz [zats] m (-es; ⁀e) **1.** ling. sentence, clause. **2.** principle, tenet, ⅃ theorem. **3.** print. a) (type)setting, composition, b) (set) matter. **4.** ♪ movement. **5.** tennis: set. **6.** set (of tools, stamps, etc). **7.** sediment, dregs, (coffee) grounds. **8.** rate: zum ~ von at the rate of. **9.** leap: e-n ~ machen (take a) leap.

'**Satz|aussage** f ling. predicate. **~ball** m tennis: set point. **~bau** m (-[e]s; no pl) ling. syntax, construction. **~gefüge** n ling. compound sentence. **~gegenstand** m ling. subject. **~lehre** f ling. syntax. **~spiegel** m print. type area. **~teil** m ling. part of sentence, clause.

'**Satzung** f (-; -en) statute, a. pl statutes and articles.

'**satzungsgemäß** adj statutory, a. in accordance with the statutes.

'**Satzzeichen** n punctuation mark.

Sau [zaʊ] f (-; ⁀e) **1.** zo. sow. **2.** V fig. a) (dirty) pig, b) slut, c) contp. swine, a. bitch: **unter aller ~** lousy; j-n (et.) zur ~ **machen** let s.o. have it (tear s.th. to pieces); **die ~ rauslassen** let one's hair down.

sauber ['zaʊbər] adj **1.** a. fig. clean, neat:

~ **sein** child: be potty-trained; **e-e ~e Lösung** a neat solution. **2.** F iro. nice, (just) great.

säuberlich ['zɔybərlɪç] adj **1.** clean, neat. **2.** careful.

'**saubermachen** v/t, v/i (sep, -ge-, h) clean (up), tidy (up).

säubern ['zɔybərn] v/t (h) **1.** clean (up), tidy (up). **2.** clear (**von** of). **3.** fig. purge.

'**Säuberung** f (-; -en) **1.** cleaning (etc). **2.** fig. purge.

'**Saubohne** f ⚹ broad bean.

Sauciere [zo'sĭɛ:rə] f (-; -n) gravy boat.

Saudi ['zaudi] m (-s; -s) saudi.

Saudi-A'rabien n (-s) Saudi Arabia.

'**sau'dumm** adj V damned stupid.

sauer ['zauər] **I** adj **1.** sour, 🜛 acid (a. drops, rain), gastr. pickled: ~ werden milk: turn (sour), curdle; **in den sauren Apfel beißen müssen** have to swallow the bitter pill. **2.** F sour, cross: ~ **werden** get cross; **j-m das Leben ~ machen** make life miserable for s.o. **II** adv **3.** ~ **verdientes Geld** hard-earned money; F ~ **reagieren auf** (acc) be annoyed (or mad) at.

'**Sauerampfer** m (-s; no pl) ⚹ sorrel.

Saue'rei f (-; -en) → **Schweinerei.**

'**Sauerkirsche** f ⚹ sour cherry.

säuerlich ['zɔyərlɪç] adj (a bit) sour.

'**Sauermilch** f curdled milk.

säuern ['zɔyərn] v/t (h) make sour.

'**Sauerstoff** m (-[e]s; no pl) oxygen. **~flasche** f oxygen cylinder. **~mangel** m lack of oxygen. **~maske** f oxygen mask. **~zelt** n ✣ oxygen tent.

'**Sauerteig** m leaven.

saufen ['zaufən] v/t, v/i (soff, gesoffen, h) **1.** animal: drink. **2.** F person: booze, guzzle. **Säufer** ['zɔyfər] m (-s; -) F alcoholic, boozer. **Saufe'rei** f (-; -en) F **1.** boozing. **2.** F drinking bout, booze-up.

'**Säuferin** f (-; -nen) → **Säufer.**

saugen ['zaugən] v/t, v/i (h) **1.** suck (**an** dat s.th.); → **Finger. 2.** vacuum.

'**Sauger** m (-s; -) teat, Am. nipple.

'**Säugetier** n mammal.

saugfähig ['zauk-] adj absorbent.

Säugling ['zɔyklɪŋ] m (-s; -e) baby.

'**Säuglings|alter** n (**im** ~ in) infancy. **~nahrung** f baby food. **~pflege** f baby care. **~schwester** f baby nurse.

~sterblichkeit f infant mortality.

'**Saugwirkung** f suction.

'**sau'kalt** adj V bloody cold.

Säule ['zɔylə] f (-; -n) column, pillar (a. fig.). '**Säulengang** m colonnade.

Saum [zaum] m (-[e]s; ⸚e) hem.

'**saumäßig** adj V awful, lousy.

säumen ['zɔymən] v/t (h) **1.** hem. **2.** fig. line, skirt.

säumig ['zɔymɪç] adj **1.** late, tardy. **2.** ✝ ~**er Zahler** (**Schuldner**) defaulter.

Sauna ['zauna] f (-; Saunen) sauna.

Säure ['zɔyrə] f (-; -n) **1.** no pl sourness, a. 🜛 acidity. **2.** 🜛 acid.

'**säure|beständig, ~fest** adj acid-proof.

'**Saure'gurkenzeit** f F (-; no pl) a) ✝ off-season, b) in the press: silly season.

'**säurehaltig** adj acid(ic).

'**säurelöslich** adj acid-soluble.

Saurier ['zauriər] m (-s; -) saurian.

Saus [zaus] m in ~ **und Braus leben** live on (or off) the fat of the land.

säuseln ['zɔyzəln] v/i, v/t (h) whisper, iro. person: purr.

sausen ['zauzən] v/i **1.** (sn) F whiz, rush, dash. **2.** (h) wind: rush, a. bullet etc: whistle, ears: buzz. '**sausenlassen** v/t (irr, sep, no -ge-, h) F a) pass up, give s.th. a miss, b) drop (s.o.).

'**Saustall** m pigsty (a. F fig.).

'**Sauwetter** n F filthy weather.

'**sau'wohl** adj F **sich ~ fühlen** feel real good.

Saxophon [zakso'fo:n] n (-s; -e) saxophone.

'**S-Bahn** f suburban (fast) train(s).

Schabe ['ʃa:bə] f (-; -n) zo. cockroach.

schaben ['ʃa:bən] v/t, v/i (h) scrape.

Schabernack ['ʃa:bərnak] m (-[e]s; -e) practical joke, hoax.

schäbig ['ʃɛ:bɪç] adj shabby, fig. a. mean. '**Schäbigkeit** f (-; no pl) shabbiness, fig. a. meanness.

Schablone [ʃa'blo:nə] f (-; -n) **1.** stencil, ⊙ template. **2.** fig. a) stereotype, cliché, b) (fixed) routine. **Scha'blonendenken** n stereotyped thinking.

scha'blonenhaft adj fig. stereotyped.

Schach [ʃax] n (-s; -s) **1.** no pl chess: ~ **spielen** play (at) chess. **2.** check: ~ **und matt!** checkmate!; **j-m ~ bieten** check s.o., fig. stand up to s.o.; **in ~ halten** keep in check (a. fig.), with gun: a. cover. **~brett** n chessboard. **~computer** m chess computer.

Schacher ['ʃaxər] m (-s; no pl) haggling. **'schachern** v/i (h) haggle (**um** over). **'Schach|fi,gur** f chessman, (chess) piece. **ℒ'matt** adj **1.** (check)mate: **~ setzen** a. fig. checkmate. **2.** F exhausted. **~par,tie** f game of chess. **~spiel** n **1.** (game of) chess. **2.** chess set. **~spieler(in** f) m chess player.

Schacht [ʃaxt] m (-[e]s; ⁀e) a) shaft (a. 𝄡), b) manhole.

Schachtel ['ʃaxtəl] f (-; -n) **1.** box, a. carton, packet. **2.** F **alte ~** old bag. **'Schachtelsatz** m involved sentence. **'Schachtur,nier** n chess tournament. **'Schachzug** m a. fig. move.

schade ['ʃaːdə] adj pred (**es ist** [**sehr**]) ~ it's a (great) pity (**um** about, **daß** that), F it's too bad (**he couldn't come** etc); **wie ~!** what a pity!; **dafür ist es** (**er**) **zu** ~ it (he) is too good for it!; **darum ist es nicht ~!** it is no great loss!

Schädel ['ʃɛːdəl] m (-s; -) skull, cranium. **~basisbruch** m fracture of the skull-base. **~bruch** m fracture of the skull. **~dach** n anat. skullcap, calvaria.

schaden ['ʃaːdən] v/i (h) (dat) damage, harm, be detrimental (to): **das schadet der Gesundheit** that's bad for your health; **das schadet nichts** a) it won't do any harm, b) it doesn't matter; iro. **das schadet ihr gar nichts!** that serves her right!; **ein Versuch kann nicht ~** there is no harm in trying.

'Schaden m (-s; ⁀) a) damage (**an** dat to), b) injury, harm, c) a. 𝄡 defect, d) disadvantage, e) loss: **~ nehmen** be damaged, person: be harmed; **durch ~ wird man klug** once bitten twice shy. **'Schadenersatz** m a) compensation, indemnification, b) damages: **~ erhalten** (**fordern, leisten**) recover (claim, pay) damages; **auf ~** (**ver**)**klagen** sue for damages. **~klage** f action for damages. **'schadenersatzpflichtig** adj liable for damages.

'Schadenfreiheitsra,batt m mot. no-claims bonus.

'Schadenfreude f (-; no pl) malicious glee, gloating: **voller ~ →** **'schadenfroh** adj gloating(ly adv): **~ sein** gloat. **'Schadenversicherung** f indemnity insurance.

schadhaft ['ʃaːt-] adj defective.

schädigen ['ʃɛːdɪɡən] v/t (h) damage, a. injure, harm, impair (a. fig.): **wir sind schwer geschädigt worden** we have suffered heavy losses. **'Schädigung** f (-; -en) (gen to) damage, harm.

schädlich ['ʃɛːtlɪç] adj (dat to) harmful, injurious, a. detrimental: **~ für die Gesundheit** bad for your health. **'Schädlichkeit** f (-; no pl) harmfulness. **'Schädling** ['ʃɛːtlɪŋ] m (-s; -e) zo. pest. **'Schädlings|bekämpfung** f pest control. **~bekämpfungsmittel** n pesticide. **'schadlos** adj **j-n** (**sich**) **~ halten** indemnify s.o. (recoup o.s.) (**für** for); **sich an j-m ~ halten** recoup one's losses from s.o.

'Schadstoff m a) harmful substance, b) pollutant.

Schaf [ʃaːf] n (-[e]s; -e) **1.** zo. sheep: fig. **schwarzes ~** black sheep. **2.** F ninny.

'Schafbock m zo. ram.

Schäfchen ['ʃɛːfçən] n (-s; -) lamb: fig. **sein ~ ins trockene bringen** feather one's nest.

Schäfer ['ʃɛːfər] m (-s; -) shepherd. **'Schäferhund** m (**deutscher**) **~** Alsatian, German shepherd (dog). **'Schäferin** f (-; -nen) shepherdess.

schaffen ['ʃafən] (schuf, geschaffen, h) **I** v/t **1.** a) create, produce, fig. a. make, b) bring about, cause, c) found, set up, establish: **er ist zum Lehrer** (**für den Posten**) **wie geschaffen** he is a born teacher (cut out for the job); → **Ordnung. 2.** take (**in** acc, **nach, zu** to), put: → **Hals, Weg, Welt. 3.** a) manage, b) F catch (**bus, train,** etc), c) set up (record): **es ~** make it, a. succeed; **das hätten wir geschafft!** we've done it!; **~ wir es bis dorthin** (**in 3 Stunden**)? can we make it there (in three hours)? **4. ich habe damit nichts zu ~** that's no business of mine, I wash my hands of it; **mit ihm will ich nichts zu ~ haben** I don't want anything to do with him. **5.** F **j-n ~** a) take it out of s.o., b) get s.o. down; **ich bin geschafft!** I've had it! **II** v/i **6.** dial. work. **7.** **etwas zu ~ machen** potter about, **an** (dat) busy o.s. (b.s. tamper) with. **8. j-m** (**viel** or **schwer**) **zu ~ machen** give (or cause) s.o. (no end of) trouble, illness: trouble s.o.

'**Schaffen** n (-s) a) work, (creative) activity, b) work(s).
'**schaffend** adj **1.** creative. **2.** working.
'**Schaffensdrang** m **1.** creative urge. **2.** zest for work. '**Schaffenskraft** f (-; no pl) **1.** creative power. **2.** vigo(u)r.
Schaffner ['ʃafnər] m (-s; -) conductor, 🚃 guard.
'**Schaffnerin** f (-; -nen) conductress.
'**Schaffung** f (-; no pl) a) creation, b) foundation, setting-up (→ **schaffen**).
'**Schafherde** f flock of sheep. '**Schafhirt** m shepherd. '**Schafleder** n sheepskin.
Schafott [ʃa'fɔt] n (-[e]s; -e) scaffold.
'**Schafpelz** m sheepskin: fig. **Wolf im ~** wolf in sheep's clothing.
'**Schafschur** f sheep shearing.
'**Schafskäse** m sheep's milk cheese.
Schaft [ʃaft] m (-[e]s; ⁓e) shaft (of axe etc), stock (of rifle), shank (of tool etc), leg (of boot). **~stiefel** m high boot.
'**Schafwolle** f sheep's wool.
'**Schafzucht** f sheep breeding.
Schah [ʃa:] m (-s; -s) Shah.
Schakal [ʃa'ka:l] m (-s; -e) zo. jackal.
schäkern ['ʃɛ:kərn] v/i (h) **1.** joke around. **2.** flirt.
schal [ʃa:l] adj stale, flat, fig. a. empty.
Schal m (-s; -s, -e) scarf.
Schale¹ ['ʃa:lə] f (-; -n) a) bowl, b) dish.
'**Schale²** f (-; -n) **1.** shell (of eggs, nuts, a. 🌰 and zo.), skin (of fruit etc), peel(ing) (of potatoes etc), husk. **2.** F **sich in ~ werfen** dress up.
schälen ['ʃɛ:lən] (h) **I** v/t peel (orange, potatoes, etc), shell (eggs, nuts), husk (peas etc), skin (tomatoes etc). **II** sich ~ skin: peel off.
'**Schalensitz** m mot. bucket seat.
'**Schalheit** f (-; no pl) a. fig. staleness.
Schall [ʃal] m (-[e]s; -e) **1.** sound: **schneller als der ~** supersonic. **2.** echo.
'**schalldämpfend** adj sound-deadening.
'**Schalldämpfer** m sound absorber, mot. silencer (a. on guns), Am. muffler.
'**schalldicht** adj soundproof.
schallen ['ʃalən] v/i (h) resound, ring: **~de Ohrfeige** resounding slap; **~des Gelächter** peals of laughter; **er lachte ~d** he roared with laughter.
'**Schallgeschwindigkeit** f sonic speed.
'**Schallmauer** f sound barrier.
'**Schallplatte** f record, disc, disk.
'**Schallplattenaufnahme** f recording.

'**schallschluckend** adj sound-absorbing.
'**Schallwelle** f sound wave.
schalt [ʃalt] pret of **schelten**.
'**Schaltauto,matik** f mot. automatic gear change.
schalten ['ʃaltən] (h) **I** v/i **1.** ⚡, ⚙ switch (**auf** acc to), shift (the levers), mot. change (or shift) the gears: **in den dritten Gang ~** change (or shift) into third (gear). **2.** F get it, catch on: **schnell ~** a) do some quick thinking, b) catch on quickly, be quick in the uptake. **3.** ~ **und walten** be in charge (of things); **j-n ~ und walten lassen** give s.o. a free hand. **II** v/t **4.** ⚙ switch, turn, shift (gear, wheel). **5.** ⚡ switch (**auf** acc to).
'**Schalter** m (-s; -) **1.** counter, 🚃 ticket window, ✉ desk. **2.** ⚡ switch. **~beamte** m (counter or booking) clerk. **~dienst** m counter duty. **~halle** f main hall. **~stunden** pl business hours.
'**Schalt|getriebe** n gear box. **~hebel** m mot. (gear)shift lever, ⚡ switch lever, ⚙ control lever: **an den ~n der Macht sitzen** be at the controls. **~jahr** n leap year: F **alle ~e** (**mal**) once in a blue moon. **~kasten** m ⚡ switchbox. **~knopf** m (control) button. **~kreis** m ⚡ circuit. **~plan** m wiring diagram. **~pult** n control desk. **~tafel** f ⚡ switchboard. **~tag** m intercalary day. **~uhr** f timer.
'**Schaltung** f (-; -en) **1.** mot. a) gearshift assembly, b) gear change (or shift). **2.** ⚡ a) circuit, b) wiring. **3.** ⚙ control(s).
Scham [ʃa:m] f (-; no pl) **1.** shame: **rot vor ~ →** **schamrot**. **2.** private parts, genitals. **~bein** n anat. pubic bone.
schämen ['ʃɛ:mən] **sich ~** (h) be (or feel) ashamed ([**wegen**] gen, **für** of); **schäme dich!** shame on you!
'**Scham|gefühl** n (-[e]s; no pl) sense of shame. **~haare** pl pubic hair.
'**schamhaft** adj bashful, modest.
'**Schamlippen** pl anat. labia.
'**schamlos** adj a) shameless, b) indecent: **~e Lüge** barefaced lie. '**Schamlosigkeit** f (-; no pl) shamelessness.
Schamottestein ['ʃa'mɔtə-] m firebrick.
'**schamrot** adj red with shame: **~ werden** blush with shame.
Schande ['ʃandə] f (-; no pl) disgrace (**für** to), a. shame: **~ machen** (dat) be a disgrace to.

schänden ['ʃɛndən] v/t (h) a) dishon-o(u)r, b) violate, rape, c) desecrate.
'**Schandfleck** m blot, eyesore.
schändlich ['ʃɛntlıç] adj disgraceful, scandalous.
Schandtat ['ʃant-] f outrage.
'**Schändung** f (-; -en) a) disgrace (gen to), b) violation, rape, c) desecration.
'**Schankstube** ['ʃaŋk-] f (public) bar.
Schanze ['ʃantsə] f (-; -n) ski-jump.
'**Schanzentisch** m ski-jump platform.
Schar [ʃaːr] f (-; -en) crowd (of people), troop (of children), flock (of birds).
scharen ['ʃaːrən] v/t/v (h) (a. sich ~) gather (or rally) (um round); e-e Menge etc um sich ~ rally a crowd etc round one.
'**scharenweise** adv in droves.

scharf [ʃarf] **I** adj **1.** sharp (a. fig. eye, criticism, tongue, etc), a. biting (wind etc, fig. words etc), a. piercing (sound), a. keen (mind, glance, etc). **2.** live (ammunition), armed (bomb etc). **3.** hot (food, pepper, etc), strong (spirits, vinegar, etc), pungent, acrid (smell), 🐍 or fig. caustic. **4.** sharp, abrupt. **5.** sharp, exact, clear: phot. ein ~es Bild a sharp(ly defined) picture. **6.** a) sharp, severe, strict, b) hard, fierce: ~e Konkurrenz stiff competition; ~er Protest fierce protest; ~es Tempo hard pace; ~e Bewachung close guard(ing); ~er Hund savage dog, F fig. tough guy. **7.** F randy, hot, a. sexy: ~ sein auf (acc) be very keen on, sexually: be hot for. **II** adv **8.** sharply (etc): ~ aufpassen pay close attention, watch out; ~ bremsen brake hard; phot. ~ einstellen focus; ~ nachdenken think hard; ~ schießen shoot with live ammunition; ~ verurteilen condemn severely.
'**Scharfblick** m (-[e]s; no pl) perspicacity.
Schärfe ['ʃɛrfə] f (-; no pl) **1.** sharpness, fig. a. severity, a. keenness (of mind), a. fierceness: in aller ~ very severely. **2.** a. gastr. hotness, a. pungency (of smell), c) 🐍 or fig. causticity. **3.** acuteness (of sight, hearing), opt., phot. sharpness.
'**Scharfeinstellung** f opt., phot. a) focus(s)ing, b) focus(s)ing control.
schärfen ['ʃɛrfən] v/t (h) a. fig. sharpen.
'**Schärfentiefe** f phot. depth of focus.
'**scharfkantig** adj sharp-edged.
'**scharfmachen** v/t (sep, -ge-, h) F j-n ~ a) gegen set s.o. against, b) auf (acc)

make s.o. keen on, c) turn s.o. on.
'**Scharfmacher** m (-s; -) F agitator.
'**Scharfschießen** n live shooting.
'**Scharfschütze** m sharpshooter, sniper.
'**scharfsichtig** adj fig. perspicacious.
'**Scharfsinn** m (-[e]s; no pl) acumen.
'**scharfsinnig** adj astute, shrewd.
Scharlach ['ʃarlax] m (-s; no pl) 🌡 scarlet fever. '**scharlachrot** adj scarlet.
Scharlatan ['ʃarlatan] m (-s; -e) charlatan, F quack, fraud.
Scharnier [ʃar'niːr] n (-s; -e) hinge.
Schärpe ['ʃɛrpə] f (-; -n) sash.
scharren ['ʃarən] v/i (h) scrape (mit den Füßen one's feet), horse etc: paw.
Scharte ['ʃartə] f (-; -en) nick: fig. die ~ (wieder) auswetzen make up for it.
schartig ['ʃartıç] adj jagged.
Schaschlik ['ʃaʃlık] m, n (-s; -s) shashlik.
Schatten ['ʃatən] m (-s; -) a) a. fig. shadow, b) shade: im ~ in the shade; fig. in den ~ stellen outshine, eclipse; in j-s ~ stehen live in s.o.'s shadow; man kann nicht über s-n (eigenen) ~ springen the leopard can't change its spots.
'**Schattendasein** n ein ~ führen live in the shadow.
'**schattenhaft** adj shadowy.
'**Schatten|kabi‚nett** n pol. shadow cabinet. ~**riß** m silhouette. ~**seite** f shady (fig. seamy) side. ~**spiel** n shadow play.
schattieren [ʃa'tiːrən] v/t (h) shade.
Schat'tierung f (-; -en) a) shading, b) a. fig. shade.
schattig ['ʃatıç] adj shady.
Schatulle [ʃa'tʊlə] f (-; -n) casket.
Schatz [ʃats] m (-es; ~e) **1.** a. fig. treasure. **2.** F darling, love.
'**Schatzamt** n pol. Treasury.
'**Schatzanweisung** f ✝ treasury bond.
'**schätzbar** adj assessable.
'**Schätzchen** ['ʃɛtsçən] n (-s; -) darling.
schätzen ['ʃɛtsən] v/t (h) **1.** estimate, guess, a. assess (damage, value, etc) (auf acc at): wie alt ~ Sie ihn? how old would you say he is?; grob geschätzt at a rough guess. **2.** suppose, Am. F guess. **3.** a) esteem, think highly of, b) appreciate: → glücklich I.
'**Schätzer** m (-s; -) ✝ valuer, assessor.
'**Schatzgräber** [-grɛːbər] m (-s; -) treasure seeker.
'**Schatz|kammer** f treasury. ~**meister** m treasurer. ~**suche** f treasure hunt.

'**Schätzung** f (-; -en) estimate, guess, ✝, ⚎ assessment.

'**schätzungsweise** adv approximately.

Schau [ʃaʊ] f (-; -en) **1.** show, exhibition: **zur ~ stellen** exhibit, display, fig. a. parade; fig. **nur zur ~** only for show. **2.** TV etc show: F **e-e ~ abziehen** put on a show; **j-m die ~ stehlen** steal the show from s.o., upstage s.o.

'**Schaubild** n chart, graph, diagram.

Schauder ['ʃaʊdər] m (-s; -) shudder, shiver. '**schauderhaft** adj horrible, dreadful. '**schaudern** v/i (h) (**vor** dat with, **bei** at) shudder, shiver.

schauen ['ʃaʊən] v/i (h) look (**auf** acc at, fig. upon): F **schau, daß du ...** mind you ...; iro. **schau, schau!** well, well!

Schauer ['ʃaʊər] m (-s; -) **1.** meteor. shower. **2.** shudder, shiver, a. thrill; → **laufen** 1. '**schauerartig** adj **~e Regenfälle** showers.

'**schauerlich** adj **1.** horrible, terrible (a. fig.). **2.** weird, F creepy.

'**Schauermärchen** n F horror story.

Schaufel ['ʃaʊfəl] f (-; -n) **1.** a) shovel, b) scoop, c) ⚙ paddle (of water wheel), blade (of turbine). **2.** hunt. palm.

'**schaufeln** v/t, v/i (h) a) shovel, b) dig.

'**Schaufenster** n shop window, fig. showcase. **~bummel** m **e-n ~ machen** go window-shopping. **~dekoration** f window dressing.

'**Schau|fliegen** n, **~flug** m air display.

'**Schaugeschäft** n show business.

'**Schaukampf** m exhibition bout.

'**Schaukasten** m showcase.

Schaukel ['ʃaʊkəl] f (-; -n) swing.

schaukeln ['ʃaʊkəln] v/t, v/i (h) swing, cradle, chair, ship: rock: F **die Sache ~** manage (or swing) it.

'**Schaukelpolitik** f seesaw politics.

'**Schaukelstuhl** m rocking chair.

'**Schaulaufen** n exhibition skating.

'**Schaulustige** m f (-n; -n) curious onlooker, contp. gaper.

Schaum [ʃaʊm] m (-[e]s; ∺e) foam (a. ⚙), froth (a. on beer); lather: gastr. **zu ~ schlagen** beat (to a froth).

'**Schaumbad** n bubble bath.

schäumen ['ʃɔʏmən] v/i (h) foam, froth: (**vor** Wut) **~** foam (with rage).

'**Schaumgummi** m, n foam rubber.

schaumig ['ʃaʊmɪç] adj frothy.

'**Schaum|krone** f white crest. **~löscher**

m foam extinguisher. **~schläger** m contp. hot-air artist. **~schläge'rei** f (-; no pl) contp. hot air. **~stoff** m ⚙ foamed material. **~teppich** m ✈ foam carpet. **~wein** m sparkling wine.

'**Schaupackung** f ✝ dummy.

'**Schauplatz** m (am ~ at the) scene.

'**Schaupro,zeß** m ⚎ show trial.

schaurig ['ʃaʊrɪç] → **schauerlich.**

'**Schauspiel** n **1.** play, drama. **2.** fig. spectacle, sight. '**Schauspieler** m (fig. play-)actor. **Schauspiele'rei** f (-; no pl) (fig. play-)acting. '**Schauspielerin** f actress. '**schauspielerisch** adj theatrical, acting (talent etc). '**schauspielern** v/i (h) fig. play-act, F put on an act.

'**Schauspielhaus** n theat/re (Am. -er).

'**Schauspielschule** f drama school.

'**Schausteller** m (-s; -) exhibitor, at fairs etc: showman.

Scheck [ʃɛk] m (-s; -s) cheque, Am. check (**über** acc for). **~buch** n, **~heft** n chequebook, Am. checkbook. **~karte** f cheque (Am. check) card.

scheel [ʃe:l] **~ ansehen** look askance at.

Scheffel ['ʃɛfəl] m (-s; -) bushel: fig. **sein Licht unter den ~ stellen** hide one's light under a bushel.

'**scheffeln** v/t (h) rake in money.

Scheibe ['ʃaɪbə] f (-; -n) **1.** disc (a. F record), ⚙ a. wheel, a. washer. **2.** (window etc) pane, mot. windscreen, Am. windshield. **3.** target. **4.** ice hockey: puck. **5.** slice (of bread etc): F **da(von) kannst du dir e-e ~ abschneiden!** you can take a leaf out of his (her etc) book!

'**Scheiben|bremse** f mot. disc brake. **~kupplung** f disc clutch. **~schießen** n target practice. **~waschanlage** f mot. windscreen (Am. windshield) washers. **~wischer** m mot. windscreen (Am. windshield) wiper.

Scheich [ʃaɪç] m (-[e]s; -s, -e) sheik(h).

'**Scheichtum** n (-s; ∺er) sheikhdom.

Scheide ['ʃaɪdə] f (-; -n) **1.** sheath (a. ⚗), a. scabbard. **2.** anat. vagina.

scheiden ['ʃaɪdən] (schied, geschieden) **I** v/t (h) separate, divide, ⚎ divorce (a married couple), dissolve (marriage): **sich ~ lassen**, a. **geschieden werden** get a divorce (**von** from). **II** v/i (sn part (**von** from): **aus dem Dienst ~** retire from service, resign; **aus e-r Firma ~**

leave a firm. **III sich ~** (h) separate; **hier ~ sich die Geister** here opinions are divided.

'**Scheide|wand** f partition, *fig.* barrier. **~weg** m *fig.* **am ~** at a crossroads.

'**Scheidung** f (-; -en) **1.** separation. **2.** divorce (**von** from), dissolution (*of marriage*): **die ~ einreichen** file a petition for divorce.

'**Scheidungs|grund** m ground for divorce. **~klage** f petition for divorce.

Schein¹ [ʃaɪn] m (-[e]s; *no pl*) **1.** light, a. glow. **2.** appearance: **et. nur zum ~ tun** pretend to do s.th.; **dem ~ nach** (**zu urteilen**) to all appearances; **den ~ wahren** keep up appearances; **der ~ trügt** appearances are deceptive.

Schein² m (-[e]s; -e) **1.** a) slip, b) a. *univ.* certificate. **2.** (bank)note, *Am. a.* bill.

'**scheinbar** adj seeming, apparent: **er ging nur ~ darauf ein** he only pretended to agree.

'**Scheinehe** f fictitious marriage.

scheinen ['ʃaɪnən] v/i (schien, geschienen, h) **1.** a) shine, b) gleam. **2.** appear, seem: **wie es scheint** as it seems; **es scheint mir** it seems to me; **er scheint nicht zu wollen; mir scheint, er will nicht** he doesn't seem to want to.

'**Schein|firma** f dummy firm. **~friede** m hollow peace. **~geschäft** n fictitious transaction.

'**scheinheilig** adj F *contp.* hypocritical. '**Scheinheiligkeit** f (-; *no pl*) hypocrisy. '**Scheintod** m suspended animation. '**scheintot** adj seemingly dead.

'**Scheinwerfer** m (-s; -) floodlight, searchlight, *mot.* headlight, *film:* klieg light, *thea.* (a. **~licht** n) spotlight.

Scheiß... [ʃaɪs-] V bloody, *sl.* fucking. '**Scheißdreck** m → **Scheiße** 2.

'**Scheiße** f (-; *no pl*) V a. *fig.* shit, crap: *fig.* **in der ~ sitzen** be in the shit; **~!** shit!; **~ bauen** foul up; **große ~ sein** be a load of crap. '**scheißen** v/i (schiß, geschissen, h) V shit, crap: **scheiß drauf!** to hell with it!, fuck it!

'**Scheißer** m (-s; -) V **1.** *kleiner ~* little shit. **2.** a. '**Scheißkerl** m bastard.

Scheit [ʃaɪt] n (-[e]s; -e) piece of wood, log.

Scheitel ['ʃaɪtəl] m (-s; -) parting: **vom ~ bis zur Sohle** from top to toe.

scheiteln ['ʃaɪtəln] v/t (h) (**sich**) **das Haar ~** part one's hair.

'**Scheitelpunkt** m A vertex, *astr.* zenith.

Scheiterhaufen ['ʃaɪtər-] m (funeral) pyre, *hist.* (**auf dem ~** at the) stake.

scheitern ['ʃaɪtərn] v/i (sn) (**an dat**) fail (because of), *negotiations:* a. break down, *sports:* be stopped (by): **daran ist er gescheitert** that was his undoing.

'**Scheitern** n (-s) failure, breakdown.

Schelle ['ʃɛlə] f (-; -n) **1.** (little) bell. **2.** ⊙ clamp, clip.

schellen ['ʃɛlən] *dial.* → **klingeln** 1.

'**Schellfisch** m haddock.

Schelm [ʃɛlm] m (-[e]s; -e) rogue.

'**schelmisch** adj roguish, impish.

schelten ['ʃɛltən] v/t (schalt, gescholten, h) scold, chide (*a. v/i*).

Schema ['ʃeːma] n (-s; -s, -ta) **1.** pattern, system: **nach e-m ~** schematically; **F nach ~ F** by rote. **2.** diagram, scheme.

schematisch [ʃeˈmaːtɪʃ] adj schematic, systematic, *contp.* mechanical.

schematisieren [ʃematiˈziːrən] v/t schematize.

Schemel ['ʃeːməl] m (-s; -) (foot)stool.

Schemen ['ʃeːmən] n (-s; -) phantom.

'**schemenhaft** adj shadowy.

Schenke ['ʃɛŋkə] f (-; -n) tavern.

Schenkel ['ʃɛŋkəl] m (-s; -) **1.** *anat.* a) thigh, b) shank. **2.** A side, leg.

schenken ['ʃɛŋkən] v/t (h) a) give (as a present), a. 🏛 donate, b) *impart:* **j-m et. ~** give s.o. s.th. (as a present) (**zum Geburtstag** for his *etc* birthday); *fig.* **sich et. ~** skip s.th., give s.th. a miss; **F geschenkt!** forget it!; → **Aufmerksamkeit** 1, **Gehör** 2, **Glaube** *etc*.

'**Schenkung** f (-; -en) donation.

'**Schenkungsurkunde** f deed of donation.

scheppern ['ʃɛpərn] v/i (h) F rattle.

Scherbe ['ʃɛrbə] f (-; -n) broken piece, fragment.

Schere ['ʃeːrə] f (-; -n) **1.** (**e-e ~** a pair of) scissors (✂ shears). **2.** *zo.* pincer. **3.** *sports:* scissors.

scheren ['ʃeːrən] **I** v/t (schor, geschoren, h) trim, cut (*a. hair*), shear (*sheep*), clip (*hedge*). **II** F *reflex.* **~ um** not to care about; **sich nach Hause** (**ins Bett**) **~** go home (to bed); **scher dich!** beat it!

'**Scherenschnitt** m silhouette.

Schererei f (-; -en) F trouble.

Scherflein [ˈʃɛrflaın] n (-s; -) **sein ~ beitragen** give one's mite, a. do one's bit.

Scherz [ʃɛrts] m (-es; -e) joke: **(s-n) ~ treiben mit** make fun of; **im ~, zum ~** as a joke, for fun; **~ beiseite** joking apart.

scherzen [ˈʃɛrtsən] v/i (h) joke: **damit ist nicht zu ~** that's not to be trifled with.

'scherzhaft adj joking, humorous.

scheu [ʃɔy] adj shy, timid: **~ machen** frighten (**horse** etc). **Scheu** f (-; no pl) a) shyness, timidity, b) awe.

scheuchen [ˈʃɔyçən] v/t (h) chase.

scheuen [ˈʃɔyən] (h) **I** v/i horse etc: shy, take fright (**vor** dat at). **II** v/t shun, avoid, shy away from: **k-e Kosten ~** spare no expense; → **Licht** 1. **III sich ~, et. zu tun** be afraid of (or shrink from) doing s.th.; **sich nicht ~ zu** inf not to be afraid to inf, b.s. have the nerve to inf.

'Scheuerbürste f scrubbing brush.

'Scheuerlappen m floor cloth.

scheuern [ˈʃɔyərn] (h) **I** v/t **1.** scour, scrub. **2.** chafe. **3.** F **j-m e-e ~** slap s.o.('s face). **II** v/i **4.** chafe.

'Scheuklappe f a. fig. blinker.

Scheune [ˈʃɔynə] f (-; -n) barn.

Scheusal [ˈʃɔyzaːl] n (-s; -e) monster (a. fig.), F beast: **kleines ~** little horror.

scheußlich [ˈʃɔyslıç] adj horrible (a. F fig.), a. hideous, revolting: **F ~es Wetter** filthy weather; **~ kalt** terribly cold.

Schi(...) [ʃiː] → **Ski(...)**.

Schicht [ʃıçt] f (-; -en) **1.** layer, a. coat(ing), geol. stratum, bed, phot. emulsion. **2.** class, pl a. social strata: **breite ~en** large sections (**of** the population). **3.** shift: **~ arbeiten** do shift work.

'Schichtarbeit f shift work.

'Schichtarbeiter(in f**)** m shift worker.

schichten [ˈʃıçtən] v/t (h) pile up, stack.

'Schichtunterricht m teaching in shifts.

'Schichtwechsel m change of shift.

'schichtweise adv **1.** in layers. **2.** work etc in shifts.

schick [ʃık] adj **1.** a) smart, chic, stylish, b) posh, c) trendy. **2.** F great, super.

Schick m (-[e]s; no pl) chic, stylishness.

schicken [ˈʃıkən] (h) **I** v/t **1.** send (**nach, zu** to). **II sich ~ 2.** befit (**für j-n** s.o.): **es schickt sich nicht!** that is not the done thing! **3. sich ~ in** (acc) resign o.s. to.

Schickeria [ʃıkəˈriːa] f (-; no pl) the chic set, the trendies. **Schickimicki** [ˈʃıkıˈmıkı] m (-s; -s) F trendy.

'schicklich adj proper, fitting.

Schicksal [ˈʃıkzaːl] n (-s; -e) fate, destiny, a. lot: **das ~ herausfordern** tempt fate. **'schicksalhaft** adj fateful.

'Schicksals|frage f vital question. **~gefährte** m, **~genosse** m companion in distress. **~schlag** m (bad) blow.

'Schiebedach n mot. sliding roof, sunroof. **'Schiebefenster** n sliding (or sash) window.

schieben [ˈʃiːbən] (schob, geschoben, h) **I** v/t **1.** a) push, b) slip, put (**in** acc into): **sich durch die Menge ~** push one's way through the crowd; → **Bank¹**. **II** v/i **2.** push. **3.** F ~ mit traffic in.

'Schieber m (-s; -) **1.** ⊙ a) slide, b) gate, c) bar, bolt. **2.** F racketeer.

'Schiebesitz m sliding seat.

'Schiebetür f sliding door.

'Schiebung f (-; -en) F put-up job, fix.

'schied [ʃiːt] pret of **scheiden**.

Schiedsgericht [ˈʃiːts-] n court of arbitration, sports etc: jury.

'Schiedsrichter m arbitrator, at competitions: judge, pl jury, sports: umpire, referee: **als ~ fungieren** → **schiedsrichtern**.

'schiedsrichterlich adj and adv sports: of (or by) the umpire (or referee).

'schiedsrichtern v/i (h) referee, umpire.

'Schiedsspruch m award, arbitration.

schief [ʃiːf] **I** adj **1.** oblique, a. slanting, lop-sided: **~e Absätze** worn-down heels; **~e Ebene** inclined plane; **der ~e Turm von Pisa** the Leaning Tower of Pisa; fig. **~es Lächeln** wry smile. **2.** fig. false, wrong, distorted, warped: → **Bahn** 1, **Licht** 1. **II** adv **3.** obliquely, aslant, at an angle: F fig. **j-n ~ ansehen** look askance at s.o.

Schiefer [ˈʃiːfər] m (-s; -) slate. **~dach** n slate roof. **~platte** f, **~tafel** f slate.

'schiefgehen v/i (irr, sep, -ge-, sn, → **gehen**) F go wrong.

'schieflachen: sich ~ (sep, -ge-, h) F laugh one's head off.

schielen [ˈʃiːlən] v/i (h) **1.** (have a) squint, be cross-eyed: **auf dem rechten Auge ~** have a squint in one's right eye. **2.** F peer: **~ auf** (acc) (or **nach**) a) steal a glance at, b) have an eye on.

schien [ʃiːn] pret of **scheinen**.

'Schienbein n anat. shin(bone), tibia. **~schützer** m sports: shin-guard.

Schiene ['ʃiːnə] f (-; -n) **1.** 🚆 etc rail, pl a. track. **2.** ⚙ bar. **3.** ⚕ splint.

schienen ['ʃiːnən] v/t (h) ⚕ put in a splint (or in splints).

'**Schienen|bus** m rail bus. **~fahrzeug** n rail vehicle. **~netz** n railway (Am. railroad) system. **~strang** m track, railway line. **~verkehr** m rail traffic.

schier [ʃiːr] **I** adj sheer, pure. **II** adv almost, nearly.

Schierling ['ʃiːrlɪŋ] m (-s; -e) ⚘ hemlock.

'**Schießbefehl** m order to fire.

'**Schießbude** f shooting gallery.

schießen ['ʃiːsən] (schoß, geschossen) **I** v/i **1.** (h) (**auf** acc at) shoot (a. sports), fire: **gut ~** be a good shot; **ein Tor ~** score (a goal); F fig. **~ Sie los!** fire away!; → **Pistole. 2.** (sn) shoot (**durch** through): **ein Gedanke schoß durch m-n Kopf** a thought flashed through my mind. **3.** (sn) shoot (or gush) (**aus** from or out of). **4.** (sn) shoot up: → **Kraut** 1, **Pilz. 5.** (h) sl. shoot, mainline. **II** v/t (h) **6.** shoot (a. sports or phot.).

Schießen n (-s) a) shooting, b) shooting match: F **es (er) ist zum ~** it (he) is a scream. **Schieße'rei** f (-; -en) **1.** gunfight. **2.** (incessant) shooting.

'**Schieß|hund** m F **aufpassen wie ein ~** watch like a hawk. **~platz** m (shooting) range. **~pulver** n gunpowder. **~scharte** f embrasure. **~scheibe** f target. **~stand** m shooting range, ⚔ rifle range.

'**schießwütig** [-vyːtɪç] adj trigger-happy.

Schiff [ʃɪf] n (-[e]s; -e) **1.** (**auf dem ~** on board) ship. **2.** △ a) nave, b) aisle.

'**Schiffahrt** f (-; no pl) navigation.

'**Schiffahrtslinie** f shipping line.

'**Schiffahrtsweg** m shipping route.

'**schiffbar** adj navigable.

'**Schiffbau** m (-[e]s; no pl) shipbuilding.

'**Schiffbruch** m shipwreck: **~ erleiden** fig. fail. '**Schiffbrüchige** m, f (-n; -n) shipwrecked person.

'**Schiffchen** n (-s; -) **1.** little ship (or boat). **2.** ⚔ forage cap.

'**Schiffer** m (-s; -) a) bargee, Am. bargeman, b) (ship's) captain, F skipper.

'**Schifferkla,vier** n accordion.

'**Schifferknoten** m sailor's knot.

'**Schiffsarzt** m ship's doctor.

'**Schiffsbesatzung** f (ship's) crew.

'**Schiffschaukel** f swingboat.

'**Schiffs|eigner** m (-s; -) shipowner.

~junge m ship's boy. **~koch** m ship's cook. **~küche** f galley. **~ladung** f a) shipload, b) cargo, freight. **~rumpf** m hull. **~schraube** f screw. **~verkehr** m shipping. **~werft** f shipyard.

Schikane [ʃiˈkaːnə] f (-; -n) harassment, pl a. persecution, mot. racing: chicane: F **mit allen ~n** with all the trimmings.

schikanieren [ʃikaˈniːrən] v/t (h) harass.

schikanös [ʃikaˈnøːs] adj harassing.

Schild[1] [ʃɪlt] m (-[e]s; -e) **1.** ⚔, a. ⚙ shield: fig. **im ~e führen** be up to s.th. **2.** peak, visor.

Schild[2] n (-[e]s; -er) a) sign, a. road (or street) sign, b) nameplate, c) label, tag.

'**Schildbürger** m Gothamite, w.s. simpleton. **~streich** m folly.

'**Schilddrüse** f anat. thyroid gland.

schildern ['ʃɪldərn] v/t (h) describe, a. relate, a. outline. '**Schilderung** f (-; -en) description, account.

'**Schilderwald** m F jungle of road signs.

'**Schildkröte** f a) tortoise, b) turtle.

'**Schildpatt** [ʃɪltpat] n (-[e]s; no pl) tortoiseshell.

Schilf [ʃɪlf] n (-[e]s; -e) ⚘ **1.** reed. **2.** reeds. '**schilfig** adj reedy. '**Schilfmatte** f rush mat. '**Schilfrohr** n ⚘ reed.

schillern ['ʃɪlərn] v/i (h) shine in various colo(u)rs, shimmer, sparkle.

'**schillernd** adj **1.** iridescent, opalescent. **2.** fig. (dazzling but) dubious.

Schimmel[1] ['ʃɪməl] m (-s; -) white horse.

'**Schimmel**[2] m (-s; no pl) mo(u)ld, mildew. '**schimm(e)lig** adj mo(u)ldy.

'**schimmeln** v/i (h) go mo(u)ldy.

'**Schimmelpilz** m mo(u)ld.

'**Schimmer** ['ʃɪmər] m (-s; no pl) gleam, glimmer (a. fig.): F **k-n (blassen) ~ haben** not to have the foggiest (idea).

'**schimmern** v/i (h) gleam, glisten.

Schimpanse [ʃɪmˈpanzə] m (-n; -n) zo. chimpanzee.

Schimpf [ʃɪmpf] m **mit ~ und Schande** ignominiously.

schimpfen ['ʃɪmpfən] (h) **I** v/i **1.** scold (**mit j-m** s.o.): **~ auf** (acc) complain about, rail at. **II** v/t **2.** scold. **3.** **j-n e-n Lügner** etc **~** call s.o. a liar etc.

'**Schimpfname** m abusive name.

'**Schimpfwort** n swearword, pl abuse.

Schindel ['ʃɪndəl] f (-; -n) shingle.

schinden ['ʃɪndən] v/t (schindete, geschunden, h) **1.** drive s.o. hard, a. mal-

treat: **sich ~** slave away. **2.** F wangle:
Eindruck ~ (**wollen**) try to impress,
show off; **Zeit ~** play for time.

'**Schinder** *m* (-s; -) slave-driver.

Schinde'rei *f* (-; -en) (real) grind.

'**Schindluder** *n* F **~ treiben mit** play fast
and loose with.

Schinken ['ʃɪŋkən] *m* (-s; -) **1.** *gastr.*
ham. **2.** F a) (great) daub, b) fat tome,
c) slushy film. **~speck** *m* bacon.

Schippe ['ʃɪpə] *f* (-; -n) shovel: F **j-n auf
die ~ nehmen** pull s.o.'s leg.

schippen ['ʃɪpən] *v/t, v/i* (h) shovel.

Schirm [ʃɪrm] *m* (-[e]s; -e) **1.** a) umbrella,
b) parasol, c) (lamp)shade, d) shield,
screen, e) peak. **2.** screen. **3.** parachute.
4. ♀ pileus. **5.** *fig.* protection.

schirmen ['ʃɪrmən] *v/t* (h) shield.

'**Schirmherr**(**in** *f*) *m* patron(ess).

'**Schirmherrschaft** *f* patronage: **unter
der ~ von ...** under the auspices of ...

'**Schirmmütze** *f* peaked cap.

'**Schirmständer** *m* umbrella stand.

schiß [ʃɪs] *pret of* **scheißen.**

Schiß *m* F **~ haben** be scared stiff; **~
bekommen** get the jitters (V shits).

schizophren [ʃitsoˈfreːn] *adj,* **Schizo-
'phrene** *m, f* (-n; -n) schizophrenic.
Schizophrenie [ʃitsofreˈniː] *f* (-; -n)
schizophrenia.

Schlacht [ʃlaxt] *f* (-; -en) battle (**bei** of):
e-e ~ liefern give battle (**dat** to).

'**schlachten** *v/t* (h) slaughter, kill.

'**Schlachtenbummler** *m* *sports:* fan,
supporter.

Schlächter ['ʃlɛçtər] *m* (-s; -) butcher.

Schlächte'rei *f* (-; -en) butcher's shop.

'**Schlacht|feld** *n* battlefield. **~hof** *m*
slaughterhouse, abattoir. **~plan** *m* a. F
fig. plan of action. **~schiff** *n* battleship.

'**Schlachtung** *f* (-; -en) slaughter(ing).

'**Schlachtvieh** *n* meat stock.

Schlacke ['ʃlakə] *f* (-; -n) **1.** a) *metall.*
dross, slag (*a. geol.*), b) cinders. **2.** *pl* ❀
a) waste products, b) roughage.

schlackern ['ʃlakərn] *v/i* (h) F wobble,
dress etc: flap, *knees:* tremble: *fig.* **mit
den Ohren ~** be flabbergasted.

Schlaf [ʃlaːf] *m* (-[e]s; *no pl*) sleep: **e-n
festen** (**leichten**) **~ haben** be a sound
(light) sleeper; F **das kann ich im ~!** I
can do that blindfold.

Schlafanzug *m* pyjamas, *Am.* pajamas.

Schläfchen ['ʃlɛːfçən] *n* (-s; -) nap.

'**Schlafcouch** *f* studio couch, sofa bed.

Schläfe ['ʃlɛːfə] *f* (-; -n) *anat.* temple.

schlafen ['ʃlaːfən] *v/i* (schlief, geschlafen, h) *a.* F *fig.* a) sleep, b) be asleep: **tief**
(*or* **fest**) **~** be sound asleep; **~ gehen** go
to bed; **im Hotel ~** stay at a hotel; **~ Sie
darüber!** sleep on it!

'**Schlafenszeit** *f* bedtime.

Schläfer ['ʃlɛːfər] *m* (-s; -), '**Schläferin** *f*
(-; -nen) sleeper.

schlaff [ʃlaf] *adj* a) slack (*rope, sail*), b)
flabby (*skin, muscles, etc*), c) limp (*body
etc, a. handshake*), d) F listless, lame:
~er Typ lame fellow.

'**Schlaffheit** *f* (-; *no pl*) slackness, flabbi-
ness, limpness, F lameness.

'**Schlaf|gelegenheit** *f* sleeping accom-
modation. **~krankheit** *f* sleeping sickness. **~lied** *n* lullaby.

'**schlaflos** *adj* sleepless: **~ liegen** lie
awake; **~e Nächte** sleepless nights.

'**Schlaflosigkeit** *f* (-; *no pl*) insomnia.

'**Schlafmittel** *n* soporific (drug).

'**Schlafmütze** *f* F *fig.* sleepyhead.

schläfrig ['ʃlɛːfriç] *adj* sleepy, drowsy.

'**Schläfrigkeit** *f* (-; *no pl*) sleepiness.

'**Schlaf|rock** *m* dressing gown. **~saal** *m*
dormitory. **~sack** *m* sleeping bag.
~stadt *f* dormitory town. **~störungen**
pl disturbed sleep. **~ta,blette** *f* sleeping
pill. **~trunk** *m* F nightcap.

'**schlaftrunken** *adj* drowsy.

'**Schlafwagen** *m* 🚃 sleeping car, sleeper.

'**schlafwandeln** *v/i* (*insep,* ge-, h *or* sn)
sleepwalk. '**Schlafwandler** [-vandlər]
m (-s; -) sleepwalker, somnambulist.

'**Schlafzimmer** *n* bedroom. '**Schlafzim-
merblick** *m* *humor.* bedroom eyes.

Schlag [ʃlaːk] *m* (-[e]s; ⸗e) **1.** a) blow (*a.
fig.*), stroke (*a.* punch, b) slap, c)
thump, thud: **j-m e-n ~ versetzen** deal
s.o. a blow, *fig.* hit s.o. hard; **~ ins
Gesicht** *a. fig.* slap in the face; **das war
ein ~ für ihn** that was a blow to him;
ein ~ ins Wasser a flop; **auf ~ ~** in rapid
succession; **auf einen ~** at a (*or* one)
stroke, in one go; **mit einem ~** abruptly. **2.** ⚔ strike. **3.** ⚡ impact, *a.* ⚡ shock.
4. *rowing, swimming:* stroke, *golf, tennis:* shot. **5.** stroke (of lightning). **6.**
beat (*of heart, pulse, etc*), stroke (*of
clock etc*). **7.** ♂ stroke: **ich dachte,
mich trifft der ~!** I was floored! **8.** F
helping. **9.** door (*of carriage etc*). **10.**

race, sort, breed: **Leute s-s ~es** men of his stamp (*contp.* his sort).

'**Schlag|abtausch** *m boxing*: exchange of punches, *fig.* crossing of swords. **~ader** *f* artery. **~anfall** *m ⚕* stroke.

'**schlagartig** *adj* abrupt.

'**Schlagbaum** *m* turnpike.

'**Schlagbohrer** *m* ⊙ percussion drill.

'**Schlagbolzen** *m* ✕ striking pin.

schlagen ['ʃlaːgən] (schlug, geschlagen) **I** *v/t* (h) **1.** strike, hit, beat, punch, slap: **e-n Nagel in die Wand ~** drive a nail into the wall; **die Trommel ~** beat the drum; **j-m et. aus der Hand ~** knock s.th. from s.o.'s hand; **j-n zu Boden ~** knock s.o. down; → **Alarm, Brücke** 1, **Flucht**[1], **geschlagen. 2.** whip (*cream*), beat (*eggs etc*): **Eier in die Pfanne ~** break eggs into the frying pan. **3.** fell (*tree*), cut (*wood*). **4.** *fig.* beat (**in** *dat* at), *a.* defeat: **sich geschlagen geben** admit defeat, give up. **II** *v/i* **5.** (h) strike, hit: **nach j-m ~** hit out at s.o.; **um sich ~** lash out. **6.** (sn) **~ an** (*acc*) (*or* **gegen**) beat against; **mit dem Kopf ~ an** (*acc*) strike (*or* bump) one's head against; **die Nachricht ist mir auf den Magen geschlagen** the news has affected my stomach; **Flammen schlugen aus dem Dach** flames leapt out of the roof; → **Art** 4, **Fach** 2 *etc*. **7.** (h) heart, *pulse*: beat, throb, *clock*: strike. **8.** (h) *bird*: sing. **III sich ~** (h) **9.** (have a) fight: **sich um et. ~** fight over s.th.; **sich gut ~** give a good account of o.s. **10.** *sich auf j-s Seite ~* side with s.o., *a.* go over to s.o.; **die Erkältung hat sich mir auf den Magen geschlagen** the cold has affected my stomach.

'**schlagend** *adj* **1.** *fig.* convincing, conclusive (*evidence*). **2.** → **Wetter** 2.

Schlager ['ʃlaːgər] *m* (-s; -) **1.** a) pop-song, b) hit (*tune*). **2.** *fig.* hit, sensation, ✝ (sales) hit, moneymaker.

Schläger ['ʃlɛːgər] *m* (-s; -) **1.** tough, *boxing etc*: slugger. **2.** *sports*: a) batsman, b) (cricket, baseball, *etc*) bat, (tennis) racket, (golf) club, (hockey) stick. **Schläge'rei** *f* (-; -en) brawl, F punch-up: **allgemeine ~** F free-for-all.

'**Schlagerfestival** *n* pop festival.

'**Schlagermu,sik** *f* pop music.

'**Schlagersänger(in** *f*) *m* pop singer.

'**schlagfertig** *adj* quick-witted: **~ sein** be

quick at repartee. '**Schlagfertigkeit** *f* (-; *no pl*) quick-wittedness, ready wit.

'**Schlag|instru,ment** *n* ♪ percussion instrument. **~kraft** *f* (-; *no pl*) **1.** *boxing or fig.* punch. **2.** ✕ combat effectiveness. **2kräftig** *adj* **1.** powerful. **2.** convincing, conclusive. **~licht** *n* (-[e]s; -er) *paint.* (*a. fig.* **ein ~ werfen auf** [*acc*]) highlight. **~loch** *n* pothole. **~mann** *m* (-[e]s; *⁻er*) *rowing*: stroke. **~obers** *n* (-; *no pl*) *Austrian*, **~rahm** *m* → **Schlagsahne. ~ring** *m* **1.** knuckleduster. **2.** ♪ plectrum, F pick. **~sahne** *f* whipped cream. **~seite** *f* ♨ list: **~ haben** be listing, F *fig.* be halfseas-over. **~stock** *m* **1.** truncheon, riot stick. **2.** ♪ drumstick. **~wechsel** *m* *boxing*: exchange of blows. **~werk** *n* striking mechanism.

'**Schlagwort** *n* **1.** catchword, slogan, *pl contp.* platitudes. **2.** (*pl* *⁻er*) catchword. **~kata,log** *m* subject catalog(ue Br.).

'**Schlagzeile** *f* headline: **~n machen, in die ~n geraten** make the headlines.

'**Schlagzeug** *n* ♪ percussion, drums. '**Schlagzeuger** [-tsɔygər] *m* (-s; -) ♪ percussionist, drummer.

schlaksig ['ʃlaːksɪç] *adj* gangling, lanky.

Schlamassel [ʃlaˈmasəl] *m, n* (-s; -) F mess.

Schlamm [ʃlam] *m* (-[e]s; -e, *⁻e*) mud. '**Schlammbad** *n* ♨ mud bath. '**schlammig** *adj* muddy. '**Schlammpackung** *f* ♨ mud pack.

Schlampe ['ʃlampə] *f* (-; -n) F slut. '**schlampen** *v/i* (h) F do a sloppy job. '**Schlamper** *m* (-s; -) F sloven, slouch. **Schlampe'rei** *f* (-; -en) F a) sloppiness, b) mess, sloppy work.

'**schlampig** *adj* F slovenly, sloppy.

schlang [ʃlaŋ] *pret of* **schlingen**[1] *and* [2].

Schlange ['ʃlaŋə] *f* (-; -n) **1.** *zo.* snake: *fig.* **falsche ~** snake in the grass. **2.** queue, *Am.* line (*of people, cars*): F **~ stehen** (**nach** for) stand in a queue (*Am.* in line), queue up, *Am.* line up. **3.** ⊙ coil.

schlängeln ['ʃlɛŋəln] **sich ~** (h) wriggle, *fig. road etc*: wind, *river*: *a.* meander; **sich ~ durch** worm one's way through.

'**Schlangen|biß** *m* snakebite. **~gift** *n* snake poison. **~haut** *f*, **~leder** *n* snakeskin. **~linie** *f* wavy line: **in ~n fahren** zigzag (along the road).

schlank [ʃlaŋk] *adj* slender, slim: *auf die ~e Linie achten* watch one's weight.
'**Schlankheit** *f* (-; *no pl*) slimness.
'**Schlankheitskur** *f* slimming (diet): *e-e ~ machen* be slimming.

schlapp [ʃlap] *adj* **1.** → *schlaff.* **2.** worn-out, listless.
'**Schlappe** *f* (-; -n) a) setback, b) beating.
'**schlappmachen** *v/i* (*sep*, -ge-, h) F wilt.
'**Schlappschwanz** *m* F softie, sissy.

Schlaraffenland [ʃla'rafən-] *n* (-[e]s; *no pl*) Cockaigne.

schlau [ʃlaʊ] *adj* a) clever, smart, b) sly, cunning, crafty: F *~e Bücher* clever books; *ich werde nicht ~ daraus* I can't make head or tail of it.

Schlauberger ['ʃlaʊbɛrgər] *m* (-s; -) F smartie.

Schlauch [ʃlaʊx] *m* (-[e]s; ~e) **1.** flexible tube, (water) hose. **2.** *mot. etc* inner tube. **3.** F hard slog. **4.** F (*room*) tunnel.
'**Schlauchboot** *n* rubber dinghy.
schlauchen ['ʃlaʊxən] (h) F I *v/t j-n ~* take it out of s.o., a. go hard with s.o. II *v/i das schlaucht!* that's tough going!

Schläue ['ʃlɔʏə] *f* → *Schlauheit.*
Schlaufe ['ʃlaʊfə] *f* (-; -n) loop.
'**Schlauheit** *f* (-; *no pl*) a) cleverness, smartness, b) slyness, cunning.

schlecht [ʃlɛçt] I *adj* bad, poor (*eyes, health, memory, quality, etc*), a. wicked: *nicht ~!* not bad!; *~e Laune* bad mood; *~e Zeiten* bad (*or* hard) times; *~ sein* (*dat*) be poor at; *~ werden* meat etc: go bad, go off; *~er werden* get worse, deteriorate; *mir ist ~* I feel sick; F *es kann e-m ~ dabei werden!* it's enough to make you sick!; → *Dienst* 1. II *adv* bad(ly): *~ aussehen* look bad, a. look ill; *~ und recht* after a fashion; *~ beraten sein* be ill-advised; *~ reden von* speak ill of; *es steht ~ um ihn* he's in a bad way; *~ daran sein* be badly off; *es bekam ihm ~ food etc*: it didn't agree with him, *fig.* it did him no good; *er kann es sich ~ leisten zu inf* he can ill afford to *inf*; *heute geht es ~* it's a bit awkward today; *ich kann ~ ablehnen* I can't very well refuse; *ich staunte nicht ~* F I wasn't half surprised.
'**schlechtgelaunt** *adj* bad-tempered.
'**schlechthin** *adv* **1.** absolutely. **2.** as such.

'**Schlechtigkeit** *f* (-; *no pl*) badness, wickedness, baseness.
'**schlechtmachen** *v/t* (*sep*, -ge-, h) run *s.o.*, *s.th.* down, knock.
Schlecht'wetter|front *f* bad weather front. *~peri,ode f* spell of bad weather.
Schlehe ['ʃle:ə] *f* (-; -n) ♣ sloe.
schleichen ['ʃlaɪçən] *v/i* (schlich, geschlichen, sn) creep, sneak, crawl (a. car, time): *auf den Zehenspitzen ~* tiptoe; *ums Haus ~* prowl around the house; *dial. schleich dich!* sl. beat it!
'**schleichend** *adj* lingering (*illness*), slow (*poison etc*), creeping (*inflation*).
'**Schleich|handel** *m* illicit trade. *~weg m* secret path: *fig. auf ~en* by secret means, surreptitiously. *~werbung f* surreptitious advertising, F plugging.
Schleier ['ʃlaɪər] *m* (-s; -) **1.** *a. fig.* veil. **2.** haze, *phot.* fog. *~eule f zo.* barn owl.
'**schleierhaft** *adj* mysterious: *das ist mir ~!* that's a mystery to me!
Schleife ['ʃlaɪfə] *f* (-; -n) **1.** bow, a. ribbon. **2.** a. ⚡, ◎ loop.
schleifen¹ ['ʃlaɪfən] *v/t* (schliff, geschliffen, h) **1.** grind, whet. **2.** ◎ smooth, sand (*wood*), cut (*glass, diamond*). **3.** ✕ F drill *s.o.* hard.
schleifen² (h) I *v/t* drag (along) (a. *fig. s.o.*), trail (*skirt etc*). II *v/i ~ lassen* drag; *die Kupplung ~ lassen* let the clutch slip.
'**Schleifer** *m* (-s; -) **1.** ◎ grinder, a. cutter. **2.** ✕ F martinet.
'**Schleif|lackausführung** *f* egg-shell finish. *~ma,schine f* grinding machine. *~mittel n* abrasive. *~pa,pier n* emery paper. *~scheibe f* grinding wheel. *~stein m* a) whetstone, b) grindstone.
Schleim [ʃlaɪm] *m* (-[e]s; -e) slime, ⚓, *physiol.* mucus, phlegm. *~beutel m anat.* bursa. *~drüse f* mucous gland. *~haut f* mucous membrane.
'**schleimig** *adj* slimy (a. *fig. contp.*).
'**schleimlösend** *adj* expectorant.
'**Schleimsuppe** *f* gruel.
schlemmen ['ʃlɛmən] *v/i* (h) feast.
'**Schlemmer** *m* (-s; -) gormandizer.
Schlemme'rei *f* (-; *no pl*) feasting.
schlendern ['ʃlɛndərn] *v/i* (sn) stroll.
Schlendrian ['ʃlɛndria:n] *m* (-s; -[e]s; *no pl*) F *contp.* a) dawdling, b) rut.
Schlenker ['ʃlɛŋkər] *m* (-s; -) (a. *e-n ~ machen*) F swerve. '**schlenkern** *v/t, v/i*

(h) swing, dangle (*mit den Armen* one's arms).

schlenzen ['ʃlɛntsən] v/t, v/i (h) scoop.

Schlepp [ʃlɛp] m in ~ nehmen (*im ~ haben*) a. fig. take (have) in tow.

'**Schleppdampfer** m tug.

Schleppe ['ʃlɛpə] f (-; -n) train, trail.

'**schleppen** (h) **I** v/t a) drag (a. fig. s.o.), ⚓, ✈, mot. tow, b) carry, F fote: F (*Kunden* s) → tout. **II sich** ~ a) drag on, b) drag o.s. (along), limp (along).

'**schleppend** adj sluggish, slow (a. ♀), labo(u)red, slow, drawling (*speech*).

'**Schlepper** m (-s; -) **1.** ⚓ tug. **2.** mot. tractor. **3.** F tout.

'**Schlepp**|**flugzeug** n towplane. ~**kahn** m lighter, barge (in tow). ~**lift** m ski tow. ~**netz** n dragnet. ~**schiff** n tug. ~**tau** n tow-rope, tow-line: F fig. j-n ins ~ nehmen take s.o. in tow. ~**zug** m **1.** ⚓ train of barges. **2.** semitrailer truck.

Schleuder ['ʃlɔʏdər] f (-; -n) **1.** catapult (a. ✈), sling, Am. slingshot. **2.** ⚙ a) → Zentrifuge, b) spin dryer.

'**Schleudergefahr** f slippery road.

schleudern ['ʃlɔʏdərn] (h) **I** v/t **1.** fling, hurl, sling, ✈ catapult. **2.** ⚙ centrifuge, strain (*honey*), spin-dry (*laundry*). **II** v/i (a. sn) mot. skid, (a. ins Schleudern geraten) go into a skid (a. fig.).

'**Schleuder**|**preis** m knockdown price. ~**sitz** m ✈ ejector seat, F fig. hot seat. ~**ware** f cut-price article(s).

schleunig ['ʃlɔʏnɪç] **I** adj quick, prompt, a. hasty. **II** adv a. '**schleunigst** quickly, promptly, a. hastily.

Schleuse ['ʃlɔʏzə] f (-; -n) sluice, floodgate (a. fig.), (canal) lock. '**schleusen** v/t (h) **1.** ⚓ lock. **2.** fig. a) channel, b) steer, c. smuggle (s.o.).

'**Schleusentor** n floodgate.

schlich [ʃlɪç] pret of **schleichen**.

Schliche ['ʃlɪçə] pl tricks: j-m auf die ~ kommen find s.o. out.

schlicht [ʃlɪçt] **I** adj simple, plain. **II** adv ~ (und einfach) (quite) simply.

schlichten ['ʃlɪçtən] **I** v/t settle (*dispute*). **II** v/i mediate (zwischen between).

'**Schlichter** m (-s; -) mediator.

'**Schlichtheit** f (-; no pl) simplicity, plainness.

'**Schlichtung** f (-; -en) a) settlement, b) arbitration.

'**Schlichtungs**|**ausschuß** m arbitration

committee. ~**versuch** m attempt at conciliation.

Schlick [ʃlɪk] m (-[e]s; -e) sludge, silt.

schlief [ʃliːf] pret of **schlafen**.

Schliere ['ʃliːrə] f (-; -n) streak.

Schließe ['ʃliːsə] f (-; -n) fastening, clasp.

schließen ['ʃliːsən] (schloß, geschlossen, h) **I** v/t **1.** close (a. ⚡ circuit), shut, a. shut down (*factory etc*): → Lücke. **2.** enter into an alliance etc, reach, come to a settlement: → Ehe, Freundschaft, Frieden etc. **3.** close, conclude, end (debate etc), a. wind up (*letter, speech* mit den Worten by saying). **II** v/i **4.** shut, close, *factory etc*: shut down. **5.** (come to a) close: er schloß mit den Worten he wound up by saying. **6.** conclude (aus from): von sich auf andere ~ judge others by o.s.; auf et. ~ lassen suggest (or point to) s.th. **III sich** ~ close, shut; → Kreis 1.

'**Schließfach** n **1.** safe deposit box. **2.** 🚉 (left-luggage) locker. **3.** → Postfach.

'**schließlich** adv a) finally, b) eventually, c) after all.

'**Schließmuskel** m anat. sphincter.

'**Schließung** f (-; -en) **1.** closing, shutting, shutdown, closure (*of factory etc*). **2.** contraction (*of marriage etc*).

schliff [ʃlɪf] pret of **schleifen**[^1].

Schliff m (-[e]s; -e) **1.** no pl grinding, a. sharpening. **2.** cut (*of glass etc*). **3.** fig. polish, refinement: den letzten ~ geben put the finishing touches (dat to).

schlimm [ʃlɪm] adj bad, F a. nasty (*wound etc*): F ~er Finger (Hals) sore finger (throat); das ist e-e ~e Sache that's a bad business; es sieht ~ aus it looks bad; das ist halb so ~! a) it's not as bad as all that!, b) it doesn't matter!, never mind!; F ist es ~, wenn ...? would you mind terribly if ...?; ~er machen (werden) → verschlimmern; es wird immer ~er things are going from bad to worse; um so ~er so much the worse; am ~sten worst of all; auf das Schlimmste gefaßt sein be prepared for the worst; es gibt Schlimmeres things could be worse.

'**schlimmstenfalls** adv if the worst comes to the worst.

Schlinge ['ʃlɪŋə] f (-; -n) loop, noose (a. fig.), a. ⚕ sling, hunt. snare (a. fig.): fig. sich aus der ~ ziehen wriggle out of it.

[^1]: schleifen[^1].

Schlingel ['ʃlɪŋəl] m (-s; -) rascal.
schlingen¹ ['ʃlɪŋən] (schlang, geschlungen, h) (**um** around) **I** v/t tie, wrap, wind. **II sich** ~ wind, coil.
'**schlingen**² (schlang, geschlungen, h) **I** v/i gobble, bolt one's food. **II** v/t gobble (up), gulp s.th. down.
schlingern ['ʃlɪŋərn] v/i (h) ♣ roll.
'**Schlingpflanze** f climbing plant.
Schlips [ʃlɪps] m (-es; -e) tie: fig. **j-m auf den ~ treten** tread on s.o.'s toes.
Schlitten ['ʃlɪtən] m (-s; -) **1.** a) sledge, Am. sled, b) sleigh, c) toboggan: ~ **fahren** sledge, toboggan; F fig. **mit j-m ~ fahren** give s.o. hell. **2.** F car: **alter** ~ crate, bus, jalopy.
'**Schlittenfahrt** f sledge (or sleigh) ride.
schlittern ['ʃlɪtərn] v/i (sn) slide (**in** acc into, a. fig.), a. slip, mot. skid.
'**Schlittschuh** m (ice-)skate: ~ **laufen** skate. ~**laufen** n (-s; -) (ice-)skating. ~**läufer(in** f) m (ice-)skater.
Schlitz [ʃlɪts] m (-es; -e) **1.** slit. **2.** slot.
'**Schlitzauge** n **1.** slit eye: ~**n haben** be slit-eyed. **2.** contp. slit-eye.
schlitzen ['ʃlɪtsən] v/t, v/i (h) slit, slash.
schloß [ʃlɔs] pret of **schließen**.
Schloß n (-sses; ⸚sser) **1.** castle, palace. **2.** a) lock, b) clasp: **hinter ~ und Riegel** behind bars.
Schloße ['ʃloːsə] f usu. pl sleet.
Schlosser ['ʃlɔsər] m (-s; -) locksmith.
Schlosse'rei f (-; -en) **1.** no pl locksmith's trade. **2.** locksmith's shop.
Schlot [ʃloːt] m (-[e]s; -e) (F **rauchen wie ein** ~ smoke like a) chimney.
schlottern ['ʃlɔtərn] v/i (h) **1.** (**vor** with) shake, tremble: **mit ~den Knien** with shaking knees. **2.** clothes: hang loosely.
Schlucht [ʃlʊxt] f (-; -en) gorge, ravine, a. canyon.
schluchzen ['ʃlʊxtsən] v/t, v/i (h) sob.
'**Schluchzen** n (-s) sobbing, sobs.
Schluck [ʃlʊk] m (-[e]s; -e) swallow, gulp: **kräftiger** ~. '**Schluckauf** m (-s; no pl) (**e-n** ~ **haben** have) the) hiccups. **Schlückchen** ['ʃlʏkçən] n (-s; -) sip. '**schlucken** (h) **I** v/t swallow (a. fig. insult etc, a. F believe), fig. swallow up (savings etc), absorb (light, sound). **II** v/i swallow. '**Schlucker** m (-s; -) **armer** ~ poor devil.
'**Schluckimpfung** f ⚕ oral vaccination.
schlud(e)rig ['ʃluːd(ə)rɪç] → **schlampig**.

schludern ['ʃluːdərn] → **schlampen**.
schlug [ʃluːk] pret of **schlagen**.
schlummern ['ʃlʊmərn] v/i (h) slumber, sleep, fig. lie dormant.
'**schlummernd** adj fig. dormant, latent.
Schlund [ʃlʊnt] m (-es; ⸚e) **1.** anat. (back of the) throat, pharynx. **2.** zo. maw. **3.** fig. abyss.
schlüpfen ['ʃlʏpfən] v/i (sn) **1.** slip (**in** acc into, **aus** out of). **2.** zo. hatch (out).
'**Schlüpfer** m (-s; -) briefs, panties.
Schlupfloch ['ʃlʊpf-] n **1.** gap. **2.** fig. loophole.
schlüpfrig ['ʃlʏpfrɪç] adj slippery, fig. lewd, risqué (joke etc).
'**Schlupfwinkel** m hideout, haunt.
schlurfen ['ʃlʊrfən] v/i (sn) shuffle.
schlürfen ['ʃlʏrfən] v/t, v/i (h) a) slurp, b) sip.
Schluß [ʃlʊs] m (-sses; ⸚sse) **1.** end, conclusion, ending (of book, film, etc): ~ (**damit**)! stop it!; F ~ **machen** a) call it a day, b) put an end to o.s.; ~ **machen mit** a) **et.** stop s.th., b) **j-m** break up with s.o.; **am** ~ at the end; **zum** ~ finally. **2.** conclusion: **voreilige Schlüsse ziehen** jump to conclusions. ~**ak,kord** m ♪ final chord. ~**akt** m **1.** thea. final act. **2.** closing ceremony. ~**bemerkung** f final comment.
Schlüssel ['ʃlʏsəl] m (-s; -) **1.** key (**zu, für** of, fig. to). **2.** ♪ clef. **3.** ratio. **4.** ⚙ spanner, Am. wrench. ~**bein** n anat. collarbone. ~**blume** f primrose, cowslip. ~**bund** m, n bunch of keys. ~**erlebnis** n crucial experience. ~**fi,gur** f key figure. ~**indu,strie** f key industry. ~**kind** n latchkey child. ~**loch** n keyhole. ~**ring** m key ring. ~**ro,man** m roman-à-clef. ~**stellung** f key position. ~**wort** n (-[e]s; ⸚er) code word, keyword, computer: a. password.
'**Schlußfeier** f closing ceremony, ped. speech day, Am. commencement.
'**Schlußfolgerung** f (-; -en) conclusion.
schlüssig ['ʃlʏsɪç] adj **1.** logical **2.** conclusive (evidence). **3.** sich ~ **werden** make up one's mind (**über** acc about).
'**Schluß|läufer(in** f) m anchor. ~**licht** n (-[e]s; -er) **1.** mot. taillight. **2.** F esp. sports: tailender: **das ~ bilden** bring up the rear. ~**pfiff** m sports: final whistle. ~**satz** m **1.** closing sentence. **2.** ♪ final movement. ~**strich** m fig. **e-n** ~ **unter**

et. **ziehen** consider the matter closed.
~verkauf *m* (end-of-season) sale.
~wort *n* (-[e]s; -e) closing words.

Schmach [ʃmaːx] *f* (-; *no pl*) disgrace.

schmächtig ['ʃmɛçtɪç] *adj* slight, thin.

schmachvoll *adj* disgraceful.

schmackhaft ['ʃmakhaft] *adj* savo(u)ry, tasty: *fig.* **j-m et. ~ machen** make s.th. palatable to s.o.

schmal [ʃmaːl] *adj* narrow, *a.* thin, slender (*a. fig.*), *fig.* meag/re (*Am.* -er).

schmälern ['ʃmɛːlərn] *v/t* (h) **1.** curtail, impair. **2.** detract from.

'Schmalfilm *m* cine-film.

'Schmalfilmkamera *f* cine-camera.

'Schmalspur *f* (-; *no pl*) narrow ga(u)ge.

'Schmalspur... F *fig.* small-time ...

Schmalz¹ [ʃmalts] *n* (-es; -e) lard.

Schmalz² *m* (-es; *no pl*) F schmaltz.

'schmalzig *adj* F schmaltzy.

schmarotzen [ʃmaˈrɔtsən] *v/i* (h) sponge (*bei* on). **Schma'rotzer** *m* (-s; -) parasite, *fig. a.* sponger.

schmatzen [ʃmatsən] *v/i* (h) eat noisily.

schmecken ['ʃmɛkən] (h) I *v/t* taste. II *v/i* **~ nach** taste of, *fig.* smack of; **es schmeckt** (*gut*) it tastes good; **sich et. ~ lassen** tuck in; **schmeckt es** (**Ihnen**)? do you like it?; *fig.* **das schmeckte ihm nicht** he didn't like it one bit.

Schmeichelei [ʃmaiçəˈlai] *f* (-; -en) flattery, (flattering) compliment.

'schmeichelhaft *adj a. fig.* flattering.

schmeicheln ['ʃmaiçəln] *v/i* (h) **j-m ~** a) flatter s.o. (*a. fig.*), b) cajole s.o.; **sich geschmeichelt fühlen** feel flattered (**durch** by); **das Bild ist geschmeichelt** the picture is flattering.

Schmeichler ['ʃmaiçlər] *m* (-s; -) flatterer. **'schmeichlerisch** *adj* a) flattering, b) cajoling.

schmeißen ['ʃmaisən] (schmiß, geschmissen, h) F I *v/t* **1.** a) throw, chuck, b) slam, bang (*door etc*). **2.** chuck up (*job etc*), *thea.* muff (*scene*). **3.** manage: **den Laden ~** run the show. **4.** *e-e Lage* **~** stand a round of drinks. II *v/i* **5.** **~ mit** throw; **mit Geld um sich ~** throw one's money around.

'Schmeißfliege *f* bluebottle.

Schmelz [ʃmɛlts] *m* (-es; -e) **1.** enamel. **2.** *fig.* mellowness, ♪ melodiousness.

'schmelzbar *adj* ⊕ fusible.

Schmelze ['ʃmɛltsə] *f* (-; -n) ⊕ melting,

molten mass. **'schmelzen** (schmolz, geschmolzen) I *v/i* (sn) liquefy, melt (*a. fig.* supply *etc*). II *v/t* (h) liquefy, melt, *metall.* smelt. **'schmelzend** *adj fig.* melting (*look*), sweet (*voice*).

'Schmelz|käse *m* soft cheese. **~punkt** *m* melting point. **~tiegel** *m a. fig.* melting pot. **~wasser** *n* melted snow and ice.

Schmerbauch ['ʃmeːr-] *m* paunch.

Schmerz [ʃmɛrts] *m* (-es; -en) a) pain, ache, b) grief, sorrow, c) agony: **~en haben** be in pain. **'schmerzen** (h) I *v/i* hurt (*a. fig.*), ache. II *v/t* hurt (*a. fig.*), pain.

'Schmerzensgeld *n* compensation for personal suffering, *Am.* smart-money.

'Schmerzensschrei *m* scream of pain.

'schmerzfrei *adj* free of pain.

'Schmerzgrenze *f* pain threshold.

'schmerzhaft *adj a. fig.* painful.

'schmerzlich I *adj* painful, *fig.* sad (*loss, smile, etc*). II *adv* badly, sadly: **j-n ~ berühren** pain s.o.

'schmerzlindernd *adj* soothing, (*a. ~es Mittel*) analgesic.

'schmerzlos *adj* painless.

'schmerzstillend *adj* painkilling.

'Schmerztablette *f* painkiller.

'Schmetterball *m tennis:* smash.

Schmetterling ['ʃmɛtərlɪŋ] *m* (-s; -e) *zo.* butterfly. **'Schmetterlingsstil** *m swimming:* butterfly (stroke).

schmettern ['ʃmɛtərn] (h) I *v/t* **1.** smash (*a. tennis*), slam. **2.** belt out (*song*). II *v/i* **3.** ring (out), *trumpet:* blare, *bird:* warble.

Schmied [ʃmiːt] *m* (-[e]s; -e) a) smith, b) blacksmith. **Schmiede** ['ʃmiːdə] *f* (-; -n) forge, smithy.

'Schmiedeeisen *n* wrought iron.

'schmiedeeisern *adj* wrought-iron.

schmieden ['ʃmiːdən] *v/t, v/i* (h) *a. fig.* forge: → *Eisen, Plan* 1.

schmiegen ['ʃmiːɡən] *sich* **~** (h) cling (*or* cuddle up) (*an acc* to). **schmiegsam** ['ʃmiːk-] *adj* pliant, flexible.

Schmiere¹ ['ʃmiːrə] *f* (-; -n) **1.** ⊕ grease, lubricant. **2.** F mess, goo.

'Schmiere² *f* F **~ stehen** keep a lookout.

schmieren ['ʃmiːrən] *v/t* (h) **1.** smear, *a.* butter (*bread*), spread (*butter etc*): F **wie geschmiert** like clockwork; **j-m e-e ~** slap s.o.('s face). **2.** ⊕ a) grease, b) lubricate, oil. **3.** *a. v/i* scrawl. **4.** F **j-n ~** grease s.o.'s palm.

'Schmierenkomödi,ant *m* ham actor.

Schmiere'rei *f* (-; -en) **1.** scribble, scrawl. **2.** daub. **3.** *pl* graffiti.

'Schmier|fett *n* ⚙ (lubricating) grease. ~fink *m* F **1.** a) scrawler, b) messy fellow. **2.** muckraker. ~geld *n* F bribe (money), payoff, *pol.* slush fund.

schmierig ['ʃmiːrɪç] *adj* **1.** greasy. **2.** messy. **3.** *fig.* a) smutty, b) F smarmy.

'Schmier|mittel *n* ⚙ lubricant. ~öl *n* ⚙ lubricating oil. ~pa,pier *n* scribbling paper. ~seife *f* soft soap.

'Schmierung *f* (-; -en) ⚙ a) lubrication, b) greasing.

Schminke ['ʃmɪŋkə] *f* (-; -n) make-up. 'schminken (h) I *v/t* make up: *sich die Lippen* ~ put on lipstick. II *sich* ~ put on make-up, make o.'s face up.

schmirgeln ['ʃmɪrgəln] *v/t* (h), 'Schmirgelpa,pier *n* ⚙ sandpaper.

schmiß [ʃmɪs] *pret of* schmeißen.

Schmiß *m* (-sses; -sse) **1.** (duelling) scar. **2.** *no pl* F *fig.* pep, zip.

'schmissig *adj* F zippy, rousing (*music*).

Schmöker ['ʃmøːkər] *m* (-s; -) F **1.** old book. **2.** light novel. 'schmökern *v/i* (h) a) do some light reading, b) browse.

schmollen ['ʃmɔlən] *v/i* (h) sulk.

'Schmollmund *m* pout.

schmolz ['ʃmɔlts] *pret of* schmelzen.

'Schmorbraten *m* pot roast.

schmoren ['ʃmoːrən] *v/t*, *v/i* (h) *gastr.* braise: F *j-n* (*in s-m eigenen Saft*) ~ *lassen* let s.o. stew (in his own juice); *in der Sonne* ~ roast in the sun.

Schmuck [ʃmʊk] *m* (-[e]s; *no pl*) **1.** decoration. **2.** jewel(le)ry, jewels.

schmücken ['ʃmʏkən] (h) I *v/t* decorate, *fig.* embroider (*speech etc*). II *sich* ~ dress up; → Feder 1.

'Schmuckkästchen *n* **1.** jewel(le)ry box. **2.** *fig.* jewel of a house.

'schmucklos *adj* plain, austere.

'Schmuckstück *n* **1.** piece of jewel(le)ry. **2.** *fig.* gem.

schmudd(e)lig ['ʃmʊd(ə)lɪç] *adj* F grubby, grimy, scruffy.

Schmuggel ['ʃmʊgəl] *m* (-s; *no pl*) smuggling. 'schmuggeln *v/t*, *v/i* (h) smuggle. 'Schmuggelware *f* smuggled goods, contraband. 'Schmuggler *m* (-s; -) smuggler.

schmunzeln ['ʃmʊntsəln] *v/i* (h) smile to o.s., grin.

Schmus [ʃmuːs] *m* (-es; *no pl*) F blarney.

schmusen ['ʃmuːzən] *v/i* (h) F cuddle, *lovers:* a. smooch.

Schmutz [ʃmʊts] *m* (-es; *no pl*) dirt, filth, mud, *fig.* a. smut: *fig. in den* ~ *ziehen* drag s.o., s.th. through the mud.

'schmutzen *v/i* (h) soil, get dirty.

'Schmutzfink *m* F **1.** pig. **2.** *fig.* dirty fellow. 'Schmutzfleck *m* smudge.

'schmutzig *adj* **1.** dirty, filthy, soiled: ~ *machen* dirty, soil; *sich* ~ *machen*, ~ *werden* get dirty; *fig.* ~*e Phantasie* dirty mind; → Wäsche 1. **2.** *contp.* a) dirty, shabby, b) smutty (*joke etc*).

Schnabel ['ʃnaːbəl] *m* (-s; ̈-) **1.** bill, beak. **2.** spout. **3.** F trap: *halt den* ~*!* shut up!

schnäbeln ['ʃnɛːbəln] *v/i* (h) *zo.* bill.

Schnake ['ʃnaːkə] *f* (-; -n) *zo.* mosquito.

Schnalle ['ʃnalə] *f* (-; -n) buckle, clasp.

schnallen ['ʃnalən] *v/t* (h) **1.** buckle, strap (*an acc* to): → Gürtel. **2.** F get: *ich schnalle das nicht!* I don't get it!

schnalzen ['ʃnaltsən] *v/i* (h) *mit der Zunge* ~ click one's tongue; *mit den Fingern* ~ snap one's fingers.

schnappen ['ʃnapən] (h) I *v/t* **1.** F catch, nab: (*sich*) *et.* ~ grab s.th.; → Luft 1. II *v/i* **2.** snap, click. **3.** ~ *nach* grab at, *dog:* snap at; *nach Luft* ~ gasp for breath.

'Schnappschuß *m phot.* snapshot: *e-n* ~ *machen von* take a snap of, snap.

Schnaps [ʃnaps] *m* (-es; ̈-e) spirits, schnapps. ~brenne'rei *f* distillery.

Schnäpschen ['ʃnɛpsçən] *n* (-s; -) F snifter.

'Schnapsi,dee *f* F *fig.* crazy idea.

schnarchen ['ʃnarçən] *v/i* (h) snore.

schnarren ['ʃnarən] *v/i* (h) **1.** rattle. **2.** *bell etc:* buzz. **3.** a. *v/t* rasp, bark.

schnattern ['ʃnatərn] *v/i* (h) **1.** *goose:* cackle, *duck:* quack. **2.** F *fig.* gabble.

schnauben ['ʃnaʊbən] *v/i*, *v/t* (h) snort: *sich* (*die Nase*) ~ blow one's nose; *vor Wut* ~ foam with rage.

schnaufen ['ʃnaʊfən] *v/i* (h) **1.** breathe hard, puff, pant. **2.** *dial.* breathe.

'Schnauzbart *m* walrus m(o)ustache.

Schnauze ['ʃnaʊtsə] *f* (-; -n) **1.** *zo.* snout, muzzle, nose. **2.** lip (*of jug etc*), ⚙ nozzle, F 🖋, *mot.* nose. **3.** V trap: *halt die* ~*!* shut up!; *die* ~ *voll haben* be fed up (to the teeth) (*von* with).

'Schnauzer *m* (-s; -) *zo.* schnauzer.

Schnecke ['ʃnɛkə] f (-; -n) **1.** zo. a) snail, b) slug: F **j-n zur ~ machen** give s.o. hell. **2.** △ scroll. **3.** gastr. Chelsea bun. **4.** pl earphones. '**Schneckenhaus** n (snail) shell. '**Schneckentempo** n im ~ at a snail's pace.

Schnee [ʃneː] m (-s; no pl) **1.** snow. **2.** Eiweiß zu ~ schlagen beat white of egg until stiff. **3.** sl. snow. **~ball** m snowball. **~ballschlacht** f snowball fight. ☨**bedeckt** adj snow-covered. **~besen** m egg-beater, whisk. ☨**blind** adj snow-blind. **~brille** f (e-e ~ a pair of) snow goggles. **~decke** f (blanket of) snow. **~fall** m snowfall. **~flocke** f snowflake. **~gestöber** n snow flurry. **~glätte** f packed snow. **~glöckchen** n ☙ snowdrop. **~grenze** f snowline. **~kette** f snowchain. **~mann** m (-[e]s; ⁻er) snowman. **~matsch** m slush. **~mo‚bil** n snowmobile. **~pflug** m snowplough, Am. snowplow. **~regen** m sleet. **~schleuder** f snowblower. **~schmelze** f thaw. **~schuh** m snowshoe. **~sturm** m snowstorm. **~treiben** n snow flurry. **~verhältnisse** pl snow conditions. **~verwehung** f, **~wehe** f snowdrift. ☨**weiß** adj snow-white.

Schneid [ʃnaɪt] m (-[e]s; no pl) F guts. '**Schneidbrenner** m cutting torch.

Schneide ['ʃnaɪdə] f (-; -n) edge.

schneiden ['ʃnaɪdən] (schnitt, geschnitten, h) **I** v/t a) cut (a. ball, curve), carve (meat), b) cut, mow (lawn), prune (tree), trim (hedge): **in Stücke ~** cut up; F **j-n** ~ fig. cut s.o. dead, mot. cut in on s.o.; → **Grimasse, Haar. 2.** edit (film, tape). **II** v/i ~ a) cut o.s., b) lines: intersect; F **da hat er sich aber geschnitten!** he is very much mistaken there! '**schneidend** adj fig. sharp (pain, voice, etc), biting (cold, sarcasm, etc).

'**Schneider** m (-s; -) tailor: F **aus dem ~ sein** be out of the woods.

Schneide'rei f (-; no pl) tailoring, dressmaking.

'**Schneiderin** f (-; -nen) dressmaker.

schneidern ['ʃnaɪdərn] (h) **I** v/i do tailoring (or dressmaking). **II** v/t make.

'**Schneidetisch** m film etc: editing table.

'**Schneidezahn** m incisor.

'**schneidig** adj plucky, snappy, dashing, w.s. brisk (a. pace), rousing (music).

schneien ['ʃnaɪən] **I** v/impers (h) **es**

schneit it's snowing. **II** v/i (sn) F **(j-m) ins Haus ~** drop in (on s.o.) unexpectedly.

Schneise ['ʃnaɪzə] f (-; -n) **1.** (forest) lane, fire-break. **2.** → **Flugschneise.**

schnell [ʃnɛl] **I** adj quick (movement, decision, etc), fast (car, runner, track, etc), a. rapid, a. prompt, speedy: **in ~er Folge** in rapid succession; **~es Handeln** prompt action; **~e Fortschritte machen** make rapid progress; F **e-e ~e Mark machen** make a fast buck; **auf dem ~sten Wege** as quickly as possible; F **auf die Schnelle** quickly, contp. slapdash; → **Brüter. II** adv fast, quick(ly), rapidly (etc): **~ fahren (handeln)** drive (act) fast; **das geht ~** that won't take long; **das ist ~ gegangen** that was quick; **~er ging es nicht** I (we etc) couldn't do it any faster; **so ~ wie möglich, schnellstens** as quickly as possible; **(mach) ~!** hurry up!, F get a move on!; **nicht so ~!** easy!; **sie ist ~ beleidigt** she is quick to take offence; **wie ~ die Zeit vergeht!** how time flies!

'**Schnellboot** n ✕ speedboat.

schnellebig [-leːbɪç] adj fast-moving (times), short-lived (fashion etc).

schnellen ['ʃnɛlən] **I** v/i (sn) bounce, pop: **in die Höhe ~** → **hochschnellen. II** v/t (h) toss, flick.

'**Schnell|feuerwaffe** f automatic weapon. **~gang** m mot. overdrive. **~gaststätte** f cafeteria. **~gericht** n **1.** ⚖ summary court. **2.** gastr. instant meal. **~hefter** m (-s; -) letter file.

'**Schnelligkeit** f (-; no pl) a) quickness, fastness, rapidity, speediness, b) speed.

'**Schnell|imbiß** m **1.** snack. **2.** → **~imbißstube** f snack bar. **~kochtopf** m pressure cooker. **~reinigung** f express dry-cleaning. **~straße** f dual carriageway, Am. divided highway. **~verband** m first-aid dressing. **~verfahren** n **1.** ⚖ summary procedure (or proceedings). **2.** ⊙ high-speed process: fig. **im ~** very quickly. **~wirkend** adj pharm. fast-acting. **~zug** m fast train.

Schnepfe ['ʃnɛpfə] f (-; -n) zo. snipe.

schneuzen ['ʃnɔʏtsən] **sich ~** (h) blow one's nose.

schniefen ['ʃniːfən] v/i (h) F sniffle.

Schnippchen ['ʃnɪpçən] n **j-m ein ~ schlagen** outwit (or fool) s.o.

schnippeln ['ʃnɪpəln] v/t, v/i (h) snip (away) (*an dat* at).

schnippen ['ʃnɪpən] (h) **I** v/i snip: (*mit den Fingern*) ~ snap one's fingers. **II** v/t flick (off).

schnippisch ['ʃnɪpɪʃ] adj pert, saucy.

Schnipsel ['ʃnɪpsəl] m, n (-s; -) shred.

schnitt [ʃnɪt] pret of **schneiden**.

Schnitt m (-[e]s; -e) **1.** no pl cutting, ✗ a. mowing, *film etc*: editing. **2.** cut, ✗ a. incision, gash: *film etc*: **harter ~** jump cut. **3.** cut (*of hair, dress, etc*), shape. **4.** pattern. **5.** ⚭ intersection. **6.** ⚙ section(al view). **7.** (a. **im ~ erreichen** *etc*) average: **im ~** on average. **8.** F profit.

'Schnittblumen pl cut flowers.

Schnitte ['ʃnɪtə] f (-; -n) **1.** slice. **2.** (open) sandwich.

'schnittfest adj firm (*tomatoes etc*).

'schnittig adj racy, sleek, streamlined.

'Schnittlauch m ❀ chives.

'Schnittmuster n pattern.

'Schnittpunkt m (point of) intersection.

'Schnittwunde f cut, gash.

'Schnittzeichnung f ⚙ section(al view).

Schnitzarbeit ['ʃnɪts-] f (wood-)carving.

Schnitzel¹ ['ʃnɪtsəl] n (-s; -) *gastr.* a. *Wiener ~* escalope.

Schnitzel² n, m (-s; -) shred, scrap.

'Schnitzeljagd f paper chase.

'Schnitzelwerk n shredder.

schnitzen ['ʃnɪtsən] v/t, v/i (h) carve.

'Schnitzer m (-s; -) **1.** (wood-)carver. **2.** F blunder.

Schnitze'rei f (-; -en) (wood-)carving.

schnodd(e)rig ['ʃnɔd(ə)rɪç] adj F snotty.

Schnorchel ['ʃnɔrçəl] m (-s; -) snorkel.

Schnörkel ['ʃnœrkəl] m (-s; -) **1.** scroll. **2.** flourish: *fig.* **ohne ~** without frills.

schnorren ['ʃnɔrən] v/i, v/t (h) scrounge (*bei j-m* off s.o.).

'Schnorrer m (-s; -) scrounger.

Schnösel ['ʃnøːzəl] m (-s; -) F snot-nose.

schnuck(e)lig ['ʃnʊk(ə)lɪç] adj F cuddly, pretty, cute.

schnüffeln ['ʃnʏfəln] v/i (h) **1.** sniff (*an dat* at). **2.** F snoop (around).

'Schnüffler m (-s; -) F snooper, sleuth.

Schnuller ['ʃnʊlər] m (-s; -) comforter, dummy, *Am.* pacifier.

Schnulze ['ʃnʊltsə] f (-; -n) F **1.** sobstuff, tearjerker. **2.** schmaltzy song.

schnupfen ['ʃnʊpfən] v/i, v/t (h) take snuff.

'Schnupfen m (-s; -) cold, F *the* sniffles.

'Schnupftabak m snuff.

schnuppe ['ʃnʊpə] → **schnurz.**

'schnuppern → **schnüffeln** 1.

Schnur [ʃnuːr] f (-; ⁓e) cord, (piece of) string, ⚡ flex: *fig.* **über die ~ hauen** overdo it.

Schnürchen ['ʃnyːrçən] n F **das ging wie am ~** it went like clockwork.

schnüren ['ʃnyːrən] v/t (h) lace up.

'schnurgerade adj *and* adv F (as) straight as an arrow, dead straight.

'Schnurrbart m m(o)ustache.

schnurren ['ʃnʊrən] v/i (h) purr.

'Schnür|riemen m strap. **~schuh** m lace-up shoe. **~senkel** [-zɛŋkəl] m (-s; -) shoelace, bootlace.

schnurstracks ['ʃnuːrʃtraks] adv F a) straight, b) straightaway.

schnurz [ʃnʊrts] adj F **das ist mir ~** I couldn't care less.

schob [ʃoːp] pret of **schieben**.

Schober ['ʃoːbər] m (-s; -) **1.** rick. **2.** barn, shed.

Schock [ʃɔk] m (-[e]s; -s) a. ⚕ shock: **e-n ~ haben** be in (a state of) shock.

'schocken v/t (h) F shock.

schockieren [ʃɔ'kiːrən] v/t (h) shock, scandalize: **~d** shocking, scandalizing.

'Schockthera,pie f ⚕ (electro-)shock therapy.

schofel ['ʃoːfəl] adj F shabby, mean.

Schöffe ['ʃœfə] m (-n; -n) lay assessor.

Schokolade [ʃoko'laːdə] f (-; -n) (**e-e Tafel ~** a bar of) chocolate.

Scholle¹ ['ʃɔlə] f (-; -n) **1.** clod (*of earth*). **2.** (ice) floe. **3.** *fig.* (native) soil.

'Scholle² f (-; -n) *zo.* plaice.

schon [ʃoːn] adv **1.** a) already, yet, b) before, c) ever, d) even: ~ *damals* even then; ~ *früher* before; ~ *immer* always, all along; ~ *oft* often (enough); ~ *wieder* again; (*nicht*) ~ *wieder!* not again!; ~ *am nächsten Tage* the very next day; ~ *im 16. Jahrhundert* as early as the 16th century; *ist er ~ da?* has he come yet?; *hast du ... (einmal) ...?* have you ever ...?; *ich habe ihn ~ einmal gesehen* I have seen him before; *ich komme (ja) ~!* (I'm) coming!; *das kennen wir ~!* that's an old story! **2.** *er wird ~ kommen* he is sure to come; don't worry, he'll come; *er wird es ~ machen* leave it to him; *das ist ~ möglich* that's quite possible; (*das ist*) ~ *wahr, aber ...*

that's (certainly) true, but ...; **er ist ~ ein guter Spieler** he really is a good player. **3. ~ gar nicht** least of all. **4. ~ der Anblick (Gedanke** etc) the very sight (idea etc); **~ deswegen** if only for that reason; **~ weil** if only because. **5.** F **na, wenn ~!** so what!; **was macht das ~?** what does it matter?; **wenn ~, denn ~!** if we do it at all, let's do it properly!

schön [ʃøːn] **I** adj **1.** beautiful: **das ~e Geschlecht** the fair sex; **die ~en Künste** the fine arts; **~es Wetter** good (or fine) weather. **2.** a) good, fine, b) pleasant, nice: **~!** all right!, okay!; **e-s ~en Tages** one of these days; **~es Wochenende!** have a nice weekend!; **~er Tod** easy death; **das ist alles ~ und gut, aber ...** that's all very well, but ...; **es war sehr ~** I (we etc) had a good time; **~ wär's!** some hope!; **das wäre ja noch ~er!** F nothing doing!; iro. **du bist mir ein ~er Freund!** a fine friend you are!; → **Dank. 3.** F handsome, nice (gift etc). **II** adv **4.** beautifully, nicely, pleasantly: **sie war ~ braun** she had a beautiful tan. **5.** F very, really, pretty: **ganz ~ teuer** pretty expensive; iro. **da wärst du ~ dumm** you'd be a fool; **sei ~ brav!** be a good boy (or girl) now!; **~ warm** nice and warm.

'**Schöne** n (-n) the beautiful: **das ~ daran** the nice thing about it; **es gibt nichts Schöneres als** there's nothing nicer (or better) than.

schonen [ˈʃoːnən] **(h) I** v/t spare (s.o., s.o.'s feelings), save (one's energy, supplies, etc), treat s.th. with care, detergent etc: a. be easy on (the carpet etc). **II** sich ~ take it easy, save one's strength for s.th.; **sich nicht ~** drive o.s. (hard). '**schonend** adj a) gentle, careful, considerate, b) mild (detergent etc): **~ umgehen mit** go easy on; → **beibringen.**

'**Schoner** m (-s; -) ⚓ schooner.
'**Schöngeist** m (-[e]s; -er) (a)esthete.
'**schöngeistig** adj (a)esthetical.
'**Schönheit** f (-; -en) beauty.
~königin f beauty queen. **~operati,on** f cosmetic operation. **~pflege** f beauty care. **~sa,lon** m beauty parlo(u)r. **~wettbewerb** m beauty contest.
'**Schonkost** f light food, bland diet.

'**schönmachen** (sep, -ge-, h) **I** v/i dog: sit up (and beg). **II** sich ~ a) dress up, b) make (o.s.) up.

'**Schonung** f (-; -en) **1.** no pl a) mercy, b) forbearance, c) good care, d) protection, e) rest: **sie braucht ~** she needs a rest; **zur ~** (gen) to protect (one's hands etc), to save (one's eyes, strength, etc). **2.** (young) forest plantation.

'**schonungsbedürftig** adj in need of rest. '**schonungslos** adj merciless.
'**Schonwaschgang** m program(me Br.) for delicate fabrics.
'**Schön'wetterlage** f period of fine weather.
'**Schonzeit** f hunt. close season.
Schopf [ʃɔpf] m (-[e]s; ⸗e) mop (of hair), of birds: tuft; → **Gelegenheit.**
schöpfen [ˈʃœpfən] v/t (h) scoop, ladle; → **Hoffnung, Kraft** 1, **Verdacht** etc.
'**Schöpfer** m (-s; -) creator, bibl. the Creator. **~geist** m creative genius.
'**schöpferisch** adj creative.
'**Schöpfkelle** f, '**Schöpflöffel** m ladle.
'**Schöpfung** f (-; -en) **1.** creation, work. **2.** no pl bibl. the Creation.
'**Schöpfungsgeschichte** f Genesis.
schor [ʃoːr] pret of **scheren.**
Schorf [ʃɔrf] m (-[e]s; -e) ⚕ scab.
Schornstein [ˈʃɔrn-] m chimney, smoke stack, ⚓, ⚒ funnel. '**Schornsteinfeger** m (-s; -) chimney sweep.
schoß [ʃɔs] pret of **schießen.**
Schoß [ʃoːs] m (-es; ⸗e) **1.** lap: → **Hand. 2.** a) womb, b) (woman's) sex.
Schößling [ˈʃœslɪŋ] m (-s; -e) ⚘ shoot.
Schote [ˈʃoːtə] f (-; -n) ⚘ husk, pod.
Schotte [ˈʃɔtə] m (-n; -n) Scot, Scotsman: **die ~n** the Scots.
Schotter [ˈʃɔtər] m (-s; -) gravel, a. (road) metal. '**schottern** v/t (h) gravel, metal.
Schottin [ˈʃɔtɪn] f (-; -nen) Scotswoman.
'**schottisch** adj Scottish: **~er Whisky** Scotch (whisky). '**Schottland** n (-s) Scotland.
schraffieren [ʃraˈfiːrən] v/t (h) hatch.
schräg [ʃrɛːk] **I** adj oblique, slanting, sloping (ground, roof, etc), diagonal (line). **II** adv cut, set, etc at an angle: **~ gegenüber** diagonally opposite.
Schräge [ˈʃrɛːgə] f (-; -n) **1.** slant. **2.** incline, slope.
'**Schrägstrich** m slash, oblique.
Schramme [ˈʃramə] f (-; -n) scratch.

'**schrammen** *v/t* (h) scratch, graze.

Schrank [ʃraŋk] *m* (-[e]s; ⸗e) a) cupboard, closet, wardrobe, b) locker: F ***er ist ein ~*** he's a hulking fellow.

'**Schrankbett** *n* foldaway bed.

Schranke ['ʃraŋkə] *f* (-; -n) **1.** barrier, 🚂 *a.* gate, ⚖ bar. **2.** *fig.* a) (*social etc, a. trade*) barrier, b) bounds, limits: ***~n setzen*** set bounds (*dat* to); (***sich***) ***in ~n halten*** keep within bounds, restrain (o.s.); ***j-n in s-e ~n weisen*** put s.o. in his place.

'**schrankenlos** *adj fig.* boundless.

'**Schrankenwärter** *m* 🚂 gatekeeper.

'**schrankfertig** *adj* washed and ironed.

'**Schrankwand** *f* wall-to-wall cupboard.

'**Schraubdeckel** *m* screw cap.

Schraube ['ʃraʊbə] *f* (-; -n) **1.** screw (*a.* ⚓), ✈ propeller: ***~ und Mutter*** bolt and nut; F ***bei ihm ist e-e ~ locker*** he has a screw loose. **2.** *gym. etc* twist.

'**schrauben** *v/t* (h) screw, *a.* twist: ***fester ~*** tighten the screw(s) of; *fig.* ***niedriger ~*** lower, scale down; (***sich***) ***in die Höhe ~*** → ***hochschrauben***; → ***geschraubt.***

'**Schraubendreher** *m* screwdriver.

'**schraubenförmig** *adj* helical, spiral.

'**Schrauben|schlüssel** *m* wrench, spanner. **~zieher** *m* (-s; -) screwdriver.

'**Schraubstock** *m* vice, *Am.* vise.

Schrebergarten ['ʃre:bər-] *m* allotment (garden).

Schreck [ʃrɛk] *m* (-[e]s; -e) fright, shock: F ***krieg k-n ~!*** don't be alarmed!; ***ach du ~!*** good God!, dear me! '**schrecken** *v/t* (h) frighten, startle: ***das schreckt mich nicht*** that can't scare me.

'**Schrecken** *m* (-s; -) fright, shock: ***in ~en versetzen*** frighten, terrify; ***mit dem ~en davonkommen*** get off with a bad fright; ***zu m-m ~en*** to my dismay; ***die ~ des Krieges*** the horrors of war.

'**Schreckens|herrschaft** *f* reign of terror. **~nachricht** *f* alarming (*or* dreadful) news. **~tat** *f* atrocity.

'**Schreckgespenst** *n fig.* nightmare.

'**schreckhaft** *adj* jumpy, nervous.

'**schrecklich I** *adj* terrible, dreadful, horrible. **II** *adv* F awfully, terribly.

'**Schreckschuß** *m* warning shot. **~pi,stole** *f* blank (cartridge) pistol.

'**Schreckse,kunde** *f mot.* reaction time.

Schrei [ʃraɪ] *m* (-[e]s; -e) cry, shout, scream, yell: *fig.* ***~ der Entrüstung*** outcry; F ***der letzte ~*** the latest rage.

Schreib|arbeit ['ʃraɪp-] *f* desk work, paperwork. **~block** *m* writing pad.

schreiben ['ʃraɪbən] *v/t, v/i* (schrieb, geschrieben, h) write (***über*** *acc* about, on), write out (*bill etc*), ⚙ record: ***j-m ~*** write to s.o., *Am. a.* write s.o.; ***j-m et. ~*** write to s.o. about s.th.; ***mit Bleistift*** *etc* **~** write in pencil *etc*; ***mit der Maschine ~*** type; ***sich mit j-m ~*** correspond with s.o.; ***noch einmal ~*** rewrite; ***gut ~*** a) write a good hand, b) be a good writer; (***richtig***) **~** spell *word* (correctly); ***falsch ~*** misspell; ***wie schreibt er sich?*** how do you spell his name?; ***an e-m Roman ~*** be working on a novel; *ped. etc* ***e-e Arbeit ~*** do a test; → ***Ohr, rein*** 1 *etc.*

'**Schreiben** *n* (-s; -) **1.** *no pl* writing. **2.** letter. '**Schreiber** *m* (-s; -) writer. **Schreibe'rei** *f* (-; -en) (endless) writing, paperwork. '**Schreiberin** *f* (-; -nen) writer. '**Schreiberling** *m* (-s; -e) *contp.* hack. '**schreibfaul** *adj* lazy about writing letters.

'**Schreib|feder** *f* pen. **~fehler** *m* a) spelling mistake, b) slip of the pen. **~gerät** *n* writing utensils, ⚙ recorder. **~heft** *n* exercise-book. **~kopf** *m* ⚙ golfball. **~kraft** *f* (shorthand) typist. **~mappe** *f* writing case. **~ma,schine** *f* typewriter: ***~ schreiben*** type; ***mit ~ geschrieben*** typewritten, typed. **~ma,schinenpa,pier** *n* typing paper. **~pa,pier** *n* writing paper. **~stube** *f* ⚔ orderly room. **~tisch** *m* (writing) desk. **~tischlampe** *f* desk lamp.

'**Schreibung** *f* (-; -en) spelling.

'**Schreibwaren** *pl* stationery. **~geschäft** *n* stationer's (shop).

'**Schreibweise** *f* **1.** style. **2.** spelling.

schreien ['ʃraɪən] *v/i, v/t* (schrie, geschrien, h) shout, yell, scream, *baby*: howl: ***~ nach*** cry for; F ***es*** (***er***) ***ist zum Schreien!*** it (he) is a scream!

'**schreiend** *adj fig.* loud (*colo[u]r*), flagrant (*injustice*), glaring (*contrast*).

'**Schreihals** *m* F **1.** loudmouth. **2.** brawler. **3.** (*baby*) bawler, (*child*) noisy brat.

Schrein [ʃraɪn] *m* (-[e]s; -e) shrine.

Schreiner ['ʃraɪnər] *m* (-s; -) *etc* → ***Tischler*** *etc.*

schreiten ['ʃraɪtən] *v/i* (schritt, geschritten, sn) **1.** walk, stride. **2.** ***zu et. ~*** proceed to (do) s.th.; ***zur Tat ~*** set to work.

schrie [ʃriː] *pret of* **schreien**.
schrieb [ʃriːp] *pret of* **schreiben**.
Schrift [ʃrɪft] *f* (-; -en) **1.** writing, hand(writing), *print*. script, type: *in lateinischer* ~ in Roman characters (*or* letters). **2.** publication, paper, pamphlet: ~**en** writings, works; *die Heilige* ~ the Holy Scripture(s). ~**art** *f* script, type. ~**bild** *n* typeface. ~**deutsch** *n* standard German. ~**führer(in** *f*) *m* secretary. ~**gelehrte** *m bibl.* scribe. ~**grad** *m* type size.
'**schriftlich I** *adj* written, in writing: ~*e Prüfung* written examination. **II** *adv* in writing, *a.* by letter: *ich kann* **F** *das kann ich dir* ~ *geben!* I can guarantee you that!
'**Schrift**|**probe** *f* specimen of *s.o.'s* handwriting. ~**satz** *m 🖶* written statement. ~**setzer** *m* (-s; -) typesetter. ~**sprache** *f* standard language.
'**Schriftsteller** *m* (-s; -) writer.
Schriftstelle'rei *f* (-; *no pl*) writing.
'**Schriftstellerin** *f* (-; -nen) writer.
'**schriftstellerisch I** *adj* literary. **II** *adv* as a writer.
'**Schriftstück** *n* document, paper.
'**Schrifttum** *n* (-s; *no pl*) literature.
'**Schriftwechsel** *m* correspondence.
'**Schriftzeichen** *n* letter, character.
schrill [ʃrɪl] *adj* shrill, piercing.
schritt [ʃrɪt] *pret of* **schreiten**.
Schritt *m* (-[e]s; -e) **1.** a) step, stride, b) footstep, c) pace: ~ *halten mit* keep pace with, *fig. a.* keep abreast of; ~ *für* ~ *a. fig.* step by step; *auf* ~ *und Tritt* at every turn, everywhere. **2.** *no pl* walk, gait: *im* ~ at a walking pace; *mot.* (*im*) ~ *fahren!* dead slow! **3.** *a.* F *anat.* crotch. **4.** *fig.* step, *a.* measure, move: *diplomatischer* ~ démarche; *Politik der kleinen* ~*e* step-by-step policy; *den ersten* ~ *tun* take the first step; *wir sind k-n* ~ *weitergekommen* we haven't made the slightest bit of progress.
'**Schrittmacher** *m* (-s; -) *sports*: pacemaker, *fig. a.* trendsetter. ~**dienste** *pl j-m* ~ *leisten sports*: make the pace for *s.o.*, *fig.* smooth the way for *s.o.*
'**schrittweise I** *adj* step-by-step, gradual. **II** *adv* step by step.
schroff [ʃrɔf] *adj* **1.** steep, precipitous. **2.** gruff, curt, abrupt: ~*e Ablehnung* flat refusal; ~*er Gegensatz* sharp contrast.
schröpfen ['ʃrœpfən] *v/t* (h) **1.** 🖶 bleed.

2. F *j-n* ~ fleece s.o. (*um* for).
Schrot [ʃroːt] *m, n* (-[e]s; -e) **1.** wholemeal. **2.** *hunt.* (small) shot. **3.** *fig. von echtem* ~ *und Korn* true.
schroten ['ʃroːtən] *v/t* (h) bruise.
'**Schrot**|**flinte** *f* shotgun. ~**korn** *n*, ~**kugel** *f* pellet. ~**säge** *f* crosscut saw.
Schrott [ʃrɔt] *m* (-[e]s; -e) **1.** scrap metal: *ein Auto zu* ~ *fahren* smash up a car. **2.** F a) junk, b) rubbish. ~**händler** *m* scrap dealer. ~**haufen** *m* scrap heap. ~**platz** *m* scrap yard. ~**reif** *adj* ready for the scrap heap. ~**wert** *m* scrap value.
schrubben ['ʃrʊbən] *v/t* (h) scrub.
'**Schrubber** *m* (-s; -) scrubbing brush.
Schrulle ['ʃrʊlə] *f* (-; -n) quirk, (cranky) whim. '**schrullig** *adj* F cranky.
schrumpf(e)lig ['ʃrʊmpf(ə)lɪç] *adj* shrivel(l)ed.
schrumpfen ['ʃrʊmpfən] *v/i* (sn) shrink (*a.* ⊙), 🖶 atrophy, *fig. a.* dwindle.
Schub [ʃuːp] *m* (-[e]s; ~e) **1.** push, *phys. a.* thrust. **2.** batch. **3.** 🖶 phase, *a.* attack, rush (*of adrenaline etc*): *in Schüben* intermittent(ly). ~**fach** *n* drawer. ~**kraft** *f phys.* thrust. ~**lade** *f* (-; -n) drawer.
Schubs [ʃʊps] *m* (-es; -e) F (*a. dat* **e-n** ~ *geben*) push, shove.
'**schubsen** *v/t* (h) F push, shove.
schubweise ['ʃuːp-] *adv* in batches.
schüchtern ['ʃʏçtərn] *adj* shy, timid, bashful. '**Schüchternheit** *f* (-; *no pl*) shyness, timidity, bashfulness.
Schuft [ʃʊft] *m* (-[e]s; -e) scoundrel.
schuften ['ʃʊftən] *v/i* (h) F slave away.
Schufte'rei *f* (-; *no pl*) F drudgery, grind.
Schuh [ʃuː] *m* (-[e]s; -e) shoe (*a.* ⊙): *fig. j-m et. in die* ~*e schieben* put the blame for s.th. on s.o.; *wo drückt dich der* ~? what's the trouble? ~**bürste** *f* shoe brush. ~**creme** *f* shoe polish. ~**geschäft** *n* shoe shop. ~**größe** *f* shoe size: *welche* ~ *haben Sie?* what size shoe(s) do you take? ~**löffel** *m* shoehorn. ~**macher** *m* (-s; -) shoemaker. ~**putzer** *m* (-s; -) shoeblack. ~**sohle** *f* sole. ~**spanner** *m* shoe tree. ~**werk** *n* (-[e]s; *no pl*) footwear, shoes.
Schukostecker ['ʃuːko-] *m* (*TM*) ⚡ shockproof plug.
'**Schul**|**abgänger** [-gɛŋər] *m* (-s; -) school-leaver. ~**alter** *n* school age. ~**anfänger** *m* (-s; -) (school) beginner.

~arbeiten *pl*, ~aufgaben *pl* homework. ~ausflug *m* school outing. ~bank *f* (-; ⸚e) desk: **die ~ drücken** go to school. ~behörde *f* education authority. ~beispiel *n* classic example (**für** of). ~besuch *m* (school) attendance. ~bildung *f* (-; *no pl*) education: **höhere ~** secondary education. ~buch *n* textbook. ~buchverlag *m* educational publishers. ~bus *m* school bus.

Schuld [ʃʊlt] *f* (-; -en) **1.** *no pl* guilt (*a.* 🝔), blame, *eccl.* sin(s): **ihn trifft die ~, er ist schuld** he is to blame for it; **die ~ auf sich nehmen** take the blame; **die ~ geben** (*dat*) blame it on; **ohne m-e ~** through no fault of mine; → **zuschieben 2. 2.** *usu. pl* debt: **~en haben, in ~en stecken** be in debt; **in ~en geraten** run into debt; *fig.* **(tief) in j-s ~ stehen** be (greatly) indebted to s.o.

'schuld**bewußt** *adj* guilty (*look etc*).

schulden ['ʃʊldən] *v/t* (h) **j-m et. ~** owe s.o. s.th.; → **Dank**.

'**Schuldenberg** *m* F enormous debt(s). '**schuldenfrei** *adj* a) free of debt, b) unencumbered (*house etc*). '**Schuldentilgung** *f* liquidation of debts. '**Schuldforderung** *f* claim, (active) debt. '**Schuldfrage** *f* question of guilt. '**Schuldgefühl(e** *pl*) *n* guilty conscience. '**schuldhaft** *adj* 🝔 culpable. '**Schuldienst** *m* (-[e]s; *no pl*) teaching: **im ~ sein** be a teacher.

schuldig ['ʃʊldɪç] *adj* **1.** (*gen a.*) 🝔 guilty (of), responsible (for): **j-n für ~ befinden** find s.o. guilty (**e-s Verbrechens** of a crime, **e-r Anklage** on a charge); **j-n ~ sprechen** pronounce s.o. guilty; **sich ~ bekennen** plead guilty. **2.** **j-m et. ~ sein** owe s.o. s.th.; **was bin ich Ihnen ~?** how much do I owe you?; **das ist man ihm ~** that's his due; **j-m die Antwort ~ bleiben** give s.o. no answer.

Schuldige ['ʃʊldɪgə] *m*, *f* (-n, -n) culprit, 🝔 guilty party, offender.

'**Schuldigkeit** *f* (-; *no pl*) duty.

'**Schuldi,rektor** *m* headmaster, *Am.* principal.

'**schuldlos** *adj* innocent (**an** *dat* of).

Schuldner ['ʃʊldnər] *m* (-s; -) debtor.

'**Schuldnerland** *n* debtor nation.

'**Schuld|schein** *m* (-[e]s; -e) promissory note, IOU (= I owe you). ~**spruch** *m*

🝔 verdict of guilty, conviction. ~**verschreibung** *f* ✝ (debenture) bond.

Schule ['ʃuːlə] *f* (-; -n) school: **höhere ~** secondary school, *Am.* senior high school; **auf** (*or* **in**) **der ~** at school; **in die** (*or* **zur**) **~ gehen** go to school; *fig.* **aus der ~ plaudern** tell tales out of school, blab; ~ **machen** set a precedent, be imitated, spread; **durch e-e harte ~ gehen** learn the hard way; → **besuchen, schwänzen**.

'**schulen** *v/t* (h) train; → **geschult**.

'**Schulenglisch** *n* school English.

Schüler ['ʃyːlər] *m* (-s; -) a) schoolboy, *a.* pupil, student, b) disciple.

'**Schüleraustausch** *m* school exchange.

'**Schülerin** *f* (-; -nen) schoolgirl (*etc*, → **Schüler**).

'**Schüler|lotse** *m* pupil acting as a school crossing warden. ~**zeitung** *f* school magazine.

'**Schul|fach** *n* subject. ~**ferien** *pl* holidays, *Am.* vacation. ~**fernsehen** *n* educational television. ~**flugzeug** *n* training aircraft, trainer. **♀frei** *adj* ~ **haben** have a holiday; **heute ist ~** there's no school today. ~**freund(in** *f*) *m* schoolmate. ~**funk** *m* school broadcasts. ~**gelände** *n* school grounds, *Am.* campus. ~**geld** *n* (-[e]s; *no pl*) school fees. ~**heft** *n* exercise book. ~**hof** *m* playground, schoolyard.

schulisch ['ʃuːlɪʃ] *adj* school (*affairs etc*): ~**e Leistungen** progress at school.

'**Schul|jahr** *n* school year: **m-e ~e** my school days. ~**junge** *m* schoolboy. ~**kame,rad(in** *f*) *m* schoolmate. ~**kenntnisse** *pl* school knowledge. ~**klasse** *f* class, *Am.* a. form, *Am.* grade. ~**leiter(in** *f*) *m* headmaster (-mistress), *Am.* principal. ~**mädchen** *n* schoolgirl. ~**mappe** *f* schoolbag. ~**medi,zin** *f* orthodox medicine. ~**meinung** *f* received opinion. ~**ordnung** *f* school regulations. ~**pflicht** *f* compulsory education.

'**schulpflichtig** *adj* school-age, of school age: ~**es Alter** school(-entering) age.

'**Schul|psycho,loge** *m* educational psychologist. ~**ranzen** *m* satchel. ~**rat** *m* school inspector. ~**schiff** *n* training ship. ~**schluß** *m* (-sses; *no pl*) a) end of school, b) end of term: **nach ~** after school. ~**schwänzer** *m* (-s; -) truant. ~**speisung** *f* school meals. ~**spre-**

cher(in f) m head boy (girl). **~stunde** f lesson, class. **~tasche** f schoolbag.

Schulter ['ʃʊltər] f (-; -n) shoulder: **~ an ~** shoulder to shoulder; **mit den ~n zuk- ken** shrug one's shoulders; **j-m auf die ~ klopfen** slap s.o.'s back; → **kalt** I, **leicht** 1. **~blatt** n anat. shoulder blade.

'**schulter|frei** adj off-the-shoulder (dress). **~lang** adj shoulder-length.

schultern ['ʃʊltərn] v/t (h) shoulder.

'**Schulung** f (-; -en) **1.** training, a. prac- tice. **2.** pol. indoctrination.

'**Schulungskurs** m course of training.

'**Schul|unterricht** m lessons, classes. **~weg** m (auf dem ~ on one's) way to school. **~weisheit** f contp. book learn- ing. **~wesen** n (-s; no pl) school system. **~zeit** f school days. **~zeugnis** n (school) report, report card.

schummeln ['ʃʊməln] v/i (h) F cheat.

schumm(e)rig ['ʃʊm(ə)rıç] adj F dim.

Schund [ʃʊnt] m (-[e]s; no pl) trash, rub- bish. '**Schundro,man** m trashy novel.

schunkeln ['ʃʊŋkəln] v/i (h) rock, sway.

Schuppe ['ʃʊpə] f (-; -n) **1.** scale: **es fiel mir wie ~n von den Augen** the scales fell from my eyes. **2.** pl dandruff.

schuppen ['ʃʊpən] (h) **I** v/t scale (fish). **II sich ~** skin: peel.

'**Schuppen** m (-s; -) **1.** shed, ✓ a. han- gar. **2.** F a) contp. hovel, b) joint.

schuppig ['ʃʊpıç] adj scaly.

Schur [ʃuːr] f (-; -en) a) shearing, b) fleece.

schürfen ['ʃʏrfən] (h) **I** v/i **1.** (nach) for) prospect, dig: fig. **tiefer ~** dig below the surface. **II** v/t **2.** prospect (or dig) for (ore etc). **3.** scrape, graze (skin).

'**Schürfwunde** f graze, abrasion.

Schurke ['ʃʊrkə] m (-n; -n) villain.

'**Schurwolle** f virgin (or new) wool.

Schurz [ʃʊrts] m (-es; -e) apron.

Schürze ['ʃʏrtsə] f (-; -n) apron.

schürzen ['ʃʏrtsən] v/t (h) gather up (skirt), purse (lips).

'**Schürzenjäger** m F womanizer.

Schuß [ʃʊs] m (-sses; «sse) **1.** shot (a. phot. or sports), round (of ammunition): **ein ~ ins Schwarze** a. fig. a bull's-eye; **e-n ~ abgeben** fire (a shot); **weit vom ~** well out of harm's way; **er** (**es**) **ist k-n ~ Pulver wert** he (it) is no good; fig. **der ~ ging nach hinten los** it backfired; → **Bug** 1. **2.** → **Schußverletzung. 3.** F

shot, sl. fix: **sich e-n ~ setzen** give o.s. a fix. **4.** skiing: (a. **im ~ fahren**) schuss. **5.** dash (a. fig.): **Tee mit e-m ~ Milch** tea with a dash of milk; **e-e Cola mit ~** a spiked coke. **6.** fig. (**gut**) **in** (or **im**) **~ sein** be in good shape; **in ~ bringen** knock s.th. into shape, bring s.o. up to the mark; **in ~ halten** keep s.o., s.th. in good shape. **7.** textil. weft.

'**schußbereit** adj ready to shoot (a. phot.), gun: at the ready.

Schussel ['ʃʊsəl] m (-s; -) F scatterbrain.

Schüssel ['ʃʏsəl] f (-; -n) bowl, basin, a. F TV dish.

'**schusselig** adj F scatterbrained.

'**Schuß|fahrt** f skiing: schuss. **~linie** f line of fire: fig. **in die ~ geraten** come under fire (gen from). **~verletzung** f gunshot wound. **~waffe** f firearm. **~wechsel** m exchange of shots. **~weite** f (firing) range: **außer ~** out of range.

Schuster ['ʃuːstər] m (-s; -) shoemaker.

Schutt [ʃʊt] m (-[e]s; no pl) rubble, geol. a. debris: **in ~ und Asche liegen** be in ruins.

'**Schüttelfrost** m 🕈 shivering fit.

schütteln ['ʃʏtəln] v/t (h) shake: **den Kopf ~** shake one's head; **j-m die Hand ~** shake hands with s.o., shake s.o. by the hand; → **Ärmel**.

schütten ['ʃʏtən] v/t (h) pour: F **es schüttet** it's pouring (with rain).

schütter ['ʃʏtər] adj thin (hair etc).

'**Schutthaufen** m heap of rubble.

Schutz [ʃʊts] m (-es; no pl) protection (**gegen**, **vor** against, from), a. shelter, esp. ✗ cover, escort, (esp. legal) safe- guard, a. preservation: **~ suchen** seek refuge (**vor** from, **bei** with); **j-n in ~ nehmen** come to s.o.'s defence, back s.o. up; **im ~e der Dunkelheit** under cover of darkness.

Schütz [ʃʏts] n (-es; -e) ⚡ contactor.

'**Schutzanzug** m protective suit.

'**Schutzbefohlene** f (-n; -n) charge.

'**Schutzblech** n mudguard, Am. fender.

'**Schutzbrille** f (safety) goggles.

Schütze ['ʃʏtsə] m (-n; -n) **1.** shot, marksman. **2.** sports: scorer. **3.** ✗ pri- vate. **4.** no pl astr. (**[ein]** ~ **sein** be [a]) Sagittarius.

'**schützen** v/t (h) (**gegen**, **vor** dat) protect (from, against), defend (against), shel- ter (from), guard (against), a. fig. shield

(from), *esp.* ✗ cover (against): **sich ~ (vor)** guard (against), protect o.s. (from): **~des Dach** shelter; → **Nässe.**
'**Schutzengel** *m* guardian angel.
'**Schützen|graben** *m* ✗ trench. **~hilfe** *f* **j-m ~ geben** back s.o. up. **~könig** *m* champion shot, *sports:* top scorer. **~panzer** *m* ✗ armo(u)red personnel carrier.
'**Schutz|gebiet** *n* protectorate. **~geld** *n* protection money. **~haft** *f* protective custody. **~heilige** *m, f* (-n; -n) patron saint. **~helm** *m* helmet. **~herrschaft** *f* protectorate. **~hülle** *f* protective cover, ⊚ sheath, *for passport etc:* holder. **~hütte** *f* shelter. **~impfung** *f* inoculation, vaccination. **~kappe** *f* protective cap, *phot.* lens cap. **~kleidung** *f* protective clothing.
Schützling ['ʃʏtslɪŋ] *m* (-s; -e) a) charge, b) protégé(e).
'**schutzlos** *adj* unprotected, defenceless, *Am.* defenseless.
'**Schutz|macht** *f pol.* protecting power. **~marke** *f* (**eingetragene ~** registered) trademark. **~maske** *f* (protective *or* safety) mask. **~maßnahme** *f* protective (*or* safety) measure, precaution. **~rechte** *pl* patent (*or* trademark) rights. **~schicht** *f* protective layer. **~schild** *m* shield. **~umschlag** *m* (dust) jacket. **~vorrichtung** *f* safety device. **~zoll** *m* protective duty.
schwabb(e)lig ['ʃvab(ə)lɪç] *adj* flabby.
Schwabe ['ʃvaːbə] *m* (-n; -n) Swabian. '**Schwaben** *n* (-s) Swabia. **Schwäbin** ['ʃveːbɪn] *f* (-; -nen) Swabian (girl *or* woman). '**schwäbisch** *adj* Swabian.
schwach [ʃvax] **I** *adj* **1.** weak (*a. ling.*), a. faint, *a.* infirm: *humor.* **das ~e Geschlecht** the weaker sex; **~ werden** weaken; **schwächer werden** weaken, *eyesight:* fail, *sound, light:* fade, ✝ *demand:* fall off; F **nur nicht ~ werden!** don't weaken!; **~e Erinnerung** faint (*or* vague) recollection; **~e Hoffnung** faint hope; → **Trost. 2.** *fig.* weak, *a.* poor (*hearing, memory, etc*), low (*battery*), low-powered (*engine*), slow (*pulse*), dim (*light*): **~e Leistung** poor performance; **~e Seite** weakness. **3.** 🝆 dilute (*solution*). **II** *adv* **~ bevölkert** sparsely populated; **~ besucht** poorly attended.
Schwäche ['ʃvɛçə] *f* (-; -n) **1.** weakness,

faintness (*a. fig.*). **2.** *fig.* weakness, failing, shortcoming, weak point. **3.** *no pl* weakness (**für** for): **e-e ~ für j-n haben** F have a soft spot for s.o. **~anfall** *m*, **~gefühl** *n* (sudden feeling of) faintness.
schwächen ['ʃvɛçən] *v/t* (h) weaken.
'**Schwachheit** *f* (-; *no pl*) weakness.
'**Schwachkopf** *m* F idiot, twit.
schwächlich ['ʃvɛçlɪç] *adj* weakly, *a.* delicate, sickly.
'**Schwächling** *m* (-s; -e) weakling.
'**schwachsichtig** *adj* 🝆 weak-sighted.
'**Schwachsinn** *m* (-[e]s; *no pl*) **1.** 🝆 mental deficiency. **2.** F *contp.* a) idiocy, b) rubbish. '**schwachsinnig** *adj* **1.** 🝆 mentally deficient. **2.** F *contp.* idiotic. '**Schwachsinnige** *m, f* (-n; -n) *a.* F *contp.* imbecile.
'**Schwachstelle** *f* weak point.
'**Schwachstrom** *m* low-voltage current.
'**Schwachstromtechnik** *f* communications engineering.
'**Schwächung** *f* (-; -en) weakening.
Schwaden ['ʃvaːdən] *m* (-s; -) cloud.
schwafeln ['ʃvaːfəln] *v/i* (h) F blether.
Schwager ['ʃvaːɡər] *m* (-s; ") brother-in-law. **Schwägerin** ['ʃveːɡərɪn] *f* (-; -nen) sister-in-law.
Schwalbe ['ʃvalbə] *f* (-; -n) *zo.* swallow.
'**Schwalbennest** *n* swallow's nest.
Schwall [ʃval] *m* (-[e]s; -e) *a. fig.* gush, flood, torrent.
schwamm [ʃvam] *pret of* **schwimmen.**
Schwamm *m* (-[e]s; "e) **1.** sponge: *fig.* **~ drüber!** (let's) forget it! **2.** a) fungus, b) → **Pilz,** c) dry rot. '**schwammig** *adj* **1.** spongy, flabby (*body*), puffy (*face*). **2.** *fig.* woolly (*idea, concept, etc*).
Schwan [ʃvaːn] *m* (-[e]s; "e) *zo.* swan.
schwand [ʃvant] *pret of* **schwinden.**
schwanen ['ʃvaːnən] *v/impers* (h) F **mir schwant** s.th. tells me; **ihr schwante nichts Gutes** she feared the worst.
schwang [ʃvaŋ] *pret of* **schwingen.**
Schwang *m* **im ~ (e) sein** be in vogue.
schwanger ['ʃvaŋər] *adj* (**im vierten** *etc* **Monat ~** four months *etc*) pregnant.
'**Schwangere** *f* (-n; -n) pregnant woman, expectant mother.
schwängern ['ʃveŋərn] *v/t* (h) **1.** make *woman* pregnant. **2.** *fig.* impregnate.
'**Schwangerschaft** *f* (-; -en) pregnancy.
'**Schwangerschafts|abbruch** *m* termination of pregnancy, induced abor-

tion. **~gym,nastik** f antenatal exercises. **~streifen** pl stretchmarks. **~test** m pregnancy test.

Schwank [ʃvaŋk] m (-[e]s; ⁺e) **1.** anecdote. **2.** thea. farce.

schwanken [ˈʃvaŋkən] v/i **1.** (h) sway, ground etc: a. shake, rock. **2.** (sn) sway, stagger, totter. **3.** (h) (**zwischen** between) waver, vacillate: **ich schwanke noch** I'm still undecided. **4.** (h) temperature, prices, etc: fluctuate, a. vary, alternate: **die Preise ~ zwischen ... und ...** a. prices range from ... to ...

'**Schwanken** n (-s) **1.** swaying (etc). **2.** vacillation. **3.** → **Schwankung** 2. '**schwankend** adj **1.** swaying (etc). a) undecided, wavering, b) unstable. '**Schwankung** f (-; -en) **1.** → **Schwanken** 1. **2.** variation, a. ✝ fluctuation.

Schwanz [ʃvants] m (-es; ⁺e) **1.** zo. tail (a. ✔ etc)**: 2.** fig. tail end. **3.** V cock, dick.

schwänzen [ˈʃvɛntsən] v/i, v/t (h) F (**die Schule**) ~ play truant (Am. hooky).
'**Schwanzfeder** f tail feather.
'**Schwanzflosse** f tail fin.
'**schwanzlastig** adj ✔ tail-heavy.

schwappen [ˈʃvapən] v/i **1.** (h) slosh around. **2.** (sn) slop, spill.

Schwarm [ʃvarm] m (-[e]s; ⁺e) **1.** swarm, a. crowd, flight (of birds), shoal (of fish). **2.** F a) heartthrob, b) dream.

schwärmen [ˈʃvɛrmən] v/i (h) **1.** swarm. **2.** enthuse (or rave) (**von** about): ~ **für** be crazy about; **für j-n ~** a. have a crush on s.o.; **ins Schwärmen geraten** go into raptures. '**Schwärmer** m (-s; -) **1.** enthusiast, dreamer. **2.** squib. **3.** zo. hawk moth. **Schwärme'rei** f (-; -en) enthusiasm, passion. '**schwärmerisch** adj enthusiastic, gushing.

Schwarte [ˈʃvartə] f (-; -n) **1.** (bacon) rind. **2.** F old book, tome.

schwarz [ʃvarts] adj **1.** black (a. coffee, tea), a. swarthy, dark-skinned, F a. dirty, a. deeply tanned: **Schwarzer Erdteil** Black Continent; **~er Humor** black humo(u)r, thea. Black Comedy; ~ **auf weiß** in black and white, in cold print; **mir wurde ~ vor den Augen** everything went black; **F sich ~ ärgern** be terribly annoyed; **da kann er warten, bis er ~ wird** he can wait till he's blue in the face; → **Brett, Liste, Schaf** 1 etc,

schwarzfahren, schwarzsehen. 2. fig. black, gloomy: **~er Tag** black day. **3.** F fig. black, illicit: **der ~e Markt** the black market. **4.** F Catholic(-Conservative).

Schwarz n (-[es]; -) black: **in ~ gehen** be dressed in black (or in mourning). **~arbeit** f illicit work, F moonlighting. **~arbeiter** m illicit worker, F moonlighter. **~brot** n brown bread.

'**Schwarze¹** m (-n; -n) **1.** black: **die ~n** the Blacks. **2.** black-haired man (or boy). **3.** F Catholic(-Conservative).
'**Schwarze²** f (-n; -n) **1.** black (woman or girl). **2.** black-haired woman (or girl).
'**Schwarze³** n (-n; -) **1.** black dress. **2.** a. fig. **ins ~ treffen** hit the bull's-eye.

Schwärze [ˈʃvɛrtsə] f (-; no pl) **1.** blackness. **2.** darkness.

schwärzen [ˈʃvɛrtsən] v/t (h) blacken.

'**schwarzfahren** v/i (irr, sep, -ge-, sn, → **fahren**) a) go without paying, b) mot. drive without a licen/ce (Am. -se).
'**Schwarzfahrer(in** f) m fare dodger.
'**schwarzhaarig** adj black-haired.

'**Schwarz|handel** m black market(eering): **im ~** on the black market. **~händler** m black marketeer. **~hörer** m (radio) licen/ce (Am. -se) dodger.

'**schwärzlich** adj blackish, swarthy.

'**Schwarz|markt** m black market. **2sehen** v/i (irr, sep, -ge-, h, → **sehen**) be pessimistic (or about): **ich sehe schwarz (für dich)**! things look bad (for you)! **~seher** m **1.** pessimist. **2.** TV-licen/ce (Am. -se) dodger. **~sender** m pirate (radio) station.

Schwarz'weiß... black-and-white (film, television, etc).
'**Schwarzwild** n hunt. wild boars.

Schwatz [ʃvats] m (-es; -e) chat.
'**schwatzen,** dial. **schwätzen** [ˈʃvɛtsən] (h) **I** v/i a) chat, b) blab. **II** v/t **dummes Zeug ~** talk rubbish.

'**Schwätzer** m (-s; -), '**Schwätzerin** f (-; -nen) chatterbox, blab(ber), F gasbag.
'**schwatzhaft** adj talkative, chatty.

Schwebe [ˈʃve:bə] f **in der ~ sein** be undecided, 🏛 be pending. **~bahn** f cableway. **~balken** m (balance) beam.

schweben [ˈʃve:bən] v/i (sn) **1.** glide, float, sail (all a. fig.), a. hover (a. fig.), a. soar, a. be suspended, hang: **in Gefahr ~** be in danger; → **Ungewißheit. 2.** be undecided, esp. 🏛 be pending.

'**schwebend** adj **1.** floating (etc, → schweben 1). **2.** esp. ⚖ pending.

Schwede ['ʃveːdə] m (-n; -n) Swede. '**Schweden** n (-s) Sweden. '**Schwedin** f (-; -nen) Swede. '**schwedisch** adj Swedish.

Schwefel ['ʃveːfəl] m (-s; no pl) sulphur, Am. sulfur. '**Schwefeldioxyd** n sulphur (Am. -f-) dioxide. '**schwefelhaltig** adj sulphur(e)ous (Am. -f-). '**schwefeln** v/t (h) 🜍 sulphurate (Am. -f-), a. ⊛ sulphurize (Am. -f-).

'**Schwefelsäure** f sulphuric (Am. -f-) acid. **Schwefel**'**wasserstoff** m hydrogen sulphide (Am. -f-).

schweflig ['ʃveːflɪç] adj sulphur(e)ous (Am. -f-).

Schweif [ʃvaɪf] m (-[e]s; -e) **1.** tail (a. astr.). **2.** fig. train.

'**schweifen** v/i (sn) a. fig. wander, roam.

'**Schweige**|**geld** n hush money. **~marsch** m silent protest march. **~mi,nute** f one minute's silence (**zu Ehren** gen in memory of).

schweigen ['ʃvaɪɡən] (schwieg, geschwiegen, h) v/i (**über** acc, **zu**) be silent (on), keep silent (about); say nothing: **ganz zu ~ von ...** to say nothing of ..., let alone ... '**Schweigen** n (-s) (a. **zum ~ bringen**) silence (a. ~ **hüllen**. '**schweigend** adj silent(ly adv), adv a. in silence: **~e Mehrheit** silent majority. '**Schweigepflicht** f secrecy, professional discretion.

'**schweigsam** adj quiet, silent, a. taciturn. '**Schweigsamkeit** f (-; no pl) quietness, silence, taciturnity.

Schwein [ʃvaɪn] n (-[e]s; -e) **1.** zo. pig, hog, swine, a. sow. **2.** gastr. pork. **3.** contp. a) F (filthy) pig, b) V bastard, swine, c) F soul: **kein ~** not a (blessed) soul; **armes ~** F poor sod! **4.** F luck: ~ **haben** be lucky.

Schweine|**braten** m roast pork. **~fi,let** n fillet of pork. **~fleisch** n pork. **~hund** m V swine, bastard: F **den inneren ~ überwinden** conquer one's weaker self. **~kote,lett** n pork chop.

Schweine'rei f (-; -en) F **1.** (awful) mess, filth. **2.** a) dirty trick, b) crying shame. **3.** → Schweinigelei.

'**Schweine**|**stall** m a. fig. pigsty. **~zucht** f pig-breeding, hog raising.

Schweinigel ['ʃvaɪnˀiːɡəl] m (-s; -) F fil-

thy pig. **Schweinige'lei** f (-; -en) F dirty joke, obscenity. '**schweinigeln** v/i (h) F **1.** mess about. **2.** talk smut.

'**schweinisch** adj F filthy.

'**Schweins**|**haxe** f (-; -n) gastr. knuckle of pork. **~leder** n pigskin.

Schweiß [ʃvaɪs] m (-es; -e) **1.** sweat, perspiration: **in ~ geraten** get into a sweat; **das hat viel ~ gekostet** that was hard work. **2.** hunt. blood. **~band** n (-[e]s; ~er) sweatband. **~blatt** n dress-shield. **~brenner** m ⊛ welding torch. **~drüse** f anat. sweat gland.

schweißen ['ʃvaɪsən] v/t (h) ⊛ weld. '**Schweißer** m (-s; -) ⊛ welder.

'**Schweißfüße** pl sweaty feet.

'**schweißgebadet** adj bathed in sweat.

'**Schweißgeruch** m smell of sweat.

schweißig ['ʃvaɪsɪç] adj sweaty.

'**Schweiß**|**naht** f (welding) seam. **~perle** f bead of perspiration. **~stelle** f weld. **⊘triefend** adj dripping with sweat. **~tropfen** m bead of perspiration.

Schweiz [ʃvaɪts] f (-) Switzerland.

Schweizer ['ʃvaɪtsər] **I** m (-s; -) Swiss: **die ~** the Swiss. **II** adj Swiss: **~ Käse** Swiss cheese. '**Schweizerdeutsch** n Swiss German. '**Schweizerin** f (-; -nen) Swiss (woman or girl).

'**schweizerisch** adj Swiss.

schwelen ['ʃveːlən] v/i (h) smo(u)lder.

schwelgen ['ʃvɛlɡən] v/i (h) revel (**in** dat in).

Schwelle ['ʃvɛlə] f (-; -n) **1.** threshold (a. fig.). **2.** 🚉 sleeper, Am. tie.

schwellen ['ʃvɛlən] v/i, v/t (schwoll, geschwollen, sn) swell.

'**Schwellenland** n emergent nation.

'**Schwellung** f (-; -en) swelling.

Schwemme ['ʃvɛmə] f (-; -n) **1.** watering place. **2.** pub. **3.** ✝ glut (**an** dat of).

schwemmen ['ʃvɛmən] v/t (h) wash.

'**Schwemmland** n alluvial land.

Schwengel ['ʃvɛŋəl] m (-s; -) handle.

Schwenk [ʃvɛŋk] m (-[e]s; -s) film: pan.

'**Schwenkarm** m ⊛ swivel arm.

'**schwenkbar** adj swivel(l)ing, slewing.

schwenken ['ʃvɛŋkən] **I** v/t (h) **1.** a) swing, ⊛ a. turn, slew, b) wave (hat, flag, etc), brandish (stick), c) film etc: pan (camera). **2.** rinse. **3.** gastr. toss. **II** v/i (sn) **4.** turn, swing (round), camera: pan, ✕ wheel. '**Schwenkung** f (-; -en) **1.** turn, swing, ✕ wheel(ing), film *etc*: pan. **2.** change of mind (*pol.* of front).

schwer [ʃveːr] **I** *adj* **1.** heavy: *100 Pfund ~ sein* weigh 100 pounds. **2.** *fig.* heavy (*storm, losses, etc*), bad (*mistake etc*), hard, difficult, F tough (*decision, struggle, work, etc*), serious (*illness, accident, etc*), onerous (*duty etc*), grave (*crime etc*): *ein ~er Schock* a bad (*or* terrible) shock; *~er Diebstahl* aggravated larceny; *~er Gegner* formidable opponent; *~es Schicksal* hard lot; *~er Tag* hard day; *~e Zeit(en)* hard times; *~en Herzens* with a heavy heart, reluctantly; *er hat es ~* he has a hard time; → *Begriff 2 etc*. **3.** rich, heavy (*food*), strong (*cigar, scent, etc*): *~er Wein* heady wine. **II** *adv* **4.** heavily (*etc*), F very much, awfully, badly: *~ arbeiten* work hard; F *~ aufpassen* watch (out) like hell; *~ zu bekommen* hard to get; F *~ beleidigt* deeply offended; *~ büßen müssen* have to pay dearly; *~ hören* be hard of hearing; *~ krank* seriously ill; *~ zu sagen* hard to say; *sie ist ~ gestürzt* she had a nasty fall; *~ zu verstehen* difficult to understand; F *da hat er sich aber ~ getäuscht* he's very much mistaken there.

'Schwer|arbeit *f* heavy labo(u)r. **~ath,let** *m* heavy athlete. **~behinderte** *m, f* ✚ severely handicapped person.

'schwerbeladen *adj* heavily laden.
'schwerbewaffnet *adj* heavily armed.
Schwere [ʃveːrə] *f* (-; *no pl*) **1.** weight, *phys.* gravity. **2.** *fig.* seriousness, gravity, severity, *a.* weightiness. **3.** heaviness (*of food etc*). **'schwerelos** *adj* weightless. **'Schwerelosigkeit** *f* (-; *no pl*) weightlessness.

Schwerenöter [ʃveːrənøːtər] *m* (-s; -) *humor.* philanderer.
'schwererziehbar *adj* difficult, recalcitrant: *~es Kind a.* problem child.
'schwerfallen *v/i* (*irr, sep, -ge-, sn,* → *fallen*) be difficult (*dat* for): *es fällt mir schwer a.* I find it hard.
'schwerfällig *adj* awkward, clumsy, heavy, ponderous (*a. fig.*), slow.
'Schwerfälligkeit *f* (-; *no pl*) clumsiness, heaviness, ponderousness.
Schwergewicht *n* (-[e]s; *no pl*) **1.** *sports*: heavyweight. **2.** *fig.* emphasis.

'schwerhalten *v/impers* (*irr, sep, -ge-, h,* → *halten*) *es hält schwer* it is difficult.
'schwerhörig *adj* hard of hearing.
'Schwerhörigkeit *f* (-; *no pl*) partial deafness.
'Schwerindu,strie *f* heavy industry.
'Schwerkraft *f* (-; *no pl*) (force of) gravity.
'schwerlich *adv* hardly.
'schwermachen *v/t* (*sep, -ge-, h*) *j-m et. ~* make s.th. difficult (*or* hard) for s.o.; *j-m das Leben ~* make life difficult for s.o; *mach es mir nicht so schwer!* don't make it so hard for me!
'Schwermut *f* (-; *no pl*) melancholy.
'schwermütig [-myːtɪç] *adj* melancholy.
'schwernehmen *v/t* (*irr, sep, -ge-, h,* → *nehmen*) *et. ~* take s.th. hard.
'Schwerpunkt *m* **1.** cent/re (*Am.* -er) of gravity. **2.** *fig.* a) focal point, b) emphasis: *~e bilden* set up priorities.
'Schwerpunktstreik *m* pinpoint strike.
'schwerreich *adj* F exceedingly rich.
Schwert [ʃvert] *n* (-[e]s; -er) sword. **~fisch** *m* swordfish. **~lilie** *f* iris.
'schwertun: *sich ~* (*irr, sep, -ge-, h,* → *tun*) have a hard time (*mit* with).
'Schwerverbrecher *m* felon, dangerous criminal.
'schwerverdaulich *adj* indigestible (*a. fig.*), heavy.
'Schwerverletzte *m, f* (-n; -n) seriously injured person. **'Schwerverwundete** *m, f* (-n; -n) seriously wounded person.
'schwerwiegend *adj* weighty, grave.
Schwester [ʃvɛstər] *f* (-; -n) **1.** *a. fig.* sister. **2.** (hospital) nurse, sister. **3.** *eccl.* sister, nun. **4.** → **'Schwesterfirma** *f* sister company.
'schwesterlich *adj* sisterly.
schwieg [ʃviːk] *pret of* **schweigen**.
Schwieger|eltern [ʃviːgər-] *pl* parents-in-law. **~mutter** *f* mother-in-law. **~sohn** *m* son-in-law. **~tochter** *f* daughter-in-law. **~vater** *m* father-in-law.
Schwiele [ʃviːlə] *f* (-; -n) callus.
'schwielig *adj* horny, callused.
schwierig [ʃviːrɪç] *adj* difficult, hard, F tough. **'Schwierigkeit** *f* (-; -en) difficulty, trouble: *(j-m) ~en machen* be a problem (to s.o.); *person:* make things difficult (for s.o.); *in ~en geraten, ~en bekommen* get into trouble; *~en haben zu inf* find it difficult to *inf*.

'Schwimm|bad n swimming pool (or bath). **~dock** n floating dock.
schwimmen ['ʃvɪmən] v/i (schwamm, geschwommen, h and sn) **1.** swim (a. v/t distance, record, etc), object: float, F floor etc: be flooded: **~ gehen** go swimming; F **im Geld ~** be rolling in money. **2.** F fig. flounder,
'Schwimmen n (-s) swimming: F fig. **ins ~ kommen** (begin to) flounder.
Schwimmer ['ʃvɪmər] m (-s; -) **1.** swimmer. **2.** fishing, ⊕ float.
'Schwimmerin f (-; -nen) swimmer.
'Schwimm|gürtel m swimming belt. **~halle** f indoor pool. **~haut** f zo. web. **~lehrer(in** f) m swimming instructor. **~sport** m swimming. **~verein** m swimming club. **~weste** f life jacket.
Schwindel ['ʃvɪndəl] m (-s; no pl) **1.** ⚕ dizziness, vertigo. **2.** F a) swindle, b) lie. **3.** F **der ganze ~** the whole lot.
'Schwindelanfall m ⚕ dizzy spell.
Schwinde'lei f (-; -en) **1.** → **Schwindel** 2. **2.** a) cheating, b) lying.
'schwindelerregend adj dizzy, giddy (a. fig.), fig. staggering (prices etc).
'schwindelfrei adj **~ sein** have a good head for heights; **nicht ~ sein** be afraid of heights.
schwind(e)lig ['ʃvɪnd(ə)lɪç] adj giddy, dizzy (a. fig.): **mir ist ~** I feel dizzy.
'schwindeln v/i (h) **1. mir schwindelt** I feel dizzy, my head reels. **2.** lie, F tell fibs. **3. in ~der Höhe** at a giddy height.
schwinden ['ʃvɪndən] v/i (schwand, geschwunden, sn) strength, supplies, etc: dwindle, colo(u)r, light, beauty, etc: fade: **~de Hoffnung** dwindling hope.
Schwindler ['ʃvɪndlər] m (-s; -) a) swindler, F con man, b) liar.
Schwinge ['ʃvɪŋə] f (-; -n) wing.
schwingen ['ʃvɪŋən] (schwang, geschwungen, h) **I** v/t **1.** swing, wave, brandish: **er schwang sich auf sein Rad** he swung himself on his bicycle; → **Rede. II** v/i **2.** a. (sn) swing. **3.** phys. oscillate, vibrate.
'Schwinger m (-s; -) boxing: swing.
'Schwingkreis m ∮ resonant circuit.
'Schwingung f (-; -en) phys. vibration, oscillation: a. fig. et. **in ~en versetzen** set s.th. vibrating. **'schwingungsfrei** adj free from vibration.
Schwips [ʃvɪps] m F **e-n ~ haben** be tipsy.

schwirren ['ʃvɪrən] v/i **1.** (sn) whir(r), insects etc: buzz, arrow etc: whizz: **Gerüchte ~ durch die Stadt** town is buzzing with rumo(u)rs. **2.** (h) **mir schwirrt der Kopf** my head is in a whirl.
schwitzen ['ʃvɪtsən] v/i, v/t (h) sweat (a. ⊕), perspire: a. fig. **ins Schwitzen kommen** get into a sweat.
Schwof [ʃvo:f] m (-[e]s; -e) F hop.
schwofen ['ʃvo:fən] v/i (h) F shake a leg.
schwoll [ʃvɔl] pret of **schwellen**.
schwören ['ʃvøːrən] v/i, v/t (schwor, geschworen, h) swear (bei by), ⚖ take the oath: F fig. **ich schwöre auf** (acc) I swear by ...; **ich schwöre dir, daß** I swear to you that; → **Eid, Rache.**
schwul [ʃvuːl] adj F gay, contp. queer.
schwül [ʃvyːl] adj a) **1.** sultry, muggy, oppressive. **2.** fig. sultry, sensuous.
'Schwule m (-n; -n) F gay, contp. queer.
'Schwüle f (-; no pl) a. fig. sultriness.
Schwulst [ʃvʊlst] m (-[e]s; no pl) bombast. **schwülstig** ['ʃvʏlstɪç] adj bombastic.
Schwund [ʃvʊnt] m (-es; no pl) dwindling, decline, ⚕, ⊕ shrinkage, ⚕ atrophy, ∮ fading.
Schwung [ʃvʊŋ] m (-[e]s; ⸚e) **1.** swing. **2.** no pl swing, impetus (a. fig.), speed: et. (j-n) in ~ bringen set s.th. (s.o.) going; (richtig) in ~ kommen get going; **im ~ sein** party etc: be in full swing, person: be in full stride. **3.** no pl verve, zest, drive, F pep. **4.** no pl F batch.
'Schwungfeder f zo. pinion.
'schwunghaft adj ✝ brisk, roaring.
'schwunglos adj spiritless, lifeless.
'Schwungrad n ⊕ flywheel.
'schwungvoll I adj a) full of drive (F go), zestful, b) bold (handwriting), c) swinging (tune). **II** adv with a swing.
Schwur [ʃvuːr] m (-[e]s; ⸚e) a) oath, b) vow. **'Schwurgericht** n jury court.
sechs [zɛks] adj six. **Sechs** f (-; -en) **1.** six. **2.** ped. very poor (mark). **'Sechseck** n (-[e]s; -e) hexagon. **'sechseckig** adj hexagonal. **Sechs'tagerennen** n six-day (cycling) race. **'sechste** adj sixth. **'Sechstel** n (-s; -) sixth (part). **'sechstens** adv sixthly.
sechzehn(te) ['zɛçtse:n(tə)] adj sixteen(th). **'Sechzehntel** n (-s; -) sixteenth (part).
sechzig ['zɛçtsɪç] adj sixty. **'Sechzig** f (-;

no pl **1.** sixty. **2.** *sie ist Anfang (der)* ~ she is in her early sixties. **sechziger** ['zɛçtsɪɡər] *adj die* ~ *Jahre* the sixties. **'Sechziger** *m* (-s; -) man in his sixties, sexagenarian: *in den* ~*n sein* be in one's sixties. **'Sechzigerin** *f* (-; -nen) woman in her sixties, sexagenarian. **'sechzigst** *adj* sixtieth.

Sediment [zedi'mɛnt] *n* (-[e]s; -e) sediment.

See¹ [ze:] *m* (-s; -n) lake.

See² *f* (-; -n) **1.** *no pl* sea, ocean: *an der* ~ by the seaside; *an die* ~ *fahren* go to the seaside; *auf* ~ at sea; *auf hoher* ~ on the high seas; *in* ~ *gehen* (or *stechen*) put to sea; *zur* ~ *gehen* go to sea; *e-e schwere* ~ a heavy sea. **2.** ⚓ big wave, surge, breaker. ~**bad** *n* seaside resort. ~**bär** *m humor.* *alter* ~ old salt. ~**beben** *n* (-s; -) seaquake. ~**Ele,fant** *m* zo. elephant seal. ~**fahrt** *f* (-; -en) **1.** *no pl* seafaring. **2.** voyage, cruise. **2fest** *adj* seaworthy: *(nicht)* ~ *sein* be a good (bad) sailor. ~**fisch** *m* saltwater fish. ~**fracht** *f* sea (or ocean) freight. ~**frachtbrief** *m* bill of lading (B/L). ~**gang** *m* (-[e]s; *no pl*) *hoher* ~ rough sea; *schwerer* ~ heavy sea. **2gestützt** *adj* ✕ sea-based. ~**gras** *n* seaweed. ~**hafen** *m* seaport. ~**handel** *m* maritime trade. ~**herrschaft** *f* (-; *no pl*) naval supremacy. ~**hund** *m* seal. ~**igel** *m* sea urchin. ~**karte** *f* nautical chart. **2klar** *adj* ⚓ ready to sail. **2krank** *adj* seasick: *leicht* ~ *werden* be a bad sailor. ~**krankheit** *f* (-; *no pl*) seasickness. ~**krieg(führung** *f*) *m* naval war(fare). ~**lachs** *m* zo. pollack.

Seele ['ze:lə] *f* (-; -n) **1.** soul, mind, *a.* heart: *e-e gute (treue)* ~ a good (faithful) soul; *k-e* ~ not a (blessed) soul; *zwei* ~*n und ein Gedanke* two minds and but a single thought; *aus tiefster* ~ wish *etc* with all one's heart, *thank etc* from the bottom of one's heart, *hate* like poison; *er ist die* ~ *des Betriebs* he is the life and soul of the firm; *es liegt mir auf der* ~ it weighs heavily on me; *es tat mir in der* ~ *weh* it hurt me deeply; *du sprichst mir aus der* ~ that's exactly how I feel (about it); *sich et. von der* ~ *reden* F get s.th. off one's chest; → *Leib etc.* **2.** core (*of cable*), bore (*of gun*).

'Seelen|arzt *m* F mind doctor, shrink. ~**frieden** *m* peace of mind. ~**größe** *f* magnanimity. ~**heil** *n* eccl. salvation. ~**leben** *n* (-s; *no pl*) inner life.

'seelenlos *adj* soulless.

'Seelen|mas,sage *f* F pep talk. ~**messe** *f* requiem. ~**qual** *f* mental anguish. ~**ruhe** *f* a) peace of mind, b) calmness: *in aller* ~ → **2ruhig** *adv* (quite) coolly. **2verwandt** *adj* congenial: ~ *sein* be kindred souls. **2voll** *adj a. iro.* soulful. ~**wanderung** *f* transmigration of souls. ~**zustand** *m* emotional state.

'Seeleute *pl* seamen, sailors.

seelisch *adj* psychological, mental, emotional, *a. eccl.* spiritual: ~**e Belastung** (⚕ *Grausamkeit*) mental strain (cruelty); ~ *bedingt sein* have psychological causes; → *Gleichgewicht.*

'Seelöwe *m* zo. sea lion.

'Seelsorge *f* (-; *no pl*) pastoral care.

'Seelsorger *m* (-s; -) pastor.

'Seeluft *f* sea air.

'Seemacht *f* naval (or sea) power.

'Seemann *m* (-[e]s; -leute) seaman, sailor. **'seemännisch** [-mɛnɪʃ] *adj* a) sailor's ..., b) nautical. **'Seemannsgarn** *n* F *ein* ~ *spinnen* spin a yarn.

'See|meile *f* nautical mile. ~**not** *f* distress at sea: *Schiffe in* ~ distressed ships. ~**not(rettungs)dienst** *m* sea rescue service. ~**pferdchen** *n* zo. seahorse. ~**räuber** *m* pirate. ~**reise** *f* voyage, cruise. ~**rose** *f* ⚘ water lily. ~**schiffahrt** *f* **1.** ocean shipping. **2.** ocean navigation. ~**schlacht** *f* naval battle. ~**stern** *m* zo. starfish. ~**streitkräfte** *pl* naval forces. ~**tang** *m* ⚘ seaweed. **2tüchtig** *adj* seaworthy. ~**wasser** *n* salt water. ~**weg** *m* sea route: *auf dem* ~ by sea. ~**wind** *m* sea breeze. ~**zunge** *f* zo. sole.

Segel ['ze:ɡəl] *n* (-s; -) sail: ~ *setzen* set sail; ~ *hissen* make sail; *die* ~ *streichen* strike sail, *fig. a.* give in; → *Wind.* ~**boot** *n* sailing boat, *Am.* sailboat, *sports:* yacht. ~**fliegen** *n* gliding. ~**flieger** *m* glider pilot. ~**flug** *m* **1.** glider flight. **2.** gliding. ~**flugplatz** *m* gliding field. ~**flugzeug** *n* glider. **2klar** *adj* ready to sail. ~**klub** *m* yachting club.

segeln ['ze:ɡəln] *v/i* **1.** (sn *and* h) sail, ⚐ glide. **2.** (sn) *fig.* sail, *bird: a.* soar. **II** *v/t* **3.** (h *and* sn) sail.

'Segeln *n* (-s) sailing.

'Segel|schiff *n* sailing ship. **~sport** *m* sailing, yachting. **~tuch** *n* (-[e]s; -e) canvas. **~tuchschuhe** *pl* canvas shoes.

Segen ['ze:gən] *m* (-s; -) **1.** blessing (*a. fig.*), *eccl. a.* benediction: ***s-n ~ geben*** give one's blessing (**zu** to); ***ein wahrer ~*** a real blessing, *iro.* (quite) a mercy. **2.** F ***der ganze ~*** the whole lot.

'segensreich *adj* beneficial: ***~ sein*** be a blessing.

'Segenswünsche *pl* good wishes.

Segler ['ze:glər] *m* (-s; -) **1.** yachtsman. **2.** → ***Segelboot, -schiff, -flugzeug.***

'Seglerin *f* (-; -nen) yachtswoman.

segnen ['ze:gnən] *v/t* (h) bless.

'Segnung *f* (-; -en) blessing (*a. fig.*), *eccl. a.* benediction.

sehen ['ze:ən] (sah, gesehen, h) **I** *v/i* **1.** see, look: ***gut*** (***schlecht***) ***~*** have good (bad *or* weak) eyes; ***sieh nur!, ~ Sie mal!*** look!; ***siehe da!*** lo and behold!; ***siehe oben*** (***unten***)***!*** see above (below)!; F ***sieh mal e-r an!*** what do you know!; F ***na, siehst du!*** there you are!, what did I tell you?; ***wir werden*** (***schon***) ***~*** we shall see, let's wait and see; ***sich gezwungen ~ zu*** *inf* find o.s. compelled to *inf.* **2.** ***~ auf*** (*acc*) set great store by. **3.** ***~ nach*** look after; ***ich muß nach dem Essen ~*** I have to see to the dinner. **II** *v/t* **4.** see, *a.* watch (*program etc*), look at, *a.* notice: ***gern ~*** like (to see); ***zu ~ sein*** a) show, b) be on show; ***es war nichts zu ~*** there was nothing to be seen; ***niemand war zu ~*** there was nobody in sight; ***man sieht's*** (***kaum***)***!*** it (hardly) shows!; ***ich habe es kommen ~*** I have seen it coming; ***sich ~ lassen*** show one's face, *a.* turn up; ***sie*** (***es***) ***kann sich ~ lassen*** she (it) isn't half bad; ***ich sehe die Sache anders*** I see it differently; ***wie ich die Dinge sehe*** as I see it; ***ich kann ihn*** (***es***) ***nicht mehr ~!*** I can't stand (the sight of) him (it) any more! **5.** see, meet: ***sich*** (*or* ***einander***) ***häufig ~*** see a lot of each other.

'Sehen *n* (-s) seeing: ***vom ~*** by sight.

'sehenswert, 'sehenswürdig *adj* worth seeing, worthwhile.

'Sehenswürdigkeit *f* (-; -en) object of interest, sight, *pl* sights: ***die ~en besichtigen*** go sightseeing.

'Sehfehler *m* eye defect.

'Sehkraft *f* (-; *no pl*) (eye)sight, vision.

Sehne ['ze:nə] *f* (-; -n) **1.** *anat.* sinew, tendon. **2.** string (*of bow*). **3.** ⩘ chord.

sehnen ['ze:nən] ***sich ~*** (h) (***nach*** for) long, yearn: ***er sehnte sich danach zu*** *inf* he was longing to *inf.*

'Sehnenzerrung *f* pulled tendon.

'Sehnerv *m* optic nerve.

sehnig ['ze:nıç] *adj* sinewy, wiry (*a. person*), stringy (*meat*).

sehnlich ['ze:nlıç] *adj* ardent.

'Sehnsucht *f* (-; ⸚e) (***nach*** for) longing, yearning. **'sehnsüchtig** *adj* longing, yearning, wistful.

sehr [ze:r] *adv* **1.** *preceding adj and adv* very, most, extremely: ***~ gern*** with pleasure, gladly; ***~ viel*** much, a lot (*better etc*). **2.** *with verb*: (very) much: ***~ vermissen*** miss *s.o., s.th.* badly (*or* a lot); ***ich freue mich ~*** I am very glad.

'Sehschärfe *f* visual power, (eye)sight.

'Sehschwäche *f* poor (eye)sight.

'Sehstörung *f* impaired vision.

'Sehtest *m* eye test: ***e-n ~ machen lassen*** have one's eyes tested.

seicht [zaıçt] *adj a. fig.* shallow.

Seide ['zaıdə] *f* (-; -n) (***reine ~*** pure) silk.

seiden ['zaıdən] *adj* (of) silk.

'Seiden|pa,pier *n* tissue paper. **~raupe** *f zo.* silkworm. **~raupenzucht** *f* sericulture. **~strümpfe** *pl* silk stockings.

'seiden'weich *adj* (as) soft as silk, silky.

seidig ['zaıdıç] *adj* silky.

Seife ['zaıfə] *f* (-; -n) soap.

seifen ['zaıfən] *v/t* (h) soap.

'Seifen|blase *f* **1.** soap bubble. **2.** *fig.* bubble. **~lauge** *f* soapsuds. **~pulver** *n* soap powder. **~schale** *f* soap dish. **~schaum** *m* lather. **~spender** *m* soap dispenser.

seifig ['zaıfıç] *adj* soapy.

seihen ['zaıən] *v/t* (h) strain, filter.

Seil [zaıl] *n* (-[e]s; -e) rope: ***~ springen*** skip. **'Seilbahn** *f* cable railway.

'Seilschaft *f* (-; -en) **1.** *mount.* rope (team). **2.** F *fig.* team.

'Seiltänzer(in *f*) *m* tightrope walker.

sein[1] [zaın] *v/i* (war, gewesen, sn) be, *as v/aux a.* have: ***bist du es?*** is that you?; ***ich bin's*** it's me; ***ich bin für e-e Reform*** I am for a reform; ***mir ist nicht nach Arbeiten*** I don't feel like working; ***mir ist, als höre ich ihn*** I think I can hear him now; ***wenn er nicht gewesen wäre*** but for him; ***er ist aus Mexiko*** he comes from Mexico; *ich bin bei m-m Anwalt gewesen* I have been to see my lawyer; *laß das ~!* stop it!; *laß es ~!* don't bother!; *muß das ~?* do I (you *etc*) have to?; *was soll das ~?* what's that supposed to be?; *(das) mag (or kann) ~* that may be, that's possible; *es sei denn, daß* unless; *nun, wie ist's?* w519ell. what about it?; *und das wäre?* and what might that be?

sein² *pos pron* 1. **~(e)** his, her, its, *of countries, ships*: her, *indefinite*: one's: **~ Glück machen** make one's fortune; *all ~ Geld* what money he had; *es kostet (gut) ~e 100 Dollar* it will easily cost a hundred dollars. 2. **~er, ~e, ~(e)s, der, die, das ~e** his, hers, its. 3. **der, die, das Seine** his (own), hers, her own, its (own); *die Seinen pl* his family; *jedem das Seine* to each his own; *das Seine tun* do one's bit.

Sein *n* (-s; *no pl*) being, existence.
seinerseits ['zaɪnərzaɪts] *adv* as far as he is concerned.
'seinerzeit *adv* then, in those days.
'seines'gleichen *indef pron* his (her) equals, F his (her) sort.
'seinet'wegen *adv* 1. for his sake. 2. on his behselbstalf. 3. because of him.
Seismograph [zaɪsmo'graːf] *m* (-en; -en) seismograph. **Seismologe** [zaɪs-mo'loːgə] *m* (-n; -n) seismologist.
seit [zaɪt] **I** *prep* 1. since: *~ wann sind Sie hier?* how long have you been here?; *~ damals → seitdem* I. 2. for: *~ drei Wochen* for the (last) three weeks; *~ langem* for a long time. **II** *conj* 3. since: *es ist ein Jahr her, ~* it is a year since.
'seit'dem I *adv* since then, ever since. **II** *conj → seit* 3.
Seite ['zaɪtə] *f* (-; -n) 1. side (*a. fig. aspect, descent, etc*), *a.* direction: *rechte (linke) ~ textil.* right (wrong) side; *fig. starke (schwache) ~* weak (strong) point; *an j-s ~* at (or by) s.o.'s side; *~ an ~* side by side; *nach allen ~n* in all directions; *von allen ~n* on all sides; *auf der e-n ~* on the one side (*fig.* hand); *auf j-s ~e sein* side with s.o.; *j-n auf s-e ~ bringen (or ziehen)* win s.o. over to one's side; *et. auf die ~ legen* put s.th. by; *j-m nicht von der ~ gehen* stick to s.o. like a leech; *von dieser ~ betrachtet* seen from that angle (or in

that light); *sich von der besten ~ zeigen* show o.s. at one's best; *j-m zur ~ stehen* stand by s.o. 2. page. 3. *auf (or von) seiten (gen)* on the part of.
'Seiten|ansicht *f* side view. **~blick** *m* sidelong glance. **~eingang** *m* side entrance. **~flügel** *m* △ wing. **~hieb** *m* (*gegen* at) cut, F sideswipe. **♀lang** *adj* pages (and pages) of. **~linie** *f* 1. *sports*: sideline. 2. *→ Nebenlinie.*
'seitens *prep* (*gen*) on the part of, by.
'Seiten|schiff *n* △ aisle. **~sprung** *m* escapade. **~stechen** *n* (-s) (*~ haben* have a) stitch. **~straße** *f* side street. **~streifen** *m* verge (*of road*). **~tasche** *f* side pocket. **~tür** *f* side door. **♀verkehrt** *adj* the wrong way round. **~wagen** *m mot.* sidecar. **~wechsel** *m sports:* change of ends. **~wind** *m* crosswind. **~zahl** *f* a) page number, b) number of pages.
'seitlich I *adj* lateral, side. **II** *adv* at the side: **✔ ~ abrutschen** sideslip.
'seitwärts *adv* 1. sideways. 2. at the side.
Sekret [ze'kreːt] *n* (-[e]s; -e) secretion.
Sekretär [zekre'tɛːr] *m* (-s; -e) 1. secretary. 2. secretary, bureau. **Sekretariat** [zekreta'rĭaːt] *n* (-[e]s; -e) (secretary's) office. **Sekre'tärin** *f* (-; -nen) secretary.
Sekt [zɛkt] *m* (-[e]s; -e) sparkling wine.
Sekte ['zɛktə] *f* (-; -n) sect.
'Sektglas *n* champagne glass.
Sektierer [zɛk'tiːrər] *m* (-s; -), **sek'tiererisch** *adj* sectarian.
Sektion [zɛk'tsĭoːn] *f* (-; -en) 1. section, division. 2. 🢒 dissection, autopsy.
Sektor ['zɛktɔr] *m* (-s; -en [-'toːrən]) sector, *fig. a.* field.
sekundär [zekʊn'dɛːr] *adj,* **Sekun'där...** secondary.
Sekunde [ze'kʊndə] *f* (-; -n) second (*a. ♪ or ♪*): *auf die ~ pünktlich* on the dot; F *(eine) ~!* just a second.
Se'kundenzeiger *m* second hand.
selb [zɛlp] *adj* same: *zur ~en Zeit* at the same time.
selber ['zɛlbər] *→ selbst* I.
selbst [zɛlbst] **I** *pron ich ~* I myself; *sie will es ~ machen* she wants to do it herself (*or* on her own); *er möchte ~ kochen* he wants to do his own cooking; *er war die Höflichkeit ~* he was politeness itself; *von ~* a) (by) itself, automatically, b) of one's own accord; *→ verstehen* 9. **II** *adv* even.

Selbst n (-; no pl) (one's own) self.
'**Selbstachtung** f self-respect.
'**selbständig I** adj independent, a. self-employed: *sich ~ machen* set up on one's own. **II** adv independently, on one's own: *~ denken* think for o.s.
'**Selbständigkeit** f (-; no pl) independence.
'**Selbst|anklage** f self-accusation. **~auslöser** m phot. selftimer. **~bedienungsrestau,rant** n self-service restaurant, cafeteria. **~befriedigung** f masturbation. **~behauptung** f self-assertion. **~beherrschung** f self-control: *die ~ verlieren* a. lose one's temper. **~bestätigung** f ego-boost: *zu s-r ~* to prove himself. **~bestimmungsrecht** n right of self-determination. **~beteiligung** f insurance: percentage excess. **~betrug** m self-deception. ²**bewußt** adj self-confident. **~bewußtsein** n self-confidence. **~bildnis** n self-portrait. **~darstellung** f promotion of one's public image, contp. showmanship. **~diszi,plin** f self-discipline. **~einschätzung** f self-assessment. **~erhaltungstrieb** m survival instinct. **~erkenntnis** f self-knowledge. ²**ernannt** adj iro. self-styled. **~fahrer** m owner-driver.
'**selbstgebacken** adj home-made.
◄**selbstgefällig** adj complacent.
'**Selbstgefälligkeit** f (-; no pl) complacency.
'**selbstgemacht** adj home-made.
'**selbstgerecht** adj self-righteous.
'**Selbstgespräch** n monologue: *~e führen* talk to o.s.
'**selbstherrlich** adj high-handed.
'**Selbst|hilfe** f (-; no pl) self-help. **~hilfegruppe** f self-help group. ²**klebend** adj (self-)adhesive. **~kon,trolle** f self-control. **~kostenpreis** m cost price. **~kri,tik** f self-criticism. **~laut** m vowel.
'**selbstlos** adj selfless, unselfish.
'**Selbst|mitleid** n self-pity. **~mord** m, **~mörder** m suicide. ²**mörderisch** adj suicidal. **~mordversuch** m attempted suicide. **~por,trät** n self-portrait. ²**sicher** adj self-confident. **~sicherheit** f (-; no pl) self-confidence.
'**Selbstsucht** f (-; no pl) selfishness.
'**selbstsüchtig** adj selfish.
'**selbsttätig** adj automatic.
'**Selbst|täuschung** f self-deception.

~überschätzung f exaggerated opinion of o.s. **~unterricht** m self-instruction. **~verlag** m im ~ published by the author. **~verleugnung** f self-denial. ²**verschuldet** adj brought about by o.s. **~versorger** m self-supplier: *Bungalows für ~* self-catering bungalows.
'**selbstverständlich I** adj self-evident, obvious, natural: *es ist ~(, daß)* it goes without saying (that); *et. als ~ betrachten* take s.th. for granted. **II** adv of course, naturally. '**Selbstverständlichkeit** f (-; -en) matter of course.
'**Selbst|verständnis** n self-image: *sein ~* a. the way he sees himself. **~verteidigung** f self-defen/ce (Am. -se). **~vertrauen** n self-confidence. **~verwaltung** f self-government. **~verwirklichung** f self-realization. **~wählferndienst** m subscriber trunk dialing, Am. direct dialing. **~wertgefühl** n (-[e]s; no pl) self-esteem. ²**zerstörerisch** adj self-destructive. ²**zufrieden** adj complacent. **~zufriedenheit** f complacency. **~zweck** m end in itself.
selektiv [zelɛk'tiːf] adj selective.
Selen [ze'leːn] n (-s; no pl) 🜛 selenium.
selig ['zeːlɪç] adj **1.** eccl. blessed. **2.** overjoyed, blissful. **3.** late. '**Seligkeit** f (-; -en) **1.** no pl eccl. salvation, everlasting life. **2.** bliss, ecstasy. '**Seligsprechung** f (-; -en) eccl. beatification.
Sellerie ['zɛləri] m (-s; -[s]) 🜨 a) celeriac, b) celery.
selten ['zɛltən] **I** adj rare (a. fig. beauty etc), scarce. **II** adv seldom, rarely: *höchst ~* very rarely.
'**Seltenheit** f (-; -en) **1.** no pl rareness, scarcity. **2.** rarity.
Selterswasser ['zɛltɐs-] n (-s; ⁀) soda water.
seltsam ['zɛltzaːm] adj strange, odd.
'**seltsamer'weise** adv oddly enough.
'**Seltsamkeit** f (-; -en) **1.** no pl oddness. **2.** oddity.
Semantik [ze'mantɪk] f (-; no pl) semantics. **se'mantisch** [-tɪʃ] adj semantic.
Semester [ze'mɛstɐ] n (-s; -) semester.
Se'mesterferien pl vacation.
Semikolon [zemi'koːlɔn] n (-s; -s, -kola) semicolon.
Seminar [zemi'naːr] n (-s; -e) **1.** univ. a) seminar, b) department. **2.** eccl. seminary.

Semit [ze'mi:t] *m* (-en; -en), **Se'mitin** *f* (-; -nen) Semite.

se'mitisch *adj* Semitic.

Semmel ['zɛməl] *f* (-; -n) roll: F **weggehen wie warme ~n** be selling like hot cakes. **'Semmelbrösel** [-brø:zəl] *pl* breadcrumbs.

Senat [ze'na:t] *m* (-[e]s; -e) **1.** *pol.*, *univ.* senate. **2.** ⅟ division(al court).

Senator [ze'na:tor] *m* (-s; -en [zena-'to:rən]) senator.

'Sende|anlage *f* transmitter. **~anstalt** *f* → *Sender* 2. **~bereich** *m* transmission range. **~folge** *f* program(me *Br*.). **~fre,quenz** *f* transmitting frequency. **~leiter(in** *f*) *m* producer.

senden¹ ['zɛndən] *v/t*, *v/i* (h) ⚡ transmit, *radio*: a. broadcast, *TV* a. telecast.

'senden² *v/t*, *v/i* (sandte, gesandt, h) send (*dat*, **an** *acc* to).

'Sender *m* (-s; -) **1.** transmitter. **2.** radio (or television) station.

'Sende|raum *m* studio. **~reihe** *f* series. **~schluß** *m* closedown. **~zeichen** *n* call sign. **~zeit** *f* broadcasting time: **zur besten ~** at prime time.

'Sendung¹ *f* (-; -en) a) transmission, b) program(me *Br*.), *radio*: a. broadcast, *TV* a. telecast: **auf ~ gehen** (**sein**) (be) on the air.

'Sendung² *f* (-; -en) **1.** ✝ consignment, shipment. **2.** parcel. **3.** *no pl fig.* mission. **'Sendungsbewußtsein** *n* sense of mission.

Senf [zɛnf] *m* (-[e]s; -e) mustard. **~gurke** *f* gherkin (pickled with mustard seeds).

sengen ['zɛŋən] (h) **I** *v/t* singe. **II** *v/i* scorch: **~de Hitze** scorching heat.

senil [ze'ni:l] *adj* senile.

Senilität [zenili'tɛ:t] *f* (-; *no pl*) senility.

senior ['ze:nior] *adj* senior (*abbr*. sen.).

'Senior *m* (-s; -en [ze'nĭo:rən]) a) senior (*a. sports*), b) senior citizen.

'Seniorchef *m* ✝ senior partner.

Senioren|heim [ze'nĭo:rən-] *n* (first-class) home for the aged. **~paß** *m* senior citizen's railcard.

Seniorin [ze'nĭo:rɪn] (-; -nen) → *Senior*.

'Senkblei *n* (-[e]s; -e) △ plumb-line.

Senke ['zɛŋkə] *f* (-; -n) *geogr.* depression. **'senken** (h) **I** *v/t* **1.** sink (*a.* ⊙), lower (*a. fig. blood pressure, voice, etc*), *fig. a.* reduce (*costs, prices, etc*): **den Kopf ~** bow one's head. **II** *sich ~* **2.**

drop (*a. voice*), *ground, building*: subside, *wall*: sag, *road etc*: dip. **3.** *fig. silence etc*: descend (**über** *acc* on).

'Senkfüße *pl* 🦶 fallen arches.

'Senkgrube *f* cesspool.

'senkrecht *adj*, **'Senkrechte** *f* (-n; -n) vertical, Å perpendicular.

'Senkrechtstarter *m* (-s; -) **1.** ✈ vertical takeoff plane. **2.** F whiz(z) kid.

'Senkung *f* (-; -en) **1.** *no pl* a) lowering, *fig. a.* reduction, b) sag(ging) (*of wall*). **2.** dip. **3.** 🦶 descent (*of organ*), sedimentation (*of blood corpuscles*). **4.** *metr.* thesis.

Sensation [zɛnza'tsĭo:n] *f* (-; -en) sensation. **sensationell** [zɛnzatsĭo'nɛl] *adj* sensational.

Sensati'ons|gier *f contp.* sensation-seeking. **~mache** *f contp.* sensationalism. **~meldung** *f* sensational report, scoop. **~presse** *f* yellow press. **~pro,zeß** *m* sensational trial.

Sense ['zɛnzə] *f* (-; -n) scythe: F **damit war ~!** that was the end of that!

sensibel [zɛn'zi:bəl] *adj* sensitive (*a. fig. problem etc*), sensitive. **Sensibilität** [zɛnzibili'tɛ:t] *f* (-; *no pl*) sensitiveness.

Sensor ['zɛnzor] *m* (-s; -en [-'zo:rən]) sensor.

sentimental [zɛntimɛn'ta:l] *adj* sentimental. **Sentimentalität** [zɛntimɛnta-li'tɛ:t] *f* (-; -en) sentimentality.

separat [zepa'ra:t] *adj* separate.

Separatismus [zepara'tɪsmʊs] *m* (-; *no pl*) separatism.

September [zɛp'tɛmbər] *m* (-[s]; -) (**im ~** in) September.

septisch ['zɛptɪʃ] *adj* septic.

serbokroatisch [zɛrbokro'a:tɪʃ] *adj ling.* Serbo-Croat(ian).

Serenade [zere'na:də] *f* (-; -n) serenade.

Serie ['ze:rĭə] *f* (-; -n) a) series, *TV etc* a. serial, b) set, line, range: ⊙ **in ~ gehen** go into production; **in ~ bauen** (or **herstellen**) produce in series.

seriell [ze'rĭɛl] *adj computer*: serial.

'Serienausstattung *f* standard fittings.

'Serienbau *m* (-[e]s; *no pl*) serial production.

'serienmäßig *adj* series(-produced), standard (*fittings etc*): **et. ~ herstellen** produce s.th. in series. **'serienreif** *adj* ready to go into production.

'Serienwagen *m* standard-type car.

seriös [ze'rjø:s] *adj* respectable, ✝ *a.* reliable, serious (*applicant, offer, etc*).
Serpentine [zɛrpɛn'ti:nə] *f* (-; -n) a) serpentine, b) double bend.
Serum ['ze:rʊm] *n* (-s; Seren) ✿ serum.
Service[1] [zɛr'vi:s] *n* (-; - ['vi:sə]) service.
Service[2] ['sœrvis] *m* (-; *no pl*) **1.** service. **2.** ✿ (after-sales) service.
servieren [zɛr'vi:rən] (h) **I** *v/t* serve: **es ist serviert!** dinner is served! **II** *v/i* serve, wait at (*Am.* on) table.
Ser'viererin *f* (-; -nen) waitress.
Ser'viertisch *m* serving table.
Ser'vierwagen *m* trolley.
Serviette [zɛr'vjɛtə] *f* (-; -n) napkin.
servil [zɛr'vi:l] *adj* servile.
Servobremse ['zɛrvo-] *f* servo (or power) brake. **'Servolenkung** *f* servo(-assisted) steering.
Sessel ['zɛsəl] *m* (-s; -) easy chair, armchair. **'Sessellift** *m* chairlift.
seßhaft ['zɛshaft] *adj* settled, *a.* resident: **~ werden** settle (down).
'Seßhaftigkeit *f* (-; *no pl*) settledness.
Set [sɛt] *n, m* (-[s]; -s) **1.** set. **2.** place mat.
'Setzei *n gastr.* fried egg.
setzen ['zɛtsən] (h) **I** *v/t* **1.** put, place, *a.* seat (*s.o.*), put, make (*comma etc*), ✎ set, plant: **an Land ~** put ashore; **das Glas an die Lippen ~** raise (or set) the glass to one's lips; **s-e Unterschrift ~ unter** (*acc*) put one's signature to; → **Bild, Denkmal, Druck**[1], **Frist** *etc.* **2. et. ~ stake** (or bet) s.th. (**auf** *acc* on). **3.** *sports:* seed (*player, team*): → **gesetzt 2. 4.** *print.* set. **II** *v/i* **5.** sit down, take a seat: **sich aufs Rad ~** mount (or get on) one's bicycle; **sich ins Auto ~** get into the car; **sich zu j-m ~** sit down beside s.o. **6.** *fig.* sink, grounds, dust, *etc*: settle, impression *etc*: sink in. **III** *v/i* **7. ~ über** (*acc*) jump (over), clear (*ditch etc*), cross (*river etc*). **8.** place one's bet: **~ auf** (*acc*) bet on, bank, *fig. a.* bank on.
'Setzer *m* (-s; -) compositor, typesetter.
Setze'rei *f* (-; -en) composing room.
'Setzling *m* (-s; -e) ✎ seedling.
'Setzmaschine *f* typesetting machine.
Seuche ['zɔʏçə] *f* (-; -n) epidemic.
'Seuchenbekämpfung *f* epidemic control.
seufzen ['zɔʏftsən] *v/i* (h) sigh (**über** *acc* at, **vor** with): **~d** with a sigh.
'Seufzer *m* (-s; -) sigh.

Sex [zɛks, sɛks] *m* (-[es]; *no pl*) sex: F **~ haben** (or **machen**) have sex. **~bombe** *f* F sexpot. **~film** *m* sex film.
Sexismus [zɛ'ksɪsmʊs] *m* (-; *no pl*) sexism. **se'xistisch** [-tʃ] *adj* sexist.
'Sexprotz *m* F sexual athlete, sexpot.
Sextett [zɛks'tɛt] *n* (-[e]s; -e) sextet(te).
sexual [zɛ'ksŏa:l] → **sexuell.**
Sexu'al... sexual, sex (*life etc*).
Sexu'alerziehung *f* sex education.
Sexualität [zɛksŭali'tɛ:t] *f* (-; *no pl*) sexuality.
Sexu'alkunde *f* (-; *no pl*) *ped.* sex education. **~täter** *m* sex offender. **~verbrechen** *n* sex crime.
sexuell [zɛ'ksŭɛl] *adj* sexual.
sexy ['zɛksi, 'sɛksi] *adj* F sexy.
sezieren [ze'tsi:rən] *v/t* (h) a) dissect (*a. fig.*), b) perform an autopsy on.
Showmaster ['ʃo:ma:stər] *m* (-s; -) *TV* compère, host.
Sibirien [zi'bi:rĭən] *n* (-s) Siberia.
Sibirier [zi'bi:rĭər] *m* (-s; -), **Si'birierin** *f* (-; -nen), **si'birisch** [-rɪʃ] *adj* Siberian.
sich [zɪç] *reflex pron* oneself, *3 sg* himself, herself, itself, *pl* themselves, *after prep* him, her, it, *pl* them, *a.* each other, one another: **~ ansehen** a) look at o.s., b) look at each other; **sie blickte hinter ~** she looked behind her.
Sichel ['zɪçəl] *f* (-; -n) sickle.
sicher ['zɪçər] **I** *adj* **1.** (**vor** *dat* from) safe, secure, b) safe (*a.* ✿), secure (*income etc*): **in ~em Abstand** at a safe distance; **~ ist ~!** better safe than sorry! **2.** reliable, good, sure (*goalkeeper, marksman, etc*), *a.* safe (*driver, method, etc*). **3.** *fig.* sure (*instinct, judg[e]ment, sign, etc*): **~es Auftreten** self-assurance; **mit ~em Blick** (**Griff**) with a sure eye (hand). **4.** certain, sure: **der ~e Sieg** (*Tod*) certain victory (death); **das ist ~** a) so much is certain, b) that's a fact; **ist das ~?** is that for certain?; **der Erfolg** (**die Stellung**) **ist ihm ~** he is sure to succeed (get the job). **5.** *pred* sure, certain: **sind Sie** (*dessen*) **~?** are you sure (about that)?; → **Sache** 2. **II** *adv* **6.** securely, safely (*etc*): **er fährt sehr ~** he is a safe driver. **7.** *a. int* certainly, surely, definitely: (**aber** or **ganz**) **~!** (but) of course!, F sure thing!; **du hast ~ kein Geld bei dir** I'm sure you have no money on you.

'**sichergehen** v/i (irr, sep, -ge-, sn, →
gehen) **er wollte ganz ~** he wanted to
be quite sure; **um sicherzugehen** to be
on the safe side.
'**Sicherheit** f (-; -en) **1.** no pl safety (a.
☺), security: **öffentliche (soziale, innere) ~** public (social, internal) security; **~ im Flugverkehr** safety in flying; **in
~ bringen** get s.o., s.th. out of harm's
way; **sich in ~ bringen** get out of danger, **durch e-n Sprung** jump to safety;
in ~ sein be safe; **zur ~** → **sicherheitshalber;** → **wiegen**[1] II. **2.** certainty: **mit
~** definitely, certainly; **man kann mit ~
sagen** it is safe to say. **3.** a) self-assurance, b) competence, skill, c) reliability. **4.** ✝, ᚕᚕ security (**gegen** on,
against): **~ leisten** give security, stand
bail; **e-m Gläubiger ~ bieten** secure a
creditor.
'**Sicherheits|abstand** m safe distance.
~beamte m security officer. **~bindung**
f skiing: safety binding. **~faktor** m factor of safety. **~glas** n (-es; ⸚er) safety
glass. **~gurt** m safety (✔, mot. a. seat)
belt.
'**sicherheitshalber** adv as a precaution,
to be on the safe side.
'**Sicherheits|kon|trolle** f security check.
~maßnahme f safety (pol. security)
measure, precaution. **~nadel** f safety
pin. **~poli|zei** f security police. **~rat** m
(-es; no pl) Security Council. **~risi-
ko** n security risk. **~schloß** n safety
lock. **~ven|til** n safety valve.
'**sicherlich** → **sicher** 7.
'**sichern** ['zɪçərn] v/t (h) **1.** (**gegen, vor**
dat) secure (a. ☺ or ✝), (safe)guard
(both: against), protect (from): **sich ~
vor** (or **gegen**) protect o.s. from, guard
against. **2.** put gun etc at safety: **gesichert sein** be at safety. **3.** secure: **sich
Karten ~** secure tickets. **4.** → **sicherstellen** 1.
'**sicherstellen** v/t (sep, -ge-, h) **1.** guarantee, a. secure. **2.** seize.
'**Sicherung** f (-; -en) **1.** no pl a) securing
(etc, → **sichern**), b) protection. **2.** ☺
safety device, safety (catch) (on gun
etc). **3.** ⚡ fuse.
'**Sicherungskasten** m ⚡ fuse box.
'**Sicht** [zɪçt] f (-; no pl) **1.** a) sight, b)
c) visibility: **in** (**außer**) **~** in (out of)
sight (a. fig.); **in ~ kommen** come into

view; fig. **auf weite** (or **lange**) **~** on a
long-term basis, a. in the long run; **auf
kurze ~** in the short term; **aus s-r ~**
from his point of view, as he sees it. **2.**
✝ (**fällig**) **bei ~** (due) at sight; **60 Tage
nach ~** payable at sixty days' sight.
'**sichtbar** adj visible, a. noticeable, evident, a. marked: **~ machen** show; **~
werden** appear, become visible.
'**Sichtbe,ton** m fair-faced concrete.
sichten ['zɪçtən] v/t (h) **1.** sight. **2.** sift,
look through, sort out.
'**Sichtflug** m contact flight.
'**Sichtgerät** n visual display unit.
'**sichtlich** adj visible, evident.
'**Sicht|verhältnisse** pl (**gute, schlechte
~** high, low) visibility. **~vermerk** m ✝
visa. **2.** ✝ endorsement. **~wechsel** m
✝ sight draft. **~weite** f visual range: **in
~** (with)in sight.
sickern ['zɪkərn] v/i (sn) seep, ooze.
sie [zi:] pers pron she, thing: it, pl they,
(acc) her, it, pl them.
Sie[1] polite address: you.
Sie[2] f (-; -s) F she, female.
Sieb [zi:p] n (-[e]s; -e) sieve, strainer, ☺
screen, ⚒ filter: **ein Gedächtnis wie ein
~** a memory like a sieve.
'**Siebdruck** m -[e]s; -e) **1.** silk-screen
print. **2.** no pl silk-screen printing.
sieben[1] ['zi:bən] v/t (h) **1.** sift, sieve. **2.**
→ **aussieben**.
'**sieben**[2] adj, **Sieben** f (-; -) seven.
'**Sieben'sachen** pl F things, belongings.
'**siebente** adj, '**Siebentel** n (-s; -) seventh. '**siebentens** adv seventh.
siebte ['zi:ptə] → **siebente**.
siebzehn(t) ['zi:p-] adj seventeen(th).
siebzig ['zi:ptsɪç] adj seventy. '**Siebzig** f
(-; -en) seventy: **er ist Mitte** (**der**) **~** he is
in his mid-seventies. **siebziger** ['zi:p-
tsɪgər] adj **die ~ Jahre** the seventies.
'**Siebziger** m (-s; -) man in his seventies, septuagenarian. '**Siebzigerin** f (-;
-nen) woman in her seventies, septuagenarian. '**siebzigst** adj seventieth.
Siechtum ['zi:çtu:m] n (-s; no pl) lingering illness, invalidism.
siedeln ['zi:dəln] v/i (h) settle.
sieden ['zi:dən] (h) **I** v/i boil: **~d heiß**
boiling hot. **II** v/t boil gently.
'**Siedepunkt** m (-[e]s; no pl) boiling
point.
Siedler ['zi:dlər] m (-s; -), '**Siedlerin** f (-;

-nen) settler. **'Siedlung** f (-; -en) a) settlement, b) housing estate.

Sieg [zi:k] m (-[e]s; -e) victory, *sports etc:* win, *fig.* triumph: **den ~ davontragen** carry the day.

Siegel ['zi:gəl] n (-s; -) a) seal, b) signet: *fig.* **unter dem ~ der Verschwiegenheit** under the seal of secrecy.

'Siegellack m sealing wax.

'siegeln ['zi:gəln] v/t (h) seal.

'Siegelring m signet ring.

siegen ['zi:gən] v/i (h) (**über** acc) be victorious (over), *sports etc:* win (against), *fig.* triumph (over), win (over).

Sieger ['zi:gər] m (-s; -) victor, *sport etc:* winner. **'Siegerehrung** f *sports:* presentation ceremony.

'Siegerin f (-; -nen) → **Sieger**.

'Siegermächte pl victorious powers.

'Siegerpo,dest n (victory) rostrum.

'sieges|bewußt, **~sicher** adj confident of victory, *fig.* sure of one's success.

'Siegeszug m *fig.* triumphant advance.

'siegreich adj victorious, triumphant.

siezen ['zi:tsən] v/t (h) *j-n* address s.o. as "Sie".

Signal [zɪ'gnaːl] n (-[e]s; -e) signal.

signalisieren [zɪgnali'zi:rən] v/t, v/i (h) signal.

Signatarmacht [zɪgna'taːr-] f pol. signatory power (**e-s Vertrages** to a treaty).

Signatur [zɪgna'tuːr] f (-; -en) **1.** signature. **2.** shelfmark (*of book*). **3.** conventional sign. **signieren** [zɪ'gniːrən] v/t (h) sign, *author:* autograph.

Silbe ['zɪlbə] f (-; -n) syllable: *fig.* **k-e ~** not a word.

'Silbentrennung f syllabification.

Silber ['zɪlbər] n (-s; *no pl*) **1.** silver. **2.** silver plate.

'Silber|besteck n silver (cutlery). **~blick** m F (slight) squint. **~distel** f 🌿 carline thistle. **~hochzeit** f silver wedding. **~me,daille** f silver medal. **~me,daillengewinner(in)** f(m) silver medal(l)ist.

'silbern adj (of) silver, *fig.* silvery.

'Silber|pa,pier n tin foil. **~streifen** m *~ am Horizont* silver lining. **~waren** pl silverware.

Silhouette [zi'lŭɛtə] f (-; -n) silhouette.

Silikat [zili'kaːt] n (-[e]s; -e) silicate.

Silikon [zili'koːn] n (-s; -e) silicon.

Silo ['zi:lo] m (-s; -s) silo.

Silvester [zɪl'vɛstər] m, n (-s; -), **~abend** m New Year's Eve.

simpel ['zɪmpəl] adj simple.

Sims [zɪms] m, n (-es; -e) **1.** ledge. **2.** sill.

Simulant [zimu'lant] m (-en; -en) malingerer. **Simulator** [zimu'laːtər] m (-s; -en [-la'toːrən]) ⊚, ✗ simulator.

simulieren [zimu'li:rən] (h) **I** v/t sham, feign, a. ⊚ simulate. **II** v/i malinger.

simultan [zimʊl'taːn] adj simultaneous.

Simul'tan|dolmetschen n (-s) simultaneous translation. **~dolmetscher** m simultaneous translator.

Sinfonie [zɪnfo'ni:] f (-; -n) symphony. **~or,chester** n symphony orchestra.

sinfonisch [zɪn'foːnɪʃ] adj symphonic.

singen ['zɪŋən] v/t, v/i (sang, gesungen, h) sing.

Single¹ ['sɪŋl] f (-; -[s]) (*record*) single.

'Single² m (-[s]; -s) single (person).

'Single³ n (-[s]; -[s]) *tennis etc:* singles.

'Singstimme f singing voice.

Singular ['zɪŋgulaːr] m (-s; -e) *ling.* (**im ~** in the) singular.

'Singvogel m songbird.

sinken ['zɪŋkən] v/i (sank, gesunken, sn) sink (a. fig.), *sun:* a. set, *fig. prices, temperature, etc:* drop (**auf** acc to), fall, go down: *fig.* **er ist tief gesunken** he has sunk very low; **~ lassen** lower, drop (a. voice); → **Mut, Wert** 1 *etc.*

Sinn [zɪn] m (-[e]s; -e) **1.** physiol. sense: *fig.* **sechster ~** sixth sense; **s-e fünf ~e beisammen haben** have one's wits about one. **2.** pl a) mind, b) consciousness: **sie war wie von ~en** she was quite beside herself (**vor** with); **bist du von ~en?** are you out of your mind? **3.** *no pl* mind: **et. im ~ haben** have s.th. in mind, intend (to do) s.th.; **damit habe ich nichts im ~** I don't want any of that; **j-m in den ~ kommen** occur to s.o. **4.** *no pl* (**für**) a) sense (of), appreciation (of), b) taste (of), c) interest (in): **~ für Musik** an ear for music; **~ für das Schöne** an eye for beauty; **~ für Humor** a sense of humo(u)r; **das ist ganz nach s-m ~** that's just what he likes; **das war ganz in m-m ~(e)** that was just what I would have done. **5.** *no pl* a) sense, meaning, b) (basic) idea: **im weiteren** (**engeren**) **~(e)** in a wider (narrower) sense; **im wahrsten ~(e) des Wortes** literally; **in gewissem ~** in a sense; **im ~e des Ge-**

setzes as defined by the law; **der ~ des Lebens** the meaning of life; **das ergibt** (F **macht**) **k-n ~** that makes no sense; **dem ~ nach** ⇒ **sinngemäß. 6.** no pl sense, purpose: **~ und Zweck** (aim and) object; **das hat k-n ~** it's no use, it's pointless; **das ist (nicht) der ~ der Sache!** that's (not) the idea!

'**Sinnbild** n symbol.

'**sinnbildlich** adj symbolic(al).

sinnen ['zɪnən] v/i (sann, gesonnen, h) (**über** acc [up]on) meditate, reflect: **~ auf** (acc) contemplate, plan, b.s. plot.

'**Sinnen** n (-s) thoughts: **all sein ~ und Trachten** his every thought and wish.

'**sinnenfroh** adj sensuous.

'**Sinnenlust** f (-; no pl) sensual pleasure.

'**sinnentstellend** adj distorting (the meaning): **~ sein** distort the meaning.

'**Sinnes|or‚gan** n sense organ. **~reiz** m sense stimulus. **~täuschung** f hallucination. **~wahrnehmung** f sensory perception. **~wandel** m change of heart.

'**sinnfällig** adj obvious, clear.

'**sinngemäß** adj giving the gist (of s.th.), esp. ⚖ analogous: **et. ~ übersetzen** give the general meaning of s.th.

sinnieren [zɪ'niːrən] v/i (h) F ruminate (**über** acc on).

'**sinnig** ['zɪnɪç] adj a. iro. clever.

'**sinnlich** adj sensual (impression, pleasure, etc), a. sensuous: **~e Wahrnehmung** sensory perception.

'**Sinnlichkeit** f (-; no pl) sensuality.

'**sinnlos** adj a) senseless, meaningless, b) absurd, c) useless: **~ betrunken** blind drunk. '**Sinnlosigkeit** f (-; no pl) senselessness (etc), absurdity.

'**sinnreich** adj ingenious, clever.

'**sinnverwandt** adj synonymous: **~es Wort** synonym.

'**sinnvoll** adj **1.** meaningful. **2.** a) useful, b) wise. **3.** ingenious, clever.

Sintflut ['zɪnt-] f (-; no pl) bibl. the Flood.

Sinus ['ziːnʊs] m (-; -, -se) **1.** Ⓐ sine. **2.** anat. sinus. '**Sinuskurve** f sine curve.

Siphon [zi'fõː] m (-s; -s) siphon.

Sippe ['zɪpə] f (-; -n) **1.** family, tribe. **2.** → '**Sippschaft** f (-; -en) contp. a) clan, b) gang, lot.

Sirene [zi're:nə] f (-; -n) siren.

Sirup ['zi:rʊp] m (-s; -e) syrup, treacle, Am. molasses.

Sitte ['zɪtə] f (-; -n) **1.** custom, a. practice,

---

habit: **~n und Gebräuche** manners and customs. **2.** pl a) morals, b) manners.

'**Sittenlehre** f ethics.

'**sittenlos** adj immoral, dissolute.

'**Sittenlosigkeit** f (-; no pl) immorality.

'**Sittenpoli‚zei** f vice squad.

'**Sittenrichter** m moralizer.

'**sittenstreng** adj puritanical.

'**sittenwidrig** adj immoral.

Sittich ['zɪtɪç] m (-s; -e) zo. parakeet.

'**sittlich** adj moral, ethical.

'**Sittlichkeit** f (-; no pl) morality, morals.

'**Sittlichkeits|verbrechen** n sex crime. **~verbrecher** m sex offender.

Situation [zituːa'tsio:n] f (-; -en) situation, position: **sich der ~ gewachsen zeigen** rise to the occasion.

Situati‚onskomik f situational comedy.

Sitz [zɪts] m (-es; -e) **1.** a) seat (a. fig.), b) (place of) residence, ✝ headquarters: **Firma mit ~ in London** London-based firm; **die Zuschauer von den ~en reißen** electrify the audience. **2.** no pl fit.

'**Sitzecke** f corner unit.

sitzen ['zɪtsən] v/i (saß, gesessen, h) **1.** sit, bird: perch: **~ bleiben** remain seated; **sie saßen beim Essen** they were having lunch; **im Parlament ~** have a seat in Parliament; **an e-r Arbeit (bei e-m Glas Wein) ~** be sitting over a task (a glass of wine); F **e-n ~ haben** be soused; **~de Lebensweise** sedentary life; → **Patsche** etc. **2.** be, firm etc: have one's headquarters (**in** dat in). **3.** sit, fit. **4.** F (**im Gefängnis**) **~** do time, be in jail. **5.** F blow, remark, etc: hit home. **6.** F stick (in the mind).

'**sitzenbleiben** v/i (irr, sep, -ge-, sn, → **bleiben**) F **1.** ped. have to repeat the year. **2.** woman: be left on the shelf. **3.** ~ **auf** (dat) be left with goods.

'**sitzenlassen** v/t (irr, sep, pp sitzenlassen, h, → **lassen**) fig. **1.** j-n ~ a) leave s.o. in the lurch, b) walk out on s.o., jilt s.o. **2.** **das lasse ich nicht auf mir sitzen!** I won't stand for that!

'**Sitz|gelegenheit** f seat. **~gruppe** f three-piece suite. **~ordnung** f seating plan. **~platz** m seat. **~streik** m sit-down strike.

'**Sitzung** f (-; -en) meeting, conference, parl. sitting, session, ⚖ hearing.

'**Sitzungs|bericht** m minutes (of the meeting). **~peri‚ode** f parl. session.

~**saal** m conference room, *parl.* chamber. ~**zimmer** n conference room.

Sizilianer [zitsi'lia:nər] m (-s; -) Sicilian. **Sizili'anerin** f (-; -nen) Sicilian (woman or girl). **sizili'anisch** adj Sicilian.

Sizilien [zi'tsi:liən] n (-s) Sicily.

Skala ['ska:la] f (-; -len, -s) 1. ♪, ⚙ scale. 2. *fig.* range.

Skalp [skalp] m (-s; -e) scalp.

Skalpell [skal'pɛl] n (-s; -e) ⚕ scalpel.

skalpieren [skal'pi:rən] v/t (h) scalp.

Skandal [skan'da:l] m (-s; -e) scandal, *a.* disgrace, shame. ~**blatt** n scandal sheet.

skandalös [skanda'lø:s] adj scandalous.

Skan'dalpresse f (-; *no pl*) gutter press.

Skandinavien [skandi'na:viən] n (-s) Scandinavia. **Skandi'navier** m (-s; -), **Skandi'navierin** f (-; -nen), **skandi'navisch** [-vɪʃ] adj Scandinavian.

Skat [ska:t] m (-[e]s; -e, -s) skat.

Skelett [ske'lɛt] n (-[e]s; -e) skeleton.

Skepsis ['skɛpsɪs] f (-; *no pl*) scepticism, *Am.* skepticism. **Skeptiker** ['skɛptikər] m (-s; -) sceptic, *Am.* skeptic.

'skeptisch adj sceptical, *Am.* skeptic.

Ski [ʃi:] m (-s; -er, -) ski: ~ **fahren**, ~ **laufen** ski.

'Ski|anzug m ski suit. ~**ausrüstung** f skiing gear. ~**bob** m skibob. ~**fahren** n skiing. ~**fahrer** m skier. ~**fliegen** n ski flying. ~**flug** m ski flying. ~**gebiet** n skiing area. ~**hütte** f ski hut, ski lodge. ~**kurs** m skiing course. ~**langlauf** m cross-country skiing. ~**lauf** m, ~**laufen** n skiing. ~**läufer** m skier. ~**lehrer** m skiing instructor. ~**lift** m ski lift. ~**piste** f ski run, piste. ~**schuh** m ski boot. ~**sport** m skiing. ~**springen** n, ~**sprung** m ski jumping. ~**stiefel** m ski boot. ~**stock** m ski pole. ~**träger** m *mot.* ski rack. ~**wandern** n ski hiking. ~**zirkus** m F ski circus (or circuit).

Skizze ['skɪtsə] f (-; -n) sketch.

'Skizzenbuch n sketchbook.

'skizzenhaft adj sketchy.

skizzieren [skɪ'tsi:rən] v/t (h) sketch, *fig. a.* outline.

Sklave ['skla:və] m (-n; -n) slave. **'Sklavenhandel** m slave trade. **Sklave'rei** f (-; *no pl*) slavery. **'Sklavin** f (-; -nen) slave. **'sklavisch** adj slavish.

Sklerose [skle'ro:zə] f (-; -n) ⚕ sclerosis.

Skonto ['skɔnto] m, n (-s; -s) ✝ (cash) discount.

Skorbut [skɔr'bu:t] m (-[e]s; *no pl*) ✱ scurvy.

Skorpion [skɔr'pĭo:n] m (-s; -e) 1. *zo.* scorpion. 2. *no pl astr.* ([**ein**] ~ **sein** be [a]) Scorpio.

Skrupel ['skru:pəl] m (-s; -) scruple.

'skrupellos adj unscrupulous.

Skulptur [skʊlp'tu:r] f (-; -en) sculpture.

skurril [skʊ'ri:l] adj bizarre.

Slalom ['sla:lɔm] m (-s; -s) *skiing:* slalom. ~**läufer(in** f) m slalom racer.

Slawe ['sla:və] m (-n; -n), **'Slawin** f (-; -nen), **'slawisch** adj Slav.

Slip [slɪp] m (-s; -s) briefs, panties.

'Slipeinlage f panty liner.

Smaragd [sma'rakt] m (-[e]s; -e), **sma'ragdgrün** adj emerald.

Smog [smɔk] m (-[s]; -s) smog.

'Smog,larm m smog alert.

Smoking ['smo:kɪŋ] m (-s; -s) dinner jacket, *Am.* tuxedo.

Snob [snɔp] m (-s; -s) snob. **Snobismus** [sno'bɪsmʊs] m (-; *no pl*) snobbery. **sno'bistisch** [-tɪʃ] adj snobbish.

so [zo:] **I** adv 1. so, so much: **nicht** ~ **einfach** not so easy; **das hat ihn ~ gefreut, daß** that pleased him so much that. 2. like this (*or* that), this (*or* that) way, thus: ~ **ist es!** that's how it is!; ~ **ist das Leben!** such is life!; ~ **oder** ~ a) one way or another, b) anyway. 3. such: ~ **etwas** such a thing; ~ **ein Trottel!** what a fool! 4. about: ~ **alle acht Tage** every week or so. **II** conj ~ **daß** so that, so as to inf; ~ **leid es mir tut** however much I regret it. **III** int ~! a) (all) right!, okay!, b) that's that!; ~, ~! well, well!; ~? really?; (**na**) ~ **was!** you don't say!; **ach** ~! oh(, I see!)

so'bald conj as soon as.

Söckchen ['zœkçən] n (-s; -) ankle sock, *Am.* anklet.

Socke ['zɔkə] f (-; -n) sock: F **sich auf die** ~**n machen** buzz off; **von den** ~**n sein** be flabbergasted, be dum(b)founded.

Sockel ['zɔkəl] m (-s; -) pedestal, *a.* ⚡, ⚙ base. ~**betrag** m basic allowance.

'Sockenhalter m suspender, *Am.* garter.

Soda ['zo:da] f (-; *no pl*), n (-s; *no pl*) soda. **'Sodawasser** n soda water.

Sodbrennen ['zo:t-] n (-s; *no pl*) ✱ heartburn.

so'eben adv just (now).

Sofa ['zo:fa] n (-s; -s) sofa, settee.

so'fern *conj* a) if, so far as, b) provided that: ~ *nicht* unless.

soff [zɔf] *pret of* **saufen.**

so'fort *adv* at once, instantly, immediately, right away: *ab* ~ a) as of now, b) *a.* (*ab*) ~ *gültig* effective immediately; ✝ ~ *zahlbar* spot cash; *er war* ~ *tot* he died instantaneously.

So'fort|bildkamera *f* instant camera. **~hilfe** *f* immediate (*or* emergency) aid.

so'fortig *adj* immediate, prompt.

So'fort|maßnahme *f* immediate action. **~pro,gramm** *n* crash program(me *Br.*).

Software ['sɔftwɛə] *f* (-; -s) software.

Sog *m* (-[e]s; -e) suction, ✈, ⚓ *a.* wake (*a. fig.*).

so'gar *adv* even.

'sogenannt *adj* so-called.

Sohle ['zoːlə] *f* (-; -n) **1.** sole. **2.** bottom (*of valley etc*), ⚒ floor.

Sohn [zoːn] *m* (-[e]s; ᵘe) son.

Soja|bohne ['zoːja-] *f* soybean. **~mehl** *n* soybean flour. **~soße** *f* soy sauce.

so'lang(e) *adv* as long as.

Solarener,gie [zo'laːr-] *f* solar energy.

Solarium [zo'laːri̯ʊm] *n* (-s; -rien) solarium.

So'larzelle *f* solar cell.

solch [zɔlç] *pron or adj* such.

'solcher'lei *adj* of such kind, such.

Sold [zɔlt] *m* (-[e]s; -e) pay.

Soldat [zɔl'daːt] *m* (-en; -en) soldier, *a.* serviceman.

Sol'datenfriedhof *m* war cemetery.

sol'datisch *adj* soldierlike, military.

'Soldbuch *n* ✕ pay book.

Söldner ['zœltnər] *m* (-s; -) mercenary.

Sole ['zoːlə] *f* (-; -n) brine.

solidarisch [zoli'daːrɪʃ] **I** *adj* solidary, ✝, ⚖ joint (and several): *sich* ~ *erklären mit* → *solidarisieren.* **II** *adv* in solidarity, ✝, ⚖ jointly (and severally). **solidarisieren** [zolidari'ziːrən] *sich* ~ *mit* (h) declare one's solidarity with, be solidly behind. **Solidarität** [zolidari-'tɛːt] *f* (-; *no pl*) solidarity.

solide [zo'liːdə] *adj* solid (*a. fig. person*), *fig. a.* steady (*person etc*), *a.* sound (*knowledge etc*), *a.* reliable (*firm*), reasonable (*price*), good (*profession*).

Solist [zo'lɪst] *m* (-en; -en), **So'listin** *f* (-; -nen) soloist.

Soll [zɔl] *n* (-[s]; -[s]) **1.** debit: ~ *und Haben* debit and credit. **2.** (*production*

etc) target, quota: *sein* ~ *erfüllen* reach the target, *fig.* do one's bit.

sollen ['zɔlən] (sollte, sollen, h) **I** *v/aux* **1.** be to: *ich soll dir ausrichten* I am to tell you; *soll ich kommen?* shall I come?; *er soll nur kommen!* just let him come!; *was soll ich tun?* what should I do? **2.** *moral obligation:* *ich hätte hingehen* ~ I ought to have gone; *ich hätte es wissen* ~ I should have known; *du hättest das nicht tun* ~ you shouldn't have done that! **3.** *intention:* *hier soll ein Schwimmbad entstehen* a swimming pool is to be built here; *es soll nicht wieder vorkommen* it won't happen again; *was soll das sein?* what's that supposed to be?; *es sollte ein Scherz sein* it was meant as (*or* supposed to be) a joke. **4.** *rumo(u)r:* *er soll reich sein* he is said to be rich; *die Rebellen* ~ *die Macht übernommen haben* the rebels are reported to have seized power. **5.** *possibility:* *sollte es wahr sein?* could it be true?; *sollte sie kommen* in case (*or* if) she should come. **6.** *fate:* *er sollte nie mehr zurückkehren* he was never to return again; *es sollte alles ganz anders kommen* things were to turn out quite differently; *ein Jahr sollte vergehen, bis ...* a year was to pass till ...; *es hat nicht* ~ *sein* it was not to be. **II** *v/i* (*pp gesollt*) *was soll ich hier?* what am I here for?; *was soll ich damit?* what am I to do with it?; *soll* (*sollte*) *ich?* shall (should) I?; *weshalb sollte ich* (*auch*)? why should I?; *was soll das?* a) what's the idea?, b) what's the use?, c) F *a.* *was soll's?* so what?

'Soll-Leistung *f* ✪ nominal output.

'Soll-Wert *m* ✪ rated value.

solo ['zoːlo] *adj* solo, F *fig. a.* alone.

'Solo *n* (-s; -s, Soli) solo, *sports:* solo attempt (*or* run).

'Solostimme *f* solo voice (*or* part).

'Solotänzer(in *f*) *m* solo dancer.

solvent [zɔl'vɛnt] *adj* ✝ solvent.

somatisch [zo'maːtɪʃ] *adj* somatic.

so'mit *adv* consequently, thus.

Sommer ['zɔmər] *m* (-s; -) summer: *im* ~ in (the) summer; *im nächsten* ~ next summer. **~ferien** *pl* summer holidays (*Am.* vacation). **~kleidung** *f* summer clothes, ✝ summer wear.

'**sommerlich** *adj* summerly, summery.
'**Sommer|loch** n F *fig.* silly season. **~rei‐
fen** *m mot.* normal tyre (*Am.* tire).
~spiele *pl Olympische* **~** Summer
Olympics. **~sprosse** f freckle.
'**sommersprossig** *adj* freckled.
'**Sommerzeit** f summer time, *a.* daylight
saving time.
Sonate [zo'naːtə] f (-; -n) ♪ sonata.
Sonde ['zɔndə] f (-; -n) ♔, *astronautics*:
probe, *meteor.*, *radar*: sonde.
Sonder... ['zɔndər-] special. **~anferti‐
gung** f special design, custom-made ar‐
ticle (*etc.*). **~angebot** n special offer.
~ausgabe f **1.** special edition. **2.** extra
(expenditure).
'**sonderbar** *adj* strange, odd, peculiar.
'**sonderbarer'weise** *adv* oddly enough.
'**Sonder|beauftragte** m, f special repre‐
sentative. **~beilage** f (special) supple‐
ment, inset. **~berichterstatter** m spe‐
cial correspondent. **~bevollmächtigte**
m, f plenipotentiary. **~druck** m (-[e]s;
-e) offprint. **~fall** m special case. **~in‐
ter,esse** n private interest.
'**sonderlich I** *adj* special: *ohne* **~e** *Mühe*
without any great effort. **II** *adv nicht* **~**
not particularly, not much, not very.
Sonderling ['zɔndərlɪŋ] m (-s; -e) eccen‐
tric, crank.
'**Sonder|marke** f special issue. **~ma‐
,schine** f ✈ special flight. **~meldung** f
special announcement. **~müll** m toxic
waste.
sondern ['zɔndərn] *conj* but: *nicht nur*
..., **~** *auch ...* not only ..., but also ...
'**Sonder|nummer** f special edition.
~recht n privilege. **~regelung** f special
arrangement. **~schule** f special school
(for handicapped or maladjusted chil‐
dren). **~sitzung** f special session.
~stempel m special postmark.
~wunsch m special request. **~zug** m
special train. **~zulage** f special bonus.
sondieren [zɔn'diːrən] (h) **I** *v/t* ♔ *or fig.*
probe, sound (out). **II** *v/i fig.* put out
feelers. **Son'dierungsgespräch** n ex‐
ploratory talk.
Sonett [zo'nɛt] n (-[e]s; -e) sonnet.
'**Sonnabend** m (*am* **~** on) Saturday.
'**sonnabends** *adv* on Saturday(s).
Sonne ['zɔnə] f (-; *no pl*) sun: *an* (*or in*)
der **~** in the sun.
sonnen ['zɔnən] *sich* **~** (h) sun o.s., bask

in the sun, *fig.* bask (*in dat* in).
'**Sonnenaufgang** m (*bei* **~** at) sunrise.
'**Sonnenbad** n sunbath: *ein* **~** *nehmen*
→ '**sonnenbaden** *v/i* (*only inf and pp*
sonnengebadet, h) sunbathe.
'**Sonnen|bank** f sun bed. **~blende** f
phot. lens hood. **~blume** f sunflower.
~brand m sunburn. **~brille** f (*e-e* **~** a
pair of) sunglasses. **~creme** f sun(tan)
cream. **~dach** n sun blind, *mot.* sun‐
shine roof. **~deck** n ⚓ sun deck. **~ener‐
,gie** f solar energy. **~finsternis** f eclipse
of the sun. **~fleck** m sunspot. **~hut** m
sunhat. **~kol,lektor** m solar panel.
~kraftwerk n solar power plant. **~licht**
n (*bei* **~** in) sunlight. **~öl** n suntan oil.
~schein m sunshine. **~schirm** m sun‐
shade, *for ladies*: parasol. **~schutz‐
creme** f sun (filter) cream. **~seite** f *a.*
fig. sunny side. **~stich** m sunstroke.
~strahl m sunbeam. **~sy,stem** n solar
system. **~uhr** f sundial. **~untergang** m
(*bei* **~** at) sunset. **~wende** f solstice.
~zelle f solar cell.
'**sonnig** *adj a. fig.* sunny.
'**Sonntag** m (*am* **~** on) Sunday. '**sonn‐
täglich** *adj* Sunday. '**sonntags** *adv* on
Sunday(s), on a Sunday.
'**Sonntags|anzug** m Sunday best. **~bei‐
lage** f Sunday supplement. **~dienst** m
~ *haben* be on Sunday duty, *pharmacy*:
be open on Sunday(s). **~fahrer** m
contp. Sunday driver. **~kind** n *er ist ein*
~ he was born on a Sunday (*fig.* under a
lucky star). **~maler** m Sunday painter.
'**sonnverbrannt** *adj* (deeply) tanned.
sonor [zo'noːr] *adj* sonorous.
sonst [zɔnst] *adv* **1.** otherwise, or, or else.
2. usually, normally: *wie* **~** as usual. **3.**
otherwise, apart from that. **4.** else: *wer*
~? who else?; **~** *noch etwas?* anything
else?; *nirgends* **~** nowhere else. **5.** al‐
ways: *alles war wie* **~** everything was
as it used to be. **~stig** *adj* other.
'**sonstjemand** *pron* F a) somebody else,
b) anybody. '**sonstwas** *pron* F a) some‐
thing else, b) anything. '**sonstwie** *adv* F
some other way. '**sonstwo(hin)** *adv* F
somewhere else.
so'**oft** *conj* whenever: **~** *du willst* as often
as you like.
Sopran [zo'praːn] m (-s; -e) soprano.
Sopranist [zopra'nɪst] m (-en; -en),
Sopra'nistin f (-; -nen) soprano.

Sorge ['zɔrgə] *f* (-; -n) **1.** a) worry, concern, b) trouble: *finanzielle (berufliche)* ~*n* financial (professional) worries (or problems); *j-m* ~*n machen* worry s.o., cause s.o. trouble; *sich* ~*n machen* a) *um* be worried about, b) *daß* be concerned that; *mach dir k-e* ~*n!*, *k-e* ~*!* don't worry!; *lassen Sie das m-e* ~ *sein!* leave that to me!; → *gering.* **2.** care: ~ *tragen für* → *sorgen* I.

sorgen ['zɔrgən] (h) **I** *v/i* ~ *für* a) see to, take care of, ensure, b) look after, c) provide; *dafür* ~, *daß* see to it that; *dafür werde ich* ~ I'll see to that; *für sich selbst* ~ fend for o.s.; *für ihn ist gesorgt* he's taken care of. **II** *sich* ~ *(um, wegen)* about) be worried, worry.

'**sorgenfrei** *adj* free from care(s), carefree. '**Sorgenkind** *n* problem child.

'**sorgenvoll** *adj* life *etc* full of worries, *a.* worried (*face, look, etc*).

'**Sorgerecht** *n* (-[e]s; *no pl*) custody (*für* of).

Sorgfalt ['zɔrkfalt] *f* (-; *no pl*) care: *große* ~ *verwenden auf* (*acc*) take great pains over. '**sorgfältig** [-fɛltɪç] *adj* careful.

'**sorglos** *adj* **1.** careless. **2.** carefree.

'**Sorglosigkeit** *f* (-; *no pl*) carelessness.

'**sorgsam** → *sorgfältig.*

Sorte ['zɔrtə] *f* (-; -n) sort, kind, type, ✚ brand, *a.* quality: ~*n* foreign exchange; *übelster* ~ of the worst kind.

sortieren [zɔr'tiːrən] *v/t* (h) sort, *a.* grade, *a.* size. **Sortiment** [zɔrti'mɛnt] *n* (-[e]s; -e) **1.** range. **2.** → **Sortiments-buchhandel** *m* retail book trade.

so'sehr *conj* ~ *(auch)* however much.

Soße ['zoːsə] *f* (-; -n) **1.** a) sauce, b) gravy, c) dressing. **2.** F juice, goo.

'**Soßenschüssel** *f* sauceboat.

Souffleur [zuˈfløːr] *m* (-s; -e) prompter. '**Souffleurkasten** *m* prompt box.

Souffleuse [zuˈfløːzə] *f* (-; -n) prompter.

soufflieren [zuˈfliːrən] *v/t*, *v/i* (h) *j-m* ~ prompt s.o.

'**sound'so** *adv* F so and so: ~ *viel* so much; ~ *viele* so and so many; ~ *oft* time and again; *Herr* ♀ Mr what's-his-name. ~*so'vielt* *adj* F **1.** *am* ~*en* on such and such a date. **2.** umpteenth.

Soutane [zuˈtaːnə] *f* (-; -n) cassock.

Souterrain [zutɛˈrɛ̃ː] *n* (-s; -s) basement.

Souvenir [zuvəˈniːr] *n* (-s; -s) souvenir.

souverän [zuvəˈrɛːn] *adj* sovereign, fig.

superior, *a. adv* in superior style.

Souveränität [zuvərɛniˈtɛːt] *f* (-; *no pl*) sovereignty.

so'viel **I** *conj* ~ *ich weiß* as far as I know; ~ *ich gehört habe* from what I have heard. **II** *adj und adv* so much: ~ *wie* as much as; *doppelt* ~ twice as much; ~ *steht fest* one thing is certain.

so'weit **I** *conj* as far as (*I know etc*). **II** *adv* ~ *sein* be ready; *es ist* ~ *fertig* it's more or less finished; *es ist* ~*!* a) it's time!, b) here goes!

so'wenig **I** *adv* not more (*als* than): ~ *wie möglich* as little as possible. **II** *conj* however little.

so'wie *conj* **1.** as soon as. **2.** as well as.

sowie'so *adv* **1.** anyway, in any case. **2.** F *(das)* ~*!* that goes without saying!

Sowjet [zɔˈvjɛt] *m* (-s; -s) *hist.* Soviet.

sowjetisch [zɔˈvjɛtɪʃ] *adj hist.* Soviet.

So'wjetuni,on *f hist.* Soviet Union.

so'wohl *conj* ~ ... *als (auch)* ... ... as well as ..., both ... and ...

sozial [zoˈtsiaːl] *adj* social: ~*e Stellung* social rank (or status); ~ *denken* be social-minded.

Sozi'al|**abgaben** *pl* social contributions. ~*amt* *n* social welfare office. ~*arbeit* *f* (-; *no pl*) social (or welfare) work. ~*arbeiter* *m* social (or welfare) worker. ~*demo,krat* *m* social democrat. ~*demo,kratie* *f* social democracy. ♀*demokratisch* *adj* social-democratic. ♀*denkend* *adj* social-minded. ~*einrichtungen* *pl* social services. ~*hilfe* *f* social security, *Am.* welfare: ~ *beziehen* be on social security (*Am.* welfare).

sozialisieren [zotsiali'ziːrən] *v/t* (h) nationalize. **Sozialismus** [zotsia'lɪsmʊs] *m* (-; *no pl*) socialism. **Sozialist** [-'lɪst] *m* (-en; -en), **Sozia'listin** *f* (-; -nen) socialist. **sozia'listisch** *adj* socialistic.

sozi'alkritisch *adj* sociocritical.

Sozi'al|**kunde** *f* (-; *no pl*) ped. social studies. ~*lasten* *pl* social expenditure. ~*leistungen* *pl* **1.** social contributions. **2.** *of company:* fringe benefits. ~*poli,tik* *f* social policy. ♀*po,litisch* *adj* socio-political. ~*pre,stige* *n* social prestige. ~*pro,dukt* *n* (gross) national product. ~*staat* *m* welfare state. ~*versicherung* *f* social security. ~*wohnung* *f* council flat.

Soziologe [zotsioˈloːgə] *m* (-n; -n) sociologist. **Soziologie** [zotsĭolo'giː] f (-; no pl) sociology. **sozio'logisch** adj sociological.

Sozius ['zoːtsĭʊs] m (-; -se) **1.** ⚭ partner. **2.** a. **~fahrer** m pillion rider. **~sitz** m (auf dem ~ mitfahren ride) pillion.

sozu'sagen adv so to speak, as it were.

Spachtel ['ʃpaxtəl] m (-s; -) **1.** spatula. **2.** → **~masse** f filler. **~messer** n putty knife.

spachteln ['ʃpaxtəln] v/t (h) surface.

Spagat [ʃpa'gaːt] m, n (-[e]s; -e) (~ machen do the) splits.

Spaghetti [ʃpa'gɛti] pl spaghetti.

spähen ['ʃpɛːən] v/i (h) peer, look out (nach for).

'Spähtrupp m ⚔ reconnaissance patrol.

Spalier [ʃpa'liːr] n (-s; -e) **1.** ⚘ trellis, espalier. **2.** a) guard of hono(u)r, b) lane, c) rows: **ein ~ bilden, ~ stehen** form a lane. **Spa'lierobst** n wall fruit.

Spalt [ʃpalt] m (-[e]s; -e) crack, gap, slit. **'spaltbar** adj phys. fissionable. **'Spalte** f (-; -n) **1.** crack, gap, split, geol. cleft, crevice, crevasse. **2.** print. column. **'spalten** v/t (spaltete, gespalten, h) split (a. atom), chop (wood), ⚗ decompose, fig. split (up), divide; → **Haar.** **'Spaltung** f (-; -en) splitting, phys. fission, fig. split, division, eccl. schism.

Span [ʃpaːn] m (-[e]s; ⁀e) chip, pl shavings, (metal) filings: **wo gehobelt wird, da fallen Späne** you can't make an omelette without breaking eggs.

'Spanferkel n sucking pig.

Spange ['ʃpaŋə] f (-; -n) a) clasp, b) buckle, c) bangle, d) (hair) slide, e) (shoe) strap, f) (dental) brace.

Spanien ['ʃpaːnĭən] n (-s) Spain. **'Spanier** m (-s; -), **'Spanierin** f (-; -nen) Spaniard. **'spanisch** adj Spanish: **~e Wand** folding screen; F **das kommt mir ~ vor!** that's strange! **Spanisch** n (auf ~ in) Spanish.

spann [ʃpan] pret of **spinnen.**

Spann m (-[e]s; -e) instep.

'Spannbe,ton m prestressed concrete.

Spanne ['ʃpanə] f (-; -n) **1.** span: fig. e-e kurze ~ a short space (of time). **2.** ⚭ margin. **'spannen** (h) **I** v/t stretch, tighten, put up (clothesline etc), cock (camera, gun), flex, tense (muscles), bend (bow), fig. strain (nerves): **e-n Bogen in die Schreibmaschine ~** insert a

sheet of paper into the typewriter; → **gespannt, Folter.** **II sich ~** stretch: **sich ~ über** (acc) span. **III** v/i dress etc be (too) tight, skin: be taut. **'spannend** adj exciting, thrilling, gripping, book, film full of suspense, suspense-packed

'Spanner m (-s; -) **1.** (racket etc) press; → **Schuhspanner. 2.** F peeping Tom

'Spannkraft f (-; no pl) energy, vigo(u)r

'Spannung f (-; -en) **1.** ⚙ tension (a. ⚡), ⚡ a. voltage, stress; ⚡ **unter ~ (stehend)** live. **2.** fig. a) excitement, suspense (a. of book etc), b) a. pol. tension: **mit** (or **voll**) **~** expect, watch, etc with bated breath; **j-n in ~ halten** keep s.o. in suspense; **in ~ versetzen** thrill, excite.

'Spannungsgebiet n pol. area of tension, trouble spot.

'spannungsgeladen adj **1.** → **spannend. 2.** (extremely) tense (atmosphere etc).

'Spannungsmesser m ⚡ voltmeter.

'Spannweite f wingspan, ⚙ span, fig scope, range.

'Spanplatte f chipboard.

'Spar|buch n savings book. **~büchse** ⚭ money box. **~einlage** f savings deposit

sparen ['ʃpaːrən] (h) **I** v/t save: **das hättest du dir ~ können!** that was unnecessary. **II** v/i a) save (up) (auf acc for), b) economize (an dat, mit on): **mit Lob etc ~** be sparing of praise etc. **'Sparer** m (-s; -), **'Sparerin** f (-; -nen) saver.

Spargel ['ʃpargəl] m (-s; -) asparagus.

'Spar|groschen m F nest egg. **~guthaben** n savings balance. **~kasse** f savings bank. **~konto** n savings account.

spärlich ['ʃpɛːrlɪç] adj scant(y), sparse thin (a. hair), poor (attendance): **~ bekleidet** scantily dressed; **~ besucht** poorly attended.

'Spar|maßnahme f economy measure **~prämie** f savings premium. **~programm** n **1.** pol. cuts (or austerity program(me Br.). **2.** washing machine energy-saving cycle.

Sparren ['ʃparən] m (-s; -) rafter.

'sparsam adj (mit) economical (of) thrifty (of, with): **~ im Verbrauch** economical; a. fig. **~ umgehen mit b** sparing of.

'Sparsamkeit f (-; no pl) economy thrift, austerity, contr. parsimony.

'Sparschwein n F piggy bank.

spartanisch [ʃparˈtaːnɪʃ] *adj* Spartan, *fig.* spartan: **~ leben** lead a spartan life.
Sparte [ˈʃpartə] *f* (-; -n) field, line.
'Sparvertrag *m* savings agreement.
Spaß [ʃpaːs] *m* (-es; ⁻e [ˈʃpɛːsə]) a) joke, b) fun: **aus** (*or* **im, zum**) **~** for fun; **er hat nur ~ gemacht!** he was only joking; **es macht (k-n) ~** it's (no) fun; **es macht ihm viel ~** he really enjoys it; **er versteht k-n ~** he can't take a joke, *w.s.* he doesn't stand for any nonsense; **~ beiseite!** joking aside; **viel ~!** have fun!; **ein teurer ~** an expensive business.
'spaßen *v/i* (h) joke: **damit ist nicht zu ~!** that's no joking matter!; **er läßt nicht mit sich ~** he doesn't stand for any nonsense. **'spaßeshalber** *adv* (just) for fun. **'spaßig** *adj* funny.
'Spaßverderber *m* (-s; -) spoilsport, killjoy. **'Spaßvogel** *m* joker, wag.
Spastiker [ˈʃpastɪkər] *m* (-s; -) 🅵 spastic.
'spastisch *adj* (*a.* **~ gelähmt**) spastic.
spät [ʃpɛːt] **I** *adj* late: **am ~en Nachmittag** late in the afternoon; **wie ~ ist es?** what time is it?; **es ist (wird) ~** it's (getting) late; **zu ~ kommen** be late (**zu** for); **er kam 5 Minuten zu ~** he was five minutes late; **zu Abend essen** have a late dinner; **bis ~ in die Nacht** till late at night; **du bist ~ dran!** you are late! **II** *adv* late, at a late hour (*a. fig.*): **zu ~ kommen** be late (**zu** for).
Spatel [ˈʃpaːtəl] *m* (-s; -) 🅵 spatula.
Spaten [ˈʃpaːtən] *m* (-s; -) spade.
'Spätentwickler *m* late developer.
'später I *adj* later. **II** *adv* later (**als** than), later on: **bis ~!** see you later!; → **früher**
II. spätestens [ˈʃpɛːtəstəns] *adv* at the latest.
'Spätherbst *m* late autumn (*Am.* fall). **~lese** *f* late vintage (wine). **~schäden** *pl* 🅵 late sequelae. **~schicht** *f* (~ haben be on) late shift. **~vorstellung** *f* late-night performance.
Spatz [ʃpats] *m* (-en, -es; -en) sparrow: F **das pfeifen die ~en von den Dächern** that's everybody's secret.
'Spätzünder *m* F **1. ein ~ sein** be slow on the uptake. **2.** → **Spätentwickler**.
'Spätzündung *f mot.* retarded ignition.
spazieren [ʃpaˈtsiːrən] *v/i* (sn) walk (around), stroll. **~fahren** (*irr, sep, -ge-, sn,* → **fahren**) **I** *v/i* take a ride. **II** *v/t* take *s.o.* for a ride. **~gehen** *v/i* (*irr, sep, -ge-, sn,* → **gehen**) go for a walk.

Spa'ziergang *m* **1.** walk, stroll: **e-n ~ machen** go for a walk. **2.** *sports etc:* walkover. **Spa'ziergänger** [-gɛŋər] *m* (-s; -) walker, stroller.
Spa'zierstock *m* walking stick.
Specht [ʃpɛçt] *m* (-[e]s; -e) woodpecker.
Speck [ʃpɛk] *m* (-[e]s; -e) **1.** *gastr.* bacon: → **Made**. **2.** F flab: **~ ansetzen** get fat.
'speckig *adj* **1.** fat. **2.** *fig.* greasy.
'Speckscheibe *f* bacon rasher.
'Speckschwarte *f* bacon rind.
'Speckseite *f* flitch (of bacon).
Spediteur [ʃpediˈtøːr] *m* (-s; -e) **1.** forwarding (⚓ shipping) agent. **2.** (furniture) remover. **Spedition** [ʃpediˈtsioːn] *f* (-; -en) **1.** forwarding (⚓ shipping) (business). **2.** → **Spediti'onsfirma** *f* **1.** forwarding (⚓ shipping) agency. **2.** removal firm. **Spediti'onskaufmann** *m* forwarding agent.
Speer [ʃpeːr] *m* (-[e]s; -e) spear, *sports:* javelin. **'Speerwerfen** *n sports:* javelin throw, *the* javelin. **'Speerwerfer(in** *f*) *m sports:* javelin thrower.
Speiche [ˈʃpaɪçə] *f* (-; -n) **1.** spoke. **2.** *anat.* radius.
Speichel [ˈʃpaɪçəl] *m* (-s; *no pl*) spittle, saliva. **~drüse** *f* salivary gland. **~lekker** *m contp.* toady, bootlicker.
Speicher [ˈʃpaɪçər] *m* (-s; -) **1.** a) granary, elevator, b) warehouse, c) reservoir. **2.** loft, attic. **3.** *computer:* store, memory. **~chip** *m computer:* memory chip. **~kapazi'tät** *f* storage (*computer:* memory) capacity.
speichern [ˈʃpaɪçərn] *v/t* (h) store (*a.* ⚡, *computer*), 🖥 *a.* stockpile. **'Speicherung** *f* (-; *no pl*) storage (*a. computer*).
Speise [ˈʃpaɪzə] *f* (-; -n) a) food, b) dish, meal. **~aufzug** *m* dumb waiter. **~eis** *n* ice cream. **~kammer** *f* larder, pantry. **~karte** *f* menu. **~leitung** *f* ⚡ feeder.
speisen [ˈʃpaɪzən] (h) **I** *v/i* eat, dine: **zu Mittag ~** (have) lunch; **zu Abend ~** have dinner, dine. **II** *v/t* feed (*a.* ⚡, ⚙).
'Speisenfolge *f* order of courses.
'Speiseöl *n* cooking oil. **~röhre** *f anat.* gullet, (o)esophagus. **~saal** *m* dining hall (*in hotel:* room, ⚓ saloon). **~wagen** *m* 🚂 dining car, *Am.* diner. **~zettel** *m* menu. **~zimmer** *n* dining room.
'Speisung *f* (-; -en) feeding, ⚙ *a.* supply.
Spektakel [ʃpɛkˈtaːkəl] *m* (-s; *no pl*) row, racket, *fig.* fuss.

Spektralana,lyse [ʃpɛk'traː-l-] *f* spectrum analysis. **Spektrum** ['ʃpɛktrʊm] *n* (-s; -tren) *a. fig.* spectrum.

Spekulant [ʃpeku'lant] *m* (-en; -en) speculator. **Spekulation** [ʃpekula'tsi̯oːn] *f* (-; -en) speculation. **Spekulati'onsgeschäft** *n* speculative operation.

spekulieren [ʃpeku'liːrən] *v/i* (h) speculate (*über acc* on); ~ *mit* in); ~ *auf* (*acc*) a) speculate on, b) F have one's eye on.

Spelunke [ʃpe'lʊŋkə] *f* (-; -n) F dive.

spendabel [ʃpɛn'daːbəl] *adj* F generous.

Spende ['ʃpɛndə] *f* (-; -n) donation, contribution. **'spenden** *v/t*, *v/i* (h) **1.** donate (*a. blood etc*), contribute. **2.** *machine*: dispense. **3.** *fig.* give (*praise etc*).

'Spenden,akti,on *f* collection campaign. **~konto** *n* account for donations.

'Spender *m* (-s; -) **1.** *a.* **'Spenderin** *f* (-; -nen) donator, contributor, *a.* ~ donor. **2.** (*machine*) dispenser.

spendieren [ʃpɛn'diːrən] *v/t* (h) F *j-m et.* ~ treat s.o. to s.th.; *j-m ein Bier* ~ stand s.o. a beer.

Sperber ['ʃpɛrbər] *m* (-s; -) *zo.* sparrow hawk.

Sperling ['ʃpɛrlɪŋ] *m* (-s; -e) *zo.* sparrow.

Sperma ['ʃpɛrma] *n* (-s; -men) sperm.

Sperre ['ʃpɛrə] *f* (-; -n) **1.** barrier, *a.* barricade, road block. **2.** ⚙ lock, stop, stoppage. **3.** *psych.* mental block. **4.** ✞ embargo, blockade: *e-e* ~ *verhängen über* (*acc*) impose a ban (✞ an embargo) on. **5.** *sports*: suspension. **'sperren** (h) **I** *v/t* **1.** shut, block (*road etc*), *police etc*: cordon off: *e-e Straße für den Verkehr* ~ close a road to traffic. **2.** ⚙ a) lock, block, stop, b) cut off (*gas etc*). **3.** ✞ a) embargo, b) freeze (*payments etc*), block (*account*), stop (*cheque*). **4.** *sports*: *j-n* ~ a) obstruct s.o. (unfairly), b) suspend s.o. **5.** *print.* space out: *gesperrt gedruckt* spaced out. **6.** *j-n* ~ *in* (*acc*) lock s.o. up in. **II** *sich* ~ balk (*gegen* at).

'Sperr|feuer *n* ✗ barrage. **~frist** *f* blocking period. **~gebiet** *n* restricted area. **~gürtel** *m* cordon. **~holz** *n* plywood.

'sperrig *adj* bulky.

'Sperr|klausel *f* restrictive clause. **~konto** *n* blocked account. **~minori,tät** *f* blocking minority. **~müll** *m* bulk rubbish. **~sitz** *m* *thea.* orchestra stalls.

~stunde *f* closing time, ✗ curfew. **~taste** *f* locking key.

'Sperrung *f* (-; -en) **1.** closing (*etc*, → *sperren* I). **2.** blockage, obstruction, stoppage, ✞ embargo.

Spesen ['ʃpeːzən] *pl* expenses. **2frei** *adj* free of charge(s). **~konto** *n* expense account. **~rechnung** *f* bill of expenses.

Spezi ['ʃpeːtsi] *m* (-s; -[s]) F chum, pal.

Spezial|ausbildung [ʃpe'tsiaː-l-] *f* special(ized) training. **~einheit** *f* task force. **~fach** *n* special subject. **~gebiet** *n* special field, speciality.

spezialisieren [ʃpetsi̯ali'ziːrən] *sich* ~ (h) specialize (*auf acc* in). **Speziali'sierung** *f* (-; *no pl*) specialization. **Spezialist** [ʃpetsi̯a'lɪst] *m* (-en; -en), **Spezia'listin** *f* (-; -nen) specialist. **Spezialität** [ʃpetsi̯ali'tɛːt] *f* (-; -en) speciality.

speziell [ʃpe'tsi̯ɛl] *adj* special, specific.

Spezies ['ʃpeːtsiɛs] *f* (-; -) species.

spezifisch [ʃpe'tsiːfɪʃ] *adj* specific: *phys.* ~*es Gewicht* specific gravity.

spezifizieren [ʃpetsifi'tsiːrən] *v/t* (h) specify, itemize.

Sphäre ['sfɛːrə] *f* (-; -n) sphere.

'sphärisch *adj* spheric.

Sphinx [sfɪŋks] *f* (-; -e) *a. fig.* sphinx.

spicken ['ʃpɪkən] *v/t* (h) **1.** *gastr.* lard. **2.** F *fig.* interlard *speech etc* (*mit* with): *gespickt mit Fehlern* full of mistakes.

Spiegel ['ʃpiːgəl] *m* (-s; -) **1.** mirror (*a. fig.*), ♣ speculum, *opt.*, ⚙ reflector. **2.** surface (*of water*), (*a. blood sugar etc*) level. **~bild** *n* **1.** mirror image. **2.** *fig.* reflection. **~ei** *n gastr.* fried egg.

'spiegel|frei *adj* nonglare. **~glatt** *adj* water (as) smooth as glass, *floor etc* like glass, *a.* icy (*road*).

spiegeln ['ʃpiːgəln] (h) **I** *v/i* shine, *a.* dazzle. **II** *v/t a. fig.* mirror, reflect. **III** *sich* ~ be reflected, *fig. a.* be mirrored.

'Spiegelre,flexkamera *f* reflex camera.

'Spiegelschrift *f* mirror writing.

'Spiegelung *f* (-; -en) **1.** reflection. **2.** mirage.

Spiel [ʃpiːl] *n* (-[e]s; -e) **1.** play (*a. fig. of colo[u]rs, muscles*), ♪ playing, *thea. a.* acting, performance. **2.** game, match, *a.* gamble: *wie steht das* ~? what's the score?; *fig. das* ~ *ist aus!* the game is up!; *gewagtes* ~ gamble; *et. ins* ~ *bringen* bring s.th. up; *gewonnenes* ~ *haben* have made it; *leichtes* ~ *haben* have little trouble (*mit* with); *die Hand im ~ haben* have one's (*or* a) finger in the pie; *ins ~ kommen* come into play; *aus dem ~ lassen* leave s.o., s.th. out of it; (*mit*) *im ~ sein* be at work, *bei et.* be involved in s.th.; *aufs ~ setzen* risk; *auf dem ~ stehen* be at stake; *mit j-m sein* play games with s.o.; *mit j-m ein falsches ~ treiben* doublecross s.o.; → *abgekartet.* 3. *thea., TV* play. 4. ~ (*Karten*) pack (*Am.* deck) (of cards). 5. ☺ a) play, b) clearance.

Spiel|anzug m playsuit. **~art** f *biol. or fig.* variety. **~auto₁mat** m a) gaming machine, b) slot machine, F one-armed bandit. **~ball** m 1. ball, *tennis*: game ball. 2. *fig.* plaything. **~bank** f (-; -en) (gambling) casino.

spielen ['ʃpiːlən] (h) **I** v/i 1. a) play (*a. fig.*), b) gamble: *~ um* play for; *hoch ~* play for high stakes; *sports*: *A. spielte gegen B.* A. played B.; *mit dem Gedanken ~ zu inf* toy with the idea of *ger*; *s-e Beziehungen ~ lassen* pull a few strings; *ins Rötliche ~* have a reddish tinge; → *Charme, Feuer* 1, *Muskel.* 2. *thea.* play, act: *~ in* (*dat*) *film, scene, etc*: be set in. **II** v/t 3. play: *Klavier ~* play the piano; *sports*: *den Ball zu j-m ~ pass* (the ball) to s.o.; → *Geige, Hand.* 4. *thea. or fig.* play, act: *fig. den Beleidigten ~* act all offended; *mit gespielter Gleichgültigkeit* with studied indifference; F *fig. was wird hier gespielt?* what's going on here?; → *Rolle²* 5. *thea. etc* play, perform: *was wird heute abend gespielt?* what's on tonight?; → *Theater.*

spielend *adv fig.* ~ (*leicht*) easily, effortlessly; *es ist ~ leicht* it's child's play; ~ *gewinnen* win hands down.

Spieler m (-s; -) a) player, b) gambler. **Spiele|rei** f (-; -en) 1. *no pl* playing around. 2. pastime. 3. *pl* a) gewgaws, b) gadgets. **Spielerin** f (-; -nen) → *Spieler.* **spielerisch** *adj* 1. *sports*: playing, *thea.* acting. 2. playful. 3. *mit ~er Leichtigkeit* effortlessly.

Spiel|feld n *sports*: field, pitch, *tennis*: a. court. **~film** m feature film. **~halle** f amusement arcade. **~hölle** f *contp.* gambling den. **~kame₁rad(in** f) m playmate. **~karte** f playing card. **~ka₁sino** n (gambling) casino. **~leiter(in** f) m →

Regisseur(in). **~macher** m *sports*: strategist. **~marke** f counter, chip. **~plan** m *thea. etc* program(me *Am.*). **~platz** m playground. **~raum** m *fig.* a) elbowroom, scope, b) time, c) margin. **~regel** f rule: *a. fig. sich an die ~n halten* play the game. **~sachen** *pl* toys. **~sa₁lon** m amusement arcade. **~schuld** f gambling debt. **~stand** m score. **~tisch** m 1. card table. 2. gambling table. **~trieb** m play instinct. **~uhr** f musical clock. **~verbot** n *sports*: suspension: ~ *haben* have been suspended. **~waren** *pl* toys. **~warengeschäft** n toy shop (*or* store). **~zeit** f *sports, thea.* season, *of match*: playing time, *of film etc*: run. **~zeug** n toy(s), *fig.* toy. **~zeugpi₁stole** f toy pistol.

Spieß [ʃpiːs] m (-es; -e) spear, *gastr.* spit, skewer: *am ~ braten* barbecue; F *fig. den ~ umdrehen* turn the tables (*gegen* on); *schreien wie am ~* scream blue murder. **Spießbürger(in** f) m, **'spießbürgerlich** *adj* petty bourgeois, F square. **'Spießer** m (-s; -), **'Spießerin** f (-; -nen), **'spießig** *adj* petty bourgeois, F square. **'Spießruten** *pl* ~ *laufen a. fig.* run the gauntlet.

Spikes [ʃpaɪks] *pl* 1. *sports*: spikes. 2. *mot.* a) studs, b) → **Spikesreifen** *pl* studded tyres (*Am.* tires).

spinal [ʃpiˈnaːl] *adj* spinal: ✦ *~e Kinderlähmung* polio(myelitis).

Spinat [ʃpiˈnaːt] m (-[e]s; -e) spinach. **Spind** [ʃpɪnt] m, n (-[e]s; -e) locker. **Spindel** ['ʃpɪndəl] f (-; -n) spindle. **Spinett** [ʃpiˈnɛt] n (-[e]s; -e) spinet. **Spinne** ['ʃpɪnə] f (-; -n) spider. **'spinnen** (spann, gesponnen, h) **I** v/t 1. spin: *fig. Ränke ~* hatch plots. **II** v/i 2. spin. 3. F a) be crazy, b) talk (a lot of) rubbish. **'Spinnennetz** n cobweb. **'Spinner** m (-s; -) 1. spinner. 2. F nut, crackpot, *Am.* screwball. **Spinne'rei** f (-; -en) 1. *no pl* spinning. 2. spinning mill. 3. F a) crazy idea, b) rubbish. **'Spinnerin** f (-; -nen) → **Spinner.**

'Spinn|gewebe n cobweb. **~rad** n spinning wheel. **~webe** f (-; -n) cobweb.

Spion [ʃpiˈoːn] m (-s; -e) 1. spy. 2. a) spyhole, b) window mirror.

Spionage [ʃpioˈnaːʒə] f (-; *no pl*) espionage, spying. **~abwehr** f counterespio-

nage, counterintelligence. **~netz** n,
~ring m spy ring. **~ro,man** m spy story.

spionieren [ʃpio'ni:rən] v/i (h) spy, fig.
contp. a. snoop (around).

Spi'onin f (-; -nen) spy.

Spirale [ʃpi'ra:lə] f (-; -n) spiral (a.
✝etc), ⊕ coil (a. ↯ pessary). **Spi'ral-
feder** f coil spring, of watch: mainspring. **spi'ralförmig** adj spiral.

Spiritismus [ʃpiri'tɪsmʊs] m (-; no pl)
spiritualism. **Spiri'tist** m (-en; -en),
spiri'tistisch adj spiritualist.

Spirituosen [ʃpiri'tǔo:zən] pl spirits,
liquor.

Spiritus ['ʃpi:ritʊs] m (-; -se) spirit.

'**Spirituskocher** m spirit stove.

spitz [ʃpɪts] adj 1. pointed, sharp: **~ zu-
laufend** tapering. **2.** ⊬ acute (angle). **3.**
F peaky. **4.** fig. pointed (remark etc),
sarcastic: **~e Zunge** sharp tongue.

Spitz m (-es; -e) (dog) Pomeranian.

'**Spitz|bart** m goatee. **~bauch** m paunch.

'**Spitze**[1] f (-; -n) **1.** point, tip (a. of finger,
nose, etc), peak, top, a. spire: fig. **die ~
des Eisbergs** the tip of the iceberg; **e-r
Sache die ~ nehmen** take the edge off
s.th.; **et. auf die ~ treiben** carry s.th.
too far. **2.** head (a. fig.), ⤬ (spear)head,
sports: lead, a. leading group: F **~ spielen** soccer: be striker; **an der ~ der
Tabelle** at the top of the table; a. fig. **an
der ~ liegen** be in front; **sich an die ~
setzen** take the lead. **3.** peak, maximum: F **das Auto macht 220 km ~** the
car does a maximum speed of 220 km
per hour; F **das ist (einsame) ~!** that's
super! **4.** a) top position, b) (top) management, c) pl leading figures, élite: **an
der ~ der Firma** at the head of the firm.
5. ⊬ apex. **6.** F dig (gegen) at.

'**Spitze**[2] f (-; -n) lace.

Spitzel ['ʃpɪtsəl] m (-s; -) a) informer, sl.
nark, b) company spy.

spitzen ['ʃpɪtsən] v/t (h) point, sharpen:
die Ohren ~ prick up one's ears, fig. a.
listen carefully.

'**Spitzen|fabri,kat** n top-quality product
(or make). **~gehalt** n top salary. **~ge-
schwindigkeit** f maximum (or top)
speed. **~gespräch** n top-level talks.
~kandi,dat(in f) m leading candidate,
front-runner. **~klasse** f top class: **Läufer (Auto) der ~** top-class runner (car).

'**Spitzenkleid** n lace dress.

'**Spitzen|kraft** f highly qualified worke**[r]**
top-level executive, thea. etc star pe**[r]**
former. **~leistung** f **1.** ⊕ maximu**[m]**
output, ⚡ peak power. **2.** sports: to**[p]**
performance, fig. a. great feat. **~lohn** **[m]**
top wage(s). **~reiter** m front-runne**[r]**
sports: leader, leading team, (film, tun**[e]**
etc) (top) hit. **~sport** m high-perfo**[r-]**
mance sports. **~sportler(in** f) m to**[p]**
athlete. **~tanz** m toe-dancing. **~techno**[-]**
lo,gie** f high technology. **~verdie**[-]**
ner(in** f) m top earner. **~wein** m vin**[-]**
tage wine. **~zeit** f **1.** sports: record tim**[e]**
2. peak hours (of traffic etc).

'**spitzfindig** adj over-subtle.

'**Spitzfindigkeit** f (-; -en) subtlety: **da**[s]**
sind ~en that's splitting hairs.

'**Spitzhacke** f pickax(e).

'**spitzkriegen** v/t (sep, -ge-, h) F **et.** **~**
cotton on to s.th.

'**Spitzname** m nickname.

'**spitzwink(e)lig** adj ⊬ acute.

Spleen [ʃpli:n] m (-s; -e, -s) F tic, quirk**[?]**

splitten ['ʃplɪtən] v/t (h) ✝, pol. split.

Splitter ['ʃplɪtər] m (-s; -) splinter, frag**[-]**
ment. **~bruch** m ⚕ chip fracture. ⅌**fre**[i]**
adj shatterproof. **~gruppe** f pol. split**[-]**
ter group.

splittern ['ʃplɪtərn] v/i **1.** (h) splinter. **2.**
(sn) glass: shatter.

'**splitternackt** adj stark naked.

'**Splitterpar,tei** f splinter party.

Spoiler ['ʃpɔylər] m (-s; -) mot. spoile**[r]**

sponsern ['ʃpɔnzərn] v/t (h) sponsor.

Sponsor ['ʃpɔnzɔr] m (-s; -s, -en [-'zo:**[-]**
rən]) sponsor.

spontan [ʃpɔn'ta:n] adj spontaneous.

sporadisch [ʃpo'ra:dɪʃ] adj sporadic.

Spore ['ʃpo:rə] f (-; -n) ♣ spore.

Sporn [ʃpɔrn] m (-[e]s; Sporen ['ʃpo:rən])
spur (a. ♥), ✈ (tail) skid: **s-m Pferd d**[ie]**
Sporen geben spur one's horse.

Sport [ʃpɔrt] m (-[e]s; no pl) **1.** sport, col**[l.]**
sports, ped. a. physical education:
treiben go in for sports; **viel ~ treibe**[n]**
do a lot of sport. **2.** fig. (als ~ as **[a]**
hobby. **~abzeichen** n sports badg**[e]**
~angler m angler. **~anlage** f spor**[ts]**
grounds (or facilities). **~art** f (kind o**[f]**
sport. **~ar,tikel** m sports article. **~arz**[t]**
m sports physician. ⅌**begeistert** a**[dj]**
sporty. **~bericht** m sports report. **~fes**[t]**
n sports day. **~flieger** m amateur pilo**[t]**
~geschäft n sports shop (or store**[)]**

~**halle** f gymnasium. ~**hochschule** f physical education college. ~**kleidung** f sportswear. ~**klub** m sports club. ~**lehrer(in** f) m ped. PE (= physical education) teacher.

'**Sportler** m (-s; -) sportsman, athlete. '**Sportlerin** f (-; -nen) sportswoman.

'**sportlich** adj sporting, sporty, a. fair (behavio[u]r, play), a. sports (meeting etc), athletic (person, figure, etc), casual (wear).

'**Sport|medi,zin** f sports medicine. ~**nachrichten** pl sports news. ~**platz** m sports ground. ~**repor,tage** f sports report, sportscast. ~**re,porter** m sports reporter, sportscaster. ~**sendung** f sports broadcast, sportscast.

'**Sportska,none** f F (sports) ace. '**Sportsmann** m sportsman.

'**Sport|tauchen** n skin (or scuba) diving. ~**veranstaltung** f sporting event, sports meeting. ~**verein** m sports club. ~**wagen** m **1.** sports car. **2.** pushchair, Am. stroller. ~**zeitung** f sporting paper.

Spott [ʃpɔt] m (-[e]s; no pl) a) mockery, ridicule, b) derision, scorn. '**spottbillig** adj F dirt-cheap. **Spötte'lei** f (-; -en) mockery, a. gibe. **spötteln** ['ʃpœtəln] v/i (h) gibe (**über** acc at). '**spotten** v/t (h) (**über** acc) mock (at), scoff (at), make fun (of); → **Beschreibung** 1. **Spötter** ['ʃpœtər] m (-s; -) **1.** mocker. **2.** cynic. '**spöttisch** adj a) mocking, b) derisive, c) sarcastic.

'**Spottlied** n satirical song. '**Spottpreis** m ridiculous(ly low) price.

sprach [ʃpra:x] pret of **sprechen**. '**sprachbegabt** adj good at languages. '**Sprachbegabung** f gift for languages. **Sprache** ['ʃpra:xə] f (-; -n) **1.** no pl speech: → **verschlagen**[1] 4. **2.** language (a. fig.), a. vernacular, idiom, a. jargon, a. diction: **heraus mit der ~!** out with it!, **et. zur ~ bringen** bring s.th. up; **ein Thema zur ~ bringen** raise a subject; **zur ~ kommen** come up (for discussion); → **herausrücken** II.

'**Sprach|ebene** f speech level. ~**eigenheit** f idiom(atic expression). '**Sprachenschule** f language school. '**Sprach|fehler** m speech defect. ~**führer** m phrasebook. ~**gebiet** n speech area: **deutsches ~** German-speaking area. ~**gebrauch** m (-[e]s; no pl) (linguistic)

usage: **im gewöhnlichen ~** in everyday usage. ~**gefühl** n (-[e]s; no pl) linguistic instinct. 2**gewandt** adj **1.** articulate. **2.** proficient in languages. ~**kenntnisse** pl knowledge of languages (or of a language): **gute deutsche ~ erwünscht** good command of German desirable. 2**kundig** adj proficient in languages, polyglot. ~**kurs** m language course. ~**la,bor** n language laboratory. ~**lehre** f **1.** grammar. **2.** grammar book. ~**lehrer** m language teacher.

'**sprachlich** adj a) linguistic, b) grammatical, c) stylistic.

'**sprachlos** adj speechless.

'**Sprach|regelung** f iro. (prescribed) phraseology. ~**rohr** n fig. mouthpiece. ~**störung** f 🐟 speech disorder. ~**studium** n language studies. ~**ta,lent** n gift for languages. ~**unterricht** m language teaching: **englischer ~** English lessons. ~**wissenschaft** f philology. ~**wissenschaftler(in** f) m philologist, linguist. 2**wissenschaftlich** adj philological, linguistic.

sprang [ʃpraŋ] pret of **springen**.

Spray [ʃpre:] m, n (-s; -s) spray.

'**Sprech|anlage** f intercom. ~**blase** f in cartoons: balloon. ~**chor** m chorus: **im ~ rufen** chant.

sprechen ['ʃprɛçən] (sprach, gesprochen, h) **I** v/i speak, a. give a speech, a. talk (**mit** j-m to s.o., **über** acc, **von** about): **~ mit** see (one's doctor etc); **über Geschäfte (Politik) ~** talk business (politics); **von et. anderem ~** change the subject; **j-n zum 2 bringen** make s.o. talk; **~ für** a) speak on behalf of s.o., b) put in a good word for, c) plead for; **das spricht für ihn** that says s.th. for him; **das spricht für sich selbst** that speaks for itself; **vieles spricht dafür (dagegen)** there is much to be said for (against) it; **alles spricht dafür, daß** there is every indication that; **auf ihn ist sie nicht gut zu ~** he's in her bad books; **wir kamen (man kam) auf ... zu ~** the subject of ... came up. **II** v/t speak (language etc), say (prayer etc): **j-n ~** speak to s.o., see s.o.; **j-n zu ~ wünschen** wish to see s.o.; **kann ich Sie kurz ~?** may I have a word with you?; **er ist nicht zu ~** he is busy; → **Recht** 1, **schuldig** 1.

'sprechend adj fig. eloquent (*gesture etc*), striking (*resemblance*).

'Sprecher m (-s; -) **1.** speaker, *radio, TV* announcer. **2.** spokesman (*gen* for).

'Sprecherin f (-; -nen) **1.** → **Sprecher** 1. **2.** spokeswoman (*gen* for).

'Sprecherziehung f speech training.

'Sprechfunk m radiotelephony. **~gerät** n a) radiotelephone, b) walkie-talkie.

'Sprechstunde f a) office hours, b) (*doctor's*) consulting hours.

'Sprechstundenhilfe f receptionist.

'Sprechzimmer n a) office, b) (*doctor's*) consulting room, surgery.

'spreizen ['ʃpraitsən] v/t (h) spread, a. straddle (*legs*).

'Spreizfuß m 🦶 splayfoot.

'Sprengbombe f high-explosive bomb.

'sprengen¹ ['ʃprɛŋən] v/t (h) sprinkle, spray.

'sprengen² v/t (h) **1.** burst open, force (*door*), break (*fetters etc*). **2.** blast, blow up. **3.** fig. break up (*meeting*): *die Bank ~ break the bank*; → *Rahmen*.

'Spreng|kapsel f detonator. **~kopf** m warhead. **~körper** m, **~ladung** f, **~satz** m explosive charge.

'Sprengstoff m explosive, fig. dynamite. **~anschlag** m bomb attack.

'Sprengung f (-; -en) **1.** blasting, blowing up. **2.** fig. breaking-up (*of meeting*).

sprenkeln ['ʃprɛŋkəln] v/t (h) dot.

Spreu [ʃprɔy] f (-; *no pl*) (fig. *die ~ vom Weizen trennen* separate the wheat from the) chaff.

'Sprichwort n proverb: *wie das ~ sagt* as the saying goes.

'sprichwörtlich adj a. fig. proverbial.

sprießen ['ʃpriːsən] v/i (sproß, gesprossen, sn) shoot up, sprout.

'Springbrunnen m fountain.

springen ['ʃprɪŋən] v/i (sprang, gesprungen, sn) **1.** a) jump, *sports*: a. dive, a. (pole)vault, b) leap, hop, skip, a. *ball etc*: bounce; → *Auge* 1, *Punkt* 2. **2.** F run, nip. **3.** F fig. et. ~ *lassen* fork out, *für j-n* treat s.o. to s.th. **4.** crack, break.

'Springen n (-s) jumping, *sports*: diving. **'Springer** m (-s; -) **1.** *sports*: a) jumper, b) diver, c) vaulter. **2.** *chess*: knight. **3.** F ✝ stand-in. **'Springerin** f (-; -nen) → *Springer* 1, 3.

'Spring|flut f spring tide. **~reiter(in** f) m show jumper. **~seil** n skipping rope.

Sprinkleranlage ['ʃprɪŋklər-]f sprinkler system.

Sprint [ʃprɪnt] m (-s; -s), **'sprinten** v/i, v/t (sn, h) sprint. **'Sprinter** m (-s; -), **'Sprinterin** f (-; -nen) sprinter.

Sprit [ʃprɪt] m (-[e]s; -e) F **1.** spirit(s), alcohol. **2.** petrol, F juice, *Am.* gas.

Spritze ['ʃprɪtsə] f (-; -n) a) syringe, b) injection, F jab, *Am.* shot, c) → *Finanzspritze.*

spritzen ['ʃprɪtsən] **I** v/t (h) **1.** squirt, spray. **2.** → *sprengen*. **3.** F a) inject (*s.o.*), b) *sl.* shoot, mainline (*drugs*). **4.** mix *drink* with (soda) water. **5.** 🔧 inject (*plastic*). **II** v/i **6.** splash, spatter, *blood*: gush. **7.** spray. **8.** F mainline (*sl.*). **'Spritzer** m (-s; -) splash, a. dash (*of rum etc*). **'Spritzguß** m 🔧 a) die-casting, b) injection mo(u)lding.

'spritzig adj **1.** sparkling (*wine etc*). **2.** fig. lively, F peppy, nippy, zippy (*car*).

'spritzlac,kieren v/t (h) spray(-paint).

'Spritzmittel n 🌱 spray. **'Spritzpi,stole** f 🔧 spray gun. **'Spritztour** f F mot. (*e-e ~ machen* go for a) spin.

spröde ['ʃprøːdə] adj **1.** brittle (*a. voice*), rough, chapped (*skin*). **2.** fig. standoffish, demure, prim (*girl*).

sproß [ʃprɔs] pret of **sprießen**.

Sproß m (-sses; -sse) **1.** 🌱 shoot. **2.** fig. scion.

Sprosse ['ʃprɔsə] f (-; -n) **1.** a. fig. rung. **2.** *hunt.* tine.

'Sprossenwand f gym. wall bars.

Sprößling ['ʃprœslɪŋ] m (-s; -e) F a) child, b) son, junior.

Sprotte ['ʃprɔtə] f (-; -n) zo. sprat.

Spruch [ʃprʊx] m (-[e]s; ⁀e) **1.** saying, dictum, a. aphorism, epigram, (bible) quotation, verse: F (*große*) *Sprüche klopfen* talk big. **2.** decision.

'Spruchband n banner.

'spruchreif adj *die Sache ist noch nicht ~* nothing has been decided yet.

Sprudel ['ʃpruːdəl] m (-s; -) (carbonated) mineral water. **'sprudeln** v/i (sn) **1.** gush (forth). **2.** bubble, *drink*: a. fizz: fig. ~ *vor* bubble (over) with.

'Sprühdose f spray can, aerosole (can).

sprühen ['ʃpryːən] (h) **I** v/t **1.** spray, sprinkle. **II** v/i **2.** (sn) spray. **3.** (a. sn) *sparks*: fly. **4.** fig. (*vor dat* with) bubble (over), *eyes*: flash: *vor Geist ~* sparkle with wit. '**sprühend** *adj fig.* sparkling (*wit etc*). '**Sprühregen** *m* drizzle.

Sprung[1] [ʃprʊŋ] *m* (-[e]s; ⁓e) jump (*a. fig.*), leap, *gym.*, *pole-vaulting*: vault, *high-diving*: dive: *fig.* **ein großer ⁓ nach vorn** a great leap forward; F **auf dem ⁓ sein zu** *inf* be about to *inf*; **j-m auf die Sprünge helfen** help s.o. along; **mit dem Gehalt kann er k-e großen Sprünge machen** he can't go far on that salary.

Sprung[2] *m* (-[e]s; ⁓e) crack: **e-n ⁓ haben** be cracked.

'**Sprung|balken** *m* *sports*: takeoff board. **⁓becken** *n* diving pool. **⁓brett** *n* springboard (*a. fig.*), *high-diving*: diving board. **⁓feder** *f* spring. **⁓federma,tratze** *f* spring (coil) mattress. **⁓grube** *f* *sports*: (jumping) pit.

'**sprunghaft** I *adj* 1. erratic. 2. rapid, *a.* sharp (*increase etc*). II *adv* rapidly: **⁓ ansteigen** go up by leaps and bounds, shoot up. '**Sprunghaftigkeit** *f* (-; *no pl*) 1. *of person*: volatility. 2. a) instability, b) rapidity.

'**Sprung|lauf** *m* ski-jumping. **⁓schanze** *f* ski jump. **⁓tuch** *n* jumping sheet. **⁓turm** *m* high-diving platforms.

Spucke ['ʃpʊkə] *f* (-; *no pl*) F spittle: **da blieb mir die ⁓ weg** I was flabbergasted. '**spucken** (h) I *v/i* 1. spit, *engine*: splutter. 2. F be sick, puke. II *v/t* 3. spit *s.th.* out: **Blut ⁓** spit blood; → **Ton**[2] 1.

Spuk [ʃpuːk] *m* (-[e]s; -e) 1. apparition, ghost, spectre, *Am.* specter, *w.s.* eerie happenings. 2. *fig.* nightmare. '**spuken** (h) I *v/i* haunt. II *v/impers* **in der Burg spukt es** the castle is haunted.

Spule ['ʃpuːlə] *f* (-; -n) 1. ⊙ spool, reel. 2. bobbin coil.

Spüle ['ʃpyːlə] *f* (-; -n) sink unit.

spulen ['ʃpuːlən] *v/t* (h) a) reel, spool, b) wind (*film etc*).

spülen ['ʃpyːlən] (h) I *v/t* 1. rinse. 2. wash (up): **Geschirr ⁓** → 4. 3. *et. ans Ufer ⁓* wash *s.th.* ashore. II *v/i* 4. wash up, wash (*or* do) the dishes. 5. flush the toilet. '**Spülmittel** *n* washing-up liquid. '**Spülung** *f* (-; -en) 1. rinse. 2. ♫ douche, irrigation. 2. a) flushing, b) flush. '**Spülwasser** *n* rinsing water, washing-up water, *a. fig. contp.*). '**Spulwurm** *m* ♫, *zo.* roundworm.

Spur [ʃpuːr] *f* (-; -en) 1. print, track(s),

trace(s), trail (*a. fig.*), *hunt. a.* scent: **e-e ⁓ aufnehmen** pick up a trail; *fig.* **auf die ⁓ kommen** (*dat*) get on to *s.o.*, *s.th.*; **auf der falschen ⁓ sein** be on the wrong track; **s-e ⁓en verwischen** cover up one's tracks; **(bei) j-m ⁓en hinterlassen** leave its mark (on s.o.). 2. *fig.* trace, *esp.* ⚖ clue: **k-e ⁓ von ...** not a trace of ...; F **k-e ⁓!** not a bit! 3. *fig.* trace, *gastr.* dash (*of pepper etc*). 4. 🚗 a) ga(u)ge, b) track(s). 5. *computer, tape*: track. 6. *mot.* a) (⁓**halten** keep) track, b) (**die ⁓ wechseln**) change lane.

'**spürbar** *adj* noticeable, marked, considerable: **⁓ sein** be felt; **⁓ werden** make itself felt.

spuren ['ʃpuːrən] *v/i* (h) 1. *skiing*: lay a track. 2. F toe the line.

spüren ['ʃpyːrən] *v/t* (h) feel, *a.* sense: **am eigenen Leibe zu ⁓ bekommen** have first-hand experience of; **von ... war nichts zu ⁓** there was no sign of ...

'**Spurene,lement** *n* trace element. '**Spürhund** *m* 1. tracker dog. 2. *humor.* sleuth.

'**spurlos** *adv* **⁓ verschwinden** disappear without a trace; **nicht ⁓ an j-m vorübergehen** leave its mark on s.o.

'**Spürnase** *f*, '**Spürsinn** *m* (-[e]s; *no pl*) (good) nose.

Spurt [ʃpʊrt] *m* (-[e]s; -s), '**spurten** *v/i* (h, sn) sprint, spurt.

'**Spurwechsel** *m* *mot.* changing lane. '**Spurweite** *f* 1. 🚗 ga(u)ge. 2. *mot.* track.

Staat[1] ['ʃtaːt] *m* (-[e]s; -en) 1. *pol.* a) state, b) country, nation, c) government: F **die ⁓en** (*USA*) the States. 2. *zo.* colony.

Staat[2] *m* (-[e]s; *no pl*) finery: *fig.* **damit kannst du k-n ⁓ machen!** that's nothing to write home about!

'**Staatenbund** *m* confederation. '**staatenlos** *adj* stateless. '**Staatenlose** *m*, *f* (-n; -n) stateless person. '**staatlich** *adj* state(-)...., government ..., national, public, state-owned (*plant etc*): **⁓e Mittel** government funds; **⁓ gefördert** state-sponsored; **⁓ gelenkt** state-run; **⁓ geprüft** qualified, registered.

'**Staats|akt** *m* a) act of state, b) state occasion. **⁓akti,on** *f* F **e-e ⁓ machen aus** (*dat*) make a big affair out of. **⁓angehörige** *m*, *f* national, citizen, *Br. a.* subject. **⁓angehörigkeit** *f* (**doppelte ⁓**

dual) nationality. **~angestellte** *m, f* state (*or* government) employee. **~anleihe** *f* government loan (*or* bond). **~anwalt** *m* 🏛 public prosecutor, *Am.* district attorney. **~anwaltschaft** *f* 🏛 a) *the* public prosecutor's office, b) *the* public prosecutors. **~beamte** *m* civil servant. **~begräbnis** *n* state funeral. **~besuch** *m* state visit. **~bürger** *m* citizen. **2bürgerlich** *adj* civic: **~e Rechte** civil rights. **~bürgerschaft** *f* → **Staatsangehörigkeit. ~chef** *m* head of state. **~dienst** *m* civil (*Am.* public) service. **2eigen** *adj* state-owned. **~ex‚amen** *n* *univ.* state examination. **~feiertag** *m* national holiday. **~feind** *m* public enemy. **2feindlich** *adj* subversive. **~form** *f* form of government. **~gebiet** *n German etc* territory. **~geheimnis** *n* state secret: F **das ist kein ~!** that's not top-secret. **~grenze** *f* border, frontier. **~haushalt** *m* (national) budget. **~hoheit** *f* (-; *no pl*) sovereignty. **~kasse** *f* (public) treasury. **~kosten** *pl* **auf ~** at (the) public expense.

'**Staatsmann** *m* (-[e]s; ¨-er) statesman. '**staatsmännisch** [-mɛnɪʃ] *adj* statesmanlike.

'**Staats|mi‚nister** *m* secretary of state, *Am.* secretary. **~mini‚sterium** *n* ministry. **~oberhaupt** *n* head of state. **~präsi‚dent** *m* president. **~rat** *m* a) council of state, *Br.* Privy Council, b) council(l)or of state. **~recht** *n* (-[e]s; *no pl*) constitutional law. **~religi‚on** *f* state religion. **~schulden** *pl* national debt. **~sekre‚tär** *m* permanent secretary. **~sicherheitsdienst** *m DDR pol. hist.* State Security (Service). **~streich** *m* coup (d'état). **2tragend** *adj* supportive of the State. **~trauer** *f* national mourning. **~verbrechen** *n* political crime. **~vertrag** *m* (international) treaty. **~wesen** *n* (-s; *no pl*) **1.** state, body politic. **2.** political system. **~wissenschaft(en** *pl*) *f* political science. **~wohl** *n* public weal. **~zuschuß** *m* government grant, subsidy.

Stab¹ [ʃtaːp] *m* (-[e]s; ¨-e) a) staff, b) stick, c) rod, bar, d) wand, e) ♪, *sports:* baton, f) *sports:* pole: *fig.* **den ~ brechen über** (*acc*) condemn.

Stab² *m* (-[e]s; ¨-e) **1.** a) (*administrative etc*) staff, b) team (*of experts etc*). **2.** ✕

a) staff, b) staff officers, c) headquarters.

Stäbchen ['ʃtɛːpçən] *n* (-s; -) chopstick.
'**Stabhochspringer** *m* pole-vaulter.
'**Stabhochsprung** *m* pole-vault(ing).
stabil [ʃtaˈbiːl] *adj* **1.** stable. **2.** solid, sturdy. **stabilisieren** [ʃtabiliˈziːrən] *v/t* (h) stabilize: **sich ~** *a.* become stabilized. **Stabili‚sierung** *f* (-; -en) stabilization. **Stabilität** [ʃtabiliˈtɛːt] *f* (-; *no pl*) stability.
'**Stabreim** *m* alliteration.
'**Stabs|arzt** *m* captain (medical corps). **~chef** *m* chief of staff. **~feldwebel** *m* warrant officer, *Am.* master sergeant.
'**Stabwechsel** *m sports:* baton change.
stach [ʃtax] *pret of* **stechen.**
Stachel ['ʃtaxəl] *m* (-s; -n) **1.** prickle, *zo. a.* spine, sting, ⚘ *a.* thorn. **2.** ⚙ spike.
'**Stachelbeere** *f* gooseberry.
'**Stacheldraht** *m* barbed wire.
'**stach(e)lig** *adj* **1.** prickly, *zo. a.* spiny, ⚘ *a.* thorny. **2.** *fig.* bristly (*chin, beard*).
'**Stachelschwein** *n* porcupine.
Stadion ['ʃtaːdiɔn] *n* (-s; -dien) stadium.
Stadium ['ʃtaːdiʊm] *n* (-s; -dien) stage, phase.
Stadt [ʃtat] *f* (-; ¨-e) **1.** town, city: **in die ~ gehen** go to town. **2.** *adm.* municipality. **~autobahn** *f* urban motorway (*Am.* expressway). **~bahn** *f* city railway. **2bekannt** *adj* known all over town, notorious. **~bevölkerung** *f* urban population. **~bewohner** *m* city dweller. **~bezirk** *m* municipal district. **~bild** *n* townscape.
Städtchen ['ʃtɛːtçən] *n* (-s; -) small town.
'**Städte|bau** ['ʃtɛːtə-] *m* (-[e]s; *no pl*) urban development. **~planung** *f* town planning.
Städter ['ʃtɛːtər] *m* (-s; -) city dweller.
'**Stadt|gas** *n* (-es; *no pl*) town gas. **~gebiet** *n* municipal area. **~gemeinde** *f* township. **~gespräch** *n fig.* **~ sein** be the talk of the town. **~gue‚rilla** *f* urban guer(r)illa. **~halle** *f* municipal hall.
städtisch ['ʃtɛːtɪʃ] *adj* town ..., city ..., urban, *adm.* municipal.
'**Stadt|kern** *m* town (*or* city) cent/re (*Am.* -er). **~leben** *n* city life. **~luft** *f* city air. **~mauer** *f* city wall. **~mitte** *f* → **Innenstadt. ~plan** *m* city map. **~planung** *f* town planning.
'**Stadtrand** *m* (*am* **~** at the) outskirts of

the town (*or* city). **~siedlung** *f* suburban estate (*or* housing development).

'Stadt|rat *m* **1.** municipal council. **2.** town (*Am.* city) council(l)or. **~rundfahrt** *f* city sightseeing tour. **~sa,nierung** *f* urban renewal. **~staat** *m* city state. **~streicher** *m* (-s; -) city vagrant. **~teil** *m* district. **~tor** *n* town gate. **~verkehr** *m* town (*or* city) traffic. **~verwaltung** *f* municipality. **~viertel** *n* district. **~zentrum** *n* → **Innenstadt.**

Staffage [ʃtaˈfaːʒə] *f* (-; -n) mere show.

Staffel ['ʃtafəl] *f* (-; -n) **1.** *sports:* relay (race *or* team). **2.** ✈, ✕ squadron.

Staffelei [ʃtafəˈlaɪ] *f* (-; -en) easel.

'Staffellauf *m sports:* relay race.

staffeln ['ʃtafəln] *v/t* (h) a) stagger, b) grade, graduate (*taxes, wages, etc*); → **gestaffelt. 'Staffelung** *f* (-; -en) a) staggering, b) graduation (*of taxes etc*), progressive rates.

Stagnation [ʃtagnaˈtsɪoːn] *f* (-; -en) stagnation.

stagnieren [ʃtaˈgniːrən] *v/i* (h) stagnate.

stahl [ʃtaːl] *pret of* **stehlen.**

Stahl *m* (-[e]s; ⸚e) steel: **~e** steel: **~e** nerves of steel. **~arbeiter** *m* steelworker. **~bau** *m* steel(-girder) construction. **~be,ton** *m* reinforced concrete. **2blau** *adj* steel-blue. **~blech** *n* sheet steel.

stählen ['ʃtɛːlən] *v/t* (h) **1.** ⚙ steel-face. **2.** *fig.* steel (*sich* o.s.). **'stählern** *adj* **1.** (of) steel. **2.** *fig.* of steel, steely.

'Stahl|gürtelreifen *m mot.* steel breaker tyre (*Am.* tire). **2hart** *adj* (as) hard as steel, steely. **~helm** *m* steel helmet. **~(rohr)möbel** *pl* tubular steel furniture. **~stich** *m* steel engraving. **~waren** *pl* steel goods. **~werk** *n* steelworks. **~wolle** *f* steel wool.

Stall [ʃtal] *m* (-[e]s; ⸚e) stable (*a. fig.*), *a.* cowshed: F **e-n ganzen ~ voll** a horde of children etc. **~bursche** *m* groom. **~gefährte** *m sports:* stable mate. **~meister** *m* riding master.

'Stallungen *pl* stabling, stables.

Stamm [ʃtam] *m* (-[e]s; ⸚e) **1.** ♣ stem (*a. ling.*), (tree) trunk. **2.** a) race, tribe, b) family. **3.** *fig.* core, nucleus. **4.** permanent staff, ✝ regular customers, *sports:* regular players. **5.** *biol.* phylum. **~aktie** *f* ordinary share, *Am.* common stock. **~baum** *m* family tree, *zo.* pedigree, *biol.* phylogenetic tree. **~buch** *n* family

register. **~burg** *f* ancestral castle. **~da,tei** *f* master file.

stammeln ['ʃtaməln] *v/t, v/i* (h) stammer.

stammen ['ʃtamən] *v/i* (h) (**von, aus**) a) come (from), b) date (from), go back (to): **der Ausspruch stammt von ihm** the word was coined by him.

'Stammform *f ling.* principal form.

'Stammgast *m* regular (guest).

'Stammhalter *m humor.* son and heir.

'Stammhaus *n* ✝ parent firm.

stämmig ['ʃtɛmɪç] *adj* stocky, burly.

'Stamm|kapi,tal *n* ordinary share capital, *Am.* common capital stock. **~kneipe** F *f* local. **~kunde** *m* regular customer, F regular. **~lo,kal** *n* favo(u)rite haunt. **~perso,nal** *n* permanent (*or* skeleton) staff. **~platz** *m* favo(u)rite seat: *sports:* **sich e-n ~ erobern** make the regular team. **~spieler** *m sports:* regular player. **~tafel** *f* genealogical table. **~tisch** *m* (table reserved for) regular guests. **~tischpo,litiker** *m* armchair politician. **~wähler** *m pol.* standing voter.

stampfen ['ʃtampfən] **I** *v/i* **1.** (sn) stamp, ⚓ pitch. **2.** (h) *mit dem Fuß* stamp one's foot. **II** *v/t* (h) a) pound, crush, mash, b) tamp: → **Boden 1.**

stand [ʃtant] *pret of* **stehen.**

Stand *m* (-[e]s; ⸚e) **1.** *no pl* a) (**aus dem ~** from a) standing position, b) footing, foothold: **k-n (festen) ~ haben** be wobbly, *person:* have no firm foothold; *fig.* (**bei j-m**) **e-n schweren ~ haben** have a hard time of it (with s.o.). **2.** *no pl* a) state, condition, b) position (*a. astr.*), c) (*a. water etc*) level, standard, d) figure, (*barometer etc*) reading, e) *sports:* score: **beim ~ von 4:2** at 4:2; **nach dem ~ vom 1. Mai** as of May 1st; **den höchsten ~ erreichen** reach its peak; *et. auf den neuesten ~ bringen* bring s.th. up to date, update s.th.; *der ~ der Dinge* the state of affairs; *nach dem ~ der Dinge* as matters stand; *der neueste ~ der Technik* (*or* *Wissenschaft*) the state of the art. **3.** *no pl* social standing, rank, (*a. legal, marital*) status. **4.** a) class, b) profession.

Stand² *m* (-[e]s; ⸚e) stall, booth.

Standard ['ʃtandart] *m* (-s; -s) standard.

standardisieren [ʃtandardiˈziːrən] *v/t*

(h) standardize. **Standardi'sierung** f (-; -en) standardization.

'**Standardwerk** n standard work.

Standarte [ʃtanˈdartə] f (-; -n) standard.

'**Standbild** n statue.

Ständchen [ˈʃtɛntçən] n (-s; -) serenade: **j-m ein ~ bringen** serenade s.o.

Stander [ˈʃtandər] m (-s; -) pennant.

Ständer [ˈʃtɛndər] m (-s; -) **1.** stand, (pipe, rifle, etc) rack. **2.** V hard-on.

'**Standes|amt** n registry office. **~amtlich** adj **~e Trauung** registry office wedding. **~beamte** m registrar. **~gemäß** adj and adv in keeping with one's station. **~unterschied** m social difference.

'**standfest** adj steady, ⚙ stable.

'**Standfestigkeit** f (-; no pl) **1.** steadiness, ⚙ stability. **2.** → **Standhaftigkeit.**

'**Stand|foto** n film: still. **~gericht** n ✗ drumhead court martial.

'**standhaft** adj steadfast, firm.

'**Standhaftigkeit** f (-; no pl) steadfastness, firmness.

'**standhalten** v/i (irr, sep, -ge-, h, → **halten**) a) hold one's ground, stand firm, b) withstand, resist (attack etc), c) stand up to (criticism etc): → **Vergleich** 1.

ständig [ˈʃtɛndɪç] **I** adj a) constant, continuous, b) permanent (abode, personnel, etc), c) fixed, regular (income), d) standing (committee): **~er Begleiter** constant companion. **II** adv permanently, constantly, always: **et. ~ tun** keep doing s.th.

'**Stand|licht** n mot. (-[e]s; no pl) parking light. **~ort** m position (a. ⚓ or fig.), location, site (of firm etc), ✗ garrison, Am. post, biol. habitat: **den ~** (gen) **bestimmen** locate. **~pauke** f F lecture: **j-m e-e ~ halten** lecture s.o. (über acc on). **~punkt** m **1.** post, point. **2.** fig. (von s-m etc ~ aus from his etc) point of view; **den ~ vertreten, auf dem ~ stehen** take the view (daß that). **~quar‚tier** n base. **~recht** n (-[e]s; no pl) martial law. **⚙rechtlich** adj and adv by order of a court martial. **~spur** f mot. hard shoulder. **~uhr** f grandfather clock.

Stange [ˈʃtaŋə] f (-; -n) **1.** pole (a. sports), (flag) staff, (metal) rod, bar, for birds: perch, (sugar, celery, etc) stick: **e-e ~ (Zigaretten)** a carton (of cigarettes):

Kleidung von der ~ clothes off the peg; F **e-e ~ Geld** a packet; **bei der ~ bleiben** stick to it, a. stick it out; **j-n bei der ~ halten** keep s.o. at it; **j-m die ~ halten** stick up for s.o. **2.** branch (on antlers).

'**Stangen|bohne** f runner (or string) bean. **~spargel** m asparagus spears.

stank [ʃtaŋk] pret of **stinken.**

stänkern [ˈʃtɛŋkərn] v/i (h) F contp. stir up trouble: **~ gegen** rail against.

Stanniol [ʃtaˈnioːl] n (-s; -e) tinfoil.

Stanze [ˈʃtantsə] f (-; -n) ⚙ stamp(ing machine). '**stanzen** v/t (h) a) punch, b) stamp.

Stapel [ˈʃtaːpəl] m (-s; -) **1.** pile, stack. **2.** ⚓ stocks: **auf ~ legen** lay down; **vom ~ lassen** launch (a. fig. project etc), fig. deliver (speech), crack (joke); **vom ~ laufen** be launched. '**Stapellauf** m launching. '**stapeln** v/t (h) **1.** stack, (a. sich ~) pile up. **2.** store, stockpile.

stapfen [ˈʃtapfən] v/i (sn) trudge.

Star¹ [ʃtaːr] m (-[e]s; -e) zo. starling.

Star² m (-[e]s; -e) 🌵 **grauer ~** cataract; **grüner ~** glaucoma.

Star³ [staːr; ʃtaːr] m (-s; -s) film etc: star.

'**Staral‚lüren** pl contp. airs and graces.

starb [ʃtarp] pret of **sterben.**

'**Stargast** m star guest.

stark [ʃtark] **I** adj **1.** strong (a. ling. or fig.), w.s. great, intense (heat, cold, etc), heavy (rain, traffic, ⬆ demand, etc): **ein ~es Polizeiaufgebot** a strong force of police; **ein 20 Mann ~er Trupp** a group of 20; **er ist ein ~er Raucher (Esser)** he is a heavy smoker (big eater); fig. **~e Seite** strong point; **sich ~ machen für** stand up for; F **das ist ein ~ Stück!** that's a bit thick! **2.** thick: **2 cm ~e Pappe** pasteboard two centimetres thick; **das Buch ist 150 Seiten ~** the book has 150 pages. **3.** in performance, a. opt., ⚙ strong, powerful, high-powered (engine): **ein ~es Medikament** a powerful (or potent) drug. **4.** stout, corpulent. **5.** bad, severe (cold, pain, etc). **6.** F (echt) ~ super, great. **II** adv strongly, highly, very much: **~ beschädigt** badly damaged; **~ übertrieben** grossly exaggerated; → **erkälten.**

Stärke¹ [ˈʃtɛrkə] f (-; -n) **1.** no pl strength, power. **2.** opt., ⚙ power, a. 🔫 strength. **3.** thickness, diameter. **4.** intensity,

force, a. heaviness (of rain, traffic, etc),
a. severity (of pain etc). **5.** fig. **j-s ~ s.o.'s**
strong point (or forte).

'Stärke² f (-; -n) 🏭 starch.

stärken¹ ['ʃtɛrkən] v/t (h) strengthen (a.
fig.), invigorate: **sich ~** fortify o.s.

'stärken² v/t (h) starch.

'stärkend adj (a. **~es Mittel**) tonic.

'Starkstrom m ⚡ high-voltage (or heavy)
current. **~leitung** f power line. **~tech-
nik** f heavy-current engineering.

'Stärkung f (-; -en) **1.** strengthening. **2.**
refreshment, F pick-me-up.

'Stärkungsmittel n tonic.

starr [ʃtar] adj rigid (a. fig.), stiff, a.
motionless: **~er Blick** (fixed) stare; **ich
war ~ (vor Staunen)** I was dum(b)-
founded.

starren¹ ['ʃtarən] v/i (h) stare (**auf** acc
at).

'starren² v/i (h) **~ vor** (or **von**) be full of;
vor Schmutz ~ be thick with dirt.

'Starrheit f (-; no pl) rigidity (a. fig.),
stiffness.

'starrköpfig [-kœpfɪç] adj pigheaded.

'Starrsinn m (-[e]s; no pl) obstinacy, pigheadedness.

Start [ʃtart] m (-[e]s; -s) start (a. fig.), ✈
takeoff, of rocket etc: liftoff: **✈ zum ~
freigeben** clear for takeoff; sports: **an
den ~ gehen** a) runner etc: take up
one's starting position, b) take part.
~automatik f mot. automatic choke
(control). **~bahn** f ✈ runway.

'startbereit adj ready to start, ✈ ready
for takeoff.

starten ['ʃtartən] **I** v/i (sn) **1.** sports:
start, a. take part (**in** dat, **bei** in). **2.** ✈
take off, rocket etc: lift off. **II** v/t (h)
start, F fig. a. launch. **'Starter** m (-s; -),
'Starterin f (-; -nen) sports: starter.

'Starterlaubnis f **1.** sports: permission
to take part. **2.** ✈ clearance for takeoff.

'Starthilfe f **1.** j-m ~ geben a) mot. give
s.o. a jump-start, b) fig. give s.o. a start
(in life). **2.** Abflug mit ~ assisted
takeoff. **~kabel** n mot. jump leads.

'Startkapi‚tal n start-up capital.

'Startschuß m sports: starting shot.

'Startverbot n sports: suspension, ✈
grounding: **~ erhalten** a) be suspended,
b) be grounded.

Stasi ['ʃtaːzi] f (-; no pl) F DDR pol. hist.
State Security (Service).

Statik ['ʃtaːtɪk] f (-; no pl) △, ⚡, phys.
statics. **Statiker** ['ʃtaːtikər] m (-s; -) △
stress analyst.

Station [ʃtaˈtsǐoːn] f (-; -en) **1.** radio, TV,
etc: station. **2.** 🚂 station, stop: **~ machen** break one's journey. **3.** (hospital)
ward. **4.** fig. stage. **stationär** [ʃtatsǐo-
ˈnɛːr] adj a. ⚕ stationary: **♂ ~e Behandlung** in-patient treatment; **~er** (or
~ behandelter) **Patient** in-patient.

stationieren [ʃtatsǐoˈniːrən] v/t (h) station, deploy (rockets etc). **Statioˈnie-
rung** f (-; -en) stationing, deployment.

Statiˈonsarzt m ward doctor. **~schwe-
ster** f ward sister. **~vorsteher** m 🚂
stationmaster.

statisch ['ʃtaːtɪʃ] adj static.

Statist [ʃtaˈtɪst] m (-en; -en), **Staˈtistin** f
(-; -nen) thea., film: extra.

Statistik [ʃtaˈtɪstɪk] f (-; -en) statistics.
Staˈtistiker [-tikər] m (-s; -) statistician.
staˈtistisch [-tɪʃ] adj statistical.

Stativ [ʃtaˈtiːf] n (-s; -e) tripod.

statt [ʃtat] → **anstatt**.

Statt f **an j-s ~** in s.o.'s place; **an Kindes
~ annehmen** adopt.

Stätte ['ʃtɛtə] f (-; -n) place, a. scene.

'stattfinden v/i (irr, sep, -ge-, h, → finden) take place, be held. **~geben** v/i
(irr, sep, -ge-, h, → geben) adm. grant.

'statthaft adj admissible: **nicht ~** not allowed.

'Statthalter m (-s; -) governor.

'stattlich adj **1.** stately, impressive. **2.**
large (sum etc). **3.** portly: **e-e ~e Erscheinung** a fine figure of a man etc.

Statue ['ʃtaːtuə] f (-; -n) statue.

statuieren [ʃtatuˈiːrən] v/t (h) → **Exempel.**

Statur [ʃtaˈtuːr] f (-; -en) stature (a. fig.).

Status [ʃtaˈtuːs] m (-; -) state, a. (legal)
status. **~symbol** n status symbol.

Stau [ʃtau] m (-[e]s; -s, -e) **1.** accumulation, pile-up. **2.** ♂ congestion. **3.** a)
traffic jam (or congestion), b) tailback.

Staub [ʃtaup] m (-[e]s; no pl) dust: **~
wischen** do the dusting; F **sich aus
dem ~(e) machen** clear off; → **aufwirbeln. 'Staubbeutel** m **1.** ♀ anther. **2.** ⚙
dust bag. **Stäubchen** ['ʃtɔypçən] n (-s;
-) speck of dust, dust particle.

'Staubecken n ⚙ reservoir.

stauben ['ʃtaubən] v/i (h) make a lot of
dust: **es staubt** it's dusty. **'Staubflocke**

f piece of fluff. **'Staubgefäß** *n* ♀ stamen. **'staubig** *adj* dusty. **'staubsaugen** *v/t, v/i* (insep, -ge-, h) vacuum, *Br.* F hoover (*TM*). **'Staubsauger** *m* (-s; -) vacuum cleaner, *Br.* F hoover (*TM*). **'Staubwolke** *f* cloud of dust.

stauchen ['ʃtauxən] *v/t* (h) ⊙ jolt, upset.
'Staudamm *m* dam.
Staude ['ʃtaudə] *f* (-; -n) herbaceous plant.
stauen ['ʃtauən] (h) **I** *v/t* dam up (water), stop (the flow of blood). **II** *sich* ~ water: build up (a. fig. anger, traffic, etc), rise, ice, fig. mail etc: accumulate, pile up, ⚓ be(come) congested.
'Stauer *m* (-s; -) ⚓ stevedore.
staunen ['ʃtaunən] *v/i* (h) (über acc at) be astonished, be amazed, marvel. **'Staunen** *n* (-s) astonishment, amazement: *in* ~ *versetzen* amaze; → **starr.** **'staunenswert** *adj* astonishing, amazing.
Staupe ['ʃtaupə] *f* (-; -n) vet. distemper.
'Stausee *m* reservoir.
'Stauung *f* (-; -en) **1.** damming up. **2.** → **Stau.**
Steak [ste:k] *n* (-s; -s) gastr. steak.
Stearin [ʃtea'ri:n] *n* (-s; -e) stearin.
stechen ['ʃtɛçən] (stach, gestochen, h) **I** *v/t* **1.** prick, wasp etc: sting, gnat: bite: *sich* ~ prick o.s.; *sich in den Finger* ~ prick one's finger; → **Hafer, gestochen. 2.** cut (asparagus, peat, etc), stick, kill (pig etc). **3.** punch (time clock). **4.** engrave (picture). **II** *v/i* **5.** prick, wasp etc: sting, gnat: bite. **6.** *nach j-m* ~ stab at s.o.; *mit et.* ~ *in* (acc) stick s.th. in(to). **7.** sun: burn. **8.** paint: stab, shoot. **9.** sports: jump (or shoot etc) off. **10.** cards: a) be trump, b) trump. **11.** F fig. *j-m in die Augen* ~ catch s.o.'s eye. **'Stechen** *n* (-s) **1.** stabbing (or shooting) pain. **2.** show jumping: jump-off. **'stechend** adj fig. piercing (look), pungent (smell), stabbing (pain), burning (sun).
'Stech|karte *f* time-punch card. **~mükke** *f* mosquito. **~palme** *f* holly. **~uhr** *f* time clock. **~zirkel** *m* dividers.
'Steckbrief *m* **1.** "wanted" circular. **2.** fig. description, fact file (gen of). **'steckbrieflich** *adv* ~ *gesucht werden* be wanted for arrest.
'Steckdose *f* ⚡ (wall) socket.

stecken ['ʃtɛkən] (h) **I** *v/t* a) put, secretly: slip, b) stick (pin etc), c) pin (fabric, paper), d) ⊙ insert (in acc into): fig. *Geld* ~ *in* (acc) put money into, invest in; *j-n ins Gefängnis (Bett)* ~ put s.o. in prison (to bed); F *wer hat ihm das gesteckt?* who told him?; → **Brand** 1, **Nase.** **II** *v/i* be stuck, bullet, splinter, etc: be lodged, person, thing: be: *der Schlüssel steckt* the key is in the lock; F *wo steckst du denn (so lange)?* where have you been (all this time)?; *da steckt 'er dahinter* he's at the bottom of it; *sie steckt mitten in den Prüfungen* she's in the middle of her exams; → **Decke** 1.
'Stecken *m* (-s; -) stick: → **Dreck** 1.
'stecken|bleiben *v/i* (irr, sep, -ge-, sn, → **bleiben**) a. fig. get stuck. **~lassen** *v/t* (irr, sep, -ge-, h, → lassen) *den Schlüssel* ~ leave the key in the lock.
'Steckenpferd *n* hobbyhorse, fig. mst hobby.
'Stecker *m* (-s; -) ⚡ plug.
'Steckkon,takt *m* ⚡ plug (connection).
'Steckling *m* (-s; -e) ♀ cutting.
'Stecknadel *f* pin. **~kopf** *m* pinhead.
'Steckschlüssel *m* ⊙ box spanner.
'Steckschuh *m* phot. accessory shoe.
Steg [ʃte:k] *m* (-[e]s; -e) **1.** footpath. **2.** a) footbridge, b) landing stage, c) gangplank. **3.** bridge (of spectacles, violin).
'Stegreif *m aus dem* ~ off the cuff; *aus dem* ~ *spielen* etc improvise; *aus dem* ~ *sprechen* extemporize, F ad-lib.
stehen ['ʃte:ən] (stand, gestanden, h) **I** *v/i* **1.** stand, be: F *wie steht's?* a) how are things?, b) *wie steht es mit dir?* how about you?, c) a. *wie steht das Spiel?* what's the score?; *wie steht's mit e-m Bier?* how about a beer?; *das Programm steht* the program(me Br.) is complete (or in the bag); *es steht zu befürchten, daß ...* it is to be feared that ...; F *mir steht's bis hier(her)!* I am fed up to here (with it); *gut (schlecht) mit j-m* ~ (not to) get on well with s.o.; *er steht sich gut (dabei)* he's not doing badly (out of it); *unter Alkohol (Drogen)* ~ be under the influence of alcohol (drugs); ~ *vor* be faced with (decision, problem, etc); *er steht vor s-r Prüfung* his exam is coming up; *zu j-m* ~ stand by s.o.; *zu s-m Versprechen* etc ~ keep one's

promise; *wie stehst du dazu?* what do you think (of it)?; *pol.* **er steht links** he belongs to the left; *die Aktie (das Thermometer etc) steht auf ...* the share (the thermometer *etc*) is at ...; *auf Diebstahl steht e-e Freiheitsstrafe* theft is punishable by imprisonment; → *Debatte,* *teuer* II. **2.** stand still, *a. clock etc:* have stopped. **3.** be written, say: *in dem Brief steht* the letter says; *wo steht das?* where does it say so? **4.** *fig. j-m ~ dress etc:* suit so., look well on s.o. II *v/t* → *Mann, Modell, Posten* 2, *Wache etc.* **'Stehen** *n* (-s) (*a. im ~*) standing; *zum ~ bringen* a) bring to a) stop, b) staunch (*bleeding*); *zum ~ kommen* come to a halt, stop.

'stehenbleiben *v/i* (*irr, sep,* -ge-, sn, → *bleiben*) **1.** stop (*a. clock etc*), engine: stall, *heart:* stop (beating); *wo waren wir stehengeblieben?* where did we leave off? **2.** umbrella *etc:* be left (behind); *fig. der Satz kann so nicht ~* the sentence cannot be left like this.

'stehend *adj* standing (*a. army, waters*), stationary; *~e Redensart* stock phrase.

'stehenlassen *v/t* (*irr, sep,* -ge-, h, → *lassen*) **1.** leave (behind): *alles stehen- und liegenlassen* drop everything. **2.** leave *food etc* untouched. **3.** overlook (*mistake*): *fig. das kann man so nicht ~* that's not quite correct. **4.** *j-n ~* leave s.o. standing there. **5.** → *Bart* 1.

'Steher *m* (-s; -) *cycling:* stayer.

'Steh|imbiß *m* stand-up snack bar. **~kragen** *m* stand-up collar. **~lampe** *f* standard (*Am.* floor) lamp.

stehlen *['ʃteːlən] v/t, v/i* (*irr* (stahl, gestohlen, h) steal: *j-m et. ~* steal s.th. from s.o.; *j-m die Zeit ~* waste s.o.'s time; F *er kann mir gestohlen bleiben!* to hell with him!

'Stehplatz *m* standing room.

'Stehvermögen *n* (-s; *no pl*) stamina, staying power.

steif *[ʃtaif] adj* stiff (*a. fig.*), *a.* ⊗ rigid: *~ vor Kälte* numb with cold; *~e Brise* (*~er Grog*) stiff breeze (grog); *gastr. ~ schlagen* beat (until stiff); F *~ und fest behaupten* insist, swear.

steifen *['ʃtaifən] v/t* (h) *fig. j-m den Nacken* (*or Rücken*) *~* stiffen s.o.'s back.

'Steifheit *f* (-; *no pl*) *a. fig.* stiffness.

'Steigbügel *m* stirrup. **'Steigeisen** *n* climbing iron, *mount. a.* crampon.

steigen *['ʃtaigən]* (stieg, gestiegen, sn) I *v/i* **1.** go up, climb (up), rise (*into the air*), ✈ climb (*auf acc* to): *auf e-n Baum* (*Berg*) *~* climb (up) a tree (mountain); *auf ein Pferd ~* mount a horse; *vom Pferd ~* dismount; *aus dem Bus etc ~* get out (*or* off) the bus *etc*; *in den Zug etc ~* get on (*or* board) a train *etc*; *~ lassen* fly (*kite*), send up (*balloon*); → *Kopf* 1. **2.** increase, grow, *temperature etc:* rise, *prices: a.* go up: → *Achtung* 1, *Wert* 1. **3.** F be on, take place: *e-e Party ~ lassen* throw a party. II *v/t* **4.** go up: *Treppen ~* climb stairs. **'Steigen** *n* (-s) **1.** climbing (*etc,* → I). **2.** rise, increase: *das ~ und Fallen* the rise and fall; *im ~ begriffen sein* be rising. **'steigend** *adj fig.* rising, increasing: *~e Tendenz* upward tendency.

'Steiger *m* (-s; -) ⚒ pit foreman.

steigern *['ʃtaigərn]* (h) I *v/t* **1.** increase, *a.* heighten (*effect, suspense, etc*), step up (*pace, production, etc*), raise (*bet, offer, etc*): *s-e Leistung ~* improve one's performance; *den Wert ~* add to the value (*gen* of). **2.** *ling.* compare. II *sich ~* **3.** a) increase, *a.* grow, *interest, suspense, etc:* rise, b) improve (one's performance). III *v/i* a) at auction: bid, b) rise the amount (*auf acc* to). **'Steigerung** *f* (-; -en) **1.** a) increase, rise, b) improvement. **2.** *ling.* comparison.

'Steigfähigkeit *f* ✈ climbing power, *mot.* hill-climbing ability.

'Steigung *f* (-; -en) rise, ascent, gradient.

steil *[ʃtail] adj a. fig.* steep: *~e Karriere* meteoric career; *~ ansteigen* rise steeply, *prices: a.* soar. **'Steilkurve** *f* steep turn. **'Steilküste** *f* steep coast. **'Steilpaß** *m* soccer: through pass.

Stein *[ʃtain] m* (-[e]s; -e) a) stone (*a.* ⚑, ⚮), ⊗ *a.* brick, b) (precious) stone, gem, jewel, *of watch:* ruby, c) *board games:* piece: *fig. den ~ ins Rollen bringen* set the ball rolling; *bei j-m e-n ~ im Brett haben* be in s.o.'s good books; *mir fällt ein ~ vom Herzen* that takes a load off my mind; → *Tropfen* 1. **~adler** *m zo.* golden eagle. **~alt** *adj* ancient. **~bock** *m* **1.** *zo.* ibex. **2.** *no pl astr.* (*[ein] ~ sein* be [a]) Capricorn. **~bruch** *m* quarry. **~butt** *m zo.* turbot. **~druck** *m*

(-[e]s; -e) **1.** *no pl* lithography. **2.** lithograph.
'steinern *adj* (of) stone, *fig.* stony.
'Steinfrucht *f* stone fruit.
'Steingarten *m* rock garden.
'Steingut *n* (-[e]s; -e) earthenware.
'steinig *adj* stony.
'Steinkohle *f* hard coal.
'Steinmetz [-mɛts] *m* (-en; -en) stonemason.
'Steinobst *n* stone fruit.
'Steinpilz *m* edible boletus.
'steinreich *adj* F filthy rich.
'Steinschlag *m* falling rocks.
'Steinzeit *f* (-; *no pl*) Stone Age.
Steiß [ʃtaɪs] *m* (-es; -e) buttocks, rump.
'Steißbein *n anat.* coccyx.
'Stelldichein *n* (-[s]; -[s]) rendezvous.
Stelle ['ʃtɛlə] *f* (-; -n) **1.** place, spot, point, position: ***an dieser ~*** here; ***an anderer ~*** elsewhere; ***an erster ~*** in the first place, first(ly); ***an erster ~ stehen*** come first; ***an ~ von*** (*or gen*) in place of, instead of; (***ich***) ***an d-r ~*** if I were you; ***an die ~ treten von*** (*or gen*) take the place of, *person*: *a.* take over from, replace; ***auf der ~*** on the spot; *fig.* ***auf der ~ treten*** mark time; ***nicht von der ~ kommen*** not to make any progress; ***er rührte sich nicht von der ~*** he didn't budge; ***zur ~ sein*** be at hand. **2.** passage (*a.* ♪). **3.** ⩚ a) digit, b) (decimal) place. **4.** situation, job, post: ***freie*** (*or* ***offene***) ***~*** vacancy. **5.** → ***Dienststelle.***
stellen ['ʃtɛlən] (h) **I** *v/t* **1.** put, place, set, arrange: → ***Antrag*** 1, ***Bedingung, Bein, Falle, Frage*** 1, ***gestellt.*** **2.** set *clock etc* (***auf*** *acc* at), adjust: ***leiser*** (*or* ***niedriger***) ***~*** turn down; ***lauter*** (*or* ***höher***) ***~*** turn up. **3.** provide, supply. **4.** hunt down (*game, criminal*). **II *sich ~*** **5.** place o.s.: ***stell dich dorthin!*** (go and) stand over there; ***auf sich selbst gestellt sein*** be on one's own; ***gut*** (***schlecht***) ***gestellt sein*** be well (badly) off; ***sich gegen ... ~*** oppose; ***sich hinter*** (***vor***) ***j-n ~*** back s.o. up (shield s.o.); ***wie stellt er sich dazu?*** what does he say (to this)? **6.** ***sich*** (***der Polizei***) ***~*** turn o.s. in; ***sich*** (***zum Wehrdienst***) ***~*** report for military service. **7.** (*dat*) take on *opponent*, face up to *criticism etc*, take up *challenge*: ***sich der Presse ~*** be prepared to meet (*or* face) the Press. **8.** ***sich krank*** *etc* ***~*** pretend to be ill *etc.*
'Stellen|angebot *n* job offer: ***~e*** *newspaper*: vacancies. **~gesuch** *n* application (for a job): ***~e*** *newspaper*: situations wanted. **~markt** *m* job market. **~suche** *f* (***auf ~ sein*** be) job-hunting. **~wechsel** *m* job change.
'stellenweise *adv* in places.
'Stellenwert *m* rating, (relative) importance: ***e-n hohen ~ haben*** rate high.
...stellig [-ʃtɛlɪç] *in cpds.* ...-digit.
'Stellplatz *m mot.* carport.
'Stellschraube *f* ⚙ adjusting screw.
'Stellung *f* (-; -en) **1.** *a.* ⚔ position: *fig.* ***die ~ halten*** hold the fort; ***~ nehmen*** (***zu***) take a stand (on), give one's view (on); ***~ nehmen für*** stand up for; ***~ nehmen gegen*** oppose. **2.** situation, job, post, position: ***e-e leitende ~*** an executive position. **3.** a) position, rank, b) status, standing.
'Stellungnahme *f* (-; -n) (***zu*** on) opinion, comment, statement.
'Stellungskrieg *m* static warfare.
'stellungslos *adj* unemployed, jobless.
'Stellungs|spiel *n sports*: positional play. **~suche** *f* search for a post (*or* job): ***auf ~ sein*** be looking for a job, be job-hunting. **~suchende** *m, f* (-n; -n) person looking for a job, job-hunter. **~wechsel** *m* change of post (*or* job): ***häufiger ~*** job-hopping.
'stellvertretend *adj* acting, deputy: ***~er Vorsitzender*** vice-chairman; ***~ für*** a) acting for, b) on behalf of.
'Stellvertreter(in *f*) *m* representative, substitute, *of doctor etc*: locum (tenens), *adm.* deputy, ✝, ⚖ proxy.
'Stellvertretung *f* representation, ✝, ⚖ proxy: ***j-s ~ übernehmen*** act as representative of s.o.
'Stellwerk *n* 🚂 signal box.
Stelze ['ʃtɛltsə] *f* (-; -n) stilt.
stelzen ['ʃtɛltsən] *v/i* (sn) stalk (along).
'Stemmbogen *m skiing*: stem turn.
'Stemmeisen *n* ⚙ mortise chisel.
stemmen ['ʃtɛmən] *v/t* (h) **1.** press: ***sich ~ gegen*** press against, *fig.* resist. **2.** heave up, *sports*: lift.
Stempel ['ʃtɛmpəl] *m* (-s; -) **1.** stamp (*a. fig.*), *a.* seal. **2.** postmark. **3.** ⚙ die. **4.** hallmark. **5.** ⚘ pistil. **~farbe** *f* stamp(ing) ink. **~kissen** *n* ink pad.
'stempeln (h) **I** *v/t* **1.** a) stamp, b) cancel:

fig. j-n ~ zu stamp (*or* label, *b.s.* brand) s.o. as. **II** *v/i* **2.** *employee:* clock in (out). **3.** F ~ *gehen* be on the dole.

'**Stempeluhr** *f* time clock.

Stengel ['ʃtɛŋəl] *m* (-s; -) stalk, stem.

Stenogramm [ʃteno'gram] *n* (-s; -e) shorthand notes. **Stenograph** [-'graːf] *m* (-en; -en) stenographer. **Stenographie** [-gra'fiː] *f* (-; -n) stenography, shorthand. **stenographieren** [-gra'fiːrən] (h) **I** *v/i* write shorthand. **II** *v/t* take down in shorthand. **stenographisch** [-'graːfiʃ] *adj* shorthand.

Stenotypistin [ʃtenoty'pistin] *f* (-; -nen) shorthand typist.

'**Steppdecke** *f* (continental) quilt.

Steppe ['ʃtɛpə] *f* (-; -n) steppe.

steppen[1] ['ʃtɛpən] *v/t* (h) backstitch.

steppen[2] *v/i* (h) tap-dance.

'**Stepptanz** *m* tap dance.

'**Sterbe|bett** *n* (*auf dem ~* on one's) deathbed. **~fall** *m* (case of) death. **~hilfe** *f* euthanasia. **~klinik** *f* hospice.

sterben ['ʃtɛrbən] *v/i* (starb, gestorben, sn) die (*an dat, fig. vor dat* of). '**Sterben** *n* (-s) dying, death: *im ~ liegen* be dying; *zum ~ langweilig* deadly dull.

'**sterbenskrank** *adj* mortally ill.

'**Sterbens|wort** *n,* **~wörtchen** *n kein ~ sagen* not to breathe a word.

'**Sterbesakra|mente** *pl* last rites.

'**Sterbeurkunde** *f* death certificate.

sterblich ['ʃtɛrplɪç] *adj* mortal: *iro. gewöhnliche* **2***e* ordinary mortals. '**Sterblichkeit** *f* (-; *no pl*) mortality.

Stereo..., **stereo...** ['ʃte:reo] stereo. '**Stereo|anlage** *f* stereo system. **~aufnahme** *f* stereo recording. **~bild** *n* stereoscopic picture. **~gerät** *n* stereo set.

stereophon [-'foːn] *adj* stereophonic. **stereoskopisch** [-'skoːpɪʃ] *adj* stereoscopic.

'**Stereoton** *m* stereo sound.

stereotyp [-'typ] *adj fig.* stereotyped.

steril [ʃteˈriːl] *adj* sterile. **sterilisieren** [ʃteriliˈziːrən] *v/t* (h) sterilize. **Sterilisation** [ʃteriliza'tsioːn] *f* (-; -en) sterilization. **Sterilität** [ʃteriliˈtɛːt] *f* (-; *no pl*) sterility.

Stern [ʃtɛrn] *m* (-[e]s; -e) *a. fig.* star: *unter e-m glücklichen* (*unglücklichen*) ~ *stehen* have fortune on one's side (be ill-fated); F *~e sehen* see stars.

'**Sternbild** *n* **1.** constellation. **2.** sign of the zodiac.

'**Sternchen** *n* **1.** little star, starlet (*a. fig. actress*). **2.** *print.* asterisk.

'**Sternenbanner:** *das ~* the Star-Spangled Banner, the Stars and Stripes.

'**Sternenhimmel** *m* starry sky.

'**Sternfahrt** *f mot.* car rally.

'**sternförmig** *adj* star-shaped.

'**sternhagel'voll** *adj* F rolling drunk.

'**sternhell,** '**sternklar** *adj* starlit.

'**Sternmarsch** *m* demonstration march from different starting points.

'**Sternschnuppe** *f* (-; -n) shooting star.

'**Sternstunde** *f fig.* great moment.

'**Sternwarte** *f* (-; -n) observatory.

stet [ʃteːt] → *stetig, Tropfen* 1.

Stethoskop [ʃtetoˈskoːp] *n* (-s; -e) ⚕ stethoscope.

'**stetig** *adj* continual, constant, steady. '**Stetigkeit** *f* (-; *no pl*) constancy, steadiness. **stets** *adv* always, constantly.

Steuer[1] ['ʃtɔyər] *n* (-s; -) ⚓ helm, rudder, *mot.* (steering) wheel, ✈ controls: *am ~* at the helm (*a. fig.*), at the wheel.

Steuer[2] *f* (-; -n) (*auf acc* on) a) tax, b) duty, c) rate, *Am.* local tax: *vor* (*nach*) *Abzug der ~n* before (after) tax.

'**Steuer|abzug** *m* tax deduction. **~aufkommen** *n* tax yield. **~ausgleich** *m* tax equalization. **~befreiung** *f* tax exemption. **2begünstigt** *adj* a) tax-privileged, b) tax-linked (*saving*). **~belastung** *f* tax burden. **~berater(in** *f*) *m* tax adviser. **~bescheid** *m* tax assessment.

'**Steuerbord** *n,* '**steuerbord(s)** *adv* ⚓ starboard.

'**Steuer|de,likt** *n* tax offen/ce (*Am.* -se). **~einnahmen** *pl* → *Steueraufkommen*. **~erklärung** *f* tax return. **~erleichterung** *f* tax relief. **~ermäßigung** *f* tax allowance. **2frei** *adj* tax-free. **~freibetrag** *m* tax-free allowance. **~hinterzieher** *m* tax dodger. **~hinterziehung** *f* tax fraud. **~karte** *f* (wage) tax card. **~klasse** *f* tax bracket.

'**Steuerknüppel** *m* ✈ control stick, F joystick.

'**steuerlich** *adj* tax ...: *aus ~en Gründen* for tax purposes; *~ günstig* with low tax liability; *~ veranlagen* assess for taxation.

'**Steuermann** *m* **1.** ⚓ helmsman (*a. fig.*). **2.** *rowing:* coxswain.

'**Steuermarke** f revenue stamp.

steuern ['ʃtɔʏərn] **I** v/t (h) steer, mot. a. drive, ✈, ⚓ a. navigate, pilot, ⚙ control. **II** v/i (h or sn) steer, mot. a. drive, ⚓ a. head (**nach Süden** southward).

'**Steuero|ase** f tax haven.
'**steuerpflichtig** adj taxable.
'**Steuer|poli,tik** f fiscal policy. **∼progressi,on** f progressive taxation.
'**Steuerpult** n ⚙ control desk.
'**Steuerrad** n ⚓, mot. (steering) wheel.
'**steuerrechtlich** adj and adv under the tax laws.
Steuer|rückerstattung f tax refund. **∼satz** m tax rate. **∼schuld** f tax(es) due. **∼senkung** f tax reduction.
'**Steuerung** f (-; -en) **1.** steering, ✈ piloting, ≴, ⚙ control (a. fig.). **2.** control system, mot. steering, ✈ controls.
'**Steuerveranlagung** f assessment.
'**Steuervorteil** m tax benefit.
'**Steuerzahler(in** f) m taxpayer.
Steward ['stju:ərt] m (-s; -s) steward.
Stewardeß ['stju:ərdes] f (-; -dessen) stewardess, air hostess.
Stich [ʃtɪç] m (-es; -e) **1.** with knife: stab, thrust, (needle) prick, (wasp etc) sting, (gnat) bite: fig. **es gab ihr e-n ∼** it cut her to the quick. **2.** sewing: stitch. **3.** (copper etc) engraving. **4.** stitch, stabbing pain. **5.** fig. cut, dig. **6. im ∼ lassen** abandon, desert, j-n a. leave s.o. in the lurch, let s.o. down; **sein Gedächtnis ließ ihn im ∼** his memory failed him. **7. e-n ∼ haben** a) milk etc: be off, b) F person: be a bit touched. **8. e-n ∼ ins Blaue** a tinge of blue. **9.** cards: **e-n ∼ machen** make a trick.
Stiche'lei f (-; -en) needling: **∼en** a. gibe(s). **sticheln** ['ʃtɪçəln] v/i (h) fig. (**gegen** at) gibe, make snide remarks.
'**Stichflamme** f jet of flame, flash.
'**stichhaltig** adj valid, sound: **das Argument ist nicht ∼** the argument doesn't hold water. '**Stichhaltigkeit** f (-; no pl) validity, soundness.
'**Stichling** m (-s; -e) zo. stickleback.
'**Stichprobe** f **e-e ∼ machen** carry out a spot check, ✝ take a random sample, customs: make a random search.
'**Stichtag** m a) effective day, b) deadline.
'**Stichwahl** f second ballot.
'**Stichwort** n (-[e]s) **1.** (pl -e) esp. thea. (**auf ∼** on) cue: **∼ „Umwelt"** à propos

"Environment". **2.** (pl ∼er) headword. **3. ∼e** pl notes: **das Wichtigste in ∼en** an outline of the main points; '**stichwortartig** adj and adv in brief outlines. '**Stichwortverzeichnis** n index.
'**Stichwunde** f stab wound.
sticken ['ʃtɪkən] v/t, v/i (h) embroider.
Sticke'rei f (-; -en) embroidery.
stickig ['ʃtɪkɪç] adj stuffy, close.
'**Sticko,xyd** n ⚗ nitrogen oxide.
'**Stickstoff** m (-[e]s; no pl) ⚗ nitrogen.
'**stickstoffhaltig** adj nitrogenous.
'**Stiefbruder** ['ʃti:f-] m stepbrother.
Stiefel ['ʃti:fəl] m (-s; -) boot. **Stiefelette** [ʃti:fə'letə] f (-; -n) ankle boot, (ladies') bootee. '**stiefeln** v/i (sn) F trudge.
'**Stiefmutter** f a. fig. stepmother. '**Stiefmütterchen** n (-s; -) ✿ pansy. '**stiefmütterlich** adv **∼ behandeln** neglect badly. '**Stiefschwester** f stepsister. '**Stiefsohn** m stepson. '**Stieftochter** f stepdaughter. '**Stiefvater** m stepfather.
stieg [ʃti:k] pret of **steigen**.
Stieglitz ['ʃti:glɪts] m (-es; -e) goldfinch.
Stiel [ʃti:l] m (-[e]s; -e) **1.** handle, stem (of glass, pipe), (broom)stick: **Eis am ∼** lolly. **2.** ⚘ stalk, stem.
'**Stielaugen** pl F **∼ machen** goggle.
Stier [ʃti:r] m (-[e]s; -e) **1.** zo. bull: fig. **den ∼ bei den Hörnern fassen** take the bull by the horns. **2.** no pl astr. ([**ein**] **∼ sein** be a]) Taurus.
'**stieren** v/i (h) stare (**auf** acc at).
'**Stierkampf** m bullfight. '**Stierkämpfer** m bullfighter.
'**stiernackig** [-nakɪç] adj bullnecked.
stieß [ʃti:s] pret of **stoßen**.
Stift¹ [ʃtɪft] m (-[e]s; -e) **1.** a) pin, b) peg, c) stud. **2.** a) pencil, b) crayon. **3.** cosmetics: stick. **4.** F apprentice.
Stift² n (-[e]s; -e) religious foundation.
stiften ['ʃtɪftən] v/t (h) **1.** found. **2.** give, donate. **3.** cause: → **Unfrieden** etc.
'**Stifter** m (-s; -) **1.** founder. **2.** donor.
'**Stiftung** f (-; -en) **1.** foundation. **2.** donation.
'**Stiftzahn** m pivot tooth.
Stil [ʃti:l] m (-[e]s; -e) style: **im großen ∼, großen ∼s** on a large scale, large-scale; **das ist schlechter ∼** that's bad style. '**Stilblüte** f howler. '**Stilbruch** m break in style. '**Stilebene** f ling. level of style.
'**stilecht** adj in period.
Stilett [ʃti'lɛt] n (-s; -e) stiletto.

'**Stilgefühl** n sense of style.

stilisieren [ʃtili'ziːrən] v/t (h) stylize.

Stilist [ʃti'lɪst] m (-en; -en) stylist (a. sports etc). **Sti'listik** [-tık] f (-; no pl) stylistics. **sti'listisch** adj stylistic.

'**Stilkunde** f → **Stilistik**.

still [ʃtıl] adj a) quiet, silent, still, b) calm, peaceful, c) secret (a. hope, love, etc): **~e Jahreszeit** dead season; **~e Reserven** hidden reserves; **~er Teilhaber** sleeping (Am. silent) partner; **~e Übereinkunft** tacit understanding; (**sei**) **~!** (be) quiet!; **im ~en** inwardly, secretly; → **Wasser** 1. **Stille** f (-; no pl) a) silence, b) quiet, calm, c) hush: **die ~ vor dem Sturm** the calm before the storm; **in aller ~** quietly, a. secretly.

'**Stilleben** n (-s; -) paint. still life.

'**stillegen** v/t (sep, -ge-, h) **1.** shut down (firm), by strike: paralyse. **2.** lay up (car), put machine etc out of operation. '**Stillegung** f (-; -en) **1.** shutdown. **2.** mot. laying-up.

stillen ['ʃtılən] v/t (h) **1.** nurse, breast-feed: **~de Mutter** nursing mother. **2.** stop, sta(u)nch (bleeding), quench (thirst), satisfy (desire), soothe (pain).

'**Stillhalteabkommen** n pol. standstill agreement. '**stillhalten** v/i (irr, sep, -ge-, h, → **halten**) **1.** keep still. **2.** fig. keep quiet. '**stilliegen** v/i (irr, sep, -ge-, h, → **liegen**) **1.** lie still. **2.** fig. lie dormant, works: lie idle.

'**stillos** adj in bad style, tasteless.

'**stillschweigen** v/i (irr, sep, -ge-, h, → **schweigen**) be quiet, be silent, say nothing. '**Stillschweigen** n (-s) silence: (**strengstes**) **~ bewahren** maintain (absolute) silence (**über** acc on).

'**stillschweigend I** adj **1.** silent. **2.** fig. tacit. **II** adv **3.** in silence, without a word. **4.** fig. tacitly.

'**Stillstand** m (-[e]s; no pl) standstill, stoppage, fig. a. stagnation, of negotiations: deadlock: **zum ~ bringen** stop; **zum ~ kommen** come to a standstill, stop, negotiations: reach a deadlock.

'**stillstehen** v/i (irr, sep, -ge-, h, → **stehen**) **1.** stand still, come to a standstill, stop, ⚙ be idle, be out of action: **~d** a. stagnant. **2.** ✗ stand to attention: **stillgestanden!** attention!

'**Stillzeit** f nursing period.

'**Stilmöbel** pl period furniture.

'**Stilvoll** adj stylish: **~ sein** have style.

'**Stimm|abgabe** f voting. **~band** n anat. vocal c(h)ord. ⚹**berechtigt** adj eligible to vote. **~bildung** f ♪ voice training. **~bruch** m (-[e]s; no pl) change of voice: **er ist im ~** his voice is breaking.

'**Stimme** ['ʃtımə] f (-; -n) **1.** (**mit lauter etc ~** in a loud etc) voice. **2.** ♪ a) voice, b) part: **gut bei ~ sein** be in good voice. **3.** fig. voice, opinion: **die ~n mehren sich, die fordern ...** there is a growing number of people calling for ... **4.** vote: **entscheidende ~** casting vote; **s-e ~ abgeben** (cast one's) vote; **sich der ~ enthalten** abstain (from voting).

stimmen ['ʃtımən] (h) **I** v/t **1.** ♪ tune (**nach** to). **2.** **j-n glücklich** (**traurig** etc) **~** make s.o. happy (sad etc). **II** v/i **3.** be right, be correct, be true: **da stimmt et. nicht** a) there is s.th. wrong here, b) there is s.th. fishy going on. **4.** **~ für** (**gegen**) vote for (against).

'**Stimmen|fang** m vote catching. **~gleichheit** f (**bei ~** in the event of a) tie. **~mehrheit** f majority (of votes).

'**Stimm|enthaltung** f abstention (from voting). **~gabel** f ♪ tuning fork.

'**stimmhaft** adj ling. voiced.

'**Stimmlage** f ♪ register, voice.

'**stimmlos** adj ling. voiceless, unvoiced.

'**Stimmrecht** n (right to) vote: **allgemeines ~** universal suffrage.

'**Stimmung** f (-; -en) **1.** mood (a. ♪, paint.), spirits, fig. a. atmosphere, ✗ etc: morale: **in guter** (**gedrückter**) **~ sein** be in high (low) spirits; **festliche ~** festive mood (or atmosphere); **nicht in der ~ sein zu** inf not to be in the mood to inf, not to feel like ger; **für ~ sorgen** liven things up. **2.** opinion.

'**Stimmungs|baro,meter** n F barometer of opinion. **~mache** f (-; no pl) F contp. propaganda. **~mu,sik** f mood music. **~umschwung** m change of mood.

'**stimmungsvoll** adj atmospheric: **~e Musik** mood music.

'**Stimmzettel** m ballot paper.

Stimulans ['ʃti:mulans] n (-; -lantia [ʃti-mu'lantsia]) ⚕ or fig. stimulant. **stimulieren** [ʃtimu'li:rən] v/t (h) stimulate.

'**Stinkbombe** f stink bomb.

stinken ['ʃtıŋkən] v/i (stank, gestunken, h) stink (**nach** of, a. fig.): F **das** (**er**) **stinkt mir!** I'm sick of it (him).

'**stink**|'**faul** *adj* F bone-lazy. **~'langwei-
lig** *adj* F deadly boring. **~'reich** *adj* F
stinking rich.
'**Stink**|**tier** *n* skunk. **~wut** *f* F **e-e ~ haben**
be hopping mad (**auf** *acc* with).
Stipendiat [ʃtipen'diaːt] *m* (-en; -en)
scholarship holder. **Stipendium** [ʃti-
'pendiʊm] *n* (-s; -dien) scholarship.
'**Stippvi**|**site** *f* F flying visit.
Stirn [ʃtɪrn] *f* (-; -en) forehead: *fig.* **die ~
haben zu** *inf* have the cheek to *inf*; **j-m
die ~ bieten** face up to s.o. squarely; →
runzeln. ~band *n* (-[e]s; ˮer) headband.
~höhle *f anat.* (frontal) sinus. **~höh-
lenentzündung** *f* frontal sinusitis.
~runzeln *n* (-s) frown(ing). **~seite** *f*
front (side *or* end). **~wand** *f* front (*or*
end) wall.
stöbern ['ʃtøːbərn] *v/i* (h) (**nach** for)
rummage (around), *dog:* hunt about.
stochern ['ʃtɔxərn] *v/i* (h) **in** (*dat*)
poke; **in den Zähnen** (**s-m Essen**) **~**
pick one's teeth (at one's food).
Stock [ʃtɔk] *m* (-[e]s; ˮe) **1.** a) stick, b)
cane, c) (billiard) cue, d) ♪ baton. **2.** ♀
stock: **über ~ und Stein** up hill and
down dale. **3.** (bee)hive. **4.** → **Stockwerk.**
'**stockbe**'**soffen** *adj* F paralytic.
'**stock**'**dunkel** *adj* F pitch-dark.
Stöckelschuhe ['ʃtœkəl-] *pl* stilettos.
stocken ['ʃtɔkən] *v/i* (h) **1.** a) stop short,
voice: falter, b) hesitate: **~d sprechen**
speak haltingly. **2.** *trade etc:* stagnate,
slacken off, *negotiations etc:* reach a
deadlock, *traffic:* be at a standstill: **ihr
stockte das Herz** (**der Atem**) her heart
missed a beat (she caught her breath).
'**Stocken** *n* (-s) **ins ~ geraten** → **stocken**.
'**Stockfisch** *m* dried cod.
...stöckig [-ʃtœkɪç] *in cpds* ...-storied.
'**stock**|**konserva**'**tiv** *adj* F ultra-conser-
vative. **~'nüchtern** *adj* F stone-cold sober. **~'sauer** *adj* F furious. **~'steif** *adj* F
(as) stiff as a poker, starchy. **~'taub** *adj*
F stone-deaf.
'**Stockung** *f* (-; -en) hold-up, interruption, *in negotiations etc:* a. deadlock, *in
talks etc:* pause, ♏ stagnation.
'**Stockwerk** *n* store(y), floor: **im ersten ~**
on the first (*Am.* second) floor.
Stoff [ʃtɔf] *m* (-[e]s; -e) **1.** ♠ substance,
stuff (*a.* F alcohol, *drug*), agent. **2.** material, *a.* fabric, cloth. **3.** *fig.* a) subject

matter, b) topic (for discussion): **~ zu
e-m Roman** material for a novel. **~mu-
ster** *n* pattern. **~tier** *n* stuffed animal.
'**Stoffwechsel** *m* metabolism. **~krank-
heit** *f* metabolic disorder.
stöhnen ['ʃtøːnən] *v/i* (h) groan.
'**Stöhnen** *n* (-s) groaning, groan(s).
stoisch ['ʃtoːɪʃ] *adj* stoical.
Stola ['ʃtoːla] *f* (-; Stolen) stole.
Stollen ['ʃtɔlən] *m* (-s; -) **1.** ⚒ tunnel. **2.**
stud (*on shoe etc*). **3.** *gastr.* fruit loaf.
stolpern ['ʃtɔlpərn] *v/i* (sn) (**über** *acc*
over) *a. fig.* stumble, trip.
'**Stolperstein** *m fig.* stumbling block.
stolz [ʃtɔlts] *adj* **1.** proud (**auf** *acc* of). **2.**
fig. proud, splendid: *iro.* **~e Preise**
(**Summe**) steep prices (tidy sum).
Stolz *m* (-es; *no pl*) pride (*a. fig.*): **voller
~, mit ~** proudly.
stolzieren [ʃtɔl'tsiːrən] *v/i* (sn) strut.
stopfen ['ʃtɔpfən] (h) **I** *v/t* **1.** darn, mend:
→ **Loch** 1. **2.** cram, stuff: **gestopft voll**
crammed (full). **3.** fill (*hole, pipe, sausage, etc*): *fig.* **j-m den Mund ~** silence
s.o. **4.** stuff (*geese etc*). **II** *v/i* **5.** ♫ cause
constipation.
'**Stopfgarn** *n* darning cotton.
stopp [ʃtɔp] *int* stop. **Stopp** *m* (-s; -s)
stop, *a.* (*price, wage, etc*) freeze.
Stoppel ['ʃtɔpəl] *f* (-; -n) stubble. **~bart** *m*
stubbly beard. **~feld** *n* stubble field.
'**stopp(e)lig** *adj* stubbly.
stoppen ['ʃtɔpən] *v/t* (h) **1.** a. *v/i* stop. **2.**
sports etc: time, clock.
'**Stopp**|**schild** *n mot.* stop sign. **~taste** *f*
stop button. **~uhr** *f* stop watch.
Stöpsel ['ʃtœpsəl] *m* (-s; -) stopper, cork,
for bathtub etc, a. ⚡ plug.
stöpseln ['ʃtœpsəln] *v/t* (h) *a.* ⚡ plug.
Stör [ʃtøːr] *m* (-[e]s; -e) *zo.* sturgeon.
'**Störakti**|**on** *f* disruptive action.
'**störanfällig** *adj* ✪ sensitive, trouble-
-prone, ⚡ interference-prone.
Storch [ʃtɔrç] *m* (-[e]s; ˮe) *zo.* stork.
Store [ʃtoːr] *m* (-s; -s) net curtain.
stören ['ʃtøːrən] (h) **I** *v/t* a) disturb, b)
bother, c) disrupt (*meeting etc*), d) jam
(*radio station*), interfere with (*reception*): **j-s Pläne ~** upset s.o.'s plans; **das
(Gesamt)Bild ~** mar the picture; **was
mich daran** (**an ihr**) **stört** what I don't
like about it (her); **lassen Sie sich
nicht ~!** don't let me disturb you; **darf
ich Sie kurz ~?** may I trouble you for a

minute?; **stört es Sie(, wenn ich rauche)?** do you mind (if I smoke)?; **das stört mich nicht** I don't mind (that); **er stört mich nicht** he doesn't bother me; → **gestört. II** *v/i* a) interfere, b) be in the way, c) be a nuisance, d) be an eyesore, e) *sports:* tackle: *„Bitte nicht ~!"* "please do not disturb!" '**störend** *adj* disturbing, troublesome, annoying.
'**Störenfried** [-fri:t] *m* (-[e]s; -e) troublemaker.
'**Störfaktor** *m* disruptive element.
'**Störfall** *m* ⚙ breakdown, accident.
stornieren [ʃtɔrˈniːrən] *v/t* (h) ✝ reverse (*entry*), cancel (*order*). **Stor'nierung** *f* (-; -en), **Storno** [ˈʃtɔrno] *n* (-s; Storni) reversal, cancellation.
Störrigkeit [ˈʃtœrɪçkaɪt] *f* (-; *no pl*) stubbornness, obstinacy, restiveness.
störrisch [ˈʃtœrɪʃ] *adj* stubborn, obstinate, restive (*horse*).
'**Störsender** *m* jamming station.
'**Störung** *f* (-; -en) disturbance, ♂ disorder, ⚙ trouble, defect, breakdown, interruption: **verzeihen Sie die ~!** sorry to disturb you; (**atmosphärische**) **~** a) statics, b) interference, c) jamming.
'**störungsfrei** *adj* undisturbed, ⚙ trouble-free, *radio, TV:* interference-free.
'**Störungsstelle** *f teleph. the* engineers.
Stoß [ʃtoːs] *m* (-es; ⁓e) **1.** a) push, b) kick, c) butt, d) dig, e) *a. fenc.* thrust, *swimming, billiards:* stroke, *shot-put:* put, f) jolt, bump, shock, *a. phys.* impact: *fig.* **j-m e-n ~ versetzen** shake s.o.; **sich** (*or* **s-m Herzen**) **e-n ~ geben** make an effort; **gib d-m Herzen e-n ~!** be a sport! **2.** ♂ massive dose (*of vitamines etc*), rush (*of adrenaline*). **3.** pile, a. stack (*of wood etc*), a. batch (*of letters*).
'**Stoßdämpfer** *m mot.* shock-absorber.
Stößel [ˈʃtøːsəl] *m* (-s; -) **1.** pestle. **2.** *mot.* tappet.
stoßen [ˈʃtoːsən] (stieß, gestoßen, h) **I** *v/t* **1.** push, poke, *a.* kick, *a.* butt, *a.* jostle: **von sich ~** push away, *fig.* reject; **er stieß ihr das Messer in die Brust** he plunged his knife into her chest. **2.** *sports:* **die Kugel ~** put the shot. **3.** pound. **II sich ~ 4.** hurt o.s.; **sich ~ an** (*dat*) a) knock (*or* bump) against, b) *fig.* object to, take exception to. **III** *v/i* **5.** push (*etc*, → 1). **6.** (sn) **~ an** (*acc*) a) **~ gegen** a) knock against, bump into, b)

border on; **er stieß mit dem Kopf an die Wand** he bumped his head against the wall; *fig.* **~ auf** (*acc*) a) come across, stumble on, b) meet with (*opposition etc*); **~ zu** join (up with) (*s.o., party, etc*); → **Horn** 2, **Kopf** 1.
'**stoßfest** *adj* shockproof.
'**Stoß|gebet** *n* quick prayer. **~kraft** *f* (-; *no pl*) *fig.* impetus, force. **~seufzer** *m* deep sigh. **~stange** *f mot.* bumper. **~trupp** *m* ✕ assault party. **~verkehr** *m* rush-hour traffic.
'**stoßweise** *adv* intermittently, sporadically, by fits and starts.
'**Stoß|zahn** *m zo.* tusk. **~zeit** *f* a) peak hours, b) rush hour.
'**Stotterer** *m* (-s; -) stutterer, stammerer.
stottern [ˈʃtɔtərn] *v/i, v/t* (h) stutter, stammer: F **auf Stottern kaufen** buy on the never-never.
'**Straf|anstalt** *f* prison, penal institution. **~antrag** *m* **1.** private application (by the injured party). **2.** sentence demanded (by the public prosecutor). **~anzeige** *f* **~ erstatten** bring a charge (**gegen** against). **~arbeit** *f ped.* extra work. **~bank** *f* (-; ⁓e) *sports:* penalty bank.
'**strafbar** *adj* a) punishable, b) criminal: **~e Handlung** (criminal) offen/ce (*Am.* -se); **sich ~ machen** make o.s. liable to prosecution.
'**Strafbefehl** *m* ⚖ order (of summary punishment).
Strafe [ˈʃtraːfə] *f* (-; -n) punishment (*a. fig.*), penalty (*a. sports*), *a.* fine, *a.* sentence: **bei ~ von** on pain (*or* penalty) of; **zur ~** as a punishment; **~ zahlen** pay a fine; → **antreten** 1, **verbüßen**.
strafen [ˈʃtraːfən] *v/t* (h) punish, *esp. sports:* penalize: **~der Blick** censorious look; → **Lüge, Verachtung**.
'**Straf|entlassene** *m, f* (-n; -n) ex-convict. **~erlaß** *m* remission (of sentence).
straff [ʃtraf] *adj* **1.** tight, taut, *a.* firm, erect (*posture*): **~ anziehen** tighten; **~ sitzen** fit tightly. **2.** *fig.* strict, tight.
'**straffällig** *adj* **~ werden** commit an offen/ce (*Am.* -se). '**Straffällige** *m, f* (-n; -n) offender, delinquent.
straffen [ˈʃtrafən] *v/t* (h) *a. fig.* tighten (up). '**Straffheit** *f* (-; *no pl*) tightness.
'**straffrei** *adj* **~ ausgehen** go unpunished.
'**Straffreiheit** *f* (-; *no pl*) immunity.
'**Straf|gebühr** *f* fine. **~gefangene** *m, f*

(-n; -n) prisoner, convict. **~gericht** n **1.** criminal court. **2.** fig. punishment. **~gesetz** n penal law. **~gesetzbuch** n penal code.

sträflich ['ʃtrɛːflɪç] **I** adj punishable, a. fig. criminal. **II** adv fig. badly.

Sträfling ['ʃtrɛːflɪŋ] m (-s; -e) prisoner, convict.

'**straflos** → **straffrei**.

'**Straf|mandat** n ticket. **~maß** n ⚖ sentence. **♀mildernd** adj mitigating. **♀mündig** adj of responsible age. **~porto** F n surcharge. **~predigt** f F lecture. **~pro,zeß** m trial, criminal case (or proceedings). **~pro,zeßordnung** f code of criminal procedure. **~punkt** m sports: penalty point. **~raum** m soccer: penalty area. **~recht** n (-[e]s; no pl) criminal law. **♀rechtlich** adj criminal, penal: **~ verfolgen** prosecute. **~re,gister** n a) criminal records, b) s.o.'s criminal record. **~sache** f criminal case. **~stoß** m soccer: penalty kick. **~tat** f (criminal) offen/ce (Am. -se), crime. **~täter** m (criminal) offender. **~verfahren** n **1.** → **Strafprozeß. 2.** criminal procedure.

'**strafverschärfend** adj aggravating.

'**strafversetzen** v/t (only inf and pp strafversetzt, h), '**Strafversetzung** f (-; -en) transfer for disciplinary reasons.

'**Straf|verteidiger(in** f) m trial lawyer; → a. **Verteidiger(in)**. **~vollzug** m **1.** a) execution of the sentence, b) imprisonment. **2.** prison system. **~vollzugsbeamte** m prison officer. **♀würdig** adj ⚖ punishable. **~zettel** m ticket.

Strahl [ʃtraːl] m (-[e]s; -en) **1.** ray (a. fig. of hope etc), a. beam (of light), flash (of fire etc). **2.** stream, jet (of water etc).

'**Strahlantrieb** m ✈ jet propulsion.

strahlen ['ʃtraːlən] v/i (h) **1.** phys. radiate, emit radiation, be radioactive. **2.** shine, sparkle: **die Sonne strahlte** the sun shone brightly. **3.** fig. beam (vor with): **sie strahlte (vor Glück)** she was radiant (with happiness).

'**Strahlen|belastung** f ☢ exposure to radiation. **~bündel** n opt., phys. pencil of rays. **~dosis** f ☢ radiation dose.

'**strahlenförmig** adj radial.

'**Strahlen|krankheit** f radiation sickness. **~schutz** m radiation protection. **~thera,pie** f radiotherapy. **~tod** m death by radiation.

'**Strahler** m (-s; -) **1.** radiator, a. heater. **2.** spotlight.

'**Strahltriebwerk** n ✈ jet engine.

'**Strahlung** f (-; -en) radiation.

'**Strahlungs|ener,gie** f radiation energy. **~wärme** f radiant heat.

Strähne ['ʃtrɛːnə] f (-; -n) a) strand, b) streak. '**strähnen** v/t (h) streak in (hair). '**strähnig** adj straggly.

stramm [ʃtram] **I** adj **1.** tight. **2.** strapping, sturdy, firm. **3.** strict (discipline), brisk (pace): F **~ Sozialist** sta(u)nch socialist. **II** adv **4.** tight(ly): **~ sitzen** fit tightly; F **~ arbeiten** work hard.

'**strammstehen** v/i (irr, sep, -ge-, h, →stehen) ⚔ stand to attention.

'**Strampelhöschen** n rompers.

strampeln ['ʃtrampəln] v/i (h) **1.** a) kick, b) struggle. **2.** F pedal (away).

'**Strampelsack** m baby's sleeping bag.

Strand [ʃtrant] m (-[e]s; -e) (sea)shore, beach. **~bad** n swimming area.

stranden ['ʃtrandən] v/i (sn) run aground: **gestrandet** a. fig. stranded.

'**Strand|gut** n (-[e]s; no pl) flotsam and jetsam (a. fig.). **~ho,tel** n seaside (or beach) hotel. **~kleidung** f beachwear. **~korb** m (canopied) beach chair. **~prome,nade** f promenade.

Strang [ʃtraŋ] m (-[e]s; -e) **1.** rope: fig. an **'einem ~ ziehen** pull together; **über die Stränge schlagen** kick over the traces; **wenn alle Stränge reißen** if all else fails. **2.** anat. cord. **3.** skein, hank.

strangulieren [ʃtraŋgu'liːrən] v/t (h) strangle.

Strapaze [ʃtra'paːtsə] f (-; -n) strain.

strapazieren [ʃtrapa'tsiːrən] v/t (h) wear s.o., s.th. out, strain (a. fig.): F **j-s Geduld ~** tax s.o.'s patience. **strapa'zierfähig** adj hardwearing, tough.

strapaziös [ʃtrapa'tsiøːs] adj strenuous, F tough: **~ sein** be a (great) strain.

Straße ['ʃtraːsə] f (-; -n) **1.** road, street: **auf der ~** on the road, in (Am. on) the street; **der Mann auf der ~** the man in the street; **j-n auf die ~ setzen** a) turn s.o. out, b) sack s.o.; **auf offener ~** in broad daylight. **2.** geogr. **die ~ von Dover** the Strait(s) of Dover. **3.** ⚙ (production etc) line.

'**Straßen|anzug** m lounge (Am. business) suit. **~arbeiten** pl roadworks. **~arbeiter** m roadman.

'Straßen|bahn f tram, Am. streetcar. **~haltestelle** f tram (Am. streetcar) stop. **~linie** f tram (Am. streetcar) line. **~wagen** m tram(car), Am. streetcar.

'Straßen|bau m (-[e]s; no pl) road construction. **~belag** m road surface. **~beleuchtung** f street lighting. **~café** n pavement (Am. sidewalk) café. **~fest** n street party. **~glätte** f slippery road(s). **~graben** m (road) ditch. **~händler** m street vendor. **~junge** m street urchin. **~kampf** m street fighting. **~karte** f road map. **~kehrer** m, **~kehrma,schine** f street sweeper. **~kreuzung** f crossroads. **~lage** f mot. roadholding. **~lärm** m noise from the street(s). **~la,terne** f street lamp. **~musi,kant** m street musician. **~name** m street name. **~netz** n road network. **~rand** m (am ~ on the) roadside. **~rennen** n road race. **~sammlung** f street collection. **~schild** n street sign. **~sperre** f road block. **~tunnel** m road tunnel. **~überführung** f flyover. **~unterführung** f underpass. **~verhältnisse** pl road conditions. **~verkehr** m (road) traffic. **~verkehrsordnung** f traffic regulations. **~zustand** m road condition(s).

Stratege [ʃtraˈteːɡə] m (-n; -n) strategist. **Strategie** [ʃtrateˈɡiː] f (-; -n) strategy. **stra'tegisch** [-ɡɪʃ] adj strategic(al).

Stratosphäre [ʃtratoˈsfɛːrə] f (-; no pl) stratosphere.

sträuben [ˈʃtrɔybən] (h) **I** v/t ruffle (up) (feathers), bristle (hair). **II sich ~** hair: stand on end, fur: bristle up; fig. **sich ~ gegen** struggle against, resist; **sich ~ zu** inf refuse to inf.

Strauch [ʃtraʊx] m (-[e]s; ⁓er) shrub, bush.

straucheln [ˈʃtraʊxəln] v/i (sn) **1.** stumble, trip. **2.** fig. go astray.

Strauß¹ [ʃtraʊs] m (-es; ⁓e) bunch of flowers.

Strauß² m (-es; -e) zo. ostrich.

'Straußenfeder f ostrich feather.

Strebe [ˈʃtreːbə] f (-; -n) strut.

streben [ˈʃtreːbən] v/i **1.** (sn) **~ zu, ~ nach** move towards, person: make for. **2.** (h) fig. **~ nach** strive (for), aim (at). **'Streben** n (-s) fig. efforts, (nach) striving (for), aspiration (for, after).

'Streber m (-s; -) contp. a) careerist, b) social climber, c) ped. swot.

'Strebertum n (-s; no pl) contp. pushiness, ped. swotting.

strebsam [ˈʃtreːp-] adj industrious, ambitious. **'Strebsamkeit** f (-; no pl) industriousness, ambition.

Strecke [ˈʃtrɛkə] f (-; -n) **1.** stretch, a. leg, a. route (a. ✈, ⚓), a. distance (a. sports), sports: (racing) course, ⚒, 🚂, teleph. line, 🔀 roadway: 🚂 **auf freier ~** between stations; **auf e-r ~ von 10 km** for a stretch of 10 km; fig. **auf der ~ bleiben** fail, come to grief. **2.** hunt. bag: **zur ~ bringen** kill, shoot down, bag, fig. hunt down, catch (criminal etc), defeat (opponent).

strecken [ˈʃtrɛkən] v/t (h) **1.** stretch: **sich** (or **s-e Glieder**) **~** stretch (o.s.) (or one's limbs); → **Decke** 1. **2.** eke out, spin out (supplies etc).

'Streckennetz n railway network.

'streckenweise adv a) in parts, in places, b) now and then, at times.

'Streckmuskel m extensor (muscle).

'Streckverband m 💉 **im ~** in traction.

Streich [ʃtraɪç] m (-[e]s; -e) trick, prank: **j-m e-n** (**bösen**) **~ spielen** play a (nasty) trick on s.o.

streichen [ˈʃtraɪçən] (strich, gestrichen, h) **I** v/t **1.** spread (butter, bread, etc), apply, put ointment etc (**auf** acc on). **2.** paint: → **gestrichen** 1. **3.** stroke. **4.** a) cross out, delete, b) cancel (order etc), cut (funds): **j-n von der Liste ~** strike s.o. off the list. **5.** strike, haul down (flag, sail). **II** v/i **6.** (mit der Hand) **~ über** (acc) stroke, pass one's hand over. **7.** (sn) **durch die Gegend ~** roam the countryside; **ums Haus ~** prowl around the house.

'Streicher pl ♩ the strings.

'Streichholz n match, matchstick.

'Streichholzschachtel f matchbox.

'Streichinstru,ment n string(ed) instrument: **die ~e** the strings.

'Streichor,chester n string orchestra.

'Streichquar,tett n string quartet.

'Streichung f (-; -en) cancel(l)ation (a. fig.), cut (of funds etc), print. deletion.

'Streichwurst f sausage spread.

'Streifband n (-[e]s; ⁓er) wrapper.

Streife [ˈʃtraɪfə] f (-; -n) ([auf] **~ gehen** go on) patrol.

streifen [ˈʃtraɪfən] (h) **I** v/t **1.** touch, brush against, car: scrape against, bul-

let: graze: **ein Thema ~** touch (up)on a subject. **2. vom Finger (Leibe) ~** slip off (*ring, dress*). **3. mit e-m Blick ~** glance at. **II** *v/i* (sn) **4. durch den Wald** *etc* **~** roam the woods *etc*.

'**Streif|licht** *n fig.* sidelight. **~schuß** *m* grazing shot. **~zug** *m a. fig.* excursion.

Streik [ʃtraɪk] *m* (-[e]s; -s) strike: **wilder ~** wildcat strike; **e-n ~ ausrufen (abbrechen)** call (call off) a strike; **in den ~ treten** go on strike. **~aufruf** *m* strike call. **~brecher** *m* strikebreaker, F blackleg, *contp.* scab.

streiken ['ʃtraɪkən] *v/i* (h) **1.** (be *or* go on) strike. **2.** F refuse, *a. stomach:* rebel, *machine etc:* refuse to work, pack up. '**Streikende** *m, f* (-n; -n) striker. '**Streik|geld** *n* strike pay. **~posten** *m* (*a.* **~ aufstellen vor, ~ stehen**) picket. **~recht** *n* right to strike. **~welle** *f* series of strikes.

Streit [ʃtraɪt] *m* (-[e]s; -e) a) quarrel, argument, F row, b) brawl, fight, c) controversy, dispute: **in ~ geraten mit** have an argument (*or* a fight) with; → **suchen, Zaun.** '**streitbar** *adj* belligerent. '**streiten** *v/i* (stritt, gestritten, h) (*a.* **miteinander** *or* **sich ~**) quarrel, have an argument (F a row), b) fight: **darüber läßt sich ~** that's a moot point. '**Streiter** *m* (-s; -) *fig.* (**für**) fighter (for), champion (of). **Streite'rei** *f* (-; -en) (constant) quarrel(l)ing, fights, F rows. '**Streitfall** *m* dispute, conflict, ⚖ case. '**Streitfrage** *f* (controversial) issue. '**Streitgespräch** *n* debate, dispute. '**streitig** *adj* **1.** ⚖ contentious. **2.** *j-m* (**das Recht auf**) **et. ~ machen** dispute s.o.'s right to s.th.; → **Rang** 1. '**Streitigkeit** *f* (-; -en) → **Streit.** '**Streitkräfte** *pl* armed forces. '**streitlustig** *adj* belligerent. '**Streitpunkt** *m* (point at) issue. '**Streitsache** *f* ⚖ case, F lawsuit. '**Streitsucht** *f* (-; *no pl*) quarrelsomeness. '**streitsüchtig** *adj* quarrelsome. '**Streitwert** *m* ⚖ value in dispute.

streng [ʃtrɛŋ] **I** *adj* severe (*a.* cold, *criticism, look, etc*), austere (*style*), strict (*discipline, regulation, etc*), harsh (*taste*), acrid (*smell etc*): (**mit** *j-m*) **~ sein** be strict (with s.o.); **~es Stillschweigen** strict secrecy. **II** *adv* severely (*etc*): **sich ~ halten an** (*acc*) ad-

here strictly to; **~ geheim** top-secret; **~ vertraulich** strictly confidential.

'**Strenge** *f* (-; *no pl*) severity, austerity, strictness, harshness.

'**strenggläubig** *adj* orthodox.

Streß [ʃtrɛs] *m* (-sses; -sse) (*im ~* under) stress. '**stressen** *v/t* (h) F *j-n ~* put s.o. under stress. '**stressig** *adj* F stressful. '**Streßkrankheit** *f* stress disease.

streuen ['ʃtrɔyən] (h) **I** *v/t* scatter, strew, spread, sprinkle: **den Gehweg ~** grit the sidewalk. **II** *v/i* ✗, *phys.* scatter.

streunen ['ʃtrɔynən] *v/i* (sn) stray, roam about: **~de Katze** stray cat.

strich [ʃtrɪç] *pret of* **streichen.**

Strich *m* (-[e]s; -e) **1.** a) stroke, b) line, c) dash, d) mark, e) (compass) point, f) stroke (of the brush): *j-m* **e-n ~ durch die Rechnung machen** thwart s.o.'s plans; **unter dem ~** on balance; **e-n (dicken) ~ unter et. machen** make a clean break with s.th.; F **auf den ~ gehen** walk the streets, be on the game. **2.** *textiles:* nap: **gegen den ~** against the nap; F **das ging mir gegen den ~** it went against the grain with me; F **nach ~ und Faden** good and proper. **3.** F cut. **4.** ♪ a) stroke, b) bowing technique.

stricheln ['ʃtrɪçəln] *v/t* (h) a) sketch in, b) hatch: **gestrichelte Linie** broken line. '**Strich|junge** *m* F male prostitute. **~kode** *m* bar code. **~liste** *f* check list. **~mädchen** *n* F streetwalker, *Am. sl.* hooker. **~männchen** *n* matchstick man. **~punkt** *m* semicolon.

'**strichweise** *adv* in parts: *meteor.* **~ Regen** scattered showers.

Strick [ʃtrɪk] *m* (-[e]s; -e) cord, rope: *fig.* **wenn alle ~e reißen** if all else fails; F *j-m* **aus e-r Sache e-n ~ drehen (wollen)** use s.th. against s.o.

stricken ['ʃtrɪkən] *v/t, v/i* (h) knit. '**Stricker** *m* (-s; -), '**Strickerin** *f* (-; -nen) knitter.

'**Strick|jacke** *f* cardigan. **~leiter** *f* rope ladder. **~ma,schine** *f* knitting machine. **~nadel** *f* knitting needle. **~waren** *pl* knitwear. **~wolle** *f* knitting wool. **~zeug** *n* knitting (things).

striegeln ['ʃtriːɡəln] *v/t* (h) curry(comb).

Strieme ['ʃtriːmə] *f* (-; -n), '**Striemen** *m* (-s; -) weal.

strikt [ʃtrɪkt] *adj* strict: **et. ~ ablehnen** refuse s.th. flatly.

Strippe ['ʃtrɪpə] f (-; -n) F cord, string: fig. **an der ~ hängen** be on the blower.
stritt [ʃtrɪt] pret of **streiten**.
strittig ['ʃtrɪtɪç] adj controversial: **der ~e Punkt** the point at issue.
Stroh [ʃtroː] n (-[e]s; no pl) **1.** straw. **2.** (a. **mit ~ decken**) thatch. 2**blond** adj flaxen(-haired). ~**blume** f immortelle. ~**dach** n thatched roof. ~**feuer** n fig. flash in the pan. ~**halm** m straw: **nach e-m ~ greifen, sich an e-n ~ klammern** clutch at a straw. ~**hut** m straw hat. ~**mann** m (-[e]s; ¨er) front. ~**witwe(r** m) f F grass widow(er).
Strom [ʃtroːm] m (-[e]s; ¨e) **1.** a) (large) river, b) torrent, c) stream, current (a. fig.), fig. flood (of blood, tears, etc), stream (of people, cars, etc): **mit dem (gegen den) ~ schwimmen** swim with (against) the current (fig. a. tide); **es gießt in Strömen** it is pouring with rain. **2.** a) (electrical) current, b) electricity: **unter ~ stehend** live.
strom'ab(wärts) adv downstream.
strom'auf(wärts) adv upstream.
'Stromausfall m power failure.
strömen ['ʃtrøːmən] v/i (sn) stream, pour, air, gas, etc: a. flow, people: a. throng, flock.
'Stromer m (-s; -) F contp. tramp.
'Strom|erzeuger m ⚡ **1.** generator. **2.** power station. ~**erzeugung** f power generation. 2**führend** adj live. ~**kreis** m (electric) circuit. ~**leitung** f power line.
'stromlinienförmig adj streamlined.
'Strom|netz n ⚡ power supply system. ~**schnelle** f (-; -n) rapid. ~**spannung** f ⚡ voltage. ~**sperre** f power cut. ~**stär-ke** f current intensity, amperage. ~**stoß** m **1.** impulse. **2.** electric shock.
'Strömung f(-; -en) current, fig. a. trend.
'Strom|verbrauch m power consumption. ~**versorgung** f power supply. ~**zähler** m electric meter.
Strophe ['ʃtroːfə] f (-; -n) stanza, verse.
strotzen ['ʃtrɔtsən] v/i (h) ~ **von**, ~ **vor** (dat) be full of, a. be teeming with (mistakes), be bursting with (energy, health, etc); **vor Dreck** ~ be caked with dirt.
Strudel ['ʃtruːdəl] m (-s; -) **1.** a. fig. whirlpool, maelstrom. **2.** gastr. strudel.
strudeln ['ʃtruːdəln] v/i (h) swirl, whirl.
Struktur [ʃtrʊk'tuːr] f (-; -en) structure.

Struk'tur... structural (change, policy, etc). **strukturell** [ʃtrʊktu'rɛl] adj (a. ~ **bedingt**) structural.
Strumpf [ʃtrʊmpf] m (-[e]s; ¨e) stocking. ~**band** n garter. ~**halter** m suspender, Am. garter. ~**hose** f (e-e ~ a pair of) tights, pantihose. ~**maske** f a stocking mask. ~**waren** pl hosiery.
Strunk [ʃtrʊŋk] m (-[e]s; ¨e) stalk.
struppig ['ʃtrʊpɪç] adj unkempt (hair), bristly (beard), shaggy (dog).
Strychnin [ʃtryç'niːn] n (-s; no pl) 🜍 strychnine.
Stube ['ʃtuːbə] f (-; -n) room.
'Stubenhocker m (-s; -) stay-at-home.
'Stubenmädchen n chambermaid.
'stubenrein adj house-broken (dog).
'Stubenwagen m bassinet.
Stuck [ʃtʊk] m (-s; no pl) stucco.
Stück [ʃtʏk] n (-[e]s; -e) **1.** piece, a. slice (of bread etc), a. lump (of sugar), a. bar (of soap), a. head (of cattle): **ein ~ Land** a piece of land, a plot; **im ~, am ~** in one piece, a. unsliced (cheese etc); **50 Cent das ~** fifty cents each; **50 ~ Vieh** 50 head of cattle; **j-n ein ~ (Weges) begleiten** accompany s.o. part of the way; **~ für ~** piece by piece; **in ~e gehen** go to pieces; **in ~e schlagen** smash (to bits); fig. **aus freien ~en** of one's own free will; **große ~e halten auf** (acc) think highly of; **wir sind ein gutes ~ weitergekommen** we have made considerable headway; **das ist ein starkes ~!** that's a bit thick. **2.** piece (of music), thea. play, passage (of book etc).
'Stückchen n (-s; -) small piece (etc, → **Stück**).
'Stückelung f (-; -en) ✝ denomination.
'Stückeschreiber(in f) m playwright.
'Stück|gut n parcel(s). ~**kosten** pl unit cost. ~**liste** f ⊕ parts list. ~**lohn** m piece rate. ~**preis** m unit price.
'stückweise adv bit by bit.
'Stück|werk n (-[e]s; no pl) contp. patchwork. ~**zahl** f number of pieces.
Student [ʃtu'dɛnt] m (-en; -en) student.
Stu'dentenausweis m student's identity card.
Stu'dentenschaft f(-; -en) the students.
Stu'denten|verbindung f fraternity. ~**wohnheim** n students' hostel.
Stu'dentin f (-; -nen) student.

Studie ['ʃtu:dïə] f (-; -n) study (a. paint. etc) (**über** acc on), sketch.

'**Studien|aufenthalt** m study visit. **~beratung** f student advisory service. **~bewerber** m university applicant. **~di,rektor** m deputy headmaster. **~fach** n subject. **~gang** m course of studies. **~gebühren** pl tuition fees.

'**studienhalber** adv for study purposes.

'**Studien|jahr** n academic year: **~e →** *Studienzeit.* **~platz** m place at a university. **~rat** m, **~rätin** [-rɛ:tın] f (-; -nen) secondary school teacher. **~refe-ren,dar(in** f) m student teacher at a secondary school. **~reise** f study trip. **~zeit** f university (Am. college) days.

studieren [ʃtu'di:rən] (h) **I** v/t study, read: **er studiert Medizin** he studies medicine, he is a medical student. **II** v/i study, go to university: **wo hat er studiert?** which university did he go to?

Studio ['ʃtu:dïo] n (-s; -s) studio.

Studium ['ʃtu:dïʊm] n (-s; -dien) studies, study (gen of).

Stufe ['ʃtu:fə] f (-; -n) **1.** step. **2.** ling., ♪ degree. **3.** fig. a) stage, b) level, standard, c) rank: **j-n auf eine ~ stellen mit** place s.o. on a level with. **4.** (income etc) bracket. **5.** stage (of rocket etc).

'**Stufen|barren** m asymmetrical bars. **~heck** n mot. notchback. **~leiter** f stepladder: **~ des Erfolgs** ladder to success.

'**stufenlos** ⚙ adj continuous: **~ regelbar** infinitely variable. '**stufenweise I** adj gradual. **II** adv step by step, by degrees.

Stuhl [ʃtu:l] m (-[e]s; ⸚e) **1.** chair, (piano etc) stool: **der Heilige ~** the Holy See; fig. **sich zwischen zwei Stühle setzen** fall between two stools; → **elektrisch** I. **2.** 𝔐 a) stool, b) → **Stuhlgang.**

'**Stuhl|bein** n leg of a chair. **~gang** m (-[e]s; no pl) bowel movement.

stülpen ['ʃtʏlpən] v/t (h) put (**auf** acc on, **über** acc over): **et. nach außen ~** turn s.th. inside out.

stumm [ʃtʊm] adj dumb, mute, fig. a. silent (a. ling.), speechless (**vor** dat with).

Stummel ['ʃtʊməl] m (-s; -) stump, butt, stub (a. of candle etc).

'**Stummfilm** m silent film.

Stumpen ['ʃtʊmpən] m (-s; -) cheroot.

Stümper ['ʃtʏmpər] m (-s; -) bungler. **Stümpe'rei** f (-; -en) **1.** no pl bungling.

2. botch. '**stümperhaft** adj bungling. '**stümpern** v/i, v/t (h) bungle, botch.

stumpf [ʃtʊmpf] adj **1.** blunt. **2.** ℳ obtuse (angle), truncated (cone). **3.** dull. **4.** fig. apathetic, dull, dulled (senses).

Stumpf m (-[e]s; ⸚e) stump: F **mit ~ und Stiel** root and branch.

'**Stumpfheit** f (-; no pl) **1.** bluntness. **2.** a. fig. dullness. '**Stumpfsinn** m (-[e]s; no pl) dullness, a. mindlessness (of work etc). '**stumpfsinnig** adj dull, a. mindless, soul-destroying (work etc).

'**stumpfwink(e)lig** adj ℳ obtuse.

Stunde ['ʃtʊndə] f (-; -n) **1.** hour: **zur ~** at this hour; **bis zur ~** as yet; mot. **50 Meilen in der ~** 50 miles per hour; **die ~ der Wahrheit** the moment of truth. **2.** ped. lesson, class, period: **bei j-m ~n nehmen** have lessons with s.o.

'**stunden** v/t (h) (**j-m**) die Zahlung **~** extend the term of payment (to s.o.).

'**Stunden|geschwindigkeit** f (average) speed per hour: **e-e ~ von 60 Meilen** an average of 60 miles per hour (abbr. mph). **~kilo,meter** pl kilomet/res (Am. -ers) per hour. ⚙**lang I** adj lasting (for) hours. **II** adv for hours (and hours). **~lohn** m hourly wage. **~plan** m timetable, Am. schedule.

'**stundenweise** adj and adv by the hour.

'**Stundenzeiger** m hour hand.

...stündig [-ʃtʏndıç] in cpds. ...-hour.

stündlich ['ʃtʏntlıç] **I** adj hourly. **II** adv a) every hour, b) any time (now).

Stunk [ʃtʊŋk] m F **~ machen** kick up a stink; **das gibt ~!** there will be trouble.

stupide [ʃtu'pi:də] adj dull, mindless.

Stups [ʃtʊps] m (-es; -e), '**stupsen** v/t (h) F prod. '**Stupsnase** f snub nose.

stur [ʃtu:r] adj F **1.** stubborn, pigheaded, stolid. **2. →** **stumpfsinnig.**

'**Sturheit** f (-; no pl) F **1.** stubbornness (etc). **2. →** **Stumpfsinn.**

Sturm [ʃtʊrm] m (-[e]s; ⸚e) **1.** storm (a. fig.), gale: **~ der Entrüstung** outcry; **~ im Wasserglas** storm in a teacup. **2.** ✕ storm, attack: a. fig. **im ~ erobern** take by storm; **~ laufen gegen** attack, assail; ✝ **~ auf** (acc) rush for (goods), run on (a bank). **3.** sports: forwards. **~angriff** m ✕ assault. **~bö** f squall.

stürmen ['ʃtʏrmən] **I** v/t (h) **1.** ✕ storm: fig. **e-e Bank ~** make a run on a bank. **II** v/i **2.** (h) ✕ or sports: attack. **3.** (sn) *fig.* rush. **III** *v/impers* (h) **es stürmt** there's a gale blowing.

'**Stürmer** *m* (-s; -) *sports:* forward.

'**stürmisch** *adj* stormy (*a. fig.* debate, love, etc), passionate (*lover*), tumultuous (*applause etc*), vehement (*protest*), turbulent (*time*), rapid (*development etc*): **nicht so ~!** easy does it!

'**Sturm|lauf** *m* ╳ assault, *fig. a.* run (*auf acc* on). **~spitze** *f soccer:* spearhead. **~tief** *n* cyclone. **~warnung** *f* gale warning. **~wolke** *f* storm cloud.

Sturz [ʃtʊrts] *m* (-es; ⸚e) **1.** (sudden) fall, plunge (*a. fig.*), *fig.* (sudden) drop (*in temperature etc*), *a.* slump (*in prices etc*). **2.** (down)fall, overthrow (*of a government*). '**Sturzbach** *m* torrent.

stürzen [ʃtʏrtsən] **I** *v/i* (sn) **1.** fall, *a. fig.* plunge: **sie ist (mit dem Fahrrad) gestürzt** she had a fall (with her bicycle). **2.** rush, dash: **er kam ins Zimmer gestürzt** he burst into the room. **II** *v/t* **3.** throw: **j-n ins Elend ~** plunge s.o. into misery. **4.** turn *s.th.* upside down, turn *pudding etc* out of the mo(u)ld: **Nicht ~!** this side up! **5.** bring down, overthrow (*government etc*). **III** *sich ~* (h) **6.** plunge (**ins Wasser** into the water); **sich aus dem Fenster ~** throw o.s. out of the window; *fig.* **sich in die Arbeit ~** throw o.s. into one's work; **sich in Schulden ~** plunge into debt; **sich in Unkosten ~** go to great expense. **7.** *sich ~ auf* (*acc*) pounce on, *a.* rush at (*s.o.*), *a.* make straight for.

'**Sturz|flug** *m* (nose)dive. **~helm** *m* crash helmet. **~regen** *m* (heavy) downpour.

Stute ['ʃtuːtə] *f* (-; -n) mare.

'**Stutenfohlen** *n* filly.

'**Stützbalken** *m* supporting beam.

Stütze ['ʃtʏtsə] *f* (-; -n) *a. fig.* support, prop, (*person*) mainstay.

stutzen¹ ['ʃtʊtsən] *v/t* (h) cut, trim (*hair, beard*), lop (*tree*), clip (*hedge, wings*), crop (*ears*), dock (*tail*).

'**stutzen²** *v/i* (h) (**bei**) a) stop short (at), b) be puzzled (by), c) become suspicious (at).

'**Stutzen** *m* (-s; -) **1.** short rifle. **2.** ☉ connecting piece. **3.** (football) sock.

stützen ['ʃtʏtsən] *v/t* (h) support (*a. fig.*), prop, *fig.* back (up) by: **die Ellbogen auf den Tisch ~** prop (*or* rest) one's elbows on the table; *fig.* **et. ~ auf** (*acc*) base

s.th. on; *sich ~ auf* (*acc*) rely on, *opinion etc:* be based on.

stutzig ['ʃtʊtsɪç] *adj* **j-n ~ machen** a) puzzle s.o., b) make s.o. suspicious; **~ werden** a) be puzzled, b) become suspicious.

'**Stütz|mauer** *f* retaining wall. **~pfeiler** *m* buttress. **~punkt** *m* ╳ *or fig.* base.

Styropor [ʃtyro'poːr] *n* (-s; *no pl*) (*TM*) polystyrene.

Subjekt [zʊp'jɛkt] *n* (-[e]s; -e) **1.** *ling.* subject. **2.** F *contp.* fellow.

subjektiv [zʊpjɛk'tiːf] *adj* subjective. **Subjektivität** [zʊpjɛktivi'tɛːt] *f* (-; *no pl*) subjectivity.

'**Subkontinent** *m* subcontinent.

'**Subkultur** *f* (-; -en) subculture.

subkutan [zʊpku'taːn] *adj* ✚ subcutaneous.

Sublimat [zubli'maːt] *n* (-[e]s; -e) 🜨 sublimate. **sublimieren** [zubli'miːrən] *v/t* (h) 🜨 *or fig.* sublimate.

Subskription [zʊpskrɪp'tsi̯oːn] *f* (-; -en) subscription. **Subskriptionspreis** *m* subscription price.

substantiell [zʊpstan'tsi̯ɛl] *adj* substantial.

Substantiv ['zʊpstanti:f] *n* (-s; -e) noun, substantive. **substantivieren** [zʊpstanti'viːrən] *v/t* (h) use as a noun. '**substantivisch** [-ti:vɪʃ] *adj* substantival, *adv a.* as a noun.

Substanz [zʊp'stants] *f* (-; -en) **1.** substance. **2.** ✝ (**von der ~ leben** live on one's) capital; F *fig.* **das geht an die ~** that really takes it out of you.

subtil [zʊp'tiːl] *adj* subtle.

subtrahieren [zʊptra'hiːrən] *v/t* (h) subtract. **Subtraktion** [zʊptrak'tsi̯oːn] *f* (-; -en) subtraction.

'**subtropisch** *adj* subtropical.

Subvention [zʊpvɛn'tsi̯oːn] *f* (-; -en) subsidy. **subventionieren** [zʊpvɛntsi̯o'niːrən] *v/t* (h) subsidize.

'**Such|akti,on** *f* search (operation). **~dienst** *m* tracing service.

Suche ['zuːxə] *f* (-; -n) (**nach** for) search, hunt: **auf der ~ nach** in search of; **auf der ~ sein nach** be looking for.

suchen ['zuːxən] (h) **I** *v/t* a) look for, search for, b) seek (*advice, happiness, etc*), c) try to trace (*person, mistake, etc*): (**mit j-m**) **Streit ~** pick a quarrel (with s.o.); **Sie haben hier nichts zu ~!**

you have no business to be here; → **gesucht, Rat** 1, **Weite**². **II** v/i look, search: **~ nach** → I; **nach Worten ~** be at a loss for words.

'**Sucher** m (-s; -) *phot.* viewfinder.

'**Sucherkamera** f rangefinder camera.

'**Such|gerät** n detector. **~hund** m tracker dog. **~lauf** m *video etc:* a) scanning, b) scanner. **~mannschaft** f search party. **~scheinwerfer** m searchlight.

Sucht [zʊxt] f (-; ⁓e) (**nach**) a) craving (for), b) a. 🟥 addiction (to).

'**suchterzeugend** adj 🟥 addictive.

süchtig ['zʏçtɪç] adj addicted (**nach** to): **~ machen** be addictive; *fig.* **~ sein nach** a) have a craving for, b) be obsessed with. '**Süchtige** m, f (-n; -n) addict.

'**Suchtmittel** n addictive drug.

'**Suchtrupp** m search party.

Süd'afrika ['zy:t-] n (-s) South Africa. '**Südafri'kaner(in** f) m, '**südafri'kanisch** adj South African.

Süda'merika n (-s) South America. '**Südameri'kaner(in** f) m, '**südameri'kanisch** adj South American.

'**süddeutsch** adj, '**Süddeutsche** m, f (-n; -n) South German.

Sude'lei f (-; -en) F *contp.* mess. **sudeln** ['zu:dəln] v/i (h) F *contp.* make a mess.

Süden ['zy:dən] m (-s; *no pl*) south, South: **im ~** in the south; **im ~ von** (*or* gen) (to) the south of; **nach ~** south(ward).

'**Südfrüchte** pl tropical fruits.

'**Südküste** f south(ern) coast.

'**Südländer** [-lɛndər] m (-s; -), '**Südländerin** f (-; -nen) Mediterranean type, Latin. '**südländisch** adj Mediterranean, Latin (*temper etc*).

'**südlich I** adj southern, south, southerly (*wind, direction*). **II** adv south(wards). **III** prep **~ von** (*or* gen) (to) the south of.

Süd'osten m southeast.

süd'östlich I adj southeast(ern), southeasterly (*wind, direction*). **II** adv (to the) southeast. **III** prep **~ von** (*or* gen) (to the) southeast of.

'**Südpol** m South Pole.

Südpo'lar... Antarctic.

'**Südsee** f (-; *no pl*) South Sea.

'**südwärts** adv southward(s).

Süd'westen m southwest.

süd'westlich I adj southwest(ern), southwesterly (*wind, direction*). **II** adv

(to the) southwest. **III** prep **~ von** (*or* gen) (to the) southwest of.

'**Südwind** m south wind.

Suff [zʊf] m (-[e]s; *no pl*) F boozing.

süffig ['zʏfɪç] adj F pleasant (to drink).

süffisant [zʏfi'zant] adj smug.

suggerieren [zʊɡe'ri:rən] v/t (h) suggest. **Suggestion** [zʊɡɛs'tio:n] f (-; -en) suggestion. **suggestiv** [zʊɡɛs'ti:f] adj suggestive. **Sugge'stivfrage** f leading question.

Sühne ['zy:nə] f (-; -n) atonement.

sühnen ['zy:nən] v/t (h) atone for.

Suite ['svi:t(ə)] f (-; -n) suite.

Sujet [sy'ʒe:] n (-s; -s) subject.

sukzessiv [zʊktsɛ'si:f] adj gradual.

Sulfat [zʊl'fa:t] n (-[e]s; -e) 🜊 sulphate (*Am.* -f-). **Sulfid** [zʊl'fi:t] n (-[e]s; -e) 🜊 sulphide (*Am.* -f-).

Sulfonamid [zʊlfona'mi:d] n (-[e]s; -e) sulphonamide (*Am.* -f-).

Sultan ['zʊlta:n] m (-s; -e) sultan.

Sultanine [zʊlta'ni:nə] f (-; -n) *gastr.* sultana.

Sülze ['zʏltsə] f (-; -n) jellied meat.

summarisch [zʊ'ma:rɪʃ] adj summary.

Summe ['zʊmə] f (-; -n) a) sum, b) (sum) total, c) amount, d) *fig.* sum total.

summen ['zʊmən] (h) **I** v/i buzz, hum, drone. **II** v/t hum (*tune etc*).

'**Summer** m (-s; -) 🎵 buzzer.

summieren [zʊ'mi:rən] v/t (a. **sich ~**) (h) add up.

Sumpf [zʊmpf] m (-[e]s; ⁓e) **1.** swamp. **2.** *fig.* (quag)mire. '**sumpfen** v/i (h) F live it up. '**sumpfig** adj marshy. '**Sumpfland** n (-[e]s; *no pl*) marshland.

Sund [zʊnt] m (-[e]s; -e) sound, strait(s).

Sünde ['zʏndə] f (-; -n) sin.

'**Sünden|erlaß** m absolution. **~fall** m the Fall (of Man). **~re,gister** n *humor.* **sein** *etc* **~** the list of his *etc* sins.

'**Sünder** m (-s; -), '**Sünderin** f (-; -nen) sinner. '**sündhaft** adj sinful: F **~ teuer** awfully expensive. '**sündig** adj sinful. **sündigen** ['zʏndɪɡən] v/i (h) **1.** sin (**gegen** against): **an j-m ~** wrong s.o. **2.** F indulge, overeat *etc*.

super ['zu:pər] adj *or int* F super.

'**Super** n (-s; *no pl*) F *mot.* super, four-star (petrol), *Am.* premium.

Superlativ ['zu:pərlati:f] m (-s; -e) *ling.* *or fig.* superlative.

'**Supermacht** f *pol.* superpower.

'**Supermarkt** *m* supermarket.
'**supermo,dern** *adj* ultramodern.
Suppe ['zʊpə] *f* (-; -n) soup: F *die ~ auslöffeln müssen* have to face the music; *j-m* (*sich*) *e-e schöne ~ einbrocken* get s.o. (o.s.) into a nice mess.
'**Suppen|fleisch** *n* meat for making soup. **~grün** *n* (bunch of) herbs and vegetables. **~huhn** *n* boiling fowl. **~kelle** *f* soup ladle. **~löffel** *m* soup spoon. **~schüssel** *f* soup tureen. **~teller** *m* soup plate. **~würfel** *m* stock cube.
Surfbrett ['sɛːf-] *n* surfboard. '**surfen** *v/i* (h, sn) do surfing, surf. '**Surfer** *m* (-s; -), '**Surferin** *f* (-; -nen) surfer.
Surrealismus [sʏrea'lɪsmʊs] *m* (-; *no pl*) surrealism.
surrea'listisch *adj* surrealist(ic).
surren ['zʊrən] *v/i* (h) whirr, hum, *insect etc*: buzz.
suspekt [zʊs'pɛkt] *adj* suspect.
suspendieren [zʊspɛn'diːrən] *v/t* (h) suspend.
Suspensorium [zʊspɛn'zoːriʊm] *n* (-s; -rien) ⚕ suspensory, *sports*: jockstrap.
süß [zyːs] *adj* sweet. '**Süße¹** *f* (-; *no pl*) sweetness. '**Süße²** *m*, *f* (-n; -n) F sweetie. '**süßen** *v/t* (h) sweeten.
'**Süßigkeiten** *pl* sweets, *Am.* candy.
'**süßlich** *adj* **1.** sweetish. **2.** *fig.* a) sugary, b) mawkish.
'**süß-'sauer** *adj gastr.* sweet and sour: F *~ lächeln* smile sourly, force a smile.
'**Süßspeise** *f* sweet, dessert.
'**Süßstoff** *m* sweetener.
'**Süßwaren** *pl* sweets, *Am.* candy. **~geschäft** *n* sweet shop, *Am.* candy store.
'**Süßwasser** *n* fresh water.
Symbiose [zʏm'biːozə] *f* (-; -n) *biol.* or *fig.* symbiosis.
Symbol [zʏm'boːl] *n* (-s; -e) symbol (*für* of), 🔔, ♣ *etc* a. (conventional) sign.
Symbolik [zʏm'boːlɪk] *f* (-; *no pl*) symbolism. **sym'bolisch** *adj* symbolic(al).
symbolisieren [zʏmboli'ziːrən] *v/t* (h) symbolize.
Symmetrie [zʏme'triː] *f* (-; -n) symmetry. **symmetrisch** [zʏ'meːtrɪʃ] *adj* symmetric(al).
Sympathie [zʏmpa'tiː] *f* (-; -n) **1.** liking: *~ empfinden für* have a liking for. **2.** sympathy: *sich j-s ~n verscherzen* lose s.o.'s sympathies (*or* support).
Sympa'thiestreik *m* sympathetic strike.

Sympathisant [zʏmpati'zant] *m* (-en; -en) sympathizer. **sympathisch** [zʏm'paːtɪʃ] *adj* **1.** likeable, F nice: *er ist mir (nicht) ~* I (don't) like him. **2.** *physiol.* sympathetic. **sympathisieren** [zʏmpati'ziːrən] *v/i* (h) sympathize.
Symphonie [zʏmfo'niː] *f* (-; -n) *etc* → *Sinfonie etc.*
Symposium [zʏm'poːziʊm] *n* (-s; -sien) symposium.
Symptom [zʏmp'toːm] *n* (-s; -e) symptom. **symptomatisch** [zʏmpto'maːtɪʃ] *adj* symptomatic (*für* of).
Synagoge [zʏna'goːgə] *f* (-; -n) synagogue.
synchron [zʏn'kroːn] *adj* synchronous, *ling.* synchronic: *~ laufen etc* be synchronized. **Syn'chron...** synchronous.
synchronisieren [zʏnkroni'ziːrən] *v/t* (h) synchronize, *film.*: a. dub.
Syndikat [zʏndi'kaːt] *n* (-[e]s; -e) syndicate.
Syndikus ['zʏndikʊs] *m* (-; -se) company lawyer, in-house legal counsel.
Syndrom [zʏn'droːm] *n* (-s; -e) ⚕ syndrome.
Synkope *f* (-; -n) **1.** ['zʏnkope] *ling.* syncope. **2.** [zʏn'koːpə] ♪ syncopation.
Synode [zʏ'noːdə] *f* (-; -n) *eccl.* synod.
synonym [zʏno'nyːm] *adj ling.* synonymous. **Syno'nym** *n* (-s; -e) synonym.
syntaktisch [zʏn'taktɪʃ] *adj ling.* syntactic(al).
Syntax ['zʏntaks] *f* (-; -en) *ling.* syntax.
Synthese [zʏn'teːzə] *f* (-; -n) synthesis.
synthetisch [zʏn'teːtɪʃ] *adj* synthetic.
Syphilis ['zyːfilɪs] *f* (-; *no pl*) ⚕ syphilis.
Syrien ['zyːriən] *n* (-s) Syria. **Syrier** ['zyːriər] *m* (-s; -), '**Syrierin** *f* (-; -nen), '**syrisch** *adj* Syrian.
System [zʏs'teːm] *n* (-s; -e) system, *of traffic etc*: a. network. **Systematik** [zʏste'maːtɪk] *f* (-; -en) systematics, system. **syste'matisch** *adj* systematic.
Sy'stemkritiker(in *f*) *m* dissident.
sy'stemlos *adj* unmethodical.
Szenario [stse'naːriọ] *n* (-s; -s) scenario.
Szene ['stseːnə] *f* (-; -n) scene; *fig.* *sich in ~ setzen* put on a show; (*j-m*) *e-e ~ machen* make (s.o.) a scene.
'**Szenen|ap,plaus** *m* applause during the scene. **~wechsel** *m* scene change.
Szenerie [stsenə'riː] *f* (-; -n) scenery, *thea.* a. setting.

T

T, t [te:] *n* (-; -) T, t.

Tabak ['ta:bak] *m* (-s; -e) tobacco.
'**Tabakpflanze** *f* tobacco (plant).
'**Tabakwaren** *pl* tobacco goods.
'**Tabakwarenladen** *m* tobacconist's.

tabellarisch [tabɛ'la:rɪʃ] *adj* tabulated, tabular. **Tabelle** [ta'bɛlə] *f* (-; -n) table. **Ta'bellen|führer** *m sports:* top team, leader. **~letzte** *m* bottom team. **~spitze** *f* (**an der ~** at) the top of the table.

Tabernakel [tabɛr'na:kəl] *n, m* (-s; -) *eccl.* tabernacle.

Tablett [ta'blɛt] *n* (-[e]s; -s, -e) tray.
Tablette [ta'blɛtə] *f* (-; -n) tablet, pill.

tabu [ta'bu:] *adj* taboo: **für ~ erklären** (put under a) taboo. **Ta'bu** *n* (-s; -s) taboo. **ta'bufrei** *adj* **~e Gesellschaft** permissive society.

Tabulator [tabu'la:tɔr] *m* (-s; -en [-la'to:-rən]) tabulator.

Tacho ['taxo] *m* (-s; -s) F, **Tachometer** [taxo'me:tər] *n* (-s; -) *mot.* speedometer.

Tadel ['ta:dəl] *m* (-s; -) reproach, rebuke, *ped.* bad mark: **ohne ~** → **tadellos** *adj* faultless, flawless, blameless, perfect, impeccable (*a. clothing*). '**tadeln** *v/t* (h) (*wegen* for) a) rebuke, reprimand, blame, b) criticize, censure. '**tadelnswert** *adj* reprehensible.

Tafel ['ta:fəl] *f* (-; -n) **1.** *ped.* a) blackboard, b) slate. **2.** notice (*Am.* bulletin) board. **3.** plate (*a. in book*). **4.** a) slab, b) tablet, plaque, c) panel. **5.** bar (*of chocolate*). **6.** (dinner) table: **die ~ aufheben** rise from table. '**tafelfertig** *adj* ready to serve. '**Tafelgeschirr** *n* dinner service.

tafeln ['ta:fəln] *v/i* (h) dine.

täfeln ['tɛ:fəln] *v/t* (h) panel.

'**Tafelobst** *n* dessert fruit.

'**Tafelsilber** *n* silver(ware).

'**Täfelung** *f* (-; -en) panel(l)ing.

'**Tafelwasser** *n* mineral (*or* table) water.

Taft [taft] *m* (-[e]s; -e) taffeta.

Tag [ta:k] *m* (-[e]s; -e) day: **am ~e, bei ~e** a) in the daytime, b) by daylight; **~ für ~** day after day, *get better etc* day by day; **am nächsten ~** the day after; **am ~ zuvor** the day before; **dieser ~e** a) one of these days, b) the other day; **e-s ~es** one day, *a.* some day; **den ganzen ~** all

day long; **alle paar ~e** every few days; **jeden zweiten ~** every other day; ⚒ **unter (über) ~e** underground (above ground); **von e-m ~ auf den anderen** overnight; **guten ~!** a) good morning!, good afternoon!, F hello!, b) how do you do!; **j-m guten ~ sagen** say hello to s.o.; **an den ~ bringen (kommen)** bring (come) to light; **an den ~ legen** display, show; **welchen ~ haben wir heute?** what's (the date) today?; → **Abend, heute** I, **heutig.**

tag'aus → **tagein.**

Tage|bau ['ta:gə-] *m* (-[e]s; *no pl*) ⚒ opencast mining. **~buch** *n* diary. **~dieb** *m* idler. **~geld(er** *pl*) *n* daily allowance.

tag'ein: **~, tagaus** day in, day out.

'**tagelang I** *adj* lasting for days. **II** *adv* for day (and days).

'**Tagelöhner** [-lø:nər] *m* (-s; -), '**Tage-löhnerin** *f* (-; -nen) day labo(u)rer.

tagen ['ta:gən] *v/i* (h) have a meeting, sit (in conference), ⚖ be in session.

Tages|anbruch ['ta:gəs-] *m* (**bei ~** at) daybreak. **~ausflug** *m* day trip. **~creme** *f* day cream. **~decke** *f* bedspread. **~einnahme(n** *pl*) *f* day's takings. **~gericht** *n gastr.* dish of the day. **~gespräch** *n* the talk of the day. **~karte** *f* **1.** day ticket. **2.** *gastr.* menu for the day. **~kasse** *f* **1.** *thea. etc* booking office. **2.** petty cash; b) → **Tageseinnahme(n). ~kurs** *m* **1.** ♦ *foreign exchange:* current rate, *stock exchange:* current price. **2.** *ped.* day course. **~leistung** *f* daily output. **~licht** *n* (-[e]s; *no pl*) daylight: *fig.* **ans ~ bringen (kommen)** bring (come) to light. **~mutter** *f* child minder. **~ordnung** *f* (**auf der ~ stehen** be on the) agenda: *a. fig.* **zur ~ übergehen** proceed to the order of the day; *fig.* **an der ~ sein** be nothing unusual. **~presse** *f* daily press. **~raum** *m* dayroom. **~rückfahrkarte** *f* day return (ticket). **~satz** *m* **1.** daily rate. **2.** daily ration. **~stätte** *f* day-care cent/re (*Am.* -er). **~tour** *f* day trip. **~zeit** *f* **1.** time of day. **2.** daytime: **zu jeder ~** at any time of the day. **~zeitung** *f* daily (newspaper).

'tageweise *adv* on a day-to-day basis.
'taghell *adj and adv* (as) light as day.
...tägig [-tɛːgɪç] *in cpds.* ...-day.
täglich ['tɛːklɪç] **I** *adj* a) daily, b) every-day. **II** *adv* every day, daily: **zweimal ~** twice a day.
tags [taːks] *adv* **~ darauf** (**zuvor**) the day after (before).
'Tagschicht *f* (**~ haben** be on) day shift.
'tagsüber *adv* during the day.
'tag'täglich *adj* day in, day out.
Tagung *f* (-; -en) conference, convention. **'Tagungsbericht** *m* proceedings. **'Tagungsort** *m* conference venue.
Taifun [taɪˈfuːn] *m* (-s; -e) typhoon.
Taille ['taljə] *f* (-; -n) waist, a. waistline.
tailliert [taˈjiːrt] *adj* waisted.
Takelage [takəˈlaːʒə] *f* (-; -n) ⚓ rigging.
takeln ['taːkəln] *v/t* h) rig.
Takt¹ [takt] *m* (-[e]s; -e) **1.** ♪ a) bar, b) beat, c) (*waltz etc*) time: **3/4-~** three-four-time; **~ halten** keep time; **den ~ schlagen** beat the time; **aus dem ~ kommen** lose the beat, *fig.* be put off one's stroke. **2.** rhythm, (*work etc*) cycle, mot. stroke: **im 15-Minuten-Takt** at 15-minute intervals.
Takt² *m* (-[e]s; *no pl*), **'Taktgefühl** *n* (-[e]s; *no pl*) tact.
taktieren [takˈtiːrən] *v/i* h) **geschickt ~** use clever tactics. **Taktik** ['taktɪk] *f* (-; -en) (**die ~ ändern** change) tactics. **'Taktiker** *m* (-s; -) tactician. **'taktisch** *adj a. fig.* tactical.
'taktlos *adj* tactless. **'Taktlosigkeit** *f* (-; *no pl*) tactlessness, indiscretion.
'Takt|stock *m* baton. **~strich** *m* ♪ bar.
'taktvoll *adj* tactful.
Tal [taːl] *n* (-[e]s; ⸚er) valley.
Talar [taˈlaːr] *m* (-s; -e) univ. gown, eccl. cassock, 🏛 robe.
Talent [taˈlɛnt] *n* (-[e]s; -e) **1.** talent (**für, zu** for). **2.** talent(ed person). **talentiert** [talɛnˈtiːrt] *adj* talented, gifted. **ta'lentlos** *adj* untalented. **Ta'lentsucher** *m* (-s; -) talent scout. **ta'lentvoll** *adj* talented, gifted.
'Talfahrt *f* **1.** descent. **2.** ⸸ downswing.
Talg [talk] *m* (-[e]s; -e) **1.** gastr. a) suet, b) tallow. **2.** physiol. sebum.
'Talgdrüse *f* sebaceous gland.
Talisman ['taːlɪsman] *m* (-s; -e) talisman, (lucky) charm, mascot.
Talk [talk] *m* (-[e]s; *no pl*) min. talc(um).

Talkmaster ['tɔːkmaːstər] *m* (-s; -) *TV* host. **Talk-Show** *f* (-; -s) *TV* chat (*esp. Am.* talk) show.
'Talsohle *f* **1.** bottom of the valley. **2.** ⸸ low. **'Talsperre** *f* dam.
Tamburin [tambuˈriːn] *n* (-s; -e) tambourine.
Tampon ['tampɔn] *m* (-s; -s), **tamponieren** [tampoˈniːrən] *v/t* (h) ♀ tampon.
Tamtam [tamˈtam] *n* (-s; *no pl*) F *contp.* fuss (**um** about).
Tandem ['tandɛm] *n* (-s; -s) tandem.
Tang [taŋ] *m* (-[e]s; -e) ⚘ seaweed.
Tangahöschen ['taŋa-] *n* G-string.
Tangente [taŋˈgɛntə] *f* (-; -n) ⊿ tangent.
tangieren [taŋˈgiːrən] *v/t* (h) **1.** ⊿ be tangent to. **2.** *fig.* affect, concern.
Tango ['taŋo] *m* (-s; -s) tango.
Tank [taŋk] *m* (-[e]s; -s) tank. **'tanken** (h) **I** *v/t* **1.** a) fill up with, b) refill, refuel. **2.** F *fig.* get (*fresh air etc*) refuel. **II** *v/i* **3.** tank up (*a.* F *drink*), refuel.
'Tanker *m* (-s; -) ⚓ (oil) tanker.
'Tank|schiff *n* → **Tanker**. **~stelle** *f* filling (*or* petrol, *Am.* gas) station. **~verschluß** *m* mot. fuel cap. **~wagen** *m* mot. tanker. **~wart** *m* (-[e]s; -e) petrol pump (*Am.* gas station) attendant.
Tanne ['tanə] *f* (-; -n) fir (tree).
'Tannen|baum *m* fir (tree). **~nadel** *f* fir needle. **~zapfen** *m* fir cone.
Tante ['tantə] *f* (-; -n) **1.** aunt: **~ Helene** Aunt Helen. **2.** F woman, bird.
Tante-'Emma-Laden *m* F corner shop, *Am.* mom-and-pop store.
Tantieme [tãˈtiɛːmə] *f* (-; -n) royalty.
Tanz [tants] *m* (-es; ⸚e) **1.** dance. **2.** F *fig.* fuss. **'Tanzbein** *n* F **das ~ schwingen** shake a leg. **tänzeln** ['tɛntsəln] *v/i* **1.** (sn) skip. **2.** (h) *horse:* prance. **'tanzen** *v/t, v/i* (h) dance. **Tänzer** ['tɛntsər] *m* (-s; -), **'Tänzerin** *f* (-; -nen) dancer, *thea.* (ballet) dancer.
'Tanz|fläche *f* dance floor. **~kurs** *m* dancing course. **~lehrer(in** *f*) *m* dancing instructor. **~lo,kal** *n* dance hall. **~mu,sik** *f* dance music. **~or,chester** *n* dance band. **~partner(in** *f*) *m* dancing partner. **~saal** *m* dance hall, ballroom. **~schule** *f* dancing school. **~stunde** *f* **in die ~ gehen** go to a dancing class. **~tur,nier** *n* dancing contest.
Tapet [taˈpeːt] F *et. aufs ~ bringen* bring s.th. up.

Tapete [ta'pe:tə] *f* (-; -n) wallpaper. **Ta'petenwechsel** *m* F *fig.* change (of scenery). **tapezieren** [tape'tsi:rən] *v/t*, *v/i* (h) (wall)paper: *neu ~* repaper.

tapfer ['tapfər] *adj* brave, courageous. **'Tapferkeit** *f* (-; *no pl*) bravery, courage.

tappen ['tapən] *v/i* **1.** (sn) a) pad, b) grope one's way. **2.** (h) grope (*or* fumble) (about) (*nach* for): *a. fig. im dunkeln ~* be groping in the dark.

Tara ['ta:ra] *f* (-; Taren) ✝ tare.

Tarantel [ta'rantəl] *f* (-; -n) tarantula.

Tarif [ta'ri:f] *m* (-s; -e) a) scale of charges, b) rate, c) charge, d) pay scale, e) tariff. **~abschluß** *m* wage settlement. **~autono,mie** *f* free collective bargaining. **~kon,flikt** *m* pay dispute.

ta'riflich *adj* tariff ..., standard ...

Ta'riflohn *m* standard wage(s). **~partner** *m* party to a wage agreement, *pl* union(s) and management. **~runde** *f* pay round. **~satz** *m* **1.** (tariff) rate. **2.** (standard) wage rate. **~verhandlungen** *pl* wage negotiations. **~vertrag** *m* wage agreement.

tarnen ['tarnən] *v/t* (h) camouflage. **'Tarn|farbe** *f* camouflage colo(u)r. **~organisati,on** *f* cover organization. **'Tarnung** *f* (-; -en) camouflage, *fig. a.* cover.

Tasche ['taʃə] *f* (-; -n) **1.** a) (shopping *etc*) bag, b) (hand)bag, *Am.* purse. **2.** pocket: *et. aus der eigenen ~ bezahlen* pay for s.th. out of one's own pocket; *den Gewinn in die eigene ~ stecken* pocket the profit; F *fig. j-n in die ~ stecken* put s.o. in one's pocket; *den Auftrag haben wir in der ~!* the order is in the bag; F *j-m auf der ~ liegen* live off s.o.; *in die eigene ~ arbeiten* line one's (own) pockets; *tief in die ~ greifen (müssen)* have to) dig deep into one's pockets.

'Taschen|buch *n* paperback. **~dieb(in** *f) m* pickpocket. **~feuerzeug** *n* pocket lighter. **~for,mat** *n* pocket size: *im ~* pocket-size(d). **~geld** *n* pocket money. **~ka,lender** *m* pocket diary. **~lampe** *f* torch, *Am.* flashlight. **~messer** *n* penknife. **~rechner** *m* pocket calculator. **~spiegel** *m* pocket mirror. **~tuch** *n* handkerchief. **~uhr** *f* fob watch. **~wörterbuch** *n* pocket dictionary.

Tasse ['tasə] *f* (-; -n) cup: *e-e ~ Tee* a cup of tea; F *contp. trübe ~* drip.

Tastatur [tasta'tu:r] *f* (-; -en) keyboard, keys. **Taste** ['tastə] *f* (-; -n) key, *a.* push button.

tasten ['tastən] (h) **I** *v/t* touch, feel. **II** *v/i* (*nach* for) *a. fig.* grope, fumble. **III** *sich ~* grope one's way. **'tastend** *adj* groping, *fig. a.* tentative. **'Tasten|instru,ment** *n* ♪ keyboard instrument. **~tele,fon** *n* push-button telephone.

'Taster *m* (-s; -) **1.** *zo.* feeler. **2.** ☉ a) key, b) sensor.

'Tastsinn *m* (-[e]s; *no pl*) sense of touch.

tat [ta:t] *pret of tun.*

Tat *f* (-; -en) **1.** a) deed, act, b) achievement, feat, c) action: *er ist ein Mann der ~* he is a man of action; → *umsetzen* **3. 2.** (criminal) offen/ce (*Am.* -se), crime: *auf frischer ~ ertappen* catch *s.o.* redhanded. **3.** *in der ~* indeed.

Tatar [ta'ta:r] *n* (-[s]; *no pl*) *gastr.* spiced raw minced beef.

'Tatbestand *m* state of affairs, ⚖ facts of the case.

'Tatendrang *m* thirst for action.

'tatenlos *adj* inactive.

Täter ['tɛ:tər] *m* (-s; -), **'Täterin** *f* (-; -nen) culprit, ⚖ offender.

tätig ['tɛ:tɪç] *adj* active (*a.* volcano), busy: *~ sein als* a) work as, b) act as; *~ sein bei* work for *a firm*, work at *an institute etc*; *~ werden* act, take action. **tätigen** ['tɛ:tɪgən] *v/t* (h) effect, transact (*business*), make (*purchases*). **'Tätigkeit** *f* (-; -en) a) activity, b) occupation, job, c) function, d) *physiol.*, ☉ *tec* action: *in ~* in action; *welche ~ üben Sie aus?* what is your job? **'Tätigkeitsfeld** *n* field of activity.

'Tatkraft *f* (-; *no pl*) energy, drive, enterprise. **'tatkräftig** *adj* energetic, active: **~e Hilfe** effective help.

tätlich ['tɛ:tlɪç] *adj* violent: ⚖ **~e Beleidigung** assault and battery; *~ werden* become violent; *gegen j-n ~ werden* assault s.o. **'Tätlichkeit** *f* (-; -en) (act of) violence, ⚖ assault (and battery).

'Tatort *m* scene of the crime.

tätowieren [tɛto'vi:rən] *v/t* (h) tattoo. **Täto'wierung** *f* (-; -en) tattoo.

'Tatsache *f* fact: *j-n vor vollendete ~n stellen* confront s.o. with a fait accompli; **~ ist, daß** the fact is that; **das ändert nichts an der ~, daß** that doesn't alter the fact that; **den ~n ins Auge blicken** face the facts.

'**Tatsachenbericht** m documentary.

'**tatsächlich I** adj actual, real. **II** adv actually, really, in fact: **~?** really?

'**tätscheln** ['tɛːtʃəln] v/t (h) pat.

'**tatterig** ['tatərɪç] adj F doddery, shaky.

'**Tatze** ['tatsə] f (-; -n) paw.

'**Tau**[1] [taʊ] n (-[e]s; -e) rope.

'**Tau**[2] m (-[e]s; no pl) dew.

taub [taʊp] adj **1.** deaf (fig. **gegen, für** to): **auf einem Ohr ~** deaf in one ear. **2.** empty (nut), dead (rock), numb (limbs).

'**Taube**[1] ['taʊbə] m, f (-n; -n) deaf person: **die ~n** the deaf.

'**Taube**[2] f (-; -n) zo. pigeon, a. pol. dove.

'**Taubenschlag** m dovecot.

'**Taubheit** f (-; no pl) **1.** deafness. **2.** numbness. '**taubstumm** adj deaf and dumb. '**Taubstumme** m, f (-n; -n) deaf-mute. '**Taubstummensprache** f deaf-and-dumb language.

tauchen ['taʊxən] **I** v/i (sn) dive (**nach** for), a. skin-dive, submarine: a. submerge. **II** v/t (h) dip, immerse: **j-n ~** duck s.o.

'**Taucher** m (-s; -) (sports: skin) diver. **~anzug** m diving suit, a. wetsuit. **~brille** f diving goggles. **~glocke** f diving bell. **~maske** f diving mask.

'**Tauch**|**sieder** m (-s; -) ⚡ immersion heater. **~sport** m skin diving.

tauen ['taʊən] **I** v/i (sn) thaw, melt. **II** v/impers (h) **es taut** a) it is thawing, b) dew is falling.

'**Taufbecken** n font. **Taufe** ['taʊfə] f (-; -n) baptism, a. christening: **aus der ~ heben** stand godfather (or godmother) to, fig. launch. '**taufen** v/t (h) **1.** baptize, christen. **2.** call. '**Täufling** m (-s; -e) child (or person) to be baptized. '**Taufname** m Christian (esp. Am. given) name. '**Taufschein** m certificate of baptism. '**Taufstein** m font.

taugen ['taʊɡən] v/i (h) (**zu, für**) be suited, be of use: **nichts ~** be no good; **taugt es (et)was?** is it any good?

'**tauglich** ['taʊklɪç] adj a) suitable (**für, zu** for), b) ✗ fit (for service). '**Tauglichkeit** f (-; no pl) a) suitability, b) fitness.

Taumel ['taʊməl] m (-s; no pl) **1.** dizziness. **2.** fig. a) whirl, b) rapture, frenzy.

taum(e)lig ['taʊm(ə)lɪç] adj dizzy.

taumeln ['taʊməln] v/i (sn) reel, stagger.

Tausch [taʊʃ] m (-[e]s; -e) exchange, F swap, barter. '**tauschen** v/t, v/i (h) exchange (a. looks etc), a. barter, F swap (**gegen** for): **ich möchte nicht mit ihr ~** I wouldn't like to be in her shoes.

täuschen ['tɔyʃən] (h) **I** v/t a) mislead, deceive, b) cheat, fool: **wenn mich nicht alles täuscht** if I am not very much mistaken; **wenn mich mein Gedächtnis nicht täuscht** if my memory serves me right; **sich ~ lassen** be taken in (**von** by). **II** v/i be deceptive, sports: feint, fake a blow etc. '**täuschend I** adj a) deceptive, b) striking: **j-m ~ ähnlich sehen** look remarkably like s.o.

'**Tausch**|**geschäft** n, **~handel** m barter, F swap. **~ob**,**jekt** n object of exchange.

'**Täuschung** f (-; -en) a) deception, b) delusion, c) mistake, d) 🕮 deceit: **optische ~** optical illusion.

'**Täuschungs**|**ma**,**növer** n feint, diversion. **~versuch** m attempt to deceive.

tausend ['taʊzənt] adj (a) thousand: **~ und aber ~** thousands and thousands of. '**Tausend** n (-s; -e) thousand: **zu ~en** by the thousand. '**Tausender** m (-s; -) F thousand mark note. '**tausendfach I** adj thousandfold. **II** adv → **tausendmal**. '**Tausendfüß**(**l**)**er** m (-s; -) zo. centipede. '**tausendjährig** adj of a thousand years, millennial. '**tausendmal** adv a thousand times. '**tausendst** adj, '**Tausendste** m, f (-n; -n) thousandth. '**Tausendstel** n (-s; -) thousandth (part).

'**Tautropfen** m dewdrop.

'**Tauwetter** n a. fig. pol. thaw.

'**Tauziehen** n a. fig. tug-of-war.

'**Taxameter** [taksa'meːtər] m (-s; -) taximeter.

Taxator [ta'ksaːtɔr] m (-s; -en [taksa'toːrən]) ✝, 🕮 valuer, assessor.

Taxe ['taksə] f (-; -n) **1.** a) rate, fee, b) tax. **2.** → **Taxi** ['taksi] n (-s; -s) taxi, cab: **~ fahren** a) drive a taxi, b) go by taxi.

taxieren [ta'ksiːrən] v/t (h) **1.** estimate, ✝, 🕮 value, assess. **2.** F size up.

'**Taxifahrer**(**in** f) m taxi driver.

'**Taxistand** *m* taxi rank.

Teak [ti:k] *n* (-s; *no pl*), **~holz** *n* teak.

Technik ['tɛçnɪk] *f* (-; -en) **1.** *no pl* a) technology, technics, b) engineering. **2.** *a. art, sports, etc*: technique.

'**Techniker** *m* (-s; -) (technical) engineer, *a. sports etc*: technician.

'**technisch** *adj* engineering (*process etc*), *a. art, sports, etc*: technical, technological (*a. age, progress, etc*): sports: **~e Disziplin** field event; **~er K.o.** technical knockout; **~es Personal** technical staff; **~e Hochschule** college (*Am.* institute) of technology; **~ begabt** gifted technically.

technisieren [tɛçni'zi:rən] *v/t* (h) mechanize.

Technokrat [tɛçno'kra:t] *m* (-en; -en) technocrat.

Technologie [tɛçnolo'gi:] *f* (-; -n) technology. **Technolo'gietrans,fer** *m* technology transfer. **technologisch** [tɛçno'lo:gɪʃ] *adj* technological.

Teddybär ['tɛdi-] *m* teddy (bear).

Tee [te:] *m* (-s; -s) **1.** tea: **e-n ~ machen** make some tea; **e-n ~ trinken** have a cup of tea; → **abwarten** II. **2.** tea party. **~beutel** *m* tea bag. **~büchse** *f* tea caddy. **~-Ei** *n* infuser, tea egg, *esp. Am.* tea ball. **~gebäck** *n* biscuits, *Am.* cookies. **~haus** *n* teahouse. **~kanne** *f* teapot. **~kessel** *m* teakettle. **~löffel** *m* teaspoon. **~ma,schine** *f* tea-urn.

Teer [te:r] *m* (-[e]s; -e) tar.

teeren ['te:rən] *v/t* (h) tar.

'**Tee|sieb** *n* tea strainer. **~stube** *f* tearoom. **~tasse** *f* teacup. **~wagen** *m* tea trolley (*Am.* wagon).

Teich [taɪç] *m* (-[e]s; -e) pond, pool.

Teig [taɪk] *m* (-[e]s; -e) dough. **teigig** ['taɪgɪç] *adj* doughy, pasty (*a. fig.*).

'**Teigwaren** *pl* pasta.

Teil [taɪl] *m, n* (-[e]s; -e) part (*a.* ⊙), share, *a.* ⊙ component, element: ⚏ **beide ~e** both sides; **ein ~ davon** part of it; **zum ~** partly; **zum großen** (*or* **größten**) **~** largely, for the most part; **der größte ~e** the greater part (*gen* of); **zu gleichen ~en** in equal shares; **sein ~ beitragen** do one's bit; **sich sein ~ denken** have one's own thoughts about it; **ich für mein ~** I for my part.

'**Teilansicht** *f* partial view.

'**teilbar** *adj* divisible.

'**Teilbetrag** *m* partial amount.

'**Teilchen** *n* (-s; -) *a. phys.* particle.

teilen ['taɪlən] (h) **I** *v/t* a) divide, b) distribute, share out, c) share: **die Kosten ~** share expenses; **Freud und Leid mit j-m ~** share s.o.'s joys and troubles. **II** *sich ~* divide, *curtain*: part; **sich in et. ~** share s.th.; → **geteilt**.

'**Teiler** *m* (-s; -) ⚏ divisor.

'**Teilerfolg** *m* partial success.

'**teilhaben** *v/i* (*irr, sep,* -ge-, h, → **haben**) (**an** *dat* in) participate, share.

Teilhaber ['taɪlha:bər] *m* (-s; -) ✝ partner, associate. '**Teilhaberschaft** *f* (-; *no pl*) partnership.

'**Teilkaskoversicherung** *f* mot. partial coverage insurance.

'**Teillieferung** *f* part delivery.

Teilnahme ['taɪlna:mə] *f* (-; *no pl*) (**an** *dat*) **1.** a) participation (in), b) attendance (at). **2.** *fig.* a) interest (in), b) sympathy (with), c) condolence(s).

'**teilnahmeberechtigt** *adj* eligible.

'**teilnahmslos** *adj* indifferent, listless, apathetic. '**Teilnahmslosigkeit** *f* (-; *no pl*) indifference, listlessness, apathy.

'**teilnahmsvoll** *adj* sympathetic.

'**teilnehmen** *v/i* (*irr, sep,* -ge-, h, → **nehmen**) (**an** *dat*) **1.** a) take part (in), b) be present (at), attend (*s.th.*). **2.** *fig.* a) take an interest (in), b) sympathize (with).

'**Teilnehmer** *m* (-s; -), '**Teilnehmerin** *f* (-; -nen) participant, *sports etc*: competitor, entrant, *teleph.* subscriber.

'**Teilpro,these** *f* partial (denture).

'**teils** [taɪls] *adv* partly.

'**Teilstrecke** *f* bus etc: (fare) stage, 🚃 section, *w.s.* stage, *a. sports*: leg.

'**Teilstrich** *m* ⊙ graduation mark.

'**Teilstück** *n* section.

Teilung *f* (-; -en) division (*a. biol.,* ⚏).

'**teilweise I** *adj* partial. **II** *adv* partly, partially, in part.

'**Teilzahlung** *f* **1.** part payment. **2.** payment by instal(l)ments: **auf ~ kaufen** buy on instal(l)ment (*or* hire purchase). '**Teilzahlungsvertrag** *m* hire-purchase contract.

'**Teilzeit|arbeit** *f*, **~beschäftigung** *f* part-time employment (*or* job).

Teint [tɛ̃:] *m* (-s; -s) complexion.

Tele ['te:lə] *n* (-[s]; -[s]) F telephoto lens.

Telefax ['te:ləfaks] *n* (-; -[e]), '**telefaxen** *v/t* (h) telefax.

Telefon [tele'fo:n] *n* (-s; -e) (tele)phone:
am ~ on the (tele)phone; *ans ~ gehen*
answer the (tele)phone; *~ haben* be on
the (tele)phone. **~appa,rat** *m* telephone.
Telefonat [telefo'na:t] *n* (-[e]s; -e) →
Telefongespräch.

Tele'fon|buch *n* phone book, telephone
directory. **~gebühr** *f* telephone charge.
~gespräch *n* telephone conversation,
phone call. **~hörer** *m* receiver.

telefonieren [telefo'ni:rən] *v/i* (h) (tel-
e)phone: *mit j-m ~* talk to s.o. over the
(tele)phone; *sie telefoniert gerade* she
is on the phone; *nach Amerika ~* make
a (tele)phone call to America; *darf ich
mal ~?* may I use your (tele)phone?

tele'fonisch I *adj* telephonic. **II** *adv* by
(or over the) (tele)phone: *~ übermitteln*
(tele)phone; *sind Sie ~ zu erreichen?*
are you on the phone?, can I call
you?

Telefonist [telefo'nɪst] *m* (-en; -en),
Telefo'nistin *f* (-; -nen) switchboard
operator.

Tele'fon|karte *f* phonecard. **~netz** *n*
telephone network. **~nummer** *f* (tele)-
phone number. **~verbindung** *f* telephone connection. **~zelle** *f* (tele)phone
box (*or* booth), call box. **~zen,trale** *f*
(telephone) exchange, *of firm*: switchboard.

Telegraf [tele'gra:f] *m* (-en; -en) telegraph. **Telegrafie** [telegra'fi:] *f* (-; *no
pl*) telegraphy: *drahtlose ~* radioteleg-
raphy. **telegrafieren** [telegra'fi:rən]
v/t, v/i (h) telegraph, wire. **Telegrafist**
[telegra'fɪst] *m* (-en; -en), **Telegra'fi-
stin** *f* (-; -nen) telegraphist.

Telegramm [tele'gram] *n* (-s; -e) telegram. **~anschrift** *f* telegraphic address.
~stil *m* (*im ~* in) telegraphese.

'Teleko,pierer *m* (-s; -) telecopier.

'Teleobjek,tiv *n* telephoto lens.

Telepathie [telepa'ti:] *f* (-; *no pl*) telep-
athy.

telepathisch [tele'pa:tɪʃ] *adj* telepathic.

Teleskop [tele'sko:p] *n* (-s; -e) telescope.
tele'skopisch *adj* telescopic.

Telespiel ['te:lə-] *n* TV game.

Telex ['te:lɛks] *n* (-; -[e]), **'telexen** *v/t* (h)
telex.

Teller ['tɛlər] *m* (-s; -) **1.** plate. **2.** ⚙, *a. on
ski stick*: disc, disk.

'Tellervoll *m* (-s; -) plateful.

Tempel ['tɛmpəl] *m* (-s; -) temple.

Temperament [tempəra'mɛnt] *n* (-[e]s;
-e) a) temperament, temper, b) verve,
vivacity, F pep: *hitziges ~* hot temper.

tempera'mentlos *adj* lifeless.

tempera'mentvoll *adj* (high-)spirited.

Temperatur [tempəra'tu:r] *f* (-; -en) (*bei
e-r ~ von* at a) temperature (of); ✚ *~
haben* have (*or* run) a temperature;
~anstieg *m* rise in temperature. **~sturz**
m sudden drop in temperature.

temperieren [tempə'ri:rən] *v/t* (h) *a.* ♩
temper.

Tempo ['tɛmpo] *n* (-s; -s, -pi) tempo (*a.
♪*), speed, rate, pace: *das ~ bestimmen
(durchhalten, forcieren or steigern)*
set (stand, force) the pace; *~!* step on
it!, go! **'Tempolimit** *n mot.* speed limit.

Tempomat [tɛmpo'ma:t] *m* (-en; -en)
mot. cruise control, speedhold.

Tendenz [tɛn'dɛnts] *f* (-; -en) tendency,
trend (*a.* ✝), *contp.* bias, slant. **tendenziös** [tɛndɛn'tsiø:s] *adj* tendentious.

tendieren [tɛn'di:rən] *v/i* (h) tend (*nach,
zu* to).

Tennis ['tɛnɪs] *n* (-; *no pl*) tennis. **~ball** *m*
tennis ball. **~halle** *f* covered court.
~platz *m* tennis court. **~schläger** *m*
tennis racket. **~spieler(in** *f)* *m* tennis
player. **~tur,nier** *n* tennis tournament.

Tenor¹ ['te:nɔr] *m* (-s; *no pl*) tenor, substance.

Tenor² [te'no:r] *m* (-s; ⸚e) ♪ **1.** (*a.* **~stim-
me** *f*, **~par,tie** *f*) tenor (voice, part). **2.**
tenor (singer *or* player).

Teppich ['tɛpɪç] *m* (-s; -e) carpet: *fig. et.
unter den ~ kehren* sweep s.th. under
the carpet; F *bleib auf dem ~!* be reasonable. **~boden** *m* fitted carpet,
wall-to-wall carpeting. **~fliese** *f* carpet
tile. **~händler** *m* carpet dealer.

Termin [tɛr'mi:n] *m* (-s; -e) **1.** a) (set)
date, time limit, b) deadline: *e-n ~ festsetzen* fix a date *etc*; *bis zu diesem ~*
by this date. **2.** (*sich e-n ~ geben lassen* make an) appointment (*bei* with
one's doctor etc). **3.** ⚖ hearing.

Ter'mindruck *m* time pressure: *unter ~
stehen* be pressed for time.

ter'mingebunden adj scheduled (*work*).
ter'mingemäß adj and adv on schedule.
Ter'minka,lender m appointments book, 🖼️ cause list, *Am.* calendar: **e-n vollen ~ haben** have a busy schedule.
Terminologie [tɛrminolo'giː] f (-; -n) terminology.
Ter'minplan m schedule.
Termite [tɛr'miːtə] f (-; -n) *zo.* termite.
Terpentin [tɛrpɛn'tiːn] n, m (-s; *no pl*) 🌲 turpentine.
Terrain [tɛ'rɛ̃ː] n (-s; -s) **1.** terrain. **2.** plot of land, (building) site.
Terrasse [tɛ'rasə] f (-; -n) terrace.
ter'rassenförmig adj terraced.
Ter'rassenhaus n stepped building.
Ter'rassentür f French window.
territorial [tɛrito'rjaːl] adj territorial.
Territorium [tɛri'toːriʊm] n (-s; -rien) territory.
Terror ['tɛrɔr] m (-s; *no pl*) terror.
'Terroranschlag m terrorist attack.
terrorisieren [tɛrori'ziːrən] v/t (h) terrorize. **Terrorismus** [tɛro'rɪsmʊs] m (-; *no pl*) terrorism. **Terrorist** [-'rɪst] m (-en; -en), **Terro'ristin** f (-; -nen) terrorist. **terro'ristisch** adj terrorist.
Terz [tɛrts] f (-; -en) **1.** ♪ third. **2.** *fenc.* tierce.
Terzett [tɛr'tsɛt] n (-[e]s; -e) ♪ trio.
Tesafilm ['teːza-] m (*TM*) sellotape (*TM*), *esp. Am.* Scotch tape (*TM*).
Test [tɛst] m (-[e]s; -s, *a.* -e) test.
Testament [tɛsta'mɛnt] n (-[e]s; -e) **1.** (last) will, 🖼️ last will and testament: **sein ~ machen** make a will. **2.** *eccl.* **Altes (Neues) ~** Old (New) Testament.
testamentarisch [tɛstamɛn'taːrɪʃ] **I** adj testamentary. **II** adv by will.
Testa'mentseröffnung f opening of the will. **~vollstrecker** m executor.
testen ['tɛstən] v/t (h) test.
'Testper,son f (test) subject.
'Teststrecke f *mot.* test track.
Tetanus(schutz)impfung ['teːtanʊs-] f 💉 tetanus vaccination.
teuer ['tɔyər] **I** adj expensive, dear: **wie ~ ist es?** how much is it?; **Fleisch ist teurer geworden** meat prices have gone up; *fig.* **j-m ~ sein** be dear to s.o. **II** adv dear(ly): **das wird ihn ~ zu stehen kommen** he will have to pay dearly for that. **'Teuerung** f (-; -en) high (*or* rising) prices, high cost of living.

'Teuerungsrate f rate of price increases.
Teufel ['tɔyfəl] m (-s; -) devil: **der ~** the Devil; F **wer (wo, was) zum ~?** who (where, what) the devil (*or* hell)?; **wie der ~, auf ~ komm raus** like blazes; **in (des) ~s Küche kommen** get into a hell of a mess; **j-n zum ~ jagen** send s.o. packing; **der ~ war los** all hell had broken loose; **das Geld ist zum ~** the money is down the drain; **mal' den ~ nicht an die Wand!** don't tempt fate; **scher dich zum ~!** go to hell!
'Teufelskerl m devil of a fellow.
'Teufelskreis m *fig.* vicious circle.
teuflisch ['tɔyflɪʃ] adj devilish, *fig. a.* hellish.
Text [tɛkst] m (-[e]s; -e) text, words, lyrics. **'Textbuch** n libretto. **'Texter** m (-s; -) **1.** copywriter. **2.** songwriter.
Textilien [tɛks'tiːljən] pl textiles.
Tex'tilindu,strie f textile industry.
'Text|kri,tik f textual criticism. **~verarbeitung** f word processing. **~verarbeitungssy,stem** n word processor.
Theater [te'aːtər] n (-s; -) **1.** theatre, *Am.* theater: **zum ~ gehen** go on the stage; **ins ~ gehen** go to the theatre. **2.** *fig.* a) play-acting, b) *contp.* farce, c) fuss: **~ spielen** put on an act; **mach kein ~!** don't make a fuss! **~abonne,ment** n theatre subscription. **~besuch** m visit to the theatre. **~besucher** m theatre/regoer (*Am.* -er.) **~karte** f theat/re (*Am.* -er) ticket. **~kasse** f box office. **~probe** f rehearsal. **~stück** n (stage) play. **~vorstellung** f theatrical performance. **~zettel** m playbill.
theatralisch [tea'traːlɪʃ] adj theatrical.
Theke ['teːkə] f (-; -n) bar, *a.* counter.
Thema ['teːma] n (-s; -men) subject, *a.* topic, ♪ *etc* theme: **beim ~ bleiben** stick to the point; **das ~ wechseln** change the subject. **Thematik** [te'maːtɪk] f (-; -en) subject (matter).
Themenkreis ['teːmən-] m subject area.
Theologe [teo'loːgə] m (-n; -n) theologian. **Theologie** [teolo'giː] f (-; -n) theology. **theo'logisch** adj theological.
Theoretiker [teo're'tiːkər] m (-s; -) theorist. **theo'retisch** adj and adv theoretical(ly), adv a. in theory. **theoretisieren** [teoreti'ziːrən] v/i (h) theorize. **Theorie** [teo'riː] f (-; -n) theory.

Therapeut [tera'pɔʏt] *m* (-en; -en), **The-ra'peutin** *f* (-; -nen) therapist.

thera'peutisch *adj* therapeutic.

Therapie [tera'pi:] *f* (-; -n) therapy.

Thermal|bad [tɛr'ma:l-] *n* **1.** thermal spa. **2.** thermal bath. **~quelle** *f* thermal spring.

Thermik ['tɛrmɪk] *f* (-; *no pl*) thermionics. **'thermisch** *adj* thermic.

Thermody'namik [tɛrmo-] *f* thermodynamics.

'Thermoele‚ment *n* thermocouple.

Thermometer [tɛrmo'me:tər] *n* (-s; -) thermometer: *das ~ zeigt 5 Grad über (unter) Null* the thermometer is at (or shows) 5 degrees above (below) zero.

thermonukle'ar *adj* thermonuclear.

Thermosflasche ['tɛrmɔs-] *f* (*TM*) Thermos (flask) (*TM*).

Thermostat [tɛrmo'sta:t] *m* (-[e]s, -en; -e[n]) thermostat.

'Thermowäsche *f* thermal underwear.

These ['te:zə] *f* (-; -n) **1.** thesis. **2.** theory.

Thrombose [trɔm'bo:zə] *f* (-; -n) ⚕ thrombosis.

Thron [tro:n] *m* (-[e]s; -e) throne.

thronen ['tro:nən] *v/i* (h) be enthroned.

'Thronerbe *m* heir to the throne.

'Thronfolge *f* succession to the throne. **'Thronfolger** *m* (-s; -), **'Thronfolgerin** *f* (-; -nen) successor to the throne.

Thunfisch ['tu:n-] *m* **1.** tunny. **2.** 🐟 tuna.

Thymian ['ty:mĭa:n] *m* (-s; -e) 🌿 thyme.

Tibet ['ti:bɛt] *n* (-s) Tibet. **Tibeter** [ti'be:tər] *m* (-s; -), **Ti'beterin** *f* (-; -nen), **ti'betisch** *adj* Tibetan.

Tick [tɪk] *m* (-[e]s; -s) quirk, tic.

ticken ['tɪkən] *v/i* (h) tick.

tief [ti:f] **I** *adj* deep (*a. fig.*), low, *fig.* profound (*knowledge etc*): *aus ~stem Herzen* from the bottom of one's heart; *im ~sten Winter* in the dead of winter. **II** *adv* deep, low, *fig.* a) deeply, b) far: *~ in Gedanken* deep in thought; *~ enttäuscht* badly disappointed; *~ schlafen* be fast asleep, sleep soundly; *bis ~ in die Nacht* far into the night.

Tief *n* (-s; -s) *meteor.* low, depression.

'Tiefbau *m* (-[e]s; *no pl*) civil engineering. **~ingeni‚eur** *m* construction engineer.

'tiefblau *adj* deep blue.

'Tiefdruck *m* (-[e]s; *no pl*) **1.** *meteor.* low pressure. **2.** intaglio (printing). **~gebiet** *n* cyclone, low-pressure area.

'Tiefe *f* (-; -n) **1.** depth, *fig. a.* profundity. **2.** *pl radio etc*: bass.

'Tiefebene *f* lowland(s).

'Tiefen|inter‚view *n* (in-)depth interview. **~psycholo‚gie** *f* depth psychology. **~regler** *m radio etc*: bass control. **~schärfe** *f phot.* depth of focus.

'tiefernst *adj* very grave.

'Tief|flug *m* low-level flight. **~gang** *m* (-[e]s; *no pl*) **1.** ⚓ draught. **2.** *fig.* depth. **~ga‚rage** *f* underground car park.

'tiefgefroren *adj* deep-frozen.

'tiefgreifend *adj* far-reaching.

'tiefgründig [-grʏndɪç] *adj* profound.

'Tiefkühlfach *n* freezing compartment.

'Tiefkühlkost *f* frozen foods.

'Tiefkühltruhe *f* freezer, deep-freeze.

'tiefliegend *adj* **1.** low(-lying). **2.** deep-set (*eyes*). **3.** *fig.* deep(-seated).

'Tiefpunkt *m fig.* low: *e-n seelischen ~ haben* feel very depressed.

'Tiefschlag *m a. fig.* hit below the belt.

'tiefschürfend *adj fig.* profound.

'tiefschwarz *adj* jet-black.

'Tiefsee *f* deep sea.

'tiefsinnig *adj* profound.

'Tiefstand *m* (-[e]s; *no pl*) low: *e-n absoluten ~ erreichen* hit an all-time low.

Tiegel ['ti:gəl] *m* (-s; -) saucepan.

Tier [ti:r] *n* (-[e]s; -e) animal (*a. fig.*), beast, *fig. contp.* brute: F *großes* (or *hohes*) *~* bigwig, big shot. **~art** *f* (animal) species. **~arzt** *m* veterinary surgeon, *Am.* veterinarian, F vet. **~freund** *m* animal lover. **~handlung** *f* pet shop. **~heim** *n* home for animals.

'tierisch I *adj* animal ..., *fig. contp. a.* brutish: **~e** *Fette* animal fats. **II** *adv* F *fig.* awfully, terribly.

'Tier|kreis *m* (-es; *no pl*) *astr.* zodiac. **~kreiszeichen** *n* sign of the zodiac. **~lieb** *adj* fond of animals. **~medi‚zin** *f* veterinary medicine. **~nahrung** *f* pet food. **~park** *m* zoological gardens, zoo. **~pfleger** *m* keeper. **~quäle‚rei** *f* cruelty to animals. **~reich** *n* animal kingdom. **~schutzverein** *m* society for the prevention of cruelty to animals. **~versuch** *m* animal experiment. **~welt** *f* animal world.

Tiger ['ti:gər] *m* (-s; -) tiger. **'Tigerfell** *n* tiger skin. **'Tigerin** *f* (-; -nen) tigress.

tigern ['ti:gərn] *v/i* (sn) F traipse, trot.

Tilde ['tɪldə] f (-; -n) ling. tilde.

tilgbar ['tɪlk-] adj ♣ redeemable. **tilgen** ['tɪlgən] v/t (h) **1.** wipe out (a. fig.), blot out (a. fig. memories etc), print. delete, cancel, a. fig. efface, erase. **2.** ♣ a) pay off, b) redeem (loan). **'Tilgung** f (-; -en) ♣ repayment, redemption.

timen ['taɪmən] v/t (h) time: **gut** (**schlecht**) **getimt** well (badly) timed.

Tinktur [tɪŋk'tu:r] f (-; -en) tincture.

Tinnef ['tɪnɛf] m (-s; no pl) F rubbish.

Tinte ['tɪntə] f (-; -n) ink: F **in der ~ sitzen** be in the soup.

'Tinten|fisch m **1.** squid. **2.** octopus. **~klecks** m inkblot. **~kuli** m stylograph. **~stift** m indelible pencil.

Tip [tɪp] m (-s; -s) tip, a. hint: **ein sicherer ~** a sure bet; **j-m e-n ~ geben** a) give s.o. a tip, b) tip s.o. off.

tippen ['tɪpən] (h) **I** v/i **1.** ~ **an** (acc) tap. **2.** F a) do the Lotto, b) do the pools. **3.** F ~ **auf** (acc) tip; **ich tippe auf ihn** my bet is on him. **4.** F type. **II** v/t **5.** F type. **'Tippfehler** m typing error.

Tippse ['tɪpsə] f (-; -n) F contp. typist.

'tipp'topp adj F first-class: ~ **gekleidet** immaculately dressed; ~ **sauber** spick and span.

'Tippzettel m lotto (or pools) coupon.

Tisch [tɪʃ] m (-es; -e) table: **er ist zu ~** he's having his lunch hour; **am ~ sitzen** sit at the table; **bei ~ sitzen** sit at table; **den ~ decken** (**abräumen**) lay (clear) the table; fig. **reinen ~ machen** make a clean sweep (or make tabula rasa) (**mit** of); **unter den ~ fallen** fall flat; **die Sache ist auf dem** (**vom**) ~ the matter is on (off) the table; → **grün. ~dame** f partner at table. **~decke** f tablecloth. **Ofertig** adj ready(-)to(-)serve. **~gebet** n **das ~ sprechen** say grace. **~karte** f place card.

Tischler ['tɪʃlər] m (-s; -) **1.** joiner. **2.** cabinetmaker. **Tischle'rei** f (-; -en) **1.** no pl joinery. **2.** joiner's workshop. **'tischlern** (h) **I** v/t make. **II** v/i do joiner's work.

'Tisch|ordnung f seating plan. **~platte** f a) tabletop, b) leaf. **~rede** f after-dinner speech. **~rücken** n table turning.

'Tischtennis n table tennis. **~ball** m table tennis ball. **~schläger** m table tennis bat (Am. paddle).

'Tisch|tuch n tablecloth. **~wein** m table

wine. **~zeit** f lunch hour (or break).

Titan [ti'ta:n] n (-s; no pl) 🜍 titanium.

Titel ['ti:təl] m (-s; -) title. **~bild** n frontispiece (of book), cover picture (of magazine). **~blatt** n title page (of book), front page (of magazine). **~geschichte** f cover story. **~halter** m sports: titleholder. **~kampf** m title match (boxing: bout). **~melo,die** f theme tune. **~rolle** f title role. **~seite** f → **Titelblatt. ~verteidiger** m sports: titleholder.

Titten ['tɪtən] pl V tits, boobs.

Toast [to:st] m (-[e]s; -e, -s) **1.** toast: **e-n ~ ausbringen** → **toasten II. 2.** gastr. toast. **'toasten** (h) **I** v/t toast (bread). **II** v/i propose (or drink) a toast (**auf** acc to). **'Toaster** m (-s; -) toaster.

toben ['to:bən] v/i (h) **1.** a. fig. rage. **2.** children: romp.

'tobsüchtig adj raving mad, frantic.

'Tobsuchtsanfall m F fig. **e-n ~ bekommen** fly into a tantrum.

Tochter ['tɔxtər] f (-; ⸚) **1.** daughter. **2.** → **~gesellschaft** f subsidiary (company).

Tod [to:t] m (-es; -e) death: **den ~ finden** be killed; fig. **et. zu ~e reiten** flog s.th. to death; F **j-n zu ~e erschrecken** (**langweilen**) frighten (bore) s.o. to death (or stiff); **auf den ~ nicht ausstehen können** loathe, hate like poison.

'tod'ernst I adj deadly serious. **II** adv in dead earnest.

Todes|angst ['to:dəs-] f **1.** fear of death. **2.** fig. mortal fear: **Todesängste ausstehen** be scared to death. **~anzeige** f obituary (notice). **~fall** m (**im ~** in case of) death. **~gefahr** f mortal danger. **~jahr** n year of s.o.'s death. **~kampf** m throes of death. **~kandi,dat** m doomed man, F goner. **~opfer** pl casualties, victims: **Zahl der ~** a. death toll. **~stoß** m death blow. **~strafe** f death penalty, capital punishment: **bei ~** on penalty of death. **~stunde** f hour of death. **~tag** m day (w.s. anniversary) of s.o.'s death. **~ursache** f cause of death. **~urteil** n death sentence (fig. warrant). **~verachtung** f defiance of death: F **mit ~** unflinchingly. **~wunsch** m death wish. **~zelle** f death cell, pl a. death row.

'Todfeind(in f) m deadly enemy.

'todgeweiht adj doomed.

'tod'krank adj fatally ill.

tödlich ['tø:tlɪç] adj a) fatal, a. fig. mortal

te mir diesen ~! don't take that tone with me; **e-n anderen** ~ **anschlagen** change one's tune; **den** ~ **angeben** call the tune, *in fashion etc*: set the trend; **es gehört zum guten** ~ **zu** *inf* it is good form to *inf*. **3.** *ling.* accent, stress: **den** ~ **legen auf** (*acc*) *a. fig.* emphasize. **4.** tone (*a. phot.*), shade: ~ **in** ~ in matching colo(u)rs; **rötlicher** ~ tinge of red.

'**tonangebend** *adj* leading, *fashion*: trend-setting.

'**Ton|arm** *m* pickup (arm). **~art** *f* ♪ key. **~aufnahme** *f* (sound) recording. **~ausfall** *m* TV loss of sound.

Tonband *n* tape: **auf** ~ **aufnehmen** tape(-record). **~aufnahme** *f* tape recording. **~gerät** *n* tape recorder.

tönen[¹] ['tø:nən] *v/i* (h) **1.** sound. **2.** F *fig.* sound off.

tönen[²] *v/t* (h) a) tint, b) tone down.

'**Tonerde** *f* argillaceous earth: **essigsaure** ~ alumin(i)um acetate.

'**tönern** *adj* (of) clay.

'**Ton|fall** *m* [-[e]s; *no pl*] intonation. **~film** *m* sound film. **~fre,quenz** *f* acoustic (*or* audio) frequency.

'**Tongeschirr** *n* earthenware, pottery.

'**Tonhöhe** *f* pitch.

Tonikum ['to:nikʊm] *n* [-s; -ka] ♣ tonic.

'**Ton|inge,ni,eur** *m* sound engineer. **~kamera** *f* sound camera. **~kopf** *m* sound (*video*: audio) head. **~lage** *f* pitch. **~leiter** *f* ♪ scale.

'**tonlos** *adj fig.* toneless, flat.

'**Tonmeister** *m* sound engineer.

Tonnage [tɔ'na:ʒə] *f* (-; -n) ♣ tonnage.

Tonne ['tɔnə] *f* (-; -n) **1.** barrel, cask. **2.** (metric) ton. **3.** ♣ a) buoy, b) (register) ton.

'**Ton|regler** *m* tone control. **~spur** *f*, **~streifen** *m film*: sound track. **~studio** *n* recording studio.

Tonsur [tɔn'zu:r] *f* (-; -en) tonsure.

'**Tontaubenschießen** *n* trap shooting.

'**Tontechniker** *m* sound engineer.

'**Tonträger** *m* sound carrier.

'**Tönung** *f* (-; -en) tinge, shade, *a. phot.* tone.

'**Tonwaren** *pl* earthenware, pottery.

Topas [to'pa:s] *m* (-es; -e) *min.* topaz.

Topf [tɔpf] *m* (-[e]s; ⸚e) pot: *fig.* **in 'einen** ~ **werfen** lump together.

Töpfchen ['tœpfçən] *n* (-s; -) pot, potty.

Töpfer ['tœpfər] *m* (-s; -) potter. **Töp-**

(**für** to), lethal (*poison, dose, etc*), b) *fig.* deadly (*accuracy etc*): ~ **verunglücken** be killed in an accident; F **sich** ~ **langweilen** be bored stiff; ~ **beleidigt** mortally offended.

'**tod'müde** *adj* dead tired. '**tod'schick** *adj* F snazzy: ~ **angezogen** *a.* dressed to kill. '**tod'sicher** F **I** *adj* dead sure, sure-fire (*method, tip, etc*): **e-e** ~**e Sache** a dead certainty, a cinch. **II** *adv* for sure: **er kommt** ~ he is sure to come.

'**Todsünde** *f* deadly (*or* mortal) sin.

Tohuwabohu [tohuva'bo:hu] *n* (-[s]; -s) complete chaos.

Toilette [tŏa'lɛtə] *f* (-; -n) **1.** lavatory, toilet, *Am.* bathroom, restroom: **öffentliche** ~**n** public conveniences. **2.** ~ **machen** make one's toilet. **3.** dress.

Toi'letten|ar,tikel *m* toilet article. **~frau** *f*, **~mann** *m* lavatory attendant. **~pa,pier** *n* toilet paper. **~seife** *f* toilet soap. **~tisch** *m* dressing table.

toi, toi, toi ['tɔy'tɔy'tɔy] *int* F **1.** (*unberufen*) ~, ~, ~! touch wood! **2.** good luck!

tolerant [tole'rant] *adj* tolerant (**gegen** of). **Toleranz** [tole'rants] *f* (-; *no pl*) tolerance (**gegen** of). **Tole'ranzschwelle** *f* tolerance threshold.

tolerieren [tole'ri:rən] *v/t* (h) tolerate.

toll [tɔl] **I** *adj* **1.** *a.* F (*crazy, mad*, b) wild: **e-e** ~**e Sache, ein** ~**es Ding** a wild affair, a wow. **2.** F terrific, fantastic: **ein** ~**er Kerl** a terrific guy; **e-e** ~**e Frau** a smasher; **er (es) ist nicht so** ~ he (it) is not so hot. **II** *adv* **3.** F (**wie**) ~ like mad; **er spielt** (**ganz**) ~ he's a fantastic player, he's terrific; → **treiben** 5.

tollen ['tɔlən] *v/i* (h, sn) romp.

'**Tollkirsche** *f* ♣ deadly nightshade.

'**tollkühn** *adj* foolhardy, daredevil.

'**Tollkühnheit** *f* (-; *no pl*) foolhardiness.

'**Tollwut** *f vet.* rabies. '**tollwütig** [-vy:tɪç] *adj* rabid.

Tolpatsch ['tɔlpatʃ] *m* (-[e]s; -e), **Tölpel** ['tœlpəl] *m* (-s; -) clumsy oaf.

Tomate [to'ma:tə] *f* (-; -n) tomato.

Tombola ['tɔmbola] *f* (-; -s) raffle.

Ton[¹] [to:n] *m* (-[e]s; -e) *geol.* clay.

Ton[²] *m* (-[e]s; ⸚e) **1.** tone, sound (*a. film, TV*): **der gute** ~ **ge,sagt** he didn't say a word; **in den höchsten Tönen loben** sing the praises of; **große Töne spukken** talk big; **hat man Töne?** can you believe it? **2.** tone (of voice): **ich verbit-**

fe'rei f (-; -en) **1.** no pl pottery. **2.** potter's workshop. **'Töpferin** f (-; -nen) potter. **'Töpferscheibe** f potter's wheel. **'Töpferwaren** pl pottery.

'top'fit adj in top form.

'Topfpflanze f potted plant.

Topographie [topogra'fi:] f (-; -n) topography.

Topp [tɔp] m (-s; -e[n], -s) ♃ top(mast).

'Toppsegel n topsail.

Tor [to:r] n (-[e]s; -e) **1.** a) gate, b) (garage etc) door, c) gateway (a. fig. **zu** to). **2.** soccer: goal: **im ~ stehen** keep goal; **ein ~ schießen** score (a goal).

'Torbogen m archway.

'Torchance f sports: chance to score.

Torf [tɔrf] m (-[e]s; no pl) peat. **~moor** n peat bog. **~mull** m peat dust.

'Torhüter(in f) m goalkeeper, F goalie.

töricht ['tø:rɪçt] adj foolish.

'Torjäger(in f) m sports: goalgetter.

torkeln ['tɔrkəln] v/i (sn) stagger, reel.

'Torlatte f crossbar.

'Torlinie f sports: goal line.

'torlos adj sports: scoreless.

Tornado [tɔr'na:do] m (-s; -s) tornado, Am. F twister.

Tornister [tɔr'nɪstər] m (-s; -) knapsack.

torpedieren [tɔrpe'di:rən] v/t (h) a. fig. torpedo.

Torpedo [tɔr'pe:do] m (-s; -s) torpedo.

'Torpfosten m sports: goalpost.

'Torraum m soccer: goal area.

'Torschlußpanik f a) last-minute panic, b) fear of being left on the shelf.

'Torschütze m sports: scorer. **'Torschützenkönig** m sports: top scorer.

Torso ['tɔrzo] m (-s; -s, -si) a. fig. torso.

Törtchen ['tœrtçən] n (-s; -) tartlet.

Torte ['tɔrtə] f (-; -n) gateau, layer cake, (fruit) tart. **'Tortenheber** m cake slice.

Tortur [tɔr'tu:r] f (-; -en) torture, fig. a. ordeal.

'Torverhältnis n sports: goal difference.

'Torwart m sports: goalkeeper, F goalie.

tosen ['to:zən] v/i (h) roar, rage: **~der Beifall** thunderous applause.

tot [to:t] adj dead (a. fig. capital, season, language, etc, **&** wire): **an e-m ~en Punkt ankommen** a) reach a low point, b) negotiations etc: reach a deadlock; **den ~en Punkt überwinden** a) get one's second wind, b) break the deadlock; **~er Winkel** blind spot, mot. blind

angle; **halb ~ vor Angst** scared stiff; **j-n für ~ erklären** declare s.o. dead; **~ umfallen** drop dead; → **Gleis, Rennen.**

total [to'ta:l] adj total, complete.

To'talausfall m dead loss.

To'talausverkauf m clearance sale.

To'tale f (-; -n) film: long shot.

totalitär [totali'tɛ:r] adj pol. totalitarian.

To'talschaden m mot. write-off.

'totarbeiten: F **sich ~** (sep, -ge-, h) work o.s. to death.

'Tote m, f (-n; -n) a) a dead man (woman), b) (dead) body: **die ~n** the dead; **bei dem Unfall gab es zwei ~** two persons were killed in the accident.

töten ['tø:tən] v/t (h) kill.

'Toten|bett n deathbed. **2blaß, 2bleich** adj deathly pale. **~gräber** [-grɛ:bər] m (-s; -) gravedigger. **~hemd** n shroud. **~kopf** m skull, death's-head (a. symbol), (poison sign) skull and crossbones. **~maske** f death mask. **~messe** f requiem. **~schein** m death certificate. **~starre** f ♄ rigor mortis. **2still** adj deathly silent. **~stille** f deathly silence.

'totgeboren adj stillborn, fig. a. abortive. **'Totgeburt** f stillbirth.

'totlachen: sich ~ (sep, -ge-, h) laugh one's head off: **es (er) ist zum 2** it's (he's) a scream.

'totlaufen: sich ~ (irr, sep, -ge-, h, → **laufen**) fig. peter out.

Toto ['to:to] m (-s; -s) (football) pools: **im ~ spielen (gewinnen)** do (win) the pools. **'Totoschein** m pools coupon.

'Totschlag m (-[e]s; no pl) ⚖ manslaughter, Am. second-degree murder. **'totschlagen** v/t (irr, sep, -ge-, h, → **schlagen**) kill, beat s.o. to death: **die Zeit ~** kill time. **'Totschläger** m **1.** killer. **2.** cosh, Am. blackjack.

'totschweigen v/t (irr, sep, -ge-, h, → **schweigen**) hush up, not to mention.

'totstellen: sich ~ (sep, -ge-, h) play dead, F play possum.

'Tötung f (-; -en) killing, ⚖ homicide.

Toupet [tu'pe:] n (-s; -s) toupee.

toupieren [tu'pi:rən] v/t (h) back-comb.

Tour [tu:r] f (-; -en) **1.** tour (**durch England** of England), trip, excursion, a. hike. **2.** usu. pl ⚙ revolution: **auf ~en bringen** a) mot. rev up, b) fig. get s.o., s.th. going; **auf ~en kommen** a) mot. pick up, rev up, b) fig. get going; **auf**

vollen **~en laufen** be going full blast; F **in 'einer ~ reden** talk incessantly. **3.** F *fig.* ploy: **auf die sanfte** (**langsame**) **~** the sweet (slow) way; → **krumm** I.

'**Touren...** touring (*bicycle, ski, car, etc*).

Tourismus [tu'rɪsmʊs] *m* (-; *no pl*) tourism. **Tou'rist** *m* (-en; -en) tourist.

Tou'risten... tourist ... **~klasse** *f* economy class.

Touristik [tu'rɪstɪk] *f* (-; *no pl*) tourism. **Tou'ristin** *f* (-; -nen) tourist. **tou'ristisch** *adj* tourist(ic).

Tournee [tur'ne:] *f* (-; -s, -n) tour.

Trab [tra:p] *m* (-[e]s; -e) (*im ~* at a) trot: **j-n auf ~ bringen** make s.o. get a move on; **j-n in ~ halten** keep s.o. on the trot.

Trabant [tra'bant] *m* (-en; -en) *astr.* satellite. **Tra'bantenstadt** *f* satellite town.

traben ['tra:bən] *v/i* (sn) trot.

'**Traber** *m* (-s; -) (*horse*) trotter.

'**Trabrennen** *n* trotting race.

Tracht [traxt] *f* (-; -en) **1.** dress, attire, (*a. traditional*) costume. **2.** (*nurse's etc*) uniform. **3.** yield (*of honey*). **4.** F **e-e** (**gehörige**) **~ Prügel** a sound thrashing.

trachten ['traxtən] *v/i* (h) **j-m nach dem Leben ~** be out to kill s.o.; → **Sinnen.**

'**Trachtengruppe** *f* (folklorist) group in traditional costume.

trächtig ['trɛçtɪç] *adj zo.* pregnant.

Tradition [tradi'tsio:n] *f* (-; -en) (**nach alter ~** by) tradition. **traditionell** [traditsio'nɛl] *adj* traditional.

traf [tra:f] *pret of* **treffen.**

Trafo ['tra:fo] *m* (-[s]; -s) transformer.

tragbar ['tra:k-] *adj* **1.** ⊙ portable. **2.** wearable (*clothes*). **3.** *fig.* a) acceptable (*price etc*), b) bearable, tolerable.

Trage ['tra:gə] *f* (-; -n) stretcher.

träge ['tra:gə] *adj* sluggish (*a.* ✝), lethargic, *phys.* inert.

tragen ['tra:gən] (trug, getragen, h) **I** *v/t* **1.** carry, *a.* support (*a. fig.*): *fig.* **zum ♀ kommen** take effect; ✝ **sich** (**selbst**) **~** pay its way. **2.** wear (*clothes, one's hair, etc*): → **getragen** 1, **Trauer. 3.** bear, yield (*fruit etc, a. interest*): → **Zins. 4.** bear (*name, title, costs, etc*): **er trägt die Schuld** he is to blame; **wer trägt das Risiko?** who takes the risk?; → **Rechnung** 2. **5.** bear, endure: **sie trägt es tapfer** she is bearing up well. **II** *v/i* **6.** carry (*a. sound, voice*), ice *etc*: hold, *water*: be buoyant: **schwer zu ~ haben**

(*an dat*) be loaded (*fig.* weighed) down (by). **7.** *zo.* be pregnant. **III sich ~ 8.** **sich gut ~** *cloth etc*: wear well. **9.** **sich mit der Absicht** (*or* **dem Gedanken**) **~ zu** *inf* be thinking of ger. '**tragend** *adj* supporting (*wall etc*), powerful (*voice*): *thea.* **~e Rolle** lead(ing part).

Träger ['trɛːgər] *m* (-s; -) **1.** carrier (*a.* 🐾, 💮), bearer (*a. of name, title*), porter, stretcher-bearer, *fig.* upholder (*of idea etc*), (*organization etc*) body responsible (*gen* for). **2.** (*shoulder*) strap. **3.** ⊙ support, △ beam, girder.

'**Trägerkleid** *n* pinafore dress.

'**trägerlos** *adj* strapless (*dress etc*).

'**Trägerrakete** *f* launcher rocket.

'**Tragetasche** *f* **1.** carrier (*Am.* tote) bag. **2.** carrycot. **~zeit** *f zo.* gestation.

'**tragfähig** *adj* **1.** ⊙ capable of bearing. **2.** *fig.* sound. '**Tragfähigkeit** *f* (-; *no pl*) load capacity.

Tragfläche *f* ✈ wing. '**Tragflächenboot** *n*, '**Tragflügelboot** *n* hydrofoil.

Trägheit ['trɛːk-] *f* (-; *no pl*) sluggishness, lethargy, *a. phys.* inertia.

Tragik ['tra:gɪk] *f* (-; *no pl*) tragedy.

Tragi'komik [tragi-] *f* tragicomedy.

tragi'komisch *adj* tragicomic.

Tragiko'mödie *f* tragicomedy.

tragisch ['tra:gɪʃ] *adj* tragic: **das Tragische daran** the tragic thing about it; F **nimm's nicht so ~!** don't take it to heart! **Tragödie** [tra'gø:diə] *f* (-; -n) *a. fig.* tragedy.

'**Tragweite** *f* (-; *no pl*) **1.** range. **2.** significance: **von großer ~** of great import.

'**Tragwerk** *n* ✈ wing unit.

'**Trainer** ['trɛːnər] *m* (-s; -), '**Trainerin** *f* (-; -nen) trainer, coach. **trainieren** [trɛ'ni:rən] *v/t*, *v/i* (h) train, coach. **Training** ['trɛːnɪŋ] *n* (-s; -s) training.

'**Trainings...** training (*camp, partner, etc*). **~anzug** *m* track suit.

Trakt [trakt] *m* (-[e]s; -e) section, wing.

Traktor ['traktɔr] *m* (-s; -en [-'to:rən]) tractor.

trällern ['trɛlərn] *v/t*, *v/i* (h) trill, warble.

Tram(bahn) ['tram-] *f* → **Straßenbahn.**

Trampel ['trampəl] *m*, *n* (-s; -) F *contp.* clod. '**trampeln** *v/i* (h) trample, stamp.

'**Trampelpfad** *m* beaten path.

trampen ['trɛmpən] *v/i* (sn) F a) hitch-hike, thumb a lift (*or* ride), b) backpack it. '**Tramper** m (-s; -), '**Tramperin** f (-; -nen) F hitchhiker.

Trampolin ['trampoli:n] n (-s; -e) trampoline.

Tran [tra:n] m (-[e]s; -e) train oil.

Trance ['trã:s(ə)] f (-; -n) trance.

tranchieren [trã'ʃi:rən] v/t (h) carve.

Tran'chiermesser n carving knife.

Träne ['trɛ:nə] f (-; -n) tear: **den ∼n nahe** on the verge of tears; **unter ∼n** in tears; **wir haben ∼n gelacht** we laughed till we cried; **ihr werde ich k-e ∼ nachweinen** I won't shed any tears over her; → **ausbrechen** 5. '**tränen** v/i (h) water.

'**Tränendrüse** f lachrymal gland: **F auf die ∼ drücken** be a real tear-jerker.

'**Tränengas** n tear gas.

'**Tränensack** m anat. lachrymal sac.

trank [traŋk] pret of **trinken.**

Trank m (-[e]s; ∼e) drink, ∦ potion.

Tränke ['trɛŋkə] f (-; -n) watering place. '**tränken** v/t (h) a) water, b) soak.

Transaktion [trans'ak'tsi̯o:n] f (-; -en) transaction.

Transat'lantik..., transat'lantisch adj transatlantic.

Transfer [trans'fe:r] m (-s; -s), **transferieren** [transfe'ri:rən] v/t (h) transfer.

Transformator [transfɔr'ma:tɔr] m (-s; -en [-ma'to:rən]) ∮ transformer. **transformieren** [-'mi:rən] v/t (h) transform.

Transfusion [transfu'zi̯o:n] f (-; -en) transfusion.

Transistor [tran'zɪstɔr] m (-s; -en [-'to:rən]) transistor.

Tran'sistorradio n transistor (radio).

Transit [tran'zi:t] m (-s; -e) transit (a. in cpds. charge, goods, road, traffic, etc).

transitiv [tranzi'ti:f] adj ling. transitive.

Tran'sitraum m ✈ transit lounge.

Transmission [transmɪ'si̯o:n] f (-; -en) ⊛ transmission.

transparent [transpa'rɛnt] adj transparent. **Transpa'rent** n (-[e]s; -e) banner.

Transplantat [transplan'ta:t] n (-[e]s; -e) ∦ transplant, graft. **Transplantation** [transplanta'tsi̯o:n] f (-; -en) transplantation, graft(ing). **transplantieren** [-'ti:rən] v/t (h) transplant, graft.

Transport [trans'pɔrt] m (-[e]s; -e) transport(ation), conveyance, ✞ shipment, haulage: **während des ∼s** in transit.

transportabel [transpɔr'ta:bəl] adj transportable, ⊛ portable, mov(e)able.

Trans'portband n (-[e]s; ∼er) ⊛ conveyor belt.

Trans'porter m (-s; -) → **Transportfahrzeug, -flugzeug, -schiff.**

Transporteur [transpɔr'tø:r] m (-s; -e) carrier.

trans'portfähig adj transportable.

Trans'portfahrzeug n transporter.

Trans'portflugzeug n transport plane.

transportieren [transpɔr'ti:rən] v/t (h) **1.** transport. **2. den Film ∼** advance the film.

Trans'port|kosten pl transport(ation) charges, ♣ freight (charges). **∼mittel** n (means of) transport(ation). **∼schaden** m damage in transit. **∼schiff** n transport ship. **∼unternehmen** n carriers, haulage contractors. **∼versicherung** f transport insurance.

Transvestit [transvɛs'ti:t] m (-en; -en) transvestite.

transzendental [trantsɛndɛn'ta:l] adj transcendental.

Trapez [tra'pe:ts] n (-es; -e) **1.** A trapezium, Am. trapezoid. **2.** gym. trapeze.

trappeln ['trapəln] v/i (sn) horse etc: clatter, child: patter.

Trara [tra'ra:] n (-s; no pl) F fuss, to-do.

Trasse ['trasə] f (-; -n) ⊛ location line.

trassieren [tra'si:rən] v/t (h) **1.** ⊛ trace (out). **2.** ✞ draw bill (auf acc on).

trat [tra:t] pret of **treten.**

Tratsch [tra:tʃ] m (-[e]s; no pl), '**tratschen** v/i (h) F contp. gossip.

Tratte ['tratə] f (-; -n) ✞ draft.

Traube ['traobə] f (-; -n) **1.** a) bunch of grapes, b) grape. **2.** fig. cluster (of people). '**Traubensaft** m grape juice. '**Traubenzucker** m glucose.

trauen¹ ['traoən] v/t (h) marry: **sich ∼ lassen** get married; → **kirchlich.**

'**trauen²** (h) **I** v/i (dat) trust (s.o., s.th.): **ich traute m-n Ohren nicht** I couldn't believe my ears; → **Weg. II sich ∼ zu inf** dare (to) inf; **du traust dich nur nicht!** you're just scared.

Trauer ['traoər] f (-; no pl) a) mourning (**um** for), b) grief (**um, wegen** at, over): **∼ tragen** be in mourning. **∼fall** m death. **∼feier** f funeral obsequies. **∼flor** m mourning band, crape. **∼kleidung** f mourning. **∼marsch** m funeral march. **trauern** ['traoərn] v/i (h) (**um**) a) mourn (for), b) grieve (for, over).

Trauer|rede f funeral oration. **~schlei-er** m mourning veil, weeper. **~spiel** n F fig. sorry affair. **~weide** f 💥 weeping willow. **~zug** m funeral procession.

Traufe ['traʊfə] f (-; -n) eaves, gutter: → **Regen**.

träufeln ['trɔyfəln] v/t (h) drip, trickle.

traulich ['traʊlɪç] adj cosy, Am. cozy.

Traum [traʊm] m (-[e]s; ⸚e) dream (a. fig.): F **das fällt mir nicht im ~ ein!** I wouldn't dream of (doing) it; → **einfallen** 1, **kühn**.

Trauma ['traʊma] n (-s; -men, -mata) 💥, psych. trauma.

traumatisch [traʊ'ma:tɪʃ] adj traumatic. '**Traumberuf** m dream job.

'**Traumbild** n a) dream vision, b) dream.

träumen ['trɔymən] (h) I v/t dream: **das hätte ich mir nicht ~ lassen** I never dreamt of such a thing. II v/i dream of (**von** about, of), a. daydream: **schlecht ~** have a bad dream. '**Träumer** m (-s; -) dreamer. **Träume'rei** f (-; -en) reverie (a. ♪), (day)dream(s). '**träumerisch** adj dreamy.

'**Traumfa,brik** f dream factory.

'**Traumfrau** f F woman of one's dreams.

'**traumhaft** adj dreamlike, (a. ~ **schön**) absolutely beautiful, a dream.

'**Traum|haus** n F dream house. **~land** n dreamland. **~mann** m F man of one's dreams. **~welt** f dream world.

traurig ['traʊrɪç] adj sad (**über** acc at, about), a. sorry: **~ stimmen** sadden; **~er Anblick** sorry sight; **~e Reste** sad remains.

'**Traurigkeit** f (-; no pl) sadness.

'**Trauring** m wedding ring (or band).

'**Trauschein** m marriage certificate.

'**Trauung** f (-; -en) marriage ceremony, wedding.

'**Trauzeuge** m, '**Trauzeugin** f witness to a marriage.

Travestie [traves'ti:] f (-; -n) travesty.

Treck [trɛk] m (-s; -s) trek. '**trecken** v/i (sn) trek. '**Trecker** m (-s; -) tractor.

Treff [trɛf] m (-s; -s) F a) meeting, b) meeting place.

treffen ['trɛfən] (traf, getroffen, h) I v/t 1. hit (**j-n am Arm** s.o.'s arm): **nicht ~** miss. F fig. **er ist gut getroffen (auf dem Bild)** that's a good photo (or painting) of him; → **Blitz** 1. **2.** a) concern, b) affect, hit s.o. hard, c) hurt:

das hat ihn hart getroffen he took it very hard, it's been a severe blow to him; → **Schuld** 1. **3.** reach, make (agreement etc); → **Anstalt** 3, **Entscheidung** etc. **4.** j-n ~ meet s.o.; **j-n zufällig ~** come across s.o. II v/i **5.** hit: **nicht ~** miss. **6. auf j-n ~** a. sports: meet s.o. **7. ~ auf** (acc) a) meet with, b) strike (or hit) on. III **sich ~ 8.** meet (**mit j-m** s.o.). **9.** F **das trifft sich gut** (**schlecht**) that suits me (or us etc) fine (that's a bit awkward); **es trifft sich gut, daß** (it's a) good thing that; **das trifft sich ja großartig!** well, that's lucky. '**Treffen** n (-s; -) meeting, sports: meet. '**treffend** adj apt (remark etc): **kurz und ~** short and to the point; **~ gesagt!** well put.

'**Treffer** m (-s; -) **1.** hit, soccer etc: goal. **2.** win. **3.** fig. lucky strike.

'**Treffpunkt** m meeting place.

treiben ['traɪbən] (trieb, getrieben) I v/t (h) **1.** drive: **die Preise in die Höhe ~** force up prices; **j-n in den Selbstmord ~** drive s.o. to suicide; **was hat sie dazu getrieben?** what made her do that? **2.** sprout (leaves etc), force (plants). **3.** physiol. produce (urine, sweat). **4.** chase (metal). **5.** do, a. go in for (sports etc): **was treibst du (zur Zeit)?** what are you doing (these days)?; **was treibst du da?** what are you up to?; F **es toll ~** carry on like mad, live it up; **es zu weit ~** go too far; → **Aufwand** 2, **Enge** 1, **Spitze**[1] 1 etc. II v/i (sn) **6.** float, a. snow, smoke, etc: drift: **sich ~ lassen** a. fig. drift; **die Dinge ~ lassen** let things drift; **~de Kraft** driving force. **7.** 💥 sprout.

'**Treiben** n (-s) a) activity, F goings-on, b) (hustle and) bustle.

'**Treiber** m (-s; -) drover, hunt. beater.

'**Treib|gas** n fuel gas, for sprays: propellent. **~haus** n hothouse. **~hausef,fekt** m meteor. greenhouse effect. **~holz** n (-es; no pl) driftwood. F fig.1. battue. **2.** fig. hunt (**auf** acc for), pol. witch hunt. **~rad** n ⚙ driving wheel. **~riemen** m ⚙ drive belt. **~satz** m propelling charge. **~stoff** m fuel.

Trend [trɛnt] m (-s; -s) trend (**zu** towards). **~wende** f change in trend.

'**trennbar** adj separable, detachable.

trennen ['trɛnən] (h) I v/t a) separate, b) divide, c) detach, cut off, 💥, teleph. a. disconnect, d) undo, e) segregate. II v/i

~ **zwischen** distinguish between. **III**
sich ~ separate, *a. fig.* part (**von** with);
getrennt leben be separated (**von**
from), live apart; **getrennt schlafen**
have separate bedrooms; → **Kasse** 4.
'**Trennschärfe** *f radio:* selectivity.
'**Trennung** *f* (-; -en) separation (*a.* 🔧,
⚙), segregation (*of races*), division, ⚡,
teleph. disconnection: 🚹 **eheliche ~**
judicial separation.
'**Trennungszeichen** *n* hyphen.
Trense ['trɛnzə] *f* (-; -n) snaffle (bit).
trepp|**auf:** ~, **treppab** up and down the
stairs. '**Treppchen** *n* F *sports:* (victory)
rostrum. **Treppe** ['trɛpə] *f* (-; -n) staircase, (**e-e ~ a** flight of) stairs (*or* steps):
zwei ~n hoch on the second floor; **die ~
hinauf** (**hinab**) up the stairs.
'**Treppen**|**absatz** *m* landing. **~geländer**
n banisters. **~haus** *n* staircase.
Tresen ['tre:zən] *m* (-s; -) bar, *a.* counter.
Tresor [tre'zo:r] *m* (-s; -e) **1.** strong-
room, vault. **2.** safe.
Tre'sorfach *n* safe deposit box.
'**Tret**|**auto** *n* pedal car. **~boot** *n* pedal
boat. **~eimer** *m* pedal bin.
treten ['tre:tən] (trat, getreten) **I** *v/i* (*sn*)
step, *cyclist etc:* pedal: **~ auf** (*acc*) step
on, tread on; **aufs Gas**(**pedal**) (**auf die
Bremse**) **~** step on the gas (brake); **ins
Zimmer ~** enter the room; **nach j-m ~**
(take a) kick at s.o.; **bitte ~ Sie näher!**
please come in!; **über die Ufer ~** overflow its banks; → **Kraft** 3, **nahe** II *etc.*
II *v/t* (*h*) tread: **j-n** (**in den Bauch**) **~**
kick s.o. (in the stomach); *fig.* **et. mit
Füßen ~** trample on s.th.
'**Tretmühle** *f a. fig.* treadmill.
treu [trɔy] *adj* (*dat* to) faithful (*a. fig.*),
loyal, devoted: **sich** (**s-n Grundsätzen**)
~ bleiben remain true to o.s. (one's
principles). '**Treue** *f* (-; *no pl*) faithful-
ness (*a. fig.*), loyalty, (*a. marital*) fidelity: **j-m die ~ halten** remain loyal to s.o.
'**Treueid** *m* oath of allegiance.
'**treuergeben** *adj* loyal, devoted.
'**Treuhänder** [-hɛndər] *m* (-s; -) trustee.
'**treuhänderisch** *adj* fiduciary: **et. ~ verwalten** hold s.th. in trust.
'**Treuhand**|**gesellschaft** *f* trust compa-
ny. **~verwaltung** *f* trusteeship.
'**treuherzig** *adj* **1.** guileless. **2.** ingen-
uous, naive. **3.** trusting.
'**treulos** *adj* disloyal (**gegen** to).

'**Treulosigkeit** *f* (-; *no pl*) disloyalty.
Tribunal [tribu'na:l] *n* (-s; -e) tribunal.
Tribüne [tri'by:nə] *f* (-; -n) **1.** (*speaker's*)
platform, rostrum. **2.** (grand)stand, *in
stadium:* **a.** terraces.
Trichine [tri'çi:nə] *f* (-; -n) *vet.* trichina.
Trichter ['trɪçtər] *m* (-s; -) **1.** ⚙ funnel. **2.**
flare, mouth. **3.** crater.
'**trichterförmig** *adj* funnel-shaped.
Trick [trɪk] *m* (-s; -s) trick. **~aufnahme** *f*
1. *film:* trick shot, *pl* trick photography. **2.** *on tape:* trick recording. **~be-
trüger** *m* trickster. **~film** *m* a) trick
film, b) animated cartoon.
'**trickreich** *adj* artful.
'**Trickskilaufen** *n* freestyle skiing.
trieb [tri:p] *pret of* **treiben**.
Trieb *m* (-[e]s; -e) **1.** 🌱 young shoot. **2.** a)
instinct, b) sexual drive, c) impulse, d)
urge. '**Triebfeder** *f fig.* mainspring.
'**triebhaft** *adj* a) instinctive, b) sexual, *a.*
highly sexed (*person*).
'**Trieb**|**kraft** *f* **1.** motive force (*or* power).
2. *fig.* driving force. **~täter** *m*, **~verbre-
cher** *m* sex offender. **~wagen** *m* tram-
car, 🚂 railcar. **~werk** *n* a) driving gear,
b) 🔩 power unit, c) drive, gear.
triefen ['tri:fən] *v/i* (*h*) drip (**von**
with), *eyes, nose:* run: **~d naß** dripping
wet.
triftig ['trɪftɪç] *adj* **1.** valid, sound. **2.**
weighty, convincing.
Trigonometrie [trigonome'tri:] *f* (-; *no
pl*) trigonometry.
Trikot [tri'ko:] **1.** *m, n* (-s; -s) *textil.* tri-
cot. **2.** *n* (-s; -s) a) leotard, tights, b)
shirt, *sports:* **a.** jersey.
Triller ['trɪlər] *m* (-s; -) trill.
trillern ['trɪlərn] *v/t, v/i* (*h*) trill, warble.
Trillion [trɪ'lio:n] *f* (-; -en) trillion, *Am.*
quintillion.
Trilogie [trilo'gi:] *f* (-; -n) trilogy.
Trimester [tri'mɛstər] *n* (-s; -) *ped., univ.*
trimester.
trimmen ['trɪmən] (*h*) **I** *v/t* **1.** trim (*a.* ✈,
⚡, ⚓). **2.** F tune *engine* up (**auf** *acc* to). **2.**
train. **II sich ~** keep fit, keep in (good)
trim. '**Trimmpfad** *m* fitness trail.
'**trinkbar** *adj* drinkable. **trinken** ['trɪŋ-
kən] *v/t, v/i* (trank, getrunken, *h*) drink,
have (*tea etc*): **~ auf** (*acc*) drink to; **was
~ Sie?** what are you having?; **er trinkt**
he drinks, he is a drinker. '**Trinker** *m*
(-s; -), '**Trinkerin** *f* (-; -nen) drinker,

alcoholic. '**trinkfest** *adj* **er** *etc* **ist ~** he *etc* holds his liquor well.

'**Trink|geld** *n* tip: *j-m* **(5 Mark) ~ geben** tip s.o. (five marks). **~halle** *f* pump room. **~halm** *m* (drinking) straw. **~kur** *f* mineral water cure. **~milch** *f* certified milk. **~spruch** *m* toast. **~wasser** *n* drinking water.

Trio ['tri:o] *n* (-s; -s) ♪ *or* F *fig.* trio.

trippeln ['trɪpəln] *v/i* (sn) trip.

Tripper ['trɪpər] *m* (-s; -) ♣ gonorrh(o)ea, F clap.

trist [trɪst] *adj* dreary, bleak, dismal.

Tritt [trɪt] *m* (-[e]s; -e) **1.** a) step, b) footstep: *~ fassen* fall in step; *aus dem ~ geraten* (*sein*) fall (be) out of step; → *Schritt* 1. **2.** footprint. **3.** kick: *j-m e-n ~ versetzen* give s.o. a kick, kick s.o. **4.** step (*of stairs etc*). **~brett** *n mot.* running board. **~leiter** *f* stepladder.

Triumph [tri'ʊmf] *m* (-[e]s; -e) triumph.

triumphal [triʊm'fa:l] *adj* triumphant.

triumphieren [triʊm'fi:rən] *v/i* (h) (*über acc over*) triumph, *contp. a.* gloat.

trivial [tri'vĭa:l] *adj* trivial.

Trivi'allitera,tur *f* light fiction.

trocken ['trɔkən] **I** *adj* dry (*a. wine etc, fig. remark, humo[u]r, etc*), *fig. a.* dull: F *fig.* **auf dem trocknen sitzen** be in a fix; → *Schäfchen*. **II** *adv fig.* drily, dryly: *sich ~ rasieren* dry-shave.

'**Trocken|dock** *n* dry dock. **~eis** *n* dry ice. **~ele,ment** *n* ⚡ dry cell. **~gewicht** *n* dry weight. **~haube** *f* hairdrier.

'**Trockenheit** *f* (-; *no pl*) **1.** dryness (*a. fig.*). **2.** drought.

'**trockenlegen** *v/t* (*sep*, -ge-, h) **1.** drain (*land etc*). **2.** *ein Baby* ~ change a baby.

'**Trocken|milch** *f* dried milk. **~obst** *n* dried fruit. **~ra,sierer** *m* dry shaver. **~schleuder** *f* spin drier. **~skikurs** *m* dry skiing (course). **~zeit** *f* dry season.

trocknen ['trɔknən] *v/t, v/i* (h) dry.

'**Trockner** *m* (-s; -) drier.

Troddel ['trɔdəl] *f* (-; -n) tassel.

Trödel ['trø:dəl] *m* (-s; *no pl*) *a. contp.* junk. '**Trödelladen** *m* junk shop. '**Trödelmarkt** *m* flea market. '**trödeln** *v/i* F a) (h) dawdle, b) (sn) saunter. **Trödler** ['trø:dlər] *m* (-s; -), '**Trödlerin** *f* (-; -nen) **1.** junk dealer. **2.** dawdler.

trog [tro:k] *pret of* **trügen.**

Trog *m* (-[e]s; ᵘe) trough.

trollen ['trɔlən] *sich ~* (h) toddle off.

Trommel ['trɔməl] *f* (-; -n) drum, ⚙ *a.* cylinder: *die ~ rühren* beat the drum (*für* for). **~bremse** *f* drumbrake. **~fell** *n* **1.** drumskin. **2.** *anat.* eardrum. **~feuer** *n a. fig.* barrage.

trommeln ['trɔməln] (h) **I** *v/i* (*auf acc* at, on) drum, *rain:* beat. **II** *v/t* drum, beat.

'**Trommel|schlegel** *m*, **~stock** *m* drumstick. **~wirbel** *m* drum roll.

Trommler ['trɔmlər] *m* (-s; -) drummer.

Trompete [trɔm'pe:tə] *f* (-; -n) trumpet. **trom'peten** *v/t, v/i* (h) trumpet.

Tropen ['tro:pən] *pl the* tropics.

'**Tropen...** tropical (*suit, fever, etc*).

'**tropenfest** *adj* tropicalized.

'**Tropenhelm** *m* pith helmet, topee.

Tropf [trɔpf] *m* (-[e]s; -e) ♣ (*am ~ hängen* be on the) drip.

Tröpfchen ['trœpfçən] *n* (-s; -) droplet.

'**tröpfchenweise** *adv* drop by drop.

tröpfeln ['trœpfəln] *v/i* (h) drip (*a. v/t*), trickle: F *es tröpfelt* it's spitting.

tropfen ['trɔpfən] *v/i* (h) drip.

'**Tropfen** *m* (-s; -) **1.** drop, *a.* bead (*of sweat*): *ein edler* (*or guter*) *~* a capital wine; *ein ~ auf den heißen Stein* a drop in the bucket; *steter ~ höhlt den Stein* little strokes fell big oaks. **2.** *pl* ♣ drops. '**tropfenweise** *adv* in drops, drop by drop.

'**Tropfflasche** *f* dropper bottle.

'**Tropfinfusi,on** *f* ♣ intravenous drip.

'**tropfnaß** *adj* dripping wet.

'**Tropfstein** *m* stalactite, stalagmite.

Trophäe [tro'fɛ:ə] *f* (-; -n) trophy.

tropisch ['tro:pɪʃ] *adj* tropical.

Trosse ['trɔsə] *f* (-; -n) cable, ⚓ hawser.

Trost [tro:st] *m* (-[e]s; *no pl*) comfort, consolation: *zum ~* as a consolation; *ein schwacher ~* cold comfort. **trösten** ['trø:stən] *v/t* (h) console (*sich* o.s.), comfort. '**tröstlich** *adj* comforting.

'**trostlos** *adj* a) disconsolate, b) hopeless (*state etc*), c) cheerless, dreary, bleak.

'**Trostlosigkeit** *f* (-; *no pl*) a) hopelessness, b) dreariness, bleakness.

'**Trost|pflaster** *n humor.* (small) consolation. **~preis** *m* consolation prize.

'**trostreich** *adj* comforting.

Trott [trɔt] *m* (-[e]s; -e) trot, *a. fig.* jogtrot: *in e-n ~ verfallen* get into a rut.

Trottel ['trɔtəl] *m* (-s; -) F dope, idiot.

trotten ['trɔtən] *v/i* (sn) trot, jog.

trotz [trɔts] *prep* (*gen*) in spite of, despite.

Trotz 574

Trotz m (-es; no pl) defiance: **aus ~** out of spite; **mir zum ~** to spite me.

'**trotzdem I** adv nevertheless, all the same, still, anyway. **II** conj although.

trotzen ['trɔtsən] v/i (h) **1.** (dat) defy (s.o., s.th.), a. brave (danger etc). **2.** be obstinate.

'**trotzig** adj defiant, obstinate.

'**Trotzreakti,on** f act of defiance.

trübe ['try:bə] adj **1.** cloudy (liquid, glass, etc), muddy: F fig. **im trüben fischen** fish in troubled waters. **2.** dull, dim, murky. **3.** dreary (day). **4.** gloomy (mood, thoughts, etc), bleak (prospects etc), sad (experience etc).

Trubel ['tru:bəl] m (-s; no pl) (hustle and) bustle.

trüben ['try:bən] (h) **I** v/t **1.** (a. sich ~) cloud (liquid, glass, etc, a. mind, relations, etc). **2.** fig. spoil (joy etc), obscure (s.o.'s view), warp (judgement), blur (sight, mind). **II sich ~ 3.** become clouded, glass etc: cloud over. **4.** fig. relations etc: become strained.

trübselig ['try:p-] adj **1.** gloomy. **2.** dreary. '**Trübseligkeit** f (-; no pl) **1.** gloominess. **2.** dreariness.

'**Trübsinn** m (-[e]s; no pl) gloom, low spirits. '**trübsinnig** adj gloomy.

'**Trübung** f (-; -en) **1.** clouding (etc, → trüben). **2.** cloudiness, dullness.

trudeln ['tru:dəln] v/i (sn) ✈ spin: **ins ~ geraten** go into a spin.

Trüffel ['tryfəl] f (-; -n) 🍫 truffle.

trug [tru:k] pret of **tragen.**

'**Trugbild** n illusion, hallucination.

trügen ['try:gən] (trog, getrogen, h) **I** v/t deceive: **wenn mein Gedächtnis mich nicht trügt** if my memory serves me right. **II** v/i be deceptive: → **Schein**¹ 2.

trügerisch ['try:gəriʃ] adj deceptive, misleading, illusive (hope etc).

'**Trugschluß** m fallacy.

Truhe ['tru:ə] f (-; -n) chest.

Trümmer ['trymər] pl **1.** ruins, rubble. **2.** debris. **3.** fragments.

'**Trümmerhaufen** m heap of rubble.

Trumpf [trumpf] m (-[e]s; ⸚e) a) trump(s), b) trump card: **was ist ~?** what's trumps?; fig. **~ sein** be the thing; a. fig. **alle Trümpfe in der Hand haben** hold all the trumps; fig. **s-n letzten ~ ausspielen** play one's trump card.

Trunk [trʊŋk] m (-[e]s; no pl) drinking.

'**Trunkenheit** f (-; no pl) drunkenness: **~ am Steuer** drunken driving.

'**Trunksucht** f (-; no pl) alcoholism.

'**trunksüchtig** adj **~ sein** be an alcoholic.

Trupp [trʊp] m (-s; -s) troop, gang, ✕ detachment. '**Truppe** f (-; -n) **1.** ✕ a) troops, pl a. forces; b) unit. **2.** thea. company, troupe. **3.** sports: team.

'**Truppen|abbau** m reduction in forces. **~abzug** m withdrawal of troops, pull-out. **~gattung** f branch (of the service), arm. **~teil** m unit. **~trans,porter** m ⚓ transport, troopship, ✈ troop carrier. **~übungsplatz** m training area.

'**Truppführer** m squad leader.

'**Truthahn** ['tru:t-] m turkey(-cock).

'**Truthenne** f turkey-hen.

Tscheche ['tʃɛçə] m (-n; -n), '**Tschechin** f (-; -nen), '**tschechisch** [-çɪʃ] adj Czech. **Tschechoslowakei** [tʃɛçoslova'kaɪ] f (-) Czechoslovakia.

tschüs [tʃy:s] int F bye!, see you!

Tube ['tu:bə] f (-; -n) tube: F mot. or fig. **auf die ~ drücken** step on it.

tuberkulös [tubɛrku'lø:s] adj tubercular, tuberculous. **Tuberkulose** [tubɛrku'lo:zə] f (-; -n) tuberculosis.

Tuch [tu:x] n (-[e]s; ⸚er) **1.** textil. cloth, fabric. **2.** a) cloth; b) scarf: **das wirkt auf ihn wie ein rotes ~** that's a red rag to him. '**Tuchfühlung** f **~ haben mit** be in close contact with.

tüchtig ['tyçtɪç] **I** adj **1.** good (in dat at), capable, competent, hard-working. **2.** F good. **II** adv **3.** F tremendously, like hell: **~ arbeiten** work hard; **~ zulangen, ~ essen** tuck in.

'**Tüchtigkeit** f (-; no pl) ability, competence, efficiency, industry.

Tücke ['tykə] f (-; -n) malice, perfidy, trick: **s-e ~n haben** be tricky, river etc: be treacherous.

tuckern ['tʊkərn] v/i (sn) F chug.

tückisch ['tykɪʃ] adj **1.** malicious, insidious (a. 🐍). **2.** treacherous (road etc).

tüfteln ['tyftəln] v/i (h) (an dat) **1.** tinker (with). **2.** puzzle (over).

'**Tüftler** ['tyftlər] m (-s; -) tinkerer.

Tugend ['tu:gənt] f (-; -en) virtue.

'**tugendhaft** adj virtuous.

Tüll [tyl] m (-s; -e) textil. tulle.

Tülle ['tylə] f (-; -n) **1.** spout. **2.** ⊙ socket.

Tulpe ['tʊlpə] f (-; -n) tulip.

tummeln ['tʊməln] **sich ~** (h) disport o.s.

'**Tummelplatz** *m* **1.** playground. **2.** *fig.* stomping ground.

Tumor ['tu:mɔr] *m* (-s; -en [tu'mo:rən]) *#* tumo(u)r.

Tümpel ['tympəl] *m* (-s; -) pool.

Tumult [tu'mʊlt] *m* (-[e]s; -e) tumult, uproar, riot.

tun [tu:n] *v/t, v/i* (tat, getan, h) a) do (→ *a.* **machen**), b) make (*vow etc*), take (*step etc*), c) put (*s.th. somewhere*), d) *F machine etc*: go, work: **höflich** *etc* ~ act (*or* do) the polite *etc*; **so** ~, **als ob** pretend to *inf*; **er tut nur so** he's only pretending; **was hat er dir getan?** what has he done to you?; **dagegen müssen wir et.** ~**!** we must do s.th. about it!; **was (ist zu)** ~**?** what's to be done?; **wir haben zu** ~ we have work to do, we are busy; **das tut nichts!** never mind!, it doesn't matter!; **was tut's!** what does it matter!; **das tut man nicht** that just isn't done!; **mit ihm** (**damit**) **habe ich nichts zu** ~ I have nothing to do with him (it); **das hat nichts damit zu** ~ that's nothing to do with it; **du wirst es mit ihm zu** ~ **bekommen** you'll get into trouble with him; *F* **es tut sich was!** there is s.th. going on.

Tun *n* (-s) doing, (*a.* ~ **und Treiben**, ~ **und Lassen**) doings, activities.

Tünche ['tynçə] *f* (-; -n) **1.** whitewash. **2.** *fig.* veneer. '**tünchen** *v/t* (h) whitewash.

Tundra ['tʊndra] *f* (-; -dren) tundra.

tunen ['tju:nən] *v/t* (h) *mot.* tune (up).

Tunesien [tu'ne:zɪən] *n* (-s) Tunisia. **Tu'nesier** *m* (-s; -), **Tu'nesierin** *f* (-; -nen), **tu'nesisch** *adj* Tunisian.

Tunke ['tʊŋkə] *f* (-; -n) sauce. **tunken** ['tʊŋkən] *v/t* (h) dip.

Tunnel ['tʊnəl] *m* (-s; -) tunnel.

tüpfeln ['typfəln] *v/t* (h) dot. '**tupfen** ['tʊpfən] *v/t* (h) **1.** *#* swab. **2.** dot. '**Tupfen** *m* (-s; -) **1.** dot, spot. '**Tupfer** *m* (-s; -) **1.** *#* swab. **2.** dot.

Tür ['ty:r] *f* (-; -en) door: **Tag der offenen** ~ Open Day; **in der** ~ in the doorway; *F fig.* **offene** ~**en einrennen** force an open door; **mit der** ~ **ins Haus fallen** blurt it out; (*dat*) ~ **und Tor öffnen** open the door to; **j-n vor die** ~ **setzen** turn s.o. out.

Turban ['tʊrba:n] *m* (-s; -e) turban.

Turbine [tʊr'bi:nə] *f* -; -n) turbine.

Turbo-Prop-Ma'schine ['tʊrbo'prɔp-] *f* *✔* turboprop (engine).

turbulent [tʊrbu'lɛnt] *adj* turbulent.

Turbulenz [tʊrbu'lɛnts] *f* (-; -en) *a.* phys. turbulence.

Türke ['tyrkə] *m* (-n; -n) **1.** Turk. **2.** *F press etc*: fake. **Türkei** [tyr'kaɪ] *f* (-) Turkey. '**türken** *v/t* (h) F fake. '**Türkin** *f* (-; -nen) Turk(ish woman).

Türkis [tyr'ki:s] *m* (-es; -e) *min.* turqoise. '**türkisch** *adj* Turkish.

'**Türklinke** *f* doorhandle.

'**Türklopfer** *m* knocker.

Turm [tʊrm] *m* (-[e]s; ⸚e) **1.** a) tower (*a. fig.*), b) steeple. **2.** *sports*: (diving) platform. **3.** *chess*: castle.

Türmchen ['tyrmçən] *n* (-s; -) turret.

türmen[1] ['tyrmən] **I** *v/t* pile (up). **II** *sich* ~ *a. fig.* pile up.

'**türmen**[2] *v/i* (sn) *F* bolt, make off.

'**Turmspitze** *f* spire.

'**Turmspringen** *n* sports: high diving.

'**Turmuhr** *f* church clock.

'**Turnanzug** *m* gymsuit. **turnen** ['tʊrnən] (h) **I** *v/i* do gymnastics. **II** *v/t* do (*an exercise*). '**Turnen** *n* (-s) gymnastics. '**Turner** *m* (-s; -), '**Turnerin** *f* (-; -nen) gymnast.

'**Turn|gerät** *n* gymnastic apparatus. ~**halle** *f* gymnasium, F gym. ~**hemd** *n* singlet, gym top. ~**hose** *f* gym shorts.

Turnier [tʊr'ni:r] *n* (-s; -e) tournament. ~**tanz** *m* ballroom dancing.

'**Turnschuhe** *pl* gym shoes, trainers.

'**Turnübung** *f* gymnastic exercise.

Turnus ['tʊrnʊs] *m* (-; -se) rotation: **im** ~ → **turnusmäßig** II. '**turnusmäßig I** *adj* a) rotational, b) regular. **II** *adv* in turns: ~ (**aus**)**wechseln** rotate.

'**Turnverein** *m* gymnastics club.

'**Tür|pfosten** *m* door post. ~**rahmen** *m* door frame. ~**schild** *n* door plate. ~**schließer** *m* ◉ door closer.

turteln ['tʊrtəln] *v/i* (h) F bill and coo. '**Turteltaube** *f* turtledove.

Tusch [tʊʃ] *m* (-[e]s; -e) ♪ flourish.

Tusche ['tʊʃə] *f* (-; -n) **1.** a) Indian ink, b) drawing ink. **2.** mascara.

tuscheln ['tʊʃəln] *v/i, v/t* (h) whisper.

tuschen ['tʊʃən] *v/t* (h) draw in Indian ink: **sich die Wimpern** ~ put some mascara on.

'**Tuschkasten** *m* paintbox.

'**Tuschzeichnung** *f* Indian drawing.

Tüte ['ty:tə] f (-; -n) **1.** (paper) bag. **2.** cone.

tuten ['tu:tən] v/i (h) F toot, *mot.* honk.

Tutor ['tu:tər] m (-s; -en [tu'to:rən]), **Tutorin** [tu'to:rɪn] f (-; -nen) *univ.* tutor.

Typ [ty:p] m (-s; -en) **1.** type, ⚙ a. model: F *sie ist mein* ~ she is my type. **2.** F fellow, chap.

Type ['ty:pə] f (-; -n) **1.** *print.* type. **2.** F *komische etc* ~ queer *etc* character.

'**Typenrad** n daisywheel.

'**Typenschild** n ⚙ type plate.

Typhus ['ty:fʊs] m (-; *no pl*) 🜩 typhoid (*a. in cpds. epidemic, patient, etc*).

typisch ['ty:pɪʃ] adj typical (**für** of): F *das ist* ~ *John!* that's John all over.

typisieren [typi'zi:rən] v/t (h) typify.

Typographie [typogra'fi:] f (-; -n) typography.

Typus ['ty:pʊs] m (-; Typen) type.

Tyrann [ty'ran] m (-en; -en) tyrant. **Tyrannei** [tyra'naɪ] f (-; -en) tyranny. **ty'rannisch** adj tyrannical. **tyrannisieren** [tyrani'zi:rən] v/t (h) tyrannize.

U

U, u [u:] n (-; -) U, u.

'**U-Bahn** f → **Untergrundbahn**.

übel ['y:bəl] adj bad, a. nasty: F (*gar*) *nicht* ~ not bad (at all); *mir ist* (*wird*) ~ I'm feeling (getting) sick; F *fig. dabei kann e-m* ~ *werden!* it's enough to make you sick; *ein übler Kerl* a bad lot; *e-e üble Sache* a bad business; ~ *riechen* smell (terrible).

'**Übel** n (-s; -) a) evil, b) illness: *das kleinere* ~ the lesser of two evils; *zu allem* ~ to top it all.

'**übelgelaunt** adj bad-tempered.

'**Übelkeit** f (-; -en) nausea.

'**übelnehmen** v/t (irr, sep, -ge-, h, → *nehmen*) et. ~ take s.th. amiss, take offen/ce (*Am.* -se) at s.th.; *j-m et.* ~ hold s.th. against s.o.; *nimm es mir nicht übel, aber ...* don't be offended but ...

'**übelriechend** adj foul-smelling, foul.

'**Übeltäter(in** f) m malefactor.

üben ['y:bən] v/t, v/i (h) practi/se (*Am.* -ce) (a. *sich* ~ *in dat*), a. train: *Klavier* ~ practise the piano; *fig. Geduld* ~ have patience; → **Nachsicht, Rache**.

über ['y:bər] **I** prep **1.** over, a. above, a. across (*the river etc*): ~ *die Straße gehen* cross the street; ~ *München nach Rom reisen* go to Rome via Munich. **2.** over (*a period*): ~ *Nacht* overnight; ~ *das Wochenende* over the weekend; ~ *die Ferien* during the holidays; ~*s Jahr* (this time) next year; ~ *der Arbeit* over

one's work. **3.** a) over, more than, b) beyond, *adm.* exceeding (*a sum etc*): *er ist* ~ *siebzig* (*Jahre alt*) he is past (*or* over) seventy; *es geht nichts* ~ *Musik!* there's nothing like music; → **Verstand. 4.** about (*a subject*), essay, *book*, *etc*: *a.* on: ~ *Geschäfte* (*Politik, den Beruf*) *reden* talk business (politics, shop). **5.** for: *e-e Rechnung* ~ *100 Mark* a bill for 100 marks. **6.** over, by: *e-e Treppe* over (*or* by) a staircase; ~ *die Auskunft* from the information; ~ *e-n Makler* through a broker. **7.** *Fehler* ~ *Fehler* one mistake after the other. **II** adv ~ *und* ~ all over; *die ganze Zeit* ~ all along; → **überhaben**.

'**überall** adv everywhere, all over: ~ *wo* wherever. '**überallher** adv from everywhere. '**überallhin** adv everywhere.

über'altert adj overaged (*population*).

'**Überangebot** n oversupply.

'**überängstlich** adj overanxious.

über'anstrengen v/t (*insep, no* -ge-, h) overexert (*sich* o.s.), strain.

Über'anstrengung f (-; *no pl*) overexertion, strain.

über'arbeiten (*insep, no* -ge-, h) **I** v/t revise (*book etc*). **II** *sich* ~ overwork. **über'arbeitet** adj **1.** revised. **2.** overworked. **Über'arbeitung** f (-; -en) **1.** a) revision, b) revised edition. **2.** *no pl* overwork.

'**überaus** adv extremely.

über'backen adj gastr. au gratin.
'**überbeanspruchen** v/t (insep, no -ge-, h) **1.** ⚙ overload, overstress. **2.** strain: **j-n ~** overtax s.o.
'**Überbein** n ✽ node, exostosis.
'**überbelegt** adj overcrowded.
'**überbelichten** v/t (insep, no -ge-, h) phot. overexpose.
'**überbesetzt** adj overstaffed.
'**überbewerten** v/t (insep, no -ge-, h) overvalue, overrate.
über'bieten v/t (irr, insep, no -ge-, h, → **bieten**) **1.** ✝ outbid (**um** by). **2.** outdo, beat (record): **sich (gegenseitig) ~ vie** with each other (**in** dat in).
'**Überbleibsel** [-blaɪpsəl] n (-s; -) a. fig. remnant.
über'blenden v/t (insep, no -ge-, h) film etc: fade over.
'**Überblick** m **1.** view (**über** acc of). fig. overall view: **e-n ~ gewinnen** get a general idea (**über** acc of); **den ~ verlieren** lose track of things, be confused.
über'blicken v/t (insep, no -ge-, h) **1.** overlook, survey. **2.** a) grasp, b) assess.
über'bringen v/t (irr, insep, no -ge-, h, → **bringen**) **j-m et. ~** deliver (or bring) s.th. to s.o. **Über'bringer** m (-s; -) bearer. **Über'bringung** f (-; no pl) delivery.
über'brücken v/t (insep, no -ge-, h) span, a. fig. bridge. **Über'brückungs·kre‚dit** m ✝ bridging loan.
über'buchen v/t (insep, no -ge-, h) ✝ overbook.
über'dacht adj roofed, covered.
über'dauern v/t (insep, no -ge-, h) outlast, survive. **~'dehnen** v/t (insep, no -ge-, h) overstretch, pull (muscle). **~'denken** v/t (irr, insep, no -ge-, h, → **denken**) think s.th. over, reconsider.
'**überdeutlich** adj all too clear.
über'dies adv besides, moreover.
'**überdimensio‚nal** adj outsize(d).
'**Überdosis** f overdose.
über'drehen v/t (insep, no -ge-, h) overspeed (engine).
'**Überdruck** m ⚙ overpressure. **~ka‚bine** f pressurized cabin. **~ven‚til** n pressure relief valve.
'**Überdruß** [-drʊs] m (-sses; no pl) weariness: **bis zum ~** ad nauseam.
'**überdrüssig** [-drʏsɪç] adj **~ sein** be weary (or tired) (gen of).

über'düngen v/t (insep, no -ge-, h) overfertilize.
'**überdurchschnittlich** adj above average.
'**Übereifer** m overzealousness.
'**übereifrig** adj overzealous, officious.
über'eignen v/t (insep, no -ge-, h) **j-m et. ~** make s.th. over to s.o. **Über'eignung** f (-; -en) transfer (**an** acc to).
über'eilen v/t (h) rush: **et. ~** a. rush things. **über'eilt** adj (over)hasty.
überein'ander adv **1.** one on top of the other. **2. ~ sprechen** talk about one another. **~schlagen** v/t (irr, sep, -ge-, h, → **schlagen**) cross (legs).
über'einkommen v/i (irr, sep, -ge-, sn, → **kommen**) (**über** acc on) agree, reach an agreement. **Über'einkommen** n (-s; -), **Über'einkunft** [-kʊnft] f (-; ⸗e) agreement.
über'einstimmen v/i (sep, -ge-, h) **1.** tally, correspond, colo(u)rs etc: match. **2. mit j-m ~** agree with s.o. (**über** acc, **in** dat on). **über'einstimmend** adj corresponding, a. concurring, matching (colo[u]rs etc). **Über'einstimmung** f (-; -en) agreement, correspondence: **in ~ mit** in accordance (or keeping) with.
'**überempfindlich** adj hypersensitive, ✽ or fig. allergic (**gegen** to).
'**überernährt** adj overfed.
über'fahren v/t (irr, insep, no -ge-, h, → **fahren**) drive through (signal etc): **j-n ~** run s.o. over, F fig. bulldoze s.o., sports: clobber s.o. '**Überfahrt** f (-; -en) ✈ crossing, passage.
'**Überfall** m (-[e]s; ⸗e) **1.** (**auf** acc) attack (on), raid (on), invasion (of). **2.** a) holdup, b) mugging. **3.** F surprise visit.
über'fallen v/t (irr, insep, no -ge-, h, → **fallen**) a) attack, assault, b) hold up, raid (bank etc), c) invade (country): F **j-n ~** descend on s.o.; **j-n mit e-r Frage** etc **~** pounce on s.o. with a question etc.
'**überfällig** adj overdue.
'**Überfallkom‚mando** n riot squad.
über'fliegen v/t (irr, insep, no -ge-, h, → **fliegen**) **1.** fly over. **2.** skim (letter etc).
'**überfließen** v/i (irr, sep, -ge-, sn, → **fließen**) overflow.
über'flügeln v/t (insep, no -ge-, h) **j-n ~** outstrip s.o.
'**Überfluß** m (-sses; no pl) abundance (**an** dat of): **~ haben an** (dat) abound in,

have plenty of; **zu allem ~** to top it all.
~gesellschaft f affluent society.

'überflüssig adj superfluous.

über'fluten v/t (insep, no -ge-, h) flood.

über'fordern v/t (insep, no -ge-, h) overtax, a. overstretch (staff etc): **j-n ~** a) expect too much of s.o., b) be too much for s.o.; **damit war sie überfordert** this was more than she could handle.

über'fragt adj F **da bin ich ~!** you've got me there.

Über'fremdung f (-; -en) foreign infiltration, ✝ control by foreign capital.

über'führen v/t (insep, no -ge-, h) 1. transport. 2. find s.o. guilty (gen of).

Über'führung f (-; -en) 1. transfer. 2. 🏛 conviction. 3. flyover, overpass.

'Überfülle f (-; no pl) (over)abundance.

über'füllt adj overcrowded, congested (streets), (jam-)packed (bus, room, etc).

'Überfunkti,on f ♞ hyperactivity.

über'füttert adj overfed.

'Übergabe f (-; -n) delivery, handing-over (a. of an office), ✕ surrender.

'Übergang m (-[e]s; ⁀e) 1. crossing, passage. 2. transition. **'übergangslos** adv without transition, directly.

'Übergangs|re,gierung f caretaker government, (jam-)**stadium** n transition(al stage). **~zeit** f transition(al period).

über'geben (irr, insep, no -ge-, h, → **geben**) **I** v/t (**j-m et.**) **~** hand over (s.th. to s.o.), present (s.o. with s.th.); **dem Verkehr ~** open s.th. to the traffic. **II sich ~** vomit, be sick.

'übergehen¹ v/i (irr, sep, -ge-, sn, → **gehen**) pass over (**zu** to): **~ auf** (acc) devolve upon (successor etc); **~ in** (acc) pass into (or turn) into; **in j-s Besitz ~** pass into s.o.'s possession; **in andere Hände ~** change hands; **in Verwesung ~** begin to putrefy; **~ zu** proceed to (s.th.).

über'gehen² v/t (irr, insep, no -ge-, h, → **gehen**) a) ignore, b) omit, skip, c) pass s.o., s.th. over.

'übergeordnet adj 1. higher (office etc). 2. of overriding importance.

'Übergepäck n ✈ excess baggage.

'übergeschnappt adj F crazy, mad.

'Übergewicht n (-[e]s; no pl) 1. (**~ haben** be) overweight. 2. fig. preponderance: **das ~ haben** predominate.

'überglücklich adj overjoyed.

'übergreifen v/i (irr, sep, -ge-, h, → **greifen**) fig. spread (**auf** acc to).

'Übergriff m (-[e]s; -e) (**in** acc) encroachment ([up]on), infringement (of).

'übergroß adj outsize(d).

'Übergröße f outsize.

'überhaben v/t (irr, sep, -ge-, h, → **haben**) F 1. have coat etc on. 2. be fed up with.

über'handnehmen v/i (irr, sep, -ge-, h, → **nehmen**) increase, spread.

'Überhang m (-[e]s; ⁀e) 1. ✓, ⚖, ⚙ overhang. 2. surplus (of money), backlog (of orders etc). **'überhängen¹** v/i (irr, sep, -ge-, h, → **hängen**) overhang, ⚖ project. **'überhängen²** v/t (sep, h) throw coat etc over one's shoulders.

über'häufen v/t (insep, no -ge-, h) **j-n mit** swamp s.o. with work etc, shower s.o. with presents etc, heap hono(u)rs etc on s.o.

über'haupt adv at all, actually, really: **was willst du ~?** what really do you want?; **~ nicht** not at all; **~ nichts** nothing at all; **er versteht davon ~ nichts** he doesn't know the first thing about it; **~ kein ...** no ... whatever; **wenn ~** if at all.

überheblich [-'he:plɪç] adj arrogant.

Über'heblichkeit f (-; no pl) arrogance.

über'hitzt adj a. fig. overheated.

über'höht adj excessive (prices etc).

über'holen v/t (insep, no -ge-, h) 1. pass, overtake, fig. outstrip. 2. ⚙ overhaul.

Über'holma,növer n overtaking manoeuvre, Am. passing maneuver.

Über'holspur f mot. passing lane.

Über'holung f (-; -en) ⚙ overhaul.

Über'holverbot n "No Passing" sign.

über'hören v/t (insep, no -ge-, h) a) not to hear, miss, not to catch, b) ignore.

'überirdisch adj supernatural.

'Überkapazi,tät f overcapacity.

über'kleben v/t (insep, no -ge-, h) **et. ~** paste s.th. over.

'überkochen v/i (sep, sn) boil over.

über'kommen v/t (irr, insep, no -ge-, h, → **kommen**) Furcht etc **~ überkam ihn** he was overcome by fear etc.

'überkonfessio,nell adj interdenominational.

über'kronen v/t (insep, no -ge-, h) crown, cap (tooth).

über'laden (irr, insep, no -ge-, h, → **laden**) **I** v/t 1. overload (a. ⚡), overburden, swamp (*mit* with *work etc*). **II** *adj* **2.** overloaded. **3.** *fig.* a) cluttered, b) overladen, florid (*style*).

über'lagern *v/t* (*insep, no* -ge-, h) superimpose, *partially*: overlap (*a.* **sich ~**), *radio*: a) heterodyne, b) jam (*station*).

'Überlandbus *m* long-distance coach.

'Überlänge *f* exceptional length.

über'lassen *v/t* (*irr, insep, no* -ge-, h, → **lassen**) **j-m et. ~** let s.o. have s.th., *a. fig.* leave s.th. to s.o.; **j-n s-m Schicksal ~** leave s.o. to his fate; **sich selbst ~ sein** be left to one's own devices; **~ Sie das mir!** leave it to me; **das bleibt ihm ~!** that's up to him.

über'lasten *v/t* (*insep, no* -ge-, h) **1.** *a.* ⚡, ⚙ overload. **2.** *fig.* a) overtax, overburden, b) overwork, overstretch.

Über'lastung *f* (-; -en) **1.** *a.* ⚡, ⚙ overload. **2.** *fig.* a) overburdening, b) strain.

'überlaufen¹ *v/i* (*irr, sep,* -ge-, sn, → **laufen**) **1.** run over. **2.** (*zu* to) desert, go over, defect. **über'laufen²** *v/t, insep, no* -ge-, h, → **laufen**) **I** *v/t* seize: *Angst überlief mich* I was seized with fear. **II** *v/impers* **es überlief mich heiß und kalt** I went hot and cold.

über'laufen³ *adj* overcrowded.

'Überläufer *m* deserter, defector.

über'leben *v/t, v/i* (*insep, no* -ge-, h) survive. **Über'leben** *n* (-s) survival.

Über'lebende *m, f* (-n; -n) survivor.

Über'lebenschance *f* chance of survival.

'überlebensgroß *adj* larger than life, larger-than-life ...

überlebt [-'le:pt] *adj* antiquated.

über'legen *v/t, v/i* (*insep, no* -ge-, h) think (*s.th.* over): **ich will es mir ~** I'll think it over; **es sich anders ~** change one's mind; **sich et. genau ~** think carefully about it; **ohne zu ~** a) without thinking, b) rashly, c) F like a shot; → **reiflich II.**

über'legen² **I** *adj* superior (*dat* to, *an dat* in), *contp. a.* supercilious: **j-m weit ~ sein** be head and shoulders above s.o. **II** *adv* a) in superior style, b) supercilously: **~ siegen** win in style.

Über'legenheit *f* (-; *no pl*) superiority.

überlegt [-'le:kt] *adj* (well-)considered.

Über'legung *f* (-; -en) consideration, reflection: **~en anstellen** a) **über** (*acc*)

think about, reflect on, b) **ob** consider if; → **reiflich I.**

'überleiten *v/i* (*sep,* h) lead over (**zu** to).

über'liefern *v/t* (*insep, no* -ge-, h) **et.** ~ hand s.th. down (*dat* to). **über'liefert** *adj* traditional. **Über'lieferung** *f* (-; -en) tradition.

über'listen *v/t* (*insep, no* -ge-, h) outwit.

'Übermacht *f* (-; *no pl*) superiority.

'übermächtig *adj* too strong, *fig.* overpowering.

über'malen *v/t* (*insep, no* -ge-, h) **et.** ~ paint this s.th. over.

'Übermaß *n* (-es; *no pl*) excess (**an** *dat* of). **'übermäßig** *adj* excessive.

'Übermensch *m* superman.

'übermenschlich *adj* superhuman.

über'mitteln *v/t* (*insep, no* -ge-, h) transmit (*dat* to).

Über'mittlung *f* (-; *no pl*) transmission.

'übermorgen *adv* the day after tomorrow.

über'müdet *adj* overtired.

'Übermut *m* (-[e]s; *no pl*) high spirits.

'übermütig [-my:tɪç] *adj* high-spirited, *pred* in high spirits.

'übernächst *adj* the next but one: **~e Woche** the week after next.

über'nachten *v/i* (*insep, no* -ge-, h) spend the night.

übernächtigt [-'nɛçtɪçt] *adj* bleary-eyed.

Über'nachtung *f* (-; -en) overnight stay: **~ und Frühstück** bed and breakfast.

Über'nachtungsmöglichkeit *f* overnight accommodation.

'Übernahme [-na:mə] *f* (-; -n) taking over, takeover (*of firm, power*), assumption (*of office, responsibility*), adoption (*of idea*). **~angebot** *n* ⚐ takeover bid.

'übernatio,nal *adj* supranational.

'überna,türlich *adj* supernatural.

über'nehmen (*irr, insep, no* -ge-, h, → **nehmen**) **I** *v/t* take over (*firm, power, etc*), *a.* accept (*goods*), take on (*responsibility, work, etc*), adopt (*ideas etc*): **es ~ zu** *inf* take it upon o.s. to *inf*; **et.** ~ take care of s.th. **II** *sich* ~ take on more than one can handle, *financially*: overreach o.s., *physically*: overdo it; *iro.* **übernimm dich nur nicht!** don't kill yourself!

'**überordnen** v/t (sep, h) (dat) set s.o., s.th. above s.o., s.th.

'**überpar,teilich** adj nonpartisan.

'**Überprodukti,on** f overproduction.

über'prüfen v/t (insep, no -ge-, h) **1.** check, examine. **2.** screen, F vet (person). **Über'prüfung** f (-; -en) check-(up), examination, a. F vetting.

'**überquellen** v/i (irr, sep, -ge-, sn, → quellen) overflow (von with).

über'queren v/t (insep, no -ge-, h) cross. **Über'querung** f (-; -en) crossing.

über'ragen v/t (insep, no -ge-, h) **1.** tower above, be taller than. **2.** fig. outclass.

über'ragend adj fig. outstanding.

überraschen [-'raʃən] v/t (insep, no -ge-, h) surprise, a. take s.o. by surprise, catch s.o. (bei at); **von e-m Gewitter überrascht werden** be caught in a thunderstorm. **über'raschend** adj a) surprising, b) unexpected, sudden.

Über'raschung f (-; -en) surprise. **Über'raschungs|mo,ment** n element of surprise. **~sieg** m unexpected win.

'**überrea,gieren** v/i (insep, h) overreact.

über'reden v/t (insep, no -ge-, h) j-n ~ persuade s.o., talk s.o. round; j-n zu et. ~ a. talk s.o. into doing s.th. **Über'redung** f (-; -en) persuasion. **Über'redungskunst** f powers of persuasion.

'**überregio,nal** adj supraregional, national (paper), nationwide (broadcast).

'**überreich** adj ~ sein an abound in.

über'reichen v/t (insep, no -ge-, h) hand s.th. over (or present s.th.) (j-m to s.o.). **Über'reichung** f (-; no pl) presentation.

'**überreif** adj overripe.

über'reizt adj overwrought: ~ sein a. be on edge.

'**Überrest** m remains, fig. a. relics.

'**Überrollbügel** m mot. rollbar. **über'rollen** v/t (insep, no -ge-, h) overrun.

über'rumpeln v/t (insep, no -ge-, h) j-n ~ take s.o. unawares (or by surprise).

über'runden v/t (insep, no -ge-, h) sports: lap, fig. outstrip.

übersät [-'zɛ:t] adj littered, fig. studded.

über'sättigen v/t (insep, no -ge-, h) oversaturate, 🜄 a. glut, 🜍 supersaturate, fig. surfeit. **Über'sättigung** f (-; no pl) surfeit, 🜄 glut, 🜍 supersaturation.

über'säuern v/t (insep, no -ge-, h) a. 🜍

overacidify. **Über'säuerung** f (-; no pl) a. 🜍 hyperacidity.

'**Überschall...** supersonic (aircraft etc).

'**Überschallknall** m sonic boom.

über'schatten v/t (insep, no -ge-, h) overshadow, fig. cast a cloud over.

über'schätzen v/t (insep, no -ge-, h) overestimate, overrate. **Über'schätzung** f (-; no pl) overestimation.

über'schaubar adj fig. clear, easy to grasp: ~, von ~er Größe of manageable size. **über'schauen** → überblicken 2.

'**überschäumen** v/i (sep, h) **1.** froth over. **2.** fig. bubble over (vor dat with).

'**Überschlag** m (-[e]s; ⸗e) **1.** gym. a) somersault, b) handspring. **2.** (rough) estimate. **3.** ⚡ flashover. **über'schlagen** (irr, insep, no -ge-, h, → schlagen) **I** v/t **1.** skip. **2.** calculate roughly. **II** sich ~ **3.** fall head over heels, mot. overturn, ✈ nose over: F fig. sich fast ~ bend over backwards; **die Ereignisse überschlugen sich** things started happening very fast. **4.** voice: crack.

'**überschnappen** v/i (sep, sn) **1.** F go mad, go crazy: → übergeschnappt. **2.** voice: crack.

über'schneiden: sich ~ (irr, insep, no -ge-, h, → schneiden) overlap (a. fig.), lines: intersect; **sich zeitlich ~** coincide. **Über'schneidung** f (-; -en) ⚕ intersection, a. fig. overlap(ping).

über'schreiben v/t (irr, insep, no -ge-, h, → schreiben) **1.** head, title. **2.** transfer (dat to): j-m et. ~ make over s.th. to s.o.

über'schreiten v/t (irr, insep, no -ge-, h, → schreiten) **1.** cross. **2.** fig. exceed.

'**Überschrift** f (-; -en) heading, title.

'**Überschuß** m (-sses; ⸗sse) surplus (an dat of).

'**überschüssig** [-ʃʏsɪç] adj surplus.

über'schütten v/t (insep, no -ge-, h) j-n ~ mit shower s.o. with (gifts etc).

'**Überschwang** m (-[e]s; no pl) exuberance.

über'schwemmen v/t (insep, no -ge-, h) flood, fig. a. inundate, 🜄 a. glut. **Über'schwemmung** f (-; -en) flooding.

'**überschwenglich** [-ʃvɛŋlɪç] adj effusive, exuberant: ~e Kritik F rave review.

'**Übersee: in** (nach) ~ overseas.

'**überseeisch** adj overseas.

über'sehbar adj **1.** open (terrain etc). **2.** foreseeable, clear. **über'sehen** v/t (irr, *insep, no* -ge-, h, → *sehen*) **1.** → **überblicken** 2. **2.** a) overlook, b) ignore.

über'senden *v/t* (*irr, insep, no* -ge-, h, → *senden*) send, forward.

'**übersetzen**¹ (*sep*, h) **I** *v/t* ferry *s.o., s.th.* over. **II** *v/i* (*a.* sn) cross the river *etc.*

über'setzen² *v/t* (*insep, no* -ge-, h) **1.** *a. v/i* translate. **2.** ⊕ transmit. **Über'setzer** *m* (-s; -). **Über'setzerin** *f* (-; -nen) translator. **Über'setzung** *f* (-; -en) **1.** translation (*aus* from, *in acc* into). **2.** ⊕ gear ratio, transmission.

Über'setzungs⌐bü⌐ro *n* translating agency. **⌐fehler** *m* error in translation.

'**Übersicht** *f* (-; -en) **1.** survey, summary, outline. **2.** → **Überblick**. '**übersichtlich** *adj* **1.** open (*terrain etc*), clear. **2.** *fig.* clear(ly arranged), lucid. '**Übersichtlichkeit** *f* (-; *no pl*) clearness.

'**übersiedeln** *v/i* (*sep*, sn) move (*nach* to). '**Übersiedler(in** *f*) *m pol. hist.* migrant (from East to West Germany). '**Übersiedlung** *f* (-; -en) move (*nach* to).

'**übersinnlich** *adj* supernatural, psychic.

über'spannen *v/t* (*insep, no* -ge-, h) **1.** span, △ vault. **2.** *fig.* exaggerate: → *Bogen* 1. **über'spannt** *adj* extravagant, eccentric. **Über'spanntheit** *f* (-; -en) extravagance, eccentricity.

über'spielen *v/t* (*insep, no* -ge-, h) **1.** rerecord (*tape etc*): *auf Band* ~ tape(-record). **2.** *fig.* cover *s.th.* up.

über'spitzt *adj* **1.** exaggerated. **2.** oversubtle.

'**überspringen**¹ *v/i* (*irr, sep*, -ge-, sn, → *springen*) ⚡ flash over.

über'springen² *v/t* (*irr, insep, no* -ge-, h, → *springen*) **1.** jump over (*or* across), clear. **2.** *fig.* skip (*page etc*).

'**überstaatlich** *adj* supranational.

'**überstehen**¹ *v/i* (*irr, sep*, -ge-, h, → *stehen*) jut out, project.

über'stehen² *v/t* (*irr, insep, no* -ge-, h, → *stehen*) get over, survive, weather, ride out (*storm, crisis, etc*): *das wäre überstanden!* that's that; *das Schlimmste ist* ~ the worst is over now.

über'steigen *v/i* (*irr, insep, no* -ge-, h, → *steigen*) **1.** climb over. **2.** *fig.* exceed.

über'steuern *v/t* (*insep, no* -ge-, h) **1.** *mot.* oversteer. **2.** ⚡ overmodulate. ~'**stimmen** *v/t* (*insep, no* -ge-, h) outvote. ~'**strahlen** *v/t* (*irr, insep, no*

-ge-, h, → *streichen*) coat (*mit* with).

'**überstreifen** *v/t* (*sep*, h) slip *s.th.* on.

'**Überstunden** *pl* (~ *machen* work *or* do) overtime.

über'stürzen *v/t* (*insep, no* -ge-, h) rush: *nur nichts* ~! don't rush things; *die Ereignisse überstürzten sich* things started happening very fast.

über'stürzt *adj* hasty, rash.

'**überta⌐riflich** *adj* in excess of the (collectively agreed) scale.

über'teuert *adj* overpriced.

über'tönen *v/t* (*insep, no* -ge-, h) drown (out).

'**Übertrag** [-tra:k] *m* (-[e]s; ⸚e) ✝ carryover. **über'tragbar** *adj* **1.** (*auf acc* to) transferable, *fig.* applicable. **2.** ✝ negotiable (*bill*). **3.** ✚ infectious, contagious. **über'tragen** (*irr, insep, no* -ge-, h, → *tragen*) **I** *v/t* **1.** (*auf acc* to) transfer, *a.* make over, give (*powers*), assign, delegate (*task etc*): *j-m et.* ~ *a.* entrust s.th. to s.o. **2.** ⚡, *phys.*, ⊕ transmit (*auf acc* to), broadcast. **3.** (*in acc* into) a) transcribe, b) translate (*a. computer*). **4.** transmit *disease* (*auf acc* to), transfuse (*blood*). **5.** *fig. et.* ~ *auf* (*acc*) apply s.th. to; *im* ~*en Sinne* in the figurative sense. **II** *sich* ~ *auf* (*acc*) *disease*: be passed on (to), *mood, panic, etc*: communicate itself (to).

Über'tragung *f* (-; -en) **1.** (*auf acc* to) transfer (*a.* ✝, ⚖), assignment (*of rights, tasks, etc*), delegation (*of powers*), conferment (*of offices, titles, etc*). **2.** ⚡, ✚, *phys.*, ⊕ transmission (*auf acc* to), *radio, TV:* a. broadcast. **3.** (*in acc* into) a) transcription, b) translation.

Über'tragungswagen *m radio, TV* outside broadcast (*or* OB) van.

über'treffen *v/t* (*irr, insep, no* -ge-, h, → *treffen*) a) (*an or in dat* in) excel (*sich selbst* o.s.), outdo, surpass, b) exceed (*expectations etc*), go beyond, beat.

über'treiben *v/t* (*irr, insep, no* -ge-, h, → *treiben*) **1.** *et.* ~ overdo *s.th.*, carry *s.th.* too far. **2.** *a. v/i* exaggerate. **Über'treibung** *f* (-; -en) exaggeration.

'**übertreten**¹ *v/i* (*irr, sep*, -ge-, sn, → *treten*) **1.** (*zu* to) *pol.* go over, *eccl.* convert: *zum Katholizismus* ~ *a.* F turn (Roman) Catholic. **2.** *sports:* foul (a jump *or* throw).

über'treten² *v/t* (*irr, insep, no* -ge-, h, →

treten) **1.** violate (*law etc*). **2.** *sich den Fuß* ~ sprain one's ankle.

Über'tretung *f* (-; -en) 🏛 a) violation, b) (petty) offen/ce (*Am.* -se).

übertrieben [-'tri:bən] *adj* exaggerated, excessive (*demands etc*).

'Übertritt *m* (-[e]s; -e) (*zu* to) change, *pol.* defection, *eccl.* conversion.

über'trumpfen *v/t* (h) *fig.* outdo.

über'tünchen *v/t* (*insep, no* -ge-, h) *a. fig.* whitewash.

über'völkert *adj* overpopulated.

über'vorteilen *v/t* (*insep, no* -ge- h) cheat.

über'wachen *v/t* (*insep, no* -ge-, h) supervise, *a.* 🎖 *etc* observe, *police:* keep under surveillance, ⚙ check, inspect, monitor. **Über'wachung** *f* (-; -en) supervision, observation, surveillance, ⚙ inspection, checking, monitoring.

überwältigen [-'vɛltɪgən] *v/t* (*insep, no* -ge-, h) *a. fig.* overpower, overwhelm. **über'wältigend** *adj fig.* overwhelming, *a.* stunning, breathtaking (*beauty*): *mit ~er Mehrheit* with an overwhelming majority; *nicht gerade ~!* nothing to write home about.

über'weisen *v/t* (*irr, insep, no* -ge-, h, → *weisen*) **1.** transfer (*auf ein Konto* to an account, *j-m* to s.o.'s account). **2.** refer *case, patient, etc* (*an acc* to). **Über'weisung** *f* (-; -en) **1.** transfer, remittance. **2.** referral (*an acc* to).

'überwerfen¹ *v/t* (*irr, sep, no* -ge-, h, → *werfen*) fling on *dress etc*.

über'werfen²: *sich* ~ (*irr, insep, no* -ge-, h, → *werfen*) fall out (*mit* with).

über'wiegen *v/t* (*insep, no* -ge-, h, → *wiegen*) predominate, prevail.

über'wiegend I *adj* predominant, prevailing: *die ~e Mehrheit* the vast majority. **II** *adv* predominantly, mainly.

über'winden (*irr, insep, no* -ge-, h, → *winden*) **I** *v/t* overcome, get over, surmount (*crisis, illness, etc*). **II** *sich* ~ *zu inf* bring o.s. to *inf.* **Über'windung** *f* (-; *no pl*) **1.** overcoming (*etc*). **2.** *es kostete mich* ~ it cost me quite an effort.

über'wintern *v/i* (*insep, no* -ge-, h) spend the winter, *zo.* hibernate.

über'wuchern *v/t* (*insep, no* -ge-, h) overgrow.

'Überzahl *f* (-; *no pl*) (*in der* ~ *sein* be in the) majority.

'überzählig [-tsɛ:lɪç] *adj* surplus, spare.

über'zeichnen *v/t* (*insep, no* -ge-, h) **1.** ✝ oversubscribe. **2.** *fig.* overdraw.

über'zeugen (*insep, no* -ge-, h) **I** *v/t* (*von*) convince (of), *esp.* 🏛 satisfy (as to). **II** *v/i* be convincing. **III** *sich* ~ satisfy o.s. (*von* as to): ~ *Sie sich selbst!* go and see for yourself. **über'zeugend** *adj* convincing: *wenig* ~ (rather) unconvincing. **über'zeugt** *adj* convinced (*von* of), ardent (*socialist etc*): *von sich selbst* (*sehr*) ~ *sein* have a high opinion of o.s. **Über'zeugung** *f* (-; -en) conviction, (*political etc*) convictions: *der* ~ *sein, daß* be convinced that; *zu der* ~ *gelangen, daß* come to the conclusion that. **Über'zeugungskraft** *f* powers of persuasion.

'überziehen¹ *v/t* (*irr, sep,* -ge-, h, → *ziehen*) put on (*coat etc*).

über'ziehen² (*irr, insep, no* -ge-, h, → *ziehen*) **I** *v/t* **1.** a) cover, b) coat, c) line. **2.** put fresh linen on (*bed*). **3.** overdraw (*account*). **4.** overrun (*air time*). **5.** *fig.* exaggerate. **II** *v/i* exceed the time limit. **III** *sich* ~ become covered (*mit* with), *sky:* become overcast. **Über'ziehung** *f* (-; *no pl*) ✝ overdraft. **Über'ziehungskre,dit** *m* overdraft credit.

'Überzug *m* a) cover, b) coat(ing).

üblich ['y:plɪç] *adj* usual, customary, normal: *wie* ~ as usual; *es ist bei uns (so)* ~, *daß* it is a custom with us that; *das Übliche* the usual (thing).

U-Boot *n* submarine.

übrig ['y:brɪç] *adj* remaining, left (over), other: *das* ~*e*, *alles* ~*e* the rest; *das* ~*e Geld* the rest of the money; *die* ~*en* the others, the rest; *im* ~*en* a) as for the rest, b) → *übrigens*; *et.* ~ *haben* have s.th. left (*fig. für* have a soft spot for); *nichts* ~ *haben für* have no time for.

'übrigbleiben *v/i* (*irr, sep,* -ge-, sn, → *bleiben*) be left, remain: *es blieb mir nichts anderes übrig* (*als*) I had no choice (but).

übrigens ['y:brɪgəns] *adv* by the way, incidentally.

'übriglassen *v/t* (*irr, sep, no* -ge-, h, → *lassen*) leave: *viel* (*nichts*) *zu wünschen* ~ leave a lot (nothing) to be desired.

'Übung *f* (-; -en) **1.** practice: *aus der* ~ *sein* (*kommen*) be (get) out of practice; *in der* ~ *bleiben* keep one's hand in; ~

macht den Meister practice makes perfect. **2.** *gym.*, ✕, ♪ exercise.

'Übungs|aufgabe *f* exercise. **~buch** *n* book of exercises. **~hang** *m* skiing: nursery slope. **~sache** *f* das ist reine **~!** it's just a matter of practice.

Ufer ['u:fər] *n* (-s; -) a) shore, b) bank: *am* **~**, *ans* **~** ashore; *über die* **~** *treten* overflow its banks. **'uferlos** *adj fig.* a) boundless, b) endless (*debate etc*): *ins* **~e** *gehen* lead nowhere.

Ufo ['u:fo] *n* (-s; -s) UFO, unidentified flying object.

Uhr [u:r] *f* (-; -en) clock, watch: *wieviel* **~** *ist es?* what time is it?; *es ist zwei* **~** it's two o'clock (*or* 2 p.m., 14.00 hours); *nach m-r* **~** by my watch; *wieviel* **~?** (at) what time?; *sports*: *ein Rennen gegen die* **~** a race against time; F *rund um die* **~** around the clock. **~armband** *n* watch strap. **~macher** *m* (-s; -) clockmaker, watchmaker. **~werk** *n* clock mechanism, works. **~zeiger** *m* hand. **~zeigersinn** *m im* **~** clockwise; *entgegen dem* **~** anticlockwise. **~zeit** *f* time.

Uhu ['u:hu] *m* (-s; -s) *zo.* eagle-owl.

Ulk [ʊlk] *m* (-[e]s; -e) joke, lark: *aus* **~** for a joke. **'ulkig** *adj* funny.

Ulme ['ʊlmə] *f* (-; -n) ♣ elm.

Ultimatum [ʊlti'ma:tʊm] *n* (-s; -ten) (*ein* **~** *stellen* deliver an) ultimatum.

Ultra ['ʊltra] *m* (-s; -s) *pol.* extremist.

Ultra'kurzwelle *f* ⚡ very high frequency (*abbr.* VHF), *a.* ☢ ultrashort wave.

'ultrarot *adj* ultrared, infrared.

'Ultraschall *m phys.* ultrasound.

'Ultraschall... ultrasonic, supersonic. **~untersuchung** *f* ☢ ultrasound scan.

'ultravio,lett *adj* ultraviolet.

um [ʊm] **I** *prep* **1.** *space*: (a)round, *time*: at, about, around: **~** *Ostern* (*herum*) some time around Easter. **2.** *denoting difference*: by: *die Hälfte billiger sein* be only half the price; **~** *so besser* so much the better; **~** *so mehr* (*weniger*) (*als* as, *weil* because) all the more (less), (so much) the more (less). **3.** for, about: *bitten* (*schreien*) **~** ask (cry) for. **4.** *es steht schlecht* **~** *ihn* he's in a bad way; *schade* **~** ... it's too bad about ... **II** *conj* **~** *zu inf* (in order) to *inf.* **III** *adv* about, around (*100 persons etc*).

'umadres,sieren *v/t* (*sep*, h) redirect.

'umarbeiten *v/t* (*sep*, h) alter, remodel

(*dress etc*), revise (*book etc*), adapt (*for the screen etc*). **'Umarbeitung** *f* (-; -en) alteration, revision, adaptation.

um'armen *v/t* (*insep*, *no* -ge-, h) (*a. sich* **~**), **Um'armung** *f* (-; -en) embrace, hug.

'Umbau *m* (-[e]s; -e, -ten) **1.** a) reconstruction, conversion (*in acc*, *zu* into), b) altered section. **2.** reorganization. **'umbauen¹** (*sep*, h) **I** *v/t* alter, *a.* redesign, remodel, convert *flat etc* (*in acc*, *zu* into). **II** *v/i thea.* change the setting. **um'bauen²** *v/t* (*insep*, *no* -ge-, h) build round: *umbauter Raum* interior space.

'umbenennen *v/t* (*irr*, *sep*, h, → *benennen*) rename.

'umbesetzen *v/t* (*sep*, h) *thea.* recast.

'umbiegen *v/t* (*irr*, *sep*, -ge-, h, → *biegen*) bend.

'umbilden *v/t* (*sep*, h) reorganize, *pol.* reshuffle (*cabinet etc*). **'Umbildung** *f* (-; -en) reorganization, *pol.* reshuffle.

'umbinden *v/t* (*irr*, *sep*, -ge-, h, → *binden*) tie round, (*a. sich* **~**) put on (*tie*, *apron, etc*).

'umblättern *v/t* (*sep*, h) turn over (the page *v/i*).

'umbrechen¹ *v/t* (*irr*, *sep*, -ge-, h, → *brechen*) break down.

um'brechen² *v/t* (*irr*, *insep*, *no* -ge-, h, → *brechen*) make up (into pages).

'umbringen (*irr*, *sep*, -ge-, h, → *bringen*) **I** *v/t* kill: F *nicht umzubringen* indestructible. **II** *sich* **~** kill o.s.; F *fig. sich* (*fast*) **~** bend over backwards.

'Umbruch *m* (-[e]s; ⁻e) **1.** *print.* makeup, *on VSU*: formatting. **2.** *fig.* upheaval.

'umbuchen *v/t* (*sep*, h) **1.** change one's booking for. **2.** ✝ transfer (*auf acc* to).

'umdenken *v/i* (*irr*, *sep*, -ge-, h, → *denken*) **~** *müssen* have to do some rethinking. **'Umdenken** *n* (-s) rethink.

'umdispo,nieren *v/i* (*sep*, h) change one's plans.

'umdrehen *v/t* (*sep*, h) turn (round) (*a. sich* **~**), twist (*arm*): *j-m den Hals* **~** wring s.o.'s neck; → *Spieß.*

Um'drehung *f* (-; -en) turn, *phys.*, ⚙ revolution, rotation: **~en** *pro Minute* revolutions per minute (*abbr.* rpm).

umein'ander *adv sich* **~** *kümmern etc* take care *etc* of each other (*or* of one another).

'Umerziehung *f* (-; *no pl*) reeducation.

'umfahren v/t (irr, sep, -ge-, h, → **fahren**) run (or knock) down.

um'fahren² v/t (irr, insep, no -ge-, h, → **fahren**) drive (or sail) round.

'umfallen v/i (irr, sep, -ge-, sn, → **fallen**) **1.** fall (down or over), collapse: **zum** ♀ **müde** ready to drop. **2.** F fig. cave in.

'Umfang m (-[e]s; no pl) a) circumference, girth, b) a. fig. extent, size, fig. scope, volume (of sales, traffic, etc): **10 Zoll im ~** 10 inches round; fig. in **vollem ~** fully; **in großem ~** on a large scale, large-scale. **'umfangreich** adj **1.** extensive. **2.** voluminous.

um'fassen v/t (insep, no -ge-, h) fig. **1.** comprise. **2.** cover (period).

um'fassend adj extensive, comprehensive (knowledge etc), complete, full (confession etc), sweeping (reforms etc).

'Umfeld n (-[e]s; -er) fig. surrounding(s).

'umformen v/t (sep, h) reshape (a. fig.), ⚡ transform, convert. **'Umformer** m (-s; -) ⚡ transformer, converter.

'Umfrage f (-; -n) a) inquiry, b) (public) opinion poll, survey.

'umfüllen v/t (sep, h) pour s.th. into another container (etc), decant (wine).

'umfunktio,nieren v/t (sep, h) et. **~ in** (acc) convert (or turn) s.th. into.

'Umgang m (-[e]s; no pl) **1.** a) social intercourse, relations, b) company, friends: **~ haben mit** associate with; **guten (schlechten) ~ haben** keep good (bad) company. **2. der ~ mit Kindern** etc dealing with children etc; **im ~ mit ...** (in) dealing with ...

umgänglich ['ʊmgɛŋlɪç] adj affable, sociable, easy to get along with.

'Umgangs|formen pl manners. **~sprache** f colloquial language: **die englische ~** colloquial English. **'umgangssprachlich** adj colloquial.

um'garnen v/t (insep, no -ge-, h) fig. ensnare.

um'geben v/t (irr, insep, no -ge-, h, → **geben**) surround (**sich** o.s.) (**mit** with).

Um'gebung f (-; -en) environs, neighbo(u)rhood, vicinity, a. biol., sociol. environment, surroundings.

'Umgegend f (-; -en) environs, vicinity.

'umgehen v/i (irr, sep, -ge-, sn, → **gehen**) **1.** disease, rumo(u)r, etc: circulate, go round. **2.** ghost: walk. **3. ~ mit** associate with (s.o.), treat, deal with, handle

(s.th., problem); **sie kann (gut) mit Leuten ~** she knows how to handle people; **er weiß mit Pferden umzugehen** he has a way with horses; **kannst du mit der Maschine ~?** do you know how to use (or handle) the machine?; → **schonend** II, **sparsam** II.

um'gehen² v/t (irr, insep, no -ge-, h, → **gehen**) **1.** bypass. **2.** fig. avoid, evade.

'umgehend adj immediate.

Um'gehung f (-; no pl) **1.** bypassing. **2.** fig. avoidance, a. ⚖ evasion.

Um'gehungsstraße f bypass, perimeter road.

'umgekehrt I adj a) reverse, b) inverse, opposite: **im ~en Falle** in the reverse case; **in ~er Reihenfolge** in reverse order; **(genau) ~!** (no,) it's exactly the other way round. **II** adv the other way round, conversely.

'umgestalten v/t (sep, h) reshape, fig. a. reorganize, ⚙ etc redesign.

'umgraben v/t (irr, sep, -ge-, h, → **graben**) dig (up), turn (over).

um'grenzen v/t (insep, no -ge-, h) fig. define.

'umgrup,pieren v/t (sep, h) regroup, pol. reshuffle. **'Umgrup,pierung** f (-; -en) regrouping, pol. reshuffle.

'Umhang m (-[e]s; ⸚e) cape, wrap.

'umhängen v/t (sep, h) **1.** put on (coat etc), sling (rifle). **2.** rehang (picture).

'Umhängetasche f shoulder bag.

'umhauen v/t (irr, sep, -ge-, h, → **hauen**) **1.** fell, cut down. **2.** F fig. **j-n ~** drink etc: knock s.o. out, news etc: bowl s.o. over.

um'her adv about, (a)round.

um'hinkönnen v/i (irr, sep, -ge-, h, → **können**) **ich kann nicht umhin zu** inf I cannot help par.

umhören: sich ~ (sep, h) keep one's ears open, ask around.

um'hüllen v/t (insep, no -ge-, h) (**mit**) wrap up (or envelop) (in), cover (with).

Um'hüllung f (-; -en) wrapping, cover.

'Umkehr f (-; no pl) **j-n zur ~ zwingen** force s.o. (to turn) back. **'umkehren** (sep) **I** v/i (sn) turn back. **II** v/t (h) turn round (a. **sich ~**), reverse (a. fig.).

'Umkehrfilm m reversal film.

'umkippen (sep) **I** v/t (h) **1.** tip over, upset. **2.** fall over, car etc: overturn, ♥ a. capsize. **3.** F faint, keel over. **4.** F *fig.* turn, change completely, *river etc*: die, *wine*: turn sour.

um'klammern *v/t* (*insep, no* -ge-, h) clutch, clinch.

'umklappen *v/t* (*sep*, h) turn down.

'Umkleideka,bine *f* changing cubicle. **'umkleiden: sich ~** (*sep*, h) change (one's clothes). **'Umkleideraum** *m* changing (*sports*: locker) room.

'umknicken *v/i* (*sep*, sn) (*mit dem Fuß*) ~ sprain one's ankle.

'umkommen *v/i* (*irr, sep,* -ge-, sn, → *kommen*) die (*a.* F *vor* with), be killed.

'Umkreis *m* (-es; *no pl*) vicinity: *im ~ von* within a radius of, for *three miles etc* round. **um'kreisen** *v/t* (*insep, no* -ge-, h) circle (*astr.* revolve) round.

'umkrempeln *v/t* (*sep*, h) **1.** roll up (*sleeve etc*). **2.** F *fig.* change completely.

'umladen *v/t* (*irr, sep,* -ge-, h, → *laden*) reload.

'Umlage *f* (-; -n) distribution of cost: *die ~ betrug ...* each person had to pay ...

'Umland *n* (-[e]s; *no pl*) environs, surrounding countryside.

'Umlauf *m* (-[e]s; ⸚e) **1.** circulation: *in ~ bringen* a) put *s.th.* in circulation, issue, b) start (*rumo[u]r*); *im ~ sein* circulate, *rumo(u)r*: *a.* be going round. **2.** *astr., phys. a.*) revolution, b) cycle, c) orbit. **3.** circular (letter). **'Umlaufbahn** *f* (*in s-e ~ bringen* or *gelangen* put or get into) orbit. **'umlaufen** *v/i* (*irr, sep,* -ge-, sn, → *laufen*) circulate.

'Umlaufkapi,tal *n* ✝ floating capital.

'Umlaut *m* (-[e]s; -e) *a*) umlaut, b) (vowel) mutation.

'umlegen *v/t* (*sep*, h) **1.** lay flat (*wheat etc*), fell (*tree*), tear down (*fence*). **2.** put on (*coat etc*). **3.** throw (*lever*). **4.** transfer (*a. teleph.*), *a.* move (*patient etc*), shift *appointment etc* (*auf acc* to). **5.** (*auf acc* among) apportion, divide (*costs etc*). **6.** *j-n ~* a) F knock s.o. down, b) bump s.o. off, c) V lay s.o.

'umleiten *v/t* (*sep*, h) divert, detour.

'Umleitung *f* (-; -en) diversion, detour.

'Umleitungsschild *n* detour sign.

'umlernen *v/i* (*sep*, h) *wir müssen sehr ~* we have a lot of relearning to do.

'umliegend *adj* surrounding.

'ummelden *v/t* (*sep*, h) (*a.* **sich ~**) register one's change of address (*bei* with).

'ummodeln *v/t* (*sep*, h) *fig.* change.

'umorgani,sieren *v/t* (*sep*, h) reorganize.

'umpacken *v/t* (*sep*, h) repack.

'umpflanzen *v/t* (*sep*, h) replant.

'umquar,tieren *v/t* (*sep*, h) move.

um'randen *v/t* (*insep, no* -ge-, h), **Um'randung** *f* (-; -en) border.

'umräumen *v/t* (*sep*, h) move *s.th.* (to another place), rearrange (*room*).

'umrechnen *v/t* (*sep*, h) convert (*in acc* into). **'Umrechnung** *f* (-; -en) conversion (*in acc* into).

'Umrechnungs|kurs *m* rate of exchange. **~ta,belle** *f* conversion table.

'umreißen¹ *v/t* (*irr, sep,* -ge-, h, → *reißen*) pull (*or* knock) down.

um'reißen² *v/t* (*irr, insep, no* -ge-, h, → *reißen*) *fig.* outline.

'umrennen *v/t* (*irr, sep,* -ge-, h, → *rennen*) run (*or* knock) down.

um'ringen *v/t* (*insep, no* -ge-, h) surround.

'Umriß *m* contour, *a. fig.* outline: *feste Umrisse annehmen* take shape.

'umrühren *v/t* (*sep*, h) stir.

'umrüsten *v/t* (*sep*, h) ⚙ change *s.th.* over (*auf acc* to).

'umsatteln *v/i* (*sep*, h) F change one's job (*student*: one's subject): ~ (*von ...*) *auf* (*acc*) switch (from ...) to.

'Umsatz *m* (-es; ⸚e) ✝ turnover, sales. **~beteiligung** *f* sales commission. **~steuer** *f* turnover tax.

'umschalten (*sep*, h) **I** *v/t, a. v/i* ⚡, ⚙ *or fig.* switch (*or* change) (over) (*auf acc* to). **II** *v/i* TV change channels.

'Umschalttaste *f typewriter*: shift key.

'umschichten *v/t* (*sep*, h) **1.** rearrange. **2.** *fig.* regroup.

'Umschichtung *f* (-; -en) *fig.* regrouping: *soziale ~* social upheaval.

um'schiffen *v/t* (*insep, no* -ge-, h) sail round, double: → *Klippe*.

'Umschlag *m* (-[e]s; ⸚e) **1.** a) envelope, b) cover, (*book or dust*) jacket. **2.** a) cuff, b) turnup. **3.** ✚ (*feuchter*) ~ compress. **4.** *no pl* ✝ a) handling (*of goods*), b) goods handled, c) transshipment.

'umschlagen (*irr, sep,* -ge-, → *schlagen*) **I** *v/i* (sn) **1.** ~ *in* → *umkippen* 2. **2.** *weather, wind, mood, etc*: change (suddenly). **II** *v/t* (h) **3.** turn up (*sleeve etc*). **4.** a) handle (*goods*), b) transship.

'Umschlag|hafen *m* port of transshipment. **~platz** m trading cent/re (Am. -er), ⚓ place of transshipment.

um'schließen v/t (irr, insep, no -ge-, h, → **schließen**) 1. surround, enclose. 2. fig. encompass.

'umschnallen v/t (sep, h) buckle on.

'umschreiben¹ v/t (irr, sep, -ge-, h, → **schreiben**) 1. rewrite. 2. transfer property (auf acc to). **um'schreiben²** v/t (irr, insep, no -ge-, h, → **schreiben**) 1. paraphrase, circumscribe (a. Ⓐ). 2. outline. **'Umschreibung¹** f (-; -en) 1. rewriting. 2. ✝ transfer. **Um'schreibung²** f (-; -en) paraphrase, circumscription (a. Ⓐ).

'Umschrift f (-; -en) transcription.

'Umschuldung f (-; -en) ✝ conversion (of a debt).

'umschulen v/t (sep, h) 1. retrain. 2. transfer student to another school.

um'schwärmen v/t (insep, no -ge-, h) 1. swarm round. 2. fig. idolize.

'Umschweife: ohne ~ a) say etc s.th. straight out, b) do s.th. straightaway.

'umschwenken v/i (sep, sn) 1. wheel round. 2. fig. veer round.

'Umschwung m (-[e]s; ⸚e) change, reversal, esp. pol. swing, about-face.

um'segeln v/t (insep, no -ge-, h) sail round, double.

'umsehen: sich ~ (irr, sep, -ge-, h, → **sehen**) 1. look back. 2. look (a)round (nach for): **sich in der Stadt ~** (have a) look (a)round the city.

'umsein v/i (irr, sep, -ge-, sn, → **sein**) F be over: **s-e Zeit ist um** his time is up.

'umseitig [-zaɪtɪç] adj and adv overleaf.

'umsetzen v/t (sep, h) 1. move, transplant, ⚕ transplant. 2. sell, turn over. 3. et. ~ **in** (acc) a. 🐾, phys. convert (or transform) s.th. into; (in die Praxis) ~ realize; **et. in die Tat ~** put s.th. into action.

'Umsicht f (-; no pl) circumspection.

'umsichtig adj circumspect.

'umsiedeln v/t (sep, h) resettle.

'Umsiedler(in f) m resettler, pol. Ethnic German repatriate (from the East).

'Umsiedlung f (-; -en) resettlement.

um'sonst adv 1. for nothing, free (of charge). 2. in vain: **nicht ~** not without (good) reason, not for nothing.

um'spannen v/t (insep, no -ge-, h) span.

'Umspannwerk n transformer station.

um'spielen v/t (insep, no -ge-, h) soccer

etc: dribble round, fig. play (a)round.

'umspringen v/i (irr, sep, -ge-, sn, → **springen**) 1. → **umschlagen** 2. 2. **mit j-m grob** etc ~ treat s.o. roughly etc.

'Umstand m 1. fact, circumstance. 2. pl circumstances, conditions, situation: **unter Umständen** possibly, perhaps; **unter allen Umständen** at all events; **unter diesen (k-n) Umständen** under the (no) circumstances; F **in anderen Umständen sein** be in the family way; → **mildern** I. 3. **ohne viel Umstände** without much fuss; **Umstände machen** a) cause trouble, b) make a fuss; **machen Sie** (sich) **k-e Umstände!** don't go to any trouble. **'umständehalber** adv owing to circumstances.

umständlich ['ʊmʃtɛntlɪç] adj a) complicated, b) long-winded, c) awkward, d) fussy: **das ist** (mir) **viel zu ~** that's far too much trouble (for me).

'Umstandskleid n maternity dress.

'Umstandskrämer m (-s; -) F fusspot.

'Umstandswort n (-[e]s; ⸚er) adverb.

'umstehend adj next (page), a. adv overleaf: **die Umstehenden** the bystanders.

'Umsteige(fahr)karte f transfer ticket.

'umsteigen v/i (irr, sep, -ge-, sn, → **steigen**) 1. change (nach for). 2. F fig. switch (auf acc to).

um'stellen¹ v/t (insep, no -ge-, h) surround.

'umstellen² (sep, h) **I** v/t a) change, b) rearrange (furniture etc), c) regroup (team), d) reset (watch), e) ⚙ change over (auf acc to), f) reorganize (firm etc): ~ **auf** (acc) switch to, convert to; **auf Computer** ~ computerize; **s-e Lebensweise** ~ readjust one's way of life. **II sich** ~ get used to new conditions, adjust (auf acc to). **'Umstellung** f (-; -en) change, rearrangement, ⚙ change-over (or switch) (auf acc to), reorganization, adjustment (auf acc to): **e-e große ~ sein** be quite a change.

'umstimmen v/t (sep, h) **j-n** ~ bring s.o. round.

'umstoßen v/t (irr, sep, -ge-, h, → **stoßen**) 1. knock over (or down). 2. fig. change (last will, plan, etc), reverse (judg[e]ment etc), upset (plan).

umstritten [ʊm'ʃtrɪtn] adj contested.

'umstruktu,rieren v/t (sep, h) restructure.

'**umstülpen** v/t (sep, h) a) turn s.th. upside down, b) turn s.th. inside out.

'**Umsturz** m (-es; ⸚e) overthrow, revolution. '**umstürzen** (sep) **I** v/t (h) upset, knock over, pol. overthrow. **II** v/i (sn) fall down (or over), overturn. '**Umstürzler** [-ʃtʏrtslər] m (-s; -) revolutionary. '**umstürzlerisch** adj subversive. '**Umsturzversuch** m attempted coup.

'**Umtausch** m (-[e]s; -e), '**umtauschen** v/t (sep, h) exchange (**gegen** for).

'**umtopfen** v/t (sep, h) ↗ repot.

'**Umtriebe** pl contp. activities, intrigues.

'**umtun**: **sich ~** (irr, sep, -ge-, h, → **tun**) look around (**nach** for).

'**umwälzen** v/t (sep, h) **1.** ⚙ circulate. **2.** fig. revolutionize.

'**umwälzend** adj fig. revolutionary.

'**Umwälzpumpe** f circulating pump.

'**Umwälzung** f (-; -en) **1.** ⚙ circulation. **2.** fig. revolution, upheaval.

'**umwandeln** v/t (sep, h) change (**in** acc, **zu** into), phys. transform, convert (a. ⚡), ⚖ commute (sentence): **sie ist wie umgewandelt** she is a completely different person. '**Umwandler** m (-s; -) ⚡, ⚙ converter. '**Umwandlung** f (-; -en) change, transformation, conversion, ⚖ commutation.

'**Umweg** m detour, roundabout way: **e-n ~ machen** make a detour; **das ist ein ~ für mich** that takes me out of my way; fig. **auf ~en** indirectly, in a roundabout way; **ohne ~e** straight.

'**Umwelt** f (-; no pl) environment: **unsere ~ a.** the world around us.

'**Umwelt...** environmental. **~belastung** f (environmental) pollution. **⚹bewußt** adj environment-conscious. **⚹feindlich** → **umweltschädlich.** **~forscher** m ecologist. **~forschung** f (-; no pl) ecology. **⚹freundlich** adj ecologically friendly, nonpolluting, a. biodegradable. **~kata,strophe** f ecocatastrophe. **~kriminali,tät** f environmental crime. **~krise** f ecological crisis, ecocrisis. **~mini,sterium** n Department of the Environment. **~poli,tik** f ecopolicy. **⚹po,litisch** adj ecopolitical. **~schäden** pl damage done by pollution. **⚹schädlich** adj harmful (to the environment), polluting. **~schutz** m environmental (or pollution) control, conservation. **~schützer** m (-s; -) environmentalist,

conservationist. **~sünder** m F polluter. **~verbrechen** n environmental crime. **~verschmutzung** f pollution. **~zerstörung** f ecocide.

'**umwenden**: **sich ~** (irr, sep, -ge-, h, → **wenden**) turn round.

um'werben v/t (irr, insep, no -ge-, h, → **werben**) court, a. fig. woo.

'**umwerfen** v/t (irr, sep, -ge-, h, → **werfen**) **1.** → umstoßen. **2.** → umhauen 2.

'**umwerfend** adj fantastic, mind-blowing: **~ komisch** too funny for words.

'**Umwertung** f (-; -en) revaluation.

um'wickeln v/t (insep, no -ge-, h) wind s.th. round, bandage s.th. (**mit** with).

'**umziehen** (irr, sep, -ge-, → **ziehen**) **I** v/i (sn) move (house). **II** v/t (h) **j-n ~** change s.o.'s clothes; **sich ~** change.

umzingeln [ʊmˈtsɪŋəln] v/t (insep, no -ge-, h) surround, encircle.

'**Umzug** m (-[e]s; ⸚e) **1.** move. **2.** procession, pol. demonstration march.

unabänderlich [ʊnˈʔapˈˀɛndərlɪç] adj unalterable, irrevocable: **sich ins ⚹e fügen** resign o.s. to the inevitable.

'**unabhängig** adj independent (**von** of): **~ von** irrespective of; **~ davon ob** regardless whether. '**Unabhängige** m, f (-n; -n) pol. independent. '**Unabhängigkeit** f (-; no pl) independence.

unab'kömmlich adj indispensable: **er ist ~** he is busy, he can't get away.

unab'lässig [ʊnˈʔapˈlɛsɪç] adj incessant.

unab'sehbar adj a) unforeseeable, b) incalculable, immense (damage etc): **auf ~e Zeit** for an indefinite period of time.

'**unabsichtlich** adj unintentional.

unab'wendbar adj unavoidable.

'**unachtsam** adj inattentive, careless. '**Unachtsamkeit** f (-; no pl) carelessness.

unähnlich adj (dat) unlike (s.o., s.th.).

unan'fechtbar adj incontestable.

'**unangebracht** adj inappropriate: **~ sein** a. be out of place.

'**unangefochten** adj and adv **1.** undisputed(ly). **2.** unhindered.

'**unangemeldet** adj unannounced.

'**unangemessen** adj **1.** inappropriate, inadequate. **2.** unreasonable (price etc).

'**unangenehm** adj unpleasant, a. nasty, awkward: **das ⚹e dabei ist** the unpleasant thing about it is.

'**unangetastet** adj untouched.

unan'greifbar adj a. fig. unassailable.

unan'nehmbar adj unacceptable.

'Unannehmlichkeiten pl (j-m ~ bereiten cause s.o.) trouble: ~ bekommen
get into trouble.

'unansehnlich adj unsightly, plain.

'unanständig adj 1. indecent, obscene.
2. unfair.

unan'tastbar adj unimpeachable, inviolable (rights), iro. sacrosanct.

'unappe‚titlich adj unappetizing, a. fig.
unsavo(u)ry.

'Unart f (-; -en) bad habit, bad trick.

'unartig adj naughty.

'unäs‚thetisch adj un(a)esthetic, w.s.
unpleasant, unsavo(u)ry, ugly.

'unaufdringlich adj unobtrusive.

'unauffällig adj 1. inconspicuous. 2.
unobtrusive, discreet.

unauf'findbar adj untraceable, pred not
to be found.

'unaufgefordert adj and adv unasked,
adv a. of one's own accord.

unaufhaltsam [ʊnʔaʊfˈhaltzaːm] adj
unstoppable.

unaufhörlich [ʊnʔaʊfˈhøːrlɪç] adj incessant, continuous.

unauf'lösbar, unauf'löslich adj indis-
soluble, a. 🜍, ⚕ insoluble.

'unaufmerksam adj 1. inattentive. 2.
thoughtless, careless.

'Unaufmerksamkeit f (-; no pl) 1. inat-
tention. 2. thoughtlessness.

'unaufrichtig adj insincere. **'Unaufrich-
tigkeit** f (-; no pl) insincerity.

unaufschiebbar [ʊnʔaʊfˈʃiːpbaːr] adj
urgent.

unausbleiblich [ʊnʔaʊsˈblaɪplɪç] adj
inevitable.

unaus'führbar adj impracticable.

'unausgefüllt adj 1. blank (form). 2. fig.
unfulfilled (life, person).

'unausgeglichen adj unbalanced, unstable. **Unausgeglichenheit** f (-; no pl)
imbalance, instability.

'unausgesprochen adj unspoken.

unauslöschlich [ʊnʔaʊsˈlœʃlɪç] adj fig.
indelible.

unaus'rottbar adj ineradicable.

unaussprechlich [ˈʊnʔaʊsʃprɛçlɪç] adj
unpronounceable, fig. unspeakable.

unausstehlich [ʊnʔaʊsˈʃteːlɪç] adj insuf-
ferable, intolerable.

unausweichlich [ʊnʔaʊsˈvaɪçlɪç] adj
unavoidable, inevitable.

unbändig [ˈʊnbɛndɪç] adj 1. unruly. 2.
fig. tremendous (rage, hate, etc).

'unbarmherzig adj merciless. **'Unbarm-
herzigkeit** f (-; no pl) mercilessness.

'unbeabsichtigt adj unintentional.

'unbeachtet adj and adv (~ bleiben go)
unnoticed: ~ lassen disregard.

'unbeanstandet adj unobjected: et. ~
lassen let s.th. pass.

'unbeantwortet adj unanswered.

'unbearbeitet adj a) untreated, unfinished, b) undealt with, c) unedited.

'unbebaut adj 1. ✓ untilled. 2. undeveloped (land).

'unbedacht adj thoughtless, rash.

unbedarft [ˈʊnbədarft] adj F naive.

'unbedenklich adj safe.

'unbedeutend adj insignificant, unimportant, a. negligible.

'unbedingt I adj a) unconditional, b)
absolute. **II** adv absolutely, at all costs:
et. ~ brauchen need s.th. badly; nicht ~
a) not necessarily, b) not exactly.

unbe'fahrbar adj impassable.

'unbefangen adj 1. unbias(s)ed, impartial. 2. uninhibited, free.

'Unbefangenheit f (-; no pl) 1. impar-
tiality. 2. naturalness.

'unbefleckt adj fig. unsullied: eccl. ~e
Empfängnis Immaculate Conception.

'unbefriedigend adj unsatisfactory.

'unbefriedigt adj unsatisfied.

'unbefristet I adj unlimited. **II** adv for
an unlimited period.

'unbefugt adj unauthorized.

'Unbefugte m, f (-n; -n) unauthorized
person: Zutritt für ~ verboten! no
unauthorized entry!

'unbegabt adj untalented.

unbegreiflich adj incomprehensible: es
ist mir völlig ~ it's beyond me.

'unbegrenzt I adj unlimited, boundless.
II adv indefinitely: ich habe ~ Zeit I
have unlimited time.

'unbegründet adj unfounded.

'Unbehagen n (-s; no pl) unease.

'unbehaglich adj uncomfortable, fig. a.
uneasy: sich ~ fühlen a. feel ill at ease.

'unbehelligt adj and adv a) unmolested,
b) unhindered.

'unbeherrscht adj unrestrained: ~ sein
have no self-control. **'Unbeherrscht-
heit** f (-; no pl) lack of self-control.

unbeholfen [ˈʊnbəhɔlfən] adj clumsy.

'**Unbeholfenheit** *f* (-; *no pl*) clumsiness.
unbe'irrbar *adj* imperturbable.
unbe'irrt *adj* unswerving, unperturbed.
'**unbekannt** *adj* unknown: *das war mir* ~ I didn't know that; ~*e Größe* → '**Unbekannte** *f* (-n; -n) ℞ *or fig.* unknown (quantity).
'**unbekleidet** *adj and adv* undressed.
'**unbekömmlich** *adj* indigestible.
'**unbekümmert** *adj* carefree: ~ *um* unconcerned about.
'**unbelastet** *adj* **1.** carefree: ~ *sein* be free from worries, *pol.* have a clean record. **2.** ℞ unencumbered (*property*).
unbe'lehrbar *adj* hopeless.
'**unbeleuchtet** *adj mot.* without lights.
'**unbeliebt** *adj* unpopular (*bei* with).
'**Unbeliebtheit** *f* (-; *no pl*) unpopularity.
'**unbemannt** *adj* unmanned, ✈ pilotless.
'**unbemerkt** *adj and adv* unnoticed.
'**unbemittelt** *adj* without means, poor.
unbenommen ['ʊnbənɔmən] *adj es ist Ihnen* ~ *zu inf* you are at liberty to *inf.*
'**unbenutzt** *adj* unused.
'**unbeobachtet** *adj and adv* unobserved.
'**unbequem** *adj* **1.** uncomfortable. **2.** *fig.* a) inconvenient, b) embarrassing (*question etc*), c) difficult (*person*). '**Unbequemlichkeit** *f* (-; -en) **1.** *no pl* uncomfortableness. **2.** *fig.* inconvenience.
unbe'rechenbar *adj* incalculable, *fig. a.* unpredictable (*person*).
'**unberechtigt** *adj* **1.** unauthorized. **2.** unjustified, unfair.
'**unberechtigter'weise** *adv* **1.** without permission. **2.** without good reason.
unbe'rücksichtigt *adj* unconsidered: *et.* ~ *lassen* leave s.th. out of account.
unbe'rufen *int* touch wood!
'**unberührt** *adj* untouched (*a. fig.*), virgin (*girl, nature, etc*): *fig.* ~ *bleiben von* not to be affected by.
unbeschadet [ʊnbə'ʃaːdət] *adj* (*gen*) a) without prejudice to, b) irrespective of.
'**unbeschädigt** *adj* undamaged, intact.
'**unbeschäftigt** *adj* unemployed, idle.
'**unbescheiden** *adj* immodest. '**Unbescheidenheit** *f* (-; *no pl*) immodesty.
unbescholten ['ʊnbəʃɔltən] *adj* blameless: ℞ ~ *sein* have no police record.
'**unbeschränkt** *adj* unrestricted, absolute (*power, right, etc*).
unbeschreiblich [ʊnbə'ʃraɪplɪç] *adj* indescribable.

'**unbeschrieben** *adj* blank (*paper*): *fig.* ~*es Blatt* unknown quantity.
'**unbeschwert** *adj fig.* a) carefree, b) light (*conscience*): ~ *von* free from.
'**unbesehen** *adv et.* ~ *kaufen* buy s.th. sight unseen; *das glaube ich dir* ~ I well believe you.
'**unbesetzt** *adj* vacant (*post*), *a.* unoccupied, free (*seat etc*).
unbe'siegbar *adj* invincible.
unbe'siegt *adj* undefeated.
'**unbesonnen** *adj* imprudent, rash.
'**Unbesonnenheit** *f* (-; *no pl*) rashness.
'**unbesorgt I** *adj* unconcerned (*wegen* about): *seien Sie* (*deswegen*) ~! don't worry! **II** *adv* safely.
'**unbespielt** *adj* blank (*tape, cassette*).
'**unbeständig** *adj* unstable, changeable, unsettled (*weather etc*). '**Unbeständigkeit** *f* (-; *no pl*) unstableness (*etc*).
'**unbestätigt** *adj* unconfirmed.
'**unbestechlich** *adj* **1.** incorruptible. **2.** unerring (*judgement etc*). '**Unbestechlichkeit** *f* (-; *no pl*) incorruptibility.
'**unbestimmt** *adj* a) vague (*idea etc*), b) indeterminate, *a. ling.* indefinite: *auf* ~*e Zeit* for an indefinite period.
'**Unbestimmtheit** *f* (-; *no pl*) vagueness.
unbe'streitbar *adj* indisputable.
unbe'stritten I *adj* undisputed. **II** *adv* indisputably, without doubt.
'**unbeteiligt** *adj* **1.** not involved (*an dat* in). **2.** indifferent.
'**unbetont** *adj* unstressed.
'**unbeträchtlich** *adj* negligible, insignificant: *nicht* ~ quite considerable.
unbeugsam [ʊn'bɔʏkzaːm] *adj fig.* uncompromising.
'**unbewacht** *adj a. fig.* unguarded.
'**unbewaffnet** *adj* unarmed.
'**unbeweglich** *adj* immobile, *a.* ℞ immovable (*possessions, holiday, etc*), motionless, ⚙ fixed, rigid (*a. fig.*), (*mentally*) inflexible: ~*e Güter* immovables. '**Unbeweglichkeit** *f* (-; *no pl*) immobility, (*mental*) inflexibility.
'**unbewegt** *adj* a) expressionless, b) unmoved (*a. adv*).
unbe'weisbar *adj* unprovable.
unbe'wiesen *adj* unproved.
unbe'wohnbar *adj* uninhabitable. '**unbewohnt** *adj* uninhabited, unoccupied.
'**unbewußt** *adj* unconscious.

unbe'zahlbar *adj* **1.** too expensive. **2.** *fig.* priceless (*a.* F *funny*).
'unbezahlt *adj* unpaid.
unbe'zähmbar *adj fig.* indomitable.
unbe'zwingbar *adj* invincible.
'Unbildung *f* (-; *no pl*) lack of education.
'unblutig I *adj* bloodless, ☞ nonoperative. **II** *adv* without bloodshed.
'unbrauchbar *adj* useless, unsuitable, impracticable (*plan etc*), ◎ unserviceable: *et. ~ machen* render s.th. useless.
'Unbrauchbarkeit *f* (-; *no pl*) uselessness, impracticability, unserviceability.
un'brennbar *adj* nonflammable.
'unbüro,kratisch *adj* unbureaucratic.
'unchristlich *adj* unchristian.
und [ʊnt] *conj* and: *~?* well?; F *~ ob!* you bet!; *na ~?* so what?; *~ so weiter* (*or fort*) and so on; *~ wenn* (*auch*) even if.
'Undank *m* (-[e]s; *no pl*) ingratitude: F *nur ~ ernten* get small thanks for it.
'undankbar *adj* **1.** ungrateful (*gegen* to). **2.** thankless (*task etc*).
'Undankbarkeit *f* (-; *no pl*) **1.** ingratitude. **2.** thanklessness.
'unda,tiert *adj* undated.
undefi'nierbar *adj* undefinable.
'undemo,kratisch *adj* undemocratic.
un'denkbar *adj* unthinkable.
undenklich [ʊn'dɛŋklɪç] *adj seit ~en Zeiten* from time immemorial.
'undeutlich *adj* indistinct, *pred* not clear, inarticulate (*speech*), blurred (*picture etc*), vague (*idea etc*).
'undicht *adj* leaking, *pred* not tight: *~e Stelle* leak (*a. fig. pol.*).
'Unding *n* (-[e]s; *no pl*) absurdity: *es ist ein ~* it is preposterous (*or* absurd).
'undiszipli,niert *adj* undisciplined.
'unduldsam *adj* intolerant.
'Unduldsamkeit *f* (-; *no pl*) intolerance.
undurch'dringlich *adj* impenetrable, *fig. a.* inscrutable.
undurch'führbar *adj* impracticable.
'undurchlässig *adj* impermeable (*für* to).
'undurchsichtig *adj* **1.** opaque. **2.** *fig.* mysterious, inscrutable.
'uneben *adj* uneven, rough (*road etc*).
'unecht *adj* **1.** *a. fig.* false, *pred* not genuine, b) artificial, c) counterfeit(ed), fake(d), F phon(e)y. **2.** ☾ improper.
'unehelich *adj* illegitimate.
'unehrenhaft *adj* dishono(u)rable.

'unehrlich *adj* dishonest, insincere.
'Unehrlichkeit *f* (-; *no pl*) dishonesty.
'uneigennützig *adj* unselfish.
'uneingeschränkt *adj* unrestricted, unqualified (*praise*), absolute (*trust etc*).
'uneingeweiht *adj* uninitiated.
'uneinheitlich *adj* nonuniform, varied.
'uneinig *adj* divided: (*sich*) *~ sein a.* be at variance, disagree. **'Uneinigkeit** *f* (-; *no pl*) disagreement, discord.
unein'nehmbar *adj* impregnable.
'unempfänglich *adj* (*für* to) insusceptible, unreceptive.
'unempfindlich *adj* **1.** insensitive (*gegen* to). **2.** durable, rugged.
'Unempfindlichkeit *f* (-; *no pl*) **1.** insensitiveness (*gegen* to). **2.** durability.
un'endlich I *adj* ☾, ♪, *phys.* infinite (*a. fig.*), endless: *phot. auf ~ einstellen* focus at infinity; *fig. bis ins ~e* ad infinitum. **II** *adv* infinitely (*etc*), *fig. a.* immensely: *~ klein* infinitesimal; *~ lang* endless; *~ viel* a tremendous amount of; *~ viele* no end of.
Un'endlichkeit *f* (-; *no pl*) infinity.
unent'behrlich *adj* indispensable (*dat, für* to).
unent'geltlich *adj and adv* free (of charge), *adv a.* for nothing.
unent'rinnbar *adj* inescapable.
'unentschieden *adj* undecided (*a. person*), *a.* open (*question*), *sports:* drawn: *~ enden* end in a draw; *~ spielen* draw.
'Unentschieden *n* (-s; -) *sports:* draw.
'unentschlossen *adj* undecided, irresolute. **'Unentschlossenheit** *f* (-; *no pl*) irresolution, indecision.
unent'schuldbar *adj* inexcusable.
'unentschuldigt *adj ~es Fehlen* unexcused absence.
unentwegt [ʊn'ɛnt've:kt] *adj* incessant.
Unent'wegte *m, f* (-n; -n) *pol.* diehard.
unent'wirrbar *adj* inextricable.
unerbittlich [ʊn'ʔɛr'bɪtlɪç] *adj* merciless.
'unerfahren *adj* inexperienced. **'Unerfahrenheit** *f* (-; *no pl*) inexperience.
unerforschlich [ʊn'ʔɛr'fɔrʃlɪç] *adj fig.* unfathomable.
'unerforscht *adj* unexplored.
'unerfreulich *adj* unpleasant.
uner'füllbar *adj* unrealizable.
'unerfüllt *adj* unfulfilled.
'unergiebig *adj* unproductive.

'**unergründlich** *adj* unfathomable, *fig. a.* inscrutable.
'**unerheblich** *adj* insignificant, *esp.* ⚖️ irrelevant (**für** to).
uner'hört *adj* **1.** a) unheard-of, b) outrageous, scandalous: *~!* what a cheek! **2.** F terrific, fantastic.
'**unerkannt** *adj* unrecognized.
'**unerklärlich** *adj* inexplicable.
unerläßlich [ʊn³ɛr'lɛslɪç] *adj* essential.
'**unerlaubt I** *adj* a) unauthorized, *pred* not allowed, b) illegal, illicit. **II** *adv* without permission.
'**unerledigt** *adj* not yet dealt with, unanswered (*mail*), unfulfilled (*orders etc*): *~e Dinge* unfinished business.
unermeßlich [ʊn³ɛr'mɛslɪç] *adj* immeasurable, immense, vast.
unermüdlich [ʊn³ɛr'my:tlɪç] *adj* indefatigable, untiring.
'**unerquicklich** *adj* unpleasant.
uner'reichbar *adj* inaccessible, *fig.* unattainable (*goal etc*): **für j-n ~** out of s.o.'s reach; **er war ~** I (*we etc*) couldn't get hold of him. '**unerreicht** *adj fig.* unequal(l)ed, unrival(l)ed, record ...
unersättlich [ʊn³ɛr'zɛtlɪç] *adj a. fig.* insatiable.
'**unerschlossen** *adj* undeveloped.
unerschöpflich [ʊn³ɛr'ʃœpflɪç] *adj* inexhaustible.
'**unerschrocken** *adj* undaunted.
unerschütterlich [ʊn³ɛr'ʃʏtərlɪç] *adj* unshak(e)able, imperturbable.
uner'schwinglich *adj* unaffordable (*goods*), exorbitant (*price*): **für j-n ~ sein** be beyond s.o.'s means.
uner'setzlich *adj* **1.** irreplaceable. **2.** irreparable (*damage*).
uner'träglich *adj* unbearable.
'**unerwähnt** *adj* unmentioned: **et. ~ lassen** make no mention of s.th.
'**unerwidert** *adj* unrequited (*love*).
'**unerwünscht** *adj* undesirable.
'**unfähig** *adj* **1.** incapable, incompetent: **~ zu** unqualified for (*a task etc*). **2.** **~ zu** *inf.* unable to *inf.*, incapable of *ger.*
'**Unfähigkeit** *f* (-; *no pl*) **1.** incompetence. **2.** inability.
'**unfair** *adj* unfair.
'**Unfall** *m* (-[e]s, ⁻e) accident. **~arzt** *m* casualty doctor. **~flucht** *f* → *Fahrerflucht.* ⚖️**frei** *adj* accident-free. ⚖️**gefährdet** *adj* accident-prone. **~krankenhaus**

n casualty hospital. **~opfer** *n* accident victim. **~quote** *f*, **~rate** *f* accident rate. **~stati‚on** *f* a) first-aid station, b) casualty ward. **~stelle** *f* scene of (the) accident. **~tod** *m* accidental death. ⚖️**trächtig** *adj* hazardous. **~ursache** *f* cause of the accident. **~verhütung** *f* prevention of accidents. **~versicherung** *f* accident insurance. **~wagen** *m* **1.** car damaged in an accident. **2.** ✈️ crash tender.
un'faßbar, un'faßlich *adj* incomprehensible, inconceivable.
un'fehlbar I *adj* infallible (*a. eccl.*), unerring. **II** *adv* infallibly, without fail.
Un'fehlbarkeit *f* (-; *no pl*) infallibility.
'**unfein** *adj* indelicate, unrefined, *pred* not nice, bad form.
'**unfertig** *adj* **1.** unfinished. **2.** *fig.* immature (*person*).
unflätig ['ʊnflɛ:tɪç] *adj* filthy, obscene.
'**unfolgsam** *adj* disobedient.
'**unförmig** ['ʊnfœrmɪç] *adj* a) shapeless, b) bulky, c) misshapen.
'**unfran‚kiert** *adj* unstamped (*letter*).
'**unfrei** *adj* **1.** not free. **2.** *fig.* inhibited.
'**unfreiwillig** *adj* a) involuntary, unintentional, b) unconscious (*humo[u]r*).
'**unfreundlich** *adj* unfriendly, inclement (*climate, weather*), cheerless (*room etc*).
'**Unfreundlichkeit** *f* (-; *no pl*) unfriendliness, inclemency, cheerlessness.
'**Unfriede** *m* (-n; *no pl*) discord.
'**unfruchtbar** *adj* infertile, *a. fig.* barren, sterile, *fig.* fruitless. '**Unfruchtbarkeit** *f* (-; *no pl*) infertility, *fig.* fruitlessness.
'**Unfug** ['ʊnfu:k] *m* (-[e]s; *no pl*) a) (*~ treiben* be up to) mischief, b) nonsense: ⚖️ **grober ~** disorderly conduct.
Ungar ['ʊŋgar] *m* (-n; -n), '**Ungarin** *f* (-; -nen), '**ungarisch** *adj* Hungarian.
'**Ungarn** *n* (-s) Hungary.
'**ungastlich** *adj* inhospitable.
'**ungeachtet** *prep* (*gen*) regardless of.
'**ungeahnt** ['ʊngəˀa:nt] *adj* undreamt-of.
'**ungebeten** *adj* unasked, uninvited.
'**ungebildet** *adj* uneducated.
'**ungeboren** *adj* unborn.
'**ungebräuchlich** *adj* unusual.
'**ungebraucht** *adj* unused.
'**ungebunden** *adj* **1.** *print.* unbound, in sheets. **2.** *fig.* unattached, independent.
'**ungedeckt** *adj* uncovered (*a. cheque*), unsecured (*credit*), *sports:* unmarked.
'**Ungeduld** *f* (-; *no pl*) impatience.

'**ungeduldig** *adj* impatient.

'**ungeeignet** *adj* (**zu** for) unsuitable, *person*: *a.* unqualified, inopportune (*time*).

ungefähr ['ʊngəfɛːr] **I** *adj* approximate, rough. **II** *adv* approximately, about, around: *so* ~ s.th. like that; *wo* ~? roughly where?

'**ungefährlich** *adj* harmless, safe.

'**ungefällig** *adj* unobliging.

'**ungehalten** *adj* annoyed (**über** *acc* at).

'**ungehemmt** **I** *adj* unchecked, *psych.* uninhibited. **II** *adv* without restraint.

'**ungeheuchelt** *adj* unfeigned.

'**ungeheuer** **I** *adj* **1.** immense, enormous. **2.** F tremendous, terrific. **II** *adv* **3.** enormously (*etc*). '**Ungeheuer** *n* (-s; -) monster. '**ungeheuerlich** *adj* monstrous, outrageous. '**Ungeheuerlichkeit** *f* (-; -en) monstrosity, outrage.

'**ungehindert** *adj and adv* unhindered.

'**ungehobelt** *adj fig.* rude, uncouth.

'**ungehörig** *adj* improper, impertinent.

'**ungehorsam** *adj* disobedient. '**Ungehorsam** *m* (-s; *no pl*) disobedience.

'**ungeklärt** *adj* **1.** unsettled (*question etc*), unsolved (*case, problem, etc*). **2.** ~**e Abwässer** untreated sewage.

'**ungekünstelt** *adj* unaffected.

'**ungekürzt** *adj* unabridged (*book*), uncut (*film*).

'**ungeladen** *adj* **1.** uninvited (*guest*). **2.** unloaded (*gun*).

'**ungelegen** *adj* inconvenient: *das kommt mir sehr* ~**!** that doesn't suit me at all! '**Ungelegenheiten** *pl j-m* ~ *machen* put s.o. out, inconvenience s.o.

'**ungelenk** *adj* clumsy, stiff.

'**ungelernt** *adj* unskilled (*worker*).

'**ungemein** *adv* immensely.

'**ungemischt** *adj* unmixed.

'**ungemütlich** *adj* uncomfortable (*a. fig.*), cheerless (*room*): F ~ *werden* get unpleasant, turn nasty. '**Ungemütlichkeit** *f* (-; *no pl*) uncomfortableness.

'**ungenannt** *adj* unnamed, anonymous.

'**ungenau** *adj* inaccurate, inexact, *fig.* vague, hazy. '**Ungenauigkeit** *f* (-; -en) inaccuracy.

'**unge,niert** **I** *adj* uninhibited. **II** *adv* without inhibition, openly.

'**ungenießbar** *adj* **1.** a) inedible, b) undrinkable. **2.** F *person*: unbearable.

'**ungenügend** *adj* insufficient, *ped.* unsatisfactory, poor.

'**ungenutzt** *adj* unused: *e-e Gelegenheit* ~ *lassen* let an opportunity slip.

'**ungepflegt** *adj* unkempt, neglected.

'**ungerade** *adj* uneven, odd (*number*).

'**ungerecht** *adj* unjust. '**ungerechtfertigt** *adj* unjustified. '**Ungerechtigkeit** *f* (-; -en) injustice (**gegen** to).

'**ungeregelt** *adj* unregulated, irregular (*life, working hours, etc*).

'**ungern** *adv* unwillingly, reluctantly: *ich tue es* ~ I don't like doing it.

'**ungerührt** *adj fig.* unmoved (**von** by).

'**ungesagt** *adj* (~ *bleiben* be left) unsaid.

'**ungesalzen** *adj* unsalted.

'**ungeschehen** *adj* ~ *machen* undo.

'**Ungeschick** *n* (-[e]s; *no pl*), '**Ungeschicklichkeit** *f* (-; *no pl*) clumsiness.

'**ungeschickt** *adj* clumsy.

'**ungeschlagen** *adj fig.* undefeated.

'**ungeschliffen** *adj* **1.** rough (*diamond*). **2.** *fig.* unpolished (*behavio[u]r etc*).

'**ungeschminkt** *adj* **1.** not made up, without makeup. **2.** *fig.* unvarnished, *a.* plain (*truth*).

'**ungeschoren** *adj* **1.** unshorn. **2.** *fig.* unmolested: *j-n* ~ *lassen* leave s.o. in peace; ~ *davonkommen* get off lightly (*or* F scot-free).

'**ungeschrieben** *adj* unwritten.

'**ungeschützt** *adj* unprotected.

'**ungesehen** *adj and adv* unseen.

'**ungesellig** *adj* unsociable. '**Ungeselligkeit** *f* (-; *no pl*) unsociableness.

'**ungesetzlich** *adj* illegal, illicit, unlawful. '**Ungesetzlichkeit** *f* (-; *no pl*) illegality.

'**ungesittet** *adj* uncivilized.

'**ungestört** *adj and adv* undisturbed.

'**ungestraft** **I** *adj* unpunished. **II** *adv* with impunity: ~ *davonkommen* go unpunished, F get off scot-free.

ungestüm ['ʊngəʃtyːm] *adj* impetuous. '**Ungestüm** *n* (-s; *no pl*) impetuosity.

'**ungesund** *adj. a. fig.* unhealthy.

'**ungeteilt** *adj a. fig.* undivided.

'**ungetrübt** ['ʊngətryːpt] *adj fig.* unspoilt.

Ungetüm ['ʊngətyːm] *n* (-s; -e) monster.

'**ungeübt** *adj* untrained.

'**ungewaschen** *adj and adv* unwashed.

'**ungewiß** *adj* uncertain: *j-n im ungewissen lassen* keep s.o. guessing. '**Ungewißheit** *f* (-; *no pl*) uncertainty: *in* ~ *schweben* be (kept) in suspense.

'**ungewöhnlich** *adj* unusual.

'**ungewohnt** *adj* strange, new (*für* to).

'**ungewollt** *adj* unintentional, unintended (*effect etc*), unwanted (*baby*).

'**ungezählt** *adj* uncounted, countless.

'**ungezähmt** *adj* untamed.

Ungeziefer ['ʊngətsiːfər] *n* (-s; *no pl*) *a. fig.* vermin.

'**ungezogen** *adj* naughty. '**Ungezogenheit** *f* (-; *no pl*) naughtiness.

'**ungezügelt** *fig.* **I** *adj* unbridled. **II** *adv* unrestrainedly.

'**ungezwungen** *adj* relaxed, informal. '**Ungezwungenheit** *f* (-; *no pl*) ease.

'**ungiftig** *adj* nontoxic.

'**Unglaube** *m* unbelief. '**unglaubhaft** ~ *unglaubwürdig*. '**ungläubig** *adj* incredulous, disbelieving, *a. eccl.* unbelieving. **un'glaublich** *adj* incredible, unbelievable. '**unglaubwürdig** *adj* untrustworthy, implausible (*reasons etc*).

'**ungleich** **I** *adj* **1.** unequal, unlike, dissimilar. **II** *adv* **2.** ~ *lang* (*groß*) unequal in length (size); ~ *verteilt* unevenly distributed. **3.** far *better etc*.

'**Ungleichgewicht** *n* imbalance.

'**Ungleichheit** *f* (-; *no pl*) **1.** dissimilarity, unlikeness. **2.** inequality.

'**ungleichmäßig** *adj* uneven, irregular.

'**Unglück** *n* (-[e]s; -e) a) misfortune, b) bad luck, c) mishap, d) disaster: *es ist* (*weiter*) *kein* ~*!* it is no tragedy!; *zu allem* ~ to crown it all; ~ *bringen* bring ill (*or* bad) luck; *in sein* ~ *rennen* head for disaster. '**unglücklich** *adj* a) unfortunate, b) unlucky, c) unhappy, miserable: ~ *enden* end badly; ~ *verliebt* crossed in love. '**unglücklicher'weise** *adv* unfortunately. '**unglückselig** *adj* a) unfortunate, b) disastrous, fatal.

'**Unglücks|fall** *m* **1.** accident. **2.** misadventure. ~**rabe** *m* unlucky fellow. ~**tag** *m* black day. ~**zahl** *f* unlucky number.

'**Ungnade** *f* (-; *no pl*) disfavo(u)r: *in* ~ *fallen* fall out of favo(u)r (*bei* with).

'**ungnädig** *adj* ungracious.

'**ungültig** *adj* invalid, (null and) void, *coin*: not legal tender, *vote*: spoilt, *goal*: disallowed: ~ *machen* cancel (*ticket etc*); *et. für* ~ *erklären* invalidate s.th., declare s.th. null and void.

'**Ungültigkeit** *f* (-; *no pl*) invalidity.

'**Ungunst** *f* (-; *no pl*) *zu j-s* ~*en* to s.o.'s disadvantage. '**ungünstig** *adj* unfavo(u)rable, inopportune (*date etc*).

'**ungut** *adj* bad: *ein* ~*es Gefühl haben* have misgivings (*bei* about); *nichts für* ~*!* no offen/ce (*Am.* -se) meant.

'**unhaltbar** *adj* **1.** untenable (*arguments etc*). **2.** intolerable (*conditions*). **3.** *sports*: unstoppable (*ball*, *shot*, *etc*).

'**unhandlich** *adj* unwieldy.

'**unhar,monisch** *adj a. fig.* discordant.

'**Unheil** *n* (-s; *no pl*) a) harm, b) disaster: ~ *anrichten* wreak havoc.

un'heilbar *adj* incurable: ~ *krank* suffering from an incurable disease.

'**unheilbringend** *adj* fatal. '**unheilvoll** *adj* **1.** disastrous. **2.** sinister (*look etc*).

'**unheimlich** **I** *adj* **1.** uncanny, weird (*both a. fig.*), eerie, F creepy. **2.** F *fig.* tremendous, terrific. **II** *adv* **3.** F *fig.* tremendously, awfully: ~ *gut* terrific, fantastic; ~ *viel* a tremendous lot of.

'**unhöflich** *adj* impolite.

'**Unhöflichkeit** *f* (-; *no pl*) impoliteness.

'**Unhold** *m* (-[e]s; -e) monster, fiend.

un'hörbar *adj* inaudible.

'**unhygi,enisch** *adj* unhygienic.

Uni ['ʊni] *f* (-; -s) F university.

Uniform [uni'form] *f* (-; -en) uniform. **uniformiert** [-'miːrt] *adj* in uniform.

Unikum ['uːnikʊm] *n* (-s; -ka) **1.** unique specimen. **2.** (*pl* -s) F character.

'**uninteres,sant** *adj* uninteresting, not interesting. '**uninteres,siert** *adj* uninterested (*an dat* in).

Union [u'niːoːn] *f* (-; -en) union: *die* ~ the Christian-Democrat Union (*or* Party).

universal [univɛr'zaːl] *adj* universal. **Univer'sal|erbe** *m* sole heir. ~**mittel** *n* universal remedy, *a. fig.* panacea.

universell [univɛr'zɛl] *adj* universal.

Universität [univɛrzi'tɛːt] *f* (-; -en) (*auf or an der* ~ at the) university; *e-e* ~ *besuchen* go to university.

Universi'täts... university (*library*, *hospital*, *studies*, *etc*).

Universum [uni'vɛrzʊm] *n* (-s; *no pl*) universe.

unken ['ʊŋkən] *v/i* (h) F *fig.* croak.

'**unkenntlich** *adj* unrecognizable.

'**Unkenntnis** *f* (-; *no pl*) ignorance: *in* ~ (*gen*) unaware of *the danger etc*, ignorant of *the facts etc*; *j-n in* ~ *lassen* keep s.o. in the dark (*über acc* about).

'**unklar** *adj* unclear, *pred* not clear, *a.* vague, obscure, muddled; *im* ~*en sein* be in the dark (*über acc* about).

'**Unklarheit** f (-; no pl) unclearness, lack of clarity, vagueness.
'**unklug** adj unwise, imprudent.
'**unkompli,ziert** adj uncomplicated.
'**unkontrol,lierbar** adj uncontrollable.
'**unkontrol,liert** adj uncontrolled.
'**Unkosten** pl costs, expenses: **allgemeine** (or **laufende**) ~ running expenses, ✝ overhead; → **stürzen** 6.
'**Unkraut** n (-[e]s; ⸚er) weed(s): fig. ~ **vergeht nicht** ill weeds grow apace. ~**vertilgungsmittel** n weed killer.
'**unkritisch** adj uncritical.
'**unkulti,viert** adj uncultivated.
'**unkündbar** adj permanent (post), contract etc: not terminable: **er ist ~** F he can't be sacked.
'**unlängst** adv lately, recently.
'**unlauter** adj fig. dubious: ✝ ~**er Wettbewerb** unfair competition.
'**unleserlich** adj illegible.
'**unlieb** adj **es ist mir nicht ~(, daß)** it suits me quite fine (that).
'**unliebenswürdig** adj unamiable, unfriendly. '**Unliebenswürdigkeit** f (-; no pl) unamiableness, unfriendliness.
'**unliebsam** [ˈʊnliːpzaːm] adj unpleasant.
'**unlini,iert** adj unruled.
'**unlogisch** adj illogical.
'**un'lösbar** adj insoluble (problem etc).
'**un'löslich** adj 🜛 insoluble.
'**Unlust** f (-; no pl) a) listlessness, b) aversion: **mit ~** with reluctance.
'**unlustig** adj listless, reluctant.
'**unma,nierlich** adj ill-mannered.
'**unmännlich** adj effeminate.
'**unmaßgeblich** adj unauthoritative: iro. **nach m-r ~en Meinung** in my humble opinion.
'**unmäßig** adj excessive, immoderate. '**Unmäßigkeit** f (-; no pl) immoderateness, excess.
'**Unmenge** f (-; -n) (**von** of) vast (or enormous) amount (or number), F loads.
'**Unmensch** m monster, brute: F **sei kein ~!** have a heart! '**unmenschlich** adj **1.** inhuman, cruel. **2.** F fig. awful. '**Unmenschlichkeit** f (-; no pl) inhumanity, cruelty.
'**unmerklich** adj imperceptible.
'**unme,thodisch** adj unmethodical.
'**unmißverständlich** I adj unmistakable. II adv a) unmistakably, b) plainly.
'**unmittelbar** I adj immediate, direct. II

adv immediately, directly: ~ **vor** (dat) a) right in front of, b) time: just before; ~ **bevorstehen** be imminent.
'**unmö,bliert** adj unfurnished.
'**unmo,dern** adj outmoded, dated.
'**unmöglich** I adj impossible (a. F fig. person, dress, situation, etc): ~**es leisten** (**verlangen**) do (ask) the impossible; fig. ~ **aussehen** look a sight; **sich ~ machen** a) compromise o.s., b) make a fool of o.s. II adv not possibly: **ich kann es ~ tun** I can't possibly do it. '**Unmöglichkeit** f (-; no pl) impossibility.
'**unmo,ralisch** adj immoral.
'**unmoti,viert** adj unmotivated.
'**unmündig** adj under age, minor.
'**unmusi,kalisch** adj unmusical.
'**Unmut** m (-[e]s; no pl) annoyance (**über** acc at).
unnachahmlich [ˈʊnnaːxˈʔaːmlɪç] adj inimitable.
'**unnachgiebig** adj unyielding.
'**unnachsichtig** adj strict, severe.
'**un'nahbar** adj unapproachable.
'**unna,türlich** adj **1.** unnatural (a. fig.). **2.** affected.
'**unnötig** adj unnecessary.
'**unnütz** [ˈʊnnʏts] adj useless, pointless.
'**unordentlich** adj disorderly, untidy.
'**Unordnung** f (-; no pl) disorder, mess: **in ~** in a mess; **in ~ bringen** mess s.th. up.
'**unor,ganisch** adj inorganic.
'**unpar,teiisch** adj impartial. '**Unpar,teiische** m (-n; -n) sports: referee.
'**unpassend** adj **1.** inappropriate, unsuitable. **2.** improper. **3.** untimely.
'**unpas,sierbar** adj impassable.
'**unpäßlich** [ˈʊnpɛslɪç] adj ~ **sein, sich ~ fühlen** be indisposed, feel unwell.
'**Unpäßlichkeit** f (-; -en) indisposition.
'**unpatri,otisch** adj unpatriotic.
'**Unper,son** f (-; -en) nonperson.
'**unper,sönlich** adj impersonal.
'**unpo,litisch** adj apolitical.
'**unpopu,lär** adj unpopular.
'**unpraktisch** adj impractical.
'**unproble,matisch** adj unproblematic.
'**unproduk,tiv** adj unproductive, ✝ nonproductive.
'**unpünktlich** adj unpunctual. '**Unpünktlichkeit** f (-; no pl) unpunctuality.
'**unqualifi,ziert** adj unqualified.
'**unra,siert** adj unshaven.

Unrat ['ʊnraːt] *m* (-[e]s; *no pl*) rubbish, *Am.* garbage: F **~ wittern** smell a rat.
'**unratio,nell** *adj* inefficient.
'**unratsam** *adj* inadvisable.
'**unrecht** *adj* wrong: *et.* **2es tun** do s.th. wrong. '**Unrecht** *n* (-[e]s; *no pl*) wrong, injustice; *j-m* **2 tun** do s.o. wrong; *im ~ sein*, **2 haben** be (in the) wrong, *a.* be mistaken; *j-m* **2 geben** disagree with s.o., *fig. result etc*: prove s.o. wrong; *j-n ins ~ setzen* put s.o. in the wrong; *zu ~* wrong(ful)ly, unjustly; *nicht zu ~* not without good reason.
'**unrechtmäßig** *adj* wrongful, unlawful.
'**unredlich** *adj* dishonest.
'**Unredlichkeit** *f* (-; *no pl*) dishonesty.
'**unre,ell** *adj* dishonest.
'**unregelmäßig** *adj* irregular. '**Unregelmäßigkeit** *f* (-; -en) irregularity.
'**unreif** *adj* 1. unripe. 2. *fig.* immature.
'**unrein** *adj* impure (*a. fig.*), bad (*skin*).
'**Unreinheit** *f* (-; -en) impurity.
'**unreinlich** *adj* unclean.
'**unren,tabel** *adj* unprofitable.
un'rettbar *adj* irrecoverable: **~ verloren** irretrievably lost, *person*: beyond help.
'**unrichtig** *adj* incorrect, wrong.
'**Unrichtigkeit** *f* (-; -en) 1. *no pl* incorrectness. 2. mistake, error.
'**Unruh** *f* (-; -en) balance wheel.
'**Unruhe** *f* (-; *no pl*) 1. restlessness. 2. uneasiness, anxiety. 3. commotion, tumult: *pol.* **~n** unrest, disturbances.
'**Unruheherd** *m fig.* trouble spot.
'**Unruhestifter(in** *f*) *m* troublemaker.
'**unruhig** *adj* 1. restless. 2. *fig.* troubled (*sleep*, *times*). 3. *fig.* uneasy, worried. 4. *fig.* noisy. 5. *fig.* choppy (*sea*).
'**unrühmlich** *adj* inglorious.
uns [ʊns] I *pers pron* 1. us, to us: *ein Freund von ~* a friend of ours; *wir sehen ~ selten* we seldom see each other. II *reflex pron* 2. ourselves: *wir waschen ~* we wash (ourselves). 3. each other, one another.
'**unsachgemäß** *adj* improper, inexpert.
'**unsachlich** *adj* unobjective, irrelevant, *pred* beside the point: **~ werden** become personal.
unsagbar [ʊn'zaːkbaːr], **unsäglich** [ʊn'zɛːklɪç] *adj* unspeakable.
'**unsanft** *adj* rough: *fig. ein ~es Erwachen* a rude awakening.
'**unsauber** *adj* 1. dirty. 2. *fig.* a) sloven-

ly, b) shady, dubious, c) *sports*: unfair.
'**unschädlich** *adj* harmless: **~ machen** render harmless, neutralize, put *s.o.* out of action, lay *criminal* by the heels.
'**unscharf** *adj* 1. *phot.* blurred: *opt.* **~ (eingestellt)** out of focus. 2. *fig.* hazy.
un'schätzbar *adj* invaluable.
'**unscheinbar** *adj* insignificant, inconspicuous, plain, *Am.* homely.
'**unschicklich** *adj* unseemly, improper.
un'schlagbar *adj* unbeatable.
'**unschlüssig** *adj* irresolute. '**Unschlüssigkeit** *f* (-; *no pl*) irresolution.
'**unschön** *adj* 1. unlovely, ugly. 2. *fig.* a) unkind, *pred* not nice, b) unpleasant.
'**Unschuld** *f* (-; *no pl*) innocence.
'**unschuldig** *adj* innocent (*an dat* of): 🕮 *sich für ~ erklären* plead not guilty.
'**unschwer** *adv* easily, without difficulty.
'**unselbständig** *adj* 1. dependent (on others), helpless. 2. employed: *Einkünfte aus ~er Arbeit* wage and salaries income. '**Unselbständigkeit** *f* (- *no pl*) lack of independence.
'**unselig** *adj* unfortunate, fatal.
unser ['ʊnzər] I *pos pron* our, ours: *der (die, das) ~e* (*or* uns[e]rige) our; *wir haben das ~e getan* we have done our bit. II *gen of* **wir**: of us.
'**unsereiner**, '**unsereins**, '**unseresgleichen** *indef pron* F people like us.
'**unser(e)twegen** *adv* 1. for our sake. 2. because of us.
'**unseri,ös** *adj* dubious.
'**unsicher** *adj* 1. unsafe, insecure, risky: F *die Gegend ~e* (*or* *reden* talk) *machen criminal etc*: prowl (*humor. tourists etc*: infest) the place. 2. uncertain. 3. unsteady, shaky (*a. fig. in dat* in). 4. insecure, unsure (of o.s.): *j-n ~ machen* make s.o. feel insecure. '**Unsicherheit** *f* (-; *no pl*) 1. unsafeness, insecurity. 2. uncertainty. 3. unsteadiness. 4. unsureness (of o.s.), insecurity. '**Unsicherheitsfaktor** *m* element of uncertainty.
'**unsichtbar** *adj* invisible.
'**Unsichtbarkeit** *f* (-; *no pl*) invisibility.
'**Unsinn** *m* (-[e]s; *no pl*) 1. (**~ reden** talk) nonsense (*or* rubbish). 2. **~ machen** fool around. '**unsinnig** *adj* 1. unreasonable, absurd. 2. F tremendous.
'**Unsitte** *f* (-; -n) bad habit.
'**unsittlich** *adj* immoral, indecent.
'**Unsittlichkeit** *f* (-; *no pl*) immorality.

'unso,lide *adj* **1.** unsolid. **2.** loose (*life, person, etc*). **3.** dubious (*firm etc*).

'unsozi,al *adj* antisocial.

'unsportlich *adj* **1.** unathletic. **2.** *fig.* unfair, unsporting.

un'sterblich **I** *adj* immortal. **II** *adv* awfully: ~ *verliebt* madly in love (*in acc* with). **Un'sterblichkeit** *f* (-; *no pl*) immortality.

'unstet *adj* **1.** inconstant. **2.** restless.

un'stillbar *adj* unquenchable (*thirst*), insatiable (*hunger*), *fig.* unappeasable.

'Unstimmigkeit *f* (-; -en) *usu. pl* **1.** discrepancy. **2.** disagreement, difference.

'unstreitig *adj* indisputable.

'Unsumme *f* (-; -n) enormous sum.

'unsym,metrisch *adj* asymmetrical.

'unsym,pathisch *adj* disagreeable, unpleasant: *er ist mir* ~ I don't like him.

'Untat *f* (-; -en) atrocity, outrage.

'untätig *adj* inactive, idle. **'Untätigkeit** *f* (-; *no pl*) inactivity, idleness.

'untauglich *adj* unfit (*a.* ✗), unsuitable. **'Untauglichkeit** *f* (-; *no pl*) unfitness.

un'teilbar *adj* indivisible.

unten ['ʊntən] *adv* a) below, b) downstairs: *da* ~ down there; *nach* ~ down(wards), *a.* downstairs; ~ *auf der Seite* at the bottom of the page; *siehe ~!* see below; (*von oben bis* ~ from top to bottom (*person:* to toe); F *er ist bei mir* ~ *durch* I am through with him.

'untenerwähnt, 'untengenannt *adj* undermentioned, mentioned below.

unter ['ʊntər] *prep* (*dat*) **1.** under, below, *a.* less than: ~ *Null* below zero; ~ *sich haben* be in charge of; *was versteht man* ~ ...? what is meant by ...?; → *Bedingung, Hand, Träne etc.* **2.** among: *einer* ~ *hundert* one in a hundred; ~ *anderem* among other things; ~ *uns gesagt* between you and me; *wir sind ganz* ~ *uns* we are quite alone. **3.** during: ~ *s-r Regierung* under (*or* during) his reign.

'Unter|abteilung *f* subdivision. **~arm** *m* forearm. **~art** *f* subspecies. **~ausschuß** *m* subcommittee. **~bau** *m* (-[e]s; -ten) **1.** substructure, foundation. **2.** *no pl fig.* base, ✝ *etc* infrastructure.

'unterbelichten *v/t* (*insep, no* -ge-, h) underexpose.

'unterbeschäftigt *adj* underemployed.

'unterbesetzt *adj* understaffed.

'unterbewerten *v/t* (*insep, no* -ge-, h) undervalue, *fig. a.* underrate.

'unterbewußt *adj* subconscious. **'Unterbewußtsein** *n* (-s; *no pl*) *the* subconscious: *im* ~ subconsciously.

'unterbezahlt *adj* underpaid.

unter'bieten *v/t* (*irr, insep, no* -ge-, h, → *bieten*) underbid, undercut (*price*), undersell (*competitors*), beat (*record*).

unter'binden *v/t* (*irr, insep, no* -ge-, h, → *binden*) *fig.* stop, prevent.

unter'bleiben *v/i* (*irr, insep, no* -ge-, sn, → *bleiben*) **1.** be left undone, not to take place. **2.** stop, cease.

Unter'bodenschutz *m mot.* underseal, *Am.* undercoat.

unter'brechen (*irr, insep, no* -ge-, h, → *brechen*) **I** *v/t* interrupt, *teleph.* cut off, hold up (*game*), ⚖ adjourn: *die Fahrt* (*or Reise*) ~ break one's journey. **II** *sich* ~ pause. **Unter'brechung** *f* (-; -en) interruption, break, *a.* stopover.

unter'breiten *v/t* (*insep, no* -ge-, h) submit (*dat* to).

'unterbringen *v/t* (*irr, sep,* -ge-, h, → *bringen*) **1.** accommodate, *a.* put *s.o.* up: *j-n* ~ *in* put s.o. into (⚖ commit s.o. to) *an institution etc; j-n* ~ *in* (*or bei*) get s.o. a job with *a firm etc;* F *fig.* *ich kann ihn nicht* ~ I can't place him. **2.** a) store, b) stow (away): *et.* ~ *in* (*dat*) get (*or* fit) s.th. into, ⚙ install s.th. in. **3.** ✝place *capital, orders* (*bei* with): *ein Buch bei e-m Verlag* ~ have a book accepted by publishers. **Unter'bringung** *f* (-; -en) accommodation, housing, ⚖ committal (*in dat* to). **'Unterbringungsmöglichkeit(en** *pl*) *f* accommodation.

'unterbuttern *v/t* (*sep,* h) F *j-n* ~ push s.o. under.

'Unterdeck *n* ⚓ lower deck.

unterder'hand *adv* secretly, on the quiet: ~ *verkaufen* sell *s.th.* privately.

unter'dessen *adv* in the meantime.

unter'drücken *v/t* (*insep, no* -ge-, h) suppress (*a. publication*), *a.* stifle (*laughter, yawn, etc*), oppress (*people*), put down, quell (*rebellion*). **Unter'drücker** *m* (-s; -) oppressor. **Unter'drückung** *f* (-; -en) suppression, oppression.

'unterdurchschnittlich *adj* below average.

'untere *adj* lower.

'untereinander[1] *adv* one below the

other. **unterein'ander**[2] *adv* among one another (*or* each other, themselves, yourselves, *etc*).

'unterentwickelt *adj* underdeveloped (*a. phot.*), *a.* backward (*child, country, etc*), *psych.* subnormal.

'unterernährt *adj* underfed, undernourished. **'Unterernährung** *f* (-; *no pl*) malnutrition, undernourishment.

Unter'fangen *n* (-s; *no pl*) **1.** venture, undertaking. **2.** attempt.

Unter'führung *f* (-; -en) a) underpass, b) subway, *Am.* pedestrian underpass.

'Unterfunkti,on *f* ✻ hypofunction.

'Untergang *m* (-[e]s; ⁓e) **1.** *astr.* setting. **2.** ⚓ sinking. **3.** *fig.* (down)fall, decline.

'Untergattung *f* subgenus.

Unter'gebene *m*, *f* (-n; -n) subordinate.

'untergehen *v/i* (*irr, sep, -ge-, sn*, → **gehen**) go down, go under (*both a. fig.*), ⚓ *a.* sink, *astr. a.* set: *fig.* **im Lärm** ⁓ be drowned out (*or* lost) by the noise.

'untergeordnet *adj* **1.** subordinate (*dat* to). **2.** *fig.* secondary (*importance etc*).

'Unter|geschoß *n* basement. **⁓gestell** *n* *mot.* underframe. **⁓gewicht** *n* (⁓ *haben* be) underweight.

unter'|gliedern *v/t* (*insep, no -ge-, h*) subdivide. **⁓'graben** *v/t* (*irr, insep, no -ge-, h*, → **graben**) *fig.* undermine.

'Untergrund *m* (-[e]s; ⁓e) **1.** *geol.* subsoil. **2.** *paint.* ground(ing). **3.** *no pl pol.* (**in den ⁓ gehen** go) underground. **⁓bahn** *f* underground, *in London: a.* tube, *Am.* subway. **⁓bewegung** *f* *pol.* underground movement. **⁓kämpfer(in** *f*) *m* *pol.* underground fighter.

'unterhalb I *prep* (*gen*) below, under. **II** *adv* below, underneath.

'Unterhalt *m* (-[e]s; *no pl*) **1.** support, maintenance. **2.** → **Lebensunterhalt.**

unter'halten (*irr, insep, no -ge-, h*, → **halten**) **I** *v/t* **1.** maintain, support. **2.** keep up (*correspondence etc*). **3.** amuse, entertain. **II** *sich* ⁓ **4.** talk (*mit* with, to). **5.** *sich* (*gut*) ⁓ enjoy o.s., have a good time. **unter'haltend** → **unterhaltsam.** **Unter'halter** *m* (-s; -) entertainer. **unter'haltsam** *adj* entertaining.

'Unterhalts|anspruch *m* maintenance claim. **⁓beihilfe** *f* maintenance grant. **Ⱡberechtigt** *adj* entitled to maintenance. **⁓kosten** *pl* maintenance costs.

Unter'haltung *f* (-; -en) **1.** entertainment. **2.** conversation, talk. **3.** *no pl* upkeep, maintenance.

Unter'haltungs... entertainment (*concert, film, industry, etc*). **⁓branche** *f* (**in der ⁓** in) show business. **⁓elek,tronik** *f* video and audio systems. **⁓litera,tur** *f* light fiction. **⁓mu,sik** *f* light music. **⁓ro,man** *m* light novel. **⁓wert** *m* (-[e]s; *no pl*) entertainment value.

'Unterhändler *m* (-s; -) negotiator.

Unter'handlung *f* (-; -en) negotiation.

'Unterhaus *n* (-es; *no pl*) *parl. Br.* House of Commons.

'Unterhemd *n* vest, *Am.* undershirt.

unter'höhlen *v/t* (*insep, no -ge-, h*) *a. fig.* undermine.

'Unterholz *n* (-es; *no pl*) undergrowth.

'Unterhose *f* (**e-e ⁓** a pair of) underpants.

'unterirdisch *adj* subterranean, underground.

unter'jochen *v/t* (*insep, no -ge-, h*) subjugate.

'unterjubeln *v/t* (*sep, h*) F *j-m et.* ⁓ foist s.th. (off) on s.o.

'Unterkiefer *m* *anat.* lower jaw.

'Unterkleid *n* (full-length) slip.

'Unterkleidung *f* underwear.

'unterkommen *v/i* (*irr, sep, -ge-, sn*, → **kommen**) find accommodation (*or* lodgings): ⁓ *in* (*dat*) find a place in; F ⁓ *bei* find a job with *a firm etc*.

'Unterkörper *m* lower part of the body.

'unterkriegen *v/t* (*sep, h*) F *j-n* ⁓ get s.o. down.

Unter'kühlung *f* (-; -en) ✻ hypothermia.

'Unterkunft *f* (-; ⁓e) accommodation, lodging(s), quarters: ⁓ *und Verpflegung* board and lodgings.

'Unterlage *f* (-; -n) **1.** ⊙ base, support. **2.** *fig.* basis. **3.** *pl* a) documents, records, b) data.

'Unterlaß *m* *ohne* ⁓ incessantly.

unter'lassen *v/t* (*irr, no -ge-, h*, → **lassen**) *et.* ⁓ a) omit (*or* fail) to do s.th., b) refrain from (doing) s.th.; *unterlaß das!* stop that!

Unter'lassung *f* (-; -en) omission.

Unter'lassungs|klage *f* ⚖ action for injunction. **⁓sünde** *f* sin of omission.

'Unterlauf *m* (-[e]s; ⁓e) lower course.

unter'laufen (*irr, insep, no -ge-*, → **laufen**) **I** *v/t* (h) F dodge. **II** *v/i* (sn) *mir ist ein Fehler* ⁓ I've made a mistake.

'unterlegen¹ *v/t* (*sep*, h) lay (*or* put) *s.th.* under. **unter'legen**² *adj* **1.** inferior (*dat* to). **2.** losing, defeated.

Unter'legene *m*, *f* (-n; -n) loser.

Unter'legenheit *f* (-; *no pl*) inferiority.

'Unterleib *m* abdomen, belly.

'Unterleibs... abdominal (*pain etc*).

unter'liegen *v/i* (*irr*, *insep*, *no* -ge-, sn, → *liegen*) **1.** (*dat*) be defeated (*or* beaten) (by), lose (to), *fig.* succumb (to). **2.** be subject (*dat* to *rule etc*): **es unterliegt k-m Zweifel, daß** there is no doubt that.

'Unterlippe *f* lower lip.

Unter'malung *f* (-; -en) background.

unter'mauern *v/t* (*insep*, *no* -ge-, h) *a. fig.* underpin.

'untermengen *v/t* (*sep*, h) mix in.

'Untermensch *m* subhuman creature.

'Untermiete *f* (-; *no pl*) **1.** subtenancy: **in** (*or* **zur**) ~ **wohnen** be a subtenant (*Am.* roomer), lodge (**bei** with). **2.** sublease: → **untervermieten**. **'Untermieter(in** *f*) *m* subtenant, lodger, *Am.* roomer.

untermi'nieren *v/t* (*insep*, h) undermine.

'U-Mu₃sik *f* light music.

unter'nehmen *v/t* (*irr*, *insep*, *no* -ge-, h, → *nehmen*) make, go on (*a trip etc*), do (*s.th.*): **et. ~ gegen** a) **j-n** take action against s.o., b) **et.** do s.th. against s.th.; **er unternahm nichts** he did nothing.

Unter'nehmen *n* (-s; -n) **1.** firm, business, enterprise, company. **2.** undertaking, enterprise, project: (**gewagtes**) ~ **venture. 3.** ✕ operation.

Unter'nehmens₃berater *m* management consultant. **₃führung** *f* (-; *no pl*) management.

Unter'nehmer *m* (-s; -) a) entrepreneur b) contractor, c) employer, d) industrialist. **unter'nehmerisch** *adj* entrepreneurial. **Unter'nehmerschaft** *f* (-; *no pl*) the employers, the management. **Unter'nehmertum** *n* (-s; *no pl*) **1.** entrepreneurship: **freies** ~ free enterprise. **2.** → **Unternehmerschaft.**

Unter'nehmungsgeist *m* (spirit of) enterprise, initiative.

unter'nehmungslustig *adj* enterprising.

'Unteroffi₃zier *m* a) noncommissioned officer (*abbr.* NCO), b) sergeant, ✓ corporal.

'unterordnen (*sep*, h) **I** *v/t* subordinate (*dat* to). **II sich** ~ submit (*dat* to).

'Unterordnung *f* (-; -en) **1.** *no pl* subordination. **2.** *biol.* suborder.

'unterprivile₃giert *adj* underprivileged.

Unter'redung *f* (-; -en) talk, conversation.

Unterricht ['ʊntərɪçt] *m* (-[e]s; *no pl*) instruction, lessons, classes: **j-m** ~ (**in Deutsch**) **geben** teach s.o. (German), give (German) lessons to s.o.

unter'richten (*insep*, *no* -ge-, h) **I** *v/t*, *v/i* **1.** teach, give lessons (*dat* to): **j-n** (**in Deutsch**) ~ teach s.o. (German); **Mathematik** ~ teach mathematics. **2.** inform (**von**, **über** *acc* of): (**gut**) **unterrichtete Kreise** (well-)informed circles. **II sich** ~ inform o.s. (**über** *acc* about).

'Unterrichts₃einheit *f* teaching unit. **₃raum** *m* classroom. **₃stunde** *f* lesson.

Unter'richtung *f* (-; *no pl*) **1.** instruction. **2.** (**zu Ihrer** ~ for your) information.

'Unterrock *m* slip.

unter'sagen *v/t* (*insep*, *no* -ge-, h) forbid, *adm.* prohibit: **j-m** ~ **zu** *inf* forbid s.o. to *inf*, prohibit s.o. from *ger*.

'Untersatz *m* (-es; ⸚e) stand, *for glasses:* mat, *for flowerpots:* saucer: F **fahrba₃rer** ~ wheels.

'Unterschall... subsonic (*speed etc*).

unter'schätzen *v/t* (*insep*, *no* -ge-, h) underestimate.

unter'scheiden (*irr*, *insep*, *no* -ge-, h, → *scheiden*) **I** *v/t*, *v/i* distinguish (**zwischen** between, **von** from): **et.** ~ **von** a. tell s.th. apart from; **das unterscheidet ihn von ...** that sets him apart from ... **II sich** ~ differ (**von** from, **dadurch daß** in *ger*). **unter'scheidend** *adj* distinctive.

Unter'scheidung *f* (-; -en) **1.** differentiation. **2.** difference. **Unter'scheidungsmerkmal** *n* distinguishing mark.

'Unterschenkel *m* anat. lower leg.

'Unterschicht *f sociol.* lower classes.

Unterschied ['ʊntərʃiːt] *m* (-[e]s; -e) difference: **e-n** ~ **machen** (**zwischen** between) distinguish (**a.** discriminate); **das macht k-n** ~ that makes no difference; **ohne** ~ indiscriminately; **zum** ~ **von** unlike, in contrast to; **das ist ein gro₃ßer** ~ that makes a great difference. **'unterschiedlich** *adj* different, varying, variable; ~ **behandeln** discriminate between. **'unterschiedslos I** *adj* indiscriminate. **II** *adv* without exception.

unter'schlagen *v/t* (*irr*, *insep*, *no* -ge-, h,

→ *schlagen*) embezzle (*money*), intercept (*letter*), suppress (*last will etc*), hold back (*facts*).
Unter'schlagung *f* (-; -en) embezzlement, interception, suppression.
'**Unterschlupf** *m* (-[e]s; -e) **1.** hiding place, F shelter. **2.** shelter, refuge.
'**unterschlüpfen** *v/i* (*sep*, sn) **1.** hide. **2.** take shelter (*bei* with).
unter'schreiben *v/t*, *v/i* (*irr*, *insep*, no -ge-, h, → *schreiben*) **1.** sign. **2.** F *fig.* subscribe (to).
unter'schreiten *v/t* (*irr*, *insep*, no -ge-, h, → *schreiten*) fall short of.
'**Unterschrift** *f* (-; -en) signature: → *setzen* 1. '**Unterschriftenmappe** *f* signature blotting book. '**unterschriftsberechtigt** *adj* authorized to sign.
'**unterschwellig** [-ʃvelɪç] *adj* subliminal.
'**Unterseeboot** *n* submarine.
'**unterseeisch** [-zeːɪʃ] *adj* submarine.
'**Unterseite** *f* underside, bottom.
untersetzt [-'zɛtst] *adj* stocky.
'**unterst** *adj* lowest: *das* ℒe *zuoberst kehren* turn everything upside down.
'**Unterstand** *m* shelter, ✕ *a.* dugout.
unter'stehen (*irr*, *insep*, no -ge-, h, → *stehen*) **I** *v/i j-m* ~ be subordinate (*or* answerable) to s.o., be under s.o.'s supervision. **II** *sich* ~ *zu inf* dare to *inf*: *was* ~ *Sie sich?* how dare you?
'**unterstellen**[1] (*sep*, h) **I** *v/t* put *s.th.* in(to *in dat*). **II** *sich* ~ take shelter.
unter'stellen[2] *v/t* (*insep*, no -ge-, h) **1.** *j-m j-n* (*et.*) ~ put s.o. in charge of s.o. (s.th.). **2.** *fig. j-m et.* ~ impute s.th. to s.o. **3.** suppose, assume. **Unter'stellung** *f* (-; -en) allegation, suggestion.
unter'streichen *v/t* (*irr*, *insep*, no -ge-, h, → *streichen*) *a. fig.* underline.
'**Unterstufe** *f* (-; -n) *ped.* lower grades.
unter'stützen *v/t* (*insep*, no -ge-, h) a) support, back (up), b) assist, aid, help.
Unter'stützung *f* (-; -en) **1.** a) support, b) aid, grant, c) subsidy, d) benefit: ~ *beziehen* be on social security. **2.** *fig.* support, backing, aid, assistance.
unter'suchen *v/t* (*insep*, no -ge-, h) examine (*a.* ✵), investigate (*a.* ⚖), inspect, check, ⚕ *or fig.* analy/se (*Am.* -ze): *et.* ~ *auf* (*acc*) test s.th. for.
Unter'suchung *f* (-; -en) examination, ✵ *a.* checkup, investigation, inspection, test, ⚕ *or fig.* analysis.

Unter'suchungs|ausschuß *m* fact-finding committee. ~**gefangene** *m, f* prisoner on remand. ~**gefängnis** *n* remand prison. ~**haft** *f* detention pending trial: *in* ~ *sein* be on remand. ~**richter(in** *f*) *m* examining magistrate.
'**Untertan** [-taːn] *m* (-s, -en; -en) subject.
'**Untertasse** *f* saucer.
'**untertauchen** *v/i* (*sep*, sn) **1.** *a. v/t* (h) duck. **2.** *fig.* disappear, go into hiding, *esp. pol.* go underground.
'**Unterteil** *n, m* lower part, base.
unter'teilen *v/t* (*insep*, no -ge-, h) subdivide (*in acc* into). **Unter'teilung** *f* (-; -en) subdivision (*in acc* into).
'**Untertitel** *m* subtitle, *film: a.* caption.
'**Unterton** *m a. fig.* undertone.
unter'treiben *v/t*, *v/i* (*irr*, *insep*, no -ge-, h, → *treiben*) understate. **Unter'treibung** *f* (-; -en) understatement.
unter'tunneln *v/t* (*insep*, no -ge-, h) tunnel through.
unter'vermieten *v/t* (*only inf and pp* untervermietet, h) sublet.
'**unterversichert** *adj* underinsured.
unter'wandern *v/t* (*insep*, no -ge-, h) infiltrate.
Unter'wanderung *f* (-; -en) infiltration.
'**Unterwäsche** *f* (-; *no pl*) underwear.
'**Unterwasser...** underwater (*camera, massage, etc*).
unterwegs [ʊntɐ've:ks] *adv* on the (*or* one's) way (*nach* to), away: *immer* ~ always on the move.
unter'weisen *v/t* (*irr*, *insep*, no -ge-, h, → *weisen*) instruct.
Unter'weisung *f* (-; -en) instruction.
'**Unterwelt** *f* (-; *no pl*) underworld.
unter'werfen *v/t* (*irr*, *insep*, no -ge-, h, → *werfen*) **I** *v/t* **1.** subdue, subjugate. **2.** subject (*dat* to *test etc*). **II** *sich* ~ *a. fig.* submit (*dat* to). **Unter'werfung** *f* (-; -en) **1.** subjugation, subjection. **2.** *fig.* submission (*unter acc* to). **unterworfen** (-*t sein*) *fig.* subject (*dat* to).
unterwürfig [ʊntɐ'vʏrfɪç] *adj* submissive, servile. **Unter'würfigkeit** *f* (-; *no pl*) submissiveness, servility.
unter'zeichnen *v/t*, *v/i* (*insep*, no -ge-, h) sign. **Unter'zeichner** *m* (-s; -) signer, *the* undersigned, signatory (*gen* to). **Unter'zeichnete** *m, f* (-n; -n) *the* undersigned. **Unter'zeichnung** *f* (-; -en) signing.

'**unterziehen**[1] *v/t* (*irr, sep,* -ge-, h, →
ziehen) put on underneath.

unter'ziehen[2] *v/t* (*irr, insep, no* -ge-, h,
→ **ziehen**) subject (*dat* to): **sich e-r
Operation ~** undergo an operation;
sich e-r Prüfung ~ take an examination.

'**Untiefe** *f* (-; -n) shallow, shoal.

'**Untier** *n* (-[e]s; -e) *a. fig.* monster.

un'tragbar *adj* intolerable (*conduct etc*),
prohibitive (*prices etc*).

un'trennbar *adj* inseparable.

untreu *adj* (*dat* to) unfaithful, disloyal.

'**Untreue** *f* (-; *no pl*) unfaithfulness, disloyalty, (*marital*) infidelity.

un'tröstlich *adj* inconsolable.

untrüglich [ʊn'try:klɪç] *adj* **1.** unerring
(*instinct etc*). **2.** sure (*sign etc*).

'**untüchtig** *adj* incapable, incompetent.

'**Untugend** *f* (-; -en) vice, bad habit.

unüber'brückbar *adj fig.* unbridgeable.

'**unüberlegt** *adj* ill-considered, unwise.

unüber'sehbar *adj* immense, vast.

unüber'setzbar *adj* untranslatable.

'**unübersichtlich** *adj* **1.** blind (*curve etc*).
2. badly arranged, unclear, confused.

unübertrefflich [-'treflɪç] *adj* matchless,
unsurpassable. **unübertroffen** [-'trɔ-
fən] *adj* unsurpassed, unmatched.

unüberwindlich [-'vɪntlɪç] *adj* invincible, *fig.* insurmountable, insuperable.

'**unumgänglich** *adj* unavoidable: **~** (*notwendig*) indispensable.

'**unumschränkt** [-'ʃrɛŋkt] *adj* unlimited,
pol. absolute.

unumstößlich [-'ʃtø:slɪç] *adj* irrefutable
(*fact etc*), irrevocable (*decision etc*).

unum'stritten *adj* undisputed.

'**unumwunden** [-vʊndən] *adv* straight
out, frankly.

'**ununterbrochen** [-brɔxən] *adj* uninterrupted, incessant.

unver'änderlich *adj* unchanging, *ling.,*
Ⓐ invariable. **unver'ändert** *adj* unchanged.

unver'antwortlich *adj* irresponsible.

unver'äußerlich *adj* inalienable.

unver'besserlich *adj* incorrigible.

'**unverbindlich** *adj offer etc* without obligation, noncommittal (*answer etc*).

'**unverblümt** *adj* plain, blunt.

'**unverbraucht** *adj* unused, *fig.* unspent.

'**unverbürgt** *adj* unconfirmed.

'**unverdächtig** *adj* unsuspicious.

'**unverdaulich** *adj. fig.* indigestible.

'**unverdaut** *adj a. fig.* undigested.

'**unverdient** *adj* undeserved. '**unver-
dienter'maßen** *adv* undeservedly.

'**unverdorben** *adj* unspoilt, *fig. a.* un-
corrupted.

'**unverdrossen** *adj* indefatigable.

'**unverdünnt** *adj* undiluted.

unver'einbar *adj* incompatible, irreconcilable.

'**unverfälscht** *adj* unadulterated, pure,
fig. a. genuine.

'**unverfänglich** *adj* harmless.

'**unverfroren** *adj* brazen, F cheeky.

'**Unverfrorenheit** *f* (-; *no pl*) brazenness,
impertinence, F cheek.

'**unvergänglich** *adj* immortal. '**Unver-
gänglichkeit** *f* (-; *no pl*) immortality.

'**unvergessen** *adj* unforgotten.

'**unvergeßlich** *adj* unforgettable.

unver'gleichlich *adj* incomparable.

'**unverhältnismäßig** *adv* disproportion-
ately: **~ hoch** excessive.

'**unverheiratet** *adj* unmarried, single.

'**unverhofft** [-hɔft] *adj a)* unhoped-for, b)
unexpected.

'**unverhohlen** [-ho:lən] *adj* undisguised.

'**unverhüllt** *adj fig.* undisguised.

'**unverkäuflich** *adj* unsal(e)able, not for
sale. '**unverkauft** *adj* unsold.

unver'kennbar *adj* unmistakable.

unver'letzlich *adj fig.* inviolable.

'**unverletzt** *adj* uninjured, unhurt.

unvermeidlich [-'maıt-] *adj* unavoidable,
inevitable (*a. iro.*): **sich ins Unvermeidliche fügen** bow to the inevitable.

'**unvermindert** *adj* undiminished.

'**unvermittelt** *adj* abrupt.

'**Unvermögen** *n* (-s; *no pl*) inability.

'**unvermutet** *adj* unexpected.

'**Unvernunft** *f* (-; *no pl*) unreasonable-
ness, folly. '**unvernünftig** *adj* unreasonable, foolish.

'**unveröffentlicht** *adj* unpublished.

'**unverrichteter'dinge** *adv* without having achieved anything.

'**unverschämt** *adj* **1.** impudent, impertinent. **2.** F barefaced (*lie*), outrageous
(*demand, price, etc*).

'**Unverschämtheit** *f* (-; -en) impudence,
impertinence: **die ~ haben zu** *inf* have
the cheek to *inf*.

'**unverschuldet** *adj and adv* through no
fault of one's own.

unversehens ['ʊnfɛrze:əns] *adv* unexpectedly, all of a sudden.

'**unversehrt** *adj* unharmed, intact.

'**unversichert** *adj* uninsured.

unver'siegbar *adj* inexhaustible.

unver'söhnlich *adj a. fig.* irreconcilable.

'**unverstanden** *adj* (*sich ~ fühlen* feel) misunderstood. '**unverständig** *adj* ignorant. '**unverständlich** *adj* (*dat* to) **1.** unintelligible. **2.** incomprehensible, obscure (*reasons etc*): *es ist mir ~, warum* (*wie etc*) I can't understand (F it beats me) why (how *etc*).

'**unversteuert** *adj* untaxed.

'**unversucht** *adj* nichts ~ *lassen* (*um zu inf*) try everything (to *inf*).

'**unverträglich** *adj* **1.** quarrelsome. **2.** indigestible. **3.** *a.* ✚ incompatible.

unver'wechselbar *adj* unmistakable.

'**unverwundbar** *adj* invulnerable.

unverwüstlich [-'vy:stlɪç] *adj* indestructible (*a. fig.*), irrepressible (*humo[u]r*).

'**unverzagt** *adj* undaunted.

unver'zeihlich *adj* inexcusable.

unver'zichtbar *adj* **1.** unrenounceable. **2.** indispensable.

unver'zinslich *adj* noninterest-bearing: *~es Darlehen* interest-free loan.

'**unverzollt** *adj* duty unpaid.

unver'züglich [ʊnfɛr'tsy:klɪç] *adj* immediate(ly *adv*), *adv a.* without delay.

'**unvollendet** *adj* unfinished.

'**unvollkommen** *adj* imperfect. '**Unvollkommenheit** *f* (-; -en) imperfection.

'**unvollständig** *adj* incomplete.

'**unvorbereitet** *adj* unprepared.

'**unvoreingenommen** *adj* unbias(s)ed, unprejudiced, objective.

'**unvorhergesehen** *adj* unforeseen.

'**unvorschriftsmäßig** *adj* irregular, contrary to (the) regulations, improper.

'**unvorsichtig** *adj* imprudent, rash, careless. '**Unvorsichtigkeit** *f* (-; *no pl*) imprudence, rashness, carelessness.

unvor'stellbar *adj* unimaginable, unthinkable, incredible.

'**unvorteilhaft** *adj* **1.** unprofitable. **2.** unbecoming (*dress etc*).

'**unwahr** *adj* untrue.

'**Unwahrheit** *f* (-; -en) untruth.

'**unwahrscheinlich** *adj* **1.** improbable, unlikely. **2.** F *fig.* incredible, fantastic. '**Unwahrscheinlichkeit** *f* (-; *no pl*) improbability.

un'wandelbar *adj* unchanging.

unwegsam ['ʊnve:kza:m] *adj* difficult.

'**unweiblich** *adj* unfeminine.

unweigerlich [ʊn'vaigərlɪç] **I** *adj* inevitable. **II** *adv* inevitably, without fail.

'**unweit** *prep* (*gen*) not far from.

'**Unwesen** *n* (-s; *no pl*) nuisance: *sein ~ treiben in* (*dat*) terrorize *a place etc*.

'**unwesentlich** *adj* **1.** irrelevant, unimportant. **2.** negligible.

'**Unwetter** *n* (-s; -) (thunder)storm.

'**unwichtig** *adj* unimportant, irrelevant.

unwider'legbar *adj* irrefutable.

unwiderruflich [-'ru:flɪç] **I** *adj* irrevocable. **II** *adv* irrevocably, definitely: *es steht ~ fest, daß* it is absolutely certain that.

unwiderstehlich [-'ʃte:lɪç] *adj* irresistible.

Unwider'stehlichkeit *f* (-; *no pl*) irresistibility.

unwiederbringlich [-'brɪŋlɪç] *adj* irretrievable.

'**Unwille** *m* (-ns; *no pl*) indignation.

'**unwillig** *adj* **1.** (*über acc* at) indignant, annoyed. **2.** unwilling, reluctant.

'**unwillkommen** *adj* unwelcome.

'**unwillkürlich** *adj* involuntary.

'**unwirklich** *adj* unreal.

'**unwirksam** *adj* ineffective, ✚ inoperative, null and void.

unwirsch ['ʊnvɪrʃ] *adj* disgruntled.

unwirtlich ['ʊnvɪrtlɪç] *adj* a) inhospitable, b) rough (*climate*).

'**unwirtschaftlich** *adj* uneconomic(al).

'**unwissend** *adj* ignorant.

'**Unwissenheit** *f* (-; *no pl*) ignorance.

'**unwissenschaftlich** *adj* unscientific.

'**unwissentlich** *adj* unknowing.

'**unwohl** *adj* **1.** unwell. **2.** *fig.* uneasy.

'**Unwohlsein** *n* (-s; *no pl*) indisposition.

'**unwürdig** *adj* unworthy (*gen* of): *das ist s-r ~* that is beneath him.

'**Unzahl** *f e-e ~ von* a host of.

unzählig [ʊn'tsɛ:lɪç] *adj* countless.

Unze ['ʊntsə] *f* (-; -n) ounce (*abbr.* oz.).

'**unzeitgemäß** *adj* old-fashioned.

'**unzerbrechlich** *adj* unbreakable.

'**unzer'reißbar** *adj* untearable.

unzer'störbar *adj* indestructible.

unzertrennlich [-'trɛnlɪç] *adj* inseparable.

'**unzivili,siert** *adj* uncivilized.

'**Unzucht** *f* (-; *no pl*) ✚ sexual offen/ce

(*Am.* -se): *gewerbsmäßige* ~ prostitution. **'unzüchtig** *adj* lewd, obscene.

'unzufrieden *adj* dissatisfied, discontented. **'Unzufriedenheit** *f* (-; *no pl*) dissatisfaction, discontent.

'unzugänglich *adj* inaccessible (*dat* to).

'unzulänglich *adj* inadequate. **'Unzulänglichkeit** *f* (-; -en) **1.** *no pl* inadequacy. **2.** shortcoming.

'unzulässig *adj* inadmissible.

'unzumutbar *adj* unreasonable: *das ist für sie ~* a) you can't expect that of her, b) she will never accept that.

'unzurechnungsfähig *adj* irresponsible (for one's actions), insane. **'Unzurechnungsfähigkeit** *f* (-; *no pl*) (*zeitweilige* ~ temporary) insanity.

'unzureichend *adj* insufficient.

'unzusammenhängend *adj* a) disconnected, b) incoherent (*speech etc*).

'unzuständig *adj* ⚖ (*für*) incompetent (for), having no jurisdiction (over).

'unzutreffend *adj* incorrect: *Unzutreffendes bitte streichen!* please delete where inapplicable.

'unzuverlässig *adj* unreliable. **'Unzuverlässigkeit** *f* (-; *no pl*) unreliability.

'unzweckmäßig *adj* unsuitable.

'unzweideutig *adj* unequivocal.

'unzweifelhaft I *adj* indubitable. **II** *adv* doubtless, without a doubt.

üppig ['ypɪç] *adj* a) luxurious, b) luxuriant (*vegetation, fig. imagination etc*), c) opulent (*meal*), d) luscious, voluptuous (*figure etc*).

Ur [uːr] *m* (-[e]s; -e) *zo.* aurochs.

'Urabstimmung *f* strike ballot.

'Urahn *m* **1.** ancestor. **2.** great-grandfather. **'Urahne** *f* (-; -n) **1.** ancestress. **2.** great-grandmother.

'uralt *adj* ancient (*a. fig. iro.*), F as old as the hills, *fig.* age-old (*problem etc*).

Uran [u'raːn] *n* (-s; *no pl*) ⚛ uranium.

u'ranhaltig *adj* uranium-bearing.

'uraufführen *v/t* (*only inf and pp* uraufgeführt, h) première, *a.* show *film* for the first time. **'Uraufführung** *f* première, first night (*or* showing).

urbar ['uːrbaːr] *adj* arable: ~ *machen* cultivate, reclaim. **'Urbarmachung** *f* (-; -en) cultivation, reclamation.

'Urbevölkerung *f* → *Ureinwohner*.

'Urbild *n* model, prototype.

'urdeutsch *adj* German to the core, *iro.* very German.

'ur'eigen *adj in Ihrem ~sten Interesse* in your own best interest.

'Ureinwohner *pl* original inhabitants, *in Australia*: Aborigines.

'Urenkel *m* great-grandson.

'Urenkelin *f* great-granddaughter.

'Urform *f* archetype.

'urge'mütlich *adj* F very cosy.

'Urgeschichte *f* (-; *no pl*) primeval history. **'urgeschichtlich** *adj* prehistoric.

'Urgestein *n* *geol.* primary rock.

'Urgewalt *f* elemental force.

'Urgroßeltern *pl* great-grandparents.

'Urgroßmutter *f* great-grandmother.

'Urgroßvater *m* great-grandfather.

'Urheber ['uːrheːbər] *m* (-s; -) author.

'Urheberrecht *n* copyright.

'urheberrechtlich *adj* copyright ...: ~ *geschützt* (protected by) copyright.

'Urheberschaft *f* (-; *no pl*) authorship.

urig ['uːrɪç] *adj* F → *urwüchsig.*

Urin [u'riːn] *m* (-s; -e) urine.

urinieren [uri'niːrən] *v/i* (h) urinate.

U'rinprobe *f* urine specimen.

U'rinuntersuchung *f* urine test.

'Urknall *m* (-[e]s; *no pl*) *phys.* big bang.

'ur'komisch *adj* F extremely funny.

'Urkunde *f* (-; -n) document, deed, record, *a.* *sports etc*: diploma. **'Urkundenfälschung** *f* forgery of documents.

'urkundlich *adj* documentary: *et. ~ belegen* document s.th.

'Urkundsbeamte *m* registrar.

'Urlaub ['uːrlaʊp] *m* (-[e]s; -e) leave (of absence) (*a.* ⚔), holiday(s), *esp. Am.* vacation: *auf ~, im ~* on holiday (vacation, ⚔ leave), *in ~ gehen* (*sein*) go (be) on holiday (*etc*); ~ *nehmen* go on leave; *e-n Tag ~ nehmen* take a day off. **'Urlauber** ['uːrlaʊbər] *m* (-s; -) holidaymaker, *esp. Am.* vacationist.

'Urlaubs|anspruch *m* holiday entitlement, *Am.* vacation privilege. **~geld** *n* holiday pay, *Am.* vacation money. **~tag** *m* (a day's) holiday (*esp. Am.* vacation). **~zeit** *f* holiday period.

'Urmensch *m* primitive man.

Urne ['ʊrnə] *f* (-; -n) **1.** urn. **2.** ballot box.

Urologe [uro'loːgə] *m* (-n; -n) urologist.

Urologie [urolo'giː] *f* (-; *no pl*) urology.

'ur'plötzlich I *adj* sudden, abrupt. **II** *adv* all of a sudden.

'**Ursache** f (-; -n) a) cause, reason, b) occasion: **keine ~!** don't mention it, that's all right. '**ursächlich** adj causal: **~er Zusammenhang** causality.

'**Urschrift** f original (text or copy).

'**Ursprung** m (-[e]s; ⁚e) origin: **s-n ~ haben in** (dat) originate in (or from); **deutschen ~s** of German origin. **ursprünglich** ['u:rʃprʏŋlɪç] adj original.

'**Ursprungsland** n country of origin.

Urteil ['ʊrtaɪl] n (-s; -e) 1. judg(e)ment, of jury: verdict (a. fig.), criminal court: sentence, divorce: decree: **das ~ verkünden** pronounce judg(e)ment (or sentence); **~ fällen** 2. 2. judg(e)ment, opinion: **sich ein ~ bilden** form a judg(e)ment (**über** acc about, on); **darüber kann ich mir kein ~ erlauben!** I am no judge of that).

urteilen ['ʊrtaɪlən] v/i (h) judge: **über j-n** (et.) ~ judge s.o. (s.th.); **ich urteile darüber anders** I take a different view (of it); ~ **Sie selbst!** judge for yourself;

nach s-m Aussehen (**s-n Worten**) **zu ~** judging by his looks (by what he says).

'**Urteils|begründung** f opinion. **⅘fähig** adj discerning. **~kraft** f (-; no pl) (power of) judg(e)ment. **~spruch** m → **Urteil** 1.

'**Urtext** m original text.

'**Urtrieb** m basic instinct.

urtümlich ['u:rty:mlɪç] adj **1.** original. **2.** archaic.

'**Urur...** great-great(-grandfather etc).

'**Urvolk** n **1.** primitive people. **2.** → **Ureinwohner**.

'**Urwald** m **1.** primeval forest. **2.** jungle.

urwüchsig ['u:rvy:ksɪç] adj **1.** original, natural. **2.** earthy, robust.

'**Urzeit** f primeval time: **vor ~en** a long, long time ago; **seit ~en** for ages.

'**Urzustand** m original state.

Utensilien [utɛn'zi:liən] pl utensils.

Uterus ['u:terʊs] m (-s; -ri) anat. uterus.

Utopie [uto'pi:] f (-; -n) a) utopia, b) wild dream. **utopisch** [u'to:pɪʃ] adj utopian, fantastic.

V

V, v [faʊ] n (-; -) V, v.

Vagabund [vaga'bʊnt] m (-en; -en) vagabond, tramp. **vagabundieren** [vagabʊn'di:rən] v/i (h) lead a vagabond life.

Vagina [va'gi:na] f (-; -nen) anat. vagina.

vakant [va'kant] adj vacant.

Vakuum ['va:kuʊm] n (-s; -kŭa) vacuum. **⅘verpackt** adj vacuum-packed.

Vakzine [vak'tsi:nə] f (-; -n) ⚕ vaccine.

Valenz [va'lɛnts] f (-; -en) valence.

Valuta [va'lu:ta] f (-; -ten) ✝ valuta, foreign currency.

Vampir ['vampi:r] m (-s; -e) vampire.

Vandale m etc → **Wandale** etc.

Vanille [va'nɪljə] f (-; no pl) ⚕ or gastr. vanilla. **~zucker** m vanilla sugar.

variabel [va'ria:bəl] adj variable.

Variable [va'ria:blə] f (-; -n) ⚕ variable.

Variante [va'riantə] f (-; -n) **1.** variant. **2.** version. **Variation** [varia'tsio:n] f (-; -en) variation.

Varieté [varie'te:] n (-s; -s), **~the͵ater** n

variety theatre, music hall, Am. vaudeville (theater).

variieren [vari'i:rən] v/t, v/i (h) vary.

Vasall [va'zal] m (-en; -en) vassal.

Va'sallenstaat m contp. satellite state.

Vase ['va:zə] f (-; -n) vase.

Vaseline [vaze'li:nə] f (-; no pl) vaseline.

Vater ['fa:tər] m (-s; ⁚) father (a. fig.), zo. sire: **er ist ~ von drei Kindern** he is a father of three (children); **er ist ganz der ~** he is a chip off the old block; humor. ~ **Staat** the State.

'**Vaterfi͵gur** f father figure.

'**Vaterland** n (-[e]s; ⁚er) one's native country. '**Vaterlandsliebe** f love of one's country, patriotism.

väterlich ['fɛ:tərlɪç] **I** adj fatherly, paternal. **II** adv like a father. '**väterlicherseits** adv on one's father's side: **Großvater** ~ paternal grandfather.

'**Vaterliebe** f paternal love.

'**vaterlos** adj fatherless.

'Vater|mord *m*, ~mörder *m* patricide.
'Vaterschaft *f* (-; *no pl*) 🚼 paternity: *Feststellung der ~* affiliation.
'Vaterschaftsklage *f* 🚼 paternity suit.
'Vater|stadt *f* hometown. ~stelle *f* ~ *vertreten* act as father (*bei* to).
Vater'unser *n* (-s; -) Lord's Prayer.
Vati ['fa:ti] *m* (-s; -s) F daddy, dad.
Vatikan [vati'ka:n] *m* (-s) vati'kanisch *adj* Vatican. Vati'kanstadt *f* Vatican City.
V-Ausschnitt ['faʊ-] *m* V-neck: *mit ~* V-necked.
Vegetarier [vege'ta:riər] *m* (-s; -) vegetarian. vege'tarisch [-rɪʃ] *adj* vegetarian: *~ leben* be a vegetarian.
Vegetation [vegeta'tsjo:n] *f* (-; -en) vegetation. vegetativ [-'ti:f] *adj* vegetative: *~es Nervensystem* autonomous nervous system. vegetieren [vege'ti:rən] *v/i* (h) *fig.* vegetate.
Vehikel [ve'hi:kəl] *n* (-s; -) F rattletrap.
Veilchen ['faɪlçən] *n* (-s; -) 1. ♀ violet: F *blau wie ein ~* drunk as a lord. 2. F *fig.* black eye. 'veilchenblau *adj* violet.
Vektor ['vɛktɔr] *m* (-s; -en [-'to:rən]) ℞ vector. ~rechnung *f* vector analysis.
Velours [və'lu:r] *m* (- [və'lu:rs]; - [və'lu:rs]) velour(s).
Ve'loursleder *n* suede (leather).
Ve'loursteppich *m* velvet-pile carpet.
Vene ['ve:nə] *f* (-; -n) *anat.* vein.
'Venenentzündung *f* 💊 phlebitis.
venerisch [ve'ne:rɪʃ] *adj* 💊 venereal.
Venezianer [vene'tsja:nər] *m* (-s; -), Vene'zianerin *f* (-; -nen), venezi'anisch *adj* Venetian.
Venezolaner [venetso'la:nər] *m* (-s; -), Venezo'lanerin *f* (-; -nen), venezo'lanisch *adj* Venezuelan.
venös [ve'nø:s] *adj* 💊 venous.
Ventil [vɛn'ti:l] *n* (-s; -e) 1. ♪, ☼ valve. 2. *fig.* outlet. Ventilation [vɛntila'tsjo:n] *f* (-; -en) a) ventilation, b) ventilating system. Ventilator [vɛnti'la:tɔr] *m* (-s; -en [-la'to:rən]) ventilator.
ver'abreden *v/t* (h) I *v/t* agree upon, arrange, *a.* fix (*date, place*): *vorher ~* prearrange. II *sich ~* (*mit j-m*) arrange to meet (s.o.), make a date (*or* an appointment) (with s.o.); *ich bin leider schon verabredet* I'm afraid I have a previous engagement. Ver'abredung *f*

(-; -en) 1. date, engagement, appointment. 2. agreement, arrangement.
ver'abreichen *v/t* (h) *j-m et.* ~ give s.o. s.th., *a.* administer s.th. to s.o.
ver'abscheuen *v/t* (h) abhor, detest.
verabschieden [vɛr'ʔapʃi:dən] (h) I *v/t* 1. say goodbye to. 2. discharge. 3. *parl.* pass (*bill etc*), adopt (*budget*). II *sich ~ von* → 1. Ver'abschiedung *f* (-; -en) 1. discharge. 2. *parl.* passing (*of bill etc*), adoption (*of budget*).
ver'achten *v/t* (h) despise, disdain, *a.* scorn: F *nicht zu ~* not to be sneezed at.
ver'achtenswert *adj* contemptible, despicable. Ver'ächter *m* (-s; -) despiser. ver'ächtlich *adj* 1. contemptuous, scornful: *~ machen* run s.o., *s.th.* down. 2. → verachtenswert.
Ver'achtung *f* (-; *no pl*) contempt, disdain, *a.* scorn: *mit ~ strafen* ignore.
ver'albern *v/t* (h) F *j-n* ~ pull s.o.'s leg.
verallgemeinern [fɛr'ʔalgə'maɪnərn] *v/t* (h) generalize. Verallge'meinerung *f* (-; -en) generalization.
ver'alten *v/t* (sn) become (out)dated (*or* obsolete, *views etc*: antiquated). ver'altet *adj* obsolete, (out)dated, *method etc*: antiquated: *~ sein* be out of date.
Veranda [ve'randa] *f* (-; -den) veranda(h).
ver'änderlich *adj* changeable, *a.* ling, ℞ variable: ℞ *~e Größe* variable.
Ver'änderlichkeit *f* (-; -en) changeability, *ling.*, ℞ variability.
ver'ändern (h) I *v/t* 1. (*an dat* on) alter, change. II *sich ~* 2. change: *sich zu s-m Vorteil (Nachteil) ~* change for the better (worse); *hier hat sich vieles verändert* there have been many changes. 3. change one's job. ver'ändert *adj* changed, different: *sie ist ganz ~* she has changed a lot. Ver'änderung *f* (-; -en) change.
verängstigt [-'ʔɛŋstɪçt] *adj* frightened.
ver'ankern *v/t* (h) ⚓, ☼ anchor: *fig. in der Verfassung verankert* laid down in the constitution.
ver'anlagen *v/t* (h) *taxation:* assess.
ver'anlagt *adj* (*zu, für* to) (💊 pre)disposed, (naturally) inclined: *künstlerisch ~ sein* have an artistic bent; *er ist praktisch ~* he is practical(ly minded); *romantisch ~ sein* have a romantic disposition. Ver'anlagung *f* (-; -en) 1.

605 **verbesserungsbedürftig**

taxation: assessment. **2.** (⚙ pre)disposition. **3.** inclination, *a.* talent(s).

ver'anlassen *v/t* (h) **1. et.** ~; ~, **daß et. getan wird** order (*or* arrange) s.th., see (to it) that s.th. is done; **das Nötige** ~ take the necessary steps. **2.** *j-n* ~ **et. zu tun** cause (*or* get) s.o. to do s.th., make s.o. do s.th.; **sich veranlaßt sehen zu** *inf* feel compelled to *inf*; **was hat ihn bloß dazu veranlaßt?** whatever made him do that? **Ver'anlassung** *f* (-; -en) **1.** (**zu, für** for) cause, motive: **ohne jede** ~ without provocation. **2.** **auf** ~ **von** (*or gen*) at the instigation of.

ver'anschaulichen [fɛr'ʔanʃaʊlɪçən] *v/t* (h) illustrate: **sich et.** ~ visualize s.th. **Ver'anschaulichung** *f* (-; -en) (**zur** ~ by way of) illustration.

ver'anschlagen *v/t* (h) ⚓ estimate (**auf** *acc* at): **zu hoch** ~ overestimate; **zu niedrig** ~ underestimate.

veranstalten [fɛr'ʔanʃtaltən] *v/t* (h) organize, arrange, stage (*a.* F *fig.*), give (*concert etc*). **Ver'anstalter** *m* (-s; -) organizer, *sports*: *a.* promoter. **Ver'anstaltung** *f* (-; -en) **1.** arrangement, organization, *fig.* staging. **2.** event, *a.* (public) function, *sports*: meeting, *Am.* meet, fixture. **Ver'anstaltungskalender** *m* calendar of events.

ver'antworten (h) **I** *v/t* answer for, take the responsibility for. **II** **sich** (*j-m gegenüber*) **für et.** ~ answer (*to s.o.*) for s.th. **ver'antwortlich** *adj* responsible (**für** for): *j-n* ~ **machen** hold s.o. responsible, *w.s.* blame s.o. (**für** for). **Ver'antwortlichkeit** *f* (; -en) responsibility. **Ver'antwortung** *f* (-; -en) (**die** ~ **tragen** bear [the] responsibility) responsibility; **auf Ihre eigene** ~**!** at your own risk; *j-n* **zur** ~ **ziehen** call s.o. to account; → **abwälzen**. **ver'antwortungsbewußt** *adj* responsible. **Ver'antwortungsbewußtsein** *n* sense of responsibility.

ver'antwortungslos *adj* irresponsible. **ver'antwortungsvoll** *adj* responsible.

veräppeln [fɛr'ʔɛpəln] *v/t* (h) F *j-n* ~ pull s.o.'s leg.

ver'arbeiten *v/t* (h) process (*a.* data), *physiol. or fig.* digest, use (*in dat, zu* in, for): **et.** ~ **zu** manufacture s.th. into; **~de Industrie** processing industries. **Ver'arbeitung** *f* (-; -en) **1.** processing, manufacture, treatment. **2.** *physiol. or*

fig. digestion. **3.** workmanship.

ver'ärgern *v/t* (h) annoy.

ver'armen *v/i* (sn) become poor. **ver'armt** *adj* impoverished. **Ver'armung** *f* (-; -en) *a. fig.* impoverishment.

ver'arschen *v/t* (h) V *j-n* ~ take the mickey out of s.o., *by satire*: send s.o. up.

verarzten [fɛr'ʔartstən] *v/t* (h) F *j-n* ~ fix s.o. up.

ver'ästeln [fɛr'ʔɛstəln] **sich** ~ (h) ramify. **Ver'ästelung** *f* (-; -en) ramification.

ver'ausgaben: sich ~ (h) **1.** overspend. **2.** *fig.* spend o.s.

ver'auslagen *v/t* (h) lay out.

ver'äußern *v/t* (h) sell, dispose of. **Ver'äußerung** *f* (-; -en) sale, disposal.

Verb [vɛrp] *n* (-s; -en) *ling.* verb.

verbal [vɛr'baːl] *adj* verbal. **verbalisieren** [vɛrbali'ziːrən] *v/t* (h) verbalize.

Verband [fɛr'bant] *m* (-[e]s; ⱨe) **1.** 🏥 bandage, dressing. **2.** union, federation. **3.** ✕ unit, ✈ formation.

Verband(s)kasten *m* 🏥 first-aid kit. **~material** *n* dressing material. **~mull** *m* surgical gauze.

ver'bannen *v/t* (h) (**aus** from) exile, banish (*a. fig.*). **Ver'bannte** *m, f* (-n; -n) exile. **Ver'bannung** *f* (-; -en) exile, banishment (*a. fig.*).

verbarrikadieren [fɛrbarika'diːrən] *v/t* (h) barricade (**sich** o.s.).

ver'bauen *v/t* (h) **1.** block up, obstruct: *fig. j-m* **sich)** **den Weg** ~ bar s.o.'s (one's) way (**zu** to). **2.** build up (*area*). **3.** use (*material*).

ver'bauern *v/i* (sn) become countrified.

ver'beamten *v/t* (h) *j-n* ~ give s.o. the rank of a civil servant.

ver'beißen (*irr, no* -ge-, h, → **beißen**) **I** *v/t* **1.** suppress (*pain etc*), *a.* bite back (*laughter, tears, etc*): **er konnte sich ein Lächeln nicht** ~ he couldn't keep a straight face. **II sich** ~ **in** (*acc*) **2.** *dog etc*: sink its teeth into. **3.** *fig. person*: get set on, keep grimly at.

ver'bergen *v/t* (*irr, no* -ge-, h, → **bergen**) conceal, hide.

ver'bessern (h) **I** *v/t* **1.** improve, better (*record*). **2.** correct (*mistake etc*). **II sich** ~ **3.** improve: **sich finanziell** ~ better o.s. **4.** correct o.s.

Ver'besserung *f* (-; -en) **1.** improvement, betterment. **2.** correction.

ver'besserungsbedürftig *adj* in need

of improvement. **~fähig** *adj* capable of improvement. **Qvorschlag** *m* suggestion for improvement.

ver'beugen: *sich* **~** (h) bow (**vor** *dat* to). **Ver'beugung** *f* (-; -en) bow (**vor** *dat* to).

ver'beulen *v/t* (h) batter, dent.

ver'biegen *v/t* (*irr, no* -ge-, h, → **biegen**) twist, bend.

ver'bieten *v/t* (*irr, no* -ge-, h, → **bieten**) **j-m das Haus (das Rauchen) ~** forbid s.o. the house (to smoke); → **verboten.**

ver'billigen *v/t* (h) reduce *s.th.* in price. **ver'billigt** *adj* reduced (*price etc*), (*tickets etc*) at reduced prices.

ver'binden *v/t* (*irr, no* -ge-, h, → **binden**) **1. ⚕** bandage: **j-n ~** dress s.o.'s wounds; **j-m die Augen ~** blindfold s.o.; → **verbunden 1. 2.** (*a. sich ~*) (*mit* with) connect (*a. ⚓, ⚙, teleph. or fig.*), combine (*a. ⚗*), unite: *teleph.* **ich verbinde Sie** I'll put you through (*mit* to); **das Angenehme mit dem Nützlichen ~** combine business with pleasure; *sich mit j-m ~* associate with s.o. **ver'bindend** *adj fig.* connecting (*text, words, etc*).

verbindlich [fɛrˈbɪntlɪç] *adj* **1.** (*für* upon) obligatory, binding: *~e Zusage* definite promise. **2.** obliging, courteous, friendly. **Ver'bindlichkeit** *f* (-; -en) **1.** *no pl* obligation, binding character. **2.** *no pl* obligingness, friendliness. **3.** *pl* courtesies. **4.** *pl* ✝ liabilities.

Ver'bindung *f* (-; -en) **1.** connection (*a. ⚙, teleph.*), combination: *in ~ mit* a) in conjunction with, b) in connection with; *in ~ bringen mit* connect (*or associate*) s.o., s.th. with. **2.** (*bus etc*) connection. **3.** a) union, association, b) students' society, *Am.* fraternity: *e-e ~ eingehen* join together (*mit* with). **4.** contact (*a. ✕*), *pl* connections: *mit j-m ~ aufnehmen* (*or in ~ treten*) contact s.o., get in touch with s.o.; *mit j-m in ~ stehen* (*bleiben*) be (keep) in touch with s.o.; *s-e ~en spielen lassen* pull a few strings.

Ver'bindungs... connecting (*cable, line, road, etc*). **~mann** *m* contact. **~offizier** *m* liaison officer. **~stück** *n* ⚙ connecting piece, ⚡ connector, *a.* adaptor.

ver'bissen *adj* grim, dogged. **Ver'bissenheit** *f* (-; *no pl*) doggedness.

ver'bitten *v/t* (*irr, no* -ge-, h, → **bitten**) *sich et. ~* not to stand for s.th.; *das*

verbitte ich mir! I won't have that.

ver'bittert *adj* embittered, bitter. **Ver'bitterung** *f* (-; *no pl*) bitterness.

ver'blassen [fɛrˈblasən] *v/i* (sn) fade.

ver'bleiben *v/i* (*irr, no* -ge-, sn, → **bleiben**) **1.** remain: *verbleibe ich ... in letter:* (I remain,) Yours faithfully ... **2.** *wir sind so verblieben, daß* we agreed (*or arranged*) that.

verbleit [fɛrˈblaɪt] *adj* leaded.

ver'blenden *v/t* (h) **1. △** face, line. **2.** *fig.* blind: *von Haß verblendet* blind with hatred. **Ver'blendung** *f* (-; -en) **1. △** facing. **2.** *no pl fig.* blindness.

verblichen [fɛrˈblɪçən] *adj* faded.

verblöden [fɛrˈbløːdən] **I** *v/i* (sn) go dotty, go daft (*bei* with). **II** *v/t* (h) dull *s.o.*'s mind, stultify.

verblüffen [fɛrˈblʏfən] *v/t* (h) amaze, baffle. **ver'blüffend** *adj* amazing. **ver'blüfft** *adj* amazed, *pred* taken aback. **Ver'blüffung** *f* (-; *no pl*) amazement.

ver'blühen *v/i* (sn) *a. fig.* fade, wither.

ver'bluten *v/i* (sn) bleed to death.

ver'bocken *v/t* (h) F bungle, botch (up).

ver'bohren: *sich ~* (h) F *fig.* become obsessed (*in acc* with). **ver'bohrt** *adj fig.* stubborn, pigheaded.

ver'borgen[1] *v/t* (h) lend (out).

ver'borgen[2] *adj* hidden: *~ halten* conceal; *sich ~ halten* hide (o.s.); *im ~en* in secret, secretly.

Verbot [fɛrˈboːt] *n* (-[e]s; -e) prohibition (*gen* of), ban (*gen, von* on). **ver'boten** *adj* a) forbidden, prohibited, banned, b) illegal: *es war uns ~ zu inf* we were forbidden (*or not allowed*) to *inf*; *ist das etwa ~?* F is there a law against it?; *Rauchen ~!* no smoking!; F *sie sah ~ aus* she looked a sight. **ver'botenerweise** *adv ~ et. tun* do s.th. although it is forbidden. **Ver'botsschild** *n* no parking (*or no smoking etc*) sign.

verbrämen [fɛrˈbrɛːmən] *v/t* (h) **1.** a) border, trim, b) fur. **2.** *fig.* gloss over. **Ver'brauch** *m* (-[e]s; *no pl*) consumption (*an dat* of).

ver'brauchen (h) **I** *v/t* consume, use up. **II** *sich ~ fig.* exhaust o.s., wear o.s. out. **Ver'braucher** *m* (-s; -) consumer. **~markt** *m* hypermarket. **~schutz** *m* consumer protection. **~umfrage** *f* consumer survey. **~verhalten** *n* consumer behavio(u)r.

Ver'brauchsgüter *pl* consumer goods.
ver'braucht *adj a. fig.* used(-)up, spent, worn(-)out: **~e Luft** stale air.
ver'brechen *v/t* (*irr, no* -ge-, h, → **brechen**) F *humor.* perpetrate: **was hat er verbrochen?** what has he done?
Ver'brechen *n* (-s; -) *a. fig.* crime.
Ver'brecher *m* (-s; -) criminal. **~album** *n* rogues' gallery. **~bande** *f* gang of criminals.
Ver'brecherin *f* (-; -nen) criminal.
ver'brecherisch *adj* criminal.
ver'breiten *v/t* (*a.* **sich ~**) (h) spread (*in dat, auf dat, über acc* over), *a.* disseminate (*ideas etc*): (**weit**) **verbreitet** widespread, *a.* widely read.
verbreitern [fɛr'braɪtərn] *v/t* (*a.* **sich ~**) (h) widen.
Ver'breitung *f* (-; *no pl*) spread(ing), *a.* dissemination.
ver'brennen (*irr, no* -ge-, h, → **brennen**) **I** *v/t* burn, burn up (*calories*), cremate (*corpse*), scorch: **sich den Mund ~** burn one's mouth, *fig.* put one's foot in it; ✗ **verbrannte Erde** scorched earth. **II** *v/i* a) burn, b) be burnt to death.
Ver'brennung *f* (-; -en) **1.** burning, ⚙ combustion. **2.** cremation. **3.** ⚕ burn: → **Grad**.
Ver'brennungs|motor *m* combustion engine. **~ofen** *m* incinerator.
verbrieft [fɛr'briːft] *adj* vested (*right*).
ver'bringen *v/t* (*irr, no* -ge-, h, → **bringen**) spend, pass.
verbrüdern [fɛr'bryːdərn] **sich ~** (h) fraternize. **Ver'brüderung** *f* (-; -en) fraternization.
ver'brühen (h) **I** *v/t* scald (**sich die Hand** one's hand). **II sich ~** scald o.s.
ver'buchen *v/t* (h) **1.** ✝ book. **2.** *fig.* achieve, F notch up (*success etc*).
ver'bummeln *v/t* (h) F **1.** waste, idle away. **2.** a) lose, b) clean forget.
Ver'bund *m* (-[e]s; -e) network, (integrated) system: **im ~ arbeiten** cooperate; → **Medien-**, **Verkehrsverbund**. **~bauweise** *f* sandwich construction.
verbunden [fɛr'bʊndən] *adj* **1.** dressed (*wound*): **mit ~en Augen** blindfold. **2.** ~ **sein mit** a) be connected with, entail (*difficulties, costs, etc*), b) be attached to; **j-m ~ sein für** be obliged to s.o. for.
verbünden [fɛr'byndən] **sich ~** (h) (**mit** with) form an alliance, ally o.s. (*a.* to).

Ver'bundenheit *f* (-; *no pl*) (**mit**) attachment (to), bond(s), solidarity (with).
Ver'bündete *m, f* (-n; -n) *a. fig.* ally.
Ver'bundglas *n* laminated glass.
ver'bürgen *v/t* (h) guarantee: **sich ~ für** *a.* answer for. **verbürgt** [-'bʏrkt] *adj* authentic, established (*fact etc*).
ver'chromen *v/t* (h) chromium-plate.
Verdacht [fɛr'daxt] *m* (-[e]s; -e) (**~ erregen** arouse) suspicion: **j-n im ~ haben** (**et. getan zu haben**) suspect s.o. (of having done s.th.); **in ~ kommen** be suspected; **~ schöpfen** become suspicious, F smell a rat; **bei ihm besteht ~ auf Krebs** he is suspected of having cancer; F **auf ~** on spec; → **lenken** 3.
verdächtig [fɛr'dɛçtɪç] *adj* suspicious, suspect, *a.* dubious, F fishy: **des Diebstahls ~ sein** be suspected of theft.
Ver'dächtige *m, f* (-n; -n) suspect.
verdächtigen [fɛr'dɛçtɪgən] *v/t* (h) **j-n ~** cast suspicion on s.o., suspect s.o. (**gen** of; **et. getan zu haben** of having done s.th.). **Ver'dächtigung** *f* (-; -en) **1.** casting suspicion (**gen** on). **2.** suspicion.
Ver'dachtsmo,ment *n* suspicious fact.
verdammen [fɛr'damən] *v/t* (h) (**zu** to) condemn, *a. eccl.* damn. **ver'dammt I** *adj* **1.** damned: **dazu ~ sein zu** *inf* be condemned (*or* doomed) to *inf*. **2.** F damn(ed), blasted, *Br. sl. a.* bloody: **~ (nochmal)!** damn (it)!, blast it (all)! **II** *adv* F damn(ed), *Br. sl.* bloody: **~ kalt** *a.* beastly cold. **Ver'dammung** *f* (-; -en) condemnation, *a. eccl.* damnation.
ver'dampfen *v/t* (h), *v/i* (sn) evaporate.
ver'danken *v/t* (h) **j-m et. ~** owe s.th. to s.o., be indebted to s.o. for s.th.; **es ist ihr zu ~, daß** it is due to her that.
verdarb [fɛr'darp] *pret of* **verderben**.
verdattert [fɛr'datərt] *adj* F dazed.
verdauen [fɛr'daʊən] *v/t* (h) digest.
ver'daulich *adj* (**leicht ~** easily) digestible; **schwer ~** hard to digest.
Ver'daulichkeit *f* (-; *no pl*) digestibility.
Ver'dauung *f* (-; *no pl*) digestion.
Ver'dauungs|appa,rat *m* digestive system. **~beschwerden** *pl* indigestion, digestive trouble.
Ver'deck *n* (-[e]s; -e) (folding) top, hood.
ver'decken *v/t* (h) cover, hide, *a.* ⚙ conceal: **verdeckte (Polizei)Aktion** undercover operation.

ver'denken v/t (irr, no -ge-, h, → **denken**) **ich kann es ihm nicht ~ (, daß)** I can't blame him (if).

verderben [fɛr'dɛrbən] (verdarb, verdorben) **I** v/i (sn) spoil, go bad, perish. **II** v/t (h) spoil, a. ruin, morally: corrupt: **sich den Magen (die Augen) ~** upset one's stomach (ruin one's eyes); **j-m die Freude (den Appetit) ~** spoil s.o.'s fun (appetite); F **es mit j-m ~** fall out with s.o.; **er will es mit niemandem ~** he tries to please everybody. **Ver'derben** n (-s; no pl) ruin: **in sein ~ rennen** rush (headlong) into disaster. **verderblich** [~pliç] adj **1.** perishable (goods). **2.** fig. ruinous (effect etc), corrupting (influence etc).

ver'deutlichen v/t (h) **j-m et. ~** make s.th. clear (or explain s.th.) to s.o.

ver'dichten (h) **I** v/t **1.** ⚙ compress, a. 🔥 condense. **II** sich **~ 2.** condense, fog: thicken. **3.** fig. suspicion etc: grow stronger. **Ver'dichtung** f (-; -en) condensation, mot. compression.

ver'dicken v/t (a. **sich ~**) (h) thicken.

ver'dienen (h) **I** v/t **1.** earn, make (money): **sich et. nebenbei ~** make some money on the side. **2.** fig. deserve (punishment, praise, etc): **er hat es nicht besser verdient!** (it) serves him right!; → **verdient. II** v/i **gut ~** earn a good salary (or wage); **an e-r Sache gut ~** make a good profit on s.th.

Ver'diener m (-s; -) (salary or wage) earner, breadwinner.

Ver'dienst¹ n (-[e]s; -e) fig. merit: **es ist ihr ~, daß** it is thanks to her that; → **erwerben.**

Ver'dienst² m (-[e]s; -e) income, earnings, salary.

Ver'dienstausfall m lost earnings.

ver'dienstvoll adj deserving (person), commendable (deed etc).

ver'dient adj fig. **1.** deserving, man etc of merit: **sich ~ machen um** do s.o., s.th. a great service. **2.** a) well-deserved, due (punishment), b) well-earned (victory).

ver'dienter'maßen adv deservedly.

ver'dolmetschen v/t (h) **j-m et. ~** translate s.th. for (fig. explain s.th. to) s.o.

ver'donnern v/t (h) F condemn s.o. (**zu** to); **j-n ~, et. zu tun** make s.o. do s.th.

ver'doppeln v/t (a. **sich ~**) (h) double. **Ver'dopplung** f (-; -en) doubling.

verdorben [fɛr'dɔrbən] **I** pp of **verderben. II** adj spoiled (a. fig.), a. bad, fig. a. ruined, morally: a. corrupt: **~er Magen** upset stomach, indigestion.

verdorren [fɛr'dɔrən] v/i (sn) wither.

verdrahten [fɛr'dra:tən] v/t (h) ⚡ wire.

ver'drängen v/t (h) **1.** → **vertreiben** 1. **2.** fig. a) displace (a. ⚓, phys.), b) supersede, replace: **j-n ~** push s.o. out (sports: **vom ersten Platz** from first place); **j-n aus s-r Stellung ~** oust s.o. from his position. **3.** psych. repress, suppress. **4.** dismiss (a problem etc). **Ver'drängung** f (-; -en) ousting, displacement (a. ⚓, phys.), fig. replacement, psych. repression, suppression.

verdreckt [fɛr'drɛkt] adj filthy, soiled.

ver'drehen v/t (h) **1.** twist (**j-m den Arm** s.o.'s arm): **die Augen ~** roll one's eyes; **j-m den Kopf ~** turn s.o.'s head. **2.** F fig. twist, distort (words etc), pervert (law). **ver'dreht** adj F fig. **1.** crazy, cranky. **2.** confused. **Ver'drehung** f (-; -en) twisting, fig. a. distortion (of facts etc).

ver'dreifachen v/t (h) treble.

verdrießen [fɛr'dri:sən] v/t (verdroß, verdrossen, h) annoy.

ver'drießlich adj morose, sullen.

verdrossen [fɛr'drɔsən] adj **1.** sullen. **2.** listless. **Ver'drossenheit** f (-; no pl) **1.** sullenness. **2.** listlessness.

ver'drücken (h) **F I** v/t polish off. **II** sich **~** slip away, beat it.

Verdruß [fɛr'drʊs] m (-sses; no pl) annoyance: **~ bereiten** cause s.o. trouble.

ver'duften v/i (sn) F beat it, scram.

verdummen [fɛr'dʊmən] **I** v/t (h) dull s.o.'s mind, stultify, brainwash (the people). **II** v/i (sn) become stultified.

ver'dunkeln v/t (h) darken (a. **sich ~**), black out, a. fig. cloud, fig. obscure. **Ver'dunklung** f (-; -en) a) darkening, b) blackout. **Ver'dunklungsgefahr** f ⚖ danger of collusion.

verdünnen [fɛr'dʏnən] v/t (h) dilute, thin (down) (paint). **Ver'dünner** m (-s; -) thinner. **Ver'dünnung** f (-; -en) dilution, thinning (down).

ver'dunsten v/t (h), v/i (sn) evaporate. **Ver'dunster** m (-s; -) humidifier. **Ver'dunstung** f (-; no pl) evaporation.

ver'dursten v/i (sn) die of thirst.

verdüstern [fɛr'dy:stərn] sich **~** (h) a. fig. darken.

verdutzt [fɛr'dʊtst] *adj* nonplussed, *pred* taken aback.

ver'ebben *v/i* (sn) *a. fig.* ebb away.

veredeln [fɛr'ʔe:dəln] *v/t* (h) **1.** ennoble. **2.** refine, ⊙ *a.* process, finish. **3.** ✗ graft, bud. **Ver'edelungsindu,strie** *f* processing industry.

ver'ehren *v/t* (h) a) revere, *a. fig.* adore, worship, b) admire: *Verehrte Anwesende!* Ladies and Gentlemen! **Ver'ehrer** *m* (-s; -), **Ver'ehrerin** *f* (-; -nen) **1.** admirer. **2.** fan. **Ver'ehrerpost** *f* fan mail. **Ver'ehrung** *f* (-; *no pl*) a) (~ *zollen* pay) reverence (*dat* to), *a. fig.* worship, adoration, b) admiration.

ver'ehrungswürdig *adj* venerable.

vereidigen [fɛr'ʔaɪdɪgən] *v/t* (h) (*auf acc* on) put *s.o.* under an oath, swear *s.o.* in. **vereidigt** [fɛr'ʔaɪdɪçt] *adj* sworn. **Ver'eidigung** *f* (-; -en) swearing-in.

Ver'ein *m* (-[e]s; -e) **1.** club: F *contp.* **ein** *netter* ~ a fine bunch. **2.** ✝ society, association. **3.** *im* ~ *mit* together with. **ver'einbar** *adj* (*mit* with) compatible, consistent. **ver'einbaren** *v/t* (h) **1.** agree (up)on, arrange: *vorher* ~ prearrange. **2.** reconcile (*mit* with). **Ver'einbarkeit** *f* (-; *no pl*) compatibility (*mit* with). **ver'einbart** *adj* agreed: *zur* ~*en Zeit* at the time agreed upon. **Ver'einbarung** *f* (-; -en) agreement, arrangement: *e-e* ~ *treffen* make an agreement; *laut* ~ as agreed; *nach* ~ by agreement; *Gehalt nach* ~ salary negotiable.

ver'einen *v/t* → **vereinigen**: *mit vereinten Kräften* → a combined effort.

ver'einfachen *v/t* (h) simplify. **Ver'einfachung** *f* (-; -en) simplification.

ver'einheitlichen *v/t* (h) standardize. **Ver'einheitlichung** *f* (-; -en) standardization.

ver'einigen *v/t* (*a. sich* ~) (h) a) unite (*zu* into), combine, join (together), ✝ amalgamate, b) assemble, *a.* rally: *Vereinigte Staaten* (*von Amerika*) United States (of America) (*abbr.* U.S.[A.]). **Ver'einigung** *f* (-; -en) **1.** *no pl* uniting (*etc*), *pol.* unification, ✝ merger. **2.** association, union.

ver'einnahmen *v/t* (h) F monopolize. **ver'einsamen** *v/i* (sn) become isolated (*or* lonely). **Ver'einsamung** *f* (-; *no pl*) (growing) isolation.

Ver'eins|haus *n* clubhouse. **~kame,rad** *m* clubmate. **~kasse** *f* club funds.

ver'einzelt I *adj* isolated, sporadic, *a.* scattered (*showers*). **II** *adv* a) sporadically, now and then, b) here and there.

ver'eisen I *v/t* (h) ✗ freeze. **II** *v/i* (sn) ice over, ✗ *etc* ice up, freeze over: *vereiste Straßen* icy roads.

ver'eiteln *v/t* (h) thwart, frustrate (*plan etc*), prevent (*deed*).

ver'eitert *adj* ✗ septic.

ver'ekeln *v/t* *j-m et.* ~ put s.o. off s.th.

verelenden [fɛr'ʔe:lɛndən] *v/i* (sn) be reduced to poverty. **Ver'elendung** *f* (-; *no pl*) impoverishment.

ver'enden *v/i* (sn) perish, die.

ver'engen *v/t* (*a. sich* ~) (h) narrow (*a. fig.*), pupil: contract. **Ver'engung** *f* (-; -en) **1.** narrowing, contraction. **2.** narrow part (*in dat* of).

ver'erben (h) **I** *v/t* *j-m et.* ~ leave (*✗* transmit) s.th. to s.o. **II** *sich* ~ *a.* ✗ *or* *fig.* be passed on (*or* down) (*auf acc* to). **vererbt** [-'ʔɛrpt] *adj biol.* inherited, hereditary. **Ver'erbung** *f* (-; *no pl*) *biol.* heredity, (hereditary) transmission.

Ver'erbungs|gesetze *pl* laws of heredity. **~lehre** *f* genetics.

verewigen [fɛr'ʔe:vɪgən] *v/t* (h) immortalize.

ver'fahren¹ (*irr, no* -ge-, → *fahren*) **I** *v/i* (sn) (*nach* on) proceed, act: ~ *mit* deal with, treat. **II** *v/t* (h) use up (*petrol*), spend *money, time* driving (around). **III** *sich* ~ get lost.

ver'fahren² *adj* muddled, tangled: *e-e* ~*e Sache* a (great) muddle.

Ver'fahren *n* (-s; -) **1.** procedure, method, process. **2.** ⚖ a) procedure, b) proceedings: *ein* ~ *einleiten* take (legal) proceedings (*gegen* against).

Ver'fahrens|frage *f* ⚖ procedural question. **~technik** *f* process technology. **~weise** *f* → **Verfahren** 1.

Ver'fall *m* (-[e]s; *no pl*) **1.** decay, *a.* dilapidation, ruin, *a.* ✝ decline, (*moral*) degeneration, corruption. **2.** ✝ expiry.

ver'fallen¹ *v/i* (*irr, no* -ge-, sn, → *fallen*) **1.** decay, dilapidate, *building etc: a.* go to ruin, *culture, empire, etc: a.* decline, *patient:* waste away. **2.** become addicted (*dat* to): *j-m* ~ become s.o.'s slave. **3.** (*wieder*) ~ *in* (*acc*) fall (back) into. **4.** ~ *auf* (*acc*) hit (up)on (*an idea etc*); *wie ist er nur darauf* ~? what on earth made him think (*or* do) that? **5.** *ticket:* expire, *pawn:* become forfeited. **ver'fallen²** *adj* **1.** decayed, *a.* dilapidated. **2.** *ticket etc:* expired, *pawn:* forfeited. **3.** addicted (*dat* to); *j-m ~ sein* be s.o.'s slave.

Ver'falls|datum *f* best-before (*Am.* pull, *pharm.* sell-by) date. **~erscheinung** *f* sign of decay. **~tag** *m* ✝ expiry date.

ver'fälschen *v/t* (h) **1.** adulterate (*food etc*). **2.** falsify, distort (*facts etc*).

Ver'fälschung *f* (-; -en) **1.** adulteration. **2.** falsification, distortion.

ver'fangen (*irr, no* -ge-, h, → *fangen*) **I** *v/i* work (*bei* with): *das verfängt bei mir nicht a.* that cuts no ice with me. **II** *sich ~ a.* fig. get caught (*in* dat in).

verfänglich [fɛrˈfɛŋlɪç] *adj* trick (*question*), compromising, awkward (*situation etc*).

ver'färben: sich ~ (h) change colo(u)r, *leaves:* turn.

ver'fassen *v/t* (h) write, compose, draw up. **Ver'fasser** *m* (-s; -), **Ver'fasserin** *f* (-; -nen) author, writer.

Ver'fassung *f* (-; -en) **1.** *no pl* a) state, condition, b) frame of mind: *in guter ~* in good condition (*or* shape), in a good state (of health). **2.** *pol.* constitution.

Ver'fassungs|änderung *f* constitutional amendment. **~beschwerde** *f* constitutional complaint. **~bruch** *m* breach of the constitution. **2feindlich** *adj* anticonstitutional. **~gericht** *n* constitutional court. **~klage** *f* complaint of unconstitutionality. **2mäßig**, **2rechtlich** *adj* constitutional. **~schutz** *m* protection of the constitution. **2widrig** *adj* unconstitutional.

ver'faulen *v/i* (sn) rot, decay.

ver'fechten *v/t* (*irr, no* -ge-, h, → *fechten*) stand up for. **Ver'fechter** *m* (-s; -), **Ver'fechterin** *f* (-; -nen) advocate.

ver'fehlen *v/t* (h) miss (*um* by): *s-n Beruf verfehlt haben* have missed one's vocation; → *Wirkung* 1, *Zweck* 1.

ver'fehlt *adj* wrong, misguided.

Ver'fehlung *f* (-; -en) offen/ce (*Am.* -se).

verfeinden [fɛrˈfaɪndən] *sich ~* (h) become enemies; *sich mit j-m ~* make an enemy of s.o. **ver'feindet** *adj* hostile: *~ sein* be enemies.

verfeinern [fɛrˈfaɪnərn] *v/t* (h) refine. **Ver'feinerung** *f* (-; -en) refinement.

ver'femen *v/t* (h) **1.** ostracize. **2.** ban.

Ver'fettung *f* (-; -en) 🜏 adiposis.

ver'feuern *v/t* (h) **1.** a) burn, b) use up. **2.** fire (*ammunition etc*).

ver'filmen *v/t* (h) film, adapt *novel etc* for the screen.

Ver'filmung *f* (-; -en) **1.** filming. **2.** film version, screen adaptation.

ver'filzen *v/i* (h) felt, *hair:* mat.

ver'finstern *v/t* (h) darken.

ver'flachen *v/i* (sn) **1.** flatten. **2.** *fig.* degenerate (*zu* into).

ver'flechten *v/t* (*irr, no* -ge-, h, → *flechten*) (*a. sich ~*) interweave (*a. fig.*), ✝ interlock: → **verflochten**. **Ver'flechtung** *f* (-; -en) interweaving (*a. fig.*), *fig.* entanglement, ✝ interlocking.

ver'fliegen (*irr, no* -ge-, → *fliegen*) **I** *v/i* (sn) **1.** *alcohol etc:* evaporate. **2.** *fig.* vanish, *time etc:* fly. **II sich ~** get lost.

verflixt [fɛrˈflɪkst] *adj* F blasted, damn(ed): *~!* blast!, damn (it)!

verflochten [fɛrˈflɔxtən] *adj* interwoven (*a. fig.*), *fig.* (en)tangled, ✝ interlocked.

ver'flossen *adj* **1.** past (*time*). **2.** F ex-...

ver'fluchen *v/t* (h) curse.

ver'flucht → **verdammt**.

verflüchtigen [fɛrˈflʏçtɪɡən] *sich ~* (h) evaporate, *fig. a.* disappear.

verflüssigen [fɛrˈflʏsɪɡən] *v/t* (*a. sich ~*) (h) liquefy. **Ver'flüssigung** *f* (-; -en) liquefaction.

ver'folgen *v/t* (h) **1.** pursue (*a. fig. policy, career, etc*), chase, *a. hunt.* track: *j-n ~ thought etc:* haunt s.o.; *strafrechtlich ~* prosecute; *gerichtlich ~* take legal steps against. **2.** follow (*trail, a. fig. events, progress, etc*). **3.** *esp. pol.* persecute. **Ver'folger** *m* (-s; -) pursuer, *pol. etc* persecutor. **Ver'folgte** *m, f* (-n; -n) victim of persecution, (political) persecutee. **Ver'folgung** *f* (-; -en) pursuit (*a. cycling or fig.*), *pol. etc* persecution: *strafrechtliche ~* (criminal) prosecution. **Ver'folgungswahn** *m* persecution complex.

ver'formen *v/t* (*a. sich ~*) (h) deform. **Ver'formung** *f* (-; -en) deformation.

ver'frachten *v/t* (h) freight, ⚓ *or Am.* ship: *F j-n in ein Taxi (ins Bett) ~* bundle s.o. off into a taxi (to bed).

verfremden [fɛrˈfrɛmdən] *v/t* (h) alienate. **Ver'fremdung** *f* (-; -en) alienation.

ver'fressen *adj* F greedy.

ver'froren *adj* ~ *sein* feel the cold (very easily); ~ *aussehen* look frozen.

ver'früht *adj* premature.

verfügbar [fɛr'fy:kbaːr] *adj* available.

Ver'fügbarkeit *f* (-; *no pl*) availability.

ver'fugen *v/t* (h) ⚙ point.

ver'fügen (h) **I** *v/t* order: *testamentarisch* ~ decree by will. **II** *v/i* ~ *über* (*acc*) have *s.th.*, *s.th.* at one's disposal, dispose of, possess, have; *frei* ~ *können über* (*acc*) be able to do what one wants with. **Ver'fügung** *f* (-; -en) **1.** order, *adm.* decree: *laut* ~ as ordered; → *einstweilig, letztwillig*. **2.** (*über acc* of) disposal, ⚖ disposition: *zur* ~ *stehen* (*stellen*) be (make) available, *j-m* be (place) at s.o.'s disposal; *sich zur* ~ *stellen* offer one's services, volunteer (*für* for); *sein Amt zur* ~ *stellen* tender one's resignation. **Ver'fügungsgewalt** *f* (-; *no pl*) control (*über acc* of).

ver'führen *v/t* (h) seduce. **Ver'führer** *m* (-s; -) seducer. **Ver'führerin** *f* (-; -nen) seductress. **ver'führerisch** *adj* **1.** seductive. **2.** *fig.* tempting. **Ver'führung** *f* (-; -en) **1.** seduction. **2.** *fig.* temptation. **Ver'führungskünste** *pl* powers of seduction.

ver'fünffachen *v/t* (*a. sich* ~) (h) quintuple.

ver'füttern *v/t* (h) feed.

Ver'gabe *f* (-; -n) placing (*of orders etc*), awarding (*of prizes*), allocation (*of funds*).

vergällen [fɛr'ɡɛlən] *v/t* (h) **1.** denature (*alcohol*). **2.** *fig.* sour, spoil.

ver'gammeln F **I** *v/i* (sn) rot, *person*: go to seed. **II** *v/t* (h) laze away (*time*). **ver'gammelt** *adj* F scruffy, seedy.

vergangen [fɛr'ɡaŋən] *adj* past: *~e Woche, in der ~en Woche* last week. **Ver'gangenheit** *f* (-; *no pl*) past (*a. fig.*), *ling.* past tense: *politische* ~ political background; → *ruhen*.

Ver'gangenheitsbewältigung *f* coming to terms with the past.

vergänglich [fɛr'ɡɛŋlɪç] *adj* transitory, transient. **Ver'gänglichkeit** *f* (-; *no pl*) transitoriness, transience.

vergasen [fɛr'ɡaːzən] *v/t* (h) **1.** 🦌 gasify. **2.** gas.

Ver'gaser *m* (-s; -) *mot.* carburet(t)or.

vergaß [fɛr'ɡaːs] *pret of* **vergessen**.

Ver'gasung *f* (-; -en) **1.** 🦌 gasification. **2.** gassing.

ver'geben¹ (*irr, no* -ge-, h, → *geben*) **I** *v/t* **1.** (*an acc*) give *s.th.* away (to), place *order etc* (with), assign *work etc* (to), award *prize* (to), allocate *funds* (to), grant *scholarship* (to). **2.** *j-m et.* ~ forgive s.o. (for doing) s.th. **3.** *e-e Chance* ~ miss (*or* give away) the chance. **II** *v/i* **4.** *j-m* ~ forgive s.o. **5.** *sports:* give away the chance, shoot wide. **ver'geben²** *adj* post: filled, *work etc:* assigned: *noch nicht* ~ open, still vacant.

ver'gebens *adj pred and adv* in vain.

vergeblich [fɛr'ɡeːplɪç] **I** *adj* vain, futile, useless. **II** *adv* in vain.

Ver'geblichkeit *f* (-; *no pl*) futility.

Ver'gebung *f* (-; *no pl*) **1.** (*j-n um* ~ *bitten* ask s.o.'s) forgiveness. **2.** → *Vergabe*.

vergegenwärtigen [fɛrɡeːɡənvɛrtɪɡən] *v/t* (h) *sich et.* ~ visualize, picture.

ver'gehen (*irr, no* -ge-, → *gehen*) **I** *v/i* (sn) pass (away) (*a. fig.*), *time:* a. go by, *pain etc:* wear off: *wie die Zeit vergeht!* how time flies; *vor Ungeduld etc* ~ be dying of impatience *etc*; *er verging fast vor Angst* he was frightened to death; *mir ist der Appetit vergangen* I've lost my appetite; F *da vergeht einem alles!* that turns you off completely. **II** *sich* ~ (h) a) *an j-m* commit indecent assault on s.o., rape s.o., b) *gegen* violate, offend against (*law etc*). **Ver'gehen** *n* (-s; -) offen/ce (*Am.* -se).

ver'gelten *v/t* (*irr, no* -ge-, h, → *gelten*) repay (*j-m et.* s.o. for s.th.). **Ver'geltung** *f* (-; *no pl*) (*als* ~ in) retaliation (*für* for, of): ~ *üben* retaliate (*an dat* on). **Ver'geltungs...** retaliatory (*measure, strike, etc*).

verge'sellschaften *v/t* (h) 🍃 socialize.

vergessen [fɛr'ɡɛsən] *v/t* (vergaß, vergessen, h) forget (*sich* o.s.), *a.* leave behind: *ich habe es* ~ *a.* it slipped my mind; *ich habe ganz* ~, *wie* I forget how; *das vergesse ich dir nie* I won't ever forget it; F *das kannst du* ~! forget it! **Ver'gessenheit** *f* (-; *no pl*) (*in* ~ *geraten* fall into) oblivion.

vergeßlich [fɛr'ɡɛslɪç] *adj* forgetful: ~ *sein a.* keep forgetting things.

Ver'geßlichkeit *f* (-; *no pl*) forgetfulness.

vergeuden [fɛr'ɡɔydən] *v/t* (h) waste,

squander. **Ver'geudung** f (-; -en) waste, squandering.

vergewaltigen [fɛrgə'valtɪgən] v/t (h) rape, a. fig. violate. **Verge'waltigung** f (-; -en) rape, a. fig. violation.

vergewissern [fɛrgə'vɪsərn] **sich ~** (h) make sure (**e-r Sache** of s.th.).

ver'gießen v/t (irr, no -ge-, h, → **gießen**) **1.** spill. **2.** shed (blood, tears).

ver'giften v/t (h) poison (**sich** o.s.), fig. a. contaminate. **Ver'giftung** f (-; -en) poisoning, fig. a. contamination.

vergilbt [fɛr'gɪlpt] adj yellowed.

Vergißmeinnicht [fɛr'gɪsmaɪnnɪçt] n (-[e]s; -[e]) ♣ forget-me-not.

ver'gittern v/t (h) bar, a. lattice.

verglasen [fɛr'glɑːzən] v/t (h) glaze.

Ver'gleich m (-[e]s; -e) **1.** (**im ~** in or by) comparison (**zu** with): **e-n ~ anstellen** draw a comparison; **dem ~** (**nicht**) **standhalten** bear (no) comparison (**mit** with); → **hinken. 2.** ⚖ settlement, with creditors: composition: **gütlicher ~** amicable arrangement; **mit e-m Gläubiger e-n ~ schließen** compound with a creditor. **ver'gleichbar** adj comparable (**mit** to, with). **ver'gleichen** (irr, no -ge-, h, → **gleichen**) **I** v/t compare (**mit** to, with): **das ist nicht zu ~ mit ...** a) that cannot be compared to ..., b) it cannot compare with ... **II sich ~ mit** come to terms (or settle, compound) with. **ver'gleichend** adj comparative. **Ver'gleichs|kampf** m sports: test. **~maßstab** m standard of comparison. **ver'gleichsweise** adv comparatively. **Ver'gleichszahl** f comparative figure.

ver'glühen v/i (sn) fire: smo(u)lder, meteor: burn out, rocket: burn up.

vergnügen [fɛr'gnyːgən] **sich ~** (h) enjoy o.s. **Ver'gnügen** n (-s; -) pleasure, fun: **mit ~** with pleasure; **viel ~!** a. iro. have fun!; (**nur**) **zum ~** (just) for fun; **vor ~ yell** etc with delight; **sein ~ haben an** (dat) enjoy; **j-m ~ machen** amuse s.o.; **ich wünsche dir viel ~** I hope you'll enjoy yourself; **es war kein** (**reines**) **~!** F it was no picnic; **ein teures ~** a costly affair. **vergnüglich** [-'gnyːklɪç] adj pleasant, amusing. **vergnügt** [-'gnyːkt] adj cheerful: **~ sein** a. be in high spirits. **Ver'gnügung** f (-; -en) usu. pl pleasure, amusement. **Ver'gnügungs|park** m amusement

park, fun fair. **~reise** f pleasure trip. **~steuer** f entertainment tax. **⊇süchtig** adj pleasure-seeking. **~viertel** n night-life district.

ver'golden v/t (h) a. fig. gild.

ver'goldet adj gold-plated (watch etc).

ver'gönnen v/t (h) gran:: **es war ihr nicht vergönnt zu inf** it was not granted to her to inf.

vergöttern [fɛr'gœtərn] v/t (h) idolize.

ver'graben v/t (irr, no -ge-, h, → **graben**) a. fig. bury (**sich** o.s.).

vergrämt [fɛr'grɛːmt] adj careworn.

ver'graulen v/t (h) F scare off.

ver'greifen (irr, no -ge-, h, → **greifen**) **1. sich ~** make a mistake, ♩ play a wrong note: fig. **sich im Ton ~** strike a false note. **2. sich ~ an** (dat) misappropriate (s.th.); **sich an j-m ~** lay hands on s.o., (sexually) assault s.o.

vergreisen [fɛr'graɪzən] v/i (sn) become senile, a. population: age. **vergreist** [-'graɪst] adj senile. **Ver'greisung** f (-; no pl) (progressive) senility, ag(e)ing.

ver'griffen adj book: out of print.

vergrößern [fɛr'grøːsərn] (h) **I** v/t a) enlarge, phot. a. blow up, opt. magnify, b) expand, extend, c) a. fig. increase. **II sich ~** grow, a. enlarge, expand, increase, organ: become enlarged.

Ver'größerung f (-; -en) **1.** enlargement, expansion, increase. **2.** phot. enlargement, blow-up, opt. magnification.

Ver'größerungs|appa,rat m phot. enlarger. **~glas** n opt. magnifying glass.

Ver'günstigung f (-; -en) privilege, (tax) allowance, (social) benefit.

vergüten [fɛr'gyːtən] v/t (h) **1.** (j-m) et. **~** a) remunerate (or pay) (s.o.) (for) s.th., b) reimburse (s.o.) for s.th., c) compensate (s.o.) for s.th. ◉ quench and temper (steel), opt. coat (lenses). **Ver'gütung** f (-; -en) **1.** remuneration, reimbursement, compensation. **2.** ◉ quenching and tempering, opt. coating.

ver'haften v/t (h) arrest: **Sie sind verhaftet!** you are under arrest!

Ver'haftete m, f (-n; -n) person arrested.

Ver'haftung f (-; -en) arrest.

ver'hallen v/i (sn) die away.

ver'halten¹: sich ~ (irr, no -ge-, h, → **halten**) behave, a. conduct s.o., act, ⚡ a. react: **sich ruhig ~** keep quiet; **ich weiß nicht, wie ich mich ~ soll** I'm not sure what to do; **wenn sich die Sache so verhält** if that is the case.

ver'halten² I *adj* 1. suppressed (*rage, laughter, etc*), restrained. **2. →** **gedämpft** 1. **II** *adv* with restraint: **~ fahren** drive cautiously; *sports*: **er lief ~** he didn't go all out; **~ spielen** *sports*: play a waiting game, *thea.* underact.

Ver'halten *n* (-s) behavio(u)r, conduct, attitude, reaction.

Ver'haltens|forscher *m* behavio(u)ral scientist. **~forschung** *f* behavio(u)ral science. **♀gestört** *adj* disturbed, maladjusted. **~(maß)regeln** *pl* instructions. **~muster** *n* behavio(u)ral pattern. **~thera,pie** *f* behavio(u)ral therapy.

Verhältnis [fɛr'hɛltnɪs] *n* (-ses; -se) 1. proportion, relation, ratio: **im ~ 1:10** in a ratio of 1:10; **in k-m ~ stehen** be out of all proportion (**zu** to). **2.** (**zu** with) relations, relationship: **ein gutes ~ zu j-m haben** get on well with s.o.; **er hat kein ~ zur Musik** he cannot relate to music. **3.** *pl* conditions, circumstances: **unter diesen ~sen** as matters stand; **in guten ~sen leben** be well off; **über s-e ~se leben** live beyond one's means. **4.** F (love) affair.

ver'hältnismäßig *adv* comparatively, relatively.

Ver'hältnis|wahl *f parl.* proportional representation. **~wort** *n* preposition.

ver'handeln (h) **I** *v/i* **1. ~ über** (*acc*) a) negotiate (about, on, for), b) discuss. **2. ♣ hold a hearing (or trial). II** *v/t* ♣ hear (*a case*), *criminal law:* try.

Ver'handlung *f* (-; -en) 1. negotiation (*über acc* about, on, for). **2.** ♣ hearing, b) trial: **zur ~ kommen** come up (for trial).

Ver'handlungs|basis *f* basis for negotiation: **♣ ~ 5000 DM** (*price*) DM 5,000 or nearest offer. **♀bereit** *adj* ready to negotiate. **~partner** *m* negotiating partner. **~runde** *f* round of negotiations. **~tisch** *m* negotiating table.

verhangen [fɛr'haŋən] *adj* cloudy (*sky*).

ver'hängen *v/t* (h) **1.** (**mit** with) cover, drape. **2.** (**über** *acc*) impose *fine etc* (on), declare *state of emergency* (in a *country etc*). **3.** *sports:* award *penalty kick* (**gegen** against).

Ver'hängnis *n* (-ses; -se) a) fate, b) disaster: **j-m zum ~ werden** be s.o.'s un-

doing. **ver'hängnisvoll** *adj* a) fateful (*day etc*), b) disastrous, fatal.

verharmlosen [fɛr'harmloːzən] *v/t* (h) play *s.th.* down.

verhärmt [fɛr'hɛrmt] *adj* careworn.

ver'harschen *v/i* (sn) crust.

ver'härten *v/t* (h) *a. fig.* harden (**sich** o.s.). **Ver'härtung** *f* (-; -en) *esp. fig.* hardening, induration (*a. ✝*).

ver'haspeln: sich ~ (h) F *fig.* get in a muddle.

ver'haßt *adj* hated, *matter: a.* hateful: **er hat sich bei allen ~ gemacht** he has turned everyone against him.

ver'hätscheln *v/t* (h) coddle, pamper.

ver'hauen *v/t* (*irr, no* -ge-, h, **→ hauen**) F **1.** beat *s.o.* up, spank. **2.** *fig.* muff.

verheddern [fɛr'hɛdɜrn] **sich ~** (h) F **1.** *a. fig.* tangle. **2. → verhaspeln.**

verheerend [fɛr'heːrənd] *adj* **1.** disastrous: **~ wirken auf** (*acc*) play havoc with. **2.** F dreadful. **Ver'heerungen** *pl* (**~ anrichten** cause) havoc.

ver'heilen *v/i* (sn) heal (up).

ver'heimlichen *v/t* (h) (*dat* from) hide, conceal, keep *s.th.* a secret.

ver'heiraten *v/t* (h) **j-n ~** marry s.o. (off) (**mit, an** *acc* to); **sich ~** marry, get married; **verheiratet sein** be married (**mit** to, *a.* F *fig.*). **Ver'heiratete** *m, f* (-n; -n) married man (woman).

ver'heißen *v/t* (*irr, no* -ge-, h, **→ heißen**), **Ver'heißung** *f* (-; -en) promise.

ver'heißungsvoll *adj* promising.

ver'helfen *v/t* (*irr, no* -ge-, h, **→ helfen**) **j-m ~ zu** help s.o. (to) find (*or* get *etc*).

ver'herrlichen *v/t* (h) glorify.

Ver'herrlichung *f* (-; -en) glorification.

ver'hexen *v/t* (h) bewitch, F jinx: **es ist wie verhext!** there is a jinx on it.

ver'hindern *v/t* (h) prevent: (**es**) **~, daß j-d et. tut** prevent s.o. from doing s.th.

ver'hindert *adj* **1. ~ sein** be unable to come. **2.** F *fig.* would-be (*artist etc*).

Ver'hinderung *f* (-; -en) prevention.

ver'höhnen *v/t* (h) deride, mock. **Ver-'höhnung** *f* (-; -en) derision, mockery.

verhökern [fɛr'høːkɜrn] *v/t* (h) F *contp.* flog, sell off.

Verhör [fɛr'høːr] *n* (-[e]s; -e) ♣ interrogation, questioning.

ver'hören (h) **I** *v/t* ♣ interrogate, question. **II sich ~** mishear.

ver'hüllen *v/t* (h) cover (up), *a. fig.* veil.

ver'hundertfachen v/t (h) centuple.
ver'hungern v/i (sn) die of starvation: *j-n ~ lassen* starve s.o. to death; F *ich bin am Verhungern!* I'm starving.
ver'hüten v/t (h) prevent.
ver'hütten v/t (h) ❂ smelt (*ore*).
Ver'hütung f (-; *no pl*) 1. prevention. 2. ⚕ contraception.
Verhütungsmittel n ⚕ contraceptive.
verhutzelt [fer'hutsəlt] *adj* F wizened.
ver'innerlichen v/t (h) internalize.
ver'irren: *sich ~* (h) lose one's way, get lost: *fig. verirrte Kugel* stray bullet.
Ver'irrung f (-; -en) *fig.* aberration.
ver'jagen v/t (h) *a. fig.* chase away.
ver'jähren v/i (sn) ⚖ come under the statute of limitation. **ver'jährt** *adj* statute-barred. **Ver'jährung** f (-; -en) 1. limitation. 2. (negative) prescription.
Ver'jährungsfrist f period of limitation.
ver'jubeln v/t (h) F blow.
verjüngen [fer'jyŋən] (h) I v/t 1. make s.o. (look) younger, rejuvenate: *sports: die Mannschaft ~* build up a younger team. II *sich ~* 2. grow (*or* look) younger. 3. ❂ taper. **Ver'jüngung** f (-; -en) 1. rejuvenation. 2. ❂ taper.
ver'kabeln v/t (h) connect to a cable TV network.
ver'kalken v/i (h) 1. calcify, F ⚕ *arteries: a.* harden, ❂ *a.* fur up. 2. F go senile: *er ist völlig verkalkt a.* he's gone completely gaga.
verkalku'lieren: *sich ~* (h) miscalculate.
Ver'kalkung f (-; -en) 1. calcification, F ⚕ *a.* hardening of the arteries, ❂ *a.* furring up. 2. F senility.
ver'kannt [fer'kant] *adj* unrecognized.
ver'kanten v/t (h) edge (*ski*).
ver'kappt *adj* disguised, in disguise.
Ver'kauf m (-[e]s; ⸚e) 1. (*zum ~* for) sale. 2. ✝ sales department. **ver'kaufen** (h) I v/t (*dat, an acc* to) sell (*a.* F *fig.*): *zu ~!* for sale! II *sich ~* sell *well, badly, etc, fig.* sell o.s. **Ver'käufer** m (-s; -) 1. ✝ seller, vendor. 2. shop assistant, *Am.* salesclerk. **Ver'käuferin** f (-; -nen) shop assistant, saleslady, *Am.* salesclerk. **ver'käuflich** *adj* a) marketable, sal(e)able, b) for sale: *gut ~* easy to sell; ⚕ *frei ~* available without prescription.
Ver'kaufs|förderung f sales promotion. **~gespräch** n sales talk. **~leiter** m sales manager. ⚖**offen** *adj* **~er Samstag**

all-day shopping on Saturday. **~preis** m selling price. **~schlager** m F money-spinner. **~stand** m stand. **~wert** m market value. **~ziffer** f sales figure.
Verkehr [fer'ke:r] m (-s; *no pl*) 1. traffic: *öffentlicher ~* public transport(ation). 2. contact, dealings: *den ~ abbrechen* break off all contact(s). 3. ✝ a) trade, b) payments, c) circulation: *aus dem ~ ziehen a.* F *fig.* withdraw from circulation. 4. (sexual) intercourse.
ver'kehren v/i (h) 1. (*a.* sn) *bus etc:* run, operate. 2. *~ in* (*dat*) frequent; *bei j-m ~* visit s.o. regularly. 3. *~ mit* associate with; *geschäftlich ~ mit* have business dealings with. 4. (*geschlechtlich*) *~ mit* have (sexual) intercourse with s.o.
Ver'kehrs|ampel f traffic lights. **~amt** n tourist office. **~aufkommen** n volume of traffic. **~behinderung** f holdup, delay. **~betriebe** pl transport services. **~chaos** n traffic chaos. **~de,likt** n traffic offen/ce (*Am.* -se). **~dichte** f traffic density. **~durchsage** f traffic announcement. **~erziehung** f road safety education. **~flugzeug** n airliner. **~fluß** m (-sses; *no pl*) traffic flow. ⚖**frei** *adj* traffic-free (*area etc*). **~funk** m information for motorists. ⚖**günstig** *adv* **~ gelegen** conveniently placed as regards transport facilities. **~insel** f traffic island. **~kon,trolle** f vehicle spot check. **~lage** f situation on the roads. **~lärm** m traffic noise. **~meldungen** pl traffic news. **~mi,nister** m minister of transport. **~mini,sterium** n ministry of transport. **~mittel** n (means of) transportation: *öffentliche ~ pl* public transport(ation *Am.*). **~netz** n traffic system. **~opfer** n road casualty. **~ordnung** f traffic regulations. **~poli,zei** f traffic police. **~poli,zist** m traffic policeman. **~regel** f traffic regulation. **~regelung** f traffic control. ⚖**reich** *adj* busy. **~schild** n road sign. ⚖**sicher** *adj* mot. roadworthy. **~sicherheit** f road safety, *mot.* roadworthiness. **~sprache** f lingua franca. **~stau** m, **~stockung** f traffic jam. **~streife** f traffic patrol. **~sünder** m traffic offender. **~teilnehmer** m road user. **~unfall** m traffic accident, (car) crash. **~unterricht** m traffic instruction. **~verbindung** f (road *or* rail) link. **~verbund** m (integrated) public

transport system. **~verein** m tourist office. **~wert** m ✝ market value. **~wesen** n (-s; no pl) public transport(ation Am.). **2widrig** adj contrary to the traffic regulations. **~zählung** f traffic census. **~zeichen** n road sign.

ver'kehrt adj and adv wrong, adv a. the wrong way: **~ herum** a) the wrong way round, b) upside down, c) inside out.

ver'kennen v/t (irr, no -ge-, h, → **kennen**) misjudge; → **verkannt**.

ver'ketten v/t (h) a. fig. link.

Ver'kettung f (-; -en) fig. concatenation.

ver'ketzern v/t (h) denounce.

ver'klagen v/t (h) ⚖ sue (**wegen**, **auf** acc for).

ver'klappen v/t (h) dump into the sea.

ver'klären v/t (h) fig. idealize.

ver'klärt adj fig. beatific.

ver'kleiden (h) **I** v/t **1.** dress s.o. up, disguise. **2.** ⚙ a) cover, b) line, c) case, d) panel, e) △ face, revet. **II** sich ~ dress (o.s.) up, disguise o.s.

Ver'kleidung f (-; -en) **1.** disguise. **2.** ⚙ covering, casing, lining, panel(l)ing, △ facing, mot. cowling, ✈ fairing.

verkleinern [fɛr'klaɪnərn] v/t (h) **1.** make s.th. smaller, reduce (scale etc), diminish. **2.** fig. detract from, belittle.

Ver'kleinerung f (-; -en) reduction.

Ver'kleinerungsform f ling. diminutive.

ver'klemmen: sich ~ (h) get stuck.

ver'klemmt adj psych. inhibited.

ver'klingen v/i (irr, no -ge-, sn, → **klingen**) a. fig. die away.

ver'knacken v/t (h) F **j-n zu zwei Jahren ~** put s.o. inside for two years.

ver'knallen: sich ~ (h) F fall for (**in** j-n s.o.); **verknallt sein in** (acc) a. be madly in love with, have a crush on.

Ver'knappung f (-; -en) shortage.

ver'kneifen v/t (irr, no -ge-, h, → **kneifen**) F **sich et. ~** do (or go) without s.th.; **ich konnte mir ein Lächeln nicht ~** I couldn't help smiling.

ver'kniffen adj pinched (face, mouth).

ver'knöchern v/i (sn) a. fig. ossify: **er ist total verknöchert** F he's an old fossil.

ver'knoten v/t (h) knot, tie (up).

ver'knüpfen v/t (h) **1.** tie (or knot) together. **2.** fig. link: **verknüpft sein mit** involve (costs, difficulties, etc); **eng verknüpft sein mit** be bound up with.

ver'kochen v/i (sn) boil away: gastr. **verkocht sein** be overboiled.

ver'kohlen I v/i (sn) char. **II** v/t (h) F fig. **j-n ~** have s.o. on, pull s.o.'s leg.

ver'kommen¹ v/i (irr, no -ge-, sn, → **kommen**) go to rack and ruin, person: go to seed, morally: sink low, fruit etc: go to waste. **ver'kommen²** adj a) run-down, dilapidated, b) person: seedy, depraved. **Ver'kommenheit** f (-; no pl) seediness, depravity.

ver'korken v/t (h) cork (up).

verkorksen [fɛr'kɔrksən] v/t (h) F mess s.th. up; **sich den Magen ~** upset one's stomach; **verkorkste Sache** mess.

verkörpern [fɛr'kœrpərn] v/t (h) personify, embody, thea. impersonate, play.

Ver'körperung f (-; -en) personification, embodiment, thea. impersonation.

verköstigen [fɛr'kœstɪgən] v/t (h) feed.

ver'krachen: sich ~ (h) F fall out (**mit** with). **ver'kracht** adj F **1.** **mit j-m ~ sein** have fallen out with s.o. **2.** failed (artist etc): **~e Existenz** failure.

verkraften [fɛr'kraftən] v/t (h) cope with, handle, mentally: bear, take.

ver'krampfen: sich ~ (h) hands: clench, muscles etc: cramp, person: tense (up).

ver'kriechen: sich ~ (irr, no -ge-, h, → **kriechen**) a. fig. hide.

ver'krümeln: sich ~ (h) F sneak off.

ver'krümmt adj ⚕ curved. **Ver'krümmung** f (-; -en) distortion: **~ der Wirbelsäule** curvature of the spine.

ver'krüppeln I v/t (h) cripple. **II** v/i (sn) become crippled (tree: stunted).

ver'krusten v/i (sn) become encrusted.

ver'kümmern v/i (sn) become stunted, a. fig. waste away, atrophy. **ver'kümmert** adj stunted, a. fig. atrophied.

verkünden [fɛr'kyndən] v/t (h) **1.** announce, adm. proclaim, ⚖ pronounce (sentence), promulgate (law etc). **2.** fig. herald. **ver'kündigen** v/t (h) **1.** lit. for **verkünden. 2.** eccl. preach.

Ver'kündigung f (-; -en) eccl. preaching.

Ver'kündung f (-; -en) announcement, proclamation, ⚖ pronouncement, promulgation.

ver'kupfern v/t (h) copper.

ver'kuppeln v/t (h) F **j-n ~** marry s.o. off (**an** acc to).

ver'kürzen (h) **I** v/t shorten (**um** by), abridge, cut short: **verkürzte Arbeits-**

zeit reduced hours. **II** v/i ~ **auf** (acc) sports: shorten to.

Ver'ladebahnhof m shipping station.

ver'laden v/t (irr, no -ge-, h, → **laden**) **1.** load, ship, ⚓ embark, ✈ emplane, 🚂 entrain, mot. entruck. **2.** F j-n ~ take s.o. for a ride, sell s.o.

Ver'ladung f (-; -en) loading (etc).

Verlag [fɛr'la:k] m (-[e]s; -e) publishing house (or company), publisher(s): **erschienen im ~ L.** published by L.

ver'lagern v/t (h) **1.** (a. **sich ~**) a. fig. interest, emphasis, etc: shift (**auf** acc to). **2.** → **verlegen** 1. **Ver'lagerung** f (-; -en) **1.** shift(ing). **2.** → **Verlegung**.

Ver'lags|anstalt f publishing house (or company). **~buchhandel** m publishing trade. **~buchhändler** m publisher. **~pro,gramm** n publisher's list. **~werk** n publication. **~wesen** n (-s; no pl) publishing.

ver'landen v/i (sn) silt up.

ver'langen (h) **I** v/t **1.** a) ask for, demand, b) expect, c) claim, d) charge: **die Rechnung ~** ask for the bill; **er verlangt viel** he's very demanding; **das ist (nicht) zuviel verlangt** that's (not) asking too much; **er verlangte den Geschäftsführer** he asked to speak to the manager; **Sie werden am Telefon verlangt** you are wanted on the phone. **2.** require, call for (patience, time, etc). **II** v/i ~ **nach** a) ask for, b) long for.

Ver'langen n (-s) **1.** (**nach** for) desire, longing: **heftiges ~** craving. **2.** demand, request: **auf ~** on request.

verlängern [fɛr'lɛŋərn] v/t (h) **1.** lengthen (a. **sich ~**), make s.th. longer, fig. prolong (life, period, etc), extend (a. credit, membership, etc), renew (contract etc). **2.** sports: touch ball etc on (**zu** to). **Ver'längerung** f (-; -en) **1.** a) lengthening, b) prolongation, extension, renewal. **2.** sports: a) pass, b) (**in die ~ gehen** go into) extra time (Am. overtime). **Ver'längerungsschnur** f ⚡ extension flex (Am. cord).

ver'langsamen v/t (a. **sich ~**) (h) slacken, slow down (a. fig. development etc).

Verlaß [fɛr'las] m **es ist (kein) ~ auf j-n** (et.) s.o. (s.th.) is reliable (unreliable).

ver'lassen[1] (irr, no -ge-, h, → **lassen**) **I** v/t leave, a. abandon, desert: **s-e Kräfte verließen ihn** his strength failed him.

II sich ~ auf (acc) rely (or count, depend) on; F **verlaß dich drauf!** take my word for it! **ver'lassen[2]** adj **1.** deserted, desolate (region etc). **2.** abandoned. **Ver'lassen** n (-s) abandonment, desertion. **Ver'lassenheit** f (-; no pl) **1.** loneliness. **2.** desolation.

ver'läßlich adj reliable, dependable.

Ver'lauf m (-[e]s; ⁓e) **1.** course (of road etc). **2.** a) course, run, b) progress, development: **im ~ von** (or gen) in the course of; **im weiteren ~** in the sequel.

ver'laufen (irr, no -ge-, → **laufen**) **I** v/i (sn) **1.** road etc: run. **2.** go, run, come off: **alles verlief wie geplant** everything went according to plan; **normal ~** take its normal course; → **ergebnislos**. **3.** paint: run, bleed. **4.** trail: disappear: → **Sand**. **5.** → **zerlaufen**. **II sich ~** (h) get lost, lose one's way.

ver'laust adj full of lice.

ver'lauten v/i (sn) be reported: **wie verlautet** as reported; **~ lassen** give to understand, hint.

ver'leben v/t (h) spend: **e-e schöne Zeit ~ a.** have a nice time. **verlebt** [fɛr'le:pt] adj dissipated, worn-out (by a fast life).

ver'legen[1] (h) **I** v/t **1.** (**nach**, **in** acc to) transfer, move. **2.** (**auf** acc) put off (to), postpone (until). **3.** mislay (key etc). **4.** lay (carpet, cable, etc). **5.** publish (book etc). **6.** → **verlagern** 1. **II sich ~ auf** (acc) take up, take to gardening etc, b) resort to pleading etc.

ver'legen[2] adj **1.** embarrassed: **~ machen** embarrass. **2.** (**nie**) ~ **um** (never) at a loss for an answer, excuse, etc.

Ver'legenheit f (-; -en) **1.** no pl embarrassment: **j-n in ~ bringen** embarrass s.o. **2.** predicament, awkward situation: **j-m aus der ~ helfen** help s.o. out. **Ver'legenheits|lösung** f makeshift solution. **~pause** f awkward silence.

ver'legerisch adj publisher's (risk etc).

Ver'leger m (-s; -) publisher.

Ver'legung f (-; -en) **1.** transfer, removal. **2.** postponement. **3.** ⊙ laying.

ver'leiden v/t (h) j-m et. ~ spoil s.th. for s.o.

Verleih [fɛr'lai] m (-[e]s; -e) **1.** no pl hiring out, film: distribution: ~ **von Autos** etc cars etc for hire. **2.** hire (or rental) service, film: distributors.

ver'leihen v/t (irr, no -ge-, h, → **leihen**)

1. (*an acc* to) a) lend (out), *esp. Am.* loan, b) hire (*Am.* rent) out. **2.** (*dat*) award *prize etc* (to), confer *title etc* (on), grant *s.o. right etc.* **3.** *fig.* give (*dat* to): **s-r Dankbarkeit Ausdruck ~** express one's gratitude. **Ver'leiher** *m* (-s; -) lender, *esp. Am.* loaner, *film:* distributor. **Ver'leihung** *f* (-; -en) **1.** lending (*etc*, → **verleihen** 1). **2.** award(ing), conferment, grant(ing).

ver'leimen *v/t* (h) glue together.

ver'leiten *v/t* (h) **j-n zu et. ~** make s.o. do s.th., lead s.o. to do s.th., seduce (*or* talk) s.o. into doing s.th.; **sich ~ lassen** (**zu** *inf*) be seduced (to *inf*).

ver'lernen *v/t* (h) unlearn, forget.

ver'lesen¹ (*irr, no -ge-, h, → lesen*) **I** *v/t* read out, call out: **die Namensliste ~** call the roll. **II sich ~** read it wrong.

ver'lesen² *v/t* (*irr, no -ge-, h, → lesen*) pick (through).

ver'letzbar, ver'letzlich *adj fig.* vulnerable, touchy. **verletzen** [fɛr'lɛtsən] (h) **I** *v/t* injure, hurt, wound, *fig. a.* offend (*s.o.*), violate (*law etc*), offend against (*good taste etc*): **er wurde tödlich verletzt** he was fatally injured; **j-n tief ~** cut s.o. to the quick; **s-e Pflicht ~** neglect one's duty. **II sich ~** hurt o.s., get hurt; **er hat sich am Arm verletzt** he hurt his arm. **ver'letzend** *adj fig.* offensive. **Ver'letzte** *m, f* (-n; -n) injured person: **die ~n** the injured; **es gab viele ~** many people were injured. **Ver'letzung** *f* (-; -en) **1.** injury, wound. **2.** *fig.* infringement, violation, breach.

Ver'letzungs|gefahr *f* danger of injuring o.s. **~pech** *n sports:* **vom ~ verfolgt** injury-ridden.

ver'leugnen *v/t* (h) deny (*fact etc*), renounce (*faith etc*), disown (*friend etc*): **es läßt sich nicht ~, daß** there's no denying that; **sich vor j-m ~ lassen** not to be at home to s.o.

Ver'leugnung *f* (-; -en) denial.

verleumden [fɛr'lɔymdən] *v/t* (h) calumniate, ⚖ slander, libel. **Ver'leumder** *m* (-s; -), **Ver'leumderin** *f* (-; -nen) slanderer, libel(l)er. **ver'leumderisch** *adj* slanderous, libel(l)ous. **Ver'leumdung** *f* (-; -en) calumny, slander, libel.

Ver'leumdungskam,pagne *f* smear campaign. **Ver'leumdungsklage** *f* ⚖ action for slander (*or* libel).

ver'lieben: sich ~ (h) fall in love (**in** *acc* with). **verliebt** [fɛr'li:pt] *adj* in love (**in** *acc* with), amorous (*look etc*): **Verliebte** people in love, lovers. **Ver'liebtheit** *f* (-; *no pl*) being in love, amorousness.

verlieren [fɛr'li:rən] (*verlor, verloren, h*) **I** *v/t* lose, *a.* shed (*leaves, hair*); *fig.* **kein Wort darüber ~** not to say a word about it; **F er hat hier nichts verloren!** he's got no business (to be) here; → **Auge** 1, **Mut, Nerv.** **II** *v/i* lose (**gegen** to, against): *fig.* **an Wert ~** go down in value; → **Reiz** 2. **III sich ~** disappear. **Ver'lierer** *m* (-s; -), **Ver'liererin** *f* (-; -nen) loser. **Ver'liererseite** *f auf der ~ sein* be on the losing side.

Verlies [fɛr'li:s] *n* (-es; -e) dungeon.

ver'loben: sich ~ (h) get engaged (**mit** to). **verlobt** [fɛr'lo:pt] *adj* engaged (to be married) (**mit** to). **Ver'lobte** *m, f* (-n; -n) fiancé(e *f*): **die ~n** the engaged couple. **Ver'lobung** *f* (-; -en) engagement.

Ver'lobungs|anzeige *f* engagement announcement. **~feier** *f* engagement party. **~ring** *m* engagement ring.

ver'locken *v/t* (h) tempt (**zu et.** into doing s.th.). **ver'lockend** *adj* tempting. **Ver'lockung** *f* (-; -en) temptation.

verlogen [fɛr'lo:gən] *adj* a) lying, b) hypocritical (*morals etc*): **du ~er Kerl!** you damned liar! **Ver'logenheit** *f* (-; -en) a) lying, b) hypocrisy.

verlor [fɛr'lo:r] *pret of* **verlieren**.

ver'loren I *pp of* **verlieren. II** *adj* lost, *fig. a.* wasted, *a.* forlorn: *gastr.* **~e Eier** poached eggs; *bibl.* **der ~e Sohn** the prodigal son; **auf ~em Posten stehen** fight a losing battle.

ver'lorengehen *v/i* (*irr, sep, -ge-, sn, → gehen*) get lost, be lost: **an ihm ist ein Lehrer verlorengegangen** he would have made a good teacher.

ver'losen *v/t* (h) **1.** draw lots for. **2.** raffle (off). **Ver'losung** *f* (-; -en) **1.** drawing lots (*gen* for). **2.** raffle, lottery.

ver'löten *v/t* (h) ⚙ solder (up).

verlottern [fɛr'lɔtərn] → **verwahrlosen**.

Ver'lust *m* (-[e]s; -e) loss (**an** *dat* of, *fig.* **für** to), *a.* bereavement: **~e** losses, *at games:* losings, ✕ casualties; **mit ~** at a loss; **mit ~ arbeiten** a. be losing money.

Ver'lust|geschäft *n* losing deal. **~meldung** *f* report of loss, ✕ casualty report. **~ziffer** *f* ✕ casualty figure.

ver'machen v/t (h) leave (*dat* to).
Vermächtnis [fɛr'mɛçtnıs] n (-ses; -se) ⚖ **1.** will. **2.** a. fig. legacy.
vermählen [fɛr'mɛːlən] **sich ~** (h) get married (*mit* to). **Ver'mählte** m, f (-n; -n) newlywed: **die ~n** the newly-married couple. **Ver'mählung** f (-; -en) marriage, wedding.
ver'männlichen v/t (h) masculinize.
vermarkten [fɛr'marktən] v/t (h) market, a. fig. sell, fig. commercialize.
Ver'marktung f (-; -en) marketing, fig. commercialization.
vermasseln [fɛr'masəln] v/t (h) F **et. ~** mess s.th. up; **j-m die Tour ~** queer s.o.'s pitch.
vermassen [fɛr'masən] **I** v/i (sn) lose one's individuality. **II** v/t (h) depersonalize. **Ver'massung** f (-; -en) loss of individuality, depersonalization.
ver'mehren (h) **I** v/t **1.** (*um* by) increase, multiply. **2.** biol. breed. **II sich ~ 3.** → 1. **4.** biol. reproduce, multiply, breed.
Ver'mehrung f (-; -en) **1.** increase. **2.** biol. reproduction, breeding.
vermeidbar [fɛr'maıtba:r] adj avoidable. **ver'meiden** v/t (irr, no -ge-, h, → **meiden**) avoid, evade, shun: **es läßt sich nicht ~** it can't be helped.
vermeintlich [fɛr'maıntlıç] adj a) supposed, b) alleged.
ver'mengen v/t (h) mix, fig. mix up.
ver'menschlichen v/t (h) humanize.
Vermerk [fɛr'mɛrk] m (-[e]s; -e) note.
ver'merken v/t (h) make a note of.
ver'messen¹ v/t (irr, no -ge-, h, → **messen**) measure, survey (*land*).
ver'messen² adj presumptuous.
Ver'messenheit f (-; -en) presumption.
Ver'messung f (-; -en) survey(ing).
Ver'messungsingeni¦eur m surveyor.
vermiesen [fɛr'mi:zən] v/t (h) F **j-m et. ~** spoil s.th. for s.o.
ver'mieten v/t (h) (**an** acc to) let, ⚖ lease, esp. Am. rent (out), hire (Am. rent) out (car etc): **zu ~ house**: to let, car: for hire, esp. Am. for rent.
Ver'mieter m (-s; -) **1.** landlord. **2.** lessor. **Ver'mieterin** f (-; -nen) landlady.
Ver'mietung f (-; -en) letting, leasing, esp. Am. renting (out), hiring (out).
ver'mindern → **verringern**.
verminen [fɛr'mi:nən] v/t (h) ✗ mine.
ver'mischen v/t (a. **sich ~**) (h) mix.

ver'mischt adj mixed, miscellaneous.
vermissen [fɛr'mısən] v/t (h) miss: **j-n sehr ~** miss s.o. badly; **vermißt werden** be missing; **ich vermisse m-e Uhr** my watch is missing; **~ lassen** lack.
Ver'mißte m, f (-n; -n) missing person.
ver'mitteln (h) **I** v/t **1.** j-m et. ~ get (or find) s.o. s.th.; **j-n ~ an** (acc) find s.o. a place with a firm etc. **2.** arrange, negotiate (deal etc). **3.** (dat to) impart (knowledge etc), convey (impression etc). **II** v/i (**zwischen** between, **in** dat in) a) mediate, b) intervene. **Ver'mittler** m (-s; -) **1.** mediator. **2.** go-between. **3.** ✝ agent. **Ver'mittlung** f (-; -en) **1.** procurement, negotiation (of deal etc), placement (of worker etc), arrangement (of meeting etc): **durch ~ von** (or gen) through. **2.** imparting (of knowledge etc), conveyance (of impression etc). **3.** a) mediation, b) intervention. **4.** agency, office. **5.** a) (telephone) exchange, in firm etc: switchboard, b) operator.
Ver'mittlungs¦gebühr f ✝ agent's commission. **~versuch** m attempt at mediation.
ver'modern v/i (sn) mo(u)lder, rot.
Ver'mögen n (-s; -) **1.** a) fortune, b) property, ✝ assets: **sie hat ~** she is wealthy; F fig. **ein ~ kosten** cost a fortune. **2.** no pl (**nach bestem ~** to the best of one's) ability.
ver'mögend adj wealthy, well-to-do.
Ver'mögens¦bildung f wealth formation. **~steuer** f property tax. **~verhältnisse** pl (financial) circumstances. **~verwalter** m custodian. **~werte** pl assets. **2wirksam** adj **~e Leistung** employer's) capital-forming payment under the employees' saving scheme.
vermummen [fɛr'mʊmən] v/t (h) **1.** wrap up. **2.** disguise.
ver'murksen v/t (h) F **et. ~** mess s.th. up.
vermuten [fɛr'mu:tən] v/t (h) **1.** think, suppose, assume, Am. F guess. **2.** expect. **3.** suspect. **ver'mutlich I** adj → **mutmaßlich**. **II** adv probably: **~!** I suppose so. **Ver'mutung** f (-; -en) a) supposition, F guess, b) suspicion, c) conjecture, speculation: **s-e ~ war richtig** his guess was right; **die ~ liegt nahe, daß** it is highly probable that; **das sind reine ~en** that's mere guesswork.

vernachlässigen [fɛr'naːxlɛsɪgən] *v/t* (h) **1.** neglect. **2.** ignore.
Ver'nachlässigung *f* (-; -en) neglect.
ver'nageln *v/t* (h) **mit Brettern ~** board up. **ver'nagelt** *adj* F *fig.* dense, thick: **ich war wie ~** my mind was a blank.
ver'nähen *v/t* (h) sew up.
ver'narben *v/i* (sn) **1.** scar over. **2.** *fig.* heal. **vernarbt** [-'narpt] *adj* scarred.
ver'narrt *adj* **~ sein in** (*acc*) F be wild about, **ein Kind** dote on a child.
ver'naschen *v/t* (h) **1.** spend on sweets. **2.** F a) lay (*sl.*), b) *sports:* clobber.
ver'nebeln *v/t* (h) **1.** ⚙ atomize. **2.** ✗ screen. **3.** *fig.* obscure.
ver'nehmbar *adj* audible. **ver'nehmen** *v/t* (*irr, ge-, h,* → *nehmen*) **1.** hear, *fig. a.* learn. **2.** ⚖ interrogate, examine: **als Zeuge vernommen werden** be called into the witness box (*Am.* stand).
Ver'nehmen *n* **dem ~ nach** from what one hears; **sicherem ~ nach** according to reliable reports.
ver'nehmlich *adj* audible, distinct.
Ver'nehmung *f* (-; -en) ⚖ interrogation, examination. **ver'nehmungsfähig** *adj* fit to be examined.
ver'neigen: sich ~ (h) bow (**vor** *dat* to).
Ver'neigung *f* (-; -en) bow (**vor** *dat* to).
verneinen [fɛr'naɪnən] *v/t* (h) **1.** *a. v/i* answer in the negative. **2.** a) deny, b) reject. **ver'neinend** *adj a. ling.* negative. **Ver'neinung** *f* (-; -en) **1.** *a. ling.* negation. **2.** a) denial, b) rejection.
vernetzen [fɛr'nɛtsən] *v/t* (h) *computer:* network. **Ver'netzung** *f* (-; -en) networking.
vernichten [fɛr'nɪçtən] *v/t* (h) **1.** destroy, annihilate, *a. fig.* exterminate, wipe out. **2.** *fig.* dash, shatter (*hopes*).
ver'nichtend *adj fig.* scathing, devastating (*look, criticism, etc*), crushing (*blow, defeat, etc*): **j-n ~ schlagen** *sports:* beat s.o. hollow.
Ver'nichtung *f* (-; -en) destruction, annihilation, *a. fig.* extermination.
Ver'nichtungs|krieg *m* war of annihilation. **~lager** *n* extermination camp. **~potenti,al** *n* destructive potential. **~schlag** *m fig.* final blow. **~waffe** *f* weapon of destruction.
ver'nickeln *v/t* (h) nickel(-plate).
ver'niedlichen *v/t* (h) play down.
ver'nieten *v/t* (h) ⚙ rivet.

Vernissage [vɛrnɪ'saːʒə] *f* (-; -n) private view.
Vernunft [fɛr'nʊnft] *f* (-; *no pl*) reason: **~ annehmen** listen to reason; **j-n zur ~ bringen** bring s.o. to his senses; **wieder zur ~ kommen** come back to one's senses. **2begabt** *adj* rational. **~ehe** *f* marriage of convenience. **~gründe** *pl* **aus ~n** for reasons of common sense.
vernünftig [fɛr'nʏnftɪç] **I** *adj* **1.** sensible, reasonable, level-headed: **sie war ~ genug, nein zu sagen** she had the good sense to say no; **sei (doch) ~!** be sensible! **2.** F reasonable, decent: **e-n ~en Beruf ergreifen** take up a proper career. **II** *adv* sensibly, reasonably: **~ reden** talk sense; F **~ essen** eat properly.
Ver'nunftmensch *m* rational person.
ver'nunftwidrig *adj* irrational.
ver'öden I *v/t* (h) ✚ sclerose, obliterate. **II** *v/i* (sn) become deserted.
ver'öffentlichen *v/t* (h) publish.
Ver'öffentlichung *f* (-; -en) publication.
ver'ordnen *v/t* (h) **1.** ✚ a) order, b) prescribe (**j-m** for s.o.). **2.** *adm.* decree.
Ver'ordnung *f* (-; -en) **1.** ✚ prescription. **2.** *adm.* ordinance, decree.
ver'pachten *v/t* (h) lease (*dat*, **an** *acc* to).
Ver'pächter(in *f*) *m* lessor.
Ver'pachtung *f* (-; -en) lease, leasing.
ver'packen *v/t* (h) pack (up), ✚ package, wrap up; → **Geschenk.**
Ver'packung *f* (-; -en) **1.** *no pl* packing, packaging. **2.** wrapping, packing material: ✚ **zuzüglich ~** plus packing.
Ver'packungs|auto,mat *m* automatic packaging machine. **~materi,al** *n* packing material.
ver'passen *v/t* (h) **1.** miss (*bus etc*), *a.* lose, waste (*chance*). **2.** F **j-m e-e Uniform** *etc* **~** fit s.o. with a uniform *etc*; **j-m ein Ding ~** land s.o. one, zap s.o.
ver'patzen *v/t* (h) F **et. ~** mess s.th. up, *sports, thea.* muff s.th.
verpesten [fɛr'pɛstən] *v/t* (h) pollute: F **die Luft ~** stink the place out.
ver'petzen *v/t* (h) F **j-n ~** sneak on s.o.
ver'pfänden *v/t* (h) pawn, pledge (*a. fig.* one's word), mortgage.
ver'pfeifen *v/t* (h) (*irr, no* -ge-, h, → *pfeifen*) F **j-n ~** squeal on s.o.; **et. ~** let s.th. out.
ver'pflanzen *v/t* (h) ⚘, ✚ transplant.
Ver'pflanzung *f* (-; -en) transplant.

ver'pflegen v/t (h) feed, ✕ supply with rations: **sich selbst ~** cook for o.s.

Ver'pflegung f (-; -en) **1.** no pl catering, food supply. **2.** food, ✕ rations.

ver'pflichten (h) **I** v/t **1.** j-n ~ oblige (by contract): obligate) s.o. (**zu inf** to inf); **j-n zum Schweigen ~** bind s.o. to silence; → **verpflichtet. 2.** engage (artist), sports: sign on (player etc). **II sich ~ 3.** commit o.s. (**et. zu tun** to do[ing] s.th.). **4.** artist, player, etc: sign on (**für** for). **ver'pflichtet** adj **j-m zu Dank ~ sein** be indebted to s.o.; **ich fühle mich ~, ihr zu helfen** I feel obliged to help her; **gesetzlich ~** (**zu inf**) bound by law (to inf). **Ver'pflichtung** f (-; -en) a obligation, duty, b) commitment, engagement, ✝, 🏛 liability.

ver'pfuschen v/t (h) F botch, mess s.th. up, ruin (a. fig. one's life etc).

ver'planen v/t (h) budget (funds), plan (holidays etc), book up (time).

ver'plappern: sich ~ (h) F blab.

verplempern [fɛr'plɛmpərn] v/t (h) F waste, fritter away.

verpönt [fɛr'pø:nt] adj disapproved-of: (**streng**) **~ sein** a. be frowned upon.

ver'prassen v/t (h) F squander, F blow.

ver'puffen v/i (sn) **1.** 🔥 detonate, blow up. **2.** fig. fizzle out, fall flat.

ver'pulvern v/t (h) F blow (money).

ver'pumpen v/t (h) F (**an acc** to) lend, esp. Am. loan.

ver'puppen: sich ~ (h) zo. pupate.

ver'pusten: sich ~ (h) F get one's breath back.

ver'putzen v/t (h) **1.** 🔺 roughcast. **2.** F polish off, put away.

ver'qualmt adj smoke-filled, pred full of smoke.

verquollen [fɛr'kvɔlən] adj puffed.

ver'ramschen v/t (h) F sell s.th. off dirt-cheap, remainder (books).

Ver'rat m [-[e]s; no pl] (**an dat**) betrayal (of), a. 🏛, ✕ treason (to), treachery (to): **~ begehen an** (dat) betray.

ver'raten (irr, no -ge-, h, → **raten**) **I** v/t betray (a. fig.), give s.o., s.th. away, fig. a. show, reveal: **F kannst du mir (mal) ~, warum?** can you tell me why?; **nicht ~!** don't tell!; **~ und verkauft** sold down the river. **II sich ~** betray o.s., give o.s. away. **Verräter** [fɛr'rɛ:tər] m (-s; -) traitor (fig. **an** dat to). **Ver'räterin** f (-;

-nen) traitress. **ver'räterisch** adj **1.** treacherous, traitorous, 🏛 treasonable. **2.** fig. revealing, telltale.

ver'rauchen v/i (sn) fig. blow over.

ver'räuchert adj smoky.

ver'rechnen (h) **I** v/t charge (to account), clear (cheque): **et. ~ mit** offset s.th. against. **II sich ~** a. fig. make a mistake; **sich um 10 Mark ~** be out by ten marks; fig. **da hast du dich aber leider verrechnet!** you are sadly mistaken there.

Ver'rechnung f (-; -en) offset, clearing: **nur zur ~** cheque: for account only.

Ver'rechnungs|einheit f clearing unit. **~konto** n offset account. **~scheck** m collection-only cheque (Am. check). **~verfahren** n clearing (system).

ver'recken v/i (sn) F perish, die, croak (sl.), fig. engine etc: conk out.

ver'regnet adj rainy.

ver'reiben v/t (irr, no -ge-, h, → **reiben**) spread s.th. by rubbing.

ver'reisen v/i (sn) go away: **~ nach** go to; **sie sind verreist** they are away.

ver'reißen v/t (irr, no -ge-, h, → **reißen**) F tear s.o., s.th. to pieces, slate, pan.

verrenken [fɛr'rɛŋkən] v/t (h) contort, 💀 dislocate (**sich den Arm** one's arm): F **sich den Hals ~** crane one's neck (**nach** to get a glimpse of), Am. rubberneck. **Ver'renkung** f (-; -en) contortion, 💀 dislocation.

ver'rennen: sich ~ (irr, no -ge-, h, → **rennen**) fig. get stuck (**in** acc on).

ver'richten v/t (h) a) do, carry out, b) say (prayer).

ver'riegeln v/t (h) bolt, bar.

verringern [fɛr'rɪŋərn] v/t (h) reduce, lower, (a. **sich ~**) diminish, decrease, lessen: **das Tempo ~** slow down. **Ver'ringerung** f (-; -en) (gen) reduction (of), lowering (of), decrease (in).

verrohen [fɛr'ro:ən] v/i (sn) become brutalized.

Ver'rohung f (-; -en) brutalization.

ver'rosten v/i (sn) rust.

ver'rostet adj rusty.

verrotten [fɛr'rɔtən] v/i (sn) a. fig. rot.

ver'rücken v/t (h) move, disarrange.

ver'rückt adj. F fig. mad, crazy, wild: **~ sein** a. be out of one's mind; **~ sein nach** (or **auf** acc) be wild about; **j-n ~ machen** drive s.o. mad; **mach dich**

doch nicht ~! don't get all worked up!; ~ **spielen** act up; **wie** ~ like mad; **ich werd'** ~! I'll be blowed!; **es ist zum Verrücktwerden!** it's enough to drive you mad.

Ver'rückte m, f (-n; -n) a. F fig. lunatic, maniac, madman (madwoman).

Ver'rücktheit f (-; -en) **1.** no pl madness. **2.** folly, craze, F crazy idea (or thing).

Ver'ruf m in ~ **bringen** (**kommen**) bring (fall) into disrepute.

ver'rufen adj disreputable, notorious.

ver'rutschen v/i (sn) slip.

Vers [fɛrs] m (-es; -e) a) verse, b) line.

ver'sachlichen v/t (h) de-emotionalize.

ver'sagen (h) **I** v/t **j-m et.** ~ refuse (or deny) s.o. s.th.; **sich et.** ~ deny o.s. s.th., forgo s.th.; → **Dienst** 1. **II** v/i fail (a. person), ☉ a. break down, gun: misfire: **ihr Gedächtnis versagte** her memory failed her. **Ver'sagen** n (-s) failure: **menschliches** ~ human error. **Ver'sager** m (-s; -) failure, F flop.

ver'salzen v/t (h) **1.** oversalt. **2.** F fig. spoil.

ver'sammeln v/t (a. **sich** ~) (h) assemble (a. ✕), gather, meet. **Ver'sammlung** f (-; -en) assembly, gathering, meeting: **gesetzgebende** ~ legislative assembly. **~raum** m assembly room.

Versand [fɛr'zant] m (-[e]s; no pl) ✝ **1.** dispatch, forwarding, shipment. **2.** → **~abteilung** f forwarding department.

versanden [fɛr'zandən] v/i (sn) **1.** silt up. **2.** fig. peter out.

ver'sandfertig adj ready for dispatch. **Ver'sand|geschäft** n, **~handel** m mail-order business. **~haus** n mail-order firm. **~kosten** pl forwarding costs. **~pa,piere** pl shipping documents.

versauen [fɛr'zauən] v/t (h) F mess s.th. up, fig. a. ruin s.th. (**j-m** for s.o.).

ver'sauern v/i (sn) F fig. rot (away).

ver'saufen v/t (irr, no -ge-, h, → **saufen**) F spend on booze.

ver'säumen v/t (h) **1.** → **verpassen** 1. **2.** neglect (**duty** etc): (**es**) ~ **zu** inf fail to inf. **Ver'säumnis** n (-ses; -se) omission, neglect. **Ver'säumnisurteil** n judg(e)ment by default.

ver'schachern v/t (h) F flog.

ver'schachtelt adj interlocked, fig. complicated, ling. involved (**sentence**).

ver'schaffen v/t (h) **1.** **j-m et.** ~ get (or find) s.o. s.th. (or s.th. for s.o.). **2.** **sich et.** ~ get, obtain, secure, raise (**money**); → **Respekt**.

verschalen [fɛr'ʃaːlən] v/t (h) ⌂ board, shutter (**concrete**). **Ver'schalung** f (-; -en) a) boarding, b) form(s).

verschämt [fɛr'ʃɛːmt] adj bashful.

verschandeln [fɛr'ʃandəln] v/t (h) F disfigure, spoil.

ver'schanzen: sich ~ (h) a. fig. entrench (**hinter** behind, **in** dat in).

ver'schärfen v/t (a. **sich** ~) (h) increase, tighten (up) (**control, law, measures,** etc), aggravate (**crisis** etc), stiffen (**penalty**): **das Tempo** ~ increase the pace; **die Spannungen** ~ **sich** tension is mounting. **Ver'schärfung** f (-; -en) increase, tightening (up), aggravation.

ver'scharren v/t (h) bury (hurriedly).

ver'schätzen: sich ~ (h) be out (**um** by).

ver'schaukeln v/t (h) F **j-n** ~ take s.o. for a ride, outtrick s.o.

ver'schenken v/t (h) a. fig. give away.

ver'scherzen v/t (h) forfeit.

ver'scheuchen v/t (h) chase away.

ver'scheuern v/t (h) F flog.

ver'schicken v/t (h) **1.** dispatch, send, ship. **2.** **j-n** ~ send s.o. away.

verschiebbar [fɛr'ʃiːpbaːr] adj mov(e)able. **ver'schieben** (irr, no -ge-, h, → **schieben**) **I** v/t **1.** (re)move, shift. **2.** postpone (**auf später** to a later date): **et.** (**von e-m Tag zum anderen**) ~ put s.th. off (from one day to the next). **3.** F ✝ sell s.th. underhand. **II sich** ~ **4.** shift, get out of place. **5.** be postponed, be put off. **Ver'schiebung** f (-; -en) **1.** shift(ing), moving. **2.** postponement.

verschieden [fɛr'ʃiːdən] adj **1.** different (**von** from): ~ **sein** a. differ, vary; **die beiden Brüder sind sehr** ~ the two brothers are quite unlike; **das ist ganz** ~ it depends; **~ groß sein** vary in size. **2.** ~**e** pl various, several; ~**es** various things; **aus den** ~**sten Gründen** for a variety of reasons. **ver'schiedenartig** adj different (kinds of) ..., various. **Ver'schiedenartigkeit** f (-; no pl) **1.** difference. **2.** variety. **Ver'schiedenheit** f (-; -en) **1.** difference (**gen** of, in). **2.** dissimilarity. **3.** diversity, variety.

ver'schiedentlich adv **1.** several times, repeatedly. **2.** occasionally.

ver'schießen (*irr, no* -ge-, → *schießen*) I *v/t* (h) **1.** shoot. **2.** *sports*: shoot wide. II *v/i* (sn) fade: → **verschossen** 1.

ver'schiffen *v/t* (h) ship.

Ver'schiffung *f* (-; -en) shipment.

ver'schimmeln *v/i* (sn) go mo(u)ldy.

ver'schlafen¹ (*irr, no* -ge-, h, → *schlafen*) I *v/i* **1.** oversleep. II *v/t* **2.** sleep through. **3.** F *fig.* miss (*chance etc*), forget (*appointment etc*). **ver'schlafen²** *adj a. fig.* sleepy. **Ver'schlafenheit** *f* (-; *no pl*) *a. fig.* sleepiness.

Ver'schlag *m* [-[e]s; ⁻e] shed, shack.

ver'schlagen¹ *v/t* (*irr, no* -ge-, h, → *schlagen*) **1.** mishit (*ball*). **2.** lose (*page in book etc*). **3.** *fig.* **es hat mich nach X ~** I ended up in X. **4.** *fig.* **j-m die Stimme** (*or* **Rede, Sprache**) **~** leave s.o. speechless; **es verschlug mir den Atem** it took my breath away.

ver'schlagen² *adj* sly, shifty.

Ver'schlagenheit *f* (-; *no pl*) shiftiness.

ver'schlampen F I *v/t* (h) a) go and lose, b) clean forget. II *v/i* (sn) go to seed.

verschlechtern [fɛrˈʃlɛçtərn] (h) I *v/t* make worse. II *sich ~* get worse, deteriorate; *sich (finanziell) ~* earn less. **Ver'schlechterung** *f* (-; -en) deterioration, *a.* change for the worse.

verschleiern [fɛrˈʃlaɪərn] *v/t* (h) veil.

ver'schleifen *v/t* (*irr, no* -ge-, h, → *schleifen¹*) *ling.*, ♪ slur.

verschleimt *adj* blocked with phlegm.

Verschleiß [fɛrˈʃlaɪs] *m* (-es; *no pl*) wear and tear (*a. fig.*), ⚙ *a.* attrition.

ver'schleißen (verschliß, verschlissen, h) I *v/t* wear out. II *sich ~* wear o.s. out. III *v/i* (sn) wear (out), become worn.

Ver'schleiß|erscheinung *f a. fig.* sign of wear. ⚙**fest** *adj* wear-resistant. **~teil** *n* ⚙ working (*or* expendable) part.

ver'schleppen *v/t* (h) **1.** carry off, *pol.* displace, ⚖ kidnap. **2.** delay, protract. **3.** ⚚ spread (*epidemic etc*), *fig.* neglect (*disease*). **Ver'schleppte** *m, f* (-n; -n) *pol.* displaced person.

Ver'schleppung *f* (-; -en) **1.** a) *pol.* displacement, b) kidnap(p)ing. **2.** protraction, delay(ing). **3.** ⚚ spreading (*of epidemic etc*), protraction (*of disease*).

Ver'schleppungstaktik *f* delaying tactics, *parl.* obstructionism.

ver'schleudern *v/t* (h) **1.** waste, squander (away). **2.** ✝ sell at a loss, dump.

ver'schließbar *adj* lockable.

ver'schließen (*irr, no* -ge-, h, → *schließen*) I *v/t* a) shut, close, b) lock (up), c) put *s.th.* under lock and key: *die Ohren ~ vor* (*dat*) turn a deaf ear to; → *Auge* 1. II *sich ~* (*dat*) shut o.s. off (from); *sich j-s Argumenten etc ~* remain inaccessible to s.o.'s arguments *etc*.

verschlimmern [fɛrˈʃlɪmərn] (h) I *v/t* make *s.th.* worse, aggravate. II *sich ~* get worse, deteriorate.

Ver'schlimmerung *f* (-; -en) deterioration, change for the worse.

verschlingen¹ *v/t* (*irr, no* -ge-, h, → *schlingen²*) wolf (down), devour (*a. book etc*), *fig.* swallow (up) (*money etc*).

verschlingen² *v/t* (*a. sich ~*) (*irr, no* -ge-, h, → *schlingen¹*) intertwine.

verschliß [fɛrˈʃlɪs] *pret,* **verschlissen** *pp of* **verschleißen.**

verschlossen [fɛrˈʃlɔsən] *adj* **1.** a) shut, closed, b) locked (up): *hinter ~en Türen* behind closed doors. **2.** reserved. **Ver'schlossenheit** *f* (-; *no pl*) reserve.

ver'schlucken (h) I *v/t* swallow. II *sich ~* choke, swallow the wrong way.

verschlungen [fɛrˈʃlʊŋən] *adj fig.* intricate (*pattern etc*), tortuous (*path etc*).

Ver'schluß *m* (-sses; ⁻sse) **1.** a) fastener, clasp, b) stopper, c) ⚙ lock, seal: *unter ~* under lock and key, *customs*: in bond. **2.** *phot.* shutter. **3.** ⚚ occlusion.

ver'schlüsseln *v/t* (h) encode: *ver-schlüsselter Text* code(d) text.

Ver'schluß|laut *m ling.* plosive. **~sache** *f pol.* classified matter.

ver'schmähen *v/t* (h) disdain, scorn.

ver'schmelzen (*irr, no* -ge-, → *schmelzen*) *v/t* (h), *v/i* (sn) (*mit, zu* into) fuse, merge (*both a.* ✝, *pol.*), *colo[u]rs etc*: blend. **Ver'schmelzung** *f* (-; -en) fusion, ✝, *pol. a.* merger.

ver'schmerzen *v/t* (h) *et.* **~** get over s.th.

ver'schmieren *v/t* (h) smear.

verschmitzt [fɛrˈʃmɪtst] *adj* roguish.

ver'schmutzen *v/t* (h) **1.** dirty, soil. **2.** pollute (*air, water, etc*).

Ver'schmutzung *f* (-; -en) **1.** a) soiling, b) dirt. **2.** (*air, water, etc*) pollution.

ver'schnaufen *v/i* (*a. sich ~*) (h) F have a breather.

ver'schneiden *v/t* (*irr, no* -ge-, h, → *schneiden*) blend (*rum etc*).

verschneit [fɛrˈʃnaɪt] *adj* snow-covered.

Ver'schnitt *m* (-[e]s; -e) blend.

ver'schnörkelt *adj* a. *fig.* ornate.

verschnupft [fɛr'ʃnʊpft] *adj* ~ *sein* have a cold, F *fig.* be in a huff.

ver'schnüren *v/t* (h) tie up.

verschollen [fɛr'ʃɔlən] *adj* **1.** missing, ⚖ presumed dead. **2.** (long-)forgotten.

ver'schonen *v/t* (h) spare: *von et. verschont bleiben* be spared s.th.; *verschone mich damit!* spare me that!

ver'schönen *v/t* (h) embellish, enhance.

verschönern [fɛr'ʃøːnərn] *v/t* (h) embellish, *a. fig.* brighten. **Ver'schönerung** *f* (-; -en) embellishment.

verschossen [fɛr'ʃɔsən] *adj* **1.** faded. **2.** F *in j-n* ~ *sein* have a crush on s.o.

verschränken [fɛr'ʃrɛŋkən] *v/t* (h) **1.** fold (*arms*), cross (*legs*). **2.** ⚙ cross.

ver'schrauben *v/t* (h) bolt, screw up.

ver'schreiben (*irr, no* -ge-, h, → *schreiben*) **I** *v/t* **1.** *j-m et.* ~ a) ⚕ prescribe s.th. for s.o., b) ⚖ make s.th. over to s.o. **II** *sich* ~ **2.** make a slip (of the pen). **3.** *fig.* devote o.s. (*dat* to).

Ver'schreibung *f* (-; -en) ⚕ prescription. **ver'schreibungspflichtig** *adj* ⚕ obtainable on prescription only.

verschroben [fɛr'ʃroːbən] *adj* eccentric. **Ver'schrobenheit** *f* (-; -en) eccentricity.

ver'schrotten *v/t* (h) scrap, *a.* junk (*car*).

ver'schrumpeln *v/i* (sn) F shrivel (up).

verschüchtert [fɛr'ʃʏçtərt] *adj* intimidated, shy.

ver'schulden (h) **I** *v/t* be responsible (*or* to blame) for. **II** *v/i* (*a. sich* ~) get into debt. **Ver'schulden** *n* (-s) fault: *ohne ihr* ~ through no fault of hers; *uns trifft kein* ~ it's not our fault. **ver'schuldet** *adj* indebted (*bei* to), *property:* encumbered. **Ver'schuldung** *f* (-; -en) indebtedness, debts, encumbrance.

ver'schütten *v/t* (h) **1.** spill. **2.** bury s.o. alive, block (*road*).

verschwägert [fɛr'ʃvɛːgərt] *adj* related by marriage.

ver'schweigen *v/t* (*irr, no* -ge-, h, → *schweigen*) (*dat* from) keep s.th. (a) secret, hide, withhold.

ver'schweißen *v/t* (h) weld together.

verschwenden [fɛr'ʃvɛndən] *v/t* (h) (*an acc, für, mit* on) waste, squander: *fig. du verschwendest d-e Worte* you are wasting your breath. **Ver'schwender** *m* (-s; -), **Ver'schwenderin** *f* (-; -nen)

spendthrift, squanderer. **ver'schwenderisch** *adj* wasteful, extravagant, lavish: ~ *umgehen mit* be lavish with. **Ver'schwendung** *f* (-; -en) waste, extravagance. **Ver'schwendungssucht** *f* extravagance, moneymania.

verschwiegen [fɛr'ʃviːgən] *adj* **1.** discreet. **2.** secret, secluded (*place*). **Ver'schwiegenheit** *f* (-; *no pl*) **1.** discretion, secrecy; → *Siegel.* **2.** seclusion.

ver'schwimmen *v/i* (*irr, no* -ge-, sn, → *schwimmen*) **1.** become blurred: *die Farben* ~ the colo(u)rs merge.

ver'schwinden (*irr, no* -ge-, sn, → *schwinden*) *v/i* **1.** disappear, vanish: *spurlos* ~ vanish into thin air; ~*d klein* infinitely small. **2.** F make o.s. scarce: *verschwinde!* beat it! **Ver'schwinden** *n* (-s) disappearance.

ver'schwitzen *v/t* (h) **1.** soak *s.th.* with sweat. **2.** F *et.* ~ clean forget about s.th. **ver'schwitzt** *adj* sweaty.

verschwollen [fɛr'ʃvɔlən] *adj* swollen.

verschwommen [fɛr'ʃvɔmən] *adj* **1.** *a. phot.* blurred. **2.** vague (*idea etc*), hazy, dim (*recollection etc*): *sich nur* ~ *erinnern* remember only dimly. **Ver'schwommenheit** *f* (-; *no pl*) vagueness, haziness, dimness.

ver'schwören: *sich* ~ (*irr, no* -ge-, h, → *schwören*) **1.** conspire (*or* plot) (*mit j-m* with s.o.) (*gegen* against). **2.** *fig.* devote o.s. (*dat* to). **Ver'schwörer** *m* (-s; -) conspirator, plotter. **Ver'schwörung** *f* (-; -en) conspiracy, plot.

ver'sehen (*irr, no* -ge-, h, → *sehen*) **I** *v/t* **1.** ~ *mit* provide (*or* furnish, equip) *s.o., s.th.* with; *mit Ratschlägen* ~ armed with advice; *mit Vollmacht* ~ authorize. **2.** perform, discharge (*duty etc*), *a.* hold (*office*): *er versieht auch das Amt des Richters a.* he acts as judge as well. **II** *sich* ~ **3.** make a mistake. **4.** provide (*or* equip) o.s. (*mit* with). **5.** *ehe man sich's versieht* F before you know it. **Ver'sehen** *n* (-s; -) oversight, mistake: *aus* ~ → **ver'sehentlich** *adv* inadvertently, by mistake.

versehrt [fɛr'zeːrt] *adj* disabled. **Ver'sehrte** *m, f* (-n; -n) disabled person.

ver'senden *v/t* (*irr, no* -ge-, h, → *senden*) send, forward, ship. **Ver'sendung** *f* (-; -en) dispatch, shipment.

ver'sengen *v/t* (h) scorch, singe.

ver'senken (h) **I** v/t sink. **II sich ~ in** (acc) fig. become absorbed in.

Ver'senkung f (-; -en) **1.** sinking. **2.** thea. trapdoor: F fig. **in der ~ verschwinden** disappear from the scene. **3.** (mental) absorption.

versessen [fɛr'zɛsən] adj **~ auf** (acc) mad about; **darauf ~ sein zu** inf be desperate to inf.

ver'setzen (h) **I** v/t **1.** remove, displace, shift, ✗ transplant. **2.** transfer (**in, auf** acc, **nach** to), ped. move s.o. up, Am. promote: → **Ruhestand**. **3.** a) pawn, b) sell. **4.** F **j-n ~** a) stand s.o. up, b) sports: outtrick s.o. **5. j-n in die Lage ~ zu** inf put s.o. in a position (or enable s.o.) to inf; **j-n in Unruhe ~** disturb s.o.; **et. in Schwingungen ~** set s.th. vibrating; → **Angst**. **6.** F **j-m e-n Schlag** etc **~** give (or deal) s.o. a blow etc. **7.** mix (**mit** with). **8.** ⚙ stagger. **II sich in j-n (j-s Lage) ~** put s.o. in s.o.'s place (or position).

Ver'setzung f (-; -en) **1.** removal, transplanting. **2.** transfer (**in, auf** acc, **nach** to). **3.** ped. remove, Am. promotion.

Ver'setzungs|zeichen n ♪ accidental. **~zeugnis** n ped. end-of-year report.

ver'seuchen v/t (h) contaminate.

Ver'seuchung f (-; -en) contamination.

Ver'sicherer m (-s; -) ✝ insurer, ⚓ underwriter. **ver'sichern** v/t (h) **1.** ✝ insure (**sich** o.s.) (**bei** with, **gegen** against). **2.** declare, protest: **ich kann dir ~, daß** I (can) assure you that. **Ver-'sicherte** m, f (-n; -n) the insured (party). **Ver'sicherung** f (-; -en) **1.** insurance: **e-e ~ abschließen** take out insurance (or an insurance policy). **2.** insurance company. **3.** assurance.

Ver'sicherungs|anstalt f insurance company. **~betrug** m insurance fraud. **~dauer** f time insured. **~gesellschaft** f insurance company. **~mathe,matiker** m actuary. **~nehmer** m (-s; -) insurant, the insured. **~nummer** f insurance policy number. **~po,lice** f insurance policy. **~prämie** f insurance premium. **~schutz** m insurance cover(age). **~summe** f sum insured. **~vertreter** m insurance agent. **~wesen** n (-s; no pl) insurance (business).

ver'sickern v/i (sn) trickle away.

ver'siegeln v/t (h) seal.

ver'siegen v/i (sn) dry up, run dry.

versiert [vɛr'ziːrt] adj (**in** dat in) experienced, (well-)versed.

ver'silbern v/t (h) **1.** ⚙ silverplate. **2.** F et. **~** turn s.th. into cash, sell s.th.

ver'sinken v/i (irr, no -ge-, sn, → **sinken**) a. fig. sink (**in** acc into).

Version [vɛr'zioːn] f (-; -en) version.

ver'sklaven v/t (h) enslave.

verslumen [fɛr'slamən] v/i (sn) become a slum.

'Versmaß n metre, Am. meter.

versnobt [fɛr'snɔpt] adj snobbish.

versoffen [fɛr'zɔfən] adj F boozy.

ver'söhnen [fɛr'zøːnən] (h) **I** v/t reconcile (**mit** with s.o., to one's fate etc). **II sich** (**wieder**) **~** be(come) reconciled, make it up. **ver'söhnlich** adj conciliatory; **~ stimmen** placate. **Ver'söhnung** f (-; -en) reconciliation.

versonnen [fɛr'zɔnən] adj pensive.

ver'sorgen v/t (h) **1.** (**mit** with) supply, provide. **2.** provide for (family etc). **3.** look after, take care of. **4.** ✗ attend to (s.o.), see to (wound). **Ver'sorgung** f (-; no pl) **1.** supply. **2.** (gen) support (of), provision (for). **3.** care.

Ver'sorgungs|betrieb m public utility. **~empfänger** (in f) m pensioner. **~güter** pl supplies. **~leitung** f supply line. **~lücke** f supply gap. **~netz** n supply system. **~technik** f utilities engineering.

ver'spannen v/t (h) ⚙ stay, brace.

ver'spannt adj cramped, tense.

verspäten [fɛr'ʃpɛːtən] sich **~** (h) be late. **ver'spätet** adj late (arrival etc), belated (thanks etc).

Ver'spätung f (-; -en) delay: **bitte entschuldigen Sie m-e ~** please excuse my being late; (**e-e Stunde**) **~ haben** be (an hour) late; **mit** (**e-r Stunde**) **~ abfahren** leave (an hour) behind schedule.

ver'speisen v/t (h) eat, consume.

ver'sperren v/t (h) bar, block (up), obstruct (a. view).

ver'spielen (h) **I** v/t lose (at play), a. fig. gamble away. **II** v/i lose: fig. **bei mir hat er verspielt!** I'm through with him.

ver'spielt adj playful.

ver'spotten v/t (h) make fun of, ridicule.

ver'sprechen (irr, no -ge-, h, → **sprechen**) **I** v/t **1.** a. fig. promise: **das Wetter verspricht schön zu werden** the weather looks promising. **2. sich et. ~**

von expect s.th. of; *ich hatte mir mehr davon versprochen* I had expected better of it. **II** *sich* ~ make a slip (of the tongue). **Ver'sprechen** *n* (-s; -) promise. **Ver'sprecher** *m* (-s; -) slip (of the tongue). **Ver'sprechung** *f* (-; -en) *f* promise: *j-m große ~en machen* promise s.o. the earth.

ver'spritzen, ver'sprühen *v/t* (h) spray.

ver'staatlichen *v/t* (h) nationalize. **Ver'staatlichung** *f* (-; -en) nationalization.

verstädtern [fɛr'ʃtɛːtərn] **I** *v/t* (h) urbanize. **II** *v/i* (sn) become urbanized. **Ver'städterung** *f* (-; -en) urbanization.

Ver'stand *m* (-[e]s; *no pl*) a) intellect, mind, b) reason, (common) sense, c) brain(s), intelligence: *scharfer ~* keen mind; *klarer (kühler) ~* clear (cool) head; *den ~ verlieren* go mad; F *hast du den ~ verloren?* are you out of your mind?; F *das geht über m-n ~!* that's beyond me; *all s-n ~ zs.-nehmen* keep all one's wits about one. **ver'standesmäßig** *adj* a) intellectual, b) rational. **Ver'standesmensch** *m* rationalist.

ver'ständig *adj* **1.** intelligent. **2.** reasonable, sensible, understanding. **verständigen** [fɛr'ʃtɛndɪɡən] (h) **I** *v/t* inform (*about*, of), call (*police, doctor, etc*). **II** *sich mit j-m ~* a) make o.s. understood by s.o., b) come to an agreement with s.o. (*über acc* on). **Ver'ständigung** *f* (-; -en) **1.** information. **2.** communication: *teleph. die ~ war schlecht* the line was bad. **3.** agreement, understanding. **Ver'ständigungsschwierigkeiten** *pl* communication problems: *ich hatte ~* I had problems to make myself understood. **verständlich** [fɛr'ʃtɛntlɪç] *adj* **1.** distinct, clear, audible. **2.** understandable, intelligible: *schwer ~* difficult to understand; *j-m et. ~ machen* explain s.th. to s.o.; *sich j-m ~ machen* make o.s. understood (*or* heard) by s.o. **ver'ständlicherweise** *adv* understandably.

Ver'ständnis [fɛr'ʃtɛntnɪs] *n* (-ses; *no pl*) **1.** (*gen* of) understanding, comprehension: *zum besseren ~ des Textes* in order to understand the text better. **2.** a) understanding, insight, b) appreciation (*für* of), c) sympathy (*für* with): (*viel*) *~ haben für* (fully) understand, *j-n* show (great) understanding for s.o.;

dafür fehlt mir jedes ~ that's beyond me. **ver'ständnislos** *adj* uncomprehending: *~e Blicke* blank looks; *e-r Sache gegenüberstehen* have no understanding (*or* appreciation) of s.th. **Ver'ständnislosigkeit** *f* (-; *no pl*) lack of understanding (*or* appreciation). **ver'ständnisvoll** *adj* understanding, sympathetic, a. knowing (*look*).

ver'stärken *v/t* (h) strengthen, a. ✗ reinforce (*both a.* ☺), 🎵 concentrate, 🎵 amplify, (*a. adj* ~) increase, intensify (*a. phot.*). **Ver'stärkung** *f* (-; -en) a) strengthening, reinforcement(s ✗), b) 🎵 amplification, c) increase, intensification (*a. phot.*).

ver'stauben *v/i* (sn) gather dust. **verstaubt** [fɛr'ʃtaʊpt] *adj* **1.** dusty. **2.** *fig.* antiquated.

ver'stauchen *v/t* (h) 🎵 sprain (*sich die Hand etc* one's wrist *etc*).

ver'stauen *v/t* (h) stow away.

Versteck [fɛr'ʃtɛk] *n* (-[e]s; -e) hiding place, hideaway: *~ spielen* play hide-and-seek. **ver'stecken** *v/t* (a. *sich ~*) (h) hide (*vor dat* from). **Ver'steckspiel** *n* (game of) hide-and-seek. **ver'steckt** *adj* hidden: *sich ~ halten* lie low; *~e Kamera* candid camera.

ver'stehen (*irr, no* -ge-, h, → *stehen*) **I** *v/t* **1.** hear, get, catch. **2.** understand, comprehend, grasp, catch, F get, realize, see, a. appreciate (*work of art etc*): *Spaß ~* take (*or* see) a joke; *falsch ~* misunderstand; *verstehe mich recht!* don't misunderstand me! **3.** understand, read, take: *was ~ Sie unter ...?* what do you understand by ...?; *wie ~ Sie das?* what do you make of it? **4.** know: *er versteht es zu inf* he knows how to *inf*; *sein Handwerk ~* know one's job; *davon versteht er gar nichts* he doesn't know the first thing about it. **5.** *j-m zu ~ geben* give s.o. to understand. **6.** *sich* (*or einander*) *~* get along (*or* on) (with each other). **II** *sich ~* **7.** *mit* get on (*or* along) with. **8.** *auf* (*acc*) be (very) good at *ger*. **9.** *das versteht sich von selbst* that goes without saying. **III** *v/i ~ Sie?* you see?, F get me?; *ich verstehe!* I see; *verstanden?* F got it?; *wenn ich recht verstanden habe, willst du kommen?* I take it that you will come?

ver'steifen v/t (a. **sich** ~) (h) stiffen: fig.
sich ~ **auf** (acc) insist on ger.
Ver'steigerer m (-s; -) auctioneer.
ver'steigern v/t (h) auction (off).
Ver'steigerung f (-; -en) (**zur** ~ **kommen**
be put up for [Am. at]) auction.
ver'steinern v/i (a. **sich** ~) (h) petrify:
fig. **wie versteinert vor Schreck** petrified with terror. **Ver'steinerung** f (-;
-en) **1.** petrifaction. **2.** fossil.
ver'stellbar adj adjustable. **ver'stellen**
(h) I v/t **1.** move, shift. **2.** disguise. **3.**
misadjust: **wer hat den Wecker ver-
stellt?** who has tampered with the
alarm? **4.** obstruct, block. II **sich** ~ fig.
a) put on an act, b) hide one's feelings.
Ver'stellung f (-; no pl) **1.** ⚙ adjustment.
2. fig. a) play-acting, b) disguise.
ver'steppen v/i (sn) turn into steppe.
ver'steuern v/t (h) pay tax on: **zu** ~(d)
taxable. **ver'steuert** adj tax-paid.
Ver'steuerung f (-; -en) payment of tax
(gen, **von** on).
verstiegen [fɛr'ʃtiːɡən] adj high-flown.
ver'stimmen v/t (h) **1.** ♪ put s.th. out of
tune. **2.** ♫ detune. **3.** j-n ~ annoy s.o.,
put s.o. in a bad mood. **ver'stimmt** adj
1. ♪ out of tune. **2.** ♫ off-tune. **3.** annoyed (**über** acc at), in a bad mood. **4.**
♫ ~er Magen upset stomach.
Ver'stimmung f (-; -en) **1.** ill humo(u)r,
ill feeling. **2.** ♫ (stomach) upset.
verstockt [fɛr'ʃtɔkt] adj stubborn, im-
penitent.
verstohlen [fɛr'ʃtoːlən] adj furtive, sur-
reptitious.
ver'stopfen v/t (h) **1.** stop (up), plug.
2. a) block (up), obstruct, b) congest, jam
(road). **3.** ♫ a) clog, occlude, b) consti-
pate: **m-e Nase ist verstopft** my nose is
plugged up; **verstopft sein** be constipated. **Ver'stopfung** f (-; -en) **1.** jam,
block(age). **2.** ♫ constipation: **an** ~ **leiden** a. be constipated.
verstorben [fɛr'ʃtɔrbən] adj deceased,
late. **Ver'storbene** m, f (-n; -n) the deceased: **die** ~n a. the dead.
verstört [fɛr'ʃtøːrt] adj badly upset, distraught, wild (look etc). **Ver'störtheit** f
(-; no pl) distraction, distraught state.
Ver'stoß m (-es; ⸚e) (**gegen**) offen-ce
(Am. -se) (against), violation (of).
ver'stoßen (irr, no -ge-, h, → **stoßen**) I
v/t reject: **j-n** ~ **aus** expel s.o. from, cast

s.o. out of. II v/i ~ **gegen** offend
against, infringe, violate.
ver'streben v/t (h) ⚙ strut.
Ver'strebung f (-; -en) ⚙ strut.
ver'streichen (irr, no -ge-, → **streichen**)
I v/i (sn) time: pass, set period: expire.
II v/t (h) spread (butter, paint, etc).
ver'streuen v/t (h) scatter.
ver'stricken (h) I v/t **1.** use (up) (wool).
2. j-n ~ **in** (acc) involve s.o. in. II **sich** ~
in (acc) get entangled (or involved) in.
verstümmeln [fɛr'ʃtʏməln] v/t (h) muti-
late, fig. a. garble (text).
Ver'stümmelung f (-; -en) mutilation.
verstummen [fɛr'ʃtʊmən] v/i (sn) become silent, a. stop talking, conversation,
noise, a. rumo(u)rs, etc: stop, die down.
Versuch [fɛr'zuːx] m (-[e]s; -e) **1.** attempt
(a. ⚖), trial (both a. sports), F try: **e-n** ~
machen mit try, give s.o., s.th. a try;
beim ersten ~ at the first attempt; **es
käme auf e-n** ~ **an** we might as well try.
2. 🌡, ⚗, phys. experiment, a. ⚙ test,
trial: ~**e anstellen** experiment. **3.** essay
(**über** acc on).
ver'suchen v/t (h) **1.** try, attempt (a. ⚖):
et. ~ a) try s.th., b) experiment with
s.th.; **es** ~ **mit** try, **j-m** give s.o. a try;
versuch's doch mal! just (have a) try!,
F have a go! **2.** fig. tempt: **ich war
versucht zu** inf I was tempted to inf. **3.**
taste, try. **Ver'sucher** m (-s; -) tempter.
Ver'sucherin f (-; -nen) temptress.
Ver'suchs|anstalt f research institute.
~**bedingung** f test condition. ~**bohrung** f trial drilling. ~**gelände** n testing
ground. ~**ingeni,eur** m research engineer. ~**ka,ninchen** n F fig. guinea pig.
~**ob,jekt** n test object. ~**per,son** f test
subject (or person). ~**pro,jekt** n pilot
project. ~**reihe** f series of tests. ~**stadium** n experimental stage. ~**strecke** f
mot. test track. ~**tier** n experimental (or
laboratory) animal.
ver'suchsweise adv a) by way of trial,
b) on trial, on a trial basis.
Ver'suchszwecke pl **zu** ~**n** for experimental purposes.
Ver'suchung f (-; -en) (**j-n in** ~ **führen**
lead s.o. into) temptation: **in** ~ **sein** (or
kommen) be tempted.
ver'sumpfen v/i (sn) **1.** become marshy.
2. F fig. a) go to seed, b) end up
boozing.

versunken [fɛr'zʊŋkən] *adj fig.* **~ in** (*acc*) absorbed in, lost in.

ver'sündigen: sich ~ (h) sin (**an** *dat* against).

ver'süßen *v/t* (h) *fig.* sweeten.

ver'tagen *v/t* (*a.* **sich ~**) (h) adjourn (**auf** *acc* until). **Ver'tagung** *f* (-; -en) adjournment.

vertäuen [fɛr'tɔyən] *v/t* (h) ⚓ moor.

ver'tauschen *v/t* (h) **1.** exchange (**mit**, **gegen** for): **mit vertauschten Rollen** with reversed roles. **2.** confuse, mix up.

verteidigen [fɛr'taɪdɪgən] (h) **I** *v/t* a) defend (**sich** o.s.) (**gegen** against, from), b) stand up for: **sich** (**vor Gericht**) **selbst ~** conduct one's own defen/ce (*Am.* -se). **II** *v/i sports:* defend.

Ver'teidiger *m* (-s; -) **1.** defender, *fig. a.* advocate, *soccer: a.* fullback. **2.** ⚖ counsel for the defence (*Am.* -se).

Ver'teidigung *f* (-; -en) defen/ce (*Am.* -se).

Ver'teidigungs|ausgaben *pl* defen/ce (*Am.* -se) expenditure. **~beitrag** *m* defen/ce (*Am.* -se) contribution. **~bereitschaft** *f* preparedness for defen/ce (*Am.* -se). **~bündnis** *n* defensive alliance. **~krieg** *m* defensive war. **~mi,ni-ster** *m* defen/ce (*Am.* -se) minister, *Br.* Defence Secretary, *Am.* Secretary of Defense. **~mini,sterium** *n* ministry of defence, *Am.* Department of Defense. **~rede** *f* (speech for the) defen/ce (*Am.* -se), *w.s.* apology. **~waffe** *f* defensive weapon.

ver'teilen (h) **I** *v/t* **1.** distribute, hand out, share out (*all:* **an** *acc* to, **unter** among), allocate, *thea.* cast (*rôles:* **an**): **die Rollen ~** cast (*rôles*): **unter sich ~** share; **mit verteilten Rollen lesen** do a play reading of. **2.** (**auf**, **über** *acc* over) distribute, spread, *w.s.* scatter. **II sich ~** spread (**auf**, **über** *acc* over), *persons:* scatter, *a.* ⚔ spread out.

Ver'teiler *m* (-s; -) **1.** distributor (*a.* ✈, ⚡, *mot.*). **2.** ⚙ *office:* distribution list. **~kasten** *m* ⚡ distributing box. **~netz** *n* **1.** ⚡ distribution system. **2.** ✈ distributing network. **~schlüssel** *m* ✚ **1.** distribution key. **2.** → **Verteiler** 2. **~tafel** *f* ⚡ distribution switchboard.

Ver'teilung *f* (-; -en) distribution.

ver'teuern (h) **I** *v/t* raise the price of. **II sich ~** go up (in price). **Ver'teuerung** *f* (-; -en) rise in price(s) (*or* costs).

ver'teufeln *v/t* (h) denounce, demonize.

ver'teufelt *adj* F devilish, tricky: **~ schwer** damned difficult.

ver'tiefen (h) **I** *v/t* **1.** (*a.* **sich ~**) deepen, *fig. a.* heighten. **2.** extend (*knowledge etc*). **II sich ~ in** (*acc*) become absorbed (*or* engrossed) in. **Ver'tiefung** *f* (-; -en) **1.** deepening, *fig. a.* heightening, extension. **2.** depression. **3.** *fig.* absorption.

vertikal [vɛrti'ka:l] *adj* vertical.

Verti'kale *f* (-; -n) vertical (line).

ver'tilgen *v/t* (h) **1.** exterminate, kill. **2.** F polish off (*food*).

Ver'tilgung *f* (-; *no pl*) extermination.

ver'tippen: sich ~ (h) make a (typing) mistake.

vertonen [fɛr'to:nən] *v/t* (h) *et.* **~ set** s.th. to music. **Ver'tonung** *f* (-; -en) setting.

vertrackt [fɛr'trakt] *adj* F tricky.

Vertrag [fɛr'tra:k] *m* (-[e]s; ⸚e) contract, agreement, *pol.* treaty, pact: **mündlicher ~** verbal agreement; **e-n ~** (**ab**)**schließen** make (*or* enter into) a contract; **j-n unter ~ nehmen** sign s.o. on.

ver'tragen (*irr, no* -ge-, h, → **tragen**) **I** *v/t* **1.** a) *a.* F *fig.* endure, bear, stand, F take, b) be able to eat (*or* drink), tolerate (*medicament*): **ich vertrage k-n Kaffee** coffee doesn't agree with me; **sie verträgt das Klima nicht** she can't stand the climate; **er kann e-e Menge ~** a) he can take a lot, b) he can hold his drink; **kannst du Kritik ~?** can you take criticism?; F **ich könnte e-e Tasse Tee ~** I could do with a cup of tea. **2. sich** (**miteinander**) **~** a) get on (well) together, b) *colo(u)rs etc:* go well together. **II sich ~ mit** a) **j-m** get on (well) with s.o., b) *fig.* go well with.

ver'traglich I *adj* contractual. **II** *adv* by contract: **sich ~** (**zu et.**) **verpflichten** contract (for s.th. *or* to do s.th.).

verträglich [fɛr'trɛ:klɪç] *adj* **1.** sociable: **~ sein** *a.* be easy to get along with. **2.** (easily) digestible, light (*food*), (*a.* **gut ~**) well-tolerated (*medicament*).

Ver'trags|abschluß *m* conclusion of a contract: **bei ~** on entering into the contract. **~bedingungen** *pl* terms of the contract. **~bruch** *m* breach of contract. **2brüchig** *adj* defaulting: **~ werden** commit a breach of contract.

ver'tragschließend *adj* contracting.

Ver'trags|entwurf *m* draft agreement.

⁀**gemäß** adv as stipulated. **~gemein-schaft** f pol. contractual union. **~händ-ler** m authorized dealer. **~par,tei** f, **~partner** m party to an agreement. **~punkt** m article of a contract. **~spie-ler(in)** f m sports: player under con-tract. **~strafe** f (contractual) penalty. **~werkstatt** f authorized repairer.

ver'tragswidrig adj contrary to (the terms of) the contract.

ver'trauen v/i (h) (dat) trust: ~ **auf** (acc) trust in, rely upon. **Ver'trauen** n (-s) (in, auf acc) trust, faith, confidence: (ganz) im ~ (gesagt) (strictly) confi-dentially, F between you and me; im ~ auf (acc) trusting in, relying on; ~ ha-ben zu have confidence, in trust; er hat wenig ~ zu Ärzten he has little faith in doctors; j-n ins ~ ziehen confide in s.o.; der Regierung das ~ ausspre-chen pass a vote of confidence.

ver'trauenerweckend adj inspiring confidence: (wenig) ~ aussehen in-spire (little) confidence.

Ver'trauens|arzt m (health insurance) medical examiner. **~beweis** m mark of confidence. **~bruch** m breach of trust. **~frage** f pol. die ~ stellen propose a vote of confidence. **~mann** m (-[e]s; -leute) a) representative, b) (pl a. ~er) spokesman. **~per,son** f reliable person. **~sache** f confidential matter: das ist ~ that's a matter of confidence. ⁀**selig** adj (too) confiding, gullible. **~seligkeit** f (-; -en) blind confidence, gullibility. **~stellung** f position of trust. **~verlust** m loss of confidence. ⁀**voll** adj trustful, trusting. **~votum** n vote of confidence. ⁀**würdig** adj trustworthy.

ver'traulich adj 1. confidential: ~e Mit-teilung a. confidence. 2. familiar, (a. plump ~) F chummy.

Ver'traulichkeit f (-; -en) 1. no pl confi-dentiality, confidence. 2. familiarity, (a. plumpe ~) F chumminess.

ver'träumt adj dreamy.

ver'traut adj 1. close, intimate. 2. famil-iar (dat to): ~ sein mit be familiar with; sich ~ machen mit acquaint (or famil-iarize) o.s. with; sich mit dem Gedan-ken ~ machen get used to the idea.

Ver'traute m, f (-n; -n) confidant(e f).

Ver'trautheit f (-; no pl) familiarity.

ver'treiben v/t (irr, no -ge-, h, → trei-

ben) 1. drive s.o., s.th. away: j-n ~ aus (dat) drive s.o. out of, expel s.o. from; sich die Zeit ~ while away the time. 2. ✝ sell, distribute.

Ver'treibung f (-; -en) expulsion.

ver'tretbar adj justifiable, acceptable.

ver'treten¹ v/t (irr, no -ge-, h, → treten) 1. substitute (or stand in, a. ⚖ act) for s.o. 2. represent (s.o., country, etc), look after (s.o.'s interests): j-s Sache ~ plead s.o.'s cause. 3. support, advocate (idea etc), hold, take (view etc): e-e andere Ansicht ~ take a different view (als from); → Standpunkt 2. 4. sich den Fuß ~ sprain one's ankle; F sich die Beine ~ stretch one's legs.

ver'treten² adj ~ sein to be represented, b) be present, esp. things: to be found.

Ver'treter m (-s; -), **Ver'treterin** f (-; -nen) 1. substitute, stand-in, deputy. 2. a) representative, ✝ a. agent, b) sales representative, c) proxy. 3. exponent. 4. advocate.

Ver'tretung f (-; -en) 1. representation, ✝ a. agency: in ~ (gen) a) as representa-tive of, b) (signed) for, c) by proxy; diplomatische ~ diplomatic mission. 2. a) substitution, b) stand-in, substitute: j-s ~ übernehmen stand in for s.o.

ver'tretungsweise adv as a stand-in.

Vertrieb [fɛr'triːp] m (-[e]s; no pl) 1. sale, distribution. 2. sales department.

Vertriebene [fɛr'triːbənə] m, f (-n; -n) expellee.

Ver'triebs|abteilung f sales depart-ment. **~kosten** pl marketing costs. **~leiter** m sales manager. **~organisa-ti,on** f marketing organization. **~weg** m distribution channel.

ver'trimmen v/t (h) F thrash.

ver'trinken v/t (irr, no -ge-, h, → trin-ken) spend on drink.

ver'trocknen v/i (sn) dry up.

ver'trödeln v/t (h) dawdle away, waste.

ver'trösten v/t (h) j-n ~ feed s.o. with hopes (auf acc of); j-n auf später ~ put s.o. off until later.

ver'trotteln v/i (sn) F go gaga.

ver'trottelt adj F senile: ~ sein be gaga.

ver'tun v/t (irr, no -ge-, h, → tun) waste.

ver'tuschen v/t (h) cover up, hush up.

verübeln [fɛr'ʔyːbəln] v/t (h) j-m et. ~ take s.th. amiss; j-m, daß take it bad-

ly that; *ich kann es ihr nicht ~(, wenn)*
I can't blame her (if).
ver'üben *v/t* (h) commit, perpetrate.
ver'ulken *v/t* (h) F make fun of.
verunglimpfen [fɛr'ʔʊnglɪmpfən] *v/t* (h)
revile, disparage.
ver'unglücken *v/i* (sn) **1.** have an accident: *tödlich ~* be killed in an accident;
mit dem Auto ~ have a car accident. **2.**
F go wrong, be a flop. **Ver'unglückte**
m, f (-n; -n) injured person, casualty.
ver'unsichern *v/t* (h) *j-n ~* make s.o. feel
insecure, F rattle s.o.
verunstalten [fɛr'ʔʊnʃtaltən] *v/t* (h) de-
face, disfigure.
veruntreuen [fɛr'ʔʊntrɔyən] *v/t* (h) embezzle. **Ver'untreuung** *f* (-; -en) embezzlement.
ver'ursachen *v/t* (h) a) cause, create,
give rise to, b) entail.
ver'urteilen *v/t* (h) (*zu* to) ⚖ sentence,
a. fig. condemn. **Ver'urteilte** *m, f* (-n;
-n) convict. **Ver'urteilung** *f* (-; -en) *a.
fig.* condemnation.
vervielfältigen [fɛr'fiːlfɛltɪgən] *v/t* (h) **1.**
(*a. sich ~*) multiply. **2.** duplicate, copy.
Ver'vielfältigung *f* (-; -en) **1.** multiplication. **2.** a) duplication, b) duplicate.
Ver'vielfältigungsappa,rat *m* duplica-
tor.
vervierfachen [fɛr'fiːrfaxən] *v/t* (*a. sich
~*) (h) quadruple.
vervollkommnen [fɛr'fɔlkɔmnən] (h) **I**
v/t perfect. **II** *sich ~* become perfect.
Ver'vollkommnung *f* (-; -en) perfection.
vervollständigen [fɛr'fɔlʃtɛndɪgən] *v/t*
(h) complete. **Ver'vollständigung** *f* (-;
-en) completion.
ver'wachsen¹ *v/i* (*irr, no* -ge-, sn, →
wachsen) (*miteinander*) *~* grow together, *bones*: unite, *organs*: fuse: *fig. ~
mit* become bound up with *one's job
etc*, feel at home in *a town etc.*
ver'wachsen² *adj* deformed, crippled.
ver'wachsen³ *v/t* (h) apply the wrong
wax to *skis*.
ver'wackeln *v/t* (h) F *phot.* blur.
ver'wählen: sich ~ (h) F dial the wrong
number.
ver'wahren (h) **I** *v/t* keep (*sicher* in a
safe place). **II** *sich ~* protest (*gegen*
against).
verwahrlosen [fɛr'vaːrloːzən] *v/i* (sn) be
neglected, *person*: go to seed: *~ lassen*

neglect. **ver'wahrlost** [-loːst] *adj* a)
neglected, run-down, dilapidated, b)
seedy, *a.* dissolute. **Ver'wahrlosung** *f*
(-; *no pl*) **1.** neglect. **2.** (moral) decline.
Ver'wahrung *f* (-; *no pl*) a) safekeeping,
b) custody (*gen* of *s.o.*): *in ~ nehmen*
take charge of, (*j-m*) *et. in ~ geben*
deposit s.th. (with s.o.).
verwaisen [fɛr'vaɪzən] *v/i* (sn) become
an orphan, be orphaned. **verwaist**
['-'vaɪst] *adj* **1.** orphan (*child etc*). **2.** *fig.*
a) deserted, b) vacant (*post*).
ver'walten *v/t* (h) administer, manage,
conduct, run. **Ver'walter** *m* (-s; -) administrator, (*a. estate*) manager, trustee. **Ver'walterin** *f* (-; -nen) manageress. **Ver'waltung** *f* (-; -en) **1.** administration, ✝ management. **2.** administra-
tive authority.
Ver'waltungs|angestellte *m, f* (-n; -n)
employee in the administration.
~appa,rat *m* administrative machinery. **~beamte** *m* civil servant. **~bezirk** *m*
administrative district. **~gebäude** *n*
administration building. **~gebühr** *f* administrative fee. **~gericht** *n* ⚖ administrative court. **~rat** *m* ✝ governing
board. **♀technisch** *adj* administrative.
~weg *m auf dem ~e* through (the) administrative channels.
ver'wandeln *v/t* (h) (*in acc* into) change
(*a. sich ~*), transform, turn, convert (*a.
sports*): *wie verwandelt* completely
changed. **Ver'wandlung** *f* (-; -en)
change, transformation, conversion.
verwandt [fɛr'vant] *adj* (*mit*) *a. fig.* related (to), *ling. a.* cognate (with).
Ver'wandte *m, f* (-n; -n) relative, relation: *der nächste ~* the next of kin.
Ver'wandtschaft *f* (-; *no pl*) **1.** relationship, *fig.* affinity. **2.** relations.
ver'wandtschaftlich *adj* relational: *~e
Beziehung(en)* relationship.
Ver'wandtschaftsgrad *m* degree of relationship.
verwanzt [fɛr'vantst] *adj* buggy.
ver'warnen *v/t* (h) warn, *a. sports*: caution. **Ver'warnung** *f* (-; -en) warning,
a. sports: caution.
ver'waschen *adj* **1.** washed(-)out, *a.*
faded. **2.** *fig.* vague, wool(l)y.
ver'wässern *v/t* (h) *a. fig.* water down.
ver'weben *v/t* (*irr, no* -ge-, h, → *weben*)
interweave.

ver'wechseln *v/t* (h) (*mit* with) confuse, mix up: *j-n* (*mit j-m*) ~ mistake s.o. for s.o. else; *sie sehen sich zum ♀ ähnlich* they are as like as two peas (in a pod). **Ver'wechslung** *f* (-; -en) **1.** confusion, mistake, F mix-up. **2.** case of mistaken identity.

ver'wegen *adj* bold, daring, reckless.

ver'wehen *v/t* (h) **1.** blow *s.th.* away, scatter. **2.** cover (up) *traces etc.*

ver'wehren *v/t* (h) refuse: *j-m den Zutritt* ~ refuse s.o. admittance (*zu* to).

ver'weichlichen I *v/t* (h) *j-n* ~ make s.o. soft. **II** *v/i* (sn) go soft.

ver'weichlicht *adj* soft, effeminate.

ver'weigern (h) **I** *v/t* refuse: *j-m et.* ~ refuse (*or* deny) s.o. s.th.; *e-n Befehl* ~ disobey an order; *die Nahrung* ~ refuse to eat. **II** *v/i horse:* refuse. **Ver'weigerung** *f* (-; -en) refusal, denial.

Ver'weildauer *f* length of stay.

verweilen [fɛr'vaɪlən] *v/i* (h) **1.** stay. **2.** *fig.* rest (*auf dat* on). **3.** ~ *bei* dwell on.

verweint [fɛr'vaɪnt] *adj* tear-stained (*face*), eyes red from crying.

Verweis [fɛr'vaɪs] *m* (-es; -e) **1.** reprimand, rebuke: *j-m e-n* ~ *erteilen* reprimand s.o. (*wegen* for). **2.** reference (*auf acc* to). **ver'weisen** *v/t* (*irr, no* -ge-, h, → *weisen*) **1.** refer (*an, auf acc* to). **2.** *j-n von der Schule* ~ expel s.o. from school; *j-n des Landes* ~ expel s.o. (from the country); → *Platz* 5.

ver'welken *v/i* (sn) *a. fig.* wither.

verwendbar [fɛr'vɛntbaːr] *adj* usable, suitable. **Ver'wendbarkeit** *f* (-; *no pl*) usability, suitability.

ver'wenden (*irr, no* -ge-, h, → *wenden*) **I** *v/t* **1.** use, employ, *a.* make use of, utilize. **2.** (*auf acc*) spend (on), *a.* devote *effort, time, etc* (to). **II** *sich* (*bei j-m*) *für j-n* ~ use one's influence (with s.o.) on s.o.'s behalf.

Ver'wendung *f* (-; -en) use, employment: *k-e* ~ *haben für* have no use for; ~ *finden* be used (*bei* in).

Ver'wendungs|bereich *m* range of use. **~möglichkeit** *f* use. **~zweck** *m* use, (intended) purpose.

ver'werfen (*irr, no* -ge-, h, → *werfen*) **I** *v/t* reject, turn down (*plan etc*), ⚖ dismiss (*appeal, action, etc*), overrule (*motion*), quash (*sentence*). **II** *sich* ~ a) *geol.* fault, b) *wood:* warp.

ver'werflich *adj* reprehensible.

Ver'werfung *f* (-; -en) **1.** rejection, ⚖ dismissal. **2.** a) *geol.* fault, b) warping.

ver'wertbar *adj* usable, ♣ realizable.

Ver'wertbarkeit *f* (-; *no pl*) usability.

ver'werten *v/t* (h) use, utilize, make use of, exploit (*patent etc*), ♣ realize (*property etc*). **Ver'wertung** *f* (-; -en) use, utilization, exploitation, ♣ realization.

ver'wesen *v/i* (sn) rot, decay: *halb verwest* putrefying. **Ver'wesung** *f* (-; *no pl*) decay, putrefaction.

ver'wetten *v/t* (h) spend *s.th.* on betting.

ver'wickeln (h) **I** *v/t* **1.** tangle *s.th.* (up). **2.** *fig. j-n* ~ *in* (*acc*) involve s.o. in, *a.* drag s.o. into. **II** *sich* ~ **3.** tangle up. **4.** *sich* ~ *in* (*acc*) *fig.* get caught in, get tangled up in *a web of contradictions etc.*

ver'wickelt *adj fig.* **1.** complicated, complex, intricate. **2.** ~ *sein* (*werden*) *in* (*acc*) be (get) involved (*or* mixed up) in.

Ver'wicklung *f* (-; -en) *fig.* **1.** involvement (*in acc* in). **2.** entanglement (*in acc* in). **3.** complication.

ver'wildern *v/i* (sn) run wild, *morals etc:* degenerate. **ver'wildert** *adj* wild, overgrown (*garden*), *fig.* degenerate.

Ver'wilderung *f* (-; *no pl*) (state of) neglect, *fig.* degeneration.

ver'wirken *v/t* (h) forfeit.

ver'wirklichen (h) **I** *v/t* realize. **II** *sich* ~ be realized, come true; *sich* (*selbst*) ~ fulfil(l) o.s. **Ver'wirklichung** *f* (-; -en) realization.

ver'wirren (h) **I** *v/t* **1.** tangle *s.th.* (up). **2.** *fig.* confuse, bewilder, muddle. **II** *sich* ~ **3.** get tangled up. **4.** *fig.* become muddled. **ver'wirrt** *adj fig.* confused, bewildered, muddled. **Ver'wirrung** *f* (-; -en) confusion, muddle, *a.* bewilderment: *es herrschte allgemeine* ~ there was general confusion; *in* ~ *bringen* → *verwirren* 2.

ver'wischen *v/t* (*a. sich* ~) (h) blur, *fig. a.* cover (up); → *Spur* 1.

ver'wittern *v/i* (sn) weather.

ver'wittert *adj* weather-beaten.

ver'witwet *adj* widowed.

verwöhnen [fɛr'vøːnən] *v/t* (h) spoil, pamper. **ver'wöhnt** *adj* **1.** spoilt. **2.** fastidious. **3.** demanding. **Ver'wöhnung** *f* (-; *no pl*) spoiling, pampering.

verworren [fɛr'vɔrən] *adj* confused,

muddled. **Ver'worrenheit** *f* (-; *no pl*) confusion, muddle.

verwundbar [fɛr'vʊntbaːr] *adj a. fig.* vulnerable. **Ver'wundbarkeit** *f* (-; *no pl*) *a. fig.* vulnerability. **verwunden** [fɛr'vʊndn] *v/t* (h) *a. fig.* wound.

ver'wunderlich *adj* surprising, astonishing. **ver'wundern** (h) **I** *v/t* surprise, astonish. **II sich ~ (über** *acc* at) be surprised, be astonished. **ver'wundert** *adj* surprised, astonished: *j-n ~ ansehen* look at s.o. in surprise.

Ver'wunderung *f* (-; *no pl*) surprise, astonishment.

Ver'wundete *m, f* (-n; -n) casualty: *die ~n* the wounded.

Ver'wundung *f* (-; -en) wound, injury.

verwunschen [fɛr'vʊnʃən] *adj* enchanted.

ver'wünschen *v/t* (h) curse.

ver'wünscht *adj* cursed, confounded.

Ver'wünschung *f* (-; -en) curse.

ver'wurzelt *adj fig.* (deeply) rooted.

ver'wüsten *v/t* (h) devastate, ravage.

Ver'wüstung *f* (-; -en) devastation, ravage(s).

ver'zagen *v/i* (h) despair (*an* *dat* of), lose heart. **verzagt** [-'tsaːkt] *adj* disheartened, despondent.

ver'zählen: sich ~ (h) miscount.

ver'zahnt *adj* ⊙ toothed: *miteinander ~ a. fig.* interlocked.

ver'zapfen *v/t* (h) **1.** ⊙ mortise. **2.** F dish out: *Unsinn ~* talk nonsense.

verzärteln [fɛr'tsɛːrtəln] *v/t* (h) pamper, (molly)coddle.

ver'zaubern *v/t* (h) cast a spell on, *fig. a.* enchant: *j-n ~ in* (*acc*) turn s.o. into.

ver'zehnfachen *v/t* (*a.* **sich ~**) (h) increase tenfold.

Verzehr [fɛr'tseːr] *m* (-[e]s; *no pl*) consumption. **ver'zehren** *v/t* (h) eat, consume (*a. fig.*). **Ver'zehrzwang** *m* (-[e]s; *no pl*) obligation to eat.

ver'zeichnen *v/t* (h) **1.** note (*or* write) down, register, record: *in e-r Liste ~* list; *er konnte e-n großen Erfolg ~* he achieved a great success; *Fortschritte sind nicht zu ~* no progress has been made. **2.** *fig.* distort, misrepresent.

Verzeichnis [fɛr'tsaɪçnɪs] *n* (-ses; -se) *a)* list, catalog(ue *Br.*), register, record, *b)* index, *c)* inventory.

verzeihen [fɛr'tsaɪən] (verzieh, verzie-

hen,) **I** *v/t* forgive, excuse, pardon: *j-m et. ~* forgive s.o. s.th., excuse (*or* pardon) s.o. (for) s.th.; *~ Sie die Störung* excuse my interrupting you. **II** *v/i* *j-m ~* forgive s.o.; *~ Sie!* (I beg your) pardon!, sorry!, *Am.* excuse me!

ver'zeihlich *adj* pardonable.

Ver'zeihung *f* (-; *no pl*) pardon: *j-n um ~ bitten* a) ask s.o.'s forgiveness, b) apologize to s.o.; *~!* (I beg your) pardon!, sorry!, *Am.* excuse me!

ver'zerren (h) **I** *v/t a. fig.* distort. **II sich ~** become distorted.

Ver'zerrung *f* (-; -en) *a. fig.* distortion.

ver'zetteln (h) **I** *v/t* fritter away. **II sich ~** waste one's time (*or* energy) (*in dat, mit* on).

Verzicht [fɛr'tsɪçt] *m* (-[e]s; -e) (*auf acc* of) renunciation, ⚖ *a.* waiver.

ver'zichten *v/i* (h) **~ auf** (*acc*) do without, F cut out, *a.* give up, ⚖ renounce, waive; *zu j-s Gunsten ~* stand aside for s.o.'s benefit.

Ver'zichterklärung *f* ⚖ waiver.

verzieh [fɛr'tsiː] *pret of* **verzeihen.**

ver'ziehen¹ *pp of* **verzeihen.**

ver'ziehen² (*irr, no -ge-, → ziehen*) **I** *v/i* (sn) **1. ~ umziehen** I. **II** *v/t* (h) **2.** distort, twist (*zu* into): *das Gesicht ~* (make a) grimace, pull a face; *→ Miene.* **3.** spoil: *→ verzogen.* **III sich ~ 4.** mouth, face, *etc:* twist (*zu* into). **5.** *wood:* warp. **6.** *clouds etc:* disperse, *storm etc:* blow over. **7.** F make o.s. scarce: *verzieht euch!* beat it!, get lost!

ver'zieren *v/t* (h) decorate.

Ver'zierung *f* (-; -en) decoration.

ver'zinken *v/t* (h) ⊙ galvanize.

ver'zinnen *v/t* (h) ⊙ tin(-plate).

verzinsen [fɛr'tsɪnzən] (h) **I** *v/t* pay interest on: *e-e Summe mit 5% ~* pay 5 per cent (*or* percent) interest on a sum. **II sich (mit 5%) ~** yield (*or* bear) (5 per cent *or* percent) interest. **ver'zinslich** *adj* interest-bearing: *~ anlegen* put out at interest. **Ver'zinsung** *f* (-; -en) **1.** (*von, gen* on) a) payment of interest, b) interest yield. **2. → Zinssatz.**

verzogen [fɛr'tsoːgən] *adj fig.* spoilt.

ver'zögern **I** *v/t* a) delay, b) slow down, c) protract. **II sich ~** be delayed. **Ver'zögerung** *f* (-; -en) delay. **Ver'zögerungstaktik** *f* delaying tactics.

ver'zollen *v/t* (h) pay duty on: *haben*

Sie et. zu ~? have you anything to declare? **ver'zollt** *adj* duty-paid.

Ver'zollung *f* (-; -en) payment of duty (*gen* on).

verzückt [fɛr'tsʏkt] *adj* enraptured, ecstatic. **Ver'zückung** *f* (-; -en) rapture, ecstasy: *in ~ geraten* go into raptures (*or* ecstasies) (*über acc* over, about).

Ver'zug *m* (-[e]s; *no pl*) **1.** delay: *ohne ~* without delay, forthwith; **✝** *im ~ sein* (*mit*) default (on), be in arrear(s) (for). **2.** *es ist Gefahr im ~* there is danger ahead.

Ver'zugszinsen *pl* interest on arrears.

ver'zweifeln *v/i* (sn) despair (*an dat* of): *es ist zum ♍* it's enough to drive you to despair; *ich bin am ♍* I'm desperate.

ver'zweifelt *adj* despairing (*look etc*), desperate (*fight, situation, etc*).

Ver'zweiflung *f* (-; *no pl*) (*j-n zur ~ bringen or treiben* drive s.o. to).

Ver'zweiflungstat *f* act of desperation.

verzweigen [fɛr'tsvaɪɡən] *sich ~* (h) branch out, *esp. fig.* ramify.

ver'zweigt *adj* branching (*network etc*).

ver'zwickt *adj* F tricky, complicated.

Veteran [vete'raːn] *m* (-en; -en) **1.** ✗ ex-serviceman, *Am. and fig.* veteran. **2.** *mot.* vintage car.

Veterinär [veteri'nɛːr] *m* (-s; -e) veterinary surgeon, *Am.* veterinarian, F vet.

Veto ['veːto] *n* (-s; -s) veto: (*s)ein ~ einlegen* put a veto on, veto.

'Vetorecht *n* veto (power).

Vetter ['fɛtɐr] *m* (-s; -n) cousin.

'Vetternwirtschaft *f* (-; *no pl*) nepotism.

Viadukt [vĭa'dʊkt] *m* (-[e]s; -e) viaduct.

Vibration [vibra'tsĭoːn] *f* (-; -en) vibration.

vibrieren [vi'briːrən] *v/i* (h) vibrate.

Video ['viːdeo] *n* → **Videotechnik.**

'Video... video (*camera, film, system, etc*). **~aufzeichnung** *f* video recording. **~band** *n* video tape. **~gerät** *n* video recorder. **~kas,sette** *f* video cassette. **~re,corder** *m* video recorder. **~spiel** *n* video game. **~technik** *f* video technology. **~text** *m* teletext.

Videothek [video'teːk] *f* (-; -en) video-tape library.

Vieh [fiː] *n* (-[e]s; *no pl*) **1.** cattle, livestock. **2.** F *contp.* animal, beast. **~bestand** *m* livestock. **~futter** *n* fodder, feed. **~händler** *m* cattle dealer.

'viehisch *adj* bestial, brutal.

'Vieh|markt *m* cattle market. **~wagen** *m* 🚚 cattle truck, *Am.* stock car. **~zeug** *n* F animals. **~zucht** *f* stockbreeding. **~züchter** *m* stockbreeder, cattleman.

viel [fiːl] *adj and adv* a **) a** lot (of), plenty (of), F lots of, **b)** (*as, how, so, too, very, not*) much: (*sehr*) **~e** (a great) many; *sehr ~ Geld* a great deal (*or* plenty) of money; *ziemlich ~* quite a lot (of); *das kommt vom ~en Rauchen* that comes from all that smoking; *ich halte nicht ~ davon* I don't think much of it; *~e hundert* hundreds and hundreds of; *~ besser* (*lieber*) much better (rather); *~ zuviel* far too much; *~ zu wenig* not nearly enough; *in ~em* in many ways.

'vielbeschäftigt *adj* very busy.

'vieldeutig [-dɔʏtɪç] *adj* ambiguous.

'vieldisku,tiert *adj* much-discussed.

'Vieleck *n* (-[e]s; -e) ♈ polygon.

'vielerlei ['fiːlɐrlaɪ] *adj* all sorts of.

'vieler'orts *adv* in many places.

'vielfach I *adj* multiple: *er ist ~er Millionär* he is a millionaire many times over; *auf ~en Wunsch* by popular request. **II** *adv* a) in many cases, b) frequently.

'Vielfalt [-falt] *f* (-; *no pl*) (great) variety.

'vielfältig [-fɛltɪç] *adj* varied, manifold.

'Vielfraß *m* (-es; -e) a. F *fig.* glutton.

'vielgeliebt *adj* much-loved.

'vielgepriesen *adj* much-praised.

'vielköpfig [-kœpfɪç] *adj* large (*family*).

vielleicht [fi'laɪçt] *adv* perhaps, maybe, possibly: *hast du ihn ~ gesehen?* have you seen him by any chance?; *~ kommen sie noch* they may yet come; *es ist ~ besser* it might be better; *könnten Sie ~ das Fenster schließen?* would you mind closing the window?; F *das ist ~ ein Trottel!* he really is an idiot!; *ich war ~ aufgeregt!* what a state I was in!; *das ist ~ ein Auto!* that's some car.

'vielmals *adv* many times: *danke ~* many thanks; *sie läßt ~ grüßen* she sends her best regards; *ich bitte ~ um Entschuldigung* I'm terribly sorry.

'vielmehr *adv* rather.

'vielsagend *adj* meaningful, knowing.

'vielschichtig [-ʃɪçtɪç] *adj fig.* complex.

'vielseitig [-zaɪtɪç] *adj* many-sided, versatile (*person*), varied (*interests etc*): *auf ~en Wunsch* by popular request; *sie ist ~ begabt* she has many talents;

er ist ~ interessiert he has varied interests; **~ verwendbar** multi-purpose.
'**Vielseitigkeit** f (-; no pl) versatility.
'**vielsprachig** [-∫praːxɪç] adj polyglot.
'**vielstimmig** [-∫tɪmɪç] adj ♪ polyphonic.
'**vielversprechend** adj (very) promising: **nicht (gerade)** ~ unpromising.
Viel'völkerstaat m multiracial state.
'**Vielweiberei** [fiːlvaɪbəˈraɪ] f (-; no pl) polygamy.
'**Vielzahl** f (-; no pl) multitude.
vier [fiːr] adj four: **unter ~ Augen** in private; **Gespräch unter ~ Augen** private talk; F **auf allen ~en** on all fours.
Vier f (-; -en) four: ped. **e-e ~ bekommen** get a D.
'**Vierbeiner** [-baɪnər] m (-s; -) F quadruped. '**vierbeinig** adj four-legged.
'**vierblätt(e)rig** [-blɛt(ə)rɪç] adj four-leaf ..., four-leaved.
Viereck n (-[e]s; -e) quadrangle, square.
'**viereckig** adj quadrangular, square.
'**Vierer** ['fiːrər] m (-s; -) rowing: four, golf: foursome. **~bob** m four-seater bob.
'**vierfach** adj fourfold.
Vier'farbendruck m four-colo(u)r printing (picture: print).
'**Vierfüßer** [-fyːsər] m (-s; -) zo. quadruped. '**vierfüßig** adj four-footed.
'**Vierganggetriebe** n mot. four-speed gear unit.
'**vierhändig** [-hɛndɪç] adj four-handed, for four hands: **~ spielen** play a duet.
'**vierhundert** adj four hundred.
'**vierjährig** [-jɛːrɪç] adj **1.** of four years, four-year (period etc). **2.** four-year-old.
'**Vierjährige** [-jɛːrɪgə] m, f (-n; -n) four-year-old.
'**Vierkant** m, n (-[e]s; -e) ⊛ square.
'**vierkantig** adj square.
'**Vierlinge** pl quadruplets.
'**viermal** adv four times.
'**viermotorig** [-moˌtoːrɪç] adj esp. ✈ four-engine(d).
'**Vierrad...** four-wheel (drive, brake).
'**vierrädrig** [-rɛːdrɪç] adj four-wheeled.
'**vierschrötig** [-∫røːtɪç] adj square-built, burly.
'**vierseitig** [-zaɪtɪç] adj four-sided, ⅋ quadrilateral.
'**viersilbig** [-zɪlbɪç] adj four-syllable.
'**Viersitzer** m (-s; -) four-seater.
'**vierspurig** [-∫puːrɪç] adj four-lane.
'**vierstellig** [-∫tɛlɪç] adj ⅋ four-digit.

'**vierstimmig** [-∫tɪmɪç] adj ♪ four-part: ~ **singen** sing in four voices.
'**vierstöckig** [-∫tœkɪç] adj four-storeyed, Am. four-storied.
'**vierstündig** [-∫tʏndɪç] adj four-hour.
viert [fiːrt] adj fourth: **sie waren zu ~** there were four of them.
Viertaktmotor m four-stroke engine.
'**vier'tausend** adj four thousand.
'**Vierte** m, f (-n; -n) fourth.
Viertel ['fɪrtəl] n (-s; -) quarter, fourth: **es ist ~ vor eins** it is a quarter to one.
'**Viertelfi,nale** n sports: quarter final.
Viertel'jahr n three months, quarter.
'**vierteljährlich** adj and adv quarterly: **~e Kündigung** three months' notice.
'**Vierteliter** m, n (-s; -) quarter of a litre (Am. liter).
vierteln ['fɪrtəln] v/t (h) quarter.
'**Viertelnote** f ♪ crotchet, Am. quarter note. **~pause** f ♪ crotchet (Am. quarter note) rest. **~pfund** n quarter of a pound. **~stunde** f quarter of an hour.
'**viertelstündlich** adj and adv every quarter of an hour (or fifteen minutes).
'**viertens** adv fourthly.
Vier'vierteltakt m ♪ four-four (or common) time.
vierzehn ['fɪr-] adj fourteen: ~ **Tage** a fortnight, Am. fourteen days; **in ~ Tagen** in two weeks' time, in a fortnight. **~jährig** [-jɛːrɪç] adj fourteen-year-old. **~tägig** [-tɛːgɪç] adj two-week.
'**Vierzeiler** [-tsaɪlər] m (-s; -) quatrain.
vierzig ['fɪrtsɪç] adj forty. '**Vierzig** f (-; -en) forty: **sie ist am Anfang (der) ~** she is in her early forties. '**vierziger** adj **die ~ Jahre** the forties. '**Vierziger** m (-s; -), '**Vierzigerin** f (-; -nen) man (woman) of forty (or in his [her] forties).
'**vierzigst** adj fortieth.
Vietnam [viɛtˈnam] n (-s) Vietnam.
Vietnamese [viɛtnaˈmeːzə] m (-n; -n), **Vietna'mesin** f (-; -nen), **vietna'mesisch** adj Vietnamese.
Vikar [viˈkaːr] m (-s; -e) curate.
Villa ['vɪla] f (-; Villen) villa.
'**Villenviertel** n residential area.
Viola ['viːola] f (-; Violen) ♪ viola.
violett [vioˈlɛt] adj violet.
Violine [vioˈliːnə] f (-; -n) ♪ violin.
Violinist [violiˈnɪst] m (-en; -en) violinist.
Vio'linschlüssel m ♪ treble clef.
Violon'cello [violɔn-] n ♪ violoncello.

Viper ['vi:pər] f (-; -n) zo. viper, adder.
Virologie [viroло'gi:] f (-; no pl) virology.
virologisch [viro'lo:gɪʃ] adj virological.
virtuos [vɪr'tŭo:s] adj virtuoso. **Virtuose** [vɪr'tŭo:zə] m (-n; -n), **Virtu'osin** f (-; -nen) virtuoso. **Virtuosität** [vɪrtŭozi'tɛ:t] f (-; no pl) virtuosity.
virulent [viru'lɛnt] adj virulent.
Virus ['vi:rus] m, n (-; Viren) ♂ virus. **~infekti,on** f virus (or viral) infection.
Visage [vi'za:ʒə] f (-; -n) F mug.
Visier [vi'zi:r] n (-s; -e) **1.** visor. **2.** on rifle: sight. **vi'sieren** v/i (h) take aim.
Vision [vi'zĭo:n] f (-; -en) vision.
visionär [vizĭo'nɛ:r] adj visionary.
Visite [vi'zi:tə] f (-; -n) (doctor's) round.
Vi'sitenkarte f (visiting) card.
visuell [vi'zŭɛl] adj visual.
Visum ['vi:zʊm] n (-s; Visa, Visen) visa.
vital [vi'ta:l] adj **1.** vigorous, fit. **2.** vital.
Vitalität [vitali'tɛ:t] f (-; no pl) vitality.
Vitamin [vita'mi:n] n (-s; -e) vitamin: F fig. **~ B** contacts. **♀arm** adj low in vitamins. **~bedarf** m vitamin requirement. **~gehalt** m vitamin content.
vita'minhaltig adj containing vitamins.
vitaminieren [vitami'ni:rən] v/t (h) vitaminize.
Vita'min|mangel m vitamin deficiency. **~präpa,rat** n vitamin preparation. **♀reich** adj rich in vitamins. **~stoß** m massive dose of vitamins.
Vitrine [vi'tri:nə] f (-; -n) glass cupboard, ♱ showcase, display case.
Vize... ['fi:tsə-] vice-(admiral, chancellor, president, etc). **~könig** m viceroy. **~meister(in** f) m sports: runner-up (**hinter** dat to).
Vogel ['fo:gəl] m (-s; ♈) **1.** bird: F fig. **e-n ~ haben** take have a screw loose; **den ~ abschießen** take the cake; **j-m den ~ zeigen** tap one's forehead at s.o. **2.** F fig. bird, fellow: **ein komischer ~** a queer customer. **~beerbaum** m rowan-(-tree). **~beere** f rowanberry. **~futter** n birdseed. **~haus** n aviary. **~käfig** m birdcage. **~kunde** f (-; no pl) ornithology. **~mist** m bird droppings.
vögeln ['fø:gəln] v/t, v/i (h) V screw.
'Vogel|nest n bird's nest. **~perspek,tive** f **Berlin aus der ~** a bird's-eye view of Berlin. **~scheuche** f (-; -n) scarecrow. **~schutzgebiet** n bird sanctuary.
Vogel-'Strauß-Poli,tik f ostrich policy.

'**Vogelwarte** f ornithological station.
'**Vogelzug** m migration of birds.
Vokabel [vo'ka:bəl] f (-; -n) word. **~heft** n vocabulary book.
Vokal [vo'ka:l] m (-s; -e) vowel.
Vo'kalmu,sik f vocal music.
Volk [fɔlk] n (-[e]s; ♈er) **1.** a) people, nation, b) the masses, contp. mob, rabble, c) crowd: **ein Mann aus dem ~** a man of the people; **sich unters ~ mischen** mingle with the crowd. **2.** zo. swarm (of bees). **3.** hunt. covey.
Völker|kunde ['fœlkər-] f (-; no pl) ethnology. **~mord** m genocide. **~recht** n (-[e]s; no pl) international law. **♀rechtlich** adj relating to (adv under) international law. **~verständigung** f international understanding. **~wanderung** f **1.** migration of peoples. **2.** fig. exodus.
'**volkreich** adj populous.
'**Volks|abstimmung** f referendum. **~aufstand** m national uprising. **~befragung** f public opinion poll. **~begehren** n petition for a referendum. **~büche,rei** f public library. **~cha,rakter** m national character. **~demokra,tie** f people's democracy. **~deutsche** m, f (-n; -n) ethnic German. **♀eigen** adj hist. DDR state-owned. **~eigentum** n national property. **~einkommen** n national income. **~entscheid** m referendum. **~feind** m public enemy. **~fest** n public festival, fair. **~gruppe** f ethnic group. **~held(in** f) m folk hero(ine f). **~herrschaft** f democracy. **~hochschule** f adult evening classes. **~kammer** f hist. DDR People's Chamber. **~kunde** f (-; no pl) folklore. **~lauf** m open cross-country race. **~lied** n folk song. **~mund** m (**im ~** in the) vernacular. **~mu,sik** f folk music. **♀nah** adj popular, people-oriented, grassroots (politician). **~poli,zist** m hist. DDR member of the people's police. **~repu,blik** f people's republic. **~schicht** f social class. **~schule** f → **Grund-, Hauptschule.** **~seele** f iro. **die ~ kocht** the populace is seething. **~sport** m popular sport. **~sprache** f vernacular. **~stamm** m tribe, race. **~stück** n thea. folk play. **~tanz** m folk dance. **~tracht** f national costume. **~trauertag** m day of national mourning.
'**Volkstum** n (-s; no pl) folklore.

'**volkstümlich** [-ty:mlıç] *adj* **1.** folkloristic. **2.** *ling.* vernacular. **3.** traditional. **4.** popular: *sich ~ geben* act folksy.
'**Volks|vermögen** *n* national wealth. **~versammlung** *f* public meeting. **~vertreter(in** *f)* *m* people's representative. **~vertretung** *f* representation of the people, parliament. **~wirt** *m* ✝ (political) economist. **~wirtschaft** *f* **1.** political economy. **2.** → **~wirtschaftslehre** *f* economics. **~zählung** *f* census.
'**voll** [fɔl] **I** *adj* **1.** full, *a.* filled, *a.* full up: *~(er), ~ von, ~ mit* full of (*a. fig.*), filled (*or* loaded) with; *e-e Kanne (~) Tee* a pot of tea; *fig.* **aus dem ~en schöpfen** draw on plentiful resources; F *~ sein* a) be full up, b) be tight. **2.** full, round (*figure*), thick, rich (*hair*): *~er werden* *a.* fill out. **3.** *fig.* full, rich (*scent, voice, etc*). **4.** full, whole: *der Mond ist ~* the moon is fully (*or* completely) filled; *e-e ~e Stunde* a full (*or* solid) hour; *~e drei Tage* fully three days; *et. in ~er Höhe bezahlen* pay the full amount, pay the amount in full; *mit ~er Lautstärke* (at) full blast; *aus ~er Brust, aus ~em Halse* at the top of one's voice; *aus ~em Herzen* from the bottom of one's heart; *~es Vertrauen* complete confidence; *die ~e Wahrheit* the whole truth. **II** *adv* fully, *a.* in full: *~ und ganz* completely, wholly; *~ arbeiten* work full time; *~ beschäftigt* fully occupied; *~ besetzt* full (up); *Sie müssen ~ bezahlen* you have to pay the full price; *~ schlagen* clock: strike the full hour; *j-n nicht für ~ nehmen* not to take s.o. seriously; F *in die ~en gehen* go flat out.
'**vollauf** *adv* quite, perfectly.
'**vollauto|matisch** *adj* fully automatic.
'**Vollbad** *n* full bath.
'**Vollbart** *m* full beard.
'**vollbeschäftigt** *adj* employed full-time.
'**Vollbeschäftigung** *f* (-; *no pl*) full employment.
'**Vollbesitz** *m* **im ~** (*gen*) in full possession of.
'**Vollblut** *n* (-[e]s; *no pl*), '**Vollblüter** [-bly:tər] *m* (-s; -), '**Vollblutpferd** *n* thoroughbred.
'**Vollbremsung** *f* full braking, crash-halt: *e-e ~ machen* F slam on the brakes.
voll'bringen *v/t* (*irr, insep, no* -ge-, h, →

bringen) a) accomplish, achieve, b) perform (*miracles etc*).
'**vollbusig** [-bu:zıç] *adj* bosomy, busty.
'**Volldampf** *m* **mit ~** at full steam, *fig.* at full blast.
'**vollelek,tronisch** *adj* fully electronic.
voll'enden *v/t* (*insep, no* -ge-, h) **1.** finish, complete. **2.** perfect. **voll'endet** *adj* perfect, accomplished: *~ schön* of perfect beauty; → *Tatsache*. **vollends** ['fɔlɛnts] *adv* completely. **Voll'endung** *f* (-; *no pl*) **1.** completion: *nach* (*or mit*) *~* (*gen*) on completion of. **2.** perfection.
'**voller** → *voll* I.
Völlerei [fœlə'raı] *f* (-; -en) gluttony.
Volleyball(spiel) ['vɔli-] *n* volleyball.
'**Vollfettkäse** *m* full-fat cheese.
voll'führen *v/t* (*insep, no* -ge-, h) perform.
'**vollfüllen** *v/t* (*sep,* h) fill (up).
'**Vollgas** *n mot.* full throttle: *mit ~* F full tilt; *~ geben* F step on the gas.
'**voll|gepackt, ~gepfropft, ~gestopft** *adj* crammed (full), F (jam-)packed.
'**vollgießen** *v/t* (*irr, sep,* -ge-, h, → *gießen*) fill (up).
'**Vollgummi** *m, n,* solid rubber.
völlig ['fœlıç] **I** *adj* total, absolute, complete: *~e Gleichberechtigung* full equality; *~er Unsinn* utter (*or* perfect) nonsense; *ein ~er Versager* a complete failure. **II** *adv* quite, fully (*etc*): *~ richtig* absolutely right; *~ am Ende sein* be completely run down; *das ist mir ~ gleichgültig* I don't give a damn.
'**volljährig** [-jɛ:rıç] *adj* of (full legal) age, major: *~ sein* (*werden*) be (come) of age; *noch nicht ~* under age.
'**Volljährigkeit** *f* (-; *no pl*) full legal age, majority.
'**Volljurist** *m* fully qualified lawyer.
'**Vollkaskoversicherung** *f* comprehensive insurance.
voll'kommen **I** *adj* perfect, total, absolute. **II** *adv* F → *völlig* II.
Voll'kommenheit *f* (-; *no pl*) perfection.
'**Vollkornbrot** *n* wholemeal bread.
'**vollmachen** *v/t* (*sep,* h) F **1.** fill (up). **2.** dirty, soil: *die Hosen ~* fill one's pants.
'**Vollmacht** *f* (-; -en) full power(s), authority, ⚖ a) power of attorney, b) proxy: *~ haben* be authorized; *j-m ~ erteilen* authorize s.o.
'**Vollma,trose** *m* able-bodied seaman.

'**Vollmilch** f full-cream milk. **~schoko-lade** f milk chocolate.

'**Vollmond** m full moon: *heute ist ~* there is a full moon tonight.

'**vollmundig** [-mʊndɪç] adj **1.** full-bodied (*wine etc*). **2.** fig. iro. pompous.

'**Vollnar,kose** f general an(a)esthesia.

'**vollpacken** v/t (sep, h) pack s.th. full (*mit* of).

'**Vollpensi,on** f (-; no pl) (full) board and lodging.

'**vollsaugen:** *sich ~* (sep, h) become saturated (*mit* with).

'**vollschlagen:** *sich ~* (irr, sep, -ge-, h, → **schlagen**) fill one's belly.

'**vollschlank** adj **~ sein** have a full figure.

'**vollschreiben** v/t (irr, sep, -ge-, h, → **schreiben**) fill.

'**vollständig I** adj complete, whole, entire: **~e Anschrift** full address. **II** adv → **völlig** II. '**Vollständigkeit** f (-; no pl) completeness.

'**vollstopfen** v/t (sep, h) stuff, cram.

Voll'streckbar adj 🄵🄳 enforceable.

voll'strecken (h) **I** v/t **1.** execute, 🄵🄳 enforce. **2.** *sports:* convert (*penalty kick etc*). **II** v/i *sports:* score. **Voll'strecker** m (-s; -) 🄵🄳 executor. **Voll'streckung** f (-; -en) 🄵🄳 execution. **Voll'streckungsbefehl** m 🄵🄳 writ of execution.

'**vollsyn,thetisch** adj all-synthetic.

'**volltanken** v/t, v/i (sep, h) fill up.

'**Volltreffer** m direct hit, a. fig. bull's-eye.

'**volltrunken** adj completely drunk.

'**Vollversammlung** f plenary assembly.

'**Vollwaise** f orphan. '**Vollwaschmittel** n all-purpose washing powder.

'**vollwertig** adj full, adequate, of high value. '**Vollwertkost** f natural food.

'**vollzählig** [-tsɛːlɪç] adj **1. ~ sein** be present in full number; **~ erscheinen** assemble in full strength. **2.** complete.

voll'ziehen (irr, insep, no -ge-, h, → **ziehen**) **I** v/t a) execute, carry out, b) perform (*marriage ceremony etc*), c) consummate (*marriage*): **~de Gewalt** executive. **II** sich ~ take place. **Voll'zieher** m (-s; -) executor. **Voll'ziehung** f (-; no pl), **Voll'zug** m (-[e]s; no pl) execution, performance (*of marriage ceremony etc*), consummation (*of marriage*). **Voll'zugs|anstalt** f penal institution, prison. **~beamte** m prison officer.

Volontär [volɔnˈtɛːr] m (-s; -e), **Volon-**

'**tärin** f (-; -nen) unpaid trainee.

Volt [vɔlt] n (-, -[e]s; -) ⚡ volt.

'**Voltmeter** n (-s; -) voltmeter.

Volumen [voˈluːmən] n (-s; -, -mina) volume, a. capacity. **voluminös** [volumiˈnøːs] adj voluminous.

von [fɔn] prep **1.** from: **~ der Seite** from the side; **~ morgen an** from (*adm.* as of) tomorrow. **2.** a) of, b) by: **e-e Freundin ~ ihr** a friend of hers; **ein Bild ~ Picasso** a painting by Picasso; **sie nahm ~ dem Kuchen** she had some of the cake; **9 ~ 10 Leuten** 9 out of (*or* in) 10 people; → **selbst** I. **3.** of: **ein Mann ~ Bildung** a man of culture. **4.** of, about: **ich habe ~ ihm gehört** I have heard of him; **weißt du ~ der Sache?** do you know about this affair?

vonein'ander adv from each other.

vonstatten [fɔnˈʃtatən] adv **~ gehen** a) take place, b) go, proceed (*well etc*).

vor [foːr] prep **1.** a) before, in front (*dat* of), b) outside, c) in the presence (*dat* of): **~ der Klasse** in front of the class; **~ der Tür** at the door; **~ dem Gesetz** before the law. **2.** before, ago: **~ 10 Jahren** (*ein paar Tagen*) ten years (a few days) ago; **~ dem Essen** before dinner; **5 Minuten ~ 12** five minutes to (*Am.* of) 12, fig. at the eleventh hour; **j-m liegen** be (*or* lie) ahead of s.o.; **et. ~ sich haben** have s.th. ahead of one, b.s. be in for s.th.; **das haben wir noch ~ uns** that's still to come. **3.** for, with: **~ Angst** for fear; **~ Kälte** with cold; **~ lauter Arbeit** for all the work. **4.** above, before: **~ allem, ~ allen Dingen** above all. **5.** from, against; → **warnen.**

vor'ab adv **1.** first, to begin with. **2.** in advance.

'**Vorabend** m (**am ~** on) the eve (*gen* of).

'**Vorahnung** f premonition, foreboding.

vor'an adv before, at the head, in front: **mit dem Kopf ~** head first.

vor'angehen v/i (irr, sep, -ge-, sn, → **gehen**) **1.** lead the way, walk at the front (*or* head) (*dat* of): **j-n ~ lassen** let s.o. go first; → **Beispiel. 2.** precede (**e-r Sache** s.th.). **3.** fig. get on, get ahead.

vor'ankommen v/i (irr, sep, -ge-, sn, → **kommen**) make progress (*or* headway): **beruflich ~** get on in one's job.

'**Vorankündigung** f previous notice.

'Voranmeldung f booking: teleph. **Gespräch mit ~** person-to-person call.
vor'antreiben v/t (irr, sep, -ge-, h, → **treiben**) fig. press ahead with.
'Voranzeige f preannouncement, film: trailer.
'Vorarbeit f preparatory work, preparations. 'vorarbeiten v/i, v/t (sep, h) work in advance: **j-m ~** pave the way for s.o. 'Vorarbeiter m foreman. 'Vorarbeiterin f forewoman.
vor'aus¹ adv a. fig. ahead (dat of).
'voraus² adv im ~ in advance.
vor'aus|ahnen v/t (sep, h) anticipate. ~berechnen v/t (sep, h) precalculate. ~bezahlen v/t (sep, h) prepay, pay s.th. in advance.
Vor'ausexem,plar n advance copy.
vor'aus|fahren v/i (irr, sep, -ge-, sn, → **fahren**) drive ahead (dat of). ~gehen v/i (irr, sep, -ge-, sn, → **gehen**) 1. go ahead (dat of). 2. precede (e-r Sache s.th.).
vor'ausgesetzt conj ~, daß provided (that), on condition that.
vor'aushaben v/t (irr, sep, -ge-, h, → **haben**) j-m einige Erfahrung etc ~ have the advantage of greater experience etc over s.o.
Vor'auskasse f † gegen ~ cash before delivery.
vor'aus|laufen v/i (irr, sep, -ge-, sn, → **laufen**) run on ahead (dat of). ~planen v/t, v/i (sep, h) plan s.th. ahead.
Vor'aussage f (-; -n) prediction, forecast. voraus'sagen v/t (sep, h) predict, forecast.
vor'ausschauend adj fig. foresighted.
vor'ausschicken v/t (sep, h) 1. send on ahead. 2. ~, daß first mention that.
vor'aussehen v/t (irr, sep, -ge-, h, → **sehen**) foresee, expect: **das war vorauszusehen** that was to be expected.
vor'aussetzen v/t (sep, h) 1. require. 2. assume, expect: **et. stillschweigend ~** take s.th. for granted; **ich setze diese Tatsachen als bekannt voraus** I assume that these facts are known; → **vorausgesetzt.**
Vor'aussetzung f (-; -en) 1. condition, prerequisite: **unter der ~, daß** on condition that; **die ~en erfüllen** meet the requirements. 2. assumption.
Vor'aussicht f (in weiser ~ with wise) foresight; **aller ~ nach** in all probability. **vor'aussichtlich I** adj prospective, expected. **II** adv probably: **er kommt ~ a.** he is likely (or expected) to come.
Vor'auszahlung f advance payment.
'Vorbau m (-[e]s; -ten) 1. front part (of a building). 2. porch. 'vorbauen (sep, h) **I** v/t build s.th. in front (or out). **II** v/i fig. take precautions.
'Vorbedeutung f (-; -en) omen.
'Vorbedingung f (-; -en) condition.
'Vorbehalt m (-[e]s; -e) reservation, proviso: **unter dem ~, daß** provided (that); **ohne ~** without reservation.
'vorbehalten v/t (irr, sep, h, → **behalten**) reserve: **Änderungen ~** subject to change (without notice); **Irrtümer ~** errors excepted; **alle Rechte ~** all rights reserved; **sich (das Recht) ~ zu** inf reserve the right to inf; **j-m ~ sein** (or **bleiben**) be left to s.o.
'vorbehaltlich prep (gen) subject to.
'vorbehaltlos adj unreserved.
'vorbehandeln v/t (sep, h) pretreat.
vor'bei adv 1. a. ~ an (dat) past, by: **~!** missed! 2. a) over, finished, b) gone, c) past: **5 Uhr ~** past five (o'clock); **es ist aus und ~** it's all over and done with.
vor'bei|fahren v/i (irr, sep, -ge-, sn, → **fahren**) ~ an (dat) drive past. ~gehen v/i (irr, sep, -ge-, sn, → **gehen**) 1. ~ an (dat) pass by, fig. miss, pass s.th. by: **im ♀ ~** in passing. 2. fig. pass. 3. shot etc: miss (the mark). ~kommen v/i (irr, sep, -ge-, sn, → **kommen**) 1. ~ an (dat) pass by, get past (or round), pass (obstacle etc). 2. F drop in (bei on). ~lassen v/t (irr, sep, -ge-, h, → **lassen**) let s.o., s.th. pass. ~mar,schieren v/i (sep, sn) ~ an (dat) march past. ~reden v/i (sep, h) aneinander ~ talk at cross-purposes; **am Thema ~** miss the point. ~schießen v/i (irr, sep, -ge-, h, → **schießen**) miss: (am Tor) ~ shoot wide. ~ziehen v/i (irr, sep, -ge-, sn, → **ziehen**) an j-m ~ 1. pass (or go past, sports: overtake) s.o. 2. fig. go through s.o.'s mind.
'vorbelastet adj erblich ~ sein have a hereditary handicap.
'Vorbemerkung f preliminary remark.
'vorbereiten v/t (a. sich ~) (sep, h) (für, auf acc for) prepare, get ready: **sich auf das Schlimmste ~** be prepared for the worst. 'vorbereitend adj preparatory.
'Vorbereitung f (-; -en) preparation

(für, zu, auf *acc* for): **~en treffen** make preparations (*or* prepare) (**für** for); **in ~** in preparation, being prepared.

'**Vorbericht** *m* preliminary report.

'**vorberuflich** *adj* prevocational.

'**Vorbesprechung** *f* preliminary discussion (*or* talk).

'**vorbestellen** *v/t* (*sep*, h) book *room, tickets, etc* in advance, reserve.

'**Vorbestellung** *f* (-; -en) advance booking, reservation.

'**vorbestraft** *adj* **~ sein** have a police record.

'**vorbeugen** (*sep*, h) **I** *v/i* **e-r Sache ~** prevent (*or* guard against) s.th. **II sich ~** bend forward. '**vorbeugend** *adj* preventive, 🍏 (*a*. **~es Mittel**) prophylactic.

'**Vorbild** *n* (-[e]s; -er) model, example: **leuchtendes ~** shining example; **sich j-n zum ~ nehmen** follow s.o.'s example; (**j-m**) **ein ~ sein** set an example (to s.o.). '**vorbildlich** *adj* exemplary, model: **er benahm sich ~** he behaved in an exemplary manner.

'**Vorbildung** *f* (-; *no pl*) (previous) training, education(al background).

'**Vorbote** *m* (-n; -n) *fig.* herald (*gen* of).

'**vorbringen** *v/t* (*irr, sep*, -ge-, h, → **bringen**) bring forward (*argument etc*), express, state (*wish, claim, etc*), offer (*excuse, reasons, etc*), raise (*objection*), enter (*protest*), ⚖ prefer (*charges*).

'**vorchristlich** *adj* pre-Christian.

'**Vordach** *n* canopy.

'**vorda,tieren** *v/t* (*sep*, h) a) postdate, b) antedate.

'**Vordenker** *m* (-s; -) thinker, brain.

vorder ['fɔrdər] *adj* front.

'**Vorder|achse** *f* front axle. **~ansicht** *f* front view. **~bein** *n* zo. foreleg. **~deck** *n* ⚓ foredeck. **~fuß** *m* zo. forefoot, front paw (*of cat, dog, etc*).

'**Vordergrund** *m* (-[e]s; *no pl*) foreground: *fig.* **in den ~ rücken** come to the fore; **et. in den ~ stellen** give s.th. special emphasis. '**vordergründig** [-grʏndɪç] *adj* (*adv* on the) surface.

'**Vorder|haus** *n* front building. **~lauf** *m* hunt. foreleg. **~mann** *m* (-[e]s; **~er**) **mein ~** the person in front of me; F *auf ~ bringen* a) **j-n** make s.o. pull his socks up, b) *et.* bring s.th. up to scratch. **~rad** *n* front wheel. **~rad...** front-wheel (*brake, drive, etc*). **~reihe** *f* front row.

~seite *f* front, 🔺, ⚙ *a.* face, obverse (*of coin*). **~sitz** *m* front seat.

vorderst ['fɔrdərst] *adj* front.

'**Vorder|teil** *m, n* front (part). **~tür** *f* front door. **~zahn** *m* front tooth.

'**vordrängen: sich ~** (*sep*, h) a) push forward, b) jump the queue, c) *fig.* put o.s. forward.

'**vordringen** *v/i* (*irr, sep*, -ge-, sn, → **dringen**) push (*or* forge) ahead: **~ in** (*acc*) *a. fig.* penetrate into; **~** (**bis**) **zu** *a. fig.* work one's way through to. '**vordringlich** *adj* urgent, priority (*task etc*): **~ behandelt werden** be given priority.

'**Vordruck** *m* (-[e]s; -e) form, *Am.* blank.

'**vorehelich** *adj* premarital.

'**voreilig** *adj* hasty, rash: **~e Schlüsse ziehen** jump to conclusions. '**Voreiligkeit** *f* (-; *no pl*) rashness, hastiness.

vorein'ander *adv* **1.** one in front of the other. **2. Achtung ~** respect for each other; **sie haben Angst ~** they are afraid of each other.

'**voreingenommen** *adj* (**gegenüber** against) prejudiced, bias(s)ed.

'**Voreingenommenheit** *f* (-; *no pl*) prejudice, bias.

'**vorenthalten** *v/t* (*irr, sep*, h, → **enthalten**) **j-m et. ~** keep s.th. from s.o.

'**Vorentscheidung** *f* preliminary decision.

'**vorerst** *adv* for the time being.

'**Vorex,amen** *n* preliminary examination.

Vorfahr ['fo:rfa:r] *m* (-en; -en) ancestor.

'**vorfahren** *v/i* (*irr, sep*, -ge-, sn, → **fahren**) drive up (**vor** *dat* before). '**Vorfahrt** *f* (-; *no pl*) priority, right of way: **~ beachten!** give way! '**vorfahrt(s)berechtigt** *adj* having the right of way.

'**Vorfahrt(s)|schild** *n* sign regulating priority. **~straße** *f* priority road.

'**Vorfall** *m* (-[e]s; **~e**) **1.** incident, occurrence. **2.** 🩺 prolapse. '**vorfallen** *v/i* (*irr, sep*, -ge-, sn, → **fallen**) happen, occur.

'**Vorfeld** *n* **1.** ✈ apron. **2.** *fig.* **im ~** (*gen*) in the run-up to.

'**Vorfilm** *m* supporting film.

'**vorfinan,zieren** *v/t* (*sep*, h) prefinance.

'**vorfinden** *v/t* (*irr, sep*, -ge-, h, → **finden**) find.

'**Vorfreude** *f* (-; -n) anticipation.

vorfristig ['fo:rfrɪstɪç] *adj and adv* ahead of time.

'**Vorfrühling** *m* early spring.
'**vorfühlen** *v/i* (*sep*, h) **bei j-m ~** sound s.o. out.
'**vorführen** *v/t* (*sep*, h) **1.** show, present, model (*clothes*), demonstrate (*machine etc*), perform (*stunt*). **2.** *j-n ~* bring s.o. before (*e-m Richter* a judge *etc*), *fig.* make s.o. look like a fool.
'**Vorführer** *m* (-s; -) projectionist.
'**Vorführraum** *m* projection room.
'**Vorführung** *f* (-; -en) **1.** showing, presentation, ☼ demonstration, performance (*of stunts etc*). **2.** *thea. etc* show.
'**Vorführwagen** *m* demonstration car.
'**Vorgabe** *f* (-; -n) **1.** *sports:* a) start, handicap, b) stagger. **2.** a) precondition, stipulation, b) target, c) given (*or* set) data. **3.** ~*zeit f* ☼ allowed time.
'**Vorgang** *m* (-[e]s; ⸚e) **1.** proceedings, *biol.,* 🐾, ☼ process. **2.** occurrence, event. **3.** *adm.* file, record.
Vorgänger ['foːrgɛŋər] *m* (-s; -), '**Vorgängerin** *f* (-; -nen) predecessor.
'**Vorgarten** *m* front garden, *Am.* frontyard.
'**vorgeben** *v/t* (*irr, sep*, -ge-, h, → *geben*) **1.** *sports:* give, allow. **2.** allege, claim, pretend. **3.** a) prescribe, stipulate, b) give, set (*data etc*).
'**Vorgebirge** *n* foothills.
'**vorgefaßt** *adj* preconceived.
'**vorgefertigt** *adj* a. *fig.* prefabricated.
'**vorgehen** *v/i* (*irr, sep, -ge-, sn,* → *gehen*) **1.** go forward, go up (**zu** to), ✗ advance, ✗ lead the way: *m-e Uhr geht (e-e Minute) vor* my watch is (one minute) fast; F *geh schon mal vor!* you go on ahead! **2.** act: ~ *gegen* take action against; *gerichtlich gegen j-n ~* proceed against s.o.; *hart ~ gegen* crack down on. **3.** happen, go on: *was geht hier vor?* what's going on here? **4.** come first, have priority. '**Vorgehen** *n* (-s) **1.** (line of) action.
'**vorgelagert** *adj* ~*e Inseln* offshore islands.
'**Vorgeschichte** *f* (-; *no pl*) **1.** prehistory. **2.** (past) history, 🩺 case history.
'**vorgeschichtlich** *adj* prehistoric.
'**Vorgeschmack** *m* (-[e]s; *no pl*) foretaste (**auf** *acc*, **von** *dat*).
'**Vorgesetzte** *m, f* (-n; -n) superior.
'**Vorgespräche** *pl* preliminary talks.
'**vorgestern** *adv* the day before

yesterday: F *von ~* → '**vorgestrig** *adj* **1.** *paper etc* of the day before yesterday. **2.** *fig.* antiquated (*views etc*).
'**vorgreifen** *v/i* (*irr, sep, -ge-, h,* → *greifen*) *j-m* (**e-r Sache**) ~ anticipate s.o. (s.th.). '**Vorgriff** *m* (*im* ~ in) anticipation (**auf** *acc etc*).
'**vorhaben** *v/t* (*irr, sep, -ge-, h,* → *haben*) ~ *zu inf* plan (*or* have in mind, intend) to *inf; e-e Reise* ~ plan to go on a journey; *was habt ihr heute vor?* what are your plans for today?; *haben Sie heute abend etwas vor?* have you got anything planned for tonight?; *morgen habe ich e-e Menge vor* I've got a lot to do tomorrow; *was hast du damit vor?* what are you going to do with it?; *was hast du jetzt wieder vor?* what are you up to now?
'**Vorhaben** *n* (-s; -) intention, plan(s), (*a. building*) project.
'**Vorhalle** *f* (entrance) hall, vestibule.
'**Vorhalt** *m* (-[e]s; -e) ♩ suspension.
'**vorhalten** *v/t* (*irr, sep, -ge-, h,* → *halten*) *j-m et.* ~ a) hold s.th. (up) in front of s.o., b) *fig.* reproach s.o. with s.th.; *mit vorgehaltener Pistole* at pistol point.
'**Vorhaltung** *f* (-; -en) reproach: *j-m ~en machen* remonstrate with s.o. (*über acc* about).
'**Vorhand** *f* (-; *no pl*) *tennis etc:* forehand.
vorhanden [foːrˈhandən] *adj* existing, available, 🛒 in stock: ~ *sein* exist; *es ist nichts mehr ~* there is nothing left.
Vor'handensein *n* (-s) existence.
'**Vorhang** *m* (-[e]s; ⸚e) curtain, drapes.
'**Vorhängeschloß** *n* padlock.
'**Vorhaut** *f* *anat.* foreskin, prepuce.
'**vorher** *adv* before: *am Abend ~* the evening before, the previous evening.
vor'herbestimmen *v/t* (*sep*, h) a) predetermine, b) predestine.
vor'hergehen *v/i* (*irr, sep, -ge-, sn,* → *gehen*) *e-r Sache* ~ precede s.th.
vor'hergehend, vorherig [foːrˈheːrɪç] *adj* preceding, previous.
'**Vorherrschaft** *f* (-; *no pl*) predominance, supremacy.
'**vorherrschen** *v/i* (*sep*, h) predominate, prevail. '**vorherrschend** *adj* predominant, prevailing (*opinion etc*).
Vor'hersage *f* (-; -n) prediction, *a.* 🌱, *meteor.* forecast.
vor'hersagen *v/t* (*sep*, h) predict.

vor'hersehen v/t (irr, sep, -ge-, h, → **sehen**) foresee.

'vorhin adv a (short) while ago.

'Vorhut f (-; -en) ✕ van(guard).

vorig ['fo:rɪç] adj former, previous: **∼e Woche** last week.

'vorindustri,ell adj pre-industrial.

'Vorjahr n previous (or last) year.

vorjährig ['fo:rjɛ:rɪç] adj of last year.

'Vorkämpfer(in f) m champion.

'vorkauen v/t (sep, h) F fig. **j-m et. ∼** spoon-feed s.th. to s.o.

'Vorkaufsrecht n right of preemption: **das ∼ haben** a. have the refusal.

'Vorkehrung f (-; -en) measure, precaution: **∼en treffen** a) take measures (or precautions) (**gegen** against), b) make arrangements (**für** for).

'Vorkenntnisse pl previous knowledge (or experience).

'vorknöpfen v/t (sep, h) F **sich j-n ∼** take s.o. to task.

'vorkommen v/i (irr, sep, -ge-, sn, → **kommen**) **1.** be found, occur. **2.** happen, occur: **so et. ist mir noch nicht vorgekommen!** F well, I never!; **das darf nicht wieder ∼!** that must not (or don't let it) happen again! **3.** seem: **es kommt mir so vor, als ob** it seems to me as if; **sich dumm ∼** feel silly; **er kommt sich sehr klug vor** he thinks he is very clever; **sie kommt mir bekannt vor** she looks familiar; **das kommt dir nur so vor** you are just imagining it; **es kommt mir merkwürdig vor** it strikes me as (rather) strange. **'Vorkommen** n (-s; -) **1.** occurrence. **2.** ⚒ deposit(s).

'Vorkommnis n (-ses; -se) incident: **k-e besonderen ∼se** no unusual occurrence(s).

'Vorkriegs... prewar ...

'vorladen v/t (irr, sep, -ge-, h, → **laden**) ⚖ summon. **'Vorladung** f (-; -en) (writ of) summons.

'Vorlage f (-; -n) **1.** model, pattern: **et. als ∼ benutzen** copy from s.th. **2.** (**gegen ∼** on) presentation (gen of). **3.** parl. bill. **4.** sports: pass.

'vorlassen v/t (irr, sep, -ge-, h, → **lassen**) **j-n ∼** a) let s.o. go first, b) let s.o. pass, c) admit s.o. (**bei** to).

'Vorlauf m (-[e]s; ∞e) **1.** sports: preliminary heat. **2.** ⊙ forward run.

'Vorläufer m forerunner (a. skiing).

'vorläufig I adj temporary, provisional. **II** adv for the time being.

'vorlaut adj pert, cheeky.

'Vorleben n (-s; no pl) former life, past.

'vorlegen (sep, h) **I** v/t **1.** a) (dat to) present, submit, b) produce, show (document etc), c) bring out, publish: pol. **den Haushalt ∼** present the budget. **2.** put chain etc on. **3.** F **ein schnelles Tempo ∼** set a fast pace. **II** **sich ∼** lean forward. **'Vorleger** m (-s; -) rug, mat.

'vorlehnen: sich ∼ (sep, h) lean forward.

'Vorleistung f (-; -en) **1.** ✝ advance (payment). **2.** pol. advance concession.

'vorlesen (irr, sep, -ge-, h, → **lesen**) **I** v/t (**j-m**) **et. ∼** read s.th. (out) (to s.o.). **II** v/i **j-m ∼** read to s.o. (**aus** dat from, out of).

'Vorleser(in f) m reader.

'Vorlesung f (-; -en) (**e-e ∼ halten** give a) lecture (**über** acc on, **vor** to): **∼en halten** lecture (**über** acc on); **∼en hören** go to lectures. **'Vorlesungsverzeichnis** n program(me Br.) of lectures.

'vorletzt adj last but one: **∼e Woche** the week before last.

'Vorliebe f (-; -n) (**für** for) preference, special liking: **et. mit ∼ tun** love doing (or to do) s.th.

'vorliebnehmen v/i (irr, sep, -ge-, h, → **nehmen**) make do (**mit** with).

'vorliegen v/i (irr, sep, h, → **liegen**) **1.** **j-m ∼** lie before s.o.; **der Antrag liegt vor** the application has been submitted; **es liegen k-e Beschwerden vor** there are no complaints; **liegt sonst noch et. vor?** is there anything else? **2.** be, exist: **es liegen Gründe vor** there are reasons; **es lag Notwehr vor** it was a case of self-defen/ce (Am. -se); **da muß ein Irrtum ∼** there must be a mistake. **3.** be available, be out: **das Ergebnis liegt noch nicht vor** the result is not yet known. **'vorliegend** adj a) existing, present, b) available: **die ∼en Probleme** the problems at issue; **im ∼en Falle** in the present case.

'vorlügen v/t (irr, sep, -ge-, h, → **lügen**) **j-m et. ∼** lie to s.o.

'vormachen v/t (sep, h) F **j-m et. ∼** a) show s.o. how to do s.th., b) fool s.o.; **sich** (**selbst**) **et. ∼** fool (F kid) o.s.

'Vormacht(stellung) f (-; no pl) supremacy.

vormalig ['fo:rma:lɪç] adj former.

'**vormals** *adv* formerly.

'**Vormarsch** *m* advance: **im** (*or* **auf dem**) ~ advancing, *fig.* on the march.

'**vormerken** *v/t* (*sep*, h) make a note of: **sich ~ lassen** put one's name down (**für** for).

'**Vormieter(in** *f*) *m* previous tenant.

'**vormittag** *adv* **heute** (**gestern**) ~ this (yesterday) morning. '**Vormittag** *m* (-s; -e) (**am** ~ in the) morning. '**vormittags** *adv* in the morning: **Montag** ~, **montags** ~ every Monday morning.

'**Vormund** *m* (-[e]s; -e, ⸚er) guardian.

'**Vormundschaft** *f* (-; -en) guardianship.

vorn [fɔrn] *adv* in front, before, ahead: **ganz** ~ a) right in front, up front, b) at the beginning; **nach** ~ to the front, forward; **von** ~ from the front; (**nochmal**) **von** ~ **anfangen** begin at the beginning; (**nochmal**) **von** ~ **anfangen** start (all over) again; **noch einmal von** ~ all over again; **von** ~ **bis hinten** a) from front to back, b) from beginning to end.

'**Vorname** *m* Christian (*or* first, *esp. Am.* given) name.

vornehm ['foːrneːm] *adj* **1.** *a. fig.* noble: ⸚**e Gesinnung** high-mindedness. **2.** a) distinguished, b) elegant, fashionable, exclusive: **e-e** ⸚**e Dame** a distinguished lady; **e-e** ⸚**e Gegend** a fashionable quarter; F ~ **tun** give o.s. airs.

'**vornehmen** *v/t* (*irr*, *sep*, -ge-, h, → **nehmen**) **1.** make (*changes etc*), carry out (*work etc*). **2. sich et.** ~ plan, make plans for; **sich** ~ **zu** *inf* decide to *inf*; **sich zuviel** ~ take on too much; F **sich** *j-n* ~ take s.o. to task (**wegen** about).

'**Vornehmheit** *f* (-; *no pl*) **1.** nobility. **2.** a) distinction, b) elegance, refinement, exclusiveness: **ihre** ~ her distinguished appearance.

'**vornherein** *adv* **von** ~ from the start.

vorn'über *adv* forward.

'**Vorort** *m* (-[e]s; -e) suburb.

'**Vorort(s)...** suburban (*traffic etc*). ⸚**bewohner(in** *f*) *m* suburbanite. ⸚**zug** *m* suburban (*or* local, commuter) train.

'**Vorplatz** *m* forecourt, square.

'**Vorposten** *m* ⚔ outpost.

'**Vorpro,gramm** *n* film: supporting program(me *Br.*). '**vorprogram,mieren** *v/t* (*sep*, h) (pre)program(me *Br.*).

'**Vorprüfung** *f* preliminary examination.

'**vorragen** *v/i* (*sep*, h) project, protrude.

'**Vorrang** *m* (-[e]s; *no pl*) precedence, priority: **den** ~ **haben vor** (*dat*) take (*or* have) priority (*or* precedence) over.

'**vorrangig** ['foːrraŋɪç] *adj* priority: ~ **behandeln** give s.th. priority treatment.

'**Vorrangstellung** *f* (-; *no pl*) (position of) pre-eminence.

'**Vorrat** *m* (-[e]s; ⸚e) (**an** *dat* of) stock (*a. fig.*), store, supply, provisions, stockpile (*of weapons etc*): **von** ~ **anlegen** lay in a stock (**von** of); **solange der** ~ **reicht** while stocks last.

vorrätig ['foːrrɛːtɪç] *adj* available, ✝ in stock: **nicht** (**mehr**) ~ out of stock; **wir haben ... nicht mehr** ~ we are out of ...

'**Vorrats|behälter** *m* storage bin (*or* tank). ⸚**kammer** *f* pantry, larder.

'**Vorraum** *m* anteroom.

'**vorrechnen** *v/t* (*sep*, h) *j-m et.* ~ calculate s.th. for s.o.

'**Vorrecht** *n* privilege, prerogative.

'**Vorredner(in** *f*) *m* previous speaker.

'**Vorrichtung** *f* (-; -en) device, F gadget.

'**vorrücken** (*sep*) **I** *v/t* (h) move s.th. forward. **II** *v/i* (sn) move on, ⚔ advance.

'**Vorrunde** *f* *sports*: preliminary round.

'**vorsagen** (*sep*) **I** *v/t* *j-m et.* ~ tell s.o. s.th. **II** *v/i* *j-m* ~ tell s.o. the answer.

'**Vorsai,son** *f* (-; -s) early season.

'**Vorsatz** *m* (-es; ⸚e) resolution, intention, ⚖ (criminal) intent: **mit** ~ with intent, wil(l)fully.

vorsätzlich ['foːrzɛtslɪç] *adj* intentional, deliberate, ⚖ wil(l)ful: ⸚**er Mord** premeditated murder.

'**Vorschau** *f* (-; -en) preview (**auf** *acc* of), *film etc*: trailer(s).

'**Vorschein** *m* **zum** ~ **bringen** produce, *fig.* bring to light; **zum** ~ **kommen** come to light, appear, emerge.

'**vorschieben** *v/t* (*irr*, *sep*, -ge-, h, → **schieben**) **1.** push (*or* move) forward, advance. **2.** shoot (*bolt*): → **Riegel** 1. **3.** *fig. et.* ~ use s.th. as an excuse; *j-n* ~ use s.o. as a dummy.

'**vorschießen** *v/t* (*irr*, *sep*, -ge-, h, → **schießen**) advance (*sum*).

'**Vorschlag** *m* (-[e]s; ⸚e) suggestion, proposal (*a. parl.*), recommendation: **darf ich e-n** ~ **machen** may I offer a suggestion; **auf** ~ **von** (*or gen*) at the suggestion of s.o. '**vorschlagen** *v/t* (*irr*, *sep*, -ge-, h, → **schlagen**) suggest, propose (*s.o.*): **ich schlage vor, nach**

Hause zu gehen I suggest going (*or* that we go) home.

'**Vorschlußrunde** *f sports:* semifinal.

'**vorschnell** *adj* hasty, rash.

'**vorschreiben** *v/t* (*irr, sep,* -ge-, h, → **schreiben**) *fig.* prescribe, dictate: *ich lasse mir nichts* ∼*!* I won't be dictated to!; *das Gesetz schreibt vor, daß* the law provides that.

'**Vorschrift** *f* (-; -en) a) rule(s), regulation(s), b) direction, instruction: *nach ärztlicher* ∼ according to doctor's orders; *Dienst nach* ∼ work-to-rule; *streng nach* ∼ **arbeiten** work to rule.

'**vorschriftsmäßig** **I** *adj* correct, (as) prescribed, regulation ... **II** *adv* correctly, according to the regulations.

'**vorschriftswidrig** *adj and adv* contrary to the regulations.

'**Vorschub** *m* (-[e]s; ⁻e) **1.** ⊙ feed. **2.** *fig.* ∼ **leisten** (*dat*) encourage (*s.th., s.o.*).

'**Vorschulalter** *n* preschool age.

'**Vorschule** *f* preschool.

'**vorschulisch** *adj* preschool.

'**Vorschuß** *m* (-sses; ⁻sse) advance (payment) (*auf acc* on).

'**vorschützen** *v/t* (*sep,* h) *et.* ∼ plead s.th. (as an excuse).

'**vorschweben** *v/i* (*sep,* h) *mir schwebt ... vor* I'm thinking of ...

'**vorsehen** (*irr, sep,* -ge-, h, → **sehen**) **I** *v/t* **1.** plan, schedule: *das war nicht vorgesehen* that was not planned. **2.** intend, designate, *a.* earmark (*funds etc*): *j-n für e-n Posten* ∼ designate s.o. for a post. **II** *sich* ∼ be careful, watch out (*vor dat* against).

'**Vorsehung** *f* (-; *no pl*) *die* ∼ Providence.

'**vorsetzen** *v/t* (*sep,* h) *j-m et.* ∼ set s.th. before s.o., *a. fig.* offer s.o. s.th.

'**Vorsicht** *f* (-; *no pl*) caution, care: ∼*!* watch out!, careful!, (*inscription*) (handle) with care!; ∼*, Stufe!* mind the step!; *zur* ∼ as a precaution; *mit äußerster* ∼ with the utmost caution.

'**vorsichtig** *adj* cautious, careful: ∼*e Schätzung* conservative estimate; (*sei*) ∼*!* be careful!; ∼ *fahren* drive carefully.

'**vorsichtshalber** *adv* as a precaution.

'**Vorsichtsmaßnahme** *f* precaution(ary measure): ∼*n treffen* take precautions.

'**Vorsilbe** *f ling.* prefix.

'**vorsingen** (*irr, sep,* -ge-, h, → **singen**) **I** *v/t j-m et.* ∼ sing s.th. to s.o. **II** *v/i*

audition (*bei* with): *j-n* ∼ *lassen* audition s.o.

'**vorsintflutlich** *adj* F *fig.* antediluvian.

'**Vorsitz** *m* (-es; *no pl*) chair(manship), presidency: *bei e-r Versammlung den* ∼ *haben* (*or* **führen**) preside over (*or* chair, be in the chair at) a meeting; *unter dem* ∼ *von ...* with ... in the chair.

'**Vorsitzende** *m, f* (-n; -n) **1.** president, chairman (chairwoman), chairperson. **2.** ⚖ presiding judge.

'**Vorsorge** *f* (-; *no pl*) provision, precaution: ∼ *treffen* take precautions (*daß* that), provide (*gegen* against).

'**vorsorgen** *v/i* (*sep,* h) (*für* for) make provisions, provide.

'**Vorsorgeuntersuchung** *f* (preventive) medical checkup.

'**vorsorglich** [-zɔrklɪç] **I** *adj* precautionary. **II** *adv* as a precaution.

'**Vorspann** *m* (-[e]s; -e) **1.** introduction. **2.** *film:* a) (title and) credits, b) pre-title sequence.

'**Vorspeise** *f* hors d'oeuvre, starter: *als* ∼ *a.* for starters.

'**Vorspiegelung** *f* (-; -en) preten/ce (*Am.* -se): *unter* ∼ *falscher Tatsachen* under false preten/ces (*Am.* -ses).

'**Vorspiel** *n* (-[e]s; -e) **1.** (*zu* to) *a. fig.* a) ♪ prelude, b) *thea.* curtain-raiser, prolog(ue *Br.*). **2.** foreplay. '**vorspielen** (*sep,* h) **I** *v/t* play: *j-m et.* ∼ play s.th. to s.o., *fig.* put on an act for s.o.'s benefit. **II** *v/i* a) play, b) audition (*bei* with): *j-n* ∼ *lassen* audition s.o.

'**vorsprechen** (*irr, sep,* -ge-, h, → **sprechen**) **I** *v/t* **1.** *j-m et.* ∼ pronounce s.th. for s.o. to repeat. **2.** recite. **II** *v/i* **3.** *thea.* audition (*bei* with): *j-n* ∼ *lassen* audition s.o. **4.** call (*bei* at).

'**vorspringen** *v/i* (*irr, sep,* -ge-, sn, → **springen**) **1.** leap forward. **2.** project, jut (out). '**vorspringend** *adj* projecting, jutting, prominent (*a. nose, chin*).

'**Vorsprung** *m* (-[e]s; ⁻e) **1.** △ projection, ledge. **2.** *a. sports:* a) start, b) lead: *ich gebe dir 5 Minuten* ∼ I'll give you a start of five minutes; *sein* ∼ *beträgt 30 Sekunden* he has a lead of 30 seconds (*vor dat* on); *mit großem* ∼ by a wide margin; *e-n* ∼ *haben a. fig.* be ahead (*vor dat* of).

'**Vorstadt** *f* suburb.

'**Vorstadtbewohner** *m* suburbanite.

'**vorstädtisch** *adj* suburban.

'**Vorstand** *m* (-[e]s; ⸗e) 1. ✝ board of directors: *im ⸗ sitzen* be on the board. 2. managing committee (*of club etc*). 3. chairman, *Am.* chief executive.

'**Vorstands|e,tage** *f* executive floor. **⸗mitglied** *n* member of the board. **⸗sitzung** *f* board meeting. **⸗vorsitzende** *m, f* (-n; -n) chairman (chairwoman) (*of the board*), *Am.* chief executive. **⸗wahl** *f* board elections.

'**vorstehen** *v/i* (*irr, sep,* -ge-, h, → **stehen**) 1. project, jut out, *eyes:* protrude. 2. (*dat*) direct, be at the head of, run (*institute etc*). '**vorstehend** *adj* projecting, protruding (*a. eyes, teeth, etc*): **⸗e Zähne** *a.* buckteeth. '**Vorsteher** *m* (-s; -) manager, director, head.

'**Vorsteherdrüse** *f anat.* prostate gland.

'**vorstellbar** *adj* conceivable, imaginable. '**vorstellen** (*sep,* h) **I** *v/t* 1. move *s.th.* forward. 2. put *clock etc* forward. 3. *j-n j-m ⸗* introduce s.o. to s.o.: *darf ich Ihnen Herrn X ⸗?* may I introduce you to Mr X, I'd like you to meet Mr X. 4. ✝ present, introduce (*new product*). 5. a) represent, b) mean: *was soll das Bild ⸗?* what's that picture supposed to be?; F *er stellt etwas vor* he's quite somebody. 6. *sich et. ⸗* fancy, imagine, picture, have *s.th.* in mind; F *stell dir vor!* fancy!, just imagine!; *du kannst dir gar nicht ⸗ ...* you've no idea ...; *man kann sich ihre Enttäuschung ⸗* you can picture her disappointment; *so stelle ich mir ... vor* that's my idea of ...; *stellt euch das nicht so leicht vor!* don't think it's so easy; *darunter kann ich mir nichts ⸗* I can't imagine anything to me. **II** *sich ⸗* introduce o.s. ([*bei*] *j-m* to s.o.), *bei* go for an interview with *a firm etc*.

'**Vorstellung** *f* (-; -en) 1. introduction, ✝ *a.* presentation (*of new product*). 2. interview (*bei* with). 3. *thea.* performance, show, *film:* show(ing). 4. idea, notion, concept: *falsche ⸗* wrong idea; misconception; *sich e-e ⸗ machen* form an idea (*or a picture*) (*von* of); F *du machst dir k-e ⸗!* you've no idea; *das entspricht nicht m-n ⸗en* that's not what I expected (*or had in mind*). 5. imagination.

'**Vorstellungsgespräch** *n* interview.

'**Vorstopper** *m* (-s; -) *soccer:* centre (*Am.* center) half.

'**Vorstoß** *m* (-es; ⸗e) ✗ advance, *sports:* attack (*a. fig.*), *pol. or fig.* démarche.

'**vorstoßen** *v/i* (*irr, sep,* -ge-, sn, → **stoßen**) ✗ advance, *sports:* attack: *fig. ⸗ in* (*acc*) venture into; *⸗ zu* reach.

'**Vorstrafe** *f* previous conviction. '**Vorstrafen(re,gister** *n*) *pl* police record.

'**vorstrecken** *v/t* (*sep,* h) 1. stretch out, stick *one's head* out. 2. advance (*sum*).

'**Vorstufe** *f* preliminary stage.

'**vorstürmen** *v/i* (*sep,* sn) rush forward.

'**Vortag** *m* previous day, day before.

'**vortasten:** *sich ⸗* (*sep,* h) grope one's way (*bis zu* to).

'**vortäuschen** *v/t* (*sep,* h) feign, simulate, fake, pretend: *Interesse ⸗* pretend to be interested.

Vorteil ['fɔrtaɪl] *m* (-[e]s; -e) a) advantage (*a. tennis*), b) benefit: *die Vor- und Nachteile e-r Sache gegeneinander abwägen* consider the pros and cons; *im ⸗ sein* have the advantage (*gegenüber* over); *auf s-n eigenen ⸗ bedacht sein* have an eye to the main chance; *⸗ ziehen aus* profit by; *sich zu s-m ⸗ verändern* change for the better.

'**vorteilhaft** *adj* advantageous, profitable, becoming (*dress etc*): *⸗ aussehen* look attractive; *sich ⸗ auswirken* have a favo(u)rable effect (*auf acc* on).

Vortrag ['fo:rtra:k] *m* (-[e]s; ⸗e) 1. lecture (*über acc* on): *e-n ⸗ halten* (*vor dat* to) give a lecture (*or* talk), read a paper; F *j-m e-n ⸗ halten* lecture s.o. 2. performance, recitation (*of poetry*), ♪ recital, execution. 3. ✝ carryover.

'**vortragen** *v/t* (*irr, sep,* -ge-, h, → **tragen**) 1. state, present, express. 2. perform, play, sing, recite. 3. ✝ carry forward. '**Vortragende** *m* (-n; -n) 1. lecturer, speaker. 2. ♪ *etc* performer.

'**Vortragsreihe** *f* series of lectures.

'**Vortragsreise** *f* lecture tour.

'**vortreten** *v/i* (*irr, sep,* -ge-, sn, → **treten**) 1. step (*or* come) forward. 2. protrude.

'**Vortritt** *m* (-[e]s; *no pl*) (*den ⸗ haben* take) precedence (*vor dat* over): *j-m den ⸗ lassen* let s.o. go first.

vor'**über** *adv* **⸗ sein** be over.

vor'**übergehen** *v/i* (*irr, sep,* -ge-, sn, → **gehen**) pass, *fig. a.* go away. vor'**über-**

gehend I *adj* temporary, passing. **II** *adv* temporarily, for a short time.
'**Vorübung** *f* preliminary exercise.
'**Voruntersuchung** *f* 🏛, ⚕ preliminary examination.
'**Vorurteil** *n* prejudice: ～**e haben gegen** be prejudiced against.
'**vorurteilsfrei**, '**vorurteilslos** *adj* unprejudiced, unbias(s)ed.
'**Vorvergangenheit** *f ling.* past perfect, pluperfect.
'**Vorverhandlung** *f* **1.** 🏛 preliminary trial. **2.** *pl* ✝, *pol.* preliminary negotiations, preliminaries.
'**Vorverkauf** *m* (-[e]s; *no pl*) advance sale (*thea.* booking): **im ～ besorgen** buy (*or* book) *tickets* in advance.
'**Vorverkaufskasse** *f*, '**Vorverkaufsstelle** *f* (advance) booking office.
'**vorverlegen** *v/t* (*sep*, h) advance.
'**Vorverstärker** *m* 🎼 pre-amplifier.
'**Vorvertrag** *m* precontract.
'**vorvorig** *adj the year etc* before last.
'**Vorwahl** *f* **1.** *pol.* preliminary election, *Am.* primary (election). **2.** → **Vorwählnummer** *f teleph.* dialling (*Am.* area) code.
'**Vorwand** *m* (-[e]s; ⁻e) pretext, excuse: **unter dem ～ von** (*or* **daß**) on the pretext of (*or* that).
'**vorwärmen** *v/t* (*sep*, h) warm, preheat.
'**Vorwarnung** *f* (advance) warning.
'**vorwärts** *adv* forward, onward, on: ～**!** let's go!
'**Vorwärtsgang** *m mot.* forward speed.
'**vorwärtsgehen** *v/i* (*irr*, *sep*, -ge-, sn, → **gehen**) F (make) progress.
'**Vorwäsche** *f* (-; -n), '**Vorwaschen** *n* (-s) prewash.
vor'weg *adv* beforehand.
Vor'wegnahme *f* (-; *no pl*) anticipation.
vor'wegnehmen *v/t* (*irr*, *sep*, -ge-, h, → **nehmen**) anticipate: **um es gleich vorwegzunehmen** to come to the point.
'**vorweihnachtlich** *adj* pre-Christmas.
'**Vorweihnachtszeit** *f* Advent season.
'**vorweisen** *v/t* (*irr*, *sep*, h, → **weisen**) produce, show.
'**vorwerfen** *v/t* (*irr*, *sep*, -ge-, h, → **werfen**) **1.** e-m *Tier et.* ～ throw s.th. to an

animal. **2.** *j-m* **Faulheit** *etc* ～ reproach s.o. with laziness (*or* for being lazy *etc*): **ich habe mir nichts vorzuwerfen** I have nothing to blame myself for.
'**vorwiegend** *adv* predominantly, mainly, chiefly: ～ **sonnig** mainly sunny.
'**Vorwort** *n* (-[e]s; -e) foreword, preface.
'**Vorwurf** *m* (-[e]s; ⁻e) reproach: *j-m* **Vorwürfe machen** reproach s.o. (**wegen** for). '**vorwurfsvoll** *adj* reproachful.
'**vorzählen** *v/t* (*sep*, h) *j-m et.* ～ count s.th. out to s.o.
'**Vorzeichen** *n* **1.** omen. **2.** ♪ accidental. **3.** ♈ sign: *fig.* **mit umgekehrtem ～** the other way round.
'**vorzeichnen** *v/t* (*sep*, h) *j-m et.* ～ draw (*fig.* trace out) s.th. for s.o.
vorzeigbar ['foːrtsaɪkbaːr] *adj* presentable. '**vorzeigen** *v/t* (*sep*, h) show.
'**Vorzeit** *f* **der Mensch der ～** prehistoric man; *fig.* **in grauer ～** ages and ages ago.
'**vorzeitig** *adj* premature.
'**Vorzen sur** *f* precensorship: **e-r ～ unterziehen** precensor.
'**vorziehen** *v/t* (*irr*, *sep*, -ge-, h, → **ziehen**) **1.** pull out. **2.** **die Vorhänge ～** pull the curtains. **3.** advance (*date etc*), deal with *s.th.* first. **4.** prefer (*dat* to): **es ～ zu** *inf* prefer to *inf*; *j-n* ～ favo(u)r s.o.
'**Vorzimmer** *n* anteroom, outer office.
'**Vorzimmerdame** *f* receptionist.
'**Vorzug** *m* (-[e]s; ⁻e) **1.** (*vor dat* over) priority, preference. **2.** (advantage, merit. **3.** privilege. **vorzüglich** [foːrˈtsyːklɪç] *adj* excellent, exquisite, first-rate.
'**Vorzugs aktien** *pl* preference shares, *Am.* preferred stock. ～**milch** *f* full-cream milk. ～**preis** *m* special price.
'**vorzugsweise** *adv* **1.** preferably. **2.** chiefly, mainly.
votieren [voˈtiːrən] *v/i* (h) vote.
Votum ['voːtʊm] *n* (-s; -ten, -ta) vote.
Voyeur [vŏaˈjøːr] *m* (-s; -e) voyeur.
vulgär [vʊlˈɡɛːr] *adj* vulgar.
Vulkan [vʊlˈkaːn] *m* (-s; -e) volcano. ～**ausbruch** *m* (volcanic) eruption.
vul'kanisch *adj geol.* volcanic.
vulkanisieren [vʊlkaniˈziːrən] *v/t* (h) ⚙ vulcanize, *mot. a.* recap.

W

W, w [ve:] *n* (-; -) W, w.

Waage ['va:gə] *f* (-; -n) **1.** (pair of) scales, balance (*a. fig.*): *fig.* **sich die ~ halten** balance each other; → **Zünglein. 2.** *astr.* (**er ist** [e-e] **~ he is** [a]) Libra.

'waagerecht *adj* horizontal.

Waagschale ['va:k-] *f* scale: *fig.* **in die ~ werfen** bring *s.th.* to bear; **s-e Worte auf die ~ legen** weigh one's words.

wabb(e)lig ['vab(ə)lıç] *adj* flabby.

wabbeln ['vabəln] *v/i* (h) wabble.

Wabe ['va:bə] *f* (-; -n) honeycomb.

'Wabenhonig *m* comb honey.

wach [vax] *adj* **1.** awake: **~ werden** *a. fig.* wake up, awake; **~ liegen** lie awake. **2.** *fig.* alert, wide-awake.

'Wachablösung *f* **1.** ✕ changing of the guard. **2.** *fig. pol.* change of power.

Wache ['vaxə] *f* (-; -n) **1.** guard: **~ halten** → **wachen 2.** ✕ a) guard, sentry, b) guardroom: **auf ~** on guard, on duty; **~ stehen**, F **~ schieben** be on guard. **3.** police station.

'wachen *v/i* (h) **1. ~ über** (*acc*) watch (over), guard; **darüber ~, daß** see (to it) that. **2. bei j-m ~** sit up with s.o.

'Wachhabende *m* (-n; -n) ✕ commander of the guard.

'Wachhalten *v/t* (*irr, sep*, -ge-, h, → **halten**) *fig. et.* **~** keep *s.th.* alive.

'Wachhund *m a. fig.* watchdog.

'Wachmannschaft *f* guard.

Wacholder [va'xɔldər] *m* (-s; -) **1.** juniper. **2.** → **Wa'cholderschnaps** *m* gin.

'Wachposten *m* guard, ✕ sentry.

'wachrufen *v/t* (*irr, sep*, -ge-, h, → **rufen**) rouse, bring back (*memories etc*). **~rütteln** *v/t* (*sep*, h) rouse (*aus* from).

Wachs [vaks] *n* (-es; -e) wax.

'Wachsabdruck *m* wax impression.

'wachsam *adj* watchful, vigilant: **ein ~es Auge haben auf** (*acc*) keep a sharp eye on. **'Wachsamkeit** *f* (-; *no pl*) vigilance, watchfulness.

wachsen¹ ['vaksən] *v/i* (wuchs, gewachsen, sn) grow, *fig. a.* increase (**an** *dat* in): → **Bart 1**, *gewachsen* II.

'wachsen² *v/t* (h) wax (*a. ski*).

'Wachsfigur *f* wax figure, *pl a.* waxwork. **~figurenkabinett** *n* waxworks.

~kerze *f* wax candle. **~tuch** *n* oilcloth.

'Wachstum *n* (-s; *no pl*) growth (*a.* ✝), *fig. a.* increase, expansion: (**noch**) **im ~ begriffen** still growing.

'wachstumsfördernd *adj* **1.** 🌿 growth-inducing. **2.** ✝ growth-stimulating. **~hemmend** *adj* growth-retarding.

'Wachstumsindustrie *f* growth industry. **~rate** *f* rate of (economic) growth.

'wachsweich *adj* **1.** *a. fig.* (as) soft as wax. **2.** medium boiled (*egg*).

Wachtel ['vaxtəl] *f* (-; -n) zo. quail.

Wächter ['vɛçtər] *m* (-s; -) a) guard, b) attendant, c) watchman.

'Wachtraum *m* daydream.

'Wach(t)turm *m* watchtower.

'Wach- und Schließgesellschaft *f* Security Corps.

wack(e)lig ['vak(ə)lıç] *adj* shaky, wobbly (*a.* F *fig.*), rickety (*chair etc*), loose (*tooth, screw*): *a. fig.* **auf ~en Beinen stehen** stand on shaky legs, be shaky.

'Wackelkontakt *m* 💡 loose contact.

wackeln ['vakəln] *v/i* (h) a) wobble, *tooth, screw, etc*: *a.* be loose, b) totter, F *fig. government, job, etc*: be shaky: **mit den Ohren ~** waggle one's ears.

Wade ['va:də] *f* (-; -n) calf.

'Wadenkrampf *m* cramp in the leg.

Waffe ['vafə] *f* (-; -n) weapon (*a. fig.*), *pl* arms: **~n tragen** bear arms; **j-n mit s-n eigenen ~n schlagen** beat s.o. at his own game.

Waffel ['vafəl] *f* (-; -n) waffle, wafer.

'Waffeleisen *n* waffle iron.

'Waffenbesitz *m* possession of firearms. **~fabrik** *f* arms factory. **~gattung** *f* arm, branch (of the service). **~gewalt** *f* (**mit ~** by) force of arms. **~handel** *m* arms trade. **~händler** *m* arms dealer. **~kammer** *f* armo(u)ry. **~lager** *n* **1.** ✕ ordnance depot. **2.** cache. **~lieferung** *f* supply of arms.

'waffenlos *adj* weaponless, unarmed.

'Waffenruhe *f* cease-fire. **~schein** *m* firearm certificate, *Am.* gun license. **~schmuggel** *m* gun-running. **~stillstand** *m* armistice, cease-fire, truce (*a. fig.*). **~system** *n* weapons system.

'wagemutig *adj* daring, bold.

wagen ['va:gən] *v/t* (h) venture (*a. sich ~*), risk, dare: *es ~* take the plunge; *es ~ mit* try; *sich ~ an* (*acc*) venture on *a task etc*; *wie können Sie es ~(, das zu sagen)?* how dare you (say that)?; *wer nicht wagt, der nicht gewinnt* nothing venture, nothing gained.

¹**Wagen** *m* (-s; -) **1.** a) vehicle, b) car, c) lorry, *Am.* truck, d) van. **2.** wag(g)on, cart: F *fig.* **j-m an den ~ fahren** tread on s.o.'s toes. **3.** 🚋 carriage, *Am.* car. **4.** *astr. der Große ~* the Great Bear, *Am.* the Big Dipper. **5.** *typewriter:* carriage. **~heber** *m mot.* jack. **~ko,lonne** *f* column of cars. **~ladung** *f* (cart)load, *Am.* truckload, 🚋 waggonload, *Am.* carload. **~pflege** *f* (car) maintenance. **~typ** *m* model. **~wäsche** *f* (-; -n) car wash.

Waggon [va'gõ:, va'gɔŋ] *m* (-s; -s) **1.** a) (railway) carriage, *Am.* (railroad) car, b) goods waggon, *Am.* freight car. **2.** waggonload, *Am.* carload.

waghalsig ['va:khalzɪç] *adj* daring.

Wagnis ['va:knɪs] *n* (-ses; -se) risk.

Wahl [va:l] *f* (-; -en) **1.** a) choice, alternative, b) selection: 🛒 *erste ~* top quality; *zweite ~* second-rate quality, seconds; *die ~ haben* have one's choice; *k-e* (*andere*) *~ haben* have no choice (*or* alternative) (*als* but); *vor der ~ stehen zu inf* be faced with the choice of *ger*; *s-e ~ treffen* make one's choice; *e-e gute ~ treffen* choose well; *wer die ~ hat, hat die Qual* the wider the choice, the greater the trouble. **2.** *pol.* a) election, b) poll(ing): **~en abhalten** hold elections; *zur ~ gehen* go to the polls; *in die engere ~ kommen* be short-listed.

Wahlalter *n* voting age.

¹**wählbar** *adj* eligible (for election).

¹**wahlberechtigt** *adj* entitled to vote.

Wahl|beteiligung *f* turnout (at the election): *hohe* (*geringe*) *~* heavy (poor) polling. **~bezirk** *m* ward, constituency, *Am.* electoral district.

wählen ['vɛ:lən] (h) **I** *v/t* **1.** choose, select. **2.** *esp. pol.* elect, vote for: *j-n zum Präsidenten ~* elect s.o. president; 🛒 *j-n in den Vorstand ~* vote s.o. on the board. **3.** *teleph.* dial. **II** *v/i* **4.** choose, make one's choice. **5.** *pol.* vote, (*a. ~ gehen*) go to the polls.

¹**Wähler** *m* (-s; -) voter.

¹**Wahlergebnis** *n* election results.

¹**Wählerin** *f* (-; -nen) voter.

¹**Wählerinitia,tive** *f* voters' initiative.

¹**wählerisch** *adj* particular, choosy: *iro. nicht gerade ~* not too particular (*in dat, mit* about).

¹**Wählerschaft** *f* (-; *no pl*) a) electorate, b) constituency, voters.

Wahl|fach *n ped.* optional subject, *Am. a.* elective. **2frei** *adj ped.* optional, *Am.* elective. **~gang** *m* (*im ersten ~* at the first) ballot. **~geschenk** *n* campaign promise. **~heimat** *f* adopted country. **~helfer(in** *f*) *m* campaign assistant. **~jahr** *n* election year. **~ka,bine** *f* polling booth. **~kampf** *m* electoral battle, election campaign. **~kreis** *m* → *Wahlbezirk.* **~leiter** *m* returning officer. **~liste** *f* electoral register. **~lo,kal** *n* polling station. **~lokomo,tive** *f* F *fig.* (great) vote-catcher.

¹**wahllos** *adj* indiscriminate.

Wahl|niederlage *f* election defeat. **~ordnung** *f* election regulations. **~pflicht** *f* electoral duty. **~pla,kat** *n* election poster. **~pro,gramm** *n* election platform. **~recht** *n* (-[e]s; *no pl*) a) right to vote, franchise, b) eligibility: *allgemeines ~* universal suffrage. **~rede** *f* electoral address. **~redner** *m* election speaker.

¹**Wählscheibe** *f teleph.* dial.

Wahl|sieg *m* election victory. **~spende** *f* election (campaign) contribution. **~spruch** *m* motto. **~stimme** *f* vote. **~tag** *m* election day. **~urne** *f* ballot box: *zur ~ gehen* go to the polls. **~versammlung** *f* election meeting. **~versprechen** *n* campaign promise. **~vorschlag** *m* election proposal.

¹**wahlweise** *adv* alternatively: *es gab ~ Fisch oder Fleisch* there was a choice of fish or meat.

Wahn [va:n] *m* (-[e]s; *no pl*) delusion, mania: *in e-m ~ befangen sein* be under a delusion. **~bild** *n* hallucination.

¹**Wahnsinn** *m* (-[e]s; *no pl*) a. F *fig.* insanity, madness. ¹**wahnsinnig I** *adj* **1.** mad, insane. **2.** F *fig.* a) mad, crazy, b) terrible (*shock, pain, etc*), c) terrific. **II** *adv* F *fig.* terribly, awfully: *~ verliebt* madly in love. **Wahnsinnige** *m, f* (-n; -n) lunatic, madman (madwoman).

¹**Wahnvorstellung** *f* delusion, idée fixe.

¹**wahnwitzig** *adj* mad, crazy.

wahr [va:r] *adj* true, real, genuine: *ein ~er Freund* a true friend; *~e Liebe* true love; *ein ~es Wunder* a real wonder; *so ~ ich lebe!* as sure as I live!; *so ~ mir Gott helfe!* so help me God!; *~ werden* come true; *F das darf doch nicht ~ sein!* I can't believe it!; *das ist nicht das Wahre* that's not the real thing.

wahren [va:rən] *v/t* (h) preserve, maintain, keep (*a. secret*), protect, safeguard (*interests*): → *Form* 1, *Schein*[1] 2.

während ['vɛ:rənt] **I** *prep* (*gen*) during, in the course of. **II** *conj* while.

'wahrhaben: nicht ~ wollen refuse to believe.

'wahrhaft I *adj* true, real. **II** *adv* ~ **wahr'haftig** *adv* truly, really, indeed.

'Wahrheit *f* (-; -en) truth: *in ~* in fact, in reality; *um die ~ zu sagen* truth to tell; *F j-m mal die ~ sagen* give s.o. a piece of one's mind.

'wahrheitsgemäß, **'wahrheitsgetreu I** *adj* truthful, true. **II** *adv* truthfully.

'Wahrheitsliebe *f* veracity. **'wahrheitsliebend** *adj* truthful, veracious.

'wahrlich *adv* truly, *bibl.* verily.

'wahrnehmbar *adj* perceptible, noticeable. **'wahrnehmen** *v/t* (*irr, sep*, -ge-, h, → *nehmen*) **1.** perceive, notice, *a.* see, *a.* hear. **2.** use, seize (*opportunity etc*), protect, safeguard (*interests etc*), observe (*deadline*). **'Wahrnehmung** *f* (-; -en) **1.** a) (*sinnliche ~* sense) perception, b) observation. **2.** *j-n mit der ~ s-r Geschäfte (Interessen) beauftragen* entrust s.o. with the care of one's business (the safeguarding of one's interests). **'Wahrnehmungsvermögen** *n* (-s; *no pl*) perceptive faculty.

'wahrsagen (*sep or insep*, h) **I** *v/t* prophesy. **II** *v/i* tell fortunes: *j-m ~* tell s.o.'s fortune. **'Wahrsager** *m* (-s; -), **'Wahrsagerin** *f* (-; -nen) fortune-teller.

wahr'scheinlich I *adj* probable, likely. **II** *adv* probably: *er wird ~ nicht kommen* he is not likely to come. **Wahr'scheinlichkeit** *f* (-; -en) (*aller ~ nach* in all) probability (*or* likelihood). **Wahr'scheinlichkeitsrechnung** *f* theory of probabilities.

'Wahrung *f* (-; *no pl*) maintenance, protection, safeguarding (*of interests etc*).

Währung ['vɛ:rʊŋ] *f* (-; -en) currency.

'Währungs|abkommen *n* monetary agreement. **~block** *m* monetary bloc. **~einheit** *f* unit of currency. **~krise** *f* monetary crisis. **~poli,tik** *f* monetary policy. **~re,form** *f* currency reform. **~sy,stem** *n* monetary system. **~uni,on** *f* monetary union.

'Wahrzeichen *n* **1.** symbol, emblem. **2.** landmark.

Waise ['vaizə] *f* (-; -n) orphan: (*zur*) *~ werden* be orphaned.

'Waisen|haus *n* orphanage. **~kind** *n* orphan. **~knabe** *m* *fig. gegen ihn sind wir die reinsten ~n* we are mere babes compared to him.

Wal [va:l] *m* (-[e]s; -e) *zo.* whale.

Wald [valt] *m* (-[e]s; *~*er) wood, forest (*a. fig.*): *er sieht den ~ vor lauter Bäumen nicht* he can't see the wood for the trees. **~bestand** *m* forest stand. **~brand** *m* forest fire. **~gebiet** *n*, **~gegend** *f* wooded area, woodland. **'Waldhorn** *n* (-[e]s; *~*er) ♪ French horn. **waldig** ['valdɪç] *adj* wooded. **'Wald|lauf** *m* cross-country race. **~meister** *m* ♀ woodruff. **~rand** *m* (*am ~* at or on the) edge of the forest. **~schäden** *pl* forest damage. **~sterben** *n* dying of forests.

Waldung ['valdʊŋ] *f* (-; -en) wood(land), forest.

'Walfang *m* (-[e]s; *no pl*) whaling.

'Walfänger *m* (-s; -) whaler (*a. ship*).

'Walfisch *m* F whale.

Waliser [va'li:zər] *m* (-s; -) Welshman: *die ~* the Welsh. **Wa'liserin** *f* (-; -nen) Welshwoman. **wa'lisisch** *adj* Welsh.

walken ['valkən] *v/t* (h) **1.** mill. **2.** knead.

Wall [val] *m* (-[e]s; *~*e) *a. fig.* rampart.

Wallach [valax] *m* (-[e]s; -e) *zo.* gelding.

'wallfahren *v/i* (*insep, sn*) (go on a) pilgrimage. **'Wallfahrer** *m* (-s; -), **'Wallfahrerin** *f* (-; -nen) pilgrim. **'Wallfahrt** *f* (-; -en) pilgrimage. **'Wallfahrtsort** *m* (-[e]s; -e) place of pilgrimage.

'Wallung *f* (-; -en) (*♂ hot*) flush: *fig. j-n in ~ bringen* make s.o.'s blood boil.

Walnuß ['valnʊs] *f* (-; *~sse*) ♀ walnut.

Walroß ['valrɔs] *n* (-sses; -sse) *zo.* walrus.

walten ['valtən] *v/i* (h) be at work: *s-s Amtes ~* do one's duty; → *schalten* 3.

'Walzblech *n* rolled steel plate.

Walze ['valtsə] *f* (-; -n) **1.** ☉ roll, roller, cylinder. **2.** *typewriter:* platen. **3.** *barrel organ:* barrel. **'walzen** *v/t* (h) ☉ roll.

wälzen ['vɛltsən] (h) **I** *v/t* **1.** roll. **2.** F pore over *books etc*, turn *problem etc* over in one's mind. **II** *sich* ~ roll, *a.* wallow (*in mud etc*); **sich hin und her** ~ toss about, toss and turn.

'**walzenförmig** *adj* cylindrical.

'**Walzer** *m* (-s; -) (*a.* ~ **tanzen**) waltz.

'**Wälzer** *m* (-s; -) F huge tome.

'**Walzertakt** *m* waltz time.

'**Walz|ma,schine** *f* rolling machine. **~stahl** *m* rolled steel. **~straße** *f* (rolling) mill train. **~werk** *n* (rolling) mill.

Wampe ['vampə] *f* (-; -n) F paunch.

wand [vant] *pret of* **winden**.

Wand *f* (-; ⸗e) a) wall (*a. fig.*), b) side, c) (rock) face: ~ **an** ~ wall to wall; **in s-n vier Wänden** within one's own four walls; F *fig.* **j-n an die** ~ **drücken** drive s.o. to the wall; **j-n an die** ~ **spielen** play s.o. into the ground; F **j-n an die** ~ **stellen** execute s.o.; **es ist, um die Wände hochzugehen** it's enough to drive you mad.

Wandale [van'daːlə] *m* (-n; -n) *hist.* Vandal, *fig.* vandal. **Wandalismus** [van-da'lɪsmʊs] *m* (-; *no pl*) vandalism.

'**Wandbehang** *m* wall hanging, tapestry.

Wandel ['vandəl] *m* (-s; *no pl*) change: **der** ~ **der Zeit** the changing times; **sich im** ~ **befinden** be changing.

'**wandelbar** *adj* changeable.

'**Wandelhalle** *f at spa:* pump room.

'**wandeln** *v/t* (*a. sich* ~) (h) change.

'**Wander|ausstellung** *f* touring exhibition. **~büche,rei** *f* travel(l)ing library, *Am. a.* bookmobile. **~bühne** *f* touring company. **~düne** *f* shifting sand dune.

'**Wanderer** *m* (-s; -), '**Wanderin** *f* (-; -nen) wanderer, hiker, rambler.

'**Wanderkarte** *f* hiking map.

'**Wanderleben** *n* (-s; *no pl*) vagrant life.

'**wandern** ['vandərn] *v/i* (sn) walk, hike, tramp, *a. fig.* thoughts *etc:* wander, *a. zo.* migrate: ~ **gehen** go hiking; F *fig.* ~ **in** (*acc*) end up in, go (in)to. '**Wandern** *n* (-s) hiking (*etc*), *zo.* migration.

'**Wanderpo,kal** *m* challenge cup.

'**Wanderpreis** *m* challenge trophy.

'**Wanderschaft** *f* (-; *no pl*) travels: **auf** ~ **sein** (**gehen**) be on (take to) the road.

'**Wandertag** *m ped.* school outing.

'**Wanderung** *f* (-; -en) walking tour, hike, ramble, *a. zo.* migration.

'**Wanderverein** *m* rambling club.

'**Wanderweg** *m* footpath.

'**Wand|gemälde** *n* mural. **~ka,lender** *m* wall calendar. **~karte** *f* wall map.

'**Wandler** ['vandlər] *m* (-s; -) converter.

'**Wandleuchte** *f* wall lamp.

'**Wandlung** *f* (-; -en) change.

'**wandlungsfähig** *adj* flexible, versatile.

'**Wand|male,rei** *f* a) mural painting, b) mural. **~schrank** *m* built-in cupboard (*Am.* closet). **~spiegel** *m* wall mirror. **~tafel** *f* blackboard.

wandte ['vantə] *pret of* **wenden**.

Wange ['vaŋə] *f* (-; -n) *a.* ◎ cheek: ~ **an** ~ cheek to cheek.

wankelmütig ['vaŋkəlmyːtɪç] *adj* fickle.

wanken ['vaŋkən] *v/i* (h) **1.** ~ **schwanken** 1. **2.** *fig.* falter, waver: **ins Wanken geraten** begin to rock (*fig.* falter *or* waver). **3.** → **weichen**[1] *v/i*.

wann [van] *adv* when, (at) what time: **seit** ~? (for) how long?, since when?; **bis** ~? till when?

Wanne ['vanə] *f* (-; -n) **1.** tub. **2.** bath(tub). '**Wannenbad** *n* (tub) bath.

Wanst [vanst] *m* (-[e]s; ⸗e) F paunch.

Wanze ['vantsə] *f* (-; -n) **1.** *zo.* bug, *Am.* bedbug. **2.** F *fig.* bug: **~n anbringen in** (*dat*) bug (*a room etc*).

Wappen ['vapən] *n* (-s; -) coat of arms. **~bild** *n* heraldic figure. **~kunde** *f* (-; *no pl*) heraldry. **~schild** *n* escutcheon, blazon. **~spruch** *m* heraldic motto. **~tier** *n* heraldic animal.

wappnen ['vapnən] *sich* ~ (h) (*gegen*) arm (against), prepare (*or* brace) o.s. (for); → **gewappnet**.

war [vaːr] *pret of* **sein**[1].

warb [varp] *pret of* **werben**.

Ware ['vaːrə] *f* (-; -n) product, article, *coll. a.* merchandise, *pl a.* goods, commodities.

'**Waren|angebot** *n* range of goods. **~bestand** *m* stock (on hand). **~börse** *f* commodity exchange. **~haus** *n* department store. **~lager** *n* **1.** stock (on hand). **2.** warehouse. **~probe** *f* sample. **~sendung** *f* consignment, ☙ trade sample. **~zeichen** *n* trademark.

warf [varf] *pret of* **werfen**.

warm [varm] **I** *adj* warm (*a. fig.*), hot (*meal, drink, etc*): **mir ist** ~ I feel warm; **et.** ~ **halten** keep s.th. warm; **sich** ~ **halten** keep warm; **et.** ~ **machen** warm s.th. up; ~ **werden** warm up; **es wird**

wärmer it's getting warmer; F *ich kann mit ihr nicht ~ werden* I can't warm to her; → *warmhalten*. **II** *adv* warmly (*a. fig.*). F *die Wohnung kostet ~ ...* the rent for the flat is ... including heating.

'**Warmblüter** [-bly:tər] *m* (-s; -) warm-blooded animal.

Wärme ['vɛrmə] *f* (-; *no pl*) warmth (*a. fig.*), *meteor.*, *phys.* heat: *zehn Grad ~* ten degrees above zero. *~behandlung f* **1.** ⚙ heat treatment. **2.** ⚕ thermotherapy. **2beständig** *adj* heat-resistant. *~dämmung f* heat insulation. *~einheit f* thermal unit. *~grad m* degree above zero. *~kraftwerk n* thermoelectric power plant. *~lehre f* thermodynamics. *~leiter m phys.* heat conductor.

wärmen ['vɛrmən] (h) **I** *v/t* warm (up), heat (up) (*food etc*): *sich die Füße ~* warm one's feet. **II** *v/i* be warm: *Wolle wärmt* wool keeps you warm. **III** *sich ~* warm o.s. (up).

'**Wärme|pumpe** *f* heat pump. *~technik f* heat engineering. *~verlust m* heat loss.

'**Wärmflasche** *f* hot-water bottle.

'**warmhalten** *v/t* (*irr, sep, -ge-, h, → halten*) F *fig. sich j-n ~* keep in with s.o.

'**Warmhalteplatte** *f* plate warmer.

'**warmherzig** *adj* warm-hearted.

'**warmlaufen** *v/i* (*irr, sep, -ge-, sn, → laufen*) *~ lassen* run *the engine* up.

'**Warmluftfront** *f meteor.* warm front.

'**Warmmiete** *f* rent including heating.

Warm'wasser|bereiter *m* water heater. *~heizung f* hot-water heating. *~speicher m* hot-water tank. *~versorgung f* hot-water supply.

'**Warn|anlage** *f* warning device. *~blinkanlage f mot.* warning flasher. *~dreieck n mot.* warning triangle.

warnen ['varnən] *v/t, v/i* (h) warn (*vor* against): *davor ~ zu inf* warn against *ger; vor ... wird gewarnt!* beware of ...!

'**Warn|kreuz** *n* warning cross. *~leuchte f, ~licht n* warning light. *~schild n* danger sign. *~schuß m* (*e-n ~ abgeben* fire a) warning shot. *~si,gnal n* warning signal. *~streik m* token strike.

'**Warnung** *f* (-; -en) warning.

'**Warnzeichen** *n* warning sign.

Warte ['vartə] *f* **1.** *fig. von hoher ~ aus* from a lofty standpoint; *von s-r ~ aus gesehen* from his point of view.

'**Warteliste** *f* (*auf der ~ stehen* be on

the) waiting list.

warten[1] ['vartən] *v/t* (h) ⚙ service.

'**warten**[2] *v/i* (h) wait (*auf acc* for): *j-n ~ lassen* keep s.o. waiting; *lange auf sich ~ lassen* be a long time in coming; *nicht lange auf sich ~ lassen* not to be long in coming; *warte (mal)!* wait a minute!; *na, warte!* you just wait!; *da kann er lange ~!* he's got a long wait coming; *das kann ~!* that'll keep!; *iro. auf ihn (darauf) haben wir gerade noch gewartet!* he (that) is all we needed. '**Warten** *n* (-s) wait(ing): *nach langem ~* after a long wait.

Wärter ['vɛrtər] *m* (-s, -), '**Wärterin** *f* (-; -nen) attendant, keeper.

'**Wartesaal** *m* 🚆 waiting room.

'**Wartezeit** *f* waiting period.

'**Wartezimmer** *n* waiting room.

'**Wartung** *f* (-; -en) maintenance, servicing.

'**Wartungsanleitung** *f* service manual.

'**wartungsfrei** *adj* maintenance-free.

warum [va'rom] *adv* why.

Warze ['vartsə] *f* (-; -n) **1.** ⚕ wart. **2.** *Brustwarze.*

was [vas] **I** *interrog pron* **1.** what (*a.* F *for wie bitte?, nanu!, nicht wahr?*): *~ gibt's?* what is it?, F what's up?; *~ gibt's zum Mittagessen?* what's for lunch?; *~ kostet das?* how much is it?; *~ für (ein) ...?* what sort of ...?; *~ für e-e Farbe?* what colo(u)r?; *~ für ein Unsinn!* what nonsense! **2.** F a) *~ mußte er auch lügen?* why did he have to lie?, b) *~ fährt er auch so e-n großen Wagen?* what does he need such a big car for? **II** *rel pron* **3.** what: *~ auch immer* whatever; *alles, ~ ich brauche* all I need; *ich weiß nicht, ~ ich tun soll* I don't know what to do. **4.** which: *er lachte nur, ~ mich ärgerte* he just laughed, which made me angry. **III** *indef pron* F something (*bad, better, etc*): *das ist ~ anderes* that's different; *ich will dir ~ sagen!* I'll tell you what; *sonst noch ~?* anything else?; *ist ~?* is anything wrong (*or* the matter)?

'**Wasch|anlage** *f mot.* car wash. *~anleitung f* washing instructions. *~auto,mat m* washing machine.

'**waschbar** *adj* washable.

'**Waschbär** *m zo.* raccoon.

'**Waschbecken** *n* washbasin.

Wäsche ['vɛʃə] f (-; no pl) **1.** wash(ing), laundry: *in der ~* in the wash; *fig. schmutzige ~ waschen* wash one's dirty linen in public. **2.** (*bed, table*) linen. **3.** (*die ~ wechseln* put on fresh) underwear. **~beutel** m laundry bag.

'**waschecht** adj **1.** a) washable, nonshrink, b) fast. **2.** F fig. true, genuine.

'**Wäsche|klammer** f clothes peg. **~korb** m laundry basket. **~leine** f clothesline.

waschen ['vaʃən] (wusch, gewaschen, h) **I** v/t wash (*sich die Hände etc* one's hands *etc*), launder (a. F fig. money): *Waschen und Legen* shampoo and set. **II** *sich ~* wash (o.s.).

Wäsche'rei f (-; -en) laundry.

'**Wäsche|schleuder** f spin-drier. **~ständer** m clotheshorse. **~tinte** f marking ink. **~trockner** m drier.

'**Wasch|gang** m cycle. **~gelegenheit** f washing facilities. **~küche** f **1.** washhouse. **2.** F fig. pea soup. **~lappen** m **1.** flannel, Am. washcloth. **2.** F fig. sissy. **~lauge** f lye. **~leder** n chamois (leather). **~ma,schine** f washing machine. ℒ**ma,schinenfest** adj machine-washable. **~mittel** n, **~pulver** n washing powder. **~raum** m washroom. **~sa,lon** m launderette, Am. laundromat. **~schüssel** f washbowl. **~straße** f car wash.

'**Waschung** f (-; -en) washing, esp. eccl., ⚕ ablution.

'**Wasch|wasser** n (-s; no pl) washing water. **~zettel** m blurb.

Wasser ['vasər] n (-s; -, ⸗) water: *fließendes (stehendes) ~* running (stagnant) water; *zu ~ und zu Land* by land and by water; *~ lassen* pass water; *sich über ~ halten* a. fig. keep one's head above water; *unter ~ setzen* flood; *fig. ins ~ fallen* fall flat; *das ist ~ auf s-e Mühle* that's grist to his mill; *da läuft e-m das ~ im Munde zusammen* it makes your mouth water; *er kann ihr nicht das ~ reichen* he's not a patch on her; *er ist mit allen ~n gewaschen* he knows all the tricks (of the trade); *das ~ steht ihm bis zum Hals* he is in bad trouble; *er ist ein stilles ~* he's a deep one; → *Schlag* 1.

'**wasser|abstoßend** adj textil. water-repellent. **~arm** adj dry, arid.

'**Wasser|aufbereitungsanlage** f water--recycling plant. **~bad** n **1.** ⚕, phot. water bath. **2.** gastr. bain-marie. **~ball** m **1.** beach ball. **2.** → **~ballspiel** n water polo. **~bau** m (-[e]s; no pl) hydraulic engineering. **~behälter** m water container (⚙ tank). **~bett** n water bed. **~bombe** f depth charge.

Wässerchen ['vɛsərçən] n er sah aus, als könne er kein ~ trüben he looked as though butter would not melt in his mouth.

'**Wasser|dampf** m steam. ℒ**dicht** adj waterproof, ⚓, ⚙ a. watertight. **~enthärter** m water softener. **~fahrzeug** n watercraft, vessel. **~fall** m waterfall, falls: F reden wie ein ~ talk nineteen to the dozen. **~farbe** f water colo(u)r. ℒ**fest** adj waterproof. **~flasche** f water bottle. **~flugzeug** n seaplane. **~gehalt** m water content. ℒ**gekühlt** adj water-cooled. **~glas** n **1.** 🝙 water glass. **2.** water glass, tumbler: → *Sturm* 1. **~graben** m ditch, sports: water jump. **~hahn** m tap, Am. faucet.

'**wasserhaltig** adj 🝙 hydrous.

'**Wasserhaushalt** m **1.** water supply. **2.** biol., 🜨 water balance.

wässerig ['vɛsərɪç] adj watery, 🝙 aqueous: *j-m den Mund ~ machen* make s.o.'s mouth water (*nach* for).

'**Wasser|kessel** m **1.** kettle. **2.** ⚙ boiler. **~klo,sett** n water closet (abbr. W.C.). **~kraft** f water power. **~kraftwerk** n hydroelectric power plant. **~kühlung** f water cooling (system). **~lauf** m watercourse. **~leitung** f water pipe(s). **~linie** f ⚓ water line. ℒ**löslich** adj water-soluble. **~mangel** m water shortage.

'**Wassermann** m (-[e]s; no pl) astr. (er ist [ein] ~ he is [an]) Aquarius.

'**Wasserme,lone** f water melon.

wassern ['vasərn] v/i (h) ⸜ touch down, spacecraft: splash down.

wässern ['vɛsərn] v/t (h) **1.** water, irrigate. **2.** soak.

'**Wasser|pfeife** f water pipe. **~pflanze** f aquatic (plant). **~pi,stole** f water pistol. **~ratte** f **1.** zo. water rat. **2.** F enthusiastic swimmer. **~rohr** n water pipe. **~rutschbahn** f water chute. **~schaden** m water damage. **~scheide** f watershed, Am. a. divide. ℒ**scheu** adj afraid of water. **~schildkröte** f turtle.

'**Wasserschutz** m prevention of water

pollution. **~gebiet** n water reserve. **~poli,zei** f river police.

¹**Wasser|ski** n (-s; no pl) water skiing: **~ laufen** go water-skiing, water-ski. **~speier** m △ gargoyle. **~spiegel** m 1. surface of the water. 2. water level. **~sport** m water (or aquatic) sports, aquatics. **~spülung** f a) flush, b) cistern. **~stand** m water level. **~standsanzeiger** m water ga(u)ge.

¹**Wasserstoff** m (-[e]s; no pl) hydrogen. ☿**blond** adj F peroxide blond(e). **~bombe** f hydrogen bomb. **~'pero,xid** n, **~'supero,xid** n hydrogen peroxide.

¹**Wasser|strahl** m jet of water. **~straße** f waterway. **~sucht** f (-; no pl) ℱ dropsy. **~tier** n aquatic (animal). **~tropfen** m drop of water. **~turm** m water tower.

¹**Wasserung** f (-; -en) ↙ touchdown on water, of spacecraft: splashdown.

¹**Wasser|verbrauch** m water consumption. **~verdrängung** f (water) displacement. **~verschmutzung** f water pollution. **~versorgung** f water supply. **~vogel** m water bird, pl a. waterfowl. **~waage** f spirit level. **~weg** m waterway: **auf dem ~** by water. **~welle** f (hairdo) water wave. **~werfer** m water cannon. **~werk(e pl)** n waterworks. **~zeichen** n watermark.

waten ['va:tən] v/i (sn) wade.

watscheln ['va:tʃəln] v/i (sn) waddle.

Watt¹ [vat] n (-[e]s; -en) geol. mud flats.

Watt² n (-s; -) ⚡ watt.

Watte ['vatə] f (-; -n) cotton wool.

¹**Wattebausch** m cotton-wool swab.

¹**Wattenmeer** n mud flats.

¹**Wattestäbchen** n cotton bud.

wattieren [va'ti:rən] v/t (h) pad, wad.

weben ['ve:bən] v/t, v/i (h) weave.

Weber ['ve:bər] m (-s; -) weaver. **Webe'rei** f (-; -en) 1. no pl weaving. 2. weaving mill.

¹**Weberknecht** m zo. daddy longlegs.

Web|fehler ['ve:p-] m flaw. **~pelz** m woven imitation fur. **~stuhl** m loom. **~waren** pl woven goods.

Wechsel ['vɛksəl] m (-s; -) 1. change, (a. ♂ crop) rotation. 2. ♦ draft, bill of exchange): **e-n ~ (auf j-n) ziehen** draw a bill (on s.o.). 3. sports: a) (baton) change, b) change of ends. 4. → **Wildwechsel. ~bäder** pl ℱ alternating hot and cold baths. **~bank** f (-; -en) discount house. **~beziehung** f interrela-

tion. **~fälle** pl vicissitudes, F the ups and downs. **~geld** n (small) change.

¹**wechselhaft** adj changeable.

¹**Wechseljahre** pl physiol. menopause.

¹**Wechselkurs** m rate of exchange.

wechseln ['vɛksəln] (h) **I** v/t 1. a) change b) exchange (rings, glances, words), c) vary, d) alternate, a. rotate: **den Arbeitsplatz (Arzt etc) ~** change jobs (doctors etc); → **Besitzer. II** v/i 2. a) change, b) vary. 3. (sn) deer etc: cross.

¹**wechselnd** adj changing, varying.

¹**Wechsel|rahmen** m interchangeable picture frame. **~schuld** f ♦ bill debt. **~seitig** [-zaitiç] adj mutual, reciprocal: **~e Abhängigkeit** interdependence.

¹**Wechselstrom** m ⚡ alternating current (abbr. A.C.). **~motor** m A.C. motor.

¹**Wechselstube** f exchange office.

¹**Wechselwähler(in** f) m floating voter.

¹**wechselweise** adv alternately, in turn.

¹**Wechselwirkung** f interaction.

wecken ['vɛkən] v/t (h) wake (up), call, a. fig. rouse, fig. awaken.

Wecker m (-s; -) alarm (clock): F **j-m auf den ~ gehen** get on s.o.'s nerves.

¹**Weckruf** m teleph. alarm call.

Wedel ['ve:dəl] m (-s; -) ♠ frond.

wedeln v/i (h) 1. **~ mit** wave (s.th.), **dem Schwanz** wag (its tail). 2. skiing: wedel.

weder ['ve:dər] conj **~ ... noch** neither ... nor.

weg [vɛk] adv F 1. a) gone, b) not in, c) away: **~ (da)!** get away!, beat it!; **~ damit!** take it away!, w.s. off with it!; **Finger (or Hände) ~!** hands off!; **ich muß ~!** I must be off!; **nichts wie ~!** let's get out of here! 2. **~ sein** a) be out cold, b) be in raptures (**von** over); **über et. ~ sein** have got over s.th.

Weg [ve:k] m (-[e]s; -e) way (a. fig.), path, route, F a. errand: **der ~ zum Erfolg** the road to success; **auf dem ~(e) der Besserung** on the road to recovery, F on the mend; **auf diesem ~e** this way; **auf diplomatischem ~e** through diplomatic channels; **auf friedlichem (legalem) ~e** by peaceful (legal) means; **auf dem besten ~e sein zu inf** be well on the way to ger; **auf dem richtigen ~e sein** be on the right track; **sich auf den ~ machen** set off; **j-m aus dem ~(e) gehen** get out of s.o.'s way; (dat) **aus**

dem ~**e gehen** steer clear of; **aus dem** ~**e räumen** (or **schaffen**) get rid of; **s-e eigenen** ~**e gehen** go one's own way; **den** ~ **ebnen** pave the way (**dat** for); **et. in die** ~**e leiten** initiate s.th., start s.th. off; **ich traue ihm nicht über den** ~ I don't trust him an inch; **im** ~**(e) stehen** (or **sein**) a) **j-m** be in s.o.'s way, b) **e-r Sache** an obstacle to s.th.; **dem steht nichts im** ~**e** there are no obstacles to that, F that's all right; → **bahnen, halb** I.

'**wegbekommen** v/t (irr, sep, h, → **bekommen**) F get s.th. off, move.

'**Wegbereiter** m (-s; -) pioneer: **der** ~ **sein** F pave the way for.

'**wegblasen** v/t (irr, sep, -ge-, h, → **blasen**) blow s.th. away; **fig. wie weggeblasen sein** be clean gone.

'**wegbleiben** v/i (irr, sep, -ge-, sn, → **bleiben**) F 1. stay away. 2. ⊙ fail, sl. conk out: → **Luft** 2, **Spucke.**

'**wegbringen** v/t (irr, sep, -ge-, h, → **bringen**) take s.th. away.

wegen ['ve:gən] prep (gen, F dat) 1. because of, on account of: ~ **Diebstahls** for larceny; → **Amt** 1, **Recht** 1. 2. for the sake of: **er hat es** ~ **s-r Kinder getan** he did it for his children's sake. 3. due to. 4. F **von** ~ that's what you think!; **von** ~ **hübsch!** pretty, my foot!

'**Wegerecht** n (-[e]s; no pl) right of way.

Wegerich ['ve:gərɪç] m (-s; -e) plantain.

'**wegfahren** v/i (irr, sep, -ge-, sn, → **fahren**) leave, drive away.

'**wegfegen** v/t (sep, h) sweep s.th. away.

Weggang m (-[e]s; no pl) leaving.

'**weggeben** v/t (irr, sep, -ge-, h, → **geben**) give s.th. away.

'**weggehen** v/i (irr, sep, -ge-, sn, → **gehen**) 1. go away (a. F fig. pain etc), leave: **geh weg!** leave me alone!; **von Berlin (der Firma)** ~ leave Berlin (the firm). 2. F fig. sell: → **Semmel.**

'**weghaben** v/t (irr, sep, -ge-, h, → **haben**) F 1. **sein Teil** etc ~ have got one's share etc. 2. **et.** ~ a) have got the hang of it, b) be good (**in** dat at).

'**wegkommen** v/i (irr, sep, -ge-, sn, → **kommen**) F 1. get away. 2. get lost. 3. fig. **gut (schlecht)** ~ come off well (badly) (**bei** at). 4. ~ **über** (acc) get over.

'**weglassen** v/t (irr, sep, -ge-, h, → **lassen**) 1. let s.o. go. 2. leave s.th. out.

Weglassung ['vɛk-] f (-; -en) omission.

'**weglaufen** v/i (irr, sep, -ge-, sn, → **laufen**) run away.

'**weglegen** v/t (sep, h) put s.th. aside.

'**wegmüssen** v/i (irr, sep, -ge-, h, → **müssen**) F **ich muß weg** I must be off; **es muß weg!** it must go!

'**wegnehmen** v/t (irr, sep, -ge-, h, → **nehmen**) remove, fig. take up (**room, time**, etc): (**j-m**) **et.** ~ take s.th. away (from s.o.); → **Gas.**

'**wegrationali,sieren** v/t (sep, h) cut jobs etc (by rationalization).

'**wegräumen** v/t (sep, h) a. fig. remove.

'**wegreißen** v/t (irr, sep, -ge-, h, → **reißen**) tear s.o., s.th. away.

'**wegscheren: sich** ~ (sep, h) F clear off.

'**wegschicken** v/t (sep, h) send s.o., s.th. away (or off).

'**wegschleppen** v/t (sep, h) drag s.o., s.th. off.

'**wegschließen** v/t (irr, sep, -ge-, h, → **schließen**) lock s.th. away.

'**wegschnappen** v/t (sep, h) F (**j-m**) **et.** ~ snatch s.th. away (from s.o.).

'**wegsehen** v/i (irr, sep, -ge-, h, → **sehen**) 1. look away, a. fig. look the other way. 2. → **hinwegsehen.**

'**wegspülen** v/t (sep, h) wash away.

'**wegstecken** v/t (sep, h) put s.th. away.

'**wegtreten** v/i (irr, sep, -ge-, sn, → **treten**) step aside, ✗ break (the) ranks: ~ **lassen (weggetreten!)** dismiss(!).

'**Wegweiser** m (-s; -) signpost, (road) sign, in buildings: directory.

'**wegwerfen** (irr, sep, -ge-, h, → **werfen**) I v/t a. fig. throw s.th. away. II **sich** ~ throw o.s. away (**an** acc on).

'**wegwerfend** adj disparaging.

Wegwerf|flasche ['vɛk-] f throwaway (or disposable) bottle. ~**gesellschaft** f contr. throwaway society.

'**wegwischen** v/t (sep, h) 1. wipe s.th. off. 2. fig. brush objection etc off.

'**wegzaubern** v/t (sep, h) spirit away.

'**wegziehen** (irr, sep, -ge-, sn, → **ziehen**) I v/t pull s.o., s.th. away. II v/i move away.

weh [ve:] adj sore: (**j-m**) ~ **tun** hurt (s.o., fig. s.o.'s feelings); **sich (am Kopf** etc) ~ hurt o.s. (one's head etc); **mir tut der Knöchel** ~ my ankle hurts.

wehe ['ve:ə] int ~ (**dir**), **wenn ...** you'll be sorry if ...

'**Wehe** f (-; -n) (sand, snow) drift.

wehen ['ve:ən] *v/i, v/t* (h) *flag etc:* wave, *wind:* blow, *scent, tune, etc:* drift, waft.

'Wehen *pl* ♣ pains, labo(u)r.

'Wehgeschrei *n a. fig.* wailing.

'wehleidig *adj* plaintive, whining: *sei nicht so ~!* don't be such a sissy!

'Wehmut *f* (-; *no pl*) melancholy, wistfulness, nostalgia. **wehmütig** ['ve:my:tɪç] *adj* melancholy, wistful, nostalgic.

Wehr[1] [ve:r] *f sich zur ~ setzen* → **wehren** I.

Wehr[2] *n* (-[e]s; -e) weir, dam.

'Wehr|beauftragte *m* ombudsman (for the Armed Forces). **~bereich** *m* military district. **~bereichskom¡mando** *n* military district command. **~dienst** *m* (-[e]s; *no pl*) (*s-n ~ ableisten* do one's) military service. **~dienstverweigerer** *m* (-s; -) conscientious objector.

wehren ['ve:rən] (h) **I** *sich ~* defend o.s. (*gegen* against); *sich ~ gegen* a) resist, fight, b) refuse to accept. **II** *v/i den Anfängen ~* nip things in the bud.

'Wehrersatzdienst *m* (-[e]s; *no pl*) alternative service (for conscientious objectors).

'wehrfähig *adj* fit for military service.

'wehrlos *adj* defen/celess (*Am.* -se-), helpless. **'Wehrlosigkeit** *f* (-; *no pl*) defen/celessness (*Am.* -se-), helplessness.

'Wehrmacht *f* (-; *no pl*) *hist.* (German) Armed Forces, Wehrmacht.

'Wehrpaß *m* service record (book).

'Wehrpflicht *f* (-; *no pl*) (*allgemeine*) ~ (universal) compulsory military service, (universal) conscription. **'wehrpflichtig** *adj* a) liable for military service, b) recruitable (*age*). **'Wehrpflichtige** *m* (-n; -n) a) person liable for military service, b) conscript, *Am.* draftee.

'Wehrsold *m* (service) pay.

'Wehrübung *f* reserve duty training.

Weib [vaip] *n* (-[e]s; -er) *a. contp.* woman.

'Weibchen *n* (-s; -) *zo.* female.

'Weiber|feind ['vaibər-] *m* woman-hater. **~geschichten** *pl* F affairs, womanizing. **~held** *m* (-en; -en) ladykiller. **~regi¡ment** *n* petticoat government.

weibisch ['vaibɪʃ] *adj* effeminate.

'weiblich *adj* female, feminine (*a. ling.*), womanly.

'Weibsbild *n* F *contp.* female, woman.

weich [vaiç] *adj* soft (*a. ling., phot.* or *fig.*), mellow (*voice, colo[u]r, etc*), ten-

der (*meat*), soft-boiled (*egg*): *~ machen* soften; *~ werden* soften, *fig. a.* give in.

'Weiche[1] *f* (-; -n) *anat.* flank, side.

'Weiche[2] *f* (-; -n) ☜ points, *Am.* switch: *fig. die ~n stellen* set the course (*für* for).

weichen[1] ['vaiçən] *v/i* (wich, gewichen, sn) **1.** (*dat* to) *a. fig.* give way, yield. **2.** go (away): *j-m nicht von der Seite ~* not to leave s.o.'s side; *er wich und wankte nicht* he didn't budge.

weichen[2] ['vaiçən] *v/i, v/t* (h) (*a. ~ lassen*) soak.

'weichgekocht *adj* soft-boiled (*egg*).

'Weichheit *f* (-; *no pl*) softness (*etc.,* → **weich**).

'weichherzig *adj* soft-hearted.

'Weichkäse *m* soft cheese.

'weichlich *adj fig.* soft, effeminate.

'Weichling *m* (-s; -e) F softie, sissy.

'Weich|macher *m* (-s; -) 🔥, ⚙ softener. **~spüler** *m* (-s; -) (fabric) softener. **~teile** *pl anat.* soft parts. **~tier** *n* mollusc. **~zeichner** *m phot.* soft-focus lens.

Weide[1] ['vaidə] *f* (-; -n) ♦ willow (tree).

Weide[2] *f* (-; -n) (*auf der ~* at) pasture.

'Weideland *n* pasturage.

weiden (h) **I** *v/i* graze. **II** *v/t a. ~ lassen* put out to pasture. **III** *sich ~ an* (*dat*) a) feast one's eyes on, b) gloat over.

'Weidenbaum *m* willow (tree).

'Weidenkätzchen *n* ♦ catkin.

weidlich ['vaitlɪç] *adv* thoroughly.

Weidmann ['vait-] *m* (-[e]s; ~er) huntsman. **'weidmännisch** [-mɛnɪʃ] **I** *adj* huntsmanlike. **II** *adv* in a huntsmanlike manner.

Weidmanns'heil *n* ~*!* good sport!

weigern ['vaigərn] *sich ~* (h) refuse.

'Weigerung *f* (-; -en) refusal.

'Weihbischof *m* suffragan (bishop).

Weihe ['vaiə] *f* (-; -n) **1.** *eccl.* a) consecration, b) ordination. **2.** *fig.* solemnity.

'weihen *v/t* (h) **1.** *eccl.* a) consecrate, b) ordain *as a priest.* **2.** (*dat* to) devote, dedicate (*both a. sich* o.s.): *dem Tode* (*or Untergang*) *geweiht* doomed.

'Weihnacht *f* (-; *no pl*) → **'Weihnachten** *pl* (*an ~, zu ~* at) Christmas (F Xmas): *Fröhliche ~!* Merry Christmas!

'weihnachtlich *adj* Christmas, F Christmassy.

'Weihnachts|abend *m* Christmas Eve. **~baum** *m* Christmas tree. **~einkäufe** *pl* Christmas shopping. **~feiertag** *m*

Christmas Day (*pl* holidays): **zweiter ~** Boxing Day. **~fest** *n* Christmas. **~geld** *n* Christmas bonus. **~lied** *n* Christmas carol. **~mann** *m* (-[e]s; ⸚er) **1.** Father Christmas, Santa Claus. **2.** F *contp.* dope. **~markt** *m* Christmas fair. **~zeit** *f* Christmas (season).

'Weihrauch *m* (-[e]s; *no pl*) incense.
'Weihwasser *n* (-s; *no pl*) holy water.
weil [vaɪl] *conj* **1.** because. **2.** since, as.
'Weilchen *n* (-s; *no pl*) **ein ~** a little while.
Weile *f* (-; *no pl*) **e-e ~** a while, a time.
Wein [vaɪn] *m* (-[e]s; -e) **1.** ♀ vine. **2.** wine: **j-m reinen ~ einschenken** tell s.o. the truth. **~bau** *m* (-[e]s; *no pl*) wine growing, viticulture. **~bauer** *m* wine grower. **~baugebiet** *n* wine growing area. **~beere** *f* grape. **~berg** *m* vineyard. **~bergschnecke** *f* (edible) snail. **~blatt** *n* vine leaf. **~brand** *m* (-[e]s; ⸚e) brandy.
weinen ['vaɪnən] *v/i, v/t* **1.** ⊙ weep (*um* over), cry: **j-n zum ⊙ bringen** make s.o. cry; **es ist zum ⊙!** it's a (crying) shame.
weinerlich ['vaɪnərlɪç] *adj* tearful, F weepy, whining (*voice, child, etc*).
'Wein|essig *m* wine vinegar. **~faß** *n* wine cask. **~flasche** *f* wine bottle. **~geist** *m* spirit(s) of wine. **~glas** *n* wine glass. **~gut** *n* wine-growing estate. **~händler** *m* wine merchant. **~handlung** *f* wine shop. **~karte** *f* wine list. **~keller** *m* wine cellar. **~kelter** *f* wine press. **~kenner** *m* wine connoisseur.

'Weinkrampf *m* crying fit.
'Wein|lese *f* grape harvest. **~lo,kal** *n* wine tavern. **~probe** *f* wine tasting. **⸚rot** *adj* wine-red. **~stock** *m* ♀ vine. **~stube** *f* wine tavern. **~traube** *f* a) bunch of grapes, b) *pl* grapes.
weise ['vaɪzə] *adj* wise.
'Weise¹ *m* (-n; -n) wise man, sage.
'Weise² *f* (-; -n) **1.** way: **auf diese ~** (in) this way; **auf jede ~** in every way; **auf die gleiche ~** the same way; **auf die e-e oder andere ~** (in) one way or another; **auf m-e (s-e) ~** my (his) way; **in k-r ~** in no way; **jeder auf s-e ~** everyone after his own fashion. **2.** ♪ tune.
weisen ['vaɪzən] (wies, gewiesen, h) I *v/t* **1.** **j-m den Weg ~** show s.o. the way. **2.** **j-n von der Schule ~** expel s.o. (from school). **3.** *et.* (*weit*) *von sich ~* repudiate s.th. (emphatically). II *v/i → zeigen* II.

'Weisheit *f* (-; -en) wisdom: **mit s-r ~ am Ende sein** be at one's wits' end.
'Weisheitszahn *m* wisdom tooth.
weismachen *v/t* (*sep*, h) **j-m ~, daß** make s.o. believe that; **mir kannst du nichts ~!** you can't fool me!; **laß dir nichts ~!** don't be fooled!

weiß [vaɪs] *adj* **1.** white: **~ machen** whiten; **~ werden** go white; **~ gekleidet** dressed in white. **2.** *fig.* blank.
Weiß *n* (-[es]; -) *a.* chess *etc*: white.
'weissagen *v/t* (*insep*, h) prophesy, foretell. **'Weissager** *m* (-s; -) prophet. **'Weissagerin** *f* (-; -nen) prophetess. **'Weissagung** *f* (-; -en) prophecy.
'Weiß|blech *n* tinplate. **⸚blond** *adj* silver-blond(e). **~brot** *n* white bread. **~buch** *n* *pol.* white paper (*Am.* book). **~dorn** *m* (-[e]s; -e) ♀ whitethorn.
'Weiße *m, f* (-n; -n) white man (woman): **die ~n** the whites, the white man.
weißen ['vaɪsən] *v/t* (h) **1.** whiten. **2.** whitewash.
'weißglühend *adj* white-hot.
'Weißglut *f* (-; *no pl*) white heat: F **j-n zur ~ bringen** make s.o. see red.
'weißhaarig *adj* white-haired.
'Weiß|kohl *m*, **~kraut** *n* white cabbage.
'weißlich *adj* whitish.
'Weißwein *m* white wine.
'Weisung *f* (-; -en) instruction, order(s).
'Weisungs|befugnis *f* authority to issue directives. **⸚gemäß** *adv* as directed.
weit [vaɪt] I *adj* **1.** a) wide, *a.* full (*skirt etc*), b) *a.* ⊙ loose. **2.** wide, extensive, vast, immense. **3.** *fig.* broad (*concept etc*): **im ~esten Sinne** in the widest sense. **4.** long: **auf ~e** (*or* **aus ~er**) **Entfernung** at a great distance. II *adv* **5.** wide(ly): **~ offen** wide open. **6.** far: **sie ist ~ über 60** she is well over sixty; **er ist ~ gereist** he has got around a good deal; **~** (*or* **bei ~em**) **das beste** by far the best; **bei ~em nicht so gut** not nearly so good; **~ gefehlt!** far from it!; F **es ist nicht ~ her mit ihm** he is not up to much; **es ~ bringen** (**im Leben**) go far; **zu ~ gehen** go too far; **das geht zu ~** that's going too far; **ich bin so ~** I'm ready; **wie ~ bist du?** how far have you got?; **wenn es so ~ ist** when the time comes; **→ entfernt, kommen** 1, 10.
'weit|ab *adv* far away (**von** from).
'weit|aus *adv* far **better** etc.

'**Weitblick** *m* (-[e]s; *no pl*) farsightedness.
'**weitblickend** *adj* farsighted, farseeing.
'**Weite¹** *f* (-; -n) **1.** *a.* ☼ a) width, b) breadth, c) size, extent: → *licht* 3. **2.** vastness, expanse. **3.** *sports*: distance.
'**Weite²**: *das ~ suchen* take to one's heels.
weiten ['vaɪtən] *v/t* (*a. sich ~*) (h) widen (*a. fig.*), stretch (*shoes etc*).
weiter ['vaɪtər] **I** *comp of* **weit.** **II** *adj* further: *nach e-r ~en Woche* after another week. **III** *adv* ~*! go on!; halt, nicht ~!* stop, no further!; *immer ~* on and on; *nichts (niemand) ~* nothing (no one) else; *und so ~* and so on (*abbr. etc*); *das ist nicht ~ schlimm* that's no tragedy; *das störte sie ~ nicht* that didn't really bother her; → *weiterhin* I.
'**weiter|arbeiten** *v/i* (*sep*, h) go on working. ~**befördern** *v/t* (*sep*, h) forward, send on. ~**bestehen** → *fortbestehen.*
'**weiterbilden** → *fortbilden.*
'**Weiterbildung** *f* → *Fortbildung.*
'**weiterbringen** *v/t* (*irr sep*, -ge-, h, → *bringen*) *das bringt mich (uns etc) nicht weiter* that's not much help.
'**Weitere, das** (-n) the rest: *bis auf weiteres* for the time being, *adm.* until further notice; *ohne weiteres* without further ado, easily.
'**weiter|empfehlen** *v/t* (*irr, sep*, h, → *empfehlen*) recommend (to others). ~**entwickeln** *v/t* (*a. sich ~*) (*sep*, h) develop (further). ~**erzählen** *v/t* (*sep*, h) tell others, repeat. ~**fahren** *v/i* (*irr, sep*, -ge-, sn, → *fahren*) go on, drive on. ~**führen** *v/t* (*sep*, h) continue, carry on. ~**geben** *v/t* (*irr, sep*, -ge-, h, → *geben*) *et. ~* pass s.th. on. ~**gehen** *v/i* (*irr, sep*, -ge-, sn, → *gehen*) **1.** go on, walk on. **2.** *fig.* go on, continue: *das kann so nicht ~!* things can't go on like this!
'**weiter|hin** **I** *adv* ~ *et. tun* continue doing (*or* to do) s.th., go on doing s.th. **II** *conj* further(more), moreover.
'**weiter|kämpfen** *v/i* (*sep*, h) continue fighting. ~**kommen** *v/i* (*irr, sep*, -ge-, sn, → *kommen*) get on, *fig. a.* make headway, get somewhere: *nicht ~ a.* be stuck; *so kommen wir nicht weiter* this won't get us any further. ~**laufen** *v/i* (*irr, sep*, -ge-, sn, → *laufen*) *payment etc*: be continued. ~**leben** *v/i* (*sep*, h) live on, *fig. a.* survive. ~**leiten** *v/t* (*sep*,

h) (*an acc* to) pass s.th. on, refer. ~**lesen** *v/t, v/i* (*irr, sep*, -ge-, h, → *lesen*) go on (reading), continue to read. ~**machen** *v/i, v/t* (*sep*, h) continue, carry (*or* go) on (with). ~**sagen** *v/t* (*sep*, h) *et. ~* pass s.th. on.
'**Weiterungen** *pl* complications.
'**weiterverarbeiten** *v/t* (*sep*, h) process.
'**Weiterverarbeitung** *f* (-; *no pl*) processing.
'**Weiterverkauf** *m* (-[e]s; *no pl*) resale.
'**weiterverkaufen** *v/t* (*sep*, h) resell.
'**weitgehend** **I** *adj* extensive, far-reaching, *a.* wide (*powers etc*): *es herrschte ~e Übereinstimmung* there was a large degree of consent. **II** *adv* largely, to a great extent.
'**weitgereist** *adj* widely travel(l)ed.
'**weit'her** *adv* from afar.
'**weit'hergeholt** *adj fig.* far-fetched.
'**weit'hin** *adv* **1.** far. **2.** to a large extent.
'**weitläufig** **I** *adj* **1.** extensive, vast, spacious. **2.** detailed, *contp.* long-winded. **3.** distant (*relatives*). **II** *adv* **4.** at great length. **5.** ~ *verwandt* distantly related.
'**weitreichend** *adj* **1.** far-reaching. **2.** ✕ long-range.
'**weitschweifig** [-ʃvaɪfɪç] *adj* long-winded.
'**weitsichtig** *adj* long-sighted, *a. fig.* farsighted. '**Weitsichtigkeit** *f* (-; *no pl*) long-sightedness, *a. fig.* farsightedness.
'**Weitspringer(in** *f*) *m* longjumper, *Am.* broadjumper. '**Weitsprung** *m* (-[e]s; *no pl*) long (*Am.* broad) jump.
'**weit|verbreitet** *adj* widespread, common. ~**verzweigt** *adj* widely ramified.
'**Weitwinkelobjektiv** *n* wide angle lens.
Weizen ['vaɪtsən] *m* (-s; -) wheat: *fig. sein ~ blüht* he is in clover.
welch [vɛlç] **I** *interrog pron* what, which: ~*er (von beiden)?* which (of the two)?; ~ *ein Anblick!* what a sight! **II** *rel pron* who, which, that. **III** *indef pron* some, any: *have you got money? ja, ich habe ~es* yes, I have some; *brauchen Sie ~es?* do you need any?
welk [vɛlk] *adj* withered, faded: ~*e Haut* wrinkled skin. '**welken** *v/i* (sn) wither.
'**Wellblech** *n* corrugated iron.
Welle ['vɛlə] *f* (-; -n) **1.** *a. fig.* wave: *fig. (hohe) ~n schlagen* cause quite a stir. **2.** ☼ shaft. **3.** *gym.* circle.

'**wellen** (h) **I** *v/t* wave (*hair*). **II sich ~** *hair*: be (*or* go) wavy.

'**Wellen|bad** *n* swimming pool with artificially produced waves. **~band** *n* ⚡ wave band. **~bereich** *m* radio: wave range. **~brecher** *m* ⚓ breakwater.

'**wellenförmig** *adj*

'**Wellen|länge** *f* (F *fig.* **die gleiche ~ haben** be on the same) wavelength. **~linie** *f* wavy line. **~reiten** *n* surfing.

'**Wellensittich** *m zo.* budgerigar.

'**wellig** ['vɛlɪç] *adj* wavy.

'**Wellpappe** *f* corrugated board.

Welpe ['vɛlpə] *m* (-n; -n) *zo.* puppy, pup.

Welt [vɛlt] *f* (-; -en) world: **die große ~** a) the big wide world, b) high society; **alle ~** everybody; **auf der ganzen ~** all over the world; **der längste Fluß der ~** the longest river in the world, the world's longest river; **was in aller ~ ...?** what on earth ...?; **nicht um alles in der ~** not on your life; **aus der ~ schaffen** a) get rid of, b) settle (*problem etc*); **in die ~ setzen** a) put *children* into the world, b) start (*rumo[u]r*); **zur ~ bringen** give birth to; **zur ~ kommen** be born.

'**Welt|all** *n* (-s; *no pl*) universe. **2anschaulich** *adj* ideological. **~anschauung** *f* philosophy (of life), world view, *a.* ideology. **~ausstellung** *f* world fair. **~bank** *f* (-; *no pl*) World Bank.

'**welt|bekannt, ~berühmt** *adj* world-famous. **~bewegend** *adj* worldshaking: *iro.* **nichts Weltbewegendes** nothing to write home about.

'**Weltbild** *n* world view.

'**Weltbürger(in** *f*) *m* cosmopolitan.

'**Weltenbummler(in** *f*) *m* globetrotter.

'**Welterfolg** *m* worldwide success.

Weltergewicht ['vɛltər-] *n* boxing: welterweight.

'**Welt|firma** *f* world-renowned firm. **2fremd** *adj* naive, unworldly, ivory-towered (*scholar etc*). **~frieden** *m* world peace. **~geschichte** *f* (-; *no pl*) world history. **2gewandt** *adj* urbane. **~handel** *m* international trade. **~herrschaft** *f* (-; *no pl*) world domination. **~karte** *f* map of the world. **~krieg** *m* world war: **der Zweite ~** World War II, the Second World War. **~kugel** *f* globe. **~lage** *f* (-; *no pl*) international situation.

'**weltlich** *adj* **1.** worldly. **2.** secular.

'**Weltlitera,tur** *f* world literature.

'**Weltmacht** *f* world power.

'**weltmännisch** [-mɛnɪʃ] *adj* man-of-the-world.

'**Welt|markt** *m* world market. **~meer** *n* ocean. **~meister(in** *f*) *m* world champion. **~meisterschaft** *f* world championship, *esp. soccer*: World Cup. **2offen** *adj* open-minded. **~öffentlichkeit** *f* world public. **~poli,tik** *f* international (*or* world) politics. **~presse** *f* international press. **~rangliste** *f* world ranking list: **er steht an dritter Stelle der ~** he is ranked third in the world. **~raum** *m* (-[e]s; *no pl*) (outer) space. **~raum... → Raum...** **~reich** *n* empire. **~reise** *f* world trip. **~reisende** *m, f* globetrotter. **~re,kord** *m* world record. **~re,kordinhaber(in** *f*) *m*, **~re,kordler(in** *f*) *m* world-record holder. **~religi,on** *f* world religion. **~ruf** *m* (*von ~ of*) worldwide renown. **~schmerz** *m* (-es; *no pl*) world-weariness. **~sicherheitsrat** *m* U.N. Security Council. **~sprache** *f* universal language. **~stadt** *f* metropolis. **~stadt..., 2städtisch** *adj* metropolitan. **~untergang** *m* end of the world. **~uraufführung** *f* world première. **~verbesserer** *m* (-s; -) world changer. **~währungsfonds** *m* International Monetary Fund. **2weit** *adj* worldwide, global. **~wirtschaft** *f* (-; *no pl*) world economy. **~wirtschaftskrise** *f* worldwide economic crisis. **~wunder** *n* wonder of the world.

wem [ve:m] *pron* (to) whom: **von ~** of whom, by whom.

wen [ve:n] *pron* whom, F who.

Wende ['vɛndə] *f* (-; -n) **1.** *a. sports*: turn. **2.** change, *pol.* change of power. **~hals** *m* **1.** *zo.* wryneck. **2.** *pol. contp.* quick-change artist. **~kreis** *m* **1.** *geogr.* tropic. **2.** *mot.* turning circle.

Wendeltreppe ['vɛndəl-] *f* spiral staircase.

wenden¹ ['vɛndən] (h) **I** *v/t* a) turn, b) turn over (*page, roast, etc*). **II** *v/i* turn (around), *sports*: turn: **bitte ~!** please turn over (*abbr.* p.t.o.). **III sich zum Guten ~** take a turn for the better.

'**wenden²** (wandte, gewandt, h) **I** *v/t* **~ an** (*acc*) spend *money* on, devote *time etc* to. **II sich ~** turn (*nach* to, *gegen* on, against); **sich ~ gegen** oppose; **sich** an j-n ~ ask (or see, consult, contact) s.o.; *sich um Rat (Hilfe)* an j-n ~ turn to s.o. for advice (help).

'**Wendepunkt** m a. fig. turning point.

wendig ['vɛndɪç] adj **1.** manoeuvrable, Am. maneuverable. **2.** nimble, agile.

'**Wendigkeit** f (-; no pl) **1.** manoeuvrability, Am. maneuverability. **2.** agility.

'**Wendung** f (-; -en) **1.** turn: fig. *e-e unerwartete ~ nehmen* take an unexpected turn. **2.** expression, phrase.

wenig ['ve:nɪç] indef pron and adv little, not much: *~e pl* few, not many, su. few (people); *nur ~e* only few; *(nur) einige ~e* (only) a few; *~er less*, Am. minus; *immer ~er* less and less; *~er als* less than; *nicht ~er als* no less than, pl no fewer than; *nichts ~er als* anything but; *~er werden* decrease; *das ~e* the little; *das ~ste* the least; *am ~sten* least of all; *ein ~* a little; *nicht ~* quite a lot; *~ beliebt* not very popular; *~ bekannt* little known; *~ begeistert* (rather) unenthusiastic; *~ hilfreich* unhelpful.

'**Wenigkeit** f F *m-e ~* yours truly.

'**wenigstens** adv at least: *wenn sie ~ zuhörte* if only she would listen.

wenn [vɛn] conj **1.** a) when, b) whenever, c) as soon as: *man ihn so reden hört* to hear him (talk). **2.** if: *~ sie doch (or nur) käme* if only she would come; *~ du nicht bezahlst* unless you pay; *~ ich das gewußt hätte* had I (but) known. **3.** *~ auch, und ~* even if; → *schon* 5. **Wenn** n *ohne ~ und Aber* no ifs or buts.

wer [ve:r] I interrog pron who, which: *von euch?* which of you? II rel pron who, which: *~ (auch immer)* whoever. III indef pron a) who, adm. any person who, b) F somebody, anybody.

'**Werbe|ab,teilung** f publicity department. **~agen,tur** f advertising agency. **~akti,on** f → **Werbekampagne**. **~fachmann** m advertising expert. **~fernsehen** n **1.** commercial television. **2.** television (or TV) commercials. **~film** m promotion(al) film. **~funk** m **1.** commercial radio. **2.** radio ads (Am. commercials). **~geschenk** n promotional gift. **~graphik** f commercial art. **~graphiker** m commercial artist. **~kam,pagne** f publicity (or advertising) campaign. **~kosten** pl advertising costs.

~leiter m publicity manager. **~mittel** pl advertising media (or funds).

werben ['vɛrbən] (warb, geworben, h) I v/t **1.** enlist (members), a. recruit (workers etc), canvass, attract (votes etc): *j-n für e-e Sache ~* win s.o. over to a cause. II v/i **2.** *~ für* advertise, promote, F plug, pol. campaign (or canvass) for. **3.** *~ um* a. fig. court, woo.

'**Werbe|pro,spekt** m publicity brochure. **~psycho,logie** f psychology of advertising. **~spot** m commercial (spot), spot. **~spruch** m (advertising) slogan. **~texter** m copywriter. **~trommel** f *die ~ rühren* → **werben** 2.

'**werbewirksam** adj effective.

Werbung (-; no pl) f **1.** enlisting (etc, → **werben** 1), recruitment. **2.** advertising, publicity: *das ist e-e gute ~ für ...* that is good publicity for ... **3.** → **Werbeabteilung**. '**Werbungskosten** pl taxation: professional outlays.

'**Werdegang** m (-[e]s; no pl) development, a. fig. or ⚙ history, of person: professional background, a. career.

werden ['ve:rdən] (wurde, geworden, sn) I v/i a) become, get, grow, b) turn, go (sour etc), turn out (well etc): *blaß ~* turn pale; *blind (verrückt) ~* go blind (mad); *böse ~* get angry; *gesund ~* get well; *wie sind die Fotos geworden?* how have the photos turned out?; *was will er (einmal) ~?* what does he want to be?; *was soll nun ~?* what are we going to do now?; *was ist aus ihm geworden?* what has become of him?; *daraus wird nichts!* a) nothing will come of it, b) nothing doing!; F *es wird schon (wieder) ~!* it will be all right!; F *wird's bald?* get a move on!; → *Mutter*[1]. II v/aux *ich werde fahren* I will (or I'll) drive, I am going to drive; *es wird gleich regnen* it's going to rain; *es ist uns gesagt worden* we have been told; *geliebt ~* be loved; *gebaut ~* be (being) built.

'**Werden** n (-s) development, growth, progress: *im ~ sein* be in the making.

werfen ['vɛrfən] (warf, geworfen, h) I v/t **1.** throw (a. fig. or zo.), cast (a. anchor, glance, shadow): (v/i mit) *a. ~ nach* throw s.th. at; *Bomben ~* drop bombs; → *Blick* 1, *Handtuch* etc. II v/i **2.** throw. **3.** → *schmeißen* 5. III sich ~ **4.**

🔘 buckle, *wood*: warp. **5. sich ~ auf** *(acc)* throw o.s. on *(fig.* into); → **Hals.**

'Werfer m (-s; -), **'Werferin** f (-; -nen) *sports*: thrower.

Werft [vɛrft] f (-; -en) **1.** shipyard. **2.** ✈ hangar. **~arbeiter** m docker.

Werg [vɛrk] n (-[e]s; *no pl*) tow.

Werk [vɛrk] n (-[e]s; -e) **1.** work, *of writer etc*: a. works, a. deed: **am ~ sein** be at work; **ans ~ gehen** set to work; **ein gutes ~ tun** do a good deed; **vorsichtig zu ~e gehen** go about it cautiously; *b.s.* **es war sein ~** it was his work (*or* doing). **2.** factory, works, plant: 🔩 **ab ~** ex works. **3.** 🔘 works, mechanism.

'Werk... works ..., factory ... **~angehörige** m, f (-n; -n) (works) employee. **~arzt** m works doctor. **~bank** f (-; ⁓e) (work)bench. **⒉eigen** adj works ..., company(-owned).

werkeln ['vɛrkəln] v/i (h) potter about.

werken ['vɛrkən] v/i (h) work, *ped.* do handicrafts.

'Werken n (-s) *ped.* handicrafts.

'Werkleiter m works manager.

'Werkmeister m foreman.

'Werks... → **Werk...**

'Werk|schutz m Security. **~spio,nage** f industrial espionage. **~statt** f (-; ⁓en) workshop. **~stoff** m material. **~stück** n workpiece. **~tag** m workday, working day. **⒉tags** adv on weekdays, during the week. **⒉tätig** adj working. **~tätige** m, f (-n; -n) working person: **die ~n** the working population. **~unterricht** m *ped.* handicrafts.

'Werkzeug n (-[e]s; -e) tool (*a. fig.*), *coll.* tools. **~kasten** m tool box, tool kit. **~macher** m toolmaker. **~ma,schine** f machine tool. **~tasche** f tool bag.

Wermut ['ve:rmu:t] m (-[e]s; *no pl*) **1.** 🍷 wormwood. **2.** vermouth. **'Wermutstropfen** m *fig.* drop of bitterness.

wert [ve:rt] adj worth: **et. ~ sein** be worth s.th.; **e-n Versuch (e-e Reise) ~** worth a try (a trip); **e-r Sache ~ sein** be worthy of s.th.; **viel ~** worth a lot, (very) valuable; **nicht viel ~** not up to much; **nichts ~** worthless, no good; **~ getan zu werden** worth doing; **das ist es (mir) nicht ~** it's not worth it.

Wert m (-[e]s; -e) **1.** a) value (*a.* 🧬, 🧪, *philos., phys.*, 🔘), *fig. a.* merit(s), b) importance, c) F use: **im ~(e) von** to the

value of; **Waren im ~(e) von 400 Dollar** 400 dollars worth of goods; **im ~ sinken (steigen)** lose (go up) in value; **e-r Sache großen ~ beimessen** attach great importance to s.th.; **(großen) ~ legen auf** *(acc)* set (great) store by; **k-n besonderen ~ legen auf** *(acc)* not to care much for; *fig. sich unter ~ verkaufen* sell o.s. short; F **es hat k-n ~!** that's no use! **2. ~e** *pl* a) data, readings, levels, b) 🔩 assets, securities, stocks.

'Wertangabe f **1.** declaration of value. **2.** declared value.

'Wertarbeit f (high-class) workmanship.

'wertbeständig adj stable, of stable (*fig.* lasting) value.

werten ['ve:rtən] v/t (h) assess, judge, *a. sports*: rate (**als Erfolg** as a success).

'wertfrei adj and adv value-free.

'Wertgegenstand m article of value, *pl* valuables.

Wertigkeit ['ve:rtɪç-] f (-; -en) 🧬 valency.

'wertlos adj worthless (*a. fig.*), valueless, useless, *pred* (of) no use, no good.

'Wertlosigkeit f (-; *no pl*) worthlessness.

'Wertmaßstab m standard (of value).

'Wertminderung f depreciation.

'Wertpa,piere *pl* securities.

'Wertsachen *pl* valuables.

'Wertsendung f 🔘 registered item.

'Wertsteigerung f 🔩 increase in value.

'Wertung f (-; -en) assessment, *a. sports*: rating, *sports*: score, points.

'Werturteil n value judgement.

'Wertverlust m 🔩 loss of value.

'wertvoll adj valuable.

'Wertvorstellungen *pl* values.

'Wertzeichen n (postage) stamp.

'Wertzuwachs m 🔩 increase in value.

Wesen ['ve:zən] n (-s; -) **1.** being, creature. **2.** *no pl* a) *philos.* essence, b) character, nature: **ihr heiteres ~** her cheerful disposition. **3.** F **viel ~s von et. machen** make a great fuss about s.th.

'Wesensart f (-; *no pl*) nature, character.

'wesensfremd adj alien (*dat* to).

'Wesenszug m (characteristic) trait.

wesentlich ['ve:zəntlɪç] **I** adj essential (**für** to), substantial: **das Wesentliche** the essence, the essential point; **nichts Wesentliches** nothing (very) important; **im ~en** essentially, on the whole; **der ~e Inhalt** the substance (*of book* *etc).* **II** *adv* essentially, considerably, a great deal, much: **~** *besser* far better.

weshalb [vɛs'halp] **I** *interrog pron* why. **II** *conj* and so, which is why.

Wespe ['vɛspə] *f* (-; -n) *zo.* wasp.

'Wespennest *n* wasps' nest: *fig. in ein ~ stechen* stir up a hornet's nest.

'Wespenstich *m* wasp sting.

wessen ['vɛsən] *interrog pron* **1.** *gen of* **wer**: whose. **2.** *gen of was*: **~** *beschuldigt man ihn?* what is he accused of?

West [vɛst] *m invar* **1.** West. **2.** west wind.

'westdeutsch *adj*, **'Westdeutsche** *m*, *f* (-n; -n) West German.

Weste ['vɛstə] *f* (-; -n) waistcoat, *Am.* vest: F *fig. e-e weiße ~ haben* have a clean record.

Westen ['vɛstən] *m* (-s; *no pl*) west, *of country*: West, *of town: a.* West End, *pol. the* West: *von ~* from the west; *nach ~* west(wards).

'Westentasche *f* waistcoat (*Am.* vest) pocket: F *et. wie s-e ~ kennen* know s.th. like the back of one's hand.

Westfale [vɛst'faːlə] *m* (-n; -n), **Westfälin** [vɛst'fɛːlɪn] *f* (-; -nen), **westfälisch** [vɛst'fɛːlɪʃ] *adj* Westphalian.

'westlich I *adj* western, west(erly) (*wind, direction*), *pol.* West(ern). **II** *adv* (to the) west (*von* of). **III** *prep* (*gen*) (to the) west of.

'Westmächte *pl pol.* Western powers.

'westwärts *adv* west(wards).

'Westwind *m* west wind.

'Wettannahme *f* betting office.

Wettbewerb ['vɛtbəvɛrp] *m* (-[e]s; -e) competition, *sports: a.* event: *↑ freier (unlauterer)* **~** free (unfair) competition; *in ~ stehen* be competing (*mit* with). **'Wettbewerber** *m* competitor.

'wettbewerbsfähig *adj* competitive.

'Wettbü,ro *n* betting office.

Wette ['vɛtə] *f* (-; -n) bet: *e-e ~ eingehen* (*or abschließen*) make a bet; *was gilt die ~?* what do you bet?; *mit j-m um die ~ laufen* (*or fahren*) race s.o.

'Wetteifer *m* emulation, rivalry.

'wetteifern *v/i* (*insep*, ge-, h) (*mit* with, *um* for) vie, compete.

wetten ['vɛtən] *v/t, v/i* (h) bet: (*mit j-m*) *um et.* **~** bet (s.o.) s.th.; *ich wette zehn zu eins, daß* I bet you ten to one that; **~** *auf* (*acc*) bet on, put one's money on, back (*horse*); F **~,** *daß ...?* want to bet?

Wetter[1] ['vɛtər] *m* (-s; -) better.

'Wetter[2] *n* (-s; -) **1.** weather, *a.* storm: *bei diesem ~* in a weather like this; → *Wind.* **2.** ⚒ *schlagende ~* firedamp.

'Wetter|amt *n* meteorological office. **~aussichten** *pl* weather outlook. **~bedingungen** *pl* weather conditions. **~bericht** *m* weather report. **~dienst** *m* weather service. **~fahne** *f* weather vane. **⚲fest** *adj* weatherproof. **~frosch** *m* humor. weatherman.

'wetterfühlig [-fyːlɪç] *adj* **~** *sein* be sensitive to changes in the weather.

'Wetter|hahn *m* weathercock. **⚲hart** *adj* weather-beaten. **~karte** *f* weather map. **~kunde** *f* (-; *no pl*) meteorology. **~lage** *f* weather situation. **~leuchten** *n* (-s) sheet lightning.

wettern ['vɛtərn] *v/i* (h) F storm (*gegen* at).

'Wetter|satel,lit *m* weather satellite. **~seite** *f* weather side. **~stati,on** *f* weather station. **~sturz** *m* sudden drop in temperature. **~umschwung** *m* (sudden) change in weather. **~vor,hersage** *f* (-; -n) weather forecast.

'wetterwendisch [-vɛndɪʃ] *adj* fickle.

'Wett|fahrt *f* race. **~kampf** *m* contest, competition, *sports: a.* event. **~kämpfer(in** *f)* *m* competitor, contestant. **~lauf** *m* race (*fig. mit der Zeit* against time). **~läufer(in** *f)* *m* runner.

'wettmachen *v/t* (*sep*, h) make up for.

'Wett|rennen *n a. fig.* race. **~rüsten** *n* arms race. **~streit** *m* contest.

wetzen ['vɛtsən] **I** *v/t* (h) sharpen, whet. **II** *v/i* (sn) F scoot.

Whisky ['vɪski] *m* (-s; -s) whisky.

wich [vɪç] *pret of* **weichen.**

wichsen ['vɪksən] (h) **I** *v/t* polish. **II** *v/i* V wank, jerk off.

Wichtel ['vɪçtəl] *m* (-s; -), **'Wichtelmännchen** *n* brownie, goblin.

wichtig ['vɪçtɪç] *adj* important (*für j-n* to s.o., *für et.* for s.th.): *~ tun, sich ~ machen* be self-important; *Wichtigeres zu tun haben* have more important things to do; *das Wichtigste* the most important thing; *das Wichtigste zuerst!* first things first.

'Wichtigkeit *f* (-; *no pl*) importance.

'Wichtigtuer *m* (-s; -) F pompous ass.

Wichtigtue'rei *f* (-; *no pl*) F pomposity.

'wichtigtuerisch *adj* pompous.

Wicke ['vɪkə] f (-; -n) ⚘ vetch, sweet pea.
Wickel ['vɪkəl] m (-s; -) ⚒ compress. **~kom,mode** f (baby's) changing table.
wickeln ['vɪkəln] (h) **I** v/t **1.** (*um* [a]round) wind, tie, wrap: *et. in Papier ~* wrap s.th. (up) in paper; → *Finger.* **2.** *ein Baby ~* change a baby's nappies (*Am.* diapers). **II** *sich ~ um* wind (*or* coil) itself around; *sich in e-e Decke ~* wrap o.s. up in a blanket.
Wickler ['vɪklər] m (-s; -) curler.
Wicklung f (-; -en) ⚙ winding.
Widder ['vɪdər] m (-s; -) **1.** zo. ram. **2.** astr. (*er ist* [*ein*] ~ he is [an]) Aries.
wider ['viːdər] prep against, contrary to: *~ Erwarten* contrary to expectation(s); → *Für, Wille.* **wider'fahren** v/i (irr, insep, no -ge-, sn, → *fahren*) *j-m ~* happen to s.o.; *j-m Gerechtigkeit ~ lassen* a) do justice to s.o., b) give s.o. his due.
'Widerhaken m (-s; -) barb.
'Widerhall m (-[e]s; -e) echo, fig. a. resonance: *k-n ~ finden* meet with no response. **'widerhallen** v/i (sep, h) (*von* with) echo, resound.
widerlegbar [-'leːkbaːr] adj refutable.
wider'legen v/t (insep, no -ge-, h) refute. **Wider'legung** f (-; -en) refutation.
'widerlich adj revolting, disgusting.
'widerna,türlich adj perverse.
'widerrechtlich adj illegal, unlawful: *~ betreten* trespass (up)on; *sich et. ~ aneignen* misappropriate s.th.
'Widerrede f (-; -n) contradiction(s), protest: *k-e ~!* no argument!
'Widerruf m (-[e]s; -e) revocation, withdrawal: (*bis*) *auf ~* until revoked.
wider'rufen v/t (irr, insep, no -ge-, h, → *rufen*) revoke, withdraw.
'Widersacher [-zaxər] m (-s; -) adversary, opponent.
'Widerschein m reflection.
wider'setzen: sich ~ (insep, no -ge-, h) put up resistance, (*dat*) oppose (s.th., s.o.). **wider'setzlich** adj recalcitrant.
'widersinnig adj absurd.
'widerspenstig [-'ʃpɛnstɪç] adj rebellious, unruly (a. fig. hair).
'Widerspenstigkeit f (-; no pl) rebelliousness, a. fig. unruliness.
'widerspiegeln (sep, h) **I** v/t a. fig. reflect. **II** *sich ~* be reflected.
wider'sprechen v/i (irr, insep, no -ge-, h, → *sprechen*) contradict (*j-m* s.o., *sich*

o.s.), (*dat*) oppose (*suggestion etc*): *sich* (*or einander*) *~* be contradictory, conflict. **'Widerspruch** m (-[e]s; ⸚e) a) contradiction (*in sich* in terms), b) protest, opposition: *im ~ zu* in contradiction to; *im ~ stehen zu* be inconsistent with, contradict; *auf ~ stoßen* meet with protest (*bei* from). **'widersprüchlich** [-'ʃpryçlɪç] adj contradictory, inconsistent, conflicting (*feelings*).
'Widerspruchsgeist m (-[e]s; no pl) spirit of contradiction.
'widerspruchslos adj and adv without contradiction (*or* protest).
'Widerstand m (-[e]s; ⸚e) **1.** no pl (*gegen* to) resistance, opposition: *~ leisten* offer resistance, fight back; *auf* (*heftigen*) *~ stoßen* meet with (stiff) opposition; *den ~ aufgeben* give in; *den Weg des geringsten ~es wählen* take the line of least resistance. **2.** ⚡ resistor.
'Widerstands|bewegung f pol. resistance movement. ⚑**fähig** adj resistant (*gegen* to), a. ⚙ robust. ⚑**fähigkeit** f (-; no pl) resistance (*gegen* to), robustness. ⚑**kämpfer(in** f) m resistance fighter. ⚑**kraft** f (powers of) resistance.
'widerstandslos adv without resistance.
wider'stehen v/i (irr, insep, no -ge-, h → *stehen*) (*dat*) resist (s.o., s.th.).
wider'streben v/i (insep, no -ge-, h) be repugnant (*dat* to): *es widerstrebt mir zu inf* I hate to inf. **Wider'streben** n (-s) reluctance. **wider'strebend** adv reluctantly.
'Widerstreit m conflict. **'widerstreitend** adj conflicting (*feelings etc*).
'widerwärtig [-vɛrtɪç] adj repulsive, disgusting, F nasty.
'Widerwille m (-n; no pl) (*gegen* to) aversion (to), disgust (at). **'widerwillig** adj unwilling, reluctant.
widmen ['vɪtmən] (h) (*dat* to) **I** v/t **1.** dedicate. **2.** devote, give (*one's time etc*). **II** *sich ~* devote o.s.; *sich ganz ... ~* give one's undivided attention to ...
widrig ['viːdrɪç] adj adverse.
widrigenfalls ['viːdrɪgən-] adv failing which, ⚖ in default of which.
wie [viː] **I** interrog adv **1.** how: *~ macht man das?* how is that done?; *~ ist er* (*es*)*?* what is he (it) like?; *~ nennt man das?* what do you call that?; *~ sagten Sie?* (sorry,) what did you say?; *~ wäre*

es mit ...? what about ...? **2. ~ schön!** how beautiful; **~ gut, daß er da war!** lucky for me *etc* that he was there; **und ~!** and how!, F you bet!; → **bitte** 3. **II** *conj* **3.** as, like: **stark ~ ein Bär** (as) strong as a bear; **ein Mann ~** a man like him; **dumm ~ er ist** fool that he is; **~ gesagt** as I said. **4.** ~ (**zum Beispiel**), **~ etwa** such as. **5.** *time:* F as, when. **6. ich sah, ~ er weglief** I saw him running away; **ich hörte, ~ er es sagte** I heard him say so. **7.** ~ (**auch**) **immer** however, no matter how; **~ dem auch sei** that as it may; **~ sie auch heißen mögen** whatever they are called.

Wiedehopf ['viːdəhɔpf] *m* (-[e]s; -e) *zo.* hoopoe.

wieder ['viːdər] *adv* again: **~ gesund** well again; **immer ~** again and again, time and again; **schon ~?** not again!; **ich bin gleich ~ da!** I'll be back in a minute!; **~ ist ein Tag vorbei!** another day's over.

Wieder|'annäherung *f pol.* rapprochement. **~'aufbau** *m* (-[e]s; *no pl*) **1.** reconstruction. **2.** recovery. **~'aufbereitung** *f* reprocessing. **~'aufbereitungsanlage** *f* reprocessing plant.

wieder|'aufführen *v/t* (*sep,* h) rerun (*film etc*). **~'aufleben** *v/i* (*sep,* sn) (*a.* **~ lassen**) revive.

Wieder'aufnahme *f* (-; *no pl*) resumption. **Wieder'aufnahmeverfahren** *n* 🏛 a) new hearing, b) retrial.

wieder'aufnehmen *v/t* (*irr, sep,* -ge-, h, → **nehmen**) resume.

Wieder'aufrüstung *f* (-; *no pl*) rearmament.

wieder|'auftauchen *v/i* (*sep,* sn) re-emerge, ⚓ *a.* resurface, *fig.* reappear, turn up again. **~'auftreten** *v/i* (*irr, sep,* -ge-, sn, → **treten**) reappear.

Wieder'ausfuhr *f* re-exportation.

'Wiederbeginn *m* (-[e]s; *no pl*) recommencement, *of school etc:* reopening.

'wiederbekommen *v/t* (*irr, sep,* h, → **bekommen**) get *s.th.* back.

'wiederbeleben *v/t* (*sep,* h) resuscitate, *a. fig.* revive. **'Wiederbelebung** *f* (-; *no pl*) resuscitation, *fig.* revival.

'Wiederbelebungsversuch *m* attempt at resuscitation.

'wiederbeschaffen *v/t* (*sep,* h) replace.

'wiederbringen *v/t* (*irr, sep,* -ge-, h, → **bringen**) bring *s.o., s.th.* back, return.

wieder'einführen *v/t* (*sep,* h) **1.** reintroduce, revive. **2.** 🕆 reimport. **Wieder'einführung** *f* (-; *no pl*) **1.** reintroduction, revival. **2.** 🕆 reimportation.

Wieder'eingliederung *f* reintegration (*in acc* into), (*social etc*) rehabilitation.

wieder'einsetzen *v/t* (*sep,* h) reinstate (*in acc* in). **Wieder'einsetzung** *f* (-; *no pl*) reinstatement.

'Wiedereintritt *m* re-entry (*in acc* into).

'wiederentdecken *v/t* (*sep,* h) rediscover.

'Wiederergreifung *f* (-; *no pl*) recapture.

'wiedererkennen *v/t* (*irr, sep,* h, → **erkennen**) recognize: **nicht wiederzuerkennen** unrecognizable.

'wiedererlangen *v/t* (*sep,* h) recover, regain.

'wiedereröffnen *v/t* (*sep,* h) reopen. **'Wiedereröffnung** *f* reopening.

'wiederfinden *v/t* (*irr, sep,* -ge-, h, → **finden**) find again.

'Wiedergabe *f* (-; *no pl*) **1.** account. **2.** ♪ rendering, interpretation. **3.** reproduction (*a.* ⊛), ♪ playback. **~gerät** *n* playback unit. **~quali͵tät** *f* fidelity of reproduction.

'wiedergeben *v/t* (*irr, sep,* -ge-, → **geben**) **1.** give *s.th.* back (*dat* to). **2.** a) describe, b) repeat, c) quote. **3.** ♪ render, interpret. **4.** reproduce (*a.* ⊛), ♪ *a.* play back.

'Wiedergeburt *f a. fig.* rebirth.

'wiedergewinnen *v/t* (*irr, sep,* h, → **gewinnen**) regain, recover (*a.* ⊛), ⊛ reclaim. **'Wiedergewinnung** *f* (-; *no pl*) recovery, ⊛ *a.* reclamation.

wieder'gutmachen *v/t* (*sep,* h) make up for, compensate for: **nicht wiedergutzumachen(d)** irreparable. **Wieder'gutmachung** *f* (-; -en) reparation.

'wiederhaben *v/t* (*irr, sep,* -ge-, h, → **haben**) F have *s.o., s.th.* back.

wieder'herstellen *v/t* (*sep,* h) restore, ⚕ *a.* cure, *a.* re-establish (*connections etc*). **Wieder'herstellung** *f* (-; -en) restoration, re-establishment, ⚕ recovery.

wieder'holbar *adj* repeatable. **wieder'holen** (*insep, no* -ge-, h) **I** *v/t* a) repeat, say (*or* do) *s.th.* (over) again, b) sum up, F recap. **II sich ~** a) repeat itself (*or o.s.*), b) recur. **wieder'holt** *adj* repeated. **Wieder'holung** *f* (-; -en) repetition, *radio, TV etc*: repeat, *TV, soccer etc*: replay.

Wieder'holungs|impfung *f* booster (shot). **~kurs** *m* refresher course. **~prüfung** *f* resit. **~spiel** *n sports*: replay. **~taste** *f* repeat key.

'**Wiederhören**: *auf* **~!** goodby(e)!

'**wiederkäuen** [-kɔyən] *(sep*, h) **I** *v/i* zo. ruminate. **II** *v/t fig*. rehash.

'**Wiederkäuer** *m* (-s; -) zo. ruminant.

'**Wiederkehr** [-keːr] *f* (-; *no pl*) **1.** return. **2.** recurrence. '**wiederkehren** *v/i* (*sep*, sn) **1.** return, come back. **2.** recur: (*regelmäßig*) **~d** recurrent.

'**wiederkommen** *v/i* (*irr, sep*, -ge-, sn, → **kommen**) a) come again, b) come back.

'**wiedersehen** *v/t* (*irr, sep*, -ge-, h, → **sehen**) see *s.o., s.th.* again: **sich ~** meet again. '**Wiedersehen** *n* (-s; -) reunion: **~ mit London** London revisited; *auf* **~!** goodby(e)!, F so long!, bye!

wiederum ['viːdərʊm] *adv* **1.** again. **2.** on the other hand.

'**wiedervereinigen** *v/t* (*a. sich ~*) (*sep*, h) reunite. '**Wiedervereinigung** *f* (-; -en) reunion, *pol. a.* reunification.

'**Wieder|verheiratung** *f* (-; -en) remarriage. **~verkäufer** *m* reseller. **~verkaufswert** *m* (-[e]s; *no pl*) resale value. **~verwendung** *f* (-; -en) reuse.

'**wiederverwerten** *v/t* (*sep*, h) recycle. '**Wiederverwertung** *f* (-; -en) recycling.

'**Wiederwahl** *f* (-; *no pl*) re-election.

'**wiederwählen** *v/t* (*sep*, h) re-elect.

'**Wiederzulassung** *f* (-; -en) **1.** readmission. **2.** *mot*. relicensing.

Wiege ['viːɡə] *f* (-; -n) *a. fig.* cradle.

wiegen[1] ['viːɡən] (h) **I** *v/t* rock, shake (*one's head*), sway (*one's hips*): *j-n in Sicherheit* **~** lull s.o. into a false sense of security. **II** *sich* **~** rock; *sich in den Hüften* **~** sway one's hips; *fig. sich in Sicherheit* **~** believe o.s. safe.

wiegen[2] (wog, gewogen, h) **I** *v/t, v/i* weigh: *fig. schwer* **~** carry (a lot of) weight. **II** *sich* **~** weigh o.s.

wiegen[3] *v/t* (h) *gastr*. chop, mince.

'**Wiegenlied** *n* lullaby.

wiehern ['viːərn] *v/i* (h) neigh: **~(d lachen)** heehaw.

Wiener[1] ['viːnər] *f* (-; -) wiener(wurst).

'**Wiener**[2] *m* (-s; -), '**Wienerin** *f* (-; -nen), '**wienerisch** *adj* Viennese.

wienern ['viːnərn] *v/t* (h) F polish.

wies [viːs] *pret of* **weisen.**

Wiese ['viːzə] *f* (-; -n) meadow.

Wiesel ['viːzəl] *n* (-s; -) zo. weasel.

wieso [viˈzoː] → **warum.**

wieviel [viˈfiːl] *interrog adv* how much: **~(e)** how many. '**wievielmal** *adv* how many times, how often. **wie'vielt** *adj* **der (die, das)** **~e** which; *zum* **~en Male?** how many times?; **den** 2**en haben wir heute?** what's the date today?

wieweit [viˈvaɪt] → **inwieweit.**

Wikinger ['viːkiŋər] *m* (-s; -) Viking.

wild [vɪlt] *adj* **1.** wild (*a.* ♀, *zo. or fig*.), *a.* savage (*dog, tribe, etc*): ♉ **~es Fleisch** proud flesh; **~e Vermutungen** wild speculation; **~ wachsen** grow wild. **2.** violent, fierce, wild: *das ist halb so* **~!** it's not all that bad. **3.** F *fig.* wild, mad: **wie ~ work** *etc* like mad; *j-n* **~ machen** make s.o. mad; **~ werden** get mad, see red; **den ~en Mann spielen** go berserk. **4.** F *ganz* **~ sein auf** (*acc*) be wild (*or* crazy) about. **5.** unauthorized (*camping etc*); → **Streik.**

Wild *n* (-[e]s; *no pl*) game, *gastr. a.* venison. **~bach** *m* torrent. **~bahn** *f* **in freier ~** in the wild. **~dieb** *m* poacher.

Wilde ['vɪldə] *m, f* (-n; -n) savage.

'**Wildente** *f* zo. wild duck.

'**Wilderer** ['vɪldərər] *m* (-s; -) poacher.

wildern ['vɪldərn] *v/i* (h) poach.

wild'fremd *adj* completely strange (*dat* to): **~er Mensch** complete stranger.

'**Wildgans** *f* zo. wild goose.

'**Wildgehege** *n* game preserve.

'**Wildheit** *f* (-; *no pl*) wildness (*a. fig*.), savagery, fury, *a.* unruliness.

'**Wildhüter** *m* (-s; -) gamekeeper.

'**Wildkatze** *f* zo. wild cat.

'**wildlebend** *adj* wild.

'**Wildleder** *n*, '**wildledern** *adj* suede.

'**Wildnis** *f* (-; -se) wilderness (*a. fig*.): *in der* **~** in the wild.

'**Wild|park** *m* game park. **~sau** *f* wild sow. **~schwein** *n* wild boar. 2**wachsend** *adj* wild. **~wasser** *n* (-s; -) torrent, whitewater. **~wechsel** *m* run.

Wild'westfilm *m* western.

Wille ['vɪlə] *m* (-ns; *no pl*) will, *philos. a.* volition, *a.* intention: **böser ~** ill will; **guter ~** good will (*or* intention); **letzter ~** (last) will, ♉ last will and testament; **aus freiem ~n** of one's own free will; **gegen m-n ~n** against my will; *j-m s-n*

~n lassen let s.o. have his (own) way;
*ich kann Ihnen beim besten ~n nicht
helfen* I can't help you, much as I
should like to; *ich kann mich beim
besten ~n nicht erinnern* I can't remember for the life of me; *wenn es
nach ihrem ~n ginge* if she had her
way; *sie mußte wider ~n lachen* she
couldn't help laughing; → *durchsetzen*[1] I. **'Willen** *m* → **Wille.**

'willenlos *adj* weak, weak-willed: *j-s
~es Werkzeug sein* be s.o.'s slave.

'willens *adj ~ sein zu inf* be willing (*or*
prepared) to *inf*.

'Willens|akt *m* act of volition. **~an-
strengung** *f* effort of will. **~äußerung**
f expression of one's will. **~erklärung** *f*
🔲 declaration of intention. **~freiheit** *f*
free will. **~kraft** *f* (-; *no pl*) **1.** willpower.
2. strong will. **2schwach** *adj* weak,
weak-willed. **2stark** *adj* strong-willed.
~stärke *f* (-; *no pl*) strong will.

'willentlich *adv* deliberately.

willfährig ['vɪlfɛːrɪç] *adj* compliant.

'willig *adj* willing.

will'kommen *adj* welcome (*dat* to): *j-n ~
heißen* welcome s.o. **Will'kommen** *n*
(-s; -) welcome, reception.

Willkür ['vɪlkyːr] *f* (-; *no pl*) arbitrariness:
j-s ~ ausgeliefert sein be at s.o.'s mercy. **~akt** *m* arbitrary act. **~herrschaft** *f*
(-; *no pl*) arbitrary rule, despotism.

'willkürlich *adj* **1.** arbitrary. **2.** random
(*selection etc*). **3.** *physiol.* voluntary.

wimmeln ['vɪməln] *v/i* (h) ~ *von* be teeming (F crawling) with.

wimmern ['vɪmərn] *v/i* (h) whimper.

Wimpel ['vɪmpəl] *m* (-s; -) pennant.

Wimper ['vɪmpər] *f* (-; -n) eyelash: *ohne
mit der ~ zu zucken* without batting an
eyelid.

'Wimpernbürste *f* eyelash brush.

'Wimperntusche *f* mascara.

Wind [vɪnt] *m* (-[e]s; -e) (*günstiger ~* fair)
wind: *fig. ein frischer ~* a breath of
fresh air; *gegen den ~* into the wind;
mit dem ~ down the wind; *bei ~ und
Wetter* in rain or storm; *fig. ~ bekommen von* get wind of; F *viel ~ machen*
a) make a great fuss (*um* of, about,
over), b) act big, talk big; *j-m den ~ aus
den Segeln nehmen* take the wind out
of s.o.'s sails; *in alle ~e zerstreut* scattered to the four winds; *in den ~ reden*

waste one's breath; *in den ~ schlagen*
cast to the winds; *wissen, woher der ~
weht* know how the wind blows; → *
Mantel* 1.

'Windbeutel *m gastr.* cream puff.

Winde[1] ['vɪndə] *f* (-; -n) ⚙ winch, hoist.

'Winde[2] *f* (-; -n) 🌿 bindweed.

'Windei *n* wind egg.

Windel ['vɪndəl] *f* (-; -n) nappy, *Am.* dia-
per. **'windelweich** *adj* F *j-n ~ schlagen*
beat s.o. to a pulp.

winden ['vɪndən] (*wand, gewunden, h*) **I**
v/t **1.** wind (*um* round). **2.** make, bind
(*wreath*). **II** *sich ~* **3.** wriggle, squirm:
sich vor Schmerzen ~ writhe with
pain. **4.** wind its way (*durch* through).
5. *sich ~ um* wind (*or* coil) itself round.

Windeseile ['vɪndəs-] *f in ~* at lightning
speed, in no time; *sich mit ~ verbreiten
rumo(u)r etc*: spread like wildfire.

'windgeschützt *adj* sheltered (from the
wind).

'Wind|hose *f meteor.* whirlwind. **~hund**
m **1.** *zo.* greyhound. **2.** F *fig.* loose fish.

'windig *adj* **1.** windy. **2.** F shady (*fellow*),
fishy (*business*), lame (*excuse etc*).

'Wind|jacke *f* windcheater. **~ka,nal** *m* ⚙
wind tunnel. **~kraft** *f* (-; *no pl*) wind
power. **~licht** *n* storm lantern. **~mühle**
f windmill. **~pocken** *pl* 🦠 chickenpox.
~richtung *f* direction of the wind. **~ro-
se** *f* compass card (*or* rose). **~sack** *m*
wind sock. **~schatten** *m* ⚓ lee, ✈ sheltered zone, *sports*: slipstream. **2schief**
adj F crooked. **2schlüpfig** [-ʃlʏpfɪç],
2schnittig *adj* streamlined. **~schutz-
scheibe** *f* windscreen, *Am.* windshield.
~stärke *f* wind force. **2still** *adj* calm.
~stille *f* calm, *a.* lull. **~stoß** *m* gust (*of*
wind). **~surfen** *n* (-s) windsurfing.
~surfer *m* wind surfer.

Windung ['vɪndʊŋ] *f* (-; -en) winding, *a.
anat.* convolution, bend (*of river etc*),
whorl (*of spiral, shell*), ⚙ thread.

Wink [vɪŋk] *m* (-[e]s; -e) a) sign, *fig.* hint,
tip, b) tip-off, warning: → *Zaunpfahl.*

Winkel ['vɪŋkəl] *m* (-s; -) **1.** Å angle: *im
rechten ~* at right angles (*zu* to). → *tot.*
2. corner. **3.** ⚔ chevron. **4.** ⚙ a) square,
b) knee, elbow. **~advo,kat** *m contr.*
pettifogger, *Am.* F shyster. **~eisen** *n* ⚙
angle iron. **~funkti,on** *f* Å goniometric
function. **~hal,bierende** *f* (-n; -n) Å
bisector of an angle. **~maß** *n* ⚙ square.

~messer m (-s; -) ⚙ protractor, surv. goniometer. **~zug** m F dodge, evasion.

winken ['vɪŋkən] (h) **I** v/i **j-m ~a)** wave to s.o., b) reward etc: be in store for s.o.; **mit dem Taschentuch ~** wave one's handkerchief; **e-m Taxi ~** hail a taxi. **II** v/t **j-n zu sich ~** beckon s.o. (to come).

Winter ['vɪntər] m (-s; -) (**im ~**) winter.

Winter... winter (coat, fashion, holiday, month, semester, etc). **~ausrüstung** f mot. winter equipment. 2**fest** adj winterproof, ⚓ hardy: **~ machen** winterize. **~garten** m conservatory. **~getreide** n winter crop. **~halbjahr** n winter.

'winterlich adj wintry.

'Winter|pause f winter break. **~reifen** m mot. winter tyre (Am. tire). **~schlaf** m zo. hibernation: **~ halten** hibernate. **~schlußverkauf** m winter sales. **~sonnenwende** f winter solstice. **~spiele** pl Olympische ~ Winter Olympics. **~sport** m winter sport(s). **~sportler(in** f) m person doing winter sports.

Winzer ['vɪntsər] m (-s; -) wine grower.

winzig ['vɪntsɪç] adj tiny, minute.

Winzling ['vɪntslɪŋ] m (-s; -e) F mite.

Wipfel ['vɪpfəl] m (-s; -) (tree) top.

Wippe ['vɪpə] f (-; -n) seesaw, Am. teeter-totter. **'wippen** v/i (h) seesaw, rock, skirt etc: bob.

wir [vi:r] pers pron we: **~ beide (alle)** both (all) of us; **~ drei** we three, the three of us.

Wirbel ['vɪrbəl] m (-s; -) **1.** whirl, eddy, vortex, turbulence. **2.** fig. a) turmoil, whirl, b) F fuss, to-do (um about): **e-n ziemlichen ~ verursachen** cause quite a stir. **3.** anat. vertebra. **4.** cowlick. **5.** (drum) roll. **6.** peg (of violin).

'Wirbelknochen m → Wirbel 3.

'wirbellos adj zo. invertebrate.

wirbeln ['vɪrbəln] v/i (sn) whirl, swirl.

'Wirbelsäule f spine, spinal column.

'Wirbelsturm m cyclone, tornado.

'Wirbeltier n vertebrate.

wirken ['vɪrkən] (h) **I** v/i **1.** take (or have) effect, be effective, work, act: **~ auf** (acc) have a depressing etc effect on, affect, 🎭, ⚙ act on; **~ gegen** be effective against; **stark ~d** potent, strong; **langsam ~d** slow-acting; **et. auf sich ~ lassen** take s.th. in; F **das wirkt immer!** it never fails (to work); **das hat gewirkt!** a) that did the trick, b) that hit

home. **2.** work (**an** dat at). **3.** seem, look: **jünger ~** look younger; **er wirkt schüchtern** he seems shy; **überzeugend ~** be convincing. **II** v/t **4. ~ be-wirken, hinwirken, Wunder. 5.** ⚙ knit.

'Wirken n (-s) **1.** activity, work. **2.** 🎭, ⚙ action. **Wirker** m (-s; -) ⚙ knitter.

'wirklich I adj real, actual, true. **II** adv really, actually: **~?** really?, is that so?

'Wirklichkeit f (-; no pl) (**die rauhe ~** harsh) reality; **in ~** in reality, actually; **~ werden** come true.

'wirklichkeits|fremd adj unrealistic, starry-eyed. **~getreu** adj realistic, faithful (copy etc).

'wirksam adj effective: **sehr ~a.** powerful, drastic; **~ gegen** good for; **~ wer-den** take effect, 🏛 come into force.

'Wirksamkeit f (-; no pl) effectiveness.

'Wirkstoff m (-[e]s; -e) active substance.

'Wirkung f (-; -en) **1.** (**auf** acc on) a) effect, operation, b) impact: **mit ~ vom** with effect from, as from, as of; **mit sofortiger ~** as of now; **~ erzielen** have an effect, a. **s-e ~ tun** work; **s-e ~ ver-fehlen** prove ineffective, have no effect; **Ursache und ~** cause and effect. **2.** phys. action. **3.** fig. appeal (**auf** acc to).

'Wirkungs|bereich m sphere of activity. **~grad** m ⚙ efficiency. **~kraft** f (-; no pl) efficacy. **~kreis** m sphere of activity.

'wirkungslos adj ineffective: **~ bleiben** have no effect. **Wirkungslosigkeit** f (-; no pl) ineffectiveness.

'wirkungsvoll adj effective.

'Wirkungsweise f (mode of) operation, function, 🎭 action, effect.

wirr [vɪr] adj **1.** dishevel(l)ed (hair), tangled (growth). **2.** fig. confused, muddleheaded (person), wild (rumo[u]r etc), incoherent (speech): **~es Zeug reden** talk wild; **mir ist ganz ~ im Kopf** my head is spinning. **'Wirren** pl turmoil, confusion. **'Wirrkopf** m muddlehead.

Wirrwarr ['vɪrvar] m (-s; no pl) muddle, chaos, F jumble.

Wirsing ['vɪrzɪŋ] m (-s; no pl), **~kohl** m (-[e]s; no pl) 🌿 savoy.

Wirt [vɪrt] m (-[e]s; -e) a) a. biol. host , b) landlord. **'Wirtin** f (-; -nen) a) hostess, b) landlady.

'Wirtschaft f (-; -en) **1.** 🎭, pol. a) economy, b) trade and industry. **2.** no pl a) management, b) housekeeping: **j-m die**

~führen keep house for s.o. **3.** *no pl* F *contp.* mess. **4.** → *Wirtshaus.*

'**wirtschaften** *v/i* (h) **1.** manage (one's affairs): *sparsam* ~ economize, be economical (*mit* with); *schlecht* ~ mismanage. **2.** be busy.

'**Wirtschafterin** *f* (-; -nen) housekeeper.

'**wirtschaftlich** *adj* **1.** a) economic, b) financial, c) business ... **2.** economical, efficient: *ein* ~*es Auto* an economical car. **3.** profitable. '**Wirtschaftlichkeit** *f* (-; no *pl*) **1.** profitability, economic efficiency. **2.** economy.

'**Wirtschafts|abkommen** *n* economic (*or* trade) agreement. **~berater** *m* economic adviser. **~beziehungen** *pl* economic (*or* trade) relations. **~führer** *m* leading industrialist. **~geld** *n* (-[e]s; no *pl*) housekeeping money. **~gemeinschaft** *f Europäische* ~ European Economic Community (*abbr. EEC*). **~gipfel** *m* economic summit. **~güter** *pl* economic goods. **~hilfe** *f* economic aid. **~jahr** *n* financial year. **~kriminali̱tät** *f* white-collar crime. **~krise** *f* economic crisis. **~macht** *f* economic power. **~mi̱nister** *m* minister for economic affairs. **~mini̱sterium** *n* economics ministry. **~poli̱tik** *f* economic policy. ₂**poli̱tisch** *adj* (politico-)economic. **~prüfer** *m* chartered (*Am.* certified public) accountant. **~re̱form** *f* economic reform. **~spio̱nage** *f* industrial espionage. **~sy̱stem** *n* economic system. **~teil** *m* business section. **~uni̱on** *f* economic union. **~verband** *m* trade association. **~wachstum** *n* economic growth. **~wissenschaft** *f* economics. **~wissenschaftler** *m* economist. **~wunder** *n* economic miracle. **~zweig** *m* branch of industry.

'**Wirtshaus** *n* inn, public house, F pub, *Am.* saloon.

'**Wirtsleute** *pl* landlord and landlady. '**Wirtstier** *n biol.* host.

Wisch [vɪʃ] *m* (-es; -e) scrap of paper.

wischen ['vɪʃən] *v/t* (h) a) wipe (*sich den Mund* one's mouth), b) mop (up).

'**Wischer** *m* (-s; -) *mot.* wiper.

'**Wischlappen** *m*, '**Wischtuch** *n* cloth.

Wisent ['vi:zɛnt] *m* (-s; -e) *zo.* bison.

wispern ['vɪspərn] *v/t, v/i* (h) whisper.

'**Wißbegier(de)** *f* **1.** thirst for knowledge. **2.** curiosity. '**wißbegierig** *adj* **1.**

eager for knowledge. **2.** curious.

wissen ['vɪsən] *v/t, v/i* (wußte, gewußt, h) know (*von* about): *man kann nie* ~ you never know; *weder ein noch aus* ~ be at one's wits' end; *ich weiß nicht recht* I'm not so sure; *nicht, daß ich wüßte* not that I know of; *woher weißt du das?* how do you know (that)?; *was weiß ich!* how should I know?; *weißt du noch?* (do you) remember?; *ich weiß nicht mehr* I don't remember; *ich will davon nichts* ~ I don't want anything to do with it; *sie will von ihm nichts mehr* ~ she is through with him; → *Bescheid.*

'**Wissen** *n* (-s) knowledge, learning, F know-how: *ohne mein* ~ without my knowing; *m-s* ~*s* as far as I know; *nach bestem* ~ *und Gewissen* to the best of one's knowledge and belief; *wider besseres* ~ against one's better judgement.

'**wissend** *adj* knowing (*look etc*).

'**Wissenschaft** *f* (-; -en) science.

'**Wissenschaftler** *m* (-s; -) scientist.

'**wissenschaftlich** *adj* **1.** scientific. **2.** academic (*career, work, etc*).

'**Wissens|durst** *m* thirst for knowledge. **~gebiet** *n* province, field of knowledge. **~lücke** *f* gap in one's knowledge. **~stand** *m* level of knowledge: *auf dem neuesten* ~ *sein* be up to date.

'**wissenswert** *adj* worth knowing: *Wissenswertes* interesting facts.

'**wissentlich I** *adj* conscious, deliberate. **II** *adv* knowingly.

wittern ['vɪtərn] *v/t* (h) scent, smell, *fig.* sense (*danger*), see (*chance*).

'**Witterung**[1] *f* (-; -en) *hunt.* scent.

'**Witterung**[2] *f* (-; -en) weather: *bei jeder* ~ in all weathers. '**witterungsbeständig** *adj* weatherproof. '**Witterungseinflüsse** *pl* influence of the weather.

Witwe ['vɪtvə] *f* (-; -n) widow.

'**Witwenrente** *f* widow's pension.

'**Witwer** ['vɪtvər] *m* (-s; -) widower.

Witz [vɪts] *m* (-es; -e) **1.** joke, quip: ~*e machen* (*or* reißen) crack jokes; F *das ist der* ~ *an der Sache* a) that's the funny thing about it, b) that's the whole point; F *mach k-e* ~*e!* you're joking. **2.** *no pl* wit. '**Witzbold** [-bɔlt] *m* (-[e]s; -e) F joker. **Witze'lei** *f* (-; -en) silly jokes. **witzeln** ['vɪtsəln] *v/i* (h) joke (*über acc* about), quip. '**witzig** *adj* witty, funny: *a. iro.* **sehr ~!** very funny!, big joke! **'witzlos** *adj* **1.** unfunny. **2.** F pointless, (of) no use.

wo [vo:] **I** *interrog and rel adv* where. **II** *conj* **wo ... (doch)** when, F although. **III** F *indef adv* somewhere. **IV** F *int* **i wo, ach wo!** nonsense!, nothing of the kind! **wo'anders** *adv* somewhere else, anywhere else. **wo'bei I** *interrog adv* **~ bist du gerade?** what are you doing right now? **II** *rel adv* in doing so: **~ mir einfällt** which reminds me.

Woche ['vɔxə] f (-; -n) week: **in e-r ~** in a week('s time); **zweimal die ~** twice a week; **auf ~n hinaus** sold out *etc* for weeks (to come); **~ um ~** week after week; F **unter der ~** during the week.

'Wochenbett *n* (-[e]s; *no pl*) childbed.

'Wochenend... weekend (*edition etc*).

'Wochenende *n* (**am ~** at the) weekend.

'Wochenkarte *f* weekly season ticket.

'wochenlang I *adj* lasting several weeks: **nach ~em Warten** after weeks of waiting. **II** *adv* for weeks.

'Wochenlohn *m* weekly wages.

'Wochenschau *f* newsreel.

'Wochentag *m* weekday.

'wochentags *adv* on weekdays.

wöchentlich ['vœçəntlɪç] *adj* weekly: **einmal ~** once a week.

'Wochenzeitung *f* weekly (paper).

Wöchnerin ['vœçnərɪn] f (-; -nen) woman in childbed.

Wodka ['vɔtka] *m* (-s; -s) vodka.

wo'durch I *interrog adv* how. **II** *rel adv* by which, through which, whereby.

wo'für I *interrog adv* what for. **II** *rel adv* for which, which ... for.

wog [vo:k] *pret of* **wiegen²**.

Woge ['vo:gə] f (-; -n) wave, surge: **die ~n glätten** pour oil on troubled waters.

wo'gegen I *interrog adv* against what, what ... against. **II** *rel adv* against which, which ... against. **III** *conj* → **wohingegen.**

wo'her I *interrog and rel adv* where (...) from: → **wissen. II** *int* F **~ denn!** nonsense!

wo'hin *interrog and rel adv* where (... to).

wohin'gegen *conj* whereas.

wohl [vo:l] *adv* **1.** well: **sich ~ fühlen** a) feel fine, feel good, be happy, b) **bei j-m** feel at home with s.o.; **ich fühle mich nicht ~** I don't feel well; F *fig.* **mir ist**

nicht **~ dabei** I don't feel happy about it; **~ oder übel** willy-nilly, whether you *etc* like it or not; → **bekommen** II. **2. sehr ~** very well; **ich bin mir dessen sehr ~ bewußt** I am well aware of that; **das kann man ~ sagen!** you can say that again. **3.** probably, I suppose: **das ist ~ möglich** that's quite possible; **ob er es ~ weiß?** I wonder if he knows (that); **~ kaum** hardly. **4. ~ 100 Leute** *etc* about 100 people *etc*. **Wohl** *n* (-[e]s; *no pl*) welfare, good, well-being: **auf j-s ~ trinken** drink to s.o.'s health; **zum ~!** to your health!, F cheers!

wohl'auf *adj* **~ sein** be well, be in good health.

'Wohlbefinden *n* (-s; *no pl*) well-being.

'wohl|behalten *adj* safe (and sound), *object*: safe, undamaged. **~bekannt** well-known, *b.s.* notorious.

'Wohlergehen *n* (-s; *no pl*) well-being.

'wohlerzogen *adj* well-behaved.

'Wohlfahrt *f* (-; *no pl*) welfare.

'Wohlfahrts|marke *f* charity stamp. **~organisati,on** *f* charitable institution. **~staat** *m* welfare state.

'wohlgeformt *adj* well-shaped, shapely.

'Wohlgefühl *n* (-[e]s; *no pl*) sense of well-being.

'wohlgemeint *adj* well-meant.

'wohlgemerkt *int* mind you!

'wohlgenährt *adj* well-fed.

'wohlgesinnt *adj* well-meaning: **j-m ~ sein** be well disposed towards s.o.

'wohlhabend *adj* well-to-do, prosperous, affluent: **~ sein** be well off.

'wohlig *adj* pleasant, cosy.

'Wohlklang *m* (-[e]s; *no pl*) melodiousness. **'wohlklingend** *adj* melodious.

'wohlmeinend *adj* well-meaning.

'wohlriechend *adj* fragrant.

'wohlschmeckend *adj* tasty.

'Wohlsein: zum ~! F cheers!

'Wohlstand *m* (-[e]s; *no pl*) prosperity, affluence. **'Wohlstandsgesellschaft** *f* affluent society.

'Wohltat *f* (-; -en) **1.** good deed. **2.** *no pl* a) relief, b) blessing. **'Wohltäter(in** *f*) *m* benefactor (benefactress). **'wohltätig** *adj* charitable. **'Wohltätigkeit** *f* (-; *no pl*) charity. **'Wohltätigkeits...** charity (*or* benefit) (*ball, concert, match, etc*).

'wohltuend *adj* **1.** pleasant. **2.** soothing.

'wohltun *v/i* (*irr, sep*, -ge-, h, → **tun**) **j-m**

Wollsachen

~ do s.o. good; *das tut wohl* that does you good.

'**wohlüberlegt** *adj* well-considered.

'**wohlverdient** *adj* well-deserved.

'**Wohlverhalten** *n* good behavio(u)r.

'**wohlweislich** [-vaislıç] *adv* wisely, for good reason: ~ *tun* be careful to do *s.th.*

'**Wohlwollen** *n* (-s; *no pl*) goodwill, favo(u)r. '**wohlwollend** *adj* benevolent, kind: *e-r Sache* ~ *gegenüberstehen* take a favo(u)rable view of s.th.

'**Wohn|anlage** *f* housing area. ~*bezirk* *m* residential district. ~*block* *m* block of flats. ~*einheit* *f* housing unit.

wohnen ['vo:nən] *v/i* (h) (*in dat* in, at, *bei* with) a) live, reside, b) stay.

'**Wohn|fläche** *f* living space. ~*gebäude* *n* residential building. ~*geld* *n* housing subsidy. ~*gemeinschaft* *f* flat-sharing community: *in e-r* ~ *leben* share a flat with s.o. (*or* several other people).

'**wohnhaft** *adj* resident (*in dat* in, at).

'**Wohn|haus** *n* residential building. ~*heim* *n* hostel, *Am.* rooming house. ~*küche* *f* kitchen-cum-living-room.

'**wohnlich** *adj* comfortable, cosy.

'**Wohnmo,bil** *n* (-s; -e) camper.

'**Wohn|ort** *m* (place of) residence. ~*raum* *m* 1. housing, accommodation. 2. → *Wohnfläche*. 3. → *Wohnzimmer*.

'**Wohn-'Schlafzimmer** *n* bedsit(ter).

'**Wohnsiedlung** *f* housing estate.

'**Wohnsitz** *m* (place of) residence.

'**Wohnung** *f* (-; -en) flat, *Am.* apartment.

'**Wohnungsamt** *n* housing office.

'**Wohnungsbau** *m* (-[e]s; *no pl*) house building. ~*mi,nister* *m* housing minister. ~*pro,gramm* *n* housing scheme.

'**Wohnungsinhaber(in** *f*) *m* tenant.

'**wohnungslos** *adj* homeless.

'**Wohnungs|markt** *m* housing market. ~*not* *f* (-; *no pl*) housing shortage. ~*schlüssel* *m* key (to the flat). ~*suche* *f* F flat-hunting. ~*suchende* *m, f* (-n; -n) F flat-hunter. ~*tür* *f* front door. ~*wechsel* *m* change of residence.

'**Wohn|verhältnisse** *pl* housing conditions. ~*viertel* *n* residential area. ~*wagen* *m* caravan, *Am.* trailer. ~*zimmer* *n* sitting (*or* living) room.

wölben ['vœlbən] *v/t* (*a. sich* ~) (h) arch: → *gewölbt*.

'**Wölbung** *f* (-; -en) 1. arch. 2. vault.

Wolf [volf] *m* (-[e]s; ⸚e) 1. *zo.* wolf: *fig. mit*

den Wölfen heulen howl with the wolves; → *Schafpelz*. 2. mincer. 3. ✻ intertrigo: *sich e-n* ~ *laufen* get sore.

Wölfin ['vœlfin] *f* (-; -nen) *zo.* she-wolf.

Wolfram ['vɔlfram] *n* (-s; *no pl*) tungsten.

'**Wolfsmilch** *f* ✿ spurge.

'**Wolfsrachen** *m* ✻ cleft palate.

Wolke ['vɔlkə] *f* (-; -n) cloud: *fig. aus allen* ~*n fallen* be thunderstruck; *in den* ~*n schweben* have one's head in the clouds.

'**Wolken|bruch** *m* cloudburst. ~*decke* *f* cloud cover. ~*kratzer* *m* skyscraper.

'**wolkenlos** *adj* cloudless, clear.

'**Wolkenwand** *f* bank of clouds.

'**wolkig** *adj* cloudy (*a.* ✻, *phot. etc*), clouded.

'**Wolldecke** *f* wool(l)en blanket.

Wolle ['vɔlə] *f* (-; -n) wool: F *sich in die* ~ *kriegen* quarrel, (have a) fight (*mit* with).

'**wollen¹** *adj* wool(l)en.

'**wollen²** *v/t, v/i* (wollte, gewollt, h) a) want, *a.* demand, b) be willing (*or* prepared) to, c) want to: *lieber* ~ prefer; *ich will lieber* I'd rather; *et. unbedingt* ~ insist on s.th.; *ich will nicht* I don't want to; *sie will, daß ich komme* she wants me to come; *was* ~ *Sie von mir?* what do you want?; *was willst du mit e-m Regenschirm?* what do you want an umbrella for?; *Verzeihung, das wollte ich nicht!* sorry, that was unintentional; *ob er will oder nicht* whether he likes it or not; *du weißt nicht, was du willst!* you don't know your own mind!; *mach, was du willst!* do what you like!; *du hast es ja so gewollt!* you asked for it!; *was (wann) du willst* whatever (whenever) you like; *wie du willst* as you like, suit yourself; *ich wollte, ich wäre (hätte)* ... I wish I were (had) ...; F *hier ist nichts zu* ~ nothing doing; → *heißen* I *etc*. II *v/t* (*pp* wollen) → *et. haben* ~ want (to have) s.th.; *et. tun* ~ want (*or* be going) to do s.th.; *er will es nicht* he refuses to do it; *was* ~ *Sie damit sagen?* what do you mean (by that)?; *er will dich gesehen haben* he says he saw you; → *heißen¹* I *etc*.

'**wollig** *adj* wool(l)y.

'**Woll|jacke** *f* cardigan. ~*knäuel* *m, n* ball of wool. ~*sachen* *pl* wool(l)ens.

~socken *pl* wool(l)en socks. **~stoff** *m* wool(l)en fabric, (broad)cloth.

wollte ['vɔltə] *pret of* **wollen²**.

Wollust ['vɔlʊst] *f* (-; *no pl*) voluptuousness, sensuality. **wollüstig** ['vɔlʏstɪç] *adj* voluptuous, sensual.

'Wollwaren *pl* wool(l)ens.

wo'mit I *interrog adv* what (...) with: **~ kann ich dienen?** what can I do for you?; **~ hab' ich das verdient?** what did I do to deserve that? II *rel adv* with which: **~ ich nicht sagen will** by which I don't mean to say.

wo'möglich *adv* if possible, possibly.

wo'nach I *interrog adv* after what: **~ fragt er?** what is he asking about? II *rel adv* what, after (*or* according to) which.

Wonne ['vɔnə] *f* (-; -n) delight, bliss: **e-e wahre ~** a real treat; F **mit ~** with relish. **'wonnig** *adj* lovely, sweet.

wor'an I *interrog adv* ~ **denken Sie?** what are you thinking about?; **~ arbeitet er?** what is he working on (*or* at)?; **~ liegt es, daß?** how is it that?; **~ hast du ihn erkannt?** how did you recognize him?; **~ sieht man, welche (ob)?** how can you tell which (if)? II *rel adv* **ich weiß nicht, ~ ich bin** I don't know where I stand, **mit ihm** I don't know what to make of him; **~ ich dich erinnern möchte** what I want to remind you of; **~ man merkte, daß** which showed that.

wor'auf I *interrog adv* what: **~ wartest du noch?** what are you (still) waiting for? II *rel adv* **et., ~ ich bestehe** s.th. (which *or* that) I insist (up)on; **~ er sagte** upon which he said; **~ alle gingen** whereupon everybody left.

wor'aus I *interrog adv* **~ ist es (gemacht)?** what is it made of?; **~ schließt du das?** what makes you think that? II *rel adv* **~ zu entnehmen war, daß** from which we understood that.

wor'in I *interrog adv* **~ liegt der Unterschied?** what (*or* where) is the difference? II *rel adv* in which.

Wort [vɔrt] *n* (-[e]s; -e, ⸚er) **1.** (*pl* ⸚er) word. **2.** (*pl* -e) word, *eccl.* Word, saying: **geflügelte ~e** familiar quotations; **in ~en** with sums: in letters; **~ für ~** word for word; **ein ernstes ~ mit j-m reden** have a good talk with s.o.; **ein gutes ~ einlegen** put in a good word;

das ~ ergreifen (begin to) speak, *parl. a.* take the floor; **mir fehlen die ~e** words fail me; **das ~ führen** do the talking; **das große ~ führen** a) do all the talking, b) talk big; **das ~ hat Herr X** the word is with Mr. X; **das letzte ~** the last word (*in dat* on); **das letzte ~ haben** have the final say; **du willst** (*or* **mußt**) **immer das letzte ~ haben** you always have to have the last word; **kein ~ darüber!** not a word of it!; **kein ~ mehr!** not another word!; F **hast du ~e?** would you believe it?; **ein ~ gab das andere** one thing led to another; → **abschneiden** 1, **entziehen** 1. **3.** *no pl* word (of hono[u]r): **sein ~ geben** (**brechen, halten**) give (break, keep) one's word; → **Mann.** **4.** **aufs ~ gehorchen** (**glauben**) obey (believe) implicitly; **j-n beim ~ nehmen** take s.o. at his word; **j-m ins ~ fallen** cut s.o. short; **in ~e fassen** put into words; **mit anderen ~en** in other words; **mit 'einem ~ in** a word; **zu ~e kommen** have one's say; **nicht zu ~e kommen** not to get a word in edgeways.

'Wortart *f ling.* part of speech.

'Wortbildung *f* word formation.

'wortbrüchig *adj* **~ werden** break one's word.

Wörterbuch ['vœrtər-] *n* dictionary.

'Wörterverzeichnis *n* list of words, vocabulary.

'Wort|führer *m* spokesman. **~gefecht** *n* battle of words, argument.

'wortgetreu *adj* literal, word-for-word.

'wortgewandt *adj* eloquent.

'wortkarg *adj* taciturn.

Wortklauberei [-klaʊbə'raɪ] *f* (-; *no pl*) hairsplitting.

'Wortlaut *m* (-[e]s; *no pl*) wording, text: **der Brief hat folgenden ~** the letter runs as follows.

wörtlich ['vœrtlɪç] *adj* literal, word-to--word: **~e Rede** direct speech.

'wortlos *adj* wordless.

'Wortmeldung *f* request to speak.

'wortreich *adj* verbose, wordy.

'Wortschatz *m* (-es; *no pl*) vocabulary.

'Wortschöpfung *f* coinage, neologism.

'Wortschwall *m* torrent of words.

'Wortspiel *n* play on words, pun.

'Wortstellung *f* word order.

'Wortwechsel *m* argument, dispute.

'**wort**'**wörtlich** → **wörtlich**.

wor'**über I** *interrog adv* ~ **lachst du?**
what are you laughing about (*or* at)? **II**
rel adv **et.,** ~ **ich sehr verärgert war**
s.th. I was very angry about (*or* at); ~ **er**
ärgerlich war which annoyed him.

wor'**um I** *interrog adv* ~ **handelt es**
sich? what is it about? **II** *rel adv* **et.,** ~
ich dich bitten möchte s.th (which *or*
that) I want to ask you.

wor'**unter I** *interrog adv* what ... under.
II *rel adv* **et.,** ~ **ich mir nichts vorstel-**
len kann s.th. which doesn't mean anything to me; ~ **ich leide** what I suffer
from (*or* under).

wo'**von** *interrog adv* ~ **leben sie?** what
do they live on?; ~ **sprecht ihr?** what
are you talking about? **II** *rel adv* **et.,** ~
ich nur zu träumen wage s.th. I can
only dream about (*or* of).

wo'**vor** *interrog adv* ~ **hast du Angst?**
what are you afraid of? **II** *rel adv* ~ **du**
dich hüten mußt, ist what you must be
careful of is.

wo'**zu I** *interrog adv* **1.** ~ **hat er sich**
entschlossen? what did he decide
upon? **2.** why. **II** *rel adv* ~ **er bereit ist**
what (*or* which) he is prepared to do.

Wrack [vrak] *n* (-[e]s; -s) *a.* *fig.* wreck.

wringen ['vrɪŋən] *v/t* (wrang, gewrungen, h) wring.

Wucher ['vu:xər] *m* (-s; *no pl*) usury.

'**Wucherer** *m* (-s; -) usurer.

'**Wuchermiete** *f* rack rent.

wuchern ['vu:xərn] *v/i* (h) **1.** ✿ grow
rampant, *a.* 🌿 proliferate, *fig.* *a.* be
rampant. **2.** practi/se (*Am.* -ce) usury.

'**Wucherpreis** *m* exorbitant price.

'**Wucherung** *f* (-; -en) 🗡 a) excrescence,
tumo(u)r, b) (tissue) proliferation.

'**Wucherzinsen** *pl* usurious interest.

wuchs [vu:ks] *pret of* **wachsen**¹.

Wuchs *m* (-es; *no pl*) **1.** growth. **2.** build,
physique: **klein von** ~ of small build.

Wucht [vʊxt] *f* (-; *no pl*) force, *a.* impact:
mit voller ~ with full force; F **das ist 'ne**
~**!** it's terrific! '**wuchten** *v/t* (h) **1.**
heave. **2.** **Räder** ~ balance wheels.

'**wuchtig** *adj* heavy (*a.* blow), powerful.

'**Wühlarbeit** *f fig.* subversive activity.

wühlen ['vy:lən] (h) **I** *v/i* **1.** dig, *animal:*
burrow, *pig:* root, grub: ~ **in** (*dat*) rummage in. **2.** *pol.* agitate. **II sich** ~ **in**
(*acc*) burrow (o.s.) into.

'**Wühler** *m* (-s; -) *pol.* agitator.

'**Wühlmaus** *f* zo. vole.

'**Wühltisch** *m* 🛒 rummage counter.

Wulst [vʊlst] *m* (-es; ⸚e) **1.** roll. **2.** pad. **3.**
bulge. **4.** (*tyre*) bead.

'**wulstig** *adj* bulging, thick (*lips*).

wund [vʊnt] *adj* sore, raw: ~ **reiben**
chafe; ~**e Stelle** sore; *fig.* ~**er Punkt**
sore point; **sich die Füße** ~ **laufen** get
sore feet, *fig.* run from pillar to post.

'**Wundbrand** *m* (-es; *no pl*) 🗡 gangrene.

Wunde ['vʊndə] *f* (-; -n) wound, cut,
gash: *fig.* **alte** ~**n wieder aufreißen**
open old sores; **die Zeit heilt alle** ~**n**
time is a great healer.

Wunder ['vʊndər] *n* (-s; -) miracle, wonder: ~ **der Technik** engineering marvel;
(es ist) kein ~**(, daß)** no wonder (that);
~ **tun,** ~ **wirken** perform miracles, *fig.*
work wonders; **es grenzt an ein** ~ it
borders on the miraculous; **F er wird**
sein blaues ~ **erleben** he's in for a
shock; **wie durch ein** ~ miraculously;
wunder wie goodness knows how; **er**
glaubt wunder was er getan hat he
thinks he's done goodness knows
what; → **Zeichen** 2.

'**wunderbar** *adj* **1.** miraculous. **2.** wonderful, marvel(l)ous.

'**wunderbarer**'**weise** *adv* miraculously.

'**Wunderding** *n* wonder.

'**Wunderdoktor** *m* iro. miracle doctor.

'**Wunderglaube** *m* belief in miracles.

'**wunder**'**hübsch** *adj* lovely.

'**Wunderkerze** *f* sparkler.

'**Wunderkind** *n* child prodigy.

'**wunderlich** *adj* strange, peculiar.

'**Wundermittel** *n* wonder drug.

wundern ['vʊndərn] (h) **I** *v/t* surprise: **es**
wundert mich I'm surprised. **II sich** ~
(*über acc* at) be surprised, wonder; **du**
wirst dich ~**!** you'll be surprised!

'**wunder**'**schön** *adj* very beautiful.

'**Wundertäter(in** *f*) *m* miracle worker.

'**wundervoll** → **wunderbar** 2.

'**Wunderwerk** *n fig.* wonder, marvel.

'**Wundfieber** *n* wound fever.

'**wundliegen: sich** ~ (*irr*, *sep*, -ge-, h, →
liegen) get bedsores.

'**Wundmal** *n eccl.* stigma.

'**Wundschmerz** *m* traumatic pain.

'**Wundstarrkrampf** *m* 🗡 tetanus.

Wunsch [vʊnʃ] *m* (-[e]s; ⸚e) **1.** wish, desire, request: **auf j-s** ~ (**hin**) at s.o.'s

request; *auf eigenen* ~ at one's own request; *auf allgemeinen* ~ by popular request; *(je) nach* ~ as desired; *es ging alles nach* ~ everything went as planned; *haben Sie noch e-n* ~? is there anything else I can do for you?; → *ablesen*[2] 3, *fromm* 1. 2. *mit den besten Wünschen* with best wishes.

'**Wunschbild** *n* ideal.

'**Wunschdenken** *n* wishful thinking.

'**Wünschelrute** ['vynʃəl-] *f* divining rod.

'**Wünschelrutengänger** [-gɛnər] *m* (-s; -) diviner.

wünschen ['vynʃən] (h) I *v/t* wish, want: *sich et.* ~ wish (*or* long) for s.th.; *was ~ Sie?* what can I do for you?; *du darfst dir et.* ~ you can make a wish; *ich wünsche mir* I'd like to have; → *gewünscht.* II *v/i Sie ~?* what can I do for you?; *wie Sie* ~ as you wish (*or* like), *iro.* suit yourself; *viel zu ~ übriglassen* leave much to be desired.

'**wünschenswert** *adj* desirable.

'**wunschgemäß** *adv* as requested.

'**Wunsch|kind** *n* planned child. **~konzert** *n* request program(me *Br.*).

'**wunschlos** *adv* ~ *glücklich* perfectly happy.

'**Wunschtraum** *m* (*iro.* pipe) dream.

'**Wunschzettel** *m* list of presents.

wurde ['vʊrdə] *pret of* **werden.**

Würde ['vʏrdə] *f* (-; -n) dignity, *a.* hono(u)r, *a.* rank, *a.* title: *akademische* ~ academic degree; *unter aller* ~ beneath contempt; *unter m-r* ~ beneath my dignity. '**würdelos** *adj* undignified.

'**Würdenträger** *m* (-s; -) dignitary.

'**würdevoll I** *adj* dignified. II *adv* with dignity.

'**würdig** *adj* 1. dignified. 2. (*gen* of) worthy, deserving: *ein ~er Nachfolger* a worthy successor; *er ist dessen nicht* ~ he doesn't deserve it.

würdigen ['vʏrdɪgən] *v/t* (h) 1. appreciate, acknowledge, recognize. 2. *j-n k-s Blickes* ~ not to deign to look at s.o.

'**Würdigung** *f* (-; -en) appreciation, acknowledgement: *in* ~ *s-r Verdienste* in recognition of his merits.

Wurf [vʊrf] *m* (-[e]s; ⁻e) 1. throw: *fig. glücklicher* ~ lucky strike; *großer* ~ great success. 2. *zo.* litter.

'**Wurfdiszi,plin** *f sports*: throwing event.

Würfel ['vʏrfəl] *m* (-s; -) 1. cube. 2. dice:

die ~ *sind gefallen* the die is cast.

'**Würfelbecher** *m* (dice) shaker.

'**würfelförmig** *adj* cubic, cube-shaped.

würfeln ['vʏrfəln] (h) I *v/i* 1. play dice: *um et.* ~ throw dice for s.th. II *v/t* 2. throw. 3. *gastr.* dice.

'**Würfelspiel** *n* game of dice.

'**Würfelzucker** *m* lump (*or* cube) sugar.

'**Wurf|geschoß** *n* projectile. **~kreis** *m* *sports*: (throwing) circle. **~pfeil** *m* dart. **~sendung(en** *pl*) *f* unaddressed advertising matter, *contp.* junk mail. **~spieß** *m* javelin. **~taube** *f sports*: clay pigeon.

'**Würgegriff** *m a. fig.* stranglehold.

würgen ['vʏrgən] (h) I *v/t* strangle, throttle, choke. II *v/i a)* choke, b) retch: ~ *an* (*dat*) choke on.

Wurm[1] [vʊrm] *m* (-[e]s; ⁻er) *zo.* worm (*a. fig.*), *a.* maggot: 🐛 *Würmer haben* suffer from worms; F *j-m die Würmer aus der Nase ziehen* drag it out of s.o.; *da ist der* ~ *drin* s.th. is wrong (with it).

Wurm[2] *n* (-[e]s; ⁻er), **Würmchen** ['vʏrmçən] *n* (-s; -) F (little) mite.

wurmen ['vʊrmən] *v/t* (h) *j-n* ~ gall (*or* get) s.o., rankle with s.o.

'**Wurm|fortsatz** *m anat.* (vermiform) appendix. **~kur** *f* 🐛 deworming. **~mittel** *n* 🐛 vermifuge.

'**wurmstichig** *adj* wormy, worm-eaten.

Wurst [vʊrst] *f* (-; ⁻e) sausage: F *es ist mir (völlig)* ~! I don't care (a damn)!; *jetzt geht's um die* ~ now or never.

Würstchen ['vʏrstçən] *n* (-s; -) 1. small sausage: *Frankfurter* ~ frankfurter; *Wiener* ~ wiener(wurst). 2. F nobody: *armes* ~ poor soul. **~bude** *f*, **~stand** *m* hot-dog stand.

wursteln ['vʊrstəln] *v/i* (h) F muddle along.

'**Wursthaut** *f* sausage skin.

'**Wurstigkeit** *f* (-; *no pl*) F couldn't-care-less attitude.

'**Wurstwaren** *pl* sausages.

Würze ['vʏrtsə] *f* (-; -n) 1. spice (*a. fig.*), seasoning, flavo(u)r. 2. wort.

Wurzel ['vʊrtsəl] *f* (-; -n) 1. root (*a. fig.*), 🄰 *a.* radical: 🄰 *zweite (dritte)* ~ square (cubic) root; *die* ~ *(aus)* e-r *Zahl ziehen* extract the (square) root of a number; *a. fig.* ~*n schlagen* take root. 2. *dial.* carrot. **~behandlung** *f* 🦷 root treatment. **~gemüse** *n* root vegetables. **~größe** *f* 🄰 radical quantity.

'wurzellos *adj a. fig.* rootless.
wurzeln ['vʊrtsəln] *v/i* (h) take root: *fig.*
~ in (*dat*) be rooted in, have its roots in.
'Wurzelwerk *n* (-[e]s; *no pl*) roots.
'Wurzelzeichen *n* ♣ radical sign.
'Wurzelziehen *n* (-s) ♣ root extraction.
würzen ['vʏrtsən] *v/t* (h) *a. fig.* spice.
'würzig *adj* spicy, *fig.* fragrant (*air*).
'Würzkräuter *pl* (pot) herbs.
wusch [vu:ʃ] *pret of* **waschen.**
wuschelig ['vʊʃəlɪç] *adj* F fuzzy.
wußte ['vʊstə] *pret of* **wissen.**
Wust [vu:st] *m* (-[e]s; *no pl*) **1.** tangled
mass. **2.** trash. **3.** jumble.
wüst [vy:st] *adj* **1.** desert, waste. **2.** a)
wild, dissolute, b) rude, c) vile: **~ aussehen** look a real mess.
Wüste ['vy:stə] *f* (-; -n) desert, *fig. a.*
waste: F *fig.* *j-n in die ~ schicken* give
s.o. the boot.
'Wüsten... desert (*sand, wind, etc*).
'Wüstling *m* (-s; -e) libertine, rake.

Wut [vu:t] *f* (-; *no pl*) rage, fury: *e-e ~
bekommen* (F *kriegen*), *in ~ geraten*
get furious (F mad), fly into a rage; *j-n
in ~ bringen* enrage (*or* infuriate) s.o.;
vor ~ kochen (*or* **schäumen**) seethe
with rage, fume; *e-e ~ auf j-n haben* F
be mad at s.o.; *s-e ~ an j-m auslassen*
take it out on s.o.
'Wutanfall *m* fit (*or* outburst) of rage:
e-n ~ bekommen blow one's top.
wüten ['vy:tən] *v/i* (h) rage (*a. fig.* storm,
epidemic, *etc*): *~ gegen* rage at (*or*
against); *~ unter* create havoc among.
'wütend *adj* **1.** furious, F mad: *auf
j-n ~ sein* be furious with (F mad at)
s.o.; *über et. ~ sein* be furious at (F
mad about) s.th.; *j-n ~ machen* infuriate (*or* enrage) s.o. **2.** *fig.* raging (*pain
etc*).
'wutentbrannt *adj* furious, infuriated.
'wutschäumend *adj* foaming with rage.
'Wutschrei *m* yell of rage.

X

X, x [ɪks] *n* (-; -) X, x: F *j-m ein X für ein U
vormachen* fool s.o.; *ich habe x Leute
gefragt* I've asked umpteen people.
'X-Achse *f* ♣ x-axis.
Xanthippe [ksan'tɪpə] *f* (-; -n) F shrew,
battle-ax(e).
'X-Beine *pl* knock-knees.
x-beinig ['ɪksbaɪnɪç] *adj* knock-kneed.
x-be'liebig *adj* F any (... you like): *jeder
~e* anybody, any Tom, Dick and Har-
ry; *et. ᵒes* anything (you like).

'X-Chromo,som *n* X chromosome.
Xenon ['kse:nɔn] *n* (-s; *no pl*) ♣ xenon.
Xerographie [kserogra'fi:] *f* (-; *no pl*)
print. xerography.
'x-fach *adv* ever so often.
x-förmig ['ɪksfœrmɪç] *adj* x-shaped.
'x-mal *adv* F umpteen times.
x-te ['ɪkstə] *adj* F *zum ᵒn Mal* for the
umpteenth time.
Xylophon [ksylo'fo:n] *n* (-s; -e) ♪ xylo-
phone.

Y

Y, y ['ʏpsilɔn] *n* (-; -) Y, y.
'Y-Achse *f* ♣ y-axis.
'Y-Chromo,som *n* Y chromosome.

Yen [jɛn] *m* (-[s]; -[s]) ✝ yen.
Yoga ['jo:ga] *m, n* (-[s]; *no pl*) yoga.
Yogi ['jo:gi] *m* (-s; -s) yogi.

Z

Z, z [tsɛt] n (-; -) Z, z; → **A.**

Zack [tsak] F **auf ~ sein** (**bringen**) be on the ball (bring *s.o.*, *s.th.* up to scratch).

Zacke ['tsakə] f (-; -n) a) (sharp) point, jag, ☉ tooth, indentation, b) prong.

zacken ['tsakən] v/t (h) a) indent, jag, b) pink (*cloth*, *paper*), c) tooth.

'**Zacken** m (-s; -) dial. → **Zacke:** F **er bricht sich k-n ~ aus der Krone, wenn er ihr hilft** it won't kill him to help her.

'**Zackenschere** f pinking shears.

'**zackig** adj **1.** a) indented, jagged, b) toothed. **2.** F fig. snappy.

zaghaft ['tsa:khaft] adj timid, cautious.

zäh [tsɛː] adj **1.** tough (*meat*), viscous (*liquid*). **2.** fig. a) tough, tenacious, b) stubborn, c) slow, sluggish, slow-moving (*traffic*): **ein ~er Bursche** a tough fellow; **~ festhalten an** (*dat*) stick doggedly to. '**zähflüssig** adj **1.** viscous. **2.** fig. sluggish, slow-moving (*traffic*).

'**Zähigkeit** f (-; *no pl*) fig. toughness.

Zahl [tsaːl] f (-; -en) a) number (*a. ling.*), b) figure, c) numeral, cipher, d) digit: **genaue ~en** exact figures; **römische ~en** Roman numerals; **sechsstellige ~** six-digit number; fig. **in großer ~** in large numbers; **an ~ übertreffen** outnumber; → **rot.**

'**zahlbar** adj payable (**an** acc to, **bei** at, with): **~ nach Erhalt** payable (up)on receipt; → **Lieferung** 1.

'**zählbar** adj countable.

'**zählebig** [-le:bɪç] adj tough, tenacious.

'**Zählebigkeit** f (-; *no pl*) tenacity of life.

zahlen ['tsaːlən] v/t, v/i (h) pay: (**Herr Ober,**) **~, bitte!** the bill (*Am.* check), please!

zählen ['tsɛːlən] (h) **I** v/t count, *sports*: score: **s-e Tage sind gezählt** his days are numbered; **ich zähle ihn zu m-n Freunden** I count him as a friend. **II** v/i count (**bis zehn** up to ten): fig. **er (es) zählt nicht** he (it) doesn't count; **~ auf** (*acc*) count on; **~ zu** rank with, belong to (*the best etc*); **er zählt zu m-n Freunden** he is a friend (of mine); → **drei** I.

'**Zahlen|angaben** pl figures. **~folge** f order of numbers. **~gedächtnis** n memory for figures. **~lotto** n → **Lotto** 2.

'**zahlenmäßig** adj numerical: **j-m ~ überlegen sein** outnumber s.o.

'**Zahlenschloß** n combination lock.

Zahler ['tsaːlər] m (-s; -) payer.

Zähler ['tsɛːlər] m (-s; -) **1.** counter, ⚡ meter. **2.** Å numerator. **3.** *sports*: point.

'**Zählerablesung** f ⚡ meter reading.

'**Zählerstand** m ⚡ count.

'**Zahlgrenze** f fare stage.

'**Zahlkarte** f ✝ paying-in slip.

'**zahllos** adj countless, innumerable.

'**Zahlmeister** m **1.** ⚓ purser. **2.** ✕ paymaster.

'**zahlreich** adj a) numerous, many, b) large: **~ versammelt sein** be present in large numbers.

'**Zahltag** m payday.

'**Zahlung** f (-; -en) (**e-e ~ leisten** make a) payment: **et. in ~ geben** trade s.th. in; **et. in ~ nehmen** take s.th. in part exchange.

'**Zählung** f (-; -en) count, *a.* census.

'**Zahlungs|abkommen** n payments agreement. **~anweisung** f **1.** order to pay. **2.** money order. **~aufforderung** f request for payment. **~aufschub** m respite. **~auftrag** m of depositor: banker's order. **~bedingungen** pl terms of payment. **~bi,lanz** f balance of payments. **~einstellung** f suspension of payment. **~empfänger(in** f) m payee. **~erleichterungen** pl easy terms (for payment). **Σfähig** adj able to pay, solvent. **~fähigkeit** f (-; *no pl*) ability to pay, solvency. **~frist** f term of payment. **Σkräftig** adj F potent, wealthy. **~mittel** n a) means of payment, b) currency: **gesetzliches ~** legal tender. **Σpflichtig** adj liable to pay. **~schwierigkeiten** pl financial difficulties. **~ter,min** m date of payment. **Σunfähig** adj unable to pay, insolvent. **~unfähigkeit** f inability to pay, insolvency. **~verpflichtung** f liability to pay): **s-n ~en pünktlich nachkommen** be punctual in one's payments. **~verzug** m default (of payment): **in ~ geraten** default. **~weise** f mode of payment. **~ziel** n date of payment.

'**Zählwerk** n counter.

'**Zahlwort** n (-[e]s; ~er) ling. numeral.

'Zahlzeichen n figure, numeral.

zahm [tsa:m] adj tame (a. fig.), domesticated, fig. tractable. **'zahmbar** adj tam(e)able. **zähmen** ['tsɛ:mən] v/t 1. a. fig. tame, domesticate. 2. control, restrain (sich o.s.). **'Zahmheit** f (-; no pl) a. fig. tameness. **'Zähmung** f (-; no pl) taming (a. fig.), domestication.

Zahn [tsa:n] m (-[e]s; ⁓e) 1. tooth (a. ☉), zo. a. fang, a. tusk: **Zähne bekommen** → **zahnen** I; humor. **die dritten Zähne** (a set of) false teeth; **der ⁓ der Zeit** the ravages of time; **bis an die Zähne bewaffnet** armed to the teeth; **sich e-n ⁓ ziehen lassen** have a tooth out; F fig. **sich an e-r Sache die Zähne ausbeißen** find s.th. too hard a nut to crack; **j-m auf den ⁓ fühlen** sound s.o. out; F **et. für den hohlen ⁓** precious little; → **fletschen, Haar, knirschen, putzen** I. 2. F speed: **er hatte e-n ziemlichen ⁓ drauf** he was going at a terrific lick; **e-n ⁓ zulegen** step on it.

'Zahn|arzt m dentist, dental surgeon. **⁓arzthelferin** f dentist's assistant. **Ặärztlich** adj dental. **⁓arztpraxis** f dental practice. **⁓behandlung** f dental treatment. **⁓belag** m plaque. **⁓bett** n anat. tooth socket. **⁓bürste** f toothbrush. **⁓creme** f toothpaste.

zähne|fletschend ['tsɛ:nə-] adj and adv snarling. **⁓klappernd** adj and adv with chattering teeth. **⁓knirschend** adv fig. gritting one's teeth.

zahnen ['tsa:nən] (h) **I** v/i teethe, cut one's teeth. **II** a. **zähnen** ['tsɛ:nən] v/t (h) ☉ tooth.

'Zahn|ersatz m dentures. **⁓fäule** f tooth decay, caries. **⁓fleisch** n gums: humor. **auf dem ⁓ gehen** be on one's last legs. **⁓fleischbluten** n bleeding of the gums. **⁓füllung** f filling. **⁓hals** m neck of a tooth. **⁓klinik** f dental clinic. **⁓kranz** m (☉ a) gear rim, b) sprocket (wheel). **⁓krone** f ⁓ crown. **⁓la‚bor** n dental laboratory. **⁓laut** m dental (sound).

'zahnlos adj toothless.

'Zahn|lücke f gap (in one's teeth). **⁓medi‚zin** f dentistry. **⁓medi‚ziner** m 1. dentist. 2. dental student. **⁓nerv** m nerve of a tooth. **⁓pasta** f toothpaste. **⁓pflege** f dental hygiene. **⁓pro‚these** f dentures.

'Zahnrad n ☉ gearwheel, toothed wheel.

⁓antrieb m gearwheel drive. **⁓bahn** f rack railway (Am. railroad). **⁓getriebe** n toothed gearing.

'Zahn|schmelz m (dental) enamel. **⁓schmerzen** pl (⁓ haben have [a]) toothache. **⁓schutz** m boxing: gumshield. **⁓seide** f dental floss. **⁓spange** f brace. **⁓stange** f ☉ rack. **⁓stein** m ⚕ tartar. **⁓stocher** m (-s; -) toothpick. **⁓stummel** m stump. **⁓technik** f dentistry. **⁓techniker** m dental technician. **⁓wechsel** m second dentition. **⁓weh** n → **Zahnschmerzen**. **⁓wurzel** f root (of a tooth). **⁓ze‚ment** m (dental) cement.

Zander ['tsandər] m (-s; -) zo. zander, pike-perch.

Zange ['tsaŋə] f (-; -n) pliers, tongs, a. zo. pincers, ⚕, zo. forceps: **e-e ⁓** a pair of tongs etc; F fig. **j-n in die ⁓ nehmen** put the screws on s.o.; **den würde ich nicht mit der ⁓ anfassen!** I wouldn't touch him with a bargepole.

Zank [tsaŋk] m (-[e]s; no pl) quarrel. **'Zankapfel** m (-s; no pl) bone of contention. **'zanken** v/i (h) **1.** (a. **sich ⁓**) quarrel (über acc about, um about, over). **2.** dial. (mit j-m) ⁓ scold (s.o.). **Zanke'rei** f (-; -en) bickering.

zänkisch ['tsɛŋkɪʃ] adj quarrelsome.

Zäpfchen ['tsɛpfçən] n (-s; -) **1.** anat. uvula. **2.** ⚕ suppository.

zapfen ['tsapfən] v/t (h) **1.** tap, draw (beer etc). **2.** ☉ mortise.

'Zapfen m (-s; -) **1.** ⚘ cone. **2.** tap, spigot, Am. faucet. **3.** ☉ a) journal, b) pivot, c) tenon, d) peg.

'Zapfenstreich m ✕ tattoo.

'Zapfer m (-s; -) tapster.

'Zapf|hahn m **1.** tap, Am. faucet. **2.** → **⁓pi‚stole** f mot. nozzle. **⁓säule** f mot. petrol (Am. gasoline) pump.

Zappe'lei f (-; no pl) F fidgets.

'zapp(e)lig adj F fidgety: **du machst mich ganz ⁓!** you give me the fidgets.

zappeln ['tsapəln] v/i (h) **1.** struggle, wriggle: F fig. **j-n ⁓ lassen** keep s.o. on tenterhooks. **2.** F fidget (**vor Aufregung** with excitement).

'Zappelphilipp [-filɪp] m (-s; -e) F fidget.

Zar [tsa:r] m (-en; -en) czar, tsar.

Zarge ['tsargə] f (-; -n) ☉ **1.** notch, groove. **2.** frame, case (of door etc).

Zarin ['tsa:rɪn] f (-; -nen) czarina, tsarina.

zart [tsart] *adj* tender (*meat etc, a. fig. age, love, etc*), delicate (*a. child, health, colo[u]r, etc*), frail (*a. fig.*), filmy (*fabric etc*), gentle (*touch etc*), soft (*skin etc*), *a.* sensitive: *das ~e Geschlecht* the gentle sex; *ein ~er Wink* a gentle hint; *nicht für ~e Ohren* not for tender (*or* sensitive) ears; (*nicht gerade*) *~ umgehen mit* handle *s.o., s.th.* (none too) gently.

'**zartbesaitet** *adj* highly sensitive.

'**zartbitter** *adj* plain (*chocolate*).

'**zartblau** *adj* pale-blue.

'**zartfühlend** *adj* **1.** sensitive. **2.** tactful, discreet. '**Zartgefühl** *n* (-[e]s; *no pl*) **1.** delicacy (of feeling), sensitivity. **2.** tact.

'**zartgliedrig** *adj* delicate, gracile.

'**Zartheit** *f* (-; *no pl*) tenderness (*a. fig.*), delicacy, delicateness, fragility, softness, gentleness.

zärtlich ['tsɛːrtlɪç] *adj* tender, affectionate (*zu* with), caressing: *~e Mutter* fond mother. '**Zärtlichkeit** *f* (-; -en) **1.** *no pl* tenderness, affection, fondness. **2.** endearment, caress.

Zaster ['tsastər] *m* (-s; *no pl*) F dough.

Zäsur [tsɛ'zuːr] *f* (-; -en) **1.** *metr., ♪* c(a)esura, break. **2.** *fig.* turning point.

Zauber ['tsaʊbər] *m* (-s; *no pl*) **1.** (*wie durch ~* as if by) magic: F *contp. fauler ~* mumbo-jumbo. **2.** *fig.* charm, magic, spell. **3.** F *contp.* a) fuss, b) nonsense: *der ganze ~* the whole bag of tricks. **Zaube'rei** *f* (-; *no pl*) **1.** magic, witchcraft. **2.** conjuring trick. '**Zauberer** *m* (-s; -) **1.** magician, sorcerer, *a. fig.* wizard. **2.** → *Zauberkünstler*.

'**Zauberformel** *f* magic formula.

'**zauberhaft** *adj* charming, enchanting.

'**Zauberin** *f* (-; -nen) *a. fig.* sorceress.

'**Zauber|kraft** *f* magic power. **~kunst** *f* magic (art). **~künstler** *m* conjurer, magician. **~kunststück** *n* conjuring trick.

zaubern ['tsaʊbərn] (h) **I** *v/t* produce *s.th.* by magic, conjure up. **II** *v/i* a) perform magic, b) conjure, do conjuring tricks, c) *soccer etc*: put on a brilliant show: *ich kann doch nicht ~!* I can't perform miracles.

'**Zauber|spruch** *m* charm, spell. **~stab** *m* (magic) wand. **~trank** *m* magic potion. **~wort** *n* (-[e]s; -e) magic word.

'**Zauderer** *m* (-s; -) waverer.

zaudern ['tsaʊdərn] *v/i* (h) hesitate, waver: *ohne Zaudern* without hesitation.

Zaum [tsaʊm] *m* (-[e]s; ⸚e) (*a. fig. im ~e halten*) bridle.

zäumen ['tsɔymən] *v/t* (h) bridle.

'**Zaumzeug** *n* headgear, bridle.

Zaun [tsaʊn] *m* (-[e]s; ⸚e) a) fence, b) hoarding: *vom ~ brechen* a) *in Streit* pick a quarrel, b) *e-n Krieg* start a war. **~gast** *m* onlooker. **~könig** *m zo.* wren. **~pfahl** *m* pale: F *ein Wink mit dem ~* a broad hint.

zausen ['tsaʊzən] *v/t* (h) ruffle, *a.* tousle.

Zebra ['tseːbra] *n* (-s; -s) *zo.* zebra.

'**Zebrastreifen** *m* zebra crossing.

Zeche[1] ['tsɛçə] *f* (-; -n) ⚒ pit, (coal) mine, colliery.

'**Zeche**[2] *f* (-; -n) bill, *Am.* check: *die ~ prellen* leave without paying; *fig. die ~ zahlen müssen* F have to pay the piper. '**Zechpreller** *m* (-s; -) bilk. **Zechprelle'rei** *f* (-; -en) bilking.

Zecke ['tsɛkə] *f* (-; -n) *zo.* tick.

Zeder ['tseːdər] *f* (-; -n) ♣ cedar.

'**Zedernholz** *n* cedar(wood).

Zeh [tse:] *m* (-s; -en) → *Zehe* **1. Zehe** ['tse:ə] *f* (-; -n) **1.** *anat., zo.* toe: *große* (*kleine*) *~* big (little) toe; *j-m auf die ~n treten a. fig.* tread on s.o.'s toes. **2.** clove (of garlic).

'**Zehen|nagel** *m* toenail. **~san,dale** *f* flip-flop. **~spitze** *f* tip of one's toe: *auf* (*den*) *~n* on tiptoe.

zehn [tse:n] *adj* ten. **Zehn** *f* (-; -en) (number) ten. '**Zehneck** *n* (-[e]s; -e) decagon.

'**Zehner**[1] *m* (-s; -) **1.** ten. **2.** F → *Zehnpfennigstück, Zehnmarkschein*.

'**Zehner**[2] *f* (-; -) → *Zehnpfennig-(brief)marke*.

'**Zehnerkarte** *f* ten-trip ticket.

'**Zehnerpackung** *f* pack(et) of ten.

'**Zehnerstelle** *f* ⓐ tens digit.

'**zehnfach** *adj und adv* tenfold.

'**Zehnfache** *n* (-n) ten times the amount: *um das ~ increase etc* tenfold.

'**Zehn'fingersy,stem** *n* touch system.

'**zehnjährig** [-jɛːrɪç] *adj* **1.** ten-year-old: *ein ~er Junge a.* a boy of ten. **2.** *~es Jubiläum etc* ten-year (*or* tenth) anniversary *etc*. **3.** *nach ~er Abwesenheit etc* after an absence *etc* of ten years.

'**Zehnkampf** *m sports*: decathlon.

'**Zehnkämpfer** *m* decathlete.

'**zehnmal** *adv* ten times.

Zehn'markschein *m* ten-mark note (*Am.* bill), F tenner.

Zehn'pfennig|(brief)marke f ten-pfennig stamp. **~stück** n ten-pfennig piece.
zehnt adj tenth.
'zehn'tausend adj ten thousand: fig. **die oberen** 2 the upper ten (thousand); **2e von ...** tens of thousands of ...
Zehntel ['tse:ntəl] n (-s; -) tenth.
'Zehntelse,kunde f tenth of a second.
zehntens ['tse:ntəns] adv tenthly.
zehren ['tse:rən] v/i (h) **1. ~ von** live on (a. fig. memories etc); **von s-m Kapital ~** live off one's capital. **2. ~ an** (dat) weaken, undermine; **an j-s Kräften ~** sap s.o.'s energy.
Zeichen ['tsaiçən] n (-s; -) **1.** a) sign, a. mark, b. characteristic, b) signal, c) symbol, computer: character: **chemisches ~** chemical symbol; **j-m ein ~ geben** give s.o. a sign (or signal), signal to s.o.; **er gab das ~ zum Aufbruch** he gave the signal to leave. **2.** fig. sign, a. mark, token, a. omen, a. symptom: **ein ~ für** (or von) a sign of; **zum ~ daß** as a proof that; **als** (or zum) **~ m-r Dankbarkeit** as a token of my gratitude; **es ist ein ~ der Zeit** it's a symptom of our times; **es geschehen noch ~ und Wunder** wonders never cease. **3.** punctuation mark. **4.** astr. sign: **im ~ des Löwen** under the sign of Leo; fig. **im ~ stehen von** (or gen) be marked by. **5.** reference (number): **✝ unser** (Ihr) **~** our (your) reference. **6. ✝** trademark.
'Zeichen|block m sketch pad. **~brett** n drawing board. **~dreieck** n set square. **~erklärung** f key (für, zu to), on maps etc: legend, in textbooks etc: signs and symbols. **~feder** f drawing pen. **~gerät** n computer: plotter. **~heft** n drawing book. **~kunst** f drawing. **~lehrer** m art teacher. **~pa,pier** n drawing paper. **~saal** m art room. **~setzung** f (-; no pl) punctuation. **~sprache** f (-; no pl) sign language. **~stift** m pencil, crayon. **~trickfilm** m (animated) cartoon. **~unterricht** m drawing lessons, ped. art.
zeichnen ['tsaiçnən] (h) **I** v/t **1.** draw (a. fig.), sketch, a. fig. delineate, design. **2.** mark: **er war von der Krankheit gezeichnet** the illness had left its mark (on him). **3.** sign (letter etc). **4. ✝** subscribe (**für Aktien** etc for shares etc, **für e-n Fonds** to a fund). **II** v/i **5.** draw (**nach der Natur** from nature). **6.** sign:

ich zeichne ... I remain ...; **verantwortlich ~ für** be responsible for.
'Zeichner m (-s; -) **1.** drawer, draughtsman, Am. draftsman. **2. ✝** subscriber (gen for, to). **'Zeichnerin** f (-; -nen) **1.** drawer, draughtswoman, Am. draftswoman. **2. → Zeichner** 2.
'zeichnerisch adj graphic: **~e Begabung haben, ~ begabt sein** have (a) talent for drawing.
'Zeichnung f (-; -en) **1.** a) drawing, ⊙ a. design, diagram, b) sketch, c) illustration. **2. ♀,** zo. marking(s), patterning. **3. ✝** subscription: **e-e Anleihe zur ~ auflegen** invite subscriptions for a loan.
'zeichnungsberechtigt adj authorized to sign, having signatory power.
'Zeigefinger m forefinger, index finger.
zeigen ['tsaigən] (h) **I** v/t show (a. fig.), a. present (film etc), a. fig. display, exhibit, a. indicate, a. demonstrate, point out: **j-m die Stadt ~** show s.o. (around) the town; **er will nur s-e Macht ~** he just wants to demonstrate his power; **großen Mut ~** display great courage; F **dem werd' ich's ~!** I'll show him. **II** v/i (**mit dem Finger**) **~ auf** (acc) point (one's finger) at; **nach Norden ~** point (to) the north; **die Uhr zeigte** (auf) **12** the clock said twelve. **III** sich **~** show (o.s.), appear, turn up; fig. **sie zeigte sich sehr großzügig** she was very generous; **sich von s-r besten Seite ~** present o.s. to best advantage; **er zeigte sich der Aufgabe nicht gewachsen** it became obvious that he wasn't equal to the task. **IV** v/impers turn out, prove: **es zeigte sich, daß er recht gehabt hatte** (**es richtig gewesen war**) he (it) turned out to have been right; **es wird sich ~, wer recht hat** we'll see who is right in the end.
'Zeiger m (-s; -) hand, ⊙ a. index, pointer, needle (of speedometer etc).
'Zeigestock m pointer.
Zeile ['tsailə] f (-; -n) **1.** line: **j-m ein paar ~n schreiben** drop s.o. a line. **2.** row.
'Zeilen|abstand m **1.** spacing. **2.** TV line advance. **~anzeige** f computer: line display. **~drucker** m computer: line printer. **~eingabe** f computer: line entry. **~raster** n TV line-scanning pattern. **~schalter** m typewriter: line spacer. **~vorschub** m computer: line feed.

'**zeilenweise** *adv* by the line.
Zeisig ['tsaızıç] *m* (-s; -e) *zo.* siskin.
Zeit [tsaıt] *f* (-; -en) **1.** *no pl* time: **~ und Raum** space and time; **freie ~** spare time; **mit der ~** in course of time, with time; **mit der ~ gehen** move with the times. **2.** time, *a.* period, space (of time), *a.* era, age, *a.* season: **schwere** (*or* **harte**) **~en** hard times; F **das waren** (**noch**) **~en!** those were the days; **die gute alte ~** the good old days; **... aller ~en** ... of all time; **seit dieser ~** since then; (**für**) **einige ~** (for) some time; (**für**) **längere ~** for quite some time, for a prolonged period; **lange ~** for a long time; **seit einiger** (*or* **längerer**) **~** for quite some time (now); **die ganze ~** (**hindurch**) all the time, all along; **in kurzer ~** in a short time; **in kürzester ~** in no time at all; **in letzter ~** lately, recently; **in nächster ~** shortly, soon, presently; **die ~ ist um!** time's up!; **um diese ~ bin ich schon im Bett** I'll be in bed already by that time; **morgen um diese ~** this time tomorrow; **von ~ zu ~** from time to time, now and then; **in der ~ vom ... bis ...** in the time between ... and ...; **vor der ~** prematurely; **vor langer ~** a long time ago; **vor nicht allzu langer ~** not so long ago; **zur ~** (*gen*) at the time of; **zu ~en der Römer** in the days of the Romans; **zu m-r ~** in my time; **alles zu s-r ~!** a) there's a time for everything, b) one thing after another; **es ist (höchste) ~ zu gehen** it is (high) time to leave; **ich habe k-e ~** I'm busy, I'm in a hurry; **das hat ~** there's no hurry; **bis morgen** that can wait till tomorrow; **laß dir ~!** take your time!; **j-m ~ lassen** give s.o. time; **sich ~ nehmen für** take (the) time for (*or* to do *s.th.*); **die ~ nutzen** make the most of one's time; *sports:* **auf ~ spielen** play for time; F **es wurde aber auch ~!** about time too!; **~ ist Geld** time is money; **andere ~en, andere Sitten** other times, other manners; **kommt ~, kommt Rat** time will bring an answer; F (**ach,**) **du liebe ~!** good heavens!; → **schinden**, **totschlagen**, **vertreiben** 1, **Wunde. 3.** *ling.* tense.
'**Zeit|abschnitt** *m* period (of time), era. **~abstand** *m* interval. **~alter** *n* age, era, epoch. **~angabe** *f* exact (date and)

time. **~ansage** *f teleph.* speaking-clock announcement. **~arbeit** *f* temporary work. **~aufnahme** *f phot.* time exposure. **~aufwand** *m* time spent (**für** on): **mit großem ~ verbunden sein** take (up) a great deal of time. **2aufwendig** *adj* time-consuming. **~begriff** *m* conception of time. **~bombe** *f a. fig.* time bomb. **~dauer** *f* 1. length of time. **2.** period, duration, term. **~doku,ment** *n* document of the times. **~druck** *m* (-[e]s; *no pl*) (time) pressure: **unter ~ stehen** be pressed for time. **~einteilung** *f* time plan: **sie hat k-e ~** she doesn't know how to organize her time.
'**Zeitenfolge** *f ling.* sequence of tenses.
'**Zeit|ersparnis** *f* saving of time. **~faktor** *m* time factor. **~folge** *f* chronological order. **~form** *f ling.* tense. **~frage** *f* 1. **es ist e-e ~** it is a question of time. **2.** topic of the day. **~gefühl** *n* (-[e]s; *no pl*) sense of time. **~geist** *m* spirit of the age, zeitgeist.
'**zeitgemäß** *adj* 1. up(-)to(-)date, modern. **2.** current, topical.
'**Zeitgenosse** *m* contemporary: F *fig.* **er ist ein übler ~** he's a nasty customer. '**zeitgenössisch** [-gənœsıʃ] *adj* contemporary.
'**Zeit|geschehen** *n* current events. **~geschichte** *f* contemporary history. **~geschmack** *m* (-[e]s; *no pl*) taste (*or* fashion) of the time(s). **~gewinn** *m* (-[e]s; *no pl*) time gained: **e-n ~ von 3 Stunden bedeuten** save three hours. **2gleich** *adj sports:* with the same time: **~ ins Ziel kommen** be clocked at the same time. **~guthaben** *n* time credit.
'**zeitig** *adj* and *adv* early.
'**Zeitkarte** *f* season (*Am.* commutation) ticket. '**Zeitkarteninhaber(in** *f*) *m* season-ticket holder, *Am.* commuter.
'**zeitkritisch** *adj* topical.
'**Zeitlang** *f*: **e-e ~** for some time.
'**zeitlebens** *adv* all one's life.
'**zeitlich I** *adj* 1. a) time ..., b) chronological: **~e Abstimmung** (*or* **Berechnung**) timing. **2.** *a. eccl.* temporary, transitory. **II** *adv* **~ abstimmen** time, synchronize; **~ begrenzt** limited in time; **~ günstig** well-timed; **es paßt mir ~ nicht** I can't fit it in(to my timetable); **ich schaffe es ~ nicht** a) I don't have the time to do it,

b) I can't make it in time; **~ zs.-fallen** coincide.

'zeitlos adj timeless, ageless.

'Zeitlupe f (-; no pl) **1.** slow-motion camera. **2.** → **Zeitlupentempo.**

'Zeitlupen|aufnahme f slow-motion shot. **~tempo** n (im ~ in) slow motion.

'Zeit|mangel m (aus ~ for) lack of time. **~maß** n tempo, ♪ a. time. **~messer** ◉ timekeeper, timer. **~messung** f timing. **⌐nah** adj topical, current. **~nehmer** m (-s; -) timekeeper, ◉ a. time-study man. **~not** f in ~ sein (geraten) be(come) pressed for time. **~plan** m schedule, timetable. **~punkt** m time, moment: zum ~ (gen) at the time of; zu e-m späteren ~ at a later date; der ~ für den Angriff war gut gewählt the attack was well timed.

'Zeitraffer... time-lapse, quick-motion (camera etc).

'zeitraubend adj time-consuming.

'Zeit|raum m period, space (of time). **~rechnung** f chronology: unserer ~ of our time. **~schalter** m, **~schaltwerk** n ◉ time switch, timer. **~schrift** f magazine, periodical. **~spanne** f period, space (of time). **⌐sparend** adj time-saving. **~strafe** f sports: time penalty. **~strömung** f trend. **~stück** n thea. period play. **~studien** pl time(-and-motion) studies. **~tafel** f chronological table. **~umstände** pl prevailing circumstances.

Zeitung ['tsaɪtʊŋ] f (-; -en) (news)paper, journal, adm. gazette: in der ~ steht, daß it says in the paper that.

'Zeitungs|abonne,ment n newspaper subscription. **~anzeige** f (newspaper) advertisement, F ad. **~ar,tikel** m newspaper article. **~ausschnitt** m newspaper clipping. **~austräger** m newspaper carrier. **~beilage** f newspaper supplement. **~ente** f F fig. hoax, canard. **~frau** f F **1.** newspaper carrier. **2.** news agent (Am. dealer). **3.** news vendor. **~händler** m news agent (Am. dealer). **~inse,rat** n → Zeitungsanzeige. **~junge** m newsboy. **~kiosk** m newsstand. **~leser** m newspaper reader. **~mann** m F → Zeitungsfrau. **~meldung** f, **~no,tiz** f press item. **~pa,pier** n newspaper, a. newsprint. **~redak,teur** m newspaper editor. **~ro,man** m novel se-

rialized in a newspaper. **~stand** m newsstand. **~ständer** m magazine (or newspaper) rack. **~stil** m journalese. **~verkäufer** m news vendor. **~verleger** m newspaper publisher. **~wesen** n (-s; no pl) journalism, the press. **~wissenschaft** f journalism.

'Zeit|unterschied m time difference, ✈ time lag. **~verlust** m (-[e]s; no pl) loss of time: den ~ aufholen make up for lost time. **~verschwendung** f waste of time. **~vertreib** [-fɛrtraɪp] m (-[e]s; -e) pastime: zum ~ as a pastime, to pass the time.

'zeitweilig [-vaɪlɪç] **I** adj **1.** temporary. **2.** occasional. **II** adv → **'zeitweise** adv **1.** for a time. **2.** from time to time, at times, occasionally.

'Zeit|wert m ✝ time (or current) value. **~wort** n (-[e]s; ⸚er) verb. **~zeichen** n radio: time signal. **~zone** f time zone. **~zünder** m time fuse.

zelebrieren [tsele'bri:rən] v/t (h) celebrate (mass etc).

Zell... cellular. **~atmung** f biol. vesicular breathing. **~bau** m (-[e]s; no pl) cell structure. **~bildung** f cell formation.

Zelle ['tsɛlə] f (-; -n) **1.** cell. **2.** airframe. **3.** (telephone) booth.

'Zellgewebe n biol. cell tissue.

'zellig adj, a. ...**zellig** biol. cellular.

'Zellkern m biol. nucleus.

Zellophan n → **Cellophan.**

'Zellstoff m cellulose, paper: pulp.

'Zellteilung f biol. cell division.

zellular [tsɛlu'laːr] adj cellular.

Zellulitis [tsɛlu'li:tɪs] f (-; -litiden [-li'ti:dən]) ⚕ cellulitis.

Zelluloid [tsɛlu'lɔyt] n (-[e]s; no pl) celluloid.

Zellulose [tsɛlu'lo:zə] f (-; -n) cellulose.

'Zell|wand f biol. cell wall. **~wolle** f rayon staple fib/re (Am. -er).

Zelt [tsɛlt] n (-[e]s; -e) a) tent, of circus: a. big top, b) marquee: ein ~ aufschlagen (abbrechen) pitch (strike) a tent; F fig. s-e ~e aufschlagen (abbrechen) settle down (pack up). **~bahn** f **1.** tent square. **2.** tarpaulin. **~dach** n **1.** tent roof. **2.** △ pyramid-type roof.

zelten ['tsɛltən] v/i (h) camp: ~ gehen go camping; ⌐ verboten! no camping!

'Zelt|lager n (tent) camp. **~leine** f guy line. **~leinwand** f canvas. **~pflock** m

tent peg. **~plane** f tarpaulin. **~stadt** f
tent city. **~stange** f tent pole.

Zement [tse'mɛnt] m (-[e]s; -e) cement.
zementieren [tsemɛn'tiːrən] v/t (h) cement (a. fig.), metall. carburize.

Ze'mentsack m cement bag.

Zenit [tse'niːt] m (-[e]s; no pl) astr. or fig. (**im ~** at the) zenith.

zensieren [tsɛn'ziːrən] v/t (h) **1.** ped. mark, Am. grade. **2.** censor. **Zensor** ['tsɛnzɔr] m (-s; -en [-'zoːrən]) censor.

Zensur [tsɛn'zuːr] f (-; -en) **1.** ped. mark, Am. grade: **gute ~en haben** a. have a good report. **2.** no pl censorship: **der ~ unterliegen** be censored.

Zensus ['tsɛnzʊs] m (-; -) census.

Zentimeter [tsɛnti'meːtər] m, n (-s; -) centimet/re (Am. -er).

Zentner ['tsɛntnər] m (-s; -) (metric) hundredweight (abbr. cwt.), centner (50 kg). **~last** f fig. heavy burden: **mir fiel e-e ~ vom Herzen** it was a great weight off my mind. **~schwer** adj fig. very heavy: **es liegt mir ~ auf der Seele** it weighs very heavily on my mind.

zentral [tsɛn'traːl] adj central: **~ gelegen sein** be centrally located; fig. **das ~e Problem** the crucial problem.

Zen'tralbank f (-; -en) central bank.

zen'tralbeheizt adj centrally heated.

Zentrale [tsɛn'traːlə] f (-; -n) **1.** central office, headquarters. **2.** telephone exchange, in firm: switchboard. **3.** ⊙ control room. **4.** fig. centre, Am. center.

Zen'tralheizung f central heating.

zentralisieren [tsɛntrali'ziːrən] v/t (h) centralize. **Zentrali'sierung** f (-; -en) centralization.

Zentralismus [tsɛntra'lɪsmʊs] m (-; no pl) pol. centralism. **zentra'listisch** [-tɪʃ] adj pol. centralist(ic).

Zen'tral|komi,tee n pol. central committee. **~nervensy,stem** n central nervous system. **~or,gan** n official party organ. **~verband** m ⚭ etc central association. **~verriegelung** f mot. central locking (system).

zentrieren [tsɛn'triːrən] v/t (h) centre, Am. center.

zentrifugal [tsɛntrifu'gaːl] adj centrifugal. **Zentrifu'galkraft** f centrifugal force. **Zentrifuge** [tsɛntri'fuːgə] f (-; -n) centrifuge.

zentrisch ['tsɛntrɪʃ] adj centric(al).

Zentrum ['tsɛntrʊm] n (-s; -tren) centre, Am. center: **im ~ von New York** Am. a. (in) downtown New York; **sie stand im ~ des Interesses** she was the centre of interest.

Zepter ['tsɛptər] n (-s; -) sceptre, Am. scepter: humor. **das ~ schwingen** rule the roost.

zer'beißen v/t (irr, no -ge-, h, → **beißen**) bite to pieces, crunch.

zerbeult [-'bɔylt] adj battered.

zerbomben [-'bɔmbən] v/t (h) bomb.

zerbombt [-'bɔmpt] adj bomb-wrecked.

zer'brechen (irr, no -ge-, h) **I** v/t break, crack, smash: → **Kopf** 2. **II** v/i break (fig. up): fig. **~ an** (dat) be crushed (or broken) by. **zerbrechlich** [-'brɛçlɪç] adj breakable, a. fig. frail, delicate, fragile: **Vorsicht, ~!** fragile, handle with care! **Zer'brechlichkeit** f (-; no pl) a. fig. fragility, frailness.

zer'bröckeln v/t (h), v/i (sn) crumble.

zer'drücken v/t (h) crush, a. mash (potatoes etc), a. crumple (clothes).

zerebral [tsere'braːl] adj cerebral.

Zeremonie [tseremo'niː] f (-; -n) ceremony. **zeremoniell** [tseremo'niɛl] adj ceremonial. **Zeremoni'ell** n (-s; -e) ceremonial, fig. a. ritual. **zeremoniös** [tseremo'niøːs] adj ceremonious.

Zer'fall m (-[e]s; no pl) disintegration, decay, a. fig. ruin, 🜍 decomposition.

zer'fallen¹ v/i (irr, no -ge-, sn, → **fallen**) **1.** disintegrate (in acc, **zu** into), decay, 🜍 decompose, building etc: crumble (a. fig. empire etc), fall to pieces. **2.** fig. **~ in** (acc) be divided into.

zer'fallen² adj **1.** decayed, in ruins. **2.** **mit j-m ~ sein** be at odds with s.o.; **mit sich und der Welt ~** disgusted with life.

Zer'falls|erscheinung f sign of decay. **~pro,dukt** n nucl. decay product. **~reihe** f nucl. family, decay chain. **~zeit** f nucl. decay period (or time).

zer'fetzen v/t (h) tear s.th. (in)to pieces, shred, slash, mangle.

zerfleddern [-'flɛdərn] v/t (h) tatter.

zerfleischen [-'flaɪʃən] (h) **I** v/t mangle, tear s.o., s.th. to pieces: fig. **einander ~** tear each other apart. **II sich ~** fig. torment o.s.

zer'fließen v/i (irr, no -ge-, sn, → **fließen**) a) run, b) melt: **sie zerfloß vor Mitleid** she was melting with pity.

zer'fressen¹ v/t (irr, no -ge-, h, → **fressen**) **1.** *moths:* eat (holes into), *mice etc:* gnaw *s.th.* to pieces. **2.** 🐾, ⚙ corrode.

zer'fressen² adj **von Motten** ~ motheaten; **vom Rost** ~ corroded; *fig.* **vom Neid** ~ eaten up with envy.

zerfurcht [-'furçt] adj a. fig. furrowed.

zer'gehen v/i (irr, no -ge-, sn, → **gehen**) dissolve, melt: **auf der Zunge** ~ melt in one's mouth.

zer'gliedern v/t (h) analy|se (Am. -ze), dissect, a. parse (sentence).

zer'hacken v/t (h) chop (a. 🎜), mince.

zer'hauen v/t (h) cut s.th. to pieces.

zer'kauen v/t (h) chew (well).

zerkleinern [-'klaɪnərn] v/t (h) reduce s.th. to small pieces, crush, cut s.th. up.

zerklüftet [-'klʏftət] adj jagged, rugged.

zer'knautschen v/t (h) F crumple.

zerknirscht [-'knɪrʃt] adj contrite: ~ **sein** feel remorse (**über** acc at).

Zer'knirschung f (-; no pl) contrition.

zer'knittern v/t (h), v/i (sn) crumple, crease.

zer'knüllen v/t (h) crumple up.

zer'kratzen v/t (h) scratch.

zer'krümeln v/t (h), v/i (sn) crumble.

zer'lassen v/t (irr, no -ge-, h, → **lassen**) melt (butter etc).

zer'laufen v/i (irr, no -ge-, sn, → **laufen**) butter etc: melt, colo[u]r: run.

zerlegbar [-'le:kbaːr] adj dismountable, knock-down ...: **... ist ...** ... can be taken apart. **zer'legen** v/t (h) **1.** take s.th. apart, ⚙ a. dismantle, knock down. **2.** cut s.th. up, dissect, carve (roast). **3.** 🖦 reduce, a. 🐾 decompose: 🖦 **in Faktoren** ~ factorize. **4.** → **zergliedern**.

zer'lesen adj well-thumbed (book etc).

zerlöchert [-'lœçərt] adj full of holes.

zerlumpt [-'lʊmpt] adj ragged, tattered.

zermalmen [-'malmən] v/t (h) crush.

zer'martern v/t (h) **sich den Kopf** ~ rack one's brain (**über** acc over).

zermürben [-'mʏrbən] v/t (h) wear s.o. down, ⚔ soften up: ~**d** trying.

Zer'mürbungskrieg m war of attrition.

zer'nagen v/t (h) gnaw s.th. to pieces.

zer'pflücken v/t (h) pick s.th. to pieces.

zer'platzen v/i (sn) burst, explode.

zer'quetschen v/t (h) crush (a. ⚙), squash, mash: F **70 Mark und ein paar Zerquetschte** 70 marks and some.

'Zerrbild n a. fig. caricature, distorted picture, fig. a. travesty.

zer'reden v/t (h) flog s.th. to death.

zer'reiben v/t (irr, no -ge-, h, → **reiben**) crush, grind: **et. zwischen den Fingern** ~ rub s.th. between one's fingers.

zer'reißen (irr, no -ge-, h, → **reißen**) **I** v/t tear s.th. up, tear s.th. to pieces (or apart), rip up, break (thread, fetters, fig. ties etc): **er hat sich die Hose zerrissen** he tore his pants; **es zerriß ihr das Herz** it broke her heart; F *fig.* **in der Luft** ~ a) tear s.o. limb from limb, b) tear s.o., s.th. to pieces. **II** v/i tear, chain, thread, etc: break, bag etc: burst. **III** **sich (fast)** ~ F bend over backwards: **ich kann mich doch nicht** ~! I can't be in two places at once.

Zer'reiß‖festigkeit f ⊘ tear resistance. **~probe** f **1.** ⊘ tension test. **2.** ordeal.

zerren ['tsɛrən] (h) **I** v/t **1.** drag, haul: **j-n hinter sich her** ~ drag s.o. along; *fig.* **et. an die Öffentlichkeit** ~ drag s.th. into the limelight. **2.** ﹟ pull, strain (**sich e-n Muskel** a muscle). **II** v/i ~ **an** (dat) pull at, tug at; **der Hund zerrte an der Leine** the dog strained at its leash.

zer'rinnen v/i (irr, no -ge-, sn, → **rinnen**) melt away (a. fig. money etc), fig. dreams etc: fade, vanish, plans etc: come to nothing: **wie gewonnen, so zerronnen** easy come, easy go.

zerrissen [-'rɪsən] adj a. fig. torn: **er ist innerlich** ~ he is torn by inner conflicts.

Zer'rissenheit f (-; no pl) fig. (**innere**) ~ inner conflicts.

'Zerrung f (-; -en) ﹟ strain.

zer'rütten [-'rʏtən] v/t (h) ruin, wreck (a. health, marriage, etc), a. unhinge, derange (mind): **ihre Nerven sind zerrüttet** her nerves are shattered; **zerrüttete Ehe** (**Familienverhältnisse**) broken marriage (home).

Zer'rüttung f (-; -en) ruin, ruinous state: ﺗﻪ (**unheilbare**) ~ **der Ehe** (irretrievable) breakdown of a marriage.

zer'sägen v/t (h) saw s.th. up.

zer'schellen v/i (sn) smash, be smashed to pieces, ✈ crash, ⚓ be wrecked.

zer'schießen v/t (irr, no -ge-, h, → **schießen**) bombard, batter.

zer'schlagen¹ (irr, no -ge-, h, → **schlagen**) **I** v/t smash (a. fig.), smash s.th. to pieces, shatter. **II** **sich** ~ hopes, plans, *etc*: come to nothing. **zer'schlagen²** *adj* F *fig*. dead-beat, whacked: **sich wie ~ fühlen** feel washed out.

zerschlissen [-'ʃlɪsən] *adj* worn-out.

zer'schmettern *v/t* (h) smash, shatter.

zer'schneiden *v/t* (*irr, no* -ge-, h, → **schneiden**) cut (*s.th.* up), carve (*roast*), slice, shred.

zer'schrammen *v/t* (h) scratch.

zer'setzen (h) **I** *v/t* **1.** 🜃 decompose. **2.** *fig*. corrupt, undermine. **II sich ~ a.** 🜃 decay, decompose, disintegrate. **zer'setzend** *adj fig*. subversive.

Zer'setzung *f* (-; *no pl*) **1.** decay, *a.* 🜃 decomposition, disintegration. **2.** *fig*. corruption, *pol*. subversion.

zer'siedeln *v/t* (h) spoil (by uncontrolled development). **Zer'sied(e)lung** *f* (-; *no pl*) urban sprawl.

zerspanen [-'ʃpaːnən] *v/t* (h) machine.

zer'splittern I *v/t* (h) shatter, *a.fig*. split (up), splinter: **s-e Kräfte ~ →** III a. **II** *v/i* (sn) shatter, *a. fig*. splinter. **III sich ~** *fig*. a) dissipate one's energies, b) do too many things at once.

zer'springen *v/i* (*irr, no* -ge-, sn, → **springen**) shatter, break.

zer'stampfen *v/t* (h) **1.** crush, pound. **2.** trample (down).

zer'stäuben *v/t* (h) **1.** spray, atomize. **2.** dust, sprinkle (*powder*).

Zer'stäuber *m* (-s; -) atomizer, sprayer.

zer'stechen *v/t* (*irr, no* -ge-, h, → **stechen**) **1.** *j-n ~ insects*: bite s.o. all over. **2.** puncture, pierce.

zer'stören *v/t* (h) *a.fig*. destroy, ruin (*a. health etc*), wreck (*a. marriage etc*): **j-s Hoffnungen ~** shatter s.o.'s hopes.

Zer'störer *m* (-s; -) *a.* ✕ destroyer.

zer'störerisch *adj* destructive.

Zer'störung *f* (-, -en) **1.** destruction (*a. fig.*), devastation. **2.** *pl* ravages.

Zer'störungs|trieb *m psych*. destruction instinct. **~werk** *n* work of destruction. **~wut** *f* destructive frenzy, vandalism.

zer'streuen (h) **I** *v/t* **1.** disperse, scatter, *a.* diffuse (*light*), *a.* break up (*crowd*). **2.** dispel, dissipate (*doubts etc*). **3.** *j-n ~* amuse s.o. **II sich ~ 4.** → 1. **5.** amuse o.s. **zer'streut** *adj fig*. absent-minded. **Zer'streutheit** *f* (-; *no pl*) *fig*. absent-mindedness. **Zer'streuung** *f* (-; -en) **1.** *no pl* a) dispersion, scattering, *a.* diffu-

sion (*of light*), b) dissipation (*of doubts etc*). **2.** (**zur ~** as a) diversion.

zer'stückeln [-'ʃtʏkəln] *v/t* (h) cut *s.th.* up, dismember (*body*).

zer'teilen *v/t* (h) **1.** (*a.* **sich ~**) divide (*or* split) (*in acc* into). **2. → zerlegen** 2. 3. (*a.* **sich ~**) disperse, break up (*clouds, fog, etc*). **4.** ✚ resolve (*tumo[u]r*).

Zertifikat [tsɛrtifi'kaːt] *n* (-[e]s; -e) certificate.

zer'trampeln *v/t* (h) trample under foot.

zer'trennen *v/t* (h) **1.** take *s.th.* apart, separate, sever. **2.** undo (*seam*).

zer'treten *v/t* (*irr, no* -ge-, h, → **treten**) crush (*a. fig.*), stamp out (*fire etc*).

zer'trümmern [-'trʏmərn] *v/t* (h) demolish, wreck, smash, ✚ crush (*stone*).

Zer'trümmerung *f* (-; -en) demolition, smashing, ✚ crushing.

Zervelatwurst [tsɛrvə'laːt-] *f* saveloy.

zer'wühlen *v/t* (h) **1.** root up, churn up. **2.** dishevel (*hair*), rumple (*a. bed*).

Zerwürfnis [-'vʏrfnɪs] *n* (-ses; -se) quarrel, split, rupture.

zer'zausen *v/t* (h) ruffle, tousle: **zerzaust** dishevel(l)ed, untidy.

Zeter ['tseːtər] F **~ und Mord(io) schreien** cry blue murder.

zetern ['tseːtərn] *v/i* (h) F **1.** wail. **2.** a) (put up a) squawk, b) nag.

Zettel ['tsɛtəl] *m* (-s; -) a) slip (of paper), b) note, c) label, *Am*. sticker, d) leaflet, e) card. **~kar,tei** *f* card index. **~kasten** *m* card index (box).

Zeug [tsɔɪk] *n* (-[e]s; *no pl*) **1.** a) things, b) tools, c) drinks, food, *etc*) stuff, d) *contp*. rubbish: **dummes ~ reden** talk nonsense, drivel. **2.** fabric, stuff: *fig*. **er hat das ~ zum Arzt** he has the makings of a doctor; **sie hat das ~ dazu** she's got what it takes; F **was das ~ hält** like mad; **sich ins ~ legen** put one's back into it, go all out (**für** for); **j-m am ~(e) flicken** find fault with s.o.

Zeuge ['tsɔɪgə] *m* (-n; -n) witness (**der Anklage** for the prosecution): **vor ~n** in the presence of witnesses; *fig*. **~n der Vergangenheit** relics of the past.

zeugen¹ ['tsɔɪgən] *v/t* (h) **1.** *biol*. procreate, father. **2.** *fig*. generate, create.

'zeugen² *v/i* (h) 🜨 give evidence: *fig*. **~ von** bespeak, be a sign of, show.

'Zeugen|aussage *f* evidence, testimony, *a.* deposition. **~bank** *f* witness box

(*Am.* stand). **~geld** *n* witness expenses. **~vernehmung** *f* hearing of witnesses.

'**Zeugin** *f* (-; -nen) (female) witness.

Zeugnis ['tsɔʏknɪs] *n* (-ses; -se) **1.** *ped.* a) report (card), b) certificate, diploma: **er hat ein gutes ~** he was given a good report. **2.** a) reference, b) credentials: **gute ~se haben** have good references; **j-m ein gutes ~ ausstellen** *a. fig.* give s.o. a good character. **3.** certificate. **4.** ♣♣♣ *or fig.* testimony (*gen* to), evidence: **zum ~** (*gen*) in witness of; *fig.* ~ **ablegen** (*or geben*) bear witness (**für** to, **von** of). **~konfe,renz** *f ped.* reports conference. **~verweigerungsrecht** *n* ♣♣ right to refuse to give evidence.

'**Zeugung** *f* (-; -en) *biol.* procreation.
'**Zeugungsakt** *m* progenitive act.
'**zeugungsfähig** *adj* fertile.
'**Zeugungsfähigkeit** *f* (-; *no pl*) fertility.
'**zeugungsunfähig** *adj* impotent, sterile.
'**Zeugungsunfähigkeit** *f* (-; *no pl*) impotence, sterility.

Zichorie [tsɪ'çoːrⁱə] *f* (-; -en) ♣ chicory.

Zicke ['tsɪkə] *f* (-; -n) **1.** *zo.* (she-)goat. **2.** → **Ziege** 2. '**Zicken** *pl* F (**mach k-e ~** none of your) silly tricks. '**zickig** *adj* F a) prim, prudish, b) silly.

'**Zicklein** *n* (-s; -) *zo.* kid.

Zickzack ['tsɪktsak] *m* (-[e]s; -e) (*a.* **im ~ gehen** *or* **fahren**) zigzag.

Ziege ['tsiːgə] *f* (-; -n) **1.** *zo.* (she-)goat. **2.** F *contp.* (**blöde ~**) silly old cow.

Ziegel ['tsiːgəl] *m* (-s; -) a) brick, b) tile.
'**Ziegeldach** *n* tiled roof.
'**Ziege'lei** *f* (-; -en) brickworks.
'**ziegelrot** *adj* brick-red.
'**Ziegelstein** *m* brick.
'**Ziegen|bock** *m* he-goat. **~fell** *n* goatskin. **~käse** *m* goat's cheese. **~leder** *n* goatskin, kid (leather). **~milch** *f* goat's milk. **~peter** *m* (-s; *no pl*) F ♣ mumps.

'**Ziehbrunnen** *m* draw well.

ziehen ['tsiːən] (zog, gezogen, h) **I** *v/t* **1.** draw, pull, drag, tug, haul: **j-n mit sich ~** drag s.o. with one; **j-n am Ärmel (Ohr) ~** pull s.o. by the sleeve (ear); **j-n an den Haaren ~** pull s.o.'s hair; **Zigaretten aus e-m Automaten ~** get some cigarettes from a machine; **sie zog den Ring vom Finger** she pulled the ring off, (her finger); *mot.* **er zog den Wagen nach links** he pulled the car to the left; **j-n an sich ~** draw s.o. close (to one);

die Aufmerksamkeit (alle Blicke) auf sich ~ attract attention (every eye); **Blasen ~** blister; **auf Flaschen ~** bottle; **den Hut ~** *a. fig.* take off one's hat (**vor j-m** to s.o.); **Perlen auf e-e Schnur ~** thread beads; → **Betracht, Bilanz, Erwägung, Fell** 2, **Länge** 1 *etc.* **2.** **nach sich ~** have (*consequences etc*), involve, entail (*costs etc*). **3.** draw, pull (out), *a.* extract (*tooth*), ♣ take out, remove (*stitches*): **er zog s-e Brieftasche** he took out his wallet; **er zog die Pistole** he drew his pistol; **j-n aus dem Wasser ~** pull s.o. from the water; → **Affäre, Gewinn** 1, **Los** 1, **Nutzen, Wurzel** 1, **Zahn** 1. **4.** draw (*circle, line, etc*): → **Parallele, Schlußstrich. 5.** ⊚ a) draw, b) stretch, c) rifle (*gun barrel*). **6.** cut, run, dig (*ditch etc*), build, erect (*wall, fence, etc*), put up (*line etc*): → **Leine. 7.** ♣ cultivate, *zo.* rear, breed. **II** *v/i* **8.** **~ an** (*dat*) pull at, tug at, **e-r Zigarette** *etc* F (have a) drag at, **der Leine** strain at its leash; F **laß mich mal ~!** give me a drag! **9.** pipe, stove, *etc, a. coffee, tea:* draw: **den Tee drei Minuten ~ lassen** *a.* let the tea stand for three minutes. **10.** move, go, march, wander, migrate, *clouds etc:* drift: **s-s Weges ~** go one's way; **in den Krieg ~** go to war; → **Feld. 11.** (re)move: **aufs Land ~** move to the country; **zu j-m ~** move in with s.o. **12.** hurt, ache: **der Schmerz** twinge. **13.** F *fig.* pretext *etc:* work, *publicity etc:* go down (well): **das zieht (bei ihm) nicht!** that won't work (with him); **das zieht immer!** that sort of thing always goes down well (**bei** with); **das zog!** that did the trick. **14.** *chess:* move: **wer zieht?** whose move is it?; **mit dem König ~** move the king (**auf** *acc* to). **15.** draw (one's pistol), pull a gun. **16.** *sports or fig.* set the pace. → **III sich ~ 17.** (*a.* **sich ~ lassen**) stretch: → **Länge 1. 18.** → **verziehen²** 5. **19.** stretch, extend, run (*a. motif etc, durch* through): F **der Weg zieht sich** the way seems endless. **IV** *v/impers* **20.** **es zieht** there is a draught (*Am.* draft). **21.** **es zieht j-n zu** s.o. feels attracted (*or* drawn) to; **es zog ihn nach Hause** he felt an urge to return home.

'**Ziehen** *n* (-s) twinge, ache.

'**Ziehhar,monika** *f* ♪ accordion.

'**Ziehung** f (-; -en) drawing, draw.

Ziel [tsiːl] n (-[e]s; -e) **1.** destination. **2.** *sports*: finish(ing line): **als Erster durchs ~ gehen** finish first; **sich ins ~ werfen** lunge into the tape. **3.** *esp.* ✕ mark, aim, *a.* target, *a.* (*tactical*) objective: **das ~ verfehlen** miss; **über das ~ hinausschießen** *a. fig.* overshoot the mark. **4.** *fig.* aim, goal, end, objective, target (*a.* ♈): **sein ~ erreichen** reach one's goal, F get there; (**nicht**) **zum ~ führen** succeed (fail); **sich das ~ setzen zu** *inf* aim to *inf*, aim at *ger*; **sein ~ aus dem Auge verlieren** (**im Auge behalten**) lose (keep) sight of one's goal.

'**Zielanflug** m approach run.

'**Zielband** n sports: tape.

'**zielbewußt** → **zielstrebig**.

'**Zieleinlauf** m sports: finish.

zielen ['tsiːlən] v/i (h) (**auf** acc at) (take) aim, level, *fig.* be aimed: → **gezielt**.

'**Ziel|fernrohr** n telescopic sight. **~flug** m homing. **~foto** n sports: photo of the finish. **~gerade** f sports: home stretch. ²**gerichtet** adj goal-directed. **~gruppe** f target group. **~kamera** f photo-finish camera. **~kurve** f sports: home bend. **~linie** f sports: finishing line.

'**ziellos** adj aimless.

'**Ziel|richter** m sports: judge (at the finish). **~scheibe** f target, *fig. a.* butt: **~ des Spottes** laughing-stock.

'**Zielsetzung** f (-; -en) target.

'**zielsicher** adj unerring.

'**Zielsprache** f target language.

'**Zielvorstellung** f objective.

'**zielstrebig** [-ʃtreːbɪç] adj purposeful, single-minded, determined.

'**Zielstrebigkeit** f (-; no pl) determination, single-mindedness.

ziemlich ['tsiːmlɪç] **I** adj **1.** F considerable, quite a: **er wird mit ~er Sicherheit kommen** he's fairly certain to come; **das ist e-e ~e Frechheit** that's rather a cheek. **II** adv **2.** rather, quite-: **~ gut** F pretty good; **~ ausführlich** in some detail; **~ viel** quite a lot (of); **~ viele** quite a few; **ich bin ~ sicher** F I'm pretty sure. **3.** almost, just about, F pretty well: **ich bin so ~ fertig** I've more or less finished; **so ~ alles** practically everything; **es ist so ~ dasselbe** F it's pretty much the same thing.

Zierde ['tsiːrdə] f (-; -n) **1.** (**zur ~** for) decoration. **2.** *fig.* credit (*gen* or **für** to).

zieren ['tsiːrən] (h) **I** v/t adorn, decorate. **II** v/refl **~ sich** make a fuss, *woman*: play coy; **er zierte sich nicht lange** he didn't need much pressing; **komm, zier dich nicht!** come on!

'**Zierfisch** m ornamental fish.

'**Ziergarten** m ornamental garden.

'**Zierleiste** f border (*a. print.*), ornamental mo(u)lding, *mot.* trim.

'**zierlich** adj **1.** delicate, dainty. **2.** graceful, gracile, *woman: a.* petite. '**Zierlichkeit** f (-; no pl) delicateness, daintiness.

'**Zierpflanze** f ornamental plant.

Ziffer ['tsɪfər] f (-; -n) **1.** a) figure, number, b) digit: **in ~n** in figures. **2.** ♈ subparagraph, *in contract etc*: item.

'**Zifferblatt** n dial, face.

zig [tsɪç] adj F umpteen.

Zigarette [tsiga'rɛtə] f (-; -n) cigarette, *Am. a.* cigaret.

Ziga'retten|anzünder m mot. cigarette lighter. **~auto,mat** m cigarette machine. **~e,tui** n cigarette case. **~marke** f brand of cigarettes. **~packung** f cigarette packet (*Am.* pack). **~pause** f (**e-e ~ machen** have a) smoke. **~raucher** m cigarette smoker. **~schachtel** f cigarette packet (*Am.* pack). **~spitze** f cigarette holder. **~stummel** m cigarette end, stub, butt.

Zigarillo [tsiga'rɪlo] m (-s; -s) cigarillo.

Zigarre [tsi'garə] f (-; -n) cigar.

Zi'garrenabschneider m cigar cutter.

Zi'garrenstummel m cigar end, butt.

Zigeuner [tsi'gɔʏnər] m (-s; -), **Zi'geunerin** f (-; -nen) gypsy, *Br. a.* gipsy.

Zi'geunerleben n *fig.* gypsy life.

zigst [tsɪçst] adj F umpteenth.

Zikade [tsi'kaːdə] f (-; -n) zo. cicada.

Zimmer ['tsɪmər] n (-s; -) room. **~an,tenne** f indoor aerial (*Am.* antenna). **~einrichtung** f **1.** furnishing, interior (decoration). **2.** furniture.

'**Zimmerhandwerk** n carpentry.

...zimm(e)rig [-tsɪm(ə)rɪç] ...-roomed.

'**Zimmer|kellner** m room waiter. **~lautstärke** f household noise level: **das Radio auf ~ stellen** turn one's radio down to moderate volume. **~mädchen** n chambermaid.

'**Zimmermann** m (-[e]s; -leute) carpenter. '**zimmern** v/t (h) carpenter (*a.* v/i), *a.* build (of wood), *fig.* shape.

'Zimmer|nachweis *m* accommodation office. **~pflanze** *f* indoor plant. **~reser,vierung** *f* room reservation(s). **~schlüssel** *m* room key. **~service** *m* room service. **~suche** *f* (**auf ~ sein**) be room-hunting. **~tempera,tur** *f* room temperature. **~the,ater** *n* small theat/re (*Am.* -er). **~vermittlung** *f* → **Zimmernachweis**.

zimperlich ['tsɪmpərlɪç] *adj* a) soft, oversensitive, b) squeamish, c) prim, prissy: **sei nicht so ~!** don't be a softie!; **F nicht gerade ~, wenig ~** none too gently, not exactly scrupulous (*in one's methods*).

'Zimperlichkeit *f* (-; *no pl*) a) softness, b) squeamishness, c) primness.

Zimt [tsɪmt] *m* (-[e]s; -e) **1.** cinnamon. **2.** F *contp.* (**red k-n** ~ don't talk) rubbish: **der ganze ~** the whole business.

Zink [tsɪŋk] *n* (-[e]s; *no pl*) zinc. **~blech** *n* a) sheet zinc, b) zinc plate.

Zinke ['tsɪŋkə] *f* (-; -n) **1.** prong. **2.** tooth (*of comb*). 'zinken *v/t* (h) mark (*cards*). 'Zinken *m* (-s; -) → **Zinke**. **2.** F conk.

Zinn [tsɪn] *n* (-[e]s; *no pl*) **1.** tin. **2.** pewter.

Zinne ['tsɪnə] *f* (-; -n) △ pinnacle, *pl* battlement.

'Zinngeschirr *n* pewter.

Zinnober [tsɪ'noːbər] *m* (-s; -) **1.** *min.* cinnabar. **2.** *no pl* F a) rubbish, b) fuss.

zin'noberrot *adj* vermilion.

Zins [tsɪns] *m* (-es; -en) interest: **~en tragen** (*or* **bringen**) bear interest; **ohne ~en** ex interest; **zu 4% ~en** at 4% interest; → **Zinseszins**.

'zinsbringend *adj* interest-bearing.

'Zinseinnahme *f* income from interest.

'Zinsen|dienst ['tsɪnzən-] *m* interest payment. **~last** *f* burden of interest.

'Zinsertrag *m* interest yield.

'Zinseszins *m* compound interest.

'Zinsfuß *m* (-es; -e) interest rate.

'zinsgünstig *adj* low-interest.

'Zinsgutschrift *f* interest credited.

'Zinsku,pon *m* interest coupon.

'zinslos *adj* interest-free.

'Zins|poli,tik *f* interest rate policy. **~rechnung** *f* **1.** calculation of interest. **2.** interest account. **~satz** *m* interest rate. **~senkung** *f* lowering of interest rates. **~verlust** *m* loss of interest.

Zionismus [tsɪo'nɪsmʊs] *m* (-; *no pl*) Zionism. **Zionist** [-'nɪst] *m* (-en; -en), **zio'nistisch** *adj* Zionist.

Zipfel ['tsɪpfəl] *m* (-s; -) a) tip, point, b) end (*of sausage etc*), c) corner.

'Zipfelmütze *f* pointed cap.

Zirbeldrüse ['tsɪrbəl-] *f* pineal gland.

zirka ['tsɪrka] *adv* about, approximately.

'Zirkapreis *m* ♥ approximate price.

Zirkel ['tsɪrkəl] *m* (-s; -) **1.** (**ein ~** a pair of) compasses, dividers. **2.** *a. fig.* circle.

'Zirkelkasten *m* compasses case.

'Zirkelschluß *m philos.* vicious circle.

'Zirkeltraining *n sports*: circuit training.

Zirkulation [tsɪrkula'tsɪoːn] *f* (-; -en) circulation. **zirkulieren** [tsɪrku'liːrən] *v/i* (sn) (*a.* **~ lassen**) circulate.

Zirkumflex ['tsɪrkʊm'flɛks] *m* (-es; -e) *ling.* circumflex (accent).

Zirkus ['tsɪrkʊs] *m* (-; -se) **1.** circus. **2.** *no pl* F fuss, carry-on.

zirpen ['tsɪrpən] *v/t, v/i* (h) chirp (*a. fig.*).

'Zirpen *n* (-s) chirp(ing).

Zirrhose [tsɪ'roːzə] *f* (-; -n) ✿ cirrhosis.

Zirrus ['tsɪrʊs] *m* (-; -, Zirren), **~wolke** *f* cirrus (cloud).

zischeln ['tsɪʃəln] *v/t, v/i* (h) hiss.

zischen ['tsɪʃən] (h) **I** *v/i* **1.** hiss (*a. fig.*), *fat:* sizzle, *bullet etc:* whiz(z). **II** *v/t* **2.** hiss (*words*). **3.** F **e-n ~** knock one back. 'Zischen *n* (-s) **1.** hiss(ing), sizzle. **2.** hisses. 'Zischlaut *m ling.* sibilant.

ziselieren [tsizə'liːrən] *v/t* (h) chase.

Zisterne [tsɪs'tɛrnə] *f* (-; -n) cistern.

Zitadelle [tsita'dɛlə] *f* (-; -n) citadel.

Zitat [tsi'taːt] *n* (-[e]s; -e) quotation.

Zither ['tsɪtər] *f* (-; -n) ♪ zither.

zitieren [tsi'tiːrən] *v/t* **1.** cite, quote: **falsch ~** misquote. **2.** summon, cite.

Zitronat [tsitro'naːt] *n* (-[e]s; -e) candied lemon peel.

Zitrone [tsi'troːnə] *f* (-; -n) lemon.

Zi'tronen|falter *m zo.* brimstone. **~li,mo,nade** *f* lemonade, *Am.* lemon soda. **~saft** *m* lemon juice. **~säure** *f* citric acid. **~schale** *f* lemon peel.

Zitrusfrucht ['tsiːtrʊs-] *f* citrus fruit.

'zitt(e)rig *adj* shaky.

zittern ['tsɪtərn] *v/i* (h) (**vor** with) tremble, shake, quiver: **vor j-m ~** be terrified of s.o.; **~ um** tremble for; **mir ~ die Knie** my knees are shaking.

'Zittern *n* (-s) tremble, shake, vibration: *fig.* **mit ~ und Zagen** trembling; F **das große ~ kriegen** get the willies.

'Zitterpappel *f* ✿ (quaking) aspen.

Zitze ['tsɪtsə] *f* (-; -n) teat, dug.

Zivi ['tsi:vi] *m* (-s; -s) F → **Zivildienstleistende**.

zivil [tsi'vi:l] *adj* **1.** a) civil, b) civilian. **2.** *fig.* a) decent, b) reasonable (*price etc*).

Zi'vil *n* (-s; *no pl*) civilian dress, *a.* plain clothes: **in ~** F *a.* in mufti; **Kriminalbeamter in ~** plain-clothes policeman. **~beruf** *m* civilian profession (*or* trade). **~bevölkerung** *f* civilian population, the civilians. **~cou,rage** *f* (-; *no pl*) courage of one's convictions.

Zi'vildienst *m* alternative (*or* community) service (*in lieu of military service*). **~leistende** *m* (-n; -n) conscientious objector doing community service.

Zi'vil|ehe *f* civil marriage. **~fahnder** *m* plain-clothes policeman. **~fahndung** *f* plain-clothes search. **~gericht** *n* civil court.

Zivilisation [tsiviliza'tsi̯o:n] *f* (-; -en) civilization.

zivilisieren [tsivili'zi:rən] *v/t* (h) civilize.

Zivilist [tsivi'lɪst] *m* (-en; -en) civilian.

Zi'vil|kammer *f* ⚖ civil division. **~klage** *f* ⚖ civil suit. **~kleidung** *f* → **Zivil**. **~luftfahrt** *f* civil aviation. **~per,son** *f* civilian. **~pro,zeß** *m* ⚖ civil action. **~pro,zeßordnung** *f* code of civil procedure. **~recht** *n* (-[e]s; *no pl*) civil law. **2rechtlich** *adj* (*adv* under) civil law. **~schutz** *m* civil defen/ce (*Am.* -se). **~stand** *m* Swiss civil (*or* marital) status. **~trauung** *f* civil marriage.

Zloty ['zloti, 'slɔti] *m* (-s; -s) zloty.

Zobel ['tso:bəl] *m* (-s; -) **1.** *zo.* sable. **2.** *a.* **'Zobelfell** *n* sable-skin. **3.** *a.* **'Zobelpelz** sable (fur).

zocken ['tsɔkən] *v/i* (h) F gamble.

'Zocker *m* (-s; -) F gambler.

Zoff [tsɔf] *m* (-s; *no pl*) F trouble.

zog [tso:k] *pret of* **ziehen**.

'zögerlich *adj* → **zögernd**. **zögern** ['tsø:gərn] *v/i* (h) hesitate, waver: **ohne zu ~** without hesitation; **er zögerte mit der Antwort** he was slow to answer; **sie zögerten mit der Entscheidung** they deferred their decision; **nicht ~ zu inf** lose no time in *ger.* **'Zögern** *n* (-s) hesitation. **'zögernd** *adj* hesitating, slow.

'Zögling ['tsø:klɪŋ] *m* (-s; -e) pupil.

Zölibat [tsøli'ba:t] *n, eccl. m* (-[e]s; *no pl*) celibacy.

Zoll¹ [tsɔl] *m* (-[e]s; -) inch.

Zoll² *m* (-[e]s; ⸚e) **1.** (customs) duty. **2.** customs. **~abfertigung** *f* customs clearance. **~amt** *n* customs office. **~beamte** *m* customs officer. **~behörde** *f* customs authorities. **~bestimmungen** *pl* customs regulations.

'zollen *v/t* (h) **Anerkennung ~** pay tribute (*dat* to); **j-m Beifall ~** applaud s.o.

'Zoll|erklärung *f* customs declaration. **~fahnder** *m* customs investigator. **~fahndung** *f* **1.** customs investigation. **2.** → **~fahndungsstelle** *f* customs investigation office. **~formali,täten** *pl* customs formalities. **2frei** *adj and adv* duty-free. **~freiheit** *f* (-; *no pl*) exemption from duty. **~gebiet** *n* customs territory. **~grenze** *f* customs frontier. **~kon,trolle** *f* customs examination.

Zöllner ['tsœlnər] *m* (-s; -) **1.** customs officer. **2.** *bibl.* publican.

'Zollpa,piere *pl* customs documents.

'zollpflichtig *adj* liable to duty, dutiable.

'Zollschranke *f* customs barrier.

'Zollstock *m* ⚙ folding rule.

'Zoll|ta,rif *m* (customs) tariff. **~uni,on** *f* customs union. **~vergehen** *n* customs offen/ce (*Am.* -se). **~wert** *m* dutiable (*or* customs) value.

Zone ['tso:nə] *f* (-; -n) **1.** zone. **2.** fare stage.

Zoo [tso:] *m* (-s; -s) zoo.

'Zoobesucher(in *f*) *m* visitor to the zoo.

'Zoodi,rektor *m* zoo director.

Zoologe [tsoo'lo:gə] *m* (-n; -n), **Zoo'login** *f* (-; -nen) zoologist.

Zoologie [tsoolo'gi:] *f* (-; *no pl*) zoology.

zoologisch [tsoo'lo:gɪʃ] *adj* zoologic(al): **~er Garten** zoological garden(s).

Zoomobjek,tiv ['zu:m-] *n* zoom lens.

Zopf [tsɔpf] *m* (-[e]s; ⸚e) **1.** plait, pigtail: F **alter ~** antiquated custom. **2.** *gastr.* twist. **~stil** *m art*: late rococo (style).

Zorn [tsɔrn] *m* (-[e]s; *no pl*) anger (**auf** *acc* at), rage, temper, fury: **in ~ geraten** become furious, fly into a rage; (**der**) **~ packte ihn** he was seized with anger.

'Zornausbruch *m* fit of anger.

'zornentbrannt *adj* incensed, furious.

'zornig *adj* (**auf, über** *acc* at) angry, furious, F mad; → *a.* **wütend**.

'Zornröte *f* flush of anger.

Zote ['tso:tə] *f* (-; -n) dirty joke: **~n reißen** talk smut.

Zotte ['tsɔtə] *f* (-; -n) *zo.* tuft (of hair).

Zottel ['tsɔtəl] *f* (-; -n) F **1.** → **Zotte**. **2.**

straggly hair. '**zott(e)lig** *adj* F straggly, unkempt (*hair*). '**zottig** *adj* shaggy.

zu [tsu:] **I** *prep* 1. a) at, b) to, towards: ~ **m-n Füßen** at my feet; ~**m Friseur gehen** go to the hairdresser; **komm ~ mir!** come to me!; **sich ~ j-m setzen** sit with s.o.; ~ **Wasser und ~ Lande** on land and sea; **von Mann ~ Mann** between men. **2.** *time*: at, *occasion*: for: ~ **Ostern** at Easter; ~ **Beginn** at the beginning; **ein Geschenk ~m Geburtstag** a present for his *etc* birthday; → **bis** 1. **3.** for: **Stoff ~m Kleid** material for a dress; *et.* ~**m Essen** s.th. to eat; **der Schlüssel** ~**m Schrank** the key to the cupboard; ~**m Preis von 100 Mark** at a price of 100 marks; **aus Liebe ~ j-m** out of love for s.o. **4.** as: ~**m Vergnügen** for fun; **j-n ~m Freund haben** have s.o. as a friend; **j-n ~m Präsidenten wählen** elect s.o. president. **5.** with: ~**m Essen Wein trinken** drink wine with one's dinner; **ich nehme k-n Zucker ~m Tee** I don't take sugar with (*or* in) my tea; **Lieder ~r Laute** songs to the lute. **6.** ~ **10 DM das Pfund** at ten marks the pound; **sie gewannen 7:5** they won 7 (to) 5; **wir sind ~ dritt** there are three of us; ~**m ersten Mal** for the first time; → **bis** 3. **7.** in(to): **werden** ~ turn into, *person*: a. become; ~ **Asche verbrennen** burn to ashes; **er hat ihn sich ~m Feind gemacht** he made him his enemy. **II** *adv* **8.** too: ~ **sehr** too much, overmuch; ~ **sehr betonen** overemphasize; ~ **dumm!** too bad!, what a nuisance! **9.** to, towards: **er ging dem Ausgang** ~ he went towards the exit. **10.** shut, closed: **(mach die) Tür ~!** shut the door! **11.** F **immer ~!, nur ~!** go on! **III** *conj* **j-n bitten ~ kommen** ask s.o. to come; **ich habe ~ arbeiten** I have work to do; **du bist ~ beneiden** you are to be envied; **nicht ~ gebrauchen** useless; **ohne es ~ wissen** unknowingly. **IV** *adj* F a) closed, shut, b) chock-a-block, c) *fig.* bombed, sloshed.

zu'aller'erst *adv* first of all.
zu'aller'letzt *adv* last of all.
'**zubauen** *v/t* (*sep*, h) **1.** build *area etc* up. **2.** block (*a. view*).
'**Zubehör** [-bəhø:r] *n* (-[e]s; -e) accessories: **mit allem** ~ with all conveniences.
'**Zubehörteil** *n* fitting, accessory.

'**zubeißen** *v/i* (*irr, sep*, -ge-, h, → **beißen**) bite, *dog*: snap.
'**zubekommen** *v/t* (*irr, sep*, h, → **bekommen**) F *et.* ~ get s.th. shut.
Zuber ['tsu:bər] *m* (-s; -) tub.
'**zubereiten** *v/t* (*sep*, h) prepare, make.
'**Zubereitung** *f* (-; -en) preparation.
'**zubilligen** *v/t* (*sep*, h) grant, concede, *a.* ⚖ allow (*j-m et.* s.o. s.th.).
'**zubinden** *v/t* (*irr, sep*, -ge-, h, → **binden**) tie (*or* bind) *s.th.* up.
'**zubleiben** *v/i* (*irr, sep*, -ge-, sn, → **bleiben**) F stay closed, stay shut.
'**zublinzeln** *v/t* (*sep*, h) *j-m* ~ wink at s.o.
'**zubringen** *v/t* (*irr, sep*, -ge-, h, → **bringen**) spend, pass (*time*).
'**Zubringer** *m* (-s; -) → **Zubringerbus, -dienst, -linie, -straße.** ~**bus** *m* feeder bus. ~**dienst** *m* feeder service. ~**linie** *f* feeder line. ~**straße** *f* feeder (road).
Zucchino [tsu'ki:no] *m* (-s; -ni) ⚘ courgette, *esp. Am.* zucchini.
Zucht [tsʊxt] *f* (-; -en) **1.** breeding, rearing, raising, ⚘ cultivation, growing, culture (*of bees, bacteria, etc*). **2.** breed. **3.** *no pl* (*a.* ~ **und Ordnung**) discipline.
'**Zuchtbuch** *n* studbook.
'**Zuchtbulle** *m* breeding bull.
züchten ['tsʏçtən] *v/t* (h) breed (*a. fig.*), *a.* rear, raise (*animals*), *a.* cultivate, grow (*plants*), culture (*bacteria etc*).
'**Züchter** *m* (-s; -) breeder, *a.* grower.
'**Zuchterfolg** *m* breeding success.
'**Zuchthaus** *n* † prison; → *a.* **Gefängnis.**
'**Zuchthengst** *m* stud horse, stallion.
züchtigen ['tsʏçtɪgən] *v/t* (h) punish, flog. '**Züchtigung** *f* (-; -en) (*körperliche* ~ corporal) punishment.
'**zuchtlos** *adj* undisciplined. '**Zuchtlosigkeit** *f* (-; *no pl*) lack of discipline.
'**Zucht|mittel** *n* disciplinary measure. ~**perle** *f* cultured pearl. ~**stier** *m* breeding bull. ~**stute** *f* stock mare. ~**tier** *n* breeding animal, *pl a.* breeding stock.
'**Züchtung** *f* (-; -en) → **Zucht** 1, 2.
'**Zuchtvieh** *n* breeding cattle.
'**Zuchtwahl** *f biol.* selection.
zuckeln ['tsʊkəln] *v/i* (sn) F trundle (*mot. etc* chug) along.
zucken ['tsʊkən] *v/i* (h) **1.** jerk, twitch, move convulsively, wince: → **Achsel, Schulter, Wimper. 2.** *lightning etc*: flash, *flames*: flicker.

zücken ['tsʏkən] v/t (h) draw (*knife etc*), F pull out, produce (*wallet etc*).

Zucker ['tsʊkər] m (-s; -) **1.** sugar. **2.** F ✱ (*er hat ~* he is suffering from) diabetes. **~brot** n F **mit ~ und Peitsche** with a stick and a carrot. **~dose** f sugar bowl. **~erbse** f ♀ sugar pea. **~guß** m icing, frosting: **mit ~ überziehen** ice, frost. **~hut** m sugar loaf.

'zuck(e)rig adj sugary.

'zuckerkrank adj, **'Zuckerkranke** m, f diabetic. **'Zuckerkrankheit** f diabetes.

zuckern ['tsʊkərn] v/t (h) sugar.

'Zucker|rohr n (-[e]s; -e) sugar cane. **~rübe** f sugar beet. ♀**süß** adj (as) sweet as sugar, *fig.* honeyed, sugary. **~watte** f candy floss. **~zange** f sugar tongs.

'Zuckung f (-; -en) a) twitch(ing), jerk, b) convulsion, spasm.

'zudecken v/t (*sep*, h) cover (up): **sich ~** cover o.s. (up); F **j-n mit Arbeit ~** swamp s.o. with work.

zu'dem adv besides, moreover.

'zudrehen v/t (*sep*, h) **1.** turn off. **2.** **j-m den Rücken ~** turn one's back on s.o.

'zudringlich adj obtrusive, F pushy: **e-r Frau gegenüber ~ werden** F make a pass at a woman. **'Zudringlichkeit** f (-; -en) **1.** *no pl* obtrusiveness, F pushiness. **2.** advances, F pass.

'zudrücken v/t (*sep*, h) close, (press) shut: → *Auge* 1.

'zueilen v/i (*sep*, sn) rush up (*auf acc* to).

zuein'ander adv to each other, to one another: **Vertrauen ~ haben** trust each other. **~halten** v/i (*irr*, *sep*, -ge-, h, → *halten*) F stick together.

'zuerkennen v/t (*irr*, *sep*, h, → *erkennen*) (*dat*) award (to), confer (on).

zu'erst adv **1.** first: **wer ~ kommt, mahlt** ~ first come, first served. **2.** first (of all). **3.** at first, at the beginning. **4.** for the first time, first.

'Zufahrt f (-; -en) **1.** access. **2.** → **'Zufahrtsstraße** f access road.

'Zufall m (-[e]s; ⁀e) chance, accident, *a.* coincidence: **durch ~** by chance; **reiner ~** pure chance; **glücklicher ~** lucky coincidence, F fluke; **unglücklicher ~** bit of bad luck; **was für ein ~!** what a coincidence!; **wie es der ~ wollte** as luck would have it; **es ist kein ~, daß** it's no accident that; **et. dem ~ überlassen** leave it to chance.

'zufallen v/i (*irr*, *sep*, -ge-, sn, → *fallen*) **1.** *eyes etc*: close, *door etc*: slam (shut): **mir fallen die Augen zu** I can't keep my eyes open. **2.** **j-m** *inheritance etc*: fall to s.o., *prize etc*: be awarded to s.o., *task etc*: be assigned to s.o.; *fig.* **ihm fällt alles nur so zu** everything comes quite naturally to him.

'zufällig I adj accidental, chance: **~es Zs.-treffen** a) chance encounter, b) coincidence; **jede Ähnlichkeit (mit ...) ist rein ~** any resemblance (to ...) is purely coincidental. **II** adv by chance, accidentally: **er war ~ zu Hause** he happened to be at home; **wir trafen uns ~** we met by chance, F we bumped into each other; **~ stoßen auf** (*acc*) chance (up)on; **rein ~** by sheer chance; **weißt du ~, wo er ist?** do you know by any chance where he is? **'Zufälligkeit** f (-; -en) **1.** *no pl* coincidence, accidentalness. **2.** fortuity, contingency.

'Zufalls|auswahl f statistics: random selection. **~bekanntschaft** f chance acquaintance. **~treffer** m lucky (F fluke) hit, *sports:* a. lucky goal.

'zufassen v/i (*sep*, h) **1.** take hold of it, grasp it. **2.** F give a hand, help.

'zufliegen v/i (*irr*, *sep*, -ge-, sn, → *fliegen*) **1.** F *door etc*: slam (shut). **2.** **~ auf** (*acc*) fly toward(s). **3.** **j-m ~** a) *bird*: fly into s.o.'s home, b) come easily to s.o.

'zufließen v/i (*irr*, *sep*, -ge-, sn, → *fließen*) a. *fig.* flow into.

'Zuflucht f (-; -en) **1.** refuge, shelter: **~ suchen (finden)** seek (find) refuge (*bei* with, *fig.* in). **2.** *fig.* (**m-e letzte ~** my last) resort: **s-e ~ nehmen zu** resort to.

'Zufluchtsort m place of refuge, retreat.

'Zufluß m (-sses; ⁀sse) **1.** influx, inflow. **2.** a) inlet, b) tributary.

'zuflüstern v/t (*sep*, h) whisper (*dat* to).

zufolge [tsu'fɔlgə] prep (*dat*) according to, in accordance with (*his request etc*).

zu'frieden adj (*mit* with) a) content(ed), b) satisfied, pleased: **ein ~es Gesicht machen** look pleased; **~es Lächeln** contented smile; **mit wenig ~** easily satisfied; **sie ist nie ~** there is no pleasing her; *iro.* **bist du nun ~?** are you satisfied now?; **~ lächeln** smile contentedly.

zu'friedengeben: sich ~ (*irr*, *sep*, -ge-, h, → *geben*) content o.s. (*mit* with).

Zu'friedenheit f (-; no pl) contentment, (**zu m-r** etc ~ to my etc) satisfaction.

zu'friedenlassen v/t (irr, sep, -ge-, h, → **lassen**) leave s.o. alone (or in peace).

zu'friedenstellen v/t (sep, h) satisfy: **sie sind schwer zufriedenzustellen** they are hard to please.

zu'friedenstellend adj satisfactory.

'zufrieren v/i (irr, sep, -ge-, sn, → **frieren**) freeze up (or over).

'zufügen v/t (sep, h) **1.** add (dat to). **2.** j-m e-n Schaden ~ harm s.o.; **j-m e-e Niederlage** etc ~ inflict defeat etc on s.o.; **j-m** (**ein**) **Unrecht** ~ wrong s.o.

'Zufuhr f (-; -en) supply, meteor. influx: **die ~ abschneiden** cut off supplies.

'zuführen (sep, h) **I** v/t (dat to) carry, bring, lead, ⚙ feed, supply: **dem Körper Nahrung ~** feed the body; **j-n s-r (gerechten) Strafe ~** punish s.o. (as he deserves), ⚙ **e-r** (acc) a. fig. lead to. **'Zuführung** f (-; -en) **1.** no pl conveyance, feeding, delivery. **2.** ⚡ lead.

Zug¹ [tsu:k] m (-[e]s; ⁓e) (**mit dem ~ fahren** go) by train: **im ~** on the train; **wir brachten sie zum ~** we saw her off at the station; F fig. **im falschen ~ sitzen** be on the wrong track; **der ~ ist abgefahren!** it's too late for that now!

Zug² m (-[e]s; ⁓e) **1.** no pl draw(ing), pull(ing), traction. **2.** ⚙ tension, tensible force. **3.** no pl draught, Am. draft **4.** a) breath, b) gulp, F swig, c) drag, puff: **in 'einem ~** a. fig. in one go; **in den letzten Zügen liegen** be breathing one's last, humor. object: be on its last legs; **et. in vollen Zügen genießen** enjoy s.th. to the full. **5.** chess: move: **wer ist am ~?** who is to move?; ~ **um ~** a) step by step, b) without delay, c) ⚡ concurrently; **er kam nicht zum ~**(e) F he didn't get a look-in. **6.** stroke (of pen etc), a. writing: fig. **in groben Zügen** in broad outline, in the rough. **7.** procession, column, ✗ etc platoon: **endlose Züge von Flüchtlingen** an endless procession of refugees. **8.** passage, migration (of birds), a. flight, movement (of clouds etc). **9.** **im ⁓e** (gen) in the course of; **im besten ⁓e sein** be well under way, person: be going strong. **10.** no pl F **~ bringen in** (acc) bring a class, team, etc up to scratch; **da ist kein ~ drin** it's a slow show, they lack the real drive. **11.**

⚙ flue. **12.** groove, pl rifling. **13.** ped. etc: stream.

Zug³ m (-[e]s; ⁓e) a) feature, b) line, look, c) characteristic, trait, b.s. streak, d) bent (**zu** for): **das war kein schöner ~ von ihr** that wasn't nice of her; **der ~ der Zeit** the trend of the times.

'Zugabe f (-; -n) **1.** extra, bonus. **2.** addition, ⚙ makeweight. **3.** ♩ etc encore.

'Zugang m (-[e]s; ⁓e) **1.** access (a. fig.), gate(way) (a. fig.), approach, access road: **ich finde k-n ~ zur modernen Musik** I'm unable to appreciate modern music. **2.** in library etc: accession, in hospital etc: admission, at university etc: intake.

'zugänglich [-gɛŋliç] adj a. fig. accessible (**für** to), get-at-able, available: **et.** (**der Allgemeinheit**) ~ **machen** open s.th. (to the public); ~ **für** open to arguments etc; **er war für neue Methoden ~** he was quite willing to try out new methods; **sie war k-n Vernunftgründen ~** she wasn't amenable to reason. **'Zugänglichkeit** f (-; no pl) (**für** to) accessibility, fig. a. amenability. **'Zugangsstraße** f access road. **'Zugbrücke** f drawbridge.

'zugeben v/t (irr, sep, -ge-, h, → **geben**) **1.** add (dat to), ⚡ give as an extra, F throw in, ♩ give s.th. as an encore. **2.** admit, confess, a. grant, concede: **zugegeben, er hat recht, aber ...** I grant you he's right but ... **3.** allow.

'zugegebener'maßen adv admittedly.

zu'gegen adj ~ **sein** be present (**bei** at).

'zugehen (irr, sep, -ge-, sn, → **gehen**) **I** v/i **1.** ~ **auf** (acc) go up to, go (or walk) towards, head for; fig. **er geht auf die Achtzig zu** he's getting on for eighty; **dem Ende ~** be drawing to a close; **man muß auf die Leute ~** you have to talk to people (openly). **2.** j-m ~ reach s.o.; **j-m et. ~ lassen** have s.th. sent to s.o. **3.** F walk faster: **geh zu!** get a move on! **4.** F door, suitcase, etc: shut. **5.** → **zulaufen** 4. **II** v/impers **6.** es **geht auf 8 Uhr zu** it's getting on for eight (o'clock); **es geht dem Winter zu** winter is drawing near (or is on its way). **7.** happen, go: **wie geht es zu, daß?** how is it that?, F how come ...?; **bei ihnen geht's vielleicht hektisch zu!** things are pretty hectic with them; → **Ding** 2.

'**Zugehörigkeit** f (-; no pl) (**zu**) membership (in), affiliation (to, with).
'**zugeknöpft** adj F fig. reserved, silent.
Zügel ['tsy:gəl] m (-s; -) rein: fig. **die ~ (fest) in der Hand halten** have things (firmly) under control; **die ~ lockern** loosen the reins; **der Phantasie etc die ~ schießen lassen** give free rein to one's imagination etc.
'**zügellos** adj fig. **1.** unrestrained. **2.** licentious. '**Zügellosigkeit** f (-; no pl) **1.** lack of restraint. **2.** licentiousness.
zügeln ['tsy:gəln] v/t (h) **1.** rein (up). **2.** fig. curb, check, bridle.
'**Zugereiste** m, f (-n; -n) newcomer.
'**Zugeständnis** n (-ses; -se) concession (**an** acc to). '**zugestehen** v/t (irr, sep, h, → **gestehen**) **1.** (dat to) concede, grant. **2.** admit.
'**zugetan** adj (dat) **~ sein** be fond of.
'**Zugewinn** m (-[e]s; -e) gain(s).
'**Zugfeder** f ⊚ tension spring, of watch: main spring.
'**Zugfestigkeit** f (-; no pl) ⊚ tensile strength.
'**Zugführer** m **1.** 🚂 guard, Am. train conductor. **2.** ✗ platoon leader.
'**Zugfunk** m 🚂 train radio.
'**zugießen** v/t (irr, sep, -ge-, h, → **gießen**) add.
zugig ['tsu:gɪç] adj draughty, Am. drafty.
zügig ['tsy:gɪç] adj quick, speedy: **~ vorankommen** make rapid progress.
'**Zugkraft** f **1.** ⊚ tractive (or tensile) force. **2.** fig. attraction, appeal, of person: magnetism. '**zugkräftig** adj fig. powerful, catchy (slogan), crowd-pulling (actor, film, etc), pol. vote-getting (candidate etc): **~ sein** a. have appeal.
zu'gleich adv at the same time.
'**Zugluft** f (-; no pl) draught, Am. draft.
'**Zugma,schine** f mot. tractor.
'**Zugmittel** n fig. draw, attraction.
'**Zugnummer** f fig. draw(ing card).
'**Zugpferd** n fig. draw, thea. etc crowd-puller, pol. a. (great) vote-getter.
'**Zugpflaster** n 🗡 blistering plaster.
'**zugreifen** v/i (irr, sep, -ge-, h, → **greifen**) **1.** → **zufassen. 2.** help o.s.: **greifen Sie bitte zu!** please help yourself! **3.** fig. seize (or jump at) the opportunity: **du brauchst nur zuzugreifen!** you may have it for the asking. **4.** fig. intervene.

'**Zugriff** m (-[e]s; -e) **1.** intervention: **er entzog sich dem ~ der Polizei** he escaped the police. **2.** computer: access.
'**Zugriffszeit** f computer: access time.
zu'grunde adv **1. ~ gehen (an** dat) a) perish (of), die (of), b) be ruined (by). **2.** (dat) **et. ~ legen** base s.th. on. **3.** (dat) **~ liegen** form the basis of, be based on. **4. ~ richten** ruin, wreck.
'**Zugschaffner** m 🚂 train conductor.
'**Zugstück** n thea. etc draw, hit.
'**Zugtele,fon** n telephone on the train.
'**Zugtier** n draught (Am. draft) animal.
'**zugucken** F → **zusehen.**
'**Zugunglück** n train accident.
zu'gunsten prep (gen) in favo(u)r of.
zu'gute adv **1. j-m et. ~ halten** a) give s.o. credit for s.th., b) pardon s.o. s.th.; **sie hielten ihm s-e Unerfahrenheit ~** they made allowances for his lack of experience. **2. ~ kommen** (dat) a) go to, be for the benefit of, b) be of advantage to, stand s.o. in good stead. **3. sich et. ~ halten (or tun) auf** (acc) pride o.s. on.
'**Zugverbindung** f train connection.
'**Zugverkehr** m train services.
'**Zugvogel** m bird of passage.
'**Zugzwang** m fig. **in ~ geraten** be forced to make a move; **unter ~ stehen** be under pressure to act.
'**zuhaben** v/i (irr, sep, -ge-, h, → **haben**) F be closed.
'**zuhalten** (irr, sep, -ge-, h, → **halten**) **I** v/t **1.** keep s.th. closed. **2.** put (or hold) one's hand(s) over (one's eyes, ears): **sich die Nase ~** hold one's nose. **II** v/i **~ auf** (acc) make for, head for.
Zuhälter ['tsu:hɛltər] m (-s; -) pimp.
Zuhälte'rei f (-; no pl) pimping.
Zuhause [tsu'haʊzə] n (-s; no pl) home.
Zu'hilfenahme f unter (ohne) ~ von (or gen) with (without) the aid of.
zu'hinterst adv at the very end.
'**zuhören** v/i (sep, h) listen (dat to).
'**Zuhörer(in** f) m listener: **die Zuhörer** a. the audience. '**Zuhörerraum** m auditorium. '**Zuhörerschaft** f (-; no pl) audience, radio: a. listeners.
'**zujubeln** v/i (sep, h) (dat) cheer.
'**zuklappen** v/t (sep, h), v/i (sn) shut, close s.th. with a snap.
'**zukleben** v/t (sep, h) seal.
'**zuklinken** v/t (sep, h) latch.
'**zuknallen** v/t (sep, h) slam s.th. (shut).

'**zuknöpfen** v/t (sep, h) button (up); → **zugeknöpft.**

'**zukommen** v/i (irr, sep, -ge-, sn, → **kommen**) 1. ~ **auf** (acc) approach, come up to; fig. **auf j-n** ~ be in store for s.o.; adm. **wir werden auf Sie** ~ we'll contact you; **die Sache auf sich** ~ **lassen** let the matter take its course, wait and see. 2. **j-m et.** ~ **lassen** send (or give) s.o. s.th. 3. **j-m** ~ a) befit s.o., b) be due to s.o.

Zukunft ['tsu:kʊnft] f (-; no pl) 1. (**in** ~ in) future: **in naher** (**nächster**) ~ in the near (immediate) future; **in die** ~ **blicken** look ahead; **dieser Beruf hat k-e** ~ there is no future in this profession; F **das hat k-e** ~**!** that has no future; **abwarten, was die** ~ **bringt** wait and see what the future has in store for us. 2. ling. future (tense). '**zukünftig** I adj future, person: a. prospective, father etc -to-be. II adv in (the) future.

'**Zukunfts|aussichten** pl future prospects. **⃝bezogen** I adj forward-looking. II adv with a view to the future. **~forscher** m futurologist. **~forschung** f futurology. **~glaube** m faith in the future. **~mu,sik** f fig. **das ist alles noch** ~ that's all still up in the air. **⃝orien,tiert** adj future-oriented. **~pläne** pl plans for the future. **⃝reich** adj with a great future, promising. **~ro,man** m science fiction novel.

'**zukunft(s)weisend** adj advanced.

'**zulächeln** v/i (sep, h) **j-m** ~ smile at s.o.

'**Zulage** f (-; -n) a) extra pay, additional allowance, b) bonus, c) rise, Am. raise.

'**zulangen** v/i (sep, h) 1. F → **zugreifen** 2. 2. → **zupacken.**

'**zulassen** v/t (irr, sep, -ge-, h, → **lassen**) 1. F leave door etc shut. 2. admit s.o. (**zu** to), adm. license, a. register (car etc): **amtlich** ~ authorize; **staatlich** ~ register; **j-n als Rechtsanwalt** ~ call (or admit) s.o. to the bar. 3. a) allow, permit, b) admit (of) (doubt etc).

'**zulässig** adj admissible, permissible, allowable: **~e** (**Höchst**)**Belastung** maximum permissible (or safe) load; **~e Höchstgeschwindigkeit** speed limit; **das ist** (**nicht**) ~ that is (not) allowed.

'**Zulassung** f (-; -en) 1. no pl admission (**zu** to). 2. mot. a) licen/ce (Am. -se), b) registration.

'**Zulassungs|beschränkung** f restriction on admissions. **~nummer** f mot. registration number. **~pa,piere** pl registration papers. **~prüfung** f entrance exam(ination). **~stelle** f registration office.

'**Zulauf** m (-[e]s; no pl) 1. a) run (of customers etc), b) custom, c) approval: **großen** ~ **haben** be much sought after, film etc: be very popular, draw large crowds. 2. ⃝ supply.

'**zulaufen** v/i (irr, sep, -ge-, sn, → **laufen**) 1. ~ **auf** (acc) run up to. 2. **j-m** ~ a) animal: stray to s.o., b) customers etc: flock to s.o., **zugelaufener Hund** stray dog. 3. flow in: ~ **lassen** add, run hot water etc in. 4. **spitz** ~ taper to a point. 5. F hurry: **lauf zu!** hurry up!

'**zulegen** (sep, h) I v/t 1. F **sich ein Auto** etc ~ buy (or get) o.s. a car etc; fig. **er hat sich e-e Freundin** (**e-n Bart**) **zugelegt** he has got himself a girlfriend (he has grown a beard). 2. add (dat to): → **Zahn** 2. II v/i F a) put on weight, b) increase the pace, c) score gains.

zuleide [tsu'laɪdə] adv **j-m et.** ~ **tun** harm (or hurt) s.o.; → **Fliege** 1.

'**zuleiten** v/t (sep, h) 1. ⃝ feed, supply, a. let in (water). 2. pass s.th. on (dat to).

'**Zuleitung** f (-; -en) 1. ⃝ supply (or feeding) pipe. 2. ⚡ a) feeder, b) lead(-in).

zu'letzt adv 1. last: **du kommst immer** ~ you are alway the last (to arrive); **ganz** ~ last of all. 2. **bis** ~ to the (very) end. 3. finally, in the end. 4. last: **wann haben Sie ihn** ~ **gesehen?** when did you see him last? 5. **nicht** ~ not least.

zu'liebe adv mir etc ~ for my etc sake.

'**Zulieferer** m (-s;-) supplier.

'**Zulieferindu,strie** f ancillary industry.

'**zumachen** (sep, h) F I v/t 1. shut, close (door etc, a. shop etc), stop up (hole), button up, do up (jacket etc), put down (umbrella), seal (envelope etc): **ich habe kein Auge zugemacht** I didn't sleep a wink. II v/i 2. shop etc: a) close, b) close down, mach zu! hurry up!

zu'mal I conj ~ (**da** or **weil**) particularly since. II adv particularly, above all.

'**zumauern** v/t (sep, h) wall up.

'**zumessen** v/t (irr, sep, -ge-, h, → **messen**) 1. (dat to) apportion, allot. 2. attach (importance etc).

zu'mindest adv at least.

zumute [tsu'mu:tə] *adv* **wie ist dir ~?** how do you feel?; **mir ist jämmerlich ~** I feel miserable; **mir ist nicht nach Essen ~** I don't feel like eating; **mir ist bei dieser Sache gar nicht wohl ~** I don't feel at all happy about it.

zumuten ['tsu:mu:tən] *v/t* (*sep*, h) **j-m et. ~** expect s.th. of s.o; **sich zuviel ~** overdo things, F bite off more than one can chew.

'Zumutung *f* (-; -en) a) unreasonable demand, b) cheek: **das ist e-e ~!** that's asking a bit much!, *a.* what a nerve!

zu'nächst *adv* **1.** first (of all), above all. **2.** to begin with, in the first place. **3.** for the present, for the time being.

'zunageln *v/t* (*sep*, h) nail up.

'zunähen *v/t* (*sep*, h) sew up.

'Zunahme ['tsu:na:mə] *f* (-; -n) increase (*gen or* **an** *dat* in).

'Zuname *m* surname, last name.

'Zündeinstellung *f mot.* ignition timing.

'zünden ['tsyndən] (h) **I** *v/t* **1.** *mot.* ignite. **2.** detonate. **3.** fire (*rocket etc*) **II** *v/i* **4.** catch fire. **5.** ⚡, *mot.* ignite, fire. **6.** *fig.* arouse enthusiasm, *idea etc:* catch on.

'zündend *adj fig.* rousing (*speech*).

Zunder ['tsundər] *m* (-s; -) (*brennen wie* **~** burn like) tinder: F *fig.* **j-m ~ geben** give s.o. hell.

'Zünder *m* (-s; -) ⚙ fuse, *Am.* fuze, ⚡ igniter.

'Zünd|funke *m mot.* (ignition) spark. **~holz** *n*, **~hölzchen** *n* match. **~kabel** *n mot.* ignition cable. **~kerze** *f mot.* spark(ing) plug. **~punkt** *m* 🔥 ignition point. **~satz** *m* primer. **~schloß** *n mot.* ignition lock. **~schlüssel** *m mot.* ignition key. **~schnur** *f* fuse, *a.* slow match wick. **~spule** *f mot.* ignition coil. **~stoff** *m* (-[e]s; *no pl*) *fig.* dynamite.

'Zündung *f* (-; -en) *mot.* ignition.

'zunehmen (*irr, sep,* -ge-, h, → **nehmen**) **I** *v/i* **1.** increase, grow: **an Wert ~** increase in value; **an Bedeutung ~** gain in importance. **2.** *moon:* wax. **3.** (**stark** *or* **sehr**) **~** put on (a lot of) weight. **II** *v/t* **sie hat 10 Pfund zugenommen** she has put on (*or* gained) ten pounds.

'zunehmend I *adj* **1.** increasing, growing: **mit ~em Alter** as one gets older; **in ~em Maße** → **II. 2.** waxing: **bei ~em Mond** when the moon is waxing. **II** *adv* increasingly, more and more.

'zuneigen (*sep*, h) **I** *v/i* **der Ansicht ~, daß** be inclined to think that. **II sich dem Ende ~** draw to a close.

'Zuneigung *f* (-; -en) affection (**für, zu** for).

Zunft [tsunft] *f* (-; ⁖e) *hist.* guild.

'zünftig ['tsynftiç] *adj* F proper, good.

Zunge ['tsuŋə] *f* (-; -n) tongue: **mit der ~ anstoßen** (have a) lisp; **sich auf die ~ beißen** bite one's tongue (*fig.* lips); (**j-m**) **die ~ herausstrecken** put one's tongue out (at s.o.); *fig.* **es lag mir auf der ~** I had it on the tip of my tongue; **sie hat e-e lose** (**scharfe**) **~** she has a loose (sharp) tongue; → **zergehen**.

züngeln ['tsyŋəln] *v/i* (h) *snake:* dart its tongue, *flames:* lick.

'Zungen|belag *m* ⚕ coat(ing) of the tongue. **~brecher** *m* F tongue twister. **⸺fertig** *adj* glib. **~kuß** *m* French (*or* deep) kiss. **~laut** *m* lingual (sound). **~spitze** *f* tip of the tongue.

'Zünglein ['tsyŋlaɪn] *n fig.* **das ~ an der Waage sein** tip the scales.

zunichte [tsu'nɪçtə] *adv* **~ machen** ruin; **~ werden** come to nothing.

'zunicken *v/i* (*sep*, h) nod (*dat* to): **j-m freundlich ~** give s.o. a friendly nod.

zunutze [tsu'nʊtsə] *adv* **sich et. ~ machen** make (good) use of s.th., *a. b.s.* take advantage of s.th.

zu'oberst *adv* (right) at the top.

'zuordnen *v/t* (*sep*, h) (*dat*) assign (to) (*a.* ♈), class (with).

'zupacken *v/i* (*sep*, h) work hard.

zupfen ['tsupfən] (h) **I** *v/t* pull, pick, *a.* ♪ pluck: **j-n am Ärmel ~** tug at s.o.'s sleeve. **II** *v/i* **~ an** (*dat*) pull at, tug at.

'Zupfinstru,ment *n* plucked instrument.

zuprosten ['tsu:pro:stən] *v/i* (*sep*, h) raise one's glass (*dat* to).

'zuraten *v/i* (*irr, sep,* -ge-, h, → **raten**) **j-m ~, et. zu tun** advise s.o. to do s.th.; **auf mein** *etc* **Zuraten** on my *etc* advice.

'zurechnen *v/t* (*sep*, h) **1.** → **zuordnen. 2.** add (*dat* to).

'zurechnungsfähig *adj* sane, of sound mind, ⚖ responsible. **'Zurechnungsfähigkeit** *f* (-; *no pl*) ⚖ (**verminderte ~** diminished) responsibility.

zu'rechtbasteln *v/t* (*sep*, h) rig up.

zu'rechtbiegen *v/t* (*irr, sep,* -ge-, h, → **biegen**) **1.** bend *s.th.* into shape. **2.** F *fig.* straighten *s.o., s.th.* out.

zu'rechtfinden: sich ~ (*irr, sep, -ge-, h, → **finden***) find one's way (around), *fig.* cope, manage: **findest du dich darin zurecht?** can you make sense of it all?

zu'rechtkommen *v/i* (*irr, sep, -ge-, sn, → **kommen***) **1.** arrive in time. **2.** (*mit* with) manage, cope: *mit j-m* (**gut**) **~** get on (well) with s.o.

zu'rechtlegen *v/t* (*sep, h*) **1.** lay *s.th.* ready, arrange. **2.** *fig. sich et.* **~** work (*or* figure) out, have *excuse etc* ready.

zu'rechtmachen (*sep, h*) F **I** *v/t* get *s.th.* ready, prepare, make, *Am.* F *a.* fix (*salad etc*), make up (*bed*). **II** *sich* **~** a) do o.s. up, b) make up.

zu'rechtrücken *v/t* (*sep, h*) adjust, *a. fig.* put *s.th.* straight.

zu'rechtstutzen *v/t* (*sep, h*) *a. fig.* trim.

zu'rechtweisen *v/t* (*irr, sep, -ge-, h, → weisen*) rebuke, reprimand. **Zu'recht·weisung** *f* (-; -en) rebuke, reprimand.

'**zureden** *v/i* (*sep, h*) *j-m* **~**(, *et. zu tun*) encourage (*or* persuade, urge) s.o. (to do s.th.); *auf ihr etc* **Zureden** upon her *etc* encouragement: *alles Zureden war umsonst* all persuasion was in vain.

'**zureiten** (*irr, sep, -ge-, → reiten*) **I** *v/t* (h) break in (*horse*). **II** *v/i* (sn) **~** *auf* (*acc*) ride up to.

'**zurichten** *v/t* (*sep, h*) **1.** ⊕ a) finish, b) shape. **2.** *print.* make ready. **3.** *übel* **~** injure (*or* persuade, urge) s.o. (to do s.th.); **zurichten** *v/t* injure (*s.o., s.th.*).

'**zuriegeln** *v/t* (*sep, h*) bolt.

'**zürnen** ['tsʏrnən] *v/i* (*h*) *j-m* **~** be angry with s.o.

Zur'schaustellung *f* (-; -en) exhibition, display, *fig. a.* parading.

zurück [tsu'rʏk] *adv* back: **~** *sein* a) be (*or* have come) back, b) F lag behind (*a. ped.*), *in one's development*: be retarded, be backward; F *mit s-r Arbeit* **~** *sein* be behind (*or* in arrears) with one's work; *sports*: **5 Punkte** (**3 Meter** *etc*) **~** *liegen* be five points down (be three metres *etc*) behind.

Zu'rück *n* **es gibt kein** **~** (**mehr**) there's no turning back (now).

zu'rück|bekommen *v/t* (*irr, sep, h, → bekommen*) get *s.th.* back. **~beordern** *v/t* (*sep, h*) order *s.o.* back. **~beugen** *v/t* (*a. sich* **~**) (*sep, h*) bend back. **~bilden: sich** **~** (*sep, h*) recede, *biol.* regress. **~bleiben** *v/i* (*irr, sep, -ge-, sn, → bleiben*) **1.** stay (*or* be left) behind. **2.** be

left. **3.** lag behind (*a. ped.*), *sports: a.* drop back, *in one's development*: be retarded: *hinter den Erwartungen* **~** fall short of expectations. **~blicken** *v/i* (*sep, h*) look back (*auf acc* at, *fig.* on). **~bringen** *v/t* (*irr, sep, -ge-, h, → bringen*) bring (*or* take) *s.o., s.th.* back, return: *j-n ins Leben* **~** bring s.o. back to life. **~da·tieren** *v/t* (*sep, h*) backdate. **~denken** *v/i* (*irr, sep, -ge-, h, → denken*) (*an acc*) think back (to), recall (*s.o., s.th.*). **~drängen** *v/t* (*sep, h*) **1.** push *s.o.* back. **2.** *fig.* repress. **~drehen** *v/t* (*sep, h*) turn (*or* put) back. **~dürfen** *v/i* (*irr, sep, -ge-, h, → dürfen*) be allowed back. **~eilen** *v/i* (*sep, h*) hurry back. **~erobern** *v/t* (*sep, h*) recapture, *fig.* win back. **~erstatten** *v/t* (*sep, h*) refund, reimburse. **~erwarten** *v/t* (*sep, h*) expect *s.o.* back. **~fahren** (*irr, sep, -ge-, → fahren*) **I** *v/i* (sn) **1.** drive (*or* travel, go) back, return. **2.** *fig.* recoil (*vor dat* from). **II** *v/t* (h) drive *s.o., s.th.* back. **~fallen** *v/i* (*irr, sep, -ge-, sn, → fallen*) **1.** fall back. **2.** fall behind (*a. ped.*), *sports: a.* drop back (*auf den dritten Platz* to third place). **3.** **~** *in* (*acc*) relapse (*or* fall back) into. **4.** *fig.* **~** *auf* (*acc*) reflect on. **~finden** *v/i* (*irr, sep, -ge-, h, → finden*) find one's way back (*zu* to). **~fließen** *v/i* (*irr, sep, -ge-, sn, → fließen*) flow back. **~fordern** *v/t* (*sep, h*) reclaim, demand *s.th.* back. **~führen** *v/t* (*sep, h*) **1.** lead *s.o.* back: (*in die Heimat*) **~** repatriate. **2.** *fig.* (*auf acc* to) reduce, trace *s.th.* (back), attribute. **~geben** *v/t* (*irr, sep, -ge-, h, → geben*) **1.** give *s.th.* back, return. **2.** *sports:* pass the *ball* back.

zu'rückgeblieben *adj fig.* retarded, backward.

zu'rückgehen *v/i* (*irr, sep, -ge-, sn, → gehen*) **1.** go back, return, retreat: *fig. et.* **~** *lassen* send s.th. back, return s.th.; *bis ins 19. Jh.* **~** go (*or* date) back to the 19th century. **2.** *fig.* go down (*a.* 🗡), fall of, decrease: *das Geschäft geht zurück* business is falling off. **3.** *fig.* **~** *auf* (*acc*) go back to, have its origin in.

zu'rückgezogen *adj* retired, secluded: **~** *leben* lead a secluded life.

zu'rückgreifen *v/i* (*irr, sep, -ge-, h, → greifen*) **~** *auf* (*acc*) fall back on.

zu'rückhalten (*irr, sep, -ge-, h, → halten*) **I** *v/t* **1.** hold *s.o., s.th.* back, withhold, *a.* suppress (*tears etc*). **II sich ~ 2.** restrain o.s.; **sich ~ mit** go easy on (*drinks etc*). **3.** be reserved, keep (*o.s.*) to o.s., *buyer:* hold back: **sich sehr ~** keep very much in the background. **III** *v/i ~ mit* keep back; **mit s-r Meinung ~** reserve judg(e)ment.

zu'rückhaltend *adj* a) reserved (*a.* ✝), b) guarded, cautious, c) reticent, d) unobtrusive: **~ sein mit** be sparing in (or with) *one's praise etc*; **er reagierte sehr ~** his reaction was very cool.

Zu'rückhaltung *f* (-; *no pl*) *fig.* a) reserve, b) caution, discretion.

zu'rück|holen *v/t* fetch *s.o.*, *s.th.* back. **~kehren** *v/i* (*sep*, sn) come back, return. **~kommen** *v/i* (*irr*, *sep*, -ge-, sn, → *kommen*) **1.** come back, return. **2. ~ auf** (*acc*) come back to, refer to (*letter etc*); **auf j-s Angebot ~** take s.o. up on his offer. **~können** *v/i* (*irr*, *sep*, -ge-, h, → *können*) F be able to go back: *fig.* **jetzt kann ich nicht mehr zurück!** I can't go back on my word (*or decision etc*) now. **~lassen** *v/t* (*irr*, *sep*, -ge-, h, → *lassen*) **1.** leave *s.o.*, *s.th.* behind. **2.** F allow *s.o.* back. **~laufen** *v/i* (*irr*, *sep*, -ge-, sn, → *laufen*) run back. **~legen** (*sep*, h) **I** *v/t* **1. et. (an s-n Platz) ~** put s.th. back (in its place). **2.** a) put *s.th.* aside, b) save, put by, lay aside (*money*): **können Sie mir den Mantel bis morgen ~?** would you keep the coat for me till tomorrow? **3.** cover, *a.* walk (*distance*): **zurückgelegte Strecke** distance covered, *mot. a.* mileage. **II sich ~** lie back. **~lehnen** *v/t* (*a. sich ~*) (*sep*, h) lean back. **~liegen** *v/i* (*irr*, *sep*, -ge-, h, → *liegen*) *das liegt zwei Jahre zurück* that was two years ago. **~melden: sich ~** (*sep*, h) report back (*bei* to). **~müssen** *v/i* (*irr*, *sep*, -ge-, h, → *müssen*) F have to go back.

Zu'rücknahme [-na:mə] *f* (-; *no pl*) taking back, ⚖ *a.* withdrawal, retraction.

zu'rück|nehmen *v/t* (*irr*, *sep*, -ge-, h, → *nehmen*) take *s.th.* back, withdraw (*troops*, ⚖ *action*), revoke (*statement*), cancel (*offer etc*). **~prallen** *v/i* (*sep*, sn) **1.** rebound. **2.** *fig.* (*vor dat* from) recoil, start back. **~rechnen** *v/i* (*sep*, h) reckon back. **~reichen** (*sep*, h) **I** *v/t* hand *s.th.* back, return. **II** *v/i ~ bis* go (or date) back to. **~reisen** *v/i* (*sep*, sn) trav-

el back, return. **~rufen** (*irr*, *sep*, -ge-, h, → *rufen*) **I** *v/t* call *s.o.* back (*a. teleph.*), recall (*a. defective cars etc*): **ins Gedächtnis ~** recall. **II** *v/i teleph.* call back. **~schalten** *v/i* (*sep*, h) change (*Am.* shift) down. **~scheuen** *v/i* (*sep*, h) shrink (back) (*vor dat* from): *fig.* **er scheut vor nichts zurück** he sticks at nothing. **~schicken** *v/t* (*sep*, h) send *s.o.*, *s.th.* back, return. **~schlagen** (*irr*, *sep*, -ge-, h, → *schlagen*) **I** *v/t* **1.** hit *s.o.* back. **2.** repulse, beat off (*attack*, *enemy*). **3.** fold back (*cover etc*), turn down (*collar*). **4.** return (*ball*). **II** *v/i* **5.** hit back. **6.** *flames:* flare back. **~schrauben** *v/t* (*sep*, h) F *fig.* cut down, reduce, lower (*expectations etc*). **~schrecken** *v/i* (*sep*, h) **1.** (*vor dat* from) recoil, start back: *fig.* **er schreckt vor nichts zurück** he sticks at nothing. **~sehnen: sich ~** (*sep*, h) long to be back.

zu'rücksetzen (*sep*, h) **I** *v/t* **1.** put *s.th.* back, back (up) (*car*). **2.** *fig.* **j-n ~** treat s.o. unfairly, slight s.o. **II** *v/i mot.* back (up). **Zu'rücksetzung** *f* (-; -en) *fig.* unfair treatment, slight.

zu'rück|spielen *v/t*, *v/i* (*sep*, h) pass (the ball) back. **~springen** *v/i* (*irr*, *sep*, -ge-, sn, → *springen*) **1.** jump back. **2.** △ recess. **~spulen** *v/t*, *v/i* (*sep*, h) rewind. **~stecken** (*sep*, h) **I** *v/t* put *s.th.* back. **II** *v/i* F *fig.* come down a peg. **~stehen** *v/i* (*irr*, *sep*, -ge-, h, → *stehen*) **1.** stand back. **2.** *fig.* a) take second place (*hinter j-m* behind s.o.), b) stand down (or aside). **~stellen** *v/t* (*sep*, h) **1.** put *s.th.* back. **2.** ✕ defer. **3.** postpone, defer. **4.** put *s.th.* aside (or last). **~stoßen** (*irr*, *sep*, -ge-, h, → *stoßen*) **I** *v/t* push *s.o.*, *s.th.* back. **II** *v/i mot.* back (up). **~stufen** *v/t* (*sep*, h) downgrade. **~treiben** *v/t* (*irr*, *sep*, -ge-, h, → *treiben*) drive *s.o.*, *s.th.* back. **~treten** *v/i* (*irr*, *sep*, -ge-, sn, → *treten*) **1.** a) step (or stand) back, b) recede. **2.** *government etc:* resign, step down: **von s-m Posten ~** resign one's post; **~ von** withdraw from, back out of (*a deal etc*). **3.** *fig.* be of secondary importance (**gegenüber** in comparison with). **~verfolgen** *v/t* (*sep*, h) *fig.* trace *s.th.* back (**zu** to). **~versetzen** *v/t* (*sep*, h) **1.** move *pupil* down, transfer *official* back. **2.** *fig.* take *s.o.* back (**in** *acc* to): **wir fühlten uns ins Mittelalter zurück-**

versetzt we felt to have stepped back into the Middle Ages. **~weichen** *v/i* (*irr, sep, -ge-, sn, → weichen*) **1.** step back, ✗ fall back. **2.** *fig.* **~ vor** (*dat*) yield to, *a.* shrink back from.

zu'rückweisen *v/t* (*irr, sep, -ge-, h, → weisen*) **1.** refuse, reject, repudiate (*accusation etc*). **2.** *j-n* ~ turn s.o. back, refuse s.o. entry. **Zu'rückweisung** *f* (-; -en) refusal, rejection.

zu'rück|werfen *v/t* (*irr, sep, -ge-, h, → werfen*) **1.** throw *s.o., s.th.* back, *a.* reflect (*light*), *a.* reverberate (*sound*). **2.** *fig.* set *s.o.* back *in one's development, work, etc* (**um 10 Jahre** [by] ten years). **~wollen** *v/i* (*irr, sep, -ge-, h, → wollen*) F want to go back. **~zahlen** *v/t* (*sep, h*) *a. fig.* pay back, repay. **~ziehen** (*irr, sep, -ge-, → ziehen*) **I** *v/t* (h) pull (*or* draw) *s.o., s.th.* back, ✗ *or fig.* withdraw. **II** *v/i* (h) (*aus, von* from) retire, withdraw, ✗ *a.* retreat; **sich ~ von** *a.* give up (*activity etc*); **sich von j-m** dissociate o.s. from s.o.; **sich zur Beratung ~** retire for deliberation. **III** *v/i* (sn) move back. **~zucken** *v/i* (*sep, sn*) flinch (**vor** *dat at*).

'Zuruf *m* (-[e]s; -e) a) shout, b) cheer: **durch ~** by acclamation.

'zurufen *v/t* (*irr, sep, -ge-, h, → rufen*) *j-m et.* ~ shout s.th. to s.o.

Zusage ['tsuːzaːgə] *f* (-; -n) **1.** promise, word. **2.** acceptance (*of invitation*). **3.** assent, consent. **'zusagen** (*sep, h*) **I** *v/t* **1.** promise (**sein Kommen** to come). **2.** F *j-m et. auf den Kopf* ~ tell s.o. s.th. to his face. **II** *v/i* **3.** accept an invitation, promise to come. **4.** agree. **5.** *j-m* ~ a) agree with s.o., b) be to s.o.'s liking.

zusammen [tsuˈzamən] *adv* together, *a.* jointly, *a.* ~ **mit** together (*or* along) with; **alle** ~ all of them; **wir alle** ~ all of us; **alles** ~ all together, (all) in all; **wir haben** ~ **100 Mark** we have one hundred marks between us; **das macht** ~ ... that amounts to (*or* totals) ...

Zu'sammenarbeit *f* (-; *no pl*) cooperation, *a.* collaboration, *a.* teamwork: **in ~ mit** in cooperation with. **zu'sammenarbeiten** *v/i* (*sep, h*) (**mit** with) cooperate, collaborate, work together.

zu'sammen|ballen (*sep, h*) **I** *v/t* form into a ball. **II** **sich ~** mass, gather. **~bauen** *v/t* (*sep, h*) ⚙ assemble. **~bei-**

ßen *v/t* (*irr, sep, -ge-, h, → beißen*) *a. fig.* **die Zähne ~** clench one's teeth. **~bekommen** *v/t* (*irr, sep, h, → bekommen*) get *s.th.* together, raise (*money*). **~binden** *v/t* (*irr, sep, -ge-, h, → binden*) bind (*or* tie) *s.th.* together. **~brauen** *v/t* (*sep, h*) concoct (*a. fig.*): *fig.* **sich ~** be brewing. **~brechen** *v/i* (*irr, sep, -ge-, sn, → brechen*) break down, collapse, *traffic:* come to a standstill. **~bringen** *v/t* (*irr, sep, -ge-, h, → bringen*) **1.** bring (*or* get) *s.o., s.th.* together, raise (*money*). **2.** F *fig.* manage, bring off, remember (*poem*).

Zu'sammenbruch *m* (-[e]s; ⸚e) breakdown, collapse.

zu'sammen|drängen *v/t* (*sep, h*) **1.** (*a.* **sich ~**) crowd (*or* huddle) together. **2.** *fig.* compress, condense. **~drücken** *v/t* (*sep, h*) compress. **~fahren** *v/i* (*irr, sep, -ge-, sn, → fahren*) **1.** → **zusammenstoßen**. **2.** *fig.* (give a) start (**bei** at). **~fallen** *v/i* (*irr, sep, -ge-, sn, → fallen*) **1.** fall in, collapse. **2.** coincide. **3.** waste away. **~falten** *v/t* (*sep, h*) fold up.

zu'sammenfassen *v/t* (*sep, h*) **1.** unite, combine: **in Gruppen** ~ group. **2.** (*a. v/i*) summarize, sum up. **zu'sammenfassend** *adj* summary: **~ kann man sagen** to sum it up it can be said.

Zu'sammenfassung *f* (-; -en) **1.** combination. **2.** summary, résumé, synopsis.

zu'sammen|finden: **sich ~** (*irr, sep, -ge-, h, → finden*) meet. **~fließen** *v/i* (*irr, sep, -ge-, sn, → fließen*) flow together, meet.

Zu'sammenfluß *m* confluence.

zu'sammen|fügen *v/t* (*sep, h*) join (together), ⚙ assemble. **~führen** *v/t* (*sep, h*) bring *persons* together: **wieder ~** reunite. **~gehen** *v/i* (*irr, sep, -ge-, sn, → gehen*) *fig.* (**mit** with) go together, make common cause.

zu'sammengehören *v/i* (*sep, h*) belong together, *a.* be a pair. **zu'sammengehörig** *adj* belonging together, *a.* matching, *fig. a.* related. **Zu'sammengehörigkeit** *f* (-; *no pl*) unity, solidarity. **Zu'sammengehörigkeitsgefühl** *n* (-[e]s; *no pl*) feeling of) solidarity.

zu'sammengesetzt *adj* ⚛ composite, *a.* *ling.* compound: **~ sein aus** be composed of; **~es Wort** compound (word).

zu'sammengewürfelt adj (bunt) ~ motley: **~e Mannschaft** scratch team.
Zu'sammenhalt m (-[e]s; no pl) **1.** a. ☼ cohesion. **2.** fig. a) bond, b) team spirit. **zu'sammenhalten** (irr, sep, -ge-, h, → **halten**) **I** v/i hold (F stick) together. **II** v/t hold s.th., persons together.
Zu'sammenhang m (-[e]s; ~e) a) connection, b) context: **in diesem** ~ in this connection; **et. in** ~ **bringen mit** connect s.th. with; **im** ~ **stehen mit** be connected with; **nicht im** ~ **stehen mit** have no connection with; **et. aus dem** ~ **reißen** divorce s.th. from its context.
zu'sammenhängen v/i (irr, sep, -ge-, h, → **hängen**) fig. be connected (mit with): **wie hängt das zusammen?** how is that linked up? **zu'sammenhängend** adj coherent (thoughts, speech, etc), connected, related (questions etc).
zu'sammenhang(s)los adj incoherent, disconnected.
zu'sammen|hauen v/t (sep, h) **1.** smash s.th. to pieces: F **j-n** ~ beat s.o. up. **2.** F fig. knock s.th. together. **~klappbar** adj folding, collapsible. **~klappen** (sep) **I** v/t (h) fold up, shut (knife etc). **II** v/i (sn) F fig. break down, collapse. **~kleben** v/t, v/i (sep, h) stick together. **~knüllen** v/t (sep, h) crumple up. **~kommen** v/i (irr, sep, -ge-, sn, → **kommen**) **1.** come (or get) together, meet, assemble. **2.** fig. combine: **heute kommt mal wieder alles zuammen!** it never rains but it pours! **3.** accumulate, mount up, money: be collected: F **da kommt ganz schön was zusammen** it comes to quite a lot in the end.
Zu'sammenkunft [-kʊnft] f (-; ~e) get-together, meeting, gathering.
zu'sammenlaufen v/i (irr, sep, -ge-, sn, → **laufen**) **1.** people: gather. **2.** roads etc: meet, converge. **3.** colo(u)rs: run.
zu'sammenleben I v/i (sep, h) live together: **mit j-m** ~ live with s.o. **II** ~ n (-s) living together: **das** ~ **mit ...** life with ...
zu'sammenlegen (sep, h) **I** v/t **1.** fold up. **2.** put things in one place, put persons together (in one room). **3.** ⊹ fuse, combine, centralize. **II** v/i club together (**für ein Geschenk** for a present).
Zu'sammenlegung f (-; -en) ⊹ fusion.
zu'sammen|nehmen (irr, sep, -ge-, h, → **nehmen**) **I** v/t gather (up): **alles**

zusammengenommen all things considered; **ich mußte all m-n Mut** ~ I had to muster up all my courage. **II sich** ~ control o.s., pull o.s. together. **~pakken** v/t (sep, h) pack up. **~passen** (sep, h) **I** v/i harmonize (with each other), colo(u)rs etc: a. go well together, partners: a. be well matched: **sie passen nicht zusammen** they are mismatched. **II** v/t ☼ adjust, match. **~pferchen** v/t (sep, h) herd (fig. a. crowd) together.
Zu'sammenprall m (-[e]s; no pl) a. fig. collision, clash. **zu'sammenprallen** v/i (sep, sn) a. fig. collide, clash.
zu'sammenpressen v/t (sep, h) compress. **~raffen** v/t (sep, h) **1.** gather up. **2.** fig. amass. **~rechnen** v/t (sep, h) add (or sum) s.th. up. **~reimen** v/t (sep, h) fig. sich et. ~ work (or figure) s.th. out, put two and two together. **~reißen:** **sich** ~ (irr, sep, -ge-, h, → **reißen**) F pull o.s. together. **~rollen** (sep, h) **I** v/t roll up. **II sich** ~ coil up, cat etc: curl up.
zu'sammenrotten: sich ~ (sep, h) gang up, form a mob. **Zu'sammenrottung** f (-; -en) a) riot(ing), b) riotous mob, ⚖ riotous assembly.
zu'sammen|rücken (sep) **I** v/t (h) move things together (or closer). **II** v/i (sn) move up, make room. **~rufen** v/t (irr, sep, -ge-, h, → **rufen**) convene, call persons together. **~sacken** v/i (sep, sn) (in sich) ~ slump (down). **~scharen: sich** ~ (sep, h) flock together. **~scharren** v/t (sep, h) scrape s.th. together. **~schiebbar** adj telescopic, sliding. **~schieben** v/t (irr, sep, -ge-, h, → **schieben**) push things together, (a. sich ~ lassen) telescope. **~schlagen** (irr, sep, -ge-, → **schlagen**) **I** v/t (h) **1.** clap (hands), click (heels etc). **2.** F smash s.th. to pieces: **j-n** ~ beat s.o. up. **II** v/i (sn) ~ **über** (dat) close over, a. fig. engulf. **~schließen I** v/t (irr, sep, -ge-, h, → **schließen**) v/t **1.** lock (or chain) together. **2.** unite, ⊹ merge. **II sich** ~ unite, join forces, team up, form an alliance.
Zu'sammenschluß m (-sses; ~sse) **1.** union (a. pol.). ⊹ merger. **2.** alliance.
zu'sammen|schnüren v/t (sep, h) tie s.th. up: **der Anblick schnürte ihr das Herz zusammen** the sight made her heart bleed. **~schrauben** v/t (sep, h) screw (or bolt) s.th. together. **~schrei-**

ben *v/t* (*irr, sep*, -ge-, h, → *schreiben*) **1.** write *s.th.* in one word: *wird das zusammengeschrieben?* is that one word? **2.** *contp.* scribble. **⸝schustern** *v/t* (*sep*, h) F *contp.* cobble together. **⸝schweißen** *v/t* (*sep*, h) *a. fig.* weld.

Zu'sammensein *n* (-s) gathering, meeting, get-together.

zu'sammensetzen (*sep*, h) **I** *v/t* **1.** put *s.th.* together, ☺ *a.* compose, *a.* 🐍, *ling.* compound. **2.** seat *persons* together. **II** *sich ⸝* **3.** sit together. **4.** get together. **5.** *sich ⸝ aus* consist of, be composed of.

Zu'sammensetzung *f* (-; -en) **1.** *no pl* composition (*a. of court, team, etc*), assembly. **2.** 🐍, *ling.* compound.

zu'sammensinken *v/i* (*irr, sep*, -ge-, sn, → *sinken*) collapse: *in sich ⸝* slump (down).

Zu'sammenspiel *n* (-[e]s; *no pl*) *sports*: teamwork.

zu'sammen|stauchen *v/t* (*sep*, h) F *j-n ⸝* haul s.o. over the coals. **⸝stecken** (*sep*, h) **I** *v/t* put *things* together. **II** *v/i* F *immer ⸝* be as thick as thieves. **⸝stehen** *v/i* (*irr, sep*, h, → *stehen*) stand (F *fig.* stick) together.

zu'sammenstellen *v/t* (*sep*, h) **1.** put *things* together. **2.** combine, draw up, compile, make (*catalogue etc*), make up, form (*team etc*), arrange: *in e-r Liste ⸝* list; *ein Menü ⸝* compose a menu. **Zu'sammenstellung** *f* (-; -en) **1.** combination, arrangement. **2.** a) survey, synopsis, b) table, c) list.

Zu'sammenstoß *m* (-[e]s; ⸚e) **1.** *mot.* collision, crash. **2.** F *fig.* clash.

zu'sammen|stoßen *v/i* (*irr, sep*, sn, → *stoßen*) collide (*mit* with): *⸝ mit a.* run (*or* crash) into. **⸝streichen** *v/t* (*irr, sep*, -ge-, h, → *streichen*) F shorten (*text etc*). **⸝strömen** *v/i* (*sep*, sn) *fig.* flock together. **⸝suchen** *v/t* (*sep*, h) gather, collect. **⸝tragen** *v/t* (*irr, sep*, -ge-, h, → *tragen*) collect (*a. fig.*), *fig.* compile (*facts etc*). **⸝treffen** **I** *v/i* (*irr, sep*, sn, → *treffen*) **1.** *mit j-m ⸝* meet s.o. **2.** coincide. **II** ♀ *n* (-s) meeting, *b.s.* encounter. **⸝treiben** *v/t* (*irr, sep*, -ge-, h, → *treiben*) round up. **⸝treten** *v/i* (*irr, sep*, -ge-, sn, → *treten*) meet, *parl.* convene. **⸝trommeln** *v/t* (*sep*, h) F call *persons* together. **⸝tun: sich ⸝** (*irr, sep*, -ge-, h, → *tun*) (*mit* with) team up, join

forces. **⸝wachsen** *v/i* (*irr, sep*, -ge-, sn, → *wachsen*) grow together. **⸝wirken** **I** *v/i* (*sep*, h) *factors etc*: combine. **II** ♀ *n* (-s) combination, interplay. **⸝zählen** *v/t* (*sep*, h) add up, sum up. **⸝ziehen** (*irr, sep*, -ge-, → *ziehen*) **I** *v/t* (h) **1.** pull *s.th.* together, *a.* 🚑 contract. **2.** concentrate, mass (*troops*). **II** *v/i* (sn) **3.** *mit j-m ⸝* move in (together) with s.o., go to live with s.o. **III** *sich ⸝* (h) **4.** contract. **5.** *storm etc*: be brewing.

Zu'sammenziehung *f* (-; -en) **1.** contraction. **2.** ✖ concentration.

zu'sammenzucken *v/i* (*sep*, sn) wince (*bei* at).

'Zusatz *m* (-es; ⸚e) a) addition, *a.* additive, admixture, b) addendum, 🚔 rider. **⸝abkommen** *n* supplementary agreement. **⸝batterie** *f* ⚡ booster battery. **⸝gerät** *n* ☺ attachment.

'zusätzlich [-zetslɪç] **I** *adj* a) additional, extra, b) supplementary, c) auxiliary. **II** *adv* in addition (*zu* to).

'Zusatzversicherung *f* supplementary insurance.

zuschanden [tsu'ʃandən] *adv* ⸝ *machen* ruin, destroy (*a. hopes etc*), thwart (*plans etc*); *⸝ fahren* ruin, smash (up).

'zuschanzen *v/t* (*sep*, h) *j-m et. ⸝* line s.o. up with s.th.

'zuschauen → *zusehen*.

'Zuschauer *m* (-s; -) onlooker, *sports, thea. etc* spectator, *TV* viewer: *die ⸝ a.* the audience. **⸝raum** *m* auditorium. **⸝reakti,on** *f* audience (*TV* viewer) response. **⸝sport** *m* spectator sport.

'zuschicken *v/t* (*sep*, h) *j-m et. ⸝* send (*or* mail, post) s.th. to s.o.

'zuschieben *v/t* (*irr, sep*, -ge-, h, → *schieben*) **1.** close, shut. **2.** *j-m et. ⸝* push s.th. over to s.o.; *j-m die Schuld* (*Verantwortung*) *⸝* put (*or* shift) the blame (responsibility) on s.o.

'zuschießen (*irr, sep*, -ge-, → *schießen*) **I** *v/t* (h) F contribute (*money*). **II** *v/i* (sn) *⸝ auf* (*acc*) rush towards, dart up to.

'Zuschlag *m* (-[e]s; ⸚e) **1.** a) extra charge, b) supplementary fare, c) extra pay. **2.** award: *er erhielt den ⸝* a) *at an auction*: the object went to him, b) 🔨 he was awarded the contract.

'zuschlagen (*irr, sep*, -ge-, h, → *schlagen*) **I** *v/t* **1.** slam *door etc* (shut), shut, close (*book etc*). **2.** *j-m et. ⸝ at an auc-*

tion: knock s.th. down to s.o.; ✝ *der Auftrag wurde ... zugeschlagen ...* was awarded the contract. **II** *v/i* **3.** (sn) slam shut. **4.** strike (*a. fig. enemy, fate, etc*), hit. **5.** F jump at it, grab it: *schwer ~ when shopping etc*: really go to town (*bei* on), *at dinner etc*: tuck in mightily.

'**zuschließen** *v/t* (*irr, sep,* -ge-, h, → *schließen*) lock (up).

'**zuschnallen** *v/t* (*sep,* h) buckle (up).

'**zuschnappen** *v/i(o)* (*sep*) **1.** (sn) snap shut. **2.** h) *dog*: snap.

'**zuschneiden** *v/t* (*irr, sep,* -ge-, h, → *schneiden*) **1.** cut out *dress etc* (*nach e-m Schnittmuster* from a pattern); *fig. zugeschnitten auf* (*acc*) tailored to. **2.** ⊙ cut up, (cut *s.th.* to) size.

'**Zuschneider(in** *f*) *m* cutter.

'**Zuschnitt** *m* (-[e]s; -e) cut, style.

'**zuschnüren** *v/t* (*sep,* h) lace up (*shoes*), tie *s.th.* up; *fig. Angst schnürte ihr die Kehle zu* she was choked with fear.

'**zuschrauben** *v/t* (*sep,* h) screw *s.th.* shut.

'**zuschreiben** *v/t* (*irr, sep,* -ge-, h, → *schreiben*) *j-m et.* ~ ascribe (*or* attribute) s.th. to s.o.; *das Bild wird Dürer zugeschrieben* the painting is ascribed to Dürer; *sie schrieben ihm die Schuld dafür zu* they blamed him for it; *das hast du dir selbst zuzuschreiben!* you've only yourself to blame.

'**Zuschrift** *f* (-; -en) letter, reply (*auf e-e Annonce etc* to an ad *etc*).

zu'schulden *adv sich et. ~ kommen lassen* do (s.th.) wrong.

'**Zuschuß** *m* (-sses; ⸱sse) **1.** contribution. **2.** allowance. **3.** subsidy, grant. *~betrieb* *m* subsidized enterprise.

'**zuschütten** *v/t* (*sep,* h) fill *s.th.* up.

'**zusehen** *v/i* (*irr, sep,* -ge-, h, → *sehen*) **1.** look on, watch: *j-m bei der Arbeit ~* watch s.o. work(ing) (*or* at work). **2.** (*untätig*) ~ sit back and watch. **3.** ~, *daß* see (to it) that.

zusehends ['tsu:ze:ənts] *adv* **1.** visibly. **2.** rapidly.

'**zusein** *v/i* (*irr, sep,* -ge-, sn, → *sein*) F be closed; → *a. zu* IV.

'**zusetzen** (*sep,* h) **I** *v/t* **1.** add (*dat* to). ⸱**2.** *Geld ~ bei* lose money on; F *fig. er hat nichts mehr zuzusetzen* he has used up all his reserves. **II** *v/i* F *j-m ~* a) press s.o. (hard), b) *fig. heat, illness, etc*: take

it out of s.o.; *j-m mit Fragen* (*Bitten*) ~ pester s.o. with questions (requests).

'**zusichern** *v/t* (*sep,* h) *j-m et.* ~ assure s.o. of s.th. '**Zusicherung** *f* (-; -en) assurance.

Zu'spätkommende *m, f* (-n; -n) latecomer.

'**Zuspiel** *n* (-[e]s; *no pl*) *sports*: pass(es).

'**zuspielen** *v/t* (*sep,* h) **1.** *j-m den Ball* ~ pass the ball to s.o. **2.** *j-m et.* ~ play s.th. into s.o.'s hands.

'**zuspitzen: sich** ~ (*sep,* h) *fig.* come to a head.

'**zusprechen** (*irr, sep,* -ge-, h, → *sprechen*) **I** *v/t* **1.** *j-m Trost* ~ comfort s.o.; *j-m Mut* ~ encourage s.o., cheer s.o. up. **2.** *j-m et.* ~ award s.th. to s.o.; ⚖ *die Kinder wurden der Mutter zugesprochen* the mother was granted custody of the children. **II** *v/i* *j-m freundlich etc* ~ speak gently *etc* to s.o.

'**zuspringen** *v/i* (*irr, sep,* -ge-, sn, → *springen*) ~ *auf* (*acc*) rush up at.

'**Zuspruch** *m* (-[e]s; *no pl*) **1.** (words of) comfort. **2.** encouragement. **3.** → *Zulauf* 1.

'**Zustand** *m* (-[e]s; ⸱e) **1.** condition, state (*a. phys.*), F shape: *ihr seelischer* ~ her mental state; *das Haus ist in gutem* ~ the house is in good condition (*or* repair); *in betrunkenem* ~ while under the influence (of alcohol); F *da kann man ja Zustände kriegen!* it's enough to drive you up the wall. **2.** state of affairs, situation: *es herrschen katastrophale Zustände* conditions are catastrophic; F *das ist doch kein ~!* that's intolerable!

zustande [tsu'ʃtandə] *adv* **1.** ~ *bringen* bring *s.th.* off, achieve, succeed in doing. **2.** ~ *kommen* a) be achieved, come off, *agreement etc*: be reached, *contract*: be signed, b) take place.

'**zuständig** *adj* relevant, competent (*authority etc*), responsible: *der ~e Beamte* the official in charge; ⚖ ~ *sein* have jurisdiction (*für* over); *dafür ist er* ~ that's his job.

'**Zuständigkeit** *f* (-; -en) competence, responsibility, powers, ⚖ jurisdiction (*für* over): *das fällt nicht in s-e* ~ that's not within his province.

'**Zuständigkeitsbereich** *m* (sphere of) responsibility, ⚖ jurisdiction.

'zustatten [tsu'ʃtatən] *adv* j-m (**sehr**) ~ **kommen** be (very) useful to s.o.

'zustecken *v/t* (*sep*, h) **j-m et.** ~ slip s.o. s.th.

'zustehen *v/i* (*irr, sep*, -ge-, h, → *stehen*) **1. et. steht j-m zu** s.o. is entitled to s.th. **2. es steht ihr** *etc* **nicht zu zu** *inf* she *etc* has no right (*or* it's not for her) to *inf*.

'zusteigen *v/i* (*irr, sep*, -ge-, sn, → *steigen*) get on *a bus etc*.

'zustellen *v/t* (*sep*, h) deliver: ɪ̸ʒ j-m e-e **Ladung** ~ serve s.o. with a summons. **'Zusteller** *m* (-s; -) postman. **'Zustellgebühr** *f* postal delivery fee. **'Zustellung** *f* (-; -en) delivery, ɪ̸ʒ service.

'zusteuern (*sep*) **I** *v/t* (h) F contribute. **II** *v/i* (sn) ~ **auf** (*acc*) a) ♨, *a. person*: make (*or* head) for, b) *fig.* be heading for *a crisis etc*, be driving at *a subject etc*.

'zustimmen *v/i* (*sep*, h) (*dat*) agree (to *s.th.*, with *s.o.*), consent (to), approve (of): **~d nicken** nod in approval; **er stimmte mir in diesem Punkt nicht zu** he disagreed with me on this point.

'Zustimmung *f* (-; -en) agreement, consent, approval: **allgemeine ~ finden** meet with universal approval.

'zustöpseln *v/t* (*sep*, h) stopper.

'zustoßen (*irr, sep*, -ge-, → *stoßen*) **I** *v/t* (h) **1.** push *door etc* shut. **II** *v/i* **2.** (h) thrust, stab. **3.** (sn) **j-m ~** happen to s.o.; **ihr muß et. zugestoßen sein** she must have had an accident.

'zustreben *v/i* (*sep*, sn) (*dat*) make for.

'Zustrom *m* (-[e]s; *no pl*) **1.** influx: *meteor*. ~ **kühler Meeresluft** inflow of fresh sea air. **2.** rush. **'zuströmen** *v/i* (*sep*, sn) *fig.* throng (*dat* towards).

'zustürzen *v/i* (*sep*, sn) ~ **auf** (*acc*) rush up to.

zutage [tsu'ta:gə] *adv* ~ **bringen**, ~ **fördern** *a. fig.* bring *s.th.* to light; ~ **treten** a) come to light, be revealed, show, b) *a. klar* ~ treten be evident, be obvious.

'Zutaten *pl* **1.** *gastr*. ingredients. **2.** *fashion*: accessories.

zu'teil *adv* j-m ~ **werden** be given to s.o.; **j-m et.** ~ **werden lassen** grant s.o. s.th.

'zuteilen *v/t* (*sep*, h) **j-m et.** ~ allot (*or* allocate, apportion) s.th. to s.o.; **j-m e-e Aufgabe** *etc* ~ assign s.o. a task *etc*.

'Zuteilung *f* (-; -en) **1.** allotment, allocation, assignment. **2.** quota.

zu'tiefst *adv* deeply, most: *fig.* ~ **verletzt** deeply hurt, cut to the quick.

'zutragen (*irr, sep*, -ge-, h, → *tragen*) **I** *v/t* (*dat* to) **1.** carry. **2.** *fig.* tell, report. **II** **sich ~** happen, take place. **'Zuträger** *m* (-s; -) *contp.* informer, talebearer.

zuträglich ['tsu:tre:klɪç] *adj* good (*dat* for): **der Gesundheit** ~ conducive to health; **nicht ~ sein** disagree (*dat* with).

'zutrauen *v/t* (*sep*, h) **j-m et.** ~ a) think s.o. capable of s.th., b) credit s.o. with s.th.; **das hätte ich dir nie zugetraut!** I never knew you had it in you; **ihm ist alles zuzutrauen!** he stops at nothing; **das ist ihr glatt zuzutrauen!** I wouldn't put it past her.

'Zutrauen *n* (-s) confidence (**zu** in).

'zutraulich *adj* trusting, confiding, friendly (*a. animal*). **'Zutraulichkeit** *f* (-; *no pl*) confidingness, friendliness.

'zutreffen *v/i* (*irr, sep*, -ge-, h, → *treffen*) be right, be correct: ~ **auf** (*acc*), ~ **für** be true (of), apply to; **die Beschreibung trifft auf ihn zu** the description fits him.

'zutreffend *adj* right, true, correct: **Zutreffendes bitte unterstreichen!** please underline where applicable!

'zutrinken *v/i* (*irr, sep*, -ge-, h, → *trinken*) (*dat* to) drink, raise one's glass.

'Zutritt *m* (-[e]s; *no pl*) access, admission: **sich gewaltsam ~ verschaffen** force one's way (**zu** into); ~ **verboten!**, **kein** ~**!** no entry!; → **Unbefugte**.

'zutun *v/t* (*irr, sep*, -ge-, h, → *tun*) → **Auge 1. 'Zutun** *n* **ohne mein** ~ a) without any help from me, b) through no fault of mine; **es geschah ohne mein ~** I had nothing to do with it.

zu'ungunsten *prep* (*gen*) to the disadvantage of.

zu'unterst *adv* right at the bottom.

zuverlässig ['tsu:fɛrlɛsɪç] *adj* a) reliable (*a.* ☺), safe (*a.* ☺), b) loyal, faithful: **aus ~er Quelle** from a reliable source. **'Zuverlässigkeit** *f* (-; *no pl*) a) *a.* ☺ reliability, safety, b) loyalty.

Zuversicht ['tsu:fɛrzɪçt] *f* (-; *no pl*) confidence: **voll(er)** ~ **sein** be quite confident (**daß** that). **'zuversichtlich** *adj* confident, optimistic: ~ **hoffen, daß** be quite confident that. **'Zuversichtlichkeit** *f* (-; *no pl*) confidence, optimism.

zu'viel *adv* too much: **eine(r)** ~ one too many; **viel ~** far too much; ~ **des Guten**

too much of a good thing; **was ~ ist, ist ~!** there's a limit to everything.

zu'vor *adv* **1.** (*kurz ~* shortly) before: **am Tag ~** the day before, (on) the previous day. **2.** first.

zu'vorkommen *v/i* (*irr, sep*, -ge-, sn, → **kommen**) (*dat*) anticipate, forestall, F *a.* beat *s.o.* to it. **zu'vorkommend** *adj* obliging, courteous. **Zu'vorkommenheit** *f* (-; *no pl*) obligingness, courtesy.

Zuwachs ['tsu:vaks] *m* (-es; *no pl*) **1.** (**an** *dat* in) increase, growth (*a.* ♥): F **auf ~ kaufen** buy *shoes etc* on the big side. **2.** F addition to the family, baby.

'zuwachsen *v/i* (*irr, sep*, -ge-, sn, → **wachsen¹**) **1.** become overgrown. **2.** ✂ heal up, close.

'Zuwachsrate *f* ♥ growth rate.

'Zuwanderer *m* (-s; -) immigrant.

'zuwandern *v/i* (*sep*, sn) immigrate.

'Zuwanderung *f* (-; -en) immigration.

zuwege [tsu've:gə] *adv* **1.** ~ **bringen** bring *s.th.* off, achieve, manage to do. **2.** F (*noch*) *gut* ~ *sein* be (still) very fit.

zu'weilen *adv* at times, occasionally.

'zuweisen *v/t* (*irr, sep*, -ge-, h, → **weisen**) assign (*dat* to).

'zuwenden (*irr, sep*, h, → **wenden²**) **I** *v/t* **1.** turn (*dat* towards): *j-m das Gesicht ~* turn one's back on *s.o.*; *j-m das Gesicht ~* face *s.o.* **2.** *j-m et. ~* give *s.o.* s.th. *fig. a.* devote *o.s.* to (*a task etc*). **'Zuwendung** *f* (-; -en) **1.** a) grant, b) allowance, c) donation. **2.** *no pl* love, (loving) care, attention.

zu'wenig *indef pron* a) too little, b) too few: *das ist ~* that's not enough; *du schläfst ~* you don't get enough sleep.

'zuwerfen *v/t* (*irr, sep*, -ge-, h, → **werfen**) **1.** slam *s.th.* (shut). **2.** (*dat* to) throw, toss: *fig. j-m e-n Blick ~* dart (*or* flash) *s.o.* a look; → **Kußhand.**

zu'wider **I** *adj j-m ist ... ~* *s.o.* hates (*or* detests) ... **II** *prep* (*dat*) contrary to, against.

zu'widerhandeln *v/i* (*sep*, h) (*dat*) act against, act contrary to, violate, contravene (*law etc*). **Zu'widerhandelnde** *m, f* (-n; -n) ⚖ offender. **Zu'widerhandlung** *f* (-; -en) ⚖ (*gegen*) offen/ce (*Am.* -se) (against), contravention (of).

zu'widerlaufen *v/i* (*irr, sep*, -ge-, sn, → **laufen**) (*dat*) run counter to.

'zuwinken *v/i* (*sep*, h) *j-m ~* wave to *s.o.*

'zuzahlen *v/t* (*sep*, h) pay *s.th.* extra.

'zuzählen *v/t* (*sep*, h) **1.** add. **2.** (*dat*) count among.

'zuziehen (*irr, sep*, -ge-, → **ziehen**) **I** *v/t* (h) **1.** pull *noose etc* tight, tighten, draw (*curtains*). **2.** *sich et. ~* a) catch (*disease etc*), suffer (*injury*), b) incur (*s.o's hatred etc*). **3.** → **hinzuziehen.** **II** *v/i* (sn) a) move in, b) settle (down). **'Zuzug** *m* (-[e]s; ⸚e) **1.** move. **2.** → **Zuwanderung.**

zuzüglich ['tsu:tsy:kliç] *prep* (*gen*) plus.

zwang [tsvaŋ] *pret of* **zwingen.**

Zwang *m* (-[e]s; ⸚e) compulsion (*a. psych.*), constraint, pressure, force: *ohne ~* without being forced to; *unter ~ handeln* ⚖ act under duress; *~ ausüben* exert pressure (*auf acc* on); *gesellschaftliche Zwänge* social constraints; *... ist ...* ... is compulsory; *iro. tu dir k-n ~ an!* just go ahead!

zwängen ['tsvɛŋən] *v/t* (h) squeeze.

'zwanglos *adj* informal, casual, unconstrained, *a.* free and easy: *in ~er Folge erscheinen* *magazine etc*: appear at irregular intervals; *sich ~ unterhalten* talk at ease; *es geht bei ihnen sehr ~ zu* things are very informal with them.

'Zwanglosigkeit *f* (-; *no pl*) informality, casualness.

'Zwangs|anleihe *f* compulsory loan. **~arbeit** *f* (-; *no pl*) forced labo(u)r. **~arbeiter(in** *f)* *m* forced labo(u)r convict. **~aufenthalt** *m* enforced stay, detention. **~bewirtschaftung** *f* (economic) control: *die ~ aufheben von* (*or gen*) decontrol. **~einweisung** *f* committal (*in acc* to). **⸗ernähren** *v/t* (h) force-feed. **~ernährung** *f* force feeding. **~handlung** *f* compulsive act. **~herrschaft** *f* despotism, tyranny. **~jacke** *f* straitjacket. **~lage** *f* predicament.

'zwangsläufig *adj* inevitable: *er mußte ~ davon erfahren* he was bound to hear of it.

'Zwangs|maßnahme *f* coercive measure, *pol.* sanction. **~neu,rose** *f* obsessional neurosis. **~pause** *f* enforced break. **~räumung** *f* eviction. **~umsiedler(in** *f)* *m* displaced person. **⸗versteigern** *v/t* (*only inf and pp* zwangsversteigert, h) put *s.th.* up for compulsory auction. **~versteigerung** *f* compulsory auction. **~verwaltung** *f* sequestration. **~vollstreckung** *f* execution. **~vorstel-**

lung f psych. obsession: **von der ~ befallen, daß** obsessed with the idea that.

'zwangsweise I adj compulsory. **II** adv compulsorily, by force.

'Zwangswirtschaft f government control, controlled economy.

zwanzig ['tsvantsɪç] adj (**~ Jahre alt**) **sein** be) twenty. **'Zwanzig** f (-; -en) twenty: **sie ist Mitte** (**der**) **~** she is in her mid-twenties. **zwanziger** ['tsvantsɪɡər] adj **die goldenen ~ Jahre** the roaring twenties. **'zwanzigfach** adj and adv twentyfold. **'zwanzigjährig** [-jɛːrɪç] adj **1.** twenty-year-old, of twenty. **2.** twentieth (jubilee etc). **'Zwanzigjährige** [-jɛːrɪɡə] m f, (-n; -n) twenty-year-old (person): **die ~n** the twenty-year-olds. **'zwanzigst** adj, **'Zwanzigstel** n (-s; -) twentieth.

zwar [tsva:r] adv **1. ~ ..., aber ...** it is true ..., but; **es ist ~ verboten, aber ...** a. it may be forbidden, but ... **2. und ~** a) namely, b) in fact.

Zweck [tsvɛk] m (-[e]s; -e) **1.** purpose, object, aim, end, use: **zu diesem ~** a) for that purpose, b) to this end; **ein Mittel zum ~** a means to an end; **der ~ heiligt die Mittel** the end justifies the means; **s-n ~ erfüllen** (**verfehlen**) serve (defeat) its purpose; **für wohltätige ~e** for charity. **2.** point, use: **es hat k-n ~ zu warten** it's no use waiting; **es hat wenig ~, daß ich hingehe** there's little point in my going; F **das ist ja** (**gerade**) **der ~ der Übung!** that's the whole point (of the exercise).

'Zweck|bau m (-[e]s; -ten) functional building. **~bindung** f earmarking of funds for specific purposes. **~denken** n (-s) pragmatism.

'zweckdienlich adj relevant, useful: **~e Hinweise** relevant information.

'zweckentfremden v/t (only inf and pp zweckentfremdet, h) use s.th. for a purpose not intended, misappropriate.

'zweckentsprechend adj appropriate.

'zweckfrei adj nonutility.

'zweckfremd adj foreign to the purpose.

'zweckgebunden adj earmarked.

'zweckgemäß adj appropriate.

'zwecklos adj useless, pointless, futile: **~ sein** a. be no use; **es ist ~, daß ich hingehe** there's no point in my going.

'Zwecklosigkeit f (-; no pl) uselessness, futility.

'zweckmäßig adj **1.** practical, functional. **2.** expedient, advisable.

'Zweckmäßigkeit f (-; no pl) **1.** practicality, functionality. **2.** advisability.

'Zweck|opti,mismus m calculated optimism. **~pessi,mismus** m calculated pessimism.

zwecks prep (gen) for the purpose of, with a view to.

'Zwecksparen n target saving.

'zweckwidrig adj inappropriate.

zwei [tsvai] adj two: **wir ~** we two, the two of us; **dazu gehören ~** it takes two. **Zwei** f (-; -en) **1.** (number) two. **2.** ped. (mark, grade) B.

'zweiachsig [-ʔaksɪç] adj **1.** ⚛ biaxial. **2.** mot. two-axle.

zweia,tomig [-ʔatomɪç] adj ⚛ diatomic.

'zweibändig [-bɛndɪç] adj two-volume.

'Zweibeiner [-bainər] m (-s; -) F man.

'Zweibettzimmer n twin-bedded room.

'zweideutig [-dɔʏtɪç] adj ambiguous, equivocal, b.s. suggestive, off-colo(u)r.

'Zweideutigkeit f (-; -en) **1.** no pl ambiguity, equivocality, b.s. suggestiveness. **2.** a) suggestive remark, b) risqué joke.

Zwei'drittelmehrheit f two thirds majority.

'zweieiig [-ʔaiɪç] adj biol. binovular: **~e Zwillinge** fraternal twins.

'Zweier m (-s; -) rowing: pair: **~ mit** (**Steuermann**) coxed pair.

'Zweierbeziehung f partnership.

'Zweierbob m (-s; -s) two-man bob.

'zweierlei adj two different (kinds of): **mit ~ Maß messen** apply double standards.

'zweifach adj double, adv a. doubly: **in ~er Ausfertigung** in duplicate.

Zweifa'milienhaus n two-family (Am. duplex) house.

'zweifarbig adj two-colo(u)red.

Zweifel ['tsvaifəl] m (-s; -) doubt (**an** dat, **wegen** about): **ohne ~** → **zweifellos**; **im ~ sein über** (acc) be in doubt (or in two minds) about; **ihm kamen ~** he was beginning to have doubts; **es bestehen berechtigte ~ an s-r Ehrlichkeit** there is good reason to doubt his honesty; **sie ließen k-n ~ daran, daß** they made it quite plain that.

'zweifelhaft adj doubtful, dubious,

questionable, F shady: **~es Vergnügen** dubious pleasure; **von ~em Wert** of debatable value (*or* merit); **es erscheint ~, ob** it seems doubtful whether.

'zweifellos *adv* undoubtedly, doubtless, without (a) doubt.

zweifeln ['tsvaɪfəln] *v/i* (h) doubt: **~ an** (*dat*) doubt (*or* question) s.th.; **daran ist nicht zu ~** there's no doubt about it.

'Zweifelsfall *m* **im ~** in case of doubt.

Zweifler ['tsvaɪflər] *m* (-s; -) doubter, sceptic, *Am.* skeptic. **'zweiflerisch** *adj* doubting, sceptical, *Am.* skeptical.

Zweig [tsvaɪk] *m* (-[e]s; -e) branch (*a. fig.*), twig; **~ grün** I. **~betrieb** *m* branch. **~bü,ro** *n* branch (office).

'zweigeschlechtig *adj* ♀ bisexual.

'zweigeteilt *adj* divided in(to) two.

'Zweiggeschäft *n* branch.

'zweigleisig [-glaɪzɪç] *adj* **1.** 🚂 double-tracked. **2.** *fig.* two-track: **~ fahren** leave both one's options open.

'Zweigniederlassung *f* (**~ im Ausland** foreign) branch.

'Zweigstelle *f* branch (office).

'zweihändig [-hɛndɪç] *adj* two-handed, ♪ for two hands.

'Zweihundert'jahrfeier *f* bicentenary.

'zweijährig [-jɛːrɪç] *adj* **1.** two-year. **2.** two-year-old. **'Zweijährige** [-jɛːrɪgə] *m, f* (-n; -n) two-year-old (child).

'Zweikampf *m* duel.

'Zweika,nal... ⚡ two-channel. **~ton** *m* TV mit **~** F with two language channels.

'zweimal *adv* twice: **das ließ sie sich nicht ~ sagen** she didn't wait to be told twice. **'zweimalig** *adj* (twice) repeated.

'Zwei'markstück *n* two-mark piece.

'zweimotorig [-mo,toːrɪç] *adj* twin-engined.

'Zweipar'teiensy,stem *n* two-party system.

'zweiphasig [-fa:zɪç] *adj* ⚡ two-phase.

'zweipolig [-po:lɪç] *adj* ⚡ two-pole, bipolar, two-pin (*plug*).

'Zweirad *n* (-[e]s; ⸚er) bicycle, F bike.

'zweirädrig [-rɛːdrɪç] *adj* two-wheeled.

'Zweireiher [-raɪər] *m* (-s; -) double-breasted suit. **'zweireihig** *adj* **1.** in two rows. **2.** double-breasted (*suit*).

'zweischneidig *adj a. fig.* double-edged.

'zweiseitig [-zaɪtɪç] *adj* **1.** bilateral. **2.** two-page (*letter*), double-page (*ad*).

'zweisilbig [-zɪlbɪç] *adj* two-syllable.

'Zweisitzer [-zɪtsər] *m* (-s; -) two-seater.

'zweispaltig [-ʃpaltɪç] *adj* two-column: **~ gedruckt** printed in two columns.

'zweisprachig [-ʃpraːxɪç] *adj* bilingual, *document etc* in two languages. **'Zweisprachigkeit** *f* (-; *no pl*) bilingualism.

'zweispurig [-ʃpuːrɪç] *adj* **1.** 🚂 double-tracked. **2.** two-lane (*road etc*).

Zwei'stärken,glas *n opt.* bifocal lens. **~brille** *f* (pair of) bifocals.

'zweistellig [-ʃtɛlɪç] *adj* two-digit (*number*), two-place (*decimal*).

'zweistimmig [-ʃtɪmɪç] *adj* ♪ for (*or* in) two voices.

'zweistöckig [-ʃtœkɪç] *adj* two-storeyed, *Am.* two-storied.

'zweistrahlig [-ʃtraːlɪç] *adj* ✈ twin-jet.

'zweistufig [-ʃtuːfɪç] *adj* ⚙ two-stage.

'zweistündig [-ʃtʏndɪç] *adj* two-hour, lasting two hours.

zweit *adj* second: **der ~e Band** volume two; **~er Mai** May 2nd, *Am.* May 2; **ein ~er Mozart** another Mozart; **jeder ~e** every other person; **zu ~** in twos, in pairs; **sie waren zu ~** there were two of them; **~er Klasse** *a. fig.* second-class; **→ Geige, Hand, Ich, Wahl 1.**

'Zweitakter *m*, **'Zweitaktmotor** *m* two-stroke engine.

'zweitältest *adj*, **Zweitälteste** *m, f* (-n; -n) second eldest.

'zwei'tausend *adj* two thousand.

'zweitbest *adj*, **'Zweitbeste** *m, f* (-n; -n) second best.

'Zweite *m, f* (-n; -n) second: *sports:* **sie wurde ~ hinter ...** she came in second behind ..., she was runner-up to ...; *fig.* **wie kein Zweiter** like nobody else.

'Zweiteiler *m* (-s; -) F **1.** two-piece (suit). **2.** *film, TV* two-parter. **'zweiteilig** [-taɪlɪç] *adj* **1.** two-piece. **2.** in two parts.

'zweitens *adv* secondly.

'Zweitfri,sur *f* wig.

'zweitgrößt *adj* second largest.

'zweithöchst *adj* second highest.

'zweitklassig [-klasɪç] *adj* second-class, *contp.* second-rate.

'zweitletzt *adj* last but one.

'zweitrangig [-raŋɪç] *adj* secondary: **~ sein** be of secondary importance.

'Zweitschlüssel *m* spare key.

'Zweitschrift *f* (-; -en) duplicate.

'Zweitstimme *f pol.* second vote.

'**Zweitstudium** *n ein ~ beginnen* begin a second course of studies.

'**zweitürig** [-ty:rıç] *adj mot.* two-door.

'**Zweitwagen** *m* second car.

'**Zweitwohnung** *f* second home.

Zwei'vierteltakt *m* ♩ two-four time.

'**zweiwertig** [-ve:rtıç] *adj* 🧪 bivalent.

'**zweiwöchig** [-vœçıç] *adj* two-week.

'**zweizeilig** [-tsailıç] *adj* double-spaced: *~ schreiben* double-space.

Zwei'zimmerwohnung *f* two-room(ed) flat (*Am.* apartment).

Zwerchfell ['tsverç-] *n* diaphragm. **~atmung** *f* abdominal breathing. ⍾**erschütternd** *adj fig.* sidesplitting.

Zwerg [tsverk] *m* -[e]s; -e) dwarf, gnome, *fig. a.* midget.

'**zwergenhaft** *adj* dwarfish.

'**Zwergpudel** *m* miniature poodle.

'**Zwergwuchs** *m biol.,* 🧪 dwarfism, 🌿 dwarf growth. '**zwergwüchsig** [-vy:k-sıç] *adj* dwarfish.

Zwetsch(g)e ['tsvetʃ(g)ə] *f* (-; -n) plum. '**Zwetsch(g)en|baum** *m* plum tree. **~wasser** *n* (-s; ⍩) plum brandy.

Zwickel ['tsvıkəl] *m* (-s; -) **1.** gusset. **2.** △ spandrel.

zwicken ['tsvıkən] *v/t, v/i* (h) pinch.

'**Zwickmühle** *f* F *fig.* (*in e-r ~ sein* or *sitzen* be on the horns of a dilemma.

Zwieback ['tsvi:bak] *m* (-[e]s; -e) rusk.

Zwiebel ['tsvi:bəl] *f* (-; -n) **1.** onion. **2.** 🌿 bulb.

'**Zwiebelkuchen** *m* onion gateau.

'**Zwiebelmuster** *n* onion pattern.

zwiebeln ['tsvi:bəln] *v/t* (h) F *j-n ~* give s.o. a hard time.

'**Zwiebel|ringe** *pl gastr.* onion rings. **~schale** *f* onion skin. **~suppe** *f* onion soup. **~turm** *m* △ onion spire.

Zwielicht ['tsvi:-] *n* (-[e]s; *no pl*) twilight: *fig. ins ~ geraten* lay o.s. open to suspicion. '**zwielichtig** [-lıçtıç] *adj fig.* dubious, F shady.

'**Zwiespalt** *m* (-[e]s; *rare* -e) conflict.

'**zwiespältig** [-ʃpɛltıç] *adj* conflicting: *er ist ein ~er Mensch* he has a conflicting personality; *mein Eindruck war ~* I came away with mixed impressions.

Zwilling ['tsvilıŋ] *m* (-s; -e) **1.** twin. **2.** *pl astr.* (*er ist* [*ein*] *~* he is [a]) Gemini.

'**Zwillings|bruder** *m* twin brother. **~paar** *n* pair of twins. **~reifen** *m mot.*

dual (*or* double, twin) tyres (*Am.* tires). **~schwester** *f* twin sister.

Zwinge ['tsvıŋə] *f* (-; -n) clamp, cramp.

zwingen ['tsvıŋən] (zwang, gezwungen, h) **I** *v/t* force, compel: *j-n ~,* *et. zu tun a.* make s.o. do s.th.; *j-n zum Rücktritt ~* force s.o. to resign; *ich sehe mich gezwungen zu verkaufen* I find myself compelled to sell; *→ a. gezwungen.* **II** *v/i ~ zu* necessitate; *die Lage zwingt zu e-r schnellen Entscheidung* the situation calls for a quick decision. **III** *sich ~* force o.s. (*et. zu tun* to do s.th.); *sie zwang sich zu e-m Lächeln* she forced a smile; *ich mußte mich dazu ~* it cost me an effort (to do that).

'**zwingend** *adj* compelling (*reason etc*), absolute, urgent (*necessity etc*), cogent, conclusive (*argument, evidence, etc*).

Zwinger ['tsvıŋər] *m* (-s; -) kennel(s).

zwinkern ['tsvıŋkərn] *v/i* (h) (*mit den Augen*) ~ a) blink, b) wink.

zwirbeln ['tsvırbəln] *v/t* (h) twist, twirl.

Zwirn [tsvırn] *m* (-[e]s; -e) twine, twist.

zwischen ['tsvıʃən] *prep* (*dat, acc*) a) between, b) among.

'**Zwischenakt** *m,* **~mu,sik** *f* entr'acte.

'**Zwischen|aufenthalt** *m* stop(over). **~bemerkung** *f* interjection. **~bericht** *m* interim report. **~bescheid** *m* provisional reply. **~bi,lanz** *f* interim balance sheet: *fig. e-e ~ ziehen* take stock in between. **~blutung** *f* 🧬 bleeding between periods, intermenstrual bleeding. **~deck** *n* ⚓ between decks.

zwischen'durch *adv* a) in between, b) in the meantime, c) now and then.

'**Zwischen|ergebnis** *n* provisional result, *sports:* interim results (*or* score). **~fall** *m* incident: *ohne Zwischenfälle* without a hitch. **~finan,zierung** *f* intermediate financing, bridging. **~frage** *f* (interposed) question. **~gericht** *n gastr.* entrée. **~geschoß** *n* △ mezzanine. **~glied** *n* link. **~größe** *f* intermediate size. **~händler** *m* intermediary. **~hoch** *n meteor.* ridge of high pressure. **~lagerung** *f nucl.* interim storage. ⍾**landen** *v/i* (*only inf and pp* zwischengelandet, sn) make an intermediate landing, stop. **~landung** *f* stop(over): *ohne ~* nonstop. **~lauf** *m sports:* intermediate heat. **~lösung** *f* interim solution. **~mahlzeit** *f* snack (between meals). **≈menschlich** adj interpersonal: **≈e Beziehungen** human relations. **≈prüfung** f intermediate examination (or test). **≈raum** m **1.** space, distance, ◎ clearance, a. gap, print. spacing: **e-e Zeile ≈ lassen** leave a space. **2.** interval. **≈ruf** m interruption: **≈e** heckling. **≈rufer** m (-s; -) heckler. **≈runde** f sports: intermediate round. **≈schalten** v/t (only inf and pp zwischengeschaltet, h) ⚡ connect s.th. in series. **≈schaltung** f ⚡ insertion. **≈speicher** m computer: buffer store (or storage). **≈spiel** n interlude. **≈spurt** m sports: (sudden) spurt: **e-n ≈ einlegen** put in a burst of speed. **≈staatlich** adj **1.** international, intergovernmental. **2.** interstate. **≈stadium** n intermediate stage. **≈stand** m (-[e]s; no pl) sports: interim score. **≈station** f stopover, (a. place) stop. **≈stecker** m ⚡ adapter. **≈stück** n ◎ intermediary, ⚡ adapter. **≈stufe** f intermediate stage. **≈summe** f subtotal. **≈text** m (inserted) caption. **≈tief** n meteor. ridge of low pressure. **≈töne** pl fig. overtones. **≈urteil** n 🏛 interlocutory judg(e)ment. **≈wand** f dividing wall, partition. **≈zeit** f **1.** time in between: **in der ≈ → zwischenzeitlich. 2.** sports: intermediate time. **≈zeitlich I** adj intermediate, interim. **II** adv meanwhile, (in the) meantime. **≈zeugnis** n intermediate report.

Zwist [tsvɪst] m (-[e]s; -e), **'Zwistigkeit** f (-; -en) quarrel.

zwitschern ['tsvɪtʃərn] v/t, v/i (h) twitter, chirp: F **e-n ≈** down one. **'Zwitschern** n (-s) twitter(ing), chirp(ing).

Zwitter ['tsvɪtər] m (-s; -) hermaphrodite.

zwo [tsvoː] F → **zwei.**

zwölf [tsvœlf] adj twelve: **um ≈ (Uhr)** at twelve (o'clock), a. at noon, a. at midnight; fig. **fünf Minuten vor ≈** at the eleventh hour.

Zwölf'fingerdarm m anat. duodenum. **≈geschwür** n 🗡 duodenal ulcer.

'Zwölfkampf m gym. twelve events.

zwölft adj, **'Zwölfte** m, f (-n; -n) twelfth.

'Zwölftonmu,sik f twelve-tone music.

Zyankali [tsyaˈnkaːli] n (-s; no pl) 🜍 potassium cyanide.

zyklisch ['tsyːklɪʃ] adj cyclic(al).

Zyklon [tsyˈkloːn] m (-s; -e) cyclone.

Zyklone [tsyˈkloːnə] f (-; -n) cyclone.

Zyklotron ['tsyːklotroːn] n (-s; -e) phys. cyclotron.

Zyklus ['tsyːklʊs] m (-; Zyklen) **1.** cycle. **2.** series (of lectures etc).

Zylinder [tsiˈlɪndər] m (-s; -) **1.** top hat. **2.** 🜍, ⚡, mot. cylinder.

Zy'linderkopf m mot. cylinder head. **≈dichtung** f mot. cylinder-head gasket. **≈schraube** f mot. cylinder-head stud.

zylindrisch [tsiˈlɪndrɪʃ] adj cylindric(al).

Zyniker ['tsyːnikər] m (-s; -) cynic.

zynisch ['tsyːnɪʃ] adj cynical.

Zynismus [tsyˈnɪsmʊs] m (-; -men) cynicism.

Zypern ['tsyːpərn] n (-s) Cyprus.

Zyprer ['tsyːprər] m (-s; -), **'Zyprerin** f (-; -nen) Cypriote.

Zypresse [tsyˈprɛsə] f (-; -n) 🜍 cypress.

zyprisch ['tsyːprɪʃ] adj Cyprian.

Zyste ['tsystə] f (-; -n) cyst.

Zystoskopie [tsystoskoˈpiː] f (-; -n) 🗡 cystoscopy.

zytologisch [tsytoˈloːgɪʃ] adj cytologic(al). **Zytostatikum** [tsytoˈstaːtikʊm] n (-s; -ka) 🗡 cytostatic agent.

German Abbreviations

A

AA *das Auswärtige Amt* Foreign Office; *Anonyme Alkoholiker* Alcoholics Anonymous

Abb. *Abbildung* ill(us)., illustration; fig., figure

Abf. *Abfahrt* dep., departure

Abk. *Abkürzung* abbr., abbreviation

ABM *Arbeitsbeschaffungsmaßnahme* job creation scheme

Abo *Abonnement* subscription

ABS *Antiblockiersystem* anti-lock braking system

Abs. *Absatz* par., paragraph; *Absender* sender

Abschn. *Abschnitt* section; ch., chapter

Abt. *Abteilung* dept, department

abzgl. *abzüglich* less, minus

a. D. *außer Dienst* retd, retired; *an der Donau* on the Danube

ADAC *Allgemeiner Deutscher Automobil-Club* General German Automobile Association

Adr. *Adresse* address

AG *Aktiengesellschaft* *Br.* PLC, Plc, plc, Ltd, public limited company; *Am.* (stock) corporation

AKW *Atomkraftwerk* nuclear power station *or* plant

allg. *allgemein* gen., general

a. M. *am Main* on the Main

am., amer(ik). *amerikanisch* Am., American

amtl. *amtlich* off., official

Anh. *Anhang* app., appendix

Ank. *Ankunft* arr., arrival

Anl. *Anlage(n)* encl., enclosure(s)

Anm. *Anmerkung* note

anschl. *anschließend* foll., following

AOK *Allgemeine Ortskrankenkasse* compulsory health insurance scheme

a. o. Prof. *außerordentlicher Professor* *Br.* senior lecturer; *Am.* associate professor

App. *Apparat* ext., extension; telephone

ARD *Arbeitsgemeinschaft der öffentlich-rechtlichen Rundfunkanstalten der Bundesrepublik Deutschland* Working Pool of the Broadcasting Corporations of the Federal Republic of Germany

a. Rh. *am Rhein* on the Rhine

Art. *Artikel* art., article

ASU *Abgassonderuntersuchung* exhaust emission test

Aufl. *Auflage* ed., edition

Ausg. *Ausgabe* ed., edition; copy

Az. *Aktenzeichen* file number

B

B *Bundesstraße* major road, federal highway

b. *bei* at; with; nr., near; c/o, care of

BAföG *Bundesausbildungsförderungsgesetz* student financial assistance scheme

BAT *Bundesangestelltentarif* salary scale for public employees

BBk *Deutsche Bundesbank* German Federal Bank

Bde. *Bände* vols, volumes

BE *Broteinheit* bread unit

beil. *beiliegend* encl., enclosed

BENELUX *Belgien, Niederlande, Luxemburg* Belgium, the Netherlands, and Luxembourg

bes. *besonders* esp., especially

Best.-Nr. *Bestellnummer* ord. no., order number

Betr. *Betreff, betrifft* ✝ re

betr. *betreffend, betreffs* conc., concerning; regarding

Bev. *Bevölkerung* pop., population

Bez. *Bezeichnung* mark; name, designation; *Bezirk* dist., district

BGB *Bürgerliches Gesetzbuch* Civil Code

BGH *Bundesgerichtshof* Federal Supreme Court

BGS *Bundesgrenzschutz* Federal Border Guard

Bhf. *Bahnhof* Sta., station

BLZ *Bankleitzahl* bank code

BND *Bundesnachrichtendienst* Federal Intelligence Service

Bq *Becquerel* Bq., Becquerel

BR *Bayerischer Rundfunk* Bavarian Broadcasting Corporation

BRD *Bundesrepublik Deutschland* FRG, Federal Republic of Germany

brit. *britisch* Br(it)., British

BRT *Bruttoregistertonnen* GRT, gross register tons

bsd. *besonders* esp., especially

Btx *Bildschirmtext* viewdata

BUND *Bund für Umwelt und Naturschutz Deutschland* the German Association for Environment Protection and Nature Conservancy

Bw. *Bundeswehr* Federal Armed Forces

b. w. *bitte wenden* PTO, p.t.o., please turn over

BWV *Bachwerkeverzeichnis* BWV, Bach catalogue

bzgl. *bezüglich* with reference to

bzw. *beziehungsweise* resp., respectively

C

C *Celsius* C, Celsius, centigrade

ca. *circa, ungefähr, etwa* c., ca, circa; about; approx., approximately

cand. *candidatus, Kandidat* cand., candidate

CD *Compact Disc* CD, compact disc

CDU *Christlich-Demokratische Union* Christian Democratic Union

cm *Zentimeter* centimetre(s)

Co. *obs. Compagnie* co., company; *Compagnon* partner

CSU *Christlich-Soziale Union* Christian Social Union

CT *Computertomographie* computer tomography

CVJM *Christlicher Verein Junger Männer* YMCA, Young Men's Christian Association

D

d. Ä. *der Ältere* Sen., sen., Snr, Sr, senior

DAAD *Deutscher Akademischer Austauschdienst* German Academic Exchange Service

DAG *Deutsche Angestelltengewerkschaft* Trade Union of German Employees

DB *Deutsche Bundesbahn* German Federal Railway

DBP *Deutsche Bundespost* German Federal Postal Services

DDR *Deutsche Demokratische Republik hist.* GDR, German Democratic Republic

DFB *Deutscher Fußball-Bund* German Football Association

DGB *Deutscher Gewerkschaftsbund* Federation of German Trade Unions

dgl. *dergleichen, desgleichen* the like

d. Gr. *der or die Große* the Great

d. h. *das heißt* i.e., that is

d. i. *das ist* i.e., that is

Di. *Dienstag* Tues., Tuesday

DIN *Deutsches Institut für Normung* German Institute for Standardization

Dipl. *Diplom* Dip., Dipl., diploma

Dipl.-Ing. *Diplomingenieur* qualified engineer

Dir. *Direktor* Dir., dir., director; *Direktion* the directors *pl*

d. J. *der Jüngere* Jun., jun., Jnr, Jr, junior; *dieses Jahres* of this year

DJH *Deutsches Jugendherbergswerk* German Youth Hostel Association

DKP *Deutsche Kommunistische Partei* German Communist Party

dkr *dänische Krone(n)* Danish crown(s)

DM *Deutsche Mark* German mark(s)

d. M. *dieses Monats* inst., instant

d. O. *der (die, das) Obige* the above--mentioned

do. *ditto* do., ditto

Do. *Donnerstag* Thurs., Thursday

Doz. *Dozent(in)* lecturer

dpa *Deutsche Presse-Agentur* German Press Agency

DR *Deutsche Reichsbahn hist. DDR* East German railway

Dr. *Doktor* Dr, Doctor; **~ jur.** *Doktor der Rechte* LLD, Doctor of Laws; **~ med.** *Doktor der Medizin* MD, Doctor of Medicine; **~ phil.** *Doktor der Philosophie* DPhil, PhD, Doctor of Philosophy; **~ rer. nat.** *Doktor der Naturwissenschaften* DSc, ScD, Doctor of Science; **~ theol.** *Doktor der Theologie* DD, Doctor of Divinity

dt. *deutsch* Ger., German

Dtzd. *Dutzend* doz., dozen(s)

DZ *Doppelzimmer* double (room)

E

E *Eilzug* fast train; *Europastraße* European Highway

ebd. *ebenda* ib(id)., ibidem, in the same place

Ed. *Edition, Ausgabe* ed., edition
ed. *edidit, hat herausgegeben* ed., edited by, published by
EDV *elektronische Datenverarbeitung* EDP, electronic data processing
EEG *Elektroenzephalogramm* EEG, electroencephalogram
e. G. *eingetragene Gesellschaft* registered (*Am.* incorporated) company
EG *Europäische Gemeinschaft* EC, European Community
e.h. *ehrenhalber* hon., honorary
eh(e)m. *ehemals* formerly; *ehemalig* former
eidg. *eidgenössisch* fed., federal, confederate, Swiss
eigtl. *eigentlich* actual(ly), real(ly), *adv a.* strictly speaking
einschl. *einschließlich* incl., inclusive (-ly), including; *einschlägig* relevant
EKD *Evangelische Kirche in Deutschland* Protestant Church in Germany
EKG *Elektrokardiogramm* ECG, electrocardiogram
engl. *englisch* Eng., English
entspr. *entsprechend* corr., corresponding
erb. *erbaut* built, erected
Erw. *Erwachsene pl* adults
Euratom *Europäische Atomgemeinschaft* Euratom, European Atomic Energy Community
ev. *evangelisch* Prot., Protestant
e. V. *eingetragener Verein* registered society *or* association
evtl. *eventuell* poss., possibly; perhaps
EWS *Europäisches Währungssystem* EMS, European Monetary System
exkl. *exklusive* exc., except(ed); excl., exclusive, excluding
Expl. *Exemplar* sample, copy
EZ *Einzelzimmer* single (room)

F

Fahrenheit *Fahrenheit* F, Fahrenheit
f. und folgende *Seite* and following *page*
Fa. *Firma* firm; *on letter:* Messrs
Fam. *Familie* family; *on letter:* Mr and Mrs ... (and family)
FC *Fußballclub* FC, Football Club
FCKW *Fluorchlorkohlenwasserstoff*

CFC, chlorofluorocarbon
F.D.P. *Freie Demokratische Partei* Liberal Democratic Party
ff. *und folgende Seiten* and following *pages*
FF *Französischer Franc* FF, French franc
FH *Fachhochschule* advanced technical college
Fig. *Figur* fig., figure; diag., diagram
fig. *figurativ, figürlich, bildlich* fig., figurative(ly)
FKK *Freikörperkultur* nudism
fl. k. u. w. W. *fließend kaltes und warmes Wasser* hot and cold running water
Fmk *Finnmark* fin(n)mark
folg. *folgend(e etc)* foll., following
Forts. *Fortsetzung* continuation; **Forts. f.** *Fortsetzung folgt* to be contd, to be continued
Fr. *Frau* Ms; (*married*) Mrs; *Freitag* Fri., Friday
Frl. *Fräulein* Miss
frz. *französisch* Fr., French
FU *Freie Universität* (*Berlin*) Free University

G

GAU *größter anzunehmender Unfall* MCA, maximum credible accident
geb. *geboren* b., born; *geborene ...* née ...; *gebunden* bd, bound
Gebr. *Gebrüder* Bros., Brothers
gegr. *gegründet* founded; est(ab)., established
gek. *gekürzt* abr., abridged
Ges. *Gesellschaft* assoc., association; co., company; soc., society; *Gesetz* law
gesch. *geschieden* div., divorced
ges. gesch. *gesetzlich geschützt* regd, registered
gest. *gestorben* d., died, deceased
Gew. *Gewicht* w., wt, weight
gez. *gezeichnet* sgd, signed
GG *Grundgesetz* constitution
Ggs. *Gegensatz* contrast; opp., opposite
ggf(s). *gegebenenfalls* should the occasion arise; if necessary; if applicable
GmbH *Gesellschaft mit beschränkter Haftung* limited liability company

GMD *Generalmusikdirektor* (chief) musical director
GUS *Gemeinschaft Unabhängiger Staaten* CIS, Commonwealth of Independent States

H

ha *Hektar* hectare(s)
Hbf. *Hauptbahnhof* cent. sta., central station; main sta., main station
h. c. *honoris causa, ehrenhalber* hon., honorary
HGB *Handelsgesetzbuch* Commercial Code
hins. *hinsichtlich* with regard to, regarding, as to
Hj. *Halbjahr* half-year, six months
hl *Hektoliter* hl, hectolitre(s)
hl. *heilig* holy
HP *Halbpension* half board
hPa *Hektopascal* hPa, hectopascal
HR *Hessischer Rundfunk* Hessian Broadcasting Corporation
Hr(n). *Herr(n)* Mr
H(rs)g. *Herausgeber* ed., editor
h(rs)g. *herausgegeben* ed., edited
Hz *Hertz* Hz, hertz
Hzg. *Heizung* heating

I

i. *im, in* in (the)
i. A. *im Auftrag* p.p., per procurationem, by proxy
i. allg. *im allgemeinen* in general, gen., generally; on the whole
i. b. *im besonderen* in particular
IC *Intercity(-Zug)* inter-city (train)
ICE *Intercity-Expresszug* intercity express (train)
i. D. *im Dienst* on duty; *im Durchschnitt* on av., on average
i. e. *im einzelnen* in detail *or* particular; *id est, das heißt, das ist* i.e., that is
IFO *Institut für Wirtschaftsforschung* Institute for Economic Research
IG *Industriegewerkschaft* industrial union
i. H. *im Hause* on the premises
IHK *Industrie- und Handelskammer* Chamber of Industry and Commerce
i. J. *im Jahre* in (the year)

i. M. *im Monat* in (the month of) *May etc*
inf. *infolge* owing to; as a result of
Ing. *Ingenieur* eng., engineer
Inh. *Inhaber* prop., propr, proprietor; *Inhalt* cont., contents
inkl. *inklusive* incl., including, included; inclusive of
IOK *Internationales Olympisches Komitee* IOC, International Olympic Committee
IQ *Intelligenzquotient* IQ, intelligence quotient
i. R. *im Ruhestand* ret., retd, retired
IRK *Internationales Rotes Kreuz* IRC, International Red Cross
ISBN *Internationale Standardbuchnummer* ISBN, international standard book number
ital. *italienisch* It., Ital., Italian
i. Tr. *in der Trockenmasse percentage of fat* in dry matter
i. V. *in Vertretung* p.p., by proxy; *in Vorbereitung* in prep., in preparation
IWF *Internationaler Währungsfonds* IMF, International Monetary Fund

J

J *Joule* joule(s)
Jan. *Januar* Jan., January
jap. *japanisch* Jap., Japanese
JH *Jugendherberge* Y.H., youth hostel
Jh. *Jahrhundert* c, cent., century
jhrl. *jährlich* yearly, ann., annual(ly)
jr., jun. *junior* Jun., jun., Jnr, Jr, junior
jur. *juristisch* leg., legal
JVA *Justizvollzugsanstalt* prison

K

Kap. *Kapitel* ch(ap)., chapter
Kat *Katalysator* cat., catalytic converter, catalyst
kath. *katholisch* C(ath)., Catholic
KB *Kilobyte(s)* KB, kilobyte(s)
kcal *Kilokalorie(n)* kcal., kilocalorie(s), kilogram(me) calorie(s)
Kffr. *Kauffrau* businesswoman
Kfm. *Kaufmann* merchant; businessman; trader; dlr, dealer; agt, agent
kfm. *kaufmännisch* com(m)., commercial

Kfz *Kraftfahrzeug* motor verhicle
kg *Kilogramm* kg, kilogramme(s)
KG *Kommanditgesellschaft* limited partnership
kgl. *königlich* royal
kHz *Kilohertz* kHz, kilohertz
kJ *Kilojoule* kJ, kilojoule(s)
k.k. *kaiserlich-königlich* imperial and royal
KKW *Kernkraftwerk* nuclear power station *or* plant
Kl. *Klasse* cl., class
km *Kilometer* km, kilometre(s)
KP *Kommunistische Partei* CP, Communist Party
Kripo *Kriminalpolizei* CID, criminal investigation department
KSZE *Konferenz über Sicherheit und Zusammenarbeit in Europa* CSCE, Conference on Security and Cooperation in Europe
Kto. *Konto* acct, a/c, account
KV *Köchelverzeichnis* K, Köchel catalogue
kW *Kilowatt* kW, kilowatt(s)
kWh *Kilowattstunde(n)* kilowatt-hour(s)
KZ *Konzentrationslager* concentration camp

L

l *Liter* litre(s)
l. *links* l., left
lat. *lateinisch* Lat., Latin
l. c. *loco citato, am angegebenen Ort* l.c., in the place cited
led. *ledig* single, unmarried
lfd. *laufend* current, running
lfde. Nr. *laufende Nummer* ser. no., serial number
Lf(r)g. *Lieferung* dely, delivery
LG *Landgericht* district court
Lkw, LKW *Lastkraftwagen* lorry, *esp. Am.* truck
log *Logarithmus* log, logarithm
LP *Langspielplatte* LP, long-playing record
LPG *landwirtschaftliche Produktionsgenossenschaft hist. DDR* collective farm
LSD *Lysergsäurediäthylamid* LSD, lysergic acid dieathylamide
lt. *laut* acc. to, according to; as per
ltd. *leitend* man., managing

Ltg. *Leitung* direction; mangt, management
luth. *lutherisch* Luth., Lutheran
LZB *Landeszentralbank* State Central Bank

M

m *Meter* m, metre(s)
MA *Mittelalter* MA, Middle Ages
M. A. *Magister Artium* MA, Master of Arts
MAD *Militärischer Abschirmdienst* Military Counter-Intelligence Service
Math. *Mathematik* math., mathematics
m. a. W. *mit anderen Worten* in other words
max. *maximal* max., maximum
MAZ *magnetische Bildaufzeichnung* VTR, video tape recording
MB *Megabyte* mb, megabyte
mbH *mit beschränkter Haftung* with limited liability
MdB *Mitglied des Bundestages* Member of the Bundestag
MdL *Mitglied des Landtages* Member of the Landtag
mdl. *mündlich* verbal, oral
m. E. *meines Erachtens* in my opinion
MEZ *mitteleuropäische Zeit* CET, Central European Time
MG *Maschinengewehr* MG, machine gun
mg *Milligramm* milligramme(s)
MHz *Megahertz* MHz, megahertz
Mi. *Mittwoch* Wed., Wednesday
Mill. *Million(en)* m, million
Min., min. *Minute(n)* min., minute(s)
min. *minimal* min., minimum
Mio. *Million(en)* m, million
Mitw. *Mitwirkung* assistance, participation, cooperation
mm *Millimeter* mm, millimetre(s)
Mo. *Montag* Mon., Monday
möbl. *möbliert* furn., furnished
mod. *modern* mod., modern
MP *Maschinenpistole* submachine gun
Mrd. *Milliarde(n)* bn, billion
MS, Ms. *Manuskript* MS, ms, manuscript
MS, m.s. *multiple Sklerose* multiple sclerosis
MT *Megatonne* megaton

MTA *medizinisch-technische Assistentin* medical laboratory assistant

mtl. *monatlich* monthly

m. ü. M. *Meter über (dem) Meer(esspiegel)* metres above sea level

mus. *musikalisch* mus., musical

m. W. *meines Wissens* as far as I know

MwSt., MWSt. *Mehrwertsteuer* VAT, value-added tax

N

N *Nord(en)* N, north

n. *nach* after

N(a)chf. *Nachfolger* successor

nachm. *nachmittags* p.m., pm, in the afternoon

näml. *nämlich* viz, i.e., namely, that is to say

NATO *Nordatlantikpakt-Organisation* NATO, North Atlantic Treaty Organization

NB *notabene* NB, note well

n. Br. *nördlicher Breite* N lat, northern latitude

n. Chr. *nach Christus* AD, anno domini

NDR *Norddeutscher Rundfunk* Northern German Broadcasting Corporation

n. J. *nächsten Jahres* of next year

nkr *norwegische Krone(n)* Nkr, Norwegian crown(s)

n. M. *nächsten Monats* of next month

N. N. *nomen nominandum* name hitherto unknown

NO *Nordost(en)* NE, northeast

No. *Nummer* No., no., number

NOK *Nationales Olympisches Komitee* National Olympic Committee

nördl. *nördlich* N, north, northern

norw. *norwegisch* Norw., Norwegian

Nov. *November* Nov., November

NPD *Nationaldemokratische Partei Deutschlands* National-Democratic Party of Germany

Nr. *Nummer* No., no., number

NS *Nachschrift* PS, postscript; *hist.* *Nationalsozialismus* National Socialism

NVA *Nationale Volksarmee* *hist.* DDR

NW *Nordwest(en)* NW, northwest

O

O *Ost(en)* E, east

o. *oben* above; *oder* or; *ohne* w/o, without

o. a. *oben angeführt* above(-mentioned)

o. ä. *oder ähnlich(e, -es etc)* or the like

ÖAMTC *Österreichischer Automobil-, Motorrad- und Touring-Club* Austrian Automobile, Motorcycling and Touring Association

OB *Oberbürgermeister* mayor

o. B. *ohne Befund* 🕭 results negative

Obb. *Oberbayern* Upper Bavaria

ÖBB *Österreichische Bundesbahnen* Austrian Federal Railways

od. *oder* or

offiz. *offiziell* off., official

OHG *offene Handelsgesellschaft* general partnership

OLG *Oberlandesgericht* Higher Regional Court

OP *Operationssaal* operating theatre (*Am.* room)

op. *Opus* ♪ op., opus

o. Prof. *ordentlicher Professor* Prof., prof., (full) professor

ORF *Österreichischer Rundfunk* Austrian Broadcasting Corporation

Orig. *Original* orig., original

orth. *orthodox* Orth., Orthodox

österr. *österreichisch* Aus., Austrian

ÖTV *(Gewerkschaft) Öffentliche Dienste, Transport und Verkehr* the (German) Public Services and Transport Union

ÖVP *Österreichische Volkspartei* Austrian People's Party

P

p. A(dr). *per Adresse* c/o, care of

PC *Personalcomputer* PC, pc, personal computer

PCB *polychlorierte Biphenyle*

PDS *Partei des demokratischen Sozialismus* Party of Democratic Socialism

pers. *persönlich* pers., personal; personally, in person

Pf *Pfennig* pf., pfennig

Pfd. *Pfund* German pound(s)

PGiroA *Postgiroamt* postal giro office

PH *Pädagogische Hochschule* college of education, *Am.* teachers' college

PIN *persönliche Identifikationsnummer* PIN, personal identification number, PIN number

Pkt. *Punkt* pt, point

Pkw, PKW *Personenkraftwagen* (motor)car

Pl. *Platz* Sq., Square; *Plural* pl., plural

PLO *Palästinensische Befreiungsorganisation* PLO, Palestine Liberation Organization

PLZ *Postleitzahl* postcode, *Am.* zip code

pol. *polizeilich* police ...

poln. *polnisch* Pol., Polish

port(ug). *portugiesisch* Port., Portuguese

pp(a). *per Prokura* p.p., per pro(c)., by proxy

PR *Public Relations, Öffentlichkeitsarbeit* PR, public relations

prakt. *praktisch* practical(ly)

Priv.-Doz. *Privatdozent(in)* unsalaried lecturer

Prof. *Professor* Prof., Professor

PS *Pferdestärke(n)* HP, hp, horsepower; *Postskriptum* PS, postscript

Pta(s) *Peseta(s)* pta(s), peseta(s)

PTT *Post, Telefon, Telegraf; Schweizerische Post-, Telefon- und Telegrafenbetriebe* Swiss Postal, Telephone and Telegraph Services

PVC *Polyvinylchlorid* PVC, polyvinyl chloride

Q

qkm *Quadratkilometer* (*obs. for* **km²**) sq. km, square kilometre(s)

qm *Quadratmeter* (*obs. for* **m²**) sq. m, square metre(s)

Qual. *Qualität* qual., quality

R

r. *rechts* r., right

RA *Rechtsanwalt* lawyer; *Br.* sol., solr, solicitor; bar., barrister; *Am.* att., atty, attorney

RAF *Rote Armee-Fraktion* Red Army Fraction

RB *Radio Bremen* Broadcasting Corporation of Bremen

Rbl *Rubel* Rbl., rbl., r(o)uble(s)

rd. *rund* roughly

Reg.-Bez. *Regierungsbezirk* administrative district

Rel. *Religion* rel., religion

Rep. *Republik* Rep., Republic

resp. *respektive* resp., respectively

RIAS *Rundfunk im* (*ehemaligen*) *amerikanischen Sektor* (*von Berlin*) Radio in the (*former*) American Sector (*of Berlin*)

rk, r.-k. *römisch-katholisch* RC, Roman Catholic

RNS *Ribonukleinsäure* RNA, ribonucleic acid

röm. *römisch* Rom., Roman

RT *Registertonne(n)* reg. t., register ton(s)

russ. *russisch* Russ., Russian

S

S *Süd(en)* S, south; *Schilling* S., schilling

s *Sekunde(n)* s, sec., second(s)

S. *Seite* p., page

s. *siehe* v., vide, see

s. a. *siehe auch* see also

SB- *Selbstbedienungs-* self-service ...

SBB *Schweizerische Bundesbahnen* Swiss Federal Railways

SC *Sportclub* sports club

schwed. *schwedisch* Swedish

schweiz. *schweizerisch* Swiss

SDR *Süddeutscher Rundfunk* Southern German Broadcasting Corporation

SED *Sozialistische Einheitspartei Deutschlands* hist. *DDR* Socialist Unity Party of Germany

Sek., sek. *Sekunde(n)* s., sec., second(s)

sen. *senior* Sen., sen., Snr, Sr, senior

Sept. *September* Sept., September

SFB *Sender Freies Berlin* Broadcasting Corporation of Free Berlin

sFr., sfr *Schweizer Franken* SF, Sfr, Swiss Franc(s)

Sg. *Singular* sing., singular

SJ *Societate Jesu, Jesuit* Jesuit

skr *schwedische Krone(n)* Kr, Skr, Swedish crown(s)

sm *Seemeile(n)* n. m., nautical mile(s)

SO *Südost(en)* SE, southeast

s.o. *siehe oben* see above

sog. *sogenannt(e, -es etc)* so-called

soz. *sozial* social
span. *spanisch* Span., Spanish
SPD *Sozialdemokratische Partei Deutschlands* Social Democratic Party of Germany
spez. *speziell* special, particular
SPÖ *Sozialistische Partei Österreichs* Austrian Socialist Party
SR *Saarländischer Rundfunk* Broadcasting Corporation of the Saarland
s. R. *siehe Rückseite* see overleaf
SRG *Schweizerische Radio- und Fernsehgesellschaft* Swiss Broadcasting Corporation
SS *Sommersemester* summer semester *or* term
St. *Sankt* St., Saint; *Stück* pc(s)., piece(s)
Std. *Stunde(n)* h., hr(s)., hour(s)
stdl. *stündlich* hourly, every hour
stellv. *stellvertretend* asst, assistant
StGB *Strafgesetzbuch* penal *or* criminal code
StPO *Strafprozeßordnung* Code of Criminal Procedure
Str. *Straße* St, Street; Rd, Road
stud. *studiosus, Student* student
StVO *Straßenverkehrsordnung* (road) traffic regulations, *Br.* Highway Code
s. u. *siehe unten* see below
SW *Südwest(en)* SW, southwest
SWF *Südwestfunk* Southwestern German Broadcasting Corporation

T

t *Tonne(n)* t, ton(s)
t(ä)gl. *täglich* daily, a *or* per day
Tb(c) *Tuberkulose* TB, tuberculosis
TEE *Trans-Europ-Express* TEE, Trans-European-Express
Tel. *Telefon* tel., (tele)phone
Telegr. *Telegramm* teleg., telegram
TH *Technische Hochschule* college of technology, technical university
TL *türkische Lira (pl Lire)* TL, Turkish lira *(pl* lire *or* liras)
TU *Technische Universität* technical university
TÜV *Technischer Überwachungsverein* Technical Control Board
TV *Turnverein* gymnastics club; *Television* TV, television

U

U *Unterseeboot* sub., submarine
u. *und* and
u. a. *und andere(s)* and others (other things); *unter anderem (anderen)* among other things, inter alia (among others)
u. ä. *und ähnliche(s)* and the like
U. *(or* u.) **A. w. g.** *um Antwort wird gebeten* RSVP, please reply
U-Bahn *Untergrundbahn* underground, *Am.* subway
u. d(er)gl. (m.) *und dergleichen (mehr)* and so on; and the like
u. d. M. *unter dem Meeresspiegel* below sea level
ü. d. M. *über dem Meeresspiegel* above sea level
u. E. *unseres Erachtens* in our opinion, as we see it
UFO, Ufo *unbekanntes Flugobjekt* UFO, unidentified flying object
U-Haft *Untersuchungshaft* custody, detention (pending trial)
UKW *Ultrakurzwelle* USW, ultrashort wave; FM, frequency modulation
U/min. *Umdrehungen pro Minute* r.p.m., revolutions per minute
U-Musik *Unterhaltungsmusik* light music
unbek. *unbekannt* unknown
unbez. *unbezahlt* unpaid
unehel. *unehelich* illegit., illegitimate
ung(ar). *ungarisch* Hung., Hungarian
ungebr. *ungebräuchlich* unusual
unverb. *unverbindlich* not binding
unverh. *unverheiratet* unm., unmarried, sgl., single
unvollst. *unvollständig* incomplete
unz. *unzählig* innumerable
urspr. *ursprünglich* orig., original(ly)
US(A) *Vereinigte Staaten (von Amerika)* US(A), United States (of America)
usw. *und so weiter* etc., and so on
u. U. *unter Umständen* poss., possibly; perh., perhaps; if need be
UV *Ultraviolett* UV, ultraviolet
u. W. *unseres Wissens* as far as we know
Ü-Wagen *Übertragungswagen* outside broadcast (OB) van *or* unit

V

V *Volt* V, volt(s)
V. *Vers* v., verse; l., line
v. *von, vom* of; from; by; *versus, gegen* v., vs., versus
VAE *Vereinigte Arabische Emirate* UAE, United Arab Emirates
VB *Verhandlungsbasis* o.n.o., or near-(est) offer
v. Chr. *vor Christus* BC, before Christ
v. D. *vom Dienst* on duty, in charge
VDE *Verein Deutscher Elektrotechniker* Association of German Electricians
VEB *volkseigener Betrieb* hist. *DDR* state-owned enterprise *or* company
Verf. *Verfasser* author
vergr. *vergriffen* out of print
verh. *verheiratet* mar., married
Verl. *Verlag* publishing house *or* company, publishers
Verw. *Verwaltung* admin, administration; mngmt, management
verw. *verwitwet* widowed
vgl. *vergleiche* cf., confer; cp., compare
v. H. *vom Hundert* pc, per cent, percent
VHS *Volkshochschule* adult education program(me); adult evening classes
v. J. *vorigen Jahres* of last year
v. l. n. r. *von links nach rechts* from left to right
v. M. *vorigen Monats* of last month
V-Mann *Vertrauensmann, Verbindungsmann* contact
Vollm. *Vollmacht* full power(s), auth., authority
vollst. *vollständig* complete(ly)
vorl. *vorläufig* temp., temporary
vorm. *vormittags* a.m., am, in the morning; *vormals* formerly
Vors. *Vorsitzende(r)* chairperson, chm., chairman, chw., chairwoman
VP *Vollpension* full board, board and lodging
VR *Volksrepublik* People's Republic
v. T. *vom Tausend* per thousand
VW *Volkswagen* VW, Volkswagen

W

W *West(en)* W, west; *Watt* W, watt(s)
WAA *Wiederaufbereitungsanlage* reprocessing plant

wbl. *weiblich* fem., female
WC *Wasserklosett* WC toilet
Wdh(lg). *Wiederholung* repetition; *TV etc* repeat
WDR *Westdeutscher Rundfunk* Western German Broadcasting Corporation
werkt. *werktags* (on) weekdays
westl. *westlich* west, western
WEU *Westeuropäische Union* WEU, Western European Union
WEZ *westeuropäische Zeit* GMT, Greenwich Mean Time
WG *Wohngemeinschaft* flat share; people sharing a flat (*esp. Am.* an apartment) *or.* a house
Whg. *Wohnung* flat, *esp. Am.* apt., apartment
wirtsch. *wirtschaftlich* econ., economic
wiss. *wissenschaftlich* academic
w. L. *westlicher Länge* W long., Western longitude
WM *Weltmeisterschaft* world championship; *soccer:* World Cup
wö. *wöchentlich* weekly, every week
WS *Wintersemester* winter semester *or* term
WSV *Winterschlußverkauf* winter sales
Wwe. *Witwe* widow
Wz. *Warenzeichen* TM, trademark; *Wasserzeichen* watermark

Z

Z. *Zeile* l., line; *Zahl* number
z. *zu, zum, zur* at; to
z. B. *zum Beispiel* e.g., for example, for instance
ZDF *Zweites Deutsches Fernsehen* Second Channel *or* Program(me) of German Television Broadcasting
zeitgen. *zeitgenössisch* contemporary
zeitl. *zeitlich* temporal, time ...
zeitw. *zeitweilig, zeitweise* occasionally, from time to time
ZH *Zentralheizung* centr. heat., central heating
z. H(d). *zu Händen* attn, attention (of)
Zi. *Zimmer* rm (no.), room (number); *Ziffer* fig., figure; No., no., number; subparagraph; *in contract etc:* item
ZK *Zentralkomitee* Central Committee
Zl *Zloty* Zl, zloty(s)
Zlg. *Zahlung* payment

ZOB *zentraler Omnibusbahnhof* bus *or* coach station
z. T. *zum Teil* partly
Ztg. *Zeitung* newspaper
Ztr. *Zentner* cwt, hundredweight(s)
Ztschr. *Zeitschrift* mag., magazine
Zub. *Zubehör* accessories, fittings

zul. *zulässig* permissible; ⊚ safe
zur. *zurück* back
zus. *zusammen* tog., together
z(u)zgl. *zuzüglich* plus
zw. *zwischen* bet., between; among
Zwgst. *Zweigstelle* branch (office)
z. Z(t). *zur Zeit* at present

Alphabetical List of the German Irregular Verbs
Infinitive — Preterite — Past Participle

backen – backte (buk) – gebacken
bedingen – bedang – (bedingte) – bedungen (*conditional*: bedingt)
befehlen – befahl – befohlen
beginnen – begann – begonnen
beißen – biß – gebissen
bergen – barg – geborgen
bersten – barst – geborsten
bewegen – bewog – bewogen
biegen – bog – gebogen
bieten – bot – geboten
binden – band – gebunden
bitten – bat – gebeten
blasen – blies – geblasen
bleiben – blieb – geblieben
bleichen – blich – geblichen
braten – briet – gebraten
brauchen – brauchte – gebraucht (*v/aux* brauchen)
brechen – brach – gebrochen
brennen – brannte – gebrannt
bringen – brachte – gebracht
denken – dachte – gedacht
dreschen – drosch – gedroschen
dringen – drang – gedrungen
dürfen – durfte – gedürft (*v/aux* dürfen)
empfehlen – empfahl – empfohlen
erlöschen – erlosch – erloschen
erschrecken – erschrak – erschrocken
essen – aß – gegessen
fahren – fuhr – gefahren
fallen – fiel – gefallen
fangen – fing – gefangen
fechten – focht – gefochten
finden – fand – gefunden
flechten – flocht – geflochten
fliegen – flog – geflogen
fliehen – floh – geflohen
fließen – floß – geflossen
fressen – fraß – gefressen
frieren – fror – gefroren
gären – gor (*esp. fig.* gärte) – gegoren (*esp. fig.* gegärt)
gebären – gebar – geboren
geben – gab – gegeben
gedeihen – gedieh – gediehen
gehen – ging – gegangen
gelingen – gelang – gelungen
gelten – galt – gegolten
genesen – genas – genesen

genießen – genoß – genossen
geschehen – geschah – geschehen
gewinnen – gewann – gewonnen
gießen – goß – gegossen
gleichen – glich – geglichen
gleiten – glitt – geglitten
glimmen – glomm – geglommen
graben – grub – gegraben
greifen – griff – gegriffen
haben – hatte – gehabt
halten – hielt – gehalten
hängen – hing – gehangen
hauen – haute (hieb) – gehauen
heben – hob – gehoben
heißen – hieß – geheißen
helfen – half – geholfen
kennen – kannte – gekannt
klimmen – klomm – geklommen
klingen – klang – geklungen
kneifen – kniff – gekniffen
kommen – kam – gekommen
können–konnte–gekonnt (*v/aux* können)
kriechen – kroch – gekrochen
laden – lud – geladen
lassen – ließ – gelassen (*v/aux* lassen)
laufen – lief – gelaufen
leiden – litt – gelitten
leihen – lieh – geliehen
lesen – las – gelesen
liegen – lag – gelegen
lügen – log – gelogen
mahlen – mahlte – gemahlen
meiden – mied – gemieden
melken–melkte (molk) – gemolken (gemelkt)
messen – maß – gemessen
mißlingen – mißlang – mißlungen
mögen – mochte – gemocht (*v/aux* mögen)
müssen–mußte–gemußt (*v/aux* müssen)
nehmen – nahm – genommen
nennen – nannte – genannt
pfeifen – pfiff – gepfiffen
preisen – pries – gepriesen
quellen – quoll – gequollen
raten – riet – geraten
reiben – rieb – gerieben
reißen – riß – gerissen
reiten – ritt – geritten
rennen – rannte – gerannt

riechen – roch – gerochen
ringen – rang – gerungen
rinnen – rann – geronnen
rufen – rief – gerufen
salzen – salzte – gesalzen (gesalzt)
saufen – soff – gesoffen
saugen – sog – gesogen
schaffen – schuf – geschaffen
schallen – schallte (scholl) – geschallt
(*for* erschallen *a.* erschollen)
scheiden – schied – geschieden
scheinen – schien – geschienen
scheißen – schiß – geschissen
schelten – schalt – gescholten
scheren – schor – geschoren
schieben – schob – geschoben
schießen – schoß – geschossen
schinden – schindete – geschunden
schlafen – schlief – geschlafen
schlagen – schlug – geschlagen
schleichen – schlich – geschlichen
schleifen – schliff – geschliffen
schleißen – schliß – geschlissen
schließen – schloß – geschlossen
schlingen – schlang – geschlungen
schmeißen – schmiß – geschmissen
schmelzen – schmolz – geschmolzen
schnauben – schnob – geschnoben
schneiden – schnitt – geschnitten
schrecken – schrak – *obs.* geschrocken
schreiben – schrieb – geschrieben
schreien – schrie – geschrie(e)n
schreiten – schritt – geschritten
schweigen – schwieg – geschwiegen
schwellen – schwoll – geschwollen
schwimmen – schwamm – geschwommen
schwinden – schwand – geschwunden
schwingen – schwang – geschwungen
schwören – schwor – geschworen
sehen – sah – gesehen
sein – war – gewesen
senden – sandte – gesandt
sieden – sott – gesotten
singen – sang – gesungen
sinken – sank – gesunken
sinnen – sann – gesonnen
sitzen – saß – gesessen
sollen – sollte – gesollt (*v/aux* sollen)

spalten – spaltete – gespalten (gespaltet)
speien – spie – gespie(e)n
spinnen – spann – gesponnen
sprechen – sprach – gesprochen
sprießen – sproß – gesprossen
springen – sprang – gesprungen
stechen – stach – gestochen
stecken – steckte (stak) – gesteckt
stehen – stand – gestanden
stehlen – stahl – gestohlen
steigen – stieg – gestiegen
sterben – starb – gestorben
stieben – stob – gestoben
stinken – stank – gestunken
stoßen – stieß – gestoßen
streichen – strich – gestrichen
streiten – stritt – gestritten
tragen – trug – getragen
treffen – traf – getroffen
treiben – trieb – getrieben
treten – trat – getreten
triefen – triefte (troff) – getrieft
trinken – trank – getrunken
trügen – trog – getrogen
tun – tat – getan
verderben – verdarb – verdorben
verdrießen – verdroß – verdrossen
vergessen – vergaß – vergessen
verlieren – verlor – verloren
verschleißen – verschliß – verschlissen
verzeihen – verzieh – verziehen
wachsen – wuchs – gewachsen
wägen – wog (wägte) – gewogen (gewägt)
waschen – wusch – gewaschen
weben – wob – gewoben
weichen – wich – gewichen
weisen – wies – gewiesen
wenden – wandte – gewandt
werben – warb – geworben
werden – wurde – geworden (worden*)
werfen – warf – geworfen
wiegen – wog – gewogen
winden – wand – gewunden
wissen – wußte – gewußt
wollen – wollte – gewollt (*v/aux* wollen)
wringen – wrang – gewrungen
zeihen – zieh – geziehen
ziehen – zog – gezogen
zwingen – zwang – gezwungen

---

* only in connection with the past participles of other verbs, *e.g.*, **er ist gesehen worden** he has been seen.

States of the Federal Republic of Germany

Baden-Württemberg Baden-Württemberg
Bayern Bayern
Berlin Berlin
Brandenburg Brandenburg
Bremen Bremen
Hamburg Hamburg
Hessen Hessen
Mecklenburg-Vorpommern Mecklenburg-Western Pomerania

Niedersachsen Lower Saxony
Nordrhein-Westfalen North Rhine-Westphalia
Rheinland-Pfalz Rhineland-Palatinate
Saarland Saarland
Sachsen Saxony
Sachsen-Anhalt Saxony-Anhalt
Schleswig-Holstein Schleswig-Holstein
Thüringen Thuringia

States of the Republic of Austria

Burgenland Burgenland
Kärnten Carinthia
Niederösterreich Lower Austria
Oberösterreich Upper Austria
Salzburg Salzburg

Steiermark Styria
Tirol Tyrol
Vorarlberg Vorarlberg
Wien Vienna

Cantons of the Swiss Confederation

(Half cantons in brackets)

Aargau Aargau
Appenzell (Inner-Rhoden; Außer-Rhoden) Appenzell (Inner Rhodes; Outer Rhodes)
Basel Basel, Basle
Bern Bern, Berne
Freiburg, Fribourg Fribourg
Genf, Genève Geneva
Glarus Glarus
Graubünden Graubünden, Grisons
Jura Jura
Luzern Lucerne
Neuenburg, Neuchâtel Neuchâtel

St. Gallen St Gallen, St Gall
Schaffhausen Schaffhausen
Schwyz Schwyz
Solothurn Solothurn
Tessin, Ticino Ticino
Thurgau Thurgau
Unterwalden (Obwalden; Nidwalden) Unterwalden (Obwalden; Nidwalden)
Uri Uri
Waadt, Vaud Vaud
Wallis, Valais Valais, Wallis
Zug Zug
Zürich Zurich

Numerals
Cardinal Numbers

0 null *nought, zero*	**41** einundvierzig *forty-one*
1 eins *one*	**50** fünfzig *fifty*
2 zwei *two*	**51** einundfünfzig *fifty-one*
3 drei *three*	**60** sechzig *sixty*
4 vier *four*	**61** einundsechzig *sixty-one*
5 fünf *five*	**70** siebzig *seventy*
6 sechs *six*	**71** einundsiebzig *seventy-one*
7 sieben *seven*	**80** achtzig *eighty*
8 acht *eight*	**81** einundachtzig *eighty-one*
9 neun *nine*	**90** neunzig *ninety*
10 zehn *ten*	**91** einundneunzig *ninety-one*
11 elf *eleven*	**100** hundert *a (or one) hundred*
12 zwölf *twelve*	**101** hundert(und)eins *a hundred and one*
13 dreizehn *thirteen*	
14 vierzehn *fourteen*	**200** zweihundert *two hundred*
15 fünfzehn *fifteen*	**300** dreihundert *three hundred*
16 sechzehn *sixteen*	**572** fünfhundert(und)zweiundsiebzig *five hundred and seventy-two*
17 siebzehn *seventeen*	
18 achtzehn *eighteen*	
19 neunzehn *nineteen*	**1000** tausend *a (or one) thousand*
20 zwanzig *twenty*	**2000** zweitausend *two thousand*
21 einundzwanzig *twenty-one*	**1 000 000** eine Million *a (or one) million*
22 zweiundzwanzig *twenty-two*	
23 dreiundzwanzig *twenty-three*	**2 000 000** zwei Millionen *two million*
30 dreißig *thirty*	
31 einunddreißig *thirty-one*	**1 000 000 000** eine Milliarde *a (or one) billion*
40 vierzig *forty*	

Ordinal Numbers

1. erste *first*	**19.** neunzehnte *nineteenth*
2. zweite *second*	**20.** zwanzigste *twentieth*
3. dritte *third*	**21.** einundzwanzigste *twenty-first*
4. vierte *fourth*	**22.** zweiundzwanzigste *twenty-second*
5. fünfte *fifth*	**23.** dreiundzwanzigste *twenty-third*
6. sechste *sixth*	
7. siebente *seventh*	**30.** dreißigste *thirtieth*
8. achte *eighth*	**31.** einunddreißigste *thirty-first*
9. neunte *ninth*	**40.** vierzigste *fortieth*
10. zehnte *tenth*	**41.** einundvierzigste *forty-first*
11. elfte *eleventh*	**50.** fünfzigste *fiftieth*
12. zwölfte *twelfth*	**51.** einundfünfzigste *fifty-first*
13. dreizehnte *thirteenth*	**60.** sechzigste *sixtieth*
14. vierzehnte *fourteenth*	**61.** einundsechzigste *sixty-first*
15. fünfzehnte *fifteenth*	**70.** siebzigste *seventieth*
16. sechzehnte *sixteenth*	**71.** einundsiebzigste *seventy-first*
17. siebzehnte *seventeenth*	**80.** achtzigste *eightieth*
18. achtzehnte *eighteenth*	

81. einundachtzigste *eighty-first*
90. neunzigste *ninetieth*
100. hundertste *(one) hundredth*
101. hundertunderste *hundred and first*
200. zweihundertste *two hundredth*
300. dreihundertste *three hundredth*

572. fünfhundertundzweiundsiebzigste *five hundred and seventy-second*
1000. tausendste *(one) thousandth*
2000. zweitausendste *two thousandth*
1 000 000. millionste *millionth*
2 000 000. zweimillionste *two millionth*

Fractions and other numerical values

$^1/_2$ ein halb *one (or a) half*
$1^1/_2$ anderthalb *one and a half*
$2^1/_2$ zweieinhalb *two and a half*
$^1/_2$ Meile *half a mile*
$^1/_3$ ein Drittel *one (or a) third*
$^2/_3$ zwei Drittel *two thirds*
$^1/_4$ ein Viertel *one (or a) fourth, one (or a) quarter*
$^3/_4$ drei Viertel *three fourths, three quarters*
$1^1/_4$ Stunden *one (or an) hour and a quarter*
$^1/_5$ ein Fünftel *one (or a) fifth*
$3^4/_5$ drei vier Fünftel *three and four fifths*
0,4 null Komma vier *(nought) point four (0.4)*
2,5 zwei Komma fünf *two point five (2.5)*

Einfach *single*
zweifach *double*
dreifach *treble, triple, threefold*
vierfach *fourfold, quadruple*
fünffach *fivefold etc*

Einmal *once*
zweimal *twice*
drei-, vier-, fünfmal *etc three, four, five times*
zweimal soviel(e) *twice as much (many)*
noch einmal *once more*

Erstens, zweitens, drittens *etc firstly, secondly, thirdly, in the first (second, third) place*

7 + 8 = 15 sieben plus (*or* und) acht ist fünfzehn *seven plus (or and) eight is fifteen*

10 – 3 = 7 zehn minus (*or* weniger) drei ist sieben *ten minus (or less) three is seven*

2 × 3 = 6 zweimal drei ist sechs *twice three is six*

20 : 5 = 4 zwanzig dividiert (*or* geteilt) durch fünf ist vier *twenty divided by five is four*

German Weights and Measures

I. Measure of length

1 mm *Millimeter* millimetre
= $^1/_{1000}$ metre
= 0.0010936 yards
= 0.0032809 feet
= 0.03937079 inches

1 cm *Zentimeter* centimetre
= $^1/_{100}$ metre
= 0.3937 inches

1 dm *Dezimeter* decimetre
= $^1/_{10}$ metre
= 3.9370 inches

1 m *Meter* metre
= 1.0936 yards
= 3.2809 feet
= 39.37079 inches

1 km *Kilometer* kilometre
= 1,000 metres
= 1,093.637 yards
= 3,280.8692 feet
= 39,370.79 inches
= 0.62138 British or Statute Miles

1 sm *Seemeile* nautical mile
= 1,852 metres

II. Surface measurements

1 mm² *Quadratmillimeter*
square millimetre
= $^1/_{1 000 000}$ square metre
= 0.000001196 square yards
= 0.0000107641 square feet
= 0.00155 square inches

1 cm² *Quadratzentimeter*
square centimetre
= $^1/_{10 000}$ square metre

1 dm² *Quadratdezimeter*
square decimetre
= $^1/_{100}$ square metre

1 m² *Quadratmeter* square metre
= 1.19599 square yards
= 10.7641 square feet
= 1,550 square inches

1 a *Ar* are
= 100 square metres
= 119.5993 square yards
= 1,076.4103 square feet

1 ha *Hektar* hectare
= 100 ares
= 10,000 square metres
= 11,959.90 square yards
= 107,641.03 square feet
= 2.4711 acres

1 km² *Quadratkilometer*
square kilometre
= 100 hectares
= 1,000,000 square metres
= 247.11 acres
= 0.3861 square miles

III. Solid measures

1 cm³ *Kubikzentimeter*
cubic centimetre
= 1,000 cubic millimetres
= 0.061 cubic inches

1 dm³ *Kubikdezimeter*
cubic decimetre
= 1,000 cubic centimetres
= 61.0253 cubic inches

1 m³ *Kubikmeter*
1 rm *Raummeter* } cubic metre
1 fm *Festmeter*
= 1,000 cubic decimetres
= 1.3079 cubic yards
= 35.3156 cubic feet

1 RT *Registertonne*
register ton
= 2.832 m³
= 100 cubic feet

IV. Measure of Capacity

1 l *Liter* litre
= 10 decilitres
= 1.7607 pints (*Br.*)
= 7.0431 gills (*Br.*)
= 0.8804 quarts (*Br.*)
= 0.2201 gallons (*Br.*)
= 2.1134 pints (*Am.*)
= 8.4534 gills (*Am.*)
= 1.0567 quarts (*Am.*)
= 0.2642 gallons (*Am*).

1 hl   ***Hektoliter*** hectolitre
- = 100 litres
- = 22.009 gallons (*Br.*)
- = 2.751 bushels (*Br.*)
- = 26.418 gallons (*Am.*)
- = 2.84 bushels (*Am.*)

V. Weights

1 mg   ***Milligramm*** milligram(me)
- = $^1/_{1000}$ gram(me)
- = 0.0154 grains

1 g   ***Gramm*** gram(me)
- = $^1/_{1000}$ kilogram(me)
- = 15.4324 grains

1 Pfd   ***Pfund*** pound (German)
- = $^1/_2$ kilogram(me)
- = 500 gram(me)s
- = 1.1023 pounds (avdp.)
- = 1.3396 pounds (troy)

1 kg   ***Kilogramm, Kilo***
kilogram(me)
- = 1,000 gram(me)s
- = 2.2046 pounds (avdp.)
- = 2.6792 pounds (troy)

1 Ztr.   ***Zentner*** centner
- = 100 pounds (German)
- = 50 kilogram(me)s
- = 110.23 pounds (avdp.)
- = 0.9842 British hundredweights
- = 1.1023 U.S. hundredweights

1 dz   ***Doppelzentner***
- = 100 kilogram(me)s
- = 1.9684 British hundredweights
- = 2.2046 U.S. hundredweights

1 t   ***Tonne*** ton
- = 1,000 kilogram(me)s
- = 0.984 British tons
- = 1.1023 U.S. tons

Phonetic Alphabet

	German	British English	American English	International	Civil Aviation (ICAO)
A	Anton	Andrew	Abel	Amsterdam	Alfa
Ä	Ärger	—	—	—	—
B	Berta	Benjamin	Baker	Baltimore	Bravo
C	Cäsar	Charlie	Charlie	Casablanca	Charlie
CH	Charlotte	—	—	—	—
D	Dora	David	Dog	Danemark	Delta
E	Emil	Edward	Easy	Edison	Echo
F	Friedrich	Frederick	Fox	Florida	Foxtrot
G	Gustav	George	George	Gallipoli	Golf
H	Heinrich	Harry	How	Havana	Hotel
I	Ida	Isaac	Item	Italia	India
J	Julius	Jack	Jig	Jerusalem	Juliett
K	Kaufmann	King	King	Kilogramme	Kilo
L	Ludwig	Lucy	Love	Liverpool	Lima
M	Martha	Mary	Mike	Madagaskar	Mike
N	Nordpol	Nellie	Nan	New York	November
O	Otto	Oliver	Oboe	Oslo	Oscar
Ö	Ökonom	—	—	—	—
P	Paula	Peter	Peter	Paris	Papa
Q	Quelle	Queenie	Queen	Québec	Quebec
R	Richard	Robert	Roger	Roma	Romeo
S	Samuel	Sugar	Sugar	Santiago	Sierra
Sch	Schule	—	—	—	—
T	Theodor	Tommy	Tare	Tripoli	Tango
U	Ulrich	Uncle	Uncle	Upsala	Uniform
Ü	Übermut	—	—	—	—
V	Viktor	Victor	Victor	Valencia	Victor
W	Wilhelm	William	William	Washington	Whiskey
X	Xanthippe	Xmas	X	Xanthippe	X-Ray
Y	Ypsilon	Yellow	Yoke	Yokohama	Yankee
Z	Zacharias	Zebra	Zebra	Zürich	Zulu

Second Part

English-German

by

Helmut Willmann

Completely revised edition 1993

LANGENSCHEIDT

NEW YORK · BERLIN · MUNICH
VIENNA · ZURICH

Guide for the User

1. English Headwords.

1.1 The alphabetical order of the headwords has been observed throughout, including the irregular forms.

1.2 Centred dots or stress marks within a headword indicate syllabification,

e.g. **cul·ti·vate ...**, **ˌcul·ti'va·tion**

1.3 In hyphenated compounds a hyphen coinciding with the end of a line is repeated at the beginning of the next.

1.4 The tilde (**~**, **~**) represents the repetition of a headword.

1.4.1 In compounds the tilde in bold type (**~**) replaces the catchword,

e.g. **af·ter ...** '**~·birth** (= afterbirth) ...

1.4.2 The simple tilde (**~**) replaces the headword immediately preceding (which itself may contain a tilde in bold type),

e.g. **dis·tance ...** *at a* **~** = at a distance.
day ... '**~·light ...** **~** *saving time* = daylight saving time.

1.5 When the initial letter changes from small to capital or vice versa, the usual tilde is replaced by **2** or **2**,

e.g. **state ...** **2** *Department* = State Department.

2. Pronunciation.

2.1 The pronunciation of English headwords is given in square brackets by means of the symbols of the International Phonetic Association.

2.2 To save space the tilde (**~**) has been made use of in many places within the phonetic transcription. It replaces any part of the preceding complete transcription which remains unchanged,

e.g. **gym·na·si·um** [dʒɪmˈneɪzjəm] ... **gym·nast** [ˈ~næst] ...

3. Subject Labels.
The field of knowledge from which an English headword or some of its meanings are taken is indicated by figurative or abbreviated labels or other labels written out in full. A figurative or abbreviated label placed immediately after the phonetic transcription of a headword refers to all translations. A label preceding an individual translation refers to this only.

4. Usage Label.
The indication of the level of usage by abbreviations such as F, *sl.* etc refers to the English headword. Wherever possible the same level of usage between headword and translation has been aimed at.

5. Grammatical References.

5.1 When the last element of a compound is a noun with an irregular plural, a reference such as (*irr man*) indicates that the plural form is given under the separate headword (in this case **man**):

fore·man (*irr man*).

5.2 An adjective marked with □ takes the regular adverbial form, i.e. by affixing ...ly to the adjective or by changing ...le into ...ly or ...y into ...ily.

5.3 (**~ally**) means that an adverb is formed by affixing ...ally to the adjective.

5.4 When there is only one adverb for adjectives ending in both ...ic and ...ical, this is indicated in the following way:

    ge·o·met·ric, ge·o·met·ri·cal □,
    i.e. geometrically is the adverb of both adjectives.

6. Translations.

6.1 The direct and indirect objects of verbs are printed in italics before the translation. Where necessary the subject of an adjective or verb is indicated in italics and in brackets after the translation,

    e.g. **a·ban·don ... 2.** *Hoffnung etc* aufgeben, *Suche etc a.* einstellen ...
    a·bate ... abklingen (*Begeisterung, Lärm, Schmerz etc*) ...
    ab·ject ... bitter (*Armut etc*) ...

6.2 Prepositions governing an English catchword (verb, adjective, noun) are given in both languages,

    e.g. **place ... 10. (with)** *Auftrag* erteilen (*dat*), vergeben (an *acc*), *Bestellung* aufgeben (bei) ...
    pose ... 3. ... *Bedrohung, Gefahr etc* darstellen (**for, to** für) ...

6.3 Where a German preposition may govern the dative or the accusative case, the case is given in brackets,

    e.g. **en·ter ...** eindringen in (*acc*) ...

7. Illustrative phrases and their translations follow the translation of the headword. When the translation can easily be gathered from the meanings of the separate words, it has occasionally been omitted, e.g.

    gain ... 4. zunehmen an (*dat*): **~ speed** schneller werden, ...
    a·board ... 1. ⚓, ✈ an Bord (*gen*): **go ~;** ...

A

A [eɪ] *s*: *from A to Z* F von A bis Z.

a [ə], *vor vokalischem Anlaut* **an** [ən] *adj od. Artikel* **1.** ein(e): *he is a doctor* er ist Arzt. **2.** der-, die-, dasselbe: *they are of an age* sie sind gleichaltrig. **3.** per, pro, je: *twice a week* zweimal wöchentlich *od.* in der Woche.

a·back [ə'bæk] *adv*: *taken ~* überrascht, verblüfft; bestürzt.

a·ban·don [ə'bændən] *v/t* **1.** *Frau etc* verlassen. **2.** *Hoffnung etc* aufgeben, *Suche etc a.* einstellen, (*Sport*) *Spiel* abbrechen.

a·base [ə'beɪs] *v/t* erniedrigen, demütigen. **a'base·ment** *s* Erniedrigung *f*, Demütigung *f*.

a·bashed [ə'bæʃt] *adj* beschämt, verlegen: *feel ~* sich schämen.

a·bate [ə'beɪt] *v/i* abklingen (*Begeisterung, Lärm, Schmerz etc*), (*a. Sturm etc*) sich legen.

ab·at·toir ['æbətwɑ:] *s* Schlachthaus *n*, -hof *m*.

ab·bess ['æbes] *s* Äbtissin *f*. **ab·bey** ['æbɪ] *s* Abtei *f*. **ab·bot** ['æbət] *s* Abt *m*.

ab·bre·vi·ate [ə'bri:vɪeɪt] *v/t* (ab-, ver)kürzen: *~d form* Kurzform *f*. **ab·bre·vi·a·tion** *s* (Ab-, Ver)Kürzung *f*.

ABC [ˌeɪbi:'si:] *s* **1.** *Am. oft pl* Abc *n*, Alphabet *n*: (*as*) *easy as ~* kinderleicht; *~ weapons pl* ✕ ABC-Waffen *pl*. **2.** *fig.* Abc *n*, Anfangsgründe *pl*.

ab·di·cate ['æbdɪkeɪt] **I** *v/i* abdanken. **II** *v/t Amt* niederlegen: *~ the throne* abdanken. **ˌab·di'ca·tion** *s* Abdankung *f*.

ab·do·men ['æbdəmen] *s anat.* Unterleib *m*. **ab·dom·i·nal** [æb'dɒmɪnl] *adj* Unterleibs...

ab·duct [əb'dʌkt] *v/t* entführen. **ab·duc·tion** [æb'dʌkʃn] *s* Entführung *f*.

ab·er·ra·tion [ˌæbə'reɪʃn] *s* **1.** Abweichung *f, ast., biol., phys. u.* Aberration *f*. **2.** geistige Verwirrung.

a·bet [ə'bet] → *aid* 3.

a·bey·ance [ə'beɪəns] *s*: *fall into ~* außer Gebrauch kommen.

ab·hor [əb'hɔː] *v/t* verabscheuen.

ab·hor·rence [əb'hɒrəns] *s* Abscheu *m, f* (*of* vor *dat*). **ab'hor·rent** *adj* □ **1.** zuwider, verhaßt (*to dat*): *it is ~ to me* es widerstrebt mir zutiefst (*to do* zu tun). **2.** abstoßend.

a·bide [ə'baɪd] **I** *v/i*: *~ by* sich halten an (*acc*); *Folgen* tragen. **II** *v/t* ertragen, aushalten: *I cannot ~ him* ich kann ihn nicht ausstehen.

a·bil·i·ty [ə'bɪlətɪ] *s* Fähigkeit *f*: *~ to pay* Zahlungsfähigkeit; *to the best of one's ~* nach besten Kräften.

ab·ject ['æbdʒekt] *adj* □ **1.** bitter (*Armut etc*), (*a. Verzweiflung etc*) tiefst. **2.** demütig, unterwürfig.

ab·jure [əb'dʒʊə] *v/t* abschwören (*dat*).

a·blaze [ə'bleɪz] *adv u. adj* **1.** *be ~* in Flammen stehen. **2.** *fig. be ~ with light* im Lichterglanz erstrahlen; *his eyes were ~ with anger* s-e Augen funkelten vor Zorn; *his face was ~ with excitement* sein Gesicht glühte vor Aufregung.

a·ble ['eɪbl] *adj* □ fähig, tüchtig, geschickt: *be ~ to* imstande *od.* in der Lage sein zu, können; *~ to pay* zahlungsfähig. *~·bod·ied* [ˌ~'bɒdɪd] *adj* körperlich leistungsfähig, kräftig: *~ seaman* ♨ Vollmatrose *m*.

ab·ne·ga·tion [ˌæbnɪ'geɪʃn] *s* Selbstverleugnung *f*.

ab·nor·mal [æb'nɔːml] *adj* □ anormal, *bsd.* ♨ abnorm.

a·board [ə'bɔːd] *adv u. prp* **1.** ♨, ✈ an Bord (*gen*): *go ~; all ~! ♨* alle Mann an Bord!; 🚌 alles einsteigen! **2.** in (*ein od. e-m Verkehrsmittel*): *~ a bus.*

a·bode [ə'bəʊd] *s a. place of ~* ♨ Wohnsitz *m*: *of (od. with) no fixed ~* ohne festen Wohnsitz.

a·bol·ish [ə'bɒlɪʃ] *v/t* abschaffen, *Gesetz etc a.* aufheben. **a·bol·ish·ment, ab·o·li·tion** [ˌæbəʊ'lɪʃn] *s* Abschaffung *f*, Aufhebung *f*.

'A-bomb *s* Atombombe *f*.

a·bom·i·na·ble [ə'bɒmɪnəbl] *adj* □ abscheulich, scheußlich: *~ snowman*

Schneemensch m. **a'bom·i·nate** [∼neɪt] v/t verabscheuen. **a,bom·i'na·tion** s 1. Abscheu m, f (**of** vor dat). 2. Scheußlichkeit f.

ab·o·rig·i·nal [,æbə'rɪdʒənl] **I** adj □ eingeboren, einheimisch, Ur... **II** s Ureinwohner m, pl a. Urbevölkerung f. **,ab·o'rig·i·ne** [∼dʒəni] → **aboriginal II**.

a·bort [ə'bɔːt] **I** v/t 1. ✝ Schwangerschaft abbrechen; Kind abtreiben. 2. Raumflug etc abbrechen. **II** v/i 3. e-e Fehlgeburt haben. 4. fig. fehlschlagen, scheitern. **a'bor·tion** s 1. ✝ Fehlgeburt f; Schwangerschaftsabbruch m, Abtreibung f: **have an** ∼ abtreiben (lassen). 2. fig. Fehlschlag m. **a'bor·tive** [∼tɪv] adj □ erfolglos, fehlgeschlagen: **prove** ∼ sich als Fehlschlag erweisen.

a·bound [ə'baʊnd] v/i 1. reichlich vorhanden sein. 2. Überfluß haben, reich sein (**in** an dat). 3. voll sein, wimmeln (**with** von).

a·bout [ə'baʊt] **I** prp 1. um (... herum). 2. herum in (dat): **wander** ∼ **the streets** in den Straßen herumwandern. 3. bei, auf (dat), an (dat): **I had no money** ∼ **me** ich hatte kein Geld bei mir. 4. um, gegen: ∼ **noon** um die Mittagszeit, gegen Mittag. 5. über (acc): **talk** ∼ **business** über Geschäfte reden. 6. im Begriff, dabei: **he was** ∼ **to go out** er wollte gerade weggehen. 7. F beschäftigt mit: **what are you** ∼? was macht ihr da? **II** adv 8. herum, umher: **all** ∼ überall. 9. ungefähr, etwa: **it's** ∼ **right** F es kommt so ungefähr hin. 10. **be** (**up and**) ∼ auf den Beinen sein. 11. in der Nähe, da: **there was no one** ∼.

a·bove [ə'bʌv] **I** prp 1. über (dat od. acc), oberhalb. 2. über (dat od. acc), mehr als: ∼ **all** vor allem; **be** ∼ **s.o.** j-m überlegen sein; **it is** ∼ **me** es ist mir zu hoch. **II** adv 3. (dr)oben: **from** ∼ von oben. 4. darüber (hinaus). **III** adj 5. a. ∼ **-mentioned** obig, obenerwähnt. **IV** s 6. **das** Obige, **das** Obenerwähnte. **a,bove'board** adv u. adj ehrlich, offen.

ab·rade [ə'breɪd] v/t 1. abschaben, -reiben, Reifen abfahren. 2. Haut etc abschürfen.

ab·ra·sion [ə'breɪʒn] s 1. Abschaben n, -reiben n. 2. (Haut)Abschürfung f. **ab'ra·sive** [∼sɪv] s ⚙ Schleifmittel n.

ab·re·act [,æbrɪ'ækt] v/t psych. abreagieren.

a·breast [ə'brest] adv: **three** ∼ zu dritt nebeneinander; **keep** ∼ **of** fig. Schritt halten mit; **keep** ∼ **of the times** auf dem laufenden bleiben.

a·bridge [ə'brɪdʒ] v/t Buch, Rede etc kürzen. **a'bridg(e)·ment** s 1. Kürzung f. 2. Kurzfassung f.

a·broad [ə'brɔːd] adv 1. im od. ins Ausland: **from** ∼ aus dem Ausland; **trip** ∼ Auslandsreise f. 2. überall(hin): **spread** ∼ (sich) verbreiten; **a rumo(u)r is** ∼ es geht das Gerücht (um); **get** ∼ ruchbar werden.

ab·ro·gate [ˈæbrəʊgeɪt] v/t Vertrag etc außer Kraft setzen, Gesetz etc a. aufheben. **,ab·ro'ga·tion** s Außerkraftsetzung f, Aufhebung f.

ab·rupt [ə'brʌpt] adj □ 1. kurz (angebunden), schroff. 2. plötzlich, abrupt: **come to an** ∼ **stop** plötzlich od. mit e-m Ruck anhalten.

ab·scess [ˈæbsɪs] s ✝ Abszeß m.

ab·scond [əb'skɒnd] v/i sich heimlich davonmachen; flüchten (**from** vor dat).

ab·sence [ˈæbsəns] s 1. Abwesenheit f: ∼ **of mind** → **absent-mindedness**. 2. Fernbleiben n (**from** von). 3. (**of**) Fehlen n (gen od. von), Mangel m (an dat): **in the** ∼ **of** in Ermangelung (gen).

ab·sent I adj [ˈæbsənt] 1. abwesend: **be** ∼ fehlen (**from school** in der Schule; **from work** am Arbeitsplatz). 2. fehlend. 3. a) (geistes)abwesend (Blick etc), b) → **absent-minded**. **II** v/t [æb'sent] ∼ **o.s.** (**from**) fernbleiben (dat od. von); sich entfernen (von, aus). **ab·sen·tee** [,æbsən'tiː] s Abwesende m, f: ∼ **ballot** bsd. Am. Briefwahl f; ∼ **voter** bsd. Am. Briefwähler(in). **,ab·sen'tee·ism** s häufiges od. längeres (unentschuldigtes) Fehlen (am Arbeitsplatz, in der Schule).

,ab·sent·'-'mind·ed adj □ geistesabwesend, zerstreut. **,∼-'mind·ed·ness** s Geistesabwesenheit f, Zerstreutheit f.

ab·so·lute [ˈæbsəluːt] adj □ absolut (a. ♠, ling., phys.): a) unumschränkt (Herrscher), b) vollkommen, völlig, c) 🜍 rein, unvermischt. **,ab·so'lu·tion** s Lossprechung f; eccl. Absolution f. **'ab·so·lut·ism** s phils., pol. Absolutismus m.

ab·solve [əb'zɒlv] v/t frei-, lossprechen (of von Sünde); entbinden (from von Verpflichtung etc); eccl. die Absolution erteilen (dat).

ab·sorb [əb'sɔːb] v/t 1. absorbieren, auf-, einsaugen, a. fig. Wissen etc aufnehmen. 2. fig. ganz in Anspruch nehmen; fesseln: ∼ed in vertieft in (acc). 3. Stoß etc dämpfen. **ab'sorb·ent** adj absorbierend: ∼ cotton ↯ Am. (Verband-)Watte f.

ab·stain [əb'steɪn] v/i sich enthalten (from gen): ∼ (from voting) sich der Stimme enthalten.

ab·ste·mi·ous [æb'stiːmjəs] adj □ 1. enthaltsam; mäßig. 2. bescheiden, kärglich (Mahlzeit).

ab·sten·tion [əb'stenʃn] s: ∼ (from voting) (Stimm)Enthaltung f.

ab·sti·nence ['æbstɪnəns] s Abstinenz f, Enthaltsamkeit f. **'ab·sti·nent** adj □ abstinent, enthaltsam.

ab·stract I adj □ ['æbstrækt] 1. abstrakt (a. ↯, paint. etc): a) theoretisch, b) schwerverständlich. II s [∼] 2. das Abstrakte: in the ∼ rein theoretisch (betrachtet), an u. für sich. 3. a. ∼ noun ling. Abstraktum n, Begriffswort n. 4. Auszug m, Abriß m. III v/t [æb'strækt] 5. abstrahieren. 6. entwenden. 7. e-n Auszug machen von. **ab'stract·ed** adj □ fig. zerstreut. **ab·strac·tion** [æb-'strækʃn] s 1. Abstraktion f. 2. Entwendung f. 3. fig. Zerstreutheit f.

ab·struse [æb'struːs] adj □ abstrus, schwerverständlich.

ab·surd [əb'sɜːd] adj □ 1. absurd, widersinnig. 2. unsinnig, albern, lächerlich.

a·bun·dance [ə'bʌndəns] s (of) Überfluß m (an dat), Fülle f (von): in ∼ in Hülle u. Fülle. **a'bun·dant** adj □ reichlich (vorhanden): 2. ∼ in reich an (dat).

a·buse I s [ə'bjuːs] 1. Mißbrauch m: ∼ of drugs Drogenmißbrauch. 2. Beschimpfungen pl: → term 1. II v/t [∼z] 3. mißbrauchen. 4. beschimpfen. **a'bu·sive** [∼sɪv] adj □ beleidigend: ∼ language Beleidigungen f, Beschimpfungen pl.

a·but [ə'bʌt] v/i (an)grenzen (on an acc). **a'but·ment** s △ Strebe-, Stützpfeiler m.

a·bys·mal [ə'bɪzml] adj □ miserabel.

a·byss [ə'bɪs] s Abgrund m (a. fig.).

a·ca·cia [ə'keɪʃə] s ↯ Akazie f.

ac·a·dem·ic [,ækə'demɪk] I adj (∼ally) 1. akademisch: a) Universitäts...: ∼ freedom akademische Freiheit: ∼ year Studienjahr n, b) (rein) theoretisch: ∼ question akademische Frage. 2. gelehrt, wissenschaftlich. II s 3. Universitätslehrer(in).

a·cad·e·my [ə'kædəmɪ] s Akademie f: ∼ of music Musikhochschule f.

ac·cede [æk'siːd] v/i (to) 1. e-m Vorschlag etc beipflichten, zustimmen. 2. Amt antreten, Macht übernehmen, Thron besteigen.

ac·cel·er·ate [æk'seləreɪt] I v/t beschleunigen. II v/i schneller werden, mot. a. Gas geben. **ac,cel·er'a·tion** s Beschleunigung f: ∼ lane mot. Beschleunigungsspur f, -streifen m. **ac'cel·er·a·tor** s mot. Gaspedal n.

ac·cent I s ['æksent] Akzent m: a) ling. Ton m, Betonung f, b) ling. Betonungs-, Tonzeichen n, c) Tonfall m, (lokale etc) Aussprache, d) fig. Nachdruck m: the ∼ is on der Akzent liegt auf (dat). II v/t [æk'sent] → accentuate.

ac·cen·tu·ate [æk'sentjueɪt] v/t akzentuieren, betonen (a. fig.). **ac,cen·tu·'a·tion** s Akzentuierung f, Betonung f.

ac·cept [ək'sept] v/t 1. an-, entgegennehmen. 2. j-n, et. akzeptieren: a) et., ↯ Wechsel annehmen, b) et. hinnehmen, sich abfinden mit. 3. Verantwortung etc auf sich nehmen. 4. aufnehmen (into in acc). **ac'cept·a·ble** adj □ 1. akzeptabel, annehmbar (a für). 2. angenehm, willkommen. **ac'cept·ance** s 1. Annahme f. 2. Akzeptierung f; Hinnahme f: win ∼ Anerkennung finden. 3. Aufnahme f. 4. ↯ Akzept n. **ac'cept·ed** adj allgemein anerkannt, üblich.

ac·cess ['ækses] s 1. Zugang m (to zu) (a. fig.): ∼ road Zufahrts- od. Zubringerstraße f. 2. fig. Zutritt m (to bei, zu): easy of ∼ zugänglich (Person). 3. Computer: Zugriff m (to auf acc).

ac·ces·sa·ry → accessory 2.

ac·ces·si·ble [ək'sesəbl] adj □ 1. (leicht) zugänglich (to für od. dat) (a. fig.). 2. um-, zugänglich (Person). 3. empfänglich (to für). **ac·ces·sion** [æk'seʃn] s 1. Antritt m (to e-s Amts): ∼ to power Machtübernahme f; ∼ to the throne

Thronbesteigung f. **2.** (Neu)Anschaffung f (**to** für). **3.** Zustimmung f (**to** zu).

ac·ces·so·ry [əkˈsesəri] s **1.** Zubehörteil n, (*Mode*) Accessoire n, pl a. Zubehör n. **2.** ⚖ Mitschuldige m, f (**to** an dat).

ac·ci·dence [ˈæksɪdəns] s ling. Formenlehre f.

ac·ci·dent [ˈæksɪdənt] s **1. by** ~ zufällig. **2.** Unglück(sfall m) n, (*in Kernkraftwerk*) Störfall m: **have** (*od.* **meet with**) **an** ~ e-n Unfall haben, verunglücken; **be killed in an** ~ bei e-m Unfall ums Leben kommen, tödlich verunglücken; ~ **insurance** Unfallversicherung f; ~-**prone** unfallgefährdet. **ac·ci·den·tal** [ˌæksɪˈdentl] adj □ **1.** zufällig. **2.** versehentlich. **3.** Unfall...

ac·claim [əˈkleɪm] **I** v/t **1.** feiern (**as** als). **2.** ~ **s.o. king** j-n zum König ausrufen. **II** s **3.** hohes Lob.

ac·cla·ma·tion [ˌækləˈmeɪʃn] s **1.** lauter Beifall m. **2.** hohes Lob. **3. by** ~ pol. durch Zuruf od. Akklamation.

ac·cli·mate [əˈklaɪmət] → **acclimatize**.

ac·cli·ma·tion [ˌæklaɪˈmeɪʃn] → **acclimatization**.

ac·cli·ma·ti·za·tion [əˌklaɪmətaɪˈzeɪʃn] s Akklimatisierung f. **ac·cli·ma·tize** v/t u. v/i (**to**) (sich) akklimatisieren (an acc), (sich) eingewöhnen (in dat) (*beide a. fig.*).

ac·cliv·i·ty [əˈklɪvətɪ] s Steigung f.

ac·com·mo·date [əˈkɒmədeɪt] v/t **1.** (**to**) anpassen (dat od. an acc); in Einklang bringen (mit). **2.** j-m aushelfen (**with** mit). **3.** unterbringen. **4.** Platz haben für, fassen. **ac·com·mo·dat·ing** adj □ gefällig, entgegenkommend. **ac·com·mo·da·tion** s **1.** Anpassung f (**to** an acc). **2.** Gefälligkeit f. **3.** Am. mst pl Unterkunft f, -bringung f; Einrichtung(en pl) f: ~ **sanitary** ~.

ac·com·pa·ni·ment [əˈkʌmpənɪmənt] s ♪ Begleitung f. **ac·com·pa·nist** s ♪ Begleiter(in). **ac·com·pa·ny** v/t begleiten (a. ♪).

ac·com·plice [əˈkʌmplɪs] s Komplice m.

ac·com·plish [əˈkʌmplɪʃ] v/t erreichen; leisten. **ac·com·plished** adj fähig, tüchtig. **ac·com·plish·ment** s Fähigkeit f, Fertigkeit f.

ac·cord [əˈkɔːd] **I** v/t **1.** gewähren, *Empfang* bereiten. **II** v/i **2.** übereinstimmen (**with** mit). **III** s **3.** Übereinstimmung f:

be in ~ → 2; **with one** ~ einstimmig. **4. of one's own** ~ aus freien Stücken, von selbst. **ac·cord·ance** s: **in** ~ **with** entsprechend (dat), gemäß (dat).

ac·cord·ing: ~ **to** prp laut; nach.

ac·cord·ing·ly adv **1.** (dem)entsprechend. **2.** also, folglich.

ac·cor·di·on [əˈkɔːdjən] s ♪ Akkordeon n, Ziehharmonika f.

ac·cost [əˈkɒst] v/t Frau (in eindeutiger Absicht) ansprechen; j-n anpöbeln.

ac·count [əˈkaʊnt] **I** v/t **1.** ansehen als, halten für. **II** v/i **2.** ~ (**to s.o.**) **for** (j-m) Rechenschaft ablegen über (acc). **3.** ~ **for** (sich) erklären, et. begründen: **there's no** ~**ing for tastes** über Geschmack läßt sich nicht streiten. **4.** ~ **for** der Grund sein für. **III** s **5.** ✝ Konto n (**with** bei): **for** ~ **only** nur zur Verrechnung; **on one's own** ~ fig. auf eigene Faust; auf eigene Gefahr; **settle** (od. **square**) ~**s with** fig. abrechnen mit. **6.** Rechenschaft(sbericht m) f: **bring** (od. **call**) **to** ~ zur Rechenschaft ziehen; **give** (**an**) ~ **of** Rechenschaft ablegen über (acc); **give a good** (**bad**) ~ **of o.s.** sich von s-r guten (schlechten) Seite zeigen; gut (schlecht) abschneiden. **7.** Bericht m, Darstellung f: **by all** ~**s** nach allem, was man hört; **give an** ~ **of** Bericht erstatten über (acc). **8. of great** (**no**) ~ von großer (ohne) Bedeutung; **on** ~ **of** um ... willen, wegen; **on my** ~ meinetwegen; **on no** ~ auf keinen Fall; **leave out of** ~ außer acht lassen; **take into** ~, **take** ~ **of** in Betracht ziehen, berücksichtigen. **9. put** (od. **turn**) **to** (**good**) ~ (aus)nutzen, Kapital schlagen aus. **ac·count·a·ble** adj verantwortlich (**to** dat; **for** für): **hold s.o.** ~ j-n verantwortlich machen. **ac·count·ant** s **1.** Buchhalter(in). **2.** Buchprüfer(in). **3.** Br. Steuerberater(in).

ac·cred·it [əˈkredɪt] v/t Botschafter etc akkreditieren (**to** bei).

ac·crue [əˈkruː] v/i **1.** erwachsen (**to** dat; **from** aus). **2.** anwachsen: ~**d interest** aufgelaufene Zinsen pl.

ac·cu·mu·late [əˈkjuːmjʊleɪt] v/t u. v/i (sich) ansammeln od. anhäufen. **ac·cu·mu·la·tion** s Anhäufung f, Ansammlung f. **ac·cu·mu·la·tor** s ⚡ Akkumulator m.

ac·cu·ra·cy [ˈækjʊrəsɪ] s Genauigkeit f.

ac·cu·rate [ˈ‿rət] adj □ genau: **be ~** genau gehen (Uhr).

ac·cu·sa·tion [ˌækjuːˈzeɪʃn] s 1. ⚖ Anklage f: **bring an ~ (of murder) against** (Mord)Anklage erheben gegen. 2. An-, Beschuldigung f. 3. Vorwurf m.

ac·cu·sa·tive [əˈkjuːzətɪv] s a. **~ case** ling. Akkusativ m, 4. Fall m.

ac·cuse [əˈkjuːz] v/t 1. ⚖ anklagen (of gen od. wegen). 2. beschuldigen (of gen): **~ s.o. of doing s.th.** j-n beschuldigen, et. getan zu haben. 3. **~ s.o. of s.th.** j-m et. zum Vorwurf machen. **ac·'cused** s: **the ~** ⚖ der od. die Angeklagte, die Angeklagten pl. **ac·'cus·ing** adj □ anklagend, vorwurfsvoll.

ac·cus·tom [əˈkʌstəm] v/t gewöhnen (to an acc): **be ~ed to doing s.th.** (es) gewöhnt sein, et. zu tun; **get ~ed to** sich gewöhnen an (acc). **ac·'cus·tomed** adj gewohnt: **~ seat** Stammplatz m.

ace [eɪs] **I** s 1. As n (Spielkarte; a. Tennis etc); Eins f (auf Würfeln): **have an ~ in the hole** (od. **up one's sleeve**) fig. (noch) e-n Trumpf in der Hand haben. 2. **he came within an ~ of losing** er hätte um ein Haar verloren. 3. F As n, Kanone f (**at** in dat). **II** adj 4. F **~ skier** Spitzenskiläufer(in); **~ reporter** Starreporter(in); **be ~** Spitze sein.

ac·e·tate [ˈæsɪteɪt] s 🜁 Acetat n. **a·ce·tic** [əˈsiːtɪk] adj essigsauer: **~ acid** Essigsäure f. **a·cet·y·lene** [əˈsetɪliːn] s Acetylen n.

ache [eɪk] **I** v/i 1. schmerzen, weh tun: **I am aching all over** mir tut alles weh. 2. sich sehnen (for nach), darauf brennen (to do zu tun). **II** s 3. anhaltende Schmerz m: **he has ~s and pains all over** ihm tut alles weh.

a·chieve [əˈtʃiːv] v/t Ziel erreichen, Erfolg erzielen. **a·'chieve·ment** s Leistung f: **~ test** Leistungstest n.

A·chil·les| heel [əˈkɪliːz] s fig. Achillesferse f. **~ ten·don** s anat. Achillessehne f.

ac·id [ˈæsɪd] **I** adj 1. sauer: **~ drops** pl saure Drops pl. 2. fig. bissig. 3. 🜁 säurehaltig, Säure...: **~ rain** saurer Regen. **II** s 4. 🜁 Säure f. 5. sl. Acid n (LSD).

ac·knowl·edge [əkˈnɒlɪdʒ] v/t 1. anerkennen. 2. zugeben: **~ having done**

s.th. zugeben, et. getan zu haben. 3. Brief, Empfang etc bestätigen. **ac·'knowl·edg(e)·ment** s 1. Anerkennung f: **in ~ of** in Anerkennung (gen). 2. (Empfangs)Bestätigung f.

ac·me [ˈækmɪ] s fig. Gipfel m, Höhepunkt m.

ac·ne [ˈæknɪ] s 🜺 Akne f.

a·corn [ˈeɪkɔːn] s 🜺 Eichel f.

a·cous·tic [əˈkuːstɪk] adj 1. akustisch, Gehör...: **~ nerve** anat. Gehörnerv m. **II** s pl Akustik f (e-s Raums).

ac·quaint [əˈkweɪnt] v/t vertraut machen (with mit): **be ~ed with** j-n, et. kennen; **we are ~ed** wir kennen uns; **become ~ed with** j-n, et. kennenlernen. **ac·'quaint·ance** s 1. Bekanntschaft f (with mit): **make s.o.'s ~** j-n kennenlernen, j-s Bekanntschaft machen. 2. Kenntnis f (with von od. gen). 3. Bekannte m, f.

ac·qui·esce [ˌækwɪˈes] v/i (zögernd) einwilligen (in in acc).

ac·quire [əˈkwaɪə] v/t erwerben (a. fig.), sich Wissen etc aneignen.

ac·qui·si·tion [ˌækwɪˈzɪʃn] s 1. Erwerb m. 2. Anschaffung f, Errungenschaft f. **ac·quis·i·tive** [əˈkwɪzɪtɪv] adj □ habgierig. **ac·'quis·i·tive·ness** s Habgier f.

ac·quit [əˈkwɪt] v/t 1. ⚖ freisprechen (of von). 2. **~ o.s. well** s-e Sache gut machen. **ac·'quit·tal** s ⚖ Freispruch m.

a·cre [ˈeɪkə] s Acre m (4047 qm).

ac·rid [ˈækrɪd] adj □ scharf, beißend (beide a. fig.).

ac·ri·mo·ni·ous [ˌækrɪˈməʊnjəs] adj □ fig. bitter; scharf, beißend; erbittert (geführt) (Diskussion etc). **ac·ri·mo·ny** [ˈækrɪmənɪ] s fig. Bitterkeit f; Schärfe f.

ac·ro·bat [ˈækrəbæt] s Akrobat(in). ˌac·ro·'bat·ic adj (~ally) akrobatisch. **II** s pl (a. sg konstruiert) Akrobatik f (a. fig.): **mental ~s** Gedankenakrobatik f.

a·cross [əˈkrɒs] **I** prp 1. (quer) über (acc); quer durch, mitten durch: **run ~ the road** über die Straße laufen; **swim ~ a river** e-n Fluß durchschwimmen. 2. jenseits (gen): **he lives ~ the street** er wohnt auf der gegenüberliegenden Straßenseite. **II** adv 3. (quer) hinüber od. herüber; (quer) durch; im Durchmesser: **go ~** hinübergehen; **saw ~** durchsägen; **a lake three miles ~** ein 3 Meilen breiter See. 4. drüben, auf der anderen Seite. **5.** waag(e)recht (*in Kreuzworträtseln*).

a‚cross-the-'board *adj* linear (*Steuersenkung etc*).

act [ækt] **I** *s* **1.** (⚖ *a.* Straf)Tat *f*, Handlung *f*, Akt *m*: **an ~ of God** höhere Gewalt; **catch in the (very) ~** auf frischer Tat ertappen; **catch s.o. in the ~ of doing s.th.** j-n (dabei) ertappen, als er et. tut. **2.** ⚘ (**of Parliament**, *Am.* **of Congress**) Gesetz *n*. **3.** *thea.* Aufzug *m*, Akt *m*. **4.** (Programm)Nummer *f*; *fig.* F Tour *f*: **put on an ~** Theater spielen. **II** *v/t* **5.** *thea. etc* Rolle spielen, *j-n a.* darstellen, *Stück a.* aufführen: **~ the fool** *fig.* sich wie ein Narr benehmen; den Dummen spielen. **III** *v/i* **6.** (Theater) spielen, *fig.* Theater spielen. **7.** handeln; tätig sein: **~ as** amtieren *od.* fungieren *od.* dienen als; **~ for s.o.** j-n vertreten; **~ on** sich richten nach. **8.** sich verhalten *od.* benehmen (**towards** *j-m* gegenüber): **~ up** F Theater machen; angeben; verrückt spielen (*Gerät etc*). **9.** (ein)wirken (**on** auf *acc*). **'act·ing I** *adj* stellvertretend, amtierend, geschäftsführend. **II** *s thea. etc* Spiel *n*; Schauspielerei *f*.

ac·tion ['ækʃn] *s* **1.** Handlung *f* (*a. thea. etc*), Tat *f*; **man of ~** Mann *m* der Tat; **put into ~** in die Tat umsetzen; **take ~** handeln. **2.** *Film etc:* Action *f*: **~ film.** *bsd.* ⚙ Funktionieren *n*: **~ of the heart** *physiol.* Herztätigkeit *f*. **4.** (Ein)Wirkung *f* (**on** auf *acc*). **5.** ⚖ Klage *f*, Prozeß *m*: **bring an ~ against** verklagen. **6.** ✗ Gefecht *n*, Einsatz *m*: **killed in ~** gefallen. **~ re·play** *s Sport, TV: Br. (bsd.* Zeitlupen)Wiederholung *f* (*e-r Spielszene*).

ac·ti·vate ['æktɪveɪt] *v/t* **1.** Alarm *etc* auslösen. **2.** *bsd.* ☢ aktivieren.

ac·tive ['æktɪv] **I** *adj* □ **1.** *allg.* aktiv, (*Vulkan a.*) tätig, (*Phantasie*) lebhaft. **2.** *ling.* aktivisch: **~ voice** → **3.** **II** *s* **3.** *ling.* Aktiv *n*, Tatform *f*. **ac'tiv·i·ty** *s* **1.** Aktivität *f*. **2.** *mst pl* Aktivität *f*, Betätigung *f*.

ac·tor ['æktə] *s* Schauspieler *m*. **ac·tress** ['æktrɪs] *s* Schauspielerin *f*.

ac·tu·al ['æktʃʊəl] *adj* wirklich, tatsächlich; eigentlich. **'ac·tu·al·ly** *adv* **1.** → **actual**. **2.** sogar.

ac·tu·ate ['æktjʊeɪt] *v/t*: **be ~d by** *fig.* getrieben werden von.

a·cu·men ['ækjʊmən] *s* Scharfsinn *m*.

ac·u·pres·sure ['ækjʊˌpreʃə] *s* ✷ Akupressur *f*. **ac·u·punc·ture** ['ækjʊˌpʌŋktʃə] ✷ **I** *s* Akupunktur *f*. **II** *v/t* akupunktieren.

a·cute [ə'kjuːt] *adj* □ **1.** A spitz (*Winkel*). **2.** scharf (*Gehör etc*). **3.** scharfsinnig. **4.** akut (*Krankheit*). **5.** stark (*Schmerzen*), erheblich (*Mangel etc*).

ad [æd] F → **advertisement**.

Ad·am ['ædəm] *npr.*: **I don't know him from ~** F ich hab' keine Ahnung, wer er ist; **~'s apple** *anat.* Adamsapfel *m*.

ad·a·mant ['ædəmənt] *adj* unnachgiebig: **be ~ that** s.o. should do s.th. darauf bestehen, daß j-d et. tut.

a·dapt [ə'dæpt] **I** *v/t* **1.** anpassen (**to** *dat*): **~ o.s** → **3**. **2.** *Text* bearbeiten (**for** für). **II** *v/i* **3.** (**to**) sich anpassen (*dat*); sich gewöhnen (an *acc*). **a'dapt·a·ble** *adj* anpassungsfähig. **ad·ap·ta·tion** [ˌædæp'teɪʃn] *s* **1.** Anpassung *f* (**to** an *acc*). **2.** Bearbeitung *f*. **a·dap·ter**, **a·dap·tor** [ə'dæptə] *s* ⚡ Adapter *m*.

add [æd] **I** *v/t* **1.** hinzuzählen, -rechnen (**to** zu). **2.** hinzufügen (**to** *dat od.* zu; **that** daß): → **fuel**. **3.** **~ up** (*od.* **together**) addieren, zs.-zählen. **4.** ✚ *etc* aufschlagen (**to** auf *acc*): **~ 5% to the price.** **II** *v/i* **5.** **~ to** hinzukommen *od.* beitragen zu, vermehren. **6.** **~ up** F aufgehen, stimmen; *fig.* e-n Sinn ergeben. **7.** **~ up to** sich belaufen auf (*acc*), betragen; *fig.* hinauslaufen auf (*acc*), bedeuten. **'ad·ded** *adj* zusätzlich.

ad·den·dum [ə'dendəm] *pl* **-da** [~də] *s* Zusatz *m*, Nachtrag *m*.

ad·der ['ædə] *s zo.* Natter *f*.

ad·dict ['ædɪkt] *s* (Drogen-, Fernseh- *etc*) Süchtige *m*, *f*, (*Fußball- etc*)Fanatiker *m*, (*Film- etc*)Narr *m*. **ad·dict·ed** [ə'dɪktɪd] *adj*: **be ~ to ...** ...süchtig sein. **ad'dic·tion** *s* Sucht *f*, (*Zustand a.*) Süchtigkeit *f*: **~ to alcohol** Alkoholsucht *f*. **ad'dic·tive** *adj* suchterzeugend: **be ~** süchtig machen; **~ drug** Suchtmittel *n*.

add·ing ma·chine ['ædɪŋ] *s* Addier-, Additionsmaschine *f*.

ad·di·tion [ə'dɪʃn] *s* **1.** Hinzufügung *f*, Zusatz *m*: **in ~** noch dazu, außerdem; **in ~ to** außer (*dat*), zusätzlich zu. **2.** Vermehrung f (**to** gen): **an ~ to the family** Familienzuwachs m. **3.** ⚕ Addition f: ~ **sign** Pluszeichen n. **ad·di·tion·al** [∼ʃənl] adj □ zusätzlich, Zusatz...

ad·di·tive [ˈædɪtɪv] s Zusatz m (a. 🜍).

ad·dress [əˈdres] **I** v/t **1.** Worte etc richten (**to** an acc), j-n anreden od. ansprechen (**as** als), Brief etc adressieren (**to** an acc). **2.** e-e Ansprache halten an (acc). **II** s **3.** Anrede f. **4.** Ansprache f, Rede f. **5.** Adresse f, Anschrift f. **ad·dress·ee** [ˌædreˈsiː] s Adressat(in), Empfänger(in).

ad·duce [əˈdjuːs] v/t Grund anführen, Beweis erbringen.

ad·e·noids [ˈædɪnɔɪdz] s pl 🜋 Polypen pl.

ad·ept [ˈædept] **I** adj erfahren, geschickt (**at, in** in dat). **II** s Meister m, Experte m (**at, in** in dat).

ad·e·qua·cy [ˈædɪkwəsɪ] s Angemessenheit f. **ad·e·quate** [∼kwət] adj □ **1.** angemessen (**to** dat). **2.** ausreichend: **be ~ for** reichen für.

ad·here [ədˈhɪə] v/i **1.** (an)kleben, (-)haften (**to** an acc), j-n anreden od. **2.** fig. (**to**) festhalten an (dat), bleiben (bei). **ad·her·ence** s **1.** (An)Kleben n, (-)Haften n. **2.** fig. Festhalten n. **ad·her·ent I** adj (an)klebend, (-)haftend. **II** s Anhänger(in).

ad·he·sion [ədˈhiːʒn] s **1.** → **adherence**. **2.** phys., ☉ Adhäsion f, Haftvermögen n.

ad·he·sive [ədˈhiːsɪv] **I** adj □ (an)haftend, klebend, Haft..., Kleb(e)...: ~ **plaster** Heftpflaster n; ~ **tape** Klebstreifen m; Am. Heftpflaster n. **II** s Klebstoff m.

ad·ja·cent [əˈdʒeɪsənt] adj □ **1.** angrenzend, -stoßend (**to** an acc). **2.** bsd. ⚕, ☉ Nachbar..., Neben...

ad·jec·ti·val [ˌædʒekˈtaɪvl] adj □ ling. adjektivisch. **ad·jec·tive** [ˈædʒɪktɪv] s Adjektiv n, Eigenschaftswort n.

ad·join [əˈdʒɔɪn] **I** v/t (an)stoßen od. (-)grenzen an (acc). **II** v/i aneinandergrenzen, nebeneinander liegen. **ad·'join·ing** adj angrenzend, -stoßend, Nachbar..., Neben...

ad·journ [əˈdʒɜːn] **I** v/t verschieben, -tagen (**till, until** auf acc; **for** um). **II** v/i sich vertagen. **ad·'journ·ment** s Vertagung f, -schiebung f.

ad·judge [əˈdʒʌdʒ] v/t **1.** ⚖ e-e Sache (gerichtlich) entscheiden; j-n für (schul-

dig etc) erklären. **2.** ⚖, Sport: zusprechen, -erkennen (**to** dat).

ad·ju·di·cate [əˈdʒuːdɪkeɪt] → **adjudge**. **ad·junct** [ˈædʒʌŋkt] s **1.** Zusatz m (**to** zu). **2.** ling. Attribut n, Beifügung f.

ad·ju·ra·tion [ˌædʒʊəˈreɪʃn] s Beschwörung f. **ad·jure** [əˈdʒʊə] v/t beschwören (**to do** zu tun).

ad·just [əˈdʒʌst] v/t **1.** (**to**) anpassen, -gleichen (dat od. an acc), abstimmen (auf acc). **2.** in Ordnung bringen, regeln. **3.** ☉ (ein)stellen, regulieren, Gewehr etc justieren, Uhr stellen. **ad·'just·a·ble** adj ☉ ein-, verstellbar, regulierbar. **ad·'just·ment** s **1.** Anpassung f, -gleichung f. **2.** Regelung f. **3.** ☉ Einstellung f, Regulierung f; Einstellvorrichtung f.

ad·ju·tant [ˈædʒʊtənt] s ✗ Adjutant m.

ad-lib [ˌædˈlɪb] v/t u. v/i F improvisieren.

ad·man [ˈædmæn] s (irr **man**) F **1.** Werbetexter m für Zeitungsanzeigen. **2.** Anzeigenvertreter m. **ad·mass** [ˈædmæs] s F **1.** Konsumbeeinflussung f. **2.** werbungsmanipulierte Gesellschaft.

ad·min·is·ter [ədˈmɪnɪstə] v/t **1.** verwalten, Amt etc ausüben. **2.** Arznei, Schlag verabreichen, Sakrament spenden, Tadel erteilen (**to** dat): ~ **justice** Recht sprechen. **ad·min·is·tra·tion** s **1.** Verwaltung f Ausübung f. **2.** Verabreichung f, Spendung f, Erteilung f: ~ **of justice** Rechtsprechung f. **3.** pol. bsd. Am. Regierung f, Amtsdauer f (e-s Präsidenten etc). **ad·min·is·tra·tive** [∼trətɪv] adj □ Verwaltungs... **ad·min·is·tra·tor** [∼treɪtə] s **1.** Verwalter m. **2.** Verwaltungsbeamte m.

ad·mi·ra·ble [ˈædmərəbl] adj □ bewundernswert, großartig.

ad·mi·ral [ˈædmərəl] s Admiral m.

ad·mi·ra·tion [ˌædməˈreɪʃn] s Bewunderung f (**for** für): **she was the ~ of all** sie wurde von allen bewundert.

ad·mire [ədˈmaɪə] v/t **1.** bewundern (**for** wegen). **2.** verehren. **ad·'mir·er** s **1.** Bewunderer m. **2.** Verehrer(in).

ad·mis·si·ble [ədˈmɪsəbl] adj zulässig, statthaft. **ad·mis·sion** s **1.** Einlaß m (**a. ☉**); Ein-, Zutritt m; Aufnahme f: ~ **free** Eintritt frei; ~ **ticket** Eintrittskarte f. **2.** Eintritt(sgeld n) m. **3.** Zulassung f. **4.** Eingeständnis n: **by** (od. **on**) **his own ~** wie er selbst zugab; ~ **of guilt** Schuldeingeständnis. **5.** Zugeständnis n. **6.** ◎ (*Luft- etc*)Zufuhr f.

ad·mit [əd'mɪt] **I** v/t **1.** j-n einlassen. **2.** (*into, to*) j-n aufnehmen (in *acc od. dat*), zulassen (zu): → **bar** 9. **3.** zulassen, gestatten. **4.** anerkennen, gelten lassen. **5.** zugeben, (ein)gestehen: ~ *doing s.th.* zugeben, et. getan zu haben. **6.** zugeben, einräumen (*that* daß). **7.** Platz haben für, fassen. **8.** ◎ einlassen, zuführen. **II** v/i **9.** ~ *of* → 3: *it ~s of no excuse* es läßt sich nicht entschuldigen. **10.** ~ *to* → 5. **ad'mit·tance** s Ein-, Zutritt m: *no* ~ (*except on business*) Zutritt (für Unbefugte) verboten. **ad'mit·ted·ly** *adv* zugegeben(ermaßen).

ad·mix·ture [æd'mɪkstʃə] s Beimischung f, Zusatz m.

ad·mon·ish [əd'mɒnɪʃ] v/t **1.** warnen (*of, against* vor *dat*). **2.** ermahnen (*for* wegen). **ad·mo·ni·tion** [ˌædməʊ'nɪʃn] s **1.** Warnung f. **2.** Ermahnung f.

a·do [ə'duː] s Getue n: *much ~ about nothing* viel Lärm um nichts; *without more* (*od. further*) ~ ohne weitere Umstände.

ad·o·les·cence [ˌædəʊ'lesns] s jugendliches Alter. **ˌad·o'les·cent I** *adj* jugendlich, heranwachsend. **II** s Jugendliche m, f.

a·dopt [ə'dɒpt] v/t **1.** adoptieren: *~ed child* Adoptivkind n; *~ed country* Wahlheimat f. **2.** *fig.* annehmen, sich zu eigen machen, *Handlungsweise* wählen, *Haltung* einnehmen. **a'dop·tion** s **1.** Adoption f: *give up for* ~ zur Adoption freigeben. **2.** Annahme f. **a'dop·tive** *adj* Adoptiv...: ~ *child* (*parents*); ~ *country* Wahlheimat f.

a·dor·a·ble [ə'dɔːrəbl] *adj* □ allerliebst, entzückend. **ad·o·ra·tion** [ˌædə'reɪʃn] s Anbetung f, Verehrung f. **a·dore** [ə'dɔː] v/t anbeten, verehren (*beide a. fig.*); F et. entzückend *od.* hinreißend finden.

a·dorn [ə'dɔːn] v/t **1.** schmücken, (ver)zieren (*beide a. fig.*). **2.** *fig.* Glanz verleihen (*dat*). **a'dorn·ment** s Schmuck m, Verzierung f.

a·dren·al·in(e) [ə'drenəlɪn] s **1.** ♣, *physiol.* Adrenalin n. **2.** *fig.* Aufputschmittel n.

a·droit [ə'drɔɪt] *adj* □ geschickt, gewandt (*at, in* in *dat*). **a'droit·ness**

s Geschicklichkeit f, Gewandtheit f.

ad·u·late [ˈædjʊlet] v/t j-m schmeicheln. **ˌad·u·la·tion** s Schmeichelei f. **ˈad·u·la·tor** s Schmeichler m. **ˈad·u·la·to·ry** *adj* schmeichlerisch.

a·dult [ˈædʌlt] **I** *adj* **1.** erwachsen. **2.** (nur) für Erwachsene (*Film etc*). **II** s **3.** Erwachsene m, f: ~ *education* Erwachsenenbildung f.

a·dul·ter·ate [ə'dʌltəreɪt] v/t *Nahrungsmittel* verfälschen, *Wein* panschen. **aˌdul·ter'a·tion** s Verfälschung f. **a'dul·ter·er** [ə'dʌltərə] s Ehebrecher m. **a'dul·ter·ess** s Ehebrecherin f. **a'dul·ter·ous** *adj* □ ehebrecherisch. **a'dul·ter·y** s Ehebruch m.

ad·um·brate [ˈædʌmbreɪt] v/t vorausahnen lassen, hindeuten auf (*acc*).

ad·vance [əd'vɑːns] **I** v/t **1.** vorrücken, -schieben, *Fuß* vorsetzen. **2.** *Zeitpunkt* vorverlegen. **3.** *Argument etc* vorbringen, geltend machen. **4.** *Projekt etc* fördern. **5.** j-n befördern, *Stellung etc* verbessern. **6.** *Preis* erhöhen. **7.** *Wachstum etc* beschleunigen. **8.** im voraus liefern; *Geld* vorauszahlen, vorschießen. **II** v/i **9.** vordringen, -rücken (*a. Zeit*). **10.** zunehmen (*in an dat*): ~ *in age* älter werden. **11.** vorankommen, Fortschritte machen. **12.** *im Rang* aufrücken, befördert werden. **13.** (an)steigen (*Preise*). **III** s **14.** Vorrücken n. **15.** Beförderung f, (*beruflicher etc*) Aufstieg. **16.** Fortschritt m, Verbesserung f. **17.** Vorsprung m: *in* ~ vorn; im voraus; *in* ~ *of* vor (*dat*); *be in* ~ e-n Vorsprung haben (*of* vor *dat*); *paid in* ~ vorausbezahlt. **18.** Vorschuß m, Vorauszahlung f. **19.** (*Preis*)Erhöhung f. **IV** *adj* **20.** Vor(aus)...: ~ *booking* Vor(aus)bestellung f; *thea. etc* Vorverkauf m; ~ *payment* Vorauszahlung f. **ad'vanced** *adj* **1.** vorgerückt (*Alter, Stunde*): *be* ~ *in years* in fortgeschrittenem Alter sein. **2.** fortgeschritten: ~ *English* Englisch für Fortgeschrittene. **3.** fortschrittlich. **ad'vance·ment** s Fortschritt m, Verbesserung f.

ad·van·tage [əd'vɑːntɪdʒ] s Vorteil m (*a. Sport*): *to* ~ günstig, vorteilhaft; *gain an* ~ *over s.o.* sich j-m gegenüber e-n Vorteil verschaffen; *have an* ~ *over s.o.* j-m gegenüber im Vorteil sein; *have the* ~ (*over s.o.*) (j-m gegenüber) den Vorteil haben (*of being* zu sein); *take ~ of* j-n, et. ausnutzen; *~ law* (*od. rule*) Vorteilsregel f. **ad·van·ta·geous** [‚ædvən'teɪdӡəs] *adj* □ vorteilhaft, günstig.

Ad·vent ['ædvənt] *s eccl.* Advent m.

ad·ven·ture [əd'ventʃə] *s* Abenteuer n: ~ *holiday* (*bsd. Am.* vacation) Abenteuerurlaub m; ~ *playground* Br. Abenteuerspielplatz m. **ad·ven·tur·er** s Abenteurer m. **ad·ven·tur·ess** s Abenteu(r)erin f. **ad·ven·tur·ous** *adj* □ **1.** abenteuerlich. **2.** abenteuerlustig.

ad·verb ['ædvɜːb] *s ling.* Adverb n, Umstandswort n. **ad·ver·bi·al** [əd'vɜːbjəl] *adj* □ adverbial: ~ *phrase* Adverbiale n, Adverbialbestimmung f.

ad·ver·sar·y ['ædvəsəri] *s* Gegner(in). **ad·verse** ['‿vɜːs] *adj* □ **1.** widrig. **2.** ungünstig, nachteilig (*to* für): ~ *balance of trade* passive Handelsbilanz. **ad·ver·si·ty** [əd'vɜːsəti] *s* **1.** Not f, Unglück n. **2.** Mißgeschick n.

ad·vert ['ædvɜːt] *s Br.* F *für* advertisement.

ad·ver·tise ['ædvətaɪz] **I** *v/t* **1.** ankündigen. **2.** Reklame machen für, werben für. **3.** *contp.* ausposaunen, an die große Glocke hängen. **II** *v/i* **4.** inserieren, annoncieren: ~ *for* durch Inserat suchen. **5.** Reklame machen, Werbung treiben. **ad·ver·tise·ment** [əd'vɜːtɪsmənt] *s* **1.** Inserat n, Annonce f. **2.** ~ *advertising* I. **ad·ver·tis·ing** **I** *s* Werbung f, Reklame f. **II** *adj* Werbe..., Reklame...: ~ *agency* Werbeagentur f; ~ *campaign* (*od.* drive) Werbekampagne f; ~ *manager* Werbeleiter m; ~ *medium* Werbeträger m.

ad·vice [əd'vaɪs] *s* **1.** Rat(schlag) m; Ratschläge *pl*: *a piece* (*od.* bit) *of* ~ ein Ratschlag; *at* (*od.* on) *s.o.'s* ~ auf j-s Rat hin; *take my* ~ *and* ... hör auf mich u. ...; *take medical* ~ e-n Arzt zu Rate ziehen. **2.** ✝ Avis m, n. **3.** *letter of* ~ Benachrichtigungsschreiben n.

ad·vis·a·ble [əd'vaɪzəbl] *adj* ratsam. **ad·vise** [əd'vaɪz] **I** *v/t* **1.** j-m raten *od.* empfehlen (*to do* zu tun), j-n beraten: ~ *against* j-m abraten von; *be well* ~*d* gut beraten sein, gut daran tun (*to do* zu tun). **2.** et. empfehlen, raten zu. **3.** ✝ avisieren (*s.o. of s.th.* j-m et.). **ad·vis·ed·ly** [‿ɪdlɪ] *adv* mit Überlegung. **ad·vis·er** s

Berater(in), Ratgeber(in). **ad·vi·so·ry** [‿ərɪ] *adj* beratend.

ad·vo·ca·cy ['ædvəkəsɪ] *s* (*of*) Eintreten n (für), Befürwortung f (gen). **ad·vo·cate** **I** s ['‿kət] Verfechter m, Befürworter m. **II** *v/t* ['‿keɪt] befürworten, eintreten für.

ae·gis ['iːdӡɪs] *s* Schirmherrschaft f: *under the* ~ *of*.

aer·ate ['eɪəreɪt] *v/t* **1.** lüften. **2.** mit Kohlensäure anreichern.

aer·i·al ['eərɪəl] **I** *adj* Luft...: ~ *cableway* Seilschwebebahn f; ~ *camera* Luftkamera f; ~ *view* Luftbild n. **II** *s bsd. Br.* Antenne f.

aer·o·drome ['eərədrəʊm] *s Br.* Flugplatz m. **aer·o·dy·nam·ic** *phys.* **I** *adj* (~*ally*) aerodynamisch. **II** *s pl* (*sg konstruiert*) Aerodynamik f. **aer·o·gram** ['‿græm] *s* **1.** Funkspruch m. **2.** Aerogramm n, Luftpostleichtbrief m. **aer·o·nau·ti·cal** *adj* □ aeronautisch: ~ *engineering* Flugzeugbau m. **aer·o·nau·tics** *s* Aeronautik f, Luftfahrtkunde f. **aer·o·plane** *s bsd. Br.* Flugzeug n. **'aer·o·space** **I** *s* **1.** Weltraum m. **II** *adj* **2.** Raumfahrt...: ~ *industry* (*medicine*). **3.** (Welt)Raum...: ~ *research* (*vehicle*).

aes·thete ['iːsθiːt] *s* Ästhet m. **aes·thet·ic**, **aes·thet·i·cal** [iːs'θetɪk(l)] *adj* □ ästhetisch. **aes·thet·ics** *s pl* (*sg konstruiert*) Ästhetik f.

a·far [ə'fɑː] *adv*: *from* ~ von weit her, aus weiter Ferne.

af·fa·bil·i·ty [‚æfə'bɪlətɪ] *s* Leutseligkeit f. **'af·fa·ble** *adj* □ leutselig.

af·fair [ə'feə] *s* **1.** Angelegenheit f, Sache f: ~ *foreign* 1. **2.** Ding n. **3.** Affäre f: a) Ereignis n, b) Skandal m, c) Verhältnis n.

af·fect¹ [ə'fekt] *v/t* **1.** e-e Vorliebe haben für. **2.** vortäuschen: *he* ~*ed not to understand* er tat so, als ob er nicht verstehe.

af·fect² [‿] *v/t* **1.** beeinflussen, in Mitleidenschaft ziehen. **2.** ✗ angreifen, befallen. **3.** bewegen, rühren: *be deeply* ~*ed*.

af·fec·ta·tion [‚æfek'teɪʃn] *s* **1.** Vorliebe f (*of* für). **2.** Affektiertheit f.

af·fec·tion [ə'fekʃn] *s* **1.** *oft pl* Liebe f, Zuneigung f (*for, towards* zu); Gefühl n: *play on s.o.'s* ~*s* mit j-s Gefühlen spielen. **2.** Gemütsbewegung *f.* **af·'fec·tion·ate** [~kʃnət] *adj* □ liebevoll, herzlich: *yours ~ly* Dein Dich liebender (*Briefschluß*).

af·fi·da·vit [ˌæfɪ'deɪvɪt] *s* 🏛 schriftliche eidliche Erklärung.

af·fil·i·ate [ə'fɪlɪeɪt] **I** *v/t* **1.** als Mitglied aufnehmen. **2.** angliedern (*to dat od.* an *acc*): *~d company* ✝ Tochtergesellschaft *f.* **II** *v/i* **3.** sich anschließen (*with dat od.* an *acc*). **af·fil·i·a·tion** *s* **1.** Aufnahme *f.* **2.** Angliederung *f.*

af·fin·i·ty [ə'fɪnətɪ] *s* **1.** Verschwägerung *f.* **2.** (geistige) Verwandtschaft. **3.** 🧪 Affinität *f.* **4.** Neigung *f* (*for, to* zu).

af·firm [ə'fɜːm] *v/t* **1.** versichern; beteuern. **2.** bekräftigen, 🏛 *Urteil* bestätigen. **3.** 🏛 an Eides Statt versichern. **af·fir·ma·tion** [ˌæfə'meɪʃn] *s* **1.** Versicherung *f.* Beteuerung *f.* **2.** Bekräftigung *f.* Bestätigung *f.* **3.** 🏛 Versicherung *f* an Eides Statt. **af·firm·a·tive** [ə'fɜːmətɪv] **I** *adj* bejahend, zustimmend. **II** *s: answer in the ~* bejahen.

af·fix **I** *v/t* [ə'fɪks] **1.** (*to*) befestigen, anbringen (an *dat*), anheften, -kleben (an *acc*). **2.** (*to*) *Unterschrift* setzen (unter *acc*). **II** *s* ['æfɪks] **3.** *ling.* Affix *n.*

af·flict [ə'flɪkt] *v/t* plagen, heimsuchen: *~ed with* geplagt von, leidend an. **af·flic·tion** *s* **1.** Kummer *m.* **2.** Gebrechen *n; pl* Beschwerden *pl: ~s of old age* Altersbeschwerden. **3.** Not *f,* Elend *n.*

af·flu·ence ['æfluəns] *s* **1.** Überfluß *m.* **2.** Reichtum *m,* Wohlstand *m.* **'af·flu·ent I** *adj* □ wohlhabend, reich (*in* an *dat*): *~ society* Wohlstandsgesellschaft *f.* **II** *s* Nebenfluß *m.*

af·flux ['æflʌks] *s* Zufluß *m.*

af·ford [ə'fɔːd] *v/t* **1.** sich leisten: *we can't ~ it* wir können es uns nicht leisten. **2.** aufbringen, *Zeit* erübrigen. **3.** *Schutz etc* gewähren, bieten, *Freude* machen. **af·ford·a·ble** *adj* **1.** erschwinglich (*Preis*). **2.** finanziell möglich *od.* tragbar.

af·for·est [æ'fɒrɪst] *v/t* aufforsten. **af·for·est·a·tion** *s* Aufforstung *f.*

af·front [ə'frʌnt] **I** *v/t* beleidigen. **II** *s* Beleidigung *f.*

a·fi·cio·na·do [əˌfɪsjə'nɑːdəʊ] *pl* **-dos** *s* Fan *m,* Liebhaber *m.*

a·field [ə'fiːld] *adv* in der *od.* die Ferne.

a·fire [ə'faɪə] *adv u. adj* in Flammen: *be ~* in Flammen stehen; *fig.* glühen (*with* vor *dat*); *set ~* in Brand stecken, anzünden; *all ~ fig.* Feuer u. Flamme.

a·flame [ə'fleɪm] → **afire.**

a·float [ə'fləʊt] *adv u. adj* **1.** flott, schwimmend: *keep ~* (sich) über Wasser halten (*a. fig.*); *set ~* ⚓ flottmachen. **2.** in Umlauf (*Gerücht etc*): *set ~* in Umlauf bringen; *there is a rumo(u)r ~ that* es geht das Gerücht (um), daß. **3.** im Gange: *set ~* in Gang setzen. **4.** überschwemmt: *be ~* unter Wasser stehen.

a·foot [ə'fʊt] → **afloat** 3.

a·fore·'men·tioned [əˌfɔː~], **~·said** [ə'fɔː~] *adj* obenerwähnt. **~·thought** [ə'fɔː~] *adj:* → **malice** 3.

a·fraid [ə'freɪd] *adj: be ~ of* sich fürchten *od.* Angst haben vor (*dat*); *be ~ to do* sich fürchten *od.* scheuen zu tun; *I'm ~ I must go* leider muß ich jetzt gehen.

a·fresh [ə'freʃ] *adv* von neuem.

Af·ri·can ['æfrɪkən] **I** *adj* afrikanisch. **II** *s* Afrikaner(in).

af·ter ['ɑːftə] **I** *adv* **1.** nach-, hinterher, darauf: *for months ~* noch monatelang; *during the weeks ~* in den (nach)folgenden Wochen; *shortly ~* kurz danach. **II** *prp* **2.** hinter (*dat*) (... her), nach: *be ~* hersein hinter. **3.** *zeitlich* nach: *~ a week; day ~ day* Tag für Tag; *the month ~ next* der übernächste Monat; *~ all* schließlich, im Grunde; immerhin, dennoch; (also) doch. **4.** nach, gemäß: *named ~ his father* nach s-m Vater genannt. **III** *adj* **5.** später: *in ~ years.* **6.** ⚓ Achter... **IV** *cj* **7.** nachdem. **'~·birth** *s* 🩺 Nachgeburt *f.* **'~·care** *s* **1.** 🩺 Nachbehandlung *f,* -sorge *f.* **2.** 🏛 Resozialisierungshilfe *f.* **'~·din·ner** *adj: ~ speech* Tischrede *f; ~ walk* Verdauungsspaziergang *m.* **'~·ef·fect** *s* 🩺 Nachwirkung *f* (*a. fig.*). **'~·glow** *s* Abendrot *n.* **'~·life** *s* **1.** Leben *n* nach dem Tode. **2.** (zu)künftiges Leben. **'~·math** [~mæθ] *s* Folgen *pl,* Nachwirkungen *pl.* **'~·noon I** *s* Nachmittag *m: in the ~* am Nachmittag; *this ~* heute nachmittag; *good ~!* guten Tag! **II** *adj* Nachmittags... **'~·play** *s* sexuelles Nachspiel.

af·ters ['ɑːftəz] *s pl* (*sg konstruiert*) *Br.* F

Nachtisch *m*: **for** ~ als *od.* zum Nachtisch.

'af·ter|-sales ser·vice *s* Kundendienst *m.* **'~taste** *s* Nachgeschmack *m* (*a. fig.*). **'~thought** *s* nachträglicher Einfall. **'~treat·ment** *s* ⚕, ⚙ Nachbehandlung *f.* **~wards** ['~wədz] *adv* später, nachher, hinterher.

a·gain [ə'gen] *adv* **1.** wieder: ~ **and** ~ immer wieder; → **now** 1, **time** 4. **2.** schon wieder: *that fool* ~*! 3.* außerdem, ferner. **4.** noch einmal: → **much** 1. **5.** and(e)rseits.

a·gainst [ə'genst] *prp* **1.** gegen: **be** ~ **s.th.** gegen et. sein; e-r Sache zuwiderlaufen. **2.** gegenüber (*dat*): (**over**) ~ **the town hall** gegenüber dem Rathaus; **my rights** ~ **the landlord** m-e Rechte gegenüber dem Vermieter. **3.** an (*dat od. acc*), gegen: ~ **the wall. 4.** *a.* **as** ~ verglichen mit, im Vergleich zu.

a·gape [ə'geɪp] *adv u. adj* mit (vor Staunen *etc*) offenem Mund.

ag·ate ['ægət] *s min.* Achat *m.*

age [eɪdʒ] **I** *s* **1.** (Lebens)Alter *n*: **at the** ~ **of** im Alter von; *I have a daughter your* ~ in Ihrem Alter; *when I was your* ~ als ich so alt war wie du; *ten years of* ~ zehn Jahre alt; *what is his* ~?, *what* ~ *is he?* wie alt ist er?; *be your* ~! sei kein Kindskopf! **2.** Reife *f*: (**come**) **of** ~ mündig *od.* volljährig (werden); *under* ~ minderjährig, unmündig. **3.** vorgeschriebenes Alter (*für ein Amt etc*): **be over** ~ die Altersgrenze überschritten haben. **4.** Zeit(alter *n*) *f*: **in our** ~ in unserer Zeit. **5.** *a.* **old** ~ (hohes) Alter: ~ *before beauty! humor.* Alter vor Schönheit! **6.** *oft pl* F Ewigkeit *f*: *I haven't seen him for* ~ **s** seit e-r Ewigkeit. **II** *v/t* **7.** alt machen (*Kleid etc*); um Jahre älter machen (*Sorgen etc*). **III** *v/i* **8.** alt werden, altern. ~ **brack·et** → **age group.**

aged¹ [eɪdʒd] *adj* im Alter von ..., ...jährig, ... Jahre alt: ~ **twenty.**

a·ged² [eɪdʒɪd] *adj* alt, betagt, bejahrt.

age| group *s* Altersgruppe *f*, -klasse *f.* **'~less** *adj* **1.** nicht alternd, ewig jung. **2.** zeitlos. ~ **lim·it** *s* Altersgrenze *f.*

a·gen·cy ['eɪdʒənsɪ] *s* **1.** (*Handels-, Nachrichten- etc*)Agentur *f*; (Handels)Vertretung *f.* **2.** *bsd. Am.* Geschäfts-, Dienststelle *f*; Amt *n*, Behörde

f. **3.** Mittel *n*: **by** (*od.* **through**) **the** ~ **of** mit Hilfe von (*od. gen*).

a·gen·da [ə'dʒendə] *s* Tagesordnung *f*: **be on the** ~ auf der Tagesordnung stehen.

a·gent ['eɪdʒənt] *s* **1.** *biol., phys. etc* Agens *n*, Wirkstoff *m*, Mittel *n*. **2.** † Agent *m* (*a. pol.*), Vertreter *m*; (*Grundstücks- etc*)Makler *m.*

ag·glom·er·ate [ə'gloməreɪt] *v/t u. v/i* (sich) zs.-ballen; (sich) (an)häufen. **ag,glom·er·a·tion** *s* Zs.-ballung *f*; Anhäufung *f.*

ag·glu·ti·nate [ə'glu:tɪneɪt] *v/t* **1.** zs.-kleben. **2.** *biol., ling.* agglutinieren. **ag,glu·ti'na·tion** *s* **1.** Zs.-kleben *n.* **2.** zs.-klebende Masse, Klumpen *m.* **3.** *biol., ling.* Agglutination *f.*

ag·gra·vate ['ægrəveɪt] *v/t* **1.** verschlimmern. **2.** F (ver)ärgern. **'ag·gra·vat·ing** *adj* **1.** verschlimmernd. **2.** F ärgerlich. **,ag·gra'va·tion** *s* **1.** Verschlimmerung *f.* **2.** F Ärger *m.*

ag·gre·gate [ə'gregət] **I** *adj* **1.** gesamt, Gesamt...: ~ **amount** → 5. **II** *v/t* ['~geɪt] **2.** anhäufen, -sammeln. **3.** sich (insgesamt) belaufen auf (*acc*). **III** *s* ['~gət] **4.** Anhäufung *f*, -sammlung *f.* **5.** Gesamtbetrag *m*, -summe *f*: **in the** ~ insgesamt, alles in allem. **6.** ⚙ *etc* Aggregat *n.* **ag·gre·ga·tion** [,~'geɪʃn] *s* (An)Häufung *f*, Ansammlung *f.*

ag·gres·sion [ə'greʃn] *s bsd.* ✕ Angriff *m*, Aggression *f* (*a. psych.*). **ag·gres·sive** [ə'gresɪv] *adj* aggressiv. **ag'gres·sive·ness** *s* Aggressivität *f.* **ag'gres·sor** *s bsd.* ✕ Angreifer *m.*

ag·grieve [ə'gri:v] *v/t* **1.** betrüben, -drücken. **2.** kränken.

ag·gro ['ægrəʊ] *s Br. sl.* Aggressivität *f.*

a·ghast [ə'gɑ:st] *adv u. adj* entgeistert, entsetzt, bestürzt (**at** über *acc*).

ag·ile ['ædʒaɪl] *adj* ☐ beweglich, wendig: *have an* ~ *mind* geistig beweglich sein. **a·gil·i·ty** [ə'dʒɪlətɪ] *s* Beweglichkeit *f*, Wendigkeit *f.*

ag·i·tate ['ædʒɪteɪt] **I** *v/t* **1.** schütteln, (um)rühren. **2.** aufregen, -wühlen. **3.** aufwiegeln, -hetzen. **II** *v/i* **4.** agitieren, hetzen (**against** gegen); Propaganda machen (**for** für). **ag·i'ta·tion** *s* **1.** Aufregung *f.* **2.** Agitation *f.* **'ag·i·ta·tor** *s* Agitator *m*, Hetzer *m.*

a·glow [ə'gləʊ] *adv u. adj* glühend.

a·go [ə'gəʊ] *adv* vor: *a year ~* vor e-m Jahr; *long ~* vor langer Zeit; *not long ~* (erst) vor kurzem.

a·gog [ə'gɒg] *adv u. adj* erpicht; gespannt (*for* auf *acc*): *all ~* ganz aus dem Häuschen; *be ~ to do s.th.* es kaum mehr erwarten können, et. zu tun.

ag·o·nize ['ægənaɪz] *v/i* 1. mit dem Tode ringen. 2. sich abquälen, verzweifelt ringen (*over* mit). **'ag·o·niz·ing** *adj* □ qualvoll. **ag·o·ny** ['ʌnɪ] *s* 1. Qual *f*: *be in an ~ of doubt* von Zweifeln gequält werden; *~ aunt* F Kummerkastentante *f*; *~ column* F Seufzerspalte *f* (*Zeitung*). 2. Todeskampf *m*.

a·grar·i·an [ə'greərɪən] *adj* landwirtschaftlich, Agrar...: *~ reform* Bodenreform *f*.

a·gree [ə'griː] I *v/t* 1. vereinbaren (*to do* zu tun; *that* daß): *~d!* einverstanden!, abgemacht!; *~ to differ* sich auf verschiedene Standpunkte einigen. 2. *bsd. Br.* sich einigen auf (*acc*); *Streit* beilegen. II *v/i* 3. (*on, about*) einig werden (über *acc*), sich einigen (auf *acc*), vereinbaren (*acc*). 4. (*to*) zustimmen (*dat*), einverstanden sein (mit). 5. sich einig sein, gleicher Meinung sein (*with* wie). 6. (*with*) übereinstimmen (mit), entsprechen (*dat*). 7. bekommen (*with dat*) (*Speise etc*). **a·gree·a·ble** [ə'grɪəbl] *adj* □ 1. angenehm (*to dat od.* für): *agreeably surprised* angenehm überrascht. 2. liebenswürdig. 3. einverstanden (*to* mit). **a·gree·a·ble·ness** *s* Liebenswürdigkeit *f*; **a'greed** *adj*: *be ~* sich einig sein, gleicher Meinung sein. **a·gree·ment** [ə'griːmənt] *s* 1. Vereinbarung *f*; *bsd. pol.* Abkommen *n*; Einigung *f*: *come to an ~* sich einigen. Einigkeit *f*. 3. Übereinstimmung *f*.

ag·ri·cul·tur·al [ˌægrɪˈkʌltʃərəl] *adj* □ landwirtschaftlich: *~ prices pl* Agrarpreise *pl*. **ag·ri·cul·ture** ['ʌtʃə] *s* Landwirtschaft *f*.

a·ground [ə'graʊnd] *adv u. adj* ⚓ gestrandet: *run ~* auflaufen, stranden; *Schiff* auf Grund setzen; *be ~* aufgelaufen sein; *fig.* auf dem trock(e)nen sitzen.

ah [ɑː] *int* ah!, ach!

a·ha [ɑːˈhɑː] I *int* aha! II *adj*: *~ experience psych.* Aha-Erlebnis *n*.

a·head [ə'hed] *adv u. adj* 1. vorn, nach

vorn zu. 2. voraus, vorwärts: *~ of* vor (*dat*), voraus (*dat*).

a·hoy [ə'hɔɪ] *int* ⚓ ahoi!

aid [eɪd] I *v/t* 1. unterstützen, *j-m* helfen (*in* bei). 2. *Verdauung etc* fördern. II *v/i* 3. **he was accused of ~ing and abetting** er wurde wegen Beihilfe angeklagt. III *s* 4. Hilfe *f* (*to* für), Unterstützung *f*: *by* (*od. with*) (*the*) *~ of* mit Hilfe von (*od. gen*); *in ~ of* zugunsten von (*od. gen*); *come to s.o.'s ~* j-m zu Hilfe kommen. 5. Hilfsmittel *n*, -gerät *n*.

AIDS [eɪdz] *s* ❀ AIDS *n* (**acquired immune deficiency syndrome**).

ail [eɪl] *v/i* kränklich sein, kränkeln (*beide a. fig. Wirtschaft etc*).

ai·ler·on ['eɪlərɒn] *s* ✈ Querruder *n*.

ail·ing ['eɪlɪŋ] *adj* kränkelnd, kränklich (*beide a. fig. Wirtschaft etc*). **'ail·ment** *s* Leiden *n*.

aim [eɪm] I *v/t* 1. zielen (*at* auf *acc*, nach). 2. beabsichtigen, bezwecken (*at acc*): *~ to do s.th.* vorhaben, et. zu tun. 3. streben (*at* nach). 4. abzielen, anspielen (*at* auf *acc*). II *v/t* 5. *Waffe* richten (*at* auf *acc*). 6. (*at*) *Bemerkung etc* richten (gegen); *Bestrebungen* richten (auf *acc*). III *s* 7. Ziel *n*: *take ~ → 1.* 8. *fig.* Ziel *n*; Absicht *f*. **'aim·less** *adj* □ ziellos.

ain't [eɪnt] *F* **are not, am not, is not, have not, has not.**

air¹ [eə] I *s* 1. Luft *f*: *by ~* auf dem Luftweg; *in the open ~* im Freien; *be in the ~* im Umlauf sein (*Gerücht etc*); *be in the air* in der Schwebe sein (*Frage etc*); *take the ~* frische Luft schöpfen; → *light²* 1, *thin* 1. 2. *Rundfunk, TV:* Äther *m:* *on the ~* im Rundfunk *od.* Fernsehen; *be on the ~* senden (*Sender*); gesendet werden (*Programm*); im Rundfunk zu hören *od.* im Fernsehen zu sehen sein (*Person*). 3. Miene *f*, Aussehen *n*: *an ~ of importance* e-e gewichtige Miene. 4. *mst pl* Getue *n*: *~s and graces* affektiertes Getue; *put on ~s, give o.s. ~s* vornehm tun. II *v/t* 5. lüften. 6. *Wäsche* zum Trocknen aufhängen. 7. *et.* an die Öffentlichkeit *od.* zur Sprache bringen.

air² [~] *s* ♪ Lied *n*, Melodie *f*.

air| bag *s mot.* Luftsack *m.* **~ base** *s* Luftstützpunkt *m.* **~ base** *s* Luftbad *n.* **'~·borne** *adj* 1. im Flugzeug befördert: *~ radar* Bordradar *m, n*; *~ troops pl* ✕ Luftlandetruppen *pl.* 2. *be ~* sich in der

Luft befinden, fliegen. ~ **brake** s ⊚ Druckluftbremse f. '~**bus** s ✈ Airbus m. ~ **car·go** s Luftfracht f. '~**con·di·tioned** adj mit Klimaanlage, klimatisiert. ~ **con·di·tion·ing** s 1. Klimatisierung f. **2.** Klimaanlage f. '~**cooled** adj luftgekühlt. '~**craft** s Flugzeug n; coll. Flugzeuge pl: ~ **car·rier** Flugzeugträger m. ~ **crash** s Flugzeugabsturz m. ~ **cush·ion** s Luftkissen n. '~**drop** s ✕ mit dem Fallschirm abwerfen; ✕ Fallschirmjäger etc absetzen. '~**field** s Flugplatz m. ~ **force** s Luftwaffe f. ~ **freight** s 1. Luftfracht f. **2.** Luftfrachtgebühr f. ~ **gun** s Luftgewehr n. ~ **host·ess** s Stewardeß f.

air·ing ['eərɪŋ] s Lüftung f: **give s.th. an** ~ et. lüften; **the room needs an** ~ das Zimmer muß (durch)gelüftet werden. **2.** Spaziergang m: **take an** ~ frische Luft schöpfen. **3. give s.th. an** ~ → **air¹** 7.

air¹ jack·et s Schwimmweste f.'~**less** adj 1. luftlos. **2.** stickig. '~**let·ter** s Luftpost(leicht)brief m. '~**lift** s Luftbrücke f. '~**line** s Fluggesellschaft f. '~**lin·er** s Verkehrsflugzeug n. '~**mail** s Luftpost f. **II** v/t per Luftpost schicken. ~ **pas·sen·ger** s Fluggast m. ~ **pho·to·graph** s Luftbild n. ~ **pi·rate** s Luftpirat(in). '~**plane** s Am. Flugzeug n. '~**pock·et** s ✈ Luftloch n. ~ **pol·lu·tion** s Luftverschmutzung f. '~**port** s Flughafen m, -platz m. ~ **pres·sure** s Luftdruck m. '~**proof** adj luftdicht. ~ **pump** s Luftpumpe f. ~ **raid** s ✕ Luftangriff m. '~**raid** adj: **precautions** s ✕ Luftschutz m; ~ **shelter** Luftschutzbunker m, -raum m. ~ **shaft** s Luftschacht m. '~**ship** s Luftschiff n. '~**sick** adj luftkrank. '~**space** s Luftraum m. '~**strip** s (behelfsmäßige) Start- u. Landebahn. ~ **ter·mi·nal** s 1. Flughafenabfertigungsgebäude n. **2.** Br. Endstation f der Zubringerlinie zum u. vom Flughafen. ~ **tick·et** s Flugticket n, -schein m. '~**tight** adj 1. luftdicht. **2.** fig. hieb- u. stichfest (Argument etc). ~ **traf·fic** s Flug-, Luftverkehr m. '~**traf·fic** adj: ~ **control** Flugsicherung f; ~ **controller** Fluglotse m. '~**way** s ✈ Luftstraße f. '~**wor·thy** adj ✈ flugtüchtig.

air·y ['eərɪ] adj □ **1.** Luft... **2.** luftig. **3.**

graziös, anmutig. **4.** lebhaft, munter. **5.** verstiegen, überspannt. **6.** vornehmtuerisch. **7.** lässig, ungezwungen.

aisle [aɪl] s **1.** △ Seitenschiff n. **2.** Gang m (zwischen Bänken etc).

a·jar [ə'dʒɑː] adv u. adj angelehnt (Tür etc).

a·kim·bo [ə'kɪmbəʊ] adv u. adj: **with arms** ~ die Arme in die Seite gestemmt.

a·kin [ə'kɪn] adj **1.** verwandt (to mit). **2.** fig. verwandt, ähnlich (to dat): **be** ~ sich ähneln; ähneln (to dat).

al·a·bas·ter [,ælə'bɑːstə] s Alabaster m.

a·lac·ri·ty [ə'lækrətɪ] s Bereitwilligkeit f, Eifer m.

a·larm [ə'lɑːm] **I** s **1.** Alarm m: **give** (od. **raise, sound) the** ~ Alarm geben; fig. Alarm schlagen. **2.** Weckvorrichtung f (e-s Weckers): ~ **(clock)** Wecker m. **3.** Alarmvorrichtung f, -anlage f. **4.** Angst f, Unruhe f. **II** v/t **5.** alarmieren. **6.** ängstigen, beunruhigen. **a'larm·ist** s Bangemacher m.

a·las [ə'læs] int ach!, leider!

Al·ba·ni·an [æl'beɪnjən] **I** adj albanisch. **II** s Albanier(in).

al·ba·tross [ælbətrɒs] s orn. Albatros m, Sturmvogel m.

al·bi·no [æl'biːnəʊ] pl **-nos** s biol. Albino m.

al·bum ['ælbəm] s Album n (a. Langspielplatte).

al·bu·men ['ælbjʊmɪn] s biol. Eiweiß n.

al·che·my ['ælkəmɪ] s hist. Alchimie f.

al·co·hol ['ælkəhɒl] s Alkohol m. ,**al·co'hol·ic I** adj (**~ally**) alkoholisch. **II** s Alkoholiker(in): **ℓs Anonymous** die Anonymen Alkoholiker. '**al·co·hol·ism** s Alkoholismus m.

al·cove ['ælkəʊv] s **1.** Alkoven m, Nische f. **2.** bsd. poet. (Garten)Laube f.

al·der ['ɔːldə] s ♣ Erle f.

al·der·man ['ɔːldəmən] s (irr man) Ratsherr m, Stadtrat m.

ale [eɪl] s Ale n (helles, obergäriges Bier).

a·lert [ə'lɜːt] **I** adj □ **1.** auf der Hut (to vor dat), wachsam. **2.** munter, flink. **3.** aufgeweckt, (hell)wach: **be** ~ **to** sich e-r Sache bewußt sein. **II** s **4.** ✕ (Alarm)Bereitschaft f: **be on the** ~ in Alarmbereitschaft sein; fig. auf der Hut sein. **5.** bsd. ✈ Alarm(signal n) m. **III** v/t **6.** alarmieren, ✕ a. in Alarmzustand versetzen. **7.** fig. aufrütteln: ~

s.o. to s.th. j-m et. (deutlich) zum Bewußtsein bringen.

al·fres·co [æl'freskəʊ] adj u. adv im Freien: ~ lunch; lunch ~.

al·ga ['ælgə] pl **-gae** ['-dʒiː] s ♣ Alge f.

al·ge·bra ['ældʒıbrə] s ♣ Algebra f. **al·ge·bra·ic** [ˌ-'breık] adj (~ally) algebraisch.

a·li·as ['eılıəs] I adv alias. II s Deck-, ⚖ a. Falschname m.

al·i·bi ['ælıbaı] s ⚖ Alibi n, fig. F a. Ausrede f, Entschuldigung f: give s.o. an ~ j-m ein Alibi geben.

al·ien ['eıljən] I adj 1. ausländisch. 2. außerirdisch. 3. fig. fremd (to dat): that is ~ to his nature das ist ihm wesensfremd. II s 4. Ausländer(in). 5. außerirdisches Wesen. **al·ien·ate** ['-eıt] v/t 1. ⚖ veräußern. 2. befremden; entfremden (from dat). ˌal·ien·a·tion s 1. ⚖ Veräußerung f. 2. Entfremdung f.

a·light¹ [ə'laıt] adv u. adj in Flammen: be ~ in Flammen stehen; fig. strahlen (with vor dat); set ~ in Brand stecken, anzünden.

a·light² [ˌ-] v/i (a. irr) 1. (from) aussteigen (aus), absteigen (von Fahrrad etc), absitzen (von Pferd). 2. (on) (sanft) fallen (auf acc) (Schnee), sich niederlassen (auf dat od. acc) (Vogel). 3. ✈ niedergehen, landen (a. allg.): ~ on one's feet auf die Füße fallen.

a·lign [ə'laın] I v/t 1. in e-e (gerade) Linie bringen, ⊚ (aus)fluchten. 2. ausrichten (with nach). 3. ~ o.s. with fig. sich anschließen (dat od. an acc). II v/i 4. sich ausrichten (with nach). **a·lign·ment** s Ausrichtung f: in ~ with in einer Linie mit, fig. a. in Übereinstimmung mit.

a·like [ə'laık] I adj gleich; ähnlich (to dat). II adv gleich, ebenso, in gleicher Weise; ähnlich: treat ~ gleich behandeln.

al·i·men·ta·ry [ˌælı'mentərı] adj 1. Nahrungs... 2. Ernährungs..., Speise...: ~ canal Verdauungskanal m.

al·i·mo·ny ['ælımənı] s ⚖ Unterhalt(szahlung f) m.

a·live [ə'laıv] adj 1. lebend, lebendig, am Leben: his grandparents are still ~ leben noch; be burnt ~ bei lebendigem Leib verbrennen. 2. in voller Kraft od. Wirksamkeit: keep ~ aufrechterhalten. 3. lebendig, lebhaft: ~ and kicking F

gesund u. munter; look ~! F mach fix! **4.** be ~ to sich e-r Sache bewußt sein. **5.** be ~ with wimmeln von.

al·ka·li ['ælkəlaı] s ♣ Alkali n, Laugensalz n. **al·ka·line** ['-laın] adj alkalisch.

all [ɔːl] I adj 1. all, gesamt, ganz: ~ day (long) den ganzen Tag (hindurch); ~ the time die ganze Zeit. 2. jeder, jede, jedes, alle pl: at ~ hours zu jeder Stunde. II adv 3. ganz, gänzlich: ~ the better um so besser; ~ in F total fertig od. erledigt; ~ over überall; that is John ~ over das ist typisch John; ~ right schon gut; in Ordnung; it's ~ right for you to talk! F du hast gut reden!; ~ round rings- od. rundherum; it's ~ up with him mit ihm ist's aus; → there 1. III pron 4. alles: ~ in ~ alles in allem; ~ of it alles, das Ganze; ~ of us wir alle; → above 2, after 3. IV s 5. his ~ sein Hab u. Gut; sein ein u. alles.

,all-A·mer·i·can adj 1. rein od. typisch amerikanisch. 2. die ganzen USA vertretend.

al·lay [ə'leı] v/t beschwichtigen; Schmerzen etc mildern, lindern.

al·le·ga·tion [ˌælı'geıʃn] s Behauptung f. **al·lege** [ə'ledʒ] v/t behaupten. **al·'leged** adj angeblich.

al·le·giance [ə'liːdʒəns] s Treue f, Loyalität f.

al·le·gor·ic, al·le·gor·i·cal [ˌælı'gɒrık(l)] adj □ allegorisch. **al·le·go·ry** ['-gərı] s Allegorie f.

al·le·lu·ia [ˌælı'luːjə] s Halleluja n.

al·ler·gic [ə'lɜːdʒık] adj (~ally) allergisch (to gegen) (a. fig. F). **al·ler·gy** ['ælədʒı] s ♬ Allergie f.

al·le·vi·ate [ə'liːvıeıt] v/t mildern, lindern. **al·le·vi·a·tion** s Milderung f, Linderung f.

al·ley ['ælı] s 1. Gasse f: → blind alley. 2. Bowling: Bahn f: that's down (od. up) my ~ F das ist et. für mich.

All Fools' Day s der 1. April.

al·li·ance [ə'laıəns] s 1. Verbindung f. 2. Bund m, Bündnis n: form an ~ ein Bündnis schließen. 3. Verschwägerung f; weitS. Verwandtschaft f. **al·lied** [ə'laıd; attr. 'ælaıd] adj 1. verbündet. 2. fig. verwandt (to mit). **Al·lies** ['ælaız] s pl hist. die Alliierten pl.

al·li·ga·tor ['ælıgeıtə] s zo. Alligator m.

,all-'in adj Gesamt..., Pauschal...

al·lit·er·a·tion [əˌlɪtəˈreɪʃn] s Alliteration f.

al·lo·cate [ˈæləʊkeɪt] v/t zuteilen, zuweisen (**to** dat). **ˌal·loˈca·tion** s Zuteilung f, Zuweisung f.

al·lop·a·thy [əˈlɒpəθɪ] s ✠ Allopathie f.

al·lot [əˈlɒt] v/t **1.** zuteilen, zuweisen (**to** dat). **2.** Geld etc bestimmen (**to, for** für). **alˈlot·ment** s **1.** Zuteilung f, Zuweisung f. **2.** Parzelle f; ~ (**garden**) bsd. Br. Schrebergarten m.

ˌallˈout adj F **1.** total: ~ **effort** äußerste Anstrengung f. **2.** Am. kompromißlos, radikal.

al·low [əˈlaʊ] **I** v/t **1.** erlauben, gestatten; bewilligen, gewähren: **be ~ed to do s.th.** et. tun dürfen; **we are ~ed ...** uns stehen ... zu. **2.** Summe geben. **3.** zugeben; anerkennen, gelten lassen. **II** v/i **4.** ~ **of** erlauben, gestatten: **it ~s of no excuse** es läßt sich nicht entschuldigen. **5.** ~ **for** in Betracht ziehen, berücksichtigen (acc). **alˈlow·a·ble** adj □ erlaubt, zulässig. **alˈlow·ance** s **1.** Erlaubnis f; Bewilligung f. **2.** Anerkennung f. **3.** Zuschuß m, Beihilfe f; Taschengeld n. **4.** ✠ Nachlaß m, Rabatt m: ~ **for cash** Skonto n. **5.** Nachsicht f: **make ~(s) for** → **allow** 5. **6.** ⚛, ⚙ Toleranz f.

al·loy ⚙ **I** s [ˈælɔɪ] Legierung f. **II** v/t [əˈlɔɪ] legieren.

ˌallˈ-ˌpur·pose adj Allzweck..., Universal... **ˌ~ˈround** adj vielseitig, Allround...

Allǀ Saints' Day s eccl. Allerheiligen n. **~ Souls' Day** s eccl. Allerseelen n.

ˈallˌtime adj bisher unerreicht, beispiellos: **~ high** Höchstleistung f, -stand m; **~ low** Tiefststand m.

al·lude [əˈluːd] v/i anspielen (**to** auf acc).

al·lure [əˈljʊə] v/t **1.** (an-, ver)locken. **2.** anziehen, verzaubern. **alˈlure·ment** s **1.** Verlockung f. **2.** Anziehungskraft f, Zauber m. **alˈlur·ing** adj □ (ver)lockend, verführerisch.

al·lu·sion [əˈluːʒn] s Anspielung f (**to** auf acc).

al·lu·vi·al [əˈluːvjəl] adj geol. angeschwemmt, Schwemm...

ˈallˌ-ˌweath·er adj Allwetter...

al·ly [əˈlaɪ] **I** v/t verbinden, -einigen (**to, with** mit): **~ o.s.** → II; → **allied.** **II** v/i sich vereinigen od. verbünden (**to, with**

mit). **III** s [ˈælaɪ] Verbündete m, f, Bundesgenosse m: → **Allies.**

al·ma·nac [ˈɔːlmənæk] s Almanach m, Kalender m.

al·might·y [ɔːlˈmaɪtɪ] adj allmächtig: **the ⦵** der Allmächtige.

al·mond [ˈɑːmənd] s ⚘ Mandel f.

al·most [ˈɔːlməʊst] adv fast, beinahe.

alms [ɑːmz] s **1.** (mst pl konstruiert) Almosen n, f, pl. Koll. Br. Kollekte f.

al·oe [ˈæləʊ] s ⚘ Aloe f.

a·lone [əˈləʊn] **I** adj allein: → **leave¹** 2, **let¹** 1. **II** adv allein, bloß, nur.

a·long [əˈlɒŋ] **I** prp **1.** entlang (dat od. acc), längs (gen, a. dat), an (dat) ... vorbei: ~ **the river** am od. den Fluß entlang, entlang dem Fluß. **II** adv **2.** vorwärts, weiter: → **get along,** etc. **3.** ~ **with** zs. mit: → **take along,** etc. **4.** F da: **I'll be ~ shortly** ich bin gleich da. **a,longˈside I** adv **1.** ⚓ längsseits. **2.** Seite an Seite. **II** prp **3.** neben (dat od. acc).

a·loof [əˈluːf] adv fern, abseits: **hold** (od. **keep**) (**o.s.**) ~, **stand** ~ sich fernhalten (**from** von), für sich bleiben. **II** adj reserviert, zurückhaltend.

a·loud [əˈlaʊd] adv laut, mit lauter Stimme.

al·pha·bet [ˈælfəbet] s Alphabet n. **ˌal·phaˈbet·ic, ˌal·phaˈbet·i·cal** adj □ alphabetisch: **in ~ order** in alphabetischer Reihenfolge, alphabetisch (an)geordnet.

Al·pine [ˈælpaɪn] adj **1.** Alpen... **2.** alpin, (Hoch)Gebirgs...

al·read·y [ɔːlˈredɪ] adv bereits, schon.

al·right [ˌɔːlˈraɪt] Br. F u. Am. für **all right** (→ **all** 3).

Al·sa·tian [ælˈseɪʃən] **I** adj **1.** elsässisch. **II** s **2.** Elsässer(in). **3.** a. ~ **dog** deutscher Schäferhund.

al·so [ˈɔːlsəʊ] adv auch, ebenfalls. **'~ran** s **1.** Sport: Teilnehmer an e-m Rennen, der sich nicht plazieren kann: **she was an ~** sie kam unter ‚ferner liefen' ein. **2.** F Versager m, Niete f.

al·tar [ˈɔːltə] s eccl. Altar m. ~ **boy** s Ministrant m.

al·ter [ˈɔːltə] **I** v/t (ver-, ab-, um)ändern. **II** v/i sich (ver)ändern. **'al·ter·a·ble** adj □ veränderlich. **ˌal·terˈa·tion** s Änderung f (**to** an dat), Ver-, Ab-, Umänderung f.

al·ter·ca·tion [ˌɔːltəˈkeiʃn] s heftige Auseinandersetzung.

al·ter·nate I adj [ɔːlˈtɜːnət] **1.** abwechselnd: **on ~ days** jeden zweiten Tag. II v/t [ˈɔːltəneit] **2.** abwechseln lassen. **3.** miteinander vertauschen. **4.** ⚡, ⊙ (periodisch) verändern. III v/i [ˈɔːltəneit] **5.** abwechseln. **al'ter·nate·ly** adv abwechselnd, wechselweise. **'al·ter·nat·ing** adj abwechselnd, Wechsel...: **~ current** ⚡ Wechselstrom m. **al·ter·na·tion** [ˌɔːltəˈneiʃn] s Abwechslung f, Wechsel m. **al·ter·na·tive** [ɔːlˈtɜːnətiv] I adj **1.** alternativ, Ersatz...: **~ airport** Ausweichflughafen m; **~ society** alternative Gesellschaft. **2.** ander(er, e, es) (von zweien). II s **3.** Alternative f (**to** zu): **have no** (**other**) **~** keine andere Möglichkeit od. Wahl haben (**but** to als zu).

al·though [ɔːlˈðəu] cj obwohl, obgleich.

al·tim·e·ter [ˈæltimiːtə] s phys. Höhenmesser m.

al·ti·tude [ˈæltitjuːd] s ast., ✈, ♈ Höhe f: **at an ~ of** in e-r Höhe von; **~ of the sun** Sonnenstand m.

al·to [ˈæltəu] pl **-tos** ♪ Alt(stimme f) m; Altistin f.

al·to·geth·er [ˌɔːltəˈgeðə] I adv **1.** insgesamt. **2.** ganz (u. gar), völlig. **3.** im ganzen genommen. II s **4. in the ~** humor. im Adams- od. Evaskostüm.

al·tru·ism [ˈæltruizəm] s Altruismus m, Selbstlosigkeit f. **'al·tru·ist** s Altruist(in). ˌal·tru'is·tic adj (**~ally**) altruistisch, selbstlos.

a·lu·min·i·um [ˌæljuˈminiəm], Am. **a·lu·mi·num** [əˈluːmənəm] s ♈ Aluminium n.

a·lum·na [əˈlʌmnə] pl **-nae** [~niː] s Am. ehemalige Schülerin od. Studentin. **a'lum·nus** [~nəs] pl **-ni** [~nai] s Am. ehemaliger Schüler od. Student.

al·ways [ˈɔːlweiz] adv immer, stets: **as ~** wie immer.

am [æm] ich bin.

a·mal·gam [əˈmælgəm] s **1.** ♈, ⊙ Amalgam n. **2.** fig. Mischung f. **a'mal·gam·ate** [~meit] v/t u. v/i **1.** ♈, ⊙ (sich) amalgamieren. **a.** fig. (sich) vereinigen, verschmelzen, **2.** fig. (sich) zs.-schließen, ♱ a. fusionieren. **a.mal·gam'a·tion** s **1.** ♈, ⊙ Amalgamieren n, a. fig. Vereinigung f, Verschmelzung f **2.** fig. Zs.-schluß m, ♱ a. Fusion f.

a·mass [əˈmæs] v/t an-, aufhäufen.

am·a·teur [ˈæmətə] s Amateur m: a) (Kunst- etc)Liebhaber(in): **~ painter** Sonntagsmaler(in), b) Amateursportler(in): **~ boxer** Amateurboxer m, c) Nichtfachmann m, contp. Dilettant(in): **~ detective** Amateurdetektiv m. **am·a·teur·ish** [ˌ~ˈtɜːriʃ] adj □ amateurhaft, dilettantisch.

a·maze [əˈmeiz] v/t in (Er)Staunen setzen, verblüffen. **a'mazed** adj □ erstaunt, verblüfft (**at** über acc). **a'maze·ment** s (Er)Staunen n, Verblüffung f: **in ~** staunend, verblüfft; **to my ~** zu m-m Erstaunen, zu m-r Verblüffung. **a'maz·ing** adj □ erstaunlich, verblüffend.

Am·a·zon [ˈæməzən] s **1.** antiq. Amazone f. **2.** a. ♀ fig. Amazone f, Mannweib n.

am·bas·sa·dor [æmˈbæsədə] s pol. Botschafter m (**to** in dat). **am'bas·sa·dress** [~dris] s Botschafterin f.

am·ber [ˈæmbə] I s **1.** min. Bernstein m. **2.** Br. Gelb(licht) n, gelbes Licht (Verkehrsampel): **at ~** bei Gelb; **the lights were at ~** die Ampel stand auf Gelb. II adj **3.** Bernstein... **4.** bernsteinfarben. **5.** **the lights were ~** Br. die Ampel stand auf Gelb.

am·bi·dex·trous [ˌæmbiˈdekstrəs] adj □ **1.** beidhändig. **2.** fig. doppelzüngig, falsch.

am·bi·gu·i·ty [ˌæmbiˈgjuːəti] s Zweideutigkeit f (a. Äußerung), Mehr-, Vieldeutigkeit f. **am'big·u·ous** [~gjuəs] adj □ zwei-, mehr-, vieldeutig.

am·bi·tion [æmˈbiʃn] s Ehrgeiz m. **am'bi·tious** adj □ ehrgeizig (a. Plan etc): **be ~ to do s.th.** den Ehrgeiz haben, et. zu tun; **be ~ for s.o.** große Dinge mit j-m vorhaben.

am·biv·a·lent [æmˈbivələnt] adj bsd. psych. ambivalent, doppelwertig.

am·ble [ˈæmbl] I v/i **1.** im Paßgang gehen od. reiten. **2.** fig. schlendern. II s **3.** Paßgang m. **4.** fig. gemächlicher Gang.

am·bu·lance [ˈæmbjuləns] s Kranken-, Sanitätswagen m.

am·bush [ˈæmbuʃ] I s Hinterhalt m: **lay an ~** e-n Hinterhalt legen; **lie** (od. **wait**) **in ~** III. II v/t aus dem Hinterhalt überfallen; auflauern (dat). III v/i im Hinterhalt liegen.

amplifier

a·me·ba Am. → **amoeba**.

a·mel·io·rate [ə'miːljəreɪt] **I** v/t verbessern, ✍ (a)meliorieren. **II** v/i besser werden. **a,mel·io·ra·tion** s Verbesserung f, ✍ (A)Melioration f.

a·men [ˌɑː'men] **I** int amen! **II** s Amen n.

a·me·na·ble [ə'miːnəbl] adj □ **(to) 1.** zugänglich (dat). **2.** verantwortlich (dat); unterworfen (dat).

a·mend [ə'mend] v/t **1.** verbessern. **2.** parl. Gesetz abändern, ergänzen. **a'mend·ment** s **1.** Verbesserung f. **2.** parl. Abänderungs-, Ergänzungsantrag m; Am. Zusatzartikel m zur Verfassung. **a'mends** s pl (mst sg konstruiert) (Schaden)Ersatz m: **make ~** Schadenersatz leisten, es wiedergutmachen; **make ~ to s.o. for s.th.** j-n für et. entschädigen.

a·men·i·ty [ə'miːnətɪ] s **1.** oft pl Liebenswürdigkeit f, Höflichkeit f: **his ~ of temper** sein angenehmes Wesen. **2.** schöne Lage (e-s Hauses etc); oft pl Annehmlichkeit(en pl) f; pl (natürliche) Vorzüge pl od. Reize pl (e-r Person, e-s Ortes etc).

A·mer·i·can [ə'merɪkən] **I** adj amerikanisch: **~ Dream** der amerikanische Traum; **~ Indian** (bes. nordamer.) Indianer(in). **II** s Amerikaner(in). **A'mer·i·can·ism** s Amerikanismus m. **A,mer·i·can·i'za·tion** s Amerikanisierung f. **A'mer·i·can·ize** v/t u. v/i (sich) amerikanisieren.

am·e·thyst ['æmɪθɪst] s min. Amethyst m.

a·mi·a·bil·i·ty [ˌeɪmjə'bɪlətɪ] s Liebenswürdigkeit f. **'a·mi·a·ble** adj □ liebenswürdig, freundlich.

am·i·ca·ble ['æmɪkəbl] adj freund(schaft)lich, friedlich, a. ⚖ gütlich. **'am·i·ca·bly** adv in Güte, gütlich: **part ~** im guten auseinandergehen.

a·mid(st) [ə'mɪd(st)] prp inmitten (gen), (mitten) in dat. → **amid** (dat od. acc).

a·miss [ə'mɪs] adj u. adv verkehrt, falsch: **take ~** übelnehmen; **there is s.th. ~ with** et. stimmt nicht mit; **it would not be ~** es würde nicht schaden (**for s.o. to do s.th.** wenn j-d et. täte).

am·i·ty ['æmətɪ] s Freundschaft f, gutes Einvernehmen.

am·me·ter ['æmɪtə] s ⚡ Amperemeter n.

am·mo·ni·a [ə'məʊnjə] s 🝆 Ammo-

niak n: **liquid ~** Salmiakgeist m.

am·mu·ni·tion [ˌæmjʊ'nɪʃn] s ✕ Munition f: **~ dump** Munitionslager n.

am·ne·sia [æm'niːzjə] s ⚕ Amnesie f, Gedächtnisschwund m.

am·nes·ty ['æmnəstɪ] **I** s Amnestie f. **II** v/t amnestieren, begnadigen.

a·moe·ba [ə'miːbə] s zo. Amöbe f.

a·mok [ə'mɒk] → **amuck**.

a·mong(st) [ə'mʌŋ(st)] prp (mitten) unter (dat od. acc), zwischen (dat od. acc), bei: **from ~** aus ... hervor; **be ~** gehören zu; **~ other things** unter anderem; **they had two pounds ~ them** sie hatten zusammen zwei Pfund.

a·mor·al [ˌeɪ'mɒrəl] adj □ amoralisch.

am·o·rous ['æmərəs] adj □ **1.** verliebt (of in acc). **2.** Liebes...: **~ song**.

a·mor·phous [ə'mɔːfəs] adj □ form-, gestaltlos.

am·or·ti·za·tion [əˌmɔːtɪ'zeɪʃn] s Amortisation f, Tilgung f, Abschreibung f. **am'or·tize** [ˌ·taɪz] v/t amortisieren: a) Schuld tilgen, b) Anlagewerte abschreiben.

a·mount [ə'maʊnt] **I** v/i **1.** (**to**) sich belaufen (auf acc), betragen (acc). **2.** fig. (**to**) hinauslaufen (auf acc), bedeuten (acc). **II** s **3.** Betrag m, Summe f; Höhe f (e-r Summe): **to the ~ of** in Höhe von; **bis zum Betrag von. 4.** Menge f.

a·mour·pro·pre [ˌæmʊə'prɒprə] s Eigenliebe f.

amp [æmp] F → **ampere, amplifier**.

am·pere ['æmpeə] s Ampere n.

am·phet·a·mine [æm'fetəmiːn] s 🝆 Amphetamin n.

am·phib·i·an [æm'fɪbɪən] adj **1.** → **amphibious**. **II** s **2.** zo Amphibie f, Lurch m. **3.** Amphibienfahrzeug n. **am'phib·i·ous** adj zo., ⊙ amphibisch, Amphibien...

am·phi·the·a·ter, bsd. Br. **am·phi·the·a·tre** ['æmfɪˌθɪətə] s Amphitheater n.

am·ple ['æmpl] adj □ **1.** weit, groß, geräumig. **2.** weitläufig, -gehend, ausführlich. **3.** reich(lich), beträchtlich. **4.** stattlich (Figur etc).

am·pli·fi·ca·tion [ˌæmplɪfɪ'keɪʃn] s **1.** Erweiterung f, Vergrößerung f, Ausdehnung f. **2.** nähere Ausführung od. Erläuterung; Weitschweifigkeit f. **3.** ⚡, phys. Verstärkung f. **am·pli·fi·er** ['ˌ·faɪə] s ⚡, phys. Verstärker m.

'**am·pli·fy** I *v/t* **1.** erweitern, vergrößern, ausdehnen. **2.** näher ausführen *od.* erläutern. **3.** *⚡, phys.* verstärken. II *v/i* **4.** sich weitläufig auslassen (*on* über *acc*). **am·pli·tude** ['~tju:d] *s* **1.** Weite *f*, Umfang *m* (*a. fig.*). **2.** Fülle *f*, Reichtum *m*. **3.** *⚡, phys.* Amplitude *f*, Schwingungsweite *f*.

am·poule ['æmpu:l] *s* 💉 Ampulle *f*.

am·pu·tate ['æmpjʊteɪt] *v/t* 💉 amputieren, abnehmen. ,**am·pu'ta·tion** *s* Amputation *f*, Abnahme *f*.

a·muck [ə'mʌk] *adv*: *run ~* Amok laufen.

am·u·let ['æmjʊlɪt] *s* Amulett *n*.

a·muse [ə'mju:z] *v/t* amüsieren; unterhalten; Spaß machen (*dat*): *be ~d* sich freuen (*at, by* über *acc*). **a'muse·ment** *s* Unterhaltung *f*; Zeitvertreib *m*: *for ~* zum Vergnügen; *~ arcade* Br. Spielsalon *m*; *~ park* Vergnügungspark *m*. **a'mus·ing** *adj* □ amüsant; unterhaltsam.

an [ən] → *a*.

a·nach·ro·nism [ə'nækrənɪzəm] *s* Anachronismus *m*.

an·a·con·da [,ænə'kɒndə] *s zo.* Anakonda *f*, Riesenschlange *f*.

a·nae·mi·a [ə'niːmjə] *s bsd. Br.* 💉 Anämie *f*, Blutarmut *f*. **a'nae·mic** *adj bsd. Br.* anämisch, blutarm.

an·aes·the·si·a [,ænɪs'θiːzjə] *s bsd. Br.* 💉 Anästhesie *f*, Narkose *f*, Betäubung *f*. **an·aes'thet·ic** [~'θetɪk] *bsd. Br.* 💉 I *adj* (*~ally*) betäubend, Narkose... II *s* Betäubungsmittel *n*. **an·aes·the·tist** [æ'niːsθətɪst] *s bsd. Br.* 💉 Anästhesist *m*, Narkosearzt *m*. **an'aes·the·tize** *v/t bsd. Br.* 💉 betäuben, narkotisieren.

an·a·log·ic, an·a·log·i·cal [,ænə'lɒdʒɪk(l)], **a·nal·o·gous** [ə'næləgəs] *adj* □ analog, entsprechend (*to, with* dat).

a'nal·o·gy [~dʒɪ] *s* Analogie *f*, Entsprechung *f*: *on the ~ of, by ~ with* analog, gemäß, entsprechend (*dat*).

an·a·lyse ['ænəlaɪz] *v/t* analysieren: a) 🜍 *etc* zerlegen, b) gründlich untersuchen, c) *ling.* zergliedern, d) Ⅎ auflösen. **a·nal·y·sis** [ə'næləsɪs] *pl -ses* [~siːz] *s* **1.** Analyse *f*, Zerlegung *f*, gründliche Untersuchung, Zergliederung *f*, Auflösung *f*. **2.** Ⅎ Analysis *f*. **3.** Psychoanalyse *f*. **an·a·lyst** ['ænəlɪst] *s* **1.** Analytiker *m*: *public ~* (behördlicher) Lebensmittelchemiker. **2.** Psy-

choanalytiker *m*. **an·a·lyt·ic, an·a·lyt·i·cal** [,ænə'lɪtɪk(l)] *adj* □ **1.** analytisch. **2.** psychoanalytisch.

an·ar·chic, an·ar·chi·cal [æ'nɑːkɪk(l)] *adj* □ anarchisch. **an·arch·ism** ['ænəkɪzəm] *s* Anarchismus *m*. '**an·arch·ist** *s* Anarchist(in). II *adj* anarchistisch. '**an·arch·y** *s* Anarchie *f*.

a·nath·e·ma [ə'næθəmə] *s* **1.** *eccl.* Bannfluch *m*, Kirchenbann *m*: *be an ~ to s.o. fig.* j-m verhaßt *od.* ein Greuel sein. **a'nath·e·ma·tize** *v/t* in den Bann tun, mit dem Kirchenbann belegen.

an·a·tom·i·cal [,ænə'tɒmɪkl] *adj* □ anatomisch. **a·nat·o·mize** [ə'nætəmaɪz] *v/t* 💉 sezieren, *fig. a.* zergliedern. **a'nat·o·my** *s* **1.** 💉 Anatomie *f*. **2.** *fig.* Zergliederung *f*, Analyse *f*.

an·ces·tor ['ænsestə] *s* Vorfahr *m*, Ahn(herr) *m*: *~ cult* Ahnenkult *m*. **an·ces·tral** [~'sestrəl] *adj* angestammt, Ahnen...: *~ home* Stammsitz *m*. **an·ces·tress** ['ænsestrɪs] *s* Ahnfrau *f*, Ahne *f*. **an·ces·try** *s* **1.** (*bsd. vornehme*) Abstammung. **2.** Vorfahren *pl*, Ahnen(reihe *f*) *pl*: *~ research* Ahnenforschung *f*.

an·chor ['æŋkə] I *s* **1.** ⚓ Anker *m*: *cast* (*od. drop*) *~* → 5a; *lie* (*od. ride*) *at ~* → 5b; *~ weigh* 3. **2.** *Rundfunk, TV: Am.* Moderator *m*, Moderatorin *f* (*e-r Nachrichtensendung*); Diskussionsleiter(in). II *v/t* **3.** ⚓, ⚙ verankern (*a. fig.*). **4.** *Rundfunk, TV: Am.* Nachrichtensendung moderieren; *Diskussion* leiten. III *v/i* **5.** ⚓ ankern: a) vor Anker gehen, b) vor Anker liegen. '**an·chor·age** *s* **1.** Ankerplatz *m*. **2.** *a. ~ dues or* Anker-, Liegegebühr *f*.

an·chor·man ['æŋkəmən] *s* (*irr man*), '**~,wom·an** *s* (*irr woman*) → **anchor** 2.

an·cho·vy ['æntʃəvɪ] *s ichth.* An(s)chovis *f*, Sardelle *f*.

an·cient ['eɪnʃənt] I *adj* **1.** alt, aus alter Zeit. **2.** uralt. **3.** altertümlich. II *s* **4.** *the ~s pl* die Alten *pl* (*Griechen u. Römer*).

an·cil·lar·y [æn'sɪlərɪ] *adj* untergeordnet (*to* dat), Zusatz..., Neben...: *~ industries pl* Zulieferbetriebe *pl*.

and [ænd] *cj* und: *better ~ better* immer besser; *thousands ~ thousands* Tausende u. aber Tausende; *there are books ~ books* es gibt gute u. schlechte Bücher; *for miles ~ miles* viele Meilen weit; *he ran ~ ran* er lief immer weiter; **bread ~ butter** Butterbrot *n*; *try ~ come* versuche zu kommen; → *nice* 4.

an·ec·do·tal [ˌænekˈdəʊtl] *adj* anekdotenhaft, anekdotisch. **an·ec·dote** [ˈænɪkdəʊt] *s* Anekdote *f*.

a·ne·mi·a, *etc Am.* → **anaemia,** *etc.*

an·e·mom·e·ter [ˌænɪˈmɒmɪtə] *s phys.* Windmesser *m*.

a·nem·o·ne [əˈnemənɪ] *s ♀* Anemone *f*.

an·es·the·si·a, *etc Am.* → **anaesthesia,** *etc.*

a·new [əˈnjuː] *adv* **1.** von neuem, noch einmal. **2.** neu.

an·gel [ˈeɪndʒəl] *s* Engel *m* (*a. fig.*): *you are an ~* du bist ein Schatz. **an·gel·ic,** **an·gel·i·cal** [ænˈdʒelɪk(l)] *adj* □ engelhaft, Engels...

an·ger [ˈæŋgə] **I** *s* Zorn *m*, Ärger *m*, Wut *f* (*at* über *acc*). **II** *v/t* erzürnen, (ver)ärgern.

an·gi·na (pec·to·ris) [ænˈdʒaɪnə (ˈpektərɪs)] *s ♣* Angina *f* pectoris.

an·gle¹ [ˈæŋgl] **I** *s* **1.** *bsd. ♣* Winkel *m*: *at an ~* schräg; *at right ~s to* im rechten Winkel zu. **2.** Ecke *f*. **3.** *fig.* Standpunkt *m*. **4.** *fig.* Seite *f*, Aspekt *m*. **II** *v/t* **5.** ab-, umbiegen. **6.** *Bericht etc* färben.

an·gle² [~] *v/i* angeln: *~ for fig.* aussein auf (*acc*); → *compliment* 1.

an·gle| i·ron [⊙] Winkeleisen *n*. '**~-park** *v/t u. v/i mot.* schräg parken.

an·gler [ˈæŋglə] *s* Angler(in).

An·gles [ˈæŋglz] *s pl hist.* Angeln *pl*.

An·gli·can [ˈæŋglɪkən] *eccl.* **I** *adj* anglikanisch. **II** *s* Anglikaner(in).

An·gli·cism [ˈæŋglɪsɪzəm] *s ling.* Anglizismus *m*.

An·glo|-A·mer·i·can [ˌæŋgləʊəˈmerɪkən] **I** *s* Angloamerikaner(in). **II** *adj* angloamerikanisch. **,~-'Sax·on I** *s* Angelsachse *m*. **II** *adj* angelsächsisch.

an·go·ra [æŋˈgɔːrə] *s a. ~ cat zo.* Angorakatze *f*. **~ wool** *s* Angorawolle *f*.

an·gry [ˈæŋgrɪ] *adj* □ (*at, about*) ärgerlich (auf, über *acc*), verärgert (über *acc*), böse (auf *j-n*, über *et.*; *with* mit *j-m*).

an·guish [ˈæŋgwɪʃ] *s* Qual *f*, Pein *f*: *be in ~* Ängste ausstehen.

an·gu·lar [ˈæŋgjʊlə] *adj* □ **1.** wink(e)lig, Winkel...: *~ point ♣* Scheitelpunkt *m*. **2.** knochig. **3.** *fig.* steif: a) linkisch, b) formell.

an·i·line [ˈænɪliːn] *s* ♣ Anilin *n*.

an·i·mal [ˈænɪml] **I** *s* Tier *n*. **II** *adj* animalisch, tierisch. **~ food** *s* **1.** Fleischnahrung *f*. **2.** Tierfutter *n*. **~ lov·er** *s* Tierfreund(in). '**~,lov·ing** *adj* tierliebend. **~ shel·ter** *s Am.* Tierheim *n*. **~ spir·its** *s pl* Lebenskraft *f*, -geister *pl*.

an·i·mate I *v/t* [ˈænɪmeɪt] **1.** beleben, mit Leben erfüllen. **2.** anregen, aufmuntern. **II** *adj* [~mət] **3.** belebt, lebend. **4.** lebhaft, munter. **an·i·mat·ed** [ˈ~meɪtɪd] *adj* **1.** lebendig: *~ cartoon* Zeichentrickfilm *m*. **2.** → *animate* 4. **an·i·ma·tion** [ˌ~ˈmeɪʃn] *s* Lebhaftigkeit *f*, Munterkeit *f*.

an·i·mos·i·ty [ˌænɪˈmɒsətɪ] *s* Feindseligkeit *f* (*against, toward*[*s*] gegen[über]; *between* zwischen *dat*).

an·ise [ˈænɪs] *s* ♀ Anis *m*. **an·i·seed** [ˈ~siːd] *s* Anis(samen) *m*.

an·kle [ˈæŋkl] *s anat.* (Fuß)Knöchel *m*. '**~-deep** *adj* knöcheltief. **~ sock** *s Br.* Söckchen *n*.

an·klet [ˈæŋklɪt] *s* **1.** Fußring *m*. **2.** *Am.* Söckchen *n*.

an·nals [ˈænlz] *s pl* **1.** Annalen *pl*, Jahrbücher *pl*. **2.** (Jahres)Bericht *m*.

an·neal [əˈniːl] *v/t* **1.** *metall.* ausglühen, *a. Kunststoffe* tempern. **2.** *Keramik:* brennen. **3.** *fig.* härten, stählen.

an·nex I *v/t* [əˈneks] **1.** (*to*) beifügen (*dat*), anhängen (an *acc*). **2.** *Gebiet* annektieren, sich einverleiben. **II** *s* [ˈæneks] **3.** Anhang *m*, Zusatz *m*. **4.** Anbau *m*, Nebengebäude *n*. **,an·nex'a·tion** *s* Annektierung *f*, Einverleibung *f* (*to* in *acc*).

an·ni·hi·late [əˈnaɪəleɪt] *v/t* vernichten. **an,ni·hi'la·tion** *s* Vernichtung *f*.

an·ni·ver·sa·ry [ˌænɪˈvɜːsərɪ] *s* Jahrestag *m*.

an·no·tate [ˈænəʊteɪt] *v/t* mit Anmerkungen versehen; kommentieren. **,an·no'ta·tion** *s* Anmerkung *f*; Kommentar *m*.

an·nounce [əˈnaʊns] *v/t* **1.** ankündigen. **2.** bekanntgeben, verkünden, *Geburt etc* anzeigen. **3.** *Rundfunk, TV:* ansagen; *über Lautsprecher* durchsagen. **an'nounce·ment** *s* **1.** Ankündigung *f*. **2.** Bekanntgabe *f* (*Geburts- etc*)Anzeige *f*. **3.** *Rundfunk, TV:* Ansage *f*; (Lautsprecher)Durchsage *f*. **an'nounc·er** *s Rundfunk, TV:* Ansager(in).

an·noy [ə'nɔɪ] v/t **1.** ärgern: *be ~ed* sich ärgern (*at s.th.* über et.; *with s.o.* über j-n). **2.** belästigen, stören. **an'noy·ance** s **1.** Ärger m. **2.** Belästigung f, Störung f. **an'noy·ing** adj □ **1.** ärgerlich. **2.** lästig, störend.

an·nu·al ['ænjʊəl] I adj □ **1.** jährlich, Jahres...: *~ ring* ♀ Jahresring m. **2.** a. ♀ einjährig. II s **3.** jährlich erscheinende Veröffentlichung. **4.** ♀ einjährige Pflanze.

an·nu·i·ty [ə'njuːɪtɪ] s (Jahres-, Leib-) Rente f.

an·nul [ə'nʌl] v/t annullieren, *Gesetz, Ehe etc* aufheben, für ungültig erklären, *Vorschrift etc* abschaffen.

an·nu·lar ['ænjʊlə] adj □ ringförmig, Ring...

an·nul·ment [ə'nʌlmənt] s Annullierung f, Aufhebung f, Ungültigkeitserklärung f, Abschaffung f.

An·nun·ci·a·tion (Day) [ə‚nʌnsɪ'eɪʃn] s eccl. Mariä Verkündigung f.

an·ode ['ænəʊd] s ⚡ Anode f, positiver Pol.

an·o·dyne ['ænəʊdaɪn] adj u. s ⚕ schmerzstillend(es Mittel).

a·noint [ə'nɔɪnt] v/t bsd. eccl. salben.

a·nom·a·lous [ə'nɒmələs] adj □ **1.** anomal. **2.** ungewöhnlich. **a'nom·a·ly** s ♀ Anomalie f.

a·non·y·mi·ty [‚ænə'nɪmətɪ] s Anonymität f. **a·non·y·mous** [ə'nɒnɪməs] adj □ anonym.

a·no·rak ['ænəræk] s Anorak m.

an·oth·er [ə'nʌðə] adj u. pron **1.** ein anderer, e-e andere, ein anderes: *~ thing* etwas anderes; *one after ~* e-r nach dem andern; → *one* 6. **2.** noch ein(er, e, es), ein zweiter od. weiterer, e-e zweite od. weitere, ein zweites od. weiteres: *~ ten years* noch od. weitere zehn Jahre; *tell me ~!* F Das kannst du deiner Großmutter erzählen!

an·swer ['ɑːnsə] I s **1.** Antwort f (a. fig. Reaktion) (*to* auf acc): *in ~ to* in Beantwortung (gen); auf (acc) hin; als Antwort auf. **2.** Lösung f (*to e-s Problems*). II v/i **3.** antworten (*to* auf acc): *~ back* freche Antworten geben; widersprechen; sich (*mit Worten etc*) verteidigen od. wehren. **4.** *~ to* → 10 u. 11. **5.** (*to s.o.*) sich (j-m gegenüber) verantworten, (j-m) Rechenschaft ablegen (*for*

für). **6.** verantwortlich sein, haften (*for* für). **7.** *~ to* hören auf (*e-n Namen*). III v/t **8.** j-m antworten: *~ s.o. back* j-m freche Antworten geben; j-m widersprechen; sich gegen j-n (*mit Worten etc*) verteidigen od. wehren. **9.** antworten auf (acc), beantworten. **10.** fig. reagieren auf (acc): a) eingehen auf: *~ the bell* (od. *door*) (*auf das Läuten od. Klopfen*) die Tür öffnen, aufmachen; *~ the telephone* ans Telefon gehen, b) ⚙ *dem Steuer etc* gehorchen, c) *e-m Befehl etc* Folge leisten, gehorchen, od. *Wunsch etc* erfüllen, *Gebet* erhören, e) sich *auf e-e Anzeige hin* melden od. bewerben. **11.** *e-r Beschreibung* entsprechen. **12.** sich *j-m gegenüber* verantworten, *j-m* Rechenschaft ablegen (*for* für). **'an·swer·a·ble** adj **1.** verantwortlich (*to dat; for* für). **2.** zu beantworten(d).

ant [ænt] s zo. Ameise f.

an·tag·o·nism [æn'tægənɪzəm] s Feindschaft f (*between* zwischen dat). **an'tag·o·nist** s Feind(in). **an‚tag·o·'nis·tic** adj (*~ally*) feindlich (*to* gegen). **an'tag·o·nize** v/t **1.** bekämpfen. **2.** sich *j-n* zum Feind machen.

ant·arc·tic [æn'tɑːktɪk] I adj antarktisch: *♀ Circle* südlicher Polarkreis. II s ♀ Antarktis f.

ant bear s zo. Ameisenbär m.

an·te·ced·ent [‚æntɪ'siːdənt] I adj **1.** (*to*) vorhergehend (*dat*), früher (als). II s **2.** pl Vorgeschichte f: *his ~s* sein Vorleben; s-e Abstammung. **3.** ling. Bezugswort n.

an·te·cham·ber ['æntɪ‚tʃeɪmbə] s Vorzimmer n.

an·te·date ['æntɪ'deɪt] v/t *Brief etc* zurückdatieren.

an·te·di·lu·vi·an [‚æntɪdaɪ'luːvjən] adj vorsintflutlich (a. fig.).

an·te·lope ['æntɪləʊp] s zo. Antilope f.

an·te me·rid·i·em [‚æntɪmə'rɪdɪəm] adv vormittags (*abbr. a.m.*): *3 a.m.* 3 Uhr morgens.

an·te·na·tal [‚æntɪ'neɪtl] I adj □ vor der Geburt: *~ examination* Mutterschaftsvorsorgeuntersuchung f; *~ exercises* pl Schwangerschaftsgymnastik f. II s F Mutterschaftsvorsorgeuntersuchung f.

an·ten·na [æn'tenə] s **1.** pl *-nae* [‚niː] zo. Fühler m. **2.** pl *-nas* bsd. Am. Antenne f.

an·te·ri·or [æn'tɪərɪə] adj **1.** (to) vorhergehend (dat), früher (als). **2.** vorder.

an·te·room ['æntɪrʊm] s Vorzimmer n.

an·them ['ænθəm] s Hymne f.

'ant·hill s Ameisenhaufen m.

an·thol·o·gy [æn'θɒlədʒɪ] s Anthologie f, (bsd. Gedicht)Sammlung f.

an·thra·cite ['ænθrəsaɪt] s min. Anthrazit m, Glanzkohle f.

an·thro·poid ['ænθrəʊpɔɪd] zo. **I** adj menschenähnlich. **II** s Menschenaffe m.

an·thro·po·log·i·cal [ˌænθrəpə'lɒdʒɪkl] adj □ anthropologisch. **an·thro·pol·o·gist** [ˌʌˈpɒlədʒɪst] s Anthropologe m. **an·thro·pol·o·gy** [ˌʌˈpɒlədʒɪ] s Anthropologie f, Menschenkunde f.

an·ti... ['æntɪ] in Zssgn Gegen..., gegen... eingestellt, anti..., Anti...

ˌan·ti'air·craft adj ✕ Flugabwehr...: ~ **gun** Flakgeschütz n.

an·ti·bi·ot·ic [ˌæntɪbaɪ'ɒtɪk] s ✿ Antibiotikum n.

'an·ti·bod·y s ✿ Antikörper m, Abwehrstoff m.

'An·ti·christ s eccl. Antichrist m.

an·tic·i·pate [æn'tɪsɪpeɪt] v/t **1.** voraussehen, (-)ahnen. **2.** erwarten, erhoffen. **3.** vorwegnehmen. **4.** j-m, e-m Wunsch etc zuvorkommen. **5.** ✝ vor Fälligkeit bezahlen od. einlösen. **an͵tic·i'pa·tion** s **1.** (Vor)Ahnung f. **2.** Erwartung f, Hoffnung f: **in ~ of** in Erwartung (gen). **3.** Vorwegnahme f: **in ~** im voraus. **an'tic·i·pa·to·ry** [ˌpeɪtərɪ] adj □ vorwegnehmend.

ˌan·ti'cler·i·cal adj □ antiklerikal, kirchenfeindlich.

ˌan·ti'cli·max s **1.** rhet. Antiklimax f. **2.** fig. enttäuschendes Abfallen; Enttäuschung f.

ˌan·ti'clock·wise adj u. adv entgegen dem od. gegen den Uhrzeigersinn.

ˌan·ti'cor'ro·sive adj **1.** korrosionsverhütend: ~ **agent** Rostschutzmittel n. **2.** rostfest.

ˌan·ti'cy·clone s meteor. Hoch(druckgebiet) n.

ˌan·ti'daz·zle adj Blendschutz...: ~ **switch** Abblendschalter m.

an·ti·dote ['æntɪdəʊt] s Gegengift n, -mittel n (a. fig.) (**against, for, to** gegen).

ˌan·ti'fas·cist I s Antifaschist(in). **II** adj antifaschistisch.

ˌan·ti'freeze s Frostschutzmittel n.

'an·ti͵he·ro s Antiheld m.

ˌan·ti'knock ✿, mot. **I** adj klopffest. **II** s Antiklopfmittel n.

an·tip·a·thy [æn'tɪpəθɪ] s Antipathie f, Abneigung f (**against, to, towards** gegen).

an·tip·o·des [æn'tɪpədiːz] s pl **1.** die diametral gegenüberliegenden Teile pl der Erde. **2.** (a. sg konstruiert) das (genaue) Gegenteil.

ˌan·ti·pol'lu·tion adj umweltschützend: ~ **device** Abgasentgiftungsanlage f.

an·ti·quar·i·an [ˌæntɪ'kweərɪən] **I** adj **1.** antiquarisch. **2.** ~ **bookseller** Antiquar m; ~ **bookshop** (bsd. Am. **bookstore**) Antiquariat n. **II** s **3.** → **antiquary** 1. **an·ti·quar·y** [ˌʌˈkwərɪ] s **1.** Altertumskenner(in), -forscher(in). **2.** Antiquitätensammler(in); -händler(in). **an·ti·quat·ed** ['ʌˈkweɪtɪd] adj antiquiert, veraltet.

an·tique [æn'tiːk] **I** adj **1.** antik, alt. **2.** F → **antiquated**. **3.** s Antiquität f: ~ **dealer** Antiquitätenhändler(in); ~ **shop** (bsd. Am. **store**) Antiquitätenladen m. **an·tiq·ui·ty** [ˌʌ'tɪkwətɪ] s **1.** Altertum n. **2.** die Antike. **3.** pl Altertümer pl.

ˌan·ti'rust adj Rostschutz...

ˌan·ti·'Sem·ite s Antisemit(in). **ˌan·ti·-Se'mit·ic** adj antisemitisch. **ˌan·ti·-Sem·i·tism** [ˌʌ'semɪtɪzəm] s Antisemitismus m.

ˌan·ti'sep·tic ✿ **I** adj □ antiseptisch. **II** s Antiseptikum n.

ˌan·ti'so·cial adj **1.** asozial, gesellschaftsfeindlich. **2.** ungesellig.

an·tith·e·sis [æn'tɪθɪsɪs] pl **-ses** [ˌsiːz] s Antithese f, Gegensatz m. **an·ti·thet·ic**, **an·ti·thet·i·cal** [ˌʌ'θetɪk(l)] adj □ gegensätzlich.

ant·ler ['æntlə] s **1.** (Geweih)Sprosse f. **2.** pl Geweih n.

an·to·nym ['æntəʊnɪm] s ling. Antonym n.

a·nus ['eɪnəs] s anat. After m.

an·vil ['ænvɪl] s Amboß m (a. anat.).

anx·i·e·ty [æŋ'zaɪətɪ] s **1.** Angst f, Sorge f (**about, for** wegen, um). **2.** ✿, psych. Beklemmung f: ~ **dream** Angsttraum m. **3.** (starkes) Verlangen (**for** nach).

anx·ious ['æŋkʃəs] adj □ **1.** ängstlich; besorgt (**about, for** wegen, um). **2.** fig.

(*for, to inf*) begierig (auf *acc*, zu *inf*), (ängstlich) bedacht (auf *acc*, darauf zu *inf*), bestrebt (zu *inf*): *I am very ~ to see him* mir liegt (sehr) viel daran, ihn zu sehen.

an·y ['enɪ] **I** *adj* **1.** (*fragend, verneinend*) (irgend)ein(e), einige *pl*, etwas: *not ~* kein. **2.** (*bejahend*) jeder, jede, jedes (beliebige): *at ~ time* jederzeit; → *case²*, *rate* 2. **II** *adv* **3.** irgend(wie), (noch) etwas: *~ more?* noch (etwas) mehr? '*~·bod·y pron* **1.** (irgend) jemand, irgendeine(r). **2.** jeder(mann): *~ who* jeder, der; wer; *hardly ~* kaum j-d, fast niemand; *not ~* niemand. '*~·how adv* **1.** irgendwie. **2.** jedenfalls. '*~·one* → *anybody*. '*~·thing pron* **1.** (irgend) etwas: *not ~* (gar *od.* überhaupt) nichts; *for ~* um keinen Preis; *take ~ you like* nimm, was du willst. **2.** alles: *~ but* alles andere als. '*~·way* → *anyhow*. '*~·where adv* **1.** irgendwo(hin): *not ~* nirgendwo(hin); *hardly ~* fast nirgends. **2.** überall.

a·or·ta [eɪ'ɔ:tə] *s anat.* Aorta *f*, Hauptschlagader *f*.

a·part [ə'pɑ:t] *adv* **1.** einzeln, für sich: *live ~* getrennt leben; → *take apart*, *tell* 4. **2.** beiseite: → *joking* II.

a·part·heid [ə'pɑ:theɪt] *s pol.* Apartheid *f*.

a·part·ment [ə'pɑ:tmənt] *s* **1.** *bsd. Am.* Wohnung *f*. **2.** *mst* Gemach *n*. **~ ho·tel** *s* Appartementhotel *n*. **~ house** *s Am.* Wohnhaus *n*.

ap·a·thet·ic [ˌæpə'θetɪk] *adj* (*~ally*) apathisch, teilnahmslos, gleichgültig. '**ap·a·thy** *s* Apathie *f*, Teilnahmslosigkeit *f*, Gleichgültigkeit *f* (*to* gegenüber).

ape [eɪp] **I** *s zo.* (*bsd. Menschen*)Affe *m*. **II** *v/t* nachäffen.

a·pe·ri·ent [ə'pɪərɪənt] *🌿, pharm.* **I** *s* Abführmittel *n*. **II** *adj* abführend.

ap·er·ture ['æpə,tjʊə] *s* **1.** Öffnung *f*. **2.** *phot.* Blende *f*.

a·pex ['eɪpeks] *pl* '**a·pex·es**, **ap·i·ces** ['eɪpɪsi:z] *s* **1.** (*Kegel-, Lungen- etc-*)Spitze *f*. **2.** *fig.* Gipfel *m*, Höhepunkt *m*.

aph·o·rism ['æfərɪzəm] *s* Aphorismus *m*.

ap·i·ces ['eɪpɪsi:z] *pl von* **apex**.

a·piece [ə'pi:s] *adv* pro Stück; pro Kopf *od.* Person.

ap·ish ['eɪpɪʃ] *adj* □ äffisch.

a·poc·a·lypse [ə'pɒkəlɪps] *s* Enthüllung *f*, Offenbarung *f*.

a·pol·o·gize [ə'pɒlədʒaɪz] *v/i* sich entschuldigen (*for* wegen; *to* bei). **a·'pol·o·gy** *s* **1.** Entschuldigung *f*: *in ~ for* zur *od.* als Entschuldigung für; *make* (*od. offer*) *s.o. an ~* sich bei j-m entschuldigen (*for* für). **2.** F minderwertiger Ersatz (*for* für): *an ~ for a meal* ein armseliges Essen.

ap·o·plec·tic [ˌæpəʊ'plektɪk] *adj*: *~ stroke* (*od. fit*) → **apoplexy**. **ap·o·plex·y** ['æpleksɪ] *s* 🩺 Schlaganfall *m*, Gehirnschlag *m*.

a·pos·tle [ə'pɒsl] *s eccl.* Apostel *m*.

a·pos·tro·phe [ə'pɒstrəfɪ] *s ling.* Apostroph *m*, Auslassungszeichen *n*. **a·'pos·tro·phize** *v/t* apostrophieren.

ap·pal [ə'pɔ:l] *v/t* erschrecken, entsetzen: *be ~led* entsetzt sein (*at* über *acc*). **ap'pal·ling** *adj* □ erschreckend, entsetzlich.

ap·pa·ra·tus [ˌæpə'reɪtəs] *pl* **-tus**, **-tus·es** *s* Apparat *m*, Gerät *n*, Vorrichtung *f*.

ap·par·el [ə'pærəl] *s* Kleidung *f*.

ap·par·ent [ə'pærənt] *adj* □ **1.** augenscheinlich, offenbar, -sichtlich: *be ~ from* hervorgehen aus; *with no ~ reason* ohne ersichtlichen Grund. **2.** anscheinend; scheinbar.

ap·pa·ri·tion [ˌæpə'rɪʃn] *s* Erscheinung *f*, Gespenst *n*, Geist *m*.

ap·peal [ə'pi:l] **I** *v/i* **1.** 🩺 Berufung *od.* Revision einlegen, *a. allg.* Einspruch erheben, Beschwerde einlegen (*against*, 🩺 *mst from* gegen; *to* bei). **2.** appellieren, sich wenden (*to* an *acc*). **3.** sich berufen (*to* auf *acc*). **4.** (*to*) Anklang finden (bei), gefallen, zusagen (*dat*), reizen (*acc*). **5.** *~ to* j-n dringend bitten (*for* um). **II** *s* **6.** 🩺 Berufung *f*, Revision *f*: *file* (*od. lodge*) *an ~* → 1. **7.** Appell *m* (*to* an *acc*). **8.** Berufung *f* (*to* auf *acc*). **9.** dringende Bitte (*to* an *acc*; *for* um). **10.** (*to*) Anziehung(skraft) *f*, Zugkraft *f*, Wirkung *f* (auf *acc*), Anklang *m* (bei). **ap'peal·ing** *adj* □ **1.** bittend, flehend. **2.** reizvoll, gefällig, ansprechend.

ap·pear [ə'pɪə] *v/i* **1.** erscheinen (*a. vor Gericht*), (*von Büchern etc a.*) herauskommen: *~ in public* sich in der Öffentlichkeit zeigen; *~ on television* im

Fernsehen auftreten. **2.** scheinen, aussehen, *j-m* vorkommen: *it ~s to me you are right* mir scheint; *he ~ed calm* er war äußerlich ruhig. **ap'pear·ance** *s* **1.** Erscheinen *n*: *public* ~ Auftreten *n* in der Öffentlichkeit; *make an ~ on television* im Fernsehen auftreten. **2.** (äußere) Erscheinung, Aussehen *n*, *das Äußere*: *have an unhealthy ~* ungesund aussehen. **3.** *mst pl* (An)Schein *m*: *to all ~(s)* allem Anschein nach; *there is every ~ that* es hat ganz den Anschein, als ob; *~s are deceptive* der Schein trügt; *keep up* (*od.* *save*) *~s* den Schein wahren.

ap·pease [əˈpiːz] *v/t* besänftigen, beschwichtigen; *Durst etc* stillen, *Neugier* befriedigen. **ap'pease·ment** *s* Besänftigung *f*, Beschwichtigung *f*: (*policy of*) ~ Beschwichtigungspolitik *f*.

ap·pend [əˈpend] *v/t* (**to**) **1.** befestigen, anbringen (an *dat*), anheften (an *acc*). **2.** bei-, hinzufügen (*dat*). **ap'pend·age** *s* Anhang *m*; Anhängsel *n*. **ap·pen·dec·to·my** [ˌæpenˈdektəmɪ] *s* 🝢 Blinddarmoperation *f*. **ap·pen·di·ci·tis** [əˌpendɪˈsaɪtɪs] *s* 🝢 Blinddarmentzündung *f*. **ap·pen·dix** [əˈpendɪks] *pl* **-dix·es**, **-di·ces** [ˌ-dɪsiːz] *s* **1.** Anhang *m* (*e-s Buchs*). **2.** (*vermiform*) ~ *anat.* Wurmfortsatz *m*, Blinddarm *m*.

ap·per·tain [ˌæpəˈteɪn] *v/i* gehören (**to** zu).

ap·pe·tite [ˈæpɪtaɪt] *s* **1.** Appetit *m* (*for* auf *acc*): *give s.o. an ~* j-m Appetit machen; *have an ~* Appetit haben; *take away* (*od.* *spoil*) *s.o.'s ~* j-m den Appetit nehmen *od.* verderben. **2.** (*for*) Verlangen *n* (nach), Lust *f* (zu). **ap·pe·tiz·er** [ˈ-taɪzə] *s* appetitanregendes Mittel *od.* Getränk *od.* Gericht. **ap·pe·tiz·ing** *adj* □ appetitanregend; appetitlich, lecker (*beide a. fig.*).

ap·plaud [əˈplɔːd] *v/i u. v/t* applaudieren (*dat*), Beifall spenden (*dat*). **ap·plause** [əˈplɔːz] *s* Applaus *m*, Beifall *m*.

ap·ple [ˈæpl] *s* Apfel *m*: ~ *of discord fig.* Zankapfel *m*; *the ~ of s.o.'s eye fig.* j-s Liebling. '**~·cart** *s* Apfelkarren *m*: *upset s.o.'s ~ fig.* j-s Pläne über den Haufen werfen. '**~·jack** *s* Am. Apfelschnaps *m*. ~ **pie** *s* gedeckter Apfelkuchen. '**~·pie or·der** *s*: *in* ~ F in bester Ordnung. '**~-,pol·ish** *v/i* Am. F

radfahren. ~ **pol·ish·er** *s* Am. F Radfahrer *m*, Speichellecker *m*. '**~·sauce** *s* **1.** Apfelmus *n*. **2.** Am. sl. Schmus *m*; Quatsch *m*. ~ **tree** *s* Apfelbaum *m*.

ap·pli·ance [əˈplaɪəns] *s* Gerät *n*; *engS.* (elektrisches) Haushaltsgerät.

ap·pli·ca·ble [ˈæplɪkəbl] *adj* □ (**to**) anwendbar (auf *acc*), passend (für): *be* ~ (**to**) → *apply* 4; *not* ~ (*in Formularen*) nicht zutreffend. '**ap·pli·cant** *s* Bewerber(in) (*for* um); Antragsteller(in). ,**ap·pli·ca·tion** *s* **1.** (**to**) Anwendung *f* (auf *acc*); Anwendbarkeit *f* (auf *acc*): *have no ~* (**to**) nicht zutreffen (auf *acc*), in keinem Zs.-hang stehen (mit). **2.** (*for*) Gesuch *n* (um), Antrag *m* (auf *acc*): *on* ~ auf Ersuchen *od.* Verlangen *od.* Wunsch. **3.** Bewerbung *f* (*for* um): (*letter of*) ~ Bewerbungsschreiben *n*.

ap·plied [əˈplaɪd] *adj* angewandt: ~ *lin·guistics* (*psychology*, *etc*).

ap·ply [əˈplaɪ] **I** *v/t* **1.** (**to**) auflegen, -tragen (auf *acc*), anbringen (an, auf *dat*). **2.** (**to**) verwenden (auf *acc*, für); anwenden (auf *acc*); betätigen: ~ *the brakes* bremsen. **3.** ~ *one's mind* to sich beschäftigen mit; ~ *o.s.* to sich widmen (*dat*). **II** *v/i* **4.** (**to**) zutreffen (auf *acc*), gelten (für). **5.** (*for*) beantragen (*acc*), nachsuchen (um). **6.** sich bewerben (*for* um).

ap·point [əˈpɔɪnt] *v/t* **1.** ernennen *od.* berufen zu: ~ *s.o. one's heir* j-n als Erben einsetzen. **2.** festsetzen, bestimmen. **3.** ausstatten, einrichten (**with** mit). **ap'point·ment** *s* **1.** Ernennung *f*, Berufung *f*. **2.** Amt *n*, Stellung *f*: *hold an* ~ e-e Stelle innehaben. **3.** Festsetzung *f*, Bestimmung *f*. **4.** Verabredung *f*, (*geschäftlich*, *beim Arzt etc*) Termin *m*: *by* ~ nach Verabredung; *make an* ~ e-e Verabredung treffen, e-n Termin ausmachen; ~ *book* Terminkalender *m*. **5.** *mst pl* Ausstattung *f*, Einrichtung *f*.

ap·por·tion [əˈpɔːʃn] *v/t* **1.** zuteilen (**to** *dat*). **2.** (proportional *od.* gerecht) verteilen; *Kosten* umlegen.

ap·po·site [ˈæpəʊzɪt] *adj* □ passend, angemessen, (*Antwort etc*) treffend.

ap·po·si·tion [ˌæpəʊˈzɪʃn] *s* Beifügung *f*, *ling. a.* Apposition *f*.

ap·prais·al [əˈpreɪzl] *s* (Ab)Schätzung *f*, Taxierung *f*. **ap'praise** *v/t* (ab)schätzen, taxieren: ~*d value* Schätzwert *m*.

ap·pre·ci·a·ble [ə'priːʃəbl] *adj* □ merklich, spürbar. **ap'pre·ci·ate** [‿ʃɪeɪt] I *v/t* **1.** (hoch)schätzen, würdigen, zu schätzen *od.* zu würdigen wissen. **2.** Gefallen finden an (*dat*); Sinn haben für. **3.** dankbar sein für. **4.** (richtig) beurteilen *od.* einschätzen. II *v/i* **5.** im Wert steigen. **ap‚pre·ci'a·tion** *s* **1.** Würdigung *f*. **2.** Sinn *m* (*of, for* für). **3.** Dankbarkeit *f* (*of* für). **4.** (richtige) Beurteilung. **ap·pre·ci·a·tive** [ə'priːʃjətɪv] *adj* □ würdigend: *be ~ of → appreciate* I.

ap·pre·hend [‚æprɪ'hend] *v/t* **1.** festnehmen, verhaften. **2.** *fig.* begreifen, erfassen. **3.** *fig.* (be)fürchten. **‚ap·pre'hen·sion** *s* **1.** Festnahme *f*, Verhaftung *f*. **2.** *fig.* Begreifen *n*, Erfassen *n*; Fassungskraft *f*. **3.** *fig.* Besorgnis *f*, *oft pl* Befürchtung *f*. **‚ap·pre'hen·sive** *adj* □ besorgt (*for* um; *that* daß): *be ~* Bedenken tragen.

ap·pren·tice [ə'prentɪs] I *s* Auszubildende *m, f*, Lehrling *m*. II *v/t* in die Lehre geben (*to* bei, zu): *be ~d to* in der Lehre sein bei. **ap'pren·tice·ship** *s* Lehrzeit *f*; Lehre *f*.

ap·pro [‚æprəʊ] *s*: *on ~* ✝ F zur Ansicht, zur Probe.

ap·proach [ə'prəʊtʃ] I *v/i* **1.** sich nähern, (heran)nahen. II *v/t* **2.** sich nähern (*dat*). **3.** *fig.* nahekommen (*dat*), (fast) erreichen. **4.** herangehen an (*acc*), *Aufgabe etc* anpacken. **5.** an *j-n* herantreten, sich an *j-n* wenden; *bsd. b.s.* sich an *j-n* heranmachen. III *s* **6.** (Heran)Nahen *n*, Annäherung *f* (*a. fig. to* an *acc*), ✈ Anflug *m*. **7.** Zugang *m*: ~ (*road*) Zufahrtsstraße *f*. **8.** *fig.* (*to*) erster Schritt (zu), (erster) Versuch (*gen*). **9.** Herantreten *n* (*to* an *acc*), *mst pl* Annäherungsversuch *m*: *make ~es to → approach* 5. **10.** Methode *f*, Verfahren *n*; Einstellung *f* (*to* zu); Behandlung *f* (*to e-s Themas etc*). **ap'proach·a·ble** *adj* zugänglich (*a. fig.*).

ap·pro·ba·tion [‚æprəʊ'beɪʃn] *s* (amtliche) Billigung, Genehmigung *f*.

ap·pro·pri·ate I *adj* [ə'prəʊprɪət] **1.** (*to, for*) passend (zu), geeignet (für zu). II *v/t* [‚ʌeɪt] **2.** *bsd. parl.* Geld bewilligen, bereitstellen. **3.** sich *et.* aneignen. **ap‚pro·pri'a·tion** [‿prɪ'eɪʃn] *s* **1.** Bewilligung *f*, Bereitstellung *f*. **2.** Aneignung *f*.

ap·prov·al [ə'pruːvl] *s* **1.** Billigung *f*, Genehmigung *f*: *on ~* ✝ zur Ansicht, zur Probe. **2.** Anerkennung *f*, Beifall *m*: *meet with ~* Beifall finden. **ap'prove** I *v/t* billigen, genehmigen. II *v/i* (*of*) billigen, genehmigen (*acc*), einverstanden sein (mit), zustimmen (*dat*).

ap·prox·i·mate I *adj* [ə'prɒksɪmət] □ annähernd, ungefähr: *~ value* Näherungswert *m*. II *v/t* [‚ʌmeɪt] sich (*e-m Wert etc*) nähern. III *v/i* [‚ʌmeɪt] sich nähern (*to dat*). **ap‚prox·i'ma·tion** [‿'meɪʃn] *s* Annäherung *f* (*to* an *acc*).

ap·pur·te·nance [ə'pɜːtɪnəns] *s mst pl* Zubehör *n*, Ausrüstung *f*.

a·pri·cot ['eɪprɪkɒt] *s* Aprikose *f*.

A·pril ['eɪprəl] *s* April *m*: *in ~* im April; *make an ~ fool of s.o.* j-n in den April schicken.

a·pron ['eɪprən] *s* **1.** Schürze *f*. **2.** ✈ (Hallen)Vorfeld *n*. **3.** *thea.* Vorbühne *f*. ~ *strings s pl* Schürzenbänder *pl*: *be tied to one's mother's (wife's) ~ fig.* an Mutters Schürzenzipfel hängen (unter dem Pantoffel stehen).

apt [æpt] *adj* □ **1.** passend, geeignet. **2.** treffend (*Bemerkung etc*). **3.** neigend, geneigt (*to do* zu tun): *he is ~ to believe it* er wird es wahrscheinlich glauben; *~ to be overlooked* leicht zu übersehen. **4.** (*at*) geschickt (in *dat*), begabt (für). **ap·ti·tude** ['‚æptɪtjuːd] *s* **1.** (*for*) Begabung *f* (für), Geschick *n* (in *dat*): ~ *test* Eignungsprüfung *f*. **2.** Neigung *f*, Hang *m* (*for* zu). **3.** Auffassungsgabe *f*.

aq·ua·ma·rine [‚ækwəmə'riːn] *s* **1.** *min.* Aquamarin *m*. **2.** Aquamarinblau *n*.

aq·ua·plan·ing ['ækwə‚pleɪnɪŋ] *s mot.* Aquaplaning *n*.

aq·ua·relle [‚ækwə'rel] *s* **1.** Aquarell *n*. **2.** Aquarellmalerei *f*. **‚aq·ua'rel·list** *s* Aquarellmaler(in).

a·quar·i·um [ə'kweərɪəm] *pl* **-i·ums, -i·a** [‿ɪə] *s* Aquarium *n*.

A·quar·i·us [ə'kweərɪəs] *s ast.* Wassermann *m*: *be (an)* ~ Wassermann sein.

a·quat·ic [ə'kwætɪk] *adj* Wasser...: ~ *plants*; ~ *sports pl* Wassersport *m*.

aq·ue·duct ['ækwɪdʌkt] *s* Aquädukt *m, a. n.*

a·que·ous ['eɪkwɪəs] *adj* wäßrig, wässerig.

aq·ui·cul·ture ['ækwɪkʌltʃə] *s* Hydrokultur *f*.

aq·ui·line ['ækwɪlaɪn] *adj* Adler..., *weitS. a.* gebogen: **~ nose** Adlernase *f*.

Ar·ab ['ærəb] **I** *s* **1.** Araber(in). **2.** *zo.* Araber *m* (*Pferd*). **II** *adj* **3.** arabisch.

ar·a·besque [͵~'besk] *s* Arabeske *f*.

A·ra·bi·an [ə'reɪbjən] **I** *adj* arabisch: **The ~ Nights** Tausendundeine Nacht. **II** *s → Arab* I. **Ar·a·bic** ['ærəbɪk] **I** *adj* arabisch: **~ numeral** arabische Ziffer. **II** *s ling.* Arabisch *n*.

ar·a·ble ['ærəbl] *adj* pflügbar, anbaufähig: **~ land** Ackerland *n*.

ar·bi·ter ['ɑːbɪtə] *s* **1.** Schiedsrichter *m*. **2.** Gebieter *m* (**of** über *acc*): **be the ~ of fashion** die Mode bestimmen *od.* diktieren. **'ar·bi·trar·y** *adj* □ willkürlich: a) beliebig (*a.* Ⓐ), b) eigenmächtig. **ar·bi·trate** [͵~treɪt] **I** *v/t* (als Schiedsrichter) entscheiden, schlichten. **II** *v/i* als Schiedsrichter fungieren. ͵**ar·bi'tra·tion** *s* **1.** Schieds(gerichts)verfahren *n*. **2.** Schiedsspruch *m*; Schlichtung *f*: **court of ~** Schiedsgericht *n*.

ar·bo(u)r ['ɑːbə] *s* Laube *f*.

arc [ɑːk] *s* Bogen *m*, Ⓐ *a.* Arkus *m*, ⚡ *a.* Lichtbogen.

ar·cade [ɑː'keɪd] *s* Arkade *f*, Bogen-, Laubengang *m*.

arch¹ [ɑːtʃ] **I** *s* **1.** △ Bogen *m*. **2.** △ überwölbter Gang, Gewölbe *n*. **3.** Bogen *m*, Wölbung *f*: **~ support** Senkfußeinlage *f*. **II** *v/t* **4.** *a.* **~ over** überwölben. **5.** wölben, krümmen: **~ one's back** e-n Buckel machen (*bsd. Katze*). **III** *v/i* **6.** sich wölben.

arch² [͵~] *adj* □ schalkhaft, schelmisch, spitzbübisch.

arch³ [͵~] *adj* Erz-.

ar·chae·o·log·i·cal [͵ɑːkɪə'lɒdʒɪkl] *adj* □ *bsd. Br.* archäologisch. **ar·chae·ol·o·gist** [͵~'ɒlədʒɪst] *s bsd. Br.* Archäologe *m.* ͵**ar·chae'ol·o·gy** *s bsd. Br.* Archäologie *f*.

ar·cha·ic [ɑː'keɪk] *adj* (□ **~ally**) archaisch: a) altertümlich, b) *ling.* veraltet.

arch·an·gel ['ɑːk͵eɪndʒəl] *s* Erzengel *m.* ͵**arch'bish·op** *s* Erzbischof *m.* ͵**arch'bish·op·ric** [͵~rɪk] *s* Erzbistum *n*. ͵**arch'duch·ess** *s* Erzherzogin *f.* ͵**arch'duch·y** *s* Erzherzogtum *n.* ͵**arch'duke** *s* Erzherzog *m*.

ar·che·o·log·i·cal, *etc Am.* → *archaeological, etc*.

arch·er ['ɑːtʃə] *s* **1.** Bogenschütze *m*. **2.** ♎

ast. Schütze *m*: **be (an)** ♎ Schütze sein. **'arch·er·y** *s* Bogenschießen *n*.

ar·che·type ['ɑːkɪtaɪp] *s* Archetyp(us) *m*, Urform *f*.

ar·chi·pel·a·go [͵ɑːkɪ'pelɪɡəʊ] *pl* **-go(e)s** *s* Archipel *m*, Inselgruppe *f*.

ar·chi·tect ['ɑːkɪtekt] *s* **1.** Architekt(in). **2.** *fig.* Urheber(in), Schöpfer(in). ͵**ar·chi'tec·tu·ral** [͵~tʃərəl] *adj* □ architektonisch, Bau..., baulich. **'ar·chi·tec·ture** *s* Architektur *f*, *a.* Baustil *m*.

ar·chive ['ɑːkaɪv] *s mst pl* Archiv *n*. **ar·chi·vist** ['ɑːkɪvɪst] *s* Archivar(in).

'arch·way *s* △ **1.** Bogengang *m*. **2.** Bogen *m* (*über e-m Tor etc*).

arc·tic ['ɑːktɪk] **I** *adj* arktisch, nördlich, Polar...: ♎ **Circle** nördlicher Polarkreis; ♎ **Ocean** Nördliches Eismeer. **II** *s* Arktis *f*.

ar·dent ['ɑːdənt] *adj* □ *fig.* **1.** heiß, feurig, glühend. **2.** leidenschaftlich, eifrig. **3.** eifrig, begeistert. **ar·do(u)r** ['ɑːdə] *s* **1.** Leidenschaft *f*, Glut *f*, Feuer *n*. **2.** Eifer *m*, Begeisterung *f*.

ar·du·ous ['ɑːdjʊəs] *adj* □ schwierig, mühsam, anstrengend.

are [ɑː] *du* bist, *wir* (*od. sie od. Sie*) sind, *ihr* seid.

a·re·a ['eərɪə] *s* **1.** (Boden-, Grund)Fläche *f*. **2.** Gebiet *n* (*a. fig.*), Gegend *f*: **~ code** *teleph. Am.* Vorwahl(nummer) *f*. **3.** *fig.* Bereich *m*.

a·re·na [ə'riːnə] *s* Arena *f*, *fig. a.* Schauplatz *m*.

aren't [ɑːnt] *F für* **are not**.

Ar·gen·tine ['ɑːdʒəntaɪn], **Ar·gen·tin·e·an** [͵~'tɪnɪən] *adj* argentinisch. **II** *s* Argentinier(in).

ar·gu·a·ble ['ɑːɡjʊəbl] *adj* □ **1.** zweifelhaft, fraglich. **2.** **it is ~ that** man kann durchaus die Meinung vertreten, daß. **ar·gue** ['ɑːɡjuː] **I** *v/i* **1.** argumentieren: **~ for** eintreten für; sprechen für (*Sache*); **~ against** Einwände machen gegen; sprechen gegen (*Sache*). **2.** streiten (**with** mit; **about** über *acc*): **don't ~!** keine Widerrede! **II** *v/t* **3.** erörtern, diskutieren. **4.** behaupten (*that* daß). **5.** *j-n* überreden (*into* zu): **~ s.o. out of s.th.** *j-n* von *et.* abbringen.

ar·gu·ment ['ɑːɡjʊmənt] *s* **1.** Argument *n*. **2.** Erörterung *f*, Diskussion *f*. **3.** Streitfrage *f*. **4.** Wortwechsel *m*, Auseinandersetzung *f*. **ar·gu·men·ta·tion**

[‚~men'teɪʃn] s **1.** Argumentation f, Beweisführung f. **2.** → **argument** 2.

ar·gu·men·ta·tive [‚~'mentətɪv] adj □ **1.** streitlustig. **2.** strittig, umstritten.

a·ri·a ['ɑːrɪə] s ♪ Arie f.

ar·id ['ærɪd] adj dürr, trocken (a. fig.). **a'rid·i·ty** s Dürre f, Trockenheit f.

Ar·ies ['eəriːz] s ast. Widder m: **be (an) ~** Widder sein.

a·rise [ə'raɪz] v/i (irr) **1. (from, out of)** entstehen, hervorgehen (aus), herrühren, stammen (von). **2.** entstehen, sich erheben, auftauchen. **a·ris·en** [ə'rɪzn] pp von **arise**.

ar·is·toc·ra·cy [‚ærɪ'stɒkrəsi] s Aristokratie f. **a·ris·to·crat** ['~stəkræt] s Aristokrat(in). **‚a·ris·to'crat·ic, ‚a·ris·to·'crat·i·cal** adj □ aristokratisch.

a·rith·me·tic [ə'rɪθmətɪk] s Arithmetik f, Rechnen n.

ar·ith·met·ic, ar·ith·met·i·cal [‚ærɪθ-'metɪk(l)] adj □ arithmetisch, Rechen...

ark [ɑːk] s: **Noah's ~** Bibl. die Arche Noah.

arm[1] [ɑːm] s **1.** Arm m (a. ☼ u. fig.): **with open ~s** mit offenen Armen; **within ~'s reach** in Reichweite; **the ~ of the law** der Arm des Gesetzes; **keep s.o. at ~'s length** sich j-n vom Leibe halten; **take s.o. in one's ~s** j-n in die Arme nehmen. **2.** Fluß-, Meeresarm m. **3.** Ast m. **4.** Arm-, Seitenlehne f (e-s Stuhls etc). **5.** Ärmel m.

arm[2] [~] **I** s **1.** mst pl Waffe f (a. fig.): **up in ~s** kampfbereit; fig. in hellem Zorn **(about, over** wegen); **take up ~s** zu den Waffen greifen; **~s control** Rüstungskontrolle f; **~s dealer** Waffenhändler m; **~s race** Wettrüsten n, Rüstungswettlauf m. **2.** ✕ Waffen-, Truppengattung f. **3.** pl Wappen(schild) n. **II** v/t **4.** bewaffnen. **5. ~ o.s.** fig. sich wappnen (**with** mit).

ar·ma·da [ɑː'mɑːdə] s (hist. ♀) Armada f.

ar·ma·ment ['ɑːməmənt] s **1.** Kriegsstärke f. **2.** Bewaffnung f. **3.** Rüstung f: **~ race** Wettrüsten n, Rüstungswettlauf m. **ar·ma·ture** ['~tjʊə] s ⚡ Anker m.

'arm·chair s Lehnstuhl m: **~ politician** Stammtischpolitiker m.

armed [ɑːmd] adj bewaffnet **(to the teeth** bis an die Zähne): **~ conflict** bewaffnete Auseinandersetzung; **~ forces**

pl Streitkräfte pl; **~ robbery** bewaffneter Raubüberfall.

...-armed [ɑːmd] ...armig, mit ... Armen.

arm·ful ['ɑːmfʊl] s Armvoll m.

ar·mi·stice ['ɑːmɪstɪs] s Waffenstillstand m.

ar·mor, etc Am. → **armour**, etc.

ar·mo·ri·al [ɑː'mɔːriəl] adj Wappen...

ar·mour ['ɑːmə] bsd. Br. **I** s **1.** Rüstung f, Panzer m (a. zo.). **2.** ✕ Panzer(fahrzeuge) pl; Panzertruppen pl. **II** v/t **3.** panzern: **~ed car** ✕ Panzerkampfwagen m; gepanzertes Fahrzeug (für Geldtransporte etc). **'~-clad, '~-,plat·ed** adj bsd. Br. gepanzert, Panzer...

ar·mour·y ['ɑːməri] s bsd. Br. Waffenfabrik f.

'arm·pit s Achselhöhle f. **'~rest** s Armlehne f.

ar·my ['ɑːmi] s Armee f, Heer n (a. fig.): **be in the ~** beim Militär sein; **join the ~** Soldat werden.

a·ro·ma [ə'rəʊmə] s Aroma n. **ar·o·mat·ic** [‚ærəʊ'mætɪk] adj (**~ally**) aromatisch.

a·rose [ə'rəʊz] pret von **arise**.

a·round [ə'raʊnd] **I** adv **1.** (rings)herum, überall(hin), nach od. auf allen Seiten. **2.** umher, (in der Gegend) herum: **look ~** sich umsehen; zurückschauen. **3.** F in der Nähe, da. **II** prp **4.** um (... herum), rund um. **5.** in (dat) ... herum. **6.** F ungefähr, etwa. **7.** F (nahe) bei.

a·rouse [ə'raʊz] v/t **1.** (auf)wecken. **2.** fig. auf-, wachrütteln, Gefühle etc wachrufen, erregen.

ar·range [ə'reɪndʒ] **I** v/t **1.** (an)ordnen, aufstellen, Angelegenheiten ordnen, regeln. **2.** festsetzen, -legen. **3.** in die Wege leiten, arrangieren. **4.** verabreden, vereinbaren. **5.** Streit schlichten, beilegen. **6.** ♪ arrangieren, a. thea. etc bearbeiten. **II** v/i **7.** sich verständigen **(with** mit; **about** über acc). **8.** Vorkehrungen treffen **(for, about** für; **to** inf zu inf): **~ for s.th. to be there** dafür sorgen, daß et. da ist. **ar'range·ment** s **1.** (An)Ordnung f. **2.** Festsetzung f. **3.** Verabredung f, Vereinbarung f: **make an ~** e-e Verabredung treffen **(with** mit). **4.** Schlichtung f, Beilegung f. **5.** ♪ Arrangement n, a. thea. etc Bearbeitung f. **6.** pl Vorkehrungen pl: **make ~s** Vorkehrungen treffen ...

ar·ray [ə'reɪ] **I** v/t **1.** *Truppen etc* aufstellen. **2.** (*o.s.* sich) kleiden, (heraus)putzen. **II** s **3.** ✗ Schlachtordnung f. **4.** fig. Phalanx f, (stattliche) Reihe. **5.** Kleidung f, Staat m.

ar·rear [ə'rɪə] s mst pl Rückstand m, -stände pl: **~s of rent** rückständige Miete; **~s of work** Arbeitsrückstände; **be in ~** im Rückstand od. Verzug sein **(for, in** mit).

ar·rest [ə'rest] **I** s **1.** Verhaftung f, Festnahme f; Haft f: **be under ~** verhaftet sein; in Haft sein; → **warrant** 2. **II** v/t **2.** an-, aufhalten, hemmen. **3.** *Aufmerksamkeit etc* fesseln. **4.** verhaften, festnehmen.

ar·riv·al [ə'raɪvl] s **1.** Ankunft f: '**~s'** pl ‚Ankunft' (*Fahrplan etc*). **2.** Erscheinen n, Auftauchen n. **3.** Ankömmling m: **new ~** Neuankömmling, F a. Familienzuwachs m. **ar·rive** [ə'raɪv] v/i **1.** (an)kommen, eintreffen. **2.** erscheinen, auftauchen. **3.** fig. (**at**) erreichen (*acc*), kommen od. gelangen (zu).

ar·ro·gance ['ærəgəns] s Arroganz f, Überheblichkeit f. '**ar·ro·gant** adj □ arrogant, überheblich.

ar·row ['ærəʊ] s Pfeil m. '**~·head** s Pfeilspitze f.

arse [ɑːs] s Br. V Arsch m (a. fig. contp.). '**~·hole** s Br. V Arschloch n (a. fig. contp.).

ar·se·nal ['ɑːsənl] s **1.** Arsenal n (a. fig.). **2.** Waffen-, Munitionsfabrik f.

ar·se·nic ['ɑːsnɪk] s 🜍 Arsen n.

ar·son ['ɑːsn] s 🜨 Brandstiftung f.

art [ɑːt] **I** s **1.** (bsd. bildende) Kunst: **work of ~** Kunstwerk n; → **fine**¹ 1. **2.** Kunst(fertigkeit) f: **the ~ of cooking** die hohe Schule des Kochens; **~s and crafts** pl Kunstgewerbe n. **3.** pl univ. Geisteswissenschaften pl: **Faculty of ~s,** Am. **~s Department** philosophische Fakultät; → **bachelor** 3, **master** 5. **4.** mst pl Kniff m, Trick m. **II** adj **5.** Kunst...: **~ critic; ~ gallery** Gemäldegalerie f.

ar·te·ri·al [ɑːˈtɪərɪəl] adj **1.** anat. arteriell, Arterien... **2. ~ road,** Am. a. **~ highway** Hauptverkehrsstraße f. **ar·te·ri·o·scle·ro·sis** [ɑːˌtɪərɪəʊsklɪəˈrəʊsɪs] s 🜨 Arteriosklerose f, Arterienverkalkung f. **ar·ter·y** ['ɑːtərɪ] s **1.** anat. Arterie f, Schlagader f. **2.**

fig. (Haupt)Verkehrsader f.

ar·te·sian well [ɑːˈtiːzjən] s Artesischer Brunnen m.

art·ful ['ɑːtfʊl] adj □ schlau, listig.

ar·thrit·ic [ɑːˈθrɪtɪk] adj 🜨 arthritisch. **ar·thri·tis** [ɑːˈθraɪtɪs] s Arthritis f, Gelenkentzündung f.

ar·ti·choke ['ɑːtɪtʃəʊk] s 🜨 Artischocke f.

ar·ti·cle ['ɑːtɪkl] **I** s **1.** (*Zeitungs- etc*)Artikel m. **2.** Artikel m, Gegenstand m. **3.** ling. Artikel m, Geschlechtswort n. **4.** Artikel m, Paragraph m, Abschnitt m (*e-s Gesetzes etc*); Punkt m, Klausel f (*e-s Vertrags etc*): **~s of apprenticeship** Lehrvertrag m; **~s** pl **of association** (*Am.* **incorporation**) Satzung f (*e-r Aktiengesellschaft*). **II** v/t **5.** in die Lehre geben (**to** bei, zu): **be ~d to** in der Lehre sein bei.

ar·tic·u·late I v/t [ɑːˈtɪkjʊleɪt] **1.** artikulieren, deutlich (aus)sprechen. **2.** äußern; zur Sprache bringen. **3.** ⊕ durch Gelenke verbinden. **II** adj [~lət] □ **4.** deutlich ausgesprochen, verständlich (*Wörter etc*). **5.** fähig, sich klar auszudrücken. **ar'tic·u·lat·ed** [~leɪtɪd] adj ⊕ Gelenk...: **~ lorry** mot. Br. Sattelschlepper m. **ar,tic·u'la·tion** s **1.** Artikulation f, deutliche Aussprache. **2.** ⊕ Gelenk(verbindung f) n.

ar·ti·fice ['ɑːtɪfɪs] s **1.** List f. **2.** Kunstgriff m, Kniff m. **ar·ti·fi·cial** [~'fɪʃl] adj □ Kunst..., künstlich: **~ flower** (*insemination, respiration, etc*) künstliche Blume (*Befruchtung, Beatmung etc*); **~ person** juristische Person; **~ silk** Kunstseide f; **~ tears** pl falsche Tränen pl.

ar·til·ler·y [ɑːˈtɪlərɪ] s Artillerie f. **ar'til·ler·y·man** [~mən] s (*irr man*) Artillerist m.

ar·ti·san [ˌɑːtɪˈzæn] s (Kunst)Handwerker m.

ar·tist ['ɑːtɪst], **ar·tiste** [ɑːˈtiːst] s Künstler(in), weitS. a. Könner(in). **ar·tis·tic, ar·tis·ti·cal** [ɑːˈtɪstɪk(l)] adj □ **1.** künstlerisch, Künstler..., Kunst... **2.** kunstverständig.

art·less ['ɑːtlɪs] adj □ **1.** aufrichtig, arglos. **2.** naiv.

art·y ['ɑːtɪ] adj F künstlerisch aufgemacht. '**~(-and)-'craft·y** adj F gewollt künstlerisch.

Ar·y·an ['eəriən] **I** *adj* arisch. **II** *s* Arier(in).

as [æz] **I** *adv* **1.** (eben- gerade)so: *I ran* ~ *fast* ~ *I could* so schnell ich konnte; *just* ~ *good* ebenso gut; *twice* ~ *large* zweimal so groß; ~ *well* ebenfalls, auch; → *much* **2. 2.** wie (z. B.): *states-men*, ~ *Churchill*. **II** *cj* **3.** (so) wie: ~ *follows* wie folgt; ~ *requested* wunsch-gemäß; ~ ... ~ (eben)so ... wie; (~) *soft* ~ *butter* butterweich; (~) *happy* ~ *can be* überglücklich; ~ *far* ~ *I know* soviel ich weiß; ~ *it were* sozusagen, gleichsam; → *good* 5, *long*[?]7, *soon*, *though* 3, *word* 1. **4.** als, während: ~ *he entered* als er eintrat, bei s-m Eintritt. **5.** da, weil: ~ *you are sorry, I'll forgive you.* **6.** ~ *for* (*od. to*) was ... (an)betrifft; ~ *from* (*vor Zeitangaben*) von ... an, ab; → *against* 4, *per* 3, *yet* 2. **III** *pron* **7.** was, wie: ~ *he himself admits.* **IV** *prp* **8.** als: *appear* ~ *Hamlet* als Hamlet auftreten.

as·bes·tos [æs'bestəs] *s* Asbest *m*.

as·cend [ə'send] **I** *v/i* **1.** (auf)steigen. **2.** ansteigen. **II** *v/t* **3.** *a.* fig. den Thron besteigen. **as'cend·an·cy** *s* Überge-wicht *n*, Überlegenheit *f* (*over* über *acc*). **as'cend·ant I** *s* **1.** *ast.* Ascendent *m*, Aufgangspunkt *m*: *in the* ~ *a. fig.* im Aufstieg *od.* Kommen. **II** *adj* **2.** (auf)steigend. **3.** überlegen (*over dat*). **as'cend·en·cy, as'cend·ent** = **as-cendancy, ascendant.**

as·cen·sion [ə'senʃn] *s* **1.** Aufsteigen *n*. **2.** *the* ♀ Christi Himmelfahrt *f*; ♀ *Day* Himmelfahrtstag *m*.

as·cent [ə'sent] *s* **1.** Aufstieg *m*. **2.** Besteigung *f*. **3.** Steigung *f*, Gefälle *n*.

as·cer·tain [ˌæsə'teɪn] *v/t* ermitteln, fest-stellen, in Erfahrung bringen. **ˌas·cer-'tain·a·ble** *adj* feststellbar. **ˌas·cer'tain-ment** *s* Ermittlung *f*, Feststellung *f*.

as·cet·ic [ə'setɪk] **I** *adj* (~*ally*) asketisch. **II** *s* Asket(in). **as'cet·i·cism** [ˌ~tɪsɪzəm] *s* Askese *f*.

as·cor·bic ac·id [ə'skɔːbɪk] *s* ♠ Ascor-binsäure *f*, Vitamin *n* C.

as·crib·a·ble [ə'skraɪbəbl] *adj* zuzu-schreiben(d). **as'cribe** *v/t* (*to*) **1.** zu-rückführen (auf *acc*), zuschreiben (*dat*). **2.** zuschreiben, beimessen (*dat*).

a·sep·tic [ˌeɪ'septɪk] *adj* (~*ally*) aseptisch, keimfrei.

a·sex·u·al [ˌeɪ'seksjʊəl] *adj* □ *biol.* ge-schlechtslos.

ash¹ [æʃ] *s* **1.** ♀ Esche *f*. **2.** Eschenholz *n*.

ash² [ˌ~] *s* **1.** *mst pl* Asche *f*: *burn to* (*od. lay in*) ~*es* einäschern, niederbrennen. **2.** *pl* Asche *f*, (sterbliche) Überreste *pl*.

a·shamed [ə'ʃeɪmd] *adj* beschämt: *be* (*od. feel*) ~ *of* sich *e-r Sache od. j-s* schämen; *be* ~ *of o.s.* sich schämen; *be* (*od. feel*) ~ *to do* (*od. of doing*) *s.th.* sich schämen, et. zu tun.

ash| bin, ~ **can** *s Am.* **1.** Abfall-, Mülleim-er *m*. **2.** Abfall-, Mülltonne *f*.

ash·en¹ ['æʃn] *adj* eschen, aus Eschen-holz.

ash·en² [ˌ~] *adj* **1.** Aschen... **2.** aschfar-ben. **3.** aschgrau, -fahl.

a·shore [ə'ʃɔː] *adv u. adj* an *od.* ans Ufer: *go* ~ an Land gehen.

'ash|·pan *s* Asche(n)kasten *m*. **'~·tray** *s* Aschenbecher *m*. ♀ **Wednes·day** *s* Aschermittwoch *m*.

ash·y ['æʃɪ] *adj* **1.** Aschen... **2.** mit Asche bedeckt. **3.** = **ashen²** 2, 3.

A·sian ['eɪʃn], **A·si·at·ic** [ˌeɪʃɪ'ætɪk] **I** *adj* asiatisch. **II** *s* Asiat(in).

a·side [ə'saɪd] **I** *adv* **1.** beiseite, auf die Seite: *step* ~ zur Seite treten. **2.** ~ *from* *bsd. Am.* abgesehen von. **II** *s* **3.** *thea.* Aparte *n*.

as·i·nine ['æsɪnaɪn] *adj* **1.** Esels... **2.** *fig.* eselhaft, dumm.

ask [ɑːsk] **I** *v/t* **1.** *j-n* fragen. **2.** *j-n* fragen nach, sich bei *j-m* nach *et.* erkundigen: ~ *s.o. the way*; ~ *s.o. a question* *j-m* e-e Frage stellen, *j-n* et. fragen. **3.** bitten um, *et.* erbitten: ~ *advice*; → *favo(u)r* 4. **4.** *j-n* bitten, fragen (*for* um): ~ *s.o. for advice.* **5.** einladen; bitten: ~ *s.o. to dinner* *j-n* zum Essen einladen; ~ *s.o. in* *j-n* hereinbitten; ~ *s.o. out* *j-n* ausfüh-ren. **6.** verlangen, fordern (*of* von): ~ *a high price for s.th.*; *that is ~ing too much* das ist zuviel verlangt. **II** *v/i* **7.** fragen, sich erkundigen (*for, about, af-ter* nach): ~ *for s.o. a.* j-n *od.* nach j-m verlangen, *j-n* zu sprechen wünschen; ~ *around* herumfragen, sich umhören. **8.** bitten (*for* um): *he ~ed for it* (*od. trou-ble*) F er wollte es ja so haben.

a·skance [ə'skæns] *adv*: *look* ~ *at s.o.* j-n von der Seite ansehen; *fig.* j-n schief *od.* mißtrauisch ansehen.

a·skew [ə'skjuː] *adv* **1.** schief: *go* ~ *fig.*

schiefgehen. **2. look ~ at s.o.** j-n verächtlich ansehen.

ask·ing [ˈɑːskɪŋ] s Fragen n, Bitten n: **to be had for the ~** umsonst od. leicht zu haben sein.

a·slant [əˈslɑːnt] **I** adv u. adj schräg, quer. **II** prp quer über (acc) od. durch.

a·sleep [əˈsliːp] adv u. adj schlafend, (Fuß etc) eingeschlafen: **be ~** schlafen; **drop** (od. **fall**) **~** einschlafen.

as·par·a·gus [əˈspærəgəs] s ♀ Spargel m: **~ tips** pl Spargelspitzen pl.

as·pect [ˈæspekt] s **1.** Aussehen n, Erscheinung f. **2.** Aspekt m (a. ling.), Seite f, Gesichtspunkt m. **3.** Beziehung f, Hinsicht f.

as·pen [ˈæspən] s ♀ Espe f: **tremble like an ~ leaf** wie Espenlaub zittern.

as·per·i·ty [æˈsperətɪ] s **1.** Rauheit f (a. fig.), Unebenheit f. **2.** fig. Schärfe f, Schroffheit f.

as·perse [əˈspɜːs] v/t verleumden. **as'per·sion** s Verleumdung f: **cast ~s on** verleumden.

as·phalt [ˈæsfælt] **I** s Asphalt m. **II** v/t asphaltieren.

as·phyx·i·a [əsˈfɪksɪə] s ⚕ Erstickung(stod m) f. **as'phyx·i·ate** [~eɪt] v/t u. v/i ersticken: **be ~d** ersticken. **as,phyx·i'a·tion** s Erstickung f.

as·pic [ˈæspɪk] s Aspik m, Gelee n.

as·pir·ant [əˈspaɪərənt] s (**to, after, for**) Bewerber(in) (um acc), Anwärter(in) (auf acc). **as·pi·ra·tion** [ˌæspəˈreɪʃn] s Streben n, Bestrebung f (**for, after** nach). **as·pire** [əˈspaɪə] v/i streben, trachten (**to, after** nach): **~ to** (od. **after**) **s.th.** a. et. erstreben.

as·pi·rin [ˈæspərɪn] s pharm. Aspirin n.

as·pir·ing [əˈspaɪərɪŋ] adj □ **1.** ehrgeizig, strebsam. **2.** auf-, emporstrebend.

ass¹ [æs] s zo. Esel m (a. fig.): **make an ~ of o.s.** sich lächerlich machen od. blamieren.

ass² [~], **~·hole** Am. V → **arse, arse-hole.**

as·sail [əˈseɪl] v/t **1.** angreifen. **2.** fig. bestürmen (**with** mit Fragen etc): **~ed by fear** von Furcht gepackt. **3.** Aufgabe etc in Angriff nehmen. **as'sail·a·ble** adj angreifbar. **as'sail·ant** s Angreifer m.

as·sas·sin [əˈsæsɪn] s (bsd. politischer) Mörder, Attentäter m. **as'sas·si·nate** [~neɪt] v/t bsd. pol. ermorden: **be ~d** e-m Attentat zum Opfer fallen. **as,sas·si·na·tion** s (**of**) (bsd. politischer) Mord, Ermordung f (gen), Attentat n (auf acc).

as·sault [əˈsɔːlt] **I** s **1.** Angriff m (auf acc) (a. fig.). **2.** ⚔ Sturm m: **take by ~** im Sturm nehmen, erstürmen. **3.** a. **~ and battery** ⚖ tätliche Beleidigung: **criminal** (od. **indecent**) **~** unzüchtige Handlung (unter Gewaltandrohung od. -anwendung). **II** v/t **4.** angreifen (a. fig.). **5.** ⚔ stürmen. **6.** ⚖ tätlich beleidigen. **7.** euphem. vergewaltigen.

as·say [əˈseɪ] **I** s **1.** Prüfung f, Untersuchung f. **II** v/t **2.** Metall etc prüfen, untersuchen. **3.** fig. versuchen, probieren.

as·sem·blage [əˈsemblɪdʒ] s **1.** Ansammlung f. **2.** Versammlung f. **3.** ☼ Montage f. **as'sem·ble I** v/t **1.** versammeln. **2.** ☼ montieren, zs.-setzen. **II** v/i **3.** sich versammeln. **as'sem·bler** s ☼ Monteur m. **as'sem·bly** s **1.** Versammlung f. **2.** ☼ Montage f: **~ line** Fließband n; **~ shop** Montagehalle f.

as·sent [əˈsent] **I** v/i (**to**) **1.** zustimmen, beipflichten (dat). **2.** billigen, genehmigen (acc). **II** s **3.** Zustimmung f, Beipflichtung f: **by common ~** mit allgemeiner Zustimmung. **4.** Billigung f, Genehmigung f.

as·sert [əˈsɜːt] v/t **1.** behaupten, erklären. **2.** Anspruch etc geltend machen, bestehen auf (dat). **3. ~ o.s.** sich behaupten od. durchsetzen; sich zu viel anmaßen. **as'ser·tion** s **1.** Behauptung f, Erklärung f: **make an ~** e-e Behauptung aufstellen. **2.** Geltendmachung f. **as'ser·tive** adj □ **1.** ausdrücklich. **2.** anmaßend.

as·sess [əˈses] v/t **1.** Geldstrafe etc festsetzen. **2.** Einkommen etc (zur Steuer) veranlagen (**at** mit). **3.** fig. ab-, einschätzen, (be)werten. **as'sess·ment** s **1.** Festsetzung f. **2.** (Steuer)Veranlagung f. **3.** Steuer(betrag m) f. **4.** fig. Ab-, Einschätzung f, (Be)Wertung f: **what is your ~ of ...?** wie beurteilen Sie ... (acc)?

as·set [ˈæset] s **1.** ♦ Aktivposten m; pl Aktiva pl: **~s and liabilities** Aktiva u. Passiva pl. **2.** pl ⚖ Vermögen(smasse f) n; Konkursmasse f. **3.** fig. Vorzug m,

Plus *n*; Gewinn *m* (**to** für): **be a great ~** viel wert sein.

as·si·du·i·ty [ˌæsɪˈdjuːətɪ] *s* Fleiß *m*, Eifer *m*. **as·sid·u·ous** [əˈsɪdjʊəs] *adj* □ fleißig, eifrig.

as·sign [əˈsaɪn] *v/t* **1.** *Aufgabe etc* zu-, anweisen, zuteilen (**to** *dat*). **2.** (**to**) *j-n* bestimmen, einteilen (zu, für *e-e Aufgabe etc*), beauftragen (mit). **3.** *Zeitpunkt etc* festsetzen, festlegen. **4.** *et. zuschreiben* (**to** *dat*). **5.** ⚖ abtreten, übertragen (**to** *dat*). **as·sign·ment** *s* **1.** Zu-, Anweisung *f* (**to** *an acc*). **2.** Bestimmung *f*, Festsetzung *f*. **3.** Aufgabe *f*, Arbeit *f* (*beide a. ped.*), Auftrag *m* **4.** ⚖ Abtretung *f*, Übertragung *f* (**to** *an acc*).

as·sim·i·late [əˈsɪmɪleɪt] **I** *v/t* **1.** assimilieren: a) angleichen (*a. ling.*), anpassen (**to**, **with** *dat*, *an acc*), b) *biol.* (sich) *Nahrung* einverleiben, c) *sociol.* aufnehmen. **II** *v/i* **2.** sich angleichen *od.* anpassen (**to**, **with** *dat*). **3.** *biol.*, *sociol.* sich assimilieren. **as·sim·i·la·tion** *s* Assimilation *f*: a) Angleichung *f*, Anpassung *f* (**to** *an acc*), b) *biol.* Einverleibung *f*.

as·sist [əˈsɪst] **I** *v/t* **1.** *j-m* helfen, beistehen, *j-n* unterstützen: **~ s.o. in doing s.th.** *j-m* (dabei) helfen, et. zu tun. **II** *v/i* **2.** mithelfen, Hilfe leisten (**in** bei). **3.** (**at**) beiwohnen (*dat*), teilnehmen (an *dat*). **as·sist·ance** *s* Hilfe *f*, Beistand *m*, Unterstützung *f*: **come to s.o.'s ~** *j-m* zu Hilfe kommen. **as·sist·ant I** *adj* **1.** stellvertretend: **~ editor** Redaktionsassistent *m*; **~ professor** *Am.* (*etwa*) Lehrbeauftragte *m, f*. **II** *s* **2.** Assistent(in), Mitarbeiter(in). **3.** Angestellte *m, f*: (**shop**) **~** *Br.* Verkäufer(in).

as·so·ci·ate [əˈsəʊʃɪeɪt] **I** *v/t* **1.** vereinigen, -binden, zs.-schließen (**with** mit): **~ o.s. with** a. sich e-r Partei, *j-s Ansichten etc* anschließen. **2.** *bsd. psych.* assoziieren, (gedanklich) verbinden (**with** mit). **II** *v/i* **3.** sich vereinigen *etc*, → **1.** **4.** verkehren (**with** mit). **III** *adj* [~ʃɪɪt] **5.** verwandt (**with** mit). **6.** beigeordnet, Mit...: **~ editor** Mitherausgeber *m*. **7.** außerordentlich (*Mitglied*). **IV** *s* [~ʃɪɪt] **8.** ⚖ Teilhaber *m*, Gesellschafter *m*. **9.** Gefährte *m*, Genosse *m*. **10.** außerordentliches Mitglied. **as·so·ci·a·tion** [əˌsəʊsɪˈeɪʃn] *s* **1.** Vereinigung *f*, -bindung *f*, Zs.-schluß *m*: **in ~ with** zusammen mit. **2.** Verein(igung *f*) *m*. **3.** ✝ Genossenschaft *f*, (Handels)Gesellschaft *f*, Verband *m*: **~ football** *Br.* Fußball *m*. **4.** Umgang *m*, Verkehr *m*. **5.** *psych.* (Ideen-, Gedanken)Assoziation *f*, Gedankenverbindung *f*.

as·sort·ed [əˈsɔːtɪd] *adj* **1.** sortiert, geordnet. **2.** zs.-gestellt, gemischt, verschiedenartig. **as·sort·ment** *s bsd.* ✝ (**of**) Sortiment *n* (von), Auswahl *f* (an *dat*).

as·sume [əˈsjuːm] *v/t* **1.** annehmen, voraussetzen: **assuming that** angenommen *od.* vorausgesetzt, daß. **2.** *Amt, Verantwortung etc* übernehmen. **3.** *Eigenschaft, Gestalt etc* annehmen. **4.** sich *Recht etc* anmaßen. **as·sum·ing** *adj* □ anmaßend. **as·sump·tion** [əˈsʌmpʃn] *s* **1.** Annahme *f*, Voraussetzung *f*: **on the ~ that** in der Annahme *od.* unter der Voraussetzung, daß. **2.** Übernahme *f*. **3.** Anmaßung *f*. **4.** 2 (**Day**) *eccl.* Mariä Himmelfahrt *f*.

as·sur·ance [əˈʃʊərəns] *s* **1.** Ver-, Zusicherung *f*. **2.** *bsd. Br.* (Lebens)Versicherung *f*. **3.** Sicherheit *f*, Gewißheit *f*. **4.** Selbstsicherheit *f*; *b.s.* Dreistigkeit *f*. **as·sure** [əˈʃɔː] *v/t* **1.** *j-m* versichern (**that** daß): **~ s.o. of s.th.** *j-m* et. zusichern. **2.** sichern, sicherstellen, bürgen für. **3.** überzeugen (**of** von): **~ o.s.** *a.* sich vergewissern (**of** *gen*). **4.** beruhigen. **5.** *bsd. Br.* Leben versichern: **~ one's life with** *e-e* Lebensversicherung abschließen bei. **as·sured** [~d] *adj* **1.** (**of**) überzeugt (von), sicher (*gen*): **you can rest ~ that** Sie können sicher sein *od.* sich darauf verlassen, daß. **2.** gesichert. **3.** selbstsicher; *b.s.* dreist. **II** *s bsd. Br.* Versicherte *m, f*. **as·sur·ed·ly** [~rɪdlɪ] *adv* ganz gewiß.

as·ter [ˈæstə] *s* ♀ Aster *f*.

as·ter·isk [ˈæstərɪsk] *s typ.* Sternchen *n*.

a·stern [əˈstɜːn] *adv* ♨ achtern.

asth·ma [ˈæsmə] *s* ♪ Asthma *n*. **asth·mat·ic** [~ˈmætɪk] **I** *adj* (~**ally**) asthmatisch: **~ attack** Asthmaanfall *m*; **be ~** Asthma haben. **II** *s* Asthmatiker(in).

a·stig·ma·tism [əˈstɪgmətɪzəm] *s* ♪, *phys.* Astigmatismus *m*.

as·ton·ish [əˈstɒnɪʃ] *v/t* in Erstaunen setzen: **be ~ed** erstaunt *od.* überrascht sein (**at** über *acc*; **to** *inf* zu *inf*), sich wundern (**at** über *acc*). **as·ton·ish·ing**

adj □ erstaunlich. **as·ton·ish·ment** *s* (Er)Staunen *n*, Verwunderung *f*: **to one's ~** zu s-r Verwunderung.

as·tound [ə'staʊnd], **as·tound·ing** → astonish, astonishing.

a·stray [ə'streɪ] *adv*: **go ~** vom Weg abkommen; *fig.* auf Abwege geraten; **lead ~** *fig.* irreführen.

as·trin·gent [ə'strɪndʒənt] **I** *adj* □ **1.** ✠ adstringierend, zs.-ziehend. **2.** *fig.* streng, hart. **II** *s* **3.** ✠ Adstringens *n*.

as·trol·o·ger [ə'strɒlədʒə] *s* Astrologe *m*. **as·tro·log·i·cal** [ˌæstrə'lɒdʒɪkl] *adj* □ astrologisch. **as·trol·o·gy** [ə'strɒlədʒɪ] *s* Astrologie *f*.

as·tro·naut ['æstrənɔːt] *s* Astronaut *m*. **'as·tro·naut·ess** *s* Astronautin *f*. **ˌas·tro·'nau·tics** *s pl* (*mst sg konstruiert*) Astronautik *f*, Raumfahrt *f*.

as·tron·o·mer [ə'strɒnəmə] *s* Astronom *m*. **as·tro·nom·i·cal** [ˌæstrə'nɒmɪkl] *adj* □ astronomisch. **as·tron·o·my** [ə'strɒnəmɪ] *s* Astronomie *f*.

as·tute [ə'stjuːt] *adj* □ **1.** scharfsinnig. **2.** schlau, gerissen. **as·'tute·ness** *s* **1.** Scharfsinn *m*. **2.** Schlauheit *f*.

a·sun·der [ə'sʌndə] *adv* auseinander, entzwei.

a·sy·lum [ə'saɪləm] *s* **1.** Asyl *n*: a) Zufluchtsort *m*, b) *fig.* Zuflucht *f*. **2.** (*politisches*) Asyl: **ask for ~** um Asyl bitten *od.* nachsuchen; **give s.o. ~** j-m Asyl gewähren; **~ seeker** Asylant(in), Asylbewerber(in).

a·sym·met·ric [ˌeɪsɪ'metrɪk], **ˌa·sym·'met·ri·cal** *adj* □ asymmetrisch, ungleichmäßig. **a·sym·me·try** [ˌeɪ'sɪmətrɪ] *s* Asymmetrie *f*, Ungleichmäßigkeit *f*.

at [æt] *prp* **1.** (*Ort*) in (*dat*), an (*dat*), bei, auf (*dat*): **~ a ball** auf e-m Ball; **~ the baker's** beim Bäcker; **~ the door** an der Tür. **2.** (*Richtung*) auf (*acc*), nach, gegen, zu: **he threw a stone ~ the door** er warf e-n Stein gegen die Tür. **3.** (*Beschäftigung*) bei, beschäftigt mit, in (*dat*): **he is still ~ it** er ist noch dabei *od.* damit beschäftigt. **4.** (*Art u. Weise, Zustand*) in (*dat*), bei, zu, unter (*dat*): **~ all** überhaupt; **not ~ all** überhaupt *od.* gar nicht; **not ~ all!** F nichts zu danken!; **nothing ~ all** überhaupt *od.* gar nichts; **no doubts ~ all** keinerlei Zweifel. **5.** (*Preis, Wert etc*) für, um: **~ 6 dollars. 6.**

(*Zeit, Alter*) um, bei: **~ 21** mit 21 (Jahren); **~ 3 o'clock** um 3 Uhr; **~ his death** bei s-m Tod.

ate [et] *pret von* eat.

a·the·ism ['eɪθɪɪzəm] *s* Atheismus *m*. **'a·the·ist** *s* Atheist(in). **ˌa·the·'is·tic**, **ˌa·the·'is·ti·cal** *adj* □ atheistisch.

ath·lete ['æθliːt] *s* **1.** Athlet *m*: a) Sportler *m*, b) Kraftmensch *m*. **2.** *Br.* Leichtathlet *m*. **ath·let·ic** [æθ'letɪk] *I adj* (**~ally**) **1.** athletisch: a) Sport...: **~ field** Sportplatz *m*, b) von athletischem Körperbau. **2.** *Br.* leichtathletisch. **II** *s pl* **3.** (*mst sg konstruiert*) Sport *m*. **4.** (*mst sg konstruiert*) *Br.* Leichtathletik *f*.

at-home [ət'həʊm] *s* zwangloser Empfang: **give an ~.**

a·thwart [ə'θwɔːt] **I** *adv* quer. **II** *prp* (quer) über (*acc*) *od.* durch.

At·lan·tic [ət'læntɪk] *adj* atlantisch.

at·las ['ætləs] *s* Atlas *m* (*Buch*).

at·mos·phere ['ætməsfɪə] *s* Atmosphäre *f* (*a. fig.*). **at·mos·pher·ic** [ˌ~'ferɪk] **I** *adj* (**~ally**) atmosphärisch. **II** *s pl* atmosphärische Störungen *pl*.

at·oll ['ætɒl] *s* Atoll *n*.

at·om ['ætəm] *s phys.* Atom *n* (*a. fig.*): **not an ~ of truth** kein Körnchen Wahrheit; **~ bomb** Atombombe *f*. **a·tom·ic** [ə'tɒmɪk] *adj* (**~ally**) atomar, Atom...: **~ age** Atomzeitalter *n*; **~ bomb** Atombombe *f*; **~ energy** Atomenergie *f*; **~ nucleus** Atomkern *m*; **~ pile** Atomreaktor *m*; **~ power** Atomkraft *f*; **~ research** Atomforschung *f*; **~-powered** mit Atomkraft betrieben, Atom...; **~ power plant** Atomkraftwerk *n*; **~ waste** Atommüll *m*; **~ weight** Atomgewicht *n*. **at·om·ize** ['ætəʊmaɪz] *v/t* **1.** atomisieren. **2.** Flüssigkeit zerstäuben. **'at·om·iz·er** *s* Zerstäuber *m* (*Gerät*).

a·tone [ə'təʊn] *v/i*: **~ for** büßen für *et.*, *et.* sühnen. **a·'tone·ment** *s* Buße *f*, Sühne *f*.

a·top [ə'tɒp] **I** *adv* oben(auf). **II** *prp a.* **~ of** (oben) auf (*dat*).

a·tro·cious [ə'trəʊʃəs] *adj* □ scheußlich, gräßlich (*beide a. fig.*). **a·troc·i·ty** [ə'trɒsətɪ] *s* **1.** Scheußlichkeit *f*, Gräßlichkeit *f*. **2.** Greueltat *f*.

at·ro·phy ['ætrəfɪ] ✠ **I** *s* Atrophie *f*, Verkümmerung *f* (*a. fig.*). **II** *v/i* verkümmern (*a. fig.*).

at·tach [ə'tætʃ] **I** *v/t* **1.** (**to**) befestigen, anbringen (an *dat*), anheften, ankleben (an *acc*). **2.** (**to**) *fig. Sinn etc* verbinden (*mit*); *Wert, Wichtigkeit etc* beimessen (*dat*); *magische Kräfte etc* zuschreiben (*dat*); *Bedingungen* knüpfen (an *acc*). **3.** *fig.* **~ o.s.** sich anschließen (**to** *dat od.* an *acc*): **be ~ed to s.o.** an j-m hängen. **4.** *fig.* (**to**) zuteilen (*dat*), ✕ *a.* abkommandieren (zu). **5.** ⚖ *j-n* verhaften; *et.* beschlagnahmen; pfänden. **II** *v/i* **6.** (**to**) anhaften (*dat*), verknüpft *od.* verbunden sein mit.

at·ta·ché [ə'tæʃeɪ] *s* Attaché *m*: **~ case** Aktentasche *f*, -koffer *m*.

at·tach·ment [ə'tætʃmənt] *s* **1.** Befestigung *f*. **2.** Anhängsel *n*, Beiwerk *n*; ⚙ Zusatzgerät *n*. **3.** *fig.* (**to**) Anhänglichkeit *f* (an *acc*); Bindung *f* (an *acc*). **4.** ⚖ Verhaftung *f*; Beschlagnahme *f*; Pfändung *f*.

at·tack [ə'tæk] **I** *v/t* **1.** (*a. v/i*) *allg.* angreifen. **2.** *fig. Arbeit etc* in Angriff nehmen, *über e-e Mahlzeit etc* herfallen. **II** *s* **3.** Angriff *m*. **4.** ⚕ Anfall *m*. **at'tack·er** *s* Angreifer *m*.

at·tain [ə'teɪn] *v/t* (*u. v/i* **~ to**) *Ziel etc* erreichen, erlangen. **at'tain·a·ble** *adj* erreichbar. **at'tain·ment** *s* **1.** Erreichung *f*, Erlangung *f*. **2.** *pl* Kenntnisse *pl*, Fertigkeiten *pl*.

at·tempt [ə'tempt] **I** *v/t* **1.** versuchen (**to do, doing** zu tun): **~ed suicide** Selbstmordversuch *m*. **2.** sich machen *od.* wagen an (*acc*), in Angriff nehmen. **II** *v/i* **3.** Versuch *m* (**to do, doing** zu tun): **~ at explanation** Erklärungsversuch; **~s** *pl* **at resuscitation** ⚕ Wiederbelebungsversuche *pl*. **4.** Anschlag *m*: **an ~ on s.o.'s life** ein Mordanschlag *od.* Attentat auf j-n.

at·tend [ə'tend] **I** *v/t* **1.** *Kranke* pflegen; (ärztlich) behandeln. **2.** *fig.* begleiten: **~ed with** (*od.* **by**) verbunden mit. **3.** teilnehmen an (*dat*), *Schule, Versammlung etc* besuchen. **II** *v/i* **4.** (**to**) sich kümmern (um); erledigen (*acc*). **6. ~ to** *j-n* (*im Laden*) bedienen: **are you being ~ed to?** werden Sie schon bedient? **7.** anwesend sein; erscheinen. **8. ~ on** *j-n* bedienen. **at'tend·ance** *s* **1.** Dienst *m*, Bereitschaft *f*: **physician in ~** diensthabender Arzt; **hours** *pl* **of ~** Dienststunden *pl*. **2.** Pflege *f* (**on** *gen*), Dienstlei-

stung *f*: **be in ~ on** → **attend** 1. **3.** Anwesenheit *f*, Erscheinen *n*: **~ list** (*od.* **record**) Anwesenheitsliste *f*. **4.** Besucher *pl*, Teilnehmer *pl*; Besuch(erzahl *f*) *m*, Beteiligung *f*. **at'tend·ant I** *adj* **1.** begleitend. **2.** *fig.* verbunden (**on** mit): **~ circumstances** *pl* Begleitumstände *pl*. **3.** anwesend. **II** *s* **4.** Begleiter(in). **5.** Aufseher(in). **6.** *pl* Dienerschaft *f*.

at·ten·tion [ə'tenʃn] *s* **1.** Aufmerksamkeit *f* (*a. fig.*): **attract** Aufmerksamkeit erregen; **call** (*od.* **draw**) **~ to** die Aufmerksamkeit lenken auf (*acc*), aufmerksam machen auf (*acc*); **pay ~ to** Beachtung schenken (*dat*), achtgeben auf (*acc*); (**for the**) **~ of** zu Händen von (*od. gen*). **2.** **give** (**prompt**) **~ to s.th.** (*rasch*) erledigen. **3. ~!** ✕ Achtung!; stillgestanden! **at'ten·tive** *adj* □ aufmerksam (**to** auf *acc*; *fig.* gegen).

at·ten·u·ate [ə'tenjʊeɪt] *v/t* **1.** *bsd.* 🝕 verdünnen. **2.** *fig.* vermindern, (ab)schwächen.

at·test [ə'test] *v/t* **1.** beglaubigen, bescheinigen. **2.** zeugen von, bestätigen. **at·tes·ta·tion** [ˌæte'steɪʃn] *s* **1.** Beglaubigung *f*, Bescheinigung *f*. **2.** Zeugnis *n*.

at·tic ['ætɪk] *s* Dachgeschoß *n*; Dachstube *f*, -kammer *f*.

at·tire [ə'taɪə] **I** *v/t* (be)kleiden. **II** *s* Kleidung *f*, Gewand *n*.

at·ti·tude ['ætɪtjuːd] *s* **1.** (*Körper*)Haltung *f*, Stellung *f*. **2.** *fig.* Haltung *f*: a) Verhalten *n*, b) Einstellung *f* (**to, toward**[s] zu, gegenüber): **what is your ~ to ...?** wie stehen Sie zu ...?

at·tor·ney [ə'tɜːnɪ] *s* ⚖ **1.** *bsd. Am.* **~** (**at law**) (*Rechts*)Anwalt *m*; **~** (**in fact**) Bevollmächtigte *m*. **2.** (**power of**) **~** Vollmacht *f*; **~-gen·er·al** *pl* **~s gen·er·al**, **gen·er·als** *pl* ⚖ **1.** *Br.* erster Kronanwalt. **2.** *Am.* Justizminister *m*.

at·tract [ə'trækt] *v/t* **1.** *phys.* anziehen (*a. fig.*). **2.** *fig. j-n* anlocken, reizen, *j-s Interesse, Blicke etc* auf sich ziehen: **be ~ed to** sich hingezogen fühlen zu; → **attention** 1. **at'trac·tion** [-kʃn] *s* **1.** *phys.* Anziehung(skraft) *f*. **2.** *fig. a*) Anziehungskraft *f*, Reiz *m*: **have little ~ for** wenig anziehend sein für, b) Attraktion *f*, *thea. etc* Zugnummer *f*. **at'trac·tive** *adj* □ **1.** *phys.* anziehend: **~ force** (*od.* **power**) Anziehungskraft *f*. **2.** *fig.* attraktiv: a) anziehend, reizvoll,

b) einnehmend (*Äußeres* etc), c) zugkräftig (*Angebot* etc).

at·trib·ute [ə'trɪbjuːt] I *v/t* **1.** zuschreiben (*to dat*). **2.** zurückführen (*to auf acc*). II *s* ['ætrɪbjuːt] **3.** Attribut *n* (*a. ling.*): a) Eigenschaft *f*, Merkmal *n*, b) (Kenn)Zeichen *n*. **at·trib·u·tive** [ə'trɪb-jʊtɪv] *ling.* I *adj* □ attributiv. II *s* Attribut *n*.

at·tri·tion [ə'trɪʃn] *s* **1.** Abnutzung *f*, Verschleiß *m* (*beide a. fig.*). **2.** *fig.* Zermürbung *f*.

au·burn ['ɔːbən] *adj* kastanienbraun (*Haar*).

auc·tion ['ɔːkʃn] I *s* Auktion *f*, Versteigerung *f*: *sell* (*buy*) *by* (*Am. at*) ~ versteigern (ersteigern); *sale by* (*Am. at*) ~, ~ *sale* Versteigerung *f*. II *v/t mst* ~ *off* versteigern. **auc·tion·eer** [,ɔːkʃə'nɪə] *s* Auktionator *m*, Versteigerer *m*: ~*s pl* Auktionshaus *n*.

au·da·cious [ɔː'deɪʃəs] *adj* □ **1.** kühn, verwegen. **2.** dreist, unverfroren. **au·dac·i·ty** [ɔː'dæsɪtɪ] *s* **1.** Kühnheit *f*, Verwegenheit *f*. **2.** Dreistigkeit *f*, Unverfrorenheit *f*.

au·di·ble ['ɔːdəbl] *adj* □ hörbar, vernehmlich.

au·di·ence ['ɔːdjəns] *s* **1.** Audienz *f* (*of, with* bei). **2.** Publikum *n*: a) Zuhörer(schaft *f*) *pl*, b) Zuschauer *pl*, c) Besucher *pl*, d) Leser(kreis *m*) *pl*.

au·di·o|·phile ['ɔːdɪəʊfaɪl] *s* Hi-Fi-Fan *m*. '~·**typ·ist** *s* Phonotypistin *f*. '~·**vis·u·al** I *adj* □ audiovisuell: ~ *aids* → II. II *s pl* audiovisuelle Unterrichtsmittel *pl*.

au·dit ['ɔːdɪt] ✝ I *s* Buch-, Rechnungsprüfung *f*. II *v/t* prüfen.

au·di·tion [ɔː'dɪʃn] I *s* **1.** *physiol.* Hörvermögen *n*, Gehör *n*. **2.** ♪, *thea.* Vorspiel(en) *n*; Vorsingen *n*; Vorsprechen *n*; Anhörprobe *f*. II *v/t u. v/i* **3.** ♪, *thea.* vorspielen *od.* vorsingen *od.* vorsprechen (lassen).

au·di·tor ['ɔːdɪtə] *s* **1.** ✝ Buch-, Rechnungsprüfer *m*. **2.** *univ. Am.* Gasthörer(in).

au·di·to·ri·um [,ɔːdɪ'tɔːrɪəm] *pl* **-ri·ums**, **-ri·a** [~ə] *s* **1.** Auditorium *n*, Zuhörer-, Zuschauerraum *m*. **2.** *Am.* Vortragssaal *m*, Konzerthalle *f*.

aug·ment [ɔːg'ment] I *v/t* vermehren, steigern, *Gehalt* etc aufbessern. II *v/i* sich vermehren, zunehmen. **,aug·men·'ta·tion** *s* Vermehrung *f*, Zunahme *f*; Aufbesserung *f*.

au·gur ['ɔːgə] I *v/t* vorher-, weissagen. II *v/i:* ~ *well* (*ill*) ein gutes (schlechtes) Zeichen sein (*for* für). **au·gu·ry** ['ɔːgjʊrɪ] *s* Vorzeichen *n*.

Au·gust ['ɔːgəst] *s* August *m*: *in* ~ im August.

auld lang syne [,ɔːldlæŋ'saɪn] *schott.* die gute alte Zeit.

aunt [ɑːnt] *s* Tante *f*.

au·pair [,əʊ'peə] *Br.* I *s a.* ~ *girl* Au-pair-Mädchen *n*. II *adv* als Au-pair-Mädchen: *work* ~. III *v/i* als Au-pair-Mädchen arbeiten.

au·ra ['ɔːrə] *s fig.* Aura *f*.

au·ral ['ɔːrəl] *adj* **1.** Ohren...: ~ *surgeon* Ohrenarzt *m*. **2.** akustisch, Hör...

au·re·ole ['ɔːrɪəʊl] *s ast.* Aureole *f*, Hof *m*.

au·ri·cle ['ɔːrɪkl] *s anat.* **1.** Ohrmuschel *f*. **2.** Herzvorhof *m*. **au·ric·u·lar** [ɔː'rɪk-jʊlə] *adj* Ohren...: ~ *confession eccl.* Ohrenbeichte *f*; ~ *witness* Ohrenzeuge *m*.

aus·cul·ta·tion [,ɔːskəl'teɪʃn] *s* ✻ Abhorchen *n*.

aus·pic·es ['ɔːspɪsɪz] *s pl:* *under the* ~ *of* unter der Schirmherrschaft von (*od. gen*). **aus·pi·cious** [ɔː'spɪʃəs] *adj* □ günstig: a) vielversprechend, b) glücklich: *be* ~ unter e-m günstigen Stern stehen.

Aus·sie ['ɒzɪ] F I *s* Australier(in). II *adj* australisch.

aus·tere [ɒ'stɪə] *adj* □ **1.** streng, ernst. **2.** enthaltsam; dürftig, karg. **3.** herb, rau, hart. **4.** nüchtern, schmucklos. **aus·ter·i·ty** [ɒ'sterətɪ] I *s* **1.** Strenge *f*, Ernst *m*. **2.** Enthaltsamkeit *f*; Dürftigkeit *f*. **3.** Herbheit *f*, Rauheit *f*. **4.** Nüchternheit *f*, Schmucklosigkeit *f*. II *adj* **5.** ✝, *pol.* Spar...: ~ *budget*; ~ *program(me)*.

Aus·tra·lian [ɒ'streɪljən] I *adj* australisch. II *s* Australier(in).

Aus·tri·an ['ɒstrɪən] I *adj* österreichisch. II *s* Österreicher(in).

au·tar·kic [ɔː'tɑːkɪk] *adj* ✝ autark. **au·tar·ky** ['~kɪ] *s* Autarkie *f*.

au·then·tic [ɔː'θentɪk] *adj* (~*ally*) **1.** authentisch: a) echt, verbürgt, b) original, urschriftlich. **2.** ⚖ gültig, rechtskräftig. **au'then·ti·cate** [~keɪt] *v/t* **1.** beglaubigen. **2.** als echt erweisen, verbürgen. **au͵then·ti·ca·tion** s Beglaubigung f. **͵au·then'tic·i·ty** [∼sətɪ] s **1.** Authentizität f, Echtheit f. **2.** ⚖ Gültigkeit f, Rechtskräftigkeit f.

au·thor ['ɔ:θə] s **1.** Urheber(in). **2.** Autor(in), Verfasser(in), a. allg. Schriftsteller(in). **'au·thor·ess** s Autorin f, Verfasserin f, a. allg. Schriftstellerin f. **au·thor·i·tar·i·an** [ɔ:͵θɒrɪ'teərɪən] adj autoritär.

au'thor·i·ta·tive [∼tətɪv] adj □ **1.** gebieterisch, herrisch. **2.** autoritativ, maßgebend, -geblich. **au'thor·i·ty** s **1.** Autorität f, (Amts)Gewalt f. **2.** Autorität f, Ansehen n (**with** bei), Einfluß m (**over** auf acc). **3.** Vollmacht f: ∼ **to sign** Unterschriftsvollmacht f; **without** ∼ unbefugt, unberechtigt. **4.** Quelle f, Beleg m: **on good** ∼ aus glaubwürdiger Quelle. **5.** Autorität f, Kapazität f (**on** in e-r Sache, auf e-m Gebiet). **6.** mst pl Behörde(n pl) f.

au·thor·i·za·tion [͵ɔ:θəraɪ'zeɪʃn] s **1.** Ermächtigung f, Bevollmächtigung f, Befugnis f. **2.** Genehmigung f. **'au·thor·ize** v/t **1.** autorisieren, ermächtigen, bevollmächtigen: ∼**d to sign** unterschriftsbevollmächtigt. **2.** billigen, genehmigen.

au·thor·ship ['ɔ:θəʃɪp] s **1.** Urheberschaft f. **2.** Autorschaft f.

au·to ['ɔ:təʊ] pl **-tos** s Am. F Auto n.

au·to... ['ɔ:təʊ] auto..., selbst..., Auto..., Selbst...

'au·to͵bi·o'graph·ic, 'au·to͵bi·o'graph·i·cal adj □ autobiographisch. **͵au·to·bi'og·ra·phy** s Autobiographie f.

au·to·cade ['ɔ:təʊkeɪd] Am. → **motor-cade.**

'au·to͵chang·er s Plattenwechsler m.

au·toc·ra·cy [ɔ:'tɒkrəsɪ] s pol. Autokratie f. **au·to·crat** ['ɔ:təʊkræt] s Autokrat m: a) pol. diktatorischer Alleinherrscher, b) selbstherrlicher Mensch. **͵au·to'crat·ic, ͵au·to'crat·i·cal** adj □ autokratisch: a) pol. unumschränkt, b) selbstherrlich.

au·to·di·dact ['ɔ:təʊdɪ͵dækt] s Autodidakt(in). **͵au·to·di'dac·tic** adj autodidaktisch.

au·to·gen·ic [͵ɔ:təʊ'dʒenɪk] adj ✿ autogen: ∼ **training.**

au·to·graph ['ɔ:təgrɑ:f] **I** s Autogramm

n: **sign** ∼**s** Autogramme geben. **II** adj Autogramm...: ∼ **album** (**hunter**, etc). **III** v/t sein Autogramm schreiben in (acc) od. auf (acc), **Buch** etc signieren.

au·to·mat ['ɔ:təʊmæt] s **1.** bsd. Am. Automatenrestaurant n. **2.** (Verkaufs)Automat m. **au·to·mate** ['ɔ:təmeɪt] v/t automatisieren. **au·to·mat·ic** [͵ɔ:tə'mætɪk] **I** adj (∼ally) **1.** automatisch: ∼ **choke** mot. Startautomatik f. **2.** ⚙ Automat m. **3.** Selbstladepistole f, -gewehr n. **4.** Auto n mit Automatik. **au·to·ma·tion** [͵ɔ:tə'meɪʃn] s **1.** Automation f. **2.** Automatisierung f. **au·tom·a·tize** [ɔ:'tɒmətaɪz] v/t automatisieren. **au'tom·a·ton** [∼tən] pl **-ta** [∼tə], **-tons** s Automat m, Roboter m (a. fig.).

au·to·mo·bile ['ɔ:təməʊbi:l] s Auto(mobil) n. **au·to·mo·tive** [͵ɔ:tə'məʊtɪv] adj **1.** selbstfahrend, mit Eigenantrieb. **2.** Auto(mobil)..., Kraftfahrzeug...

au·ton·o·mous [ɔ:'tɒnəməs] adj autonom. **au'ton·o·my** s Autonomie f.

'au·to͵pi·lot s ✈ Autopilot m, automatische Steuerungsanlage.

au·top·sy ['ɔ:tɒpsɪ] s ✚ Autopsie f.

au·tumn ['ɔ:təm] s **1.** Herbst m (a. fig.): **the** ∼ **of life**; **in (the)** ∼ im Herbst. **II** adj Herbst... **au·tum·nal** [ɔ:'tʌmnəl] adj □ herbstlich, Herbst...

aux·il·ia·ry [ɔ:g'zɪljərɪ] **I** adj **1.** Hilfs..., ✿ a. Zusatz...: ∼ **verb** → **3. II** s **2.** Helfer(in), Hilfskraft f. **3.** ling. Hilfsverb n, -zeitwort n.

a·vail [ə'veɪl] **I** v/t: ∼ **o.s. of** sich e-r Sache bedienen, sich et. zunutze machen. **II** v/i nützen. **III** s Nutzen m: **of no** ∼ nutzlos; **to no** ∼ vergeblich. **a͵vail·a·'bil·i·ty** s Verfügbarkeit f. **a'vail·a·ble** adj □ **1.** verfügbar, vorhanden: **make** ∼ zur Verfügung stellen. **2.** ✝ lieferbar, vorrätig, erhältlich: **no longer** ∼ nicht mehr lieferbar, vergriffen; → **prescription. 3.** erreichbar, abkömmlich.

av·a·lanche ['ævəlɑ:nʃ] s **1.** Lawine f. **2.** fig. Flut f: **an** ∼ **of letters.**

av·a·rice ['ævərɪs] s Habsucht f, Habgier f. **͵av·a'ri·cious** adj □ habsüchtig, habgierig.

a·venge [ə'vendʒ] v/t rächen: ∼ **o.s., be** ∼**d** sich rächen (**on** an dat; **for** für). **a'veng·er** s Rächer(in).

av·e·nue ['ævənju:] s **1.** Allee f. **2.** Hauptstraße f. **3.** fig. Weg m (**to** zu).

av·er·age ['ævərɪdʒ] **I** *s* **1.** Durchschnitt *m*: *be above (the)* ~ über dem Durchschnitt liegen; *be below (the)* ~ unter dem Durchschnitt liegen; *on (an od. the)* ~ durchschnittlich, im Durchschnitt. **2.** ♏, ♏ Havarie *f*, Seeschaden *m*. **II** *adj* **3.** durchschnittlich, Durchschnitts... **III** *v/t* **4.** a. ~ *out* den Durchschnitt ermitteln *od.* nehmen von (*od. gen*). **5.** ⚓ anteil(s)mäßig aufteilen (*among* unter *dat*). **6.** durchschnittlich betragen *od.* haben *od.* leisten *etc*. **IV** *v/i* **7.** ~ *out at* → 6.

a·verse [ə'vɜːs] *adj* □ abgeneigt (*to*, *bsd. Br. a. from dat*). **a·ver·sion** *s* **1.** Abneigung *f*, Aversion *f* (*to*, *for*, *from* gegen). **2.** ... *is my* ~ ... ist mir ein Greuel.

a·vert [ə'vɜːt] *v/t* abwenden (*a. fig*.).

a·vi·a·tion [ˌeɪvɪ'eɪʃn] *s* Luftfahrt *f*.

av·id ['ævɪd] *adj* □ gierig (*for*, *a. of* nach); ~ *for fame* ruhmsüchtig. **a·vid·i·ty** [ə'vɪdətɪ] *s* Gier *f*.

a·void [ə'vɔɪd] *v/t* (ver)meiden, ausweichen (*dat*), aus dem Wege gehen (*dat*), *Pflicht etc* umgehen, *e-r Gefahr* entgehen: ~ *s.o.* j-n meiden; ~ *doing s.th.* es vermeiden, et. zu tun. **a·void·a·ble** *adj* vermeidbar; **a·void·ance** *s* (Ver)Meiden *n*, Umgehung *f*: *in* ~ *of* um zu vermeiden.

av·oir·du·pois [ˌævədə'pɔɪz] *s a.* ~ *weight* ⚓ Handelsgewicht *n* (= *16 Unzen*).

a·vow [ə'vaʊ] *v/t* bekennen, (ein)gestehen. **a·vow·al** *s* Bekenntnis *n*, (Ein)Geständnis *n*. **a·vowed** *adj* erklärt (*Gegner, Prinzip etc*). **a·vow·ed·ly** [~ɪdlɪ] *adv* eingestandenermaßen.

a·wait [ə'weɪt] *v/t* erwarten (*a. fig*.).

a·wake [ə'weɪk] **I** *v/t* (*irr*) **1.** (auf)wecken. **2.** *fig.* auf-, wachrütteln (*from* aus): ~ *s.o. to s.th.* j-m et. zum Bewußtsein bringen. **II** *v/i* (*irr*) **3.** auf-, erwachen. **4.** ~ *to s.th.* sich e-r Sache bewußt werden. **III** *adj* **5.** wach: *wide* ~ hellwach, *fig. a.* aufgeweckt: *be* ~ *to s.th. fig.* sich e-r Sache bewußt sein. **a·wak·en** → *awake* 1–4. **a·wak·en·ing** *s* Erwachen *n*: *a rude* ~ *fig.* ein unsanftes *od.* böses Erwachen.

a·ward [ə'wɔːd] **I** *v/t* **1.** zuerkennen, zusprechen, *Preis etc a.* verleihen. **II** *s* **2.** Urteil *n*, *bsd.* Schiedsspruch *m*. **3.** Auszeichnung *f*, Preis *m*. **4.** (*Preis- etc-*)

Verleihung *f*. **5.** *univ.* Stipendium *n*.

a·ware [ə'weə] *adj*: *be* ~ *of s.th.* et. wissen *od.* kennen, sich e-r Sache bewußt sein; *become* ~ *of s.th.* et. merken; *make s.o.* ~ *of s.th.* j-m et. bewußt machen. **a'ware·ness** *s* Bewußtsein *n*, Kenntnis *f*.

a·way [ə'weɪ] **I** *adv u. adj* **1.** weg, fort (*from* von): *go* ~ weg-, fortgehen. **2.** (weit) entfernt *od.* weg: *six miles* ~ sechs Meilen entfernt. **3.** fort, abwesend, verreist: ~ *on business* geschäftlich unterwegs. **4.** d(a)rauflos, immer weiter (→ *Verben*). **II** *adj* **5.** *Sport*: Auswärts...: ~ *match*.

awe [ɔː] **I** *s* (Ehr)Furcht *f*, Scheu *f*: *hold s.o. in* ~ → II; *stand in* ~ *of* e-e (heilige) Scheu *od.* großen Respekt haben vor (*dat*). **II** *v/t* j-m (Ehr)Furcht *od.* großen Respekt einflößen. '~·in·spir·ing *adj* ehrfurchtgebietend.

awe·some ['ɔːsəm] *adj* □ **1.** furchteinflößend. **2.** ehrfurchtgebietend.

'**awe·struck** *adj* von Ehrfurcht ergriffen.

aw·ful ['ɔːfʊl] *adj* furchtbar, schrecklich (*beide a.* F). '**aw·ful·ly** *adv* F furchtbar, schrecklich: ~ *nice* furchtbar *od.* riesig nett; *thanks* ~*!* tausend Dank!

awk·ward ['ɔːkwəd] *adj* □ **1.** ungeschickt, unbeholfen, linkisch: *be* ~ *with* ungeschickt umgehen mit. **2.** verlegen (*a. Schweigen etc*): *feel* ~ verlegen sein. **3.** peinlich, unangenehm. **4.** unhandlich, sperrig. **5.** unangenehm, schwierig: *an* ~ *customer* F ein unangenehmer Zeitgenosse. **6.** ungünstig (*Zeitpunkt etc*).

awl [ɔːl] *s* ⚙ Ahle *f*, Pfriem *m*.

awn·ing ['ɔːnɪŋ] *s* **1.** Plane *f*. **2.** Markise *f*. **3.** ♏ Sonnensegel *n*. **4.** Vorzelt *n*.

a·woke [ə'wəʊk] *pret u. pp von* **awake**. **a'wok·en** *pp von* **awake**.

a·wry [ə'raɪ] *adv u. adj* schief: *go* ~ *fig.* schiefgehen.

ax(e) [æks] **I** *s* Axt *f*, Beil *n*: *have an* ~ *to grind fig.* eigennützige Zwecke verfolgen; *get the* ~ F rausfliegen, entlassen werden. **II** *v/t* F *Ausgaben etc* rücksichtslos kürzen *od.* (zs-)streichen; *Beamte, Dienststellen* abbauen, *Leute* feuern, entlassen.

ax·es ['æksiːz] *pl von* **axis**.

ax·i·om ['æksɪəm] *s* Axiom *n*, Grundsatz *m*.

ax·is [ˈæksɪs] *pl* **ax·es** [ˈ⁓siːz] *s* ♈ *etc*
Achse *f* (*a. pol.*).
ax·le [ˈæksl] *s* ☉ (Rad)Achse *f*, Welle *f*.
ay(e) [aɪ] *s parl.* Jastimme *f*: *the* ⁓*s*

have it die Mehrheit ist dafür.
a·zal·ea [əˈzeɪljə] *s* ♣ Azalee *f*.
az·ure [ˈæʒə] **I** *adj* himmelblau. **II** *s* Himmelblau *n*.

B

baa [bɑː] *v/i* blöken.
Bab·bitt [ˈbæbət] *s Am.* selbstzufriedener
Spießer.
bab·ble [ˈbæbl] **I** *v/i* **1.** *a. v/t* stammeln.
2. *a.* plappern, schwatzen: ⁓ (*out*)
ausplaudern. **3.** plätschern. **II** *s* **4.** Geplapper *n*, Geschwätz *n*. **5.** Geplät-
scher *n*.
babe [beɪb] *s* **1.** Baby *n*: → *innocent* b. **1.**
bsd. Am. sl. Puppe *f* (*Mädchen*).
ba·bel [ˈbeɪbl] *s* Wirrwarr *m*, Durcheinander *n*; Stimmengewirr *n*.
ba·boon [bəˈbuːn] *s zo.* Pavian *m*.
ba·by [ˈbeɪbɪ] **I** *s* **1.** Baby *n*, Säugling *m*:
be left holding the ⁓ F der Dumme
sein; *that's your* ⁓ *sl.* das ist dein Bier
od. deine Sache. **2.** Benjamin *m* (*der Familie etc*). **3.** *contp.* Kindskopf *m*; Heulsuse *f*. **4.** *sl.* Puppe (*Mädchen*); Schatz
m, Liebling *m*. **5.** Baby..., Säuglings... **6.** Klein... **III** *v/t* **7.** verhätscheln. ⁓ *boom s* Babyboom *m*. ⁓ *car s*
Kleinwagen *m*. ⁓ *car·riage s Am.* Kinderwagen *m*.
ba·by·hood [ˈbeɪbɪhʊd] *s* Säuglingsalter
n. **'ba·by·ish** *adj* **1.** kindisch. **2.** kindlich.
'ba·by-,mind·er *s Br.* Tagesmutter *f*.
'⁓-sit *v/i* (*irr sit*) babysitten. **'⁓-,sit·ter**
s Babysitter(in). ⁓ *talk s* kindlich-
(tuend)es Gebabbel.
bach·e·lor [ˈbætʃələ] *s* **1.** Junggeselle *m*:
⁓ *girl* Junggesellin *f*. **2.** *univ.* Bakkalaureus *m*: ☿ *of Arts* (*Science*) Bakkalaureus der philosophischen Fakultät (*der
Naturwissenschaften*). **bach·e·lor·ette**
[⁓ˈret] *s* Junggesellin *f*. **bach·e·lor·
hood** [ˈ⁓hʊd] *s* **1.** Junggesellenstand *m*.
2. *univ.* Bakkalaureat *n*.
ba·cil·lus [bəˈsɪləs] *pl* **-li** [⁓ˌlaɪ] *s* ♠ Bazillus *m*.

back [bæk] **I** *s* **1.** *anat.*, *zo.* Rücken *m*: *at
the* ⁓ *of* hinter (*dat*); hinten in (*dat*); *be
at the* ⁓ *of s.th. fig.* hinter et. stecken;
behind s.o.'s ⁓ *fig.* hinter j-s Rücken; ⁓
to ⁓ Rücken an Rücken; *be on one's* ⁓
bettlägerig sein; *break s.o.'s* ⁓ j-m das
Kreuz brechen (*a. fig.*); *break the* ⁓ *of
s.th. fig.* das Schwierigste e-r Sache
hinter sich bringen; *have one's* ⁓ *to the
wall fig.* mit dem Rücken zur Wand
stehen; *put* (*od.* *get*) *s.o.'s* ⁓ *up fig.* j-n
auf die Palme bringen; *put one's* ⁓ *into
s.th. fig.* sich in e-e Sache hineinknien;
turn one's ⁓ *on* j-m den Rücken zuwenden
(*dat*); *fig.* den Rücken kehren (*dat*). **2.**
Hinter-, Rückseite *f*, (*Buch-, Hand- etc*)
Rücken *m*, (Rück)Lehne *f* (*e-s Stuhls*),
linke Seite (*e-s Stoffs*). **3.** hinterer *od.*
rückwärtiger Teil: ⁓ *of the head* Hinterkopf *m*; *in the* ⁓ *of the car* auf dem
Rücksitz *od.* im Fond des Autos. **4.**
Rückenteil *m* (*e-s Kleidungsstücks*):
have one's pullover on ⁓ *to front* den
Pullover verkehrt herum anhaben. **5.**
Sport: Verteidiger *m*. **II** *adj* **6.** rückwärtig, Hinter...: ⁓ *entrance.* **7.** fern, abgelegen: ⁓ *country* Hinterland *n*. **8.** rückständig (*Zahlung*). **9.** alt, zurücklie-
gend (*Zeitung etc*). **III** *adv* **10.** zurück,
rückwärts: ⁓ *and forth* hin u. her, vor u.
zurück; *move* ⁓ zurückgehen. **11.** (wieder) zurück: *he is* ⁓ (*again*) er ist wieder da. **12.** zurück, vorher: *20 years* ⁓
vor 20 Jahren; ⁓ *in 1900* (noch *od.*
schon) im Jahre 1900. **13.** F zurück, im
Rückstand: *be* ⁓ *in one's rent* mit der
Miete im Rückstand sein. **IV** *v/t* **14.** *a.*
⁓ *up* unterstützen, j-m den Rücken
stärken, ♥ *Währung etc* stützen. **15.** *a.*
⁓ *up* zurückbewegen, rückwärts fahren
od. laufen lassen: ⁓ *the car out of the*

garage den Wagen rückwärts aus der Garage fahren. **16.** wetten *od.* setzen auf (*acc*). **V** *v/i* **17.** *oft* ~ *up* sich rückwärts bewegen, zurückgehen od. *-fahren, mot. a.* zurückstoßen: ~ *out* (*of*) rückwärts herausfahren (aus). **18.** ~ *out* (*of*) zurücktreten *od.* abspringen (von), aussteigen (aus).

'**back|·ache** *s* Rückenschmerzen *pl.* ~ **al·ley** *s Am.* finsteres Seitengäßchen. ͵~'**bench·er** *s parl. Br.* Hinterbänkler *m.* '~**bite** *v/t* (*irr bite*) lästern über *j-n.* '~**bone** *s* Rückgrat *n* (*a. fig.*), Wirbelsäule *f:* **to the** ~ *fig.* bis auf die Knochen, durch u. durch. '~**breaking** *adj* zermürbend, mörderisch. '~**chat** *s* freche Antwort(en *pl*). ~ **cloth** *s thea. bsd. Br.* Prospekt *m.* '~**date** *v/t* (zu)rückdatieren. ~ **door** *s* Hintertür *f; fig.* Hintertürchen *n.* '~**door** *adj* geheim, heimlich, *fig.* ~ **drop** *s thea.* Prospekt *m:* **be the** ~ **for** *fig.* den Hintergrund (*gen*) bilden.

back·er ['bækə] *s* Unterstützer(in), Helfer(in); Geldgeber(in).

͵**back**'**fire I** *v/i* **1.** ⚙ früh-, fehlzünden. **2.** *fig.* fehlschlagen, ins Auge gehen. **II** *s* **3.** ⚙ Früh-, Fehlzündung *f.* ~ **for·mation** *s ling.* Rückbildung *f.* '~**gam·mon** *s* Backgammon *n* (*Spiel*). '~**ground** *s* **1.** Hintergrund *m* (*a. fig.*): **against the** ~ **of** vor dem Hintergrund (*gen*); **keep in the** ~ im Hintergrund bleiben; ~ **music** musikalische Untermalung, Hintergrundsmusik *f.* **2.** *fig.* Hintergrund *m,* Umstände *pl;* Umwelt *f,* Milieu *n;* Werdegang *m;* Erfahrung *f,* Wissen *n:* ~ **information** Hintergrundinformationen *pl; educational* ~ Vorbildung *f.* '~**hand I** *s Sport:* Rückhand(schlag *m*) *f.* **II** *adj* → **backhanded.** '~**hand·ed** *adj* **1.** *Sport:* Rückhand... **2.** indirekt (*Zensur etc*). **3.** unredlich (*Methode etc*). **4.** zweifelhaft (*Kompliment etc*).

back·ing ['bækɪŋ] *s* Unterstützung *f.*

'**back|·lash** *s* (heftige) Reaktion (**to** auf *acc*). '~**log** *s* (*Arbeits-, Auftrags- etc*)Rückstand *m;* Überhang *m* (**of** an *dat*): ~ **demand** Nachholbedarf *m.* ~ **num·ber** *s* **1.** alte Nummer (*e-r Zeitung etc*). **2.** F rückständige Person *od.* Sache. '~**pack** *s bsd. Am.* Rucksack *m.* '~**pack·ing** *s bsd. Am.* Rucksacktou-

rismus *m.* ͵~'**ped·al** *v/i pret u. pp* -**aled,** *bsd. Br.* -**alled 1.** rückwärts treten (*Radfahrer*). **2.** *fig.* e-n Rückzieher machen. '~**seat** *s Bildsatz m:* **take a** ~ F in den Hintergrund treten (**to** gegenüber). '~**seat driv·er** *s* F Besserwisser(in). ͵~'**side** *s* **1.** Kehr-, Rückseite *f.* **2.** F Hintern *m.* ͵~'**slide** *v/i* (*irr slide*) rückfällig werden. '~**stage** *adj u. adv thea.* hinter den Kulissen (*a. fig.*). '~**stair** → **backstairs II.** ͵~'**stairs I** *s pl* **1.** Hintertreppe *f.* **II** *adj* **2.** *gossip* (*talk*) (bösartige) Anspielungen *pl* (*about* auf *acc*). **3.** ~ *influence* Protektion *f.* ~ *street* s Seitenstraße *f.* '~**street** *adj* heimlich: ~ *abortion* illegale Abtreibung; ~ *abortionist* Engelmacher(in). '~**stroke** *s* Rückenschwimmen *n.* ~ **talk** *s bsd. Am.* F freche Antwort(en *pl*). '~**track** *v/i* **1.** denselben Weg zurückgehen. **2.** *fig.* sich zurückziehen (**from** von), e-n Rückzieher machen; e-e Kehrtwendung machen. '~**up** *s* **1.** Unterstützung *f.* **2.** *mot. Am.* (Rück)Stau *m.* **3.** *fig.* Rückzieher *m* (**on** hinsichtlich). **4.** ⚙ Ersatzgerät *n.*

back·ward ['bækwəd] **I** *adj* **1.** rückwärts gerichtet, Rückwärts...: ~ *flow* Rückfluß *m; a* ~ *glance* ein Blick zurück *od.* nach hinten. **2.** *fig.* in der Entwicklung *etc* zurück(geblieben). **3.** rückständig: *be* ~ *in one's work* mit s-r Arbeit in Rückstand liegen. **II** *adv* **4.** rückwärts, zurück: ~ *and forward* hin u. her, vor u. zurück. **back·wards** ['~dz] → **backward II.**

'**back|·wash** *s* **1.** Rückströmung *f,* ⚓ *a.* Kielwasser *n.* **2.** *fig.* Aus-, Nachwirkung(en *pl*) *f.* '~**wa·ter** *s* **1.** → **backwash** 1. **2.** Stauwasser *n.* **3.** *fig.* Ort *m od.* Zustand *m* der Rückständigkeit u. Stagnation. '~**woods** *s pl* **1.** unerschlossenes Waldgebiet. **2.** *contp.* Provinz *f.* '~**woods·man** ['~mən] *s* (*irr man*) *contp.* Hinterwäldler *m.* ͵~'**yard** *s* **1.** *Br.* Hinterhof *m.* **2.** *Am.* Garten *m* hinter dem Haus.

ba·con ['beɪkən] *s* Frühstücks-, Schinkenspeck *m:* **bring home the** ~ F die Brötchen verdienen; Erfolg haben; **save one's** ~ *Br.* F mit heiler Haut davonkommen.

bac·te·ri·al [bæk'tɪərɪəl] *adj* □ bakteriell. **bac·te·ri·o·log·i·cal** [bæk͵tɪərɪə-

'lɒdʒɪkl] *adj* □ bakteriologisch, Bakterien... **bac·te·ri·ol·o·gist** [ˌtɪərɪˈɒlədʒɪst] *s* Bakteriologe *m*. **bac·te·ri·um** [ˌtɪərɪəm] *pl* **-ri·a** [ˌtɪərɪə] *s* Bakterie *f*.

bad [bæd] **I** *adj comp* **worse** [wɜːs] *sup* **worst** [wɜːst] (□ → *badly*) **1.** *allg.* schlecht: a) fehler-, mangelhaft (*Qualität, Zustand etc*): **not** ~ nicht schlecht *od.* übel; ~ **trip** *sl.* Bad Trip *m* (*Drogenrausch mit Angstzuständen*), b) ungünstig (*Nachricht etc*), c) schädlich, ungesund (*for* für): ~ *for one's health* ungesund, d) verdorben (*Nahrungsmittel*): **go** ~ schlecht werden, verderben, e) angegriffen (*Gesundheit*), f) widerlich (*Geruch*), g) schwach (*at* in e-m Fach). **2.** böse: a) schlimm, schwer (*Verbrechen, Erkältung etc*), b) ungezogen (*Junge etc*). **3.** unanständig, unflätig, (*Wort u.*) häßlich: ~ *language* unanständige Ausdrücke *pl*; beleidigende Äußerungen *pl*. **4.** ungedeckt (*Scheck*), ungültig (*Münze etc*): ~ *debts pl* ✝ zweifelhafte Forderungen *pl*. **5.** unangenehm, ärgerlich: *that's too* ~ das ist (doch) zu dumm. **6.** unwohl, krank: **she is** (*od.* **feels**) **very** ~ *today* es geht ihr heute sehr schlecht; *he felt* ~ *at* (*od.* *about*) *it* er war (sehr) deprimiert darüber. **II** *s* **7.** *das Schlechte:* **go from** ~ *to* **worse** immer schlimmer werden; **go to the** ~ auf die schiefe Bahn geraten; **be in the** ~ **with** F schlecht angeschrieben sein bei. **8.** ✝ Defizit *n*: **be £ 100 to the** ~ ein Defizit *od.* e-n Verlust von 100 Pfund haben. **III** *adv* **9.** F → *badly*.

bade [bæd] *pret u. pp von* bid.

badge [bædʒ] *s* **1.** (✕ Rang)Abzeichen *n*. **2.** *fig.* Kennzeichen *n*.

badg·er ['bædʒə] **I** *s zo.* Dachs *m*. **II** *v/t* plagen, *j-m* zusetzen (*for* wegen).

bad·ly ['bædlɪ] *adv* **1.** schlecht, schlimm: *he is* ~ *off* es geht ihm sehr schlecht; *do* ~ schlecht fahren (*in* bei, mit). **2.** dringend, sehr: ~ *needed* dringend nötig. **3.** schwer: ~ *wounded*.

bad·min·ton ['bædmɪntən] *s* Federball(spiel *n*) *m*, *Sport:* Badminton *n*.

‚bad-'tem·pered *adj* schlechtgelaunt.

baf·fle ['bæfl] *v/t* **1.** verwirren, -blüffen: **be** ~ *d* vor e-m Rätsel stehen. **2.** *Plan etc* durchkreuzen, vereiteln: *it* ~ *s* (*all*) *description* es spottet jeder Beschreibung.

bag [bæg] **I** *s* **1.** Sack *m*; Beutel *m*; Tasche *f*; Tüte *f*: ~ *and baggage* mit Sack u. Pack; ~ *s of* F jede Menge (*Geld etc*). **2.** *hunt.* (Jagd)Beute *f*, Strecke *f*. **3.** (*pair of*) ~ *s pl bsd. Br.* F Hose *f*. **II** *v/t* **4.** in e-n Sack *od.* Säcke stecken; in Beutel verpacken *od.* abfüllen. **5.** *hunt.* zur Strecke bringen. **6.** F klauen, stehlen. **III** *v/i* **7.** a. ~ *out* sich bauschen.

bag·a·telle [ˌbægəˈtel] *s* Bagatelle *f*.

bag·gage ['bægɪdʒ] *s bsd. Am.* (Reise)Gepäck *n*. ~ *al·low·ance s* ✈ *bsd. Am.* Freigepäck *n*. ~ *car s* 🚃 *Am.* Gepäckwagen *m*. ~ *check s bsd. Am.* Gepäckschein *m*. ~ *in·sur·ance s bsd. Am.* Reisegepäckversicherung *f*. ~ *lock·er s bsd. Am.* Gepäckschließfach *n*. ~ *re·claim s* ✈ *bsd. Am.* Gepäckausgabe *f*.

bag·gy ['bægɪ] *adj* **1.** bauschig. **2.** ausgebeult (*Hose*).

'bag‚pip·er *s* Dudelsackpfeifer *m*. **'~‚pipes** *s pl* ♪ Dudelsack *m*. **'~‚snatch·er** *s* Handtaschenräuber *m*.

bah [bɑː] *int contp.* bah!

bail¹ [beɪl] ⚖ **I** *s* **1.** Bürge(n *pl*) *m*. **2.** (Haft)Kaution *f*, Sicherheitsleistung *f*: **be out on** ~ gegen Kaution auf freiem Fuß sein; **go** (*od.* **stand**) ~ *for s.o.* für j-n Kaution stellen. **II** *v/t* **3.** ~ *s.o.* **out** j-s Freilassung gegen Kaution erwirken.

bail² [~] **I** *v/t mst* ~ *out* Wasser, Boot etc ausschöpfen. **II** *v/i:* ~ *out* ✈ aussteigen (*a.* F *fig.* of aus), (mit dem Fallschirm) abspringen.

bail³ [~] *s* Henkel *m* (*e-s Eimers etc*).

bail·iff ['beɪlɪf] *s Br.* **1.** ⚖ Gerichtsvollzieher *m*. **2.** (Guts)Verwalter *m*.

bait [beɪt] **I** *s* **1.** Köder *m* (*a. fig.*): **rise to** (*od.* **swallow, take**) **the** ~ anbeißen (*a. fig.*). **II** *v/t* **2.** mit e-n Köder versehen. **3.** *fig.* ködern. **4.** *hunt.* (mit Hunden) hetzen. **5.** *fig.* quälen, peinigen.

bake [beɪk] **I** *v/t* **1.** backen: ~ *d beans pl* Baked Beans *pl* (*in Tomatensoße gekochte Bohnen*); ~ *d potatoes pl* ungeschälte, im Ofen gebackene Kartoffeln. **2.** dörren, härten; *Ziegel* brennen; *Lack* einbrennen. **II** *v/i* **3.** backen, *mst fig.* (*in der Sonne*) braten. **4.** zs.- *od.* festbacken. **'bak·er** *s* Bäcker *m*: **at the** ~ *'s* beim Bäcker; ~ *'s dozen* dreizehn. **'bak·er·y** *s* Bäckerei *f*; **‚bak·ing-'hot** *adj* glühendheiß (*Tag etc*).

ban

bak·ing pow·der s Backpulver n.
bal·ance ['bæləns] **I** s **1.** Waage f. **2.** Gleichgewicht n: a) Balance f, b) a. ~ *of mind* Fassung f: *in the* ~ *fig.* in der Schwebe; *hold the* ~ *fig.* das Zünglein an der Waage bilden; *keep one's* ~ das Gleichgewicht halten; *fig.* sich nicht aus der Fassung bringen lassen; *lose one's* ~ das Gleichgewicht od. (*fig.*) die Fassung verlieren; *strike a* ~ *between ... and fig.* e-n Mittelweg finden zwischen (*dat*) ... u.; *throw s.o. off* (*his*) ~ *fig.* j-n aus der Fassung bringen; ~ *of power pol.* Gleichgewicht der Kräfte. **3.** *bsd. fig.* (*to*) Gegengewicht n (zu), Ausgleich m (für). **4.** † Bilanz f; Saldo m, Guthaben n; Restbetrag m: ~ *of payments* Zahlungsbilanz; ~ *of trade* Handelsbilanz; *on* ~ *fig.* alles in allem. **II** v/t **5.** *fig.* ab-, erwägen. **6.** (*o.s.* sich) im Gleichgewicht halten; balancieren. **7.** ins Gleichgewicht bringen, ausbalancieren. **8.** † *Konten, Rechnungen* ausgleichen, saldieren. **III** v/i **9.** sich im Gleichgewicht halten (*a. fig.*); balancieren. **10.** † sich ausgleichen. **'bal·anced** *adj fig.* ausgewogen, -geglichen.
bal·ance| **sheet** s † Bilanz f. ~ **wheel** s ☉ Unruh f (e-r Uhr).
bal·anc·ing ['bælənsɪŋ] *adj* Balance..., Balancier...: ~ *act* Balanceakt m (*a. fig.*); ~ *pole* Balancierstange f.
bal·co·ny ['bælkənɪ] s Balkon m, *thea. a.* zweiter Rang.
bald [bɔːld] *adj* □ **1.** kahl: *go* ~ e-e Glatze bekommen, kahl werden. **2.** (völlig) abgefahren (*Reifen*).
bal·der·dash ['bɔːldədæʃ] s Quatsch m, Unsinn m.
'bald·head s Kahl-, Glatzkopf m; **,~'head·ed** *adj* kahl-, glatzköpfig.
bale¹ [beɪl] **I** s † Ballen m: *in* ~*s* ballenweise. **II** v/t in Ballen verpacken.
bale² [~] → **bail²**.
balk [bɔːk] v/i **1.** stocken, stutzen. **2.** scheuen (*at* vor *dat*) (*Pferd*). **3.** (*at*) sträuben (gegen); zurückschrecken (vor *dat*).
ball¹ [bɔːl] **I** s **1.** Ball m; Kugel f; Knäuel m, n: *be on the* ~ F auf Draht sein; *the* ~ *is with you* (*od. in your court*) du bist an der Reihe od. am Zug; *have the* ~ *at one's feet Br.* s-e große Chance haben; *keep the* ~ *rolling* das Gespräch od. die

Sache in Gang halten; *play* ~ F mitmachen, spuren; *set* (*od. start*) *the* ~ *rolling* den Stein ins Rollen bringen. **2.** *anat.* ~ *of the eye* Augapfel m; ~ *of the foot* Fußballen m; ~ *of the thumb* Handballen m. **3.** *pl* V Eier pl (*Hoden*). **II** v/t u. v/i **4.** (sich) zs.-ballen.
ball² [~] s Ball m (*Tanzveranstaltung*): *have a* ~ *bsd. Am.* F sich köstlich amüsieren.
bal·lad ['bæləd] s Ballade f.
,ball-and-'sock·et *adj*: ~ *joint anat.*, ☉ Kugelgelenk n.
bal·last ['bæləst] *bsd.* ⚓, ⚓ **I** s Ballast m. **II** v/t mit Ballast beladen.
ball| **bear·ing** s ☉ Kugellager n. ~ **boy** s Sport: Balljunge f.
bal·let ['bæleɪ] s Ballett n. ~ **danc·er** s Balletttänzer(in).
bal·lis·tics [bə'lɪstɪks] s pl (*meist sg konstruiert*) ✕, *phys.* Ballistik f.
bal·loon [bə'luːn] **I** s **1.** (Frei-, Fessel-, Luft)Ballon m. **2.** Sprech-, Denkblase f. **II** v/i **3.** sich (auf)blähen. **bal'loon·ist** s Ballonfahrer(in).
bal·lot ['bælət] **I** s **1.** Stimmzettel m. **2.** Gesamtzahl f der abgegebenen Stimmen: *large* ~ hohe Wahlbeteiligung. **3.** (*bsd.* geheime) Wahl *od.* Abstimmung: *have* (*od. hold, take*) *a* ~ abstimmen (*on* über *acc*). **4.** Wahlgang m. **II** v/i **5.** (*for*) stimmen (für), (*bsd.* in geheimer Wahl) wählen (*acc*). ~ **box** s Wahlurne f. ~ **card**, ~ **pa·per** s Stimmzettel m.
'ball|·point (**pen**) s Kugelschreiber m. **'~·room** s Ball-, Tanzsaal m.
bal·ly·hoo [,bælɪ'huː] s F **1.** Wirbel m, Tamtam n, Getue n (*about* um). **2.** marktschreierische Reklame.
balm [bɑːm] s Balsam m (*a. fig.*). **'balm·y** *adj* □ **1.** balsamisch. **2.** lind, mild (*Wetter*). **3.** *bsd. Am. sl.* bekloppt, verrückt: *go* ~ überschnappen.
ba·lo·ney → **boloney**.
bal·us·trade [,bælə'streɪd] s Balustrade f.
bam·boo [bæm'buː] s Bambus m.
bam·boo·zle [bæm'buːzl] v/t F **1.** betrügen (*out of* um), übers Ohr hauen: ~ *s.o. into doing s.th.* j-n so einwickeln, daß er et. tut. **2.** irremachen, verwirren.
ban ['bæn] **I** v/t **1.** verbieten: ~ *s.o. from speaking* j-m Rede- *od.* Sprechverbot erteilen. **2.** *Sport:* sperren. **II** s **3.** (amt-

liches) Verbot (**on** *gen*), Sperre *f* (*a. Sport*): **import** ~ Einfuhrverbot, -sperre.

ba·nal [bə'nɑːl] *adj* □ banal, abgedroschen.

ba·nan·a [bə'nɑːnə] *s* 1. ✿ Banane *f*. 2. *sl.* **be ~s** bekloppt *od.* verrückt sein; **go ~s** überschnappen. ~ **re·pub·lic** *s* Bananenrepublik *f*.

band¹ [bænd] **I** *s* 1. Schar *f*, Gruppe *f*; *b.s.* (*bsd. Räuber*)Bande *f*. 2. (Musik)Kapelle *f*, (*Jazz-, Rock- etc*)Band *f*: **big** ~ Big Band. **II** *v/i* 3. *mst* ~ **together** sich zs.-tun, *b.s.* sich zs.-rotten.

band² [~] **I** *s* 1. Band *n*; Gurt *m*; (*Hosen- etc*)Bund *m*; Bauchbinde *f* (*e-r Zigarre*); *andersfarbiger od. -artiger Streifen.* 2. *Radio*: (Frequenz)Band *n*. 3. Ring *m*. 4. ⚙ Treibriemen *m*; Band *n*. **II** *v/t* 5. mit e-m Band zs.-binden.

band·age ['bændɪdʒ] **I** *s* ⚕ Bandage *f*; Binde *f*; Verband *m*. **II** *v/t* bandagieren; verbinden.

'band-aid *s Am.* Heftpflaster *n*.

ban·dit ['bændɪt] *s* Bandit *m*.

'band|,lead·er *s* ♪ Bandleader *m*. **'~ ,mas·ter** *s* ♪ Kapellmeister *m*. **'~,wag-(g)on** *s* Wagen *m* mit e-r Musikkapelle: **climb** (*od.* **get, jump**) **on the** ~ *fig.* zur erfolgreichen Partei umschwenken.

ban·dy¹ ['bændɪ] *v/t* 1. sich *e-n* Ball *etc* zuwerfen. 2. sich *Geschichten etc* erzählen. 3. sich *Beleidigungen etc* an den Kopf werfen, sich (gegenseitig) *Komplimente, Vorwürfe* machen: ~ **blows** sich schlagen; ~ **words** sich streiten. **I** *a.* ~ **about** (*od.* **around**) *Gerücht etc* in Umlauf setzen; weitererzählen: **he has his name bandied about** sein Name fällt dauernd (**in connection with it** in Zs.-hang mit); *b.s.* er ist ins Gerede gekommen.

ban·dy² [~] *adj* 1. krumm, nach außen gebogen: ~ **legs** *pl* Säbelbeine *pl*, O-Beine *pl*. 2. → **bandy-legged.** **'~-legged** *adj* säbelbeinig, O-beinig.

bang [bæŋ] **I** *s* 1. heftiger *od.* schallender Schlag. 2. Bums *m*, Krach *m*, Knall *m*: **shut the door with a** ~ zuschlagen; zuknallen. 3. *sl.* Schuß *m* (*Heroin etc*). **II** *v/t* 4. knallen mit, *Tür etc* zuschlagen, zuknallen: ~ **one's fist on the table** mit der Faust auf den Tisch schlagen; ~ **one's head** sich den Kopf anschlagen

(**against, on** an *dat*); ~ **sense into s.o.** *fig.* j-m Vernunft einhämmern. 5. V bumsen. **III** *v/i* 6. knallen: a) krachen, b) zuschlagen (*Tür etc*), c) schießen: ~ **away** drauflosknallen; ~ **into** stoßen *od.* prallen gegen *od.* an (*acc*); *fig.* F zufällig treffen. 7. *sl.* sich e-n Schuß (*Heroin etc*) setzen *od.* drücken. 8. V bumsen. **IV** *adv* 9. mit lautem Knall: **go** ~ explodieren. 10. peng; genau: ~ **in the eye** peng ins Auge. **V** *int* 11. peng!, bum(s)! **'bang·er** *s Br.* 1. Feuerwerks-, Knallkörper *m*. 2. F (alter) Klapperkasten (*Auto*). 3. F (Brat)Wurst *f*, Würstchen *n*.

'bang-up *adj bsd. Am.* F prima.

ban·ish ['bænɪʃ] *v/t* 1. verbannen (*a. fig.*), ausweisen (**from** aus). 2. *Sorgen etc* verscheuchen, -treiben. **'ban·ish-ment** *s* Verbannung *f*, Ausweisung *f*.

ban·is·ters ['bænɪstəz] *s pl* Treppengeländer *n*.

ban·jo ['bændʒəʊ] *pl* **-jo(e)s** *s* ♪ Banjo *n*.

bank¹ [bæŋk] **I** *s* 1. ✝ Bank *f*. 2. Bank *f* (*bei Glücksspielen*): **break** (**be** *od.* **keep**) **the** ~ die Bank sprengen (halten). 3. (*Blut-, Daten- etc*)Bank *f*. **II** *v/i* 4. ein Bankkonto haben (**with** bei). 5. die Bank halten (*bei Glücksspielen*). 6. ~ **on** bauen *od.* sich verlassen auf (*acc*). **III** *v/t* 7. *Geld* bei e-r Bank einzahlen, auf die Bank bringen.

bank² [~] **I** *s* 1. (Erd)Wall *m*; Böschung *f*; Überhöhung *f* (*e-r Straße etc in Kurven*). 2. (*Fluß- etc*)Ufer *n*. 3. (*Sand*)Bank *f*. 4. Zs.-ballung *f*: ~ **of clouds** Wolkenbank *f*; ~ **of snow** Schneewall *m*, -wächte *f*. **II** *v/t* 5. mit e-m Wall umgeben. 6. *Straße etc* (*in der Kurve*) überhöhen. 7. ~ **up** aufhäufen, zs.-ballen. **III** *v/i* 8. ~ **up** sich aufhäufen, sich zs.-ballen. 9. überhöht sein (*Straße, Kurve*).

bank·a·ble ['bæŋkəbl] *adj fig.* zuverlässig, verläßlich.

bank| ac·count *s* Bankkonto *n*. ~ **bill** *Am.* → **bank note.** **'~-book** *s* Sparbuch *n*. ~ **card** *s* Scheckkarte *f*. ~ **clerk** *s* Bankangestellte *m, f*.

bank·er ['bæŋkə] *s* 1. ✝ Bankier *m*. 2. Bankhalter *m* (*bei Glücksspielen*).

bank| hold-up *s* Banküberfall *m*. ~ **hol·i·day** *s Br.* Bankfeiertag *m*.

bank·ing ['bæŋkɪŋ] ✝ **I** s Bankwesen n. **II** adj Bank...: **~ hours** pl Öffnungszeiten pl (e-r Bank).

bank| man·ag·er s Bankdirektor m. **~ note** s Banknote f, Geldschein m. **~ raid** s Banküberfall m, -raub m. **~ raid·er** s Bankräuber m. **~ rate** s ✝ Diskontsatz m. **~ rob·ber** s Bankräuber m. **~ rob·ber·y** s Bankraub m, -überfall m.

bank·rupt ['bæŋkrʌpt] ⚖ **I** s **1.** Konkurs-, Gemeinschuldner m: **~'s estate** (od. **property**) Konkursmasse f. **2.** (betrügerischer) Bankrotteur. **II** adj **3.** bankrott: **go ~** in Konkurs gehen, Bankrott machen; **declare o.s. ~** Konkurs anmelden. **bank·rupt·cy** ['~rəptsɪ] s ⚖ Bankrott m, Konkurs m.

ban·ner ['bænə] s **1.** Standarte f; Banner n. **2.** Spruchband n, Transparent n. **3.** a. **~ headline** Balkenüberschrift f, breite Schlagzeile. **II** adj **4.** Am. hervorragend.

banns [bænz] s pl eccl. Aufgebot n: **have one's ~ called** das Aufgebot bestellen.

ban·quet ['bæŋkwɪt] **I** s Bankett n, Festessen n. **II** v/i tafeln.

ban·tam·weight ['bæntəmweɪt] (Sport) **I** s Bantamgewicht(ler m) n. **II** adj Bantamgewichts...

ban·ter ['bæntə] v/t u. v/i necken. **II** s Neckerei f.

bap·tism ['bæptɪzəm] s eccl. Taufe f. **bap·tis·mal** [~'tɪzml] adj Tauf...: **~ font** Taufbecken n. **'Bap·tist** s Baptist(in).

bap·tize [~'taɪz] v/t taufen.

bar [ba:] **I** s **1.** Stange f, Stab m: **~s** od. Gitter n; **behind ~s** fig. hinter Schloß u. Riegel. **2.** Riegel m. **3.** Schranke f, Sperre f; fig. Hindernis n (to für). **4.** Riegel m, Stange f: **a ~ of soap** ein Riegel od. Stück Seife; **a ~ of chocolate** ein Riegel (weitS.) e-e Tafel) Schokolade. **5.** (Gold- etc)Barren m. **6.** (dicker) Strich. **7.** ♪ Taktstrich m; ein Takt m. **8.** ⚖ (Gerichts)Schranke f: **prisoner at the ~** Angeklagte m,f. **9.** ⚖ Anwaltsberuf m; coll. Anwaltschaft f, Br. Stand m der **barristers: be admitted** (Br. **called**) **to the ~** als Anwalt (Br. **barrister**) zugelassen werden; **read for the ~** Br. Jura studieren. **10.** (Tor-, Quer-, Sprung)Latte f. **11.** Bar f; Lokal n, Imbißstube f; Bar f, Theke f. **II** v/t **12.**

verriegeln. **13.** a. **~ up** vergittern. **14.** a. **~ in** einsperren: **~ out** aussperren. **15.** hemmen; (from) hindern (an dat), abhalten (von). **III** prp **16.** außer, abgesehen von: **~ none** (alle) ohne Ausnahme.

barb [ba:b] s **1.** Widerhaken m; Stachel m. **2.** fig. Spitze f.

bar·bar·i·an [ba:'beərɪən] **I** s Barbar(in). **II** adj barbarisch. **bar·bar·ic** [~'bærɪk] adj (~ally) barbarisch. **bar·ba·rism** ['~bərɪzəm] s **1.** Barbarismus m, Sprachwidrigkeit f. **2.** Barbarei f. **bar·bar·i·ty** [~'bærətɪ] s Barbarei f. **bar·ba·rize** ['~baraɪz] v/t barbarisieren. **'bar·ba·rous** adj □ barbarisch.

bar·be·cue ['ba:bɪkju:] **I** v/t auf dem Rost od. am Spieß braten, grillen. **II** s Barbecue n: a) Grillfest n, b) Bratrost m, Grill m, c) auf dem Rost od. Grill gebratenes Fleisch.

barbed [ba:bd] adj **1.** mit Widerhaken od. Stacheln: **~ wire** Stacheldraht m. **2.** fig. spitz (Bemerkung etc).

bar·ber ['ba:bə] s (Herren)Friseur m: **~('s) shop** Friseurgeschäft n.

bar·bi·tu·rate [ba:'bɪtjʊrət] s ⚗ etc Barbiturat n.

bare [beə] **I** adj (□ → **barely**) **1.** nackt: a) entblößt: **on one's ~ feet** barfuß; **in one's ~ skin** nackt, b) kahl (Wand etc), c) fig. ungeschminkt: **~ facts** pl nackte Tatsachen pl. **2.** fig. unverhüllt: **~ nonsense** blanker Unsinn; **lay ~** → **13.**. **3.** **~ of** arm an (dat); ohne, ...los. **4.** knapp (Mehrheit etc): **earn a ~ living** knapp das Nötigste zum Leben verdienen. **5.** bloß: **the ~ thought** allein od. schon der Gedanke. **II** v/t **6.** entblößen, weitS. Zähne zeigen. **7.** fig. enthüllen, bloßlegen. **'~·back(ed)** adj u. adv ungesattelt, ohne Sattel. **'~-faced** adj unverschämt, schamlos. **'~foot**, **'~foot·ed** adj u. adv barfuß, -füßig. **'~head·ed** adj u. adv barhäuptig.

bare·ly ['beəlɪ] adv **1.** kaum, knapp. **2.** ärmlich, spärlich.

bar·gain ['ba:gɪn] **I** s **1.** Handel m, Geschäft n (a. fig.): **it's a ~!** abgemacht!; **into the ~** noch dazu, obendrein; **make the best of a bad ~** sich so gut wie möglich aus der Affäre ziehen; **strike a ~** ein Geschäft abschließen; → **drive 12.**. **2.** vorteilhaftes Geschäft, Gelegenheitskauf m. **II** v/i **3.** handeln, feilschen (**for** um). **4.** verhandeln (**for** über *acc*): ~ **on** vereinbaren (*acc*). **5.** (**for**) rechnen (mit), gefaßt sein (auf *acc*). **III** *v/t* **6.** aushandeln. ~ **base·ment** *s* Niedrigpreisabteilung *f* im Tiefgeschoß (*e-s Kaufhauses*). ~ **count·er** *s* Wühltisch *m*. ~ **price** *s* Gelegenheits-, Sonderpreis *m*. ~ **sale** *s* **1.** Verkauf *m* zu herabgesetzten Preisen. **2.** Ausverkauf *m*.

barge [bɑːdʒ] **I** *s* **1.** Last-, Schleppkahn *m*. **II** *v/i* **2.** sich schwerfällig bewegen. **3.** F (*into*) stoßen, prallen, bumsen (gegen, an *acc*). **4.** ~ **in(to)** F hereinplatzen (in *acc*); sich einmischen (in *acc*).

bar·i·tone ['bærɪtəʊn] *s* ♪ Bariton *m*.

bark[1] [bɑːk] **I** *s* **1.** (Baum)Rinde *f*, Borke *f*. **II** *v/t* **2.** abrinden. **3.** sich *die Knie etc* auf-, abschürfen: ~ **one's knees.**

bark[2] [~] **I** *v/i* bellen (*a.* F *husten*): ~ **at s.o.** j-n anbellen; *fig.* j-n anschnauzen; *,ing dogs never bite* Hunde, die bellen, beißen nicht; ~ **up the wrong tree** F auf dem Holzweg sein; an der falschen Adresse sein. **II** *s* Bellen (*a.* F *Husten*): *his* ~ *is worse than his bite* er bellt nur(, aber beißt nicht).

'**bar,keep·er** *s* Barkeeper *m*: a) Barbesitzer *m*, b) Barmann *m*, -mixer *m*.

bar·ley ['bɑːlɪ] *s* ♀ Gerste *f*.

'**bar|·maid** *s bsd. Br.* Bardame *f*. ~·**man** ['~mən] *s* (*irr man*) Barmann *m*, -keeper *m*, -mixer *m*.

barm·y ['bɑːmɪ] *adj sl.* bekloppt, verrückt: *go* ~ überschnappen.

barn [bɑːn] *s* **1.** Scheune *f*. **2.** (Vieh-) Stall *m*.

ba·rom·e·ter [bə'rɒmɪtə] *s* Barometer *n* (*a. fig.*).

bar·on ['bærən] *s* **1.** Baron *m*. **2.** (*Industrie- etc*)Baron *m*, Magnat *m*. '**bar·on·ess** *s* Baronin *f*. **bar·on·et** ['~nɪt] *s* Baronet *m*.

ba·roque [bə'rɒk] **I** *adj* barock. **II** *s* Barock *n*, *m*.

bar·racks ['bærəks] *s pl (meist sg konstruiert)* **1.** Kaserne *f*. **2.** *contp.* Mietskaserne *f*.

bar·rage ['bærɑːʒ] *s* **1.** (Stau)Damm *m*, Talsperre *f*. **2.** ✕ Sperrfeuer *n*. **3.** *fig.* Hagel *m*, Schwall *m*.

bar·rel ['bærəl] **I** *s* **1.** Faß *n*, (*Rohölmaß mst*) Barrel *n*: ~**s** (*od.* **a** ~) **of** F ein Haufen (*Geld etc*). **2.** (Gewehr)Lauf *m*, (Geschütz)Rohr *n*. **II** *v/t pret u. pp*

-**reled**, *bsd. Br.* -**relled 3.** in Fässer füllen: ~(*l*)**ed beer** Faßbier *n*. ~ **or·gan** *s* ♪ Drehorgel *f*, Leierkasten *m*.

bar·ren ['bærən] *adj* □ **1.** unfruchtbar (*Lebewesen, Land etc*). **2.** geistig unproduktiv. **3.** ~ **of** arm an (*dat*), ...los. **4.** nutzlos, ✝ tot (*Kapital*).

bar·rette [bæ'ret] *s Am.* Haarspange *f*.

bar·ri·cade [ˌbærɪ'keɪd] **I** *s* Barrikade *f*: **go to** (*od.* **mount**) **the** ~**s** *fig.* auf die Barrikaden gehen *od.* steigen. **II** *v/t* verbarrikadieren.

bar·ri·er ['bærɪə] *s* **1.** Schranke *f*, Barriere *f*, Sperre *f*. **2.** Schlag-, Grenzbaum *m*. **3.** *phys.* (*Schall*)Grenze *f*. **4.** *fig.* Hindernis *n* (**to** für). ~ **cream** *s* Schutzcreme *f*.

bar·ring ['bɑːrɪŋ] *prp* ausgenommen, abgesehen von: **a miracle** falls *od.* wenn kein Wunder geschieht.

bar·ris·ter ['bærɪstə] *s* ✐ **1.** *Br.* Barrister *m* (*vor höheren Gerichten plädierender Anwalt*). **2.** *Am. allg.* Rechtsanwalt *m*.

bar·row ['bærəʊ] *s* (Hand-, Schub)Karre(n *m*) *f*.

'**bar,tend·er** *bsd. Am.* → **barman.**

bar·ter ['bɑːtə] **I** *v/t* **1.** (ein)tauschen (**against, for** gegen). **II** *v/i* verhandeln (**for** über *acc*). **III** *s* Tausch(handel *m*, -geschäft *n*) *m*.

ba·salt ['bæsɔːlt] *s geol.* Basalt *m*.

base[1] [beɪs] *adj* □ **1.** gemein, niederträchtig. **2.** minderwertig, (*Metall*) unedel.

base[2] [~] **I** *s* **1.** *a. fig.* Basis *f*, Grundlage *f*, Fundament *n* (*a.* △). **2.** Grundstoff *m*, Hauptbestandteil *m*. **3.** *fig.* Ausgangspunkt *m*, -basis *f*. **4.** ✕ Standort *m*; Basis *f*, Stützpunkt *m*. **5.** *Baseball:* Mal *n*. **II** *v/t* stützen, gründen (**on** auf *acc*): **be** ~**d on** beruhen *od.* basieren auf (*dat*).

'**base|·ball** *s Sport:* Baseball(spiel *n*) *m*. '~·**board** *s Am.* Fuß(boden)-, Scheuerleiste *f*. '~·**less** *adj* □ grundlos. ~ **line** *s* Grundlinie *f*.

base·ment ['beɪsmənt] *s* Kellergeschoß *n*.

base·ness ['beɪsnɪs] *s* **1.** Gemeinheit *f*, Niedertracht *f*. **2.** Minderwertigkeit *f*.

ba·ses ['beɪsiːz] *pl von* **basis.**

bash [bæʃ] F **I** *v/t* **1.** heftig schlagen, j-n verprügeln: ~ **in** einschlagen. **II** *s* **2.** heftiger Schlag: **give s.o. a** ~ (**on the**

nose) *j-m* ein Ding (auf die Nase) verpassen. **3.** Versuch *m*: **have a ~ at s.th.** es mit et. probieren.

bash·ful ['bæʃful] *adj* □ scheu, schüchtern.

bas·ic ['beɪsɪk] **I** *adj* grundlegend, Grund...: **~ fact** grundlegende Tatsache; **~ fee** (*law, salary, etc*) Grundgebühr *f* (-gesetz *n*, -gehalt *n etc*). **II** *s pl* Grundlagen *pl*. **'bas·i·cal·ly** *adv* **1.** im Grunde. **2.** im wesentlichen.

ba·sil·i·ca [bə'zɪlɪkə] *s* △ Basilika *f*.

ba·sin ['beɪsn] *s allg.* Becken *n* (*a. geol. etc*); *engS.* Schale *f*, Schüssel *f*.

ba·sis ['beɪsɪs] *pl* **-ses** [-siːz] *s* **1.** ✕ Basis *f*, Stützpunkt *m*. **2.** *fig.* Basis *f*, Grundlage *f*: **on the ~ of** auf der Basis von (*od. gen*); **~ of discussion** Diskussionsgrundlage; **take as a ~** zugrunde legen.

bask [bɑːsk] *v/i* sich sonnen (*a. fig.*): **~ in the sun** ein Sonnenbad nehmen.

bas·ket ['bɑːskɪt] *s* Korb *m*. **'~·ball** *s Sport*: Basketball(spiel *n*) *m*.

bass [beɪs] *s* ♪ Baß(stimme *f*) *m*; Bassist *m*.

bas·soon [bə'suːn] *s* ♪ Fagott *n*.

bas·tard ['bɑːstəd] **I** *s* **1.** Bastard *m* (*a. biol.*). **2.** *sl.* Scheißkerl *m*, Kerl *m*: **poor ~** armes Schwein; **a ~ of a headache** verfluchte Kopfschmerzen *pl*. **II** *adj* **3.** unehelich. **4.** *biol.* Bastard...

baste¹ [beɪst] *v/t* Braten mit Fett begießen.

baste² [~] *v/t* verprügeln.

baste³ [~] *v/t* (an)heften.

bas·tion ['bæstɪən] *s* ✕ Bastion *f*.

bat¹ [bæt] *s zo.* Fledermaus *f*: **(as) blind as a ~** stockblind; **have ~s in the belfry** F e-n Vogel haben.

bat² [~] **I** *s* **1.** *Baseball, Kricket*: Schlagholz *n*, Schläger *m*: **off one's own ~** *fig.* selbständig; auf eigene Faust. **2.** *Br.* F Tempo *n*: **at a fair ~** mit e-m ganz schönen Zahn. **3.** *Am. sl.* Sauferei *f*: **go on a ~** e-e Sauftour machen. **II** *v/i* **4.** *Baseball, Kricket*: am Schlagen sein.

bat³ [~] *v/t*: **without ~ting an eyelid** ohne mit der Wimper zu zucken.

batch [bætʃ] *s* Stapel *m*, Stoß *m*.

bat·ed ['beɪtɪd] *adj*: **with ~ breath** mit angehaltenem Atem, gespannt.

bath [bɑːθ] **I** *pl* **baths** ['~ðz] *s* **1.** (Wannen)Bad *n*: **have** (*od. take*) **a ~** ein Bad

nehmen, baden. **2.** Badewanne *f*. **3.** Bad(ezimmer) *n*. **4.** *mst pl* Bad *n*: a) Badeanstalt *f*, b) Badeort *m*. **5.** 🏵, *phot.* Bad *n*. **II** *v/t* **6.** *Br. Kind etc* baden. **III** *v/i* **7.** *Br.* baden, ein Bad nehmen.

bathe [beɪð] **I** *v/t* **1.** *Wunde etc, bsd. Am. a. Kind etc* baden. **2.** **~d in sunlight** (**sweat, tears**) *fig.* sonnenüberflutet (schweißgebadet, tränenüberströmt). **II** *v/i* **3.** *bsd. Am.* baden, ein Bad nehmen. **4.** baden, schwimmen. **III** *s* **5.** Bad *n* (*im Freien*): **have** (*od. take*) **a ~ → 4.**

bath·ing ['beɪðɪŋ] **I** *s* Baden *n*. **II** *adj* Bade...: **~ accident** (**cap, costume od. dress od. suit, trunks**) Badeunfall *m* (-mütze *f od.* -kappe *f*, -anzug *m*, -hose *f*).

'bath·robe *s* **1.** Bademantel *m*. **2.** *Am.* Morgen-, Schlafrock *m*. **~·room** ['~rʊm] *s* **1.** Badezimmer *n*. **2.** Toilette *f*. **~ tow·el** *s* Badetuch *n*. **'~·tub** *s* Badewanne *f*.

ba·tik [bə'tiːk] *s* Batik(druck) *m*.

ba·tiste [bæ'tiːst] *s* Batist *m*.

ba·ton ['bætən] *s* **1.** (Amts-, Kommando)Stab *m*. **2.** ♪ Taktstock *m*. **3.** *Leichtathletik*: (Staffel)Stab *m*. **4.** Schlagstock *m*, Gummiknüppel *m* (*der Polizei*).

bats·man ['bætsmən] *s* (*irr man*) *Kricket*: Schläger *m*, Schlagmann *m*.

bat·tal·ion [bə'tæljən] *s* ✕ Bataillon *n*.

bat·ten¹ ['bætn] **I** *s* Latte *f*, Leiste *f*. **II** *v/t*: **~ down the hatches** ♻ die Luken schalken; *fig.* alles dichtmachen.

bat·ten² [~] *v/i mst fig.* dick u. fett werden (**on** auf Kosten *gen*).

bat·ter¹ ['bætə] *v/t* **1.** wiederholt heftig schlagen; *Frau, Kind etc* (wiederholt) mißhandeln: **~ down** (*od. in*) einschlagen; **~ed wives' refuge** Frauenhaus *n*. **2.** abnutzen. **3.** (*arg*) lädieren *od.* zerbeulen, *a. fig.* arg in Mitleidenschaft ziehen. **II** *v/i* **4.** wiederholt heftig schlagen *od.* stoßen (**against** gegen; **at** an *acc*): **~ (away) at the door** gegen die Tür hämmern. **III** *s* **5.** *gastr.* Eierkuchenteig *m*.

bat·ter² [~] *s Baseball, Kricket*: Schläger *m*, Schlagmann *m*.

bat·ter·y ['bætərɪ] *s* **1.** ⚡ Batterie *f*. **2.** Batterie *f*, Reihe *f*, Satz *m*. **3.** ✒ Legebatterie *f*. **4.** ⚖ Tätlichkeit *f*; Körper-

verletzung f. **~ hen** s ✔ Batteriehenne f.
'**~,op·er·at·ed** adj batteriebetrieben,
Batterie...

bat·tle ['bætl] **I** s **1.** ✕ Schlacht f (**of** bei).
2. fig. Kampf m (**for** um). **II** v/i **3.** bsd.
fig. kämpfen: **~ for breath** um Atem
ringen. '**~·ax(e)** s **1.** ✕ hist. Streitaxt f.
2. F alter Drachen. '**~·field**, '**~·ground**
s ✕ Schlachtfeld n: **~ country** kriegführendes Land. '**~·ship** s Schlacht-
schiff n.

bat·tue [bæ'tu:] s Treibjagd f.

bat·ty ['bætɪ] adj sl. bekloppt, verrückt.

baulk → **balk**.

baux·ite ['bɔːksaɪt] s min. Bauxit m.

Ba·var·i·an [bə'veərɪən] **I** adj bay(e)-
risch. **II** s Bayer(in).

bawd·y ['bɔːdɪ] adj unflätig, obszön.

bawl [bɔːl] **I** v/i schreien, brüllen: **~ at
s.o.** j-n anbrüllen; **~ for help** um Hilfe
schreien. **II** v/t oft **~ out** (heraus)schrei-
en, (-)brüllen.

bay¹ [beɪ] s Bai f, Bucht f.

bay² [~] s ⚒ Erker m.

bay³ [~] s ♣ Lorbeer(baum) m.

bay⁴ [~] **I** v/i bellen: **~ at s.o.** j-n anbellen;
fig. j-n anschreien. **II** s Gebell n: **be** (od.
stand) **at ~** gestellt sein (Wild); fig. in
die Enge getrieben sein; **bring to ~** Wild
stellen; fig. in die Enge treiben; **hold**
(od. **keep**) **at ~** j-n in Schach halten;
Krankheit etc von sich fernhalten; Feuer, Seuche etc unter Kontrolle halten.

bay·o·net ['beɪənɪt] s ✕ Bajonett n, Sei-
tengewehr n.

bay win·dow s **1.** Erkerfenster n. **2.** Am.
humor. Vorbau m (Bauch).

ba·zaar [bə'zɑː] s (a. Wohltätigkeits)Ba-
sar m.

be [biː] (irr) **I** v/aux **1.** Zustand: sein: **he
is gone** er ist weg. **2.** Passiv: werden: **I
was cheated** ich wurde betrogen. **3.**
sollen, müssen, dürfen, können: **he is
to be piloted** er ist zu begleiten; **it is not
to be seen** es ist nicht zu sehen; **it was
not to be** es sollte nicht sein. **4.** Verlaufsform: **he is reading** er liest (gerade); **he was watching TV when the
telephone rang** er sah gerade fern, als
das Telefon läutete. **5.** nahe Zukunft: **I
am leaving tomorrow** ich reise morgen
ab; → **go** 27. **6.** Kopula: sein: **he is my
father. II** v/i **7.** sein, der Fall sein: **how
is it that ...?** wie kommt es, daß ...?; **it is**

I (F **me**) ich bin es. **8.** sein, bestehen: **to
be or not to be: that is the question**
Sein oder Nichtsein, das ist hier die
Frage. **9.** sein, stattfinden (Versammlung etc); gehen, fahren (Bus etc). **10.**
sein, sich befinden: **have you ever
been to London?** sind Sie schon einmal
in London gewesen?; **has anyone
been?** F ist j-d dagewesen? **11.** (beruflich) werden: **I'll be an engineer** ich
werde einmal Ingenieur. **12.** gehören:
this book is mine. 13. sein, stammen
(**from** aus). **14.** kosten: **how much are
these gloves?** **15.** dauern (Veranstaltung etc).

beach [biːtʃ] **I** s Strand m: **on the ~** am
Strand. **II** v/t Schiff auf den Strand
setzen od. ziehen. **~ ball** s Wasserball
m. **~ bug·gy** s mot. Strandbuggy m. **~
tow·el** s Bade-, Strandlaken n. '**~·wear**
s Strandkleidung f.

bea·con ['biːkən] s **1.** Leucht-, Signal-
feuer n. **2.** → **Belisha beacon.**

bead [biːd] **I** s (Glas-, Schweiß-, Tau-
etc)Perle f. **2.** pl eccl. Rosenkranz m:
say (od. **tell**) **one's ~s** den Rosenkranz
beten. **II** v/t **3.** mit Perlen besetzen. **III**
v/i **4.** perlen.

beak [biːk] s **1.** orn. Schnabel m. **2.** ⚙
Tülle f. **beaked** adj **1.** schnabelförmig.
2. vorspringend, spitz.

beak·er ['biːkə] s Becher m.

beam [biːm] **I** s **1.** Balken m. **2.** Strahl m,
⚓, phys. a. Bündel n: **~ of rays** Strahlen-
bündel; **~ of hope** Hoffnungsstrahl. **3.**
Peil-, Leit-, Richtstrahl m: **be off** (the) **~**
✈, ⚓ vom Kurs abgekommen sein; F
auf dem Holzweg sein; **be on** (the) **~** ✈,
⚓ auf Kurs sein; F auf dem richtigen
Weg sein. **4.** strahlendes Lächeln. **II** v/t
5. ausstrahlen (a. phys. u. Rundfunk,
TV). **III** v/i **6.** strahlen (a. fig. with vor
dat): **~ing with joy** freudestrahlend.
'**~·ends** s pl: **be on one's ~** fig. auf
dem letzten Loch pfeifen.

bean [biːn] s **1.** ♣ Bohne f: **be full of ~s** F
aufgekratzt sein; voller Leben(skraft)
stecken; **spill the ~s** F alles ausplaudern. **2.** Am. sl. Birne f (Kopf).

bear¹ [beə] **I** s **1.** zo. Bär m. **2.** fig.
Brummbär m; Tolpatsch m. **3.** ✝ Baiss-
sespekulant m. **II** v/i **4.** ✝ auf Baisse
spekulieren.

bear² [~] (irr) **I** v/t **1.** Last, a. fig. Datum,

Verantwortung, Verlust etc tragen: → *fruit* 2a, *interest* 6, *resemblance, etc.* **2.** zur Welt bringen, gebären. **3.** *Gefühl* hegen: → *grudge* 3. **4.** *Gehorsam etc* leisten: → *company* 1. **5.** ertragen, aushalten, -stehen: → *comparison* 1. **II** *v/i* **6.** tragen, halten (*Balken, Eis etc*). **7.** (**on**) sich beziehen (**auf** *acc*), betreffen (*acc*): → *pressure.* **8.** ~ (**to the**) *left* sich links halten.

Verbindungen mit Adverbien:

~ **a·way** *v/t* **1.** forttragen. **2.** *Sieg etc* davontragen. ~ **down** *I v/t* überwinden, -wältigen, *Widerstand* brechen. **II** *v/i* (**on**) sich (schnell) nähern (*dat*); sich stürzen (auf *acc*); *fig.* lasten (auf *dat*), bedrücken (*acc*); *e-r Sache* zu Leibe gehen. ~ **in** *v/t*: *it was borne in on him* es wurde ihm klar (*that* daß). ~ **out** *v/t* bekräftigen, bestätigen; *j-m* recht geben. ~ **up** **I** *v/t* **1.** ermutigen. **II** *v/i* **2.** (**against, under**) sich behaupten (gegen), (tapfer) ertragen (*acc*). **3.** *Br.* Mut fassen, (wieder) fröhlich werden: ~*!* Kopf hoch!

bear·a·ble ['beərəbl] *adj* □ erträglich.
beard [bɪəd] *I s* Bart *m*: *laugh in one's* ~ sich ins Fäustchen lachen. **II** *v/t*: ~ *the lion in his den fig.* sich in die Höhle des Löwen wagen. '**beard·ed** *adj* bärtig. '**beard·less** *adj* bartlos.
bear·er ['beərə] *s* **1.** Träger(in). **2.** Überbringer(in) (*a.* ✝ *e-s Schecks etc*). **3.** ✝ Inhaber(in) (*e-s Wertpapiers*).
bear·ing ['beərɪŋ] *s* **1.** Ertragen *n*: *beyond* (*od.* *past*) ~ unerträglich. **2.** Betragen *n*, Verhalten *n*. **3.** (Körper)Haltung *f*. **4.** (**on**) Beziehung *f* (zu), Bezug *m* (auf *acc*). **5.** ⚓︎, ⚓ Lage *f*, Position *f*; (*a.* Funk)Peilung *f*, *a. fig.* Orientierung *f*: *take one's* ~*s* e-e Peilung vornehmen; *sich orientieren; lose one's* ~*(s)* die Orientierung verlieren; *find* (*od.* *get*) *one's* ~*s* sich zurechtfinden. **6.** ⚙ (*Achsen-, Kugel- etc*)Lager *n*.
bear·ish ['beərɪʃ] *adj* **1.** bärenhaft. **2.** *fig.* brummig; tolpatschig. **3.** ✝ flau; Baisse...
bear| **paw** *s Am.* Radkralle *f*, Parkriegel *m.* '~**·skin** *s* Bärenfell *n.*
beast [bi:st] *s* **1.** (*a.* wildes) Tier: ~ *of burden* Lasttier; ~ *of prey* Raubtier. **2.** *fig.* Bestie *f*; *F* Biest *n*, Ekel *n.* '**beast·ly**

adj **1.** *fig.* tierisch. **2.** ekelhaft, gemein; scheußlich.
beat [bi:t] **I** *s* **1.** (*Herz-, Trommeletc*)Schlag *m*. **2.** ♪ Takt *m*; (*Jazz*) Beat *m*; Beat(musik *f*) *m*: *in* ~ im Takt; *out of* ~, *off* (**the**) ~ aus dem Takt. **3.** Runde *f*, Revier *n* (*e-s Schutzmanns etc*): *be on one's* ~ s-e *od.* die Runde machen; *that is out of my* ~ *fig.* das schlägt nicht in mein Fach. **II** *adj* **4.** *F* wie erschlagen, fix u. fertig. **5.** ♪ Beat...: ~ *group* (*music, etc*). **III** *v/t* (*irr*) **6.** schlagen, (ver)prügeln. **7.** *a)* schlagen; *Teppich etc* (aus)klopfen; *Metall* hämmern *od.* schmieden, *b)* → *beat up* 3. **8.** *Weg* treten, sich bahnen: → *it F* abhauen, verduften. **9.** *j-n* schlagen, besiegen (*at* in *dat*); *et.* übertreffen, -bieten: *that* ~*s all* (*od.* *everything*)*!* das ist doch die Höhe! **10.** verblüffen: *that* ~*s me* das ist mir zu hoch. **IV** *v/i* **11.** schlagen: ~ *at* (*od.* *on*) *the door* gegen die Tür hämmern.

Verbindungen mit Adverbien:

beat| **back** *v/t* Gegner zurückschlagen. ~ **down** **I** *v/t* **1.** *Aufstand etc* niederschlagen. **2.** *Preis* drücken, *a. j-n* herunterhandeln (*to auf acc*). **II** *v/i* **3.** herunterbrennen (**on** *auf acc*) (*Sonne*); herunter-, niederprasseln (**on** *auf acc*) (*Regen*). ~ **off** *v/t Angriff*, *Gegner* zurückschlagen. ~ **in** *v/t Tür* einschlagen. ~ **out** *v/t Feuer* ausschlagen. ~ **up** *v/t* **1.** aufrütteln (*a. fig.*). **2.** *j-n* zs.-schlagen. **3.** *Eier etc* (zu Schaum *od.* Schnee) schlagen.

beat·en ['bi:tn] **I** *pp von* **beat.** **II** *adj* **1.** ⚙ gehämmert: ~ *gold* Blattgold *n.* **2.** vielbegangen (*Weg*): *off the* ~ *track* ungewohnt, ungewöhnlich. '**beat·er** *s* **1.** ⚙ Stampfe *f*; Stößel *m*; Klopfer *m.* **2.** *gastr.* Schneebesen *m.* '**beat·ing** *s* Prügel *pl*; *fig.* Niederlage *f*: *give s.o. a sound* ~ *j-m* e-e tüchtige Tracht Prügel verabreichen; *j-m* e-e böse Schlappe zufügen.
beat·nik ['bi:tnɪk] *s* Beatnik *m.*
beau·ti·cian [bju:'tɪʃn] *s* Kosmetiker(in).
beau·ti·ful ['bju:təfʊl] *adj* □ schön: *the* ~ *people pl* die Schickeria.
beau·ti·fy ['bju:tɪfaɪ] *v/t* verschönern.
beau·ty ['bju:tɪ] *s* **1.** Schönheit *f* (*a.* Frau). **2.** *F* das Schön(st)e. **3.** *F* Gedicht

n, Prachtstück *n* (*of* von). ~ **com-pe·ti·tion**, ~ **con·test** *s* Schönheitswettbewerb *m*. ~ **farm** *s* Schönheitsfarm *f*. ~ **par·lo(u)r** *s* Schönheitssalon *m*. ~ **patch** → *beauty spot* 1. ~ **queen** *s* Schönheitskönigin *f*. ~ **sa·lon**, *Am.* ~ **shop** → *beauty parlo(u)r*. ~ **sleep** *s* F Schlaf *m* vor Mitternacht. ~ **spot** *s* 1. Schönheitspflästerchen *n*. 2. schönes Fleckchen Erde.

bea·ver ['biːvə] *s zo.* Biber *m*.

be·came [bɪ'keɪm] *pret von* **become**.

be·cause [bɪ'kɒz] I *cj* weil, da. II *prp:* ~ *of* wegen (*gen*).

beck [bek] *s: be at s.o.'s ~ and call* j-m auf den leisesten Wink gehorchen, nach j-s Pfeife tanzen. **beck·on** ['~ən] *v/t j-m* (zu)winken, *j-m* ein Zeichen geben.

be·come [bɪ'kʌm] (*irr*) I *v/i* 1. werden: *what has become of him?* was ist aus ihm geworden? II *v/t* 2. sich ziemen für. 3. *j-m* stehen, passen zu.

be'com·ing *adj* □ 1. passend, kleidsam: *be very ~ to s.o.* j-m sehr gut stehen. 2. schicklich, geziemend.

bed [bed] I *s* 1. (*a. Fluß- etc*)Bett *n*: *go to ~* ins Bett gehen (*with* mit); *keep one's ~* das Bett hüten; *make the ~* das Bett machen; *as you make your ~ so you must lie on it* wie man sich bettet, so liegt man; *put to ~* ins Bett bringen; *take to one's ~* sich (krank) ins Bett legen; *~ and breakfast* Zimmer *n* mit Frühstück. 2. (Garten)Beet *n*. 3. ⚙ Bett(ung *f*) *n*, Unterlage *f*. II *v/t* 4. ins Bett bringen 5. ~ *out* auspflanzen, -setzen.

be·daub [bɪ'dɔːb] *v/t* beschmieren: *~ed with clay* lehmbeschmiert.

'**bed·bug** *s zo.* Wanze *f*. '**~·clothes** *s pl* Bettwäsche *f*. '**~·cov·er** *s* Bettdecke *f*.

bed·ding ['bedɪŋ] *s* Bettzeug *n*.

be·deck [bɪ'dek] *v/t* schmücken.

be·dev·il [bɪ'devl] *v/t* *pret u. pp* -**iled**, *bsd. Br.* -**illed** durcheinanderbringen, verwirren.

bed·lam ['bedləm] *s fig.* Tollhaus *n*.

bed| lin·en *s* Bettwäsche *f*. '**~·pan** *s* Stechbecken *n*, Bettpfanne *f*, -schüssel *f*. '**~·post** *s* Bettpfosten *m*: → *between* 2.

be·drag·gled [bɪ'dræɡld] *adj* 1. durchnäßt; verdreckt. 2. *fig.* heruntergekom-

men (*Haus etc*); ungepflegt (*Erscheinung etc*).

bed| rest *s* Bettruhe *f*. '**~·rid·den** *adj* bettlägerig. '**~·rock** *s geol.* Grund-, Muttergestein *n*: *get down to the ~ of a matter fig.* e-r Sache auf den Grund gehen. ~ **room** ['~rʊm] *s* Schlafzimmer *n*: ~ **suburb** (*od. town*) Schlafstadt *f*. '**~·side** *s: at the ~* am Bett; *have a good ~ manner* gut mit Kranken umgehen können; ~ *lamp* Nachttischlampe *f*; ~ *rug* Bettvorleger *m*; ~ *table* Nachttisch(chen) *n* (*m*). '**~·sit**, ~'**sit·ter**, '~·'**sit·ting room** *s Br.* 1. möbliertes Zimmer. 2. Einzimmerapartment *n*. '**~·sore** ✿ wundgelegene Stelle: *get ~s* sich durch- *od.* wundliegen. '**~·space** *s* Bettenzahl *f*, -kapazität *f* (*in Klinik, Hotel etc*). '**~·spread** *s* Tagesdecke *f*. '**~·stead** *s* Bettgestell *n*. '**~·tick** *s* Inlett *n*. '**~·time** *s* Schlafenszeit *f*: ~ *reading* Bettlektüre *f*; ~ *story* Gutenachtgeschichte *f*.

bee [biː] *s zo.* Biene *f*: (*as*) *busy as a ~* bienenfleißig; *have a ~ in one's bonnet* F e-n Fimmel *od.* Tick haben.

beech [biːtʃ] *s* ✿ Buche *f*. '**~·nut** *s* Buchecker *f*.

beef [biːf] I *s* 1. Rindfleisch *n*. 2. F (Muskel)Kraft *f*. 3. *sl.* Meckerei *f*, Nörgelei *f*. II *v/i* 4. *sl.* meckern, nörgeln (*about* über *acc*). '**~·bur·ger** ['~bɜːɡə] *s gastr.* Hamburger *m*. '**~·eat·er** *s Br.* Beefeater *m*, Tower-Wächter *m*. '**~·steak** *s* Beefsteak *n*. ~ **tea** *s* (Rind)Fleischbrühe *f*, Bouillon *f*.

beef·y ['biːfɪ] *adj* F bullig.

'**bee·line** *s: make a ~ for* schnurstracks zu- *od.* losgehen auf (*acc*).

been [biːn] *pp von* **be**.

beer [bɪə] *s* Bier *n*: → *small* I. ~ **gar·den** *s* Biergarten *m*.

beer·y ['bɪərɪ] *adj* 1. bierselig. 2. nach Bier riechend: ~ *breath* Bierfahne *f*.

'**bees·wax** *s* Bienenwachs *n*.

beet [biːt] *s* ✿ Runkelrübe *f*, *Am. a.* rote Bete *od.* Rübe.

bee·tle ['biːtl] *s zo.* Käfer *m*.

be·fore [bɪ'fɔː] I *adv* 1. *räumlich:* vorn, voran: *go ~* vorangehen. 2. *zeitlich:* vorher, zuvor: *the year ~* das vorhergehende Jahr. II *prp* 3. *räumlich:* vor (*acc od. dat*): ~ *my eyes* vor m-n Augen. 4. vor (*dat*), in Gegenwart von (*od. gen*): ~

witnesses vor Zeugen. **5.** *zeitlich:* vor (*dat*): *the week ~ last* vorletzte Woche; *~ long* in Kürze, bald. **6.** *Reihenfolge, Rang:* voraus, vor (*acc od. dat*): *be ~ the others* den anderen voraus sein. **III** *cj* **7.** bevor, ehe: *not ~* erst als *od.* wenn.

be·fore·hand *adv* **1.** zu'vor, (im) voraus: *know s.th. ~* et. im voraus wissen. **2.** zuvor, früher. **3.** zu früh, verfrüht.

be·friend [bɪ'frend] *v/t j-m* behilflich sein; *j-s* annehmen.

beg [beg] **I** *v/t* **1.** *et.* erbitten (*of s.o.* von *j-m*): *~ leave* (*of s.o.*) (j-n) um Erlaubnis bitten; → *pardon* **3. 2.** erbetteln, betteln um. **3.** *j-n* bitten (*to do* zu tun). **II** *v/i* **4.** betteln: *go ~ging* betteln gehen; *fig.* keinen Interessenten *od.* Abnehmer finden. **5.** (dringend) bitten (*for* um; *of s.o.* j-n). **6.** sich erlauben *od.* gestatten (*to do* zu tun).

be·gan [bɪ'gæn] *pret von* **begin**.

be·get [bɪ'get] *v/t (irr)* **1.** *Kind* zeugen. **2.** *fig.* erzeugen.

beg·gar ['begə] **I** *s* **1.** Bettler(in). **2.** F *Kerl m: lucky ~* Glückspilz *m*. **II** *v/t* **3.** an den Bettelstab bringen. **4.** *~ description* sich nicht mit Worten beschreiben lassen; jeder Beschreibung spotten. '**beg·gar·ly** *adj* **1.** bettelarm. **2.** *fig.* armselig, kümmerlich. '**beg·gar·y** *s* Bettelarmut *f*.

be·gin [bɪ'gɪn] *v/t u. v/i (irr)* beginnen, anfangen: *to ~ with* zunächst (einmal); erstens (einmal); *~ on s.th.* et. in Angriff nehmen; *~* (*on*) *a new bottle* e-e neue Flasche anbrechen. **be·gin·ner** *s* Anfänger(in): *~'s luck* Anfängerglück *n*. **be·gin·ning** *s* **1.** Beginn *m*, Anfang *m*: *at* (*od. in*) *the ~* am Anfang; *from the ~* (ganz) von Anfang an. **2.** *pl* (erste) Anfänge *pl*.

be·go·ni·a [bɪ'gəʊnjə] *s* ⚘ Begonie *f*.

be·got [bɪ'gɒt] *pret von* **beget**. **be·got·ten** [~tn] *pp von* **beget**.

be·grudge [bɪ'grʌdʒ] *v/t* **1.** *~ s.o. s.th.* j-m et. mißgönnen. **2.** *~ doing s.th.* et. nur widerwillig tun.

be·guile [bɪ'gaɪl] *v/t* **1.** betrügen (*of, out of* um), täuschen. **2.** verleiten (*into doing* zu tun). **3.** sich *die Zeit* (angenehm) vertreiben (*by, with* mit).

be·gun [bɪ'gʌn] *pp von* **begin**.

be·half [bɪ'hɑːf] *s: on* (*Am. a. in*) *~ of* zugunsten von (*od. gen*), für; im Na-

men *od.* Auftrag von (*od. gen*), für.

be·have [bɪ'heɪv] **I** *v/i* **1.** sich (gut) benehmen. **2.** sich verhalten *od.* benehmen (*to, towards* zu, gegenüber). **3.** sich verhalten (*Sache*), arbeiten, funktionieren (*Maschine etc*). **II** *v/t* **4.** *~ o.s.* → **1: *~ yourself!*** benimm dich!

be·hav·io(u)r [~jə] *s* Benehmen *n*, Betragen *n*, Verhalten *n: be on one's best ~* sich von s-r besten Seite zeigen; *put s.o. on his best ~* j-m einschärfen, sich gut zu benehmen; *~ pattern psych.* Verhaltensmuster *n*. **be·hav·io(u)r·al** *adj psych.* Verhaltens...: *~ disturbance* Verhaltensstörung *f*. **be·hav·io(u)r·ism** *s psych.* Behaviorismus *m*.

be·head [bɪ'hed] *v/t* enthaupten.

be·hind [bɪ'haɪnd] **I** *prp* **1.** *räumlich u. zeitlich:* hinter (*acc od. dat*): *get s.th. ~ one* et. hinter sich bringen. **2.** *Reihenfolge, Rang:* hinter (*acc od. dat*): *~ s.o.* j-m nachstehen (*in* in *dat*). **II** *adv* **3.** hinten, dahinter: *walk ~* hinterhergehen. **4.** nach hinten: *look ~* zurückblicken. **III** *adj* **5.** im Rückstand *od.* Verzug (*in, with* mit). **IV** *s* **6.** F Hintern *m*. **be'hind·hand** *adv u. adj* **1.** im Rückstand *od.* Verzug (*with* mit). **2.** rückständig.

beige [beɪʒ] *adj* beige.

be·ing ['biːɪŋ] *s* **1.** (Da)Sein *n*, Existenz *f: in ~* existierend, wirklich (vorhanden); *call into ~* ins Leben rufen; *come into being* entstehen. **2.** *j-s* Wesen *n*, Natur *f*. **3.** (Lebe)Wesen *n*, Geschöpf *n*.

be·la·bo(u)r [bɪ'leɪbə] *v/t* mit Worten bearbeiten, *j-m* zusetzen.

be·lat·ed [bɪ'leɪtɪd] *adj* verspätet: *~ best wishes* nachträglich herzlichen Glückwunsch.

belch [beltʃ] **I** *v/i* **1.** aufstoßen, rülpsen. **2.** quellen (*from* aus) (*Rauch etc*). **II** *v/t* **3.** *a. ~ out* (*od. forth*) *Feuer, Rauch etc* speien, *a. fig. Beleidigungen etc* ausstoßen. **III** *s* **4.** Aufstoßen *n*, Rülpsen *n*; Rülpser *m*. **5.** *fig.* (Rauch-, Flammen-*etc*)Stoß *m*. **6.** *fig.* Schwall *m* (*von Beleidigungen etc*).

bel·fry ['belfrɪ] *s* Glockenstuhl *m*; Glockenturm *m*: → *bat*¹.

Bel·gian ['beldʒən] **I** *adj* belgisch. **II** *s* Belgier(in).

be·lie [bɪ'laɪ] *v/t* **1.** *j-n, et.* Lügen strafen. **2.** hinwegtäuschen über (*acc*). **3.** *Hoff-*

nung etc enttäuschen, *e-r Sache* nicht entsprechen.

be·lief [bɪˈliːf] *s* **1.** Glaube *m* (*in* an *acc*): *beyond* ~ unglaublich. **2.** Vertrauen *n* (*in* auf *e-e Sache*, zu *j-m*). **3.** Anschauung *f*, Überzeugung *f*: *to the best of my* ~ nach bestem Wissen u. Gewissen.

be·liev·a·ble [bɪˈliːvəbl] *adj* **1.** glaubhaft. **2.** glaubwürdig.

be·lieve [bɪˈliːv] *I v/i* **1.** glauben (*in* an *acc*). **2.** (*in*) vertrauen (auf *acc*), Vertrauen haben (zu). **3.** viel halten (*in* von): *not* ~ *in doing s.th.* nichts *od.* nicht viel davon halten, et. zu tun. *II v/t* **4.** glauben: ~ *it or not!* ob Sie es glauben oder nicht!; *would you* ~ *it!* ist das denn die Möglichkeit!; *he is* ~*d to be rich* man hält ihn für reich; → *reason* 1. **5.** glauben (*dat*). **be'liev·er** *s* Gläubige *m*, *f*: *be a great* ~ *in* fest glauben an (*acc*); viel halten von.

Be·li·sha bea·con [bɪˈliːʃə] *s Br.* Blinklicht *n* (*an Fußgängerüberwegen*).

be·lit·tle [bɪˈlɪtl] *v/t* **1.** herabsetzen, schmälern. **2.** verharmlosen, bagatellisieren.

bell [bel] *I s* **1.** Glocke *f*, Klingel *f*, Schelle *f*: *that rings a* ~ F das kommt mir bekannt vor, das erinnert mich an et. **2.** Glockenzeichen *n*, Läuten *n*, Klingeln *n*: → *answer* 10. **3.** *teleph.* Wecker *m*. **4.** Taucherglocke *f*. *II v/t* **5.** ~ *the cat fig.* der Katze die Schelle umhängen. '~**boy** *s bsd. Am.* (Hotel)Page *m*. '~**flow·er** *s* ⚘ Glockenblume *f*. '~**hop** *s Am.* (Hotel)Page *m*.

bel·li·cose [ˈbelɪkəʊs] *adj* ☐ **1.** kriegslustig, kriegerisch. **2.** → *belligerent* 3.

bel·lied [ˈbelɪd] *adj* bauchig.

bel·lig·er·ent [bɪˈlɪdʒərənt] *I adj* ☐ **1.** → *bellicose* 1. **2.** kriegführend. **3.** *fig.* streitlustig, aggressiv. *II s* **4.** kriegführendes Land.

bel·low [ˈbeləʊ] *I v/i* **1.** brüllen (*with* vor *dat*). **2.** grölen. *II v/t* **3.** a. ~ *out* **3.** Befehl *etc* brüllen. **4.** *Lied etc* grölen. *III s* **5.** Brüllen *n*. **6.** Grölen *n*.

bel·lows [ˈbeləʊz] *s pl* (*a. sg konstruiert*) Blasebalg *m*.

bell‖ push *s* Klingelknopf *m*. '~**weth·er** *s* Leithammel *m* (*a. fig.*).

bel·ly [ˈbelɪ] *I s* **1.** Bauch *m* (*a. e-s Schiffs etc*). **2.** Magen *m*. *II v/i u.v/t* **3.** *a.* ~ *out* (an)schwellen (lassen). '~**ache** *I s* F

Bauchweh *n*. *II v/i sl.* meckern, nörgeln (*about* über *acc*). ~ **but·ton** *s* F Bauchknöpfchen *n*. ~ **danc·er** *s* Bauchtänzerin *f*.

bel·ly·ful [ˈbelɪfʊl] *s* F **1.** *have a* ~ *of* sich den Bauch vollschlagen mit. **2.** *have had a* ~ (*od. one's*) ~ *of* die Nase voll haben von.

bel·ly land·ing *s* ✈ Bauchlandung *f*.

be·long [bɪˈlɒŋ] *v/i* **1.** gehören (*to dat*). **2.** gehören (*to* zu; *in* in *acc*). **3.** angehören (*to dat*). **be'long·ings** *s pl* Habseligkeiten *pl*, Habe *f*; F Angehörige *pl*.

be·lov·ed [bɪˈlʌvd; -ɪd] *I adj* (innig) geliebt. *II s* Geliebte *m*, *f*.

be·low [bɪˈləʊ] *I adv* **1.** unten. **2.** hinunter, nach unten. *II prp* **3.** unter (*acc od. dat*), unterhalb (*gen*): ~ *s.o.* unter j-s Rang, Würde *dat*.

belt [belt] *I s* **1.** Gürtel *m*: *hit below the* ~ (*Boxen*) tief schlagen; → *tighten* 1. **2.** (Sicherheits)Gurt *m*. **3.** Gürtel *m*, Gebiet *n*, Zone *f*. **4.** ⚙ (Treib)Riemen *m*. *II v/t* **5.** ~ *on* an-, umschnallen. **6.** *a.* ~ *out Lied etc* schmettern. *III v/i* **7.** ~ *up mot. etc* sich anschnallen. **8.** *bsd. mot.* F rasen. **9.** ~ *up! sl.* halt die Schnauze!

be·moan [bɪˈməʊn] *v/t* betrauern, beklagen.

be·mused [bɪˈmjuːzd] *adj* **1.** verwirrt. **2.** gedankenverloren.

bench [bentʃ] *s* **1.** (Sitz)Bank *f*. **2.** Werkbank *f*, -tisch *m*.

bend [bend] *I s* **1.** Biegung *f*, Krümmung *f*, (*e-r Straße a.*) Kurve *f*: *drive s.o. round the* ~ *Br.* F j-n verrückt machen. *II v/t* (*irr*) **2.** biegen, krümmen: ~ *out of shape* verbiegen. **3.** *Kopf* neigen, *Knie* beugen. **4.** *Bogen*, *Feder etc* spannen. **5.** ⚖ *Recht* beugen. **6.** *Blicke*, *Gedanken etc* richten, *Anstrengungen etc* konzentrieren (*on*, *to* auf *acc*). *III v/i* (*irr*) **7.** sich biegen *od.* krümmen; *e-e* Biegung machen (*Fluß*), (*Straße a.*) *e-e* Kurve machen. **8.** *a.* ~ *down* sich bücken; sich nach unten biegen; sich verbeugen (*to*, *before* vor *dat*).

be·neath [bɪˈniːθ] *I adv* **1.** unten. **2.** darunter. *II prp* **3.** unter (*acc od. dat*), unterhalb (*gen*): ~ *him* (*od. his dignity*) unter s-r Würde; → *contempt* 1.

ben·e·dic·tion [ˌbenɪˈdɪkʃn] *s eccl.* **1.** Segen *m*. **2.** Segnung *f*.

best man

ben·e·fac·tion [ˌbenɪˈfækʃn] s 1. Wohltat f. 2. wohltätige Gabe. **ben·e·fac·tor** [ˈ‿tə] s Wohltäter m. **ben·e·fac·tress** [ˈ‿trɪs] s Wohltäterin f.

be·nef·i·cence [bɪˈnefɪsns] s Wohltätigkeit f. **be·nef·i·cent** adj □ wohltätig.

ben·e·fi·cial [ˌbenɪˈfɪʃl] adj □ (**to**) nützlich, zuträglich (dat), vorteilhaft, günstig (für).

ben·e·fit [ˈbenɪfɪt] I s 1. Vorteil m, Nutzen m, Gewinn m: **be of ~ to** nützen (dat); **for the ~ of** zugunsten (gen); **derive** (od. **get**) **~** (**from**) → 5; → **reap.** 2. (Arbeitslosen- etc)Unterstützung f; (Kranken- etc)Geld n; (Sozial-, Versicherungs- etc)Leistung f. 3. Wohltätigkeitsveranstaltung f. II v/t pret u. pp **-ed,** bsd. Am. **-ted** 4. nützen (dat), fördern (acc), im Interesse (gen) sein od. liegen. III v/i 5. (**by, from**) Vorteil haben (von, durch), Nutzen ziehen (aus).

be·nev·o·lence [bɪˈnevələns] s 1. Wohltätigkeit f. 2. Wohlwollen n. 3. Wohltat f. **be·nev·o·lent** adj □ 1. wohltätig. 2. wohlwollend.

be·nign [bɪˈnaɪn] adj □ 1. gütig, freundlich. 2. mild: ~ **climate.** 3. 🌿 gutartig: ~ **tumo(u)r.**

bent [bent] I pret u. pp von **bend.** II adj 1. entschlossen (**on doing** zu tun); erpicht (**on** auf acc), darauf aus (**on doing** zu tun). III s 2. Neigung f, Hang m (**for** zu): **to the top of one's ~** nach Herzenslust. 3. Veranlagung f: **have a ~ for art** künstlerisch veranlagt sein; ~ **for languages** Sprachbegabung f.

be·numbed [bɪˈnʌmd] adj 1. gefühllos, starr (**with cold** vor Kälte). 2. fig. gelähmt.

ben·zene [ˈbenziːn] s 🧪 Benzol n.

ben·zine [ˈbenziːn] s 🧪 Leichtbenzin n.

be·queath [bɪˈkwiːð] v/t hinterlassen, vermachen (**s.th. to s.o.** j-m et.).

be·quest [bɪˈkwest] s Vermächtnis n.

be·rate [bɪˈreɪt] v/t auszanken (**about, for** wegen).

be·reave [bɪˈriːv] v/t (a. irr) berauben (**of** gen): ~ **s.o. of speech** j-m die Sprache rauben; **the ~d** die Hinterbliebene, die Hinterbliebenen pl. **be'reavement** s 1. schmerzlicher Verlust (**durch** Tod). 2. Trauerfall m.

be·reft [bɪˈreft] I pret u. pp von **bereave.** II adj mst fig. beraubt (**of** gen): ~ **of all hope.**

ber·ry [ˈberɪ] s 🍓 Beere f.

ber·serk [ˈbɜːˈzɜːk] adj: **go ~** wild werden; Amok laufen.

berth [bɜːθ] s 1. ⚓ Liege-, Ankerplatz m. 2. ⚓ Koje f. 3. 🚃 (Schlafwagen)Bett n. 4. **give a wide ~ to** e-n großen Bogen machen um. 5. F Stellung f, Pöstchen n: **he's got a good ~.** II v/i 6. ⚓ festmachen, anlegen.

be·seech [bɪˈsiːtʃ] v/t (a. irr) 1. j-n anflehen (**for** um; **to do** zu tun). 2. et. erflehen (**of** von). **be'seech·ing** adj flehend. **be'seech·ing·ly** adv flehentlich.

be·set·ting [bɪˈsetɪŋ] adj hartnäckig: ~ **sin** Gewohnheitslaster n.

be·side [bɪˈsaɪd] prp 1. neben (acc od. dat). 2. außerhalb: → **point** 11. 3. **be ~ o.s.** außer sich sein (**with** vor dat). **be'sides** [‿dz] I adv außerdem. II prp außer, neben (dat).

be·siege [bɪˈsiːdʒ] v/t 1. ⚔ belagern (a. fig.). 2. fig. bestürmen, bedrängen (**with** mit).

be·sought [bɪˈsɔːt] pret u. pp von **beseech.**

be·spec·ta·cled [bɪˈspektəkld] adj bebrillt.

be·spoke [bɪˈspəʊk] adj Br. Maß...: ~ **tailor** Maßschneider m.

best [best] I (sup von **good**) adj 1. best. 2. größt, meist: **the ~ part of** der größte Teil (gen). II (sup von **well²**) adv 3. am besten: **the ~hated man** der meistgehaßte Mann; **as ~ they could** so gut sie konnten; **you had ~ go** es wäre das beste, wenn Sie gingen. III s 4. **der, die, das** Beste: **at ~** bestenfalls, höchstens; **do one's ~** sein möglichstes tun; **have** (od. **get**) **the ~ of** übertreffen; F übers Ohr hauen; **make the ~ of** sich zufriedengeben mit; sich abfinden mit; voll ausnutzen; das beste machen aus; **all the ~!** alles Gute!; → **ability, belief** 3, etc.

bes·tial [ˈbestjəl] adj □ tierisch, fig. a. bestialisch, viehisch. **bes·ti·al·i·ty** [ˌbestɪˈælɪtɪ] s 1. Bestialität f (a. fig.). 2. Sodomie f.

be·stir [bɪˈstɜː] v/t: ~ **o.s. to do s.th.** sich dazu aufraffen, et. zu tun.

best man s (irr **man**) Freund des Bräuti-

gams, der bei der Ausrichtung der Hochzeit e-e wichtige Rolle spielt.

be·stow [bɪˈstəʊ] *v/t* Preis, Titel verleihen (**on** *dat*). **be'stow·al** *s* Verleihung *f*.

best| sell·er *s* **1.** Bestseller *m*. **2.** Bestsellerautor *m*. '~,**sell·ing** *adj*: ~ *novel* Bestseller *m*; ~ *author* Bestsellerautor *m*.

bet [bet] **I** *s* **1.** Wette *f*; Wetteinsatz *m*: *have* (*od. make*) *a* ~ *e-e* Wette abschließen *od.* eingehen (**on** auf *acc*). **2.** *my* ~ *is that* ich würde sagen, daß; *it's a safe* ~ *that* es steht so gut wie fest, daß. **3.** *your best* ~ *is to take the car* F du nimmst am besten den Wagen. **II** *v/t* (*a. irr*) **4.** *Geld* wetten, setzen (**on** auf *acc*): *I'll* ~ *you £ 10 that* ich wette mit dir (um) 10 Pfund, daß; *you can* ~ *your boots* (*od. bottom dollar, shirt*) *that* F du kannst Gift darauf nehmen, daß. **5.** ~ (*s.o.*) *that fig.* (mit j-m) wetten, daß. **III** *v/i* (*a. irr*) **6.** wetten, setzen (**on** auf *acc*): *you* ~*!* F das kann man wohl sagen.

be·tray [bɪˈtreɪ] *v/t* verraten (**to** *dat od.* an *acc*) (*a. fig.*). **be'tray·al** *s* Verrat *m*.

bet·ter¹ [ˈbetə] **I** (*comp von good*) *adj* besser: *I am* ~ es geht mir (*gesundheitlich*) besser; *get* ~ besser werden; sich erholen. **II** *s das* Bessere: *for* ~ *for worse* in Freud u. Leid (*Trauformel*); *was auch (immer) geschieht; get the* ~ *of j-n* besiegen, ausstechen; *et.* überwinden. **III** (*comp von well²*) *adv* besser: ~ *off* besser daran; (*finanziell*) bessergestellt; *think* ~ *of it* sich anders überlegen; *you had* ~ *go* es wäre besser, du gingst; *you had* ~ *not!* laß das lieber sein! → *know* 6, *like²* 1. **IV** *v/t Beziehungen, Rekord etc* verbessern: ~ *o.s.* sich (*finanziell*) verbessern; sich weiterbilden. **V** *v/i* besser werden.

bet·ter² [~] *s* Wetter(in).

bet·ter·ment [ˈbetəmənt] *s* **1.** (Ver)Besserung *f*. **2.** ⚖ Wertsteigerung *f*, -zuwachs *m*.

bet·ting [ˈbetɪŋ] *s* Wetten *n*: ~ *office* (*Br. shop*) Wettbüro *n*.

be·tween [bɪˈtwiːn] **I** *prp* **1.** *räumlich u. zeitlich*: zwischen (*dat od. acc*): → *devil* 1, *stool* 1. **2.** unter (*dat od. acc*): *you and me* (*and the bedpost od. gatepost od. lamppost* F) unter uns *od.* im Vertrauen (gesagt); *we had ten pounds* ~

us wir hatten zusammen zehn Pfund. **II** *adv* **3.** dazwischen: *the space* ~ der Zwischenraum; *in* ~ dazwischen.

bev·el [ˈbevl] **I** *s* Schräge *f*, Abschrägung *f*. **II** *v/t pret u. pp* -**eled**, *bsd. Br.* -**elled** abschrägen. **III** *adj* abgeschrägt, schräg.

bev·er·age [ˈbevərɪdʒ] *s* Getränk *n*.

bev·y [ˈbevɪ] *s orn.* Schwarm *m*, Schar *f*.

be·wail [bɪˈweɪl] *v/t* beklagen.

be·ware [bɪˈweə] *v/i* sich hüten, sich in acht nehmen (**of** vor *dat*): ~ *of the dog!* Vorsicht, bissiger Hund!; ~ *of pickpockets!* vor Taschendieben wird gewarnt!

be·wil·der [bɪˈwɪldə] *v/t* irremachen, verwirren. **be'wil·der·ment** *s* Verwirrung *f*.

be·witch [bɪˈwɪtʃ] *v/t* bezaubern, behexen.

be·yond [bɪˈjɒnd] **I** *adv* **1.** darüber hinaus. **II** *prp* **2.** jenseits. **3.** über ... (*acc*) hinaus: *that is* ~ *me* F das ist mir zu hoch, das geht über m-n Verstand; → *belief* 1, *endurance* 1, *measure* 1, *word* 1, *etc.*

bi... [baɪ] zwei...

bi'an·nu·al *adj* zweimal jährlich vorkommend *od.* erscheinend. **bi'an·nu·al·ly** *adv* zweimal im Jahr.

bi·as [ˈbaɪəs] **I** *s* **1.** (*towards*) Neigung *f*, Hang *m* (zu); Vorliebe *f* (für). **2.** Vorurteil *n*, ⚖ Befangenheit *f*: *free from* ~ unvoreingenommen. **II** *adj u. adv* **3.** schräg. **III** *v/t pret u. pp* -**as(s)ed 4.** (*mst ungünstig*) beeinflussen, j-n einnehmen (*against* gegen). '**bi·as(s)ed** *adj* voreingenommen, ⚖ befangen.

bib [bɪb] *s* **1.** Lätzchen *n*. **2.** Schürzenlatz *m*.

Bi·ble [ˈbaɪbl] *s* Bibel *f*. **bib·li·cal** [ˈbɪblɪkl] *adj* □ biblisch, Bibel...

bib·li·o·graph·ic, bib·li·o·graph·i·cal [ˌbɪblɪəʊˈgræfɪk(l)] *adj* □ bibliographisch. **bib·li·og·ra·phy** [~ˈɒgrəfɪ] *s* Bibliographie *f*. **bib·li·o·phile** [~əʊfaɪl] *s* Bücherfreund *m*, Bibliophile *m*.

bi'car·bon·ate *s* 🧪 Bikarbonat *n*: ~ *of soda* Natriumbikarbonat.

bi·ceps [ˈbaɪseps] *pl* -**ceps(·es)** *s anat.* Bizeps *m*.

bick·er [ˈbɪkə] **I** *v/i* sich zanken *od.* streiten (*about, over* um). **II** *s* Zank *m*, Streit *m*. '**bick·er·ing** *s* Gezänk *n*.

billiard

bi·cy·cle ['baɪsɪkl] **I** s Fahrrad n. **II** v/i radfahren; mit dem Rad fahren.

bid [bɪd] **I** s 1. ✝ Gebot n (*bei Versteigerungen*); ✝ Angebot n (*bei Ausschreibungen*); ✝ *Am.* Kostenvoranschlag m; fig. Bewerbung f (*for* um), Versuch m (*to do* zu tun): *highest* ~ Meistgebot n; *make a* ~ *for* sich bemühen um; ~ *for power* Griff m nach der Macht. **II** v/t (*irr*) **2.** ✝ *bei Versteigerungen* bieten. **3.** j-m e-n guten Morgen etc wünschen: ~ *s.o. good morning;* ~ *farewell* Lebewohl sagen. **III** v/i (*irr*) **4.** ✝ *bei Versteigerungen* bieten; ✝ *Am.* e-n Kostenvoranschlag maehen; fig. sich bemühen (*for* um): ~ *for power* nach der Macht greifen. '**bid·den** pp *von* bid. '**bid·der** s ✝ Bieter m (*bei Versteigerungen*): *highest* ~ Meistbietende m, f. '**bid·ding** s ✝ Gebot n (*bei Versteigerungen*).

bide [baɪd] v/t (*a. irr*): ~ *one's time* den rechten Augenblick abwarten *od.* abpassen.

bi·en·ni·al [baɪ'enɪəl] adj □ **1.** zweijährlich. **2.** zweijährig.

bier [bɪə] s (Toten)Bahre f.

bi·fur·cate ['baɪfəket] **I** v/i sich gabeln. **II** adj gegabelt, gabelförmig. ,**bi·fur·'ca·tion** s Gabelung f.

big [bɪg] **I** adj **1.** *allg.* groß: a) dick, stark: *the* ~*gest party* die stärkste Partei; *earn* ~ *money* f das große Geld verdienen, b) breit, weit: *the coat is too* ~ *for me* der Mantel ist mir zu groß; *get too* ~ *for one's boots* (*od. breeches, bsd. Am. pants*) F größenwahnsinnig werden, c) hoch: ~ *trees,* d) Mords...: ~ *rascal* Erzgauner m; ~ *eater* starker Esser, e) erwachsen, f) wichtig, bedeutend: → *shot* 3. **2.** ausgiebig, reichlich: → *meal.* **3.** F aufgeblasen, eingebildet: *have* ~ *ideas* große Rosinen im Kopf haben; ~ *talk* große Töne pl. **4.** *that's very* ~ *of you* das ist sehr großzügig od. nobel von Ihnen. **5.** *be* ~ *on* F stehen auf (*acc*) II adv **6.** F mächtig, mordsmäßig. **7.** F großspurig: *talk* ~ große Töne spucken.

big·a·mist ['bɪgəmɪst] s Bigamist(in).

'**big·a·my** s Bigamie f, Doppelehe f.

big| bang s Kosmologie: Urknall m. '~·,**cir·cu·'la·tion** adj auflagenstark (*Zeitung*). '~·**mouth** s F Großmaul n.

big·ness ['bɪgnɪs] s Größe f.

big·ot ['bɪgət] s **1.** selbstgerechte *od.* intolerante Person. **2.** Frömmler(in). '**big·ot·ed** adj **1.** selbstgerecht, intolerant. **2.** bigott, frömmlerisch. '**big·ot·ry** s **1.** Selbstgerechtigkeit f, Intoleranz f. **2.** Bigotterie f, Frömmelei f.

'**big·wig** s F großes *od.* hohes Tier.

bike [baɪk] F **I** s Rad n (*Fahrrad*); Maschine f (*Motorrad*). **II** v/i radeln, Motorrad fahren; mit dem Motorrad fahren.

,**bi'lat·er·al** adj bilateral, zweiseitig.

bil·ber·ry ['bɪlbərɪ] s ♀ Blau-, Heidelbeere f.

bile [baɪl] s **1.** physiol. Galle f. **2.** fig. Gereiztheit f; Reizbarkeit f. '~·**stone** s physiol. Gallenstein m.

bilge [bɪldʒ] s **1.** ⚓ Kielraum m. **2.** F Quatsch m, Mist m.

bi'lin·gual adj □ zweisprachig.

bil·ious ['bɪljəs] adj □ **1.** ♣ gallig; Gallen...: ~ *attack* Gallenkolik f. **2.** fig. gereizt; reizbar.

bill¹ [bɪl] **I** s zo. Schnabel m. **II** v/i a. ~ *and coo* (miteinander) turteln.

bill² [~] **I** s **1.** pol. (Gesetzes)Vorlage f, Gesetzentwurf m. **2.** ⚖ (An)Klageschrift f. **3.** a. ~ *of exchange* ✝ Wechsel m. **4.** Rechnung f: *waiter, the* ~, *please* (Herr) Ober, bitte zahlen! **5.** Liste f, Aufstellung f: ~ *of fare* Speise(n)karte f. **6.** Bescheinigung f: ~ *of delivery* ✝ Lieferschein m. **7.** Plakat n. **8.** thea. etc Programm(zettel m) n; weitS. Programm n: *be on the* ~ auftreten; → *top¹* 12. **9.** *Am.* Banknote f, (Geld)Schein m. **II** v/t **10.** j-m e-e Rechnung ausstellen *od.* schicken: ~ *s.o. for s.th.* j-m et. in Rechnung stellen. **11.** (durch Plakate) ankündigen *od.* bekanntgeben.

'**bill·board** s bsd. Am. **1.** Reklametafel f. **2.** Film, TV: Vorspann m.

bil·let ['bɪlɪt] **I** s **1.** ✗ (Privat)Quartier n. **2.** Unterkunft f. **II** v/t **3.** ✗ einquartieren (*with, on* bei). **4.** unterbringen. **III** v/i **5.** ✗ einquartiert sein. **6.** (*bsd.* vorübergehend) wohnen.

'**bill·fold** s Am. Scheintasche f; Brieftasche f.

bil·liard ['bɪljəd] **I** s pl (mst sg konstruiert) Billard(spiel) n. **II** adj Billard...: ~ *ball* (*table*); ~ *cue* Queue f.

bil·lion ['bɪljən] s **1.** Milliarde f. **2.** Br. obs. Billion f.

bil·low ['bɪləʊ] **I** s **1.** Woge f. **2.** (Nebel-, Rauch)Schwaden m. **II** v/i **3.** wogen. **4.** a. ~ **out** sich bauschen od. blähen (Segel, Vorhänge etc). **III** v/t **5.** bauschen, blähen. **'bil·low·y** adj **1.** wogend. **2.** in Schwaden ziehend. **3.** gebauscht, gebläht.

'bill,post·er, '~,stick·er s Plakatkleber m.

bil·ly ['bɪlɪ] s Am. (Polizei)Knüppel m. ~ **goat** s Ziegenbock m.

,bi'month·ly adj u. adv zweimonatlich.

bin [bɪn] s Behälter m.

bi·na·ry ['baɪnərɪ] adj ℞, ⚙ etc binär, Binär...

bind [baɪnd] **I** v/t (irr) **1.** binden (to an acc): ~ **together** zs.-binden; ~ **up** aneinander-, zs.-binden; Wunde verbinden. **2.** Saum einfassen. **3.** ℞ etc (mit e-m Bindemittel) binden. **4.** Buch (ein)binden. **5.** fig. (a. vertraglich) binden, verpflichten (s.o. j-n zu et.; to do zu tun). **II** v/i (irr) **6.** ℞ etc binden. **7.** fest od. hart werden. **8.** fig. binden(d sein). **III** s **9.** be in a ~ F in Schwulitäten sein. **'bind·er** s **1.** (Buch- etc)Binder(in). **2.** (Akten- etc)Deckel m, Umschlag m. **3.** ℞ Bindemittel n. **'bind·ing I** adj □ **1.** fig. bindend, verbindlich (on für): legally ~ rechtsverbindlich; not ~ unverbindlich. **II** s **2.** (Buch)Einband m. **3.** Einfassung f, Borte f. **4.** (Ski)Bindung f. **5.** → binder 3.

binge [bɪndʒ] s F Sauf- od. Freßgelage n: go (out) on a ~ e-e Sauf- od. Freßtour machen; go on a buying (od. shopping, spending) ~ wie verrückt einkaufen.

bin·go ['bɪŋgəʊ] s Bingo n (ein Glücksspiel).

bin·oc·u·lars [bɪ'nɒkjʊləz] s pl (a pair of ein) Fernglas n.

bi·o·chem·i·cal [,baɪəʊ'kemɪkl] adj □ biochemisch. **,bi·o'chem·ist** s Biochemiker(in). **,bi·o'chem·is·try** s Biochemie f.

bi·o·graph·ic, bi·o·graph·i·cal [,baɪəʊ'græfɪk(l)] adj □ biographisch. **bi·og·ra·phy** [~'ɒgrəfɪ] s Biographie f.

bi·o·log·i·cal [,baɪəʊ'lɒdʒɪkl] adj □ biologisch. **bi·ol·o·gist** [~'ɒlədʒɪst] s Biologe m. **bi'ol·o·gy** s Biologie f.

bi·par·ti·san [,baɪpɑːtɪ'zæn] adj pol. Zweiparteien...

birch [bɜːtʃ] s ❀ Birke f.

bird [bɜːd] s **1.** Vogel m: ~ **of passage** Zugvogel (a. fig.); ~ **of prey** Raubvogel; a ~ **in the hand is worth two in the bush** besser ein Spatz in der Hand als e-e Taube auf dem Dach; tell a child about the ~s and the bees ein Kind aufklären; that's (strictly) for the ~s F das ist für die Katz; das taugt nichts; give s.o. the ~ j-n ausgfeifen od. ausbuhen; → early 4, feather I, fly¹ 2, kill 1. **2.** F Kerl m: queer ~ komischer Kauz. **'~cage** s Vogelkäfig m. **'~house** s Nistkasten m.

bird·ie ['bɜːdɪ] s Vögelchen n.

bird| sanc·tu·a·ry s Vogelschutzgebiet n. **'~seed** s Vogelfutter n.

'bird's-eye adj: ~ **view** (Blick m aus der) Vogelschau; fig. allgemeiner Überblick (of über acc); ~ **perspective** Vogelperspektive f. ~ **nest** s Vogelnest n.

bird strike s ✈ Vogelschlag m.

bi·ro ['baɪərəʊ] pl -ros (TM) s Br. Kugelschreiber m.

birth [bɜːθ] s **1.** Geburt f: at ~ bei der Geburt; from (od. since) (one's) ~ von Geburt an; give ~ to gebären, zur Welt bringen; fig. hervorbringen, -rufen. **2.** Abstammung f, Herkunft f: he's a man of (good) ~ er stammt aus gutem Hause; she's English by ~ sie ist gebürtige Engländerin. **3.** Ursprung m, Entstehung f. ~ **cer·tif·i·cate** s Geburtsurkunde f. ~ **con·trol** s Geburtsregelung f, -kontrolle f. **'~day I** s Geburtstag m: when is your ~? wann hast du Geburtstag?; happy ~! alles Gute od. herzlichen Glückwunsch zum Geburtstag! **II** adj Geburtstags...: ~ **party** (present, etc); ~ **honours** pl Titelverleihungen pl anläßlich des Geburtstags des Königs od. der Königin; in one's ~ **suit** im Adams- od. Evaskostüm. **'~mark** s Muttermal n. **~pill** s ⚕ Antibabypille f. **'~place** s Geburtsort m. **'~rate** s Geburtenziffer f: falling ~ Geburtenrückgang m.

bis·cuit ['bɪskɪt] s **1.** Br. Keks m, n. **2.** Am. kleines weiches Brötchen n.

bi·sect [baɪ'sekt] v/t **1.** in zwei Teile (zer)schneiden. **2.** ℞ halbieren. **,bi'sec·tion** s ℞ Halbierung f.

,bi·sex·u·al *adj* □ bisexuell.
bish·op ['bɪʃəp] *s* **1.** *eccl.* Bischof *m.* **2.** *Schach:* Läufer *m.* **bish·op·ric** ['ʌrɪk] *s eccl.* Bistum *n.*
bit¹ [bɪt] *s* **1.** Gebiß *n* (*am Pferdezaum*): **take the ~ between one's teeth** durchgehen (*Pferd*); *fig.* störrisch werden; *fig.* sich reinknien. **2.** ⊕ Backe *f*, Maul *n* (*e-r Zange etc*); (*Schlüssel*)Bart *m.* **3.** Mundstück *n* (*e-r Tabakspfeife etc*).
bit² [ʌ] *s* **1.** Bissen *m*, Happen *m.* **2.** Stück(chen) *n* (*a. fig.*): **fall to ~s** entzweigehen, zerbrechen; **a ~** ein bißchen; ziemlich; **not a ~** überhaupt nicht; **a ~ of a coward** ziemlich feig; **a ~ of a fool** ein bißchen dumm; **~ by ~** Stück für Stück, nach u. nach; **do one's ~** s-e Pflicht (u. Schuldigkeit) tun; s-n Beitrag leisten. **3.** F Augenblick *m*, Moment *m*: **after a ~** nach e-m Weilchen. **4.** F kleine Münze.
bit³ [ʌ] *s Computer:* Bit *n.*
bit⁴ [ʌ] *pret von* bite.
bitch [bɪtʃ] *s* **1.** *zo.* Hündin *f.* **2.** *sl.* Schlampe *f*; Miststück *n*: → **son** 1.
bite [baɪt] **I** *v/t* (*irr*) **1.** beißen: **~ back** sich e-e Äußerung *etc* verkneifen; **~ off** abbeißen; **~ off more than one can chew** F sich zuviel zumuten; **~ the dust** (*Am. a. ground*) F ins Gras beißen; **~ one's nails** an den Nägeln kauen; *fig.* nervös sein; → **lip** 1, **tongue** 1. **2.** beißen, stechen (*Insekt*). **II** *v/i* (*irr*) **3.** (zu)beißen: **~ into** (hinein)beißen in (*acc*). **4.** anbeißen (*a. fig.*), schnappen (*at* nach) (*Fisch*). **5.** beißen, stechen (*Insekt*). **6.** beißen (*Rauch, Gewürz etc*). **7.** fassen, greifen (*Rad, Schraube etc*). **8.** *fig.* beißend *od.* verletzend sein. **9.** sich (*bsd. negativ*) auswirken (*Maßnahme*). **III** *s* **10.** Biß *m*, (*e-s Insekts a.*) Stich *m.* **11.** Biß(wunde *f*) *m.* **12.** Bissen *m*, Happen *m* (*a. weitS. Imbiß, Nahrung*). **13.** Fassen *n*, Greifen *n* (*von Rädern, Schrauben etc*): **s.th. has lost its ~** et greift *od.* zieht nicht mehr. **14.** Schärfe *f* (*a. fig.*).
bit·ing ['baɪtɪŋ] *adj* beißend (*Rauch etc*), schneidend (*Wind, Kälte etc*) (*beide a. Worte etc*).
bit·ten ['bɪtn] **I** *pp von* bite. **II** *adj:* **once ~ twice shy** (ein) gebranntes Kind scheut das Feuer.
bit·ter ['bɪtə] **I** *adj* □ **1.** bitter (*a. fig.*): **to**

the ~ end bis zum bitteren Ende; **weep ~ly** bitterlich weinen. **2.** *fig.* scharf, heftig (*Kritik etc*). **3.** *fig.* erbittert (*Feinde etc*); verbittert (*about* wegen). **II** *adv* **4.** **~ cold** bitterkalt. **III** *s* **5.** Bitterkeit *f.* **6.** *fig.* das Bittere. **7.** *Br.* stark gehopftes (*Faß*)Bier. **8.** *mst pl* Magenbitter *m.*
bit·ter·ness ['bɪtənɪs] *s* **1.** Bitterkeit *f* (*a. fig.*). **2.** *fig.* Verbitterung *f.*
bi·tu·men ['bɪtjʊmɪn] *s min.* Bitumen *n.*
bi·tu·mi·nous [bɪ'tjuːmɪnəs] *adj:* **~ coal** Steinkohle *f.*
biz [bɪz] F *für* business.
bi·zarre [bɪ'zɑː] *adj* bizarr.
blab [blæb] **I** *v/t* **1.** *oft* **~ out** ausplaudern. **II** *v/i* **2.** schwatzen. **3.** *fig.* eiausplaudern.
black [blæk] **I** *adj* **1.** *allg.* schwarz (*a. fig.*): **~ coffee; ~ humo(u)r; ~ man** Schwarze *m*; **in the face** dunkelrot im Gesicht (*vor Aufregung etc*); **beat s.o. ~ and blue** j-n grün u. blau schlagen; **look ~ at s.o., give s.o. a ~ look** j-n (böse) anfunkeln; **he's not so ~ as he's painted** er ist besser als sein Ruf. **2.** ✝ *bsd. Br.* boykottiert. **II** *s* **3.** Schwarz *n*: **dressed in ~** schwarz *od.* in Schwarz gekleidet; **be in ~** (*od. wear* ~) Trauer tragen. **4.** *oft* ♋ Schwarze *m*, *f.* **5.** **be in the ~** ✝ mit Gewinn arbeiten; aus den roten Zahlen herauskommen. **III** *v/t* **6.** → **blacken** I. **7.** ✝ *bsd. Br.* boykottieren. **8.** **~ out** abdunkeln, *a.* ✕ verdunkeln. **9.** **~ out** Nachrichten *etc* unterdrücken. **IV** *v/i* **10.** schwarz werden. **11.** **~ out** ein Blackout haben. **12.** **~ out** bewußtlos werden.
black| and white *pl* **black and whites** *s* **1.** **in ~** schwarz auf weiß, schriftlich. **2.** Schwarzweißbild *n.* **3.** **depict s.th. in ~** *fig.* et. schwarzweißmalen. **~-and-'white** *adj* **1.** schriftlich. **2.** Schwarzweiß...: **~ television;** ~ **depiction** Schwarzweißmalerei *f.* '**~·ball** *v/t* stimmen gegen. '**~·ber·ry** *f* ['ʌbərɪ] *s* ♣ Brombeere *f.* '**~·bird** *s orn.* Amsel *f.* '**~·board** *s* (Schul-, Wand)Tafel *f.* **~ box** *s* ✈ F Flugschreiber *m.*
black·en ['blækən] **I** *v/t* **1.** schwarz machen, schwärzen. **2.** *fig.* **~ s.o.'s character** j-n verunglimpfen; **~ s.o.'s name** (*od. reputation*) j-n schlechtmachen. **II** *v/i* **3.** schwarz werden.
black| eye *s* blaues Auge, Veilchen *n*: **give s.o. a ~** j-m ein blaues Auge schla-

gen. **~guard** ['blæga:d] s Schuft m, Lump m. **~ ice** s Glatteis n.

black·ish ['blækɪʃ] adj schwärzlich.

'black·jack s **1.** Siebzehnundvier n. **2.** bsd. Am. Totschläger m (Waffe). **~ lead** [led] s min. Graphit m. **'~·leg** s bsd. Br. Streikbrecher m. **,~'let·ter day** s schwarzer Tag, Unglückstag m. **'~·list I** s schwarze Liste. **II** v/t auf die schwarze Liste setzen. **~ mag·ic** s Schwarze Magie. **'~·mail I** s Erpressung f. **II** v/t j-n erpressen (**over** mit). **'~·mail·er** s Erpresser(in). **⚥ Ma·ri·a** [məˈraɪə] s F grüne Minna. **~ mar·ket** s schwarzer Markt, Schwarzmarkt m. **~ mar·ket·eer** [ˌmɑːkəˈtɪə] s Schwarzhändler(in). **~ mass** s Schwarze Messe.

black·ness ['blæknɪs] s Schwärze f.

'black·out s **1.** ✕, ✈, thea. etc Blackout n, m. **2.** ✶ Ohnmacht f, Bewußtlosigkeit f. **3.** (bsd. Nachrichten)Sperre f: draw a ~ over e-e Nachrichtensperre verhängen über (acc). **~ pud·ding** s Blutwurst f. **~ sheep** s (irr sheep) fig. schwarzes Schaf.

blad·der ['blædə] s anat. Blase f.

blade [bleɪd] s **1.** 🌾 Halm m. **~ of grass** Grashalm m. **2.** ❀ Blatt n (e-r Säge, e-s Ruders etc). **3.** ⚙ Flügel m (e-s Propellers); Schaufel f (e-r Turbine etc). **4.** ❀ Klinge f (e-r Messers etc).

blah [blɑː], a. **,blah'blah** s F Blabla n, Geschwafel n.

blame [bleɪm] **I** v/t **1.** tadeln (**for** wegen). **2.** ~ s.o. for s.th., ~ s.th. on s.o. j-n verantwortlich machen für et., j-m die Schuld geben an et.; he is to ~ for it er ist daran schuld; he has only himself to ~ er hat es sich selbst zuzuschreiben. **II** s **3.** Tadel m. **4.** Schuld f, Verantwortung f: lay (od. put, cast) the ~ on s.o. j-m die Schuld geben; bear (od. take) the ~ die Schuld auf sich nehmen. **'blame·less** adj □ **1.** untadelig. **2.** schuldlos (**of** an acc).

blanch [blɑːntʃ] **I** v/t **1.** bleichen. **2.** gastr. blanchieren. **3.** erbleichen lassen. **II** v/i **4.** erbleichen, bleich werden (**with** vor dat).

blanc·mange [bləˈmɒndʒ] s Pudding m.

blan·dish ['blændɪʃ] v/t j-m schmeicheln, schöntun. **'blan·dish·ment** s mst pl Schmeichelei f.

blank [blæŋk] **I** adj □ **1.** leer, unbe-

schrieben: leave ~ frei lassen. **2.** ✝, ⚰ Blanko...: ~ check (Br. cheque) Blankoscheck m, Scheckformular n; ~ signature Blankounterschrift f. **3.** inhaltslos, unausgefüllt (Leben etc); ausdruckslos (Gesicht etc). **4.** verdutzt, verblüfft; verständnislos. **5.** ~ cartridge → 9. **II** s **6.** freier Raum, Lücke f. **7.** unbeschriebenes Blatt (a. fig.); Formular n, Vordruck m. **8.** Lotterie: Niete f: draw a ~ e-e Niete ziehen, fig. a. kein Glück haben. **9.** ✕ Platzpatrone f.

blan·ket ['blæŋkɪt] **I** s (eng S. Bett)Decke f: ~ of snow (clouds) Schnee-(Wolken)decke; → wet 1. **II** v/t zudecken. **~ed in** (od. with) fog in Nebel eingehüllt. **III** adj umfassend, Gesamt..., Pauschal...

blare [bleə] **I** v/i schmettern (Trompete); brüllen, plärren (Radio etc). **II** s Schmettern n; Brüllen n, Plärren n.

blar·ney ['blɑːnɪ] **I** s Schmeichelei f. **II** v/t u. v/i (j-m) schmeicheln.

bla·sé ['blɑːzeɪ] adj gleichgültig.

blas·pheme [blæsˈfiːm] **I** v/t **1.** Gott etc lästern. **2.** allg. schmähen. **II** v/i **3.** Gott lästern: ~ against → I. **blas'phem·er** s (Gottes)Lästerer m. **blas·phe·mous** ['blæsfəməs] adj □ blasphemisch, (gottes)lästerlich. **'blas·phe·my** s **1.** Blasphemie f, (Gottes)Lästerung f. **2.** allg. Schmähung f.

blast [blɑːst] **I** s **1.** Windstoß m. **2.** (at) full ~ ⚙ u. fig. auf Hochtouren (laufen od. arbeiten). **3.** Explosion f, Detonation f; Druckwelle f. **4.** Sprengung f; Sprengladung f. **II** v/t **5.** sprengen. **6.** fig. zunichte machen, vereiteln. **7.** ~ off (into space) in den Weltraum schießen. **8.** sl. verfluchen: ~ed verdammt, verflucht; ~ed idiot Vollidiot m; ~ him (all)! verdammt (noch mal); ~ it! der Teufel soll ihn holen! ~ him! s **fur·nace** s ⚙ Hochofen m. **'~·off** s Start m (e-r Rakete).

bla·tant ['bleɪtənt] adj □ **1.** lärmend, laut. **2.** marktschreierisch; aufdringlich. **3.** offenkundig, eklatant.

blath·er ['blæðə] **I** v/i quatschen. **II** s Gequatsche n.

blaze [bleɪz] **I** s **1.** (lodernde) Flamme: be in a ~ in hellen Flammen stehen. **2.** Glanz m (a. fig.): ~ of colo(u)rs Farbenpracht f. **3.** fig. plötzlicher Ausbruch: ~ *of anger* Wutanfall *m.* **4.** F *go to ~s!* scher dich zum Teufel!; *like ~s* wie verrückt; *what the ~s ...?* was zum Teufel ...? II *v/i* **5.** lodern: ~ *up* aufflammen, -lodern, *fig. a.* entbrennen. **6.** *a. fig.* leuchten, glühen (*with* vor *dat*). III *v/t* **7.** *a.* ~ *abroad* verkünden, *contr.* ausposaunen. **'blaz·er** *s* Blazer *m,* Klub-, Sportjacke *f.* **'blaz·ing** *adj* **1.** glühend. **2.** auffällig, schreiend, (*Farben a.*) grell.

bla·zon ['bleɪzn] I *v/t* **1.** Wappen *n.* II *v/t mst* ~ *abroad* → **blaze** 7.

bleach [bli:tʃ] I *v/t* bleichen. II *s* Bleichmittel *n.*

bleak [bli:k] *adj* □ **1.** kahl, öde. **2.** ungeschützt, windig. **3.** *fig.* trost-, freudlos (*Dasein etc*), trüb, düster (*Aussichten etc*).

blear·y ['blɪərɪ] *adj* **1.** verschwommen. **2.** trüb (*Augen*). **'~-eyed** *adj* **1.** mit trüben Augen. **2.** *fig.* kurzsichtig.

bleat [bli:t] I *v/i* blöken (*Schaf*), meckern (*Ziege*). II *v/t et.* in weinerlichem Ton sagen. III *s* Blöken *n,* Meckern *n.*

bled [bled] *pret u. pp von* **bleed.**

bleed [bli:d] (*irr*) I *v/i* **1.** bluten: ~ *to death* verbluten. II *v/t* **2.** ~ zur Ader lassen. **3.** F schröpfen: ~ *s.o. for s.th.* j-m et. abknöpfen. **4.** ❂ *Bremsen* entlüften. **'bleed·er** *s* ❦ Bluter *m:* ~*'s disease* Bluterkrankheit *f.* **'bleed·ing** I *s* **1.** Blutung *f:* ~ *of the nose* Nasenbluten *n.* **2.** ❦ Aderlaß *m.* II *adj u. adv* **3.** *sl.* verdammt, verflucht.

bleep [bli:p] I *s* **1.** Piepton *m.* **2.** F Piepser *m* (*Funkrufempfänger*). II *v/i* **3.** piepen. III *v/t* **4.** j-n anpiepsen. **'bleep·er** *s* → **bleep** 2.

blem·ish ['blemɪʃ] I *v/t* verunstalten; *fig.* beflecken. II *s* Fehler *m,* Mangel *m; fig.* Makel *m.*

blend [blend] I *v/t* **1.** vermengen, (ver-)mischen; e-e (*Tee- etc*)Mischung zs.-stellen aus, *Wein* verschneiden. II *v/i* **2.** (*with*) sich vermischen (mit), gut passen (zu). **3.** verschmelzen, ineinander übergehen (*Farben, Klänge, Kulturen etc*): ~ *into* sich vereinigen zu. III *s* **4.** Mischung *f;* Verschnitt *m.*

bless [bles] *v/t* (*a. irr*) **1.** segnen (*a. fig.*): *be ~ed with* gesegnet sein mit; ~ *me!,* ~ *my soul!* F du-me-Güte!; (*God*) ~ *you!* Gesundheit! **2.** ~ *o.s.* sich glücklich

schätzen. **3.** ~ *him!* *euphem.* der Teufel soll ihn holen! **bless·ed** ['blesɪd] *adj* **1.** gesegnet, selig: *the* ♀ *Virgin* die heilige Jungfrau. **2.** *euphem.* verwünscht, verflixt: *not a ~ soul* keine Menschenseele. **'bless·ed·ness** *s* Seligkeit *f.* **'bless·ing** *s* Segen *m* (*a. fig.* **to** für): *it turned out to be a ~ in disguise* es stellte sich im nachhinein als Segen heraus.

blest [blest] *pret u. pp von* **bless.**

bleth·er ['bleðə] → **blather.**

blew [blu:] *pret von* **blow¹.**

blight [blaɪt] I *s* **1.** ❦ Mehltau *m.* **2.** *fig.* schädlicher Einfluß. II *v/t* **3.** *fig.* zunichte machen, zerstören. **'blight·er** *s Br.* F Kerl *m:* **lucky** ~ Glückspilz *m;* **poor** ~ armer Hund.

bli·mey ['blaɪmɪ] *int bsd. Br. sl.* Mensch Meier! (*überrascht*): verdammt!

blind [blaɪnd] I *adj* **1.** blind (*a. fig.* **to** gegenüber; **with** vor *dat*): ~ *in one eye* auf e-m Auge blind; **turn a** ~ *eye* ein Auge zudrücken (**to** bei). **2.** ~ unübersichtlich (*Kurve etc*). II *adv* **3.** ~ *drunk* F sternhagelvoll. III *v/t* **4.** blenden (*a. fig.*); blind machen (*a. fig.* **to** für, gegen). IV *s* **5.** Rolladen *m;* Rouleau *n; bsd. Br.* Markise *f;* → **Venetian.** ~ **al·ley** *s* Sackgasse *f* (*a. fig.*): **lead up a** ~ in e-e Sackgasse führen. ~ **flight** *s* ✈ Blindflug *m.* **'~-fold** I *adj* mit verbundenen Augen. II *adv fig.* blindlings. III *v/t* j-m die Augen verbinden. IV *s* Augenbinde *f.* **,~-man's 'buff** *s* Blindekuh(spiel *n*) *f.*

blind·ness ['blaɪndnɪs] *s* Blindheit *f* (*a. fig.*).

blind| spot *s* **1.** *mot.* toter Winkel (*im Rückspiegel*). **2.** *fig.* schwacher Punkt. **'~-worm** *s zo.* Blindschleiche *f.*

blink [blɪŋk] I *v/i* **1.** blinzeln, zwinkern: ~ *at* a) j-m zublinzeln, b) *fig.* sich maßlos wundern über (*acc*), c) → **4.** **2.** flimmern; blinken. II *v/t* **3.** ~ *one's eyes* (mit den Augen) zwinkern. **4.** *a.* ~ *away fig.* ignorieren. III *s* **5.** Blinzeln *n.* **'blink·er** *s* Blinklicht *n; mot.* Blinker *m.* **'blink·ing** *adj u. adv Br.* F verdammt.

bliss [blɪs] *s* (Glück)Seligkeit *f.* **bliss·ful** ['~fʊl] *adj* □ (glück)selig.

blis·ter ['blɪstə] I *s* ❦, ❂ Blase *f.* II *v/t* Blasen hervorrufen auf (*dat*). III *v/i* Blasen ziehen *od.* ❂ werfen.

blith·er·ing ['blɪðərɪŋ] *adj Br.* F verdammt: ~ *idiot* Vollidiot *m.*

blitz [blɪts] ⚔ **I** *s* **1.** heftiger Luftangriff. **2.** Blitzkrieg *m.* **II** *v/t* **3.** schwer bombardieren: *~ed* zerbombt.

bliz·zard ['blɪzəd] *s* Blizzard *m,* Schneesturm *m.*

bloat·ed ['bləʊtɪd] *adj* aufgeblasen (*a. fig. Person*), aufgebläht (*a. fig. Budget etc*), aufgedunsen (*Gesicht etc*).

bloat·er ['bləʊtə] *s gastr.* Bückling *m.*

blob [blɒb] *s* Klecks *m.*

bloc [blɒk] *s* ✝, *pol.* Block *m.*

block [blɒk] *s* **1.** (*a. Motor- etc*)Block *m,* Klotz *m;* Baustein *m,* (Bau)Klötzchen *n* (*für Kinder*). **2.** (*Schreib-, Notiz*)Block *m.* **3.** *bsd. Am.* (Häuser)Block *m:* ~ (*of flats*) *Br.* Wohnhaus *n.* **4.** *fig.* Block *m,* Gruppe *f.* **II** *v/t* **5.** *a.* ~ *up* (ab-, ver)sperren, blockieren, verstopfen. **6.** ✝ *Konto* sperren: *~ed account* Sperrkonto *n.*

block·ade [blɒ'keɪd] **I** *s* Blockade *f.* **II** *v/t* blockieren.

'**block|·head** *s* Dummkopf *m.* '~·**house** *s* Blockhaus *n.* ~ **let·ters** *s pl* Blockschrift *f.*

bloke [bləʊk] *s bsd. Br.* F Kerl *m.*

blond [blɒnd] *adj* **1.** blond (*Haar*), hell (*Haut*). **2.** blond(haarig). **blonde** [blɒnd] **I** *s* Blondine *f.* **II** *adj* → **blond.**

blood [blʌd] *s* **1.** Blut *n* (*a. fig.*): *his ~ froze* das Blut erstarrte ihm in den Adern; *related by* ~ blutsverwandt; → *cold* 1, *sweat* 2. **2.** Geblüt *n,* Abstammung *f.* ~ **al·co·hol** *s* ✿ Blutalkohol *m.* ,~-**and-'thun·der** *adj:* ~ *novel* Reißer *m.* ~ **bank** *s* ✿ Blutbank *f.* '~-**bath** *s* Blutbad *n.* ~ **clot** *s* ✿ Blutgerinnsel *n.* '~-**cur·dling** *adj* grauenhaft. ~ **do·nor** *s* ✿ Blutspender(in). ~ **group** *s* Blutgruppe *f.* '~-**hound** *s* Bluthund *m.*

blood·less ['blʌdlɪs] *adj* □ **1.** blutlos, -leer (*a. fig.*). **2.** unblutig (*Kampf etc*).

blood| **or·ange** *s* Blutorange *f.* ~ **poi·son·ing** *s* ✿ Blutvergiftung *f.* ~ **pres·sure** *s* ✿ Blutdruck *m.* ~ **pud·ding** *s* Blutwurst *f.* ~ **re·la·tion,** ~ **re·la·tive** *s* Blutsverwandte, *m, f.* ~ **re·venge** *s* Blutrache *f.* ~ **sam·ple** *s* ✿ Blutprobe *f.* '~-**shed** *s* Blutvergießen *n.* '~-**shot** *adj* blutunterlaufen. '~-**stained** *adj* blutbefleckt. '~-**suck·er** *s zo.* Blutsauger *m* (*a. fig.*). ~ **sug·ar** *s physiol.* Blutzucker *m.*

'~,**thirst·y** *adj* blutdürstig. ~ **trans·fu·sion** *s* ✿ Bluttransfusion *f,* -übertragung *f.* ~ **ves·sel** *s anat.* Blutgefäß *n.*

blood·y ['blʌdɪ] **I** *adj* **1.** blutig. **2.** *Br. sl.* verdammt, verflucht: ~ *fool* Vollidiot *m; not a* ~ *soul* kein Schwanz. **II** *adv* **3.** *Br. sl.* ~ 2: ~ *awful* saumäßig.

bloom [bluːm] **I** *s* → *blossom* I. **II** *v/i* blühen (*a. fig.*).

bloom·er ['bluːmə] *s bsd. Br.* F grober Fehler, Schnitzer *m.*

bloom·ing ['bluːmɪŋ] *adj* **1.** blühend (*a. fig.*). **2.** (*a. adv*) F verflixt.

blos·som ['blɒsəm] **I** *s* **1.** Blüte *f: be in full* ~ in voller Blüte stehen. **2.** *fig.* Blüte (-zeit) *f.* **II** *v/i* **3.** blühen (*a. fig.*): ~ (*out*) erblühen (*into* zu).

blot [blɒt] **I** *s* **1.** Klecks *m.* **2.** *fig.* Makel *m.* **II** *v/t* **3.** beklecksen. **4.** *fig.* beflecken. **5.** *Familie, Erinnerungen etc* auslöschen. **6.** *mit Löschpapier* (ab)löschen.

blotch [blɒtʃ] *s* → *blot* 1–3.

blot·ter ['blɒtə] *s Am.* Kladde *f.*

blot·ting pa·per ['blɒtɪŋ] *s* Löschpapier *n.*

blot·to ['blɒtəʊ] *adj sl.* (stink)besoffen.

blouse [blaʊz] *s* Bluse *f.*

blow¹ [bləʊ] *s* **1.** Blasen *n,* Wehen *n.* **2.** Luftzug *m.* **3.** Blasen *n:* ~ *on a whistle* Pfiff *m; give one's nose a* ~ sich schneuzen. **II** *v/i* (*irr*) **4.** blasen, wehen. **5.** ertönen (*Pfiff etc*). **6.** keuchen, schnaufen. **7.** explodieren; platzen (*Reifen*); ✿ durchbrennen (*Sicherung*). **III** *v/t* (*irr*) **8.** blasen, wehen. **9.** *Suppe etc* blasen, *Feuer* anfachen. **10.** (auf-, aus)blasen: ~ *bubbles* Seifenblasen machen; ~ *glass* Glas blasen; ~ *one's nose* sich schneuzen. **11.** ~ *one's lid* (*od. top, stack*) F an die Decke gehen. **12.** *sl. Geld* verpulvern (*on* für); *Chance* vergeben.

Verbindungen mit Adverbien:

blow| **a·way** *v/t* fort-, wegblasen. ~ **down** *v/t* um-, herunterwehen. ~ **in** *v/i* F hereinschneien (*Besucher*). ~ **off** → *blow away.* ~ **out** *v/t* **1.** *Licht etc* ausblasen. **2.** *e-m* Reifen etc ~ e-e Kugel durch den Kopf jagen. ~ **up I** *v/t* **1.** (in die Luft) sprengen. **2.** aufblasen, -pumpen. **3.** *phot.* vergrößern. *Bild, fig.* aufbauschen (*into* zu). **4.** F *j-n* anschnauzen. **II** *v/i* **5.** in die Luft fliegen; explodieren (*a. fig.* F): ~ *at* → 4. **6.** losbrechen (*Sturm etc*), ausbrechen (*Streit etc*).

blow² [~] s (a. Schicksals)Schlag m, Stoß m: **at one** (*od. a* [*single*]) ~ mit 'einem Schlag; **come to** ~**s** handgreiflich werden.

'**blow**|**-dry** v/t **1.** j-m die Haare fönen: ~ **s.o.'s hair. 2.** j-m die Haare fönen: ~ **s.o.** ~ **dry·er** s Haartrockner m.

blow·er ['bləʊə] s ⚙ Gebläse n.

'**blow**|**·fly** s zo. Schmeißfliege f. '~**·gun** s ⚙ Spritzpistole f. '~**·lamp** s ⚙ Lötlampe f.

blown [bləʊn] pp von **blow¹.**

'**blow**|**-out** s mot. Reifenpanne f. '~**·torch** s ⚙ Lötlampe f. '~**·up** s **1.** Explosion f (a. fig. F). **2.** F Krach m, Streit m. **3.** phot. Vergrößerung f.

blow·y ['bləʊɪ] adj windig.

blowz·y ['blaʊzɪ] adj schlampig (bsd. Frau).

blub·ber ['blʌbə] v/i flennen, plärren.

bludg·eon ['blʌdʒən] I s **1.** Knüppel m. II v/t **2.** niederknüppeln. **3.** ~ **s.o. into doing s.th.** j-n zwingen, et. zu tun.

blue [blu:] I adj **1.** blau: → **moon** I. **2.** F melancholisch, traurig. **3.** unanständig, schlüpfrig: ~ **jokes**; → **funk** I, **murder** I. II s **5.** Blau n: **dressed in** ~ blau od. in Blau gekleidet; **out of the** ~ fig. aus heiterem Himmel. **6.** pl (a. sg konstruiert) F Melancholie f: **have** (od. **be in**) **the** ~**s** den Moralischen haben. **7.** → **blues.** III v/t **8.** blau färben. ~**·ber·ry** ['~bərɪ] s ♥ Blau-, Heidelbeere f. '~**·blood·ed** adj blaublütig, adlig. '~**,bot·tle** s **1.** zo. Schmeißfliege f. **2.** ♥ Kornblume f. ~ **jeans** s pl Blue jeans pl. ~ **pen·cil** s **1.** Blaustift m. **2.** fig. Rotstift m, Zensur f. ,~**'pen·cil** v/t pret u. pp **-ciled,** bsd. Br. **-cilled** zensieren. ~**'print** I s **1.** phot. Blaupause f. **2.** fig. Plan m, Entwurf m: ~ **stage** Planungsstadium n. II v/t **3.** e-e Blaupause machen von. **4.** planen, entwerfen.

blues [blu:z] s pl **1.** → **blue** 6. **2.** (a. sg konstruiert) ♪ Blues m.

'**blue,stock·ing** s bsd. contp. Blaustrumpf m.

bluff [blʌf] I v/t u. v/i bluffen. II s Bluff m. '**bluff·er** s Bluffer m.

blu·ish ['blu:ɪʃ] adj bläulich.

blun·der ['blʌndə] I s **1.** (grober) Fehler. II v/i **2.** e-n (groben) Fehler machen. **3.** pfuschen, stümpern. **4.** stolpern, tappen (**into** in acc) (beide a. fig.). III v/t **5.** verpfuschen, verpatzen. '**blun·der·er** s Pfuscher m, Stümper m. '**blun·der·ing** adj stümperhaft.

blunt [blʌnt] I adj **1.** stumpf. **2.** fig. abgestumpft (**to** gegen). **3.** fig. ungehobelt. **4.** fig. offen, schonungslos. II v/t **5.** stumpf machen, abstumpfen (a. fig. **to** gegen). '**blunt·ly** adv fig. frei heraus: **to put it** ~ um es ganz offen zu sagen; **refuse** ~ glatt ablehnen.

blur [blɜ:] I v/t **1.** verwischen: a) Schrift etc verschmieren, b) a. fig. undeutlich od. verschwommen machen. **2.** phot. verwackeln. **3.** Sinne etc trüben. II v/i **4.** verschwimmen (a. undeutlich werden). **5.** fig. sich verwischen (Unterschiede etc).

blurt [blɜ:t] v/t: ~ **out** herausplatzen mit.

blush [blʌʃ] I v/i **1.** erröten, rot werden (**at** bei): ~ **for** (od. **with**) **shame** schamrot werden. II s Erröten n, (Scham)Röte f. '**blush·er** s Rouge n.

boar [bɔ:] s zo. Eber m, (Wildschwein) Keiler m.

board [bɔ:d] I s **1.** Brett n, Diele f, Planke f. **2.** (Anschlag-, Schach- etc)Brett n; (Wand)Tafel f: → **sweep** 4. **3.** pl thea. Bretter pl, Bühne f: **tread** (od. **walk**) **the** ~**s** auf den Brettern stehen. **4.** Kost f, Verpflegung f: ~ **and lodging** Kost u. Logis, Wohnung u. Verpflegung. **5.** Ausschuß m, Kommission f; Amt n, Behörde f: ~ **of examiners** Prüfungskommission; ♀ **of Trade** Br. Handelsministerium n, Am. Handelskammer f. **6.** on ~ an Bord (e-s Schiffs, Flugzeugs); im Zug od. Bus; **on** ~ (a) **ship** an Bord e-s Schiffs; **go on** ~ an Bord gehen; einsteigen. **7.** Pappe f: (bound) **in** ~**s** kartoniert. II v/t **8.** dielen, täfeln, verschalen. **9.** an Bord (e-s Schiffs od. Flugzeugs) gehen, ♣, ✗ entern; einsteigen in (e-n Zug od. Bus). '**board·er** s **1.** Kostgänger(in); Pensionsgast m. **2.** Br. Internatsschüler(in).

board game s Brettspiel n.

board·ing ['bɔ:dɪŋ] s Dielenbelag m, Täfelung f, Verschalung f. ~ **card** s ✈ Bordkarte f. '~**·house** s Pension f, Fremdenheim n. ~ **pass** s ✈ Bordkarte f. ~ **school** s Internat n, Pensionat n.

board room s Sitzungssaal m.

boast [bəʊst] **I** s **1.** Prahlerei f. **2.** Stolz m (*Gegenstand des Stolzes*). **II** v/i **3.** prahlen (*of, about* mit). **III** v/t **4.** sich des Besitzes (gen) rühmen (können), aufzuweisen haben. **'boast·er** s Prahler(in). **boast·ful** ['-fʊl] adj □ prahlerisch.

boat [bəʊt] **I** s **1.** Boot n; Schiff n: *be in the same ~* fig. im selben Boot sitzen; *burn one's ~s* (*behind one*) fig. alle Brücken hinter sich abbrechen; *take to the ~s* ♏ in die (Rettungs)Boote gehen; → *miss¹* **1**, *rock²* **2**. **2.** (*bsd.* Soßen)Schüssel f. **II** v/i **3.** Boot fahren: *go ~ing* e-e Bootsfahrt machen. **'~house** s Bootshaus n.

boat·ing ['bəʊtɪŋ] s **1.** Bootfahren n. **2.** Bootsfahrt f.

boat¦ race s Bootrennen n. **~swain** ['bəʊsn] s ♏ Bootsmann m. **~ train** s Zug m mit Schiffsanschluß.

bob [bɒb] **I** s **1.** Knicks m. **2.** Sport: Bob m. **II** v/t **3.** Haare etc kurz schneiden, stutzen. **III** v/i **4.** sich auf u. ab bewegen: *~ up* (plötzlich) auftauchen (*a. fig.*). **5.** knicksen (*at, before,* to vor dat).

bob·bin ['bɒbɪn] s Spule f (a. ⚡).

bob·by ['bɒbɪ] s Br. F Bobby m (*Polizist*). **~ pin** s bsd. Am. Haarklammer f, -klemme f.

'bob¦·sled, **'~sleigh** s Sport: Bob m.

bode¹ [bəʊd] v/t: *~ ill* Unheil verkünden; *~ well* Gutes versprechen.

bode² [~] pret von **bide**.

bod·ice ['bɒdɪs] s **1.** Mieder n. **2.** Oberteil n (*e-s Kleids etc*).

bod·i·ly ['bɒdɪlɪ] **I** adj **1.** körperlich: *~ harm* (*od. injury*) ⚖ Körperverletzung f; *~ needs* (*od. wants*) pl leibliche Bedürfnisse pl. **II** adv **2.** leibhaftig. **3.** als Ganzes; geschlossen.

bod·y ['bɒdɪ] s **1.** Körper m, Leib m, engS. Rumpf m. **2.** oft dead ~ Leiche f. **3.** ♏, ✈ Rumpf m; mot. Karosserie f. **4.** Gesamtheit f: *in a ~* geschlossen, wie ein Mann. *~ of laws* Gesetz(es)sammlung f. **5.** Körper(schaft f) m, Gruppe f, Gremium n: → *diplomatic, governing* **2**. **6.** fig. Kern m, das Wesentliche. **7.** Hauptteil m, Text(teil) m (*e-s Briefs etc*). **8.** phys. etc Körper m: → *celestial, heavenly.* **9.** fig. Körper m, Gehalt m (*von Wein*), (Klang)Fülle f. *~*

build·ing s Bodybuilding n. **'~guard** s **1.** Leibwächter m. **2.** Leibgarde f, -wache f. **~ lan·guage** s Körpersprache f. **~ o·do(u)r** s (bsd. unangenehmer) Körpergeruch. **~ search** s Leibesvisitation f. **'~work** s mot. Karosserie f.

bog [bɒg] **I** s Sumpf m, Morast m (*beide a. fig.*). **II** v/t: *~ down* fig. zum Stocken bringen; *get ~ged* (*down*) → **III**. **III** v/i sich festfahren, steckenbleiben (*beide a. fig.*).

bo·gey → **bogy**.

bog·gle ['bɒgl] v/i fassungslos sein: *imagination* (*od. the mind*) *~s at the thought* es wird e-m schwindlig bei dem Gedanken.

bog·gy ['bɒgɪ] adj sumpfig, morastig.

bo·gie → **bogy**.

bo·gus ['bəʊgəs] adj **1.** falsch, unecht. **2.** Schwindel..., Schein...

bo·gy ['bəʊgɪ] s Kobold m; (Schreck-)Gespenst n (a. fig.).

boil¹ [bɔɪl] s ✖ Geschwür n, Furunkel m, n.

boil² [~] **I** s Kochen n, Sieden n: *bring to the ~* zum Kochen bringen. **II** v/i kochen (*a. fig.* with vor dat), sieden: → *kettle, pot* **1.** **III** v/t kochen (lassen). *Verbindungen mit Adverbien:*

boil¦ a·way **I** v/i **1.** kochen, sieden. **2.** verdampfen. **II** v/t **4.** verdampfen lassen. **~ down** **I** v/t **1.** einkochen lassen. **2.** fig. zs.-fassen (*to a few sentences* in ein paar Sätzen). **II** v/i **3.** einkochen. **4.** *~ to* fig. hinauslaufen auf (acc). **~ o·ver** v/i **1.** überkochen, -laufen. **2.** fig. vor Wut kochen. **3.** fig. Situation etc: außer Kontrolle geraten; sich auswachsen (*into* zu).

boil·er ['bɔɪlə] s **1.** ⚙ Dampfkessel m. **2.** Boiler m, Heißwasserspeicher m. **3.** Suppenhuhn n. **~ suit** s Overall m.

boil·ing ['bɔɪlɪŋ] **I** adj siedend, kochend. **II** adv: *~ hot* kochendheiß. **~ point** s Siedepunkt m (a. fig.): *reach* → den Siedepunkt erreichen.

bois·ter·ous ['bɔɪstərəs] adj □ **1.** stürmisch (*Meer, Wetter etc*). **2.** lärmend, laut. **3.** ausgelassen, wild (*Person, Party etc*).

bold [bəʊld] adj □ **1.** kühn: a) mutig, unerschrocken, b) gewagt, c) fortschrittlich. **2.** dreist, frech: *make ~ to* sich erdreisten *od.* es wagen zu. **3.** scharf hervortretend: *in ~ outline* in deutlichen Umrissen.

bole [bəʊl] *s* Baumstamm *m.*

bo·lo·ney [bə'ləʊnɪ] *s sl.* Quatsch *m.*

bol·ster ['bəʊlstə] *I s* **1.** Keilkissen *n;* Nackenrolle *f.* **2.** Polster *n,* Kissen *n,* Unterlage *f* (a. ☉). **II** *v/t* **3.** (aus)polstern. **4.** *mst ~ up fig.* unterstützen.

bolt¹ [bəʊlt] *I s* **1.** Bolzen *m: he has shot his ~ fig.* er hat sein Pulver verschossen. **2.** Blitz(strahl) *m: a ~ from the blue fig.* ein Blitz aus heiterem Himmel. **3.** ☉ Riegel *m.* **4.** ☉ (Schrauben)Bolzen, Schraube *f* (mit Mutter): *~ nut* Schraubenmutter *f.* **5.** plötzlicher Satz *od.* Sprung: *he made a ~ for the door* er machte e-n Satz zur Tür. **II** *adv* **6.** *~ upright* bolzen-, kerzengerade. **III** *v/i* **7.** durchbrennen, ausreißen. **8.** durchgehen (*Pferd*). **IV** *v/t* **9.** ver-, zuriegeln. **10.** *oft ~ down Essen* hinunterschlingen, *Getränk* hinunterstürzen.

bolt² [~] *v/t Mehl* sieben.

bomb [bɒm] *I s* Bombe *f.* **II** *v/t* bombardieren: *~ed out* ausgebombt. *~ a·lert s* Bombenalarm *m.*

bom·bard [bɒm'bɑːd] *v/t* bombardieren (*a. fig. with* mit). **bom'bard·ment** *s* Bombardement *n,* Bombardierung *f.*

bom·bast ['bɒmbæst] *s* Bombast *m,* Schwulst *m.* **bom'bas·tic** *adj* (*~ally*) bombastisch, schwülstig.

bombed [bɒmbd] *adj sl.* **1.** besoffen. **2.** high (*im Drogenrausch*).

bomb·er ['bɒmə] *s* **1.** ✈ Bomber *m.* **2.** Bombenleger *m.*

'**bomb|·proof I** *adj* bombensicher: *~ shelter → 1.* **II** *s* Bunker *m.* '*~·shell s:* *be a ~* wie e-e Bombe einschlagen. *~ threat s* Bombendrohung *f.*

bo·nan·za [bəʊ'nænzə] **I** *s fig.* Goldgrube *f.* **II** *adj* sehr einträglich.

bond [bɒnd] **I s 1.** *pl fig.* Bande *pl: the ~s of love.* **2.** Bund *m,* Verbindung *f.* **3.** ✝ Zollverschluß *m: in ~* unter Zollverschluß. **4.** ✝ Schuldverschreibung *f,* Obligation *f.* **II** *v/t* **5.** ✝ unter Zollverschluß legen: *~ed warehouse* Zollspeicher *m.* '*~·hold·er s* ✝ Obligationsinhaber *m.*

bone [bəʊn] *I s* **1.** Knochen *m, pl a.* Gebeine *pl: make no ~s about* (*od. of*) nicht viel Federlesens machen mit; *feel*

s.th. in one's ~s et. in den Knochen *od.* instinktiv spüren; *have a ~ to pick with s.o.* mit j-m ein Hühnchen zu rupfen haben; *chilled* (*od. frozen*) *to the ~* völlig durchgefroren; *→ contention* 1. **2.** (*Fisch*)Gräte *f.* **II** *v/t* **3.** entbeinen; *Fisch* entgräten. **III** *v/i* **4.** *~ up on s.th.* F et. pauken *od.* büffeln. *~·dry adj* knochentrocken. '*~·head s* F Holzkopf *m.* '*~·la·zy adj* stinkfaul. '*~·shak·er s* F Klapperkasten *m* (*Bus etc*).

bon·fire ['bɒn·faɪə] *s* **1.** Freudenfeuer *n.* **2.** Feuer *n* im Freien (*zum Unkrautverbrennen etc*).

bonk [bɒŋk] *v/t u. v/i sl.* bumsen.

bon·kers ['bɒŋkəz] *adj sl.* übergeschnappt: *go ~* überschnappen.

bon·net ['bɒnɪt] *s* **1.** ☉ (Schutz)Kappe *f,* Haube *f.* **2.** *mot. Br.* Motorhaube *f.*

bo·nus ['bəʊnəs] *s* **1.** ✝ Bonus *m,* Prämie *f.* **2.** Gratifikation *f.* **3.** ✝ *bsd. Br.* Extradividende *f.*

bon·y ['bəʊnɪ] *adj* **1.** (stark-, grob)knochig. **2.** voll(er) Knochen; voll(er) Gräten (*Fisch*). **3.** knochendürr.

boo [buː] **I** *int* buh! **II** *s* Buh(ruf *m*) *n.* **III** *v/i* buhen. **IV** *v/t* ausbuhen.

boob [buːb] *sl.* **I** *s* **1.** Blödmann *m,* Idiot *m.* **2.** *Br.* Schnitzer *m.* **II** *v/i* **3.** *Br.* e-n Schnitzer machen.

boo·by ['buːbɪ] *s* **1.** Trottel *m,* Dummkopf *m.* **2.** *Sport etc:* Letzte *m, f,* Schlechteste *m, f.* '*~·hatch s Am. sl.* Klapsmühle *f.* *~ prize s Sport etc:* Scherzpreis *für den Letzten od. Schlechtesten.* *~ trap s* **1.** versteckte Sprengladung; *Auto etc,* in dem e-e Sprengladung versteckt ist. **2.** grober Scherz (*bsd. über halbgeöffneter Tür angebrachter Wassereimer*).

book [bʊk] **I s 1.** Buch *n: the* 2 die Bibel; *a closed ~ fig.* ein Buch mit sieben Siegeln (*to für*); *an open ~ fig.* ein offenes *od.* aufgeschlagenes Buch (*to für*); *be at one's ~s* über s-n Büchern sitzen; *speak* (*od. talk*) *like a ~* geschraubt *od.* gestelzt reden; *→ suit* 5. **2.** ✝ Geschäftsbuch *n: be deep in s.o.'s ~s* bei j-m tief in der Kreide stehen. **3.** Liste *f,* Verzeichnis *n: be on the ~s* auf der (Mitglieder- *etc*)Liste stehen. **4.** Notizbuch *n,* -block *m;* (Schreib-, Schul)Heft *n: be in s.o.'s good* (*bad*)*~s* bei j-m gut (schlecht) angeschrieben sein. **5.**

Heft(chen) n: ~ **of stamps** (**tickets**) Marken-(Fahrschein)heft(chen); ~ **of matches** Streichholzbriefchen n. **II** v/t **6.** ✝ (ver)buchen; *Auftrag* notieren. **7.** aufschreiben, *Sport: a.* verwarnen. **8.** verpflichten, engagieren. **9.** *Zimmer etc* bestellen, *Reise etc* buchen, *Eintritts-, Fahrkarte* lösen: ~**ed up** ausgebucht (*Künstler, Hotel, Veranstaltung*). **10.** *Gepäck* aufgeben (**to** nach). **III** v/i **11.** *Br. a.* ~ **up** e-e (*Fahr- etc*)Karte lösen (**to, for** nach): ~ **through** durchlösen (**to** bis, nach). **12.** sich (*für e-e Fahrt etc*) vormerken lassen, e-n Platz *etc* bestellen, buchen. **13.** ~ **in** *bsd. Br.* sich (*im Hotel*) eintragen, ~ **in at** absteigen in (*dat*).

book·a·ble ['bʊkəbl] *adj* im Vorverkauf erhältlich.

'**book**|**bind·er** s Buchbinder m. '~·**case** s Bücherschrank m. ~ **club** s Buchgemeinschaft f. ~ **end** s Bücherstütze f.

book·ie ['bʊkɪ] s F Buchmacher m.

book·ing ['bʊkɪŋ] s Buchung f, (Vor)Bestellung f: **make a** (**firm**) ~ (fest) buchen. ~ **clerk** s Fahrkartenverkäufer m. ~ **of·fice** s **1.** (Fahrkarten)Schalter m. **2.** (*Theater- etc*)Kasse f, Vorverkaufsstelle f.

book·ish ['bʊkɪʃ] *adj* **1.** belesen. **2.** papieren (*Stil*).

'**book**|**keep·er** s ✝ Buchhalter(in). '~·**keep·ing** s ✝ Buchhaltung f, -führung f. '~·**mak·er** s Buchmacher m. '~·**mark**, '~·**mark·er** s Lesezeichen n. '~·**mo·bile** ['~məʊ,biːl] s Am. Wanderbücherei f. '~·**sell·er** s Buchhändler(in). '~·**shop** s Buchhandlung f. '~·**stall** s **1.** Bücherstand m. **2.** bsd. Br. Zeitungskiosk m, -stand m. '~·**store** s bsd. Am. Buchhandlung f. '~·**worm** s zo. Bücherwurm m (a. fig.).

boom¹ [buːm] **I** v/i dröhnen (*Stimme etc*), donnern (*Geschütz etc*), brausen (*Wellen etc*). **II** s Dröhnen, Donner m, Brausen n.

boom² [~] s **1.** ♫ Baum m, Spiere f. **2.** ☼ (*Kran*)Ausleger m. **3.** *Film, TV:* (*Mikrophon*)Galgen m.

boom³ [~] ✝ **I** s Boom m: a) Hochkonjunktur f, b) Börse: Hausse f, **II** v/i e-n Boom erleben.

boom·er·ang ['buːməræŋ] **I** s Bumerang

m (a. fig.). **II** v/i fig. sich als Bumerang erweisen (**on** für).

boon [buːn] s fig. Segen m (**to** für).

boor [bʊə] s ungehobelter Kerl. **boor·ish** ['bʊərɪʃ] adj □ ungehobelt. '**boor·ish·ness** s ungehobeltes Benehmen od. Wesen.

boost [buːst] **I** v/t **1.** F Preise in die Höhe treiben. **2.** F Auftrieb geben (dat), Produktion etc ankurbeln, Moral heben. **3.** ⚙ Druck erhöhen; ⚡ Spannung verstärken. **II** s **4.** F Auftrieb m. **5.** ⚙ Erhöhung f; ⚡ Verstärkung f. '**boost·er** s **1.** a. ~ **shot** ✚ Wiederholungsimpfung f. **2.** Zündstufe f (e-r Rakete): ~ **rocket** Startrakete f.

boot¹ [buːt] **I** s **1.** Stiefel m: **the ~ is on the other foot** (od. leg) die Sache liegt umgekehrt; → beat 4, lick 1. **2.** F (Fuß)Tritt m: **give s.o. a** ~ → 4; **get the** ~ rausgeschmissen (entlassen) werden. **3.** mot. Br. Kofferraum m. **II** v/t **4.** F j-m e-n (Fuß)Tritt geben: ~ (**out**) rausschmeißen (entlassen).

boot² [~] s: **to** ~ obendrein, noch dazu.

'**boot·black** s Schuhputzer m.

booth [buːð] s **1.** (Markt-, Schau)Bude f, (Messe)Stand m. **2.** (Telefon)Zelle f; (Wahl)Kabine f, (-)zelle f.

'**boot**|**lace** s Schnürsenkel m. '~·**lick** v/t u. v/i F (vor j-m) kriechen. '~·**lick·er** s F Kriecher m.

boots [buːts] pl **boots** s Br. Hausdiener m (im Hotel).

boo·ty ['buːtɪ] s (fig. a. Aus)Beute f.

booze [buːz] F **I** v/i saufen. **II** s Zeug n (alkoholisches Getränk); Sauferei f; (Br. a. ~**up**) Sauftour f; (Br. a. ~**up**) Besäufnis n. '**booz·er** s F **1.** Säufer(in). **2.** Kneipe f. '**booz·y** adj F versoffen.

bor·der ['bɔːdə] **I** s **1.** Rand m. **2.** Einfassung f, Saum m, Umrandung f. **3.** (Gebiets-, Landes)Grenze f: ~ **incident** Grenzzwischenfall m. **II** v/t **4.** einfassen. **5.** begrenzen, grenzen an (acc). **III** v/i **6.** grenzen (**on** an acc) (a. fig.).

'**bor·der·er** s Grenzbewohner m.

'**bor·der**|**land** s Grenzgebiet n. '~·**line** s **1.** Grenzlinie f. **2.** fig. Grenze f. **II** adj **3.** fig. Grenz...: ~ **case** Grenzfall m.

bore¹ [~] **I** s **1.** Bohrung f: a) Bohrloch n, b) ⚙ Kaliber n. **II** v/t (bsd. aus)bohren. **III** v/i bohren (**for** nach).

bore² [~] **I** s **1.** langweilige Sache; bsd.

Br. lästige Sache. **2.** Langweiler *m; bsd. Br.* lästiger Kerl. **II** *v/t* **3.** *j-n* langweilen; *bsd. Br. j-m* lästig sein: **be ~d** sich langweilen; **be ~d stiff** F sich zu Tode langweilen.

bore³ [~] *pret von* **bear².**

bore·dom ['bɔːdəm] *s* **1.** Lang(e)weile *f*. **2.** Langweiligkeit *f*.

bor·er ['bɔːrə] *s* ⚙ Bohrer *m.*

bo·ric ac·id ['bɔːrɪk] *s* 🜊 Borsäure *f*.

bor·ing ['bɔːrɪŋ] *adj* langweilig.

born [bɔːn] **I** *pp von* **bear²** 2. **II** *adj* geboren (*a. fig.*): **a ~ poet.**

borne [bɔːn] *pp von* **bear².**

bo·ron ['bɔːrɒn] *s* 🜊 Bor *n.*

bor·ough ['bʌrə] *s* **1.** *Br.* Stadt *f* (*mit Selbstverwaltung*); (*a.* **parliamentary ~**) Stadt *f zur* städtischer Wahlbezirk mit eigener Vertretung im Parlament; Stadtteil *m* (*von Groß-London*). **2.** *Am.* Stadtbezirk *m* (*in New York*).

bor·row ['bɒrəʊ] **I** *v/t* **1.** (sich) *et.* (aus)borgen *od.* leihen (*from* von). **2.** *fig.* entlehnen (*from* von): **~ed word** Lehnwort *n.* **II** *v/i* **3.** 🏦 Kredit aufnehmen. **'bor·row·er** *s* **1.** Entleiher(in). **2.** 🏦 Kreditnehmer(in).

bosh [bɒʃ] *s* F Blödsinn *m*, Quatsch *m.*

bos·om ['bʊzəm] *s* **1.** Busen *m* (*a. fig.*): **~ friend** Busenfreund(in). **2.** *fig.* Schoß *m:* **in the ~ of one's family.**

boss¹ [bɒs] *s* Buckel *m*, Knauf *m.*

boss² [~] F **I** *s* Boß *m*, Chef *m.* **II** *v/t:* **~ about** (*od.* **around**) herumkommandieren.

boss·y ['bɒsɪ] *adj* F herrisch.

bo·tan·i·cal [bə'tænɪkl] *adj* ☐ botanisch: **~ garden(s** *pl*) botanischer Garten. **bot·a·nist** ['bɒtənɪst] *s* Botaniker(in). **'bot·a·ny** *s* Botanik *f*.

botch [bɒtʃ] **I** *s* Pfusch(arbeit *f*) *m:* **make a ~ of** → II. **II** *v/t* verpfuschen. **III** *v/i* pfuschen. **'botch·er** *s* Pfuscher *m.*

both [bəʊθ] **I** *adj u. pron* beide(s): **~ my brothers** m-e beiden Brüder; **~ of them** alle beide; → **sex** 1. **II** *adv od. cj:* **~ ... and** sowohl ... als (auch).

both·er ['bɒðə] **I** *s* Belästigung *f*, Störung *f*. **II** *v/t* belästigen, stören: **don't ~ me!** laß mich in Ruhe!; **I can't be ~ed** ich habe keine Lust (**to do** zu tun). **III** *v/i* (*about*) sich kümmern (um); sich aufregen (über *acc*).

bot·tle ['bɒtl] **I** *s* Flasche *f:* → **hit** 7. **II** *v/t*

in Flaschen abfüllen: **~d beer** Flaschenbier *n;* **~ up** Gefühle *etc* unterdrücken; **~d-up** aufgestaut. **'~·neck** *s* Flaschenhals *m*, Engpaß *m* (*e-r Straße*) (*a. fig.*). **~·o·pen·er** *s* Flaschenöffner *m.* **~ post** *s* Flaschenpost *f.*

bot·tom ['bɒtəm] **I** *s* **1.** Boden *m* (*e-s Gefäßes etc*), Fuß *m* (*e-s Bergs etc*), Sohle *f* (*e-s Tals etc*), Unterseite *f:* **at the ~ of the street** am Ende der Straße; **from the ~ of one's heart** aus tiefstem Herzen; **~s up!** F ex! **2.** Boden *m*, Grund *m:* **~ of the sea** Meeresboden, -grund. **3.** Grund(lage *f*) *m:* **be at the ~ of** der Grund sein für, hinter *e-r Sache* stecken; **get to the ~ of s.th.** e-r Sache auf den Grund gehen *od.* kommen; **knock the ~ out of s.th.** *et. fig.* widerlegen. **4.** (Stuhl)Sitz *m.* **5.** F Popo *m.* **II** *adj* **6.** unterst: **~ line** letzte Zeile; → **bet** 4, **rung².** **'bot·tom·less** *adj* ☐ *fig.* unergründlich; unerschöpflich.

bough [baʊ] *s* Ast *m*, Zweig *m.*

bought [bɔːt] *pret u. pp von* **buy.**

bouil·lon ['buːjɒn] *s* Fleischbrühe *f*, Bouillon *f.*

bou·le·vard ['buːləvɑːd] *s* Boulevard *m.*

bounce [baʊns] **I** *s* **1.** Elastizität *f.* **2.** Sprung *m*, Satz *m.* **3.** F Schwung *m*, Schmiß *m.* **4.** F Rausschmiß *m* (*a. Entlassung*): **give** *s.o.* **the ~** → 6; **get the ~** rausgeschmissen werden. **II** *v/t* **5.** Ball *etc* aufprallen *od.* aufspringen lassen. **6.** F *j-n* rausschmeißen (*a. entlassen*). **III** *v/i* **7.** aufprallen, -springen (*Ball etc*): **~ off** abprallen (von). **8.** federn, elastisch sein (*Gummi etc*); springen (*Ball*). **9.** a) springen, hüpfen (*over* über *acc*), b) stürmen, stürzen (*into* in *acc*). **10.** F platzen (*Scheck*). **'bounc·er** *s* F **1.** Rausschmeißer *m.* **2.** ungedeckter Scheck. **'bounc·ing** *adj* stramm (*Baby etc*).

bound¹ [baʊnd] **I** *pret u. pp von* **bind.** **II** *adj:* **be ~ to do s.th.** (zwangsläufig) *et.* tun müssen; **he was ~ to be late** er mußte ja zu spät kommen.

bound² [~] *adj* unterwegs (**for** nach): **where are you ~ for?** wohin reisen *od.* gehen Sie?

bound³ [~] **I** *s mst pl* Grenze *f*, *fig. a.* Schranke *f:* **keep within ~s** in (vernünftigen) Grenzen halten; **beyond all ~s** maß-, grenzenlos; **the park is out of ~s**

(to) das Betreten des Parks ist (für *od. dat*) verboten; *within the ~s of possibility* im Bereich des Möglichen. **II** *v/t* begrenzen.

bound⁴ [~] **I** *s* → **bounce** 2. **II** *v/i* → **bounce** 7, 9 a.

bound·a·ry ['baʊndərɪ] *s* Grenze *f*.

bound·en ['baʊndən] *adj*: *my ~ duty* meine Pflicht u. Schuldigkeit.

bound·less ['baʊndlɪs] *adj* □ grenzenlos (*a. fig.*).

boun·te·ous ['baʊntɪəs], **boun·ti·ful** ['~tɪfʊl] *adj* □ **1.** freigebig (*of* mit). **2.** reichlich.

boun·ty ['baʊntɪ] *s* **1.** Freigebigkeit *f*. **2.** großzügige Spende. **3.** Prämie *f*: a) Belohnung *f*, b) ✠ Zuschuß *m* (*on* auf *acc*, für).

bou·quet [bʊ'keɪ] *s* Bukett *n*: a) (Blumen)Strauß *m*, b) Blume *f* (*von Wein*).

bour·bon ['bɜːbən] *s* Bourbon *m* (*amerikanischer Maiswhisky*).

bout [baʊt] *s* **1.** *fenc.* Gefecht *n*; (*Box-, Ring*)Kampf *m*. **2.** ✠ Anfall *m*: *~ of rheumatism* Rheumaanfall.

bou·tique [buː'tiːk] *s* Boutique *f*.

bo·vine ['bəʊvaɪn] *adj* (*a. geistig*) träge, schwerfällig.

bov·ver ['bɒvə] *Br. sl.* **I** *s* Straßenkämpfe *pl* (*bsd. unter Rockerbanden*): *~ boots pl* schwere Stiefel, mit denen Rocker aufeinander eintreten; *~ boy* Rocker *m*. **II** *v/i* sich Straßenkämpfe liefern (*with* mit).

bow¹ [baʊ] **I** *s* Verbeugung *f*. **II** *v/t* beugen, *Kopf* neigen. **III** *v/i* sich verbeugen (*to* vor *dat*): *have a ~ing acquaintance with s.o.* j-n flüchtig kennen.

bow² [~] *s* ✠ Bug *m*.

bow³ [bəʊ] *s* **1.** (Schieß)Bogen *m*: → **string** 3 a. **2.** ♪ (*Violin- etc*)Bogen *m*. **3.** Knoten *m*, Schleife *f*.

bowd·ler·ize ['baʊdləraɪz] *v/t Text* von anstößigen Stellen reinigen.

bow·el ['baʊəl] *s anat.* Darm *m*, *pl a.* Eingeweide *pl*. **~ move·ment** *s physiol.* Stuhl(gang) *m*.

bowl¹ [bəʊl] *s* **1.** Schüssel *f*; (*Obstetc*)Schale *f*; (*Zucker*)Dose *f*; Napf *m* (*für Tiere etc*). **2.** (*Wasch*)Becken *n*. **3.** (*Pfeifen*)Kopf *m*.

bowl² [~] **I** *s* **1.** (*Bowling-, Kegel*)Kugel *f*. **2.** Wurf *m*. **II** *v/t* **3.** *~ over* umwerfen, *fig. a.* j-m die Sprache verschlagen.

bow·legged ['bəʊlegd] *adj* O-beinig. *~ legs s pl* O-Beine *pl*.

bowl·er ['bəʊlə] *s* **1.** Bowlingspieler(in); Kegler(in). **2.** *a. ~ hat bsd. Br.* Bowler *m*, Melone *f*.

bowl·ing ['bəʊlɪŋ] *s* Bowling *n*; Kegeln *n*. **~ al·ley** *s* Bowling-, Kegelbahn *f*.

bow·man ['bəʊmən] *s* (*irr man*) Bogenschütze *m*. **~sprit** ['~sprɪt] *s* ✠ Bugspriet *n*. '**~string** *s* Bogensehne *f*. **~ tie** *s* (*Frack*)Schleife *f*, Fliege *f*.

bow-wow I *int* [,bəʊ'waʊ] wauwau! **II** *s* ['baʊwaʊ] *Kindersprache:* Wauwau *m* (*Hund*).

box¹ [bɒks] *s* **1.** Kasten *m*, Kiste *f*. **2.** Schachtel *f*: *~ of chocolates* Bonbonniere *f*. **3.** Büchse *f*, Dose *f*, Kästchen *n*. **4.** Behälter *m*. **5.** ⊙ Gehäuse *n*. **6.** Briefkasten *m*; Postfach *n*. **7.** (Wahl)Urne *f*. **8.** *Br.* (Telefon)Zelle *f*. **9.** → *Christmas box*. **10.** → *box junction*. **11.** *thea. etc* Loge *f*. **12.** ⚖ Zeugenstand *m*; Geschworenenbank *f*. **13.** Box *f*: a) *Pferdestand*, b) *abgeteilter Einstellplatz in e-r Großgarage.* **14.** → *box number*. **15.** F Kasten *m* (*Fernseher*): Fernsehen *n*: *on the ~* im Fernsehen. **II** *v/t* **16.** *oft ~ in* (*od. up*) in Schachteln *etc* packen, ver-, einpacken; *parkendes Fahrzeug* einklemmen. **17.** *oft ~ up* einschließen, -sperren.

box² [~] **I** *s* **1.** *~ on the ear* Ohrfeige *f*. **II** *v/t* **2.** *~ s.o.'s ears* j-n ohrfeigen. **3.** *Sport:* boxen mit *od.* gegen. **III** *v/i* **4.** boxen.

box·er ['bɒksə] *s Sport:* Boxer *m* (*a. zo.*).

box·ing ['bɒksɪŋ] *s* Boxen *n*, Boxsport *m*. **~ box** *s* Boxkampf *m*. **2 Day** *s Br.* der 2. Weihnachtsfeiertag. **~ gloves** *s pl* Boxhandschuhe *pl*. **~ match** *s* Boxkampf *m*.

box junc·tion *s Br.* gelbmarkierte Kreuzung, *in die bei stehendem Verkehr nicht eingefahren werden darf.* **~ num·ber** *s* Chiffre(nummer) *f*. **~ of·fice** *s thea. etc* **1.** Kasse *f*. **2.** *be a good ~* ein Kassenerfolg *od.* -schlager sein. '**~of·fice** *adj*: *~ success thea. etc* Kassenerfolg *m*, -schlager *m*.

boy [bɔɪ] *s* Junge *m* (*a.* F *Sohn*), Knabe *m*.

boy·cott ['bɔɪkɒt] **I** *v/t* boykottieren. **II** *s* Boykott *m*.

'**boy·friend** *s* Freund *m* (*e-s Mädchens*).

boy·hood ['bɔɪhʊd] s Knabenjahre pl, Jugend(zeit) f.

boy·ish ['bɔɪʃ] adj □ **1.** jungenhaft: *his ~ laughter*. **2.** knabenhaft: *her ~ movements*. **3.** Jungen...: *~ games*.

boy scout s Pfadfinder m.

bra [brɑː] s F BH m (*Büstenhalter*).

brace [breɪs] I s **1.** ⊕ Strebe f, △ a. Stützbalken m. **2.** pl Br. Hosenträger pl. **3.** mst pl ✻ (Zahn)Klammer f, (-)Spange f. **4.** (pl **brace**) Paar n. II v/t **5.** ⊕ verstreben. **6.** fig. (a. v/i) erfrischen; kräftigen, stärken. **7.** *~ o.s. for* fig. sich gefaßt machen auf (acc).

brace·let ['breɪslɪt] s Armband n.

brack·et ['brækɪt] I s **1.** ⊕ Träger m, Stütze f. **2.** ✗, typ. Klammer f: *in ~s*; *round* (*square*) *~s* runde (eckige) Klammern. **3.** (*Alters-, Steuer*)Klasse f, (*Einkommens- etc*)Gruppe f, (-)Stufe f. II v/t **4.** einklammern.

brag [bræg] I s **1.** Prahlerei f. **2.** Prahler m. II v/i **3.** prahlen (*about, of* mit).

brag·gart ['brægət] I s Prahler m. II adj prahlerisch.

braid [breɪd] I v/t **1.** Haar, Bänder flechten. **2.** mit Litze od. Borte besetzen. II s **3.** Zopf m. **4.** Borde f, Litze f, bsd. ✗ Tresse f.

braille [breɪl] s Blindenschrift f.

brain [breɪn] s **1.** anat. Gehirn n. **2.** oft pl fig. F Köpfchen n, Grips m, Verstand m: *cudgel* (od. *rack*) *one's ~s* sich das Hirn zermartern, sich den Kopf zerbrechen; → *blow out* **2.** *~·case* s anat. Hirnschale f, Schädeldecke f. *~ child* s (*irr* **child**) F Geistesprodukt n. *~ death* s ✻ Hirntod m. *~ drain* s Brain-Drain m (*Abwanderung von Wissenschaftlern ins Ausland*). '*~·fag* s geistige Erschöpfung.

brain·less ['breɪnlɪs] adj □ hirn-, geistlos.

'**brain|·pan** → **braincase**. '*~·storm* s F **1.** *have a ~* Br. geistig weggetreten sein. **2.** Am. a) hirnverbrannte Idee, b) → *brain wave*. '*~·storm·ing* s Brainstorming n (*Sammeln von spontanen Einfällen zur Lösung e-s Problems*).

brains trust [breɪnz] s Br. **1.** Teilnehmer pl an e-r Podiumsdiskussion. **2.** → *brain trust*.

'**brain|·teas·er** → **brain twister**. *~ trust* s Am. Brain-Trust m (*bsd. politische*

od. *wirtschaftliche Beratergruppe*). *~ twist·er* s F harte Nuß. '*~·wash* v/t j-n e-r Gehirnwäsche unterziehen. '*~ ·wash·ing* s Gehirnwäsche f. *~ wave* s F Geistesblitz m, tolle Idee. '*~·work·er* s Geistes-, Kopfarbeiter m.

brain·y ['breɪnɪ] adj F gescheit (a. Vorschlag etc).

braise [breɪz] v/t gastr. schmoren.

brake [breɪk] I s ⊕ Bremse f. II v/t u. v/i bremsen. *~ flu·id* s Bremsflüssigkeit f. *~ lin·ing* s Bremsbelag m. *~ ped·al* s Bremspedal n.

brak·ing dis·tance ['breɪkɪŋ] s Bremsweg m.

bram·ble ['bræmbl] s ♣ bsd. Br. Brombeerstrauch m; Brombeere f.

branch [brɑːntʃ] I s **1.** Ast m, Zweig m. **2.** fig. Zweig m, Linie f (e-r Familie). **3.** fig. Zweig m, Sparte f (e-r Wissenschaft etc); ✝ Branche f. **4.** ✝ Filiale f. **5.** → *branch line* **1.** **6.** geogr. Arm m (e-s Gewässers); Am. Nebenfluß m. II v/i **7.** oft *~ off* (od. *out*) sich verzweigen od. verästeln; abzweigen od. sich gabeln (*Straße etc*). *~ line* s **1.** 🚆 Neben-, Zweiglinie f. **2.** Seitenlinie f (e-r Familie). *~ man·ag·er* s Filialleiter m. *~ of·fice* s ✝ Filiale f.

brand [brænd] I s **1.** ✝ (Handels-, Schutz)Marke f, Warenzeichen n; Markenname m; Sorte f, Klasse f (e-r Ware). **2.** fig. Sorte f, Art f. **3.** Brandmal n, -zeichen n. II v/t **4.** mit e-m Warenzeichen etc versehen: *~ed goods* pl Markenartikel pl. **5.** fig. unauslöschlich einprägen (*on s.o.'s mind* j-m).

bran·dish ['brændɪʃ] v/t (*bsd.* drohend) schwingen.

,**brand-'new** adj (funkel)nagelneu.

bran·dy ['brændɪ] s **1.** Weinbrand m, Kognak m, Brandy m. **2.** Obstwasser n: *plum ~* Zwetschgenwasser n.

bran-new [,bræn'njuː] → **brand-new**.

brash [bræʃ] adj □ **1.** ungestüm; draufgängerisch; unüberlegt; taktlos, ungezogen; frech, unverfroren. **2.** aufdringlich, laut (*Musik etc*); grell, schreiend (*Farben*).

brass [brɑːs] s **1.** Messing n. **2.** *the ~* ♪ das Blech (*im Orchester*), die Blechbläser pl. **3.** Br. F Knete f (*Geld*). **4.** F Frechheit f, Unverschämtheit f. *~ band* s Blaskapelle f.

bras·sière ['bræsıə] *s* Büstenhalter *m*.
brass tacks *s pl*: ***get down to*** ~ F zur Sache *od*. auf den Kern der Sache kommen.
bras·sy ['brɑːsı] *adj* □ **1.** messingartig *od*. -farben. **2.** blechern (*Klang*). **3.** F frech, unverschämt. **4.** unangenehm laut.
brat [bræt] *s contp*. Balg *m*, *n*, Gör *n*.
brave [breıv] **I** *adj* □ tapfer, mutig. **II** *v/t* die Stirn bieten, trotzen (*dat*): ~ ***it out*** es (tapfer) durchstehen. **'brav·er·y** *s* Tapferkeit *f*, Mut *m*.
bra·vo [ˌbrɑː'vəʊ] **I** *int* bravo! **II** *pl* **-vos** *s* Bravo(ruf *m*) *n*.
brawl [brɔːl] **I** *v/i* **1.** e-e laute Auseinandersetzung haben. **2.** raufen, sich schlagen. **3.** tosen, rauschen (*Fluß etc*). **II** *s* **4.** laute Auseinandersetzung. **5.** Rauferei *f*, Schlägerei *f*. **6.** Tosen *n*, Rauschen *n*.
brawn [brɔːn] *s* **1.** Muskeln *pl*. **2.** Muskelkraft *f*. **3.** *gastr*. *Br*. (Schweine)Sülze *f*. **'brawn·y** *adj* muskulös.
bray [breı] **I** *v/i* **1.** schreien (*Esel*, *a. Person*): ~ ***at s.o.*** j-n anschreien. **2.** schmettern (*Trompete*). **3.** lärmen, tosen (*Verkehr etc*). **II** *s* **4.** Schrei *m*. **5.** Schmettern *n*. **6.** Lärmen *n*, Tosen *n*.
bra·zen ['breızn] **I** *adj* □ **1.** Messing... **2.** metallisch (*Klang*). **3.** *fig*. unverschämt, unverfroren. **II** *v/t* **4.** ~ ***it out*** sich mit großer Unverfrorenheit behaupten. **'~-faced** → ***brazen*** 3.
breach [briːtʃ] **I** *s* **1.** *fig*. Bruch *m*, Verletzung *f*: ~ ***of confidence*** Vertrauensbruch; ~ ***of contract*** ⚖ Vertragsbruch; ~ ***of the peace*** ⚖ öffentliche Ruhestörung; → ***duty*** 1, ***promise*** 1. **2.** ⚔ Bresche *f* (*a. fig*.): ***fill*** (*od*. ***step into***) ***the*** ~ in die Bresche springen (***for*** für). **II** *v/t* **3.** ⚔ e-e Bresche schlagen in (*acc*).
bread [bred] **I** *s* **1.** Brot *n* (*a. Lebensunterhalt*): ~ ***and butter*** Butterbrot; ***earn*** (*od*. ***make***) ***one's*** ~ sein Brot verdienen; ***know which side one's*** ~ ***is buttered*** (***on***) F s-n Vorteil (er)kennen; ***take the*** ~ ***out of s.o.'s mouth*** j-n brotlos machen. **2.** *sl*. Knete *f* (*Geld*). **II** *v/t* **3.** *gastr*. panieren. **'~ˌbas·ket** *s* **1.** Brotkorb *m*. **2.** *sl*. Magen *m*. ~ **bin** *s* Brotkasten *m*. ~ **crumb** *s* Brotkrume *f*, -krümel *m*: ~**s** *pl* Paniermehl *n*. **'~-crumb** → ***bread*** 3.
breadth [bretθ] *s* Breite *f*: ***ten yards in*** ~ 10 Yards breit; ***what*** ~ ***is it?*** wie breit ist es?
'breadˌwin·ner *s* Ernährer *m*, (Geld-)Verdiener *m* (*e-r Familie*).
break [breık] **I** *s* **1.** Bruch(stelle *f*) *m*. **2.** *fig*. Bruch *m* (***from, with*** mit; ***between*** zwischen *dat*): ***make a*** ~ ***from*** brechen mit. **3.** Pause *f*, Unterbrechung *f*: ***without a*** ~ ununterbrochen; ***take a*** ~ ***for a cigarette*** e-e Zigarettenpause machen. **4.** (plötzlicher) Wechsel, Umschwung *m*: ~ ***in the weather*** Wetterumschlag *m*; ***at*** ~ ***of day*** bei Tagesanbruch. **5.** F ***bad*** ~ Pech *n*; ***lucky*** ~ Dusel *m*, Schwein *n*. **6.** F Chance *f*: ***give s.o. a*** ~. **II** *v/t* (*irr*) **7.** (ab-, auf-, durch-, zer)brechen; *Schallmauer* durchbrechen: ~ ***one's arm*** sich den Arm brechen; ~ ***s.o.'s resistance*** j-s Widerstand brechen; → ***heart*** 1, ***ice*** 1. **8.** zerschlagen, -trümmern, kaputtmachen: → ***bank***[1] 2. **9.** ~ ***s.o. of s.th.*** j-m et. abgewöhnen. **10.** *Speise*, *Ware*, *Geldschein* anbrechen; *Geldschein* kleinmachen, wechseln. **11.** a) *Tiere* zähmen, abrichten, *Pferd* zureiten, *a. j-n* gewöhnen (***to*** an *acc*), b) → ***break in*** 3 b, c. **12.** *Gesetz*, *Vertrag etc* brechen. **13.** ~ ***the bad news gently to s.o.*** j-m die schlechte Nachricht schonend beibringen. **14.** *Code etc* knacken, entschlüsseln. **III** *v/i* (*irr*) **15.** brechen (*a. fig. Widerstand etc*): ~ ***into*** einbrechen in (*ein Haus etc*); ~ ***with*** brechen mit (*j-m*, *e-r Tradition etc*). **16.** (zer)brechen, (-)reißen, kaputtgehen. **17.** umschlagen (*Wetter*); anbrechen (*Tag*). **18.** *fig*. ausbrechen (***into*** in *Tränen etc*).
Verbindungen mit Adverbien:
break| a·way **I** *v/t* **1.** ab-, losbrechen (***from*** von). **II** *v/i* **2.** ab-, losbrechen (***from*** von). **3.** *fig*. sich lossagen *od*. trennen (***from*** von). ~ **down** **I** *v/t* **1.** ein-, niederreißen, *Haus* abbrechen, abreißen. **2.** *Maschine* zerlegen. **3.** *fig*. aufgliedern, -schlüsseln. **II** *v/i* **4.** zs.-brechen (*a. fig*.). **5.** versagen (*Maschine*, *Stimme etc*), kaputtgehen, *mot*. e-e Panne haben. **6.** scheitern (*Ehe*, *Verhandlungen etc*). ~ **in** **I** *v/i* **1.** einbrechen, -dringen: ~ ***on*** bei *j-m* hereinplatzen; sich in *e-e Unterhaltung etc* einmischen. **II** *v/t* **2.** einschlagen, *Tür* aufbrechen. **3.** a) → ***break*** 10 a, b) *Auto etc* einfahren, *Schuhe* einlaufen, c) *j-n* ein-

arbeiten, anlernen. **~ off** I v/t **1.** →
break away 1. **2.** Rede, Verhandlungen
etc abbrechen, Verlobung (auf)lösen:
break it off sich entloben. II v/i **3.** →
break away 2. **~ out** v/i ausbrechen
(Gefangener, Krieg etc): **~ in laughter**
(**tears**) in Gelächter (Tränen) ausbrechen; **he broke out in a cold sweat**
ihm brach der Angstschweiß aus. **~
through** I v/t **1.** durchbrechen. II v/i **2.**
durchbrechen, (Sonne a.) hervorkom-
men. **3.** fig. den Durchbruch schaffen.
~ up I v/t **1.** Straße, Eis etc aufbrechen.
2. Sitzung etc aufheben, Versammlung,
Haushalt etc auflösen. II v/i **3.** aufbrechen (Straße, Eis etc). **4.** aufgehoben
werden (Sitzung etc), sich auflösen
(Versammlung). **5.** zerbrechen, auseinandergehen (Ehe etc); sich trennen
(Ehepaar etc).

break·a·ble ['breɪkəbl] adj zerbrechlich.
'**break·age** s Bruch(stelle f) m.
'**break·|a·way** s Trennung f (**from** von).
'**~·down** s **1.** Zs.-bruch m (a. fig.): **ner·
vous ~** Nervenzusammenbruch. **2.**
mot. Panne f: **~ service** Br. Pannen-,
Straßendienst m; **~ van** Br. Abschleppwagen m. '**~·fast** ['brekfəst] I s Frühstück n: **have ~** → II; **~ television**
Frühstücksfernsehen n. II v/i frühstücken. '**~·in** s **1.** 🚉 Einbruch m. **2.**
Abrichten, Einfahren n etc (→ **break**
10 a, **break in** 2 b, c). '**~·neck** adj halsbrecherisch (Geschwindigkeit). '**~·out** s
Ausbruch m (aus dem Gefängnis etc).
'**~·through** s ✕ Durchbruch m (a. fig.).
'**~·up** s Aufhebung f (e-r Sitzung etc),
Auflösung f (e-r Versammlung, e-s
Haushalts etc).

breast [brest] I s Brust f (a. gastr.): **make
a clean ~ of s.th.** sich. von der Seele
reden. II v/t: **~ the tape** (Sport) das
Zielband durchreißen, weitS. durchs
Ziel gehen. '**~·bone** s anat. Brustbein n.
'**~·feed** v/t u. v/i (irr **feed**) stillen. '**~·pin**
s Brosche f, Ansteckenadel f. '**~·pock·et** s
Brusttasche f. '**~·stroke** s Sport: Brust-
schwimmen n.

breath [breθ] s **1.** Atem(zug) m: **bad ~**
Mundgeruch m; **in the same ~** im gleichen Atemzug; **under** (od. **below**)
one's ~ im Flüsterton, leise; **be out of ~**
außer Atem sein; **get one's ~ back** wieder zu Atem kommen; **waste one's ~**

in den Wind reden. **2.** fig. Hauch m,
Spur f. **3.** a. **~ of air** Lufthauch m,
Lüftchen n.

breath·a·lys·er ['breθəlaɪzə] s mot. Al-
koholtestgerät n, Röhrchen n.
breathe [briːð] I v/i **1.** atmen: **~ in** (**out**)
ein-(aus)atmen. II v/t **2.** atmen: **~ in**
(**out**) ein-(aus)atmen; → **sigh** II. **3.** flüstern, hauchen. '**breath·er** s F Atem-,
Verschnaufpause f: **have** (od. **take**) **a ~**
verschnaufen. '**breath·ing** s Atmen
n, Atmung f: **~ space** Atem-, Verschnaufpause f.
breath·less ['breθlɪs] adj □ atemlos (a.
fig.).
'**breath|·tak·ing** adj □ atemberaubend.
~ test s mot. Br. Alkoholtest m.
bred [bred] pret u. pp von **breed**.
breech·es ['brɪtʃɪz] s pl (**a pair of** e-e)
Kniebund-, Reithose f.
breed [briːd] I v/t (irr) **1.** Tiere, Pflanzen
züchten. **2.** fig. hervorrufen, verursachen. II v/i (irr) **3.** sich fortpflanzen od.
vermehren. **4.** Rasse f, Zucht f. **5.**
Art f, (Menschen)Schlag m. '**breed·er** s
1. Züchter(in). **2.** Zuchttier n. **3.** phys.
Brüter m: **~ reactor** Brutreaktor m.
'**breed·ing** s **1.** Fortpflanzung f, Zucht f. **3.** Ausbildung f,
Erziehung f. **4.** (gutes) Benehmen, (gu-
te) Manieren pl.
breeze [briːz] I s Brise f. II v/i F schweben (Person): **~ in** hereingeweht kommen. '**breez·y** adj □ **1.** luftig, windig.
2. heiter, unbeschwert.
breth·ren ['breðrən] pl von **brother** 2.
bre·vi·a·ry ['briːvjərɪ] s eccl. Brevier n.
brev·i·ty ['brevətɪ] s Kürze f.
brew [bruː] I v/t **1.** Bier brauen, Tee etc
a. zubereiten. II v/t **2.** fig. aushecken, -brü-
ten. II v/i **3.** fig. sich zs.-brauen, im
Anzug sein (Gewitter, Unheil). III s **4.**
Gebräu n. '**brew·er** s Brauer m.
'**brew·er·y** s Brauerei f.
brib·a·ble ['braɪbəbl] adj bestechlich.
bribe I v/t bestechen. II s Bestechungs-
geld n, -geschenk n: **accept** (od. **take**)
~s sich bestechen lassen. '**brib·er·y** s
Bestechung f: **open to ~** bestechlich.
bric-a-brac ['brɪkəbræk] s Nippsachen
pl.
brick [brɪk] I s **1.** Ziegel(stein) m, Back-
stein m: **drop a ~** Br. F ins Fettnäpfchen
treten. **2.** Br. Baustein m, (Bau)Klötz-

chen *n* (*für Kinder*): **box of ~s** Baukasten *m*. **3.** F Pfundskerl *m*, feiner Kerl. **II** *v/t* **4.** ~ **up** (*od.* **in**) zumauern. **'~,lay·er** *s* Maurer *m*.

brid·al ['braɪdl] *adj* Braut...: ~ **dress** Braut-, Hochzeitskleid *n*; ~ **ceremony** Hochzeitsfeier *f*.

bride [braɪd] *s* Braut *f*: **give away the ~** die Braut zum Altar führen. **~groom** ['~grʊm] *s* Bräutigam *m*.

brides·maid ['braɪdzmeɪd] *s* Brautjungfer *f*.

bridge¹ [brɪdʒ] *s* **1.** (♣ *a.* Kommando)Brücke *f*: **burn one's ~s** (**behind one**) *fig.* alle Brücken hinter sich abbrechen. **2.** ~ **of the nose** *anat.* Nasenrücken *m*. **II** *v/t* **3.** e-e Brücke schlagen über (*acc*). **4.** *oft* ~ **over** ⚡ überbrücken (*a. fig.*).

bridge² [~] *s* Bridge *n* (*Kartenspiel*). **'bridge·head** *s* ✗ Brückenkopf *m*.

bri·dle ['braɪdl] **I** *s* **1.** Zaum(zeug *n*) *m*; Zügel *m*. **II** *v/t* **2.** (auf)zäumen. **3.** zügeln, im Zaum halten (*beide a. fig.*). **III** *v/i* **4.** *oft* ~ **up** den Kopf zurückwerfen.

brief [briːf] **I** *adj* □ **1.** kurz: **be ~!** fasse dich kurz! **2.** kurz angebunden (**with** mit). **3.** knapp (*Bikini etc*) **I** *s* **4.** **in ~** kurz(um). **5.** ⚖ *Br.* schriftliche Beauftragung u. Information (*des Barristers durch den Solicitor*) zur Vertretung des Falles vor Gericht, *weitS.* Mandat *n*: **abandon** (*od.* **give up**) **one's ~** sein Mandat niederlegen; **hold a ~ for** *j-n od. j-s* Sache vor Gericht vertreten; *fig.* sich einsetzen für. **6.** *pl* → **briefs**. **II** *v/t* **7.** *j-n* instruieren, *j-m* genaue Anweisungen geben. **8.** ⚖ *Br. Barrister* mit der Vertretung des Falles betrauen; *Anwalt* über den Sachverhalt informieren. **'~case** *s* Aktentasche *f*.

brief·ness ['briːfnɪs] *s* Kürze *f*.

briefs [briːfs] *s pl* (**a pair of** ein) Slip *m* (*kurze Unterhose*).

bri·gade [brɪ'geɪd] *s* ✗ Brigade *f*.

bright [braɪt] *adj* □ **1.** hell, glänzend, leuchtend, strahlend. **2.** heiter (*Wetter etc*). **3.** gescheit, hell. **4.** günstig, vielversprechend (*Aussichten*). **'bright·en I** *v/t oft* ~ **up 1.** hell(er) machen, aufhellen (*a. fig.*). **2.** *j-n* fröhlich stimmen, aufheitern. **II** *v/i* **3.** *oft* ~ **up** sich aufhellen (*Gesicht, Wetter etc*), aufleuchten (*Augen*). **'bright·ness** *s* **1.**

Helligkeit *f* (*a.* TV), Glanz *m*. **2.** Heiterkeit *f*. **3.** Gescheitheit *f*.

bril·liance ['brɪljəns], **'bril·lian·cy** *s* **1.** Leuchten *n*, Glanz *m*, Helligkeit *f*. **2.** *fig.* Brillanz *f*. **'bril·liant I** *adj* □ **1.** leuchtend, glänzend, hell. **2.** *fig.* brillant. **II** *s* **3.** Brillant *m*.

brim [brɪm] **I** *s* **1.** Rand *m* (*bsd. e-s Gefäßes*): **full to the ~** randvoll. **2.** (Hut-) Krempe *f*. **II** *v/i* **3.** voll sein: ~ **over** übervoll sein (**with** von) (*a. fig.*); überfließen (**with** von) (*a. fig.*). **,brim'ful(l)** *adj* randvoll.

brine [braɪn] **I** *s* **1.** Sole *f*; Lake *f*. **2.** Salzwasser *n*. **II** *v/t* **3.** (ein)salzen.

bring [brɪŋ] *v/t* (*irr*) **1.** (mit-, her)bringen: **what ~s you here?** was führt Sie zu mir?; → **bacon, home** 9, **light¹** 1e. **2.** *fig.* Gewinn etc (ein)bringen. **3.** nach sich ziehen, bewirken. **4.** *j-n* dazu bringen *od.* bewegen (**to do** zu tun): **I can't ~ myself to do it** ich kann mich nicht dazu durchringen(, es zu tun):

Verbindungen mit Adverbien:

bring| a·bout *v/t* **1.** zustande bringen. **2.** bewirken, verursachen. ~ **a·long** *v/t* mitbringen. ~ **back** *v/t* **1.** zurückbringen. **2.** *Erinnerungen* wachrufen (**of** an *acc*); Erinnerungen wachrufen an (*acc*). **3.** ~ **to life** *j-n* wieder zu(m) Bewußtsein bringen; (*a.* ~ **to health**) *j-n* wieder gesund machen. ~ **down** *v/t* **1.** herunterbringen. **2.** *Regierung etc* zu Fall bringen, stürzen. **3.** *Preis etc* herabsetzen. **4.** ~ **the house** *thea. etc* F stürmischen Beifall auslösen; Lachstürme entfesseln. ~ **forth** *v/t* hervorbringen. ~ **for·ward** *v/t* **1.** *Entschuldigung etc* vorbringen. **2.** ♠ *Betrag* übertragen. **3.** *Versammlung etc* vorverlegen (**to** auf *acc*); *Uhr* vorstellen (**one hour** um e-e Stunde). ~ **in** *v/t* **1.** hereinbringen. **2.** *Kapital, Gesetzesvorlage etc* einbringen. **3.** → **verdict**. ~ **off** *v/t* zustande bringen. ~ **on** *v/t* **1.** *bsd. Krankheit* verursachen. **2.** in Gang bringen. ~ **out** *v/t allg.*, *a. Buch, Auto etc* herausbringen. ~ **o·ver** *v/t* **1.** herüberbringen. **2.** → **bring round 3.** ~ **round** *v/t* **1.** her-, vorbeibringen. **2.** a) *Ohnmächtigen* wieder zu sich bringen, b) *Kranken* wieder auf die Beine bringen. **3.** *j-n* umstimmen, herumkriegen. ~ **through** *v/t* *Kranken* durchbringen. ~ **to** → **bring**

round 2 a. **~ up** v/t **1.** heraufbringen. **2.** *Kind* auf-, großziehen; erziehen: **~ s.o. up to do s.th.** j-n dazu erziehen, et. zu tun. **3.** *et.* (er)brechen. **4.** zum Stillstand *od.* Halten bringen.

bring·er ['brɪŋə] *s* Überbringer(in).

brink [brɪŋk] *s* Rand *m* (*a. fig.*): **be on the ~ of war** am Rande e-s Krieges stehen; **bring s.o. to the ~ of ruin** j-n an den Rand des Ruins bringen. **~·man-ship** ['~mənʃɪp] *s* Politik *f* des äußersten Risikos.

brin·y ['braɪnɪ] *adj* salzig.

bri·quet(te) [brɪ'ket] *s* Brikett *n*.

brisk [brɪsk] *adj* □ **1.** flott. **2.** lebhaft, munter. **3.** frisch (*Luft etc*).

bris·ket ['brɪskɪt] *s gastr.* Brust(stück *n*) *f*.

bris·tle ['brɪsl] **I** *s* **1.** Borste *f*; (Bart)Stoppel *f*. **II** v/i **2.** a. **~ up** sich sträuben. **3.** a. **~ up** zornig werden. **4.** strotzen, wimmeln (*with* von). '**bris·tly** *adj* **1.** borstig; stopp(e)lig: **~ beard** Stoppelbart *m*. **2.** *fig.* kratzbürstig.

Brit·ish ['brɪtɪʃ] **I** *adj* britisch. **II** *s*: **the ~** *pl* die Briten *pl*. '**Brit·ish·er** *s Am.* Brite *m*, Britin *f*.

Brit·on ['brɪtn] *s* Brite *m*, Britin *f*.

brit·tle ['brɪtl] *adj* **1.** spröde, zerbrechlich. **2.** brüchig (*Metall etc*) (*a. fig.*).

broach [brəʊtʃ] v/t **1.** *Faß* anstechen. **2.** *Thema* anschneiden.

broad [brɔːd] *adj* (□ → **broadly**) **1.** breit. **2.** weit, ausgedehnt. **3.** → **daylight. 4.** weitreichend, -gehend: *in the **~est sense*** im weitesten Sinne. **5.** → **broad-minded. 6.** derb; anstößig, schlüpfrig. **7.** klar, deutlich: → **hint** 1. **8.** allgemein: **in ~ outline** in großen Zügen, in groben Umrissen. **9.** breit, stark (*Akzent*). '**~·cast I** v/t (*a. irr*) **1.** *Nachricht* verbreiten, *contp.* ausposaunen. **2.** im Rundfunk *od.* Fernsehen bringen; übertragen. **II** v/i (*a. irr*) **3.** im Rundfunk *od.* Fernsehen auftreten. **4.** senden. **III** *s* **5.** *Rundfunk, TV*: Sendung *f*; Übertragung *f*. '**~·cast·er** *s* Rundfunk-, Fernsehsprecher(in). '**~·cast·ing I** *s* **1.** → **broadcast** 5. **2.** Sendebetrieb *m*. **3.** Rundfunk *m*, Fernsehen *n*. **II** *adj* **4.** Rundfunk..., Fernsehen...: **~ station** Sender *m*.

broad·en ['brɔːdn] v/t verbreitern: **~ one's horizons** (*od.* **mind**) s-n Horizont erweitern. **II** v/i a. **~ out** sich verbreitern (*into* zu), sich erweitern (*a. fig.*).

broad| jump *s Leichtathletik: Am.* Weitsprung *m*. **~ jump·er** *s Am.* Weitspringer(in).

broad·ly ['brɔːdlɪ] *adv* **1.** a. **~ speaking** allgemein (gesprochen). **2.** in großen Zügen.

,**broad·**'**mind·ed** *adj* □ großzügig, tolerant. '**~·side** *s ⚓* Breitseite *f* (*a. fig.*).

bro·cade [brəʊ'keɪd] *s* Brokat *m*.

bro·chure ['brəʊʃə] *s* Broschüre *f*.

brogue [brəʊg] *s* derber Straßenschuh.

broil[1] [brɔɪl] **I** v/t **1.** (auf dem Rost) braten, grillen. **2. get ~ed** vor Hitze fast umkommen. **II** v/i **3. be ~ing in the sun** in der Sonne schmoren. **4.** vor Wut kochen.

broil[2] [~] *s* laute Auseinandersetzung.

broil·ing ['brɔɪlɪŋ] **I** *adj* glühendheiß: **a ~ day.** **II** *adv*: **~ hot** glühend heiß.

broke[1] [brəʊk] *pret von* **break.**

broke[2] [~] *adj* F pleite (*a.* ✝), abgebrannt: **go ~** pleite gehen.

bro·ken ['brəʊkən] **I** *pp von* **break. II** *adj* **1.** zerbrochen, entzwei, kaputt. **2.** gebrochen (*a. fig.*): **a ~ leg** (*promise, etc*). **3.** unterbrochen, gestört: **~ sleep. 4.** (*seelisch od. körperlich*) gebrochen. **5.** zerrüttet: **~ marriage; ~ health; ~ home** zerrüttete Familienverhältnisse *pl*. **6.** *ling.* gebrochen: **speak ~ English** gebrochen Englisch sprechen.

bro·ker ['brəʊkə] *s* ✝ Makler *m*. **2.** Vermittler *m*. '**bro·ker·age** *s* Maklergebühr *f*.

brol·ly ['brɒlɪ] *s Br.* F (Regen)Schirm *m*.

bro·mide ['brəʊmaɪd] *s* **1.** ◈ Bromid *n*. **2.** *fig.* Gemeinplatz *m*. **bro·mine** ['~miːn] *s* ◈ Brom *n*.

bron·chi ['brɒŋkaɪ] *s pl anat.* Bronchien *pl*. **bron·chi·al** ['~kjəl] *adj anat.*, *⚕* Bronchial... **bron·chi·tis** [~'kaɪtɪs] *s ⚕* Bronchitis *f*.

bronze [brɒnz] **I** *s* **1.** Bronze *f*. **II** *adj* **2.** bronzefarben. **3.** Bronze...: ⚲ **Age** Bronzezeit *f*; **~ medal** Bronzemedaille *f*; **~ medal(l)ist** Bronzemedaillengewinner(in).

brooch [brəʊtʃ] *s* Brosche *f*.

brood [bruːd] **I** *s* Brut *f* (*a. fig. contp.*). **II** v/t ausbrüten (*a. fig.*). **III** v/i brüten (*a. fig.* **on, over, about** über *dat*). **IV** *adj*

Brut...: ~ **hen**. '**brood·er** s Brutapparat m, -kasten m.

brook [brʊk] s Bach m.

broom [bruːm] s Besen m: *a new ~ sweeps clean* neue Besen kehren gut. '**~stick** s Besenstiel m.

broth [brɒθ] s (Kraft-, Fleisch)Brühe f.

broth·el ['brɒθl] s Bordell n.

broth·er ['brʌðə] s **1.** Bruder m: **~s** pl *and sisters* pl Geschwister pl; *Smith* **2s** ~ Gebrüder Smith. **2.** eccl. pl **brethren** Bruder m. **broth·er·hood** ['~hʊd] s eccl. Bruderschaft f.

broth·er-in-law pl '**broth·ers-in-law** s Schwager m.

broth·er·ly ['brʌðəlɪ] adj brüderlich.

brought [brɔːt] pret u. pp von **bring**.

brow [braʊ] s **1.** (Augen)Braue f. **2.** Stirn f. **3.** Miene f. Gesichtsausdruck m. '**~beat** v/t (irr **beat**) einschüchtern.

brown [braʊn] **I** adj braun: ~ **bread** Misch-; Vollkorn-; Schwarzbrot n; ~ **coal** Braunkohle f; ~ **paper** Packpapier n; ~ **study** 1. **II** s Braun n: *dressed in* ~ braun od. in Braun gekleidet. **III** v/t Haut etc bräunen, Fleisch etc (an)bräunen. **IV** v/i braun werden. **brown·ie** ['~nɪ] s Heinzelmännchen n. '**brown·ish** adj bräunlich.

browse [braʊz] v/i **1.** grasen, weiden. **2.** a. ~ **around** sich umsehen: ~ **through** a *book* in e-m Buch schmökern od. blättern; ~ **in** (od. **around**) a *shop* (od. Am. **store**) sich (unverbindlich) in e-m Laden umsehen.

bruise [bruːz] **I** v/t **1.** sich e-n Körperteil quetschen; *Früchte* anstoßen. **II** v/i **2.** e-e Quetschung od. e-n blauen Fleck bekommen. **III** s **3.** Quetschung f, blauer Fleck. **4.** Druckstelle f (auf *Früchten*).

brunch [brʌntʃ] s F Brunch n (*spätes reichliches Frühstück*).

bru·nette [bru'net] **I** s Brünette f. **II** adj brünett.

brunt [brʌnt] s: *bear the* ~ fig. die Hauptlast tragen.

brush¹ [brʌʃ] **I** s **1.** Bürste f. **2.** Pinsel m: → **tar** II. **3.** *give s.th. a* ~ et. ab- od. ausbürsten. **4.** ⚔ Scharmützel n (a. fig.): *have a* ~ *with s.o.* mit j-m aneinandergeraten. **II** v/t **5.** bürsten: *brush one's teeth* sich die Zähne putzen; ~ *aside* (od. *away*) zur Seite schieben,

wegschieben; fig. (mit e-r Handbewegung) abtun, wegwischen: ~ *away* (od. *off*) wegbürsten; ~ *down* abbürsten; ~ *off* sl. j-n abwimmeln; j-m e-e Abfuhr erteilen; ~ *up* *Kenntnisse* aufpolieren, -frischen. **6.** streifen, leicht berühren. **III** v/i **7.** ~ *past s.o.* j-n streifen od. leicht berühren; an j-m vorbeihuschen; an j-m (gerade noch) vorbeikommen.

brush² [~], a. '**~wood** s Gestrüpp n, Unterholz n.

brusque [bruːsk] adj □ brüsk, barsch, schroff.

Brus·sels sprouts [ˌbrʌslˈspraʊts] s pl ⚘ Rosenkohl m.

bru·tal ['bruːtl] adj □ brutal. **bru·tal·i·ty** [~ˈtælɪtɪ] s Brutalität f. **bru·tal·ize** ['~təlaɪz] v/t **1.** brutalisieren. **2.** brutal behandeln. **brute** [bruːt] **I** s **1.** Vieh n, fig. a. Untier n, Scheusal n. **II** adj **2.** brutal: ~ **force** (od. **strength**) rohe Gewalt. **3.** hirnlos, dumm. '**brut·ish** adj □ → **brute** II.

bub·ble ['bʌbl] **I** s **1.** (Luft- etc)Blase f: ~ **bath** Schaumbad n; ~ **gum** Bubble-gum m, Ballon-, Knallkaugummi m. **2.** fig. Seifenblase f. **II** v/i **3.** sprudeln, brodeln (*kochendes Wasser etc*); sprudeln, perlen (*Sekt etc*); in Blasen aufsteigen (*Gas*): ~ *over* übersprudeln (a. fig. with vor dat). '**bub·bly I** adj **1.** sprudelnd. **2.** fig. temperamentvoll. **II** s **3.** bsd. Br. F Champus m.

buck¹ [bʌk] **I** s **1.** zo. Bock m, engS. Rehbock, allg. Männchen n. **2.** *pass the* ~ F den Schwarzen Peter weitergeben; *pass the* ~ *to s.o.* F j-m den Schwarzen Peter zuschieben. **II** v/i **3.** bocken (*Pferd etc*). **4.** ~ *up* F aufleben; sich ranhalten: ~ *up!* Kopf hoch! **III** v/t **5.** ~ *up* F j-n aufmuntern; j-m Dampf machen.

buck² [~] s Am. sl. Dollar m.

buck·et ['bʌkɪt] **I** s **1.** Eimer m, Kübel m: *kick the* ~ F den Löffel weglegen (*sterben*). **II** v/t schöpfen: ~ *out* ausschöpfen. **III** v/i: *it's* (od. *the rain's*) *~ing* (*down*) Br. F es gießt wie aus od. mit Kübeln. **buck·et·ful** ['~fʊl] s ein Eimer(voll) m.

buck·et seat s mot. Schalensitz m.

buck·le ['bʌkl] **I** s **1.** Schnalle f, Spange f. **II** v/t **2.** a. ~ *up* zu-, festschnallen: ~ *on* anschnallen. **III** v/i **3.** ~ *up* mot., ✈ sich anschnallen. **4. ~ down** F sich dahinterklemmen: **~ down to a task** sich hinter e-e Aufgabe klemmen.

'**buck·skin** s Wildleder n.

bud [bʌd] **I** s Knospe f: **be in ~** knospen; **nip in the ~** fig. im Keim ersticken. **II** v/i knospen: **~ding lawyer** angehender Jurist.

Bud·dhism ['budɪzəm] s Buddhismus m. '**Bud·dhist I** s Buddhist m. **II** adj buddhistisch.

bud·dy ['bʌdɪ] s bsd. Am. F Kumpel m, Spezi m.

budge [bʌdʒ] mst neg **I** v/i sich (von der Stelle) rühren: **~ from** fig. von et. abrücken. **II** v/t (vom Fleck) bewegen: **~ from** fig. j-n abbringen von.

bud·ger·i·gar ['bʌdʒərɪgɑː] s orn. Wellensittich m.

budg·et ['bʌdʒɪt] s Budget n, Etat m: **for the low ~** für den schmalen Geldbeutel; **~-conscious** preisbewußt; **~(-priced)** preisgünstig. '**budg·et·a·ry** adj Budget..., Etat...

bud·gie ['bʌdʒɪ] F → **budgerigar**.

buff [bʌf] s F **1. in the ~** im Adams- od. Evaskostüm. **2.** in Zssgn ...fan m; ...experte m.

buf·fa·lo ['bʌfələu] pl **-lo(e)s** s zo. Büffel m.

buff·er ['bʌfə] s ⚙ Stoßdämpfer m; Puffer m (a. fig.); Prellbock m (a. fig.). **~ state** s pol. Pufferstaat m. **~ zone** s ✕ Pufferzone f.

buf·fet¹ ['bʌfɪt] **I** s **1.** (Faust)Schlag m; Ohrfeige f. **II** v/t **2.** j-m e-n (Faust)Schlag versetzen; j-m e-e Ohrfeige geben. **3.** ankämpfen gegen.

buf·fet² s **1.** ['bʌfɪt] Büfett n, Anrichte f. **2.** ['bʊfeɪ] Büfett n, Theke f.

buf·foon [bə'fuːn] s Possenreißer m, Hanswurst m (a. fig. contp.).

bug [bʌg] **I** s **1.** zo. Wanze f (a. F Minispion); bsd. Am. allg. Insekt n. **2.** F Bazillus m, fig. a. Fieber n: **he got bitten by** (od. **he's got**) **the ~** ihn hat's gepackt. **3.** ⚙ F Defekt m, pl Mucken pl. **II** v/t **4.** Am. F j-n wütend machen; j-m auf den Wecker fallen. **5.** F Wanzen anbringen in (dat). '**~-bear** s (Schreck-) Gespenst n.

bug·ger ['bʌgə] V **I** s Scheißkerl m; allg. Kerl m: **poor ~** armes Schwein. **II** v/t: **~ up** versauen; **~ed up** im Arsch. **III**

v/i: **~ off** Br. (mst imp) sich verpissen.

bug·gy¹ ['bʌgɪ] adj verwanzt.

bug·gy² [~] s mot. Buggy m (geländegängiges Freizeitauto).

bu·gle ['bjuːgl] s (Wald-, Jagd)Horn n; ✕ Signalhorn n: **~ call** Hornsignal n. '**bu·gler** s Hornist m.

build [bɪld] **I** v/t (irr) **1.** bauen: a) errichten, b) herstellen: **~ in(to)** einbauen (in acc). **2. ~ up** Gelände bebauen. **3. ~ up** Geschäft etc aufbauen: **~ up a reputation** sich e-n Namen machen. **4. ~ up** j-n (in der Presse etc) aufbauen. **5. ~ one's hope on** s-e Hoffnung setzen auf (acc). **II** v/i (irr) **6.** bauen: **be ~ing** im Bau sein. **7.** fig. bauen (**on** auf acc). **III** s **8.** Körperbau m, Statur f. '**build·er** s **1.** Erbauer m. **2.** Bauunternehmer m. '**build·ing** s **1.** Bauwesen n. **2.** Gebäude n, Bau(werk n) m. **II** adj **3.** Bau...: **~ contractor → builder 2; ~ freeze** Baustopp m; **~ industry** Baugewerbe n, -wirtschaft f; **~ site** Baustelle f; **~ society** Br. Bausparkasse f.

built [bɪlt] pret u. pp von **build**. '**~-'in** adj eingebaut, Einbau... '**~-'up** adj: **~ area** bebautes Gelände od. Gebiet; (Verkehr) geschlossene Ortschaft.

bulb [bʌlb] s **1.** ♣ Knolle f, Zwiebel f. **2.** ⚡ Glühbirne f. '**bulb·ous** (od.) knollenförmig: **~ nose** Knollennase f.

Bul·gar·i·an [bʌl'geərɪən] **I** s **1.** Bulgare m, Bulgarin f. **2.** ling. Bulgarisch n. **II** adj **3.** bulgarisch.

bulge [bʌldʒ] **I** s **1.** (Aus)Bauchung f, Ausbuchtung f. **2.** fig. (rapide) Zunahme. **II** v/i **3.** a. **~ out** sich (aus)bauchen, hervorquellen (a. Augen). **III** v/t **4.** Backen aufblähen. **5.** Taschen etc vollstopfen (**with** mit).

bulk [bʌlk] s **1.** Umfang m, Größe f, Masse f. **2.** Großteil m, Mehrheit f. **3. in ~** ⚓ lose, unverpackt; en gros. '**bulk·y** adj **1.** massig. **2.** unhandlich, sperrig: **~ refuse** (od. **waste**) Sperrmüll m.

bull [bʊl] **I** s **1.** zo. Bulle m, (Zucht)Stier m: **take the ~ by the horns** fig. den Stier bei den Hörnern packen; **like a ~ in a china shop** wie ein Elefant im Porzellanladen; → **shoot 5a.** ⚓ Haussespekulant m. **II** v/i **3.** ⚓ auf Hausse spekulieren. '**~-dog** s zo. Bulldogge f. '**~-doze** v/t **1.** planieren. **2.** F einschüchtern;

zwingen (*into doing* zu tun). '**~·doz·er**
s ☉ Bulldozer *m*, Planierraupe *f*.
bul·let ['bʊlɪt] *s* (*Gewehr-, Pistolen*)Kugel *f*.
bul·le·tin ['bʊlətɪn] *s* **1.** Bulletin *n*: a)
Tagesbericht *m*, b) ✚ Krankenbericht
m, c) offizielle Bekanntmachung: ~
board Am. Schwarzes Brett. **2.** Mitteilungsblatt *n*.
'**bul·let⟩·proof** *adj* kugelsicher: ~ *glass*
Panzerglas *n*. ~ *wound* *s* Schußwunde
f, -verletzung *f*.
'**bull⟩·fight** *s* Stierkampf *m*. '**~⟩·fight·er** *s*
Stierkämpfer *m*.
bul·lion ['bʊljən] *s* (*Gold-, Silber*)Barren
m.
bull·ish ['bʊlɪʃ] *adj* ✝ Hausse...
bull·ock ['bʊlək] *s zo.* Ochse *m*.
'**bull·ring** *s* Stierkampfarena *f*.
'**bull's-eye** *s* **1.** △, ⚓ Bullauge
n. **2.** Zentrum *n*, *das* Schwarze (*e-r Zielscheibe*): *hit the ~* ins Schwarze treffen
(*a. fig.*).
'**bull⟩·shit** *s* V Scheiß *m*: *talk ~* Scheiß
reden. ~ *ter·ri·er* *s zo.* Bullterrier *m*.
bul·ly ['bʊlɪ] **I** *s* brutaler *od.* tyrannischer
Kerl. **II** *v/t* tyrannisieren, schikanieren: ~ *about* (*od. around*) *j-n* herumkommandieren.**III** *adj u. int* F prima: ~
for you! na und?; *iro.* gratuliere!
bul·wark ['bʊlwək] *s* Bollwerk *n*.
bum¹ [bʌm] *s bsd. Br.* F Hintern *m*.
bum² [~] *bsd. Am.* F **I** *s* **1.** Gammler *m*;
Tippelbruder *m*. **2.** Schnorrer *m*, Nassauer *m*. **3.** Saukerl *m*. **II** *v/i* **4.** ~ *about* (*od. around*) herumgammeln. **5.**
schnorren, nassauern (*off* bei). **6.** tippeln (*through* durch). **III** *adj* **7.** mies;
kaputt.
bum·ble·bee ['bʌmblbi:] *s zo.* Hummel
f.
bump [bʌmp] **I** *v/t* **1.** (heftig) stoßen. **2.**
mit *et.* rennen (*against* gegen), *et.* rammen, auf *ein Auto* auffahren. **3.** ~ *off* F
umlegen (*umbringen*). **II** *v/i* **4.** (*against,
into*) stoßen, prallen (gegen, an *acc*),
zs.-stoßen (mit): ~ *into* fig. *j-n* zufällig
treffen. **5.** rumpeln, holpern (*Fahrzeug*). **III** *s* **6.** heftiger Ruck *od.* Stoß. **7.**
Beule *f*. **8.** Unebenheit *f*.
bump·er¹ ['bʌmpə] **I** *s et.* Riesiges. **II** *adj*
riesig: ~ *crop* Rekordernte *f*.
bump·er² [~] *s* **1.** *mot.* Stoßstange *f*. **2.** 🚃
etc Am. Puffer *m*.

bump·er⟩ car *s* (Auto)Skooter *m*. ~
stick·er *s* Autoaufkleber *m*.
bump·kin ['bʌmpkɪn] *s a. country ~
contp.* Bauer *m*, Provinzler *m*.
bump⟩ start *s Br.* Anschieben *n*. '**~·start**
v/t Br. Auto anschieben.
bump·tious ['bʌmpʃəs] *adj* □ F aufgeblasen, wichtigtuerisch.
bump·y ['bʌmpɪ] *adj* □ **1.** holp(e)rig,
uneben. **2.** unruhig (*Flug*).
bun [bʌn] *s* **1.** süßes Brötchen: *she has a
~ in the oven* F bei ihr ist was unterwegs. **2.** (Haar)Knoten *m*.
bunch [bʌntʃ] **I** *s* **1.** Bündel *n*, Bund *n*: ~
of flowers Blumenstrauß *m*; ~ *of
grapes* Weintraube *f*; ~ *of keys* Schlüsselbund *m, n*. **2.** F Verein *m*, Haufen *m*.
II *v/t* **3.** *a.* ~ *up* bündeln. **III** *v/i* **4.** *oft* ~
up (*od. together*) Grüppchen *od.* Haufen bilden.
bun·combe *bsd. Am.* → *bunkum*.
bun·dle ['bʌndl] **I** *s* **1.** Bündel *n*, Bund *n*.
2. F (*Energie-, Nerven- etc*)Bündel *n*. **II**
v/t **3.** *oft* ~ *up* bündeln. **4.** stopfen (*into*
in *acc*). **5.** *mst* ~ *off* eilig *od.* ohne viel
Federlesens fortschaffen. **III** *v/i* **6.** *mst*
~ *off* sich packen *od.* eilig davonmachen.
bung [bʌŋ] **I** *s* **1.** a) Spund(zapfen) *m*, b)
→ *bunghole*. **II** *v/t* **2.** *Faß* verspunden.
3. *mst* ~ *up* F Öffnung *etc* verstopfen:
my nose is ~ed up m-e Nase ist zu.
bun·ga·low ['bʌŋɡələʊ] *s* Bungalow *m*.
'**bung·hole** *s* Spundloch *n*.
bun·gle ['bʌŋɡl] **I** *v/i* **1.** pfuschen. **II** *v/t*
2. verpfuschen. **III** *s* Pfusch(arbeit *f*) *m*.
'**bun·gler** *s* Pfuscher(in). '**bun·gling**
adj □ stümperhaft.
bunk¹ [bʌŋk] *s* ⚓ Koje *f*.
bunk² [~] F → *bunkum*.
bunk³ [~] *s*: *do a ~ Br.* F verduften, türmen.
bunk bed *s* Etagenbett *n*.
bunk·er ['bʌŋkə] *s* **1.**, ✕ Bunker *m*.
bun·kum ['bʌŋkəm] *s* Blödsinn *m*, Gewäsch *n*.
bun·ny ['bʌnɪ] *s* Häschen *n* (*a.* F *attraktives Mädchen*).
buoy [bɔɪ] **I** *s* **1.** ⚓ Boje *f*, Bake *f*. **2.**
Rettungsring *m*. **II** *v/t* **3.** *mst* ~ *up* fig.
Auftrieb geben (*dat*).
buoy·an·cy ['bɔɪənsɪ] *s* **1.** *phys.*
Schwimm-, Tragkraft *f*. **2.** ✈ Auftrieb
m. **3.** *fig.* Spannkraft *f*; Schwung *m*.

bushy

'**buoy·ant** *adj* **1.** federnd (*Schritt*). **2.** schwungvoll.

bur [bɜː] *s* ✿ Klette *f* (*a. fig.*).

bur·den¹ ['bɜːdn] **I** *s* Last *f*, *fig. a.* Bürde *f*: **~ of proof** ⚖ Beweislast; **be a ~ to** (*od. on*) **s.o.** j-m zur Last fallen. **II** *v/t* belasten (*a. fig.*): **~ s.o. with s.th.** j-m et. aufbürden.

bur·den² [~] *s* **1.** Kehrreim *m*, Refrain *m*. **2.** Hauptgedanke *m*.

bur·den·some ['bɜːdnsəm] *adj* lästig, beschwerlich.

bu·reau ['bjʊərəʊ] *pl* **-reaus, -reaux** ['~rəʊz] *s* **1.** *Br.* Schreibtisch *m*, -pult *n*. **2.** *Am.* (*od.* Spiegel)Kommode *f*. **3.** Büro *n*. **4.** Auskunfts- *od.* Vermittlungsstelle *f*. **bu·reauc·ra·cy** [~'rɒkrəsɪ] *s* Bürokratie *f*. **bu·reau·crat** ['~kræt] *s* Bürokrat *m*. ,**bu·reau'crat·ic** *adj* (**~ally**) bürokratisch. **bu·reauc·ra·tize** [~'rɒkrətaɪz] *v/t* bürokratisieren.

burg·er ['bɜːgə] *s gastr. bsd. Am.* F Hamburger *m*.

bur·glar ['bɜːglə] *s* Einbrecher *m*: **we had ~s** bei uns wurde eingebrochen; **~ alarm** Alarmanlage *f*. **bur·glar·ize** ['~raɪz] *Am.* → **burgle**. '**bur·glar·proof** *adj* einbruch(s)sicher. **bur·gla·ry** ['bɜːglərɪ] *s* Einbruch *m*. **bur·gle** ['bɜːgl] *v/t u. v/i* einbrechen (in *acc od. dat*): **he was ~d** bei ihm wurde eingebrochen.

bur·i·al ['berɪəl] *s* Begräbnis *n*, Beerdigung *f*. **~ ground** *s* Friedhof *m*. **~ place** *s* Grabstätte *f*. **~ ser·vice** *s* Trauerfeier *f*.

bur·lesque [bɜː'lesk] **I** *adj* burlesk, possenhaft. **II** *s* Burleske *f*, Posse *f*.

bur·ly ['bɜːlɪ] *adj* stämmig.

burn [bɜːn] **I** *s* **1.** verbrannte Stelle. **2.** 𝟉 Verbrennung *f*, Brandwunde *f*. **II** *v/i* (*a. irr*) **1.** *allg.* brennen (*Feuer, Licht, Haus, Wunde etc*): **~ down** ab-, niederbrennen. **4.** *fig.* brennen (**with** vor *dat*): **~ing with anger** wutentbrannt; **be ~ing to do s.th.** darauf brennen, et. zu tun. **5.** ver-, anbrennen (*Speise etc*). **III** *v/t* (*a. irr*) **6.** verbrennen: **~ down** ab-, niederbrennen; **his house was ~t** sein Haus brannte ab; **be ~t to death** verbrennen; → **boat** 1, **bridge** 1, **candle**. **7.** verbrennen, -sengen, *Speise* anbrennen (lassen): **~ one's fingers** sich die Finger verbrennen (*a. fig.*); **~ a hole in** ein

Loch brennen in (*acc*). **8.** *Ziegel, Porzellan etc* brennen. '**burn·er** *s* Brenner *m* (*Person u. Gerät*). '**burn·ing** *adj* brennend (*a. fig.*): **take a ~ interest in** brennend interessiert sein an (*dat*); **~ sensation** 𝟉 Brennen *n*.

bur·nish ['bɜːnɪʃ] *v/t* polieren.

burnt [bɜːnt] **I** *pret u. pp von* **burn**. **II** *adj*: **~ almonds** *pl* gebrannte Mandeln *pl*.

burp [bɜːp] F **I** *v/i* rülpsen, aufstoßen, (*Baby*) ein Bäuerchen machen. **II** *s* Rülpser *m*, Bäuerchen *n*.

burr → **bur**.

bur·row ['bʌrəʊ] **I** *s* (*Fuchs- etc*)Bau *m*. **II** *v/i* (**into**) sich eingraben (in *acc*); *fig.* sich vertiefen (in *acc*).

burst [bɜːst] **I** *v/i* (*irr*) **1.** bersten (*Eis etc*), (zer)platzen (*Luftballon etc*): **~ (open)** aufplatzen (*Wunde etc*), aufspringen (*Tür etc*); → **seam** 1. **2.** explodieren. **3.** *fig.* ausbrechen (**into** *in acc*): **~ into laughter (tears)** in Gelächter (Tränen) ausbrechen; **~ into flame(s)** in Flammen aufgehen. **4.** **~ out** *fig.* herausplatzen. **5.** **~ with** zum Bersten voll sein von; *fig.* strotzen vor (*dat*) *od.* von; *fig.* platzen vor (*dat*). **6.** **~ in** (**out**) herein-(hinaus)stürmen; **~ into sight** (*od.* **view**) plötzlich sichtbar werden. **II** *v/t* (*irr*) **7.** (auf)sprengen, zum Platzen bringen: **~ open** aufbrechen; **the car ~ a tire** (*bsd. Br.* **tyre**) ein Reifen am Wagen platzte. **III** *s* **8.** Bersten *n*, Platzen *n*. **9.** Explosion *f*. **10.** *fig.* Ausbruch *m*: **~ of applause** Beifallssturm *m*; **~ of laughter** Lachsalve *f*. **11.** *a.* **~ of fire** Feuerstoß *m*, Salve *f*.

bur·y ['berɪ] *v/t* **1.** begraben: a) beerdigen, b) verschütten, c) *Streit etc* vergessen: **~ o.s. in** sich vertiefen in (*acc*); **buried in thought(s)** gedankenversunken. **2.** ver-, eingraben, ⚷, ✿ in die Erde verlegen: → **hatchet**.

bus [bʌs] *pl* **-(s)es** *s* (Omni-, Auto)Bus: → **miss²** 1.

bush¹ [bʊʃ] *s* **1.** Busch *m*, Strauch *m*: **beat about** (*od.* **around**) **the ~** *fig.* wie die Katze um den heißen Brei herumgehen, um die Sache herumreden. **2.** Gebüsch *n*. **3.** Busch *m*; Waldland *n*.

bush² [~] *s* ✿ Buchse *f*.

bush·el ['bʊʃl] *s* Bushel *m*, Scheffel *m* (*Br. 36, 37 l, Am. 35, 24 l*): → **light¹** 1d.

bush·y ['bʊʃɪ] *adj* □ buschig.

busi·ness ['bɪznɪs] s **1.** Geschäft n, Beruf m, Tätigkeit f: **on** ~ geschäftlich, beruflich. **2.** ♣ Geschäft(sgang m) n: **how is** ~? wie gehen die Geschäfte? **3.** ♣ Geschäft n, Unternehmen n. **4.** Arbeit f, Beschäftigung f: ~ **before pleasure** erst die Arbeit, dann das Vergnügen; → **mix** 2. **5.** Sache f, Aufgabe f: **make it one's** ~ **to do s.th.** es sich zur Aufgabe machen, et. zu tun. **6.** Angelegenheit f, Sache f: **get down to** ~ zur Sache kommen; **that's none of your** ~ das geht Sie nichts an; **send s.o. about his** ~ j-m heimleuchten; → **mean³** 1, **mind** 5. **7.** Anlaß m, Berechtigung f: **have no** ~ **doing** (od. **to do**) **s.th.** kein Recht haben, et. zu tun. **8.** Geschäft n (*Notdurft*): **do one's** ~ sein Geschäft erledigen od. machen. ~ **ad·dress** s Geschäftsadresse f. ~ **hours** s pl Geschäftsstunden pl, -zeit f: **after** ~ nach Geschäftsschluß. ~ **let·ter** s Geschäftsbrief m. '~**·like** adj sachlich, nüchtern. '~**·man** s (irr **man**) Geschäftsmann m. ~ **se·cret** s Betriebs-, Geschäftsgeheimnis n. ~ **trip** s Geschäftsreise f. '~**·wom·an** s (irr **woman**) Geschäftsfrau f. ~ **year** s ♣ Geschäftsjahr n.

bus·ker ['bʌskə] s Br. Straßenmusikant(in); -sänger(in).

bus·man ['bʌsmən] s (irr **man**) (Omni)Busfahrer m: ~**'s holiday** Urlaub, der mit der üblichen Berufsarbeit verbracht wird. ~ **ser·vice** s Busverbindung f. ~ **stop** s Bushaltestelle f.

bust¹ [bʌst] s Büste f.

bust² [~] F **I** v/i (a. irr) **1.** kaputtgehen. **2.** pleite gehen. **II** v/t (a. irr) **3.** kaputtmachen. **III** s **4.** Pleite f, a. weitS. Reinfall m. **5.** Sauferei f; Sauftour f: **go on a** ~ e-e Sauftour machen. **IV** adj **6.** kaputt. **7.** pleite: **go** ~ → 2.

bus·tle ['bʌsl] **I** v/i **1.** a. ~ **about** (od. **around**) geschäftig hin u. her eilen. **2.** sich beeilen; eilen, hasten. **3.** **the streets were bustling with life** auf den Straßen herrschte geschäftiges Treiben. **II** v/t **4.** a. ~ **up** antreiben, hetzen. **III** s **5.** Geschäftigkeit f; geschäftiges Treiben. '**bus·tler** s geschäftiger Mensch. '**bus·tling** adj **1.** geschäftig. **2.** belebt (*Straße etc*).

bus·y ['bɪzɪ] **I** adj □ **1.** beschäftigt: **be** ~ **doing s.th.** damit beschäftigt sein, et. zu tun. **2.** geschäftig, fleißig: **get** ~! an die Arbeit!; → **bee**. **3.** Straße etc: belebt; verkehrsreich. **4.** arbeitsreich (*Tag etc*). **5.** übereifrig, aufdringlich. **6.** teleph. bsd. Am. besetzt: ~ **signal** Besetztzeichen n. **II** v/t **7.** (*o.s.* sich) beschäftigen (**with** mit): ~ **o.s. doing s.th.** sich damit beschäftigen, et. zu tun. '~**·bod·y** s j-d, der sich in alles einmischt.

bus·y·ness ['bɪzɪnɪs] s Geschäftigkeit f.

but [bʌt] **I** cj **1.** aber, jedoch: ~ **then** (**again**) and(e)rerseits. **2.** sondern: **not only ...** ~ **also** nicht nur ..., sondern auch. **3.** als, außer: ~ **for** ohne; ~ **for my parents** wenn m-e Eltern nicht (gewesen) wären. **II** prp **4.** außer: **nothing** ~ nichts als, nur; **the last** ~ **one** (**two**) der vorletzte (drittletzte); → **anything** 2. **5.** all ~ fast, beinahe. **III** s **6.** no ~s about it kein Aber; → **if** 4.

bu·tane ['bjuːteɪn] s ♣ Butan n.

butch·er ['bʊtʃə] **I** s **1.** Fleischer m, Metzger m: **at the** ~**'s** beim Fleischer. **II** v/t **2.** schlachten. **3.** abschlachten, niedermetzeln. '**butch·er·y** s **1.** Fleischer-, Metzgerhandwerk n. **2.** Gemetzel n.

but·ler ['bʌtlə] s Butler m.

butt¹ [bʌt] **I** s **1.** (*Gewehr- etc*)Kolben m. **2.** (Zigarren-, Zigaretten-, Kerzen-)Stummel m, (Zigaretten)Kippe f. **3.** fig. Zielscheibe f. **4.** Kopfstoß m; Stoß mit den Hörnern. **5.** j-m e-n Kopfstoß od. e-n Stoß mit den Hörnern versetzen. **6.** Zigarre, Zigarette ausdrücken. **III** v/i **7.** ~ **in** F sich einmischen: ~ **in on**, ~ **into** sich einmischen in (acc).

but·ter ['bʌtə] **I** s **1.** Butter f: **he looks as if** ~ **would not melt in his mouth** er sieht aus, als könnte er nicht bis drei zählen od. als könnte er kein Wässerchen trüben. **II** v/t **2.** mit Butter bestreichen. **3.** ~ **up** F j-m schöntun, j-m Honig ums Maul schmieren. ~ **dish** s Butterdose f, -schale f. '~**·fin·gered** adj F tolpatschig. '~**·fin·gers** pl -, '**·fin·gers** s F Tolpatsch m. '~**·fly** s zo. Schmetterling m: **have butterflies in one's stomach** F ein flaues Gefühl in der Magengegend haben. **2.** a. ~ **stroke** (Schwimmen) Schmetterlingsstil m. '~**·milk** s Buttermilch f.

but·tock ['bʌtək] s anat. Gesäßbacke f: ~s pl Gesäß n.

byword

but·ton ['bʌtn] **I** s **1.** (Kleider-, a. Klingel-etc)Knopf m. **2.** (Ansteck)Plakette f, Abzeichen n. **3.** pl (sg konstruiert) bsd. Br. F Hotelpage m. **II** v/t **4.** mst ~ **up** zuknöpfen: ~**ed up** F zugeknöpft, zurückhaltend. **III** v/i **5.** hinten etc geknöpft werden. '~**hole** s **1.** Knopfloch n. **2.** bsd. Br. Blume f im Knopfloch.

but·tress ['bʌtrɪs] **I** s **1.** △ Strebe-, Stützpfeiler m. **2.** fig. Stütze f. **II** v/t a. ~ **up 3.** stützen. **4.** fig. (unter)stützen.

bux·om ['bʌksəm] adj drall.

buy [baɪ] **I** s **1.** F Kauf m: a good ~. **II** v/t (irr) **2.** (ein)kaufen (of, from von; at bei): ~ s.th. from s.o. j-m et. abkaufen. **3.** Fahrkarte etc lösen. **4.** fig. Sieg etc erkaufen (with et.): dearly bought teuer erkauft. **5.** j-n kaufen, bestechen. **6.** bsd. Am. F et. glauben: I won't ~ that! das kauf ich dir etc nicht ab!
Verbindungen mit Adverbien:
buy| back v/t zurückkaufen. ~ **in** v/t sich eindecken mit. ~ **off** → buy 5. ~ **out** v/t Teilhaber etc abfinden, auszahlen. ~ **up** v/t aufkaufen.

buy·er ['baɪə] s Käufer(in).

buzz [bʌz] **I** v/i summen, surren, schwirren: ~ **off** F (mst imp) abschwirren, abhauen; ~ **for** → **II** a. **II** v/t a) j-n mit dem Summer rufen, b) teleph. F j-n anrufen. **III** s Summen n, Surren n, Schwirren n: give s.o. a ~ → **II**.

buz·zard ['bʌzəd] s orn. Bussard m.

buzz·er ['bʌzə] s ⚡ Summer m.

'**buzz·word** s Modewort n.

by [baɪ] **I** prp **1.** örtlich: (nahe od. dicht) bei od. an (dat), neben (dat): side ~ side Seite an Seite. **2.** vorbei od. vorüber an (dat), an (dat) ... entlang. **3.** Verkehrsmittel: per, mit: → **air**¹ 1, etc. **4.** zeitlich: bis um od. spätestens: be here ~ 4.30 sei um 4 Uhr 30 hier; → **now** 1. **5.** Tageszeit: während, bei: → **day** 1, etc.

6. nach, ...weise: **sold by the yard** yardweise verkauft; → **hour** 1, etc. **7.** nach, gemäß: **it is ten ~ my watch** nach od. auf m-r Uhr ist es zehn. **8.** von: ~ **nature** 2, **trade** 4. **9.** Urheberschaft: von, durch: a play ~ Shaw ein Stück von Shaw; → **oneself** 1. **10.** mit Hilfe von, mit, durch: ~ **listening** durch Zuhören; → **force** 1, 3, 4. **11.** Größenverhältnisse: um: (too) **short ~ an inch** um e-n Zoll zu kurz. **12.** Ⓐ a) mal: **3 ~ 4; the size is 9 feet ~ 6** die Größe ist 9 auf 6 (od. 9 x 6) Fuß; → **multiply** 2, b) durch: **6 ~ 2;** → **divide** 4, 6. **13.** an (dat), bei: → **root**¹, etc. **II** adv **14.** nahe: ~ **and large** im großen u. ganzen; ~ **and** ~ bald, demnächst; nach u. nach; → **close** 9, **hard** 13. **15.** vorbei, vorüber: → **go by**, etc. **16.** beiseite: → **put by**, etc.

by(e)... Neben..., Seiten...

bye [baɪ] → **bye-bye** **II**.

bye-bye I s ['baɪbaɪ]: **go to ~(s)** in die Heia gehen; einschlafen. **II** int [ˌbaɪ'baɪ] F Wiedersehen!, Tschüs!; teleph. Wiederhören!

'**by|-ef·fect** s Nebenwirkung f. '**~-e-ˌlec·tion** s Nachwahl f. '**~-gone I** adj vergangen. **II** s: let ~s be ~s laß(t) das Vergangene ruhen. '**~-law** s bsd. Br. Ortsstatut n, städtische Verordnung. '**~-name** s Beiname m. '**~-pass** s **1.** Umleitung f, Umgehungsstraße f. **2.** ⚕ Bypass m: ~ **operation** Bypassoperation f. '**~-prod·uct** s Nebenprodukt n (a. fig.). '**~-road** s Seiten-, Nebenstraße f. '**~-stand·er** s Umstehende m, f, Zuschauer(in). '**~-street** → **byroad**.

byte [baɪt] s Computer: Byte n, Binärwort n.

'**by|-way** → **byroad**. '**~-word** s Inbegriff m (for gen): be a ~ for stehen für, gleichbedeutend sein mit.

C

cab [kæb] *s* **1.** Taxi *n*, Taxe *f*. **2.** 🚂 Führerstand *m*; Fahrerhaus *n* (*e-s Lastkraftwagens*), (*a. e-s Krans*) Führerhaus *n*.

cab·a·ret ['kæbəreɪ] *s a.* ~ **show** Varietédarbietungen *pl* (*in e-m Restaurant od. Nachtklub*).

cab·bage ['kæbɪdʒ] *s* ♣ Kohl *m*.

cab·bie, cab·by ['kæbɪ] *s bsd. Am.* F Taxifahrer(in).

'cab,driv·er *s bsd. Am.* Taxifahrer(in).

cab·in ['kæbɪn] *s* **1.** Häuschen *n*, Hütte *f*. **2.** ⚓ Kabine *f*, Kajüte *f*. **3.** ✈ Kabine *f* (*a. e-r Seilbahn etc*). ~ **class** *s* ⚓ Kabinen-, Kajütsklasse *f*. ~ **cruis·er** *s* ⚓ Kabinenkreuzer *m*.

cab·i·net ['kæbɪnɪt] *s* **1.** *oft* ⚖ *pol.* Kabinett *n*. **2.** Vitrine *f*. **3.** (*Büro-, Kartei- etc*)Schrank *m*. **4.** (*Radio- etc*)Gehäuse *n*.

ca·ble ['keɪbl] **I** *s* **1.** Kabel *n* (*a. ⚡*), (Draht)Seil *n*. **2.** → **cablegram**. **II** *v/t* **3.** *TV:* Gegend *mit* Kabeln versorgen. **4.** *j-m et.* telegrafieren; *j-n* telegrafisch benachrichtigen. **5.** *j-m* Geld telegrafisch an- *od.* überweisen. **III** *v/i* **6.** telegrafieren. ~ **ad·dress** *s* Telegrammadresse *f*. ~ **car** *s* Seilbahn: Kabine *f*; Wagen *m*.

ca·ble·gram ['keɪblgræm] *s* (Übersee-) Telegramm *n*.

ca·ble tel·e·vi·sion *s* Kabelfernsehen *n*.

cab·man ['kæbmən] *s* (*irr* **man**) Taxifahrer *m*.

ca·boo·dle [kə'buːdl] *s*: **the whole** ~ F die ganze Chose.

ca·boose [kə'buːs] *s* ⚓ Kombüse *f*.

cab| rank, '~stand *s bsd. Am.* Taxistand *m*.

cache [kæʃ] **I** *s* Versteck *n*, geheimes Lager. **II** *v/t* verstecken.

cack·le ['kækl] **I** *v/i* gackern (*Huhn*), schnattern (*Gans*), *fig. a.* gackernd lachen. **II** *s* Gegacker *n*, Geschnatter *n*, *fig. a.* gackerndes Lachen.

ca·coph·o·ny [kæ'kɒfənɪ] *s* ♪ Kakophonie *f*, Mißklang *m*.

cac·tus ['kæktəs] *pl* **-ti** ['~taɪ], **-tus·es** ♣ Kaktus *m*.

ca·das·tre [kə'dæstə] *s* Grundbuch *n*.

ca·dav·er·ous [kə'dævərəs] *adj* ☐ leichenblaß.

cad·die ['kædɪ] *s* Golf: Caddie *m* (*Schlägerträger*).

cad·dy ['kædɪ] *s* (*bsd.* Tee)Büchse *f*, (-)Dose *f*.

ca·dence ['keɪdəns] *s* **1.** (Vers-, Sprech-) Rhythmus *m*. **2.** ♪ Kadenz *f*.

ca·det [kə'det] *s* **1.** ✕ Kadett *m*. **2.** (*Polizei- etc*)Schüler *m*: ~ **nurse** Schwesternschülerin *f*.

cadge [kædʒ] *v/t u. v/i* schnorren (**from** bei). **'cadg·er** *s* Schnorrer(in).

cad·mi·um ['kædmɪəm] *s* 🜊 Cadmium *n*.

cad·re ['kɑːdə] *s* ✠, ✕, *pol.* Kader *m*.

Cae·sar·e·an, a. c. ♪ [siː'zeərɪən] **I** *adj:* ~ **section** → **II**. **II** *s* ⚕ Kaiserschnitt *m*.

cae·su·ra [sɪ'zjʊərə] *s* Zäsur *f*.

ca·fé ['kæfeɪ] *s* **1.** Café *n*. **2.** Restaurant *n*. **3.** *Am.* Kneipe *f*; Nachtklub *m*.

caf·e·te·ri·a [ˌkæfɪ'tɪərɪə] *s* Cafeteria *f*, Selbstbedienungsrestaurant *n*, *a.* Kantine *f*, *univ.* Mensa *f*.

caf·feine ['kæfiːn] *s* 🜊 Koffein *n*.

cage [keɪdʒ] **I** *s* **1.** Käfig *m*. **2.** Kabine *f* (*e-s Aufzugs*); ✕ Förderkorb *m* **II** *v/t* **3.** in e-n Käfig sperren, einsperren.

cage·y ['keɪdʒɪ] *adj* ☐ F **1.** verschlossen. **2.** vorsichtig. **3.** *Am.* gerissen, schlau.

ca·jole [kə'dʒəʊl] *v/t* ✕ j-m schmeicheln. **2.** *j-n* beschwatzen (**into doing** zu tun); ~ **s.o. out of s.th.** j-m et. ausreden; ~ **s.th. out of s.o.** j-m et. abbetteln.

cake [keɪk] *s* **1.** Kuchen *m*, Torte *f*: **go** (*od.* **sell**) **like hot** ~**s** weggehen wie die warmen Semmeln; **take the** ~ F den Vogel abschießen; **you can't have your** ~ **and eat it** du kannst nur eines von beiden tun *od.* haben; → **piece** 1. **2.** Tafel *f* Schokolade, Riegel *m* Seife. **II** *v/i* **3.** klumpen.

ca·lam·i·tous [kə'læmɪtəs] *adj* ☐ verheerend, katastrophal. **ca'lam·i·ty** *s* **1.** Katastrophe *f*: **in the** ~ bei der Katastrophe; ~ **of nature** Naturkatastrophe; ~ **howler** *bsd. Am.* Schwarzseher(in), Panikmacher(in). **2.** Elend *n*, Misere *f*.

cal·cif·er·ous [kæl'sɪfərəs] *adj* kalkhal-

tig. **cal·ci·fy** ['↘faɪ] v/t u. v/i verkalken.
cal·ci·um ['↘sɪəm] s ♫ Kalzium n.
cal·cu·la·ble ['kælkjʊləbl] adj □ **1.** be-
rechen-, kalkulierbar: ~ risk kalkulier-
bares Risiko. **2.** verläßlich. **cal·cu·late**
['↘leɪt] I v/t **1.** be-, ausrechnen: ~ that
damit rechnen, daß. **2.** Preise, Entfernung etc kalkulieren, Chancen etc abwägen. **3.** Am. F vermuten, glauben
(that daß). II v/i **4.** ~ on rechnen mit od.
auf (acc), zählen od. sich verlassen auf
(acc). **cal·cu·lat·ed** adj **1.** gewollt, beabsichtigt, (Indiskretion) gezielt, (Beleidigung) bewußt, (Risiko) kalkuliert. **2.**
gedacht, bestimmt (for für; to do zu
tun): it was ~ to impress es sollte Eindruck machen. **'cal·cu·lat·ing** adj □ **1.**
(kühl) überlegend; berechnend. **2.**
Rechen...: ~ machine. **,cal·cu·la·tion** s **1.**
Berechnung f (a. fig.), Ausrechnung f:
be out in one's ~ sich verrechnet haben. **2.** Kalkulation f: ~ of profits ✝
Gewinnkalkulation. **3.** Überlegung
f: after much ~ nach reiflicher Überlegung. **'cal·cu·la·tor** s Rechner m
(Gerät). **cal·cu·lus** ['↘ləs] pl -li ['↘laɪ],
-lus·es a ♫ Rechnungsart f, (Dif-
ferential- etc)Rechnung f: ~ of probabilities Wahrscheinlichkeitsrech-
nung.
cal·en·dar ['kælɪndə] s **1.** (engS. Termin)Kalender m, fig. a. Zeitrechnung f.
2. Liste f, Register n.
cal·ends ['kælɪndz] s pl: on the Greek ~
am St. Nimmerleinstag.
calf¹ [kɑːf] pl calves [kɑːvz] s **1.** Kalb n.
2. Kalb(s)leder n.
calf² [↘] pl calves [↘] s anat. Wade f.
calf│ love s F kindische Schwärmerei.
'~·skin → calf¹ 2.
cal·i·ber Am. → calibre. **cal·i·brate**
['kælɪbreɪt] v/t ⚙ kalibrieren, eichen.
cal·i·bre ['↘bə] s Kaliber n, fig. a. Format n (e-s Menschen).
call [kɔːl] I s **1.** Ruf m (for nach): ~ for
help Hilferuf; within ~ in Rufweite. **2.**
teleph. Anruf m: give s.o. a ~ j-n anrufen; make a ~ telefonieren. **3.**
(Lock)Ruf m (e-s Tiers). **4.** fig. Ruf m
(der Natur etc). **5.** Berufung f (to auf e-n
Lehrstuhl, an e-e Universität, in ein
Amt). **6.** Aufruf m: make a ~ for s.th.
zu et. aufrufen. **7.** thea. Herausruf m,
Vorhang m. **8.** (kurzer) Besuch m (on

s.o., at s.o.'s [house] bei j-m): make
(od. pay) a ~ on s.o. j-n besuchen, j-m
e-n Besuch abstatten. **9.** ✝ Zahlungs-
aufforderung f; Abruf m, Kündigung f
(von Geldern). II v/t **10.** j-n (herbei)ru-
fen, Arzt etc kommen lassen: → attention 1, being 1. **11.** zu e-m Streik etc
aufrufen. **12.** Versammlung etc einberufen. **13.** j-n wecken. **14.** teleph. anrufen. **15.** j-n berufen (to → 5). **16.** j-n, et.
nennen: be ~ed heißen; → spade¹. **17.**
nennen, bezeichnen (als): what do you
~ this? wie nennt man od. heißt das? **18.**
nennen, finden, halten für: I ~ that stupid. **19.** et. schimpfen: he ~ed me a
fool. III v/i **20.** rufen (a. fig. Pflicht etc):
~ for um Hilfe rufen; nach j-m, et. rufen; fig. erfordern. **21.** e-n (kurzen) Besuch machen (on s.o., at s.o.'s [house]
bei j-m): call on s.o. j-n besuchen, j-m
e-n Besuch abstatten; ~ for et. anfordern; j-n, et. abholen. **22.** ~ on sich
wenden an (acc) (for s.th. um et., wegen
e-r Sache); j-n bitten (to do zu tun). **23.**
~ at ⚓ anlegen in (dat), Hafen anlaufen; ⭐ halten in (dat); ✈ Flughafen
anfliegen. **24.** anrufen, telefonieren.
Verbindungen mit Adverbien:
call│ a·way v/t **1.** wegrufen (from von).
2. Gedanken etc ablenken (from von). ~
back I v/t **1.** a. teleph. zurückrufen. **2.**
defekte Autos etc (in die Werkstatt) zurückrufen. II v/i **3.** a. teleph. zurückrufen. **4.** noch einmal vorbeikommen. ~
down v/t **1.** Segen etc herabflehen, -ru-
fen. **2.** sich j-s Zorn zuziehen. **3.** Am. F
zs.-stauchen (for wegen). ~ **forth** v/t
hervorrufen, auslösen, Fähigkeiten etc
wachrufen, wecken. ~ **in I** v/t **1.** hinein-,
hereinrufen. **2.** Arzt etc (hin)zuziehen,
zu Rate ziehen. **3.** Schulden einfordern,
Forderungen etc einziehen. II v/i **4.**
(kurz) vorbeischauen (on s.o., at s.o.'s
[house] bei j-m). ~ **off** v/i **1.** zum Streik
etc rufen. **5.** rufen (for um Hilfe). ~
o·ver v/t Namen, Liste etc verlesen. ~
up v/t **1.** teleph. anrufen. **2.** Erinnerungen etc wachrufen, wecken. **3.** ✕ einberufen.

'call|·back s Rückruf(aktion f) m. **~ box** s Br. Telefonzelle f.

call·er ['kɔːlə] s **1.** Rufer(in). **2.** teleph. Anrufer(in). **3.** Besucher(in). **4.** Abholer(in).

call| girl s Callgirl n. **'~-in** Am. → **phone-in**.

call·ing ['kɔːlɪŋ] s **1.** Beruf m: **what is his ~?** was ist er von Beruf? **2.** bsd. eccl. Berufung f: **have a ~ to** do s.th. sich berufen fühlen, et. zu tun. **~ card** s Am. Visitenkarte f.

cal·lis·then·ics [ˌkælɪs'θenɪks] s pl Gymnastik f, Freiübungen pl.

cal·los·i·ty [kæ'lɒsətɪ] s **1.** Schwiele f. **2.** fig. Gefühllosigkeit f. **'cal·lous** adj □ **1.** schwielig. **2.** fig. abgestumpft, gefühllos (**to** gegenüber).

'call-up s ✕ Einberufung f.

cal·lus ['kæləs] s Schwiele f.

calm [kɑːm] **I** s **1.** Stille f, Ruhe f (a. fig.): **the ~ before the storm; ~ (of mind)** Gelassenheit f, Gemütsruhe. **2.** Windstille f. **II** adj □ **3.** still, ruhig. **4.** windstill. **5.** fig. ruhig, gelassen. **III** v/t **6.** oft **~ down** beruhigen, besänftigen. **IV** v/i **7.** oft **~ down 7.** sich beruhigen. **8.** sich legen (Sturm, Zorn etc).

cal·o·rie ['kælərɪ] s Kalorie f. **'~-,con·scious** adj □ kalorienbewußt.

ca·lum·ni·ate [kə'lʌmnɪeɪt] v/t verleumden. **ca'lum·ni·a·tor** s Verleumder(in). **ca'lum·ni·ous** adj □ verleumderisch. **cal·um·ny** ['kæləmnɪ] s Verleumdung f.

calve [kɑːv] v/i kalben.

calves [kɑːvz] pl von **calf**[1] u. [2].

ca·lyp·so [kə'lɪpsəʊ] pl **-sos** s ♪ Calypso m.

cam [kæm] s ⊙ Nocken m.

cam·ber ['kæmbə] **I** v/t u. v/i **1.** (sich) wölben. **II** s **2.** (leichte) Wölbung. **3.** mot. Sturz m.

came [keɪm] pret von **come**.

cam·el ['kæml] s zo. Kamel n.

cam·el's| hair ['kæmlz] s Kamelhaar(stoff m) n. **'~-hair** adj Kamelhaar...

cam·er·a ['kæmərə] s **1.** (a. Film-, Fernseh)Kamera f, Fotoapparat m. **2.** ⚖ unter Ausschluß der Öffentlichkeit; fig. geheim. **'~·man** s (irr **man**) **1.** Kameramann m. **2.** Pressefotograf m. **'~-shy** adj kamerascheu.

cam·i·on ['kæmɪən] s Last(kraft)wagen m.

cam·o·mile ['kæməmaɪl] s ❀ Kamille f: **~ tea** Kamillentee m.

cam·ou·flage ['kæməflɑːʒ] **I** s ✕, zo. Tarnung f, fig. a. Verschleierung f. **II** v/t ✕ tarnen, fig. a. verschleiern.

camp¹ [kæmp] **I** s **1.** (Zelt- etc)Lager n (fig. a. Partei): **~ bed** (Am. a. **cot**) Feldbett n; Campingliege f; **~ chair** Klapp-, Campingstuhl m. **II** v/i **2.** sein Lager aufschlagen, kampieren. **3.** oft **~ out** zelten, campen.

camp² [~] **F I** adj **1.** künstlich, gewollt; aufgemotzt, thea. etc a. überzogen. **2.** tuntenhaft. **II** v/i **3.** sich tuntenhaft benehmen. **III** v/t **4.** **~ it up**) a) → 3, b) eine Sache aufmotzen, thea. etc a. überziehen.

cam·paign [kæm'peɪn] **I** s **1.** ✕ Feldzug m, fig. a. Kampagne f. **2.** pol. Wahlkampf m: **~ pledge** (od. **promise**) Wahlversprechen n. **II** v/i **3.** ✕ an e-m Feldzug teilnehmen. **4.** fig. kämpfen (**for** für; **against** gegen). **cam'paign·er** s **1.** ✕ Feldzugteilnehmer m: **old ~** Veteran m; fig. alter Praktikus. **2.** fig. Kämpfer m.

camp·er ['kæmpə] s **1.** Zeltler(in), Camper(in). **2.** Am. Wohnanhänger m, -wagen m; Wohnmobil n.

'camp|·fire s Lagerfeuer n. **'~·ground** s **1.** Lagerplatz m. **2.** Zelt-, Campingplatz m.

cam·phor ['kæmfə] s ⚘ Kampfer m: **~ ball** Mottenkugel f.

camp·ing ['kæmpɪŋ] s Camping n, Zelten n: **~ ground** (od. **site**) → **campground**.

'camp·site → **campground**.

cam·pus ['kæmpəs] s Campus m (Gesamtanlage e-r Universität, e-s College od. e-r Schule).

'cam·shaft s ⊙ Nockenwelle f.

can¹ [kæn] v/aux (irr) ich kann etc.

can² [~] **I** s **1.** (Blech)Kanne f: **have to carry the ~** F den Kopf hinhalten müssen (**for** für). **2.** (Blech-, Konserven-) Dose f, (-)Büchse f: **~ opener** Dosen-, Büchsenöffner m. **3.** Kanister m. **4.** Am. Müll-, Abfalleimer m; Müll-, Abfalltonne f. **II** v/t **5.** einmachen, -dosen: → **canned** 1. **6.** F (auf Band etc) aufnehmen: → **canned** 2.

Ca·na·di·an [kəˈneɪdjən] **I** *adj* kanadisch. **II** *s* Kanadier(in).

ca·nal [kəˈnæl] *s* Kanal *m*, *anat. a.* Gang *m*, Röhre *f*. **ca·nal·i·za·tion** [ˌkænəlaɪˈzeɪʃn] *s* Kanalisation *f*, Kanalisierung *f*. '**ca·nal·ize** *v/t* kanalisieren.

can·a·pé [ˈkænəpeɪ] *s gastr.* Appetit-, Cocktailhappen *m*.

ca·nard [kæˈnɑːd] *s* (Zeitungs)Ente *f*, Falschmeldung *f*.

ca·nar·y [kəˈneərɪ] *s* Kanarienvogel *m*.

can·cel [ˈkænsl] **I** *v/t pret u. pp* **-celed**, *bsd. Br.* **-celled** **1.** (durch-, aus)streichen. **2.** *Erlaubnis etc* widerrufen, *Beschluß etc* rückgängig machen, *Abonnement etc* kündigen, *Auftrag etc* stornieren. **3.** *Verabredung etc* absagen, *Veranstaltung etc* ausfallen lassen. **4.** *Briefmarke, Fahrschein* entwerten. **5.** ⅍ kürzen. **6.** *a.* ~ **out** ausgleichen, kompensieren. **II** *v/t* **7.** ⅍ sich kürzen lassen. **8.** *a.* ~ **out** sich (gegenseitig) aufheben. **can·cel·(l)a·tion** [ˌkænsəˈleɪʃn] *s* **1.** Streichung *f*. **2.** Widerrufung *f*, Rückgängigmachung *f*, Kündigung *f*, Stornierung *f*. **3.** Absage *f*. **4.** Entwertung *f*. **5.** ⅍ Kürzung *f*.

can·cer [ˈkænsə] **I** *s* **1.** ⚕ Krebs *m*. **2.** *fig.* Krebsgeschwür *n*. **3.** ⚹ *astr.* Krebs *m*. **II** *adj* **4.** Krebs...: ~ *cells* (**research**, *etc*). '**can·cer·ous** *adj* ⚕ krebsbefallen; Krebs...; krebsartig.

can·de·la·bra [ˌkændɪˈlɑːbrə] *s* **1.** *pl* **-bras** → **candelabrum**. **2.** *pl von* **candelabrum**. ˌ**can·de·la·brum** [~brəm] *pl* **-bra** [~brə], **-brums** *s* Kandelaber *m*, Armleuchter *m*.

can·did [ˈkændɪd] *adj* □ **1.** offen, aufrichtig. **2.** unvoreingenommen. **3.** *phot.* ungestellt: ~ *camera* versteckte Kamera; ~ *picture* Schnappschuß *m*.

can·di·da·cy [ˈkændɪdəsɪ] *s bsd. Am.* Kandidatur *f*, Bewerbung *f*, Anwartschaft *f* (*on* auf *acc*). **can·di·date** [~dət] *s* (**for**) Kandidat(in) (für), Anwärter(in) (auf *acc*), Bewerber(in) (um). **can·di·da·ture** [~tʃə] *bsd. Br.* → **candidacy**.

can·died [ˈkændɪd] *adj* kandiert. **2.** *fig.* honigsüß, schmeichlerisch.

can·dle [ˈkændl] *s* Kerze *f*: **burn the** ~ **at both ends** Raubbau mit s-r Gesundheit treiben; **not to be fit** (*od.* **able**) **to hold a** ~ **to** j-m nicht das Wasser reichen können; **the game is not worth the** ~

die Sache ist nicht der Mühe wert. '~**light** *s* Kerzenlicht *n*: **by** ~ bei Kerzenlicht; ~ **dinner** Essen *n* bei Kerzenlicht.

Can·dle·mas [ˈkændlməs] *s eccl.* (Mariä) Lichtmeß *f*.

'**can·dle·stick** *s* Kerzenleuchter *m*, -ständer *m*.

can·do(u)r [ˈkændə] *s* **1.** Offenheit *f*, Aufrichtigkeit *f*. **2.** Unvoreingenommenheit *f*.

can·dy [ˈkændɪ] **I** *s* **1.** Kandis(zucker) *m*. **2.** *bsd. Am.* Süßigkeiten *pl*: (**hard**) ~ Bonbon *m*, *n*. **II** *v/t* **3.** kandieren. '~**floss** *s Br.* Zuckerwatte *f*.

cane [keɪn] **I** *s* **1.** Spazierstock *m*. **2.** (Rohr)Stock *m*. **3.** (*Bambus-, Zucker-, Schilf*)Rohr *n*. **II** *v/t* **4.** (mit dem Stock) züchtigen. ~ **sug·ar** *s* Rohrzucker *m*.

ca·nine [ˈkeɪnaɪn] **I** *adj* **1.** Hunde..., Hunds... **2.** *contp.* hündisch: ~ *devotion* hündische Ergebenheit. **II** *s* **3.** *a.* ~ **tooth** Eckzahn *m*.

can·is·ter [ˈkænɪstə] *s* Blechbüchse *f*, -dose *f*.

can·ker [ˈkæŋkə] *s* **1.** ⚕ Soor *m*; Lippengeschwür *n*. **2.** ⚘ Baumkrebs *m*. **3.** *fig.* Krebsgeschwür *n*.

can·na·bis [ˈkænəbɪs] *s* Cannabis *m*: a) ⚘ Hanf *m*, b) Haschisch *n*.

canned [kænd] *adj* **1.** Dosen-, Büchsen...: ~ *fruit* Obstkonserven *pl*; ~ *meat* Büchsenfleisch *n*. **2.** *F* ~ *music* Musik *f* aus der Konserve; ~ *program(me)* (*Rundfunk, TV*) Programmkonserve *f*. **3.** *sl.* blau, betrunken.

can·ni·bal [ˈkænɪbl] *s* Kannibale *m*, Menschenfresser *m*. **can·ni·bal·ism** [~bəlɪzəm] *s* Kannibalismus *m*. ˌ**can·ni·bal·is·tic** *adj* (~*ally*) kannibalisch. '**can·ni·bal·ize** *v/t Auto etc* ausschlachten.

can·non [ˈkænən] *pl* **-non(s)** *s* ✕ (✔ Bord)Kanone *f*, (-)Geschütz *n*. **can·non·ade** [~ˈneɪd] *s* ✕ Kanonade *f*. '**can·non·ball** *s* Kanonenkugel *f*. ~ **fod·der** *s* Kanonenfutter *n*.

can·not [ˈkænɒt] kann *etc* nicht.

can·ny [ˈkænɪ] *adj* □ schlau, gerissen.

ca·noe [kəˈnuː] **I** *s* Kanu *n*, Paddelboot *n*: **paddle one's own** ~ *fig.* auf eigenen Beinen *od.* Füßen stehen. **II** *v/i* paddeln.

can·on [ˈkænən] *s* **1.** Kanon *m* (*a. eccl.*),

Regel f. **2.** Grundsatz m. **3.** ♪ Kanon m.
can·on·i·za·tion [ˌ~naɪˈzeɪʃn] s eccl.
Heiligsprechung f. **'can·on·ize** v/t heiligsprechen.

can·on law s Kirchenrecht n.

ca·noo·dle [kəˈnuːdl] v/i sl. knutschen, schmusen (**with** mit).

can·o·py [ˈkænəpɪ] s **1.** Baldachin m (a. △). **2.** △ Vordach n. **3.** ✈ Kabinenhaube f.

cant[1] [kænt] I s **1.** Schrägung f. **2.** Neigung f. II v/t **3.** kanten, kippen: **~ over** umkippen. **4.** ◉ abschrägen. III v/i **5.** a. **~ over** umkippen.

cant[2] [~] I s **1.** Jargon m. **2.** Kauderwelsch n. **3.** (leere) Phrase(n pl). II v/i **4.** Jargon reden. **5.** Phrasen dreschen.

can't [kɑːnt] F → **cannot**.

can·tan·ker·ous [kænˈtæŋkərəs] adj □ giftig, streitsüchtig.

can·teen [kænˈtiːn] s **1.** bsd. Br. Kantine f. **2.** ✕ Feldflasche f; Kochgeschirr n. **3.** Erfrischungsstand m. **4.** Besteckkasten m; Besteck n.

can·ter [ˈkæntə] I s Kanter m: **win at a ~** fig. mühelos siegen. II v/i kantern.

can·ti·le·ver [ˈkæntɪliːvə] s **1.** △ Konsole f. **2.** ◉ Ausleger m.

can·vas [ˈkænvəs] s **1.** Segeltuch n. **2.** Zeltleinwand f. **3.** paint. Leinwand f.

can·vass [ˈkænvəs] I v/t **1.** eingehend erörtern od. prüfen. **2.** pol. um Stimmen werben. **3.** † Geschäftsbezirk bereisen; Aufträge hereinholen, Abonnenten, Inserate sammeln. II v/i **4.** pol. e-n Wahlfeldzug veranstalten. **5.** † werben (**for** um, für), e-n Werbefeldzug durchführen. III s **6.** eingehende Erörterung od. Prüfung. **7.** pol. Wahlfeldzug m. **8.** † Werbefeldzug m. **'can·vass·er** s **1.** pol. Stimmenwerber m. **2.** † Handelsvertreter m.

can·yon [ˈkænjən] s Cañon m.

caou·tchouc [ˈkaʊtʃʊk] s Kautschuk m.

cap [kæp] I s **1.** Mütze f, Haube f: **~ in hand** demütig, unterwürfig; **set one's ~ at** (od. **for**) s.o. F j-n zu angeln suchen (Frau). **2.** ◉ (Schutz-, Verschluß)Kappe f, (Abdeck-, Schutz-) Haube f; Deckel m. II v/t **3.** Flasche etc verschließen. **4.** krönen: a) oben liegen auf (dat), b) fig. abschließen. **5.** fig. übertreffen, -trumpfen: **~ everything** allem die Krone aufsetzen, alles über-

treffen; **to ~ it all** als Krönung des Ganzen.

ca·pa·bil·i·ty [ˌkeɪpəˈbɪlətɪ] s **1.** Fähigkeit f (**of** zu). **2.** a. pl Befähigung f, Begabung f. **ca·pa·ble** [ˈ~bl] adj □ **1.** fähig, tüchtig. **2.** fähig (**of** zu od. gen; **of doing** zu tun), imstande (**of doing** zu tun). **3.** be **~ of** s.th. et. zulassen: **~ of being divided** teilbar.

ca·pa·cious [kəˈpeɪʃəs] adj □ **1.** geräumig (Saal, Tasche etc), groß (Flasche, Topf etc). **2.** aufnahmefähig (Verstand). **ca·pac·i·tate** [kəˈpæsɪteɪt] v/t befähigen. **ca'pac·i·tor** [ˌ~tə] s ⚡ Kondensator m. **ca'pac·i·ty** I s **1.** (Raum)Inhalt m; Fassungsvermögen n, Kapazität f (a. ⚡): **filled to ~** ganz voll, thea. etc ausverkauft; → **measure** 1. **2.** (a. ⚡, ◉ Leistungs)Fähigkeit f. fig. Auffassungsgabe f: **that is beyond his ~** das ist zu hoch für ihn. **3.** Eigenschaft f, Stellung f: **in his ~ as** in s-r Eigenschaft als. II adj **5.** Höchst..., maximal. **6.** **~ audience** thea. etc ausverkauftes Haus.

cape[1] [keɪp] s Kap n, Vorgebirge n.

cape[2] [~] s Cape n, Umhang m.

ca·per[1] [ˈkeɪpə] s Kaper f: **~ sauce** Kapernsoße f.

ca·per[2] [~] I s Kapriole f: a) Freuden-, Luftsprung m: **cut ~s** → II, b) übermütiger Streich. II v/i Freuden- od. Luftsprünge machen; herumtollen, -hüpfen.

cap·il·lar·y [kəˈpɪlərɪ] I adj haarförmig, -fein: **~ vessel** → II. II s anat. Kapillargefäß n.

cap·i·tal[1] [ˈkæpɪtl] s △ Kapitell n.

cap·i·tal[2] [~] I s **1.** Hauptstadt f. **2.** Großbuchstabe f. **3.** † Kapital n: **make ~ out of** → **capitalize** 3. II adj **4.** Kapital...: **~ crime** Kapitalverbrechen n; **~ error** Kapitalfehler m; **~ punishment** Todesstrafe f. **5.** Haupt..., wichtigst...: **~ city** → **1. 6.** großartig, prima: **~ fellow** ein Prachtkerl. **7.** **~ letter** → 2; **B ~** großes B.

cap·i·tal as·sets s pl † Kapitalvermögen n; (Bilanz) Anlagevermögen n. **~ flight** s Kapitalflucht f. **~ goods** s pl Investitionsgüter pl. **'~·in,ten·sive** adj □ kapitalintensiv. **~ in·vest·ment** s Kapitalanlage f.

cap·i·tal·ism [ˈkæpɪtəlɪzəm] s Kapitalismus *m.* '**cap·i·tal·ist** I *s* Kapitalist *m.* II *adj* kapitalistisch. ‚**cap·i·tal'is·tic** *adj* (**~ally**) kapitalistisch. '**cap·i·tal·ize** I *v/t* 1. ✝ kapitalisieren. 2. groß schreiben. II *v/i* 3. **~ on** Kapital schlagen aus.

cap·i·tal mar·ket *s* ✝ Kapitalmarkt *m.*

Cap·i·tol ['kæpɪtl] *s* Kapitol *n* (*Kongreßhaus in Washington*).

ca·pit·u·late [kə'pɪtʃʊleɪt] *v/i* ✗ kapitulieren (**to** vor *dat*) (*a. fig.*). **ca‚pit·u'la·tion** *s* Kapitulation *f.*

ca·price [kə'priːs] *s* 1. Laune *f.* 2. Launenhaftigkeit *f.* **ca·pri·cious** [kə'prɪʃəs] *adj* □ launenhaft, launisch, kapriziös.

Cap·ri·corn ['kæprɪkɔːn] *s ast.* Steinbock *m.*

cap·size [kæp'saɪz] I *v/i* kentern. II *v/t* zum Kentern bringen.

cap·sule ['kæpsjuːl] *s allg.* Kapsel *f.*

cap·tain ['kæptɪn] I *s* 1. (An)Führer *m*: **~ of industry** Industriekapitän *m.* 2. ✗ Hauptmann *m.* 3. ✲ (✈ Flug)Kapitän *m.* 4. *Sport:* (Mannschafts)Kapitän *m.*, Mannschaftsführer *m.* II *v/t* 5. Kapitän (*gen*) sein, *Schiff a.* befehligen.

cap·tion ['kæpʃn] *s* 1. Überschrift *f.* 2. Bildunterschrift *f*, -text *m*; (*Film*) Untertitel *m.*

cap·tious ['kæpʃəs] *adj* □ kritt(e)lig, spitzfindig.

cap·ti·vate ['kæptɪveɪt] *v/t fig.* gefangennehmen, fesseln. '**cap·tive** I *adj* gefangen (*a. fig.* **to** von), in Gefangenschaft: **hold ~** gefangenhalten (*a. fig.*); **take ~** gefangennehmen (*a. fig.*); **~ balloon** Fesselballon *m.* II *s* Gefangene *m, f* (*a. fig.* **to, of** *gen*).

cap·ture ['kæptʃə] I *v/t* 1. fangen, gefangennehmen. 2. ✗ erobern (*a. fig.*); erbeuten. 3. ✲ kapern, aufbringen. 4. *Stimmung* einfangen. II *s* 5. Gefangennahme *f.* 6. ✗ Eroberung *f* (*a. fig.*); Erbeutung *f.* 7. ✲ Kapern *n*, Aufbringen *n*; Beute *f*, Prise *f.*

car [kaː] *s* 1. Auto *n*, Wagen *m*: **by ~** mit dem Auto. 2. *Am. allg.* Wagen *m*, Waggon *m*, *Br.* (*nur in Zssgn*) Personenwagen *m*: → **dining car**, *etc.* 3. (Straßenbahn- *etc*)Wagen *m*; Gondel *f* (*e-s Ballons etc*); Kabine *f* (*e-s Aufzugs*).

ca·rafe [kə'ræf] *s* Karaffe *f.*

car·a·mel ['kærəmel] *s* 1. Karamel *m.* 2. Karamelle *f* (*Bonbon*).

car·at ['kærət] *s* Karat *n*: **18-~ gold** 18karätiges Gold.

car·a·van ['kærəvæn] *s* 1. Karawane *f.* 2. Wohnwagen *m* (*von Schaustellern etc*); *Br.* Caravan *m*, Wohnwagen *m*, -anhänger *m*: **~ site** (*od. park*) Platz *m* für Wohnwagen. '**car·a·van·(n)er** *s Br.* Caravaner *m.*

car·a·way ['kærəweɪ] *s* ✿ Kümmel *m* (*a. Gewürz*).

car·bide ['kaːbaɪd] *s* 🜍 Karbid *n.*

car·bine ['kaːbaɪn] *s* Karabiner *m.*

car·bo·hy·drate [‚kaːbəʊ'haɪdreɪt] *s* 🜍 Kohle(n)hydrat *n.*

car bomb *s* Autobombe *f.*

car·bon ['kaːbən] *s* 1. 🜍 Kohlenstoff *m*: **~ dioxide** Kohlendioxyd *n*; **~ monoxide** Kohlenmonoxyd *n.* 2. a) a. **~ paper** Kohlepapier *n*, b) a. **~ copy** Durchschlag *m.* **car·bon·ate** ['~bənɪt] *s* 🜍 Karbonat *n*, kohlensaures Salz. **car·bon·at·ed** ['~bəneɪtɪd] *adj* kohlensäurehaltig. **car·bon·ic** [~'bɒnɪk] *adj* 🜍 kohlenstoffhaltig: **~ acid** Kohlensäure *f.* '**car·bon·ize** *v/t u. v/i* verkohlen.

car·bu·ret·(t)er, **car·bu·ret·(t)or** [‚kaːbə'retə] *s mot.* Vergaser *m.*

car·case, **car·cass** ['kaːkəs] *s* 1. Kadaver *m*, *contp.* Leiche *f.* 2. *humor.* Leichnam *m* (*Körper*). 3. Rumpf *m* (*e-s ausgeweideten Tiers*): **~ meat** frisches (*Ggs. konserviertes*) Fleisch. 4. Gerippe *n*, Skelett *n* (*e-s Schiffs etc*).

car| cem·e·ter·y *s* Autofriedhof *m.* **~ chase** *s* Verfolgungsjagd *f* im Auto.

car·ci·no·gen·ic [‚kaːsɪnəʊ'dʒenɪk] *adj* ⚚ karzinogen, krebserzeugend.

car·ci·no·ma [~'nəʊmə] *pl* **-ma·ta** [~mətə], **-mas** *s* ⚚ Karzinom *n*, Krebsgeschwulst *f.*

card [kaːd] *s* 1. (Spiel-, Post-, Visiten- *etc*)Karte *f*: **house of ~s** Kartenhaus *n* (*a. fig.*); **have a ~ up one's sleeve** *fig.* (noch) e-n Trumpf in der Hand haben; **at ~s** beim Kartenspiel; → **stack** 6. 2. *pl* (Arbeits)Papiere *pl*: **get one's ~s** entlassen werden. '**~board** *s* Karton *m*, Pappe *f*: **~ box** Pappschachtel *f*, -karton *m.* **~ game** *s* Kartenspiel *n.*

car·di·ac ['kaːdɪæk] I *adj* ⚕, *anat.*, *physiol.* Herz...: **~ arrest** Herzstillstand *m*; **~ pacemaker** Herzschrittmacher *m.* II *s pharm.* Herzmittel *n.*

car·di·gan ['kaːdɪgən] *s* Strickjacke *f.*

car·di·nal [ˈkɑːdɪnl] **I** adj □ **1.** hauptsächlich, Haupt...: ~ *number* → **4**. **2.** scharlachrot. **II** s **3.** eccl. Kardinal m. **4.** Kardinal-, Grundzahl f.

'card|,sharp·er s Falschspieler m. ~ **trick** s Kartenkunststück n.

care [keə] **I** s **1.** Kummer m, Sorge f: *be free from* ~(*s*) keine Sorgen haben. **2.** Sorgfalt f, Vorsicht f: *have a* ~! Br. Paß (doch) auf!; *take* ~ vorsichtig sein, aufpassen; sich Mühe geben; darauf achten, nicht vergessen (*to do* zu tun; *that* daß); *take* ~! F mach's gut! **3.** Obhut f, Fürsorge f, Betreuung f: ~ *and custody* ✠ Sorgerecht n; *take* ~ *of* aufpassen auf (*acc.*). **4.** (*Körperetc*)Pflege f. **II** v/i u. v/t **5.** sich sorgen (*about* über *acc*, um): *I couldn't* ~ *less* das ist mir völlig egal. **6.** ~ *for* sorgen für, sich kümmern um, betreuen. **7.** (*for*) Interesse haben (an *dat*), (*j-n, et.*) gern mögen: *I don't* ~ *for* tea mache mir nichts aus. **8.** *I don't* ~ *if* ich habe nichts dagegen od. es macht mir nichts aus, wenn; *I don't* ~ *if I do!* F von mir aus!

ca·reer [kəˈrɪə] s **1.** Karriere f, Laufbahn f: *enter upon a* ~ e-e Laufbahn einschlagen; *make a* ~ *for o.s.* Karriere machen. **2.** Beruf m: ~ *diplomat* Berufsdiplomat m; ~ *girl* (*od. woman*) Karrierefrau f. **ca·reer·ist** [kəˈrɪərɪst] s Karrieremacher m.

'care·free s sorgenfrei.

care·ful [ˈkeəful] adj □ **1.** vorsichtig, achtsam: *be* ~! paß auf!, gib acht!; *be* ~ *to do* darauf achten od. nicht vergessen zu tun. **2.** sorgfältig, gründlich. **3.** sorgsam, bedacht (*of, for, about* auf *acc*): *be* ~ *with* Br. sparsam umgehen mit. **'care·ful·ness** s **1.** Vorsicht f. **2.** Sorgfalt f, Gründlichkeit f.

care·less [ˈkeəlɪs] adj □ **1.** nachlässig. **2.** unüberlegt. **3.** *be* ~ *of* nicht achten auf (*acc*), unachtsam umgehen mit. **4.** unvorsichtig, leichtsinnig. **5.** sorglos. **'care·less·ness** s **1.** Nachlässigkeit f. **2.** Unüberlegtheit f. **3.** Unvorsichtigkeit f, Leichtsinn m. **4.** Sorglosigkeit f.

ca·ress [kəˈres] **I** s Liebkosung f. **II** v/t liebkosen, streicheln.

'care|,tak·er s Hausmeister m; (*Hausetc*)Verwalter m. **II** adj Interims...: ~ *government* geschäftsführende Regierung. '~**worn** adj abgehärmt.

'car|,fare s Am. Fahrgeld n (*für Bus etc*). ~ **fer·ry** s Autofähre f.

car·go [ˈkɑːɡəʊ] **I** pl -**go(e)s** s Ladung f, Fracht f. **II** adj Fracht...; Transport...

car·i·ca·ture [ˈkærɪkəˌtjʊə] **I** s Karikatur f (*a. fig.*). **II** v/t karikieren. **'car·i·ca·,tur·ist** s Karikaturist m.

car·i·es [ˈkeəriːz] s 🦷 Karies f: a) Knochenfraß m, b) Zahnfäule f.

car·il·lon [ˈkærɪljən] s (Turm)Glockenspiel n.

car·i·ous [ˈkeərɪəs] adj 🦷 kariös, von Karies befallen.

car| jack s ⚙ Wagenheber m. '~**load** s **1.** Wagenladung f. **2.** 🚃 Am. Waggonladung f.

car·mine [ˈkɑːmaɪn] adj karminrot.

car·nage [ˈkɑːnɪdʒ] s Blutbad n, Gemetzel n.

car·nal [ˈkɑːnl] adj □ fleischlich, sinnlich.

car·na·tion [kɑːˈneɪʃn] s ⚘ Nelke f.

car·ni·val [ˈkɑːnɪvl] s **1.** Karneval m, Fasching m. **2.** Volksfest n.

car·ni·vore [ˈkɑːnɪvɔː] s zo., ⚘ Fleischfresser m. **car·niv·o·rous** [~ˈnɪvərəs] adj □ fleischfressend.

car·ol [ˈkærəl] **I** s Weihnachtslied n. **II** v/i pret u. pp -**oled**, *bsd.* Br. -**olled** Weihnachtslieder singen.

ca·rot·id [kəˈrɒtɪd] s anat. Halsschlagader f.

car·ou·sel [ˌkærəˈsel] s *bsd. Am.* Karussell n.

car own·er s Autobesitzer(in).

carp[1] [kɑːp] s ichth. Karpfen m.

carp[2] [~] v/i (herum)nörgeln, (-)kritteln (*at* an *dat*).

car| park s *bsd. Br.* **1.** Parkplatz m. **2.** Parkhaus n. ~ **pas·sen·ger** s Autoinsasse m.

car·pen·ter [ˈkɑːpəntə] **I** s Zimmermann m, (Bau)Tischler m: ~'**s bench** Hobelbank f. **II** v/i u. v/t zimmern.

car·pet [ˈkɑːpɪt] **I** s **1.** Teppich m (*a. fig.*): *sweep* (*od. brush*) *under the* ~ Br. fig. et. unter den Teppich kehren. **II** v/t **2.** mit e-m Teppich auslegen. **3.** *bsd.* Br. F j-n zs.-stauchen. '~**bag** s Reisetasche f.

car·pet·ing [ˈkɑːpɪtɪŋ] s **1.** Teppichstoff m, -material n. **2.** coll. Teppiche pl.

car·pet| square s Teppichfliese f. ~

sweep·er s Teppichkehrmaschine f. **~ tile** s Teppichfliese f.

car| pool s **1.** Fahrbereitschaft f, Fuhrpark m. **2.** Fahrgemeinschaft f. '**~·port** s Einstellplatz m (im Freien).

car·riage ['kærɪdʒ] s **1.** Wagen m, Kutsche f. **2.** 🚂 Br. (Personen)Wagen m. **3.** Beförderung f, Transport m. **4.** ✝ Transport-, Beförderungskosten pl, Fracht(gebühr) f: **~ free** (od. **paid**) frachtfrei. **5.** ⚙ Wagen m (e-r Schreibmaschine etc); Schlitten m (e-r Werkzeugmaschine). **6.** (Körper)Haltung f: **~ of head** Kopfhaltung f. '**~·way** s Fahrbahn f.

car·ri·er ['kærɪə] s **1.** Überbringer m, Bote m. **2.** Spediteur m. **3.** 🌿 Keimträger m, (Krankheits)Überträger m. **4.** Gepäckträger m (am Fahrrad); mot. Dachgepäckträger m. **5.** Transportbehälter m. **6.** Flugzeugträger m. **7.** → **carrier pigeon**. **~ bag** s Br. Einkaufsbeutel m, -tasche f. **~ pi·geon** s Brieftaube f.

car·ri·on ['kærɪən] **I** s Aas n. **II** adj aasfressend, Aas...

car·rot ['kærət] s **1.** 🥕 Karotte f, Mohrrübe f. **2.** F a) pl rotes Haar, b) Rotkopf m. '**car·rot·y** adj **1.** gelbrot. **2.** rothaarig.

car·ry ['kærɪ] **I** v/t **1.** tragen. **2.** bringen, tragen, befördern: → **coal**. **3.** Nachricht etc (über)bringen; Bericht etc bringen (Medien). **4.** mitführen, mit od. bei sich tragen: **~ s.th. in one's head** fig. et. im Kopf haben. **5.** fig. (an sich od. zum Inhalt) haben: **~ conviction** überzeugen(d sein od. klingen); **~ weight** Gewicht od. Bedeutung haben (**with** bei). **6.** fig. nach sich ziehen, zur Folge haben: **~ interest** Zinsen tragen. **7.** fig. treiben: **~ s.th. too far** (od. **to excess**) et. übertreiben od. zu weit treiben. **8.** fig. erreichen, durchsetzen; parl. Antrag etc durchbringen: **be carried** durchgehen. **9.** a) → **carry off** 3, b) siegreich hervorgehen aus (e-r Wahl etc): → **day** 2. **10.** Mineralien etc führen. **11.** ✝ Ware führen. **II** v/i **12.** weit tragen, reichen (Stimme, Schußwaffe etc).

Verbindungen mit Adverbien:

car·ry| a·bout v/t herumtragen: **~ with one** mit sich herumtragen, Paß etc bei

sich haben. **~ a·way** v/t **1.** weg-, forttragen. **2.** wegreißen (Sturm etc), (Flut etc a.) wegspülen. **3.** fig. mitreißen. **~ for·ward** v/t ✝ Summe, Saldo vor-, übertragen. **~ off** v/t **1.** weg-, forttragen. **2.** wegraffen (Krankheit). **3.** Preis etc erringen, gewinnen. **~ on I** v/t **1.** fortführen, -setzen. **2.** Geschäft betreiben. **II** v/i **3.** weitermachen (**with** mit). **4.** F e-e Szene machen (**about** wegen). **~ out** v/t Plan etc aus-, durchführen, Drohung wahrmachen. **~ o·ver** → **carry forward**. **~ through** v/t aus-, durchführen.

car·ry·all s bsd. Am. Reisetasche f. '**~·cot** s Br. (Baby)Tragetasche f. **~·on** ✈ **I** s Bordcase n, m. **II** adj: **~ baggage** (bsd. Br. **luggage**) Bordgepäck n. '**~·out** → **takeaway**.

'**car·ri·sick** adj: **she gets easily ~** ihr wird beim Autofahren leicht übel od. schlecht. **~ sick·ness** s Übelkeit f beim Autofahren. **~ stick·er** s Autoaufkleber m.

cart [kɑːt] s **1.** Karren m: **put the ~ before the horse** fig. das Pferd beim Schwanz aufzäumen. **2.** (Hand)Wagen m.

car·tel [kɑːtel] s ✝ Kartell n.

car·ti·lage ['kɑːtɪlɪdʒ] s anat. Knorpel m. '**cart·load** s Fuhre f.

car·tog·ra·pher [kɑːtɒɡrəfə] s Kartograph(in). **car·tog·ra·phy** s Kartographie f.

car·ton ['kɑːtən] s (Papp)Karton m, (-)Schachtel f; Tüte f (Milch); Stange f (Zigaretten).

car·toon [kɑː'tuːn] s **1.** Cartoon m, n, Karikatur f. **2.** Zeichentrickfilm m. **3.** Cartoon m, Bilderfortsetzungsgeschichte f. **car·toon·ist** s Cartoonist m, Karikaturist m.

car·tridge ['kɑːtrɪdʒ] s **1.** ✗ Patrone f. **2.** phot. (Film)Patrone f, (-)Kassette f. **3.** Tonabnehmer m (e-s Plattenspielers). **4.** Patrone f (e-s Füllhalters). **~ case** s Patronenhülse f.

'**cart·wheel** s **1.** Wagenrad n. **2.** Sport: Rad n: **turn ~s** radschlagen. **3.** Am. F Silberdollar m.

carve [kɑːv] v/t **1.** (in) Holz schnitzen, (in) Stein meißeln: **~ out of stone** aus Stein meißeln od. hauen; **~ one's name on a tree** s-n Namen in e-n Baum schnitzen. **2.** (mit Schnitzereien) verzieren. **3.** *Fleisch etc* zerlegen, tranchieren. **'carv·er** *s* **1.** (Holz)Schnitzer *m*, Bildhauer *m*. **2.** Tranchiermesser *n*: (*pair of*) **~s** *pl* Tranchierbesteck *n*. **'carv·ing** *s* **1.** Schnitzen *n*, Meißeln *n*. **2.** Schnitzerei *f*. **3.** Tranchieren *n*: **~ knife** Tranchiermesser *n*.

car wash *s* **1.** Autowäsche *f*. **2.** Waschanlage *f*, -straße *f*.

cas·cade [kæ'skeɪd] *s* Kaskade *f*, (*bsd. mehrstufiger*) Wasserfall.

case¹ [keɪs] **I** *s* **1.** Kiste *f*, Kasten *m*. **2.** *allg.* Behälter *m*: a) Schachtel *f*, b) (*Brillen- etc*)Etui *n*, (-)Futteral *n*, c) (*Schreib- etc*)Mappe *f*, d) (*Kissen*)Bezug *m*, Überzug *m*. **3.** ⊙ Verkleidung *f*, Mantel *m*. **II** *v/t* **4.** in ein Futteral *etc* stecken. **5.** ⊙ verkleiden, ummanteln.

case² [~] *s* Fall *m* (*a.* ⚕, ⚖): **it is a ~ of** es handelt sich um; **in any ~** auf jeden Fall, jedenfalls; **in no ~** auf keinen Fall, keinesfalls; **in ~ (that)** falls; **in ~ of** im Falle von (*od. gen*); **in ~ of need** nötigenfalls, im Notfall.

'case·book *s* ⚕ Patientenbuch *n*. **'~·hard·ened** *adj fig.* hartgesotten. **'~·his·to·ry** *s* **1.** *bsd.* ⚕ Vorgeschichte *f* (*e-s Falls*). **2.** ⚕ Krankengeschichte *f*.

case·ment ['keɪsmənt] *s* Fensterflügel *m*: **~ (window)** Flügelfenster *n*.

case stud·y *s sociol.* Fallstudie *f*.

cash [kæʃ] **I** *s* **1.** (Bar)Geld *n*. **2.** † Barzahlung *f*, Kasse *f*: **for ~,** **~ down** gegen bar *od.* Barzahlung; **in ~** bar; **in advance** gegen Vorauszahlung; **~ with order** zahlbar bei Bestellung; **be in (out of) ~** (nicht) bei Kasse sein; **short of ~** knapp bei Kasse; **~ delivery** 1. *u.* 3. **~ in** 3. Scheck *etc* einlösen. **4.** zu Geld machen. **III** *v/i* **5.** **~ in on** F profitieren von; ausnutzen. **~ and car·ry** *s econ.* Cash-and-carry-Geschäft *n*. **~ cheque** *s* † *Br.* Barscheck *m*. **~ desk** *s* Kasse *f* (*im Warenhaus etc*). **~ dis·count** *s* † Barzahlungsrabatt *m*. **~ dis·pens·er** *s bsd. Br.* Geldautomat *m*.

cash·ier [kæ'ʃɪə] *s* Kassierer(in): **~'s desk** (*od. office*) Kasse *f*.

cash·less ['kæʃlɪs] *adj* bargeldlos.

cash ma·chine *s bsd. Am.* Geldautomat *m*.

cash·mere [kæʃ'mɪə] *s* Kaschmir(wolle *f*) *m*.

cash| pay·ment *s* Barzahlung *f*. **~ price** *s* Bar(zahlungs)preis *m*. **~ vouch·er** *s* Kassenbeleg *m*, -zettel *m*.

cas·ing ['keɪsɪŋ] *s* **1.** → **case¹** 3. **2.** (*Fenster-, Tür*)Futter *n*. **3.** (*Wurst*)Haut *f*.

ca·si·no [kə'siːnəʊ] *pl* **-nos** *s* Kasino *n*.

cask [kɑːsk] *s* Faß *n*.

cas·ket ['kɑːskɪt] *s* **1.** Schatulle *f*, Kästchen *n*. **2.** *bsd. Am.* Sarg *m*.

cas·se·role ['kæsərəʊl] *s* Kasserolle *f*.

cas·sette [kə'set] *s* (*Film- etc*)Kassette *f*. **~ deck** *s* Kassettendeck *n*. **~ ra·di·o** *s* Radiorecorder *m*. **~ re·cord·er** *s* Kassettenrecorder *m*.

cas·sock ['kæsək] *s eccl.* Soutane *f*.

cast [kɑːst] **I** *s* **1.** Wurf *m*. **2.** *thea. etc* Besetzung *f*: a) Rollenverteilung *f*, b) Ensemble *n*. **3.** Schattierung *f*, Anflug *m* (*a. fig.*). **4.** ⊙ Guß(form *f*) *m*; Abdruck *m*. **5.** ⚕ Gips(verband) *m*. **6.** Typ *m*, Gattung *f*. **II** *v/t* (*irr*) **7.** werfen: → **die²** 1, **doubt** 5, **light¹** 1, **spell³** 2. **8.** *Angel, Netz etc* auswerfen. **9.** *zo.* Haut, Gehörn abwerfen. **10.** *Stimmzettel, Stimme* abgeben; → **vote** 2. **11.** *Blick* werfen (**at, on** auf *acc*); *Schatten etc* werfen (**on** auf *acc*). **12.** ⊙ *Metall, Statue etc* gießen, formen. **13.** *thea. etc* *Stück etc* besetzen; *Rollen* verteilen (**to** an *acc*). **III** *v/i* (*irr*) **14.** sich werfen (*Holz*).

Verbindungen mit Adverbien:

cast| a·bout, ~ a·round *v/i*: **~ for** suchen (nach), *fig. a.* sich umsehen nach. **~ a·side** *v/t* **1.** *Möbel etc* ausrangieren, *Kleidung a.* ablegen. **2.** *Gewohnheit etc* ablegen, *Freund etc* fallenlassen. **~ a·way** *v/t* wegwerfen. **~ down** *v/t* **1.** entmutigen: **be ~** niedergeschlagen *od.* deprimiert sein. **2.** *Augen* niederschlagen. **~ off** *v/t* **1.** *Kleidung* ablegen, ausrangieren. **2.** *Freund etc* fallenlassen. **~ out** *v/t* verstoßen, vertreiben (**from** aus), *Dämonen etc* austreiben. **~ up** *v/t* **1.** *Augen* aufschlagen. **2.** zs.-zählen, ausrechnen.

'cast·a·way **I** *s* et. Ausrangiertes, *bsd.* abgelegtes Kleidungsstück. **II** *adj* ausrangiert (*Möbel etc*), (*Kleidung a.*) abgelegt.

caste [kɑːst] *s* **1.** Kaste *f*. **2.** gesellschaftliche Stellung, Ansehen *n*.

cas·ter → **castor**.

cas·ti·gate ['kæstɪgeɪt] *v/t* **1.** züchtigen.

catch

2. scharf kritisieren. **ˌcas·ti·'ga·tion** s 1. Züchtigung f. 2. scharfe Kritik (*of* an *dat*).

cast·ing ['kɑːstɪŋ] I s 1. ⊙ Guß(stück n) m. 2. → cast 2a. II adj 3. Wurf... 4. entscheidend (*Stimme*).

cast| i·ron s ⊙ Gußeisen n. **ˌ~-'i·ron** adj 1. gußeisern. 2. *fig.* eisern (*Wille, Konstitution*), hieb- u. stichfest (*Alibi*).

cas·tle ['kɑːsl] I s 1. Burg f; Schloß n: **build ~s in the air** (*od.* **in Spain**) Luftschlösser bauen. 2. *Schach:* Turm m. II v/i 3. *Schach:* rochieren.

cas·tling ['kɑːslɪŋ] s *Schach:* Rochade f.

ˌcast|-'off adj abgelegt, ausrangiert (*Kleidungsstück*). **ˌ~-'off** s abgelegtes *od.* ausrangiertes Kleidungsstück.

cas·tor ['kɑːstə] s 1. Laufrolle f. 2. (*Salz-etc*)Streuer m. **~ oil** s Rizinusöl n.

cas·trate [kæ'streɪt] v/t kastrieren. **cas·'tra·tion** s Kastrierung f, Kastration f.

cast steel s ⊙ Gußstahl m.

cas·u·al ['kæʒʊəl] adj □ 1. zufällig. 2. gelegentlich: **~ customer** Laufkunde m; **~ labo(u)rer** Gelegenheitsarbeiter m. 3. beiläufig (*Bemerkung*); flüchtig (*Blick*). 4. lässig (*Art etc*). 5. sportlich, salopp (*Kleidung*): **~ wear** Freizeitkleidung f.

cas·u·al·ty ['kæʒʊəltɪ] s 1. Unfall m. 2. Verunglückte m, f; ✕ Verwundete m, Gefallene m: **casualties** *pl* Opfer *pl* (*e-r Katastrophe etc*), ✕ *mst* Verluste *pl*. 3. a. **~ ward** (*od.* **department**) Unfallstation f.

cat [kæt] s 1. *zo.* Katze f: **let the ~ out of the bag** die Katze aus dem Sack lassen; **play ~ and mouse with** Katz u. Maus spielen mit; **it is raining ~s and dogs** es gießt in Strömen; **see which way the ~ jumps** sehen, wie der Hase läuft. 2. *fig.* Katze f, falsches Frauenzimmer: **old ~** boshafte Hexe.

cat·a·comb ['kætəkuːm] s *mst pl* Katakombe f.

cat·a·logue, *Am. a.* **cat·a·log** ['kætəlɒg] I s 1. Katalog m. 2. (*univ. Am.* Vorlesungs)Verzeichnis n, (*Preis- etc*)Liste f. II v/t 3. katalogisieren.

ca·tal·y·sis [kə'tæləsɪs] s 🜊 Katalyse f. **cat·a·lyst** ['kætəlɪst] s Katalysator m (*a. fig.*). **cat·a·lyt·ic** [ˌkætə'lɪtɪk] adj ka-

talytisch (*a. fig.*): **~ converter** *mot.* Katalysator m.

ˌcat-and-'dog adj: **lead a ~ life** wie Hund u. Katze leben.

cat·a·pult ['kætəpʌlt] I s Katapult n, m: **~ seat** ✈ Schleudersitz m. II v/t katapultieren.

cat·a·ract ['kætərækt] s 1. Katarakt m, Wasserfall m. 2. 🜋 grauer Star.

ca·tarrh [kə'tɑː] s ✚ Katarrh m.

ca·tas·tro·phe [kə'tæstrəfɪ] s Katastrophe f. **cat·a·stroph·ic** [ˌkætə'strɒfɪk] adj (**~ally**) katastrophal.

cat| bur·glar s Fassadenkletterer m. **'~-call** I s Buh(ruf m) n; Pfiff m. II v/i buhen; pfeifen. III v/t ausbuhen; -pfeifen.

catch [kætʃ] I s 1. Fangen n. 2. Fang m, Beute f (*beide a. fig.*). 3. ⊙ Haken m (*a. fig.*), (*Tür*)Klinke f; Verschluß m (*e-r Brosche etc*). II v/t (*irr*) 4. *allg.* fangen; Blick, Flüssigkeit auffangen, Tier etc (ein)fangen: → sight 2. 5. kriegen, bekommen, erwischen. 6. *j-n* einholen. 7. erwischen, ertappen (*s.o. at s.th.* j-n bei et.): **~ s.o. lying** j-n bei e-r Lüge ertappen; **~ me** (**doing that**)! *Br.* F denkste! → nap 1, unawares. 8. *a. fig.* packen, ergreifen, erfassen: → hold 1. 9. sich *e-e Krankheit etc* holen, sich *e-e Erkältung etc* zuziehen: **~** (**a**) **cold** sich erkälten; **~ it** *sl.* sein Fett (ab)kriegen; → fire 1. 10. *fig.* **~ the eye** ins Auge fallen; **~ the eye** ins Auge fallen; **~ s.o.'s eye** (*od.* **attention**) j-s Aufmerksamkeit auf sich lenken. 11. verstehen, mitkriegen. 12. *Gewohnheit, Aussprache* annehmen. 13. hängenbleiben *od.* sich verfangen mit et. (**in** *in dat*): **my fingers were caught in the door** ich klemmte mir die Finger in der Tür. III v/i (*irr*) 14. **~ at** greifen *od.* schnappen nach, *Gelegenheit* ergreifen. 15. einschnappen, -rasten (*Schloß etc*); klemmen, festsitzen. 16. sich verfangen, hängenbleiben (**on** an *dat*; **in** in *dat*). 17. anspringen (*Motor*).

Verbindungen mit Adverbien:

catch| on v/i F 1. **~ to s.th.** et. kapieren. 2. Anklang finden, einschlagen. **~ out** v/t ertappen; überführen. **~ up I** v/t 1. *Br.* einholen (*a. bei der Arbeit*). 2. **be caught up in** vertieft sein in (*acc*); verwickelt sein in (*acc*). II v/i 3. aufholen:

~ with einholen (*a. bei der Arbeit*); **~ on** (*od.* **with**) *Arbeitsrückstand etc* aufholen; **~ on one's sleep** Schlaf nachholen.

'catch·all *s bsd. Am.* **1.** Tasche *f od.* Behälter *m* für alles mögliche. **2.** *fig.* Sammelbezeichnung *f*: **~ term** Sammelbegriff *m*. **'~-as-.catch-'can** *s Sport*: Catchen *n*: **~ wrestler** Catcher *m*.

catch·er ['kætʃə] *s* Fänger *m*; **'catch·ing** *adj* □ **1.** ✱ ansteckend (*a. fig. Lachen etc*). **2.** *fig.* anziehend, fesselnd. **3.** → **catchy** **1.**

catch·ment ['kætʃmənt] *s geol.* Reservoir *n*. **~ a·re·a** *s* **1.** *geol.* Einzugsgebiet *n* (*e-s Flusses*). **2.** *fig.* Einzugsbereich *m*, -gebiet *n* (*e-s Krankenhauses etc*). **ba·sin → catchment area** **1.** **'catch·phrase** *s* Schlagwort *n*. **'~-up** *bsd. Am.* → **ketchup**. **'~-word** *s* **1.** Stichwort *n* (*im Lexikon etc; a. thea.*). **2.** Schlagwort *n*.

catch·y ['kætʃɪ] *adj* **1.** eingängig (*Melodie etc*). **2.** → **catching** **2.** **3.** Fang...: **~ question.**

cat·e·chism ['kætɪkɪzəm] *s eccl.* Katechismus *m*.

cat·e·gor·i·cal [,kætə'gɒrɪkl] *adj* □ kategorisch. **cat·e·go·ry** ['~gərɪ] *s* Kategorie *f*, Klasse *f*.

ca·ter ['keɪtə] *v/i* **1.** Speisen u. Getränke liefern (*for* für). **2.** sorgen (*for* für). **3.** *fig.* (*for, to*) befriedigen (*acc*), *bsd. b.s.* Nahrung liefern (*dat*). **'ca·ter·er** *s* Lieferant *m od.* Lieferfirma *f* für Speisen u. Getränke.

cat·er·pil·lar ['kætəpɪlə] *s* **1.** *zo.* Raupe *f*. **2.** (*TM*) ⊕ Raupenfahrzeug *n*.

cat·er·waul ['kætəwɔːl] **I** *v/i* **1.** jaulen (*Katze*). **2.** *fig.* (sich an)keifen. **II** *s* **3.** Jaulen *n*. **4.** *fig.* Keifen *n*.

'cat·gut *s* Darmsaite *f*.

ca·the·dral [kə'θiːdrəl] **I** *s* Dom *m*, Kathedrale *f*. **II** *adj* Dom...

cath·e·ter ['kæθɪtə] *s* ✱ Katheter *m*.

cath·ode ['kæθəʊd] *s* ⚡ Kathode *f*.

Cath·o·lic ['kæθəlɪk] *eccl.* **I** *adj* katholisch. **II** *s* Katholik(in). **Ca·thol·i·cism** [kə'θɒlɪsɪzəm] *s* Katholizismus *m*.

cat·kin ['kætkɪn] *s* ♀ (Blüten)Kätzchen *n*.

'cat|·lick *s F* Katzenwäsche *f*: **have a ~** Katzenwäsche machen. **~ lit·ter** *s* Katzenstreu *f*. **'~·nap** *s* Nickerchen *n*: **have** (*od.* **take**) **a ~** ein Nickerchen machen.

'cat's-eye *s* ⊕ Katzenauge *n*, Rückstrahler *m*; Leuchtnagel *m*.

cat suit *s* einteiliger Hosenanzug.

cat·tish ['kætɪʃ] *adj* □ **1.** katzenhaft. **2.** *fig.* falsch, boshaft.

cat·tle ['kætl] *s coll.* (*mst pl konstruiert*) (Rind)Vieh *n*: **ten head of ~** zehn Stück Vieh, zehn Rinder. **~ breed·ing** *s* Viehzucht *f*.

cat tray *s* Katzenklosett *n*.

cat·ty ['kætɪ] → **cattish.**

'cat·walk *s* **1.** ⊕ Laufplanke *f*, Steg *m*. **2.** Laufsteg *m* (*bei Modeschauen*).

caught [kɔːt] *pret u. pp von* **catch.**

caul·dron ['kɔːldrən] *s* großer Kessel.

cau·li·flow·er ['kɒlɪˌflaʊə] *s* ♀ Blumenkohl *m*.

caus·al ['kɔːzl] *adj* □ ursächlich, kausal: **~ connection** *od.* **causality** **2**; **~ law** Kausalgesetz *n*. **cau·sal·i·ty** [~'zælətɪ] *s* **1.** Ursächlichkeit *f*, Kausalität *f*: **law of ~** Kausalgesetz *n*. **2.** Kausalzs.-hang *m*.

caus·a·tive ['~zətɪv] *adj* □ verursachend (*of acc*).

cause [kɔːz] **I** *s* **1.** Ursache *f*: **~ of death** Todesursache. **2.** Grund *m*, Anlaß *m* (*for* für): **~ for complaint** Grund zur Klage. **3.** Sache *f*: **make common ~ with** gemeinsame Sache machen mit. **4.** ⚖ Rechtsstreit *m*; Gegenstand *m* (*e-s Rechtsstreits*): **~ of action** Klagegrund *m*. **II** *v/t* **5.** veranlassen. **6.** verursachen, bewirken. **7.** bereiten, zufügen. **'~·less** *adj* □ grundlos, unbegründet.

caus·tic ['kɔːstɪk] **I** *adj* (*~ally*) 🔥 ätzend, *fig. a.* beißend, sarkastisch. **II** *s* Ätzmittel *n*.

cau·ter·ize ['kɔːtəraɪz] *v/t* **1.** ✱, ⊕ (aus-)brennen, (ver)ätzen. **2.** *fig. Gefühl etc* abstumpfen.

cau·tion ['kɔːʃn] **I** *s* **1.** Vorsicht *f*. **2.** Warnung *f*. **3.** Verwarnung *f*. **II** *v/t* **4.** warnen (*against* vor *dat*). **5.** verwarnen.

cau·tious ['kɔːʃəs] *v/t* □ **1.** vorsichtig. **2.** achtsam. **3.** verhalten, gedämpft (*Optimismus etc*).

cav·al·cade [,kævl'keɪd] *s* Kavalkade *f*.

cav·al·ry ['kævlrɪ] *s* ✕ **a)** *bsd. hist.* Kavallerie *f*, **b)** Panzertruppe(n *pl*) *f*. **~ man** [~mən] *s* (*irr man*) ✕ **a)** *bsd. hist.* Kavallerist *m*, **b)** Angehörige *m* e-r Panzertruppe.

cave [keɪv] **I** *s* **1.** Höhle *f*. **II** *v/t* **2.** aushöhlen. **3.** *mst* **~ in** eindrücken, zum Einsturz bringen. **III** *v/i mst* **~ in 4.** einstürzen, -sinken. **5.** F zs.-klappen, schlappmachen; nachgeben (**to** *dat*), klein beigeben. **~ dwell·er** *s* Höhlenbewohner(in).

cav·ern ['kævən] *s* (große) Höhle.

cav·i·ar(e) ['kævɪɑː] *s* Kaviar *m*: **~ to the general** *fig.* Kaviar fürs Volk.

cav·il ['kævl] **I** *v/i pret u. pp* **-iled,** *bsd.* *Br.* **-illed** nörgeln: **~ at** (*od.* **about**) herumnörgeln an (*dat*). **II** *s* Nörgelei *f*. **'cav·il·(l)er** *s* Nörgler(in).

cav·i·ty ['kævətɪ] *s* **1.** (Aus)Höhlung *f*, Hohlraum *m*. **2.** *anat.* Höhle *f*: **abdominal ~** Bauchhöhle; → **oral 2. 3.** ✮ Loch *n* (*im Zahn*).

ca·vort [kə'vɔːt] *v/i* F herumhüpfen, -tanzen.

cay·enne [keɪ'en], *a.* **~ pep·per** ['keɪen] *s* Cayennepfeffer *m*.

cease [siːs] **I** *v/i* aufhören, enden. **II** *v/t* aufhören (**to do, doing** zu tun): **~ fire** ✕ das Feuer einstellen; **~ payment** ✝ die Zahlungen einstellen. **~·'fire** *s* ✕ Feuereinstellung *f*; Waffenstillstand *m*. **'~·less** *adj* □ unaufhörlich.

cede [siːd] *v/t* **1.** (**to**) abtreten, abgeben (*dat od.* an *acc*), überlassen (*dat*). **2. ~ a point** in e-m Punkt nachgeben.

ceil [siːl] *v/t* e-e Decke einziehen in (*acc*). **'ceil·ing** *s* **1.** Decke *f* (*e-s Raums*). **2.** Höchstmaß *n*; ✝ Höchstgrenze *f* (*von Preisen etc*), Plafond *m* (*e-s Kredits*): **~ price** Höchstpreis *m*. **3.** ✈ Gipfelhöhe *f*; Wolkenhöhe *f*.

cel·e·brate ['selɪbreɪt] **I** *v/t* **1.** Fest *etc* feiern, begehen; → **occasion 3. 2.** j-n feiern. **3.** *eccl.* Messe *etc* zelebrieren. **II** *v/i* **4.** feiern. **'cel·e·brat·ed** *adj* berühmt (**for** für, wegen). **,cel·e·'bra·tion** *s* **1.** Feier *f*. **2.** Feiern *n*: **in ~ of** zur Feier (*gen*). **3.** *eccl.* Zelebrieren *n*.

ce·leb·ri·ty [sɪ'lebrətɪ] *s* Berühmtheit *f* (*a. Person*).

cel·er·y ['selərɪ] *s* ✿ Sellerie *m*, *f*.

ce·les·tial [sɪ'lestjəl] *adj* □ himmlisch, Himmels... (*a. astr.*): **~ body** Himmelskörper *m*.

cel·i·ba·cy ['selɪbəsɪ] *s* Zölibat *m*, Ehelosigkeit *f*. **cel·i·bate** ['selɪbət] **I** *adj* unverheiratet. **II** *s* Unverheiratete *m*, *f*.

cell [sel] *s allg.* Zelle *f*, ⚡ *a.* Element *n*.

cel·lar ['selə] **I** *s* **1.** Keller *m*. **2.** → **salt-**

cellar. II *v/t* **3.** *a.* **~ in** einkellern, -lagern.

cell di·vi·sion *s biol.* Zellteilung *f*.

cel·list ['tʃelɪst] *s* ♪ Cellist(in).

cell nu·cle·us *s* (*mst irr* **nucleus**) *biol.* Zellkern *m*.

cel·lo ['tʃeləʊ] *pl* **-los** *s* ♪ Cello *n*.

cel·lo·phane ['seləʊfem] *s* Zellophan *n*.

cell ther·a·py *s* ✮ Zelltherapie *f*.

cel·lu·lar ['seljʊlə] *adj* Zell(en)...: **~ therapy** ✮ Zelltherapie *f*. **cel·lu·loid** ['~jʊlɔɪd] *s* Zelluloid *n*. **cel·lu·lose** ['~jʊləʊs] *s* Zellulose *f*, Zellstoff *m*.

Celt [kelt] *s* Kelte *m*, Keltin *f*. **'Celt·ic I** *adj* keltisch. **II** *s ling.* Keltisch *n*.

ce·ment [sɪ'ment] **I** *s* **1.** Zement *m*. **2.** Kitt *m*. **II** *v/t* **3.** zementieren, *fig. a.* festigen. **4.** (ver)kitten. **~ mix·er** *s* Betonmischmaschine *f*.

cem·e·ter·y ['semɪtrɪ] *s* Friedhof *m*.

cen·ser ['sensə] *s eccl.* Weihrauchfaß *n*.

cen·sor ['sensə] **I** *s* Zensor *m*. **II** *v/t* zensieren. **cen·so·ri·ous** [~'sɔːrɪəs] *adj* □ **1.** kritisch, streng. **2.** krittelig (**of** gegenüber). **'cen·sor·ship** *s* Zensur *f*: **~ of the press** Pressezensur.

cen·sure ['senʃə] **I** *s* **1.** Tadel *m*, Rüge *f*: **vote of ~** Mißtrauensvotum *n*. **2.** (**of**) Kritik *f* (an *dat*), Mißbilligung *f* (*gen*). **II** *v/t* **3.** tadeln (**for** wegen). **4.** kritisieren, mißbilligen.

cen·sus ['sensəs] *s* (*bsd.* Volks)Zählung *f*: **traffic ~** Verkehrszählung.

cent [sent] *s Am.* Cent *m*.

cen·te·nar·i·an [,sentɪ'neərɪən] **I** *adj* hundertjährig. **II** *s* Hundertjährige *m*, *f*. **cen·te·nar·y** [sen'tiːnərɪ] **I** *adj* hundertjährig. **II** *s* Hundertjahrfeier *f*, hundertjähriges Jubiläum.

cen·ten·ni·al [sen'tenjəl] **I** *adj* hundertjährig. **II** *s bsd. Am.* → **centenary** II.

cen·ter *etc Am.* → **centre,** *etc.*

cen·ti·grade ['sentɪgreɪd] *adj*: **... degrees ~** ... Grad Celsius; **~ ther·mometer** Celsiusthermometer *n*. **'~·gram(me)** *s* Zentigramm *n*. **'~·me·ter,** *bsd. Br.* **'~·me·tre** *s* Zentimeter *m*, *n*.

cen·tral ['sentrəl] **I** *adj* □ **1.** zentral (gelegen). **2.** Mittel(punkts)... **3.** Haupt..., Zentral...: **~ bank** ✝ Zentralbank *f*; **~ figure** Schlüssel-, Hauptfigur *f*. **II** *s* **4.** (*Am.* Telefon)Zentrale *f*. ♀ **A·mer·i·can** *adj* zentral-, mittelamerikanisch. ♀ **Eu·ro·pe·an Time** *s* mitteleuropäische

Zeit. **~ heat·ing** s Zentralheizung f.

cen·tral·ize ['sentrəlaɪz] v/t u. v/i (sich) zentralisieren.

cen·tral‖ lock·ing s mot. Zentralverrieg(e)lung f. **~ ner·vous sys·tem** s physiol. Zentralnervensystem n. **~ reserve** s Br. Mittelstreifen m (e-r Autobahn). **~ sta·tion** s Hauptbahnhof m.

cen·tre ['sentə] **I** s **1.** Mitte f, a. fig. Zentrum n, Mittelpunkt m: **in** (od. **at**) **the ~** in der Mitte; **~ of gravity** phys. Schwerpunkt m; **be the ~ of interest** im Mittelpunkt des Interesses stehen. **2.** Fußball: Flanke f. **II** v/t **3.** fig. konzentrieren (**on** auf acc). **4.** ⊙ zentrieren. **III** v/i **5.** fig. sich konzentrieren (**in, on** auf acc), sich drehen (**round** um). **6.** Fußball: flanken. **~ for·ward** s Sport: Mittelstürmer(in).

cen·trif·u·gal [sen'trɪfjʊgl] adj □ phys. zentrifugal: **~ force** Flieh-, Zentrifugalkraft f. **cen·tri·fuge** ['~fju:dʒ] s ⊙ Zentrifuge f.

cen·tu·ry ['sentʃʊrɪ] s Jahrhundert n.

ce·ram·ic [sɪ'ræmɪk] **I** adj **1.** keramisch. **II** s **2.** Keramik f, pl a. keramische Erzeugnisse pl. **3.** pl (mst sg konstruiert) Keramik f (Technik).

ce·re·al ['sɪərɪəl] **I** adj **1.** Getreide... **II** s **2.** Getreidepflanze f. **3.** Getreide n. **4.** Getreideflocken pl, Frühstückskost f (aus Getreide).

cer·e·bel·lum [ˌserɪ'beləm] s anat. Kleinhirn n.

ce·re·bral ['serɪbrəl] adj anat. Gehirn...: **~ death** ⚕ Hirntod m.

ce·re·brum ['serɪbrəm] s anat. Großhirn n.

cer·e·mo·ni·al [ˌserɪ'məʊnjəl] **I** adj □ **1.** zeremoniell, feierlich. **2.** → ceremonious 2, 3. **II** s **3.** Zeremoniell n. **ˌcer·e·mo·ni·ous** adj □ **1.** feierlich. **2.** förmlich. **3.** rituell. **4.** umständlich.

cer·e·mo·ny ['serɪmənɪ] s **1.** Zeremonie f, Feier(lichkeit) f: **master of ceremonies** Zeremonienmeister m; thea. etc bsd. Am. Conférencier m. **2.** Förmlichkeit(en pl) f: **without ~** ohne Umstände; → **stand on** 2.

cert [sɜːt] s Br. F sichere Sache: **it's a dead ~** das ist todsicher, das.

cer·tain ['sɜːtn] adj **1.** sicher: a) (mst von Sachen) bestimmt: **it is ~ to happen** es wird mit Sicherheit geschehen; **for ~**

mit Sicherheit, b) (mst von Personen) überzeugt: **make ~ of** sich (gen) vergewissern; sich et. sichern; **make ~ (that)** dafür sorgen, daß, c) zuverlässig. **2.** (ganz) bestimmt: **a ~ day. 3.** gewiß: **a ~ Mr Brown; for ~ reasons** aus bestimmten Gründen. **'cer·tain·ly** adv **1.** sicher, bestimmt. **2.** Antwort: aber sicher, natürlich. **'cer·tain·ty** s Sicherheit f, Bestimmtheit f: **it is a ~ that** es ist sicher, daß.

cer·tif·i·cate I s [sə'tɪfɪkət] **1.** Bescheinigung f, Attest n: **~ of (good) conduct** Führungszeugnis n. **2.** ped. Zeugnis n. **3.** Gutachten n. **II** v/t [sə'tɪfɪkeɪt] **4.** et. bescheinigen. **5.** j-m e-e Bescheinigung od. ein Zeugnis geben: **~d** (amtlich) zugelassen; diplomiert. **cer·ti·fy** ['sɜːtɪfaɪ] v/t **1.** bescheinigen, attestieren: **this is to ~ that** hiermit wird bescheinigt, daß. **2.** beglaubigen. **3.** amtlich für geisteskrank erklären.

cer·ti·tude ['sɜːtɪtjuːd] s Sicherheit f, Bestimmtheit f.

ces·sa·tion [se'seɪʃn] s Aufhören n, Einstellung f.

ces·sion ['seʃn] s Abtretung f.

cess‖·pit ['sespɪt], **'~·pool** s Senkgrube f.

chafe [tʃeɪf] **I** v/t **1.** warmreiben, frottieren. **2.** auf-, durchreiben, wund reiben. **3.** fig. ärgern, reizen. **II** v/i **4.** (sich durch)reiben, scheuern. **5.** fig. sich ärgern (**at, against** über acc).

chaff [tʃɑːf] s Spreu f: → **wheat**.

cha·grin ['ʃægrɪn] **I** v/t verdrießen. **II** s Verdruß m.

chain [tʃeɪn] **I** s allg. Kette f (a. fig.): **~ of evidence** Beweiskette f; **~ of mountains** Gebirgskette. **II** v/t (an)ketten (**to** an acc): **~ (up)** Hund an die Kette legen. **~ re·ac·tion** s phys. Kettenreaktion f (a. fig.). **~ smok·er** s Kettenraucher(in). **~ store** s Kettenladen m.

chair [tʃeə] **I** s **1.** (Am. F elektrischer) Stuhl, Sessel m: **on a ~** auf e-m Stuhl; **in a ~** in e-m Sessel; **take a ~** Platz nehmen. **2.** fig. Vorsitz m: **be in the ~** den Vorsitz führen. **3.** univ. Lehrstuhl m (**of** für). **II** v/t **4.** bestuhlen. **5.** den Vorsitz führen bei: **~ed by** unter dem Vorsitz von (od. gen). **~ lift** s Sessellift m.

chair·man ['tʃeəmən] s (irr man) Vorsitzende m. **'chair·man·ship** s Vorsitz m: **under the ~ of** unter dem Vorsitz von (*od.* gen). **'chair·wom·an** *s* (*irr* **wom-an**) Vorsitzende *f.*

chal·ice ['tʃælɪs] *s eccl.* (Abendmahls-) Kelch *m.*

chalk [tʃɔːk] **I** *s* **1.** Kreide *f.:* (**as**) **different** (*od.* **like**) **as ~ and cheese** verschieden wie Tag u. Nacht. **II** *v/t* **2.** mit Kreide markieren. **3. ~ out** Plan *etc* entwerfen, skizzieren.

chal·lenge ['tʃælɪndʒ] **I** *s* **1.** Herausforderung *f* (**to** gen *od.* an *acc*) (*a. fig.*): **~ cup** (*bsd. Sport*) Wanderpokal *m.* **2.** (schwierige *od.* reizvolle) Aufgabe. **3.** ⅏ Ablehnung *f.* **II** *v/t* **4.** herausfordern. **5.** ⅏ Geschworenen, Richter ablehnen. **6.** *j-n* fordern *od.* reizen (*Aufgabe*). **7.** stark anzweifeln, in Frage stellen. **'chal·leng·er** *s bsd. Sport:* Herausforderer *m.* **'chal·leng·ing** *adj* □ **1.** herausfordernd. **2.** schwierig; reizvoll (*Aufgabe*).

cham·ber ['tʃeɪmbə] *s* ⚙, *parl. etc* Kammer *f:* **~ of commerce** Handelskammer. '**~·maid** *s* Zimmermädchen *n.* **~ mu·sic** *s* Kammermusik *f.* **~ pot** *s* Nachtgeschirr *n,* -topf *m.*

cha·me·le·on [kə'miːljən] *s zo.* Chamäleon *n.*

cham·fer ['tʃæmfə] **I** *s* **1.** ⊿ Auskehlung *f.* **2.** ⊿ Abschrägung *f.* **II** *v/t* **3.** ⊿ auskehlen. **4.** ⊿ abschrägen.

cham·ois ['ʃæmwɑː] *s* **1.** zo. Gemse *f.* **2.** *a.* **~ leather** [*mst* 'ʃæmɪ] Sämischleder *n.* **3.** Polier-, Fensterleder *n.*

champ¹ [tʃæmp] *v/i u. v/t* (heftig *od.* geräuschvoll) kauen: **~ at the bit** *fig.* ungeduldig sein, es kaum mehr erwarten können (**to do** zu tun).

champ² [~] F ⇨ **champion** 2.

cham·pagne [ʃæm'peɪn] *s* Champagner *m;* Sekt *m.*

cham·pi·on ['tʃæmpjən] **I** *s* **1.** Verfechter *m,* Fürsprecher *m* (**of** von *od.* gen). **2.** Sport: Meister *m.* **II** *v/t* **3.** verfechten, eintreten für. '**cham·pi·on·ship** *s* Sport: Meisterschaft *f.*

chance [tʃɑːns] **I** *s* **1.** Zufall *m:* **by ~** zufällig; **game of ~** Glücksspiel *n.* **2.** Möglichkeit *f,* Wahrscheinlichkeit *f:* **the ~s are that** es besteht Aussicht, daß. **3.** Chance *f,* (günstige) Gelegenheit; Aussicht *f* (**of** auf *acc*): **stand a ~** Aussichten *od.* e-e Chance haben. **4.** Risiko *n:* **take a ~** es darauf ankommen

lassen, es riskieren (**on** mit); **take no ~s** nichts riskieren (wollen). **II** *v/i* **5.** *I ... d to meet her* ich traf sie zufällig. **6. ~ on** zufällig begegnen (*dat*) *od.* treffen (*acc*); zufällig stoßen auf (*acc*). **III** *v/t* **7.** riskieren: **~ missing him** es riskieren, ihn zu verfehlen; **~ it** F es darauf ankommen lassen. **IV** *adj* **8.** zufällig, Zufalls...

chan·cel·lor ['tʃɑːnsələ] *s pol.* Kanzler *m:* **♀ of the Exchequer** *Br.* Schatzkanzler *m,* Finanzminister *m.*

chanc·y ['tʃɑːnsɪ] *adj* F riskant.

chan·de·lier [ˌʃændə'lɪə] *s* Kronleuchter *m,* Lüster *m.*

change [tʃeɪndʒ] **I** *v/t* **1.** (ver)ändern, verwandeln (**into** in *acc*): → **subject** 1. **2.** wechseln, (ver)tauschen: **~ one's shirt** ein anderes Hemd anziehen; **~ places with s.o.** mit j-m den Platz tauschen; **~ trains** (**planes**) umsteigen; **~ it** F es darauf ankommen lassen; **~ hand** 1, **mind** 4. **3.** Bettzeug *etc* wechseln, Bett frisch beziehen, Baby wickeln. **4.** Geld (um)wechseln (**into** in *acc*). **5.** ⚙ Teile (aus)wechseln, Öl wechseln. **6.** *mot.,* ⚙ schalten: **~ over** umschalten; Maschine, *a.* Industrie *etc* umstellen (**to** auf *acc*); → **gear** 1. **II** *v/i* **7.** sich (ver)ändern, wechseln. **8.** sich verwandeln (**to, into** in *acc*). **9.** übergehen (**to** zu). **10.** sich umziehen (**for dinner** zum Abendessen). **11.** 🚌, ✈ umsteigen. **12.** wechseln, umspringen (**from ... to** von ... auf *acc*) (*Verkehrsampel*). **13.** *mot.,* ⚙ schalten: **~ up** (**down**) hinauf- (herunter)schalten; → **gear** 1. **III** *s* **14.** (Ver)Änderung *f,* Wechsel *m, weitS. a.* Umschwung *m:* **~ of air** Luftveränderung; **~ of life** *physiol.* Wechseljahre *pl;* **~ in weather** Witterungsumschlag *m;* → **scene** 1a. **15.** (Aus)Tausch *m.* **16.** *et.* Neues, Abwechslung *f:* **for a ~** zur Abwechslung. **17.** Wechselgeld *n;* Kleingeld *n:* **can you give me ~ for a pound?** können Sie mir auf ein Pfund herausgeben?; können Sie mir ein Pfund wechseln?; → **small** I. '**change·a·ble** *adj* □ unbeständig: a) wankelmütig (*Person*), b) veränderlich (*Wetter*).

chan·nel ['tʃænl] *s* Kanal *m* (*a. fig.*), (Rundfunk, *TV a.*) Programm *n:* **switch ~s** umschalten; **through official ~s** auf dem Dienst- *od.* Instanzenweg.

chant [tʃɑːnt] I s 1. Gesang m. 2. Singsang m. 3. Sprechchor m. II v/t 4. singen. 5. herunterleiern. 6. in Sprechchören rufen.

cha·os ['keɪɒs] s Chaos n. **cha'ot·ic** adj (**~ally**) chaotisch.

chap¹ [tʃæp] I v/t Haut rissig machen. II v/i rissig werden, aufspringen. III s Riß m.

chap² [~] s F Bursche m, Kerl m.

chap·el ['tʃæpl] s Kapelle f.

chap·er·on ['ʃæpərəʊn] I s 1. Anstandsdame f. 2. Aufsichts-, Begleitperson f. II v/t 3. (als Anstandsdame) begleiten. 4. beaufsichtigen.

chap·fall·en ['tʃæp͵fɔːlən] adj niedergeschlagen, bedrückt.

chap·lain ['tʃæplɪn] s Kaplan m.

chapped [tʃæpt], **chap·py** ['tʃæpɪ] adj aufgesprungen, rissig.

chap·ter ['tʃæptə] s Kapitel n (a. fig.).

char¹ [tʃɑː] v/t u. v/i verkohlen.

char² [~] s Br. F → *charwoman*. II v/i putzen: *go out ~ring* putzen gehen.

char·ac·ter ['kærəktə] I s 1. allg. Charakter m. 2. Ruf m, Leumund m. 3. Eigenschaft f, Stellung f: *in one's ~ as* in s-r Eigenschaft als. 4. Figur f, Gestalt f (*e-s Romans etc*), pl a. Charaktere pl. 5. Schriftzeichen n, Buchstabe m. II adj 6. Charakter...: ~ *actor* (study, etc); ~ *assassination* Rufmord m. ͵**char·ac·ter'is·tic** I adj (**~ally**) charakteristisch (**of** für). II s charakteristisches Merkmal. '**char·ac·ter·ize** v/t charakterisieren.

char·coal ['tʃɑːkəʊl] s Holzkohle f.

charge [tʃɑːdʒ] I v/t 1. Gewehr etc laden, Batterie etc (auf)laden. 2. beauftragen (**with** mit): ~ *s.o. to be careful* j-m einschärfen, vorsichtig zu sein. 3. (**with**) j-m (et.) zur Last legen od. vorwerfen, a. ⛓ j-n (*e-r Sache*) beschuldigen od. anklagen. 4. (**with**) ✝ j-n belasten (mit *e-m Betrag*), j-m (et.) in Rechnung stellen. 5. berechnen, verlangen, fordern (**for** für). 6. ✕ angreifen; stürmen. II v/i 7. ~ *at* losgehen auf (acc). III s 8. Ladung f (*e-s Gewehrs etc*). 9. Preis m; Forderung f; Gebühr f; a. pl Unkosten pl, Spesen pl: *free of* ~ kostenlos, gratis. 10. Beschuldigung f, a. ⛓ Anklage(punkt m) f: *be on a ~ of murder* unter Mordanklage stehen. 11. Verant-

wortung f: *the person in* ~ der od. die Verantwortliche; *be in* ~ *of* verantwortlich sein für, leiten (acc); *be in* (od. *under*) *s.o.'s* ~ von j-m betreut werden; *take* ~ *of* die Leitung od. Aufsicht (gen) übernehmen. 12. Schützling m, Mündel m, n; j-m anvertraute Sache. ~ **ac·count** ✝ 1. Kundenkreditkonto n. 2. Abzahlungskonto n (*bei Teilzahlungen*).

char·gé d'af·faires [͵ʃɑːʒeɪdæ'feə] pl **char·gés d'af·faires** [~ʒeɪz~] s Geschäftsträger m.

charg·er ['tʃɑːdʒə] s ⚡ Ladegerät n.

char·is·ma [kə'rɪzmə] s Charisma n, Ausstrahlung(skraft) f. **char·is·mat·ic** [͵kærɪz'mætɪk] adj charismatisch.

char·i·ta·ble ['tʃærətəbl] adj □ 1. wohltätig, karitativ. 2. gütig, nachsichtig (**to** gegenüber). **char·i·ty** ['~tɪ] s 1. Nächstenliebe f. 2. Wohltätigkeit f. 3. Güte f, Nachsicht f. 4. Almosen n, milde Gabe.

char·la·tan ['ʃɑːlətən] s Scharlatan m. '**char·la·tan·ry** s Scharlatanerie f.

char·ley horse s Am. F Muskelkater m.

charm [tʃɑːm] I s 1. Charme m, Zauber m. 2. Zauber(formel f; -mittel n) m. 3. Talisman m, Amulett n. II v/t 4. bezaubern, entzücken. 5. verzaubern, *Schlangen* beschwören: ~ *away* wegzaubern, *Sorgen etc* zerstreuen. '**charm·er** s 1. Zauberer m, Zauberin f. 2. reizvolles Geschöpf (*Frau*); Charmeur m. '**charm·ing** adj □ charmant, bezaubernd.

chart [tʃɑːt] I s 1. (See-, Himmels-, Wetter)Karte f. 2. Diagramm n, Schaubild n, Kurve(nblatt n) f. 3. pl Charts pl, Hitliste(n pl) f. II v/t 4. auf e-r Karte etc einzeichnen od. verzeichnen.

char·ter ['tʃɑːtə] s 1. Urkunde f. 2. Konzession f. 3. pol. Charta f. 4. Chartern n. II v/t 5. konzessionieren. 6. chartern: ~**ed** Charter... ~ **flight** s Charterflug m.

'**char͵wom·an** s (irr *woman*) Putzfrau f, Raumpflegerin f.

char·y ['tʃeərɪ] adj □ 1. vorsichtig (**in, of** in dat, bei). 2. sparsam, zurückhaltend (**of** mit).

chase¹ [tʃeɪs] v/t 1. jagen, Jagd machen auf, (a. fig. *e-m Traum etc*) nachjagen;

F *e-m Mädchen etc* nachlaufen. **2.** *hunt.* hetzen, jagen: **~ up** (*od.* **down**) *mst fig.* aufstöbern. **3.** *a.* **~ away** verjagen, -treiben. **II** *v/i* **4. ~ after s.o.** j-m nachjagen. **5.** F rasen, rennen. **III** *s* **6.** *hunt.* (Hetz-)Jagd *f, fig. a.* Verfolgung(sjagd) *f*: **give ~ to** verfolgen (*acc*), nachjagen (*dat*).

chase² [~] *v/t* ziselieren.

chas·er² ['tʃeɪsə] *s* Jäger *m*, Verfolger *m*.

chas·er² [~] *s* Ziseleur *m*.

chasm ['kæzəm] *s* **1.** Kluft *f*, Abgrund *m* (*a. fig.*). **2.** Schlucht *f*, Klamm *f*. **3.** Riß *m*, Spalte *f*. **4.** *fig.* Lücke *f*.

chas·sis ['ʃæsɪ] *pl* **-sis** ['~sɪz] *s* ✓, *mot.* Chassis *n*, Fahrgestell *n*.

chaste [tʃeɪst] *adj* □ **1.** keusch, züchtig. **2.** bescheiden, schlicht (*Mahl etc*).

chas·ten ['tʃeɪsn] *v/t* **1.** züchtigen. **2.** *fig.* läutern. **3.** *fig.* ernüchtern, nachdenklich stimmen.

chas·tise [tʃæ'staɪz] *v/t* **1.** züchtigen. **2.** *fig.* geißeln, scharf tadeln.

chas·ti·ty ['tʃæstətɪ] *s* **1.** Keuschheit *f*. **2.** Schlichtheit *f*.

chat [tʃæt] **I** *v/i* plaudern. **II** *v/t*: **~ up** *Br.* F einreden auf (*acc*); sich ranmachen an (*ein Mädchen etc*), anquatschen. **III** *s* Plauderei *f*: **have a ~** plaudern.

chat show *s Br.* Talk-Show *f*.

chat·tels ['tʃætlz] *s pl* 🏛 bewegliches Eigentum: → **good** 3.

chat·ter ['tʃætə] **I** *v/i* **1.** schnattern, schwatzen, plappern. **2.** klappern. **II** *s* **3.** Geschnatter *n*, Geplapper *n*. **4.** Klappern *n*. '**~·box** *s* Plaudertasche *f*, Plappermaul *n*.

chat·ty ['tʃætɪ] *adj* □ **1.** geschwätzig, gesprächig. **2.** *fig.* wortreich, ausführlich; im Plauderton (geschrieben).

chauf·feur ['ʃəʊfə] **I** *s* Chauffeur *m*, Fahrer *m*. **II** *v/t* chauffieren, fahren: **~ed** mit Chauffeur.

chau·vi ['ʃəʊvɪ] *s* F Chauvi *m*. '**chau·vin·ism** *s* Chauvinismus *m*: **male ~** männlicher Chauvinismus. '**chau·vin·ist** *s* Chauvinist *m*: **male ~** männlicher Chauvinist; **male ~ pig** F a) *contp.* Chauvischwein *n*, b) *humor.* Chauvi *m*. ˌ**chau·vin'ist·ic** *adj* (**~ally**) chauvinistisch.

cheap [tʃiːp] **I** *adj* □ **1.** billig, Billig... **2.** billig, minderwertig. **3.** schäbig, gemein: **feel ~** sich schäbig vorkommen. **II** *adv* **4.** billig: **buy s.th. ~**. **III** *s* **5.** **on**

the ~ billig. '**cheap·en** *v/t u. v/i* (sich) verbilligen. '**cheap·ness** *s* Billigkeit *f*.

'**cheap·skate** *s* F Knicker *m*, Geizkragen *m*.

cheat [tʃiːt] **I** *s* **1.** Betrüger(in), Schwindler(in). **2.** Betrug *m*, Schwindel *m*. **II** *v/t* **3.** betrügen (**of, out of** um). **III** *v/i* **4.** betrügen, schwindeln. **5. ~ on** F *s-e Frau etc* betrügen. '**cheat·ing** *adj*: **~ pack** Mogelpackung *f*.

check [tʃek] **I** *s* **1.** Schach(stellung *f*) *n*: **give ~** Schach bieten; **hold** (*od.* **keep**) **in ~** *fig.* in Schach halten. **2.** Hemmnis *n*, Hindernis *n* (**on** für). **3.** Einhalt *m*: **give a ~ to** Einhalt gebieten (*dat*). **4.** Kontrolle *f*, Überprüfung *f*: **keep a ~ on** unter Kontrolle halten (*acc*). **5.** *Am.* Häkchen *n* (*auf Liste etc*). **6.** ✝ *Am.* Scheck *m* (**for** über *acc*). **7.** *bsd. Am.* Kassenzettel *m*, Rechnung *f*. **8.** Kontrollabschnitt *m*, -schein *m*. **9.** *bsd. Am.* Garderobenmarke *f*; Gepäckschein *m*. **10.** Schachbrett-, Karomuster *n*; Karo *n*, Viereck *n*; karierter Stoff. **11.** Poker *etc*: Spielmarke *f*: **pass** (*od.* **hand**) **in one's ~s** *Am.* F den Löffel weglegen (*sterben*). **II** *v/t* **12.** Schach bieten (*dat*). **13.** hemmen, hindern. **14.** ⊕ drosseln, bremsen (*a. fig.*). **15.** zurückhalten, zügeln: **~ o.s.** sich beherrschen. **16.** checken, kontrollieren, überprüfen (**for** auf *acc* hin). **17.** *Am. auf Liste etc* abhaken. **18.** *bsd. Am.* (zur Aufbewahrung *od.* in der Garderobe) abgeben; (als Reisegepäck) aufgeben. **19.** *a.* **~ out** *Am. Geld* mittels Scheck abheben. **III** *v/i* **20.** (plötzlich) innehalten, stutzen. **21.** *Am. e-n* Scheck ausstellen (**for** über *acc*). *Verbindungen mit Adverbien:*

check| back *v/i* rückfragen (**with** bei). **~ in** *v/i* **1.** sich (*in e-m Hotel*) anmelden. **2.** einstempeln. **3.** ✓ (*a. v/t*) einchecken. **~ off** → **check** 17. **~ out** **I** *v/t* **1.** → **check** 19. **2.** sich erkundigen nach, sich informieren über (*acc*). **II** *v/i* **3.** *aus e-m Hotel* abreisen. **4.** ausstempeln. **~ up** *v/i*: **~ on** *et.* nachprüfen *et.*, j-n überprüfen.

'**check|·back** *s* Rückfrage *f*. '**~·book** *s Am.* Scheckbuch *n*, -heft *n*. **~ card** *s Am.* Scheckkarte *f*.

checked [tʃekt] *adj* kariert: **~ pattern** Karomuster *n*.

check·er¹ ['tʃekə] *s* **1.** *Am.* a) (Dame)Stein *m*, b) *pl* (*sg konstruiert*) Dame(spiel *n*) *f*. **2.** Karomuster *n*.

check·er² [~] *s bsd. Am.* **1.** Kassiererin *f* (*bsd. im Supermarkt*). **2.** Garderobenfrau *f*. **3.** 🎏 Angestellte *m*, *f* in e-r Gepäckaufbewahrung.

'check·er·board *s Am.* Schach-, Damebrett *n*.

check·ered ['tʃekəd] *adj* **1.** kariert. **2.** bunt (*a. fig.*). **3.** *fig.* wechselvoll, bewegt (*Geschichte etc*).

'check·in *s* **1.** Anmeldung *f* (*in e-m Hotel*). **2.** Einstempeln *n*. **3.** ✔ Einchecken *n*: ~ **counter** Abfertigungsschalter *m*.

'check·ing ac·count [ˈtʃekɪŋ] *s* ✝ *Am.* Girokonto *n*.

check| list *s* Check-, Kontrolliste *f*. **'~·mate I** *s* (Schach)Matt *n*, Mattstellung *f*. **II** *v/t* (schach)matt setzen (*a. fig.*). **'~·out** *s* **1.** Abreise *f* (*aus e-m Hotel*): ~ (**time**) Zeit, zu der ein Hotelzimmer geräumt sein muß. **2.** Ausstempeln *n*. **3.** *a.* ~ **counter** Kasse *f* (*bsd. im Supermarkt*). **'~·point** *s* Kontrollpunkt *m* (*an der Grenze*). **'~·room** *s bsd. Am.* **1.** 🎏 Gepäckaufbewahrung(sstelle) *f*. **2.** Garderobe(nraum *m*) *f*. **'~·up** *s* **1.** Überprüfung *f*. **2.** ✚ Check-up *m*, Vorsorgeuntersuchung *f*.

cheek [tʃiːk] **I** *s* **1.** Backe *f* (*a.* ⚙), Wange *f*: **be ~ by jowl** Tuchfühlung haben (**with** mit) (*a. fig.*). **2.** *F* Frechheit *f*. **II** *v/t* **3.** *F* frech sein zu. **'~·bone** *s* Backenknochen *m*.

cheek·y ['tʃiːki] *adj* □ *F* frech (**to** zu).

cheep [tʃiːp] **I** *v/i u. v/t* piepsen. **II** *s* Piepsen *n*; Pieps(er) *m* (*a. fig.*).

cheer [tʃɪə] **I** *s* **1.** Beifall(sruf) *m*, Hoch(ruf *m*) *n*: **give three ~s for s.o.** j-n dreimal hochleben lassen. **2.** Auf-, Ermunterung *f*, Aufheiterung *f*: **words pl of ~** aufmunternde Worte *pl*; **~s!** → **cheerio. 3.** (*gute*) Laune: **be of good ~** guter Laune *od.* Dinge sein. **II** *v/t* **4.** Beifall spenden (*dat*), hochleben lassen. **5.** *a.* ~ **on** anspornen, anfeuern. **6.** *a.* ~ **up** auf-, ermuntern, aufheitern. **III** *v/i* **7.** Beifall spenden, jubeln. **8.** *mst* ~ **up** Mut fassen, (wieder) fröhlich werden: ~ **up!** Kopf hoch!, laß den Kopf nicht hängen! **cheer·ful** ['~ful] *adj* □ **1.** fröhlich (*a. Lied etc*), vergnügt. **2.** freundlich (*Raum, Wetter etc*).

cheer·i·o [ˌtʃɪərɪˈəʊ] *int bsd. Br. F* **1.** mach's gut!, tschüs! **2.** prost!

'cheer,lead·er *s Sport:* Einpeitscher *m*.

cheer·less ['tʃɪəlɪs] *adj* □ **1.** freudlos. **2.** unfreundlich (*Raum, Wetter etc*).

'cheer·y *adj* □ fröhlich, vergnügt.

cheese [tʃiːz] *s* Käse *m*: **say ~!** *phot.* bitte recht freundlich!; **hard ~!** *sl.* Künstlerpech!; **the ~** *sl.* genau das Richtige. **'~·cake** *s* **1.** *ein* Käsekuchen *m*. **2.** *sl.* Zurschaustellung *f* weiblicher Reize (*bsd. auf Fotografien*). **'~,par·ing** *s* Knauserei *f*. **II** *adj* knaus(e)rig. ~ **spread** *s* Streichkäse *m*.

chees·y ['tʃiːzi] *adj* käsig.

chef [ʃef] *s* Küchenchef *m*.

chem·i·cal ['kemɪkl] **I** *adj* □ chemisch: ~ **fiber** (*bsd. Br.* **fibre**) Chemie-, Kunstfaser *f*; ~ **warfare** chemische Kriegsführung. **II** *s* Chemikalie *f*.

chem·ist ['kemɪst] *s* **1.** Chemiker(in). **2.** *Br.* Apotheker(in); Drogist(in): ~**'s shop** Apotheke *f*; Drogerie *f*. **'chem·is·try** *s* Chemie *f*.

chem·o·ther·a·py [ˌkiːməʊˈθerəpi] *s* ✚ Chemotherapie *f*.

cheque [tʃek] *s* ✝ *Br.* Scheck *m*. ~ **ac·count** *s* ✝ *Br.* Girokonto *n*. **'~·book** *s Br.* Scheckbuch *n*, -heft *n*. ~ **card** *s* Scheckkarte *f*.

chequ·er, cheq·uer·board, cheq·uered *bsd. Br.* → **checker¹**, **checkerboard**, **checkered.**

cher·ish ['tʃerɪʃ] *v/t* **1.** j-s Andenken in Ehren halten. **2.** *Gefühle* hegen. **3.** festhalten an (*dat*).

che·root [ʃəˈruːt] *s* Stumpen *m* (*Zigarre ohne Spitzen*).

cher·ry ['tʃeri] **I** *s* ♣ Kirsche *f*. **II** *adj* kirschrot. ~ **bran·dy** *s* Cherry Brandy *m*, Kirschlikör *m*.

cher·ub ['tʃerəb] *pl* **-ubs, -u·bim** ['~əbɪm] *s* **1.** Cherub *m*, Engel *m*. **2.** geflügelter Engelskopf.

chess [tʃes] *s* Schach(spiel) *n*. **'~·board** *s* Schachbrett *n*. **'~·man** *s* (*irr* **man**), ~ **piece** *s* Schachfigur *f*.

chest [tʃest] *s* **1.** Kiste *f*, Kasten *m*; Truhe *f*: ~ (**of drawers**) Kommode *f*. **2.** *anat.* Brust(kasten *m*) *f*: **get s.th. off one's ~** *F* sich *etc.* von der Seele reden.

chest·nut ['tʃesnʌt] *s* **1.** ♣ Kastanie *f*: **pull the ~s out of the fire (for s.o.)** *fig.* (für j-n) die Kastanien aus dem Feuer holen. **2.** F alte *od.* olle Kamelle, alter Witz. **II** *adj* **3.** kastanienbraun.

chest·y ['tʃestɪ] *adj* F **1.** mit viel Holz vor der Hütte (*vollbusig*). **2.** tiefsitzend (*Husten*).

chev·ron ['ʃevrən] *s* ✕ Winkel *m* (*Rangabzeichen*).

chew [tʃuː] **I** *v/t* **1.** (zer)kauen: ~ *one's nails* an den Nägeln kauen; → *cud* 1, *fat* 3. **II** *v/i* **2.** kauen: ~ *on* herumkauen auf (*dat*). **3.** nachsinnen, grübeln (*on, over* über *acc*).

chew·ing gum ['tʃuːɪŋ] *s* Kaugummi *m, a. n.*

chic [ʃiːk] **I** *s* Schick *m,* Eleganz *f.* **II** *adj* schick, elegant.

chick [tʃɪk] *s* **1.** Küken *n,* junger Vogel. **2.** F Huhn(chen) *n* (*Kind; oft Anrede*). **3.** *sl.* Biene *f,* Puppe *f* (*Mädchen*).

chick·en ['tʃɪkɪn] **I** *s* **1.** Küken *n* (*a.* F *junge Person*), Hühnchen *n,* Hähnchen *n: she's no ~* F sie ist (auch) nicht mehr die Jüngste. **2.** Huhn *n.* **3.** F Feigling *m.* **II** *adj* **4.** F feig. **III** *v/i* **5.** ~ *out* F kneifen (*of, on* vor *dat*). ~ **broth** *s* Hühnerbrühe *f.* ~ **farm·er** *s* Geflügelzüchter *m.* ~ **feed** *s* **1.** Hühnerfutter *n.* **2.** *sl. contp.* ein paar Pfennige *pl, a.* Hungerlohn *m.* '~**heart·ed,** '~**liv·ered** *adj* furchtsam, feig. ~ **pox** *s* ❀ Windpocken *pl.*

chic·o·ry ['tʃɪkərɪ] *s* ♣ Chicorée *f, a. m.*

chief [tʃiːf] **I** *s* **1.** (Ober)Haupt *n,* (An)Führer *m,* Chef *m: ~ of the department* Abteilungsleiter *m;* ~ *of state* Staatschef, -oberhaupt. **2.** Häuptling *m: ~ of the tribe* Stammeshäuptling. **II** *adj* **3.** erst, oberst, Ober..., Haupt...: ~ *designer* Chefkonstrukteur *m.* **4.** hauptsächlich, wichtigst. '**chief·ly** *adv* hauptsächlich, vor allem.

chif·fon ['ʃɪfɒn] *s* Chiffon *m.*

child [tʃaɪld] *pl* **chil·dren** ['tʃɪldrən] *s* Kind *n: from a ~* von Kindheit an; *be a good ~!* sei artig *od.* brav!; *that's ~'s play fig.* das ist ein Kinderspiel. '~**bed** *s: be in ~* im Wochenbett liegen; *fever* ⚕ Kindbettfieber *n.* ~ **ben·e·fit** *s* Br. Kindergeld *n.* '~**birth** *s* Geburt *f,* Niederkunft *f,* Entbindung *f.*

child·hood ['tʃaɪldhʊd] *s* Kindheit *f: from ~* von Kindheit an; → *second*¹ 1.

child·ish ['tʃaɪldɪʃ] *adj* ☐ **1.** kindlich. **2.** kindisch.

child·less ['tʃaɪldlɪs] *adj* kinderlos.

'**child·like** *adj* kindlich. ~ **mind·er** *s* Tagesmutter *f.* ~ **prod·i·gy** *s* Wunderkind *n.* '~**proof** *adj* kindersicher: ~ *lock mot.* Kindersicherung *f.*

chil·dren ['tʃɪldrən] *pl von* **child:** ~'s clin·ic Kinderklinik *f.*

chil·e ['tʃɪlɪ] *s,* '**chil·i** *pl* -**ies** ♣ Chili *m* (*a. Cayennepfeffer*): ~ *sauce* Chili(soße *f*) *m.*

chill [tʃɪl] *s* **1.** Kältegefühl *n,* Frösteln *n.* **2.** Kälte *f,* Kühle *f* (*beide a. fig.*): *take the ~ off et.* leicht anwärmen. **3.** Erkältung *f: catch a ~* sich erkälten. **4.** *fig.* gedrückte Stimmung: *cast* (*od.* *put*) *a ~ on* (*od.* *over*) → 8. **II** *adj* **5.** kalt, frostig, kühl (*alle a. fig.*). **III** *v/i* **6.** abkühlen. **IV** *v/t* **7.** *j-n* frösteln lassen; abkühlen (lassen), *Lebensmittel etc* kühlen: ~*ed meat* Kühlfleisch *n.* **8.** *fig.* abkühlen, dämpfen; entmutigen.

chil·li *pl* -**lies** → **chile.**

chil·ly ['tʃɪlɪ] *adj* → **chill** 5: *feel* ~ frösteln.

chime [tʃaɪm] **I** *s* **1.** *oft pl* Glockenspiel *n,* (Glocken)Geläute *n.* **2.** (Glocken-) Schlag *m.* **II** *v/i* **3.** läuten; ertönen; schlagen (*Uhr*). **4.** *fig.* harmonieren, übereinstimmen (*with* mit): ~ *in* sich (ins Gespräch) einmischen, einfallen (*a.* ♪); ~ *in with* zustimmen, beipflichten (*dat*); übereinstimmen mit. **III** *v/t* **5.** *Glocken* läuten; *die Stunde* schlagen.

chim·ney ['tʃɪmnɪ] *s* Schornstein *m,* Kamin *m.* '~**piece** *s* Kaminsims *m, n.* ~ **sweep** *s* Schornsteinfeger(in), Kaminkehrer(in).

chim·pan·zee [ˌtʃɪmpən'ziː] *s zo.* Schimpanse *m.*

chin [tʃɪn] *s* Kinn *n:* (*keep your*) ~ *up!* F Kopf hoch!, halt die Ohren steif! **II** *v/t:* ~ *o.s.* (*up*), ~ *the bar* e-n Klimmzug machen. **III** *v/i Am.* F schwatzen, plappern.

chi·na ['tʃaɪnə] *s* **1.** Porzellan *n.* **2.** (Porzellan)Geschirr *n.* **♀·man** ['~mən] *s* (*irr man*) *mst contp.* Chinese *m.* '**♀·town** *s* Chinesenviertel *n.* '~**ware** *s* Porzellan(waren *pl*) *n.*

Chi·nese [ˌtʃaɪ'niːz] **I** *s* **1.** Chinese *m,* Chinesin *f: the ~ pl* die Chinesen *pl.* **2.** *ling.* Chinesisch *n.* **II** *adj* **3.** chinesisch.

chink¹ [tʃɪŋk] *s* Riß *m,* Ritze *f,* Spalt *m,* Spalte *f.*

chink² [~] **I** v/i u. v/t klingen od. klirren (lassen), klimpern (mit). **II** s Klirren n, Klimpern n.

'chin-wag F **I** s **1.** Plauderei f, Plausch m. **2.** Klatsch m, Tratsch m. **II** v/i **3.** plaudern, plauschen. **4.** klatschen, tratschen.

chip [tʃɪp] **I** s **1.** Splitter m, Span m, Schnitzel n, m: **be a ~ off the old block** ganz der Vater sein; **have a ~ on one's shoulder** F sich ständig angegriffen fühlen; e-n Komplex haben (**about** wegen). **2.** angeschlagene Stelle. **3.** pl Br. Pommes frites pl; Am. (Kartoffel-) Chips pl. **4.** Chip m (a. 🖥). Spielmarke f. **II** v/t s. **5. a. ~ off** abbrechen. **6.** Geschirr etc ausschlagen. **7. ~ in** F im Gespräch einwerfen. **8. ~ in** F Geld etc beisteuern. **III** v/i **9. a. ~ off** abbrechen, abbröckeln. **10. ~ in** F dazu beisteuern: **~ in with** → 8. **11. ~ in** F sich (in ein Gespräch) einmischen. **~ pan** s Friteuse f.

chi·rop·o·dist [kɪ'rɒpədɪst] s Fußpfleger(in), Pediküre f. **chi'rop·o·dy** s Fußpflege f, Pediküre f.

chi·ro·prac·tor ['kaɪrəʊˌpræktə] s 🖋 Chiropraktiker m.

chirp [tʃɜːp] **I** v/i u. v/t **1.** zirpen (Grille etc); zwitschern, piepsen (Vogel) (alle a. fig. Person etc). **II** s **2.** Zirpen n; Zwitschern n, Piepsen n. **3.** Piepser m. **'chirp·y** adj □ F quietschvergnügt.

chir·rup ['tʃɪrəp] → chirp.

chis·el ['tʃɪzl] **I** s **1.** Meißel m. **II** v/t pret u. pp **-eled**, bsd. Br. **-elled 2.** (aus)meißeln. **3.** fig. (stilistisch) ausfeilen. **4.** sl. betrügen (**out of** um); et. ergaunern.

chit¹ [tʃɪt] s: **a ~ of a girl** ein junges Ding; contp. ein Fratz.

chit² [~] s **1.** vom Gast abgezeichnete Rechnung. **2.** (kurze) Notiz; beschriebener Zettel.

chit-chat ['tʃɪttʃæt] s **1.** Plauderei f, Plausch m. **2.** Klatsch m, Tratsch m.

chiv·al·rous ['ʃɪvlrəs] adj □ **1.** ritterlich, galant. **2.** tapfer; loyal; großzügig. **'chiv·al·ry** s **1.** Ritterlichkeit f. **2.** hist. Rittertum n; ~stand m.

chives [tʃaɪvz] s pl ♣ Schnittlauch m.

chlo·ric ['klɔːrɪk] adj 🜍 chlorhaltig, Chlor... **chlo·rin·ate** ['klɔːrɪneɪt] v/t chloren. **chlo·rine** ['~riːn] s 🜍 Chlor n.

chlo·ro·form ['klɒrəfɔːm] **I** s 🜍 Chloroform n. **II** v/t chloroformieren.

chlo·ro·phyll ['klɔːrəfɪl] s ♣ Chlorophyll n, Blattgrün n.

choc ice [tʃɒk] s Br. Eis n mit Schokoladeüberzug.

chock [tʃɒk] **I** s Bremsklotz m. **II** v/t festkeilen. **,~-a-'block** adj vollgestopft (**with** mit). **,~-'full** adj zum Bersten voll (**of** mit).

choc·o·late ['tʃɒkələt] **I** s **1.** Schokolade f (a. Getränk). **2.** Praline f: **~s** pl Pralinen pl, Konfekt n; → **box¹** 2. **II** adj **3.** schokolade(n)braun.

choice [tʃɔɪs] **I** s **1.** (a. freie) Wahl: **make a ~** wählen, e-e Wahl treffen; **take one's ~** s-e Wahl treffen, sich et. aussuchen; **at ~** nach Belieben; **have no ~** keine andere Wahl haben. **2.** (große) Auswahl (**of** an dat). **3.** Auslese f, das Beste. **II** adj **4.** auserlesen, ausgesucht (gut). **5.** humor. deftig (Sprache): **~ word** Kraftausdruck m.

choir ['kwaɪə] s ♪, ⌂ Chor m.

choke [tʃəʊk] **I** s **1.** Würgen n. **2.** mot. Choke m: **pull out the ~** den Choke ziehen. **II** v/t **3.** würgen. **4.** erwürgen, erdrosseln, a. weitS. Feuer ersticken. **5.** a. **~ back** (od. **down**) Bemerkung, Ärger etc unterdrücken, hinunterschlucken, Tränen zurückhalten. **6.** Motor, Strom drosseln; F Motor abwürgen. **7.** a. **~ off** Diskussion etc abwürgen; j-s Redefluß stoppen. **8.** a. **~ up** verstopfen; vollstopfen. **III** v/i **9.** würgen. **10.** ersticken (**on** an dat). **'chok·ing** adj **1.** stickig (Luft). **2.** erstickt (Stimme). **'chok·y** → choking 1.

chol·er·a ['kɒlərə] s 🖋 Cholera f. **'chol·er·ic** adj □ (~ally) cholerisch.

cho·les·ter·in [kə'lestərɪn], **cho'les·ter·ol** [~rɒl] s physiol. Cholesterin n.

choose [tʃuːz] (irr) **I** v/t **1.** (aus)wählen, (sich et.) aussuchen. **2. ~ to do s.th.** es vorziehen od. beschließen, et. zu tun. **II** v/i **3.** wählen: **there are three versions to ~ from** es stehen drei Ausführungen zur Auswahl. **'choos·(e)y** adj F wählerisch, heikel.

chop¹ [tʃɒp] **I** s **1.** Hieb m, Schlag m. **2.** gastr. Kotelett n **II** v/t **3.** (zer)hacken: **~ wood** Holz hacken; **~ away** (od. **off**) abhacken; **~ down** fällen.

chop² [~] v/i oft **~ about** (od. **round**) plötzlich umschlagen (Wind etc): **~ and**

change dauernd s-e Meinung *od.* s-e Pläne ändern.

chop·per ['tʃɒpə] *s* **1.** Hackmesser *n.* **2.** F Hubschrauber *m.*

chop·py ['tʃɒpɪ] *adj* **1.** kabbelig (*Meer*). **2.** böig (*Wind*). **3.** *fig.* abgehackt; zusammenhang(s)los.

'**chop·stick** *s* Eßstäbchen *n.*

cho·ral ['kɔːrəl] *adj* □ Chor..., chorartig: ~ **society** Gesangverein *m.* **cho·ral(e)** [kɒ'rɑːl] *s* Choral *m.*

chord¹ [kɔːd] *s* ♪ Saite *f* (*a. fig.*): **strike the right** ~ den richtigen Ton treffen; **does that strike a ~?** erinnert das an etwas?

chord² [~] *s* ♪ Akkord *m.*

chore [tʃɔː] *s* **1.** *pl* Hausarbeit *f:* **do the ~s** den Haushalt machen. **2.** schwierige *od.* unangenehme Aufgabe.

cho·re·og·ra·pher [ˌkɒrɪ'ɒɡrəfə] *s* Choreograph(in). **cho·re·og·ra·phy** *s* Choreographie *f.*

cho·rus ['kɔːrəs] **I** *s* **1.** Chor *m* (*a. fig.*): ~ **of protest** Protestgeschrei *n;* **in** ~ im Chor. **2.** Tanzgruppe *f* (*bsd. e-r Revue*). **II** *v/t u. v/i* **3.** im Chor singen *od.* sprechen *od.* rufen. ~ **girl** *s* (Revue)Tänzerin *f.*

chose [tʃəʊz] *pret von* choose. **cho·sen** ['~] *pp von* choose.

chow [tʃaʊ] *s* **1.** *zo.* Chow-Chow *m.* **2.** *sl.* Futter *n,* Essen *n.*

chow·der ['tʃaʊdə] *s gastr. bsd. Am.* dikke Suppe *aus Meeresfrüchten.*

Christ [kraɪst] **I** *s* Christus *m: before* ~ vor Christi Geburt. **II** *int sl.* verdammt *od.* Herrgott noch mal!

chris·ten ['krɪsn] *v/t j-n, a.* Schiff *etc* (auf den Namen ...) taufen. '**chris·ten·ing** *s* Taufe *f.*

Chris·tian ['krɪstʃən] **I** *adj* □ christlich: ~ **Era** christliche Zeitrechnung; ~ **name** → first name. **II** *s* Christ(in). **Chris·ti·an·i·ty** [ˌ~tɪ'ænətɪ] *s* **1.** Christenheit *f.* **2.** Christentum *n.* **Chris·tian·ize** ['~jənaɪz] *v/t* christianisieren.

Christ·mas ['krɪsməs] *s* Weihnachten *n u. pl: at* ~ zu Weihnachten; → **merry** 1. ~ **bo·nus** *s* Weihnachtsgratifikation *f.* ~ **box** *s Br.* Geldgeschenk *n* zu Weihnachten (*für Briefträger etc*). ~ **car·ol** *s* Weihnachtslied *n.* ~ **Day** *s* erster Weihnachtsfeiertag. ~ **Eve** *s* Heiliger Abend. ~ **pud·ding** *s* Plumpudding *m.* '~**tide,**

'~**time** *s* Weihnachtszeit *f.* ~ **tree** *s* Christ-, Weihnachtsbaum *m.*

chro·mat·ic [krəʊ'mætɪk] *phys.* **I** *adj* (~**ally**) chromatisch, Farben... **II** *s pl* (*sg konstruiert*) Chromatik *f,* Farbenlehre *f.*

chrome [krəʊm] *s* ♔ **I** *s* Chrom *n.* **II** *v/t a.* ~**plate** verchromen.

chro·mi·um ['krəʊmɪəm] *s* ♔ Chrom *n.* ,~'**plate** *v/t* verchromen.

chro·mo·some ['krəʊməsəʊm] *s biol.* Chromosom *n.*

chron·ic ['krɒnɪk] *adj* (~**ally**) **1.** ständig, (an)dauernd: ~ **unemployment** Dauerarbeitslosigkeit *f.* **2.** eingewurzelt; unverbesserlich. **3.** ♣ chronisch. **4.** *Br.* F scheußlich, miserabel.

chron·i·cle ['krɒnɪkl] **I** *s* Chronik *f.* **II** *v/t* aufzeichnen. '**chron·i·cler** *s* Chronist *m.*

chron·o·log·i·cal [ˌkrɒnə'lɒdʒɪkl] *adj* □ chronologisch: **in** ~ **order,** ~**ly** in chronologischer Reihenfolge. **chro·nol·o·gy** [krə'nɒlədʒɪ] *s* **1.** Chronologie *f,* Zeitrechnung *f.* **2.** Zeittafel *f.* **3.** chronologische Aufstellung.

chrys·an·the·mum [krɪ'sænθəməm] *s* ❀ Chrysantheme *f.*

chub·by ['tʃʌbɪ] *adj* **1.** dicklich, rundlich: ~ **cheeks** *pl* Pausbacken *pl.* **2.** pausbäkig.

chuck¹ [tʃʌk] **I** *s* **1.** F Wurf *m: give s.o. the* ~ *Br.* j-n rausschmeißen (*entlassen*). **II** *v/t* **2.** F schmeißen, werfen. **3.** *a*) Schluß machen mit (*e-r Freundin etc*): ~ **it!** laß das!, *b*) → **chuck up. 4.** ~ **s.o. under the chin** j-n *od.* j-m zärtlich unters Kinn fassen.

Verbindungen mit Adverbien:

chuck a·way *v/t* F **1.** wegschmeißen. **2.** *Geld* verschwenden. **3.** *Gelegenheit etc* verpassen, verschenken. ~ **in** → **chuck up.** ~ **out** *v/t* F *j-n* rausschmeißen, *et. Altes etc a.* wegschmeißen. ~ **up** *v/t* F *Job etc* hinschmeißen.

chuck² [~] *s* ⊛ **1.** Spann-, Klemmfutter *n.* **2.** Spannvorrichtung *f.*

chuck·er-out [ˌtʃʌkər'aʊt] *s* F Rausschmeißer *m.*

chuck·le ['tʃʌkl] **I** *v/i* **1.** glucksen: ~ (**to o.s.**) (still)vergnügt in sich hineinlachen. **2.** glucken (*Henne*). **II** *s* **3.** Glucksen *n.*

chug [tʃʌg] **I** s Tuckern n (*des Motors*). **II** v/i tuckern(d fahren).

chum [tʃʌm] F **I** s Kumpel m: *be great ~s* dicke Freunde sein. **II** v/i: *~ up with s.o.* enge Freundschaft mit j-m schließen.

chump [tʃʌmp] s **1.** Holzklotz m. **2.** dickes Ende (*e-r Hammelkeule etc*). **3.** F Trottel m. **4.** *Br. sl.* Birne f (*Kopf*): *be off one's ~* e-n Vogel haben.

chunk [tʃʌŋk] s F (Holz)Klotz m; (dickes) Stück: *a ~ of bread* ein Runken. **'chunk·y** adj F klobig, klotzig.

church [tʃɜːtʃ] **I** s Kirche f: *at (od. in) ~* in der Kirche; *go to ~* in die Kirche gehen. **II** adj Kirchen..., kirchlich. **'~go·er** s Kirchgänger(in). **~ wed·ding** s kirchliche Trauung. **'~yard** s Kirch-, Friedhof m.

churl [tʃɜːl] s **1.** Flegel m. **2.** Geizhals m. **'churl·ish** adj □ **1.** flegelhaft. **2.** geizig.

churn [tʃɜːn] **I** s **1.** Butterfaß n, -maschine f. **2.** *Br.* Milchkanne f. **II** v/t **3.** zu Butter verarbeiten. **4.** *a. ~ up* Flüssigkeiten heftig schütteln, *Wellen* aufwühlen, peitschen. **III** v/i **5.** buttern. **6.** sich heftig bewegen.

chute [ʃuːt] s **1.** Stromschnelle f. **2.** Rutsche f (*a. ⊙*), Rutschbahn f. **3.** Müllschlucker m. **4.** F Fallschirm m.

chut·ney ['tʃʌtni] s *gastr.* Chutney n (*scharf gewürzte Paste aus Früchten*).

ci·ce·ro·ne [ˌtʃitʃəˈrəʊni] pl **-ni** [ˌni:], **-nes** s Cicerone m, Fremdenführer m.

ci·der ['saidə] s (*Am. hard ~*) Apfelwein m: (*sweet*) *~ Am.* Apfelmost m, -saft m.

ci·gar [si'gɑː] s Zigarre f. *~ cut·ter* s Zigarrenabschneider m.

cig·a·rette, *Am. a.* **cig·a·ret** [ˌsigəˈret] s Zigarette f. *~ case* s Zigarettenetui n. *~ end* s Zigarettenstummel m. *~ hold·er* s Zigarettenspitze f. *~ pa·per* s Zigarettenpapier n.

cig·a·ril·lo [ˌsigəˈriləʊ] pl **-los** s Zigarillo m, n.

cig·ar light·er s *mot.* Zigarren-, Zigarettenanzünder m.

cinch [sintʃ] s *sl.* todsichere Sache; Kinderspiel n.

cin·der ['sində] s **1.** Schlacke f: *burnt to a ~* verkohlt, verbrannt. **2.** pl Asche f. **Cin·der·el·la** [ˌsindəˈrelə] s Aschenbrödel n, -puttel n (*a. fig.*).

cin·der track s *Sport:* Aschenbahn f. **cin·e·cam·er·a** [ˈsiniˌkæmərə] s

(Schmal)Filmkamera f. **'cin·e·film** s Schmalfilm m.

cin·e·ma ['sinəmə] s **1.** *bsd. Br.* Kino n. **2.** Film(kunst f) m. **'~go·er** s *bsd. Br.* Kinobesucher(in).

cin·na·mon ['sinəmən] s Zimt m.

ci·pher ['saifə] **I** s **1.** A Null f (*Ziffer*). **2.** (arabische) Ziffer, Zahl f. **3.** *fig.* Null f (*Person*); Nichts n (*Sache*). **4.** Chiffre f: *in ~* chiffriert. **5.** *fig.* Schlüssel m (*zu e-r Geheimschrift*). **II** v/t **6.** chiffrieren, verschlüsseln.

cir·cle ['sɜːkl] **I** s **1.** (*a. Familien-, Freundes- etc*)Kreis m: *go (od. run) round in ~s fig.* sich im Kreis bewegen; → *vicious circle.* **2.** *thea.* Rang m: *upper ~* zweiter Rang; → *dress circle.* **3.** *fig.* Kreislauf m, Zyklus m. **II** v/t **4.** umringen. **5.** umkreisen. **6.** einkreisen, umzingeln. **7.** einringeln. **III** v/i **8.** kreisen (*a. ✈*), die Runde machen (*a. Pokal etc*).

cir·cuit ['sɜːkit] **I** s **1.** Umfang m, Umkreis m. **2.** Runde f, Rundreise f, -flug m: *make (od. do) the (od. a) ~ of* die Runde od. e-e Rundreise machen in (*dat*). **3.** *⚡* Strom-, Stromkreis m; Schaltung f, Schaltsystem n: *~ closed* 1, *integrate* Ia, *short circuit.* **II** v/t **4.** umkreisen. *~ break·er* s *⚡* Unterbrecher m (*a. mot.*). *~ di·a·gram* s *⚡* Schaltplan m.

cir·cu·i·tous [səˈkjuːitəs] adj □ **1.** gewunden (*Flußlauf etc*). **2.** *fig.* weitschweifig, umständlich.

cir·cuit train·ing s *Sport:* Zirkel-, Circuittraining n.

cir·cu·lar ['sɜːkjʊlə] **I** adj □ **1.** (kreis)rund, kreisförmig. **2.** Kreis..., Rund...: *~ letter* → 4a; *~ saw ⊙* Kreissäge f. **3.** → *circuitous* 2. **II** s **4.** a) Rundschreiben n, b) Umlauf m, c) (Post)Wurfsendung f.

cir·cu·late ['sɜːkjʊleit] **I** v/i zirkulieren: a) kreisen, b) im Umlauf sein, kursieren (*Geld, Nachricht etc*). **II** v/t in Umlauf setzen (*a. fig.*), zirkulieren lassen. **'cir·cu·lat·ing** adj zirkulierend: *~ library* Leihbücherei f. **ˌcir·cu·la·tion** s **1.** (*physiol. a.* Blut)Kreislauf m, Zirkulation f. **2.** ⚡ Umlauf m: *bring (od. put) into ~* in Umlauf setzen (*a. fig.*); *withdraw from ~* aus dem Verkehr ziehen; *out of ~* außer Kurs (gesetzt). **3.** Auflage f (e-r Zeitung etc).

cir·cu·la·to·ry ['sɜːkjəlætərɪ] adj ≉, physiol. (Blut-)Kreislauf...: ~ **collapse** Kreislaufkollaps m; ~ **disturbances** pl Kreislaufstörungen pl; ~ **system** Kreislauf m.

cir·cum·cise ['sɜːkəmsaɪz] v/t ≉, eccl. beschneiden. **cir·cum·ci·sion** [ˌ~'sɪʒn] s Beschneidung f.

cir·cum·fer·ence [səˈkʌmfərəns] s A Umfang m.

cir·cum·lo·cu·tion [ˌsɜːkəmləˈkjuːʃn] s **1.** Umschreibung f. **2.** Umschweife pl; Weitschweifigkeit f.

cir·cum·nav·i·gate [ˌsɜːkəmˈnævɪgeɪt] v/t umschiffen, umsegeln. **'cir·cum·nav·i'ga·tion** s Umschiffung f, Umseg(e)lung f: ~ **of the globe** Weltumseg(e)lung.

cir·cum·scribe ['sɜːkəmskraɪb] v/t **1.** begrenzen, einschränken. **2.** umschreiben (a. A). definieren.

cir·cum·scrip·tion [ˌ~'skrɪpʃn] s **1.** Begrenzung f, Einschränkung f. **2.** Umschreibung f. **3.** Umschrift f (e-r Münze etc).

cir·cum·spect ['sɜːkəmspekt] adj □ **1.** umsichtig. **2.** vorsichtig. **cir·cum·spec·tion** [ˌ~'spekʃn] s **1.** Umsicht f. **2.** Vorsicht f.

cir·cum·stance ['sɜːkəmstəns] s **1.** Umstand m. **2.** mst pl (Sach)Lage f, Umstände pl: **in** (od. **under**) **no** ~s unter keinen Umständen, auf keinen Fall; **in** (od. **under**) **the** ~s unter diesen Umständen. **3.** pl Verhältnisse pl: **live in easy** ~s in gesicherten Verhältnissen leben. **cir·cum·stan·tial** [ˌ~'stænʃl] adj □ **1.** umstandsbedingt. **2.** ausführlich. **3.** umständlich. **4.** ~ **evidence** ᚱᚱᚱ Indizienbeweis m. **5.** nebensächlich.

cir·cus ['sɜːkəs] s **1.** Zirkus m. **2.** Br. runder, von Häusern umschlossener Platz.

cir·rho·sis [sɪˈrəʊsɪs] s ≉ Zirrhose f.

cir·rus ['sɪrəs] pl **-ri** ['~raɪ] s meteor. Zirrus-, Federwolke f.

cis·sy → **sissy**.

cis·tern ['sɪstən] s **1.** Wasserbehälter m, (in Toilette) Spülkasten m. **2.** Zisterne f.

cit·a·del ['sɪtədəl] s ✕ Zitadelle f.

ci·ta·tion [saɪˈteɪʃn] s **1.** Zitieren n; Zitat n. **2.** ᚱᚱᚱ Vorladung f. **3.** ✕ lobende Erwähnung.

cite [saɪt] v/t **1.** zitieren. **2.** ᚱᚱᚱ vorladen. **3.** ✕ lobend erwähnen.

cit·i·zen ['sɪtɪzn] s **1.** Bürger(in). **2.** Städter(in). **3.** Staatsangehörige m, f. **'cit·i·zen·ship** s Staatsangehörigkeit f.

cit·ric ac·id ['sɪtrɪk] s ⚗ Zitronensäure f.

cit·rus ['sɪtrəs] s ♀ Zitrusgewächs n. ~ **fruit** s Zitrusfrucht f.

cit·y ['sɪtɪ] s (Groß)Stadt f: **the** ⚹ die (Londoner) City. ~ **cen·tre** s Br. Innenstadt f, City f. ~ **fa·thers** s pl Stadtväter pl. ~ **hall** s Rathaus n. ~ **plan·ning** s Stadtplanung f. ~ **state** s Stadtstaat n.

civ·ic ['sɪvɪk] **I** adj (ally) **1.** → **civil 1**. **2.** städtisch, Stadt... **II** s pl (sg konstruiert) Staatsbürgerkunde f.

civ·il ['sɪvl] adj □ **1.** staatlich, Staats... **2.** (a. staats)bürgerlich, Bürger... **3.** zivil, Zivil... (Ggs. militärisch, kirchlich etc): ~ **aviation** Zivilluftfahrt f; ~ **marriage** standesamtliche Trauung. **4.** höflich. **5.** ᚱᚱᚱ zivilrechtlich: ~ **case** (od. **suit**) Zivilprozeß m. ~ **en·gi·neer** s Bauingenieur m.

ci·vil·ian [sɪˈvɪljən] **I** s Zivilist m. **II** adj zivil, Zivil...

civ·i·li·za·tion [ˌsɪvɪlaɪˈzeɪʃn] s Zivilisation f, Kultur f: **disease of** ~ ≉ Zivilisationskrankheit f. **'civ·i·lize** v/t zivilisieren: ~**d nations** pl Kulturvölker pl.

civ·il | **law** s **1.** römisches Recht. **2.** Zivilrecht n, bürgerliches Recht. ~ **rights** s pl bürgerliche Ehrenrechte pl, (Staats)Bürgerrechte pl: ~ **activist** Bürgerrechtler(in); ~ **movement** Bürgerrechtsbewegung f. ~ **ser·vant** s Staatsbeamte m. ~ **ser·vice** s Staatsdienst m. ~ **war** s Bürgerkrieg m.

clack [klæk] **I** v/i **1.** klappern. **2.** plappern. **II** s **3.** Klappern n. **4.** Geplapper n.

clad [klæd] **I** pret u. pp von **clothe**. **II** adj gekleidet.

claim [kleɪm] **I** v/t **1.** verlangen, a. Todesopfer etc fordern: ~ **back** zurückfordern. **2.** in Anspruch nehmen, (er)fordern. **3.** behaupten (s.th. et.; that daß); (von sich) behaupten (to be zu sein), Anspruch erheben auf (acc); aufweisen (können), haben; sich bekennen zu (e-m Terroranschlag etc). **II** s **4.** Forderung f (on, against gegen): **make a** ~ e-e Forderung erheben. **5.** Anrecht n (to auf acc): ~ **for damages** Schadener-

satzanspruch *m*. **6.** Behauptung *f*.
'claim·ant *s* **1.** Antragsteller(in): *rightful* ~ Anspruchsberechtigte *m, f*. **2.** Anwärter(in) (*to* auf *acc*).

clair·voy·ance [kleə'vɔɪəns] *s* Hellsehen *n*. **clair'voy·ant** I *adj* hellseherisch. II *s* Hellseher(in).

clam [klæm] *s zo*. eßbare Muschel: *hard* (*od. round*) ~ Venusmuschel.

clam·ber ['klæmbə] I *v/i* (mühsam) klettern. II *v/t* erklettern.

clam·my ['klæmɪ] *adj* □ feuchtkalt, klamm.

clam·or·ous ['klæmərəs] *adj* □ **1.** lärmend. **2.** *fig*. lautstark (*Forderungen etc*) **'clam·o·u(r** I *s* **1.** Lärm *m*, Geschrei *n*. **2.** *fig*. lautstarker Protest (*against* gegen), *fordernder* Schrei (*for* nach). II *v/i* **3.** lärmen, schreien. **4.** *fig*. lautstark protestieren (*against* gegen), lautstark verlangen (*for* nach).

clamp [klæmp] I *s* ⊛ Klemme *f*, Klammer *f*. II *v/t* festklemmen, mit Klammern befestigen. III *v/i*: ~ *down* F scharf vorgehen (*on* gegen).

clan [klæn] *s* **1.** Clan *m*: a) *schott*. Stamm *m*, b) *allg*. Sippe *f*, Geschlecht *n*. **2.** Gruppe *f*, *bsd. contp*. Clique *f*.

clan·des·tine [klæn'destɪn] *adj* □ heimlich, verstohlen.

clang [klæŋ] I *v/i* klingen, klirren. II *v/t* erklingen lassen. III *s* Klang *m*, Geklirr *n*. **'clang·er** *s*: *drop a* ~ *Br*. F ins Fettnäpfchen treten. **clang·or·ous** ['klæŋgərəs] *adj* □ klirrend.

clang·o·u(r [klæŋə] → **clang** III.

clank [klæŋk] I *v/i u. v/t* klirren *od*. rasseln (mit). II *s* Geklirr *n*, Gerassel *n*.

clap¹ [klæp] I *s* **1.** (*a*. Hände-, Beifall)Klatschen *n*. **2.** Klaps *m*. **3.** Krachen *n*: ~ *of thunder* Donnerschlag *m*. II *v/t* **4.** zs.-schlagen: ~ *one's hands* in die Hände klatschen. **5.** *j-m* Beifall klatschen, applaudieren, *a. et*. beklatschen. **6.** *j-m auf die Schulter etc* klopfen. III *v/i* **7.** klatschen. **8.** (Beifall) klatschen, applaudieren.

clap² [~] *s* ⚥ *sl*. Tripper *m*.

clap·per ['klæpə] *s* **1.** Klöppel *m* (*e-r Glocke*). **2.** Klapper *f*.

'clap·trap *s* F **1.** Effekthascherei *f*. **2.** Gewäsch *n*.

clar·et ['klærət] *s* roter Bordeaux(wein); *allg*. Rotwein *m*.

clar·i·fi·ca·tion [ˌklærɪfɪ'keɪʃn] *s* **1.** (Auf)Klärung *f*, Klarstellung *f*. **2.** ⊛ (Abwasser)Klärung *f*, Abklärung *f*: ~ *plant* Kläranlage *f*. **clar·i·fy** ['~faɪ] I *v/t* **1.** (auf)klären, klarstellen. **2.** ⊛ (ab)klären. II *v/i* **3.** sich (auf)klären, klar werden. **4.** sich (ab)klären.

clar·i·net [ˌklærə'net] *s* ♪ Klarinette *f*. **ˌclar·i'net·(t)ist** *s* Klarinettist *m*.

clar·i·ty ['klærətɪ] *s* Klarheit *f*.

clash [klæʃ] I *v/i* **1.** prallen, stoßen (*into* gegen), (*a. feindlich*) zs.-prallen, -stoßen (*with* mit). **2.** *fig*. (*with*) kollidieren: a) im Widerspruch stehen (zu), unvereinbar sein (mit), b) (zeitlich) zs.-fallen (mit). **3.** nicht zs.-passen (*with* mit), (*Farben a*.) sich beißen. II *v/t* **4.** (*a. feindlicher*) Zs.-prall *od*. -stoß, Kollision *f* (*a. fig*.): ~ *of interests* Interessenkollision. **5.** *fig*. Widerspruch *m*. **6.** (zeitliches) Zs.-fallen.

clasp [klɑːsp] I *v/t* **1.** ein-, zuhaken, zu-, festschnallen. **2.** ergreifen, umklammern: ~ *s.o.'s hand* j-m die Hand drücken; *j-s* Hand umklammern; ~ *one's hands* die Hände falten. II *s* **3.** Haken *m*, Schnalle *f*; Schloß *n*, Schließe *f* (*e-r Handtasche etc*). **4.** Umklammerung *f*: *by* ~ *of hands* durch Händedruck *od*. Handschlag. ~ *knife* *s* (*irr knife*) Klapp-, Taschenmesser *n*.

class [klɑːs] I *s* **1.** Klasse *f* (*a*. ♜, *biol. etc*). **2.** (Wert-, Güte)Klasse; *engS*. F Klasse *f* (*Erstklassigkeit*): *in the same* ~ *with* gleichwertig mit; *in a* ~ *by o.s.* (*od. of one's own*) e-e Klasse für sich; *have* ~ F (große) Klasse sein. **3.** gesellschaftlicher Rang, soziale Stellung; (Gesellschafts)Klasse *f*, (Bevölkerungs)Schicht *f*. **4.** *ped*. (Schul)Klasse *f*; (Unterrichts)Stunde *f*: *attend* ~*es* am Unterricht teilnehmen. II *v/t* **5.** klassifizieren: ~ *with* gleichstellen mit; ~ *as* ansehen *od*. betrachten als. ~ *con·flict* *s* Klassenkonflikt *m*. '~*con·scious* *adj* klassenbewußt. ~ *dis·tinc·tion* *s* Klassenunterschied *m*. '~*fel·low* *s* Klassenkamerad(in), Mitschüler(in). '~*ha·tred* *s* Klassenhaß *m*. ~ *hour* *s ped*. Unterrichtsstunde *f*.

clas·sic ['klæsɪk] I *adj* (~*ally*) **1.** klassisch, vollendet: ~ *example* klassisches Beispiel. **2.** klassisch: a) *das klassische Altertum betreffend*, b) *die klassische*

Literatur etc betreffend. **3.** klassisch: a) herkömmlich, b) typisch, c) zeitlos. **II** *s*
4. Klassiker *m* (*Person u. Werk*). **5.** *pl* Altphilologie *f*. **clas·si·cal** ['~kl] *adj* □
1. → *classic* **I.** **2.** klassisch: a) humanistisch (gebildet), b) *die klassische Kunst od. Literatur betreffend:* ~ *education* humanistische Bildung; *the* ~ *languages* die alten Sprachen; ~ *scholar* Altphilologe *m*. **3.** klassisch (*Musik*).

clas·si·fi·ca·tion [ˌklæsɪfɪ'keɪʃn] *s* Klassifikation *f*, Klassifizierung *f*. **clas·si·fied** ['~faɪd] *adj* **1.** klassifiziert: ~ *ad*(*vertisement*) Kleinanzeige *f*; ~ *directory* Branchenverzeichnis *n*. **2.** ✕, *pol.* geheim. **clas·si·fy** ['~faɪ] *v/t* **1.** klassifizieren. **2.** ✕, *pol.* für geheim erklären.

class·less ['klɑːslɪs] *adj* klassenlos (*Gesellschaft*). **'~mate** → *classfellow*. **~room** ['~rʊm] *s* Klassenzimmer *n*. **~ strug·gle, ~ war** *s* Klassenkampf *m*.

class·y ['klɑːsɪ] *adj* F Klasse, Klasse..

clat·ter ['klætə] *I* *v/i* **1.** klappern, rasseln. **2.** poltern: ~ *about* (*od. around*) herumtrampeln. **II** *v/t* **3.** klappern *od.* rasseln mit. **III** *s* **4.** Geklapper *n*, Gerassel *n*.

clause [klɔːz] *s* **1.** *ling.* Satz(teil) *m.* **2.** ⚖ Klausel *f*, Abschnitt *m*, Absatz *m*.

claus·tro·pho·bi·a [ˌklɔːstrəˈfəʊbjə] *s* ✚ Klaustrophobie *f*, Platzangst *f*.

clav·i·cle ['klævɪkl] *s* *anat.* Schlüsselbein *n*.

claw [klɔː] *I* *s* **1.** Klaue *f*, Kralle *f* (*beide a.* ⊙ *u. fig.*), Schere *f* (*e-s Krebses etc*). **II** *v/t* **2.** zerkratzen. **3.** umkrallen, packen. **III** *v/i* **4.** kratzen. **5.** reißen, zerren (*at an dat*). **6.** greifen (*at, for* nach).

clay [kleɪ] *s* Ton *m*, Lehm *m*: ~ *pigeon* (*Sport*) Ton-, Wurftaube *f*. **clay·ey** ['~ɪ] *adj* Ton..., Lehm...

clean [kliːn] *I* *adj* □ **1.** rein, sauber: → *breast* **I**, *heel* ² **I**, *sweep* **1**, **2.** sauber, frisch (*gewaschen*). **3.** einwandfrei, rein. **4.** makellos (*a. fig.*): ~ *record* tadellose Vergangenheit. **5.** anständig, sauber: ~ *living!* bleib sauber! **6.** glatt (*Schnitt, Bruch*). **7.** *sl.* clean (*nicht mehr drogenabhängig*). **8.** *sl.* sauber (*unbewaffnet*). **II** *adv* **9.** rein, sauber: *sweep* ~ rein ausfegen; → *broom* **10.** völlig, total. **III** *v/t* **11.** reinigen, säubern, putzen: ~ *down* (*od. up*) gründlich reini-

gen. **,~·'cut** *adj* klar (umrissen), deutlich.

clean·er ['kliːnə] *s* **1.** *pl* Reinigung(sanstalt) *f*: *take to the* ~*s* zur Reinigung bringen; F *j-n* ausnehmen. **2.** Rein(e)machefrau *f*, (*Fenster- etc*)Putzer *m*. **'clean·ing** *I* *s*: *do the* ~ saubermachen, putzen. **II** *adj* Reinigungs...: ~ *cloth*; ~ *woman* (*od. lady*) Rein(e)machefrau *f*.

clean·li·ness ['klenlɪnɪs] *s* Reinlichkeit *f*. **'clean·ly** *adj* reinlich: a) sauber, b) sauberkeitsliebend.

clean·ness ['kliːnnɪs] *s* Reinheit *f*, Sauberkeit *f*.

cleanse [klenz] *v/t* reinigen, säubern, reinwaschen (*from, of* von) (*alle a. fig.*). **'cleans·er** *s* Reinigungsmittel *n*.

,clean·'shav·en *adj* glattrasiert.

clear [klɪə] *I* *adj* (□ *~ly*) **1.** klar, hell. **2.** klar, heiter (*Wetter etc*). **3.** klar, rein, hell (*Stimme etc*). **4.** klar, verständlich, deutlich: *make s.th.* ~ (*to s.o.*) (j-m) et. klarmachen; *make o.s.* ~ sich klar ausdrücken, sich verständlich machen. **5.** klar, unvermischt: ~ *soup gastr.* klare Suppe. **6.** deutlich, scharf (*Foto, Umrisse etc*). **7.** klar, offensichtlich: *a* ~ *win* ein klarer Sieg; *for no* ~ *reason* ohne ersichtlichen Grund. **8.** klar: a) sicher, b) in Ordnung. **9.** frei (*of* von) (*a. fig.*): ~ *of snow* (*debt*) schneefrei (schuldenfrei); *a* ~ *conscience* ein reines Gewissen. **10.** ♥ Netto..., Rein...: ~ *gain* (*od. profit*) Reingewinn *m*. **II** *adv* **11.** hell, klar. **12.** klar, deutlich: *speak* ~. **13.** los, weg (*of* von): *keep* (*od. steer*) ~ *of* sich fernhalten von, meiden; *get* ~ *of* loskommen von; *stand* ~ *of* Tür etc freihalten. **III** *v/t* **14.** oft ~ *away* wegräumen (*from* von), *Geschirr* abräumen. **15.** *Straße etc* freimachen, *Saal etc* räumen. **16.** reinigen, säubern: ~ *one's throat* sich räuspern. **17.** frei-, lossprechen (*of* von), *Gewissen* entlasten, *Namen* reinwaschen. **18.** *Verbrechen etc* (auf)klären. **IV** *v/i* **19.** klar *od.* hell werden. **20.** aufklaren (*Wetter*). **21.** oft ~ *away* sich verziehen (*Nebel etc*). **'clear·ance** *s* Räumung *f*: ~ *sale* Räumungs-, Ausverkauf *m*. **,clear·'cut** *adj* **1.** klargeschnitten. **2.** *fig.* klar, deutlich. **,~·'head·ed** *adj* klardenkend, intelligent.

clear·ly ['klɪəlɪ] *adv* **1.** klar, deutlich. **2.**

offensichtlich. **'clear·ness** s 1. Klarheit f. 2. Reinheit f. 3. Schärfe f.

cleav·age ['kliːvɪdʒ] s 1. Spaltung f. 2. Spalt m.

cleave [kliːv] (mst irr) v/t 1. (zer)spalten. 2. Luft, Wasser etc durchschneiden. 3. Weg bahnen.

clef [klef] s ♩ (Noten)Schlüssel m.

cleft [kleft] **I** pret u. pp von **cleave**. **II** s 1. Spalt m, Spalte f. 2. fig. Kluft f. ~ **pal·ate** s ✚ Wolfsrachen m. ~ **stick** s: **be in a ~** in der Klemme sitzen od. stecken.

clem·en·cy ['klemənsɪ] s Milde f, Nachsicht f. **'clem·ent** adj □ mild (a. Wetter), nachsichtig.

clench [klentʃ] v/t 1. zs.-pressen, Faust ballen, Zähne zs.-beißen. 2. fest packen od. anfassen.

cler·gy ['klɜːdʒɪ] s eccl. Klerus m, die Geistlichen pl. **~·man** ['~mən] s (irr **man**) Geistlicher m.

cler·i·cal ['klerɪkl] adj □ 1. klerikal, geistlich. 2. Schreib..., Büro...: ~ **error** Schreibfehler m; ~ **work** Büroarbeit f.

clerk [klɑːk] s 1. Schriftführer m, Sekretär m. 2. (Büro- etc)Angestellte m, f, (Bank- etc)Beamte m, (-)Beamtin f. 3. Am. Verkäufer(in).

clev·er ['klevə] adj □ 1. clever: a) geschickt, gewandt (at in dat), b) gerissen, raffiniert (a. Gerät etc): ~ **dick** bsd. Br. sl. Schlaumeier m. 2. geschickt: a) clever, klug, b) geistreich (Bemerkung etc). 3. begabt (at in dat, für). **'clev·er·ness** s 1. Cleverness f. 2. Gescheitheit f.

cli·ché ['kliːʃeɪ] s Klischee n, Gemeinplatz m.

click [klɪk] **I** s 1. Klicken n. 2. ✚ Einschnappen n. 3. ⚙ Sperrklinke f, -vorrichtung f. 4. Schnalzer m. **II** v/i 5. klicken. 6. mit der Zunge schnalzen. 7. zu-, einschnappen: ~ **shut** ins Schloß fallen. 8. F einschlagen, Erfolg haben (**with** bei). 9. F sofort Gefallen aneinander finden; sich sofort ineinander verknallen. **III** v/t 10. klicken od. einschnappen lassen: ~ **one's heels** die Hacken zs.-schlagen. 11. ~ **glasses** anstoßen. 12. mit der Zunge schnalzen.

cli·ent ['klaɪənt] s 1. ⚖ Klient(in), Mandant(in). 2. Kunde m, Kundin f. **cli·en·tele** [ˌkliːənˈtel] s 1. ⚖ Klientel f, Klienten pl. 2. Kundschaft f, Kunden pl.

cliff [klɪf] s 1. Klippe f, Felsen m. 2. steiler Abhang. **'~ˌhang·er** s 1. spannender Fortsetzungsroman (der immer im spannendsten Moment aufhört); (Rundfunk, TV) spannender Mehrteiler. 2. fig. spannende Sache.

cli·mac·ter·ic [klaɪˈmæktərɪk] s physiol. Wechseljahre pl.

cli·mate ['klaɪmɪt] s Klima n, fig. a. Atmosphäre f. **cli·mat·ic** [~ˈmætɪk] adj (**~ally**) klimatisch, Klima...

cli·max ['klaɪmæks] **I** s Höhepunkt m, physiol. a. Orgasmus m. **II** v/t auf den Höhepunkt bringen. **III** v/i den Höhepunkt erreichen.

climb [klaɪm] **I** s 1. Aufstieg m, Besteigung f. 2. Berg-, Klettertour f. **II** v/i 3. klettern: ~ **up** (**down**) **a tree** auf e-n Baum klettern (von e-m Baum herunterklettern). 4. (auf-, empor)steigen. 5. (an)steigen (Straße etc). **III** v/t 6. er-, besteigen, erklettern, klettern auf (acc).

clinch [klɪntʃ] **I** v/t 1. Spiel etc entscheiden: **that ~ed it** damit war die Sache entschieden. 2. ⚙ sicher befestigen; (ver)nieten. 3. Boxen: umklammern. **II** v/i 4. Boxen: clinchen. **III** s 5. ⚙ Vernietung f. 6. Boxen: Clinch m (a. sl. Umarmung).

cling [klɪŋ] v/i (irr) 1. kleben, haften (**to** an dat): ~ **together** zs.-halten (a. fig.). 2. a. fig. (**to**) hängen (an dat), anhaften (dat). 3. a. fig. (**to**) sich klammern (an acc), festhalten (an dat). 4. sich (an-) schmiegen (**to** an acc). ~ **film** s Frischhaltefolie f.

clin·ic ['klɪnɪk] s Klinik f. **clin·i·cal** [~kl] adj □ klinisch: ~ **death**; ~ **thermometer** Fieberthermometer n.

clink[^1] [klɪŋk] **I** v/i klingen, klirren. **II** v/t klingen od. klirren lassen: ~ **glasses** anstoßen. **III** s Klingen n, Klirren n.

clink[^2] [~] s sl. Kittchen n: **in ~** im Knast.

clip[^1] [klɪp] **I** v/t 1. (be)schneiden, stutzen (a. fig.). 2. fig. kürzen, beschneiden. 3. a. ~ **off** abschneiden. 4. aus der Zeitung ausschneiden. 5. Haare schneiden. 6. Schaf etc scheren. 7. Fahrschein etc lochen. 8. Silben verschlucken. 9. F j-m e-n Schlag versetzen. 10. sl. j-n erleichtern (**for** um Geld); j-n neppen. **II** s 11. Haarschnitt m. 12. Schur f.

clip[^2] [~] **I** v/t a. ~ **on** anklammern. **II** s (Heft-, Büro- etc)Klammer f.

clip joint *s sl.* Nepplokal *n*.

clip·pers ['klɪpəz] *s pl, a.* **pair of ~** (*Nagel- etc*)Schere *f*, Haarschneidemaschine *f*.

'**clip·ping** *s* **1.** *bsd. Am.* (Zeitungs)Ausschnitt *m*. **2.** *pl* Schnitzel *pl*, Abfälle *pl*.

clique [kli:k] *s* Clique *f*, Klüngel *m*.

clit·o·ris ['klɪtərɪs] *s anat.* Kitzler *m*.

cloak [kləʊk] **I** *s* (loser) Mantel, Umhang *m*: **under the ~ of** *fig.* unter dem Deckmantel der *Freundschaft etc*, im Schutz der *Dunkelheit etc*. **II** *v/t fig.* bemänteln, verhüllen. **~room** [~rom] *s* **1.** Garderobe *f*: **~ attendant** Garderobenfrau *f*; **~ ticket** (*bsd. Am.* **check**) Garderobenmarke *f*, -zettel *m*. **2.** *Br.* Toilette *f*.

clob·ber¹ ['klɒbə] *s Br. sl.* Klamotten *pl*; Plunder *m*, Kram *m*.

clob·ber² [~] *v/t sl.* **1.** zs.-schlagen. **2.** *Sport:* überfahren (hoch besiegen).

clock [klɒk] **I** *s* **1.** (*Wand-, Turm-, Stand*)Uhr *f*: **(a)round the ~** rund um die Uhr, 24 Stunden (lang); **five o' ~** 5 Uhr; **put** (*od.* **turn) the ~ back** *fig.* das Rad der Zeit zurückdrehen. **2.** F Kontroll-, Stoppuhr *f*; Fahrpreisanzeiger *m* (*Taxi*). **II** *v/t bsd. Sport:* (ab)stoppen: **~ (up)** *Zeit* erreichen (**for** über *e-e Distanz*). **III** *v/i* **4. ~ in** (*out*) einstempeln (ausstempeln). **~ card** *s* Steckkarte *f*. '**~face** *s* Zifferblatt *n*. **~ ra·di·o** *s* Radiowecker *m*. '**~wise** *adj u. adv* im Uhrzeigersinn. '**~work** *s* Uhrwerk *n*: **like ~** wie am Schnürchen, wie geschmiert.

clod [klɒd] *s* **1.** (Erd)Klumpen *m*. **2.** Trottel *m*.

clog [klɒg] **I** *s* **1.** (Holz)Klotz *m*. **2.** *fig.* Hemmschuh *m*, Klotz *m* am Bein. **3.** Holzschuh *m*. **II** *v/t* **4.** (be)hindern, hemmen. **5.** *a.* **~ up** verstopfen. **III** *v/i* **6.** sich verstopfen.

clois·ter ['klɔɪstə] *s* **1.** Kloster *n*. **2.** △ Kreuzgang *m*.

close I *adj* [kləʊs] □ **1.** geschlossen. **2.** verschlossen, verschwiegen. **3.** eng(anliegend). **4.** nah: **~ fight** Handgemenge *n*, *weitS.* zähes Ringen; **~ to tears** den Tränen nahe. **5.** eng (*Freund*); nah (*Verwandter*). **6.** knapp (*Sieg etc*): **~ shave** 5. **7.** gespannt (*Aufmerksamkeit*). **8.** gründlich (*Untersuchung etc*). **II** *adv* [kləʊs] **9.** eng, nahe, dicht: **~ by**

ganz in der Nähe; nahe *od.* dicht bei; **~ at hand** nahe bevorstehend; **come ~ to** fast ... sein; → **wind¹** 1. **III** *s* [kləʊz] **10.** Abschluß *m*: **come** (*od.* **draw) to a ~** sich dem Ende nähern. **IV** *v/t* [kləʊz] **11.** (ab-, ver-, zu)schließen, zumachen. **12.** *Betrieb etc* schließen; *Straße etc* sperren (**to** für). **13.** beenden, beschließen. **V** *v/i* [kləʊz] **14.** sich schließen (*a. Wunde etc*). **15.** geschlossen werden. **16.** schließen, zumachen. **17.** enden, aufhören, zu Ende gehen. **18.** schließen (**with the words** mit den Worten). **19.** sich verringern (*Abstand etc*).

Verbindungen mit Adverbien:

close| down I *v/t* **1.** *Geschäft etc* schließen, *Betrieb* stillegen. **II** *v/i* **2.** schließen, stillgelegt werden. **3.** *fig.* scharf vorgehen (**on** gegen). **~ in** *v/i* **1.** sich heranarbeiten (**on** an *acc*). **2.** kürzer werden (*Tage*). **3.** hereinbrechen (*Dunkelheit, Nacht*). **~ up I** *v/t* **1.** → **close** 11, 12. **2.** abschließen, beenden. **II** *v/i* **3.** → **close down** 2. **4.** aufschließen, -rücken (**on** zu).

closed [kləʊzd] *adj* **1.** geschlossen: **behind ~ doors** hinter verschlossenen Türen; **~ circuit** ⚡ geschlossener Stromkreis; → **book** 1. **2.** gesperrt (**to** für).

'**close-down** *s* Schließung *f*, Stillegung *f*.

closed shop *s* ⚓ gewerkschaftspflichtiger Betrieb.

,**close|'fist·ed** *adj* geizig. ,**~'fit·ting** *adj* enganliegend. '**~-knit** *adj fig.* engverbunden.

close·ness ['kləʊsnɪs] *s* **1.** Nähe *f*. **2.** Knappheit *f*. **3.** Gründlichkeit *f*.

close sea·son *s hunt.* Schonzeit *f*.

clos·et ['klɒzɪt] *s* **1.** (Wand-, Einbau)Schrank *m*. **2.** Klosett *n*.

'**close-up** *s phot.*, *Film:* Nah-, Großaufnahme *f*.

clos·ing| date ['kləʊzɪŋ] *s* letzter Termin (**for** für). **~ time** *s* Laden-, Geschäftsschluß *m*; Ende *n* der Schalterstunden; Polizeistunde *f*.

clo·sure ['kləʊʒə] *s* **1.** Schließung *f* (*e-s Betriebes etc*). **2.** ⚙ Verschluß *m*. **3.** Schluß *m*, Beendigung *f* (*e-r Debatte etc*).

clot [klɒt] **I** *s* **1.** Klumpen *m*, Klümpchen *n*: **~ of blood** 🔬 Blutgerinnsel *n*. **2.** *Br.* F Trottel *m*. **II** *v/i* **3.** gerinnen. **4.** Klumpen bilden.

cloth [klɒθ] *s* **1.** Tuch *n*, Stoff *m*. **2.** Tuch *n*, Lappen *m*.

clothe [kləʊð] *v/t* (*a. irr*) **1.** (an-, be)kleiden. **2.** einkleiden. **3.** *fig.* umhüllen, einhüllen.

clothes [kləʊðz] *s pl* **1.** Kleider *pl*, Kleidung *f*: *change one's ~* sich umziehen. **2.** (*a.* Bett)Wäsche *f*. **~ bas·ket** *s* Wäschekorb *m*. **~ brush** *s* Kleiderbürste *f*. **~ hang·er** *s* Kleiderbügel *m*. '**~horse** *s* Wäscheständer *m*. '**~line** *s* Wäscheleine *f*. **~ peg** *s Br.*, '**~pin** *s Am.* Wäscheklammer *f*. **~ tree** *s* Garderoben-, Kleiderständer *m*.

cloth·ing ['kləʊðɪŋ] *s* Kleidung *f*: **~ indus·try** Bekleidungsindustrie *f*.

cloud [klaʊd] **I** *s* **1.** Wolke *f*: *~ of dust* Staubwolke; *have one's head in the ~s fig.* in höheren Regionen schweben; in Gedanken vertieft sein; *be on ~ nine* F im siebten Himmel sein. **2.** *fig.* Schatten *m*: *cast a ~ on* e-n Schatten werfen auf (*acc*). **II** *v/t* **3.** be-, umwölken. **4.** *fig.* verdunkeln, trüben. **III** *v/i a. ~ over* **5.** sich bewölken. **6.** *fig.* sich trüben. **~ bank** *s* Wolkenbank *f*. '**~burst** *s* Wolkenbruch *m*. ,**~'cuck·oo-land** *s* Wolkenkuckucksheim *n*.

cloud·less ['klaʊdlɪs] *adj* □ **1.** wolkenlos. **2.** *fig.* ungetrübt. '**cloud·y** *adj* □ **1.** wolkig, bewölkt. **2.** *fig.* nebelhaft, unklar.

clout [klaʊt] F **I** *s* **1.** Schlag *m*: *give s.o. a ~* j-m e-e runterhauen. **2.** *bsd. pol. Am.* Einfluß *m* (*with* auf *acc*). **II** *v/t* **3.** schlagen: *~ s.o.* j-m e-e runterhauen.

clove[1] [kləʊv] *s* (Gewürz)Nelke *f*.

clove[2] [~] *s*: *~ of garlic* Knoblauchzehe *f*.

clove[3] [~] *pret von* **cleave**.

clo·ven ['kləʊvn] *pp von* **cleave**: *show the ~ foot* (*od.* **hoof**) *fig.* sein wahres Gesicht zeigen.

clo·ver ['kləʊvə] *s* ♣ Klee *m*: *be* (*od.* **live**) *in ~* wie Gott in Frankreich leben. '**~leaf** *s* (*irr* **leaf**) **1.** Kleeblatt *n*. **2.** *a. ~ intersection mot.* Kleeblatt *n*.

clown [klaʊn] **I** *s* Clown *m* (*a. fig.*). **II** *v/i a. ~ about* (*od.* **around**) herumkaspern. '**clown·ish** *adj* □ clownisch.

club [klʌb] *s* **1.** Keule *f*, Knüppel *m*. **2.** *Sport:* Schlagholz *n*; (*Golf*)Schläger *m*. **3.** Klub *m*, Verein *m*: *join the ~!* *bsd. Br.* F du auch? **4.** *Spielkarten:* a) *pl*

Kreuz *n*, Eichel *f* (*Farbe*), b) Kreuz(karte *f*) *n*. **II** *v/t* **5.** einknüppeln auf (*acc*), (nieder)knüppeln. **6.** sich teilen in (*acc*); *Geld* zs.-legen. **III** *v/i* **7.** *mst ~ together* sich zs.-tun: a) e-n Verein *etc* bilden, b) (Geld) zs.-legen. **~ chair** *s* Klubsessel *m*. ,**~'foot** *s* (*irr* **foot**) ⚕ Klumpfuß *m*. '**~house** *s* Klub-, Vereinshaus *n*.

cluck [klʌk] *v/i* gackern; glucken.

clue [kluː] **I** *s* **1.** (*to*) Hinweis *m* (auf *acc*), Anhaltspunkt *m* (für), Fingerzeig *m*. **2.** Schlüssel *m* (*to zu* e-m Rätsel *etc*): *I haven't a ~* F ich hab' keinen Schimmer. **II** *v/t* **3.** *~ in* j-m e-n Hinweis geben. **4.** *~ up* informieren (*on, about* über *acc*): *all ~d up* vollkommen im Bild.

clump [klʌmp] **I** *s* **1.** (Baum-, Häuser)Gruppe *f*. **2.** (Holz)Klotz *m*; (*Erde etc*)Klumpen *m*. **II** *v/i* **3.** trampeln: *~ about* (*od.* **around**) herumtrampeln. **4.** sich zs.-ballen. **III** *v/t* **5.** zs.-ballen, anhäufen.

clum·si·ness ['klʌmzɪnɪs] *s* Plumpheit *f*. '**clum·sy** *adj* □ plump: a) ungeschickt, unbeholfen, b) schwerfällig, c) taktlos, d) unförmig.

clung [klʌŋ] *pret u. pp von* **cling**.

clus·ter ['klʌstə] **I** *s* **1.** ♣ Büschel *n*, Traube *f*. **2.** Haufen *m*, Schwarm *m*, Gruppe *f*. **II** *v/i* **3.** e-e Gruppe *od.* Gruppen bilden, sich versammeln *od.* drängen (*round* um).

clutch [klʌtʃ] **I** *v/t* **1.** packen, (er)greifen. **2.** umklammern. **II** *v/i* **3.** (gierig) greifen (*at* nach): → *straw* 2. **II** *s* **4.** (gieriger) Griff. **5.** *zo.* Klaue *f*, Kralle *f* (*beide a. fig.*): *in s.o.'s ~es* in j-s Klauen *od.* Gewalt. **6.** ⚙ Kupplung *f*: *~ disk* Kupplungsscheibe *f*; *~ facing* (*od.* **lining**) Kupplungsbelag *m*; *~ pedal* Kupplungspedal *n*.

clut·ter ['klʌtə] **I** *v/t* **1.** *a. ~ up* (unordentlich) vollstopfen. **2.** durcheinanderwerfen, herumstreuen. **II** *s* **3.** Wirrwarr *m*, Durcheinander *n*. **4.** Unordnung *f*: *in a ~* in Unordnung.

coach [kəʊtʃ] **I** *s* **1.** Kutsche *f*. **2.** 🚌 *Br.* (Personen)Wagen *m*. **3.** *Br.* Reisebus *m*. **4.** Nachhilfe-, Hauslehrer *m*. **5.** *Sport:* Trainer *m*. **II** *v/t* **6.** *j-m* Nachhilfeunterricht geben: *~ s.o. in s.th.* j-m et. einpauken. **7.** *Sport:* trainieren. **~man**

['‿mən] *s* (*irr* **man**) Kutscher *m*. '**‿work** *s mot.* Karosserie *f*.

co·ag·u·late [kəʊˈægjʊleɪt] *v/i u. v/t* gerinnen (lassen). **co,ag·u·la·tion** *s* Gerinnung *f*.

coal [kəʊl] *s* Kohle *f*; *engS.* Steinkohle *f*: **carry** (*od.* **take**) **‿s to Newcastle** *fig.* Eulen nach Athen tragen; **haul** (*od.* **drag**) *s.o.* **over the ‿s** *fig.* j-m die Hölle heiß machen.

co·a·li·tion [ˌkəʊəˈlɪʃn] **I** *s* **1.** *pol.* Koalition *f*: **form a ‿** e-e Koalition eingehen *od.* bilden, koalieren. **2.** Bündnis *n*, Zs.-schluß *m*. **II** *adj* **3.** *pol.* Koalitions...

coal mine, '**‿pit** *s* Kohlenbergwerk *n*, -grube *f*, -zeche *f*. **‿ pow·er sta·tion** *s* Kohlekraftwerk *n*.

coarse [kɔːs] *adj* □ grob: a) rauh, b) grobkörnig, c) *fig.* ungenau, d) *fig.* derb, ungehobelt.

coast [kəʊst] **I** *s* **1.** Küste *f*: *the ‿ is clear fig.* die Luft ist rein. **II** *v/i* **2.** ⚓ die Küste entlangfahren. **3.** im Leerlauf (*Auto*) *od.* im Freilauf (*Fahrrad*) fahren. **coast·al** ['‿tl] *adj* Küsten... '**coast·er** *s* **1.** *Am.* Berg-u.-Tal-Bahn *f* (*im Vergnügungspark*). **2.** *bes. Am.* Untersatz *m* (*für Gläser etc*).

coast guard *s Br.* Küsten(zoll)wache *f*.

coat [kəʊt] **I** *s* **1.** Jacke *f*, Jackett *n*. **2.** Mantel *m*: **turn one's ‿** *fig.* sein Mäntelchen nach dem Wind hängen. **3.** *zo.* Pelz *m*, Fell *n*. **4.** (*Farb- etc*) Überzug *m*, Anstrich *m*, Schicht *f*. **II** *v/t* **5.** (an)streichen, überstreichen, -ziehen, beschichten. **6.** bedecken, umhüllen, umgeben (**with** mit). '**coat·ed** *adj* **1.** mit ... überzogen *od.* beschichtet: **sugar-‿** mit Zuckerüberzug; **‿ tablet** Dragée *n*. **2.** 🖋 belegt (*Zunge*).

coat hang·er *s* Kleiderbügel *m*. **‿ hook** *s* Kleiderhaken *m*.

coat·ing ['kəʊtɪŋ] *s* **1.** Mantelstoff *m*. **2.** → **coat** 4.

coat of arms *s* Wappen(schild *m*, *n*) *n*.

coax [kəʊks] *v/t* überreden, beschwatzen (**to do, into doing** zu): **‿ s.th. out of** (*od.* **from**) *s.o.* j-m et. abschwatzen.'

cob [kɒb] *s* Maiskolben *m*.

co·balt [kəʊˈbɔːlt] *s min.* Kobalt *n*: **‿** (**blue**) Kobaltblau *n*.

cob·ble¹ [ˈkɒbl] **I** *s* Kopfstein *m*: **‿s** *pl* Kopfsteinpflaster *n*. **II** *v/t* mit Kopf-

steinen pflastern: **‿d street** Straße *f* mit Kopfsteinpflaster.

cob·ble² [‿] *v/t* **1.** Schuhe flicken. **2.** *a.* **‿ up** zs.-pfuschen, zs.-schustern.

cob·bler [ˈkɒblə] *s* **1.** (Flick)Schuster *m*. **2.** Pfuscher *m*.

'**cob·ble·stone** *s* Kopfstein *m*: **‿ pave·ment** Kopfsteinpflaster *n*.

co·bra [ˈkəʊbrə] *s zo.* Kobra *f*.

'**cob·web** *s* Spinnwebe *f*, Spinnennetz *n*.

co·cain(e) [kəʊˈkeɪn] *s* 💊 Kokain *n*.

cock [kɒk] **I** *s* **1.** *orn.* Hahn *m*. **2.** Männchen *n*, Hahn *m* (*von Vögeln*). **3.** Wetterhahn *m*. **4. ‿ of the walk** (*od.* **roost**) *oft contp.* der Größte. **5.** ⚙ (*Absperr-, Gewehr- etc*)Hahn *m*. **6.** V Schwanz *m* (*Penis*). **II** *v/t* **7.** aufrichten: **‿ one's ears** die Ohren spitzen; **‿ one's hat** den Hut schief aufsetzen; → **snook**.

Cock·aigne [kɒˈkeɪn] *s* Schlaraffenland *n*.

,**cock-and-'bull sto·ry** *s* F Ammenmärchen *n*.

cock·a·too [ˌkɒkəˈtuː] *s orn.* Kakadu *m*.

'**cock,chaf·er** *s zo.* Maikäfer *m*.

cocked hat [kɒkt] *s* Dreispitz *m*: **knock** (*od.* **beat**) **into a ‿** *sl.* j-n, et. weit in den Schatten stellen; *Plan etc* völlig über den Haufen werfen.

cock·er¹ [ˈkɒkə] → **cocker spaniel**.

cock·er² [‿] *v/t* verhätscheln, verwöhnen: **‿ up** aufpäppeln.

cock·er span·iel *s zo.* Cockerspaniel *m*.

'**cock·eyed** *adj* F **1.** schielend: **be ‿** schielen. **2.** blau (*betrunken*). '**‿fight**, '**‿,fight·ing** *s* Hahnenkampf *m*.

cock·ney [ˈkɒknɪ] *s* **1.** Cockney *m*, waschechter Londoner. **2.** Cockney-(dialekt) *m*) *n*. '**cock·ney·ism** *s* Cockneyausdruck *m*.

'**cock·pit** *s* **1.** ✈, ⚓ Cockpit *n* (*a. e-s Rennwagens*). **2.** Hahnenkampfplatz *m*. '**‿roach** *s zo.* (Küchen)Schabe *f*. ,**‿sure** *adj* □ **1.** vollkommen überzeugt (**of, about** von), ganz sicher. **2.** übertrieben selbstsicher. '**‿tail** *s* Cocktail *m*.

cock·y [ˈkɒkɪ] *adj* □ F großspurig, anmaßend.

co·co [ˈkəʊkəʊ] **I** *pl* **-cos** 🌴 Kokospalme *f*; Kokosnuß *f*. **II** *adj* Kokos...: **‿ matting** Kokosmatte *f*.

co·coa [ˈkəʊkəʊ] *s* Kakao(pulver *n*) *m*.

co·co·nut ['kəʊkənʌt] s Kokosnuß f. ~ **palm** s ♀ Kokospalme f.

co·coon [kə'ku:n] s zo. Kokon m, Puppe f (der Seidenraupe).

cod [kɒd] s ichth. Kabeljau m, Dorsch m.

cod·dle ['kɒdl] v/t verhätscheln, verzärteln: ~ **up** aufpäppeln.

code [kəʊd] s 1. Kodex m: a) ⚖ Gesetzbuch n, b) Regeln pl: ~ **of** hono(u)r Ehrenkodex; → **moral** 4. **2.** (Telegramm)Schlüssel m. **3.** Code m; Chiffre f; Code m, Schlüssel m: ~ **number** Code-, Kennziffer f; ~ **word** Code-, Schlüsselwort n. II v/t **4.** verschlüsseln, chiffrieren.
'**cod-fish** → **cod.**

cod·i·fy ['kɒdɪfaɪ] v/t ⚖ kodifizieren.
'**cod·,liv·er oil** s Lebertran m.

co·ed [ˌkəʊ'ed] ped. F I s **1.** Am. Studentin f od. Schülerin f e-r gemischten Schule. **2.** Br. gemischte Schule. II adj **3.** gemischt.

co·ed·u·ca·tion [ˌkəʊedju'keɪʃn] s ped. Gemeinschaftserziehung f. ˌco·ed·u'ca·tion·al [~ʃənl] adj: ~ **school** gemischte Schule; ~ **teaching** → **coeducation.**

co·ef·fi·cient [ˌkəʊɪ'fɪʃnt] s A, phys. Koeffizient m.

co·erce [kəʊ'ɜ:s] v/t **1.** zwingen (**into** zu). **2.** erzwingen. **co'er·cion** [~ʃn] s Zwang m: **by** ~ → **coercively. co'er·cive** [~sɪv] adj **1.** Zwangs..., zwingend: ~ **measure** Zwangsmaßnahme f. **2.** überzeugend, zwingend (Gründe etc). **co'er·cive·ly** adv durch Zwang, zwangsweise.

co·ex·ist [ˌkəʊɪg'zɪst] v/i gleichzeitig od. nebeneinander bestehen od. leben. ˌco·ex'ist·ence s Koexistenz f: **peace·ful** ~ **pol.** friedliche Koexistenz. ˌco·ex'ist·ent adj gleichzeitig od. nebeneinander bestehend.

cof·fee ['kɒfɪ] s Kaffee m. ~ **bar** s Br. Café n; Imbißstube f. ~ **bean** s Kaffeebohne f. ~ **break** s Kaffeepause f. ~ **cup** s Kaffeetasse f. ~ **grind·er** s Kaffeemühle f. ~ **grounds** s pl Kaffeesatz m. '~**house** s Kaffeehaus n, Café n. ~ **ma·chine** s Kaffeeautomat m. '~,**mak·er** s Kaffeemaschine f. ~ **mill** s Kaffeemühle f. '~**pot** s Kaffeekanne f. ~ **set** s Kaffeeservice n. ~ **shop** Am. → **coffee bar.** ~ **ta·ble** s Couchtisch m.

cof·fin ['kɒfɪn] s Sarg m.

cog [kɒg] s ⚙ (Rad)Zahn m; Zahnrad n: **be just a** ~ **in the machine** (od. **wheel**) fig. nur ein Rädchen im Getriebe sein.

co·gent ['kəʊdʒənt] adj ☐ zwingend, überzeugend (Gründe etc).

cogged [kɒgd] adj ⚙ gezahnt.

cog·i·tate ['kɒdʒɪteɪt] I v/t nachdenken über (acc). II v/i (nach)denken: ~ **on** (od. **about**) → I.

cog·nate ['kɒgneɪt] adj **1.** (bluts)verwandt (**with** mit). **2.** fig. (art)verwandt (**with** mit).

cog·ni·tion [kɒg'nɪʃn] s Erkenntnis f.

cog·ni·zance ['kɒgnɪzəns] s **1.** Kenntnis f: **have** (**take**) ~ **of s.th.** von et. Kenntnis haben (nehmen). **2.** ⚖ Zuständigkeit f: **have** ~ **over** zuständig sein für (a. weitS.). '**cog·ni·zant** adj unterrichtet (**of** über acc od. von): **be** ~ **of s.th.** a. von et. Kenntnis haben.

cog·no·men [kɒg'nəʊmen] pl **-mens, -nom·i·na** [~'nɒmɪnə] s **1.** Familien-, Zuname m. **2.** Spitz-, Beiname m.
'**cog-wheel** s ⚙ Zahnrad n.

co·hab·it [kəʊ'hæbɪt] v/i (unverheiratet) zs.-leben. ˌco·hab·i'ta·tion s Zs.-leben n.

co·here [kəʊ'hɪə] v/i zs.-hängen (a. fig.). **co'her·ence, co'her·en·cy** s **1.** Zs.-halt m (a. fig.). **2.** phys. Kohärenz f. **3.** fig. Zs.-hang m. **co'her·ent** adj **1.** zs.-hängend (a. fig.). **2.** phys. kohärent.

co·he·sion [kəʊ'hi:ʒn] s **1.** Zs.-halt m (a. fig.). **2.** phys. Kohäsion f. **co'he·sive** adj ☐ **1.** (fest) zs.-haltend (a. fig.). **2.** phys. Kohäsions..., Binde-...

coil [kɔɪl] I v/t **1.** a. ~ **up** aufrollen, (auf)wickeln. **2.** ⚡ wickeln. II v/i **3.** a. ~ **up** sich zs.-rollen. III s **4.** Spirale f (a.⚙ u. ♂). **5.** Rolle f, Spule f.

coin [kɔɪn] I s Münze f: **pay s.o. back in his own** (od. **in the same**) ~ fig. es j-m mit od. in gleicher Münze heimzahlen; **the other side of the** ~ fig. die Kehrseite der Medaille. II v/t Münzen, fig. Wort etc prägen: ~ **money** F Geld wie Heu verdienen. '**coin·age** s **1.** Prägen n. **2.** coll. Münzen pl. **3.** fig. Prägung f (e-s Worts etc); Neuprägung f (Wort etc).

'**coin-box tel·e·phone** s Münzfernsprecher m.

co·in·cide [ˌkəʊɪn'saɪd] v/i **1.** örtlich od. zeitlich zs.-treffen, -fallen (**with** mit). **2.**

übereinstimmen, sich decken (**with** mit). **co'in·ci·dence** [~sɪdəns] s **1.** Zs.-treffen n, -fallen n. **2.** zufälliges Zs.-treffen, Zufall m: **by mere** ~ rein zufällig. **co'in·ci·dent** adj □ **1.** zs.-fallend, -treffend. **2.** übereinstimmend, sich deckend. **co,in·ci'den·tal** adj □ **1.** → **coincident** 2. **2.** zufällig.

coin|-op [ˈkɔɪnɒp] s F **1.** Waschsalon m. **2.** Münztankstelle f. '**~-,op·er·at·ed** adj mit Münzbetrieb, Münz...

coke¹ [kəʊk] **I** s Koks m. **II** v/t u. v/i verkoken.

coke² [~] s sl. Koks m (Kokain).

co·la [ˈkəʊlə] v/on **colon¹**.

cold [kəʊld] **I** adj □ **1.** kalt: (**as**) ~ **as ice** eiskalt; **I feel** (od. **am**) ~ mir ist kalt, ich friere; **in** ~ **blood** kaltblütig; ~ **snap** Kälteeinbruch m; **get** ~ **feet** F kalte Füße (Angst) bekommen; → **shoulder** 1, **sweat, water** 1. **2.** fig. kalt, kühl: a) frostig, unfreundlich (Empfang etc), b) nüchtern, sachlich: **the** ~ **facts** die nackten Tatsachen, c) ruhig, gelassen: **it left me** ~ es ließ mich kalt. **3.** (gefühls)kalt, frigid. **II** s **4.** Kälte f: **be left out in the** ~ fig. kaltgestellt sein, ignoriert werden. **5.** # Erkältung f: (**common**) ~, ~ (**in the head**) Schnupfen m; → **catch** 9. ,~-'**blood·ed** adj □ **1.** zo. kaltblütig (a. fig.). **2.** F kälteempfindlich: **be** ~ a. leicht frieren. ,~-'**heart·ed** adj □ kalt-, hartherzig.

cold·ish [ˈkəʊldɪʃ] adj ziemlich kalt. '**cold·ness** s Kälte f (a. fig.).

cold| room s Kühlraum m. ,~-'**shoul·der** v/t F j-m die kalte Schulter zeigen, j-n kühl od. abweisend behandeln. ~ **stor·age** s Kühlraumlagerung f: **put into** ~ fig. auf Eis legen. ~ **tur·key** s sl. radikale Entziehungskur: **go** ~ e-e radikale Entziehungskur machen. ~ **war** s pol. kalter Krieg. ~ **wave** s **1.** meteor. Kältewelle f. **2.** Kaltwelle f (Frisur).

cole·slaw [ˈkəʊlslɔː] s Krautsalat m.

col·ic [ˈkɒlɪk] s # Kolik f.

col·lab·o·rate [kəˈlæbəreɪt] v/i **1.** zs.-arbeiten (**with** mit; **in, on** bei), mitarbeiten. **2.** pol. kollaborieren. **col,lab·o'ra·tion** s **1.** Zs.-arbeit f: **in** ~ **with** gemeinsam mit. **2.** pol. Kollaboration f. **col'lab·o·ra·tor** s **1.** Mitar-

beiter(in). **2.** pol. Kollaborateur m.

col·lage [kɒˈlɑːʒ] s Kunst: Collage f.

col·lapse [kəˈlæps] **I** v/i **1.** zs.-brechen, -stürzen. **2.** fig. zs.-brechen, scheitern. **3.** moralisch od. physisch zs.-brechen. **4.** # e-n Kollaps erleiden. **5.** zs.-legbar sein, sich zs.-klappen lassen. **II** v/t **6.** zum Einsturz bringen. **7.** zs.-legen, -klappen. **III** s **8.** Einsturz m. **9.** fig. Zs.-bruch m. **10.** # Kollaps m: **nervous** ~ Nervenzusammenbruch m. **col'laps·i·ble** adj zs.-klappbar, Klapp...: → **chair**.

col·lar [ˈkɒlə] s **1.** Kragen m. **2.** (Hundeetc)Halsband n. **3.** Hals-, Amts-, Ordenskette f. **4.** Kollier n: ~ **of pearls** Perlenkollier. **II** v/t **5.** j-n beim Kragen packen. **6.** F j-n schnappen, verhaften, festnehmen; sich et. schnappen; sich et. unter den Nagel reißen. '~**bone** s anat. Schlüsselbein n.

col·lat·er·al [kɒˈlætərəl] adj □ **1.** seitlich, Seiten... **2.** parallel (laufend). **3.** begleitend, Neben...: ~ **circumstances** pl Begleit-, Nebenumstände pl.

col·league [ˈkɒliːg] s Kollege m, Kollegin f.

col·lect [kəˈlekt] **I** v/t **1.** Briefmarken etc sammeln. **2.** (ein)sammeln. **3.** auflesen, -sammeln. **4.** Fakten etc sammeln, zs.-tragen. **5.** j-n, et. abholen. **6.** Geld etc (ein)kassieren. **7.** Gedanken etc sammeln: ~ **o.s.** sich sammeln od. fassen. **8.** versammeln. **II** v/i **9.** sich (ver)sammeln. **10.** sich ansammeln. **III** adj **11.** Am. Nachnahme...: ~ **call** teleph. R-Gespräch n. **IV** adv **12.** a. ~ **on delivery** Am. per Nachnahme: **call** ~ teleph. ein R-Gespräch führen. **col'lect·ed** adj □ **1.** gesammelt: ~ **works.** **2.** fig. gefaßt. **col'lec·tion** s **1.** (Ein)Sammeln n. **2.** (Briefmarkenetc)Sammlung f. **3.** Kollekte f, (Geld-)Sammlung f. **4.** † Inkasso n. **5.** † (Muster)Kollektion f. **6.** Abholung f. **7.** fig. Fassung f, Gefaßtheit f. **col'lec·tive** adj **1.** gesammelt, zs.-gefaßt. **2.** kollektiv: ~ **agreement** † Tarifabkommen n; ~ **bargaining** † Tarifverhandlungen pl; ~ **noun** Sammelbegriff m. **col'lec·tive·ly** adv gemeinsam, gemeinschaftlich. **col'lec·tor** s **1.** Sammler(in): ~'s **item** Sammlerstück n. **2.** Kassierer m. **3.** ⚡ Stromabnehmer m.

col·lege ['kɒlɪdʒ] s **1.** College n: ~ **of education** Br. pädagogische Hochschule. **2.** Akademie f. **3.** Kollegium n (a. eccl.). **col·le·gi·ate** [kə'liːdʒɪət] adj College..., akademisch: ~ **dictionary** Schulwörterbuch n.

col·lide [kə'laɪd] v/i (**with**) kollidieren (mit): a) zs.-stoßen (mit) (a. fig.), b) fig. im Widerspruch stehen (zu).

col·lie ['kɒlɪ] s zo. Collie m (langhaariger schottischer Schäferhund).

col·li·sion [kə'lɪʒn] s **1.** Kollision f, Zs.-stoß m (beide a. fig.): be **on a** ~ **course** auf Kollisionskurs sein. **2.** fig. Widerspruch m: **bring s.o. into** ~ **with the law** j-n mit dem Gesetz in Konflikt bringen.

col·lo·qui·al [kə'ləʊkwɪəl] adj □ umgangssprachlich: ~ **English** Umgangsenglisch n. **col'lo·qui·al·ism** s Ausdruck m der Umgangssprache.

col·lu·sion [kə'luːʒn] s ♣ **1.** geheimes Einverständnis n. **2.** Verdunk(e)lung f: **risk** (od. **danger**) **of** ~ Verdunklungsgefahr f.

col·ly·wob·bles ['kɒlɪ,wɒblz] s pl (a. sg konstruiert): **have the** ~ F ein flaues Gefühl in der Magengegend haben.

co·lon¹ ['kəʊlən] pl **-lons, -la** [~lə] s anat. Dickdarm m.

co·lon² [~] s ling. Doppelpunkt m.

colo·nel ['kɜːnl] s ✕ Oberst m.

co·lo·ni·al [kə'ləʊnjəl] adj □ kolonial, Kolonial...: ~ **masters** pl Kolonialherren pl. **co'lo·ni·al·ism** s pol. Kolonialismus m. **co·lo·nist** ['kɒlənɪst] s Kolonist(in), (An)Siedler(in). **col·o·ni·za·tion** [,kɒlənaɪ'zeɪʃn] s Kolonisation f, Besiedlung f. **'col·o·nize** I v/t **1.** kolonisieren, besiedeln. **2.** ansiedeln. II v/i **3.** sich ansiedeln. **4.** e-e Kolonie bilden.

col·on·nade [,kɒlə'neɪd] s △ Säulengang m, Kolonnade f.

col·o·ny ['kɒlənɪ] s (a. Ausländer-, Künstler- etc)Kolonie f.

col·or, etc Am. → **colour**, etc.

Col·o·ra·do bee·tle [,kɒlə'rɑːdəʊ] s zo. Kartoffelkäfer m.

co·los·sal [kə'lɒsl] adj □ kolossal, riesig, Riesen... (alle a. fig. F).

co·los·sus [~səs] pl **-si** [~saɪ], **-sus·es** s Koloß m.

col·our ['kʌlə] bsd. Br. I s **1.** Farbe f: **what** ~ **is ...?** welche Farbe hat ...?; **to** **paint in bright** (**glowing, gloomy**) **~s** et. in rosigen (glühenden, düsteren) Farben schildern; **local** ~ fig. Lokalkolorit m. **2.** (a. gesunde) Gesichtsfarbe f: **lose** (**all**) ~ (ganz) blaß werden. **3.** (bsd. dunkle) Hautfarbe: **people** pl **of** ~ Farbige pl. **4.** fig. Färbung f, Ton m. **5.** pl ✕ Fahne f: **call to the** ~**s** einberufen; **pass** (**fail**) **an examination with flying** ~**s** e-e Prüfung mit Glanz u. Gloria bestehen (mit Pauken u. Trompeten durch e-e Prüfung fallen). **6.** pl ♣ Flagge f: **sail under false** ~**s** unter falscher Flagge segeln (a. fig.); **show one's true** ~**s** fig. sein wahres Gesicht zeigen; Farbe bekennen. II v/t **7.** färben (a. fig.), kolorieren. III v/i **8.** sich (ver)färben. **9.** a. ~ **up** erröten, rot werden (**with** vor dat). ~**bar** s Rassenschranke f. '~**-blind** adj ❀ farbenblind.

col·oured ['kʌləd] adj bsd. Br. **1.** farbig, bunt (beide a. fig.): ~ **pencil** Bunt-, Farbstift m. **2.** farbig: **a** ~ **man** ein Farbiger. **3.** fig. gefärbt.

col·our|·fast adj bsd. Br. farbecht. ~ **film** s phot. Farbfilm m.

col·our·ful ['kʌləfʊl] adj □ bsd. Br. **1.** farbenfreudig, -prächtig. **2.** fig. farbig, bunt. '**col·our·ing I** s **1.** Färbung f (a. fig.), Farbgebung f. **2.** Gesichtsfarbe f. **II** adj **3.** Farb...: ~ **matter** Farbstoff m; ~ **book** Malbuch n.

'**col·our·in,ten·sive** adj □ bsd. Br. farbintensiv.

col·our·less ['kʌləlɪs] adj □ bsd. Br. **1.** farblos (a. fig.). **2.** fig. neutral, unparteiisch.

col·our| line s bsd. Br. Rassenschranke f. ~ **or·gan** s Lichtorgel f. ~ **prob·lem** s Rassenproblem n. ~ **set** s Farbfernseher m. ~ **sup·ple·ment** s Farbbeilage f (e-r Zeitung). ~ **tel·e·vi·sion** s Farbfernsehen n.

colt [kəʊlt] s **1.** Fohlen n. **2.** fig. Grünschnabel m.

col·umn ['kɒləm] s **1.** △ (a. Rauch-, Wasser- etc)Säule f. **2.** typ. Spalte f: **in double** ~**s** zweispaltig. **3.** Zeitung: Kolumne f. **4.** ♣, ✕ Kolonne f. **co·lum·nar** [kə'lʌmnə] adj **1.** säulenartig, -förmig. **2.** säulenartig. **col·um·nist** ['kɒləmnɪst] s Kolumnist(in).

co·ma ['kəʊmə] s ❀ Koma n: **be in a** ~ im Koma liegen.

comb [kəʊm] **I** s **1.** Kamm m (a. des Hahns, e-r Welle etc). **II** v/t **2.** kämmen: **~ one's hair** (od. **o.s.**) sich kämmen. **3.** fig. Gegend durchkämmen. **4.** mst **~ out** fig. sieben, sichten; aussondern, -suchen.

com·bat ['kɒmbæt] **I** v/t bekämpfen, kämpfen gegen (beide a. fig.). **II** v/i kämpfen (**with** mit) (a. fig.). **III** s Kampf m, ✕ a. Gefecht n. **IV** adj Kampf...

com·bi·na·tion [ˌkɒmbɪˈneɪʃn] s **1.** Verbindung f (a. 🐝), Kombination f: **~ lock** Kombinationsschloß n. **2.** 🐝 Konzern m; Kartell n, Ring m. **3.** Zs.-schluß m, Bündnis n. **com·bine** [kəmˈbaɪn] **I** v/t **1.** verbinden (a. 🐝), kombinieren: **business with pleasure** das Nützliche mit dem Angenehmen verbinden. **2.** in sich vereinigen. **II** v/i **3.** sich verbinden (a. 🐝). **4.** zs.-wirken: **everything ~d against him** alles verschwor sich gegen ihn. **III** s ['kɒmbaɪn] **5.** Verbindung f. **6.** pol. Interessengemeinschaft f; 🐝 a. Verband m; Konzern m; Kartell n. **com·bined** [kəm~] adj gemeinsam, gemeinschaftlich.

com·bus·ti·ble [kəmˈbʌstəbl] **I** adj □ **1.** brennbar, (leicht)entzündlich. **2.** fig. leichterregbar. **II** s **3.** Brennstoff m, -material n. **com·bus·tion** [~ˈbʌstʃən] s Verbrennung f (a. biol., 🐝): **~ engine** ⚙ Verbrennungsmotor m.

come [kʌm] **I** v/i (irr) **1.** kommen (a. sl. e-n Orgasmus haben): **s.o. is coming** es kommt j-d; **he came to see us** er besuchte uns. **2.** (dran)kommen, an die Reihe kommen. **3.** kommen, erscheinen: **~ and go** kommen u. gehen; erscheinen u. verschwinden. **4.** kommen, gelangen (**to** zu). **5.** kommen, abstammen (**of, from** von). **6.** kommen, herrühren (**of** von). **7.** kommen, geschehen, sich ereignen: **~ what may** (od. **will**) komme, was da wolle; **how ~s it that ...?**, F **how ~ that ...?** wie kommt es, daß ...? **8.** sich erweisen: **it ~s expensive** es kommt teuer. **9.** vor inf: dahin od. dazu kommen: **~ to know s.o.** j-n kennenlernen; **~ to know s.th.** et. erfahren; **I have ~ to believe that** ich bin zu der Überzeugung gekommen, daß. **10.** bsd. vor adj: werden: **~ true** sich bewahrheiten od. erfüllen, eintreffen. **11.** **to ~** (als adj) zukünftig, kommend: **for**

all time to ~ für alle Zukunft. **II** v/t (irr) **12.** F sich aufspielen als, j-n, et. spielen. **III** int **13.** na!, komm!: **~, ~!** nicht so wild!, immer langsam!; na komm schon!, auf geht's!

Verbindungen mit Präpositionen:

come| a·cross v/i zufällig treffen od. finden od. sehen, stoßen auf (acc). **~ at** v/i. erreichen, bekommen, Wahrheit etc herausfinden. **2.** losgehen auf (acc). **~ for** v/i **1.** et. abholen kommen, kommen wegen. **2.** losgehen auf (acc). **~ in·to** v/i **1.** kommen in (acc). **2. ~ a fortune** ein Vermögen erben; → **fashion** 1, **own** 5, **use** 5. **~ near** v/i **1.** fig. nahekommen (dat). **2. ~ doing s.th.** et. beinahe tun. **~ off** v/i **1.** herunterfallen von. **2. ~ it!** F hör schon auf damit! **~ on** → **come upon**. **~ over** v/i überkommen, befallen: **what has ~ you?** was ist mit dir los? **~ through** v/i Krankheit etc überstehen, -leben. **~ to** v/i **1.** j-m (bsd. durch Erbschaft) zufallen. **2. when it comes to paying** wenn es ans Bezahlen geht. **3.** sich belaufen auf (acc). **~ un·der** v/i **1.** unter ein Gesetz etc fallen. **2.** geraten unter (acc). **~ up·on** v/i **1.** → **come over.** **2.** → **come across.**

Verbindungen mit Adverbien:

come| a·bout v/i geschehen, passieren. **~ a·cross** v/i **1.** herüberkommen. **2.** verstanden werden; an-, rüberkommen (Rede etc). **3.** F damit herausrücken: **~ with** mit Informationen herausrücken; Geld herausrücken. **~ a·long** v/i **1.** mitkommen, -gehen: **~!** F dalli! **2.** kommen, sich ergeben (Chance etc). **~ a·part** v/i auseinanderfallen. **~ a·way** v/i sich lösen, - losgehen (Knopf etc). **~ back** v/i **1.** zurückkommen: **~ to s.th.** auf e-e Sache zurückkommen; **it came back to him** es fiel ihm wieder ein. **2.** wieder in Mode kommen. **3.** ein Come-back feiern. **~ by** v/i vorbeikommen (Besucher). **~ down** v/i **1.** herunterkommen, (Regen, Schnee) fallen. **2.** (ein)stürzen, (ein)fallen. **3.** fig. herunterkommen (Person): **she has ~ quite a bit** sie ist ganz schön tief gesunken. **4.** überliefert werden. **5.** F sinken (Preise); billiger werden (Ware). **6. ~ on** sich stürzen auf (acc); j-m aufs Dach steigen. **7. ~ with** F Geld herausrücken. **8. ~ with** erkranken an (dat). **9. ~ to** hinauslaufen auf (*acc*). **~ for·ward** *v/i* sich (freiwillig) melden, sich anbieten. **~ home** *v/i* **1.** nach Hause kommen, heimkommen. **2. ~ to s.o.** j-m schmerzlich bewußt werden. **~ in** *v/i* **1.** hereinkommen; **~!** herein!; (*Funk*) (bitte) kommen! **2.** eingehen, -treffen (*Nachricht etc*), *Sport*, ⚓ einkommen, 🚂 einlaufen: **~ second** den zweiten Platz belegen. **3.** aufkommen, in Mode kommen. **4.** an die Macht kommen. **5.** sich als *nützlich etc* erweisen: → **handy** 4. **6.** Berücksichtigung finden: **where do I ~?** wo bleibe ich? **7. ~ for** Bewunderung *etc* erregen, auf *Kritik etc* stoßen. **8. ~ on** mitmachen bei, sich beteiligen an (*dat*). **~ off** *v/i* **1.** → **come away. 2.** herunterfallen. **3.** auslaufen (*Stück*), enden (*Ausstellung*). **4.** F stattfinden, über die Bühne gehen. **5.** F abschneiden; erfolgreich verlaufen, glücken. **~ on** *v/i* **1.** herankommen: **~!** komm (mit)!; komm her!; los!; F na, na! **2.** an die Reihe kommen. **3.** *thea.* auftreten; aufgeführt werden. **~ out** *v/i* **1.** herauskommen. **2.** *a.* **~ on strike** *bsd. Br.* streiken. **3.** herauskommen: a) erscheinen (*Buch etc*), b) an den Tag kommen (*Wahrheit etc*). **4.** ausgehen (*Haare, Farbe*), herausgehen (*Fleck etc*). **5.** ausbrechen (*Ausschlag*): **~ in a rash** e-n Ausschlag bekommen. **6.** *phot. etc* gut *etc* werden (*Bild*); gut *etc* herauskommen (*in auf dat*). **7. ~ with** F mit *der Wahrheit etc* herausrücken; *Flüche etc* vom Stapel lassen. **8. ~ against** (*for*) sich aussprechen gegen (für). **~ o·ver** → **come across** 1, 2. **~ round** *v/i* **1.** vorbeikommen (**to** bei). **2.** wieder zu sich kommen; sich erholen. **~ through** *v/i* durchkommen (*Funkspruch, Patient etc*). **~ to** → **come round** 2. **~ up** *v/i* **1.** heraufkommen. **2.** herankommen: **~ to s.o.** auf j-n zukommen. **3.** ⚖️ zur Verhandlung kommen. **4.** *a.* **~ for dis·cussion** zur Sprache kommen. **5. ~ for** zur *Abstimmung, Entscheidung* kommen. **6.** aufkommen, Mode werden. **7. ~ to** reichen bis an (*acc*) od. zu; erreichen (*acc*); *fig.* heranreichen an (*acc*): → **expectation. 8. his supper came up again** das Abendessen kam ihm wieder hoch. **9. ~ with** daherkommen mit, auftischen, präsentieren.

come|-at-a·ble [ˌkʌmˈætəbl] *adj* F erreichbar, zugänglich. **'~back** *s* Comeback *n*: **stage** (*od.* **make**) **a ~** ein Comeback feiern.

co·me·di·an [kəˈmiːdjən] *s* **1.** Komödienschauspieler *m*; Komiker *m* (*a. contp.*). **2.** Spaßvogel *m*, Witzbold *m* (*beide a. contp.*).

'come-down *s fig.* **1.** Niedergang *m*, Abstieg *m*. **2.** F Enttäuschung *f*.

com·e·dy [ˈkɒmədɪ] *s* **1.** Komödie *f* (*a. fig.*), Lustspiel *n*. **2.** Komik *f*.

come·ly [ˈkʌmlɪ] *adj* attraktiv, schön.

com·er [ˈkʌmə] *s* Ankömmling *m*.

com·et [ˈkɒmɪt] *s ast.* Komet *m*.

com·fort [ˈkʌmfət] **I** *v/t* **1.** trösten. **2.** beruhigen. **II** *s* **3.** Trost *m*: **cold ~** ein schwacher Trost. **4.** Behaglichkeit *f*: **to live in ~** sorgenfrei leben. **5.** *a. pl* Komfort *m*: **with every modern ~** (*od. all modern ~s*) mit allem Komfort; **~ sta·tion** *Am.* öffentliche Bedürfnisanstalt. **'com·fort·a·ble** *adj* ☐ **1.** komfortabel, bequem, behaglich: **make o.s. ~** es sich bequem machen; **are you ~?** haben Sie es bequem?, sitzen *od.* liegen *etc* Sie bequem?; **feel ~** sich wohl fühlen. **2.** bequem, sorgenfrei (*Leben etc*). **3.** ausreichend, recht gut (*Einkommen etc*): **to be ~** (*od. comfortably off*) einigermaßen wohlhabend sein. **'com·fort·er** *s* **1.** Tröster *m*. **2.** *bsd. Br.* Wollschal *m*. **3.** *Am.* Steppdecke *f*. **4.** *bsd. Br.* Schnuller *m*. **'com·fort·ing** *adj* tröstlich. **'com·fort·less** *adj* **1.** unbequem. **2.** trostlos.

com·fy [ˈkʌmfɪ] *F* → **comfortable** 1.

com·ic [ˈkɒmɪk] **I** *adj* (**~ally**) **1.** Komödien..., Lustspiel...: **~ actor** Komödienschauspieler *m*; Komiker *m*; **~ opera** ♪ komische Oper; **~ tragedy** Tragikomödie *f* (*a. fig.*). **2.** komisch, humoristisch: **~ paper** Witzblatt *n*; **~ strips** *pl* Comics *pl*. **3.** → **comical** 1. **II** *s* **4.** → **comedian** 1. **5.** F Witzblatt *n*: **~s** *pl* Comics *pl*. **'com·i·cal** *adj* ☐ **1.** komisch, ulkig, spaßig. **2.** F komisch, sonderbar.

com·ing [ˈkʌmɪŋ] **I** *adj* kommend: a) zukünftig: **the ~ man** der kommende Mann, b) nächst: **~ week** nächste Woche. **II** *s* Kommen *n*, Ankunft *f*: **the ~s and goings** das Kommen u. Gehen.

com·ma [ˈkɒmə] *s* Komma *n*, Beistrich *m*.

com·mand [kəˈmɑːnd] **I** *v/t* **1.** befehlen

commit

(*s.o. to do* j-m zu tun). **2.** fordern, verlangen: **~ silence** sich Ruhe erbitten. **3.** ✕ kommandieren, befehligen. **4.** *Gefühle, Lage etc* beherrschen. **5.** *Vertrauen etc* einflößen: **~ (s.o.'s) admiration** (j-m) Bewunderung abnötigen; **~ respect** Achtung gebieten. **6.** zur Verfügung haben, verfügen über (*acc*). **II** *v/i* **7.** befehlen. **8.** ✕ das Kommando führen, den Befehl haben. **III** *s* **9.** Befehl *m*: **at s.o.'s ~** auf j-s Befehl. **10.** Verfügung *f*: **be at s.o.'s ~** j-m zur Verfügung stehen; **have at ~** → 6. **11.** Beherrschung *f* (*e-r Sprache etc*): **have ~ of** *Fremdsprache etc* beherrschen; **his ~ of English** s-e Englischkenntnisse *pl.* **12.** ✕ Kommando *n*: a) (Ober)Befehl *m*: **be in ~** → 8; **~ module** (*Raumfahrt*) Kommandokapsel *f*, b) Befehl *m*. **com·man·dant** [ˌkɒmənˈdænt] *s* ✕ Kommandant *m*. **com·mand·er** [kəˈmɑːndə] *s* ✕ Kommandeur *m*, Befehlshaber *m*; Kommandant *m*: **~ in chief** Oberbefehlshaber *m*. **com'mand·ing** *adj* □ **1.** ✕ kommandierend, befehlshabend. **2.** herrisch, gebieterisch. **3.** *die Gegend beherrschend.* **4.** weit (*Aussicht*). **com'mand·ment** *s* Gebot *n*, Vorschrift *f*: **the Ten ⁊s** *Bibl.* die Zehn Gebote. **com'man·do** [ˌ~dəʊ] *pl* **-do(e)s** ✕ Kommando *n*: **~ squad** Kommandotrupp *m*.

com·mem·o·rate [kəˈmeməreɪt] *v/t* **1.** erinnern an (*acc*). **2.** (ehrend) gedenken (*gen*). **com·mem·o'ra·tion** *s* Gedenk-, Gedächtnisfeier *f*: **in ~ of** zum Gedenken *od.* Gedächtnis an (*acc*). **com'mem·o·ra·tive** [ˌ~rətɪv] *adj* **1.** **be ~ of** erinnern an (*acc*). **2.** Gedenk..., Gedächtnis..., Erinnerungs...: **~ issue** Gedenkausgabe *f* (*Briefmarken etc*); **~ plaque** Gedenktafel *f*.

com·mence [kəˈmens] *v/i* u. *v/t* anfangen, beginnen (**to do, doing** zu tun). **com'mence·ment** *s·* Anfang *m*, Beginn *m*.

com·mend [kəˈmend] *v/t* **1.** empfehlen. **2.** loben (**on** wegen). **3.** anvertrauen (**to** *dat*). **com'mend·a·ble** *adj* □ **1.** empfehlenswert. **2.** lobenswert, löblich. **com·men·da·tion** [ˌkɒmenˈdeɪʃn] *s* **1.** Empfehlung *f*. **2.** Lob *n*. **com'men·da·to·ry** [ˌ~dətərɪ] *adj* **1.** Empfehlungs...: **~ letter** Empfehlungsbrief *m*,

-schreiben *n*. **2.** lobend, anerkennend. **com·men·su·ra·ble** [kəˈmenʃərəbl] *adj* □ vergleichbar (**to, with** mit). **com'men·su·rate** [ˌ~rət] *adj* (**to, with** im Einklang stehend (mit), entsprechend *od.* angemessen (*dat*). **com·ment** [ˈkɒment] **I** *s* (**on**) Kommentar *m* (zu): a) Bemerkung *f* (zu): **no ~!** kein Kommentar!, b) Anmerkung *f* (zu). **II** *v/i*: **~ on** e-n Kommentar abgeben zu, *et.* kommentieren. **III** *v/t* bemerken (**that** daß). **com·men·ta·tor** [ˈ~mənteɪtə] *s* Kommentator *m*.

com·merce [ˈkɒmɜːs] *s* Handel *m*. **com·mer·cial** [kəˈmɜːʃl] **I** *adj* □ **1.** Geschäfts..., Handels...: **~ attaché** Handelsattaché *m*; **~ correspondence** Geschäfts-, Handelskorrespondenz *f*; **~ letter** Geschäftsbrief *m*; **~ travel(l)er** Handlungsreisende *m*. **2.** handelsüblich (*Qualität etc*). **3.** *Rundfunk, TV:* Werbe..., Reklame...: **~ broadcasting** Werbefunk *m*; kommerzieller Rundfunk; **~ television** Werbefernsehen *n*; kommerzielles Fernsehen. **4.** kommerziell: a) auf finanziellen Gewinn abzielend, b) finanziell. **II** *s* **5.** *Rundfunk, TV:* Werbespot *m*; von e-m Sponsor finanzierte Sendung. **com'mer·cial·ize** [ˌ~ʃəlaɪz] *v/t* kommerzialisieren, vermarkten.

com·mie [ˈkɒmɪ] *s* F Kommunist(in). **com·mis·er·ate** [kəˈmɪzəreɪt] *v/t* u. *v/i* (**with**) bemitleiden. **com·mis·er'a·tion** *s* Mitleid *n*.

com·mis·sion [kəˈmɪʃn] **I** *s* **1.** Auftrag *m*. **2.** Kommission *f*, Ausschuß *m*: **be on the ~** Mitglied der Kommission sein. **3.** ✝ a) Kommission *f*: **on ~** in Kommission, b) Provision *f*: **on ~** gegen Provision; **on a ~ basis** auf Provisionsbasis. **4.** Begehung *f*, Verübung *f* (*e-s Verbrechens etc*). **II** *v/t* **5.** beauftragen. **6.** *et.* in Auftrag geben: **~ed work** Auftragsarbeit *f*. **com·mis·sion·aire** [kəˌmɪʃəˈneə] *s bsd. Br.* (livrierter) Portier (*Theater, Hotel etc*). **com'mis·sion·er** [ˌ~ʃnə] *s* Beauftragte *m*.

com·mit [kəˈmɪt] *v/t* **1.** anvertrauen, übergeben (**to** *dat*): **~ to paper** zu Papier bringen. **2.** ✝✝ einweisen (**to** in *acc*). **3.** *Verbrechen etc* begehen, verüben. **4.** (**to**) verpflichten (zu), festlegen (auf *acc*): **~ted** engagiert (*Schriftsteller etc*).

com·mit·ment [~] s 1. Übergabe f. 2. → **committal** 2. 3. Begehung f, Verübung f. 4. Verpflichtung f, Festlegung f, (a. politisches etc) Engagement: **without any ~** ganz unverbindlich. **com'mit·tal** [~tl] s 1. → **commitment** 1, 3, 4. 2. ⚖️ Einweisung f. **com'mit·tee** [~tɪ] s Komitee n, Ausschuß m: **be** (od. **sit**) **on a ~** in e-m Ausschuß sein.

com·mode [kə'məʊd] s (Wasch)Kommode f. **com'mo·di·ous** [~djəs] adj □ geräumig.

com·mod·i·ty [kə'mɒdətɪ] s ⭢ Ware f, (Handels)Artikel m. **~ ex·change** s Warenbörse f.

com·mo·dore ['kɒmədɔː] s ⚓ Kommodore m.

com·mon ['kɒmən] I adj (□ → **commonly**) 1. gemeinsam (a. Ⓐ), gemeinschaftlich: **~ to all** allen gemeinsam; **~ room** Gemeinschaftsraum m; → **cause** 3, **denominator**. 2. allgemein: **by ~ consent** mit allgemeiner Zustimmung. 3. allgemein (bekannt), alltäglich: **it is ~ knowledge** (**usage**) es ist allgemein bekannt (üblich); **~ name** häufiger Name; **~ sight** alltäglicher od. vertrauter Anblick. 4. bsd. biol. gemein: **~ or garden** F Feld-Wald-u.-Wiesen-...; → **cold** 5. 5. gewöhnlich, ohne Rang: the **~ people** pl das einfache Volk; **~ soldier** einfacher Soldat. II s 6. Gemeinsamkeit f: **in ~** gemeinsam (**with** mit). 7. das Gewöhnliche: **out of the ~** außergewöhnlich, -ordentlich. 8. → **commons**. '**com·mon·er** s Bürger(liche) m.

com·mon law s 1. Br. Gewohnheitsrecht n. 2. das anglo-amerikanische Rechtssystem.

com·mon·ly ['kɒmənlɪ] adv gewöhnlich, im allgemeinen.

Com·mon| Mar·ket s Gemeinsamer Markt. '**~·place** I s 1. Gemeinplatz m. 2. alltägliche Sache. II adj 3. alltäglich, abgedroschen. **~ Prayer** s eccl. anglikanische Liturgie.

com·mons ['kɒmənz] s pl 1. the ♌ parl. Br. das Unterhaus. 2. **be kept on small ~** auf schmale Kost gesetzt sein.

com·mon| sense s gesunder Menschenverstand. '**~·wealth** s: the ♌ (**of Nations**) das Commonwealth.

com·mo·tion [kə'məʊʃn] s 1. Aufregung f. 2. Aufruhr m, Tumult m.

com·mu·nal ['kɒmjʊnl] adj □ 1. Gemeinde..., Kommunal... 2. gemeinschaftlich: **~ aerial** (bsd. Am. **antenna**) TV Gemeinschaftsantenne f.

com·mune¹ [kə'mjuːn] v/i 1. sich (vertraulich) unterhalten (**with** mit): **~ with o.s.** mit sich zu Rate gehen. 2. bsd. Am. → **communicate** 6.

com·mune² ['kɒmjuːn] s Gemeinde f, Kommune f (a. sociol.).

com·mu·ni·ca·ble [kə'mjuːnɪkəbl] adj □ 1. mitteilbar. 2. ⚕️ übertragbar. **com·'mu·ni·cate** [~keɪt] I v/t 1. mitteilen (**to** dat). 2. ⚕️, phys. übertragen (**to** auf acc) (a. fig.). II v/i 3. kommunizieren, sich besprechen, in Verbindung stehen (**with** mit). 4. sich in Verbindung setzen (**with** mit). 5. miteinander (durch e-e Tür etc) verbunden sein: **communicating door** Verbindungstür f. 6. eccl. das Abendmahl empfangen, kommunizieren. **com·mu·ni·ca·tion** s 1. Mitteilung f (**to** an acc): **~ cord** 🚂 Br. Notbremse f. 2. Übertragung f: **~ of power** phys. Kraftübertragung f. 3. Verbindung f: **be in ~ with** in Verbindung stehen mit. 4. pl Ⓜ 🛰 Fernmeldewesen n: **~s satellite** 🛰 Nachrichtensatellit m; **~ system** Fernmeldenetz n. **com·'mu·ni·ca·tive** [~kətɪv] adj □ mitteilsam, gesprächig, kommunikativ.

com·mun·ion [kə'mjuːnjən] s 1. (eccl. Religions)Gemeinschaft f. 2. eccl. Abendmahl n, Kommunion f: **go to ~** zum Abendmahl gehen; **~ cup** Abendmahlskelch m.

com·mu·ni·qué [kə'mjuːnɪkeɪ] s Kommuniqué n.

com·mu·nism ['kɒmjʊnɪzəm] s Kommunismus m. '**com·mu·nist** I s Kommunist(in). II adj kommunistisch. **,com·mu·'nis·tic** adj (~**ally**) kommunistisch.

com·mu·ni·ty [kə'mjuːnətɪ] s 1. Gemeinschaft f: **~ of heirs** Erbengemeinschaft; **~ singing** gemeinsames Singen; **~ spirit** Gemeinschaftsgeist m. 2. Gemeinde f. 3. Gemeinsamkeit f, gemeinsamer Besitz: **~ of goods** (od. **property**) Gütergemeinschaft f. **~ cen·ter**, bsd. Br. **~ cen·tre** s Gemeinschaftszentrum n. **~ home** s Br. Erziehungsheim n.

com·mut·a·ble [kə'mjuːtəbl] adj umwandelbar. **com·mu·ta·tion** [,kɒmjuː-

'teɪʃn] s **1.** Umwandlung f. **2.** Ablösung f; Ablöse(summe) f. **3.** ⚖️ (Straf)Umwandlung f. **4.** 🚂, etc Pendeln n: ~ **ticket** Am. Dauer-, Zeitkarte f. **com-mute** [kə'mjuːt] **I** v/t **1.** eintauschen (**for** für). **2.** ⚖️ Strafe umwandeln (**to, into** in acc). **3.** Verpflichtung etc umwandeln (**into** in acc), ablösen (**for, into** durch). **II** v/i **4.** 🚂, etc Pendeln. **com'mut·er** s a) Am. Zeitkarteninhaber(in), b) Pendler(in): ~ **train** Pendler-, Nahverkehrszug m.

com·pact [kəm'pækt] **I** adj □ **1.** kompakt: ~ **cassette** Kompaktkassette f. **2.** eng, klein (Wohnung etc). **3.** gedrungen (Gestalt). **4.** knapp, gedrängt (Stil etc). **II** v/t **5.** zs.-drängen, fest miteinander verbinden. **III** s ['kɒmpækt] **6.** kompakte Masse. **7.** Puderdose f. **com-'pact·ness** s **7.** Kompaktheit f. Knappheit f, Gedrängtheit f.

com·pan·ion [kəm'pænjən] s **1.** Begleiter(in) (a. fig.). **2.** Kamerad(in), Genosse m, Genossin f. **3.** Gesellschafterin f. **4.** Gegenstück n, Pendant n. **5.** Handbuch n, Leitfaden m. **com'pan·ion·a·ble** adj □ umgänglich, gesellig. **com'pan·ion·ship** s Begleitung f, Gesellschaft f.

com·pa·ny ['kʌmpəni] s **1.** Gesellschaft f: **in** ~ (**with**) in Gesellschaft od. Begleitung (gen od. von); **be in good** ~ sich in guter Gesellschaft befinden; **keep** (od. **bear**) s.o. ~ j-m Gesellschaft leisten; **part** ~ (**with**) sich trennen (von); fig. anderer Meinung sein (als) (on in dat). **2.** Gesellschaft f, Besuch m, Gäste pl: **be fond of** ~ die Gesellschaft lieben; **present** ~ **excepted!** Anwesende ausgenommen! **3.** Gesellschaft f, Umgang m: **keep good** ~ guten Umgang pflegen; **keep** ~ **with** verkehren mit. **4.** ✝ Gesellschaft f, Firma f: ~ **car** Firmenwagen m; ~ **pension** Betriebsrente f. **5.** ✕ Kompanie f. **6.** thea. Truppe f.

com·pa·ra·ble ['kɒmpərəbl] adj □ vergleichbar (**with, to** mit). **com·par·a·tive** [kəm'pærətɪv] **I** adj **1.** vergleichend. **2.** verhältnismäßig, relativ. **3.** ~ **degree** → **4. II** s **4.** ling. Komparativ m. **com·par·a·tive·ly** adv verhältnismäßig: a) vergleichsweise, b) ziemlich. **com·pare** [~'peə] **I** v/t **1.** vergleichen (**with, to** mit): ~d **with** (od. **to**) im Ver-

gleich zu, gegenüber (dat). **2.** vergleichen, gleichsetzen, -stellen: **not to be** ~d **with** (od. **to**) nicht zu vergleichen mit. **3.** ling. steigern. **II** v/i **4.** sich vergleichen (lassen): ~ **favo(u)rably with** den Vergleich mit ... nicht zu scheuen brauchen. **III** s **5.** **beyond** (od. **past, without**) ~ unvergleichlich. **com·par·i·son** [~'pærɪsn] s **1.** Vergleich m: **by** ~ vergleichsweise; **in** ~ **with** im Vergleich mit od. zu; **bear** (od. **stand**) ~ **with** e-n Vergleich aushalten mit; **without** ~, **beyond** (**all**) ~ unvergleichlich. **2.** ling. Steigerung f.

com·part·ment [kəm'pɑːtmənt] s **1.** Fach n. **2.** 🚂 Abteil n.

com·pass ['kʌmpəs] s **1.** Kompaß m. **2.** pl, a. **pair of** ~**es** Zirkel m.

com·pas·sion [kəm'pæʃn] s Mitleid n, -gefühl n: **have** (od. **take**) ~ **on** (od. **for**) Mitleid mit j-m haben. **com'pas·sion·ate** [~ʃənət] adj □ mitleidsvoll, -fühlend.

com·pat·i·ble [kəm'pætəbl] adj □ **1.** vereinbar (**with** mit), miteinander vereinbar. **2.** verträglich: **be** ~ (**with**) sich vertragen (mit), passen (zu), zs.-passen.

com·pa·tri·ot [kəm'pætrɪət] s Landsmann m, -männin f.

com·pel [kəm'pel] v/t **1.** zwingen: **be** ~**led to do** (od. **into doing**) s.th. gezwungen sein, et. zu tun, et. tun müssen. **2.** et. erzwingen. **3.** a. Bewunderung etc abnötigen (**from** dat).

com·pen·di·um [kəm'pendɪəm] pl **-ums, -a** [~ə] s **1.** Kompendium n, Handbuch n. **2.** Zs.-fassung f, Abriß m.

com·pen·sate ['kɒmpenseɪt] **I** v/t **1.** kompensieren (a. psych.), ausgleichen. **2.** j-n entschädigen (**for** für); et. ersetzen, vergüten, für et. Ersatz leisten (**to** dat). **3.** Am. j-n bezahlen, entlohnen. **II** v/i **4.** Ersatz leisten (**for** für). **5.** ~ **for** → **1.** **com·pen·sa·tion** s **1.** Kompensation f, Ausgleich m: **in** ~ **for** als Ausgleich für. **2.** (Schaden)Ersatz m, Entschädigung f; Vergütung f: **pay** ~ Schadenersatz leisten; **as** (od. **by way of**) ~ als Ersatz. **3.** Am. Bezahlung f, Gehalt n, Lohn m. **4.** psych. Kompensation f, Ersatzhandlung f.

com·père, com·pere ['kɒmpeə] bsd. Br. **I** s Conférencier m, Ansager(in). **II** v/t konferieren, ansagen. **III** v/i konferieren, als Conférencier fungieren.

com·pete [kəm'pi:t] *v/i* **1.** sich (mit)bewerben (*for* um). **2.** ✝ *u. weitS.* konkurrieren (*with* mit). **3.** wetteifern, sich messen (*with* mit). **4.** *Sport:* (am Wettkampf) teilnehmen; *a. weitS.* kämpfen (*for* um; *against* gegen).

com·pe·tence, com·pe·ten·cy ['kɒmpɪtəns(ɪ)] *s* **1.** Fähigkeit *f*, Tüchtigkeit *f*. **2.** ⚖ Zuständigkeit *f*, Kompetenz *f* (*beide a. weitS.*); Zulässigkeit *f*. **'com·petent** *adj* □ **1.** fähig (*to do* zu tun), tüchtig. **2.** fach-, sachkundig. **3.** gut(gemacht), gekonnt. **4.** ⚖ zuständig, kompetent (*beide a. weitS.*); zulässig (*Beweise, Zeuge*).

com·pe·ti·tion [ˌkɒmpɪ'tɪʃn] *s* **1.** *allg.* Wettbewerb *m* (*for* um). **2.** Konkurrenz *f*: a) ✝ Wettbewerb *m*, Konkurrenzkampf *m*: *unfair* ~ unlauterer Wettbewerb, b) ✝ Konkurrenzfirma *f*, -firmen *pl*, c) *weitS.* Gegner *pl*, Rivalen *pl*. **3.** Preisausschreiben *n*. **com·pet·itive** [kəm'petətɪv] *adj* □ **1.** konkurrierend. **2.** Wettbewerbs..., Konkurrenz..., ✝ *a.* konkurrenzfähig. **com·'pet·i·tor** [ˌ~tɪtə] *s* **1.** Mitbewerber(in) (*for* um). **2.** *bsd.* ✝ Konkurrent(in). **3.** *bsd. Sport:* Teilnehmer(in).

com·pi·la·tion [ˌkɒmpɪ'leɪʃn] *s* Kompilation *f* (*a. Werk*). **com·pile** [kəm'paɪl] *v/t* Verzeichnis etc kompilieren, zs.-stellen; *Material* zs.-tragen. **com·'pil·er** *s* Kompilator *m*.

com·pla·cence, com·pla·cen·cy [kəm'pleɪsns(ɪ)] *s* Selbstzufriedenheit *f*, Gefälligkeit *f*. **com·pla·cent** *adj* □ selbstzufrieden, -gefällig.

com·plain [kəm'pleɪn] *v/i* **1.** sich beklagen *od.* beschweren (*of, about* über *acc*; *to* bei): *~ing letter* Beschwerdebrief *m*. **2.** klagen (*of* über *acc*). **3.** ✝ reklamieren: *~ about* et. reklamieren *od.* beanstanden. **com·'plaint** *s* **1.** Klage *f*, Beschwerde *f*: *make* (*od.* lodge) *a* ~ (*about*) → *complain* 1; *~ book* Beschwerdebuch *n*. **2.** ✝ Reklamation *f*, Beanstandung *f*. **3.** ✚ Leiden *n*, *pl a.* Beschwerden *pl*.

com·plai·sance [kəm'pleɪzəns] *s* Gefälligkeit *f*, Entgegenkommen *n*. **com·'plai·sant** *adj* □ gefällig, entgegenkommend.

com·ple·ment I *s* ['kɒmplɪmənt] **1.** (*to*

gen) Ergänzung *f* (*a. ling.*); Vervollkommnung *f*. **2.** Ergänzungsstück *n*. **II** *v/t* ['~ment] **3.** ergänzen *od.* vervollkommnen. **com·ple·men·ta·ry** [ˌ~'mentərɪ] *adj* □ (sich) ergänzend: *be ~ to s.th.* et. ergänzen; *~ colo(u)rs pl* Komplementärfarben *pl*.

com·plete [kəm'pli:t] **I** *adj* □ **1.** komplett, vollständig. **2.** vollzählig, komplett. **3.** beendet, vollendet. **II** *v/t* **4.** vervollständigen. **5.** vollenden, abschließen. **6.** *fig.* vollenden, vollkommen machen. **7.** *Formular* ausfüllen. **com·'plete·ness** *s* Vollständigkeit *f*. **com·'ple·tion** *s* **1.** Vervollständigung *f*. **2.** Vollendung *f*: *bring to* ~ zum Abschluß bringen. **3.** Ausfüllung *f*.

com·plex ['kɒmpleks] **I** *adj* □ **1.** zs.-gesetzt (*a. ling.*). **2.** komplex, vielschichtig. **II** *s* **3.** Komplex *m*, *das* Ganze. **4.** (*Gebäude- etc*)Komplex *m*. **5.** *psych.* Komplex *m*.

com·plex·ion [kəm'plekʃn] *s* **1.** Gesichtsfarbe *f*, Teint *m*. **2.** *fig.* Aussehen *n*, Anstrich *m*. **3.** *fig.* Couleur *f*, (politische) Richtung.

com·plex·i·ty [kəm'pleksətɪ] *s* **1.** Komplexität *f*, Vielschichtigkeit *f*. **2.** et. Komplexes.

com·pli·ance [kəm'plaɪəns] *s* **1.** (*with*) Einwilligung *f* (in *acc*); Befolgung *f* (*gen*): *in* ~ *with e-r Vorschrift etc* gemäß. **2.** Willfährigkeit *f*. **com·'pli·ant** *adj* □ willfährig.

com·pli·cate ['kɒmplɪkeɪt] *v/t* komplizieren. **'com·pli·cat·ed** *adj* □ kompliziert. **com·pli·ca·tion** *s* **1.** Komplikation *f* (*a.* ✚). **2.** Kompliziertheit *f*.

com·plic·i·ty [kəm'plɪsətɪ] *s* Mitschuld *f*, Mittäterschaft *f* (*in an dat*): ~ *in murder* ⚖ Beihilfe *f* zum Mord.

com·pli·ment I *s* ['kɒmplɪmənt] **1.** Kompliment *n*: *angle* (*od. fish*) *for* ~*s* nach Komplimenten fischen; *pay s.o. a* ~ j-m ein Kompliment machen. **2.** Empfehlung *f*, Gruß *m*: *with the* ~*s of the season* mit den besten Wünschen zum Fest. **II** *v/t* ['~ment] **3.** j-m ein Kompliment *od.* Komplimente machen (*on* wegen). **com·pli·men·ta·ry** [ˌ~'tərɪ] *adj* **1.** höflich, Höflichkeits...: ~ *close* Gruß-, Schlußformel *f* (*in Briefen*). **2.** Ehren..., Frei..., Gratis...: ~ *ticket* Ehren-, Freikarte *f*.

com·ply [kəmˈplaɪ] v/i (**with**) einwilligen (**in** acc); (e-m Wunsch od. Befehl) nachkommen (od. Folge leisten, erfüllen (acc); (e-e Abmachung) befolgen, einhalten: **~ with the law** sich an die Gesetze halten.

com·po·nent [kəmˈpəʊnənt] **I** adj Teil...: **~ part** Bestandteil m. **II** s (Bestand)Teil m, a. ⚓, phys. Komponente f.

com·pose [kəmˈpəʊz] **I** v/t **1.** zs.-setzen od. -stellen: **be ~d of** bestehen od. sich zs.-setzen aus. **2.** Satz etc bilden. **3.** Gedicht etc verfassen. **4.** ♪ komponieren. **5.** Gemälde etc entwerfen. **6.** typ. (ab)setzen. **7.** besänftigen: **~ o.s.** sich beruhigen od. fassen. **8.** Streit etc beilegen, schlichten. **9.** Gedanken sammeln. **II** v/i **10.** ♪ komponieren. **com'posed** adj, **com'pos·ed·ly** [~zɪdlɪ] adv ruhig, gelassen. **com'pos·er** s **1.** ♪ Komponist m. **2.** Verfasser(in). **com·po·site** [ˈkɒmpəzɪt] adj zs.-gesetzt. **com·po-'si·tion** s **1.** Zs.-setzung f. **2.** Verfassen n. **3.** Schrift(stück n) f. **4.** ped. Aufsatz m. **5.** Komposition f: a) Musikstück n, b) (künstlerische) Anordnung od. Gestaltung, Aufbau m. **6.** Beschaffenheit f, Art f. **7.** typ. Setzen n, Satz m. **com·pos·i·tor** [kəmˈpɒzɪtə] s (Schrift-)Setzer m. **com·post** [ˈkɒmpɒst] **I** s Kompost m: **~ heap** Komposthaufen m. **II** v/t kompostieren. **com·po·sure** [kəmˈpəʊʒə] s (Gemüts)Ruhe f, Fassung f, Gelassenheit f.

com·pote [ˈkɒmpɒt] s Kompott n.

com·pound¹ [ˈkɒmpaʊnd] **I** v/t **1.** zs.-setzen od. -stellen: **~ interest** Zinseszins pl; **~ word** → **11. 6.** ⚕ kompliziert (Bruch). **7.** ⚡, ⚙ Verbund... **IV** s [ˈkɒmpaʊnd] **8.** Zs.-setzung f, Mischung f. **9.** Mischung f, Masse f. **10.** ⚛ Verbindung f. **11.** ling. Kompositum n, zs.-gesetztes Wort.

com·pound² [ˈkɒmpaʊnd] s **1.** Lager n. **2.** Gefängnishof m. **3.** (Tier)Gehege n.

com·pre·hend [ˌkɒmprɪˈhend] v/t **1.** umfassen, einschließen. **2.** begreifen, verstehen. **com·pre·hen·si·ble** adj begreiflich, verständlich. **com·pre·hen-**

si·bly adv verständlicherweise. **com·pre'hen·sion** s **1.** Begriffsvermögen n, Verstand m: **past ~** unfaßbar, unfaßlich. **2.** (of) Begreifen n (gen), Verständnis n (für). **com·pre'hen·sive** [~sɪv] **I** adj □ **1.** umfassend: **~ school** → **3. 2.** Begriffs...: **~ faculty** Fassungskraft f, Begriffsvermögen n. **II** s **3.** Br. Gesamtschule f.

com·press I v/t [kəmˈpres] zs.-drücken, -pressen, phys., ⚙ komprimieren (a. fig.), verdichten: **~ed air** Preß-, Druckluft f. **II** s [ˈkɒmpres] ⚕ Kompresse f. **com·pres·sion** [kəmˈpreʃn] s **1.** Zs.-drücken n, -pressen n. **2.** phys., ⚙ Druck m, Kompression f, Verdichtung f. **com'pres·sor** [~sə] s ⚙ Kompressor m.

com·prise [kəmˈpraɪz] v/t **1.** einschließen, umfassen. **2.** bestehen od. sich zs.-setzen aus.

com·pro·mise [ˈkɒmprəmaɪz] **I** s **1.** Kompromiß m: **make a ~** e-n Kompromiß schließen; **~ formula** Kompromißformel f; **~ settlement** (od. **solution**) Kompromißlösung f. **II** v/t **2.** Ruf, Leben etc gefährden, aufs Spiel setzen. **3.** bloßstellen, kompromittieren. **III** v/i **4.** e-n Kompromiß od. (a. fig. contp.) Kompromisse schließen.

com·pul·sion [kəmˈpʌlʃn] s Zwang m (a. psych.): **under ~** unter Zwang, zwangsweise. **com'pul·sive** [~sɪv] adj □ **1.** zwingend, Zwangs... **2.** psych. zwanghaft. **com'pul·so·ry** [~sərɪ] adj □ **1.** zwangsweise: **~ auction** Zwangsversteigerung f; **~ measures** pl Zwangsmaßnahmen pl. **2.** obligatorisch, Pflicht...: **~ education** allgemeine Schulpflicht; **~ military service** allgemeine Wehrpflicht; **~ subject** ped. univ. Pflichtfach n.

com·punc·tion [kəmˈpʌŋkʃn] s Gewissensbisse pl; Reue f; Bedenken pl: **without ~** a. bedenkenlos.

com·pu·ta·tion [ˌkɒmpjuːˈteɪʃn] s **1.** Berechnung f. **2.** Schätzung f. **com·pute** [kəmˈpjuːt] v/t **1.** berechnen. **2.** schätzen, veranschlagen (**at** auf acc). **com'put·er** s Computer m: **~ centre** (Am. **center**) Rechenzentrum n; **~·controlled** computergesteuert; **~ language** Computersprache f; **~ science** Informatik f. **com'put·er·ize** [~təraɪz] **I** v/t

Werk etc computerisieren, auf Computer umstellen; *System etc* mit e-m Computer durchführen; computerisieren, mit Hilfe e-s Computers errechnen *od.* zs.-stellen. **II** *v/i* sich auf Computer umstellen.

com·rade ['kɒmreɪd] *s* **1.** Kamerad *m*, Gefährte *m*. **2.** *pol.* (Partei)Genosse *m*. **'com·rade·ship** *s* Kameradschaft *f*.

con¹ [kɒn] **I** *s* **1.** Nein-Stimme *f*. **2.** Gegenargument *n*: → *pro¹.* **II** *adv* **3.** F dagegen: the ~.

con² [⁓] *sl.* **I** *adj* betrügerisch: ~ **man** Betrüger *m*; Hochstapler *m*; ~ **game** aufgelegter Schwindel; Hochstapelei *f*. **II** *v/t* betrügen (*out of* um), reinlegen.

con·cat·e·nate [kɒn'kætɪneɪt] *v/t* verknüpfen. **con,cat·e·na·tion** *s* **1.** Verkettung *f*. **2.** Kette *f*, Reihe *f*.

con·cave ['kɒnkeɪv] *adj* □ konkav, hohl: ~ *mirror* Hohlspiegel *m*.

con·ceal [kən'siːl] *v/t* (*from* vor *dat*) verbergen: a) verstecken, b) geheimhalten, c) verschweigen, verheimlichen. **con'ceal·ment** *s* **1.** Verbergung *f*, Geheimhaltung *f*, Verheimlichung *f*. **2.** Verborgenheit *f*: stay in ~ sich verborgen halten.

con·cede [kən'siːd] *v/t* zugestehen, einräumen: a) gewähren, bewilligen, b) anerkennen (*a. that* daß). **con'ced·ed·ly** *adv* zugestandenermaßen.

con·ceit [kən'siːt] *s* Einbildung *f*, Dünkel *m*: be full of ~ völlig von sich eingenommen sein. **con'ceit·ed** *adj* □ eingebildet, dünkelhaft.

con·ceiv·a·ble [kən'siːvəbl] *adj* □ denk-, vorstellbar: the best plan ~ der denkbar beste Plan. **con'ceive** **I** *v/t* **1.** *biol.* Kind empfangen. **2.** begreifen. **3.** sich *et.* vorstellen *od.* denken, sich e-n Begriff *od.* e-e Vorstellung machen von. **4.** ersinnen, ausdenken. **II** *v/i* **5.** *biol.* empfangen, schwanger werden (*Mensch*); aufnehmen, trächtig werden (*Tier*). **6.** ~ *of* → 3.

con·cen·trate ['kɒnsəntreɪt] **I** *v/t* konzentrieren: a) zs.-ziehen, -ballen, massieren, b) *Gedanken etc* richten (*on* auf *acc*), c) 🝪 anreichern. **II** *v/i* sich konzentrieren. **III** *s* Konzentrat *n*. **,con·cen'tra·tion** *s* Konzentration *f*: a) Zs.-ziehung *f*, -ballung *f*, Massierung *f*; ~ *camp* Konzentrationslager *n*, b) ge-

spannte Aufmerksamkeit: *power of ~* Konzentrationsfähigkeit *f*, c) 🝪 Anreicherung *f*.

con·cen·tric [kən'sentrɪk] *adj* (**~ally**) konzentrisch.

con·cept ['kɒnsept] *s* **1.** *phls.* Begriff *m*. **2.** Gedanke *m*, Auffassung *f*. **con·cep·tion** [kən'sepʃn] *s* **1.** *biol.* Empfängnis *f*. **2.** Begreifen *n*; Begriffsvermögen *n*; Begriff *m*, Vorstellung *f* (*of* von); Konzeption *f*, Idee *f*. **3.** Entwurf *m*, Konzept *n*. **con'cep·tu·al** [⁓tʃʊəl] *adj* begrifflich, Begriffs...

con·cern [kən'sɜːn] **I** *v/t* **1.** angehen: a) betreffen, b) von Wichtigkeit *od.* Interesse sein für. **2.** beunruhigen. **3.** ~ *o.s. with* sich beschäftigen *od.* befassen mit. **II** *s* **4.** Angelegenheit *f*, Sache *f*: that is no ~ of mine das geht mich nichts an. **5.** ✝ Geschäft *n*, Unternehmen *n*. **6.** Unruhe *f*, Sorge *f* (*at, about, for* wegen, um). **7.** Wichtigkeit *f*: a matter of national ~ ein nationales Anliegen. **8.** Beziehung *f* (*with* zu): have no ~ with nichts zu tun haben mit. **9.** (*at, about, for, in, with*) Teilnahme *f* (an *dat*), Rücksicht *f* (auf *acc*), Anteil *m* (an *dat*), Interesse *n* (für). **10.** F Ding *n*, Geschichte *f*. **con'cerned** *adj* **1.** betroffen, betreffend. **2.** (*in*) beteiligt, interessiert (an *dat*); verwickelt (in *acc*). **3.** (*with, in*) befaßt, beschäftigt (mit); handelnd (von). **4.** (*about, at, for*) besorgt (um), beunruhigt (wegen). **con'cern·ing** *prp* betreffend, hinsichtlich, was ... (an)betrifft.

con·cert *s* **1.** ['kɒnsət] ♩ Konzert *n*: ~ *hall* Konzertsaal *m*; ~ *pianist* Konzertpianist(in). **2.** ['kɒnsɜːt] *in* ~ *with* in Übereinstimmung *od.* gemeinsam mit. **con·cert·ed** [kən'sɜːtɪd] *adj* gemeinsam: ~ *action* gemeinsames Vorgehen; ✝, *pol.* konzertierte Aktion. **con·cer·to** [kən'tʃeətəʊ] *pl* -tos, -ti [⁓tɪ] *s* ♩ (Solo)Konzert *n* (*mit Orchesterbegleitung*): piano ~ Klavierkonzert *n*.

con·ces·sion [kən'seʃn] *s* **1.** Konzession *f*, Zugeständnis *n*. **2.** Genehmigung *f*, Bewilligung *f*; (amtliche *od.* staatliche) Konzession.

con·cil·i·ate [kən'sɪlɪeɪt] *v/t* **1.** aus-, versöhnen, versöhnlich stimmen. **2.** *Gunst etc* gewinnen. **3.** in Einklang bringen. **con,cil·i'a·tion** *s* Aus-, Versöhnung *f*: ~

committee Schlichtungsausschuß *m.*
con·cil·i·a·tor *s* Schlichter *m,* Vermittler *m.* **con·cil·i·a·to·ry** [~ətərɪ] *adj* □ versöhnlich, vermittelnd.

con·cise [kən'saɪs] *adj* □ kurz, knapp, prägnant. **con·cise·ness** *s* Kürze *f,* Prägnanz *f.*

con·clave ['kɒŋkleɪv] *s eccl.* Konklave *n.*
con·clude [kən'kluːd] **I** *v/t* **1.** beenden, (be-, ab)schließen (**with** mit): **to be ~d** Schluß folgt. **2.** *Vertrag etc* abschließen. **3.** *et.* Folgerung *f:* schließen (**from** aus): **~ that** zu dem Schluß kommen, daß. **II** *v/i* **4.** enden, schließen (**with** mit). **con·clud·ing** *adj* abschließend, Schluß...

con·clu·sion [kən'kluːʒn] *s* **1.** (Ab-) Schluß *m,* Ende *n:* **in ~** zum Abschluß bringen; **in ~** zum Schluß. **2.** Abschluß *m* (*e-s Vertrags etc*). **3.** (Schluß)Folgerung *f:* **come to** (*od.* **arrive at**) **the ~ that** zu dem Schluß kommen, daß; **draw a ~** e-n Schluß ziehen; **jump at** (*od.* **to**) **~s, leap to ~s, rush at ~s** voreilig(e) Schlüsse ziehen. **con·clu·sive** [~sɪv] *adj* □ **1.** → **concluding. 2.** schlüssig (*Beweis*).

con·coct [kən'kɒkt] *v/t* **1.** (zs.-)brauen. **2.** *fig.* aushecken, -brüten. **con·coc·tion** *s* **1.** (Zs.-)Brauen *n.* **2.** Gebräu *n* (*a. contp.*). **3.** *fig.* Ausbrüten *n,* -hecken *n.* **4.** *fig.* Erfindung *f.*

con·course ['kɒŋkɔːs] *s* **1.** Zs.-treffen *n;* Zs.-fluß *m.* **2.** (Menschen)Auflauf *m,* (-)Menge *f.* **3.** freier Platz (*für Versammlungen etc*); *Am.* Bahnhofshalle *f.*

con·crete I *v/t* **1.** [kən'kriːt] konkretisieren. **2.** ['kɒŋkriːt] betonieren: **~ over** zubetonieren. **II** *adj* ['kɒŋkriːt] □ **3.** konkret (*a. ling., ♪ etc*). **4.** betoniert, Beton...: **~ jungle** Betonwüste *f;* **~ mixer** Betonmischmaschine *f;* **~ pile** Betonklotz *m,* -silo *m.* **III** *s* ['kɒŋkriːt] **5.** Beton *m.*

con·cu·bine ['kɒŋkjʊbaɪn] *s* Nebenfrau *f.*

con·cur [kən'kɜː] *v/i* **1.** zs.-fallen, -treffen. **2.** zs.-wirken. **3.** übereinstimmen (**with** mit; **in** in *dat*): **~ with s.o.** *a.* j-m beipflichten. **con·cur·rence** [~'kʌrəns] *s* **1.** Zs.-treffen *n.* **2.** Zs.-wirken *n.* **3.** Übereinstimmung *f.* **con·cur·rent** *adj* □ **1.** zs.-treffend. **2.** zs.-wirkend. **3.** übereinstimmend.

con·cuss [kən'kʌs] *v/t* erschüttern: **be ~ed** ✿ e-e Gehirnerschütterung erleiden. **con·cus·sion** [~ʃn] *s* Erschütterung *f:* **~** (**of the brain**) ✿ Gehirnerschütterung.

con·demn [kən'dem] *v/t* **1.** verdammen, verurteilen. **2.** ⚖ verurteilen (**to death** zum Tode): **~ed cell** Todeszelle *f.* **3.** für unbrauchbar *od.* unbewohnbar *od.* gesundheitsschädlich erklären. **4.** *Kranken* aufgeben. **con·dem·na·tion** [ˌkɒndem'neɪʃn] *s* Verdammung *f,* Verurteilung *f* (*a.* ⚖).

con·den·sa·tion [ˌkɒnden'seɪʃn] *s* **1.** *phys.* Kondensation *f* (*a.* 🌡), Verflüssigung *f;* Kondensat *n,* Kondenswasser *n:* **~ trail** ✈ Kondensstreifen *m.* **2.** Zs.-fassung *f.* **con·dense** [kən'dens] **I** *v/t* **1.** *phys.* Gase, Dämpfe kondensieren, verflüssigen. **2.** 🌡 *Milch etc* eindicken, konzentrieren: **~d milk** Kondensmilch *f.* **3.** zs.-fassen, gedrängt darstellen. **II** *v/i* **4.** *phys.* kondensieren, sich verflüssigen. **con·dens·er** *s phys.* Kondensator *m* (*a.* ⚡), Verflüssiger *m.*

con·de·scend [ˌkɒndɪ'send] *v/i* **1.** sich herablassen (**to do** zu tun; **to** zu). **2.** herablassend *od.* gönnerhaft sein (**to** gegen, zu). **con·de·scend·ing** *adj* □ herablassend, gönnerhaft.

con·di·ment ['kɒndɪmənt] *s* Gewürz *n,* Würze *f.*

con·di·tion [kən'dɪʃn] **I** *s* **1.** Bedingung *f:* **on ~ that** unter der Bedingung *od.* vorausgesetzt, daß; **on no ~** unter keinen Umständen, keinesfalls; **make s.th. a ~** et. zur Bedingung machen. **2.** Verfassung *f:* a) Zustand *m,* Beschaffenheit *f,* b) (körperlicher *od.* Gesundheits)Zustand *m,* (*Sport*) Form *f:* **out of ~** in schlechter Verfassung, in schlechtem Zustand; **the ~ of her health** ihr Gesundheitszustand. **3.** *pl* Bedingungen *pl,* Verhältnisse *pl:* **living ~s** Lebensbedingungen, -verhältnisse; **weather ~s** Witterungs-, Wetterverhältnisse. **II** *v/t* **4.** zur Bedingung machen, die Bedingung stellen (**that** daß). **5.** *j-n* programmieren (**to, for** auf *acc*). **con·di·tion·al** [~ʃənl] *adj* □ **1.** (on *od.* *upon*) bedingt (durch), abhängig (von): **be ~ on** abhängen von; **make ~ on** abhängig machen von. **2.** *ling.* Konditional...: **~ clause** (*od.* **sentence**) Konditional-, Bedingungssatz *m.* **con·di·tioned** [-∫nd] *adj* **1.** (*on*) bedingt (durch), abhängig (von): *be ~ on* abhängen von; *~ response* (*od. reflex*) *psych.* bedingter Reflex. **2.** beschaffen, geartet.

con·dole [kənˈdəʊl] *v/i* sein Beileid ausdrücken, kondolieren (*with s.o. on s.th.* j-m zu et.). **con·do·lence** *s* Beileid *n*: *please accept my ~s* mein herzliches *od.* aufrichtiges Beileid; *register of ~* Kondolenzliste *f.*

con·dom [ˈkɒndəm] *s* Kondom *n*, *m*, Präservativ *n.*

con·do·min·i·um [ˌkɒndəˈmɪnɪəm] *s Am.* Eigentumswohnanlage *f*: *~* (*apartment*) Eigentumswohnung *f.*

con·done [kənˈdəʊn] *v/t* **1.** verzeihen, vergeben: *she ~d his infidelity* sie verzieh ihm s-e Untreue. **2.** wettmachen, wiedergutmachen.

con·duce [kənˈdjuːs] *v/i* (*to, toward[s]*) beitragen (zu), dienlich *od.* förderlich sein, dienen (*dat*). **con·du·cive** *adj* dienlich, förderlich (*to dat*).

con·duct **I** *s* [ˈkɒndʌkt] **1.** Führung *f*, Leitung *f.* **2.** Betragen *n*, Verhalten *n*: → *certificate* **1. II** *v/t* [kənˈdʌkt] **3.** führen, geleiten: *~ed tour* Führung *f* (*of* durch). **4.** *Prozeß, Verhandlungen etc* führen, *Geschäft a.* betreiben, leiten. **5.** ♪ leiten, dirigieren. **6.** *~ o.s.* sich betragen *od.* verhalten. **7.** *phys.* leiten. **con·duct·i·ble** [kənˈdʌktəbl], **con·duc·tive** *adj phys.* leitfähig. **con·duc·tor** *s* **1.** Führer *m*, Leiter *m.* **2.** (*Bus-*, *Straßenbahn*)Schaffner *m*; *Am.* Zugbegleiter *m.* **3.** ♪ Dirigent *m.* **4.** *phys.* Leiter *m*; ⚡ *a.* Blitzableiter *m.* **con·duc·tress** *s* Schaffnerin *f.*

cone [kəʊn] **I** *s* **1.** ⚲ u. *fig.* Kegel *m.* **2.** ⚘ (*Tannen- etc*)Zapfen *m.* **3.** kegelförmiger Gegenstand, *z. B.* a) Waffeltüte *f* (*für Speiseeis*), b) Pylon(e *f*) *m*, Leitkegel *m.* **II** *v/t* **4.** *~ off* mit Leitkegeln absperren.

con·fec·tion [kənˈfek∫n] *s* Konfekt *n.* **con·fec·tion·er** *s* Konditor *m.* **con·fec·tion·er·y** *s* **1.** Süßwaren *pl.* **2.** Süßwarengeschäft *n*; Konditorei *f.*

con·fed·er·a·cy [kənˈfedərəsɪ] *s* **1.** (Staaten)Bund *m.* **2.** Komplott *n*, Verschwörung *f.* **con·fed·er·ate** [ˌ~rət] **I** *adj* verbündet (*with* mit), Bundes... **II** *s* Verbündete *m*, Bundesgenosse *m.* **III** *v/t u.*

v/i [ˌ~reɪt] (sich) verbünden *od.* zs.-schließen. **con·fed·er·a·tion** *s* **1.** Bund *m*, Bündnis *n.* **2.** (Staaten)Bund *m.*

con·fer [kənˈfɜː] **I** *v/t* Titel *etc* verleihen (*on dat*). **II** *v/i* sich beraten (*with* mit). **con·fer·ence** [ˈkɒnfərəns] *s* Konferenz *f*: a) Tagung *f*, b) Besprechung *f*: *be in ~* in e-r Besprechung sein.

con·fess [kənˈfes] **I** *v/t* **1.** bekennen, (ein)gestehen. **2.** zugeben (*a. that* daß). **3.** *eccl.* beichten; j-m die Beichte abnehmen. **II** *v/i* **4.** (*to*) (ein)gestehen (*acc*), sich schuldig bekennen (*gen od.* an *acc*), sich bekennen (zu): *~ to doing s.th.* (ein)gestehen, et. getan zu haben; *he has ~ed* 🔪 er hat gestanden, er ist geständig. **5.** *eccl.* beichten (*to dat*). **con·fessed** *adj* erklärt. **con·fess·ed·ly** [ˌ~ɪdlɪ] *adv* zugestandener-, eingestandenermaßen. **con·fes·sion** [ˌ~∫n] *s* **1.** Geständnis *n* (*a.* 🔪): *make a full ~* ein volles Geständnis ablegen. **2.** *eccl.* Beichte *f*: *go to ~* zur Beichte gehen; → *auricular.* **3.** *eccl.* Konfession *f*: a) Glaubensbekenntnis *n*, b) Glaubensgemeinschaft *f.* **con·fes·sion·al** [ˌ~∫ənl] **I** *adj* **1.** konfessionell, Konfessions... **2.** Beicht... **II** *s* **3.** Beichtstuhl *m*: *secret of the ~* Beichtgeheimnis *n.* **con·fes·sor** [ˌ~sə] *s eccl.* Beichtvater *m.*

con·fet·ti [kənˈfetɪ] *s pl* (*sg konstruiert*) Konfetti *n.*

con·fi·dant [ˌkɒnfɪˈdænt] *s* Vertraute *m.* **con·fi·dante** [ˌ~ˈdænt] *s* Vertraute *f.*

con·fide [kənˈfaɪd] **I** *v/i* **1.** sich anvertrauen (*in dat*). **2.** vertrauen (*in dat od.* auf *acc*). **II** *v/t* **3.** *~ s.th. to s.o.* j-m et. anvertrauen.

con·fi·dence [ˈkɒnfɪdəns] *s* **1.** (*in*) Vertrauen *n* (auf *acc*, zu), Zutrauen *n* (zu): *have ~ in* Vertrauen haben zu; *take s.o. into one's ~* j-n ins Vertrauen ziehen; *in ~*, → *confidentially*; → *strict.* **2.** *a. ~ in o.s.* Selbstvertrauen *n.* **3.** vertrauliche Mitteilung *f. a.* Vertraulichkeiten *pl. ~ game Am.* → *confidence trick.* *~ man* (*s irr man*) Betrüger *m*; Hochstapler *m. ~ trick s* aufgelegter Schwindel; Hochstapelei *f. ~ trick·ster* → *confidence man.*

con·fi·dent [ˈkɒnfɪdənt] *adj* □ **1.** (*of*; *that*) überzeugt (von; daß), sicher (*gen*; daß). **2.** *a. ~ in o.s.* selbstsicher. **con·fi·den·tial** [ˌ~ˈden∫l] *adj* **1.** vertraulich, geheim. **2.** vertraut, Vertrauens...: ~ *clerk* ✝ Prokurist(in). **,con·fi'den·tial·ly** [~ʃəlɪ] *adv* vertraulich, im Vertrauen.

con·fine I *s* ['kɒnfaɪn] **1.** *mst pl* Grenze *f*, Grenzgebiet *n*, *fig*. Rand *m*, Schwelle *f*. **II** *v/t* [kən'faɪn] **2.** begrenzen, be-, einschränken (*to* auf *acc*). **3.** einschließen, einsperren: ~*d to bed* ans Bett gefesselt. **4. *be* ~*d* (*of*) niederkommen (mit), entbunden werden (von). **con'fine·ment** *s* **1.** Be-, Einschränkung *f*. **2.** Haft *f*: *solitary* ~ Einzelhaft. **3.** Niederkunft *f*, Entbindung *f*.

con·firm [kən'fɜːm] *v/t* **1.** bestätigen. **2.** *Entschluß* bekräftigen; *j-n* bestärken (*in* in *dat*). **3.** *eccl*. konfirmieren; firmen. **con·fir·ma·tion** [ˌkɒnfə'meɪʃn] *s* **1.** Bestätigung *f*. **2.** Bekräftigung *f*; Bestärkung *f*. **3.** *eccl*. Konfirmation *f*; Firmung *f*. **con'firmed** *adj* **1.** fest (*Gewohnheit etc*). **2.** erklärt, überzeugt: ~ *bachelor* eingefleischter Junggeselle.

con·fis·cate ['kɒnfɪskeɪt] *v/t* beschlagnahmen, konfiszieren. **,con·fis'ca·tion** *s* Beschlagnahme *f*, Konfiszierung *f*.

con·flict I *s* ['kɒnflɪkt] *s* Konflikt *m*: a) Zs.-stoß *m*: → *armed*, b) Widerstreit *m*: *come into* ~ *with* in Konflikt geraten mit; ~ *of interests* Interessenkonflikt *m*, -kollision *f*. **II** *v/i* [kən'flɪkt] (*with*) kollidieren (mit), im Widerspruch od. Gegensatz stehen (zu). **con'flict·ing** *adj* widersprüchlich.

con·form [kən'fɔːm] **I** *v/t* **1.** anpassen (*to* dat *od*. an *acc*). **2.** in Einklang bringen (*to* mit). **II** *v/i* **3.** sich anpassen (*to* dat). **4.** übereinstimmen (*to* mit). **con'form·i·ty** *s* **1.** Übereinstimmung *f*: *be in* ~ übereinstimmen (*with* mit); *in* ~ *with* in Übereinstimmung mit, gemäß (*dat*). **2.** Anpassung *f* (*to* an *acc*).

con·found [kən'faʊnd] *v/t* **1.** verwechseln, durcheinanderbringen (*with* mit). **2.** verwirren, durcheinanderbringen. ~ *it!* verdammt! **con'found·ed** *adj* □ F verdammt.

con·front [kən'frʌnt] *v/t* **1.** (*oft feindlich*) gegenübertreten, -stehen (*dat*): *be* ~*ed with Schwierigkeiten etc* gegenüberstehen, sich gegenübersehen (*dat*). **2.** sich *e-r Gefahr etc* stellen. **3.** *a.* ⚛ (*with*) konfrontieren (mit), gegenüberstellen (*dat*): ~ *s.o. with s.th.* j-m et. entge-

genhalten. **con·fron·ta·tion** [ˌkɒnfrʌn'teɪʃn] *s* Konfrontation *f* (*a. pol. etc*).

con·fuse [kən'fjuːz] *v/t* **1.** verwechseln, durcheinanderbringen (*with* mit). **2.** verwirren: a) in Unordnung bringen, b) aus der Fassung bringen, verlegen machen. **con'fused** *adj* **1.** verwirrt: a) konfus, verworren, wirr, b) verlegen, bestürzt. **2.** undeutlich, verworren. **con'fu·sion** [~ʒn] *s* **1.** Verwechs(e)lung *f*: ~ *of names* Namensverwechslung. **2.** Verwirrung *f*: a) Durcheinander *n*: *cause* ~ Verwirrung stiften od. anrichten; *throw everything into* ~ alles durcheinanderbringen, b) Verlegenheit *f*, Bestürzung *f*: *in* ~ → *confused* 1b; *put to* ~ in Verlegenheit bringen.

con·fu·ta·tion [ˌkɒnfjuː'teɪʃn] *s* Widerlegung *f*. **con·fute** [kən'fjuːt] *v/t* widerlegen.

con·geal [kən'dʒiːl] *v/t u. v/i* gefrieren *od*. gerinnen *od*. erstarren (lassen).

con·gen·ial [kən'dʒiːnjəl] *adj* □ **1.** gleichartig, (geistes)verwandt (*with* mit *od*. *dat*). **2.** sympathisch, angenehm (*to dat*): *be* ~ *to s.o.* j-m zusagen. **3.** zuträglich (*to dat od*. für): ~ *to one's health* gesund.

con·gen·i·tal [kən'dʒenɪtl] *adj* angeboren: ~ *defect* Geburtsfehler *m*. **con'gen·i·tal·ly** [~təlɪ] *adv* **1.** von Geburt (an). **2.** von Natur (aus).

con·gest·ed [kən'dʒestɪd] *adj* **1.** verstopft: ~ *streets*. **2.** überfüllt (*with* von): ~ *area* übervölkertes Gebiet, Ballungsgebiet *n*. **con'ges·tion** *s* **1.** Anhäufung *f*. ~ *of population* Übervölkerung *f*; ~ *of traffic* Verkehrsstockung *f*, -stauung *f*, -stau *m*. **2.** ⚛ Blutandrang *m* (*of the brain* zum Gehirn).

con·glom·er·ate I *v/t u. v/i* [kən'glɒməreɪt] (sich) zs.-ballen (*to* zu). **II** *adj* [~rət] *fig*. zs.-gewürfelt. **III** *s* [~rət] Konglomerat *n*, zs.-gewürfelte Masse, Gemisch *n*. **con,glom·er'a·tion** → *conglomerate* III.

con·grats [kən'græts] *int bsd. Br.* F gratuliere!

con·grat·u·late [kən'grætʃʊleɪt] *v/t* j-m gratulieren, j-n beglückwünschen (*on* zu). **con,grat·u'la·tion** *s* Gratulation *f*, Glückwunsch *m*: ~*s!* ich gratuliere!, herzlichen Glückwunsch! **con'grat·u·la·tor** *s* Gratulant(in). **con'grat·u·la-**

to·ry [∪lətəri] *adj* Glückwunsch...: ~ *tel-egram.*

con·gre·gate ['kɒŋgrɪgeɪt] *v/t u. v/i* (sich) versammeln. **,con·gre'ga·tion** *s* **1.** Versammlung *f.* **2.** (Kirchen)Gemeinde *f.* **con·gre'ga·tion·al** [∪ʃənl] *adj eccl.* Gemeinde...

con·gress ['kɒŋgres] *s* **1.** Kongreß *m,* Tagung *f.* **2.** ♀ *pol. Am.* der Kongreß. **♀·man** ['∪mən] *s (irr* man*) pol. Am.* Mitglied *n* des Repräsentantenhauses.

con·gru·ence ['kɒŋgruəns] *s* **1.** Übereinstimmung *f.* **2.** Å Kongruenz *f (a. fig.).* **'con·gru·ent** [∪∪] *adj* □ **1.** übereinstimmend **(to, with** mit). **2.** Å kongruent *(a. fig.).* **con·gru·i·ty** [∪'gru:ɪtɪ] → *congruence.* **con·gru·ous** ['∪gruəs] → *congruent.*

con·ic, con·i·cal ['kɒnɪk(l)] *adj* □ konisch, kegelförmig: **conic section** Å Kegelschnitt *m.*

co·ni·fer ['kɒnɪfə] *s* ♣ Nadelbaum *m.* **co·nif·er·ous** [kəʊ'nɪfərəs] *adj* zapfentragend; Nadel...: ~ *tree.*

con·jec·tur·al [kən'dʒektʃərəl] *adj* □ mutmaßlich. **con'jec·ture I** *s* Vermutung *f,* Mutmaßung *f:* **be reduced to ~** auf Vermutungen angewiesen sein. **II** *v/t* vermuten, mutmaßen. **III** *v/i* Vermutungen anstellen, mutmaßen **(of, about** über *acc).*

con·ju·gal ['kɒndʒʊgl] *adj* □ ehelich: ~ **life** Eheleben *n.* **con·ju·gate** ['∪geɪt] *ling.* **I** *v/t* konjugieren, beugen. **II** *v/i* konjugiert *od.* gebeugt werden. **,con·ju'ga·tion** *s ling.* Konjugation *f,* Beugung *f.*

con·junc·tion [kən'dʒʌŋkʃn] *s* **1.** Verbindung *f:* **in ~ with** in Verbindung *od.* zusammen mit. **2.** Zs.-treffen *n (von Ereignissen etc).* **3.** *ling.* Konjunktion *f,* Bindewort *n.* **con·junc·ti·va** [,kɒn-dʒʌŋk'taɪvə] *pl* -**vas,** -**vae** [∪vi:] *s anat.* Bindehaut *f.* **con·junc·ti·vi·tis** [kən-,dʒʌŋktɪ'vaɪtɪs] *s* ⚕ Bindehautentzündung *f.*

con·jure ['kʌndʒə] **I** *v/t* **1.** [kən'dʒʊə] beschwören **(to do** zu tun). **2.** *Teufel etc* beschwören, anrufen: ~ **up** heraufbeschwören *(a. fig.).* **3.** ~ **away** wegzaubern; ~ **up** hervorzaubern *(a. fig.).* **II** *v/i* **4.** zaubern. **'con·jur·er** *s* **1.** Zauberer *m.* **2.** Zauberkünstler *m.* **'con·jur·ing**

trick *s* Zauberkunststück *n,* -trick *m.* **'con·jur·or** → *conjurer.*

conk¹ [kɒŋk] *s sl.* Riecher *m (Nase);* Birne *f (Kopf).*

conk² [∪] *v/i sl. mst* ~ **out 1.** streiken, den Geist aufgeben *(Fernseher etc),* absterben *(Motor).* **2.** a) umkippen *(ohnmächtig werden),* b) *vor Erschöpfung etc* zs.-klappen, c) *a.* ~ **off** einpennen. **3.** den Löffel weglegen *(sterben).*

con·nect [kə'nekt] **I** *v/t* **1.** verbinden **(with** mit) *(a. fig.).* **2.** *fig.* in Zs.-hang *od.* Verbindung bringen **(with** mit). **3.** ⚙ **(to)** verbinden (mit), *Wagen etc* anhängen, ankuppeln (an *acc).* **4.** ⚡ **(to)** anschließen (an *acc),* zuschalten *(dat).* **5.** *teleph.* verbinden **(to, with** mit): *s.o. further* j-n weiterverbinden. **II** *v/i* **6.** 🚂 *etc* Anschluß haben **(with** an *acc).* **con'nect·ed** *adj* **1.** verbunden. **2.** (logisch) zs.-hängend. **3.** verwandt: ~ **by marriage** verschwägert; **be well ~** einflußreiche Verwandte *od.* gute Beziehungen haben. **4.** *(with)* verwickelt (in *acc),* beteiligt (an *dat).* **con'nect·ing** *adj* Verbindungs...: ~ **door;** ~ **flight** Anschlußflug *m;* ~ **train** Anschlußzug *m.* **con'nec·tion** *s* **1.** Verbindung *f.* **2.** ⚙ *allg.* Verbindung *f,* Anschluß *m (a.* ⚡, 🚂 *etc).* **3.** Zs.-hang *m:* **in this ~** in diesem Zs.-hang; **in ~ with** in Zs.-hang mit; mit Bezug auf *(acc).* **4.** *pl* geschäftliche, gute etc Beziehungen *od.* Verbindungen *pl;* Bekannten-, Kundenkreis *m.* **con'nec·tive I** *adj* □ verbindend: ~ **tissue** *anat.* Bindegewebe *f;* ~ **word** →II. **II** *s ling.* Bindewort *n.*

con·nex·ion *bsd. Br.* → *connection.*

con·nois·seur [,kɒnə'sɜ:] *s (Wein- etc)* Kenner *m.*

con·no·ta·tion [,kɒnəʊ'teɪʃn] *s* Nebenbedeutung *f.* **con·note** [kə'nəʊt] *v/t* (zugleich) bedeuten.

con·quer ['kɒŋkə] *v/t* **1.** erobern *(a. fig.).* **2.** besiegen, *fig. a.* bezwingen. **'con·quer·or** *s* Eroberer *m.*

con·quest ['kɒŋkwest] *s* **1.** Eroberung *f (a. fig. Person):* **make a ~ of** *s.o.* j-n erobern. **2.** Besiegung *f, fig. a.* Bezwingung *f.*

con·san·guin·e·ous [,kɒnsæŋ'gwɪnɪəs] *adj* blutsverwandt. **,con·san'guin·i·ty** *s* Blutsverwandtschaft *f.*

con·science ['kɒnʃəns] *s* Gewissen *n:* **a**

good (*guilty*) ~ ein gutes (schlechtes) Gewissen; *for ~'s sake* um das Gewissen zu beruhigen; *act on* ~ nach s-m Gewissen handeln, s-m Gewissen folgen; *have s.th. on one's* ~ Gewissensbisse *od.* ein schlechtes Gewissen haben wegen et.

con·sci·en·tious [ˌkɒnʃɪˈenʃəs] *adj* □ **1.** gewissenhaft. **2.** Gewissens...: ~ *objector* Kriegs-, Wehrdienstverweigerer *m* (*aus Gewissensgründen*). **ˌcon·sci·en·tious·ness** *s* Gewissenhaftigkeit *f*.

con·scious [ˈkɒnʃəs] *adj* □ **1.** bei Bewußtsein. **2.** *be* ~ *of* sich bewußt sein (*gen*), sich im klaren sein über (*acc*). **3.** bewußt, absichtlich. **'con·scious·ness** *s* Bewußtsein *n*: *lose* ~ das Bewußtsein verlieren; *regain* ~ wieder zu sich kommen; ~*expanding* bewußtseinserweiternd.

con·script ✕ **I** *v/t* [kənˈskrɪpt] **1.** einziehen, -berufen. **II** *s* [ˈkɒnskrɪpt] **2.** Wehr(dienst)pflichtige *m*. **3.** Einberufene *m*. **con·scrip·tion** [kənˈskrɪpʃn] *s* **1.** Einziehung *f*, -berufung *f*. **2.** Wehrpflicht *f*.

con·se·crate [ˈkɒnsɪkreɪt] *v/t* **1.** *eccl.* weihen. **2.** weihen, widmen (*to dat*). **ˌcon·se·cra·tion** *s* **1.** *eccl.* Weihe *f*, Weihung *f*. **2.** Hingabe *f* (*to an acc*).

con·sec·u·tive [kənˈsekjʊtɪv] *adj* **1.** aufeinanderfolgend: *for two* ~ *days* zwei Tage hintereinander. **2.** (fort)laufend (*Nummer*). **3.** ~ *clause ling.* Konsekutiv-, Folgesatz *m*. **con·sec·u·tive·ly** *adv* **1.** nach-, hintereinander. **2.** (fort)laufend.

con·sen·sus [kənˈsensəs] *s a.* ~ *of opinion* (allgemein) übereinstimmende Meinung, (allgemeine) Übereinstimmung.

con·sent [kənˈsent] **I** *v/i* **1.** (*to*) zustimmen (*dat*), einwilligen (in *acc*). **2.** sich bereit erklären (*to do* zu tun). **II** *s* **3.** (*to*) Zustimmung *f* (zu), Einwilligung *f* (in *acc*): *with the* ~ *of* mit Zustimmung von (*od. gen*); *with one* ~ einstimmig, -mütig.

con·se·quence [ˈkɒnsɪkwəns] *s* **1.** Folge *f*, Konsequenz *f*: *in* ~ folglich, daher; *in* (*od. as a*) ~ *of* infolge von (*od. gen*); *take the* ~*s* die Folgen tragen; *with the* ~ *that* mit dem Ergebnis, daß. **2.** Folgerung *f*, Schluß *m*. **3.** Bedeutung *f*,

Wichtigkeit *f*: *of* (*no*) ~ von (ohne) Bedeutung, (un)bedeutend, (un)wichtig (*to* für); *a person of great* ~ e-e bedeutende *od.* einflußreiche Persönlichkeit. **'con·se·quent** *adj* (*on*) folgend (*dat od.* auf *acc*); sich ergebend (aus). **'con·se·quent·ly** *adv* folglich, daher.

con·ser·va·tion [ˌkɒnsəˈveɪʃn] *s* **1.** Erhaltung *f*, Bewahrung *f*. **2.** Natur- *od.* Umweltschutz *m*: ~ *area* Naturschutzgebiet *n*. **3.** Konservieren *n*, Haltbarmachen *n*. **ˌcon·ser·va·tion·ist** *s* Natur- *od.* Umweltschützer(in). **con·serv·a·tive** [kənˈsɜːvətɪv] **I** *adj* □ **1.** konservativ (*pol. mst* ≈). **2.** vorsichtig (*Schätzung etc*). **II** *s* **3.** *mst* ≈ *pol.* Konservative *m*, *f*. **4.** konservativer Mensch. **con·serv·a·toire** [kənˈsɜːvətwɑː] *s* Konservatorium *n*, Musik(hoch)schule *f*. **con·serv·a·to·ry** [kənˈsɜːvətrɪ] *s* **1.** Treib-, Gewächshaus *n*, Bot. Wintergarten *m*. **2.** → *conservatoire*. **con·serve** **I** *v/t* **1.** erhalten, bewahren. **2.** konservieren, haltbar machen, *Obst etc* einmachen. **II** *s* **3.** *mst pl* Eingemachte *n*.

con·sid·er [kənˈsɪdə] **I** *v/t* **1.** nachdenken über (*acc*). **2.** betrachten *od.* ansehen als, halten für: ~ *s.th.* (*to be*) *a mistake*; *be* ~*ed rich* als reich gelten. **3.** sich überlegen, erwägen (*doing* zu tun). **4.** berücksichtigen, in Betracht ziehen. **5.** Rücksicht nehmen auf (*acc*), denken an (*acc*). **6.** finden, meinen, denken (*that* daß). **II** *v/i* **7.** nachdenken, überlegen. **con·sid·er·a·ble** *adj* □ **1.** beachtlich, beträchtlich. **2.** bedeutend, wichtig (*beide a.* Person). **con·sid·er·ate** [~rət] *adj* □ aufmerksam, rücksichtsvoll (*to, toward*[s] gegen): *be* ~ *of* Rücksicht nehmen auf (*acc*). **con·sid·er·a·tion** [~ˈreɪʃn] *s* **1.** Erwägung *f*, Überlegung *f*: *take into* ~ in Erwägung *od.* Betracht ziehen; *leave out of* ~ ausklammern; *on* (*od. under*) *no* ~ unter keinen Umständen. **2.** Berücksichtigung *f*: *in* ~ *of* in Anbetracht (*gen*). **3.** Rücksicht(nahme) *f* (*for, of* auf *acc*): *lack of* ~ Rücksichtslosigkeit *f*. **4.** (zu berücksichtigender) Grund: *money is no* ~ Geld spielt keine Rolle. **con·sid·er·ing I** *prp* in Anbetracht (*gen*). **II** *cj*: ~ *that* in Anbetracht der Tatsache, daß. **III** *adv* F alles in allem.

con·sign [kənˈsaɪn] *v/t* **1.** übergeben (*to*

dat). **2.** ✝ *Waren* übersenden, zusenden (**to** *dat*). **con·sig·nee** [ˌkɒnsaɪˈniː] *s* ✝ Empfänger *m.* **con·sign·er** [kənˈsaɪnə] *s* → **consignor.** **con·sign·ment** *s* ✝ **1.** Übersendung *f*, Zusendung *f*: **~ note** Frachtbrief *m.* **2.** (Waren)Sendung *f.* **con·sign·or** *s* ✝ Übersender *m.*

con·sist [kənˈsɪst] *v/i* **1.** ~ *in* bestehen *od.* sich zs.-setzen aus. **2.** ~ *in* bestehen in (*dat*). **con·sist·ence, con·sist·en·cy** *s* **1.** Konsistenz *f*, Beschaffenheit *f*, (Grad *m* der) Festigkeit *f od.* Dichtigkeit *f.* **2.** *fig.* Konsequenz *f*, Folgerichtigkeit *f.* **3.** *fig.* Übereinstimmung *f*, Einklang *m.* **con·sist·ent** *adj* □ **1.** konsistent, fest, dicht. **2.** *fig.* konsequent, folgerichtig. **3.** *fig.* übereinstimmend, vereinbar, in Einklang stehend (**with** mit). **4.** *fig.* beständig (*Leistung etc*).

con·so·la·tion [ˌkɒnsəˈleɪʃn] *s* Trost *m*: ~ **goal** (*Sport*) Ehrentor *n*; ~ **prize** Trostpreis *m.* **con·sol·a·to·ry** [kənˈsɒlətərɪ] *adj* tröstend, tröstlich.

con·sole[1] [ˈkɒnsəʊl] *s* **1.** Konsole *f*: ~ **table** Konsoltischchen *n.* **2.** (Fernseh-, Musik)Truhe *f*, (Radio)Schrank *m.* **3.** ♪ Schalt-, Steuerpult *n.*

con·sole[2] [kənˈsəʊl] *v/t* trösten: ~ **s.o. for s.th.** j-n über et. hinwegtrösten.

con·sol·i·date [kənˈsɒlɪdeɪt] **I** *v/t* **1.** (ver)stärken, festigen (*beide a. fig.*). **2.** ✗ *Truppen* zs.-ziehen. **3.** ✝ *Gesellschaften* zs.-schließen, -legen. **4.** ◉ verdichten. **II** *v/i* **5.** ✝ sich zs.-schließen. **6.** ◉ sich verdichten. **con·sol·i·da·tion** *s* **1.** (Ver)Stärkung *f*, Festigung *f.* **2.** ✗ Zs.-ziehung *f.* **3.** ✝ Zs.-legung *f*; Zs.-schluß *m.* **4.** ◉ Verdichtung *f.*

con·som·mé [kənˈsɒmeɪ] *s* Consommé *f* (*klare Kraftbrühe*).

con·so·nant [ˈkɒnsənənt] **I** *adj* □ **1.** gleichlautend. **2.** übereinstimmend (**with** mit). **II** *s* **3.** *ling.* Konsonant *m.*

con·sort [ˈkɒnsɔːt] *s* Gemahl(in): *prince* ~ Prinzgemahl. **con·sor·ti·um** [~tjəm] *pl* **-ti·a** [~ə] *s* ✝ Konsortium *n*: ~ **of banks** Bankenkonsortium.

con·spic·u·ous [kənˈspɪkjʊəs] *adj* □ **1.** deutlich sichtbar: **be** ~ *a.* in die Augen fallen. **2.** auffallend, -fällig: **make o.s.** ~ sich auffällig benehmen, auffallen. **3.** bemerkenswert (**for** wegen): **be** ~ **by one's absence** durch Abwesenheit

glänzen; **render o.s.** ~ sich hervortun.

con·spir·a·cy [kənˈspɪrəsɪ] *s* Verschwörung *f.* **con·spir·a·tor** *s* Verschwörer *m.* **con·spire** [~ˈspaɪə] *v/i* **1.** sich verschwören (**against** gegen) (*a. fig.*). **2.** *fig.* zs.-wirken.

con·sta·ble [ˈkʌnstəbl] *s bsd. Br.* Polizist *m*, Wachtmeister *m.* **con·stab·u·lar·y** [kənˈstæbjʊlərɪ] *s bsd. Br.* Polizei *f* (*e-s Bezirks*).

con·stan·cy [ˈkɒnstənsɪ] *s* **1.** Konstanz *f*, Beständigkeit *f.* **2.** Bestand *m*, Dauer *f.* **3.** *fig.* Standhaftigkeit *f.* **'con·stant I** *adj* □ **1.** konstant (*a. phys., ♣ etc*), beständig, gleichbleibend. **2.** (be)ständig, (an)dauernd: ~ **rain** anhaltender Regen. **3.** *fig.* standhaft, beharrlich. **II** *s* **4.** *phys., ♣* Konstante *f.*

con·stel·la·tion [ˌkɒnstəˈleɪʃn] *s ast.* Konstellation *f* (*a. fig.*), Sternbild *n.*

con·ster·na·tion [ˌkɒnstəˈneɪʃn] *s* Bestürzung *f*: **in** ~ konsterniert, bestürzt; **to my** ~ zu m-r Bestürzung.

con·sti·pate [ˈkɒnstɪpeɪt] *v/t* ✽ verstopfen: **be** ~**d** an Verstopfung leiden. **ˌcon·sti·ˈpa·tion** *s* Verstopfung *f.*

con·stit·u·en·cy [kənˈstɪtjʊənsɪ] *s* **1.** Wählerschaft *f.* **2.** Wahlbezirk *m*, -kreis *m.* **con·stit·u·ent I** *adj* **1.** e-n (Bestand)Teil bildend: ~ **part** → **a. 2.** *pol.* Wähler..., Wahl...: ~ **body** Wählerschaft *f.* **3.** ~ **assembly** *pol.* verfassunggebende Versammlung. **II** *s* **4.** (wesentlicher) Bestandteil. **5.** *pol.* Wähler(in).

con·sti·tute [ˈkɒnstɪtjuːt] *v/t* **1.** ernennen, einsetzen: ~ **s.o. a judge** j-n als Richter einsetzen *od.* zum Richter ernennen. **2.** *Gesetz* erlassen, in Kraft setzen. **3.** einrichten, gründen, *Ausschuß etc* einsetzen. **4.** ausmachen, bilden, darstellen. **ˌcon·sti·ˈtu·tion** *s* **1.** Zs.-setzung *f.* **2.** Konstitution *f*, körperliche Veranlagung. **3.** Natur *f*, Wesen *n*: **by** ~ von Natur (aus). **4.** Einrichtung *f*, Gründung *f*, Einsetzung *f.* **5.** *pol.* Verfassung *f.* **ˌcon·sti·ˈtu·tion·al I** *adj* □ **1.** ✽ konstitutionell, anlagebedingt. **2.** *pol.* a) verfassungsgemäß, Verfassungs...: → **monarchy**, b) rechtsstaatlich: ~ **state** Rechtsstaat *m.* **II** *s* **3.** F Gesundheitsspaziergang *m.*

con·strain [kənˈstreɪn] *v/t* **1.** *j-n* zwingen, nötigen: **feel** ~**ed to do s.th.** sich gezwungen fühlen, et. zu tun. **2.** *et.* erzwingen. **con'straint** [⁓'streınt] *s* Zwang *m*, Nötigung *f*: *under* ⁓ unter Zwang, gezwungen.

con·struct [kən'strʌkt] *v/t* **1.** errichten, bauen. **2.** ⊕ konstruieren (*a. ling.*, ⚕), bauen. **3.** *fig.* gestalten, ausarbeiten. **con'struc·tion** [⁓kʃn] *s* **1.** Errichtung *f*, Konstruktion *f* (*a.* ⊕, ⚕, *ling.*): *under* ⁓ im Bau (befindlich); ⁓ *industry* Baugewerbe *n*, -wirtschaft *f*; ⁓ *site* Baustelle *f*. **2.** Bauweise *f*: *steel* ⁓ Stahlkonstruktion *f*. **3.** Bau(werk *n*) *m*. **4.** *fig.* Aufbau *m*, Gestaltung *f*. **con'struc·tion·al** [⁓ʃənl] *adj* Konstruktions..., baulich. **con'struc·tive** [⁓] □ **1.** konstruktiv (*a. Kritik*), schöpferisch. **2.** → *constructional*. **con'struc·tor** *s* Erbauer *m*; Konstrukteur *m*.

con·strue [kən'struː] *v/t ling.* konstruieren.

con·sul ['kɒnsəl] *s* Konsul *m*: ⁓ *general* Generalkonsul *m*. **con·su·lar** ['⁓sjʊlə] *adj* Konsulats..., Konsular..., konsularisch. **con·su·late** ['⁓lət] *s* Konsulat *n* (*a. Gebäude*): ⁓ *general* Generalkonsulat.

con·sult [kən'sʌlt] **I** *v/t* **1.** um Rat fragen, zu Rate ziehen, konsultieren (*about* wegen). **2.** in *e-m Buch* nachschlagen *od.* -sehen. **3.** berücksichtigen. **II** *v/i* **4.** (sich) beraten (*about* über *acc*). **con'sult·ant** *s* **1.** (fachmännischer) Berater. **2.** ⚕ facharztlicher Berater; Facharzt *m* (*an e-m Krankenhaus*). **con·sul·ta·tion** [ˌkɒnsəl'teıʃn] *s* Beratung *f*, Konsultation *f*: *on* ⁓ *with* nach Rücksprache mit; ⁓ *hour* Sprechstunde *f*. **con'sult·ing** *adj* beratend: ⁓ *room* Sprechzimmer *n*.

con·sume [kən'sjuːm] *v/t* **1.** zerstören, vernichten: *be* ⁓*d by fire* ein Raub der Flammen werden. **2.** *fig.* verzehren: *be* ⁓*d with hatred* von Haß verzehrt werden. **3.** auf-, verzehren. **4.** auf-, verbrauchen, konsumieren. **5.** verschwenden, -geuden (*on* für). **6.** *Aufmerksamkeit etc* in Anspruch nehmen. **con'sum·er** *s* Verbraucher(in), Konsument(in): ⁓ *goods pl* Konsumgüter *pl*; ⁓ *protection* Verbraucherschutz *m*. **con·sum·mate I** *v/t* ['kɒnsʌmeıt] **1.** vollenden; *Ehe* vollziehen. **2.** vollkommen machen. **II** *adj* [kən'sʌmıt] **3.** vollendet,

vollkommen. **con·sum·ma·tion** [ˌkɒnsə'meıʃn] *s* Vollendung *f*; Vollziehung *f*.

con·sump·tion [kən'sʌmpʃn] *s* **1.** Verbrauch *m* (*of* an *dat*), ⚕ *a.* Konsum *m*. **2.** Verzehr *m*: *(un)fit for human* ⁓ für den menschlichen Verzehr (un)geeignet.

con·tact ['kɒntækt] **I** *s* **1.** Kontakt *m* (*a.* ⚡ *u. fig.*), Berührung *f*: *make* ⁓ ⚡ Verbindungen anknüpfen *od.* herstellen; *business* ⁓*s pl* Geschäftsverbindungen *pl*; ⁓ *lens* Haftlinse *f*, -schale *f*, Kontaktlinse *f*, -schale *f*. **2.** ✿ Kontaktperson *f*. **3. a.** ⁓ *man* Verbindungs-, Kontaktmann *m*. **II** *v/t* **4.** Kontakt aufnehmen mit, sich in Verbindung setzen mit.

con·ta·gion [kən'teıdʒən] *s* ✿ Ansteckung *f* (*durch Berührung*); ansteckende Krankheit. **con'ta·gious** *adj* □ ✿ ansteckend (*a. fig.*).

con·tain [kən'teın] *v/t* **1.** enthalten. **2.** aufnehmen, fassen. **3.** *fig.* zügeln, zurückhalten: ⁓ *o.s.* (an) sich halten, sich beherrschen. **con'tain·er** *s* **1.** Behälter *m*, (*Benzin- etc*)Kanister *m*. **2.** ✝ Container *m*: ⁓ *ship* Containerschiff *n*. **con'tain·er·ize** *v/t* **1.** auf Containerbetrieb umstellen. **2.** in Containern transportieren.

con·tam·i·nate [kən'tæmıneıt] *v/t* **1.** verunreinigen. **2.** infizieren, vergiften (*beide a. fig.*), (*a. radioaktiv*) verseuchen. **con·tam·i·na·tion** *s* **1.** Verunreinigung *f*. **2.** Infizierung *f*, Vergiftung *f* (*beide a. fig.*), (*a. radioaktive*) Verseuchung.

con·tem·plate ['kɒntempleıt] **I** *v/t* **1.** (nachdenklich) betrachten. **2.** nachdenken über (*acc*). **3.** erwägen, beabsichtigen (*doing* zu tun). **4.** erwarten, rechnen mit. **II** *v/i* **5.** nachdenken (*about, on* über *acc*). **con·tem·pla·tion** *s* **1.** (nachdenkliche) Betrachtung. **2.** Nachdenken *n*. **3.** Erwägung *f*: *be in* ⁓ erwogen werden. **'con·tem·pla·tive** *adj* □ nachdenklich.

con·tem·po·ra·ne·ous [kənˌtempə'reınjəs] *adj* □ gleichzeitig: *be* ⁓ *with* zeitlich zs.-fallen mit. **con'tem·po·ra·ry I** *adj* □ **1.** zeitgenössisch. **2.** → *contemporaneous*. **3.** gleichalt(e)rig. **II** *s* **4.** Zeitgenosse *m*, -genossin *f*. **5.** Altersgenosse *m*, -genossin *f*.

con·tempt [kən'tempt] *s* **1.** Verachtung *f*: ~ *of death* Todesverachtung; *feel* ~ *for, hold in* ~ verachten; *feel nothing but* ~ *for* nur Verachtung übrig haben für; *beneath* ~ unter aller Kritik; einfach lächerlich. **2.** Mißachtung *f*: ~ (*of court*) ⚖ Mißachtung des Gerichts. **con'tempt·i·ble** *adj* □ verächtlich, verachtenswert. **con'temp·tu·ous** [~t∫υəs] *adj* □ verächtlich, geringschätzig: *be* ~ *of s.th.* et. verachten.

con·tend [kən'tend] **I** *v/i* **1.** kämpfen, ringen (*with* mit; *for* um). **2.** *mit Worten* streiten (*about* über *acc*). **3.** wetteifern, sich bewerben (*for* um). **II** *v/t* **4.** behaupten (*that* daß).

con·tent¹ ['kɒntent] *s* **1.** *e-s Buchs etc*: a) Gehalt *m*, Aussage *f*, b) *pl* Inhalt *m* (*a. e-r Tasche etc*): (*table of*) ~s Inhaltsverzeichnis *n*. **2.** 🝣 Gehalt *m* (*of an dat*): *gold* ~ Goldgehalt.

con·tent² [kən'tent] **I** *adj* zufrieden (*with* mit): *have to be* ~ *with* sich begnügen müssen mit. **II** *v/t* zufriedenstellen: ~ *o.s. with* sich zufrieden geben *od.* begnügen mit. **III** *s* Zufriedenheit *f*: → *heart* 1. **con'tent·ed** *adj* □ zufrieden (*with* mit).

con·ten·tion [kən'ten∫n] *s* **1.** Streit *m*, Zank *m*: *bone of* ~ *fig.* Zankapfel *m*. **2.** Streitpunkt *m*. **3.** Behauptung *f*: *my* ~ *is that* ich behaupte, daß. **con'tentious** *adj* □ **1.** umstritten, strittig: ~ *point* Streitpunkt *m*.

con·tent·ment [kən'tentmənt] *s* Zufriedenheit *f*.

con·test I *s* ['kɒntest] **1.** (Wett)Kampf *m*; Wettbewerb *m* (*for* um). **II** *v/t* [kən'test] **2.** kämpfen um, sich bewerben um. **3.** bestreiten, *a.* ⚖ anfechten: ~ *s.o.'s right to do s.th.* j-m das Recht streitig machen, et. zu tun. **III** *v/i* [kən'test] **4.** wetteifern (*with, against* mit). **con'test·ant** *s* **1.** (Wettkampf-)Teilnehmer(in). **2.** (Mit)Bewerber(in). **con'test·ed** → *contentious* 2.

con·text ['kɒntekst] *s* Zs.-hang *m*, Kontext *m*: *in this* ~ in diesem Zs.-hang; *out of* ~ aus dem Zs.-hang gerissen.

con·ti·nent ['kɒntinənt] *s* **1.** Kontinent *m*, Erdteil *m*. **2.** *the* 🝣 *Br.* das (europäische) Festland. **con·ti·nen·tal** [~-'nentl] **I** *adj* **1.** kontinental, Kontinental... **2.** *mst* 🝣 *Br.* kontinental(europä-

isch): ~ *breakfast* kleines Frühstück; ~ *quilt* Federbett *n*. **II** *s* **3.** 🝣 *Br.* Kontinentaleuropäer(in).

con·tin·gen·cy [kən'tındʒənsɪ] *s* **1.** Zufälligkeit *f*. **2.** Möglichkeit *f*, Eventualität *f*: ~ *plan* Notplan *m*. **con'tin·gent I** *adj* □ **1.** (*on*) abhängig (von), bedingt (durch). **2.** möglich, eventuell. **3.** zufällig. **II** *s* **4.** (✕ Truppen)Kontingent *n*, Anteil *m*.

con·tin·u·al [kən'tınjυəl] *adj* □ **1.** (an)dauernd, ständig. **2.** immer wiederkehrend, sich wiederholend: *a* ~ *knocking* ein wiederholtes Klopfen. **con·'tin·u·ance** → *continuation*. **con·tin·u·a·tion** *s* **1.** Fortsetzung *f*. **2.** Fortbestand *m*, -dauer *f*. **con'tin·ue** [~ju:] **I** *v/i* **1.** fortfahren, weitermachen. **2.** andauern, anhalten. **3.** (fort)bestehen. **4.** (ver)bleiben: ~ *in office* im Amt bleiben. **5.** a) ~ *to do, ~ doing* (auch) weiterhin tun: ~ *to sing* weitersingen, b) ~ *to be, ~ being* weiterhin *od.* noch immer ... sein. **II** *v/t* **6.** fortsetzen, -führen, -fahren mit: *to be* ~*d* Fortsetzung folgt. **7.** beibehalten, erhalten. **con·ti·nu·i·ty** [ˌkɒntɪ'nju:ətɪ] *s* **1.** Kontinuität *f*. **2.** *Film:* Drehbuch *n*; *Rundfunk, TV:* Manuskript *n*: ~ *girl* Scriptgirl *n*. **con·tin·u·ous** [kən'tınjυəs] *adj* □ **1.** ununterbrochen, unaufhörlich. **2.** kontinuierlich: ~ *current* ≴ Gleichstrom *m*. **3.** ~ *form* *ling.* Verlaufsform *f*.

con·tort [kən'tɔ:t] **I** *v/t* **1.** *Glieder* verdrehen, verrenken. **2.** *Gesicht* verzerren, -ziehen (*with vor dat*): *face with pain* schmerzverzerrt. **3.** *fig.* *Tatsachen etc* verdrehen. **II** *v/i* **4.** sich verzerren *od.* verziehen (*with vor dat*; *in a grimace* zu e-r Grimasse). **con'tor·tion** *s* **1.** Verrenkung *f*. **2.** Verzerrung *f*. **3.** *fig.* Verdrehung *f*. **con'tor·tion·ist** *s* **1.** Schlangenmensch *m*. **2.** *a. verbal* ~ Wortverdreher(in).

con·tour ['kɒnˌtυə] *s* Kontur *f*, Umriß *m*.

con·tra·band ['kɒntrəbænd] *s* **1.** Schmuggelware *f*. **2.** Schmuggel *m*.

con·tra·cep·tion [ˌkɒntrə'sep∫n] *s* ✻ Empfängnisverhütung *f*. **con·tra·cep·tive** *adj u. s* empfängnisverhütend(es Mittel).

con·tract I *s* ['kɒntrækt] **1.** Vertrag *m*: ~ *of employment* Arbeitsvertrag; ~ *of* *sale* Kaufvertrag; *enter into* (*od.* *make*) *a* ~ e-n Vertrag abschließen; *by* ~ vertraglich; *be under* ~ unter Vertrag stehen (*with, to* bei). **II** *v/t* [kən'trækt] **2.** *Muskel etc* zs.-ziehen, *Stirn* runzeln. **3.** *Gewohnheit* annehmen; *sich e-e Krankheit* zuziehen. **4.** *Schulden* machen. **5.** *Verpflichtung* eingehen; *Ehe etc* schließen. **III** *v/i* [kən'trækt] **6.** sich zs.-ziehen. **7.** e-n Vertrag abschließen; sich vertraglich verpflichten (*to do* zu tun; *for* zu): *~ for s.th.* et. vertraglich festsetzen. con'trac·tion *s* Zs.-ziehung *f.* con'trac·tor *s* (*bsd.* Bau)Unternehmer *m*; (Vertrags)Lieferant *m*. con-'trac·tu·al [~t∫υəl] *adj* □ vertraglich, Vertrags...

con·tra·dict [ˌkɒntrə'dɪkt] *v/t* **1.** *j-m, e-r Sache* widersprechen, *et.* bestreiten. **2.** widersprechen (*dat*), im Widerspruch stehen zu, unvereinbar sein mit. ˌcon·tra'dic·tion *s* **1.** Widerspruch *m*, -rede *f.* **2.** Unvereinbarkeit *f*: *be in* ~ *to* im Widerspruch stehen zu; ~ *in terms* Widerspruch *m* in sich selbst. ˌcon·tra'dic·to·ry *adj* □ **1.** (*to*) widersprechend (*dat*), im Widerspruch stehend (zu), unvereinbar (mit). **2.** sich widersprechend, widersprüchlich.

con·tral·to [kən'træltəʊ] *pl* **-tos** *s* ♪ Alt(stimme *f*) *m*; Altistin *f.*

con·trap·tion [kən'træp∫n] *s* F (komischer) Apparat.

con·tra·ry ['kɒntrərɪ] **I** *adj* **1.** entgegengesetzt (*to dat*). **2.** einander entgegengesetzt, gegensätzlich. **3.** widrig, ungünstig (*Wind, Wetter*). **4.** (*to*) verstoßend (gegen), im Widerspruch (zu). **II** *adv* **5.** im Widerspruch (*to* zu): ~ *to expectations* wider Erwarten; *act* ~ *to* zuwiderhandeln (*dat*); → *law* 1. **III** *s* **6.** Gegenteil *n*: *on the* ~ im Gegenteil; *be the* ~ *to* das Gegenteil sein von; *to the* ~ gegenteilig; *proof to the* ~ Gegenbeweis *m.*

con·trast **I** *s* ['kɒntrɑːst] **1.** Kontrast *m* (*a. TV etc*), Gegensatz *m* (*between* zwischen *dat*): *form a* ~ e-n Kontrast bilden (*to* zu); *by* ~ *with* im Vergleich mit; *in* ~ *to* (*od. with*) im Gegensatz zu. **II** *v/t* [kən'trɑːst] **2.** entgegensetzen, gegenüberstellen (*with dat*). **III** *v/i* [kən'trɑːst] **3.** sich abheben, abstechen (*with* von, gegen): *~ing* colo(u)rs *pl*

Kontrastfarben *pl.* **4.** e-n Gegensatz bilden, im Gegensatz stehen (*with* zu).

con·tra·vene [ˌkɒntrə'viːn] *v/t* **1.** zuwiderhandeln (*dat*), *Gesetz* übertreten, verstoßen gegen. **2.** im Widerspruch stehen zu. ˌcon·tra'ven·tion [~'ven∫n] *s* (*of*) Zuwiderhandlung *f* (gegen), Übertretung *f* (von *od. gen*): *in* ~ *to* entgegen (*dat*).

con·trib·ute [kən'trɪbjuːt] **I** *v/t* **1.** beitragen, -steuern (*to* zu). **2.** *Artikel etc* beitragen (*to* für *e-e Zeitung etc*). **3.** spenden (*to* für). **4.** ✝ *Kapital* (*in e-e Firma*) einbringen. **II** *v/i* **5.** (*to*) beitragen, -steuern, e-n Beitrag leisten (zu), mitwirken (an *dat*): ~ *to* (*od. toward*[s]) *the expenses* sich an den Unkosten beteiligen; ~ *to a newspaper* für e-e Zeitung schreiben. **6.** spenden (*to* für). con·tri·bu·tion [ˌkɒntrɪ'bjuː∫n] *s* **1.** Beitrag *m* (*a. für Zeitung etc*), Beisteuer *f*: ~ *to* (*od. toward*[s]) *the expenses* Unkostenbeitrag. **2.** Spende *f*: *a small* ~, *please.* **3.** ✝ Einlage *f.* con·trib·u·tor [kən'trɪbjʊtə] *s* **1.** Beitragende *m, f.* **2.** Mitarbeiter(in) (*to a newspaper* bei *od.* an e-r Zeitung). con'trib·u·to·ry *adj* beitragend.

con·trite ['kɒntraɪt] *adj* □ zerknirscht, reuevoll. con·tri·tion [kən'trɪ∫n] *s* Zerknirschung *f*, Reue *f.*

con·triv·ance [kən'traɪvns] *s* **1.** ❂ Vorrichtung *f*; Gerät *n*, Apparat *m.* **2.** Erfindung *f.* **3.** Erfindungsgabe *f.* **4.** Plan *m.* **5.** Kunstgriff *m*, Kniff *m.* con'trive *v/t* **1.** erfinden, sich ausdenken. **2.** *et. Böses* aushecken, *Pläne* schmieden. **3.** zustande bringen; es fertigbringen, es verstehen (*to do* zu tun).

con·trol [kən'trəʊl] **I** *v/t* **1.** beherrschen, die Herrschaft *od.* Kontrolle haben über (*acc*). **2.** in Schranken halten, (erfolgreich) bekämpfen: ~ *o.s.* sich beherrschen. **3.** kontrollieren: a) überwachen, beaufsichtigen, b) (nach)prüfen. **4.** leiten, führen, verwalten. **5.** ✝ *Absatz etc* lenken, *Preise* binden. **6.** ⚡, ❂ steuern, regeln, regulieren. **II** *s* **7.** (*of, over*) Beherrschung *f* (*gen*), Macht *f*, Gewalt *f*, Kontrolle *f*, Herrschaft *f* (über *acc*): *bring* (*od. get*) *under* ~ unter Kontrolle bringen; *get out of* ~ außer Kontrolle geraten; *lose* ~ *of* (*od. over*) die Herrschaft *od.* Kontrolle verlieren über (acc); **lose ~ of o.s.** die (Selbst)Beherrschung verlieren. **8.** Aufsicht f, Kontrolle f (**of, over** über acc): **be in ~ of** et. leiten od. unter sich haben; **be under s.o.'s ~** j-m unterstehen od. unterstellt sein. **9.** Leitung f, Verwaltung f. **10.** mst pl ⚙ Steuerung f, Steuervorrichtung f; Kontroll-, Betätigungshebel m: **be at the ~s** fig. das Sagen haben; an den (Schalt)Hebeln der Macht sitzen. **11.** ⚡, ⚙ Reg(e)lung f, Regulierung f; Regler m. **~ cen·tre** (Am. **cen·ter**) s Kontrollzentrum n. **~ desk** s **1.** ⚡ Schaltpult n. **2.** Rundfunk, TV: Regiepult n.

con·trol·la·ble [kən'trəʊləbl] adj **1.** kontrollierbar. **2.** ⚡, ⚙ steuer-, regel-, regulierbar. **con'trol·ler** s **1.** Kontrolleur m, Aufseher m. **2.** ✝ Controller m (Fachmann für Kostenrechnung u. -planung).

con·trol| le·ver s **1.** ⚙ Schalthebel m. **2.** → **control stick. ~ room** s Rundfunk, TV: Regieraum m. **~ stick** s ✈ Steuerknüppel m. **~ tow·er** s ✈ Kontrollturm m, Tower m.

con·tro·ver·sial [ˌkɒntrə'vɜːʃl] adj □ **1.** strittig, umstritten. **2.** polemisch. **3.** streitsüchtig. **con·tro·ver·sy** ['~sɪ] s **1.** Kontroverse f: **beyond ~** unstreitig. **2.** a. **point in ~** Streitfrage f, -punkt m.

con·tuse [kən'tjuːz] v/t 𝕗 sich et. quetschen. **con'tu·sion** [~ʒn] s Quetschung f.

co·nun·drum [kə'nʌndrəm] s Scherzfrage f, (Scherz)Rätsel n.

con·ur·ba·tion [ˌkɒnɜː'beɪʃn] s Ballungsraum m, -zentrum n.

con·va·lesce [ˌkɒnvə'les] v/i gesund werden. **con·va'les·cence** s Rekonvaleszenz f, Genesung f. **con·va'les·cent I** adj rekonvaleszent, genesend. **II** s Rekonvaleszent(in), Genesende m, f.

con·vene [kən'viːn] **I** v/i zs.-kommen, sich versammeln. **II** v/t versammeln, zs.-rufen, Versammlung einberufen.

con·ven·ience [kən'viːnjəns] s **1.** Annehmlichkeit f, Bequemlichkeit f: **all** (**modern**) **~s** aller Komfort; **at your ~** wenn es Ihnen gerade paßt; **at your earliest ~** so bald wie möglich. **2.** bsd. Br. Toilette f. **con'ven·ient** adj □ **1.** bequem, praktisch. **2.** günstig, passend: **be ~ for s.o.** j-m passen.

con·vent ['kɒnvənt] s (bsd. Nonnen)Kloster n.

con·ven·tion [kən'venʃn] s **1.** Zs.-kunft f, Tagung f, Versammlung f. **2.** a) pol. Am. Parteiversammlung f, -tag m, b) Kongreß m: **~ centre** (Am. **center**) Kongreßzentrum n. **3.** bilaterales Abkommen; multilaterales Übereinkommen, Konvention f. **4.** (gesellschaftliche) Konvention, Sitte f. **con'ven·tion·al** [~ʃənl] adj □ **1.** konventionell, herkömmlich (beide a. ✕). **2.** contp. schablonenhaft, unoriginell. **3.** konventionell, förmlich.

con·verge [kən'vɜːdʒ] v/i zs.-laufen (Straßen, Flüsse), 𝔸 konvergieren (a. fig.), fig. sich annähern. **con'vergence, con'ver·gen·cy** s **1.** Zs.-laufen n. **2.** 𝔸 Konvergenz f (a. fig.). **con'ver·gent** adj 𝔸 konvergent, fig. a. sich annähernd.

con·ver·sa·tion [ˌkɒnvə'seɪʃn] s Konversation f, Unterhaltung f, Gespräch n: **in ~ with** im Gespräch mit; **get into ~ with s.o.** mit j-m ins Gespräch kommen; **make ~** Konversation machen. **con·ver'sa·tion·al** [~ʃənl] adj □ **1.** gesprächig. **2.** Unterhaltungs..., Gesprächs...: **~ English** Umgangsenglisch n; **~ tone** Plauderton m. **con·ver'sa·tion·al·ly** [~ʃnəlɪ] adv im Plauderton.

con·verse [kən'vɜːs] v/i sich unterhalten (**with** mit; **on, about** über acc).

con·ver·sion [kən'vɜːʃn] s **1.** Um-, Verwandlung f (**into, to** in acc). **2.** 🏗, ⚙ Umbau m (**into** zu). **3.** ⚙, a. ✝ Umstellung f (**to** auf acc). **4.** 𝔸 Umrechnung f (**into, to** in acc): **~ table** Umrechnungstabelle f. **5.** Bekehrung f, eccl. a. Konversion f, Übertritt m (a. pol. etc) (**to** zu).

con·vert I v/t [kən'vɜːt] **1.** allg., a. 🦃 um-, verwandeln (**into, to** in acc). **2.** 🏗, ⚙ umbauen (**into** zu). **3.** ⚙, a. ✝ umstellen (**to** auf acc). **4.** 𝔸 umrechnen (**into, to** in acc). **5.** eccl. etc bekehren (**to** zu). **II** v/i [kən'vɜːt] **6.** sich umwandeln od. verwandeln (**into, to** in acc). **7.** sich bekehren, eccl. a. konvertieren, übertreten (a. pol. etc) (**to** zu). **III** s ['kɒnvɜːt] **8.** Bekehrte m, f, eccl. a. Konvertit(in). **con'vert·i·ble I** adj □ **1.** um-, verwandelbar. **2.** 𝔸 umrechenbar. **II** s **3.** mot. Kabriolett n.

con·vex [kɒn'veks] *adj* □ konvex: **~** *mir·ror* Konvex-, Wölbspiegel *m*.

con·vey [kən'veɪ] *v/t* **1.** *Waren etc* befördern, transportieren (*beide a.* ⚙). **2.** *Grüße etc* überbringen, -mitteln. **3.** *Ideen etc* mitteilen, vermitteln, *Meinung, Sinn* ausdrücken. **con'vey·ance** *s* **1.** Beförderung *f*, Transport *m*. **2.** Transport-, Verkehrsmittel *n*. **3.** Überbringung *f*, -mittlung *f*. **4.** Mitteilung *f*, Vermittlung *f*. **con'vey·er, con'vey·or** *s a.* **~** *belt* ⚙ Förderband *n*.

con·vict I *v/t* [kən'vɪkt] **1.** ⚖ (*of*) überführen, für schuldig erklären (*gen*); verurteilen (*wegen*). **2.** überzeugen (*of* von). **II** *s* ['kɒnvɪkt] **3.** Verurteilte *m, f*. **4.** Strafgefangene *m, f*, Sträfling *m*. **con'vic·tion** *s* **1.** ⚖ Überführung *f*, Schuldspruch *m*; Verurteilung *f*: → *previous* 1. **2.** Überzeugung *f*: *from* **~** aus Überzeugung; → *carry* 5.

con·vince [kən'vɪns] *v/t* überzeugen (*of* von; *that* daß). **con'vinc·ing** *adj* □ überzeugend: **~** *proof* schlagender Beweis.

con·voy ['kɒnvɔɪ] *I* **s** **1.** Geleit *n*, Begleitung *f*. **2.** Konvoi *m*: a) ✕, *a. allg.* (Wagen)Kolonne *f*, b) ⚓ Geleitzug *m*. **II** *v/t* **3.** Geleitschutz geben (*dat*).

con·vulse [kən'vʌls] *I* *v/t* **1.** in Zuckungen versetzen: *be* **~***d with* → 4. **2.** *Muskeln etc* krampfhaft zs.-ziehen: **~***d fea·tures pl* verzerrte Züge *pl*. **3.** in Lachkrämpfe versetzen. **II** *v/i* **4.** **~** *with* sich krümmen vor (*Lachen, Schmerzen etc*). **con'vul·sion** *s* **1.** *bsd.* ✚ Krampf *m*, Zuckung *f*: *nervous* **~***s pl* nervöse Zuckungen *pl*. **2.** *pl* Lachkrampf *m*: *they were in* **~***s* sie krümmten sich vor Lachen. **con'vul·sive** *adj* □ krampfhaft.

coo [kuː] *I* *v/i* gurren (*a. fig.*). **II** *s* Gurren *n*.

cook [kʊk] *I* **s** **1.** Koch *m*, Köchin *f*: *too many* **~***s spoil the broth* viele Köche verderben den Brei. **II** *v/t* **2.** kochen. **3.** *a.* **~** *up* F *Geschichte etc* erfinden, sich ausdenken. **4.** F *Rechnung etc* frisieren. **III** *v/i* **5.** kochen. **6.** kochen, gekocht werden: *what's* **~***ing?* F was ist los? **'~·book** *s bsd. Am.* Kochbuch *n*.

cook·er ['kʊkə] *s* Kocher *m*, Kochgerät *n*; *Br.* Herd *m*: **~** *hood Br.* Abzugshaube *f*. **'cook·er·y** *s* Kochen *n*, Kochkunst *f*: **~** *book bsd. Br.* Kochbuch *n*.

cook·ie ['ʊkɪ] *s Am.* (süßer) Keks, Plätzchen *n*. **'cook·ing I** *s* **1.** Kochen *n*. **2.** Küche *f*, Art *f* zu kochen: *Italian* **~** die italienische Küche. **II** *adj* **3.** Koch... **'cook·y** → *cookie*.

cool [kuːl] *I* *adj* □ **1.** kühl, frisch: *get* **~** sich abkühlen. **2.** *fig.* kühl: a) gelassen, kalt(blütig): *keep* **~** e-n kühlen Kopf behalten, sich nicht aufregen; → *cu·cumber*, b) gleichgültig, c) abweisend. **3.** F glatt: *a* **~** *thousand pounds* glatte *od.* die Kleinigkeit von tausend Pfund. **4.** *bsd. Am.* F klasse, prima. **II** *s* **5.** Kühle *f*, Frische *f* (*der Luft*). **6.** F (Selbst)Beherrschung *f*: *blow* (*od. lose*) *one's* **~** hochgehen; *keep one's* **~** ruhig bleiben. **III** *v/t* **7.** (ab)kühlen, abkühlen lassen: **~** *it!* F immer mit der Ruhe!; reg dich ab! **IV** *v/i* **8.** kühl werden, sich abkühlen: **~** *down* F sich abregen. **~** *bag s* F Kühltasche *f.* **~** *box s* Kühlbox *f.*

cool·er ['kuːlə] *s* **1.** (*Wein- etc*)Kühler *m*. **2.** *sl.* Kittchen *n*. **,cool'head·ed** *adj* □ besonnen. **cool·ing** ['kuːlɪŋ] *adj* **1.** (ab)kühlend. **2.** ⚙ Kühl... **'cool·ness** *s* **1.** Kühle *f* (*a. fig.*). **2.** Kaltblütigkeit *f*.

co-op ['kəʊɒp] *s* F Co-op *m* (*Genossenschaft u. Laden*).

co·op·er·ate [kəʊ'ɒpəreɪt] *v/i* **1.** zs.-arbeiten (*with* mit; *in* bei; *to, toward*[*s*] zu e-m Zweck). **2.** (*in*) mitwirken (an *dat*), helfen, behilflich sein (bei). **co,op·er'a·tion** *s* **1.** Zs.-arbeit *f*. **2.** Mitwirkung *f*, Hilfe *f*. **co'op·er·a·tive** [~ətɪv] *I* *adj* □ **1.** zs.-arbeitend. **2.** mitwirkend. **3.** kooperativ, hilfsbereit. **4.** ✚ Gemeinschafts...; Genossenschafts...: **~** *society* → 5; **~** *store* → 6. **II** *s* **5.** Co-op *m*: a) Genossenschaft *f*, b) Konsumverein *m*. **6.** Co-op *m*, Konsumladen *m*.

co·or·di·nate *I* *v/t* [kəʊ'ɔːdɪneɪt] koordinieren, bei-, gleichordnen, aufeinander abstimmen. **II** *adj* [~dnət] □ koordiniert, bei-, gleichgeordnet. **III** *s* [~dnət] ✚ Koordinate *f*. **co,or·di'na·tion** *s* Koordinierung *f*, Koordination *f*, Bei-, Gleichordnung *f*, Abstimmung *f*.

cop [kɒp] *sl.* **I** *v/t* **1.** erwischen (*at* bei): **~** *it* sein Fett (ab)kriegen; → *packet* 3. **II** *s* **2.** *no great* **~**, *not much* **~** *Br.* nicht so toll. **3.** Bulle *m* (*Polizist*).

co·part·ner [ˌkəʊˈpɑːtnə] *s* Teilhaber *m*,

Mitinhaber *m*. ,**co'part·ner·ship** *s* **1.** Teilhaberschaft *f*. **2.** *Br*. Gewinn- *od*. Mitbeteiligung *f* (*of labour* der Arbeitnehmer).

cope [kəʊp] *v/i* (*with*) gewachsen sein (*dat*), fertig werden (mit).

cop·i·lot ['kəʊpaɪlət] *s* Kopiergerät *n*, Kopierer *m*.

co·pi·lot ['kəʊpaɪlət] *s* ✈ Kopilot *m*.

co·pi·ous ['kəʊpjəs] *adj* □ **1.** reich(lich), ausgiebig. **2.** wortreich, weitschweifig. **3.** produktiv (*Schriftsteller etc*).

cop·per¹ ['kɒpə] *s* **1.** *min*. Kupfer *n*. **2.** Kupfermünze *f*; ⹂**s** *pl* Kupfergeld *n*. **II** *adj* **3.** kupfern, Kupfer... **4.** kupferrot.

cop·per² [⹂] *s sl*. Bulle *m* (*Polizist*).

cop·per| ore *s min*. Kupfererz *n*. '⹂**plate** *s* Kupferstich(platte *f*) *m*: **like ⹂** wie gestochen (*Schrift*). '⹂**smith** *s* Kupferschmied *m*.

cop·u·la ['kɒpjʊlə] *s ling*. Kopula *f*. **cop·u·late** ['⹂leɪt] *v/i* kopulieren: a) koitieren, b) *zo*. sich paaren. ,**cop·u'la·tion** *s* Kopulation *f*: a) Koitus *m*, b) Paarung *f*.

cop·y ['kɒpɪ] **I** *s* **1.** Kopie *f*, Abschrift *f*: *fair* (*od. clean*) ⹂ Reinschrift *f*; *rough* (*od. foul*) ⹂ Rohentwurf *m*, Konzept *n*. **2.** Durchschlag *m*, -schrift *f*. **3.** *phot*. Abzug *m*. **4.** Nachbildung *f*, Kopie *f*. **5.** *typ*. (Satz)Vorlage *f*. **6.** Exemplar *n* (*e-s Buchs etc*). **7.** (Werbe-, Zeitungs-*etc*)Text *m*. **II** *v/t* **8.** abschreiben (*off*, *from* von), e-e Kopie anfertigen (von, *Kassette etc* überspielen. **9.** durch-, abpausen; kopieren. **10.** *phot*. e-n Abzug machen von. **11.** nachbilden. **12.** kopieren, nachahmen, -machen. **III** *v/i* **13.** abschreiben (*from* von). '⹂**cat** F **I** *s* (*bsd*. sklavischer *od*. gedankenloser) Nachahmer. **II** *v/t* (*bsd*. sklavisch *od*. gedankenlos) nachahmen *od*. -machen. ⹂ **ed·i·tor** *s* Zeitungsredakteur(in); Lektor(in).

cop·y·ing| ma·chine ['kɒpɪɪŋ] *s* Kopiergerät *n*. ⹂ **pa·per** *s* Kopierpapier *n*.

'**cop·y| read·er** *Am*. → **copy editor**. '⹂**right** ⛌⛌ **I** *s* Urheberrecht *n*, Copyright *n* (*in*, *on*, *of*, *for* für, von). **II** *v/t* das Urheberrecht erwerben für *od*. von; urheberrechtlich schützen. **III** *adj* urheberrechtlich geschützt. '⹂**writ·er** *s* Werbetexter *m*.

cor·al ['kɒrəl] *s* **1.** *zo*. Koralle *f*. **II** *adj* **2.** Korallen... **3.** korallenrot.

cord [kɔːd] **I** *s* **1.** Schnur *f* (*a*. ⚡), Kordel *f*, Strick *m*. **2.** gerippter Stoff, *bsd*. Kordsamt *m*. **II** *v/t* **3.** festbinden; ver-, zuschnüren.

cor·dial ['kɔːdjəl] **I** *adj* □ **1.** herzlich. **2.** ⚕ belebend, stärkend. **II** *s* **3.** ⚕ Stärkungsmittel *n*. **4.** Fruchtsaftgetränk *n*. **5.** Likör *m*. **cor·dial·i·ty** [,kɔː'dʒælətɪ] *s* Herzlichkeit *f*.

cor·don ['kɔːdn] **I** *s* Kordon *m*, Postenod. Absperrkette *f*. **II** *v/t* a. ⹂ *off* (mit Posten *od*. Seilen) absperren *od*. abriegeln.

cor·du·roy ['kɔːdərɔɪ] *s* **1.** Kordsamt *m*. **2.** *pl*, *a. pair of* ⹂**s** Kord(samt)hose *f*.

core [kɔː] **I** *s* **1.** ⚘ Kerngehäuse *n*; Kern *m*. **2.** *fig*. Kern *m*, das Innerste: *to the* ⹂ bis ins Innerste; durch u. durch. **II** *v/t* **3.** *Obst* entkernen. ⹂ **time** *s* Kernzeit *f*.

cork [kɔːk] **I** *s* **1.** Kork *m*. **2.** Korken *m*, Pfropfen *m*. **II** *v/t* **3.** *oft* ⹂ *up* zu-, verkorken.

'**cork·screw** *s* Korkenzieher *m*.

corn¹ [kɔːn] **I** *s* **1.** Korn *n*, Getreide *n*: *bsd*. a) *Br*. Weizen *m*, b) *schott*., *ir*. Hafer *m*. **2.** *a. Indian* ⹂ *Am*. Mais *m*. **II** *v/t* **3.** pökeln: *⹂ed beef* Corned beef *n*, gepökeltes Rindfleisch.

corn² [⹂] *s* ⚕ Hühnerauge *n*: *tread on s.o.'s* ⹂**s** *fig*. j-m auf die Hühneraugen treten.

corn| bread *s Am*. Maisbrot *n*. '⹂**cob** *s Am*. Maiskolben *m*.

cor·ne·a ['kɔːnɪə] *pl* **-as**, **-ae** [⹂iː] *s* Hornhaut *f* (*des Auges*).

cor·ner ['kɔːnə] **I** *s* **1.** Ecke *f*, *bsd*. *mot*. Kurve *f*: *take a* ⹂ → **5**; *turn the* ⹂ um die Ecke biegen; *he's turned the* ⹂ *fig*. er ist über den Berg. **2.** Winkel *m*, Ecke *f*: ⹂ *of the mouth* Mundwinkel; *look at s.o. from the* ⹂ *of one's eye* j-n aus den Augenwinkeln (heraus) ansehen; *drive* (*od. force, put*) *into a* ⹂ → **4**; *be in a tight* ⹂ in der Klemme sein *od*. sitzen *od*. stecken. **3.** *Fußball*: Eckball *m*, Ecke *f*. **II** *v/t* **4.** in die Enge treiben. **III** *v/i* **5.** *mot*. e-e Kurve nehmen: ⹂ *well* gut in der Kurve liegen, e-e gute Kurvenlage haben. **IV** *adj* **6.** Eck...: ⹂ *house*; ⹂ *seat* Eckplatz *m*. '**cor·nered** *adj*; *in Zssgn* ...eckig.

cor·ner| kick *s Fußball*: Eckstoß *m*.

'**~stone** s 1. △ Eckstein m; Grundstein m. 2. fig. Eckpfeiler m.

'**corn|·field** s 1. Br. Korn-, Getreidefeld n. 2. Am. Maisfeld n. '**~flakes** s pl Corn-flakes pl. '**~flow·er** s ♀ Kornblume f.

Cor·nish ['kɔːnɪʃ] adj kornisch, aus Cornwall.

corn pop·py s ♀ Klatschmohn m.

corn·y ['kɔːnɪ] adj sl. sentimental, schmalzig; kitschig; abgedroschen: **a ~ joke** ein Witz mit Bart.

cor·o·nar·y ['kɒrənərɪ] adj anat. Koronar...: **~ vessel** (Herz)Kranzgefäß n.

cor·o·na·tion [ˌkɒrə'neɪʃn] s Krönung(sfeier) f.

cor·o·ner ['kɒrənə] s ⚖ Coroner m (richterlicher Beamter zur Untersuchung der Todesursache in Fällen gewaltsamen od. unnatürlichen Todes): **~'s inquest** gerichtliches Verfahren zur Untersuchung der Todesursache.

cor·po·ral[1] ['kɔːpərəl] s ✕ Unteroffizier m.

cor·po·ral[2] [~] adj □ körperlich, leiblich: **~ punishment** körperliche Züchtigung.

cor·po·rate ['kɔːpərət] adj □ 1. a) ⚖ körperschaftlich, Körperschafts...: **~ body → corporation** 1, b) ✝ Am. Gesellschafts..., Firmen...: **~ planning** Unternehmensplanung f. 2. gemeinsam, kollektiv. **cor·po·ra·tion** [~'reɪʃn] s 1. ⚖ Körperschaft f, juristische Person: **~ tax** Körperschaftssteuer f. 2. a. **stock ~** ✝ Am. Kapital- od. Aktiengesellschaft f. 3. Br. Innung f. 4. Br. Stadtverwaltung f. 5. F Schmerbauch m.

corps [kɔː] pl **corps** [~z] s 1. ✕ Korps n, Truppe f. 2. Korps n: **→ diplomatic.**

corpse [kɔːps] s Leichnam m, Leiche f.

cor·pu·lence, cor·pu·len·cy ['kɔːpjʊləns(ɪ)] s Beleibtheit f, Korpulenz f. '**cor·pu·lent** adj □ beleibt, korpulent.

Cor·pus Chris·ti [ˌkɔːpəs'krɪstɪ] s eccl. Fronleichnam(sfest n) m.

cor·ral [kə'rɑːl] Am. I s 1. Pferch m. II v/t 2. in e-n Pferch treiben. 3. fig. einpferchen, -sperren. 4. F sich et. schnappen.

cor·rect [kə'rekt] I v/t 1. korrigieren, verbessern, berichtigen: **I stand ~ed** ich nehme alles zurück. 2. Mängel etc

abstellen. 3. zurechtweisen, tadeln; (be)strafen (**for** wegen). II adj 4. korrekt: a) richtig: **be ~** stimmen; recht haben, b) einwandfrei (Benehmen). **cor·rec·tion** s 1. Korrektur f, Verbesserung f, Berichtigung f. 2. Zurechtweisung f, Tadel m; Bestrafung f. **cor·rec·tive** adj □ korrigierend, verbessernd, berichtigend. **cor·rect·ness** s Korrektheit f, Richtigkeit f.

cor·re·late ['kɒrɪleɪt] I v/t 1. in Wechselbeziehung bringen (**with** mit). 2. in Übereinstimmung bringen (**with** mit), aufeinander abstimmen. II v/i 3. in Wechselbeziehung stehen (**with** mit), sich aufeinander beziehen. 4. übereinstimmen (**with** mit). **cor·re·la·tion** s 1. Wechselbeziehung f. 2. Übereinstimmung f.

cor·re·spond [ˌkɒrɪ'spɒnd] v/i 1. (**to, with**) entsprechen (dat), übereinstimmen (mit). 2. (**to**) entsprechen (dat), das Gegenstück sein (von). 3. korrespondieren, in Briefwechsel stehen (**with** mit). **cor·re·spond·ence** s 1. Entsprechung f, Übereinstimmung f. 2. Korrespondenz f: a) Briefwechsel m: **be in ~** (**with**) → **correspond** 3; **~ course** Fernkurs m; **~ school** Fernlehrinstitut n, b) Briefe pl. **cor·re·spond·ent** I s 1. Korrespondent(in): **be a good** (**bad**) **~** fleißig schreiben (schreibfaul sein). 2. ✝ (auswärtiger) Geschäftsfreund. 3. Korrespondent(in), Berichterstatter(in) (e-r Zeitung etc): **foreign ~** Auslandskorrespondent(in). II adj □ 4. entsprechend, gemäß (**to** dat). **cor·re·spond·ing → correspondent** 4.

cor·ri·dor ['kɒrɪdɔː] s Korridor m, Gang m. **~ train** s D-Zug m.

cor·rode [kə'rəʊd] I v/t 1. 🔥, ⚙ korrodieren, an-, zerfressen, angreifen. 2. fig. zerfressen, untergraben. II v/i 3. korrodieren. 4. rosten. **~d** rostig. **cor·ro·sion** [~ʒn] s 1. 🔥, ⚙ Korrosion f. 2. Rostfraß m, -bildung f. 3. fig. Untergrabung f. **cor·ro·sive** [~sɪv] adj □ 1. 🔥, ⚙ korrodierend, Korrosions... fig. nagend, quälend.

cor·ru·gat·ed ['kɒrʊgeɪtɪd] adj gewellt: **~ cardboard** Wellpappe f; **~ iron** (od. **sheet**) Wellblech n.

cor·rupt [kə'rʌpt] I adj □ 1. (moralisch) verdorben. 2. unredlich, unlauter. 3.

korrupt: a) bestechlich, b) Bestechungs... **II** v/t **4.** (moralisch) verderben. **5.** korrumpieren, bestechen. **III** v/i **6.** (moralisch) verderben, -kommen.

cor·rupt·i·ble → **corrupt** 3a. **cor·rup·tion** s **1.** Verdorbenheit f. **2.** Unredlichkeit f, Unlauterkeit f. **3.** Korruption f: a) Bestechlichkeit f, b) Bestechung f. **cor·rup·tive** adj verderblich (Einfluß etc).

cor·set ['kɔːsɪt] s a. pl Korsett n.

cosh [kɒʃ] s Br. F Totschläger m (Waffe).

co·sig·na·to·ry [ˌkəʊˈsɪɡnətərɪ] s Mitunterzeichner(in).

co·sine ['kəʊsaɪn] s A Kosinus m.

co·si·ness ['kəʊzɪnɪs] s Behaglichkeit f, Gemütlichkeit f.

cos·met·ic [kɒzˈmetɪk] **I** adj (~ally) kosmetisch (a. fig.): ~ surgery Schönheitschirurgie f. **II** s kosmetisches Mittel. **cos·me·ti·cian** [ˌkɒzməˈtɪʃn] s Kosmetiker(in).

cos·mic ['kɒzmɪk] adj □ kosmisch.

cos·mo·naut ['kɒzmənɔːt] s (Welt-) Raumfahrer m, Kosmonaut m.

cos·mo·pol·i·tan [ˌkɒzməˈpɒlɪtən] **I** adj kosmopolitisch, weltbürgerlich, weitS. weltoffen. **II** s Kosmopolit(in), Weltbürger(in).

cos·mos ['kɒzmɒs] s Kosmos m, Weltall n.

cost [kɒst] **I** s **1.** Kosten pl, Aufwand m: ~ of living Lebenshaltungskosten. **2.** Kosten pl, Schaden m: at s.o.'s ~ auf j-s Kosten; at the ~ of his health auf Kosten s-r Gesundheit. **3.** Opfer n, Preis m: at all ~s, at any ~ um jeden Preis; at a heavy ~ unter schweren Opfern. **4.** ✝ (Selbst-, Gestehungs)Kosten pl: ~ abatement Kostendämpfung f; ~ increase Kostensteigerung f; ~ inflation Kosteninflation f; ~ price Selbstkostenpreis m; at ~ zum Selbstkostenpreis. **5.** pl ⚖️ (Gerichts-, Prozeß)Kosten pl: with ~s kostenpflichtig. **II** v/t (irr) **6.** Preis kosten: it ~ me one pound es kostete mich ein Pfund. **7.** kosten, bringen um: it ~ him his life es kostete ihn das Leben. **8.** et. Unangenehmes verursachen: it ~ me a lot of trouble es verursachte mir od. kostete mich große Mühe. **9.** pret u. pp **'cost·ed** ✝ den Preis od. die Kosten kalkulieren von

(od. gen). **III** v/i (irr) **10.** it ~ him dearly bsd. fig. es kam ihm teuer zu stehen.

co-star ['kəʊstɑː] **I** v/t: the film ~red X X spielte in dem Film e-e der Hauptrollen. **II** v/i: ~ with die Hauptrolle spielen neben (dat).

'cost|-,con·scious adj □ kostenbewußt. **'~-,cov·er·ing** adj □ kostendeckend.

cos·ter(·mon·ger) ['kɒstə(ˌmʌŋɡə)] s Br. Straßenhändler(in) für Obst, Gemüse etc.

cost es·ti·mate s Kostenvoranschlag m.

cost·ly ['kɒstlɪ] adj **1.** kostspielig, teuer. **2.** teuer erkauft (Sieg etc). **3.** prächtig.

cost-of-'liv·ing| al·low·ance, ~ bo·nus s ✝ Teuerungszulage f. **~ in·dex** s (a. irr index) ✝ Lebenshaltungs(kosten)index m.

cos·tume ['kɒstjuːm] s **1.** Kostüm n, Kleidung f, Tracht f. **2.** thea. etc Kostüm n: ~ ball Kostümball m; ~ de·signer Kostümbildner(in); ~ jew·el(le)ry Modeschmuck m.

co·sy ['kəʊzɪ] **I** adj □ behaglich, gemütlich. **II** s Wärmer m: → egg cosy, tea cosy.

cot [kɒt] s **1.** Feldbett n. **2.** Br. Kinderbett(chen) n.

cot·tage ['kɒtɪdʒ] s **1.** Cottage n, (kleines) Landhaus. **2.** Am. Ferienhaus n, -häuschen n. **3.** Am. Wohngebäude n, (e-s Krankenhauses etc) Einzelgebäude n, (e-s Hotels) Dependance f. **~ cheese** s Hüttenkäse m. **~ in·dus·try** s Heimgewerbe n, -industrie f.

cot·ton ['kɒtn] **I** s **1.** Baumwolle f: → absorbent. **II** adj **2.** baumwollen, Baumwoll... **III** v/i **3.** Am. F (with) gut auskommen (mit); sich anfreunden (mit). **4.** F ~ to Am. sich anfreunden mit (e-r Idee etc); ~ on to et. kapieren. ~ pad s Wattestäbchen n. ~ wool s Br. (Verband)Watte f.

couch [kaʊtʃ] **I** s Couch f, Liege(sofa n) f. **II** v/t abfassen, formulieren; Gedanken etc in Worte fassen, ausdrücken.

cou·chette [kuːˈʃet] s 🚄 Platz m (im Liegewagen).

cough [kɒf] **I** s **1.** Husten m: have a ~ Husten haben; give a (slight) ~ hüsteln, sich räuspern. **2.** Husten n. **3.** mot. Stottern n. **II** v/i **4.** husten. **5.** mot. stottern, husten (Motor). **III** v/t **6.** mst

~ **out**, ~ **up** aushusten: ~ **up blood** Blut husten. **7.** ~ **up** *sl.* herausrücken mit (*der Wahrheit etc*); Geld herausrücken, ausspucken. ~ **drop** *s* Hustenbonbon *m, n.*

cough·ing bout ['kɒfɪŋ] *s* Hustenanfall *m.*

cough| loz·enge → **cough drop.** ~ **syr·up** *s* Hustensaft *m,* -sirup *m.*

could [kʊd] *v/aux* **1.** *pret von* **can¹. 2.** *konditional, vermutend od. fragend:* könnte *etc:* **that ~ be right** das könnte stimmen.

couldn't ['kʊdnt] F *für* **could not.**

coun·cil ['kaʊnsl] *s* **1.** Rat(sversammlung *f*) *m:* **be in** ~ zu Rate sitzen; **family** ~ Familienrat *m.* **2.** Rat *m* (*Körperschaft*); *engS.* Gemeinderat *m:* **♀ of Europe** Europarat; **municipal** ~ Stadtrat. ~ **es·tate** *s Br.* soziale Wohnsiedlung (*e-r Gemeinde*). ~ **house** *s Br.* gemeindeeigenes Wohnhaus (*mit niedrigen Mieten*).

coun·cil·(l)or ['kaʊnsələ] *s* Ratsmitglied *n,* Stadtrat *m,* -rätin *f.*

coun·sel ['kaʊnsl] **I** *s* **1.** Rat(schlag) *m:* **take ~ of s.o.** von j-m (e-n) Rat annehmen. **2.** Beratung *f:* **hold** (*od.* **take**) ~ **with** sich beraten mit; sich Rat holen bei. **3.** ⚖ *Am.* Rechtsberater *m,* -beistand *m; Br.* (Rechts)Anwalt *m:* ~ **for the defence** Verteidiger *m;* ~ **for the prosecution** Anklagevertreter *m.* **II** *v/t pret u. pp* **-seled,** *bsd. Br.* **-selled 4.** *j-m* raten, *j-m* e-n Rat geben *od.* erteilen: ~ **s.o. against** j-m abraten von. **5.** zu *et.* raten: ~ **s.th. to s.o.** j-m *et.* raten. **III** *v/i* **6.** ~ **against** abraten von. '**coun·sel·(l)or** (*of Berufs- etc*)Berater(in).

count¹ ['kaʊnt] **I** *s* **1.** Zählen *n,* (Ab-, Auf-, Aus)Zählung *f:* **keep ~** *of et.* genau zählen; **fig.** die Übersicht behalten über (*acc*); **lose ~** sich verzählen; **fig.** die Übersicht verlieren (*of* über *acc*); **by this** ~ nach dieser Zählung *od.* Berechnung. **2.** Endzahl *f,* Ergebnis *n.* **3.** ⚖ Anklagepunkt *m:* **on all ~s** in allen Anklagepunkten; **fig.** in jeder Hinsicht. **4. leave out of** ~ unberücksichtigt lassen; **take no ~ of** nicht berücksichtigen. **II** *v/t* **5.** (ab-, auf-, aus-, zs.-)zählen, *Wechselgeld* nachzählen. **6.** aus-, berechnen. **7.** zählen bis: ~ **ten. 8.** (mit)zählen, mit einrechnen: (**not**) ~**ing**

the persons present die Anwesenden (nicht) mitgerechnet; *without* (*od.* **not**) ~**ing** abgesehen von. **9.** halten für, betrachten als, zählen (**among** zu): ~ **o.s. lucky** (*od.* **fortunate**) sich glücklich schätzen. **III** *v/i* **10.** zählen (**fig.** **among** zu): ~ **up to ten** bis 10 zählen; ~ **ing from today** von heute an (gerechnet). **11.** (**on**) zählen, sich verlassen (*acc*), sicher rechnen (mit). **12.** zählen: a) von Wert sein, ins Gewicht fallen, b) gelten: ~ **for much** viel gelten *od.* wert sein; ~ **against** sprechen gegen; sich nachteilig auswirken auf (*acc*).

Verbindungen mit Adverbien:

count| down *v/t* **1.** Geld hinzählen. **2.** den Countdown durchführen für, a. *weitS.* letzte (Start)Vorbereitungen treffen für. ~ **in** *v/t* → **count¹ 8: count me in!** ich bin dabei!, ich mache mit! ~ **off** *v/t u. v/i bsd.* ✕ abzählen. ~ **out** *v/t* **1.** Münzen *etc* (langsam) abzählen. **2.** ausschließen, unberücksichtigt lassen: **count me out!** ohne mich! **3.** Boxen, Kinderspiel: auszählen. ~ **o·ver** *v/t* nachzählen. ~ **up** *v/t* zs.-zählen.

count² [~] *s nichtbritischer* Graf.

count·a·ble ['kaʊntəbl] *adj* zählbar (a. *ling.*).

'**count·down** *s* Countdown *m,* a. *weitS.* letzte (Start)Vorbereitungen *pl.*

coun·te·nance ['kaʊntənəns] *s* **1.** Gesichtsausdruck *m,* Miene *f:* **change one's** ~ s-n Gesichtsausdruck ändern. **2.** Fassung *f,* Haltung *f:* **in** ~ gefaßt; **keep one's** ~ die Fassung bewahren; **put s.o. out of** ~ j-n aus der Fassung bringen.

count·er¹ ['kaʊntə] **I** *s* **1.** Ladentisch *m:* **under the** ~ unter dem Ladentisch *verkaufen etc; fig.* unter der Hand, heimlich. **2.** Theke *f.* **3.** (*Bank-, Post*)Schalter *m.* **II** *adj* **4.** rezeptfrei (*Medikament*).

count·er² [~] *s* **1.** ◉ Zähler *m.* **2.** Spielmarke *f,* Jeton *m.*

coun·ter³ [~] **I** *adv* **1.** in entgegengesetzter Richtung. **2.** *a. fig.* wider (*acc*), zuwider (*dat*), entgegen (*dat*): **run** ~ **to** zuwiderlaufen (*dat*). **II** *adj* **3.** Gegen..., entgegengesetzt. **III** *v/t* **4.** entgegenwirken (*dat*). **IV** *v/i* **5.** *bsd. Sport:* kontern.

coun·ter... [kaʊntə] *in Zssgn* Gegen...

,**coun·ter'act** *v/t* **1.** entgegenwirken

(dat). **2.** Wirkung kompensieren, neutralisieren. ˌcoun·ter'ac·tive adj □ entgegenwirkend, Gegen...

'coun·terˌar·gu·ment s Gegenargument n.

'coun·terˌat·tack s Gegenangriff m.

coun·ter·bal·ance fig. I s ['kaʊntəˌbæləns] Gegengewicht n (to zu). II v/t [ˌ~'bæləns] ein Gegengewicht bilden zu, ausgleichen.

'coun·ter·blast s heftige Reaktion.

'coun·ter·charge s **1.** ⚖ Gegenklage f. **2.** ✕ Gegenangriff m.

'coun·ter·check I s Gegen-, Nachprüfung f. II v/t gegen-, nachprüfen.

'coun·ter·claim s ✝, ⚖ Gegenanspruch m, -forderung f.

ˌcoun·ter'clock·wise Am. → anticlockwise.

'coun·terˌdem·on'stra·tion s Gegendemonstration f.

ˌcoun·ter·es·pi·o·nage s Spionageabwehr f.

'coun·ter·ex·am·ple s Gegenbeispiel n.

coun·ter·feit ['kaʊntəfɪt] I adj **1.** falsch: a) gefälscht: ~ money Falschgeld n, b) vorgetäuscht. II s **2.** Fälschung f. III v/t **3.** Geld, Unterschrift etc fälschen. **4.** vortäuschen, simulieren.

'coun·ter·foil s bsd. Br. (Kontroll)Abschnitt m.

'coun·terˌin·tel·li·gence s Spionageabwehr(dienst m) f.

coun·ter·mand [ˌkaʊntə'mɑːnd] I v/t **1.** Befehl etc widerrufen, rückgängig machen: ~ Auftrag stornieren: **until ~ed** bis auf Widerruf. **2.** Ware abbestellen. II s **3.** Widerrufung f, ✝ Stornierung f.

'coun·terˌmeas·ure s Gegenmaßnahme f.

'coun·ter·move s Gegenzug m.

'coun·ter·ofˌfen·sive s ✕ Gegenoffensive f.

'coun·terˌof·fer s Gegenangebot n.

'coun·terˌor·der s bsd. ✕ Gegenbefehl m.

'coun·ter·pane s Tagesdecke f.

'coun·ter·part s **1.** Gegenstück n (to zu). **2.** Pendant n, genaue Entsprechung f. Ebenbild n (Person).

'coun·ter·point s ♪ Kontrapunkt m.

'coun·ter·poise s Gegengewicht n (to zu) (a. fig.).

ˌcoun·ter·pro'duc·tive adj kontrapro-

duktiv: **be ~** nicht zum gewünschten Ziel führen, das Gegenteil bewirken.

'coun·ter·proˌpos·al s Gegenvorschlag m.

'coun·ter·rev·oˌlu·tion s pol. Konter-, Gegenrevolution f.

'coun·ter·sign v/t gegenzeichnen.

'coun·ter·weight s Gegengewicht n (to zu) (a. fig.).

count·ess ['kaʊntɪs] s Gräfin f.

count·less ['kaʊntlɪs] adj zahllos, unzählig.

coun·try ['kʌntrɪ] I s **1.** Gegend f, Landschaft f: **flat ~** Flachland n. **2.** Land n, Staat m: **in this ~** hierzulande; **~ of birth** Geburtsland. **3.** Land n (Ggs. Stadt): **in the ~** auf dem Lande. II adj **4.** ländlich, Land... **~ home, ~ house** s **1.** Landhaus n. **2.** Landsitz m. '**~·man** s ['~mən] s (irr man) **1.** Landsmann m. **2.** Landbewohner m; Bauer m. **~ mu·sic** s Country-music f. **~ road** s Landstraße f. **~ seat** s Landsitz m. '**~·side** s **1.** Landstrich m, (ländliche) Gegend. **2.** Landschaft f. ˌ~'wide adj landesweit. '~·ˌwom·an s (irr woman) **1.** Landsmännin f. **2.** Landbewohnerin f; Bäuerin f.

coun·ty ['kaʊntɪ] s **1.** Br. Grafschaft f. **2.** Am. (Land)Kreis m (einzelstaatlicher Verwaltungsbezirk).

coup [kuː] s **1.** Coup m: **make** (od. **pull off**) **a ~** e-n Coup landen. **2.** Staatsstreich m, Putsch m. **~ d'é·tat** [ˌkuːdeɪ'tɑː] pl **coups d'é·tat** [ˌkuːz~] → **coup** 2.

cou·pé ['kuːpeɪ] s mot. Coupé n.

cou·ple ['kʌpl] I s **1.** Paar n: **a ~ of** zwei; **F** ein paar; **in ~s** paarweise. **2.** (Ehe-, Liebes- etc)Paar n. II v/t **3.** (zs.-)koppeln, verbinden (a. fig. **with** mit). **4.** ⚡ koppeln: ~ **back** rückkoppeln; ~ **out** auskoppeln.

cou·pon ['kuːpɒn] s **1.** Gutschein m, Bon m; Berechtigungsschein m. **2.** Kupon m, Bestellzettel m (in Zeitungsinseraten etc). **3.** Br. Tippzettel m (Fußballtoto).

cour·age ['kʌrɪdʒ] s Mut m, Tapferkeit f: **lose ~** den Mut verlieren; **muster up** (od. **pluck up, take**) ~ Mut od. sich ein Herz fassen. **cou·ra·geous** [kə'reɪdʒəs] adj □ mutig, tapfer.

cour·gette [ˌkɔː'ʒet] s ♀ Br. Zucchini f.

cou·ri·er ['kʊrɪə] s **1.** Eilbote m, (a. diplomatischer) Kurier m. **2.** Reiseleiter m.

cowardice

course [kɔːs] *s* **1.** ✍, ⚓ Kurs *m* (*a. fig.*): *change one's* ~ s-n Kurs ändern; ~ *correction* Kurskorrektur *f*. **2.** *Sport*: (*Renn*)Bahn *f*, (-)Strecke *f*, (*Golf*)Platz *m*. **3.** (*zeitlicher, natürlicher*) (Ver-)Lauf *m*: *in the* ~ *of* im (Ver)Lauf (*gen*); *in the* ~ *of time* im Laufe der Zeit; *of* ~ natürlich, selbstverständlich; *the* ~ *of events* der Gang der Ereignisse, der Lauf der Dinge; *take* (*od. run*) *its* ~ s-n Lauf nehmen; → *due* 6, *matter* 3. **4.** Gang *m* (*Speisen*): *a four-*~ *meal* e-e Mahlzeit mit 4 Gängen. **5.** Zyklus *m*, Reihe *f*: ~ *of lectures* Vortragsreihe. **6.** Kurs *m*, Lehrgang *m*: *English* ~ Englischkurs; ~ *of study* *univ.* Kurs; Lehrplan *m*.

court [kɔːt] **I** *s* **1.** Hof *m*: *in the* ~ auf dem Hof. **2.** *Sport*: (*Tennis- etc*)Platz *m*; (*Spiel*)Feld *n*. **3.** (*fürstlicher etc*) Hof: *at* ~ bei Hofe. **4.** *pay* (*one's*) ~ *to* a) → 6, b) *j-m* s-e Aufwartung machen. **5.** 📖 Gericht *n*: *in* ~ vor Gericht; *bring into* ~ vor Gericht bringen; *come to* ~ vor Gericht *od.* zur Verhandlung kommen; *go to* ~ vor Gericht gehen; *out of* ~ außergerichtlich; → *arbitration* 2. **II** *v/t* **6.** e-r Dame den Hof machen. **7.** ~ *death* mit s-m Leben spielen; ~ *disaster* das Schicksal herausfordern. **III** *v/i* **8.** miteinander gehen: ~*ing couple* Liebespaar *n*. ~ *card* *s* Kartenspiel: Bild(karte *f*) *n*.

court·e·ous ['kɜːtjəs] *adj* □ höflich, liebenswürdig.

court·e·sy ['kɜːtɪsɪ] *s* **1.** Höflichkeit *f*, Liebenswürdigkeit *f*: *by* ~ aus Höflichkeit; ~ *light* *mot.* Innenbeleuchtung *f*. ~ *visit* Höflichkeits-, Anstandsbesuch *m*. **2.** Gefälligkeit *f*: *by* ~ aus Gefälligkeit; *by* ~ *of* mit freundlicher Genehmigung von (*od. gen*).

'**court**|**·house** *s* Gerichtsgebäude *n*. ~ **mar·tial** *pl* **court mar·tials, courts mar·tial** *s* Kriegsgericht *n*. '~**·mar·tial** *v/t pret u. pp* '~**·mar·tialed,** *bsd.* Br. -'**mar·tialled** vor ein Kriegsgericht stellen. ~ **or·der** *s* 📖 Gerichtsbeschluß *m*, richterliche Verfügung. '~**·room** *s* Gerichtssaal *m*. '~**·yard** → **court** 1.

cous·in ['kʌzn] *s* Cousin *m*, Vetter *m*; Cousine *f*.

cov·er ['kʌvə] **I** *s* **1.** (*weitS. a.* Schnee-, Wolken- *etc*)Decke *f*. **2.** Deckel *m*. **3.** (*Buch*)Deckel *m*, Einband *m*; Umschlag-, Titelseite *f*; (*Schutz*)Umschlag *m*: *from* ~ *to* ~ von der ersten bis zur letzten Seite. **4.** Hülle *f*, Futteral *n*. **5.** Überzug *m*, Bezug *m*. **6.** Abdeck-, ⚙ Schutzhaube *f*. **7.** Briefumschlag *m*: *under separate* ~ mit getrennter Post; *under plain* ~ in neutralem Umschlag. **8.** ✗ *u. allg.* Deckung *f* (*from* vor *dat*): *take* ~ in Deckung gehen. **9.** Schutz *m* (*from* vor *dat*): *get under* ~ sich unterstellen; *under* (*the*) ~ *of night* im Schutze der Nacht. **10.** *fig.* Tarnung *f*: *under* ~ *of* unter dem Deckmantel (*gen*). **11.** Gedeck *n* (*bei Tisch*). **12.** ♣ ⓐ) Deckung *f*, Sicherheit *f*, b) → *coverage* 2. **II** *v/t* **13.** be-, zudecken (*with* mit), Dach decken: ~*ed with* vollig ~; ~*ed court* (*Sport*) Hallenplatz *m*. **14.** Fläche bedecken, sich über *e-e Fläche, a.* e-n *Zeitraum* erstrecken. **15.** *Seite etc* vollschreiben. **16.** einwickeln, -schlagen (*in, with* in *acc*). **17.** verbergen (*a. fig.*): ~ (*up*) *fig.* verheimlichen, -tuschen. **18.** decken, schützen (*from, against* vor *dat*, gegen) (*beide a.* ✗ *u. fig.*): ~ *o.s. fig.* sich absichern. **19.** → ♣ (ab)decken; versichern. **20.** *Thema* erschöpfend behandeln. **21.** *Presse, Rundfunk etc*: berichten über (*acc*). **22.** *Strecke* zurücklegen. **23.** *Sport*: *Gegenspieler* decken. **24.** *j-n* beschatten. **25.** *zo.* decken. ~ **ad·dress** *s* Deckadresse *f*.

cov·er·age ['kʌvərɪdʒ] *s* **1.** erschöpfende Behandlung (*e-s Themas*). **2.** ♣ Versicherungsschutz *m*, (*Schadens*)Deckung *f*. **3.** *Presse, Rundfunk etc*: Berichterstattung *f* (*of* über *acc*).

cov·er| **charge** *s* pro Gedeck berechneter Betrag. ~ **girl** *s* Covergirl *n*, Titelblattmädchen *n*.

cov·er·ing ['kʌvərɪŋ] *s* **1.** → *cover* 4. **2.** (*Fußboden*)Belag *m*. ~ **let·ter** *s* Begleitbrief *m*, -schreiben *n*.

cov·er·let ['kʌvəlɪt] *s* Tagesdecke *f*.

cov·er sto·ry *s* Titelgeschichte *f*.

cov·ert ['kʌvət] *adj* □ heimlich, verborgen.

'**cov·er-up** *s* Vertuschung *f* (*for gen*).

cow¹ [kaʊ] *s* Kuh *f* (*a. fig. contp.*): *till the* ~*s come home* F bis in alle Ewigkeit.

cow² [~] *v/t* einschüchtern.

cow·ard ['kaʊəd] *s* Feigling *m*. **cow-**

ard·ice ['~dɪs] s Feigheit f. **'cow·ard·ly** adj feig.

'cow·boy s Cowboy m.

cow·er ['kaʊə] v/i **1.** kauern, (zs.-gekauert) hocken. **2.** a. ~ **down** sich ducken.

'cow|·hide s **1.** Kuhhaut f. **2.** Rind(s)leder n. **'~house** s Kuhstall m.

cowl [kaʊl] s **1.** Mönchskutte f. **2.** Kapuze f. **3.** Schornsteinkappe f.

'cow|·pat s Kuhfladen m. **'~pox** s Kuh-, Impfpocken pl. **'~shed** s Kuhstall m. **'~skin** → **cowhide**. **'~slip** s **1.** Br. Schlüsselblume f. **2.** Am. Sumpfdotterblume f.

cox [kɒks] → **coxswain**. **~swain** ['kɒksn] **I** s **1.** Rudern: Steuermann m. **2.** Boot(s)führer m. **II** v/t u. v/i **3.** steuern.

coy [kɔɪ] adj □ **1.** schüchtern, scheu. **2.** neckisch-verschämt.

co·zi·ness, co·zy Am. → **cosiness, cosy**.

crab¹ [kræb] s **1.** zo. Krabbe f; Taschenkrebs m: **catch a** ~ (Rudern) e-n Krebs fangen. **2.** ⊕ Winde f; Laufkatze f. **3.** → **crab louse**.

crab² [~] **I** s **1.** Nörgler(in); Nörgelei f. **II** v/i **2.** nörgeln. **III** v/t **3.** (herum)nörgeln an (dat). **4.** Am. verpatzen.

crab·bed ['kræbɪd] adj □ **1.** mürrisch, verdrießlich. **2.** verworren, unklar. **3.** unleserlich. **'crab·by** → **crabbed 1.**

crab louse *(irr* **louse)** zo. Filzlaus f.

crack [kræk] **I** s **1.** Krach m, Knall m: **at the** ~ **of dawn** im Morgengrauen, in aller Frühe; **in a** ~ F im Nu; **give s.o. a fair** ~ **of the whip** F j-m e-e faire Chance geben. **2.** F (heftiger) Schlag: **give s.o. a** ~ **on the head** j-m eins auf den Kopf geben. **3.** Sprung m, Riß m. **4.** Spalt(e f) m, Ritz(e f) m: **be open a** ~ e-n Spalt (breit) offenstehen. **5.** F Knacks m (geistiger Defekt). **6.** sl. Versuch m: **have a** ~ **at s.th., give s.th. a** ~ es (einmal) mit et. versuchen. **7.** sl. a) Witz m: **make ~s about** Witze machen über (acc), b) Seitenhieb m, Stichelei f. **8.** Br. F Crack m, As n (bsd. Sportler). **II** adj **9.** erstklassig, großartig: ~ **shot** Meisterschütze m. **III** v/t **10.** krachen, knallen mit. **11.** (zer)springen, (-)platzen, rissig werden, e-n Sprung od. Sprünge bekommen. **12.** überschnappen (Stimme). **13.** fig.

(F ~ **up**) zs.-brechen. **14.** **get** ~**ing** F loslegen. **15.** ~ **down on** F scharf vorgehen gegen, durchgreifen bei. **IV** v/t **16.** knallen mit (Peitsche), knacken mit (Fingern): → **joke 1.** **17.** zerbrechen, Ei aufschlagen, e-r Flasche den Hals brechen. **18.** e-n Sprung machen in (dat); sich e-e Rippe etc anbrechen. **19.** F a) schlagen, hauen: ~ **s.o. over the head** j-m eins auf den Kopf geben, b) ein-, zerschlagen. **20.** Nuß, F Code, Safe etc knacken. **21.** ~ **up** F hochjubeln. **'~brained** adj F verrückt. **'~down** s F (on) scharfes Vorgehen (gegen), Durchgreifen n (bei).

cracked [krækt] adj **1.** gesprungen, rissig: **be** ~ e-n Sprung haben. **2.** F verrückt.

crack·er ['krækə] s **1.** Cracker m, Kräker m: a) ungesüßtes, keksartiges Kleingebäck, b) Schwärmer m, Frosch m (Feuerwerkskörper), c) Knallbonbon m, n. **2.** pl Nußknacker m. **crack·ers** ['~əz] adj Br. F übergeschnappt: **go** ~ überschnappen.

'crack·jaw I adj zungenbrecherisch. **II** s Zungenbrecher m.

crack·le ['krækl] **I** v/i knistern, prasseln, knattern. **II** s Knistern n, Prasseln n, Knattern n.

'crack|·pot F **I** s Verrückte m, Spinner m. **II** adj verrückt. **'~up** s fig. F Zs.-bruch m.

crack·y ['krækɪ] → **cracked**.

cra·dle ['kreɪdl] **I** s **1.** Wiege f (a. fig.): **from the** ~ **to the grave** von der Wiege bis zur Bahre; **from the** ~ von Kindheit od. von Kindesbeinen an. **2.** teleph. Gabel f: **put the receiver in the** ~ den Hörer auf die Gabel legen. **II** v/t **3.** wiegen, schaukeln: ~ **to sleep** in den Schlaf wiegen. **4.** (zärtlich) halten. **5.** teleph. Hörer auflegen.

craft [krɑːft] s **1.** (Hand- od. Kunst)Fertigkeit f, Geschicklichkeit f: → **art 2.** **2.** Gewerbe n, Beruf m, Handwerk n. **3.** → **craftiness. 4.** Boot(e pl) n, Schiff(e pl) n; Flugzeug(e pl) n. **'craft·i·ness** s Schlauheit f, Verschlagenheit f, List f.

crafts·man ['krɑːftsmən] s *(irr* **man)** Handwerker m. **'crafts·man·ship** s Kunstfertigkeit f, handwerkliches Können.

crazy

craft·y ['krɑːftɪ] *adj* □ schlau, verschlagen, listig.

crag [kræg] *s* Felsenspitze *f*, Klippe *f*. **crag·ged** ['krægɪd] *adj Am.*, **'crag·gy** *adj* **1.** felsig, schroff. **2.** runz(e)lig, zerfurcht (*Gesicht*); knorrig, rauh (*Person*).

cram [kræm] **I** *v/t* **1.** vollstopfen, *a. fig.* vollpacken (**with** mit). **2.** (hinein)stopfen, (-)zwängen (*into* in *acc*). **3.** F a) mit *j-m* pauken od. büffeln, b) *mst* ~ *up Fach* pauken, büffeln. **II** *v/i* **4.** sich vollstopfen. **5.** F pauken, büffeln (**for** für): ~ *up on* → 3b. **III** *s* **6.** F Pauken *n*, Büffeln *n*: ~ *course* Paukkurs *m*. **,~'full** *adj* vollgestopft (*of* mit), zum Bersten voll.

cram·mer ['kræmə] *s* F **1.** Paukstudio *n*. **2.** Einpauker *m*. **3.** Paukbuch *n*. **4** *j-d, der für e-e Prüfung paukt.*

cramp¹ [kræmp] *s* ✝ Krampf *m*.

cramp² [~] **I** *s* **1.** ☉ Krampe *f*, Klammer *f*. **II** *v/t* **2.** ☉ ankrampen, anklammern. **3.** *a.* ~ *up* einzwängen, -engen: *be ~ed for space* (*od. room*) (zu) wenig Platz haben, räumlich beschränkt sein.

cran·ber·ry ['krænbərɪ] *s* ♠ Preiselbeere *f*.

crane [kreɪn] **I** *s* **1.** *orn.* Kranich *m*. **2.** ☉ Kran *m*. **II** *v/t* **3.** ~ *one's neck* sich den Hals verrenken (**for** nach), e-n langen Hals machen, den Hals recken. **III** *v/i* **4.** *a.* ~ *forward* den Hals recken. ~ **driv·er** *s* Kranführer *m*.

crank [kræŋk] **I** *s* **1.** ☉ Kurbel *f*. **2.** F wunderlicher Kauz, Spinner *m*; *Am.* Miesepeter *m*. F fixe Idee, Marotte *f*. **II** *v/t* **4.** *oft* ~ *up* ankurbeln. **'~·shaft** *s* ☉ Kurbelwelle *f*.

crank·y ['kræŋkɪ] *adj* □ F **1.** verschroben, wunderlich. **2.** *Am.* reizbar, schlechtgelaunt. **3.** wack(e)lig, unsicher, baufällig.

cran·nied ['krænɪd] *adj* rissig. **'cran·ny** *s* Riß *m*, Ritze *f*, Spalt *m*: → **nook.**

crape [kreɪp] *s* **1.** Krepp *m*. **2.** Trauerflor *m*.

crash [kræʃ] **I** *v/t* **1.** zertrümmern, -schmettern. **2.** F uneingeladen kommen zu, hineinplatzen in (*acc*): ~ *a party;* ~ *the gate* → **gate-crash. II** *v/i* **3.** (krachend) zerbersten. **4.** krachend einstürzen, zs.-krachen. **5.** *bsd.* ✝ zs.-brechen. **6.** krachen (*against, into* gegen):

~ *open* krachend auffliegen (*Tür*). **7.** stürmen, platzen: ~ *in*(*to the room*) hereinplatzen. **8.** *mot.* zs.-stoßen, verunglücken; ✈ abstürzen. **III** *s* **9.** Krach(en *n*) *m*. **10.** *bsd.* ✝ Zs.-bruch *m*, (Börsen)Krach *m*. **11.** *mot.* Unfall *m*, Zs.-stoß *m*; ✈ Absturz *m.* ~ **bar·ri·er** *s Br.* Leitplanke *f.* ~ **course** *s* Schnell-, Intensivkurs *m.* ~ **di·et** *s* radikale Schlankheitskur. ~ **hel·met** *s* Sturzhelm *m.*

crash·ing ['kræʃɪŋ] *adj* F fürchterlich. **'crash|-land** *v/i* ✈ Bruch *od.* e-e Bruchlandung machen, bruchlanden. ~ **land·ing** *s* ✈ Bruchlandung *f.* ~ **pro·gram**(**me**) *s* Sofortprogramm *n.* ~ **test** *s mot.* Crashtest *m.*

crass [kræs] *adj* □ **1.** grob, kraß (*Fehler etc*). **2.** derb, unfein (*Benehmen etc*).

crate [kreɪt] *s* **1.** (Latten)Kiste *f.* **2.** (*Bieretc*)Kasten *m.* **3.** *sl.* Kiste *f* (*Auto, Flugzeug*).

cra·ter ['kreɪtə] *s* **1.** *geol.* Krater *m*: ~ *lake* Kratersee *m.* **2.** (*Bomben-, Granat*)Trichter *m.*

cra·vat [krə'væt] *s* Halstuch *n.*

crave [kreɪv] **I** *v/t* **1.** *et.* ersehnen. **2.** (inständig) bitten *od.* flehen um. **II** *v/i* **3.** sich sehnen (**for, after** nach). **4.** ~ *for* → 2. **'crav·ing** *s* Sehnsucht *f* (for nach).

crawl [krɔːl] **I** *v/i* **1.** kriechen: a) krabbeln, b) *fig.* sich dahinschleppen (*Zeit etc*), c) im Schneckentempo gehen *od.* fahren, d) F unterwürfig sein: ~ *to s.o.* vor *j-m* kriechen. **2.** wimmeln (**with** von). **3.** kribbeln: *the sight made her flesh* ~ bei dem Anblick bekam sie e-e Gänsehaut. **4.** *Schwimmen:* kraulen. **II** *s* **5.** Kriechen *n*: *go at a* ~ → 1c. **6.** *Schwimmen:* Kraul(en) *n*, Kraulstil *m.* **'crawl·er** *s* **1.** Kriechtier *n.* **2.** *Br.* F Kriecher(in). **3.** *Schwimmen:* Krauler(in).

cray·fish ['kreɪfɪʃ] *s zo.* **1.** Flußkrebs *m.* **2.** Languste *f.*

cray·on ['kreɪən] *s* **1.** Zeichenkreide *f.* **2.** Zeichen-, Bunt-, Pastellstift *m*: *blue* ~ Blaustift. **3.** Kreide-, Pastellzeichnung *f.* **II** *v/t* **4.** mit Kreide *etc* zeichnen.

craze [kreɪz] *s* Manie *f*, Verrücktheit *f*: *be the* ~ große Mode sein; *the latest* ~ der letzte Schrei. **'cra·zi·ness** *s* Verrücktheit *f.* **'cra·zy** *adj* □ **1.** *a. fig.*

verrückt, wahnsinnig (**with** vor *dat*): **drive s.o. ~** j-n wahnsinnig machen; **~ bone** *Am.* Musikantenknochen *m.* **2** F (*about*) hingerissen (von), vernarrt in (*acc*); versessen, scharf (auf *acc*), wild, verrückt (nach): **be ~ to do s.th.** darauf versessen sein, et. zu tun.

creak [kriːk] **I** *v/i* knarren (*Treppe etc*), quietschen (*Bremsen etc*). **II** *s* Knarren *n*, Quietschen *n*. **'creak·y** *adj* knarrend, quietschend.

cream [kriːm] **I** *s* **1.** Rahm *m*, Sahne *f*. **2.** Creme(speise) *f*. **3.** (*Haut-, Schuhetc*)Creme *f*. **4.** *fig.* Creme *f*, Auslese *f*, Elite *f*: **the ~ of the ~** die Crème de la crème. **II** *v/t* **5.** den Rahm abschöpfen von (*a. fig.*). **6.** zu Schaum schlagen; schaumig rühren. **7.** sich *das Gesicht etc* eincremen: **~ one's face. III** *adj* **8.** creme(farben). **~ cheese** *s* Rahm-, Vollfettkäse *m.* **'~·col·o(u)red** → **cream** 8. **~ puff** *s* Windbeutel *m.*

crease [kriːs] **I** *s* **1.** Falte *f*. **2.** Bügelfalte *f*. **3.** Knick *m*, *a.* Eselsohr *n*. **II** *v/t* **4.** falten, knicken. **5.** Falten bügeln in (*e-e Hose*). **6.** zerknittern. **III** *v/i* **7.** knittern. **'~·proof, '~·re·sist·ant** *adj* knitterfrei, -fest.

cre·ate [kriːˈeɪt] *v/t* **1.** (er)schaffen. **2.** ins Leben rufen, *Arbeitsplätze* schaffen; hervorrufen, verursachen. **3.** *thea. etc, Mode:* kreieren. **4.** j-n machen *od.* ernennen zu. **cre·a·tion** *s* **1.** (Er)Schaffung *f*. **2.** Hervorrufung *f*, Verursachung *f*. **3. the** 2 *eccl.* die Schöpfung. **4.** *thea. etc, Mode:* Kreierung *f*. **5.** (Kunst-, Mode)Schöpfung *f*, (*Mode a.*) Kreation *f*. **6.** Ernennung *f*. **cre·a·tive** *adj* □ schöpferisch, kreativ. **cre·a·tor** *s* Schöpfer *m*, Urheber *m*: **the** 2 *eccl.* der Schöpfer.

crea·ture [ˈkriːtʃə] *s* **1.** Geschöpf *n*, (Lebe)Wesen *n*, Kreatur *f*: **dumb ~** stumme Kreatur; **good ~** gute Haut; **lovely ~** süßes Geschöpf; **poor (silly) ~** armes (dummes) Ding; **~ of habit** Gewohnheitstier *n*. **2.** Produkt *n*: **~ of the imagination** Phantasieprodukt *n*. **~ com·forts** *s pl* leibliches Wohl.

crèche [kreɪʃ] *s* **1.** (Kinder)Krippe *f*. **2.** *Am.* (Weihnachts)Krippe *f*.

cre·dence [ˈkriːdəns] *s*: **give** (*od.* **attach**) **~ to** Glauben schenken (*dat*).

cre·den·tials [krɪˈdenʃlz] *s pl* **1.** Beglau-

bigungs- *od.* Empfehlungsschreiben *n*. **2.** (Leumunds)Zeugnis *n*. **3.** Ausweis(papiere *pl*) *m*.

cred·i·bil·i·ty [ˌkredəˈbɪlətɪ] *s* Glaubwürdigkeit *f*. **'cred·i·ble** *adj* □ glaubwürdig.

cred·it [ˈkredɪt] **I** *s* **1.** Glaube(n) *m*: **give ~ to** Glauben schenken (*dat*). **2.** Ansehen *n*, Achtung *f*: **be in high ~ with** in hohem Ansehen stehen bei. **3.** Ehre *f*: **be a ~ to s.o.**, **be to s.o.'s ~**, **do s.o. ~** j-m Ehre machen *od.* einbringen; **to his ~ it must be said** zu s-r Ehre muß man sagen; **where ~ is due** Ehre, wem Ehre gebührt. **4.** Anerkennung *f*, Lob *n*: **get ~ for** Anerkennung finden für; **that's very much to his ~** das ist sehr anerkennenswert *od.* verdienstvoll von ihm. **5.** Verdienst *n*: **give s.o. (the) ~ for** j-m et. hoch anrechnen; j-m et. zutrauen; j-m et. zuschreiben. **6.** ✝ Kredit *m*: **on ~** auf Kredit; **give s.o. ~ for £1,000** j-m e-n Kredit von 1000 Pfund geben; **~ card** Kreditkarte *f*. **7.** ✝ Guthaben *n*, Kredit(seite *f*) *n*, Haben *n*: **your ~** Saldo zu Ihren Gunsten; **enter** (*od.* **place, put**) **a sum to s.o.'s ~** j-m e-n Betrag gutschreiben. **II** *v/t* **8.** Glauben schenken (*dat*), glauben (*dat*). **9.** **~ s.o. with** j-m et. zutrauen; j-m et. zuschreiben. **10.** ✝ *Betrag* zuschreiben (**to s.o.** j-m). **'cred·it·a·ble** *adj* □ (**to**) ehrenvoll (für), anerkennenswert (von). **'cred·i·tor** *s* ✝ Gläubiger *m*.

'cred·it·wor·thy *adj* ✝ kreditwürdig.

cre·du·li·ty [krɪˈdjuːlətɪ] *s* Leichtgläubigkeit *f*. **cred·u·lous** [ˈkredjʊləs] *adj* □ leichtgläubig.

creed [kriːd] *s* **1.** *eccl.* Glaubensbekenntnis *n*; Glaube *m*, Konfession *f*. **2.** *fig.* Überzeugung *f*, Weltanschauung *f*.

creek [kriːk] *s* **1.** *Am.* Bach *m*. **2.** *bes. Br.* kleine Bucht. **3. be up the ~** F in der Klemme sein *od.* sitzen *od.* stecken.

creep [kriːp] **I** *v/i* (*irr*) **1.** kriechen: a) krabbeln, b) *fig.* sich dahinschleppen (*Zeit etc*), c) im Schneckentempo gehen *od.* fahren, d) unterwürfig sein. **2.** schleichen: **~ in** (sich) hinein- *od.* einschleichen; *fig.* sich einschleichen (*Fehler etc*). **3.** kribbeln: **the sight made her flesh ~** bei dem Anblick bekam sie e-e Gänsehaut. **II** *s* **4.** Kriechen *n*, Schleichen *n*: **go at a ~** → 1c. **5. the**

sight gave her the ∼s F bei dem Anblick bekam sie e-e Gänsehaut. **6.** F Kriecher(in). **'creep·er** *s* **1.** Kriechtier *n*. **2.** Kriech- *od*. Kletterpflanze *f*. **'creep·ing** *adj* □ kriechend: *∼ inflation* ✝ schleichende Inflation. **'creep·y** *adj* grus(e)lig.

cre·mate [krɪˈmeɪt] *v/t bsd. Leichen* verbrennen, einäschern. **cre'ma·tion** *s* Verbrennung *f*, Einäscherung *f*, Feuerbestattung *f*. **crem·a·to·ri·um** [ˌkremə-ˈtɔːrɪəm] *pl* **-ums, -a** [∼ə], *bsd. Am.* **cre·ma·to·ry** [ˈ∼tərɪ] *s* Krematorium *n*.

crept [krept] *pret u. pp von* creep.
cres·cent [ˈkresnt] *s* Halbmond *m*, Mondsichel *f*.
cress [kres] *s* ♣ Kresse *f*.
crest [krest] *s* **1.** *orn.* Büschel *n*, Haube *f*; Kamm *m*. **2.** *zo.* Mähne *f*. **3.** Bergrücken *m*, Kamm *m*. **4.** (*Wellen*)Kamm *m*: *be riding (along) on the ∼ of a wave fig.* im Augenblick ganz oben schwimmen. **5.** *fig.* Gipfel *m*, Scheitelpunkt *m*: *at the ∼ of his fame* auf dem Gipfel s-s Ruhms. **'∼ˌfall·en** *adj fig.* niedergeschlagen, geknickt.
cre·tin [ˈkretɪn] *s* 🗡 Kretin *m* (*a. fig. contp.*).
cre·vasse [krɪˈvæs] *s* **1.** tiefer Spalt *od.* Riß. **2.** Gletscherspalte *f*.
crev·ice [ˈkrevɪs] *s* Riß *m*, Spalt *m*, (Fels)Spalte *f*.
crew¹ [kruː] *s* **1.** (*Arbeits*)Gruppe *f*, (*Bauetc*)Trupp *m*, (*Arbeiter*)Kolonne *f*. **3.** ✈, ⚓ (*Bedienungs*)Mannschaft *f*. **3.** ✈, ⚓ Besatzung *f*; ⚓ *engS.* Mannschaft *f* (*a. Sport*).
crew² [∼] *pret von* crow².
crew cut *s* Bürstenschnitt *m*.
crib [krɪb] *s* **1.** Kinderbettchen *n*. **2.** (*Futter*)Krippe *f*. **3.** *bsd. Br.* (Weihnachts)Krippe *f*. **4.** F kleiner Diebstahl; Anleihe *f*, Plagiat *n*. **5.** *ped.* F Eselsbrücke *f*, Klatsche *f*; Spickzettel *m*. **II** *v/t u. v/i* **6.** F klauen (*a. fig. plagiieren*). **7.** *ped.* F abschreiben, spicken (*off, from* von).
crick [krɪk] *s*: *a ∼ in one's neck* ein steifer Hals.
crick·et¹ [ˈkrɪkɪt] *s zo.* Grille *f*.
crick·et² [∼] (*Sport*) **I** *s* Kricket *n*: *not ∼* F nicht fair. **II** *v/i* Kricket spielen. **'crick·et·er** *s* Kricketspieler *m*.
cri·er [ˈkraɪə] *s* Schreier *m*, Schreihals *m*.

crime [kraɪm] *s* **1.** Verbrechen *n*, *coll. a. pl*: *∼ prevention* Verbrechensverhütung *f*; *∼ syndicate* Verbrechersyndikat *n*; *∼ wave* Welle *f* von Verbrechen. **2.** → **criminality**. **3.** F Verbrechen *n*; Jammer *m*, Zumutung *f*.
crim·i·nal [ˈkrɪmɪnl] **I** *adj* **1.** kriminell, verbrecherisch (*beide a. fig.* F): *∼ act* Straftat *f*, strafbare Handlung; *∼ association* kriminelle Vereinigung; → *record¹* **2.** **2.** strafrechtlich, Straf..., Kriminal...: *∼ code* Strafgesetzbuch *n*; *∼ law* Strafrecht *n*; *∼ proceedings pl* Strafprozeß *m*, -verfahren *n*. **II** *s* **3.** Verbrecher(in), Kriminelle *m, f*. **crim·i·nal·i·ty** [ˌ∼ˈnælətɪ] *s* Kriminalität *f*, Verbrechertum *n*. **crim·i·nol·o·gy** [ˌ∼ˈnɒlədʒɪ] *s* Kriminologie *f*.
crimp [krɪmp] *v/t* **1.** kräuseln. **2.** falteln, fälteln. **3.** *Haar* wellen, locken.
crim·son [ˈkrɪmzn] *adj* **1.** karmin-, karmesinrot. **2.** puterrot (*from* vor *dat*).
cringe [krɪndʒ] *v/i* **1.** sich ducken *od.* (zs.-)krümmen: *∼ at* zurückschrecken vor (*dat*). **2.** *fig.* kriechen, katzbuckeln (*to* vor *dat*). **'cring·ing** *adj* □ kriecherisch, unterwürfig.
crin·kle [ˈkrɪŋkl] **I** *v/i* **1.** Falten werfen. **2.** knittern. **3.** rascheln, knistern. **II** *v/t* **4.** zerknittern. **III** *s* **5.** Falte *f*, (*im Gesicht*) Fältchen *n*.
crip·ple [ˈkrɪpl] **I** *s* Krüppel *m* (*a. fig.*). **II** *v/t* zum Krüppel machen; lähmen, *fig. a.* lahmlegen.
cri·sis [ˈkraɪsɪs] *pl* **-ses** [∼siːz] *s* Krise *f* (*a. thea., ⚕*): *economic ∼* Wirtschaftskrise; *∼ of confidence* Vertrauenskrise; *∼ staff* Krisenstab *m*.
crisp [krɪsp] **I** *adj* □ **1.** knusp(e)rig (*Gebäck etc*). **2.** kraus (*Haar*). **3.** frisch, knackig, fest (*Gemüse*). **4.** forsch, schneidig (*Benehmen etc*). **5.** klar (*Stil etc*). **6.** scharf, frisch (*Luft etc*). **II** *s* **7.** *pl bsd. Br.* (*Kartoffel*)Chips *pl*. **III** *v/t* **8.** knusp(e)rig backen *od.* braten. **IV** *v/i* **9.** knusp(e)rig werden.
criss·cross [ˈkrɪskrɒs] **I** *adj* kreuzweise, Kreuz... **II** *adv* kreuzweise, kreuz u. quer. **III** *s* Gewirr *n*. **IV** *v/t* kreuz u. quer ziehen durch. **V** *v/i* kreuz u. quer (ver)laufen.
cri·te·ri·on [kraɪˈtɪərɪən] *pl* **-ri·a** [∼ə], **-ri·ons** *s* Kriterium *n*: a) Maßstab *m*, b) (Unterscheidungs)Merkmal *n*.

crit·ic [ˈkrɪtɪk] s Kritiker(in): a) Beurteiler(in), b) Rezensent(in), c) Krittler(in).
crit·i·cal [ˈ~kl] adj □ kritisch: a) anspruchsvoll, b) mißbilligend, tadelnd (*of acc*): **be ~ of** et. auszusetzen haben an (*dat*), kritisch gegenüberstehen (*dat*), kritisieren (*acc*), c) entscheidend (*Augenblick etc*), d) gefährlich, bedenklich (*Situation etc*): **he is in (a) ~ condition** ✗ sein Zustand ist kritisch. **crit·i·cism** [ˈ~sɪzəm] s Kritik f: a) kritische Beurteilung, b) Tadel m, Vorwurf m: **open to ~** anfechtbar; **above ~** über jede Kritik *od.* jeden Tadel erhaben, c) → **critique** a. **crit·i·cize** [ˈ~saɪz] v/t kritisieren: a) kritisch beurteilen, b) Kritik üben an (*dat*), bekritteln, tadeln: **~ s.o. for doing s.th.** j-n kritisieren, weil er et. getan hat, c) besprechen, rezensieren. **cri·tique** [krɪˈtiːk] s Kritik f: a) Rezension f, Besprechung f, b) kritische Untersuchung.
croak [krəʊk] **I** v/i **1.** quaken (*Frosch*); krächzen (*Rabe etc, a. Mensch*). **2.** sl. abkratzen. **II** s **3.** Quaken n; Krächzen n.
cro·chet [ˈkrəʊʃeɪ] **I** s a. ~ **work** Häkelarbeit f, Häkelei f: ~ **hook** Häkelnadel f. **II** v/t u. v/i häkeln.
crock¹ [krɒk] s irdener Topf *od.* Krug.
crock² [~] s sl. Wrack n (*Person od. Sache*); Klapperkasten m (*Auto*).
crock·er·y [ˈkrɒkərɪ] s Steingut n, Töpferware f.
croc·o·dile [ˈkrɒkədaɪl] s zo. Krokodil n.: ~ **tears** pl f Krokodilstränen pl.
cro·cus [ˈkrəʊkəs] s ♣ Krokus m.
crook [krʊk] **I** s **1.** Haken m. **2.** Krümmung f, Biegung f: ~ **of one's arm** Armbeuge f. **3.** F Gauner m; Gaunerei f: **on the ~** auf betrügerische Weise. **II** v/t u. v/i **4.** (sich) krümmen *od.* biegen. **crook·ed** [ˈ~ɪd] adj □ **1.** gekrümmt, gebogen, krumm. **2.** F betrügerisch.
croon [kruːn] v/t u. v/i **1.** schmachtend singen. **2.** leise singen *od.* summen. **ˈcroon·er** s Schnulzensänger(in).
crop [krɒp] **I** s **1.** Ernte f: ~ **failure** Mißernte f. **2.** fig. Ertrag m, Ausbeute f (*of* an *dat*); große Menge, Masse f. **3.** kurzer Haarschnitt; kurzgeschnittenes Haar. **II** v/t **4.** stutzen, beschneiden. **5.** *Haar* kurz scheren. **III** v/i **6.** mst ~ **up** (*od.* **out**) fig. plötzlich auftauchen *od.*

eintreten. **ˈcrop·per** s F **1.** schwerer Sturz: **come a ~** schwer stürzen. **2.** Mißerfolg m, Fehlschlag m: **come a ~** Schiffbruch erleiden.
cro·quet [ˈkrəʊkeɪ] s Sport: Krocket n.
cross [krɒs] **I** s **1.** eccl. Kreuz n: **the** ☨ **das Kreuz** (Christi), das Kruzifix. **2.** Kreuz(zeichen) n: **make the sign of the ~** sich bekreuzigen; **mark with a ~** ankreuzen. **3.** fig. Kreuz n, Leiden n: **bear** (*od.* **carry**) **one's ~** sein Kreuz tragen. **4.** Querstrich m. **5.** biol. Kreuzung(sprodukt n) f. **6.** fig. Mittel-, Zwischending n. **II** v/t **7.** das Kreuzzeichen machen auf (*acc*) *od.* über (*dat*): ~ **o.s.** sich bekreuzigen. **8.** kreuzen: ~ **one's arms** die Arme kreuzen *od.* verschränken; *fig.* die Hände in den Schoß legen; ~ **one's legs** die Beine kreuzen *od.* über(einander)schlagen; → **finger** I, **sword.** **9.** *Grenze, Meer, Straße etc* überqueren: ~ **s.o.'s path** *fig.* j-m in die Quere kommen. **10.** kreuzen, schneiden. **11.** sich kreuzen mit (*Brief*). **12.** ankreuzen. **13.** *oft* ~ **off** (*od.* **out**) ausdurchstreichen: ~ **off** *fig.* abschreiben (*as* als). **14.** *Plan etc* durchkreuzen, vereiteln. **15.** *biol.* kreuzen. **III** v/i **16.** sich kreuzen (*a. Briefe*) *od.* schneiden. **17.** *oft* ~ **over** (*to*) hinübergehen, -fahren (nach), übersetzen (nach). **18.** *biol.* sich kreuzen (lassen). **IV** adj **19.** schräg, Schräg... **20.** (*to*) entgegengesetzt (*dat*), im Widerspruch (zu). **21.** F böse (*with* auf *acc*, mit), mürrisch. **ˈ~·bar** s Sport: Tor-, Querlatte f. **ˈ~·beam** ⊙ Querträger m, -balken m. **ˈ~·bones** s pl → **skull.** **ˈ~·breed** biol. **I** s Mischling m, Kreuzung f. **II** v/t (*irr* **breed**) kreuzen. **ˈ~·check I** v/t von verschiedenen Gesichtspunkten aus überprüfen. **II** s Überprüfung f von verschiedenen Gesichtspunkten aus. **ˌ~·ˈcoun·try** adj Querfeldein..., Gelände..., *mot. a.* geländegängig: ~ **skiing** Skilanglauf m. **ˈ~ˌcur·rent** s Gegenströmung f (*a. fig.*). **ˈ~ˌdress·ing** s Transvestismus m.
crossed [krɒst] adj gekreuzt: ~ **cheque** ☨ Br. Verrechnungsscheck m.
ˈcrossˌ-exˌam·iˈna·tion s ☎ Kreuzverhör n. **ˌ~·exˈam·ine** v/t ☎ ins Kreuzverhör nehmen. **ˈ~-eyed** adj schielend: **be ~** schielen. **ˈ~ˌfire** s ✗ Kreuzfeuer n (*a. fig.*). **ˈ~-grained** adj **1.** quergefasert.

2. *fig.* widerspenstig (*a. Sache*); kratzbürstig.

cross·ing ['krɒsɪŋ] *s* **1.** Überquerung *f*: ~ **point** Grenzübergang *m.* **2.** ♣ Überfahrt *f*: **rough** ~ stürmische Überfahrt. **3.** (*Straßen- etc*)Kreuzung *f.* **4.** Straßenübergang *m*; *Br.* Fußgängerüberweg *m*: → **grade** 4, **level** 5. **5.** *biol.* Kreuzung *f.*

'**cross-legged** *adj u. adv* mit gekreuzten *od.* über(einander)geschlagenen Beinen, (*am Boden a.*) im Schneidersitz.

'**cross·ness** ['krɒsnɪs] *s* F Mürrischkeit *f*, schlechte Laune.

'**cross|·patch** *s* F Brummbär *m.* ,~'**pur·pos·es** *s pl*: **talk at** ~ aneinander vorbeireden. ~ **ref·er·ence** *s* Kreuz-, Querverweis *m.* '~**road** *s* **1.** *Am.* Quer*od.* Seitenstraße *f.* **2.** *pl* (*mst sg konstruiert*) (Straßen)Kreuzung *f*; *fig.* Scheideweg *m.* ~ **sec·tion** *s* ⚓, ⚙ *u. fig.* Querschnitt *m* (*of* durch). '~**walk** *s Am.* Fußgängerüberweg *m.* '~**ways**, '~'**wise** *adv* quer, kreuzweise. '~**word** (**puz·zle**) *s* Kreuzworträtsel *n.*

crotch [krɒtʃ] *s* **1.** Gab(e)lung *f.* **2.** Schritt *m* (*der Hose od. des Körpers*).

crotch·et ['krɒtʃɪt] *s* **1.** ♪ *bsd. Br.* Viertelnote *f.* **2.** *fig.* Grille *f*, Marotte *f.* '**crotch·et·y** *adj* **1.** grillenhaft. **2.** mürrisch.

crouch [kraʊtʃ] **I** *v/i* **1.** a. ~ **down** sich bücken *od.* ducken. **2.** hocken; kauern. **II** *s* **3.** Hocke *f*: **in a** ~ gebückt; in der Hocke.

crou·pi·er ['kruːpɪə] *s* Croupier *m.*

crow[1] [krəʊ] *s* **1.** *orn.* Krähe *f*: **as the** ~ **flies** (in der) Luftlinie; **eat** ~ *bsd. Am.* F zu Kreuze kriechen; **have a** ~ **to pluck** (*od. pull, pick*) **with** F ein Hühnchen zu rupfen haben mit. **2.** → **crowbar**.

crow[2] [~] **I** *v/i pret* **crowed** *u.* (*für* 1) **crew** [kruː], *pp* **crowed 1.** krähen (*Hahn*). **2.** (*fröhlich*) krähen. **3.** jubeln, frohlocken (*over* über *acc*). **4.** protzen, prahlen (*over, about* mit). **II** *s* **5.** Krähen *n.* **6.** Jubel(schrei) *m.*

'**crow·bar** *s* ⚙ Brecheisen *n*, -stange *f.*

crowd [kraʊd] **I** *s* **1.** dichte (Menschen)Menge, Masse *f*: ~**s** *pl* od *pop* Menschenmassen *pl.* **2. the** ~ die Masse, das (gemeine) Volk: **one of the** ~ ein Mann aus dem Volk; **follow** (*od. move*

with) **the** ~ mit der Masse gehen. **3.** F Gesellschaft *f*, Haufen *m*, Verein *m.* **4.** Ansammlung *f*, Haufen *m.* **II** *v/i* **5.** (zs.-)strömen; sich drängen (*into* in *acc*; **round** um). **III** *v/t* **6.** *Straßen etc* bevölkern. **7.** sich drängen in (*acc od. dat*) *od.* um. **8.** zs.-drängen, -pressen. **9.** hineinpressen, -stopfen (*into* in *acc*). **10.** vollstopfen (*with* mit). '**crowd·ed** *adj* **1.** (**with**) überfüllt (von), voll (von): ~ **street** stark befahrene *od.* verkehrsreiche Straße. **2.** (zs.-)gedrängt. **3.** *fig.* voll ausgefüllt, ereignisreich.

crowd| pull·er *s* Zuschauermagnet *m.* ~ **scene** *s Film, TV*: Massenszene *f.*

crown [kraʊn] **I** *s* **1.** Krone *f* (*a. fig.*), (*Sport a.*) (Meister)Titel *m*: **the** ♛ die Krone, der König, die Königin. **2.** Krone *f* (*Währung*). **3.** *Zahnmedizin*: Krone *f.* **4.** *fig.* Krönung *f*, Höhepunkt *m.* **II** *v/t* **5.** *j-n* krönen (**king** zum König): ~**ed heads** *pl* gekrönte Häupter *pl.* **6.** *fig.* krönen: a) ehren, auszeichnen, b) schmücken, zieren, c) den Höhepunkt bilden von (*od. gen*): ~ **all** allem die Krone aufsetzen (*a. iro.*); **to** ~ **it all** zu allem Überfluß *od.* Unglück, **d)** erfolgreich abschließen: ~**ed with success** von Erfolg gekrönt. **7.** *Zahn* überkronen. ~ **col·o·ny** *s Br.* Kronkolonie *f.*

crown·ing ['kraʊnɪŋ] **I** *adj fig.* krönend. **II** *s* Krönung *f* (*a. fig.*).

crown| jew·els *s pl* Kronjuwelen *pl.* ~ **prince** *s* Kronprinz *m* (*a. fig.*). ~ **prin·cess** *s* Kronprinzessin *f.* ~ **wit·ness** *s* ⚖ *Br.* Belastungszeuge *m.*

'**crow's|·feet** *s pl* Krähenfüße *pl*, Fältchen *pl.* ~ **nest** *s* ♣ Krähennest *n.*

cru·ces ['kruːsiːz] *pl von* **crux**.

cru·cial ['kruːʃl] *adj* □ kritisch, entscheidend (**to, for** für): ~ **point** springender Punkt.

cru·ci·fix ['kruːsɪfɪks] *s* Kruzifix *n.* **cru·ci·fix·ion** [,~'fɪkʃn] *s* Kreuzigung *f.* **cru·ci·fy** ['~faɪ] *v/t* kreuzigen.

crude [kruːd] *adj* □ **1.** roh, unver-, unbearbeitet: ~ **oil** Rohöl *n.* **2.** *fig.* roh, grob. **3.** nackt, ungeschminkt. '**crude·ness, cru·di·ty** ['~dɪtɪ] *s* Roheit *f* (*a. fig.*).

cru·el ['krʊəl] *adj* □ **1.** grausam (**to** zu, gegen). **2.** unmenschlich, unbarmherzig. **3.** schrecklich, mörderisch. '**cru·**

el·ty *s* Grausamkeit *f*: **~ to animals** Tierquälerei *f*.

cru·et ['kruːɪt] *s* **1.** Essig-, Ölfläschchen *n*. **2.** *a.* **~ stand** Menage *f*, Gewürzständer *m*.

cruise [kruːz] **I** *v/i* **1.** ⚓ kreuzen, e-e Kreuzfahrt *od.* Seereise machen. **2.** ✈, *mot.* mit Reisegeschwindigkeit fliegen *od.* fahren: **cruising speed** Reisegeschwindigkeit *f*. **II** *v/t* **3.** Kreuzfahrt *f*, Seereise *f*. **~ mis·sile** *s* ✗ Marschflugkörper *m*.

cruis·er ['kruːzə] *s* **1.** ⚓ a) ✗ Kreuzer *m* (*a. allg.*), b) Kreuzfahrtschiff *n*. **2.** *Am.* (Funk)Streifenwagen *m*.

crumb [krʌm] **I** *s* **1.** Krume *f*, Krümel *m*, Brösel *m*. **2.** *fig.* Brocken *m*: **a few ~s of information** ein paar Informationsbrocken; **~ of comfort** Trostpflaster *m*, -pflästerchen *n*. **II** *v/t* **3.** *gastr.* panieren. **4.** zerkrümeln. **crum·ble** ['~bl] **I** *v/t* **1.** zerkrümeln, -bröckeln. **II** *v/i* **2.** *a.* **~ away** zerbröckeln, -fallen: **~ to dust** (*od. nothing*) *fig.* sich in nichts auflösen. **3.** ✝ abbröckeln (*Kurse*). '**crum·bling**, '**crum·bly** *adj* **1.** krüm(e)lig, bröck(e)lig. **2.** zerbröckelnd, -fallend.

crum·my ['krʌmɪ] *adj sl.* lausig, miserabel.

crum·ple ['krʌmpl] **I** *v/t* **1.** *a.* **~ up** zerknittern, -knüllen. **2.** zerdrücken. **II** *v/i* **3.** knittern. **4.** *a.* **~ up** zs.-brechen (*a. fig.*). **III** *s* **5.** (Knitter)Falte *f*.

crunch [krʌntʃ] **I** *v/t* **1.** knirschend (zer-) kauen. **2.** zermalmen. **II** *v/i* **3.** knirschend kauen. **4.** knirschen. **III** *s* **5.** Knirschen. **6.** **when it comes to the ~, when the ~ comes** F wenn es hart auf hart geht.

cru·sade [kruː'seɪd] **I** *s hist.* Kreuzzug *m* (*a. fig.*). **II** *v/i hist.* e-n Kreuzzug unternehmen, *fig. a.* zu Felde ziehen (**against** gegen; **for** für). **cru'sad·er** *s* **1.** *hist.* Kreuzfahrer *m*, -ritter *m*. **2.** *fig.* Kämpfer *m*.

crush [krʌʃ] **I** *s* **1.** Gedränge *n*, Gewühl *n*. **2.** *bsd. Br.* Getränk *aus ausgepreßten Früchten*: **orange ~**. **3. have a ~ on s.o.** F in j-n verknallt sein. **II** *v/t* **4.** zerquetschen, -malmen, -drücken: **~ out** *Zigarette etc* ausdrücken. **5.** zerdrücken, -knittern. **6.** ⚙ zerkleinern, -mahlen. **7.** auspressen, -drücken, -quetschen: **~**

the juice from *Zitrone etc* auspressen. **8.** *fig.* nieder-, zerschmettern; *Aufstand etc* niederwerfen, unterdrücken: **~ing blow** vernichtender Schlag; **~ing majority** erdrückende Mehrheit. **III** *v/i* **9.** zerquetscht werden. **10.** sich drängen (**into** in *acc*). **11.** (zer)knittern. '**crush·a·ble** *adj* **1.** knitterfest, -frei. **2.** **~ zone** *mot.* Knautschzone *f*.

crush·| bar·ri·er *s Br.* Barriere *f*, Absperrung *f*. '**~·re,sist·ant** → **crushable** 1.

crust [krʌst] **I** *s* **1.** (Brot)Kruste *f*, (-)Rinde *f*. **2.** Knust *m*, hartes *od.* trockenes Stück Brot. **3.** *geol.* (Erd)Kruste *f*. **4.** ✿ Kruste *f*, Schorf *m*. **5.** *sl.* Unverschämtheit *f*. **II** *v/i a.* **~ over 6.** verkrusten. **7.** verharschen: **~ed snow** Harsch *m*. '**crust·y** *adj* ☐ **1.** verkrustet, krustig. **2.** *fig.* barsch.

crutch [krʌtʃ] *s* **1.** Krücke *f*: **walk on ~es** auf *od.* an Krücken gehen. **2.** *fig.* Stütze *f*, Hilfe *f*.

crux [krʌks] *pl* '**crux·es, cru·ces** ['kruːsiːz] *s* Crux *f*, Schwierigkeit *f*, Haken *m*; schwieriges Problem, harte Nuß.

cry [kraɪ] **I** *s* **1.** Schrei *m*, Ruf *m* (**for** nach): **~ for help** Hilferuf; **within ~** in Rufweite (**of** von); **a far** (*od. long*) **~ from** *fig.* (himmel)weit entfernt von; **et. ganz anderes als. 2.** Geschrei *n*. **3.** Weinen *n*: **have a good ~** sich (richtig) ausweinen. **4.** (Schlacht)Ruf *m*, Schlag-, Losungswort *n*. **II** *v/i* **5.** schreien, rufen (**for** nach): **~ for help** (**vengeance**) um Hilfe rufen (nach Rache schreien). **6.** weinen (**for joy** vor Freude); heulen, jammern (**over** wegen, über *acc*; **for** um): → **milk** I. **III** *v/t* **7.** *et.* schreien, (aus)rufen: → **wolf** 1. **8.** *Tränen* weinen: **~ o.s. to sleep** sich in den Schlaf weinen; → **eye** 1, **head** 8, **heart** 1.

Verbindungen mit Adverbien:

cry| down *v/t* **1.** heruntersetzen, -machen. **2.** niederschreien. **~ off** *v/t* (*a. bsd. Br.*) *v/i* (plötzlich) absagen, zurücktreten (von). **~ out** **I** *v/t* ausrufen. **II** *v/i* aufschreien: **~ against** heftig protestieren gegen; **~ (for)** → **cry** 5. **~ up** *v/t* rühmen: **he's not all he's cried up to be** so gut ist er auch wieder nicht.

'**cry·ba·by** *s* Heulsuse *f*.

cry·ing ['kraɪɪŋ] *adj* **1.** (himmel)schreiend: **it's a ~ shame** es ist jammerschade *od.* ein Jammer. **2.** dringend (*Bedürfnis etc*).

crypt [krɪpt] *s* △ Krypta *f.* '**cryp·tic** *adj* (**~ally**) **1.** geheim, verborgen. **2.** rätselhaft, dunkel.

crys·tal ['krɪstl] *I s* **1.** Kristall *m* (*a.* 🔬, *etc*): (**as**) **clear as ~** kristallklar; *fig.* sonnenklar. **2.** *a.* **~ glass** Kristall(glas) *n.* **3.** Uhrglas *n.* **II** *adj* **4.** kristallen: a) Kristall...), b) kristallklar. **crys·tal·li·za·tion** *f*, [ˌ~təlaɪˈzeɪʃn] *s* Kristallisation *f*, Kristallbildung *f.* '**crys·tal·lize** *v/t* **1.** kristallisieren. **2.** *fig.* konkrete od. feste Form geben (*dat*). **3.** *Früchte* kandieren. **II** *v/i* **4.** kristallisieren. **5.** *fig.* konkrete od. feste Form annehmen, sich kristallisieren (*into* zu): **~ out** sich herauskristallisieren.

cub [kʌb] *I s* **1.** *zo.* Junge *n* (*des Fuchses, Bären etc*). **2.** *a.* **unlicked ~** grüner Junge. **3.** Anfänger *m.* **II** *v/i* **4.** (Junge) werfen.

cube [kjuːb] *I s* **1.** Würfel *m*: **~ sugar** Würfelzucker *m.* **2.** Å Kubikzahl *f*, dritte Potenz: **~ root** Kubikwurzel *f.* **II** *v/t* **3.** Å zur dritten Potenz erheben. **4.** würfeln, in Würfel schneiden *od.* pressen. '**cu·bic** *adj* (**~ally**) **1.** Kubik..., Raum...: **~ content** Rauminhalt *m*; **~ metre** (*Am. meter*) Kubikmeter *m, n.* **2.** würfelförmig, Würfel... **3.** Å kubisch: **~ equation** Gleichung *f* dritten Grades.

cu·bi·cle ['kjuːbɪkl] *s* Kabine *f.*

cuck·old ['kʌkəʊld] *I s* betrogener Ehemann. **II** *v/t j-m* Hörner aufsetzen.

cuck·oo ['kʊkuː] *I s orn.* Kuckuck *m.* **II** *adj* F bekloppt, plemplem. **~ clock** *s* Kuckucksuhr *f.*

cu·cum·ber ['kjuːkʌmbə] *s* Gurke *f*: (**as**) **cool as a ~** F eiskalt, kühl u. gelassen.

cud [kʌd] *s* **1.** Klumpen *m* wiedergekäuten Futters: **chew the ~** wiederkäuen; *fig.* überlegen, nachdenken. **2.** F Streifen *m* (*Kaugummi*).

cud·dle ['kʌdl] *I v/t* **1.** an sich drücken, hätscheln. **2.** schmusen mit. **II** *v/i* **3.** **~ up** sich kuscheln od. schmiegen (**to** an *acc*): **~ up together** sich aneinanderkuscheln. **4.** schmusen. **III** *s* **5.** enge Umarmung.

cudg·el ['kʌdʒəl] *I s* Knüppel *m*: **take up the ~s for s.o.** *fig.* für j-n eintreten. **II**

v/t perf. u. pp **-eled**, *bsd. Br.* **-elled** prügeln: → **brain** 2.

cue¹ [kjuː] *I s* **1.** *thea. etc, a. fig.* Stichwort *n*, ♩ Einsatz *m.* **2.** Wink *m*, Fingerzeig *m*: **take the ~ from s.o.** sich nach j-m richten. **II** *v/t* **3.** *a.* **~ in** *thea. etc, a. fig. j-m* das Stichwort geben, ♩ *j-m* den Einsatz geben.

cue² [~] *s* Queue *n*, Billardstock *m.*

cuff¹ [kʌf] *s* **1.** (Ärmel-, *Am. a.* Hosen)Aufschlag *m*, Manschette *f* (*a.* ⚙): **~ link** Manschettenknopf *m*; **off the ~** F aus dem Stegreif. **2.** *pl* F Manschetten *pl* (*Handschellen*).

cuff² [~] *I v/t j-m* e-n Klaps geben. **II** *s* Klaps *m.*

cui·sine [kwɪˈziːn] → **cooking** 2.

cul-de-sac ['kʌldəsæk] *pl* **cul-de-sacs**, **culs-de-sac** *s* Sackgasse *f* (*a. fig.*).

cu·li·nar·y ['kʌlɪnərɪ] *adj* □ kulinarisch, Koch...: **~ art** Kochkunst *f*; **~ herbs** *pl* Küchenkräuter *pl.*

cull [kʌl] *v/t* **1.** pflücken. **2.** auslesen, -suchen. **3.** *Minderwertiges* aussortieren.

cul·mi·nate ['kʌlmɪneɪt] *v/i* **1.** *ast.* kulminieren: **culminating point** Kulminations-, *fig. a.* Höhepunkt *m.* **2.** *fig.* den Höhepunkt erreichen; kulminieren, gipfeln (**in** in *dat*). **cul·mi·na·tion** *s* **1.** *ast.* Kulmination *f.* **2.** *fig.* Gipfel *m*, Höhepunkt *m.*

cu·lottes [kjuːˈlɒts] *s pl* Hosenrock *m.*

cul·pa·ble ['kʌlpəbl] *adj* □ **1.** tadelnswert, sträflich. **2.** ♯♯ strafbar, schuldhaft.

cul·prit ['kʌlprɪt] *s* **1.** ♯♯ Angeklagte *m, f*; Täter(in), Schuldige *m, f.* **2.** Missetäter(in).

cult [kʌlt] *s* **1.** *eccl.* Kult(us) *m* (*a.* ♯♯). Kult *m.*

cul·ti·vate ['kʌltɪveɪt] *v/t* **1.** *Boden* bebauen, bestellen. **2.** *Pflanzen* züchten, anbauen. **3.** *fig.* entwickeln, ausbilden; verfeinern. **4.** *fig.* kultivieren: a) fördern, b) *Freundschaft etc* pflegen, c) sich widmen (*dat*). **5.** freundschaftlichen Verkehr pflegen mit. '**cul·ti·vat·ed** → **cultured** 2. ,**cul·ti·va·tion** *s* **1.** Bebauung *f*, Bestellung *f.* **2.** Züchtung *f*, Anbau *m.* **3.** *fig.* a) Kultivierung *f*, b) Pflege *f.* **4.** → **culture** 4. '**cul·ti·va·tor** *s* Pflanzer *m*, Züchter *m.*

cul·tur·al ['kʌltʃərəl] *adj* □ kulturell, Kultur...

cul·ture ['kʌltʃə] *s* **1.** → cultivation 1, 2. **2.** (*Tier*)Züchtung *f*, (-)Zucht *f*. **3.** *biol.* Kultur *f*. **4.** Kultur *f*: a) (Geistes)Bildung *f*, b) Kultiviertheit *f*. **5.** Kultur *f*: a) Kulturkreis *m*, b) Kulturform *f*, -stufe *f*. '**cul·tured** *adj* **1.** gezüchtet: ~ *pearl* Zuchtperle *f*. **2.** kultiviert, gebildet.

cum·ber·some ['kʌmbəsəm] *adj* □ **1.** lästig, hinderlich. **2.** klobig, unhandlich, sperrig.

cu·mu·la·tive ['kjuːmjʊlətɪv] *adj* □ **1.** sich (an)häufend, anwachsend. **2.** † kumulativ. **cu·mu·lus** ['~ləs] *pl* **-li** ['~laɪ] *s* Haufenwolke *f*.

cun·ning ['kʌnɪŋ] **I** *adj* □ **1.** klug, geschickt; schlau, listig, gerissen. **2.** *Am.* F niedlich, süß; drollig. **II** *s* **3.** Klugheit *f*, Geschicktheit *f*; Schlauheit *f*, List(igkeit) *f*, Gerissenheit *f*.

cunt [kʌnt] *s* V Fotze *f* (*Vagina*).

cup [kʌp] **I** *s* **1.** Tasse *f*: *that's not my ~ of tea Br.* F das ist nicht mein Fall. **2.** *Sport:* Cup *m*, Pokal *m*: ~ *final* Pokalendspiel *n*; ~ *tie* Pokalspiel *n*, -paarung *f*; ~ *winner* Pokalsieger *m*. **3.** (*Wein-etc*)Becher *m*: *be fond of the ~* gern trinken. **4.** *eccl.* Kelch *m*, *fig. a.* Becher *m*. **5.** ♀ Blüten-, Fruchtbecher *m*. **II** *v/t* **6.** *Hand* hohl machen: ~*ped hand* hohle Hand. ~**board** ['kʌbəd] *s* (Geschirr-, Speise-, *bsd. Br. a.* Kleider-, Wäsche-) Schrank *m*: ~ *bed* Schrankbett *n*. ~**ful** ['~fʊl] *s e-e* Tasse(voll).

cu·po·la ['kjuːpələ] *s* △ Kuppel *f*.

cup·pa, cup·per ['kʌpə] *s Br.* F Tasse *f* Tee.

cur [kɜː] *s* **1.** Köter *m*. **2.** *fig.* (Schweine)Hund *m*.

cur·a·ble ['kjʊərəbl] *adj* heilbar.

curb [kɜːb] *s* **1.** Kandare *f*. **2.** *bsd. Am.* Bord-, Randstein *m*. **II** *v/t* **3.** *Pferd* an die Kandare nehmen. **4.** *fig.* zügeln, im Zaum halten. ~**stone** → curb **2**.

curd [kɜːd] *s oft pl* geronnene *od.* dicke Milch, Quark *m*.

cur·dle ['kɜːdl] **I** *v/t Milch* gerinnen lassen: ~ *s.o.'s blood* j-m das Blut in den Adern erstarren lassen. **II** *v/i* gerinnen, dick werden (*Milch*): *the sight made my blood ~* bei dem Anblick erstarrte mir das Blut in den Adern.

cure [kjʊə] **I** *s* **1.** ❦ Kur *f*, Heilverfahren

n (*for* gegen): *under ~* in Behandlung. **2.** ❦ Heilung *f*: *past ~* unheilbar krank (*Person*); unheilbar (*Krankheit*); *fig.* hoffnungslos (*Lage etc*). **3.** ❦ (Heil-) Mittel *n* (*for* gegen) (*a. fig.*). **II** *v/t* ❦ *j-n* heilen, kurieren, *fig. a.* abbringen (*of* von); ❦ *Krankheit* heilen; *fig. Mißstände etc* abstellen. **5.** haltbar machen: a) räuchern, b) trocknen, c) einpökeln, -salzen. **III** *v/i* **6.** Heilung bringen, heilen. '~**all** *s* Allheilmittel *n*.

cur·few ['kɜːfjuː] *s* ✕ Ausgangsverbot *n*, -sperre *f*.

cu·ri·o ['kjʊərɪəʊ] *pl* **-os** → curiosity 2a, c. **cu·ri·os·i·ty** [,~'ɒsətɪ] *s* **1.** Neugier *f*; Wißbegierde *f*. **2.** Kuriosität *f*: a) Rarität *f*, b) Sehenswürdigkeit *f*, c) Kuriosum *n*. '**cu·ri·ous** *adj* □ **1.** neugierig; wißbegierig: *I am ~ to know if* ich möchte gern wissen, ob. **2.** kurios, seltsam: *~ly enough* merkwürdigerweise. **3.** F komisch, wunderlich.

curl [kɜːl] **I** *v/t* **1.** *Haar etc* locken; kräuseln. **II** *v/i* **2.** sich locken *od.* kräuseln: ~ *up* in Ringen hochsteigen (*Rauch*); sich zs.-rollen; ~ *up on the sofa* es sich auf dem Sofa gemütlich machen. **3.** *Sport:* Curling spielen. **III** *s* **4.** Locke *f*. **5.** (Rauch)Ring *m*. '**curl·er** *s* **1.** *Sport:* Curlingspieler(in). **2.** Lockenwickel *m*, -wickler *m*. '**curl·ing** *s Sport:* Curling *n*: ~ *stone* Curlingstein *m*. '**curl·y** *adj* lockig; gelockt; gekräuselt, kraus.

cur·rant ['kʌrənt] *s* **1.** Korinthe *f*. **2.** △ Johannisbeere *f*.

cur·ren·cy ['kʌrənsɪ] *s* **1.** Umlauf *m*: *give ~ to Gerücht etc* in Umlauf setzen. **2.** † Währung *f*; Zahlungsmittel *pl*: *foreign ~* Devisen *pl*; ~ *reform* Währungsreform *f*. **3.** †, ⚖ Laufzeit *f*. '**cur·rent** **I** *adj* □ **1.** laufend (*Monat, Ausgaben etc*): ~ *account* † Girokonto *n*. **2.** gegenwärtig, augenblicklich, aktuell: ~ *events pl* Tagesereignisse *pl*. **3.** üblich, gebräuchlich: *not in ~ use* nicht allgemein üblich. **II** *s* **4.** Strömung *f*, Strom *m* (*beide a. fig.*): *against the ~* gegen den Strom; ~ *of air* Luftstrom, -zug *m*. **5.** ⚡ Strom *m*: ~ *meter* Stromzähler *m*.

cur·ric·u·lum [kə'rɪkjələm] *pl* **-la** [~lə], **-lums** *s* Lehr-, Studienplan *m*. ~ **vi·tae** ['viːtaɪ] *pl* **-la** - *s* Lebenslauf *m*.

cur·ry¹ ['kʌrɪ] **I** *s* Curry *m, n*. **II** *v/t* mit

Curry zubereiten: *curried* Curry...

cur·ry² [~] *v/t* **1.** *Pferd* striegeln. **2.** *Leder* zurichten. **3.** ~ *favo(u)r with s.o.*, ~ *s.o.'s favo(u)r* sich bei j-m lieb Kind machen (wollen).

curse [kɜːs] **I** *s* **1.** Fluch *m*: *there is a* ~ *on the house, the house is under a* ~ auf dem Haus lastet *od.* liegt ein Fluch. **2.** Fluch(wort *n*) *m*, Verwünschung *f*. **3.** Fluch *m*, Unglück *n* (*to* für). **II** *v/t* **4.** verfluchen: a) mit e-m Fluch belegen, b) verwünschen, fluchen auf (*acc*) *od.* über (*acc*). **5.** *be* ~*ed with* bestraft *od.* geplagt sein mit. **curs·ed** [~sɪd] *adj* □ verflucht, F a. verdammt.

cur·so·ry [ˈkɜːsərɪ] *adj* □ flüchtig, oberflächlich.

curt [kɜːt] *adj* □ **1.** kurz(gefaßt), knapp. **2.** (*with*) barsch, schroff (gegen), kurz angebunden (zu).

cur·tail [kɜːˈteɪl] *v/t* **1.** (ab-, ver)kürzen. **2.** beschneiden, stutzen. **3.** *fig. Ausgaben etc* kürzen, *Rechte etc* beschneiden, einschränken. **cur·tail·ment** *s* **1.** (Ab-, Ver)Kürzung *f*. **2.** *fig.* Beschneidung *f*, Einschränkung *f*.

cur·tain [ˈkɜːtn] **I** *s* **1.** Vorhang *m* (*a. thea. u. fig.*), Gardine *f*: *draw the* ~ die Vorhänge auf- *od.* zuziehen; *the* ~ *rises (falls)* der Vorhang geht auf (fällt); *lift the* ~ den Schleier lüften. **2.** *thea.* Hervorruf *m*: *get (od. take) ten* ~*s* zehn Vorhänge haben. **II** *v/t* **3.** mit Vorhängen versehen. ~ *off* mit Vorhängen abteilen *od.* abschließen. ~ *call* → **curtain** 2. ~ **lec·ture** *s* Gardinenpredigt *f*. ~ **rais·er** *s* **1.** *thea.* kurzes Vorspiel. **2.** *fig.* Vorspiel *n*, Ouvertüre *f* (*to* zu).

curt·s(e)y [ˈkɜːtsɪ] **I** *s* Knicks *m*: *drop a* ~ (*to*) → **II. II** *v/i* e-n Knicks machen, knicksen (*to vor dat*).

cur·va·ture [ˈkɜːvətʃə] *s* Krümmung *f*: ~ *of the earth* Erdkrümmung *f*.

curve [kɜːv] **I** *s* Kurve *f* (*a. ◊*): a) Krümmung *f*, Biegung *f*, b) (Straßen)Kurve *f*, (-)Biegung *f*, c) Rundung *f* (*pl* F a. e-r Frau). **II** *v/t u. v/i* (sich) krümmen *od.* biegen.

cush·ion [ˈkʊʃn] **I** *s* **1.** Kissen *n*, Polster *n* (*a. fig.*). **2.** ◎ Puffer *m*, Dämpfer *m*. **II** *v/t* **3.** polstern (*a. fig.*). **4.** Stoß, *Fall etc* dämpfen, *a. fig.* abmildern. **5.** ◎ abfedern.

cush·y [ˈkʊʃɪ] *adj* F gemütlich, ruhig (*Job etc*).

cuss [kʌs] *s* F **1.** Fluch *m*. **2.** Kerl *m*: *queer* ~ komischer Kauz.

cus·tard [ˈkʌstəd] *s* Vanillesoße *f*.

cus·to·di·an [kʌˈstəʊdjən] *s* **1.** Aufseher *m*, Wächter *m*. **2.** (*Haus- etc*)Verwalter *m*. **3.** ⚖ (Vermögens)Verwalter *m*.

cus·to·dy [~tədɪ] *s* **1.** Obhut *f*, Schutz *m*: *in s.o.'s* ~ in j-s Obhut. **2.** Aufsicht *f* (*of* über *acc*). **3.** ⚖ (*a.* Untersuchungs)Haft *f*: *take into* ~ verhaften; → *remand* I. **4.** ⚖ Sorgerecht *n*.

cus·tom [ˈkʌstəm] **I** *s* **1.** Brauch *m*, Gewohnheit *f*, Sitte *f*, *pl a.* Brauchtum *n*. **2.** ⚖ Gewohnheitsrecht *n*. **3.** † Kundschaft *f*: a) Kunden *pl*, b) Kundesein *n*: *get s.o.'s* ~ j-n als Kunden gewinnen; *have withdrawn one's* ~ *from* nicht mehr (ein)kaufen bei. **4.** *pl* Zoll *m*: ~*s clearance* Zollabfertigung *f*; ~*s ex·amination* (*od.* **inspection**) Zollkontrolle *f*; ~*s officer* (*od.* **official**) Zollbeamte *m*. **II** *adj* **5.** → **custom-made**. **'cus·tom·ar·y** *adj* üblich, gebräuchlich. **'cus·tom·er** *s* **1.** Kunde *m*, Kundin *f*. **2.** F Kerl *m*, Kunde *m*: → *queer* 1.

‚cus·tom-'made *adj bsd. Am.* maßgefertigt, Maß...

cut [kʌt] **I** *s* **1.** Schnitt *m*; Schnittwunde *f*. **2.** Haarschnitt *m*. **3.** Schnitte *f*, Stück *n* (*bsd. Fleisch*): *cold* ~ *s pl bsd. Am.* Aufschnitt *m*. **4.** F Anteil *m* (*of*, *in* an *dat*). **5.** (Zu)Schnitt *m* (*von Kleidung*). **6.** Schnitt *m*, Schliff *m* (*von Edelsteinen*). **7.** Kürzung *f*, Senkung *f*: ~ *in salary* Gehaltskürzung *f*. **8.** *Kartenspiel*: Abheben *n*; abgehobene Karte(n *pl*). **II** *adj* **9.** ge-, beschnitten: ~ *flowers pl* Schnittblumen *pl*. **III** *v/t* (*irr*) **10.** (ab-, be-, durch-, zer)schneiden: ~ *one's finger* sich in den Finger schneiden; ~ *to pieces* zerstückeln; ~ *one's teeth* Zähne bekommen, zahnen; ~ *one's teeth in* (*od.* **on**) *s.th. fig.* s-e ersten Erfahrungen mit et. sammeln; → *throat.* **11.** *Gras* mähen, *Bäume* fällen, *Holz* hacken. **12.** *Hecke etc* (be)schneiden, stutzen: ~ *s.o.'s hair* j-m die Haare schneiden. **13.** *Kleid etc* zuschneiden, *et.* zurechtschneiden; *Stein* behauen, *Glas, Edelsteine* schleifen. **14.** *mot. Kurve* schneiden. **15.** a) *Löhne etc* kürzen, *Text etc a.* zs.-streichen (**to** auf *acc*), b) *Film* schneiden. **16.** *Preise* herabsetzen, senken. **17.** (*auf Tonband*) mitschneiden. **18.** *fig. j-m* weh tun, *j-n* kränken. **19.** F *j-n* schneiden: ~ **dead** völlig ignorieren. **20.** *ped. univ.* F *Stunde etc* schwänzen. **21.** *Karten* abheben. **22.** *Tennis etc: Ball* (an)schneiden. **23.** F *Gewinne* teilen. **IV** *v/i (irr)* **24.** schneiden (**in, into** in *acc*): ~ **into** *Kuchen etc* abschneiden; einschneiden in (*acc*) (*a. fig.*); ~ **into s.o.'s time** *j-n* Zeit kosten; ~ **into s.o.'s savings** ein Loch in *j-s* Ersparnisse reißen; ~ **into a conversation** sich in ein Gespräch einmischen; *it* ~**s both ways** es ist ein zweischneidiges Schwert. **25.** einschneiden (*Kragen etc*). **26.** sich schneiden lassen. **27.** *fig.* weh tun, kränken. **28.** F abhauen. **29.** *Kartenspiel:* abheben. **30.** F die Gewinne teilen.

Verbindungen mit Adverbien:

cut| back I *v/t* **1.** *Hecke etc* beschneiden, stutzen. **2.** → *cut* 15a. **II** *v/i* **3.** *bsd. Am.* (zu)rückblenden (**to** auf *acc*) (*Film, Roman etc*). **4.** ~ **on** *et.* einschränken. ~ **down I** *v/t* **1.** *Bäume* fällen, *Wald* abholzen. **2.** zurückschneiden, -stutzen (*a. fig.*): → *size* 2. **3.** *Ausgaben* verringern, einschränken. **4.** *j-n* herunterhandeln (**by** um; **to** auf *acc*). **II** *v/i* **5.** → *cut back* 4. ~ **in I** *v/t* **1.** F *j-n* beteiligen (**on** an *dat*). **II** *v/i* **2.** sich einmischen. **3.** ~ **on s.o.** *mot.* j-n schneiden. ~ **off** *v/t* **1.** abschneiden. **2.** *Strom etc* absperren, abdrehen, *Verbindung, Versorgung, Weg etc* abschneiden: *he had his electricity* ~ ihm wurde der Strom gesperrt. **3.** *teleph. Teilnehmer* trennen. ~ **out I** *v/t* **1.** (her)ausschneiden. **2.** *Kleid etc* zuschneiden. **3.** *be* ~ **for** wie geschaffen sein für. **4.** *Rivalen* ausstechen, verdrängen. **5.** *cut it out!* F hör auf (damit)! **6.** F *j-n* betrügen (**of** um *s-n Anteil*). **II** *v/i* **7.** *mot.* aussetzen. ~ **un-der** *v/t* ♥ *j-n* unterbieten. ~ **up** *v/t* **1.** zerschneiden. **2.** F verreißen.

'**cut·a·way I** *adj* Schnitt...: ~ **model.** **II** *s a.* ~ **coat** Cut(away) *m.* '~**-back** *s* **1.** Kürzung *f,* Zs.-streichung *f.* **2.** *Film etc: bsd. Am.* Rückblende *f.*

cute [kjuːt] *adj* □ F **1.** schlau, clever. **2.** niedlich, süß.

cut·ler·y ['kʌtlərɪ] *s* (Tisch-, Eß)Besteck *n.*

cut·let ['kʌtlɪt] *s* **1.** Schnitzel *n.* **2.** Hacksteak *n.*

'**cut|·out** *s* **1.** Ausschnitt *m.* **2.** Ausschneidefigur *f.* ,~**-'price** *adj Br.,* ,~**-'rate** *adj Am.* ♥ ermäßigt, herabgesetzt: ~ **offer** Billigangebot *n.*

cut·ter ['kʌtə] *s* **1.** Zuschneider *m;* (*Glas-, Diamant*)Schleifer *m.* **2.** ☼ Schneidemaschine *f,* -werkzeug *n.* **3.** *Film:* Cutter(in). **4.** ♣ Kutter *m.*

'**cut·throat I** *s* Mörder *m;* (professioneller) Killer. **II** *adj* mörderisch, *fig. a.* halsabschneiderisch: ~ **price** Wucherpreis *m.*

cut·ting ['kʌtɪŋ] **I** *s* **1.** (Ab-, Aus-, Be-, Zu)Schneiden *n.* **2.** *bsd. Br.* (Zeitungs)Ausschnitt *m.* **3.** (*Hobel etc*)Späne *pl;* Abfälle *pl,* Schnitzel *pl.* **II** *adj* **4.** schneidend (*a. fig. Schmerz, Wind*), Schneid(e)..., Schnitt...: ~ **blow-pipe** (*od. torch*) ☼ Schneidbrenner *m;* ~ **edge** Schneide *f;* ~ **nippers** *pl* Kneifzange *f.*

cy·a·nide ['saɪənaɪd] *s:* ~ **of potash** 🜍 Zyankali *n.*

cy·ber·net·ics [ˌsaɪbə'netɪks] *s pl (sg konstruiert)* Kybernetik *f.*

cyc·la·men ['sɪkləmən] *s* ❀ Alpenveilchen *n.*

cy·cle ['saɪkl] **I** *s* **1.** Zyklus *m,* Kreis(lauf) *m.* **2.** (*Gedicht-, Lieder*)Zyklus *m.* **3.** a) Fahrrad *n:* ~ **lane** (*od. path*) Rad(fahr)weg *m;* ~ **race** (*Sport*) Radrennen *n,* b) Motorrad *n.* **4.** ☼ Arbeitsgang *m;* Takt *m:* **four-~ engine** Viertaktmotor *m.* **5.** ⚡, *phys.* (Schwingungs)Periode *f.* **II** *v/i* **6.** radfahren, radeln. '**cy·cler** *Am.* → *cyclist.*

'**cy·cle·way** *s* Rad(fahr)weg *m.*

cy·clic, cy·cli·cal ['saɪklɪk(l)] *adj* □ **1.** zyklisch. **2.** ♥ konjunkturbedingt, Konjunktur... **cy·cling** ['saɪklɪŋ] *s* **1.** Radfahren *n:* ~ **tour** Radtour *f.* **2.** Radrennsport *m.* '**cy·clist** *s* Rad- *od.* Motorradfahrer(in).

cy·clone ['saɪkləʊn] *s* Zyklon *m,* Wirbelsturm *m.*

cyl·in·der ['sɪlɪndə] *s* ⚙ Zylinder *m,* ☼ *a.* Walze *f,* Trommel *f.* **cy'lin·dri·cal** [~drɪkl] *adj* □ ⚙ zylindrisch, Zylinder..., ☼ *a.* walzenförmig.

cyn·ic ['sɪnɪk] **I** *s* Zyniker *m.* **II** *adj* (~**ally**)

zynisch. **cyn·i·cal** ['ˌkl] → **cynic** II.
cyn·i·cism ['ˌsɪzəm] s Zynismus m, a.
zynische Bemerkung.
cy·press ['saɪprəs] s ♀ Zypresse f.
Cyp·ri·ot ['sɪprɪət], **Cyp·ri·ote** ['ˌəʊt] I s
Zyprer(in). II adj zyprisch.
cyst [sɪst] s ⚕ Zyste f.

czar [zɑ:] s hist. Zar m.
Czech [tʃek] I s 1. Tscheche m, Tschechin f. 2. ling. Tschechisch n. II adj 3.
tschechisch.
Czech·o·slo·vak [ˌtʃekəʊˈsləʊvæk] I s
Tschechoslowake m, -slowakin f. II adj
tschechoslowakisch.

D

'd F für **had, should, would.**
dab¹ [dæb] I v/t 1. antippen. 2. be-, abtupfen (**with** mit). 3. Farbe etc (leicht)
auftragen (**on** auf acc). II s 4. Klecks m,
Spritzer m.
dab² [ˌ] s a. ~ **hand** bsd. Br. F Könner m:
be a ~ at et. aus dem Effeff können; ~ **at
tennis** Tennisas n.
dab·ble ['dæbl] I v/t 1. bespritzen. II v/i
2. plan(t)schen. 3. ~ **at** (od. **in**) fig. sich
oberflächlich od. aus Liebhaberei od.
dilettantisch beschäftigen mit: ~ **in politics** ein bißchen in der Politik mitmischen.
dachs·hund ['dækshʊnd] s zo. Dackel
m.
dad [dæd] s F Vati m, Papa m.
dad·dy ['dædɪ] → **dad.** ~ **long·legs** pl
-dy -legs s zo. F 1. Schnake f. 2. Am.
Weberknecht m.
daf·fo·dil ['dæfədɪl] s ♀ gelbe Narzisse,
Osterglocke f.
daft [dɑ:ft] adj □ F 1. doof, dämlich. 2.
be ~ about verrückt nach.
dag·ger ['dægə] s Dolch m: **be at ~s
drawn** auf Kriegsfuß stehen (**with** mit);
look ~s at s.o. j-n mit Blicken durchbohren.
da·go ['deɪgəʊ] pl **-go(e)s** s Schimpfwort
für Italiener, Spanier u. Portugiesen.
dahl·ia ['deɪljə] s ♀ Dahlie f.
dai·ly ['deɪlɪ] I adj/adv 1. täglich (a. adv),
Tage(s)....: ~ **help** → 4; ~ **newspaper**
→ 3; ~ **press** Tagespresse f; → **dozen.**
2. alltäglich: **be a ~ occurrence** an der
Tagesordnung sein. II s 3. Tageszei-
tung f. 4. Br. Putzfrau f (die jeden Tag
kommt).

dain·ty ['deɪntɪ] I adj 1. zierlich, niedlich,
reizend. 2. wählerisch, verwöhnt (bsd.
im Essen). 3. schmackhaft, lecker. II s
4. Leckerbissen m (a. fig.).
dair·y ['deərɪ] s 1. Molkerei f. 2. Milch-
geschäft n. ~ **prod·uce** s Molkereipro-
dukte pl.
da·is ['deɪɪs] s Podium n.
dai·sy ['deɪzɪ] s ♀ Gänseblümchen n:
push up the daisies sl. sich die Radieschen von unten ansehen od. betrachten.
dal·ly ['dælɪ] I v/i 1. schäkern: ~ **with** a.
spielen mit (j-s Gefühlen). 2. spielen,
liebäugeln (**with** mit e-r Idee etc). 3. a. ~
about (od. **around**) herumtrödeln,
bummeln. II v/t 4. ~ **away** Zeit vertrödeln; Gelegenheit verspielen.
dam [dæm] I s 1. (Stau)Damm m, Talsperre f. 2. Stausee m. II v/t 3. a. ~ **up**
stauen, ab-, eindämmen; Gefühle aufstauen: ~ **back** Tränen zurückhalten.
dam·age ['dæmɪdʒ] I s 1. Schaden m (to
an dat). 2. pl ⚖ Schadenersatz m: **sue
for ~s** auf Schadenersatz verklagen. 3.
what's the ~? F was kostet es? II v/t 4.
beschädigen. 5. j-m, j-s Ruf etc schaden.
dam·ask ['dæməsk] s Damast m.
dame [deɪm] s 1. ♀ Br. Ordens- od. Adelstitel. 2. bsd. Am. sl. Weib n.
damn [dæm] I v/t 1. eccl. u. weitS. verdammen. 2. verurteilen. 3. verwerfen,
ablehnen. 4. F ~ **it!, ~ me!** verflucht!,
verdammt!; ~ **you!** der Teufel soll dich
holen!; **I'll be ~ed if I do that** ich denk'
ja gar nicht daran, das zu tun. II s 5. F
I don't care a ~ das ist mir völlig egal;

not worth a ~ keinen Pfifferling wert. **III** *int* **6.** F verflucht!, verdammt! **IV** *adj u. adv* **7.** → **damned** 2, 4.

dam'na·tion I *s* Verdammung *f*; *eccl.* Verdammnis *f*. **II** *int* → **damn** 6.

damned [dæmd] **I** *adj* **1.** verdammt: *the* ~ *pl eccl.* die Verdammten *pl*. **2.** F verflucht, verdammt: ~ *fool* Vollidiot *m*. **3.** F *Bekräftigung:* **a** ~ *sight better* viel besser. **II** *adv* **4.** F verdammt: ~ *cold*. **5.** F *Bekräftigung:* **he** ~ *well ought to know it* das müßte er wahrhaftig wissen.

Dam·o·cles ['dæməkli:z] *s:* *sword of* ~ Damoklesschwert *n*; *hang over s.o. like a sword of* ~ über j-m wie ein Damoklesschwert hängen.

damp [dæmp] **I** *adj* □ **1.** feucht, (*Raum etc a.*) klamm: ~ *squib Br.* F Pleite *f*, Reinfall *m*. **II** *s* **2.** Feuchtigkeit *f*: ~ *in the air* Luftfeuchtigkeit. **3.** *fig.* Dämpfer *m*: *cast* (*od. strike*) **a** ~ *on* (*od. over*) *et.* dämpfen *od.* lähmen. **III** *v/t* **4.** an-, befeuchten. **5.** *Begeisterung etc* dämpfen; *j-n* entmutigen. '**damp·en** → *damp* III. '**damp·er** *s fig.* Dämpfer *m*: *cast* (*od. put, strike*) **a** ~ *on et.* dämpfen *od.* lähmen. '**damp·ness** *s* Feuchtigkeit *f*.

dance [dɑ:ns] **I** *v/i* **1.** tanzen: ~ *to* (*od. after*) *s.o.'s pipe* (*od. tune, whistle*) *fig.* nach j-s Pfeife tanzen. **2.** tanzen, hüpfen (*with, for* vor *dat*). **II** *v/t* **3.** *Tanz* tanzen: ~ *attendance on s.o. fig.* um j-n scharwenzeln. **III** *s* **4.** Tanz *m*: *lead s.o. a* (*pretty*) ~ *Br.* j-n zum Narren halten. **5.** Tanz(veranstaltung *f*) *m*. **IV** *adj* **6.** Tanz...: ~ *music*. '**danc·ing** *s* Tanzen *n*. **II** *adj* Tanz...: ~ *lesson* Tanzstunde *f*, *pl a.* Tanzunterricht *m*; ~ *master* Tanzlehrer *m*; ~ *partner* Tanzpartner(in); ~ *school* Tanzschule *f*.

dan·de·li·on ['dændilaiən] *s* ♣ Löwenzahn *m*.

dan·der ['dændə] *s* F: *get s.o.'s* ~ *up* j-n auf die Palme bringen; *get one's* ~ *up* auf die Palme gehen.

dan·druff ['dændrʌf] *s* (Kopf-, Haar-) Schuppen *pl*.

dan·dy ['dændi] **I** *s* Dandy *m*. **II** *adj* F prima.

Dane [dein] *s* Däne *m*, Dänin *f*.

dan·ger ['deindʒə] **I** *s* Gefahr *f* (*to* für): ~ *of infection* ✱ Infektionsgefahr; *be in* ~

of one's life in Lebensgefahr sein *od.* schweben; *without* ~ gefahrlos. **II** *adj* Gefahr...: ~ *area* (*od. zone*) Gefahrenzone *f*, -bereich *m*; ~ *money* (*od. pay*) Gefahrenzulage *f*. '**dan·ger·ous** *adj* □ gefährlich (*to, for* für).

dan·gle ['dæŋgl] **I** *v/i* baumeln: *keep s.o. dangling* F j-n im unklaren lassen. **II** *v/t* baumeln lassen: ~ *s.th. before s.o.* j-m et. (verlockend) in Aussicht stellen, j-m mit et. winken.

Dan·ish ['deiniʃ] **I** *adj* **1.** dänisch. **II** *s* **2.** *ling.* Dänisch *n*. **3.** *the* ~ *pl* die Dänen *pl*.

dank [dæŋk] *adj* □ (*unangenehm*) feucht, naß(kalt).

dap·per ['dæpə] *adj* □ **1.** adrett, elegant. **2.** flink, (*a. Benehmen*) gewandt.

dap·ple ['dæpl] *v/t* sprenkeln.

dare [deə] **I** *v/i* es wagen, sich (ge)trauen: *who* ~*s wins* wer wagt, gewinnt; *how* ~ *you!* unterstehe dich!; was fällt dir ein!; *how* ~ *you say that?* wie können Sie das sagen?; *don't* (*you*) ~ (*to*) *touch it!* rühr es ja nicht an!; *I* ~ *say* ich glaube wohl; allerdings. **II** *v/t* et. wagen, riskieren. '~·**dev·il** *s* Draufgänger *m*.

dar·ing ['deəriŋ] **I** *adj* **1.** wagemutig, kühn. **2.** gewagt, verwegen (*beide a. fig.*). **3.** unverschämt, dreist **II** *s* **4.** Wagemut *m*, Kühnheit *f*.

dark [dɑ:k] **I** *adj* □ **1.** dunkel, finster. **2.** dunkel (*Farbe*). **3.** *fig.* düster, trüb (*Aussichten etc*): *the* ~ *side of things* die Schattenseite der Dinge; *one's* ~ *est hour* s-e schwärzeste Stunde. **4.** *fig.* düster, finster (*Blick etc*). **5.** finster, böse (*Gedanken etc*). **6.** *fig.* geheim(nisvoll), verborgen: *keep s.th.* ~ et. geheimhalten. **II** *s* **7.** Dunkel(heit *f*) *n*, Finsternis *f*: *in the* ~ im Dunkel(n); *after* ~ nach Einbruch der Dunkelheit. **8.** *fig.* das Ungewisse *od.* Dunkle: *be in the* ~ im dunkeln tappen; *keep s.o. in the* ~ j-n im ungewissen lassen (*about* über *acc*). ♀ **Ag·es** *s pl* das (frühe *od.* finstere) Mittelalter. ♀ **Con·ti·nent** *s* der dunkle Erdteil, Afrika *n*.

dark·en ['dɑ:kən] **I** *v/t* **1.** verdunkeln, -düstern (*beide a. fig.*). **2.** dunkel *od.* dunkler färben. **II** *v/i* **3.** dunkel werden, sich verdunkeln. **4.** *fig.* sich verdüstern.

dark horse *s* **1.** *Sport:* unbekannte Größe (*Person*). **2.** *pol. Am.* unbeschriebenes Blatt.

dark·ness ['dɑːknɪs] *s* Dunkelheit *f*, Finsternis *f*: **be in complete ~** völlig dunkel sein.

'dark·room *s phot.* Dunkelkammer *f*.

'~-skinned *adj* dunkelhäutig.

dar·ling ['dɑːlɪŋ] **I** *s* Liebling *m*. **II** *adj* reizend, goldig.

darn¹ [dɑːn] → **damn** 4–6.

darn² [~] *v/t* stopfen.

darned [dɑːnd] → **damned** 2–5.

dart [dɑːt] **I** *s* **1.** (Wurf)Pfeil *m*. **2.** Satz *m*, Sprung *m*: **make a ~ for** losstürzen auf (*acc*). **3.** *pl* (*sg konstruiert*) Darts *n* (*Wurfpfeilspiel*). **II** *v/t* **4.** Speer werfen, schleudern, *Pfeil* schießen: **~ a look at s.o.** j-m e-n Blick zuwerfen. **III** *v/i* **5.** sausen, flitzen: **~ at** losstürzen auf (*acc*). **6.** zucken, schnellen (*Schlange, Zunge etc*), huschen (*Augen, Blick*). **'~-board** *s* Dartsscheibe *f*.

dash [dæʃ] **I** *v/t* **1.** schleudern, schmettern: **~ to pieces** zerschmettern. **2.** **~ down** (*od. off*) *Getränk* hinunterstürzen; *Aufsatz, Zeichnung etc* schnell hinhauen. **3.** *Hoffnungen etc* zerstören, zunichte machen; *j-n* deprimieren. **II** *v/i* **4.** stürmen: **~ off** davonstürzen. **III** *s* **5.** Schlag *m*: **at one ~** mit 'einem Schlag (*a. fig.*). **6.** Schuß *m* (*Rum etc*), Prise *f* (*Salz etc*). **7.** *fig.* Anflug *m* (*of von*); Stich *m* (*of green* ins Grüne). **8.** Gedankenstrich *m*. **9. make a ~ at** (*od. for*) losstürzen auf (*acc*). **10.** Schwung *m*, Schmiß *m*, Elan *m*. **11.** *Leichtathletik*: Sprint *m*, Kurzstreckenlauf *m*; **'~-board** *s mot.* Armaturen-, **⤴** *a.* Instrumentenbrett *n*.

dash·ing ['dæʃɪŋ] *adj* □ schneidig, forsch.

da·ta ['deɪtə] *s pl* **1.** (*oft sg konstruiert*) (*a. technische*) Daten *pl od.* Angaben *pl*: **~ protection** Datenschutz *m*. **2.** *Computer*: Daten *pl*: **~ bank** Datenbank *f*; **~ processing** Datenverarbeitung *f*; **~ transmission** Datenübertragung *f*; **~ typist** Datentypistin *f*.

date¹ [deɪt] *s* **⚘** Dattel *f*.

date² [~] **I** *s* **1.** Datum *n*: a) Tag *m*: **what is the ~ today?** der Wievielte ist heute?, welches Datum haben wir heute?, b) Zeit(punkt *m*) *f*: **of recent ~** neu(eren Datums), c) Datumsangabe *f*, d) **✝**, **📅**

Tag *m*, Termin *m*: **~ of delivery** Liefertermin; **~ of maturity** Fälligkeitstag. **2.** heutiges Datum, heutiger Tag: **to ~** bis heute; **out of ~** veraltet, unmodern; **go out of ~** veralten; **(up) to ~** zeitgemäß, modern, auf dem laufenden; **bring up to ~** auf den neuesten Stand bringen, modernisieren. **3.** Verabredung *f*, Rendezvous *n*: **have a ~ with s.o.** mit j-m verabredet sein; **make a ~** sich verabreden. **4.** (Verabredungs)Partner(in): **who is your ~?** mit wem bist du verabredet? **II** *v/t* **5.** datieren. **6.** sich verabreden mit; gehen mit. **III** *v/i* **7. ~ back to** a) **~ from** stammen aus, entstanden sein in (*dat*), b) bis in *e-e Zeit* zurückreichen, auf *e-e Zeit* zurückgehen. **8.** veralten. **'dat·ed** *adj* **1.** datiert. **2.** veraltet, überholt. **'date·less** *adj* **1.** undatiert. **2.** zeitlos.

date| line *s geogr.* Datumsgrenze *f*. **~ stamp** *s* Datums-, *a.* Poststempel *m*.

da·tive ['deɪtɪv] *s a.* **~ case** *ling.* Dativ *m*, 3. Fall.

daub [dɔːb] **I** *v/t* **1.** be-, verschmieren: **~ed with oil** ölverschmiert. **2.** schmieren (*on* auf *acc*). **3.** *contp. Bild* zs.-klecksen. **II** *s* **4.** *paint. contp.* (Farb-) Kleckserei *f*.

daugh·ter ['dɔːtə] *s* Tochter *f*: **~ (company ✝)** Tochter(gesellschaft) *f*. **'~-in--law** *pl* **'daugh·ters-in-law** *s* Schwiegertochter *f*.

daunt [dɔːnt] *v/t* **1.** einschüchtern, erschrecken. **2.** entmutigen. **'daunt·less** *adj* □ unerschrocken.

dav·en·port ['dævnpɔːt] *s* **1.** kleiner Schreibtisch. **2.** *Am.* (*bsd.* Bett)Couch *f*.

daw·dle ['dɔːdl] **I** *v/i* (herum)trödeln, (-)bummeln. **II** *v/t oft* **~ away** *Zeit* vertrödeln. **'daw·dler** *s* Trödler(in), Bummler(in).

dawn [dɔːn] **I** *v/i* **1.** dämmern (*Morgen, Tag*). **2. ~ on** *fig.* j-m dämmern, klarwerden. **3.** *fig.* sich zu entwickeln beginnen, erwachen. **II** *s* **4.** (Morgen)Dämmerung *f*: **at ~** bei Tagesanbruch. **5.** *fig.* Beginn *m*.

day [deɪ] *s* **1.** Tag *m* (*Ggs. Nacht*): **by ~** bei Tag(e). **2.** Tag *m* (*Zeitraum*): **~ after ~** Tag für Tag; **the ~ after tomorrow**, *Am.* **~ after tomorrow** übermorgen; **~ in, ~ out** tagaus, tagein; **let's call it a ~!**

F Feierabend!, Schluß für heute!; *carry* (*od. win*) *the* ~ den Sieg davontragen. **3.** (*bestimmter, festgesetzter*) Tag: ~ *of delivery* Liefertermin *m*. **4.** *oft pl* (Lebens)Zeit *f*, Zeiten *pl*, Tage *pl*: *in my young* ~s in m-n Jugendtagen; *in those* ~s damals. **5.** *oft pl* (*beste*) Zeit (*des Lebens*), Glanzzeit *f*: *he has had his* ~ s-e beste Zeit ist vorüber; *those were the* ~*s!* das waren noch Zeiten! '~**break** *s* Tagesanbruch *m*: *at* ~ bei Tagesanbruch. '~**dream** **I** *s* Tag-, Wachtraum *m*. **II** *v/i* (*a. irr dream*) (mit offenen Augen) träumen. '~**dream·er** *s* Träumer(in). '~**light** *s* Tageslicht *n*: *by* (*od. in*) ~ bei Tag(eslicht); *in broad* ~ am hellichten Tag; *beat* (*od. knock*) *the* (*living*) ~s *out of s.o.* F j-n fürchterlich verdreschen; ~ *saving time* Sommerzeit *f*. ~ *nurs·er·y s* Tagesheim *n*, -stätte *f*. ~ *re·turn* (*tick·et*) → day ticket. ~ *shift s* Tagschicht *f*: *be* (*od. work*) *on* ~ Tagschicht haben. ~ *tick·et s Br*. Tagesrückfahrkarte *f*. '~**time** *s*: *in the* ~ bei Tag(e). '~-*to-'day adj* (tag)täglich. **day| *trip** *s* Tagesausflug *m*. ~ *trip·per s* Tagesausflügler(in).

daze [deɪz] **I** *v/t* benommen machen. **II** *s* Benommenheit *f*: *in a* ~ benommen.

daz·zle ['dæzl] **I** *v/t* **1.** blenden (*a. fig.*). **II** *s* **2.** Blenden *n*: *in a* ~ geblendet. **3.** blendender Glanz.

dea·con ['diːkən] *s eccl.* Diakon *m*. **dea·con·ess** [͵~'nes] *s* Diakonisse *f*.

dead [ded] **I** *adj* (□ → **deadly** II) **1.** tot, gestorben: *shoot* ~ erschießen; → *body* **2.** *fig.* tot: a) leblos: ~ *matter* tote Materie, b) ausgestorben: ~ *language* tote Sprache, c) überlebt (*Brauch etc*). **3.** gefühllos, abgestorben (*Finger etc*). **4.** *fig.* (*to*) unempfänglich (für); gleichgültig, abgestumpft (gegen). **5.** *bsd.* ✝ flau. **6.** tot (*Kapital, Wissen etc*). **7.** ⚡ tot, stromlos. **8.** erloschen (*Vulkan, Gefühle etc*). **9.** matt, stumpf (*Farben, Blick etc*). **10.** völlig, total: ~ *certainty* absolute Gewißheit; ~ *silence* Totenstille *f*; → *cert, earnest* 4, *loss* 1a. **II** *s* **11.** *the* ~ *pl* die Toten *pl*. **12.** *in the* ~ *of night* mitten in der Nacht; *in the* ~ *of winter* im tiefsten Winter. **III** *adv* **13.** völlig, total: *be* ~ *asleep* im tiefsten Schlaf liegen; ~ *drunk* sinnlos betrunken; ~ *slow! mot*. Schritt fahren!; ~

straight schnurgerade; ~ *tired* todmüde; → *set* 8. **14.** plötzlich, abrupt: *stop* ~ (*in one's tracks*) plötzlich *od.* abrupt stehenbleiben. **15.** genau, direkt: ~ *against* genau gegenüber von (*od. dat*). '~-'**beat** *adj* F todmüde, völlig kaputt. ~ **cen·tre** (*Am.* **cen·ter**) *s* genaue Mitte.

dead·en ['dedn] *v/t* **1.** Geräusch abdämpfen, *a. Schlag etc* (ab)schwächen. **2.** *Schmerz* stillen; *Gefühl* abtöten, abstumpfen (*to* gegen).

dead| end *s* Sackgasse *f* (*a. fig.*): *come to a* ~ in e-e Sackgasse geraten. '~-**end** *adj* **1.** ~ *street* Sackgasse *f*. **2.** ohne Aufstiegschancen (*Stellung*). ~ *heat s Sport*: totes Rennen. '~-**line** *s* **1.** letzter (Ablieferungs)Termin, Anzeigen-, Redaktionsschluß *m*: ~ *pressure* Termindruck *m*; *meet the* ~ den Termin einhalten. **2.** Stichtag *m*. '~-**lock** **I** *s* völliger Stillstand, toter Punkt: *come to* (*od. reach*) *a* ~ → II. **II** *v/i* sich festfahren, an e-m toten Punkt anlangen (*Verhandlungen etc*). '~-**locked** *adj* festgefahren.

dead·ly ['dedlɪ] **I** *adj* **1.** tödlich; Tod...: ~ *enemy* Todfeind *m*; ~ *fight* mörderischer Kampf; ~ *sin* Todsünde *f*. **2.** totenähnlich: ~ *pallor* Leichen-, Todesblässe *f*. **3.** F schrecklich, äußerst. **II** *adv* **4.** totenähnlich: ~ *pale* leichen-, totenblaß. **5.** F schrecklich, äußerst: *be* ~ *afraid of* e-e Sterbensangst haben vor (*dat*); ~ *dull* sterbenslangweilig; ~ *tired* todmüde.

dead| march *s* ♩ Trauermarsch *m*. ~ *pan s* F ausdrucksloses Gesicht. '~-*pan adj* F **1.** ausdruckslos (*Gesicht*); mit ausdruckslosem Gesicht (*Person*). **2.** trocken (*Humor*).

deaf [def] **I** *adj* □ **1.** taub (*a. fig. to* gegen): ~ *and dumb* taubstumm; ~ *in one ear* auf einem Ohr taub; → *ear*¹ 1. **2.** schwerhörig. **II** *s* **3.** *the* ~ *die* Tauben *pl*. ~ *aid s* Hörgerät *n*. '~-*and-'dumb adj* **1.** taubstumm. **2.** Taubstummen...: ~ *language*.

deaf·en ['defn] *v/t* taub machen. '**deaf·en·ing** *adj* ohrenbetäubend.

'**deaf-'mute** **I** *adj* taubstumm. **II** *s* Taubstumme *m*, *f*.

deaf·ness ['defnɪs] *s* **1.** Taubheit *f* (*a. fig. to* gegen). **2.** Schwerhörigkeit *f*.

debt

deal¹ [di:l] **I** v/i (irr) **1.** ~ **with** sich befassen od. beschäftigen mit; handeln von; et. behandeln od. zum Thema haben; et. erledigen, mit et., j-m fertig werden. **2.** ~ **with** ✝ Handel treiben od. Geschäfte machen mit. **3.** ~ **in** ✝ handeln od. Handel treiben mit: ~ **in paper** Papier führen. **4.** sl. dealen (mit Drogen handeln). **5.** Kartenspiel: geben. **II** v/t **6.** oft ~ **out** et. aus-, verteilen, Karten a. geben. **III** s **7.** F Handlungsweise f, Verfahren n. **8.** F Geschäft n, Handel m: **it's a ~!** abgemacht!; → **raw 6. 9.** Abkommen n: **make a ~** ein Abkommen treffen. **10.** Kartenspiel: Geben n: **it is my ~** ich muß geben.

deal² [~] s Menge f: **a great ~** sehr viel; **a good ~** e-e ganze Menge, ziemlich viel; **a ~ worse** F viel schlechter.

deal·er ['di:lə] s **1.** Händler(in): ~ **in antiques** Antiquitätenhändler. **2.** sl. Dealer m (Drogenhändler). **3.** Kartenspiel: Geber(in). **'deal·ing** s **1.** mst pl Umgang m, Beziehungen pl: **have ~s with** zu tun haben mit. **2.** ✝ Handel m (in in dat, mit).

dealt [delt] pret u. pp von **deal¹**.

dean [di:n] s eccl., univ. Dekan m.

dear [dɪə] **I** adj **1.** lieb, teuer (**to** dat): 2 **Sir**, (in Briefen) sehr geehrter Herr (Name); **run for ~ life** um sein Leben rennen. **2.** teuer, kostspielig. **II** adv **3.** teuer: **it cost him** ~ es kam ihm od. ihn teuer zu stehen. **III** s **4.** Liebste m, f, Schatz m: **there's a ~** sei (so) lieb. **IV** int **5.** (oh) ~!, ~ **me!** du liebe Zeit!, ach je! **'dear·ly** adv **1.** innig, herzlich. **2.** teuer: → **buy 4. 'dear·ness** s hoher Preis.

dearth [dɜ:θ] s Mangel m (**of** an dat).

death [deθ] s **1.** Tod m: **to** ~ zu Tode; (**as**) **sure as** ~ todsicher; **catch one's** ~ sich den Tod holen (engS. durch Erkältung); **put to** ~ hinrichten. **2.** Todesfall m. ~ **ag·o·ny** s Todeskampf m. **'~bed** s Sterbebett n. **'~blow** s fig. Todesstoß m (**to** für). ~ **cell** s Todeszelle f. ~ **du·ty** s Br. Erbschaftsteuer f.

death·less ['deθlɪs] adj □ unsterblich (Ruhm etc). **'death·like** adj totenähnlich: ~ **pallor** Leichen-, Todesblässe f; ~ **stillness** Totenstille f. **'death·ly** → **deadly:** ~ **silence** eisiges Schweigen; ~ **stillness** Totenstille f.

death| mask s Totenmaske f. ~ **pen·al·ty** s Todesstrafe f. ~ **rate** s Sterblichkeitsziffer f.

'death's-head s Totenkopf m (Symbol).

death| threat s Morddrohung f. ~ **toll** s Zahl f der Toten: **the ~ on the roads** die Zahl der Verkehrstoten. ~ **trap** s Todesfalle f. ~ **war·rant** s **1.** ✠ Hinrichtungsbefehl m. **2.** fig. Todesurteil n (**of** für): **sign one's** ~ sein (eigenes) Todesurteil unterschreiben.

de·ba·cle [deɪˈbɑːkl] s Debakel n, Zs.-bruch m.

de·bar [dɪˈbɑː] v/t j-n ausschließen (**from** von).

de·base [dɪˈbeɪs] v/t **1.** entwürdigen. **2.** im Wert mindern; Wert mindern.

de·bat·a·ble [dɪˈbeɪtəbl] adj strittig, umstritten. **de'bate I** v/i **1.** debattieren, diskutieren (**on, about** über acc). **II** v/t **2.** et. debattieren, diskutieren. **3.** et. erwägen, sich et. überlegen. **III** s **4.** Debatte f, Diskussion f: **be under** ~ zur Debatte stehen.

de·bauch [dɪˈbɔːtʃ] **I** v/t sittlich verderben. **II** s Ausschweifung f, Orgie f. **de'bauch·er·y** [~tʃərɪ] s Ausschweifung f.

de·ben·ture [dɪˈbentʃə] s **1.** Schuldschein m. **2.** ✝ a) Br. a. ~ **bond** Obligation f, Schuldverschreibung f, b) Br. Pfandbrief m.

de·bil·i·tate [dɪˈbɪlɪteɪt] v/t schwächen, entkräften. **de·bil·i'ta·tion** s Schwächung f, Entkräftung f. **de'bil·i·ty** s Schwäche f, Kraftlosigkeit f.

deb·it ['debɪt] ✝ **I** s **1.** Soll n: ~ **and credit** Soll u. Haben n. **2.** Belastung f: **to the** ~ **of** zu Lasten von (od. gen); **charge** (od. **place**) **a sum to s.o.'s** ~ j-s Konto mit e-r Summe belasten; ~ **entry** Lastschrift f. **II** v/t **3.** j-n, Konto belasten (**with** mit): ~ **£ 100 against s.o.('s ac-count**) j-n (j-s Konto) mit £ 100 belasten.

de·bouch [dɪˈbaʊtʃ] v/i sich ergießen, (ein)münden (**into** in acc) (Fluß).

de·brief [ˌdiːˈbriːf] v/t sich informieren lassen von (e-m Piloten, Diplomaten etc).

de·bris ['deɪbriː] s Trümmer pl, Schutt m.

debt [det] s Schuld f: ~ **of hono(u)r** Ehrenschuld f; **be in** ~ Schulden haben, verschuldet sein; *be in ~ to s.o. for £100* j-m £100 schulden; *be in s.o.'s ~* in j-s Schuld stehen; *be out of ~* schuldenfrei sein. **'debt·or** *s* Schuldner *m*.

de·bug [ˌdiːˈbʌg] *v/t* **1.** entwanzen (*a. F von Minispionen befreien*). **2.** ⊕ F Fehler *e-r Maschine* beheben; (*Computer*) *Programm* austesten.

de·bu·reauc·ra·tize [ˌdiːbjʊəˈrɒkrətaɪz] *v/t* entbürokratisieren.

de·but [ˈdeɪbjuː] *s* Debüt *n:* *make one's ~* sein Debüt geben.

deb·u·tant [ˈdebjuːtɑːŋ] *s* Debütant *m.* **deb·u·tante** [ˈ~tɑːnt] *s* Debütantin *f.*

dec·ade [ˈdekeɪd] *s* Jahrzehnt *n.*

de·ca·dence [ˈdekədəns] *s* Dekadenz *f.* **'de·ca·dent** *adj* dekadent.

de·caf·fein·at·ed [ˌdiːˈkæfɪneɪtɪd] *adj* koffeinfrei (*Kaffee*).

de·cal [ˈdiːkæl] *s bsd. Am.* Abziehbild *n.*

de·camp [dɪˈkæmp] *v/i* F sich aus dem Staub machen.

de·cant [dɪˈkænt] *v/t* **1.** dekantieren. **2.** ab-, umfüllen. **de'cant·er** *s* Karaffe *f.*

de·cap·i·tate [dɪˈkæpɪteɪt] *v/t* enthaupten, köpfen. **de,cap·i'ta·tion** *s* Enthauptung *f.*

de·car·tel·i·za·tion [ˈdiːˌkɑːtələˈzeɪʃn] *s* † Entkartellisierung *f*, Entflechtung *f.* **'de·car·tel·ize** *v/t* entkartellisieren, entflechten.

de·cath·lete [dɪˈkæθliːt] *s Leichtathletik:* Zehnkämpfer *m.* **de'cath·lon** [ˌ~lɒn] *s* Zehnkampf *m.*

de·cay [dɪˈkeɪ] **I** *v/i* **1.** zerfallen (*a. phys.*), vermodern. **2.** verfaulen, -wesen; kariös *od.* schlecht werden (*Zahn*). **3.** abnehmen, schwinden; schwach *od.* kraftlos werden. **4.** zugrunde gehen. **5.** *geol.* verwittern. **II** *s* **6.** Zerfall *m* (*a. phys.*). **7.** Verfaulen *n.* **8.** *geol.* Verwitterung *f.*

de·cease [dɪˈsiːs] *s* Ableben *n.* **de'ceased** **I** *adj* verstorben. **II** *s: the ~* der *od.* die Verstorbene, die Verstorbenen *pl.*

de·ceit [dɪˈsiːt] *s* Betrug *m*, Täuschung *f.* **de'ceit·ful** *adj* □ **1.** betrügerisch. **2.** falsch, hinterlistig.

de·ceive [dɪˈsiːv] **I** *v/t* täuschen (*Person*), (*Sache a.*) trügen: *be ~d* sich täuschen (lassen); *be ~d in s.o.* sich in j-m täuschen; *~ o.s.* sich et. vormachen. **II** *v/i*

täuschen, trügen (*Sache*). **de'ceiv·er** *s* Betrüger(in).

de·cel·er·ate [ˌdiːˈseləreɪt] **I** *v/t* verlangsamen; die Geschwindigkeit herabsetzen von (*od. gen*). **II** *v/i* sich verlangsamen; s-e Geschwindigkeit verringern.

De·cem·ber [dɪˈsembə] *s* Dezember *m:* *in ~* im Dezember.

de·cen·cy [ˈdiːsnsɪ] *s* Anstand *m*, *pl a.* Anstandsformen *pl: for ~'s sake* anstandshalber. **'de·cent** *adj* □ **1.** anständig. **2.** passabel, annehmbar. **3.** F salonfähig (*angezogen*).

de·cen·tral·i·za·tion [diːˌsentrəlaɪˈzeɪʃn] *s* Dezentralisierung *f.* **de'cen·tral·ize** *v/t* dezentralisieren.

de·cep·tion [dɪˈsepʃn] *s* Täuschung *f.* **de'cep·tive** *adj* □ täuschend, trügerisch: *be ~* → *deceive* II; → *appearance* 3.

de·cide [dɪˈsaɪd] **I** *v/t* **1.** *et.* entscheiden; *et.* bestimmen. **2.** *~ s.o. to do s.th.* j-n veranlassen *od.* dazu bringen, et. zu tun. **II** *v/i* **3.** beschließen, sich entscheiden *od.* entschließen (*to do, on doing* zu tun; *against doing* nicht zu tun): *~ in favo(u)r of* (*od. on*) (*against*) sich entscheiden für (gegen). **4.** entscheiden, den Ausschlag geben. **de'cid·ed** *adj* □ entscheiden, entschlossen. **de'cid·ing** *adj* entscheidend, ausschlaggebend.

de·cid·u·ous [dɪˈsɪdjʊəs] *adj: ~ tree* Laubbaum *m.*

dec·i·mal [ˈdesɪml] **I** *adj* □ **1.** dezimal, Dezimal...: *go ~* das Dezimalsystem einführen; *~ fraction* → 2; *~ point* Komma *n* (*in GB u. USA Punkt*) vor der ersten Dezimalstelle; *~ system* Dezimalsystem *n.* **II** *s* **2.** Dezimalbruch *m.* **3.** Dezimalzahl *f.* **dec·i·mal·ize** [ˈ~məlaɪz] *v/t* auf das Dezimalsystem umstellen.

dec·i·mate [ˈdesɪmeɪt] *v/t* dezimieren.

de·ci·pher [dɪˈsaɪfə] *v/t* entziffern.

de·ci·sion [dɪˈsɪʒn] *s* **1.** Entscheidung *f:* *make* (*od.* *take*) *a ~* e-e Entscheidung treffen (*on, over* über *acc*). **2.** Entschluß *m: arrive at* (*od.* *come to*) *a ~* zu e-m Entschluß kommen. **3.** Entschlußkraft *f*, Entschlossenheit *f.* **de'ci·sive** [dɪˈsaɪsɪv] *adj* □ **1.** → *deciding: be ~ of et.* entscheiden. **2.** → *decided.*

deck [dek] **I** *s* **1.** ⚓ Deck *n: on ~* an Deck; *bsd. Am.* F auf dem Posten. **2.**

Stock(werk *n*) *m*, (*e-s Busses a.*) Deck *n*. **3.** *bsd. Am.* Spiel *n*, Pack *m* (Spiel)Karten. **II** *v/t* **4.** *oft ~ out* herausputzen; schmücken. **~ chair** *s* Liegestuhl *m*.

de·claim [dɪ'kleɪm] *v/i* **1.** deklamieren, (*v/t a.*) vortragen. **2.** eifern, wettern (**against** gegen).

dec·la·ra·tion [ˌdeklə'reɪʃn] *s* **1.** Erklärung *f:* a) Aussage *f:* **make a ~** e-e Erklärung abgeben; **~ of intent** Absichtserklärung, b) Verkündung *f:* **~ of independence** Unabhängigkeitserklärung; **~ of war** Kriegserklärung *f*. **2.** (Zoll)Deklaration *f*, Zollerklärung *f*.

de·clare [dɪ'kleə] *v/t* **1.** erklären, verkünden: **~ open** für eröffnet erklären; **~ s.o. the winner** j-n zum Sieger erklären; → **war. 2.** deklarieren: **have you anything to ~?** haben Sie et. zu verzollen? **II** *v/i* **3.** sich erklären *od.* entscheiden (**for** für; **against** gegen). **de'clared** *adj* erklärt.

de·clen·sion [dɪ'klenʃn] *s ling.* Deklination *f*.

de·cline [dɪ'klaɪn] **I** *v/i* **1.** sich neigen *od.* senken. **2.** zur Neige *od.* zu Ende gehen. **3.** abnehmen, zurückgehen; fallen, sinken (*Preise*); verfallen. **4.** (höflich) ablehnen. **II** *v/i* **5.** (höflich) ablehnen: **~ doing** (*od.* **to do**) es ablehnen zu tun. **6.** *ling.* deklinieren. **III** *s* **7.** Neigung *f*, Senkung *f*. **8.** Neige *f:* **be on the ~** zur Neige gehen; im Niedergang begriffen sein. **9.** Abnahme *f*, Rückgang *m:* **~ of** (*od.* **in**) **strength** Kräfteverfall *m;* **~ in value** Wertminderung *f*.

de·cliv·i·tous [dɪ'klɪvɪtəs] *adj* abschüssig. **de'cliv·i·ty** [ˌ~vətɪ] *s* **1.** Abschüssigkeit *f*. **2.** (Ab)Hang *m*.

de·clutch [ˌdiː'klʌtʃ] *v/i mot.* auskuppeln.

de·code [ˌdiː'kəʊd] *v/t* entschlüsseln.

dé·colle·tage [ˌdeɪkɒl'taːʒ] , **dé·colle·té** [ˌ~teɪ] *s* Dekolleté *n*.

de·com·pose [ˌdiː·kəm'pəʊz] **I** *v/t* **1.** 🝆, *phys.* zerlegen, spalten. **2.** zersetzen. **II** *v/i* **3.** sich auflösen, zerfallen (**into** in *acc*). **4.** sich zersetzen. **de·com·po·si·tion** [ˌdiː·kɒmpə'zɪʃn] *s* **1.** 🝆, *phys.* Zerlegung *f*, Spaltung *f*. **2.** Zersetzung *f*, Zerfall *m*.

de·con·tam·i·nate [ˌdiː·kən'tæmɪneɪt] *v/t* entgasen, -seuchen, -strahlen. **'de·con-**

tam·i·na·tion *s* Entgasung *f*, -seuchung *f*, -strahlung *f*.

de·con·trol [ˌdiː·kən'trəʊl] ✝ **I** *v/t* freigeben, die Zwangsbewirtschaftung aufheben von (*od. gen*). **II** *s* Freigabe *f*, Aufhebung *f* der Zwangsbewirtschaftung.

dé·cor, de·cor [ˈdeɪkɔː] *s* **1.** Ausstattung *f* (*e-s Raums*). **2.** *thea.* Dekor *m*, *n*, Ausstattung *f*, Dekoration *f*.

dec·o·rate [ˈdekəreɪt] *v/t* **1.** schmücken, verzieren; ausschmücken, dekorieren. **2.** tapezieren; (an)streichen. **3.** dekorieren, (*mit Orden etc*) auszeichnen. **dec·o·ra·tion** *s* **1.** (Aus)Schmückung *f*, Dekorierung *f*. **2.** Schmuck *m*, Dekoration *f*, Verzierung *f*. **3.** Orden *m*, Ehrenzeichen *n*. **dec·o·ra·tive** [ˈdekərətɪv] *adj* dekorativ, Schmuck...: **~ plant** Zierpflanze *f*. **dec·o·ra·tor** [ˈ~reɪtə] *s* **1.** Dekorateur *m:* → **interior** 1. **2.** Maler *m u.* Tapezierer *m*.

dec·o·rous [ˈdekərəs] *adj* □ anständig, schicklich. **de·co·rum** [dɪ'kɔːrəm] *s* Anstand *m*, Schicklichkeit *f*.

de·coy **I** *s* [ˈdiːkɔɪ] Lockvogel *m*, *fig. a.* Köder *m*. **II** *v/t* [dɪ'kɔɪ] (an)locken, ködern; *fig. a.* verleiten (**into** zu).

de·crease [diː'kriːs] **I** *v/i* abnehmen, sich vermindern *od.* verringern: **~ in length** kürzer werden. **II** *v/t* vermindern, -ringern, herabsetzen. **III** *s* [ˈdiːkriːs] Abnahme *f*, Verminderung *f*, -ringerung *f*: **be on the ~** → I; **~ in value** Wertminderung *f*.

de·cree [dɪ'kriː] **I** *s* **1.** Dekret *n*, Erlaß *m*, Verfügung *f*. **2.** 🜊 Entscheid *m*, Urteil *n*. **II** *v/t* **3.** verfügen. **~ ni·si** ['naɪsaɪ] *s* 🜊 vorläufiges Scheidungsurteil.

de·crep·it [dɪ'krepɪt] *adj* altersschwach (*Person, Auto etc*).

de·cry [dɪ'kraɪ] *v/t* schlecht-, heruntermachen, herabsetzen.

ded·i·cate [ˈdedɪkeɪt] *v/t* **1.** Buch, Leben, Zeit etc widmen (**to** dat). **2.** Am. feierlich eröffnen *od.* einweihen. **'ded·i·cat·ed** *adj* treusorgend (*Vater etc*), einsatzfreudig (*Angestellter etc*), engagiert (*Verfechter etc*). **ded·i·ca·tion** *s* **1.** Widmung *f*. **2.** Hingabe *f*. **3.** *Am.* feierliche Eröffnung *od.* Einweihung.

de·duce [dɪ'djuːs] *v/t* **1.** folgern, schließen (**from** aus). **2.** ab-, herleiten (**from** von).

de·duct [dɪ'dʌkt] v/t (**from**) Betrag a) abziehen (von): *after ~ing charges, charges ~ed* nach Abzug der Kosten, b) einbehalten (von), c) (*von der Steuer*) absetzen. **de'duct·i·ble** adj (*steuerlich*) absetzbar. **de'duc·tion** s 1. Abzug m; Einbehaltung f; Absetzung f. 2. ♣ Nachlaß m. 3. (Schluß)Folgerung f, Schluß m.

deed [diːd] s 1. Tat f: *do a good ~* e-e gute Tat vollbringen; → *will* 1, *word* 1. 2. Helden-, Großtat f. 3. ⚖ (Übertragungs)Urkunde f.

dee·jay ['diːdʒeɪ] s F Diskjockey m.

deem [diːm] v/t halten od. erachten für, betrachten als.

deep [diːp] **I** adj □ 1. tief (a. fig.): *~ breath* tiefer Atemzug; *~ disappointment* schwere od. bittere Enttäuschung; *~ly disappointed* schwer enttäuscht; *~ poverty* tiefste Armut; *~ silence* tiefes od. völliges Schweigen; *~ sleep* tiefer Schlaf, Tiefschlaf m; *~ voice* tiefe od. dunkle Stimme; *in ~ water(s)* in Schwierigkeiten. 2. schwerverständlich, schwierig: *that is too ~ for me* das ist mir zu hoch. **II** adv 3. tief (a. fig.): *~ into the night* (bis) tief in die Nacht (hinein); *~ in thought* tief in Gedanken (versunken); *~ in winter* im tiefen Winter; → *water* 2. **III** s 4. Tiefe f. 5. *in the ~ of night* mitten in der Nacht; *in the ~ of winter* im tiefen Winter. **'deep·en** v/t u. v/i (sich) vertiefen, fig. a. (sich) steigern od. verstärken.

'deep|-felt adj tiefempfunden. **,~·'freeze I** s Tiefkühl-, Gefriergerät n. **II** adj Tiefkühl-..., Gefrier-...: *~ cabinet* Tiefkühl-, Gefriertruhe f. **III** v/t (*mst irr freeze*) tiefkühlen, einfrieren: *deep-frozen food* Tiefkühlkost f. **~·freez·er** → *deep-freeze* I. **,~·'fry** v/t fritieren. **~ fry·er**, **'~·,fry·ing pan** s Friteuse f.

deep·ness ['diːpnɪs] s Tiefe f (a. fig.). **,deep|-'root·ed** adj tief verwurzelt (a. fig.). **~·'sea** adj Tiefsee-...: *~ fishing* Hochseefischerei f. **~·'seat·ed** adj fig. tiefsitzend. **'~-set** adj tiefliegend (Augen).

deer [dɪə] pl **deer(s)** s zo. Hirsch m; Reh n.

de·es·ca·late [ˌdiː'eskəleɪt] **I** v/t 1. Krieg etc deeskalieren. 2. Erwartungen etc herunterschrauben. **II** v/i 3. deeskalieren. **,de·es·ca·la·tion** s Deeskalation f.

de·face [dɪ'feɪs] v/t 1. entstellen, verunstalten. 2. aus-, durchstreichen, unleserlich machen.

def·a·ma·tion [ˌdefə'meɪʃn] s Verleumdung f, Diffamierung f. **de·fam·a·to·ry** [dɪ'fæmətərɪ] adj □ verleumderisch, diffamierend. **de·fame** [dɪ'feɪm] v/t verleumden, diffamieren.

de·fault [dɪ'fɔːlt] **I** s 1. Unterlassung f, (Pflicht)Versäumnis n. 2. ♣ Nichterfüllung f, Verzug m: *be in ~* in Verzug sein (*on* mit). 3. ⚖ Nichterscheinen n vor Gericht: *judg(e)ment by ~* Versäumnisurteil n. 4. Sport: Nichtantreten n. 5. *in ~ of* in Ermangelung von (*od. gen*), mangels (*gen*). **II** v/i 6. s-n Verpflichtungen nicht nachkommen, ♣ a. im Verzug sein: *~ on s.th.* mit et. in Rückstand sein. 7. ⚖ nicht vor Gericht erscheinen. 8. Sport: nicht antreten. **III** v/t 9. e-r Verpflichtung nicht nachkommen, in Verzug geraten mit.

de·feat [dɪ'fiːt] **I** v/t 1. Gegner besiegen, schlagen. 2. Hoffnung, Plan etc vereiteln, zunichte machen. **II** s 3. Besiegung f. 4. Niederlage f: *admit ~* sich geschlagen geben. 5. Vereit(e)lung f.

de·fect I s ['diːfekt] 1. Defekt m, Fehler *m*: *~ in character* Charakterfehler; *~ of vision* Sehfehler. 2. Mangel m (*of od. dat*): *~ of memory* Gedächtnisschwäche f. **II** v/i [dɪ'fekt] 3. abtrünnig werden (*from dat*); übergehen, -laufen (*to* zu). **de'fec·tion** s Überlaufen n. **de'fec·tive** adj □ 1. mangelhaft, unzulänglich: *he is ~ in* es mangelt ihm an (*dat*). 2. schadhaft, defekt: *mentally ~* schwachsinnig. **de'fec·tor** s Überläufer m.

de·fence [dɪ'fens] s Br. Verteidigung f (a. ✕, ⚖, Sport), Schutz m: *in ~ of* zur Verteidigung od. zum Schutz von (*od. gen*); *come to s.o.'s ~* j-m zu Hilfe kommen; → *counsel* 3, *witness* 1. **de'fence·less** adj □ schutz-, wehrlos.

de·fend [dɪ'fend] v/t 1. (*from, against*) verteidigen (gegen), schützen (vor *dat*, gegen). 2. Meinung etc verteidigen, rechtfertigen. **de'fend·ant** s ⚖ Beklagte m, f; Angeklagte m, f.

de·fend·er s **1.** Verteidiger(in). **2.** *Sport*: Abwehrspieler(in).

de·fense, *etc Am.* → **defence**, *etc.*

de·fen·sive I *adj* defensiv, Verteidigungs..., Abwehr... II *s* Defensive *f*: **on the ~** in der Defensive.

de·fer¹ [dɪ'fɜː] *v/t* **1.** auf-, verschieben (**to** auf *acc*). **2.** hinausschieben, verzögern. **3.** ✕ *Am.* (vom Wehrdienst) zurückstellen.

de·fer² [~] *v/i* sich fügen (**to** *dat*). **def·er·ence** ['defərəns] s **1.** Ehrerbietung *f*, (Hoch)Achtung *f*: **in** (*od.* **out of**) ~ **to** aus Achtung vor (*dat*). **2.** Rücksicht(nahme) *f*: **in** (*od.* **out of**) ~ **to** mit *od.* aus Rücksicht auf (*acc*). **def·er·en·tial** [~'renʃl] *adj* □ **1.** ehrerbietig. **2.** rücksichtsvoll.

de·fer·ment [dɪ'fɜːmənt] s **1.** Aufschub *m*, Verschiebung *f*. **2.** ✕ *Am.* Zurückstellung *f* (*vom Wehrdienst*).

de·fi·ance [dɪ'faɪəns] s **1.** Trotz *m*: **in ~ of** ungeachtet, trotz (*gen*), e-m Gebot *etc* zuwider, j-m zum Trotz. **2.** Herausforderung *f*. **de·fi·ant** *adj* □ **1.** trotzig. **2.** herausfordernd.

de·fi·cien·cy [dɪ'fɪʃnsɪ] s **1.** (**of**) Mangel *m* (an *dat*), Fehlen *n* (von): **~ of blood** Blutarmut *f*; **~ disease** ♣ Mangelkrankheit *f*. **2.** → **deficit. de·fi·cient** *adj* □ unzureichend, mangelhaft, ungenügend: **be ~ in** Mangel leiden an (*dat*); **he is ~ in** ihm fehlt es an (*dat*).

def·i·cit ['defɪsɪt] s Defizit *n*, Fehlbetrag *m*.

de·file [dɪ'faɪl] *v/t* beschmutzen, besudeln (*beide a. fig.*).

de·fine [dɪ'faɪn] *v/t* **1.** definieren: a) *Wort etc* erklären, b) *Begriff* bestimmen. **2.** abgrenzen. **3.** **~ itself against** sich scharf *od.* deutlich abheben von *od.* gegen. **def·i·nite** ['defɪnɪt] *adj* **1.** bestimmt (*a. ling.*). **2.** endgültig, definitiv. **'def·i·nite·ly** *adv* → **definite:** ~ **not!** ganz bestimmt nicht! **def·i·ni·tion** [,defɪ'nɪʃn] s Definition *f*: a) Erklärung *f*, b) Bestimmung *f*. **de·fin·i·tive** [dɪ'fɪnɪtɪv] *adj* □ **1.** → **definite. 2.** maßgeblich.

de·flate [dɪ'fleɪt] *v/t* **1.** (die) Luft ablassen aus. **2.** † deflationieren. **de·fla·tion** s † Deflation *f*.

de·flect [dɪ'flekt] I *v/t* ablenken (**from** von). II *v/i* abweichen (**from**·von) (*a.*

fig.). **de·flec·tion** s **1.** Ablenkung *f*. **2.** Abweichung *f*.

de·fo·li·ate [,diː'fəʊlɪeɪt] *v/t* entblättern, -lauben.

de·for·est [dɪ'fɒrɪst] *v/t* abholzen.

de·form [dɪ'fɔːm] *v/t* **1.** deformieren, verformen (*beide a. phys.*, ☉). **2.** verunstalten, entstellen: **~ed by anger** wutverzerrt (*Gesicht*). **de·for·ma·tion** [,diːfɔː'meɪʃn] s **1.** Deformierung *f*, Verformung *f*. **2.** Verunstaltung *f*, Entstellung *f*. **de·form·i·ty** [dɪ'fɔːmətɪ] s **1.** Entstelltheit *f*. **2.** Mißbildung *f*.

de·fraud [dɪ'frɔːd] *v/t* betrügen (**of** um).

de·fray [dɪ'freɪ] *v/t Kosten* tragen, bestreiten.

de·frost [,diː'frɒst] I *v/t* von Eis befreien, *Windschutzscheibe etc* abtauen, *Kühlschrank etc* abtauen, *Tiefkühlkost etc* auftauen. II *v/i* ab-, auftauen.

deft [deft] *adj* □ gewandt, geschickt.

de·fuse [,diː'fjuːz] *v/t Bombe, Lage etc* entschärfen.

de·fy [dɪ'faɪ] *v/t* **1.** trotzen (*dat*); sich widersetzen (*dat*): **~ description** unbeschreiblich sein, jeder Beschreibung spotten. **2.** herausfordern.

de·gen·er·ate *v/i* [dɪ'dʒenəreɪt] degenerieren, entarten (**into** zu). II *adj* [~rət] degeneriert, entartet. **de·gen·er·a·tion** [~'reɪʃn] s Degeneration *f*, Entartung *f*.

deg·ra·da·tion [,degrə'deɪʃn] s **1.** Degradierung *f*. **2.** Erniedrigung *f*. **de·grade** [dɪ'greɪd] *v/t* **1.** degradieren. **2.** erniedrigen (**into, to** zu).

de·gree [dɪ'griː] s **1.** Grad *m*, Stufe *f*: **by ~s** allmählich, nach u. nach; **by slow ~s** ganz allmählich; **to some** (*od.* **a certain**) ~ ziemlich, bis zu e-m gewissen Grade; **to a high ~** in hohem Maße; **~ of comparison** *ling.* Steigerungsstufe *f*; **~ of priority** Dringlichkeitsstufe *f*. **2.** ⒜, ☉, *ast., geogr etc* Grad *m*: **~ of latitude** (*longitude*) Breiten-(Längen)grad. **3.** *univ.* Grad *m*: **take one's ~** e-n akademischen Grad erwerben; → **doctor** 2.

de·hu·man·ize [,diː'hjuːmənaɪz] *v/t* entmenschlichen.

de·hy·drate [,diː'haɪdreɪt] *v/t* das Wasser entziehen (*dat*): **~d vegetables** *pl* Trockengemüse *n*.

de·ice [,diː'aɪs] *v/t* enteisen.

deign [deɪn] I *v/i* sich herablassen, geruhen (**to do** zu tun). **II** v/t sich herablassen zu.

de·i·ty ['di:ɪtɪ] s Gottheit f.

de·ject·ed [dɪ'dʒektɪd] adj □ niedergeschlagen.

de·jec·tion s Niedergeschlagenheit f.

de·lay [dɪ'leɪ] **I** v/t **1.** a) ver-, auf-, hinausschieben: ~ **doing s.th.** es verschieben, et. zu tun, b) verzögern, -schleppen: **be ~ed** sich verzögern. **2.** aufhalten: **be ~ed (for two hours)** 🚂, etc (zwei Stunden) Verspätung haben. **II** v/i **3.** zögern. **4.** Zeit zu gewinnen suchen. **III** s **5.** Verschiebung f, Aufschub m; Verzögerung f, Verschleppung f: **without ~** unverzüglich. **6.** 🚂, etc Verspätung f. **de·lay·ing** adj: ~ **tactics** pl Hinhalte-, Verzögerungstaktik f.

de·lec·ta·ble [dɪ'lektəbl] adj □ köstlich (bsd. Speise). **de·lec·ta·tion** [ˌdi:lek-'teɪʃn] s Vergnügen n: **for the ~ of** zum Ergötzen s.

del·e·gate I s ['delɪɡət] **1.** Delegierte m, f, bevollmächtigter Vertreter. **II** v/t [~ɡeɪt] **2.** abordnen, delegieren. **3.** Vollmachten etc übertragen (**to** dat). **del·e·ga·tion** [~'ɡeɪʃn] s **1.** Übertragung f. **2.** Abordnung f, Delegation f.

de·lete [dɪ'li:t] **I** v/t (aus)streichen. **II** v/i: ~ **where inapplicable** Nichtzutreffendes bitte streichen. **de·le·tion** [dɪ'li:ʃn] s Streichung f.

de·lib·er·ate I adj [dɪ'lɪbərət] □ **1.** überlegt. **2.** bewußt, absichtlich, vorsätzlich. **3.** bedächtig, besonnen. **II** v/t [~reɪt] **4.** überlegen, erwägen. **III** v/i [~reɪt] **5.** nachdenken (**on** über acc), überlegen. **6.** beratschlagen, sich beraten (**on** über acc). **de·lib·er·a·tion** [~'reɪʃn] s **1.** Überlegung f. **2.** Beratung f. **3.** Bedächtigkeit f.

del·i·ca·cy ['delɪkəsɪ] s **1.** Zartheit f. **2.** Fein-, Zartgefühl n, Takt m. **3.** Empfindlichkeit f. **4. of great ~** sehr heikel. **5.** Delikatesse f, Leckerbissen m.

del·i·cate ['~kət] adj □ **1.** zart: a) fein (Farben etc), b) zierlich (Figur etc), c) zerbrechlich: **of** (od. **in**) ~ **health** von zarter Gesundheit, d) sanft, leise: ~ **hint** zarter Wink. **2.** delikat, heikel (Frage etc). **3.** fein, empfindlich (Instrument etc). **4.** feinfühlig, zartfühlend, taktvoll. **5.** delikat, schmackhaft. **del·i·ca·tes·sen** [ˌdelɪkə'tesn] s pl **1.** Deli-

katessen pl, Feinkost f. **2.** (sg konstruiert) Feinkostgeschäft n.

de·li·cious [dɪ'lɪʃəs] adj □ köstlich.

de·light [dɪ'laɪt] **I** s Vergnügen n, Entzücken n: **to my ~** zu m-r Freude; **take ~ in** → **III**. **II** v/t erfreuen, entzücken. **III** v/i: ~ **in** (große) Freude haben an (dat), sich ein Vergnügen machen aus. **de·light·ful** [~fʊl] adj □ entzückend, köstlich.

de·lim·it [di:'lɪmɪt], **de·lim·i·tate** [~teɪt] v/t abgrenzen.

de·lin·e·ate [dɪ'lɪnɪeɪt] v/t **1.** skizzieren, entwerfen. **2.** beschreiben, schildern.

de·lin·quen·cy [dɪ'lɪŋkwənsɪ] s Kriminalität f: → **juvenile I**. **de·lin·quent I** adj straffällig. **II** s Delinquent(in), Straffällige m, f: → **juvenile I**.

de·lir·i·ous [dɪ'lɪrɪəs] adj □ **1.** 🩺 im Delirium, phantasierend. **2.** fig. rasend (**with** vor dat): ~ **with joy** in e-m Freudentaumel; ~**ly happy** vor Glück außer sich. **de·lir·i·um** [~əm] pl **-i·ums**, **-i·a** [~ɪə] s **1.** 🩺 Delirium n: ~ **tremens** ['tri:menz] Delirium tremens, Säuferwahn(sinn) m. **2.** fig. Taumel m: ~ **of joy** Freudentaumel.

de·liv·er [dɪ'lɪvə] v/t **1.** a) ~ **up** (od. **over**) übergeben, ausliefern: ~ **o.s. up to s.o.** sich j-m stellen od. ergeben. **2.** Waren liefern; Brief etc zustellen; Nachricht etc bestellen. **3.** Rede etc halten (**to** dat). **4.** befreien, erlösen (**from** von, aus). **5. be ~ed of** entbinden: **be ~ed of** entbunden werden von. **de·liv·er·y** s **1.** 🏺 Lieferung f: **on** ~ bei Lieferung od. Empfang; **cash** (Am. **collect**) **on** ~ per Nachnahme; ~ **note** Lieferschein m. **2.** 🕊 Zustellung f: ~ **charge** Zustellgebühr f. **3.** Halten n (e-r Rede); Vortrag(sweise f) m. **4.** 🩺 Entbindung f: ~ **room** Kreißsaal m.

de·louse [ˌdi:'laʊs] v/t entlausen.

del·ta ['deltə] s (Fluß)Delta n.

de·lude [dɪ'lu:d] v/t **1.** täuschen, irreführen: ~ **o.s.** sich et. vormachen. **2.** verleiten (**into** zu).

del·uge ['delju:dʒ] **I** s **1.** Überschwemmung f: **the** ♌ Bibl. die Sintflut. **2.** fig. Flut f, (Un)Menge f. **II** v/t **3.** überschwemmen, -fluten (beide a. fig. **with** mit).

de·lu·sion [dɪ'lu:ʒn] s **1.** Täuschung f, Irreführung f. **2.** Wahn m (a. psych.):

be under the ~ *that* in dem Wahn leben, daß; ~*s pl of grandeur* Größenwahn. **de'lu·sive** [~sɪv] *adj* □ **1.** täuschend, irreführend. **2.** Wahn...

de luxe [də'lʌks] *adj* Luxus..., De-Luxe-...

delve [delv] *v/i* angestrengt suchen (*for* nach): ~ *into* sich vertiefen in (*acc*); erforschen.

dem·a·gog·ic [ˌdeməˈgɒgɪk] *adj* (~*ally*) demagogisch. **dem·a·gogue** ['~gɒg] *s* Demagoge *m*. **'dem·a·gog·y** *s* Demagogie *f*.

de·mand [dɪ'mɑːnd] **I** *v/t* **1.** fordern, verlangen (*of, from* von). **2.** (*fordernd*) fragen nach. **3.** *fig.* erfordern, verlangen. **II** *s* **4.** Forderung *f* (*for* nach): *on* ~ auf Verlangen; *make* ~*s on s.o.* Forderungen an j-n stellen. **5.** (*on*) Anforderung *f* (an *acc*), Beanspruchung *f* (*gen*): *make great* ~*s on* stark in Anspruch nehmen (*acc*), große Anforderungen stellen an (*acc*). **6.** ✝ *u. allg.* (*for*) Nachfrage *f* (nach), Bedarf *m* (an *dat*): *be in great* ~ sehr gefragt sein. **de'mand·ing** *adj* anspruchsvoll.

de·mar·cate ['diːmɑːkeɪt] *v/t* abgrenzen (*from* gegen, von) (*a. fig.*). ˌ**de·mar·'ca·tion** *s* Abgrenzung *f*: ~ *line* Grenz-, *pol.* Demarkationslinie *f*; *fig.* Trennungslinie *f*, -strich *m*.

demi... [demɪ] *in Zssgn* Halb..., halb... **'dem·i·god** *s* Halbgott *m* (*a. fig.*). **'dem·i·john** *s* große Korbflasche.

de·mil·i·ta·rize [ˌdiːˈmɪlɪtəraɪz] *v/t* entmilitarisieren.

de·mist [ˌdiːˈmɪst] *v/t Windschutzscheibe* freimachen. ˌ**de'mist·er** *s mot.* Gebläse *n.*

dem·o ['deməʊ] *pl* **-os** *s* F Demo *f* (*De-monstration*).

de·mo·bi·lize [diːˈməʊbɪlaɪz] *v/t* demobilisieren.

de·moc·ra·cy [dɪ'mɒkrəsɪ] *s* Demokratie *f.* **'dem·o·crat**, *pol. Am.* 2 ['deməkræt] *s* Demokrat(in). ˌ**dem·o'crat·ic**, *pol. Am.* 2 *adj* (~*ally*) demokratisch.

de·mog·ra·phy [diːˈmɒgrəfɪ] *s* Demographie *f.*

de·mol·ish [dɪ'mɒlɪʃ] *v/t* **1.** ab-, ein-, niederreißen, abbrechen. **2.** *fig.* zerstören. **3.** F *Essen* verdrücken. **dem·o·li·tion** [ˌdeməˈlɪʃn] *s* **1.** Niederreißen *n*, Abbruch *m*. **2.** *fig.* Zerstörung *f.*

de·mon ['diːmən] *s* **1.** Dämon *m.* **2.** ~ *for work* Arbeitsfanatiker *m.* **de·mo·ni·ac** [dɪ'məʊnɪæk], **de·mon·ic** [diːˈmɒnɪk] *adj* (~*ally*) dämonisch.

dem·on·strate ['demənstreɪt] **I** *v/t* **1.** demonstrieren: a) beweisen, b) darlegen, veranschaulichen, zeigen. **2.** *Auto etc* vorführen. **II** *v/i* **3.** *pol. etc* demonstrieren. ˌ**dem·on'stra·tion** *s* **1.** Demonstrierung *f*, Veranschaulichung *f.* **2.** Vorführung *f*: ~ *car* Vorführwagen *m.* **3.** Demonstration *f*, Kundgebung *f.* **de·mon·stra·tive** [dɪ'mɒnstrətɪv] *adj* □ **1.** anschaulich: *be* ~ *of* → *demonstrate* 1. **2.** *be* ~ s-e Gefühle (offen) zeigen. **3.** demonstrativ, betont. **4.** ~ *pronoun ling.* Demonstrativpronomen *n*, hinweisendes Fürwort.

dem·on·stra·tor ['demənstreɪtə] *s* **1.** Vorführer(in), Propagandist(in). **2.** Demonstrant(in).

de·mor·al·ize [dɪ'mɒrəlaɪz] *v/t* demoralisieren.

de·mo·ti·vate [ˌdiːˈməʊtɪveɪt] *v/t* demotivieren.

den [den] *s* **1.** *zo.* Höhle *f* (*a. fig.*): ~ *of vice* Lasterhöhle. **2.** F Bude *f.*

de·na·tion·al·ize [ˌdiːˈnæʃnəlaɪz] *v/t* ✝ reprivatisieren, entstaatlichen.

de·na·ture [ˌdiːˈneɪtʃə] *v/t* 🜂 denaturieren.

de·ni·al [dɪ'naɪəl] *s* **1.** Ablehnung *f.* **2.** (Ab)Leugnung *f*: *official* ~ Dementi *n.*

den·im ['denɪm] *s* **1.** Köper *m.* **2.** *pl* Jeans *pl.*

de·nom·i·nate [dɪ'nɒmɪneɪt] *v/t* nennen, bezeichnen als. **de·nom·i·na·tion** *s* **1.** Bezeichnung *f.* **2.** *eccl.* Konfession *f*, Bekenntnis *n.* **3.** ✝ Nennwert *m.* **de·nom·i·na·tion·al** [~'neɪʃənl] *adj* □ konfessionell, Konfessions... **de'nom·i·na·tor** *s* ⅍ Nenner *m*: *common* ~ gemeinsamer Nenner (*a. fig.*); *reduce to a common* ~ auf e-n gemeinsamen Nenner bringen.

de·note [dɪ'nəʊt] *v/t* **1.** bedeuten, anzeigen. **2.** kenn-, bezeichnen.

de·nounce [dɪ'naʊns] *v/t* **1.** (öffentlich) anprangern. **2.** *j-n* anzeigen, *contp.* denunzieren (*to* bei). **3.** *Vertrag* kündigen.

dense [dens] *adj* □ **1.** *allg.* dicht: ~*ly populated* dichtbevölkert. **2.** *fig.* beschränkt, begriffsstutzig. **'dense·ness**

s **1.** → *density.* **2.** *fig.* Beschränktheit *f*, Begriffsstutzigkeit *f.* **'den·si·ty** *s* Dichte *f*, Dichtheit *f*: ~ *of population* Bevölkerungsdichte; ~ *of traffic* Verkehrsdichte.

dent [dent] **I** *s* Beule *f*, Delle *f*, Einbeulung *f*: *make a* ~ *in fig.* ein Loch reißen in (*Ersparnisse etc*); *j-s Ruf etc* schaden, *j-s Stolz etc* verletzen. **II** *v/t* ein-, verbeulen.

den·tal ['dentl] *adj* **1.** Zahn...: ~ *hygiene* Zahnpflege *f*; ~ *plaque* Zahnbelag *m*; ~ *surgeon* → *dentist*; ~ *treatment* Zahnbehandlung *f.* **2.** Zahnarzt...: ~ *assistant* Zahnarzthelferin *f.* **'den·tist** *s* Zahnarzt *m*, -ärztin *f.* **'den·tist·ry** *s* Zahnmedizin *f.* **den·ture** ['~tʃə] *s mst pl* (Zahn)Prothese *f.*

de·nude [dɪ'njuːd] *v/t* (*of*) entblößen (von *od.* gen); *fig.* berauben (gen).

de·nun·ci·a·tion [dɪˌnʌnsɪ'eɪʃn] *s* **1.** (öffentliche) Anprangerung. **2.** Anzeige *f*, *contp.* Denunziation *f.* **3.** Kündigung *f* (*of e-s Vertrags*).

de·ny [dɪ'naɪ] *v/t* **1.** ab-, bestreiten, (ab)leugnen: *it cannot be denied, there is no ~ing (the fact)* es läßt sich nicht bestreiten, es ist nicht zu leugnen (*that* daß). **2.** *Bitte etc* ablehnen, *j-m et.* abschlagen, verweigern. **3.** *Glauben, j-n etc* verleugnen.

de·o·dor·ant [diːˈəʊdərənt] **I** *s* De(s)odorant *n*, Deo *n.* **II** *adj* de(s)odorierend. **de·o·dor·ize** [~raɪz] *v/t* de(s)odorieren.

de·part [dɪ'pɑːt] *v/i* **1.** abreisen, abfahren (*for* nach). **2.** 🚆, *etc* abfahren, ✈ abfliegen. **3.** abweichen (*from* von *-er Regel, der Wahrheit etc*). **de·part·ed I** *adj* verstorben. **II** *s*: *the* ~ der *od.* die Verstorbene, der Verstorbenen *pl.* **de·'part·ment** *s* **1.** Fach *n*, Gebiet *n.* **2.** Abteilung *f*, *univ. a.* Fachbereich *m*: ~ *store* Kauf-, Warenhaus *n.* **3.** *pol.* Ministerium *n*: ♀ *of Defense Am.* Verteidigungsministerium; ♀ *of the Interior Am.* Innenministerium; ♀ *of State Am.* Außenministerium. **de·part·men·tal** [ˌdiːpɑːt'mentl] *adj* Abteilungs..., **de·par·ture** [dɪ'pɑːtʃə] *s* **1.** Abreise *f.* **2.** 🚆, *etc* Abfahrt *f*, ✈ Abflug *m*: ~*s pl* ,Abfahrt' (*Fahrplan etc*); ~ *lounge* Abflughalle *f.* **3.** Abweichen *n.*

de·pend [dɪ'pend] *v/i* **1.** sich verlassen (*on* auf *acc*). **2.** (*on*) abhängen, abhängig sein (von): a) angewiesen sein (auf *acc*), b) ankommen (auf *acc*): *that* ~*s* das kommt darauf an, je nachdem; ~*ing on whether* je nachdem, ob. **de·'pend·a·ble** *adj* □ verläßlich, zuverlässig. **de·'pen·dance** *Am.* → *de·pendence.* **de·'pen·dant I** *s* (Familien)Angehörige *m, f.* **II** *adj Am.* → *dependent* I. **de·'pen·dence** *s* **1.** Vertrauen *n* (*on* auf *acc*). **2.** (*on*) Abhängigkeit *f* (von), Angewiesensein *n* (auf *acc*). **de·'pen·dent I** *adj* (*on*) abhängig (von): a) angewiesen (auf *acc*), b) bedingt (durch): ~ *on weather conditions* wetter-, witterungsbedingt. **II** *s bsd. Am.* → *dependant* I.

de·pict [dɪ'pɪkt] *v/t* **1.** (bildlich) darstellen. **2.** schildern, beschreiben.

de·pil·a·to·ry [dɪ'pɪlətərɪ] *s* Enthaarungsmittel *n.*

de·plete [dɪ'pliːt] *v/t* **1.** leeren. **2.** *fig.* Raubbau treiben mit, *Kräfte, Vorräte etc* erschöpfen, *Bestand* dezimieren.

de·plor·a·ble [dɪ'plɔːrəbl] *adj* □ **1.** bedauerlich, bedauerns-, beklagenswert. **2.** erbärmlich, kläglich. **de·'plore** *v/t* bedauern, beklagen.

de·ploy [dɪ'plɔɪ] *v/t* **1.** ✕ *u. allg.* verteilen, einsetzen. **2.** ✕ *Truppen* stationieren, *Raketen etc a.* aufstellen.

de·pop·u·late [ˌdiːˈpɒpjʊleɪt] *v/t u. v/i* (sich) entvölkern.

de·port [dɪ'pɔːt] *v/t* **1.** des Landes verweisen, ausweisen, *Ausländer a.* abschieben. **2.** deportieren. **de·por·ta·tion** [ˌdiːpɔːˈteɪʃn] *s* **1.** Ausweisung *f*, Abschiebung *f.* **2.** Deportation *f.*

de·pose [dɪ'pəʊz] **I** *v/t* **1.** *j-n* absetzen: ~ *s.o. from office j-n* s-s Amtes entheben. **2.** ⚖ eidlich bezeugen *od.* erklären. **II** *v/i* **3.** ~ *to* → 2.

de·pos·it [dɪ'pɒzɪt] **I** *v/t* **1.** absetzen, abstellen. **2.** 🐾, *geol.* ablagern, absetzen. **3.** deponieren, hinterlegen. **4.** ✝ *Betrag* anzahlen. **II** *v/i* **5.** 🐾 sich absetzen *od.* ablagern. **III** *s* **6.** 🐾 Ablagerung *f*, *geol. a.* (Erz- *etc*)Lager *n.* **7.** Deponierung *f*, Hinterlegung *f.* **8.** Anzahlung *f*: *make (od. pay) a* ~ e-e Anzahlung leisten (*on* für). ~ *ac·count s bsd. Br.* Sparkonto *n.*

dep·o·si·tion [ˌdepə'zɪʃn] *s* **1.** Absetzung *f.* **2.** 🐾, *geol.* Ablagerung *f.* **3.** ⚖ eidliche Aussage.

descend

de·pot s 1. ['depəʊ] Depot n (a. ✕, ✗). 2. ['diːpəʊ] Am. Bahnhof m.

de·prave [dɪ'preɪv] v/t moralisch verderben. **de·prav·i·ty** [dɪ'prævətɪ] s Verderbtheit f.

dep·re·cate ['deprɪkeɪt] v/t 1. mißbilligen. 2. → **depreciate** 2. **'dep·re·cat·ing** adj □ 1. mißbilligend. 2. entschuldigend. ,**dep·re'ca·tion** s Mißbilligung f. **dep·re·ca·to·ry** ['-kətərɪ] → **deprecating**.

de·pre·ci·ate [dɪ'priːʃɪeɪt] I v/t 1. geringschätzen, verachten. 2. herabsetzen, herunterwürdigen. 3. im Preis od. Wert herabsetzen; Währung abwerten. II v/i 4. an Wert verlieren. **de'pre·ci·at·ing** adj □ geringschätzig, verächtlich. **de,pre·ci'a·tion** s 1. Geringschätzung f, Verachtung f. 2. Herabsetzung f. ✝ Wertminderung f; Abwertung f.

dep·re·da·tion [,deprɪ'deɪʃn] s Verwüstung f.

de·press [dɪ'pres] v/t 1. Pedal, Taste etc (nieder)drücken. 2. j-n deprimieren, bedrücken. 3. Preis, Stimmung etc drücken. **de'pres·sant** s ✠ Beruhigungsmittel n. **de'pressed** adj 1. deprimiert, niedergeschlagen, bedrückt. 2. gedrückt. 3. ✝ flau (Markt etc), notleidend (Industrie). 4. ~ **area** Notstandsgebiet n. **de·pres·sion** [dɪ'preʃn] s 1. Depression f, Niedergeschlagenheit f. 2. Senkung f, Vertiefung f; geol. Landsenke f. 3. ✝ Depression f, Flaute f. 4. meteor. Tief(druckgebiet) n.

dep·ri·va·tion [,deprɪ'veɪʃn] s 1. Beraubung f, Entzug m. 2. (empfindlicher) Verlust. **de·prive** [dɪ'praɪv] v/t (of s.th.) j-n od. et. (e-r Sache) berauben, j-m (et.) entziehen od. nehmen: be ~d of s.th. et. entbehren (müssen). **de'prived** adj benachteiligt.

depth [depθ] I s Tiefe f (a. fig.): at a ~ of in e-r Tiefe von; five feet in ~ fünf Fuß tief; in ~ bis in alle Einzelheiten, eingehend; in the ~(s) of winter im tiefsten Winter; be out of one's ~ nicht mehr stehen können; fig. ratlos od. unsicher sein, schwimmen; get out of one's ~ den Boden unter den Füßen verlieren (a. fig.); ~ (of field od. focus) phot. Tiefenschärfe f. II adj psych. etc Tiefen...: ~ psychology.

dep·u·tize ['depjʊtaɪz] I v/t (als Vertreter) ernennen. II v/i: ~ for j-n vertreten.

'dep·u·ty I s 1. (Stell)Vertreter(in). 2. parl. Abgeordnete m, f. 3. a. ~ sheriff Am. Hilfssheriff m. II adj 4. stellvertretend, Vize...

de·rail [dɪ'reɪl] I v/t entgleisen lassen: be ~ed → II. II v/i entgleisen.

de·range [dɪ'reɪndʒ] v/t in Unordnung bringen, durcheinanderbringen. **de'ranged** adj 1. in Unordnung, durcheinander. 2. a. mentally ~ geistesgestört. **de'range·ment** s 1. Unordnung f. 2. a. mental ~ Geistesgestörtheit f.

der·by ['daːbɪ] s 1. Sport: Derby n: → local 1. 2. a. ~ hat Am. Bowler m, Melone f.

der·e·lict ['derəlɪkt] adj heruntergekommen, baufällig.

de·ride [dɪ'raɪd] v/t verhöhnen, -spotten. **de·ri·sion** [dɪ'rɪʒn] s Hohn m, Spott m. **de·ri·sive** [dɪ'raɪsɪv] adj □, **de'ri·so·ry** [-sərɪ] adj 1. höhnisch, spöttisch: ~ laughter Hohngelächter n. 2. fig. lächerlich.

der·i·va·tion [,derɪ'veɪʃn] s 1. Ab-, Herleitung f. 2. Herkunft f, Abstammung f. **de·riv·a·tive** [dɪ'rɪvətɪv] I adj □ abgeleitet. II s et. Abs od. Hergeleitetes, a. ling. Ableitung f. **de·rive** [dɪ'raɪv] I v/t 1. herleiten (from von): be ~d (from), ~ itself (from) → 4. 2. Nutzen ziehen, Gewinn schöpfen (from aus): ~ pleasure from Freude finden od. haben an (dat). 3. ling., ♟, etc ableiten. II v/i 4. (from) abstammen (von); sich ab- od. herleiten (von).

der·ma·tol·o·gist [,dɜːmə'tɒlədʒɪst] s Dermatologe m, Hautarzt m. ,**der·ma'tol·o·gy** s Dermatologie f.

de·rog·a·to·ry [dɪ'rɒgətərɪ] adj □ 1. (from, to) nachteilig (für), abträglich (dat). 2. abfällig, geringschätzig.

der·rick ['derɪk] s 1. Derrick-, Mastenkran m. 2. Bohrturm m.

de·scale [,diː'skeɪl] v/t Boiler etc entkalken.

de·scend [dɪ'send] I v/i 1. herunter-, hinuntersteigen, -gehen, -kommen, -fahren, -fallen. 2. ✈ niedergehen; (mit dem Fallschirm) abspringen. 3. abfallen (Straße etc). 4. abstammen, herkommen (from von j-m, aus e-r Familie). 5. (to) übergehen, sich vererben (auf acc), zufallen (dat). 6. (on) herfallen (über *acc*), sich stürzen (auf *acc*), *a. fig.* überfallen (*acc*) (*Besuch etc*). **7.** *ast.* sinken. **II** *v/t* **8.** *Treppe etc* herunter-, hinuntersteigen, -gehen. **9.** *be* ~ed (*from*) → 4. **de·scend·ant** *s* Nachkomme *m*, Abkömmling *m*.

de·scent [dɪ'sent] *s* **1.** Herunter-, Hinuntersteigen *n*, -gehen *n*, -fahren *n*. **2.** ✈ Niedergehen *n*; (Fallschirm)Absprung *m*. **3.** Abfallen *n*, Gefälle *n*. **4.** Abstammung *f*, Herkunft *f*: *of French* ~ französischer Herkunft. **5.** Vererbung *f* (*to* auf *acc*). **6.** Überfall *m* (*on* auf *acc*) (*a. fig.*).

de·scribe [dɪ'skraɪb] *v/t* **1.** beschreiben, schildern (*s.th. to s.o.* j-m et.). **2.** bezeichnen (*as* als).

de·scrip·tion [dɪ'skrɪpʃn] *s* **1.** Beschreibung *f* (*a.* ⊚), Schilderung *f*: *beyond* ~ unbeschreiblich; → *beggar* 4. **2.** Art *f*, Sorte *f*. **de·scrip·tive** *adj* □ **1.** beschreibend. **2.** anschaulich.

des·e·crate ['desɪkreɪt] *v/t* entweihen.

de·seg·re·gate [ˌdiː'segrɪgeɪt] *v/t* die Rassentrennung aufheben in (*dat*). **ˌde·seg·re·ga·tion** *s* Aufhebung *f* der Rassentrennung (*in* in *dat*).

de·sen·si·tize [ˌdiː'sensɪtaɪz] *v/t* ✶ unempfindlich *od.* immun machen (*to* gegen).

de·sert¹ [dɪ'zɜːt] *v/t* verlassen, im Stich lassen; ⚖️ *Ehegatten* (böswillig) verlassen. **II** *v/i* ✕ desertieren.

de·sert² [~] *s mst pl* verdienter Lohn (*a. iro. Strafe*).

des·ert³ ['dezət] **I** *s* Wüste *f*. **II** *adj* Wüsten-.

de·sert·ed [dɪ'zɜːtɪd] *adj* **1.** verlassen, unbewohnt (*Insel etc*), (wie) ausgestorben, menschenleer (*Straßen etc*). **2.** verlassen, einsam (*Person*). **de·sert·er** *s* ✕ Deserteur *m*. **de·ser·tion** *s* **1.** (*a.* ⚖️ böswilliges) Verlassen. **2.** ✕ Desertion *f*, Fahnenflucht *f*.

de·serve [dɪ'zɜːv] *v/t* verdienen, verdient haben. **de·serv·ed·ly** [~ɪdlɪ] *adv* verdientermaßen. **de·serv·ing** *adj* verdienstvoll.

des·ic·cat·ed ['desɪkeɪtɪd] *adj*: ~ *fruit* Dörrobst *n*; ~ *milk* Trockenmilch *f*.

de·sign [dɪ'zaɪn] **I** *v/t* **1.** entwerfen, ⊚ konstruieren. **2.** gestalten, anlegen. **3.** ausdenken, ersinnen. **4.** bestimmen, vorsehen (*for* für; *as* als): ~ed to do

s.th. dafür bestimmt, et. zu tun. **II** *v/i* **5.** Entwürfe machen (*for* für). **III** *s* **6.** Design *n*, Entwurf *m*, (⊚ Konstruktions)Zeichnung *f*. **7.** Design *n*, Muster *n*. **8.** Gestaltung *f*. **9.** (*a.* böse) Absicht: *by* ~ mit Absicht; *have* ~s *on* (*od. against*) et. im Schilde führen gegen, *a. humor.* e-n Anschlag vorhaben auf (*acc*).

des·ig·nate ['dezɪgneɪt] **I** *v/t* **1.** et. bestimmen, festlegen. **2.** j-n designieren, bestimmen (*to, for* für ein Amt etc, zu e-m Amtsträger etc). **3.** et. bestimmen, vorsehen (*for* für). **II** *adj* **4.** nachgestellt: designiert.

de·sign·ed·ly [dɪ'zaɪnɪdlɪ] *adv* absichtlich. **de·sign·er** *s* Designer(in); ⊚ Konstrukteur *m*; (*Mode*)Schöpfer(in).

de·sir·a·ble [dɪ'zaɪərəbl] *adj* □ **1.** wünschenswert, erwünscht. **2.** begehrenswert. **de·sire** [dɪ'zaɪə] **I** *v/t* **1.** wünschen: *if* ~d auf Wunsch; *leave much* (*nothing*) *to be* ~d viel (nichts) zu wünschen übriglassen. **2.** begehren. **II** *s* **3.** Wunsch *m*: *at his* ~ auf s-n Wunsch. **4.** Verlangen *n*, Begierde *f* (*for* nach): ~ *for knowledge* Wissensdurst *m*. **de·sir·ous** [dɪ'zaɪərəs] *adj*: *be* ~ *to know s.th.* et. (sehr) gern wissen wollen.

de·sist [dɪ'zɪst] *v/i* Abstand nehmen (*from* von).

desk [desk] **I** *s* **1.** Schreibtisch *m*. **2.** (*Schreib-, Noten- etc*)Pult *n*. **3.** Kasse *f* (*im Restaurant etc*). **4.** Empfang *m*, Rezeption *f* (*im Hotel*): ~ *clerk Am.* Empfangschef *m*, -dame *f*. **II** *adj* **5.** Schreibtisch...; Büro... '~·top *adj*: ~ *computer* Tischcomputer *m*.

des·o·late ['desələt] *adj* □ **1.** einsam, verlassen. **2.** trostlos. **des·o·la·tion** [~'leɪʃn] *s* **1.** Einsamkeit *f*, Verlassenheit *f*. **2.** Trostlosigkeit *f*.

de·spair [dɪ'speə] **I** *v/i* verzweifeln (*of* an *dat*). **II** *s* Verzweiflung *f* (*at* über *acc*): *a look of* ~ ein verzweifelter Blick; *drive s.o. to* ~, *be the* ~ *of s.o.* j-n zur Verzweiflung bringen. **de·spair·ing** *adj* □ verzweifelt.

des·patch → *dispatch*.

des·per·ate ['despərət] *adj* □ **1.** verzweifelt (*Mensch, Anstrengung, Lage etc*): ~ *deed* Verzweiflungstat *f*; *be* ~ *for s.th.* et. dringend nötig haben; *be* ~ *to do s.th.* et. unbedingt tun wollen; →

strait. **2.** F hoffnungslos, schrecklich.
des·per·a·tion [͵~'reɪʃn] s Verzweiflung f: **in ~** verzweifelt; **drive s.o. to ~** j-n zur Verzweiflung bringen.
des·pi·ca·ble [dɪ'spɪkəbl] adj □ verachtenswert, verabscheuungswürdig.
de·spise [dɪ'spaɪz] v/t verachten, *Speise etc a.* verschmähen: **not to be ~d** nicht zu verachten.
de·spite [dɪ'spaɪt] prp trotz (*gen od. dat*).
de·spond·ent [dɪ'spɒndənt] adj □ mutlos, verzagt.
des·pot ['despɒt] s Despot m. **des·pot·ic** adj (**~ally**) despotisch. **des·pot·ism** ['~pətɪzəm] s Despotismus m.
des·sert [dɪ'zɜːt] **I** s Dessert n, Nachtisch m. **II** adj Dessert...: **~ wine.** **des·'sert·spoon** s Dessertlöffel m.
des·ti·na·tion [͵destɪ'neɪʃn] s **1.** Bestimmungsort m; Reiseziel n: **country of ~** Bestimmungsland n. **2.** Bestimmung f, (End)Zweck m, Ziel n. **des·tine** ['~tɪn] v/t bestimmen, vorsehen (**for** für): **~d for** unterwegs nach (*Schiff etc*); **be ~d to** (*inf*) dazu bestimmt od. dafür vorgesehen sein zu (*inf*); **he was ~d to** (*inf*) er sollte (*früh sterben etc*). **'des·ti·ny** s Schicksal n: **he met his ~** sein Schicksal ereilte ihn.
des·ti·tute ['destɪtjuːt] adj **1.** mittellos, (völlig) verarmt. **2.** (**of**) bar (*gen*), ohne (*acc*). ͵**des·ti·tu·tion** s **1.** Mittellosigkeit f, (völlige) Armut. **2.** (völliger) Mangel (**of** an *dat*).
de·stroy [dɪ'strɔɪ] v/t **1.** zerstören, *a. Insekten etc* vernichten. **2.** Tier töten, einschläfern. **3.** j-n, j-s Ruf, *Gesundheit etc* ruinieren, *Hoffnungen etc* zunichte machen, zerstören. **de'stroy·er** s **1.** Zerstörer(in), Vernichter(in). **2.** ⚓, ✕ Zerstörer m.
de·struc·tion [dɪ'strʌkʃn] s **1.** Zerstörung f, Vernichtung f. **2.** Tötung f, Einschläferung f. **de'struc·tive** adj □ **1.** zerstörend, vernichtend. **2.** schädlich, verderblich: **~ to health** gesundheitsschädlich. **3.** destruktiv (*Kritik*). **de·'struc·tive·ness** s zerstörende od. vernichtende Wirkung.
des·ul·to·ry ['desəltərɪ] adj □ **1.** unzusammenhängend. **2.** oberflächlich.
de·tach [dɪ'tætʃ] v/t (ab-, los)trennen, (los)lösen, *a.* ⚙ abnehmen (**from** von). **de'tached** adj □ **1.** (ab)getrennt: be-

come ~ sich (los)lösen. **2.** einzeln, frei-, alleinstehend: **~ house** Einzelhaus n. **3.** separat, gesondert. **4.** *fig.* unvoreingenommen; uninteressiert (**about** an *dat*); distanziert. **de'tach·ment** s **1.** (Ab-) Trennung f, (Los)Lösung f. **2.** *fig.* Unvoreingenommenheit f; Distanz f.
de·tail ['diːteɪl] **I** s **1.** Detail n, Einzelheit f: **~s** pl Näheres n; (**down**) **to the smallest ~** bis ins kleinste Detail; **in ~** ausführlich, in allen Einzelheiten; **go into ~** ins einzelne gehen, auf Einzelheiten eingehen. **II** v/t **2.** ausführlich berichten; einzeln aufzählen od. -führen. **3.** ✕ abkommandieren (**for** zu). **'de·tailed** adj detailliert, ausführlich, eingehend.
de·tain [dɪ'teɪn] v/t **1.** j-n aufhalten. **2.** *a.* **~ in custody** ⚖ in (Untersuchungs-) Haft behalten. **3.** *ped.* nachsitzen lassen.
de·tect [dɪ'tekt] v/t **1.** entdecken, (heraus)finden, ermitteln. **2.** wahrnehmen. **3.** *Verbrechen etc* aufdecken. **de'tec·tion** s **1.** Entdeckung f, Ermittlung f. **2.** Wahrnehmung f. **3.** Aufdeckung f. **de'tec·tive I** adj Detektiv...: **~ story** (*od. novel*) Kriminalroman m. **II** s Detektiv m, Kriminalbeamte m. **de'tec·tor** s ⚡ Detektor m.
dé·tente [deɪ'tɑ̃ːnt] s pol. Entspannung f.
de·ten·tion [dɪ'tenʃn] s **1.** ⚖ Haft f: **~** (**pending trial**) Untersuchungshaft. **2.** *ped.* Nachsitzen n: **keep in ~** → **detain** 3.
de·ter [dɪ'tɜː] v/t abschrecken (**from** von).
de·ter·gent [dɪ'tɜːdʒənt] s Reinigungs-, Wasch-, Geschirrspülmittel n.
de·te·ri·o·rate [dɪ'tɪərɪəreɪt] **I** v/i sich verschlechtern, schlechter werden, (*Material*) verderben. **II** v/t verschlechtern. **de͵te·ri·o·ra·tion** s Verschlechterung f.
de·ter·mi·na·ble [dɪ'tɜːmɪnəbl] adj □ bestimmbar. **de'ter·mi·nant I** adj **1.** bestimmend, entscheidend. **II** s **2.** entscheidender Faktor (**in** bei). **3.** *biol.,* ✗ Determinante f. **de'ter·mi·nate** [~nət] adj □ bestimmt, festgelegt. **de͵ter·mi·'na·tion** [~'neɪʃn] s **1.** Entschluß m. **2.** Bestimmung f, Festsetzung f. **3.** Feststellung f, Ermittlung f. **4.** Bestimmtheit f, Entschlossenheit f. **de·'ter·mine I** v/t **1.** *Streitfrage etc* ent-

scheiden. **2.** *et.* beschließen (*a.* **to do** zu tun), *Zeitpunkt etc* bestimmen, festsetzen. **3.** feststellen, ermitteln, bestimmen. **4.** *j-n* bestimmen, veranlassen (**to do** zu tun). **II** *v/i* **5.** (**on**) sich entscheiden (für), sich entschließen (zu). **de'ter·mined** *adj* □ entschlossen.

de·ter·rence [dɪ'terəns] *s* Abschreckung *f.* **de'ter·rent** **I** *adj* abschreckend, Abschreckungs... **II** *s* Abschreckungsmittel *n* (**to** für).

de·test [dɪ'test] *v/t* verabscheuen, hassen: ~ *having to do s.th.* es hassen, et. tun zu müssen. **de'test·a·ble** *adj* □ abscheulich. ‚**de·tes'ta·tion** [‚diː~] *s* (*of*) Verabscheuung *f* (*gen*), Abscheu *m* (vor *dat*, gegen).

de·throne [dɪ'θrəʊn] *v/t* entthronen (*a. fig.*).

det·o·nate ['detəneɪt] **I** *v/t* zünden. **II** *v/i* detonieren, explodieren. ‚**det·o'na·tion** *s* Detonation *f*, Explosion *f*; Zündung *f.* ‚**det·o·na·tor** *s* Zünd-, Sprengkapsel *f.*

de·tour ['diː‚tʊə] **I** *s* **1.** Umweg *m*: *make a ~* → **3. 2.** Umleitung *f.* **II** *v/i* **3.** e-n Umweg machen. **III** *v/t* **4.** e-n Umweg machen um. **5.** *Verkehr etc* umleiten.

de·tract [dɪ'trækt] **I** *v/t Aufmerksamkeit etc* ablenken (**from** von). **II** *v/i* (**from**) Abbruch tun (*dat*), herabsetzen, schmälern (*acc*).

det·ri·ment ['detrɪmənt] *s* Nachteil *m*, Schaden *m* (**to** für): *to the ~ of* zum Nachteil *od.* Schaden (*gen*). ‚**det·ri·men·tal** [‚~'mentl] *adj* □ nachteilig, schädlich (**to** für).

de·tri·tus [dɪ'traɪtəs] *s geol.* Geröll *n*, Schutt *m.*

deuce [djuːs] *s* **1.** *Kartenspiel, Würfeln:* Zwei *f.* **2.** *Tennis:* Einstand *m.* **3.** F Teufel *m*: *who* (*what*) *the ~?* wer (was) zum Teufel?

de·val·u·ate [‚diː'væljʊeɪt] *v/t* ✝ abwerten (**against** gegenüber). ‚**de·val·u·a·tion** *s* Abwertung *f.* ‚**de'val·ue** [~juː] → **devaluate.**

dev·as·tate ['devəsteɪt] *v/t* verwüsten, -nichten. '**dev·as·tat·ing** *adj* □ **1.** verheerend, vernichtend (*a. Kritik etc*). **2.** F toll, phantastisch. **3.** F umwerfend (*Humor etc*). ‚**dev·as'ta·tion** *s* Verwüstung *f.*

de·vel·op [dɪ'veləp] **I** *v/t* **1.** *phot. u. fig.*

allg. entwickeln. **2.** *Krankheit, Fieber* bekommen. **3.** *Naturschätze, Bauland* erschließen, *Altstadt etc* sanieren. **II** *v/i* **4.** sich entwickeln (**from** aus; **into** zu). **de'vel·op·er** *s* **1.** *phot.* Entwickler *m* (*a. Flüssigkeit*). **2.** *late* ~ *bsd. ped.* Spätentwickler *m.* **3.** (*Stadt*)Planer *m.* **de'vel·op·ing** *adj* Entwicklungs...: ~ *country.* **de'vel·op·ment** *s* **1.** Entwicklung *f*: ~ *aid* ✝ Entwicklungshilfe *f*; ~ *country* ✝ Entwicklungsland *n.* **2.** Erschließung *f*, Sanierung *f.*

de·vi·ate ['diːvɪeɪt] *v/i* abweichen (**from** von). ‚**de·vi'a·tion** *s* Abweichung *f.* ‚**de·vi'a·tion·ist** [~ʃənɪst] *s pol.* Abweichler(in).

de·vice [dɪ'vaɪs] *s* **1.** Vorrichtung *f*, Gerät *n.* **2.** Einfall *m*; Kunstgriff *m*, Trick *m*: *leave s.o. to his own ~s* j-n sich selbst überlassen.

dev·il ['devl] **I** *s* **1.** Teufel *m*: *poor* ~ armer Teufel *od.* Schlucker; *be between the ~ and the deep blue sea* sich zwischen zwei Feuern befinden, in e-r bösen Zwickmühle sein *od.* sitzen; *like the ~* F wie der Teufel, wie verrückt; *go to the ~* F vor die Hunde gehen; *go to the ~!* scher dich zum Teufel!; *speak* (*od.* *talk*) *of the ~!* wenn man vom Teufel spricht!; *who* (*what*) *the ~?* F wer (was) zum Teufel? **2.** *a.* ~ *of a fellow* F Teufelskerl *m.* **II** *v/t pret u. pp* **-iled,** *bsd. Br.* **-illed 3.** F schikanieren, piesacken. '**dev·il·ish** *adj* □ **1.** teuflisch. **2.** (*a. adv*) F verteufelt, höllisch.

‚**dev·il-may-'care** *adj* leichtsinnig.

‚**dev·il·ry** ['devlrɪ] *s* **1.** Teufelei *f.* **2.** Übermut *m.*

de·vi·ous ['diːvjəs] *adj* □ **1.** abwegig, falsch. **2.** gewunden (*a. fig.*): ~ *route* Umweg *m.* **3.** verschlagen, unaufrichtig: *by ~ means* auf krummen Wegen.

de·vise [dɪ'vaɪz] *v/t* (sich) ausdenken, ersinnen.

de·void [dɪ'vɔɪd] *adj*: ~ *of* ohne (*acc*), bar (*gen*), ...los.

de·vo·lu·tion [‚diːvə'luː[n] *s* **1.** Übertragung *f.* **2.** *pol.* Dezentralisierung *f.* **de·volve** [dɪ'vɒlv] **I** *v/t Rechte etc* übertragen (**on** *dat od.* auf *acc*). **II** *v/i* (**on**, **to**) übergehen (auf *acc*), zufallen (*dat*).

de·vote [dɪ'vəʊt] *v/t Zeit etc* widmen (**to** *dat*): ~ *o.s. to* sich *j-m* widmen, sich e-r

Sache widmen *od.* verschreiben. **de·'vot·ed** *adj* □ hingebungsvoll: a) aufopfernd, b) anhänglich, c) eifrig, begeistert. **dev·o·tee** [ˌdevəʊˈtiː] *s* begeisterter Anhänger; glühender Verehrer *od.* Verfechter. **de·vo·tion** [dɪˈvəʊʃn] *s* **1.** Hingabe *f:* a) Aufopferung *f,* b) Anhänglichkeit *f.* **2.** Frömmigkeit *f: ~s pl* Gebet *n,* Andacht *f.*

de·vour [dɪˈvaʊə] *v/t* **1.** Essen, *fig.* Buch *etc* verschlingen. **2.** *fig. j-n* verzehren (*Leidenschaft etc*).

de·vout [dɪˈvaʊt] *adj* □ **1.** fromm. **2.** innig. **3.** herzlich.

dew [djuː] *s* Tau *m. '~·drop s* **1.** Tautropfen *m.* **2.** *Br. humor.* Nasentropfen *m.*

dew·y [ˈdjuːɪ] *adj* □ taufeucht, *a. fig.* taufrisch. **'~-eyed** *adj* blauäugig, naiv.

dex·ter·i·ty [dekˈsterətɪ] *s* Gewandtheit *f,* Geschicklichkeit *f.* **dex·ter·ous** [ˈ~stərəs] *adj* □ gewandt, geschickt.

dex·trose [ˈdekstrəʊs] *s* Traubenzucker *m.*

dex·trous [ˈdekstrəs] → **dexterous.**

di·a·be·tes [ˌdaɪəˈbiːtiːz] *s ☛* Diabetes *m,* Zuckerkrankheit *f: suffer from ~* Zucker haben. **di·a·bet·ic** [ˌ~ˈbetɪk] **I** *adj* diabetisch: a) zuckerkrank, b) Diabetes...: *~ chocolate* Diabetikerschokolade *f.* **II** *s* Diabetiker(in).

di·a·bol·ic, di·a·bol·i·cal [ˌdaɪəˈbɒlɪk(l)] *adj* □ **1.** diabolisch, teuflisch. **2.** F scheußlich, widerlich.

di·a·dem [ˈdaɪədem] *s* Diadem *n.*

di·ag·nose [ˈdaɪəgnəʊz] *v/t ☛* diagnostizieren (*as* als) (*a. fig.*). **di·ag·no·sis** [ˌ~sɪs] *pl* **-ses** [ˌ~siːz] *s* Diagnose *f* (*a. fig.*): *give* (*od.* **make**) *a ~* e-e Diagnose stellen.

di·ag·o·nal [daɪˈægənl] **I** *adj* □ diagonal. **II** *s ✗* Diagonale *f.*

di·a·gram [ˈdaɪəgræm] *s* Diagramm *n,* graphische Darstellung.

di·al [ˈdaɪəl] **I** *s* **1.** *a. ~ plate* Zifferblatt *n* (*Uhr*). **2.** *a. ~ plate ⊙* Skala *f,* Skalenscheibe *f.* **3.** *teleph.* Wählscheibe *f.* **4.** *Br. sl.* Visage *f* (*Gesicht*). **II** *v/t pret u. pp* **-aled,** *bsd. Br.* **-alled 5.** *teleph. Nummer* wählen, *Stadt* anwählen. **III** *v/i* **6.** *teleph.* wählen: *~ direct* durchwählen (*to* nach).

di·a·lect [ˈdaɪəlekt] *s* Dialekt *m,* Mundart *f.* **,di·a·lec·tal** □ Dialekt..., mundartlich.

di·al·ling| **code** [ˈdaɪəlɪŋ] *s teleph. Br.* Vorwahl(nummer) *f. ~ tone s teleph. Br.* Wählton *m,* -zeichen *n.*

di·a·logue, *Am. a.* **di·a·log** [ˈdaɪəlɒg] *s* Dialog *m.*

di·al tone *Am.* → **dialling tone.**

di·am·e·ter [daɪˈæmɪtə] *s* Durchmesser *m: be ... in ~* e-n Durchmesser von ... haben.

di·a·met·ri·cal [ˌdaɪəˈmetrɪkl] *adj* □ **1.** diametrisch. **2.** *fig.* diametral, genau entgegengesetzt.

di·a·mond [ˈdaɪəmənd] *s* **1.** *min.* Diamant *m:* → *rough* 4. **2.** *✗* Raute *f,* Rhombus *m.* **3.** *Kartenspiel:* a) *pl* Karo *n* (*Farbe*), b) Karo(karte *f*) *n. ~·cut·ter s* Diamantschleifer *m. ~ wed·ding s* diamantene Hochzeit.

di·a·per [ˈdaɪəpə] *s Am.* Windel *f.*

di·a·phragm [ˈdaɪəfræm] *s* **1.** *anat.* Zwerchfell *n.* **2.** *teleph. etc* Membran(e) *f.* **3.** *opt. phot.* Blende *f.*

di·ar·rh(o)e·a [ˌdaɪəˈrɪə] *s ☛* Durchfall *m.*

di·a·ry [ˈdaɪərɪ] *s* **1.** Tagebuch *n.* **2.** Notizbuch *n,* Taschenkalender *m.* **3.** Terminkalender *m.*

dice [daɪs] **I** *s* **1.** *pl von* **die².** **2.** *pl* **dice** → **die².** **II** *v/t* **3.** *gastr.* in Würfel schneiden. **4.** *mit j-m* würfeln. **III** *v/i* **5.** würfeln, knobeln (*for* um): *~ with death* mit s-m Leben spielen. *~ cup s* Würfel-, Knobelbecher *m.*

dic·ey [ˈdaɪsɪ] *adj* F prekär, heikel (*Situation etc*).

dick [dɪk] *s* **1.** *bsd. Br. sl.* Kerl *m:* → *clever* 1. **2.** *bsd. Am. sl.* Schnüffler *m* (*Detektiv*).

dick·ens [ˈdɪkɪnz] *s* F Teufel *m: who* (*what*) *the ~?* wer (was) zum Teufel?

dick·er [ˈdɪkə] *v/i* feilschen, schachern (*with* mit; *for* um).

dick·(e)y [ˈdɪkɪ] *adj* F schwach (*Herz*), wack(e)lig (*Leiter etc*).

dic·tate [dɪkˈteɪt] **I** *v/t* (*to dat*) **1.** *Brief etc* diktieren. **2.** diktieren: a) vorschreiben, b) aufzwingen. **II** *v/i* **3.** *~ to s.o.* j-m Vorschriften machen. **III** *s* [ˈdɪkteɪt] **4.** Gebot *n,* Diktat *n.* **dic'ta·tion** *s* Diktat *n.* **dic'ta·tor** *s* Diktator *m.* **dic·ta·to·ri·al** [ˌdɪktəˈtɔːrɪəl] *adj* □ diktatorisch. **dic'ta·tor·ship** *s* Diktatur *f.*

dic·tion [ˈdɪkʃn] *s* Diktion *f,* Ausdrucksweise *f,* Sprache *f.*

dictionary

dic·tion·ar·y ['dɪkʃənrɪ] *s* Wörterbuch *n*.

did [dɪd] *pret von* **do**.

di·dac·tic [dɪ'dæktɪk] *adj* (**~ally**) didaktisch.

did·dle ['dɪdl] *v/t* F betrügen (**out of** um), übers Ohr hauen.

didn't ['dɪdnt] F = **did not**.

die¹ [daɪ] **I** *v/i* (*pres p* **dying**) **1.** sterben (**of** an *dat*): **~ of hunger** (**thirst**) verhungern (verdursten); **never say ~!** nur nicht nach- *od*. aufgeben! **2.** eingehen (*Pflanze, Tier*), verenden (*Tier*). **3. be dying** (**for; to do**) sich sehnen (nach; danach, zu tun), brennen (auf *acc*; darauf, zu tun). **II** *v/t* **4.** *e-s* Todes sterben: → **natural** 1, **violent** 2.

Verbindungen mit Adverbien:

die| a·way *v/i* sich legen (*Wind*), verhallen, -klingen (*Ton*). **~ down** *v/i* **1.** → **die away. 2.** sich legen (*Aufregung etc*). **~ out** *v/i* aussterben (*a. fig.*).

die² [~] *pl* **dice** [daɪs] *s* Würfel *m* (*a. gastr. etc*): **the ~ is cast** *fig.* die Würfel sind gefallen.

die·sel ['diːzl] **I** *s* Diesel *m* (*Motor, Fahrzeug, Kraftstoff*). **II** *adj* Diesel...

di·et ['daɪət] **I** *s* **1.** Nahrung *f*, Ernährung *f*, Kost *f*. **2.** ✒ Diät *f*: **be** (**put**) **on a ~** auf Diät gesetzt sein, diät leben (müssen). **II** *v/i* **3.** *j-n auf* Diät setzen: **~ o.s.** → 4. **III** *v/i* **4.** Diät halten.

dif·fer ['dɪfə] *v/i* **1.** sich unterscheiden, verschieden sein (**from** von). **2.** auseinandergehen (*Meinungen*). **3.** (**from, with**) nicht übereinstimmen (mit), anderer Meinung sein (als): → **agree** 1 **4.** sich nicht einig sein (**on, about, over** über *acc*). **dif·fer·ence** ['dɪfrəns] *s* **1.** Unterschied *m*: a) Unterscheidung *f*: **make no ~ between** keinen Unterschied machen zwischen (*dat*); **make no ~** nichts ausmachen (**to** *dat*), b) Verschiedenheit *f*: **~ of opinion** Meinungsverschiedenheit *f*, c) Differenz *f* (*a.* ♇): **~ in price, price ~** Preisunterschied; → **split** 2. **2.** Differenz *f*, Meinungsverschiedenheit *f*. **3.** Besonderheit *f*: **with a ~** (von) ganz besonderer Art, mit Pfiff. **'dif·fer·ent** *adj* □ **1.** verschieden(artig). **2.** (**from**) verschieden (von), anders (als): **he is ~** er ist anders. **dif·fer·en·tial** [ˌdɪfə'renʃl] **I** *adj* □ **1.** unterschiedlich. **2.** ♇, ⊘, *etc* Differential...: **~ calculus** Differentialrechnung *f*; **~**

gear → 4. **II** *s* 3. ♇ Differential *n*. **4.** ⊘ Differential-, Ausgleichsgetriebe *n*.

dif·fer·en·ti·ate [~ʃɪeɪt] **I** *v/t* **1.** unterscheiden (**from** von); voneinander unterscheiden. **II** *v/i* **2.** sich unterscheiden (**from** von). **3.** differenzieren, unterscheiden (**between** zwischen *dat*). **dif·fer·en·ti·a·tion** *s* Differenzierung *f*, Unterscheidung *f*.

dif·fi·cult ['dɪfɪkəlt] *adj* schwierig (*a. Person*), schwer: **it was quite ~ for me to** *inf* es fiel mir schwer, zu *inf.* **'dif·fi·cul·ty** *s* **1.** Schwierigkeit *f*: a) Mühe *f*: **with ~** mühsam, (nur) schwer; **have ~** (**in**) **doing s.th.** Mühe haben, et. zu tun, b) schwierige Sache, c) Hindernis *n*, Widerstand *m*: **make** (*od.* **raise**) **difficulties** Schwierigkeiten machen. **2.** *oft pl* (*a.* Geld)Schwierigkeiten *pl*, Verlegenheit *f*.

dif·fi·dence ['dɪfɪdəns] *s* Schüchternheit *f*, Mangel *m* an Selbstvertrauen. **'dif·fi·dent** *adj* □ schüchtern, ohne Selbstvertrauen: **be ~ about doing s.th.** et. nur zögernd *od.* zaghaft tun.

dif·fuse **I** *v/t u. v/i* [dɪ'fjuːz] **1.** *bsd. fig.* (sich) verbreiten: **a widely ~d opinion** e-e weitverbreitete Meinung. **2.** ﹖, *phys.* (sich) zerstreuen. **II** *adj* [~s] **3.** diffus: a) weitschweifig, langatmig (*Stil, Autor*), b) unklar, ungeordnet (*Gedanken etc*), c) ﹖, *phys.* zerstreut: **~ light** diffuses Licht, Streulicht *n*. **dif·'fu·sion** [~ʒn] *s* **1.** *bsd. fig.* Verbreitung *f*. **2.** ﹖, *phys.* (Zer)Streuung *f*.

dig [dɪg] **I** *s* **1.** Puff *m*, Stoß *m*: **~ in the ribs** Rippenstoß *m*. **2.** *fig.* (Seiten)Hieb *m* (**at** auf *acc*). **3.** *pl Br.* F Bude *f*. **II** *v/t* (*irr*) **4.** *Loch etc* graben: a) (**up**) umgraben; **~** (**up** *od.* **out**) ausgraben (*a. fig.*); → **grave². 5.** *j-m* e-n Stoß geben: **~ s.o. in the ribs** j-m e-n Rippenstoß geben. **6.** F kapieren. **7.** F stehen *od.* abfahren auf (*acc*). **III** *v/i* **8.** (**for**) graben (nach); *fig.* forschen (nach). **9.** **~ in(to)** F reinhauen (in *e-n Kuchen etc*). **10.** *Br.* F s-e Bude haben, wohnen.

di·gest [dɪ'dʒest] **I** *v/t* verdauen (*a. fig.*). **II** *v/i* sich verdauen lassen: **~ well** leicht verdaulich sein. **III** *s* ['daɪdʒest] (**of**) Auslese *f* (*a. Zeitschrift*), Auswahl *f* (aus); Abriß *m* (*gen*). **di·gest·i·ble** [dɪ'dʒestəbl] *adj* □ verdaulich. **di·'ges·tion** *s* Verdauung *f* (*a. fig.*). **di·'ges·tive**

I *adj* □ **1.** verdauungsfördernd. **2.** Verdauungs...: ~ *system* Verdauungsapparat *m*; ~ *tract* Verdauungstrakt *m*. **II** *s* **3.** ✻ verdauungsförderndes Mittel.

dig·ger ['dɪɡə] *s* **1.** (*bsd.* Gold)Gräber *m*; Erdarbeiter *m*. **2.** Grabgerät *n*, -maschine *f*.

dig·it ['dɪdʒɪt] *s* **1.** *anat. zo.* Finger *m*, Zehe *f*. **2.** ⅍ Ziffer *f*; Stelle *f*. **dig·i·tal** ['~tl] *adj* **1.** Finger...: ~ *telephone* Tastentelefon *n*. **2.** Digital...: ~ *clock* (*watch*); ~ *computer* Digitalrechner *m*.

dig·ni·fied ['dɪɡnɪfaɪd] *adj* würdevoll, würdig. **dig·ni·fy** ['~faɪ] *v/t* Würde verleihen (*dat*).

dig·ni·tar·y ['dɪɡnɪtərɪ] *s* Würdenträger(in). **'dig·ni·ty** *s* **1.** Rang *m*, (hohe) Stellung. **2.** Würde *f*: → *beneath* 3.

di·gress [daɪ'ɡres] *v/i* abschweifen (*from* von; *into* in *acc*). **di·gres·sion** *s* Abschweifung *f*.

dike¹ [daɪk] **I** *s* **1.** Deich *m*, Damm *m*. **2.** Graben *m*. **II** *v/t* **3.** eindämmen, -deichen.

dike² [~] *s sl.* Lesbe *f* (*Lesbierin*).

di·lap·i·dat·ed [dɪ'læpɪdeɪtɪd] *adj* verfallen, baufällig (*Haus etc*), klapp(e)rig (*Auto etc*).

di·late [daɪ'leɪt] **I** *v/t u. v/i* (sich) ausdehnen *od.* (-)weiten *od.* erweitern: *with ~d eyes* mit aufgerissenen Augen; *his eyes ~d with terror* seine Augen weiteten sich vor Entsetzen. **II** *v/i*: ~ *on fig.* sich (ausführlich) verbreiten *od.* auslassen über (*acc*).

dil·a·to·ry ['dɪlətərɪ] *adj* □ **1.** verzögernd, hinhaltend: ~ *tactics pl* Verzögerungs-, Verschleppungs-, Hinhaltetaktik *f*. **2.** langsam: *be ~ in doing s.th.* sich mit et. Zeit lassen.

di·lem·ma [dɪ'lemə] *s* Dilemma *n*, Klemme *f*: *be on the horns of a ~* in e-r Zwickmühle sein *od.* sitzen.

dil·et·tante [ˌdɪlɪ'tæntɪ] *mst contp.* **I** *pl* -**ti** [~tɪː], -**tes** Dilettant(in). **II** *adj* dilettantisch.

dil·i·gence ['dɪlɪdʒəns] *s* **1.** Fleiß *m*. **2.** Sorgfalt *f*. **'dil·i·gent** *adj* □ **1.** fleißig. **2.** sorgfältig, gewissenhaft.

dill [dɪl] *s* ❧ Dill *m*.

dil·ly·dal·ly ['dɪlɪdælɪ] *v/i* F (herum)trödeln.

di·lute [daɪ'ljuːt] **I** *v/t* **1.** verdünnen. **2.** *fig.* verwässern, abschwächen. **II** *adj* **3.**

verdünnt. **4.** *fig.* verwässert, abgeschwächt. **di·lu·tion** *s* **1.** Verdünnung *f*. **2.** *fig.* Verwässerung *f*, Abschwächung *f*.

dim [dɪm] **I** *adj* □ **1.** (halb)dunkel, düster (*a. fig.*): → *view* 4. **2.** undeutlich, verschwommen, schwach. **3.** schwach, trüb (*Licht*): ~*ly lit* schwacherleuchtet. **4.** matt (*Farbe*). **5.** *fig.* schwer von Begriff. **II** *v/t* **6.** verdunkeln, -düstern. **7.** trüben (*a. fig.*). **8.** *a.* ~ *out Licht* abblenden: ~ *the headlights mot. Am.* abblenden. **III** *v/i* **9.** sich verdunkeln *od.* -düstern. **10.** undeutlich werden. **11.** sich trüben (*a. fig.*).

dime [daɪm] *s Am.* Zehncentstück *n*: ~ *novel* Groschenroman *m*.

di·men·sion [dɪ'menʃn] *s* Dimension *f* (*a. Å*): a) Ausdehnung *f*, Maß *n*, Abmessung *f*, b) *pl oft fig.* Ausmaß *n*, Umfang *m*. **di'men·sion·al** [~ʃənl] *adj* □ *in Zssgn*: ...dimensional.

di·min·ish [dɪ'mɪnɪʃ] *v/t u. v/i* (sich) vermindern *od.* verringern: ~ *in numbers* weniger werden; ~ *in value* an Wert verlieren. **dim·i·nu·tion** [ˌdɪmɪ'njuːʃn] *s* Verminderung *f*, Verringerung *f*. **di·'min·u·tive** [~jʊtɪv] **I** *adj* **1.** klein, winzig. **2.** *ling.* Diminutiv..., Verkleinerungs... **II** *s* **3.** *ling.* Diminutiv *n*, Verkleinerungsform *f od.* -silbe *f*.

dim·mer ['dɪmə] *s* **1.** Dimmer *m* (*Helligkeitsregler*). **2.** *pl mot. Am.* Abblend-*od.* Standlicht *n*. **'dim·ness** *s* **1.** Dunkelheit *f*, Düsterkeit *f*. **2.** Undeutlichkeit *f*. **3.** Mattheit *f*.

dim·ple ['dɪmpl] *s* Grübchen *n*.

din [dɪn] **I** *s* Lärm *m*, Getöse *n*: *kick up* (*od. make*) *a ~* Krach machen. **II** *v/t*: ~ *s.th. into s.o.* j-m et. einhämmern. **III** *v/i* lärmen, (*Motoren etc*) dröhnen (*in s.o.'s ears* j-m in den Ohren).

dine [daɪn] **I** *v/i* speisen, essen (*off, on acc*): ~ *in* (*out*) zu Hause (auswärts) essen. **II** *v/t* bewirten. **'din·er** *s* **1.** Speisende *m*, *f*. **2.** Gast *m* (*im Restaurant*). **3.** 🚂 Speisewagen *m*. **4.** *Am.* Eß-, Speiselokal *n*. **di·nette** [daɪ'net] *s* Eßecke *f*.

din·ghy ['dɪŋɡɪ] *s* **1.** ⚓ Ding(h)i *n*; Beiboot *n*. **2.** Schlauchboot *n*.

din·gy ['dɪndʒɪ] *adj* □ schmutzig, schmudd(e)lig.

din·ing| car ['daɪnɪŋ] *s* 🚂 Speisewagen

m. **~ room** *s* Speise-, Eßzimmer *n.* **~ ta·ble** *s* Eßtisch *m.*

dink·y ['dɪŋkɪ] *adj* F **1.** *Br.* niedlich. **2.** *Am.* klein, unbedeutend.

din·ner ['dɪnə] *s* **1.** (Mittag-, Abend-) Essen *n* (*Hauptmahlzeit*): **after ~** nach dem Essen, nach Tisch; **at ~** bei Tisch. **2.** Diner *n*, Festessen *n*: **at a ~** auf *od.* bei e-m Diner. **~ coat** *s bsd. Am.,* **jack·et** *s* Smoking *m.* **~ par·ty** *s* Diner *n*, Abendgesellschaft *f.* **~ ser·vice,** **~ set** *s* Speiseservice *n*, Tafelgeschirr *n.* **~ ta·ble** *s* Eßtisch *m.* '**~·time** *s* Essens-, Tischzeit *f.*

di·no·saur ['daɪnəʊsɔː] *s zo.* Dinosaurier *m.*

di·o·cese ['daɪəsɪs] *s eccl.* Diözese *f.*

di·ode ['daɪəʊd] *s ⚡ Diode f.*

di·ox·ide [daɪˈɒksaɪd] *s 🔬 Dioxyd n.*

dip [dɪp] **I** *v/t* **1.** (ein)tauchen (**in, into** *in acc*): **~ one's hand into one's pocket** in die Tasche greifen. **2. ~ the headlights** *mot. bsd. Br.* abblenden. **II** *v/i* **3.** unter-, eintauchen. **4. ~ into** a) sich flüchtig befassen mit, e-n Blick werfen in (*ein Buch etc*), b) *Reserven etc* angreifen: **~ into one's pocket** (*od. purse*) fig. tief in die Tasche greifen. **III** *s* **5.** (Unter-, Ein)Tauchen *n.* **6.** kurzes Bad: **have a ~** mal schnell ins Wasser springen.

diph·the·ri·a [dɪfˈθɪərɪə] *s ✚ Diphtherie f.*

diph·thong ['dɪfθɒŋ] Diphthong *m*, Doppelvokal *m.*

di·plo·ma [dɪˈpləʊmə] *s* Diplom *n.*

di·plo·ma·cy [dɪˈpləʊməsɪ] *s pol.* Diplomatie *f* (*a. fig.*). **dip·lo·mat** ['dɪpləmæt] *s* Diplomat *m.* ,**dip·lo·mat·ic** *adj* (**~ally**) diplomatisch: **~ corps** (*a. body*) diplomatisches Korps; **~ relations** *pl* diplomatische Beziehungen *pl.*

'**dip·stick** *s* (*Öl- etc*)Meßstab *m.*

dire ['daɪə] *adj* **1.** gräßlich, schrecklich. **2.** äußerst, höchst: **be in ~ need of s.th.** et. ganz dringend brauchen; → **strait.**

di·rect [dɪˈrekt] **I** *v/t* **1.** *Aufmerksamkeit etc* richten, lenken (**to, toward[s]** *auf acc*): **~ away** *j-n, et.* ablenken (**from** von). **2.** *Betrieb etc* führen, leiten; Regie führen bei (*e-m Film od. Stück*): **~ed by** unter der Regie von. **3.** *Worte* richten, *Brief etc* adressieren, richten (**to** an *acc*). **4.** anweisen, beauftragen, *j-m* Anweisungen geben (**to do** zu tun).

5. anordnen, verfügen: **~ s.th. to be done** anordnen, daß et. geschieht. **6.** (**to**) *j-m* den Weg zeigen (zu, nach); *fig.* *j-n* verweisen (an *acc*). **II** *adj* □ **7.** direkt, gerade. **8.** direkt, unmittelbar: **~ current** *⚡* Gleichstrom *m*; **~ flight** Direktflug *m*; **~ train** durchgehender Zug. **9.** direkt, genau: **the ~ contrary** das genaue Gegenteil. **10.** *ling.* **~ speech** (*bsd. Am.* **discourse**) direkte Rede; **~ object** direktes Objekt, Akkusativobjekt *n.* **III** *adv* **11.** direkt, unmittelbar: → **dial** 6. **di·rec·tion** *s* **1.** Richtung *f*: **in the ~ of** in Richtung auf (*acc*) *od.* nach; **from** (*in*) **all ~s** aus (nach) allen Richtungen *od.* Seiten; **sense of ~** Orts-, Orientierungssinn *m*; **~ indicator** *mot.* (Fahrt)Richtungsanzeiger *m*, Blinker *m.* **2.** Führung *f*, Leitung *f.* (*Film etc*) Regie *f.* **3.** Anweisung *f*, Anleitung *f*: **~s pl for use** Gebrauchsanweisung. **4.** Anweisung *f*, Anordnung *f*: **by** (*od.* **at**) **~ of** auf Anweisung von (*od. gen*). **di·rec·tion·al** [**~**ʃənl] *adj* **1.** Richtungs... **2.** *⚡* Peil...; Richt...: **~ aerial** (*bsd. Am.* **antenna**) Richtantenne *f.* **di·rec·tive** *s* Direktive *f*, Anweisung *f.* **di·rec·tor** *s* **1.** Direktor *m* (*a.* **✝**), Leiter *m*: **~'s secretary** Chefsekretärin *f*; **~-general** Generaldirektor. **2.** *Film etc*: Regisseur *m.* **di·rec·to·rate** [**~**rət] *s* **1.** Direktorat *n*, Direktor-, Direktorenposten *m.* **2.** Direktorium *n.* **di·rec·tor·ship** *s* → **directorate** 1. **di·rec·to·ry** *s* **1.** Adreßbuch *n*; Telefonbuch *n*; Branchenverzeichnis *n.* **di·rec·tress** *s* Direktorin *f*, Leiterin *f.*

dirt [dɜːt] *s* Schmutz *m* (*a. fig.*), Dreck *m*: **fling** (*od.* **throw**) **~ at s.o.** *fig. j-n* mit Schmutz bewerfen; **treat s.o. like ~** *j-n* wie (den letzten) Dreck behandeln. ,**~-'cheap** *adj u. adv* F spottbillig. **~ road** *s Am.* unbefestigte Straße.

dirt·y [dɜːtɪ] **I** *adj* □ **1.** schmutzig (*a. fig.*), dreckig: **~ look** böser Blick; **~ mind** schmutzige Gedanken *pl*; schmutzige Phantasie; **~ word** Reizwort *n*; **~ work** Dreck(s)arbeit *f* (*a. fig.*); → **linen** 2. **2.** gemein, niederträchtig: → **trick** 1. **3.** schlecht, *bsd.* **⚓** stürmisch (*Wetter*). **II** *v/t* **4.** beschmutzen (*a. fig.*): **~ one's hands** sich die Hände schmutzig machen (*a. fig.*). **III** *v/i* **5.** schmutzig werden, schmutzen.

dis·a·bil·i·ty [ˌdɪsəˈbɪlətɪ] s **1.** Unvermögen n, Unfähigkeit f. **2.** Arbeits-, Erwerbsunfähigkeit f, Invalidität f: ~ *benefit* Invaliditätsrente f. **3.** ✝ Gebrechen n.

dis·a·ble [dɪsˈeɪbl] v/t **1.** unfähig machen, außerstand setzen (*from doing* zu tun). **2.** unbrauchbar *od.* untauglich machen (*for* für, zu). **3.** arbeits- *od.* erwerbsunfähig machen. **dis·a·bled** adj **1.** arbeits-, erwerbsunfähig, invalid. **2.** kriegsversehrt. **3.** (*körperlich od. geistig*) behindert. **dis·a·ble·ment** s **1.** → *disability* **2.** (*körperliche od. geistige*) Behinderung.

dis·ad·van·tage [ˌdɪsədˈvɑːntɪdʒ] **I** s Nachteil m (*to* für): *to s.o.'s* ~ zu j-s Nachteil *od.* Schaden; *be at a* ~ im Nachteil *od.* benachteiligt sein; *put at a* ~ → **II**; *sell at a* ~ mit Verlust verkaufen. **II** v/t benachteiligen. **dis·ad·van·ta·geous** [ˌædvɑnˈteɪdʒəs] adj □ nachteilig, ungünstig, unvorteilhaft (*to* für).

dis·af·fect·ed [ˌdɪsəˈfektɪd] adj □ unzufrieden (*to, toward*[s] mit), verdrossen. **dis·af·fec·tion** s Unzufriedenheit f, (*a.* Staats)Verdrossenheit f.

dis·a·gree [ˌdɪsəˈgriː] v/i **1.** (*with*) nicht übereinstimmen (mit), im Widerspruch stehen (zu, mit). **2.** (*with*) anderer Meinung sein (als), nicht zustimmen (*dat*). **3.** (sich) streiten (*on, about* über *acc*). **4.** nicht einverstanden sein (*with* mit). **5.** nicht bekommen (*with dat*) (*Essen*). **dis·a·gree·a·ble** [ˌ~ˈgrɪəbl] adj □ unangenehm. **dis·a·gree·ment** s **1.** Unstimmigkeit f, Verschiedenheit f: *be in* ~ (*with*) → *disagree* 1. **2.** Widerspruch m (*between* zwischen *dat*). **3.** Meinungsverschiedenheit f (*over, on* über *acc*).

dis·al·low [ˌdɪsəˈlaʊ] v/t nicht anerkennen, nicht gelten lassen.

dis·ap·pear [ˌdɪsəˈpɪə] v/i verschwinden (*from* von, aus): → *thin* 1. **dis·ap·'pear·ance** s Verschwinden n.

dis·ap·point [ˌdɪsəˈpɔɪnt] v/t j-n enttäuschen, j-s *Hoffnungen etc a.* zunichte machen: *be ~ed* enttäuscht sein (*at, st.h.* von, über *acc*; *in, with s.o.* von). **dis·ap·'point·ment** s Enttäuschung f.

dis·ap·prov·al [ˌdɪsəˈpruːvl] s (*of*) Mißbilligung f (*gen*), Mißfallen n (über

acc): *in* ~ mißbilligend. **dis·ap·'prove** v/t mißbilligen. **II** v/i dagegen sein: ~ *of* → I.

dis·arm [dɪsˈɑːm] **I** v/t entwaffnen (*a. fig.*). **II** v/i ✕, pol. abrüsten. **dis·ar·ma·ment** s **1.** Entwaffnung f. **2.** ✕, pol. Abrüstung f. **dis·arm·ing** adj □ fig. entwaffnend.

dis·ar·range [ˌdɪsəˈreɪndʒ] v/t in Unordnung bringen, durcheinanderbringen (*beide a. fig.*).

dis·ar·ray [ˌdɪsəˈreɪ] **I** v/t in Unordnung bringen (*a. fig.*). **II** s Unordnung f (*a. fig.*).

dis·as·sem·ble [ˌdɪsəˈsembl] v/t auseinandernehmen, zerlegen, demontieren. **dis·as·'sem·bly** s **1.** Zerlegung f, Demontage f. **2.** zerlegter Zustand.

dis·as·ter [dɪˈzɑːstə] s **1.** Unglück n (*to* für). **2.** Unglück n, Katastrophe f: ~ *area* Katastrophengebiet n. **dis·as·trous** adj □ katastrophal, verheerend.

dis·be·lief [ˌdɪsbɪˈliːf] s **1.** Unglaube m. **2.** Zweifel m (*in* an *dat*). **dis·be·lieve** [ˌ~ˈliːv] **I** v/t *et.* nicht glauben, bezweifeln; *j-m* nicht glauben. **II** v/i nicht glauben (*in* an *dat*). **dis·be·liev·er** s Ungläubige m, f (*a. eccl.*).

dis·bur·den [dɪsˈbɜːdn] v/t entlasten (*of, from* von): ~ *one's mind* sein Herz ausschütten *od.* erleichtern.

dis·burse [dɪsˈbɜːs] v/t **1.** Geld aus(be)zahlen. **2.** Geld auslegen, verauslagen.

disc, *etc* → **disk,** *etc.*

dis·card I v/t [dɪˈskɑːd] **1.** Spielkarten ablegen, *Kleidung etc a.* ausrangieren, *Gewohnheit etc a.* aufgeben. **2.** *Freund etc* fallenlassen. **II** s [ˈdɪskɑːd] **3.** abgelegte Karte(n pl). **4.** *et.* Abgelegtes.

dis·cern [dɪˈsɜːn] v/t wahrnehmen, erkennen. **dis·cern·ing** adj □ scharfsichtig, kritisch (urteilend). **dis·cern·ment** s **1.** Wahrnehmen n, Erkennen n. **2.** Scharfblick m.

dis·charge [dɪsˈtʃɑːdʒ] **I** v/t **1.** ausladen: a) *Schiff etc* entladen, b) *Ladung* löschen, c) *Passagiere* ausschiffen. **2.** *Gewehr, Geschoß etc* abfeuern, abschießen. **3.** ~ *itself* → 9. **4.** ausströmen, -stoßen, ✝, physiol. absondern: ~ *matter* eitern. **5.** Angestellten, Patienten, Strafgefangenen etc entlassen (*from* aus). **6.** ⚖ freisprechen (*of* von). **7.** befreien, entbinden (*of, from* von; *from*

disci   886

doing s.th. davon, et. zu tun). **8.** *Ver-pflichtungen etc* erfüllen, nachkommen (*dat*). **II** *v/i* **9.** sich ergießen, münden (*into* in *acc*). **10.** ✱ eitern. **11.** ⚡ sich entladen. **III** *s* ['~t∫ɑ:dʒ] **12.** Entladung *f*; Löschung *f*. **13.** Abfeuern *n*. **14.** ✱, *physiol.* Absonderung *f*. **15.** Entlassung *f*. **16.** ⚖ Freisprechung *f*. **17.** Befreiung *f*, Entbindung *f*. **18.** Erfüllung *f*.

dis·ci ['dɪskaɪ] *pl von* **discus.**

dis·ci·ple [dɪ'saɪpl] *s Bibl.* Jünger *m*, *fig. a.* Schüler *m*.

dis·ci·pli·na·ry ['dɪsɪplɪnərɪ] *adj* diszipli-narisch, Disziplinar... **'dis·ci·pline I** *s* **1.** Disziplin *f*: *keep* ~ Disziplin halten. **2.** Disziplin *f*, Wissenschaftszweig *m*. **II** *v/t* **3.** disziplinieren, an Disziplin ge-wöhnen: *badly* ~*d* disziplinlos, undiszi-pliniert.

dis·claim [dɪs'kleɪm] *v/t* **1.** ab-, bestrei-ten. **2.** jede Verantwortung ablehnen für; *Verantwortung* ablehnen. **3.** wider-rufen, dementieren. **4.** ⚖ verzichten *od.* keinen Anspruch erheben auf (*acc*), *Erbschaft* ausschlagen. **dis'claim·er** *s* **1.** Widerruf *m*, Dementi *n*. **2.** (*of*) Ver-zicht *m* (auf *acc*), Ausschlagung *f* (*gen*).

dis·close [dɪs'kləʊz] *v/t* **1.** bekanntge-ben, -machen. **2.** enthüllen, aufdecken. **3.** zeigen, enthüllen. **dis'clo·sure** [~ʒə] *s* **1.** Bekanntgabe *f*. **2.** Enthüllung *f*.

dis·co ['dɪskəʊ] *pl* **-cos** *s* F Disko *f* (*Dis-kothek*).

dis·col·o·(u)r [dɪs'kʌlə] *v/t u. v/i* (sich) verfärben.

dis·com·fit [dɪs'kʌmfɪt] *v/t* aus der Fas-sung bringen, verwirren; in Verlegen-heit bringen. **dis'com·fi·ture** [~t∫ə] *s* Verwirrung *f*; Verlegenheit *f*.

dis·com·fort [dɪs'kʌmfət] *s* **1.** Unan-nehmlichkeit *f*, Verdruß *m*. **2.** Unbeha-gen *n*.

dis·con·cert [ˌdɪskən'sɜːt] *v/t* **1.** aus der Fassung bringen, verwirren. **2.** beunru-higen.

dis·con·nect [ˌdɪskə'nekt] *v/t* **1.** trennen (*from* von) (*a. teleph. Teilnehmer*). **2.** ⚡ *Gerät, Stecker etc* ausstecken. **3.** *Gas, Strom, Telefon* abstellen: *we have been* ~*ed* uns ist das Gas *etc* abgestellt worden. **dis·con'nect·ed** *adj* □ zs.-hang(s)los.

dis·con·so·late [dɪs'kɒnsəlɪt] *adj* □ un-tröstlich (*about, at* über *acc*).

dis·con·tent [ˌdɪskən'tent] **I** *adj* → **dis-contented.** **II** *s* Unzufriedenheit *f*. **ˌdis·con'tent·ed** *adj* □ unzufrieden (*with* mit).

dis·con·tin·ue [ˌdɪskən'tɪnjuː] *v/t* **1.** un-terbrechen. **2.** einstellen (*a.* ⚖); *Ge-wohnheit etc* aufgeben; *Beziehungen* abbrechen; *Zeitung etc* abbestellen. **3.** aufhören (*doing* zu tun). **ˌdis·con-'tin·u·ous** [~jʊəs] *adj* □ **1.** unterbro-chen. **2.** zs.-hang(s)los.

dis·cord ['dɪskɔːd] *s* **1.** Uneinigkeit *f*. **2.** Zwietracht *f*, Zwist *m*: → **apple. 3.** ♪ Mißklang *m* (*a. fig.*), Dissonanz *f*. **dis'cord·ant** *adj* □ **1.** sich widerspre-chend. **2.** ♪ mißtönend (*a. weitS. u. fig.*).

dis·co·theque ['dɪskəʊtek] *s* Diskothek *f*.

dis·count ['dɪskaʊnt] **I** *s* **1.** ✳ Preisnach-laß *m*, Rabatt *m*, Skonto *m*, *n* (*on auf acc*). **2.** ✳ Diskont *m*: ~ (*rate*) Diskont-satz *m*. **3.** ✳ Abzug *m* (*vom Nominal-wert*): *at a* ~ unter Pari; *fig.* nicht ge-schätzt *od.* gefragt; *sell at a* ~ mit Ver-lust verkaufen. **II** *v/t* **4.** ✳ abziehen, abrechnen; e-n Abzug gewähren auf (*acc*). **5.** ✳ *Wechsel* diskontieren. **6.** *Geschichte etc* mit Vorsicht *od.* Vorbe-halt aufnehmen.

dis·cour·age [dɪs'kʌrɪdʒ] *v/t* **1.** entmuti-gen. **2.** abschrecken, abhalten, j-m ab-raten (*from* von). **dis'cour·age·ment** *s* **1.** Entmutigung *f*. **2.** Abschreckung *f*.

dis·course I *s* ['dɪskɔːs] **1.** Unterhaltung *f*, Gespräch *n*. **2.** Vortrag *m*. **II** *v/i* [dɪ'skɔːs] **3.** sich unterhalten (*on* über *acc*). **4.** e-n Vortrag halten (*on* über *acc*).

dis·cour·te·ous [dɪs'kɜːtjəs] *adj* □ un-höflich. **dis'cour·te·sy** [~tɪsɪ] *s* Unhöf-lichkeit *f*.

dis·cov·er [dɪ'skʌvə] *v/t* entdecken, *fig. a.* ausfindig machen, (heraus)finden. **dis'cov·er·er** *s* Entdecker(in). **dis-'cov·er·y** *s* Entdeckung *f*.

dis·cred·it [dɪs'kredɪt] **I** *v/t* **1.** in Verruf *od.* Mißkredit bringen (*with* bei). **2.** anzweifeln, keinen Glauben schenken (*dat*). **II** *s* **3.** Mißkredit *m*: *bring into* ~, *bring* ~ *on* → 1. **4.** Zweifel *m*.

dis·creet [dɪ'skriːt] *adj* □ **1.** umsichtig, besonnen. **2.** diskret: a) taktvoll, b) ver-schwiegen, c) dezent, unaufdringlich.

dis·crep·an·cy [dɪ'skrepənsɪ] s Diskrepanz f, Widerspruch m.

dis·crete [dɪ'skriːt] adj □ getrennt, einzeln.

dis·cre·tion [dɪ'skreʃn] s 1. Ermessen n, Gutdünken n: *at ~* nach Belieben; *it is at* (od. *within*) *your ~* es steht Ihnen frei; *leave s.th. to s.o.'s ~* j-m et. anheimstellen. 2. Umsicht f, Besonnenheit f. 3. Diskretion f.

dis·crim·i·nate [dɪ'skrɪmɪneɪt] **I** v/i (scharf) unterscheiden, e-n Unterschied machen (*between* zwischen dat): *~ between* unterschiedlich behandeln (acc); *~ against* j-n benachteiligen, diskriminieren. **II** v/t (scharf) unterscheiden (*from* von). **dis'crim·i·nat·ing** adj □ scharfsinnig, urteilsfähig. **dis,crim·i'na·tion** s 1. unterschiedliche Behandlung; Diskriminierung f: *~ against s.o.* Benachteiligung f e-r Person. 2. Scharfsinn m, Urteilsfähigkeit f. **dis'crim·i·na·tive** [~nətɪv], **dis'crim·i·na·to·ry** [~nətərɪ] adj diskriminierend.

dis·cur·sive [dɪ'skɜːsɪv] adj □ weitschweifig.

dis·cus ['dɪskəs] pl **-cus·es, -ci** ['~kaɪ] s Leichtathletik: a) Diskus m: *~ throw →* b; *~ thrower* Diskuswerfer(in), b) Diskuswerfen n.

dis·cuss [dɪ'skʌs] v/t diskutieren, besprechen, erörtern. **dis'cus·sion** s Diskussion f, Besprechung f, Erörterung f: *be under ~* zur Diskussion stehen; *matter for ~* Diskussionsgegenstand m.

dis·dain [dɪs'deɪn] **I** v/t verachten, geringschätzen. **II** s Verachtung f, Geringschätzung f. **dis'dain·ful** [~ful] adj □ verächtlich, geringschätzig: *be ~ of* (od. *toward*[s]) *→ disdain* I.

dis·ease [dɪ'ziːz] s Krankheit f (a. fig.). **dis'eased** adj krank.

dis·em·bark [,dɪsɪm'baːk] **I** v/t ✈, ⚓ *Passagiere* von Bord gehen lassen, ⚓ a. ausschiffen, *Waren* ausladen. **II** v/i ✈, ⚓ von Bord gehen, ⚓ a. sich ausschiffen. **dis,em·bar'ka·tion** [~em~] s Ausschiffung f, -ladung f.

dis·en·chant [,dɪsɪn'tʃɑːnt] v/t desillusionieren, ernüchtern.

dis·en·gage [,dɪsɪn'geɪdʒ] **I** v/t 1. los-, freimachen, befreien (*from* von). 2. ☉ loskuppeln: *~ the clutch* auskuppeln; *~ the gears* in den Leergang schalten. **II**

v/i 3. sich freimachen, loskommen (*from* von). **dis·en'gaged** adj 1. frei, unbeschäftigt. 2. ungebunden. **dis·en·'gage·ment** s 1. Befreiung f. 2. Ungebundenheit f. 3. Muße(stunden pl) f.

dis·en·tan·gle [,dɪsɪn'tæŋgl] **I** v/t 1. entwirren, -flechten (*beide a. fig.*). 2. befreien (*from* von, aus). **II** v/i 3. sich befreien.

dis·e·qui·lib·ri·um [,dɪsekwɪ'lɪbrɪəm] s bsd. ✝ Ungleichgewicht n.

dis·fa·vo(u)r [,dɪs'feɪvə] s 1. Mißbilligung f, -fallen n. 2. Ungnade f: *be in* (*fall into*) *~* in Ungnade stehen (fallen) (*with* bei).

dis·fig·ure [dɪs'fɪgə] v/t entstellen, verunstalten (*with* durch).

dis·gorge [dɪs'gɔːdʒ] **I** v/t 1. *Essen* ausspeien, *Lava* speien. 2. (widerwillig) wieder herausgeben. **II** v/i 3. sich ergießen, fließen (*into* in acc).

dis·grace [dɪs'greɪs] **I** s 1. Schande f (*to* für): *bring ~ on →* 3. 2. *→ disfavo(u)r* 2. **II** v/t 3. Schande bringen über (acc). **dis'grace·ful** [~ful] adj □ schändlich.

dis·grun·tled [dɪs'grʌntld] adj verärgert, -stimmt (*at* über acc).

dis·guise [dɪs'gaɪz] **I** v/t 1. (*o.s.* sich) verkleiden od. maskieren (*as* als). 2. *Handschrift, Stimme* verstellen. 3. *Absichten, Fakten etc* verschleiern, *Gefühle etc* verbergen. **II** s 4. Verkleidung f: *in ~* verkleidet, maskiert; *fig.* verkappt; *in the ~ of* verkleidet als; *→ blessing*. 5. Verstellung f. 6. Verschleierung f: *make no ~ of* kein Hehl machen aus.

dis·gust [dɪs'gʌst] **I** v/t 1. anekeln, anwidern: *be ~ed with* (od. *at, by*) Ekel empfinden über (acc). 2. empören, entrüsten: *be ~ed with* empört od. entrüstet sein über (acc). **II** s 3. Ekel m (*at, for* vor dat). **dis'gust·ing** adj □ ekelhaft, widerlich.

dish [dɪʃ] **I** s 1. flache Schüssel, (Servier)Platte f; pl Geschirr n: *wash* (od. *do*) *the ~es* abspülen. 2. Gericht n, Speise f. **II** v/t 3. *oft ~ up Speisen* anrichten; auftragen. 4. *oft ~ up* F *Geschichte etc* auftischen. 5. *~ out* F austeilen.

dis·har·mo·ny [,dɪs'hɑːmənɪ] s Disharmonie f.

'dish·cloth s Geschirrtuch n.

dis·heart·en [dɪs'hɑːtn] v/t entmutigen.

di·shev·el(l)ed [dɪˈʃevld] adj **1.** zerzaust (*Haar*). **2.** unordentlich, ungepflegt.

dis·hon·est [dɪsˈɒnɪst] adj □ unehrlich, unredlich. **dis·hon·es·ty** s Unredlichkeit *f*: a) Unehrlichkeit *f*, b) unredliche Handlung.

dis·hon·o(u)r [dɪsˈɒnə] I s **1.** Unehre *f*, Schande *f* (**to** für). II v/t **2.** entehren. **3.** ✝ *Wechsel* etc nicht honorieren od. einlösen. **dis·hon·o(u)r·a·ble** adj □ schändlich, unehrenhaft.

'dish|·rag s Br., ~ **tow·el** s bsd. Am. Geschirrtuch n. '~**wash·er** s **1.** Tellerwäscher(in), Spüler(in). **2.** Geschirrspülmaschine *f*, -spüler m. '~**wa·ter** s Abwasch-, Spülwasser n.

dish·y [ˈdɪʃɪ] adj bsd. Br. F dufte, toll (*Person*).

dis·il·lu·sion [ˌdɪsɪˈluːʒn] I s Ernüchterung *f*, Desillusion *f*. II v/t ernüchtern, desillusionieren. **dis·il·lu·sion·ment** n. **dis·il·lu·sion** → **disillusion** I.

dis·in·cli·na·tion [ˌdɪsɪnklɪˈneɪʃn] s Abneigung *f* (**for** gegen; **to do** zu tun). **dis·in·clined** [ˌ~ˈklaɪnd] adj abgeneigt.

dis·in·fect [ˌdɪsɪnˈfekt] v/t desinfizieren. **dis·in·fect·ant** s Desinfektionsmittel n. **dis·in·fec·tion** s Desinfektion *f*, Desinfizierung *f*.

dis·in·gen·u·ous [ˌdɪsɪnˈdʒenjʊəs] adj □ unaufrichtig.

dis·in·her·it [ˌdɪsɪnˈherɪt] v/t enterben.

dis·in·te·grate [dɪsˈɪntɪgreɪt] I v/t **1.** auflösen, fig. a. zersetzen. II v/i **2.** sich auflösen (a. fig.). **3.** ver-, zerfallen (a. fig.). **4.** geol. verwittern. **dis·in·te·gra·tion** s **1.** Auflösung *f*, Zerfall m. **3.** geol. Verwitterung *f*.

dis·in·ter·est·ed [dɪsˈɪntrəstɪd] adj □ **1.** uneigennützig. **2.** objektiv. **3.** un-, desinteressiert (**in** an dat).

dis·joint·ed [dɪsˈdʒɔɪntɪd] adj □ zs.-hang(s)los.

disk [dɪsk] s **1.** allg. Scheibe *f*. **2.** (Schall)Platte *f*. ~ **brake** s ⊙ Scheibenbremse *f*.

disk·ette [dɪˈsket] s *Computer:* Diskette *f*.

disk jock·ey s Diskjockey m.

dis·like [dɪsˈlaɪk] I v/t nicht leiden können, nicht mögen: ~ **doing s.th.** et. nicht gern od. (nur) ungern tun; **get o.s.** ~**d** sich unbeliebt machen. II s Abneigung *f*, Widerwille m (**of, for** gegen):

take a ~ **to** e-e Abneigung fassen gegen.

dis·lo·cate [ˈdɪsləʊkeɪt] v/t **1.** verrücken. **2.** ✿ sich *den Arm* etc ver- od. ausrenken. **dis·lo·ca·tion** s **1.** Verrückung *f*. **2.** ✿ Verrenkung *f*; Dislokation *f*.

dis·loy·al [ˌdɪsˈlɔɪəl] adj □ (**to**) untreu (dat), treulos (gegen). **dis·loy·al·ty** s Untreue *f*, Treulosigkeit *f*.

dis·mal [ˈdɪzməl] I adj □ düster, trüb, trostlos, bedrückend. II s: **be in the** ~s F Trübsal blasen.

dis·man·tle [dɪsˈmæntl] v/t **1.** demontieren, abbauen; *Gebäude* abbrechen; ⚓ abwracken. **2.** zerlegen, auseinandernehmen.

dis·may [dɪsˈmeɪ] I v/t erschrecken, bestürzen. II s Schreck(en) m, Bestürzung *f*: **in** (od. **with**) ~ bestürzt; **to one's** ~ zu s-r Bestürzung.

dis·mem·ber [dɪsˈmembə] v/t **1.** zerstückeln; bsd. ✿ zergliedern. **2.** *Land* etc zersplittern, aufteilen.

dis·miss [dɪsˈmɪs] v/t **1.** entlassen, gehen lassen. **2.** entlassen (**from** aus e-m Amt etc). **3.** *Thema* etc fallenlassen; *Frage* etc abtun (**as** als). **4.** a. ⚖ abweisen. **dis·miss·al** s **1.** Entlassung *f*. **2.** a. ⚖ Abweisung *f*.

dis·mount [ˌdɪsˈmaʊnt] I v/i **1.** absteigen, absitzen (**from** von). II v/t **2.** *Reiter* abwerfen. **3.** abmontieren.

dis·o·be·di·ence [ˌdɪsəˈbiːdjəns] s Ungehorsam m. **dis·o·be·di·ent** adj □ ungehorsam (**to** gegen[über]). **dis·o·bey** [ˌ~ˈbeɪ] I v/t **1.** j-m nicht gehorchen. **2.** *Gesetz* etc nicht befolgen, mißachten. II v/i **3.** nicht gehorchen, ungehorsam sein.

dis·o·blige [ˌdɪsəˈblaɪdʒ] v/t ungefällig sein gegen. **dis·o·blig·ing** adj □ ungefällig, unfreundlich.

dis·or·der [dɪsˈɔːdə] I s **1.** Unordnung *f*, Durcheinander n: **in** ~ durcheinander; **throw into** ~ → 4. **2.** Aufruhr m, Unruhen pl. **3.** ✿ Störung *f*: **mental** ~ Geistesstörung. II v/t **4.** in Unordnung bringen, durcheinanderbringen. **dis·or·dered** adj **1.** unordentlich, durcheinander. **2.** ✿ gestört. **dis·or·der·ly** adj **1.** unordentlich. **2.** schlampig, (a. *Leben* etc) liederlich. **3.** ⚖ ordnungswidrig.

dis·or·gan·ize [dɪsˈɔːgənaɪz] → **disorder** 4.

dis·own [dɪs' əʊn] v/t **1.** nichts zu tun haben wollen mit, ablehnen. **2.** ableugnen.

dis·par·age [dɪ'spærɪdʒ] v/t **1.** herabsetzen, verächtlich machen. **2.** verachten, geringschätzen. **dis'par·age·ment** s **1.** Herabsetzung f, Verächtlichmachung f. **2.** Verachtung f, Geringschätzung f. **dis'par·ag·ing** adj □ herabsetzend, verächtlich, geringschätzig.

dis·pa·rate ['dɪspərət] adj □ ungleich(artig), (grund)verschieden. **dis'par·i·ty** [dɪ'spærətɪ] s Verschiedenheit f: ~ *in* (od. *of*) *age* (zu großer) Altersunterschied.

dis·pas·sion·ate [dɪ'spæʃnət] adj □ leidenschaftslos, kühl, sachlich.

dis·patch [dɪ'spætʃ] I v/t **1.** (ab)senden, (ab)schicken, *Telegramm* aufgeben. **2.** rasch erledigen. **3.** ins Jenseits befördern, töten. **4.** F wegputzen, schnell aufessen. II s **5.** Absendung f, Versand m: ~ *by rail* Bahnversand. **6.** rasche Erledigung. **7.** Tötung f. ~ **box**, ~ **case** s bsd. Br. Aktenkoffer m.

dis·pel [dɪ'spel] v/t *Menge etc, a. fig. Befürchtungen etc* zerstreuen, *Nebel* zerteilen.

dis·pen·sa·ble [dɪ'spensəbl] adj □ entbehrlich. **dis'pen·sa·ry** s Werks-, Krankenhausapotheke f. **dis·pen·sa·tion** [ˌ~'seɪʃn] s **1.** Aus-, Verteilung f. **2.** Zuteilung f, Gabe f. **3.** (göttliche) Fügung f. **4.** Verzicht m (*with* auf acc). **dis·pense** [dɪ'spens] I v/t **1.** aus-, verteilen; *Sakrament* spenden: ~ *justice* Recht sprechen. **2.** *Arzneien* dispensieren, zubereiten u. abgeben. **3.** befreien, entbinden (*from* von). II v/i **4.** ~ *with* verzichten auf (acc); überflüssig machen (acc). **dis'pens·er** s **1.** Austeiler m. **2.** Ⓒ Spender m, (für Klebestreifen etc a.) Abroller m, (Briefmarken- etc)Automat m. **dis'pens·ing** adj: ~ *chemist* Br. Apotheker m.

dis·per·sal [dɪ'spɜːsl] s **1.** Zerstreuung f (a. fig.). **2.** Verteilung f. **dis·perse** I v/t **1.** verstreuen (*over* über acc). **2.** → *dispel.* **3.** *Nachrichten etc* verbreiten. **4.** 🐾, phys. dispergieren, zerstreuen. II v/i **5.** sich zerstreuen (*Menge*). **6.** sich verteilen. **dis'per·sion** s **1.** → *dispersal.* **2.** 🐾, phys. Dispersion f, (Zer-)Streuung f.

dis·pir·it·ed [dɪ'spɪrɪtɪd] adj mutlos, niedergeschlagen.

dis·place [dɪs'pleɪs] v/t **1.** versetzen, -rücken, -schieben. **2.** verdrängen (a. ⚓, phys., Sport). **3.** j-n ablösen (*as* als). **4.** j-n verschleppen: ~*d person* Verschleppte m, f, Zwangsumsiedler(in). **dis'place·ment** s **1.** Versetzung f, -schiebung f. **2.** Verdrängung f. **3.** Ablösung f. **4.** Verschleppung f.

dis·play [dɪ'spleɪ] I v/t **1.** *Aktivität etc* zeigen, entfalten, an den Tag legen. **2.** *Waren* auslegen, -stellen. **3.** zur Schau stellen, hervorkehren. II s **4.** Entfaltung f. **5.** Ausstellung f: *be on* ~ ausgestellt sein. **6.** Display n: a) (Sichtbild)Anzeige f, b) a. ~ *unit* Sichtbildgerät n. III adj **7.** Ausstellungs..., Schau...: ~ *cabinet* (od. *case*) Schaukasten m, Vitrine f; ~ *window* Auslage(n)-, Schaufenster n.

dis·please [dɪs'pliːz] v/t **1.** j-m mißfallen: *be* ~*d at* (od. *with*) unzufrieden sein mit. **2.** j-n ärgern, verstimmen. **dis·'pleas·ing** adj □ unangenehm. **dis·pleas·ure** [~'pleʒə] s Mißfallen n (*at* über acc).

dis·pos·a·ble [dɪ'spəʊsəbl] adj **1.** (frei) verfügbar. **2.** Einweg..., Wegwerf... **dis'pos·al** s **1.** Erledigung f. **2.** Beseitigung f. **3.** Übergabe f, -tragung f: ~ (*by sale*) Veräußerung f, Verkauf m. **4.** Verfügung(srecht n) f (*of* über acc): *be at s.o.'s* ~ j-m zur Verfügung stehen; *place* (od. *put*) *s.th. at s.o.'s* ~ j-m et. zur Verfügung stellen; *have the* ~ *of* verfügen (können) über (acc). **dis'pose** I v/t **1.** anordnen, aufstellen. **2.** geneigt machen, bewegen (*to* zu; *to do* zu tun). II v/i **3.** ~ *of* (frei) verfügen über (acc); (endgültig) erledigen; wegschaffen, beseitigen; verkaufen, veräußern; übergeben, -tragen. **dis'posed** adj **1.** *be well* ~ *to*(*ward*[*s*]) j-m wohlgesinnt sein, j-m wohlwollen; *e-m Plan etc* wohlwollend gegenüberstehen; → *ill-disposed.* **2.** geneigt (*to do* zu tun): *feel* ~ *to do s.th.* et. tun wollen. **dis·po·si·tion** [ˌ~pə'zɪʃn] s **1.** Disposition f, Veranlagung f; Art f. **2.** Neigung f, Hang m (*to* zu); ⚕ Anfälligkeit f (*to* für): *have a* ~ *to* neigen zu; anfällig sein für. **3.** → *disposal* 4.

dis·pos·sess [ˌdɪspə'zes] v/t enteignen.

dis·pro·por·tion·ate [ˌdɪsprəˈpɔːʃnət] *adj* □ unverhältnismäßig (groß *od.* klein); unangemessen; übertrieben: **be ~ to** in keinem Verhältnis stehen zu.

dis·prove [ˌdɪsˈpruːv] *v/t* widerlegen.

dis·pu·ta·ble [dɪˈspjuːtəbl] *adj* □ strittig. ˌ**dis·pu·ta·tion** *s* 1. Disput *m*. 2. Disputation *f*. ˌ**dis·pu·ta·tious** *adj* □ streitsüchtig. **dis·pute** [dɪˈspjuːt] I *v/i* 1. streiten (**on, about** über *acc*). II *v/t* 2. streiten über (*acc*). 3. in Zweifel ziehen, bezweifeln: **~d** umstritten. 4. kämpfen um. 5. (an)kämpfen gegen. III *s* 6. Disput *m*: **in** (*od.* **under**) ~ umstritten; **beyond** (*od.* **past, without**) ~ fraglos, unbestritten.

dis·qual·i·fi·ca·tion [dɪsˌkwɒlɪfɪˈkeɪʃn] *s* 1. Disqualifikation *f*, Disqualifizierung *f*. 2. Untauglichkeit *f* (**for** für). **dis·qual·i·fy** *v/t* 1. disqualifizieren. 2. untauglich machen (**for** für). 3. für untauglich erklären.

dis·qui·et [dɪsˈkwaɪət] I *v/t* beunruhigen. II *s* Unruhe *f*, Besorgnis *f*. **dis·qui·et·ing** *adj* □ beunruhigend, besorgniserregend.

dis·re·gard [ˌdɪsrɪˈgɑːd] I *v/t* 1. nicht beachten, ignorieren. 2. mißachten. II *s* 3. Nichtbeachtung *f*, Ignorierung *f* (**of, for** gen). 4. Mißachtung *f* (**of, for** gen).

dis·re·pair [ˌdɪsrɪˈpeə] *s* Baufälligkeit *f*: **be in** (**a state of**) ~ baufällig sein; **fall into** ~ baufällig werden.

dis·rep·u·ta·ble [dɪsˈrepjʊtəbl] *adj* □ verrufen. **dis·re·pute** [ˌ~rɪˈpjuːt] *s* schlechter Ruf: **be in** ~ verrufen sein; **bring** (**fall, sink**) **into** ~ in Verruf bringen (kommen).

dis·re·spect [ˌdɪsrɪˈspekt] *s* Respektlosigkeit *f*. ˌ**dis·re·spect·ful** [ˌ~fʊl] *adj* □ respektlos (**to** gegenüber).

dis·rupt [dɪsˈrʌpt] *v/t* 1. auseinanderreißen, (zer)spalten. 2. *Gespräch, Verkehr etc* unterbrechen. 3. *Land etc* zerrütten; *Koalition etc* sprengen. **dis·rup·tion** *s* 1. Spaltung *f*. 2. Unterbrechung *f*. 3. Zerrüttung *f*; Sprengung *f*.

dis·sat·is·fac·tion [ˈdɪsˌsætɪsˈfækʃn] *s* Unzufriedenheit *f*. ˈ**dis·sat·is·fac·to·ry** [ˌ~tərɪ] *adj* unbefriedigend (**to** für). ˌ**dis·sat·is·fied** [ˌ~faɪd] *adj* unzufrieden (**at, with** mit).

dis·sect [dɪˈsekt] *v/t* 1. ⚕ sezieren. 2. *fig.* zergliedern.

dis·sem·ble [dɪˈsembl] *v/t* verbergen, -hehlen, sich *et.* nicht anmerken lassen.

dis·sem·i·nate [dɪˈsemɪneɪt] *v/t* 1. ausstreuen. 2. *fig.* verbreiten. **dis·sem·i·na·tion** *s* 1. Ausstreuung *f*. 2. *fig.* Verbreitung *f*.

dis·sen·sion [dɪˈsenʃn] *s* Meinungsverschiedenheit(en *pl*) *f*.

dis·sent [dɪˈsent] I *v/i* 1. (**from**) anderer Meinung sein (als), nicht übereinstimmen (mit). 2. *eccl.* von der Staatskirche abweichen. II *s* 3. Meinungsverschiedenheit *f*. **dis·sent·er** *s* 1. Andersdenkende *m*, *f*. 2. *eccl.* Dissident *m*; Dissenter *m*.

dis·ser·ta·tion [ˌdɪsəˈteɪʃn] *s* 1. (wissenschaftliche) Abhandlung. 2. *univ.* Diplomarbeit *f*.

dis·ser·vice [ˌdɪsˈsɜːvɪs] *s*: **do s.o. a** ~ j-m e-n schlechten Dienst erweisen.

dis·si·dent [ˈdɪsɪdənt] I *adj* 1. (**from**) andersdenkend (als), abweichend (von). II *s* 2. Andersdenkende *m*, *f*. 3. *eccl.* Dissident(in), *pol. a.* Regime-, Systemkritiker(in).

dis·sim·i·lar [ˌdɪˈsɪmɪlə] *adj* □ (**to, from**) verschieden (von), unähnlich (dat). **dis·sim·i·lar·i·ty** [ˌ~ˈlærətɪ] *s* Verschiedenheit *f*, Unähnlichkeit *f*.

dis·sim·u·late [dɪˈsɪmjʊleɪt] → **dissemble**.

dis·si·pate [ˈdɪsɪpeɪt] I *v/t* 1. zerstreuen (*a. fig.*); *Nebel* zerteilen. 2. *Kräfte* verzetteln, -geuden; *Vermögen etc* durchbringen, verschwenden. II *v/i* 3. sich zerstreuen (*a. fig.*); sich zerteilen. ˈ**dis·si·pat·ed** *adj* □ ausschweifend: a) zügellos (*Leben*), b) leichtlebig (*Person*). ˌ**dis·si·pa·tion** *s* 1. Zerstreuung *f* (*a. fig.*); Zerteilung *f*. 2. Vergeudung *f*. 3. Ausschweifung *f*: **a life of** ~ ein ausschweifendes *od.* zügelloses Leben.

dis·so·ci·ate [dɪˈsəʊʃɪeɪt] *v/t* 1. trennen (**from** von). 2. ~ **o.s.** sich distanzieren, abrücken (**from** von). **dis·so·ci·a·tion** [ˌ~sɪˈeɪʃn] *s* Trennung *f*.

dis·so·lute [ˈdɪsəluːt] → **dissipated**.

dis·so·lu·tion [ˌdɪsəˈluːʃn] *s* 1. Auflösung *f* (*a. fig.*). 2. 🏛 Annullierung *f*, Aufhebung *f*.

dis·solve [dɪˈzɒlv] I *v/t* 1. auflösen (*a. fig.*): **~ in the mouth** *Tablette etc* im Mund zergehen lassen; **~d in tears** in Tränen aufgelöst. 2. 🏛 annullieren,

district

aufheben. **II** v/i **3.** sich auflösen (a. fig.): **~ in the mouth** im Mund zergehen; **~ in(to) tears** in Tränen zerfließen.

dis·so·nance ['dɪsənəns] s Dissonanz f: a) ♪ Mißklang m (a. fig.), b) fig. Unstimmigkeit f. **'dis·so·nant** adj □ **1.** ♪ dissonant. **2.** mißtönend. **3.** fig. unstimmig.

dis·suade [dɪ'sweɪd] v/t **1.** j-m abraten (**from** von; **from doing** [davon,] et. zu tun). **2.** abbringen (**from** von; **from doing** davon, et. zu tun). **3.** abraten von.

dis·tance ['dɪstəns] **I** s **1.** Entfernung f: **at a ~** in einiger Entfernung; von weitem, von fern; **from a ~** aus einiger Entfernung; **keep one's ~** Abstand halten (**from** von); fig. Distanz wahren. **2.** Ferne f: **from (in) the ~** aus (in) der Ferne. **3.** Strecke: a) Entfernung f: **go the ~** fig. durchhalten, über die Runden kommen, b) Sport: Distanz f: **~ runner** (Leichtathletik) Langstreckenläufer(in), Langstreckler(in). **4.** (a. zeitlicher) Abstand: **at this ~ of** (od. **in**) **time** nach all dieser Zeit. **II** v/t **5.** überholen, (weit) hinter sich lassen (Sport a.) distanzieren. **6.** fig. überflügeln, -treffen. **7.** **~ o.s.** sich distanzieren (**from** von). **'dis·tant** adj □ **1.** entfernt (a. fig.). **2.** fern (a. zeitlich), Fern...: **~ heating** Fernheizung f. **3.** (weit) voneinander entfernt. **4.** fig. distanziert.

dis·taste [ˌdɪs'teɪst] s **1.** Ekel m (**for** vor dat). **2.** fig. Widerwille m, Abneigung f (**for** gegen). **dis'taste·ful** [~fʊl] adj □ **1.** ekelerregend. **2.** fig. unangenehm: **be ~ to** j-m zuwider sein.

dis·tend [dɪ'stend] **I** v/t **1.** (aus)dehnen. **2.** Bauch etc aufblähen. **II** v/i **3.** sich (aus)dehnen. **4.** sich aufblähen. **5.** sich weiten (**with** vor dat) (Augen).

dis·til [dɪ'stɪl] v/t **1.** 🜊 destillieren: **~ out** herausdestillieren (**from** aus) (a. fig.). **2.** Branntwein brennen (**from** aus). **dis·til·la·tion** [ˌ~'leɪʃn] s **1.** 🜊 Destillation f. **2.** 🜊 Destillat n. **3.** Brennen n. **dis'till·er·y** s (Branntwein)Brennerei f.

dis·tinct [dɪ'stɪŋkt] adj □ **1.** verschieden (**from** von): **as ~ from** im Unterschied zu. **2.** ausgeprägt, klar, deutlich. **dis'tinc·tion** s **1.** Unterscheidung f. **2.** Unterschied m: **in ~ from** im Unterschied

zu; **draw** (od. **make**) **a ~ between** e-n Unterschied machen zwischen (dat). **3.** Auszeichnung f, Ehrung f. **4.** (hoher) Rang: **of ~** von Rang (u. Namen). **dis'tinc·tive** adj □ **1.** Unterscheidungs... **2.** kennzeichnend (**of** für): → **mark**² **3.**

dis·tin·guish [dɪ'stɪŋgwɪʃ] **I** v/t **1.** unterscheiden (**from** von), auseinanderhalten. **2.** wahrnehmen, erkennen. **3.** kennzeichnen: **~ing mark** Kennzeichen n. **4.** **~ o.s.** sich auszeichnen (a. iro.). **II** v/i **5.** unterscheiden, e-n Unterschied machen (**between** zwischen dat). **dis'tin·guished** adj **1.** hervorragend, ausgezeichnet. **2.** vornehm.

dis·tort [dɪ'stɔːt] v/t **1.** verdrehen. **2.** Gesicht etc verzerren: **~ed with** (od. **by**) **pain** schmerzverzerrt. **3.** Tatsachen etc verdrehen, entstellen, verzerren. **dis'tor·tion** s **1.** Verdrehung f. **2.** Verzerrung f. **3.** Entstellung f.

dis·tract [dɪ'strækt] v/t Aufmerksamkeit, Person etc ablenken (**from** von). **dis'tract·ed** adj □ **1.** beunruhigt, besorgt. **2.** (**with, by**) außer sich (vor dat); wahnsinnig (vor dat). **dis'trac·tion** s **1.** Ablenkung f. **2.** oft pl Zerstreuung f, Ablenkung f. **3.** Wahnsinn m: **drive s.o. to ~** j-n zur Raserei od. zum Wahnsinn treiben.

dis·traught [dɪ'strɔːt] → **distracted** 1.

dis·tress [dɪ'stres] **I** s **1.** Leid n, Kummer m, Sorge f. **2.** Not f, Elend n. **3.** Notlage f, -stand m. **4.** ⚓ Seenot f: **in ~** in Seenot; **~ call** SOS-Ruf m. **II** v/t **5.** mit Sorge erfüllen. **dis'tressed** adj **1.** besorgt (**about** um). **2.** notleidend: **~ area** Br. Notstandsgebiet n. **dis'tress·ing** adj □ besorgniserregend.

dis·trib·ute [dɪ'strɪbjuːt] v/t **1.** ver-, austeilen (**among** unter dat od. acc; **to** an acc). **2.** zuteilen (**to** dat). **3.** ♣ Waren vertreiben, absetzen; Filme verleihen; Dividende, Gewinn ausschütten. **dis·tri'bu·tion** s **1.** Ver-, Austeilung f: **~ of seats** parl. Sitzverteilung. **2.** Zuteilung f; Gabe f, Spende f. **3.** ♣ Vertrieb m, Absatz m; Verleih m; Ausschüttung f. **dis'trib·u·tor** s **1.** Verteiler m (a. ⊙). **2.** ♣ Großhändler m; Generalvertreter m; pl (Film)Verleih m.

dis·trict ['dɪstrɪkt] s **1.** Distrikt m, (Verwaltungs)Bezirk m, Kreis m. **2.** (Stadt-)

Bezirk *m*, (-)Viertel *n*. **3.** Gegend *f*, Gebiet *n*.

dis·trust [dɪs'trʌst] **I** *s* Mißtrauen *n*: **with** ~ mißtrauisch. **II** *v/t* mißtrauen (*dat*). **dis'trust·ful** [~fʊl] *adj* □ mißtrauisch (**of** gegen).

dis·turb [dɪ'stɜːb] *v/t u. v/i allg.* stören. **dis'turb·ance** *s* **1.** Störung *f* (*a.* ☉ *etc*). **2.** *politische od.* Unruhe; Ruhestörung *f*: **cause** (*od.* **create**) **a** ~ für Unruhe sorgen; ruhestörenden Lärm machen. **dis'turb·er** *s* **1.** Störer(in), Störenfried *m*. **2.** Unruhestifter(in).

dis·u·nite [ˌdɪsjuː'naɪt] *v/t u. v/i* (sich) trennen *od.* entzweien. **dis·u·ni·ty** [~nətɪ] *s* Uneinigkeit *f*, Zwietracht *f*.

dis·use [ˌdɪs'juːs] *s*: **fall into** ~ ungebräuchlich werden. **dis'used** [~zd] *adj* nicht mehr benutzt (*Maschine etc*), stillgelegt (*Bergwerk etc*), leerstehend (*Haus*).

ditch [dɪtʃ] **I** *s* **1.** Graben *m*. **II** *v/t* **2.** Gräben ziehen durch *od.* in (*dat*). **3.** *Fahrzeug* in den Straßengraben fahren. **4.** *sl. Wagen etc* stehenlassen; *j-m* entwischen; *dem Freund etc* den Laufpaß geben; *er. wegschmeißen; Am. die Schule* schwänzen.

dith·er ['dɪðə] **I** *v/i* **1.** (*bsd.* vor Kälte) zittern. **2.** schwanken, sich nicht entscheiden können (**between** zwischen *dat*). **3.** aufgeregt sein. **II** *s* **4.** Schwanken *n*. **5.** Aufregung *f*: **throw into a** ~ in Aufregung versetzen; **be all of a** ~, **be in a** ~, *bsd. Br.* F **have the** ~**s** aufgeregt sein.

di·ur·nal [daɪ'ɜːnl] *adj* □ täglich (wiederkehrend).

di·va·gate ['daɪvəgeɪt] *v/i* abschweifen (**from** von), nicht bei der Sache bleiben.

di·van [dɪ'væn] *s* Diwan *m*: ~ (**bed**) Bettcouch *f*.

dive [daɪv] **I** *v/i* **1.** tauchen (**for** nach; **into** in *acc*). **2.** (unter)tauchen (*a. U-Boot*). **3.** *e-n Hecht- od.* Kopfsprung machen; (*Wasserspringen*) springen; (*bsd. Sport*) sich werfen, hechten (**for the ball** nach dem Ball): ~ **for cover** sich in Deckung werfen. **4.** ✈ *e-n Sturzflug* machen. **II** *s* **5.** (Unter)Tauchen *n*, ♣ *a.* Unterwasser-, Tauchfahrt *f*. **6.** Kopfsprung *m*, Hechtsprung *m* (*a. des Tormanns etc*); (*Wasserspringen*) Sprung *m*: **make a** ~ **for** hechten nach; **make a**

~ **for cover** sich in Deckung werfen. **7.** ✈ Sturzflug *m*. **8.** F Spelunke *f*. **'div·er** *s* **1.** Taucher(in). **2.** *Sport*: Wasserspringer(in).

di·verge [daɪ'vɜːdʒ] *v/i* **1.** divergieren (*a.* &, *phys.*), auseinandergehen, -laufen. **2.** abweichen (**from** von); voneinander abweichen. **di'ver·gent** *adj* □ **1.** divergierend (*a.* &, *phys.*). **2.** abweichend (**from** von).

di·verse [daɪ'vɜːs] *adj* □ verschieden, ungleich, andersartig. **di,ver·si·fi·ca·tion** [~fɪ'keɪʃn] *s* **1.** abwechslungsreiche Gestaltung. **2.** *a.* ~ **of risk** Risikoverteilung *f*. **3.** † *Unternehmen* Diversifizierung *f*. **di'ver·si·fy** [~faɪ] *v/t* **1.** abwechslungsreich gestalten. **2.** *Risiko* verteilen. **3.** † *Unternehmen* diversifizieren. **di'ver·sion** [~ʃn] *s* **1.** Ablenkung *f*. **2.** Zerstreuung *f*, Zeitvertreib *m*. **3.** † (Verkehrs)Umleitung *f*. **di'ver·si·ty** [~sətɪ] *s* Verschiedenheit *f*, Ungleichheit *f*. **di'vert** *v/t* **1.** ablenken, abwenden (**from** von), lenken (**to** auf *acc*). **2.** *Br. Verkehr* umleiten. **3.** zerstreuen, unterhalten (**with** mit, durch).

di·vide [dɪ'vaɪd] **I** *v/t* **1.** teilen (**s.th. with** *s.o.* et. mit j-m): ~ **in halves** halbieren. **2.** (zer)teilen, spalten, *fig. a.* entzweien: **opinion is** ~**d** die Meinungen sind geteilt (**on** über *acc*). **3.** ver-, austeilen (**among, between** unter *dat od. acc*). **4.** & dividieren, teilen (**by** durch): **20** ~**d by 5 is 4** 20 (geteilt) durch 5 ist 4; ~**s into 20** 20 durch 5 teilen. **II** *v/i* **5.** sich aufteilen, zerfallen (**into** in *acc*). **6.** & sich dividieren *od.* teilen lassen (**by** durch). **div·i·dend** ['dɪvɪdend] *s* **1.** & Dividend *m*. **2.** † Dividende *f*. **di·vid·ers** [dɪ'vaɪdəz] *s pl.* **a. pair of** ~ Stechzirkel *m*. **di'vid·ing** *adj* Trennungs...

div·i·na·tion [ˌdɪvɪ'neɪʃn] *s* Weissagung *f*. **di·vine** [dɪ'vaɪn] **I** *adj* □ **1.** göttlich (*a. fig.* F), Gottes... **II** *v/t* **2.** weissagen. **3.** mit der Wünschelrute suchen (nach). **di'vin·er** *s* **1.** Wahrsager(in). **2.** (Wünschel)Rutengänger(in).

div·ing ['daɪvɪŋ] *s* **1.** Tauchen *n*. **2.** *Sport*: Wasserspringen *n*. ~ **bell** *s* Taucherglocke *f*. ~ **board** *s* Sprungbrett *n*. ~ **hel·met** *s* Taucherhelm *m*. ~ **suit** *s* Taucheranzug *m*. ~ **tow·er** *s* Sprungturm *m*.

di·vin·ing rod [dɪˈvaɪnɪŋ] s Wünschelrute f.

di·vin·i·ty [dɪˈvɪnətɪ] s **1.** Göttlichkeit f. **2.** Gottheit f. **3.** Theologie f.

di·vis·i·ble [dɪˈvɪzəbl] adj □ teilbar (A· **by** durch). **di·vi·sion** [~ʒn] s **1.** (Ver-, Aus)Teilung f: ~ **of labo(u)r** Arbeitsteilung. **2.** Zerteilung f, Spaltung f, fig. a. Entzweiung f. **3.** A· Division f: ~ **sign** Teilungszeichen n. **4.** parl. Br. (Abstimmung f durch) Hammelsprung m. **5.** Abteilung f. **6.** ✕ Division f. **7.** Sport: Liga f. **di·vi·sor** [dɪˈvaɪzə] s A· Divisor m, Teiler m.

di·vorce [dɪˈvɔːs] **I** s **1.** ⚖ (Ehe)Scheidung f: **get** (od. **obtain**) a ~ geschieden werden, sich scheiden lassen (**from** von). **2.** fig. (völlige) Trennung (**from** von; **between** zwischen dat). **II** v/t **3.** ⚖ j-n, Ehe scheiden: ~ **s.o.** j-s Ehe scheiden; **he has ~d his wife** er hat sich (von s-r Frau) scheiden lassen. **4.** fig. (völlig) trennen (**from** von).

diz·zi·ness [ˈdɪzɪnɪs] s Schwindel(anfall) m. **'diz·zy I** adj □ **1.** schwind(e)lig. **2.** schwindelnd, schwindelerregend; schwindelnd hoch. **II** v/t **3.** schwind(e)lig machen.

do¹ [duː] (irr) **I** v/t **1.** tun, machen; ausführen, Arbeiten verrichten; anfertigen, herstellen: ~ **one's best** sein Bestes tun, sich alle Mühe geben. **2.** j-m et. tun, zufügen, erweisen: → **disservice**, **favo(u)r** 4, etc. **3.** Speisen zubereiten. **4.** Zimmer aufräumen, machen. **5.** (her)richten: → **face** 1, **hair**. **6.** zurücklegen, schaffen: **the car does 100 m.p.h.** der Wagen fährt 160 km/h. **7.** F besichtigen, die Sehenswürdigkeiten besichtigen von (od. gen). **8.** F betrügen (**out of** um), übers Ohr hauen. **9.** F Strafe abbrummen: → **time** 1. **II** v/i **10.** handeln, sich verhalten. **11.** weiter-, vorankommen: ~ **well** gut abschneiden (**in** bei, in dat); s-e Sache gut machen. **12.** sich befinden: ~ **well** gesund sein; in guten Verhältnissen leben; sich gut erholen; **how ~ you ~?** guten Tag! (bei Vorstellung). **13.** genügen, reichen (**for** für). **III** v/t u. v/i **14.** (Ersatzverb zur Vermeidung von Wiederholungen; mst unübersetzt) **you know it as well as I ~** du weißt es so gut wie ich; **I take a bath. So ~ I** Ich nehme ein Bad. Ich auch; **he**

works hard, doesn't he? er arbeitet viel, nicht wahr?; **Did he buy it? He did** Kaufte er es? Ja(wohl); **He sold his car. Did he?** Er verkaufte sein Auto. Wirklich?, So? **IV** v/aux **15.** in Fragesätzen: ~ **you know him?** kennst du ihn? **16.** in verneinten Sätzen: **I ~ not believe it** ich glaube es nicht. **17.** zur Verstärkung: **I did like it** mir gefiel es wirklich.

Verbindungen mit Präpositionen:

do| by v/i behandeln, handeln an (dat). ~ **for** v/i F **1.** erledigen, ruinieren. **2.** j-m den Haushalt führen; putzen bei od. für. **3.** → **do¹** 13. ~ **with** v/t u. v/i **1. I can't do anything with him** (it) ich kann nichts mit ihm (damit) anfangen; **I won't have anything to ~ it** ich will nichts damit zu tun od. schaffen haben; **it has nothing to ~ you** es hat nichts mit dir zu tun. **2.** auskommen od. sich begnügen mit. **3.** F **he could ~ the money** er kann das Geld (sehr gut) brauchen; **I could ~ a glass of beer** ich könnte ein Glas Bier vertragen. ~ **with·out** v/i **1.** auskommen od. sich behelfen ohne. **2.** verzichten auf (acc).

Verbindungen mit Adverbien:

do| a·way with v/i **1.** beseitigen: a) wegschaffen, b) abschaffen. **2.** Geld durchbringen. **3.** umbringen, töten. ~ **down** v/t Br. F **1.** heruntermachen, schlechtmachen. **2.** → **do in** 2. ~ **in** v/t F **1.** erledigen: a) erschöpfen: **I'm done in** ich bin geschafft, b) zugrunde richten, ruinieren, c) um die Ecke bringen, umbringen. **2.** reinlegen, übers Ohr hauen. ~ **up** v/t **1.** zs.-schnüren; Päckchen etc zurechtmachen, verschnüren; einpakken; Kleid, Reißverschluß etc zumachen: **do s.o. up** j-m das Kleid etc zumachen. **2. do o.s. up** sich zurechtmachen; → **face** 1.

do² [∿] pl **dos, do's** [duːz] s **1.** sl. Schwindel m, Gaunerei f. **2. fair ~s!** F sei nicht unfair!; gleiches Recht für alle. **3.** ~**s and don'ts** F Gebote u. Verbote, (Spiel)Regeln.

doc [dɒk] F → **doctor** 1.

doc·ile [ˈdəʊsaɪl] adj □ **1.** fügsam, gefügig. **2.** gelehrig. **do·cil·i·ty** [~ˈsɪlətɪ] s **1.** Fügsamkeit f. **2.** Gelehrigkeit f.

dock¹ [dɒk] s **1.** Dock n. **2.** Hafenbekken n, Anlegeplatz m. **3.** Kai m, Pier m.

4. *pl* Docks *pl*, Hafenanlagen *pl.* **II** *v/t*
5. *Schiff* (ein)docken. **6.** *Raumschiffe*
koppeln. **III** *v/i* **7.** docken. **8.** im Hafen
od. am Kai anlegen. **9.** andocken
(*Raumschiff*).

dock² [~] *v/t* **1.** *Schwanz* stutzen; *e-m Tier*
den Schwanz stutzen. **2.** *j-s Lohn etc*
kürzen: ~ **£5 off** (*od.* **from**) **s.o.'s
wages** j-s Lohn um 5 Pfund kürzen.

dock³ [~] *s* 🕮 Anklagebank *f*: **be in the ~**
auf der Anklagebank sitzen.

dock·er ['dɔkə] *s* Dock-, Hafenarbeiter
m, Schauermann *m*.

'**dock·yard** *s* Werft *f.*

doc·tor ['dɔktə] I *s* **1.** Doktor *m*, Arzt *m*,
(*Anrede*) Herr Doktor: **be under the ~**
F in Behandlung sein (**for** wegen); **~'s
certificate** ärztliches Attest. **2.** *univ.*
Doktor *m*: ♀ **of Divinity** (**Laws**, **Medicine**) Doktor der Theologie (Rechte,
Medizin); **take one's ~'s degree**
promovieren. **II** *v/t* **3.** (ärztlich) behandeln, verarzten.
4. zs.-flicken, (notdürftig) ausbessern.
5. *a.* ~ **up** F *Wein etc* (ver)panschen,
Abrechnung etc frisieren. '**doc·tor·al**
adj: ~ **thesis** → **thesis 2. doc·tor·ate**
['~rət] *s* Doktorwürde *f*, -titel *m.*

doc·tri·naire [,dɔktri'neə] *adj* doktrinär.
doc·trine ['~trin] *s* Doktrin *f*: a) Lehre
f, b) *bsd. pol.* Grundsatz *m*: **party ~**
Parteiprogramm *n.*

doc·u·ment I *s* ['dɔkjumənt] Dokument
n: a) Urkunde *f*, b) amtliches Schriftstück, *pl* Akten *pl.* **II** *v/t* ['~mənt] dokumentieren, dokumentarisch *od.* urkundlich belegen. **doc·u·men·ta·ry**
[,~'mentəri] I *adj* □ **1.** dokumentarisch,
urkundlich. **2.** Dokumentar...: ~ **film**
→ 3; ~ **novel** Tatsachenroman *m.* **II** *s*
3. Dokumentar-, Tatsachenfilm *m.*
,**doc·u·men'ta·tion** *s* Dokumentation
f.

dod·der ['dɔdə] *v/i* F **1.** (*bsd. vor Altersschwäche*) zittern. **2.** wack(e)lig gehen.
'**dod·der·er** *s* F Tattergreis *m.* '**dod-
der·ing**, '**dod·der·y** *adj* F dattlig.

dodge [dɔdʒ] I *v/i* **1.** (rasch) zur Seite
springen, ausweichen. **2.** Ausflüchte
machen; sich drücken. **II** *v/t* **3.** ausweichen (*dat*). **4.** sich drücken vor (*dat*).
III *s* **5.** Sprung *m* zur Seite. **6.** Kniff *m*,
Trick *m.* **dodg·em** (**car**) ['dɔdʒəm] *s*
(Auto)Skooter *m.* '**dodg·er** *s* **1.** gerie-

bener Kerl. **2.** Gauner *m*, Schwindler
m. **3.** Drückeberger *m.* '**dodg·y** *adj* F **1.**
verschlagen, gerieben. **2.** *Br.* unsicher:
a) wack(e)lig, b) riskant.

doe [dəʊ] *s zo.* (Reh)Geiß *f.*

do·er ['duːə] *s* Tatmensch *m*, Macher *m.*

does [dʌz] *er, sie, es* tut (→ **do¹**).

'**doe·skin** *s* Rehleder *n.*

doesn't ['dʌznt] F = **does not** (→ **do¹**).

dog [dɔg] I *s* **1.** Hund *m*; *engS.* Rüde *m*:
~ **in the manger** j-d, der anderen et.
mißgönnt, womit er selbst gar nichts anfangen kann; ~ **does not eat** ~ e-e Krähe
hackt der anderen kein Auge aus; **go
to the ~s** vor die Hunde gehen; **lead a
~'s life** ein Hundeleben führen; **let
sleeping ~s lie** schlafende Hunde soll
man nicht wecken. **2.** *contp.* Schuft *m*:
dirty ~ Mistkerl *m.* **3.** F Kerl *m*: **lazy ~**
fauler Hund; **lucky ~** Glückspilz *m.* **4.**
the ~s *pl Br.* F das Windhundrennen. **II**
v/t **5.** *j-n* verfolgen (*a. Pech etc*). ~
bis·cuit *s* Hundekuchen *m.* ,~**·'cheap**
adj u. adv spottbillig. ~ **col·lar** *s* **1.**
Hundehalsband *n.* **2.** F steifer, hoher
Kragen (*e-s Geistlichen*). ~ **days** *s pl*
Hundstage *pl.* '~**·ear** *s* Eselsohr *n* (*in
Buch etc*). '~**·eared** *adj* mit Eselsohren.

dog·ged ['dɔgid] *adj* □ verbissen, hartnäckig.

dog·gie ['dɔgi] → **doggy.** '**dog·gish** *adj*
□ **1.** hundeartig, Hunde... **2.** bissig;
mürrisch. **dog·go** ['dɔgəʊ] *adv*: **lie ~** sl.
sich mäuschenstill verhalten; sich versteckt halten. '**dog·gy** *s* Hündchen *n*,
(*Kindersprache*) Wauwau *m*: ~ **bag**
*Beutel für Essensreste, die aus e-m
Restaurant mit nach Hause genommen
werden.*

dog·ma ['dɔgmə] *pl* **-mas**, **-ma·ta**
['~mətə] *s* Dogma *n*, Glaubens- *od.*
Grund- *od.* (*contp.* starrer) Lehrsatz.
dog·mat·ic [~'mætik] *adj* (~**ally**) dogmatisch.

,**dog·'poor** *adj* F bettelarm. ,~**·'tired** *adj*
hundemüde.

doi·ly ['dɔili] *s* (Zier)Deckchen *n.*

do·ing ['duːiŋ] *s* **1.** Tun *n*: **it was your** ~
du hast es getan, das war dein Werk. **2.**
pl Taten *pl*, Tätigkeit *f*, Begebenheiten
pl, Vorfälle *pl*; Treiben *n.* **3.** *pl* (*sg konstruiert*) *Br.* F Dingsbums *n.*

,**do-it-your'self** I *s* Heimwerken *n.* **II** *adj*
Heimwerker...: ~ **kit** Heimwerkeraus-

rüstung f; Bausatz m (für Radio etc); ~ **movement** Do-it-yourself-Bewegung f. **'do-it-your'self·er** s Heimwerker m.

dol·drums ['dɒldrəmz] s pl: **be in the ~** deprimiert od. niedergeschlagen sein, Trübsal blasen.

dole [dəʊl] **I** s **1.** milde Gabe. **2.** a. ~ **money** Br. F Stempelgeld n: **be** (od. **go**) **on the ~** stempeln gehen. **II** v/t **3.** ~ **out** sparsam ver- od. austeilen.

dole·ful ['dəʊlfʊl] adj □ traurig, (Gesicht etc a.) trübselig.

doll [dɒl] **I** s Puppe f (a. F hübsches, aber dummes Mädchen): ~**'s house** Br. Puppenhaus n; ~**'s pram** bsd. Br. F Puppenwagen m. **II** v/t: ~ **o.s. up** → III. **III** v/i: ~ **up** F sich feinmachen, sich in Schale werfen.

dol·lar ['dɒlə] s Dollar m.

doll‖ bug·gy s Am. F, ~ **car·riage** s Am. Puppenwagen m. '**~·house** s Am. Puppenhaus n.

dol·lop ['dɒləp] s F **1.** Klumpen m. **2.** Schlag m (Essensportion), Am. Schuß m (Alkohol etc, a. fig. Ironie etc).

doll·y ['dɒlɪ] s **1.** Kindersprache: Püppchen n. **2.** Film, TV: Kamerawagen m. **3.** a. ~ **bird** bsd. Br. F Püppchen n (hübsches, aber dummes Mädchen).

dol·phin ['dɒlfɪn] s zo. Delphin m.

dolt [dəʊlt] s Dummkopf m, Tölpel m.

do·main [dəʊ'meɪn] s Domäne f, fig. a. Gebiet n, Bereich m.

dome [dəʊm] s △ Kuppel f.

do·mes·tic [dəʊ'mestɪk] **I** adj (~ally) **1.** häuslich, Haus(halts)...: ~ **appliance** Haushaltsgerät n; ~ **science** ped. Hauswirtschaftslehre f; ~ **servant** (od. **help**) → 6. **2.** häuslich (veranlagt). **3.** Haus...: ~ **animal. 4.** inländisch, Inlands...: ~ **flight** Inlandsflug m; ~ **products** → 7; ~ **trade** Binnenhandel m. **5.** inner, Innen..., innenpolitisch: ~ **policy** Innenpolitik f. **II** s **6.** Hausangestellte m, f, pl a. (Dienst)Personal n. **7.** pl ✝ Landesprodukte pl, inländische Erzeugnisse pl. **do'mes·ti·cate** [~keɪt] v/t **1.** an häusliches Leben gewöhnen. **2.** Tier zähmen.

dom·i·cile ['dɒmɪsaɪl] **I** s **1.** (st̲s ständiger) Wohnsitz. **2.** ✝ Sitz m (e-r Gesellschaft); Zahlungsort m (für e-n Wechsel). **II** v/t **3.** ansässig od. wohnhaft machen. **4.** ✝ Wechsel domizilieren.

'dom·i·ciled adj ansässig, wohnhaft.

dom·i·nance ['dɒmɪnəns] s **1.** (Vor-) Herrschaft f. **2.** Macht f, Einfluß m. **'dom·i·nant I** adj □ **1.** dominierend, (vor)herrschend. **2.** beherrschend: a) bestimmend, tonangebend, b) emporragend, weithin sichtbar. **II** s **3.** ♪ Dominante f. **dom·i·nate** ['~neɪt] **I** v/t beherrschen (a. fig.): a) herrschen über (acc), b) emporragen über (acc), c) dominieren od. (vor)herrschen in (dat). **II** v/i dominieren, vorherrschen: ~ **over** herrschen über (acc). **,dom·i'na·tion** s (Vor)Herrschaft f. **dom·i·neer** [~'nɪə] v/i **1.** (over) despotisch herrschen (über acc). **2.** anmaßend sein od. auftreten. **,dom·i'neer·ing** adj □ **1.** tyrannisch, despotisch. **2.** anmaßend.

do·min·ion [dəʊ'mɪnjən] s **1.** (Ober)Herrschaft f; Regierungsgewalt f. **2.** (Herrschafts)Gebiet n. **3.** oft ⊆ obs. Dominion n (im Commonwealth).

dom·i·no ['dɒmɪnəʊ] pl **-no(e)s** s a) pl (mst sg konstruiert) Domino(spiel) n, b) Dominostein m.

don [dɒn] v/t et. anziehen, Hut aufsetzen.

do·nate [dəʊ'neɪt] v/t schenken (a. st̲s), a. Blut etc spenden (**to s.o.** j-m). **do'na·tion** s Schenkung f, Spende f.

done [dʌn] **I** pp **von do'. II** adj **1.** getan: **it isn't ~** (od. **the ~ thing**) so et. tut man nicht, das gehört sich nicht. **2.** erledigt: **get s.th. ~** erledigen (lassen). **3.** gastr. gar: **well ~** durchgebraten. **4.** F fertig: **have ~ with** fertig sein mit (a. fig.); nichts mehr zu tun haben wollen mit; nicht mehr brauchen. **5.** ~**!** abgemacht!

don·key ['dɒŋkɪ] s zo. Esel m (a. fig. contp.): ~**'s years** Br. F e-e Ewigkeit. '~·**work** s F Dreck(s)arbeit f.

do·nor ['dəʊnə] s Schenker(in) (a. st̲s), (a. Blut- etc)Spender(in): ~**('s) card** Organspenderausweis m.

don't [dəʊnt] **I** F = **do not** (→ **do'**). **II** s pl → **do²** 3.

doo·dle ['duːdl] **I** s Gekritzel n, gedankenlos hingekritzelte Figur(en pl). **II** v/i Männchen malen.

doom [duːm] **I** s Schicksal n, Geschick n, Verhängnis n: **he met his ~** sein Schicksal ereilte ihn. **II** v/t verurteilen, verdammen (beide a. fig.): ~**ed to failure** (od. **to fail**) zum Scheitern verurteilt.

dooms·day ['du:mzdeɪ] s Jüngstes Gericht, Jüngster Tag.

door [dɔ:] s 1. Tür f: from ~ to ~ von Haus zu Haus; out of ~s ins Freie, hinaus; im Freien, draußen; two ~s down the street zwei Häuser weiter; bang (od. close, shut) the ~ on j-n abweisen; et. unmöglich machen; lay s.th. at s.o.'s ~ j-m et. zur Last legen; show s.o. the ~ j-m die Tür weisen. 2. Tor n, Pforte f (to zu) (beide a. fig.). '~·bell s Türklingel f, -glocke f: ring the ~ (an der Tür) klingeln od. läuten. ~·chain s Sicherheitskette f. '~·frame s Türrahmen m. ~·han·dle s Türgriff m, -klinke f. '~·keep·er s Pförtner m. '~·knock·er s Türklopfer m. '~·man s (irr man) (livrierter) Portier. ~ mat s (Fuß)Abtreter m. '~·plate s Türschild n. '~·post s Türpfosten m. '~·step s Türstufe f: at (od. on) s.o.'s ~ vor j-s Tür (a. fig.). ~-to-'~ adj von Haus zu Haus; Verkauf an der Haustür: ~ collection Haussammlung f; ~ salesman Hausierer m; Vertreter m. '~·way s 1. Türöffnung f. 2. fig. Weg m (to zu). '~·yard s Am. Vorgarten m.

dope [dəʊp] I s I. F Stoff m (Rauschgift). 2. a) Sport: Dopingmittel n, b) Betäubungsmittel n. 3. sl. Trottel m. 4. sl. a) oft inside ~ (vertrauliche) Informationen pl, Geheimtip(s pl) m, b) allg. Information(en pl) f, Material n. II v/t 5. F j-m Stoff geben. 6. a) Sport: dopen, b) Getränk etc präparieren, ein Betäubungsmittel untermischen (dat). ~ ad·dict, ~ fiend s F Rauschgiftsüchtige m, f. ~ test s Sport: Dopingkontrolle f. dop·ey ['dəʊpɪ] adj F 1. benommen, benebelt. 2. dämlich, doof.

dorm [dɔ:m] F → dormitory.

dor·mant ['dɔ:mənt] adj 1. schlafend. 2. fig. ruhend, (a. Vulkan) untätig. 3. fig. schlummernd, verborgen, latent: lie ~ schlummern.

dor·mer ['dɔ:mə] s a) (Dach)Gaupe f, (-)Gaube f, b) a. ~ window stehendes Dachfenster.

dor·mi·to·ry ['dɔ:mɪtərɪ] s 1. Schlafsaal m. 2. (bsd. Studenten)Wohnheim n. ~ sub·urb, ~ town s Schlafstadt f.

dor·sal ['dɔ:sl] adj Rücken...: ~ fin Rückenflosse f.

dos·age ['dəʊsɪdʒ] s 1. Dosierung f. 2.

→ dose 1. **dose** [dəʊs] I s 1. ✿ Dosis f (a. fig.). II v/t 2. Arznei etc dosieren. 3. j-m Arznei geben.

doss [dɒs] bsd. Br. sl. I s 1. Schlafplatz m. 2. Schlaf m. 3. Penne f. II v/i 4. oft ~ down pennen. 'doss·er s bsd. Br. sl. 1. Pennbruder m. 2. Penne f.

'**doss·house** s bsd. Br. sl. Penne f.

dos·si·er ['dɒsɪeɪ] s Dossier n, Akten pl: keep a ~ on ein Dossier angelegt haben über (acc).

dot [dɒt] I s 1. Punkt m, Pünktchen n; Tupfen m: on the ~ F auf die Sekunde pünktlich; at 8 o'clock on the ~ F Punkt 8 Uhr; → year. II v/t 2. punktieren, punkteln: sign on the ~ted line unterschreiben; (formell od. bedingungslos) zustimmen. 3. sprenkeln, übersäen (with mit).

dot·age ['dəʊtɪdʒ] s 1. Senilität f: be in one's ~ kindisch od. senil sein. 2. Vernarrtheit f (on in acc). **dote** [dəʊt] v/i vernarrt sein (on in acc). 'dot·ing adj □ 1. vernarrt (on in acc). 2. kindisch, senil.

dou·ble ['dʌbl] I adj □ 1. doppelt, Doppel..., zweifach: ~ bottom doppelter Boden; ~ murder Doppelmord m. 2. Doppel..., verdoppelt, verstärkt: ~ beer Starkbier n. 3. Doppel... (für 2 bestimmt): ~ bed Doppelbett n; ~ room Doppel-, Zweibettzimmer n. 4. zweideutig. II adv 5. doppelt: ~ as long noch einmal so lang. 6. doppelt, zweifach: play (at) ~ or quit(s) alles riskieren od. aufs Spiel setzen; see ~ doppelt sehen. III s 7. das Doppelte od. Zweifache. 8. Doppel n, Duplikat n. 9. Doppelgänger(in). 10. Film, TV: Double n. 11. mst pl Tennis etc: Doppel n: a ~ match ein Doppel; men's ~s Herrendoppel. IV v/t 12. verdoppeln. 13. oft ~ up Papier etc kniffen, falten, Bettdecke etc um-, zurückschlagen; zs.-falten, -legen. 14. ♣ umsegeln, umschiffen. 15. Film, TV: j-n doubeln. V v/i 16. sich verdoppeln. 17. sich (zs.-)falten (lassen); ~ up sich krümmen vor (dat). 18. plötzlich kehrtmachen; e-n Haken schlagen. '~-bar·rel(l)ed adj 1. doppelläufig: ~ gun Doppelflinte f, Zwilling m. 2. zweifach: ~ name Doppelname m. 3. zweideutig. ~ bend s S-Kurve f. ~'breast·ed adj zweireihig (Anzug).

~ check s genaue Nachprüfung. ,**~·'check** v/t u. v/i genau nachprüfen. **~ chin** s Doppelkinn n. **~ cross** s F doppeltes od. falsches Spiel. ,**~·'cross** v/t F ein doppeltes od. falsches Spiel treiben mit. ,**~·'deal·er** s Betrüger m. ,**~·'deal·ing I** adj betrügerisch. **II** s Betrug m. ,**~·'deck·er** s 1. Doppeldecker m (Autobus, Flugzeug etc). 2. F Etagenbett n; Doppelsandwich n. **~ Dutch** s F Kauderwelsch n. ,**~·'edged** adj 1. zweischneidig (a. fig.). 2. fig. zweideutig. '**~·faced** adj heuchlerisch, unaufrichtig. **~ fea·ture** s Doppelprogramm n (2 Spielfilme in jeder Vorstellung). **~ life** s (irr life) Doppelleben n. ,**~·'park** v/t u. v/i mot. in zweiter Reihe parken. ,**~·'quick I** s → **double time. II** adj: in **~ time** → III. **III** adv F im Eiltempo, fix. **~ stand·ard** s: apply ~s mit zweierlei Maß messen. **~ talk** s hinhaltendes od. nichtssagendes Gerede; doppelzüngiges Gerede; Augen(aus)wischerei f. **~ time** s 1. ✕ Am. Schnellschritt m: in ~ F im Eiltempo, fix. 2. doppelter Lohn (für Feiertagsarbeit etc).

doubt [daut] **I** v/t 1. zweifeln (of an e-r Sache). 2. Bedenken haben. **II** v/t 3. bezweifeln (a. that daß), anzweifeln. 4. mißtrauen (dat). **III** s 5. Zweifel m (of an dat; about hinsichtlich): no (od. without, beyond) ~ zweifellos, fraglos; be in ~ Zweifel haben (about an dat); ungewiß sein; unschlüssig sein; cast (od. throw) ~ on et. in Zweifel ziehen; if (od. when) in ~ im Zweifelsfall; leave no ~s about keinen Zweifel lassen an (dat). '**doubt·er** s Zweifler(in). **doubt·ful** ['~ful] adj □ 1. allg. zweifelhaft. 2. be ~ of (od. about) zweifeln an (dat), im Zweifel sein über (acc). '**doubt·less** adv zweifellos, sicherlich.

dough [dəu] s 1. Teig m. 2. bsd. Am. sl. Kohlen pl (Geld). '**~·nut** s Krapfen m, Berliner (Pfannkuchen).

dough·y ['dəuɪ] adj 1. teigig. 2. fig. teigig, wächsern (Gesicht).

dour [duə] adj 1. mürrisch. 2. hart, streng. 3. hartnäckig, halsstarrig.

douse [daus] v/t 1. ins Wasser tauchen, eintauchen; Wäsche etc einweichen; Wasser schütten über (acc). 2. F Licht ausmachen.

dove [dʌv] s 1. orn. Taube f: ~ of peace fig. Friedenstaube f. 2. pol. Taube f (gemäßigter Politiker).

dow·dy ['daudɪ] adj □ nachlässig gekleidet; unelegant; unmodern.

dow·el ['dauəl] s ⊙ Dübel m.

down¹ [daun] **I** adv 1. nach unten, her-, hinunter, abwärts, (in Kreuzworträtseln) senkrecht. 2. go ~ to the country (von London) aufs Land fahren. 3. ~ with ...! nieder mit ...! 4. (dr)unten: ~ there dort unten; ~ under F in od. nach Australien od. Neuseeland (→ **down under**). 5. untergegangen (Sonne etc). 6. gefallen (Preise, Thermometer etc): ~ by 10 degrees um 10 Grad gefallen. 7. niedergeschlagen, down: ~ mouth 1. 8. bettlägerig: be ~ with influenza mit Grippe im Bett liegen. 9. they were 2 points (goals) ~ (Sport) sie lagen 2 Punkte (Tore) zurück. **II** adj 10. nach unten (gerichtet), Abwärts... 11. von London abfahrend od. kommend: ~ platform Abfahrtsbahnsteig m (in London). **III** prp 12. her-, hinunter: ~ the river flußabwärts. **IV** s 13. have a ~ on F j-n auf dem Kieker haben. **V** v/t 14. zu Fall bringen (a. Sport u. fig.). 15. niederlegen: ~ tools die Arbeit niederlegen. 16. Flugzeug abschießen. 17. F Getränk runterkippen.

down² [~] s 1. orn. Daunen pl: ~ quilt Daunendecke f. 2. (a. Bart)Flaum m. '**down|·cast** adj 1. niedergeschlagen: a) gesenkt (Blick), b) deprimiert. '**~·fall** s 1. fig. Sturz m. 2. starker Regenguß, Platzregen m, a. starker Schneefall. '**~·grade** v/t 1. niedriger einstufen. 2. degradieren. ,**~·'heart·ed** adj □ niedergeschlagen, entmutigt. ,**~·'hill** I adv 1. abwärts, bergab (beide a. fig.), den Berg hinunter: he is going ~ es geht bergab mit ihm; the rest was ~ (all the way) alles andere ging wie von selbst. **II** adj 2. abschüssig. 3. Skisport: Abfahrts...: ~ race Abfahrtslauf m. ~ pay·ment s 1. Barzahlung f. 2. Anzahlung f. '**~·pour** s Platzregen m. '**~·right** adj u. adv völlig, absolut, ausgesprochen: a ~ lie e-e glatte Lüge. ,**~·'stairs I** adv 1. die Treppe her- od. hinunter, nach unten. 2. unten, im unteren Stockwerk. 3. e-e Treppe tiefer. **II** adj ['~steəz] 4. im unteren Stockwerk (gelegen), unter. ,**~·'stream** adv fluß-

ab(wärts). **~-to-'earth** *adj* realistisch.
~town *Am.* **I** *adv* [~'taʊn] im *od.* ins
Geschäftsviertel. **II** *adj* ['~taʊn] im Geschäftsviertel (gelegen *od.* tätig): *in ~
Los Angeles* in der Innenstadt von Los
Angeles. **III** *s* ['~taʊn] Geschäftsviertel
n, Innenstadt *f*, City *f.* '**~,trod·den** *adj*
unterdrückt. **~ un·der** *s* F Australien *n*;
Neuseeland *n.*

down·ward ['daʊnwəd] **I** *adv* **1.** nach
unten: *face ~* mit dem Gesicht nach
unten. **2.** *fig.* abwärts, bergab: *he went
~ in life* es ging bergab mit ihm. **3.** *from
... ~ (zeitlich)* von ... ab, seit. **II** *adj* **4.**
Abwärts..., (*Preise*) sinkend. **down·
wards** ['~wədz] → **downward** I.

down·y ['daʊnɪ] *adj* **1.** Daunen... **2.** flaumig.

dow·ry ['daʊərɪ] *s* Mitgift *f*, Aussteuer *f.*

dowse¹ → **douse.**

dowse² [daʊz] *v/i* mit der Wünschelrute
(Wasser *etc*) suchen. '**dows·er** *s* (Wün-
schel)Rutengänger *m.* '**dows·ing rod** *s*
Wünschelrute *f.*

doy·en [dɔɪ'en] *s* **1.** Rangälteste *m.* **2.**
Doyen *m.* **3.** Nestor *m.*

doze [daʊz] **I** *v/i* dösen, ein Nickerchen
machen *od.* halten: **~ off** einnicken, -dö-
sen. **II** *s* Nickerchen *n*: *have a ~* → I.

doz·en ['dʌzn] *s* Dutzend *n*: *~s of times*
F x-mal; *do one's daily ~* Früh-*od.*
Morgengymnastik machen; *talk nineteen (od. twenty, forty) to the ~* Br. wie
ein Wasserfall reden; → **baker.**

doz·y ['daʊzɪ] *adj* □ **1.** schläfrig, verschlafen, dösig. **2.** *Br.* F schwer von
Begriff.

drab [dræb] *adj* **1.** graubraun. **2.** *fig.*
trist: a) grau (*Stadt etc*), b) düster (*Farben etc*), c) langweilig (*Abend etc*), d)
freudlos (*Dasein etc*)

Dra·co·ni·an [drə'kəʊnjən] *adj* drakonisch.

draft [drɑːft] **I** *s* **1.** Entwurf *m.* **2.** (Luft-
etc)Zug *m*: *feel the draught Br.* F den
Wind im Gesicht spüren. **3.** *make a ~
on* Geld abheben von; *fig.* in Anspruch
nehmen. **4.** ✝ Tratte *f*, Wechsel *m.* **5.**
✕ *Am.* Einberufung *f*, Einziehung *f.* **6.**
→ **draught** I. **II** *v/t* **7.** entwerfen,
Schriftstück abfassen. **8.** ✕ *Am.* einziehen (*into* zu), einberufen.

drafts·man ['drɑːftsmən] *s* (*irr man*)
1. *j-d*, der *et.* *entwirft od. aufsetzt.*

2. ⊙ (Konstruktions)Zeichner *m.*

draft·y ['drɑːftɪ] *adj* zugig.

drag [dræg] **I** *s* **1.** Schleppen *n*, Zerren *n.*
2. Hemmschuh *m* (*a. fig. on* für). **3.** F a)
et. Langweiliges *od.* Lästiges: *be a ~!*
langweilig sein; *what a ~!* so ein Mist!,
b) Langweiler *m*; lästiger Kerl. **4.** *Am.* F
Einfluß *m*: *use one's ~* s-e Beziehungen spielen lassen. **5.** F Zug *m* (*at, on* an
e-r Zigarette *etc*): *give me a ~* laß mich
mal ziehen. **6.** F (*von Männern, bsd. von
Transvestiten, getragene*) Frauenklei-
dung. **II** *v/t* **7.** schleppen, zerren, schleifen, ziehen: → **mire, mud.** **2.** **~** *one's
feet* a) schlurfen, b) *a. ~ one's heels
fig.* sich Zeit lassen (*over, in, about*
mit, bei). **9.** *fig.* hineinziehen (*into* in
acc). **10.** F *j-n* langweilen; *j-m* lästig
sein. **III** *v/t* **11.** (am Boden) schleppen
od. schleifen. **12.** → **drag behind. 13.**
zerren (*at* an *dat*). **14.** F ziehen (*at, on*
an e-r Zigarette *etc*).
Verbindungen mit Adverbien:

drag| a·long I *v/t* wegschleppen, -zer-
ren. **II** *v/i* sich dahinschleppen. **~ a·way**
v/t → **drag along** I: *drag o.s. away
from fig.* sich losreißen von. **~ be·hind**
v/i zurückbleiben, nachhinken. **~ down**
v/t **1.** herunter-, hinunterziehen; *fig.* in
den Schmutz ziehen. **2.** *fig.* zermürben
(*Krankheit etc*); entmutigen. **~ in** *v/t* **1.**
herein-, hineinziehen. **2.** *fig.* (mit) hineinziehen. **~ off** *v/t* → **drag away.** **~ on** I
v/t **drag s.o. off to a party** F *j-n* auf e-e
Party schleppen. **~ on** I *v/t* weiter-
schleppen. **II** *v/i* *fig.* sich dahinschleppen; sich in die Länge ziehen: *the
speech dragged on for two hours* die
Rede zog sich über zwei Stunden hin. **~
out** *v/t* **1.** heraus-, hinausziehen. **2.** *fig.*
hinausziehen, in die Länge ziehen. **~ up**
v/t **1.** hochziehen. **2.** F *Kind* lieblos aufziehen. **3.** F *Skandal etc* ausgraben.

dra·gée [dræ'ʒeɪ] *s* Dragée *n* (*a. pharm.*).

'**drag|·lift** *s* Schlepplift *m.* '**~·net** *s* **1.**
Schleppnetz *n*: *~ operation* Schlepp-
netzfahndung *f.* **2.** *fig.* Netz *n* (*der Polizei etc*).

drag·on ['drægən] *s* Drache *m.* '**~·fly** *s*
zo. Libelle *f.*

drain [dreɪn] **I** *v/t* **1.** *a. ~ off (od. away)
Flüssigkeit* abfließen lassen: **~ off** ab-
tropfen lassen; *Gemüse* abgießen. **2.** ✍
Eiter etc drainieren. **3.** austrinken, lee-

ren: → **dreg** 1. **4.** *Land* entwässern. **5.** *Gebäude etc* kanalisieren. **6.** *j-n, Vorräte etc* erschöpfen. **II** *v/i* **7.** ~ **off** (*od.* **away**) abfließen, ablaufen. **8.** leerlaufen. **9.** abtropfen. **10.** *a.* ~ **away** *fig.* dahinschwinden. **III** *v/i* **11.** → **drainage** 1–3. **12.** Abzugskanal *m,* Entwässerungsgraben *m.* **13.** *pl* Kanalisation *f.* **14.** *fig.* Abfluß *m.* **15.** *fig.* Belastung *f* (**on** *gen*). '**drain·age** *s* **1.** Ableitung *f.* **2.** Abfließen *n,* Ablaufen *n.* **3.** Entwässerung *f.* **4.** Kanalisation *f.* **5.** ⚕ Drainage *f.*

'**drain·pipe** *s* **1.** Abflußrohr *n:* ~ **trousers** → 3. **2.** Fallrohr *n* (*der Dachrinne*). **3.** *pl, a.* **pair of** ~**s** F Röhrenhose(n *pl*) *f.*

drake [dreɪk] *s orn.* Enterich *m,* Erpel *m.*

dram [dræm] *s* F Schluck *m* (*Alkohol*): **be fond of a** ~ gern einen trinken.

dra·ma ['drɑːmə] *s* Drama *m* (*a. fig.*): ~ **critic** Theaterkritiker(in); ~ **school** Schauspielschule *f.* **dra·mat·ic** [drə'mætɪk] **I** *adj* (~**ally**) **1.** dramatisch (*a.* ♪ *u. fig.*), Schauspiel..., Theater...: ~ **critic** Theaterkritiker(in). **2.** *fig.* dramatisch (*Beispiel, Veränderungen etc*); aufsehenerregend (*Rede etc*). **II** *s pl* **3.** (*a. sg konstruiert*) Dramaturgie *f.* **4.** theatralisches Getue.

dram·a·tis per·so·nae [ˌdrɑːmətɪspɜː'səʊnaɪ] *s pl* Personen *pl* der Handlung. **dram·a·tist** ['dræmətɪst] *s* Dramatiker *m.* **dram·a·tize** ['~taɪz] *v/t* dramatisieren: a) für die Bühne bearbeiten, b) *fig.* aufbauschen, (*a. v/i*) übertreiben.

drank [dræŋk] *pret von* **drink.**

drape [dreɪp] *v/t* **1.** drapieren (**with** mit): a) (mit Stoff) behängen, b) in (dekorative) Falten legen. **2.** *Mantel etc* hängen (**over** über *acc*). '**drap·er** *s Br.* Textilkaufmann *m.* '**drap·er·y** *s* **1.** Textilien *pl.* **2.** *bsd. Am.* Vorhänge *pl,* Vorhangstoffe *pl.*

dras·tic ['dræstɪk] *adj* (~**ally**) drastisch.

draught [drɑːft] **I** *s* **1.** Zug *m,* Schluck *m:* **at a** ~ in einem Zug. **2.** **beer on** ~, ~ **beer** Bier *n* vom Faß, Faßbier. **3.** *Br.* a) *pl* (*sg konstruiert*) Dame(spiel *n*) *f,* b) → **draughtsman** 1. **4.** a) *bsd. Br. für* **draft** 2, b) *selten bsd. Br. für* **draft** 1, 4. **II** *v/t* **5.** *selten bsd. Br. für* **draft** 7. '~**·board** *s Br.* Damebrett *n.*

draughts·man *s* (*irr man*) **1.** ['drɑːfts-

mæn] *Br.* Damestein *m.* **2.** ['drɑːftsmən] *selten bsd. Br. für* **draftsman.**

draught·y ['drɑːftɪ] *bsd. Br. für* **drafty.**

draw [drɔː] **I** *s* **1.** Ziehen *n;* Zug *m* (*a. an der Pfeife etc*). **2.** Ziehung *f,* Verlosung *f.* **3.** *fig.* Zugkraft *f.* **4.** *fig.* Attraktion *f* (*a. Person*), Zugstück *n.* **5.** *Sport:* Unentschieden *n:* **end in a** ~ unentschieden ausgehen. **II** *v/t* (*irr*) **6.** *Waffe, Zahn etc, fig. Schluß etc* ziehen; *Vorhänge* auf- *od.* zuziehen; *Bogen* spannen: ~ *s.o.* **into** *fig.* j-n hineinziehen in (*acc*). **7.** bringen (**on** über *acc*): ~ *s.o.'s* **anger on o.s.** sich j-s Zorn zuziehen. **8.** *Atem* holen: ~ **a sigh** aufseufzen. **9.** *Tee* ziehen lassen. **10.** auslosen. **11.** *fig.* anziehen: **feel** ~**n to(ward[s])** *s.o.* sich zu j-m hingezogen fühlen. **12.** *Linie, Grenze etc, fig. Vergleich etc* ziehen. **13.** zeichnen. **14.** *Schriftstück* abfassen, aufsetzen; *Scheck* ausstellen, *Wechsel* a. ziehen (**on** auf *acc*). **15.** *Geld* abheben (**from** von); *Rente etc* beziehen. **16.** entlocken (**from** *dat*): ~ **applause** Beifall hervorrufen; ~ (**information from**) *s.o.* j-n aushorchen. **17.** entnehmen (**from** *dat*): ~ **consolation from** Trost schöpfen aus; ~ **inspiration from** sich Anregung holen von *od.* bei *od.* durch. **III** *v/i* (*irr*) **18.** ziehen (*a. Tee, Kamin etc*). **19.** (**to**) sich nähern (*dat*), herankommen (**an** *acc*): → **end** 8. **20.** (**on**) in Anspruch nehmen (*acc*), Gebrauch machen (**von**), (*Vorräte etc*) angreifen. **21.** *Sport:* unentschieden kämpfen *od.* spielen (**with** gegen), sich unentschieden trennen. **22.** losen (**for** um).

Verbindungen mit Adverbien:

draw| **a·part I** *v/t* auseinanderziehen. **II** *v/i* sich entfernen (**from** von), sich voneinander entfernen, *fig.* a. sich auseinanderleben. ~ **a·side** *v/t* j-n beiseite nehmen. ~ **a·way I** *v/t* **1.** wegziehen. **2.** *j-s Aufmerksamkeit* ablenken. **II** *v/i* **3.** sich entfernen; (*Sport*) sich lösen (**from** von). ~ **down** *v/t* **1.** herabziehen, *Jalousien* herunterlassen. **2.** → **draw** 7. ~ **in I** *v/t* **1.** *Luft* einziehen. **2.** *j-n* (mit) hineinziehen. **II** *v/i* **3.** einfahren (*Zug*), vorfahren (*Wagen etc*). **4.** zu Ende gehen (*Tag*); abnehmen, kürzer werden (*Tage*). ~ **off** *v/t* *Handschuhe etc* ausziehen. ~ **on** *v/t* *Handschuhe etc* anziehen. ~ **out I** *v/t* **1.** herausziehen. **2.** *fig.* Aussage *etc* herausholen (*of, from* aus); *j-n* aushorchen. **3.** *fig.* hinausziehen, in die Länge ziehen. **II** *v/i* **4.** länger werden (*Tage*). **~ up** *v/t* **1.** aufrichten. **2.** *Schriftstück* abfassen, aufsetzen. **II** *v/i* **3.** (an)halten (*Wagen etc*). **4.** vorfahren (**to** vor *dat*).

'draw|-back *s* Nachteil *m* (**to** für). **'~-bridge** *s* Zugbrücke *f*.

draw·ee [drɔːˈiː] *s* ✝ Bezogene *m*.

draw·er [*1, 2:* drɔː; *3, 4:* ˈdrɔːə] *s* **1.** Schublade *f*, -fach *n* **2.** *pl, a.* **pair of ~s** Unterhose *f*. **3.** Zeichner *m*. **4.** ✝ Aussteller *m*.

draw·ing [ˈdrɔːɪŋ] *s* **1.** Zeichnen *n*. **2.** Zeichnung *f*. *~s* Zeichenblock *m*. **~ board** *s* Reiß-, Zeichenbrett *n*: **go back to the ~** *fig.* noch einmal von vorne anfangen. **~ pin** *s* *Br.* Reißzwecke *f*, -nagel *m*. **~ room** *s* Gesellschaftszimmer *n*, Salon *m*.

drawl [drɔːl] **I** *v/t u. v/i* gedehnt *od.* schleppend sprechen. **II** *s* gedehntes Sprechen.

drawn [drɔːn] **I** *pp von* **draw**. **II** *adj* *Sport:* unentschieden: **~ game** Unentschieden *n*.

dread [dred] **I** *v/t etc.*, *j-n* sehr fürchten, sich fürchten (**to do, doing** zu tun), (große) Angst haben *od.* sich fürchten vor (*dat*). **II** *s* (große) Angst, Furcht *f* (**of** vor *dat*). **dread·ful** [ˈ~fʊl] **I** *adj* □ furchtbar, schrecklich (*beide a. fig.* F). **II** *s* → **penny dreadful**.

dream [driːm] **I** *s* **1.** Traum *m*: **have a ~ about** träumen von; **pleasant ~s!** träum was Schönes! **2.** *fig.* Traum *m*: **a)** Wunschtraum *m*: **that's beyond my wildest ~s** das übertrifft me kühnsten Träume, **b)** Ideal *n*: **a ~ of a hat** ein Gedicht *n* von e-m Hut; **a perfect ~** traumhaft schön. **II** *v/i* (*a. irr*) **3.** träumen (*of, about* von) (*a. fig.*): **~ of doing s.th.** davon träumen, et. zu tun; daran denken, et. zu tun (*a. irr*) **4.** träumen (*a. fig.*): **~ away** verträumen; **~ up** F sich ausdenken *od.* einfallen lassen. **'dream·er** *s* Träumer(in) (*a. fig.*).

dream read·er *s* Traumdeuter(in).

dream·y [dremt] *pret u. pp von* **dream**.

dream·y [ˈdriːmɪ] *adj* □ **1.** verträumt (*a. Augen*), träumerisch. **2.** dunkel, verschwommen (*Erinnerung*). **3.** zum Träumen: **~ music**.

drear·y [ˈdrɪərɪ] *adj* □ **1.** trübselig (*Ort etc*). **2.** trüb (*Tag etc*). **3.** langweilig (*Person, Arbeit etc*).

dredge¹ [dredʒ] ⚙ **I** *s* Bagger *m*. **II** *v/t* ausbaggern.

dredge² [~] *v/t* **1.** bestreuen (**with** mit). **2.** *Mehl etc* streuen (**over** über *acc*).

dredg·er¹ [ˈdredʒə] *s* ⚙ Bagger *m*.

dredg·er² [~] *s* Streubüchse *f*, Streuer *m*.

dreg [dreg] *s mst pl* **1.** (Boden)Satz *m*: **drain to the ~s** bis auf den letzten Tropfen *od.* bis zur Neige leeren. **2.** *fig.* Abschaum *m*.

drench [drentʃ] *v/t* durchnässen: **~ed in tears** in Tränen aufgelöst; → **skin** 1.

dress [dres] **I** *s* **1.** Kleidung *f*. **2.** (Damen)Kleid *n*. **II** *v/t* **3.** an-, bekleiden, anziehen: **~ o.s., get ~ed** sich anziehen; → **kill** 9. **4.** einkleiden. **5.** schmücken, dekorieren. **6.** zurechtmachen, (her-)richten, *bsd. Speisen* zubereiten: *Salat* anmachen; *Haar* frisieren. **7.** ⚕ *Wunde etc* verbinden. **III** *v/i* **8.** sich anziehen: **~ well (badly)** weit*S.* sich geschmackvoll (geschmacklos) kleiden.

Verbindungen mit Adverbien:

dress| down *v/t* F *j-m* e-e Standpauke halten, *j-m* aufs Dach steigen. **II** *v/i* sich unauffällig kleiden. **~ up** *v/t* **1.** feinmachen; herausputzen. **2.** *Fakten etc* verpacken (**in** in *acc*); beschönigen; ausschmücken (**with** mit). **II** *v/i* **3.** feinmachen; sich herausputzen. **4.** sich kostümieren *od.* verkleiden (**as** als).

dress| cir·cle *s* *thea. etc* erster Rang. **~ coat** *s* Frack *m*.

dress·er [ˈdresə] *s* **1.** *thea.* Garderobiere *f*. **2.** **be a fashionable ~** immer modisch gekleidet sein. **3.** Küchen-, Geschirrschrank *m*. **4.** → **dressing table**.

dress·ing [ˈdresɪŋ] *s* **1.** Ankleiden *n*. **2.** Zubereitung *f*. **3.** Dressing *n* (*Salatsoße*). **4.** ⚕ Verband *m*. **,~'down** *s* F Standpauke *f*: **give** *s.o.* **a ~** → **dress down** I; **get a ~** eins aufs Dach bekommen. **~ gown** *s* Morgenmantel *m*, (*für Damen a.*) Morgenrock *m*. **~ room** *s* Ankleidezimmer *n*; (*Künstler*)Garderobe *f*; (*Sport*) (Umkleide)Kabine *f*. **~ ta·ble** *s* Toilettentisch *m*, Frisierkommode *f*.

'dress|,mak·er *s* (*bsd.* Damen)Schneider(in). **~ re·hears·al** *s* *thea.* Generalprobe *f* (*a. fig.*); Kostümprobe *f*. **~ shirt**

s Frackhemd *n*. ~ **suit** *s* Abend-, Gesellschaftsanzug *m*.

dress·y ['dresɪ] *adj* □ F **1.** geschniegelt, aufgetakelt. **2.** elegant, schick.

drew [druː] *pret von* **draw**.

drib·ble ['drɪbl] I *v/i* **1.** tröpfeln: ~ *away fig.* allmählich zu Ende gehen (*Geld etc*). **2.** sabbern, geifern. **3.** *Sport*: dribbeln: ~ *past j-n* umdribbeln. II *v/t* **4.** tröpfeln lassen, träufeln. III *s* **5.** → **drib(b)let. 6.** *Sport*: Dribbling *n*.

drib·(b)let ['drɪblɪt] *s* kleine Menge *od.* Summe: *in (od. by)* ~s in kleinen Mengen *od.* Raten.

dribs and drabs [drɪbz] *s pl*: *in* ~ F kleckerweise.

dried [draɪd] *adj* Dörr..., getrocknet: ~ *fruit* Dörrobst *n*; ~ *milk* Trockenmilch *f.* Trockner *m*.}

dri·er ['draɪə] *s* Trockenapparat *m*,}

drift [drɪft] I *s* **1.** Treiben *n*; *fig.* (Sich-)Treibenlassen *n*, Ziellosigkeit *f.* **2.** ✈ ⚓ Abtrift *f.* **3.** *fig.* Strömung *f*, Tendenz *f*; Absicht *f*; Gedankengang *m*. **4.** (*Schnee*)Verwehung *f*, (*Schnee-, Sand-*)Wehe *f.* II *v/i* **5.** getrieben werden, treiben (*a. fig.* intr in *e-n Krieg etc*): *let things* ~ den Dingen ihren Lauf lassen. **6.** *fig.* sich (willenlos) treiben lassen. **7.** sich häufen (*Sand, Schnee*). III *v/t* **8.** (dahin)treiben. **'drift·er** *s* ziellos herumwandernder Mensch.

drift| ice *s* Treibeis *n*. **'~·wood** *s* Treibholz *n*.

drill¹ [drɪl] I *s* **1.** ⚙ Bohrer *m*. **2.** ✗ Drill *m* (*a. fig.*); Exerzieren *n*. II *v/t* **3.** *Loch* bohren (*in* in *acc*). **4.** ✗ drillen (*a. fig.* in *dat*). **5.** ~ *s.th. into s.o.* j-m et. eindrillen *od.* einpauken. III *v/i* **6.** bohren (*for* nach).

drill² [~] *s* Drillich *m*.

drink [drɪŋk] I *s* **1.** Getränk *n*; *coll.* Getränke *pl*. **2.** das Trinken, der Alkohol: *take to* ~ sich das Trinken angewöhnen. **3.** Schluck *m*. II *v/t* (*irr*) **4.** trinken, (*Tier a.*) saufen: ~ *away* Geld *etc* vertrinken; *Sorgen etc* im Alkohol ertränken; ~ *down* j-n unter den Tisch trinken; ~ *in fig.* (gierig) in sich aufnehmen, verschlingen; ~ *off* (*od. up*) austrinken; → *table.* **5.** trinken *od.* anstoßen auf (*acc*): → *health* **3.** III *v/i* (*irr*) **6.** trinken, *weitS. a.* (ein) Trinker sein, (*Tier a.*) saufen: ~ *off* (*od. up*) austrinken. **7.**

trinken, anstoßen (*to* auf *acc*): ~ *to s.o.* j-m zuprosten *od.* zutrinken; → *health* **3.** **'drink·a·ble** *adj* trinkbar, Trink... **'drink·er** *s* **1.** Trinkende *m, f.* **2.** Trinker(in).

drink·ing ['drɪŋkɪŋ] I *s* Trinken *n*. II *adj* Trink...: ~ *song* (*water, etc*); ~ *straw* Trinkhalm *m*.

drip [drɪp] I *v/i* **1.** tropfen (*a.* Hahn *etc*), tröpfeln. **2.** triefen (*with* von, *vor dat*) (*a. fig.*). II *v/t* **3.** tropfen *od.* tröpfeln lassen. **4.** ~ *sweat* vor Schweiß triefen. III *s* **5.** → *dripping* **1. 6.** ✚ Tropf(infusion *f*) *m*: *be on the* ~ am Tropf hängen. **7.** F Nulpe *f*; Flasche *f*. **'~·dry** I *adj* bügelfrei. II *v/t* tropfnaß aufhängen.

drip·ping ['drɪpɪŋ] I *s* **1.** Tropfen *n* (*a.* Geräusch), Tröpfeln *n*. **2.** (abtropfendes) Bratenfett. II *adj* **3.** tropfend (*a.* Hahn *etc*), tröpfelnd. **4.** triefend (*with* von, *vor dat*) (*a. fig.*). **5.** triefend (naß), tropf-, triefnaß. III *adv* **6.** ~ *wet* → **5.**

drive [draɪv] I *s* **1.** Treiben *n*; *engS.* Aus-, Spazierfahrt *f*: *an hour's* ~ e-e Autostunde. **2.** Fahrweg *m*; Zufahrt(sstraße) *f*; (*private*) Auffahrt **3.** *Golf, Tennis*: Drive *m*, Treibschlag *m*. **4.** *Kampagne f*, Feldzug *m*. **5.** *fig.* Schwung *m*, Elan *m* **6.** *psych.* Trieb *m*. **7.** ⚙ Antrieb *m*. **8.** *mot.* (*Links- etc*) Steuerung *f.* II *v/t* (*irr*) **9.** treiben (*a. fig.*); *Nagel etc* schlagen, *Pfahl* rammen (*into* in *acc*): ~ *s.th. into s.o.* j-m et. einbleuen; → *bend* **1,** *corner* **2,** *home* **9,** *wall* **1,** *etc.* **10.** *j-n* veranlassen (*to, into* zu; *to do* zu tun), dazu bringen (*to do* zu tun): *driven by hunger* vom Hunger getrieben. **11.** *Auto etc* lenken, steuern, fahren; (im *Auto etc*) fahren, befördern, bringen (*to* nach). **12.** ⚙ (an)treiben. **13.** zielbewußt durchführen: ~ *a hard bargain* hart verhandeln; überzogene Forderungen stellen. III *v/i* (*irr*) **14.** treiben, getrieben werden. **15.** jagen, stürmen. **16.** (Auto) fahren: ~ *into a wall* gegen e-e Mauer fahren. **17.** *fig.* abzielen (*at* auf *acc*): *what is he driving at?* worauf will er hinaus? *Verbindungen mit Adverbien:*

drive| a·way *v/t a. fig.* Sorgen *etc* vertreiben, -jagen; *Bedenken etc* zerstreuen. ~ *in v/t* Nagel *etc* einschlagen, *Pfahl* einrammen. ~ *up* I *v/t* Preise *etc* in die Höhe treiben. **II** v/i (*to*) vorfahren (vor *dat*); heranfahren (an *acc*).

'**drive-in I** *adj* Auto...: ~ *cinema* (*Am. motion-picture theater*) → IIa; ~ *restaurant* → IIb; ~ *window* → IIc. **II** *s* a) Autokino *n*, Drive-in-Kino *n*, b) Drive-in-Restaurant *n*, c) Autoschalter *m*, Drive-in-Schalter *m* (*e-r Bank*).

driv-el ['drɪvl] **I** v/i pret u. pp -**eled**, *bsd. Br.* -**elled** 1. sabbern, geifern. **2.** faseln. **II** *s* **3.** Geifer *m*. **4.** Gefasel *n*.

driv-en ['drɪvn] *pp von* **drive**.

driv-er ['draɪvə] s (*Auto- etc*)Fahrer *m*; (*Kran- etc, Br. Lokomotiv*)Führer *m*. ~'**s cab** s Führerhaus *n* (*e-s Lastwagens od. Krans*), 🚂 *Br.* Führerstand *m*. ~'**s li-cense** s *Am.* Führerschein *m*.

'**drive-way** s Zufahrt(sstraße) *f*; (private) Auffahrt.

driv-ing ['draɪvɪŋ] **I** *adj* **1.** (an)treibend: ~ *force* treibende Kraft. **2.** ⚙ Treib..., Antriebs... **II** *s* **3.** Autofahren *n*. **4.** *mot.* Fahrweise *f*, -stil *m*. ~ **in-struc-tor** s Fahrlehrer(in). ~ **les-son** s Fahrstunde *f*: *take* ~**s** Fahrunterricht nehmen, den Führerschein machen. ~ **li-cence** s *Br.* Führerschein *m*. ~ **mir-ror** s *mot.* Rückspiegel *m*. ~ **school** s Fahrschule *f*. ~ **test** s Fahrprüfung *f*: *take one's* ~ die Fahrprüfung *od.* den Führerschein machen.

driz-zle ['drɪzl] **I** v/impers nieseln. **II** s Sprüh-, Nieselregen *m*.

droll [drəʊl] *adj* □ drollig, spaßig.

drom-e-dar-y ['drɒmədərɪ] s zo. Dromedar *n*.

drone¹ [drəʊn] s zo. Drohne *f*, *fig. a.* Schmarotzer *m*.

drone² [~] **I** v/i brummen, summen. **II** v/t her(unter)leiern. **III** s Brummen *n*, Summen *n*.

drool [druːl] **I** v/i 1. → **drivel** I. **2.** ~ *over* (*od. about*) sich begeistern für, vernarrt sein in (*acc*). **II** s 3. → **drivel** II.

droop [druːp] **I** v/i 1. (schlaff) herabhängen *od.* -sinken. **2.** ermatten, erschlaffen (*from, with* vor *dat*). **3.** sinken (*Mut etc*), erlahmen (*Interesse etc*). **4.** den Kopf hängenlassen (*a. Blume*). **II** v/t 5. (schlaff) herabhängen lassen. **6.** *Kopf* hängenlassen. **III** s 7. Herabhängen *n*.

drop [drɒp] **I** s 1. Tropfen *m*: *a* ~ *in the bucket* (*od. ocean*) *fig.* ein Tropfen auf den heißen Stein; *empty to the last* ~ bis auf den letzten Tropfen leeren; *he has had a* ~ *too much* er hat e-n über den Durst getrunken. **2.** Bonbon *m, n*: *fruit* ~ Drops *m*. **3.** Fall(tiefe *f*) *m*: *a* ~ *of ten yards* ein Fall aus 10 Yards Höhe. **4.** *fig.* (Ab)Fall *m*, Sturz *m*: ~ *in prices* ✝ Preissturz; ~ *in* (the) *temperature* Temperatursturz, -abfall. **5.** Falltür *f*. **6.** *bsd. Am.* (*Brief- etc*)Einwurf *m*. **II** v/i **7.** (herab)tropfen, herabtröpfeln. **8.** (herunter)fallen. *let s.th.* ~ et. fallen lassen. **9.** sinken, fallen (*beide a. Preise etc*): ~ *into a chair* sich in e-n Sessel fallen lassen. **10.** a) (ohnmächtig) zu Boden sinken, umfallen: *be fit* (*od. ready*) *to* ~ (*with fatigue*) zum Umfallen müde sein, b) a. ~ *dead* tot umfallen: ~ *dead! sl.* geh zum Teufel! **11.** leiser werden (*Stimme*); sich legen (*Wind*). **III** v/t **12.** tropfen *od.* tröpfeln lassen. **13.** fallen lassen: ~ *everything* alles liegen- u. stehenlassen. **14.** (hinein)werfen (*into* in *acc*). **15.** *Bemerkung* fallenlassen: ~ *s.o. a line* (*od. note*) j-m ein paar Zeilen schreiben. **16.** *j-n, Absicht etc* fallenlassen. **17.** *Tätigkeit* aufgeben, aufhören mit: ~ *it!* hör auf damit! **18.** *Last, a. Passagiere* absetzen. **19.** *Buchstaben etc* auslassen: → **H** 1. **20.** *Sport:* *Punkt etc* abgeben (*to* gegen). **21.** *Augen, a. Stimme* senken (*to a whisper* zu e-m Flüstern).

Verbindungen mit Adverbien:

drop| **a-way** v/i immer weniger werden. ~ **back**, ~ **be-hind** v/i 1. zurückfallen. **2.** sich zurückfallen lassen. ~ **in** v/i 1. hereinkommen (*a. fig. Aufträge etc*). **2.** (kurz) hereinschauen (*on* bei). ~ **off** I v/i 1. zurückgehen (*Umsatz etc*), nachlassen (*Interesse etc*). **2.** einschlafen, -nicken. **II** v/t 3. → **drop** 18. ~ **out** v/i 1. aussteigen (*of* aus *Politik etc*). **2.** die Schule *od.* das Studium abbrechen.

drop-let ['drɒplɪt] s Tröpfchen *n*.

'**drop-out** s 1. Aussteiger *m* (*aus der Gesellschaft*). **2.** (Schul-, Studien)Abbrecher *m*.

drop-pings ['drɒpɪŋz] s pl (Tier)Kot *m*.

drop-sy ['drɒpsɪ] s 🩺 Wassersucht *f*.

drought [draʊt] s Trockenheit *f*, Dürre(periode) *f*.

drove¹ [drəʊv] pret von **drive**.

drove² [~] s Schar *f* (*Menschen*): *in* ~**s** in

(großen od. hellen) Scharen, scharen-weise.

drown [draʊn] **I** v/i **1.** ertrinken. **II** v/t **2.** ertränken: **be drowned** → 1; **~ one's sorrows** s-e Sorgen im Alkohol ertränken. **3.** überschwemmen: **be ~ed in tears** in Tränen schwimmen od. zerfließen. **4.** a. **~ out** bsd. Stimme übertönen.

drowse [draʊz] **I** v/i **1.** dösen: **~ off** eindösen. **II** v/t **2.** schläfrig machen. **3. ~ away** Zeit verdösen. **III** s **4.** Dösen n. '**drows·y** adj □ **1.** schläfrig; verschlafen. **2.** einschläfernd. **3.** fig. verschlafen, -träumt.

drudge [drʌdʒ] **I** s **1.** fig. Kuli m, Last-, Packesel m; Arbeitstier n. **2.** → **drudgery**. **II** v/i **3.** sich (ab)placken od. (ab)schinden. '**drudg·er·y** s (stumpfsinnige) Plackerei od. Schinderei.

drug [drʌg] **I** s **1.** Arzneimittel n, Medikament n. **2.** Droge f (a. fig.), Rauschgift n: **be on** (off) **~s** rauschgift- od. drogensüchtig (clean) sein. **3.** Betäubungsmittel n (a. fig.). **4. ~ on** (Am. a. **in**) **the market** ✝ schwerverkäufliche Ware, (im Laden a.) Ladenhüter m. **II** v/t **5.** j-m Medikamente geben. **6.** j-n unter Drogen setzen. **7.** ein Betäubungsmittel beimischen (dat). **8.** betäuben (a. fig.): **~ged with sleep** schlaftrunken. **~ a·buse** s **1.** Drogenmißbrauch m. **2.** Medikamentenmißbrauch m. **~ ad·dict** s **1.** Drogen-, Rauschgiftsüchtige m, f. **2.** Medikamentensüchtige m, f. '**~ad·dict·ed** adj **1.** drogen-, rauschgiftsüchtig. **2.** medikamentensüchtig. **~ ad·dic·tion** s **1.** Drogen-, Rauschgiftsucht f. **2.** Medikamentensucht f. **~ clin·ic** s Drogenklinik f. **~ deal·er** s Drogen-, Rauschgifthändler m. **~ de·pend·ence** s **1.** Drogenabhängigkeit f. **2.** Medikamentenabhängigkeit f.

drug·gist ['drʌgɪst] s Am. Inhaber(in) e-s Drugstores.

'**drug**͵**push·er** s F Pusher m (Rauschgifthändler). **~ scene** s Drogenszene f.

drug·ster ['drʌgstə] → **drug addict** 1.

'**drug·store** s Am. Drugstore m.

drum [drʌm] **I** s **1.** ♪ Trommel f (a. ⚙, ⊙); ~s pl Schlagzeug n. **2.** Trommeln n (a. weitS. des Regens etc). **3.** anat. Mittelohr n; Trommelfell n. **II** v/t **4.** Rhythmus trommeln: **~ s.th. into s.o.** fig. j-m

et. einhämmern. **5.** trommeln auf (acc); trommeln mit (on auf acc). **6. ~ up** fig. zs.-trommeln, (an)werben; Aufträge etc hereinholen; sich et. ausdenken. **III** v/i **7.** a. weitS. trommeln (at an acc; on auf acc). '**~beat** s Trommelschlag m. **~ brake** s ⊙ Trommelbremse f. '**~͵fire** s Trommelfeuer n. '**~head** s ♪, a. anat. Trommelfell n.

drum·mer ['drʌmə] s ♪ Trommler m; Schlagzeuger m.

'**drum·stick** s **1.** Trommelstock m, -schlegel m. **2.** Unterschenkel m (von zubereitetem Geflügel).

drunk [drʌŋk] **I** pp von **drink**. **II** adj pred **1.** betrunken: **get ~** sich betrinken; **(as) ~ as a lord** F total blau. **2.** fig. berauscht (**with** von): **~ with joy** freudetrunken. **III** s **3.** a) Betrunkene m, f, b) → **drunkard. drunk·ard** ['~əd] s (Gewohnheits)Trinker(in), Säufer(in). '**drunk·en** adj attr **1.** betrunken: **a ~ man** ein Betrunkener; **~ driving** Trunkenheit f am Steuer; **~ stupor.** **2.** Sauf...: **~ party.** '**drunk·en·ness** s **1.** Betrunkenheit f. **2.** Trunksucht f.

dry [draɪ] **I** adj □ **1.** allg. trocken (a. fig. Humor etc): **rub ~** trockenreiben. **2.** F durstig. **3.** durstig machend (Arbeit). **4.** trocken (ohne Aufstrich). **5.** trocken, langweilig: **(as) ~ as dust** F stinklangweilig. **6.** trocken, herb (Wein etc). **7.** F trocken, weg vom Alkohol. **II** v/t **8.** trocknen. **9.** → o.s. (one's hands) sich (sich die Hände) abtrocknen (on an dat). **10.** oft **~ up** Geschirr abtrocknen. **11.** Obst etc dörren. **III** v/i **12.** trocknen, trocken werden. **13. ~ up** ein-, aus-, vertrocknen; F die Klappe halten; F steckenbleiben (Schauspieler etc). **~ bat·ter·y** s ⚡ Trockenbatterie f. **~ cell** s ⚡ Trockenelement n. **~ clean** v/t chemisch reinigen. **~ clean·er('s)** s chemische Reinigung(sanstalt). **~ clean·ing** s chemische Reinigung.

dry·er → **drier**.

dry| **goods** s pl ✝ Textilien pl. **~ ice** s 🜄 Trockeneis n.

dry·ness ['draɪnɪs] s Trockenheit f.

dry nurse s Säuglingsschwester f.

du·al ['djuːəl] adj **1.** doppelt, zweifach: **~ carriageway** mot. Br. Schnellstraße f.

dub[1] [dʌb] v/t nennen, j-m den (Spitz-) Namen ... geben.

dub² [~] v/t Film synchronisieren.
du·bi·ous ['dju:bjəs] adj □ **1.** zweifelhaft: a) unklar, zweideutig, b) ungewiß, unbestimmt, c) fragwürdig, dubios: ~ *pleasure* zweifelhaftes Vergnügen, d) unzuverlässig. **2.** unschlüssig, schwankend; unsicher, im Zweifel (*of*, *about* über *acc*).
du·cal ['dju:kl] adj □ herzoglich, Herzogs...
duch·ess ['dʌtʃis] s Herzogin f.
duch·y ['dʌtʃi] s Herzogtum n.
duck¹ [dʌk] s **1.** orn. Ente f: *look like a dying* ~ (*in a thunderstorm*) F dumm aus der Wäsche schauen. **2.** Br. F Schatz m.
duck² [~] **I** v/i **1.** (rasch) (unter)tauchen. **2.** a. fig. sich ducken (*to* vor *dat*). **3.** ~ *out* F verduften; fig. sich drücken (*of* vor *dat*). **II** v/t **4.** (unter)tauchen. **5.** *Kopf* ducken, einziehen. **6.** F sich drücken vor (*dat*).
duct [dʌkt] s **1.** ☉ Röhre f, Rohr n, Leitung f. **2.** anat. Gang m, Kanal m.
duc·tile ['dʌktail] adj □ **1.** phys., ☉ dehn-, streckbar. **2.** fig. fügsam.
dud [dʌd] s F **1.** ✗ Blindgänger m (a. fig.). **2.** Niete f, Versager m. **3.** ungedeckter Scheck.
dude [dju:d] s Am. F **1.** Dandy m. **2.** Stadtmensch m.
due [dju:] **I** adj (□ → *duly*) **1.** ✝ fällig: *fall* (*od.* **become**) ~ fällig werden; *when* ~ bei Fälligkeit; ~ *date* Fälligkeitstermin m. *zeitlich* fällig: *the train is* ~ *at* ... der Zug soll um ... ankommen. **3.** *be* ~ *to* zuzuschreiben sein (*dat*), zurückzuführen sein auf (*acc*): *it is* ~ *to him* es ist ihm zu verdanken. **4.** gebührend, geziemend: *be* ~ *to s.o.* j-m gebühren *od.* zukommen; → *credit* 3, *hono(u)r* 4. **5.** gebührend, angemessen: *after* ~ *consideration* nach reiflicher Überlegung. **6.** passend, richtig: *in* ~ *course* zur rechten *od.* gegebenen Zeit; *in* ~ *time* rechtzeitig, termingerecht; *in* ~ *form* ordnungsgemäß, vorschriftsmäßig. **7.** ~ *to* wegen (*gen*), infolge *od.* auf Grund (*gen od.* von). **II** s **8.** *das* Gebührende: *give s.o. his* ~ j-m Gerechtigkeit widerfahren lassen. **9.** pl Gebühren pl.
du·el ['dju:əl] **I** s Duell n (a. fig.). **II** v/i pret u. pp **-eled**, bsd. Br. **-elled** sich duellieren.

du·et [dju:'et] s ♪ **1.** Duett n. **2.** Duo n.
duff·er ['dʌfə] s F (alter) Trottel.
dug [dʌg] pret u. pp von **dig**. '~**out** s **1.** ✗ Unterstand m. **2.** Einbaum m.
du·i ['dju:i:] pl von **duo**.
duke [dju:k] s Herzog m.
dull [dʌl] **I** adj □ **1.** schwer von Begriff, dumm. **2.** schwerfällig, träge. **3.** teilnahmslos. **4.** langweilig, fad(e). **5.** ✝ flau, schleppend. **6.** stumpf (*Klinge etc*). **7.** matt, glanzlos (*Augen, Farben*). **8.** dumpf (*Klang, Schmerz etc*). **II** v/t **9.** abstumpfen. **10.** (ab)schwächen. **11.** mildern, dämpfen. **12.** *Schmerz* betäuben. **dull·ard** ['~əd] s Dummkopf m. **'dul(l)·ness** s **1.** Dummheit f. **2.** Trägheit f. **3.** Teilnahmslosigkeit f. **4.** Langweiligkeit f. **5.** ✝ Flaute f. **6.** Stumpfheit f. **7.** Mattheit f. **8.** Dumpfheit f.
du·ly ['dju:li] adv **1.** ordnungsgemäß. **2.** rechtzeitig.
dumb [dʌm] adj □ **1.** stumm (a. fig.): *strike s.o.* ~ j-m die Sprache verschlagen *od.* rauben; (*struck*) ~ sprachlos (*with* vor *dat*); *the* ~ *masses* pl die stumme Masse. **2.** bsd. Am. F doof, dumm. '~**bell** s **1.** *Sport:* Hantel f. **2.** bsd. Am. sl. Trottel m. '~**found** v/t verblüffen. .'~**found·ed** adj verblüfft, sprachlos. ~ *show* s Pantomime f. ,~**wait·er** s **1.** stummer Diener, Serviertisch m. **2.** Speiseaufzug m.
dum·found, etc → **dumbfound**, etc.
dum·my ['dʌmi] **I** s **1.** Attrappe f, ✝ a. Leer-, Schaupackung f. **2.** Kleider-, Schaufensterpuppe f. **3.** ✝, ⚏ Strohmann m. **4.** Br. Schnuller m. **II** adj **5.** Schein...
dump [dʌmp] **I** v/t **1.** (hin)plumpsen *od.* (-)fallen lassen, hinwerfen. **2.** *Schutt etc* auskippen, abladen; *Karren etc* (um-) kippen, entladen. **3.** ✝ zu Dumpingpreisen verkaufen. **II** v/i **4.** plumpsen. **5.** (s-n) Schutt abladen. **III** s **6.** a) Schutt-, Abfallhaufen m, b) (Schutt-, Müll)Abladeplatz m, Müllkippe f, -halde f. '**dump·er** (**truck**) s mot. Dumper m, Kipper m. '**dump·ing** s **1.** (Schutt)Abladen n: ~ *ground* → **dump** 6b. **2.** ✝ Dumping n.
dump·ling ['dʌmplin] s **1.** Knödel m, Kloß m. **2.** F Dickerchen n.
dumps [dʌmps] s pl: (**down**) *in the* ~ F down, niedergeschlagen.

dump truck → *dumper* (**truck**).

dun [dʌn] *v/t bsd. Schuldner* mahnen.

dune [dju:n] *s* Düne *f.* **~ bug·gy** *s mot.* Strandbuggy *m.*

dung [dʌŋ] *s* Mist *m,* Dung *m.*

dun·ga·rees [ˌdʌŋgəˈri:z] *s pl* Arbeitsanzug *m:* (**pair of**) **~** Arbeitshose *f.*

dun·geon [ˈdʌndʒən] *s* Verlies *n.*

'dung·hill *s* Misthaufen *m.*

dunk [dʌŋk] *v/t Brot etc* eintunken, stippen.

du·o [ˈdju:əʊ] *pl* **-os,** **du·i** [ˈ~i:] → **duet**.

du·o·de·num [ˌdju:əʊˈdi:nəm] *pl* **-na** [~nə], **-nums** *s anat.* Zwölffingerdarm *m.*

dupe [dju:p] **I** *s* Betrogene *m, f.* **II** *v/t* betrügen.

du·plex [ˈdju:pleks] **I** *adj* doppelt, Doppel..., zweifach: **~ apartment** → IIa; **~ house** → IIb. **II** *s Am.* a) Maison(n)ette *f,* b) Zweifamilienhaus *n.*

du·pli·cate [ˈdju:plɪkət] **I** *adj* **1.** doppelt, Doppel..., zweifach. **2.** genau gleich *od.* entsprechend: **~ key** → **II 3. 3.** Duplikat *n,* Ab-, Zweitschrift *f,* Kopie *f:* **in ~** in zweifacher Ausfertigung. **4.** (genau gleiches) Seitenstück, Kopie *f.* **5.** Zweit- *od.* Nachschlüssel *m.* **III** *v/t* [ˈ~keɪt] **6.** ein Duplikat anfertigen von, kopieren, vervielfältigen. **7.** *Experiment etc* (beliebig) wiederholen. **du·pli·ca·tor** [ˈ~keɪtə] *s* Vervielfältigungsapparat *m.*

du·ra·bil·i·ty [ˌdjʊərəˈbɪlətɪ] *s* a) Haltbarkeit *f,* b) Dauerhaftigkeit *f.* **'du·ra·ble I** *adj* □ a) haltbar, ✝ langlebig: **~ goods** → II, b) dauerhaft. **II** *s pl* ✝ Gebrauchsgüter *pl.* **du·ra·tion** [~ˈreɪʃn] *s* Dauer *f:* **for the ~ of** für die Dauer von (*od. gen*).

du·ress [djʊəˈres] *s* Zwang *m* (*a.* ✝✝).

du·ring [ˈdjʊərɪŋ] *prp* während.

dusk [dʌsk] *s* (Abend)Dämmerung *f:* **at ~** bei Einbruch der Dunkelheit. **'dusk·y** *adj* □ dämmerig, düster (*a. fig.*).

dust [dʌst] **I** *s* **1.** Staub *m:* **throw** (*od.* **cast**) **~ in s.o.'s eyes** *fig.* j-m Sand in die Augen streuen; **raise a ~** a) *a.* Staubwolke aufwirbeln, b) *a.* **kick up a ~** *fig.* viel Staub aufwirbeln; **the ~ has settled** die Aufregung hat sich gelegt, die Wogen haben sich geglättet; → **bite** 1, **kiss** 2. **II** *v/t* **2.** abstauben. **3.** bestreuen, bestäuben. **III** *v/i* **4.** Staub wi-

schen. **5.** staubig werden, verstauben. **'~bin** *s Br.* Abfall-, Mülleimer *m;* Abfall-, Mülltonne *f:* **~ man** Müllmann *m.* **'~cart** *s Br.* Müllwagen *m.* **~ cov·er** *s* Schutzumschlag *m.*

dust·er [ˈdʌstə] *s* Staubtuch *n.*

dust| jack·et *s* **dust cover.** **~man** [ˈ~mən] *s (irr man) Br.* Müllmann *m.* **~ storm** *s* Staubsturm *m.* **~ trap** *s* Staubfänger *m.* **'~up** *s* F **1.** Krach *m.* **2.** handgreifliche Auseinandersetzung.

dust·y [ˈdʌstɪ] *adj* staubig: **not so ~** *Br.* F gar nicht so übel.

Dutch [dʌtʃ] **I** *adj* **1.** holländisch, niederländisch. **II** *adv* **2. go ~** getrennte Kasse machen. **II** *s* **3.** *ling.* Holländisch *n,* Niederländisch *n.* **4. the ~** *pl* die Holländer *pl,* die Niederländer *pl.* **~ cour·age** *s* F angetrunkener Mut. **'~man** [ˈ~mən] *s (irr man)* Holländer *m,* Niederländer *m.* **'~wom·an** *s (irr woman)* Holländerin *f,* Niederländerin *f.*

du·te·ous [ˈdju:tjəs] → **dutiful. du·ti·a·ble** [ˈ~tjəbl] *adj* zollpflichtig. **du·ti·ful** [ˈ~tɪfʊl] *adj* □ pflichtgetreu, -bewußt.

du·ty [ˈdju:tɪ] *s* **1.** Pflicht *f:* a) Schuldigkeit *f* (**to, toward[s]** gegen[über]), b) Aufgabe *f:* **do one's ~** s-e Pflicht tun; **breach of ~** Pflichtverletzung *f.* **2.** Dienst *m:* **be on ~** Dienst haben, im Dienst sein; **be off ~** nicht im Dienst sein, dienstfrei haben; **do ~ for** benutzt werden *od.* dienen als; *j-n* vertreten. **3.** ✝ Zoll *m.* **II** *adj* **4. ~ call** Höflichkeits-, Pflichtbesuch *m.* **5. ~ chemist** *Br.* dienstbereite Apotheke; **~ doctor** Bereitschaftsarzt *m;* **~ officer** ✕ Offizier *m* vom Dienst; **~ roster** Dienstplan *m* (*od. pl*). **'~free I** *adj u. adv* zollfrei: **~ shop** Duty-free-Shop *m.* **II** *s pl* F zollfreie Ware(*n pl*).

dwarf [dwɔ:f] **I** *pl* **dwarfs, dwarves** [~vz] *s* Zwerg(in) (*a. fig.*). **II** *adj* zwergenhaft, *bsd.* ♈, *zo.* Zwerg... **III** *v/t* klein erscheinen lassen; *fig.* in den Schatten stellen. **'dwarf·ish** *adj* □ zwergenhaft.

dwarves [dwɔ:vz] *pl von* **dwarf.**

dwell [dwel] *v/i (irr)* **1.** wohnen, leben. **2. ~ on** *fig.* (im Geiste) verweilen bei. **'dwell·er** *s mst in Zssgn* Bewohner(in). **'dwell·ing** *s* Wohnung *f:* **~ house** Wohnhaus *n.*

dwelt [dwelt] *pret u. pp von* **dwell.**

dwin·dle ['dwɪndl] *v/i* abnehmen, schwinden.

dye [daɪ] **I** *s* **1.** Farbstoff *m*. **2.** Färbung *f*: *of the deepest (od. blackest)* ~ *fig.* von der übelsten Sorte. **II** *v/t* **3.** färben.

‚dyed-in-the-'wool *adj* eingefleischt, ... durch u. durch.

'dye·works *s pl (oft sg konstruiert)* Färberei *f*.

dy·ing ['daɪɪŋ] *adj* **1.** sterbend: *be* ~ im Sterben liegen. **2.** Sterbe...: ~ *hour* Todesstunde *f*; ~ *wish* letzter Wunsch.

dyke → **dike**[1] *u.* [2].

dy·nam·ic [daɪ'næmɪk] **I** *adj* (~*ally*) dynamisch (*a. fig.*). **II** *s pl (sg konstruiert)* Dynamik *f (a. fig.)*.

dy·na·mite ['daɪnəmaɪt] **I** *s* Dynamit *n*. **II** *v/t (mit Dynamit)* sprengen.

dy·na·mo ['daɪnəməʊ] *pl* **-mos** *s* ⚡ Dynamo *m*.

dy·nas·ty ['dɪnəstɪ] *s* Dynastie *f*.

dys·en·ter·y ['dɪsntrɪ] *s* 🐾 Ruhr *f*.

dys·func·tion [dɪs'fʌŋkʃn] *s* 🐾 Funktionsstörung *f*.

E

each [iːtʃ] **I** *adj* jede(r, -s): ~ *one* jede(r) einzelne. **II** *pron:* ~ *of us* jede(r) von uns; ~ *other* einander, sich. **III** *adv* je, pro Person *od.* Stück.

ea·ger ['iːgə] *adj* □ **1.** eifrig: ~ *beaver* F Übereifrige *m, f*. **2.** *(for)* begierig (nach), erpicht, gespannt (auf *acc*): *be* ~ *to do s.th.* darauf brennen, et. zu tun. **3.** gespannt (*Aufmerksamkeit, Blick etc*). **'ea·ger·ness** *s* **1.** Eifer *m*. **2.** Begierde *f*.

ea·gle ['iːgl] *s orn.* Adler *m*.

ear[1] [ɪə] *s* **1.** *anat.* Ohr *n*: *be all* ~*s* ganz Ohr sein; *be up to the (od. one's)* ~*s in debt (work)* bis über die Ohren in Schulden (Arbeit) sitzen *od.* stecken; *fall on deaf* ~*s* auf taube Ohren stoßen; *have (od. keep) an (od. one's)* ~ *to the ground* die Ohren offenhalten; *turn a deaf* ~ *to* die Ohren verschließen vor (*dat*). → *flea, prick* 7, *thick* 1, *wet* 1. **2.** *fig.* Gehör *n*, Ohr *n*: *play by* ~ nach dem Gehör spielen; *fig.* improvisieren.

ear[2] [~] *s* (Getreide)Ähre *f*.

ear·ache ['ɪəreɪk] *s* Ohrenschmerzen *pl*. **~drum** ['ɪədrʌm] *s anat.* Trommelfell *n*.

earl [ɜːl] *s britischer* Graf.

'ear·lobe *s anat.* Ohrläppchen *n*.

ear·ly ['ɜːlɪ] **I** *adv* **1.** früh(zeitig): *as* ~ *as May* schon im Mai. **2.** bald: *as* ~ *as possible* so bald wie möglich. **3.** zu früh; früher. **II** *adj* **4.** früh(zeitig): ~

riser, humor. ~ *bird* Frühaufsteher(in); *the* ~ *bird catches the worm* Morgenstunde hat Gold im Munde; *Thursday is* ~ *closing* am Donnerstag schließen die Geschäfte früher; *in his* ~ *days* in s-r Jugend; *at an* ~ *hour* zu früher Stunde; ~ *warning system* ✕ Frühwarnsystem *n*; *at the (very) earliest* (aller-) frühestens; → *convenience* 1. **5.** vorzeitig: *his* ~ *death* sein früher Tod. **6.** zu früh: *be* ~ zu früh (daran) sein. **7.** anfänglich, Früh...: ~ *Christian* frühchristlich. **8.** baldig.

'ear·mark I *s* **1.** Ohrmarke *f (e-s Haustiers)*. **2.** *fig.* Kennzeichen *n*. **II** *v/t* **3.** kennzeichnen. **4.** *bsd.* ✝ bestimmen, vorsehen (*for* für): ~*ed* zweckbestimmt, -gebunden (*Mittel*). **'~muff** *s* Ohrenschützer *m*.

earn [ɜːn] *v/t* **1.** Geld etc verdienen: → *living* 6. **2.** Zinsen etc einbringen. **3.** *fig.* j-m et. einbringen, -tragen.

ear·nest ['ɜːnɪst] **I** *adj* □ **1.** ernst. **2.** ernst-, gewissenhaft. **3.** ernstlich. **II** *s* **4.** *in* ~ im Ernst; *in good (od. dead, perfect)* ~ in vollem Ernst; *are you in* ~? ist das dein Ernst?; *be in* ~ *about* es ernst meinen mit.

earn·ings ['ɜːnɪŋz] *s pl* Verdienst *m*, Einkommen *n*.

'ear·phones *s pl, a. pair of* ~ Kopfhörer *m*. **'~piece** *s teleph.* Hörmuschel *f*. **'~,pierc·ing** → *earsplitting*. **'~plug** *s*

Wattepfropf m. '**~·ring** s Ohrring m. '**~·shot** s: *within* (*out of*) ~ in (außer) Hörweite. '**~·split·ting** adj ohrenbetäubend.

earth [ɜːθ] **I** s **1.** Erde f: a) a. ⚲ Erdball m, b) Welt f: *on* ~ auf Erden; *what* (*why*) *on* ~? warum (was) in aller Welt? **2.** Erde f, (Erd)Boden m: *come back* (*od. down*) *to* ~ fig. auf den Boden der Wirklichkeit zurückkehren. **3.** (Fuchs*etc*)Bau m. **4.** ⚡ bsd. Br. Erde f, Erdung f: **~·cable** Massekabel n. **II** v/t **5.** ⚡ bsd. Br. erden. '**earth·en** adj irden. '**earth·en·ware** s Steingut(geschirr) n. '**earth·ly** adj **1.** irdisch, weltlich. **2.** F *there's no* ~ *reason* es gibt nicht den geringsten Grund; *of no* ~ *use* völlig unnütz; *not to have an* ~ (*chance*) nicht die geringste Chance haben.

'**earth|·quake** s Erdbeben n. '**~·quake-proof** adj erdbebensicher. '**~·shak·ing**, '**~·shat·ter·ing** adj fig. welterschütternd. **~ sta·tion** s Raumfahrt: Bodenstation f. **~·trem·or** s leichtes Erdbeben. '**~·worm** s zo. Regenwurm m.

earth·y ['ɜːθɪ] adj **1.** erdig, Erd... **2.** weltlich od. materiell (eingestellt). **3.** derb (Humor etc).

'**ear|·wax** s physiol. Ohrenschmalz n. '**~·wig** s zo. Ohrwurm m. '**~·wit·ness** s Ohrenzeuge m.

ease [iːz] **I** s **1.** Bequemlichkeit f, Behaglichkeit f. **2.** a. ~ *of mind* (Gemüts)Ruhe f, Ausgeglichenheit f: *at* (*one's*) ~ ruhig, entspannt; unbefangen; *be* (*od. feel*) *at* ~ sich wohl fühlen; *ill at* ~ unruhig; befangen; *be* (*od. feel*) *ill at* ~ sich (in s-r Haut) nicht wohl fühlen. **3.** Sorglosigkeit f: *live at* ~ in guten Verhältnissen leben. **4.** Leichtigkeit f, Mühelosigkeit f: *with* ~ leicht, mühelos. **5.** Erleichterung f, Befreiung f: *give s.o.* ~ j-m Erleichterung verschaffen. **II** v/t **6.** erleichtern, beruhigen: ~ *one's mind* sich erleichtern. **7.** Schmerzen lindern. **III** v/i **8.** mst ~ *off* (*od. up*) nachlassen, sich abschwächen; sich entspannen (Lage); (bei der Arbeit) kürzertreten; weniger streng sein (*on* zu).

ea·sel ['iːzl] s paint. Staffelei f.

eas·i·ly ['iːzɪlɪ] adv **1.** leicht, mühelos. **2.** ohne Zweifel; mit Abstand, bei weitem.

east [iːst] **I** s **1.** Osten m: *in the* ~ *of* im

Osten von (*od. gen*); *to the* ~ *of* → 5. **2.** a. ⚲ Osten, östlicher Landesteil: *the* ⚲ Br. Ostengland n; Am. die Oststaaten pl; pol. der Osten; der Orient. **II** adj **3.** Ost..., östlich. **III** adv **4.** ostwärts, nach Osten. **5.** ~ *of* östlich von (*od. gen*). '**~·bound** adj nach Osten gehend od. fahrend.

East·er ['iːstə] **I** s Ostern n od. pl, Osterfest n: *at* ~ zu Ostern; *happy* ~ frohe Ostern! **II** adj Oster...: ~ *egg*; ~ *Sunday* (*od. Day*) Ostersonntag m.

east·er·ly ['iːstəlɪ] **I** adj östlich, Ost... **II** adv von od. nach Osten. **east·ern** ['iːstən] adj östlich, Ost... '**east·ern·er** s **1.** Bewohner(in) des Ostens (*e-s Landes*). **2.** ⚲ Am. Oststaatler(in). '**east·ern·most** ['iːstənməʊst] adj östlichst.

east·ward ['iːstwəd] adj u. adv östlich, ostwärts, nach Osten: *in an* ~ *direction* in östlicher Richtung, Richtung Osten. '**east·wards** ['~z] adv → *eastward*.

eas·y ['iːzɪ] **I** adj (□ → *easily*) **1.** leicht, mühelos: *it is* ~ *for him to talk* er hat gut reden. **2.** leicht, einfach (*for* für): ~ *money* leichtverdientes Geld. **3.** bequem, angenehm: *live in* ~ *circumstances*, F *be on* ~ *street* in guten Verhältnissen leben. **4.** gemächlich, gemütlich (Tempo, Spaziergang etc): ~ *stage* 2. **5.** günstig, erträglich (Strafe): *on* ~ *terms* auf Raten. **6.** leichtfertig; locker, frei (Moral etc). **7.** ungezwungen, natürlich: *be free and* ~ sich ganz ungezwungen benehmen. **II** adv **8.** leicht, bequem: *go* ~, *take it* ~ sich Zeit lassen; sich nicht aufregen; *take it* ~! immer mit der Ruhe!; keine Bange!; *go* ~ *on* j-n, et. sachte anfassen; schonend od. sparsam umgehen mit; *easier said than done* leichter gesagt als getan; ~ *come*, ~ *go* wie gewonnen, so zerronnen. ~ *chair* s Sessel m. '**~·go·ing** adj **1.** gelassen. **2.** unbeschwert.

eat [iːt] **I** s **1.** pl F Fressalien pl. **II** v/t (irr) **2.** essen (Mensch), fressen (Tier): ~ *one's words* alles(, was man gesagt hat,) zurücknehmen; *what's* ~*ing him?* F was hat er denn?; ~ *up* aufessen, -fressen; Reserven etc völlig aufbrauchen; *be* ~*en up with* fig. sich verzehren vor (*dat*), zerfressen werden von; → *cake* 1, *dog* 1, *hat*, *humble* Ia. **3.** zerfressen: ~*en by worms* wurmstichig. **4.** Loch fressen (*into* in *acc*). **III** *v/i* (*irr*) **5.** essen (*Mensch*), fressen (*Tier*): **~ out** auswärts essen, essen gehen. **6. ~ into** sich (hin)einfressen in (*acc*); *Reserven etc* angreifen. **'eat·a·ble I** *adj* eß-, genießbar. **II** *s pl* Eßwaren *pl*. **eat·en** ['i:tn] *pp von* **eat**. **'eat·er** *s* Esser(in) (*Mensch*), Fresser *m* (*Tier*): → **big** 1d, **small** 7. **'eat·ing I** *s* Essen *n*. **II** *adj* Eß...: **~ apple** Eß-, Speiseapfel *m*.

eau de Co·logne [ˌəʊdəkə'ləʊn] *s* Kölnischwasser *n*.

eaves [i:vz] *s pl* Traufe *f*. **'~·drop** *v/i* (heimlich) lauschen *od.* horchen: **~ on** belauschen. **'~·drop·per** *s* Lauscher(in), Horcher(in).

ebb [eb] **I** *s* **1.** a. **~ tide** Ebbe *f*. **2.** *fig.* Tiefstand *m*: **be at a low ~** auf e-m Tiefpunkt angelangt sein. **II** *v/i* **3.** zurückgehen (a. *fig.*). **4.** a. **~ away** *fig.* abnehmen, verebben.

eb·on·y ['ebənɪ] *s* Ebenholz *n*.

e·bul·li·ent [ɪ'bʌljənt] *adj* □ *fig.* sprudelnd, überschäumend (*with* von); überschwenglich.

ec·cen·tric [ɪk'sentrɪk] **I** *adj* (**~ally**) Ⓐ, ☉ exzentrisch, *fig. a.* überspannt. **II** *s* Exzentriker(in). **ec·cen·tric·i·ty** [ˌeksen'trɪsətɪ] *s* Ⓐ, ☉ Exzentrizität *f*, *fig. a.* Überspanntheit *f*.

ec·cle·si·as·ti·cal [ɪˌkli:zɪ'æstɪkl] *adj* □ kirchlich: **~ law** Kirchenrecht *n*.

ech·e·lon ['eʃəlɒn] ⚓, ✕ **I** *s* Staffelung *f*: **in ~** staffelförmig. **II** *v/t* staffeln.

ech·o ['ekəʊ] **I** *pl* **-oes** *s* **1.** Echo *n*, Widerhall *m* (*beide a. fig.*). **II** *v/t* **2.** widerhallen (*with* von). **3.** nach-, widerhallen, zurückgeworfen werden (*Ton*). **III** *v/t* **4.** a. **~ back** *Ton* zurückwerfen. **5.** *Worte* nachbeten; *j-m* alles nachbeten. **~ sound·er** *s* ⚓ Echolot *n*.

é·clat ['eɪklɑ:] *s* **1.** durchschlagender Erfolg. **2.** (allgemeiner) Beifall.

e·clipse [ɪ'klɪps] **I** *s* **1.** *ast.* (Sonnen-, Mond)Finsternis *f*. **2.** *fig.* Niedergang *m*: **be in ~** im Sinken sein; in der Versenkung verschwunden sein. **II** *v/t* **3.** *ast.* verfinstern. **4.** *fig.* in den Schatten stellen: **be ~d by** verblassen neben (*dat*).

e·co·cide ['i:kəʊsaɪd] *s* Umweltzerstörung *f*. **e·co·cri·sis** ['i:kəʊˌkraɪsɪs] *s* (*irr crisis*) Umweltkrise *f*.

e·co·log·i·cal [ˌi:kə'lɒdʒɪkl] *adj* □ öko-

logisch, Umwelt...: **~ balance** ökologisches Gleichgewicht; **~ly beneficial** (**harmful**) umweltfreundlich (umweltfeindlich). **e·col·o·gist** [i:'kɒlədʒɪst] *s* Ökologe *m*. **e·col·o·gy** [i:'kɒlədʒɪ] *s* Ökologie *f*.

e·co·nom·ic [ˌi:kə'nɒmɪk] **I** *adj* (**~ally**) **1.** (staats-, volks)wirtschaftlich, Wirtschafts...: **~ aid** Wirtschaftshilfe *f*. **2.** rentabel, wirtschaftlich. **II** *s pl* (*sg construiert*) **3.** Volkswirtschaft(slehre) *f*. **e·co·nom·i·cal** [ˌkl] *adj* □ **1.** wirtschaftlich, sparsam, (*Person a.*) haushälterisch: **be ~ with** → **economize** 1. **2.** Spar... **3.** → **economic** 1. **e·con·o·mist** [ɪ'kɒnəmɪst] *s* Volkswirt(schaftler) *m*. **e·con·o·mize** [ɪ'kɒnəmaɪz] **I** *v/t* sparsam umgehen *od.* wirtschaften mit. **II** *v/i* sparsam wirtschaften: **~ on** *od.* **~ in** I. **e·con·o·my** [ɪ'kɒnəmɪ] *s* **1.** Wirtschaftlichkeit *f*, Sparsamkeit *f*. **2.** Sparmaßnahme *f*; Einsparung *f*. **3.** Wirtschafts(system *n*) *f*. **II** *adj* **4.** Spar...: **~ class** ✈ Economyklasse *f*; **~ drive** Sparmaßnahmen *pl*; **~ price** günstiger *od.* niedriger Preis.

e·co·sys·tem ['i:kəʊˌsɪstəm] *s* Ökosystem *n*.

ec·sta·size ['ekstəsaɪz] **I** *v/t* in Ekstase versetzen. **II** *v/i* in Ekstase geraten. **'ec·sta·sy** *s* Ekstase *f*: **be in an ~** außer sich sein (**of** vor *dat*); **in an ~ of joy** in e-m Freudentaumel; **go into ecstasies over** in Verzückung geraten über (*acc*). **ec·stat·ic** [ɪk'stætɪk] *adj* (**~ally**) ekstatisch, verzückt.

e·cu·men·i·cal [ˌi:kju:'menɪkl] *adj* □ ökumenisch.

ec·ze·ma ['eksɪmə] *s* 🩺 Ekzem *n*.

ed·dy ['edɪ] **I** *s* Wirbel *m*, Strudel *m*. **II** *v/i* wirbeln.

edge [edʒ] **I** *s* **1.** Schneide *f*; Schärfe *f*: **have no ~** stumpf sein, nicht schneiden; **take the ~ off** *Klinge* stumpf machen; *fig. e-r Sache* die Schärfe nehmen. **2.** Ecke *f*, scharfe Kante. **3.** (äußerster) Rand, Saum *m*; **on the ~ of** *fig.* kurz vor (*dat*); **be on the ~ of despair** am Rande der Verzweiflung sein; **be on the ~ of doing s.th.** im Begriff sein, et. zu tun. **4.** Kante *f*, Schmalseite *f*: **set** (**up**) **on ~** hochkant stellen; **on ~** nervös; gereizt; **set s.o.'s teeth on ~** j-n nervös machen. **5.** F Vorteil *m*: **give s.o. an ~** j-m e-n Vorteil verschaffen; **have the ~ on s.o.**

j-m über sein. **II** v/t **6.** schärfen. **7.** umsäumen, einfassen. **8.** schieben, drängen: **~ on** antreiben, drängen. **III** v/i **9.** sich schieben od. drängen. **edged** adj **1.** scharf. **2.** in Zssgn ...schneidig; ...kantig.

'**edge|·ways**, **~·wise** ['~waɪz] adv hochkant: **I could hardly get a word in ~** fig. ich bin kaum zu Wort gekommen.

edg·y ['edʒɪ] adj □ nervös; gereizt.

ed·i·ble ['edɪbl] **I** adj eß-, genießbar: **~ oil** Speiseöl n. **II** s pl Eßwaren pl.

e·dict ['iːdɪkt] s Erlaß m, hist. Edikt n.

ed·i·fice ['edɪfɪs] s Gebäude n (a. fig.).

ed·i·fy ['~faɪ] v/t fig. erbauen. '**ed·i·fy·ing** adj □ erbaulich.

ed·it ['edɪt] v/t **1.** Texte etc a) herausgeben, b) redigieren. **2.** Film schneiden. **3.** Zeitung etc als Herausgeber leiten. **e·di·tion** [ɪ'dɪʃn] s **1.** Ausgabe f: **first ~** Erstausgabe; **morning ~** Morgenausgabe (Zeitung). **2.** Auflage f. **ed·i·tor** ['edɪtə] s **1.** a. **~ in chief** Herausgeber(in) (e-s Buchs etc). **2.** Zeitung: a) a. **~ in chief** Chefredakteur(in): → **letter** 2, b) Redakteur(in): **the ~s** pl die Redaktion. **3.** Film, TV: Cutter(in). **ed·i·to·ri·al** [~'tɔːrɪəl] **I** adj □ redaktionell, Redaktions...: **~ department** Redaktion f; → **staff** 1. **II** s Leitartikel m.

ed·u·cate ['edʒʊkeɪt] v/t **1.** erziehen, (aus)bilden: **he was ~d at** er besuchte die (Hoch)Schule in (dat). **2.** weitS. (**to**) erziehen (zu); gewöhnen (an acc). '**ed·u·cat·ed** adj □ gebildet. **2. ~ guess** mehr als e-e bloße Vermutung. **ed·u·ca·tion** s **1.** Erziehung f, (Aus)Bildung f: → **compulsory** 2, **university** 1. **2.** Bildung(sstand m) f: → **general** 2, **3.** Bildungs-, Schulwesen n. **4.** Pädagogik f. **ed·u·ca·tion·al** [~ʃənl] adj □ **1.** a) pädagogisch, Unterrichts...: **~ film** Lehrfilm m; **~ television** Schulfernsehen n, b) lehrreich (Erfahrung etc), c) pädagogisch wertvoll (Spielzeug). **2.** Bildungs...: **~ level** (od. **standard**) Bildungsniveau n.

eel [iːl] s ichth. Aal m: (**as**) **slippery as an ~** fig. aalglatt.

ee·rie, **ee·ry** ['ɪərɪ] adj □ unheimlich, (Schrei etc) schaurig.

ef·face [ɪ'feɪs] v/t wegwischen, -reiben, a. fig. (aus)löschen.

ef·fect [ɪ'fekt] **I** s **1.** Wirkung f (**on** auf acc): a) Erfolg m: **of no ~**, **without ~** erfolg-, wirkungslos, b) Auswirkung f, c) Effekt m, Eindruck m: **have an ~ on** wirken auf (acc); e-n Eindruck hinterlassen bei. **2.** Inhalt m, Sinn m: **a letter to the ~ that** ein Brief des Inhalts, daß; **inform s.o. to that ~** j-n entsprechend informieren. **3.** (Rechts)Wirksamkeit f, (~)Kraft f: **be in ~** in Kraft sein; **take ~**, **come** (od. **go**) **into ~** in Kraft treten; **with ~ from** mit Wirkung vom. **4.** **carry into ~**, **give ~ to** verwirklichen, ausführen; **in ~** in Wirklichkeit, tatsächlich. **5.** ✪ (Nutz)Leistung f. **6.** pl ✝ Effekten pl; Vermögen(swerte pl) n. **II** v/t **7.** bewirken. **8.** ausführen, tätigen. **ef'fec·tive** adj □ **1.** wirksam, erfolgreich. **2.** eindrucks-, wirkungs-, effektvoll. **3.** (rechts)wirksam, rechtskräftig: **be ~** in Kraft sein; **become ~** in Kraft treten; **~ from** (od. **as of**) mit Wirkung vom. **4.** tatsächlich, effektiv: **~ salary** Effektivgehalt n. **ef'fec·tive·ness** s Wirksamkeit f. **ef'fec·tu·al** [~tʃʊəl] adj □ **1.** wirksam. **2.** → **effective** 3. **ef'fec·tu·ate** [~tʃʊeɪt] v/t bewirken.

ef·fem·i·nate [ɪ'femɪnət] adj □ **1.** weibisch, unmännlich. **2.** verweichlicht, weichlich.

ef·fer·vesce [ˌefə'ves] v/i **1.** sprudeln, schäumen, moussieren. **2.** fig. (über-)sprudeln, überschäumen (**with** vor dat). **ef·fer·ves·cent** [~snt] adj □ **1.** sprudelnd, schäumend, moussierend: **~ powder** Brausepulver n. **2.** fig. (über-)sprudelnd, überschäumend.

ef·fi·ca·cious [ˌefɪ'keɪʃəs] adj □ wirksam. **ef·fi·ca·cy** ['~kəsɪ] s Wirksamkeit f.

ef·fi·cien·cy [ɪ'fɪʃənsɪ] s Effizienz f: a) Tüchtigkeit f, (Leistungs)Fähigkeit f: **~ rating** Leistungsbewertung f; → **principle** 1, b) rationelle Arbeitsweise, Wirtschaftlichkeit f: **~ expert** ✝ Rationalisierungsfachmann m. **ef'fi·cient** adj □ effizient: a) tüchtig, (leistungs-)fähig, b) rationell, wirtschaftlich.

ef·fi·gy ['efɪdʒɪ] s **1.** Steinplastik f; Bildnis n (auf e-r Münze). **2.** Puppe od. bildhafte Darstellung e-r verhaßten Person: **burn** (**hang**) **s.o. in ~** j-n symbolisch verbrennen (hängen).

ef·fort ['efət] s Anstrengung f: a) Bemühung *f*, b) Mühe *f*: **make an** ~ sich bemühen *od.* anstrengen; **make every** ~ sich alle Mühe geben; **spare no** ~ keine Mühe scheuen; **without** ~ mühelos; ~ **of will** Willensanstrengung. **'ef·fort·less** *adj* □ mühelos.

ef·fron·ter·y [ɪ'frʌntərɪ] *s* Frechheit *f*, Unverschämtheit *f*: **have the** ~ die Unverschämtheit haben *od.* besitzen (**to do** zu tun).

ef·fu·sive [ɪ'fjuːsɪv] *adj* □ überschwenglich.

egg[1] [eg] *s* Ei *n*: **in the** ~ *fig.* im Anfangsstadium, im Entstehen; (**as**) **sure as** ~**s is** (*od.* **are**) ~**s** F so sicher wie das Amen in der Kirche, todsicher; → **like**[1] 4.

egg[2] [~] *v/t mst* ~ **on** anstacheln, antreiben.

'egg|**·beat·er** *s* Schneebesen *m*. ~ **co·sy** (*Am.* **co·zy**) *s* Eierwärmer *m*. **'~·cup** *s* Eierbecher *m*. **'~·head** *s* F Eierkopf *m* (*Intellektueller*). **'~·shaped** *adj* eiförmig. **'~·shell** *s* Eierschale *f*. ~ **tim·er** *s* Eieruhr *f*. ~ **whisk** *s* Schneebesen *m*. ~ **white** *s* Eiweiß *n*.

e·go ['egəʊ] *pl* -**gos** *s phls.*, *psych.* Ich *n*, Ego *n*; *weitS.* Selbst(wertgefühl *n*): **boost s.o.'s**, **give s.o. an** ~ **boost** F j-s Selbstwertgefühl (an)heben. **e·go·cen·tric** [~'sentrɪk] *adj* (**~ally**) egozentrisch. ~ *s* Egozentriker(in). **'e·go·ism** *s* Egoismus *m*. **'e·go·ist** *s* Egoist(in). **,e·go·is·tic, ,e·go·is·ti·cal** [~kl] *adj* □ egoistisch. **e·go·tism** ['~tɪzəm] *s* 1. Egotismus *m*, Geltungsbedürfnis *n*, Selbstgefälligkeit *f*. 2. → **egoism**. **'e·go·tist** *s* 1. Egotist(in). 2. → **egoist**. **,e·go·tis·tic, ,e·go·tis·ti·cal** [~kl] *adj* □ 1. egotistisch, geltungsbedürftig, selbstgefällig. 2. → **egoistic**.

e·go trip *s* F Egotrip *m* (*Akt geistiger Selbstbefriedigung*): **be off on an** ~ auf e-m Egotrip sein.

E·gyp·tian [ɪ'dʒɪpʃn] I *adj* ägyptisch. II *s* Ägypter(in).

ei·der ['aɪdə] *s* 1. → **eider duck**. 2. → **eiderdown** 1. **'~·down** *s* 1. *coll.* Eiderdaunen *pl*. 2. Daunendecke *f*. ~ **duck** *s orn.* Eiderente *f*.

eight [eɪt] I *adj* 1. acht: **~·hour day** Achtstundentag *m*. II *s* 2. Acht *f*: ~ **of hearts** Herzacht. 3. *Rudern*: Achter *m* (*Boot*, *Mannschaft*). **eight·een** [,eɪ'tiːn] *adj* achtzehn. **,eight'eenth** [~θ] *adj* acht-

zehnt. **eight·fold** ['~fəʊld] I *adj* achtfach. II *adv* achtfach, um das Achtfache: **increase** ~ (sich) verachtfachen. **eighth** [eɪtθ] I *adj* 1. achte(r, -s). II *s* 2. der, die, das Achte: **the** ~ **of May** der 8. Mai. 3. Achtel *n*. **'eighth·ly** *adv* achtens. **eight·i·eth** ['~ɪəθ] *adj* achtzigst. **'eight-time** *adj* achtmalig. **eight·y** ['eɪtɪ] I *adj* achtzig. II *s* Achtzig *f*: **be in one's eighties** in den Achtzigern sein; **in the eighties** in den achtziger Jahren (*e-s Jahrhunderts*).

ei·ther ['aɪðə] I *adj* 1. jede(r, -s) (*von zweien*): **on** ~ **side** auf beiden Seiten. 2. irgendein (*von zweien*): ~ **way** auf die e-e *od.* die andere Art. II *pron* 3. irgendein (*von zweien*): **I haven't seen** ~ ich habe beide nicht gesehen, ich habe keinen (von beiden) gesehen. 4. beides: ~ **is possible.** III *cj* 5. ~ ... **or** entweder ... oder. 6. *neg.*: ~ ... **or** weder ... noch: **it isn't enough** ~ **for you or for me** es reicht weder für mich noch für dich. IV *adj* 7. **not** ~ auch nicht.

e·jac·u·late [ɪ'dʒækjʊleɪt] I *v/t* 1. *physiol.* Samen ausstoßen. 2. Worte etc aus-, hervorstoßen. II *v/i* 3. *physiol.* ejakulieren, e-n Samenerguß haben. **e·,jac·u·la·tion** *s* 1. *physiol.* Ejakulation *f*, Samenerguß *m*. 2. Ausruf *m*; Stoßseufzer *m*.

e·ject [ɪ'dʒekt] I *v/t* 1. (**from**) *j-n* hinauswerfen (aus); vertreiben (aus, von). 2. entlassen, entfernen (**from** aus *e-m Amt*). 3. ☉ ausstoßen, -werfen. II *v/i* 4. ✈ den Schleudersitz betätigen. **e·jec·tion** *s* 1. Vertreibung *f*. 2. Entfernung *f*. 3. ☉ Ausstoßen *n*, -werfen *n*: ~ **seat** ✈ Schleudersitz *m*. **e·jec·tor** *s* ☉ Auswerfer *m*: ~ **seat** ✈ Schleudersitz *m*.

eke [iːk] *v/t*: ~ **out** Flüssigkeit, Vorräte etc strecken; Einkommen aufbessern (**with** mit): ~ **out a living** sich (mühsam) durchschlagen.

e·lab·o·rate I *adj* [ɪ'læbərət] 1. sorgfältig *od.* kunstvoll gearbeitet *od.* ausgeführt. 2. (wohl)durchdacht. 3. umständlich. II *v/t* [~reɪt] 4. sorgfältig ausarbeiten. 5. *Theorie etc* entwickeln. III *v/i* [~reɪt] 6. nähere Angaben machen: ~ **on** näher eingehen auf (*acc*).

e·lapse [ɪ'læps] *v/i* vergehen, -streichen (*Zeit*), ablaufen (*Frist*).

e·las·tic [ɪˈlæstɪk] **I** adj (~ally) **1.** allg. elastisch (a. fig.): ~ conscience weites Gewissen; ~ word dehnbarer Begriff. **2.** Gummi...: ~ band Gummiring m, -band n, (Dichtungs)Gummi m; ~ stocking Gummistrumpf m. **II** s **3.** bsd. Am. Gummiring m, -band n, (Dichtungs)Gummi m. **e·las·tic·i·ty** [ˌelæˈstɪsətɪ] s allg. Elastizität f (a. fig.).

e·lat·ed [ɪˈleɪtɪd] adj □ begeistert (at von), in Hochstimmung. **e·la·tion** s Begeisterung f, Hochstimmung f.

el·bow [ˈelbəʊ] **I** s **1.** Ell(en)bogen m: at one's ~ in Reichweite; bsd. fig. an s-r Seite; out at ~(s) schäbig, abgetragen (Kleidung); schäbig gekleidet; Am. knapp bei Kasse. **2.** (scharfe) Biegung od. Krümmung. **3.** (Rohr)Krümmer m, Kniestück n. **II** v/t **4.** mit dem Ellbogen stoßen, drängen (a. fig.): ~ out hinausdrängen; ~ one's way through sich den Weg bahnen durch. ~ grease s humor. **1.** Armschmalz n (Kraft). **2.** Schufterei f. ~room s **1.** Ellbogenfreiheit f. **2.** fig. Bewegungsfreiheit f, Spielraum m.

eld·er¹ [ˈeldə] **I** adj **1.** älter (Bruder, Schwester etc). **2.** ~ statesman Staatsmann im Ruhestand, der die politischen Führer inoffiziell berät; weitS. großer alter Mann (e-r Berufsgruppe etc). **II** s **3.** my ~s Leute, die älter sind als ich.

eld·er² [~] s ♀ Holunder m. ~·ber·ry s Holunderbeere f.

eld·er·ly [ˈeldəlɪ] adj ältlich, älter.

eld·est [ˈeldɪst] adj ältest (Bruder, Schwester etc).

e·lect [ɪˈlekt] **I** v/t j-n wählen ([as, to be] president zum Präsidenten). **II** adj (nachgestellt) designiert, zukünftig. **e·lec·tion I** s Wahl f: → stand for 4. **II** adj Wahl...: ~ campaign Wahlkampf m. **e·lec·tion·eer** [~ʃəˈnɪə] v/i Wahlkampf betreiben: ~ for Wahlpropaganda treiben für. **e·lec·tion·eer·ing** s Wahlkampf m; -propaganda f. **e·lec·tive I** adj **1.** gewählt, Wahl... **2.** wahlberechtigt. **3.** ped., univ. bsd. Am. fakultativ: ~ subject → 4. **II** s **4.** ped. univ. bsd. Am. Wahlfach n. **e·lec·tor** s Wähler(in); Am. Wahlmann m. **e·lec·tor·al** adj Wähler..., Wahl...: ~ college Am. Wahlmänner pl. **e·lec·to·rate** [~tərət] s Wähler(schaft f) pl.

e·lec·tric [ɪˈlektrɪk] adj (~ally) **1.** a) elektrisch: ~ chair elektrischer Stuhl; ~ cushion Heizkissen n; ~ shock Stromschlag m; ✳ etc Elektroschock m; ~ torch bsd. Br. Taschenlampe f, b) Elektro..., c) Elektrizitäts..., d) elektrotechnisch. **2.** fig. elektrisierend (Wirkung etc); spannungsgeladen (Atmosphäre). **e·lec·tri·cal** [~kl] adj □ → electric: ~ engineer Elektroingenieur m; -techniker m; ~ engineering Elektrotechnik f.

e·lec·tri·cian [ˌɪlekˈtrɪʃn] s Elektrotechniker m, Elektriker m. **e·lec·tric·i·ty** [~sətɪ] s Elektrizität f; Strom m. **e·lec·tri·fy** [~faɪ] v/t **1.** elektrisieren (a. fig.). **2.** elektrifizieren.

e·lec·tro·car·di·o·gram [ɪˌlektrəʊˈkɑːdɪəʊɡræm] s ✳ Elektrokardiogramm n. **e·lec·tro·cute** [ɪˈlektrəkjuːt] v/t **1.** auf dem elektrischen Stuhl hinrichten. **2.** be ~d e-n tödlichen Stromschlag erhalten. **e·lec·tro·cu·tion** s Hinrichtung f auf dem elektrischen Stuhl. **e·lec·trode** [ɪˈlektrəʊd] s ∮ Elektrode f. **e·lec·tron** [ɪˈlektrɒn] phys. **I** s Elektron n. **II** adj Elektronen...: ~ microscope. **e·lec·tron·ic** [ˌɪlekˈtrɒnɪk] **I** adj (~ally): ~ data processing elektronische Datenverarbeitung; ~ flash phot. Elektronenblitz m. **II** s pl (sg konstruiert) Elektronik f.

e·lec·tro·plate [ɪˈlektrəʊpleɪt] v/t galvanisieren. **e·lec·tro·ther·a·py** s ✳ Elektrotherapie f.

el·e·gance [ˈelɪɡəns] s Eleganz f. **'el·e·gant** adj □ elegant.

el·e·ment [ˈelɪmənt] s **1.** allg. Element n. **2.** pl Anfangsgründe pl. **3.** grundlegender Umstand, wesentlicher Faktor: ~ of uncertainty Unsicherheitsfaktor; ~ of surprise Überraschungselement n. **4.** fig. Körnchen n, Fünkchen n (Wahrheit etc). **5.** (Lebens)Element n: be in one's ~ in s-m Element sein; be out of one's ~ sich fehl am Platz fühlen. **6.** pl Elemente pl, Naturkräfte pl. **el·e·men·tal** [~ˈmentl] adj □ **1.** elementar: a) ursprünglich, natürlich, b) urgewaltig, c) wesentlich, grundlegend. **2.** Elementar..., Ur... **3.** → elementary 2, 3. **el·e·men·ta·ry** adj □ **1.** → elemental 1, 2. **2.** elementar, Einführungs...: ~ school Am. Grundschule f. **3.** 🜍, ♣, *phys.* Elementar...: **~ particle** Elementarteilchen *n*.

e·le·phant ['elɪfənt] *s zo.* Elefant *m*. **el·e·phan·tine** [,~'fæntaɪn] *adj* **1.** elefantenartig: **an ~ memory** ein Gedächtnis wie ein Elefant. **2.** plump, schwerfällig.

el·e·vate ['elɪveɪt] *v/t* **1.** (hoch-, auf)heben. **2.** *j-n* erheben (**to peerage** in den Adelsstand), befördern (**to** zu). **'el·e·vat·ed** *adj* **1.** erhöht: **~ railway** (*Am.* **railroad**) Hochbahn *f*. **2.** gehoben (*Position, Stil etc*), erhaben (*Gedanken*). **3.** übersteigert (*Meinung etc*). **,el·e·'va·tion** *s* **1.** (Boden)Erhebung *f*, (An-)Höhe *f*. **2.** Erhebung *f*, Beförderung *f*. **3.** △, ✏ Aufriß *m*. **'el·e·va·tor** *s Am.* Aufzug *m*, Fahrstuhl *m*: **~ shaft** Aufzugschacht *m*.

e·lev·en [ɪ'levn] **I** *adj* elf. **II** *s* Elf *f* (*a. Sport*). **e·lev·en·ses** [,~zɪz] *s pl Br.* F zweites Frühstück. **e·lev·enth** [,~θ] *adj* elft: **at the ~ hour** *fig.* in letzter Minute.

elf *pl* **elves** [elvz] *s* **1.** Elf *m*, Elfe *f*. **2.** Kobold *m*. **'elf·ish** *adj* □ **1.** elfenhaft. **2.** koboldhaft, schelmisch.

e·lic·it [ɪ'lɪsɪt] *v/t* **1.** (**from**) *et.* entlocken (*dat*); *Wahrheit* herausholen, -lokken (aus). **2.** *Applaus, Gelächter etc* hervorrufen.

el·i·gi·bil·i·ty [,elɪdʒə'bɪlətɪ] *s* **1.** Eignung *f*. **2.** Berechtigung *f*. **3.** Wählbarkeit *f*. **'el·i·gi·ble** *adj* □ (**for**) in Frage kommend (für): a) geeignet, annehmbar (für): **~ bachelor** begehrter Junggeselle, b) berechtigt, befähigt (zu), qualifiziert (für): **be ~ for** Anspruch haben auf (*acc*); **~ to vote** wahlberechtigt, c) teilnahmeberechtigt (an *dat*), (*Sport a.*) start- od. spielberechtigt (für), d) wählbar (für).

e·lim·i·nate [ɪ'lɪmɪneɪt] *v/t* **1.** beseitigen, entfernen, eliminieren (**from** aus). **2.** ✏, *physiol.* ausscheiden. **3.** *Gegner* ausschalten: **be ~d** (*Sport*) ausscheiden. **e,lim·i·'na·tion** *s* **1.** Beseitigung *f*, Eliminierung *f*. **2.** ✏, *physiol.* Ausscheidung *f* (*a. Sport*): **~ contest** Ausscheidungswettbewerb *m*. **3.** Ausschaltung *f*.

e·lite, *Br. a.* **é·lite** [eɪ'liːt] *s* Elite *f*.

e·lix·ir [ɪ'lɪksə] *s* Elixier *n*.

elk [elk] *s zo.* Elch *m*.

el·lipse [ɪ'lɪps] *s* ✏ Ellipse *f*. **el'lip·sis**

[,sɪs] *pl* **-ses** [,siːz] *s ling.* Ellipse *f*. **el'lip·tic, el'lip·ti·cal** [,kl] *adj* □ ✏, *ling.* elliptisch.

elm [elm] *s* ♣ Ulme *f*, Rüster *f*.

e·lo·cu·tion [,elə'kjuːʃn] *s* **1.** Vortrag(sweise *f*) *m*. **2.** Vortrags-, Redekunst *f*. **3.** Sprechtechnik *f*.

e·lon·gate ['iːlɒŋgeɪt] *v/t* (*u. v/i* sich) verlängern. **,e·lon'ga·tion** *s* Verlängerung *f*.

e·lope [ɪ'ləʊp] *v/i* **1.** (mit s-m *od.* s-r Geliebten) ausreißen *od.* durchbrennen. **2.** sich davonmachen.

el·o·quence ['eləkwəns] *s* Beredsamkeit *f*, Redegewandtheit *f*. **'el·o·quent** *adj* □ beredt, redegewandt.

else [els] *adv* **1.** (*in Fragen u. Verneinungen*) sonst, weiter, außerdem: **anything ~?** sonst noch etwas?; **what ~ can we do?** was können wir sonst noch tun?; **no one ~** sonst *od.* weiter niemand. **2.** ander: **that's s.th. ~** das ist et. anderes; **everybody ~** alle anderen; **s.o. ~** j-d anders. **3.** *mst* **or ~** sonst, andernfalls. **,~'where** *adv* **1.** sonst-, anderswo. **2.** anderswohin.

e·lu·ci·date [ɪ'luːsɪdeɪt] *v/t* *Text, Gründe etc* erklären, *Geheimnis etc* aufklären.

e·lu·sive [ɪ'luːsɪv] *adj* □ **1.** schwerfaßbar (*Dieb etc*), ausweichend (*Antwort*). **2.** schwer(er)faßbar *od.* -bestimmbar. **3.** unzuverlässig, schlecht (*Gedächtnis*).

elves [elvz] *pl von* **elf**.

e·ma·ci·at·ed [ɪ'meɪʃɪeɪtɪd] *adj* abgemagert, ausgemergelt.

em·a·nate ['eməneɪt] **I** *v/i* **1.** ausströmen (*Gas etc*), ausstrahlen (*Licht*) (**from** von). **2.** stammen, ausgehen (**from** von). **II** *v/t* **3.** ausströmen, -strahlen (*beide a. fig.*).

e·man·ci·pate [ɪ'mænsɪpeɪt] *v/t* emanzipieren, selbständig *od.* unabhängig machen (**from** von). **e'man·ci·pat·ed** *adj* emanzipiert (*Frau etc*), mündig (*Bürger*). **e,man·ci·'pa·tion** *s* Emanzipation *f*.

em·balm [ɪm'bɑːm] *v/t* (ein)balsamieren.

em·bank [ɪm'bæŋk] *v/t* eindämmen, -deichen. **em'bank·ment** *s* **1.** Eindämmung *f*, -deichung *f*. **2.** (Erd)Damm *m*. **3.** (Bahn-, Straßen)Damm *m*.

em·bar·go [em'bɑːɡəʊ] **I** *pl* **-goes** *s* **1.** ✏ Embargo *n*: **lay** (*od.* **place, put**) **an ~ on**

→ 3. **2.** ✝ a) Handelssperre f, -verbot n, b) a. allg. Sperre f, Verbot n (**on** auf dat od. acc): **~ on imports** Einfuhrsperre. **II** v/t **2.** ein Embargo verhängen über (acc).

em·bark [ɪmˈbɑːk] **I** v/t **1.** ✈, ⚓ Passagiere an Bord nehmen, ⚓ a. einschiffen, Waren a. verladen (**for** nach). **II** v/i **2.** ✈, ⚓ an Bord gehen, ⚓ a. sich einschiffen (**for** nach). **3.** anfangen, unternehmen (**on** acc). **em·bar·ka·tion** [ˌembaːˈkeɪʃn] s Einschiffung f, Verladung f.

em·bar·rass [ɪmˈbærəs] v/t **1.** in (a. Geld)Verlegenheit bringen, verlegen machen. **em'bar·rassed** adj **1.** verlegen. **2.** in Geldverlegenheit. **em'bar·rass·ing** adj □ unangenehm, peinlich (**to** dat). **em'bar·rass·ment** s (a. Geld)Verlegenheit f: **be an ~ to** j-n in Verlegenheit bringen; j-m peinlich sein.

em·bas·sy [ˈembəsɪ] s pol. Botschaft f.

em·bed [ɪmˈbed] v/t **1.** (ein)betten (**in** in acc): **~ded in concrete** einbetoniert. **2.** verankern (**in** in acc od. dat) (a. fig.).

em·bel·lish [ɪmˈbelɪʃ] v/t **1.** verschöne(r)n, (aus)schmücken. **2.** Erzählung etc ausschmücken, Wahrheit beschönigen.

em·ber [ˈembə] s **1.** glühendes Stück Holz od. Kohle. **2.** pl Glut(asche) f.

em·bez·zle [ɪmˈbezl] v/t veruntreuen, unterschlagen. **em'bez·zle·ment** s Veruntreuung f, Unterschlagung f. **em'bez·zler** s Veruntreuer(in).

em·bit·ter [ɪmˈbɪtə] v/t **1.** j-n verbittern. **2.** Lage etc (noch) verschlimmern.

em·blem [ˈembləm] s **1.** Emblem n, Symbol n: **national ~** Hoheitszeichen n. **2.** Kennzeichen n.

em·bod·y [ɪmˈbɒdɪ] v/t **1.** verkörpern: a) konkrete Form geben (dat), b) personifizieren. **2.** umfassen, (in sich) vereinigen: **be embodied in** enthalten od. vereinigt sein in (dat).

em·bo·lism [ˈembəlɪzəm] s ⚕ Embolie f.

em·brace [ɪmˈbreɪs] **I** v/t **1.** umarmen. **2.** fig. einschließen, umfassen. **3.** Beruf, Gelegenheit ergreifen; Angebot, Religion etc annehmen. **II** v/i **4.** sich umarmen. **III** s **5.** Umarmung f.

em·broi·der [ɪmˈbrɔɪdə] **I** v/t **1.** Muster sticken; Stoff besticken. **2.** Bericht etc ausschmücken. **II** v/i **3.** sticken.

em'broi·der·y s **1.** Sticken n: **~ needle** Sticknadel f. **2.** Stickerei(arbeit) f: **do ~** sticken. **3.** fig. Ausschmückung f.

em·bry·o [ˈembrɪəʊ] pl **-os** s biol. Embryo m: **in ~** fig. im Entstehen od. Werden. **em·bry·on·ic** [ˌ~ˈɒnɪk] adj **1.** biol. embryonal. **2.** fig. (noch) unentwickelt.

em·cee [ˌemˈsiː] bsd. Am. F **I** s Conférencier m. **II** v/t u. v/i als Conférencier leiten (fungieren).

e·mend [ɪˈmend] v/t bsd. Texte verbessern, korrigieren.

em·er·ald [ˈemərəld] **I** s min. Smaragd m. **II** adj smaragdgrün.

e·merge [ɪˈmɜːdʒ] v/i **1.** auftauchen (a. fig.). **2.** hervorkommen (**from behind** hinter den Wolken etc). **3.** sich herausstellen od. ergeben (Tatsache). **e·mer·gence** [iːˈm~] s Auftauchen n (a. fig.).

e·mer·gen·cy [ɪˈmɜːdʒənsɪ] s plötzliche Notlage, kritische Lage: **in an ~, in case of ~** im Ernst- od. Notfall; **state of ~** Notstand m, pol. a. Ausnahmezustand m. **~ call** s teleph. Notruf m. **~ door, ~ ex·it** s Notausgang m. **~ land·ing** s ✈ Notlandung f: **make an ~** notlanden. **~ meet·ing** s Dringlichkeitssitzung f. **~ num·ber** s teleph. Notruf(nummer f) m. **~ op·er·a·tion** s ⚕ Notoperation f. **~ ra·tion** s eiserne Ration. **~ stop** s mot. Vollbremsung f: **do** (od. **make**) **an ~** e-e Vollbremsung machen.

e·mer·gent [iːˈmɜːdʒənt] adj □ **1.** auftauchend (a. fig.). **2.** fig. (jung u.) aufstrebend: **~ countries** pl Schwellenländer pl.

em·er·y [ˈemərɪ] adj Schmirgel...: **~ paper.**

e·met·ic [ɪˈmetɪk] s Brechmittel n.

em·i·grant [ˈemɪgrənt] s Auswanderer m, bsd. pol. Emigrant(in). **em·i·grate** [ˈ~greɪt] v/i auswandern, bsd. pol. emigrieren (**from** aus, von; **to** nach). **em·i·gra·tion** s Auswanderung f, bsd. pol. Emigration f.

em·i·nence [ˈemɪnəns] s **1.** (An)Höhe f. **2.** Berühmtheit f: **reach** (od. **win**) **~** Bedeutung erlangen (**as** als). **3.** eccl. Eminenz f. **'em·i·nent** adj **1.** hervorragend, berühmt. **2.** bedeutend. **3.** überragend, außergewöhnlich. **'em·i·nent·ly** adv in hohem Maße, überaus.

e·mis·sion [ı'mıʃn] s **1.** Ausstoß m, -strahlung f, Aus-, Verströmen n. **2.** ✝ Ausgabe f, Emission f.

e·mit [ı'mıt] v/t **1.** Lava, Rauch ausstoßen, Licht, Wärme ausstrahlen, Gas, Wärme aus-, verströmen. **2.** Ton, Meinung von sich geben; Schrei, Fluch etc ausstoßen. **3.** Banknoten ausgeben, Wertpapiere a. emittieren.

e·mo·tion [ı'məʊʃn] s **1.** Emotion f, Gefühl n. **2.** Erregung f. **3.** Rührung f, Ergriffenheit f. **e'mo·tion·al** [~ʃənl] adj □ **1.** emotional, emotionell: a) gefühlsmäßig, -bedingt, b) gefühlsbetont, empfindsam, c) Gemüts..., seelisch: ~ balance inneres od. seelisches Gleichgewicht. **2.** gefühlvoll, rührselig. **e'mo·tion·al·ize** [~ʃənlaız] v/t emotionalisieren, unterstreichen. **e'mo·tion·less** adj gefühllos. **e'mo·tive** [~tıv] adj **1.** gefühlvoll. **2.** gefühlsbetont: ~ term (od. word) emotionsgeladenes Wort; Reizwort n.

em·pa·thy ['empəθı] s Einfühlung(svermögen n) f: feel ~ for sich hineinversetzen in (acc).

em·per·or ['empərə] s Kaiser m.

em·pha·sis ['emfəsıs] pl **-ses** [~siːz] s ling. Betonung f, fig. a. Schwerpunkt m; Nachdruck m: lay (od. place, put) ~ on → emphasize; with ~ nachdrücklich, mit Nachdruck. **em·pha·size** ['~saız] v/t (nachdrücklich) betonen, Nachdruck legen auf (acc), hervorheben, unterstreichen. **em·phat·ic** [ım-'fætık] adj (~ally) nachdrücklich; eindringlich.

em·pire ['empaıə] s **1.** Reich n, Imperium n (beide a. ✝ u. fig.). **2.** Kaiserreich n.

em·pir·i·cal [em'pırıkl] adj □ empirisch, Erfahrungs...

em·ploy [ım'plɔı] I v/t **1.** j-n beschäftigen (as als); an-, einstellen. **2.** Gewalt etc anwenden, gebrauchen. **3.** (in) Energie etc widmen (dat), Zeit verbringen (mit): be ~ed in doing s.th. damit beschäftigt sein, et. zu tun. II s **4.** Dienst(e pl) m, Beschäftigung(sverhältnis n) f: in s.o.'s ~ bei j-m beschäftigt. **em·ploy-ee** [ˌemplɔı'iː] s Arbeitnehmer(in), Angestellte m, f, Arbeiter(in): the ~s pl die Belegschaft. **em·ploy·er** [ım'plɔıə] s Arbeitgeber(in); Unternehmer(in). **em·ploy·ment** s **1.** Beschäftigung f,

Arbeit f, (An)Stellung f: full ~ Vollbeschäftigung; ~ agency Br. Stellenvermittlung(sbüro n) f; ~ contract Arbeitsvertrag m; ~ market Arbeits-, Stellenmarkt m; ~ service agency Br. Arbeitsamt n. **2.** An-, Einstellung f.

em·pow·er [ım'paʊə] v/t bevollmächtigen, ermächtigen (to do zu tun).

em·press ['emprıs] s Kaiserin f.

emp·ti·ness ['emptınıs] s Leere f (a. fig.). **'emp·ty** I adj □ **1.** allg. leer (a. fig. Versprechungen, Worte etc), (Haus etc a.) leerstehend: feel ~ sich (innerlich) leer fühlen; F Kohldampf schieben; ~ stand ~ leerstehen; ~ of ohne; ~ of meaning nichtssagend; ~ stomach 1. II v/t **2.** leeren (into in acc), Fach etc a. ausräumen, Glas etc a. austrinken. **3.** Haus etc räumen. III v/i **4.** sich leeren. **5.** sich ergießen, münden (into in acc). IV s **6.** pl Leergut n. **,~'hand·ed** adj mit leeren Händen, unverrichteterdinge.

em·u·late ['emjʊleıt] v/t **1.** wetteifern mit. **2.** nacheifern (dat), es gleichtun wollen (dat).

e·mul·sion [ı'mʌlʃn] s ✿, etc Emulsion f.

en·a·ble [ı'neıbl] v/t **1.** j-n berechtigen, ermächtigen (to do zu tun). **2.** j-n befähigen, es j-m möglich machen (to do zu tun). **3.** et. möglich machen, ermöglichen: ~ s.th. to be done es ermöglichen, daß et. getan wird.

en·act [ı'nækt] v/t **1.** ✄ Gesetz erlassen; verfügen, -ordnen. **2.** thea. etc Stück aufführen; Person, Rolle darstellen, spielen. **en'act·ment** s Verfügung f, -ordnung f.

en·am·el [ı'næml] I s **1.** Email(le f) n. **2.** Glasur f. **3.** anat. Zahnschmelz m. II v/t pret u. pp **-eled**, bsd. Br. **-elled 4.** emaillieren. **5.** glasieren.

en·am·o·u(r) [ı'næmə] v/t: be ~ed of (od. with) verliebt sein in (acc); fig. gefesselt od. verzaubert sein von.

en·case [ın'keıs] v/t: ~d in gehüllt in (acc), umhüllt von.

en·chant [ın'tʃɑːnt] v/t **1.** verzaubern. **2.** fig. bezaubern, entzücken: be ~ed entzückt sein (by, with von). **en'chant·er** s Zauberer m. **en'chant·ing** adj □ bezaubernd, entzückend. **en'chant·ment** s **1.** Verzauberung f. **2.** Zauber m (a.

endorsement

fig.). **3.** Zauberei *f.* **en'chant·ress** *s* **1.** Zauberin *f.* **2.** *fig.* bezaubernde Frau.

en·ci·pher [ɪn'saɪfə] → *encode.*

en·cir·cle [ɪn'sɜːkl] *v/t* **1.** umgeben: **~d by** (*od.* **with**) umgeben von. **2.** umfassen. **3.** einkreisen, umzingeln, ✕ *a.* einkesseln. **en'cir·cle·ment** *s* Einkreisung *f*, Umzing(e)lung *f*, ✕ *a.* Einkesselung *f*.

en·close [ɪn'kləʊz] *v/t* **1.** (*in*) einschließen (in *acc od. dat*), umgeben (mit). **2.** umringen. **3.** *mit der Hand etc* umfassen. **4.** beilegen, -fügen (*in*, **with** *dat*): **~d please find** in der Anlage erhalten Sie. **en'clo·sure** [~ʒə] *s* Anlage *f* (*zu e-m Brief etc*).

en·code [en'kəʊd] *v/t Text* verschlüsseln, chiffrieren.

en·com·pass [ɪn'kʌmpəs] *v/t* **1.** umgeben (**with** mit). **2.** *fig.* umfassen.

en·core I *int* [ɒŋ'kɔː] **1.** da capo!; Zugabe! II *s* ['ɒŋkɔː] **2.** Dakapo(ruf *m*) *n*. **3.** Wiederholung *f* (*e-r Arie etc*); Zugabe *f*. III *v/t* ['ɒŋkɔː] **4.** die Wiederholung (*gen*) verlangen *od.* erzwingen; von *j-m* e-e Zugabe verlangen *od.* erzwingen.

en·coun·ter [ɪn'kaʊntə] I *v/t* **1.** *j-m, e-r Sache* begegnen, *j-n* treffen, auf *j-n*, *Widerstand etc* stoßen. **2.** *mit j-m* (*feindlich*) zs.-stoßen. II *v/i* **3.** sich begegnen *od.* treffen. III *s* **4.** Begegnung *f* (**of, with** mit). **5.** *feindlicher* Zs.-stoß *m*.

en·cour·age [ɪn'kʌrɪdʒ] *v/t j-n* ermutigen, ermuntern (**to** zu), *j-m* Mut machen. **2.** *j-n* unterstützen, bestärken (*in* in *dat*). **3.** *et.* fördern, unterstützen. **en'cour·age·ment** *s* **1.** Ermutigung *f*, Ermunterung *f*. **2.** Unterstützung *f*, Bestärkung *f*. **3.** Förderung *f*.

en·croach [ɪn'krəʊtʃ] *v/i* **1.** (**on**) eingreifen (*in j-s Besitz od. Recht*), unberechtigt eindringen (*in acc*), sich Übergriffe leisten (*in*, auf *acc*). **2.** über Gebühr in Anspruch nehmen, mißbrauchen (**on** *acc*). **en'croach·ment** *s* Ein-, Übergriff *m*.

en·crust → *incrust.*

en·cum·ber [ɪn'kʌmbə] *v/t Grundstück etc* belasten: **~ed with mortgages** hypothekarisch belastet. **en'cum·brance** *s* Belastung *f*.

en·cy·clo·p(a)e·di·a [en,saɪkləʊ'piːdjə] *s*

Enzyklopädie *f*. **en,cy·clo'p(a)e·dic** *adj* (~ally) enzyklopädisch.

end [end] I *v/t* **1.** beenden, zu Ende bringen *od.* führen. **2.** *a.* **~ up** *et.* ab-, beschließen (**with** mit), b) *den Rest s-r Tage* zu-, verbringen, *s-e Tage* beschließen. II *v/i* **3.** enden, aufhören. III *v/i* **4.** *a.* **~ up** enden, ausgehen: **~ happily** gut ausgehen; **~ in disaster** (*od.* **a fiasco**) mit e-m Fiasko enden. **4.** a) enden, landen (**in prison** im Gefängnis), b) enden (**as** als). III *v/i* **6.** (*örtlich*) Ende *n*: **go off** (**at**) **the deep ~** F hochgehen, wütend werden; **make** (**both**) **~s meet** durchkommen, finanziell über die Runden kommen. **7.** Ende *n*, Rest *m*: → *thick* 1, *thin* 1. **8.** (*zeitlich*) Ende *n*: **in the ~** am Ende, schließlich; **at the ~ of May** Ende Mai; **without ~** unaufhörlich; **come** (*od.* **draw**) **to an ~** zu Ende gehen; **make an ~ of, put an ~ to** *e-r Sache* ein Ende setzen. **9.** Tod *m*, Ende *n*. **10.** *oft pl* Absicht *f*, (End)Zweck *m*, Ziel *n*: **the means** der Zweck heiligt die Mittel; **to this ~** zu diesem Zweck; **to no ~** vergebens.

en·dan·ger [ɪn'deɪndʒə] *v/t* gefährden.

end con·sum·er *s* ✝ End-, Letztverbraucher *m*.

en·dear·ing [ɪn'dɪərɪŋ] *adj* □ **1.** gewinnend (*Lächeln etc*). **2.** liebenswert (*Eigenschaft etc*). **en'dear·ment** *s*: (**term of**) **~** Kosename *m*, -wort *n*; **words** *pl* **of ~, ~s** *pl* liebe *od.* zärtliche Worte *pl*.

en·deav·o(u)r [ɪn'devə] I *v/i* bemüht *od.* bestrebt sein (**to do** zu tun). II *s* Bemühung *f*, Bestrebung *f*: **make every ~** sich nach Kräften bemühen.

end·ing ['endɪŋ] *s* **1.** Ende *n*, Schluß *m*: **happy ~** Happy-End *n*. **2.** *ling.* Endung *f*.

en·dive ['endɪv] *s* ✿ (Winter)Endivie *f*.

end·less ['endlɪs] *adj* □ *allg.* endlos.

en·dorse [ɪn'dɔːs] *v/t* **1.** *Erklärung etc* vermerken (**on** auf *dat*); *bsd.* Br. e-e Strafe vermerken auf (*e-m Führerschein*). **2.** ✝ *Scheck etc* indossieren, girieren. **3.** *Plan etc* billigen. **en·dor·see** [,endɔː'siː] *s* ✝ Indossat *m*. **en·dorse·ment** [ɪn'dɔːsmənt] *s* **1.** Vermerk *m*; *bsd.* Br. Strafvermerk *m* (*auf e-m Führerschein*). **2.** ✝ Indossament *n*,

Giro n. **3.** Billigung f. **en'dors·er** s ✝ Indossant m.

en·dow [ɪn'daʊ] v/t **1.** e-e Stiftung machen (dat). **2.** et. stiften: ~ **s.o. with s.th.** j-m et. stiften. **3.** fig. ausstatten (**with** mit). **en'dow·ment** s **1.** Stiftung f. **2.** Begabung f, Talent n.

end prod·uct s **1.** ✝, ⚙ Endprodukt n. **2.** fig. (End)Produkt n.

en·dur·a·ble [ɪn'djʊərəbl] adj □ erträglich. **en'dur·ance I** s **1.** Standhaftigkeit f, Ausdauer f; Aushalten n, Ertragen n: **beyond** (od. **past**) ~ unerträglich. **2.** ⚙ Dauerleistung f. **II** adj ⚙ Dauer...: ~ **test** ⚙ Belastungsprobe f. **en'dure I** v/i **1.** andauern, Bestand haben. **2.** durchhalten. **II** v/t **3.** aushalten, ertragen, erdulden. **4.** neg. ausstehen, leiden.

end us·er → **end consumer.**

en·e·ma ['enɪmə] pl **-mas, -ma·ta** [~mətə] s ✗ Klistier n, Einlauf m: **give s.o. an** ~ j-m e-n Einlauf machen.

en·e·my ['enəmɪ] **I** s ✗ Feind m, weitS. a. Gegner m (**of, to gen**): ~ **to reform** Reformgegner; **make an** ~ **of s.o.** sich j-n zum Feind machen. **II** adj feindlich, Feind(es)...

en·er·get·ic [¸enə'dʒetɪk] adj (~**ally**) energisch. **'en·er·gy** s Energie f (a. phys.): ~**saving** energiesparend.

en·er·vate ['enɜːveɪt] v/t entkräften, schwächen (a. fig.); entnerven.

en·fee·ble [ɪn'fiːbl] v/t entkräften, schwächen (a. fig.).

en·fold [ɪn'fəʊld] v/t **1.** einhüllen (**in** in acc), umhüllen (**with** mit) (beide a. fig.). **2.** umfassen: ~ **s.o. in one's arms** j-n in die Arme schließen.

en·force [ɪn'fɔːs] v/t **1.** Argument, ✝, ⚖ Forderung geltend machen; e-r Sache Geltung verschaffen, Gesetz etc durchführen; Urteil vollstrecken. **2.** durchsetzen, erzwingen: ~ **s.th. on s.o.** et. von j-m erzwingen; j-m et. aufzwingen. **en'force·ment** s **1.** ✝, ⚖ Geltendmachung f, ⚖ Vollstreckung f. **2.** Durchsetzung f, Erzwingung f.

en·fran·chise [ɪn'fræntʃaɪz] v/t das Wahlrecht verleihen (dat).

en·gage [ɪn'geɪdʒ] v/t **1.** (**o.s.** sich) verpflichten (**to do** zu tun). **2.** **become** (od. **get**) ~**d** sich verloben (**to** mit). **3.** j-n ein-, anstellen, Künstler etc engagieren

(**as** als). **4.** fig. j-n in Anspruch nehmen, j-s Aufmerksamkeit a. auf sich ziehen. **5.** ⚙ einrasten lassen, Kupplung etc einrücken, Gang einlegen. **II** v/i **6.** sich verpflichten (**to do** zu tun). **7.** ~ **in** sich einlassen auf (acc) od. in (acc); sich beschäftigen mit. **8.** ⚙ einrasten. **en'gaged** adj **1.** a. ~ **to be married** verlobt: ~ **to** verlobt mit. **2.** beschäftigt (**in, on** mit): ~ **in doing s.th.** damit beschäftigt sein, et. zu tun. **3.** in Anspruch genommen: **my time is fully** ~ ich bin zeitlich voll ausgelastet. **4.** teleph. Br. besetzt: ~**tone** Besetztton m, -zeichen n. **en'gage·ment** s **1.** Verpflichtung f: **without** ~ unverbindlich, ✝ a. freibleibend. **2.** Verabredung f: **have an** ~ verabredet sein. **3.** Verlobung f (**to** mit): ~ **ring** Verlobungsring m. **4.** (An)Stellung f, thea. etc Engagement n. **en'ga·ging** adj □ einnehmend (Wesen etc), gewinnend (Lächeln etc).

en·gen·der [ɪn'dʒendə] v/t Neid etc erzeugen, hervorrufen (**in** bei).

en·gine ['endʒɪn] s **1.** Motor m. **2.** 🚂 Lokomotive f. ~ **block** s Motorblock m. ~ **driv·er** s 🚂 Lokomotivführer m.

en·gi·neer [¸endʒɪ'nɪə] **I** s **1.** Ingenieur m; Techniker m; Mechaniker m. **2.** 🚂 Am. Lokomotivführer m. **II** v/t **3.** fig. (geschickt) in die Wege leiten, organisieren. **¸en·gi'neer·ing** s allg. Technik f, engS. Ingenieurwesen n, (a. **mechanical** ~) Maschinen- u. Gerätebau m.

Eng·lish ['ɪŋglɪʃ] **I** adj **1.** englisch. **II** s **2.** **the** ~ pl die Engländer pl. **3.** ling. Englisch n; **in** ~ auf englisch; **in plain** ~ unverblümt; auf gut deutsch; **Queen's** (od. **King's**) ~ hochsprachliches Englisch. ~**man** ['~mən] s (irr **man**) Engländer m. '~**wom·an** s (irr **woman**) Engländerin f.

en·grave [ɪn'greɪv] v/t (**on**) (in Metall, Stein etc) (ein)gravieren, (-)meißeln, (in Holz) einschnitzen: **it is** (od. **has**) **been** (**in**) **his memory** (od. **mind**) ~**d** es hat sich ihm tief od. unauslöschlich eingeprägt. **en'grav·er** s Graveur m: ~ **on copper** Kupferstecher m. **en'grav·ing** s **1.** Gravieren n. **2.** Gravierung f, (Kupfer-, Stahl)Stich m, (Holz)Schnitt m.

en·gross [ɪn'grəʊs] v/t j-s Aufmerksamkeit etc in Anspruch nehmen, Macht, Unterhaltung etc an sich reißen.

en·grossed *adj* (*in*) (voll) in Anspruch genommen (von), vertieft, versunken (in *acc*).

en·gulf [ɪnˈgʌlf] *v/t* verschlingen (*a. fig.*).

en·hance [ɪnˈhɑːns] *v/t* Wert etc erhöhen, steigern, heben.

e·nig·ma [ɪˈnɪgmə] *s fig.* Rätsel *n*. **en·ig·mat·ic** [ˌenɪgˈmætɪk] *adj* (~*ally*) rätselhaft.

en·joy [ɪnˈdʒɔɪ] *v/t* **1.** Vergnügen *od.* Gefallen finden *od.* Freude haben an (*dat*): ~ **doing s.th.** daran Vergnügen finden, et. zu tun; *I* ~ **dancing** ich tanze gern, Tanzen macht mir Spaß; *did you* ~ **the play?** hat dir das Stück gefallen?; ~ **o.s.** sich amüsieren *od.* gut unterhalten; ~ **yourself!** viel Spaß! **2.** genießen, sich *et.* schmecken lassen. **3.** sich *e-s Besitzes* erfreuen, *j-s Vertrauen etc* genießen: ~ **good health** sich e-r guten Gesundheit erfreuen. **en·joy·a·ble** *adj* ☐ angenehm, erfreulich. **en·joy·ment** *s* **1.** Vergnügen *n*, Freude *f* (*of* an *dat*). **2.** Genuß *m*: *be in the* ~ *of* → *enjoy* 3.

en·large [ɪnˈlɑːdʒ] *I v/t* **1.** vergrößern (*a. phot.*), *Kenntnisse etc* a. erweitern, *Einfluß etc* a. ausdehnen. **II** *v/i* **2.** sich vergrößern *od.* erweitern *od.* ausdehnen. **3.** sich verbreiten *od.* (weitläufig) auslassen (*on* über *acc*). **en·large·ment** *s* Vergrößerung *f* (*a. phot.*).

en·light·en [ɪnˈlaɪtn] *v/t* aufklären, belehren (*on, as to* über *acc*). **en·light·en·ment** *s* Aufklärung *f*.

en·list [ɪnˈlɪst] *I v/t* **1.** *Soldaten* anwerben, *Rekruten* einstellen. **2.** *fig.* heranziehen, *j-s Dienste* in Anspruch nehmen. **II** *v/i* **3.** ✕ Soldat werden, sich (freiwillig) melden (*to* zu). **4.** (*in*) mitwirken (bei), sich beteiligen (an *dat*).

en·liv·en [ɪnˈlaɪvn] *v/t* beleben, in Schwung bringen.

en·mesh [ɪnˈmeʃ] *v/t*: *be* ~*ed in one's own lies* sich in s-n eigenen Lügen verstrickt *od.* verfangen haben.

en·mi·ty [ˈenmɪtɪ] *s* Feindschaft *f*: *be at* ~ *with* verfeindet sein mit.

e·nor·mous [ɪˈnɔːməs] *adj* ☐ enorm, ungeheuer, gewaltig.

e·nough [ɪˈnʌf] *I adj* ausreichend, genug: *be* ~ (aus)reichen, genügen. **II** *s: I have had* ~, *thank you* danke, ich bin satt!; ~ *of that!* genug davon!, Schluß damit! **III** *adv* genug, genügend: *be kind* (*od.*

good) ~ *to do this for me* sei so freundlich *od.* gut u. erledige das für mich; *curiously* (*od.* *strangely*) ~ merkwürdigerweise.

en·quire, en·quir·y → *inquire, inquiry.*

en·rage [ɪnˈreɪdʒ] *v/t* wütend machen. **en·raged** *adj* wütend, aufgebracht (*at, by* über *acc*).

en·rap·ture [ɪnˈræptʃə] *v/t* hinreißen, entzücken. **en·rap·tured** *adj* hingerissen, entzückt (*at, by* von).

en·rich [ɪnˈrɪtʃ] *v/t* **1.** bereichern (*a. fig.*). **2.** 🔭, *etc* anreichern.

en·rol(l) [ɪnˈrəʊl] **I** *v/t* **1.** *j-n, j-s Namen* einschreiben, -tragen (*in* in *dat od. acc*), *univ. j-n* immatrikulieren: ~ **o.s.** → **3. 2.** *j-n* aufnehmen (*in* in e-n *Verein etc*): ~ **o.s.** → **4. II** *v/i* **3.** sich einschreiben (lassen), *univ.* sich immatrikulieren: ~ *for a course* e-n Kurs belegen. **4.** ~ **in** beitreten (*dat*). **en·rol(l)·ment** *s* **1.** Einschreibung *f*, -tragung *f*, *univ.* Immatrikulation *f*. **2.** (Gesamt)Zahl *f* der Eingetragenen *od. univ.* Immatrikulierten.

en route [ɑ̃ːˈruːt] *adv* unterwegs (*for* nach).

en·sem·ble [ɑ̃ːˈsãːmbl] *s* **1.** das Ganze, Gesamteindruck *m*. **2.** ♪, *thea.*, *Mode:* Ensemble *n*.

en·sign [ˈensaɪn] *s* ⚓ (*bsd.* National-) Flagge *f*.

en·slave [ɪnˈsleɪv] *v/t* zum Sklaven machen (*a. fig.*), versklaven.

en·snare [ɪnˈsneə] *v/t* **1.** in e-r *Schlinge* fangen. **2.** *fig.* bestricken, umgarnen.

en·sue [ɪnˈsjuː] *v/i* **1.** (darauf-, nach)folgen: *the ensuing years* die (darauf)folgenden Jahre. **2.** folgen, sich ergeben (*from* aus).

en·sure [ɪnˈʃɔː] *v/t* **1.** (*against, from*) sichern (vor *dat*, gegen), schützen (vor *dat*). **2.** sicherstellen, garantieren (*s.th.* et.); *that* daß; *s.o. being* daß j-d ist). **3.** sorgen für *et.*: ~ *that* dafür sorgen, daß.

en·tail [ɪnˈteɪl] *v/t* mit sich bringen *od.* zur Folge haben, nach sich ziehen, *Kosten etc* verursachen, erfordern.

en·tan·gle [ɪnˈtæŋgl] *v/t* **1.** *Haare, Garn etc* verwirren, -filzen. **2.** (*o.s.* sich) verwickeln, -heddern (*in* in *dat*). **3.** *fig.* verwickeln, -stricken (*in* in *acc*).

en·ter [ˈentə] *I v/t* **1.** (hinein-, herein)gehen, (-)kommen, (-)treten in (*acc*), eintreten, -steigen in (*acc*), betreten; einreisen in (*acc*); ♣, 🚂 einlaufen, -fahren in (*acc*); eindringen in (*acc*): *it ~ed my mind* es kam mir in den Sinn. **2.** *fig.* eintreten in (*acc*), beitreten (*dat*). **3.** *Namen etc* eintragen, -schreiben, *j-n* aufnehmen, zulassen: ~ *one's name* (*od.* **o.s.**) → 7a. **4.** *Sport:* melden, nennen (*for* für): ~ **o.s.** → 7b. **5.** *Vorschlag etc* einreichen, -bringen: ~ *a protest* Protest erheben *od.* einlegen. **II** *v/i* **6.** eintreten, herein- *od.* hineinkommen, -gehen; *thea.* auftreten: ♀ *Hamlet* Hamlet tritt auf. **7.** *a) eintreten od.* -schreiben *b) (Sport)* melden, nennen (*for* für).

Verbindungen mit Präpositionen:

en·ter| in·to *v/i* **1.** → **enter** 1, 2. **2.** anfangen, beginnen; sich einlassen auf (*acc*); eingehen auf (*acc*): ~ *into correspondence with* in Briefwechsel treten mit. **3.** *Verpflichtung, Partnerschaft etc* eingehen. ~ **on** (*od.* **upon**) **1.** *Thema* anschneiden; sich in *ein Gespräch etc* einlassen. **2.** *Amt, Erbschaft* antreten; *Laufbahn* einschlagen; in *ein neues Stadium etc* treten.

en·ter·i·tis [ˌentəˈraɪtɪs] *s* 🔬 Darmkatarrh *m.*

en·ter·prise [ˈentəpraɪz] *s* **1.** Unternehmen *n,* -nehmung *f.* **2.** ✝ Unternehmen *n,* Betrieb *m;* Unternehmertum *m.* **3.** Unternehmungsgeist *m.* **'en·ter·pris·ing** *adj* □ unternehmungslustig.

en·ter·tain [ˌentəˈteɪn] *v/t* **1.** *(angenehm)* unterhalten. **2.** bewirten. **3.** *Furcht, Hoffnung etc* hegen. **4.** *Vorschlag etc* in Betracht *od.* Erwägung ziehen: ~ *an idea* sich mit e-m Gedanken tragen. **en·ter·tain·er** *s* Entertainer(in). **en·ter·tain·ing** *adj* □ unterhaltend, -haltsam. **en·ter·tain·ment** *s* **1.** Unterhaltung *f: much* (*od.* **greatly**) *to his* ~ sehr zu s-r Belustigung. **2.** *(öffentliche)* Unterhaltung, *(professionell dargebotene a.)* Entertainment *n:* ~ *industry* Unterhaltungsindustrie *f;* ~ *tax* Vergnügungssteuer *f.*

en·thral(l) [ɪnˈθrɔːl] *v/t fig.* bezaubern, fesseln.

en·thuse [ɪnˈθjuːz] *v/i* F (*about, over*) begeistert sein (von), schwärmen (von, für).

en·thu·si·asm [ɪnˈθjuːzɪæzəm] *s* Enthusiasmus *m,* Begeisterung *f* (*for* für;

about über *acc*). **en·thu·si·ast** [~æst] *s* Enthusiast(in). **en·thu·si·as·tic** *adj* (~**ally**) begeistert (*about, over* von), enthusiastisch.

en·tice [ɪnˈtaɪs] *v/t* **1.** locken (*into* in *acc*): ~ *away* weglocken (*from* von); ✝ abwerben; ~ **s.o.'s** *girlfriend away* j-m die Freundin abspenstig machen. **2.** verlocken, -leiten, -führen (*into* zu *et.*): ~ **s.o. to do** *s.th.* j-n dazu verleiten, et. zu tun. **en·tice·ment** *s* **1.** (Ver)Lockung *f,* (An)Reiz *m.* **2.** Verführung *f,* -leitung *f.* **en·tic·ing** *adj* □ verlockend, -führerisch.

en·tire [ɪnˈtaɪə] *adj* **1.** ganz: a) vollzählig, -ständig, b) gesamt, Gesamt..., c) unversehrt, unbeschädigt. **2.** *fig.* voll, uneingeschränkt (*Vertrauen etc*): *be in* ~ *agreement* voll u. ganz *od.* völlig übereinstimmen mit. **en·tire·ly** *adv* völlig, gänzlich. **en·tire·ty** *s: in its* ~ in s-r Gesamtheit, als (ein) Ganzes.

en·ti·tle [ɪnˈtaɪtl] *v/t* **1.** *Buch etc* betiteln: *~d ...* mit dem Titel ... **2.** *j-n* berechtigen (*to* zu): *be ~d to* ein Anrecht *od.* (e-n) Anspruch haben auf (*acc*); *be ~d to do s.th.* (dazu) berechtigt sein *od.* das Recht haben, et. zu tun; *~d to vote* wahl-, stimmberechtigt.

en·ti·ty [ˈentɪtɪ] *s* **1.** Einheit *f.* **2.** 🎓 Rechtspersönlichkeit *f: legal* ~ juristische Person.

en·trails [ˈentreɪlz] *s pl anat.* Eingeweide *pl.*

en·trance¹ [ˈentrəns] *s* **1.** Eintreten *n,* -tritt *m;* ♣, 🚂 Einlaufen *n,* -fahrt *f.* **2.** Ein-, Zugang *m* (*to* zu); Zufahrt *f:* ~ *hall* (Eingangs-, Vor)Halle *f,* (Haus-) Flur *m.* **3.** *fig.* Antritt *m* (*on an inheritance* e-r Erbschaft): ~ *on an office* Amtsantritt *m.* **4.** Einlaß *m,* Ein-, Zutritt *m:* ~ *fee* Eintritt(sgeld *n*); Aufnahmegebühr *f; no* ~! Zutritt verboten! **5.** *thea.* Auftritt *m: make one's* ~ auftreten.

en·trance² [ɪnˈtrɑːns] *v/t* entzücken, hinreißen: *~d* entzückt, hingerissen (*at, by* von).

en·trant [ˈentrənt] *s* **1.** (Berufs)Anfänger(in) (*to in dat*). **2.** neues Mitglied. **3.** *Sport:* Teilnehmer(in) (*a. allg. an e-m Wettbewerb*).

en·treat [ɪnˈtriːt] *v/t* **1.** inständig *od.* dringend bitten, anflehen (*for* um). **2.**

et. erflehen (*of* von). **en'treat·ing** *adj*
□ flehentlich. **en'treat·y** *s* dringende
Bitte: *at s.o.'s* ~ auf j-s Bitte (hin).

en·trée ['ɒntrɪ] *s* **1.** *bsd. fig.* Zutritt *m*
(*into* zu). **2.** *gastr.* Zwischen-, *Am.*
Hauptgericht *n*.

en·trench [ɪn'trentʃ] *v/t* ✕ (*o.s.* sich)
verschanzen (*behind* hinter *dat*) (*a.
fig.*). **en'trenched** *adj fig.* eingewurzelt.

en·tre·pre·neur [ˌɒntrəprə'nɜː] *s* ✝ Unternehmer *m*.

en·trust [ɪn'trʌst] *v/t* **1.** *et.* anvertrauen
(*to s.o.* j-m). **2.** *j-n* betrauen (*with* mit).

en·try ['entrɪ] *s* **1.** → *entrance*[1] **2.**
Einreise *f*, Zuzug *m*: ~ *visa* Einreisevi-
sum *n*. **3.** → *entrance*[1] **5.** **4.** Beitritt *m*
(*into* zu). **5.** Einlaß *m*, Zutritt *m*: *gain*
(*od. obtain*) ~ Einlaß finden; *force an* ~
into, make a forcible ~ *into* gewaltsam
eindringen in (*acc*); *no* ~*!* Zutritt verboten. **6.** Zu-, Eingang(stür *f*) *m*, Ein-
fahrt(stor *n*) *f*; (Eingangs-, Vor)Halle *f*,
(Haus)Flur *m*. **7.** Eintrag(ung *f*) *m*, ✝
a. Buchung *f*; Stichwort *n* (*im Lexikon
etc*). **8.** *Sport:* a) Nennung *f*, Meldung
f, b) → *entrant* 3. **'~·phone** *s* Tür-
sprechanlage *f*.

en·twine [ɪn'twaɪn] *v/t* winden, schlingen ([*a*]*round* um), umwinden (*with*
mit).

e·nu·mer·ate [ɪ'njuːməreɪt] *v/t* aufzählen. **e·nu·mer·a·tion** *s* Aufzählung *f*.

e·nun·ci·ate [ɪ'nʌnsɪeɪt] **I** *v/t* **1.** ausdrük-
ken, -sprechen. **2.** formulieren. **3.** (*bsd.
deutlich*) aussprechen. **II** *v/i* **4.** ~ *clearly* e-e deutliche Aussprache haben,
deutlich sprechen.

en·vel·op [ɪn'veləp] *v/t* **1.** einschlagen,
-wickeln, (ein)hüllen (*in* in *acc*). **2.** *fig.*
ver-, einhüllen: ~*ed in mystery* geheim-
nisumhüllt. **en·ve·lope** ['envələʊp] *s* **1.**
Hülle *f*, Umschlag *m*. **2.** Briefumschlag
m, Kuvert *n*.

en·vi·a·ble ['envɪəbl] *adj* □ beneidenswert. **'en·vi·er** *s* Neider(in). **'en·vi·ous**
adj □ neidisch (*of* auf *acc*).

en·vi·ron·ment [ɪn'vaɪərənmənt] *s* **1.**
Umgebung *f*, *sociol. a.* Milieu *n*. **2.** Umwelt *f*. **en·vi·ron·men·tal** [~'mentl] *adj*
□ **1.** *sociol.* Milieu... **2.** Umwelt...: ~
pollution Umweltverschmutzung *f*; ~
protection Umweltschutz *m*; **~·ly** *beneficial* (*harmful*) umweltfreundlich

(-feindlich). **en·vi·ron·men·tal·ist**
[~'təlɪst] *s* Umweltschützer(in). **en'vi-
rons** *s pl* Umgebung *f* (*e-s Ortes
etc*).

en·vis·age [ɪn'vɪzɪdʒ] *v/t* **1.** gedenken
(*doing* zu tun), in Aussicht nehmen, ins
Auge fassen. **2.** sich *et.* vorstellen.

en·vi·sion [ɪn'vɪʒn] → **envisage** 2.

en·voy ['envɔɪ] *s* **1.** *pol.* Gesandte *m*. **2.**
Abgesandte *m*, Bevollmächtigte *m*.

en·vy ['envɪ] **I** *s* **1.** Neid *m* (*of* auf *acc*). **2.**
Gegenstand *m* des Neides: *his car is
the* ~ *of everybody* alle beneiden ihn
um s-n Wagen. **II** *v/t* **3.** *j-n* beneiden
(*s.th.* um etwas).

en·zyme ['enzaɪm] *s Biochemie:* Enzym
n.

e·phem·er·al [ɪ'femərəl] *adj* □ flüchtig,
kurzlebig.

ep·ic ['epɪk] **I** *adj* (*~ally*) **1.** episch. **2.**
heldenhaft. **II** *s* **3.** Epos *n*.

ep·i·cure ['epɪkjʊə] *s* **1.** Epikureer *m*,
Genußmensch *m*. **2.** Feinschmecker *m*.

ep·i·dem·ic [ˌepɪ'demɪk] ✻ **I** *adj* (*~ally*)
epidemisch (*a. fig.*). **II** *s* Epidemie *f*,
Seuche *f* (*beide a. fig.*).

ep·i·der·mis [ˌepɪ'dɜːmɪs] *s anat.* Ober-
haut *f*.

ep·i·gram ['epɪgræm] *s* Epigramm *n*.

ep·i·lep·sy ['epɪlepsɪ] *s* ✻ Epilepsie *f*.
ep·i·lep·tic **I** *adj* (*~ally*) epileptisch: ~
fit epileptischer Anfall. **II** *s* Epilepti-
ker(in).

ep·i·logue ['epɪlɒg] *s* Epilog *m*: a) Nachwort *n* (*e-s Buchs etc*), b) *fig.* Nachspiel
n, Ausklang *m*.

E·piph·a·ny [ɪ'pɪfənɪ] *s eccl.* Dreikönigs-
fest *n*.

e·pis·co·pal [ɪ'pɪskəpl] *adj* □ bischöflich, Bischofs... **e'pis·co·pate** [~kəʊ-
pət] *s* Episkopat *m, n*, Bistum *n*.

ep·i·sode ['epɪsəʊd] *s* **1.** Episode *f*. **2.**
Rundfunk, TV etc: Folge *f*. **ep·i·sod·ic**
[~'sɒdɪk] *adj* (*~ally*) **1.** episodisch. **2.**
episodenhaft.

e·pis·tle [ɪ'pɪsl] *s eccl.* Epistel *f*.

ep·i·taph ['epɪtɑːf] *s* Grabschrift *f*.

ep·i·thet ['epɪθet] *s* **1.** Beiwort *n*, Attribut
n. **2.** Beiname *m*.

e·pit·o·me [ɪ'pɪtəmɪ] *s* **1.** Auszug *m*, Abriß *m*; kurze Darstellung: *in* ~ auszugsweise; in gedrängter Form. **2.** *fig.* Verkörperung *f*, Inbegriff *m*. **e'pit·o·mize**
v/t verkörpern.

ep·och ['i:pɒk] *s* Epoche *f.* '~·,mak·ing *adj* epochemachend.

equa·bil·i·ty [,ekwə'bɪlətɪ] *s* **1.** Gleichförmigkeit *f.* **2.** Ausgeglichenheit *f*, Gleichmut *m.* '**equa·ble** *adj* □ **1.** gleich(förmig). **2.** ausgeglichen (*a. Klima*), gleichmütig.

equal ['i:kwəl] **I** *adj* (□ → **equally**) **1.** gleich: *be ~ to* gleichen, gleich sein (*dat*); entsprechen, gleichkommen (*dat*); *~ opportunities pl* Chancengleichheit *f*; *~ rights pl for women* Gleichberechtigung *f* der Frau; *~ in size, of ~ size* (von) gleicher Größe, gleich groß. **2.** *be ~ to e-r Aufgabe etc* gewachsen sein. **3.** ebenbürtig (*to dat*), gleichwertig: *be on ~ terms (with)* auf gleicher Stufe stehen (mit); gleichberechtigt sein (mit) **I** *s* **4.** Gleichgestellte *m, f*: *your ~s pl* deinesgleichen; *~s pl in age* Altersgenossen *pl*; *he has no (od. is without) ~* er hat nicht *od.* sucht seinesgleichen. **III** *v/t pret u. pp* **-qualed,** *bsd. Br.* **-qualled 5.** (*dat*) gleichen, gleichkommen (*in an dat*). **6.** *Sport:* Rekord einstellen. **equal·i·ty** [ɪ'kwɒlətɪ] *s* Gleichheit *f*: *~ (of rights)* Gleichberechtigung *f*; *~ of opportunity (od. opportunities)* Chancengleichheit. **equal·i·za·tion** [,i:kwəlaɪ'zeɪʃn] *s* Gleichstellung *f.* '**equal·ize I** *v/t* **1.** gleichmachen, -setzen, -stellen. **2.** ausgleichen. **II** *v/i* **3.** *Sport:* ausgleichen. '**equal·iz·er** *s Sport:* Ausgleich(stor *n*) *m.* '**equal·ly** *adv* gleich (*groß etc*).

equa·nim·i·ty [,ekwə'nɪmətɪ] *s* Ausgeglichenheit *f*, Gleichmut *m.*

equate [ɪ'kweɪt] *v/t* **1.** gleichsetzen, -stellen (*to, with dat*). **2.** als gleich(wertig) ansehen *od.* behandeln. **equa·tion** [~ʒn] *s* **1.** ⚕ Gleichung *f.* **2.** Gleichsetzung *f*, -stellung *f.* **equa·tor** [~tə] *s* Äquator *m.* **equa·to·ri·al** [,ekwə'tɔːrɪəl] *adj* äquatorial, Äquator...

ques·tri·an [ɪ'kwestrɪən] **I** *adj* Reit(er)-...: *~ sports pl* Reit-, Pferdesport *m*; *~ statue* Reiterstatue *f*; -standbild *n.* **II** *s* (*a.* Kunst)Reiter(in).

equi·dis·tant [,i:kwɪ'dɪstənt] *adj* □ gleich weit entfernt. **equi·lat·er·al** [,~'lætərəl] *adj* □ *bsd. Å* gleichseitig.

equi·lib·ri·um [,i:kwɪ'lɪbrɪəm] *pl* **-ri·ums, -ri·a** [~rɪə] *s* Gleichgewicht *n* (*a. fig.*).

equi·nox ['i:kwɪnɒks] *s* Tagundnachtgleiche *f.*

equip [ɪ'kwɪp] *v/t* **1.** ausrüsten, -statten (*with* mit), *Krankenhaus etc* einrichten. **2.** *fig.* j-m das (geistige *od.* nötige) Rüstzeug geben (*for* für): *be well ~ped for* das nötige Rüstzeug haben (*for* für). **e'quip·ment** *s* **1.** a) Ausrüstung *f*, -stattung *f*, b) *mst pl* Ausrüstung(sgegenstände *pl*) *f*, c) ⚙ Einrichtung *f*, Maschine(n *pl*) *f.* **2.** *fig.* (geistiges *od.* nötiges) Rüstzeug.

equi·poise ['ekwɪpɔɪz] **I** *s* **1.** Gleichgewicht *n* (*a. fig.*). **2.** *mst fig.* Gegengewicht *n* (*to* zu). **II** *v/t* **3.** im Gleichgewicht halten (*a. fig.*). **4.** *mst fig.* ein Gegengewicht bilden zu.

eq·ui·ta·ble ['ekwɪtəbl] *adj* □ gerecht, (recht u.) billig. **eq·ui·ty** ['ekwətɪ] *s* **1.** Gerechtigkeit *f*, Billigkeit *f.* **2.** *a. ~ law* ⚖ (*ungeschriebenes*) Billigkeitsrecht.

equiv·a·lence [ɪ'kwɪvələns] *s* Gleichwertigkeit *f*, ⚛ *etc a.* Äquivalenz *f.* **e'quiv·a·lent I** *adj* □ **1.** gleichbedeutend (*to* mit). **2.** gleichwertig, ⚛ *etc a.* äquivalent: *be ~ to* gleichkommen, entsprechen (*dat*). **II** *s* **3.** (*of*) Äquivalent *n* (für), (genaue) Entsprechung (zu).

equiv·o·cal [ɪ'kwɪvəkl] *adj* □ **1.** zweideutig, doppelsinnig. **2.** unbestimmt, ungewiß, fraglich. **3.** fragwürdig.

e·ra ['ɪərə] *s* Ära *f*, Zeitalter *n.*

e·rad·i·cate [ɪ'rædɪkeɪt] *v/t* ausrotten (*a. fig.*). **e,rad·i'ca·tion** *s* Ausrottung *f.*

e·rase [ɪ'reɪz] *v/t* **1.** *Schrift etc* ausstreichen, -radieren, löschen (*from* von); *Tonband(aufnahme) etc*, *ped. Am. a.* *Tafel* löschen. **2.** *fig.* (aus)löschen (*from* aus). **e'ras·er** *s* Radiergummi *m*; *ped. Am.* Tafelwischer *m.* **e'ra·sure** [~ʒə] *s* **1.** Ausradieren *n*; Löschen *n.* **2.** ausradierte *od.* gelöschte Stelle.

e·rect [ɪ'rekt] **I** *v/t* **1.** aufrichten. **2.** *Gebäude etc* errichten; *Maschine etc* aufstellen. **II** *adj* **3.** aufgerichtet, aufrecht: *with head ~* erhobenen Hauptes. **4.** *physiol.* erigiert. **e'rec·tion** *s* **1.** Errichtung *f*; Aufstellung *f.* **2.** Bau *m*, Gebäude *n.* **3.** *physiol.* Erektion *f.*

er·e·mite ['erɪmaɪt] *s* Eremit *m*, Einsiedler *m.*

er·mine ['ɜːmɪn] *s zo.* Hermelin *n.*

e·rode [ɪ'rəʊd] *v/t* **1.** an-, zer-, wegfressen. **2.** *geol.* erodieren. **3.** *fig.* aushöhlen, untergraben.

e·rog·e·nous [ɪˈrɒdʒɪnəs] *adj physiol.* erogen: ~ **zone.**

e·ro·sion [ɪˈrəʊʒn] *s* **1.** *geol.* Erosion *f.* **2.** *fig.* Aushöhlung *f.*

e·rot·ic [ɪˈrɒtɪk] *adj* (~**ally**) erotisch. **e'rot·i·cism** [~sɪzəm], *bsd. Am.* **er·o·tism** [ˈerətɪzəm] *s* Erotik *f.*

err [ɜː] *v/i* (sich) irren: **to ~ is human** Irren ist menschlich.

er·rand [ˈerənd] *s* Botengang *m,* Besorgung *f:* **go on** (*od.* **run**) **an ~** e-n Botengang *od.* e-e Besorgung machen. ~ **boy** *s* Laufbursche *f.*

er·ra·ta [eˈrɑːtə] *pl von* **erratum.**

er·rat·ic [ɪˈrætɪk] *adj* (~**ally**) sprunghaft, unberechenbar.

er·ra·tum [eˈrɑːtəm] *pl* **-ta** [~tə] *s* **1.** Druckfehler *m.* **2.** *pl* Errata *pl,* Druckfehlerverzeichnis *n.*

er·ro·ne·ous [ɪˈrəʊnjəs] *adj* irrig, falsch: ~ **belief** Irrglaube(n) *m.* **er'ro·ne·ous·ly** *adv* irrtümlicher-, fälschlicherweise.

er·ror [ˈerə] *s* Irrtum *m,* Fehler *m,* Versehen *n:* **in ~** irrtümlicherweise; **be in ~** im Irrtum sein, sich im Irrtum befinden; ~ **of judg(e)ment** falsche Beurteilung; ~**s excepted** † Irrtümer vorbehalten.

e·rupt [ɪˈrʌpt] *v/i* **1.** ausbrechen (*Aufruhr, Streit, Vulkan etc*): ~ **in** (*od.* **with**) **anger** e-n Wutanfall bekommen. **e'rup·tion** *s* **1.** Ausbruch *m:* **angry ~** Wutausbruch. **2.** *⚕* Ausschlag *m.*

es·ca·late [ˈeskəleɪt] **I** *v/t* **1.** *Krieg etc* eskalieren. **2.** *Erwartungen etc* höherschrauben. **II** *v/i* **3.** eskalieren. **4.** steigen, in die Höhe gehen (*Preise etc*). **‚es·ca·la·tion** *s* Eskalation *f.* **'es·ca·la·tor** *s* Rolltreppe *f.*

es·ca·lope [eˈskæləp] *s gastr.* (*bsd.* Wiener) Schnitzel *n.*

es·ca·pade [‚eskəˈpeɪd] *s* Eskapade *f.*

es·cape [ɪˈskeɪp] **I** *v/t* **1.** *j-m* entfliehen, -kommen; *e-r Sache* entgehen: **I cannot ~ the impression that** ich kann mich des Eindrucks nicht erwehren, daß; → **notice 1. 2.** *fig. j-m* entgehen, übersehen *od.* nicht verstanden werden von. **3.** *dem Gedächtnis* entfallen: **his name ~s me** sein Name ist mir entfallen. **4.** *j-m* entschlüpfen, -fahren (*Fluch etc*). **II** *v/i* **5.** (ent)fliehen, entkommen (*from* aus, *dat*). **6.** sich retten (*from* vor *dat*),

davonkommen (**with a fright** mit dem Schrecken; **with one's life** mit dem Leben). **7.** ausfließen (*Flüssigkeit*); entweichen, ausströmen (*from* aus) (*Gas etc*). **III** *s* **8.** Entkommen *n,* Flucht *f:* **have a narrow** (*od.* **near**) ~ mit knapper Not davonkommen *od.* entkommen; **that was a narrow ~!** das war knapp! **9.** Entweichen *n,* Ausströmen *n.* ~ **chute** *s ✓* Notrutsche *f.*

es·cort *s* [ˈeskɔːt] **1.** ✗ Eskorte *f,* Begleitmannschaft *f.* **2.** ✓, ⚓ Geleit(schutz *m*) *n;* ⚓ Geleitschiff *n.* **3.** Geleit *n,* Schutz *m;* Gefolge *n,* Begleitung *f;* Begleiter(in). **II** *v/t* [ɪˈskɔːt] **4.** ✗ eskortieren. **5.** ✓, ⚓ *Schiff* Geleitschutz geben. **6.** geleiten; begleiten.

Es·ki·mo [ˈeskɪməʊ] *pl* **-mos** *s* Eskimo *m.*

e·soph·a·gus *Am.* → **oesophagus.**

es·o·ter·ic [‚esəʊˈterɪk] *adj* (~**ally**) esoterisch.

es·pe·cial [ɪˈspeʃl] *adj* besonder. **es'pe·cial·ly** [~ʃəlɪ] *adv* besonders, hauptsächlich.

Es·pe·ran·to [‚espəˈræntəʊ] *s* Esperanto *n.*

es·pi·o·nage [ˈespɪənɑːʒ] *s* Spionage *f.*

es·pla·nade [‚espləˈneɪd] *s* **1.** (*bsd.* Strand-, Ufer)Promenade *f.* **2.** Esplanade *f.*

es·pres·so [eˈspresəʊ] *pl* **-sos** *s* **1.** Espresso *m.* **2.** Espressomaschine *f.* ~ **bar** *s* Espresso *n.*

Es·quire [ɪˈskwaɪə]: **John Smith, Esq.** *bsd. Br.* (*auf Briefen*) Herrn John Smith.

es·say [ˈeseɪ] *s* Essay *m, n, a. ped.* Aufsatz *m.* **'es·say·ist** *s* Essayist(in).

es·sence [ˈesns] *s* **1.** *das* Wesen(tliche), Kern *m* (*e-r Sache*): **in ~** im wesentlichen. **2.** Essenz *f,* Extrakt *m.*

es·sen·tial [ɪˈsenʃl] **I** *adj* (□ → **essentially**) **1.** wesentlich: a) grundlegend, b) unentbehrlich, unbedingt erforderlich (**to** für): ~ (**to life**) lebensnotwendig, -wichtig. **2.** 🌿 ätherisch: ~ **oil.** **II** *s mst pl* **3.** *das* Wesentliche, Hauptsache *f.* **4.** (wesentliche) Voraussetzung (**to** für). **es'sen·tial·ly** [~ʃəlɪ] *adv* im wesentlichen.

es·tab·lish [ɪˈstæblɪʃ] *v/t* **1.** ein-, errichten, *Konto* eröffnen, *Gesetz etc* einführen, erlassen, *Rekord, Theorie* aufstellen, *Ausschuß etc* bilden, einsetzen, *Verbindung* herstellen, *diplomatische Beziehungen etc* aufnehmen. **2. ~ o.s. †** sich (*a. beruflich*) etablieren *od.* niederlassen. **3.** *Ruhm etc* begründen: ~ *one's reputation as* sich e-n Namen machen als. **4.** *Ansicht, Forderung etc* durchsetzen, *Ordnung* schaffen. **5.** be-, nachweisen. **es'tab·lished** *adj* **1.** bestehend. **2.** feststehend, unzweifelhaft. **3.** ♀ *Church* Staatskirche *f.* **es'tab·lish·ment** *s* **1.** Ein-, Errichtung *f*, Einführung *f*, Aufstellung *f*, Bildung *f*, Herstellung *f*, Aufnahme *f.* **2.** *the* ♀ das Establishment. **3.** † Unternehmen *n*, Firma *f*; Niederlassung *f.* **4.** Anstalt *f*, (öffentliches) Institut.

es·tate [ɪ'steɪt] *s* **1.** *sociol.* Stand *m.* **2.** ⚖ Besitz(tum *n*) *m*; (Erb-, Konkurs)Masse *f*, Nachlaß *m*; → *real* **3.** **3.** Landsitz *m*, Gut *n.* **4.** *Br.* (Wohn)Siedlung *f*; Industriegebiet *n.* ~ **a·gent** *s Br.* **1.** Grundstücksverwalter *m.* **2.** Grundstücks-, Immobilienmakler *m.* ~ **car** *s Br.* Kombiwagen *m.*

es·teem [ɪ'sti:m] **I** *v/t* **1.** achten, (hoch)schätzen. **2.** erachten *od.* ansehen als, *et.* halten für. **II** *s* **3.** Achtung *f* (*for, of* vor *dat*): **hold in** (**high**) ~ → 1.

es·thete, *etc. Am.* → **aesthete**, *etc.*

es·ti·ma·ble ['estɪməbl] *adj* □ **1.** achtens-, schätzenswert. **2.** (ab)schätzbar.

es·ti·mate ['estɪmeɪt] **I** *v/t* **1.** (ab-, ein)schätzen, veranschlagen (*at* auf *acc*): ~*d value* Schätzwert *m*; *an* ~*d 200 people* schätzungsweise 200 Leute. **2.** beurteilen, bewerten. **II** *v/i* **3.** schätzen, e-n Kostenvoranschlag machen (*for* für). **III** *s* ['~mət] **5.** Schätzung *f*, Veranschlagung *f*, Kostenvoranschlag *m*: *rough* ~ grober Überschlag; *at a rough* ~ grob geschätzt. **6.** Beurteilung *f*, Bewertung *f.* **es·ti·ma·tion** [~'meɪʃn] *s* **1.** Meinung *f*: *in my* ~ nach m-r Ansicht. **2.** Achtung *f*, Wertschätzung *f.*

es·trange [ɪ'streɪndʒ] *v/t* j-n entfremden (*from dat*): *become* ~*d* sich entfremden (*from dat*); sich auseinanderleben. **es'trange·ment** *s* Entfremdung *f.*

es·tro·gen *Am.* → **oestrogen.**

es·tu·ar·y ['estjʊərɪ] *s* **1.** (*den Gezeiten ausgesetzte*) Flußmündung. **2.** Meeresbucht *f*, -arm *m.*

et cet·er·a [ɪt'setərə] et cetera, und so weiter.

etch [etʃ] *v/t* **1.** ätzen. **2.** in Kupfer stechen; radieren: *be* ~*ed on* (*od.* **in**) **s.o.'s memory** sich j-s Gedächtnis (unauslöschlich) eingeprägt haben. **'etch·ing** *s* Kupferstich *m*; Radierung *f.*

e·ter·nal [ɪ'tɜ:nl] *adj* □ **1.** ewig. **2.** ewig, unaufhörlich. **e·ter·nal·ize** [~nəlaɪz] *v/t* verewigen (*a. fig.*). **e·ter·ni·ty** *s* Ewigkeit *f* (*a. fig.*).

e·ther ['i:θə] *s* 🜊 Äther *m.* **e·the·re·al** [ɪ'θɪərɪəl] *adj* ätherisch (*a. fig.*).

eth·i·cal ['eθɪkl] *adj* □ **1.** ethisch. **2.** *pharm.* rezeptpflichtig. **'eth·ics** *s pl* **1.** (*sg konstruiert*) Ethik *f.* **2.** (*Berufs- etc*)Ethos *m.*

eth·nic ['eθnɪk] *adj* (~*ally*) ethnisch: ~ *group* Volksgruppe *f.*

eth·yl ['eθɪl] *s* 🜊 Äthyl *n.*

et·i·quette ['etɪket] *s* Etikette *f*, Anstands-, Verhaltensregeln *pl.*

et·y·mo·log·i·cal [ˌetɪmə'lɒdʒɪkl] *adj* □ etymologisch. **et·y·mol·o·gy** [~'mɒlədʒɪ] *s* Etymologie *f.*

eu·ca·lyp·tus [ˌjuːkə'lɪptəs] *pl* **-ti** [~taɪ], **-tus·es** *s* ♀ Eukalyptus *m.*

eu·lo·gy ['juːlədʒɪ] *s* **1.** Lob(preisung *f*) *n.* **2.** Lobrede *f*, -schrift *f* (*on* auf *acc*)

eu·nuch ['juːnək] *s* Eunuch *m.*

eu·phe·mism ['juːfəmɪzəm] *s* Euphemismus *m.* **eu·phe·mis·tic** *adj* (~*ally*) euphemistisch, beschönigend, verhüllend.

eu·pho·ri·a [juː'fɔːrɪə] *s* Euphorie *f.* **eu·phor·ic** [~'fɒrɪk] *adj* (~*ally*) euphorisch.

Eu·ro·cheque ['jʊərəʊtʃek] *s Br.* Euroscheck *m.*

Eu·ro·pe·an [ˌjʊərə'piːən] **I** *adj* europäisch: ~ (*Economic*) *Community* Europäische (Wirtschafts)Gemeinschaft; ~ *champion* (*Sport*) Europameister(in); ~ *championship* (*Sport*) Europameisterschaft *f.* **II** *s* Europäer(in).

Eu·ro·vi·sion ['jʊərəʊˌvɪʒn] *TV* **I** *s* Eurovision *f.* **II** *adj* Eurovisions-.

eu·tha·na·si·a [ˌjuːθə'neɪʒə] *s* Sterbehilfe *f*: *active* (*passive*) ~.

e·vac·u·ate [ɪ'vækjʊeɪt] *v/t Personen* evakuieren; *Gebiet etc* evakuieren, *a. Haus etc* räumen. **e·vac·u·a·tion** [~]

Evakuierung f; Räumung f. **e·vac-u·ee** [~ju:'i:] s Evakuierte m, f.

e·vade [ɪ'veɪd] v/t **1.** e-m Schlag etc ausweichen. **2.** sich e-r Pflicht etc entziehen, et. umgehen, vermeiden, Steuern hinterziehen: ~ (**answering**) **a question** e-r Frage ausweichen.

e·val·u·ate [ɪ'væljʊeɪt] v/t **1.** Wert etc schätzen, Schaden etc festsetzen (**at** auf acc). **2.** abschätzen, bewerten. **e·val-u·a·tion** s **1.** Schätzung f, Festsetzung f. **2.** Abschätzung f, Bewertung f.

e·vap·o·rate [ɪ'væpəreɪt] **I** v/t **1.** verdampfen od. verdunsten lassen. **2.** eindampfen: **~d milk** Kondensmilch f. **II** v/i **3.** verdampfen, verdunsten. **4.** fig. sich verflüchtigen, verfliegen. **e·vap-o'ra·tion** s Verdampfung f, Verdunstung f.

e·va·sion [ɪ'veɪʒn] s **1.** Umgehung f, Vermeidung f, (Steuer)Hinterziehung f. **2.** Ausflucht f, Ausrede f. **e·va·sive** [~sɪv] adj □ **1.** ausweichend (Antwort): **be** ~ ausweichen. **2.** schwer feststell- od. faßbar.

eve [i:v] s **1.** mst ♀ Vorabend m, -tag m (e-s Festes). **2.** fig. Vorabend m: **on the ~ of** am Vorabend von (od. gen), kurz od. unmittelbar vor (dat).

e·ven¹ [ˈiːvn] adv **1.** sogar, selbst: **not ~ he** nicht einmal er; ~ **if** selbst wenn; ~ **though** obwohl; ~ **as a child he was ...** schon als Kind war er ... **2.** noch: ~ **better** (sogar) noch besser.

e·ven² [~] **I** adj **1.** eben, flach, gerade. **2.** auf od. in gleicher Höhe (**with** mit). **3.** waag(e)recht. **4.** fig. ausgeglichen (of an ~ temper ausgeglichen; ~ voice ruhige Stimme. **5.** gleichmäßig (Atmen etc). **6.** ♱ ausgeglichen (a. Sport): **be ~ with** quitt sein mit (a. fig.). **7.** gleich, identisch. **8.** gerade (Zahl). **II** v/t **9.** a. ~ **out** (ein)ebnen, glätten; ausgleichen; (gleichmäßig) verteilen. **10.** ~ **up** Rechnung aus-, begleichen: ~ **things up** sich revanchieren. **III** v/i **11.** a. ~ **out** eben werden (Gelände); sich ausgleichen; sich (gleichmäßig) verteilen.

eve·ning [ˈiːvnɪŋ] s Abend m: **in the** ~ abends, am Abend; **on the ~ of** am Abend (gen); **last** (**this, tomorrow**) ~ gestern (heute, morgen) abend. ~ **class·es** s pl ped. Abendunterricht m. ~ **dress** s **1.** Abendkleid n. **2.** Frack m;

Smoking m. ~ **pa·per** s Abendzeitung f. ~ **star** s ast. Abendstern m.

e·ven·ness [ˈiːvnnɪs] s **1.** Ausgeglichenheit f. **2.** Gleichmäßigkeit f.

e·vent [ɪ'vent] s **1.** Fall m: **at all ~s** auf alle Fälle; **in any ~** in jedem Fall; **in the ~ of** im Falle (gen). **2.** Ereignis n: **before the ~** vorher, im voraus; **after the ~** hinterher, im nachhinein. **3.** Sport: Disziplin f; Wettbewerb m.

e·ven·tem·pered adj ausgeglichen.

e·vent·ful [ɪ'ventfʊl] adj □ ereignisreich.

e·ven·tu·al·i·ty [ɪˌventʃʊ'ælətɪ] s Möglichkeit f, Eventualität f. **e'ven·tu·al·ly** [~əlɪ] adv schließlich.

ev·er [ˈevə] adv **1.** immer (wieder), ständig: ~ **after**(**wards**) (od. **since**) seit der Zeit, seitdem; **Yours ~, ...** viele Grüße, Dein(e) etc Ihr(e) ... (Briefschluß); → **forever. 2.** immer (vor comp): ~ **larger. 3.** je(mals): **have you ~ been to London?** bist du schon einmal in London gewesen?; **hardly** (od. **seldom if**) ~ fast nie. **4.** ~ **so** bsd. Br. F sehr, noch so: ~ **so simpdd** ganz einfach; ~ **so many** unendlich viele; **thank yge ~ so much** tausend Dank! **5.** F denn, überhaupt: **what$ᶜ does he want?** was will er denn überhaupt? '**~green** s **1.** ♀ immergrüne Pflanze. **2.** ♪ Evergreen m, n. **~'last·ing** adj □ **1.** ewig. **2.** fig. unaufhörlich. **3.** unverwüstlich, unbegrenzt haltbar. **~'more** adj: (**for**) ~ für immer.

ev·er·y [ˈevrɪ] adv jede(r, -s): ~ **day** jeden Tag, alle Tage; → **now** 1, **other** 4, **second¹** 1. **2.** jede(r, -s) einzelne od. erdenkliche: **her ~ wish** jeder ihrer ad. alle ihre Wünsche; ~ **bit as much** F ganz genau so viel; **have ~ reason** allen Grund haben. '**~·bod·y** pron **everyone.** '**~·day** adj **1.** (all)täglich. **2.** Alltags... **3.** gewöhnlich, Durchschnitts... '**~·one** pron jeder(mann): **in ~'s mouth** in aller Munde; **to ~'s amazement** zum allgemeinen Erstaunen. '**~·thing** pron **1.** alles (**that** was). **2.** F die Hauptsache, alles (**to** für). **3. and ~** F und so. '**~·where** adv überall(hin): ~ **he goes** wo er auch hingeht.

ev·i·dence [ˈevɪdəns] s **1.** ⚖ Beweis(stück n, -material n) m, Beweise pl: **for lack of** ~ mangels Beweisen. **2.** ⚖ (Zeugen)Aussage f: **give** ~ aussagen (**for** für; **against** gegen); **give** ~ **of**

aussagen über (acc); fig. zeugen von; **turn queen's** (od. **king's**, Am. **state's**) ~ als Kronzeuge auftreten. **3.** (An)Zeichen n, Spur f (**of** von od. gen).

ev·i·dent adj □ augenscheinlich, offensichtlich.

e·vil ['iːvl] **I** adj □ übel, böse, schlimm: ~ **day** Unglückstag m; ~ **eye** der böse Blick. **II** s Übel n, das Böse: **do** ~ Böses tun; **the lesser** ~ das kleinere Übel. ‚~'**do·er** s Übeltäter(in). ‚~'**mind·ed** adj □ bösartig.

e·voc·a·tive [ɪ'vɒkətɪv] adj: **be** ~ **of** erinnern an (acc).

e·voke [ɪ'vəʊk] v/t **1.** Geister beschwören, herbeirufen. **2.** Bewunderung etc hervorrufen; Erinnerungen wachrufen, wecken.

ev·o·lu·tion [ˌiːvə'luːʃn] s **1.** Entfaltung f, -wicklung f: **the** ~ **of events** die Entwicklung (der Dinge). **2.** biol. Evolution f.

e·volve [ɪ'vɒlv] v/t u. v/i (sich) entfalten od. -wickeln (**into** zu).

ex¹ [eks] prp ✝ ab: ~ **works** ab Werk.

ex² [~] s F Verflossene m, f.

ex- [eks] in Zssgn: Ex..., ehemalig.

ex·ac·er·bate [ɪg'zæsəbeɪt] v/t **1.** j-n verärgern. **2.** Krankheit, Schmerzen verschlimmern, Situation verschärfen.

ex·act [ɪg'zækt] **I** adj (□ → **exactly**) **1.** exakt, genau. **2.** genau, tatsächlich. **3.** methodisch, gewissenhaft (Person). **II** v/t **4.** Gehorsam, Geld etc fordern, verlangen (**from** von). **5.** Zahlung eintreiben, -fordern (**from** von). **ex'act·ing** adj □ **1.** streng, genau. **2.** aufreibend, anstrengend. **3.** anspruchsvoll: **be** ~ hohe Anforderungen stellen. **ex'act·i·tude** [~tɪtjuːd] → **exactness**. **ex'act·ly** adv **1.** → **exact**. **2.** als Antwort: ganz recht, genau: **not** ~ nicht ganz od. direkt. **3.** wo, wann etc eigentlich. **ex'act·ness** s **1.** Exaktheit f, Genauigkeit f. **2.** Gewissenhaftigkeit f.

ex·ag·ger·ate [ɪg'zædʒəreɪt] v/t u. v/i übertreiben. **ex‚ag·ger'a·tion** s Übertreibung f.

ex·alt [ɪg'zɔːlt] v/t **1.** im Rang etc erheben, erhöhen (**to** zu). **2.** (lob)preisen: ~ **to the skies** in den Himmel heben. **ex·al·ta·tion** [ˌegzɔːl'teɪʃn] s **1.** Erhebung f, Erhöhung f. **2.** Begeisterung f: **fill with** ~ in Begeisterung versetzen.

ex·alt·ed [ɪg'zɔːltɪd] adj **1.** hoch (Rang, Ideal etc). **2.** begeistert. **3.** F übertrieben hoch (Meinung etc).

ex·am [ɪg'zæm] F → **examination** 2.

ex·am·i·na·tion [ɪgˌzæmɪ'neɪʃn] s **1.** Untersuchung f (a. ✷), Prüfung f: **on** ~ bei näherer Prüfung; **be under** ~ untersucht od. geprüft werden. **2.** ped. etc Prüfung f, bsd. univ. Examen n: ~ **paper** schriftliche Prüfung; Prüfungsarbeit f. **3.** ⚖ Vernehmung f, Verhör n. **ex'am·ine** v/t **1.** untersuchen (a. ✷), prüfen (**for** auf acc). **2.** ped. etc prüfen (**in** in dat; **on** über acc). **3.** ⚖ vernehmen; verhören. **ex‚am·i'nee** s ped. etc Prüfling m, (Prüfungs-, bsd. univ. Examens)Kandidat(in). **ex'am·in·er** s ped. etc Prüfer(in).

ex·am·ple [ɪg'zɑːmpl] s **1.** Beispiel n (**of** für): **for** ~ zum Beispiel; **without** ~ beispiellos. **2.** Vorbild n, Beispiel n: **set a good** ~ ein gutes Beispiel geben, mit gutem Beispiel vorangehen; **take** ~ **by**, **take as an** ~ sich ein Beispiel nehmen an (dat); → **hold up** 2. **3.** (warnendes) Beispiel: **make an** ~ **(of s.o.)** (an j-m) ein Exempel statuieren; **let this be an** ~ **to you** laß dir das e-e Warnung sein.

ex·as·per·ate [ɪg'zæspəreɪt] v/t aufbringen (**against** gegen), wütend machen. **ex·as·per·at·ed** adj wütend, aufgebracht (**at, by** über acc). **ex‚as·per'a·tion** s Wut f: **in** ~ wütend, aufgebracht.

ex·ca·vate ['ekskəveɪt] v/t **1.** aushöhlen. **2.** ausgraben, -baggern. **‚ex·ca'va·tion** s **1.** Aushöhlung f. **2.** Ausgrabung f. **'ex·ca·va·tor** s Bagger m.

ex·ceed [ɪk'siːd] v/t **1.** Tempolimit etc überschreiten. **2.** hinausgehen über (acc): ~ **the limit** den Rahmen sprengen. **3.** et., j-n übertreffen (**in** an dat). **ex'ceed·ing·ly** adv überaus, äußerst: ~ **kind** überfreundlich.

ex·cel [ɪk'sel] **I** v/t übertreffen (**o.s.** sich selbst). **II** v/i sich auszeichnen (od. hervortun (**in, at** in dat; **as** als). **ex·cel·lence** ['eksələns] s **1.** Vorzüglichkeit f. **2.** pl Vorzüge pl. '**Ex·cel·len·cy** s Exzellenz f (Titel). '**ex·cel·lent** adj □ ausgezeichnet, hervorragend, vorzüglich.

ex·cept [ɪk'sept] **I** v/t **1.** ausnehmen, -schließen (**from** von): **present compa·ny** ~**ed** Anwesende ausgenommen; **no-**

body **~ed** ohne Ausnahme. **2.** sich *et.* vorbehalten: → *error.* **II** *prp* **3.** ausgenommen, außer, mit Ausnahme von (*od. gen*): **~ for** abgesehen von, bis auf (*acc*). **III** *cj* **4.** außer: **~ that** außer, daß.

ex·cept·ing *prp* → *except* 3. **ex·ception** *s* **1.** Ausnahme *f* (**to the rule** von der Regel): **by way of ~** ausnahmsweise; **without ~** ohne Ausnahme, ausnahmslos; **make an ~** (**in s.o.'s case**) (bei j-m *od.* in j-s Fall) e-e Ausnahme machen. **2.** Einwand *m* (**to** gegen): **take ~ to** Einwendungen machen gegen; Anstoß nehmen an (*dat*). **ex·cep·tion·al** [~ʃənl] *adj* **1.** Ausnahme..., Sonder... **2.** außer-, ungewöhnlich. **ex·cep·tion·al·ly** [~ʃnəlɪ] *adv* **1.** außergewöhnlich. **2.** ausnahmsweise.

ex·cerpt ['eksɜːpt] *s* Exzerpt *n*, Auszug *m* (**from** aus).

ex·cess [ɪk'ses] **I** *s* **1.** Übermaß *n*, -fluß *m* (**of** *an dat*): **in ~ of** mehr als, über (*acc*) (... hinaus); **to ~** übermäßig; → *carry* 7. **2.** *pl* Exzesse *pl*: a) Ausschweifungen *pl*, b) Ausschreitungen *pl*. **3.** Überschuß *m*. **II** *adj* **4.** überschüssig, Über...: **~ baggage** (*bsd. Br. luggage*) **☆** Übergepäck *n*; **~ fare** (Fahrpreis)Zuschlag *m*; **~ postage** Nachporto *n*, -gebühr *f*. **ex'cess·ive** *adj* □ übermäßig, -trieben.

ex·change [ɪks'tʃeɪndʒ] **I** *v/t* **1.** (**for**) aus-, umtauschen (gegen), vertauschen (mit). **2.** eintauschen, *Geld a.* (um)wechseln (**for** gegen). **3.** *Blicke, die Plätze etc* tauschen, *Blicke* wechseln, *Gedanken, Gefangene etc* austauschen: **~ blows** aufeinander einschlagen; **☆ words** e-n Wortwechsel haben. **4. ☆** auswechseln. **II** *v/i* **5.** (Aus-, Um)Tausch *m*: **in ~** als Ersatz, dafür; **in ~ for** (im Austausch) gegen, (als Entgelt) für; **~ of letters** Brief-, Schriftwechsel *m*; **~ of shots** Schußwechsel *m*; **~ of views** Gedanken-, Meinungsaustausch *m*. **6. ✝** (Um)Wechseln: **rate of ~, ~ rate** Wechselkurs *m*; → *bill*[2] 3, *foreign* 1. **7. ✝** Börse *f*. **8.** *a. ~ office* Wechselstube *f*. **9.** (Fernsprech)Amt *n*, Vermittlung *f*. **ex'change·a·ble** *adj* **1.** aus-, umtauschbar (**for** gegen). **2.** Tausch...

Ex·cheq·uer [ɪks'tʃekə] *s Br.* Finanzministerium *n*: → *chancellor.*

ex·cit·a·ble [ɪk'saɪtəbl] *adj* reizbar,

(leicht) erregbar. **ex'cite** *v/t* **1.** j-n er-, aufregen: **get ~d** sich aufregen (**over** über *acc*). **2.** j-n (an-, auf)reizen, aufstacheln. **3.** *Interesse etc* erregen, (er)wecken, *Appetit, Phantasie* anregen. **ex'cit·ed** *adj* □ erregt, aufgeregt. **ex'cite·ment** *s* Er-, Aufregung *f*. **ex'cit·ing** *adj* □ er-, aufregend, spannend.

ex·claim [ɪk'skleɪm] **I** *v/i* (auf)schreien. **II** *v/t et.* (aus)rufen.

ex·cla·ma·tion [ˌekskləˈmeɪʃn] *s* Ausruf *m*, (Auf)Schrei *m*: **~ of pain** Schmerzensschrei; **~ mark** (*Am. a.* **point**) Ausrufe-, Ausrufungszeichen *n*.

ex·clude [ɪk'skluːd] *v/t* j-n, *Möglichkeit etc* ausschließen (**from** von, aus). **ex'clud·ing** *prp* ausgenommen, nicht inbegriffen.

ex·clu·sion [ɪk'skluːʒn] *s* Ausschluß *m* (**from** von, aus): **to the ~ of** unter Ausschluß von (*od. gen*). **ex'clu·sive I** *adj* □ **1.** ausschließend: **~ of** ausschließlich, abgesehen von, ohne; **be ~ of** sich ausschließen; **be mutually ~** einander ausschließen. **2.** ausschließlich, Allein... **; Exclusiv... 3.** exklusiv. **II** *s* **4.** Exklusivbericht *m.*

ex·com·mu·ni·cate [ˌekskəˈmjuːnɪkeɪt] *v/t eccl.* exkommunizieren. **'ex·com·ˌmu·ni'ca·tion** *s* Exkommunikation *f.*

ex·cre·ment ['ekskrɪmənt] *s* Kot *m*, Exkremente *pl.*

ex·crete [ɪk'skriːt] *v/t* absondern, ausscheiden. **ex'cre·tion** *s* Absonderung *f*, Ausscheidung *f.*

ex·cru·ci·at·ing [ɪk'skruːʃɪeɪtɪŋ] *adj* □ qualvoll (**to** für).

ex·cur·sion [ɪk'skɜːʃn] *s* Ausflug *m*, *fig. a.* Abstecher *m* (**into politics** in die Politik): **go on an ~** e-n Ausflug machen. **ex'cur·sion·ist** *s* Ausflügler(in).

ex·cus·a·ble [ɪk'skjuːzəbl] *adj* □ entschuldbar, verzeihlich. **ex'cuse I** *v/t* [ɪk'skjuːz] **1.** j-n, *et.* entschuldigen, j-m, *et.* verzeihen: **~ me** entschuldigen Sie!, Verzeihung!; **~ me for being late, ~ my being late** entschuldige mein Zuspätkommen; **~ o.s.** sich entschuldigen. **2.** für *et.* e-e Entschuldigung finden: **I cannot ~ his conduct** ich kann sein Verhalten nicht gutheißen. **3. ~ s.o. from s.th.** j-n von et. befreien, j-m et. erlassen: **he begs to be ~d** er läßt sich entschuldigen. **II** *s* [ɪk'skjuːs] **4.** Entschuldigung *f*: *offer* (*od.* *make*) *an* ~ sich entschuldigen; *in* ~ *of* als Entschuldigung für. **5.** Entschuldigung(sgrund *m*) *f*, Rechtfertigung *f*: *without* (*good*) ~ unentschuldigt. **6.** Ausrede *f*, -flucht *f*.

ex·di·rec·to·ry [ˌeksdɪ'rektərɪ] *adj*: ~ *number* *teleph.* *Br.* Geheimnummer *f*.

ex·e·cute ['eksɪkjuːt] *v/t* **1.** *Auftrag, Plan etc* aus-, durchführen, *Vertrag* erfüllen. **2.** ♪ vortragen, spielen. **3.** ⚖ *Urteil* vollziehen, -strecken; *j-n* hinrichten (*for* wegen). **ˌex·e'cu·tion** *s* **1.** Aus-, Durchführung *f*, Erfüllung *f*: *carry* (*od.* *put*) *into* ~ → *execute* 1. **2.** ♪ Vortrag *m*, Spiel *n*. **3.** ⚖ Vollziehung *f*, -streckung *f*; Hinrichtung *f*. **ˌex·e'cu·tion·er** *s* Henker *m*, Scharfrichter *m*.

ex·ec·u·tive [ɪg'zekjʊtɪv] **I** *adj* □ **1.** ausübend, vollziehend, *pol.* Exekutiv...: ~ *power* (*od.* *authority*) → 3. **2.** ⚹ geschäftsführend, leitend: ~ *board* Vorstand *m*; ~ *post* (*od.* *position*) leitende Stellung; ~ *staff* leitende Angestellte *pl.* **II** *s* **3.** *pol.* Exekutive *f*. **4.** *a.* *senior* ~ ⚹ leitender Angestellter.

ex·em·pla·ry [ɪg'zemplərɪ] *adj* □ **1.** exemplarisch: a) beispiel-, musterhaft, b) warnend, abschreckend. **2.** typisch, Muster...

ex·em·pli·fy [ɪg'zemplɪfaɪ] *v/t* veranschaulichen: a) durch Beispiele erläutern, b) als Beispiel dienen für.

ex·empt [ɪg'zempt] **I** *v/t* *j-n* befreien (*from* von *Steuern, Verpflichtungen etc*), freistellen (*from military service* vom Wehrdienst): ~*ed amount* ⚹ (Steuer)Freibetrag *m*. **II** *adj* befreit, ausgenommen (*from* von): ~ *from taxation* steuerfrei. **ex'emp·tion** *s* Befreiung *f*, Freistellung *f*: ~ *from taxes* Steuerfreiheit *f*.

ex·er·cise ['eksəsaɪz] **I** *s* **1.** Ausübung *f*, Geltendmachung *f*. **2.** ⚹ (*körperliche od. geistige*) Übung, (körperliche) Bewegung: *do one's* ~*s* Gymnastik machen; *take* ~ sich Bewegung machen; ~ *bicycle* Zimmerfahrrad *n*; ~ *therapy* ⚕ Bewegungstherapie *f*. **3.** *mst pl* ✕ Übung *f*, Manöver *n*. **4.** Übung(sarbeit) *f*, Schulaufgabe *f*: ~ *book* Schul-, Schreibheft *n*. **5.** ♪ Übung(sstück *n*) *f*. **II** *v/t* **6.** *Amt, Recht, Macht etc* ausüben, *Einfluß, Macht etc* geltend machen. **7.** *Körper, Geist* üben, trainieren. **8.** *Geduld etc* üben, trainieren. **III** *v/i* **9.** sich Bewegung machen. **10.** *Sport etc*: üben, trainieren. **11.** ✕ exerzieren. **'ex·er·cis·er** *s* Trainingsgerät *n*.

ex·ert [ɪg'zɜːt] *v/t* **1.** *Druck, Einfluß etc* ausüben (*on* auf *acc*), *Autorität* geltend machen. **2.** ~ *o.s.* sich bemühen (*for* um; *to do* zu tun), sich anstrengen. **ex'er·tion** *s* **1.** Ausübung *f*, Geltendmachung *f*. **2.** Anstrengung *f*.

ex·e·unt ['eksɪʌnt] *thea.* Bühnenanweisung: (sie gehen) ab: ~ *omnes* alle ab.

ex·ha·la·tion [ˌekshə'leɪʃn] *s* **1.** Ausatmen *n*. **2.** Verströmen *n*. **3.** Gas *n*; Rauch *m*. **ex'hale** [~'heɪl] *v/t* **1.** (*a. v/i*) ausatmen. **2.** *Gas, Geruch etc* verströmen, *Rauch* ausstoßen.

ex·haust [ɪg'zɔːst] **I** *v/t* erschöpfen: a) *Vorräte* ver-, aufbrauchen, b) *j-n* ermüden, entkräften, c) *j-s Kräfte* strapazieren: ~ *s.o.'s patience* j-s Geduld erschöpfen, d) *Thema* erschöpfend abod. behandeln: ~ *all possibilities* alle Möglichkeiten ausschöpfen. **II** *s* ⚙ *a.* ~ *fumes pl* Auspuff-, Abgase *pl*, b) Auspuff *m*: ~ *pipe* Auspuffrohr *n*. **ex'haust·ed** *adj* **1.** verbraucht, erschöpft, aufgebraucht (*Vorräte*), vergriffen (*Auflage*). **2.** erschöpft, entkräftet. **ex'haust·ing** *adj* erschöpfend, strapaziös. **ex'haus·tion** *s* Erschöpfung *f*: a) völliger Verbrauch, b) Entkräftung *f*. **ex'haus·tive** *adj* □ *fig.* erschöpfend.

ex·hib·it [ɪg'zɪbɪt] **I** *v/t* **1.** *Bilder etc* ausstellen. **2.** *fig.* zeigen, an den Tag legen; zur Schau stellen. **II** *v/i* **3.** ausstellen (*at a fair* auf e-r Messe). **III** *s* **4.** Ausstellungsstück *n*, Exponat *n*. **5.** ⚖ Beweisstück *n*. **ex·hi·bi·tion** [ˌeksɪ'bɪʃn] *s* **1.** Ausstellung *f*: *be on* ~ ausgestellt *od.* zu sehen sein; *make an* ~ *of o.s.* sich lächerlich *od.* zum Gespött machen. **2.** *fig.* Zurschaustellung *f*. **3.** *univ. Br.* Stipendium *n*. **ˌex·hi'bi·tion·ism** *s* *psych.* *u. fig.* Exhibitionismus *m*. **ˌex·hi'bi·tion·ist** *psych.* *u. fig.* **I** *s* Exhibitionist *m*. **II** *adj* exhibitionistisch. **ex·hib·i·tor** [ɪg'zɪbɪtə] *s* Aussteller *m*.

ex·hort [ɪg'zɔːt] *v/t* ermahnen (*to* zu; *to do* zu tun). **ex·hor·ta·tion** [ˌegzɔː'teɪʃn] *s* Ermahnung *f*.

ex·hu·ma·tion [ˌekshjuːˈmeɪʃn] s Exhumierung f. **ex'hume** v/t Leiche exhumieren.

ex·i·gence, ex·i·gen·cy [ˈeksɪdʒəns,-ɪ)] s 1. Dringlichkeit f. 2. Not(lage) f. 3. mst pl Erfordernis n. '**ex·i·gent** adj 1. dringend, drängend. 2. anspruchsvoll.

ex·ig·u·ous [egˈzɪgjʊəs] adj □ dürftig.

ex·ile [ˈeksaɪl] **I** s 1. Exil n; Verbannung f: **go into ~** ins Exil gehen; **live in ~** im Exil od. in der Verbannung leben; **send into ~** → 3; **government in ~** Exilregierung f. 2. im Exil Lebende m, f; Verbannte m, f. **II** v/t 3. ins Exil schicken; verbannen (**from** aus), in die Verbannung schicken.

ex·ist [ɪgˈzɪst] v/i 1. existieren, vorkommen: **do such things ~?** gibt es so et was?; **right to ~** Existenzberechtigung f. 2. existieren, leben (**on** von). 3. existieren, bestehen. **ex'ist·ence** s 1. Existenz f, Vorkommen n: **call into ~** ins Leben rufen; **come into ~** entstehen; **be in ~** → **exist** 3; **remain in ~** weiterbestehen. 2. Existenz f, Leben n, Dasein n. 3. Existenz f, Bestand m. **ex'ist·ent** adj 1. existierend, bestehend, vorhanden. 2. gegenwärtig, augenblicklich. **ex·is·ten·tial·ism** [ˌegzɪˈstenʃəlɪzəm] s phls. Existentialismus m.

ex·it [ˈeksɪt] **I** s 1. Ausgang m. 2. thea. Abgang m. 3. (Autobahn)Ausfahrt f. 4. Ausreise f: **~ visa** Ausreisevisum n. **II** v/i 5. thea. Bühnenanweisung: (er, sie, es geht) ab: **~ Macbeth** Macbeth ab.

ex·o·dus [ˈeksədəs] s Ab-, Auswanderung f: **rural ~** Landflucht f.

ex·on·er·ate [ɪgˈzɒnəreɪt] v/t 1. Angeklagten entlasten (**from** von). 2. j-n befreien, entbinden (**from** von e-r Pflicht etc). **ex·on·er·a·tion** s 1. Entlastung f. 2. Befreiung f, Entbindung f.

ex·or·bi·tance [ɪgˈzɔːbɪtəns] s Unverschämtheit f, Maßlosigkeit f. **ex'or·bi·tant** adj □ unverschämt (a.) astronomisch: **~ price** Phantasiepreis m (a.) übertrieben, maßlos (Forderung etc).

ex·or·cism [ˈeksɔːsɪzəm] s Exorzismus m, Geisterbeschwörung f, Teufelsaustreibung f. '**ex·or·cist** s Exorzist m, Geisterbeschwörer m, Teufelsaustreiber m. **ex·or·cize** [ˈ-saɪz] v/t 1. böse Geister austreiben, beschwören. 2. j-n, e-n Ort von bösen Geistern befreien, j-m den Teufel austreiben.

ex·ot·ic [ɪgˈzɒtɪk] adj (**~ally**) exotisch (a. fig.).

ex·pand [ɪkˈspænd] **I** v/t 1. ausbreiten, -spannen. 2. ♣, phys. etc, a. fig. ausdehnen, -weiten, erweitern. **II** v/i 3. ♣, phys. etc, a. fig. sich ausdehnen od. erweitern, ♣ a. expandieren. 4. fig. (vor Stolz etc) aufblühen; aus sich herausgehen. 5. fig. sich ausdehnen od. verbreiten (**on** über acc). **ex'pand·er** s Sport: Expander m. **ex·panse** [ˈ-ˈspæns] s weite Fläche, Weite f. **ex'pan·sion** s 1. Ausbreitung f. 2. ♣, phys. etc, a. fig. Ausdehnung f, -weitung f, Erweiterung f; pol. Expansion f. **ex'pan·sive** adj □ 1. ausdehnungsfähig. 2. ausgedehnt, weit. 3. fig. mitteilsam.

ex·pa·tri·ate I v/t ausbürgern. **II** adj [ˈ-ət] ausgebürgert. **III** s [ˈ-ət] Ausgebürgerte m, f. **ex·pa·tri·a·tion** s Ausbürgerung f

ex·pect [ɪkˈspekt] **I** v/t 1. j-n, et. erwarten: **~ s.o. to do s.th.** erwarten, daß j-d et. tut; **~ s.th. of** (od. **from**) **s.o.** et. von j-m erwarten. 2. F vermuten, glauben: **I ~ so** ich nehme es an. **II** v/i 3. **be ~ing** F in anderen Umständen sein. **ex'pec·tan·cy** s Erwartung f: **look of ~** erwartungsvoller Blick. **ex'pec·tant** adj □ 1. **~ mother** werdende Mutter. 2. erwartungsvoll. **ex·pec·ta·tion** [ˌekspekˈteɪʃn] s Erwartung f: **in ~ of** in Erwartung (gen); **beyond** (**all**) **~(s)** über Erwarten; **against all** (od. **contrary to** [**all**]) **~(s)** wider Erwarten; **come up to ~s** den Erwartungen entsprechen; **fall short of s.o.'s ~s** hinter j-s Erwartungen zurückbleiben; **~ of life** Lebenserwartung.

ex·pe·di·ence, ex·pe·di·en·cy [ɪkˈspiːdjəns(ɪ)] s 1. Zweckdienlichkeit f, Nützlichkeit f. 2. Eigennutz m. **ex'pe·di·ent I** adj 1. ratsam, angebracht. 2. zweckdienlich, -mäßig, nützlich. 3. eigennützig. **II** s 4. (Hilfs)Mittel n, (Not)Behelf m. **ex'pe·di·ent·ly** adv zweckmäßigerweise.

ex·pe·dite [ˈekspɪdaɪt] v/t beschleunigen. **ex·pe·di·tion** [ˌ-ˈdɪʃn] s 1. Expedition f: **on an ~** auf e-r Expedition. 2. Eile f, Schnelligkeit f. **ex·pe·di·tious** adj □ schnell, rasch, prompt.

ex·pel [ɪkˈspel] v/t (**from**) 1. vertreiben

(aus). **2.** ausweisen (aus), verweisen (*des Landes*). **3.** ausschließen (aus, von).

ex·pen·di·ture [ɪkˈspendɪtʃə] *s* **1.** Aufwand *m*, Verbrauch *m* (*of* an *dat*). **2.** Ausgaben *pl*, (Kosten)Aufwand *m*.

ex·pense [ɪkˈspens] *s* **1.** → *expenditure* 2: *at s.o.'s ~* auf j-s Kosten (*a. fig.*); *spare no ~* keine Kosten scheuen. **2.** *pl* Unkosten *pl*, Spesen *pl*: *travel(l)ing ~s* Reisespesen; *~ account* Spesenkonto *n*. **ex'pen·sive** *adj* □ teuer, kostspielig.

ex·pe·ri·ence [ɪkˈspɪərɪəns] I *s* **1.** Erfahrung *f*: a) (Lebens)Praxis *f*: *by* (*od. from*) *~* aus Erfahrung; *in my ~* nach m-r Erfahrung, b) Fach-, Sachkenntnis *f*; Routine *f*. **2.** Erlebnis *n*. II *v/t* **3.** erfahren: a) kennenlernen, b) erleben, c) *Schmerzen, Verluste etc* erleiden, *et.* durchmachen, *Vergnügen etc* empfinden. **ex'pe·ri·enced** *adj* erfahren, routiniert.

ex·per·i·ment I *s* [ɪkˈsperɪmənt] Experiment *n*, Versuch *m* (*on* an *dat*; *with* mit): *~ on animals* Tierversuch. II *v/i* [~ment] experimentieren, Versuche anstellen (*on* an *dat*; *with* mit). **ex·per·i·men·tal** [ek͵sperɪˈmentl] *adj* □ experimentell, Versuchs...: *~ animal* Versuchstier *n*. **ex͵per·i·men'ta·tion** *s* Experimentieren *n*. **ex'per·i·ment·er** *s* Experimentator *m*.

ex·pert [ˈekspɜːt] I *adj* **1.** (*at, in* in *dat*) erfahren; geschickt: *be ~ at* Erfahrung haben in. **2.** fachmännisch, fach-, sachkundig: *~ knowledge* Fach-, Sachkenntnis *f*; *~ opinion* Gutachten *n*. II *s* **3.** (*at, in* in *dat*; *on* auf dem Gebiet *gen*) Fachmann *m*, Experte *m*; Sachverständige *m*, Gutachter *m*: *~ on disarmament* Abrüstungsexperte. **ex·per·tise** [͵~ˈtiːz] *s* **1.** Expertise *f*, Gutachten *n*. **2.** Fach-, Sachkenntnis *f*.

ex·pi·ate [ˈekspɪeɪt] *v/t* sühnen, (ab)büßen. **ex·pi·a·tion** *s* Sühne *f*, Buße *f*.

ex·pi·ra·tion [͵ekspɪˈreɪʃn] *s* **1.** Ablauf *m*, Erlöschen *n*, Ende *n*: *at* (*od. on*) *the ~ of* nach Ablauf (*gen*). **2.** Verfall *m*: *~ date* Verfallstag *m*, -datum *n*. **3.** † Fälligwerden *n*. **ex·pire** [ɪkˈspaɪə] *v/i* **1.** ablaufen (*Frist, Paß etc*), erlöschen (*Konzession, Patent etc*), enden. **2.** ungültig werden, verfallen. **3.** † fällig werden. **ex'pi·ry** → *expiration* 1.

ex·plain [ɪkˈspleɪn] *v/t* erklären: a) erläutern (*s.th. to s.o.* j-m et.), b) begründen, rechtfertigen: *~ s.th. away* e-e einleuchtende Erklärung für et. finden; sich aus et. herausreden; *~ o.s.* sich erklären; sich rechtfertigen.

ex·pla·na·tion [͵ekspləˈneɪʃn] *s* Erklärung *f* (*for, of* für *od. gen*): a) Erläuterung *f*: *in ~ of* als Erklärung für, b) Begründung *f*, Rechtfertigung *f*. **ex·plan·a·to·ry** [ɪkˈsplænətərɪ] *adj* □ erklärend, erläuternd.

ex·ple·tive [ɪkˈspliːtɪv] *s* **1.** *ling.* Füllwort *n*. **2.** Fluch *m*; Kraftausdruck *m*.

ex·pli·ca·ble [ɪkˈsplɪkəbl] *adj* erklärbar, erklärlich.

ex·plic·it [ɪkˈsplɪsɪt] *adj* □ **1.** ausdrücklich, deutlich. **2.** ausführlich. **3.** offen, deutlich (*about, on* in bezug auf *acc*): (*sexually*) *~* freizügig (*Film etc*).

ex·plode [ɪkˈspləʊd] I *v/t* **1.** zur Explosion bringen; (in die Luft) sprengen. **2.** *Gerüchten etc* den Boden entziehen, *Theorie etc* widerlegen, *Mythos etc* zerstören. II *v/i* **3.** explodieren; (in die Luft fliegen. **4.** *fig.* ausbrechen (*into, with* in *acc*), platzen (*with, in* vor *dat*). **5.** *fig.* sprunghaft ansteigen, sich explosionsartig vermehren (*bsd. Bevölkerung*).

ex·ploit I *s* [ˈeksplɔɪt] **1.** (Helden)Tat *f*. **2.** Großtat *f*, große Leistung. II *v/t* [ɪkˈsplɔɪt] **3.** *et.* auswerten, *Patent etc* (kommerziell) verwerten, *Erzvorkommen etc* ausbeuten, abbauen; *bsd. j-n, et.* ausbeuten. **ex·ploi'ta·tion** [͵eks~] *s* Auswertung *f*, Verwertung *f*, Ausbeutung *f*, Abbau *m*.

ex·plo·ra·tion [͵ekspləˈreɪʃn] *s* **1.** Erforschung *f*. **2.** Untersuchung *f*. **ex·plor·a·to·ry** [ekˈsplɔːrətərɪ] *adj* Forschungs...: *~ talks pl* Sondierungsgespräche *pl*. **ex·plore** [ɪkˈsplɔː] *v/t* **1.** *Land* erforschen. **2.** erforschen, untersuchen, sondieren. **ex'plor·er** *s* Forscher(in).

ex·plo·sion [ɪkˈspləʊʒn] *s* **1.** Explosion *f*; Sprengung *f*. **2.** *fig.* Widerlegung *f*, Zerstörung *f*. **3.** *fig.* Ausbruch *m*: *~ of loud laughter* Lachsalve *f*. **4.** *fig.* sprunghafter Anstieg, (*Bevölkerungs*)Explosion *f*. **ex'plo·sive** [~sɪv] I *adj* **1.** explosiv (*a. fig.*), Spreng...: *~ problem* brisantes Problem. **2.** *fig.* aufbrausend (*Temperament*). II *s* **3.** Sprengstoff *m*.

ex·po·nent [ık'spəʊnənt] *s* **1.** *Ar* Exponent *m*, Hochzahl *f*. **2.** Vertreter(in); Verfechter(in).

ex·port I *v/t u. v/i* [ık'spɔːt] **1.** exportieren, ausführen: *~ing country* Ausfuhrland *n*; *~ing firm* Exportfirma *f*. **II** *s* ['ekspɔːt] **2.** Export *m*, Ausfuhr *f*. **3.** *pl* (Gesamt)Export *m*, (-)Ausfuhr *f*; Exportgüter *pl*, Ausfuhrware *f*. **III** *adj* ['eks-] **4.** Export..., Ausfuhr...: *~ trade* Exportgeschäft *n*, Ausfuhrhandel *m*. **ex'port·er** [ık'sp~] *s* Exporteur *m*.

ex·pose [ık'spəʊz] *v/t* **1.** *Kind* aussetzen. **2.** *Waren* ausstellen (*for sale* zum Verkauf). **3.** *~ to fig.* dem *Wetter, e-r Gefahr etc* aussetzen, *der Lächerlichkeit etc* preisgeben: *~ o.s.* sich exponieren; *~ o.s. to ridicule* sich zum Gespött (der Leute) machen. **4.** *fig.* j-n bloßstellen; j-n entlarven, *Spion a.* enttarnen; *et.* aufdecken, entlarven, enthüllen. **5.** entblößen. **6.** *phot.* belichten. **ex'posed** *adj* ungeschützt (*Haus, Lage etc*), (*a. fig. Stellung etc*) exponiert.

ex·po·si·tion [ˌekspəʊ'zıʃn] *s* **1.** Ausstellung *f*. **2.** Exposition *f* (*e-s Dramas*). **ex·po·sure** [ık'spəʊʒə] *s* **1.** (Kindes-) Aussetzung *f*. **2.** *fig.* Aussetzen *n*, Preisgabe *f* (*to dat*). **3.** *fig.* Ausgesetztsein *n* (*to dat*): *die of ~* an Unterkühlung sterben. **4.** Bloßstellung *f*; Entlarvung *f*, Enttarnung *f*; Aufdeckung *f*, Enthüllung *f*. **5.** Entblößung *f*. **6.** ungeschützte *od.* exponierte Lage. **7.** *phot.* a) Belichtung *f*: *~ meter* Belichtungsmesser *m*, b) Aufnahme *f*. **8.** Lage *f* (*e-s Gebäudes*): *southern ~* Südlage.

ex·pound [ık'spaʊnd] *v/t* erklären, erläutern, *Theorie etc* entwickeln (*to s.o.* j-m).

ex·press [ık'spres] **I** *v/t* **1.** ausdrücken, äußern: *~ the hope that* der Hoffnung Ausdruck geben, daß; *~ o.s.* sich äußern; sich ausdrücken. **2.** bezeichnen, bedeuten. **3.** *Br.* durch Eilboten *od.* als Eilgut schicken. **II** *adj* □ **4.** ausdrücklich. **5.** Expreß..., Schnell...: *~ letter Br.* Eilbrief *m*; *~ train → 9*. **III** *adv* **6.** eigens. **7.** *Br.* durch Eilboten, als Eilgut. **IV** *s* **8.** *Br.* Eilbote *m*; -beförderung *f*. **9.** D-Zug *m*, Schnellzug *m*. **ex·pres·sion** [ık'spreʃn] *s* **1.** Ausdruck *m*, Äußerung *f*: *find ~ in* sich ausdrücken *od.* äußern in (*dat*); *give ~ to e-r Sache* Ausdruck

verleihen; *beyond* (*od. past*) *~* unsagbar. **2.** Ausdruck *m*, Redensart *f*. **3.** (Gesichts)Ausdruck *m*. **4.** Ausdruck(skraft *f*) *m*. **ex'pres·sion·ism** *s Kunst*: Expressionismus *m*. **ex'pres·sion·ist** (*Kunst*) **I** *s* Expressionist(in). **II** *adj* expressionistisch. **ex'pres·sion·less** *adj* ausdruckslos. **ex'pres·sive** *adj* □ **1.** *be ~ of et.* ausdrücken. **2.** ausdrucksvoll. **ex'press·way** *s bsd Am.* Schnellstraße *f*.

ex·pro·pri·ate [eks'prəʊprıeıt] *v/t* ₺ enteignen. **ex·pro·pri·a·tion** *s* Enteignung *f*.

ex·pul·sion [ık'spʌlʃn] *s* (*from*) **1.** Vertreibung *f* (aus). **2.** Ausweisung *f* (aus). **3.** Ausschluß *m* (aus, von).

ex·qui·site ['ekskwızıt] *adj* □ **1.** exquisit, köstlich, erlesen. **2.** gepflegt, erlesen (*Wein etc*). **3.** äußerst fein (*Gehör etc*). **4.** heftig (*Schmerz*), groß (*Vergnügen*).

ex·ser·vice·man [ˌeks'sɜːvısmən] *s* (*irr man*) ✕ *bsd. Br.* Veteran *m*.

ex·tant [ek'stænt] *adj* noch vorhanden *od.* bestehend.

ex·tem·po·ra·ne·ous [ekˌstempə'reınjəs], **ex·tem·po·rar·y** [ık'stempərərı] *adj* □ improvisiert, aus dem Stegreif, Stegreif... **ex·tem·po·re** [ek'stempərı] *adj u. adv* improvisiert, aus dem Stegreif. **ex·tem·po·rize** [ık'stempəraız] *v/t* aus dem Stegreif darbieten *od.* vortragen, (*a. v/i*) improvisieren.

ex·tend [ık'stend] **I** *v/t* **1.** (aus)dehnen, (-)weiten. **2.** *Betrieb etc* vergrößern, erweitern, ausbauen. **3.** *Hand etc* ausstrecken. **4.** *Besuch, Macht, Vorsprung etc* ausdehnen (*to* auf *acc*), *Frist, Paß etc* verlängern, ✝ *a.* prolongieren, *Angebot etc* aufrechterhalten. **5.** *~ o.s.* sich völlig ausgeben. **II** *v/i* **6.** sich ausdehnen *od.* erstrecken (*over* über *acc*; *to* bis zu); hinausgehen (*beyond* über *acc*).

ex·ten·sion [ık'stenʃn] *s* **1.** Ausdehnung *f* (*a. fig.*: *to* auf *acc*). **2.** Vergrößerung *f*, Erweiterung *f*. **3.** (Frist)Verlängerung *f*, ✝ *a.* Prolongation *f*. **4.** △ Erweiterung *f*, Anbau *m*. **5.** *teleph.* Nebenanschluß *m*, Apparat *m*. *~ ca·ble s* ✦ *bsd. Br.* Verlängerungsschnur *f*. *~ cord Am.* → **extension cable**. *~ lad·der s* Ausziehleiter *f*. *~ lead* → **extension cable**.

ex·ten·sive [ık'stensıv] *adj* □ **1.** ausgedehnt (*a. fig.*). **2.** *fig.* umfassend; eingehend; beträchtlich.

ex·tent [ɪkˈstent] *s* **1.** Ausdehnung *f.* **2.** *fig.* Umfang *m,* (Aus)Maß *n,* Grad *m:* *to a large ~* in hohem Maße, weitgehend; *to some* (*od. a certain*) *~* bis zu e-m gewissen Grade; *to such an ~ that* so sehr, daß.

ex·ten·u·ate [ɪkˈstenjʊeɪt] *v/t* abschwächen, mildern: *extenuating circumstances pl* ⚖ mildernde Umstände *pl.* **ex.ten·u·a·tion** *s* Abschwächung *f,* Milderung *f.*

ex·te·ri·or [ɪkˈstɪərɪə] **I** *adj* □ **1.** äußer, Außen... **II** *s* **2.** *das* Äußere: a) Außenseite *f,* b) äußere Erscheinung (*e-r Person*). **3.** Film, TV: Außenaufnahme *f.*

ex·ter·mi·nate [ɪkˈstɜːmɪneɪt] *v/t* ausrotten (*a. fig.*), vernichten, *Ungeziefer, Unkraut etc a.* vertilgen. **ex.ter·mi·na·tion** *s* Ausrottung *f,* Vernichtung *f,* Vertilgung *f.*

ex·ter·nal [ɪkˈstɜːnl] **I** *adj* □ äußer, äußerlich, Außen...: *for ~ use* ✗ zum äußerlichen Gebrauch; *~ to* außerhalb (*gen*). **II** *s pl* Äußerlichkeiten *pl.*

ex·ter·ri·to·ri·al [ˈeksˌterɪˈtɔːrɪəl] *adj* □ exterritorial.

ex·tinct [ɪkˈstɪŋkt] *adj* **1.** erloschen (*Vulkan*) (*a. fig.*). **2.** ausgestorben (*Pflanze, Tier etc*), untergegangen (*Reich etc*): *become ~* aussterben. **ex·ˈtinc·tion** *s* **1.** Erlöschen *n.* **2.** Aussterben *n,* Untergang *m.*

ex·tin·guish [ɪkˈstɪŋgwɪʃ] *v/t* **1.** Feuer, Licht (aus)löschen, Zigarette ausmachen. **2.** Leben, Gefühl auslöschen, ersticken, Hoffnungen, Pläne etc zunichte machen. **3.** Schuld tilgen. **ex·ˈtin·guish·er** *s* (Feuer)Löscher *m.*

ex·tol [ɪkˈstəʊl] *v/t* (lob)preisen, rühmen: → **sky.**

ex·tort [ɪkˈstɔːt] *v/t* Geld, Geständnis etc erpressen (*from* von). **ex·ˈtor·tion** *s* **1.** Erpressung *f.* **2.** Wucher *m.* **ex·ˈtor·tion·ate** [~ʃnət] *adj* □ **1.** erpresserisch. **2.** Wucher...: *~ price.* **ex·ˈtor·tion·er, ex·ˈtor·tion·ist** *s* **1.** Erpresser *m.* **2.** Wucherer *m.*

ex·tra [ˈekstrə] **I** *adj* **1.** zusätzlich, Extra..., Sonder...: *be ~* gesondert berechnet werden; *~ charge* Zuschlag *m;* *~ charges pl* Nebenkosten *pl;* *~ pay* Zulage *f;* *if you pay an ~ two pounds* wenn Sie noch zwei Pfund dazulegen. **2.** besonder. **II** *adv* **3.** extra, besonders: *charge ~ for et.* gesondert berechnen. **III** *s* **4.** Sonderleistung *f;* bsd. mot. Extra *n, pl a.* Sonderausstattung *f;* Zuschlag *m:* *be an ~* gesondert berechnet werden. **5.** Extrablatt *n,* -ausgabe *f.* **6.** Film: Statist(in).

ex·tract I *v/t* [ɪkˈstrækt] **1.** herausziehen, -holen (*from* aus). **2.** Zahn, ✗ Wurzel ziehen. **3.** *fig.* (*from*) Geld, Geständnis etc herausholen (aus), entlocken (*dat*). **II** *s* [ˈekstrækt] **4.** 🦌, gastr. Extrakt *m,* (*from* aus e-m Buch etc a.) Auszug *m.* **ex·ˈtrac·tion** *s* **1.** ✗, ✗ Ziehen *n.* **2.** Herkunft *f,* Abstammung *f.*

ex·tra·cur·ric·u·lar [ˌekstrəkəˈrɪkjələ] *adj* □ ped. univ. außerhalb des Stunden- od. Lehrplans. **2.** außerplanmäßig.

ex·tra·dite [ˈekstrədaɪt] *v/t* Verbrecher ausliefern. **ex·tra·di·tion** [~ˈdɪʃn] *s* Auslieferung *f.*

ex·tra·mar·i·tal [ˌekstrəˈmærɪtl] *adj* außerehelich.

ex·tra·ne·ous [ɪkˈstreɪnjəs] *adj* **1.** fremd (*to dat*): *~ to reality* realitätsfremd. **2.** nicht dazugehörig: *be ~ to* nicht gehören zu.

ex·traor·di·nar·y [ɪkˈstrɔːdnrɪ] *adj* □ **1.** außerordentlich, -gewöhnlich. **2.** ungewöhnlich, seltsam.

ex·tra·sen·so·ry [ˌekstrəˈsensərɪ] *adj:* *~ perception* außersinnliche Wahrnehmung. **ex·ter·ˈres·tri·al** *adj* außerirdisch. **ex·ter·ri·to·ri·al** *adj* □ exterritorial. **~ time** *s* Sport: Verlängerung *f: after ~* nach Verlängerung; *the game went into ~* das Spiel ging in die Verlängerung.

ex·trav·a·gance [ɪkˈstrævəgəns] *s* **1.** Verschwendung(ssucht) *f.* **2.** Übertriebenheit *f,* Extravaganz *f.* **3.** Ausschweifung *f,* Zügellosigkeit *f.* **ex·ˈtrav·a·gant** *adj* □ **1.** verschwenderisch. **2.** übertrieben, -spannt, extravagant. **3.** ausschweifend, zügellos.

ex·treme [ɪkˈstriːm] **I** *adj* (□ → **extremely**) **1.** äußerst, extrem. **2.** äußerst, höchst: *~ necessity* zwingende Notwendigkeit; *~ penalty* Höchststrafe *f.* **3.** extrem, radikal. **II** *s* **4.** äußerstes Ende: *at the other ~* am entgegengesetzten Ende. **5.** *das* Äußerste, Extrem *n:* *in the ~* extrem, höchst; *go to ~s* vor nichts zurückschrecken. **ex·ˈtreme·ly**

adv äußerst, höchst. **ex'trem·ism** *s bsd. pol.* Extre'mismus *m.* **ex'trem·ist** *bsd. pol.* **I** *s* Extremist(in). **II** *adj* extremistisch. **ex·trem·i·ty** [ɪk'stremətɪ] *s* **1.** äußerstes Ende. **2.** *das* Äußerste: *drive s.o. to extremities* j-n bis zum Äußersten treiben. **3.** *be reduced to extremities* in größter Not sein. **4.** *mst pl* Gliedmaße *f*, Extremität *f*.
ex·tri·cate ['ekstrɪkeɪt] *v/t (from)* herausziehen (aus), befreien (aus, von).
ex·tro·vert ['ekstrəʊvɜːt] *adj psych.* extra-, extrovertiert.
ex·u·ber·ance [ɪg'zjuːbərəns] *s* **1.** *(of)* Fülle *f* (von *od. gen*), Reichtum *m* (an *dat*). **2.** *fig.* Überschwang *m.* **ex'u·ber·ant** *adj* □ **1.** üppig, (über)reich. **2.** *fig.* überschwenglich; (-)sprudelnd.
ex·ude [ɪg'zjuːd] *v/t* **1.** ausschwitzen, absondern. **2.** *Duft, Charme etc* verströmen.
ex·ult [ɪg'zʌlt] *v/i* frohlocken, jubeln (*at, over, in* über *acc*). **ex'ult·ant** *adj* □ frohlockend, jubelnd. **ex·ul·ta·tion** [ˌegzʌl'teɪʃn] *s* Frohlocken *n*, Jubel *m*.
eye [aɪ] **I** *s* **1.** Auge *n*: *before (od. under) s.o.'s ~s* vor j-s Augen; *all ~s were waiting etc*; *be up to the ~s in work* bis über die Ohren in Arbeit sitzen *od.* stecken; *cry one's ~s out* sich die Au-

gen ausweinen; → *peel* I, *skin* 5. **2.** *fig.* Blick *m*, Auge(nmerk) *n*: *have an ~ for* Sinn *od.* ein (offenes) Auge *od.* e-n Blick haben für; → *catch* 10. **3.** *fig.* Ansicht *f*: *in my ~s* in m-n Augen, m-r Ansicht nach. **4.** *(Nadel)*Öhr *n*; Öse *f*. **5.** *Auge n.* **II** *v/t* **6.** betrachten; mustern. '**~·ball** *s anat.* Augapfel *m.* '**~·black** *s* Wimperntusche *f.* '**~·brow** *s* (Augen-)Braue *f*: *raise one's ~s (od. an ~)* die Stirn runzeln (*at* über *acc*). '**~·catch·er** *s* Blickfang *m.* '**~·con·tact** *s* Blickkontakt *m.* **~·ful** ['~fʊl] *s*: *get an ~* F was zu sehen bekommen. '**~·glass·es** *s pl, a. pair of ~* bsd. Am. Brille *f.* '**~·lash** *s* Augenwimper *f.* **~ lev·el** *s*: *on ~* in Augenhöhe. '**~·lid** *s* Augenlid *n*: → *bat³.* **~ lin·er** *s* Eyeliner *m.* **~ o·pen·er** *s*: *be an ~ to (od. for) s.o.* F j-m die Augen öffnen. **~ shad·ow** *s* Lidschatten *m.* '**~·shot** *s* Sicht-, Sehweite *f*: *(with)in (beyond, out of) ~* in (außer) Sichtweite. '**~·sight** *s* Sehkraft *f*: *good (poor) ~* gute (schlechte) Augen *pl.* '**~·sore** *s et.* Unschönes, Schandfleck *m.* '**~·strain** *s* Überanstrengung *f* der Augen. '**~·wit·ness** *s* Augenzeuge *m (to gen)*: *~ account* Augenzeugenbericht *m.* **II** *v/t* Augenzeuge sein *od.* werden von (*od. gen*).

F

fa·ble ['feɪbl] *s* **1.** Fabel *f*; Sage *f.* **2.** *fig.* Märchen *n.* **fa·bled** ['~bld] *adj* sagenhaft (*a. fig.*).
fab·ric ['fæbrɪk] *s* **1.** Gewebe *n*, Stoff *m.* **2.** *fig.* Gefüge *n*, Struktur *f.* **fab·ri·cate** ['~keɪt] *v/t* **1.** fabrizieren (*a. fig.*), herstellen. **2.** *fig.* erfinden. ˌ**fab·ri·ca·tion** *s* **1.** Fabrikation *f*, Herstellung *f.* **2.** *fig.* Erfindung *f*, Märchen *n.*
fab·u·lous ['fæbjʊləs] *adj* □ sagenhaft (*a. fig.*).
fa·cade, fa·cade [fə'sɑːd] *s* △ Fassade *f (a. fig.).*
face [feɪs] **I** *s* **1.** Gesicht *n*: *in (the) ~ of* angesichts; trotz; *~ to ~ with* Auge in

Auge mit; *do (up) one's ~* sich schminken; *say s.th. to s.o's ~* j-m et. ins Gesicht sagen; → *stare* II. **2.** Gesicht(sausdruck *m*) *n*, Miene *f*: *make (od. pull) a ~* ein Gesicht machen *od.* schneiden; *have the ~ to inf* die Stirn haben *od.* so unverfroren sein zu *inf*; → *straight* 1. **3.** *das* Äußere: *on the ~ of it* oberflächlich (betrachtet). **4.** Ansehen *n*: *save one's ~* das Gesicht wahren; *lose ~* das Gesicht verlieren. **5.** Bildseite *f (e-r Spielkarte).* **6.** Zifferblatt *n.* **7.** → *façade.* **II** *v/t* **8.** ansehen, j-m ins Gesicht sehen. **9.** gegenüberstehen, -liegen, -sitzen (*dat*); nach *Osten etc* blicken *od.* liegen

(*Raum etc*). **10.** *j-m, e-r Sache* mutig entgegentreten *od.* begegnen, sich stellen: → *music* 1. **11.** *oft be ~d with* sich e-r *Gefahr etc* gegenüberschen, gegenüberstehen: *be ~d with ruin* vor dem Ruin stehen. **III** *v/i* **12.** sich wenden: ~ *about* kehrtmachen; ~ *away* sich abwenden. **13.** blicken, liegen (*to, toward*[*s*]) nach; *south* nach Süden). **14.** ~ *up to* → 10. ~ **card** *s Kartenspiel*: Bild(karte *f*) *n*. '~*cloth s* Waschlappen *m*. ~ **cream** *s* Gesichtscreme *f*. '~‚**lift**(**·ing**) *s* Facelifting *n*, Gesichtsstraffung *f*: *have a ~* sich das Gesicht liften lassen.

fa·ce·tious [fəˈsiːʃəs] *adj* □ witzig, spaßig.

face val·ue *s* † Nenn-, Nominalwert *m*: *take s.th. at* (*its*) ~ *fig.* et. unbesehen glauben; et. für bare Münze nehmen.

fa·cial [ˈfeɪʃl] *adj* Gesichts...

fa·cil·i·tate [fəˈsɪlɪteɪt] *v/t* erleichtern.

fa·cil·i·ty *s* **1.** Leichtigkeit *f*. **2.** (günstige) Gelegenheit, Möglichkeit *f* (*for* für). **3.** *pl* Einrichtungen *pl*, Anlagen *pl*. **4.** *pl* Erleichterungen *pl*, Vergünstigungen *pl*.

fac·sim·i·le [fækˈsɪmɪlɪ] *s* Faksimile *n*.

fact [fækt] *s* Tatsache *f*, Faktum *n*: *be founded on* ~ auf Tatsachen beruhen; *know s.th. for a* ~ et. (ganz) sicher wissen; *tell s.o. the ~s of life* j-n (*sexuell*) aufklären; → *matter* 3. '~‚**find·ing** *adj* Untersuchungs...

fac·tion [ˈfækʃn] *s bsd. pol.* Splittergruppe *f*.

fac·ti·tious [fækˈtɪʃəs] *adj* □ künstlich, (*Freundlichkeit etc a.*) gekünstelt.

fac·tor [ˈfæktə] *s* Faktor *m*.

fac·to·ry [ˈfæktərɪ] *s* Fabrik *f*. ~ **hand**, ~ **work·er** *s* Fabrikarbeiter(in).

fac·to·tum [fækˈtəʊtəm] *s* Faktotum *n*, Mädchen *n* für alles.

fac·tu·al [ˈfæktʃʊəl] *adj* □ **1.** Tatsachen...: → *report* 2. sachlich.

fac·ul·ty [ˈfækltɪ] *s* **1.** Fähigkeit *f*, Vermögen *n*: ~ *of hearing* Hörvermögen; (*mental*) *faculties pl* Geisteskräfte *pl*; *be in possession of one's faculties* im (Voll)Besitz s-r Kräfte sein. **2.** Gabe *f*, Talent *n*. **3.** *univ.* Fakultät *f*.

fad [fæd] *s* Mode(erscheinung, -torheit) *f*; (vorübergehende) Laune.

fade [feɪd] **I** *v/i* **1.** (ver)welken. **2.** verschießen, -blassen (*Farbe etc*). **3.** *a.* ~ *away* sich auflösen (*Menge*), ♬ immer schwächer werden (*Person*), verklingen (*Lied etc*), verblassen (*Erinnerung*), verrauchen (*Zorn etc*), zerrinnen (*Hoffnungen*). **4.** *Radio:* schwinden (*Ton, Sender*). **5.** nachlassen (*Bremsen*), (*Sportler a.*) abbauen. **6.** *a.* ~ *out* (*Film, Rundfunk, TV*) aus- *od.* abgeblendet werden (*Ton, Bild*): ~ *in* (*od. up*) auf- *od.* eingeblendet werden. **II** *v/t* **7.** (ver)welken lassen. **8.** *Farbe etc* ausbleichen. **9.** *a.* ~ *out Ton, Bild* aus- *od.* abblenden: ~ *in* (*od. up*) auf- *od.* einblenden. '**fad·ed** *adj* verwelkt, welk.

fae·ces [ˈfiːsiːz] *s pl* Fäkalien *pl*, Kot *m*.

fag¹ [fæg] *s* F Glimmstengel *m*.

fag² [~] **I** *v/i* sich abarbeiten *od.* (ab)schinden (*at* mit). **II** *v/t a.* ~ *out* ermüden, fertigmachen. **III** *s* Schinderei *f*.

fag³ [~] → *faggot²*.

fag end *s* **1.** letzter *od.* schäbiger Rest. **2.** *Br.* F Kippe *f* (*Zigarettenstummel*).

fag·got¹, *bsd. Am.* **fag·ot** [ˈfægət] *s gastr.* Frikadelle *f* (*bsd. aus Schweineleber*).

fag·got² [~] *s bsd. Am. sl.* Schwule *m*. '**fag·got·y** *adj bsd. Am. sl.* schwul.

Fahr·en·heit [ˈfærənhaɪt]: *10° ~* zehn Grad Fahrenheit.

fail [feɪl] **I** *v/i* **1.** versagen (*a. Stimme, Motor etc*); keinen Erfolg haben; *ped.* durchfallen (*in in dat*); † Bankrott machen: *he ~ed in his attempt* sein Versuch schlug fehl. **2.** mißlingen, fehlschlagen, scheitern: *if everything else ~s* wenn alle Stricke reißen. **3.** nachlassen, schwinden (*Kräfte etc*); ausgehen, zu Ende gehen (*Vorräte etc*); abnehmen, schwächer werden (*Sehkraft etc*). **4.** ~ *to inf* es unterlassen *od.* versäumen zu *inf*: ~ *to do s.th.* et. nicht tun; *I ~ to see* ich sehe nicht ein. **II** *v/t* **5.** *j-m* versagen: *his courage ~ed him* ihm sank der Mut; *words ~ me* mir fehlen die Worte (*to inf zu inf*). **6.** *j-n* im Stich lassen. **7.** *ped. j-n* durchfallen lassen; durchfallen in (*e-r Prüfung*). **III** *s* **8.** *without* ~ mit Sicherheit, ganz bestimmt.

'**fail·ing** *prp* in Ermang(e)lung (*gen*): ~ *this* andernfalls.

'**fail-safe** *adj* störungs-, *a. fig.* pannensicher.

fail·ure ['feɪljə] s **1.** Versagen n. **2.** Unterlassung f, Versäumnis f: ~ *to pay* Nichtzahlung f. **3.** Fehlschlag(en n) m, Mißerfolg m. **4.** ped. Durchfallen n (*in* in dat). **5.** ✝ Bankrott m. **6.** Versager m (*Person, Sache*).

faint [feɪnt] **I** adj □ schwach, matt (*Person, Farbe etc*; a. fig.): *I haven't the ~est idea* ich habe nicht die leiseste Ahnung. **II** s Ohnmacht f: *in a ~* ohnmächtig. **III** v/i ohnmächtig werden, in Ohnmacht fallen (*with, from* vor dat). ,~'heart·ed adj □ zaghaft, furchtsam.

fair¹ [feə] **I** adj (□ → **fairly**) **1.** schön, hübsch: → *sex* 1. **2.** hell (*Haut, Haar, Teint*), blond (*Haar*), zart (*Teint, Haut*); hellhäutig. **3.** klar, heiter (*Himmel*), schön, trocken (*Wetter, Tag*). **4.** sauber: → *copy* 1. **5.** reell (*Chance*). **6.** gerecht, fair: → *play* 2. **7.** anständig, fair: *play* ~ fair spielen, a. fig. sich an die Spielregeln halten. **8.** direkt, genau: → *in the face* mitten ins Gesicht.

fair² [~] s **1.** Jahrmarkt m; Volksfest n. **2.** Messe f. '~·ground s **1.** Rummelplatz m. **2.** Messegelände n.

fair·ly ['feəlɪ] adv **1.** gerecht(erweise). **2.** ziemlich. '**fair·ness** s Gerechtigkeit f, Anständigkeit f, Fairneß f: *in ~ to him* um ihm Gerechtigkeit widerfahren zu lassen.

'**fair·way** s **1.** ✈ Fahrwasser n, -rinne f. **2.** Golf: Fairway n. '~·,weath·er adj: ~ *friend* Freund m nur in guten Zeiten.

fair·y ['feərɪ] s **1.** Fee f. **2.** sl. Schwule m. '~·sto·ry, ~ **tale** s Märchen n (a. fig.).

faith [feɪθ] s **1.** (*in*) Glaube(n) m (an acc) (a. eccl.), Vertrauen n (auf acc, zu): *have ~ in* e-r *Sache* Glauben schenken, an et. glauben; zu j-m Vertrauen haben. **2.** Redlichkeit f: *in good ~* in gutem Glauben, gutgläubig (*beide a. 🏛*). ~·**ful** ['~fʊl] adj □ **1.** treu (*to* dat): *Yours ~ly* Hochachtungsvoll (*Briefschluß*). **2.** wahrheits- od. wortgetreu. **3.** eccl. gläubig. **faith heal·ing** s Gesundbeten n.

faith·less ['feɪθlɪs] adj □ **1.** treulos (*to* gegenüber). **2.** eccl. ungläubig.

fake [feɪk] **I** v/t **1.** a. ~ *up* Bilanz etc frisieren. **2.** Paß etc fälschen. **3.** Interesse etc vortäuschen, Krankheit a. simulieren. **II** s **4.** Fälschung f. **5.**

Schwindel m. **6.** Schwindler m; Simulant m.

fa·kir ['feɪˌkɪə] s Fakir m.

fal·con ['fɔːlkən] s orn. Falke m.

fall [fɔːl] **I** s **1.** Fall m, Sturz m: *have a (bad od. heavy)* ~ (schwer) stürzen. **2.** bsd. Am. Herbst m: *in (the)* ~ im Herbst. **3.** (Regen-, Schnee)Fall m. **4.** fig. Fallen n, Sinken n: ~ *in temperature* Temperatursturz m. **5.** Gefälle n (*des Geländes*). **6.** Fall m (*e-r Stadt etc*). **7.** Einbruch m (*der Nacht etc*). **8.** mst pl Wasserfall m. **II** v/i (*irr*) **9.** (um-, herunter-, hinunter)fallen; (ab)stürzen; (ab-)fallen (*Blätter*): *he fell to his death* er stürzte tödlich ab. **10.** a. ~ *apart* zerfallen. **11.** fig. fallen: a) (*im Krieg*) umkommen, b) erobert werden (*Stadt*), c) gestürzt werden (*Regierung*). **12.** fig. fallen, sinken (*Preise, Temperatur etc*): *his face fell* er machte ein langes Gesicht. **13.** abfallen (*Gelände etc*). **14.** hereinbrechen (*Nacht etc*). **15.** krank, fällig etc werden.

Verbindungen mit Präpositionen:

fall| be·hind v/i zurückbleiben hinter (dat), zurückfallen hinter (acc) (*beide a. fig.*). ~ **down** v/i die Treppe etc hinunterfallen. ~ **for** v/i **1.** hereinfallen auf (acc). **2.** ~ *s.o.* sich verknallen in (acc). ~ **in·to** v/i **1.** kommen od. geraten in (acc): ~ *difficulties*; → *line¹* 11, *trap* 2. **2.** sich et. angewöhnen: ~ *a habit* e-e Gewohnheit annehmen. **3.** fallen in (*ein Gebiet od. Fach*). ~ **on** v/i **1.** fallen auf (acc) (*a. zeitlich*): *his glance fell on me; Christmas falls on a Monday this year;* → *ear¹* 1. **2.** herfallen über (acc). **3.** j-m zufallen (*to do* zu tun). ~ **out of** v/i sich abgewöhnen: ~ *a habit* e-e Gewohnheit ablegen. ~ **o·ver** v/i: ~ *o.s. to do s.th.* F sich fast umbringen, et. zu tun. ~ **to** v/i **1.** beginnen mit: ~ *doing s.th.* sich daranmachen, et. zu tun. **2.** → *fall on* 3. ~ **un·der** v/i unter *ein Gesetz etc* fallen.

Verbindungen mit Adverbien:

fall| a·bout v/i: ~ (*laughing od. with laughter*) F sich (vor Lachen) kugeln. ~ **a·way** → *fall off*. ~ **back** v/i zurückweichen. ~ **on** zurückgreifen auf (acc). ~ **be·hind** v/i zurückbleiben, -fallen (*beide a. fig.*). ~ **with** (od. **on**) in Rückstand od. Verzug geraten mit. ~

down v/i **1.** umfallen, einstürzen. **2.** F (**on**) enttäuschen, versagen (bei); Pech haben (mit). ~ **in** v/i **1.** einfallen, -stürzen. **2.** ~ **with** beipflichten, zustimmen (*dat*); sich anpassen (*dat*); entsprechen (*dat*). ~ **off** v/i **1.** zurückgehen (*Geschäfte, Zuschauerzahlen etc*), nachlassen (*Begeisterung etc*). **2.** (**from**) abfallen (von), abtrünnig werden (*dat*). ~ **out** v/i **1.** *gut etc* ausfallen, -gehen. **2.** sich ereignen, geschehen. **3.** (sich) streiten (**with** mit; *over* über *acc*). ~ **o·ver** v/i hinfallen (*Person*), umfallen (*Vase etc*): ~ **backwards to do s.th.** F sich fast umbringen, et. zu tun. ~ **through** v/i **1.** durchfallen (*a. fig.*). **2.** mißglücken, ins Wasser fallen. ~ **to** v/i reinhauen, (tüchtig) zugreifen (*beim Essen*).

fal·la·cious [fəˈleɪʃəs] *adj* □ **1.** trügerisch, irreführend. **2.** irrig, falsch.

fal·la·cy [ˈfæləsɪ] *s* Trugschluß *m*, Irrtum *m*.

fall·en [ˈfɔːlən] I *pp von* **fall.** II *adj* gefallen (*a. Mädchen*).

fall guy *s bsd. Am.* F **1.** Opfer *n* (*e-s Betrügers*); Gimpel *m* (*leichtgläubiger Mensch*). **2.** Sündenbock *m*.

fal·li·ble [ˈfæləbl] *adj* □ fehlbar.

fall·ing star [ˈfɔːlɪŋ] *s* Sternschnuppe *f*.

'fall·out Fallout *m*, radioaktiver Niederschlag.

fal·low [ˈfæləʊ] *adj* ↗ brach(liegend) (*a. fig.*): **lie** ~ brachliegen.

false [fɔːls] I *adj* □ *allg.* falsch: ~ **alarm** falscher *od.* blinder Alarm (*a. fig.*); ~ **bottom** doppelter Boden; ~ **key** Dietrich *m*, Nachschlüssel *m*; ~ **teeth** *pl* (*künstliches*) Gebiß; → **pretence** 2. II *adv*: **play s.o.** ~ ein falsches Spiel mit j-m treiben. **false·hood** [ˈ~hʊd] *s* **1.** Unwahrheit *f*. **2.** Falschheit *f*. **'false·ness** *s allg.* Falschheit *f*.

fal·si·fi·ca·tion [ˌfɔːlsɪfɪˈkeɪʃn] *s* (Ver-) Fälschung *f*. **fal·si·fy** [ˈ~faɪ] v/t **1.** fälschen. **2.** verfälschen, falsch darstellen *od.* wiedergeben. **3.** widerlegen. **fal·si·ty** [ˈ~ətɪ] → **falsehood.**

fal·ter [ˈfɔːltə] I v/i schwanken: a) taumeln, b) zögern, zaudern, c) stocken (*a. Stimme*). II v/t stammeln.

fame [feɪm] *s* Ruhm *m*. **famed** *adj* berühmt (**for** für, wegen).

fa·mil·iar [fəˈmɪljə] I *adj* □ **1.** vertraut, bekannt, geläufig (**to** *dat*): **a** ~ **sight** ein gewohnter Anblick. **2.** vertraut, bekannt (**with** mit): **be** ~ **with** *a.* sich auskennen in (*dat*); **make o.s.** ~ **with** sich vertraut machen mit. **3.** a) vertraulich, ungezwungen (*Ton etc*), b) plump-vertraulich, aufdringlich. **4.** vertraut, eng (*Freund etc*): **be on** ~ **terms with** auf vertrautem Fuß stehen mit. II *s* **5.** Vertraute *m, f.* **fa·mil·i·ar·i·ty** [ˌʌlɪˈærətɪ] *s* **1.** Vertrautheit *f.* **2.** a) Vertraulichkeit *f*, b) *oft pl* plumpe Vertraulichkeit, Aufdringlichkeit *f.* **fa·mil·iar·ize** [fəˈmɪljəraɪz] v/t vertraut *od.* bekannt machen (**with** mit).

fam·i·ly [ˈfæmɪlɪ] I *s* Familie *f*, *fig. a.* Herkunft *f*: **a** ~ **of four** e-e vierköpfige Familie; **of good** ~ aus gutem Haus; → **run** 11. II *adj* Familien...: ~ **allowance** Kindergeld *n*; ~ **doctor** Hausarzt *m*; ~ **man** Familienvater *m*; häuslicher Mensch; ~ **name** → **surname**; ~ **planning** Familienplanung *f*; ~ **problems** *pl* familiäre Probleme *pl*; ~ **tree** Stammbaum *m*.

fam·ine [ˈfæmɪn] *s* Hungersnot *f*.

fa·mous [ˈfeɪməs] *adj* □ berühmt (**for** wegen, für).

fan¹ [fæn] I *s* **1.** Fächer *m*. **2.** Ventilator *m*: ~ **belt** ⊙ Keilriemen *m*. II v/t **3.** j-m Luft zufächeln. **4.** anfachen, *fig. a.* entfachen, -flammen. III v/i **5.** *oft* ~ **out** sich fächerförmig ausbreiten; ausschwärmen.

fan² [~] *s* (*Sport- etc*)Fan *m*: ~ **club** Fanklub *m*; ~ **mail** Verehrerpost *f*.

fa·nat·ic [fəˈnætɪk] I *s* Fanatiker(in). II *adj* (~**ally**) fanatisch. **fa·nat·i·cism** [~sɪzəm] *s* Fanatismus *m*.

fan·ci·er [ˈfænsɪə] *s* (*Tier-, Blumen- etc*-) Liebhaber(in) *od.* (-)Züchter(in).

fan·ci·ful [ˈfænsɪfʊl] *adj* □ **1.** phantasiereich. **2.** phantastisch, wirklichkeitsfremd.

fan·cy [ˈfænsɪ] I *s* **1.** Phantasie *f*, Einbildung *f*: → **tickle** I. **2.** Idee *f*, plötzlicher Einfall. **3.** Laune *f*, Grille *f*. **4.** (**for**) Neigung *f* (zu), Vorliebe *f* (für), Gefallen *n* (an *dat*): **have a** ~ **for** gern haben; Lust haben auf (*acc*); **take a** ~ **to** (*od.* **for**) Gefallen finden an (*dat*), sympathisch finden. II *adj* **5.** Phantasie..., phantastisch: ~ **name** Phantasiename *m*; ~ **price** Liebhaberpreis *m*. **6.** phantasie-, kunstvoll. III v/t **7.** sich j-n, et.-

vorstellen: ~ *that!* stell dir vor!, denk nur!; sieh mal einer an! **8.** annehmen, glauben. **9.** ~ *o.s.* sich einbilden (**to be** zu sein), sich halten ([*as*] für): ~ *o.s.* (*very important*) sich sehr wichtig vorkommen. **10.** gern haben *od.* mögen. **11.** Lust haben (auf *acc; doing* zu tun). **12.** *Tiere, Pflanzen* (aus Liebhaberei) züchten. ~ **ball** *s* Kostümfest *n*, Maskenball *m.* ~ **dress** *s* (Masken)Kostüm *n.* '**~-dress** *adj:* ~ *ball* → *fancy ball.* ,**~-'free** *adj* frei u. ungebunden. ~ **goods** *s pl* **1.** Modeartikel *pl.* **2.** kleine Geschenkartikel *pl*; Nippes *pl.*

fan·fare ['fænfeə] *s* **1.** Fanfare *f*, Tusch *m.* **2.** *fig. contp.* Trara *n*, Tamtam *n.*

fang [fæŋ] *s* Reiß-, Fangzahn *m*, Fang *m* (*e-s Raubtiers etc*), Hauer *m* (*e-s Ebers*), Giftzahn *m* (*e-r Schlange*).

fan·ta·sia [fæn'teɪʒə] *s* ♩ Fantasie *f.* **fan·tas·tic** [~'tæstɪk] *adj* (**~ally**) phantastisch: a) unwirklich, b) absurd, c) F toll. **fan·ta·sy** ['fæntəsɪ] *s* Phantasie *f*: a) Einbildungskraft *f*, b) Phantasievorstellung *f*, c) Tag-, Wachtraum *m.*

far [fɑː] **I** *adj* **1.** fern, (weit)entfernt, weit: → *cry* **1.** **2.** (*vom Sprecher aus*) entfernter: *at the ~ end* am anderen Ende. **II** *adv* **3.** fern, weit: ~ *away* (*od. off*) weit weg *od.* entfernt; *as ~ as* soweit *od.* soviel (wie); bis (nach); *so ~ so good* so weit, so gut. **4.** *fig.* (*from*) weit entfernt (von), alles andere (als): ~ *from completed* noch lange *od.* längst nicht fertig. **5.** ~ *into* weit in (*acc*): ~ *into the night* bis spät *od.* tief in (die) Nacht (hinein). **6.** *a. by* ~ weit(aus), bei weitem, wesentlich. '**~-a·way** → *far* **1.**

farce [fɑːs] *s thea.* Farce *f* (*a. fig.*), Posse *f*, Schwank *m.* **far·ci·cal** [~'sɪkl] *adj* □ **1.** farcen-, possenhaft. **2.** *fig.* absurd, lächerlich.

fare [feə] **I** *s* **1.** Fahrpreis *m*, -geld *n*; Flugpreis *m*: *what's the ~?* was kostet die Fahrt *od.* der Flug?; *any more ~s, please?* noch j-d zugestiegen?; ~ *dodger* (*od. evader*) Schwarzfahrer(in); ~ *stage Br.* Fahrpreiszone *f*, Teilstrecke *f.* **2.** Fahrgast *m* (*bsd. e-s Taxis*). **3.** Kost *f* (*a. fig.*), Nahrung *f.* **II** *v/i* **4.** (er)gehen: *how did you ~?* wie ist es dir ergangen?; *he ~d ill, it ~d ill with him* es erging ihm schlecht. ,**~-'well I** *int* leb(t)

wohl. **II** *s* Lebewohl *n*, Abschied(s-gruß) *m*: *make one's ~s* sich verabschieden. **III** *adj* Abschieds... **far-'fetched** *adj fig.* weitherholt, an den Haaren herbeigezogen.

farm [fɑːm] **I** *s* **1.** (*a. Geflügel- etc*)Farm *f*, Bauernhof *m.* **II** *v/t* **2.** *Land* bebauen, bewirtschaften. **3.** *Geflügel etc* züchten. **4.** ~ *out* ♣ *Arbeit* vergeben (*to* an *acc*). **III** *v/i* **5.** Landwirtschaft betreiben. '**farm·er** *s* **1.** Bauer *m*, Landwirt *m*, Farmer *m.* **2.** (*Geflügel- etc*)Züchter *m.* '**farm·house** *s* Bauernhaus *n.*

farm·ing ['fɑːmɪŋ] *s* **1.** Landwirtschaft *f.* **2.** (*Geflügel- etc*)Zucht *f.* ,**far-|'off** → *far* **1.** ~-'**out** *adj sl.* **1.** toll, super. **2.** exzentrisch. ~-'**reach·ing** *adj* weitreichend, *fig. a.* folgenschwer. ~-'**see·ing** *adj fig.* weitblickend, umsichtig. ~-'**sight·ed** *adj* **1.** → *farseeing.* **2.** ✻ weitsichtig.

fart [fɑːt] V **I** *s* **1.** Furz *m.* **2.** *fig.* Arschloch *n.* **II** *v/i* **3.** furzen.

far·ther ['fɑːðə] **I** *adj* **1.** *comp von far.* **2.** weiter weg liegend, entfernter. **3.** → *further* **5.** **II** *adv* **4.** weiter: *so far and no ~* bis hierher u. nicht weiter. **5.** → *further* **2**, **3.** **far·thest** ['~ðɪst] **I** *adj* **1.** *sup von far.* **2.** weitest, entferntest. **3.** → *furthest* **2.** **II** *adv* **4.** am weitesten *od.* entferntesten. **5.** → *further* **4.**

fas·ci·nate ['fæsɪneɪt] *v/t* faszinieren. ,**fas·ci·'na·tion** *s* Faszination *f.*

fas·cism, *oft* ♀ ['fæʃɪzəm] *s pol.* Faschismus *m.* '**fas·cist**, *a.* ♀ **I** *s* Faschist(in). **II** *adj* faschistisch.

fash·ion ['fæʃn] **I** *s* **1.** Mode *f*: *come into ~* in Mode kommen, modern werden; *go out of ~* aus der Mode kommen, unmodern werden; ~ *parade* (*od. show*) Mode(n)schau *f.* **2.** Art *f* u. Weise *f*, Stil *m*: *after* (*od. in*) *a ~* schlecht u. recht, so lala. **II** *v/t* **3.** formen, gestalten. '**fash·ion·a·ble** *adj* □ **1.** modisch, elegant. **2.** a) in Mode: *be very ~* große Mode sein (*to do* zu tun), b) Mode...: ~ *complaint* Modekrankheit *f.*

fast¹ [fɑːst] **I** *adj* **1.** schnell: ~ *train* Schnell-, D-Zug *m; my watch is* (*ten minutes*) ~ m-e Uhr geht (10 Minuten) vor. **2.** *phot.* hochempfindlich (*Film*); lichtstark (*Objektiv*). **II** *adv* **3.** schnell.

fast² [~] **I** *adj* **1.** fest: *make ~* festmachen; ~ *friends pl* unzertrennliche Freunde *pl.* **2.** widerstandsfähig (**to** gegen): ~ **colo(u)r** (wasch)echte Farbe; ~ **to light** lichtecht. **II** *adv* **3.** fest: *be* ~ *asleep* fest *od.* tief schlafen; *play* ~ *and loose with* Schindluder treiben mit.

fast² [~] **I** *v/t* **1.** fasten. **II** *s* **2.** Fasten *n.* **3.** Fastenzeit *f*: ~ (**day**) Fastentag *m.*

'fast·back *s mot.* (Wagen *m* mit) Fließheck *n.* ~ **breed·er,** ~'**breed·er re·ac·tor** *s phys.* schneller Brüter.

fas·ten ['fɑːsn] **I** *v/t* **1.** befestigen, festmachen (**to, on** an *acc*): → **seat belt. 2.** *a.* ~ **up** (ab-, ver)schließen, *Jacke etc* zuknöpfen, *Paket etc* zu-, verschnüren: ~ *s.o. down to* j-n festnageln auf (*acc*). **3.** ~ *on fig.* Blick, *Aufmerksamkeit etc* richten auf (*acc*); *j-m e-e Straftat etc* in die Schuhe schieben, anhängen. **II** *v/i* **4.** sich festmachen *od.* schließen lassen.

'fas·ten·er *s* Verschluß *m.*

'fast-food re·stau·rant Schnellimbiß *m,* -gaststätte *f.*

fas·tid·i·ous [fə'stɪdɪəs] *adj* □ anspruchsvoll, wählerisch, heikel (**about** in *dat*).

fast·ness ['fɑːstnɪs] *s* Widerstandsfähigkeit *f* (**to** gegen), Echtheit *f* (*von Farben*).

fat [fæt] **I** *adj* □ **1.** dick (*a. fig. Bankkonto etc*), *contp.* fett. **2.** fett(ig), fetthaltig. **II** *s* **3.** Fett *n*: *the* ~ *is in the fire* der Teufel ist los; *chew the* ~ F quatschen, plaudern; *live on* (*od. off*) *the* ~ *of the land* in Saus u. Braus *od.* wie Gott in Frankreich leben.

fa·tal ['feɪtl] *adj* □ **1.** tödlich. **2.** fatal, verhängnisvoll (**to** für). **'fa·tal·ism** ['~təlɪzəm] *s* Fatalismus *m.* **'fa·ta·list** *s* Fatalist(in). **,fa·tal'is·tic** *adj* (~*ally*) fatalistisch. **fa·tal·i·ty** [fə'tælətɪ] *s* **1.** Verhängnis *n.* **2.** tödlicher Unfall; (Todes)Opfer *n.*

fate [feɪt] *s* **1.** Schicksal *n*: *he met his* ~ das Schicksal ereilte ihn; (*as*) *sure as* ~ *is* ~ garantiert, mit Sicherheit; → *tempt* **2.** Verhängnis *n,* Verderben *n.* **'fat·ed** *adj* **1.** *he was* ~ *to inf* es war ihm (vom Schicksal) bestimmt zu *inf.* **2.** → *fateful* **2. 'fate·ful** ['~fʊl] *adj* □ **1.** verhängnisvoll. **2.** schicksalhaft, Schicksals...

fa·ther ['fɑːðə] **I** *s* **1.** Vater *m, fig. a.* Begründer *m*: *like* ~ *like son* der Apfel fällt nicht weit vom Stamm; ♀'*s Day* Vatertag *m.* **2.** *pl* Ahnen *pl,* Vorfahren *pl,* Väter *pl.* **3.** *eccl.* a) Pater *m,* b) *the Holy* ♀ der Heilige Vater. **II** *v/t* **4.** *et.* ins Leben rufen. **5.** ~ *s.th. on s.o.* j-m die Schuld für *et.* zuschreiben. ♀ *Christmas s bsd. Br.* der Weihnachtsmann. ~ *fig·ure s psych.* Vaterfigur *f.*

'fa·ther·hood ['fɑːðəhʊd] *s* Vaterschaft *f.* **'fa·ther-in-law** *pl* **'fa·thers-in-law** *s* Schwiegervater *m.* **'~land** *s* Vaterland *n.*

fa·ther·less ['fɑːðəlɪs] *adj* vaterlos. **'fa·ther·ly** *adj* väterlich.

fath·om ['fæðəm] *v/t* ♄ ausloten, *fig. a.* ergründen. **'fath·om·less** *adj* □ unergründlich (*a. fig.*).

fa·tigue [fə'tiːg] **I** *s* **1.** Ermüdung *f* (*a.* ⊙). **2.** *pl* Strapazen *pl.* **II** *v/t u. v/i* **3.** ermüden (*a.* ⊙).

fat·less ['fætlɪs] *adj* fettlos. **'fat·ness** *s* Dicke *f, contp.* Fettheit *f.* **fat·ten** ['~tn] *v/t* **1.** *a.* ~ **up** dick *od. contp.* fett machen. **2.** *Tier,* F *a. j-n* mästen. **II** *v/i* **3.** dick *od. contp.* fett werden. **'fat·ty I** *adj* fettig, Fett... **II** *s* F Dickerchen *n.*

fa·tu·i·ty [fə'tjuːətɪ] *s* Albernheit *f.* **fat·u·ous** ['fætjʊəs] *adj* □ albern.

fau·cet ['fɔːsɪt] *s Am.* (Wasser)Hahn *m.*

fault [fɔːlt] *s* **1.** Schuld *f,* Verschulden *n*: *it is my* ~ es ist me-e Schuld; *be at* ~ schuld sein. **2.** Fehler *m* (*a. Tennis etc*): *find* ~ *with et.* auszusetzen haben an (*dat*); *be at* ~ sich irren. **3.** ⊙ Defekt *m.* **'~,find·er s** Nörgler(in), Kritt(e)ler(in). **'~,find·ing I s** Nörgelei *f,* Krittelei *f.* **II** *adj* nörglerisch, kritt(e)lig.

fault·less ['fɔːltlɪs] *adj* □ fehlerfrei, -los. **'fault·y** *adj* □ fehlerhaft, ⊙ *a.* defekt, (*Argumentation etc* a.) falsch.

fau·na ['fɔːnə] *pl* **-nas, -nae** ['~niː] *s* Fauna *f,* Tierwelt *f.*

fa·vo(u)r ['feɪvə] **I** *v/t* **1.** begünstigen: a) favorisieren, bevorzugen, b) günstig sein für, fördern, c) unterstützen, für *et.* sein. **2.** *bsd. Sport:* favorisieren, zum Favoriten erklären. **II** *s* **3.** Gunst *f,* Wohlwollen *n*: *in* ~ *of* zugunsten von (*od. gen*); *in my* ~ zu m-n Gunsten; *be in* ~ *of et.* sein; *be in* (*out of*) *s.o.'s* ~ *be in* (*out of*) ~ *with* s.o. bei j-m gut (schlecht) angeschrieben sein. **4.** Gefallen *m,* Gefälligkeit *f*: *ask s.o. a* ~ (*od. a* ~ *of s.o.*) j-n um e-n Gefallen bitten; *do s.o. a* ~ j-m e-n Gefallen tun. **'fa-**

vo(u)r·a·ble *adj* □ günstig: a) vorteilhaft (**to**, **for** für), b) positiv, zustimmend (*Antwort etc*). **'fa·vo(u)red** *adj* **1.** begünstigt. **2.** bevorzugt, Lieblings... **3.** *bsd. Sport*: favorisiert. **fa·vo(u)r·ite** ['ⁿrɪt] **I** *s* **1.** Liebling *m*, *contp*. Günstling *m*. **2.** *bsd. Sport*: Favorit(in). **II** *adj* **3.** Lieblings...: ~ **dish** Lieblingsgericht *n*, Leibspeise *f*. **fa·vo(u)r·it·ism** *s* Günstlings-, Vetternwirtschaft *f*.

fawn [fɔːn] *v/i*: ~ **on** *fig*. katzbuckeln vor (*dat*). **'fawn·ing** *adj* □ kriecherisch.

fax [fæks] *v/t* faxen.

fear [fɪə] **I** *s* **1.** Furcht *f*, Angst *f* (**of** vor *dat*; **that** daß): **for** ~ **that** aus Furcht, daß; **be in** ~ (**of** *s.o.*) sich (vor j-m) fürchten, (vor j-m) Angst haben. **2.** Befürchtung *f*, Sorge *f*: **for** ~ **of hurting him** um ihn nicht zu verletzen. **3.** Ehrfurcht *f* (**of** *od.* **for** vor *dat*): ~ **of God** Gottesfurcht *f*. **II** *v/t* **4.** fürchten, sich fürchten *od.* Angst haben vor (*dat*). **5.** *das Schlimmste etc* (be)fürchten. **6.** *Gott* fürchten. **III** *v/i* **7.** ~ **for** fürchten um. **fear·ful** ['ⁿfʊl] *adj* □ **1.** furchtbar, fürchterlich (*beide a. fig*. F). **2.** **be** ~ **in** (großer) Sorge sein, sich ängstigen (**of**, **for** um; **that** daß). **3.** furchtsam, angsterfüllt: **be** ~ **of** → **fear** 4. **'fear·less** *adj* □ furchtlos: **be** ~ **of** sich nicht fürchten *od.* keine Angst haben vor (*dat*).

fea·si·bil·i·ty [ˌfiːzə'bɪlətɪ] *s* Durchführbarkeit *f*, Durchführbarkeit *f*. **'fea·si·ble** *adj* □ machbar, (*Plan etc*) durchführbar.

feast [fiːst] **I** *s* **1.** *eccl.* Fest *n*, Feiertag *m*. **2.** Festessen *n*, -mahl *n*. **3.** *fig*. (Hoch-)Genuß *m*: ~ **for the eyes** Augenweide *f*. **II** *v/t* **4.** festlich bewirten (**on** mit). **5.** ergötzen (**on** mit): ~ **one's eyes on** s-e Augen weiden an (*dat*). **III** *v/i* **6.** sich gütlich tun (**on** an *dat*). **7.** sich weiden (**on** an *dat*).

feat [fiːt] *s* **1.** Helden-, Großtat *f*. **2.** Kunst-, Meisterstück *n*, Kraftakt *m*. **3.** (*technische etc*) Großtat, große Leistung.

feath·er ['feðə] **I** *s* Feder *f*, *pl* Gefieder *n*: **birds of a** ~ Leute vom gleichen Schlag; **birds of a** ~ **flock together** gleich u. gleich gesellt sich gern; **that is a** ~ **in his cap** darauf kann er stolz sein; → **light**² 1. **II** *v/t* mit Federn polstern *od.* schmücken, *Pfeil* fiedern: ~ **one's nest** *fig*. sein(e) Schäfchen ins trockene

bringen. ~ **bed** *s* Matratze *f* mit Federod. Daunenfüllung. **'~bed** *v/t* j-n verhätscheln. **'~brained** *adj* **1.** hohlköpfig. **2.** leichtsinnig. **'~weight** *s* **1.** *Sport*: Federgewicht(ler *m*) *n*. **2.** Leichtgewicht *n* (*Person*). **II** *adj* **3.** *Sport*: Federgewichts... **4.** leichtgewichtig.

fea·ture ['fiːtʃə] **I** *s* **1.** (Gesichts)Zug *m*. **2.** Merkmal *n*, Charakteristikum *n*. **3.** (Haupt)Attraktion *f*. **4.** a) ~ **pro·gram(me)** (*Rundfunk, TV*) Feature *n*, b) a. ~ **article** (*od.* **story**) (*Zeitung*) Feature *n*, c) a. ~ **film** Feature *n*, Haupt-, Spielfilm *m*. **II** *v/t* **5.** als (Haupt-)Attraktion zeigen *od.* bringen, groß herausbringen *od.* -stellen. **6.** in der Hauptrolle zeigen: **a film featuring X** ein Film mit X in der Hauptrolle. **7.** sich auszeichnen durch.

fe·brile ['fiːbraɪl] *adj ✶* fieb(e)rig, fieberhaft, Fieber...

Feb·ru·ar·y ['februərɪ] *s* Februar *m*: **in** ~ im Februar.

fe·ces *bsd. Am.* → **faeces**.

fed [fed] *pret u. pp von* **feed**.

fed·er·al ['fedərəl] *adj pol.* Bundes...: 2 **Bureau of Investigation** *Am.* Bundeskriminalpolizei *f*. **'fed·er·al·ism** *mst* '2 *s pol.* Föderalismus *m*. **'fed·er·al·ist** *adj* föderalistisch. **II** *s mst* '2 Föderalist *m*. **fed·er'a·tion** *s* **1.** *pol.* Bundesstaat *m*; Föderation *f*, Staatenbund *m*. **2.** (*Sport- etc*)Verband *m*.

fee [fiː] *s* (*Anwalts- etc*)Honorar *n*, (*Mitglieds- etc*)Beitrag *m*, (*Eintritts- etc*)Geld *n*, (*Aufnahme- etc*)Gebühr *f*.

fee·ble ['fiːbl] *adj* □ schwach (*a. fig.*). **~'mind·ed** *adj* □ schwachsinnig, geistesschwach.

fee·ble·ness ['fiːblnɪs] *s* Schwäche *f*.

feed [fiːd] **I** *v/t* (*irr*) **1.** *Tier, Kind* füttern (**on**, **with** mit): **be fed up with** F die Nase voll haben von, *et*. satt haben. **2.** *Familie etc* ernähren, unterhalten. **3.** ☉ *Maschine* speisen, beschicken, a. j-n versorgen (**with** mit): ~ **s.th. into a computer** *et*. in e-n Computer eingeben *od.* einspeisen. **4.** ~ **back** a) *⚡, Kybernetik*: rückkoppeln, b) *Informationen etc* zurückleiten (**to** an *acc*). **5.** *Gefühl* nähren. **II** *v/i* (*irr*) **6.** fressen (*Tier*); F futtern (*Mensch*). **7.** sich ernähren, leben (**on** von). **III** *s* **8.** Füttern *n*, Fütterung *f*. **9.** F Mahlzeit *f*. **'~back** *s* **1.** ⚡,

feeder 938

Kybernetik: Feedback *n*, Rückkopp(e)-lung *f*. **2.** a) *Rundfunk, TV*: Feedback *n*, b) Zurückleitung *f (von Informationen)* (**to** an *acc*).

feed·er ['fiːdə] *s* **1.** *a heavy* ~ ein starker Fresser (*Tier*) *od.* F Esser (*Mensch*). **2.** → *feeding bottle*. **3.** *Br.* Lätzchen *s*. ~ **road** *s* Zubringerstraße *f*.

feed·ing ['fiːdɪŋ] *s* Füttern *n*, Fütterung *f*. ~ **bot·tle** *s* (Säuglings-, Saug)Flasche *f*.

feel [fiːl] I *v/t (irr)* **1.** (an-, be)fühlen: ~ *one's way* sich tasten (*through* durch). **2.** fühlen, (ver)spüren: *make itself felt* spürbar werden, sich bemerkbar machen. **3.** *Freude etc* empfinden. **4.** a) finden, glauben (*that* daß), b) halten für: *I* ~ *it (to be)* my duty ich halte es für m-e Pflicht. II *v/i (irr)* **5.** fühlen (*whether, if* ob; *how* wie): ~ *for* tasten nach. **6.** sich fühlen: ~ *ill;* ~ *up to s.th.* sich e-r Sache gewachsen fühlen; ~ *like* (*doing*) *s.th.* Lust haben zu e-r *od.* auf e-e Sache (et. zu tun); → *cold* 1, *warm* 1. **7.** *how do you* ~ *about it?* was meinst du dazu? **8.** sich *weich etc* anfühlen. III *s* **9.** *klebriges etc* Gefühl. **10.** *be soft to the* ~, *have a soft* ~ sich weich anfühlen. **'feel·er** *s zo.* Fühler *m (a. fig.)*: *put out* ~*s* (*od. a* ~) s-e Fühler ausstrecken. **'feel·ing** *s* Gefühl *n*: a) Gefühlssinn *m*, b) (Gefühls)Eindruck *m*: *have a* ~ *that* das Gefühl haben, daß, c) Empfindung *f*: ~*s pl of guilt* Schuldgefühle *pl*, d) Feingefühl *n*: *have a* ~ *for* Gefühl haben für.

feet [fiːt] *pl von* **foot.**

feign [feɪn] I *v/t* Interesse etc vortäuschen, *Krankheit a.* simulieren: ~ *death* (*od. to be dead*) sich totstellen. II *v/i* sich verstellen, simulieren.

feint [feɪnt] *s Sport:* Finte *f (a. fig.)*.

fell¹ [fel] *pret von* **fall.**

fell² [~] *v/t* **1.** *Baum* fällen. **2.** *Gegner etc* fällen, niederstrecken.

fel·loe ['feləʊ] *s* ⊙ Felge *f*.

fel·low ['feləʊ] I *s* **1.** Gefährte *m*, Gefährtin *f*, Genosse *m*, Genossin *f*, Kamerad(in). **2.** Mitmensch *m*, Zeitgenosse *m*. **3.** F Kerl *m: old* ~ alter Knabe; a ~ man. II *adj* **4.** Mit...: ~ *being* Mitmensch *m;* ~ *citizen* Mitbürger *m;* ~ *countryman* Landsmann *m;* ~ *feeling* Mitgefühl *n;* Zs.-gehörigkeitsgefühl *n;*

~ *student* Studienkollege *m*, Kommilitone *m;* ~ *travel(l)er* Mitreisende *m; pol.* Mitläufer *m*. **'fel·low·ship** *s* **1.** Kameradschaft *f*. **2.** Gesellschaft *f*, Gruppe *f*.

felt¹ [felt] *pret u. pp von* **feel.**

felt² [~] I *s* Filz *m*. II *adj* Filz... ~ *tip, *~*-tip(ped) pen* *s* Filzschreiber *m*, -stift *m*.

fe·male ['fiːmeɪl] I *s contp.* Weib(sbild) *n*. **2.** *zo.* Weibchen *n*. II *adj* **3.** weiblich: ~ *dog* Hündin *f;* ~ *screw* Schraubenmutter *f*. **4.** Frauen...

fem·i·nine ['femɪnɪn] *adj* □ **1.** weiblich (*a. ling.*), Frauen... **2.** fraulich. **3.** weibisch, feminin. **fem·i'nin·i·ty** *s* **1.** Weiblichkeit *f*. **2.** Fraulichkeit *f*. **3.** weibische *od.* feminine Art. **'fem·i·nism** *s* Feminismus *m*, Frauenrechtsbewegung *f*. **'fem·i·nist** I *s* Feminist(in), Frauenrechtler(in). II *adj* feministisch.

fe·mur ['fiːmə] *pl* **-murs, fem·o·ra** ['femərə] *s anat.* Oberschenkel(knochen) *m*.

fen [fen] *s* Fenn *n*, Sumpf-, Marschland *n*.

fence [fens] I *s* **1.** Zaun *m: sit on the* ~ sich neutral verhalten; unentschlossen sein. **2.** *sl.* Hehler *m*. II *v/t* **3.** *a.* ~ *in* einzäunen; ~ *off* abzäunen. III *v/i* **4.** *Sport:* fechten. **'fenc·er** *s Sport:* Fechter(in). **'fenc·ing** I *s* **1.** Zaun *m*, Einzäunung *f*. **2.** *Sport:* Fechten *m*. **3.** *sl.* Hehlerei *f*. II *adj* **4.** *Sport:* Fecht...: ~ *master* Fechtmeister *m*.

fend [fend] I *v/t oft* ~ *off* Angreifer, Fragen etc abwehren. II *v/i:* ~ *for o.s.* für sich selbst sorgen. **'fend·er** *s mot. Am.* Kotflügel *m*.

fen·nel ['fenl] *s* ♣ Fenchel *m*.

fer·ment [fə'ment] I *v/t* **1.** ♠ in Gärung bringen (*a. fig.*), gären lassen, vergären; *fig.* in Wallung bringen. II *v/i* **2.** ♠ gären, in Gärung sein (*beide a. fig.*). III *s* ['fɜːment] **3.** ♠ Gärstoff *m*, Ferment *n*. **4.** a) ♠ Gärung *f (a. fig.)*, b) *fig.* innere Unruhe, Aufruhr *m*. **fer·men·ta·tion** [,fɜːmen'teɪʃn] *s* **1.** ♠ Gärung *f (a. fig.)*, Gärungsprozeß *m*. **2.** → *ferment* 4b.

fern [fɜːn] *s* ♣ Farn(kraut *n*) *m*.

fe·ro·cious [fə'rəʊʃəs] *adj* □ **1.** wild (*Tier etc*). **2.** wild, grimmig (*Blick etc*), grausam (*Strafe etc*), heftig, scharf (*Auseinandersetzung*).

fer·ret ['ferɪt] **I** s *zo.* Frettchen *n*. **II** *v/t* mst ~ **out** *et.* aufspüren, -stöbern, *Wahrheit* herausfinden, hinter *ein Geheimnis* kommen. **III** *v/i* mst ~ **about** (*od.* **around**) herumstöbern (**among** in *dat*; **for** nach).

fer·rous ['ferəs] *adj* eisenhaltig, Eisen...

fer·ry ['ferɪ] **I** s **1.** Fähre *f*, Fährschiff *n*, -boot *n*. **2.** Fährdienst *m*, -betrieb *m*. **II** *v/t* **3.** (in e-r Fähre) übersetzen. '~**boat** → **ferry** 1. '~**man** ['~mən] s (*irr* **man**) Fährmann *m*. ~ **ser·vice** → **ferry** 2.

fer·tile ['fɜːtaɪl] *adj* ☐ fruchtbar, *fig. a.* produktiv, schöpferisch. **fer·til·i·ty** [fə'tɪlətɪ] s Fruchtbarkeit *f*, *fig. a.* Produktivität *f*. **fer·ti·li·za·tion** [ˌfɜːtɪlaɪ'zeɪʃn] s **1.** Befruchtung *f* (*a. fig.*). **2.** Düngung *f*. '**fer·ti·lize** *v/t* **1.** befruchten (*a. fig.*). **2.** düngen. '**fer·ti·liz·er** s (*bsd.* Kunst)Dünger *m*.

fer·vent ['fɜːvənt], **fer·vid** ['~vɪd] *adj* ☐ glühend, leidenschaftlich (*Haß*, *Verehrer etc*), inbrünstig (*Gebet*, *Verlangen etc*). '**fer·vo(u)r** s Leidenschaft *f*, Inbrunst *f*.

fes·ter ['festə] *v/i* **1.** eitern. **2.** ~ *in s.o.'s mind* an j-m nagen *od.* fressen.

fes·ti·val ['festəvl] s **1.** Festtag (tag *m*) *n*. **2.** Festival *n*, Festspiele *pl*. **fes·tive** ['~tɪv] *adj* ☐ festlich, Fest...: ~ *season* Fest-, *bsd.* Weihnachtszeit *f*. **fes·tiv·i·ty** s *oft pl* Festlichkeit *f*.

fes·toon [fe'stuːn] **I** s Girlande *f*. **II** *v/t* mit Girlanden schmücken.

fetch [fetʃ] *v/t* **1.** (herbei)holen, (her)bringen: *go and* ~ *a doctor* e-n Arzt holen. **2.** *Seufzer etc* ausstoßen. **3.** *Preis etc* erzielen, einbringen. **4.** F *j-m e-n Schlag od. Tritt* versetzen: ~ *s.o. one* j-m e-e langen *od.* kleben. '**fetch·ing** *adj* F bezaubernd: a) reizend, entzückend (*Kleid etc*), b) gewinnend, einnehmend (*Lächeln etc*).

fet·id ['fetɪd] *adj* ☐ stinkend.

fe·tish ['fiːtɪʃ] s Fetisch *m* (*a. psych.*). '**fe·tish·ism** s Fetischismus *m*. '**fe·tish·ist** s Fetischist(in).

fet·ter ['fetə] **I** s **1.** Fußfessel *f*. **2.** *pl fig.* Fesseln *pl*. **II** *v/t* **3.** *j-m* Fußfesseln anlegen. **4.** *fig.* behindern.

fet·tle ['fetl] s: *in fine* (*od.* **good**) ~ (gut) in Form.

fe·tus ['fiːtəs] s ⚕ Fötus *m*.

feud [fjuːd] **I** s Fehde *f* (*a. fig.*): *be at* ~ (**with**) → **II.** **II** *v/i* sich befehden, in Fehde liegen (**with** mit) (*beide a. fig.*).

feu·dal ['fjuːdl] *adj* ☐ Feudal..., Lehns... **feu·dal·ism** ['~dəlɪzəm] s Feudalismus *m*, Feudal-, Lehnssystem *n*.

fe·ver ['fiːvə] s ⚕ Fieber *n* (*a. fig.*): *have a* ~ Fieber haben; ~ *blister* Fieberbläschen *n*; ~ *heat* Fieberhitze *f*; *fig.* fieberhafte Auf- *od.* Erregung; *be in a* ~ (*of excitement*) in fieberhafter Aufregung sein, vor Aufregung fiebern. '**fe·ver·ish** *adj* ☐ **1.** ⚕ a) fieberkrank: *be* ~ Fieber haben, b) fieb(e)rig, Fieber...: ~ *cold* fiebrige Erkältung. **2.** *fig.* fieberhaft: *be* ~ *with excitement* vor Aufregung fiebern.

few [fjuː] *adj u. pron* **1.** wenige: *some* ~ einige wenige. **2.** *a* ~ einige, ein paar: *a good* ~, *quite a* ~ ziemlich viele, e-e ganze Menge; *every* ~ *days* alle paar Tage.

fi·an·cé [fɪ'ɑ̃ːŋseɪ] s Verlobte *m*. **fi·an·cée** [fɪ'ɑ̃ːŋseɪ] s Verlobte *f*.

fi·as·co [fɪ'æskəʊ] *pl* -cos s Fiasko *n*.

fib [fɪb] F **I** s Flunkerei *f*, Schwindelei *f*. **II** *v/i* flunkern, schwindeln. '**fib·ber** s F Flunkerer *m*, Schwindler *m*.

fi·ber, *bsd. Br.* **fi·bre** ['faɪbə] s **1.** *biol.*, ⊙ Faser *f*. **2.** *fig.* Charakter *m*; Kraft *f*: *moral* ~ Charakterstärke *f*. '~**glass** s ⊙ Fiberglas *n*.

fib·u·la ['fɪbjʊlə] s *anat.* Wadenbein *n*.

fick·le ['fɪkl] *adj* launenhaft, launisch, unbeständig (*Wetter*), (*Person a.*) wankelmütig.

fic·tion ['fɪkʃn] s **1.** (freie) Erfindung, Fiktion *f*. **2.** *coll.* Prosa-, Romanliteratur *f*. **fic·tion·al** ['~ʃənl] *adj* erdichtet, erfunden.

fic·ti·tious [fɪk'tɪʃəs] *adj* ☐ (frei) erfunden, fiktiv.

fid·dle ['fɪdl] F **I** s **1.** ♪ Fiedel *f*, Geige *f*: *play first* (**second**) ~ *fig.* die erste (zweite) Geige spielen; (*as*) *fit as a* ~ kerngesund. **II** *v/i* **2.** a. ~ *away* fiedeln, geigen. **3.** ~ *about* (*od.* **around**) herumtrödeln. **4.** a. ~ *about* (*od.* **around**) (**with**) herumfummeln (an *dat*), spielen (mit). **III** *v/t* **5.** fiedeln. **6.** *Br.* frisieren, manipulieren. '**fid·dler** s F **1.** Fiedler *m*, Geiger *m*. **2.** *Br.* Schwindler *m*, Betrüger *m*. '**fid·dling** *adj* F läppisch, geringfügig.

fidelity

fi·del·i·ty [fɪ'delətɪ] *s* **1.** Treue *f* (*to* gegenüber, zu). **2.** Genauigkeit *f* (*a. e-r Übersetzung*). **3.** *⚡* Klangtreue *f*.

fidg·et ['fɪdʒɪt] **I** *s* **1.** *oft pl* nervöse Unruhe, Zappelei *f*: **give s.o. the** ~**s** → 3; **have the** ~**s** → 4. **2.** Zappelphilipp *m*. **II** *v/t* **3.** *j-n* nervös od. zapp(e)lig machen. **III** *v/i* **4.** (herum)zappeln, unruhig od. nervös sein. **'fidg·et·y** *adj* zapp(e)lig, nervös.

fi·du·ci·ar·y [fɪ'dju:ʃjərɪ] *st* **I** *s* Treuhänder *m*. **II** *adj* treuhänderisch, Treuhand...

field [fi:ld] **I** *s* **1.** *⚼* Feld *n* (*a. ♘, phys. etc*): **in the** ~ auf dem Feld; ~ **of vision** Blick-, Gesichtsfeld *n*: Gesichtskreis *m*, Horizont *m*. **2.** *fig.* Bereich *m*, (Fach-, Sach)Gebiet *n*: *in his* ~ auf s-m Gebiet, in s-m Fach; ~ **of application** Anwendungsbereich. **3.** *Sport:* Spielfeld *n*, -fläche *f*; Feld *n* (*Läufer etc*). **II** *v/t* **4.** *Sport:* Spieler aufs Feld schicken, bringen; *Kandidaten etc* ins Rennen schicken. ~ **day** *s:* **have a** ~ riesigen Spaß haben (*with* mit); s-n großen Tag haben. ~ **e·vents** *s pl Leichtathletik:* Sprung- u. Wurfdisziplinen *pl.* ~ **glass·es** *s pl,* **a. pair of** ~ Feldstecher *m.* ~ **hock·ey** *s Sport:* bsd. Am. (Feld)Hockey *n.* ~ **mar·shal** *s* ✕ Feldmarschall *m.* **'~·work** *s* **1.** praktische (wissenschaftliche) Arbeit, (*Archäologie etc a.*) Arbeit *f* im Gelände. **2.** *Markt-, Meinungsforschung:* Feldarbeit *f.* ~ **work·er** *s Markt-, Meinungsforschung:* Befrager(in), Interviewer(in).

fiend [fi:nd] *s* **1.** Satan *m,* Teufel *m, fig. a.* Unhold *m.* **2.** F (*Frischluft- etc*)Fanatiker *m.* **'fiend·ish** *adj* □ **1.** teuflisch, unmenschlich. **2.** F verteufelt, höllisch.

fierce [fɪəs] *adj* □ **1.** wild (*Tier etc*). **2.** böse, grimmig (*Gesicht etc*), wild (*Blick, Haß etc*). **3.** scharf (*Rede, Wettbewerb etc*); heftig (*Angriff, Schmerz etc*). **'fierce·ness** *s* **1.** Wildheit *f.* **2.** Schärfe *f;* Heftigkeit *f.*

fi·er·y ['faɪərɪ] *adj* □ **1.** brennend, glühend. **2.** feurig, hitzig (*Person, Temperament*). **3.** feurig, scharf (*Gewürz etc*). **4.** leidenschaftlich (*Rede, Affäre etc*).

fif·teen [,fɪf'ti:n] *adj* fünfzehn. **,fif'teenth** [~θ] *adj* fünfzehnt. **fifth** [fɪfθ] **I** *adj* **1.** fünft: ~ **column** *pol.* Fünfte Kolonne; ~

wheel *fig.* fünftes Rad am Wagen. **II** *s* **2.** *der, die, das* Fünfte: **the** ~ **of May** der 5. Mai. **3.** Fünftel *n.* **'fifth·ly** *adv* fünftens. **fif·ti·eth** ['fɪftɪəθ] *adj* fünfzigst.

fif·ty ['fɪftɪ] **I** *adj* fünfzig. **II** *s* Fünfzig *f:* **be in one's fifties** in den Fünfzigern sein; **in the fifties** in den fünfziger Jahren (*e-s Jahrhunderts*). **,~·'fif·ty** *adj u. adv* F fifty-fifty: **go** ~ (*with*) halbe-halbe machen (mit).

fig [fɪg] *s* ♣ Feige *f:* **I don't care a** ~ F das ist mir völlig egal.

fight [faɪt] **I** *s* **1.** Kampf *m* (*for* um; **against** gegen) (*a. fig.*): **put up a good** ~ sich tapfer schlagen. **2.** *a)* Boxen: Kampf *m,* *b)* Rauferei *f,* Schlägerei *f:* **have a** ~ (**with**) → 7. **3.** Kampf(es)lust *f:* **show** ~ sich zur Wehr setzen. **II** *v/t* (*irr*) **4.** *j-n, et.* bekämpfen. **5.** kämpfen gegen *od.* mit: ~ **back** (*od.* **down**) Enttäuschung, Tränen *etc* unterdrücken; ~ **off** *j-n, et.* abwehren. **III** *v/i* (*irr*) **6.** kämpfen (**for** um; **against** gegen): ~ **back** sich zur Wehr setzen *od.* wehren, zurückschlagen; → **shy** 2. **7.** sich raufen *od.* schlagen *od.* prügeln (*with* mit). **'fight·er** *s* **1.** Kämpfer *m.* **2.** *Sport:* Boxer *m.* **3.** Schläger *m,* Raufbold *m.* **4.** *a.* ~ **plane** ✈, ✕ Jagdflugzeug *n.* **'fight·ing** *s* Kampf *m,* Kämpfe *pl.* **II** *adj* Kampf...: ~ **chance** reelle Chance (*wenn man sich anstrengt*); ~ **spirit** Kampfgeist *m.*

fig·ment ['fɪgmənt] *s oft* ~ **of the imagination** reine Erfindung.

fig tree *s* Feigenbaum *m.*

fig·u·ra·tive ['fɪgərətɪv] *adj* □ bildlich, übertragen.

fig·ure ['fɪgə] **I** *s* **1.** Zahl *f,* Ziffer *f:* **run into three** ~**s** in die Hunderte gehen; **five-~ income** fünfstelliges Einkommen. **2.** Summe *f,* Preis *m:* **at a high** (**low**) ~ teuer (billig). **3.** Figur *f* (*a. Sport etc*), Gestalt *f.* **4.** *fig.* Figur *f,* Persönlichkeit *f:* ~ **of fun** komische Figur, *contp.* Witzfigur; **cut** (*od.* **make**) **a poor** ~ e-e traurige Figur abgeben. **5.** *a.* ~ **of speech** (Rede-, Sprach)Figur *f.* **II** *v/t* **6.** *oft* ~ **to o.s.** sich *et.* vorstellen *od.* ausmalen. **7.** ~ **out** F ausrechnen; ausknobeln, rauskriegen; kapieren. **8.** *Am.* F meinen, glauben. **III** *v/i* **9.** erscheinen, auftauchen, vorkommen. **10.** ~ **on** *bsd. Am.* F rechnen mit; sich verlassen auf (*acc*). **'~head** *s* ⚓ Galionsfigur *f*, *fig. a.* Aushängeschild *n*. **~ skat·ing** *s* Sport: Eiskunstlauf *m*.

filch [fɪltʃ] *v/t* klauen, stibitzen.

file¹ [faɪl] **I** *s* **1.** (Akten- *etc*)Ordner *m*. **2.** a) Akte *f*: **keep** (*od.* **have**) **a ~ on** e-e Akte führen über (*acc*); **~ number** Aktenzeichen *n*, b) Akten *pl*, Ablage *f*: **on ~** bei den Akten. **3.** Reihe *f*: → **Indian file, single file. II** *v/t* **4.** *a.* **~ away** Briefe *etc* ablegen, zu den Akten nehmen. **5.** *Antrag etc* einreichen, *Forderung* anmelden.

file² [~] **I** *s* **1.** ⚙ Feile *f*. **II** *v/t* **2.** (zu)feilen, *sich die Nägel* feilen: **~ away** (*od.* **down**) abfeilen. **3.** *fig. Stil etc* (zurecht)feilen.

fil·i·al ['fɪljəl] *adj* Kindes...

fil·i·bus·ter ['fɪlɪbʌstə] *parl. bsd. Am.* **I** *s* Obstruktion *f*; Obstruktionspolitiker *m*. **II** *v/i* Obstruktion treiben.

fil·i·gree ['fɪlɪgriː] *s* Filigran(arbeit *f*) *n*.

fil·ing cab·i·net ['faɪlɪŋ] *s* Aktenschrank *m*.

fil·ings ['faɪlɪŋz] *s pl* Feilspäne *pl*.

fill [fɪl] **I** *s* **1. eat one's ~** sich satt essen; **have had one's ~ of** von *et.*, *j-m* genug haben, *et.*, *j-n* satt haben. **2.** Füllung *f*. **II** *v/t* **3.** (an-, aus-, voll)füllen; *Pfeife* stopfen; *Zahn* füllen, plombieren. **4.** erfüllen (**with** mit) (*a. fig.*): **~ed with envy** neiderfüllt. **5.** *Posten, Amt* besetzen; *ausfüllen*, bekleiden: **~ s.o.'s place** j-s Stelle einnehmen, j-n ersetzen. **6.** *Auftrag, Bestellung* ausführen; *Rezept* ausfertigen. **III** *v/i* **7.** sich füllen.
Verbindungen mit Adverbien:
fill· in I *v/t* **1.** *Loch etc* auf-, ausfüllen. **2.** *Br. Formulare etc* ausfüllen. **3.** *Namen etc* einsetzen; *Fehlendes* ergänzen. **4.** F *j-n* informieren (**on** über *acc*). **II** *v/i* **5.** einspringen (**for** für). **~ out** **I** *v/t* **1.** *bsd. Am.* → **fill in** 2. **2.** *Bericht etc* abrunden. **II** *v/i* **3.** fülliger werden (*Figur*, (*Person a.*) zunehmen, (*Gesicht etc*) runder *od.* voller werden. **~ up I** *v/t* **1.** vollfüllen. **2.** → **fill in** 1, 2. **II** *v/i* **3.** → **fill** 7.

fill·er ['fɪlə] *s* **1.** Trichter *m*. **2.** *Zeitungswesen etc:* Füller *m*, Füllsel *n*. **3.** *ling.* Füllwort *n*.

fil·let ['fɪlɪt] *s gastr.* Filet *n*. **~ steak** *s* Filetsteak *n*.

fill·ing ['fɪlɪŋ] **I** *s* **1.** Füllung *f*, Füllmasse *f*. **2.** *Zahnmedizin:* Füllung *f*, Plombe *f*.

II *adj* **3.** sättigend. **~ sta·tion** *s* Tankstelle *f*.

fil·lip ['fɪlɪp] *s* **1.** Schnalzer *m*, Schnipser *m* (*mit den Fingern*). **2.** *fig.* Ansporn *m*, Auftrieb *m*.

film [fɪlm] **I** *s* **1.** Film *m* (*a. phot.*). **2.** (hauch)dünne Schicht, Film *m*; (Plastik)Folie *f*. **II** *adj* **3.** Film... **III** *v/t* **4.** *Roman etc* verfilmen; *Szene etc* filmen.

fil·ter ['fɪltə] **I** *s* **1.** Filter *m*, ⊙ *etc mst n.* **II** *v/t* **2.** filtern. **III** *v/i* **3.** durchsickern (**through** durch). **4.** **~ out** (*od.* **through**) *fig.* durchsickern (*Nachricht etc*). **5.** *mot. Br.* die Spur wechseln; sich einordnen (**to the left** links). **~ tip** *s* Filter *m*. **2.** Filterzigarette *f*. **'~-tipped** *adj* Filter...: **~ cigarette.**

filth [fɪlθ] *s* **1.** Schmutz *m* (*a. fig.*), Dreck *m*. **2.** unflätige Sprache *od.* Ausdrücke *pl.* **'filth·y** *adj* □ **1.** schmutzig (*a. fig.*), dreckig. **2.** *fig.* unflätig. **3.** *bsd. Br.* F ekelhaft, scheußlich: **~ weather** Sauwetter *n*.

fin [fɪn] *s* **1.** *ichth.* Flosse *f*. **2.** Schwimmflosse *f*.

fi·nal ['faɪnl] **I** *adj* (□ → **finally**) **1.** letzt; End..., Schluß...: **~ examination** (Ab-)Schlußprüfung *f*; **~ whistle** (Sport) Schluß-, Abpfiff *m*. **2.** endgültig. **II** *s* **3.** Sport: Finale *n*. **4.** *mst pl bsd. univ.* (Ab)Schlußexamen *n*, -prüfung *f*. **5.** F Spätausgabe *f* (*e-r Zeitung*). **fi·na·le** [fɪ'nɑːlɪ] *s* ♪, *thea.* Finale *n*. **fi·nal·ist** ['faɪnəlɪst] *s* Sport: Finalist(in). **fi·nal·i·ty** [~'nælətɪ] *s* **1.** Endgültigkeit *f*. **2.** Entschiedenheit *f*. **fi·nal·ize** ['~nəlaɪz] *v/t* **1.** be-, vollenden, abschließen. **2.** endgültige Form geben (*dat*). **'fi·nal·ly** *adv* **1.** endlich, schließlich, zuletzt. **2.** zum (Ab)Schluß. **3.** endgültig.

fi·nance [faɪ'næns] **I** *s* **1.** Finanz(wesen *n*) *f*: **~ company** Finanzierungsgesellschaft *f*. **2.** *pl* Finanzen *pl*. **II** *v/t* **3.** finanzieren. **fi·nan·cial** [~ʃl] *adj* □ finanziell, Finanz..., Geld...: **~ year** *Br.* Geschäftsjahr *n*. **fin·an·cier** [~sɪə] *s* Finanzier *m*.

finch [fɪntʃ] *s orn.* Fink *m*.

find [faɪnd] **I** *s* **1.** Fund *m*. **II** *v/t* (*irr*) **2.** *allg.* finden. **3.** bemerken, feststellen, (heraus)finden. **4.** ⚖ für *schuldig* erklären *od.* befinden. **5.** **~ out** *et.* herausfinden; *j-n* ertappen; *j-n*, *et.* durchschauen. **III** *v/i* (*irr*) **6.** ~ *out* es herausfinden. **7.** ~ *against* (*for*) *the defendant* 🏛 den Angeklagten verurteilen (freisprechen). 'find·er *s* Finder(in): ~'s *reward* Finderlohn *m.* 'find·ing *s* **1.** *mst pl* Befund *m* (*a.* 🏥). **2.** 🏛 Feststellung *f* (*des Gerichts*), (*der Geschworenen a.*) Spruch *m.*

fine¹ [faɪn] **I** *adj* □ **1.** *allg.* fein: ~ *arts pl* die schönen Künste *pl*; *one* ~ *day* e-s schönen Tages. **2.** großartig, ausgezeichnet. **3.** F fein, schön: *that's all very* ~ *but* das ist ja alles gut u. schön, aber. **II** *adv* **4.** F sehr gut, bestens: *that will suit me* ~ das paßt mir ausgezeichnet.

fine² [~] **I** *s* Geldstrafe *f*, Bußgeld *n.* **II** *v/t* mit e-r Geldstrafe belegen, zu e-r Geldstrafe verurteilen: *he was* ~*d £ 50* er mußte 50 Pfund Strafe bezahlen, er wurde zu e-r Geldstrafe von 50 Pfund verurteilt.

fine·ness ['faɪnnɪs] *s allg.* Feinheit *f.*

fi·nesse [fɪ'nes] *s* **1.** Finesse *f.* **2.** Raffinesse *f*, Schlauheit *f.*

fin·ger ['fɪŋgə] **I** *s* Finger *m*: *first* (*second*, *third*) ~ Zeige- (Mittel-, Ring)finger; *fourth* (*od. little*) ~ kleiner Finger; *have a* (*od. one's*) ~ *in the pie* die Hand im Spiel haben; *keep one's* ~*s crossed for s.o.* j-m die Daumen drücken *od.* halten; *not to lift* (*od. raise*, *stir*) *a* ~ keinen Finger rühren; → *burn* 7, *twist* 2. **II** *v/t* betasten, befühlen; herumfingern an (*dat*), spielen mit. **III** *v/i* herumfingern (*at* an *dat*), spielen (*with* mit). ~ **al·pha·bet** *s* Fingeralphabet *n.* '~**mark** *s* Fingerabdruck *m* (*Schmutzfleck*). '~**nail** *s* Fingernagel *m.* '~**print** *s* Fingerabdruck *m*: *take s.o.'s* ~*s* → **II. II** *v/t j-m* Fingerabdrücke abnehmen, von *j-m* Fingerabdrücke abnehmen, von *j-m* Fingerabdrücke machen. '~**tip** *s* Fingerspitze *f*: *have at one's* ~*s* Kenntnisse parat haben; *et.* aus dem Effeff beherrschen.

fin·ick·y ['fɪnɪkɪ] *adj* **1.** pedantisch. **2.** wählerisch (*about* in *dat*). **3.** geziert, affektiert.

fin·ish ['fɪnɪʃ] **I** *v/t* **1.** beenden, aufhören mit: ~ *reading* aufhören zu lesen. **2.** *a.* ~ *off* vollenden, zu Ende führen, erledigen, *Buch etc* auslesen. **3.** *a.* ~ *off* (*od.*

up) *Vorräte* aufbrauchen; aufessen, austrinken. **4.** *a.* ~ *off j-n* erledigen, fertigmachen. **5.** *a.* ~ *off* (*od. up*) vervollkommnen, den letzten Schliff geben (*dat*). **II** *v/i* **6.** *a.* ~ *off* (*od. up*) enden, aufhören (*with* mit): *have you* ~*ed?* bist du fertig? **7.** enden, zu Ende gehen. **8.** ~ *with* mit *j-m*, *et.* aufgeben: *I am* ~*ed with him* ich bin mit ihm fertig. **9.** ~ *third* (*Sport*) Dritter werden; *allg.* als dritter fertig sein. **III** *s* **10.** Ende *n*, Schluß *m.* **11.** *Sport*: Endspurt *m*, Finish *n*; Ziel *n.* **12.** Vollendung *f*; letzter Schliff. 'fin·ished *adj* **1.** beendet, fertig: ~ *goods* (*od. products*) *pl* Fertigwaren *pl.* **2.** *fig.* vollendet, vollkommen. 'fin·ish·ing *adj* abschließend: ~ *line* (*Sport*) Ziellinie *f*; → *touch* 4.

fink [fɪŋk] *s bsd. Am. sl.* **1.** Streikbrecher *m.* **2.** Spitzel *m.*

Finn [fɪn] *s* Finne *m*, Finnin *f.* 'Finn·ish **I** *adj* finnisch. **II** *s ling.* Finnisch *n.*

fiord [fjɔːd] *s geogr.* Fjord *m.*

fir [fɜː] *s* ♣ Tanne *f*; Fichte *f.* ~ *cone s* Tannenzapfen *m.*

fire ['faɪə] **I** *s* **1.** Feuer *n* (*a.* ✗ *u. fig.*), Brand *m*: *be on* ~ in Flammen stehen, brennen; *come under* ~ unter Beschuß geraten (*a. fig.*); *catch* (*od. take*) ~ Feuer fangen, in Brand geraten; *play with* ~ *fig.* mit dem Feuer spielen; *set on* ~, *set* ~ *to* → 2; → *chestnut* 1, *Thames.* **II** *v/t* **2.** anzünden, in Brand stecken. **3.** *Kessel* heizen, *Ofen* (be)feuern, beheizen. **4.** *j-n*, *j-s Gefühle* entflammen, *j-s Phantasie* beflügeln. **5.** *a.* ~ *off Schußwaffe* abfeuern, abschießen; *Schuß* (ab)feuern, abgeben (*at*, *on* auf *acc*). **6.** F feuern, rausschmeißen. **III** *v/i* **7.** feuern, schießen (*at*, *od. auf acc*). **8.** zünden (*Motor*). ~ **a·larm** *s* **1.** Feueralarm *m.* **2.** Feuermelder *m.* '~**arm** *s* Feuer-, Schußwaffe *f.* '~**ball** *s* Feuerball *m.* ~ **bri·gade** *s Br.* Feuerwehr *f.* '~**bug** *s* Feuerteufel *m.* ~ **de·part·ment** *s Am.* Feuerwehr *f.* '~**eat·er** *s* **1.** Feuerschlucker *m*, -fresser *m.* **2.** *fig.* aggressiver Mensch. ~ **en·gine** *s* Löschfahrzeug *n.* ~ **es·cape** *s* **1.** Feuerleiter *f*, -treppe *f.* **2.** *Br.* Feuerwehrleiter *f.* ~ **ex·tin·guish·er** *s* Feuerlöscher *m.* ~ **fight·er** *s* Feuerwehrmann *m.* ~ **house** *s Am.* Feuerwache *f.* ~ **hy·drant** *s Br.*

Hydrant *m*. **~·man** ['~mən] *s* (*irr* **man**) **1.** Feuerwehrmann *m*, *pl a.* Löschtrupp *m*. **2.** Heizer *m*. **'~·place** *s* (offener) Kamin. **'~·plug** *s Am.* Hydrant *m.* **pre·ven·tion** *s* Brandverhütung *f.* **'~·proof** *adj* feuerfest, -sicher. **~ rais·er** *s Br.* Brandstifter(in). **~ rais·ing** *s Br.* Brandstiftung *f.* **~ ser·vice** *s Br.* Feuerwehr *f.* **'~·side** *s* **1.** (offener) Kamin: **by the ~** am Kamin. **2.** *fig.* häuslicher Herd, Daheim *n.* **~ sta·tion** *s* Feuerwache *f.* **'~·wa·ter** *s* F Feuerwasser *n.* **'~·wood** *s* Brennholz *n.* **'~·work** *s* **1.** Feuerwerkskörper *m.* **2.** *pl* Feuerwerk *n* (*a. fig.: a. sg* konstruiert).

fir·ing ['faɪərɪŋ] *s* **1.** Heizen *n.* **2.** (Ab)Feuern *n*, (Ab)Schießen *n.* **~ line** *s* ✗ Feuer-, Frontlinie *f*: **be in** (*Am. on*) **the ~** *fig.* an vorderster Front stehen; in der Schußlinie stehen. **~ par·ty, ~ squad** *s* Exekutionskommando *n.*

firm¹ [fɜːm] **I** *adj* □ fest: a) hart, gastr. steif, b) standhaft, c) sicher (*Beweise etc*), d) *bsd.* ✝, ♣ bindend. **II** *adv*: **stand ~** *fig.* festbleiben, hart bleiben.

firm² [~] *s* Firma *f.*

fir·ma·ment ['fɜːməmənt] *s* Firmament *n.*

firm·ness ['fɜːmnɪs] *s* Festigkeit *f.*

first [fɜːst] **I** *adj* (□ *a. firstly*) **1.** erst: **at ~ hand** aus erster Hand; **~ offender, place** 6, **sight** 2, **thing** 2, **view** 1. **2.** *fig.* erst, best: → **fiddle** 1. **II** *adv* **3.** zuerst: **go ~** vorangehen. **4.** (zu)erst (einmal). **5.** als erst(er, e, es), an erster Stelle: **~ come, ~ served** wer zuerst kommt, mahlt zuerst; **~ of all** vor allen Dingen, zu allererst. **III** *s* **6.** der, die, das Erste *od.* (*fig.*) Beste: **the ~ of May** der 1. Mai; **at ~** (zu)erst, anfangs; **from the (very) ~** von (allem) Anfang an. **7.** *mot.* erster Gang. **~ aid** *s* Erste Hilfe: **give** (*od. render*) **s.o. ~** j-m Erste Hilfe leisten. **,~·'aid** *adj*: **~ box** (*od. kit*) Verband(s)kasten *m*; **~ post** (*od.* **station**) Unfallstation *f.* **'~·born** *adj* erstgeboren. **~·'class I** *adj* **1.** erstklassig, -rangig. **2.** 🚃 *etc* erster Klasse. **II** *adv* **3.** 🚃 *etc* erste(r) Klasse. **'~·day cov·er** *s* Philatelie: Ersttagsbrief *m.* **,~·de'gree** *adj* Verbrennungen ersten Grades. **,~·'hand** *adj u. adv* aus erster Hand.

first·ly ['fɜːstlɪ] *adv* erstens.

first| name *s* Vorname *m*: **what is his ~?**

wie heißt er mit Vornamen? **~ night** *s* Premiere *f*, Uraufführung *f*. **,~·'rate** → **first-class** 1. **'~·time** *adj*: **~ voter** Erstwähler(in).

firth [fɜːθ] *s* Meeresarm *m*, Förde *f.*

fis·cal ['fɪskl] *adj* □ fiskalisch, Finanz...: **~ year** *Am.* Geschäftsjahr *n.*

fish [fɪʃ] **I** *pl* **fish**, (*bsd. Fischarten*) **'fish·es** *s* **1.** Fisch *m*: **drink like a ~** F saufen wie ein Loch; **have other ~ to fry** F Wichtigeres zu tun haben; **queer ~** F komischer Kauz; → **kettle**. **2.** ♓︎es *pl ast.* Fische *pl.* **II** *v/t* **3.** fischen, angeln. **4.** *fig.* fischen (**from, out of** aus): **~ out** herausholen. **III** *v/i* **5.** fischen (*a. fig.: for* nach); angeln: → **trouble** 4. **~ and chips** *s Br.* paniertes Fischfilet mit Pommes frites. **~ ball** *s gastr.* Fischfrikadelle *f.* **'~·bone** *s* Gräte *f.* **~ cake** *s* → **fish ball.**

fish·er·man ['fɪʃəmən] *s* (*irr* **man**) *s* Fischer *m*, Angler *m.*

fish·er·y ['fɪʃərɪ] *s* **1.** Fischerei *f*, Fischfang *m.* **2.** Fischgründe *pl*, Fanggebiet *n.*

fish| fin·ger *s gastr. Br.* Fischstäbchen *n.* **'~·hook** *s* Angelhaken *m.*

fish·ing ['fɪʃɪŋ] *s* **1.** Fischen *n*, Angeln *n.* **2.** → **fishery** 1. **~ boat** *s* Fischerboot *n.* **~ grounds** *s pl* → **fishery** 2. **~ line** *s* Angelschnur *f.* **~ net** *s* Fisch(er)netz *n.* **~ rod** *s* Angelrute *f.* **~ tack·le** *s* Angelgerät(e *pl*) *n.* **~ vil·lage** *s* Fischerdorf *n.* **'fish|·mon·ger** *s bsd. Br.* Fischhändler(in). **~ stick** *Am.* → **fish finger.**

fis·sile ['fɪsaɪl] *adj* spaltbar. **fis·sion** ['fɪʃn] *s* **1.** Spaltung *f* (*a. fig.*). **2.** *biol.* (Zell)Teilung *f.* **fis·sure** ['fɪʃə] *s* Spalt(e *f*) *m*, Riß *m* (*a. fig.*), Ritz(e *f*) *m.*

fist [fɪst] *s* Faust *f.*

fis·tu·la ['fɪstjʊlə] *pl* **-las, -lae** ['~liː] *s* ✚ Fistel *f.*

fit¹ [fɪt] **I** *adj* □ **1.** passend, geeignet; fähig, tauglich: **~ for service** *bsd.* ✗ dienstfähig, (-)tauglich; **~ to drink** trinkbar; **~ to eat** eß-, genießbar; **~ to drive** fahrtüchtig; → **consumption** 2, **drop** 10a. **2.** angemessen, angebracht: **see** (*od. think*) **~** es für richtig *od.* angebracht halten (**to do** zu tun). **3.** schicklich, geziemend. **4.** fit, (gut) in Form: **keep ~** sich fit halten; → **fiddle** 1. **II** *s* **5.** Paßform *f*, Sitz *m*: **be a perfect ~** genau passen, tadellos sitzen; **be a tight ~** sehr eng sein. **III** v/t **6.** passend machen (**for** für), anpassen (**to** dat). **7.** a. ~ **up** ausrüsten, -statten, einrichten (**with** mit). **8.** j-m passen, sitzen (**Kleid** etc). **9.** zutreffen auf (acc) (**Beschreibung** etc), passen zu (**Name** etc). **10.** ◎ einpassen, -bauen (**into** in acc); anbringen (**to** an dat): ~ (**up**) montieren, installieren. **11.** ~ **in** j-m e-n Termin geben, j-n, et. einschieben. **IV** v/i **12.** passen, sitzen (**Kleid** etc).

fit² [~] s **1.** 🐟 Anfall m, Ausbruch m: ~ **of coughing** Hustenanfall; ~ **of anger** (od. F **temper**) Wutanfall, Zornausbruch; ~ **of laughter** Lachkrampf m; **give s.o. a** ~ F j-m e-n Schock versetzen; j-n auf die Palme bringen. **2.** fig. (plötzliche) Anwandlung od. Laune: **by** (od. **in**) ~**s** (**and starts**) stoß-, ruckweise; dann u. wann, sporadisch.

fit-ful ['fɪtfʊl] adj □ **1.** unruhig (**Schlaf** etc). **2.** sprung-, launenhaft. **'fit-ness** s **1.** Eignung f, Fähigkeit f, Tauglichkeit f: ~ **to drive** Fahrtüchtigkeit f; ~ **test** Eignungsprüfung f. **2.** Fitneß f, (gute) Form: ~ **test** Fitneßtest m; ~ **trail** Am. Trimmpfad m. **'fit-ted** adj **1.** zugeschnitten: ~ **carpet** Spannteppich m, Teppichboden m. **2.** Einbau...: ~ **kitch-en.** '**fit-ter** s ◎ Monteur m, Installateur m. **'fit-ting I** adj **1.** passend, geeignet. **2.** schicklich. **II** s **3.** ◎ Montage f, Installation f. **4.** Zubehörteil n, pl Ausstattung f, Einrichtung f.

five [faɪv] **I** adj fünf: ~**day week** Fünftagewoche f. **II** s Fünf f: ~ **of hearts** Herzfünf f. **five-fold** ['~fəʊld] **I** adj fünffach. **II** adv fünffach, um das Fünffache: **increase** ~ (sich) verfünffachen. '**fiv-er** s F Br. Fünfpfundschein m, Am. Fünfdollarschein m.

'five-time adj fünfmalig.

fix [fɪks] **I** v/t **1.** befestigen, festmachen, anbringen (**to** an dat). **2.** Preis etc festsetzen, -legen (**at** auf acc): ~ (**up**) Termin etc festsetzen. **3.** Blick, Aufmerksamkeit etc richten, heften (**on** auf acc). **4.** fixieren, anstarren. **5.** j-s Aufmerksamkeit etc fesseln. **6.** Schuld etc zuschieben (**on** dat). **7.** reparieren. **8.** bsd. Am. et. zurechtmachen, Essen zubereiten: ~ **one's face** sich schminken; ~ **one's hair** sich frisieren. **9.** F Wettkampf etc manipulieren; j-n schmieren.

II v/i **10.** sich entscheiden od. entschließen (**on** für, zu). **11.** sl. fixen. **III** s **12.** F Klemme f: **be in a** ~ in der Klemme sein od. stecken. **13.** F abgekartete Sache, Schiebung f; Bestechung f. **14.** sl. Fix m: **give o.s. a** ~ sich e-n Schuß setzen. **fix-ate** ['~eɪt] v/t: **be** ~**d on** psych. fixiert sein an od. auf (acc). **fix'a-tion** s psych. (**Mutter-** etc)Bindung f, (-)Fixierung f.

fixed [fɪkst] adj (□ → **fixedly**) **1.** ◎ fest, Fest... **2.** unverwandt, starr (**Blick**). **3.** fest, unveränderlich: ~ **cost** Fixkosten pl; ~ **idea** psych. fixe Idee; ~ **star** ast. Fixstern m. ~**in-ter-est(-,bear-ing)** adj ✝ festverzinslich.

fix-ed-ly ['fɪksɪdlɪ] adv starr, unverwandt.

fix-ing ['fɪksɪŋ] s **1.** Reparatur f. **2.** pl bsd. Am. Geräte pl; Zubehör n; gastr. Beilagen pl. **fix-ture** ['~tʃə] s **1.** Inventarstück n: **lighting** ~ Beleuchtungskörper m. **2.** bsd. Sport: bsd. Br. (Termin m für e-e) Veranstaltung.

fizz [fɪz] **I** v/i **1.** zischen. **2.** sprudeln, moussieren (**Getränk**). **3.** fig. sprühen (**with** vor dat). **II** s **4.** Zischen n. **5.** Sprudeln n, Moussieren n. **6.** Sprudel m; Fizz m. **7.** F Schampus m. **fiz-zle** ['fɪzl] **I** v/i **1.** → **fizz** 1. **2.** a. ~ **out** fig. verpuffen, im Sand verlaufen. **II** s **3.** → **fizz** 4, 5. **4.** F Pleite f, Mißerfolg m.

flab-ber-gast ['flæbəgɑːst] v/t F verblüffen: **be** ~**ed** platt sein.

flab-by ['flæbɪ] adj □ **1.** schlaff (**Muskeln** etc). **2.** schwammig (**Person** etc). **3.** fig. schwach (**Charakter** etc).

flac-cid ['flæksɪd] → **flabby** 1.

flag¹ [flæg] **I** s **1.** Fahne f, Flagge f: **be** (**like**) **a red** ~ **to a bull to s.o.** Am. F wie ein rotes Tuch für j-n sein od. auf j-n wirken; **keep the** ~ **flying** die Fahne hochhalten; **show the** ~ fig. Flagge zeigen; sich sehen lassen od. zeigen. **II** v/t **2.** beflaggen. **3.** ~ **down** Fahrzeug anhalten, Taxi herbeiwinken.

flag² [~] **I** s (**Stein**)Platte f, Fliese f. **II** v/t mit (**Stein**)Platten od. Fliesen belegen, fliesen.

flag³ [~] v/i **1.** schlaff herabhängen. **2.** fig. nachlassen, erlahmen (**Interesse** etc).

'flag-pole → **flagstaff.**

fla-grant ['fleɪɡrənt] adj □ **1.** schamlos, schändlich. **2.** eklatant, kraß.

'**flag·staff** s Fahnenstange f, Fahnen-, Flaggenmast m.

flair [fleə] s **1.** Veranlagung f: **have a ~ for art** künstlerisch veranlagt sein. **2.** (feines) Gespür (**for** für).

flake [fleɪk] **I** s (Schnee- etc)Flocke f; (Haut)Schuppe f. **II** v/i a) mst ~ **off** abblättern, b) schuppen. '**flak·y** adj **1.** flockig; schuppig. **2.** blätt(e)rig: ~ **pastry** Blätterteig m.

flam·boy·ant [flæm'bɔɪənt] adj □ **1.** extravagant. **2.** grell, leuchtend. **3.** pompös, bombastisch.

flame [fleɪm] **I** s **1.** Flamme f: **be in ~s** in Flammen stehen; **an old ~ of mine** F e-e alte Flamme von mir. **2.** fig. Feuer n, Glut f. **II** v/i **3.** lodern: ~ **up** auflodern, in Flammen aufgehen; fig. aufbrausen. '**flam·ing** adj **1.** lodernd, brennend. **2.** fig. flammend, feurig. **3.** Br. F verdammt.

flam·ma·ble ['flæməbl] → **inflammable**.

flan [flæn] s Obst-, Käsekuchen m.

flange [flændʒ] s ⚙ **1.** Flansch m. **2.** Spurkranz m (e-s Rads).

flank [flæŋk] **I** s **1.** Flanke f, Weiche f (e-s Tiers); Seite f (e-s Menschen, Gebäudes etc). **2.** ✕ Flanke f, Flügel m (beide a. Sport). **II** v/t **3.** flankieren (a. ✕).

flan·nel ['flænl] s **1.** Flanell m. **2.** pl, a. **pair of ~s** Flanellhose f. **3.** Br. Waschlappen m. **4.** Br. F Schmus m.

flap [flæp] **I** s **1.** Flattern n, (Flügel)Schlag m. **2.** Schlag m, Klaps m. **3.** Klappe f (e-r Tasche etc). **4. be in a ~** F in heller Aufregung sein. **II** v/t **5.** mit den Flügeln etc schlagen. **III** v/i **6.** flattern. **7.** F in heller Aufregung sein; in helle Aufregung geraten. '**~·jack** s bsd. Am. Pfannkuchen m.

flare [fleə] **I** s **1.** Flackern n, Lodern n, Leuchten n. **2.** Leuchtfeuer n; Licht-, Feuersignal n. **3.** → **flare-up**. **II** v/i **4.** flackern (Kerze etc), (Feuer etc a.) lodern, (Licht) leuchten: ~ **up** aufflammen, -flackern, -lodern (alle a. fig.); fig. aufbrausen; ~ **up at s.o.** j-n anfahren. '**~·up** s **1.** Aufflammen n, -flackern n, -lodern n (alle a. fig.). **2.** fig. Ausbruch m: ~ **of fury** Wutausbruch.

flash [flæʃ] **I** s **1.** Aufblitzen n, -leuchten n, Blitz m: **a ~ of lightning** ein Blitz; ~ **of wit** Geistesblitz; **give s.o. a ~** mot. j-n

anblinken. **2.** Stichflamme f: ~ **in the pan** fig. Eintagsfliege f; Strohfeuer n. **3.** Augenblick m: **in a ~** im Nu, sofort. **4.** Rundfunk etc: Kurzmeldung f. **II** v/t **5.** aufleuchten od. (auf)blitzen lassen. **III** v/i **6.** aufflammen, (auf)blitzen; zucken (Blitz). **7.** rasen, flitzen: **it ~ed** od. **across, through) my mind that** plötzlich schoß es mir durch den Kopf, daß. **8.** ~ **back** (in e-m Film etc) zurückblenden (**to** auf acc). '**~·back** s Film etc: Rückblende f. ~ **bulb** s phot. Blitz(licht)lampe f. ~ **cube** s phot. Blitzwürfel m.

flash·er ['flæʃə] s **1.** mot. Blinker m. **2.** Br. F Exhibitionist m.

'**flash·light** s **1.** phot. Blitzlicht n: ~ **photograph** Blitzlichtaufnahme f. **2.** bsd. Am. Taschenlampe f.

flash·y ['flæʃɪ] adj □ **1.** prunkvoll, protzig. **2.** auffallend. **3.** aufbrausend (Temperament).

flask [flɑːsk] s **1.** Taschenflasche f. **2.** Thermosflasche f.

flat¹ [flæt] s **1.** Fläche f, Ebene f. **2.** flache Seite: ~ **of the hand** Handfläche f. **3.** Flachland n, Niederung f. **4.** mot. bsd. Am. Reifenpanne f. **II** adj □ **5.** flach, eben, Flach... **6.** flach, offen (Hand). **7.** mot. platt (Reifen). **8.** entschieden, kategorisch: **and that's ~** damit basta! **9.** einheitlich, Einheits...; Pauschal... **III** adv **10. fall ~** der Länge nach hinfallen; fig. F danebengehen, mißglücken; durchfallen (Theaterstück etc). **11.** ♪ zu tief: **sing ~**. **12. in five minutes** ~ in sage u. schreibe fünf Minuten. **13.** ~ **broke** F total abgebrannt od. pleite.

flat² [~] s bsd. Br. Wohnung f: → **block** 3.

'**flat·foot** s (irr foot) **1.** mst pl ✎ Plattfuß m. **2.** pl a. **-foots** od. **-feet** Bulle m (Polizist). '**~·foot·ed** adj **1.** ✎ plattfüßig: **be ~** Plattfüße haben. **2.** F entschieden.

flat·let ['flætlɪt] s bsd. Br. Kleinwohnung f. '**flat·ness** s Flachheit f. **flat·ten** ['~·tn] **I** v/t **1.** (ein)ebnen. **2.** Ä, ⚙ abflachen. **3.** ⚙ ausbeulen. **II** v/i **3.** a. ~ **out** flach(er) werden.

flat·ter ['flætə] v/t j-m schmeicheln (a. fig. Bild etc): **be ~ed** sich geschmeichelt fühlen (**at, by** durch). '**flat·ter·er** s Schmeichler(in). '**flat·ter·ing** adj □ **1.** schmeichlerisch. **2.** schmeichelhaft (**to**

für). '**flat·ter·y** s Schmeichelei(en pl) f: → **obtain** I.

flat·u·lence ['flætjʊləns] s ⚕ Blähung(en pl) f: **cause** (od. **produce**) ~ blähen.

flaunt [flɔːnt] v/t zur Schau stellen, protzen mit.

flau·tist ['flɔːtɪst] s ♪ Flötist(in).

fla·vo(u)r ['fleɪvə] I s 1. Geschmack m, Aroma n. 2. fig. Beigeschmack m. II v/t 3. würzen (a. fig.). '**fla·vo(u)r·ing** s Würze f, Aroma n (beide a. fig.).

flaw [flɔː] s 1. (⊕ Material-, ⚖ Form-) Fehler m, ⊙ a. Defekt m. 2. fig. schwache Stelle. '**flaw·less** adj □ einwandfrei, tadellos.

flax [flæks] s ♀ Flachs m. '**flax·en** adj 1. Flachs... 2. flachsen, flachsfarben.

flay [fleɪ] v/t Tier abhäuten: ~ s.o. **alive** F kein gutes Haar an j-m lassen, j-m gehörig s-e Meinung sagen.

flea [fliː] s zo. Floh m: **send s.o. away with a** ~ **in his ear** F j-m heimleuchten. '**~bite** s 1. Flohbiß m. 2. fig. Bagatelle f. ~ **cir·cus** s Flohzirkus m. ~ **mar·ket** s Flohmarkt m.

fled [fled] pret u. pp von **flee**.

fledged [fledʒd] adj flügge. **fledg(e)·ling** ['∼lɪŋ] s 1. eben flügge gewordener Vogel. 2. fig. Grünschnabel m.

flee [fliː] (irr) I v/i fliehen, flüchten (**from** vor dat; aus). II v/t fliehen vor (dat) od. aus.

fleece [fliːs] I s 1. Vlies n, bsd. Schaffell n. II v/t 2. Schaf etc scheren. 3. F j-n schröpfen (**of** um), ausnehmen.

fleet[1] [fliːt] s 1. ♣ Flotte f. 2. ~ **of cars** Wagenpark m.

fleet[2] [∼] adj □ schnell, flink.

fleet·ing ['fliːtɪŋ] adj □ flüchtig, vergänglich.

Fleet Street s das Londoner Presseviertel; fig. die (Londoner) Presse.

flesh [fleʃ] s 1. Fleisch n: **put on** ~ zunehmen; **lose** ~ abmagern, abnehmen; → **creep** 3. 2. Körper m, Leib m: **my own** ~ **and blood** mein eigen Fleisch u. Blut; **in the** ~ leibhaftig, höchstpersönlich; in natura, in Wirklichkeit. 3. (Frucht-) Fleisch n. '~**col·o(u)red** adj fleischfarben. '~**eat·ing** adj ♀, zo. fleischfressend. ~ **wound** s ✚ Fleischwunde f.

flew [fluː] pret von **fly**[1].

flex [fleks] I v/t bsd. anat. biegen, beugen. II s ⚡ bsd. Br. (Anschluß-, Verlänge-

rungs)Kabel n, (-)Schnur f. '**flex·i·ble** adj □ flexibel: a) elastisch, b) fig. anpassungsfähig, beweglich.

flex·i·time ['fleksɪtaɪm] s Br. gleitende Arbeitszeit: **be on** ~ gleitende Arbeitszeit haben.

flick [flɪk] I s 1. Klaps m. 2. Knall m, Schnalzer m. 3. Schnipser m. II v/t 4. j-m e-n Klaps geben. 5. schnalzen mit (**Fingern**), (**mit Peitsche** a.) knallen mit. 6. schnippen, schnipsen: ~ **away** (od. **off**) wegschnippen.

flick·er ['flɪkə] I s 1. Flackern n. 2. TV Flimmern n. II v/i 3. flackern. 4. flimmern (**Fernsehbild**).

flick knife s (irr **knife**) Br. Schnappmesser n.

flight[1] [flaɪt] s 1. (a. **Gedanken-** etc)Flug m: **in** ~ im Flug. 2. Schwarm m (**Vögel**): **in the first** ~ fig. in vorderster Front. 3. a. ~ **of stairs** Treppe f.

flight[2] [∼] s Flucht f: **in his** ~ auf s-r Flucht; **put to** ~ in die Flucht schlagen; **take** (to) ~ die Flucht ergreifen; ~ **of capital** ✝ Kapitalflucht.

flight| en·gi·neer s Bordingenieur m. ~ **re·cord·er** s Flug(daten)schreiber m.

flight·y ['flaɪtɪ] adj □ flatterhaft.

flim·sy ['flɪmzɪ] I adj 1. dünn, zart. 2. fig. fadenscheinig (**Ausrede**). II s 3. Durchschlagpapier n.

flinch [flɪntʃ] v/i 1. zurückschrecken (**from**, **at** vor dat). 2. (zurück)zucken, zs.-fahren: **without** ~**ing** ohne mit der Wimper zu zucken.

fling [flɪŋ] I s 1. Wurf m: (**at**) **full** ~ mit voller Wucht. 2. **have one's** (od. **a**) ~ sich austoben. 3. F Versuch m: **have** (od. **take**) **a** ~ **at** es versuchen od. probieren mit. II v/t (irr) 4. werfen, schleudern (**at** nach): ~ **open** (**to**) Tür etc aufreißen (zuschlagen); ~ **away** wegwerfen; ~ **o.s.** sich stürzen (**at s.o.** auf j-n; **into s.th.** in od. auf e-e Sache).

flint [flɪnt] s Feuerstein m.

flip [flɪp] I v/t 1. → **flick** 6. 2. a. ~ **over** Pfannkuchen, Schallplatte etc wenden, umdrehen. II v/i 3. a. ~ **out** bsd. Am. sl. ausflippen, durchdrehen (**for**, **over** bei). III s 4. Schnipser m. 5. Flip m (**Getränk**). '~**flop** s Zehensandale f.

flip·pant ['flɪpənt] adj □ respektlos, schnodd(e)rig.

flip·per ['flɪpə] *s* **1.** *zo.* Flosse *f.* **2.** Schwimmflosse *f.*

flip side *s* B-Seite *f* (*e-r Single*).

flirt [flɜːt] **I** *v/i* flirten, *fig. a.* spielen, liebäugeln (**with** mit). **II** *s*: **be a ~** gern flirten. **flir'ta·tion** *s* Flirt *m, fig. a.* Spielen *n,* Liebäugeln *n.* **flir'ta·tious** *adj* □ kokett.

flit [flɪt] *v/i* flitzen, huschen.

float [fləʊt] **I** *v/i* **1.** (auf dem Wasser) schwimmen, (im Wasser) treiben. **2.** ⚓ flott sein *od.* werden. **3.** schweben, ziehen. **4.** *a.* ⚓ in Umlauf sein. **II** *v/t* **5.** schwimmen *od.* treiben lassen. **6.** ⚓ flottmachen. **7.** ✝ *Wertpapiere etc* in Umlauf bringen; *Anleihe* auflegen; *Gesellschaft* gründen. **8.** ✝ *Währung* floaten, den Wechselkurs (*gen*) freigeben. **9.** *Gerücht etc* in Umlauf setzen. **III** *s* **10.** flacher Plattformwagen, *bsd.* Festwagen *m.* **'float·er** *s pol.* Wechselwähler(in). **'float·ing I** *adj* **1.** treibend, schwimmend: **~ ice** Treibeis *n.* **2.** ✝ umlaufend (*Geld etc*); frei konvertierbar (*Währung*). **3. ~ voter** → **floater.**

flock [flɒk] **I** *s* **1.** Herde *f* (*bsd. Schafe od. Ziegen*); Schwarm *m* (*Vögel*). **2.** Menge *f,* Haufen *m*: **come in ~s** in (hellen) Scharen herbeiströmen. **3.** *eccl.* Herde *f,* Gemeinde *f.* **II** *v/i* **4.** *fig.* strömen: **~ together** zs.-strömen.

floe [fləʊ] *s* **1.** Treibeis *n.* **2.** Eisscholle *f.*

flog [flɒg] *v/t* **1.** prügeln, schlagen: **~ a dead horse** *fig.* offene Türen einrennen; s-e Zeit verschwenden. **2.** auspeitschen. **3.** *Br.* F verkloppen, -scheuern. **'flog·ging** *s* **1.** Tracht *f* Prügel. **2.** 🔨 Prügelstrafe *f.*

flood [flʌd] **I** *s* **1.** *a.* **~ tide** Flut *f.* **2.** Überschwemmung *f* (*a. fig.*), Hochwasser *n.* **3.** *fig.* Flut *f,* Strom *m,* Schwall *m*: **~ of tears** Tränenstrom *m.* **II** *v/t* **4.** überschwemmen, -fluten (*beide a. fig. with* mit). **5.** unter Wasser setzen. **6.** *Fluß etc* anschwellen *od.* über die Ufer treten lassen. **III** *v/i* **7.** fluten, strömen, sich ergießen (*alle a. fig.*). **8.** anschwellen; über die Ufer treten. **'~·light** *s* Scheinwerfer-, Flutlicht *n*: **by ~** unter Flutlicht. **II** *v/t* (*irr light*[1]) (mit Scheinwerfern) beleuchten *od.* anstrahlen: **floodlit match** (*Sport*) Flutlichtspiel *n.*

floor [flɔː] **I** *s* **1.** (Fuß)Boden *m*: → **wipe** II. **2.** Tanzfläche *f*: **take the ~** auf die Tanzfläche gehen. **3.** Stock(werk *n*) *m,* Geschoß *n.* **4.** *parl.* Sitzungs-, Plenarsaal *m*: **take the ~** das Wort ergreifen. **II** *v/t* **5.** e-n (Fuß)Boden legen in (*dat*). **6.** zu Boden schlagen, (*Boxen a.*) auf die Bretter schicken. **7.** F a) *j-n* umhauen, *j-m* die Sprache verschlagen: **~ed** platt, sprachlos, b) *j-n* schaffen (*Problem etc*). **'~·board** *s* Diele *f.* **~ ex·er·cis·es** *s pl Sport:* Bodenturnen *n.*

floor·ing ['flɔːrɪŋ] *s* (Fuß)Bodenbelag *m.*

floor| lamp *s* Stehlampe *f.* **~ lead·er** *s parl. Am.* Fraktionsführer *m.* **~ show** *s* Varietévorstellung *f* (*in Nachtclub etc*). **~ wait·er** *s* Etagenkellner *m.* **~ vase** *s* Bodenvase *f.*

floo·zy ['fluːzɪ] *s sl.* Flittchen *n.*

flop [flɒp] **I** *v/i* **1.** plumpsen; sich plumpsen lassen (*into* in *acc*). **2.** F durchfallen (*Prüfling, Theaterstück etc*); *allg.* e-e Pleite *od.* ein Reinfall sein. **II** *s* **3.** Plumps *m.* **4.** F a) *thea. etc* Flop *m,* Durchfall *m,* b) Reinfall *m,* Pleite *f,* c) Versager *m.* **'flop·py** *adj* □ **1.** schlaff, schlott(e)rig. **2. ~ disk** (*Computer*) Diskette *f.*

flo·ra ['flɔːrə] *pl* **-ras, -rae** [-riː] *s* 🌿 Flora *f,* Pflanzenwelt *f.* **'flo·ral** *adj* Blumen..., Blüten...: **~ pattern** Blumenmuster *n.*

flor·id ['flɒrɪd] *adj* □ **1.** blühend (*Gesichtsfarbe, Gesundheit*). **2.** blumig (*Stil*).

flo·rist ['flɒrɪst] *s* **1.** Blumenhändler(in). **2.** Blumenzüchter(in).

flot·sam ['flɒtsəm] *s a.* **~ and jetsam** ⚓ Treibgut *n*: **~ and jetsam** Strandgut *n* (*a. fig.*), Wrackgut *n.*

flounce [flaʊns] *v/i* erregt stürmen *od.* stürzen.

floun·der[1] ['flaʊndə] *s ichth.* Flunder *f.*

floun·der[2] [~] *v/i* **1.** zappeln; strampeln. **2.** *fig.* sich verhaspeln, ins Schwimmen kommen.

flour ['flaʊə] **I** *s* Mehl *n.* **II** *v/t* mit Mehl bestreuen.

flour·ish ['flʌrɪʃ] **I** *v/i* **1.** gedeihen, *fig. a.* blühen, florieren. **2.** auf der Höhe s-r Macht *od.* s-s Ruhms stehen; s-e Blütezeit haben. **II** *v/t* **3.** *Fahne etc* schwenken. **III** *s* **4.** ♪ Tusch *m.* **5.** Schnörkel *m.*

flout [flaʊt] *v/t Befehl etc* mißachten.

flow [fləʊ] **I** *v/i* **1.** fließen, strömen (*beide a. fig.*): **~ freely** in Strömen fließen

(*Sekt etc*); ~ **over its banks** über die Ufer treten. **2.** lose herabhängen. **II** *s* **3.** Fluß *m*, Strom *m* (*beide a. fig.*): ~ **of information** Informationsfluß; ~ **of tears** Tränenstrom *m*; ~ **of traffic** Verkehrsfluß, -strom. ~ **chart**, ~ **di·a·gram** *s* Flußdiagramm *n*.

flow·er ['flauə] **I** *s* **1.** Blume *f*. **2.** Blüte(zeit) *f* (*a. fig.*): **be in** ~ in Blüte stehen, blühen. **II** *v/i* **3.** blühen, *fig. a.* in höchster Blüte stehen. **~ bed** *s* Blumenbeet *n*.

flow·ered ['flauəd] *adj* **1.** geblümt. **2.** *in Zssgn* ...blütig; ...blühend.

flow·er pot *s* Blumentopf *m*.

flow·er·y ['flauərɪ] *adj* **1.** blumen-, blütenreich. **2.** geblümt. **3.** *fig.* blumig (*Stil*).

flown [fləun] *pp von* **fly**[1].

flu [flu:] *s* ⚕ F Grippe *f*: **he's got (the)** ~ er hat Grippe.

fluc·tu·ate ['flʌktʃueɪt] *v/i* schwanken (**between** zwischen *dat*) (*a. fig.*), fluktuieren. **,fluc·tu·a·tion** *s* Schwankung *f*, Fluktuation *f*: ~ **in prices** ✝ Preisschwankung.

flu·en·cy ['flu:ənsɪ] *s* **1.** Flüssigkeit *f* (*des Stils etc*). **2.** (Rede)Gewandtheit *f*. **'flu·ent** *adj* □ **1.** fließend: **speak ~ German, be ~ in German** fließend Deutsch sprechen. **2.** flüssig (*Stil etc*). **3.** gewandt (*Redner etc*).

fluff [flʌf] **I** *s* **1.** Staubflocke *f*, Fussel(n *pl*) *f*. **2.** Flaum *m* (*a. erster Bartwuchs*). **3.** *thea. etc* F Patzer *m*. **II** *v/t* **4.** *thea. etc* F verpatzen: ~ **one's lines** steckenbleiben. **'fluff·y** *adj* □ flaumig.

flu·id ['flu:ɪd] **I** *s* Flüssigkeit *f*. **II** *adj* □ flüssig (*a. Stil etc*).

fluke [flu:k] *s* F Dusel *m*: **by a** ~ mit Dusel.

flung [flʌŋ] *pret u. pp von* **fling**.

flunk [flʌŋk] *ped. bsd. Am.* F **I** *v/t* **1.** *Schüler* durchrasseln lassen. **2.** durchrasseln in (*dat*). **II** *v/i* durchrasseln.

flu·o·res·cent [flɔː'resnt] *adj* 🔆, *phys.* fluoreszierend, Leucht(stoff)...

flur·ry ['flʌrɪ] **I** *s* **1.** Windstoß *m*. **2.** (*Regen-, Schnee*)Schauer *m*. **3.** *fig.* Hagel *m*, Wirbel *m*: ~ **of blows** Schlaghagel. **4.** *fig.* Aufregung *f*, Unruhe *f*: **in a** ~ aufgeregt, unruhig. **II** *v/t* **5.** aufregen, beunruhigen.

flush [flʌʃ] **I** *s* **1.** Erröten *n*; Röte *f* **2.**

(Wasser)Schwall *m*, Strom *m*. **II** *v/t* **3.** *a.* ~ **out** (aus)spülen: ~ **down** hinunterspülen; ~ **the toilet** spülen. **III** *v/i* **4.** *a.* ~ **up** erröten, rot werden. **5.** spülen (*Toilette[nbenutzer]*).

flus·ter ['flʌstə] **I** *v/t* nervös machen, durcheinanderbringen. **II** *v/i* nervös werden. **III** *s* Nervosität *f*: **get in a** ~ nervös werden; **all in a** ~ ganz durcheinander.

flute [flu:t] ♪ **I** *s* Flöte *f*. **II** *v/i* flöten, Flöte spielen. **III** *v/t* flöten, auf der Flöte spielen. **'flut·ist** *s bsd. Am.* Flötist(in).

flut·ter ['flʌtə] **I** *v/i* **1.** flattern (*a.* 🫀 *Herz, Puls*). **II** *v/t* **2.** wedeln mit. **3.** → **fluster** I. **III** *s* **4.** Flattern *n* (*a.* 🫀). **5.** → **fluster** III.

flux [flʌks] *s* **1.** Fließen *n*, Fluß *m*. **2.** ⚕ Ausfluß *m*. **3. in** (**a state of**) ~ *fig.* im Fluß, in Bewegung.

fly[1] [flaɪ] **I** *s* **1.** Hosenschlitz *m*. **II** *v/i* (*irr*) **2.** fliegen: **the bird is flown** *fig.* der Vogel ist ausgeflogen; ~ **open** auffliegen (*Tür etc*). **3.** fliegen, stieben (*Funken etc*): → **spark** I. **4.** stürmen, stürzen: ~ **at s.o.** auf j-n losgehen; → **temper** 3. **5.** (ver)fliegen (*Zeit*). **6.** flattern, wehen. **III** *v/t* **7.** fliegen lassen: → **kite**. **8.** ✈ *Flugzeug, j-n, et., Strecke* fliegen; *Ozean etc* überfliegen; mit *e-r Fluggesellschaft* fliegen: ~ **in** (**out**) ein-(aus)fliegen. **9.** *Fahne* hissen, wehen lassen.

fly[2] [~] *s zo.* Fliege *f*: **a** ~ **in the ointment** *fig.* ein Haar in der Suppe; **he would not hurt** (*od.* **harm**) **a** ~ er tut keiner Fliege et. zuleide.

fly·ing ['flaɪɪŋ] *adj* **1.** fliegend, Flug...: ~ **saucer** fliegende Untertasse; ~ **squad** *Br.* Überfallkommando *n*; ~ **start** (*Sport*) fliegender Start; → **colour** 5. **2.** kurz, flüchtig (*Eindruck etc*): ~ **visit** Stippvisite *f*, Blitzbesuch *m*. **II** *s* **3.** Fliegen *n*.

'fly | o·ver *s Br.* (Straßen-, Eisenbahn-) Überführung *f*. ~ **sheet** *s* Flugblatt *n*, Reklamezettel *m*. **'~·swat·ter** → **swatter**. **'~·weight** (*Sport*) *s* Fliegengewicht(ler *m*) *n*. **II** *adj* Fliegengewichts...

foal [fəul] *s zo.* Fohlen *n*, Füllen *n*: **in** (*od.* **with**) ~ trächtig.

foam [fəum] **I** *s* Schaum *m*. **II** *v/i* schäumen (*a. fig.* **with rage** vor Wut).

~ rub·ber s Schaumgummi m, n.

foam·y ['fəʊmɪ] adj schäumend, schaumig.

fob [fɒb] v/t **1.** ~ **s.th. off on s.o.** j-m et. andrehen od. aufhängen. **2.** ~ **s.o. off** j-n abspeisen od. abwimmeln (**with** mit).

fo·cal ['fəʊkl] adj A, ⊙, phys. im Brennpunkt stehend (a. fig.), Brenn(-punkt)...: ~ **point** Brennpunkt m (a. fig.). **fo·cus** ['~kəs] I pl **-cus·es, -ci** ['~saɪ] s **1.** A, ⊙, phys. Brenn-, fig. a. Mittelpunkt m; opt., phot. Scharfeinstellung f: **in** ~ scharf; fig. klar u. richtig; **out of** ~ unscharf, verschwommen (a. fig.); **be the** ~ **of attention** im Mittelpunkt des Interesses stehen; **bring into** ~ → 2, b) fig. in den Brennpunkt rücken. II v/t pret u. pp **-cus(s)ed 2.** phys. im Brennpunkt vereinigen, Strahlen bündeln; opt., phot. scharf einstellen. **3.** fig. konzentrieren, richten (**on** auf acc). III v/i **4.** fig. sich konzentrieren od. richten (**on** auf acc).

fod·der ['fɒdə] s (Trocken)Futter n.

fog [fɒg] I s (dichter) Nebel. II v/t in Nebel hüllen, einnebeln. III v/i a. ~ **up** (sich) beschlagen (Glas). ~ **bank** s Nebelbank m.

fo·gey → **fogy.**

fog·gy ['fɒgɪ] adj ☐ **1.** neb(e)lig: ~ **day** Nebeltag m. **2.** fig. nebelhaft: **I haven't got the foggiest (idea)** F ich hab' keinen blassen Schimmer.

'fog·horn s Nebelhorn n. ~ **lamp,** ~ **light** s mot. Nebelscheinwerfer m, -lampe f.

fo·gy ['fəʊgɪ] s mst **old** ~ verknöcherter (alter) Kerl.

foi·ble ['fɔɪbl] s fig. **1.** (kleine) Schwäche. **2.** (vorübergehende) Laune.

foil[1] [fɔɪl] v/t Plan etc vereiteln, durchkreuzen, j-m e-n Strich durch die Rechnung machen.

foil[2] [~] s **1.** (Metall)Folie f. **2.** fig. Hintergrund m (**to** für).

foil[3] [~] s fenc. Florett n.

foist [fɔɪst] v/t: ~ **s.th. (off) on s.o.** j-m et. andrehen od. aufhängen; ~ **o.s. (od. one's company) on s.o.** sich j-m aufdrängen.

fold [fəʊld] I v/t **1.** Tuch, Hände falten, Arme verschränken, kreuzen. **2.** oft ~ **up** zs.-legen, -falten; zs.-klappen: ~ **away** zs.-klappen (u. verstauen). **3.** ein-

wickeln, -schlagen (**in** in acc): ~ **s.o. in one's arms** j-n in die Arme nehmen od. schließen. II v/i **4.** sich (zs.-)falten od. zs.-legen od. zs.-klappen (lassen). **5.** mst ~ **up** F zs.-brechen (**with** vor dat); ✝ eingehen. III v/i **6.** (anat. Haut-, geol. Boden)Falte f. **'fold·er** s **1.** Faltprospekt m, -blatt n, Broschüre f. **2.** Aktendeckel m, Mappe f. **3.** Schnellhefter m. **'fold·ing** adj zs.-legbar, -faltbar; zs.-klappbar: ~ **bed** Klappbett n; ~ **bi·cycle** Klapprad n; ~ **boat** Faltboot n; ~ **chair** Klappstuhl m; ~ **door(s** pl) Falttür f; ~ **table** Klapptisch m; ~ **umbrella** Taschenschirm m.

fo·li·age ['fəʊlɪɪdʒ] s Laub(werk) n, Blätter(werk n) pl: ~ **plant** Blattpflanze f.

folk [fəʊk] I s pl **1.** a. **folks** Leute pl. **2.** (nur **folks**) F m-e etc Leute od. Verwandte od. Angehörigen pl; (bsd. als Anrede) Leute pl, Herrschaften pl. II adj **3.** Volks...: ~ **dance** (**etymology, music,** etc).

fol·low ['fɒləʊ] I v/t **1.** folgen (dat): a) nachfolgen (dat), sich anschließen (dat), b) (zeitlich) folgen auf (acc), nachfolgen (dat), c) Ratschlag etc befolgen, sich richten nach, d) Mode etc mitmachen, e) folgen können (dat), verstehen. **2.** Ziel, Zweck verfolgen: ~ **up** e-r Sache nachgehen; Sache weiterverfolgen. **3.** e-r Beschäftigung etc nachgehen, Beruf ausüben. III v/t **4.** (zeitlich od. räumlich) (nach)folgen: **letter to** ~ Brief folgt; **as** ~**s** wie folgt, folgendermaßen; → **footstep 2. 5.** mst impers folgen, sich ergeben (**from** aus): **it** ~**s from this** hieraus folgt (**that** daß). **'fol·low·er** s Anhänger(in): ~**s** pl → **following** 1. **'fol·low·ing** I s **1.** Gefolge n, Anhang m; Anhänger(schaft f) pl, Gefolgschaft f. **2.** das Folgende; die Folgenden pl. II adj **3.** folgend: ~ **wind** Rückenwind m. III prp **4.** im Anschluß an (acc).

'fol·low-up s **1.** Weiterverfolgen n (e-r Sache). **2.** ✆ Nachbehandlung f.

fol·ly ['fɒlɪ] s Torheit f.

fond [fɒnd] adj ☐ **1. be** ~ **of** mögen, gern haben: **be** ~ **of doing s.th.** et. gern tun. **2.** zärtlich, liebevoll. **3.** allzu nachsichtig (Mutter etc).

fon·dle ['fɒndl] v/t (liebevoll) streicheln.

fond·ness ['fɒndnɪs] s **1.** Zärtlichkeit f.

2. Zuneigung *f* (**of** zu). **3.** Vorliebe *f* (**for** für).

font [fɒnt] *s eccl.* Taufstein *m*, -becken *n*.

food [fuːd] *s* **1.** Nahrung *f* (*a. fig.*), Essen *n*, Verpflegung *f*: **~ for thought** (*od.* **reflection**) Stoff *m* zum Nachdenken. **2.** Nahrungs-, Lebensmittel *pl.* ~: **poi·son·ing** *s ☞* Lebensmittelvergiftung *f*. **'~stuff** → **food** 2.

fool [fuːl] **I** *s* **1.** Narr *m*, Närrin *f*, Dummkopf *m*: **make a ~ of** → 2; **make a ~ of o.s.** sich lächerlich machen; **I am a ~ to him** gegen ihn bin ich ein Waisenknabe. **II** *v/t* **2.** zum Narren halten. **3.** betrügen (**out of** um); verleiten (**into doing** zu tun). **4. ~ away** Zeit, Geld etc vergeuden. **III** *v/i* **5.** *a.* **~ about** (*od.* **around**) Unsinn machen, herumalbern. **6.** *oft* **~ about** (*od.* **around**) spielen (**with** mit); sich herumtreiben; herumtrödeln. **'fool·er·y** *s* Torheit *f*.

'fool·har·dy *adj* □ tollkühn, verwegen.

fool·ish ['fuːlɪʃ] *adj* □ dumm, töricht.

'fool·proof *adj* **1.** ☺ betriebssicher. **2.** todsicher (*Plan etc*). **3.** narren-, idiotensicher (*Gerät etc*).

foot [fʊt] **I** *pl* **feet** [fiːt] *s* **1.** Fuß *m*: **on ~** zu Fuß; **be on ~** im Gange sein; **set on ~** in die Wege leiten, in Gang bringen; **be on one's feet** (**again**) (wieder) auf den Beinen sein; **put one's ~ in it** ins Fettnäpfchen treten; → **sweep** 6. **2.** (*pl a.* **foot**) Fuß *m* (= 0,3048 m). **3.** Fuß *m* (*e-s Berges, Strumpfes etc*), Fußende *n* (*e-s Bettes etc*): **at the ~** am Fuß (*gen*), unten an (*dat*). **II** *v/t* **4.** ~ **it** F zu Fuß gehen. **5.** *Rechnung* bezahlen. **,~-and-'mouth dis·ease** *s vet.* Maulu. Klauenseuche *f*. **'~ball** (*Sport*) **I** *s* **1.** *Br.* Fußball(spiel *n*) *m*; *Am.* Football(spiel *n*) *m*. **2.** *Br.* Fußball *m*; *Am.* Football-Ball *m*. **II** *adj* **3.** *Br.* Fußball...; *Am.* Football...: **~ pools** *pl* Fußballtoto *n*, *m*. **'~bridge** *s* Fußgängerbrücke *f*. **'~fall** *s* Schritt *m*, Tritt *m* (*Geräusch*). **'~hills** *s pl* Vorgebirge *n*. **'~hold** *s* Stand *m*: **safe ~** fester Stand, sicherer Halt; **gain** (*od.* **get**) **a ~** *fig.* (festen) Fuß fassen (**in** in *dat*; **as** als).

foot·ing ['fʊtɪŋ] *s* **1.** Stand *m*: **lose** (*od.* **miss**) **one's ~** den Halt verlieren. **2.** *fig.* Basis *f*, Grundlage *f*: **place on a** (*od.* **the same**) ~ gleichstellen (**with** *dat*); **be**

on a friendly ~ auf freundschaftlichem Fuße stehen (**with** mit).

'foot·lights *s pl thea.* **1.** Rampenlicht(er *pl*) *n*. **2.** *fig. die* Bühne, *das* Theater.

foot·ling ['fuːtlɪŋ] *adj* F läppisch (*Sache*), (*a. Person*) albern.

'foot·loose *adj* frei, ungebunden: **~ and fancy-free** frei u. ungebunden. **'~note I** *s* Fußnote *f* (**to** zu). **II** *v/t* mit Fußnoten versehen. **~ pas·sen·ger** *s Am.* Fußgänger(in). **'~path** *s* **1.** (Fuß)Pfad *m*, (-)Weg *m*. **2.** *bsd. Br.* Bürgersteig *m*. **'~print** *s* Fußabdruck *m*.

foot·sie ['fʊtsɪ] *s*: **play ~** F füßeln (**with** mit).

'foot·slog *v/i* F latschen. **'~sore** *adj* fußwund, *bsd.* ✗ fußkrank. **~ spray** *s* Fußspray *m*, *n*. **'~step** *s* **1.** Tritt *m*, Schritt *m*. **2.** Fußstapfe *f*: **follow in s.o.'s ~s** *fig.* in j-s Fußstapfen treten. **'~wear** *s* Schuhwerk *n*. **'~work** *s Sport:* Beinarbeit *f*.

for [fɔː] **I** *prp* **1.** für: a) zugunsten von: *a gift ~ him* ein Geschenk für ihn, b) (mit der Absicht) zu: *come ~ dinner* zum Essen kommen, c) (*passend od. geeignet*) für; (*bestimmt*) für, zu: *tools pl ~ cutting* Schneidewerkzeuge *pl*; *the right man ~ the job* der richtige Mann für diesen Posten, d) (*als Belohnung od. Entgelt*) für, e) (*als Strafe etc*) wegen, f) in Anbetracht (*gen*), im Hinblick auf (*acc*): *he is tall ~ his age* er ist groß für sein Alter, g) (*Begabung, Neigung*) für, (*Hang*) zu, h) (*zeitlich*) auf (*acc*), für die Dauer von, seit: *~ hours* stundenlang; *he has been here ~ a week* er ist schon seit e-r Woche hier, i) an Stelle von (*od. gen*), (an)statt; in Vertretung od. im Namen von (*od. gen*). **2.** (*Wunsch, Ziel*) nach, auf (*acc*). **3.** (*Mittel*) gegen. **4.** dank, wegen: *if it wasn't ~ him* wenn er nicht wäre, ohne ihn. **5.** (*Strecke*) weit: *run ~ a mile* e-e Meile (weit) laufen. **6.** nach: *the train ~ London.* **7.** trotz: *~ all that* trotz alledem. **8.** was ... betrifft: *as ~ me* was mich betrifft *od.* anbelangt; *as all I know* soviel ich weiß. **9.** *nach adj u. vor inf*: *it is impossible ~ me to come* ich kann unmöglich kommen. **10.** *mit s od. pron u. inf*: *it is time ~ you to go home* es ist Zeit für dich heimzugehen; *it is ~ you to decide* die Entscheidung liegt bei Ihnen. **II** *cj* **11.** denn, weil.

fo·ra ['fɔːrə] *pl von* **forum**.

for·ay ['fɔreɪ] *s* **1.** Beute-, Raubzug *m*. **2.** *bsd.* ✕ Ein-, Überfall *m*.

for·bad(e) [fə'bæd] *pret von* **forbid**.

for·bear → **forebear**.

for·bid [fə'bɪd] (*irr*) **I** *v/t* **1.** verbieten, untersagen: ~ *s.o. the house* j-m das Haus verbieten. **2.** ausschließen, unmöglich machen. **II** *v/i* **3.** *God* (*od. heaven*) ~*!* Gott behüte *od.* bewahre! **for·bid·den** [~dn] *pp von* **forbid**. **for·bid·ding** *adj* □ **1.** abstoßend, abschreckend. **2.** bedrohlich.

force [fɔːs] **I** *s* **1.** Stärke *f*, Kraft *f*, Wucht *f* (*a. fig.*): ~ *of gravity phys.* Schwerkraft; *by* ~ *of* kraft, vermittels; *by* ~ *of arms* mit Waffengewalt; *join* ~*es* sich zs.-tun (*with* mit). **2.** *fig.* Kraft *f*: ~*s pl of nature* Naturkräfte *pl*, -gewalten *pl*. **3.** Gewalt *f*: *by* ~ gewaltsam. **4.** Zwang *m* (*a.* ⚖): *by* ~ zwangsweise. **5.** (Rechts)Kraft *f*, (-)Gültigkeit *f*: *come* (*put*) *into* ~ in Kraft treten (setzen). **6.** Einfluß *m*, Wirkung *f*: ~ *of habit* Macht *f* der Gewohnheit. **7.** *pl*, *a.* **armed** ~*es* ✕ Streitkräfte *pl*. **II** *v/t* **8.** *j-n* zwingen, nötigen (*to do* zu tun). **9.** *et.* erzwingen, durchsetzen. **10.** zwängen, drängen: ~ *one's way* sich (durch)drängen (*through* durch). **11.** ~ *s.th. on s.o.* j-m et. aufzwingen *od.* -drängen; ~ *o.s. on s.o.* sich j-m aufdrängen; → **throat**. **12.** *a.* ~ *up Preise* in die Höhe treiben. **13.** *Tempo* beschleunigen, forcieren. **14.** *a.* ~ *open Tür etc* aufbrechen. **forced** *adj* **1.** erzwungen, Zwangs...: ~ *landing* ✈ Notlandung *f*. **2.** gezwungen, gequält. **forc·ed·ly** ['~ɪdlɪ] *adv* **1.** → **forced** **2.** gezwungenermaßen.

'force-feed *v/t* (*irr* **feed**) zwangsernähren.

force·ful ['fɔːsfʊl] *adj* □ **1.** energisch, kraftvoll (*Person*). **2.** eindrucksvoll, -dringlich (*Rede etc*). **3.** zwingend, überzeugend (*Argument etc*).

for·ceps ['fɔːseps] *pl* **-ceps**, **-ci·pes** ['~sɪpiːz] *s* **1.** ✄, *zo.* Zange *f*: ~ *delivery* Zangengeburt *f*. **2.** Pinzette *f*.

for·ci·ble ['fɔːsəbl] *adj* □ **1.** gewaltsam; zwangsweise. **2.** → **forceful**.

for·ci·pes ['fɔːsɪpiːz] *pl von* **forceps**.

ford [fɔːd] **I** *s* Furt *f*. **II** *v/t* durchwaten.

fore [fɔː] **I** *adj* **1.** vorder, Vorder... *od.* früher. **II** *adv* **3.** ⚓ vorn. **III** *s* **4.** Vorderteil *m*, -seite *f*, Front *f*: *come to the* ~ *fig.* sich hervortun. **'~·arm** *s* Unterarm *m*. **'~·bear** *s mst pl* Vorfahr *m*, Ahn *m*. **'~·bode** *v/t* **1.** *Schlimmes* ahnen, voraussehen. **2.** ein (böses) Vorzeichen *od.* Omen sein für. **'~·bod·ing** *s* **1.** (böse) (Vor)Ahnung. **2.** (böses) Vorzeichen *od.* Omen. **'~·cast** **I** *v/t pret u. pp* **-cast**(**·ed**) **1.** voraussagen, vorhersehen. **2.** *Wetter etc* vorhersagen. **II** *s* **3.** Voraussage *f*. **4.** (Wetter)Vorhersage *f*. **'~·fa·ther** *s* Ahn *m*, Vorfahr *m*. **'~·fin·ger** *s* Zeigefinger *m*. **'~·front** *s* vorderste Reihe (*a. fig.*). **'~·go** *v/t u. v/i* (*irr* **go**) vorangehen (*dat*), (*zeitlich a.*) vorhergehen (*dat*). **~·gone** *adj*: ~ *conclusion* ausgemachte Sache; *be a* ~ *conclusion a.* von vornherein feststehen. **'~·ground** *s* Vordergrund *m* (*a. fig.*). **'~·hand** (*Sport*) **I** *s* Vorhand(schlag *m*) *f*. **II** *adj* Vorhand... **~·head** ['fɒrɪd] *s* Stirn *f*.

for·eign ['fɒrən] *adj* **1.** fremd, ausländisch, Auslands...: ~ *affairs pl* Außenpolitik *f*, auswärtige Angelegenheiten *pl*; ~ *currency* (*od.* **exchange**) ✝ Devisen *pl*; ~ *language* Fremdsprache *f*; ⚲ **Office** *pol. Br.* Außenministerium *n*; ~ *policy* Außenpolitik *f*; ⚲ **Secretary** *pol. Br.* Außenminister *m*; ~ *trade* Außenhandel *m*; ~ *word* Fremdwort *n*; ~ *worker* Gastarbeiter *m*; → **correspondent 3.** **2.** fremd (*to dat*): *this is* ~ *to his nature* das ist ihm wesensfremd; ~ *body* (*od.* **matter**) ✿ Fremdkörper *m*. **'for·eign·er** *s* Ausländer(in).

ˌfore·'knowl·edge *s* Vorwissen *n*, vorherige Kenntnis. **~·man** ['~mən] *s* (*irr* **man**) **1.** Vorarbeiter *m*, (*am Bau*) Polier *m*. **2.** ⚖ Obmann *m* (*der Geschworenen*). **'~·most** **I** *adj* **1.** vorderst, erst. **2.** *fig.* herausragendst. **II** *adv* **3.** zuerst. **~·name** *s* Vorname *m*.

fo·ren·sic [fə'rensɪk] *adj* Gerichts...: ~ *medicine*.

'fore·play *s* (*sexuelles*) Vorspiel. **'~·run·ner** *s fig.* **1.** Vorläufer *m*. **2.** Vorbote *m*; (*erstes*) Anzeichen. **~·'see** *v/t* (*irr* **see**[1]) vorher-, voraussehen. **~·'see·a·ble** *adj*: *in the* ~ *future* in absehbarer Zeit. **~·'shad·ow** *v/t* ahnen lassen, andeuten. **'~·sight** *s* Weitblick *m*; (*weise*) Voraussicht *f*. **'~·skin** *s anat.* Vorhaut *f*.

for·est ['fɒrɪst] *s* (*a. fig. Antennen- etc*)Wald *m*; Forst *m*.

fore·stall [fɔː'stɔːl] *v/t* **1.** *j-m, e-r Sache* zuvorkommen. **2.** *Einwand etc* vorwegnehmen.

for·est·er ['fɒrɪstə] *s* Förster *m*. **'for·est·ry** *s* Forstwirtschaft *f*.

'fore|·taste *s* Vorgeschmack *m* (*of* von). **~'tell** *v/t* (*irr* **tell**) vorher-, voraussagen: **~ s.o.'s future** j-m die Zukunft vorhersagen.

for·ev·er, *Br. a.* **for ev·er** [fə'revə] *adv* **1.** für *od.* auf immer. **2.** ständig, (an)dauernd.

fore|'warn *v/t* vorher warnen (*of* vor *dat*). **~·wom·an** *s* (*irr* **woman**) Vorarbeiterin *f*. **'~·word** *s* Vorwort *n* (*to* zu).

for·feit ['fɔːfɪt] **I** *s pl* (*sg konstruiert*) Pfänderspiel *n*: **play ~s** ein Pfänderspiel machen. **II** *v/t* verwirken, verlustig gehen (*gen*); einbüßen. **III** *adj* verwirkt, verfallen. **for·fei·ture** ['~tʃə] *s* Verlust *m*; Einbuße *f*.

forge¹ [fɔːdʒ] *v/t* fälschen.

forge² [~] *v/i mst* **~ ahead** sich (mühsam) vorankämpfen: **~ ahead** *fig.* allmählich Fortschritte machen.

forg·er ['fɔːdʒə] *s* Fälscher *m*. **'forg·er·y** *s* Fälschen *n*; Fälschung *f*: **~ of a document** 🏛 Urkundenfälschung.

for·get [fə'get] (*irr*) **I** *v/t* **1.** *allg.* vergessen: **I ~ his name** sein Name fällt mir im Moment nicht ein. **2. ~ o.s.** sich vergessen; (*nur*) an andere denken. **II** *v/i* **3.** *a.* **~ about it** es vergessen. **for'get·ful** [~fʊl] *adj* □ vergeßlich.

for'get-me-not *s* ♣ Vergißmeinnicht *n*.

for·give [fə'gɪv] *v/t* (*irr* **give**) **1.** *j-m et.* verzeihen, -geben. **2.** *j-m e-e* Schuld *etc* erlassen. **for'giv·ing** *adj* □ **1.** versöhnlich. **2.** verzeihend.

for·go [fɔː'gəʊ] *v/t* (*irr* **go**) verzichten auf (*acc*).

for·got [fə'gɒt] *pret u. pp von* **forget**. **for'got·ten** [~tn] *pp von* **forget**.

fork [fɔːk] **I** *s* **1.** Gabel *f*. **2.** Gab(e)lung *f*, Abzweigung *f*. **II** *v/t* **3. ~ out** (*od. up*) F *Geld* herausrücken, lockermachen. **III** *v/i* **4.** sich gabeln (*Fluß*, *Straße a.*) abzweigen. **forked** *adj* gegabelt, (*Zunge*) gespalten.

'fork·lift (truck) *s* ☉ Gabel-, Hubstapler *m*.

for·lorn [fə'lɔːn] *adj* **1.** verlassen, einsam.

2. verzweifelt (*Versuch*): **~ hope** aussichtsloses *od.* verzweifeltes Unternehmen.

form [fɔːm] **I** *s* **1.** Form *f*, Gestalt *f*: **take ~** Form *od.* Gestalt annehmen (*a. fig.*); **in the ~ of** in Form von (*od. gen*); **in tablet ~** in Tablettenform. **2.** ☉ Form *f*, Schablone *f*. **3.** Form *f*, Art *f*: **~ of government** Regierungsform; → **due** 6. **4.** *a. printed* ~ Formular *n*, Vordruck *m*: **~·letter** Schemabrief *m*. **5.** Form *f* (*a. ling.*), Fassung *f* (*e-s Textes etc*). **6. good** (**bad**) ~ guter (schlechter) Ton: **it is good** (**bad**) ~ es gehört sich (nicht). **7.** Formalität *f*: → **matter** 3. **8.** Verfassung *f*: **in** (**out of, off one's**) ~ (nicht) in Form. **9.** *bsd. Br.* (*Schul*)Klasse *f*: ~ **master** (**mistress**) Klassenlehrer(in). **II** *v/t* **10.** formen, gestalten (*into* zu; **after, on** nach), *Regierung etc* bilden, *Gesellschaft* gründen. **11.** *Charakter etc* formen, bilden. **12.** sich *e-e* Meinung bilden. **III** *v/i* **13.** Form *od.* Gestalt annehmen (*a. fig.*).

for·mal ['fɔːml] *adj* (□ → **formally**) **1.** förmlich, formell: ~ **call** Höflichkeitsbesuch *m*; ~ **dress** Gesellschaftskleidung *f*. **2.** formal, formell: ~ **defect** 🏛 Formfehler *m*. **for·mal·ism** ['~məlɪzəm] *s* Formalismus *m*. **for·mal·i·ty** [~'mælətɪ] *s* **1.** Förmlichkeit *f*. **2.** Formalität *f*, Formsache *f*. **for·mal·ize** ['~məlaɪz] *v/t* **1.** formalisieren. **2.** *e-e* feste Form geben (*dat*). **for·mal·ly** *adv* formell, in aller Form.

for·mat ['fɔːmæt] *s typ.* Aufmachung *f*; Format *n*.

for·ma·tion [fɔː'meɪʃn] *s* **1.** Formung *f*, Gestaltung *f*. **2.** ✈, ✗, *geol.*, *Sport*: Formation *f*. **form·a·tive** ['~mətɪv] *adj* formend, gestaltend: ~ **years** *pl* Entwicklungsjahre *pl*.

for·mer ['fɔːmə] *adj* **1.** früher, vorig; ehemalig: **in ~ times** früher. **2.** erstwähnt, -genannt: **the ~, the latter** ersterer, letzterer. **'for·mer·ly** *adv* früher, ehemals.

for·mi·da·ble ['fɔːmɪdəbl] *adj* □ **1.** furchterregend. **2.** gefährlich (*Gegner etc*), gewaltig, riesig (*Schulden etc*), schwierig (*Frage etc*).

form·less ['fɔːmlɪs] *adj* □ formlos.

for·mu·la ['fɔːmjʊlə] *pl* **-las, -lae** ['~liː] *s* **1.** ⚗, *mot. etc* Formel *f* (*a. fig.*). **2.**

pharm. Rezept *n* (*zur Anfertigung*).
for·mu·late ['~leıt] *v/t* formulieren.
for·mu·la·tion *s* Formulierung *f*.
for·sake [fə'seık] *v/t* (*irr*) **1.** *j-n* verlassen, im Stich lassen. **2.** *et.* aufgeben. **for·'sak·en** *pp von* **forsake**. **for·sook** [fə'sʊk] *pret von* **forsake**.
for·swear [fɔː'sweə] *v/t* (*irr* **swear**) **1.** unter Eid verneinen. **2.** abschwören (*dat*). **3. ~ o.s.** e-n Meineid leisten.
fort [fɔːt] *s* ⚔ Fort *n*: **hold the ~** *fig.* die Stellung halten.
for·te ['fɔːteı] *j-s* Stärke *f*, starke Seite.
forth [fɔːθ] *adv* **1.** weiter, fort: **and so ~** und so weiter. **2.** (her)vor. **,~'com·ing** *adj* **1.** bevorstehend, kommend. **2.** in Kürze erscheinend (*Buch*) *od.* anlaufend (*Film*).
for·ti·eth ['fɔːtıəθ] *adj* vierzigst.
for·ti·fi·ca·tion [,fɔːtıfı'keıʃn] *s* **1.** ⚔ Befestigung *f*: **~s** *pl* Festungswerk *n*. **2.** Verstärkung *f*; Anreicherung *f*. **3.** *fig.* Untermauerung *f*. **for·ti·fy** ['~faı] *v/t* **1.** ⚔ befestigen. **2.** *Wein etc* verstärken; *Nahrungsmittel* anreichern. **3.** *Theorie etc* untermauern (**with** mit).
for·ti·tude ['fɔːtıtjuːd] *s* (innere) Kraft *od.* Stärke.
fort·night ['fɔːtnaıt] *s bsd. Br.* vierzehn Tage: **in a ~** in 14 Tagen. **'fort,night·ly** *bsd. Br.* **I** *adj* vierzehntägig, halbmonatlich. **II** *adv* vierzehntäglich, alle 14 Tage.
for·tress ['fɔːtrıs] *s* ⚔ Festung *f*.
for·tu·i·tous [fɔː'tjuːıtəs] *adj* □ zufällig.
for·tu·nate ['fɔːtʃnət] *adj* glücklich: **be ~** Glück haben; **be ~ in having s.th., be ~ enough to have s.th.** das Glück haben, et. zu besitzen. **'for·tu·nate·ly** *adv* glücklicherweise, zum Glück: **~ for me** zu m-m Glück.
for·tune ['fɔːtʃuːn] *s* **1.** Vermögen *n*: **come into a ~** ein Vermögen erben; **make a ~** ein Vermögen verdienen; **marry a ~** e-e gute Partie machen, reich heiraten. **2.** (glücklicher) Zufall, Glück(sfall *m*) *n*. **3.** Geschick *n*, Schicksal *n*: **good ~** Glück *n*; **bad** (*od.* **ill**) **~** Unglück *n*; **tell ~s** wahrsagen; **read s.o.'s ~** j-m die Karten legen; j-m aus der Hand lesen. **~** *oft* 2 Fortuna *f*, das Glück, die Glücksgöttin. **~ hunt·er** ['~tʃən] *s* Mitgiftjäger *m*. **~ tell·er** ['~tʃən] *s* Wahrsager(in).

for·ty ['fɔːtı] **I** *adj* vierzig: **have ~ winks** F ein Nickerchen machen. **II** *s* Vierzig *f*: **be in one's forties** in den Vierzigern sein; **in the forties** in den vierziger Jahren (*e-s Jahrhunderts*).
fo·rum ['fɔːrəm] *pl* **-rums, -ra** ['~rə] *s* Forum *n* (*a. fig.*).
for·ward ['fɔːwəd] **I** *adv* **1.** nach vorn, vorwärts. **II** *adj* □ **2.** Vorwärts...: **~ planning** Vorausplanung *f*. **3.** fortschrittlich. **4.** vorlaut, dreist. **III** *s* **5.** *Sport*: Stürmer *m*: **~ line** Sturmreihe *f*. **IV** *v/t* **6.** fördern, begünstigen. **7.** (ver)senden, schicken; befördern; *Brief etc* nachsenden. **'for·ward·er** *s* Spediteur *m*.
'for·ward·ing *s* Versand *m*; Beförderung *f*; Nachsendung *f*: **~ address** Nachsendeadresse *f*; **~ agent** Spediteur *m*.
'for·ward-,look·ing *adj* vorausschauend, fortschrittlich.
for·wards ['fɔːwədz] → **forward** I.
fos·sil ['fɒsl] *geol.* **I** *s* Fossil *n* (*a. fig.* F), Versteinerung *f*. **II** *adj* fossil (*a. fig.* F), versteinert.
fos·ter ['fɒstə] **I** *v/t* **1.** *Kind* in Pflege haben *od.* nehmen; *bsd. Br.* in Pflege geben (**with** bei). **2.** *Gefühle, Plan etc* hegen. **II** *adj* **3.** Pflege...: **~ mother.**
fought [fɔːt] *pret u. pp von* **fight**.
foul [faʊl] **I** *adj* □ **1.** stinkend, widerlich. **2.** verpestet, schlecht (*Luft*); verdorben, faul (*Lebensmittel etc*). **3.** schmutzig, verschmutzt. **4.** schlecht, stürmisch (*Wetter*). **5.** *fig.* schmutzig, zotig. **6.** *Sport*: regelwidrig. **II** *adv* **7. fall ~ of** ⚓ kollidieren mit, *a. fig.* zs.-stoßen mit: **fall ~ of the law** mit dem Gesetz in Konflikt geraten. **III** *s* **8.** *Sport*: Foul *n*: **commit a ~ on** ein Foul begehen an (*dat*). **IV** *v/t* **9.** *a.* **~ up** beschmutzen (*a. fig.*), verschmutzen: **~ one's (own) nest** das eigene Nest beschmutzen. **10.** *Sport*: foulen. **11. ~ up** F verpatzen, -sauen. **~-mouthed** ['~maʊðd] *adj* unflätig.
found¹ [faʊnd] *pret u. pp von* **find**.
found² [~] *v/t* **1.** (be)gründen, *Schule etc* stiften. **2.** gründen, stützen (**on** auf *acc*): **be ~ed on** sich gründen auf (*acc*), beruhen auf (*dat*).
found³ [~] *v/t* ⊙ gießen.
foun·da·tion [faʊn'deıʃn] *s* **1.** △ Fundament *n*: **lay the ~(s) of** *fig.* den

Grund(stock) legen zu. **2.** Gründung *f.* **3.** Stiftung *f.* **4.** Grundlage *f,* Basis *f.* ~ **stone** *s* **1.** △ Grundstein *m (a. fig.).* **2.** → **foundation** 4.

found·er¹ ['faʊndə] *s* (Be)Gründer(in), Stifter(in): ~ **member** Gründungsmitglied *n.*

found·er² [~] *s* ⊙ Gießer *m.*

found·er³ *v/i* scheitern, *(Koalition etc a.)* zerbrechen, *(Ehe etc a.)* in die Brüche gehen.

found·ry ['faʊndrɪ] *s* ⊙ Gießerei *f.*

foun·tain ['faʊntɪn] *s* **1.** Quelle *f (a. fig.).* **2.** Fontäne *f:* a) *(Wasser- etc)*Strahl *m,* b) Springbrunnen *m.* **3.** Trinkbrunnen *m.* ~ **pen** *s* Füll(feder)halter *m.*

four [fɔː] **I** *adj* **1.** vier. **II** *s* **2.** Vier *f:* ~ **of hearts** Herzvier; **on all** ~**s** auf allen vieren. **3.** *Rudern:* Vierer *m.* **four·fold** ['fɔːfəʊld] **I** *adj* vierfach. **II** *adv* vierfach, um das Vierfache: *increase* ~ (sich) vervierfachen.

,**four**|-**hand·ed** *adj* □ ♪ vierhändig. '~**leaf clo·ver** *s* ♣ vierblätt(e)riges Kleeblatt. '~**legged** *adj* vierbeinig. '~,**let·ter word** *s* unanständiges Wort. ~ **star** *s mot. Br.* F Super *n (Benzin).* '~**star** *adj:* ~ **petrol** *mot. Br.* Superbenzin *n.*

four·teen [,fɔː'tiːn] *adj* vierzehn. ,**four·teenth** [~θ] *adj* vierzehnt. **fourth** [fɔːθ] **I** *adj* **1.** viert. **II** *s* **2.** der, die, das Vierte: *the* ~ *of May* der 4. Mai. **3.** Viertel *n.* '**fourth·ly** *adv* viertens.

'**four-time** *adj* viermalig.

fowl [faʊl] *s coll.* Geflügel *n.*

fox [fɒks] **I** *s* **1.** *zo.* Fuchs *m.* **2.** *oft sly old* ~ gerissener *od.* verschlagener Kerl. **II** *v/t* **3.** verblüffen. **4.** täuschen, reinlegen. ~ **hunt(·ing)** *s* Fuchsjagd *f.* ~ **ter·ri·er** *s zo.* Foxterrier *m.* '~**trot** *s* ♪ Foxtrott *m.*

fox·y ['fɒksɪ] *adj* □ gerissen, verschlagen.

foy·er ['fɔɪeɪ] *s* Foyer *m.*

fra·cas ['fræka:] *pl* **-cas** [-ka:z], *Am.* **-cas·es** ['freɪkəsɪz] *s* Aufruhr *m,* Tumult *m.*

frac·tion ['frækʃn] *s* **1.** Å Bruch *m:* ~ **bar** *(od. line, stroke)* Bruchstrich *m.* **2.** Bruchteil *m.* **frac·tion·al** ['~ʃənl] *adj* □ **1.** Å Bruch... **2.** *fig.* minimal, geringfügig.

frac·tious ['frækʃəs] *adj* □ mürrisch, reizbar.

frac·ture ['fræktʃə] **I** *s* Bruch *m,* ✻ *a.* Fraktur *f.* **II** *v/t* (zer)brechen: ~ *one's arm* sich den Arm brechen; ~**d skull** ✻ Schädelbruch *m; speak* ~**d English** *fig.* gebrochen Englisch sprechen. **III** *v/i* (zer)brechen.

frag·ile ['frædʒaɪl] *adj* □ **1.** zerbrechlich *(a. fig.).* **2.** schwach, zart *(Gesundheit);* gebrechlich *(Person).* **fra·gil·i·ty** [frə'dʒɪlətɪ] *s* **1.** Zerbrechlichkeit *f.* **2.** Zartheit *f;* Gebrechlichkeit *f.*

frag·ment ['frægmənt] *s* **1.** *literarisches etc* Fragment. **2.** Bruchstück *n,* -teil *m.* '**frag·men·ta·ry** *adj* □ fragmentarisch, bruchstückhaft.

fra·grance ['freɪɡrəns] *s* Wohlgeruch *m,* Duft *m.* '**fra·grant** *adj* □ wohlriechend, duftend.

frail [freɪl] *adj* □ zart, schwach *(Gesundheit, Stimme etc);* gebrechlich *(Person);* *(charakterlich od. moralisch)* schwach. '**frail·ty** *s* Zartheit *f;* Gebrechlichkeit *f;* Schwäche *f.*

frame [freɪm] **I** *s* **1.** *(Bilder- etc)*Rahmen *m.* **2.** *(Brillen- etc)*Gestell *n.* **3.** *fig.* Rahmen *m: within the* ~ *of* im Rahmen *(gen).* **4.** *bsd.* ~ *of mind* (Gemüts)Verfassung *f,* (-)Zustand *m.* **II** *v/t* **5.** Bild *etc* (ein)rahmen; *fig.* umrahmen. **6.** *Plan* schmieden, *Politik etc* abstecken. **7.** *a.* ~ *up* F *Sache* drehen, schaukeln, *Spiel* (vorher) absprechen; *j-m* et. anhängen. **III** *v/i* **8.** sich entwickeln. '~**up** *s* F **1.** Komplott *n,* Intrige *f.* **2.** abgekartetes Spiel, Schwindel *m.* '~**work** → **frame** 3.

franc [fræŋk] *s* Franc *m;* Franken *m.*

fran·chise ['fræntʃaɪz] *s* **1.** *pol.* Wahlrecht *n.* **2.** ✝ *bsd. Am.* Konzession *f.*

Fran·co- ['fræŋkəʊ] *in Zssgn* französisch, franko-.

frank [fræŋk] **I** *adj* □ offen(herzig), aufrichtig, frei(mütig): *to be* ~, ~*ly (speaking)* offen gestanden *od.* gesagt; *be* ~ *with s.o.* ehrlich zu j-m sein. **II** *v/t* ✉ frankieren, *(maschinell a.)* freistempeln: ~*ing machine* Frankiermaschine *f,* Freistempler *m.*

frank·furt·er ['fræŋkfɜːtə] *s* Frankfurter (Würstchen *n*) *f.*

frank·in·cense ['fræŋkɪn,sens] *s* Weihrauch *m.*

frank·ness ['fræŋknɪs] *s* Offenheit *f,* Freimütigkeit *f.*

fran·tic ['fræntɪk] adj (~ally) **1.** außer sich, rasend (**with** vor dat). **2.** verzweifelt. **3.** hektisch.

fra·ter·nal [frə'tɜ:nl] adj □ brüderlich. **fra'ter·ni·ty** s **1.** Brüderlichkeit f. **2.** Vereinigung f, Zunft f: **the medical** ~ die Ärzteschaft. **3.** Am. (Studenten-) Verbindung f. **frat·er·ni·za·tion** [,frætənaɪ'zeɪʃn] s Verbrüderung f. '**frat·er·nize** v/i sich verbrüdern.

fraud [frɔ:d] s **1.** ⚖ Betrug m (**on** an dat); arglistige Täuschung: **obtain by** ~ sich et. erschleichen. **2.** Schwindel m (a. Sache). **3.** F Betrüger m, Schwindler m. **fraud·u·lence** ['-jʊləns] s Betrügerei f. '**fraud·u·lent** adj □ betrügerisch.

fray¹ [freɪ] **I** v/t a. ~ **out** ausfransen, durchscheuern: ~**ed nerves** pl verschlissene od. strapazierte Nerven pl. **II** v/i a. ~ **out** ausfransen, sich durchscheuern.

fray² [~] s Rauferei f, Schlägerei f.

freak [fri:k] **I** s **1.** Mißgeburt f, Monstrosität f. **2.** Grille f, Laune f. **3.** sl. ...fan m, ...fanatiker m. **4.** sl. Freak m, irrer Typ. **II** v/i **5.** ~ **out** sl. allg. ausflippen (**for, over** bei).

freck·le ['frekl] s Sommersprosse f. '**freck·led** ['-ld] adj sommersprossig.

free [fri:] **I** adj □ **1.** frei: a) unabhängig, b) selbständig, c) ungebunden, d) ungehindert, e) uneingeschränkt, f) in Freiheit (befindlich): **he is** ~ **to go** es steht ihm frei zu gehen; **give s.o. a** ~ **hand** j-m freie Hand lassen; → **set** 13, **will¹** 1. **2.** frei: a) unbeschäftigt, b) ohne Verpflichtungen, c) unbesetzt. **3.** frei (*nicht wörtlich od. an Regeln gebunden*): ~ **translation**; ~ **skating** (*Eis-, Rollkunstlauf*) Kür(laufen n) f. **4.** (**from, of**) frei (von), ohne (acc): ~ **from error** fehlerfrei. **5.** frei, befreit (**from, of** von): ~ **from pain** schmerzfrei; ~ **of debt** schuldenfrei; → **charge** 9. **6.** ungezwungen, natürlich: → **easy** 7. **7.** offen(herzig), freimütig; unverblümt; dreist; plump-vertraulich: **make** ~ **with** sich Freiheiten herausnehmen gegen j-n; sich (ungeniert) gütlich tun an e-r Sache. **8.** frei, kostenlos, unentgeltlich: ~ **copy** Freiexemplar n; **for** ~ F umsonst. **9.** freigebig: **be** ~ **with** großzügig sein od. umgehen mit. **II** adv **10.** allg. frei. **III** v/t **11.** befreien

(**from** von, aus) (a. fig.). **12.** freilassen.

free·bee, free·bie ['fri:bi:] s sl. et., was es gratis gibt, z. B. Freikarte f.

'**free,boot·er** s Freibeuter m.

free·dom ['fri:dəm] s **1.** Freiheit f: ~ **of the press** Pressefreiheit. **2.** Freisein n: ~ **from pain** Schmerzfreiheit f.

free|en·ter·prise s freies Unternehmertum. ~ **fall** s ✈, phys. freier Fall. '~**hand·ed** adj □ freigebig, großzügig. ~ **kick** s Fußball: Freistoß m: (**in**)**direct** ~ '~**lance I** s Freiberufler m, Freischaffende m; freier Mitarbeiter. **II** adj frei(beruflich tätig), freischaffend. **III** adv freiberuflich: **work** ~ → IV. **IV** v/i freiberuflich arbeiten (**for** für). '~**lanc·er** → **freelance** I. '~**load** v/i Am. F schnorren (**off, of** bei), nassauern. '~**load·er** s Am. F Schnorrer m, Nassauer m. ~ **mar·ket e·con·o·my** s freie Marktwirtschaft. ~ **port** s Freihafen m. ,~**'spo·ken** adj □ freimütig, offen. ~ **state** s Freistaat m. '~**style** (*Sport*) **I** s Freistil m. **II** adj Freistil... ~ **trade** s Freihandel m. ,~**'trade a·re·a** s Freihandelszone f.

freeze [fri:z] **I** v/i (irr) **1.** impers frieren: **it is freezing hard** es herrscht starker Frost. **2.** frieren: ~ **to death** erfrieren; **I am freezing** mir ist eiskalt. **3.** (ge)frieren, zu Eis werden; ~ **blood** 1. **4.** a. ~ **up** (od. **over**) zufrieren (See etc), vereisen (Windschutzscheibe etc): ~ (**up**) einfrieren (*Türschloß etc*); ~ **to** fest-od. anfrieren an (dat). **5.** fig. erstarren. **II** v/t (irr) **6.** zum Gefrieren bringen. **7.** Fleisch etc einfrieren, tiefkühlen. **8.** ✈ vereisen. **9.** ✝ Preise etc, pol. diplomatische Beziehungen einfrieren. **III** s **10.** Frost(periode f) m. **11.** ✝, pol. Einfrieren n: ~ **on wages** Lohnstopp m. '**freez·er** s a) Kühltruhe, -fach, b) Gefrierfach n (e-s Kühlschranks). '**freez·ing** adj **1.** Gefrier..., Kälte...: ~ **compartment** → **freezer** b; ~ **point** Gefrierpunkt m. **2.** eisig kalt, eiskalt.

freight [freɪt] **I** s **1.** Fracht(gebühr) f. **2.** ⚓ (Am. a. ✈, mot.) Fracht f, Ladung f. **II** v/t **3.** Schiff, Am. a. Güterwagen etc befrachten, beladen. **4.** Güter verfrachten. ~ **car** s ⚓ Am. Güterwagen m.

freight·er ['freɪtə] s Frachter m, Frachtschiff n; Transportflugzeug n.

freight train s Am. Güterzug m.

French [frentʃ] **I** adj **1.** französisch: ~ **beans** pl ♣ bsd. Br. grüne Bohnen pl; ~ **fried potatoes,** F ~ **fries** pl bsd. Am. Pommes frites pl; ~ **kiss** Zungenkuß m; **take** ~ **leave** sich (auf) französisch empfehlen; ~ **letter** Br. F Pariser m (Kondom); ~ **window**(s pl) Terrassen-, Balkontür f. **II** s **2.** the ~ pl die Franzosen pl. **3.** ling. Französisch n: in ~ auf französisch. **-man** [´-mən] s (irr man) Franzose m. '~,**wom·an** s (irr woman) Französin f.

fre·net·ic [frə´netɪk] adj (**~ally**) **1.** a) ausgelassen, b) → **frenzied** 2. **2.** → **frenzied** 3.

fren·zied [´frenzɪd] adj **1.** außer sich, rasend (**with** vor dat). **2.** frenetisch (Geschrei etc), (Beifall a.) rasend. **3.** wild, hektisch. **'fren·zy** s **1.** helle Aufregung. **2.** wildes od. hektisches Treiben. **3.** Wahnsinn m, Raserei f.

fre·quen·cy [´fri:kwənsɪ] s **1.** Häufigkeit f. **2.** ≵, phys. Frequenz f. **fre·quent I** adj [´fri:kwənt] häufig. **II** v/t [frɪ´kwent] häufig besuchen.

fres·co [´freskəʊ] pl **-co(e)s** s Fresko(gemälde) n.

fresh [freʃ] **I** adj □ **1.** allg. frisch: ~ **butter** ungesalzene Butter; ~ **meat** Frischfleisch n; ~ **shirt** sauberes Hemd. **2.** neu: ~ **ground²** 1, **start** 9. **3.** grün, unerfahren: **be** ~ **to** noch keine Erfahrung haben in (dat). **4.** F frech (**with** zu): **don't get** ~ **with me!** werd bloß nicht pampig! **II** adv **5.** frisch: ~ **from the oven** ofenfrisch; ~ **from the press** druckfrisch; ~**laid eggs** pl frisch gelegte Eier pl. **'fresh·en I** v/t **1.** mst ~ **up** erfrischen: ~ **o.s.** (**up**) sich frisch machen. **2.** ~ **s.o.** (**up**) j-m nachgießen od. -schenken. **II** v/i mst ~ **up 3.** sich frisch machen. **4.** auffrischen (Wind). **'fresh·er** Br. F → **freshman.**

fresh·man [´freʃmən] s (irr man) Student(in) im ersten Jahr.

fresh·ness [´freʃnɪs] s Frische f.

fret [fret] **I** v/t **1.** j-m Sorgen machen. **2.** j-n ärgern, reizen. **3.** abscheuern, abnutzen; reiben od. scheuern an (dat): ~ **s.o.'s nerves** an j-s Nerven zerren. **II** v/i **4.** sich Sorgen machen (**about, at, for, over** wegen). **5.** sich ärgern (**about, at, for, over** über acc): ~ **and fume** vor Wut schäumen. **6.** sich abscheuern od.

abnutzen. **III** s **7.** **be in a** ~ → 4, 5.

fret·ful [´-fʊl] adj □ verärgert, gereizt.

Freud·i·an [´frɔɪdɪən] adj Freudsch: ~ **slip** Freudsche Fehlleistung.

fri·a·ble [´fraɪəbl] adj bröck(e)lig, krümelig.

fric·as·see [´frɪkəsi:] s gastr. Frikassee n: ~ **of chicken** Hühnerfrikassee.

fric·tion [´frɪkʃn] s **1.** ☉, phys. Reibung f. **2.** fig. Reiberei(en pl) f. **fric·tion·al** [´-ʃənl] adj ☉, phys. Reibungs...

Fri·day [´fraɪdɪ] s Freitag m: **on** ~ (am) Freitag; **on** ~**s** freitags.

fridge [frɪdʒ] s bsd. Br. F Kühlschrank m. ~**'freez·er** s bsd. Br. F Kühl- u. ~Gefrierkombination f.

friend [frend] s **1.** Freund(in): **be** ~**s** with befreundet sein mit; **make** ~**s with** sich anfreunden mit; **make** ~**s again** sich wieder vertragen. **2.** Bekannte m, f. **'friend·li·ness** s Freundlichkeit f. **'friend·ly I** adj **1.** freundlich (a. fig. Zimmer etc). **2.** freundschaftlich: ~ **game** (od. **match**) (Sport) Freundschaftsspiel n; → **term** 5. **3.** befreundet (**with** mit). **II** s **4.** Sport: F Freundschaftsspiel n. **'friend·ship** s Freundschaft f.

frieze [fri:z] s △ Fries m.

frig·ate [´frɪgət] s ♣ Fregatte f.

frige → **fridge.**

fright [fraɪt] s **1.** Schreck(en) m: **get** (od. **have**) **a** ~ e-n Schreck bekommen, erschrecken; **get off with a** ~ mit dem Schrecken davonkommen; **give s.o. a** ~ j-m e-n Schrecken einjagen, j-n erschrecken. **2.** **look a** ~ F verboten od. zum Abschießen aussehen. **'fright·en I** v/t **1.** j-n erschrecken (**to death** zu Tode); j-m Angst einjagen: **be** ~**ed** erschrecken (**at, by, of** vor dat); Angst haben (**of** vor dat). **2.** mst ~ **away** (od. **off**) vertreiben, -scheuchen. **II** v/i **3.** ~ **easily** leicht erschrecken, schreckhaft sein. **fright·ful** [´-fʊl] adj □ schrecklich, fürchterlich (beide a. fig.).

frig·id [´frɪdʒɪd] adj □ **1.** kalt, frostig, eisig (alle a. fig.). **2.** psych. frigid. **fri'gid·i·ty** s **1.** Kälte f, Frostigkeit f (beide a. fig.). **2.** psych. Frigidität f.

frill [frɪl] s **1.** Krause f, Rüsche f. **2.** pl Verzierungen pl, Kinkerlitzchen pl.

fringe [frɪndʒ] **I** s **1.** Franse f, Besatz m. **2.** Rand m, Einfassung f, Umrandung *f.* **II** *v/t* **3.** mit Fransen besetzen. **4.** umsäumen. **~ ben·e·fits** *s pl* ✝ (Gehalts-, Lohn)Nebenleistungen *pl.* **~ group** *s sociol.* Randgruppe *f.*

frisk [frɪsk] **I** *v/i* herumtollen. **II** *v/t* F *j*-*n* filzen, durchsuchen. **'frisk·y** *adj* □ **1.** lebhaft, munter. **2.** ausgelassen.

frit·ter ['frɪtə] *v/t mst* **~ away** *Geld, Gelegenheit* vertun, *Zeit a.* vertrödeln, *Geld, Kräfte* vergeuden.

fri·vol·i·ty [frɪ'vɒlətɪ] *s* Frivolität *f:* a) Leichtsinnigkeit *f*, -fertigkeit *f*, Oberflächlichkeit *f*, b) leichtfertige Rede *od.* Handlung. **friv·o·lous** ['~ələs] *adj* □ **1.** frivol, leichtfertig, -sinnig. **2.** nicht ernst zu nehmen(d).

friz·zy ['frɪzɪ] *adj* gekräuselt, kraus: **~ hair** Kraushaar *n.*

fro [frəʊ] *adv:* → **to.**

frock [frɒk] *s* **1.** (Mönchs)Kutte *f.* **2.** (Kinder-, Arbeits)Kittel *m.* **3.** Kleid *n.*

frog [frɒg] *s zo.* Frosch *m:* **have a ~ in the** (*od.* **one's**) **throat** *fig.* e-n Frosch im Hals haben. **~·man** ['~mən] *s* (*irr man*) Froschmann *m,* ✕ *a.* Kampfschwimmer *m.*

frol·ic ['frɒlɪk] *v/i pret u. pp* **-icked** *a.* **~ about** (*od.* **around**) herumtoben, -tollen. **frol·ic·some** ['~səm] *adj* □ ausgelassen, übermütig.

from [frɒm] *prp* **1.** von, aus, von ... aus *od.* her: **he took it ~ me** er nahm es mir weg; **~ what he said** nach dem, was er sagte. **2.** von (... an), seit: **~ 2 to 4 o'clock** von 2 bis 4 Uhr; **~ day to day** von Tag zu Tag. **3.** von ... aus: **~ £ 5** von 5 Pfund an (aufwärts). **4.** (weg *od.* entfernt) von: **~ dish·wash·er to millionaire** vom Tellerwäscher zum Millionär. **5.** von (*Unterscheidung*): **he does not know black ~ white** er kann Schwarz u. Weiß nicht auseinanderhalten. **6.** von (*Geben etc*): **a letter ~ his son. 7.** aus, vor (*dat*), an (*dat*) (*Grund*): **he died ~ fatigue** er starb vor Erschöpfung.

front [frʌnt] **I** *s* **1.** *allg.* Vorder-, Stirnseite *f,* Front *f:* **at the ~** auf der Vorderseite, vorn. **2.** △ (Vorder)Front *f,* Fassade *f* (*a. fig.* F): **maintain a ~** den Schein wahren. **3.** ✕ Front *f:* **to the ~** an die Front; **on all ~s** an allen Fronten (*a. fig.*). **4.** Vordergrund *m:* **in ~** an der *od.* die Spitze, vorn; **in ~ of** vor (*dat*); **to the**

~ nach vorn. 5. *fig.* Bereich *m,* Sektor *m:* **on the educational ~** auf dem Erziehungssektor. **6.** *fig.* Frechheit *f,* Unverschämtheit *f:* **have the ~ to do s.th.** die Stirn haben, et. zu tun. **7.** *meteor.* Front *f.* **II** *adj* **8.** Front..., Vorder...: **~ entrance** Vordereingang *m;* **~ row** vorder(st)e Reihe; **~ tooth** Vorderzahn *m.* **III** *v/t* **9.** gegenüberstehen, -liegen: **the windows ~ the street** die Fenster gehen auf die Straße (hinaus). **IV** *v/i* **10. ~ on** (*od.* **to, toward[s]**) → 9. **'front·age** *s* △ (Vorder)Front *f.* **'fron·tal** *adj* **1.** Frontal... **2.** *anat.,* ◎ Stirn...

‚front|'bench·er *s parl. Br.* führendes Fraktionsmitglied. **~ door** *s* Haus-, Vordertür *f:* **by** (*od.* **through**) **the ~** *fig.* direkt, ohne Umschweife; legal.

fron·tier ['frʌn‚tɪə] **I** *s* Grenze *f* (*a. fig.*). **II** *adj* Grenz...: **~ town.**

front| line *s* ✕ Front(linie) *f:* **be in the ~** an vorderster Front stehen (*a. fig.*). **~ page** *s* erste Seite, Titelseite *f* (*e-r Zeitung*): **hit the ~s** die Schlagzeilen machen. **'~-page** *adj* wichtig, aktuell: **~ news.** **~ pas·sen·ger** *s mot.* Beifahrer(in). **'~‚pas·sen·ger seat** *s mot.* Beifahrersitz *m.* **~ rank** *s:* **be in the ~** *fig.* zur Spitze gehören *od.* zählen. **'~-seat pas·sen·ger** *s mot.* Beifahrer(in). **'~-wheel drive** *s* ◎ Vorderrad-, Frontantrieb *m.*

frost [frɒst] **I** *s* **1.** Frost *m.* **2.** Reif *m.* **II** *v/t* **3.** mit Reif überziehen. **4.** ◎ *Glas* mattieren: **~ed glass** Matt-, Milchglas *n.* **5.** *gastr. bsd. Am.* glasieren, mit Zuckerguß überziehen; mit (Puder)Zucker bestreuen. **'~·bite** *s* Erfrierung *f.* **'~‚bit·ten** [‚ʌtn] *adj* erfroren.

frost·ing ['frɒstɪŋ] *s gastr. bsd. Am.* Zuckerguß *m,* Glasur *f.* **'frost·y** *adj* □ **1.** eisig, frostig (*beide a. fig.*). **2.** mit Reif bedeckt. **3.** (eis)grau: **~ hair.**

froth [frɒθ] **I** *s* Schaum *m.* **II** *v/t a.* **~ up** zum Schäumen bringen; zu Schaum schlagen. **III** *v/i* schäumen. **'froth·y** *adj* □ **1.** schaumig, schäumend. **2.** *fig.* seicht.

frown [fraʊn] **I** *v/i* die Stirn runzeln (**at** über *acc*) (*a. fig.*): **~ on** et. mißbilligen. **II** *s* Stirnrunzeln *n:* **with a ~** stirnrunzelnd.

frowst [fraʊst] *s bsd. Br.* F Mief *m:* **there's a ~ in here** hier mieft es.

'frowst·y adj bsd. Br. F miefig, vermieft.

frowz·y ['fraʊzɪ] adj **1.** schlampig, ungepflegt. **2.** muffig.

froze [frəʊz] pret von freeze. **'fro·zen I** pp von freeze. **II** adj Gefrier...: ~ **meat**; ~ **food** Tiefkühlkost f.

fru·gal ['fruːgl] adj □ **1.** sparsam: a) haushälterisch (**of** mit, in dat), b) wirtschaftlich (Auto etc). **2.** genügsam, bescheiden. **3.** einfach, bescheiden (Mahlzeit).

fruit [fruːt] s **1.** Frucht f. **2.** coll. a) Früchte pl: **bear** ~ Früchte tragen (a. fig.), b) Obst n. **3.** mst pl fig. Früchte pl. '~**cake** s englischer Kuchen. ~ **cock·tail** s Frucht-, Früchtecocktail m.

fruit·er·er ['fruːtərə] s bsd. Br. Obsthändler m. **fruit·ful** ['~fʊl] adj □ **1.** fruchtbar (a. fig.). **2.** fig. erfolgreich.

fru·i·tion [fruːˈɪʃn] s: **bring to** ~ verwirklichen; **come to** ~ sich verwirklichen; Früchte tragen.

fruit knife s (irr knife) Obstmesser n.

fruit·less ['fruːtlɪs] adj □ **1.** unfruchtbar. **2.** fig. frucht-, erfolglos.

fruit‖ **ma·chine** s Br. (Geld)Spielautomat m. ~ **sal·ad** s Obstsalat m. ~ **tree** s Obstbaum m.

fruit·y ['fruːtɪ] adj **1.** fruchtartig. **2.** fruchtig (Wein). **3.** Br. F saftig, gepfeffert (Witz etc). **4.** Am. F schmalzig: ~ **song** Schnulze f.

frump [frʌmp] s: **old** ~ alte Schachtel.

frus·trate [frʌˈstreɪt] v/t **1.** Plan etc vereiteln, durchkreuzen; Hoffnungen zunichte machen. **2.** j-n frustrieren. **frus-ˈtra·tion** s **1.** Vereit(e)lung f, Durchkreuzung f. **2.** Frustration f (a. psych.).

fry[1] [fraɪ] v/t u. v/i braten: **fried eggs** pl Spiegeleier pl; **fried potatoes** pl Bratkartoffeln pl.

fry[2] [~] s: **small** ~ ein kleiner Fisch, kleine Fische pl (Person[en]).

fry·ing pan ['fraɪɪŋ] s Bratpfanne f: **jump** (od. leap) **out of the** ~ **into the fire** fig. vom Regen in die Traufe kommen.

fuck [fʌk] v/t u. v/i V ficken, vögeln: ~ **off!** verpiß dich! **'fuck·ing** adj V Scheiß..., verflucht.

fud·dled ['fʌdld] adj F **1.** benebelt. **2.** verwirrt, durcheinander.

fuel ['fjʊəl] s Brennstoff m: a) Heiz-, Brennmaterial n, b) mot. etc Treib-,

Kraftstoff m: ~ **ga(u)ge** Benzinuhr f; ~ **injection engine** Einspritzmotor m; **add** ~ **to the fire** (od. flames) fig. Öl ins Feuer gießen.

fug [fʌg], **'fug·gy** → frowst, frowsty.

fu·gi·tive ['fjuːdʒətɪv] **I** s a) Flüchtige m, b) pol. etc Flüchtling m, c) Ausreißer m. **II** adj flüchtig: a) entflohen, b) fig. vergänglich.

ful·fil, -fill, a. **ful·fill** [fʊlˈfɪl] v/t Bedingung, Versprechen etc erfüllen, Befehl etc ausführen: ~ **o.s.** sich (selbst) verwirklichen; **be fulfilled** sich erfüllen. **ful·ˈfil(l)·ment** s Erfüllung f, Ausführung f.

full [fʊl] **I** adj (□ → fully) **1.** allg. voll: ~ **of** voll von, voller; → **stomach** 1. **2.** voll, ganz: **a** ~ **hour** e-e volle od. geschlagene Stunde. **3.** voll (Gesicht), vollschlank (Figur). **4.** voll, besetzt: ~ (**up**) (voll) besetzt (Bus etc); **house** ~! thea. ausverkauft! **5.** fig. (ganz) erfüllt (**of** von): ~ **of o.s.** (ganz) von sich eingenommen. **6.** reichlich (Mahlzeit). **7.** voll, unbeschränkt: ~ **power** Vollmacht f; **have** ~ **power to do s.th.** bevollmächtigt sein, et. zu tun. **8.** voll(berechtigt): ~ **member** Vollmitglied n. **9.** a. ~ **up** F voll, satt. **II** adv **10.** völlig, ganz: **know** ~ **well** that ganz genau wissen, daß. **11.** ~ **out** mit Vollgas fahren, auf Hochtouren arbeiten. **III** s **12.** **in** ~ vollständig, ganz: **spell** (od. write) **in** ~ ausschreiben; **to the** ~ vollständig, bis ins letzte od. kleinste.

full age s: **of** ~ mündig, volljährig. '~**back** s Fußball: (Außen)Verteidiger m. **~-'blood·ed** adj **1.** vollblütig, Vollblut... (beide a. fig.). **2.** eindringlich (Argument etc). **~-'blown** adj **1.** ganz aufgeblüht. **2.** voll entwickelt, ausgereift (Idee etc). **3.** ausgemacht (Skandal etc). **~-'fledged** bsd. Am. → fully fledged. **~-'grown** adj ausgewachsen. **~-'length** adj **1.** in voller Größe, lebensgroß. **2.** abendfüllend (Film); ausgewachsen (Roman). ~ **moon** s Vollmond m: **at** ~ bei Vollmond.

full·ness ['fʊlnɪs] s (♪ Klang)Fülle f: **feeling of** ~ Völlegefühl n.

full‖-**page** adj ganzseitig. '~-**scale** adj **1.** in Originalgröße, im Maßstab 1:1. **2.** fig. großangelegt, Groß... ~ **stop** s ling. Punkt m. '~-**time I** adj ganztägig,

Ganztags... **II** *adv* ganztags: *work* ~.
ful·ly ['foli] *adv* voll, völlig, ganz: ~ *automatic* vollautomatisch; ~ *two hours* volle *od.* geschlagene zwei Stunden. ~ *fledged adj* **1.** flügge (*Vogel*). **2.** *fig.* richtig.
ful·mi·nate ['fʌlmineit] *v/i* donnern, wettern (*against, at* gegen).
ful·ness *bsd. Am.* → **fullness**.
ful·some ['fulsəm] *adj* □ übertrieben; überschwenglich (*Lob etc*).
fum·ble ['fʌmbl] **I** *v/i a.* ~ *about* (*od. around*) herumtappen, -tasten; (herum)fummeln (*at* an *dat*); ungeschickt umgehen (*with* mit); tastend suchen (*for, after* nach): ~ *in one's pockets* in s-n Taschen (herum)wühlen; ~ *for words* nach Worten suchen. **II** *v/t* verpatzen. **'fum·bler** *s* Patzer(in).
fume [fju:m] **I** *s* *oft pl* Dampf *m*, Rauch *m*. **II** *v/i* **2.** dampfen, rauchen. **3.** *fig.* wütend *od.* aufgebracht sein (*at* über *acc*).
fu·mi·gate ['fju:migeit] *v/t* ausräuchern.
fun [fʌn] *s* Spaß *m* für ~ aus *od.* zum Spaß; *in* ~ im *od.* zum Scherz; *make* ~ *of* sich lustig machen über (*acc*); → *poke* **V**.
func·tion ['fʌŋkʃn] **I** *s* **1.** *allg.* Funktion *f*: *out of* ~ ✪ außer Betrieb. **II** *v/i* **2.** ~ *as* tätig sein *od.* fungieren als; dienen als (*Sache*). **3.** ✪ *etc* funktionieren. **'function·al** *adj* □ **1.** *allg.* funktionell, Funktions...: ~ *disorder* ✿ Funktionsstörung *f*. **2.** zweckbetont, -mäßig, praktisch. **'func·tion·ar·y** *s bsd. pol.* Funktionär *m*.
fund [fʌnd] *s* **1.** ✝ Kapital *n*, Vermögen *n*; Fonds *m*. **2.** *pl* ✝ (Geld)Mittel *pl*: *no* ~*s* (*Scheck*) keine Deckung; *be in* (*out of*) ~*s* (nicht) bei Kasse sein, zahlungs(un)fähig sein. **3.** *fig.* Vorrat *m* (*of* an *dat*).
fun·da·men·tal [ˌfʌndə'mentl] **I** *adj* (□ → *fundamentally*) **1.** grundlegend, wesentlich, fundamental (*to* für). **2.** grundsätzlich, elementar. **3.** Grund..., Fundamental...: ~ *research* Grundlagenforschung *f*. **II** *s* **4.** Grundlage *f*, -prinzip *n*, -begriff *m*. **ˌfun·da'men·tal·ly** *adv* im wesentlichen.
fu·ner·al ['fju:nərəl] **I** *s* Begräbnis *n*, Beerdigung *f*: *that's your* ~ F das ist dein Problem. **II** *adj* Begräbnis...: ~ *march*

♪ Trauermarsch *m*; ~ *parlo(u)r* Leichenhalle *f*; ~ *service* Trauergottesdienst *m*.
'fun·fair *s bsd. Br.* Vergnügungspark *m*, Rummelplatz *m*.
fun·gus ['fʌŋgəs] *pl* **-gi** ['~gai], **-gus·es** *s* ✿ Pilz *m*, Schwamm *m*.
fu·nic·u·lar (**rail·way**) [fju:'nikjolə] *s* (Draht)Seilbahn *f*.
funk [fʌŋk] F **I** *s* Schiß *m*, Bammel *m*: *be in a blue* ~ *of* e-n mächtigen Schiß *od.* Bammel haben vor (*dat*). **II** *v/t* kneifen *od.* sich drücken vor (*dat*).
fun·nel ['fʌnl] *s* **1.** Trichter *m*. **2.** ⚓, 🚂 Schornstein *m*.
fun·nies ['fʌniz] *s pl bsd. Am.* F *Zeitung:* Comics *pl*; Comic-Teil *m*.
fun·ny ['fʌni] *adj* □ komisch: a) spaßig, lustig, b) sonderbar, merkwürdig. ~ *bone s anat.* Musikantenknochen *m*.
fur [fɜ:] *s* **1.** Pelz *m*, Fell *n*: *make the* ~ *fly fig.* Stunk machen (*Person*), (a. *Sache*) für helle Aufregung sorgen. **2.** a) Pelzfutter *n*, -besatz *m*: ~ *collar* Pelzkragen *m*, b) a. ~ *coat* Pelzmantel *m*.
fur·bish ['fɜ:biʃ] *v/t* **1.** polieren, blank reiben. **2.** *oft* ~ *up* herrichten, *Gebäude etc a.* renovieren; *fig.* Kenntnisse auffrischen.
fu·ri·ous ['fjʊəriəs] *adj* □ **1.** wütend, zornig (*with s.o.* auf, *about acc*; *at s.th.* über *acc*). **2.** wild, heftig (*Kampf etc*).
furl [fɜ:l] *v/t* Fahne, Transparent etc auf-, einrollen, Schirm zs.-rollen.
fur·nace ['fɜ:nis] *s* ✪ (Schmelz-, Hoch-) Ofen *m*.
fur·nish ['fɜ:niʃ] *v/t* **1.** versorgen, ausrüsten, -statten (*with* mit): ~ *s.o. with s.th.* a.-n mit et. beliefern. **2.** *Informationen etc* liefern; ~ *proof* den Beweis liefern *od.* erbringen. **3.** *Wohnung etc* einrichten, möblieren: ~*ed room* möbliertes Zimmer. **'fur·nish·ings** *s pl* Einrichtung *f*, Mobiliar *n*.
fur·ni·ture ['fɜ:nitʃə] *s* Möbel *pl*: *piece of* ~ Möbelstück *n*; → *stick*[1] *4*.
furred [fɜ:d] *adj* **1.** Pelz... **2.** mit Pelz besetzt. **3.** ✿ belegt (*Zunge*).
fur·row ['fʌrəʊ] **I** *s* **1.** (Acker)Furche *f*. Runzel *f*, Furche *f*. **II** *v/t* **3.** *Land* furchen; *Wasser* durchfurchen. **4.** *Gesicht, Stirn* furchen, runzeln.
fur·ther ['fɜ:ðə] **I** *adv* **1.** *comp von* **far**. **2.** *fig.* mehr, weiter. **3.** *fig.* ferner, weiter-

hin. **4.** → **farther** 4. II *adj* **5.** *fig.* weiter: ~ **education** *Br.* Fort-, Weiterbildung *f*; **anything ~?** (sonst) noch etwas? **6.** → **farther** 2. III *v/t* **7.** fördern, unterstützen. ,**fur·ther'more** → **further** 3. '**further·most** *adj fig.* äußerst. **fur·thest** ['~ðɪst] **I** *sup von* **far.** 2. *fig.* weitest, meist: **at** (**the**) ~ höchstens. **3.** → **farthest** 2. II *adv* **4.** *fig.* am weitesten, am meisten. **5.** → **farthest** 4.

fur·tive ['fɜːtɪv] *adj* □ heimlich, (*Blick a.*) verstohlen.

fu·ry ['fjʊərɪ] *s* Wut *f*, Zorn *m*: **for** ~ vor lauter Wut; **fly into a** ~ wütend *od.* zornig werden.

fuse [fjuːz] **I** *s* **1.** Zünder *m*. **2.** ⚡ Sicherung *f*: ~ **box** Sicherungskasten *m*. **II** *v/t* **3.** *phys.*, ⊙ schmelzen. **4.** *fig.* verschmelzen, ✝, *pol. a.* fusionieren. **III** *v/i* **5.** ⊙ schmelzen. **6.** *fig.* verschmelzen, ✝, *pol. a.* fusionieren.

fu·se·lage ['fjuːzəlɑːʒ] *s* (Flugzeug-) Rumpf *m*.

fu·sion ['fjuːʒn] *s* **1.** *phys.*, ⊙ Schmelzen *n*. **2.** *biol.*, *opt.*, *phys.* Fusion *f*: ~ **bomb** Wasserstoffbombe *f*. **3.** *fig.* Verschmelzung *f*, ✝, *pol. a.* Fusion *f*.

fuss [fʌs] **I** *s* **1.** (unnötige) Aufregung:

get into a ~ → **3.** **2.** Wirbel *m*, Theater *n*: **make a** ~ → **4.** II *v/i* **3.** sich (unnötig) aufregen (**about** über *acc*): **don't ~!** nur keine Aufregung. **4.** viel Wirbel machen (**about**, **over** um). **5.** ~ **about** (*od.* **around**) herumfuhrwerken. '~**budg·et** *s* *Am.* F, '~**pot** *s* F Kleinlichkeitskrämer *m*. **fuss·y** ['fʌsɪ] *adj* □ **1.** (unnötig) aufgeregt. **2.** kleinlich, pedantisch. **3.** heikel, wählerisch (**about** in *dat*).

fust·y ['fʌstɪ] *adj* □ **1.** mod(e)rig, muffig. **2.** *fig.* verstaubt, -altet; rückständig.

fu·tile ['fjuːtaɪl] *adj* □ **1.** nutzlos, vergeblich. **2.** unbedeutend, geringfügig. **fu·til·i·ty** [~'tɪlətɪ] *s* **1.** Nutzlosigkeit *f*. **2.** Geringfügigkeit *f*.

fu·ture ['fjuːtʃə] **I** *s* **1.** Zukunft *f*: **in** ~ in Zukunft. **2.** *ling.* Futur *n*, Zukunft *f*. **II** *adj* **3.** (zu)künftig, Zukunfts... **4.** *ling.* futurisch: ~ **perfect** Futurum *n* exaktum, zweites Futur; ~ **tense** → 2.

fuze *bsd. Am.* → **fuse.**

fuzz¹ [fʌz] *s* feiner Flaum.

fuzz² [~] *s sl.* Bulle *m* (*Polizist*): **the** ~ *coll.* die Bullen.

fuzz·y ['fʌzɪ] *adj* □ **1.** flaumig. **2.** kraus, wuschelig. **3.** unscharf, verschwommen.

G

gab [gæb] *s* F Gequassel *n*, Gequatsche *n*: **have the gift of the** ~ (*Am.* **of** ~) ein flottes Mundwerk haben. **gab·ble** ['gæbl] **I** *v/i* **1.** *a.* ~ **away** brabbeln. **2.** schnattern (*Gänse*). **II** *v/t* **3.** *Gebet etc* herunterleiern, -rasseln. **4.** *et.* brabbeln. **III** *s* **5.** Gebrabbel *n*. **6.** Geschnatter *n*.

gab·er·dine [,gæbə'diːn] *s* Gabardine *m*.

ga·ble ['geɪbl] *s* Giebel *m*: ~ **window** Giebelfenster *n*. '**ga·bled** *adj* Giebel...

gad [gæd] *v/i*: ~ **about** (*od.* **around**) (viel) unterwegs sein (in *dat*); (viel) herumkommen (in *dat*); sich herumtreiben (in *dat*).

gadg·et ['gædʒɪt] *s* ⊙ F Apparat *m*, Gerät *n*; *oft contp.* technische Spielerei.

Gael·ic ['geɪlɪk] **I** *s ling.* Gälisch *n*. **II** *adj* gälisch: ~ **coffee** Irish coffee *m*.

gaff [gæf] *s sl.*: **blow the** ~ alles verraten, plaudern; **blow the** ~ **on s.th.** *et.* ausplaudern.

gaffe [gæf] *s* Fauxpas *m*, *bsd.* taktlose Bemerkung.

gag [gæg] **I** *v/t* **1.** knebeln (*a. fig.*). **2.** *fig.* mundtot machen. **II** *s* **3.** Knebel *m* (*a. fig.*). **4.** F Gag *m*.

ga·ga ['gɑːgɑː] *adj sl.* verkalkt, -trottelt; plemplem.

gage *Am.* → **gauge.**

gag·gle ['gægl] **I** *v/i* **1.** schnattern (*Gänse*) (*a. fig.*). **II** *s* **2.** Geschnatter *n* (*a. fig.*). **3.** Gänseherde *f*; F schnatternde Schar.

gai·e·ty ['geɪətɪ] s **1.** Fröhlichkeit f. **2.** oft pl Vergnügung f.

gain [geɪn] **I** v/t **1.** Zeit, j-s Vertrauen etc gewinnen: → **ground²** 2, **upper** I. 2. erreichen, erwerben, Erfahrungen sammeln: → **advantage. 3.** j-m et. einbringen, -tragen. **4.** zunehmen an (dat): ~ **speed** schneller werden; **he ~ed 10 pounds** er nahm 10 Pfund zu; ~ **weight** I. **5.** vorgehen (um) (Uhr). **II** v/i **6.** Einfluß od. Boden gewinnen. **7.** zunehmen (**in** an dat). **8.** vorgehen (**by two minutes** zwei Minuten) (Uhr). **III** s **9.** Gewinn (**to** für) (a. ✝). **10.** Zunahme f (**in** an dat): ~ **in weight** Gewichtszunahme. **gain·ful** ['~fʊl] adj □ einträglich, gewinnbringend: ~ **employment** Erwerbstätigkeit f; **~ly employed** erwerbstätig. **'gain·ings** s pl Gewinn(e pl) m.

gait [geɪt] s **1.** Gang(art f) m. **2.** Gangart f (des Pferdes).

gal [gæl] s F Mädchen n.

ga·la [ˈgɑːlə] **I** adj **1.** festlich, Gala... **II** s **2.** Festlichkeit f. **3.** Gala(veranstaltung) f.

ga·lac·tic [gəˈlæktɪk] adj ast. Milchstraßen..., galaktisch.

gal·ax·y [ˈgæləksɪ] s ast. Milchstraße f.

gale [geɪl] s Sturm m (a. fig. F): **a ~ of laughter** e-e Lachsalve, stürmisches Gelächter.

gall¹ [gɔːl] **I** s **1.** wund geriebene od. wunde Stelle. **II** v/t **2.** wund reiben od. scheuern. **3.** fig. (ver)ärgern.

gall² [~] s **1.** Bitterkeit f, Erbitterung f. **2.** F Frechheit f.

gal·lant [ˈgælənt] adj □ **1.** tapfer. **2.** prächtig, stattlich. **3.** galant. **'gal·lant·ry** s **1.** Tapferkeit f. **2.** Galanterie f.

gall blad·der s anat. Gallenblase f.

gal·ler·y [ˈgælərɪ] s **1.** △ Galerie f, Empore f (in Kirchen). **2.** thea. Galerie f (a. Publikum): **play to the ~** für die Galerie spielen (a. weitS.). **3.** (Gemälde- etc-) Galerie f.

gal·ley [ˈgælɪ] s **1.** ♧ hist. Galeere f. **2.** ♧ Kombüse f.

Gal·li·cism [ˈgælɪsɪzəm] s ling. Gallizismus m.

gal·lon [ˈgælən] s Gallone f (GB: 4,55 l, USA: 3,79 l).

gal·lop [ˈgæləp] **I** v/i galoppieren (a. Pferd), (im) Galopp reiten: **~ing infla-**

tion ✝ galoppierende Inflation. **II** s Galopp m: **at a ~** im Galopp.

gal·lows [ˈgæləʊz] pl **-lows·es, -lows** s Galgen m. ~ **bird** s F Galgenvogel m. ~ **hu·mo(u)r** s Galgenhumor m.

'gall·stone s ✿ Gallenstein m.

Gal·lup poll [ˈgæləp] s Meinungsumfrage f.

ga·lore [gəˈlɔː] adv F in rauhen Mengen: **money** ~ Geld wie Heu.

ga·lumph [gəˈlʌmf] v/i F stampfen, stapfen.

gal·va·nize [ˈgælvənaɪz] v/t **1.** ⊕ galvanisieren. **2.** fig. elektrisieren.

gam·ble [ˈgæmbl] **I** v/i (um Geld) spielen: ~ **with s.th.** fig. mit et. spielen, et. aufs Spiel setzen. **II** v/t mst ~ **away** verspielen (a. fig.). **III** s Hasardspiel n (a. fig.), Glücksspiel n. **'gam·bler** s **1.** (Glücks)Spieler m. **2.** fig. Hasardeur m. **'gam·bling** adj Spiel...: ~ **casino;** ~ **den** Spielhölle f.

gam·bol [ˈgæmbl] **I** v/i pret u. pp **-boled,** bsd.Br. **-bolled** (herum)tanzen, (-)hüpfen, Freuden- od. Luftsprünge machen. **II** s Freuden-, Luftsprung m.

game [geɪm] **I** s **1.** (Karten-, Ball- etc-) Spiel n: **play the ~** sich an die Spielregeln halten (a. fig.); → **chance** 1, **skill** 1. **2.** (einzelnes) Spiel: **a ~ of chess** e-e Partie Schach. fig. Spiel n, Plan m: **the ~ is up** das Spiel ist aus; **play a double ~** ein doppeltes Spiel treiben; **beat s.o. at his own ~** j-n mit s-n eigenen Waffen schlagen. **4.** F Branche f: **be in the advertising ~** in Werbung machen. **5.** pl ped. Sport m. **6.** Wild(bret) n. **II** adj □ **7.** mutig. **8.** a) aufgelegt (**for** zu): **be ~ to do s.th.** dazu aufgelegt sein, et. zu tun, b) bereit (**for** zu; **to do** zu tun). **'~keep·er** s bsd. Br. Wildhüter m. ~ **park** s Wildpark m. ~ **pre·serve** s Wildgehege n.

gam·ma rays [ˈgæmə] s pl phys. Gammastrahlen pl.

gam·mon [ˈgæmən] s schwachgepökelter od. -geräucherter Schinken m.

gamp [gæmp] s Br. F (bsd. großer) Regenschirm m.

gam·ut [ˈgæmət] s **1.** ♩ Tonleiter f. **2.** fig. Skala f.

gan·der [ˈgændə] s Gänserich m.

gang [gæŋ] **I** s **1.** (Arbeiter)Kolonne f, (-)Trupp m. **2.** Gang f, Bande f. **3.** Cli-

que *f* (*a. contp.*). **4.** *contp.* Horde *f*. **II** *v/i*
5. *mst ~ up* sich zs.-tun, *bsd. contp.* sich
zs.-rotten: *~ up against* (*od. on*) sich
verbünden *od.* verschwören gegen.

gan·grene ['gæŋgriːn] *s ⚕* Brand *m*.

gang·ster ['gæŋstə] *s* Gangster *m*, Verbrecher *m*.

'gang·way *s* **1.** Durchgang *m*, Passage *f*.
2. ⚓, ✈ Gangway *f*. **3.** *Br. thea. etc*
(Zwischen)Gang *m*.

gaol [dʒeɪl], *etc bsd. Br.* → *jail, etc*.

gap [gæp] *s* **1.** Lücke *f* (*a. fig.*): *fill in a ~
in one's education* e-e Bildungslücke
schließen. **2.** *fig.* Kluft *f*.

gape [geɪp] **I** *v/i* **1.** den Mund aufreißen
(*vor Staunen etc*). **2.** (mit offenem
Mund) gaffen *od.* glotzen: *~ at s.o.* j-n
angaffen *od.* anglotzen. **II** *s* **3.** Gaffen
n, Glotzen *n*. **4.** gähnender Abgrund.
'gap·ing *adj* □ **1.** gaffend, glotzend. **2.**
klaffend (*Wunde*), gähnend (*Abgrund*).

ga·rage ['gærɑːʒ] **I** *s* **1.** Garage *f*. **2.**
Reparaturwerkstätte *f* (u. Tankstelle
f). **II** *v/t* **3.** *Auto* in die Garage fahren.

gar·bage ['gɑːbɪdʒ] *s* **1.** *bsd. Am.* Abfall
m, Müll *m*: *~ can* Abfall-, Mülleimer
m; Abfall-, Mülltonne *f*; *~ chute* Müllschlucker *m*; *~ collection* Müllabfuhr
f; *~ collector* (*od. man*) Müllmann *m*; *~
truck* Müllwagen *m*. **2.** *fig.* Schund *m*;
Unfug *m*.

gar·ble ['gɑːbl] *v/t Text etc* durcheinán-
derbringen (*durch Auslassungen etc*)
verfälschen.

gar·den ['gɑːdn] **I** *s* **1.** Garten *m*. **2.** *oft pl*
Garten(anlagen *pl*) *m*: → *botanical,
zoological*. **II** *adj* **3.** Garten...: *~ center*
(*bsd. Br. centre*) Gartencenter *n*; *~ city
Br.* Gartenstadt *f*; *~ party* Gartenfest *n*,
-party *f*; *lead s.o. up the ~ path* j-n
hinters Licht führen; *~ suburb Br.* Gar-
tenvorstadt *f*. **III** *v/i* **4.** im Garten arbeiten. **'gar·den·er** *s* Gärtner(in).
'gar·den·ing *s* Gartenarbeit *f*.

gar·gan·tu·an [gɑː'gæntjʊən] *adj* riesig,
gewaltig.

gar·gle ['gɑːgl] **I** *v/t* **1.** gurgeln mit. **II** *v/i*
2. gurgeln (*with* mit). **III** *s* **3.** Gurgeln *n*:
have a ~ gurgeln. **4.** Gurgelmittel *n*.

gar·ish ['geərɪʃ] *adj* □ grell (*Licht*), (*Farben a.*) schreiend, (*Parfüm a.*) aufdringlich.

gar·land ['gɑːlənd] **I** *s* Girlande *f*, (*a.

Sieges*)Kranz *m*. **II** *v/t* bekränzen.

gar·lic ['gɑːlɪk] *s* ♣ Knoblauch *m*.

gar·ment ['gɑːmənt] *s* Kleidungsstück *n*,
pl a. Kleidung *f*.

gar·net ['gɑːnɪt] *s min.* Granat *m*.

gar·nish ['gɑːnɪʃ] **I** *v/t* **1.** (*with* mit)
schmücken, verzieren; *fig.* ausschmük-
ken. **2.** *gastr.* garnieren (*with* mit). **II** *s*
3. Verzierung *f*; *fig.* Ausschmückung *f*.
4. *gastr.* Garnierung *f*.

gar·ret ['gærət] *s* Dachkammer *f*.

gar·ri·son ['gærɪsn] ✕ **I** *s* **1.** Garnison *f*:
~ town Garnison(s)stadt *f*. **II** *v/t* **2.** Ort
mit e-r Garnison belegen. **3.** *Truppen* in
Garnison legen.

gar·ru·li·ty [gæ'ruːlətɪ] *s* Geschwätzig-
keit *f*. **gar·ru·lous** ['gærələs] *adj* □ geschwätzig.

gar·ter ['gɑːtə] *s* Strumpfband *n*; Sok-
kenhalter *m*; *Am.* Strumpfhalter *m*,
Straps *m*.

gas [gæs] **I** *pl* **-(s)es 1.** Gas *n*. **2.** F a) *Am.*
Benzin *n*, Sprit *m*, b) *step on the ~* Gas
geben, auf die Tube drücken (*beide a.
fig.*). **3.** F Gewäsch *n*, Blech *n*. **II** *v/t* **4.**
vergasen: *be ~sed a.* e-e Gasvergiftung
erleiden. **III** *v/i* **5.** F faseln. *'~·bag* s F
Quatscher(in). *~ cham·ber* s Gaskam-
mer *f*. *~ cook·er* s Gasherd *m*.

gas·e·ous ['gæsjəs] *adj* **1.** gasförmig. **2.**
Gas...

gas ex·plo·sion *s* Gasexplosion *f*.

gash [gæʃ] **I** *s* klaffende Wunde, tiefer
Riß *od.* Schnitt. **II** *v/t* j-m e-e klaffende
Wunde beibringen, *Haut* aufreißen,
-schlitzen.

gas heat·ing *s* Gasheizung *f*.

gas·ket ['gæskɪt] *s* ⊙ Dichtung(sman-
schette) *f*.

'gas·man *s* (*irr man*) Gasmann *m*, -ab-
leser *m*. *~ mask* s Gasmaske *f*. *~ me·ter*
s Gaszähler *f*, -zähler *m*.

gas·o·lene, gas·o·line ['gæsəʊliːn] *s*
Am. Benzin *n*: *~ attendant* Tankwart
m; *~ bomb* Molotowcocktail *m*; *~ station* Tankstelle *f*.

gasp [gɑːsp] **I** *v/i* **1.** keuchen, schwer
atmen: *~ for breath* nach Luft schnappen. **2.** den Atem anhalten (*with, in* vor
dat): *make s.o. ~* j-m den Atem neh-
men *od.* verschlagen. **II** *v/t* **3.** *mst ~ out*
Worte keuchen, (keuchend) hervorsto-
ßen. **III** *s* **4.** Keuchen *n*, schweres Atmen: *be at one's last ~* in den letzten

gelatinous

Zügen liegen; **to the last** ~ bis zum letzten Atemzug.

gas| sta·tion s Am. F Tankstelle f. ~ **stove** s Gasofen m, -herd m.

gas·sy ['gæsɪ] adj **1.** gasartig. **2.** kohlensäurehaltig. **3.** F geschwätzig.

gas·tric ['gæstrɪk] adj ∦, physiol. Magen...: ~ **acid** Magensäure f; ~ **ulcer** Magengeschwür n. **gas·tri·tis** [gæ-'straɪtɪs] s ∦ Gastritis f, Magenschleimhautentzündung f.

gas·tro·nom·ic [,gæstrə'nɒmɪk] adj (~**ally**) gastronomisch, feinschmeckerisch. **gas·tron·o·my** [~'strɒnəmɪ] s **1.** Gastronomie f (feine Kochkunst). **2.** fig. Küche f: the Italian ~.

'**gas·works** s pl (mst sg konstruiert) Gaswerk n.

gate [geɪt] s **1.** Tor n (a. Skisport), Pforte f. **2.** fig. Tor n, Zugang m (**to** zu). **3.** ⊙ Sperre f, Schranke f; ∦ Flugsteig m. **4.** Sport: a) Zuschauer(zahl f) pl, b) (Gesamt)Einnahmen pl. '~**crash** v/i u. v/t F uneingeladen kommen (zu); sich ohne zu bezahlen hineinschmuggeln (in acc). '~**house** s Pförtnerhaus n. '~**,keep·er** s **1.** Pförtner m. **2.** Bahn-, Schrankenwärter m. '~**leg(ged) ta-ble** s Klapptisch m. ~**man** ['~mən] s (irr man) bsd. Am. → **gatekeeper.** ~ **mon·ey** → **gate** 4b. '~**post** s Torpfosten m: → **between** 2. '~**way** s **1.** Torweg m, Einfahrt f. **2.** → **gate** 2.

gath·er ['gæðə] I v/t **1.** Reichtümer, Erfahrungen etc sammeln, Informationen einholen, -ziehen. **2.** Personen versammeln. **3.** erwerben, gewinnen: ~ **dust** verstauben; ~ **speed** schneller werden. **4.** a. ~ **up** auflesen, (vom Boden) aufheben. **5.** Blumen etc pflücken. **6.** fig. folgern, schließen (**from** aus). II v/i **7.** sich (ver)sammeln od. scharen (**round** s.o. um j-n). **8.** sich (an)sammeln. '**gath·er·ing** s (Menschen)Ansammlung f; Versammlung f, Zs.-kunft f.

gauche [gəʊʃ] adj ∘ **1.** linkisch. **2.** taktlos.

gaud·y ['gɔːdɪ] adj ∘ auffällig bunt, (Farben) grell, schreiend, (Einrichtung etc) protzig.

gauge [geɪdʒ] I v/t **1.** (ab-, aus)messen. **2.** ⊙ eichen. **3.** fig. (ab)schätzen, beurteilen. II s **4.** ⊙ Eichmaß n. **5.** fig. Maßstab m, Norm f (**of** für). **6.** ⊙ Meß-

gerät n, Lehre f. **7.** ⊙ Stärke f, Dicke f (bsd. von Blech od. Draht). **8.** 🚋 Spur(weite) f.

gaunt [gɔːnt] adj ∘ hager, ausgemergelt, -gezehrt.

gaunt·let¹ ['gɔːntlɪt] s fig. Fehdehandschuh m: **fling** (od. **throw**) **down the** ~ (**to** s.o.) (j-m) den Fehdehandschuh hinwerfen, (j-n) herausfordern; **pick** (od. **take**) **up the** ~ den Fehdehandschuh aufnehmen, die Herausforderung annehmen.

gaunt·let² [~]: **run the** ~ Spießruten laufen (a. fig.).

gauze [gɔːz] s Gaze f, ∦ a. (Verband[s])Mull m: ~ **bandage** Mullbinde f. '**gauz·y** adj ∘ gazeartig, hauchdünn.

gave [geɪv] pret von **give.**

gav·el ['gævl] s Hammer m (e-s Auktionators, Vorsitzenden etc).

gawk [gɔːk] v/i glotzen: ~ **at** glotzen auf (acc), anglotzen.

gay [geɪ] I adj ∘ **1.** lustig, fröhlich. **2.** bunt, (farben)prächtig; fröhlich, lebhaft (Farben). **3.** lebenslustig. **4.** F schwul (homosexuell); Schwulen... II s **5.** F Schwule m.

gaze [geɪz] I v/i starren: ~ **at** starren auf (acc), anstarren. II s starrer Blick, Starren n.

ga·zette [gə'zet] s Br. Amtsblatt n, Staatsanzeiger m.

gear [gɪə] I s **1.** mot. a) Gang m: **change** (bsd. Am. **shift**) ~(**s**) schalten; **change** (bsd. Am. **shift**) **into second** ~ den zweiten Gang einlegen, in den zweiten Gang schalten, b) pl Getriebe n. **2.** Vorrichtung f, Gerät n. **3.** F Kleidung f, Aufzug m. II v/t **4.** ~ **up** (down) fig. steigern (drosseln). **5.** fig. (**to, for**) anpassen (dat od. an acc), abstimmen (auf acc). '~**box** s mot. Getriebe n. ~ **change** s mot. Br. (Gang)Schaltung f. ~ **le·ver** s mot. Br. Schalthebel m. '~**shift** s mot. Am. **1.** (Gang)Schaltung f. **2.** a. ~ **lever** Schalthebel m. '~**wheel** s ⊙ Getriebe-, Zahnrad n.

gee [dʒiː] int Am. F na so was!, Mann!

geese [giːs] pl von **goose.**

Gei·ger count·er ['gaɪgə] s phys. Geigerzähler m.

gei·sha ['geɪʃə] pl -**sha**(**s**) s Geisha f.

gel·a·tin ['dʒelətɪn], **gel·a·tine** [~'tiːn] s **1.** Gelatine f. **2.** Gallerte f. **ge·lat·i-**

nous [dʒə'læti:nəs] *adj* □ gallertartig.

geld [geld] *v/t (a. irr)* Tier, *bsd.* Hengst kastrieren, verschneiden. **'geld·ing** *s* kastriertes Tier, *bsd.* Wallach *m*.

gelt [gelt] *pret u. pp von* **geld**.

gem [dʒem] *s* **1.** Edelstein *m*. **2.** *fig.* Perle *f*, Juwel *n* (*beide a. Person*), Prachtstück *n*.

Gem·i·ni ['dʒemɪnaɪ] *s pl (mst sg konstruiert)* *ast.* Zwillinge *pl*.

gen·der ['dʒendə] *s ling.* Genus *n*, Geschlecht *n*: **what ~ is ...?** welches Genus hat ...? '~,**bend·er** *v/t* Transvestit *m*.

gene [dʒi:n] *s biol.* Gen *n*, Erbfaktor *m*.

gen·e·a·log·i·cal [,dʒi:njə'lɒdʒɪkl] *adj* □ genealogisch: **~ tree** Stammbaum *m*. **gen·e·al·o·gy** [,dʒi:nɪ'ælədʒɪ] *s* Genealogie *f*.

gen·er·a ['dʒenərə] *pl von* **genus**.

gen·er·al ['dʒenərəl] **I** *adj* (□ → **generally**) **1.** allgemein (gebräuchlich *od.* verbreitet), üblich, gängig: **as a ~ rule** meistens, üblicherweise. **2.** allgemein, generell: **~ education** (*od.* **knowledge**) Allgemeinbildung *f*; **the ~ public** die breite Öffentlichkeit; **~ term** Allgemeinbegriff *m*. **3.** allgemein (*nicht spezialisiert*): **the ~ reader** der Durchschnittsleser. **4.** allgemein (gehalten); ungefähr: **a ~ idea** e-e ungefähre Vorstellung. **5.** Haupt..., General...: **~ manager** Generaldirektor *m*. **II** *s* **6.** ✕ General *m*. **7.** **in ~** im allgemeinen, im großen u. ganzen. **~ e·lec·tion** *s* Parlamentswahlen *pl*.

gen·er·al·i·ty [,dʒenə'rælɪtɪ] *s* **1.** *mst pl* allgemeine Redensart, Gemeinplatz *m*. **2.** Allgemeingültigkeit *f*.

gen·er·al·ize ['dʒenərəlaɪz] *v/t* verallgemeinern.

gen·er·al·ly ['dʒenərəlɪ] *adv a.* **~ speaking** im allgemeinen, allgemein.

gen·er·al| prac·ti·tion·er *s* praktischer Arzt. **~ staff** *s* ✕ Generalstab *m*. **~ strike** *s* ☩ Generalstreik *m*.

gen·er·ate ['dʒenəreɪt] *v/t* **1.** *Elektrizität etc* erzeugen. **2.** *biol.* zeugen. **3.** *fig.* bewirken, erzeugen, verursachen. **,gen·er'a·tion** *s* **1.** Generation *f* (*a.* ☺ *etc*). **2.** Erzeugung *f*. **3.** *biol.* Zeugung *f*, Fortpflanzung *f*. **,gen·er'a·tion·al** [~ʃənl] *adj* Generations...: **~ conflict** (*od.* **clash**) Generationskonflikt *m*. **gen·er·a·tive** ['~rətɪv] *adj biol.* Zeu-

gungs..., Fortpflanzungs...: **~ power** Zeugungskraft *f*. **gen·er·a·tor** ['~reɪtə] *s* ⚡ Generator *m*.

ge·ner·ic [dʒɪ'nerɪk] *adj*: **~ term** (*od.* **name**) *biol.* Gattungsname *m*; *allg.* Oberbegriff *m*.

gen·er·os·i·ty [,dʒenə'rɒsɪtɪ] *s* Großzügigkeit *f*, Freigebigkeit *f*. **'gen·er·ous** *adj* □ **1.** großzügig, freigebig. **2.** reichlich, üppig.

gen·e·sis ['dʒenəsɪs] *pl* **-es·es** ['~si:z] *s* Entstehung *f*.

ge·net·ic [dʒɪ'netɪk] **I** *adj* (**~ally**) genetisch: **~ engineering** Gentechnologie *f*; **~ factor** Erbfaktor *m*. **II** *s pl (sg konstruiert)* Genetik *f*, Vererbungslehre *f*.

gen·ial ['dʒi:njəl] *adj* □ freundlich (*a. fig. Klima etc*). **ge·ni·al·i·ty** [,~nɪ'ælətɪ] *s* Freundlichkeit *f*.

gen·i·tals ['dʒenɪtlz] *s pl* Genitalien *pl*, Geschlechtsteile *pl*.

gen·i·tive ['dʒenɪtɪv] *s a.* **~ case** *ling.* Genitiv *m*, zweiter Fall.

gen·ius ['dʒi:njəs] *s* **1.** Genie *n*: a) genialer Mensch, b) Genialität *f*. **2.** (natürliche) Begabung: **have a ~ for languages** sprachbegabt sein.

gen·o·cide ['dʒenəʊsaɪd] *s* Völkermord *m*.

genre ['ʒɑ̃:rə] *s* Genre *n*, Gattung *f*. **~ paint·ing** *s* Genremalerei *f*.

gent [dʒent] *s* **1.** F *od. humor. für* **gentleman**: **~s' hairdresser** Herrenfriseur *m*. **2.** *pl (sg konstruiert)* Br. F Herrenklo *n*.

gen·teel [dʒen'ti:l] *adj* □ **1.** vornehm. **2.** vornehm tuend, affektiert.

gen·tle ['dʒentl] *adj* □ **1.** freundlich, liebenswürdig. **2.** sanft, zart: **~ hint** zarter Wink; **→ sex** 1. **'~·folk(s)** *s pl* vornehme *od.* feine Leute *pl*.

gen·tle·man ['dʒentlmən] *s (irr man)* **1.** Gentleman *m*: **~ 's** (*od.* **gentlemen's**) **agreement** Gentleman's *od.* Gentlemen's Agreement *n*. **2.** Herr *m*: **gentlemen** (*Anrede*) m-e Herren; (*in Briefen*) Sehr geehrte Herren. **'gen·tleman--like**, **'gen·tle·man·ly** *adj* gentlemanlike.

gen·tle·ness ['dʒentlnɪs] *s* **1.** Freundlichkeit *f*, Liebenswürdigkeit *f*. **2.** Sanftheit *f*, Zartheit *f*.

gen·try ['dʒentrɪ] *s* **1.** Oberschicht *f*. **2.** Br. niederer Adel.

gen·u·ine ['dʒenjʊɪn] *adj* □ **1.** echt: a)

authentisch (*Unterschrift etc*), b) ernsthaft (*Angebot etc*), c) aufrichtig (*Mitgefühl etc*). **2.** natürlich, ungekünstelt (*Lachen*, *Person*).

ge·nus [ˈdʒiːnəs] *pl* **gen·er·a** [ˈdʒenərə] *s* ♀, *zo.* Gattung *f*.

ge·og·ra·pher [dʒiˈɒgrəfə] *s* Geograph(in). **ge·o·graph·ic**, **ge·o·graph·i·cal** [ˌ~əˈgræfɪk(l)] *adj* □ geographisch. **ge·og·ra·phy** [ˌ~ˈɒgrəfɪ] *s* Geographie *f*, Erdkunde *f*.

ge·o·log·ic, **ge·o·log·i·cal** [ˌdʒiəʊˈlɒdʒɪk(l)] *adj* □ geologisch. **ge·ol·o·gist** [ˌ~ˈɒlədʒɪst] *s* Geologe *m*. **ge·ol·o·gy** [~] Geologie *f*.

ge·o·met·ric, **ge·o·met·ri·cal** [ˌdʒiəʊˈmetrɪk(l)] *adj* □ geometrisch. **ge·om·e·try** [ˌ~ˈɒmətrɪ] *s* Geometrie *f*.

ge·ra·ni·um [dʒɪˈreɪnjəm] *s* ♀ Geranie *f*.

ger·i·at·rics [ˌdʒerɪˈætrɪks] *s pl* (*sg konstruiert*) ♂ Geriatrie *f*, Altersheilkunde *f*.

germ [dʒɜːm] *s* **1.** *biol.*, ♀ Keim *m* (*a. fig.*): **in ~** im Keim, im Werden. **2.** ♂ Bazillus *m*, Bakterie *f*, (Krankheits)Erreger *m*.

Ger·man [ˈdʒɜːmən] **I** *adj* **1.** deutsch: **~ measles** *pl* (*sg konstruiert*) ♂ Röteln *pl*. **II** *s* **2.** Deutsche *m*, *f*. **3.** *ling.* Deutsch *n*: **in ~** auf deutsch.

ger·mane [dʒɜːˈmeɪn] *adj*: **~ to** gehörig zu, betreffend (*acc*).

Ger·man·ic [dʒɜːˈmænɪk] *adj* germanisch. **Ger·man·ism** [ˈ~mənɪzəm] *s ling.* Germanismus *m*.

'germ-free *adj* ♂ keimfrei.

ger·mi·nate [ˈdʒɜːmɪneɪt] *v/i u. v/t* keimen (lassen) (*a. fig.*).

germ war·fare *s* ⚔ bakteriologische Kriegführung.

ger·on·tol·o·gy [ˌdʒerɒnˈtɒlədʒɪ] *s* ♂ Gerontologie *f*, Altersforschung *f*.

ger·und [ˈdʒerənd] *s ling.* Gerundium *n*.

ges·ta·tion [dʒeˈsteɪʃn] *s* Schwangerschaft *f*; *zo.* Trächtigkeit *f*: **~ period** Trag(e)zeit *f*.

ges·tic·u·late [dʒeˈstɪkjʊleɪt] *v/i* gestikulieren. **ges·tic·u·la·tion** *s* Gestikulation *f*.

ges·ture [ˈdʒestʃə] *s* Geste *f* (*a. fig.*), Gebärde *f*.

get [get] (*irr*) **I** *v/t* **1.** bekommen, erhalten. **2.** sich *et.* verschaffen *od.* besorgen: **~ s.th. for s.o.** j-m et. besorgen.

3. erringen, erwerben, sich *Wissen etc* aneignen. **4.** erwischen; (*a. telefonisch*) erreichen. **5.** holen. **6.** schaffen, bringen. **7.** machen: **~ s.th. ready** et. fertigmachen. **8.** (*mit pp*) lassen: **~ one's hair cut** sich die Haare schneiden lassen. **9.** *j-n* dazu bringen (**to do** zu tun): **~ s.o. to speak** j-n zum Sprechen bringen. **10.** **~ going** *Maschine etc*, *fig.* Verhandlungen *etc* in Gang bringen; *fig.* Schwung bringen in (*acc*). **11. have got** haben: **have got to** müssen. **12.** F kapieren, (*a. akustisch*) verstehen: **don't ~ me wrong** versteh mich nicht falsch. **II** *v/i* **13.** kommen, gelangen: **~ home** nach Hause kommen. **14.** dahin kommen (**to do** zu tun): **~ to know s.th.** et. erfahren *od.* kennenlernen. **15.** (*mit pp od. adj*) werden: **~ tired** müde werden, ermüden. **16.** beginnen, anfangen (**doing** zu tun): **~ going** in Gang kommen (*Maschine etc*, *fig.* Verhandlungen *etc*); *fig.* in Schwung kommen.

Verbindungen mit Präpositionen:

get| at *v/i* **1.** herankommen an (*acc*), erreichen. **2.** an *j-n* herankommen, *j-m* beikommen. **3. what is he getting at?** worauf will er hinaus? **~ off** *v/i* absteigen von; aussteigen aus. **~ o·ver** *v/i* hinwegkommen über (*acc*), *fig. a.* sich erholen von. **~ through** *v/i* **1.** kommen durch (*e-e Prüfung etc*). **2.** Geld durchbringen. **~ to** *v/i* **1.** kommen nach, erreichen. **2.** **~ talking about** zu sprechen kommen auf (*acc*).

Verbindungen mit Adverbien:

get| a·bout *v/i* **1.** herumkommen. **2.** sich herumsprechen *od.* verbreiten (*Gerücht etc*). **~ a·cross** I *v/t* **1.** verständlich machen; *Idee etc* an den Mann bringen. **II** *v/i* **2.** ankommen; sich verständlich machen. **3.** ankommen, einschlagen; klarwerden (**to s.o.** j-m). **~ a·long** *v/i* **1.** vorwärts-, weiterkommen (*a. fig.*). **2.** auskommen, sich vertragen (**with** mit *j-m*). **3.** zurechtkommen (**with** mit *et.*). **~ a·round** *v/i* **1.** → **get about. 2.** → **get round I.** **~ a·way** *v/i* **1.** loskommen, sich losmachen. **2.** entkommen, -wischen: **~ with** davonkommen mit. **~ back I** *v/t* **1.** zurückbekommen: **get one's own back** F sich rächen; **get one's own back on s.o.** → 3; → **breath** 1. **II** *v/i* **2.** zurückkommen. **3.** **~ at s.o.** F

sich an j-m rächen, es j-m heimzahlen.
~ be·hind v/i in Rückstand kommen
(**with** mit). **~ by** v/i 1. aus-, durchkommen (**on** mit). **2.** gerade noch annehmbar sein (*Arbeit etc*), gerade noch ausreichen (*Kenntnisse*). **~ down** I v/t 1.
Essen etc runterkriegen. II v/i 2. aus-,
absteigen. **3. ~ to** sich machen an (*acc*):
→ **brass tacks, business** 6. **~ in** I v/t 1.
Bemerkung etc anbringen. **2.** *Speziali-
sten etc* (hin)zuziehen. II v/i 3. hinein-,
hereinkommen. **4.** einsteigen. **5. ~ on** F
mitmachen bei. **~ off** v/i 1. (**from**) absteigen (von), aussteigen (aus). **2.** davonkommen (**with** mit). **~ on** v/i 1. vor-
wärts-, vorankommen (*a. fig.*): **he is
getting on for sixty** er geht auf die
Sechzig zu; **it is getting on for 5 o'clock**
es geht auf 5 Uhr (zu). **2.** → **get along**
2, 3. **~ out** I v/t 1. herausbekommen (*a.
fig.*). **2.** *Worte etc* herausbringen. II v/i
3. aussteigen. **4.** *fig.* durchsickern, herauskommen (*Geheimnis etc*). **~ o·ver**
v/t hinter sich bringen. **~ round** I v/t *j-n*
herumkriegen. II v/i dazu kommen (**to
doing** zu tun). **~ through** I v/t 1. durchbringen, -bekommen (*a. fig.*). **2.** → **get
over.** II v/i 3. durchkommen (*a. fig.*). **~
to·geth·er** I v/t 1. *Menschen etc*
zs.-bringen. **2.** zs.-tragen. II v/i 3.
zs.-kommen. **~ up** I v/t 1. *j-n* herausputzen. **2.** *Buch etc* ausstatten, *Waren*
(hübsch) aufmachen. II v/i 3. aufstehen, (*von e-m Stuhl etc a.*) sich erheben.
get·at·a·ble [get'ætəbl] *adj* F 1. erreichbar (*Ort, Sache*). **2.** zugänglich (*Ort,
Person*). **'~·a·way** s Flucht f: **~ car**
Fluchtauto n. **'~·to,geth·er** s F (zwang-
lose) Zs.-kunft: **have a ~** sich treffen,
zs.-kommen. **'~·up** s F Aufmachung f:
a) Ausstattung f, b) Aufzug m (*Kleidung*).
gey·ser s 1. ['gaɪzə] Geysir m. **2.** ['gi:zə]
Br. Durchlauferhitzer m.
ghast·ly ['gɑ:stlɪ] I *adj* 1. gräßlich, entsetzlich (*beide a. fig.* F). **2.** gespenstisch.
II *adv* 3. **~ pale** totenblaß.
gher·kin ['gɜ:kɪn] s Gewürz-, Essiggurke f.
ghet·to ['getəʊ] *pl* **-to(e)s** s G(h)etto n.
~ blast·er s *sl.* Ghetto-Blaster m
(*tragbarer Stereo-Kassettenrecorder*). **~
dwell·er** s G(h)ettobewohner(in).
ghost [gəʊst] s 1. Geist m, Gespenst n. **2.**

give up the ~ den Geist aufgeben. **3.**
fig. Spur f. **'ghost·ly** *adj* geister-, ge-
spensterhaft.
ghost| sto·ry s Geister-, Gespensterge-
schichte f. **~ town** s Geisterstadt f. **~
train** s Geisterbahn f: **go on the ~** Geisterbahn fahren. **~ writ·er** s Ghostwriter m.
gi·ant ['dʒaɪənt] I s Riese m. II *adj* riesig:
~ slalom (*Skisport*) Riesenslalom m.
gib·ber ['dʒɪbə] v/i schnattern (*Affen,
Personen*). **gib·ber·ish** ['~rɪʃ] s Geschnatter n.
gibe [dʒaɪb] v/i: **~ at** (*od. about*) spotten über (*acc*), verhöhnen, -spotten. II
s höhnische Bemerkung.
gib·lets ['dʒɪblɪts] s pl Innereien pl (*vom
Geflügel*).
gid·di·ness ['gɪdɪnɪs] s 1. Schwindel(gefühl n) m. **2.** *fig.* Leichtsinn m. **'gid·dy**
adj □ 1. **I am** (*od. feel*) **~** mir ist
schwind(e)lig. **2.** schwindelerregend (*a.
fig.*). **3.** *fig.* leichtsinnig.
gift [gɪft] I s 1. Geschenk n: **I wouldn't
have it as a ~** das möchte ich nicht
(mal) geschenkt; **at £ 10 it's a ~** für 10
Pfund ist es geschenkt. **2.** *fig.* Begabung f, Talent n (**for, of** für): **~ for
languages** Sprachtalent; → **gab.** II *adj*
3. geschenkt, Geschenk...: **don't look a
~ horse in the mouth** e-m geschenkten
Gaul schaut man nicht ins Maul.
'gift·ed *adj* begabt, talentiert.
gi·gan·tic [dʒaɪ'gæntɪk] *adj* (**~ally**) gigantisch, riesig.
gig·gle ['gɪgl] I v/i kichern. II s Gekicher n.
gild [gɪld] v/t (*a. irr*) 1. vergolden. **2.** *fig.*
versüßen; beschönigen: → **pill** 1.
gill [gɪl] s 1. *ichth.* Kieme f. **2.** ♀ Lamelle f.
gilt [gɪlt] I *pret u. pp von* **gild.** II s Vergol-
dung f: **take the ~ off the gingerbread**
fig. der Sache den Reiz nehmen. **,~-
-'edged** *adj* 1. mit Goldschnitt. **2. ~
securities** pl ✝ mündelsichere (Wert-)
Papiere pl.
gim·crack ['dʒɪmkræk] *adj* 1. wertlos;
kitschig. **2.** wack(e)lig.
gim·mick ['gɪmɪk] s F 1. → **gadget. 2.**
(*bsd.* Reklame)Trick m, (-)Dreh m.
gin [dʒɪn] s Gin m.
gin·ger ['dʒɪndʒə] I s 1. Ingwer m. **2.** F
Schmiß m, Schwung m. II *adj* 3. röt-

lich- *od.* gelblichbraun. **III** *v/t* **4.** mit
Ingwer würzen. **5.** *mst* ~ **up** F *j-n* aufmöbeln, -muntern; *et.* ankurbeln, in
Schwung bringen. ~ **ale** *s* Ginger-ale *n.*
~ **beer** *s* Ginger-beer *n,* Ingwerbier *n.*
'**~bread** *s* Leb-, Pfefferkuchen *m (mit
Ingwergeschmack):* → **gilt** II.

gin·ger·ly ['dʒɪndʒəlɪ] *adj u. adv* **1.** behutsam, vorsichtig. **2.** zimperlich.

gin·gi·vi·tis [ˌdʒɪndʒɪ'vaɪtɪs] *s* ✛ Zahn-
fleischentzündung *f.*

gip·sy ['dʒɪpsɪ] *s* Zigeuner(in).

gi·raffe [dʒɪ'rɑːf] *pl* -'**raffes,** *bsd. coll.*
-'**raffe** *s zo.* Giraffe *f.*

gird·er ['gɜːdə] *s* ⊚ Balken *m,* Träger *m.*

gir·dle ['gɜːdl] *s* **1.** Gürtel *m,* Gurt *m.* **2.**
Hüfthalter *m,* -gürtel *m.*

girl [gɜːl] *s* **1.** Mädchen *n.* **2.** (Dienst-)
Mädchen *n.* '**~friend** *s* Freundin *f
(e-s Jungen).* ~ **guide** *s Br.* Pfadfinderin *f.*

girl·hood ['gɜːlhʊd] *s* Mädchenjahre *pl,*
Jugend(zeit) *f.*

girl·ish ['gɜːlɪʃ] *adj* □ **1.** mädchenhaft. **2.**
Mädchen...: ~ **games.**

girl scout *s Am.* Pfadfinderin *f.*

gi·ro ['dʒaɪərəʊ] *s Br.* Postgirodienst *m:* ~
account Postgirokonto *n;* ~ **cheque**
Postscheck *m.*

girth [gɜːθ] *s* **1.** (a. Körper)Umfang *m.* **2.**
(Sattel-, Pack)Gurt *m.*

gist [dʒɪst] *s das* Wesentliche, Kern *m.*

give [gɪv] (*irr*) **I** *v/t* **1.** geben; schenken;
Blut etc spenden. **2.** geben, reichen: ~
s.o. one's hand j-m die Hand geben. **3.**
Auskunft, Rat *etc* geben, erteilen. **4.**
sein Wort geben. **5.** *Aufmerksamkeit
etc* widmen (*to dat*): → **attention** 2. **6.**
sein Leben hingeben, opfern (*for* für). **7.**
geben, gewähren: ~ *s.o. until* j-m ...
Zeit geben *od.* lassen (*to do* zu tun). **8.**
Befehl, Auftrag etc geben, erteilen. **9.**
Hilfe gewähren, leisten, *Schutz* bieten.
10. *Grüße etc* übermitteln: ~ *him my
love* bestelle ihm herzliche Grüße von
mir. **11.** *j-m e-n Schlag etc* geben, versetzen. **12.** *j-m e-n Blick* zuwerfen. **13.**
Lebenszeichen etc von sich geben: ~ *a
cry* (*od.* **shout**) e-n Schrei ausstoßen,
aufschreien; ~ *a laugh* auflachen. **14.**
Grund etc (an)geben. **15.** *Konzert etc*
geben, veranstalten, *Theaterstück etc*
geben, aufführen, *Vortrag* halten. **16.**
Schmerzen etc bereiten, verursachen.

17. *j-m zu tun etc* geben: *I was ~n to
understand* man gab mir zu verstehen.
II *v/i* **18.** geben, spenden (*to dat*). **19.**
nachgeben (*a. Preise*). **20.** *what ~s? sl.*
was gibt's? **21.** führen (*into in acc;
on*[*to*] auf *acc,* nach) (*Straße etc*);
gehen (*on*[*to*] nach) (*Fenster etc*).
Verbindungen mit Adverbien:

give| a·way *v/t* **1.** her-, weggeben; ver-
schenken: → **bride.** **2.** *j-n, et.* verraten.
3. *Chance etc* vertun. ~ **back** *v/t* **1.**
zurückgeben (*a. fig.*), *Blick* erwidern.
2. *Schall* zurückwerfen; *Licht* etc reflektieren. ~ **in I** *v/t* **1.** *Gesuch etc* einreichen, *Prüfungsarbeit etc* abgeben. **II** *v/i*
2. (*to*) nachgeben (*dat*); sich anschließen (*dat*). **3.** aufgeben, sich geschlagen
geben. ~ **off** *v/t Geruch* verbreiten, ausströmen, *Rauch etc* ausstoßen, *Gas,
Wärme etc* aus-, verströmen. ~ **out I** *v/t*
1. aus-, verteilen. **2.** bekanntgeben. **3.**
give o.s. out to be s.th. sich als et.
ausgeben. **4.** → *give off.* **II** *v/i* **5.** zu
Ende gehen (*Kräfte, Vorräte*). **6.** versagen (*Maschine, Nieren etc*). ~ **o·ver I**
v/t **1.** übergeben (*to dat*). **2.** et. aufgeben: ~ *doing s.th.* aufhören, et. zu tun.
3. *give o.s. over to* sich hingeben (*dat*).
II *v/i* **4.** aufhören. ~ **up I** *v/t* **1.** aufgeben, aufhören mit: ~ *smoking* das Rau-
chen aufgeben. **2.** *Plan, Patienten etc*
aufgeben: → *adoption* 1. **3.** *j-n* ausliefern: *give o.s. up* sich stellen (*to dat*). **4.**
(*to*) *Posten etc* abgeben, abtreten (*an
acc*); *Sitzplatz etc* freimachen (*für*). **5.**
give o.s. up to sich hingeben (*dat*); sich
widmen (*dat*). **II** *v/i* **6.** → *give in* 3. **7.**
resignieren.

,**give-and-'take** *s* **1.** beiderseitiges Entgegenkommen *od.* Nachgeben, Kom-
promiß(bereitschaft *f*) *m.* **2.** Mei-
nungs-, Gedankenaustausch *m.* '**~a-
way I** *s bsd. Am.* Werbegeschenk *n.* **II**
adj: ~ *price* Schleuderpreis *m.*

giv·en ['gɪvn] **I** *pp von* **give.** **II** *adj* **1.**
gegeben: ~ *name bsd. Am.* → *first
name; at the ~ time* zur festgesetzten
Zeit; *within a ~ time* innerhalb e-r bestimmten Zeit. **2.** *be ~ to* neigen zu: ~
to doing s.th. die (An)Gewohnheit
haben, et. zu tun. **3.** vorausgesetzt. **4.** in
Anbetracht (*gen*): ~ *that* in Anbetracht
der Tatsache, daß. '**giv·er** *s* Geber(in),
Spender(in).

gla·cé ['glæseɪ] *adj* **1.** glasiert; kandiert. **2.** Glacé...

gla·cial ['gleɪsjəl] *adj* □ **1.** eiszeitlich: ~ **epoch** (*od.* **era**) Eiszeit *f.* **2.** eisig (*a. fig.*). **gla·cier** ['glæsjə] *s* Gletscher *m.*

glad [glæd] *adj* (□ → **gladly**) **1.** froh, erfreut (*of, about, at* über *acc*): *be* ~ *of* sich freuen über; *I am* ~ *to hear* es freut mich zu hören; *I am* ~ *to go* ich gehe gern. **2.** freudig, froh, erfreulich. **glad·den** ['glædn] *v/t* erfreuen.

glad·i·a·tor ['glædɪeɪtə] *s hist.* Gladiator *m.*

glad·i·o·lus [ˌglædɪ'əʊləs] *pl* **-li** [ˌlaɪ], **-lus·es** *s* ♀ Gladiole *f.*

glad·ly ['glædlɪ] *adv* mit Freuden, gern. **'glad·ness** *s* Freude *f.*

glam·or·ize ['glæmər[aɪz] *v/t* verherrlichen, glorifizieren. **'glam·or·ous** *adj* □ bezaubernd (schön). **glam·our** ['~mə] *s* Zauber *m*, (*contp.* falscher) Glanz: ~ *girl* Glamourgirl *n*, Film-, Reklameschönheit *f.*

glance [glɑːns] **I** *v/i* **1.** e-n (schnellen) Blick werfen, (rasch *od.* flüchtig) blicken (*at* auf *acc*): ~ *over* (*od.* *through*) *a letter* e-n Brief überfliegen; ~ *at a problem* ein Problem streifen. **2.** ~ *off* abprallen (von) (*Kugel etc*), abgleiten (von) (*Messer etc*). **II** *s* **3.** (schneller *od.* flüchtiger) Blick (*at* auf *acc*): *at a* ~ auf 'einen Blick; *at first* ~ auf den ersten Blick; *take a* ~ *at* → 1; → **steal** 1.

gland [glænd] *s anat.* Drüse *f.* **glan·du·lar** ['~djʊlə] *adj* Drüsen...

glare [gleə] **I** *v/i* **1.** grell scheinen (*Sonne etc*), grell leuchten (*Scheinwerfer etc*). **2.** wütend starren: ~ *at s.o.* j-n wütend anstarren, j-n anfunkeln. **II** *s* **3.** greller Schein, grelles Leuchten. **4.** wütender *od.* funkelnder Blick. **glar·ing** ['~rɪŋ] *adj* □ **1.** grell. **2.** grell, schreiend (*Farben*). **3.** eklatant, kraß (*Fehler, Unterschied etc*), (himmel)schreiend (*Unrecht etc*). **4.** wütend, funkelnd (*Blick*).

glass [glɑːs] **I** *s* **1.** Glas *n.* **2.** *coll.* Glas(waren *pl*) *n.* **3.** (Trink)Glas *n*; Glas(gefäß) *n.* **4.** (Fern-, Opern)Glas. **5.** *pl*, *a. pair of ~es* Brille *f.* **II** *adj* **6.** Glas...: ~ *eye.* ~ *blow·er s* Glasbläser *m.* ~ *case s* Glaskasten *m*, Vitrine *f.*

glass·ful ['glɑːsfʊl] *s ein* Glasvoll *n.* **'glass|·house** *s* **1.** *bsd. Br.* Gewächs-, Glas-, Treibhaus *n.* **2.** *people who live*

in ~*s should not throw stones* wer (selbst) im Glashaus sitzt, soll nicht mit Steinen werfen. **'~ware** *s* Glaswaren *pl.*

glass·y ['glɑːsɪ] *adj* □ **1.** gläsern. **2.** glasig (*Augen*).

glau·co·ma [glɔː'kəʊmə] *s* ♣ grüner Star.

glaze [gleɪz] **I** *v/t* **1.** verglasen: ~ *in* einglasen; ~*d veranda* Glasveranda *f.* **2.** ⚙, *a. gastr.* glasieren: ~*d tile* Kachel *f.* **II** *v/i* **3.** *a.* ~ *over* glasig werden (*Augen*). **glaz·ier** ['~jə] *s* Glaser *m.* **'glaz·ing** *s* **1.** Verglasung *f.* **2.** ⚙, *a. gastr.* Glasur *f.*

gleam [gliːm] **I** *s* schwacher Schein, Schimmer *m* (*a. fig.*): ~ *of hope* Hoffnungsschimmer. **II** *v/i* scheinen, schimmern.

glean [gliːn] *v/t fig.* sammeln, zs.-tragen; herausfinden, in Erfahrung bringen: ~ *from* schließen (*od.* entnehmen) aus. **'glean·ings** *s pl das* Gesammelte.

glee [gliː] *s* **1.** Freude *f.* **2.** Schadenfreude *f.* **glee·ful** ['~fʊl] *adj* □ **1.** fröhlich. **2.** schadenfroh.

glib [glɪb] *adj* □ **1.** schlagfertig (*a. Antwort etc*). **2.** oberflächlich.

glide [glaɪd] **I** *v/i* **1.** gleiten. **2.** ✈ gleiten, e-n Gleitflug machen; segelfliegen. **II** *s* **3.** Gleiten *n.* **4.** ✈ Gleitflug *m.* **'glid·er** *s* ✈ a) Segelflugzeug *n*, b) *a.* ~ *pilot* Segelflieger(in). **'glid·ing** *s* ✈ Segelfliegen *n.*

glim·mer ['glɪmə] **I** *v/i* **1.** glimmen. **2.** schimmern. **II** *s* **3.** Glimmen *n.* **4.** Schimmer *m* (*a. fig.*): ~ *of hope* Hoffnungsschimmer.

glimpse [glɪmps] **I** *s* flüchtiger Blick: *catch* (*od.* *get*) *a* ~ *of* → III. **II** *v/i* flüchtig blicken (*at* auf *acc*). **III** *v/t* (nur) flüchtig zu sehen bekommen.

glint [glɪnt] **I** *v/i* glänzen, glitzern. **II** *s* Glanz *m*, Glitzern *n.*

glis·ten ['glɪsn] → **glint.**

glit·ter ['glɪtə] **I** *v/i* **1.** glitzern, funkeln, glänzen: *all that* ~*s is not gold, all is not gold that* ~*s* es ist nicht alles Gold, was glänzt. **II** *s* **2.** Glitzern *n*, Funkeln *n*, Glanz *m.* **3.** *fig.* Glanz *m*, Pracht *f.* **'glit·ter·ing** *adj* □ **1.** glitzernd, funkelnd, glänzend. **2.** *fig.* glänzend, prächtig.

gloat [gləʊt] *v/i* (**over, at**) sich weiden (**an** *dat*): a) verzückt betrachten (*acc*), b) sich hämisch *od.* diebisch freuen (über *acc*). **'gloat·ing** *adj* □ hämisch, schadenfroh.

glob·al ['gləʊbl] *adj* □ global: a) weltumspannend, Welt..., b) umfassend, Gesamt...

globe [gləʊb] *s* **1.** Kugel *f*. **2.** Erde *f*, Erdball *m*, -kugel *f*. **3.** *geogr.* Globus *m*. **'~,trot·ter** *s* Globetrotter(in), Weltenbummler(in).

glob·u·lar ['glɒbjʊlə] *adj* □ kugelförmig: ~ **lightning** Kugelblitz *m*. **glob--ule** ['~ju:l] *s* **1.** Kügelchen *n*. **2.** Tröpfchen *n*.

gloom [glu:m] *s* **1.** Düsterkeit *f*. **2.** *fig.* düstere *od.* gedrückte Stimmung: **throw a ~ over** e-n Schatten werfen auf (*acc*). **'gloom·y** *adj* □ **1.** düster (*a. fig.*). **2.** hoffnungslos: **feel ~ about the future** schwarzsehen.

glo·ri·fi·ca·tion [ˌglɔːrɪfɪˈkeɪʃn] *s* **1.** Verherrlichung *f*. **2.** *eccl.* Lobpreisung *f*. **glo·ri·fied** ['~faɪd] *adj* F besser. **glo·ri--fy** ['~faɪ] *v/t* **1.** verherrlichen, glorifizieren. **2.** *eccl.* lobpreisen. **3.** F aufmotzen. **'glo·ri·ous** *adj* □ **1.** ruhm-, glorreich. **2.** herrlich, prächtig. **3.** *iro.* schön, großartig.

glo·ry ['glɔːrɪ] **I** *s* **1.** Ruhm *m*. **2.** Zier(de) *f*, Stolz *m*. **3.** Herrlichkeit *f*, Glanz *m*. **II** *v/i* **4.** sich freuen, glücklich sein (**in** über *acc*). **5.** sich sonnen (**in** in *dat*). **~ hole** *s* F Rumpelkammer *f*.

gloss¹ [glɒs] *s* Glosse *f*, Erläuterung *f*, Anmerkung *f*.

gloss² [~] **I** *s* **1.** Glanz *m*. **2.** *fig.* (äußerer) Glanz. **II** *v/t* **3.** *mst* ~ **over** beschönigen; vertuschen.

glos·sa·ry ['glɒsərɪ] *s* Glossar *n*.

gloss·y ['glɒsɪ] *adj* □ glänzend: **be ~** glänzen; **~ magazine** Hochglanzmagazin *n*. **II** *s* F Hochglanzmagazin *n*.

glove [glʌv] *s* Handschuh *m*: **fit (s.o.) like a ~** (j-m) wie angegossen passen; *fig.* (zu j-m *od.* auf j-n) ganz genau passen. **~ box, ~ com·part·ment** *s mot.* Handschuhfach *n*. **~ pup·pet** *s* Handpuppe *f*.

glow [gləʊ] **I** *v/i* glühen (*a. fig.* **with** vor *dat*). **II** *s* Glühen *n*, Glut *f* (*beide a. fig.*).

glow·er ['glaʊə] *v/i* finster blicken: ~ **at**

s.o. j-n finster anblicken. **'glow·er·ing** *adj* □ finster.

'glow·worm *s zo.* Glühwürmchen *n*.

glu·cose ['glu:kəʊs] *s* 🜩 Glukose *f*, Traubenzucker *m*.

glue [glu:] **I** *s* Leim *m*; Klebstoff *m*. **II** *v/t* leimen, kleben (**on** auf *acc*; **to** an *acc*): **be ~d to** *fig.* kleben an (*dat*). **'glue·y** *adj* klebrig.

glum [glʌm] *adj* □ bedrückt, niedergeschlagen.

glut [glʌt] **I** *v/t* **1.** übersättigen (*a. fig.*): ~ **o.s. with** (*od.* **on**) sich überessen mit *od.* an (*dat*). **2.** ✝ *Markt* überschwemmen. **II** *s* **3.** ✝ Schwemme *f*.

glu·ti·nous ['glu:tɪnəs] *adj* □ klebrig.

glut·ton ['glʌtn] *s* **1.** Vielfraß *m*. **2.** *fig.* Unersättliche *m, f*: ~ **for books** Leseratte *f*, Bücherwurm *m*; ~ **for work** Arbeitstier *n*. **'glut·ton·ous** *adj* □ gefräßig, unersättlich (*a. fig.*). **'glut·ton·y** *s* Gefräßigkeit *f*, Unersättlichkeit *f* (*a. fig.*).

glyc·er·in(e) ['glɪsərɪn('~riːn)] *s* 🜩 Glyzerin *n*.

G-man ['dʒiːmæn] *s* (*irr* **man**) G-man *m*, FBI-Agent *m*.

gnarled [nɑːld] *adj* **1.** knorrig. **2.** schwielig (*Hände*).

gnash [næʃ] *v/t*: ~ **one's teeth** mit den Zähnen knirschen.

gnat [næt] *s zo.* Br. (Stech)Mücke *f*.

gnaw [nɔː] (*a. irr*) **I** *v/t* **1.** Loch etc nagen (**into** in *acc*). **2.** nagen an (*dat*) (*a. fig.*). **II** *v/i* **3.** nagen (**at** an *dat*) (*a. fig.*).

gnome [nəʊm] *s* Gnom *m*, Zwerg *m* (*beide a. contp. Mensch*).

go [gəʊ] **I** *s pl* **goes 1.** F Schwung *m*, Schmiß *m*. **2. be all the ~** F große Mode sein. **3. it's a ~!** F abgemacht! **4.** F Versuch *m*: **have a ~ at s.th.** et. probieren; **at one ~** auf 'einen Schlag, auf Anhieb. **II** *v/i* (*irr*) **5.** gehen, fahren, reisen (**to** nach): ~ **on foot** zu Fuß gehen; ~ **by plane** (*od.* **air**) mit dem Flugzeug reisen. **6.** (fort)gehen: **I must be ~ing** ich muß gehen *od.* weg. **7.** anfangen: ~**!** (*Sport*) los! **8.** gehen (**to** nach) (*Straße etc*). **9.** sich erstrecken; gehen (**to** bis). **10.** verkehren, fahren (*Bus etc*). **11.** *fig.* gehen: **let it ~ at that** laß es dabei bewenden. **12.** gehen, passen (**into** in *acc*). **13.** (**to**) gehen (an *acc*) (*Preis etc*), zufallen (*dat*) (*Erbe*). **14.** ◉

gehen, laufen, funktionieren (*alle a. fig.*): *keep* (*set*) *s.th. ~ing* et. in Gang halten (bringen); → *get* 10, 16. **15.** werden: ~ *cold*; ~ *blind* erblinden. **16.** (*with*) gehen (mit), sich anschließen (an *acc*): → *tide* 2. **17.** sich halten (*by, on* an *acc*); gehen, sich richten (*on* nach): *~ing by her clothes* ihrer Kleidung nach (zu urteilen). **18.** kursieren, im Umlauf sein (*Gerücht etc*): *the story ~es* es heißt, man erzählt sich. **19.** gehen, -streichen: *one minute to ~* noch eine Minute. **20.** gelten (*for* für): *it ~es without saying* es versteht sich von selbst. **21.** verkauft werden (*at, for* für): → *cake* 1. **22.** dazu beitragen od. dienen (*to do* zu tun): *it ~es to show* dies zeigt, daran erkennt man. **23.** ausgehen, -fallen (*Entscheidung etc*). **24.** (*with*) harmonieren (mit), passen (zu). **25.** lauten (*Worte etc*). **26.** sterben. **27.** (*im pres p mit inf*) *zum Ausdruck e-r Zukunft, bsd.* a) e-r *Absicht,* b) *et. Un-abänderlichen: it is ~ing to rain* es gibt Regen; *she is ~ing to have a baby* sie bekommt ein Kind; *I am ~ing to tell him* ich werde *od.* will es ihm sagen. **28.** (*mit ger*) gehen: ~ *swimming* schwimmen gehen. **29.** (daran)gehen (*to do* zu tun): *he went to find her* er ging sie suchen; *she went to see him* sie besuchte ihn. **III** *v/t* (*irr*) **30.** *Weg, Strecke etc* gehen: ~ *it alone* F es ganz allein machen.

Verbindungen mit Präpositionen:

go| a·bout *v/i* **1.** in Angriff nehmen, sich machen an (*acc*). ~ **af·ter** *v/i* **1.** nachlaufen (*dat*). **2.** sich bemühen um. ~ **a·gainst** *v/i* **1.** *j-m* widerstreben. **2.** *e-m Verbot etc* zuwiderhandeln, sich widersetzen (*dat*). ~ **at** *v/i* **1.** losgehen auf (*acc*). **2.** → *go about*. ~ **be·tween** *v/i* vermitteln zwischen (*dat*). ~ **be·yond** *v/i fig.* überschreiten, hinausgehen über (*acc*). ~ **by** → *go* 17. ~ **for** *v/i* **1.** holen (gehen). **2.** *Spaziergang etc* machen. **3.** a) gelten als *od.* für, b) → *go* 20. ~ **in·to** *v/i* **1.** in die Politik *etc* gehen. **2.** geraten in (*acc*). **3.** (genau) untersuchen *od.* prüfen. ~ **off** *v/i* aufgeben: *have gone off j-n, et.* nicht mehr mögen. ~ **on** *v/i* **1.** → *go* 17. **2.** → *strike* 1. ~ **o·ver** *v/i* **1.** → *go into* 3. **2.** → *go through* 1. ~ **through** *v/i* **1.** durchgehen, -nehmen,

-sprechen. **2.** → *go into* 3. **3.** erleiden, durchmachen; erleben. ~ **with** *v/i* **1.** begleiten. **2.** mit *e-m Mädchen etc* gehen. **3.** → *go* 24. ~ **with·out** *v/i* **1.** auskommen *od.* sich behelfen ohne. **2.** verzichten auf (*acc*).

Verbindungen mit Adverbien:

go| a·bout *v/i* **1.** herumgehen, -fahren, -reisen. **2.** a) → *go* 18, b) umgehen (*Grippe etc*). ~ **a·head** *v/i* **1.** voran-, vorausgehen (*of s.o.* j-m): *~! fig.* nur zu!; ~ **with** *fig.* weitermachen *od.* fortfahren mit. **2.** vorankommen (*Person, Arbeit*). ~ **a·long** *v/i* **1.** weitergehen. **2.** *fig.* weitermachen, fortfahren. **3.** ~ **with** einverstanden sein mit; *j-m* beipflichten. ~ **a·round** *v/i* **1.** → *go about*. **2.** → *go round*. ~ **back** *v/i* **1.** zurückgehen. **2.** (*to*) *fig.* zurückgehen (auf *acc*), zurückreichen (bis). **3.** ~ **on** *fig.* j-n im Stich lassen; *sein Wort etc* nicht halten; *Entscheidung* rückgängig machen. ~ **by** *v/i* vorbeigehen (*a. Chance etc*); vergehen (*Zeit*). ~ **down** *v/i* **1.** hinuntergehen. **2.** untergehen, sinken (*Schiff, Sonne etc*). **3.** → *go back* 2. **4.** (hinunter)rutschen (*Essen*). **5.** *fig.* (*with*) Anklang finden, ankommen (bei); geschluckt werden (von). **6.** zurückgehen, sinken, fallen (*Fieber, Preise etc*), billiger werden. **7.** ~ **in history** in die Geschichte eingehen. **8.** sich im Niedergang befinden. ~ **in** *v/i* **1.** hineingehen. **2.** verschwinden (*Sonne etc*). **3.** ~ **for** sich befassen mit, betreiben, *Sport* treiben; mitmachen (bei), sich beteiligen an (*dat*), *Prüfung* machen; sich einsetzen für; sich begeistern für. ~ **off** *v/i* **1.** fort-, weggehen. **2.** losgehen (*Gewehr etc*). **3.** verfallen, geraten (*in, into* in *acc*): ~ **in a fit** e-n Anfall bekommen. **4.** nachlassen (*Schmerz etc*). **5.** gut *etc* verlaufen. **6.** verderben (*Nahrungsmittel*). ~ **on** *v/i* **1.** weitergehen, -fahren. **2.** angehen (*Licht etc*). **3.** weitermachen, fortfahren (*doing* zu tun; *with* mit): ~ **talking** weiterreden; *he went on to say* sagte er. **4.** weitergehen (*Verhältnisse etc*). **5.** vor sich gehen, passieren, vorgehen. **6.** *it is going on for 5 o'clock* es geht auf 5 Uhr zu; *he is going on for 60* er geht auf die Sechzig zu. ~ **out** *v/i* **1.** hinausgehen. **2.** ausgehen. **3.** ausgehen, erlöschen (*Licht, Feuer*). **4.** in den Streik

treten, streiken: → *strike* 1. ~ **o·ver** *v/i*
1. hinübergehen (*to* zu). 2. *fig.* übergehen (*into* in *acc*). 3. *fig.* übergehen, -treten (*from* von; *to* zu). ~ **round** *v/i* 1. herumgehen (*a. fig.*). 2. (für alle) (aus)reichen: *there are enough chairs to* ~ es sind genügend Stühle da. ~ **through** *v/i* 1. durchgehen, angenommen werden (*Antrag*). 2. ~ **with** durchführen, zu Ende führen. ~ **to·geth·er** *v/i* 1. zs.-passen (*Farben etc*). 2. F miteinander gehen (*Liebespaar*). ~ **up** *v/i* 1. hinaufgehen. 2. steigen (*Fieber etc*), (*Preise a.*) anziehen. 3. ~ *in flames* in Flammen aufgehen; ~ *in smoke* in Rauch aufgehen (u. Flammen) aufgehen; *fig.* in Rauch aufgehen, sich in Rauch auflösen.

goad [gəʊd] *v/t a.* ~ *on* anstacheln (*to do s.th., into doing s.th.* dazu, et. zu tun).

'go·a·head F I *adj* mit Unternehmungsgeist *od.* Initiative. II *s*: *get the* ~ grünes Licht bekommen (*on* für).

goal [gəʊl] *s* 1. Ziel *n* (*a. fig.*). 2. *Sport*: (*a. erzieltes*) Tor: *keep* ~ im Tor stehen, das Tor hüten. ~ **a·re·a** *s Sport*: Torraum *m*. '~**get·ter** *s* Torjäger(in).

goal·ie ['gəʊlɪ] F → *goalkeeper*.

'goal|**keep·er** *s Sport*: Torwart *m*, -mann *m*, -frau *f*, -hüter(in). ~ **kick** *s Fußball*: Abstoß *m*. ~ **line** *s Sport*: Torlinie *f*. ~ **post** *s* Torpfosten *m*.

goat [gəʊt] *s zo.* Ziege *f*: *act* (*od. play*) *the* (*giddy*) ~ *fig.* herumalbern, -kaspern; *get s.o.'s* ~ F j-n auf die Palme bringen. **goat·ee** *s* Spitzbart *m*.

gob·ble ['gɒbl] *v/t mst* ~ *up* verschlingen (*a. fig. Buch etc*), hinunterschlingen.

'go-be·tween *s* Vermittler(in): *act as a* ~ vermitteln.

gob·lin ['gɒblɪn] *s* Kobold *m*.

go·by ['gəʊbaɪ] *s*: *give s.o. the* ~ F j-n schneiden *od.* ignorieren.

'go-cart *s* 1. *bes. Am.* Laufstuhl *m* (*für Kinder*). 2. *bes. Am.* Sportwagen *m* (*für Kinder*). 3. *Sport*: Go-Kart *m*.

god [gɒd] *s* 1. Gott *m*, Gottheit *f*. 2. ♀ *eccl.* Gott *m*: *so help me* ♀! so wahr mir Gott helfe!; *thank* ♀ Gott sei Dank; → *act* 1, *bless* 1, *forbid* 3, *sake*, *willing* 1. '~**child** *s* (*irr child*) Patenkind *n*.

god·dess ['gɒdɪs] *s* Göttin *f* (*a. fig.*).

'god|**fa·ther** *s* Pate *m*: *stand* ~ *to* Pate stehen bei (*a. fig.*). '♀-**fear·ing** *adj* gott-

tesfürchtig. '~**for·sak·en** *adj* contp. gottverlassen. '~**less** *adj* □ gottlos. '~**like** *adj* gottähnlich, göttergleich.

god·ly ['gɒdlɪ] *adj* fromm.

'god|**moth·er** *s* Patin *f*. '~**par·ent** *s* Pate *m*, Patin *f*. '~**send** *s* Geschenk *n* des Himmels.

,go-'get·ter *s* F Draufgänger *m*.

gog·gle ['gɒgl] I *v/i* glotzen: ~ *at s.o.* j-n anglotzen. II *s pl, a.* **pair of** ~**s** Schutzbrille *f*. '~**box** *s Br.* F Glotze *f*, Glotzkiste *f* (*Fernseher*).

go·ing ['gəʊɪŋ] I *s* 1. Boden-, Straßenzustand *m*, (*Pferderennsport*) Geläuf *n*; Tempo *n*. II *adj* 2. ~ *concern* gutgehendes Geschäft. 3. ~, ~, *gone!* (*bei Versteigerungen*) zum ersten, zum zweiten, zum dritten! **,go·ings-'on** *s pl mst b.s.* Treiben *n*, Vorgänge *pl*: *there were strange* ~ es passierten merkwürdige Dinge.

goi·ter, *bsd. Br.* **goi·tre** ['gɔɪtə] *s* ✻ Kropf *m*.

go-kart ['gəʊkɑːt] *s Sport*: Go-Kart *m*.

gold [gəʊld] I *s* Gold *n*: → *glitter* 1. II *adj* golden, Gold... ~ **dig·ger** *s* 1. Goldgräber *m*. 2. F Frau, *die nur hinter dem Geld der Männer her ist.*

gold·en ['gəʊldən] *adj* 1. *mst fig.* golden: ~ *days pl* glückliche Tage *pl*; ~ *opportunity* einmalige Möglichkeit; ~ *wedding* goldene Hochzeit. 2. golden, goldgelb: ~ *hamster zo.* Goldhamster *m*.

'gold|**fish** *s* Goldfisch *m*. ~ **med·al** *s* Goldmedaille *f*. ~ **med·al·(l)ist** *s* Goldmedaillengewinner(in). ~ **mine** *s* Goldgrube *f* (*a. fig.*), -mine *f*, -bergwerk *n*. '~**plat·ed** *adj* vergoldet. '~**smith** *s* Goldschmied(in).

golf [gɒlf] (*Sport*) I *s* Golf(spiel) *n*. II *v/i* Golf spielen. ~ **ball** *s* 1. *Sport*: Golfball *m*. 2. ◎ Kugel-, Schreibkopf *m* (*der Schreibmaschine*). ~ **club** *s* (*Sport*) 1. Golfschläger *m*. 2. Golfclub *m*. ~ **course** *s Sport*: Golfplatz *m*.

golf·er ['gɒlfə] *s Sport*: Golfer(in), Golfspieler(in).

golf links *s pl* (*a. sg konstruiert*) *Sport*: Golfplatz *m*.

Go·li·ath [gəʊ'laɪəθ] *s fig.* Goliath *m*.

gon·do·la ['gɒndələ] *s* Gondel *f*.

gone [gɒn] I *pp von* **go**. II *adj* 1. fort, weg. 2. F verknallt (*on* in *acc*). 3. *she's* *six months* ~ F sie ist im 6. Monat (*schwanger*).

gong [gɒŋ] *s* Gong *m*.

gon·or·rh(o)e·a [ˌgɒnəˈrɪə] *s* 🗲 Tripper *m*.

goo [guː] *s* F **1.** Papp *m*, klebriges Zeug. **2.** Schmalz *m*, sentimentales Zeug.

good [gʊd] **I** *s* **1.** Nutzen *m*, Wert *m*: *for one's own* ~ zu s-m eigenen Vorteil; *what* ~ *is it?* wozu soll das gut sein?; *it is no* ~ *trying* es hat keinen Sinn *od.* Zweck, es zu versuchen. **2.** *das Gute*, Gutes *n*: *do s.o.* ~ j-m Gutes tun; j-m guttun; *be up to no* ~ nichts Gutes im Schilde führen. **3.** *pl* bewegliches Vermögen: *~s and chattels* Hab *n* u. Gut *n*; F Siebensachen *pl*. **4.** *pl* 🗲 Güter *pl*, Ware(n *pl*) *f*: *~s lift* Br. Lastenaufzug *m*; *~s train* Br. Güterzug *m*. **II** *adj* **5.** *allg.* gut: *as* ~ *as* so gut wie, praktisch; *have a* ~ *time* sich (gut) amüsieren; es sich gutgehen lassen. **6.** gut, lieb: *be so* ~ *as to fetch it* sei so gut u. hol es; → *enough* III. **7.** gut, geeignet: *~ for colds* gut gegen *od.* für Erkältungen; ~ *for one's health* gesund. **8.** gut, richtig: *in* ~ *time* zur rechten Zeit, (gerade) rechtzeitig; *all in* ~ *time* alles zu s-r Zeit. **9.** gut, reichlich: *a* ~ *hour* e-e gute Stunde; *a* ~ *many* ziemlich viele. **10.** (*vor adj*) verstärkend: *a* ~ *long time* sehr lange (*Zeit*); ~ *and* ... F ganz schön, mordsmäßig; ~ *and tired* F hundemüde. **11.** gut, triftig (*Grund*). **12.** gut, tüchtig (*at* in *dat*). **,~'by(e)** **I** *s* Abschiedsgruß *m*: *wish s.o.* ~, *say* ~ *to s.o.* j-m auf Wiedersehen sagen, sich von j-m verabschieden. **II** *adj* Abschieds...: *~ kiss.* **III** *int* auf Wiedersehen!, *teleph.* auf Wiederhören! **'~-for-,noth·ing** *adj* **I** nichtsnutzig. **II** *s* Taugenichts *m*, Nichtsnutz *m*. **♀ Fri·day** *s eccl.* Karfreitag *m*. **,~-'hu·mo(u)red** *adj* □ **1.** gutgelaunt. **2.** gutmütig. **,~-'look·ing** *adj* gutaussehend. **,~-'na·tured** *adj* □ gutmütig.

good·ness ['gʊdnɪs] *s* **1.** Güte *f*. **2.** *thank* ~ Gott sei Dank; *(my)* ~!, ~ *gracious!* du m-e Güte!, du lieber Himmel!; → sake.

,good·'tem·pered *adj* □ gutmütig. **,~'will** *s* **1.** gute Absicht, guter Wille: ~ *tour bsd. pol.* Goodwillreise *f*, -tour *f*. **2.** Goodwill *m*: a) guter Ruf (*e-r Instituti-*

on *etc*), b) 🗲 ideeller Firmen- *od.* Geschäftswert.

good·y ['gʊdɪ] **I** *s* F **1.** Bonbon *m*, *n*: *goodies pl* Süßigkeiten *pl*. **2.** Film, TV *etc*: Gute, Held *m*. **3.** Tugendbold *m*. **II** *adj* **4.** F (betont) tugendhaft. **III** *int* **5.** *bsd. Kindersprache*: prima! **'~,good·y** → *goody* 3, 4.

goo·ey ['guːɪ] *adj* F **1.** pappig, klebrig. **2.** schmalzig, sentimental: *~ song* Schnulze *f*.

goof [guːf] F **I** *s* **1.** Schnitzer *m*. **2.** Trottel *m*. **II** *v/t* **3.** *oft ~up* vermasseln. **III** *v/i* **4.** Mist bauen. **'goof·y** *adj* F **1.** vertrottelt. **2.** Br. vorstehend (*Zähne*).

goose [guːs] *pl* **geese** [giːs] *s* **1.** *orn.* Gans *f*: *all his geese are swans* bei ihm ist immer alles besser als bei anderen; *cook s.o.'s* ~ F j-m alles kaputtmachen. **2.** *fig.* (*dumme*) Gans. **~·ber·ry** ['gʊzbərɪ] *s* **1.** ♀ Stachelbeere *f*. **2.** *play* ~ *bsd. Br.* das fünfte Rad am Wagen sein. **~ flesh** *s*, **~ pim·ples** *s pl* Gänsehaut *f*.

goos·(e)y ['guːsɪ] *adj* **1.** *get* ~ e-e Gänsehaut bekommen. **2.** dumm.

Gor·di·an ['gɔːdjən] *adj*: *cut the* ~ *knot fig.* den gordischen Knoten durchhauen.

gore [gɔː] *s* Zwickel *m*, Keil *m*.

gorge [gɔːdʒ] **I** *s* **1.** enge Schlucht. **2.** *it makes my* ~ *rise, my* ~ *rises at it* mir wird übel davon *od.* dabei; mir kommt die Galle dabei hoch. **II** *v/i* **3.** schlemmen: ~ *on* (*od.* *with*) → 5. **III** *v/t* **4.** gierig verschlingen. **5.** ~ *o.s. on* (*od.* *with*) sich vollstopfen mit.

gor·geous ['gɔːdʒəs] *adj* □ **1.** prächtig, prachtvoll (*beide a. fig.* F). **2.** F großartig, wunderbar.

go·ril·la [gəˈrɪlə] *s zo.* Gorilla *m* (*a. fig.* F Leibwächter).

gor·mand·ize ['gɔːməndaɪz] *v/i* schlemmen. **'gor·mand·iz·er** *s* Schlemmer(in).

gor·y ['gɔːrɪ] *adj* □ blutrünstig.

gosh [gɒʃ] *int* F Mensch!, Mann!

,go-'slow *s* ❀ Br. Bummelstreik *m*.

gos·pel, *mst* ♀ ['gɒspl] *s* Evangelium *n* (*a. fig.*): *gospel truth* reine Wahrheit.

gos·sa·mer ['gɒsəmə] *s* **1.** Altweibersommer *m*. **2.** feine Gaze.

gos·sip ['gɒsɪp] **I** *s* **1.** Klatsch *m*, Tratsch *m*: *~ column* Klatschspalte *f*. **2.** Plaude-

rei f, Schwatz m: *have a ~ → 5.* **3.**
Klatschbase f, -maul n. **II** v/i **4.** klatschen, tratschen. **5.** plaudern, schwatzen (*with* mit; *about* über acc).

got [gɒt] pret u. pp von **get.**
Goth·ic ['gɒθɪk] **I** adj (**~ally**) **1.** gotisch. **2.** *~ novel* Schauerroman m. **II** s **3.** △ Gotik f.

got·ten ['gɒtn] Am. pp von **get.**
gou·lash ['gu:læʃ] s gastr. Gulasch n.
gourd [gʊəd] s ♀ Kürbis m.
gour·mand ['gʊəmənd] s Schlemmer m.
gour·met ['gʊəmeɪ] s Feinschmecker m.
gout [gaʊt] s ♂ Gicht f.
gov·ern ['gʌvn] **I** v/t **1.** regieren (a. ling.). **2.** leiten, verwalten. **3.** fig. bestimmen, regeln: *be ~ed by* sich leiten lassen von. **4.** fig. zügeln, beherrschen: *~ o.s.* (od. *one's temper*) sich beherrschen. **II** v/i **5.** regieren. **'gov·ern·ing** adj **1.** regierend, Regierungs... **2.** leitend, Vorstands...: *~ body* Leitung f, Direktion f, Vorstand m. **3.** fig. leitend, bestimmend: *~ idea* Leitgedanke m. **'gov·ern·ment** s **1.** oft ♀ Regierung f: *~ spokesman* Regierungssprecher m; *~ exile* 1. **2.** Regierung(sform) f. **3.** Leitung f, Verwaltung f. **4.** Staat m: *~ monopoly* Staatsmonopol n. **gov·ern·men·tal** [\~'mentl] adj **1.** Regierungs... **2.** Staats..., staatlich. **gov·er·nor** ['gʌvənə] s **1.** Gouverneur m. **2.** Direktor m, Leiter m. **3.** F der Alte: a) alter Herr (*Vater*), b) Chef m (a. *Anrede*).

gown [gaʊn] s **1.** mst in Zssgn Kleid n. **2.** ♣, eccl., univ. Talar m, Robe f.
grab [græb] **I** v/t **1.** (hastig od. gierig) ergreifen, packen. **2.** fig. an sich reißen; *Gelegenheit* beim Schopf ergreifen. **3.** F *Zuhörer etc* packen, fesseln. **II** v/i **4.** *~ at* (gierig od. hastig) greifen nach, schnappen nach. **III** s **5.** (hastiger od. gieriger) Griff: *make a ~ at →* 1, 4. **6.** *be up for ~s* F (für jeden) zu haben od. zu gewinnen sein.
grace [greɪs] s **1.** Anmut f, Grazie f. **2.** Anstand m. **3.** mst pl gute Eigenschaft: *→ saving* 3. **4.** Gunst f, Wohlwollen n: *be in s.o.'s good* (**bad**) *~s* in j-s Gunst stehen (bei j-m in Ungnade sein). **5.** (a. göttliche) Gnade, Barmherzigkeit f. **6.** Tischgebet n: *say ~* das Tischgebet sprechen. **II** v/t **7.** zieren, schmücken.

8. (be)ehren. **grace·ful** ['~fʊl] adj □ **1.** anmutig, graziös. **2.** würde-, taktvoll. **'grace·less** adj □ ungraziös.

gra·cious ['greɪʃəs] **I** adj □ **1.** wohlwollend. **2.** gnädig, barmherzig (*Gott*). **II** int **3.** *good ~!, ~ me!* du m-e Güte!, lieber Himmel!

gra·da·tion [grə'deɪʃn] s Abstufung f.
grade [greɪd] **I** s **1.** Grad m, Stufe f. **2.** ✕ bsd. Am. (Dienst)Grad m. **3.** ♣ Qualität f, Handelsklasse f. **4.** bsd. Am. Steigung f, Gefälle n: *make the ~* fig. es schaffen, Erfolg haben; *~ crossing* schienengleicher (Bahn)Übergang. **5.** ped. Am. Klasse f; Note f, Zensur f. **II** v/t **6.** sortieren, einteilen. **7.** abstufen, staffeln. **~ school** s Am. Grundschule f.
gra·di·ent ['greɪdjənt] s Steigung f, Gefälle n.
grad·u·al ['grædʒʊəl] adj □ allmählich, stufen-, schrittweise: *~ly* a. nach u. nach.
grad·u·ate **I** s ['grædʒʊət] **1.** univ. Hochschulabsolvent(in), Akademiker(in); Graduierte m, f. **2.** Am. Schulabgänger(in). **II** adj ['grædʒʊət] **3.** univ. Akademiker...; graduiert. **III** v/i ['~jʊeɪt] **4.** univ. graduieren. **5.** ped. Am. die Abschlußprüfung bestehen (*from* an dat): *~ from* a. e-e Schule absolvieren. **V** v/t ['~jʊeɪt] **6.** → **grade** 7. **grad·u·a·tion** [,grædʒʊ'eɪʃn] s **1.** Abstufung f, Staffelung f. **2.** univ. Graduierung f. **3.** ped. Am. Absolvieren n (*from* e-r Schule).
graf·fi·ti [grə'fi:tɪ] s pl Wandschmierereien pl.
graft¹ [grɑ:ft] ♂ **I** s Transplantat n. **II** v/t *Gewebe* verpflanzen, transplantieren.
graft² [~] **I** s **1.** *hard ~* Schufterei f. **2.** bsd. Am. Schmiergelder pl. **II** v/i **3.** *~ hard* schuften. **4.** bsd. Am. Schmiergelder zahlen.
grain [greɪn] s **1.** ♀ (Samen-, bsd. Getreide)Korn n. **2.** coll. Getreide n, Korn n. **3.** (Sand- etc)Körnchen n, (-)Korn n: *→ salt* 1. **4.** fig. Spur f: *not a ~ of hope* kein Funke Hoffnung. **5.** Maserung f (*vom Holz*): *it goes* (od. *is*) *against the ~* (*with* [od. *for*] *me*) fig. es geht mir gegen den Strich.
gram [græm] s Gramm n.
gram·mar ['græmə] s Grammatik f: *bad ~* grammatisch falsch; *~ (book)* Grammatik. **gram·mat·i·cal** [grə'mætɪkl]

adj □ grammatisch, Grammatik...

gramme [græm] *s bsd. Br.* Gramm *n.*

gram·o·phone ['græməfəʊn] *s Br.* Plattenspieler *m.*

grand [grænd] **I** *adj* □ **1.** großartig, grandios, prächtig. **2.** groß, bedeutend, wichtig. **3.** Haupt...: **~** *prize*; **~** *total* Gesamt-, Endsumme *f.* **4.** F großartig, glänzend. **II** *s* **5.** ♩ Flügel *m.* **6.** *pl* **grand** *Am. sl.* Riese *m* (*$ 1000*).

gran·dad → **granddad**.

grand·child ['græntʃaild] *s* (*irr child*) Enkelkind *n.* '**~dad** *s* F Opa *m* (*a. alter Mann*), Großpapa *m.* '**~daugh·ter** *s* Enkelin *f.*

gran·deur ['grændʒə] *s* **1.** Pracht *f.* **2.** Größe *f*, Wichtigkeit *f.*

'**grand·fa·ther** *s* Großvater *m:* **~('s) clock** Standuhr *f.*

gran·dil·o·quent [græn'dɪləkwənt] *adj* □ **1.** schwülstig, hochtrabend. **2.** großsprecherisch.

gran·di·ose ['grændɪəʊs] *adj* □ großartig, grandios.

grand·ma ['grænmɑː] *s* F Oma *f*, Großmama *f.* '**~moth·er** *s* Großmutter *f.* '**~pa** *s* F Opa *m*, Großpapa *m.* '**~par·ents** *s pl* Großeltern *pl.* '**~son** *s* Enkel *m.* **~stand** ['grænd~] *s Sport:* Haupttribüne *f.*

gran·ite ['grænɪt] *s geol.* Granit *m.*

gran·ny ['grænɪ] *s* F Oma *f.*

grant [grɑːnt] **I** *v/t* **1.** bewilligen, gewähren. **2.** *Erlaubnis etc* geben, erteilen. **3.** *Bitte etc* erfüllen, *a.* ⚖ *e-m Antrag etc* stattgeben. **4.** ⚖ (*bsd. formell*) übertragen, übereignen. **5.** zugeben, zugestehen: *I* **~** *you that* ich gebe zu, daß; *take s.th. for* **~***ed et.* als erwiesen *od.* gegeben ansehen; *et.* als selbstverständlich betrachten *od.* hinnehmen. **II** *s* **6.** Bewilligung *f*, Gewährung *f.* **7.** Stipendium *n.* **8.** ⚖ Übertragung *f*, Übereignung *f.*

gran·u·lar ['grænjʊlə] *adj* gekörnt, körnig, granuliert. **gran·u·lat·ed** ['~leɪtɪd] *adj* → **granular:** **~** *sugar* Kristallzucker *m.* **gran·ule** ['~juːl] *s* Körnchen *n.*

grape [greɪp] *s* Weintraube *f*, -beere *f.* '**~fruit** *s* ♣ Grapefruit *f*, Pampelmuse *f.* **~** *juice s* Traubensaft *m.* **~** *sug·ar s* Traubenzucker *m.* '**~vine** *s* **1.** ♣ Weinstock *m.* **2.** *I heard on the* **~** *that* F mir ist zu Ohren gekommen, daß.

graph [græf] **I** *s* **1.** Diagramm *n*, Schaubild *n*, graphische Darstellung. **2.** *bsd.* & Kurve *f:* **~** *paper* Millimeterpapier *n.* **II** *v/t* **3.** graphisch darstellen. '**graph·ic** *adj* (**~***ally*) **1.** anschaulich, plastisch. **2.** graphisch: **~** *artist* Graphiker(in); **~** *arts pl* Graphik *f.*

graph·ite ['græfaɪt] *s min.* Graphit *m.*

graph·ol·o·gist [græ'fɒlədʒɪst] *s* Graphologe *m.* **graph·ol·o·gy** *s* Graphologie *f.*

grap·ple ['græpl] *v/i:* **~** *with* kämpfen mit, *fig. a.* sich herumschlagen mit.

grasp [grɑːsp] **I** *v/t* **1.** packen, (er)greifen, *Gelegenheit* ergreifen; an sich reißen. **2.** *fig.* verstehen, begreifen. **II** *v/i* **3.** zugreifen, zupacken: **~** *at* greifen nach (*a. fig.*). **III** *s* **4.** Griff *m.* **5.** Reichweite *f* (*a. fig.*). **6.** *fig.* Verständnis *n: be beyond s.o.'s* **~** über j-s Verstand gehen.

grass [grɑːs] **I** *s* **1.** ♣ Gras *n: hear the* **~** *grow fig.* das Gras wachsen hören; *not let the* **~** *grow under one's feet fig.* keine Zeit verschwenden; *keep off the* **~** Betreten des Rasens verboten! **3.** *sl.* Gras(s) *n* (*Marihuana*). **4.** *Br. sl.* Spitzel *m.* **II** *v/i* **5.** grasen, weiden. **6.** *Br. sl.* singen (*to* bei): **~** *on j-n* verpfeifen. **~** *blade s* Grashalm *m.* '**~hop·per** *s zo.* Heuschrecke *f*, Grashüpfer *m.* **~** *roots s pl* (*a. sg konstruiert*) **1.** *fig.* Wurzel *f: attack a problem at the* **~** ein Problem an der Wurzel packen. **2.** *pol.* Basis *f* (*e-r Partei*). **~** *snake s zo.* Ringelnatter *f.* **~** *wid·ow s* Strohwitwe *f.* **~** *wid·ow·er s* Strohwitwer *m.*

grass·y ['grɑːsɪ] *adj* grasbedeckt, Gras...

grate¹ [greɪt] **I** *s* **1.** Gitter *n.* **2.** (Feuer)Rost *m.* **II** *v/t* **3.** vergittern.

grate² [~] **I** *v/t* **1.** *Käse etc* reiben, *Gemüse etc a.* raspeln. **2.** knirschen *od.* kratzen *od.* quietschen mit. **3.** *et.* krächzen(d sagen). **II** *v/i* **4.** knirschen; kratzen; quietschen. **5.** *fig.* weh tun (*on s.o.* j-m): **~** *on s.o.'s ears* j-m in den Ohren weh tun.

grate·ful ['greɪtfʊl] *adj* □ dankbar (*to s.o. for s.th.* j-m für et.).

grat·er ['greɪtə] *s* Reibe *f*, Reibeisen *n*, Raspel *f.*

grat·i·fi·ca·tion [ˌgrætɪfɪ'keɪʃn] *s* **1.** Befriedigung *f*, Genugtuung *f* (*at* über *acc*). **2.** Freude *f*, Genuß *m.* **grat·i·fy**

['faɪ] v/t **1.** j-n, Verlangen etc befriedigen. **2.** erfreuen: **be gratified** sich freuen (**at** über acc); **I am gratified to hear** ich höre mit Befriedigung od. Genugtuung. **'grat·i·fy·ing** adj □ erfreulich (**to** für).

grat·ing ['greɪtɪŋ] s Gitter(werk) n.

gra·tis ['greɪtɪs] **I** adv gratis, umsonst. **II** adj unentgeltlich, Gratis...

grat·i·tude ['grætɪtjuːd] s Dankbarkeit f: **in** ~ **for** aus Dankbarkeit für.

gra·tu·i·tous [grə'tjuːɪtəs] adj □ **1.** → **gratis** II. **2.** freiwillig. **3.** grundlos, unbegründet. **gra'tu·i·ty** s **1.** Zuwendung f, Gratifikation f. **2.** Trinkgeld n.

grave² [~] s Grab n: **dig one's own** ~ sich sein eigenes Grab schaufeln; **turn (over) in one's** ~ sich im Grab (her)umdrehen. '~**dig·ger** s Totengräber m (a. fig.).

grav·el ['grævl] **I** s Kies m. **II** v/t pret u. pp -**eled,** bsd. Br. -**elled** mit Kies bestreuen: ~(l)**ed path** Kiesweg m. ~ **pit** s Kiesgrube f.

'grave·stone s Grabstein m. '~**yard** s Friedhof m.

grav·i·tate ['grævɪteɪt] v/i: ~ **toward(s)** sich hingezogen fühlen zu, neigen zu. ,**grav·i'ta·tion** s phys. Gravitation f, Schwerkraft f. ,**grav·i'ta·tion·al** adj phys. Gravitations...: ~ **force** Schwerkraft f; ~ **pull** Anziehungskraft f.

grav·i·ty ['grævətɪ] s **1.** Ernst m. **2.** phys. Gravitation f, Schwerkraft f: → **centre** 1, **force** 1, **specific** 1.

gra·vy ['greɪvɪ] s **1.** Braten-, Fleischsaft m. **2.** (Braten)Soße f. ~ **boat** s Soßenschüssel f.

gray, etc Am. → **grey,** etc.

graze¹ [greɪz] v/i weiden, grasen.

graze² [~] **I** v/t **1.** streifen. **2.** das Knie etc (ab-, auf)schürfen od. (auf)schrammen. **II** s **3.** Abschürfung f, Schramme f. **4.** a. grazing shot Streifschuß m.

grease [s griːs] **I** s **1.** (zerlassenes) Fett. **2.** ⊙ Schmierfett n, Schmiere f. **II** v/t [griːz] **3.** (ein)fetten, ⊙ (ab)schmieren: **like** ~**d lightning** F wie ein geölter Blitz; → **palm¹** 1. **greas·y** ['griːzɪ] adj □ fett(ig).

great [greɪt] adj (□ → **greatly**) **1.** groß,

beträchtlich: **a** ~ **many** sehr viele. **2.** groß, bedeutend, wichtig. **3.** ausgezeichnet, großartig. **4.** F **be** ~ **at** gut od. groß sein in (dat); **be** ~ **on** sich begeistern für. **5.** F großartig, herrlich. ,~'**grand·child** s (irr **child**) Urenkel(in). ,~'**grand,daugh·ter** s Urenkelin f. ,~'**grand,fa·ther** s Urgroßvater m. ,~'**grand,moth·er** s Urgroßmutter f. ,~'**grand,par·ents** s pl Urgroßeltern pl. ,~'**grand·son** s Urenkel m.

great·ly ['greɪtlɪ] adv sehr, überaus. '**great·ness** s Größe f, Bedeutung f.

greed [griːd] s **1.** Gier f (**for** nach): ~ **for power** Machtgier. **2.** Habgier f, -sucht f. **3.** Gefräßigkeit f. '**greed·i·ness** s **1.** Gierigkeit f. **2.** Gefräßigkeit f. '**greed·y** adj □ **1.** gierig (**for** auf acc, nach): ~ **for power** machtgierig. **2.** habgierig, -süchtig. **3.** gefräßig.

Greek [griːk] **I** s **1.** Grieche m, Griechin f. **2.** ling. Griechisch n: **that's** ~ **to me** fig. das sind für mich böhmische Dörfer. **II** adj **3.** griechisch.

green [griːn] **I** adj □ **1.** grün: **have** ~ **fingers** fig. e-e grüne Hand haben; **the lights are** ~ die Ampel steht auf Grün; **give s.o. the** ~ **light** fig. j-m grünes Licht geben (**on, to** für); ~ **with envy** grün od. gelb vor Neid. **2.** fig. grün, unerfahren. **II** s **3.** Grün n: **dressed in** ~ grün od. in Grün gekleidet; **at** ~ bei Grün; **the lights are at** ~ die Ampel steht auf Grün. **4.** pl grünes Gemüse. '~,**gro·cer** s bsd. Br. Obst- u. Gemüsehändler m. '~**horn** s F Grünschnabel m; Neuling m. '~**house** s Gewächs-, Treibhaus n.

green·ish ['griːnɪʃ] adj grünlich.

Green·wich (Mean) Time ['grenɪdʒ] s Greenwicher Zeit f.

greet [griːt] v/t **1.** grüßen. **2.** begrüßen, empfangen. **3.** Nachricht etc aufnehmen. '**greet·ing** s **1.** Gruß m, Begrüßung f. **2.** pl Grüße pl; Glückwünsche pl: ~**s card** Glückwunschkarte f. **3.** Am. Anrede f (im Brief).

gre·gar·i·ous [grɪ'geərɪəs] adj □ **1.** gesellig. **2.** zo. in Herden lebend, Herden...

gre·nade [grə'neɪd] s ✕ (Hand-, Gewehr)Granate f.

grew [gruː] pret von **grow.**

grey [greɪ] bsd. Br. **I** adj □ **1.** grau: ~

area Grauzone *f;* ~ *eminence* graue Eminenz; ~ *matter anat.* graue Substanz; F Grips *m.* **2.** grau(haarig), ergraut. **3.** *fig.* trüb, düster, grau: ~ *prospects pl* trübe Aussichten *pl.* **II** *s* **4.** Grau *n: dressed in* ~ grau *od.* in Grau gekleidet. **III** *v/i* **5.** grau werden, ergrauen; ~*ing* angegraut, graumeliert (*Haare*). ,~·**'haired** *adj* grauhaarig. '~·**hound** *s zo.* Windhund *m.*

grey·ish ['greiʃ] *adj* grau-, gräulich.

grid [grid] *s* **1.** Gitter *n,* (Eisen)Rost *m.* **2.** *≠ etc* Versorgungsnetz *n.* **3.** *geogr.* Gitter(netz) *n* (*auf Karten*). **4.** Bratrost *m.*

grid·dle ['gridl] *s* (rundes) Backblech.

'**grid,i·ron** *s* Bratrost *m.*

grief [gri:f] *s* Gram *m,* Kummer *m: come to* ~ zu Schaden kommen; fehlschlagen, scheitern.

griev·ance ['gri:vns] *s* **1.** Beschwerde(grund *m*) *f;* Mißstand *m.* **2.** *nurse a* ~ *against* e-n Groll hegen gegen. **grieve** **I** *v/t* betrüben, bekümmern. **II** *v/i* bekümmert sein, sich grämen (*at, about, over über acc,* wegen): ~ *for* trauern um. '**griev·ous** *adj* □ **1.** schmerzlich, bitter. **2.** schwer, schlimm (*Fehler, Verlust etc*): ~ *bodily harm ⚖ Br.* schwere Körperverletzung.

grill [gril] **I** *s* **1.** Grill *m.* **2.** Grillen *n.* **3.** Gegrillte *n: a* ~ *of meat* gegrilltes Fleisch. **4.** Grillroom *m.* **II** *v/t* **5.** grillen. **6.** ~ *o.s.* → **9. 7.** F *j-n* in die Mange nehmen (*bsd. Polizei*): ~ *s.o. about j-n* ausquetschen über (*acc*). **III** *v/i* **8.** gegrillt werden. **9.** sich (*in der Sonne*) grillen (*lassen*).

grille [gril] *s* **1.** (Schalter-, Sprech)Gitter *n.* **2.** *mot.* (Kühler)Grill *m.*

grill-room ['~rʊm] *s* Grillroom *m.*

grim [grim] *adj* □ **1.** grimmig. **2.** erbittert, verbissen. **3.** hart, unerbittlich. **4.** grausig.

gri·mace [gri'meis] **I** *s* Grimasse *f.* **II** *v/i* e-e Grimasse *od.* Grimassen schneiden.

grime [graim] **I** *s* (dicker) Schmutz *m.* Ruß. **II** *v/t* beschmutzen. '**grim·y** *adj* □ schmutzig, rußig.

grin [grin] **I** *v/i* grinsen: ~ *at s.o. j-n* angrinsen; ~ *and bear it* gute Miene zum bösen Spiel machen. **II** *s* Grinsen *n.*

grind [graind] **I** *v/t* (*irr*) **1.** Messer etc schleifen; → *ax(e)* 1. **2.** *a.* ~ *down*

(zer)mahlen, zerreiben, -kleinern. **3.** *Kaffee etc* mahlen; *Fleisch* durchdrehen. **4.** ~ *one's teeth* mit den Zähnen knirschen. **II** *v/i* (*irr*) **5.** knirschen. **6.** F schuften; pauken, büffeln (*for* für). **III** *s* **7.** Knirschen. **8.** F Schufterei *f;* Pauken *n,* Büffeln *n.* '**grind·er** *s* **1.** (*Messer etc*)Schleifer *m.* **2.** (*Kaffee*)Mühle *f;* (*Fleisch*)Wolf *m.* **3.** *anat.* Backenzahn *m.*

'**grind·stone** *s* Schleifstein *m: keep* (*od.* have) *one's nose to the* ~ *fig.* schuften.

grip [grip] **I** *s* **1.** Griff *m: come* (*od.* get) *to* ~*s with* aneinandergeraten mit; *fig.* sich auseinandersetzen mit. **2.** *fig.* Herrschaft *f,* Gewalt *f: have* (*od.* keep) *a* ~ *on et.* in der Gewalt haben, *Zuhörer etc* fesseln. ~ *on et.* (a.) ~ *of Koffers etc*). **II** *v/t* (*Am. a. irr*) **4.** ergreifen, packen. **5.** *fig. j-n* packen (*Furcht etc*), *Zuhörer etc* fesseln.

gripe [graip] **I** *v/t* **1.** *Am.* F ärgern. **II** *v/i* **2.** Bauchschmerzen haben. **3.** F (*about*) meckern (über *acc*), nörgeln (an *dat,* über *acc*): ~ *at j-n* anmeckern. **III** *s* **4.** *mst pl* Bauchschmerzen *pl.*

'**grip·ping** ['gripiŋ] *adj* □ packend, fesselnd.

gript [gript] *Am. pret u. pp von* **grip.**

gris·ly ['grizli] *adj* gräßlich, schrecklich.

grist [grist] *s* Mahlgut *n: all is* ~ *that comes to his mill fig.* er weiß aus allem Kapital zu schlagen.

gris·tle ['grisl] *s* Knorpel *m.* '**gris·tly** *adj* knorp(e)lig.

grit [grit] **I** *s* **1.** (grober) Sand, Kies *m.* **2.** Streusand *m.* **3.** *fig.* Mut *m.* **II** *v/t* **4.** *Straße etc* sanden, streuen. **5.** ~ *one's teeth* die Zähne zs.-beißen (*a. fig.*).

griz·zle ['grizl] *v/i Br.* F **1.** quengeln. **2.** sich beklagen (*about* über *acc*).

griz·zly ['grizli] **I** *adj* grau(haarig). **II** *s a.* ~ *bear zo.* Grizzly(bär) *m.*

groan [grəʊn] **I** *v/i* **1.** stöhnen, ächzen (*with* vor *dat; fig. under* unter *dat*). **2.** ächzen, knarren (*under* unter *dat*) (*Fußboden etc*). **II** *s* **3.** Stöhnen *n,* Ächzen *n.*

groats [grəʊts] *s pl* Hafergrütze *f.*

gro·cer ['grəʊsə] *s* Lebensmittelhändler *m.* '**gro·cer·y** *s* **1.** Lebensmittelgeschäft *n.* **2.** *pl* Lebensmittel *pl.*

grog [grɒg] *s* Grog *m.*

grog·gy ['grɒgɪ] *adj* F **1.** groggy (*a. Boxen*). **2.** wacklig (*Tisch etc*).

groin [grɔɪn] *s anat.* Leiste(ngegend) *f*.

groom [gru:m] **I** *s* **1.** Pferdepfleger *m*, Stallbursche *m.* **2.** Bräutigam *m.* **II** *v/t* **3.** *Pferde* versorgen, pflegen. **4.** *Person, Kleidung* pflegen.

groove [gru:v] **I** *s* **1.** Rinne *f*, Furche *f*. **2.** ⚙ Rille *f* (*a. e-r Schallplatte*), Nut *f*. **3.** *fig.* ausgefahrenes Gleis. **II** *v/t* ⚙ rillen, nuten.

grope [grəʊp] **I** *v/i* tasten (**for** nach): ~ **about** (*od.* **around**) herumtappen, -tasten; ~ **in the dark** *fig.* im dunkeln tappen. **II** *v/t*: ~ **one's way** sich vorwärtstasten.

gross [grəʊs] **I** *adj* □ **1.** Brutto...: ~ **national product** Bruttosozialprodukt *n.* **2.** schwer, grob (*Fehler etc*), schreiend (*Ungerechtigkeit*), stark, maßlos (*Übertreibung*): ~ **negligence** ⚖ grobe Fahrlässigkeit. **3.** unfein, derb. **4.** dick, feist. **II** *s* **5.** *das Ganze:* **in (the)** ~ im ganzen. **6.** *pl* **gross** Gros *n* (*12 Dutzend*). **III** *v/t* **7.** brutto verdienen *od.* einnehmen.

gro·tesque [grəʊ'tesk] *adj* □ grotesk.

grot·to ['grɒtəʊ] *pl* **-to(e)s** *s* Grotte *f*.

grouch [graʊtʃ] F **I** *v/i* (**about**) nörgeln (an *dat*, über *acc*), meckern (über *acc*). **II** *s* Nörgler(in). '**grouch·y** *adj* □ F nörglerisch.

ground¹ [graʊnd] *I pret u. pp von* **grind**. **II** *adj* gemahlen (*Kaffee etc*): ~ **meat** Hackfleisch *n*.

ground² [~] **I** *s* **1.** (Erd)Boden *m*, Erde *f*: **above** ~ oberirdisch; ⚒ über Tage; **below** ~ ⚒ unter Tage; **break new** (*od.* **fresh**) ~ Land urbar machen, *a. fig.* Neuland erschließen; **fall to the** ~ zu Boden fallen; *fig.* sich zerschlagen, ins Wasser fallen. **2.** Boden *m*, Gebiet *n* (*a. fig.*): **on German** ~ auf deutschem Boden; **gain** ~ (an) Boden gewinnen, *fig. a.* um sich fassen. **3.** Grundbesitz *m. 4. oft pl Sport:* Platz *m.* **5.** *fig.* Standpunkt *m:* **hold** (*od.* **stand**) **one's** ~ sich *od.* s-n Standpunkt behaupten. **6.** *pl* (Beweg)Grund *m:* **on the** ~**(s) of** auf Grund von (*od. gen*); **on** ~**s of age** aus Altersgründen; **on the** ~**(s) that** mit der Begründung, daß. **7.** *pl* (Boden)Satz *m*. **8.** ⚡ *Am.* Erde *f*, Erdung *f*. **II** *v/t* **9.** gründen, stützen (**on, in** auf *acc*): ~**ed**

in fact auf Tatsachen beruhend. **10.** ✈ Startverbot erteilen (*dat*). **11.** ⚡ *Am.* erden. **III** *v/i* **12.** ⚓ auflaufen.

'**ground**|**-break·ing** *adj* bahnbrechend, wegweisend. ~ **ca·ble** *s* ⚡ *Am.* Massekabel *n.* ~ **crew** *s* ✈ Bodenpersonal *n.* ~ **floor** *s* Erdgeschoß *n.* ~ **fog** *s* Bodennebel *m.* ~ **frost** *s* Bodenfrost *m.*

ground·less ['graʊndlɪs] *adj* □ grundlos, unbegründet.

'**ground**|**nut** *s* ♣ Erdnuß *f.* ~ **plan** *s* △ Grundriß *m.* ~ **staff** *s* ✈ *Br.* Bodenpersonal *n.* ~ **sta·tion** *s* Raumfahrt: Bodenstation *f.* ~ **wa·ter** *s* Grundwasser *n.* '~**,wa·ter lev·el** *s* Grundwasserspiegel *m.* '~**work** *s* △ Fundament *n* (*a. fig.*).

group [gru:p] **I** *s* **1.** Gruppe *f:* ~ **of islands** Inselgruppe. **2.** ✝ Gruppe *f*, Konzern *m.* **II** *v/t* **3.** eingruppieren (**into** in *acc*). **4.** zu e-r Gruppe zs.-stellen. **III** *v/i* **5.** sich gruppieren. ~ **dynam·ics** *s pl* (*sg konstruiert*) *Sozialpsychologie:* Gruppendynamik *f.* ~ **sex** *s* Gruppensex *m.* ~ **ther·a·py** *s* ✚, *psych.* Gruppentherapie *f.*

grouse [graʊs] → **grouch** I.

grove [grəʊv] *s* Wäldchen *n*, Gehölz *n*.

grov·el ['grɒvl] *v/i pret u. pp* **-eled**, *bsd. Br.* **-elled:** ~ **before** (*od.* **to**) *s.o. fig.* vor j-m kriechen. '**grov·el·(l)er** *s* Kriecher *m.* '**grov·el·(l)ing** *adj* □ kriecherisch.

grow [grəʊ] (*irr*) **I** *v/i* **1.** wachsen: ~ **up** auf-, heranwachsen; ~ **out of** a) herauswachsen aus (*e-m Kleidungsstück*), b) e-r *Angewohnheit etc* entwachsen. **2.** *fig.* zunehmen (**in** an *dat*), anwachsen. **3.** *fig.* (*bsd.* allmählich) werden: ~ **less** sich vermindern. **II** *v/t* **4.** *Gemüse etc* anbauen, anpflanzen, *Blumen etc* züchten. **5.** ~ **a beard** sich e-n Bart wachsen lassen. '**grow·er** *s* Pflanzer *m*, Züchter *m*, **in** *Zssgn* ...bauer *m*.

growl [graʊl] **I** *v/i* **1.** knurren (*Hund*), brummen (*Bär*) (*beide a. Person*): ~ **at** j-n anknurren. **2.** (g)rollen (*Donner*). **II** *v/t* **3.** *oft* ~ **out** *Worte* knurren, brummen. **III** *s* **4.** Knurren *n*, Brummen *n.* **5.** (G)Rollen *n.*

grown [grəʊn] *pp von* **grow**. '~**-up I** *adj* [*a.* ~'ʌp] **1.** erwachsen. **2.** (nur) für Erwachsene; Erwachsenen... **II** *s* **3.** Erwachsene *m*, *f*.

growth [grəʊθ] *s* **1.** Wachsen *n*, Wachstum *n.* **2.** Wuchs *m*, Größe *f.* **3.** *fig.*

Zunahme f, Anwachsen n (**in** gen). **4.** Anbau m. **5.** 🐾 Gewächs n, Wucherung f. **~in·dus·try** s ⚕ Wachstumsindustrie f. **~ rate** s ⚕ Wachstumsrate f.

grub [grʌb] **I** v/i **1.** graben. **2.** stöbern, wühlen (**among, in** in dat; **for** nach). **II** v/t **3.** oft **~ up** (od. **out**) ausgraben, fig. a. aufstöbern. **III** s **4.** zo. Made f, Larve f. **5.** sl. Futter n (Essen).

'**grub·by** adj schmudd(e)lig, schmutzig.

grudge [grʌdʒ] **I** v/t **1.** mißgönnen (**s.o. s.th.** j-m et.). **2.** **~ doing s.th.** et. nur widerwillig od. ungern tun. **II** s **3.** Groll m: **bear s.o. a ~** e-n Groll auf j-n haben. '**grudg·ing** adj □ **1.** mißgünstig. **2.** widerwillig.

gru·el ['grʊəl] s Haferschleim m. '**gru·el·(l)ing** adj fig. aufreibend, zermürbend.

grue·some ['gru:səm] adj □ grausig, schauerlich.

gruff [grʌf] adj □ **1.** schroff, barsch. **2.** rauh (Stimme).

grum·ble ['grʌmbl] **I** v/i **1.** murren (**at, about, over** über acc). **2.** → growl 2. **II** v/t **3.** oft **~ out** et. murren. **III** s **4.** Murren n. **5.** → growl 5.

grump·y ['grʌmpɪ] adj □ mißmutig, mürrisch.

grunt [grʌnt] **I** v/i **1.** grunzen (Schwein, a. Person). **2.** murren, brummen (**at** über acc). **II** v/t **3.** oft **~ out** et. grunzen, murren, brummen. **III** s **4.** Grunzen n.

guar·an·tee [ˌɡærən'tiː] **I** s **1.** Garantie f (**on** auf acc, für): **the watch is still under ~** auf der Uhr ist noch Garantie. **2.** (**card**) Garantiekarte f, -schein m. **2.** Kaution f, Sicherheit f. **3.** Bürge m, Bürgin f, Garant(in). **II** v/t **4.** (sich ver)bürgen für, Garantie leisten für. **5.** garantieren. **guar·an·tor** [ˌ~'tɔː] → guarantee 3.

guard [gɑːd] **I** v/t **1.** bewachen, wachen über (acc); behüten, beschützen (**against, from** vor dat): **a closely ~ed secret** ein streng gehütetes Geheimnis. **2.** bewachen, beaufsichtigen. **3.** sich hüten (**against** vor dat). **III** s **4.** Wache f, (Wach)Posten m, Wächter m; Aufseher m, Wärter m. **5.** Wache f, Bewachung f: **be on ~** Wache stehen; **keep ~ over** et. bewachen. **6.** 🚂 Br. Schaffner m; Am. Bahnwärter m. **7.**

Garde f: **~ of hono(u)r** Ehrengarde. **8.** fig. Wachsamkeit f: **be on (off) one's ~** (nicht) auf der Hut sein (**against** vor dat). **9.** Boxen etc: Deckung f. **~ dog** s Wachhund m. **~ du·ty** s Wachdienst m: **be on ~** Wache haben.

guard·ed ['gɑːdɪd] adj □ vorsichtig, zurückhaltend, (Optimismus) verhalten, gedämpft.

guard·i·an ['gɑːdjən] s **1.** Hüter m, Wächter m: **~ angel** Schutzengel m. **2.** 🔏 Vormund m. '**guard·i·an·ship** s 🔏 Vormundschaft f (**of** über acc, für): **be (place) under ~** unter Vormundschaft stehen (stellen).

'**guard·rail** s **1.** Handlauf m. **2.** mot. Leitplanke f. **~ rope** s Absperrseil n.

guards·man ['gɑːdzmən] s (irr man) ✕ Gardist m.

gue(r)·ril·la [ɡə'rɪlə] s ✕ Guerilla m: **war(fare)** Guerillakrieg m.

guess [ɡes] **I** v/t **1.** schätzen (**at** auf acc). **2.** (er)raten. **3.** ahnen, vermuten. **4.** bsd. Am. F glauben, meinen, annehmen. **II** v/i **5.** schätzen (**at s.th.** et.). **6.** raten: **~ing game** Ratespiel n. **III** s **7.** Schätzung f, Vermutung f: **at a ~** schätzungsweise; **I'll give you three ~es** dreimal darfst du raten; → educated 2, rough 5, wild 5. '**~work** s (reine) Vermutung(en pl).

guest [ɡest] **I** s Gast m. **II** adj a) Gast...: **~ speaker** Gastredner m, b) Gäste...: **~ list.** '**~house** s **1.** Gästehaus n. **2.** Pension f, Fremdenheim n. **~ room** s Gast-, Gäste-, Fremdenzimmer n.

guf·faw [ɡʌ'fɔː] **I** s schallendes Gelächter. **II** v/i schallend lachen.

guid·ance ['gaɪdns] s **1.** Leitung f, Führung f. **2.** Anleitung f, Unterweisung f: **for your ~** zu Ihrer Orientierung. **3.** (Berufs-, Ehe- etc)Beratung f.

guide [gaɪd] **I** v/t **1.** j-n führen, j-m den Weg zeigen. **2.** fig. lenken, leiten. **3.** et., a. j-n bestimmen: **be ~d by** sich leiten lassen von. **4.** anleiten. **II** s **5.** (Reise-, Berg- etc)Führer m. **6.** (Reise- etc)Führer m (**to** durch, von) (Buch): **~ to London** London-Führer m. **7.** (**to**) Leitfaden m (gen), Einführung f (**in** acc), Handbuch n (gen). '**~book** → guide 7.

guid·ed ['gaɪdɪd] adj **1.** **~ tour** Führung f (**of** durch). **2.** ✕, ⚙ (fern)gelenkt, (-)gesteuert: **~ missile** Lenkflugkörper m.

guide| dog s Blindenhund m. '**~·lines** s pl Richtlinien pl (**on** gen).

guid·ing [ˈgaɪdɪŋ] adj leitend: **~ principle** Leitprinzip n.

guild [gɪld] s **1.** hist. Gilde f, Zunft f. **2.** Vereinigung f, Gesellschaft f.

guild·less adj □ arglos.

guile [gaɪl] s (Arg)List f, Tücke f. **guile·ful** [ˈ~fʊl] adj □ arglistig, tückisch. '**guile·less** adj □ arglos.

guil·lo·tine [ˌgɪləˈtiːn] **I** s Guillotine f, Fallbeil n. **II** v/t durch die Guillotine od. mit dem Fallbeil hinrichten.

guilt [gɪlt] s Schuld f: **~ complex** Schuldkomplex m. '**guilt·less** adj □ schuldlos, unschuldig (**of** an dat). '**guilt·y** adj □ **1.** schuldig (**of** gen): → **plea** 2, **plead** 2. **2.** schuldbewußt: **a ~ conscience** ein schlechtes Gewissen (**about** wegen).

guin·ea pig [ˈgɪnɪ] s **1.** zo. Meerschweinchen n. **2.** fig. Versuchskaninchen n.

guise [gaɪz] s: **in the ~ of** als ... (verkleidet); **under** (od. **in**) **the ~ of** fig. in der Maske (gen), unter dem Deckmantel (gen).

gui·tar [gɪˈtɑː] s ♪ Gitarre f. **gui·tar·ist** s Gitarrist(in).

gulch [gʌltʃ] s bsd. Am. (Berg)Schlucht f.

gulf [gʌlf] s **1.** Golf m, Meerbusen m. **2.** Abgrund m (a. fig.). **3.** fig. Kluft f.

gull [gʌl] s orn. Möwe f.

gul·let [ˈgʌlɪt] s **1.** anat. Speiseröhre f. **2.** Gurgel f, Kehle f.

gul·li·ble [ˈgʌləbl] adj □ leichtgläubig.

gul·ly [ˈgʌlɪ] s **1.** (Wasser)Rinne f. **2.** ◎ Gully m: **~ (drain)** Abzugskanal m.

gulp [gʌlp] **I** v/t **1.** oft **~ down** Getränk hinunterstürzen, Speise hinunterschlingen. **2.** oft **~ back** Tränen etc hinunterschlucken, unterdrücken. **II** s **3.** (großer) Schluck: **at one ~** auf 'einen Zug.

gum[1] [gʌm] s oft pl anat. Zahnfleisch n.

gum[2] [~] **I** s **1.** Gummi m, n, Kautschuk m. **2.** Klebstoff m, bsd. Am. Gummilösung f. **II** v/t **3.** gummieren. **4.** (an-, ver)kleben. '**gum·my** adj klebrig.

gump·tion [ˈgʌmpʃn] s F **1.** Grips m. **2.** Mumm m, Schneid m.

gun [gʌn] **I** s **1.** ✕ Geschütz n, Kanone f: **stand** (od. **stick**) **to one's ~s** festbleiben, nicht nachgeben. **2.** Gewehr n; Pistole f, Revolver m. **3.** Sport: Startpistole f; Startschuß m: → **jump** 9. **4.** Tankstelle: Zapfpistole f. **II** v/t **5.** a. **~ to**

death erschießen: **~ down** niederschießen. **~ bat·tle** s Feuergefecht n, Schießerei f, Schußwechsel m. '**~-fight** → **gun battle**. **~ li·cence** (Am. **li·cense**) s Waffenschein m. '**~·man** [ˈ~mən] s (irr **man**) **1.** Bewaffnete m. **2.** Revolverheld m. '**~·point** s: **at ~** mit vorgehaltener Waffe, mit Waffengewalt. '**~·pow·der** s Schießpulver n. '**~·run·ner** s Waffenschmuggler m. '**~·run·ning** s Waffenschmuggel m. '**~-shot** s **1.** Schuß m. **2.** a. **~ wound** Schußwunde f, -verletzung f. **3.** Schußweite f: **within** (**out of**) **~** in (außer) Schußweite.

gur·gle [ˈgɜːgl] **I** v/i gurgeln: a) gluckern (Wasser), b) glucksen (**with** vor dat) (Person, Stimme). **II** s Gurgeln n, Gluckern n, Glucksen n.

gush [gʌʃ] **I** v/i **1.** strömen, schießen (**from** aus). **2.** F schwärmen (**over** von). **II** s **3.** Schwall m, Strom m (beide a. fig.). **4.** F Schwärmerei f. '**gush·er** s **1.** F Schwärmer(in). **2.** Springquelle f (Erdöl). '**gush·ing**, '**gush·y** adj □ F schwärmerisch.

gus·set [ˈgʌsɪt] s Schneiderei: Zwickel m, Keil m.

gust [gʌst] s **1.** Windstoß m, Bö f. **2.** fig. (Gefühls)Ausbruch m: **~ of anger** Wutanfall m.

gus·to [ˈgʌstəʊ] s Begeisterung f, Genuß m.

gus·ty [ˈgʌstɪ] adj □ **1.** böig. **2.** stürmisch (a. fig.).

gut [gʌt] **I** s **1.** pl bsd. zo. Eingeweide pl, Gedärme pl: **hate s.o.'s ~s** F j-n hassen wie die Pest. **2.** anat. Darm m. **3.** oft pl F Bauch m. **4.** pl F Mumm m, Schneid m. **II** v/t **5.** ausweiden, -nehmen. '**gut·less** adj F ohne Mumm od. Schneid. '**guts·y** adj F **1.** mutig. **2.** verfressen.

gut·ter [ˈgʌtə] **I** s **1.** Gosse f (a. fig.), Rinnstein m. **2.** Dachrinne f. **II** v/i **3.** tropfen (Kerze). **~ press** s Skandal-, Sensationspresse f. '**~-snipe** s Gassenkind n.

gut·tur·al [ˈgʌtərəl] **I** adj □ Kehl..., guttural (beide a. ling.), kehlig. **II** s ling. Guttural m, Kehllaut m.

guy [gaɪ] s F Kerl m, Typ m.

guz·zle [ˈgʌzl] v/t v/i **1.** (a. v/i) saufen; fressen. **2.** oft **~ away** Geld verprassen, bsd. versaufen.

gym [dʒɪm] F → **gymnasium; gymnastic:** ~ **shoes** *pl* Turnschuhe *pl.*
gym·na·si·um [dʒɪm'neɪzjəm] *pl* **-si-
-ums, -si·a** [~zɪə] *s* Turn-, Sporthalle *f.*
gym·nast ['~næst] *s* Turner(in). **gym-
'nas·tic** I *adj* (**~ally**) **1.** turnerisch,
Turn..., gymnastisch, Gymnastik... **II** *s*
2. *pl* (*sg* konstruiert) Turnen *n*, Gymnastik *f.* **3.** *mental* **~s** *pl* Gehirnakroba-
tik *f.*
gyn·(a)e·co·log·i·cal [ˌgaɪnəkə'lɒdʒɪkl]
adj □ ♂ gynäkologisch. **gyn·(a)e·**

col·o·gist [ˌ~'kɒlədʒɪst] *s* Gynäkologe
m, Gynäkologin *f*, Frauenarzt *m*, -ärz-
tin *f.* **,gyn·(a)e'col·o·gy** *s* Gynäkologie *f.*
gyp [dʒɪp] *sl.* I *v/t u.* v/i **1.** bescheißen. **II** *s*
2. Gauner(in). **3.** Beschiß *m.*
gyp·sum ['dʒɪpsəm] *s min.* Gips *m.*
gyp·sy *bsd. Am.* → **gipsy.**
gy·rate [ˌdʒaɪə'reɪt] *v/i* kreisen, sich (im
Kreis) drehen. **,gy'ra·tion** *s* Kreisbewe-
gung *f*, Drehung *f.* **gy·ra·to·ry** ['~rətərɪ]
adj kreisend, sich (im Kreis) drehend.

H

H [eɪtʃ] *pl* **H's** ['eɪtʃɪz] *s* **1.** drop one's H's
das H nicht aussprechen (*Zeichen der
Unbildung*). **2.** *sl.* H [eɪtʃ] *n* (*Heroin*).
ha [hɑː] *int* ha!, ah!
ha·be·as cor·pus [ˌheɪbjəs'kɔːpəs] *s a.*
writ of ~ ♂♂ gerichtliche Anordnung e-s
Haftprüfungstermins.
hab·er·dash·er ['hæbədæʃə] *s* **1.** *Br.*
Kurzwarenhändler *m.* **2.** *Am.* Herrenausstatter *m.* **'hab·er·dash·er·y** *s* **1.**
Br. Kurzwarengeschäft *n*; Kurzwaren
pl. **2.** *Am.* Herrenmodengeschäft *n*;
Herrenbekleidung *f.*
hab·it ['hæbɪt] *s* **1.** (An)Gewohnheit *f*:
out of (*od. by*) ~ aus Gewohnheit; get
into (out of) a ~ e-e Gewohnheit annehmen (ablegen); get into (out of) the ~ of
smoking sich das Rauchen angewöhnen (abgewöhnen); be in the ~ of doing
s.th. die (An)Gewohnheit haben, et. zu
tun. **2.** oft ~ of mind Geistesverfassung
f. **3.** (*bsd.* Ordens)Tracht *f.*
hab·it·a·ble ['hæbɪtəbl] □ bewohnbar.
hab·i·tat ['hæbɪtæt] *s* ♀, *zo.* Standort *m*,
Heimat *f.*
ha·bit·u·al [hə'bɪtʃʊəl] *adj* □ **1.** gewohn-
heitsmäßig, Gewohnheits...: ~ criminal
Gewohnheitsverbrecher *m.* **2.** gewohnt, ständig: be ~ly late ständig zu
spät kommen. **ha'bit·u·ate** [~eɪt] *v/t*
(o.s. sich) gewöhnen (to an *acc*): ~ o.s.
to doing s.th. sich daran gewöhnen, et.
zu tun.

hack¹ [hæk] I *v/t* **1.** (zer)hacken: ~ to
pieces (*od. bits*) in Stücke hacken; *fig.*
Ruf etc zerstören. **II** *v/i* **2.** *a.* ~ away
einhauen (auf *acc*). **3.** trocken u. stoßweise husten: ~ing cough → **5. III** *s* **4.**
Hieb *m.* **5.** trockener, stoßweiser Husten.
hack² [~] *Am.* F I *s* **1.** Taxi *n.* **II** *v/i* **2.** in
e-m Taxi fahren. **3.** ein Taxi fahren.
hack·ie ['hækɪ] *s Am.* F Taxifahrer(in).
hack·le ['hækl] *s*: get s.o.'s ~ up j-n
wütend machen.
hack·neyed ['hæknɪd] *adj* abgedroschen.
had [hæd] *pret u. pp von* **have.**
had·dock ['hædək] *pl* **-docks**, *bsd. coll.*
-dock *s ichth.* Schellfisch *m.*
hae·mo·glo·bin [ˌhiːməʊ'gləʊbɪn] *s*
physiol. bsd. Br. Hämoglobin *n.*
hae·mo·phile ['hiːməʊfaɪl] *s* ♂ *bsd. Br.*
Bluter *m.* **hae·mo·phil·i·a** [ˌ~'fɪlɪə] *s*
♂ *bsd. Br.* Bluterkrankheit *f.*
haem·or·rhage ['heməʊrɪdʒ] *s* ♂ *bsd. Br.*
Blutung *f.* **haem·or·rhoids** ['~rɔɪdz] *s*
pl ♂ *bsd. Br.* Hämorrhoiden *pl.*
haft [hɑːft] *s* Griff *m*, Heft *n* (*bsd. e-r
Stichwaffe*), Stiel *m* (*e-r Axt*).
hag [hæg] *s* häßliches altes Weib, Hexe *f.*
hag·gard ['hægəd] *adj* □ **1.** wild (*Blick*).
2. abgehärmt; abgespannt; abgezehrt,
hager.
hag·gle ['hægl] *v/i* feilschen, handeln,
schachern (*about, over* um).

hail[1] **I** s **1.** Hagel m (a. fig. von Flüchen, Fragen etc): ~ of bullets Geschoßhagel. **II** v/i **2.** impers hageln. **3.** ~ down fig. niederhageln, -prasseln (on auf acc).

hail[2] [~] **I** v/t **1.** j-m zujubeln. **2.** j-n, Taxi etc herbeirufen od. -winken. **3.** fig. et. begrüßen. **II** s **4.** (Zu)Ruf m: within ~ in Rufweite.

'**hail·stone** s Hagelkorn n, (Hagel-) Schloße f. '**~storm** s Hagelschauer m.

hair [heə] s (einzelnes). ~**breadth** ['~bretθ] s **1.** Haar n, Haare pl: to a ~ aufs Haar, haargenau; do one's ~ sich die Haare richten, sich frisieren; keep your ~ on! F reg dich ab!; let one's ~ down sich ungezwungen benehmen; aus sich herausgehen; split ~s Haarspalterei treiben; tear one's ~ (out) sich die Haare raufen; without turning a ~ ohne mit der Wimper zu zucken. ~**breadth** ['~bretθ] s: by a ~ um Haaresbreite; have a ~ escape mit knapper Not entkommen. '~**brush** s Haarbürste f. '~**cut** s Haarschnitt m: have a ~ sich die Haare schneiden lassen. '~**do** pl -**dos** s F Frisur f. '~**dress·er** s Friseur m, Friseuse f. '~**dress·ing** s Frisieren n: ~ salon Friseur-, Frisiersalon m. '~**dri·er** s Haartrockner m.

haired [heəd] adj **1.** behaart. **2.** in Zssgn ...haarig. '**hair·less** adj unbehaart, kahl.

'**hair**|**·line** s **1.** Haaransatz m. **2.** a. ~ crack ⊙ Haarriß m. '~**piece** s Haarteil n (für Frauen), Toupet n (für Männer). '~**pin** s **1.** Haarnadel f. **2.** a. ~ bend Haarnadelkurve f. '~**rais·ing** adj haarsträubend. ~ **re·stor·er** s Haarwuchsmittel n. ~ **slide** s Br. Haarspange f. '~**split·ting I** s Haarspalterei f. **II** adj haarspalterisch. ~ **spray** s Haarspray m, n. '~**style** s Frisur f. ~ **styl·ist** s Hair-Stylist(in).

hair·y ['heərɪ] adj **1.** haarig, behaart. **2.** F haarig, schwierig; gefährlich.

hale [heɪl] adj gesund, kräftig, rüstig: ~ and hearty gesund u. munter.

half [hɑːf] **I** adj **1.** halb: a mile e-e halbe Meile; two pounds and a ~, two and a ~ pounds zweieinhalb Pfund; → mind 5. **II** adv **2.** halb, zur Hälfte: ~ as long halb so lang; ~ past two halb drei. **3.** halb(wegs), fast, nahezu: ~ dead halbtot; not ~ bad F gar nicht übel; I ~ suspect ich vermute fast. **III** pl halves [hɑːvz] s **4.** Hälfte f: cut in(to) halves (od. in ~) halbieren; go halves with s.o. in (od. on) s.th. et. mit j-m teilen. **5.** Sport: a) (Spiel)Hälfte f, Halbzeit f, b) (a. ~ of the field Spielfeld)Hälfte f. ~**baked** adj F nicht durchdacht, unausgegoren (Plan etc); grün (Person). '~**breed** s Mischling m, Halbblut n. ~**broth·er** s Halbbruder m. ~**caste** ['~kɑːst] → half-breed. ~ **face** s part., phot. Profil n. ~**heart·ed** adj □ halbherzig. ~**mast** s: fly at ~ a) a. put at ~ auf halbmast setzen, b) auf halbmast wehen. ~ **meas·ure** s Halbheit f, halbe Sache. ~ **moon** s Halbmond m. ~**pen·ny** ['heɪpnɪ] s F pl half-pence ['heɪpəns] halber Penny. **2.** pl '**half·pen·nies** Halbpennystück n. ~'**price** adj u. adv zum halben Preis. ~**seas-o·ver** s F blau, betrunken. ~**sis·ter** s Halbschwester f. '~**tim·ber(ed)** adj △ Fachwerk... ~ **time** s Sport: Halbzeit f (Pause): at ~ bei od. zur Halbzeit. ~**time I** adj **1.** Halbtags...: ~ job. **2.** Sport: Halbzeit...: ~ interval Halbzeitpause f; ~ score Halbzeitstand m. **II** adv **3.** halbtags: work ~. '~**truth** s Halbwahrheit f. ~**way I** adj **1.** auf halbem Weg od. in der Mitte (liegend). **2.** fig. halb, teilweise: ~ measure → half measure. **II** adv **3.** auf halbem Weg, in der Mitte: meet s.o. ~ bsd. fig. j-m auf halbem Weg entgegenkommen. **4.** teilweise, halb(wegs). '~**wit** s Schwachkopf m, Trottel m. ~**year·ly** adj u. adv halbjährlich.

hal·i·but ['hælɪbət] pl -**buts**, bsd. coll. -**but** s ichth. Heilbutt m.

hal·i·to·sis [ˌhælɪˈtəʊsɪs] s übler Mundgeruch.

hall [hɔːl] s **1.** Halle f, Saal m. **2.** Diele f, Flur m. **3.** univ. a) a. ~ of residence Studentenheim n, b) Speisesaal m.

hal·le·lu·jah [ˌhælɪˈluːjə] **I** s Halleluja n. **II** int halleluja!

'**hall·mark I** s **1.** Br. Feingehaltsstempel m. **2.** fig. (Kenn)Zeichen n, Merkmal n. **II** v/t **3.** Br. Gold, Silber stempeln. **4.** fig. kennzeichnen.

hal·lo bsd. Br. → hello.

hal·low ['hæləʊ] v/t heiligen.

hall¦ por·ter s bsd. Br. Hausdiener m (im Hotel). **'~stand** s Garderoben-, Kleiderständer m; (Flur)Garderobe f.

hal·lu·ci·nate [hə'luːsɪneɪt] v/i halluzinieren. **hal¦lu·ci'na·tion** s Halluzination f.

ha·lo ['heɪləʊ] pl **-lo(e)s** s 1. Heiligenschein m. 2. ast. Hof m.

hal·o·gen ['hæledʒen] s ⚗ Halogen n.

halt [hɔːlt] I s Halt m: **bring to a ~** → II; **come to a ~** → III. II v/t anhalten, a. fig. zum Stehen od. Stillstand bringen. III v/i anhalten, a. fig. zum Stehen od. Stillstand kommen.

hal·ter ['hɔːltə] s 1. Halfter m, n. 2. Strick m, Strang m (zum Hängen).

halve [hɑːv] v/t halbieren. **halves** [~z] pl von **half**.

ham [hæm] s 1. Schinken m: **~ and eggs** Schinken mit (Spiegel)Ei. 2. a. **~ actor** F Schmierenkomödiant m. 3. F Funkamateur m, Amateurfunker m.

ham·burg·er ['hæmbɜːgə] s gastr. Hamburger m.

¦ham¦-'fist·ed adj bsd. Br. F, **'~-¦hand·ed** adj F tolpatschig, ungeschickt.

ham·let ['hæmlɪt] s Weiler m, Dörfchen n.

ham·mer ['hæmə] I s 1. Hammer m: **come** (od. **go**) **under the ~** unter den Hammer kommen; **go at it ~ and tongs** F sich mächtig ins Zeug legen; (sich) streiten, daß die Fetzen fliegen. 2. Leichtathletik: Hammer m: **~ throw** Hammerwerfen n; **~ thrower** Hammerwerfer m. II v/t 3. hämmern: **~ in** einhämmern; **~ s.th. into s.o.'s head** fig. j-m et. einhämmern od. -bleuen. III v/i 4. hämmern (a. Puls etc): **~ at** einhämmern auf (acc).

ham·mock ['hæmək] s Hängematte f.

ham·per¹ ['hæmpə] v/t (be)hindern.

ham·per² [~] s 1. (Deckel)Korb m. 2. Geschenk-, Freßkorb m. 3. Am. Wäschekorb m.

ham·ster ['hæmstə] s zo. Hamster m.

'ham·string I s anat. Kniesehne f. II v/t (irr string) fig. vereiteln; lähmen.

hand [hænd] I s 1. Hand f: **at ~** in Reichweite; nahe (bevorstehend); bei der od. zur Hand; **by ~** mit der Hand, manuell; **~s down** spielend, mühelos (gewinnen etc); **~s off!** Hände weg!; **~s up!** Hände hoch!; **be ~ in glove** (**with**) ein Herz u.

e-e Seele sein (mit); unter 'einer Decke stecken (mit); **change ~s** den Besitzer wechseln; **give** (od. **lend**) **a** (**helping**) **~** mit zugreifen, j-m helfen (**with** bei); **have a ~ in** s-e Hand im Spiel haben bei, beteiligt sein an (dat); **hold ~s** Händchen halten; **not to lift** (od. **raise**) **a ~** keinen Finger rühren; **live from ~ to mouth** von der Hand in den Mund leben; **shake ~s with** j-m die Hand schütteln od. geben; → **tie** 7a. 2. oft pl Hand f, Macht f, Gewalt f: **be entirely in s.o.'s ~s** ganz in j-s Hand sein; **fall into s.o.'s ~s** j-m in die Hände fallen. 3. pl Hände pl, Obhut f: **in good ~s**. 4. Seite f: **on the right ~** rechts; **on the one ~ ..., on the other ~** fig. einerseits ..., andererseits. 5. oft in Zssgn Arbeiter m. 6. Fachmann m, Routinier m: **an old ~** ein alter Praktikus od. Hase; **be a good ~** at sehr geschickt od. geübt sein in (dat). 7. Hand f, Quelle f: **at first ~** aus erster Hand. 8. Handschrift f. 9. Unterschrift f: **set one's ~ to** s-e Unterschrift setzen unter (acc), unterschreiben. 10. Applaus m, Beifall m: **get a big ~** stürmischen Beifall bekommen. 11. (Uhr)Zeiger m. 12. Kartenspiel: Spieler m; Blatt n, Karten pl: **show one's ~** fig. s-e Karten aufdecken. II v/t 13. aushändigen, (über)geben, (-)reichen.

Verbindungen mit Adverbien:

hand¦ a·round v/t herumreichen, herumgeben lassen. **~ back** v/t zurückgeben. **~ down** v/t 1. hinunter-, herunterreichen, -langen (**from** von; **to** dat). 2. (**to**) Tradition etc weitergeben (an acc), Bräuche etc überliefern (dat). **~ in** v/t 1. hinein-, hereinreichen, -langen (**to** dat). 2. Prüfungsarbeit etc abgeben, Gesuch etc einreichen (**to** bei): → **check** 11. **~ on** v/t 1. weiterreichen, -geben (**to** dat, an acc). 2. → **hand down** 2. **~ out** v/t 1. aus-, verteilen (**to** an acc). 2. Ratschläge, Komplimente etc verteilen. **~ o·ver** v/t (**to** dat) 1. übergeben. 2. geben, aushändigen. **~ round** → **hand around**. **~ up** v/t hinauf-, heraufreichen, -langen (**to** dat).

'hand·bag s Handtasche f. **~ bag·gage** s bsd. Am. Handgepäck n. **'~·bill** s Handzettel m, Flugblatt n. **'~·book** s 1. Handbuch n. 2. Reiseführer m (**of** durch; von): **a ~ of London** ein London-Führer. **~ brake** s ⊙ Handbremse f. **~breadth** ['ˌbretθ] s Handbreit f. **'~carved** adj handgeschnitzt. **~ cream** s Handcreme f. **'~cuff** I s mst pl Handschelle f. II v/t j-m Handschellen anlegen: **~ed** in Handschellen.

hand·ful ['hændfʊl] s **1.** e-e Handvoll (a. fig. Personen). **2.** F Plage f (Person, Sache), Nervensäge f.

hand gre·nade s ✗ Handgranate f.

hand·i·cap ['hændɪkæp] I s Handikap s: a) Vorgabe(rennen n, -spiel n) f, b) fig. Behinderung f, Nachteil m (**to** für): → **mental** 1, **physical** 1. II v/t behindern, benachteiligen: → **mentally** 1, **physically**.

hand·i·craft ['hændɪkrɑft] s **1.** Handfertigkeit f. **2.** (bsd. Kunst)Handwerk n. **'hand·i·crafts·man** [~mən] s (irr man) (bsd. Kunst)Handwerker m.

hand·i·work ['hændɪwɜːk] s **1.** Handarbeit f. **2.** fig. Werk n.

hand·ker·chief ['hæŋkətʃɪf] s Taschentuch n.

han·dle ['hændl] I s **1.** (Hand)Griff m; Stiel m; Henkel m; Klinke f, Drücker m: **fly off the ~** F hochgehen, wütend werden. **2.** fig. Handhabe f (**against** gegen). II v/t **3.** anfassen, berühren. **4.** hantieren od. umgehen mit, Maschine bedienen. **5.** Thema etc behandeln; et. erledigen, durchführen; mit et., j-m fertigwerden. **6.** j-n behandeln, umgehen mit: → **kid glove.** III v/i **7. glass – ~ with care!** Vorsicht, Glas! **'~bar** s mst pl Lenkstange f.

hand| lug·gage s Handgepäck n. **'~made** adj handgearbeitet. **'~op·er·at·ed** adj handbedient, Hand... **'~out** s **1.** Almosen n, milde Gabe. **2.** Prospekt m, Hand-, Werbezettel m. **3.** Handout n (für Pressevertreter etc). **'~rail** s Handlauf m. **'~set** s teleph. Hörer m. **'~shake** s Händedruck m: **give s.o. a firm ~** j-m kräftig die Hand schütteln.

hand·some ['hænsəm] adj □ **1.** gutaussehend (bsd. Mann). **2.** beträchtlich, ansehnlich (Summe etc). **3.** großzügig, nobel.

'hand|·stand s Handstand m: **do a ~** e-n Handstand machen. **'~to-'mouth** adj: **lead a ~ existence** von der Hand in den Mund leben. **'~work** s Handarbeit

f. **'~writ·ing** s (Hand)Schrift f. **'~written** adj handgeschrieben.

hand·y ['hændɪ] adj □ **1.** zur od. bei der Hand: **keep s.th. ~** et. griffbereit aufbewahren. **2.** geschickt, gewandt. **3.** handlich, praktisch. **4.** nützlich: **come in ~** sich als nützlich erweisen; (sehr) gelegen kommen. **'~man** s (irr man) Mädchen n für alles, Faktotum n.

hang [hæŋ] I s **1.** Sitz m (e-s Kleids etc). **2. get the ~ of s.th.** F et. rauskriegen od. kapieren. II v/t (irr) **3.** (auf)hängen; Tür etc einhängen: **~ on a hook** an e-n Haken hängen. **4.** pret u. pp **hanged** j-n (auf)hängen: **~ o.s.** sich erhängen. **5.** Kopf hängen lassen od. senken. **6.** behängen (**with** mit). **7.** Tapeten ankleben. III v/i (irr) **8.** hängen (**by, on** an dat): **~ by a thread** fig. an e-m (dünnen od. seidenen) Faden hängen; **~ over** fig. hängen od. schweben über (dat). **9.** **~ about** (od. around) herumlungern od. sich herumtreiben in (dat).

Verbindungen mit Adverbien:

hang| a·bout, **~ a·round** v/i herumlungern, sich herumtreiben. **~ back** v/i zögern (**from doing** zu tun). **~ down** v/i hinunter-, herunterhängen (**from** von). **~ on** v/i **1.** (**to**) sich klammern (an acc) (a. fig.), festhalten (acc). **2.** warten; teleph. am Apparat bleiben. **3.** nicht nachlassen (Krankheit etc). **~ out** I v/t **1.** (hin-, her)aushängen, Wäsche (draußen) aufhängen. II v/i **2.** heraushängen. **3.** aushängen, ausgehängt sein. **~ o·ver** I v/i andauern, existieren (from seit). II v/t: **be hung over** F e-n Kater haben. **~ to·geth·er** v/i **1.** zs.-halten (Personen). **2.** e-n (logischen) Zs.-hang haben, zs.-hängen. **~ up** I v/t **1.** aufhängen. **2.** aufschieben. **3. be hung up on** F e-n Komplex haben wegen; besessen sein von. II v/i **4.** teleph. einhängen, auflegen.

hang·ar ['hæŋə] s Hangar m, Flugzeughalle f.

hang·er ['hæŋə] s Kleiderbügel m; Schlaufe f, Aufhänger m.

hang| glid·er s (Sport) **1.** (Flug)Drachen m. **2.** Drachenflieger(in). **~ glid·ing** s Drachenfliegen n.

hang·ing ['hæŋɪŋ] I adj Hänge...: **~ bridge.** II s mst pl Wandbehang m.

hang|·man ['hæŋmən] s (irr man) Hen-

ker m. '**~nail** s ✲ Nied-, Neidnagel m.
'**~o·ver** s 1. Überbleibsel n, -rest m. 2.
F Katzenjammer m, Kater m (beide a.
fig.). '**~up** s F 1. Komplex m. 2. Problem n, Schwierigkeit f.

han·ker ['hæŋkə] v/i sich sehnen, Verlangen haben (**after, for** nach): **~ to do
s.th.** sich danach sehnen, et. zu tun.
'**han·ker·ing** s Sehnsucht f, Verlangen n.

han·kie, han·ky ['hæŋkı] s F Taschentuch n.

han·ky-pan·ky [,hæŋkı'pæŋkı] s F 1.
Hokuspokus m, fauler Zauber. 2.
Techtelmechtel n.

hap·haz·ard [,hæp'hæzəd] adj □ u. adv
plan-, wahllos, adv a. aufs Geratewohl.

hap·pen ['hæpən] v/i 1. geschehen, sich
ereignen, passieren: **it will not ~ again**
es wird nicht wieder vorkommen. 2.
zufällig geschehen, sich zufällig ergeben: **it ~ed that** es traf od. ergab sich,
daß. 3. **if you ~ to see it** wenn du es
zufällig siehst od. sehen solltest; **it ~ed
to be cold** zufällig war es kalt. 4. **~ to**
geschehen od. passieren mit (od. dat),
zustoßen (dat), werden aus. 5. **~ on**
zufällig begegnen (dat) od. treffen
(acc); zufällig stoßen auf (acc).
hap·pen·ing ['hæpnɪŋ] s 1. Ereignis n.
2. Kunst: Happening n.

hap·pi·ly ['hæpɪlı] adv 1. glücklich. 2.
glücklicherweise, zum Glück. '**hap·pi-
ness** s Glück n.

hap·py ['hæpı] adj (□ → **happily**) 1. allg.
glücklich (**at, about** über acc; **with** mit):
I am ~ to see you es freut mich (sehr),
Sie zu sehen; → **birthday** I, **Easter** I,
new year 1. 2. F beschwipst. 3. in
Zssgn: a) ...begeistert: → **trigger-happy**, b) F ...süchtig. ,**~go-'luck·y** adj
unbekümmert, sorglos. **~ hour** s F Zeit,
in der in Pubs etc alkoholische Getränke
verbilligt ausgeschenkt werden.

har·ass ['hærəs] v/t 1. ständig belästigen
(**with** mit). 2. aufreiben, zermürben. 3.
schikanieren.

har·bin·ger ['ha:bɪndʒə] fig. I s Vorläufer m; Vorbote m; (erstes) Anzeichen.
II v/t ankündigen.

har·bo(u)r ['ha:bə] I s 1. Hafen m. 2.
Zufluchtsort m, Unterschlupf m. II v/t
3. j-m Zuflucht od. Unterschlupf gewähren. 4. Gedanken, Groll etc hegen.

hard [ha:d] I adj 1. allg. hart. 2. schwer,
schwierig: **~ work** harte Arbeit; **~ to
believe** kaum zu glauben; **~ to please**
schwer zufriedenzustellen; **~ to imagine** schwer vorstellbar. 3. heftig, stark:
a ~ blow ein harter Schlag, fig. a. ein
schwerer Schlag. 4. hart (Winter), (a.
Frost) streng, (Klima) rauh. 5. hart,
streng: **be ~ on s.o.** j-n hart od. ungerecht behandeln; j-m hart zusetzen. 6.
hart, drückend: **~ times** pl schwere Zeiten pl; **it is ~ on him** es ist hart für ihn,
es trifft ihn schwer. 7. hart, nüchtern:
the ~ facts pl die nackten Tatsachen pl.
8. hart (Droge), (Getränk a.) stark. 9. **~
of hearing** schwerhörig. 10. **~ up** f in
(Geld)Schwierigkeiten; in Verlegenheit
(**for** um). II adv 11. hart, fest: **frozen ~**
hartgefroren. 12. hart, schwer: **work ~;
brake ~** scharf bremsen; **think ~** scharf
nachdenken; **try ~** sich große Mühe geben. 13. nahe, dicht: **~ by** ganz in der
Nähe. '**~back** s gebundene Ausgabe.
,**~'boiled** adj 1. hart(gekocht) (Ei). 2.
fig. hart, unsentimental; nüchtern,
sachlich. **~ core** s harter Kern (e-r Bande etc): '**~core** adj 1. zum harten Kern
gehörend. 2. hart (Pornographie).
'**~cov·er → hardback.** ,**~'earned** adj
hartverdient.

hard·en ['ha:dn] I v/t 1. härten (a. ✪),
hart machen. 2. fig. hart machen, abstumpfen (**to** gegen): **~ed** verstockt, abgebrüht. 3. fig. abhärten (**to** gegen). II
v/i 4. erhärten (a. ✪), hart werden. 5.
fig. hart werden, abstumpfen (**to** gegen). 6. fig. sich abhärten (**to** gegen). 7.
✝ anziehen (Preise).

,**hard'head·ed** adj nüchtern, realistisch. ,**~'heart·ed** adj □ hartherzig. **~
line** s 1. bsd. pol. harter Kurs: **follow**
(od. **adopt**) **a ~** e-n harten Kurs einschlagen. 2. pl bsd. Br. Pech n (**on** für).
hard·ly ['ha:dlı] adv 1. kaum, fast nicht:
~ ever fast nie. 2. (wohl) kaum, schwerlich. 3. (zeitlich) kaum. '**hard·ness** s 1.
Härte f (a. fig.). 2. Schwierigkeit f.
'**hard·ship** s 1. Not f, Elend n. 2. Härte
f: **~ case** Härtefall m.

hard| shoul·der s mot. Br. Standspur f.
'**~top** s mot. Hardtop n, m (a. Wagen).
'**~ware** s 1. Metall-, Eisenwaren pl;
Haushaltswaren pl. 2. Computer:
Hardware f. ,**~'wear·ing** adj Br. stra-

pazierfähig. ~·'**work·ing** *adj* fleißig, arbeitsam.

har·dy ['hɑːdɪ] *adj* □ **1.** zäh, ausdauernd, robust; abgehärtet. **2.** ♀ winterfest.

hare [heə] *s zo.* Hase *m:* **(as) mad as a March ~** F total verrückt; **play ~ and hounds** e-e Schnitzeljagd machen. '**~·bell** *s* ♀ Glockenblume *f.* '**~·brained** *adj* verrückt. ~·'**lip** *s ♣* Hasenscharte *f.*

ha·rem ['hɑːriːm] *s* Harem *m (a. fig. humor.).*

harm [hɑːm] **I** *s* Schaden *m:* **there is no ~ in doing s.th.** es kann nicht(s) schaden, et. zu tun; **there is no ~ in trying** ein Versuch kann nicht schaden; **come to ~** zu Schaden kommen; **do s.o. ~** j-m schaden *od.* et. antun; → **bodily** 1, **mean³** 1. **II** *v/t* j-n verletzen *(a. fig.)*, j-m, j-s *Ruf etc* schaden. **harm·ful** ['~fʊl] *adj* □ schädlich (**to** für): **~ to one's health** gesundheitsschädlich. '**harm·less** *adj* □ *allg.* harmlos.

har·mon·ic [hɑːˈmɒnɪk] *adj (~ally)* harmonisch. **har'mon·i·ca** [~kə] *s* ♪ Mundharmonika *f.* **har·mo·ni·ous** [~ˈməʊnjəs] *adj* □ harmonisch. **har·mo·ni·um** [~ˈməʊnjəm] *s* ♪ Harmonium *n.* **har·mo·nize** ['~mənaɪz] **I** *v/i* harmonieren, zs.-passen, in Einklang sein (**with** mit). **II** *v/t* harmonieren, in Einklang bringen (**with** mit). **har·mo·ny** ['~mənɪ] *s* ♪ Harmonie *f, fig. a.* Einklang *m,* Eintracht *f.*

har·ness ['hɑːnɪs] **I** *s* **1.** *(Pferde- etc)* Geschirr *n:* **die in ~** *fig.* in den Sielen sterben. **2.** *mot.* (Sicherheits)Gurt *m.* **II** *v/t* **3.** Pferd *etc* anschirren; anspannen (**to** an *acc*).

harp [hɑːp] **I** *s* **1.** ♪ Harfe *f.* **II** *v/i* **2.** Harfe spielen. **3.** *fig.* (**on, on about**) herumreiten (auf *dat*), dauernd reden (von). '**harp·er,** '**harp·ist** *s* Harfenist(in).

har·poon [hɑːˈpuːn] **I** *s* Harpune *f.* **II** *v/t* harpunieren.

harp·si·chord ['hɑːpsɪkɔːd] *s* ♪ Cembalo *n.*

har·row ['hærəʊ] **I** *s* **1.** ✓ Egge *f.* **II** *v/t* **2.** ✓ eggen. **3.** *fig.* quälen, peinigen.

harsh [hɑːʃ] *adj* □ rauh *(Stoff, Stimme);* grell *(Farbe);* barsch, schroff *(Art etc);* streng *(Disziplin etc),* hart *(Worte etc).*

har·um-scar·um [ˌheərəmˈskeərəm] *adj* unbesonnen, leichtsinnig.

har·vest ['hɑːvɪst] **I** *s* Ernte *f:* a) Erntezeit *f,* b) Ernten *n,* c) (Ernte)Ertrag *m.* **II** *v/t* ernten, *fig. a.* einheimsen. ~ **fes·ti·val** *s* Erntedankfest *n.*

has [hæz] *er, sie, es* hat. '**~·been** *s* F **1.** *et.* Überholtes. **2.** *j-d, der den Höhepunkt s-r Karriere überschritten hat.* **3.** *pl* alte Zeiten *pl.*

hash¹ [hæʃ] *v/t* **1.** a. ~ **up** Fleisch zerhacken, -kleinern. **2.** a. ~ **up** *fig.* durcheinanderbringen; verpfuschen. **I** *s* **3.** *gastr.* Haschee *n.* **4.** *fig. et.* Aufgewärmtes. **5. make a ~ of** → 2.

hash² [~] *s* F Hasch *n (Haschisch).*

hash·ish ['hæʃiːʃ] *s* Haschisch *n.*

has·sle ['hæsl] F **I** *s* **1.** Krach *m, (a.* handgreifliche) Auseinandersetzung. **2.** Mühe *f:* **it was quite a ~** es war ganz schön mühsam (**doing, to do** zu tun). **II** *v/i* **3.** Krach *od.* e-e (handgreifliche) Auseinandersetzung haben.

haste [heɪst] *s* Hast *f,* Eile *f:* **make ~** sich beeilen; **more ~, less speed** eile mit Weile. **has·ten** ['heɪsn] **I** *v/t* j-n antreiben; *et.* beschleunigen. **II** *v/i* (sich be)eilen, hasten. **hast·y** ['heɪstɪ] *adj* □ **1.** eilig, hastig, *(Abreise)* überstürzt. **2.** voreilig, -schnell, übereilt.

hat [hæt] *s* Hut *m:* **I'll eat my ~ if ...** F ich fresse e-n Besen, wenn ...; **talk through one's ~** F dummes Zeug reden; **~s off!** Hut ab!, alle Achtung! (**to** vor *dat*); → **cocked hat, old** 1.

hatch¹ [hætʃ] *s* **1.** ✓, ♣ Luke *f, allg. a.* Bodentür *f,* -öffnung *f.* **2.** Durchreiche *f.*

hatch² [~] **I** *v/t* **1.** a. ~ **out** Eier, Junge ausbrüten. **2.** a. ~ **out** (*od.* **up**) Racheplan etc ausbrüten, -hecken; Programm etc entwickeln. **II** *v/i* **3.** brüten. **4.** a. ~ **out** (*aus dem Ei*) ausschlüpfen. **III** *s* **5.** Brut *f.*

hatch³ [~] *v/t* schraffieren.

'**hatch·back** *s mot.* (Wagen *m* mit) Hecktür *f.*

hatch·et ['hætʃɪt] *s* Beil *n:* **bury** (**take up**) **the ~** *fig.* das Kriegsbeil begraben (ausgraben).

hate [heɪt] **I** *v/t* **1.** hassen: **~d** verhaßt. **2.** nicht ausstehen können: → **gut** 1. **3.** nicht wollen *od.* mögen: **~ doing** (*od.* **to do**) *s.th.* et. (nur) äußerst ungern tun.

II *s* **4.** Haß *m* (*of, for* auf *acc*, gegen): *full of ~* haßerfüllt. **5.** *et.* Verhaßtes: *... is my pet ~* F ... kann ich auf den Tod nicht ausstehen *od.* leiden.
ha·tred ['heɪtrɪd] *s* → **hate** 4.
hat·ter ['hætə] *s* Hutmacher *m*: (*as*) *mad as a ~* total verrückt.
hat trick *s Sport:* Hattrick *m*.
haugh·ty ['hɔːtɪ] *adj* □ hochmütig, überheblich.
haul [hɔːl] **I** *s* **1.** Ziehen *n*, Zerren *n*; kräftiger Zug. **2.** Fischzug *m, fig. a.* Fang *m*, Beute *f*: *make a big ~* e-n guten Fang machen. **3.** a) Beförderung *f*, Transport *m*, b) Transportweg *m*. **II** *v/t* **4.** ziehen, zerren: *~ down* Flagge *etc* ein-, niederholen; *~ up* F sich *j-n* vorknöpfen; *j-n* schleppen (*before vor acc*); → **coal.** 5. befördern, transportieren. **III** *v/i* **6.** *~ away* ziehen, zerren (*at, on* an *dat*). **'haul·age** *s* → **haul** 3a.
'haul·er, *bsd. Br.* **haul·i·er** ['~jə] *s* Transportunternehmer *m*.
haulm [hɔːm] *s* Halm *m*, Stengel *m*.
haunch [hɔːntʃ] *s gastr.* Lendenstück *n*, Keule *f*: *~ of beef* Rindslende *f*.
haunt [hɔːnt] **I** *v/t* **1.** spuken *od.* umgehen in (*dat*): *this room is ~ed* in diesem Zimmer spukt es; *~ed castle* Spukschloß *n.* **2.** *fig.* a) verfolgen, quälen: *~ed look* gehetzter Blick, b) *j-m* nicht mehr aus dem Kopf gehen, *j-n* nicht mehr loslassen. **3.** häufig besuchen. **II** *s* **4.** häufig besuchter Ort. **'haunt·ing** *adj* □ **1.** quälend. **2.** unvergeßlich: *~ melody* (*od. tune*) Ohrwurm *m.*
have [hæv] **I** *v/t* (*irr*) **1.** *allg.* haben: *~ on* Kleidungsstück anhaben, Hut aufhaben; → **get** 11. **2.** haben, erleben. **3.** Kind bekommen; *zo.* Junge werfen. **4.** behalten: *may I ~ it?* **5.** *Gefühle, Verdacht etc* haben, hegen. **6.** erhalten, bekommen: *~ back* zurückbekommen. **7.** essen, trinken: → **breakfast** I, *etc.* **8.** haben, machen: → **look** 1, **try** 1, **walk** 1, **wash** 1. **9.** *a. ~ on* F *j-n* reinlegen. **10.** *~ on et.* vorhaben. **11.** *vor inf:* müssen: *I ~ to go now;* → **get** 11. **12.** *mit Objekt u. pp:* lassen: *I had a suit made* ich ließ mir e-n Anzug machen. **13.** *mit Objekt u. inf:* (veran)lassen: *I had him sit down* ich ließ ihn Platz nehmen. **14.** *I had rather go than stay* ich möchte lieber gehen als bleiben; *you had best*

go du tätest am besten daran zu gehen. **II** *v/aux* (*irr*) **15.** haben, (*bei vielen v/i*) sein: *I have come* ich bin gekommen. **III** *s* **16.** *the ~s and the ~-nots* die Begüterten u. die Habenichtse.
ha·ven ['heɪvn] *s* **1.** *mst fig.* (sicherer) Hafen. **2.** *fig.* Zufluchtsort *m.*
'have-not *s mst pl* Habenichts *m:* → **have** 16.
hav·oc ['hævək] *s* Verwüstung *f*, Zerstörung *f*: *cause ~* schwere Zerstörungen *od.* (*a.* (*fig.*)) ein Chaos verursachen; *play ~ with, make ~ of* verwüsten, zerstören; *fig.* verheerend wirken auf (*acc*).
haw [hɔː] *v/i* → **hem²** II, **hum** 2.
hawk¹ [hɔːk] *s orn.* Falke *m* (*a. pol.*), Habicht *m.*
hawk² [~] *v/t* **1.** hausieren mit; auf der Straße verkaufen. **2.** *a. ~ about* (*od. around*) *Gerücht etc* verbreiten. **'hawk·er** *s* Hausierer(in); Straßenhändler(in).
haw·ser ['hɔːzə] *s* ⚓ Kabeltau *n*, Trosse *f.*
haw·thorn ['hɔːθɔːn] *s* ♣ Weißdorn *m.*
hay [heɪ] *s* Heu *n*: *make ~ while the sun shines fig.* das Eisen schmieden, solange es heiß ist; *hit the ~ sl.* sich in die Falle *od.* Klappe hauen. *~ fe·ver s* 🏥 Heuschnupfen *m.* '~*wire adj* F kaputt (*Gerät*); (völlig) durcheinander (*Pläne etc*); übergeschnappt (*Person*): *go ~* kaputtgehen; (völlig) durcheinandergeraten; überschnappen.
haz·ard ['hæzəd] **I** *s* **1.** Gefahr *f*, Risiko *n*: *at all ~s* unter allen Umständen; *at the ~ of one's life* unter Lebensgefahr, unter Einsatz s-s Lebens; *~ to health* Gesundheitsrisiko; *~ warning lights pl mot.* Warnblinkanlage *f.* **2.** Zufall *m*: *by ~* durch Zufall, zufällig. **II** *v/t* **3.** riskieren: a) aufs Spiel setzen, b) (zu sagen) wagen, sich *e-e Bemerkung etc* erlauben. **'haz·ard·ous** *adj* □ gewagt, gefährlich, riskant.
haze [heɪz] *s* **1.** Dunst(schleier) *m.* **2.** *fig.* Nebel *m*, Schleier *m.*
ha·zel ['heɪzl] *adj* □ (hasel)nußbraun. '~*-nut s* ♣ Haselnuß *f.*
ha·zy ['heɪzɪ] *adj* □ **1.** dunstig, diesig. **2.** *fig.* verschwommen, nebelhaft (*Vorstellung etc*): *be rather ~ about* nur e-e ziemlich verschwommene *od.* vage Vorstellung haben von.

'H-bomb s ⚔ H-Bombe f, Wasserstoffbombe f.

he [hi:] **I** pron er: ~ **who** wer; derjenige, welcher. **II** s Er m: a) Junge m, Mann m, b) zo. Männchen n. **III** adj in Zssgn zo. ...männchen n: ~**goat** Ziegenbock m.

head [hed] **I** v/t **1.** anführen, an der Spitze stehen von (od. gen). **2.** voran-, vorausgehen (dat). **3.** (an)führen, leiten: ~**ed by** unter der Leitung von. **4.** Fußball: köpfen. **5.** (for) gehen, fahren (nach); sich bewegen (auf acc ... zu), lossteuern, -gehen (auf acc); ♣ Kurs halten (auf acc). **II** adj **6.** Kopf... **7.** Chef..., Haupt..., Ober...: ~ **cook** Chefkoch m; ~ **nurse** Oberschwester f. **IV** s **8.** Kopf m: **above** (od. over) s.o.'s ~ zu hoch für j-n; **from** ~ **to foot** von Kopf bis Fuß; ~ **over heels** kopfüber (die Treppe hinunterstürzen); bis über beide Ohren (verliebt sein); **be** ~ **over heels in debt** bis über die Ohren in Schulden stecken; **bury one's** ~ **in the sand** den Kopf in den Sand stecken; **cry one's** ~ **off** F sich die Augen ausweinen; **go to s.o.'s** ~ j-m in den od. zu Kopf steigen (Alkohol, Erfolg etc); **keep one's** ~ **above water** sich über Wasser halten (a. fig.); **lose one's** ~ den Kopf od. die Nerven verlieren; → **snap** 5. **9.** (Ober)Haupt n: ~ **of the family** Familienvorstand m, -oberhaupt; ~ **of state** Staatsoberhaupt; → **crown** 5. **10.** (An)Führer m, Leiter m: ~ **of government** Regierungschef m. **11.** Spitze f, führende Stellung: **at the** ~ **of** an der Spitze (gen). **12.** Kopf(ende n) m (e-s Bettes etc); Kopf m (e-s Briefs, Nagels etc). **13.** Kopf m, (einzelne) Person: **one pound a** ~ ein Pfund pro Kopf od. Person. **14.** pl Vorderseite f (e-r Münze): ~**s or tails?** Wappen od. Zahl?; **I cannot make** ~ **or tail of it** ich kann daraus nicht schlau werden. **15.** ❡ (Salat- etc)Kopf m. **16.** Schaum(krone f) m (vom Bier etc). **17.** Quelle f (e-s Flusses). **18.** Überschrift f, Titelkopf m. **19.** in Zssgn F ...süchtige m, f. '~**ache** s Kopfschmerz(en pl) m, -weh n: **be a bit of a** ~ **for s.o., give s.o. a** ~ F j-m Kopfschmerzen od. Sorgen machen. '~**band** s Kopf-, Stirnband n.

head·er ['hedə] s **1.** Kopfsprung m. **2.** Fußball: Kopfball m.

,**head|'first** → **headlong**. '~,**hunt·er** s Kopfjäger m.

head·ing ['hedɪŋ] s **1.** Überschrift f, Titel(zeile f) m. **2.** Thema n, (Gesprächs)Punkt m.

'**head·lamp** → **headlight**. ~**land** ['~lənd] s Landspitze f, -zunge f. '~**light** s mot. etc Scheinwerfer m: ~ **flasher** Lichthupe f. '~**line** s **1.** Schlagzeile f: **hit the** ~**s** Schlagzeilen machen. **2.** Überschrift f. '~**long I** adv **1.** kopfüber, mit dem Kopf voran. **2.** fig. a) Hals über Kopf, b) ungestüm, stürmisch. **II** adj **3.** mit dem Kopf voran. **4.** fig. a) voreilig, -schnell, b) → 2b. ,~'**mas·ter** s ped. (Di)Rektor m. ,~'**mis·tress** s ped. (Di)Rektorin f. ~**of·fice** s Hauptbüro n, -sitz m, Zentrale f. ,~'**on** adj **1.** frontal (a. adv), Frontal... **2.** fig. direkt (Art etc). '~**phones** s pl Kopfhörer m. ,~'**quar·ters** s pl (oft sg konstruiert) **1.** ⚔ Hauptquartier n. **2.** (Polizei)Präsidium n. **3.** → **head office.** '~**rest** s Kopfstütze f. '~**set** s Kopfhörer m. '~**shrink·er** s sl. Psychiater m. ~**start** s Sport: Vorsprung m (a. fig.): **have a** ~ **on** (od. **over**) **s.o.** j-m gegenüber im Vorteil sein. '~**strong** adj eigensinnig, halsstarrig. ~ **voice** s ♪ Kopfstimme f. ,~'**wait·er** s Oberkellner m. '~**way** s: **make** ~ (**with**) (gut) vorankommen (mit), Fortschritte machen (bei). ~ **wind** s ✈, ♣ Gegenwind m. '~**work** s geistige Arbeit.

head·y ['hedɪ] adj □ **1.** → **headlong** 4a. **2.** berauschend (a. fig.).

heal [hi:l] **I** v/t heilen (of von) (a. fig.). **II** v/i oft ~ **up** (od. **over**) (zu)heilen. '**heal·ing** s **1.** Heilung f. **II** adj heilsam (a. fig.), heilend: ~ **process** Heil(ungs)prozeß m.

health [helθ] s **1.** Gesundheit f: ~ **certificate** ärztliches Attest; ~ **club** Fitneßclub m; ~ **food** Reform- od. Biokost f; **on** ~ **grounds** aus gesundheitlichen Gründen; ~ **hazard** Gesundheitsrisiko n; ~ **insurance** Krankenversicherung f; ~ **resort** Kurort m; ~ **service** Gesundheitsdienst m. **2.** a. **state of** ~ Gesundheitszustand m: **in good** (**poor**) ~ gesund, bei guter Gesundheit (kränklich, bei schlechter Gesundheit). **3.** Gesundheit f, Wohl n: **drink (to)** (od. **propose**) **s.o.'s** ~ auf j-s Wohl trinken; **your (very good)** ~! auf Ihr Wohl! '**health·y** adj □ **1.** allg. gesund (a. fig.). **2.** F gesund, kräftig (Appetit).

heap [hi:p] **I** s **1.** Haufen m: **in** ~s haufenweise. **2.** F Haufen m, Menge f: ~**s of time** e-e Menge Zeit; ~**s of times** unzählige Male; ~**s better** sehr viel besser. **II** v/t **3.** häufen: ~ **up** auf-, fig. a. anhäufen. **4.** fig. überhäufen (**with** mit).

hear [hɪə] (irr) **I** v/t **1.** hören: **I** ~**d him laugh(ing)** ich hörte ihn lachen; **make o.s.** ~**d** sich Gehör verschaffen. **2.** et. hören, erfahren (**about, of** von, über acc). **3.** j-n anhören, j-m zuhören: ~ **s.o. out** j-n ausreden lassen. **4.** (an)hören, sich et. anhören. **5.** Bitte etc erhören. **6.** Schüler, Gelerntes abhören. **7.** ⚖ verhören, -nehmen; Fall verhandeln. **II** v/i **8.** hören: ~ **say** sagen hören; **he would not** ~ **of it** er wollte davon nichts hören od. wissen; ~! ~! bravo!, sehr richtig!, iro. hört, hört! **9.** hören, erfahren (**about, of** von). **heard** [hɜ:d] pret u. pp von **hear**. '**hear·ing** s **1.** Hören n: **within (out of)** ~ in (außer) Hörweite; ~ **aid** Hörgerät n. **2.** Gehör(sinn m) n: → **hard** 9. **3.** gain (od. get) **a** ~ sich Gehör verschaffen. **4.** ⚖ Verhör n, Vernehmung f; Verhandlung f. **5.** bsd. pol. Hearing n, Anhörung f.

'**hear·say** s: **by** ~ vom Hörensagen.

hearse [hɜ:s] s Leichenwagen m.

heart [hɑ:t] s **1.** anat. Herz n (a. fig. Gemüt, Mitgefühl, Empfindung etc): **my** ~ auswendig; **to one's ~'s content** nach Herzenslust; **with all one's** (od. **one's whole**) ~ von ganzem Herzen; **break s.o.'s** ~ j-m das Herz brechen; **cry** (od. **sob**) **one's** ~ **out** sich die Augen ausweinen; **have no** ~ kein Herz haben, herzlos sein; **my** ~ **sank** ich wurde deprimiert; **take s.th. to** ~ sich et. zu Herzen nehmen; → **bottom** 1, **stone** 1. **2.** fig. Kern m. **3.** Kartenspiel: a) pl Herz n (Farbe), b) Herz(karte f) f n. '~**·ache** s Kummer m, Gram m. ~ **at·tack** s ⚕ Herzanfall m; Herzinfarkt m. '~**·beat** s physiol. Herzschlag m. '~**·break·ing** adj □ herzzerreißend. '~**·burn** s ⚕ Sodbrennen n. ~ **con·di·tion** s ⚕ Herzleiden n.

heart·en ['hɑ:tn] v/t ermutigen.

heart| **fail·ure** s ⚕ Herzversagen n. '~**·felt** adj tiefempfunden, aufrichtig.

hearth [hɑ:θ] s **1.** Kamin m. **2.** a. ~ **and home** fig. häuslicher Herd, Heim n.

heart·i·ly ['hɑ:tɪlɪ] adv **1.** herzlich, von Herzen. **2.** herzhaft.

heart·less ['hɑ:tlɪs] adj □ herzlos.

,**heart**|**·lung ma·chine** s ⚕ Herz-Lungen-Maschine f. ~ **pace·mak·er** s ⚕ Herzschrittmacher m. '~**·rend·ing** adj □ herzzerreißend. ,~**·to-** '~ adj aufrichtig, offen. ~ **trans·plant** s ⚕ Herzverpflanzung f.

heart·y ['hɑ:tɪ] adj (□ → **heartily**) **1.** herzlich. **2.** → **hale** 3. herzhaft, kräftig (Appetit, Mahlzeit etc).

heat [hi:t] **I** s **1.** allg. Hitze f; a. phys. Wärme f. **2.** fig. Ungestüm n; Eifer m: **in the** ~ **of the moment** im Eifer od. in der Hitze des Gefechts; **in the** ~ **of passion** ⚖ im Affekt. **3.** Sport: (Einzel)Lauf m: **(preliminary)** ~ Vorlauf f. **the** ~ Am. coll. F die Bullen pl (Polizei). **5.** zo. Läufigkeit f: **in** ~ läufig. **II** v/t **6.** a. ~ **up** erhitzen, Speisen a. aufwärmen. **7.** heizen. **8.** ~ **up** Diskussion etc anheizen. **III** v/i **9.** sich erhitzen (a. fig.). '**heat·ed** adj **1.** geheizt. **2.** erhitzt, fig. a. erregt, hitzig. '**heat·er** s Heizgerät n, -körper m.

heath [hi:θ] s **1.** bsd. Br. Heide(land n) f. **2.** ♀ a) Erika f, b) → **heather**.

hea·then ['hi:ðn] **I** s **1.** Heide m, Heidin f: **the** ~ coll. die Heiden pl. **2.** Barbar m. **II** adj **3.** heidnisch, Heiden... **4.** unzivilisiert, barbarisch. **hea·then·ish** ['~ənɪʃ] → **heathen** II.

heath·er ['heðə] s ♀ Heidekraut n.

heat·ing ['hi:tɪŋ] **I** s Heizung f. **II** adj Heiz...: ~ **pad** Heizkissen n.

heat| **light·ning** s Wetterleuchten n. '~**·proof** adj hitzebeständig, -fest. ~ **rash** s ⚕ Hitzeausschlag m. '~**·re**,**sist·ant** → **heatproof**. '~**·stroke** s ⚕ Hitzschlag m. ~ **wave** s Hitzewelle f.

heave [hi:v] **I** s **1.** Hochziehen n, -winden n. **2.** F Wurf m. **3.** Wogen n: ~ **of the sea** ♣ Seegang m. **II** v/t (bsd. ♣ irr) **4.** (hoch)stemmen, (-)hieven. **5.** hochziehen, -winden, Anker lichten. **6.** F schmeißen, werfen. **7.** Seufzer etc ausstoßen: → **sigh** II. **8.** F auskotzen. **III** v/i (bsd. ♣ irr) **9.** sich heben u. senken, wogen. **10.** F würgen, Brechreiz haben:

hell

~ **(up)** kotzen. **11.** ~ **to** ⚓ beidrehen.

heav·en ['hevn] *s* **1.** Himmel(reich *n*) *m*: **move** ~ **and earth** *fig.* Himmel u. Hölle in Bewegung setzen; **in the seventh** ~ **(of delight)** *fig.* im sieb(en)ten Himmel; **thank** ~**!** Gott sei Dank!; **what in** ~ **...?** was in aller Welt ...?; → **forbid** 3, **sake**, **stink** 1. **2.** ♀ Himmel *m*, Gott *m*. '**heav·en·ly** *adj* himmlisch (*a. fig.*): ~ **body** *ast.* Himmelskörper *m*.

heav·i·ly ['hevɪlɪ] *adv* schwer (*a. fig.*): ~ **armed** schwerbewaffnet; **suffer** ~ schwere (finanzielle) Verluste erleiden.

heav·y ['hevɪ] **I** *adj* (□ → **heavily**) **1.** *allg.* schwer. **2.** schwer (*Sturz, Verluste etc*), stark (*Regen, Trinker, Verkehr etc*), wuchtig (*Schlag*), hoch (*Geldstrafe, Steuern etc*): ~ **current** ⚡ Starkstrom *m*. **3.** schwer (*Wein etc*), (*Nahrung a.*) schwerverdaulich: ~ **beer** Starkbier *n*. **4.** drückend, lastend (*Stille etc*). **5.** (**with**) (schwer)beladen (mit); *fig.* überladen, voll (von): ~ **with meaning** bedeutungsvoll, -schwer. **6.** begriffsstutzig, dumm. **7.** benommen (**with** von): ~ **with sleep** schlaftrunken. **8. with a** ~ **heart** schweren Herzens. **II** *adv* **9. hang** ~ dahinschleichen (*Zeit*); **lie** ~ **on s.o.** schwer auf j-m lasten. '~·**du·ty** *adj* **1.** ⚙ Hochleistungs... **2.** strapazierfähig. '~·**weight** (*Sport*) **I** *s* Schwergewicht(ler *m*) *n*. **II** *adj* Schwergewichts...

heck·le ['hekl] *v/t* Redner durch Zwischenrufe *od.* -fragen aus dem Konzept bringen *od.* in die Enge treiben. '**heck·ler** *s* Zwischenrufer *m*.

hec·tic ['hektɪk] *adj* (~**ally**) hektisch (*a.* 🩺).

hec·to·li·ter, *bsd. Br.* **hec·to·li·tre** ['hektəʊˌliːtə] *s* Hektoliter *m, n*.

he'd [hiːd] F *für* **he had; he would.**

hedge [hedʒ] **I** *s* **1.** Hecke *f*. **2.** *fig.* (Ab)Sicherung *f* (**against** gegen). **II** *v/t* **3.** *a.* ~ **in** (*od.* **round**) mit e-r Hecke einfassen; ~ **off** mit e-r Hecke abgrenzen *od.* abtrennen. **4.** *fig.* (ab)sichern (**against** gegen). **III** *v/i* **5.** *fig.* ausweichen, sich nicht festlegen (wollen). '~·**hog** *s zo.* Igel *m*; *Am.* Stachelschwein *n*.

heed [hiːd] **I** *v/t* beachten, Beachtung schenken (*dat*). **II** *s*: **give** (*od.* **pay**) ~ **to, take** ~ **of** → I. '**heed·ful** ['~fʊl] *adj* □ achtsam: **be** ~ **of** → **heed** I. '**heed·less**

adj □ achtlos, unachtsam: **be** ~ **of** nicht beachten, keine Beachtung schenken (*dat*), *Warnung etc* in den Wind schlagen.

hee-haw [ˌhiːˈhɔː] **I** *s* **1.** Iah *n* (*Eselsschrei*). **2.** *fig.* wieherndes Gelächter, Gewieher *n*. **II** *v/i* **3.** iahen. **4.** *fig.* wiehernd lachen, wiehern.

heel[1] [hiːl] *v/i* ⚓ sich auf die Seite legen, krängen.

heel[2] [~] **I** *s* **1.** *anat.* Ferse *f* (*a. vom Strumpf etc*); Absatz *m*, Hacken *m* (*vom Schuh*): **down at** ~ a) mit schiefen Absätzen, b) *a.* **out at** ~**s** *fig.* heruntergekommen (*Hotel etc*), (*Person a.*) abgerissen; **on the** ~**s of** unmittelbar auf (*acc*), gleich nach; **follow at s.o.'s** ~**s, follow s.o. at** (*od.* **on**) **his** ~**s** j-m auf den Fersen folgen, sich j-m an die Fersen heften; **show a clean pair of** ~**s, take to one's** ~**s** die Beine in die Hand *od.* unter den Arm nehmen. **II** *v/t* **2.** Absätze machen auf (*acc*). **3.** *Fußball:* Ball mit dem Absatz kicken.

heft·y ['heftɪ] *adj* □ **1.** schwer. **2.** kräftig, stämmig. **3.** F mächtig, gewaltig (*Schlag etc*), stattlich (*Mehrheit etc*), saftig (*Preise etc*).

he·gem·o·ny [hɪ'gemənɪ] *s bsd. pol.* Hegemonie *f*.

height [haɪt] *s* **1.** Höhe *f*: **10 feet in** ~ 10 Fuß hoch. **2.** (Körper)Größe *f*: **what is your** ~**?** wie groß sind Sie? **3.** Anhöhe *f*, Erhebung *f*. **4.** *fig.* Höhe(punkt *m*) *f*, Gipfel *m*: **at the** ~ **of one's fame** auf der Höhe s-s Ruhms; **at the** ~ **of summer** im Hochsommer. '**height·en I** *v/t* **1.** erhöhen (*a. fig.*). **2.** *fig.* vergrößern, steigern. **II** *v/i* **3.** *fig.* sich erhöhen, (an)steigen, zunehmen.

hei·nous ['heɪnəs] *adj* □ abscheulich, scheußlich.

heir [eə] *s* ⚖ Erbe *m* (**to, of** gen): ~ **to the throne** Thronerbe *m*, -folger *m*; → **universal** 1. '**heir·ess** *s* Erbin *f*.

held [held] *pret u. pp von* **hold.**

hel·i·cop·ter ['helɪkɒptə] *s* Hubschrauber *m*.

hel·i·port ['helɪpɔːt] *s* Hubschrauberlandeplatz *m*.

he·li·um ['hiːliəm] *s* 🧪 Helium *n*.

hell [hel] *s* Hölle *f* (*a. fig.*): **like** ~ F wie verrückt *arbeiten etc*; **a** ~ **of a noise** ein Höllenlärm; **what the** ~ **...?** F was zum Teufel ...?; **give** s.o. ~ F j-m die Hölle heiß machen; **go to** ~! F scher dich zum Teufel!; **raise** ~ F e-n Mordskrach schlagen; **suffer** ~ **on earth** die Hölle auf Erden haben.

he'll [hi:l] F *für he will.*

,**hell**|'**bent** *adj* F ganz versessen, wie wild (**on, for** auf *acc*). '~**cat** *s* Xanthippe *f*.

hell·ish ['helɪʃ] *adj* □ **1.** höllisch (*a. fig.* F). **2.** F verteufelt, scheußlich.

hel·lo [hə'ləʊ] **I** *int* **1.** hallo!, (*überrascht a.*) nanu! **II** *pl* -**los** *s* **2.** Hallo *n.* **3.** Gruß *m:* **say** ~ (**to** s.o.) (j-m) guten Tag sagen.

helm [helm] *s* ⚓ Ruder *n* (*a. fig.*), Steuer *n:* **be at the** ~ am Ruder *od.* an der Macht sein; **take the** ~ das Ruder übernehmen.

helms·man ['helmzmən] *s* (*irr man*) ⚓ Steuermann *m* (*a. fig.*).

help [help] **I** *s* **1.** Hilfe *f:* **come to** s.o.'s ~ j-m zu Hilfe kommen. **2.** Abhilfe *f.* **3.** (*bsd.* Haus)Angestellte *f.* **II** *v/t* **4.** *j-m* helfen *od.* behilflich sein (**in** [*od.* with] bei): ~ s.o. **out** j-m aushelfen (**with** mit); → **god** 2. **5.** ~ s.o. **to** s.th. j-m zu et. verhelfen; ~ **o.s.** sich bedienen, zugreifen. **6.** *mit can:* **I cannot** ~ **it** ich kann es nicht ändern; ich kann nichts dafür; **it cannot be** ~**ed** da kann man nichts machen, es ist nicht zu ändern; **I could not** ~ **laughing** ich mußte einfach lachen. **III** *v/i* **7.** helfen: ~ **out** aushelfen (**with** mit). '**help·er** *s* Helfer(in). **help·ful** ['~fʊl] *adj* □ **1.** hilfsbereit. **2.** hilfreich. '**help·ing I** *adj* hilfreich: → **hand** 1. **II** *s* Portion *f* (*Essen*): **have** (*od.* **take**) **a second** ~ sich nachnehmen. '**help·less** *adj* □ hilflos.

hel·ter-skel·ter [,heltə'skeltə] **I** *adv* holterdiepolter, Hals über Kopf. **II** *adj* hastig, überstürzt. **III** *s* (wildes) Durcheinander, (wilde) Hast.

hem[1] [hem] **I** *s* **1.** Saum *m.* **2.** Rand *m,* Einfassung *f.* **II** *v/t* **3.** *Kleid etc* (ein)säumen. **4.** ~ **in** a) a. ~ **about** (*od.* **around**) umranden, einfassen, b) ✕ einschließen, c) *fig.* einengen.

hem[2] [~] **I** *int* h(e)m! **II** *v/i* sich (*verlegen*) räuspern: ~ **and haw** herumdrucksen, nicht recht mit der Sprache herauswollen.

'**he-man** *s* (*irr man*) F He-man *m* (*bsd. männlich wirkender Mann*).

hem·i·sphere ['hemɪˌsfɪə] *s geogr.* Halbkugel *f,* Hemisphäre *f.*

'**hem·line** *s* Saum *m:* ~**s are going up again** die Kleider werden wieder kürzer.

he·mo·glo·bin, hem·or·rhoids *etc bsd. Am.* → **haemoglobin, haemorrhoids** *etc.*

hemp [hemp] *s* Hanf *m.*

hen [hen] *s orn.* **1.** Henne *f,* Huhn *n.* (*Vogel*)Weibchen *n.*

hence [hens] *adv* **1.** a **week** ~ in e-r Woche. **2.** folglich, daher, deshalb. **3.** hieraus, daraus: ~ **it follows that** daraus folgt, daß. ,~'**forth,** ,~'**for·ward(s)** *adv* von nun an, fortan.

hench·man ['hentʃmən] *s* (*irr man*) *bsd. pol.* Anhänger *m; contp.* Handlanger *m.*

hen| **par·ty** *s* F Damengesellschaft *f,* Kaffeeklatsch *m.* '~**pecked** *adj* unter dem Pantoffel stehend: ~ **husband** Pantoffelheld *m.*

hep [hep] → **hip**[4].

hep·a·ti·tis [,hepə'taɪtɪs] *s* 🕮 Leberentzündung *f.*

her [hɜ:] **I** *personal pron* **1.** sie (*acc von* **she**): **I know** ~. **2.** ihr (*dat von* **she**): **I gave** ~ **the book**. **3.** F sie (*nom*): **he's younger than** ~; **it's** ~ sie ist es. **II** *possessive pron* **4.** ihr(e). **III** *reflex pron* **5.** sich: **she looked about** ~ sie sah sich um.

her·ald ['herəld] **I** *s* **1.** *hist.* Herold *m.* **2.** *fig.* Vorbote *m.* **II** *v/t* **3.** ankündigen (*a. fig.*). **he·ral·dic** [he'rældɪk] *adj* (~**ally**) heraldisch, Wappen... **her·ald·ry** ['herəldrɪ] *s* Heraldik *f,* Wappenkunde *f.*

herb [hɜ:b] *s* ♃ Kraut *n; engS.* Heilkraut; Gewürz-, Küchenkraut. **herb·al** ['~bl] *adj* Kräuter..., Pflanzen... **her·bar·i·um** [~'beərɪəm] *s* Herbarium *n.* **her·biv·o·rous** [~'bɪvərəs] *adj* □ *zo.* pflanzenfressend.

herd [hɜ:d] **I** *s* **1.** Herde *f,* (*wildlebender Tiere a.*) Rudel *n* (*a. von Menschen*). **2.** *contp.* Herde *f,* Masse *f* (*Menschen*): **the** (**common od. vulgar**) ~ die große *od.* breite Masse. **II** *v/i* **3.** a. ~ **together** in Herden leben; sich zs.-drängen (*a. Menschen*). **4.** sich zs.-tun (**with** mit). **III** *v/t* **5.** Vieh hüten. **6.** *Vieh, a. Menschen* treiben: ~ **together** zs.-treiben. '**herd·er** *s bsd. Am.* Hirt *m.*

herd in·stinct *s zo.* Herdeninstinkt *m, (a. bei Menschen)* Herdentrieb *m.*

herds·man ['hɜːdzmən] *s (irr man) bsd. Br.* Hirt *m.*

here [hɪə] *adv* hier; (hier)her: **come ~** komm her; **~ and there** hier u. da, da u. dort; hierhin u. dorthin; **~'s to you!** auf dein Wohl!; **~ you** (*od.* **we**) **are!** hier (bitte)! (*da hast du es*). '**~a,bouts** *adv* hier herum, in dieser Gegend. **,~'af·ter I** *adv* **1.** nachstehend, im folgenden. **2.** künftig, in Zukunft. **II** *s* **3.** Jenseits *n.* **,~'by** *adv* hiermit.

he·red·i·ta·ry [hɪ'redɪtərɪ] *adj* □ **1.** (ver)erblich, Erb...: **~ disease** Erbkrankheit *f.* **2.** *fig.* althergebracht, Erb...: **~ enemy** Erbfeind *m.*

,here|'in *adv* hierin. **,~'of** *adv* hiervon.

her·e·sy ['herəsɪ] *s* Ketzerei *f.*

her·e·tic ['herətɪk] *s* Ketzer(in). **he·ret·i·cal** [hɪ'retɪkl] *adj* □ ketzerisch.

,here|·up'on *adv* hierauf, darauf(hin). **,~'with** *adv* hiermit.

her·it·a·ble ['herɪtəbl] *adj* □ erblich, vererbbar. **'her·it·age** *s* Erbe *n.*

her·maph·ro·dite [hɜː'mæfrədaɪt] *s biol.* Zwitter *m.*

her·met·ic [hɜː'metɪk] *adj* (**~ally**) hermetisch, ⊙ luftdicht: **~ally sealed** luftdicht verschlossen.

her·mit ['hɜːmɪt] *s* Einsiedler *m (a. fig.)*, Eremit *m.* **'her·mit·age** *s* Einsiedelei *f.*

her·ni·a ['hɜːnjə] *s ✻* Bruch *m.*

he·ro ['hɪərəʊ] *pl* **-roes** *s* Held *m, thea. etc a.* Hauptperson *f.* **he·ro·ic** [hɪ'rəʊɪk] *adj* (**~ally**) **1.** heroisch, heldenhaft, Helden... **2.** hochtrabend, bombastisch (*Sprache, Stil*).

her·o·in ['herəʊɪn] *s* Heroin *n.*

her·o·ine ['herəʊɪn] *s* Heldin *f, thea. etc a.* Hauptperson *f.* **'her·o·ism** *s* Heldentum *n.*

her·on ['herən] *s orn.* Reiher *m.*

her·pes ['hɜːpiːz] *s ✻* Herpes *m.*

her·ring ['herɪŋ] *pl* **-rings,** *bsd. coll.* **-ring** *s ichth.* Hering *m.* '**~·bone** *s a.* **~ design** (*od.* **pattern**) Fischgrätenmuster *n.*

hers [hɜːz] *possessive pron:* **it is ~** es gehört ihr; **a friend of ~** e-e Freundin von ihr; **my mother and ~** m-e u. ihre Mutter.

her'self *pron* **1.** *verstärkend:* sie (*nom od. acc*) selbst, ihr (*dat*) selbst: **she did it ~,**

she ~ **did it** sie hat es selbst getan. **2.** *reflex* sich: **she killed ~. 3.** sich (selbst): **she wants it for ~.**

he's [hiːz] F *für* **he is; he has.**

hes·i·tate ['hezɪteɪt] *v/i* **1.** zögern, zaudern, Bedenken haben (**to do** zu tun), unschlüssig sein (**over** hinsichtlich). **2.** (*beim Sprechen*) stocken. **hes·i'ta·tion** *s* Zögern *n,* Zaudern *n,* Unschlüssigkeit *f:* **without** (**any**) ~ ohne zu zögern. **2.** Stocken *n.*

het·er·o·dox ['hetərəʊdɒks] *adj* heterodox, anders-, irrgläubig. **het·er·o·ge·ne·ous** [,~'dʒiːnjəs] *adj* □ heterogen, ungleichartig, verschiedenartig. **het·er·o'sex·u·al I** *adj* □ heterosexuell. **II** *s* Heterosexuelle *m, f.*

het¹ [het] *adj:* **be ~ up** F aufgeregt *od.* nervös sein (**about** wegen).

het² [~] F **I** *adj* hetero (*heterosexuell*). **II** *s* Hetero *m, f.*

hew [hjuː] *v/t (a. irr)* **1.** hauen, hacken: ~ **down** umhauen; ~ **off** abhauen; ~ **up** zerhauen, -hacken. **2.** Steine etc behauen. **hewn** [hjuːn] *pp von* **hew.**

hex·a·gon ['heksəgən] *s* Sechseck *n.* **hex·ag·o·nal** [~'sægənl] *adj* □ sechseckig.

hey [heɪ] *int* **1.** → **presto. 2.** he!

hey·day ['heɪdeɪ] *s* a) Höhepunkt *m,* Gipfel *m:* **in the ~ of one's power** auf dem Gipfel der Macht, b) Blüte(zeit) *f:* **in one's ~** in s-r Glanzzeit.

hi [haɪ] *int* F hallo!

hi·ber·nate ['haɪbəneɪt] *v/i* überwintern: a) *zo.* Winterschlaf halten, b) den Winter verbringen. **,hi·ber'na·tion** *s* Überwinterung *f,* Winterschlaf *m.*

hi·bis·cus [hɪ'bɪskəs] *s ✻* Hibiskus *m,* Eibisch *m.*

hic·cough, hic·cup ['hɪkʌp] **I** *s* **1. have** (**the**) **~s** e-n Schluckauf haben. **2.** *fig.* Panne *f.* **II** *v/i* **3.** hicksen.

hick [hɪk] *bsd. Am.* F **I** *s* Bauer *m,* Provinzler *m.* **II** *adj* Bauern..., provinziell: ~ **town** (Provinz)Nest *n,* (Bauern-) Kaff *n.*

hick·o·ry ['hɪkərɪ] *s* **1. ✻** Hickory(baum) *m.* **2.** Hickory(holz) *n.*

hid [hɪd] *pret u. pp von* **hide². 'hid·den I** *pp von* **hide². II** *adj* □ geheim, verborgen.

hide¹ [haɪd] **I** *s* **1.** Haut *f,* Fell *n (beide a. fig.):* **save one's own ~** die eigene Haut retten; **tan s.o.'s ~** F j-m das Fell gerben. II v/t 2. abhäuten. 3. F verprügeln.

hide² [~] (irr) I v/t (from) verbergen (vor dat): a) verstecken (vor dat), b) verheimlichen (dat od. vor dat), c) verhüllen, -decken. II v/i a. **~ out** (bsd. Am. up) sich verbergen od. verstecken. **~-and-'seek** s Versteckspiel n: **play ~** Verstecken spielen. **'~-a-way** s 1. Versteck n. 2. Zufluchtsort m.

hid·e·ous ['hɪdɪəs] adj □ abscheulich, scheußlich.

'hide-out s Versteck n.

hid·ing¹ ['haɪdɪŋ] s F Tracht f Prügel.

hid·ing² [~] s a. **~ place** Versteck n: **be in ~** sich versteckt halten; **go into ~** untertauchen.

hi·er·arch·y ['haɪərɑːkɪ] s Hierarchie f.

hi·er·o·glyph ['haɪərəʊglɪf] → **hieroglyphic** 1, 3. **,hi·er·o·'glyph·ic** s 1. Hieroglyphe f. 2. pl (mst sg konstruiert) Hieroglyphenschrift f. 3. pl humor. Hieroglyphen pl, unleserliches Gekritzel.

hi·fi ['haɪfaɪ] F I s 1. Hi-Fi n. 2. Hi-Fi-Anlage f; -Gerät n. II adj 3. Hi-Fi-...

hig·gle·dy-pig·gle·dy [,hɪgldɪ'pɪgldɪ] F I adv drunter u. drüber, (wie Kraut u. Rüben) durcheinander. II adj kunterbunt.

high [haɪ] I adj (□ → **highly**) 1. allg. hoch; engS. a. hochgelegen: → **horse**. 2. hoch (Geschwindigkeit, Preise etc), groß (Hoffnungen, Lob etc). 3. (rang-od. stellungsmäßig) hoch: **~ society** High-Society f. 4. hoch: **~ season** Hochsaison f; **~ summer** Hochsommer m; **it is ~ time** es ist höchste Zeit. 5. hoch, erstklassig (Qualität etc). 6. a) gehoben: → **spirit** 4, b) blau (betrunken), c) F high. 7. F scharf (on auf acc). II adv 8. hoch: **aim ~** fig. sich hohe Ziele setzen od. stecken: **search ~ and low** überall suchen. 9. hoch, mit hohem Einsatz (spielen). III s 10. (An)Höhe f: **on ~** hoch oben, droben; im Himmel. 11. meteor. Hoch n. 12. fig. Höchststand m. 13. Am. F High-School f. **~ al·tar** s Hochaltar m. **,~'al·ti·tude** adj Höhen... **~ and dry** adj: **leave s.o. ~** j-n im Stich lassen. **~ and might·y** adj F anmaßend, arrogant. **'~ball** s Am. Highball m (Whiskycocktail). **~ beam** s mot. Am. Fernlicht n. **'~brow** oft contp. I s Intellektuelle m, f. II adj (betont) intellektuell. **'~chair** s (Kinder)Hochstuhl m. **~ Church** s anglikanische Hochkirche. **,~cir·cu'la·tion** adj auflagenstark. **,~'class** adj erstklassig. **,~'du·ty** adj ⊕ Hochleistungs... **~ fi·del·i·ty** s High-Fidelity f. **,~fi'del·i·ty** adj High-Fidelity-... **'~flown** adj 1. bombastisch, hochtrabend (Worte etc). 2. (allzu) hochgesteckt (Ziele etc), (allzu) hochfliegend (Pläne etc). **~ gear** s mot. hochwertig. 2. a. ♃ erstklassig. **,~ 'hand·ed** adj □ anmaßend, willkürlich. **,~'heeled** adj hochhackig (Schuhe). **~ jump** s Leichtathletik: Hochsprung m. **~ jump·er** s Hochspringer(in). **,~talks** pl Gespräche pl auf höherer Ebene. **'~light** I s Höhe-, Glanzpunkt m; pl Querschnitt m (of durch e-e Oper etc). II v/t hervorheben.

high·ly ['haɪlɪ] adv 1. fig. hoch: **~ gifted** hochbegabt; **~ interesting** hochinteressant; **~ paid** hochbezahlt; teuer bezahlt. 2. lobend, anerkennend: **think ~ of** viel halten von.

High¦ Mass s eccl. Hochamt n. **,~'necked** adj hochgeschlossen (Kleid). **high-ness** ['haɪnɪs] s 1. mst fig. Höhe f. 2. ♀ Hoheit f (Titel).

,high¦-'pow·er(ed) adj 1. ⊕ Hochleistungs... 2. fig. dynamisch, energisch. **,~'pres·sure** adj ⊕, meteor. Hochdruck... **~ priest** s eccl. Hohepriester m (a. fig.). **,~'qual·i·ty** adj hochwertig. **'~rank·ing** adj hochrangig: **~ officer** ✕ hoher Offizier. **'~rise** s Hochhaus n. **~ school** s Am. High-School f. **,~'sea** adj Hochsee... **'~sound·ing** adj hochtönend, -trabend. **~ street** s Br. Hauptstraße f. **~ tea** s Br. frühes Abendessen. **~tech** [,~'tek] adj High-Tech-... **~ tech·nol·o·gy** s Hochtechnologie f. **~ ten·sion** s ⚡ Hochspannung f. **,~'ten·sion** adj Hochspannungs... **~ trea·son** s Hochverrat m. **~ wa·ter** s Hochwasser n. **'~way** s Highway m, Haupt(verkehrs)straße f: **~ code** Br. Straßenverkehrsordnung f.

hi·jack ['haɪdʒæk] I v/t 1. Flugzeug entführen. 2. j-n, Geldtransport etc überfallen. II s 3. (Flugzeug)Entführung f. 4. Überfall m. **'hi·jack·er** s 1. (Flug-

zeug)Entführer *m*. **2.** Räuber *m*.
'**hi·jack·ing** → **hijack** II.

hike [haɪk] **I** *v/i* wandern. **II** *s* Wanderung *f*: **go on a** ~ e-e Wanderung machen. '**hik·er** *s* Wanderer *m*.

hi·lar·i·ous [hɪˈleərɪəs] *adj* □ **1.** vergnügt, ausgelassen, übermütig. **2.** lustig (*Geschichte etc*). **hi·lar·i·ty** [hɪˈlærətɪ] *s* Vergnügtheit *f*, Ausgelassenheit *f*, Übermütigkeit *f*.

hill [hɪl] *s* Hügel *m*, Anhöhe *f*: (**as**) **old as the** ~**s** uralt, (*Person a*.) steinalt; **be over the** ~ F s-e besten Jahre *od*. s-e beste Zeit hinter sich haben; *bsd*. ⚓ über den Berg sein. '~**bil·ly** *s Am. mst contp*. Hillbilly *m*, Hinterwäldler *m*.

hill·ock [ˈhɪlək] *s* kleiner Hügel.

ˌ**hill**'**side** *s* (Ab)Hang *m*. ˌ~'**top** *s* Hügelspitze *f*. ~ **walk** *s* Bergwanderung *f*.

hilt [hɪlt] *s* Heft *n*, Griff *m* (*Schwert, Dolch*): (**up**) **to the** ~ bis ans Heft; *fig*. durch u. durch, ganz u. gar.

him [hɪm] **I** *personal pron* **1.** ihn (*acc von* **he**): **I know** ~. **2.** ihm (*dat von* **he**): **I gave** ~ **the book. 3.** F er (*nom*): **she's younger than** ~; **it's** ~ er ist es. **II** *reflex pron* **4.** sich: **he looked about** ~ er sah sich um.

him'self *pron* **1.** *verstärkend*: er *od*. ihm *od*. ihn selbst: **he did it** ~, **he** ~ **did it** er hat es selbst getan. **2.** *reflex* sich: **he killed** ~. **3.** sich (selbst): **he wants it for** ~.

hind [haɪnd] *adj* hinter, Hinter...: ~ **wheel** Hinterrad *n*.

hind·er [ˈhɪndə] *v/t* **1.** *j-n, et*. aufhalten (**in** bei); behindern. **2.** (**from**) hindern (**an** *dat*), abhalten (**von**).

hind·most [ˈhaɪndməʊst] *sup von* **hind**.

ˌ**hind**'**quar·ters** *s pl* Hinterhand *f* (*vom Pferd*); Hinterteil *n*.

hin·drance [ˈhɪndrəns] *s* **1.** Behinderung *f*: **be a** ~ **to** → **hinder** 1. **2.** Hindernis *n* (**to** für).

'**hind·sight** *s*: **with** ~ im nachhinein (betrachtet).

Hin·du [ˌhɪnˈduː] *eccl*. **I** *s* Hindu *m*. **II** *adj* Hindu... '**Hin·du·ism** *s* Hinduismus *m*.

hinge [hɪndʒ] **I** *s* **1.** *a*. ~ **joint** ⚙ Scharnier *n*, (Tür)Angel *f*. **2.** *fig*. Angelpunkt *m*. **II** *v/t* **3.** Tür etc einhängen. **III** *v/i* **4.** (**on** *fig*. abhängen (**von**), ankommen (**auf** *acc*); sich drehen (**um**).

hint [hɪnt] **I** *s* **1.** Wink *m*, Andeutung *f*:

drop a ~ e-e Andeutung machen; **broad** ~ Wink mit dem Zaunpfahl. **2.** Fingerzeig *m*, Tip *m* (**on** für). **3.** Anspielung *f* (**at** auf *acc*). **4.** Anflug *m*, Spur *f* (**of** von). **II** *v/t* **5.** andeuten. **III** *v/i* **6.** (**at**) andeuten (*acc*); anspielen (**auf** *acc*).

hin·ter·land [ˈhɪntəlænd] *s* **1.** Hinterland *n*. **2.** Umland *n*.

hip¹ [hɪp] *s anat*. Hüfte *f*.

hip² [~] *s* ♣ Hagebutte *f*.

hip³ [~] *int*: ~, ~, **hurrah!** hipp, hipp, hurra!

hip⁴ [~] *adj sl*. **1. be** ~ alles mitmachen, was gerade in ist. **2. be** ~ auf dem laufenden sein (**to** über *acc*).

'**hip**·**bath** *s* Sitzbad *n*. '~**bone** *s anat*. Hüftbein *n*, -knochen *m*. ~ **flask** *s* Taschenflasche *f*, Flachmann *m*. ~ **joint** *s anat*. Hüftgelenk *n*.

hip·pie [ˈhɪpɪ] *s* Hippie *m*.

hip pock·et *s* Gesäßtasche *f*.

hip·po·pot·a·mus [ˌhɪpəˈpɒtəməs] *pl* -**mus·es**, -**mi** [~maɪ] *s zo*. Fluß-, Nilpferd *n*.

hip·py → **hippie**.

hire [ˈhaɪə] **I** *v/t* **1.** *Auto etc* mieten, *Flugzeug etc* chartern: ~**d car** Leih-, Mietwagen *m*; ~**d plane** Charterflugzeug *n*. **2.** *a*. ~ **on** *j-n* ein-, anstellen, ⚓ (an)heuern; *j-n* engagieren; *bsd. b.s*. anheuern: ~**d killer** gekaufter Mörder, Killer *m*. *mst* ~ **out** vermieten. **II** *s* **4.** Miete *f*: ~ **company** Verleih(firma *f*) *m*; **on** ~ mietweise; **for** ~ zu vermieten; (*Taxi*) frei. **5.** Lohn *m*, Entgelt *n*. ~ **pur·chase** *s*: **on** ~ *bsd. Br*. auf Abzahlung *od*. Raten.

his [hɪz] *possessive pron*: **it is** ~ es gehört ihm; **a friend of** ~ ein Freund von ihm; **my mother and** ~ m-e u. s-e Mutter.

hiss [hɪs] **I** *v/i* **1.** zischen, (*Katze*) fauchen: ~ **at** → **2**. **II** *v/t* **2.** auszischen. **3.** *et*. zische(l)n. **III** *s* **4.** Zischen *n*, Fauchen *n*.

his·to·ri·an [hɪˈstɔːrɪən] *s* Historiker *m*.

his·tor·ic [hɪˈstɒrɪk] *adj* (~**ally**) **1.** historisch, geschichtlich (berühmt *od*. bedeutsam). **2.** → **historical**. **his·tor·i·cal** [~kl] *adj* □ **1.** → **historic** 1. **2.** historisch: a) geschichtlich (belegt *od*. überliefert) b) Geschichts..., c) geschichtlich(en Inhalts): ~ **novel** historischer Roman. **his·to·ry** [ˈ~tərɪ] *s* **1.** Geschichte *f*: *contemporary* ~ Zeitgeschichte; ~ *of art* Kunstgeschichte; *go down in* ~ in die Geschichte eingehen; *make* ~ Geschichte machen. **2.** (Entwicklungs-) Geschichte *f*, Werdegang *m*. **3.** *allg.*, *a.* *⚚* Vorgeschichte *f*: → *case history*.

hit [hɪt] **I** *s* **1.** Hieb *m* (*a. fig. at* gegen), Schlag *m*: *that was a* ~ *at me* das ging gegen mich. **2.** Treffer *m* (*a. Sport u. fig.*): *make* (*od. score*) *a* ~ e-n Treffer erzielen; *fig.* gut ankommen (*with* bei). **3.** Hit *m* (*Buch, Schlager etc*): *it was a big* ~ es hat groß eingeschlagen. **4.** *sl.* Schuß *m* (*Drogeninjektion*): *give o.s. a* ~ sich e-n Schuß setzen *od.* drücken. **5.** *bsd. Am. sl.* (*von e-m* **hit man** *ausgeführter*) Mord. **II** *v/t* (*irr*) **6.** schlagen. *~ the nail on the head fig.* den Nagel auf den Kopf treffen; *~ the bottle* F saufen; → *hay, road, sack* [1] **3. 8.** *mot. etc j-n, etc.* anfahren, *et.* rammen: ~ *one's head against* (*od. on*) sich den Kopf anschlagen an (*dat*), mit dem Kopf stoßen gegen. **9.** *et.* erreichen, schaffen: → *front page, headline* 1. **10.** *bsd. fig.* stoßen auf (*acc*), finden. **11.** *a.* ~ *up bsd. Am.* F anhauen, anpumpen (*for* um). **12.** F ankommen in (*dat*), erreichen. **13.** *bsd. Am. sl. j-n* umlegen (**hit man**). **14.** *v/i* (*irr*) **14.** treffen. **15.** schlagen (*at* nach). **16.** stoßen, schlagen (*against* gegen; *on* auf *acc*). **17.** ~ *on* → 10.
Verbindungen mit Adverbien:

hit *back v/i* zurückschlagen (*a. fig.*). ~ *off v/t*: *hit it off* F sich gut vertragen (*with* mit). ~ *out v/i* **1.** um sich schlagen: ~ *at s.o.* auf j-n einschlagen. **2.** *fig.* her-, losziehen (*at, against* über *acc*).

,**hit-and-'run** *adj*: ~ *accident* Unfall *m* mit Fahrerflucht; ~ *driver* (unfall-) flüchtiger Fahrer.

hitch [hɪtʃ] **I** *s* **1.** Ruck *m*, Zug *m*. **2.** Schwierigkeit *f*, Haken *m*: *without a* ~ glatt, reibungslos. **3.** *get a* ~ F im Auto mitgenommen werden. **II** *v/t* **4.** rücken, ziehen: ~ *up* hochziehen. **5.** befestigen, festhaken (*to* an *acc*): *get* ~*ed* F heiraten. **6.** ~ *a ride* → 3. **III** *v/i* **7.** sich festhaken, hängenbleiben (*on* an *dat*). **8.** F → *hitchhike*.

'**hitch·er** F → *hitchhiker*.

'**hitch**|·**hike** *v/i* per Anhalter fahren,

trampen. '~**,hik·er** *s* Anhalter(in), Tramper(in).

hith·er ['hɪðə] *adv* hierher. ,~'**to** *adv* bisher, bis jetzt.

hit| **list** *s*: *be on the* ~ *bsd. Am. sl.* auf der Abschußliste stehen (*a. fig.*). ~ **man** *s* (*irr* **man**) *bsd. Am. sl.* Killer *m* (*e-s Verbrechersyndikats*). ~ **or miss** *adv* aufs Geratewohl, auf gut Glück. ~ **pa·rade** *s* Hitparade *f*. ~ **song** *s* Hit *m*.

hive [haɪv] **I** *s* **1.** Bienenkorb *m*, -stock *m*. **2.** Bienenvolk *n*; *fig.* Schwarm *m* (*Menschen*). **II** *v/i* **3.** ~ *off fig.* abschwenken (*from* von); sich selbständig machen; *bsd. Br.* F sich aus dem Staub machen. **4.** sich zs.-drängen.

hives [haɪvz] *s pl* (*a. sg* konstruiert) *⚚* Nesselausschlag *m*.

hoard [hɔːd] **I** *s* Vorrat *m* (*of* an *dat*). **II** *v/t a.* ~ *up* horten, hamstern. **III** *v/i* hamstern, sich Vorräte anlegen.

hoard·ing ['hɔːdɪŋ] *s* **1.** Bau-, Bretterzaun *m*. **2.** *Br.* Reklametafel *f*.

hoar·frost [,hɔː'frɒst] *s* (Rauh)Reif *m*.

hoarse [hɔːs] *adj* □ heiser. '**hoarse-ness** *s* Heiserkeit *f*.

hoar·y ['hɔːrɪ] *adj* □ **1.** weiß(grau). **2.** (alters)grau.

hoax [həʊks] **I** *s* **1.** (Zeitungs)Ente *f*. **2.** Streich *m*, (übler) Scherz: *play a* ~ *on s.o.* j-m e-n Streich spielen, sich mit j-m e-n Scherz erlauben. **II** *v/t* **3.** *j-m* e-n Bären aufbinden.

hob·ble ['hɒbl] *v/i* hinken, humpeln.

hob·by ['hɒbɪ] *s* Hobby *n*, Steckenpferd *n*. ~ **room** *s* Hobbyraum *m*.

hob·gob·lin ['hɒbgɒblɪn] *s* Kobold *m*.

hob·nob ['hɒbnɒb] *v/i* freundschaftlich verkehren, auf du u. du sein (*with* mit).

ho·bo ['həʊbəʊ] *pl* -**bo(e)s** *s Am.* Landstreicher *m*, Tippelbruder *m*.

Hob·son's choice ['hɒbsnz] *s*: *it was (a case of)* ~ es gab nur 'eine Möglichkeit; *he had to take* ~ es blieb ihm keine andere Wahl.

hock[1] [hɒk] *s* weißer Rheinwein.

hock[2] [~] *bsd. Am.* F **I** *s*: *be in* ~ versetzt sein; Schulden haben (*to* bei); im Kittchen sein *od.* sitzen; *put into* ~ → II. **II** *v/t* versetzen, ins Leihhaus tragen.

hock·ey ['hɒkɪ] *s bsd. Br.* Hockey *n*; *bsd. Am.* Eishockey *n.*

ho·cus-po·cus [,həʊkəs'pəʊkəs] *s* Hokuspokus *m*, fauler Zauber.

hodge·podge ['hɒdʒpɒdʒ] → **hotch-potch.**

hoe [həʊ] I s Hacke f. II v/t Boden hak-ken: ~ (**up**) Unkraut aushacken.

hog [hɒg] I s **1.** (Haus-, Schlacht-) Schwein n: **go the whole ~** F aufs Ganze gehen. **2.** F rücksichtsloser Kerl; gieriger od. gefräßiger Kerl; Schmutzfink m, Ferkel n. II v/t **3.** F rücksichtslos an sich reißen: ~ **the road** mot. die ganze Straße für sich brauchen; rücksichtslos fahren.

Hog·ma·nay ['hɒgmənei] s schott. Silvester(abend m) m, n.

'hog·wash I s **1.** Schweinefutter n. **2.** F Spülwasser n (dünner Kaffee etc). **3.** fig. Gewäsch n, Geschwätz n.

hoi pol·loi [,hɔɪ'pɒlɔɪ] s contp. breite Masse, Pöbel m.

hoist [hɔɪst] I v/t **1.** hochziehen; Flagge, Segel hissen. II s **2.** Hochziehen n. **3.** ⊙ (Lasten)Aufzug m.

hoi·ty-toi·ty [,hɔɪtɪ'tɔɪtɪ] adj hochnäsig, eingebildet.

hold [həʊld] I s **1.** Griff m (a. Ringen), Halt m: **catch** (od. **get, take**) **~ of s.th.** et. ergreifen od. zu fassen bekommen; **get ~ of s.o.** j-n erwischen; **keep ~ of** festhalten; **let go one's ~ of s.th.** et. loslassen. **2.** Halt m, Stütze f: **lose one's ~** den Halt verlieren. **3.** (**on, over, of**) Gewalt f, Macht f (über acc), Einfluß m (auf acc): **have a** (**firm**) **~ on s.o.** j-n in s-r Gewalt haben; **lose ~ o/o.s.** die Fassung verlieren. II v/t (irr) **4.** (fest)halten. **5.** sich die Nase, die Ohren zuhalten: ~ **one's nose** (**ears**). **6.** Gewicht etc tragen, (aus)halten. **7.** (in e-m Zustand) halten: ~ **o.s. erect** sich geraderhalten: ~ (**o.s.**) **ready** (sich) bereithalten. **8.** zurück-, abhalten (**from** von): ~ **s.o. from doing s.th.** j-n davon abhalten, et. zu tun; **there was no ~ing him** er war nicht zu halten. **9.** Wahlen, Pressekonferenz etc abhalten; Fest etc veranstalten. **10.** ✕ u. fig. Stellung halten, behaupten: ~ **one's own** (**with**) sich behaupten (gegen), bestehen (neben). **11.** Aktien, Rechte etc besitzen; Amt etc bekleiden. **12.** Platz etc (inne)halten; Rekord halten; Titel führen. **13.** fassen: a) enthalten, b) Platz bieten für. **14.** Bewunderung, Sympathie etc hegen, haben (**for** für).

15. der Ansicht sein (**that** daß). **16.** halten für: **I ~ him to be a liar** ich halte ihn für e-n Lügner. **17.** halten: ~ **responsible** verantwortlich machen; ~ **contempt** 1, **esteem** 3. **18.** bsd. ⚖ entscheiden (**that** daß). **19.** Publikum, j-s Aufmerksamkeit fesseln. **20.** ~ **s.th. against s.o.** j-m et. vorhalten od. vorwerfen; j-m et. übelnehmen od. nachtragen. III v/i (irr) **21.** halten, nicht (zer)reißen od. (zer)brechen. **22.** (sich) festhalten (**by, to** an dat). **23.** a. ~ **good** (weiterhin) gelten, gültig sein od. bleiben. **24.** anhalten, andauern.

Verbindungen mit Adverbien:

hold| back I v/t **1.** zurückhalten. **2.** → **hold in** I. **3.** fig. zurückhalten mit, verschweigen. II v/i **4.** fig. sich zurückhalten. **5.** nicht mit der Sprache herausrücken. ~ **down** v/t **1.** niederhalten, fig. a. unterdrücken. **2.** F Posten haben; sich in e-r Stellung etc halten. ~ **in** I v/t zügeln, zurückhalten: **hold o.s. in** a) → II, b) den Bauch einziehen. II v/i sich zurückhalten od. beherrschen. ~ **off** I v/t **1.** ab-, fernhalten, abwehren. **2.** et. aufschieben, j-n hinhalten. II v/i **3.** sich fernhalten (**from** von). **4.** zögern; warten (**from** mit). **5.** ausbleiben (Regen etc). ~ **on** v/i **1.** festhalten (**to** an dat) (a. fig.). **2.** sich festhalten (**to** an dat) (a. fig.). **3.** aus-, durchhalten. **4.** andauern, anhalten. **5.** teleph. am Apparat bleiben. ~ **out** I v/t **1.** Hand etc ausstrecken: **hold s.th. out to s.o.** j-m et. hinhalten. II v/i **2.** reichen (Vorräte). **3.** aus-, durchhalten. ~ **o·ver** v/t **1.** Sitzung, Entscheidung etc vertagen, -schieben (**till, until** auf acc). **2.** Film etc verlängern (**for** um). ~ **to·geth·er** v/t u. v/i zs.-halten (a. fig.). ~ **up** I v/t **1.** hochhalten. **2.** fig. hinstellen (**as an example** als Beispiel). **3.** j-n, et. aufhalten; et. verzögern: **be held up** sich verzögern. **4.** j-n, Bank etc überfallen. II v/i **5.** sich halten (Preise, Wetter etc).

'hold·all s bsd. Br. Reisetasche f.

hold·er ['həʊldə] s **1.** oft in Zssgn Halter m, ⊙ a. Halterung f. **2.** Inhaber(in).

'hold·ing s oft pl Besitz m (an Effekten etc): ~ **company** ✝ Holding-, Dachgesellschaft f.

'hold·up s (bewaffneter) (Raub)Überfall.

hole [həʊl] **I** s **1.** Loch n: **be in a ~** F in der Klemme sein od. sitzen od. stecken; **make a ~ in** fig. ein Loch reißen in (*Vorräte*); **pick** (od. **knock**) **~s in** fig. an e-r Sache herumkritteln, *Argument etc* zerpflücken; **j-m** am Zeug flicken. **2.** Höhle f, Bau m (e-s Tiers), Loch n (e-r Maus). **3.** F a) a. **~ in the wall** Loch n, (Bruch)Bude f, b) Kaff n, Nest n. **II** v/t **4.** ein Loch od. Löcher machen in (acc); durchlöchern. **5.** Golf: *Ball* einlochen. **III** v/i **6.** oft **~ out** (Golf) einlochen.

hol·i·day ['hɒlədeɪ] **I** s **1.** Feiertag m: → **public 3b. 2.** freier Tag: **take a ~** (sich) e-n Tag frei nehmen. **3.** mst pl bsd.Br. Ferien pl, Urlaub m: **be on ~** im Urlaub sein, Urlaub machen. **II** adj **4.** bsd. Br. Ferien..., Urlaubs... **III** v/i **5.** bsd. Br. Urlaub machen , die Ferien verbringen. **~·mak·er** ['~ˌdɪ~] s bsd. Br. Urlauber(in).

hol·ler ['hɒlə] v/i u. v/t F schreien, brüllen: **~ for help** um Hilfe schreien; **~ at** j-n anbrüllen.

hol·low ['hɒləʊ] **I** s **1.** (Aus)Höhlung f, Hohlraum m: **~ of the hand** hohle Hand. **II** adj □ **2.** hohl: **beat s.o. ~** Br. F j-n haushoch schlagen; **feel ~** Hunger haben. **3.** hohl, dumpf (*Klang, Stimme*). **4.** fig. hohl, leer; falsch, unaufrichtig: → **ring²** 2, 6. **5.** hohl: a) eingefallen (*Wangen*), b) tiefliegend (*Augen*). **III** adv **6.** hohl: **ring ~** fig. hohl klingen (*Versprechen etc*), unglaubwürdig klingen (*Protest etc*). **IV** v/t **7.** oft **~ out** aushöhlen.

hol·ly ['hɒlɪ] s ⚘ Stechpalme f.

hol·o·caust ['hɒləkɔːst] s Massenvernichtung f, -sterben n, (bsd. Brand)Katastrophe f: **the 2** hist. der Holocaust.

hol·ster ['həʊlstə] s (Pistolen)Halfter f, n.

ho·ly ['həʊlɪ] adj heilig, (*Hostie etc*) geweiht. **2 Ghost** s eccl. der Heilige Geist. **2 Scrip·ture** s eccl. die Heilige Schrift. **2 Spir·it** → **Holy Ghost. ~ ter·ror** s F Nervensäge f. **2 Thurs·day** s eccl. Gründonnerstag m. **~ wa·ter** s eccl. Weihwasser n. **2 Week** s eccl. Karwoche f.

hom·age ['hɒmɪdʒ] s Huldigung f, Reverenz f: **do** (od. **pay**) **~ to s.o.** j-m huldigen, j-m (die od. s-e) Reverenz erweisen od. bezeigen.

home [həʊm] **I** s **1.** Heim n: a) Haus n, (*eigene*) Wohnung f, b) Zuhause n, Daheim n, c) Elternhaus n: **at ~** zu Hause, daheim (*beide a. Sport*); **at ~ in** fig. zu Hause in (dat), bewandert in (dat); **make o.s. at ~** es sich bequem machen; **away from ~** abwesend, verreist, (bsd. Sport) auswärts; **his ~ is in London** er ist in London zu Hause. **2.** Heimat f (a. fig.): **at ~ and abroad** im In- u. Ausland. **3.** Heim n: **~ for the aged** Alters-, Altenheim n. **II** adj **4.** häuslich, Heim...: **~ address** Privatanschrift f; **~ life** häusliches Leben, Familienleben n. **5.** inländisch, Inlands...: **~ affairs** pl innere Angelegenheiten pl, Innenpolitik f; **~ market** ✝ Inlands-, Binnenmarkt m; **~ trade** ✝ Binnenhandel m. **6.** Heimat...: **~ town.** 7. Sport: Heimat...: **~ match. III** adv **8.** heim, nach Hause: **way ~** Heimweg m; **that's nothing to write ~ about** F das ist nichts Besonderes; → **come home. 9.** zu Hause, daheim. **10.** fig. ins Ziel: **bring** (od. **drive**) **s.th. ~ to s.o.** j-m et. klarmachen; **the thrust went ~** der Hieb saß. **'~·com·ing** s Heimkehr f. **~·com·pu·ter** s Heimcomputer m. **,~·'grown** adj selbstangebaut (*Obst*), (*Gemüse a.*) selbstgezogen. **'~·land** s Heimatland n.

home·less ['həʊmlɪs] adj **1.** heimatlos. **2.** obdachlos: **be left ~** heimatlos werden. **'home·like** adj wie zu Hause, gemütlich. **'home·ly** adj **1.** einfach (*Mahlzeit, Leute*). **2.** Am. unscheinbar, reizlos.

,home'made adj haus-, selbstgemacht, Hausmacher...

homeo... → **homoeo...**

Home| Of·fice s Br. Innenministerium n. **2 rule** s pol. Selbstverwaltung f. **~ Sec·re·tar·y** s Br. Innenminister m. **'2·sick** adj: **be ~** Heimweh haben. **'2·sick·ness** s Heimweh n. **'2·spun** adj schlicht, einfach. **2 truth** s unangenehme Wahrheit.

home·ward ['həʊmwəd] **I** adv heimwärts, nach Hause. **II** adj Heim..., Rück... **'~·wards** → **homeward** I. **'home|·work** s **1.** ✝ Heimarbeit f. **2.** ped. Hausaufgabe(n pl) f: **do one's ~** s-e Hausaufgaben machen (a. fig.). **'~·work·er** s ✝ Heimarbeiter (-in).

hom·i·cide ['hɒmɪsaɪd] s ⚖ Mord m; Totschlag m.

ho·mo ['həʊməʊ] pl **-mos** s F Homo m (*Homosexuelle*).

ho·moe·o·path ['həʊmjəʊpæθ] s ✚ Homöopath(in). **,ho·moe·o'path·ic** (~*ally*) homöopathisch. **ho·moe·op·a·thy** [,həʊmɪ'ɒpəθɪ] s Homöopathie f.

ho·mo·ge·ne·ous [,hɒməʊ'dʒiːnjəs] adj □ homogen, gleichartig. **ho·mog·e·nize** [hɒ'mɒdʒənaɪz] v/t homogenisieren.

hom·o·graph ['hɒməʊgrɑːf] s ling. Homograph n. **hom·o·nym** ['~nɪm] s ling. Homonym n. **hom·o·phone** ['~fəʊn] s ling. Homophon n.

ho·mo·sex·u·al [,hɒməʊ'sekʃʊəl] I adj □ homosexuell. II s Homosexuelle m, f. **ho·mo·sex·u·al·i·ty** [~ʃʊ'ælətɪ] s Homosexualität f.

hom·y ['həʊmɪ] adj F gemütlich, behaglich.

hon·est ['ɒnɪst] adj ehrlich: a) redlich, b) aufrichtig. **'hon·est·ly** I adv → *honest*. II int F ganz bestimmt!, ehrlich! **'hon·es·ty** s Ehrlichkeit f: a) Redlichkeit f, b) Aufrichtigkeit f.

hon·ey ['hʌnɪ] s 1. Honig m: (*as*) *sweet as* ~ honigsüß (a. fig.). 2. bsd. Am. F Liebling m, Schatz m. '~*bee* s Honigbiene f. '~*dew* s Honigtau m: ~ *melon* Honigmelone f.

hon·eyed ['hʌnɪd] adj honigsüß (a. fig.). **'hon·ey·moon** I s Flitterwochen pl: ~ (*trip*) Hochzeitsreise f. II v/i in den Flitterwochen sein, s-e Flitterwochen verbringen; s-e Hochzeitsreise machen, auf Hochzeitsreise sein. '~**moon·er** s Flitterwöchner m; Hochzeitsreisende m, f.

honk [hɒŋk] mot. I s Hupsignal n. II v/i hupen.

hon·or, etc Am. → **honour,** etc.

hon·or·ar·y ['ɒnərərɪ] adj 1. Ehren... 2. ehrenamtlich.

hon·our ['ɒnə] bsd. Br. I v/t 1. ehren. 2. ehren, auszeichnen: ~ *s.o. with* j-m et. verleihen; j-n beehren mit. 3. ✝ *Scheck etc* honorieren, einlösen. II s 4. Ehre f: (*sense of*) ~ Ehrgefühl n; ~ *to whom* ~ *is due* Ehre, wem Ehre gebührt; *guest of* ~ Ehrengast m; *do s.o.* ~ j-m zur Ehre gereichen, j-m Ehre machen; → *debt.* 5. Ehrung f, Ehre(n pl) f: *in s.o.'s* ~ zu

j-s Ehren, j-m zu Ehren. 6. *Your* ⚅ bsd. ⚖ Euer Gnaden. **'hon·our·a·ble** adj □ bsd. Br. 1. achtbar, ehrenwert. 2. ehrenvoll, -haft. 3. ⚅ der, die Ehrenwerte (*Titel*).

hood [hʊd] s 1. Kapuze f. 2. mot. Br. Verdeck n; Am. (Motor)Haube f. 3. ☯ (Schutz)Haube f.

hood·lum ['huːdləm] s F 1. Rowdy m; Schläger m. 2. Ganove m; Gangster m. **'hood·wink** v/t hinters Licht führen.

hoo·ey ['huːɪ] s bsd. Am. sl. Krampf m, Quatsch m.

hoof [huːf] pl **hoofs, hooves** [huːvz] s zo. Huf m.

hook [hʊk] I s 1. Haken m: *by* ~ *or* (*by*) *crook* unter allen Umständen, mit allen Mitteln; *on one's own* ~ F auf eigene Faust. 2. Angelhaken m: ~, *line and sinker* F voll (u. ganz); *be on the* ~ F in der Patsche sein od. sitzen od. stecken. 3. *Boxen:* Haken m. II v/t 4. an-, ein-, fest-, zuhaken. 5. angeln (a. fig. F): ~ *a husband* sich e-n Mann angeln. 6. ~ *it* F Leine ziehen, verschwinden. III v/i 7. sich (zu)haken lassen. **hooked** [hʊkt] adj 1. hakenförmig, Haken... 2. mit (e-m) Haken (versehen). 3. F süchtig (*on* nach) (a. fig.): ~ *on TV* fernsehsüchtig. **'hook·er** s Am. sl. Nutte f. **'hook·y** s: *play* ~ bsd. Am. F (die Schule) schwänzen.

hoo·li·gan ['huːlɪgən] s Rowdy m. **'hoo·li·gan·ism** s Rowdytum n.

hoop [huːp] s allg. Reif(en) m: *put through the* ~(*s*) fig. durch die Mangel drehen, in die Mangel nehmen.

hoo·ray [hʊ'reɪ] → **hurah.**

hoot [huːt] I v/i 1. (*höhnisch*) johlen: ~ *at s.o.* j-n verhöhnen. 2. bsd. Br. heulen (*Fabriksirene etc*); mot. hupen. II v/t 3. auszischen, -pfeifen: ~ *down* niederschreien. III s 4. (*höhnischer, johlender*) Schrei: *I don't care a* ~ (od. *two* ~*s*) F das ist mir völlig egal. 5. bsd. Br. Heulen n; mot. Hupen n. **'hoot·er** s bsd. Br. Sirene f; mot. Hupe f.

Hoo·ver ['huːvə] *TM* I s Staubsauger m. II v/t mst ⚅ (staub)saugen, *Teppich etc a.* absaugen: ⚅ *up* aufsaugen. III v/i mst ⚅ (staub)saugen.

hooves [huːvz] pl von **hoof.**

hop¹ [hɒp] I s ♣ Hopfen m. II v/t Bier hopfen.

hop² [~] **I** v/i **1.** hüpfen: ~ **off** Br. F abschwirren. **2.** F schwofen, tanzen. **II** v/t **3.** hüpfen über (acc): ~ **it** F abschwirren. **III** s **4.** Sprung m: **keep s.o. on the** ~ F j-n in Trab halten. **5.** F Schwof m, Tanz(veranstaltung f) m.

hope [həup] **I** s Hoffnung f (of auf acc): **past** (od. **beyond**) (**all**) ~ hoffnungs-, aussichtslos; **in the** ~ auf gut Glück; **in** der Hoffnung (**of getting** zu bekommen); **no** ~ **of success** keine Aussicht auf Erfolg; ~**s** pl **of victory** Siegeshoffnungen pl. **II** v/i hoffen (**for** auf acc): ~ **for the best** das Beste hoffen; **I** ~ **so** hoffentlich; **I** ~ **not** hoffentlich nicht. **III** v/t hoffen (**that** daß). **hope·ful** ['həufʊl] adj hoffnungsvoll: **be** ~ **that** hoffen, daß. **'hope·ful·ly** adv **1.** → hopeful. **2.** hoffentlich. **'hope·less** adj □ hoffnungslos.

hop·ping ['hɒpɪŋ] adv: **be** ~ **mad** F e-e Stinkwut (im Bauch) haben.

horde [hɔːd] s Horde f, (wilder) Haufen.

ho·ri·zon [hə'raɪzn] s Horizont m: **appear on the** ~ am Horizont auftauchen, fig. a. sich abzeichnen; → **broaden** I. **hor·i·zon·tal** [ˌhɒrɪˈzɒntl] adj □ horizontal, waag(e)recht: ~ **bar** (Turnen) Reck n; ~ **line** → II. **II** s ⅋ Horizontale f, Waag(e)rechte f.

hor·mone ['hɔːməʊn] s biol. Hormon n.

horn [hɔːn] **I** s **1.** zo. Horn n, pl a. Geweih n: **show one's** ~**s** fig. die Krallen zeigen; → **bull** 1, **dilemma**, **2.** zo. Fühler m, Fühlhorn n. **3.** (Pulver-, Trink)Horn n: ~ **of plenty** Füllhorn n. **4.** Horn n (Substanz). **5.** ♪ Horn n. **6.** mot. Hupe f. **II** v/i **7.** ~ **in** sl. sich eindrängen od. einmischen (**on** in acc).

hor·net ['hɔːnɪt] s zo. Hornisse f: **stir up a** ~**'s nest** fig. in ein Wespennest stechen.

'horn-rimmed adj: ~ **spectacles** pl Hornbrille f.

horn·y ['hɔːnɪ] adj **1.** hornig, schwielig. **2.** aus Horn, Horn...

hor·o·scope ['hɒrəskəʊp] s Horoskop n: **cast a** ~ ein Horoskop stellen.

hor·ren·dous [hɒˈrendəs] → horrific.

hor·ri·ble ['hɒrəbl] adj □ schrecklich, furchtbar, scheußlich (alle a. fig. F).

hor·rid ['hɒrɪd] → horrible. **hor·rif·ic** [hɒˈrɪfɪk] adj (~ally) schrecklich, entsetzlich. **hor·ri·fy** ['~faɪ] v/t entsetzen:

be horrified at (od. **by**) entsetzt sein über (acc); ~**ing** → horrible.

hor·ror ['hɒrə] s **1.** Entsetzen n: **to one's** ~ zu s-m Entsetzen; **in** ~ entsetzt. **2.** Abscheu f, Horror m (**of** vor dat). **3.** Schrecken m, Greuel m. **4.** F Greuel m (Person od. Sache). **II** adj **5.** Horror...: ~ **film.** '~**strick·en,** '~**struck** adj von Entsetzen gepackt.

horse [hɔːs] s Pferd n (a. Turnen): **back the wrong** ~ fig. aufs falsche Pferd setzen; **eat like a** ~ wie ein Scheunendrescher essen; **get** (od. **come**) **off one's high** ~ fig. von s-m hohen Roß herunterkommen; **a** ~ **of another** (od. **a different**) **colo(u)r** fig. et. (ganz) anderes; (**straight od. right**) **from the** ~**'s mouth** F aus erster Hand; → **cart** 1, **dark horse, flog** 1, **gift** 3. '~**back** s: **on** ~ zu Pferd; **go on** ~ reiten. ~**chest·nut** s ⅋ Roßkastanie f. '~**hair** s Roßhaar n. '~**laugh** s wieherndes Gelächter. ~**man** ['~mən] s (irr **man**) (geübter) Reiter. ~ **op·er·a** s F Western m (Film). '~**pow·er** s phys. Pferdestärke f. ~ **race** s Sport: Pferderennen n. '~**rad·ish** s ⅋ Meerrettich m. ~ **sense** s gesunder Menschenverstand. ~**shoe** ['hɔːʃuː] s Hufeisen n. ~ **trad·ing** s bsd. pol. F Kuhhandel m. '~**wom·an** s (irr **woman**) (geübte) Reiterin.

hor·ti·cul·tur·al [ˌhɔːtɪˈkʌltʃərəl] adj Garten(bau)...: ~ **show** Gartenschau f. **'hor·ti·cul·ture** s Gartenbau m.

ho·san·na [həʊˈzænə] **I** int hos(i)anna! **II** s Hos(i)anna n.

hose¹ [həʊz] s (pl konstruiert) Strümpfe pl, Strumpfwaren pl.

hose² [~] **I** s Schlauch m. **II** v/t spritzen: ~ **down** abspritzen.

ho·sier·y ['həʊzɪərɪ] s coll. Strumpfwaren pl.

hos·pice ['hɒspɪs] s Sterbeklinik f.

hos·pi·ta·ble [hɒˈspɪtəbl] adj □ gast(freund)lich (Person); gastlich, gastfrei (Haus etc).

hos·pi·tal ['hɒspɪtl] s Krankenhaus n, Klinik f: **in** (Am. **in the**) ~ im Krankenhaus.

hos·pi·tal·i·ty [ˌhɒspɪˈtælɪtɪ] s Gastfreundschaft f, Gastlichkeit f.

hos·pi·tal·ize ['hɒspɪtlaɪz] v/t ins Krankenhaus einliefern od. einweisen.

host¹ [həʊst] **I** s **1.** Gastgeber m. **2.** biol.

Wirt *m* (*Tier od. Pflanze*). **3.** *Rundfunk, TV:* Talkmaster *m*; Showmaster *m*; Moderator *m*. **II** *v/t* **4.** *Rundfunk, TV: Sendung* moderieren.

host² [~] *s* Menge *f*, Masse *f*: **a ~ of questions** e-e Unmenge Fragen.

Host³ [~] *s eccl.* Hostie *f*.

hos·tage ['hɒstɪdʒ] *s* Geisel *f*: **take s.o. ~** j-n als Geisel nehmen.

hos·tel ['hɒstl] *s* **1.** *mst youth ~* Jugendherberge *f*. **2.** *bsd. Br.* (*Studenten-, Arbeiter- etc*)Wohnheim *n*.

host·ess ['hɒʊstɪs] *s* **1.** Gastgeberin *f*. **2.** Hostess *f* (*Betreuerin auf Messen etc*). **3.** ✈ Hostess *f*, Stewardeß *f*. **4.** Animier-, Tischdame *f*.

hos·tile ['hɒstaɪl] *adj* □ **1.** feindlich, Feind(es)... **2.** (**to**) feindselig (gegen), feindlich gesinnt (*dat*): **~ to foreigners** ausländerfeindlich. **hos·til·i·ty** [hɒ'stɪlətɪ] *s* **1.** Feindschaft *f*, Feindseligkeit *f*: **~ to foreigners** Ausländerfeindlichkeit *f*. **2.** *pl* ✗ Feindseligkeiten *pl*.

hot [hɒt] **I** *adj* □ **1.** *allg.* heiß (*a. fig.*): **I am ~** mir ist heiß; **I went ~ and cold** es überlief mich heiß u. kalt; **~ favo(u)rite** F (*bsd. Sport*) heißer od. hoher Favorit; **~ music** *sl.* heiße Musik; **~ tip** F heißer Tip; **be in ~ water** F in Schwulitäten sein. **2.** warm, heiß (*Speisen*): **~ meal** warme Mahlzeit; → **potato. 3.** scharf (gewürzt). **4. be ~ for** (*od.* **on**) F brennen *od.* scharf sein auf (*acc*). **5.** ganz neu *od.* frisch: **~ from the press** frisch aus der Presse (*Nachrichten*), soeben erschienen (*Buch etc*); **~ scent** (*od. trail*) *hunt.* warme od. frische Fährte *od.* Spur (*a. fig.*). **6.** F toll, großartig, (*Nachrichten*) sensationell. **7.** F heiß (*gestohlen, geschmuggelt etc*). **II** *adv* **8.** heiß: **give it s.o. ~** (*and strong*) F j-m gründlich einheizen (→ **track** 1, **trail** 7. **III** *v/t* **9.** *mst ~ up bsd. Br.* heiß machen, *Speisen a.* warm machen, aufwärmen. **10. ~ up** *fig.* F an-, aufheizen; Schwung bringen in (*acc*); *Auto, Motor* frisieren. **IV** *v/i* **11. ~ up** F sich verschärfen; schwungvoller werden. **~ air** *s* **1.** ⊗ Heißluft *f*. **2.** F heiße Luft, leeres Geschwätz. **,~·'air** *adj* ⊗ Heißluft... **~-bed** *s* **1.** ✔ Mist-, Frühbeet *n*. **2.** *fig.* Brutstätte *f*. **,~·'blood·ed** *adj* heißblütig.

hotch·potch ['hɒtʃpɒtʃ] *s* **1.** *gastr.* Eintopf *m*, *bsd.* Gemüsesuppe *f* mit

Fleisch. **2.** *fig.* Mischmasch *m*, Durcheinander *n*.

hot dog *s* Hot dog *m*, *n*.

ho·tel [həʊ'tel] **I** *s* Hotel *n*. **II** *adj* Hotel... **ho·tel·ier** [həʊ'telɪeɪ], **ho'tel,keep·er** *s* Hotelier *m*.

'hot|·foot F **I** *adv* schleunigst, schnell. **II** *v/i u. v/t*: **~** (**it**) rennen. **'~·head** *s* Hitzkopf *m*. **,~·'head·ed** *adj* □ hitzköpfig. **'~·house** *s* Treib-, Gewächshaus *n*. **~ line** *s bsd. pol.* heißer Draht. **~ pants** *s pl* Hot pants *pl*, heiße Höschen *pl*. **'~·plate** *s* **1.** Koch-, Heizplatte *f*. **2.** Warmhalteplatte *f*. **~ rod** *s bsd. Am. sl.* frisierter Wagen. **~ spot** *s* **1.** *bsd. Am.* F Nachtklub *od.* Amüsierbetrieb, in dem *et. los ist.* **,~·'wa·ter** *adj* Heißwasser...: **~ bottle** Wärmflasche *f*.

hound [haʊnd] **I** *s* **1.** Jagdhund *m*. **2.** *contp.* Hund *m*, gemeiner Kerl. **II** *v/t* **3.** (*bsd. mit Hunden, a. fig. j-n*) jagen, verfolgen.

hour ['aʊə] *s* **1.** Stunde *f*: **by the ~** stundenweise; **for ~s** (**and ~s**) stundenlang; **on the ~** (immer) zur vollen Stunde; **24 ~s a day** Tag u. Nacht. **2.** (*Tages*)Zeit *f*, Stunde *f*: **at all ~s** zu jeder Zeit, jederzeit; **at what ~?** um wieviel Uhr?; → **early** 4, **eleventh** 1, **late** 1, **small** 1. **3.** Zeitpunkt *m*, Stunde *f*. **4.** Stunde *f*, Tag *m*: **the man of the ~** der Mann des Tages. **5.** *pl* (*Arbeits*)Zeit *f*, (*Geschäfts*)Stunden *pl*: **after ~s** nach Geschäftsschluß; nach der Polizeistunde; nach der Arbeit; *fig.* zu spät. **~ hand** *s* Stundenzeiger *m*.

hour·ly ['aʊəlɪ] *adj u. adv* stündlich.

house I *s* [haʊs] *pl* **hous·es** ['haʊzɪz] **1.** Haus *n* (*a.* ✔, *parl., thea.*): → **bring down** 4, **card** 1. **2.** Haus(halt *m*) *n*: **keep ~** den Haushalt führen (**for s.o.** j-m); **put** (*od.* **set**) **one's ~ in order** *fig.* s-e Angelegenheiten in Ordnung bringen. **3.** Haus *n*, Geschlecht *n*: **the ♀ of Hanover** das Haus Hannover. **II** *v/t* [haʊz] **4.** unterbringen; beherbergen (*a. fig. enthalten*). **~ a·gent** *s* Br. Häusermakler *m*. **~ ar·rest** *s* Hausarrest *m*: **be under ~** unter Hausarrest stehen. **'~·boat** *s* Hausboot *n*. **'~·bound** *adj fig.* ans Haus gefesselt. **'~·break·er** *s* Einbrecher *m*. **'~·break·ing** *s* Einbruch *m*. **'~·bro·ken** *adj Am.* stubenrein (*Hund* *etc*, F *a. Witz etc*). '~**clean** *v/i* Hausputz machen. '~**clean·ing** *s* Hausputz *m*. '~**coat** *s* Morgenrock *m*, -mantel *m*. '~**fly** *s zo.* Stubenfliege *f*.

house·hold ['haʊshəʊld] **I** *s* **1.** Haushalt *m*. **II** *adj* **2.** Haushalts..., häuslich: ~ *remedy* Hausmittel *n*. **3.** ~ *word* (fester *od.* geläufiger) Begriff. '**house·hold·er** *s* Haushaltsvorstand *m*. '**house|·hunt** *v/i* auf Haussuche sein: *go* ~*ing* auf Haussuche gehen. '~**keep·er** *s* Haushälterin *f*, Wirtschafterin *f*. '~**keep·ing** *s* Haushaltung *f*, Haushaltsführung *f*: ~ (*money*) Haushalts-, Wirtschaftsgeld *n*. '~**maid** *s* Hausangestellte *f*, -mädchen *n*. 2 *of Com·mons* *s parl.* Unterhaus *n* (*GB*). 2 *of Lords* *s parl.* Oberhaus *n* (*GB*). 2 *of Rep·re·sent·a·tives* *s parl.* Repräsentantenhaus *n* (*USA*). '~**proud** *adj* übertrieben ordentlich (*Hausfrau*). ~ *rules* *s pl* Hausordnung *f*. ~ **search** 🏛 Haussuchung *f*. '~**to·**'~ *adj* von Haus zu Haus: ~ *collection* Haussammlung *f*; ~ *salesman* Hausierer *m*; Vertreter *m*. '~**top** *s* Dach *n*: *cry* (*od. proclaim, shout*) *from the* ~*s et.* öffentlich verkünden, *et. Vertrauliches* an die große Glocke hängen. '~**trained** *adj bsd. Br.* stubenrein (*Hund etc*). '~**warm·ing** (**par·ty**) *s* Einzugsparty *f* (*im neuen Haus*). '~**wife** *s* (*irr wife*) Hausfrau *f*. '~**work** *s* Hausarbeit *f*.

hous·ing ['haʊzɪŋ] *s* **1.** Wohnung *f*: ~ *development* *bsd. Am.*, ~ *estate* *Br.* Wohnsiedlung *f*; ~ *market* Wohnungsmarkt *m*; ~ *shortage* Wohnungsnot *f*. **2.** *coll.* Häuser *pl.* **3.** Wohnen *n*: ~ *conditions* *pl* Wohnverhältnisse *pl.*

hove [həʊv] *pret u. pp von* **heave**.

hov·el ['hɒvl] *s contp.* Bruchbude *f*, Loch *n*.

hov·er ['hɒvə] *v/i* **1.** schweben (*a. fig. between* zwischen *Leben u. Tod etc*). **2.** sich herumtreiben (*about* in der Nähe von). **3.** *fig.* schwanken (*between* zwischen *dat*). '~**craft** *pl* -**craft** *s* Luftkissenfahrzeug *n*.

how [haʊ] *adv* **1.** *fragend:* wie: ~ *are you?* wie geht es dir?; ~ *is your toothache?* was machen die Zahnschmerzen?; ~ *about ...?* wie steht *od.* wäre es mit ...?; ~ *do you know?* woher wissen Sie das?; ~ *much?* wieviel?; ~ *many?*

wieviel?, wie viele?; → *be* 7, *come* 7, *do*[1] 12. **2.** *ausrufend u. relativ:* wie: ~ *absurd!* wie absurd!; *he knows* ~ *to ride* er kann reiten; *I know* ~ *to do it* ich weiß, wie man es macht; *and* ~! F u. ob! ~'**ev·er** **I** *adv* wie auch (immer): ~ *it* (*may*) *be* wie dem auch sei; ~ *you do it* wie du es auch machst. **II** *cj* jedoch.

howl [haʊl] **I** *v/i* **1.** heulen (*Wölfe, Wind etc*). **2.** brüllen, schreien (*in agony* vor Schmerzen; *with laughter* vor Lachen). **II** *v/t* **3.** brüllen, schreien: ~ *down j-n* niederschreien, -brüllen. **III** *s* **4.** Heulen *n*. '**howl·er** *s* F grober Schnitzer. '**howl·ing** *adj* **1.** heulend. **2.** F Mords...: ~ *success* Bombenerfolg *m*.

hub [hʌb] *s* **1.** ⊙ (Rad)Nabe *f*. **2.** *fig.* Mittel-, Angelpunkt *m*.

hub·bub ['hʌbʌb] *s* **1.** Stimmengewirr *n*. **2.** Tumult *m*.

'**hub·cap** *s mot.* Radkappe *f*.

huck·le·ber·ry ['hʌklberɪ] *s* 🌿 Amer. Heidelbeere *f*.

huck·ster ['hʌkstə] → *hawker*.

hud·dle ['hʌdl] **I** *v/t* **1.** *mst* ~ *together* (*od. up*) zs.-werfen, auf e-n Haufen werfen; zs.-drängen; ~ *s.th. into bsd. Br.* et. stopfen in (*acc*). **II** *v/i* **2.** (sich) kauern: ~ *up* sich zs.-kauern. **3.** *mst* ~ *together* (*od. up*) sich zs.-drängen. **4.** ~ (*up*) *against* (*od. to*) sich kuscheln *od.* schmiegen an (*acc*). **III** *s* **5.** (wirrer) Haufen; Wirrwarr *m*, Durcheinander *n*. **6.** *go into a* F die Köpfe zs.-stecken; sich beraten (*with mit*).

hue[1] [hju:] *s* **1.** Farbe *f*. **2.** (Farb)Ton *m*, Tönung *f*, *a. fig.* Färbung *f*, Schattierung *f*.

hue[2] [~] *s*: *raise a* ~ *and cry against* lautstark protestieren gegen.

huff [hʌf] **I** *v/i* keuchen, schnaufen. **II** *s*: *be in a* ~ muffeln; *go into a* ~ muff(e)lig werden. '**huff·y** *adj* □ **1.** muff(e)lig. **2.** übelnehmerisch.

hug [hʌg] *v/t* **1.** umarmen, (*a.* ~ *to one*) an sich drücken. **2.** *fig.* (zäh) festhalten an (*dat*). **3.** sich umarmen. **III** *s* **4.** Umarmung *f*: *give s.o. a* ~ j-n umarmen.

huge [hju:dʒ] *adj* riesig, riesengroß (*beide a. fig.*). '**huge·ly** *adv* ungeheuer, gewaltig. '**huge·ness** *s* ungeheure *od.* gewaltige Größe.

hulk [hʌlk] *s* Koloß *m*: a) *Gebilde von gewaltigem Ausmaß*, b) klotziges *od.* sperriges *od.* unhandliches Ding, c) ungeschlachter Kerl, schwerfälliger Riese. **'hulk·ing**, **'hulk·y** *adj* **1.** klotzig, sperrig, unhandlich. **2.** ungeschlacht, schwerfällig.

hull¹ [hʌl] **I** *s* ♀ Schale *f*, Hülse *f*. **II** *v/t* schälen, enthülsen.

hull² [ʌ] *s* ♣ Rumpf *m*.

hul·la·ba·(l)·loo [ˌhʌlǝbǝ'luː] *s* Lärm *m*, Getöse *n*.

hul·lo → hello.

hum [hʌm] **I** *v/i* **1.** *allg.* summen: **my head is ～ing** mir brummt der Kopf; **～ (with activity)** F voller Leben *od.* Aktivität sein. **2.** *～ and haw* herumdrucksen, nicht recht mit der Sprache herauswollen. **II** *v/t* **3.** *Lied* summen. **III** *s* **4.** Summen *n*.

hu·man ['hjuːmǝn] **I** *adj* (□ → *humanly*) menschlich, Menschen...: *～ being* Mensch *m*; **～ chain** Menschenkette *f*; **～ dignity** Menschenwürde *f*; **～ medicine** Humanmedizin *f*; **～ race** Menschengeschlecht *n*; **～ rights** *pl* Menschenrechte *pl*; → **err. II** *s* Mensch *m*. **hu·mane** [hjuː'meɪn] *adj* □ **1.** human, menschlich. **2.** humanistisch. **hu·man·ism** ['hjuːmǝnɪzǝm] *s* Humanismus *m*. **'hu·man·ist** *s* Humanist(in). **ˌhu·man·'is·tic** *adj* (*～ally*) humanistisch. **hu·man·i·tar·i·an** [hjuːˌmænɪ'teǝrɪǝn] *adj* humanitär, menschenfreundlich. **hu·'man·i·ty** *s* **1.** die Menschheit. **2.** Humanität *f*, Menschlichkeit *f*. **3.** *pl* Altphilologie *f*; Geisteswissenschaften *pl*. **hu·man·ize** ['hjuːmǝnaɪz] *v/t* **1.** humanisieren, humaner *od.* menschenwürdiger gestalten. **2.** vermenschlichen, personifizieren. **hu·man·kind** [ˌ～'kaɪnd] → *humanity* **1.** **'hu·man·ly** *adv*: *do everything ～ possible* alles menschenmögliche *od.* sein menschenmöglichstes tun.

hum·ble ['hʌmbl] **I** *adj* □ bescheiden: a) demütig: *in my ～ opinion* m-r unmaßgeblichen Meinung nach; *eat ～ pie fig.* klein beigeben; → *self*, b) anspruchslos, einfach, c) niedrig: *of ～ birth* von niederer Geburt. **II** *v/t* demütigen, erniedrigen. **'hum·ble·ness** *s* Bescheidenheit *f*, Demut *f*.

hum·bug ['hʌmbʌg] *s* **1.** Humbug *m*: a)

Schwindel *m*, Betrug *m*, b) Unsinn *m*, dummes Zeug. **2.** *Br.* Pfefferminzbonbon *m*, *n*.

hum·ding·er [ˌhʌm'dɪŋǝ] *s bsd. Am.* F **1.** Mordskerl *m*. **2.** tolles Ding.

hum·drum ['hʌmdrʌm] **I** *adj* **1.** eintönig, langweilig. **II** *s* **2.** Eintönigkeit *f*, Langweiligkeit *f*. **3.** eintönige *od.* langweilige Arbeit; Langweiler *m*.

hu·mid ['hjuːmɪd] *adj* □ feucht. **hu·'mid·i·fi·er** [～dɪfaɪǝ] *s* ⊙ (Luft)Befeuchter *m*. **hu·'mid·i·fy** [～faɪ] *v/t* befeuchten. **hu·'mid·i·ty** *s* Feuchtigkeit *f*: *～ of the air* Luftfeuchtigkeit.

hu·mil·i·ate [hjuː'mɪlɪeɪt] *v/t* demütigen, erniedrigen. **hu·mil·i·'a·tion** *s* Demütigung *f*, Erniedrigung *f*.

hum·ming·bird ['hʌmɪŋbɜːd] *s orn.* Kolibri *m*.

hum·mock ['hʌmǝk] *s* Hügel *m*.

hu·mor *Am.* → humour.

hu·mor·ist ['hjuːmǝrɪst] *s* **1.** Humorist(in). **2.** Spaßvogel *m*. **ˌhu·mor·'is·tic** *adj* (*～ally*) humoristisch.

hu·mor·ous ['hjuːmǝrǝs] *adj* □ humorvoll, humorig.

hu·mour ['hjuːmǝ] *bsd. Br.* **I** *s* **1.** Humor *m*: (*a. good*) *sense of ～* (Sinn *m* für) Humor. **2.** Komik *f*, *das Komische*. **3.** (*Gemüts*)Verfassung *f*: *in a good* (*bad*) *～* (*bei*) guter (schlechter) Laune; *out of ～* schlecht gelaunt. **II** *v/t* **4.** *j-m* s-n Willen tun *od.* lassen; *j-n*, *et.* hinnehmen. **'hu·mour·less** *adj bsd. Br.* humorlos.

hump [hʌmp] **I** *s* **1.** Buckel *m*, (*e-s Kamels*) Höcker *m*. **2.** (*kleiner*) Hügel: *be over the ～ fig.* über den Berg sein. **II** *v/t* **3.** *～ one's back* e-n Buckel machen. **4.** *bsd. Br.* F auf den Rücken *od.* die Schulter nehmen; tragen. **'～·back** *s* **1.** Buckel *m*. **2.** Buck(e)lige *m*, *f*. **'～·backed** *adj* buck(e)lig.

humph [hʌmf] *int* hm!

Hun [hʌn] *s* **1.** *hist.* Hunne *m*. **2.** F *contp.* Deutsche *m*.

hu·mus ['hjuːmǝs] *s* Humus *m*.

hunch [hʌntʃ] **I** *s* **1.** → *hump* 1. **2.** dickes Stück. **3.** (Vor)Ahnung *f*: *have a ～ that* das Gefühl *od.* den Verdacht haben, daß. **II** *v/t* **4.** *～ up* → *hump* 3: *～ one's shoulders* die Schultern hochziehen. **'～·back** → *humpback.* **'～·backed** → *humpbacked.*

hun·dred ['hʌndrəd] **I** adj **1.** hundert: a (one) ~ (ein)hundert. **II** s **2.** Hundert n: ~s of times hundertmal; ~s pl of thousands Hunderttausende pl. **3.** & Hunderter m. **hun·dred·fold** ['-fəʊld] **I** adj u. adv hundertfach. **II** s das Hundertfache. **hun·dredth** ['-tθ] **I** adj **1.** hundertst. **II** s **2.** der, die, das Hundertste. **3.** Hundertstel n: a ~ of a second e-e Hundertstelsekunde.

hung [hʌŋ] pret u. pp von **hang**.

Hun·gar·i·an [hʌŋ'geəriən] **I** adj **1.** ungarisch. **II** s **2.** Ungar(in). **3.** ling. Ungarisch n.

hun·ger ['hʌŋgə] **I** s Hunger m (a. fig. for, after nach): ~ for knowledge Wissensdurst m. **II** v/i fig. hungern (for, after nach). ~ strike s Hungerstreik m: go on (a) ~ in den Hungerstreik treten.

hun·gry ['hʌŋgri] adj □ hungrig (a. fig. for nach): be (od. feel) (very) ~ (sehr) hungrig sein, (großen) Hunger haben; go ~ hungern; ~ for knowledge wissensdurstig.

hunk [hʌŋk] s großes Stück.

hunt [hʌnt] **I** s **1.** Jagd f, Jagen n. **2.** fig. Jagd f: a) Verfolgung f, b) Suche f (for, after nach): be on the ~ for auf der Jagd sein nach. **II** v/t **3.** (a. fig. j-n) jagen, Jagd machen auf (acc): erlegen, zur Strecke bringen (a. fig.); ~ed look gehetzter Blick. **4.** verfolgen. **5.** ~ away (od. off) wegjagen, vertreiben. **6.** ~ out (od. up) heraussuchen; aufstöbern, -spüren. **III** v/i **7.** jagen: go ~ing auf die Jagd gehen; ~ for Jagd machen auf (acc) (a. fig.). **8.** suchen (for, after nach). '**hunt·er** s Jäger m (a. fig.). '**hunt·ing I** s Jagen n, Jagd f. **II** adj Jagd...: ~ licence (Am. license) Jagdschein m; ~ season Jagdzeit f.

hur·dle ['hɜːdl] s Hürde f (a. Leichtathletik u. fig.): ~ race Hürdenlauf m. '**hur·dler** m Leichtathletik: Hürdenläufer(in).

hur·dy-gur·dy ['hɜːdɪˌgɜːdɪ] s Leierkasten m.

hurl [hɜːl] v/t schleudern: ~ down zu Boden schleudern; ~ o.s. sich stürzen (on, at auf acc); ~ abuse at s.o. j-m Beleidigungen ins Gesicht schleudern.

hurl·y-burl·y ['hɜːlɪˌbɜːlɪ] s Tumult m, Aufruhr m.

hur·rah [hʊ'rɑː], **hur·ray** [hʊ'reɪ] **I** int hurra! **II** s Hurra(ruf m) n.

hur·ri·cane ['hʌrɪkən] s Hurrikan m, Wirbelsturm m; Orkan m, fig. a. Sturm m: rise to a ~ zum Orkan anschwellen.

hur·ried ['hʌrɪd] adj □ eilig, hastig, übereilt.

hur·ry ['hʌrɪ] **I** s **1.** Hast f, Eile f: be in a ~ es eilig haben (to do zu tun), in Eile sein; be in no ~ es nicht eilig haben; do s.th. in a ~ et. eilig od. hastig tun; there is no ~ es eilt nicht. **2.** Hetze f. **II** v/t **3.** schnell od. eilig befördern od. bringen. **4.** oft ~ up j-n antreiben, hetzen; et. beschleunigen. **III** v/i **5.** eilen, hasten: ~ (up) sich beeilen; ~ up! (mach) schnell!

hurt [hɜːt] (irr) **I** v/t **1.** (a. fig. j-n, j-s Gefühle etc) verletzen: ~ one's knee sich das od. am Knie verletzen; feel ~ gekränkt sein; → fly². **2.** schmerzen, j-m weh tun (beide a. fig.). **3.** schaden (dat). **II** v/i **4.** schmerzen, weh tun (beide a. fig.). **hurt·ful** ['-fʊl] adj □ **1.** verletzend. **2.** schmerzlich. **3.** schädlich (to für).

hus·band ['hʌzbənd] **I** s (Ehe)Mann m, Gatte m. **II** v/t haushalten od. sparsam umgehen mit. '**hus·band·ry** s Landwirtschaft f.

hush [hʌʃ] **I** int **1.** still!, pst! **II** v/t **2.** zum Schweigen bringen. **3.** mst ~ up vertuschen. **III** v/i **4.** still werden, verstummen. **IV** s **5.** Stille f, Schweigen n: ~ money Schweigegeld n.

husk [hʌsk] **I** s ♀ Hülse f, Schale f, Schote f. **II** v/t enthülsen, schälen.

husk·y¹ ['hʌskɪ] adj □ **1.** heiser, rauh (Stimme). **2.** F stämmig, kräftig.

hus·ky² [~] s zo. Husky m, Eskimohund m.

hus·sy ['hʌsɪ] s **1.** Fratz m, Göre f. **2.** Flittchen n.

hus·tle ['hʌsl] **I** v/t **1.** stoßen, drängen: (an)rempeln. **2.** hetzen, (an)treiben; drängen (into doing zu tun). **3.** (in aller Eile) wohin bringen od. schicken. **4.** sich beeilen mit. **5.** bsd. Am. F ergattern; (sich) et. ergaunern. **II** v/i **6.** sich drängen. **7.** hasten, hetzen. **8.** sich beeilen. **III** s **9.** mst ~ and bustle Gedränge n; Gehetze n; Betrieb m, Wirbel m. '**hus·tler** s bsd. Am. F Nutte f.

hut [hʌt] s Hütte f.

hy·a·cinth ['haɪəsɪnθ] s ❦ Hyazinthe f.
hy·ae·na → **hyena.**
hy·brid ['haɪbrɪd] s biol. Hybride f, m, Kreuzung f.
hy·dran·gea [haɪ'dreɪndʒə] s ❦ Hortensie f.
hy·drant ['haɪdrənt] s Hydrant m.
hy·drate ['haɪdreɪt] s ✿ Hydrat n.
hy·drau·lic [haɪ'drɔ:lɪk] **I** adj (~ally) phys., ⊕ hydraulisch. **II** s pl (sg konstruiert) phys. Hydraulik f.
hy·dro... ['haɪdrəʊ] Wasser...
hy·dro·car·bon s ✿ Kohlenwasserstoff m. **~'chlo·ric** adj: ~ acid ✿ Salzsäure f. **~·e'lec·tric** adj: ~ power station Wasserkraftwerk n. **'~foil** s Tragflächen-, Tragflügelboot n.
hy·dro·gen ['haɪdrədʒən] s ✿ Wasserstoff m: ~ bomb ✗ Wasserstoffbombe f.
hy·dro'pho·bi·a s **1.** psych. Hydrophobie f. **2.** vet. Tollwut f. **'~·plane** s Wasserflugzeug n.
hy·e·na [haɪ'i:nə] s zo. Hyäne f (a. fig.).
hy·giene ['haɪdʒi:n] s Hygiene f, Gesundheitspflege f. **hy'gien·ic** (~ally) hygienisch.
hy·grom·e·ter [haɪ'grɒmɪtə] s Hygrometer n, Luftfeuchtigkeitsmesser m.
hymn [hɪm] s Kirchenlied n, Choral m. **hym·nal** ['~nəl], **'hymn·book** s Gesangbuch n.
hy·per... ['haɪpə] hyper..., übermäßig.
hy·per·bo·la [haɪ'pɜ:bələ] pl **-las, -lae** [~i:] s A Hyperbel f. **hy'per·bo·le** [~lɪ] s rhet. Hyperbel f, Übertreibung f. **hy·per·bol·ic** [ˌhaɪpə'bɒlɪk] adj (~ally) A hyperbolisch, rhet. a. übertreibend.
hy·per'crit·i·cal adj □ hyperkritisch. **'~ˌmar·ket** s Br. Groß-, Verbrauchermarkt m. **'~'sen·si·tive** adj □ hypersensibel, a. ✗ überempfindlich (**to** gegen). **~'ten·sion** s ✗ erhöhter Blutdruck.

hy·phen ['haɪfn] s **1.** Bindestrich m. **2.** Trennungszeichen n. **hy·phen·ate** ['~fəneɪt] v/t **1.** mit Bindestrich schreiben. **2.** trennen.
hyp·no·sis [hɪp'nəʊsɪs] pl **-ses** [~si:z] s Hypnose f. **hyp·not·ic** [~'nɒtɪk] adj (~ally) hypnotisch. **hyp·no·tist** ['~nətɪst] s Hypnotiseur m. **hyp·no·tize** ['~taɪz] v/t hypnotisieren.
hy·po... ['haɪpəʊ] Unter..., Sub...
hy·po·chon·dri·a [ˌhaɪpəʊ'kɒndrɪə] s Hypochondrie f. **hy·po·chon·dri·ac** [~drɪæk] **I** adj □ hypochondrisch. **II** s Hypochonder m.
hy·poc·ri·sy [hɪ'pɒkrəsɪ] s Heuchelei f. **hyp·o·crite** ['hɪpəkrɪt] s Heuchler(in). **ˌhyp·o'crit·i·cal** adj □ heuchlerisch.
hy·po·der·mic [ˌhaɪpəʊ'dɜ:mɪk] ✗ **I** adj (~ally) subkutan, unter od. die Haut: ~ injection ✗. **II** s subkutane Injektion od. Einspritzung.
ˌhy·po'ten·sion s ✗ zu niedriger Blutdruck.
hy·pot·e·nuse [haɪ'pɒtənju:z] s A Hypotenuse f.
hy·po·ther·mi·a [ˌhaɪpəʊ'θɜ:mɪə] s ✗ Unterkühlung f.
hy·poth·e·sis [haɪ'pɒθɪsɪs] pl **-ses** [~si:z] s Hypothese f. **hy·po·thet·i·cal** [ˌhaɪpə-'θetɪkl] adj □ hypothetisch.
hys·te·ri·a [hɪ'stɪərɪə] s Hysterie f. **hys·ter·ic** [hɪ'sterɪk] **I** s **1.** Hysteriker(in). **2.** pl (mst sg konstruiert) hysterischer Anfall: **go (off) into ~s** hysterisch werden. **II** adj **3.** → **hysterical. hys'ter·i·cal** adj □ hysterisch.

I

I [aɪ] pron ich: **it is ~** ich bin es.
i·bex ['aɪbeks] pl **i·bex·es, ib·i·ces** ['ɪbɪsi:z] s zo. Steinbock m.
ice [aɪs] **I** s **1. be (skating) on thin ~** fig. sich auf gefährlichem Boden bewegen;

break the ~ fig. das Eis brechen; **cut no ~ (with)** F keinen Eindruck machen (auf acc), nicht ziehen (bei); **put on ~** kalt stellen; fig. F auf Eis legen. **2.** a) Am. Fruchteis n, b) Br. → **ice cream.**

3. → **icing**. **II** v/t **4.** gefrieren lassen. **5.** Getränk etc mit od. in Eis kühlen. **6.** gastr. glasieren. **III** v/i **7.** gefrieren. **8.** mst ~ **up** (od. **over**) zufrieren; vereisen. **9.** ~ **out** auftauen (Gewässer). ♀ **Age** s geol. Eiszeit f. ~ **ax(e)** s Eispickel m. ~ **bag** s ♣ Eisbeutel m. ~**berg** ['~bɜːɡ] s Eisberg m (a. fig. Person): **the tip of the** ~ die Spitze des Eisbergs (a. fig.). '~**bound** adj eingefroren (Schiff); zugefroren (Hafen). '~**box** s **1.** Eisfach n (e-s Kühlschranks). **2.** Am. Eis-, Kühlschrank m. '~**break·er** s ⚓ Eisbrecher m. ~ **buck·et** s Eiskübel m. ,~'**cold** adj eiskalt. ~ **cream** s (Speise)Eis n, Eiscreme f: **chocolate** ~ Schokoladeneis. '~**cream** adj Eis...: ~ **parlo(u)r** Eisdiele f. ~ **cube** s Eiswürfel m.

iced [aɪst] adj **1.** eisgekühlt. **2.** gefroren. **3.** gastr. glasiert, mit Zuckerguß.
ice| **floe** → **floe**. ~ **hock·ey** s Sport: Eishockey n.
Ice·land·er ['aɪsləndə] s Isländer(in).
Ice·lan·dic [~'lændɪk] **I** adj isländisch. **II** s ling. Isländisch n.
ice| **lol·ly** s Br. Eis n am Stiel. '~**man** s (irr **man**) Am. Eismann m, -verkäufer m. ~ **pack** s **1.** Packeis n. **2.** ♣ Eisbeutel m. ~ **pail** s Eiskübel m. ~ **rink** s (Kunst)Eisbahn f. ~ **wa·ter** s Eiswasser n.
ich·thy·ol·o·gy [ˌɪkθɪˈɒlədʒɪ] s Fischkunde f.
i·ci·cle ['aɪsɪkl] s Eiszapfen m.
i·ci·ness ['aɪsɪnɪs] s eisige Kälte (a. fig.).
ic·ing ['aɪsɪŋ] s gastr. Glasur f, Zuckerguß m.
i·con ['aɪkɒn] s Ikone f.
i·cy ['aɪsɪ] adj eisig (a. fig.).
I'd [aɪd] F für **I had**; **I would**.
i·de·a [aɪˈdɪə] s **1.** Idee f, Vorstellung f, Begriff m: **form an** ~ **of** sich et. vorstellen, sich e-n Begriff machen von; **have no** ~ keine Ahnung haben; **put** ~**s into s.o.'s head** j-m Flausen in den Kopf setzen. **2.** Absicht f, Gedanke m, Idee f: **the** ~ **is** ... der Zweck der Sache ist, ...; es geht darum, ...; **the** ~ **entered my mind** mir kam der Gedanke. **3. I have an** ~ **that** ich habe so das Gefühl, daß; es kommt mir (so) vor, als ob.
i·de·al [aɪˈdɪəl] **I** adj (□ ~ **ideally**) **1.** ideal. **2.** ideell. **II** s **3.** Ideal n.
i·de·al·ism s Idealismus m. **i·de·al·ist** s

Idealist(in). **i,de·al'is·tic** adj (~**ally**) idealistisch. **i'de·al·ize** v/t u. v/i idealisieren. **i'de·al·ly** adv **1.** → **ideal** I. **2.** im Idealfall.
i·den·ti·cal [aɪˈdentɪkl] adj □ identisch (**to, with** mit): ~ **twins** pl eineiige Zwillinge pl.
i·den·ti·fi·ca·tion [aɪˌdentɪfɪˈkeɪʃn] s **1.** Identifizierung f: ~ **card** (Personal-)Ausweis m; ~ **papers** pl Ausweispapiere pl; ~ **parade** ⚖ Br. Gegenüberstellung f. **2.** Ausweis m, Legitimation f: **he didn't have any** ~ er konnte sich nicht ausweisen. **i'den·ti·fy** [~faɪ] **I** v/t **1.** identifizieren, gleichsetzen (**with** mit): ~ **o.s. with** → **4. 2.** identifizieren, erkennen (**as** als). **3.** ~ **o.s.** sich ausweisen od. legitimieren. **II** v/i **4.** ~ **with** sich identifizieren mit.
i·den·ti·kit (**pic·ture**) [aɪˈdentɪkɪt] s ⚖ Br. Phantombild n.
i·den·ti·ty [aɪˈdentətɪ] s Identität f: a) (völlige) Gleichheit f, b) Persönlichkeit f: **prove one's** ~ → **identify** 3; **loss of** ~ Identitätsverlust m; ~ **mistaken** (2 **card** s (Personal)Ausweis m. ~ **cri·sis** s (irr **crisis**) Identitätskrise f. ~ **pa·rade** s ⚖ Gegenüberstellung f.
i·de·o·log·i·cal [ˌaɪdɪəˈlɒdʒɪkl] adj □ ideologisch. **i·de·ol·o·gy** [~'ɒlədʒɪ] s Ideologie f.
id·i·o·cy ['ɪdɪəsɪ] s ♣ Idiotie f, contp. a. Blödheit f.
id·i·om ['ɪdɪəm] s ling. Idiom n, idiomatischer Ausdruck, Redewendung f.
id·i·o·mat·ic [~'mætɪk] adj (~**ally**) idiomatisch.
id·i·ot ['ɪdɪət] s ♣ Idiot m, contp. a. Trottel m. **id·i·ot·ic** [~'ɒtɪk] adj (~**ally**) adj ♣ idiotisch, contp. a. vertrottelt.
i·dle ['aɪdl] **I** adj □ **1.** untätig, müßig. **2.** ruhig, still: ~ **hours** pl Mußestunden pl. **3.** faul, träge. **4.** ◎ stillstehend, außer Betrieb; leer laufend, im Leerlauf: **run** ~ → **8. 5.** nutz-, sinn-, zwecklos; vergeblich. **6.** leer, hohl: ~ **gossip** (od. **talk**) leeres Geschwätz. **II** v/i **7.** faulenzen: ~ **about** (od. **around**) herumtrödeln. **8.** ◎ leer laufen. **III** v/t **9.** mst ~ **away** Zeit vertrödeln. '**i·dler** s Müßiggänger(in).
i·dol ['aɪdl] s Idol n (a. fig.); Gottesstatue f, Götterbild n; contp. Götze(nbild n) m: **make an** ~ **of** → **idolize** b.
i·dol·a·trous [aɪˈdɒlətrəs] adj □ ♣

im·mov·a·ble [ɪˈmuːvəbl] *adj* □ **1.** unbeweglich. **2.** *fig.* fest, unerschütterlich; hart, unnachgiebig. **3.** (*zeitlich*) unveränderlich: ~ *feast* eccl. unbeweglicher Feiertag.

im·mune [ɪˈmjuːn] *adj* **1.** ✻ *u. fig.* (*against, from, to*) immun (gegen), unempfänglich (für). **2.** geschützt, gefeit (*against, from, to* gegen). **3.** befreit, ausgenommen (*from* von). **imˈmuˈniˈty** *s* ✻, ᴢᴛᴢ *u. fig.* Immunität *f*: *diplomatic* ~. **imˈmuˈnize** [ˈnaɪz] *v/t* immunisieren, immun machen (*against* gegen) (*a. fig.*).

im·mu·ta·ble [ɪˈmjuːtəbl] *adj* □ unveränderlich.

imp [ɪmp] *s* **1.** Kobold *m*. **2.** F Racker *m*.

im·pact [ˈɪmpækt] *s* **1.** Zs-, Anprall *m*; Aufprall *m*; ✗ Auf-, Einschlag *m*. **2.** *fig.* (Ein)Wirkung *f*, (starker) Einfluß (*on auf acc*).

im·pair [ɪmˈpeə] *v/t* beeinträchtigen.

im·pale [ɪmˈpeɪl] *v/t* aufspießen (*on auf acc*), durchbohren.

im·pal·pa·ble [ɪmˈpælpəbl] *adj* □ **1.** unfühlbar. **2.** äußerst fein. **3.** *fig.* kaum (er)faßbar *od.* greifbar.

im·part [ɪmˈpɑːt] *v/t* (*to dat*) **1.** Eigenschaft *etc* verleihen. **2.** mitteilen; *Kenntnisse etc* vermitteln.

im·par·tial [ɪmˈpɑːʃl] *adj* □ unparteiisch, unvoreingenommen. **ˈim͵parˈtiˈalˈiˈty** [͵ʃɪˈælɪtɪ] *s* Unparteilichkeit *f*, Unvoreingenommenheit *f*.

im·pass·a·ble [ɪmˈpɑːsəbl] *adj* □ **1.** unpassierbar. **2.** *bsd. fig.* unüberwindbar (*Hindernis etc*).

im·passe [ˈæmpɑːs] *s fig.* Sackgasse *f*: *reach an* ~ in e-e Sackgasse geraten.

im·pas·sioned [ɪmˈpæʃnd] *adj* leidenschaftlich.

im·pas·sive [ɪmˈpæsɪv] *adj* □ **1.** teilnahmslos; ungerührt. **2.** gelassen.

im·pa·tience [ɪmˈpeɪʃns] *s* **1.** Ungeduld *f*. **2.** Unduldsamkeit *f*. **im·pa·tient** *adj* □ **1.** ungeduldig: *be* ~ *with* keine Geduld haben mit. **2.** *be* ~ *for et.* nicht erwarten können; *be* ~ *to do s.th.* es nicht erwarten können, et. zu tun. **3.** unduldsam (*of* gegenüber).

im·peach [ɪmˈpiːtʃ] *v/t* **1.** ᴢᴛᴢ anklagen (*for, of, with gen*); *Am. bsd. Präsidenten* unter Amtsanklage stellen. **2.** ᴢᴛᴢ anfechten. **3.** in Frage stellen, in Zweifel ziehen. **imˈpeachˈment** *s* **1.** ᴢᴛᴢ Anklage *f*; *Am.* Impeachment *n*. **2.** ᴢᴛᴢ Anfechtung *f*. **3.** Infragestellung *f*.

im·pec·ca·ble [ɪmˈpekəbl] *adj* □ untadelig, einwandfrei.

im·pede [ɪmˈpiːd] *v/t* **1.** *j-n, et.* (be)hindern: ~ *s.o.'s doing s.th.* j-n daran hindern, et. zu tun. **2.** *et.* erschweren.

im·ped·i·ment [ɪmˈpedɪmənt] *s* **1.** Behinderung *f*. **2.** Hindernis *n* (*to* für). **3.** ✻ (*bsd.* angeborener) Fehler: → *speech* 1.

im·pel [ɪmˈpel] *v/t* **1.** antreiben (*a. fig.*). **2.** zwingen: *I felt* ~*led* ich sah mich gezwungen *od.* fühlte mich genötigt (*to do* zu tun).

im·pend·ing [ɪmˈpendɪŋ] *adj* **1.** nahe bevorstehend: *his* ~ *death* sein naher Tod. **2.** drohend (*Gefahr etc*).

im·pen·e·tra·ble [ɪmˈpenɪtrəbl] *adj* □ **1.** undurchdringlich (*by* für) (*a. fig.*). **2.** *fig.* unergründlich, unerforschlich.

im·pen·i·tent [ɪmˈpenɪtənt] *adj* □ verstockt; *eccl.* unbußfertig.

im·per·a·tive [ɪmˈperətɪv] **I** *adj* □ **1.** gebieterisch. **2.** unumgänglich, unbedingt erforderlich. **3.** *ling.* Imperativ..., Befehls...: ~ *mood* → 4. **II** *s* **4.** *ling.* Imperativ *m*, Befehlsform *f*.

im·per·cep·ti·ble [͵ɪmpəˈseptəbl] *adj* □ **1.** nicht wahrnehmbar, unmerklich. **2.** verschwindend klein.

im·per·fect [ɪmˈpɜːfɪkt] **I** *adj* □ **1.** unvollkommen: a) unvollständig, b) mangel-, fehlerhaft. **2.** ~ *tense* → 3. **II** *s* **3.** *ling.* Imperfekt *n*, unvollendete Vergangenheit *f*. **im·per·fec·tion** [͵~pəˈfekʃn] *s* **1.** Unvollkommenheit *f*. **2.** Mangel *m*, Fehler *m*.

im·pe·ri·al [ɪmˈpɪərɪəl] *adj* □ **1.** kaiserlich, Kaiser... **2.** *Br.* gesetzlich (*Maße u. Gewichte*). **im·pe·ri·al·ism** *s pol.* Imperialismus *m*. **im·pe·ri·al·ist** **I** *s* Imperialist *m*. **II** *adj* imperialistisch. **im͵pe·ri·al·is·tic** *adj* (~*ally*) imperialistisch.

im·per·il [ɪmˈperəl] *v/t* gefährden.

im·pe·ri·ous [ɪmˈpɪərɪəs] *adj* □ **1.** gebieterisch. **2.** dringend: ~ *necessity* zwingende Notwendigkeit.

im·per·ish·a·ble [ɪmˈperɪʃəbl] *adj* □ **1.** unverderblich. **2.** *fig.* unvergänglich.

im·per·ma·nent [͵ɪmˈpɜːmənənt] *adj* □ vorübergehend, nicht von Dauer.

im·per·me·a·ble [ɪmˈpɜːmjəbl] *adj* □

undurchlässig (**to** für): **~ to water** wasserdicht.

im·per·son·al [ɪmˈpɜːsnl] *adj* □ unpersönlich (*a. ling.*).

im·per·son·ate [ɪmˈpɜːsəneɪt] *v/t* **1.** *thea. etc* verkörpern, darstellen. **2.** *j-n* imitieren, nachahmen.

im·per·ti·nence [ɪmˈpɜːtɪnəns] *s* **1.** Unverschämtheit *f*, Frechheit *f*. **2.** Belanglosigkeit *f*. **im·per·ti·nent** *adj* □ **1.** unverschämt, frech. **2.** belanglos (**to** für).

im·per·turb·a·ble [ˌɪmpəˈtɜːbəbl] *adj* □ unerschütterlich.

im·per·vi·ous [ɪmˈpɜːvjəs] *adj* □ **1.** → **impermeable**. **2.** *fig.* unzugänglich (**to** für *od. dat*).

im·pet·u·ous [ɪmˈpetʃʊəs] *adj* □ **1.** heftig, ungestüm. **2.** impulsiv. **3.** übereilt, vorschnell.

im·pe·tus [ˈɪmpɪtəs] *s* **1.** *phys.* Triebkraft *f*, Schwung *m* (*a. fig.*). **2.** *fig.* Antrieb *m*, Impuls *m*: **give an ~ to** Auftrieb *od.* Schwung verleihen (*dat*).

im·pi·e·ty [ɪmˈpaɪətɪ] *s* **1.** Gottlosigkeit *f*. **2.** (**to** gegenüber) Pietätlosigkeit *f*; Respektlosigkeit *f*.

im·pinge [ɪmˈpɪndʒ] *v/i* **1.** auftreffen (**on** auf *acc*). **2.** *fig.* (**on**) sich auswirken (auf *acc*), beeinflussen (*acc*).

im·pi·ous [ˈɪmpɪəs] *adj* □ **1.** gottlos. **2.** (**to** gegenüber) pietätlos; respektlos.

imp·ish [ˈɪmpɪʃ] *adj* □ schelmisch, spitzbübisch.

im·plac·a·ble [ɪmˈplækəbl] *adj* □ unversöhnlich, unnachgiebig.

im·plant *v/t* [ɪmˈplɑːnt] **1.** 🩺 implantieren, einpflanzen (**in, into** *dat*). **2.** *fig.* einprägen (**in, into** *dat*): **deeply ~ed hatred** tiefverwurzelter Haß. **II** *s* [ˈɪmplɑːnt] **3.** 🩺 Implantat *n*.

im·plau·si·ble [ˌɪmˈplɔːzəbl] *adj* □ unglaubwürdig.

im·ple·ment I *s* [ˈɪmplɪmənt] Werkzeug *n* (*a. fig.*), Gerät *n*. **II** *v/t* [ˈ~ment] aus-, durchführen. **im·ple·men·ta·tion** [ˌ~menˈteɪʃn] *s* Aus-, Durchführung *f*.

im·pli·cate [ˈɪmplɪkeɪt] *v/t* **1.** *j-n* verwickeln, hineinziehen (**in** *in acc*). **2.** → **imply** 1, 3. **ˌim·pli·ˈca·tion** *s* **1.** Verwicklung *f*. **2.** Folgerung *f*. **3.** Folge *f*, Auswirkung *f*. **4.** Andeutung *f*.

im·plic·it [ɪmˈplɪsɪt] *adj* **1.** → **implied**. **2.** vorbehalt-, bedingungslos: **~ faith** (**obedience**) blinder Glaube (Gehor-

sam). **im·plic·it·ly** *adv* **1.** stillschweigend. **2.** → **implicit** 2.

im·plied [ɪmˈplaɪd] *adj* impliziert, (stillschweigend *od.* mit) inbegriffen.

im·plode [ɪmˈpləʊd] *v/i* *phys.* implodieren.

im·plore [ɪmˈplɔː] *v/t* **1.** *j-n* anflehen. **2.** *et.* erflehen, flehen um.

im·plo·sion [ɪmˈpləʊʒn] *s* *phys.* Implosion *f*.

im·ply [ɪmˈplaɪ] *v/t* **1.** implizieren, (sinngemäß *od.* stillschweigend) beinhalten. **2.** andeuten, zu verstehen geben. **3.** mit sich bringen, zur Folge haben.

im·po·lite [ˌɪmpəˈlaɪt] *adj* □ unhöflich.

im·pol·i·tic [ɪmˈpɒlətɪk] *adj* □ undiplomatisch, unklug.

im·pon·der·a·ble [ɪmˈpɒndərəbl] **I** *adj* unwägbar. **II** *s* *pl* Imponderabilien *pl*, Unwägbarkeiten *pl*.

im·port I *v/t u. v/i* [ɪmˈpɔːt] **1.** importieren, einführen: **~ing country** Einfuhrland *n*; **~ing firm** Importfirma *f*. **II** *s* [ˈɪmpɔːt] **2.** Import *m*, Einfuhr *f*. **3.** *pl* (Gesamt)Import *m*, (-)Einfuhr *f*; Importgüter *pl*, Einfuhrware *f*. **III** *adj* [ˈɪmpɔːt] **4.** Import..., Einfuhr...: **~ trade** Importgeschäft *n*, Einfuhrhandel *m*.

im·por·tance [ɪmˈpɔːtns] *s* Bedeutung *f*: a) Wichtigkeit *f*: **attach ~ to** Bedeutung beimessen (*dat*); **be of no ~** unwichtig *od.* belanglos sein (**to** für), b) Ansehen *n*, Gewicht *n*: **a person of ~** e-e gewichtige Persönlichkeit. **im·por·tant** *adj* □ bedeutend: a) wichtig, von Belang (**to** für), b) angesehen, gewichtig.

im·port·er [ɪmˈpɔːtə] *s* Importeur *m*.

im·por·tu·nate [ɪmˈpɔːtjʊnət] *adj* □ lästig, zu-, aufdringlich. **im·por·tune** [ˌ~tjuːn] *v/t* belästigen, dauernd (*bsd.* mit Bitten) behelligen.

im·pose I *v/t* **1.** (**on** *et.* auferlegen, -bürden (*dat*); *Strafe* verhängen (gegen). **2.** (**on** *acc*) *et.* aufdrängen, -zwingen (*dat*): **~ o.s.** (*od.* **one's presence**) **on s.o.** sich j-m aufdrängen; **~ one's will on s.o.** j-m s-n Willen aufzwingen, b) *et.* (**mit** *Gewalt*) einführen *od.* durchsetzen (bei). **II** *v/i* **3.** ausnutzen, *b.s. a.* mißbrauchen (**on** *acc*). **4.** (**on** *acc*) sich aufdrängen; zur Last fallen. **im·pos·ing** *adj* □ imponierend, imposant. **im·po·si·tion** [ˌɪmpəˈzɪʃn],

1. Auferlegung *f*, -bürdung *f*; Verhängung *f*. **2.** Auflage *f*, Pflicht *f*. **3.** Abgabe *f*, Steuer *f*. **4.** Ausnutzung *f*, *b.s. a.* Mißbrauch *m* (**on** *gen*).

im·pos·si·bil·i·ty [ɪm‚pɒsə'bɪlətɪ] *s* Unmöglichkeit *f*. **im·pos·si·ble** *adj* unmöglich (*a.* F *unglaublich, unerträglich etc*): **it is ~ for me to come** ich kann unmöglich kommen. **im'pos·si·bly** *adv* unglaublich.

im·post·er, im·post·or [ɪm'pɒstə] *s* Betrüger(in), *bsd.* Hochstapler(in).

im·po·tence [ɪmpətəns] *s* **1.** Unvermögen *n*, Unfähigkeit *f*; Hilflosigkeit *f*, Ohnmacht *f*. **2.** ♀ Impotenz *f*. **'im·po·tent** *adj* □ **1.** unfähig (**in doing, to do** zu tun); hilflos, ohnmächtig. **2.** ♀ impotent.

im·pov·er·ish [ɪm'pɒvərɪʃ] *v/t* arm machen: **be ~ed** verarmen; verarmt sein.

im·prac·ti·ca·ble [ɪm'præktɪkəbl] *adj* □ **1.** undurchführbar. **2.** unpassierbar (*Straße etc*).

im·prac·ti·cal [ɪm'præktɪkl] *adj* □ **1.** unpraktisch (*Person*). **2.** undurchführbar.

im·preg·nate ['ɪmpregneɪt] *v/t* **1.** *biol.* schwängern; befruchten (*a. fig.*). **2.** ♀, ◎ imprägnieren, tränken. **3.** *fig.* durchdringen, erfüllen (**with** mit).

im·pre·sa·ri·o [‚ɪmprɪ'sɑːrɪəʊ] *pl* **-os** *s* Impresario *m*, Theater-, Konzertagent *m*.

im·press I *v/t* [ɪm'pres] **1.** beeindrucken, Eindruck machen auf (*acc*), imponieren (*dat*). **2.** (auf)drücken (**on** auf *acc*), (ein)drucken (**in, into** in *acc*). II *s* ['ɪmpres] **3.** Ab-, Eindruck *m*. **im·'pres·sion** [~ʃn] *s* **1.** Eindruck *m* (**of** von): **give s.o. a wrong ~** bei j-m e-n falschen Eindruck erwecken; **make a good** (**bad**) **~** e-n guten (schlechten) Eindruck machen. **2.** Eindruck *m*, Vermutung *f*: **I have an** (*od.* **the**) **~** (*od.* **I am under the** (*od.* **the**) **~**) **that** ich habe den Eindruck, daß; **under the ~ that** in der Annahme, daß. **3.** Abdruck *m* (*a.* ✏). **4.** *typ.* (*bsd.* unveränderte) Auflage, Nachdruck *m*. **im·'pres·sion·a·ble** *adj* leicht zu beeinflussen(d). **im·'pres·sion·ism** *s* Impressionismus *m*. **im·'pres·sion·ist** I *s* Impressionist(in). II *adj* impressionistisch. **im·pres·sion·'is·tic** [~ʃə'nɪ~] *adj* (**~ally**) impressioni-

stisch. **im·'pres·sive** [~sɪv] *adj* □ eindrucksvoll.

im·print I *s* ['ɪmprɪnt] **1.** Ab-, Eindruck *m*. **2.** *fig.* Stempel *m*, Gepräge *n*. **3.** *typ.* Impressum *n*. II *v/t* [ɪm'prɪnt] **4.** (auf)drücken (**on** auf *acc*). **5. ~ s.th. on** (*od.* **in**) **s.o.'s memory** j-m et. ins Gedächtnis einprägen.

im·pris·on [ɪm'prɪzn] *v/t* ⚖ inhaftieren, *a. weitS.* einsperren. **im·'pris·on·ment** *s* a) Freiheitsstrafe *f*, Gefängnis(strafe *f*) *n*, Haft *f*: **he was given 10 years ~** er wurde zu e-r zehnjährigen Freiheitsstrafe verurteilt, b) Inhaftierung *f*.

im·prob·a·bil·i·ty [ɪm‚prɒbə'bɪlətɪ] *s* Unwahrscheinlichkeit *f*. **im·'prob·a·ble** *adj* □ unwahrscheinlich.

im·promp·tu [ɪm'prɒmptjuː] I *s* ♪ Impromptu *n*. II *adj u. adv* aus dem Stegreif, Stegreif...

im·prop·er [ɪm'prɒpə] *adj* □ **1.** ungeeignet, unpassend. **2.** unanständig, unschicklich. **3.** unrichtig. **4.** A unecht (*Bruch*). **im·pro·pri·e·ty** [‚ɪmprə'praɪətɪ] *s* **1.** Unschicklichkeit *f*. **2.** Unrichtigkeit *f*.

im·prove [ɪm'pruːv] I *v/t* **1.** verbessern. **2.** *Wert etc* erhöhen, steigern. II *v/i* **3.** sich (ver)bessern, besser werden, Fortschritte machen (*a. Patient*), sich erholen (*gesundheitlich od.* ↟ *Preise etc*): **he is improving** (**in health**) es geht ihm besser; **~ in strength** kräftiger werden. **im·'prove·ment** *s* **1.** (Ver)Besserung *f* (**in** *gen*; **on** gegenüber, im Vergleich zu): **~ in the weather** Wetterbesserung *f*. **2.** Erhöhung *f*, Steigerung *f*.

im·prov·i·dent [ɪm'prɒvɪdənt] *adj* □ **1.** sorglos: **be ~ of** nicht vorsorgen für. **2.** verschwenderisch.

im·pro·vi·sa·tion [‚ɪmprəvaɪ'zeɪʃn] *s* Improvisation *f*. **im·pro·vise** ['~vaɪz] *v/t u. v/i* improvisieren.

im·pru·dence [ɪm'pruːdəns] *s* **1.** Unklugheit *f*. **2.** Unvorsichtigkeit *f*. **im·'pru·dent** *adj* □ **1.** unklug. **2.** unvorsichtig.

im·pu·dence ['ɪmpjʊdəns] *s* Unverschämtheit *f*. **'im·pu·dent** *adj* □ unverschämt.

im·pugn [ɪm'pjuːn] *v/t* bestreiten; anfechten.

im·pulse ['ɪmpʌls] *s* **1.** *phys.*, ♀, ⚡ *etc* Impuls *m*. **2.** *fig.* Impuls *m*: a) Anstoß *m,* Anreiz *m,* b) plötzliche Regung *od.* Eingebung: **act on ~** impulsiv *od.* spontan handeln; **on the ~ of the moment, on ~** e-r plötzlichen Eingebung folgend. **im'pul·sion** *s* **1.** Triebkraft *f (a. fig.).* **2.** *psych.* Zwang *m.* **im'pul·sive** *adj* □ *fig.* impulsiv.

im·pu·ni·ty [ɪm'pjuːnətɪ] *s* Straflosigkeit *f:* **with ~** straflos.

im·pure [ɪm'pjʊə] *adj* □ **1.** unrein (*a. eccl.*), unsauber. **2.** *fig.* schlecht, unmoralisch. **im'pur·i·ty** *s* **1.** Unreinheit *f.* **2.** *fig.* Schlechtheit *f.*

im·pu·ta·tion [ˌɪmpjuː'teɪʃn] *s* Bezichtigung *f.* **im'pute** *v/t* zuschreiben (**to** *dat*): a) beimessen, b) anlasten: **~ s.th. to s.o.** j-n e-r Sache bezichtigen.

in [ɪn] **I** *prp* **1.** *räumlich:* a) (*wo?*) in (*dat*), an (*dat*), auf (*dat*): **~ London** in London; → **country 3, field 1, sky, street,** *etc,* b) (*wohin?*) in (*acc*): **put it ~ your pocket** steck es in die Tasche. **2.** *zeitlich:* in (*dat*), an (*dat*): **~ 1988** 1988; **~ two hours** in zwei Stunden; → **April, beginning 1, evening,** *etc.* **3.** *Zustand, Beschaffenheit, Art u. Weise:* in (*dat*), auf (*acc*), mit: → **brief 4, cash 2, English 3,** *etc.* **4.** *Tätigkeit, Beschäftigung:* in (*dat*), bei, auf (*dat*): **~ crossing the river** beim Überqueren des Flusses; → **accident 2, search 4.** **5.** bei (*Schriftstellern*): **~ Shakespeare. 6.** *Richtung:* in (*acc, dat*), auf (*acc, dat*), zu: → **confidence 1,** *etc.* **7.** *Zweck:* in (*dat*), zu, als: → **answer 1, defence,** *etc.* **8.** *Grund:* in (*dat*), aus, zu: → **honour 5, sport 3,** *etc.* **9.** *Hinsicht, Beziehung:* in (*dat*), an (*dat*): **the latest thing ~** das Neueste auf dem Gebiet (*gen*); → **equal 1, number 3,** *etc.* **10.** nach, gemäß: → **opinion 1, probability,** *etc.* **11.** *Material:* in (*dat*), aus, mit: → **black 3, oil 3,** *etc.* **12.** *Zahl, Betrag:* in (*dat*), von, aus, zu: **five ~ all** insgesamt *od.* im ganzen fünf; **one ~ ten Americans** einer von zehn Amerikanern; → **all 4, two,** *etc.* **II** *adv* **13.** (dr)innen: **be ~ for s.th.** *et.* zu erwarten haben; **be ~ on** eingeweiht sein in (*acc*); beteiligt sein an (*dat*); **know ~ and out** in- u. auswendig kennen. **14.** hinein; herein: → **come in 1,** *etc.* **15.** da, (an)gekommen. **16.** da, zu Hause. **17.** *pol.* an der Macht, an der Regierung. **III** *adj* **18. ~**

party *pol.* Regierungspartei *f.* **19. ~ restaurant** Restaurant, das gerade in ist. **IV** *s* **20. know the ~s and outs of** in- u. auswendig kennen.

in·a·bil·i·ty [ˌɪnə'bɪlətɪ] *s* Unfähigkeit *f,* Unvermögen *n:* **~ to pay ✝** Zahlungsunfähigkeit.

in·ac·ces·si·ble [ˌɪnæk'sesəbl] *adj* □ unzugänglich (**to** für *od. dat*) (*a. fig.*).

in·ac·cu·ra·cy [ɪn'ækjʊrəsɪ] *s* Ungenauigkeit *f.* **in'ac·cu·rate** [~rət] *adj* □ ungenau: **be ~** falsch gehen (*Uhr*).

in·ac·tion [ɪn'ækʃn] *s* **1.** Untätigkeit *f.* **2.** Trägheit *f,* Faulheit *f.*

in·ac·tive [ɪn'æktɪv] *adj* □ **1.** untätig. **2.** träge (*a. phys.*), faul. **3. ✝** lustlos, flau. **in·ac'tiv·i·ty** [~'tɪvətɪ] *s.* → **inaction. 2.** Lustlosigkeit *f,* Flauheit *f.*

in·ad·e·quate [ɪn'ædɪkwət] *adj* □ **1.** unzulänglich, ungenügend: **be ~ for** nicht reichen für. **2.** unangemessen (**to** *dat*): **feel ~ to the occasion** sich der Situation nicht gewachsen fühlen.

in·ad·mis·si·ble [ˌɪnəd'mɪsəbl] *adj* □ unzulässig, unstatthaft.

in·ad·vert·ent [ˌɪnəd'vɜːtənt] *adj* □ unabsichtlich, versehentlich: **~ly** *a.* aus Versehen.

in·ad·vis·a·ble [ˌɪnəd'vaɪzəbl] *adj* nicht ratsam *od.* empfehlenswert.

in·al·ien·a·ble [ɪn'eɪljənəbl] *adj* □ unveräußerlich.

in·ane [ɪ'neɪn] *adj* □ geistlos, albern.

in·an·i·mate [ɪn'ænɪmət] *adj* □ **1.** leblos, unbelebt. **2.** *fig.* schwunglos, langweilig.

in·ap·pli·ca·ble [ɪn'æplɪkəbl] *adj* □ nicht anwendbar *od.* zutreffend (**to** auf *acc*): → **delete** II.

in·ap·pre·ci·a·ble [ˌɪnə'priːʃəbl] *adj* □ unmerklich.

in·ap·pro·pri·ate [ˌɪnə'prəʊprɪət] *adj* □ unpassend, ungeeignet (**to, for** für).

in·apt [ɪn'æpt] *adj* □ **1.** unpassend, ungeeignet. **2.** ungeschickt. **3.** unfähig, außerstande (**to do** zu tun). **in'apt·i·tude** [~tɪtjuːd] *s* **1.** Ungeschicktheit *f.* **2.** Unfähigkeit *f.*

in·ar·tic·u·late [ˌɪnɑː'tɪkjʊlət] *adj* □ **1.** undeutlich (ausgesprochen), unverständlich. **2.** unfähig(, deutlich) zu sprechen. **3.** unfähig, sich klar auszudrücken. **4.** sprachlos (**with** *vor dat*).

is ~ *to it* es ist ihm gleichgültig. **2.** mittelmäßig.

in·dig·e·nous [ɪnˈdɪdʒɪnəs] *adj* □ **1.** einheimisch (**to** in *dat*) (*a.* 🌱, *zo.*). **2.** *fig.* angeboren (**to** *dat*).

in·di·gest·i·ble [ˌɪndɪˈdʒestəbl] *adj* □ un-, schwerverdaulich (*a. fig.*). **,in·di-'ges·tion** *s* 🐍 Magenverstimmung *f*, verdorbener Magen.

in·dig·nant [ɪnˈdɪgnənt] *adj* □ entrüstet, empört (**at** *s.th.*, **with** *s.o.* über *acc*). **,in·dig'na·tion** *s* Entrüstung *f*, Empörung *f*: **to my** ~ zu m-r Entrüstung.

in·di·rect [ˌɪndɪˈrekt] *adj* □ *allg.* indirekt: **by** ~ **means** *fig.* auf Umwegen; ~ **object** *ling.* Dativobjekt *n*; ~ **speech** (*bsd. Am.* **discourse**) *ling.* indirekte Rede.

in·dis·cern·i·ble [ˌɪndɪˈsɜːnəbl] *adj* □ nicht wahrnehmbar, unmerklich.

in·dis·creet [ˌɪndɪˈskriːt] *adj* □ **1.** unbesonnen, unbedacht. **2.** indiskret. **in·dis·cre·tion** [ˌ~ˈskreʃn] *s* **1.** Unbesonnenheit *f*. **2.** Indiskretion *f*.

in·dis·crim·i·nate [ˌɪndɪˈskrɪmɪnət] *adj* □ **1.** nicht wählerisch; urteils-, kritiklos. **2.** wahl-, unterschiedslos; ungeordnet.

in·dis·pen·sa·ble [ˌɪndɪˈspensəbl] *adj* □ unentbehrlich (*a. Person*), unerläßlich (**to** für).

in·dis·posed [ˌɪndɪˈspəʊzd] *adj* **1.** indisponiert, unpäßlich. **2.** abgeneigt (**for** *dat*; **to do** zu tun): **be** ~ **to do s.th.** *a.* et. nicht tun wollen. **,in·dis·po·si·tion** [ˌɪndɪspəˈzɪʃn] *s* **1.** Unpäßlichkeit *f*. **2.** Abgeneigtheit *f* (**for** gegenüber; **to do** zu tun).

in·dis·pu·ta·ble [ˌɪndɪˈspjuːtəbl] *adj* □ unstrittig, unstreitig.

in·dis·so·lu·ble [ˌɪndɪˈsɒljʊbl] *adj* □ **1.** unlöslich. **2.** *fig.* unauflösbar.

in·dis·tinct [ˌɪndɪˈstɪŋkt] *adj* □ **1.** undeutlich; unscharf. **2.** verschwommen (*Erinnerung etc*).

in·dis·tin·guish·a·ble [ˌɪndɪˈstɪŋgwɪʃəbl] *adj* □ nicht zu unterscheiden(d) (**from** von).

in·di·vid·u·al [ˌɪndɪˈvɪdʃʊəl] **I** *adj* (□ → **individually**) **1.** individuell, einzeln, Einzel...: ~ **case** Einzelfall *m*; ~ **traffic** Individualverkehr *m*. **2.** individuell, persönlich (*Stil etc*). **II** *s* **3.** Individuum *n* (*a. contp.*), Einzelne *m, f.* **,in·di-**

'**vid·u·al·ism** *s* Individualismus *m.* **,in·di'vid·u·al·ist** *s* Individualist(in). **II** *adj* individualistisch. **'in·di,vid·u·al'is·tic** *adj* (~**ally**) individualistisch. **'in·di,vid·u·al·i·ty** [ˌ~ˈælətɪ] *s* Individualität *f.* **,in·di'vid·u·al·ize** [ˌ~əlaɪz] *v/t* **1.** individualisieren. **2.** individuell gestalten. **,in·di'vid·u·al·ly** *adv* **1.** individuell. **2.** einzeln, jede(r, -s) für sich.

in·di·vis·i·ble [ˌɪndɪˈvɪzəbl] *adj* □ unteilbar.

in·doc·tri·nate [ɪnˈdɒktrɪneɪt] *v/t* **1.** *contp. bsd. pol.* indoktrinieren. **2.** unterweisen, schulen (**in** in *dat*). **in,doc·tri'na·tion** *s* **1.** Indoktrination *f.* **2.** Unterweisung *f*, Schulung *f.*

in·do·lence [ˈɪndələns] *s* Trägheit *f.* **'in·do·lent** *adj* □ träg; träg machend (*Hitze etc*).

in·dom·i·ta·ble [ɪnˈdɒmɪtəbl] *adj* □ **1.** unbezähmbar, nicht unterzukriegen(d). **2.** unbeugsam.

in·door [ˈɪndɔː] *adj* Haus..., Zimmer..., (*Sport*) Hallen...: ~ **aerial** (*bsd. Am.* **antenna**) Zimmerantenne *f*; ~ **dress** Hauskleid *n*; ~ **plant** Zimmerpflanze *f*; ~ **shot** *phot.* Innenaufnahme *f*; ~ **swimming pool** Hallenbad *n.* **,in'doors** *adv* **1.** im Haus, drinnen. **2.** ins Haus (hinein). **3.** *Sport:* in der Halle.

in·du·bi·ta·ble [ɪnˈdjuːbɪtəbl] *adj* □ unzweifelhaft, *adv a.* zweifel-, fraglos.

in·duce [ɪnˈdjuːs] *v/t* **1.** j-n veranlassen, bewegen (**to do** zu tun). **2.** herbeiführen, verursachen, auslösen: ~ **labo(u)r** 🩺 die Geburt einleiten. **3.** 🔌 *etc* induzieren: ~**d current** Induktionsstrom *m.* **in'duce·ment** *s* Veranlassung *f*; Anreiz *m*: ~ **to buy** Kaufanreiz.

in·duc·tion [ɪnˈdʌkʃn] *s* **1.** Herbeiführung *f*, Auslösung *f.* **2.** 🔌 *etc* Induktion *f.*

in·dulge [ɪnˈdʌldʒ] **I** *v/t* **1.** nachsichtig sein gegen: ~ **o.s. in s.th.** → **4. 2.** *Kinder* verwöhnen. **3.** *e-r Neigung etc* nachgeben, frönen. **II** *v/i* **4.** ~ **in s.th.** sich et. gönnen *od.* leisten. **5.** (**in**) schwelgen (in *dat*), frönen (*dat*). **in'dul·gence** *s* **1.** Nachsicht *f.* **2.** Verwöhnung *f.* **3.** Schwelgen *n* (**in** in *dat*). **4.** Luxus *m*; Genuß *m.* **in'dul·gent** *adj* □ nachsichtig (**to** gegen).

in·dus·tri·al [ɪnˈdʌstrɪəl] *adj* □ industriell, Industrie...: ~ **action** *Br.* Arbeitskampf *m*; ~ *disease* Berufskrankheit *f*; ~ *espionage* Industrie-, Werkspionage *f*. **2.** industrialisiert, Industrie... **3.** Betriebs...: ~ *management* Betriebsführung *f*. **4.** industriell erzeugt, Industrie...: ~ *products pl* gewerbliche Erzeugnisse *pl*. **in·dus·tri·al·ist** *s* Industrielle *m*, *f*. **in·dus·tri·al·ize** *v/t* industrialisieren.

in·dus·tri·ous [ɪn'dʌstrɪəs] *adj* □ fleißig.

in·dus·try ['ɪndəstrɪ] *s* **1.** Industrie *f*; Industrie(zweig *m*) *f*: *steel* ~ Stahlindustrie. **2.** Fleiß *m*.

in·ed·i·ble [ɪn'edəbl] *adj* ungenießbar.

in·ef·fa·ble [ɪn'efəbl] *adj* □ unbeschreiblich, unsagbar.

in·ef·face·a·ble [ˌɪnɪ'feɪsəbl] *adj* □ **1.** unlöschbar. **2.** *fig.* unauslöschlich.

in·ef·fec·tive [ˌɪnɪ'fektɪv], **in·ef·fec·tu·al** [~'fektʃʊəl] *adj* □ **1.** unwirksam, wirkungslos. **2.** unfähig, untauglich.

in·ef·fi·cient [ˌɪnɪ'fɪʃnt] *adj* □ ineffizient: a) untüchtig, b) unrationell, unwirtschaftlich.

in·el·e·gant [ɪn'elɪɡənt] *adj* □ unelegant.

in·el·i·gi·ble [ɪn'elɪdʒəbl] *adj* □ (*for*) nicht in Frage kommend (für): a) ungeeignet, unannehmbar (für), b) nicht berechtigt *od.* befähigt (zu): *be* ~ *for* keinen Anspruch haben auf (*acc*), c) nicht teilnahmeberechtigt (an *dat*), (*Sport a.*) nicht start- *od.* spielberechtigt (für).

in·ept [ɪ'nept] *adj* □ **1.** unpassend. **2.** ungeschickt, unbeholfen; unfähig.

in·e·qual·i·ty [ˌɪnɪ'kwɒlətɪ] *s* Ungleichheit *f*, Verschiedenheit *f*.

in·eq·ui·ta·ble [ɪn'ekwɪtəbl] *adj* □ ungerecht. **in'eq·ui·ty** [~wətɪ] *s* Ungerechtigkeit *f*.

in·e·rad·i·ca·ble [ˌɪnɪ'rædɪkəbl] *adj* □ unausrottbar (*a. fig.*).

in·ert [ɪ'nɜːt] *adj* □ *phys.* träg (*a. fig.*). **in·er·tia** [ɪ'nɜːʃə] *s* Trägheit *f*.

in·es·cap·a·ble [ˌɪnɪ'skeɪpəbl] *adj* □ unvermeidlich: a) unabwendbar, b) unweigerlich.

in·es·sen·tial [ˌɪnɪ'senʃl] **I** *adj* unwesentlich. **II** *s et.* Unwesentliches, Nebensache *f*.

in·es·ti·ma·ble [ɪn'estɪməbl] *adj* □ unschätzbar.

in·ev·i·ta·ble [ɪn'evɪtəbl] **I** *adj* □ unvermeidlich. **II** *s das* Unvermeidliche.

in·ex·act [ˌɪnɪɡ'zækt] *adj* □ ungenau.

in·ex·cus·a·ble [ˌɪnɪk'skjuːzəbl] *adj* □ unverzeihlich, unentschuldbar.

in·ex·haust·i·ble [ˌɪnɪɡ'zɔːstəbl] *adj* □ unerschöpflich (*Thema etc*).

in·ex·o·ra·ble [ɪn'eksərəbl] *adj* □ unerbittlich.

in·ex·pe·di·ent [ˌɪnɪk'spiːdjənt] *adj* □ **1.** nicht ratsam, unangebracht. **2.** unzweckmäßig.

in·ex·pen·sive [ˌɪnɪk'spensɪv] *adj* □ billig, nicht teuer.

in·ex·pe·ri·ence [ˌɪnɪk'spɪərɪəns] *s* Unerfahrenheit *f*. **in·ex·pe·ri·enced** *adj* unerfahren.

in·ex·pert [ɪn'ekspɜːt] *adj* □ **1.** unerfahren (*at, in* in *dat*). **2.** unfachmännisch. **3.** ungeschickt, unbeholfen (*at, in* in *dat*).

in·ex·pli·ca·ble [ˌɪnɪk'splɪkəbl] *adj* □ ·unerklärlich.

in·ex·press·i·ble [ˌɪnɪk'spresəbl] *adj* □ unaussprechlich, unsäglich.

in·ex·tin·guish·able [ˌɪnɪk'stɪŋɡwɪʃəbl] *adj* □ **1.** unlöschbar. **2.** *fig.* unauslöschlich.

in·ex·tri·ca·ble [ɪn'ekstrɪkəbl] *adj* □ **1.** unentwirrbar (*a. fig.*). **2.** *fig.* ausweglos.

in·fal·li·bil·i·ty [ɪnˌfælə'bɪlətɪ] *s* Unfehlbarkeit *f* (*a. eccl.*). **in·fal·li·ble** *adj* □ unfehlbar. **in'fal·li·bly** *adv* **1.** unfehlbar. **2.** F todsicher, ganz bestimmt.

in·fa·mous ['ɪnfəməs] *adj* □ **1.** verrufen, berüchtigt (*for* wegen). **2.** infam, niederträchtig. **'in·fa·my** *s* **1.** Verrufenheit *f*. **2.** Infamie *f*: a) Niedertracht *f*, b) niederträchtige Handlung.

in·fan·cy ['ɪnfənsɪ] *s* frühe Kindheit, *bsd.* Säuglingsalter *n*: *be still in its* ~ *fig.* noch in den Anfängen *od.* Kinderschuhen stecken. **'in·fant I** *s* Säugling *m*; kleines Kind. **II** *adj* Säuglings...: ~ *mortality* Säuglingssterblichkeit *f*; ~ *prodigy* Wunderkind *n*.

in·fan·ti·cide [ɪn'fæntɪsaɪd] *s* **1.** Kind(es)tötung *f*. **2.** Kind(es)-, Kindermörder(in).

in·fan·tile ['ɪnfəntaɪl] *adj* **1.** infantil, kindisch. **2.** kindlich. **3.** Kinder..., Kindes...

in·fan·try ['ɪnfəntrɪ] *s* ✕ Infanterie *f*. **~man** ['~mən] *s* (*irr man*) Infanterist *m*.

in·farct [ɪnˈfɑːkt] s 🩺 Infarkt m.

in·fat·u·at·ed [ɪnˈfætjʊeɪtɪd] adj vernarrt (**with** in acc).

in·fect [ɪnˈfekt] v/t **1.** 🩺 infizieren, anstecken (**with** mit; **by** durch): **become ~ed** sich anstecken. **2.** Luft verpesten; fig. Atmosphäre vergiften. **3.** fig. anstecken (**with** mit). **in·fec·tion** s **1.** 🩺 Infektion f, Ansteckung f. **2.** Verpestung f; fig. Vergiftung f. **in·fec·tious** adj □ **1.** 🩺 ansteckend (a. fig. Lachen etc), infektiös: **~ disease** Infektionskrankheit f; **be ~** fig. ansteckend.

in·fe·lic·i·tous [ˌɪnfɪˈlɪsɪtəs] adj □ unglücklich (a. fig. Ausdruck etc).

in·fer [ɪnˈfɜː] v/t schließen, folgern (**from** aus). **in·fer·ence** [ˈɪnfərəns] s (Schluß-) Folgerung f, (Rück)Schluß m.

in·fe·ri·or [ɪnˈfɪərɪə] I adj **1.** (**to**) untergeordnet (dat), niedriger (als): **be ~ to** j-m untergeordnet sein; j-m unterlegen sein. **2.** weniger wert (**to** als). **3.** minderwertig, mittelmäßig. II s **4.** Untergebene m, f. **in·fe·ri·or·i·ty** [ˌ~ˈɒrətɪ] s **1.** Unterlegenheit f. **2.** Minderwertigkeit f, Mittelmäßigkeit f: **~ complex** psych. Minderwertigkeitskomplex m.

in·fer·nal [ɪnˈfɜːnl] adj □ **1.** höllisch, Höllen..., infernalisch. **2.** teuflisch. **in·fer·no** [~ˈnəʊ] pl **-nos** s Inferno n, Hölle f.

in·fer·tile [ɪnˈfɜːtaɪl] adj unfruchtbar. **in·fer·til·i·ty** [ˌɪnfəˈtɪlətɪ] s Unfruchtbarkeit f.

in·fest [ɪnˈfest] v/t **1.** verseuchen, befallen (Parasiten etc): **~ed with lice** verlaust. **2.** fig. überschwemmen, -laufen: **be ~ed with** wimmeln von.

in·fi·del [ˈɪnfɪdəl] eccl. I s Ungläubige m, f. II adj ungläubig. **in·fi·del·i·ty** [ˌ~ˈdelətɪ] s **1.** eccl. Unglaube m. **2.** (bsd. eheliche) Untreue f.

in·fight·ing [ˈɪnˌfaɪtɪŋ] s **1.** Boxen: Infight m, Nahkampf m. **2.** (partei- etc)interne Kämpfe pl od. Streitereien pl.

in·fil·trate [ˈɪnfɪltreɪt] I v/t **1.** einsickern in (acc). **2.** einschleusen, -schmuggeln (**into** in acc). **3.** pol. unterwandern. II v/i **4.** einsickern (**into** in acc). **in·fil·'tra·tion** s **1.** Einsickern n. **2.** pol. Unterwanderung f.

in·fi·nite [ˈɪnfɪnɪt] adj □ **1.** unendlich (a. 🅰), grenzenlos (beide a. fig.). **2.** gewaltig, ungeheuer. **in·fin·i·tes·i·mal** [ˌɪnfɪ-

'tesɪml] adj □ **1.** unendlich klein. **2.** 🅰 infinitesimal: **~ calculus** Infinitesimalrechnung f. **in·fin·i·tive** [~ˈtɪv] s ling. Infinitiv m. **in·fin·i·ty** s **1.** Unendlichkeit f, Grenzenlosigkeit f (beide a. fig.). **2.** unendliche Menge od. Größe (a. 🅰): **an ~ of people** unendlich viele Leute.

in·firm [ɪnˈfɜːm] adj □ schwach, gebrechlich. **in·fir·ma·ry** s **1.** Krankenhaus n. **2.** Krankenzimmer n, -stube f (in Internat etc). **in·fir·mi·ty** s Schwäche f, Gebrechlichkeit f; Gebrechen n.

in·flame [ɪnˈfleɪm] I v/t **1.** entzünden (a. 🩺): **become ~d** → 3. **2.** fig. Gefühle etc entfachen, -flammen; j-n entflammen, erregen: **~d with rage** wutentbrannt. II v/i **3.** sich entzünden (a. 🩺). **4.** fig. entbrennen (**with** vor dat); in Wut geraten.

in·flam·ma·ble [ɪnˈflæməbl] adj □ **1.** brennbar, leichtentzündlich; feuergefährlich. **2.** fig. reizbar, leichterregbar. **in·flam·ma·tion** [ˌɪnfləˈmeɪʃn] s 🩺 Entzündung f. **in·flam·ma·to·ry** [ɪnˈflæmətərɪ] adj **1.** 🩺 entzündlich, Entzündungs... **2.** fig. aufrührerisch, Hetz...

in·flate [ɪnˈfleɪt] v/t aufblasen, Reifen etc aufpumpen. **in·flat·ed** adj **1.** aufgeblasen: **~ with pride** fig. stolzgeschwellt. **2.** fig. schwülstig, bombastisch. **in·fla·tion** [~ʃn] s **1.** Aufblasen n, -pumpen n. **2.** 🟎 Inflation f: → **creeping, gallop** n, **runaway** 3. **in·fla·tion·ar·y** adj 🟎 Inflations..., inflationär.

in·flect [ɪnˈflekt] v/t **1.** beugen. **2.** ling. flektieren, beugen. **in·flec·tion** s **1.** Beugung f. **2.** ling. Flexion f, Beugung f.

in·flex·i·ble [ɪnˈfleksəbl] adj □ inflexibel: a) unbiegsam, b) fig. unbeweglich. **in·flex·ion** bsd. Br. → **inflection**.

in·flict [ɪnˈflɪkt] v/t (**on**) **1.** Leid, Schaden etc zufügen (dat), Niederlage, Wunde etc beibringen (dat), Strafe auferlegen (dat), verhängen (über acc). **2.** aufbürden (dat): **~ o.s. on s.o.** sich j-m aufdrängen. **in·flic·tion** s **1.** Zufügung f; Auferlegung f. **2.** Plage f, Last f.

'in·flight adj ✈ Bord...: **~ fare** Bordverpflegung f. **2.** während des Flugs.

in·flow [ˈɪnfləʊ] → **influx**.

in·flu·ence [ˈɪnflʊəns] I s Einfluß m (**on**, **over** auf acc; **with** bei): **be under s.o.'s ~** unter j-s Einfluß stehen; **under the ~**

of drink (od. alcohol) unter Alkoholeinfluß; *under the* ~ F alkoholisiert. **II** *v/t* beeinflussen. **in·flu·en·tial** [ˌ~'enʃl] *adj* □ einflußreich.

in·flu·en·za [ˌɪnfluˈenzə] *s* ⚕ Grippe *f.*

in·flux ['ɪnflʌks] *s* Zustrom *m (a. fig.),* (*Kapital- etc)*Zufluß *m:* ~ *of visitors* Besucherstrom *m.*

in·fo ['ɪnfəʊ] F → *information.*

in·form [ɪnˈfɔːm] **I** *v/t (of, about)* benachrichtigen, unterrichten (von), informieren (über *acc):* **keep** *s.o.* **~ed** j-n auf dem laufenden halten; ~ *s.o.* **that** j-n davon in Kenntnis setzen, daß. **II** *v/i:* ~ **against** *(od. on) s.o.* j-n anzeigen; *b.s.* j-n denunzieren.

in·for·mal [ɪnˈfɔːml] *adj* □ **1.** formlos, ⚖ *a.* formfrei. **2.** zwanglos, ungezwungen. **3.** inoffiziell.

in·form·ant [ɪnˈfɔːmənt] *s* **1.** Informant *m,* Gewährsmann *m.* **2.** → *informer.*

in·for·mat·ics [ˌɪnfəˈmætɪks] *s pl (sg konstruiert)* Informatik *f.*

in·for·ma·tion [ˌɪnfəˈmeɪʃn] *s* **1.** Benachrichtigung *f,* Unterrichtung *f;* Nachricht *f,* Mitteilung *f,* Bescheid *m.* **2.** Auskünfte *pl,* Auskunft *f,* Information *f:* **for your** ~ zu Ihrer Information *od.* Kenntnisnahme. **3.** *coll.* Nachrichten *pl,* Informationen *pl:* **bit** *(od.* **piece)** **of** ~ Nachricht *f,* Information *f.* **4.** *coll.* Erkundigungen *pl:* **gather** ~ Erkundigungen einziehen. **in·form·a·tive** [ɪnˈfɔːmətɪv] *adj* □ informativ, aufschlußreich. **in·form·er** *s* **1.** Denunziant(in). **2.** Spitzel *m.*

in·fra| dig [ˌɪnfrəˈdɪg] *adj:* **it is** ~ **for him** F es ist unter s-r Würde *(to do* zu tun). **'~·red** *adj phys.* infrarot. **'~·struc·ture** *s* Infrastruktur *f.*

in·fre·quent [ɪnˈfriːkwənt] *adj* □ **1.** selten. **2.** spärlich.

in·fringe [ɪnˈfrɪndʒ] *v/t u. v/i (~ **on**) Gesetz, Vertrag etc* brechen, verletzen, verstoßen gegen. **in·fringe·ment** *s* Verletzung *f;* Verstoß *m* (*of* gegen).

in·fu·ri·ate [ɪnˈfjʊərɪeɪt] *v/t* wütend machen.

in·fuse [ɪnˈfjuːz] *v/t* **1.** *Tee etc* aufgießen; ziehen lassen. **2.** *fig. Mut etc* einflößen (*into* dat); *j-n* erfüllen (*with* mit). **in·fu·sion** [ˌ~ʒn] *s* **1.** ⚕ Infusion *f.* **2.** Aufguß *m.* **3.** *fig.* Einflößung *f.*

in·gen·ious [ɪnˈdʒiːnjəs] *adj* □ genial: a)

erfinderisch, einfallsreich, b) sinnreich, raffiniert. **in·ge·nu·i·ty** [ˌɪndʒɪˈnjuːətɪ] *s* Genialität *f,* Einfallsreichtum *m.*

in·gen·u·ous [ɪnˈdʒenjʊəs] *adj* □ **1.** offen(herzig), aufrichtig. **2.** naiv, kindlich-unbefangen.

in·gle-nook ['ɪŋglnʊk] *s Br.* Kaminecke *f.*

in·glo·ri·ous [ɪnˈglɔːrɪəs] *adj* □ unrühmlich, schmählich.

in·go·ing ['ɪnˌɡəʊɪŋ] *adj* nachfolgend, neu (*Mieter etc*). **2.** ~ **mail** Posteingang *m.*

in·got ['ɪŋgət] *s (Gold- etc)*Barren *m:* ~ **of gold.**

in·gra·ti·ate [ɪnˈgreɪʃɪeɪt] *v/t:* ~ **o.s. with** *s.o.* sich bei j-m einschmeicheln.

in·grat·i·tude [ɪnˈgrætɪtjuːd] *s* Undank (-barkeit *f) m.*

in·gre·di·ent [ɪnˈgriːdjənt] *s* **1.** Bestandteil *m (a. fig.).* **2.** *gastr.* Zutat *f.*

in·hab·it [ɪnˈhæbɪt] *v/t* bewohnen. **'in·hab·it·a·ble** *adj* bewohnbar. **in·hab·it·ant** *s* Einwohner(in) (*e-s Orts, Landes*), Bewohner(in) (*bsd. e-s Hauses*).

in·hale [ɪnˈheɪl] **I** *v/t* **1.** einatmen, ⚕ *a.* inhalieren. **II** *v/i* **2.** einatmen. **3.** inhalieren, Lungenzüge machen.

in·har·mo·ni·ous [ˌɪnhɑːˈməʊnjəs] *adj* □ unharmonisch.

in·here [ɪnˈhɪə] *v/i* innewohnen (*in* dat). **in·her·ent** [ɪnˈhɪərənt] *adj* innewohnend.

in·her·it [ɪnˈherɪt] *v/t* erben (*from* von) (*a. fig.).* **in·her·i·tance** *s* Erbe *n (a. fig.).*

in·hib·it [ɪnˈhɪbɪt] *v/t* **1.** hemmen (*a. psych.),* (ver)hindern. **2.** *j-n* hindern (*from* an *dat):* ~ *s.o.* **from doing s.th.** j-n daran hindern, et. zu tun. **in·hi·bi·tion** [ˌɪnhɪˈbɪʃn] *s psych.* Hemmung *f.*

in·hos·pi·ta·ble [ˌɪnhɒˈspɪtəbl] *adj* □ wenig gastfreundlich; ungastlich.

in·hu·man [ɪnˈhjuːmən], **in·hu·mane** [ˌ~ˈmeɪn] *adj* □ inhuman, unmenschlich. **in·hu·man·i·ty** [ˌ~ˈmænətɪ] *s* Unmenschlichkeit *f.*

in·im·i·cal [ɪˈnɪmɪkl] *adj* □ **1.** feindselig (*to* gegen). **2.** (*to*) nachteilig (für), abträglich (*dat*).

in·im·i·ta·ble [ɪˈnɪmɪtəbl] *adj* □ unnachahmlich.

in·iq·ui·tous [ɪˈnɪkwɪtəs] *adj* □ **1.** ungerecht. **2.** schändlich. **in·iq·ui·ty** *s* **1.** Ungerechtigkeit f. **2.** Schändlichkeit f; Schandtat f.

in·i·tial [ɪˈnɪʃl] **I** adj anfänglich, Anfangs... **II** s Initiale f, (großer) Anfangsbuchstabe. **III** v/t pret u. pp **-tialed**, bsd. Br. **-tialled** abzeichnen, pol. paraphieren. **in'i·tial·ly** [~ʃəlɪ] adv anfänglich, am Anfang. **in·i·ti·ate I** v/t [ɪˈnɪʃɪeɪt] **1.** einleiten, ins Leben rufen. **2.** j-n einführen (**into** in acc): a) einweihen, b) aufnehmen, c) einarbeiten. **II** s [~ʃɪət] **3.** Eingeweihte m, f. **in,i·ti·a·tion** s **1.** Einleitung f. **2.** Einführung f: a) Einweihung f, b) Aufnahme f, c) Einarbeitung f. **in'i·ti·a·tive** [~ətɪv] s Initiative f: **take the** ~ die Initiative ergreifen; **on one's own** ~ aus eigenem Antrieb. **in'i·ti·a·tor** [~eɪtə] s Initiator m, Urheber m.

in·ject [ɪnˈdʒekt] v/t 🏥 injizieren, einspritzen (a. ⚙): ~ **s.th. into s.o.**, ~ **s.o. with s.th.** j-m et. einflößen. **in'jec·tion** s 🏥 Injektion f: a) Einspritzung f (a. ⚙), Spritze f, b) eingespritztes Medikament.

in·ju·di·cious [ˌɪndʒuːˈdɪʃəs] adj □ unklug, unvernünftig.

in·junc·tion [ɪnˈdʒʌŋkʃn] s **1.** ⚖ gerichtliches Verbot: (**interim**) ~ einstweilige Verfügung. **2.** ausdrücklicher Befehl.

in·jure [ˈɪndʒə] v/t **1.** verletzen: ~ **one's leg** sich am Bein verletzen. **2.** fig. kränken, verletzen. **3.** fig. schaden (dat), schädigen. **in·ju·ri·ous** [ɪnˈdʒʊərɪəs] adj □ (**to**) schädlich (für), abträglich (dat): **be** ~ (**to**) a. schaden (dat). **in·ju·ry** [ˈɪndʒərɪ] s **1.** 🏥 Verletzung f (**to** an dat): ~ **to the head** Kopfverletzung, -wunde f. **2.** fig. Kränkung f, Verletzung f (**to** gen).

in·jus·tice [ɪnˈdʒʌstɪs] s Unrecht n, Ungerechtigkeit f: **do s.o. an** ~ j-m unrecht tun; **suffer an** ~ ungerecht behandelt werden.

ink [ɪŋk] s **1.** Tinte f. **2.** Tusche f. **3.** typ. (Drucker)Schwärze f.

ink·ling [ˈɪŋklɪŋ] s **1.** Andeutung f, Wink m. **2.** dunkle Ahnung: **give s.o. an** ~ **of** (od. **as to**) j-m e-e ungefähre Vorstellung geben von.

'ink·pad s Stempelkissen n. ~ **stain** s Tintenklecks m, -fleck m.

ink·y [ˈɪŋkɪ] adj **1.** tinten-, pechschwarz. **2.** tintig, voller Tinte.

in·land I adj [ˈɪnlənd] **1.** binnenländisch, Binnen... **2.** inländisch, einheimisch: ⁓ **Revenue** Br. F Finanzamt n. **II** adv [ɪnˈlænd] **3.** landeinwärts.

in·laws [ˈɪnlɔːz] s pl F angeheiratete Verwandte pl, engS. Schwiegereltern pl.

in·lay I v/t (irr **lay**) [ˌɪnˈleɪ] **1.** einlegen (**with** mit): **inlaid work** → **3. 2.** parkettieren: **inlaid floor** Parkett(fußboden m) n. **II** s [ˈɪnleɪ] **3.** Einlegearbeit f.

in·let [ˈɪnlet] s **1.** Eingang m. **2.** Einlaß m (a. ⚙). **3.** schmale Bucht; Meeresarm m.

in·mate [ˈɪnmeɪt] s Insasse m, Insassin f (e-r Anstalt, e-s Gefängnisses etc).

in·most [ˈɪnməʊst] adj innerst, fig. a. tiefst, geheimst.

inn [ɪn] s **1.** Gasthaus n, -hof m. **2.** Wirtshaus n.

in·nards [ˈɪnədz] s pl F Eingeweide pl: **his** ~ **were rumbling** es rumorte in s-m Bauch.

in·nate [ˌɪˈneɪt] adj angeboren (**in** dat).

in·ner [ˈɪnə] adj **1.** inner, Innen...: ~ **door** Innentür f; ~ **life** Innen-, Seelenleben n; ~ **man** Seele f; Geist m; humor. Magen m. **2.** fig. tiefer, verborgen (Sinn etc). **in·ner·most** [ˈ~məʊst] → **inmost**.

'inn,keep·er s Gast(wirt)in.

in·no·cence [ˈɪnəsns] s Unschuld f: a) Schuldlosigkeit f, b) Unberührtheit f: **lose one's** ~ s-e Unschuld verlieren, c) Harmlosigkeit f, d) Arglosigkeit f, Naivität f. **in·no·cent** [ˈ~snt] adj □ unschuldig: a) schuldlos (**of** an dat), b) sittlich rein, (Mädchen a.) unberührt: (**as**) ~ **as a newborn babe** so unschuldig wie ein neugeborenes Kind, c) harmlos: ~ **air** Unschuldsmiene f; d) arglos, naiv.

in·noc·u·ous [ɪˈnɒkjʊəs] adj □ unschädlich, harmlos.

in·no·vate [ˈɪnəʊveɪt] v/i Neuerungen einführen (**on**, **in** bei, in dat). **in·no'va·tion** s Neuerung f.

in·nu·en·do [ˌɪnjuːˈendəʊ] pl **-do(e)s** s (**about**, **at**) versteckte Andeutung (über acc) od. Anspielung (auf acc).

in·nu·mer·a·ble [ɪˈnjuːmərəbl] adj □ unzählig, zahllos.

in·oc·u·late [ɪˈnɒkjʊleɪt] v/t 🏥 impfen (**against** gegen): ~ **s.o. with s.th.** fig. j-m et. einimpfen. **in,oc·u'la·tion** s 🏥 Impfung f.

in·o·dor·ous [ɪnˈəʊdərəs] adj geruchlos.

in·of·fen·sive [ˌɪnəˈfensɪv] *adj* □ harmlos.

in·op·er·a·ble [ɪnˈɒpərəbl] *adj* **1.** undurchführbar. **2.** ♣ inoperabel.

in·op·er·a·tive [ɪnˈɒpərətɪv] *adj* unwirksam: a) wirkungslos, b) ⅟₁₂ ungültig.

in·op·por·tune [ɪnˈɒpətjuːn] *adj* □ ungünstig, unpassend.

in·or·di·nate [ɪnˈɔːdɪnət] *adj* □ un-, übermäßig, (*Forderung etc a.*) überzogen.

in·or·gan·ic [ˌɪnɔːˈɡænɪk] *adj* (**~ally**) **1.** anorganisch. **2.** 🜨 anorganisch.

in·pa·tient [ˈɪnˌpeɪʃnt] *s* stationärer Patient: **~ treatment** stationäre Behandlung.

in·put [ˈɪnpʊt] *s* Input *m*: a) ⚕ eingesetzte Produktionsmittel *pl*, b) ⚡ Eingangsleistung *f*, c) ⊙ eingespeiste Menge, d) *Computer*: (Daten)Eingabe *f*.

in·quest [ˈɪnkwest] *s* ⅟₁₂ gerichtliche Untersuchung: → **coroner**.

in·qui·e·tude [ɪnˈkwaɪətjuːd] *s* Unruhe *f*, Besorgnis *f*.

in·quire [ɪnˈkwaɪə] **I** *v/t* **1.** **~ s.th. (of s.o.)** sich (bei j-m) nach et. erkundigen. **II** *v/i* **2.** (nach)fragen, sich erkundigen (*of s.o.* bei j-m; *after, for* nach; *about* wegen): **~ within** Näheres im Hause (zu erfragen). **3. ~ into** et. untersuchen, prüfen. **in·quir·y** *s* **1.** Erkundigung *f*, (An-, Nach)Frage *f*: **on ~** auf An- *od.* Nachfrage; **make inquiries** Erkundigungen einziehen (*of s.o.* bei j-m; *about, after* über *acc*, wegen). **2.** Untersuchung *f*, Prüfung *f* (*of, into gen*), Nachforschung *f*, Ermittlung *f*, Recherche *f*. **3.** *pl* ⚕ *etc* Auskunft *f* (*Büro, Schalter*).

in·qui·si·tion [ˌɪnkwɪˈzɪʃn] *s* **1.** (*a.* gerichtliche *od.* amtliche) Untersuchung (*into gen*). **2.** ⚑ *eccl. hist.* Inquisition *f*. **in·quis·i·tive** [ɪnˈkwɪzɪtɪv] *adj* □ **1.** wißbegierig. **2.** neugierig.

in·quo·rate [ɪnˈkwɔːrət] *adj* beschlußunfähig.

in·road [ˈɪnrəʊd] *s bsd. pl* **1.** *bsd.* ✗ Einfall *m* (*in, into, on* in *acc*). **2.** *fig.* (*in, into, on*) Eingriff *m* (*in* (*acc*), Übergriff *m* (auf *acc*). **3.** *a.* **heavy ~** *fig.* übermäßige Inanspruchnahme (*in, into, on gen*): **make ~s on s.o.'s free time** j-s Freizeit stark einschränken; **make ~s**

into s.o.'s savings ein großes Loch in j-s Ersparnisse reißen.

in·rush [ˈɪnrʌʃ] *s* **1.** (Her)Einströmen *n*. **2.** *fig.* Flut *f*, (Zu)Strom *m*: **~ of tourists** Touristenstrom.

in·sa·lu·bri·ous [ˌɪnsəˈluːbrɪəs] *adj* □ ungesund.

in·sane [ɪnˈseɪn] *adj* □ wahn-, irrsinnig, ♣ *a.* geisteskrank.

in·san·i·tar·y [ɪnˈsænɪtərɪ] *adj* unhygienisch, gesundheitsschädlich.

in·san·i·ty [ɪnˈsænətɪ] *s* Wahn-, Irrsinn *m*, ♣ *a.* Geisteskrankheit *f*.

in·sa·ti·a·ble [ɪnˈseɪʃəbl] *adj* □ unersättlich (*Person*), unstillbar (*Durst etc*) (*beide a. fig.*).

in·scrip·tion [ɪnˈskrɪpʃn] *s* **1.** In- *od.* Aufschrift *f*. **2.** (persönliche) Widmung.

in·scru·ta·ble [ɪnˈskruːtəbl] *adj* □ unerforschlich, unergründlich.

in·sect [ˈɪnsekt] *s zo.* Insekt *n*: **~ spray** Insektenspray *n*. **in·sec·ti·cide** [ˌɪntɪsaɪd] *s* Insektizid *n*, Insektenvernichtungsmittel *n*.

in·se·cure [ˌɪnsɪˈkjʊə] *adj* □ **1.** ungesichert, nicht fest. **2.** *fig.* unsicher. **in·se·cu·ri·ty** [ˌrətɪ] *s* Unsicherheit *f*.

in·sem·i·nate [ɪnˈsemɪneɪt] *v/t biol.* befruchten, *zo. a.* besamen. **in·sem·i·'na·tion** *s* Befruchtung *f*, Besamung *f*.

in·sen·si·ble [ɪnˈsensəbl] *adj* □ **1.** unempfindlich (**to** gegen): **~ to pain** schmerzunempfindlich. **2.** bewußtlos. **3.** *fig.* unempfänglich (für), gleichgültig (gegen). **4.** unmerklich.

in·sen·si·tive [ɪnˈsensətɪv] *adj* □ **1.** *a. phys.*, ⊙ unempfindlich (**to** gegen): **~ to light** lichtunempfindlich. **2.** → **insensible** 1, 3.

in·sep·a·ra·ble [ɪnˈsepərəbl] *adj* □ **1.** untrennbar (*a. ling.*). **2.** unzertrennlich (**from** von).

in·sert **I** *v/t* [ɪnˈsɜːt] **1.** einfügen, -setzen, -schieben, *Instrument etc* einführen, *Schlüssel etc* (hinein)stecken, *Münze etc* einwerfen (**in, into** in *acc*). **2. ~ an advertisement in(to) a newspaper** e-e Anzeige in e-e Zeitung setzen, in e-r Zeitung inserieren. **II** *s* [ˈɪnsɜːt] **3.** *a.* **insertion** 2-4. **in·ser·tion** *s* **1.** Einsetzen *n*, Einführung *f*, Einwurf *m*. **2.** Einsatz(stück *n*) *m*. **3.** Anzeige *f*, Inserat *n*. **4.** (Zeitungs)Beilage *f*, (Buch)Einlage *f*.

in·shore [ˌɪnˈʃɔː] *adj* an *od.* nahe der

Küste: ~ **fishing** Küstenfischerei f.

in·side I s [ˌɪnˈsaɪd] **1.** Innenseite f; *das* Innere: **on the ~** innen; **from the ~** von innen; **turn ~ out** umdrehen, umstülpen; *fig.* (völlig) umkrempeln; **know ~ out** in- u. auswendig kennen. **II** adj [ˈɪnsaɪd] **2.** inner, Innen...: **~ lane** (*Sport*) Innenbahn f; *mot. Br.* äußere Fahrspur; **overtake s.o. on the ~ lane** (*in GB etc*) j-n links überholen, (*in Deutschland etc*) j-n rechts überholen. **3. ~ information** (F **stuff**) Insiderinformationen pl, interne od. vertrauliche Informationen pl. **III** adv [ˌɪnˈsaɪd] **4.** im Inner(e)n, (dr)innen. **5.** hinein, herein. **6. ~ of** a) *zeitlich:* innerhalb (*gen*), b) *Am.* → **7. IV** prp [ˌɪnˈsaɪd] **7.** innerhalb, im Inner(e)n (*gen*): **~ the house** im Hause. **in·sid·er** s Insider(in), Eingeweihte m, f.

in·sid·i·ous [ɪnˈsɪdɪəs] adj □ hinterhältig, heimtückisch.

in·sight [ˈɪnsaɪt] s **1.** (**into**) Einblick m (in acc); Verständnis n (für). **2.** Einsicht f.

in·sig·ni·a [ɪnˈsɪgnɪə] pl **-a(s)** s **1.** Insignie f, Amts-, Ehrenzeichen n. **2.** ✕ Abzeichen n.

in·sig·nif·i·cant [ˌɪnsɪgˈnɪfɪkənt] adj □ **1.** bedeutungslos. **2.** geringfügig, unerheblich (*Betrag*). **3.** unbedeutend (*Person*).

in·sin·cere [ˌɪnsɪnˈsɪə] adj □ unaufrichtig, falsch.

in·sin·u·ate [ɪnˈsɪnjʊeɪt] v/t andeuten, anspielen auf (acc): **are you insinuating that ...?** wollen Sie damit sagen, daß ...? **in·sin·u·a·tion** s (**about**) Anspielung f (auf acc), Andeutung f (über acc): **by ~** andeutungsweise.

in·sip·id [ɪnˈsɪpɪd] adj □ fad (a. fig.).

in·sist [ɪnˈsɪst] **I** v/i **1.** darauf bestehen: **~ on** bestehen auf (dat), verlangen (acc); **~ on doing s.th.** darauf bestehen, et. zu tun; et. unbedingt tun wollen. **2.** (**on**) beharren (auf dat), bleiben bei. **3.** (**on**) Gewicht legen (auf acc), (nachdrücklich) betonen (acc). **II** v/t **4.** darauf bestehen (**that** daß). **5.** darauf beharren, dabei bleiben (**that** daß). **in·sist·ence** s **1.** Bestehen n, Beharren n (**on** auf dat). **2.** Betonung f (**on** gen): **with great ~** mit großem Nachdruck. **3.** Beharrlichkeit f, Hartnäckigkeit f. **in·sist·ent** adj □ **1.** beharrlich, hartnäckig: **be ~ (on)** →

insist I; be ~ that darauf bestehen, daß. **2.** eindringlich, nachdrücklich.

in·so·far adv: **~ as** soweit.

in·sole [ˈɪnsəʊl] s **1.** Brandsohle f. **2.** Einlegesohle f.

in·so·lence [ˈɪnsələns] s Unverschämtheit f, Frechheit f. **in·so·lent** adj □ unverschämt, frech.

in·sol·u·ble [ɪnˈsɒljʊbl] adj □ **1.** 🧪 un(auf)löslich. **2.** fig. unlösbar.

in·sol·ven·cy [ɪnˈsɒlvənsɪ] s ✝ Zahlungsunfähigkeit f, Insolvenz f. **in·sol·vent** adj zahlungsunfähig, insolvent.

in·som·ni·a [ɪnˈsɒmnɪə] s Schlaflosigkeit f.

in·so·much adv: **~ that** dermaßen od. so sehr, daß.

in·spect [ɪnˈspekt] v/t **1.** untersuchen, prüfen (**for** auf acc). **2.** besichtigen, inspizieren. **in·spec·tion** s **1.** Untersuchung f, Prüfung f: **on ~** bei näherer Prüfung; **for ~** ✝ zur Ansicht. **2.** Besichtigung f, Inspektion f. **in·spec·tor** s **1.** Inspektor m, Aufsichtsbeamte m, Kontrolleur m (a. 🎬 etc). **2.** police ~ Br. Polizeiinspektor m, -kommissar m.

in·spi·ra·tion [ˌɪnspəˈreɪʃn] s Inspiration f: a) (*eccl.* göttliche) Eingebung, (plötzlicher) Einfall, b) Anregung f: **be s.o.'s ~, be an ~ to** (od. **for**) **s.o.** j-n inspirieren. **in·spire** [ɪnˈspaɪə] v/t **1.** inspirieren, anregen (**to** zu; **to do** zu tun). **2.** Gefühl etc erwecken, auslösen (**in** in dat). **3.** erfüllen (**with** mit).

in·sta·bil·i·ty [ˌɪnstəˈbɪlətɪ] s **1.** mangelnde Festigkeit od. Stabilität. **2.** bsd. 🧪, ⚙ Instabilität f. **3.** fig. Unbeständigkeit f. **4.** (**emotional**) ~ fig. Labilität f.

in·stall [ɪnˈstɔːl] v/t **1.** ⚙ installieren: a) Bad etc einbauen, b) Leitung etc legen, c) Telefon etc anschließen. **2.** j-n einsetzen (**interim president**) als Interimspräsidenten). **in·stal·la·tion** [ˌɪnstəˈleɪʃn] s **1.** ⚙ Installation f, Einbau m, Anschluß m. **2.** ⚙ Anlage f, Einrichtung f. **3.** (Amts)Einsetzung f.

in·stall·ment, bsd. Br. **in·stal·ment** [ɪnˈstɔːlmənt] s **1.** ✝ Rate f: **by** (od. **in**) **~s** in Raten, ratenweise; **first ~** Anzahlung f (**toward[s]** auf acc); **monthly ~** Monatsrate; **buy on** (od. **by**) **the ~ plan** Am. auf Raten kaufen. **2.** (Teil)Lieferung f (e-s Buchs etc). **3.** a) Fortsetzung f: **novel by** (od. **in**) **~s** Fortsetzungsroman *m*, b) *Rundfunk, TV*: Folge *f*.

in·stance ['ɪnstəns] *s* **1.** (*einzelner*) Fall: *in this ~* in diesem (besonderen) Fall. **2.** Beispiel *n*: *for ~* zum Beispiel; *as an ~ of* als Beispiel für. **3.** *at s.o.'s ~* auf j-s Veranlassung (hin), auf j-s Betreiben *od.* Drängen. **4.** ⚖ Instanz *f*: *in the last ~* in letzter Instanz; *fig.* letztlich; *in the first ~* *fig.* in erster Linie; zuerst.

in·stant ['ɪnstənt] **I** *s* **1.** Moment *n*, Augenblick *m*: *in an ~, on the ~* sofort, augenblicklich; *at this ~* in diesem Augenblick. **II** *adj* (□ → *instantly*) **2.** sofortig, augenblicklich: *~ camera phot.* Sofortbildkamera *f*; *~ coffee* Pulverkaffee *m*; *~ meal* Fertig-, Schnellgericht *n*. **3.** *the 10th ~* ✝ der 10. dieses Monats. **4.** dringend: *be in ~ need of et.* dringend brauchen.

in·stan·ta·ne·ous [ˌɪnstən'teɪnjəs] *adj* sofortig, augenblicklich: *his death was ~* er war auf der Stelle tot. **in·stan'ta·ne·ous·ly** *adv* sofort, auf der Stelle.

in·stant·ly ['ɪnstəntlɪ] *adv* sofort, augenblicklich.

in·stead [ɪn'sted] *adv* **1.** *~ of* an Stelle von (*od. gen*), (an)statt (*gen*): *~ of me* an m-r Stelle; *~ of going* (an)statt zu gehen. **2.** statt dessen, dafür.

in·step ['ɪnstep] *s anat.* Rist *m*, Spann *m*.

in·sti·gate ['ɪnstɪgeɪt] *v/t* **1.** j-n aufhetzen, *a.* anstiften (*to* zu; *to do* zu tun). **2.** *et. Böses* anstiften, anzetteln; *et.* in Gang setzen, in die Wege leiten. **ˌin·sti'ga·tion** *s* **1.** Aufhetzung *f*, Anstiftung *f*. **2.** *at s.o.'s ~* → *instance* 3.

in·stil(l) [ɪn'stɪl] *v/t* **1.** einträufeln (*into dat*). **2.** *fig.* einflößen (*into dat*).

in·stinct ['ɪnstɪŋkt] *s* Instinkt *m*: *by* (*od. from*) *~* instinktiv; *~ for self-preservation* Selbsterhaltungstrieb *m*. **in'stinc·tive** *adj* □ instinktiv.

in·sti·tute ['ɪnstɪtjuːt] **I** *v/t* **1.** gründen, ins Leben rufen. **2.** in Gang setzen, in die Wege leiten. **II** *s* **3.** Institut *n*. **ˌin·sti'tu·tion** *s* **1.** Institution *f*, Einrichtung *f* (*beide a. sociol.*); Institut *n*; Anstalt *f*. **2.** Sitte *f*, Brauch *m*. **3.** Gründung *f*. **ˌin·sti'tu·tion·al** [~ʃənl] *adj* **1.** Instituts...; Anstalts... **2.** *bsd. contp.* Einheits..., **ˌin·sti'tu·tion·al·ize** *v/t* **1.** institutionalisieren. **2.** in e-e Anstalt einweisen.

in·struct [ɪn'strʌkt] *v/t* **1.** (*in* in *dat*) unterrichten; ausbilden, schulen. **2.** informieren, unterrichten. **3.** instruieren, anweisen, beauftragen (*to do* zu tun).

in·struc·tion *s* **1.** Unterricht *m*; Ausbildung *f*, Schulung *f*. **2.** Informierung *f*, Unterrichtung *f*. **3.** Instruktion *f*, Anweisung *f*, (*Computer*) Befehl *m*: *according to ~s* auftragsgemäß; vorschriftsmäßig; *~s pl for use* Gebrauchsanweisung, -anleitung *f*. **in'struc·tive** *adj* □ instruktiv, lehrreich. **in'struc·tor** *s* Lehrer *m*; Ausbilder *m*. **in'struc·tress** *s* Lehrerin *f*.

in·stru·ment ['ɪnstrʊmənt] **I** *s* **1.** ☉ Instrument *n* (*a.* ♪): a) Werkzeug *n*: *~ of torture* Foltergerät *n*, -instrument, -werkzeug; b) (*bsd.* Meß)Gerät *n*. **2.** ♪ Instrument *n*. **3.** ✝, ⚖ Dokument *n*, Urkunde *f*. **4.** *fig.* Werkzeug *n*: a) (Hilfs)Mittel *n*, Instrument *n*, b) Handlanger(in). **II** *v/t* **5.** ♪ instrumentieren. **in·stru·men·tal** [~'mentl] *adj* □ **1.** ☉ Instrumenten... **2.** ♪ Instrumental...: *~ music.* **3.** behilflich, förderlich: *be ~ in* beitragen zu.

in·sub·or·di·nate [ˌɪnsə'bɔːdnət] *adj* □ aufsässig.

in·sub·stan·tial [ˌɪnsəb'stænʃl] *adj* □ **1.** unkörperlich. **2.** unwirklich. **3.** wenig *od.* nicht gehaltvoll (*Essen etc*). **4.** nicht *od.* wenig stichhaltig (*Argument etc*); gegenstandslos (*Befürchtung etc*).

in·suf·fer·a·ble [ɪn'sʌfərəbl] *adj* □ unerträglich, unausstehlich.

in·suf·fi·cien·cy [ˌɪnsə'fɪʃnsɪ] *s* **1.** Unzulänglichkeit *f*. **2.** Untauglich-, Unfähigkeit *f*. **3.** 🩺 Insuffizienz *f*. **ˌin·suf'fi·cient** *adj* □ **1.** unzulänglich, ungenügend. **2.** untauglich, unfähig (*to do* zu tun).

in·su·lar ['ɪnsjʊlə] *adj* □ **1.** Insel... **2.** *fig.* engstirnig.

in·su·late ['ɪnsjʊleɪt] *v/t* ⚡, ☉ isolieren (*a. fig. from* von): *insulating tape Br.* Isolierband *n*. **ˌin·su'la·tion** *s* Isolierung *f*.

in·su·lin ['ɪnsjʊlɪn] *s* 🩺 Insulin *n*.

in·sult **I** *v/t* [ɪn'sʌlt] beleidigen. **II** *s* ['ɪnsʌlt] Beleidigung *f* (*to* für *od. gen*).

in·su·per·a·ble [ɪn'suːpərəbl] *adj* □ unüberwindlich (*a. fig.*).

in·sup·port·a·ble [ˌɪnsə'pɔːtəbl] *adj* □ unerträglich, unausstehlich.

in·sur·ance [ɪn'ʃɔːrəns] *s* **1.** ✝ Versicherung *f*: **~ agent** Versicherungsvertreter *m*; **~ company** Versicherungs(gesellschaft *f*); **~ policy** Versicherungspolice *f*, -schein *m*. **2.** ✝ Versicherungssumme *f*; -prämie *f*. **3.** *fig.* (Ab)Sicherung *f* (**against** gegen). **in'sure** *v/t* ✝ versichern (**against** gegen; **for** mit e-r Summe). **in'sured** *s* Versicherte *m,f*, Versicherungsnehmer(in). **in'sur·er** *s* Versicherer *m*, Versicherungsträger *m*: **~s** *pl* Versicherung(sgesellschaft) *f*.

in·sur·mount·a·ble [ˌɪnsəˈmaʊntəbl] *adj* □ *fig.* unüberwindlich.

in·sur·rec·tion [ˌɪnsəˈrekʃn] *s* Aufstand *m*, Revolte *f*.

in·sus·cep·ti·ble [ˌɪnsəˈseptəbl] *adj* □ **1.** unempfindlich (**to** gegen): **~ to pain** schmerzunempfindlich. **2.** unempfänglich (**to** für).

in·tact [ɪnˈtækt] *adj* intakt: a) unversehrt, unbeschädigt, b) ganz, vollständig.

in·take [ˈɪnteɪk] *s* **1.** ⚙ Einlaß(öffnung *f*) *m*. **2.** (*Nahrungs- etc*)Aufnahme *f*. **3.** aufgenommene Menge, Zufuhr *f*; (Neu)Aufnahme(n *pl*) *f*, (Neu)Zugänge *pl*.

in·tan·gi·ble [ɪnˈtændʒəbl] *adj* □ **1.** nicht greifbar. **2.** *fig.* unbestimmt, vage.

in·te·ger [ˈɪntɪdʒə] *s* A ganze Zahl.

in·te·gral [ˈɪntɪɡrəl] *adj* □ **1.** integral (*Bestandteil etc*). **2.** ganz, vollständig. **3.** A Integral...: **~ calculus** Integralrechnung *f*.

in·te·grate [ˈɪntɪɡreɪt] **I** *v/t* integrieren: a) zs.-schließen (**into** zu): **~d circuit** ⚡ integrierter Schaltkreis, b) eingliedern (**into** in *acc*), c) einbeziehen, einbauen (**into, with** in *acc*). **II** *v/i* sich integrieren (→ Ia, b); sich einbeziehen *od.* einbauen lassen. **ˌin·te'gra·tion** *s* Integration *f*, Integrierung *f*.

in·teg·ri·ty [ɪnˈtegrətɪ] *s* **1.** Integrität *f*. **2.** Vollständigkeit *f*; Einheit *f*.

in·tel·lect [ˈɪntəlekt] *s* Intellekt *m*, Verstand *m*. **ˌin·tel'lec·tu·al** [ˌ~tjʊəl] **I** *adj* □ intellektuell: a) geistig, Geistes...: **~ property** 1, b) verstandesbetont. **II** *s* Intellektuelle *m,f*.

in·tel·li·gence [ɪnˈtelɪdʒəns] *s* **1.** Intelligenz *f*: **~ quotient** Intelligenzquotient *m*; **~ test** Intelligenztest *m*. **2.** nachrichtendienstliche Information *f*. **3.** a. **~ service** Nachrichten-, Geheimdienst *m*. **in'tel·li·gent** *adj* □ **1.** intelligent. **2.**

vernünftig. **in·tel·li'gent·si·a** [~ˈdʒentsɪə] *s* (*pl konstruiert*) *coll.* die Intelligenz, die Intellektuellen *pl*.

in·tel·li·gi·ble [ɪnˈtelɪdʒəbl] *adj* □ verständlich (**to** für *od. dat*).

in·tem·per·ate [ɪnˈtempərət] *adj* □ unmäßig.

in·tend [ɪnˈtend] *v/t* **1.** beabsichtigen, vorhaben (**s.th.** et.; **doing, to do** zu tun): **was this ~ed?** war das Absicht? **2.** bestimmen (**for** für, **dat**): **it was ~ed for you** es war für dich (bestimmt *od.* gedacht). **3.** sagen wollen, meinen (**by** mit). **4.** bedeuten, sein sollen: **it was ~ed for** (*od.* **as, to be**) **a compliment** es sollte ein Kompliment sein. **in'tend·ed I** *adj* **1.** beabsichtigt. **2.** absichtlich. **3.** *her.* **~ husband** F ihr Zukünftiger. **II** *s* **4.** F Zukünftige *m,f*.

in·tense [ɪnˈtens] *adj* □ intensiv: a) stark, heftig: **~ heat** starke Hitze, b) hell, grell (*Licht*), c) satt (*Farben*), d) durchdringend (*Geräusch, Geruch*), e) angestrengt, f) sehnlich, dringend. **in'tense·ness** *s* Intensität *f*.

in·ten·si·fi·ca·tion [ɪnˌtensɪfɪˈkeɪʃn] *s* Verstärkung *f*, Intensivierung *f*. **in'ten·si·fy** [~faɪ] *v/t* (*a. v/i* sich) verstärken, intensivieren.

in·ten·sive [ɪnˈtensɪv] *adj* □ intensiv: a) → **intense** a, b) gründlich, erschöpfend: **~ course** Intensivkurs *m*; **be in** (*od.* **at**) **the ~ care unit** 🏥 auf der Intensivstation liegen.

in·tent [ɪnˈtent] **I** *s* **1.** Absicht *f*, Vorsatz *m* (*a.* ⚖): **with ~** absichtlich, mit Absicht, *bsd.* ⚖ vorsätzlich. **II** *adj* □ **2.** **be ~ on doing s.th.** fest entschlossen sein, et. zu tun; et. unbedingt tun wollen. **3.** aufmerksam, gespannt (*Blick etc*). **in'ten·tion** *s* Absicht *f*, Vorsatz *m* (**of doing, to do** zu tun): **with the best** (**of**) **~s** in bester Absicht; **good ~s** *pl* gute Vorsätze *pl*. **in'ten·tion·al** [~ʃənl] *adj* absichtlich, *bsd.* ⚖ vorsätzlich: **~ly** *a.* mit Absicht.

in·ter... [ˈɪntə] Zwischen...; Wechsel...

ˌin·ter'act *v/i* aufeinander (ein)wirken. **ˌin·ter'ac·tion** *s* Wechselwirkung *f*.

ˌin·ter'breed *v/t u. v/i* (*irr* **breed**) *biol.* (sich) kreuzen.

in·ter·ca·lar·y [ɪnˈtɜːkələrɪ] *adj* Schalt...: **~ day**; **~ year**.

in·ter·cede [ˌɪntəˈsiːd] *v/i* sich verwenden *od.* einsetzen (**with** bei; **for, on behalf of** für).

in·ter·cept [͵ɪntə'sept] *v/t* Brief, Boten, Funkspruch *etc* abfangen. ͵**in·ter·cep·tion** *s* Abfangen *n*. ͵**in·ter'cep·tor** *s a.* ~ **plane** ✈, ⚔ Abfangjäger *m*.

in·ter·ces·sion [͵ɪntə'seʃn] *s* Fürsprache *f*.

in·ter·change I *v/t* [͵~'tʃ~] **1.** gegen- *od.* untereinander austauschen, auswechseln. **2.** *Geschenke, Meinungen etc* austauschen, *Briefe* wechseln (**with** mit). **II** *s* ['~tʃ~] **3.** Austausch *m*: ~ **of ideas** Gedankenaustausch. **4.** *mot.* Autobahnkreuz *n*. **5.** *a.* ~ **station** Umsteig(e)bahnhof *m*, -station *f*. ͵**in·ter'cit·y·s** 🚆 *Br.* Intercity *m*: ~ **train** Intercityzug *m*.

in·ter·com ['ɪntəkɒm] *s* (Gegen-, Haus-, ⚓, ✈) Sprechanlage *f*. ͵**in·ter·com'mu·ni·cate** *v/i* **1.** miteinander in Verbindung stehen. **2.** miteinander (durch *e-e* Tür *etc*) verbunden sein. ͵**in·ter͵con·ti'nen·tal** *adj* interkontinental, Interkontinental...: ~ **ballistic missile** ⚔ Interkontinentalrakete *f*. '**in·ter·course** *s* **1.** Verkehr *m*, Umgang *m* (**with** mit): **commercial** ~ Geschäfts-, Handelsverkehr. **2.** (Geschlechts)Verkehr *m*. ͵**in·ter·de͵nom·i'na·tion·al** *adj* interkonfessionell, konfessionsübergreifend. ͵**in·ter·de'pend·ence** *s* gegenseitige Abhängigkeit. ͵**in·ter·de'pend·ent** *adj* voneinander abhängig.

in·ter·dict I *s* ['ɪntədɪkt] (amtliches) Verbot. **II** *v/t* [͵ɪntə'dɪkt] (amtlich) verbieten.

in·ter·est ['ɪntrəst] **I** *s* **1.** Interesse *n* (**in** an *dat*, für): **take** (*od.* **have**) **an** ~ **in** sich interessieren für. **2.** Reiz *m*, Interesse *n*: **be of** ~ (**to**) reizvoll sein (für), interessieren (*acc*). **3.** Wichtigkeit *f*, Bedeutung *f*: **of great** (**little**) ~ von großer Wichtigkeit (von geringer Bedeutung). **4.** *bsd.* ✝ Beteiligung *f*, Anteil *m* (**in** an *dat*): **have an** ~ **in** s.th. an *od.* bei et. beteiligt sein. **5.** Interesse *n*, Vorteil *m*, Nutzen *m*: **be in** (*od.* **to**) **s.o.'s** ~ in j-s Interesse liegen; **in your** (**own**) ~ zu Ihrem (eigenen) Vorteil. **6.** ✝ Zins(en *pl*) *m*: **bear** (*od.* **carry**) ~ Zinsen tragen, sich verzinsen (**at 4%** mit 4%); ~ **rate, rate of** ~

Zinssatz *m*. **II** *v/t* **7.** interessieren (**in** für). '**in·ter·est·ed** *adj* interessiert (**in** an *dat*): **be** ~ **in** sich interessieren für. '**in·ter·est·ing** *adj* □ interessant.

'**in·ter·face** *s* ⚡ Schnittstelle *f*, (*Computer a.*) Nahtstelle *f*.

in·ter·fere [͵ɪntə'fɪə] *v/i* **1.** (**in** in *acc*) eingreifen; sich einmischen. **2.** ~ **with** *j-n, et.* stören, behindern; sich zu schaffen machen an (*dat*). ͵**in·ter'fer·ence** *s* **1.** Eingriff *m*; Einmischung *f*. **2.** Störung *f*, Behinderung *f* (**with** *gen*).

in·ter·im ['ɪntərɪm] **I** *s*: **in the** ~ in der Zwischenzeit, inzwischen. **II** *adj* Interims..., Zwischen...: ~ **aid** Überbrükkungshilfe *f*; ~ **government** Interims-, Übergangsregierung *f*; ~ **report** Zwischenbericht *m*.

in·te·ri·or [ɪn'tɪərɪə] **I** *adj* **1.** inner..., Innen...: ~ **decorator** a) Innenausstatter(in), b) *a.* ~ **designer** Innenarchitekt(in). **2.** binnenländisch, Binnen...; inländisch, Inlands... **II** *s* **3.** *oft pl das* Innere. **4.** Innenraum *m*, -seite *f*. **5.** *phot.* Innenaufnahme *f*, (*Film, TV a.*) Studioaufnahme *f*. **6.** Binnenland *n*, *das* Innere. **7.** *pol.* innere Angelegenheiten *pl*: → **department** 3.

in·ter·ject [͵ɪntə'dʒekt] *v/t Bemerkung etc* dazwischen-, einwerfen. ͵**in·ter'jec·tion** *s ling.* Interjektion *f*.

͵**in·ter'lace I** *v/t* **1.** verflechten, -schlingen, *a. fig.* verweben. **2.** durchflechten (**with** mit) (*a. fig.*). **II** *v/i* **3.** sich verflechten.

in·ter·loc·u·tor [͵ɪntə'lɒkjʊtə] *s* Gesprächspartner *m*.

in·ter·lop·er ['ɪntələʊpə] *s* Eindringling *m*.

in·ter·lude ['ɪntəluːd] *s* **1.** (*kurze*) Zeit, Periode *f*. **2.** Unterbrechung *f* (**in** *gen*). **3.** *thea.,* ♪ Zwischenspiel *n*, Intermezzo *n* (*beide a. fig.*).

͵**in·ter'mar·riage** *s* **1.** Mischehe *f*. **2.** Heirat *f* innerhalb der Familie *od.* zwischen Blutsverwandten. ͵**in·ter'mar·ry** *v/i* **1.** *e-e* Mischehe eingehen; untereinander heiraten. **2.** innerhalb der Familie heiraten.

in·ter·me·di·ar·y [͵ɪntə'miːdjərɪ] **I** *adj* **1.** → **intermediate**. **2.** vermittelnd. **II** *s* **3.** Vermittler(in), Mittelsmann *m*. **4.** ✝ Zwischenhändler *m*. ͵**in·ter·me·di·ate** [͵~djət] *adj* □ **1.** Zwischen... **2.**

ped. für fortgeschrittene Anfänger.

in·ter·mez·zo [ˌɪntəˈmetsəʊ] *pl* **-zi** [ˌtsiː], **-zos** *s* ♪ Intermezzo *n*, Zwischenspiel *n*.

in·ter·mi·na·ble [ɪnˈtɜːmɪnəbl] *adj* □ endlos.

ˌin·terˈmin·gle *v/t u. v/i* (sich) vermischen.

ˌin·terˈmis·sion *s* Pause *f* (*a. thea. etc*), Unterbrechung *f*: *without* ~ pausenlos.

ˌin·terˈmit·tent [ˌɪntəˈmɪtənt] *adj* □ mit Unterbrechungen, periodisch (auftretend); ♣ *etc* intermittierend: ~ *fever* ♣ Wechselfieber *n*.

in·tern [ɪnˈtɜːn] *v/t* internieren.

in·ter·nal [ɪnˈtɜːnl] *adj* □ **1.** inner, Innen...: ~ *injury* (*medicine*) innere Verletzung (Medizin); *he was bleeding ~ly* er hatte innere Blutungen. **2.** ♣, *pharm.* innerlich anzuwenden(d). **3.** einheimisch, Inlands...: ~ *trade* Binnenhandel *m*. **4.** *pol.* innenpolitisch, Innen...: ~ *affairs pl* innere Angelegenheiten *pl*. **5.** (♣ *a.* betriebs)intern.

inˌter·nal-comˈbus·tion enˈgine *s* ⊚ Verbrennungsmotor *m*.

in·ter·nal·ize [ɪnˈtɜːnəlaɪz] *v/t* verinnerlichen.

ˌin·terˈna·tion·al I *adj* □ **1.** international: ~ *law* Völkerrecht *n*; ♀ *Monetary Fund* Internationaler Währungsfonds; ~ *reply coupon* ♥ internationaler Antwortschein. **2.** Auslands...: ~ *call teleph.* Auslandsgespräch *n*; ~ *flight* Auslandsflug *m*. **II** *s* **3.** *Sport:* Internationale *m, f*, Nationalspieler(in); Länderkampf *m*, -spiel *n*. **ˌin·terˈna·tion-al·ize** *v/t* internationalisieren.

in·tern·ee [ˌɪntɜːˈniː] *s* Internierte *m, f*.

in·tern·ist [ɪnˈtɜːnɪst] *s* ♣ Internist(in).

in·tern·ment [ɪnˈtɜːnmənt] *s* Internierung *f*: ~ *camp* Internierungslager *n*.

ˈin·terˈphone → **intercom**.

ˌin·terˈplan·e·ta·ry *adj* interplanetar(isch).

ˈin·terˈplay *s* Wechselspiel *n*.

in·ter·pret [ɪnˈtɜːprɪt] **I** *v/t* **1.** auslegen, interpretieren (*as* als). **2.** dolmetschen. **3.** *Daten etc* auswerten. **II** *v/i* **4.** dolmetschen (*for s.o.* j-m). **inˌter·preˈta·tion** *s* **1.** Auslegung *f*, Interpretation *f*. **2.** Dolmetschen *n*. **3.** Auswertung *f*. **inˈter·pret·er** *s* Dolmetscher(in).

ˌin·ter·reˈlat·ed *adj* in Wechselbeziehung stehend, zs.-hängend. **ˌin·ter·reˈla·tion** *s* Wechselbeziehung *f*.

ˌin·ter·ro·gate [ɪnˈterəʊgeɪt] *v/t* verhören, -nehmen. **inˌter·roˈga·tion** *s* **1.** Verhör *n*, Vernehmung *f*. **2.** Frage *f* (*a. ling.*): ~ *mark* (*od.* **point**) Fragezeichen *n*. **in·ter·rog·a·tive** [ˌɪntəˈrɒgətɪv] *adj* □ **1.** fragend. **2.** *ling.* Interrogativ..., Frage...: ~ *pronoun* Interrogativpronomen *n*, Fragefürwort *n*. **ˌin·terˈrog·a·to·ry** [ˌtərɪ] *adj* fragend.

in·ter·rupt [ˌɪntəˈrʌpt] **I** *v/t* unterbrechen (*a.* ∮), *j-m* ins Wort fallen. **II** *v/i*: *don't ~!* unterbrich mich *etc* nicht! **ˌin·terˈrupt·ed·ly** *adv* mit Unterbrechungen. **ˌin·terˈrupt·er** *s* ∮ Unterbrecher *m*. **ˌin·terˈrup·tion** *s* Unterbrechung *f*: *without* ~ ununterbrochen.

in·ter·sect [ˌɪntəˈsekt] **I** *v/t* (durch)schneiden, (-)kreuzen. **II** *v/i* sich schneiden *od.* kreuzen. **ˌin·terˈsec·tion** *s* **1.** ⅄ Schnitt *m*: (*point of*) ~ Schnittpunkt *m*. **2.** (Straßen)Kreuzung *f*.

ˌin·terˈsperse [ˌɪntəˈspɜːs] *v/t* **1.** einstreuen. **2.** durchsetzen (*with* mit).

in·ter·state *adj Am.* zwischenstaatlich: ~ *highway* (*zwei od. mehrere Bundesstaaten verbindende*) Autobahn.

in·ter·stice [ɪnˈtɜːstɪs] *s* **1.** Zwischenraum *m*. **2.** Lücke *f*, Spalt *m*.

ˌin·terˈtwine , **ˌin·terˈtwist** *v/t u. v/i* (sich) verflechten *od.* verschlingen.

ˌin·terˈur·ban *adj* zwischen mehreren Städten (*bestehend od. verkehrend*): ~ *traffic* Überlandverkehr *m*.

in·ter·val [ˈɪntəvl] *s* **1.** (*zeitlicher od. räumlicher*) Abstand, (*zeitlich a.*) Intervall *n*: *at regular* ~*s* in regelmäßigen Abständen. **2.** *Br.* Pause *f* (*a. thea. etc*), Unterbrechung *f*: ~ *signal* (*Rundfunk, TV*) Pausenzeichen *n*. **3.** ♪, ♠ Intervall *n*.

in·ter·vene [ˌɪntəˈviːn] *v/i* **1.** eingreifen, -schreiten, *bsd.* ✕, *pol.* intervenieren. **2.** (*zeitlich*) dazwischenliegen. **3.** sich inzwischen ereignen; dazwischenkommen: *if nothing* ~*s* wenn nichts dazwischenkommt. **in·ter·ven·tion** [ˌˈvenʃn] *s* Eingreifen *n*, -schreiten *n*, Intervention *f*.

in·ter·view [ˈɪntəvjuː] **I** *s* **1.** Interview *n*: *give s.o. an* ~. **2.** Einstellungsgespräch *n*. **II** *v/t* **3.** interviewen. **4.** ein Einstellungsgespräch führen mit. **in·ter·view-**

ee [‿'i:] s Interviewte m, f. 'in·ter·view·er s Interviewer(in).

,in·ter'weave v/t (irr weave) **1.** (miteinander) verweben od. verflechten (a. fig.). **2.** vermengen, -mischen (**with** mit) (beide a. fig.).

in·tes·tate [ın'testeıt] adj: die ~ 🔧 sterben ohne Hinterlassung e-s Testaments sterben.

in·tes·tine [ın'testın] s anat. Darm m: ~s pl Gedärme pl; **large** ~ Dickdarm; **small** ~ Dünndarm.

in·ti·ma·cy ['ıntıməsı] s Intimität f: a) Vertrautheit f, b) (a. contp. plumpe) Vertraulichkeit, c) intime (sexuelle) Beziehungen pl, d) Gemütlichkeit f.

in·ti·mate¹ ['ıntımət] adj □ intim: a) vertraut, eng (**Freund** etc), b) vertraulich (Mitteilung etc), contp. a. plump-vertraulich, c) in sexuellen Beziehungen stehend (**with** mit), d) anheimelnd, gemütlich (Atmosphäre etc), e) innerst (Wünsche etc), f) gründlich, genau (Kenntnisse etc): **be on ~ terms** (**with**) auf vertrautem Fuße stehen (mit); intime Beziehungen haben (zu).

in·ti·mate² ['ıntımeıt] v/t **1.** andeuten: ~ **to s.o. that** j-m zu verstehen geben, daß. **2.** ankündigen; mitteilen. in·ti·'ma·tion s **1.** Andeutung f. **2.** Ankündigung f; Mitteilung f.

in·tim·i·date [ın'tımıdeıt] v/t einschüchtern: ~ **s.o. into doing s.th.** j-n nötigen, et. zu tun. in,tim·i'da·tion s Einschüchterung f.

in·to ['ıntʊ] prp **1.** in (acc), in (acc) ... hinein. **2.** gegen: → **crash** 6, etc. **3.** Zustandsänderung: → **ice. 4.** Ⓐ in (acc): → **divide** 4. **5.** be ~ F stehen auf (acc).

in·tol·er·a·ble [ın'tɒlərəbl] adj □ unerträglich. in'tol·er·ance s Intoleranz f. in'tol·er·ant adj □ intolerant (**of** gegenüber): **be ~ of s.th.** et. nicht dulden od. tolerieren.

in·to·na·tion [,ıntəʊ'neıʃn] s **1.** ling. Intonation f, Satzmelodie f. **2.** Tonfall m. **3.** ♪ Intonation f. in'tone v/t ♪ intonieren: a) Lied etc anstimmen, b) Ton angeben.

in·tox·i·cant [ın'tɒksıkənt] **I** adj berauschend (a. fig.). **II** s Rauschmittel n, bsd. berauschendes Getränk. in'tox·i·cate [‿keıt] v/t berauschen (a. fig.). in,tox·i·ca·tion s Rausch m (a. fig.).

in·trac·ta·ble [ın'træktəbl] adj □ **1.** eigensinnig. **2.** hartnäckig (Krankheit, Problem etc).

in·tran·si·gent [ın'trænsıdʒənt] adj □ unnachgiebig.

in·tran·si·tive [ın'trænsətıv] adj □ ling. intransitiv.

in·tra·ve·nous [,ıntrə'vi:nəs] adj □ anat., 🔬 intravenös.

in·tre·pid [ın'trepıd] adj □ unerschrocken.

in·tri·ca·cy ['ıntrıkəsı] s **1.** Kompliziertheit f. **2.** Verworrenheit f. in·tri·cate ['‿kət] adj □ **1.** verwickelt, kompliziert. **2.** verworren.

in·trigue [ın'tri:g] **I** v/t faszinieren; interessieren; neugierig machen. **II** v/i intrigieren (**against** gegen). **III** s Intrige f. in'tri·guer s Intrigant(in). in'tri·guing adj □ **1.** faszinierend; interessant. **2.** intrigant. □

in·trin·sic [ın'trınsık] adj **1.** inner. **2.** wesentlich.

in·tro·duce [,ıntrə'dju:s] v/t **1.** neue Methode etc einführen. **2.** (**to**) j-n bekannt machen (mit), vorstellen (dat). **3.** (**to**) j-n einführen (in ein Fach etc), bekannt machen (mit). **4.** Redner, Programm etc ankündigen. **5.** Gedanken, Gesetzesvorlage etc einbringen (**into** in acc). **6.** (**into** in acc) einfügen; (hinein)stecken, einführen. in·tro·duc·tion [,‿'dʌkʃn] s **1.** Einführung f. **2.** Vorstellung f. **3.** Einleitung f, Vorwort n. **4.** Leitfaden m (**to** gen). **5.** Einbringung f. in·tro·'duc·to·ry [‿tərı] adj **1.** Einführungs...: ~ **price. 2.** einleitend, Einleitungs...

in·tro·spec·tion [,ıntrəʊ'spekʃn] s Selbstbeobachtung f. in·tro·'spec·tive [‿tıv] adj □ introspektive.

in·tro·vert ['ıntrəʊvɜ:t] adj psych. introvertiert.

in·trude [ın'tru:d] **I** v/t **1.** ~ **o.s.** → 3. **2.** aufdrängen (**s.th. on s.o.** j-m et.; **o.s. on s.o.** sich j-m). **II** v/i **3.** sich eindringen (**into** in acc) (a. fig.). **4.** sich aufdrängen (**on** dat). **5.** stören (**on s.o.** j-n). in'trud·er s **1.** Eindringling m. **2.** Störenfried m.

in·tru·sion [ın'tru:ʒn] s Störung f (**on** gen). in'tru·sive [‿sıv] adj □ aufdringlich.

in·tu·i·tion [,ıntjυ'ıʃn] s Intuition f. in'tu·i·tive [‿tıv] adj □ intuitiv.

in·un·date ['ɪnʌndeɪt] v/t überschwemmen, -fluten (*beide a. fig.*). ,**in·un·da·tion** s Überschwemmung f, -flutung f.

in·ure [ɪ'njuə] v/t (*to*) abhärten (gegen), *fig. a.* gewöhnen (an *acc*).

in·vade [ɪn'veɪd] v/t 1. einfallen *od.* eindringen in (*acc*), ✕ *a.* einmarschieren in (*acc*). 2. sich ausbreiten über (*acc*) *od.* in (*dat*), erfüllen. 3. *fig.* überlaufen, -schwemmen. 4. *j-s Privatsphäre etc* verletzen, in *j-s Rechte* eingreifen. **in'vad·er** s 1. Eindringling m. 2. pl ✕ Invasoren pl.

in·va·lid¹ ['ɪnvəlɪd] I adj 1. krank, gebrechlich; invalid, arbeits-, erwerbsunfähig; kriegsbeschädigt. 2. Kranken... II s 3. Kranke m, f; Gebrechliche m, f; Invalide m, Arbeits-, Erwerbsunfähige m, f; Pflegefall m. III v/t ['ɪnvəli:d] 4. zum Invaliden machen.

in·val·id² [ɪn'vælɪd] adj □ (rechts)ungültig, unwirksam. **in·val·i·date** [~deɪt] v/t für ungültig erklären. **in,val·i'da·tion** s Ungültigkeitserklärung f.

in·va·lid·i·ty [,ɪnvə'lɪdətɪ] s Invalidität f, Arbeits-, Erwerbsunfähigkeit f.

in·va·lid·i·ty² [~] s (Rechts)Ungültigkeit f.

in·val·u·a·ble [ɪn'væljuəbl] adj □ unschätzbar, von unschätzbarem Wert (*beide a. fig.*): **be ~ to s.o.** für j-n von unschätzbarem Wert sein.

in·var·i·a·ble [ɪn'veərɪəbl] adj □ unveränderlich, gleichbleibend.

in·va·sion [ɪn'veɪʒn] s 1. (*of*) Einfall m (in *acc*), Eindringen n (in *acc*), ✕ *a.* Invasion f (*gen*), Einmarsch m (in *acc*): **~ of tourists** Touristeninvasion. 2. *fig.* (*of*) Verletzung f (*gen*), Eingriff m (in *acc*).

in·vec·tive [ɪn'vektɪv] s Beschimpfung(en pl) f, Schmähung(en pl) f.

in·veigh [ɪn'veɪ] v/i (*against*) schimpfen (über *od.* auf *acc*), herziehen (über *acc*).

in·vei·gle [ɪn'veɪgl] v/t verleiten, -führen (*into* zu; *into doing s.th.* dazu, et. zu tun).

in·vent [ɪn'vent] v/t erfinden, *et. Unwahres a.* erdichten. **in'ven·tion** s Erfindung f. **in'ven·tive** [~tɪv] adj □ 1. erfinderisch. 2. einfallsreich. **in'ven·tor** s Erfinder(in).

in·ven·to·ry ['ɪnvəntrɪ] ✝ I s 1. Inventar n: a) Bestandsliste f: **make** (*od.* **take**) **an ~ of** → 3, b) (Waren-, Lager)Be-

stand m. 2. Inventur f. II v/t 3. e-e Bestandsliste machen von.

in·verse [,ɪn'vɜːs] adj □ umgekehrt: *in ~ order* in umgekehrter Reihenfolge. **in·'ver·sion** s 1. Umkehrung f. 2. ♏, *ling. etc* Inversion f.

in·vert [ɪn'vɜːt] v/t 1. umkehren: *~ed commas* pl bsd. Br. Anführungszeichen pl. 2. umwenden, umstülpen: *~ s.th. over* et. stülpen über (*acc*).

in·ver·te·brate [ɪn'vɜːtɪbreɪt] zo. I adj wirbellos. II s wirbelloses Tier.

in·vest [ɪn'vest] I v/t 1. ✝ (*in*) investieren (in *acc od.* dat), anlegen (in *dat*). 2. *~ s.o. with* j-m et. verleihen; j-n mit *Befugnissen etc* ausstatten. II v/i 3. *~ in a)* ✝ investieren in (*acc od.* dat), sein Geld anlegen in (*dat*), b) F sich et. kaufen *od.* zulegen.

in·ves·ti·gate [ɪn'vestɪgeɪt] I v/t *Verbrechen etc* untersuchen, Ermittlungen *od.* Nachforschungen anstellen über (*acc*), *Fall* recherchieren, *j-n, Anspruch etc* überprüfen, *e-r Beschwerde etc* nachgehen, *Gebiet etc (wissenschaftlich)* erforschen. II v/i ermitteln, recherchieren, Ermittlungen *od.* Nachforschungen anstellen (*into* über *acc*): *investigating committee* Untersuchungsausschuß m. **in,ves·ti'ga·tion** s Untersuchung f (*into, of gen*), Nachforschung f, Recherche f, Überprüfung f: *be under ~* untersucht werden.

in·vest·ment [ɪn'vestmənt] s ✝ Investition f, (Kapital)Anlage f; Anlagekapital n: *~ adviser* (*od.* **consultant**) Anlageberater(in); *~ trust* Kapitalanlagegesellschaft f. **in'ves·tor** s Investor m, Kapitalanleger m.

in·vet·er·ate [ɪn'vetərət] adj □ 1. eingewurzelt, unausrottbar. 2. ♈ hartnäckig; chronisch. 3. eingefleischt, unverbesserlich.

in·vid·i·ous [ɪn'vɪdɪəs] adj □ gehässig, boshaft.

in·vig·or·ate [ɪn'vɪgəreɪt] v/t stärken, kräftigen; beleben, anregen; er-, aufmuntern.

in·vin·ci·ble [ɪn'vɪnsəbl] adj □ 1. ✕, *Sport:* unbesiegbar. 2. *fig.* unüberwindlich.

in·vis·i·ble [ɪn'vɪzəbl] adj □ unsichtbar (*to* für).

in·vi·ta·tion [,ɪnvɪ'teɪʃn] s 1. Einladung f

(**to** an *acc;* zu): **at the ~ of** auf Einladung von (*od. gen*). **2.** (höfliche) Aufforderung, Ersuchen *n.* **3.** Herausforderung *f:* **be an ~ for** → **invite** 4. **in'vite** *v/t* **1.** einladen (**to dinner** zum Essen). **2.** (höflich) auffordern, ersuchen (**to do** zu tun). **3.** bitten *od.* ersuchen um, erbitten. **4.** herausfordern (zu), einladen zu.

in·vo·ca·tion [ˌɪnvəʊ'keɪʃn] *s* **1.** Anrufung *f* (**to gen**). **2.** Beschwörung *f.*

in·voice ['ɪnvɔɪs] ✝ **I** *s* (Waren)Rechnung *f*, Faktura *f.* **II** *v/t* fakturieren, in Rechnung stellen.

in·voke [ɪn'vəʊk] *v/t* **1.** flehen um, erflehen. **2.** *Gott etc* anrufen. **3.** *Geist* beschwören.

in·vol·un·tar·y [ɪn'vɒləntərɪ] *adj* □ **1.** unfreiwillig. **2.** unabsichtlich. **3.** unwillkürlich.

in·volve [ɪn'vɒlv] *v/t* **1.** a) *j-n* verwickeln, hineinziehen (**in** in *acc*): **~d in an accident** in e-n Unfall verwickelt, b) *j-n, et.* angehen, betreffen: **the persons ~d** die Betroffenen. **2. be ~d** zu tun haben (**with** mit). **3.** zur Folge haben, nach sich ziehen; verbunden sein mit; erfordern, nötig machen. **in'volved** *adj* kompliziert; verworren.

in·vul·ner·a·ble [ɪn'vʌlnərəbl] *adj* □ **1.** unverwundbar (*a.* fig.). **2.** fig. unanfechtbar, hieb- u. stichfest.

in·ward ['ɪnwəd] **I** *adv* **1.** einwärts, nach innen. **2.** → **inwardly** 1, 2. **II** *adj* **3.** innerlich, inner (*beide a.* fig.), Innen... **'in·ward·ly** *adv* **1.** innerlich, im Inner(e)n (*beide a.* fig.). **2.** fig. im stillen, insgeheim. **3.** → **inward** I. **in·wards** ['~z] → **inward** I.

i·o·dine ['aɪəʊdiːn] *s* 🜍 Jod *n.*

i·on ['aɪən] *s* 🜍, *phys.* Ion *n.* **i·on·ic** [aɪ'ɒnɪk] *adj* Ionen...

i·o·ta [aɪ'əʊtə] *s* Jota *n:* **not an ~ of truth** kein Körnchen Wahrheit.

IOU [ˌaɪəʊ'juː] *s* Schuldschein *m* (= **I owe you**).

i·ras·ci·ble [ɪ'ræsəbl] *adj* □ jähzornig, reizbar.

i·rate [aɪ'reɪt] *adj* zornig, wütend.

ir·i·des ['aɪrɪdiːz] *pl von* **iris**.

ir·i·des·cent [ˌɪrɪ'desnt] *adj* □ (*in den Regenbogenfarben*) schillernd.

i·ris ['aɪərɪs] *pl* **'i·ris·es**, **ir·i·des** ['aɪrɪdiːz] *s* **1.** *anat.* Iris *f*, Regenbogen-

haut *f.* **2.** ✿ Iris *f*, Schwertlilie *f.*

I·rish ['aɪərɪʃ] **I** *adj* **1.** irisch: **~ coffee** Irish Coffee *m.* **II** *s* **2. the ~** *pl* die Iren *pl.* **3.** *ling.* Irisch *n.* **~·man** ['~mən] *s* (*irr* **man**) Ire *m.* **~·wom·an** *s* (*irr* **woman**) Irin *f.*

irk [ɜːk] *v/t* **1.** ärgern, verdrießen. **2.** ermüden, langweilen. **irk·some** ['ɜːksəm] *adj* □ **1.** ärgerlich, verdrießlich. **2.** ermüdend, langweilig.

i·ron ['aɪən] **I** *s* **1.** Eisen *n:* **have several ~s in the fire** *fig.* mehrere Eisen im Feuer haben; **strike while the ~ is hot** *fig.* das Eisen schmieden, solange es heiß ist; **will of ~** eiserner Wille. **2.** Bügeleisen *n.* **II** *adj* **3.** eisern (*a.* fig.), Eisen...: **≈ Curtain** *pol.* Eiserner Vorhang; **~ lung** 🝘 eiserne Lunge; **~ ore** *min.* Eisenerz *n.* **III** *v/t* **1.** bügeln: **~ out** ausbügeln; *fig.* Meinungsverschiedenheiten *etc* aus der Welt schaffen, beseitigen.

i·ron·ic, i·ron·i·cal [aɪ'rɒnɪk(l)] *adj* □ ironisch.

i·ron·ing board ['aɪənɪŋ] *s* Bügelbrett *n.*

'i·ron·work *s* **1.** Eisenbeschläge *pl.* **2.** *pl* (*oft sg konstruiert*) Eisenhütte *f.*

i·ro·ny ['aɪərənɪ] *s* Ironie *f:* **~ of fate** Ironie des Schicksals.

ir·ra·tion·al [ɪ'ræʃənl] *adj* □ **1.** irrational, unvernünftig. **2.** ⅍ irrational.

ir·rec·og·niz·a·ble [ɪ'rekəgnaɪzəbl] *adj* □ nicht zu erkennen(d) *od.* wiederzuerkennen(d), unkenntlich.

ir·rec·on·cil·a·ble [ɪ'rekənsaɪləbl] *adj* □ **1.** unvereinbar (**with** mit). **2.** unversöhnlich.

ir·re·cov·er·a·ble [ˌɪrɪ'kʌvərəbl] *adj* □ nicht wiedergutzumachen(d), unersetzlich, -bar (*Verlust etc*).

ir·re·deem·a·ble [ˌɪrɪ'diːməbl] *adj* □ **1.** ✝ unkündbar (*Obligation etc*). **2.** nicht wiedergutzumachen(d) (*Verlust etc*).

ir·ref·u·ta·ble [ɪ'refjʊtəbl] *adj* □ unwiderlegbar.

ir·reg·u·lar [ɪ'regjʊlə] *adj* □ **1.** unregelmäßig (*a.* ling.). **2.** regel- od. vorschriftswidrig. **ir·reg·u·lar·i·ty** [~'lærətɪ] *s* **1.** Unregelmäßigkeit *f.* **2.** Regelod. Vorschriftswidrigkeit *f.*

ir·rel·e·vance, ir·rel·e·van·cy [ɪ'reləvəns(ɪ)] *s* Irrelevanz *f*, Unerheblichkeit *f*, Belanglosigkeit *f.* **ir'rel·e·vant** *adj* □ irrelevant, unerheblich, belanglos (**to** für).

ir·re·me·di·a·ble [ˌɪrɪˈmiːdjəbl] *adj* □ nicht behebbar *od.* abstellbar.

ir·re·mis·si·ble [ˌɪrɪˈmɪsəbl] *adj* □ unverzeihlich.

ir·re·mov·a·ble [ˌɪrɪˈmuːvəbl] *adj* □ unabsetzbar.

ir·rep·a·ra·ble [ɪˈrepərəbl] *adj* □ irreparabel, nicht wieder gutzumachen(d).

ir·re·place·a·ble [ˌɪrɪˈpleɪsəbl] *adj* □ unersetzlich, -bar.

ir·re·press·i·ble [ˌɪrɪˈpresəbl] *adj* □ un(be)zähmbar.

ir·re·proach·a·ble [ˌɪrɪˈprəʊtʃəbl] *adj* □ untadelig, tadellos.

ir·re·sist·i·ble [ˌɪrɪˈzɪstəbl] *adj* □ unwiderstehlich.

ir·res·o·lute [ɪˈrezəluːt] *adj* □ unentschlossen, unschlüssig.

ir·re·spec·tive [ˌɪrɪˈspektɪv] *adj* □: ~ **of** ohne Rücksicht auf (*acc*).

ir·re·spon·si·ble [ˌɪrɪˈspɒnsəbl] *adj* □ **1.** verantwortungslos: a) unzuverlässig, b) unverantwortlich. **2.** ₰₷ unzurechnungsfähig; nicht haftbar (**for** für).

ir·re·triev·a·ble [ˌɪrɪˈtriːvəbl] *adj* □ unersetzlich, -bar.

ir·rev·er·ence [ɪˈrevərəns] *s* Respektlosigkeit *f*. **ir·rev·er·ent** *adj* □ respektlos.

ir·re·vers·i·ble [ˌɪrɪˈvɜːsəbl] → *irrevocable.*

ir·rev·o·ca·ble [ɪˈrevəkəbl] *adj* □ unwiderruflich, unumstößlich.

ir·ri·gate [ˈɪrɪgeɪt] *v/t* **1.** ✔ bewässern. **2.** ✿ *Wunde etc* ausspülen. **ˌir·riˈga·tion** *s* **1.** ✔ Bewässerung *f*: ~ **ditch** Bewässerungsgraben *m*. **2.** ✿ Ausspülung *f*.

ir·ri·ta·ble [ˈɪrɪtəbl] *adj* □ reizbar.

ir·ri·tate [ˈ~teɪt] *v/t* reizen, (ver)ärgern: ~**d at** (**by, with**) verärgert *od.* ärgerlich über (*acc*). **ˈir·ri·tat·ing** *adj* □ ärgerlich. **ˌir·riˈta·tion** *s* Verärgerung *f*; Ärger *m* (**at** über *acc*).

is [ɪz] *er, sie, es* ist.

Is·lam [ˈɪzlɑːm] *s* Islam *m*. **Is·lam·ic** [ɪzˈlæmɪk] *adj* islamisch.

is·land [ˈaɪlənd] *s* **1.** Insel *f*. **2.** Verkehrsinsel *f*. **ˈis·land·er** *s* Inselbewohner(in).

isn't [ˈɪznt] F *für is not.*

i·so·late [ˈaɪsəleɪt] *v/t* **1.** *a.* ✿ isolieren, absondern (**from** von). **2.** ⚛ *etc* isolieren. **3.** *fig.* a) isoliert *od.* einzeln betrachten, b) trennen (**from** von). **ˈi·so·lat·ed** *adj* **1.** isoliert, abgesondert. **2.**

einzeln, vereinzelt: ~ **case** Einzelfall *m*. **3.** abgeschieden. **ˌi·soˈla·tion** *s* **1.** Isolierung *f*, Absonderung *f*: ~ **ward** ✿ Isolierstation *f*. **2. consider in** ~ → *isolate* 3a. **3.** Abgeschiedenheit *f*: **live in** ~ zurückgezogen leben.

i·so·met·rics [ˌaɪsəʊˈmetrɪks] *s pl* (*a. sg konstruiert*) Isometrik *f*.

i·sos·ce·les [aɪˈsɒsɪliːz] *adj* ⅍ gleichschenk(e)lig (*Dreieck*).

i·so·tope [ˈaɪsəʊtəʊp] *s phys.* Isotop *n*.

Is·rae·li [ɪzˈreɪlɪ] **I** *adj* israelisch. **II** *s* Israeli *m*, *f*.

is·sue [ˈɪʃuː] **I** *s* **1.** Ausgabe *f*, Erlaß *m*. **2.** ✝ Ausgabe *f*, Emission *f*, Begebung *f*, Auflegung *f*, Ausstellung *f*. **3.** Ausgabe *f* (*e-r Zeitung etc*). **4.** Streitfrage *f*, -punkt *m*: **be at** ~ zur Debatte stehen; **point at** ~ strittige Frage. **5.** Ausgang *m*, Ergebnis *n*: **bring to an** ~ zur Entscheidung bringen; **force an** ~ e-e Entscheidung erzwingen. **6.** ₰₷ Nachkommen(schaft *f*) *pl*: **die without** ~ kinderlos sterben. **II** *v/t* **7.** *Befehle etc* ausgeben, *a.* ₰₷ *Haftbefehl* erlassen. **8.** ✝ *Banknoten, Wertpapiere* ausgeben, *Anleihe* begeben, auflegen, *Dokument, Wechsel etc* ausstellen. **9.** *Zeitung etc* herausgeben. **10.** *bsd.* ✕ *Munition etc* ausgeben. **III** *v/i* **11.** heraus-, hervorkommen. **12.** herausfließen, -strömen. **13.** herrühren (**from** von).

isth·mus [ˈɪsməs] *pl* **-mus·es, -mi** [ˈ~maɪ] *s* Landenge *f*, Isthmus *m*.

it [ɪt] *pron* **1.** es (*nom od. acc*). **2.** *auf schon Genanntes bezogen*: es, er, ihn, sie. **3.** *unpersönliches od. grammatisches Subjekt*: es: ~ **is raining; oh,** ~ **was you** oh, Sie waren es *od.* das. **4.** *unbestimmtes Objekt* (*oft unübersetzt*) es: → *foot* 4, *etc*. **5.** *verstärkend*: ~ **is to him that you should turn** an ihn solltest du dich wenden.

I·tal·ian [ɪˈtæljən] **I** *adj* **1.** italienisch. **II** *s* **2.** Italiener(in). **3.** *ling.* Italienisch *n*.

i·tal·ic [ɪˈtælɪk] *typ.* **I** *adj* kursiv. **II** *s oft pl* Kursivschrift *f*: **in** ~**s** kursiv. **i·tal·i·cize** [ˈ~saɪz] *v/t* kursiv drucken.

itch [ɪtʃ] **I** *s* **1.** Jucken *n*, Juckreiz *m*. **2.** ✿ Krätze *f*. **3.** *fig.* Verlangen *n* (**for** nach): **have** (*od.* **feel**) **an** ~ **to do s.th.** große Lust haben *od.* darauf brennen, *etc* zu tun. **II** *v/i* **4.** jucken, (*Pullover etc a.*) kratzen. **5.** *fig.* F **be** ~**ing for s.th.** st.

unbedingt (haben) wollen; *he's ~ing to try it* es reizt *od.* juckt ihn, es zu versuchen. **III** *v/t* **6.** *j-n* jucken, kratzen. **'itch·y** *adj* juckend; kratzend: → **palm¹** 1.

i·tem ['aɪtəm] *s* **1.** Punkt *m* (*der Tagesordnung etc*), (*Bilanz- etc*)Posten *m.* **2.** (Waren)Artikel *m; weitS.* Gegenstand *m,* Ding *m.* **3.** (*Presse-, Zeitungs*)Notiz *f,* (*a. Rundfunk, TV*) Nachricht *f,* Meldung *f.* **i·tem·ize** ['~maɪz] *v/t Rechnungsposten* einzeln aufführen, *a. Rechnung* spezifizieren, *Kosten etc* aufgliedern.

i·tin·er·ant [ɪ'tɪnərənt] *adj* □ (*beruflich*) reisend, Reise..., Wander... **i·tin·er·ar·y** [aɪ'tɪnərərɪ] *s* **1.** Reiseweg *m,* -route *f;* Reiseplan *m.* **2.** Reiseführer *m* (*Buch*). **i·tin·er·ate**

[ɪ'tɪnəreɪt] *v/i* (herum)reisen.

it'll ['ɪtl] F *für it will.*

its [ɪts] *pron* sein, s-e, ihr, ihre.

it's [ɪts] F *für it is; it has.*

it·self [ɪt'self] *pron* **1.** *reflex* sich. **2.** sich selbst. **3.** *verstärkend:* selbst: *by ~* (für sich) allein; von allein *od.* selbst.

it·sy-bit·sy [ˌɪtsɪ'bɪtsɪ] *adj* F klitzeklein, winzig.

I've [aɪv] F *für I have.*

i·vo·ry ['aɪvərɪ] **I** *s* **1.** Elfenbein *n.* **2.** *pl sl.* (*bsd.* Klavier)Tasten *pl: tickle the ivories* (auf dem Klavier) klimpern. **II** *adj* **3.** elfenbeinern, Elfenbein...: *live in an ~ tower fig.* in e-m Elfenbeinturm leben *od.* sitzen.

i·vy ['aɪvɪ] *s* ⚘ Efeu *m:* ♀ *League* Eliteuniversitäten *im Osten der USA.*

J

jab [dʒæb] **I** *v/t* **1.** (hinein)stechen, (-)stoßen (*into* in *acc*). **II** *v/i* **2.** stechen, stoßen (*at* nach; *with* mit). **I 3.** Stich *m,* Stoß *m.* **4.** *Boxen:* Jab *m.* **5.** ✻ F Spritze *f.*

jab·ber ['dʒæbə] **I** *v/t a. ~ out* (daher)plappern, *Gebet etc* herunterrasseln. **II** *v/i a. ~ away* plappern, schwatzen. **III** *s* Geplapper *n,* Geschwätz *n.*

jack [dʒæk] **I** *s* **1.** ♀ F *für John: before you could say* ♀ *Robinson* im Nu, im Handumdrehen; *every man ~* jeder, alle. **2.** *Kartenspiel:* Bube *m: ~ of hearts* Herzbube *m.* **3.** ⊚ Hebevorrichtung *f;* (*car*) *~* Wagenheber *m.* **II** *v/t* **4.** hochheben, *Auto* aufbocken.

jack·al ['dʒækɔːl] *s zo.* Schakal *m.*

'jack·ass *s* **1.** (männlicher) Esel. **2.** *fig.* Esel *m,* Dummkopf *m.* **'~boot** *s* **1.** Stulp(en)stiefel *m.* **2.** Wasserstiefel *m.* **~daw** ['~dɔ:] *s orn.* Dohle *f.*

jack·et ['dʒækɪt] *s* **1.** Jacke *f,* Jackett *n.* **2.** ⊚ Mantel *m.* **3.** (Schutz)Umschlag *m,* (*Buch-, Am. a. Schallplatten*)Hülle *f.* **4.** Schale *f: potatoes pl (boiled) in their*

~s, ~ potatoes *pl* Pellkartoffeln *pl.* **~ crown** *s* ✻ Jacketkrone *f.*

'jack|**·ham·mer** *s* ⊚ Preßlufthammer *m.* **'~-in-the-box** *pl* **'~-in-the-₋box·es,** **'~s-in-the-box** *s* Schachtelmännchen *n,* -teufel *m.* **'~knife** *s* (*irr knife*) Klappmesser *m.* **,~of-'all-trades** *s a. contp.* Hansdampf *m* in allen Gassen. **'~pot** *s* *Poker etc:* Jackpot *m: hit the ~* F den Jackpot gewinnen; *fig.* das große Los ziehen (*with* mit).

jade [dʒeɪd] *s min.* Jade *m, f.*

jad·ed ['dʒeɪdɪd] *adj* **1.** erschöpft, ermattet. **2.** abgestumpft, übersättigt. **3.** schal, reizlos geworden.

jag [dʒæg] **I** *s* **1.** Zacke *f.* **2.** Loch *n,* Riß *m.* **II** *v/t* **3.** auszacken. **4.** ein Loch reißen in (*acc*). **jag·ged** ['~gɪd], **'jag·gy** *adj* □ **1.** (aus)gezackt, zackig. **2.** zerklüftet (*Steilküste etc*).

jag·uar ['dʒægjʊə] *s zo.* Jaguar *m.*

jail [dʒeɪl] **I** *s* Gefängnis *n: in ~* im Gefängnis; *put in ~* → **II. II** *v/t* einsperren. **'~bird** *s* F Knastbruder *m,* Knacki *m.* **'~break** *s* Ausbruch *m* (aus dem Gefängnis). **'~break·er** *s* Ausbrecher *m,*

jail·er ['dʒeɪlə] s Gefängniswärter m, -aufseher m.

ja·lop·(p)y [dʒə'lɒpɪ] s F alte Kiste od. Mühle (Auto, Flugzeug).

jam¹ [dʒæm] s Marmelade f.

jam² [~] I v/t 1. (hinein)pressen, (-)quetschen, (-)zwängen, Menschen a. (-)pferchen (**into** in acc): ~ **in** hineinpressen etc. 2. (ein)klemmen, (-)quetschen: **he** *~med his finger* (od. **got his finger** *~med*) **in the door** er quetschte sich den Finger in der Tür; **be** *~med in* eingekeilt sein (**between** zwischen dat). 3. a. ~ **up** blockieren, verstopfen. 4. a. ~ **up** (Funk etc) Empfang (durch Störsender) stören. 5. ~ **on the brakes** mot. voll auf die Bremse treten. II v/i 6. sich (hinein)drängen od. (-)quetschen (-)zwängen (**into** in acc): ~ **in** sich hineindrängen etc. 7. ⊗ sich verklemmen, (Bremsen) blockieren; Ladehemmung haben (Pistole etc). III s 8. Gedränge n. 9. Verstopfung f: → **traffic jam**. 10. ⊗ Verklemmung f, Blockierung f; Ladehemmung f. 11. F Klemme f: **be in a** ~ in der Klemme sein od. sitzen od. stecken.

Ja·mai·ca (rum) [dʒə'meɪkə] s Jamaikarum m.

jamb [dʒæm] s (Tür-, Fenster)Pfosten m.

jam·bo·ree [,dʒæmbə'riː] s 1. Jamboree n, (internationales) Pfadfindertreffen. 2. große (Partei- etc)Veranstaltung. 3. F ausgelassene Feier.

jam·my ['dʒæmɪ] adj Br. sl. 1. (kinder)leicht. 2. Glücks...: ~ **fellow** Glückspilz m.

jam-'packed adj F vollgestopft (**with** mit), (Stadion etc) bis auf den letzten Platz besetzt.

jan·gle ['dʒæŋɡl] I v/i klimpern (Münzen etc), klirren, rasseln (Ketten etc). II v/t klimpern od. klirren mit. III s Klimpern n, Klirren n.

jan·i·tor ['dʒænɪtə] s 1. Pförtner m. 2. bsd. Am. Hausmeister m.

Jan·u·ar·y ['dʒænjʊərɪ] s Januar m: **in** ~ im Januar.

Jap [dʒæp] s F Japs m (Japaner).

Jap·a·nese [,dʒæpə'niːz] I s 1. pl -nese Japaner(in). 2. ling. Japanisch n. II adj 3. japanisch.

jar¹ [dʒɑː] s 1. (irdenes od. gläsernes) Gefäß, Krug m. 2. (Marmelade-, Einmach)Glas n. 3. Br. F Glas n Bier.

jar² [~] I v/i 1. kratzen, kreischen, quietschen (**on** auf dat). 2. sich beißen (Farben); sich widersprechen (Meinungen etc); ♩ dissonieren: *~ring tone* Mißton m (a. fig.). 3. ~ **on** weh tun (dat) (Farbe, Geräusch etc), Auge etc beleidigen. 4. wackeln: ~ **loose** sich lockern. II v/t 5. kratzen od. quietschen mit. 6. erschüttern, fig. a. er-, aufregen. 7. → 3. III s 8. Kratzen n etc (→ 1). 9. Erschütterung f (a. fig.); Stoß m. 10. ♩ Mißklang m, Dissonanz f (beide a. fig.).

jar·gon ['dʒɑːɡən] s Jargon m.

jas·min(e) ['dʒæsmɪn] s ♣ Jasmin m.

jas·per ['dʒæspə] s min. Jaspis m.

jaun·dice ['dʒɔːndɪs] s 1. ✻ Gelbsucht f. 2. fig. Neid m, Eifersucht f. **'jaun·diced** adj 1. ✻ gelbsüchtig. 2. fig. neidisch, eifersüchtig.

jaunt [dʒɔːnt] I v/i e-n Ausflug od. e-e Spritztour machen. II s Ausflug m, mot. Spritztour f: **go for** (od. **on**) **a** ~ → I.

jaun·ty ['dʒɔːntɪ] adj □ 1. fesch, flott (Hut etc). 2. unbeschwert, unbekümmert (Einstellung, Person). 3. flott, schwungvoll (Melodie).

jave·lin ['dʒævlɪn] s Leichtathletik: Speer m: ~ **throw** Speerwerfen n; ~ **thrower** Speerwerfer(in).

jaw [dʒɔː] I s 1. anat. Kiefer m: **lower** ~ Unterkiefer; **upper** ~ Oberkiefer. 2. mst pl Mund m; zo. Rachen m (a. fig.), Maul n. 3. ⊗ (Klemm)Backe f, Klaue f. 4. F Geschwätz n. II v/i 5. F schwatzen. '~·bone s anat. Kieferknochen m. '~·break·er s F Zungenbrecher m.

jay [dʒeɪ] s orn. Eichelhäher m. '~·walk·er s unachtsamer Fußgänger.

jazz [dʒæz] I s 1. ♩ Jazz m. 2. **and all that** ~ F u. so ein Zeug(s). II adj 3. ♩ Jazz... III v/t 4. oft ~ **up** ♩ verjazzen. 5. mst ~ **up** F Schmiß od. Schwung bringen in (acc); j-n, et. aufmöbeln. **'jaz·zy** adj □ 1. jazzartig. 2. F knallig (Farben), (a. Kleidung etc) poppig.

jeal·ous ['dʒeləs] adj □ 1. eifersüchtig (**of** auf acc). 2. neidisch (**of** auf acc): **be** ~ **of s.o.'s success** j-m s-n Erfolg mißgönnen. 3. eifersüchtig besorgt (**of** um). **'jeal·ous·y** s 1. Eifersucht f; pl Eifersüchteleien pl. 2. Neid m.

jeans [dʒiːnz] s pl Jeans pl.

jeep [dʒiːp] s mot. Jeep m.

jeer [dʒɪə] **I** *v/i* (*at*) höhnische Bemerkungen machen (über *acc*); höhnisch lachen (über *acc*): **~ at** → *a*. **II**. **II** *v/t* verhöhnen. **III** *s* höhnische Bemerkung; Hohngelächter *n*. **'jeer·ing** *adj* □ höhnisch: **~ laughter** Hohngelächter *n*.

Je·ho·va's Wit·ness [dʒɪˈhəʊvəz] *s eccl.* Zeuge *m* Jehovas.

jell [dʒel] **I** *v/i* **1.** gelieren. **2.** *fig.* Gestalt annehmen. **II** *v/t* **3.** gelieren lassen, zum Gelieren bringen.

jel·lied ['dʒelɪd] *adj* in Aspik *od.* Sülze.

jel·ly ['dʒelɪ] **I** *s* Gallert(e *f*) *n*; Gelee *m*; Aspik *n*, Sülze *f*; Götterspeise *f*. **II** *v/i* → *jell* I. **III** *v/t* → *jell* II. **~ ba·by** *s Br.* Gummibärchen *n*. **'~·fish** *s* **1.** *zo.* Qualle *f*. **2.** *fig.* F Waschlappen *m*.

jem·my ['dʒemɪ] *Br.* **I** *s* Brech-, Stemmeisen *n*. **II** *v/t* **a. ~ open** aufbrechen, -stemmen.

jeop·ard·ize ['dʒepədaɪz] *v/t j-n, et.* gefährden, in Gefahr bringen, et. in Frage stellen. **'jeop·ard·y** *s* Gefahr *f*: **put** (*od.* **place**) **in ~** → *jeopardize*.

jerk [dʒɜːk] **I** *s* **1.** Ruck *m*; Sprung *m*, Satz *m*: **by ~s** sprung-, ruckweise; **give a ~** rucken, e-n Satz machen (*Auto etc*), zs.-zucken (*Person*). **2.** ϟ Zuckung *f*; (*bsd.* Knie)Reflex *m*. **3.** *Am. sl.* Trottel *m*. **II** *v/t* **4.** ruckartig ziehen an (*dat*): **~ o.s. free** sich losreißen. **III** *v/i* **5.** sich ruckartig *od.* ruckweise bewegen: **~ to a stop** ruckweise *od.* mit e-m Ruck stehenbleiben. **6.** (zs.-)zucken. **'jerk·y** *adj* □ **1.** ruckartig, (*Bewegungen*) fahrig; stoß-, ruckweise. **2.** *Am. sl.* blöd.

jer·ry ['dʒerɪ] *s Br.* F Pott *m* (*Nachttopf*). **'~·built** *adj* schlampig gebaut: **~ house** Bruchbude *f*.

jer·sey ['dʒɜːzɪ] *s* **1.** Pullover *m*. **2.** *Sport:* Trikot *n*. **3.** Jersey *m* (*Stoff*).

jest [dʒest] **I** *s* Spaß *m*: **in ~** im *od.* zum Scherz. **II** *v/i* spaßen: **~ with** (s-n) Spaß treiben mit. **'jest·er** *s* **1.** Spaßvogel *m*. **2.** *hist.* (Hof)Narr *m*. **'jest·ing** *adj* spaßend; spaßhaft. **'jest·ing·ly** *adv* im *od.* zum Scherz.

Jes·u·it ['dʒezjʊɪt] *s eccl.* Jesuit *m*. **,Jes·u·it·ic, ,Jes·u·it·i·cal** *adj* □ jesuitisch, Jesuiten...

jet [dʒet] **I** *s* **1.** (Feuer-, Wasseretc)Strahl *m*. **2.** ϙ Düse *f*. **3.** ✈ Jet *m*. **II** *v/i* **4.** (heraus-, hervor)schießen

(*from* aus). **5.** ✈ jetten. **~ age** *s* Düsenzeitalter *n*. **~ en·gine** *s* Strahlmotor *m*, -triebwerk *n*. **'~·fight·er** *s* ✈, ⚔ Düsenjäger *m*. **~ lag** *s* Störung *f* des gewohnten Alltagsrhythmus durch die Zeitverschiebung bei Langstreckenflügen. **'~·lin·er** *s* Jetliner *m*, Düsenverkehrsflugzeug *n*. **~ plane** *s* Düsenflugzeug *n*. **'~·pro,pelled** *adj bsd.* ✈ mit Düsen- *od.* Strahlantrieb. **~ pro·pul·sion** *s bsd.* ✈ Düsen-, Strahlantrieb *m*.

jet·sam ['dʒetsəm] *s* ⚓ **1.** Seewurfgut *n*. **2.** Strandgut *n*: → *flotsam*.

jet | **set** *s* Jet-set *m*. **'~·set·ter** *s* Angehörige *m, f* des Jet-set.

jet·ti·son ['dʒetɪsn] *v/t* **1.** ⚓ über Bord werfen (*a. fig.*). **2.** ✈ (im Notwurf) abwerfen, *Treibstoff* ablassen. **3.** *ausgebrannte Raketenstufe* absprengen.

jet·ty ['dʒetɪ] *s* ⚓ **1.** Hafendamm *m*, Mole *f*. **2.** Strombrecher *m* (*an Brükken*).

Jew [dʒuː] *s* Jude *m*, Jüdin *f*.

jew·el ['dʒuːəl] **I** *s* **1.** Juwel *n* (*a. fig.*), Edelstein *m*: **~ box** Schmuckkassette *f*. **2.** ϙ Stein *m* (*e-r Uhr*). **II** *v/t pret u. pp* **-eled**, *bsd. Br.* **-elled 3.** mit Juwelen schmücken *od.* besetzen. **'jew·el·(l)er** *s* Juwelier *m*, *bsd. Br.* **jew·el·le·ry** ['~·əlrɪ] *s* Juwelen *pl*, *weitS.* Schmuck *m*: **piece of ~** Schmuckstück *n*.

Jew·ish ['dʒuːɪʃ] *adj* jüdisch, Juden...

jib¹ [dʒɪb] *s* **1.** ⚓ Klüver *m*. **2.** ϙ Ausleger *m* (*e-s Krans*).

jib² [~] *v/i* **1.** scheuen, bocken (*at* vor *dat*). **2.** *fig.* störrisch *od.* bockig sein: **~ at** sich sträuben gegen; streiken bei.

jif·fy ['dʒɪfɪ] *s* F Augenblick *m*: **in a ~** im Nu, im Handumdrehen.

jig·gered ['dʒɪgəd] *adj* F **1.** *I'm ~ if* der Teufel soll mich holen, wenn. **2.** *be ~* *Br.* baff *od.* platt sein: *well, I'm ~!* da bin ich aber baff!

jig·gle ['dʒɪgl] **I** *v/t* wackeln mit; schütteln; rütteln an (*dat*). **II** *v/i* wackeln.

jig·saw (**puz·zle**) ['dʒɪgsɔː] *s* Puzzle (-spiel) *n*.

jilt [dʒɪlt] *v/t Mädchen* sitzenlassen (*for* wegen *e-s anderen Mädchens*); *e-m Liebhaber, e-m Mädchen* den Laufpaß geben.

jim·jams ['dʒɪmdʒæmz] *s pl* F **1.** Säuferwahn *m*. **2.** → *jitter* I.

jim·my ['dʒɪmɪ] *Am.* → **jemmy**.

jin·gle ['dʒɪŋgl] **I** *v/i* klimpern (*Münzen etc*), bimmeln (*Glöckchen etc*). **II** *v/t* klimpern mit, bimmeln lassen. **III** *s* Klimpern *n*, Bimmeln *n*.

jin·go ['dʒɪŋgəʊ] *pl* **-goes** *s* Chauvinist(in). **'jin·go·ism** *s* Chauvinismus *m*. **,jin·go·'is·tic** *adj* (**~ally**) chauvinistisch.

jinks [dʒɪŋks] *s pl*: **high ~** Ausgelassenheit *f*; **they were having high ~** bei ihnen ging es hoch her.

jinx [dʒɪŋks] F **I** *s* **1.** Unglücksbringer *m*. **2.** Unglück *n*: **put a ~ on →** 3. **II** *v/t* **3.** Unglück bringen (*dat*); verhexen.

jit·ter ['dʒɪtə] F **I** *s*: **the ~s** *pl* Bammel *m*, e-e Heidenangst (*about* vor *dat*): **have the ~s →** II. **II** *v/i* Bammel *od.* e-e Heidenangst haben; furchtbar nervös sein. **'jit·ter·y** *adj* F furchtbar nervös.

jiu·jit·su [dʒuː'dʒɪtsuː] → **jujitsu**.

job¹ [dʒɒb] **I** *s* **1.** (einzelne) Arbeit: **make a good (bad) ~ of s.th.** et. gut (schlecht) machen; **→ odd** 5. **2.** *a.* **~ work** Akkordarbeit *f*: **by the ~** im Akkord. **3.** Stellung *f*, Tätigkeit *f*, Arbeit *f*, Job *m*; Arbeitsplatz *m*: **~ creation** Arbeits(platz)beschaffung *f*; **~ description** Arbeits(platz)beschreibung *f*; **computers are ~ killers** Computer vernichten Arbeitsplätze; **know one's ~** s-e Sache verstehen. **4.** Sache *f*: a) Aufgabe *f*, Pflicht *f*, b) Geschmack *m*: **this is not everybody's ~** das ist nicht jedermanns Sache, das liegt nicht jedem. **5.** F Sache *f*, Angelegenheit *f*: **make the best of a bad ~** gute Miene zum bösen Spiel machen; das Beste daraus machen. **6.** F Ding *n*, krumme Sache: **pull a ~** ein Ding drehen. **II** *v/i* **7.** Gelegenheitsarbeiten machen, jobben. **8.** (im) Akkord arbeiten. **III** *v/t* **9.** *a.* **~ out** Arbeit in Auftrag vergeben; im Akkord vergeben.

Job² [dʒəʊb] *npr Bibl.* Hiob *m*: **have the patience of ~, be (as) patient as ~** e-e Engelsgeduld haben; **~'s comforter** *j-d*, *der durch s-n Trost alles nur noch schlimmer macht*.

job·ber ['dʒɒbə] *s* **1.** Gelegenheitsarbeiter *m*, Jobber *m*. **2.** Akkordarbeiter *m*. **3.** *Börse*: *Br.* Jobber *m*.

'job·hunt *v/i* auf Arbeitssuche sein: **go ~ing** auf Arbeitssuche gehen.

jock·ey ['dʒɒkɪ] **I** *s* **1.** *Pferderennsport*: Jockey *m*. **II** *v/t* **2.** Pferd (*als Jockey*)

reiten. **3.** manövrieren (*a. fig.*): **~ out of** *j-n* hinausbugsieren aus (*e-r Stellung etc*); *j-n* betrügen um. **III** *v/i* **4.** **~ for** rangeln um (*a. fig.*): **~ for position** (*Sport etc, a. fig.*) sich e-e günstige (Ausgangs)Position zu verschaffen suchen.

jo·cose [dʒəʊ'kəʊs], **joc·u·lar** ['dʒɒkjʊlə] *adj* □ **1.** ausgelassen (*Person*). **2.** witzig, spaßig (*Bemerkung etc*).

jog [dʒɒg] **I** *v/t* **1.** stoßen an (*acc*) *od.* gegen, *j-n* anstoßen, stupsen: **~ s.o.'s memory** *fig.* *j-s* Gedächtnis nachhelfen. **II** *v/i* **2.** trotten (*Person, Tier*), zuckeln (*Bus etc*); (*Sport*) joggen. **III** *s* **3.** Stoß *m*, Stups *m*. **4.** Trott *m*; (*Sport*) Trimmtrab *m*. **'jog·ger** *s Sport*: Jogger(in). **'jog·ging** *s Sport*: Joggen *n*, Jogging *n*.

jog·gle ['dʒɒgl] *v/t* (leicht) schütteln, rütteln an (*dat*).

jog| trot *s* gemächlicher Trab, Trott *m* (*a. fig.*). **'~-trot** *v/i* gemächlich traben (*bsd. Pferd*), trotten (*Person, Tier*).

john [dʒɒn] *s Am.* F Klo *n*: **in the ~** auf dem *od.* im Klo. ♀ **Bull** *s* England *n*, die Engländer *pl*; ein typischer Engländer. ♀ **Han·cock** ['hænkɒk] *s Am.* F Friedrich Wilhelm *m* (*Unterschrift*).

join [dʒɔɪn] **I** *v/t* **1.** *et.* verbinden, -einigen, zs.-fügen (**to** mit): **~ hands** die Hände falten; sich die Hand *od.* die Hände reichen; *fig.* sich zs.-tun (**with** mit). **2.** Personen vereinigen, zs.-bringen (**with, to** mit). **3.** sich anschließen (*dat od.* an *acc*), stoßen *od.* sich gesellen zu: **I'll ~ you later** ich komme später nach. **4.** eintreten in (*e-e Firma, e-n Verein etc*). **5.** teilnehmen *od.* sich beteiligen an (*dat*), mitmachen bei. **6.** einmünden in (*acc*) (*Fluß, Straße*). **II** *v/i* **7.** sich vereinigen *od.* verbinden (**with** mit). **8.** **~ in** a) teilnehmen, sich beteiligen, mitmachen, b) **→** 5. **9.** zs.-kommen (*Straßen*), (*Flüsse a.*) zs.-fließen. **'join·er** *s* Tischler *m*, Schreiner *m*: **~'s bench** Hobelbank *f*. **'join·er·y** *s* **1.** Tischler-, Schreinerhandwerk *n*. **2.** Tischler-, Schreinerarbeit *f*.

joint [dʒɔɪnt] **I** *s* **1.** Verbindung(sstelle) *f*, *bsd.* a) (Löt)Naht *f*, Nahtstelle *f*, b) *anat.*, ⊙ Gelenk *n*: **out of ~** ausgerenkt, *fig.* aus den Fugen; **put out of ~** sich *et.* ausrenken; **→ nose** 1. **2.** *gastr.*

Braten(stück *n*) *m.* **3.** *sl.* Laden *m*, Bude *f* (*Lokal*, *Firma etc*): → **clip** joint. **4.** *sl.* Joint *m* (*Haschisch*- *od.* *Marihuanazigarette*). **II** *adj* □ **5.** gemeinsam, gemeinschaftlich: **take ~ action** gemeinsam vorgehen; **~ venture** ✝ Gemeinschaftsunternehmen *n.* **,~'stock com·pa·ny** *s* **1.** *Br.* Kapital- *od.* Aktiengesellschaft *f.* **2.** *Am.* Offene Handelsgesellschaft auf Aktien.

joist [dʒɔɪst] *s* △ **1.** Deckenträger *m*, -balken *m.* **2.** I-Träger *m.*

joke [dʒəʊk] **I** *s* **1.** Witz *m*: **crack ~s** Witze reißen. **2.** a) Scherz *m*, Spaß *m*: in (*od. for a*) **~** im *od.* zum Spaß; **that's going beyond a ~** das ist kein Spaß mehr, das ist nicht mehr lustig; **he can't take a ~** er versteht keinen Spaß, b) *mst* **practical ~** Streich *m*: **play a ~ on s.o.** j-m e-n Streich spielen. **II** *v/i* **3.** scherzen, Witze *od.* Spaß machen: **I'm not joking** ich meine das ernst; **you must be joking, are you joking?** das ist doch nicht dein Ernst! **'jok·er** *s* **1.** Spaßvogel *m*, Witzbold *m.* **2.** Joker *m* (*Spielkarte*). **3.** *sl.* Typ *m*, Kerl *m.* **'jok·ing I** *adj* □ scherzhaft, spaßend: **~ly** a. im Spaß. **II** *s* Witze *pl*: **~ apart** Scherz *od.* Spaß beiseite.

jol·li·fi·ca·tion [,dʒɒlɪfɪ'keɪʃn] *s* F (feucht)fröhliches Fest, Festivität *f.*

jol·ly¹ ['dʒɒlɪ] **I** *adj* □ **1.** lustig, fröhlich, vergnügt. **2.** F angeheitert: **be ~** e-n Schwips haben. **II** *adv* **3.** *Br.* F ganz schön, ziemlich: **a ~ good fellow** ein prima Kerl.

jol·ly² [~], **~ boat** *s* ♣ Jolle *f.*

Jol·ly Rog·er [,dʒɒlɪ'rɒdʒə] *s* Totenkopf-, Piratenflagge *f.*

jolt [dʒəʊlt] **I** *v/t* **1.** e-n Ruck *od.* Stoß geben (*dat*); *Passagiere* durchrütteln, -schütteln. **2.** *fig.* j-m e-n Schock versetzen; *j-n* auf- *od.* wachrütteln: **~ s.o. out of a ~** j-n reißen aus. **II** *v/i* **3.** e-n Ruck machen; rütteln, holpern (*Fahrzeug*). **III** *s* **4.** Ruck *m*, Stoß *m.* **5.** *fig.* Schock *m*: **give s.o. a ~** j-m e-n Schock versetzen.

josh [dʒɒʃ] *v/t Am.* F *j-n* aufziehen, veräppeln.

joss stick [dʒɒs] *s* Räucherstäbchen *n.*

jos·tle ['dʒɒsl] **I** *v/t* **1.** anrempeln. **2.** dränge(l)n: **~ one's way through** sich (durch)drängen durch. **II** *v/i* **3.** **~**

against rempeln gegen, anrempeln (*acc*). **4.** (sich) dränge(l)n.

jot [dʒɒt] **I** *s fig.* Spur *f*: **not a ~ of truth** kein Funke *od.* Körnchen Wahrheit. **II** *v/t mst* **~ down** sich *et.* notieren. **'jot·ter** *s* Notizbuch *n*, -block *m.* **'jot·ting** *s mst pl* Notiz *f.*

joule [dʒuːl] *s phys.* Joule *n.*

jour·nal ['dʒɜːnl] *s* **1.** Journal *n*, Zeitschrift *f.* **2.** Tagebuch *n.* **3.** *Buchhaltung*: Journal *n*: **cash ~** Kassenbuch *n.* **4.** ♣ Logbuch *n.* **jour·nal·ese** [,~nə'liːz] *s* Zeitungsstil *m.* **'jour·nal·ism** *s* Journalismus *m.* **'jour·nal·ist** *s* Journalist(in). **,jour·nal'is·tic** *adj* (**~ally**) journalistisch.

jour·ney ['dʒɜːnɪ] *s* **1.** Reise *f*: **go on a ~** verreisen. **2.** Reise *f*, Entfernung *f*: **a two days' ~** zwei Tagesreisen (**to** nach). **~·man** ['~mən] *s* (*irr man*) Geselle *m*: **~ tailor** Schneidergeselle.

jo·vi·al ['dʒəʊvjəl] *adj* □ lustig, fröhlich, vergnügt. **jo·vi·al·i·ty** [,~vɪ'ælətɪ] *s* Lustigkeit *f*, Fröhlichkeit *f.*

jowl [dʒaʊl] *s* **1.** (Unter)Kiefer *m.* **2.** Wange *f*, Backe *f*; Hängebacke *f*: → **cheek** 1.

joy [dʒɔɪ] *s* **1.** Freude *f* (**at** über *acc*; **in** *dat*): **for ~** vor Freude *weinen etc*; **tears** *pl* **of ~** Freudentränen *pl*; **to s.o.'s ~** j-s Freude. **2.** *Br.* F Erfolg *m*: **I didn't have any ~** ich hatte kein Glück. **'joy·ful** [*'~fʊl*] *adj* □ **1.** freudig, erfreut: **be ~** sich freuen, froh sein. **2.** erfreulich, freudig (*Ereignis etc*). **'joy·less** *adj* □ **1.** freudlos. **2.** unerfreulich. **'joy·ous** → **joyful**.

joy| **ride** *s* F Spritztour *f* (*bsd. in e-m gestohlenen Wagen*): **go on a ~** e-e Spritztour machen. **~ stick** *s* F **1.** ✈ Steuerknüppel *m.* **2.** *Computer*: Joystick *m.*

ju·bi·lant ['dʒuːbɪlənt] *adj* □ **1.** überglücklich. **2.** jubelnd: **~ shout** Jubelschrei *m.* **ju·bi·late** ['~leɪt] *v/i* jubilieren, jubeln. **ju·bi'la·tion** *s* Jubel *m.* **ju·bi·lee** ['~liː] *s* Jubiläum *n.*

judge [dʒʌdʒ] **I** *s* **1.** ⚖ Richter *m*: → **sober** I. **2.** Schiedsrichter *m*; Preisrichter *m*; (*Sport a.*) Kampfrichter *m*, (*Boxen*) Punktrichter *m.* **3.** Kenner *m*: **a (good) ~ of wine** ein Weinkenner. **II** *v/t* **4.** ⚖ *Fall* verhandeln; die Verhandlung führen gegen. **5.** *Wettbewerbsteil-*

nehmer, Leistungen etc beurteilen (**on** nach); als Schiedsrichter (*etc*, → 2) fungieren bei. **6.** entscheiden (*s.th.* et; *that* daß). **7.** beurteilen, einschätzen (**by** nach). **III** *v/i* **8.** als Schiedsrichter (*etc*, → 2) fungieren (**at** bei). **9.** urteilen (**of** über *acc*): *judging by his words* s-n Worten nach zu urteilen.

judg(e)·ment ['dʒʌdʒmənt] *s* **1.** ⚖ Urteil *n.* **2.** Urteilsvermögen *n:* **against** (**one's**) **better ~** wider bessere Einsicht. **3.** Meinung *f,* Ansicht *f,* Urteil *n* (**on** über *acc*): *in my ~* m-s Erachtens; *form a* (*final*) *~ on* sich ein (abschließendes *od.* endgültiges) Urteil bilden über. **4.** göttliches (Straf)Gericht: *the Last* ♀ das Jüngste Gericht; *Day of* ♀, ♀ *Day* Jüngster Tag.

ju·di·ca·ture ['dʒuːdɪkətʃə] *s* ⚖ **1.** Rechtsprechung *f,* Rechtspflege *f.* **2.** Gerichtswesen *n.* **3.** → *judiciary* 3.

ju·di·cial [dʒuːˈdɪʃl] *adj* □ **1.** ⚖ gerichtlich, Gerichts...: **~ error** Justizirrtum *m;* **~ murder** Justizmord *m.* **2.** ⚖ richterlich. **3.** kritisch.

ju·di·ci·a·ry [dʒuːˈdɪʃərɪ] ⚖ **I** *adj* **1.** → *judicial* 1, 2. **II** *s* **2.** → *judicature* 2. **3.** *coll.* Richter(schaft *f*) *pl.*

ju·di·cious [dʒuːˈdɪʃəs] *adj* □ **1.** vernünftig, umsichtig. **2.** wohlüberlegt.

ju·do ['dʒuːdəʊ] *s Sport:* Judo *n.* **ju·do·ka** ['~kɑː] *s* Judoka *m.*

jug [dʒʌɡ] **I** *s* **1.** Krug *m; bsd. Br.* Kanne *f;* Kännchen *n.* **2.** *sl.* Knast *m* (*Gefängnis*). **II** *v/t* **3.** *sl.* einlochen.

jug·ger·naut ['dʒʌɡənɔːt] *s* **1.** *mot. Br.* Schwerlastzug *m.* **2.** *fig.* Moloch *m.*

jug·gins ['dʒʌɡɪnz] *s bsd. Br.* F Trottel *m.*

jug·gle ['dʒʌɡl] **I** *v/i* **1.** jonglieren (mit). **2.** *fig.* jonglieren mit (*Fakten, Worten etc*); *Fakten, Worte etc* verdrehen; *Konten etc* fälschen, frisieren. **II** *v/i* **3.** jonglieren. **4. ~ with** → 2. '**jug·gler** *s* **1.** Jongleur *m.* **2. ~ of words** Wortverdreher *m.* **3.** Schwindler *m.*

Ju·go·slav → *Yugoslav.*

juice [dʒuːs] **I** *s* **1.** Saft *m:* **let s.o. stew in his own ~** F j-n im eigenen Saft schmoren lassen. **2.** *sl.* ⚡ Saft *m; mot.* Sprit *m.* **II** *v/t* **3.** entsaften. '**juic·y** *adj* □ **1.** saftig. **2.** F knackig (*Mädchen*); saftig (*Gewinn etc*); lukrativ (*Vertrag etc*); pikant (*Einzelheiten etc*).

ju·jit·su [dʒuːˈdʒɪtsuː] *s Sport:* Jiu-Jitsu *n.*

juke·box ['dʒuːkbɒks] *s* Jukebox *f,* Musikautomat *m.*

Ju·ly [dʒuːˈlaɪ] *s* Juli *m:* **in ~** im Juli.

jum·ble ['dʒʌmbl] **I** *v/t a.* **~ together** (*od.* **up**) *Sachen* durcheinanderwerfen; *Fakten etc* durcheinanderbringen. **II** *s* Durcheinander *n.* **~ sale** *s Br.* Wohltätigkeitsbasar *m.*

jum·bo ['dʒʌmbəʊ] **I** *pl* **-bos** *s* **1.** Koloß *m* (*Sache, Person*). **2.** ✈ Jumbo *m.* **II** *adj* **3.** riesig, Riesen...: **~ jet** ✈ Jumbo-Jet *m.* '**~-sized** → *jumbo* 3.

jump [dʒʌmp] **I** *s* **1.** Sprung *m:* **make** (*od.* **take**) **a ~** e-n Sprung machen; **have the ~ on s.o.** F j-m vorausein. **2.** *Sport:* (*Hoch-, Ski- etc*)Sprung *m.* **3.** **give a ~** → 6; **it gives me the ~s** F es macht mich ganz nervös *od.* unruhig; **have the ~s** F ganz nervös *od.* aufgeregt sein. **II** *v/i* **4.** springen: **~ at** *fig.* sich stürzen auf (*acc*); **~ off** abspringen (von); **~ out of one's skin** *fig.* aus der Haut fahren; **~ to one's feet** aufspringen; → *conclusion* 3. **5.** hüpfen, springen: **~ for joy** Freudensprünge machen. **6.** zs.-zucken, auf-, zs.-fahren (**at** bei). **7.** *fig.* abrupt übergehen, überspringen, -wechseln (**to** zu). **III** *v/t* **8.** springen über (*acc*). **9.** *fig.* überspringen, auslassen: **~ the gun** (*Sport*) e-n Fehlstart verursachen; *fig.* voreilig sein *od.* handeln; **~ the line** (*bsd. Br. queue*) sich vordräng(el)n (*beim Schlangestehen u. fig.*); *mot.* aus e-r Kolonne ausscheren u. überholen; → *rail¹* 3. **10.** (heraus)springen aus: → *rail¹* 3, *track* 3.

jump·er¹ ['dʒʌmpə] *s Sport:* (*Hoch-etc*)Springer(in).

jump·er² ['~] *s* **1.** *bsd. Br.* Pullover *m.* **2.** *Am.* Trägerrock *m,* -kleid *n.*

jump·er ca·bles *v/t pl Am.* → *jump leads.*

jump| leads [liːdz] *s pl Br. mot.* Starthilfekabel *n.* **~ rope** *s Am.* Spring-, Sprungseil *n.* **~ seat** *s* Klapp-, Notsitz *m.* **~ suit** *s* Overall *m.*

jump·y ['dʒʌmpɪ] *adj* □ nervös; schreckhaft.

junc·tion ['dʒʌŋkʃn] *s* **1.** Verbindung *f,* -einigung *f.* ⚙ Knotenpunkt *m.* **3.** (Straßen)Kreuzung *f,* (-)Einmündung *f.*

junc·ture ['dʒʌŋktʃə] *s:* **at this ~** in die-

sem Augenblick, zu diesem Zeitpunkt.
June [dʒuːn] *s* Juni *m: in ~* im Juni.
jun·gle ['dʒʌŋgl] *s* Dschungel *m (a. fig.).*
jun·ior ['dʒuːnjə] **I** *adj* **1.** junior. **2.** *(to)* jünger (als); untergeordnet *(dat):* **~ partner** ✝ Junior(partner) *m;* → **man·agement** 2. **3.** *ped.* **~ high** *(school)* Am. die unteren Klassen der High-School; **~ school** *Br.* Grundschule *f (für Kinder von 7 - 11).* **4.** *Sport:* Junioren... **II** *s* **5.** Jüngere *m, f: he is my ~ by two years, he is two years my ~* er ist 2 Jahre jünger als ich. **6.** *Sport:* Junior(in).
ju·ni·per ['dʒuːnipə] *s* ✿ Wacholder *m.*
junk¹ [dʒʌŋk] *s* ♣ Dschunke *f.*
junk² [~] *s* **1.** Trödel *m;* Altmaterial *n;* Schrott *m.* **2.** Gerümpel *n,* Abfall *m.* **3.** *contp.* Schund *m,* Mist *m.* **4.** *sl.* Stoff *m, bsd.* Heroin *n.* **II** *v/t* **5.** *et.* unbrauchbar Gewordenes ausrangieren, *Auto etc* verschrotten.
junk·et ['dʒʌŋkit] *s* (Sahne)Quark *m;* Dickmilch *f.*
junk food *s* Junk-food *m (kalorienreiche Nahrung von geringem Nährwert).*
junk·ie ['dʒʌŋki] *s sl.* Junkie *m (Rauschgiftsüchtiger, bsd.* H-Fixer *m.*
'junk·yard *s* Schuttabladeplatz *m;* Schrottplatz *m.*
jun·ta ['dʒʌntə] *s pol.* Junta *f.*
ju·rid·i·cal [,dʒuə'ridikl] *adj* □ **1.** gerichtlich, Gerichts... **2.** juristisch, Rechts...
ju·ris·dic·tion [,dʒuəris'dikʃn] *s* Gerichtsbarkeit *f;* (örtliche u. sachliche) Zuständigkeit *f* (*of, over* für): **come** *(od. fall)* **under** *(od.* **within)** **the ~** *of* unter die Zuständigkeit fallen von *(od. gen)* **have ~ over** zuständig sein für.
ju·ris·pru·dence [,dʒuəris'pruːdəns] *s* Rechtswissenschaft *f.*
ju·rist ['dʒuərist] *s* **1.** Jurist *m,* Rechtsgelehrte *m.* **2.** *Br.* Rechtsstudent *m.* **3.** *Am.* Rechtsanwalt *m.*
ju·ror ['dʒuərə] *s* **1.** ⚖ Geschworene *m, f.* **2.** Preisrichter(in).
ju·ry ['dʒuəri] *s* **1.** ⚖ die Geschworenen *pl:* → **trial** 1. **2.** Jury *f,* Preis-, *(Sport a.)*

Kampfgericht *n.* **~ box** *s* ⚖ Geschworenenbank *f.* **~·man** ['~mən] *s (irr man)* ⚖ Geschworene *m.* **'~·wom·an** *s (irr woman)* Geschworene *f.*
just [dʒʌst] **I** *adj* (□ **~** *justly)* **1.** gerecht *(to* gegen). **2.** gerecht, angemessen: *it was only ~* es war nur recht u. billig. **3.** rechtmäßig *(Anspruch etc);* berechtigt, gerechtfertigt *(Zorn etc).* **II** *adv* **4.** gerade, (so)eben: → **now** 1. **5.** gerade, genau, eben: *~ as* gerade als; *that is ~ like you* das sieht dir ähnlich; → **well¹** 1. **6.** gerade (noch), ganz knapp. **7.** nur, lediglich, bloß: *~ moment* 1, *etc* **8.** *~ about* ungefähr, etwa; gerade noch.
jus·tice ['dʒʌstis] *s* **1.** Gerechtigkeit *f (to* gegen): **do ~ to** gerecht werden *(dat);* *et.* richtig würdigen. **2.** ⚖ Gerechtigkeit *f,* Recht *n:* **do ~** der Gerechtigkeit Genüge tun; **bring to ~** vor die Richter bringen; → **administer** 2. **3.** ⚖ Richter *m:* **~ of the peace** Friedensrichter.
jus·ti·fi·a·ble ['dʒʌstifaiəbl] *adj* zu rechtfertigen(d), berechtigt, vertretbar. **'jus·ti·fi·a·bly** *adv* berechtigterweise, mit gutem Grund, mit Recht.
jus·ti·fi·ca·tion [,dʒʌstifi'keiʃn] *s* Rechtfertigung *f: in ~ of* zur Rechtfertigung von *(od. gen).*
jus·ti·fy ['dʒʌstifai] *v/t* rechtfertigen *(before, to* vor *dat,* gegenüber): *be justified in doing s.th.* et. mit gutem Recht tun; berechtigt sein, et. zu tun.
just·ly ['dʒʌstli] *adv* mit *od.* zu Recht.
jut [dʒʌt] *v/i a.* **~ out** vorspringen; herausragen.
jute [dʒuːt] *s* Jute(faser) *f.*
ju·ve·nile ['dʒuːvənail] **I** *adj* jugendlich; Jugend...: **~ court** Jugendgericht *n;* **~ delinquency** Jugendkriminalität *f;* **~ delinquent** *(od.* **offender)** straffälliger Jugendlicher. **II** *s* Jugendliche *m, f.*
jux·ta·pose [,dʒʌkstə'pəuz] *v/t* nebeneinanderstellen *(a. fig.).* **jux·ta·po·si·tion** [,~pə'ziʃn] *s* **1.** Nebeneinanderstellung *f.* **2.** Nebeneinanderstehen *n:* **be in ~** nebeneinanderstehen.

K

kale [keɪl] *s* **1.** ♣ Grün-, Braunkohl *m.* **2.** *Am. sl.* Kies *m* (Geld).

ka·lei·do·scope [kə'laɪdəskəʊp] *s* Kaleidoskop *n* (*a. fig.*).

kan·ga·roo [ˌkæŋgə'ruː] *s zo.* Känguruh *n.*

ka·put [kæ'pʊt] *adj pred* F kaputt.

kar·at *bsd. Am.* → **carat.**

ka·ra·te [kə'rɑːtɪ] *s* Karate *n*: ~ **chop** Karateschlag *m.*

kar·ma ['kɑːmə] *s* Buddhismus, Hinduismus: Karma(n) *n.*

ka·yak ['kaɪæk] *s* Kajak *m, n* (*a. Sport*).

keck [kek] *v/i bsd. Am.* **1.** würgen (*beim Erbrechen*). **2.** *fig.* sich ekeln (*at* vor *dat*).

keel [kiːl] ♣ **I** *s* ✡ Kiel *m*: **on an even** ~ *fig.* gleichmäßig, ruhig. **II** *v/i mst* ~ **over** (*od.* **up**) umschlagen, kentern.

keen [kiːn] *adj* □ **1.** scharf (geschliffen). **2.** schneidend (*Kälte*), scharf (*Wind*). **3.** scharf (*Sinne, Verstand etc*). **4.** ✝ scharf (*Wettbewerb*); lebhaft, stark (*Nachfrage*). **5.** heftig, stark (*Gefühl*): ~ **interest** starkes *od.* lebhaftes Interesse. **6.** begeistert, leidenschaftlich (*Schwimmer etc*). **7.** versessen, scharf (**on**, **about** *auf acc*): **be** ~ **on a** sth. begeistert sein von; **be** ~ **on doing** (*od.* **to do**) **s.th.** et. unbedingt tun wollen.

keep [kiːp] **I** *s* **1.** (Lebens)Unterhalt *m*. **for** ~**s** F für *od.* auf immer, endgültig: **it's yours for** ~**s** du kannst *od.* darfst es behalten. **II** *v/t* (*irr*) **3.** (be)halten. **4.** *j-n, et.* lassen, (*in e-m bestimmten Zustand*) (er)halten: ~ **closed** Tür etc geschlossen halten; ~ **s.th. a secret** et. geheimhalten (**from** vor *dat*); → **wait** 1, *etc.* **5.** (*im Besitz*) behalten: ~ **the change** (den Rest *des Geldes*) ist für Sie; ~ **your seat, please** bitte behalten Sie Platz. **6.** *j-n* aufhalten: **don't let me** ~ **you** laß dich nicht aufhalten. **7.** aufheben, -bewahren: **can you** ~ **a secret?** kannst du schweigen? **8.** Beziehungen etc unterhalten (**with** zu). **9.** Ware führen. **10.** Laden etc haben, betreiben. **11.** Versprechen, Wort halten. **12.** Bett, Haus, Zimmer hüten. **13.** ernähren, er-, unterhalten: **have a family to** ~ e-e Familie ernähren müssen. **14.** *Tiere* halten; sich *ein Auto etc* halten. **III** *v/i* (*irr*) **15.** bleiben: ~ **in sight** in Sicht(weite) bleiben; ~ **still** stillhalten. **16.** sich halten, (*in e-m bestimmten Zustand*) bleiben: ~ **friends** (weiterhin) Freunde bleiben. **17.** *mit ger* weiter...: ~ **smiling!** immer nur lächeln!; ~ **(on) trying** es weiterversuchen, es immer wieder versuchen.

Verbindungen mit Präpositionen:

keep| at *v/i* **1.** weitermachen mit. **2.** *j-m* zusetzen (*to do* zu tun). ~ **from** I *v/t* **1.** abhalten von: **keep s.o. from doing s.th.** j-n davon abhalten, et. zu tun. **2.** bewahren vor (*dat*). **3.** *et.* vorenthalten, verschweigen. **II** *v/i* **4.** vermeiden (*acc*): ~ **doing s.th.** es vermeiden *od.* sich davor hüten, et. zu tun; **I could hardly** ~ **laughing** ich konnte mir kaum das Lachen verkneifen. ~ **off** *v/t u. v/i* (sich) fernhalten von: **keep your hands off it!** Hände weg (davon)!; → **grass** 2. ~ **on** *v/i* leben *od.* sich ernähren von. ~ **to** I *v/i* **1.** bleiben in (*dat*): → **left** 3, **right** 9. **2.** *fig.* festhalten an (*dat*), bleiben bei. **II** *v/t* **3.** **keep s.th. to a** (*od.* **the**) **minimum** et. auf ein Minimum beschränken. **4.** **keep s.th. to o.s.** et. für sich behalten.

Verbindungen mit Adverbien:

keep| a·way *v/t u. v/i* (sich) fernhalten (**from** von). ~ **back** *v/t* **1.** zurückhalten: **keep s.o. back from doing s.th.** j-n davon abhalten *od.* daran hindern, et. zu tun. **2.** *fig.* zurückhalten: a) *Lohn etc* einbehalten, b) *Tränen etc* unterdrükken, c) *et.* verschweigen. ~ **down** I *v/t* **1.** *Kopf etc* unten behalten. **2.** *Kosten etc* niedrig halten. **3.** unter Kontrolle halten, *Volk, Gefühle etc a.* unterdrücken. **4.** *Nahrung etc* bei sich behalten. **II** *v/i* **5.** unten bleiben; sich geduckt halten. ~ **in** I *v/t* **1.** nicht heraus- *od.* hinauslassen; *ped.* nachsitzen lassen. **2.** *Atem* anhalten. **3.** *Gefühle* zurückhalten, unterdrücken. **II** *v/i* **4.** drin bleiben, nicht herauskommen. **5.** sich mit *j-m* gut stellen. ~ **off** *v/t u. v/i* (sich) fernhalten: **keep your hands off!** Hände weg!; ~**!** Berühren verboten!; Betreten verbo-

ten! **~ on I** v/t **1.** *Kleidungsstück* anbehalten, anlassen, *Hut* aufbehalten: →
shirt. 2. *Licht* brennen lassen, anlassen.
II v/i **3.** a) weitermachen, b) nicht lok-
kerlassen, c) → **keep** 17. **4. ~ at →** **keep**
at 2. **~ out I** v/t **1.** (**of**) nicht hinein- *od.*
hereinlassen (in *acc*), fern-, abhalten
(von). **2.** *fig.* heraushalten (**of** aus). **II**
v/i **3.** draußen bleiben: **~!** Zutritt verboten! **4.** *fig.* sich heraushalten (**of** aus): **~**
of sight sich nicht blicken lassen. **~**
to-geth-er I v/t *Dinge, fig. Mannschaft*
etc zs.-halten. **II** v/i zs.-bleiben (*a. fig.*
Mannschaft etc), zs.-halten (*a. fig.*
Freunde etc). **~ up I** v/t **1.** oben halten,
hochhalten: **→ chin** 1. **2.** *fig.* aufrechterhalten, *Brauch etc a.* weiterpflegen,
Tempo halten, *Preise etc* (hoch)halten,
Mut nicht sinken lassen: **→ appear-**
ance 3. **3.** in gutem Zustand *od.* in
Ordnung halten. **II** v/i **4.** oben bleiben.
5. *fig.* sich halten, (*Preise etc a.*) sich
behaupten; andauern, nicht nachlas-
sen. **6. ~ with** a) Schritt halten mit (*a.*
fig.): **~ with the Joneses** es den Nachbarn gleichtun (wollen); **→ time** 1, b)
sich auf dem laufenden halten über
(*acc*), c) in Kontakt bleiben mit.

keep·er ['kiːpə] s **1.** Wächter m, Aufseher m. **2.** *mst in Zssgn* Inhaber m, Besitzer m; Halter m, Züchter m. **3.** Betreuer
m, Verwalter m.

keep-'fresh bag s Frischhaltebeutel m.

keep·ing ['kiːpɪŋ] s **1.** Verwahrung f: **put**
in s.o.'s ~ j-n in j-s Obhut geben; j-m
et. zur Aufbewahrung geben. **2. be in**
(**out of**) **~ with** (nicht) übereinstimmen
mit; (nicht) passen zu; (nicht) entsprechen (*dat*).

keep·sake ['kiːpseɪk] s (*Geschenk zum*)
Andenken n: **as** (*od.* **for**) **a ~** als *od.* zum
Andenken.

keg [keg] s Fäßchen n.

ken [ken] s: **this is beyond** (*od.* **outside**)
my ~ das entzieht sich m-r Kenntnis;
das ist mir zu hoch.

ken·nel ['kenl] s **1.** Hundehütte f. **2.** *oft*
pl (*sg konstruiert*) Hundezwinger m;
Hundeheim n.

kept [kept] *pret u. pp von* **keep.**

kerb [kɜːb], **'~·stone** s Br. Bord-, Randstein m.

ker·chief ['kɜːtʃɪf] s Hals-, Kopftuch n.

ker·nel ['kɜːnl] s **1.** Kern m (*a. fig.*).

2. (*Hafer-, Mais- etc*)Korn n.

ker·o·sene ['kerəsiːn] s **~** Kerosin n.

ketch·up ['ketʃəp] s Ketchup m, n.

ket·tle ['ketl] s Kessel m: **a pretty** (*od.*
fine) **~ of fish** iro. e-e schöne Besche-
rung; **that's a different ~ of fish** das ist
et. ganz anderes; **keep the ~ boiling**
sich über Wasser halten; die Sache in
Schwung halten.

key [kiː] **I** s **1.** Schlüssel m (*a. fig. to* zu).
2. Taste f (*e-s Klaviers, e-r Schreibma-*
schine etc). **3.** ♪ Tonart f: **major** (**mi-**
nor) **~** Dur n (Moll n); **off** (*od.* **out of**) **~**
falsch singen *etc.* **II** *adj* **4.** Schlüssel...
(*a. fig.*). **III** v/t **5.** ♪ stimmen. **6. ~ in**
(*Computer*) *Daten* eintasten, -tippen. **7.**
~ (up) to, ~ in with *fig.* abstimmen auf
(*acc*). **8. ~ up** j-n in nervöse Spannung
versetzen: **~ed up** nervös, aufgeregt
(**about** wegen). **'~·board** s **1.** Tastatur f
(*e-s Klaviers, e-r Schreibmaschine etc*):
~ instrument Tasteninstrument n. **2.**
Schlüsselbrett n. **'~·hole** s Schlüssel-
loch n. **'~·man** s (*irr man*) **1.** Schlüssel-
figur f. **2.** Mann m in e-r Schlüsselstellung. **'~·note** s **1.** ♪ Grundton m. **2.**
fig. Grund-, Leitgedanke m: **~ address**
(*od.* **speech**) *pol.* programmatische
Rede. **'~·phone** s *Br.* Tastentelefon n. **~**
sig·na·ture s ♪ Vorzeichen n u. pl
'~·stone s △ Schlußstein m. **2.** *fig.*
Grundpfeiler m.

kha·ki ['kɑːkɪ] **I** s **1.** Khaki n (*Farbe*). **2.**
Khaki m (*Stoff*); mst pl Khakiuniform
f. **II** *adj* **3.** Khaki...: a) khakifarben, b)
aus Khaki.

kib·itz·er ['kɪbɪtsə] s F **1.** Kiebitz m. **2.**
fig. Besserwisser m.

kick [kɪk] **I** s **1.** (Fuß)Tritt m, Stoß m:
give s.o. a ~ j-m e-n Tritt geben *od.*
versetzen; **get the ~** F (raus)fliegen (*ent-*
lassen werden). **2.** *Fußball:* Schuß m. **3.**
Schwimmen: Beinschlag m. **4.** F
Schwung m: **give s.th. a ~** et. in
Schwung bringen. **5.** F *or* **~s** zum
Spaß; **he gets a ~ out of** es macht ihm
e-n Riesenspaß. **II** v/t **6.** (mit dem Fuß)
stoßen, treten, e-n Tritt geben *od.* versetzen (*dat*): **I could have ~ed myself**
ich hätte mich ohrfeigen *od.* mir in den
Hintern beißen können; **~ bucket** 1. **7.**
loskommen von (*e-r Droge, Gewohn-*
heit etc). **III** v/i **8.** (mit dem Fuß) stoßen, treten (**at** nach); strampeln; aus-

schlagen (*Pferd etc*): → **trace²**. **9.** ~ **about** (*od.* **around**) F sich herumtreiben in (*dat*). **10.** F meutern, rebellieren (**against**, **at** gegen).

Verbindungen mit Adverbien:

kick| a·bout, ~ a·round F I *v/t* **1.** j-n herumkommandieren. **2.** j-n, *et.* herumstoßen, -schubsen. II *v/i* **3.** sich herumtreiben. **~ back** *v/i* **1.** zurücktreten. **2.** *fig.* unangenehme Folgen haben (**at** für); zurückschlagen. **~ in** *v/t* **1.** Tür eintreten. **2.** *Am.* F *et.* beisteuern (**for** zu). **~ off** I *v/i* **1.** *Fußball:* anstoßen. **2.** F anfangen. II *v/t* **3.** *et.* wegtreten, *Schuhe* wegschleudern. **~ out** I *v/i* um sich treten; ausschlagen (*Pferd etc*) II *v/t* F j-n rausschmeißen (**of** aus) (*a. fig.*). **~ o·ver** *v/t* mit dem Fuß umstoßen. **~ up** *v/t* mit dem Fuß hochschleudern, *Staub* aufwirbeln: → **din** I, **dust** 1, **row³** I, *etc.*

'kick·back *s* unangenehme Folge(n *pl*). **'~·off** *s* *Fußball:* Anstoß *m*. **'~·out** *s* F Rausschmiß *m* (*a. fig.*). **~ start·er** *s* Kickstarter *m* (*e-s Motorrads*).

kid¹ [kɪd] *s* **1.** Zicklein *n*, Kitz *n*. **2.** *a.* ~ **leather** Ziegen-, Glacéleder *n*. **3.** F a) Kind *n*: **my ~ brother** mein kleiner Bruder, b) *bsd. Am.* Jugendliche *m*, *f*.

kid² [~] F I *v/t* j-n auf den Arm nehmen. II *v/i* albern; Spaß machen, schwindeln: **he was only ~ding** er hat nur Spaß gemacht, er hat es nicht ernst gemeint; **no ~ding?** im Ernst?, ehrlich?

kid glove *s* Glacéhandschuh *m*: **handle s.o. with ~s** *fig.* j-n mit Samt- *od.* Glacéhandschuhen anfassen.

kid·nap ['kɪdnæp] *v/t pret od. pp* **-naped**, *bsd. Br.* **-napped** kidnappen, entführen. **'kid·nap·(p)er** *s* Kidnapper *m*, Entführer *m*. **'kid·nap·(p)ing** *s* Kidnapping *n*, Entführung *f*.

kid·ney ['kɪdnɪ] *s* **1.** *anat.* Niere *f*. **2.** *fig.* Art *f*, Schlag *m*. **~ bean** *s* ♀ Weiße Bohne. **~ ma·chine** *s* ✄ künstliche Niere: **put on a ~** j-n an e-e künstliche Niere anschließen. **~ stone** *s* ✄ Nierenstein *m*. **~ trans·plant** *s* ✄ Nierenverpflanzung *f*.

kill [kɪl] I *v/t* **1.** töten, umbringen, ermorden: ~ **two birds with one stone** *fig.* zwei Fliegen mit 'einer Klappe schlagen; **be ~ed** *a.* ums Leben kommen, umkommen; → **accident** 2, **action** 6. **2.**

Tier schlachten. **3.** (fast) umbringen: **my feet are ~ing me** m-e Füße bringen mich (noch) um. **4.** *a.* ~ **off** *Knospen, Rost etc* vernichten. **5.** *Gefühle* (ab)töten, ersticken; *Schmerzen* stillen. **6.** *Zeit* totschlagen. **7.** F *Flasche etc* vernichten, austrinken. II *v/i* **8.** töten. **9.** **dressed to ~** F todschick gekleidet, *contp.* aufgedonnert. **'kill·er** I *s* **1.** Mörder *m*, (*kaltblütiger, professioneller*) Killer *m*. **2.** *bsd. in Zssgn* Vertilgungs- *od.* Vernichtungsmittel *n*. II *adj* **3.** tödlich: ~ **whale** *zo.* Schwert-, Mordwal *m*. **'kill·ing** *adj* □ **1.** tödlich. **2.** vernichtend (*a. fig. Blick*), mörderisch (*a. fig. Tempo etc*). **3.** F umwerfend, hinreißend.

'kill·joy *s* Spielverderber(in), Miesmacher(in).

kiln [kɪln] *s* Brenn- *od.* Trockenofen *m*.

ki·lo ['kiːləʊ] *pl* **-los** *s* Kilo *n*.

ki·lo|·gram(me) ['kɪləʊɡræm] *s* Kilogramm *n*. **'~·me·ter**, *bsd. Br.* **'~·me·tre** *s* Kilometer *m*. **'~·watt** *s* ⚡ Kilowatt *n*.

kilt [kɪlt] *s* Kilt *m*, Schottenrock *m*.

ki·mo·no [kɪ'məʊnəʊ] *pl* **-nos** *s* Kimono *m*.

kin [kɪn] *s coll.* (*pl konstruiert*) Blutsverwandtschaft *f*, Verwandte *pl*: **be of no ~ to** nicht verwandt sein mit; → **next** 5.

kind¹ [kaɪnd] *s* **1.** Art *f*, Sorte *f*: **all ~s of** alle möglichen, allerlei; **nothing of the ~** nichts dergleichen. **2.** Art *f*, Wesen *n*: **different in ~** der Art *od.* dem Wesen nach verschieden. **3.** ~ **of** F ein bißchen, irgendwie: **I've ~ of promised it** ich habe es halb u. halb versprochen. **4.** **in ~** in Naturalien *zahlen*.

kind² [~] *adj* (□ *a.* **kindly** II) **1.** freundlich, liebenswürdig, nett (**to** zu): ~ **to animals** tierlieb; **would you be so ~ as to do this for me?** sei so gut *od.* freundlich u. erledige das für mich, erledige das doch bitte für mich; → **enough** III. **2.** herzlich: → **regard** 4.

kin·der·gar·ten ['kɪndəˌɡɑːtn] *s* Kindergarten *m*: **~ teacher** Kindergärtnerin *f*. **kind'heart·ed** *adj* □ gütig, herzig.

kin·dle ['kɪndl] I *v/t* **1.** an-, entzünden. **2.** *Haß etc* entfachen, -flammen, *Interesse etc* wecken. II *v/i* **3.** sich entzünden, Feuer fangen. **4.** *fig.* entbrennen, -flammen.

kin·dling ['kɪndlɪŋ] *s* Anzündmaterial *n*.

kind·ly ['kaɪndlɪ] **I** adj **1.** freundlich, liebenswürdig. **II** adv **2.** → **kind²** 1. **3.** freundlicher-, liebenswürdiger-, netterweise: ~ **tell me** sagen Sie mir bitte. **4.** **take** ~ **to** sich mit et. an- od. befreunden.

kind·ness ['kaɪndnɪs] s **1.** Freundlichkeit f, Liebenswürdigkeit f. **2.** Gefälligkeit f: **do s.o. a** ~ j-m e-e Gefälligkeit erweisen.

kin·dred ['kɪndrɪd] **I** s **1.** (Bluts)Verwandtschaft f. **2.** coll. (pl konstruiert) Verwandte pl, Verwandtschaft f. **II** adj **3.** (bluts)verwandt. **4.** fig. verwandt, ähnlich.

ki·net·ic [kɪ'netɪk] phys. **I** adj (~ally) kinetisch. **II** s pl (sg konstruiert) Kinetik f.

king [kɪŋ] s **1.** König m (a. Schach u. Kartenspiel): ~ **of hearts** Herzkönig; → **English** 3, **evidence** 2. **2.** Damespiel: Dame f. '**king·dom** s **1.** Königreich n. **2.** a. ℒ eccl. Reich n (Gottes). **3.** fig. Reich n: **animal** (**mineral**, **vegetable** od. **plant**) ~ Tier-(Mineral-, Pflanzen)reich. '**king·ly** adj königlich.

'**king·pin** s F wichtigster Mann; Drehu. Angelpunkt m. '~-**size(d)** adj Riesen...: ~ **cigarettes** pl King-size-Zigaretten pl.

kink [kɪŋk] s **1.** Knick m (in Draht etc). **2.** fig. Spleen m, Tick m. **3.** **have a** ~ **in one's back** (**neck**) e-n steifen Rücken (Hals) haben. '**kink·y** adj **1.** kraus (Haar). **2.** fig. spleenig. **3.** F abartig, pervers.

kins·folk ['kɪnzfəʊk] s pl Verwandtschaft f, (Bluts)Verwandte pl.

kin·ship ['kɪnʃɪp] s (Bluts)Verwandtschaft f.

kins·man ['kɪnzmən] s (irr **man**) (Bluts)Verwandte m. '**kins·wom·an** s (irr **woman**) (Bluts)Verwandte f.

ki·osk ['ki:ɒsk] s **1.** Kiosk m. **2.** Br. Telefonzelle f.

kip [kɪp] sl. **I** s **1.** Schlaf m: **have a** ~ pennen. **2.** Schlafstelle f. **II** v/i **3.** pennen. **4.** ~ **down** sich hinhauen.

kip·per ['kɪpə] s Kipper m (Räucherhering).

kiss [kɪs] **I** s **1.** Kuß m: ~ **of life** Br. Mund-zu-Mund-Beatmung f. **II** v/t **2.** küssen: ~ **s.o. good night** j-m e-n Gutenachtkuß geben; ~ **the dust** F ins Gras

beißen. **3.** leicht berühren. **III** v/i **4.** sich küssen. **5.** sich leicht berühren. '**kiss·er** s sl. Schnauze f, Fresse f; Visage f.

'**kiss-proof** adj kußecht.

kit [kɪt] **I** s **1.** (Reise-, Reit- etc)Ausrüstung f, (-)Sachen pl. **2.** ✗ Montur f; Gepäck n. **3.** Arbeitsgerät n, Werkzeug(e pl) n; Werkzeugtasche f, -kasten m. **4.** Baukasten m; Bastelsatz m. **5.** a. **press** ~ Pressemappe f. **II** v/t **6.** oft ~ **out** (od. **up**) ausstatten (**with** mit). ~**bag** s **1.** ✗ Kleider-, Seesack m. **2.** Reisetasche f.

kitch·en ['kɪtʃɪn] **I** s Küche f. **II** adj Küchen...: ~ **knife** (**table**, etc); ~ **garden** (Obst- u.) Gemüsegarten m; ~ **help** Küchenhilfe f; ~ **sink** Ausguß m, Spüle f; **with everything but the** ~ **sink** humor. mit Sack u. Pack. **kitch·en·et(te)** [ˌ~'net] s Kochnische f.

kite [kaɪt] s Drachen m: **fly a** ~ e-n Drachen steigen lassen od. fig. e-n Versuchsballon steigen lassen.

kith [kɪθ] s: **with** ~ **and kin** mit Kind u. Kegel.

kit·ten ['kɪtn] s Kätzchen n: **have** ~**s** Br. F Zustände kriegen. '**kit·ten·ish** adj **1.** (kindlich) verspielt od. ausgelassen. **2.** kokett.

kit·ty ['kɪtɪ] s Kätzchen n.

ki·wi ['ki:wi:] s **1.** orn. Kiwi m. **2.** ℒ Kiwi f. **3.** mst ℒ F Neuseeländer(in). **II** adj **1.** mst ℒ F neuseeländisch.

klax·on ['klæksn] s mot. Hupe f.

klep·to·ma·ni·a [ˌkleptəʊ'meɪnjə] s psych. Kleptomanie f. **klep·to·ma·ni·ac** [~nɪæk] s Kleptomane m, -manin f.

knack [næk] s **1.** Kniff m, Trick m: **get the** ~ **of doing s.th.** dahinterkommen od. herausbekommen, wie man et. tut; **have the** ~ **of s.th.** den Dreh von od. bei et. heraushaben. **2.** Geschick n: **have the** (od. **a**) ~ **of doing s.th.** Geschick od. das Talent haben, et. zu tun.

knack·er ['nækə] s Br. **1.** Abdecker m: ~**'s yard** Abdeckerei f. **2.** Abbruchunternehmer m. '**knack·ered** adj Br. F geschlachtet, kaputt. '**knack·er·y** s Br. Abdeckerei f.

knag [næg] s Knorren m.

knap·sack ['næpsæk] s **1.** ✗ Tornister m. **2.** Rucksack m.

knave [neɪv] s **1.** obs. Schurke m. **2.** Kar-

tenspiel: Bube *m*: ~ *of hearts* Herzbube *m*.

knead [niːd] *v/t* Teig etc (durch)kneten, *Muskeln a.* massieren.

knee [niː] *s* **1.** Knie *n*: *on one's ~s* kniefällig, auf Knien; *bring s.o. to his ~s* j-n auf *od.* in die Knie zwingen; *go (down)* (*od. fall) on one's ~s to* niederknien vor (*dat*), *fig. a.* in die Knie gehen vor (*dat*). **2.** ⚙ Knie(stück) *n*; (Rohr)Krümmer *m.* ~ *bend* s Kniebeuge *f.* '~*cap* s anat. Kniescheibe *f.* ~·'*deep*, ~·'*high adj* knietief, -hoch. ~ *joint* s anat., ⚙ Kniegelenk *n*.

kneel [niːl] *v/i* (*mst irr*) **1.** *a.* ~ *down* (sich) hinknien, niederknien (*to* vor *dat*). **2.** knien, auf den Knien liegen (*before* vor *dat*).

'**knee·pad** s Knieschützer *m.* '~·*pan* → *kneecap.* '~·*room* s ✓, *mot.* Kniefreiheit *f*.

knelt [nelt] *pret u. pp von* **kneel**.

knew [njuː] *pret von* **know**.

knick·er·bock·ers ['nɪkəbɒkəz] *s pl, a. pair of* ~ Knickerbocker *pl*.

knick·ers ['nɪkəz] *s pl, a. pair of* ~ **1.** → *knickerbockers.* **2.** *bsd. Br.* (Damen)Schlüpfer *m*: *get one's* ~ *in a twist* F, *oft humor.* sich ins Hemd machen.

knick-knack ['nɪknæk] *s* **1.** Nippsache *f.* **2.** billiges Schmuckstück. **3.** Spielerei *f*, Schnickschnack *m*.

knife [naɪf] **I** *pl* **knives** [naɪvz] *s* Messer *n*: *before you can say* ~ *bsd. Br.* im Handumdrehen; *to the* ~ bis aufs Messer ~ *into s.o.* j-n auf den Kieker haben; *go under the* ~ ✄ unters Messer kommen. **II** *v/t* mit e-m Messer stechen *od.* verletzen; ~ (*to death*) erstechen. ~ *blade* s Messerklinge *f.* ~ *edge* s Messerschneide *f*: *be balanced on a* ~ *fig.* auf des Messers Schneide stehen. ~ *point* s Messerspitze *f*: *at* ~ mit vorgehaltenem Messer.

knight [naɪt] **I** *s* **1.** *hist.* Ritter *m* (*Br. a. Adelsstufe*). **2.** *Schach*: Springer *m*, Pferd *n*. **II** *v/t* **3.** zum Ritter schlagen. '**knight·ly** *adj u. adv* ritterlich.

knit [nɪt] (*a. irr*) **I** *v/t* **1.** stricken. **2.** *a.* ~ *together* zs.-fügen, verbinden (*a. fig.*). **3.** *fig.* verknüpfen. **4.** *Stirn* runzeln; *Augenbrauen* zs.-ziehen. **II** *v/i* **5.** stricken. '**knit·ting I** *s* **1.** Stricken *n.* **2.**

Strickarbeit *f*, -zeug *n*. **II** *adj* **3.** Strick...: ~ *needle*.

'**knit·wear** s Strickwaren *pl*.

knives [naɪvz] *pl von* **knife**.

knob [nɒb] *s* **1.** (*runder*) Kniff, Knauf *m*. **2.** Beule *f*, Höcker *m*. **3.** *bsd. Br.* Stück(chen) *n* (*Zucker etc*).

knock [nɒk] **I** *s* **1.** Schlag *m*, Stoß *m*. **2.** Klopfen *n* (*a. mot.*): *there is a* ~ (*at* [*Am.* on] *the door*) es klopft. **II** *v/t* **3.** schlagen, stoßen: ~ *one's head against* sich den Kopf anschlagen an (*dat*); ~ *one's head against a brick wall fig.* mit dem Kopf gegen die Wand rennen. **III** *v/i* **4.** schlagen, klopfen: ~ *at* (*Am.* on) *the door* an die Tür klopfen. **5.** schlagen, prallen, stoßen (*against, into* gegen; *on* auf *acc*). **6.** ⚙ klopfen (*Motor, Brennstoff*). **7.** ~ *about* (*od. around*) F sich herumtreiben in (*dat*); herumliegen in (*dat*) (*Gegenstand*).

Verbindungen mit Adverbien:

knock| a·bout, ~ a·round I *v/t* **1.** herumstoßen. **II** *v/i* **2.** F sich herumtreiben: ~ *with a.* gehen mit (*e-m Mädchen etc*). **3.** F herumliegen (*Gegenstand*). ~ *back v/t* **1.** *Stuhl* zurückstoßen. **2.** *bsd. Br.* F *Getränk* runterkippen. ~ *down v/t* **1.** a) umstoßen, umwerfen, b) niederschlagen, c) an-, umfahren, b) überfahren, d) F umhauen, sprachlos machen. **2.** *Gebäude etc* abreißen, abbrechen. **3.** (*to* auf *acc*; £2 *um* 2 *Pfund*) j-n, *Preis* herunterhandeln; *mit dem Preis* heruntergehen. **4.** *knock s.th. down to s.o.* (*Auktion*) j-m et. zuschlagen (*at, for* für). ~ *in v/t* **1.** *Nagel* einschlagen. ~ *off* I *v/t* **1.** herunter-, abschlagen. **2.** F aufhören mit: *knock it off!* hör auf (*damit*)! ~ *work*(*ing*) → 6b. **3.** F *Arbeit* erledigen. **4.** F j-n umlegen. **5.** F *Essen* wegputzen. **II** *v/i* **6.** F a) *allg.* aufhören, b) Feierabend *od.* Schluß machen. ~ *out v/t* **1.** herausschlagen, -klopfen (*of* aus), *Pfeife* ausklopfen; → *bottom* 3. **2.** a) bewußtlos schlagen, b) *Boxen*: k.o. schlagen, ausknocken, c) betäuben (*Droge etc*), d) F umhauen (*sprachlos machen, hinreißen*). ~ *to·geth·er v/t* **1.** F et. schnell zs.-zimmern, *Essen etc* (her)zaubern. ~ *o·ver v/t* **1.** umstoßen, -werfen, b) an-, umfahren, umstoßen. **2.** überfahren. ~ *up* I *v/t* **1.** hochschlagen, in die Höhe schlagen. **2.**

Br. F herausklopfen, *(durch Klopfen)* wecken. **3.** *Br.* F *Geld* verdienen. **4.** *sl. Mädchen* anbumsen. **II** *v/i* **5.** *Tennis etc:* sich einschlagen *od.* einspielen.

'knock·a·bout *adj* **1.** strapazierfähig *(Kleidung etc).* **2.** *thea. etc* Klamauk...: **~ comedy** Klamaukstück *n.* '**~·down I** *adj* **1.** niederschmetternd *(a. fig.).* **2. ~ price** Schleuderpreis *m:* **at a ~** spottbillig. **II** *s* **3.** *Boxen:* Niederschlag *m.*

knock·er ['nɒkə] *s* **1.** (Tür)Klopfer *m.* **2.** *pl sl.* Titten *pl.*

‚knock|-'kneed *adj* X-beinig: **be ~** X-Beine haben. **‚~-'knees** *s pl* X-Beine *pl.* '**~-out I** *s* **1.** *Boxen:* K.o. *m:* **win by a ~** durch K.o. gewinnen. **2.** F tolle Person *od.* Sache; Attraktion *f;* Bombenerfolg *m.* **II** *adj* **3.** *Boxen:* K.-o.-...: **~ system** *(Sport)* K.-o.-System *n.* '**~-up** *s Tennis etc:* Einschlagen *n,* -spielen *n.*

knoll [nəʊl] *s* Hügel *m.*

knot [nɒt] **I** *s* **1.** Knoten *m:* **make** *(od.* **tie) a ~** e-n Knoten machen; **tie s.o.** *(up)* **in ~s** F j-n völlig durcheinanderbringen. **2.** Astknoten *m,* Knorren *m.* **3.** ♣ Knoten *m,* Seemeile *f.* **4.** *fig.* Knoten *m,* Schwierigkeit *f:* **cut the ~** den Knoten durchhauen. **II** *v/t* **5.** (e-n) Knoten machen in *(acc).* **6.** (ver)knoten, (-)knüpfen. **III** *v/i* **7.** sich verknoten. '**knot·ty** *adj* **1.** knotig. **2.** knorrig *(Holz).* **3.** *fig.* verwickelt, kompliziert.

know [nəʊ] **I** *v/t* (*irr*) **1.** *allg.* wissen. **2.** können: **~ how to do s.th.** et. tun können. **3.** kennen: a) sich auskennen in *(dat),* b) vertraut sein mit *(c),* c) bekannt sein mit. **4.** erfahren, erleben: **he has ~n better days** er hat schon bessere Tage gesehen. **5.** (wieder)erkennen *(by* an *dat);* unterscheiden (können) *(from* von): **~ apart** auseinanderhalten. **II** *v/i*

(*irr*) **6.** wissen *(of* von, um), Bescheid wissen *(about* über *acc):* **you never ~** man kann nie wissen; **~ better than to do s.th.** sich davor hüten, et. zu tun. **III** *s* **7. be in the ~** Bescheid wissen. '**~-all** *s* Besserwisser *m.* '**~-how** *s* Know-how *n* *(a.* ✝): **industrial ~** praktische Betriebserfahrung.

know·ing ['nəʊɪŋ] *adj* **1.** klug, gescheit. **2.** schlau, durchtrieben. **3.** verständnisvoll, wissend *(Blick).* '**know·ing·ly** *adv* **1.** → **knowing.** **2.** wissentlich, bewußt, absichtlich.

knowl·edge ['nɒlɪdʒ] *s* **1.** Kenntnis *f:* **bring s.th. to s.o.'s ~** j-n von et. in Kenntnis setzen; **it has come to my ~** ich habe erfahren *(that* daß); **(not)** *(to)* **my ~** m-s Wissens (nicht); **without my ~** ohne mein Wissen. **2.** Wissen *n,* Kenntnisse *pl:* **have a good ~ of** viel verstehen von, sich gut auskennen in *(dat).*

known [nəʊn] **I** *pp von* **know.** **II** *adj* bekannt *(as* als; *for* für; *to s.o.* j-m): **~ to the police** polizeibekannt; **make ~** bekanntmachen; **make o.s. ~ to s.o.** sich vorstellen.

knuck·le ['nʌkl] **I** *s* **1.** *anat.* (Finger)Knöchel *m:* → **rap¹** 1, 3. **2.** *(Kalbs-, Schweins)*Haxe *f,* (-)Hachse *f:* **near the ~** F reichlich gewagt *(Witz etc).* **II** *v/i* **3. ~ down** sich anstrengen *od.* dahinterklemmen: **~ down to work** sich an die Arbeit machen, sich hinter die Arbeit klemmen. **4. ~ under** sich unterwerfen *od.* beugen *(to* dat), klein beigeben. '**~·dust·er** *s* Schlagring *m.*

kook [kuːk] *s Am.* F Spinner *m.*

Ko·ran [kɒ'rɑːn] *s eccl.* Koran *m.*

kraut [kraʊt] *s sl. contp.* Deutsche *m, f.*

Krem·lin ['kremlɪn] *npr* Kreml *m.*

L

lab [læb] *s* F Labor *n.*

la·bel ['leɪbl] **I** *s* **1.** Etikett *n,* (Klebe-, Anhänge)Zettel *m,* (-)Schild(chen) *n.* **II** *v/t pret u. pp* **-beled,** *bsd. Br.* **-belled**

2. etikettieren, beschriften. **3.** als ... bezeichnen, zu ... stempeln: **be ~(l)ed a criminal** zum Verbrecher gestempelt werden.

la·bi·al ['leɪbjəl] *s ling.* Lippen-, Labiallaut *m*.

la·bor ['leɪbə] *Am.* **I** → **labour**, *etc.* **II** *adj* **1.** Gewerkschafts... **2.** *~ union* Gewerkschaft *f*.

la·bor·a·to·ry [lə'bɒrətərɪ] *s* Labor(atorium) *n*: *~ assistant* Laborant(in).

la·bo·ri·ous [lə'bɔːrɪəs] *adj* □ **1.** mühsam. **2.** schwerfällig (*Stil*). **3.** arbeitsam, fleißig.

la·bour ['leɪbə] *bsd. Br.* **I** *s* **1.** (schwere) Arbeit. **2.** Mühe *f*, Plage *f*: *lost ~* vergebliche Mühe. **3.** ✝ Arbeiterschaft *f*; Arbeiter *pl*, Arbeitskräfte *pl*. **4.** ♀ *pol.* die Labour Party (*Großbritanniens etc*). **5.** ♂ Wehen *pl*: *be in ~* in den Wehen liegen. **II** *v/i* **6.** (schwer) arbeiten (*at* an *dat*), sich bemühen (*for* um), sich anstrengen (*to do* zu tun). **7.** *a. ~ along* sich mühsam fortbewegen: *~ through* sich kämpfen durch (*Schlamm, Buch etc*). **8.** (*under*) zu leiden haben (unter *dat*), zu kämpfen haben (mit): befangen sein (in *dat*). **9.** ♂ in den Wehen liegen. **III** *v/t* **10.** ausführlich *od.* umständlich behandeln, breitwalzen. **IV** *adj* **11.** Arbeits...; Arbeiter... **12.** ♀ *pol.* Labour...: *~ Party* Labour Party *f*. **'la·bour·er** *s bsd. Br.* (*bsd.* Hilfs)Arbeiter *m*.

'la·bour|-in,ten·sive ['læsəreɪt] *adj* □ *bsd. Br.* arbeitsintensiv. **'~,sav·ing** *adj bsd. Br.* arbeitssparend.

lab·y·rinth ['læbərɪnθ] *s* Labyrinth *n*, *fig. a.* Gewirr *n*.

lace [leɪs] **I** *s* **1.** *Textilwesen:* Spitze *f*. **2.** Litze *f*, Tresse *f*, Borte *f*. **3.** Schnürband *n*, -senkel *m*. **4.** Schuß *m* Alkohol (*in Getränken*): *with a ~ of rum* mit e-m Schuß Rum. **II** *v/t* **5.** *a. ~ up* (zu-, zs.-)schnüren. **6.** mit Spitzen *od.* Litzen besetzen. **7.** *~ one's tea with rum* sich e-n Schuß Rum in den Tee geben; *~ s.o.'s beer with vodka* j-m heimlich Wodka ins Bier schütten; *tea ~d with rum* Tee mit e-m Schuß Rum. **III** *v/i* **8.** *~ into s.o.* F über j-n herfallen (*a. mit Worten*).

lac·er·ate ['læsəreɪt] *v/t Gesicht etc* aufreißen; zerschneiden; zerkratzen. **,lac·er'a·tion** *s* Riß-; Schnitt-, Kratzwunde *f*.

lach·ry·mal ['lækrɪml] *adj* **1.** Tränen...: *~ gland anat.* Tränendrüse *f*. **2.** → **lach-**

---

ry·mose 1, 2. **lach·ry·mose** ['~məʊs] *adj* □ **1.** tränenreich. **2.** weinerlich. **3.** traurig, ergreifend.

lack [læk] **I** *s* **1.** Mangel *m* (*of* an *dat*): *~ of sleep* fehlender Schlaf; *for* (*od. through*) *~ of time* aus Zeitmangel. **II** *v/t* **2.** nicht haben, Mangel haben *od.* leiden an (*dat*): *we ~ coal* es fehlt uns an Kohle. **3.** es fehlen lassen an (*dat*). **III** *v/i* **4.** a) *be ~ing* fehlen, b) *~ in* Mangel haben *od.* leiden an (*dat*): *he ~ing in courage* ihm fehlt der Mut. **5.** *~ for nothing* von allem genug haben: *he ~s for nothing* es fehlt ihm an nichts.

lack·a·dai·si·cal [,lækə'deɪzɪkl] *adj* □ **1.** lustlos. **2.** nachlässig (*about* in *dat*).

lack·ey ['lækɪ] *s* Lakai *m* (*a. fig. contp.*).

lack·ing ['lækɪŋ] *adj* **1.** *be found ~* sich nicht bewähren. **2.** *Br.* F beschränkt, dumm.

'lack|,lus·ter *adj Am.*, **'~,lus·tre** *adj bsd. Br.* glanzlos, matt.

la·con·ic [lə'kɒnɪk] *adj* (*~ally*) **1.** lakonisch. **2.** wortkarg.

lac·quer ['lækə] **I** *s* **1.** (Farb)Lack *m*. **2.** (Haar)Festiger *m*. **II** *v/t* **3.** lackieren.

la·crosse [lə'krɒs] *s Sport:* Lacrosse *n* (*Ballspiel*).

lad [læd] *s* **1.** junger Kerl *od.* Bursche. **2.** *a bit of a ~ Br.* F ein ziemlicher Draufgänger.

lad·der ['lædə] **I** *s* **1.** Leiter *f* (*a. fig.*). **2.** *bsd. Br.* Laufmasche *f*. **II** *v/i* **3.** *bsd. Br.* Laufmaschen bekommen. **'~-proof** *adj* maschenfest.

lad·en ['leɪdn] *adj* **1.** (schwer) beladen (*with* mit). **2.** *fig.* bedrückt (*with* von): *~ with guilt* schuldbeladen.

la-di-da [,lɑːdɪ'dɑː] *adj* F affektiert, affig.

la·dies' *choice* → Damenwahl *f*. **~ man** *s* (*irr man*) Frauenheld *m*. **~ room** *s* Damentoilette *f*.

la·dle ['leɪdl] **I** *s* **1.** Schöpflöffel *m*, -kelle *f*. **2.** ⚙ Schaufel *f* (*e-s Baggers etc*). **II** *v/t* **3.** *a. ~ out* (aus)schöpfen. **4.** *a. ~ out* austeilen (*a. fig.*).

la·dy ['leɪdɪ] **I** *s* **1.** Dame *f*: *ladies and gentlemen* m-e Damen u. Herren. **2.** ♀ Lady *f* (*Titel*). **3.** ♀ *eccl.* Unsere Liebe Frau, die Mutter Gottes. **4.** *Ladies pl* (*sg konstruiert*) Damentoilette *f*. **II** *adj* **5.** weiblich: *~ doctor* Ärztin *f*. **'~-bird**, *Am.* **'~-bug** *s zo.* Marienkäfer *m*. **,~-in-'wait·ing** *pl* **la·dies-in-**

-'wait·ing s Hofdame f. '∼‚kill·er s F Ladykiller m, Herzensbrecher m. '∼-like adj damenhaft.

la·dy's man → ladies' man.

lag¹ [læg] I v/i 1. mst ∼ behind zurückbleiben, nicht mitkommen (beide a. fig.): ∼ behind s.o. hinter j-m zurückbleiben. 2. mst ∼ behind sich verzögern. II s 3. → time lag.

lag² [∼] v/t ⊙ verschalen; isolieren, ummanteln.

la·ger ['lɑ:gə] s Lagerbier n.

la·goon [lə'gu:n] s Lagune f.

laid [leɪd] pret u. pp von lay¹.

lain [leɪn] pp von lie².

lair [leə] s 1. zo. Lager n; Bau m; Höhle f. 2. Versteck n.

la·i·ty ['leɪətɪ] s Laien pl.

lake [leɪk] s See m. ∼ dwell·ings s pl Pfahlbauten pl.

lam [læm] sl. I v/t verdreschen, -möbeln. II v/i: ∼ into s.o. auf j-n eindreschen; über j-n herfallen (a. mit Worten).

la·ma ['lɑ:mə] s eccl. Lama m.

lamb [læm] I s 1. Lamm n: (as) gentle (od. meek) as a ∼ lammfromm. 2. Lamm n: a) gastr. Lammfleisch n: ∼ chop Lammkotelett n, b) → lambskin. II v/i 3. lammen.

lam·baste [læm'beɪst] v/t sl. 1. → lam I. 2. fig. herunterputzen, zs.-stauchen.

'lamb|·like adj lammfromm. '∼·skin s 1. Lammfell n. 2. Schafleder n.

'lamb's wool s Lambswool f, Lammwolle f.

lame [leɪm] I adj □ 1. a) lahm: walk ∼ly hinken (Tier a.) lahmen, b) gelähmt. 2. fig. lahm: a) faul (Ausrede), b) schwach (Argument), c) matt, schwach (Anstrengungen). II v/t 3. lähmen (a. fig.). ∼ duck s F 1. Niete f, Versager m (a. Sache). 2. pol. Am. nicht wiedergewähltes Kongreßmitglied bis zum Ablauf s-r Amtszeit.

la·mel·la [lə'melə] pl -lae [∼li:], -las s Lamelle f.

lame·ness ['leɪmnɪs] s Lahmheit f (a. fig.).

la·ment [lə'ment] I v/i 1. jammern, (weh)klagen, contp. lamentieren (for, over um). 2. trauern (for, over um). II v/t 3. beklagen: a) bejammern, bedauern, b) betrauern. III s Jammer m, (Weh)Klage f. 5. Klagelied n.

lam·en·ta·ble ['læməntəbl] adj □ 1. beklagenswert, bedauerlich. 2. contp. erbärmlich, kläglich. lam·en·ta·tion [∼men'teɪʃn] s 1. (Weh)Klage f. 2. contp. Lamento n, Lamentieren n.

lam·i·nat·ed ['læmɪneɪtɪd] adj ⊙ laminiert, geschichtet: ∼ glass Verbundglas n.

lamp [læmp] s Lampe f, (Straßen)Laterne f.

lam·poon [læm'pu:n] I s Spott-, Schmähschrift f. II v/t (schriftlich) verspotten.

'lamp-post s Laternenpfahl m: → between 2.

'lamp-shade s Lampenschirm m.

lance [lɑ:ns] I s Lanze f. II v/t ✠ Geschwür etc (mit e-r Lanzette) öffnen.

lan·cet ['lɑ:nsɪt] s 1. ✠ Lanzette f. 2. △ a) a. ∼ arch Spitzbogen m, b) a. ∼ window Spitzbogenfenster n.

land [lænd] I s 1. Land n (Ggs. Wasser, Luft): by ∼ auf dem Landwege; by ∼ and sea zu Wasser u. zu Lande; see (od. find out) how the ∼ lies fig. die Lage peilen; sich e-n Überblick verschaffen. 2. Land n, Boden m: ploughed ∼ Akkerland. 3. Land n, Staat m. 4. fig. Land n, Reich n: → milk I. II v/i 5. ✈ landen, ♨ a. anlegen. 6. oft ∼ up landen, (an)kommen: ∼ up in prison im Gefängnis landen. III v/t 7. Personen, Güter, Flugzeug landen, Güter ausladen, ♨ a. löschen. 8. j-n bringen: ∼ o.s. (od. be ∼ed) in trouble in Schwierigkeiten geraten od. kommen. 9. F Schlag, Treffer landen, anbringen: he ∼ed him one er knallte ihm eine. 10. F j-n, et. kriegen, erwischen, Preis ergattern. 11. ∼ s.o. s.th. F j-m et. einbringen.

land·ed ['lændɪd] adj Land-, Grund...: ∼ property Land-, Grundbesitz m.

land forc·es s pl ✕ Landstreitkräfte pl.

land·ing ['lændɪŋ] s 1. ✈ Landung f, Landen n, ♨ a. Anlegen n. 2. (Treppen)Absatz m. ∼ ap·proach s ✈ Landeanflug m. ∼ field s ✈ Landeplatz m. ∼ gear s ✈ Fahrgestell n, -werk n. ∼ per·mit s ✈ Landeerlaubnis f.

land|·la·dy ['læn‚leɪdɪ] s (Haus-, Gast-, Pensions)Wirtin f. ∼·lord ['læn∼] s 1. Grundeigentümer m, -besitzer m. 2. (Haus-, Gast-, Pensions)Wirt m. ∼·lub·ber ['lænd‚∼] s ♨ Landratte f. '∼·mark s

1. Grenzstein *m*, -zeichen *n*. **2.** ♣ Landmarke *f*, Seezeichen *n*. **3.** Wahrzeichen *n* (*e-r Stadt etc*). **4.** *fig.* Mark-, Meilenstein *m*. **~ of·fice** *s Am.* Grundbuchamt *n*. **'~,own·er** *s* Grundbesitzer(in), -eigentümer(in). **~ reg·is·ter** *s Br.* Grundbuch *n*. **~ reg·is·try** *s Br.* Grundbuchamt *n*. **~·scape** ['lænskeɪp] *s* Landschaft *f* (*a. paint.*): **~ architect** Landschaftsarchitekt *m*; **~ gardener** Landschaftsgärtner *m*; **~ painter** Landschaftsmaler *m*. **'~·slide** *s* **1.** Erdrutsch *m*. **2.** *a.* **~ victory** (*od.* **win**) *pol.* überwältigender Wahlsieg.

land·ward(s) ['lændwəd(z)] *adv* land(ein)wärts.

lane [leɪn] *s* **1.** (Feld)Weg *m*. **2.** Gasse *f*: a) Sträßchen *n*, b) Durchgang *m* (*zwischen Menschenreihen etc*): **form a ~** Spalier stehen, e-e Gasse bilden. **3.** Schneise *f*. **4.** ♣ Fahrrinne *f*. **5.** ✈ Flugschneise *f*. **6.** *mot.* (Fahr)Spur *f*: **change ~s** die Spur wechseln; **get in ~** sich einordnen. **7.** *Sport:* (einzelne) Bahn.

lan·guage ['læŋgwɪdʒ] *s* **1.** Sprache *f*. **2.** Sprache *f*, Ausdrucks-, Redeweise *f*: → **bad** 3, **strong** 7. **3.** (Fach)Sprache *f*. **~ course** *s* Sprachkurs *m*. **~ la·bo·ra·to·ry** *s* Sprachlabor *n*. **~ school** *s* Sprachenschule *f*.

lan·guid ['læŋgwɪd] *adj* □ **1.** schwach, matt. **2.** *fig.* lau, interesselos.

lan·guish ['læŋgwɪʃ] *v/i* **1.** ermatten, erschlaffen. **2.** erlahmen (*Interesse etc*). **3.** sich sehnen, schmachten (**for** nach). **'lan·guish·ing** *adj* □ **1.** sehnsüchtig, schmachtend (*Blick etc*).

lan·guor ['læŋgə] *s* **1.** Schwachheit *f*, Mattigkeit *f*. **2.** *fig.* Lauheit *f*, Interesselosigkeit *f*. **3.** einschläfernde Schwüle. **'lan·guor·ous** *adj* □ **1.** → **languid**. **2.** einschläfernd schwül.

lank [læŋk] *adj* □ **1.** hager, mager. **2.** glatt (*Haar*). **'lank·y** *adj* □ schlaksig.

lan·tern ['læntən] *s* Laterne *f*.

lap¹ [læp] *s* Schoß *m* (*a. fig.*): **drop** (*od.* **fall**) **into s.o.'s ~** j-m in den Schoß fallen.

lap² [~] **I** *s* **1.** wickeln ([a]round um). **2.** einschlagen, -wickeln (**in** *in acc*). **3.** hinausragen über (*acc*). **4.** *Sport:* überrunden. **II** *v/i* **5.** überstehen, hinausragen (**over** über *acc*). **6.** sich überlappen. **III**

s **7.** *Sport:* Runde *f*: **~ of hono(u)r** Ehrenrunde.

lap³ [~] **I** *v/t* **1.** (sch)lecken: **~ up** a) auf(sch)lecken, b) *fig.* F fressen, schlucken (*kritiklos glauben*), c) *fig.* F Komplimente *etc* gierig aufnehmen. **II** *v/i* **2.** plätschern (**against** gegen, an *acc*). **3.** (sch)lecken: **take a ~ at** (sch)lecken an (*dat*). **4.** Plätschern *n*.

lap belt *s* ✈, *mot.* Beckengurt *m*.

la·pel [lə'pel] *s* Aufschlag *m*, Revers *n*, *m*.

lapse [læps] **I** *s* **1.** Versehen *n*, (kleiner) Fehler *od.* Irrtum. **2.** Vergehen *n*, Entgleisung *f*. **3.** Zeitspanne *f*. **4.** ⚖ Verfall *m*, Erlöschen *n*. **II** *v/i* **5.** vergehen, -streichen (*Zeit*); ablaufen (*Frist*). **6.** verfallen, -sinken (**into** in *acc*). **7.** ⚖ verfallen, erlöschen (*Anspruch etc*).

lar·ce·ny ['lɑːsənɪ] *s* ⚖ Diebstahl *m*: **grand** (**petty**) **~** schwerer (einfacher) Diebstahl.

larch [lɑːtʃ] *s* ♣ Lärche *f*.

lard [lɑːd] **I** *s* **1.** Schweinefett *n*, -schmalz *n*. **II** *v/t* **2.** einfetten. **3.** *Fleisch* spicken: **~ing needle** (*od.* **pin**) Spicknadel *f*. **4.** *fig.* spicken, (aus)schmücken (**with** mit).

lard·er ['lɑːdə] *s* **1.** Speisekammer *f*. **2.** Speiseschrank *m*.

large [lɑːdʒ] *adj* (□ → **largely**) **1.** *allg.* groß: (**as**) **~ as life** in voller Lebensgröße; **~r than life** überlebensgroß. **2.** groß (*Familie etc*), (*Einkommen etc a.*) beträchtlich, (*Mahlzeit*) ausgiebig, reichlich. **3.** umfassend, weitgehend (*Vollmachten etc*). **4.** Groß...: **~ consumer** Großverbraucher *m*. **5.** F großspurig. **II** *adv* **6.** **talk ~** F große Töne spucken. **III** *s* **7.** *at* **~** a) in Freiheit, auf freiem Fuß: **set at ~** auf freien Fuß setzen; b) (sehr) ausführlich, c) in der Gesamtheit: **the nation at ~** die ganze Nation.

'large·ly *adv* **1.** großen-, größtenteils. **2.** allgemein.

large-'mind·ed *adj* □ aufgeschlossen, tolerant.

large·ness ['lɑːdʒnɪs] *s* **1.** Größe *f*. **2.** F Großspurigkeit *f*.

'large-scale *adj* groß(angelegt), Groß...: **~ experiment** Großversuch *m*.

lar·gess(e) [lɑː'dʒes] *s* Freigebigkeit *f*, Großzügigkeit *f*.

lar·go ['lɑːgəʊ] *pl* **-gos** *s* ♪ Largo *n*.

lar·i·at ['læriət] *s bsd. Am.* Lasso *n*, *m*.

lark¹ [lɑːk] *s orn.* Lerche *f*.

lark² [~] F **I** *s* Jux *m*, Ulk *m*: **for a** ~ zum Spaß, aus Jux. **II** *v/i mst* ~ **about** (*od. around*) Blödsinn machen, herumalbern.

lark·spur ['lɑːkspɜː] *s* ♣ Rittersporn *m*.

lar·va ['lɑːvə] *pl* **-vae** ['~viː] *s zo.* Larve *f*.

lar·yn·gi·tis [,lærin'dʒaitis] *s* ♣ Kehlkopfentzündung *f*. **lar·ynx** ['læriŋks] *pl* **la·ryn·ges** [lə'rindʒiːz], **'lar·ynx·es** *s anat.* Kehlkopf *m*.

las·civ·i·ous [lə'siviəs] *adj* □ **1.** geil, lüstern. **2.** lasziv, schlüpfrig.

la·ser ['leizə] *s phys.* Laser *m*. ~ **beam** *s* Laserstrahl *m*.

lash¹ [læʃ] **I** *s* **1.** Peitschenschnur *f*. **2.** Peitschenhieb *m*. **3.** *fig.* (Peitschen-)Hieb *m* (*at gegen*). **4.** Peitschen *n* (*a. fig.*). **5.** (Augen)Wimper *f*. **II** *v/t* **6.** (aus)peitschen. **7.** *fig.* a) peitschen, b) peitschen an (*acc*) *od.* gegen. **8.** peitschen mit: ~ **its tail** mit dem Schwanz um sich schlagen. **9.** *fig.* aufpeitschen (**into** zu): ~ **o.s. into a fury** sich in Wut hineinsteigern. **10.** *fig.* geißeln, vom Leder ziehen gegen. **III** *v/i* **11.** ~ **against** → 7b; ~ **down** niederprasseln (*Regen*). **12.** schlagen (**at** nach): ~ **a·bout** (*od. around*) (wild) um sich schlagen; ~ **into** a) einschlagen auf (*acc*), b) *fig.* j-n zs.-stauchen; ~ **out** (wild) um sich schlagen; ausschlagen (*Pferd*); ~ **out at** a) einschlagen auf (*acc*), b) *a.* ~ **out against** → 10.

lash² [~] *v/t* **1.** a. ~ **down** (fest)binden (**to**, **on** an *dat*). **2.** ♣ (fest)zurren.

lash·ing ['læʃiŋ] *s* **1.** Auspeitschung *f*. **2.** *pl bsd. Br.* F e-e Unmenge (**of** von, an *dat*): ~**s of** (*od.* **to**) **drink** jede Menge zu trinken.

lass [læs], **las·sie** ['læsi] *s* **1.** Mädchen *n*. **2.** Freundin *f*, Schatz *m*.

las·si·tude ['læsitjuːd] *s* Mattigkeit *f*, Abgespanntheit *f*.

las·so [læ'suː] **I** *pl* **-so(e)s** *s* Lasso *n*, *m*. **II** *v/t* mit e-m Lasso (ein)fangen.

last¹ [lɑːst] **I** *adj* (□ → **lastly**) **1.** letzt: ~ **but one** vorletzt; ~ **but two** drittletzt. **2.** letzt, vorig: ~ **Monday** (am) letzten *od.* vorigen Montag; ~ **night** gestern abend; letzte Nacht. **3.** letzt (*allein übrigbleibend*): **my** ~ **hope.** **4.** letzt (*am wenigsten erwartet od. geeignet*): **the** ~ **thing I would do** das letzte, was ich tun würde. **II** *adv* **5.** zuletzt, an letzter Stelle: **he came** ~ er kam als letzter; ~ **but not least** nicht zuletzt, nicht zu vergessen. **6.** zuletzt, zum letzten Mal. **7.** *in Zssgn:* ~**mentioned** letztgenannt, -erwähnt. **III** *s* **8.** *at* ~ endlich, schließlich, zuletzt. **9.** *der, die, das* Letzte: **the** ~ **to arrive** der letzte, der ankam; **to the** ~ bis zum äußersten; bis zum Ende *od.* Schluß.

last² **I** *v/i* **1.** (an-, fort)dauern. **2.** *a.* ~ **out** durch-, aushalten. **3.** (sich) halten. **4.** *a.* ~ **out** (aus)reichen (*Geld etc*). **II** *v/t* **5.** *j-m* reichen (*Geld etc*). **6.** *mst* ~ **out** überdauern, -leben.

last³ [~] *s* Leisten *m*: **stick to one's** ~ *fig.* bei s-m Leisten bleiben.

'last-ditch *adj* allerletzt: ~ **attempt** a. letzter verzweifelter Versuch.

last·ing ['lɑːstiŋ] *adj* □ **1.** dauerhaft: a) andauernd, beständig: ~ **peace** dauerhafter Friede; ~ **effect** anhaltende Wirkung; ~ **memories** *pl* bleibende Erinnerungen *pl*, b) haltbar. **2.** nachhaltig (*Eindruck etc*).

last·ly ['lɑːstli] *adv* zuletzt, zum Schluß.

latch [lætʃ] **I** *s* **1.** Schnappriegel *m*. **2.** Schnappschloß *n*. **II** *v/t* **3.** ein-, zuklinken. **III** *v/i* **4.** einschnappen. **5.** ~ **on** F kapieren: ~ **on to** (*od.* **onto**) **s.th.** *etc.* kapieren. '~**key** *s* Haus-, Wohnungsschlüssel *m*: ~ **child** (F **kid**) Schlüsselkind *n*.

late [leit] **I** *adj* (□ → **lately**) **1.** spät: **at a** ~ **hour** spät (*a. fig.*), zu später Stunde; ~ **shift** ✝ Spätschicht *f*; **it's getting** ~ es ist schon spät. **2.** vorgerückt, Spät...: ~ **summer** Spätsommer *m*. **3.** verspätet: **be** ~ zu spät kommen (**for dinner** zum Essen), sich verspäten; Verspätung haben (*Zug etc*). **4.** **the latest fashion** die neueste Mode. **5.** letzt, früher, ehemalig; verstorben. **II** *adv* **6.** spät: **as** ~ **as last year** erst *od.* noch letztes Jahr; **see you** ~ auf bald, bis später; ~ **on** später; ~ **sleep** II. **7.** zu spät: **the train came** ~ der Zug hatte Verspätung. '~**com·er** *s* Zuspätkommende *m*, *f*; Zuspätgekommene *m*, *f*.

late·ly ['leitli] *adv* **1.** vor kurzem, kürzlich. **2.** in letzter Zeit, neuerdings. '**late·ness** *s* **1.** späte Zeit: **the** ~ **of his arrival**

law

s-e späte Ankunft. **2.** Verspätung *f*, Zu-spätkommen *n*.

la·tent ['leɪtənt] *adj* □ latent (*a. ✹ etc*), verborgen.

lat·er·al ['lætərəl] *adj* seitlich, Seiten... **'lat·er·al·ly** *adv* **1.** seitlich, seitwärts. **2.** von der Seite.

la·test ['leɪtɪst] *I adj u. adv sup von* **late**. **II** *s at the* **~** spätestens.

lath [lɑ:θ] *s* **1.** Latte *f*, Leiste *f*: (**as**) **thin as a ~** spindeldürr. **2.** *coll.* Latten *pl*, Leisten *pl*.

lathe [leɪð] *s* ⚙ Drehbank *f*.

lath·er ['lɑ:ðə] *s* **1.** (Seifen)Schaum *m*. **2. get in a ~, work o.s. up into a ~** F außer sich geraten (**over** wegen). **II** *v/t* **3.** einseifen. **4.** F verprügeln. **III** *v/i* **5.** schäumen.

Lat·in ['lætɪn] *ling.* **I** *adj* lateinisch. **II** *s* Latein(isch) *n*. **~ A·mer·i·can** *adj* la-teinamerikanisch. **II** *s* Lateinamerika-ner(in).

Lat·in·ism ['lætɪnɪzəm] *s ling.* Latinis-mus *m*.

lat·i·tude ['lætɪtju:d] *s* **1.** *geogr.* Breite *f*: **in these ~s** in diesen Breiten *od.* Ge-genden; → **degree** 2, **parallel** 3. **2.** *fig.* Spielraum *m*, (Bewegungs)Freiheit *f*.

la·trine [lə'tri:n] *s* Latrine *f*.

lat·ter ['lætə] *adj* **1.** letzterwähnt, -ge-nannt (*von zweien*): → **former** 2. **2.** letzt, später: **the ~ half of June** die zweite Junihälfte.

lat·tice ['lætɪs] *I s* Gitter(werk) *n*. **II** *v/t* vergittern.

laud·a·ble ['lɔ:dəbl] *adj* □ löblich, lo-benswert. **laud·a·to·ry** ['.dətərɪ] *s* lo-bend: **~ speech** Lobrede *f*, Laudatio *f*.

laugh [lɑ:f] *I s* Lachen *n*, Gelächter *n*: **with a ~** lachend; **have a good ~** herz-lich lachen; **have the last ~** am Ende recht haben. **II** *v/i* lachen (**at** über *acc*): **~ at s.o.** a. j-n auslachen; **~ to o.s.** in sich hineinlachen; **~ out** auf- *od.* her-auslachen; → **beard**, **sleeve** 1. **III** *v/t*: **~ away** (*od.* **off**) *et.* lachend *od.* mit e-m Scherz abtun. **'laugh·a·ble** *adj* □ lä-cherlich, lachhaft. **'laugh·er** *s* La-cher(in).

laugh·ing ['lɑ:fɪŋ] *I s* **1.** Lachen *n*, Ge-lächter *n*. **II** *adj* □ **2.** lachend. **3.** lustig: **it is no ~ matter** es ist nicht(s) zum Lachen. **~ gas** *s* ✹ Lachgas *n*. **'~·stock** *s* Zielscheibe *f* des Spotts: **make s.o.**

the **~ of** j-n zum Gespött (*gen*) machen.

laugh·ter ['lɑ:ftə] *s* Lachen *n*, Geläch-ter *n*.

launch¹ [lɔ:ntʃ] *I v/t* **1.** *Boot* zu Wasser lassen; *Schiff* vom Stapel lassen: **be ~ed** vom Stapel laufen. **2.** *Geschoß, Torpedo* abschießen, *Rakete, Raum-fahrzeug a.* starten. **3.** *Rede, Kritik etc* vom Stapel lassen; *Drohungen etc* aus-stoßen. **4.** *Projekt etc* in Gang setzen, starten. **5. ~ o.s. on a task (into work)** sich auf e-e Aufgabe (in die Arbeit) stürzen. **II** *v/i* **6. ~ out** *fig.* sich stürzen (*into* in *acc*). **III** *s* **7.** ⚓ Stapellauf *m*. **8.** Abschuß *m*, Start *m*.

launch² [~] *s* ⚓ Barkasse *f*.

launch·ing ['lɔ:ntʃɪŋ] → **launch** III. **~ pad** *s* Abschußrampe *f*. **~ site** *s* Ab-schußbasis *f*.

laun·der ['lɔ:ndə] *I v/t Wäsche* waschen (u. bügeln). **II** *v/i* sich waschen (lassen).

laun·der·ette [~'ret] *s* Waschsalon *m*.

laun·dro·mat ['lɔ:ndrəmæt] *s bsd. Am.* Waschsalon *m*.

laun·dry ['lɔ:ndrɪ] *s* **1.** Wäscherei *f*. **2.** Wäsche *f*. **~ bas·ket** *s* Wäschekorb *m*.

lau·rel ['lɒrəl] *s* **1.** ♀ Lorbeer(baum) *m*. **2.** Lorbeerkranz *m*. **3. rest on one's ~s** *fig.* (sich) auf s-n Lorbeeren ausruhen.

lav [læv] *s* F Klo *n*: **in the ~** auf dem *od.* im Klo.

la·va ['lɑ:və] *s* Lava *f*.

lav·a·to·ry ['lævətərɪ] *s* **1.** Waschraum *m*. **2.** Toilette *f*, Klosett *n*: **in the ~** auf *od.* auf der Toilette. **~ at·tend·ant** *s* Toilet-tenfrau *f*. **~ pa·per** *s Br.* Toiletten-, Klosettpapier *n*.

lav·en·der ['lævəndə] *s* ♀ Lavendel *m*.

lav·ish ['lævɪʃ] *I adj* □ **1.** sehr freigebig, verschwenderisch (*of* mit; *in* in *dat*): **be ~ of a.** verschwenderisch umgehen mit. **2.** überschwenglich (*Lob etc*), großzü-gig (*Geschenk etc*), luxuriös, aufwendig (*Einrichtung etc*). **3.** verschwen-den: **~ s.th. on s.o.** j-n mit et. überhäu-fen.

law [lɔ:] *s* **1.** (*objektives*) Recht, Gesetz(e *pl*) *n*: **contrary to ~, against the ~** ge-setz-, rechtswidrig; **under German ~** nach deutschem Recht; **~ and order** Recht *od.* Ruhe u. Ordnung. **2.** (*einzel-nes*) Gesetz. **3.** *Recht n:* a) Rechts-system *n*, b) (*einzelnes*) Rechtsgebiet: → **international** 1. **4.** Rechtswissenschaft *f*, Jura *pl*: **read** (*od.* **study**) ~ Jura studieren. **5.** Gericht *n*, Rechtsweg *m*: **at** ~ vor Gericht; **go to** ~ vor Gericht gehen, prozessieren; **go to** ~ **with** *j-n* verklagen, belangen. **6.** F Bullen *pl* (*Polizei*); Bulle *m* (*Polizist*). **7.** *allg.* Gesetz *n*, Vorschrift *f*. **8.** a) *a.* ~ **of nature, natural** ~ Naturgesetz *n*, b) (wissenschaftliches) Gesetz, c) (Lehr)Satz *m*. '~-a,bid·ing *adj* gesetzestreu. '~,break·er *s* Gesetzesübertreter(in), Rechtsbrecher(in). ~ **court** *s* Gerichtshof *m*.

law·ful ['lɔ:fʊl] *adj* □ **1.** gesetzlich, legal. **2.** rechtmäßig, legitim. **3.** gesetzlich anerkannt, rechtsgültig. '**law·less** *adj* □ **1.** gesetzlos. **2.** rechts-, gesetzwidrig. **3.** zügellos.

lawn [lɔ:n] *s* Rasen *m*. ~ **chair** *s Am.* Liegestuhl *m*. ~ **mow·er** *s* Rasenmäher *m*.

'**law·suit** *s* ♊ (Zivil)Prozeß *m*, Verfahren *n*.

law·yer ['lɔ:jə] *s* **1.** (Rechts)Anwalt *m*. **2.** Jurist *m*.

lax [læks] *adj* □ **1.** schlaff, lose, locker. **2.** *fig.* lax, lasch (*Einstellung etc*), locker (*Sitten etc*). **3.** *fig.* unklar, verschwommen (*Vorstellung etc*). **lax·a·tive** ['~ətɪv] *s pharm.* mildes Abführmittel. '**lax·i·ty, 'lax·ness** *s* **1.** Schlaffheit *f*. Laxheit *f*, Laschheit *f*.

lay¹ [leɪ] *(irr)* **I** *v/t* **1.** legen, *Teppich* verlegen. **2.** Eier legen. **3.** *fig.* Hinterhalt *etc* legen, *Hoffnungen etc* setzen (*on auf acc*). **4.** (her)richten, *Tisch* decken. **5.** be-, auslegen (*with* mit). **6.** (*before*) vorlegen (*dat*), bringen (vor *dat*). **7.** *Anspruch etc* geltend machen. **8.** *Schuld etc* zuschreiben, zur Last legen (*to dat*). **II** *v/i* **9.** (Eier) legen. **10.** ~ **about one** → **lay about**; ~ **into s.o.** über j-n herfallen (*a. mit Worten*). **11.** ~ **off** *f j-n*, *et.* in Ruhe lassen; aufhören mit: ~ **off it!** hör auf (damit)!

Verbindungen mit Adverbien:

lay| a·bout *v/i* (wild) um sich schlagen (**with** mit). **~ a·side** *v/t* **1.** beiseite legen, weglegen. **2.** Angewohnheit *etc* ablegen, aufgeben. **3.** (*für die Zukunft*) beiseite *od.* auf die Seite legen, zurücklegen. **~ a·way** *v/t* **1.** → **lay aside** 3. **2.** angezahlte Ware zurücklegen. **~ down** *v/t* **1.** hinlegen. **2.** *Amt*, *Waffen etc* niederle-

gen. **3.** *sein Leben* hingeben, opfern. **4.** planen, entwerfen; *Straße etc* anlegen. **5.** *Grundsatz etc* aufstellen, *Regeln etc* festlegen, -setzen, *Bedingungen* (*in e-m Vertrag*) niederlegen, vereinbaren. **6.** *in v/t* sich eindecken mit; einlagern. **~ off I** *v/t* **1.** *Arbeiter* (*bsd.* vorübergehend) entlassen. **2.** *Arbeit* einstellen. **3.** F aufhören mit: ~ **smoking** *a.* das Rauchen aufgeben. **II** *v/i* **4.** F Feierabend machen; *Ferien* machen, ausspannen; aufhören; e-e Pause machen. ~ **on** *v/t* **1.** *Farbe etc* auftragen: **lay it on** F dick auftragen; → **thick** 6, **trowel**. **2.** *Br. Gas etc* installieren. **3.** *Br. Busse etc* einsetzen. ~ **o·pen** *v/t* **1.** bloß-, freilegen. **2.** *fig.* offen darlegen; aufdecken, enthüllen. ~ **out** *v/t* **1.** ausbreiten, -legen. **2.** ausstellen. **3.** *Toten* aufbahren. **4.** planen, entwerfen. **5.** *typ.* aufmachen, das *Layout* (*gen*) machen. **6.** **lay o.s. out** F sich mächtig anstrengen. ~ **o·ver** *Am.* **I** *v/i* Zwischenstation machen. **II** *v/t* verschieben, -tagen (*until auf acc*, bis). ~ **to** *v/i* ♧ beidrehen. ~ **up** *v/t* **1.** anhäufen, (an)sammeln: ~ **trouble for o.s.** sich Schwierigkeiten einbrocken *od.* einhandeln. **2.** **be laid up** das Bett hüten müssen, bettlägerig sein: **be laid up with influenza** mit Grippe im Bett liegen.

lay² [~] *pret von* **lie²**.

lay³ [~] *adj* Laien...: a) *eccl.* weltlich: ~ **preacher** Laienprediger *m*, b) laienhaft, nicht fachmännisch.

'**lay|·a·bout** *s bsd. Br.* F Faulenzer *m*, Tagedieb *m*. '~**·a,way** *s* angezahlte u. zurückgelegte Ware. '~**·by** *s mot. Br.* Park-, Rastplatz *m* (*Autobahn*), Parkbucht *f* (*Landstraße*).

lay·er ['leɪə] **I** *s* **1.** Schicht *f* (*a. geol.*), Lage *f*: **in** ~**s** schicht-, lagenweise. **2.** *in Zssgn* ...leger *m*. **3.** ♪, ♣ Ableger *m*. **II** *v/t* **4.** schicht- *od.* lagenweise anordnen, schichten.

lay·ette [leɪ'et] *s* Babyausstattung *f*.

'**lay|·man** ['leɪmən] *s* (*irr man*) Laie *m*. '~**·off** *s* **1.** (*bsd.* vorübergehende) Entlassung. **2.** F Pause *f*. '~**·out** *s* **1.** Grundriß *m*, Lageplan *m*. **2.** *typ.* Layout *n*. '~**·o,ver** *s Am.* Zwischenstation *f*.

laze [leɪz] F **I** *v/i* faulenzen. **II** *v/t mst* ~ **away** Zeit vertrödeln. '**la·zi·ness** *s* Faulheit *f*; Trägheit *f*.

la·zy ['leɪzɪ] *adj* □ **1.** faul; träg. **2.** träg, langsam. '**~.bones** *s pl* (*sg konstruiert*) F Faulpelz *m*.

lead¹ [led] **I** *s* **1.** 🜨 Blei *n*. **2.** ⚓ Senkblei *n*, Lot *n*. **3.** (Bleistift)Mine *f*. **4.** Blei *n*, Kugeln *pl*. **II** *v/t* **5.** verbleien; **~ed** verbleit, (*Benzin a.*) bleihaltig. **6.** mit Blei beschweren.

lead² [liːd] **I** *s* **1.** Führung *f*: a) Leitung *f*: *under s.o.'s ~*, b) führende Stelle, Spitze *f*: *be in the ~* an der Spitze stehen, führend sein, (*Sport etc*) in Führung liegen, führen; *take the ~* die Führung übernehmen, an die Spitze setzen (*from* vor *dat*) (*beide a. Sport*). **2.** Vorsprung *m* (*over* vor *dat*) (*a. Sport*). **3.** Vorbild *n*, Beispiel *n*: *follow s.o.'s ~* j-s Beispiel folgen; *give s.o. a ~* j-m ein gutes Beispiel geben. **4.** Hinweis *m*, Wink *m*; Anhaltspunkt *m*. **5.** *thea. etc* Hauptrolle *f*; Hauptdarsteller(in). **6.** (Hunde)Leine *f*: *keep on the ~* an der Leine führen *od.* halten. **II** *adj* **7.** Leit..., Führungs...: **~ guitarist** ♪ Leadgitarrist *m*. **III** *v/t* (*irr*) **8.** führen: **~ the way** vorangehen; → **garden 3**, **nose 1. 9.** führen, bringen (*a. Straße etc*). **10.** dazu bringen, veranlassen (*to do* zu tun). **11.** (an)führen, leiten. **12.** Leben führen. **IV** *v/i* (*irr*) **13.** führen: a) vorangehen, b) die erste Stelle einnehmen, c) (*Sport*) an der Spitze *od.* in Führung liegen. **14.** führen (*Straße etc*): **~ to** fig. führen zu.

Verbindungen mit Adverbien:

lead| a·stray *v/t fig.* irreführen; verführen. **~ a·way** *v/t* **1.** wegführen, *Verhafteten etc* abführen. **2.** *fig.* abbringen (*from* von). **~ off** *v/t* **1.** → **lead away**. **2.** einleiten, beginnen (*with* mit). **II** *v/i* **3.** anfangen, beginnen. **~ on** *v/t* j-m etwas vor- *od.* weismachen: *lead s.o. on to think that* j-n glauben machen, daß. **~ up** *v/i fig.* (*to*) (allmählich) führen (zu); hinauswollen (auf *acc*)

lead·en ['ledn] *adj* □ bleiern: a) Blei..., b) bleigrau, c) *fig.* schwer: **~ limbs** *pl* bleischwere Glieder *pl*; **~ sleep** bleierner Schlaf.

lead·er ['liːdə] *s* **1.** Führer(in). **2.** (An)Führer *m*, (*Delegations-*, *Oppositions- etc*)Führer *m*. **3.** ♪ a) *bsd. Am.* Leiter *m*, Dirigent *m*, b) *bsd. Br.* Konzertmeister *m*, c) (*Band*)Leader *m*. **4.**

bsd. Br. Leitartikel *m*. **5.** *Sport etc*: Spitzenreiter *m*. **6.** 🜨 Zug-, Lockartikel *m*. '**lead·er·ship** *s* **1.** Führung *f*, Leitung *f*. **2.** *a.* **~ qualities** *pl* Führungsqualitäten *pl*.

lead-free ['led~] *adj* bleifrei (*Benzin*).

lead·ing ['liːdɪŋ] *adj* **1.** führend: a) Leit..., leitend, b) Haupt..., erst. **~ ar·ti·cle** → **leader 4. ~ la·dy** *s thea. etc* Hauptdarstellerin *f*. **~ light** *s* führende *od.* wichtige Persönlichkeit. **~ man** *s* (*irr man*) *thea. etc* Hauptdarsteller *m*. **~ ques·tion** *s* Suggestivfrage *f*. **~ strings** *s pl* Gängelband *n* (*a. fig.*): *keep s.o. in* ~ j-n am Gängelband führen *od.* haben *od.* halten.

leaf [liːf] **I** *pl* **leaves** [liːvz] *s* **1.** 🌿 Blatt *n*: *come into* ~ ausschlagen. **2.** Blatt *n* (*Buch*): *take a* ~ *out of s.o.'s book fig.* sich an j-m ein Beispiel nehmen; *turn over a new* ~ *fig.* ein neues Leben beginnen. **3.** (*Fenster-*, *Tür*)Flügel *m*; (*Tisch*)Klappe *f*; Ausziehplatte *f* (*e-s Tisches*): *pull out the leaves* den Tisch ausziehen. **II** *v/t* **4.** *Am.* durchblättern. **III** *v/i* **5.** **~ through** durchblättern. '**leaf·let** ['~lɪt] *s* Flugblatt *n*, Hand-, Reklamezettel *m*; Prospekt *m*.

league [liːg] *s* **1.** Liga *f*, Bund *m*. **2.** Bündnis *n*, Bund *m*: *be in* ~ *with* gemeinsame Sache machen mit. **3.** *Sport*: Liga *f*: **~ game** Punktspiel *n*.

leak [liːk] **I** *s* **1.** a) ⚓ Leck *n* (*a. in Tank etc*): *spring a* ~ ein Leck bekommen, b) undichte Stelle (*a. fig.*). **2.** Auslaufen *n*; *fig.* Durchsickern *n*. **II** *v/i* **3.** lecken, leck sein. **4.** tropfen (*Wasserhahn*). **5.** **~ out** auslaufen, -treten; *fig.* durchsickern. **III** *v/t* **6.** *fig.* durchsickern lassen. '**leak·age** *s* **1.** → **leak 2. 2.** 🜨 Leckage *f*. '**leak·y** *adj* leck, undicht (*a. fig.*).

lean¹ [liːn] **I** *adj* □ mager (*a.* ⊙ *u. fig.*). **II** *s* das Magere (*des Fleisches*).

lean² [~] **I** *v/i* (*bsd. Br. a. irr*) **1.** sich neigen, schief sein *od.* stehen. **2.** sich beugen (*over* über *acc*): **~ back** sich zurücklehnen; **~ forward** sich vorbeugen; **~ over backward(s)** F sich fast umbringen (*to do* zu tun). **3.** (*against*) sich lehnen (an *acc*, gegen); lehnen (an *dat*). **4.** (*on*) sich stützen (auf *acc*); *fig.* sich verlassen (auf *acc*). **5.** **~ to(ward[s])** *fig.* (hin)neigen *od.* tendieren zu. **II** *v/t* (*bsd. Br. a. irr*) **6.** lehnen (**against** an *acc*, gegen). **III** *s* 7. Neigung *f*. **'lean·ing** I *adj* schräg, schief. II *s fig.* Neigung *f*, Tendenz *f* (**to, toward[s]** zu).

leant [lent] *bsd. Br.* pret u. pp von **lean²**.

leap [li:p] I *v/i* (*a. irr*) springen: ~ **at** *fig.* sich stürzen auf (*ein Angebot etc*); ~ **for joy** Freudensprünge machen; ~ (**in)to fame** schlagartig berühmt werden; ~ **out** ins Auge springen (**to s.o.** j-m); ~ **up** aufspringen; *fig.* sprunghaft anwachsen; → **conclusion** 3. II *v/t* (*a. irr*) überspringen (*a. fig.*), springen über (*acc*). **III** *s* Sprung *m* (*a. fig.*): **take a** ~ e-n Sprung machen; **by** (*od. in*) ~**s and bounds** *fig.* sprunghaft. **IV** *adj* Schalt...: ~ **year.** '**~·frog** I *s* Bockspringen. II *v/i* bockspringen.

leapt [lept] *pret u. pp* von **leap**.

learn [lɜːn] (*a. irr*) I *v/t* 1. (er)lernen: ~ (**how**) **to swim** schwimmen lernen. 2. (**from**) erfahren, hören (von); ersehen, entnehmen (aus *e-m Brief etc*). II *v/i* 3. lernen. 4. hören, erfahren (**about, of** von). **learn·ed** ['~nid] *adj* gelehrt (*Mensch*), (*Abhandlung etc a.*) wissenschaftlich. **'learn·er** *s* 1. Anfänger(in). 2. Lernende *m, f*: **be a fast** (**slow**) ~ schnell (langsam) lernen. **learnt** [lɜːnt] *pret u. pp* von **learn**.

lease [li:s] I *s* 1. Pacht-, Mietvertrag *m*. 2. Verpachtung *f*, Vermietung *f* (**to** an *acc*); Pacht *f*, Miete *f*: **put out to** (*od. let out on*) ~ → 5; **take on** ~ → 5. 3. Pacht-, Mietzeit *f*. II *v/t* 4. ~ **out** verpachten, -mieten (**to** an *acc*). 5. pachten, mieten, leasen.

leash [li:ʃ] *s* (Hunde)Leine *f*: **keep on the** ~ an der Leine halten *od.* führen; **keep** (*od. hold*) **in** ~ *fig.* im Zaum halten; → **strain** 5.

least [li:st] I *adj* (*sup* von **little**) 1. geringst, mindest, wenigst: ~ **resistance** 1. 2. geringst, unbedeutendst: **at the** ~ **thing** bei der geringsten Kleinigkeit. II *s* 3. das Mindeste, das Wenigste: **at** ~ wenigstens, zumindest; **at** (**the**) ~ mindestens; **not in the** ~ nicht im geringsten *od.* mindesten; **to say the** ~ (**of it**) gelinde gesagt. III *adv* 4. am wenigsten: ~ **of all** am allerwenigsten.

leath·er ['leðə] I *s* Leder *n* (*a. humor. Haut; a. Sport: Ball*): → **tough** 1. II *v/t*

F versohlen. '**~·neck** *s* ✕ *Am. sl.* Ledernacken *m*.

leath·er·y ['leðəri] *adj* lederartig, zäh.

leave¹ [li:v] (*irr*) I *v/t* 1. verlassen: a) von *j-m, e-m Ort etc* fort-, weggehen, b) abreisen, abfahren *etc* von, c) von *der Schule* abgehen, d) *j-n, et.* im Stich lassen, *et.* aufgeben: **she left him for another man** sie verließ ihn wegen e-s anderen Mannes. 2. lassen: ~ **alone** allein lassen; *j-n, et.* in Ruhe lassen; ~ **it at that** es dabei belassen *od.* (bewenden) lassen; ~ **s.o. to himself** j-n sich selbst überlassen; → **cold 4, lurch².** 3. übriglassen: **be left** übrigbleiben *od.* übrig sein. 4. *Narbe etc* zurücklassen, *Nachricht, Spur etc* hinterlassen. 5. hängen-, liegen-, stehenlassen, vergessen. 6. überlassen, anheimstellen (**to s.o.** j-m). 7. vermachen, -erben. II *v/i* 8. (fort-, weg)gehen, abreisen, abfahren (**for** nach). 9. gehen (*die Stellung aufgeben*).

Verbindungen mit Adverbien:

leave| be·hind *v/t* 1. zurücklassen. 2. → **leave¹** 4, 5. 3. *Gegner etc* hinter sich lassen (*a. fig.*). ~ **on** *v/t Radio etc* anlassen, *Kleidungsstück a.* anbehalten. ~ **out** *v/t* 1. draußen lassen. 2. weglassen (**of** von, bei). ~ **o·ver** *v/t Br.* 1. → **leave¹** 3. 2. verschieben (**until** auf *acc*, bis).

leave² [~] *s* 1. Erlaubnis *f*, Genehmigung *f*: **ask** ~ **of s.o., ask s.o.'s** ~ j-n um Erlaubnis bitten. 2. Urlaub *m*: **on** ~ auf Urlaub. 3. Abschied *m*: **take** (**one's**) ~ Abschied nehmen (**of** von).

leav·en ['levn] I *s* 1. Sauerteig *m*; Treibmittel *n*. II *v/t* 2. *Teig* säuern; (auf)gehen lassen. 3. *fig.* auflockern (**with** mit, durch).

leaves [li:vz] *pl* von **leaf**.

leav·ing ['li:vɪŋ] *s* 1. *mst pl* Überbleibsel *n*, Rest *m*. 2. *pl* Abfall *m*.

lech·er ['letʃə] *s* Lüstling *m*. '**lech·er·ous** *adj* □ geil, lüstern. '**lech·er·y** *s* Geilheit *f*, Lüsternheit *f*.

lec·ture ['lektʃə] I *s* 1. (**on** über *acc*; **to** vor *dat*) Vortrag *m*; *univ.* Vorlesung *f*: ~ **hall** (*od. theater, bsd. Br. theatre*) Hörsaal *m*. 2. Strafpredigt *f*: **give** (*od. read*) **s.o. a** ~ → 4. II *v/i* 3. (**on** über *acc*; **to** vor *dat*) e-n Vortrag *od.* Vorträge halten; *univ.* e-e Vorlesung *od.* Vorlesungen halten. **III** *v/t* **4.** *j-m* e-e Strafpredigt halten. **'lec·tur·er** *s* **1.** Vortragende *m, f.* **2.** *univ.* Dozent(in).

led [led] *pret u. pp von* **lead²**.

ledge [ledʒ] *s* Leiste *f*, Sims *m, n.*

ledg·er ['ledʒə] *s* ✝ Hauptbuch *n.*

lee [liː] *s* ⚓ Lee(seite) *f.*

leech [liːtʃ] *s* **1.** *zo.* Blutegel *m.* **2.** *fig.* Klette *f*; Blutsauger *m.*

leek [liːk] *s* ♣ Lauch *m*, Porree *m.*

leer [lɪə] **I** *s* höhnisches *od.* boshaftes *od.* anzügliches Grinsen; lüsterner Seitenblick. **II** *v/i* höhnisch *od.* boshaft *od.* anzüglich grinsen; lüstern schielen (**at** *nach*).

lees [liːz] *s pl* Bodensatz *m.*

lee·ward ['liːwəd] *adv* ⚓ leewärts.

'lee·way *s* **1.** ✈, ⚓ Abtrift *f.* **2.** *fig.* Rückstand *m*, Zeitverlust *m*: **make up ~** (den Rückstand *od.* Zeitverlust) aufholen. **3.** *fig.* Spielraum *m.*

left¹ [left] *pret u. pp von* **leave¹**.

left² [~] **I** *adj* **1.** link, Links... **II** *s* **2.** die Linke, linke Seite: **on** (*od.* **at, to**) **the ~** (**of**) links (*von*), linker Hand (*von*); **on our ~** zu unserer Linken; **the second turning to** (*od.* **on**) **the ~** die zweite Querstraße links; **keep to the ~** sich links halten; *mot.* links fahren. **3. the ~** *pol.* die Linke. **III** *adv* **4.** links (**of** *von*): **turn ~** sich nach links wenden; *mot.* links abbiegen. **'~·hand** *adj* **1.** link: **~ bend** Linkskurve *f.* **2.** ⚙ linksgängig, -läufig: **~ drive** Linkssteuerung *f.* **~·'hand·ed** *adj* **1.** linkshändig: **be ~** Linkshänder(in) sein. **2.** linkisch, ungeschickt. **3.** zweifelhaft, fragwürdig (*Kompliment etc*). **~·'hand·er** *s* Linkshänder(in).

left·ist ['leftɪst] *adj pol.* linksgerichtet, -stehend.

left·'lug·gage lock·er *s* 🚉 *Br.* (Gepäck)Schließfach *n.* **~·'lug·gage office** *s* 🚉 *Br.* Gepäckaufbewahrung(sstelle) *f.* **'~·o·ver** *s mst pl* Überbleibsel *n*, Rest *m.*

'left-wing *adj pol.* dem linken Flügel angehörend, links...

leg [leg] **I** *s* **1.** (*a. Hosen-, Stuhl- etc*)Bein *n*: **be on one's last ~** auf dem letzten Loch pfeifen; **give s.o. a ~ up** *j-m* (hin)aufhelfen; *fig.* *j-m* unter die Arme greifen; **pull s.o.'s ~** F *j-n* auf den Arm nehmen; **stretch one's ~s** sich die Bei-

ne vertreten; → **shake** 7. **2.** (*Hammel-etc*)Keule *f*: → **of mutton. 3.** ♣ Kathete *f*, Schenkel *m* (*e-s Dreiecks*). **4.** Etappe *f*, Abschnitt *m* (*e-r Reise etc*). **II** *v/i* **5.** **mst ~ it** F zu Fuß gehen.

leg·a·cy ['legəsɪ] *s* ⚖ Vermächtnis *n*, *fig. a.* Erbe *n.*

le·gal ['liːgl] *adj* □ **1.** gesetzlich, rechtlich: **~ holiday** *Am.* gesetzlicher Feiertag; → **tender²** 4. **2.** legal, gesetzmäßig, rechtsgültig. **3.** Rechts..., juristisch: **~ adviser** Rechtsberater *m*; **~ aid** Prozeßkostenhilfe *f.* **4.** gerichtlich: **take ~ action** (*od.* **steps**) **against s.o.** gerichtlich gegen *j-n* vorgehen. **le·gal·i·ty** [liː'gælətɪ] *s* Legalität *f.* **le·gal·i·za·tion** [ˌliːgəlaɪ'zeɪʃn] *s* Legalisierung *f.* **'le·gal·ize** *v/t* legalisieren.

le·ga·tion [lɪ'geɪʃn] *s* Gesandtschaft *f.*

leg·end ['ledʒənd] *s* **1.** Legende *f* (*a. fig.*), Sage *f.* **2.** Legende *f*: a) erläuternder Text, Bildunterschrift *f*, b) Zeichenerklärung *f* (*auf Karten etc*), c) Inschrift *f* (*auf Münzen etc*).

leg·er·de·main [ˌledʒədə'meɪn] *s* **1.** Taschenspielerei *f* (*a. fig.*). **2.** Schwindel *m.*

leg·gy ['legɪ] *adj* langbeinig.

leg·i·ble ['ledʒəbl] *adj* □ leserlich, lesbar.

le·gion ['liːdʒən] *s* Legion *f.* **'le·gion·ar·y** *s* Legionär *m.*

leg·is·late ['ledʒɪsleɪt] *v/i* Gesetze erlassen. **'leg·is·la·tion** *s* Gesetzgebung *f.* **leg·is·la·tive** ['~lətɪv] **I** *adj* □ **1.** gesetzgebend, legislativ: **~ assembly** gesetzgebende Versammlung; **~ body** → 3b; **~ power** → 3a. **2.** gesetzgeberisch, Legislatur...: **~ period** Legislaturperiode *f.* **II** *s* **3.** Legislative *f*: a) gesetzgebende Gewalt, b) gesetzgebende Körperschaft. **'leg·is·la·tor** ['~leɪtə] *s* Gesetzgeber *m.* **leg·is·la·ture** ['~leɪtʃə] → **legislative** 3b.

le·git·i·ma·cy [lɪ'dʒɪtɪməsɪ] *s* Legitimität *f*: a) Gesetzmäßigkeit *f*, Gesetzlichkeit *f*, b) Rechtmäßigkeit *f*, Berechtigung *f*, c) Ehelichkeit *f.* **le·git·i·mate** [~mət] *adj* □ legitim: a) gesetzmäßig, gesetzlich, b) rechtmäßig, berechtigt, c) ehelich. **le·git·i·mize** *v/t* legitimieren.

leg-room ['legrʊm] *s* ✈, *mot.* Beinfreiheit *f.*

leg·ume ['legjuːm] *s* ♣ Hülsenfrucht *f.*

lei·sure ['leʒə] **I** s freie Zeit: *at* ~ mit Muße, in (aller) Ruhe; frei, unbeschäftigt; *at your* ~ wenn es Ihnen (gerade) paßt, bei Gelegenheit. **II** *adj* Freizeit...: ~ *activities pl* Freizeitgestaltung *f*; ~ *facilities pl* Freizeiteinrichtungen *pl*; ~ *hours pl* Mußestunden *pl*; ~ *occupation* Freizeitbeschäftigung *f*; ~ *time* Freizeit *f*; ~ *wear* Freizeitkleidung *f*. **'lei·sure·ly** *adj u. adv* gemächlich, gemütlich.

lem·on ['lemən] **I** s **1.** Zitrone *f*. **2.** *sl.* Niete *f* (*Sache, Person*). **II** *adj* **3.** Zitronen...: ~ *juice*; ~ *soda* Am. Zitronenlimonade *f*; ~ *squash* Br. *Getränk aus Zitronenkonzentrat u. Wasser*; ~ *squeezer* Zitronenpresse *f*. **4.** zitronengelb.

lend [lend] *v/t* (*irr*) **1.** (ver-, aus)leihen. **2.** *fig.* Nachdruck, Würde etc verleihen (*to dat*). **3.** *fig.* leihen, gewähren; ~ *o.s. to s.th.* sich zu et. hergeben; ~ *itself to s.th.* sich für *od.* zu et. eignen; → *hand* 1. **'lend·er** s Aus-, Verleiher(in). **'lend·ing** *adj*: ~ *library* Leihbücherei *f*.

length [leŋθ] s **1.** Länge *f*: a) *Dimension*: *two feet* ~ 2 Fuß lang; *what* ~ *is it?* wie lang ist es?, b) *Strecke f*: *go to great* ~*s* sich sehr bemühen, c) Umfang *m* (*e-s Buchs etc*), d) Dauer *f*: *at* ~ ausführlich; *at full* ~ in allen Einzelheiten. **2.** Bahn *f* (*Stoff etc*). **3.** *Sport*: Länge *f* (Vorsprung). **'length·en I** *v/t* verlängern, länger machen, *Kleidungsstück a.* auslassen. **II** *v/i* sich verlängern, länger werden. **'length·ways, length·wise** ['~waɪz] *adv* der Länge nach, längs. **'length·y** *adj* □ ermüdend lang, langatmig.

le·ni·ence, le·ni·en·cy ['li:njəns(ɪ)] s Milde *f*, Nachsicht *f*. **'le·ni·ent** *adj* □ mild, nachsichtig (*to, toward[s]* gegenüber).

lens [lenz] s **1.** *anat., phot., phys.* Linse *f*: ~ *aperture* phot. Blende *f*. **2.** *phot., phys.* Objektiv *n*. **3.** (*einzelnes*) Glas (*e-r Brille*).

lent¹ [lent] *pret u. pp von* **lend.**

Lent² [~] s Fastenzeit *f*.

len·til ['lentɪl] s ⚘ Linse *f*.

Leo ['li:əʊ] s *ast.* Löwe *m*.

leop·ard ['lepəd] s *zo.* Leopard *m*.

le·o·tard ['li:əʊtɑːd] s **1.** Trikot *n*. **2.** Gymnastikanzug *m*.

les·bi·an ['lezbɪən] **I** *adj* lesbisch. **II** s Lesbierin *f*.

lese maj·es·ty [ˌliːz'mædʒɪstɪ] s **1.** Majestätsbeleidigung *f* (*a. fig.*). **2.** Hochverrat *m*.

le·sion ['li:ʒn] s Verletzung *f*, Wunde *f*.

less [les] **I** *adv* (*comp von little*) weniger: ~ *and* ~ immer weniger; *the* ~ *so as* (dies) um so weniger, als. **II** *adj* (*comp von little*) geringer, kleiner, weniger: *in* ~ *time* in kürzerer Zeit; *no* ~ *man than* kein geringerer als. **III** s weniger, e-e kleinere Menge *od.* Zahl: *little* ~ *than* so gut wie, schon fast; *no* ~ *than* nicht weniger als. **IV** *prp* weniger, minus, abzüglich.

less·en ['lesn] **I** *v/i* **1.** sich vermindern *od.* verringern, abnehmen. **II** *v/t* **2.** vermindern, verringern. **3.** *fig.* herabsetzen, schmälern; bagatellisieren.

less·er ['lesə] *adj* kleiner, geringer; → *evil* 2.

les·son ['lesn] s **1.** Lektion *f* (*a. fig.*): → *teach* 2. **2.** (Lehr-, Unterrichts)Stunde *f*; *pl* Unterricht *m*, Stunden *pl*: *give* ~*s* Unterricht erteilen, unterrichten; *take* ~*s from* Stunden *od.* Unterricht nehmen bei. **3.** *fig.* Lehre *f*: *this was a* ~ *to me* das war mir e-e Lehre.

lest [lest] *cj* **1.** (*mst mit folgendem should*) daß *od.* damit nicht: *he ran away* ~ *he should be seen* er lief weg, um nicht gesehen zu werden. **2.** (*nach Ausdrücken des Befürchtens*) daß.

let¹ [let] (*irr*) *v/t* **1.** lassen: ~ *alone et.* seinlassen; *j-n, et.* in Ruhe lassen; geschweige denn, ganz zu schweigen von; ~ *s.th. go* et. loslassen; ~ *o.s. go* sich gehenlassen; aus sich herausgehen; ~ *it go at that* laß es dabei bewenden; ~*'s go* gehen wir!; ~ *s.o. know* j-n wissen lassen, j-m Bescheid geben; ~ *into* (her-, hin)einlassen in (*acc*); *j-n* einweihen in (*ein Geheimnis*). **2.** *bsd. Br.* vermieten, -pachten (*to* an *acc*; *for* auf *ein Jahr etc*): "*to* ~" „zu vermieten". **II** *v/i* **3.** ~ *go* loslassen (*of s.th.* et.). **4.** ~ *into* auf *j-n* herfallen.

Verbindungen mit Adverbien:

let| by *v/t* vorbeilassen. ~ *down v/t* **1.** hinunter-, herunterlassen; → *hair.* **2.** im Stich lassen; enttäuschen. ~ *in v/t* **1.** (her-, hin)einlassen. **2.** Stück etc einlassen, -setzen. **3.** *j-n* einweihen (*on* in *ein*

Geheimnis). **4. let o.s. in for s.th.** sich et. einbrocken, sich auf et. einlassen. ~ **off** *v/t* **1.** *Feuerwerk* abbrennen, *Gewehr etc* abfeuern. **2.** *Gas etc* ablassen: → **steam** 1. ~ **on** F I *v/i* **1.** sich et. anmerken lassen (*about* von). **II** *v/t* **2.** zugeben (*that* daß). **3.** vorgeben. ~ **out** I *v/t* **1.** heraus-, hinauslassen (*of* aus): **let the air out of** die Luft lassen aus. **2.** *Kleidungsstück* auslassen. **3.** *Schrei etc* ausstoßen. **4.** *Geheimnis* ausplaudern, verraten. **5.** → **let**' **2. II** *v/i* **6.** herfallen (*at* über *acc*) (*a.* mit *Worten*). ~ **through** *v/t* durchlassen. ~ **up** *v/i* F nachlassen; aufhören.

let² [~] *s* Tennis: Netzaufschlag *m*: ~**!** Netz!

'**let-down** *s* Enttäuschung *f*.

le·thal ['li:θl] *adj* □ tödlich; Todes...

le·thar·gic [ləˈθɑːdʒɪk] *adj* (~**ally**) lethargisch, teilnahmslos. **leth·ar·gy** ['leθədʒɪ] *s* Lethargie *f*, Teilnahmslosigkeit *f*.

let's [lets] F *für* **let us.**

let·ter ['letə] I *s* **1.** Buchstabe *m*: **to the** ~ wortwörtlich, buchstäblich; *fig.* peinlich genau. **2.** Brief *m*, Schreiben *n* (**to** an *acc*): **by** ~ brieflich; ~ **of application** Bewerbungsschreiben; ~ **of complaint** Beschwerdebrief; ~ **to the editor** Leserbrief. **3.** *typ.* Letter *f*, Type *f*. **4.** *pl* (a. *as konstruiert*) (schöne) Literatur; Bildung *f*. **II** *v/t* **5.** beschriften. ~ **bomb** *s* Briefbombe *f*. ~ **box** *s bsd. Br.* Briefkasten *m*. ~ **file** *s* Briefordner *m*. '~**head** *s* (gedruckter) Briefkopf *m*. ~ **o·pen·er** *s* Brieföffner *m*. ~ **pa·per** *s* Briefpapier *n*. ~ **scales** *s pl* Briefwaage *f*. '~**weight** *s* Briefbeschwerer *m*.

let·tuce ['letɪs] *s* (*bsd.* Kopf)Salat *m*.

'**let-up** *s* F Nachlassen *n*; Aufhören *n*.

leu·co·cyte ['luːkəʊsaɪt] *s* Leukozyt *m*, weißes Blutkörperchen.

leu·k(a)e·mi·a [luːˈkiːmɪə] *s* Leukämie *f*.

lev·el ['levl] I *s* **1.** Libelle *f*, Wasserwaage *f*. **2.** Ebene *f* (*a.* *fig.*), ebene Fläche: **at government** ~ auf Regierungsebene. **3.** Höhe *f* (*a. geogr.*), (*Wasser-etc*)Spiegel *m*, (-)Stand *m*, (-)Pegel *m*; *fig.* (*a. geistiges*) Niveau, Stand *m*, Stufe *f*: ~ **of sound** Geräuschpegel, Tonstärke *f*; **be on a** ~ **with** auf gleicher Höhe sein mit; genauso hoch sein wie;

fig. auf dem gleichen Niveau *od.* auf der gleichen Stufe stehen wie. **II** *adj* □ **4.** eben (*Straße etc*): **a** ~ **teaspoon** ein gestrichener Teelöffel(voll). **5.** gleich (*a. fig.*): ~ **crossing** *Br.* schienengleicher (Bahn)Übergang; **be** ~ **on points** (*Sport*) punktgleich sein; **be** ~ **with** auf gleicher Höhe sein mit; genauso hoch sein wie; *fig.* auf dem gleichen Niveau *od.* auf der gleichen Stufe stehen wie; **draw** ~ (*Sport*) ausgleichen; **draw** ~ **with** *j-n* einholen; **make** ~ **with the ground** → 9b. **6.** a) gleichmäßig: ~ **stress** *ling.* schwebende Betonung, b) ausgeglichen (*Rennen etc*). **7. do one's ** ~ **best** sein möglichstes tun. **8. have (keep) a** ~ **head** e-n kühlen Kopf haben (bewahren), sich nicht aus der Ruhe bringen lassen; **give s.o. a** ~ **look** *j-n* ruhig *od.* fest anschauen. **III** *v/t pret u. pp* -**eled**, *bsd. Br.* -**elled 9.** a) (ein)ebnen, planieren, b) *a.* ~ **to** (*od.* **with**) **the ground** dem Erdboden gleichmachen. **10.** *fig.* gleichmachen, nivellieren; *Unterschiede* beseitigen, ausgleichen.

Verbindungen mit Adverbien:

lev·el| **down** *v/t* Preise, Löhne *etc* drücken, herabsetzen. ~ **off** I *v/t* **1.** → **level** 9a, 10. **2.** Flugzeug abfangen. **II** *v/i* **3.** flach werden *od.* auslaufen (*Gelände etc*). **4.** *fig.* sich stabilisieren *od.* einpendeln (**at** bei). ~ **out** I *v/t* **1.** → **level** 10. **2.** → **level off** 2. **II** *v/i* **3.** → **level off** II. ~ **up** *v/t* Preise, Löhne *etc* hinaufschrauben.

,**lev·el·'head·ed** *adj* □ vernünftig.

le·ver ['liːvə] I *s* **1.** *phys.*, © Hebel *m*. **2.** Brechstange *f*. **3.** Anker *m* (*e-r Uhr*). **4.** *fig.* Druckmittel *n*. **II** *v/t* **5.** ~ **out** (*of*) herausstemmen (aus); *fig.* *j-n* verdrängen (aus).

lev·i·ty ['levətɪ] *s* Leichtfertigkeit *f*.

lev·y ['levɪ] I *s* **1.** ✝ Erhebung *f*. **2.** ✝ Steuer *f*, Abgabe *f*. **3.** ✗ Aushebung *f*. **II** *v/t* **4.** *Steuern etc* a) erheben, b) (**on**) legen (auf *acc*), auferlegen (*dat*). **5.** ✗ *Truppen* ausheben.

lewd [ljuːd] *adj* □ **1.** geil, lüstern. **2.** unanständig, obszön. '**lewd·ness** *s* **1.** Geilheit *f*, Lüsternheit *f*. **2.** Unanständigkeit *f*, Obszönität *f*.

lex·i·cog·ra·pher [,leksɪˈkɒɡrəfə] *s* Lexikograph(in). **lex·i·co·graph·ic** [,leksɪkəʊˈɡræfɪk] *adj* (~**ally**) lexikographisch.

lex·i·cog·ra·phy [͵~'kɒɡrəfɪ] s Lexiko-graphie f.

li·a·bil·i·ty [͵laɪə'bɪlətɪ] s 1. ✝, ⚖ Ver-pflichtung f, Verbindlichkeit f; Haf-tung f, Haftpflicht f: **~ insurance** Haftpflichtversicherung f; → **limit** 4. 2. pl ✝ Passiva pl. 3. allg. Verantwortung f, Verantwortlichkeit f. 4. ~ **to penalty** Strafbarkeit f; **~ to taxation** Steuer-pflicht f. 5. **(to)** Hang m, Neigung f (zu), Anfälligkeit f (für).

li·a·ble ['laɪəbl] adj 1. ✝, ⚖ haftbar, -pflichtig **(for** für): **be ~ for** a. haften für. 2. unterworfen (zu gen od. für Sache): **be ~ to s.th.** a. e-r Sache unterliegen; **~ to penalty** strafbar; **~ to taxation** steuerpflichtig. 3. **be ~ to** neigen zu, anfällig sein für. 4. **be ~ to do s.th.** et. gern od. leicht tun; et. wahrscheinlich tun: **he is ~ to come** er kommt wahr-scheinlich; **that is ~ to happen** das kann durchaus od. leicht passieren.

li·aise [lɪ'eɪz] v/i 1. Verbindung aufneh-men **(with** mit). 2. sich verbünden **(with** mit). 3. zs.-arbeiten **(with** mit). **li·ai-son** [lɪ'eɪzɒn] s 1. Verbindung f: **~ man** Verbindungsmann m. 2. Bündnis n. 3. Zs.-arbeit f. 4. Liaison f, (Liebes)Ver-hältnis n.

li·ar ['laɪə] s Lügner(in).

li·bel ['laɪbl] ⚖ I s (schriftliche) Ver-leumdung od. Beleidigung **(of, on** gen). II v/t pret u. pp **-beled,** bsd. Br. **-belled** (schriftlich) verleumden od. beleidigen. **'li·bel·(l)ous** adj □ verleumderisch.

lib·er·al ['lɪbərəl] I adj □ 1. liberal, auf-geschlossen. 2. mst ⚌ pol. liberal. 3. großzügig: a) freigebig **(of** mit), b) reichlich (bemessen): **~ gift** großzügiges Geschenk. 4. **~ arts** pl Geisteswissen-schaften pl. II s 5. mst ⚌ pol. Liberale m, f. **'lib·er·al·ism** s Liberalismus m. **lib-er·al·i·ty** [͵~'rælətɪ] s 1. Liberalität f. 2. Großzügigkeit f. **lib·er·al·ize** ['lɪbərəlaɪz] v/t liberalisieren.

lib·er·ate ['lɪbəreɪt] v/t 1. befreien **(from** von, aus) (a. fig.); Sklaven etc freilas-sen. 2. Gase etc, fig. Kräfte etc freiset-zen: **be ~d** a. frei werden. ͵**lib·er'a·tion** s 1. Befreiung f; Freilassung f. 2. Frei-setzung f.

lib·er·tine ['lɪbətiːn] s Wüstling m.

lib·er·ty ['lɪbətɪ] s 1. Freiheit f: a) persön-liche etc Freiheit f: **religious ~** Reli-gionsfreiheit; **~ of the press** Pressefrei-heit; **~ of speech** Redefreiheit; **at ~** frei, in Freiheit, auf freiem Fuß, b) freie Wahl, Erlaubnis f: **be at ~ to do s.th.** et. tun dürfen, (c) mst pl Privileg n, Vor-recht n. 2. Dreistigkeit f, (plumpe) Ver-traulichkeit f: **take liberties with** sich Freiheiten gegen j-n herausnehmen; willkürlich mit et. umgehen.

li·bid·i·nous [lɪ'bɪdɪnəs] adj □ libidinös, triebhaft. **li·bi·do** [lɪ'biːdəʊ] s Libido f, Geschlechtstrieb m.

Li·bra ['laɪbrə] s ast. Waage f.

li·brar·i·an [laɪ'breərɪən] s Bibliothe-kar(in). **li·brar·y** ['~brərɪ] s 1. Biblio-thek f: a) öffentliche Bücherei: **~ ticket** Leserausweis m, b) private Bücher-sammlung, c) Bibliothekszimmer n. 2. (Bild-, Zeitungs)Archiv n: **~ picture** Ar-chivbild n.

li·bret·tist [lɪ'bretɪst] s Librettist m, Text-dichter m. **li·bret·to** [͵~tǝʊ] pl **-tos, -ti** [͵~tɪ] s Libretto (n) a) Textbuch (n, b) (Opern- etc)Text m.

lice [laɪs] pl von **louse** 1.

li·cence ['laɪsəns] s 1. Lizenz f, Konzes-sion f, behördliche Genehmigung (Führer-, Jagd-, Waffen- etc)Schein m: **~ number** mot. Kennzeichen n. 2. dich-terische Freiheit. 3. Zügellosigkeit f. II v/t 4. Am. → **license** I.

li·cense ['laɪsəns] I v/t 1. lizensieren, konzessionieren, behördlich genehmi-gen: **fully ~d** voller Schankkonzes-sion. 2. j-m e-e Lizenz od. Konzession erteilen; (es) j-m (offiziell) erlauben **(to do** zu tun). II s 3. Am. → **licence** I: **~ plate** mot. Nummern-, Kennzeichen-schild n.

li·cen·tious [laɪ'senʃəs] adj □ ausschwei-fend, zügellos.

li·chen ['laɪkən] s 1. ♧ Flechte f. 2. ⚕ Knötchenflechte f.

lick [lɪk] I v/t 1. (ab)lecken: **~ up (out)** auf-(aus)lecken; **~ s.o.'s boots** fig. vor j-m kriechen; **~ one's lips** sich die Lip-pen lecken (a. fig.). 2. F verprügeln, -dreschen; übertreffen: **this ~s me** das geht über m-n Horizont. II v/i 3. lecken **(at** an dat). III s 4. Lecken n: **give s.th. a ~** an etwas lecken. 5. F Tempo n: **at full ~** mit voller Geschwindigkeit. **'lick·ing** s F Prügel pl, Dresche f.

lic·o·rice ['lɪkərɪs] s ♧ Lakritze f.

lid [lɪd] *s* **1.** Deckel *m*: *put the ~ on Br.* F *e-r Sache* die Krone aufsetzen; *e-r Sache* ein Ende machen. **2.** (*Augen-*) Lid *n*.

li·do ['liːdəʊ] *pl* **-dos** *s Br.* Frei- *od.* Strandbad *n*.

lie¹ [laɪ] I *s* Lüge *f*: *tell ~s* (*od. a ~*) lügen; *give the ~ to et., j-n* Lügen strafen; → *white lie.* II *v/i* lügen: *~ to s.o.* j-n belügen.

lie² [~] I *s* **1.** Lage *f* (*a. fig.*): *the ~ of the land fig. Br.* die Lage (der Dinge). II *v/i* (*irr*) **2.** liegen: a) *allg.* im Bett, im Hinterhalt etc liegen; *ausgebreitet, tot etc* daliegen, b) begraben sein, ruhen, c) gelegen sein, sich befinden: *the town ~s on a river* die Stadt liegt an e-m Fluß; *~ second* (*Sport etc*) an zweiter Stelle liegen, d) begründet liegen (*in* in *dat*). **3.** a) *~ heavy on s.o.'s stomach* j-m schwer im Magen liegen, b) *fig.* lasten (*on auf der Seele etc*). **4.** *fig.* stecken (*behind* hinter *dat*).
Verbindungen mit Adverbien:

lie| **a·bout** *v/i* herumliegen. **~ a·head** *v/i: what lies ahead of us* was vor uns liegt, was uns bevorsteht. **~ a·round** → **lie about. ~ back** *v/i* sich zurücklegen *od.* -lehnen; *fig.* sich ausruhen. **~ down** *v/i* **1.** sich hin- *od.* niederlegen: **~ on** sich legen auf (*acc*). **2.** *take lying down* Beleidigung *etc* widerspruchslos hinnehmen, sich *e-e Beleidigung etc* gefallen lassen. **~ in** *v/i Br.* (*morgens*) lang im Bett bleiben. **~ low** *v/i* sich verstecken *od.* versteckt halten; sich ruhig verhalten. **~ o·ver** *v/i* liegenbleiben, unerledigt bleiben; aufgeschoben *od.* zurückgestellt werden. **~ up** *v/i* **1.** das Bett *od.* das Zimmer hüten (müssen). **2.** nicht benutzt werden, (*Maschine etc*) außer Betrieb sein.

'lie·a·bed *s* Langschläfer(in).
lie de·tec·tor *s* Lügendetektor *m*.
'lie|**-down** *s* F Schläfchen *n: have a ~* ein Schläfchen machen; sich (kurz) hinlegen. **'~-in** *s: have* (*od. take*) *a ~* F → **lie in.**

lieu [ljuː] *s: in ~* statt dessen; *in ~ of* an Stelle von (*od. gen*), (an)statt (*gen*); → **oath** 1.

lieu·ten·ant [lefˈtenənt] *s* ⚔ a) Leutnant *m*, b) *Br.* (*Am. first ~*) Oberleutnant *m*.

life [laɪf] *pl* **lives** [laɪvz] *s* **1.** Leben *n*: a)

organisches Leben, b) Lebenskraft *f*, c) Lebewesen *n*, d) Menschenleben *n: they lost their lives* sie kamen ums Leben; *a matter of ~ and death* e-e lebenswichtige Angelegenheit; *early in ~* in jungen Jahren; *late in ~* in vorgerücktem Alter, e) Lebenszeit *f*, -dauer *f: all his ~* sein ganzes Leben lang; *for ~* fürs (ganze) Leben, für den Rest s-s Lebens; *bsd.* ⚖, *pol.* lebenslänglich, auf Lebenszeit, f) menschliches Tun u. Treiben, g) Lebensweise *f*, -wandel *m*, h) Schwung *m: full of ~* voller Leben. **2.** ⚖ Laufzeit *f* (*e-s Wechsels, Vertrags etc*); ✝ Haltbarkeit *f*, Lagerfähigkeit *f*. **3.** ⚖ F lebenslängliche Freiheitsstrafe: *he is doing ~* er sitzt lebenslänglich; *he got ~* er bekam lebenslänglich. **~ an·nu·i·ty** *s* Leibrente *f*. **~ as·sur·ance** *s bsd. Br.* Lebensversicherung *f*. '**~-boat** *s* ⚓ Rettungsboot *n*. **~ buoy** *s* ⚓ Rettungsring *m*. **~ ex·pect·an·cy** *s* Lebenserwartung *f*. '**~·guard** *s* Rettungsschwimmer *m*; Bademeister *m*. **~ im·pris·on·ment** *s* ⚖ lebenslängliche Freiheitsstrafe. **~ in·sur·ance** *s* Lebensversicherung *f*. **~ jack·et** *s* ⚓ Rettungs-, Schwimmweste *f*.

life·less ['laɪflɪs] *adj* □ **1.** leblos: a) tot, b) unbelebt. **2.** *fig.* matt, schwunglos.

'**life**|**·like** *adj* lebensecht, naturgetreu. '**~·line** *s* **1.** ⚓ Rettungsleine *f*. **2.** *fig.* Rettungsanker *m*. **3.** Lebenslinie *f* (*in der Hand*). '**~·long** *adj* lebenslang. **~ mem·ber** *s* Mitglied *n* auf Lebenszeit. **~ peer** *s* Peer *m* auf Lebenszeit. **~ pre·serv·er** *s* **1.** *Am.* Rettungs-, Schwimmweste *f*; Rettungsgürtel *m*. **2.** *bsd. Br.* Totschläger *m* (*Waffe*).

lif·er ['laɪfə] *s* ⚖ F Lebenslängliche *m*, *f*.

life| **raft** *s* ⚓ Rettungsfloß *n*. '**~·sav·er** *s* **1.** Lebensretter *m*. **2.** → **lifeguard. 3.** F rettender Engel; Rettung *f*. '**~·sav·ing** *adj* lebensrettend. **~ sen·tence** *s* ⚖ lebenslängliche Freiheitsstrafe. '**~-size(d)** *adj* lebensgroß, in Lebensgröße. '**~·time** I *s* Lebenszeit *f: once in a ~* sehr selten, einmal im Leben; *during* (*od. in*) *s.o.'s ~* zu j-s Lebzeiten *od.* Zeit; *in* j-s Leben. II *adj* auf Lebenszeit, lebenslang. **~ work** *s* Lebenswerk *n*.

lift [lɪft] I *s* **1.** (Hoch-, Auf)Heben *n*. **2.** ⚙ Hub(höhe *f*) *m*. **3.** Luftbrücke *f*. **4.** ✈

phys. Auftrieb *m, fig. a.* Aufschwung *m:* **give s.o. a ~** → 10. **5. give s.o. a ~** j-n (im Auto) mitnehmen; **get a ~ from s.o.** von j-m mitgenommen werden; → **thumb** II. **6.** *bsd. Br.* Lift *m,* Aufzug *m,* Fahrstuhl *m.* **7.** *(Ski- etc)*Lift *m.* **8.** ✈ Lift *m, n,* Lifting *n:* **have a ~** sich liften lassen. II *v/t* **9.** *a.* **~ up** (hoch-, auf)heben; *Stimme etc* erheben: **~ one's eyes** aufschauen, -blicken; → **finger** I, **hand** 1. **10.** *a.* **~ up** *j-n* aufmuntern, *j-m* Auftrieb *od.* Aufschwung geben. **11.** F klauen (*a. plagiieren*). **12.** *Gesicht etc* liften, straffen. III *v/i* **14.** sich heben, steigen (*a. Nebel*); **~ off** starten (*Rakete*); abheben (*Flugzeug*). **15.** sich (hoch)heben lassen. **'~·boy** *s bsd. Br.* Liftboy *m.* **'~·man** *s (irr man) bsd. Br.* Fahrstuhlführer *m.* **'~·off** *s* Start *m (e-r Rakete*); Abheben *n (e-s Flugzeugs).*

lig·a·ment ['lɪgəmənt] *s anat.* Band *n.*

lig·a·ture ['lɪgətʃə] *s 1.* Ligatur *f.* ♪ Ligatur *f.*

light¹ [laɪt] I *s 1.* Licht *n:* a) Helligkeit *f:* **stand** *(od.* **be***)* **in s.o.'s ~** j-m im Licht *(fig.* im Weg) stehen, b) Beleuchtung *f:* **in subdued ~** bei gedämpftem Licht, c) Schein *m:* **by the ~ of a candle** bei Kerzenschein, d) Lichtquelle *f:* **hide one's ~ under a bushel** sein Licht unter den Scheffel stellen, e) Sonnen-, Tageslicht *n:* **bring (come) to ~** *fig.* ans Licht bringen (kommen); **see the ~ (of day)** das Licht der Welt erblicken; *fig.* herauskommen, auf den Markt kommen; *fig.* bekannt *od.* veröffentlicht werden, f) *fig.* Aspekt *m:* **in the ~ of** unter dem Aspekt *od.* in Anbetracht (*gen*), g) *fig.* Erleuchtung *f:* **cast** *(od.* **shed, throw***)* **~ on** Licht auf *e-e Sache* werfen; zur Lösung *e-r Sache* beitragen; **I see the ~** mir geht ein Licht auf. **2.** *mot.* Scheinwerfer *m.* **3.** *Br. mst pl* (Verkehrs)Ampel *f:* **jump** *(od.* **shoot***)* **the ~s** bei Rot über die Kreuzung fahren; → **amber** 2, **green** 1, 3, **red** 1, 3, **yellow** 3. **4.** Feuer *n (zum Anzünden), bsd.* Streichholz *n:* **have you got a ~?** haben Sie Feuer? **5.** *a.* **shining ~** *fig.* Leuchte *f,* großes Licht *(Person):* → **leading light.** II *adj* **6.** hell, licht: **~ red** Hellrot *n.* III *v/t (a. irr lit)* **7.** *a.* **~ up** anzünden: **~ a cigarette** sich e-e Zigarette anzünden. **8.** be-, erleuchten,

erhellen: **~ up** hell beleuchten. **9.** *j-m* leuchten. IV *v/i (a. irr lit)* **10.** *a.* **~ up** sich entzünden. **11.** *mst* **~ up** *fig.* aufleuchten (*Augen etc*). **12.** **~ up** Licht machen; *mot.* die Scheinwerfer einschalten; F sich e-e (*Zigarette etc*) anzünden.

light² [~] I *adj* (□ → **lightly**) **1.** *allg.* leicht (*z. B. Last; Kleidung; Mahlzeit, Wein; Schlaf; Fehler, Strafe*): (**as**) **~ as air** *(od.* **a feather***)* federleicht; **~ current** ≴ Schwachstrom *m;* **no ~ matter** keine Kleinigkeit; **~ metal** Leichtmetall *n;* **~ reading** Unterhaltungslektüre *f;* **make ~ of** auf die leichte Schulter nehmen; verharmlosen, bagatellisieren. **2.** lokker (*Erde, Schnee*), locker gebacken (*Brot etc*). **3.** *Sport:* Halb...: **~ heavyweight** Halb-, Leichtschwergewicht(ler *m*) *n.* II *adv* **4.** **travel ~** mit leichtem Gepäck reisen.

light‖ bar·ri·er *s* ≴ Lichtschranke *f.* **~ bulb** *s* ≴ Glühbirne *f.*

light·en¹ ['laɪtn] I *v/i* **1.** sich aufhellen, hell(er) werden. **2.** *impers* blitzen. II *v/t* **3.** (*a.* blitzartig) erhellen.

light·en² [~] I *v/t* **1.** leichter machen, erleichtern (*beide a. fig.*): **~ s.o.'s heart** j-m das Herz leichter machen. **2.** *j-n* aufheitern. II *v/i* **3.** leichter werden: **her heart ~ed** *fig.* ihr wurde leichter ums Herz.

light·er ['laɪtə] *s 1.* Anzünder *m (a. Gerät).* **2.** Feuerzeug *n.*

'light‖-,fin·gered *adj* **1.** fingerfertig, geschickt. **2.** langfing(e)rig, diebisch. **'~--foot·ed** *adj* □ leichtfüßig. **'~-,head·ed** *adj* □ **1.** leichtsinnig, -fertig. **2.** **feel ~** (leicht) benommen sein; wie auf Wolken schweben. **'~-,heart·ed** *adj* □ unbeschwert. **'~·house** *s* Leuchtturm *m.*

light·ing ['laɪtɪŋ] *s* Beleuchtung *f.*

light·ly ['laɪtlɪ] *adv* **1.** leicht. **2.** wenig: **eat ~.** **3.** leichthin. **4.** geringschätzig.

,light-'mind·ed *adj* □ leichtfertig, -sinnig; unbeständig, flatterhaft.

light·ness¹ ['laɪtnɪs] *s* Helligkeit *f.*

light·ness² [~] *s 1.* Leichtheit *f,* Leichtigkeit *f (a. fig.).* **2.** Lockerheit *f.*

light·ning ['laɪtnɪŋ] I *s* Blitz *m:* (**as**) **quick as ~** blitzschnell; **struck by ~** vom Blitz getroffen; **like ~** wie der Blitz; → **flash** 1, **grease** 3, **streak** 1, **stroke** 2. II *adj* blitzschnell, Blitz...: **with ~ speed** mit

Blitzesschnelle. **~ con·duc·tor**, **~ rod** *s* ⚡ Blitzableiter *m*.

light| pen *s* Computer: Lichtstift *m*. **'~proof** *adj* lichtundurchlässig.

lights [laɪts] *s pl zo*. Lunge *f*.

'light·ship *s* ⚓ Feuer-, Leuchtschiff *n*. **'~weight** I *adj* leicht(gewichtig). II *s* Sport: Leichtgewicht(ler *m*) *n*. **~ year** *s ast*. Lichtjahr *n*.

lig·ne·ous ['lɪɡnɪəs] *adj* holzig, holzartig, Holz...

lik·a·ble ['laɪkəbl] *adj* liebenswert, -würdig, sympathisch.

like[1] [laɪk] I *adj u. prp* **1.** gleich (*dat*), wie (*a. adv*): **a man ~ you** ein Mann wie du; **what is he ~?** wie ist er?; **what does it look ~?** wie sieht es aus?; → **feel** 6. **2.** ähnlich (*dat*), bezeichnend für: **that is just ~ him!** das sieht ihm ähnlich. **3.** gleich (*Menge etc*): **in ~ manner** auf gleiche Weise; gleichermaßen. **4.** ähnlich: **they are (as) ~ as two eggs** sie gleichen sich wie ein Ei dem anderen. **5.** ähnlich, gleich-, derartig. II *s* **6.** der, die, das gleiche: **his ~** seinesgleichen; **the ~** dergleichen; **the ~s pl of me** F meinesgleichen, Leute pl wie ich.

like[2] [~] I *v/t* gern haben, mögen: **I ~ it** es gefällt mir; **I ~ him** ich kann ihn gut leiden; **how do you ~ it?** wie gefällt es dir?, wie findest du es?; **what do you ~ better?** was hast du lieber?, was gefällt dir besser?; **~ doing** (*bsd. Am. a.* **to do**) **s.th.** et. gern tun; **I should** (*od.* **would**) **~ to know** ich möchte gern wissen. II *v/i* wollen: (*just*) **as you ~** (ganz) wie du willst; **do as you ~** mach, was du willst; **if you ~** wenn du willst. III *s* Neigung *f*, Vorliebe *f*: **~s pl and dislikes** *pl* Neigungen *pl u.* Abneigungen *pl*.

like·a·ble → **likable**.

like·li·hood ['laɪklɪhʊd] *s* Wahrscheinlichkeit *f*: **in all ~** aller Wahrscheinlichkeit nach, höchstwahrscheinlich. **'like·ly** I *adj* **1.** wahrscheinlich, voraussichtlich: **he is** (**not**) **~ to come** er kommt wahrscheinlich (es ist unwahrscheinlich, daß er kommt). **2.** glaubhaft: **a ~ story!** *iro.* das soll glauben, wer mag! **3.** in Frage kommend, geeignet. II *adv* **4.** wahrscheinlich: **most ~** höchstwahrscheinlich; (**as**) **~ as not** (sehr) wahrscheinlich; **not ~!** F wohl kaum!

,like-'mind·ed *adj* □ gleichgesinnt.

lik·en ['laɪkən] *v/t* vergleichen (**to** mit).

like·ness ['laɪknɪs] *s* **1.** Ähnlichkeit *f* (**between** zwischen *dat*; **to** mit). **2.** Abbild *n* (**of** gen).

like·wise ['laɪkwaɪz] *adv* desgleichen, ebenso.

lik·ing ['laɪkɪŋ] *s* Vorliebe *f* (**for** für): **this is not** (**to**) **my ~** das ist nicht nach m-m Geschmack.

li·lac ['laɪlək] I *s* ♀ Flieder *m*. II *adj* lila(farben).

Lil·li·pu·tian [ˌlɪlɪˈpjuːʃn] I *adj* winzig, zwergenhaft; Liliput..., Klein(st)... II *s* Liliputaner(in).

li·lo ['laɪləʊ] *pl* **-los** *Br*. F Luftmatratze *f*.

lilt [lɪlt] *s* flotter Rhythmus; flotte *od.* schwungvolle Melodie.

lil·y ['lɪlɪ] *s* ♀ Lilie *f*: **~ of the valley** Maiglöckchen *n*. **,~'liv·ered** *adj* feig.

limb [lɪm] *s* **1.** (*Körper*)Glied *n*, *pl a*. Gliedmaßen *pl*. **2.** Hauptast *m* (*e-s Baums*): **be out on a ~** F in e-r gefährlichen Lage sein; *Br*. allein (da)stehen.

lim·ber ['lɪmbə] I *adj* **1.** biegsam, geschmeidig. **2.** beweglich, gelenkig. II *v/t* **3.** *mst* **~ up** biegsam *od.* geschmeidig machen, *Muskeln a.* auflockern: **~ o.s. up** → 4. II *v/i* **4.** *mst* **~ up** sich auflockern, Lockerungsübungen machen.

lime[1] [laɪm] I *s* 🧪 Kalk *m*. II *v/t* kalken.

lime[2] [~] *s* ♀ Linde *f*.

lime[3] [~] *s* ♀ Limonelle *f* (*Baum*); Limone *f*, Limonelle *f* (*Frucht*).

lime·light *s*: **be in the ~** im Rampenlicht *od.* im Licht der Öffentlichkeit stehen.

lim·er·ick ['lɪmərɪk] *s* Limerick *m*.

'lime|·stone *s geol*. Kalkstein *m*. **'~-wash** I *v/t* kalken, weißen, tünchen. II *s* (Kalk)Tünche *f*.

lim·it ['lɪmɪt] I *s* **1.** *fig*. Grenze *f*, Beschränkung *f*, (*Zeit- etc*)Limit *n*: **to the ~** bis zum Äußersten *od*. Letzten; **within ~s** in (gewissen) Grenzen; **there is a ~ to everything** alles hat s-e Grenzen; **off ~s** Zutritt verboten (**to** für); **that's the ~!** F das ist (doch) die Höhe! **2.** ✚, ⚙ Grenzwert *m*. **3.** ✚ Limit *n*, Preisgrenze *f*. II *v/t* **4.** beschränken, begrenzen (**to** auf *acc*); *Auflage*, *Preise etc* limitieren: **~ed in time** befristet; **~ed** (**liability**) **company** ✚ *Br*. Aktiengesellschaft *f*. **lim·i·'ta·tion** *s* **1.** *fig*. Grenze *f*: **know one's** (**own**) **~s** s-e Grenzen kennen. **2.** Begrenzung *f*, Beschränkung *f*: **~ of liability** 🏛 Haftungsbeschränkung. **3.** 🏛 Verjährung *f*: **~ (period)** Verjährungsfrist *f*.

lim·ou·sine ['lɪməziːn] *s mot.* **1.** *Br.* Luxuslimousine *f*. **2.** *Am.* Kleinbus *m*.

limp¹ [lɪmp] **I** *v/i* hinken (*a. fig. Vers etc*), humpeln. **II** *s* Hinken *n*: **walk with a ~** hinken, humpeln.

limp² [~] *adj* schlaff, schlapp: **go ~** erschlaffen.

lim·pet ['lɪmpɪt] *s zo.* Napfschnecke *f*: **hold on (od. hang on, cling) to s.o. like a ~** *fig.* wie e-e Klette an j-m hängen.

lim·pid ['lɪmpɪd] *adj* □ klar (*a. fig. Stil etc*), durchsichtig.

lim·y ['laɪmɪ] *adj* kalkig, Kalk...

lin·age ['laɪnɪdʒ] *s* **1.** Zeilenzahl *f*. **2.** Zeilenhonorar *n*.

linch·pin ['lɪntʃpɪn] *s* **1.** ⚙ Achsnagel *m*. **2.** *fig.* Stütze *f*.

lin·den ['lɪndən] *s* ♣ Linde *f*.

line¹ [laɪn] **I** *s* **1.** Linie *f* (*a. Sport*), Strich *m*: → **toe** II. **2.** a) (*Hand- etc*)Linie *f*, b) Falte *f*, Runzel *f*: **~s pl of worry** Sorgenfalten *pl*, c) Zug *m* (*im Gesicht*). **3.** Zeile *f* (*a. TV*): **read between the ~s** *fig.* zwischen den Zeilen lesen; → **hot line. 4.** *pl thea. etc* Rolle *f*, Text *m*. **5.** *pl* (*mst sg konstruiert*) *bsd. Br.* F Trauschein *m*. **6.** Linie *f*, Richtung *f*: **~ of sight** Blickrichtung. **7.** *pl* Grundsätze *pl*, Richtlinien *pl*: **along these ~s** nach diesen Grundsätzen; folgendermaßen. **8.** Art *f* u. Weise *f*, Methode *f*: **~ of thought** Auffassung *f*; Gedankengang *m*; **take a strong ~** energisch auftreten *od.* werden (**with s.o.** gegenüber j-m). **9.** Grenze *f* (*a. fig.*), Grenzlinie *f*: **draw the ~** die Grenze ziehen, haltmachen (**at** bei). **10.** Reihe *f*, Kette *f*; *bsd. Am.* (Menschen-, *a.* Auto)Schlange *f*: **stand in ~** anstehen, Schlange stehen (**for** um, nach); **drive in ~** *mot.* Kolonne fahren. **11.** Reihe *f*, Linie *f*: **be in (out of) ~** *fig.* (nicht) übereinstimmen (**with** mit); **bring (od. get) into ~** *fig.* in Einklang bringen (**with** mit); **fall into ~** sich einordnen (*fig.* sich anschließen (**with** *dat*); **keep s.o. in ~** *fig.* j-n bei der Stange halten. **12.** (Abstammungs)Linie *f*: **in the direct ~** in direkter Linie. **13.** Fach *n*, Gebiet *n*: **~ (of business)** Branche *f*; **that's not in**

my **~** das schlägt nicht in mein Fach; das liegt mir nicht. **14.** (*Verkehrs-, Eisenbahn- etc*)Linie *f*, Strecke *f*, Route *f*, engS. 🚃 Gleis *n*: **the end of the ~** *fig.* das (bittere) Ende. **15.** (*Flug- etc*)Gesellschaft *f*. **16.** *bsd. teleph.* Leitung *f*: **the ~ is busy** (*Br.* **engaged**) die Leitung ist besetzt; **hold the ~** bleiben Sie am Apparat; → **hot line. 17.** 𝕏 (Rohr)Leitung *f*. **18.** 𝕏 a) Linie: **behind the enemy ~s** hinter den feindlichen Linien, b) Front *f*: **all along the ~, down the ~** *fig.* auf der ganzen Linie. **19.** *geogr.* Längen- *od.* Breitenkreis *m*: **the ⚋** der Äquator. **20.** Leine *f*; Schnur *f*; Seil *n*. **II** *v/t* **21.** → **line up** I. **III** *v/t* **22.** lini(i)eren. **23.** zeichnen; skizzieren. *Gesicht* (zer)furchen. **25.** *Straße* etc säumen.

Verbindungen mit Adverbien:

line| off *v/t* abgrenzen. **~ up** *v/i* **1.** sich in e-r Reihe *od.* Linie aufstellen, (*Sport*) sich aufstellen. **2.** *bsd. Am.* sich anstellen (**for** um, nach). **II** *v/t* **3.** in e-r Reihe *od.* Linie aufstellen. **4.** F auf die Beine stellen, organisieren.

line² [~] *v/t* **1.** *Kleid etc* füttern. **2.** *bsd.* ⚙ auskleiden, -schlagen (**with** mit), *Bremsen, Kupplung* belegen. **3.** (an)füllen: **~ one's pocket(s)** (*od.* **purse**) sich bereichern.

lin·e·age¹ ['lɪnɪɪdʒ] *s* **1.** geradlinige Abstammung. **2.** Stammbaum *m*. **3.** Geschlecht *n*.

line·age² → **linage.**

lin·e·al ['lɪnɪəl] *adj* □ geradlinig, direkt (*Nachkomme etc*).

lin·e·a·ment ['lɪnɪəmənt] *s mst pl* (Gesichts)Zug *m*.

lin·e·ar ['lɪnɪə] *adj* □ **1.** 𝔸, ⚙ *etc* linear. **2.** Längen...

lin·en ['lɪnɪn] **I** *s* **1.** Leinen *n*. **2.** (*Bett-, Unter- etc*)Wäsche *f*: **wash one's dirty ~ in public** *fig.* s-e schmutzige Wäsche in der Öffentlichkeit waschen. **II** *adj* **3.** Leinen... **~ bas·ket** *s bsd. Br.* F Wäschekorb *m*.

lin·er ['laɪnə] *s* **1.** ⚓ Linienschiff *n*. **2.** ✈ Verkehrsflugzeug *n*. **3.** → **eye liner.**

lines|·man ['laɪnzmən] *s* (*irr man*) *Sport*: Linienrichter *m*. **~ wom·an** *s* (*irr woman*) Linienrichterin *f*.

'line·up *s* **1.** *Sport*: Aufstellung *f*. **2.** *bsd. Am.* (Menschen)Schlange *f*.

lin·ger ['lɪŋgə] v/i **1.** verweilen, sich aufhalten (*beide a. fig.* **over, on** bei e-m *Thema etc*): ~ **on** noch dableiben; nachklingen (*Ton*); *fig.* fortleben, bestehen (*Tradition etc*). **2.** *fig.* (zurück)bleiben (*Verdacht etc*). **3.** trödeln: ~ **about** (*od.* **around**) herumtrödeln. '**lin·ger·ing** *adj* □ **1.** nachklingend. **2.** schleichend (*Krankheit*).

lin·go ['lɪŋgəʊ] *pl* **-goes** s F **1.** Kauderwelsch n. **2.** (Fach)Jargon m.

lin·gual ['lɪŋgwəl] *adj* Zungen...

lin·guist ['lɪŋgwɪst] s **1.** Linguist(in), Sprachwissenschaftler(in). **2.** Sprachkundige m, f: **be a good** ~ (sehr) sprachbegabt sein. **lin'guist·ic** I *adj* (~**ally**) **1.** linguistisch, sprachwissenschaftlich. **2.** Sprach(en)... II *s pl* (*mst sg konstruiert*) **3.** Linguistik f, Sprachwissenschaft f.

lin·i·ment ['lɪnɪmənt] s 🧪 Einreibemittel n.

lin·ing ['laɪnɪŋ] s **1.** Futter(stoff m) n. **2.** *bsd.* ⚙ Auskleidung f, (Brems-, Kupplungs)Belag m.

link [lɪŋk] I s **1.** (Ketten)Glied n; *fig.* Glied n (*in e-r Kette von Ereignissen etc*); Bindeglied n; Verbindung f, Zs.-hang m. **2.** Manschettenknopf m. II v/t **3.** a. ~ **up** verketten, -binden (**to, with** mit): ~ **arms** sich unter- od. einhaken (**with** bei). **4.** a. ~ **up** *fig.* in Verbindung od. Zs.-hang bringen (**with** mit), e-n Zs.-hang herstellen zwischen (*dat*). III v/i **5.** a. ~ **up** sich verketten od. verbinden (**to, with** mit). **6.** a. ~ **up** *fig.* sich zs.-fügen.

links [lɪŋks] → **golf links**.

'**link-up** s Verbindung f, Zs.-hang m.

li·no·le·um [lɪ'nəʊljəm] s Linoleum n.

lin·seed ['lɪnsiːd] s 🌿 Leinsamen m. ~ **oil** s Leinöl n.

lin·tel ['lɪntl] s △ Oberschwelle f, (Tür-, Fenster)Sturz m.

li·on ['laɪən] s **1.** *zo.* Löwe m (*a. ast.* ♌): **go into the** ~'**s den** *fig.* sich in die Höhle des Löwen wagen; **the** ~'**s share** der Löwenanteil; → **beard** II. **2.** *fig.* Größe f, Berühmtheit f (*Person*). **li·on·ess** ['~es] s Löwin f.

lip [lɪp] s **1.** *anat.* Lippe f: **lower** (**upper**) ~ Unter-(Ober)lippe; **keep a stiff upper** ~ *fig.* Haltung bewahren; sich nichts anmerken lassen; **bite one's** ~ *fig.* sich

auf die Lippen beißen; → **smack**² **2. 2.** F Unverschämtheit f: **none of your** ~**!** sei nicht so unverschämt *od.* frech! **3.** Rand m (*e-r Wunde, e-s Kraters etc*). '**~-read** v/t u. v/i (*irr* **read**) von den Lippen ablesen. ~ **ser·vice** s Lippenbekenntnis n. '**~-stick** s Lippenstift m: **put on** ~ sich die Lippen schminken.

liq·ue·fy ['lɪkwɪfaɪ] v/t u. v/i **1.** (sich) verflüssigen. **2.** schmelzen.

li·queur [lɪ'kjʊə] s Likör m.

liq·uid ['lɪkwɪd] I *adj* □ **1.** flüssig. **2.** Flüssigkeits...: ~ **measure** Flüssigkeitsmaß n. **3.** 🌿 liquid, flüssig. II *s* **4.** Flüssigkeit f.

liq·ui·date ['lɪkwɪdeɪt] v/t **1.** 🌿 liquidieren: a) *Gesellschaft* auflösen, b) *Sachwerte etc* realisieren, zu Geld machen, c) *Schulden etc* tilgen. **2.** *fig.* liquidieren, beseitigen. **liq·ui'da·tion** s **1.** 🌿 Liquidation f: a) Auflösung f, b) Realisierung f, c) Tilgung f. **2.** *fig.* Liquidierung f, Beseitigung f.

li·quid·i·ty [lɪ'kwɪdətɪ] s **1.** flüssiger Zustand. **2.** 🌿 Liquidität f, Flüssigkeit f.

liq·ui·dize ['lɪkwɪdaɪz] v/t **1.** (v/i sich) verflüssigen. **2.** (im Mixer) zerkleinern od. pürieren. '**liq·ui·diz·er** s Mixer m, Mixgerät n.

liq·uor ['lɪkə] s a) Br. alkoholische Getränke pl, Alkohol m: **hard** ~ → b), b) Am. Schnaps m, Spirituosen pl: ~ **cabinet** Hausbar f.

liq·uo·rice → **licorice**.

li·ra ['lɪərə] pl **-re** ['~rɪ], **-ras** s Lira f.

lisp [lɪsp] I v/i lispeln (*a.* v/t), mit der Zunge anstoßen. II s Lispeln n: **speak with a** ~ → I.

list¹ [lɪst] I s **1.** Liste f, Verzeichnis n: **be on the** ~ auf der Liste stehen; ~ **price** Listenpreis m. II v/t **2.** (in e-r Liste) verzeichnen, erfassen, registrieren: ~**ed building** Br. Gebäude n unter Denkmalschutz. **3.** in e-r Liste eintragen.

list² [lɪst] ⚓ I s Schlagseite f. II v/i Schlagseite haben *od.* bekommen.

lis·ten ['lɪsn] v/i **1.** hören, horchen (**to** auf *acc*): ~ **to** a) j-m zuhören, j-n anhören: ~**!** hör mal!), b) auf j-n, j-s Rat hören, c) e-m *Rat etc* folgen; → **reason** 3. **2.** ~ **in** Radio hören: ~ **in to a concert** sich ein Konzert im Radio anhören. '**lis·ten·er** s **1.** Horcher(in). **2.** Zuhörer(in): **be a**

good ~ (gut) zuhören können. **3.** *Radio:* Hörer(in).

list-less ['lɪstlɪs] *adj* □ lust-, teilnahmslos.

lit [lɪt] *pret u. pp von* **light¹**.

lit·a·ny ['lɪtənɪ] *s eccl.* Litanei *f (a. fig.).*

li·ter *Am. →* **litre.**

lit·er·a·cy ['lɪtərəsɪ] *s* **1.** Fähigkeit *f* zu lesen u. zu schreiben. **2.** (literarische) Bildung, Belesenheit.

lit·er·al ['lɪtərəl] *adj* □ **1.** wörtlich (*Übersetzung etc*): **take s.th. ~ly** et. wörtlich nehmen. **2.** genau, wahrheitsgetreu. **3.** nüchtern, trocken, prosaisch. **4.** wörtlich, eigentlich (*Bedeutung e-s Worts etc*). **5.** buchstäblich: **he did ~ly nothing.**

lit·er·ar·y ['lɪtərərɪ] *adj* □ **1.** literarisch, Literatur...: **~ critic** Literaturkritiker(in); **~ history** Literaturgeschichte *f*. **2.** gewählt, hochgestochen (*Ausdruck etc*).

lit·er·ate ['lɪtərət] *adj* □ **1. be ~** lesen u. schreiben können. **2.** (literarisch) gebildet, belesen. **lit·er·a·ture** ['~ətʃə] *s* **1.** Literatur *f.* **2.** F Informationsmaterial *n.*

lith·o·graph ['lɪθəʊɡrɑːf] *s* Lithographie *f,* Steindruck *m.*

lit·i·gant ['lɪtɪɡənt] 📖 I *adj* streitend, prozeßführend. II *s* Prozeßführende *m, f,* streitende Partei. **lit·i·gate** ['~ɡeɪt] *v/i (u. v/t)* prozessieren *od.* streiten (um). **lit·i·ga·tion** *s* Rechtsstreit *m,* Prozeß *m.*

li·to·tes ['laɪtəʊtiːz] *s rhet.* Litotes *f.*

li·tre ['liːtə] *s bsd. Br.* Liter *m, a. n.*

lit·ter ['lɪtə] I *s* **1.** (herumliegender) Abfall. **2.** Streu *f (für Tiere),* (a. *für Pflanzen*) Stroh *n*. **3.** *zo.* Wurf *m*. **4.** Trage *f;* Sänfte *f.* II *v/t* **5.** Abfall herumliegen lassen in (*dat*) *od.* auf (*dat*); *Park etc* verschandeln (**with** mit). **6.** *mst* **~ down** Streu legen für; *Stall* einstreuen. **7.** *Pflanzen* mit Stroh abdecken. **8.** *zo.* *Junge* werfen. III *v/i* **9.** *zo.* (Junge) werfen. **~ bas·ket**, '**~·bin** *s* Abfallkorb *m.* '**~·bug** *s bsd. Am.* F, '**~·lout** *s bsd. Br.* F *j-d, der Straßen etc mit Abfall verschandelt.*

lit·tle ['lɪtl] I *adj* **1.** klein (*Kind etc*): **the ~ ones** *pl* die Kleinen *pl;* → **finger** I. **2.** kurz (*Strecke od. Zeit*). **3.** wenig (*Hoffnung etc*): **a ~ jam** ein wenig *od.* ein

bißchen Marmelade. **4.** klein, gering(-fügig). II *adv* **5.** wenig, kaum: **think ~ of** wenig halten von; **for as ~ as £10** für nur 10 Pfund. **6.** wenig, selten: **I see him very ~.** III *s* **7.** Kleinigkeit *f, das* wenige, *das* bißchen: **a ~** ein wenig, ein bißchen; **~ by ~** (ganz) allmählich, nach u. nach. **8. in ~** im kleinen, in kleinem Maßstab.

lit·ur·gy ['lɪtədʒɪ] *s eccl.* Liturgie *f.*

liv·a·ble ['lɪvəbl] *adj* **1.** wohnlich, bewohnbar. **2.** lebenswert (*Leben*). **3.** *a.* **~ with** erträglich (*Schmerzen etc*): **not ~** (**with**) unerträglich. **4.** *a.* **~ with** umgänglich (*Person*).

live¹ [lɪv] I *v/i* leben: a) am Leben sein, am Leben bleiben: **~ through the night** die Nacht überleben; **you ~ and learn** man lernt nie aus; **~ on** bsd. fig. weiter-, fortleben, c) sich ernähren (**on** von): **he ~s on his wife** er lebt auf Kosten *od.* von (den Einkünften) s-r Frau, d) ein *ehrliches etc* Leben führen: **~ honestly; ~ up to** s-n *Grundsätzen etc* gemäß leben, *s-m* Ruf etc gerecht werden, *den Erwartungen etc* entsprechen, e) wohnen (**with** bei): **~ with** zs.-leben mit; **~ together** zs.-leben, f) das Leben genießen: **~ and let ~** leben u. leben lassen. II *v/t* ein *bestimmtes Leben* führen.

live² [laɪv] I *adj* **1.** lebend, lebendig: **~ weight** Lebendgewicht *n;* **a real ~ lord** F ein richtiger *od.* echter Lord. **2.** aktuell (*Frage etc*). **3.** scharf (*Munition etc*). **4.** ⚡ stromführend: **~ wire** F Energiebündel *n.* **5.** *Rundfunk, TV:* Direkt..., Original..., Live-... II *adv* **6.** direkt, original, live.

live·a·ble → **livable.**

live·li·hood ['laɪvlɪhʊd] *s* Lebensunterhalt *m:* **earn** (*od.* **gain, make**) **a** (*od.* **one's**) **~** s-n Lebensunterhalt verdienen.

live·li·ness ['laɪvlɪnɪs] *s* **1.** Lebhaftigkeit *f.* **2.** Lebendigkeit *f.* '**live·ly** *adj* □ **1.** lebhaft (*Interesse, Person, Phantasie etc*). **2.** lebendig (*Schilderung etc*). **3.** aufregend (*Zeiten*): **make it** (*od.* **things**) **~ for s.o., give s.o. a ~ time** j-m (*kräftig*) einheizen. **4.** schnell, flott (*Tempo etc*).

liv·en ['laɪvn] *mst* **~ up** I *v/t* beleben, Leben bringen in (*acc*). II *v/i* in Schwung kommen.

liv·er¹ ['lɪvə] s anat. Leber f (a. gastr.).

liv·er² [~] s: **be a fast ~** ein flottes Leben führen; **loose ~** liederlicher Mensch.

liv·er·ied ['lɪvərɪd] adj livriert.

liv·er·ish ['lɪvərɪʃ] adj **1. be ~** F es mit der Leber haben. **2.** mürrisch.

liv·er| **sau·sage** s Leberwurst f. **~ spot** s Leberfleck m. **~·wurst** ['~wɜːst] s bsd. Am. Leberwurst f.

liv·er·y ['lɪvərɪ] s Livree f: **in ~** in Livree.

lives [laɪvz] pl von **life**.

live·stock ['laɪvstɒk] s Vieh(bestand m) n.

liv·id ['lɪvɪd] adj □ **1.** blau, bläulich (verfärbt). **2.** bleifarben, graublau. **3.** fahl, aschgrau, bleich (**with** vor dat). **4.** F fuchsteufelswild.

liv·ing ['lɪvɪŋ] **I** adj **1.** lebend (a. Sprache): **while ~** bei od. zu Lebzeiten; **within ~ memory** seit Menschengedenken; → **daylight**. **2.** Lebens...: **~ conditions** pl Lebensbedingungen pl. **II** s **3. the ~** pl die Lebenden pl. **4.** das Leben: → **cost 1**. **5.** Leben(sweise f) n: **loose ~** lockerer Lebenswandel; → **clean 5**. **6.** Lebensunterhalt m: **earn** (od. **gain, get, make**) **a ~** s-n Lebensunterhalt verdienen (**as** als; **out of** durch, mit). **~ room** s Wohnzimmer n. **~ space** s Wohnfläche f, -raum m.

liz·ard ['lɪzəd] s zo. Eidechse f.

lla·ma ['lɑːmə] s zo. Lama n.

load [ləʊd] **I** s **1.** Last f, fig. a. Bürde f: **his decision took a ~ off my mind** bei s-r Entscheidung fiel mir ein Stein vom Herzen. **2.** Ladung f (a. e-r Schußwaffe): **get a ~ of** F sich ansehen od. anhören; et. zu sehen od. zu hören bekommen; **get a ~ of this!** F hör od. schau dir das mal an! **3.** pl (od. F) Massen pl (von Geld etc), e-e Unmasse (Leute etc): **there were ~s to eat** es gab massenhaft zu essen. **4.** ⚡, ⊕ Belastung f. **II** v/t **5.** a. **~ up** Fahrzeug etc beladen (**with** mit). **6.** Gegenstand etc laden (**into** in acc; **onto** auf acc), Güter verladen. **7.** Schußwaffe laden: **~ the camera** e-n Film (in die Kamera) einlegen. **8.** j-n überhäufen (**with** mit Arbeit, Vorwürfen etc). **9.** beschweren, schwerer machen, engS. Würfel sinnvoll fälschen od. präparieren. **III** v/t **10.** mst **~ up** (auf-, ein)laden. **11.** (das Gewehr etc) laden, phot. e-n Film einlegen.

'load·ed adj **1.** be-, geladen etc, → **load** **II**. **2. ~ question** Fang- od. Suggestivfrage f; **~ word** emotionsgeladenes Wort; vorbelastetes Wort; Reizwort n. **3.** F stinkreich: **be ~ a.** Geld wie Heu haben.

loaf¹ [ləʊf] pl **loaves** [ləʊvz] s **1.** Laib m (Brot); weitS. Brot n. **2.** a. **meat ~** gastr. Hackbraten m. **3. use one's ~** Br. sl. sein Hirn anstrengen, (nach)denken.

loaf² [~] F **I** v/i **1.** a. **~ about** (od. **around**) herumlungern; **~ about** (od. **around**) **the streets** auf den Straßen herumlungern. **2.** faulenzen. **II** v/t **3. ~ away** Zeit verbummeln. **'loaf·er** s F **1.** Müßiggänger(in). **2.** Faulenzer(in). **3.** bsd. Am. leichter Slipper.

loam [ləʊm] s Lehm m. **'loam·y** adj lehmig, Lehm...

loan [ləʊn] **I** s **1.** (Ver)Leihen n: **on ~** leihweise; **a book on ~** ein geliehenes Buch; **may I have the ~ of ...?** darf ich (mir) ... (aus)leihen? **2.** ✝ Anleihe f (a. fig.): **take up a ~** e-e Anleihe aufnehmen (**on** auf acc). **3.** ✝ Darlehen n, Kredit m. **4.** Leihgabe f (für e-e Ausstellung). **II** v/t **5.** bsd. Am. (**to**) (aus)leihen (dat), ver-, ausleihen (an acc). **~ shark** s F Kredithai m. **'~·word** s ling. Lehnwort n.

loath [ləʊθ] adj: **be ~ to do s.th.** et. nur (sehr) ungern od. widerwillig tun.

loathe [ləʊð] v/t verabscheuen, hassen: **~ doing s.th.** es hassen, et. zu tun. **'loath·ing** s Abscheu m. **loath·some** ['~səm] adj □ widerlich, abscheulich.

loaves [ləʊvz] pl von **loaf¹**.

lob [lɒb] (bsd. Tennis) **I** s Lob m. **II** v/t a) **~ a ball →** III, b) Gegner überlobben. **III** v/i lobben, e-n Lob spielen od. schlagen.

lob·by ['lɒbɪ] **I** s **1.** Vor-, Eingangshalle f; Wandelhalle f; thea. Foyer n. **2.** pol. Lobby f, Interessengruppe f, -verband m. **II** v/t **3.** a. **~ through** Gesetzesvorlage mit Hilfe e-r Lobby durchbringen. **4.** Abgeordnete beeinflussen. **'lob·by·ist** s Lobbyist m.

lobe [ləʊb] s ⚕, anat. Lappen m: **~** (**of the ear**) Ohrläppchen n.

lob·ster ['lɒbstə] s zo. Hummer m: (**as**) **red as a ~** krebsrot.

lo·cal ['ləʊkl] **I** adj □ **1.** lokal, örtlich: **~ call** teleph. Ortsgespräch n; **~ derby**

(*Sport*) Lokalderby *n*; **~ elections** *pl* Kommunalwahlen *pl*; **~ hero** (*bsd. Sport*) Lokalmatador *m*; **~ news** Lokalnachrichten *pl*; **~ time** Ortszeit *f*; **~ traffic** Lokal-, Orts-, Nahverkehr *m*; → **colour** 1. **2.** Orts-..., ansässig, hiesig. **3.** lokal, örtlich (beschränkt): **~ an(a)esthesia** örtliche Betäubung; **~ custom** ortsüblicher Brauch. **II s 4.** *mst pl* Ortsansässige *m, f*, Einheimische *m, f*. **5.** *Br.* F (nächstgelegene) Kneipe, *bsd.* Stammkneipe *f*.

lo·cale [ləʊˈkɑːl] *s* Schauplatz *m*, Szene *f*.

lo·cal·i·ty [ləʊˈkælətɪ] *s* **1.** a) Örtlichkeit *f*, Ort *m*: **sense of ~** Ortssinn *m*, b) Gegend *f*. **2.** (*örtliche*) Lage.

lo·cal·ize [ˈləʊkəlaɪz] *v/t* lokalisieren (**to** auf *acc*).

lo·cate [ləʊˈkeɪt] **I** *v/t* **1.** ausfindig machen, aufspüren; ✤ *etc* orten; ✕ *Ziel* ausmachen. **2.** *Büro etc* errichten. **3.** (*an e-m bestimmten Ort*) an- *od.* unterbringen; (*an e-m Ort*) verlegen: **be ~d** gelegen sein, liegen, sich befinden. **II** *v/i* **4.** *Am.* sich niederlassen. **lo·ca·tion** *s* **1.** Ausfindigmachen *n*; ✤ *etc* Ortung *f*; ✕ Ausmachen *n*. **2.** Stelle *f*, Platz *m*; Lage *f*, Standort *m*. **3.** *Film, TV:* Gelände *n* für Außenaufnahmen: **~ shooting, shooting on ~** Außenaufnahmen *pl*.

loch [lɒx] *s schott.* **1.** See *m*. **2.** Bucht *f*.

lock¹ [lɒk] **I** *s* **1.** (*Tür-, Gewehr- etc-*) Schloß *n*: **under ~ and key** hinter Schloß u. Riegel; unter Verschluß; **~, stock and barrel** *fig.* mit allem Drum u. Dran; mit Stumpf u. Stiel; mit Sack u. Pack. **2.** Verschluß *m*; Sperrvorrichtung *f*. **3.** Schleuse(nkammer) *f*. **II** *v/t* **4.** *a.* **~ up** zu-, verschließen, zu-, versperren. **5.** *a.* **~ up** einschließen, (ein)sperren (**in, into** in *acc*): **~ away** wegschließen; **~ out** ausschließen (*a.* ✦). **6.** umschlingen, umfassen, *in die Arme* schließen. **7.** ⚙ sperren. **III** *v/i* **8.** schließen: **~ up** abschließen. **9.** ab- *od.* verschließbar sein. **10.** *mot. etc* blockieren (*Räder*).

lock² [~] *s* (*Haar*)Locke *f*, (-)Strähne *f*.

lock·er [ˈlɒkə] *s* **1.** Schließfach *n*. Spind *m, n*.

lock·et [ˈlɒkɪt] *s* Medaillon *n*.

'lock·jaw *s* 🜥 **1.** Kiefersperre *f*. Wundstarrkrampf *m.* **~ keep·er** *s* Schleusenwärter *m.* **'~·out** *s* ✦ Aus-

sperrung *f*. **'~·up** *s* **1.** Arrestzelle *f*; F Kittchen *n*. **2.** *bsd. Br.* (Einzel)Garage *f*.

lo·co [ˈləʊkəʊ] *bes. Am. sl.* verrückt (*a. Ideen etc*).

lo·co·mo·tion [ˌləʊkəˈməʊʃn] *s* Fortbewegungs... **'lo·co·mo·tive** [~tɪv] **I** *adj* Fortbewegungs... **II** *s* 🚂 Lokomotive *f*.

lo·cust [ˈləʊkəst] *s zo.* Heuschrecke *f*.

lo·cu·tion [ləʊˈkjuːʃn] *s* **1.** Ausdrucks-, Redeweise *f*. **2.** Redewendung *f*, Ausdruck *m*.

lodge [lɒdʒ] **I** *s* **1.** Sommer-, Gartenhaus *n*; (*Jagd- etc*)Hütte *f*; Gärtner-, Pförtnerhaus *n*. **2.** Portier-, Pförtnerloge *f*. **II** *v/i* **3.** logieren, (*bsd.* vorübergehend *od.* in Untermiete) wohnen. **4.** übernachten. **5.** stecken(bleiben) (*Kugel, Bissen etc*). **III** *v/t* **6.** aufnehmen, beherbergen, (für die Nacht) unterbringen. **7.** *Antrag, Beschwerde etc* einreichen, *Anzeige* erstatten, *Berufung, Protest* einlegen (**with** bei). **'lodg·er** *s* Untermieter(in): **take ~s** Zimmer vermieten. **'lodg·ing** *s* **1.** Wohnen *n*. **2.** *a. pl* Unterkunft *f*: **night's ~, ~ for the night** Nachtquartier *n*; **~ house** Fremdenheim *n*, Pension *f*; → **board** 4. **3.** *pl* möbliertes Zimmer: **live in ~s** möbliert wohnen.

loft [lɒft] *s* **1.** Dachboden *m*; Speicher *m*. **2.** 🜨 Empore *f*, (*Orgel*)Chor *m*. **'loft·y** *adj* □ **1.** hoch(ragend). **2.** hochfliegend (*Pläne etc*), hochgesteckt (*Ziele etc*), erhaben (*Gedanken, Stil etc*). **3.** stolz, hochmütig.

log [lɒg] **I** *s* **1.** (Holz)Klotz *m*; (*gefällter*) Baumstamm; (*großes*) (Holz)Scheit: → **sleep** II. 2. → **logbook. II** *v/t* **3.** *a.* **~ up** in das Logbuch *etc* eintragen; *allg.* *Ereignisse etc* aufzeichnen, festhalten.

log·a·rithm [ˈlɒgərɪðəm] *s* ⅍ Logarithmus *m*.

'log·book *s* **1.** ✤ Logbuch *n*. **2.** ✈ Flugbuch *n*. **3.** *mot.* Bord-, Fahrtenbuch *n*. **4.** *mot. Br.* Kraftfahrzeugbrief *m*. **~ cab·in** *s* Blockhaus *n*, -hütte *f*.

log·ger·heads [ˈlɒgəhedz] *s pl*: **be at ~** Streit haben (**with** mit), sich in den Haaren liegen.

log·ic [ˈlɒdʒɪk] *s phls. u. allg.* Logik *f*. **'log·i·cal** *adj* □ logisch.

lo·gis·tics [ləʊˈdʒɪstɪks] *s pl* (*oft sg konstruiert*) ✕, ✦ Logistik *f*.

loin [lɔɪn] *s* **1.** *mst pl anat.* Lende *f*. **2.**

gastr. Lende(nstück *n*) *f.* '**~·cloth** *s* Lendenschurz *m.*

loi·ter ['lɔɪtə] **I** *v/i* **1.** bummeln: a) schlendern, b) trödeln. **2.** *a.* **~ about** (*od.* **around**) herumlungern. **II** *v/t* **3.** **~ away** *Zeit* vertrödeln. '**loi·ter·er** *s* Bummler(in).

loll [lɒl] **I** *v/i* **1.** sich rekeln *od.* räkeln: **~ about** (*od.* **around**) herumlümmeln. **2.** **~ out** heraushängen (*Zunge*). **II** *v/t* **3.** **~ out** *Zunge* heraushängen lassen.

lol·li·pop ['lɒlɪpɒp] *s* **1.** Lutscher *m.* **2.** *Br.* Eis *n* am Stiel. **~ man** *s* (*irr* **man**) *Br.* F (*etwa*) Schülerlotse *m.* **~ wom·an** *s* (*irr* **woman**) *Br.* F (*etwa*) Schülerlotsin *f.*

lol·lop ['lɒləp] *v/i* hoppeln (*Hase, Fahrzeug*), latschen (*Person*).

lol·ly ['lɒlɪ] *s* **1.** F → *lollipop* 1. **2.** → *lollipop* 2. **3.** *Br. sl.* Kies *n* (*Geld*).

Lon·don·er ['lʌndənə] *s* Londoner(in).

lone [ləʊn] *adj* **1.** einzeln: **play a ~ hand** *fig.* e-n Alleingang machen; → *wolf* 1. **2.** alleinstehend, einzeln (*Haus etc*). **lone·li·ness** ['~lɪnɪs] *s* Einsamkeit *f.* '**lone·ly** *adj* einsam. '**lon·er** *s* Einzelgänger *m* (*a. zo.*). **lone·some** ['~səm] *adj* □ *bsd. Am.* einsam.

long¹ [lɒŋ] **I** *adj* **1.** *allg.* lang (*a. fig.*): → *run* 1. **2.** weit, lang (*Weg*), weit (*Entfernung*). **3.** zu lang: **the coat is ~ on him** der Mantel ist ihm zu lang. **4.** weitreichend (*Gedanken*), gut (*Gedächtnis*). **5.** ♱ langfristig. **6.** **be ~ on** F e-e Menge ... haben. **II** *adv* **7.** lang(e): **~ dead** schon lange tot; **as** (*od.* **so**) **~ as** solange wie; vorausgesetzt, daß; falls; **~ after** lange danach; **as ~ ago as 1900** schon 1900; **so ~!** F bis dann!; → *ago, all* 1. **III** *s* **8.** (e-e) lange Zeit: **at (the) ~est** längstens; **for ~** lange (Zeit); **take ~ (to do s.th.)** lange brauchen(, um et. zu tun); → *before* 5.

long² [~] *v/i* sich sehnen (*for* nach): **~ to do s.th.** sich danach sehnen, et. zu tun.

long-'dis·tance *adj* **1.** Fern...: **~ call** *teleph.* Ferngespräch *n*; **~ driver** Fernfahrer *m.* **2.** ✔, *Sport:* Langstrecken... **~ drink** *s* Longdrink *m.* **~'haired** *adj* langhaarig.

long·ing ['lɒŋɪŋ] **I** *adj* □ sehnsüchtig. **II** *s* Sehnsucht *f* (*for* nach).

long·ish ['lɒŋɪʃ] *adj* **1.** ziemlich lang. **2.** länglich.

lon·gi·tude ['lɒndʒɪtjuːd] *s geogr.* Länge *f:* → *degree* 2.

long johns *s pl* F lange Unterhose. **~ jump** *s Leichtathletik: bsd. Br.* Weitsprung *m.* **~ jump·er** *s Leichtathletik: bsd. Br.* Weitspringer(in). **~'lived** *adj* **1.** langlebig. **2.** dauerhaft. **~·play·ing rec·ord** *s* Langspielplatte *f.* **~'range** *adj* **1.** ✗, ✔ Fern...; Langstrecken... langfristig. **2.** dauerhaft. **~·shore·man** ['~mən] *s* (*irr* **man**) *bsd. Am.* Dock-, Hafenarbeiter *m.* **~ shot** *s* **1.** *Sport:* Weitschuß *m.* **2.** *fig.* riskante Angelegenheit. **3.** *not by a* **~** *fig.* bei weitem nicht, nicht im entferntesten. **~'sight·ed** *adj* □ ⚕ weitsichtig, *fig. a.* weitblickend. **~'stand·ing** *adj* seit langer Zeit bestehend, alt. '**~·term** *adj* langfristig: **~ memory** Langzeitgedächtnis *n.* '**~·time** *adj* langjährig. **long·standing. ~ wave** *s* ⚡, *phys.* Langwelle *f.* '**~·wave** *adj* ⚡, *phys.* Langwellen... **~·wind·ed** [~'wɪndɪd] *adj* □ **1.** ausdauernd (*Person*). **2.** langatmig, weitschweifig (*Erzählung etc*), (*a. Person*) umständlich.

loo· [luː] *s bsd. Br.* F Klo *n:* **in the ~** auf dem *od.* im Klo; **~ attendant** Klofrau *f*; **~ paper** Klopapier *n.*

look [lʊk] **I** *s* **1.** Blick *m* (*at auf acc*): **cast** (*od.* **throw**) *a* **~** e-n Blick werfen auf; **give s.o. an angry ~** j-m e-n wütenden Blick zuwerfen, j-n wütend ansehen; **have a ~ at s.th.** (sich) et. ansehen; **have a ~ round** sich umschauen in (*dat*). **2.** Miene *f*, (*Gesichts*)Ausdruck *m:* **the ~ on his face** sein Gesichtsausdruck. **3.** *oft pl* Aussehen *n:* **have the ~ of** aussehen wie. **II** *v/i* **4.** schauen: **don't ~!** nicht hersehen!; **~ who is coming!** schau (mal), wer da kommt. **5.** (nach-) schauen, nachsehen. **6.** ausschauen, -sehen (*beide a. fig.*): **~ well on s.o.** j-m stehen (*Hut etc*); **it ~s like snow(ing)** es sieht nach Schnee aus. **7.** liegen *od.* (hinaus)gehen nach: **my room ~s north.** **III** *v/t* **8.** j-m (*in die Augen etc*) sehen *od.* schauen *od.* blicken: **~ s.o. in the eyes.** **9.** aussehen wie: **she does not ~ her age** man sieht ihr ihr Alter nicht an; **~ an idiot** *fig.* wie ein Idiot dastehen. **10.** durch Blicke ausdrücken: **~ one's surprise** überrascht blicken *od.* dreinschauen; → *dagger.*

Verbindungen mit Präpositionen:
look| a·bout → **look around. ~ af·ter**
v/i **1.** nachblicken, -schauen, -sehen
(*dat*). **2.** aufpassen auf (*acc*), sich kümmern um. **~ a·round** *v/i* **1.** sich umschauen *od.* umsehen in (*dat*). **2. ~ one**
sich umsehen *od.* umblicken. **~ at** *v/i*
1. ansehen, anschauen, betrachten; **~**
one's watch auf die Uhr schauen; **to ~**
him wenn man ihn (so) ansieht. **2.** sich
et. ansehen, *et.* prüfen. **~ for** *v/i* suchen (nach). **~ in·to** *v/i* **1.** (hinein-)
schauen *od.* (-)sehen in (*acc*): **~ the**
mirror in den Spiegel schauen. **2.** untersuchen, prüfen. **~ on** *v/i* ansehen,
betrachten (**as** als). **~ on·to** *v/i* (hinaus)gehen auf (*acc*) *od.* nach: **my room**
looks onto the garden. ~ o·ver *v/i* **1.**
schauen *od.* blicken über (*acc*). **2.** (sich)
et. (flüchtig) ansehen *od.* anschauen,
et. (flüchtig) überprüfen. **~ round** →
look around. ~ through *v/i* **1.** blicken
durch. **2.** (hin)durchsehen *od.* (-)durchschauen durch. **3.** *fig.* j-n, *et.* durchschauen. **4.** *et.* (flüchtig) durchsehen
od. -schauen. **~ to** *v/i* **1.** achten *od.* achtgeben auf (*acc*): **~ it that** achte darauf,
daß; sieh zu, daß. **2. ~ s.o. to do s.th.**
von j-m erwarten, daß er et. tut: **I ~ you**
to help me (*od.* **for help**) ich erwarte
Hilfe von dir. **~ to·ward(s)** → **look** 7.
Verbindungen mit Adverbien:
look| a·bout → **look around. ~ a·head**
v/i **1.** nach vorne sehen *od.* blicken *od.*
schauen. **2.** *fig.* vorausschauen (**two**
years um zwei Jahre). **~ a·round** *v/i*
sich umblicken *od.* -sehen *od.* -schauen
(**for** nach). **~ a·way** *v/i* wegblicken, -sehen, -schauen. **~ back** *v/i* **1.** sich umsehen. **2.** *a. fig.* zurückblicken, -schauen
(**on, to** auf *acc*). **~ down** *v/i* **1.** hinunterblicken, -sehen, -schauen, herunterblicken, -sehen, -schauen (**on** auf *acc*):
~ on *fig.* a) herabschauen auf (*acc*), b)
→ **look onto. 2.** zu Boden blicken. **~**
for·ward *v/i* sich freuen (**to** auf *acc*): **~**
to doing s.th. sich darauf freuen, et. zu
tun. **~ in** *v/i* **1.** hineinsehen, -schauen,
hereinsehen, -schauen. **2.** e-n kurzen
Besuch machen, vorbeischauen (**on**
bei). **~ on** *v/i* zusehen, zuschauen. **~ out**
I *v/i* **1.** hinausblicken, -sehen, -schauen,
herausblicken, -sehen, -schauen (**of**

zu): **~ of the window** aus dem Fenster
blicken. **2.** (**for**) aufpassen (auf *acc*), auf
der Hut sein (vor *dat*): **~!** paß auf!,
Vorsicht! **3.** Ausschau halten (**for**
nach). **4. ~ on** (*od.* **over**) → **look onto.**
II *v/t* **5.** *bsd. Br. et.* heraussuchen; sich
et. aussuchen: **look s.th. out for** j-m et.
et. aussuchen. **~ o·ver** *v/t* (sich)
et. (flüchtig) ansehen *od.* anschauen, et.
(flüchtig) (über)prüfen. **~ round** →
look around. ~ through *v/t et.* (flüchtig) durchsehen *od.* -schauen. **~ up I** *v/i*
1. hinaufblicken, -sehen, -schauen, hinaufblicken, -sehen, -schauen. **2.** aufblicken, -sehen, -schauen (**from** von;
fig. **to** zu). **II** *v/t* **3.** *Wort etc* nachschlagen (**in** in *dat*). **4. look s.o. up and**
down j-n von oben bis unten mustern.
'look·a,like *s:* **she's a real ~** sie sieht
einfach klasse aus. **,~'on** *pl* **,lookers-'on** *s* Zuschauer(in).

look·er ['lʊkə] *s:* **she's a real ~** sie sieht
einfach klasse aus. **,~'on** *pl* **,lookers-'on** *s* Zuschauer(in).

'look-in *s* **1.** kurzer Besuch. **2.** F (Erfolgs- *etc*)Chance *f:* **I don't get a ~** ich
hab' keine Chance.

look·ing glass ['lʊkɪŋ] *s* Spiegel *m.*
'look|·out *s* **1. be on the ~ (for)** → **look**
out 3. **2.** Wache *f*, Beobachtungsposten
m: **act as ~** Schmiere stehen. **3.** a) durch.
✕ Beobachtungsstand *m:* **~ tower**
Wachturm *m*, b) ♣ Krähennest *n.* **4.** F
Angelegenheit *f*, Sache *f:* **'~,o·ver** *s:*
give s.th. a ~ → **look over** (*adv*). **'~
through** *s:* **give s.th. a ~** → **look**
through (*adv*).

loom¹ [luːm] *s* Webstuhl *m.*

loom² [~] *v/i* **1.** *a.* **~ up** undeutlich *od.*
drohend sichtbar werden; *fig.* bedrohlich näherrücken. **2.** *a.* **~ up** (drohend)
aufragen: **~ large** *fig.* sich auftürmen
(*Schwierigkeiten etc*); e-e große Rolle
spielen.

loon·y ['luːnɪ] *sl.* **I** *adj* bekloppt, verrückt. **II** *s* Verrückte *m*, *f.* **~ bin** *s sl.*
Klapsmühle *f.*

loop [luːp] *s* **1.** Schlinge *f*, Schleife *f.* **2.**
Schleife *f*, Windung *f* (*a. e-s Flusses etc*).
3. Schlaufe *f*; Öse *f.* **4.** ✈ Looping *m*, *a.*
n. **II** *v/t* **5.** *Schnur etc* schlingen
([a]**round** um). **6. ~ the ~** ✈ loopen, e-n
Looping fliegen *od.* ausführen. **III** *v/i*
7. sich schlingen ([a]**round** um). **8. ~**
6. **'~·hole** *s* **1.** ✕ Schießscharte *f.* **2.** *fig.*

Schlupfloch *n*, Hintertürchen *n*: **~ in the law, legal ~** Gesetzeslücke *f*.

loose [lu:s] **I** *adj* □ **1.** los(e), locker; frei, nicht eingesperrt od. eingesperrt: **break ~** sich losreißen (**from** von); **come** (*od.* **get**) **~** abgehen (*Knopf etc*), sich lockern (*Schraube etc*), sich ablösen, abblättern (*Farbe etc*); **let ~ Hund** von der Leine lassen, *a.* Flüche *etc* loslassen, *s-m* Ärger *etc* Luft machen, freien Lauf lassen; **~ connection** ⚡ Wackelkontakt *m*; **→ screw** 1. **2.** a) lose (*Haar, Geldscheine etc*): **~ money** Kleingeld *n*, Münzen *pl*, b) offen, lose, unverpackt (*Ware*). **3.** lose sitzend, weit (*Kleidungsstück*). **4.** *fig.* lose (*Abmachung, Zs.-hang etc*); frei, ungenau (*Übersetzung etc*); unkonzentriert, nachlässig (*Spielweise etc*); unkontrolliert: **have a ~ tongue** den Mund nicht halten können. **5.** locker (*Moral, Lebenswandel etc*): **→ liver², living** 5. **I** *s* **6. be on the ~** a) auf freiem Fuß sein, b) *a.* **go on the ~** F auf den Putz hauen. **'~·fit·ting** → **loose** 3. **'~·leaf** *adj* Loseblatt...: **~ binder** Schnellhefter *m*.

'loos·en I *v/t* **1.** Knoten, Fesseln *etc* a. ✄ Husten, *fig.* Zunge lösen: **~ s.o.'s tongue** j-m die Zunge lösen. **2.** Schraube, Griff *etc* a. *fig.* Disziplin etc lockern: **~ one's hold of** et. loslassen. **3.** *a.* **~ up** Muskeln *etc* a. *fig.* j-n auflockern. **II** *v/i* **4.** sich lösen *od.* lockern. **5.** **~ up** (*bsd. Sport*) sich auflockern.

loot [lu:t] **I** *s* (*Kriegs-, Diebes*)Beute *f.* **II** *v/t u. v/i* plündern.

lop [lɒp] *v/t* **1.** Baum *etc* beschneiden, (zu)stutzen. **2.** *oft* **~ off** abhauen, abhacken. **,~·sid·ed** *adj* □ **1.** schief, nach 'einer Seite hängend, ⚓ mit Schlagseite. **2.** *fig.* einseitig.

lo·qua·cious [ləʊˈkweɪʃəs] *adj* □ geschwätzig, redselig.

lord [lɔ:d] **I** *s* **1.** Herr *m*, Gebieter *m* (**of** über *acc*). **2.** *fig.* Magnat *m*. **3. the** ♀ a) *a.* ♀ **God** Gott *m* (der Herr); ♀ (**only**) **knows where ...** Gott *od.* der Himmel weiß, wo ..., b) *a.* **our** ♀ (Christus *m*) der Herr: ♀**'s Prayer** Vaterunser *m*; ♀**'s Supper** (heiliges) Abendmahl. **4.** *Br.* Lord *m*: **the** ♀**s** das Oberhaus; **→ drunk** 1. **II** *v/t* **5.** **~ it** den Herren spielen (**over s.o.** j-m gegenüber). ♀ **Chan·cel·lor** *s*

Br. Lordkanzler *m.* ♀ **May·or** *s Br.* Oberbürgermeister *m.*

lor·ry [ˈlɒrɪ] *s Br.* Last(kraft)wagen *m*, Lastauto *m*.

lose [lu:z] (*irr*) **I** *v/t* **1.** Sache, Interesse *etc* verlieren, Geld, Stellung *etc* a. einbüßen: **~ o.s.** sich verirren; **~ 10 pounds** 10 Pfund abnehmen; **→ life** 1d, **sight** 2, *etc*. **2.** Spiel, Prozeß *etc* verlieren. **3.** Zug *etc, fig.* Chance *etc* versäumen, -passen. **4.** Gelerntes vergessen. **5.** 5 Minuten *etc* nachgehen (*Uhr*). **6.** Gewohnheit, Krankheit *etc* loswerden, Verfolger a. abschütteln. **7.** **~ s.o. s.th.** j-n et. kosten, j-n um et. bringen. **II** *v/i* **8.** *a.* **~ out** (to) verlieren (gegen), unterliegen (*dat*). **9.** *a.* **~ out** verlieren, draufzahlen (**on** bei). **10.** nachgehen (*Uhr*). **'los·er** *s* Verlierer(in): **good** (**bad**) **~, be a bad ~** *a.* nicht verlieren können; **be a born ~** der geborene Verlierer sein. **'los·ing** *adj* **1.** verlustbringend, Verlust... **2.** verloren, aussichtslos: **fight a ~ battle** *fig.* auf verlorenem Posten stehen.

loss [lɒs] *s* **1.** Verlust *m*: a) Einbuße *f*: **~ of blood** (**memory, time**) Blut-(Gedächtnis-, Zeit)verlust; **dead ~** Totalverlust; *fig.* hoffnungsloser Fall (*Person*); **sell s.th. at a ~** et. mit Verlust verkaufen; **work at a ~** mit Verlust arbeiten; **→ identity**, b) Schaden *m*, c) verlorene Sache *od.* Person, d) Abnahme *f*, Schwund *m*: **~ in weight** Gewichtsverlust, -abnahme. **2.** *pl* ✗ Verluste *pl*, Ausfälle *pl*. **3.** an Verlegenheit sein (**for** um): **be at a ~ for words** keine Worte finden.

lost [lɒst] **I** *pret u. pp von* **lose. II** *adj* **1.** verloren: **~ cause** *fig.* aussichtslose Sache; **be a ~ cause** *a.* aussichtslos; **be a ~ cause** *a.* aussichtslos **2.** verloren(gegangen): **~ property** ①, **→ property** 3. **3.** verirrt: **be ~** verirrt haben, sich nicht mehr zurechtfinden (*a. fig.*); **get ~** sich verirren; **get ~!** F hau ab! **4. be ~ on s.o.** keinen Eindruck auf j-n machen, j-n kaltlassen. **5.** *in* vertieft *od.* versunken in (*acc*): **~ in thought** in Gedanken versunken, *fig. adv a.* gedankenversunken, -verloren. **,~-and-'found (of·fice)** *s Am.* Fundbüro *n*.

lot [lɒt] *s* **1.** Los *n*: *cast* (*od.* *draw*) ~**s** losen (*for* um); *the* ~ *fell on* (*od.* *to*) *me* das Los fiel auf mich. **2.** Los *n*, Schicksal *n*. **3.** Anteil *m*. **4.** Parzelle *f*, Grundstück *n*. **5.** ♣ Partie *f*, Posten *m*. **6.** Gruppe *f*, Gesellschaft *f*: *the whole* ~ a) die ganze Gesellschaft, b) → 7. **7.** *the* ~ alles, das Ganze. **8.** F Menge *f*, Haufen *m*: *a* ~ *of*, ~*s of* viel, e-e Menge; *a* ~ (*od.* ~*s*) *better* (*far*) viel besser. **9.** *a bad* ~ F ein mieser Typ; ein mieses Pack.

loth → *loath*.

lo·tion ['ləʊʃn] *s* Lotion *f*, (Haut-, Rasier)Wasser *n*.

lot·ter·y ['lɒtərɪ] *s* **1.** Lotterie *f*: ~ *ticket* Lotterielos *n*. **2.** *fig*. Glückssache *f*, Lotteriespiel *n*.

lo·tus ['ləʊtəs] *s* ♣ Lotos(blume *f*) *m*.

loud [laʊd] *adj* □ **1.** (*a.* *adv*) laut. **2.** *fig*. grell, schreiend (Farben), auffallend (Kleidung, Benehmen). **'~·mouth** *s* F Großmaul *n*. **'~·speak·er** *s* Lautsprecher *m*.

lounge [laʊndʒ] **I** *s* **1.** Wohnzimmer *n*. **2.** Gesellschaftsraum *m*, Salon *m* (e-s Hotels, Schiffs). **3.** Foyer *n* (e-s Theaters). **4.** Wartehalle *f* (e-s Flughafens). **5.** *Br.* vornehmerer u. teurerer Teil e-s Lokals. **II** *v/i* **6.** → *loll* 1. **III** *v/t* **7.** *mst* ~ *away* Zeit vertrödeln, -bummeln. ~ *bar* → *lounge* 1. ~ *chair* *s* Klubsessel *m*, *suit* *s* *bsd.* *Br.* Straßenanzug *m*.

lour, **lour·ing** → *lower¹*, *lowering*.

louse **I** *s* [laʊs] **1.** *pl* **lice** [laɪs] *zo.* Laus *f*. **2.** *pl* **'lous·es** *sl.* Scheißkerl *m*. **II** *v/t* [laʊz] **3.** ~ *up sl.* versauen, -murksen. **lous·y** ['laʊzɪ] *adj* □ **1.** verlaust. **2.** *sl.* fies, hundsgemein; lausig, mies. **3.** *be* ~ *with sl.* wimmeln von (*dat*) od. von: *be* ~ *with money* vor Geld stinken.

lout [laʊt] *s* Flegel *m*, Rüpel *m*. **'lout·ish** *adj* □ flegel-, rüpelhaft.

lov·a·ble ['lʌvəbl] *adj* □ liebenswert, reizend.

love [lʌv] **I** *s* **1.** Liebe *f* (*of*, *for*, *to toward*[*s*] zu): ~ *herzliche Grüße* (Briefschluß); *be in* ~ verliebt sein (*with* in *acc*); *fall in* ~ sich verlieben (*with* in *acc*); *not for* ~ *or money* nicht für Geld u. gute Worte; *um nichts in der Welt*; *make* ~ sich (*körperlich*) lieben; *make* ~ *to s.o.* j-n (*körperlich*) lieben; *there is no* ~ *lost between them* sie können sich nicht leiden; ~ *of adventure* Abenteuerlust *f*; ~ *of one's country* Vaterlandsliebe *f*; → *give* 10. **2.** F a) (Anrede, *oft* unübersetzt) Schatz, b) Schatz *m*: *he's a real* ~ er ist ein richtiger Schatz; *a* ~ *of a car* ein süßer Wagen. **3.** *bsd.* *Tennis*: null. **II** *v/t* **4.** j-n (*a.* *körperlich*) lieben, liebhaben. **5.** *et.* lieben, gerne mögen: ~ *doing* (*bsd.* *Am. a.* *to do*) *s.h.* et. sehr gern tun.

love·a·ble → *lovable*.

love| **af·fair** *s* (Liebes)Affäre *f*, (-)Verhältnis *n*. ~ *bite* *s* F Knutschfleck *m*. ~ *du·et* *s* ♪ Liebesduett *n*. **'~·hate** (**re·la·tion·ship**) *s* Haßliebe *f*.

love·less ['lʌvlɪs] *adj* □ **1.** lieblos. **2.** ungeliebt.

love| **let·ter** *s* Liebesbrief *m*. ~ *life* *s* (irr *life*) Liebesleben *n*.

love·ly ['lʌvlɪ] *adj* □ **1.** (wunder)schön. **2.** nett, reizend. **3.** F prima, großartig.

'love| **mak·ing** *s* **1.** (körperliche) Liebe. **2.** Liebeskunst *f*. ~ *match* *s* Liebesheirat *f*. ~ *po·em* *s* Liebesgedicht *n*.

lov·er ['lʌvə] *s* **1.** Liebhaber *m*, Geliebte *m*; Geliebte *f*. **2.** *pl* Liebende *pl*, Liebespaar *n*: *they are* ~*s* sie lieben sich. **3.** (Musik- *etc*)Liebhaber(in), (-)Freund (-in): ~ *of music*, *music* ~.

love| **scene** *s* *thea*. *etc* Liebesszene *f*. **'~·sick** *adj* liebeskrank: *be* ~ Liebeskummer haben. ~ *song* *s* Liebeslied *n*. ~ *sto·ry* *s* Liebesgeschichte *f*, (bsd. rührselige a.) Love-Story *f*.

lov·ing ['lʌvɪŋ] *adj* □ liebevoll, zärtlich: *your* ~ *father* Dein Dich liebender Vater (Briefschluß).

low¹ [ləʊ] **I** *adj* u. *adv* **1.** *allg*. niedrig (*a.* *fig*. Löhne *etc*): ~ *in fat* fettarm; → *low, profile* 1. **2.** tief (*a.* *fig*.): *a* ~ *bow* e-e tiefe Verbeugung; ~ *shot* (Sport) Flachschuß *m*; *the sun is* ~ die Sonne steht tief; *sunk thus* ~ *fig*. so tief gesunken. **3.** tiefgelegen. **4.** knapp (Vorrat *etc*): *get* (*od.* *run*) ~ knapp werden, zur Neige gehen; *we are getting* (*od.* *running*) ~ *on money* uns geht allmählich das Geld aus; ~ *on funds* knapp bei Kasse. **5.** schwach (*a.* Puls); niedergeschlagen, deprimiert: *feel* ~ in gedrückter Stimmung sein; sich elend fühlen; → *spirit* 4. **6.** gering(schätzig): → *opinion* 2. **7.** ordinär, vulgär (Ausdruck *etc*); gemein, niederträchtig (Trick *etc*);

feel ~ sich gemein vorkommen. **8.** tief (*Ton* etc); leise (*Ton, Stimme* etc): **in a** ~ **voice** leise. **II** *s* **9.** *meteor.* Tief *n.* **10.** *fig.* Tief(punkt *m,* -stand *m*) *n:* **be at a new** ~ e-n neuen Tiefpunkt erreicht haben.

low² [~] **I** *v/i* brüllen, muhen (*Rind*). **II** *s* Brüllen *n,* Muhen *n.*

,low'bred *adj* ungebildet, gewöhnlich. '**~·brow** [~] *s* geistig Anspruchslose *m, f,* Unbedarfte *m, f.* **II** *adj* geistig anspruchslos, unbedarft. **,~·'cal·o·rie** *adj* kalorienarm. ~ **com·e·dy** *s* Posse *f,* (derber) Schwank. '**~·cost** *adj* kostengünstig. '**~·down** *adj* F fies, hundsgemein. '**~·down** *s* F: **give s.o. the** ~ j-n aufklären (**on** über *acc*); **get the** ~ aufgeklärt werden (**on** über *acc*).

low·er¹ ['ləʊə] *v/i* **1.** finster *od.* drohend blicken: ~ **at s.o.** j-n finster *od.* drohend ansehen. **2.** sich auftürmen (*Wolken*); sich mit schwarzen Wolken überziehen (*Himmel*).

low·er² ['ləʊə] **I** *v/t* **1.** niedriger machen. **2.** *Augen, Preis, Stimme* etc senken. **3.** *fig.* erniedrigen: ~ **o.s.** sich herablassen. **4.** herunter-, herablassen, *Fahne, Segel* niederholen, streichen. **II** *v/i* **5.** niedriger werden. **6.** *fig.* sinken, fallen.

low·er³ ['ləʊə] **I** *comp. von* **low¹. II** *adj* **1.** niedriger (*a. fig.*). **2.** unter, Unter...: the ~ **class(es** *pl*) *sociol.* die Unterschicht; ~ **court** ⚖ untergeordnetes Gericht; ~ **deck** ♣ Unterdeck (*n*). → **jaw** 1, **lip** 1.

low·est ['ləʊɪst] **I** *sup von* **low¹. II** *adj* **1.** niedrigst (*a. fig.*): ~ **bid** ✝ Mindestgebot *n.* **2.** unterst. **III** *s* **3. at the** ~ wenigstens, mindestens.

'**low·fat** *adj* fettarm. **,~·'in·come** *adj* einkommensschwach. **,~·'key(ed)** *adj* **1.** gedämpft (*Farbe*), (*Ton a.*) leise. **2.** zurückhaltend (*Empfang* etc). **~·land** ['~lənd] *s* Tief-, Flachland *n.* 2 **Mass** *s eccl.* Stille Messe. **,~·'necked** *adj* tief ausgeschnitten, mit tiefem Ausschnitt (*Kleid*). **,~·'noise** *adj* rauscharm (*Tonband* etc). **,~·'pres·sure** *adj:* ~ **area** Tiefdruckgebiet *n.* '**~·rise** *s* Flachbau *m.* '**~·sea·son** *s* Vor- *od.* Nachsaison *f.* '**~·shoe** *s* Halbschuh *m.* **,~·'spir·it·ed** *adj* □ niedergeschlagen, deprimiert.

loy·al ['lɔɪəl] *adj* □ **1.** loyal (**to** gegenüber). **2.** (ge)treu (**to** dat). '**loy·al·ty** *s* Loyalität *f* (**to** zu).

loz·enge ['lɒzɪndʒ] *s* **1.** A Raute *f,*

Rhombus *m.* **2.** *pharm.* Pastille *f,* Tablette *f.*

lub·ber ['lʌbə] *s* Flegel *m,* Rüpel *m;* Trottel *m;* Tolpatsch *m.*

lu·bri·cant ['luːbrɪkənt] *s* ⚙ Schmiermittel *n.* **lu·bri·cate** ['~keɪt] *v/t* schmieren. **,lu·bri'ca·tion** *s* Schmieren *n.*

lu·cid ['luːsɪd] *adj* □ klar (*Auskunft, Gedanke, Verstand* etc); hell, (*geistig*) klar: ~ **interval** (*od.* **moment**) bsd. *psych.* heller *od.* lichter Augenblick.

luck [lʌk] *s* **1.** Schicksal *n,* Zufall *m:* **as** ~ **would have it** wie es der Zufall wollte, (un)glücklicherweise; **bad** (*od.* **hard, ill**) ~ Pech *n* (**on** für), Unglück *n;* **good** ~ Glück *m;* **good** ~! viel Glück! **2.** Glück *n:* **for** ~ als Glücksbringer; **be in** (**out of**) ~ (kein) Glück haben; **try one's** ~ sein Glück versuchen. '**luck·i·ly** *adv* zum Glück, glücklicherweise: ~ **for me** zu m-m Glück. '**luck·less** *adj* □ glück-, erfolglos. '**luck·y** *adj* (□ → **luckily**) **1.** Glücks..., glücklich: **be (very)** ~ (großes) Glück haben; ~ **day** Glückstag *m;* ~ **fellow** Glückspilz *m.* **2.** glückbringend, Glücks...: **be** ~ Glück bringen; ~ **penny** Glückspfennig *m;* → **star** 1.

lu·cra·tive ['luːkrətɪv] *adj* □ einträglich, lukrativ.

lu·cre ['luːkə] *s: filthy* ~ *oft humor.* schnöder Mammon.

lu·di·crous ['luːdɪkrəs] *adj* □ lächerlich, absurd.

lu·do ['luːdəʊ] *s Br.* Mensch, ärgere dich nicht *n* (*Spiel*).

lug [lʌg] *v/t* zerren, schleifen; schleppen.

lug·gage ['lʌgɪdʒ] *s* (Reise)Gepäck *n.* ~ **al·low·ance** *s* ✈ Freigepäck *n.* ~ **com·part·ment** *s mot. Br.* Kofferraum *m.* ~ **in·sur·ance** *s* Reisegepäckversicherung *f.* ~ **lock·er** *s* Gepäckschließfach *n.* ~ **re·claim** *s* ✈ Gepäckausgabe *f.*

luke·warm [,luːk'wɔːm] *adj* □ lau(-warm) (*a. fig.* Zustimmung etc), (*Unterstützung* etc *a.*) halbherzig, (*Applaus* etc) lau, mäßig.

lull [lʌl] **I** *v/t* **1.** *mst* ~ **to sleep** einlullen. **2.** *fig.* j-n beruhigen, beschwichtigen, j-s *Argwohn* zerstreuen: ~ **s.o. into** (**a false sense of**) **security** j-n in Sicherheit wiegen. **II** *v/i* **3.** sich legen, nachlassen (*Sturm*). **III** *s* **4.** (Ruhe)Pause *f* (**in** in *dat*): ~ (**in the wind**) Flaute *f;* **the** ~

before the storm die Stille vor dem Sturm (a. fig.).
lull·a·by ['lʌləbaɪ] s Wiegenlied n.
lum·ba·go [lʌm'beɪgəʊ] s ℱ Hexenschuß m.
lum·ber¹ ['lʌmbə] **I** s **1.** bsd. Am. Bau-, Nutzholz n. **2.** Gerümpel n. **II** v/t **3.** a. ~ **up** Zimmer etc vollstopfen, a. Erzählung etc überladen (**with** mit). **4.** ~ **s.o. with s.th.** Br. F j-m et. aufhängen od. aufhalsen.
lum·ber² [~] v/i sich (dahin)schleppen, schwerfällig gehen; (dahin)rumpeln (Wagen).
'lum·ber|·jack s bsd. Am. Holzfäller m, -arbeiter m. ~ **mill** s bsd. Am. Sägewerk n. ~ **room** s Rumpelkammer f.
lu·mi·nar·y ['luːmɪnərɪ] s fig. Leuchte f.
lu·mi·nos·i·ty [ˌ~'nɒsətɪ] s **1.** Leuchtkraft f; ast., phys. Lichtstärke f, Helligkeit f. **2.** fig. Brillanz f.
lu·mi·nous ['luːmɪnəs] adj □ **1.** leuchtend: ~ **paint** Leuchtfarbe f. **2.** fig. intelligent, brillant; klar, einleuchtend.
lump¹ [lʌmp] **I** s **1.** Klumpen m: **have a ~ in one's** (od. **the**) **throat** fig. e-n Kloß im Hals haben. **2.** Schwellung f, Beule f; ℱ Geschwulst f, (in der Brust) Knoten m. **3.** Stück n Zucker etc. **4.** fig. Gesamtheit f, Masse f: **in the ~** in Bausch u. Bogen, pauschal; im großen u. ganzen. **5.** F Klotz m (ungeschlachter, dummer Mensch). **II** adj **6.** Stück...: ~ **sugar** Würfelzucker m. **7.** Pauschal... **III** v/t **8.** oft ~ **together** zs.-ballen; fig. zs.-werfen, in 'einen Topf werfen (**with** mit). **IV** v/i **9.** Klumpen bilden, klumpen.
lump² [~] v/t: ~ **it** F sich damit abfinden.
lu·na·cy ['luːnəsɪ] s ℱ Wahnsinn m (a. fig.).
lu·nar ['luːnə] adj Mond...: ~ **eclipse** ast. Mondfinsternis f; ~ **landing** Mondlandung f; ~ **module** Mond(lande)fähre f.
lu·na·tic ['luːnətɪk] **I** adj a) ~ wahnsinnig, geistesgestört: ~ **asylum** contp. Irrenanstalt f, b) fig. verrückt. **II** s a) ℱ Wahnsinnige m, f, Geistesgestörte m, f, b) fig. Verrückte m, f.
lunch [lʌntʃ] **I** s Mittagessen n: **have ~** → II; ~ **hour** a) a. ~ **break** Mittagspause f, b) → **lunchtime**. **II** v/i (zu) Mittag essen: ~ **out** auswärts od. im Restaurant zu Mittag essen.

lunch·eon| meat ['lʌntʃən] s Frühstücksfleisch n. ~ **vouch·er** s Essen(s)-bon m.
'lunch·time s Mittagszeit f: **at** ~ zur Mittagszeit; ~ **train** Mittagszug m.
lung [lʌŋ] s anat. Lungenflügel m: ~**s** pl Lunge f.
lunge [lʌndʒ] **I** s a) bsd. fenc. Ausfall m, b) Sprung m vorwärts, Satz m: **make a ~** → II. **II** v/i a) bsd. fenc. e-n Ausfall machen, b) a. ~ **out** e-n Sprung vorwärts od. e-n Satz machen, c) sich stürzen (**at** auf acc).
lurch¹ [lɜːtʃ] **I** s **1.** Taumeln n, Torkeln n. **2.** ⊕ Schlingern n. **3.** Ruck m: **give a ~** → 6. **II** v/i **4.** taumeln, torkeln. **5.** ⊕ schlingern. **6.** rucken, e-n Ruck machen.
lurch² [~] s: **leave in the** ~ im Stich lassen.
lure [lʊə] **I** s **1.** Köder m (**to** für) (a. fig.). **2.** fig. Lockung f, Reiz m. **II** v/t **3.** (an)locken, ködern (beide a. fig.): ~ **away** weglocken; ~ **into** locken in (acc); verlocken od. -führen zu.
lu·rid ['lʊərɪd] adj □ **1.** fahl, gespenstisch (Beleuchtung etc). **2.** grell (Farben). **3.** gräßlich, schauerlich.
lurk [lɜːk] v/i **1.** lauern (a. fig.): ~ **for** s.o. j-m auflauern. **2.** schleichen: ~ **about** (od. **around**) herumschleichen.
lus·cious ['lʌʃəs] adj □ **1.** köstlich, lekker; süß (u. saftig). **2.** sinnlich (Lippen etc), üppig (Figur, Frau etc), knackig (Mädchen).
lush [lʌʃ] adj □ saftig (Gras etc), üppig (Vegetation).
lust [lʌst] **I** s **1.** sinnliche Begierde. **2.** Gier f (**of**, **for** nach): ~ **for power** Machtgier f. **II** v/i **3.** gieren (**for**, **after** nach).
lus·ter Am. → **lustre**.
lust·ful ['lʌstfʊl] adj □ lüstern.
lus·tre ['lʌstə] s bsd. Br. **1.** Glanz m (a. fig.). **2.** Lüster m, Kronleuchter m.
lus·trous ['lʌstrəs] adj □ **1.** glänzend (a. fig.). **2.** fig. illuster.
lust·y ['lʌstɪ] adj □ **1.** kräftig, robust. **2.** tatkräftig.
lute¹ [luːt] s ♪ Laute f.
lute² [~] **I** s Kitt m. **II** v/t (ver)kitten.
lux·ate ['lʌkseɪt] v/t ℱ sich die Schulter etc aus- od. verrenken: **he ~d his left**

shoulder. lux'a·tion *s* Luxation *f*, Aus-, Verrenkung *f*.

lux·u·ri·ant [lʌgˈʒʊərɪənt] *adj* □ **1.** üppig (*Vegetation*) (*a. fig.*). **2.** *fig.* (über)reich, verschwenderisch, (*Phantasie*) blühend. **lux'u·ri·ate** [ˌ~eɪt] *v/i* schwelgen (*in in dat*). **lux'u·ri·ous** *adj* □ **1.** luxuriös, Luxus... **2.** verschwenderisch, genußsüchtig. **lux·u·ry** [ˈlʌkʃərɪ] **I** *s* **1.** *allg.* Luxus *m*. **2.** Luxusartikel *m*. **II** *adj* **3.** Luxus..., der Luxusklasse.

lye [laɪ] *s* 🜂 Lauge *f*.

ly·ing [ˈlaɪɪŋ] **I** *pres p von* **lie¹. II** *adj* lügnerisch, verlogen.

lymph [lɪmf] *s physiol.* Lymphe *f*. **~ gland, ~ node** *s anat.* Lymphknoten *m*.

lynch [lɪntʃ] *v/t* lynchen. **~ law** *s* Lynchjustiz *f*.

lynx [lɪŋks] *s zo.* Luchs *m*. **'~-eyed** *adj fig.* mit Augen wie ein Luchs.

lyr·ic [ˈlɪrɪk] **I** *adj* (**~ally**) **1.** lyrisch (*a. fig.* gefühlvoll). **II** *s* **2.** lyrisches Gedicht: **~s** *pl* Lyrik *f*. **3.** *pl* (Lied)Text *m*. **lyr·i·cal** *adj* □ **1.** → **lyric** 1. **2.** schwärmerisch: **get ~** ins Schwärmen geraten. **lyr·i·cist** [ˈ~sɪst] *s* **1.** Lyriker(in). **2.** Texter(in), Textdichter(in).

M

ma [mɑː] *s* F Mama *f*, Mutti *f*.

ma'am [mæm] F → **madam**.

mac [mæk] F → **mackintosh**.

ma·ca·bre [məˈkɑːbrə] *adj* □ makaber.

mac·(c)a·ro·ni [ˌmækəˈrəʊnɪ] *s pl* (*sg konstruiert*) Makkaroni *pl*.

mace¹ [meɪs] *s* Amtsstab *m*.

mace² [ˌ~] *s* Muskatblüte *f*.

Mach [mæk] *s*: **fly at ~ two** ✈, *phys.* mit e-r Geschwindigkeit von zwei Mach fliegen.

ma·che·te [məˈtʃetɪ] *s* Machete *f*, Buschmesser *n*.

ma·chine [məˈʃiːn] **I** *s* **1.** Maschine *f* (F *a.* Flugzeug, Motorrad *etc*). **2.** Apparat *m*; Automat *m*. **3.** *pol.* (Partei- *etc*)Apparat *m*. **II** *v/t* **4.** maschinell herstellen. **~ gun** *s* Maschinengewehr *n*.

ma'chine|-made *adj* maschinell hergestellt. **~read·a·ble** *adj* maschinell lesbar, maschinenlesbar.

ma·chin·er·y [məˈʃiːnərɪ] *s* **1.** Maschinen *pl*; Maschinerie *f*. **2.** *fig.* a) Maschinerie *f*, Räderwerk *n*, b) → **machine** 3.

ma'chine| tool *s* ⚙ Werkzeugmaschine *f*. **~ trans·la·tion** *s* maschinelle Übersetzung.

ma·chin·ist [məˈʃiːnɪst] *s* **1.** Maschinenschlosser *m*. **2.** Maschinist *m*.

ma·chis·mo [məˈtʃɪzməʊ] *s* Machismo *m*, Männlichkeitswahn *m*. **ma·cho** [ˈmætʃəʊ] *pl* **-chos** *s* Macho *m*.

mack·er·el [ˈmækrəl] *pl* **-el** *s ichth.* Makrele *f*.

mack·in·tosh [ˈmækɪntɒʃ] *s bsd. Br.* Regenmantel *m*.

mac·ro·cosm [ˈmækrəʊkɒzəm] *s* Makrokosmos *m*, Weltall *n*.

mad [mæd] *adj* (□ → **madly**) **1.** wahnsinnig, verrückt (*beide a. fig.*): **go ~** verrückt werden; **drive s.o. ~** j-n verrückt machen; **like ~** wie verrückt. **2.** (*after, about, for on*) wild, versessen (auf *acc*), verrückt (nach), vernarrt (in *acc*): **~ about soccer** fußballverrückt. **3.** F außer sich, verrückt (**with** vor *dat*). **4.** *bsd. Am.* F wütend (**at, about** über *acc*, auf *acc*). **5.** wild (geworden) (*Stier etc*). **6.** *vet.* tollwütig.

mad·am [ˈmædəm] *s* gnädige Frau (*Anrede, oft unübersetzt*).

'mad·cap I *s* verrückter Kerl. **II** *adj* verrückt.

mad·den [ˈmædn] *v/t* verrückt machen (*a. fig.*). **'mad·den·ing** *adj* □ unerträglich: **it is ~** es ist zum Verrücktwerden.

made [meɪd] **I** *pret u. pp von* **make. II** *adj*: **a ~ man** ein gemachter Mann. **ˌ~-to-'meas·ure** *adj* **1.** nach Maß angefertigt, Maß...: **~ suit** maßgeschneiderter Anzug, Maßanzug *m*. **ˌ~-to-'or·der** *adj* **1.** → **made-to-measure. 2.** *fig.*

maßgeschneidert, nach Maß. '**~-up** *adj* **1.** (frei) erfunden. **2.** geschminkt.

'**mad·house** *s* Irrenhaus *n*, *fig. a.* Tollhaus *n*.

mad·ly ['mædlɪ] *adv* **1.** wie verrückt. **2.** F wahnsinnig, schrecklich.

mad·man ['mædmən] *s* (*irr* **man**) Verrückte *m*.

mad·ness ['mædnɪs] *s* **1.** Wahnsinn *m* (*a. fig.*): **sheer ~** heller *od.* blanker Wahnsinn. **2.** *bsd. Am.* F Wut *f*.

'**mad,wom·an** *s* (*irr* **woman**) Verrückte *f*.

mael·strom ['meɪlstrɒm] *s* Strudel *m*, Sog *m* (*beide a. fig.*).

Ma·fi·a ['mæfɪə] *s* Mafia *f* (*a. fig.*).

ma·fi·o·so [ˌ~ɒˈəʊsəʊ] *pl* **-sos, -si** [ˌ~sɪ] *s* Mafioso *m* (*a. fig.*).

mag [mæg] F → **magazine** 3.

mag·a·zine [ˌmægəˈziːn] *s* **1.** Magazin *n* (*e-r Feuerwaffe, e-s Fotoapparats*). **2.** Magazin *n*, Lagerhaus *n*. **3.** Magazin *n*, Zeitschrift *f*. **~ rack** *s* Zeitungsständer *m*.

mag·got ['mægət] *s* zo. Made *f*. '**mag·got·y** *adj* madig.

Ma·gi ['meɪdʒaɪ] *s pl*: **the** (**three**) **~** die (drei) Weisen aus dem Morgenland, die Heiligen Drei Könige.

mag·ic ['mædʒɪk] **I** *s* **1.** Magie *f*, Zauberei *f*: **as if by ~, like ~** wie durch Zauberei. **2.** Zauber(kraft *f*) *m*, magische Kraft (*a. fig.*). **II** *adj* (*~ally*) **3.** magisch, Zauber...: **~ carpet** fliegender Teppich; **~ eye** *⚡* magisches Auge; **~ trick** Zaubertrick *m*, -kunststück *n*; **~ wand** Zauberstab *m*. **4.** zauberhaft. **ma·gi·cian** [məˈdʒɪʃn] *s* **1.** Magier *m*, Zauberer *m*. **2.** Zauberkünstler *m*.

mag·is·trate ['mædʒɪstreɪt] *s* ⚖ Richter *m* (*an e-m* **magistrates' court**): **~s' court** *Br.*, **~'s court** *Am.* erstinstanzliches Gericht für Straf- u. Zivilsachen niederer Ordnung.

mag·na·nim·i·ty [ˌmægnəˈnɪmətɪ] *s* Großmut *f*. **mag·nan·i·mous** [~ˈnænɪməs] *adj* □ großmütig.

mag·nate ['mægneɪt] *s* Magnat *m*.

mag·ne·sia [mægˈniːʃə] *s* 🜊 Magnesia *f*. **mag·ne·si·um** [~ˈniːzɪəm] *s* 🜊 Magnesium *n*.

mag·net ['mægnɪt] *s* Magnet *m* (*a. fig.*).

mag·net·ic [~ˈnetɪk] *adj* (*~ally*) **1.** magnetisch, Magnet...: **~ field** *phys.* Ma-

gnetfeld *n*; **~ pole** *phys.* magnetischer Pol, Magnetpol *m*. **2.** *fig.* magnetisch, faszinierend. **mag·net·ism** ['~nɪtɪzəm] *s* **1.** *phys.* Magnetismus *m*. **2.** *fig.* Anziehungskraft *f*. '**mag·ne·tize** *v/t* **1.** magnetisieren. **2.** *fig.* anziehen, fesseln.

mag·nif·i·cence [mægˈnɪfɪsns] *s* Großartigkeit *f*, Herrlichkeit *f*. **mag·nif·i·cent** *adj* □ großartig, prächtig, herrlich (*alle a. Fig.*).

mag·ni·fy ['mægnɪfaɪ] *v/t* **1.** (*a. v/i*) vergrößern: **~ing glass** Vergrößerungsglas *n*, Lupe *f*. **2.** *fig.* aufbauschen.

mag·ni·tude ['mægnɪtjuːd] *s* Größe(nordnung) *f*, *fig. a.* Ausmaß *n*, Schwere *f*: **of the first ~** von äußerster Wichtigkeit.

mag·no·lia [mægˈnəʊljə] *s* 🜚 Magnolie *f*.

mag·pie ['mægpaɪ] *s* **1.** *orn.* Elster *f*. **2.** *fig.* Schwätzer(in). **3.** *Br. fig.* sammelwütiger Mensch.

ma·hog·a·ny [məˈhɒgənɪ] *s* Mahagoni(holz) *n*.

maid [meɪd] *s* **1.** **old ~** alte Jungfer; **~ of hono(u)r** Hofdame *f*; *Am.* (erste) Brautjungfer. **2.** (Dienst)Mädchen *n*, Hausangestellte *f*: **~ of all work** *bsd. fig.* Mädchen für alles.

maid·en ['meɪdn] *adj* **1.** **~ name** Mädchenname *m* (*e-r Frau*). **2.** unverheiratet. **3.** Jungfern...: **~ flight** *✈* Jungfernflug *m*; **~ speech** *parl.* Jungfernrede *f*; **~ voyage** *⚓* Jungfernfahrt *f*.

mail [meɪl] **I** *s* **1.** Post(sendung) *f*: **by ~** *bsd. Am.* mit der Post; → **incoming** 3, **outgoing** 2. **II** *v/t bsd. Am.* aufgeben, Brief einwerfen; (zu)schicken (**to** *dat.*). '**~·box** *s bsd. Am.* Briefkasten *m*. **~ car·ri·er** *s bsd. Am.*, '**~·man** *s* (*irr* **man**) *bsd. Am.* Postbote *m*, Briefträger *m*. '**~,or·der** *adj*: **~ catalog(ue)** Versandhauskatalog *m*; **~ firm** (*od.* **house**) Versandhaus *n*.

maim [meɪm] *v/t* verstümmeln (*a. fig. Text*).

main [meɪn] **I** *adj* (□ → **mainly**). **1.** Haupt..., wichtigst: **~ clause** *ling.* Hauptsatz *m*; **~ office** Hauptbüro *n*, Zentrale *f*; **~ reason** Hauptgrund *m*; **~ thing** Hauptsache *f*. **II** *s* **2.** *mst pl* Haupt(gas-, -wasser)leitung *f*; (Strom-) Netz *n*: **~s cable** Netzkabel *n*. **3. in** (*Am. a. for*) **the ~** hauptsächlich, in der Hauptsache. '**~·land** ['~lənd] *s* Festland *n*.

main·ly ['meɪnlɪ] *adv* hauptsächlich, vorwiegend.

'**main·spring** *s fig.* (Haupt)Triebfeder *f.* '**~stay** *s fig.* Hauptstütze *f.*

main·tain [meɪn'teɪn] *v/t* **1.** *Zustand* (aufrecht)erhalten, beibehalten, (be-)wahren; ✝ *Preis* halten. **2.** instand halten, pflegen, ☢ *a.* warten. **3.** (*in e-m bestimmten Zustand*) lassen. **4.** *Familie etc* unterhalten, versorgen. **5.** behaupten (*that* daß; *to inf* zu *inf*). **6.** *Meinung, Recht etc* verfechten; auf *e-r Forderung* bestehen: ~ **one's ground** *bsd. fig.* sich behaupten.

main·te·nance ['meɪntənəns] *s* **1.** (Aufrecht)Erhaltung *f,* Beibehaltung *f.* **2.** Instandhaltung *f,* Pflege *f,* ☢ *a.* Wartung *f:* **~-free** wartungsfrei. **3.** Unterhalt *m:* **~ grant** Unterhaltszuschuß *m.*

mai·son·(n)ette [ˌmeɪzə'net] *s* **1.** Maison(n)ette *f.* **2.** Einliegerwohnung *f.*

maize [meɪz] *s* ✿ *bsd. Br.* Mais *m.*

ma·jes·tic [mə'dʒestɪk] *adj* (*~ally*) majestätisch. **maj·es·ty** ['mædʒəstɪ] *s* Majestät *f (a. fig.):* **His** (**Her**) ⚶ Seine (Ihre) Majestät.

ma·jor ['meɪdʒə] **I** *s* **1.** ✕ Major *m.* **2.** *univ. Am.* Hauptfach *n.* **3.** ⚖ Volljährige *m, f:* **become a ~** volljährig werden. **4.** ♪ Dur *n.* **II** *adj* **5.** größer, *fig. a.* bedeutend, wichtig. **6.** ⚖ volljährig. **III** *v/i* **7.** ~ **in** *univ. Am.* als *od.* im Hauptfach studieren. **ma·jor·i·ty** [mə'dʒɒrətɪ] *s* **1.** Mehrheit *f:* **by a large ~** mit großer Mehrheit; **in the ~ of cases** in der Mehrzahl der Fälle; **~ of votes** Stimmenmehrheit *f;* **be in the ~** (*od.* **a**) ~ in der Mehrzahl sein; **~ decision** Mehrheitsbeschluß *m.* **2.** ⚖ Volljährigkeit *f:* **reach one's ~** volljährig werden.

make [meɪk] **I** *s* **1.** Machart *f,* Ausführung *f;* Erzeugnis *n,* Fabrikat *n,* Produkt *n.* **II** *v/t* (*irr*) **2.** *allg. z. B. Reise, Versuch* machen: ~ **a speech** e-e Rede halten. **3.** machen: a) anfertigen, herstellen, erzeugen (*from, of, out of* von, aus), b) verarbeiten, formen (*to, into* in acc, zu), c) *Tee etc* zubereiten. **4.** (er)schaffen: **he is made for this job** er ist für diese Arbeit wie geschaffen. **5.** ergeben, bilden. **6.** *Geräusch, Schwierigkeiten etc* machen, b) bewirken, (mit sich) bringen. **7.** machen *od.* ernennen zu: ~ **s.o.** (**a**) **gen-**

eral j-n zum General ernennen. **8.** *mit adj, pp etc:* machen: ~ **angry** zornig machen, erzürnen. **9.** sich erweisen als (*Person*): **he would ~ a good teacher** er würde e-n guten Lehrer abgeben. **10.** *mit inf: j-n* lassen, veranlassen *od.* bringen zu: ~ **s.o. wait** j-n warten lassen; ~ **s.o. talk** j-n zum Sprechen bringen; ~ **s.th. do,** ~ **do with s.th.** mit et. auskommen, sich mit et. behelfen. **11.** ~ **much of** viel Wesens machen um; viel halten von. **12.** sich e-e Vorstellung machen von, halten für: **what do you ~ of it?** was halten Sie davon? **13.** schätzen auf (*acc*). **14.** sich *Vermögen etc* erwerben, *Geld, Profit* machen, *Gewinn* erzielen. **15.** schaffen a) *Strecke* zurücklegen, b) *Geschwindigkeit* erreichen, machen. **16.** F *Zug* erwischen: ~ **it** es schaffen. **17.** sich belaufen auf (*acc*), ergeben: **two and two ~ four** 2 u. 2 macht *od.* ist 4. **III** *v/i* (*irr*) **18.** ~ **as if** (*od.* **as though**) so tun als ob *od.* als wenn: ~ **believe** (**that; to do**) vorgeben (daß; zu tun).

Verbindungen mit Präpositionen:

make at *v/i* losgehen *od.* sich stürzen auf (*acc*). ~ **for** *v/i* **1.** zugehen *od.* lossteuern auf (*acc*); sich aufmachen nach; sich stürzen auf (*acc*). **2.** förderlich sein, dienen (*dat*), beitragen zu.

Verbindungen mit Adverbien:

make a·way *v/i* sich davonmachen (**with** mit). ~ **make away.** ~ **out I** *v/t* **1.** *Scheck etc* ausstellen; *Urkunde etc* ausfertigen; *Liste etc* aufstellen. **2.** ausmachen, erkennen. **3.** aus *j-m, e-r Sache* klug werden. **4. make s.o. out to be bad** (**a liar**) j-n als schlecht (als Lügner) hinstellen. **5.** *bsd. Am.* auskommen (**with** mit *j-m*). **6.** *bsd. Am.* F *gut etc* zurechtkommen. ~ **o·ver** *v/t* **1.** *Eigentum* übertragen, vermachen (**to** *dat*). **2.** umarbeiten; umbauen (**into** zu). ~ **up I** *v/t* **1.** bilden: **be made up of** bestehen *od.* sich zs.-setzen aus. **2.** *Schriftstück etc* abfassen, aufsetzen; *Liste etc* anfertigen, *Tabelle* aufstellen, *Arznei, Bericht etc* zs.-stellen. **3.** sich *e-e Geschichte etc* ausdenken, *a. b.s.* erfinden. **4.** *Paket etc* (ver)packen, (-)schnüren. **5.** → **mind** 5. **6.** *Versäumtes* nachholen, wettmachen. **7. make it up** sich versöhnen *od.* wieder vertragen (**with** mit). **II** *v/i* **8.** sich schminken. **9.** ~

for wiedergutmachen, wettmachen. **10.**
→ 7. **11. ~ to s.o.** F j-m schöntun; sich
an j-n heranmachen.

'make-be,lieve *adj* Phantasie...,
Schein...: **~ world.**

mak·er ['meɪkə] *s* **1.** ♱ Hersteller *m*,
Erzeuger *m*. **2. the** ⚕ *eccl.* der Schöpfer.

'make|·shift I *s* Notbehelf *m*. **II** *adj* be-
helfsmäßig, provisorisch, Behelfs...
'~-up *s* **1.** Make-up *n*: **without ~** *a.*
ungeschminkt. **2.** Aufmachung *f*,
(Ver)Kleidung *f*. **3.** *Film etc:* Maske *f*.
4. Zs.-setzung *f*.

mak·ing ['meɪkɪŋ] *s* **1.** Erzeugung *f*, Herstellung *f*, Fabrikation *f*: **be in the ~** im
Werden *od.* Kommen sein; noch in Arbeit sein. **2. have the ~s of** das Zeug
haben zu.

mal·ad·just·ed [ˌmælə'dʒʌstɪd] *adj*
psych. nicht angepaßt, milieugestört.

mal·ad·min·is·tra·tion ['mælədˌmɪnɪ-
'streɪʃn] *s* schlechte Verwaltung.

mal·a·droit [ˌmælə'drɔɪt] *adj* □ **1.** ungeschickt. **2.** taktlos.

ma·laise [mæ'leɪz] *s* **1.** Unpäßlichkeit *f*,
Unwohlsein *n*. **2.** *fig.* Unbehagen *n*.

ma·lar·i·a [mə'leərɪə] *s* ♣ Malaria *f*.

mal·con·tent ['mælkən,tent] **I** *adj* unzufrieden. **II** *s* Unzufriedene *m*, *f*.

male [meɪl] **I** *adj* männlich: **~ choir** Männerchor *m*; **~ cousin** Vetter *m*; **~ model**
Dressman *m*; **~ nurse** (Kranken)Pfle-
ger *m*; **~ prostitute** Strichjunge *m*; →
chauvinism, chauvinist. II *s* Mann *m*;
zo. Männchen *n*.

mal·e·dic·tion [ˌmælɪ'dɪkʃn] *s* Fluch *m*,
Verwünschung *f*.

mal·ev·o·lence [mə'levələns] *s* Böswilligkeit *f*. **ma·lev·o·lent** *adj* □ übelwol-
lend (**to** *dat*), böswillig.

mal·for·ma·tion [ˌmælfɔː'meɪʃn] *s* *bsd.* ♣
Mißbildung *f*.

mal·func·tion [ˌmæl'fʌŋkʃn] **I** *s* **1.** ♣
Funktionsstörung *f*. **2.** ⚙ schlechtes
Funktionieren *od.* Arbeiten; Versagen
n. **II** *v/i* **3.** ♣ schlecht funktionieren *od.*
arbeiten; versagen.

mal·ice ['mælɪs] *s* **1.** Böswilligkeit *f*. **2.**
Groll *m*: **bear s.o. ~** e-n Groll auf j-n
haben *od.* gegen j-n hegen, j-m grollen.
3. ⚖ böse Absicht, Vorsatz *m*: **with ~**
(**aforethought**) vorsätzlich.

ma·li·cious [mə'lɪʃəs] *adj* □ **1.** böswillig,
⚖ *a.* vorsätzlich. **2.** arglistig.

ma·lig·nant [mə'lɪgnənt] *adj* □ **1.** bösartig (*a.* ♣), böswillig. **2.** arglistig.

ma·lin·ger [mə'lɪŋgə] *v/i* sich krank stellen, simulieren. **ma·lin·ger·er** *s* Simu-
lant(in).

mall [mɔːl] *s* **1.** Allee *f*. **2.** *Am.* Einkaufszentrum *n*.

mal·le·a·ble ['mælɪəbl] *adj* **1.** ⚙ ver-
formbar. **2.** *fig.* formbar.

mal·let ['mælɪt] *s* Holzhammer *m*, Schle-
gel *m*.

mal·low ['mæləʊ] *s* ♣ Malve *f*.

mal·nu·tri·tion [ˌmælnjuː'trɪʃn] *s* **1.** Unterernährung *f*. **2.** Fehlernährung *f*.

mal·o·dor·ous [ˌmæl'əʊdərəs] *adj* □
übelriechend.

mal·prac·tice [ˌmæl'præktɪs] *s* Vernachlässigung *f* der beruflichen Sorgfalt;
(ärztlicher) Kunstfehler.

malt [mɔːlt] **I** *s* Malz *n*. **II** *v/t* mälzen.

Mal·tese [ˌmɔːl'tiːz] **I** *s* Malteser(in): **the**
~ pl die Malteser *pl.* **II** *adj* maltesisch: **~**
cross Malteserkreuz *n*.

mal·treat [ˌmæl'triːt] *v/t* **1.** schlecht behandeln. **2.** mißhandeln. **mal·treat·**
ment *s* **1.** schlechte Behandlung *f*. **2.**
Mißhandlung *f*.

mam·mal ['mæml] *s* *zo.* Säugetier *f*.

mam·mon ['mæmən] *s* Mammon *m*.

mam·moth ['mæməθ] **I** *s* *zo.* Mammut *n*.
II *adj* Mammut..., Riesen...

man [mæn] **I** *pl* **men** [men] *s* **1.** Mensch
m. **2.** *oft* ⚕ *coll.* der Mensch, die Menschen *pl.* **3.** Mann *m*: **the ~ in** (*Am. a.*
on) **the street** der Mann auf der Straße; **~ of straw** *fig.* Strohmann; **be**
one's own ~ sein eigener Herr sein. Be-
weitS. Mann *m*, Person *f*; jemand;
man: **every ~** jeder(mann); **no ~** niemand; **~ by ~** Mann für Mann; **to a ~**
bis auf den letzten Mann; → **jack** 1. **5.**
(*Dame*)Stein *m*, (*Schach*)Figur *f*. **II** *v/t*
6. (*Raum*)Schiff *etc* bemannen.

man·age ['mænɪdʒ] **I** *v/t* **1.** Betrieb *etc*
leiten, führen. **2.** *Künstler, Sportler etc*
managen. **3.** *et.* zustande bringen, bewerkstelligen; es fertigbringen (**to do** *a.*
tun). **4.** umgehen (können) mit (*Werk-*
zeug, Tieren etc); mit *j-m*, *et.* fertig werden, *j-n* zu nehmen wissen. **5.** F *Arbeit,*
Essen etc bewältigen, schaffen. **II** *v/i* **6.**
auskommen (**with** mit; **without** ohne).
7. F es schaffen, zurechtkommen; es
einrichten *od.* ermöglichen. **'man·age-**

a·ble adj □ **1.** lenk-, fügsam. **2.** handlich. **'man·age·ment** s **1.** (Haus- etc-) Verwaltung f. **2.** ✝ Management n, Unternehmensführung f: **junior** (**middle, top**) ~ untere (mittlere, obere) Führungskräfte pl; ~ **consultant** Betriebs-, Unternehmensberater m. **3.** ✝ Geschäftsleitung f, Direktion f: **under new** ~ unter neuer Leitung, (Geschäft etc) neu eröffnet. **'man·ag·er** s **1.** (Haus- etc)Verwalter m. **2.** ✝ Manager m; Führungskraft f; Geschäftsführer m, Leiter m, Direktor m. **3.** Manager m (e-s Schauspielers etc). **4. be a good** ~ gut od. sparsam wirtschaften können. **5.** Fußball: (Chef)Trainer m. **man·ag·er·ess** [~'res] s **1.** (Haus- etc)Verwalterin f. **2.** ✝ Managerin f; Geschäftsführerin f, Leiterin f, Direktorin f. **3.** Managerin f (e-s Schauspielers etc). **man·a·ger·i·al** [~ə'dʒɪərɪəl] adj ✝ geschäftsführend, leitend: ~ **position** leitende Stellung; ~ **staff** leitende Angestellte pl. **man·ag·ing** [~'ɪdʒɪŋ] adj ✝ geschäftsführend, leitend: ~ **director** Generaldirektor m, leitender Direktor.

man·da·rin(e) ['mændərɪn] s ⚘ Mandarine f.

man·date ['mændeɪt] s **1.** ⚖ Mandat n, (Prozeß)Vollmacht f. **2.** parl. Mandat n, Auftrag m. **man·da·to·ry** ['~dətərɪ] adj □ obligatorisch, zwingend, verbindlich.

man·di·ble ['mændɪbl] s anat. Unterkiefer(knochen) m.

man·do·lin ['mændəlɪn], **man·do·line** [~'liːn] s ♪ Mandoline f.

mane [meɪn] s Mähne f (a. fig. e-s Menschen).

'man·eat·er s **1.** Menschenfresser m. **2.** menschenfressendes Tier. **3.** F männermordendes Wesen (Frau).

ma·neu·ver, etc Am. → **manoeuvre**, etc.

man·ga·nese ['mæŋgəniːz] s 🝆 Mangan n.

mange [meɪndʒ] s vet. Räude f.

man·ger ['meɪndʒə] s Krippe f, Futtertrog m: → **dog** 1.

man·gle¹ ['mæŋgl] I s (Wäsche)Mangel f. II v/t mangeln.

man·gle² [~] v/t **1.** zerfleischen, -reißen, -fetzen. **2.** fig. Text verstümmeln.

man·go ['mæŋgəʊ] pl **-go(e)s** s ⚘ **1.**

Mango(frucht, -pflaume) f. **2.** Mangobaum m.

man·gy ['meɪndʒɪ] adj □ **1.** vet. räudig. **2.** fig. schmutzig, eklig. **3.** fig. schäbig, heruntergekommen.

'man|·han·dle v/t **1.** mißhandeln. **2.** mit Menschenkraft bewegen. **'~·hole** s ⚒ Kanal-, Einsteigeschacht m: ~ **cover** Schachtdeckel m.

man·hood ['mænhʊd] s **1.** Mannesalter n: **reach** ~ ins Mannesalter kommen. **2.** euphem. Manneskraft f.

'man|·hour s ⚒ Arbeitsstunde f. **'~·hunt** s (Groß)Fahndung f.

ma·ni·a ['meɪnjə] s **1.** 🝆 Manie f, Wahn(sinn) m: → **persecution** 1. **2.** fig. (**for**) Sucht f (nach), Leidenschaft f (für), Manie f, Fimmel m: **collector's** ~ Sammelwut f, -leidenschaft; ~ **for cleanliness** Sauberkeitsfimmel m; **have a** ~ **for** verrückt sein nach. **ma·ni·ac** ['~nɪæk] I s **1.** 🝆 Wahnsinnige m, f, Verrückte m, f. **2.** fig. (Sportetc)Fanatiker(in): **car** ~ Autonarr m. II adj (~**ally**) **3.** ✝ wahnsinnig, verrückt. **man·ic-de·pres·sive** [ˌmænɪkdɪ'presɪv] psych. I adj manisch-depressiv. II s 🝆 Manisch-Depressive m, f: **be a** ~ manisch-depressiv sein.

man·i·cure ['mænɪˌkjʊə] I s Maniküre f. II v/t maniküren.

man·i·fest ['mænɪfest] I adj □ offenkundig, augenscheinlich. II v/t offenbaren, manifestieren. III s ✔ bsd. Am. Passagierliste f. **man·i·fes'ta·tion** s **1.** Offenbarung f, Manifestation f. **2.** Anzeichen n, Symptom n. **man·i·fes·to** [~təʊ] pl **-to(e)s** s Manifest n.

man·i·fold ['mænɪfəʊld] I adj □ **1.** mannigfaltig, vielfältig. **2.** ⚙ Mehr-, Vielfach...; Kombinations... II s **3.** ⚙ Verteiler m. III v/t **4.** vervielfältigen.

ma·nip·u·late [mə'nɪpjʊleɪt] v/t **1.** j-n, Preise etc manipulieren. **2.** ⚙ bedienen, betätigen. **3.** Konten etc frisieren. **ma·ˌnip·u'la·tion** s **1.** Manipulation f. **2.** ⚙ Bedienung f, Betätigung f. **3.** Frisieren n. **ma'nip·u·la·tor** s Manipulator m (a. Zauberkünstler).

man·kind [mæn'kaɪnd] s die Menschheit, die Menschen pl. **'man·ly** adj männlich; Männer...

'man·made adj vom Menschen geschaffen od. verursacht; künstlich: ~ **fibers**

(bsd. Br. fibres) pl Kunst-, Chemiefasern pl.

man·ne·quin [ˈmænɪkɪn] s **1.** Mannequin n. **2.** Kleider- od. Schaufensterpuppe f.

man·ner [ˈmænə] s **1.** Art f (u. Weise f): *in this ~* auf diese Art od. Weise, so; *in such a ~ (that)* so od. derart (daß); *adverb of ~* Umstandswort n der Art u. Weise, Modaladverb n; *in a ~ of speaking* sozusagen. **2.** Betragen n, Auftreten n: *it's just his ~* das ist so s-e Art. **3.** pl Benehmen n, Umgangsformen pl, Manieren pl: *it is bad ~s* es gehört od. schickt sich nicht *(to do zu tun)*. **4.** pl Sitten pl (u. Gebräuche pl). **'man·ner·ism** s **1.** paint. etc Manierismus m. **2.** Manieriertheit f. **3.** manierierte Wendung (in Rede etc).

ma·noeu·vra·ble [məˈnuːvrəbl] adj bsd. Br. manövrierfähig; lenk-, steuerbar; weitS. wendig (Fahrzeug). **ma'noeu·vre** [~və] s **1.** a. pl ⚓, ⚔ Manöver n: *be on ~s* im Manöver sein; *room for ~* fig. Handlungsspielraum m. **2** fig. Manöver n, Schachzug m, List f. **II** v/i **3.** ⚓, ⚔ manövrieren (a. fig.). **II** v/t **4.** manövrieren (a. fig.): *~ s.o. into s.th.* j-n in et. hineinmanövrieren.

man·or [ˈmænə] s Br. (Land)Gut n: *~ (house)* Herrenhaus n.

'man,pow·er s **1.** menschliche Arbeitskraft od. -leistung. **2.** (verfügbare) Arbeitskräfte pl: *~ shortage* Arbeitskräftemangel m.

'man,ser·vant pl **'men,ser·vants** s Diener m.

man·sion [ˈmænʃn] s **1.** herrschaftliches Wohnhaus. **2.** pl bsd. Br. (großes) Mietshaus.

'man,slaugh·ter [~] ⚖ Totschlag m.

man·tel·piece [ˈmæntl~] s, **'~,shelf** s (irr **shelf**) Kaminsims m.

,man·to·'man adj von Mann zu Mann: *'~trap* s Fußangel f.

man·u·al [ˈmænjʊəl] **I** adj □ **1.** Hand..., manuell: *~ work* körperliche Arbeit; *~ worker* (Hand)Arbeiter(in). **2.** handschriftlich. **II** s **3.** Handbuch n, Leitfaden m.

man·u·fac·ture [ˌmænjʊˈfæktʃə] **I** s **1.** Fertigung f, Erzeugung f, Herstellung f: *year of ~* Herstellungs-, Baujahr n. **2.** Erzeugnis n, Fabrikat n. **II** v/t **3.** erzeu-

gen, herstellen. **4.** verarbeiten *(into* zu). **5.** fig. Ausrede etc erfinden. **,man·u'fac·tur·er** s Hersteller m, Erzeuger m. **,man·u'fac·tur·ing** adj Herstellungs...: *~ cost* Herstellungskosten pl.

ma·nure [məˈnjʊə] **I** s *(bsd. natürlicher)* Dünger. **II** v/t düngen.

man·u·script [ˈmænjʊskrɪpt] s Manuskript n.

man·y [ˈmenɪ] **I** adj **1.** viel(e): *~ times* oft; *as ~ as forty* nicht weniger als vierzig; *we had one chair too ~* wir hatten e-n Stuhl zuviel. **2.** *~ a* manch (ein): *~ a time* so manches Mal. **II** s **3.** viele: *~ of us* viele von uns; *a good ~* ziemlich viel(e); *a great ~* sehr viele. *,~'sid·ed* adj **1.** vielseitig (a. fig.). **2.** fig. vielschichtig (Problem etc).

map [mæp] **I** s **1.** (Land- etc)Karte f; (Stadt- etc)Plan m: *be off the ~* F hinter dem Mond liegen; *put on the ~* F Stadt etc bekannt machen. **II** v/t **2.** e-e Karte machen von, Gebiet kartographisch erfassen; in e-e Karte eintragen. **3.** *mst ~ out* fig. (bis in die Einzelheiten) (vor)aus)planen.

ma·ple [ˈmeɪpl] s ♣ Ahorn m.

mar [mɑː] v/t **1.** beschädigen; verunstalten. **2.** fig. Pläne etc stören, beeinträchtigen; Spaß etc verderben.

mar·a·thon [ˈmærəθn] *(Leichtathletik)* **I** s a. *~ race* Marathonlauf m. **II** adj Marathon..., fig. a. Dauer...

ma·raud [məˈrɔːd] **I** v/i plündern. **II** v/t (aus)plündern. **ma'raud·er** s Plünderer m.

mar·ble [ˈmɑːbl] **I** s **1.** Marmor m. **2.** a) Murmel f, b) pl (sg konstruiert) Murmelspiel n: *play ~s* mit) Murmeln spielen. **II** adj **3.** marmorn (a. fig.).

March¹ [mɑːtʃ] s März m: *in ~* im März.

march² [~] **I** v/i **1.** ⚔ etc marschieren: *~ off* abrücken; *~ past (s.o.)* (an j-m) vorbeiziehen od. -marschieren; *time is ~ing on* es ist schon spät; → *time* 1. **II** v/t **2.** Strecke marschieren, zurücklegen. **3.** *~ s.o. off* j-n abführen. **III** s **4.** ⚔ Marsch m (a. ♪); allg. (Fuß)Marsch m. **5.** Marsch(strecke f) m: *a day's ~* ein Tage(s)marsch; *steal a ~ on s.o.* fig. j-m zuvorkommen. **6.** fig. (Ab)Lauf m, (Fort)Gang m.

march·ing or·ders [ˈmɑːtʃɪŋ] s pl ⚔ Marschbefehl m: *get one's ~* fig. F den

Laufpaß bekommen (*von Firma od. Freundin*); (*Sport*) vom Platz fliegen.

mare [meə] *s* zo. Stute *f*: **~'s nest** *fig.* Windei *n*, *a.* (Zeitungs)Ente *f*.

mar·ga·rine [ˌmɑːdʒəˈriːn] *s*, **marge** [mɑːdʒ] *s* Br. F Margarine *f*.

mar·gin [ˈmɑːdʒɪn] *s* **1.** Rand *m* (*a. fig.*). **2.** (Seiten)Rand *m*: **in the ~** am Rand. **3.** Grenze *f* (*a. fig.*): **~ of income** Einkommensgrenze. **4.** *fig.* Spielraum *m*: **allow** (*od.* **leave**) **a ~ for** Spielraum lassen für. **5.** ✝ (*Gewinn-*, *Verdienst-*) Spanne *f*. **6.** Sport: Abstand *m*, (*a.* Punkt)Vorsprung *m*: **by a wide ~** mit großem Vorsprung. **~·al** [ˈ~l] *adj* **1.** Rand...: **~ note** Randbemerkung *f*. **2.** Grenz... (*a. fig.*). **3.** *fig.* geringfügig. **~·al·ly** [ˈ~əlɪ] *adv fig.* **1.** geringfügig. **2.** (nur) am Rand.

mar·gue·rite [ˌmɑːgəˈriːt] *s* ⚘ **1.** Gänseblümchen *n*. **2.** Margerite *f*.

mar·i·hua·na, mar·i·jua·na [ˌmærɪˈjuːɑːnə] *s* Marihuana *n*.

ma·ri·nade [ˌmærɪˈneɪd] *s* Marinade *f*. **mar·i·nate** [ˈ~neɪt] *v/t* marinieren.

ma·rine [məˈriːn] **I** *adj* **1.** a) See...: **~ chart** Seekarte *f*, b) Meeres...: **~ animal**. **II** *s* **2.** Marine *f*. **3.** ✕ Marineinfanterist *m*: **tell that to the ~s!** F das kannst du deiner Großmutter erzählen!

mar·i·o·nette [ˌmærɪəˈnet] *s* Marionette *f*: **~ play** Puppenspiel *n*.

mar·i·tal [ˈmærɪtl] *adj* □ ehelich, Ehe...: **~ duties** *pl* (**rights** *pl*) eheliche Pflichten *pl* (Rechte *pl*); **~ status** Familienstand *m*.

mar·i·time [ˈmærɪtaɪm] *adj* **1.** See...: **~ blockade** Seeblockade *f*. **2.** seefahrend. **3.** Küsten...

mar·jo·ram [ˈmɑːdʒərəm] *s* ⚘ Majoran *m*.

mark¹ [mɑːk] *s* (deutsche) Mark.

mark² [~] **I** *s* **1.** Markierung *f*, bsd. ⚙ Marke *f*, Zeichen *n* (*a. fig.*): **~ of confidence** Vertrauensbeweis *m*; **~ of respect** Zeichen der Hochachtung. **3.** (Kenn)Zeichen *n*, Merkmal *n*: **distinctive ~** Kennzeichen *n*. **4.** Narbe *f* (*a.* ⚘); Kerbe *f*, Einschnitt *m*. **5.** Ziel *n* (*a. fig.*): **hit the ~** (das Ziel) treffen; *fig.* ins Schwarze treffen; **miss the ~** das Ziel verfehlen, danebenschießen (*a. fig.*); **be off** (**wide of**) **the ~** (weit) danebenschießen; *fig.* sich (gewaltig) irren; (weit)

danebenliegen (*Schätzung etc*). **6.** *fig.* Norm *f*: **be up to the ~** den Anforderungen gewachsen sein (*Person*) od. genügen (*Leistungen etc*); *gesundheitlich* auf der Höhe sein. **7.** a) (*Fuß-*, *Brems-etc*)Spur *f* (*a. fig.*): **leave one's ~** on s-n Stempel aufdrücken (*dat*); bei *j-m* s-e Spuren hinterlassen, b) Fleck *m*. **8.** ✝ (*Fabrik-*, *Waren*)Zeichen *n*, (*Schutz-*, *Handels*)Marke *f*. **9.** *ped.* Note *f* (*a. Sport*), Zensur *f*: **get** (*od.* **obtain**) **full ~s** die beste Note bekommen, die höchste Punktzahl erreichen. **10.** a) *Fußball*: Elfmeterpunkt *m*, b) *Laufsport*: Startlinie *f*: **on your ~s!** auf die Plätze!; **be quick** (**slow**) **off the ~** e-n guten (schlechten) Start haben; *fig.* schnell (langsam) schalten *od.* reagieren. **II** *v/t* **11.** markieren, anzeichnen, *a. fig.* kennzeichnen; *Wäsche* zeichnen; *Waren* auszeichnen; *Preis* festsetzen; *Temperatur etc* anzeigen; *fig.* ein Zeichen sein für: **to ~ the occasion** zur Feier des Tages, aus diesem Anlaß; **~ time** ✕ auf der Stelle treten (*a. fig.*); *fig.* abwarten. **12.** Spuren hinterlassen auf (*dat*); *fig. j-n* zeichnen (*Krankheit etc*). **13.** bestimmen (**for** für). **14.** *ped.* benoten, zensieren, (*Sport*) bewerten. **15.** *Sport*: *Gegenspieler* decken, markieren. **III** *v/i* **16. ~ easily** leicht schmutzen.

Verbindungen mit Adverbien:

mark| down *v/t* **1.** ✝ (*im Preis*) herunter-, herabsetzen. **2.** bestimmen, vormerken (**for** für). **~ off** *v/t* **1.** abgrenzen, abstecken. **2.** (*auf e-r Liste*) abhaken. **~ out** *v/t* **1.** → **mark²** 13. **2.** abgrenzen, markieren. **~ up** *v/t* ✝ (*im Preis*) hinauf-, heraufsetzen.

'mark·down *s* ✝ Preissenkung *f* (**of** um).

marked [mɑːkt] *adj* deutlich, merklich, ausgeprägt. **mark·ed·ly** [ˈ~kɪdlɪ] *adv* deutlich, ausgesprochen.

mark·er [ˈmɑːkə] *s* **1.** Markierstift *m*. **2.** Lesezeichen *n*. **3.** *Sport*: Bewacher(in).

mar·ket [ˈmɑːkɪt] ✝ **I** *s* **1.** Markt *m*: a) *Handel*: **be on the ~** auf dem Markt od. im Handel sein; **put** (*od.* **place**) **on the ~** auf den Markt od. in den Handel bringen; zum Verkauf anbieten, b) *Handelszweig*, c) Marktplatz *m*: **in the ~** auf dem Markt, d) Wochen-, Jahrmarkt *m*, e) *Absatzgebiet*: **hold the ~** den Markt beherrschen, f) Absatz *m*, Verkauf *m*:

meet with a ready ~ schnellen Absatz finden; **there is no** ~ **for** ... lassen sich nicht absetzen. **2.** *Am.* (Lebensmittel)Geschäft *n*, Laden *m*. **II** *v/t* **3.** auf den Markt *od.* in den Handel bringen. **4.** vertreiben. **III** *adj* **5.** Markt... **a·nal·y·sis** *s* (*irr* **analysis**) Marktanalyse *f*. ~ **e·con·o·my** *s: free* (*social*) ~ freie (soziale) Marktwirtschaft.

mar·ket·ing ['maːkɪtɪŋ] *s* ✝ Marketing *n*: ~ **research** Absatzforschung *f*.

mar·ket | **place** *s* Marktplatz *m*. ~ **re·search** *s* Marktforschung *f*.

mark·ing ['maːkɪŋ] *s* **1.** Markierung *f*, *a. fig.* Kennzeichnung *f*. **2.** *zo.* Musterung *f*, Zeichnung *f*. **3.** *ped.* Benotung *f*, Zensierung *f*, (*Sport*) Bewertung *f*. **4.** *Sport:* Deckung *f*.

marks·man ['maːksmən] *s* (*irr* **man**) guter Schütze.

'mark·up *s* ✝ Preiserhöhung *f* (**of** um).

mar·ma·lade ['maːməleɪd] *s* (*bsd.* Orangen)Marmelade *f*.

mar·mot ['maːmət] *s zo.* Murmeltier *n*.

ma·roon [mə'ruːn] *adj* kastanienbraun.

mar·quee [maː'kiː] *s* großes Zelt.

mar·riage ['mærɪdʒ] *s* **1.** Heirat *f*, Vermählung *f*, Hochzeit *f* (**to** mit). **2.** Ehe *f*: **by** ~ angeheiratet; **related by** ~ verschwägert. ~ **bu·reau** (*a. irr bureau*) Heiratsinstitut *n*. ~ **cer·tif·i·cate** *s* Trauschein *m*. ~ **guid·ance cen·ter** (*bsd. Br.* **cen·tre**) *s* Eheberatungsstelle *f*. ~ **lines** *s pl* (*mst sg konstruiert*) *bsd. Br.* Trauschein *m*.

mar·ried ['mærɪd] *adj* verheiratet, ehelich, Ehe...: ~ **couple** Ehepaar *n*; ~ **life** Eheleben *n*.

mar·row ['mærəʊ] *s* **1.** *anat.* (Knochen)Mark *n*: **be frozen to the** ~ völlig durchgefroren sein. **2.** *fig.* Mark *n*, Kern *m*, das Innerste.

mar·ry ['mærɪ] **I** *v/t* **1.** heiraten: **be married** verheiratet sein (**to** mit); heiraten. **2.** *a.* ~ **off** Tochter *etc* verheiraten (**to** an *acc*, mit). **3.** *Paar* trauen. **II** *v/i* **4.** heiraten: ~ **into** einheiraten in (*acc*).

Mars [maːz] *s ast.* Mars *m*.

marsh [maːʃ] *s* Sumpf(land *n*) *m*, Marsch *f*.

mar·shal ['maːʃl] **I** *s* **1.** ✗ Marschall *m*. **2.** *Am.* Bezirkspolizeichef *m*. **II** *v/t pret u. pp* **-shaled**, *bsd. Br.* **-shalled 3.** (an)ordnen, arrangieren.

marsh·y ['maːʃɪ] *adj* sumpfig, Sumpf...

mar·ten ['maːtɪn] *s zo.* Marder *m*.

mar·tial ['maːʃl] *adj* □ **1.** kriegerisch. **2.** Kriegs..., Militär...: ~ **law** Kriegsrecht *n*. **3.** ~ **arts** *pl* asiatische Kampfsportarten *pl*.

Mar·tian ['maːʃn] *s* Marsmensch *m*, -bewohner(in).

mar·ti·ni [maː'tiːnɪ] *s* Martini *m* (*Cocktail*).

Mar·tin·mas ['maːtɪnməs] *s* Martinstag *m* (*11. November*).

mar·tyr ['maːtə] **I** *s* **1.** Märtyrer(in): **make a** ~ **of o.s.** sich (auf)opfern; *iro.* den Märtyrer spielen. **II** *v/t* **2.** zum Märtyrer machen. **3.** zu Tode martern. **'mar·tyr·dom** *s* Martyrium *n* (*a. fig.*).

mar·vel ['maːvl] **I** *s* Wunder *n* (**of** an *dat*): **work** (*od.* **do**) ~**s** Wunder wirken. **II** *v/i pret u. pp* **-veled**, *bsd. Br.* **-velled** sich wundern, staunen (**at** über *acc*). **mar·vel·(l)ous** ['maːvələs] *adj* □ **1.** erstaunlich, wunderbar. **2.** F fabelhaft, phantastisch.

Marx·ism ['maːksɪzəm] *s* Marxismus *m*. **'Marx·ist** *s* Marxist(in). **II** *adj* marxistisch.

mar·zi·pan [ˌmaːzɪ'pæn] *s* Marzipan *n*, *m*.

mas·ca·ra [mæ'skaːrə] *s* Wimperntusche *f*.

mas·cot ['mæskət] *s* Maskottchen *n*: a) Glücksbringer(in), b) Talisman *m*.

mas·cu·line ['mæskjʊlɪn] *adj* □ **1.** männlich (*a. ling.*), Männer... **2.** unfraulich, maskulin.

mash [mæʃ] **I** *s* **1.** breiige Masse, Brei *m*. **2.** *Br.* F Kartoffelbrei *m*. **II** *v/t* **3.** zerdrücken, -quetschen: ~**ed potatoes** *pl* Kartoffelbrei *m*.

mask [maːsk] **I** *s* **1.** *allg.* Maske *f* (*a. fig.*): **throw off the** ~ die Maske fallen lassen, sein wahres Gesicht zeigen. **II** *v/t* **2.** maskieren: ~**ed ball** Maskenball *m*. **3.** *fig.* verschleiern: ~**ed advertising** ✝ Schleichwerbung *f*.

mas·o·chism ['mæsəʊkɪzəm] *s psych.* Masochismus *m*. **'mas·o·chist** *s* Masochist(in). ˌ**mas·o'chis·tic** *adj* (~**ally**) masochistisch.

ma·son ['meɪsn] *s* **1.** Steinmetz *m*. **2.** *oft* ♘ Freimaurer *m*.

mas·quer·ade [ˌmæskə'reɪd] *s* Maskerade *f* (*a. fig.*).

1077 match point

mass¹ [mæs] *s eccl.* Messe *f*: **go to ~** zur Messe gehen.

mass² [~] I *s* 1. *allg.* Masse *f* (*a. phys.*): **a ~ of errors** e-e (Un)Menge Fehler; **~es** *pl* **of ice** Eismassen *pl*; **the ~es** *pl* die (breite) Masse. 2. Mehrzahl *f*, überwiegender Teil. II *v/t u. v/i* 3. (sich) (an)sammeln *od.* (an)häufen. III *adj* 4. Massen...: **~ demonstration**, *etc.*

mas·sa·cre ['mæsəkə] I *s* Massaker *n.* II *v/t* niedermetzeln.

mas·sage ['mæsɑːʒ] I *s* Massage *f.* II *v/t* massieren.

mas·seur [mæ'sɜː] *s* Masseur *m.* **masseuse** [~'sɜːz] *s* Masseurin *f*, Masseuse *f.*

mas·sive ['mæsɪv] *adj* □ *allg.* massiv (*a. fig.*): **on a ~ scale** in ganz großem Rahmen.

mass| me·di·a *s pl* (*a. sg konstruiert*) Massenmedien *pl.* **'~pro·duce** *v/t* serienmäßig herstellen. **~ pro·duc·tion** *s* Massen-, Serienproduktion *f.*

mast¹ [mɑːst] *s* ♣ (*a. Antennen- etc-*) Mast *m.*

mast² [~] *s* Mast(futter *n*) *f.*

mas·ter ['mɑːstə] I *s* 1. Meister *m*, Herr *m*: **be ~ of s.th.** *et.* (*a. e-e Sprache etc*) beherrschen; **be ~ of the situation** Herr der Lage sein; **be one's own ~** sein eigener Herr sein; **find one's ~** s-n Meister finden (**in s.o.** in j-m). 2. (dazu) passende Sache *od.* Person, Gegenstück *n* (**to** zu). 3. *Br.* Lehrer *m.* 4. *paint. etc* Meister *m*: **an old ~** ein alter Meister. 5. *univ.* Magister *m*: ♀ **of Arts** Magister Artium *od.* der Geisteswissenschaften; ♀ **of Science** Magister der Naturwissenschaften. 6. → **ceremony** 1. II *v/t* 7. Herr sein über (*acc*), *a. Sprache etc* beherrschen. 8. *Aufgabe, Schwierigkeit etc* meistern, *Temperament etc* zügeln. III *adj* 9. meisterhaft, -lich, Meister... 10. Haupt... **~ cop·y** *s* Originalkopie *f* (*a. e-s Films etc*).

mas·ter·ful ['mɑːstəfʊl] *adj* □ 1. herrisch, gebieterisch. 2. → **master** 9.

mas·ter| fuse *s* ⚡ Hauptsicherung *f.* **~ key** *s* Hauptschlüssel *m.*

mas·ter·ly ['mɑːstəlɪ] → **master** 9.

'mas·ter·mind I *s* 1. überragender Geist, Genie *n.* 2. (führender) Kopf: **be the ~ behind** stecken hinter (*dat*). II *v/t*

3. der Kopf (*gen*) sein, stecken hinter (*dat*). **'~piece** *s* 1. Haupt-, Meisterwerk *n.* 2. Meisterstück *n.* **~ plan** *s* Gesamtplan *m.* **'~stroke** *s* Meisterstück *n*, -leistung *f.*

mas·ter·y ['mɑːstərɪ] *s* 1. Herrschaft *f*, Gewalt *f* (**of, over** über *acc*): **gain the ~ over** die Oberhand gewinnen über. 2. Beherrschung *f* (*e-r Sprache etc*).

mas·ti·cate ['mæstɪkeɪt] *v/t* (zer)kauen. **mas·ti·ca·tion** *s* (Zer)Kauen *n.*

mas·tiff ['mæstɪf] *s zo.* Bulldogge *f.*

mas·tur·bate ['mæstəbeɪt] *v/i* masturbieren, onanieren. **mas·tur·ba·tion** *s* Masturbation *f*, Onanie *f.*

mat¹ [mæt] I *s* 1. Matte *f* (*a. Ringen etc*). 2. Untersetzer *m*, -satz *m.* 3. Vorleger *m*, Abtreter *m.* 4. verfilzte Masse. II *v/i* 5. sich verfilzen.

mat² [~] I *adj* matt (*a. phot.*), mattiert. II *v/t* mattieren.

match¹ [mætʃ] *s* Streich-, Zündholz *n.*

match² [~] I *s* 1. der, die, das gleiche *od.* Ebenbürtige: **his ~** seinesgleichen; sein Ebenbild; j-d, der es mit ihm aufnehmen kann; **be a (no) ~ for s.o.** j-m (nicht) gewachsen sein; **find (od. meet) one's ~** s-n Meister finden (**in s.o.** in j-m). 2. (dazu) passende Sache *od.* Person, Gegenstück *n* (**to** zu): **they are an excellent ~** sie passen ausgezeichnet zueinander. 3. (*Fußball-* etc)Spiel *n*, (*Box- etc*)Kampf *m.* 4. Heirat *f*; **gute etc** Partie (*Person*). II *v/t* 6. j-m, e-r Sache ebenbürtig *od.* gewachsen sein, gleichkommen: **no one can ~ her in cooking** niemand kann so gut kochen wie sie; **... cannot be ~ed** ... ist unerreicht *od.* nicht zu übertreffen. 7. j-m, e-r Sache (*a. farblich etc*) entsprechen, passen zu. 8. j-n, et. vergleichen (**with** mit): **~ one's strength against s.o.('s)** s-e Kräfte mit j-m messen. III *v/i* 9. zs.-passen, übereinstimmen (**with** mit), entsprechen (**to** dat).

'match·box *s* Streich-, Zündholzschachtel *f.*

match·ing ['mætʃɪŋ] *adj* (dazu) passend.

'match·less *adj* □ unvergleichlich, einzigartig.

'match|·mak·er *s* 1. Ehestifter(in). 2. *b.s.* Kuppler(in). **~ point** *s* Tennis *etc*: Matchball *m.*

mate¹ [meɪt] → *checkmate.*

mate² [~] I *s* **1.** (Arbeits)Kamerad *m*, (-)Kollege *m*; (*Anrede*) Kamerad!, Kumpel! **2.** *zo., bsd. orn.* Männchen *n od.* Weibchen *n.* **3.** ✣ Maat *m.* II *v/t* **4.** *Tiere* paaren. III *v/i* **5.** *zo.* sich paaren.

ma·te·ri·al [məˈtɪərɪəl] I *adj* □ **1.** materiell, physisch; Material...: ~ *damage* Sachschaden *m*; ~ *defect* Materialfehler *m.* **2.** materiell: a) leiblich (*Wohlergehen*), b) wirtschaftlich: ~ *wealth* materieller Wohlstand. **3.** wesentlich, ausschlaggebend (*to* für); ⚖ erheblich, relevant. II *s* **4.** Material *n*, Stoff *m* (*beide a. fig. for* zu e-m *Buch etc*). **ma·ˈte·ri·al·ism** *s* Materialismus *m.* **ma·ˈte·ri·al·ist** *s* Materialist(in). **ma·ˌte·ri·al·ˈis·tic** *adj* (*~ally*) materialistisch. **ma·ˈte·ri·al·ize** *v/t* **1.** *et.* verwirklichen. II *v/i* **2.** sich verwirklichen. **3.** erscheinen, sich materialisieren (*Geist*).

ma·ter·nal [məˈtɜːnl] *adj* □ **1.** mütterlich, Mutter... **2.** *Großvater etc* mütterlicherseits.

ma·ter·ni·ty [məˈtɜːnətɪ] I *s* Mutterschaft *f.* II *adj:* ~ *allowance* (*od. benefit*) Mutterschaftsbeihilfe *f*; ~ *dress* Umstandskleid *n*; ~ *leave* Mutterschaftsurlaub *m*; ~ *ward* Entbindungsstation *f.*

mat·ey [ˈmeɪtɪ] *adj* kameradschaftlich: *be ~ with s.o.* mit j-m auf du u. du stehen.

math [mæθ] *s Am.* F Mathe *f.*

math·e·mat·i·cal [ˌmæθəˈmætɪkl] *adj* □ mathematisch; Mathematik... **math·e·ma·ti·cian** [ˌ~məˈtɪʃn] *s* Mathematiker(in). **math·e·mat·ics** [ˌ~ˈmætɪks] *s pl* (*mst sg konstruiert*) Mathematik *f.*

maths [mæθs] *s pl* (*mst sg konstruiert*) *Br.* F Mathe *f.*

mat·i·née [ˈmætɪneɪ] *s thea.* Nachmittagsvorstellung *f.*

mat·ing [ˈmeɪtɪŋ] *s zo.* Paarung *f*: ~ *season* Paarungszeit *f.*

ma·tri·arch·y [ˈmeɪtrɪɑːkɪ] *s sociol.* Matriarchat *n.*

ma·tri·ces [ˈmeɪtrɪsiːz] *pl von* **matrix.**

ma·tric·u·late [məˈtrɪkjoleɪt] I *v/t u. v/i* (sich) immatrikulieren. II *s* [~lət] Immatrikulierte *m, f.* **ma·ˌtric·u·ˈla·tion** *s* Immatrikulation *f.*

mat·ri·mo·ni·al [ˌmætrɪˈməonjəl] *adj* □ ehelich, Ehe...: ~ *agency* Heiratsinsti-

tut *n.* **mat·ri·mo·ny** [ˈ~mənɪ] *s* Ehe(-stand *m*) *f.*

ma·trix [ˈmeɪtrɪks] *pl* **ma·tri·ces** [ˈ~trɪsiːz], **'ma·trix·es** *s* **1.** ⚙ Matrize *f.* **2.** A Matrix *f.*

ma·tron [ˈmeɪtrən] *s* **1.** Matrone *f.* **2.** *Br.* Oberschwester *f*, Oberin *f.* **'ma·tron·ly** *adj* matronenhaft.

mat·ter [ˈmætə] I *s* **1.** Materie *f* (*a. phys.*), Substanz *f*, Stoff *m.* **2.** ✣ Eiter *m.* **3.** Sache *f*, Angelegenheit *f*: *this is an entirely different* ~ das ist et. ganz anderes; *a ~ of course* e-e Selbstverständlichkeit; *as a ~ of course* selbstverständlich, natürlich; *a ~ of fact* e-e Tatsache; *as a ~ of fact* tatsächlich, eigentlich; *a ~ of form* e-e Formsache; *as a ~ of form* der Form halber; *a ~ of taste* (e-e) Geschmackssache; *a ~ of time* e-e Frage der Zeit; *it is a ~ of life and death* es geht um Leben u. Tod; → *laughing* **3. 4.** *pl* die Sache, die Dinge *pl*: *to make ~s worse* was die Sache noch schlimmer macht; *as ~s stand* wie die Dinge liegen. **5.** *what's the ~* (*with him*)*?* was ist los (mit ihm)?; *it's no ~ whether* es spielt keine Rolle, ob; *no ~ what he says* ganz gleich, was er sagt; *no ~ who* gleichgültig, wer. II *v/i* **6.** von Bedeutung sein (*to* für): *it doesn't* ~ es macht nichts; *it hardly ~s to me* es macht mir nicht viel aus; *it little ~s* es spielt kaum e-e Rolle. **7.** ✣ eitern. **‚~-of-'course** *adj* selbstverständlich, natürlich. **‚~-of-'fact** *adj* sachlich, nüchtern.

mat·tress [ˈmætrɪs] *s* Matratze *f.*

ma·ture [məˈtjoə] I *adj* □ **1.** *allg.* reif (*a. fig.*). **2.** *fig.* ausgereift (*Pläne etc*): *after ~ reflection* nach reiflicher Überlegung. **3.** ✣ fällig (*Wechsel*). II *v/t* **4.** reifen lassen (*a. fig.*). III *v/i* **5.** (heran)reifen (*into* zu), reif werden (*beide a. fig.*). **6.** ✣ fällig werden. **ma·ˈtur·i·ty** *s* **1.** Reife *f* (*a. fig.*). **2.** ✣ Fälligkeit *f.*

maud·lin [ˈmɔːdlɪn] *adj* **1.** weinerlich (*Stimme*). **2.** rührselig.

maul [mɔːl] *v/t* **1.** *j-n, et.* übel zurichten. **2.** *fig.* herunter-, verreißen (*Kritiker*).

Maun·dy Thurs·day [ˈmɔːndɪ] *s* Gründonnerstag *m.*

mau·so·le·um [ˌmɔːsəˈlɪəm] *pl* **-le·ums, -le·a** [ˌ~ˈlɪə] *s* Mausoleum *n.*

mauve [məov] *adj* malvenfarbig, mauve.

mav·er·ick [ˈmævərɪk] *s pol.* (abtrünniger) Einzelgänger; *allg.* Außenseiter *m*.

mawk·ish ['mɔːkɪʃ] *adj* □ **1.** (unangenehm) süßlich. **2.** *fig.* rührselig, süßlich.

max·im ['mæksɪm] *s* Maxime *f*, Grundsatz *m*.

max·i·ma ['mæksɪmə] *pl von* **maximum**.

max·i·mal ['ˌml] *adj* □ → **maximum** II.

max·i·mize ['ˌmaɪz] *v/t* ✝, ☯ maximieren.

max·i·mum ['ˌməm] **I** *pl* **-ma** ['ˌmə], **-mums** *s* Maximum *n*. **II** *adj* maximal, Maximal..., Höchst...: **~** (*permissible*) *speed* (zulässige) Höchstgeschwindigkeit.

May[1] [meɪ] *s* Mai *m*: *in ~* im Mai.

may[2] [ˌ] *v/aux* (*irr*) **1.** *Möglichkeit, Gelegenheit:* ich kann, du kannst *etc*, ich mag, du magst *etc*: *it ~ happen any time* es kann jederzeit geschehen; *it might happen* es könnte geschehen; *you ~ be right* du magst recht haben, vielleicht hast du recht. **2.** *Erlaubnis:* ich kann, du kannst *etc*, ich darf, du darfst *etc*. **3.** *you ~ well say so* du hast gut reden; *we might as well go* da könnten wir (auch) ebensogut gehen. **4.** *ungewisse Frage:* *how old ~ she be?* wie alt mag sie wohl sein? **5.** *Aufforderung:* *you might help me* du könntest mir (eigentlich) helfen.

may·be ['meɪbiː] *adv* vielleicht.

May| bee·tle, **~ bug** *s zo.* Maikäfer *m.* **~ Day** *s* der 1. Mai. **'2-day** *int* ✈, ⚓ Mayday! (*internationaler Funknotruf*).

may·hem ['meɪhem] *s* **1.** ⚖ *bsd. Am.* schwere Körperverletzung. **2.** *fig.* Chaos *n*: *cause* (*od. create*) *~* ein Chaos auslösen.

may·on·naise [ˌmeɪə'neɪz] *s* Mayonnaise *f*.

may·or [meə] *s* Bürgermeister *m*.

'may·pole *s* Maibaum *m*.

maze [meɪz] *s* Irrgarten *m*, Labyrinth *n* (*a. fig.*): *~ of streets* Straßengewirr *n*; *be in a ~* verwirrt sein.

me [miː] **I** *personal pron* **1.** mich (*acc von* I): *he knows ~.* **2.** mir (*dat von* I): *he gave ~ the book*. **3.** F ich (*nom*): *he's younger than ~*; *it's ~* ich bin's. **II** *reflex pron* **4.** mich: *I looked about ~* ich sah mich um.

mead·ow ['medəʊ] *s* Wiese *f*, Weide *f*: *in the ~* auf der Wiese *od.* Weide.

mea·ger *Am.*, **mea·gre** *bsd. Br.* ['miːgə]

adj □ **1.** mager, dürr, (*Gesicht*) hager. **2.** *fig.* dürftig, kärglich: *~ attendance* spärlicher Besuch.

meal[1] [miːl] *s* Mahl(zeit *f*) *n*, Essen *n*: *~s pl on wheels* Essen auf Rädern.

meal[2] [ˌ] *s* Schrotmehl *n*.

'meal·time *s* Essenszeit *f*.

meal·y ['miːlɪ] *adj* mehlig. **~-mouthed** ['ˌmaʊðd] *adj* schönfärberisch, heuchlerisch (*Person*), (*Äußerung etc a.*) verschlüsselt.

mean[1] [miːn] *adj* □ **1.** gemein, niederträchtig. **2.** schäbig, geizig. **3.** F (*charakterlich*) schäbig: *feel ~* sich schäbig *od.* gemein vorkommen (*about* wegen).

mean[2] [ˌ] **I** *adj* **1.** mittler, Mittel..., durchschnittlich, Durchschnitts... **II** *s* **2.** Mitte *f*, Mittel(weg *m*) *n*, Durchschnitt *m*. **3.** *pl* (*a. sg konstruiert*) Mittel *n od. pl*, Weg *m*: *by all ~s* auf alle Fälle, unbedingt; *by no ~s* keineswegs, auf keinen Fall; *by ~s of* mittels, durch, mit; *find the ~s* Mittel u. Wege finden; *a ~s of communication* ein Kommunikationsmittel; → *end* 10. **4.** *pl* Mittel *pl*, Vermögen *n*: *live within* (*beyond*) *one's ~s* s-n Verhältnissen entsprechend (über s-e Verhältnisse) leben.

mean[3] [ˌ] (*irr*) **I** *v/t* **1.** beabsichtigen, vorhaben: *~ to do s.th.* et. tun wollen; *I ~ it* es ist mir Ernst damit; *~ business* es ernst meinen; *~ no harm* es nicht böse meinen; *no harm ~t!* nichts für ungut (*od.* übel). **2.** *be ~t for* bestimmt sein für, (*Bemerkung etc*) gemünzt sein auf (*acc*). **3.** meinen, sagen wollen: *what do you ~ by this?* was wollen Sie damit sagen?; was verstehen Sie darunter? **4.** *e-e Menge Arbeit etc* bedeuten, heißen (*Wort etc*): *does this ~ anything to you?* ist Ihnen das ein Begriff?, sagt Ihnen das et.? **5.** F **6.** *~ well* (*ill*) *by* (*od.* *to*) *s.o.* j-m wohlgesinnt (übel gesinnt) sein. **7.** *~ everything* (*little*) *to s.o.* j-m alles (wenig) bedeuten.

me·an·der [mɪ'ændə] *v/i* sich winden *od.* schlängeln.

mean·ing ['miːnɪŋ] **I** *s* **1.** Sinn *m*, Bedeutung *f*: *full of ~* → 3; *do you get* (*od.* *take*) *my ~?* verstehst du, was ich meine? **2.** Sinn *m*, Inhalt *m*: *give one's life a new ~* s-m Leben e-n neuen Sinn geben. **II** *adj* □ **3.** bedeutungsvoll, bedeutsam (*Blick etc*). **mean·ing·ful**

['ˑfʊl] *adj* □ **1.** bedeutungsvoll (*Blick*, *Ereignis etc*). **2.** sinnvoll (*Arbeit etc*). '**mean·ing·less** *adj* □ sinnlos.

mean·ness ['miːnnɪs] *s* **1.** Gemeinheit *f*, Niederträchtigkeit *f*. **2.** Schäbigkeit *f*, Geiz *m*.

meant [ment] *pret u. pp von* **mean³**.

,mean·'time I *adv* inzwischen, unterdessen, in der Zwischenzeit. II *s*: *in the* ~ → I. **,~'while** → **meantime** I.

mea·sles ['miːzlz] *s pl* (*mst sg konstruiert*) *§* Masern *pl*: → **German** I.

meas·ur·a·ble ['meʒərəbl] *adj* □ **1.** meßbar. **2.** merklich.

meas·ure ['meʒə] I *s* **1.** Maß(einheit *f*) *n*: ~ *of capacity* Hohlmaß; ~ *of length* Längenmaß. **2.** *fig.* (richtiges *od.* vernünftiges) Maß, Ausmaß *n*: *set* ~*s to* Grenzen setzen (*dat*); *know no* ~ kein Maß kennen; *beyond* (*all*) ~ über alle Maßen, grenzenlos; *in a great* (*od. large*) ~ in großem Maße; großenteils; *in some* ~, *in a* (*certain*) ~ bis zu e-m gewissen Grade. **3.** Maß *n*, Meßgerät *n*: *weigh with two* ~*s fig.* mit zweierlei Maß messen. **4.** *§* Takt *m*. **5.** *Metrik:* Versmaß *n*. **6.** Maßnahme *f*: *take* ~*s* Maßnahmen treffen *od.* ergreifen. II *v/t* **7.** (ver)messen, ab-, ausmessen: ~ *s.o.* j-m Maß nehmen (*for* für); ~ *one's length* fig. der Länge nach hinfallen. **8.** *fig.* messen (*by* an *dat*). **9.** *fig.* vergleichen, messen (*against*, *with* mit): ~ *one's strength with* s-e Kräfte messen mit. III *v/i* **10.** messen, groß sein: *it* ~*s 7 inches* es mißt 7 Zoll, es ist 7 Zoll lang. '**meas·ure·ment** *s* **1.** (Ver)Messung *f*. **2.** Maß *n*; *pl a.* Abmessungen *pl*: *take s.o.'s* ~*s* j-m Maß nehmen (*for* für). '**meas·ur·ing** *adj* Meß...: ~ *instrument* Meßgerät *n*.

meat [miːt] *s* **1.** Fleisch *n*: *cold* ~ kalter Braten. **2.** *fig.* Substanz *f*, Gehalt *m*. '**~·ball** *s* Fleischklößchen *n*.

me·chan·ic [mɪ'kænɪk] *s* Mechaniker *m*. **me'chan·i·cal** *adj* □ mechanisch (*a. fig.*): ~ *engineering* Maschinenbau *m*; ~ *pencil Am.* Drehbleistift *m*.

mech·a·nism ['mekənɪzəm] *s* Mechanismus *m* (*a. fig.*). '**mech·a·nize** *v/t* mechanisieren.

med·al ['medl] *s* **1.** Medaille *f*. **2.** Orden *m*. **med·al·ist** *Am.* → **medallist.** **me·dal·lion** [mɪ'dæljən] *s* Medaillon *n*.

med·al·list ['medlɪst] *s bsd. Br.* Medaillengewinner(in).

med·dle ['medl] *v/i* sich einmischen (*with*, *in* in *acc*). **med·dle·some** ['ˑsəm] *adj* aufdringlich.

me·di·a ['miːdjə] I *pl von* **medium**. II *s pl* (*a. sg konstruiert*) Medien *pl*: ~ *event* Medienereignis *s*; ~*shy* medienscheu.

me·di·ae·val → **medieval**.

me·di·ate ['miːdɪeɪt] I *v/i* vermitteln (*between* zwischen *dat*). II *v/t* (durch Vermittlung) zustande bringen *od.* beilegen. **,me·di·'a·tion** *s* Vermittlung *f*. '**me·di·a·tor** *s* Vermittler *m*.

med·ic ['medɪk] *s* → **medico.**

med·i·cal ['medɪkl] *adj* □ **1.** medizinisch, ärztlich, Kranken...: ~ *certificate* ärztliches Attest; ~ *examination* ärztliche Untersuchung; *on* ~ *grounds* aus gesundheitlichen Gründen; ~ *student* Medizinstudent(in). **2.** internistisch: ~ *ward* innere Abteilung (*e-r Klinik*). II *s* **3.** F ärztliche Untersuchung.

med·i·ca·ment [məˈdɪkəmənt] *s* Medikament *n*.

med·i·cate ['medɪkeɪt] *v/t* medizinisch *od.* medikamentös behandeln. **,med·i·'ca·tion** *s* medizinische *od.* medikamentöse Behandlung.

me·dic·i·nal [məˈdɪsɪnl] *adj* □ heilkräftig, Heil...: ~ *herbs pl* Heilkräuter *pl*.

med·i·cine ['medsɪn] *s* **1.** Medizin *f*, Arznei *f*: *give s.o. a dose* (*od. taste*) *of his own* ~ fig. es j-m in *od.* mit gleicher Münze heimzahlen. **2.** Medizin *f*, Heilkunde *f*; innere Medizin. ~ *ball s Sport:* Medizinball *m*. ~ *chest s* Hausapotheke *f*. ~ *man s* (*irr man*) Medizinmann *m*.

med·i·co ['medɪkəʊ] *pl* -**cos** *s* F Mediziner *m* (*Arzt u. Student*).

me·di·e·val [,medɪ'iːvl] *adj* □ mittelalterlich.

me·di·o·cre [,miːdɪ'əʊkə] *adj* mittelmäßig. **me·di·oc·ri·ty** [,ˑ'ɒkrətɪ] *s* Mittelmäßigkeit *f*.

med·i·tate ['medɪteɪt] I *v/i* (*on*) nachdenken (über *acc*), grübeln (über *acc*, *dat*), *a. engS.* meditieren (über *acc*). II *v/t* erwägen: ~ *revenge* auf Rache sinnen. **,med·i·'ta·tion** *s* Nachdenken *n*, Grübeln *n*; *engS.* Meditation *f*.

me·di·um ['miːdjəm] I *pl* -**di·a** ['ˑdjə],

-di·ums *s* **1.** *fig.* Mitte *f*, Mittelweg *m*. **2.** *biol. etc* Medium *n*, Träger *m*. **3.** ♀ (*a. künstlerisches etc*) Medium *n*, Mittel *n*: ~ *advertising* II. **4.** *Hypnose, Parapsychologie*: Medium *n*. **II** *adj* **5.** mittler, Mittel..., *a.* mittelmäßig. **6.** *gastr.* englisch (*Steak*). '~**-priced** *adj* der mittleren Preislage. '~**-range** *adj*: ~ *missile* ✠ Mittelstreckenrakete *f*. '~**-size(d)** *adj* mittelgroß: ~ *car mot.* Mittelklassewagen *m*. '~**-term** *adj* mittelfristig (*Planung etc*). ~ *wave s ♪* Mittelwelle *f*: *on* ~ auf Mittelwelle.

med·ley ['medlɪ] *s* **1.** Gemisch *n*, contp. Mischmasch *m*, Durcheinander *n*. **2.** ♪ Medley *n*, Potpourri *n*.

meek [miːk] *adj* □ **1.** sanft(mütig). **2.** bescheiden; *contp.* unterwürfig: *be* ~ *and mild* sich alles gefallen lassen. '**meek·ness** *s* **1.** Sanftmut *f*. **2.** Bescheidenheit *f*; *contp.* Unterwürfigkeit *f*.

meet [miːt] (*irr*) **I** *v/t* **1.** begegnen (*dat*); treffen, sich treffen mit. **2.** j-n kennenlernen: *when I first met him* als ich s-e Bekanntschaft machte; *pleased to* ~ *you* F sehr erfreut; (*Sie kennenzulernen*). **3.** j-n abholen (*at the station* von der Bahn). **4.** → *halfway* 3. **5.** (*feindlich*) zs.-treffen mit, (*Sport a.*) treffen auf (*acc*): → *fate* 1. **6.** *fig.* entgegentreten (*dat*). **7.** münden in (*acc*) (*Straße etc*), stoßen *od.* treffen auf (*acc*) (*there is more to it than* ~*s the eye* da steckt mehr dahinter). **8.** *j-s Wünschen* entgegenkommen, entsprechen, *e-r Forderung, Verpflichtung* nachkommen, *Unkosten* bestreiten, decken. **II** *v/i* **9.** zs.-kommen, -treten. **10.** sich begegnen, sich (*a. verabredungsgemäß*) treffen: ~ *again* sich wiedersehen; *our eyes met* unsere Blicke trafen sich. **11.** (*feindlich*) zs.-stoßen, (*Sport*) aufeinandertreffen. **12.** sich kennenlernen: *we have met before* wir kennen uns schon. **13.** sich vereinigen (*Straßen etc*); sich berühren (*a. Interessen etc*). **14.** genau zs.-passen, sich decken: → *end* 6. **15.** ~ *with* zs.-treffen mit; sich treffen mit; erleben, erleiden: ~ *with an accident* e-n Unfall erleiden, verunglücken; ~ *with a refusal* auf Ablehnung stoßen; → *approval* 2.

meet·ing ['miːtɪŋ] *s* **1.** Begegnung *f*,

Zs.-treffen *n*, -kunft *f*. **2.** Versammlung *f*, Konferenz *f*, Tagung *f*: *at a* ~ auf e-r Versammlung; ~ *of members* Mitgliederversammlung. **3.** *Sport*: Veranstaltung *f*. ~ *place s* **1.** Tagungs-, Versammlungsort *m*. **2.** Treffpunkt *m*.

meg·a·lo·ma·ni·a [ˌmeɡələʊˈmeɪnjə] *s* Größenwahn *m*. ˌ**meg·a·lo·ˈma·ni·ac** [~nɪæk] *adj* größenwahnsinnig.

meg·a·phone ['meɡəfəʊn] *s* Megaphon *f*.

mel·an·chol·y ['melənkəlɪ] **I** *s* **1.** Melancholie *f*, Schwermut *f*. **II** *adj* **2.** melancholisch, schwermütig. **3.** traurig, schmerzlich (*Pflicht etc*).

mel·low ['meləʊ] **I** *adj* □ **1.** reif, weich (*Obst*). **2.** ausgereift, lieblich (*Wein*). **3.** sanft, mild (*Licht*), zart (*Farbton*). **4.** *fig.* gereift, abgeklärt (*Person*). **5.** angeheitert, beschwipst. **II** *v/t* **6.** reifen lassen (*a. fig.*). **III** *v/i* **7.** reifen (*a. fig.*).

me·lo·di·ous [mɪˈləʊdjəs] *adj* □ melodisch, melodiös.

mel·o·dra·ma ['meləʊˌdrɑːmə] *s* Melodram(a) *n* (*a. fig.*). **mel·o·dra·mat·ic** [~drəˈmætɪk] *adj* (~*ally*) melodramatisch.

mel·o·dy ['melədɪ] *s* Melodie *f*.

melt [melt] (*a. irr*) **I** *v/i* **1.** (zer)schmelzen, sich auflösen: ~ *in the mouth* auf der Zunge zergehen; ~ *away fig.* sich auflösen (*Menge*); dahinschmelzen (*Geld*); ~ *into tears fig.* in Tränen zerfließen; ~ *butter* 1. **2.** verschmelzen (*Farben, Ränder etc*): ~ *into* übergehen in (*acc*). **II** *v/t* **3.** schmelzen, *Butter* zerlassen: ~ *down* einschmelzen. **4.** *fig. j-s Herz* erweichen.

melt·ing ['meltɪŋ] *adj* weich, angenehm (*Stimme*). ~ *fur·nace s* ☉ Schmelzofen *m*. ~ *point s phys.* Schmelzpunkt *m*. ~ *pot s* Schmelztiegel *m* (*a. fig.*).

mem·ber ['membə] *s* **1.** Mitglied *n*, Angehörige *m*, *f*: ~ *of the family* Familienmitglied; ♀ *of Parliament Br.* Unterhausabgeordnete *m*, *f*; ♀ *of Congress Am.* Mitglied des Repräsentantenhauses; ~*s only* (Zutritt) nur für Mitglieder; ~ *country* Mitgliedsland *n*. **2.** *anat.* Glied(maße *f*) *n*; (*männliches*) Glied. '**mem·ber·ship** *s* **1.** (*of*) Mitgliedschaft *f* (bei), Zugehörigkeit *f* (zu): ~ *card* Mitgliedsausweis *m*; ~ *fee* Mitgliedsbeitrag *m*. **2.** Mitgliederzahl *f*: *have* *a ~ of 200* 200 Mitglieder haben.

mem·brane ['membreɪn] *s* Membran(e) *f*.

mem·o ['meməʊ] *pl* **-os** *s* F Memo *n* (→ *memorandum* 1).

mem·oirs ['memwɑːz] *s pl* Memoiren *f*.

mem·o·ra·ble ['memərəbl] *adj* □ **1.** denkwürdig. **2.** einprägsam. **3.** unvergeßlich.

mem·o·ran·dum [ˌmemə'rændəm] *pl* **-da** [~də], **-dums** *s* **1.** (*a.* Akten)Vermerk *m*, (-)Notiz *f*; (*geschäftliche*) Kurzmitteilung. **2.** *pol.* Memorandum *n*, Denkschrift *f*.

me·mo·ri·al [mɪ'mɔːrɪəl] **I** *adj* **1.** Gedenk..., Gedächtnis...: ≈ *Day Am.* Gedenktag *m* für die Gefallenen (*30. Mai*); ~ *service* Gedenkgottesdienst *m*. **II** *s* **2.** Denk-, Ehrenmal *n*, Gedenkstätte *f* (*to* für). **3.** Gedenkfeier *f* (*to* für).

mem·o·rize ['meməraɪz] *v/t* auswendig lernen, sich *et.* einprägen.

mem·o·ry ['memərɪ] *s* **1.** Gedächtnis *n*: *from* (*od. by*) ~ aus dem Gedächtnis, auswendig; ~ *for names* Namensgedächtnis; *to the best of my* ~ soweit ich mich erinnern kann; *call to* ~ sich *et.* ins Gedächtnis zurückrufen; → *sieve* I. **2.** Andenken *n*, Erinnerung *f* (*of* an *acc*): *in* ~ *of* zum Andenken an. **3.** *mst pl* Erinnerung *f*: *childhood memories* Kindheitserinnerungen. **4.** *Computer:* Speicher *m*.

men [men] *pl von* **man**: ~*'s magazine* Herrenmagazin *n*; ~*'s room Am.* Herrentoilette *f*.

men·ace ['menəs] **I** *v/t* bedrohen. **II** *s* Drohung *f*; Bedrohung *f* (*to gen*).

mend [mend] **I** *v/t* **1.** ausbessern, reparieren, flicken, *Strümpfe etc* flicken; *fig. Freundschaft etc* kitten. **2.** (ver)bessern: ~ *one's ways* sich bessern. **II** *v/i* **3.** sich bessern (*a. Person*). **4.** *be ~ing* auf dem Weg der Besserung sein. **III** *s* **5.** Besserung *f*: *be on the* ~ → 4. **6.** ausgebesserte Stelle.

men·da·cious [men'deɪʃəs] *adj* □ lügnerisch, verlogen. **men·dac·i·ty** [~'dæsətɪ] *s* Verlogenheit *f*.

me·ni·al ['miːnjəl] *adj* □ untergeordnet, niedrig (*Arbeit*).

men·in·gi·tis [ˌmenɪn'dʒaɪtɪs] *s* ⚕ Hirnhautentzündung *f*.

men·o·pause ['menəʊpɔːz] *s physiol.*

Wechseljahre *pl*: *go through the* ~ in den Wechseljahren sein.

men·stru·ate ['menstrʊeɪt] *v/i physiol.* menstruieren. ˌ**men·stru·a·tion** *s* Menstruation *f*.

men·tal ['mentl] *adj* (□ → *mentally*) **1.** geistig, Geistes...: ~ *arithmetic* Kopfrechnen *n*; ~ *deficiency* (*od. derangement*) Geistesstörung *f*; ~ *disease* (*od. illness*) Geisteskrankheit *f*; ~ *handicap* geistige Behinderung; ~ *hospital* psychiatrische Klinik, Nervenheilanstalt *f*; *make a ~ note of s.th.* sich *et.* (vor)merken; ~ *state* Geisteszustand *m*. **2.** seelisch, psychisch: ~ *cruelty* 🏛 seelische Grausamkeit. **men·tal·i·ty** [~'tælətɪ] *s* Mentalität *f*. **men·tal·ly** ['~təlɪ] *adv* **1.** geistig, geistes...: ~ *deficient* (*od. deranged*) geistesgestört; ~ *handicapped* geistig behindert; ~ *ill* geisteskrank. **2.** im Geist, in Gedanken.

men·thol ['menθɒl] *s* 🜊 Menthol *n*.

men·tion ['menʃn] **I** *s* Erwähnung *f*: *get* (*od. be given*) *a* ~ erwähnt werden. **II** *v/t* erwähnen (*to* gegenüber); *don't* ~ *it!* bitte (sehr)!, gern geschehen!; *not to* ~ ganz abgesehen *od.* zu schweigen von; nicht zu vergessen; → *worth* I.

men·u ['menjuː] *s* Speise(n)karte *f*.

mer·can·tile ['mɜːkəntaɪl] *adj* Handels...: ~ *law* Handelsrecht *n*.

mer·ce·nar·y ['mɜːsɪnərɪ] *s* ✗ Söldner *m*.

mer·chan·dise ['mɜːtʃəndaɪz] *s* Ware(n *pl*) *f*.

mer·chant ['mɜːtʃənt] **I** *s* (Groß)Händler *m*, (Groß)Kaufmann *m*. **II** *adj* Handels...: ~ *ship*.

mer·ci·ful ['mɜːsɪfʊl] *adj* □ (*to*) barmherzig (gegen), gnädig (*dat*). **mer·ci·less** *adj* □ unbarmherzig, erbarmungslos.

mer·cu·ri·al [mɜː'kjʊərɪəl] *adj* □ **1.** Quecksilber... **2.** *fig.* quecksilb(e)rig, quicklebendig; sprunghaft.

mer·cu·ry ['mɜːkjʊrɪ] *s* **1.** ≈ *ast.*, *myth.* Merkur *m*. **2.** 🜍 Quecksilber *n*.

mer·cy ['mɜːsɪ] *s* **1.** Barmherzigkeit *f*, Erbarmen *n*, Gnade *f*: *without* ~ *od. merciless*; *be at s.o.'s* ~ j-m (auf Gedeih u. Verderb) ausgeliefert sein; *have* ~ *on* Mitleid *od.* Erbarmen haben mit. **2.** (wahres) Glück, (wahrer) Segen. ~ *kill·ing s* Sterbehilfe *f*.

mere [mɪə] *adj* bloß, nichts als: *a ~ ex-*

method

cuse nur e-e Ausrede; **~ imagination** bloße *od.* reine Einbildung. **'mere·ly** *adv* bloß, nur, lediglich.

merge [mɜːdʒ] **I** *v/i* **1.** (*in, into*) verschmelzen (mit), aufgehen (in *dat.*). **2.** zs.-laufen (*Straßen etc*). **3.** ✝ fusionieren. **II** *v/t* **4.** verschmelzen (*in, into* mit). **5.** ✝ fusionieren. **'merg·er** *s* ✝ Fusion *f*.

me·rid·i·an [məˈrɪdɪən] *s* **1.** *geogr.* Meridian *m*, Längenkreis *m*. **2.** *ast.* Kulminationspunkt *m*; *fig.* Gipfel *m*, Zenit *m*, Höhepunkt *m*.

mer·it [ˈmerɪt] **I** *s* **1.** Verdienst *n*: *a man of ~* ein verdienter *od.* verdienstvoller Mann. **2.** Wert *m*; Vorzug *m*: *work of ~* bedeutendes Werk; *of artistic ~* von künstlerischem Wert. **3.** Lohn, Strafe *etc* verdienen. **mer·i·toc·ra·cy** [~ˈtɒkrəsɪ] *s* Leistungsgesellschaft *f*.

mer·maid [ˈmɜːmeɪd] *s* Meerjungfrau *f*, Nixe *f*.

mer·ri·ment [ˈmerɪmənt] *s* **1.** Fröhlichkeit *f*, Lustigkeit *f*, Ausgelassenheit *f*. **2.** Gelächter *n*, Heiterkeit *f*.

mer·ry [ˈmerɪ] *adj* □ **1.** lustig (*a. Streich etc*), fröhlich, ausgelassen: *~ Christmas!* fröhliche *od.* frohe Weihnachten! **2.** F beschwipst, angeheitert: *get ~* sich e-n anudeln.

mesh [meʃ] **I** *s* **1.** Masche *f*. **2.** *mst pl fig.* Netz *n*, Schlingen *pl*: *~ of lies* Lügennetz, -gespinst *n*; *be caught in the ~es of the law* sich in den Schlingen des Gesetzes verfangen (haben). **II** *v/t* **3.** in e-m Netz fangen. **III** *v/i* **4.** ineinandergreifen (*Zahnräder; a. fig.*). **5.** *fig.* passen (*with* zu), zs.-passen.

mess [mes] **I** *s* **1.** Unordnung *f*, *a. fig.* Durcheinander *n*; Schmutz *m*; *fig.* Patsche *f*, Klemme *f*: *in a ~* in Unordnung; schmutzig; *be in a nice ~* ganz schön in der Klemme sein *od.* sitzen *od.* stecken; *make a ~ of* → 3. **2.** ✕ Messe *f*: *officers' ~* Offiziersmesse, -kasino *n*. **II** *v/t* **3.** *a. ~ up* in Unordnung bringen, *a. fig.* durcheinanderbringen; schmutzig machen; *fig.* verpfuschen, Pläne *etc* über den Haufen werfen. **III** *v/i* **4.** *~ about* (*od. around*) herumspielen, *b.s. a.* herumbasteln (*with* an *dat*).

mes·sage [ˈmesɪdʒ] *s* **1.** Mitteilung *f*, Nachricht *f*: *can I give him a ~?* kann ich ihm et. ausrichten?; *leave a ~* (*for*

s.o.) (j-m) e-e Nachricht hinterlassen; *can I take a ~?* kann ich et. ausrichten?; *get the ~* F kapieren. **2.** *fig.* Anliegen *n* (*e-s Künstlers etc*); Aussage *f* (*e-s Romans etc*).

mes·sen·ger [ˈmesɪndʒə] *s* **1.** Bote *m*: *by ~* durch Boten. **2.** *fig.* (Vor)Bote *m*. **~ boy** *s* Laufbursche *m*, Botenjunge *m*.

Mes·si·ah [mɪˈsaɪə] *s eccl. der* Messias.

'mess-up *s* Durcheinander *n* (*a. fig.*).

mess·y [ˈmesɪ] *adj* □ **1.** schmutzig (*a. fig.*). **2.** *fig.* verfahren.

met [met] *pret u. pp von* **meet.**

met·a·bol·ic [ˌmetəˈbɒlɪk] *adj physiol.* Stoffwechsel... **me·tab·o·lism** [meˈtæbəlɪzəm] *s* Stoffwechsel *m*.

met·al [ˈmetl] **I** *s* Metall *n*. **II** *adj* → **metallic 1. me·tal·lic** [mɪˈtælɪk] *adj* (*~ally*) **1.** metallen, Metall... **2.** metallisch (glänzend *od.* klingend). **met·al·lur·gy** [meˈtælədʒɪ] *s* Metallurgie *f*, Hüttenkunde *f*.

'met·al-ˌpro·cess·ing *adj* metallverarbeitend.

met·a·mor·pho·sis [ˌmetəˈmɔːfəsɪs] *pl* **-ses** [~siːz] *s* Metamorphose *f*, Verwandlung *f*.

met·a·phor [ˈmetəfə] *s* Metapher *f*. **met·a·phor·i·cal** [~ˈfɒrɪkl] *adj* □ metaphorisch, bildlich.

met·a·phys·i·cal [ˌmetəˈfɪzɪkl] *adj* □ **1.** *phls.* metaphysisch. **2.** übersinnlich. **met·a·phys·ics** [~siks] *s pl* (*sg konstruiert*) *phls.* Metaphysik *f*.

me·tas·ta·sis [məˈtæstəsɪs] *pl* **-ses** [~siːz] *s ✱* Metastase *f*; Metastasenbildung *f*.

me·te·or [ˈmiːtɪɔː] *s ast.* Meteor *m*. **me·te·or·ic** [ˌmiːtɪˈɒrɪk] *adj* (*~ally*) **1.** *ast.* meteorisch, Meteor... **2.** *fig.* kometenhaft (*Aufstieg etc*). **me·te·or·ite** [ˈmiːtɪəraɪt] *s ast.* Meteorit *m*.

me·te·or·o·log·i·cal [ˌmiːtɪərəˈlɒdʒɪkl] *adj* □ meteorologisch, Wetter..., Witterungs...: *~ office* Wetteramt *n*. **me·te·or·ol·o·gist** [ˌmiːtɪəˈrɒlədʒɪst] *s* Meteorologe *m*. **me·te·or·ol·o·gy** [~dʒɪ] *s* Meteorologie *f*.

me·ter¹ [ˈmiːtə] *Am.* → **metre.**

me·ter² [~] *s* ⊛ Meßgerät *n*, Zähler *m*: *~ maid bsd. Am.* F Politesse *f*; *~ reader* Gas- *od.* Stromableser *m*.

meth·od [ˈmeθəd] *s* **1.** Methode *f*, Verfahren *n*: *the ~ of doing s.th.* die Art u. Weise, et. zu tun. **2.** Methode *f*, System *n*, Planmäßigkeit *f*: **work with** ~ methodisch arbeiten. **me·thod·i·cal** [mɪ-ˈθɒdɪkl] *adj* □ methodisch, systematisch, planmäßig.

meth·yl [ˈmeθɪl] *s* ⚗ Methyl *n*: ~ **alcohol** Methylalkohol *m*.

me·tic·u·lous [mɪˈtɪkjʊləs] *adj* □ peinlich genau, akribisch.

me·tre [ˈmiːtə] *s bsd. Br.* 1. Meter *m*, *n*. 2. Versmaß *n*.

met·ric [ˈmetrɪk] I *adj* (~*ally*) metrisch: ~ **system** metrisches (Maß- u. Gewichts)System. II *s pl (sg konstruiert)* Metrik *f*, Verslehre *f*.

me·trop·o·lis [mɪˈtrɒpəlɪs] *s* Metropole *f*, Hauptstadt *f*. **me·tro·pol·i·tan** [ˌmetrəˈpɒlɪtən] I *adj* ... der Hauptstadt. II *s* Bewohner(in) der Hauptstadt.

met·tle [ˈmetl] *s* Mut *m*; Eifer *m*, Feuer *n*: **put s.o. on his** ~ j-n zur Aufbietung all s-r Kräfte zwingen. **met·tle·some** [ˈ~səm] *adj* mutig; eifrig, feurig.

mew [mjuː] *v/i* miauen.

Mex·i·can [ˈmeksɪkən] I *adj* mexikanisch. II *s* Mexikaner(in).

mez·za·nine [ˈmetsəniːn] *s* △ Zwischen-, Halbgeschoß *n*.

mi·aow [miːˈaʊ] *v/i* miauen.

mice [maɪs] *pl von* **mouse**.

mick·ey [ˈmɪkɪ] *s*: **take the** ~ **out of s.o.** *bsd. Br.* F j-n auf den Arm nehmen.

mi·cro... [ˈmaɪkrəʊ] *in Zssgn* Mikro..., (sehr) klein.

mi·crobe [ˈmaɪkrəʊb] *s biol.* Mikrobe *f*.

'mi·cro|·chip *s* ⚡ Mikrochip *m*. **'~·com·put·er** *s* Mikrocomputer *m*. **'~·fiche** [ˈ~fiːʃ] *s* Mikrofiche *m*. **'~·film** I *s* Mikrofilm *m*. II *v/t* auf Mikrofilm aufnehmen. **,~·or·gan·ism** *s biol.* Mikroorganismus *m*.

mi·cro·phone [ˈmaɪkrəfəʊn] *s* Mikrophon *f*: **at the** ~ am Mikrophon.

mi·cro·scope [ˈmaɪkrəskəʊp] I *s* Mikroskop *n*. II *v/t* mikroskopisch untersuchen. **mi·cro·scop·ic** [ˌ~ˈskɒpɪk] *adj* (~*ally*) 1. mikroskopisch. 2. mikroskopisch klein.

mi·cro·wave [ˈmaɪkrəweɪv] *s* ⚡ Mikrowelle *f*: ~ **oven** Mikrowellenherd *m*.

mid [mɪd] *adj attr. od. in Zssgn* mittler..., Mittel...: **in** ~**April** Mitte April; **be in one's** ~**forties** Mitte vierzig sein. **,~'air** *s*: **in** ~ in der Luft; ~ **collision** Zs.-stoß *m* in der Luft. **'~·day** I *s* Mit-

tag *m*. II *adj* mittägig, Mittag(s)...

mid·dle [ˈmɪdl] I *adj* 1. mittler, Mittel...: ~ **classes** *pl* Mittelstand *m*; ~ **ear** *anat.* Mittelohr *n*; ~ **finger** Mittelfinger *m*; ~ **name** zweiter Vorname; → **manage·ment** 2. II *s* 2. Mitte *f*: **in the** ~ in der Mitte; **in the** ~ **of** in der Mitte (*gen*), mitten in (*dat*); **in the** ~ **of July** Mitte Juli; **in the** ~ **of the street** mitten auf der Straße. 3. Taille *f*. 4. mittlerer Teil, Mittelstück *n*. ~ **age** *s* mittleres Alter: **be in** ~ mittleren Alters sein. **,~'aged** *adj* mittleren Alters. ♀ **Ag·es** *s pl das* Mittelalter *n*. **,~'dis·tance** *adj Sport:* Mittelstrecken... ♀ **East** *s geogr. der* Nahe Osten. **'~·man** *s (irr man) s* 1. Mittelsmann *m*. 2. ♥ Zwischenhändler *m*. **,~-of-the-'road** *adj bsd. pol.* gemäßigt. **'~·weight** *s Sport:* Mittelgewicht(ler *m*) *n*.

mid·dling [ˈmɪdlɪŋ] I *adj* von mittlerer Größe *od.* Güte, mittelmäßig (*a. contp.*): **how are you? fair to** ~ so einigermaßen, mittelprächtig. II *adv* F leidlich, einigermaßen.

,mid·field *s bsd. Fußball:* Mittelfeld *n*: **in** ~ im Mittelfeld; ~ **man** (*od.* **player**) Mittelfeldspieler *m*.

midge [mɪdʒ] *s zo.* Mücke *f*.

midg·et [ˈmɪdʒɪt] I *s* Zwerg *m*, Knirps *m*. II *adj* Zwerg..., Miniatur..., Kleinst...

mid|·land [ˈmɪdlənd] *s*: **the** ♀*s pl* Mittelengland *n*. **'~·life cri·sis** *s (irr crisis) psych.* Midlife-crisis *f*. **'~·night** I *s* Mitternacht *f*: **at** ~ um Mitternacht. II *adj* Mitternachts...: ~ **sun; burn the** ~ **oil** bis spät in die Nacht arbeiten *od.* aufbleiben. **'~·point** *s*: **be at** ~ die Hälfte hinter sich haben. **'~·sum·mer** I *s* 1. Hochsommer *m*. 2. *ast.* Sommersonnenwende *f*. II *adj* 3. hochsommerlich, Hochsommer... **'~'way** *adj a. fig.* auf halbem Weg (*between* zwischen *dat*). **'~·wife** *s (irr wife)* Hebamme *f*. **,~'win·ter** I *s* 1. Mitte *f* des Winters. 2. *ast.* Wintersonnenwende *f*.

might¹ [maɪt] *s*: **with** ~ **and main** mit aller Kraft *od.* Gewalt.

might² [~] *pret von* **may²**.

might·y [ˈmaɪtɪ] I *adj* □ mächtig, gewaltig (*beide a. fig.*). II *adv* F ungeheuer: ~ **easy** kinderleicht; ~ **fine** prima.

mi·graine [ˈmiːgreɪn] *s* ⚕ Migräne *f*.

mi·grant [ˈmaɪgrənt] → **migratory**.

mi·grate [maɪˈɡreɪt] *v/i* (ab-, aus)wandern, (*a. orn.* fort)ziehen. **mi·gra·tion** *s* **1.** Wanderung *f* (*a.* 🐾, *zo.*). **2.** Abwandern *m*, Fortziehen *n*. **mi·gra·to·ry** [ˈ‿ɡrətərɪ] *adj* Wander..., Zug...: **~ bird** Zugvogel *m*; **~ worker** Wanderarbeiter *m*.

mike [maɪk] *s* F Mikro *n* (*Mikrophon*).

mild [maɪld] *adj* □ mild (*Strafe, Wein, Wetter etc*), (*Licht etc a.*) sanft, (*Fieber, Zigarre etc a.*) leicht: **to put it ~ly** gelinde gesagt; **that's putting it ~ly** das ist gar kein Ausdruck.

mil·dew [ˈmɪldjuː] I *s* **1.** 🌾 Mehltau *m*. **2.** Schimmel *m*, Stockfleck *m*. II *v/i* **3.** schimm(e)lig *od.* mod(e)rig werden.

mile [maɪl] *s* Meile *f*: **~s apart** meilenweit auseinander; *fig.* himmelweit (voneinander) entfernt; **~s better** F wesentlich besser; **for ~s** meilenweit; **it sticks out a ~** F das sieht ja ein Blinder; **talk a ~ a minute** F wie ein Maschinengewehr *od.* Wasserfall reden.

mile·age [ˈmaɪldʒ] *s* **1.** zurückgelegte Meilenzahl *od.* Fahrtstrecke, Meilenstand *m*: **~ indicator** (*od. recorder*) *mot.* Meilenzähler *m*. **2.** *a.* **~ allowance** Meilengeld *n*.

mile·om·e·ter [maɪˈlɒmɪtə] *s mot.* Meilenzähler *m*.

'mile·stone *s* Meilenstein *m* (*a. fig.*).

mil·i·tant [ˈmɪlɪtənt] I *adj* □ **1.** kriegführend. **2.** militant. II *s* **3.** militante Person, militantes Mitglied. **mil·i·ta·rism** [ˈ‿tərɪzəm] *s* Militarismus *m*. **'mil·i·ta·rist** *s* Militarist *m*. **ˌmil·i·ta·ris·tic** *adj* (**~ally**) militaristisch. **'mil·i·tar·y** I *adj* □ militärisch, Militär...: **~ academy** Militärakademie *f*; **of ~ age** in wehrpflichtigem Alter; **~ cemetery** Soldatenfriedhof *m*; **~ dictatorship** Militärdiktatur *f*; **~ government** Militärregierung *f*; **~ police** Militärpolizei *f*; **do one's ~ service** s-n Militärdienst ableisten. II *s* (*pl konstruiert*): **the ~** das Militär.

mi·li·tia [mɪˈlɪʃə] *s* Miliz *f*, Bürgerwehr *f*. **mi·li·tia·man** [‿mən] *s* (*irr man*) Milizsoldat *m*.

milk [mɪlk] I *s* Milch *f* (*a.* 🌾, 🐾): **land of ~ and honey** *fig.* Schlaraffenland *n*; **it's no use crying over spilt ~** geschehen ist geschehen. II *v/t* melken (*a. fig.*). III *v/i*

Milch geben. **~ bar** *s* Milchbar *f*. **~ choc·o·late** *s* Vollmilchschokolade *f*. **~ float** *s* Br. Milchwagen *m*. **~ glass** *s* Milchglas *n*. **~·man** [ˈ‿mən] *s* (*irr man*) Milchmann *m*. **~ pow·der** *s* Milchpulver *n*, Trockenmilch *f*. **~ shake** *s* Milchshake *m*. **'~·sop** *s* Weichling *m*, Muttersöhnchen *n*. **~ tooth** *s* (*irr tooth*) Milchzahn *m*.

milk·y [ˈmɪlkɪ] *adj* □ **1.** milchig. **2.** mit (viel) Milch (*Kaffee etc*). ♀ **Way** *s ast.* Milchstraße *f*.

mill [mɪl] I *s* **1.** *allg.* Mühle *f*: **go through the ~** *fig.* e-e harte Schule durchmachen; **put s.o. through the ~** *fig.* j-n hart rannehmen. **2.** Fabrik *f*, Werk *n*: → **rolling mill, spinning mill.** II *v/t* **3.** Korn etc mahlen. 🛠 *allg.* verarbeiten. III *v/i* **5.** *a.* **~ about** (*od. around*) herumlaufen: **~ing crowd** wogende Menge, (Menschen)Gewühl *n*.

mil·len·ni·um [mɪˈlenɪəm] *pl* **-ums, -a** [‿ə] *s* Jahrtausend *n*.

mil·le·pede [ˈmɪlɪpiːd] *s zo.* Tausendfüßer *m*.

mill·er [ˈmɪlə] *s* Müller *m*.

mil·li·gram(me) [ˈmɪlɪɡræm] *s* Milligramm *n*.

mil·li·me·ter *Am.*, **mil·li·me·tre** *bsd. Br.* [ˈmɪlɪˌmiːtə] *s* Millimeter *m*, *n*.

mil·lion [ˈmɪljən] *s* Million *f*: **feel like a ~ dollars** F sich ganz prächtig fühlen. **mil·lion·aire** [‿ˈneə] *s* Millionär(in).

'mill·pond *s* Mühlteich *m*: **(as) smooth as a ~** spiegelglatt (*Meer etc*). **'~·stone** *s* Mühlstein *m*: **be a ~ round s.o.'s neck** *fig.* j-m ein Klotz am Bein sein.

mime [maɪm] I *s* **1.** Pantomime *f*. **2.** Pantomime *m*. II *v/t* **3.** (panto)mimisch darstellen. **4.** mimen, nachahmen. III *v/i* **5.** *TV etc* Playback singen *od.* spielen. **'mim·ic·ry** I *s* **1.** Nachahmung *f*. **2.** *zo.* Mimikry *f*.

mim·ing [ˈmaɪmɪŋ] *s* *TV etc* Playback *n*.

mim·ic [ˈmɪmɪk] I *adj* **1.** mimisch. **2.** nachgeahmt, Schein... II *s* **3.** Nachahmer *m*, Imitator *m*. III *v/t pret u. pp* **-icked** **4.** nachahmen (*a. biol.*).

mi·mo·sa [mɪˈməʊzə] *s* ♀ Mimose *f*.

min·a·ret [ˈmɪnəret] *s* △ Minarett *n*.

mince [mɪns] I *v/t* zerhacken, (zer-) schneiden: **~ meat** Fleisch durchdrehen, Hackfleisch machen; **~d meat** Hackfleisch *n*; **not to ~ matters** (*od.*

one's words) *fig.* kein Blatt vor den Mund nehmen. **II** *v/i* geziert *od.* affektiert sprechen; tänzeln, trippeln. **III** *s bsd. Br.* Hackfleisch *n.* '**~meat** *s* **1.** Hackfleisch *n:* **make ~ of** *fig.* aus j-m Hackfleisch machen; *Argument etc* (in der Luft) zerreißen. **2.** Pastetenfüllung *f.* **~ pie** *s* gefüllte Pastete.

minc·er ['mɪnsə] *s* Fleischwolf *m.* '**minc·ing** *adj* □ **1. ~ machine** Fleischwolf *m.* **2.** geziert, affektiert; tänzelnd, trippelnd.

mind [maɪnd] **I** *s* **1.** Sinn *m,* Gemüt *n,* Herz *n:* **have s.th. on one's ~** et. auf dem Herzen haben. **2.** Verstand *m,* Geist *m: before one's ~'s eye* vor s-m geistigen Auge; *be out of one's ~* nicht (recht) bei Sinnen sein; *enter s.o.'s ~* j-m in den Sinn kommen; *lose one's ~* den Verstand verlieren; *put s.th. out of one's ~* sich et. aus dem Kopf schlagen; *read s.o.'s ~* j-s Gedanken lesen; → *presence.* **3.** Kopf *m,* Geist *m* (*Person*). **4.** Ansicht *f,* Meinung *f: to my ~* m-r Ansicht nach, m-s Erachtens; *change one's ~* es sich anders überlegen, s-e Meinung ändern; *give s.o. a piece of one's ~* j-m gründlich die Meinung sagen; *speak one's ~ (to s.o.)* (j-m) s-e Meinung sagen. **5.** Neigung *f,* Lust *f,* Absicht *f: have s.th. in ~* et. im Sinn haben; *have a good (half a) ~ to do s.th.* gute (nicht übel) Lust haben, et. zu tun; *make up one's ~* sich entschließen, e-n Entschluß fassen; zu der Überzeugung kommen (*that* daß), sich klarwerden (*about* über *acc*). **6.** Erinnerung *f,* Gedächtnis *n:* **bear** (*od.* **keep**) *in* ~ (immer) denken an (*acc*), et. nicht vergessen; → *stick²* 7. **II** *v/t* **7.** achtgeben auf (*acc*): **~** *the step!* Vorsicht, Stufe!; *~ your head!* stoß dir den Kopf nicht an! **8.** sehen nach, aufpassen auf (*acc*): *~ your own business!* kümmere dich um deine eigenen Dinge! **9.** et. haben gegen: *do you ~ my smoking* (*od.* **if I smoke**)*?* haben Sie et. dagegen *od.* stört es Sie, wenn ich rauche?; *would you ~ coming?* würden Sie so freundlich sein zu kommen? **III** *v/i* **10.** aufpassen: *~* (*you*) wohlgemerkt; allerdings; *never ~!* macht nichts!, ist schon gut! **11.** et. dagegen haben: *I don't ~* meinetwegen, von mir aus

(gern). '**~·bend·ing** *adj* F (nahezu) unfaßbar *od.* unverständlich. '**~·blow·ing,** '**~·bog·gling** *adj* F irr.el.

mind·ed ['maɪndɪd] *adj* in *Zssgn* ...gesinnt; *religiös, technisch etc* veranlagt; ...begeistert. '**mind·er** *s* Aufseher *m;* Aufpasser *m.*

'**mind·ex·pand·ing** *adj* bewußtseinserweiternd.

mind·ful ['maɪndfʊl] *adj* □ **1.** aufmerksam, achtsam: *be ~ of* achten auf (*acc*). **2.** eingedenk (*of gen*): *be ~ of* denken an (*acc*), bedenken. '**mind·less** *adj* □ **1.** (*of*) unbekümmert (um), ohne Rücksicht (auf *acc*). **2.** gedankenlos, blind.

mind read·er *s* Gedankenleser(in).

mine¹ [maɪn] *possessive pron: it is ~* es gehört mir; *a friend of ~* ein Freund von mir; *his mother and ~* s-e u. m-e Mutter.

mine² [~] **I** *v/i* **1.** schürfen, graben (*for* nach). **II** *v/t* **2.** *Erz, Kohle* abbauen, gewinnen. **3.** ♺, ✗ verminen. **4.** *fig.* untergraben, -minieren. **III** *s* **5.** Bergwerk *n,* Zeche *f,* Grube *f.* **6.** ♺, ✗ Mine *f.* **7.** *fig.* Fundgrube *f* (*of an dat*): *he is a ~ of information* er ist e-e Quelle *od.* reiche Informationsquelle. **~ de·tec·tor** *s* ✗ Minensuchgerät *n.*

min·er ['maɪnə] *s* Bergmann *m,* Kumpel *m.*

min·er·al ['mɪnərəl] **I** *s* **1.** Mineral *n.* **2.** *mst pl Br.* Mineralwasser *n.* **II** *adj* **3.** Mineral...: *~ oil; ~ water; ~ coal* Steinkohle *f; ~ resources pl* Bodenschätze *pl.*

min·er·al·og·i·cal [,mɪnərə'lɒdʒɪkl] *adj* □ mineralogisch. **min·er·al·o·gist** [,~ 'rælədʒɪst] *s* Mineraloge *m.* ,**min·er·al·o·gy** [,~dʒɪ] *s* Mineralogie *f.*

min·gle ['mɪŋgl] **I** *v/i* **1.** sich (ver)mischen (*with* mit). **2.** sich (ein)mischen (*in* in *acc*); sich mischen (*among, with* unter *acc*). **II** *v/t* **3.** (ver)mischen (*with* mit).

min·i... ['mɪnɪ] *in Zssgn* Mini...

min·i·a·ture ['mɪnətʃə] **I** *s* **1.** Miniatur(gemälde *n*) *f.* **2.** *fig.* Miniaturausgabe *f: in ~* en miniature, im kleinen. **II** *adj* **3.** Miniatur...

'**min·i·bus** *s* Kleinbus *m.* '**~dress** *s* Minikleid *n.*

min·im ['mɪnɪm] *s* ♩ halbe Note.

min·i·ma ['mɪnɪmə] *pl von* **minimum.**

min·i·mal ['~ml] *adj* □ **1.** minimal. **2.** → *minimum* II. **'min·i·mize** *v/t* **1.** auf ein Minimum herabsetzen, möglichst gering halten. **2.** bagatellisieren, herunterspielen. **min·i·mum** ['~məm] **I** *pl* **-ma** ['~mə] *s* Minimum *n*: **with a ~ of** mit e-m Minimum an (*dat*); → *keep to* 3. **II** *adj* Minimal..., Mindest...

min·ing ['mainiŋ] **I** *s* Bergbau *m*. **II** *adj* Bergwerks..., Berg(bau)...: **~ disaster** Grubenunglück *n*.

'min·i·skirt *s* Minirock *m*.

min·is·ter ['ministə] **I** *s* **1.** *eccl.* Geistliche *m*, Pfarrer *m*. **2.** *pol. bsd. Br.* Minister *m*: **♀ of Defence** Verteidigungsminister. **II** *v/i* **3. ~ to** s.o. sich um j-n kümmern, für j-n sorgen. **min·is·te·ri·al** [,~'stiəriəl] *adj* □ **1.** *eccl.* geistlich. **2.** *pol. bsd. Br.* ministeriell, Minister... **min·is·tra·tion** [,mini'streiʃn] *s mst pl* Dienst *m* (*to* an *dat*). **min·is·try** ['ministri] *s* **1.** *eccl.* geistliches Amt. **2.** *pol. bsd. Br.* Ministerium *n*: **♀ of Defence** Verteidigungsministerium.

mink [miŋk] *s zo.* Nerz *m*.

mi·nor ['mainə] **I** *s* **1.** *univ. Am.* Nebenfach *n*. **2.** ♫ Minderjährige *m*, *f*. **3.** ♪ Moll *n*. **II** *adj* **4.** kleiner, *fig.* a. unbedeutend, unwichtig. **5.** ♫ minderjährig. **III** *v/i* **6. ~ in** *univ. Am.* als od. im Nebenfach studieren. **mi·nor·i·ty** [mai-'nɒrəti] *s* **1.** Minderheit *f*: **be in the** (*od.* **a**) **~** in der Minderheit sein; **~ government** *pol.* Minderheitsregierung *f*. **2.** ♫ Minderjährigkeit *f*.

mint¹ [mint] *s* **1.** ♀ Minze *f*: **~ sauce** Minzsoße *f*. **2.** Pfefferminz *n* (*Bonbon*).

mint² [~] **I** *s* **1.** Münze *f*, Münzanstalt *f*. **2.** **a ~** (*of money*) F ein Heidengeld. **II** *adj* **3.** ungebraucht (*Münze*), postfrisch (*Briefmarke*): **in ~ condition** in einwandfreiem od. tadellosem Zustand. **III** *v/t* **4.** Geld, a. *fig.* Wort *etc* prägen.

min·u·et [,minju'et] *s* ♪ Menuett *n*.

mi·nus ['mainəs] **I** *prp* **1.** ♫ minus, weniger. **2.** F ohne. **II** *adj* **3.** Minus...: **~ amount** → 5a; **~ sign** → 4. **III** *s* **4.** Minus(zeichen) *n*. **5.** Minus *n*: a) Fehlbetrag *m*, b) Nachteil *m*, c) Mangel *m* (*of* an *dat*).

min·ute¹ ['minit] **I** *s* **1.** Minute *f*: **to the ~** auf die Minute (genau); **I won't be a ~** ich bin gleich wieder da; ich bin gleich fertig; **ten~** zehnminütig; → *silence* I.

2. Augenblick *m*: **at the last ~** in letzter Minute; **in a ~** sofort; **just a ~!** Moment mal! **3.** *pl* (Sitzungs)Protokoll *n*: **keep the ~s** das Protokoll führen. **II** *v/t* **4.** protokollieren.

mi·nute² [mai'nju:t] *adj* □ **1.** winzig. **2.** peinlich genau, minuziös.

min·ute| **hand** *s* Minutenzeiger *m* (*e-r Uhr*). **~ steak** *s gastr.* Minutensteak *n*.

minx [miŋks] *s* (kleines) Biest.

mir·a·cle ['mirəkl] *s* Wunder *n* (*a. fig.* of an *dat*): **as if by** (**a**) **~** wie durch ein Wunder; **work** (**perform**) **~s** Wunder tun (vollbringen). **mi·rac·u·lous** [mi'rækjuləs] *adj* wunderbar (*a. fig.*), Wunder... **mi'rac·u·lous·ly** *adv* wie durch ein Wunder.

mi·rage ['mira:ʒ] *s* **1.** *phys.* Luftspieg(e)lung *f*, Fata Morgana *f* (*a. fig.*). **2.** *fig.* Illusion *f*.

mire ['maiə] *s* Schlamm *m*: **drag through the ~** *fig.* in den Schmutz ziehen.

mir·ror ['mirə] **I** *s* **1.** Spiegel *m*: **hold up the ~ to** s.o. j-m den Spiegel vorhalten. **2.** *fig.* Spiegel(bild *n*) *m*. **II** *v/t* **3.** (wider)spiegeln (*a. fig.*): **be ~ed** sich spiegeln (*in* in *dat*). **~ im·age** *s* Spiegelbild *n*. **'~·in,vert·ed** *adj* seitenverkehrt. **~ writ·ing** *s* Spiegelschrift *f*.

mirth [mɜ:θ] *s* Fröhlichkeit *f*, Heiterkeit *f*, Freude *f*. **mirth·ful** ['~ful] *adj* □ fröhlich, heiter, lustig. **'mirth·less** *adj* □ freudlos.

mis... [mis] *in Zssgn* miß..., falsch.

mis·ad'ven·ture *s* **1.** Unfall *m*, Unglück(sfall *m*) *n*. **2.** Mißgeschick *n*: **he's had a ~** ihm ist ein Mißgeschick passiert.

mis·an·thrope ['misənθrəʊp] *s* Menschenfeind(in), -hasser(in). **mis·an·throp·ic** [,~'θrɒpik] *adj* (**~ally**) menschenfeindlich. **mis·an·thro·py** [mi-'sænθrəpi] *s* Menschenfeindlichkeit *f*, -haß *m*.

mis·ap'ply *v/t* **1.** falsch verwenden. **2.** → *misappropriate* 1.

'mis,ap·pre'hend *v/t* mißverstehen. **'mis,ap·pre'hen·sion** *s* Mißverständnis *n*: **be** (*od.* **labo[u]r**) **under a ~** sich in e-m Irrtum befinden.

mis·ap'pro·pri·ate *v/t* **1.** unterschlagen, veruntreuen. **2.** zweckentfremden. **'mis·ap,pro·pri'a·tion** *s* **1.** Unterschlagung f, Veruntreuung f. **2.** Zweckentfremdung f.

mis·be'have v/i sich schlecht benehmen, sich danebenbenehmen, (Kind) ungezogen sein. **mis·be'hav·io(u)r** s schlechtes Benehmen, Ungezogenheit f.

mis·cal·cu·late I v/t falsch berechnen, sich verrechnen in (dat). **II** v/i sich verrechnen od. verkalkulieren. **'mis·cal·cu'la·tion** s Rechenfehler m, Fehlkalkulation f.

mis·car·riage s **1.** Fehlschlag(en n) m, Mißlingen n: ~ of justice ⚖ Fehlurteil n, Justizirrtum m. **2.** ✱ Fehlgeburt f. **mis·car·ry** v/i **1.** fehlschlagen, mißlingen. **2.** ✱ e-e Fehlgeburt haben.

mis·cel·la·ne·ous [ˌmɪsə'leɪnjəs] adj □ ge-, vermischt; verschiedenartig. **mis·cel·la·ny** [mɪ'selənɪ] s **1.** Gemisch n. **2.** Sammlung f, Sammelband m.

mis'chance s: **by ~** durch e-n unglücklichen Zufall.

mis·chief ['mɪstʃɪf] s **1.** Unheil n, Schaden m: **do ~** Unheil od. Schaden anrichten; **make ~** Unfrieden stiften (**between** zwischen dat); **mean ~** Böses im Schilde führen. **2.** Unfug m, Dummheiten pl: **be up to ~** et. aushecken. **3.** Übermut m, Ausgelassenheit f: **be full of ~** immer zu Dummheiten aufgelegt sein. **'~·mak·er** s Unruhestifter(in).

mis·chie·vous ['mɪstʃɪvəs] adj □ **1.** boshaft, mutwillig. **2.** schelmisch.

mis·con'ceive v/t falsch auffassen, mißverstehen. **mis·con'cep·tion** s Mißverständnis n.

mis·con·duct I v/t [ˌmɪskən'dʌkt] **1.** schlecht führen. **2. ~ o.s.** sich schlecht benehmen. **II** s [ˌmɪs'kɒndʌkt] **3.** schlechte Führung. **4.** schlechtes Benehmen. **5.** Verfehlung f.

mis·con'struc·tion s Mißdeutung f, falsche Auslegung. **mis·con'strue** v/t mißdeuten, falsch auslegen.

mis'count I v/t falsch (aus)zählen. **II** v/i sich verzählen.

mis'deal v/t u. v/i (irr deal): ~ **(the cards)** (Kartenspiel) sich vergeben.

mis'deed s Missetat f.

mis·de·mean·o(u)r [ˌmɪsdɪ'miːnə] s ⚖ Vergehen n.

mis·di'rect v/t **1.** j-n, et. fehl-, irreleiten (a. fig.), j-m den falschen Weg zeigen. **2.** Brief etc falsch adressieren.

mi·ser ['maɪzə] s Geizhals m.

mis·er·a·ble ['mɪzərəbl] adj □ **1.** jämmerlich, erbärmlich, kläglich, contp. a. miserabel. **2.** traurig, unglücklich.

mi·ser·ly ['maɪzəlɪ] adj geizig.

mis·er·y ['mɪzərɪ] s **1.** Elend n, Not f. **2.** Trübsal f, Jammer m.

mis'fire I v/i **1.** versagen (Schußwaffe). **2.** mot. fehlzünden, aussetzen. **3.** fig. danebengehen (Witz etc), fehlschlagen (Plan etc). **II** s **4.** mot. Fehlzündung f.

mis'fit s **1.** schlechtsitzendes Kleidungsstück. **2.** Außenseiter(in).

mis'for·tune s **1.** schweres Schicksal, Unglück n. **2.** Unglücksfall m; Mißgeschick n.

mis'giv·ing s Befürchtung f, Zweifel m.

mis'gov·ern v/t schlecht regieren od. verwalten.

mis'guid·ed adj irrig (Entscheidung etc), unangebracht (Optimismus etc).

mis'han·dle v/t **1.** et. falsch behandeln od. handhaben. **2.** fig. falsch anpacken.

mis·hap ['mɪshæp] s Unglück(sfall m) n; Mißgeschick n: **he's had a ~** ihm ist ein Mißgeschick passiert; **without ~** ohne Zwischenfälle.

mis'hear (irr hear) I v/t falsch hören. **II** v/i sich verhören.

mish·mash ['mɪʃmæʃ] s Mischmasch m.

mis·in'form v/t j-n falsch informieren (**about** über acc). **mis·in·for'ma·tion** s Fehlinformation f.

mis·in'ter·pret v/t mißdeuten, falsch auffassen od. auslegen. **'mis·in·ter·pre'ta·tion** s Mißdeutung f, falsche Auslegung.

mis'judge v/t **1.** falsch beurteilen, verkennen. **2.** falsch einschätzen.

mis'lay v/t (irr lay) et. verlegen.

mis'lead v/t (irr lead) **1.** irreführen, täuschen: **be misled** sich täuschen lassen. **2.** verführen, -leiten (**into doing** zu tun).

mis'man·age v/t schlecht verwalten od. führen. **mis'man·age·ment** s Mißwirtschaft f.

mis·no·mer [ˌmɪs'nəʊmə] s falsche Benennung od. Bezeichnung.

mi·sog·a·mist [mɪ'sɒɡəmɪst] s Ehefeind m.

mi·sog·y·nist [mɪ'sɒdʒɪnɪst] s Frauenfeind m.

ˌmisˈplace v/t **1.** et. verlegen. **2.** et. an e-e falsche Stelle legen od. setzen: **~d** fig. unangebracht, deplaziert.

misˈprint I v/t [ˌmisˈprint] verdrucken. II s [ˈmisprint] Druckfehler m.

ˌmisproˈnounce v/t falsch aussprechen. 'misproˌnunciˈaˈtion s falsche Aussprache.

ˌmisquoˈtation s falsches Zitat. ˌmisˈquote v/t falsch zitieren.

ˌmisˈread v/t (irr read) **1.** falsch lesen. **2.** mißdeuten.

'misˌrepˈreˈsent v/t **1.** falsch darstellen. **2.** entstellen, verdrehen. 'misˌrepˈreˈsenˈtaˈtion s **1.** falsche Darstellung. **2.** Entstellung f, Verdrehung f.

miss¹ [mis] s **1.** ♀ (mit folgendem Namen) Fräulein n: ♀ America Miß f Amerika. **2.** (ohne folgenden Namen) Fräulein n (Anrede für Lehrerinnen, Kellnerinnen etc).

miss² [~] ~ I v/t **1.** Chance, Zug etc verpassen, Beruf, Ziel etc verfehlen, sich et. entgehen lassen: **~ the boat** (od. bus) F den Anschluß od. s-e Chance verpassen; **~ doing s.th.** versäumen, et. zu tun. **2.** a. **~ out** auslassen, übergehen, -springen. **3.** überhören; übersehen, nicht bemerken; nicht verstehen od. begreifen. **4.** vermissen: **we ~ her very much** sie fehlt uns sehr. II v/i **5.** nicht treffen: a) danebenschlagen etc, b) danebengehen (Schuß etc). **6.** mißglücken, -lingen. **7.** **~ out on** et. verpassen; et. weglassen od. nicht berücksichtigen. III s **8.** Fehlschuß m, -wurf m etc. **9.** Verpassen n, Verfehlen n: → **near** 9.

ˌmisˈshapˈen adj mißgebildet, ungestalt.

misˈsile [ˈmisail] v s **1.** (Wurf)Geschoß n. **2.** ✕ Rakete f: **~ base** (od. site) Raketen(abschuß)basis f.

missˈing [ˈmisiŋ] adj **1.** fehlend: **be ~** fehlen; verschwunden od. weg sein. **2.** (✕ a. **~ in action**) vermißt: **be ~** vermißt sein od. werden.

misˈsion [ˈmiʃn] s **1.** (Militär- etc)Mission f. **2.** bsd. pol. Auftrag m, Mission f. **3.** eccl. Mission f. **4.** (innere) Berufung: **~ in life** Lebensaufgabe f. **5.** ✈, ✕ Einsatz m.

ˌmisˈspell v/t (a. irr spell) falsch schrei-

ben. ˌmisˈspellˈing s Rechtschreibfehler m.

ˌmisˈstate v/t falsch angeben. ˌmisˈstateˈment s falsche Angabe.

mist [mist] I s **1.** (feiner) Nebel. **2.** fig. Nebel m, Schleier m: **see things through a ~** alles wie durch e-n Schleier sehen; **through a ~ of tears** durch e-n Tränenschleier. **3.** Beschlag m (auf Glas). II v/i **4.** a. **~ up** (od. over) (sich) beschlagen (Glas).

misˈtakˈaˈble [miˈsteikəbl] adj **1.** leicht zu verwechseln(d). **2.** mißverständlich.

misˈtake I v/t (irr take) **1.** verwechseln (for mit); verkennen, sich irren in (dat). **2.** falsch verstehen, mißverstehen. II s **3.** Irrtum m, Versehen n, Fehler m: **by ~** irrtümlich, aus Versehen; **make a ~** einen Fehler machen; sich irren. **4.** (Rechen- etc)Fehler m. misˈtakˈen I pp von **mistake.** II adj **1.** be **~** sich irren: **be ~ in s.o.** sich in j-m täuschen; **unless I am very much ~** wenn mich nicht alles täuscht. **2.** irrig, falsch (Meinung etc), unangebracht (Freundlichkeit etc): **a case of ~ identity** e-e (Personen)Verwechslung.

ˌmisˈtime v/t e-n schlechten Zeitpunkt wählen für.

misˈtleˈtoe [ˈmisltəu] s ♀ **1.** Mistel f. **2.** Mistelzweig m.

ˌmisˈtransˈlate v/t falsch übersetzen. ˌmisˈtransˈlaˈtion s Übersetzungsfehler m.

misˈtress [ˈmistris] s **1.** Herrin f (a. fig.). **2.** bsd. Br. Lehrerin f. **3.** Mätresse f, Geliebte f.

ˌmisˈtrust I s Mißtrauen n (of gegen). II v/t mißtrauen (dat). misˈtrustˈful [~fʊl] adj □ mißtrauisch (of gegen).

mistˈy [ˈmisti] adj □ **1.** (leicht) neb(e)lig. **2.** fig. unklar, verschwommen (Vorstellung etc): **have only ~ memories of s.th.** sich nur schwach od. undeutlich an et. erinnern können. **3.** beschlagen (Glas).

ˌmisˈunˈderˈstand v/t (irr stand) **1.** mißverstehen: **don't ~ me** versteh mich nicht falsch. **2.** j-n nicht verstehen: **his wife ~s him.** ˌmisˈunˈderˈstandˈing s Mißverständnis n, weitS. a. Meinungsverschiedenheit f, Differenz f.

misˈuse I s [ˌmisˈjuːs] **1.** Mißbrauch m: **~ of power** Machtmißbrauch m. **2.** falscher

Gebrauch. **II** v/t [␣'ju:z] **3.** mißbrauchen. **4.** falsch od. zu unrechten Zwecken gebrauchen.

mite¹ [maɪt] s zo. Milbe f.

mite² [␣] s **1** kleines Ding, Würmchen n. **2.** a ␣ F ein bißchen.

mit·i·gate ['mɪtɪgeɪt] v/t Schmerzen etc lindern, Strafe etc mildern, Zorn etc besänftigen: **mitigating circumstances** pl ⚖ mildernde Umstände pl. **ˌmit·i·ˈga·tion** s Linderung f, Milderung f, Besänftigung f.

mitt [mɪt] s **1.** Halbhandschuh m. **2.** Baseball: Fanghandschuh m. **3.** → **mitten** 1. **4.** sl. Flosse f, Pfote f (Hand). **5.** sl. Boxhandschuh m.

mit·ten ['mɪtn] s **1.** Fausthandschuh m, Fäustling m. **2.** → **mitt** 5.

mix [mɪks] **I** v/t **1.** (ver)mischen, vermengen (**with** mit), Cocktail etc mixen, Teig anrühren: ␣ **into** mischen in (acc), beimischen (dat): ␣ **up** zs.-, durcheinandermischen; gründlich mischen; (völlig) durcheinanderbringen; verwechseln (**with** mit); **be ␣ed up** verwickelt sein od. werden (**in** in acc); (geistig) ganz durcheinander sein. **2.** fig. verbinden: ␣ **business with pleasure** das Angenehme mit dem Nützlichen verbinden. **II** v/i **3.** sich (ver)mischen. **4.** sich mischen lassen. **5.** ␣ **well** kontaktfreudig sein: ␣ **well with s.o.** gut mit j-m auskommen. **6.** verkehren (**with** mit; **in** in dat). **III** s **7.** (a. Back- etc)Mischung f. **8.** F Durcheinander n. **mixed** [mɪkst] adj gemischt (a. fig. Gefühle etc); vermischt, Misch...: ␣ **blessing** zweifelhaftes Vergnügen; ␣ **double(s** pl) (Tennis etc) gemischtes Doppel, Mixed n; **a ␣ doubles match** ein gemischtes Doppel; ␣ **grill** Mixed grill m; ␣ **pickles** pl Mixed Pickles pl, Mixpickles pl. **ˈmix·er** s **1.** Mixer m (a. Küchengerät). **2.** ⚙ Mischmaschine f. **3.** TV etc Mischpult n. **4. be a good (bad)** ␣ F kontaktfreudig (kontaktarm) sein. **mix·ture** ['␣tʃə] s Mischung f, a. ⚗ Gemisch n (**of ... and** aus ... u.): ␣ **of teas** Teemischung.

ˈmix-up s F **1.** Durcheinander n. **2.** Verwechslung f. **3.** Handgemenge n.

mne·mon·ic [niː'mɒnɪk] s Gedächtnishilfe f, -stütze f.

mo [məʊ] pl **mos** s F Moment m, Augenblick m.

moan [məʊn] **I** v/i stöhnen, ächzen. **II** s Stöhnen n, Ächzen n.

moat [məʊt] s (Burg-, Stadt)Graben m.

mob [mɒb] **I** s **1.** Mob m. **2.** Pöbel m, Gesindel n. **3.** sl. (Verbrecher)Bande f. **II** v/t **4.** herfallen über (acc); Filmstar etc bedrängen, belagern.

mo·bile ['məʊbaɪl] adj allg. beweglich, ⚙ a. fahrbar, ✗ a. motorisiert: ␣ **home** Wohnwagen m; ␣ **library** Wanderbücherei, Autobücherei f. **mo·bil·i·ty** [␣'bɪlətɪ] s Beweglichkeit f. **mo·bi·li·za·tion** [ˌ␣balaɪ'zeɪʃn] s Mobilisierung f, ✗ a. Mobilmachung f. **'mo·bi·lize** [␣] v/t mobilisieren, ✗ a. mobil machen. **II** v/i ✗ mobil machen.

moc·ca·sin ['mɒkəsɪn] s Mokassin m.

mo·cha ['mɒkə] s Mokka m.

mock [mɒk] **I** v/t **1.** verspotten, lächerlich machen. **2.** nachäffen. **II** v/i **3.** sich lustig machen, spotten (**at** über acc). **III** adj **4.** nachgemacht, Schein... **'mock·er** s **1.** Spötter(in). **2.** Nachäffer(in). **'mock·er·y** s **1.** Spott m, Hohn m: **hold up to** ␣ j-n lächerlich machen; et. ins Lächerliche ziehen. **2.** fig. Hohn m (**of** auf acc). **3.** Gespött n: **make a ␣ of** zum Gespött (der Leute) machen; ad absurdum führen. **'mock·ing** adj □ spöttisch.

'mock-up s Modell n (in natürlicher Größe), Attrappe f.

mod·al ['məʊdl] **I** adj □ ling. etc modal: ␣ **auxiliary** modales Hilfsverb. **II** s ling. F modales Hilfsverb. **mo·dal·i·ty** [␣'dælətɪ] s Modalität f.

mode [məʊd] s **1.** (Art f u.) Weise f: ␣ **of address** Anrede f; ␣ **of life** Lebensweise. **2.** ling. Modus m, Aussageweise f.

mod·el ['mɒdl] **I** s **1.** Muster n, Vorbild n (**for** für): **after** (od. **on**) **the** ␣ **of** nach dem Muster von (od. gen); **he is a** ␣ **of self-control** er ist ein Muster an Selbstbeherrschung. **2.** (fig. Denk)Modell n. **3.** Muster n, Vorlage f. **4.** paint. etc Modell n. **5.** Mode: Mannequin n. **6.** ⚙ Modell n, Typ(e f) m. **II** adj **7.** vorbildlich, musterhaft: ␣ **husband** Mustergatte m. **8.** Modell...: ␣ **builder** Modellbauer m. **III** v/t pret u. pp **-eled**, bsd. Br. **-elled 9.** modellieren. **10.** fig. formen (**after, on** nach [dem Vorbild *gen*)): ~ **o.s. on** sich *j-n* zum Vorbild nehmen. **11.** *Kleider etc* vorführen. **IV** *v/i* **12.** Modell stehen *od.* sitzen (*for dat*). **13.** als Mannequin *od.* Dressman arbeiten.

mod·er·ate ['mɒdərət] **I** *adj* □ **1.** mäßig: a) gemäßigt (*a. pol.*), maßvoll, b) mittelmäßig, c) gering: **~ly successful** mäßig erfolgreich, d) vernünftig, angemessen: **~ demands** *pl* maßvolle Forderungen *pl.* **2.** mild (*Strafe, Winter etc*). **II** *s* **3.** *bsd. pol.* Gemäßigte *m, f.* **III** *v/t* ['~reɪt] **4.** mäßigen: **~ one's language** sich mäßigen. **mod·er·a·tion** [‚~'reɪʃn] *s* Mäßigung *f*: **in ~** in *od.* mit Maßen, maßvoll.

mod·ern ['mɒdən] *adj* □ modern. **'mod·ern·ize** *v/t* modernisieren.

mod·est ['mɒdɪst] *adj* □ bescheiden: a) zurückhaltend, b) anspruchslos, c) maßvoll, vernünftig. **'mod·es·ty** *s* Bescheidenheit *f*: a) Zurückhaltung *f*: **in all ~** bei aller Bescheidenheit, b) Anspruchslosigkeit *f*.

mod·i·cum ['mɒdɪkəm] *s* kleine Menge: **a ~ of sense** ein Funke Verstand.

mod·i·fi·a·ble ['mɒdɪfaɪəbl] *adj* modifizierbar. **mod·i·fi·ca·tion** [‚~fɪ'keɪʃn] *s* Modifikation *f*, (Ab-, Ver)Änderung *f.* **mod·i·fy** ['~faɪ] *v/t* **1.** (ab-, ver)ändern, modifizieren. **2.** *ling.* näher bestimmen.

mod·u·lar ['mɒdjʊlə] *adj* ❂ Modul...
mod·u·late ['mɒdjʊleɪt] *v/t u. v/i* ♪ *etc* modulieren. **‚mod·u'la·tion** *s* Modulation *f.*

mod·ule ['mɒdjuːl] *s* **1.** ❂ Modul *n, ⚡ etc* Baustein *m.* **2.** *Raumfahrt:* (*Kommando- etc*)Kapsel *f.*

mo·hair ['məʊheə] *s* Mohair *m.*

Mo·ham·med·an [məʊ'hæmɪdən] **I** *adj* mohammedanisch. **II** *s* Mohammedaner(in).

moist [mɔɪst] *adj* □ feucht (**with** von): **~ with tears** tränenfeucht. **mois·ten** ['mɔɪsn] **I** *v/t* an-, befeuchten. **II** *v/i* feucht werden. **mois·ture** ['~tʃə] *s* Feuchtigkeit *f.* **mois·tur·iz·er** ['~tʃəraɪzə] *s* ❂ Luftbefeuchter *m.*

mo·lar ['məʊlə] **I** *adj*: **~ tooth** → II. **II** *s* Backenzahn *m.*

mo·las·ses [məʊ'læsɪz] *s pl Am.* Sirup *m.*

mold, *etc Am.* → **mould**, *etc.*

mole¹ [məʊl] *s zo.* Maulwurf *m* (F *a.* Spionage).

mole² [~] *s* Muttermal *n*, Leberfleck *m.*

mole³ [~] *s* Mole *f*, Hafendamm *m.*

mo·lec·ular [məʊ'lekjʊlə] *adj* 🔬, *phys.* Molekular... **mol·e·cule** ['mɒlɪkjuːl] *s* Molekül *n.*

'mole·hill *s* Maulwurfshügel *m*: → **mountain** I.

mo·lest [məʊ'lest] *v/t* (*a. unsittlich*) belästigen. **mo·les·ta·tion** [‚~le'steɪʃn] *s* Belästigung *f.*

moll [mɒl] *s sl.* **1.** Gangsterbraut *f.* **2.** Nutte *f.*

mol·li·fy ['mɒlɪfaɪ] *v/t* besänftigen, beschwichtigen.

mol·lusc, mol·lusk ['mɒləsk] *s zo.* Molluske *f*, Weichtier *n.*

mol·ly·cod·dle ['mɒlɪˌkɒdl] **I** *s* Weichling *m.* **II** *v/t* verhätscheln.

Mol·o·tov cock·tail ['mɒlətɒf] *s* Molotowcocktail *m.*

mol·ten ['məʊltən] *pp von* **melt.**

mom [mɒm] *s bsd. Am.* F Mami *f*, Mutti *f.* **~-and-'pop store** *s Am.* F Tante-Emma-Laden *m.*

mo·ment ['məʊmənt] *s* **1.** Moment *m*, Augenblick *m*: **at the ~** im Augenblick; **at the last ~** im letzten Augenblick; (**not**) **for a ~** (k)einen Augenblick (lang); **just a ~!** a) *a.* **wait a ~!** Moment mal!, b) Augenblick! **the ~ of truth** die Stunde der Wahrheit. **2.** Bedeutung *f*, Belang *m* (**to** für): **of great** (**little**) **~** von großer (geringer) Bedeutung; **of no ~** bedeutungs-, belanglos. **3.** *phys.* Moment *n*: **~ of inertia** Trägheitsmoment.

mo·men·tar·i·ly ['~tərəlɪ] *adv* **1.** momentan, e-n Augenblick (lang). **2.** jeden Augenblick. **'mo·men·tar·y** *adj* momentan. **mo·men·tous** [~'mentəs] *adj* □ bedeutsam, folgenschwer. **mo'men·tum** [~təm] *s* **1.** *phys.* Moment *n*, Impuls *m.* **2.** Wucht *f*, Schwung *m*: **gather** (*od.* **gain**) **~** in Fahrt kommen; *fig. a.* an Boden gewinnen (*Bewegung etc*); **lose ~** an Schwung verlieren (*a. fig.*).

mon·arch ['mɒnək] *s* Monarch(in), Herrscher(in). **mo·nar·chic** [mɒ'nɑːkɪk] *adj* (**~ally**) **1.** monarchisch. **2.** monarchistisch. **mon·arch·ism** ['mɒnəkɪzəm] *s* Monarchismus *m.* **'mon·arch·ist I** *s* Monarchist(in). **II** *adj* monarchistisch. **'mon·arch·y** *s* Monar-

chie f: *constitutional* ~ konstitutionelle
Monarchie.

mon·as·ter·y ['mɒnəstəri] s (Mönchs-)
Kloster n. **mo·nas·tic** [mə'næstɪk] adj
(*~ally*) **1.** klösterlich, Kloster... **2.** mön-
chisch, Mönchs...

Mon·day ['mʌndɪ] s Montag m: *on* ~
(am) Montag; *on* ~*s* montags.

mon·e·tar·y ['mʌnɪtəri] adj □ **1.** Wäh-
rungs...: ~ *reform*. **2.** Geld..., finanziell.

mon·ey ['mʌnɪ] s Geld n: *be out of* ~ kein
Geld (mehr) haben; *be in the* ~ F reich
od. vermögend sein; *be short of* ~
knapp bei Kasse sein; *I'll bet you any* ~
that F ich wette mit dir um jeden Betrag, daß; *get one's money's worth* et.
für sein Geld bekommen; *have* ~ *to*
burn F Geld wie Heu haben; *for* ~ *rea-*
sons aus finanziellen Gründen; → *roll*
7. '~·bags s pl (sg konstruiert) F Geld-
sack m (reiche Person). ~ *box* s Spar-
büchse f. '~·chang·er s **1.** (Geld-)
Wechsler m. **2.** bsd. Am. Wechselauto-
mat m.

mon·eyed ['mʌnɪd] adj wohlhabend,
vermögend.

'**mon·ey**|**·lend·er** s Geldverleiher m.
'~·**mak·er** s **1.** guter Geschäftsmann. **2.**
gutes Geschäft, einträgliche Sache. ~
or·der s Post- od. Zahlungsanweisung
f. ~ **spin·ner** F bsd. Br. → *money-*
maker 2.

mon·ger ['mʌŋgə] s in Zssgn **1.** ...händ-
ler m. **2.** fig. contp. → *scandalmonger*,
scaremonger, etc.

mon·go·li·an [mɒŋ'gəʊljən] adj ✿ mongoloid.

mon·gol·ism ['mɒŋgəlɪzəm] s ✿ Mongolismus m. '**mon·gol·oid** adj ✿ mongoloid.

mon·grel ['mʌŋgrəl] s biol. Bastard m,
bsd. Promenadenmischung f.

mon·i·tor ['mɒnɪtə] I s **1.** Monitor m: a)
Abhörgerät n, b) Kontrollgerät n,
-schirm m. II v/t **2.** abhören. **3.** überwachen.

monk [mʌŋk] s Mönch m.

mon·key ['mʌŋkɪ] I s **1.** zo. Affe m: *make*
a ~ (*out*) *of s.o.* F j-n zum Deppen
machen. **2.** (kleiner) Schlingel. II v/i **3.**
~ *about* (od. *around*) herumalbern. **4.**
a. ~ *about* (od. *around*) (*with*) F herumspielen (mit), herumpfuschen an (dat).
~ *busi·ness* s F **1.** krumme Tour. **2.**

Blödsinn m, Unfug m. ~ *wrench* s ⊕
Engländer m: *throw a* ~ *into s.th.* Am. f
et. behindern od. beeinträchtigen.

mon·o ['mɒnəʊ] I pl -os s **1.** Mono n. **2.**
F Monogerät n od. -schallplatte f. II adj
3. Mono...

mon·o... [~] in Zssgn ein..., mono...

mon·o·cle ['mɒnəkl] s Monokel n.

mo·nog·a·mous [mɒ'nɒgəməs] adj □
monogam(isch). **mo'nog·a·my** s Mo-
nogamie f, Einehe f.

mon·o·gram ['mɒnəgræm] s Monogramm n.

mon·o·lith ['mɒnəʊlɪθ] s Monolith m.
,**mon·o'lith·ic** adj (*~ally*) **1.** monoli-
thisch (a. fig.). **2.** fig. gigantisch.

mon·o·logue ['mɒnəlɒg] s Monolog m,
Selbstgespräch n.

mo·nop·o·lize [mə'nɒpəlaɪz] v/t **1.** ✝
monopolisieren. **2.** fig. a) an sich reißen, *Unterhaltung* a. ganz allein bestreiten, b) j-n, et. mit Beschlag belegen. **mo'nop·o·ly** s ✝ Monopol n (*of*
auf acc) (a. fig.).

,**mon·o·syl'lab·ic** adj (*~ally*) ling. einsilbig (a. fig. *Antworten* etc).

mo·not·o·nous [mə'nɒtnəs] adj □ monoton, eintönig, fig. a. einförmig.
mo'not·o·ny [~tnɪ] s Monotonie f, Eintönigkeit f, fig. a. Einförmigkeit f, (ewiges) Einerlei.

mon·ox·ide [mɒ'nɒksaɪd] s ✿ Mon-
oxyd n.

mon·soon [,mɒn'suːn] s Monsun m.

mon·ster ['mɒnstə] I s **1.** Monster n,
Ungeheuer n (beide a. fig.). **2.** Mon-
strum n (a. fig.). II adj **3.** Riesen...,
Monster...: ~ *film* Monsterfilm m.

mon·strance ['mɒnstrəns] s eccl. Monstranz f.

mon·stros·i·ty [mɒn'strɒsətɪ] s **1.** Ungeheuerlichkeit f. **2.** → *monster* 2.

mon·strous ['~strəs] adj □ monströs:
a) ungeheuer, riesig, b) unförmig, ungestalt, c) fig. ungeheuerlich, scheußlich.

month [mʌnθ] s Monat m: *we haven't*
seen each other in a ~ *of Sundays* F
wir haben uns schon seit einer Ewigkeit
nicht mehr gesehen. '**month·ly** I adj □
(a. adv) monatlich. **2.** Monats...: ~ *sea-*
son ticket Monatskarte f. II s **3.** Mo-
natsschrift f.

mon·u·ment ['mɒnjʊmənt] s a. fig. Mo-

nument *n*, Denkmal *n* (**to** für *od. gen*).
mon·u·men·tal [͵ˈmentl] *adj* □ **1.** monumental (*a. fig.*). **2.** F kolossal: ~ **stupidity** Riesendummheit *f*.

moo [muː] **I** *v/i* muhen. **II** *s* Muhen *n*.

mood¹ [muːd] *s ling.* Modus *m*.

mood² [~] *s* **1.** Stimmung *f*, Laune *f*: **be in a good (bad)** ~ gute (schlechte) Laune haben, gut (schlecht) aufgelegt sein; **be in the (in no)** ~ **to do** (nicht) dazu aufgelegt sein zu tun, (keine) Lust haben zu tun; **be in the** ~ **for** aufgelegt sein zu; **I am in no laughing** ~ (*od.* ~ **for laughing**) mir ist nicht nach *od.* zum Lachen zumute. **2. be in a** ~ schlechte Laune haben, schlecht aufgelegt sein; **he is in one of his** ~**s again** er hat wieder einmal schlechte Laune.

mood·y [ˈmuːdɪ] *adj* □ **1.** launisch, launenhaft. **2.** schlechtgelaunt.

moon [muːn] **I** *s* Mond *m*: **there is a (no)** ~ der Mond scheint (nicht); **be over the** ~ F überglücklich sein (**about, at** über *acc*); **cry for the** ~ nach et. Unmöglichem verlangen; **promise s.o. the** ~ j-m das Blaue vom Himmel (herunter)versprechen; **once in a blue** ~ F alle Jubeljahre (einmal). **II** *v/i:* ~ **about** (*od.* **around**) herumtrödeln; ziellos herumstreichen. **III** *v/t:* ~ **away** Zeit vertrödeln, -träumen. 'ˌ~·beam *s* Mondstrahl *m*. 'ˌ~·light **I** *s* Mondlicht *n*, -schein *m*: ~ **walk** Mondscheinspaziergang *m*. **II** *v/i* F schwarzarbeiten. 'ˌ~·light·er *s* F Schwarzarbeiter(in). 'ˌ~·lit *adj* mondhell: ~ **night** Mondnacht *f*. 'ˌ~·shine *s* **1.** Mondschein *m*. **2.** F Unsinn *m*, Quatsch *m*.

moon·y [ˈmuːnɪ] *adj* □ F verträumt.

moor¹ [mɔː] *s* (Hoch)Moor *n*.

moor² [~] *v/t* ⚓ vertäuen, festmachen.

moor·ings [ˈmɔːrɪŋz] *s pl* ⚓ **1.** Vertäuung *f*. **2.** Liegeplatz *m*.

moose [muːs] *pl* **moose** *s zo.* Elch *m*.

moot [muːt] *adj* strittig (*Punkt*): ~ **question** Streitfrage *f*.

mop [mɒp] **I** *s* **1.** Mop *m*. **2.** (Haar)Wust *m*. **II** *v/t* **3.** wischen: ~ **up** aufwischen; ~ **one's face** sich das Gesicht (ab)wischen. **4.** *Blut etc* abwischen (**from** von).

mope [məʊp] *v/i* den Kopf hängen lassen: ~ **about** (*od.* **around**) mit e-r Leichenbittermiene herumlaufen.

mo·ped [ˈməʊped] *s Br.* Moped *n*.

mo·raine [mɒˈreɪn] *s geol.* Moräne *f*.

mor·al [ˈmɒrəl] **I** *adj* □ **1.** moralisch: a) sittlich, b) geistig, innerlich: ~ **obligation** moralische Verpflichtung; ~ **support** moralische Unterstützung; ~ **victory** moralischer Sieg, c) sittenstreng, tugendhaft. **2.** Moral..., Sitten...: ~ **theology** Moraltheologie *f*. **II** *s* **3.** Moral *f* (*e-r Geschichte etc*): **draw the** ~ **from** die Lehre ziehen aus. **4.** *pl* Moral *f*, Sitten *pl*: **code of** ~**s** Sittenkodex *m*. **mo·rale** [mɒˈrɑːl] *s* Moral *f*, Stimmung *f*: **raise (lower) the** ~ die Moral heben (senken). **mor·al·ist** [ˈmɒrəlɪst] *s* Moralist(in). **mo·ral·i·ty** [məˈrælɪtɪ] *s* **1.** Moral *f*, Tugend(haftigkeit) *f*. **2.** Ethik *f*, Moral *f*. **mor·al·ize** [ˈmɒrəlaɪz] *v/i* moralisieren (**about, on** über *acc*).

mor·a·to·ri·um [͵mɒrəˈtɔːrɪəm] *pl* **-ri·a** [~rɪə], **-ri·ums** *s* ✝, ✗, *pol.* Moratorium *n*.

mor·bid [ˈmɔːbɪd] *adj* □ **1.** morbid, krankhaft (*beide a. fig.*). **2.** gräßlich, grauenerregend. **3.** trübsinnig, pessimistisch. **mor·bid·i·ty** *s* **1.** Morbidität *f*, Krankhaftigkeit *f* (*beide a. fig.*). **2.** Trübsinn *m*; Pessimismus *m*.

mor·dant [ˈmɔːdənt] *adj* □ *fig.* ätzend, beißend.

more [mɔː] **I** *adj* **1.** mehr: **they are** ~ **than we are** sie sind zahlreicher als wir. **2.** mehr, noch (mehr): **some** ~ **tea** noch et. Tee; **two** ~ **miles** noch zwei Meilen. **II** *adv* **3.** mehr: ~ **and** ~ immer mehr; ~ **and** ~ **difficult** immer schwieriger; ~ **or less** mehr od. weniger; ungefähr; **the** ~ **so because** um so mehr, da. **4.** *zur Bildung des comp:* ~ **important** wichtiger; ~ **often** öfter. **5.** noch: **once** ~ noch einmal. **III** *s* **6.** Mehr *n* (**of** an *dat*): **some** ~ noch et. (mehr); **a little** ~ et. mehr; **what** ~ **do you want?** was willst du denn noch?

mo·rel [mɒˈrel] *s* ❦ Morchel *f*.

mo·rel·lo [məˈreləʊ] *pl* **-los** *s a.* ~ **cherry** ❦ Morelle *f*.

more·o·ver [mɔːˈrəʊvə] *adv* außerdem, überdies, weiter, ferner.

morgue [mɔːɡ] *s* **1.** Leichenschauhaus *n*. **2.** F Archiv *n* (*e-s Zeitungsverlags etc*).

Mor·mon [ˈmɔːmən] **I** *s* Mormone *m*, Mormonin *f*. **II** *adj* mormonisch.

morn·ing [ˈmɔːnɪŋ] **I** *s* Morgen *m*; Vormittag *m*: *in the ~* morgens, am Morgen; vormittags, am Vormittag; *early in the ~* frühmorgens, früh am Morgen; *this ~* heute morgen *od.* vormittag; *tomorrow ~* morgen früh *od.* vormittag. **II** *adj* Morgen...; Vormittags...; Früh... **~ coat** *s* Cut(away) *m*. **~ pa·per** *s* Morgenzeitung *f*. **~ star** *s ast.* Morgenstern *m*.

mo·rose [məˈrəʊs] *adj* □ mürrisch, verdrießlich.

mor·pheme [ˈmɔːfiːm] *s ling.* Morphem *n*.

mor·phi·a [ˈmɔːfjə], **mor·phine** [ˈmɔːfiːn] *s* Morphium *n*.

mor·pho·log·i·cal [ˌmɔːfəˈlɒdʒɪkl] *adj* □ *biol.*, *ling.* morphologisch. **mor·phol·o·gy** [~ˈfɒlədʒɪ] *s* Morphologie *f*.

Morse code [mɔːs] *s* Morsealphabet *n*.

mor·sel [ˈmɔːsl] *s* **1.** Bissen *m*, Happen *m*. **2.** *a ~ of* ein bißchen: *a ~ of sense* ein Funke Verstand.

mor·tal [ˈmɔːtl] **I** *adj* □ **1.** sterblich. **2.** tödlich (*to* für). **3.** Tod(es)...: *~ fear* Todesangst *f*; *~ hour* Todesstunde *f*; *~ sin* Todsünde *f*. **4.** auf Leben u. Tod: *~ enemy* Todfeind *m*; *~ hatred* tödlicher Haß. **5.** F *of no ~ use* absolut zwecklos; *every ~ thing* alles menschenmögliche; *I'm in a ~ hurry* ich hab's furchtbar eilig. **6.** F ewig (lang): *three ~ hours pl* drei endlose Stunden *pl*. **II** *s* **7.** Sterbliche *m*, *f*: *an ordinary ~* ein gewöhnlicher Sterblicher. **mor·tal·i·ty** [~ˈtælətɪ] *s* **1.** Sterblichkeit *f*. **2.** *a. ~ rate* Sterblichkeit(sziffer) *f*.

mor·tar¹ [ˈmɔːtə] *s* **1.** Mörser *m*. **2.** ✕ Granatwerfer *m*.

mor·tar² [~] *s* Mörtel *m*.

mort·gage [ˈmɔːgɪdʒ] **I** *s* Hypothek *f*: *raise a ~* e-e Hypothek aufnehmen (*on* auf *acc*). **II** *v/t* mit e-r Hypothek belasten, e-e Hypothek aufnehmen auf (*acc*).

mor·ti·cian [mɔːˈtɪʃən] *s Am.* Leichenbestatter *m*.

mor·ti·fi·ca·tion [ˌmɔːtɪfɪˈkeɪʃn] *s* **1.** Demütigung *f*, Kränkung *f*. **2.** Ärger *m*, Verdruß *m*: *to one's ~* zu s-m Verdruß. **3.** Kasteiung *f*. **4.** Abtötung *f*. **5.** ⚕ Absterben *n*. **mor·ti·fy** [ˈ~faɪ] **I** *v/t* **1.** demütigen, kränken. **2.** ärgern, verdrießen. **3.** *Fleisch etc* kasteien. **4.** Lei-

denschaften abtöten. **II** *v/i* **5.** ⚕ absterben (*Gewebe*).

mor·tu·ar·y [ˈmɔːtʃʊərɪ] *s* Leichenhalle *f*. **II** *adj* Begräbnis..., Leichen...

mo·sa·ic [məʊˈzeɪɪk] *s* Mosaik *n*.

Mos·lem [ˈmɒzləm] **I** *s* Moslem *m*. **II** *adj* moslemisch.

mosque [mɒsk] *s* Moschee *f*.

mos·qui·to [məˈskiːtəʊ] *pl* **-to(e)s** *s zo.* Moskito *m*; *allg.* Stechmücke *f*. **~ net** *s* Moskitonetz *n*.

moss [mɒs] *s* Moos *n*. **'moss·y** *adj* moosig, bemoost.

most [məʊst] **I** *adj* **1.** meist, größt: *for the ~ part* größten-, meistenteils. **2.** (*vor e-m s im pl*, *mst ohne Artikel*) die meisten: *~ people* die meisten Leute. **II** *s* **3.** *das meiste*, *das Höchste*: *at (the) ~* höchstens, bestenfalls; *make the ~ of et.* nach Kräften ausnützen, das Beste herausholen aus. **4.** das meiste, der größte Teil: *he spent ~ of his time there* er verbrachte die meiste Zeit dort. **5.** die meisten *pl*: *better than ~* besser als die meisten; *~ of my friends* die meisten m-r Freunde. **III** *adv* **6.** am meisten: *~ of all* am allermeisten. **7.** *zur Bildung des sup*: *the ~ important point* der wichtigste Punkt. **8.** (*vor adj*) höchst, äußerst: *~ agreeable* äußerst angenehm; *he is ~ likely to come* er kommt höchstwahrscheinlich. **'most·ly** *adv* **1.** größtenteils. **2.** meist(ens).

MOT [ˌeməʊˈtiː] *s Br.* a) *a. ~ test* (*etwa*) TÜV-Prüfung *f*: *my car has failed* (*od. hasn't got through*) *its* (*od. the*) *~* mein Wagen ist nicht durch den TÜV gekommen, b) *a. ~ certificate* (*etwa*) TÜV-Bescheinigung *f*.

mo·tel [məʊˈtel] *s* Motel *n*.

moth [mɒθ] *s zo.* **1.** Nachtfalter *m*. **2.** Motte *f*. **'~·ball** *s* Mottenkugel *f*: *put in ~s* einmotten (*a. fig.*). **'~·eat·en** *adj* **1.** mottenzerfressen. **2.** *fig.* veraltet.

moth·er [ˈmʌðə] **I** *s* Mutter *f* (*a. fig.*): ♀'*s Day* Muttertag *m*; *~'s milk* Muttermilch *f*; *a ~ of four* e-e Mutter von vier Kindern. **II** *adj* Mutter...: *~ ship.* **III** *v/t* bemuttern. **~ coun·try** *s* **1.** Mutterland *n*. **2.** Vater-, Heimatland *n*.

moth·er·hood [ˈmʌðəhʊd] *s* Mutterschaft *f*.

'moth·er|-in-law *pl* **'moth·ers-in-law** *s* Schwiegermutter *f*: *~ joke* Schwiegermutterwitz *m*. '**~·land** → *mother country*.

moth·er·less ['mʌðəlɪs] *adj* mutterlos. '**moth·er·ly** *adj* mütterlich.

,**moth·er|-of-'pearl** *s* Perlmutter *f, n*, Perlmutt *n*. ,**~-to-'be** *pl* ,**moth·ers--to-'be** *s* werdende Mutter. **~ tongue** *s* Muttersprache *f*. **~ wit** *s* Mutterwitz *m*.

mo·tif [məʊ'tiːf] *s Kunst*: Motiv *n*.

mo·tion ['məʊʃn] **I** *s* **1.** Bewegung *f (a. phys. etc)*: **be in ~** in Gang sein *(a. fig.)*, in Bewegung sein; **put** *(od.* **set)** **in ~** in Gang bringen *(a. fig.)*, in Bewegung setzen; **go through the ~s** of doing s.th. *fig.* et. mechanisch *od.* pro forma tun. **2.** Bewegung *f*, Geste *f*, Wink *m*: **~ of the head** Kopfbewegung; **make a ~ with one's hand** e-e Handbewegung machen. **3.** *parl. etc* Antrag *m*: **on the ~ of** auf Antrag von *(od. gen)*. **II** *v/i* **4.** winken (**with** mit; **to, at** *dat*). **III** *v/t* **5.** *j-n* durch e-n Wink auffordern, *j-m* ein Zeichen geben (**to do** zu tun): **~ s.o. into the room** *j-n* ins Zimmer winken. '**mo·tion·less** *adj* □ bewegungs-, regungslos.

mo·tion| pic·ture *s Am.* Film *m.* **~·ther·a·py** *s ✻* Bewegungstherapie *f*.

mo·ti·vate ['məʊtɪveɪt] *v/t* motivieren, anspornen. ,**mo·ti·va·tion** *s* Motivation *f*, Ansporn *m*, Antrieb *m*.

mo·tive ['məʊtɪv] **I** *s* Motiv *n*, Beweggrund *m* (**for** zu). **II** *adj* treibend *(a. fig.)*: **~ power** Antriebskraft *f*, *bsd. fig.* Triebkraft *f*.

mot·ley ['mɒtlɪ] *adj* (kunter)bunt *(a. fig.)*.

mo·tor ['məʊtə] **I** *s* **1.** ✿ Motor *m, fig. a.* treibende Kraft. **II** *adj* **2.** Motor... **3.** *physiol.* motorisch, Bewegungs...: **~ nerve.** '**~·bike** *s* F Motorrad *n.* '**~·boat** *s* Motorboot *n.* **~·cade** ['~keɪd] *s* Auto-, Wagenkolonne *f.* '**~·car** *s* Kraftfahrzeug *n.* **~ car·a·van** *s Br.* Wohnmobil *n.* '**~·cy·cle** *s* Motorrad *n.* '**~·cy·clist** *s* Motorradfahrer(in).

mo·tor·ing ['məʊtərɪŋ] **I** *s* Autofahren *n*: **~ school** *od.* **~** Fahrschule *f.* **II** *adj* Verkehrs..., Auto... '**mo·tor·ist** *s* Autofahrer(in).

,**mo·tor·i·za·tion** [,məʊtəraɪ'zeɪʃn] *s* Motorisierung *f.* '**mo·tor·ize** *v/t* motorisieren.

mo·tor| scoot·er *s* Motorroller *m.* '**~·way** *s Br.* Autobahn *f*.

mot·tled ['mɒtld] *adj* gesprenkelt.

mot·to ['mɒtəʊ] *pl* **-to(e)s** *s* Motto *n*.

mould¹ [məʊld] *bsd. Br.* **I** *s* **1.** ✿ (Gieß-, Guß-, Press)Form *f*: **be cast** *(od.* **made) in the same (a different) ~** *fig.* aus demselben (e-m anderen) Holz geschnitzt sein. **II** *v/t* **2.** ✿ gießen. **3.** formen *(a. fig. Charakter etc)*, bilden (**out of** aus), gestalten (**on** nach dem Muster *gen*); formen (**into** zu).

mould² [~] *s bsd. Br.* Schimmel *m*; Moder *m*.

mould·er ['məʊldə] *v/i a.* **~ away** *bsd. Br.* vermodern, zerfallen.

mould·y ['məʊldɪ] *adj bsd. Br.* **1.** a) verschimmelt, schimm(e)lig: **get** *(od.* **go)** **~** (ver)schimmeln, b) mod(e)rig: **~ smell** Modergeruch *m.* **2.** *sl.* schäbig *(Person, Summe etc)*.

mound [maʊnd] *s* Erdwall *m*, -hügel *m*: **~ of work** *fig.* Berg *m* Arbeit.

mount¹ [maʊnt] **I** *v/t* **1.** *Pferd etc, fig.* Thron besteigen; *Treppen* hinaufgehen: **~ one's bicycle** auf sein Fahrrad steigen. **2.** *Kind etc* setzen (**on** auf *ein Pferd etc*). **3.** errichten, *a. Maschine* aufstellen. **4.** anbringen, befestigen; *Bild etc* aufkleben; *Edelstein* fassen. **II** *v/i* **5.** aufsitzen *(Reiter).* **6.** steigen, *fig. a.* (an)wachsen. **7.** *oft* **~ up** *fig.* sich belaufen *(to auf acc).* **III** *s* **8.** Gestell *n*; Fassung *f.* **9.** Reittier *n*.

Mount² [~] *s in Eigennamen*: a) Berg *m*: **~ Sinai**, b) Mount *m*: **~ Everest**.

moun·tain ['maʊntɪn] **I** *s* Berg *m (a. fig.)*, *pl a.* Gebirge *n*: **in the ~s** im Gebirge; **make a ~ out of a molehill** aus e-r Mücke e-n Elefanten machen. **II** *adj* Berg..., Gebirgs... **~ chain** *s* Berg-, Gebirgskette *f.* **~ crys·tal** *s min.* Bergkristall *m*.

moun·tain·eer [,maʊntɪ'nɪə] *s* Bergsteiger(in). ,**moun·tain·eer·ing** *s* Bergsteigen *n*. '**moun·tain·ous** *adj* □ **1.** bergig, gebirgig. **2.** *fig.* riesig, *(Wellen a.)* haushoch.

moun·tain range *s* Gebirgszug *m*.

mount·ed ['maʊntɪd] *adj* beritten: **~ po·lice.**

mourn [mɔːn] **I** *v/i* **1.** trauern (**at, over** über *acc*; **for, over** um). **2.** Trauer(kleidung) tragen. **II** *v/t* **3.** betrauern, trau-

ern um. '**mourn·er** s Trauernde m, f.
mourn·ful ['ᴗfʊl] adj □ traurig.
'**mourn·ing** s 1. Trauer f: ~ **band** Trauerband n, -flor m. 2. Trauer(kleidung) f: **go into** ~ Trauerkleidung anlegen.

mouse [maʊs] pl **mice** [maɪs] s 1. zo. Maus f. 2. fig. schüchterne od. ängstliche Person. '**ᴗhole** s Mauseloch n. '**ᴗtrap** s Mausefalle f.

mous·tache [məˈstɑːʃ] s Schnurrbart m.

mous·y ['maʊsɪ] adj □ 1. mausgrau. 2. schüchtern; ängstlich.

mouth I s [maʊθ] pl **mouths** [maʊðz] 1. Mund m: **down in the** ~ F deprimiert; **keep one's** ~ **shut** F den Mund halten; **take the words out of s.o.'s** ~ j-m das Wort aus dem Mund nehmen; → **stop** 12, **word** 1. 2. zo. Maul n, Schnauze f: → **horse.** 3. Mündung f (e-s Flusses etc); Öffnung f (e-r Flasche etc), Ein-, Ausfahrt f (e-s Hafens etc). II v/t [maʊð] 4. Worte (unhörbar) mit den Lippen formen. **mouth·ful** ['ᴗfʊl] s 1. ein Mundvoll m, Bissen m. 2. fig. Bandwurm m, ellenlanges Wort; Zungenbrecher m.

mouth| or·gan s ♪ Mundharmonika f. '**ᴗpiece** s 1. Mundstück n (e-s Blasinstruments, e-r Pfeife etc). 2. fig. Sprachrohr n (a. Person). **,~-to-'~ res·pi·ra·tion** s ✚ Mund-zu-Mund-Beatmung f. '**ᴗwash** s ✚ Mundwasser n. '**ᴗwa·ter·ing** adj appetitlich, lecker.

mov·a·ble ['muːvəbl] I adj □ beweglich (a. eccl., ✚); transportierbar. II s pl ✚ Mobilien pl, bewegliches Vermögen.

move [muːv] I v/t 1. (von der Stelle) bewegen, rücken; transportieren; Körperteil bewegen, rühren: ~ **one's car** s-n Wagen wegfahren; → **heaven** 1. 2. a) Wohnsitz etc verlegen (**to** nach): ~ **house** umziehen, b) Angestellten etc versetzen (**to** nach). 3. ~ **on** vorwärtstreiben; j-n auffordern weiterzugehen. 4. fig. bewegen, rühren: **be ᴗd to tears** zu Tränen gerührt sein. 5. bewegen, veranlassen (**to** zu): **feel ᴗd to say s.th.** sich veranlaßt fühlen, et. zu sagen. 6. Schach etc: ziehen a/so. e-n Zug machen mit. 7. parl. etc beantragen (a. **that** daß). II v/i 8. sich bewegen od. rühren; fig. sich ändern (Ansichten etc): **begin to ~, ~ off** sich in Bewegung setzen; ~ **on** weitergehen; → **time** 1. 9. umziehen: ~

to a. ziehen nach; ~ **in** (**out, away**) ein-(aus-, weg)ziehen. 10. handeln, et. unternehmen. 11. (**in** in guter Gesellschaft etc) verkehren (a. **with** mit), sich bewegen. 12. Schach etc: e-n Zug machen, ziehen. III s 13. Bewegung f: **on the** ~ in Bewegung; auf den Beinen; **get a** ~ **on!** F Tempo!, mach(t) schon! 14. Umzug m. 15. a) Schach etc: Zug m: **it is your** ~ Sie sind am Zug, b) fig. Schritt m: a **clever** ~ ein kluger Schachzug; **make the first** ~ den ersten Schritt tun. 16. Sport: Kombination f; Spielzug m. '**move·ment** s 1. Bewegung f (a. fig.): **without** ~ bewegungslos. 2. ♪ Satz m.

mov·ie ['muːvɪ] bsd. Am. F I s 1. Film m. 2. Kino n. 3. **go to the** ~**s** ins Kino gehen. II adj 4. Film..., Kino...: ~ **cam·era** Filmkamera f; ~ **star** Filmstar m.

mov·ing ['muːvɪŋ] adj □ 1. beweglich, sich bewegend, (Verkehr) fließend: ~ **staircase** Rolltreppe f. 2. fig. bewegend, rührend.

mow [məʊ] v/t u. v/i (a. irr) mähen: ~ **down** niedermähen (a. fig.). '**mow·er** s a) Mähmaschine f, b) Rasenmäher m. **mown** pp von **mow.**

much [mʌtʃ] I adj 1. viel: **as** ~ **again** noch einmal soviel. II adv 2. sehr: ~ **to my regret** sehr zu m-m Bedauern; ~ **to my surprise** zu m-r großen Überraschung; **I thought as** ~ das habe ich mir gedacht. 3. (in Zssgn) viel...: ~ **admired** vielbewundert. 4. (vor comp) viel: ~ **better.** 5. fast, mehr od. weniger: ~ **the same.** III s 6. große Sache: **nothing** ~ nichts Besonderes; **think ~ of** viel halten von; **he is not** ~ **of a dancer** er ist kein großer od. berühmter Tänzer; → **make** 11.

muck [mʌk] I s 1. Mist m, Dung m. 2. Kot m, Dreck m, Schmutz m. 3. **make a** ~ **of** → 6b. II v/t 4. düngen. 5. a. ~ **out** ausmisten. 6. oft ~ **up** a) schmutzig machen, b) bsd. Br. F verpfuschen, -masseln. III v/i 7. mst ~ **about** (od. **around**) bsd. Br. F a) herumgammeln, b) herumpfuschen (**with** an dat), c) herumalbern. '**ᴗheap,** '**ᴗhill** s Misthaufen m. '**ᴗrake** v/i Skandale aufdecken; im Schmutz wühlen.

muck·y ['mʌkɪ] adj □ schmutzig, dreckig.

mu·cous ['mjuːkəs] adj schleimig: ~

membrane *anat.* Schleimhaut *f.* **mucus** ['kəs] *s* Schleim *m.*

mud [mʌd] *s* **1.** Schlamm *m*, Matsch *m.* **2.** Schmutz *m* (*a. fig.*): **drag through the ~** *fig.* in den Schmutz ziehen *od.* zerren; **sling** (*od.* **throw**) **~ at** *s.o. fig.* j-n mit Schmutz bewerfen.

mud-dle ['mʌdl] **I** *s* Durcheinander *n*, Unordnung *f*; Verwirrung *f*: **be in a ~** durcheinander sein (*Dinge*), (*Person a.*) konfus sein; **get in(to) a ~** durcheinandergeraten (*Dinge*); konfus werden (*Person*); **make a ~** → IIa. **II** *v/t* **1.** durcheinanderbringen: a) in Unordnung bringen, b) konfus machen, c) verwechseln (**with** mit). **III** *v/i*: **~ through** sich durchwursteln. '**~headed** *adj* wirr(köpfig), konfus.

mud-dy ['mʌdɪ] *adj* □ **1.** schlammig, trüb. **2.** schmutzig. **3.** *fig.* wirr; unklar, verschwommen.

'**mud|guard** *s mot.* Kotflügel *m*; Schutzblech *n* (*e-s Fahrrads*). **~ pack** *s* 🏥 Fango-, Schlammpackung *f.* '**~sling·er** *s* Verleumder(in). '**~sling-ing** *s* Verleumdung *f.*

muf·fin ['mʌfɪn] *s* Muffin *m*: a) *Br.* Hefeteigsemmel *f*, b) *Am. kleine süße Semmel.*

muf·fle ['mʌfl] *v/t* **1.** *oft* **~ up** einhüllen, -wickeln. **2.** Ton *etc* dämpfen: **~d voices** *pl* gedämpfte Stimmen *pl.* '**muf·fler** *s* **1.** dicker Schal. **2.** *mot. Am.* Auspufftopf *m.*

muf·ti ['mʌftɪ] *s*: **in ~** in Zivil.

mug [mʌg] **I** *s* **1.** Krug *m*; Becher *m*; große Tasse. **2.** *sl.* Visage *f* (*Gesicht*); Fresse *f* (*Mund*). **II** *v/t* F **3.** (*bsd. auf der Straße*) überfallen u. ausrauben. **4.** *a.* **~ up** *Br. et.* büffeln. **III** *v/i* **5.** *Br.* F büffeln. '**mug·ger** *s* F (*bsd.* Straßen)Räuber *m.* '**mug·ging** *s* F Raubüberfall *m*, *bsd.* Straßenraub *m.*

mug·gy ['mʌgɪ] *adj* □ schwül.

mule¹ [mju:l] *s zo.* Maultier *n*; Maulesel *m*: (**as**) **stubborn** (*od.* **obstinate**) **as a ~** (so) störrisch wie ein Maulesel.

mule² [~] *s* Pantoffel *m.*

mul·ish ['mju:lɪʃ] *adj* □ störrisch, stur.

mull¹ [mʌl] *s* (*s* Verband[s])Mull *m.*

mull² [~] *v/i u. v/t*: **~ over** *s.th.*, **~** *s.th.* **over** nachdenken *od.* -grübeln über (*acc*).

mulled [mʌld] *adj*: **~ wine** Glühwein *m.*

mul·ti... ['mʌltɪ] *in Zssgn* viel..., mehr..., Mehrfach..., Multi...

mul·ti·far·i·ous [,mʌltɪ'feərɪəs] *adj* □ mannigfaltig, vielfältig. **,mul·ti'lat·er·al** *adj* □ **1.** vielseitig. **2.** *pol.* multilateral, mehrseitig. **,mul·ti'lin·gual** *adj* mehrsprachig. **,mul·ti·mil·lion'aire** *s* Multimillionär *m.* **,mul·ti'na·tion·al** ✝ **I** *adj* multinational (*Konzern*). **II** *s* F Multi *m.*

mul·ti·ple ['mʌltɪpl] **I** *adj* □ **1.** viel-, mehrfach: **~ sclerosis** 🏥 multiple Sklerose. **2.** mannigfaltig, vielfältig. **3.** 🔬, ⚙ Mehr(fach)..., Vielfach... **II** *s* **4.** *das* Vielfache (*a.* 🅐).

mul·ti·pli·ca·tion [,mʌltɪplɪ'keɪʃn] *s* **1.** Vermehrung *f* (*a. biol.*). **2.** 🅐 Multiplikation *f*: **~ sign** Mal-, Multiplikationszeichen *n*; **~ table** Einmaleins *n.* **mul·ti·plic·i·ty** [,~'plɪsətɪ] *s* **1.** Vielfalt *f.* **2.** Vielzahl *f.* **mul·ti·pli·er** ['~plaɪə] *s* 🅐 Multiplikator *m.* **mul·ti·ply** ['~plaɪ] **I** *v/t* **1.** vermehren, -vielfachen. **2.** 🅐 multiplizieren, malnehmen (**by** mit): **6 multiplied by 5 is 30** 6 mal 5 ist 30. **II** *v/i* **3.** sich vermehren (*a. biol.*), sich vervielfachen.

,mul·ti'pur·pose *adj* Mehrzweck... **,multi'sto·r(e)y** *adj* vielstöckig: **~ car park** Park(hoch)haus *n.*

mul·ti·tude ['mʌltɪtju:d] *s* **1.** große Zahl, Vielzahl *f*: **for a ~ of reasons** aus vielerlei Gründen. **2.** *the* **~(s** *pl) die* Masse. **mul·ti·tu·di·nous** [,~'tju:dɪnəs] *adj* □ zahlreich.

mum¹ [mʌm] **I** *int*: **~'s the word** Mund halten!, kein Wort darüber! **II** *adj*: **keep ~** nichts verraten (**about, on** von), den Mund halten.

mum² [~] *s bsd. Br.* F Mami *f*, Mutti *f.*

mum·ble ['mʌmbl] *v/t u. v/i* (vor sich hin) murmeln.

mum·bo jum·bo [,mʌmbəʊ'dʒʌmbəʊ] *s* **1.** Hokuspokus *m*, fauler Zauber. **2.** Kauderwelsch *n.*

mum·mi·fi·ca·tion [,mʌmɪfɪ'keɪʃn] *s* Mumifizierung *f.* **mum·mi·fy** ['~faɪ] **I** *v/t* mumifizieren. **II** *v/i* vertrocknen.

mum·my¹ ['mʌmɪ] *s* Mumie *f.*

mum·my² [~] → **mum.**

mumps [mʌmps] *s pl* (*sg konstruiert*) 🏥 Mumps *m*, Ziegenpeter *m.*

munch [mʌntʃ] *v/t u. v/i* mampfen: **~ away at** *et.* mampfen.

mun·dane [ˌmʌnˈdeɪn] *adj* □ **1.** weltlich. **2.** alltäglich, profan; prosaisch, sachlich-nüchtern.

mu·nic·i·pal [mjuːˈnɪsɪpl] *adj* □ städtisch, Stadt..., kommunal, Gemeinde...: **~ council** Stadt-, Gemeinderat *m*; **~ elections** *pl* Kommunalwahlen *pl.* **mu·nic·i·pal·i·ty** [~ˈpælətɪ] *s* **1.** Gemeinde *f.* **2.** Kommunalbehörde *f*, -verwaltung *f.*

mu·ral [ˈmjʊərəl] **I** *adj* Mauer..., Wand...: **~ painting** → II. **II** *s* Wandgemälde *n.*

mur·der [ˈmɜːdə] **I** *s* **1.** (of) Mord *m* (an *dat*), Ermordung *f* (*gen*): **cry** (*od.* **scream**) **blue ~** F zetermordio schreien; **get away with ~** F sich alles erlauben können. **II** *adj* **2.** Mord...: **~ trial** Mordprozeß *m*; **~ victim** Mordopfer *n*; **~ weapon** Mordwaffe *f.* **III** *v/t* **3.** ermorden. **4.** *fig.* verschandeln, verhunzen. **'mur·der·er** *s* Mörder *m.* **'mur·der·ess** *s* Mörderin *f.* **'mur·der·ous** *adj* □ mörderisch (*a. fig.*).

murk·y [ˈmɜːkɪ] *adj* □ dunkel, finster (*beide a. fig.*).

mur·mur [ˈmɜːmə] **I** *s* **1.** Murmeln *n.* **2.** Murren *n*: **without a ~** ohne zu murren. **II** *v/i* **3.** murmeln. **4.** murren (**at**, **against** gegen). **III** *v/t* **5.** *et.* murmeln.

mus·cle [ˈmʌsl] **I** *s anat.* Muskel *m*: **not to move a ~** *fig.* nicht mit der Wimper zucken. **II** *v/i*: **~ in on** *fig.* F sich eindrängen in (*acc*). **'~·man** *s* (*irr man*) Muskelmann *m*, -paket *n.*

mus·cu·lar [ˈmʌskjʊlə] *adj* □ **1.** Muskel...: **~ atrophy** ♂ Muskelschwund *m.* **2.** muskulös.

muse [mjuːz] *v/i* (nach)sinnen, (-)grübeln (**on**, **over** über *acc*).

mu·se·um [mjuːˈzɪəm] *s* Museum *n.*

mush [mʌʃ] *s* **1.** Brei *m*, Mus *n.* **2.** *Am.* Maisbrei *m.*

mush·room [ˈmʌʃrʊm] **I** *s* **1.** ♀ (eßbarer) Pilz, *engS.* Champignon *m.* **2.** Pilz...; pilzförmig: **~ cloud** Atompilz *m.* **III** *v/i* **3.** Pilze sammeln: **go ~ing** in die Pilze gehen. **4.** *oft* **~ up** *fig.* wie Pilze aus dem Boden schießen.

mush·y [ˈmʌʃɪ] *adj* □ **1.** breiig, weich. **2.** F rührselig.

mu·sic [ˈmjuːzɪk] *s* **1.** Musik *f*: **that's ~ to my ears** das ist Musik in m-n Ohren; **face the ~** F dafür geradestehen; **put**

(*od.* **set**) **to ~** vertonen. **2.** Noten *pl.* **'mu·si·cal I** *adj* □ **1.** Musik...: **~ instrument.** **2.** musikalisch. **II** *s* **3.** Musical *n.*

mu·sic| book *s* Notenheft *n*, -buch *n.* **~ cen·tre** (*Am.* **cen·ter**) *s* Kompaktanlage *f.* **~ hall** *s bsd. Br.* Varieté(theater) *n.*

mu·si·cian [mjuːˈzɪʃn] *s* Musiker(in).

mu·sic| pa·per *s* Notenpapier *n.* **~ stand** *s* Notenständer *m.* **~ stool** *s* Klavierstuhl *m.*

muss [mʌs] *Am.* F **I** *s* Durcheinander *n*, Verhau *m.* **II** *v/t oft* **~ up** durcheinanderbringen, *Haar* zerwühlen.

mus·sel [ˈmʌsl] *s* (Mies)Muschel *f.*

must¹ [mʌst] **I** *v/aux* ich muß, du mußt *etc*: **you ~ not smoke here** du darfst hier nicht rauchen. **II** *s* Muß *n*: **this book is a(n absolute) ~** dieses Buch muß man (unbedingt) gelesen haben.

must² [~] *s* Most *m.*

mus·tache *Am.* → **moustache.**

mus·tang [ˈmʌstæŋ] *s zo.* Mustang *m.*

mus·tard [ˈmʌstəd] *s* Senf *m.*

mus·ter [ˈmʌstə] **I** *v/t* **1.** ✕ (zum Appell) antreten lassen; *allg.* zs.-rufen, versammeln. **2.** *j-n*, *et.* auftreiben. **3.** *a.* **~ up** *s-e Kraft etc* aufbieten: → **courage.** **II** *v/i* **4.** ✕ (zum Appell) antreten; *allg.* sich versammeln. **III** *s* **5.** ✕ (Antreten *n* zum) Appell: **pass ~** *fig.* durchgehen (**with** bei); ganz passabel sein, den Anforderungen genügen.

mustn't [ˈmʌsnt] F *für* must not.

mus·ty [ˈmʌstɪ] *adj* □ **1.** muffig. **2.** mod(e)rig.

mu·ta·tion [mjuːˈteɪʃn] *s* **1.** (Ver)Änderung *f.* **2.** Umwandlung *f.* **3.** *biol.* Mutation *f.*

mute [mjuːt] **I** *adj* □ **1.** stumm (*a. ling.*), *weitS. a.* sprachlos. **II** *s* **2.** Stumme *m*, *f.* **3.** ♪ Dämpfer *m.* **II** *v/t* **4.** ♪ dämpfen.

mu·ti·late [ˈmjuːtɪleɪt] *v/t* verstümmeln (*a. fig.*). **ˌmu·ti·ˈla·tion** *s* Verstümm(e)lung *f.*

mu·ti·neer [ˌmjuːtɪˈnɪə] **I** *s* Meuterer *m.* **II** *v/i* meutern. **'mu·ti·nous** *adj* □ **1.** meuternd. **2.** meuterisch. **'mu·ti·ny I** *s* Meuterei *f.* **II** *v/i* meutern.

mut·ter [ˈmʌtə] **I** *v/i* **1.** murmeln: **~ (away) to o.s.** vor sich hin murmeln. **2.** murren (**about** über *acc*). **II** *v/t* **3.** murmeln. **III** *s* **4.** Murmeln *n.* **5.** Murren *n.*

mut·ton [ˈmʌtn] *s* Hammelfleisch *n*: (as)

dead as ~ F mausetot. **~ chop** s Hammelkotelett n. **,~'chops** s pl Koteletten pl.

mu·tu·al ['mju:t∫ʊəl] adj □ **1.** gegen-, wechselseitig: **be ~** auf Gegenseitigkeit beruhen; **by ~ consent** (od. **agreement**) in gegenseitigem Einvernehmen. **2.** gemeinsam.

muz·zle ['mʌzl] **I** s **1.** zo. Maul n, Schnauze f. **2.** Maulkorb m (a. fig.). **3.** Mündung f (e-r Feuerwaffe). **II** v/t **4.** e-n Maulkorb anlegen (dat), fig. a. mundtot machen.

my [maɪ] possessive pron mein(e).

my·o·pi·a [maɪ'əʊpjə] s ✻ Kurzsichtigkeit f (a. fig.). **my·op·ic** [~'ɒpɪk] adj (~ally) ✻ kurzsichtig (a. fig.).

myr·i·ad ['mɪrɪəd] **I** s Myriade f, fig. a. Unzahl f: **a ~ of → II. II** adj: **a ~** unzählige, zahllose.

myrrh [mɜː] s ✿ Myrrhe f.

myr·tle ['mɜːtl] s ✿ Myrte f.

my·self [maɪ'self] pron **1.** verstärkend: ich, mich od. mir selbst: **I did it ~, I ~ did it** ich habe es selbst getan. **2.** reflex mich: **I cut ~. 3.** mich (selbst): **I want it for ~.**

mys·te·ri·ous [mɪ'stɪərɪəs] adj mysteriös: a) geheimnisvoll: **be very ~ about** ein großes Geheimnis machen aus, b) rätsel-, schleierhaft, unerklärlich. **mys·'te·ri·ous·ly** adv auf mysteriöse Weise, unter mysteriösen Umständen.

mys·ter·y ['mɪstərɪ] s **1.** Geheimnis n, Rätsel n (to für od. dat): **it is a (complete) ~ to me** es ist mir (völlig) schleierhaft; **make a ~ of** ein Geheimnis machen aus; **wrapped in ~** in geheimnisvolles Dunkel gehüllt. **2.** eccl. Mysterium n.

mys·tic ['mɪstɪk] **I** adj (~ally) mystisch. **II** s Mystiker(in). **'mys·ti·cal → mystic I. mys·ti·cism** ['~sɪzəm] s Mystizismus m; Mystik f.

mys·ti·fy ['mɪstɪfaɪ] v/t verwirren, vor ein Rätsel stellen: **be mystified** vor e-m Rätsel stehen.

myth [mɪθ] s **1.** Mythos m, Mythus m, fig. a. Märchen n. **myth·i·cal** ['mɪθɪkl] adj □ mythisch, sagenhaft, fig. a. erdichtet.

myth·o·log·i·cal [ˌmɪθə'lɒdʒɪkl] adj □ mythologisch. **my·thol·o·gy** [mɪ'θɒlədʒɪ] s Mythologie f.

N

nab [næb] v/t F **1.** schnappen, erwischen. **2.** sich et. schnappen.

na·bob ['neɪbɒb] s Nabob m, Krösus m.

na·dir ['neɪ,dɪə] s **1.** ast. Nadir m, Fußpunkt m. **2.** fig. Tief-, Nullpunkt m: **reach its ~** den Nullpunkt erreichen.

nag [næɡ] **I** v/t **1.** herumnörgeln an (dat). **2. ~ s.o. for s.th.** j-m wegen et. in den Ohren liegen; **~ s.o. into doing s.th.** j-m so lange zusetzen, bis er et. tut; **~ s.o. to do s.th.** j-m zusetzen, damit er et. tut. **II** v/i **3.** nörgeln: **~ at → 1. III** s **4.** Nörgler(in). **'nag·ger** s Nörgler(in). **'nag·ging I** s **1.** Nörgelei f. **II** adj □ **2.** nörgelnd. **3.** fig. nagend, bohrend (Schmerzen etc).

nail [neɪl] **I** s **1.** (Finger-, Zehen)Nagel m. **2.** ⊙ Nagel m: **(as) hard as ~s** a) a. **(as)**

tough as ~s von eiserner Gesundheit, b) eisern, unerbittlich; **→ hit 7. II** v/t **3.** (an)nageln (**on** auf acc; **to** an acc): **~ed to the spot** fig. wie angenagelt; **~ down** ver-, zunageln; fig. j-n festnageln (**to** auf acc). **~ brush** s Nagelbürste f. **~ file** s Nagelfeile f. **~ pol·ish** s Nagellack m. **~ scis·sors** s pl, a. **pair of ~** Nagelschere f. **~ var·nish** s bsd. Br. Nagellack m.

na·ive, na·ïve [nɑː'iːv] adj □ naiv (a. Kunst). **na·ive·ty** s Naivität f.

na·ked ['neɪkɪd] adj □ allg. nackt (a. fig. Wahrheit etc), (Wand etc a.) kahl: **with the ~ eye** mit bloßem Auge. **'na·ked·ness** s Nacktheit f.

nam·by-pam·by [ˌnæmbɪ'pæmbɪ] **I** adj **1.** sentimental. **2.** verweichlicht. **II**

s **3.** Mutterkind *n*, -söhnchen *n*.

name [neɪm] **I** *v/t* **1.** (be)nennen (*after, Am. a.* **for** nach): *~d* genannt, namens. **2.** beim Namen nennen. **3.** nennen, erwähnen. **4.** ernennen zu; nominieren, vorschlagen (**for** für); wählen zu; benennen, bekanntgeben. **5.** *Datum etc* festsetzen, bestimmen. **II** *s* **6.** Name *m*: **what is your ~?** wie heißen Sie?; **by ~** mit Namen, namentlich; dem Namen nach; **in the ~ of** im Namen *des Gesetzes etc*; auf *j-s* Namen *bestellen etc*; **put one's ~ down for** kandidieren für; sich anmelden für; sich vormerken lassen für. **7.** Name *m*, Bezeichnung *f*. **8.** Schimpfname *m*: **call s.o. ~s** j-n beschimpfen *od.* verspotten. **9.** Name *m*, Ruf *m*: **get a bad ~** in Verruf kommen; **have a bad ~** in schlechtem Ruf stehen. **10.** (berühmter) Name, (guter) Ruf: **a man of ~** ein Mann von Ruf; **have a ~ for being ...** im Rufe stehen, ... zu sein; **make a ~ for o.s.** sich e-n Namen machen (**as** als). **~ day** *s* Namenstag *m*. **'~·drop·per** *s* F *j-d, der dadurch Eindruck schindet, daß er ständig (angebliche) prominente Bekannte erwähnt.*

name·less ['neɪmlɪs] *adj* □ **1.** namenlos, unbekannt. **2.** ungenannt, unerwähnt. **3.** *fig.* namenlos, unbeschreiblich; unaussprechlich.

name·ly ['neɪmlɪ] *adv* nämlich.

name| plate *s* Namensschild *n*. **'~·sake** *s* Namensvetter *m*, -schwester *f*. **~ tag** *s* (*am Revers etc getragenes*) Namensschild.

nan·ny ['nænɪ] *s bsd. Br.* **1.** Kindermädchen *n*. **2.** Oma *f*, Omi *f*. **~ goat** *s* Geiß *f*, Ziege *f*.

nap [næp] **I** *v/i* ein Schläfchen *od.* Nikkerchen machen: **catch s.o. ~ping** j-n überrumpeln *od.* -raschen. **II** *s* Schläfchen *n*, Nickerchen *n*: **have** (*od.* **take**) **a ~** → **I.**

na·palm ['neɪpɑːm] *s* Napalm *n*: **~ bomb** ✕ Napalmbombe *f*.

nape [neɪp] *s mst* **~ of the neck** Genick *n*.

nap·kin ['næpkɪn] *s* **1.** Serviette *f*: **~ ring** Serviettenring *m*. **2.** *bsd. Br.* Windel *f*.

nap·py ['næpɪ] *s bsd. Br.* F Windel *f*.

nar·cis·si [nɑːˈsɪsaɪ] *pl von* **narcissus.**

nar·cis·sism ['nɑːsɪsɪzəm] *s psych.* Narzißmus *m*. **'nar·cis·sist** *s* Narzißt(in). **nar·cis·sis·tic** *adj* (*~ally*) narzißtisch.

nar·cis·sus [nɑːˈsɪsəs] *pl* -'**cis·sus·es,** -'**cis·si** [-saɪ] *s* ♀ Narzisse *f*.

nar·co·sis [nɑːˈkəʊsɪs] *pl* -**ses** [-siːz] *s* ⚕ Narkose *f*.

nar·cot·ic [nɑːˈkɒtɪk] **I** *adj* (*~ally*) **1.** narkotisch, betäubend, einschläfernd (*a. fig.*). **2.** Rauschgift...: **~ addiction** Rauschgiftsucht *f*. **II** *s* **3.** Narkotikum *n*, Betäubungsmittel *n*. **4.** *oft pl* Rauschgift *n*.

nark [nɑːk] *Br. sl.* **I** *s* (Polizei)Spitzel *m*. **II** *v/t* ärgern.

nar·rate [nəˈreɪt] *v/t* **1.** erzählen. **2.** berichten, schildern. **nar·ra·tion** *s* Erzählung *f*. **nar·ra·tive** ['nærətɪv] **I** *s* **1.** Erzählung *f*. **2.** Bericht *m*, Schilderung *f*. **II** *adj* **3.** erzählend: **~ perspective** Erzählperspektive *f*. **4.** Erzählungs...

nar·row ['nærəʊ] **I** *adj* □ **~ a. narrow·ly**) **1.** eng, schmal. **2.** eng (*a. fig.*), (*räumlich*) beschränkt: **in the ~est sense** im engsten Sinne. **3.** zs.-gekniffen (*Augen*). **4.** *fig.* eingeschränkt, beschränkt. **5.** *fig.* knapp, dürftig (*Einkommen etc*). **6.** *fig.* knapp (*Mehrheit, Sieg etc*): **by a ~ margin** knapp, mit knappem Vorsprung; **win by a ~ majority** knapp gewinnen; → **escape** 9, **squeak** 6. **7.** *fig.* gründlich, eingehend (*Untersuchung etc*). **II** *v/i* **8.** enger *od.* schmäler werden, sich verengen (*[in]to* zu): **his eyes ~ed to slits** s-e Augen wurden zu Schlitzen. **9.** *fig.* knapp(er) werden, zs.-schrumpfen (*to auf acc*). **10.** *fig.* sich annähern (*Standpunkte etc*). **III** *v/t* **11.** enger *od.* schmäler machen, verenge(r)n, *Augen* zs.-kneifen. **12.** *a.* **~ down** *fig.* be-, einschränken (*to auf acc*); eingrenzen. **'nar·row·ly** *adv* mit knapper Not: **he ~ escaped death** er ist gerade noch mit dem Leben davongekommen; **he ~ escaped drowning** er wäre beinahe *od.* um ein Haar ertrunken.

na·sal ['neɪzl] **I** *adj* □ **1.** *anat.* Nasen...: **~ bone** Nasenbein *n*. **2.** a) näselnd (*Stimme*): → **twang**, b) *ling.* nasal, Nasal... **II** *s* **3.** *ling.* Nasal(laut) *m*.

nas·ty ['nɑːstɪ] *adj* □ **1.** ekelhaft, eklig, widerlich (*Geschmack etc*); abscheulich (*Verbrechen, Wetter etc*). **2.** schmutzig, zotig (*Buch etc*). **3.** bös, schlimm (*Unfall etc*). **4.** a) häßlich (*Charakter, Benehmen etc*), b) gemein, fies (*Person,*

Trick etc), c) übelgelaunt: **turn ~** unangenehm werden. **II s 5.** *Br.* F *pornographische od. gewaltverherrlichende Videokassette.*

na·tal ['neɪtl] *adj* Geburts...

na·tion ['neɪʃn] *s* Nation *f:* a) Volk *n,* b) Staat *m.*

na·tion·al ['næʃənl] **I** *adj* □ **1.** national, National..., Landes..., Volks...: **~ anthem** Nationalhymne *f;* ~ **championship** (*Sport*) Landesmeisterschaft *f;* ~ **currency** ✝ Landeswährung *f;* ♀ **Guard** *Am.* Nationalgarde *f;* ~ **language** Landessprache *f;* ~ **park** Nationalpark *m;* ~ **team** (*Sport*) Nationalmannschaft *f.* **2.** staatlich, öffentlich, Staats...: ♀ **Health Service** *Br.* Staatlicher Gesundheitsdienst. **3.** national (*Streik etc*), überregional (*Sender, Zeitung etc*); inländisch: ~ **call** *teleph.* Inlandsgespräch *n.* **II s 4.** Staatsangehörige *m, f.* **na·tion·al·ism** ['næʃnəlɪzəm] *s* Nationalismus *m.* **'na·tion·al·ist I** *s* Nationalist(in). **II** *adj* nationalistisch. **na·tion·al·is·tic** *adj* (**~ally**) nationalistisch. **na·tion·al·i·ty** [ˌnæʃə'næləti] *s* Nationalität *f,* Staatsangehörigkeit *f:* **have French ~** die französische Staatsangehörigkeit besitzen *od.* haben. **na·tion·al·i·za·tion** [ˌnæʃnəlaɪ'zeɪʃn] *s* ✝ Verstaatlichung *f.* **'na·tion·al·ize** *v/t* ✝ verstaatlichen.

'na·tion-wide *adj u. adv* landesweit.

na·tive ['neɪtɪv] **I** *adj* □ **1.** eingeboren, Eingeborenen... **2.** einheimisch, inländisch, Landes... **3.** heimatlich, Heimat...: ~ **country** Heimat *f,* Vaterland *n;* ~ **language** Muttersprache *f;* ~ **speaker** Muttersprachler(in); ~ **speaker of English** englischer Muttersprachler; ~ **town** Heimat-, Vaterstadt *f.* **II s 4.** Eingeborene *m, f.* **5.** Einheimische *m, f:* **a ~ of London** ein gebürtiger Londoner; **are you a ~ here?** sind Sie von hier?

Na·tiv·i·ty [nə'tɪvəti] *s* die Geburt Christi (*a. Kunst*): ~ **play** Krippenspiel *n.*

nat·ter ['nætə] *bsd. Br.* F **I** *v/i* **1.** ~ **away** schwatzen, plaudern. **II** *s* Schwatz *m,* Plausch *m:* **have a ~** e-n Schwatz *od.* Plausch halten.

nat·u·ral ['nætʃrəl] **I** *adj* (□ → **naturally**) **1.** natürlich, Natur...: ~ **blonde** echte Blondine; **die a ~ death** e-s natürlichen

Todes sterben; ~ **disaster** Naturkatastrophe *f;* ~ **gas** Erdgas *n;* ~ **resources** *pl* Naturschätze *pl;* ~ **science** Naturwissenschaft *f;* ~ **scientist** Naturwissenschaftler(in). **2.** naturgemäß, -bedingt. **3.** angeboren, eigen (**to** *dat*): ~ **talent** natürliche Begabung. **4.** natürlich, selbstverständlich. **5.** natürlich, ungekünstelt (*Benehmen etc*). **6.** naturgetreu, natürlich wirkend. **7.** Natur..., Roh..., (*Lebensmittel*) naturbelassen. **8.** leiblich (*Eltern etc*). **II s 9.** ♩ Auflösungszeichen *n.* **10.** F Naturtalent *n* (*Person*). **'nat·u·ral·ism** *s* Naturalismus *m.* **'nat·u·ral·ist** *s* Naturalist(in). **ˌnat·u·ral·is·tic** *adj* (**~ally**) naturalistisch. **nat·u·ral·i·za·tion** [ˌnætʃrəlaɪ'zeɪʃn] *s* Naturalisierung *f,* Einbürgerung *f.* **'nat·u·ral·ize** *v/t* **1.** naturalisieren, einbürgern: **become ~d** *fig.* sich einbürgern (*Wort etc*). **2.** ♀, *zo.* heimisch machen: **become ~d** heimisch werden. **'nat·u·ral·ly** *adv* **1.** *a.* int natürlich. **2.** von Natur (aus). **3.** instinktiv, spontan: **learning comes ~ to him** das Lernen fällt ihm leicht. **4.** auf natürliche Wege.

na·ture ['neɪtʃə] *s* **1.** *allg.* Natur *f:* **back to ~** zurück zur Natur. **2.** Natur *f,* Wesen *n,* Veranlagung *f:* **by ~** von Natur (aus); **it is (in) her ~** es liegt in ihrem Wesen; → **alien** 3, **second**¹ 1. **3.** Art *f,* Sorte *f:* **of a grave ~** ernster Natur. **4.** (natürliche) Beschaffenheit.

naught·y ['nɔːtɪ] *adj* □ **1.** ungezogen, unartig. **2.** unanständig (*Witz etc*).

nau·se·a ['nɔːsjə] *s* Übelkeit *f,* Brechreiz *m.* **nau·se·ate** ['~sɪeɪt] *v/t* Übelkeit erregen in (*dat*); *fig.* anwidern.

nau·ti·cal ['nɔːtɪkl] *adj* nautisch, See(fahrts)...: ~ **mile** Seemeile *f.*

na·val ['neɪvl] *adj* **1.** Flotten..., Marine...: ~ **base** Flottenstützpunkt *m;* ~ **officer** Marineoffizier *m;* ~ **power** Seemacht *f;* ~ **review** Flottenparade *f.* **2.** See..., Schiffs...: ~ **battle** Seeschlacht *f.*

nave [neɪv] *s* △ Mittel-, Hauptschiff *n.*

na·vel ['neɪvl] *s anat.* Nabel *m, fig. a.* Mittelpunkt *m.* ~ **or·ange** *s* Navelorange *f.*

nav·i·ga·ble ['nævɪgəbl] *adj* ♣ schiffbar. **nav·i·gate** ['~geɪt] *v/i* **1.** ♣ befahren; durchfahren. **2.** ✈, ♣ steuern, lenken. **ˌnav·i'ga·tion** *s* **1.** Schiffahrt *f,* Seefahrt *f.* **2.** ✎, ⚓ Navigation *f.* '**nav-i·ga·tor** *s* ✎, ⚓ Navigator *m.*

nav·vy ['nævı] *s* Erd- *od.* Bauarbeiter *m.*

na·vy ['neıvı] *s* **1.** (Kriegs)Marine *f.* **2.** Kriegsflotte *f.* ~ **blue** *s* Marineblau *n.*

nay [neı] *s parl.* Gegen-, Neinstimme *f:* **the ~s have it** die Mehrheit ist dagegen.

near [nıə] **I** *adv* **1.** *a.* ~ **at hand** nahe, (ganz) in der Nähe. **2.** *a.* ~ **at hand** bevorstehend) (*Zeitpunkt etc*). **3.** nahezu, beinahe, fast: ~ *impossible*; *she came* ~ *to tears* sie war den Tränen nahe; → *nowhere* 1. **II** *adj* (□ → *near-ly* 4). nahe(gelegen): ♀ *East geogr.* der Nahe Osten. **5.** kurz, nahe (*Weg*). **6.** nahe (*Zukunft etc*). **7.** nahe (verwandt): *the ~est relations pl* die nächsten Verwandten *pl.* **8.** eng (befreundet): *a ~ friend* ein guter *od.* enger Freund. **9.** knapp: ~ *miss* ✎ Beinahezusammenstoß *m*; *that was a ~ thing* F das hätte ins Auge gehen können, das ist gerade noch einmal gutgegangen. **10.** genau, wörtlich (*Übersetzung etc*). **III** *prp* **11.** nahe (*dat*), in der Nähe von (*od. gen*): ~ *here* nicht weit von hier; hier in der Nähe. **IV** *v/t u. v/i* **12.** sich nähern, näherkommen (*dat*): *be ~ing completion* der Vollendung entgegengehen. ~**·by I** *adv* [ˌnıə'baı] in der Nähe. **II** *adj* ['nıəbaı] nahe(gelegen).

near·ly ['nıəlı] *adv* **1.** beinahe, fast. **2.** annähernd: *not* ~ bei weitem nicht, nicht annähernd.

ˌ**near**|'**sight·ed** *adj* □ ✎ kurzsichtig. ~'**sight·ed·ness** *s* Kurzsichtigkeit *f.*

neat [niːt] *adj* □ **1.** sauber: a) ordentlich, reinlich: *keep* ~ *et.* sauberhalten, b) übersichtlich, c) geschickt: *a ~ solution* e-e saubere *od.* elegante Lösung. **2.** pur: *drink one's whisky* ~; *two* ~ *whiskies* zwei Whisky pur.

neb·u·lous ['nebjʊləs] *adj* □ *fig.* verschwommen, nebelhaft.

nec·es·sar·i·ly ['nesəsərəlı] *adv* **1.** notwendigerweise. **2.** *not* ~ nicht unbedingt. '**nec·es·sar·y I** *adj* □ **1.** notwendig, nötig, erforderlich (*to, for* für): *it is* ~ *for me to do it* ich muß es tun; *a* ~ *evil* ein notwendiges Übel; *if* ~ nötigenfalls. **2.** unvermeidlich, zwangsläufig, notwendig (*Konsequenz etc*). **II** *s* **3.** *neces-saries pl of life* Lebensbedürfnisse *pl.*

ne·ces·si·tate [nı'sesıteıt] *v/t et.* notwendig *od.* erforderlich machen, erfordern: ~ *doing s.th.* es notwendig machen, et. zu tun. **ne·ces·si·ty** *s* **1.** Notwendigkeit *f:* *of* (*od. by*) ~ notgedrungen; *be under the* ~ *of doing s.th.* gezwungen sein, et. zu tun. **2.** (dringendes) Bedürfnis: *ne-cessities pl of life* lebensnotwendiger Bedarf; *be a* ~ *of life* lebensnotwendig sein. **3.** Not *f:* ~ *is the mother of invention* Not macht erfinderisch; *in case of* ~ im Notfall; → *virtue* 2.

neck [nek] **I** *s* **1.** Hals *m* (*a. e-r Flasche etc*): *be* ~ *and* ~ Kopf an Kopf liegen (*a. fig.*); *be up to one's* ~ *in debt* bis an den Hals in Schulden stecken; *it is* ~ *or nothing* es geht um alles *od.* nichts; *risk one's* ~ Kopf u. Kragen riskieren; *save one's* ~ den Kopf aus der Schlinge ziehen; *stick out one's* ~ einiges riskieren. **2.** Genick *n:* *break one's* ~ sich das Genick brechen; *get it in the* ~ F eins aufs Dach bekommen. **3.** → *neckline.* **4.** *gastr.* Halsstück *n* (*of lamb* vom Lamm). **II** *v/i* **5.** F knutschen, schmusen. ˌ~**-and-**'~ *adj:* ~ *race* Kopf-an-Kopf-Rennen *n* (*a. fig.*).

neck·lace ['nekləs] *s* Halskette *f.* **neck·let** ['~lıt] *s* Halskettchen *n.*

'**neck·line** *s* Ausschnitt *m* (*e-s Kleids etc*): *with a low* (*od. plunging*) ~ tief ausgeschnitten. '~·**tie** *s Am.* Krawatte *f*, Schlips *m.*

nec·tar ['nektə] *s* ⚕ Nektar *m.*

née, nee [neı] *adj bei Frauennamen*: geborene.

need [niːd] **I** *s* **1.** (*of, for*) (dringendes) Bedürfnis (nach), Bedarf *m* (an *dat*): *in* ~ *of help* hilfs-, hilfebedürftig; *in* ~ *of repair* reparaturbedürftig; *be in* ~ *of s.th.* et. dringend brauchen. **2.** Mangel *m* (*of, for* an *dat*). **3.** dringende Notwendigkeit: *there is no* ~ *for you to come* du brauchst nicht zu kommen. **4.** Not(lage) *f:* *if* ~ *be* nötigen-, notfalls. **5.** Armut *f*, Not *f:* *in* ~ in Not. **6.** *pl* Bedürfnisse *pl*, Erfordernisse *pl.* **II** *v/t* **7.** benötigen, brauchen: *your hair* ~*s cutting* du mußt dir wieder einmal die Haare schneiden lassen. **8.** erfordern. **III** *v/aux* **9.** brauchen, müssen: *she* ~ *not do it* sie braucht es nicht zu tun; *you* ~ *not have come* du hättest nicht zu kommen brauchen.

nee·dle ['niːdl] I s 1. *allg.* Nadel f, ⚙ a. Zeiger m: **a ~ in a haystack** *fig.* e-e Stecknadel im Heuhaufen. II v/t 2. F *j-n* aufziehen, hänseln (**about** wegen). 3. ~ **one's way through** sich (durch-) schlängeln durch.

need·less ['niːdlɪs] *adj* unnötig, überflüssig: ~ **to say** selbstverständlich, natürlich. '**need·less·ly** *adv* unnötig(er-weise).

'**nee·dle·work** s Hand-, Nadelarbeit f: **do ~** handarbeiten; ~ **magazine** Handarbeitsheft n.

neg [neg] s *phot.* F Negativ n.

ne·gate [nɪ'geɪt] v/t 1. verneinen. 2. *Wirkung etc* neutralisieren, aufheben. **ne'ga·tion** s 1. Verneinung f. 2. Neutralisierung f, Aufhebung f.

neg·a·tive ['negətɪv] I *adj* □ 1. negativ (a. ⚡, ⚗, ⚕ *etc*): a) verneinend: **he was ~** ⚕ sein Befund war negativ; ~ **pole** ⚡ Minuspol m; ~ **sign** Minuszeichen n, negatives Vorzeichen; b) abschlägig, ablehnend. II s 2. Verneinung f (a. *ling.*): **answer in the ~** verneinen; **his answer was in the ~** s-e Antwort fiel negativ aus. 3. abschlägige Antwort. 4. negative Eigenschaft. 5. *phot.* Negativ n.

ne·glect [nɪ'glekt] I v/t 1. vernachlässigen: ~**ed** ungepflegt (*Erscheinung etc*), verwahrlost (*Kind etc*). 2. es versäumen *od.* unterlassen (**doing, to do** zu tun). II s 3. Vernachlässigung f: **be in a state of ~** vernachlässigt *od.* verwahrlost sein. 4. Versäumnis n, Unterlassung f: ~ **of duty** Pflichtversäumnis n. **ne'glect·ful** [~fʊl] → **negligent** 1.

neg·li·gee, neg·li·gé(e) ['neglɪʒeɪ] s Negligé n.

neg·li·gence ['neglɪdʒəns] s 1. Nachlässigkeit f, Unachtsamkeit f: **dress with ~** sich nachlässig kleiden. 2. ⚖ Fahrlässigkeit f. '**neg·li·gent** *adj* □ 1. nachlässig, unachtsam: **be ~ of** *j-n, et.* vernachlässigen, *et.* außer acht lassen. 2. ⚖ fahrlässig. 3. lässig, salopp.

neg·li·gi·ble ['neglɪdʒəbl] *adj* □ 1. nebensächlich, unwesentlich. 2. geringfügig, unbedeutend, nicht der Rede wert.

ne·go·ti·a·ble [nɪ'gəʊʃjəbl] *adj* □ 1. ✝ verkäuflich; übertragbar, begebbar. 2. passier-, befahrbar (*Straße etc*).

ne·go·ti·ate [nɪ'gəʊʃɪeɪt] I v/i 1. verhan-

deln (**with** mit; **for, about, on** über *acc*): **negotiating skills** *pl* Verhandlungsgeschick n; **negotiating table** Verhandlungstisch m. II v/t 2. *Vertrag etc* aushandeln (**with** mit). 3. verhandeln über (*acc*). 4. ✝ verkaufen; *Wechsel* begeben. 5. *Straße etc* passieren, *Hindernis etc* überwinden, *Steigung etc* schaffen; *Musikstück etc* meistern. **ne·go·ti'a·tion** s 1. Verhandlung f: **by way of ~** auf dem Verhandlungsweg; **it is still under ~** darüber wird noch verhandelt. 2. Aushandeln n. 3. ✝ Verkauf m; Begebung f. 4. Passieren n, Überwindung f.

Ne·gress ['niːgrɪs] s Negerin f. **Ne·gro** ['~grəʊ] *pl* -**groes** s Neger m.

neigh [neɪ] I v/i wiehern. II s Wiehern n.

neigh·bo(u)r ['neɪbə] s Nachbar(in): ~ **at table** Tischnachbar(in). II v/t (a. v/i ~ **on**) (an)grenzen an (*acc*). **neigh·bo(u)r·hood** ['~hʊd] s 1. Nachbarschaft f, *coll. a.* Nachbarn *pl*: **in the ~ of** in der Umgebung *od.* Gegend von (*od. gen*); *fig.* um (... herum). 2. Gegend f, Viertel n. '**neigh·bo(u)r·ing** *adj* benachbart, angrenzend; Nachbar... '**neigh·bo(u)r·ly** *adj* 1. (gut)nachbarlich. 2. Nachbarschafts...: → **help.**

nei·ther ['naɪðə] I *adj u. pron* 1. kein (von beiden): ~ **of you** keiner von euch (beiden). II *cj* 2. ~ ... **nor** weder ... noch. 3. auch nicht: **he does not know, ~ do I** er weiß es nicht, u. ich auch nicht.

ne·ol·o·gism [niː'ɒlədʒɪzəm] s *ling.* Neologismus m, Neuwort n.

ne·on ['niːɒn] s 🜚 Neon n: ~ **lamp** Neonlampe f; ~ **sign** 🜚 Neon-, Leuchtreklame f.

neph·ew ['nevjuː] s Neffe m.

ne·phri·tis [nɪ'fraɪtɪs] s ⚕ Nierenentzündung f.

nep·o·tism ['nepətɪzəm] s Vetternwirtschaft f.

nerve [nɜːv] I s 1. Nerv m: **get on s.o.'s ~s** j-m auf die Nerven gehen *od.* fallen; **get ~s** F Nerven bekommen; **have ~s of iron** (**steel**) eiserne Nerven (Nerven aus Stahl) haben; **hit** (*od.* **touch**) **a ~** e-n wunden Punkt treffen; **bag** (*od.* **bundle**) **of ~s** F Nervenbündel n. 2. *fig.* Stärke f, Energie f; Mut m; Selbstbeherrschung f; F Frechheit f: **have the ~ to do s.th.** den Nerv haben, et. zu tun; **lose one's ~** den Mut *od.* die Nerven verlieren. **II** *v/t* **3.** ~ *o.s.* sich moralisch *od.* seelisch vorbereiten (**for** auf *acc*). ~ **cell** *s* Nervenzelle *f.* ~ **cen·tre** (*Am.* **cen·ter**) *s* **1.** Nervenzentrum *n.* **2.** *fig.* Schaltzentrale *f.*

nerve·less ['nɜːvlɪs] *adj* □ **1.** kraft-, energielos; mutlos. **2.** ohne Nerven, kaltblütig. **'nerve-,rack·ing** *adj* nervenaufreibend.

nerv·ous ['nɜːvəs] *adj* □ **1.** Nerven..., nervös: ~ *system* Nervensystem *n*; → *breakdown* 1, *collapse* 10. **2.** nervös: *make s.o.* ~ j-n nervös machen (**with** mit). **'nerv·ous·ness** *s* Nervosität *f.*

nerv·y ['nɜːvɪ] *adj* □ F **1.** *Br.* nervös, ängstlich. **2.** *Am.* frech, unverfroren.

nest [nest] **I** *s* **1.** *orn., zo.* Nest *n*: → *feather* II, *foul* 9. **2.** *fig.* Brutstätte *f.* **3.** Serie *f,* Satz *m* (*ineinanderpassender Dinge*). **II** *v/i* **4.** nisten. ~**egg** *s* **1.** Nestei *n.* **2.** *fig.* Spar-, Notgroschen *m.*

nes·tle ['nesl] **I** *v/i* **1.** *a.* ~ *down* sich behaglich niederlassen, es sich bequem machen (**in** in *dat*). **2.** sich schmiegen *od.* kuscheln (**against, to** an *acc*). **II** *v/t* **3.** schmiegen, kuscheln (**against, to** an *acc*).

net¹ [net] **I** *s* **1.** Netz *n* (*a. fig.*): ~ *curtain* Store *m.* **II** *v/t* **2.** mit e-m Netz fangen. **3.** *fig.* einfangen. **4.** mit e-m Netz abdecken.

net² [~] **✝** **I** *adj* **1.** netto, Netto..., Rein... **II** *v/t* **2.** netto einbringen. **3.** netto verdienen *od.* einnehmen.

net·ting ['netɪŋ] *s* Netz(werk) *n,* Geflecht *n.*

net·tle ['netl] **I** *s* **✿** Nessel *f:* *grasp the* ~ *fig.* den Stier bei den Hörnern packen. **II** *v/t* ärgern, reizen (**with** mit). ~ *rash* *s* **✚** Nesselausschlag *m.*

'net·work *s* **1.** Netz(werk) *n,* Geflecht *n.* **2.** *fig.* (*Händler-, Straßen- etc*) Netz *n*: *social* ~ soziales Netz. **3.** *Rundfunk, TV:* Sendernetz *n.*

neu·ral·gia [ˌnjuəˈrældʒə] *s* **✚** Neuralgie *f.* **,neu·ral·gic** *adj* (**~ally**) neuralgisch.

neu·ri·tis [ˌnjuəˈraɪtɪs] *s* **✚** Nervenentzündung *f.*

neu·ro·log·i·cal [ˌnjuərəˈlɒdʒɪkl] *adj* ✚ neurologisch. **neu·rol·o·gist** [ˌ~ˈrɒl-ədʒɪst] *s* Neurologe *m,* Nervenarzt *m.* **,neu·rol·o·gy** *s* Neurologie *f.*

neu·ro·sis [ˌnjuəˈrəʊsɪs] *pl* **-ses** [~siːz] *s* ✚ Neurose *f.* **neu·rot·ic** [ˌ~ˈrɒtɪk] **I** *adj*

(**~ally**) neurotisch (*a. contp.*). **II** *s* Neurotiker(in).

neu·ter ['njuːtə] *adj* **1.** *ling.* neutral, sächlich. **2.** *biol.* geschlechtslos, ungeschlechtlich. **II** *s* **3.** *ling.* Neutrum *n.* **III** *v/t* **4.** *zo.* kastrieren.

neu·tral ['njuːtrəl] **I** *adj* □ **1.** *allg.* neutral. **II** *s* **2.** Neutrale *m, f.* **3.** *mot.* Leerlaufstellung *f:* *the car is in* ~ es ist kein Gang eingelegt; *put the car in* ~ den Gang herausnehmen. **neu·tral·i·ty** [~ˈtræləti] *s* Neutralität *f.* **neu·tral·i·za·tion** [ˌ~trəlaɪˈzeɪʃn] *s* Neutralisierung *f, a.* **⚛** Neutralisation *f.* **'neu·tral·ize** *v/t* neutralisieren: ~ *each other* sich gegenseitig aufheben.

neu·tron ['njuːtrɒn] *s phys.* Neutron *n:* ~ *bomb* **✗** Neutronenbombe *f.*

nev·er ['nevə] *adv* **1.** nie(mals): → *die¹* 1. **2.** durchaus nicht, ganz u. gar nicht: → *mind* 10. **'~,end·ing** *adj* endlos, nicht enden wollend. **,~'nev·er** *s:* *buy s.th. on the* ~ *Br.* F et. auf Pump od. Stottern kaufen.

,nev·er·the'less *adv* nichtsdestoweniger, dennoch, trotzdem.

new [njuː] *adj* (□ → *newly*) *allg.* neu: *nothing* ~ nichts Neues; *this is not* ~ *to me* das ist mir nichts Neues; *be* ~ *to s.o.* j-m neu *od.* ungewohnt sein; *be* ~ *to s.th.* (noch) nicht vertraut sein mit et.; *feel a* ~ *man* sich wie neugeboren fühlen; ~ *moon* Neumond *m*; ~ *publications* *pl* Neuerscheinungen *pl*; ~ *snow* Neuschnee *m*; **♀** *Testament* das Neue Testament; **♀** *World* die Neue Welt; ~ *broom, leaf* 2. **'~·born** *adj* neugeboren. **'~,com·er** *s* **1.** Neuankömmling *m.* **2.** Neuling *m* (*to* auf *od.* e-m Gebiet). **~·fan·gled** [ˌ~ˈfæŋgld] *adj contp.* neumodisch.

new·ly ['njuːlɪ] *adv* **1.** kürzlich, jüngst: ~ *married* jungverheiratet, -vermählt. **2.** neu: ~ *arranged furniture* umgestellte Möbel *pl*; ~ *raised hope* neuerweckte Hoffnung. **'~·weds** *s pl* die Jungverheirateten *pl od.* -vermählten *pl.*

news [njuːz] *s pl* (*sg konstruiert*) Neuigkeit(en *pl*) *f,* Nachricht(en *pl*) *f:* *a bit* (*od. piece*) *of* ~ e-e Neuigkeit *od.* Nachricht; *at this* ~ bei dieser Nachricht; *what's the* ~? was gibt es Neues?; *this is* ~ *to me* das ist mir (ganz) neu; *have* ~ *from s.o.* Nachricht von j-m haben; **I**

haven't had any ~ from her for two months ich habe schon seit zwei Monaten nichts mehr von ihr gehört; *I heard it on the ~* ich hörte es in den Nachrichten. **~ a·gen·cy** s Nachrichtenagentur f. **'~‚a·gent** s Zeitungshändler(in). **black·out** s Nachrichtensperre f: *order a ~ on* e-e Nachrichtensperre verhängen über (acc). **'~‚boy** s Zeitungsjunge m. **'~‚cast** s Rundfunk, TV: Nachrichtensendung f. **'~‚cast·er** s Rundfunk, TV: Nachrichtensprecher(in). **~ con·fer·ence** → **press conference**. **~ deal·er** s Am. Zeitungshändler(in). **~ flash** s Rundfunk, TV: Kurzmeldung f. **'~‚let·ter** s Rundschreiben n, Mitteilungsblatt n. **~ mag·a·zine** s Nachrichtenmagazin n. **~‚pa·per** ['nju:s‚peɪpə] s Zeitung f: **~ publisher** Zeitungsverleger(in); **~ rack** Zeitungsständer m. **'~‚read·er** Br. → **newscaster**. **'~‚stand** s Zeitungskiosk m, -stand m. **~ ven·dor** s Zeitungsverkäufer(in).

new| year s oft **New Year** das neue Jahr: *happy New Year!* gutes neues Jahr!, Prosit Neujahr! ♀ **Year's Day** s Neujahr(stag m) n. ♀ **Year's Eve** s Silvester(abend m) m, n.

next [nekst] **I** adj **1.** allg. nächst: *(the) ~ day* am nächsten Tag; *the ~ room* nebenan, im nächsten Raum od. Haus; *be ~ door to* fig. grenzen an (acc); *~ month* nächsten Monat; *~ time* das nächste Mal; *~ but one* übernächst: *~ to* gleich neben (dat od. acc); gleich nach (Rang, Reihenfolge); beinahe, fast *unmöglich etc*, so gut wie *nichts etc*, praktisch *zwecklos etc*. **II** adv **2.** als nächste(r, -s): *you will be ~* du wirst der nächste sein. **3.** demnächst, das nächste Mal. **4.** dann, darauf. **III** s **5.** der, die, das nächste: *the next of kin* die nächsten Angehörigen pl od. Verwandten pl. **‚~'door** adj (von) nebenan: *we are ~ neighbo(u)rs* wir wohnen Tür an Tür.

NHS [‚eneɪtʃ'es] Br. **I** s Staatlicher Gesundheitsdienst: *get s.th. on the ~* et. auf Krankenschein od. Rezept bekommen. **II** adj a) Kassen...: *~ glasses*, b) Behandlung etc auf Krankenschein: *~ treatment*.

nib·ble ['nɪbl] **I** v/t **1.** knabbern an (dat). **2.** Loch etc knabbern, nagen (in in acc). **II** v/i **3.** knabbern (at an dat): *~ at one's*

food im Essen herumstochern. **III** s **4.** Knabbern n.

nice [naɪs] adj **1.** fein (Unterschied etc). **2.** fein, lecker (Speise etc). **3.** nett, freundlich (to zu j-m). **4.** nett, hübsch, schön: *~ and warm* schön warm; → **mess** 1. **'nice·ly** adv **1.** gut, fein: *that will do ~* das genügt vollauf; das paßt ausgezeichnet; *she is doing ~* es geht ihr gut od. besser, sie macht gute Fortschritte. **2.** genau, sorgfältig. **ni·ce·ty** ['~sətɪ] s **1.** Feinheit f. **2.** peinliche Genauigkeit: *to a ~* peinlich od. äußerst genau. **3.** pl feine Unterschiede pl, Feinheiten pl.

niche [nɪtʃ] s **1.** Nische f. **2.** fig. Platz m, wo man hingehört: *he has finally found his ~ in life* er hat endlich s-n Platz im Leben gefunden.

nick [nɪk] **I** s **1.** Kerbe f, Einkerbung f. **2.** *in the ~ of time* gerade noch rechtzeitig, im letzten Moment. **3.** Br. F Kittchen n: *in the ~* im Kittchen. **4.** *be in good ~* Br. F gut in Schuß sein. **II** v/t **5.** a) (ein)kerben: *~ o.s. while shaving* sich beim Rasieren schneiden, b) j-n streifen (Kugel). **6.** Br. F klauen. **7.** Br. F j-n schnappen. **8.** *~ s.o. (for) $100* Am. F j-m 100 Dollar abknöpfen.

nick·el ['nɪkl] **I** s **1.** 🜍, min. Nickel n. **2.** Am. Fünfcentstück n. **II** v/t pret u. pp **-eled**, bsd. Br. **-elled 3.** vernickeln. **'~‚plate** v/t vernickeln.

nick·name ['nɪkneɪm] **I** s Spitzname m. **II** v/t j-m den Spitznamen ... geben.

nic·o·tine ['nɪkəti:n] s Nikotin n.

niece [ni:s] s Nichte f.

niff [nɪf] s Br. F Gestank m. **'niff·y** adj Br. F stinkend: *be ~* stinken.

nif·ty ['nɪftɪ] adj □ F **1.** flott, fesch (Kleidung, Person). **2.** praktisch (Gerät).

nig·gard ['nɪgəd] s Knicker(in), Geizhals m. **'nig·gard·ly** adj **1.** geizig, knick(e)rig. **2.** schäbig, kümmerlich.

nig·gle ['nɪgl] v/i **1.** herumnörgeln (about, over an dat). **2.** ~ at fig. nagen an (dat), plagen, quälen.

night [naɪt] s **1.** Nacht f: *at (od. by, in the) ~* in der od. bei Nacht, nachts; *~ and day* Tag u. Nacht; *have a good (bad) ~* gut (schlecht) schlafen; *make a ~ of it* bis zum Morgen feiern, durchmachen; *stay the ~* übernachten (at in dat; at s.o.'s bei j-m). **2.** Abend m: *last ~* gestern abend; *the ~ before last* vorgestern nacht; *on the ~ of May 5th* am Abend des 5. Mai. **3.** Nacht *f*, Dunkelheit *f*. **~ bird** *s* **1.** *orn.* Nachtvogel *m.* **2.** *fig.* Nachtmensch *m*; Nachtschwärmer *m.* '**~blind** *adj* **𝄐** nachtblind. **~ blindness** *s* **𝄐** Nachtblindheit *f.* '**~cap** *s* Schlummertrunk *m.* '**~club** *s* Nachtklub *m*, -lokal *n.* '**~dress** *s* Nachthemd *n.* '**~fall** *s*: *at ~* bei Einbruch der Dunkelheit. **~ flight** *s* Nachtflug *m.* '**~gown** *s* Nachthemd *n.*

night·ie ['naɪtɪ] *s* F Nachthemd *n.*

night-in·gale ['naɪtɪŋɡeɪl] *s orn.* Nachtigall *f.*

night life *s* Nachtleben *n.*

night·ly ['naɪtlɪ] **I** *adj* (all)nächtlich; (all)abendlich. **II** *adv* jede Nacht; jeden Abend.

night·mare ['naɪtmeə] *s* Alptraum *m* (*a. fig.*).

night nurse *s* Nachtschwester *f.* **~ owl** *s* F Nachteule *f*, -mensch *m*; Nachtschwärmer *m.* **~ por·ter** *s* Nachtportier *m.* **~ school** *s* Abendschule *f.* **~ shift** *s* Nachtschicht *f*: *be* (*od. work*) *on a ~* Nachtschicht haben. '**~shirt** *s* Nachthemd *n.* '**~spot** *s* F *nightclub.* '**~stick** *s Am.* Gummiknüppel *m*, Schlagstock *m* (*der Polizei*). '**~time** *s*: *in the* (*od. at*) *~* zur Nachtzeit, nachts. **~ watch** *s* Nachtwache *f.* **~ watch·man** *s* (*irr man*) Nachtwächter *m.*

ni·hil·ism ['naɪlɪzəm] *s* Nihilismus *m.* '**ni·hil·ist** *s* **I** *s* Nihilist(in). **II** *adj* nihilistisch. **,ni·hil'is·tic** *adj* (**~ally**) nihilistisch.

nil [nɪl] *s*: *our team won three to ~* (*od. by three goals to ~*) (*3-0*) unsere Mannschaft gewann drei zu null (3 : 0).

nim·bi ['nɪmbaɪ] *pl von* **nimbus.**

nim·ble ['nɪmbl] *adj* □ **1.** flink, gewandt. **2.** *fig.* geistig beweglich: *~ mind* beweglicher Geist.

nim·bus ['nɪmbəs] *pl* **-bi** ['~baɪ], **-bus·es** *s* Nimbus *m*, Heiligenschein *m.*

nin·com·poop ['nɪŋkəmpuːp] *s* Einfaltspinsel *m*, Trottel *m.*

nine [naɪn] **I** *adj* neun: *~ times out of ten* in neun von zehn Fällen, fast immer; → **wonder 5.** **II** *s* Neun *f*: *~ of hearts* Herzneun *f*; *be dressed* (*up*) *to the ~s* F in Schale sein. **nine·fold** ['~fəʊld] **I** *adj* neunfach. **II** *adv* neunfach, um das Neunfache: *increase ~* (sich) verneun-

fachen. **nine·teen** [,~'tiːn] *adj* neunzehn: → **dozen. ,nine'teenth** [~θ] *adj* neunzehnt. **nine·ti·eth** ['~tɪɪθ] *adj* neunzigst. '**nine·time** *adj* neunmalig. **nine·ty** ['naɪntɪ] **I** *adj* neunzig. **II** *s* Neunzig *f*: *be in one's nineties* in den Neunzigern sein; *in the nineties* in den neunziger Jahren (*e-s Jahrhunderts*).

nin·ny ['nɪnɪ] *s* F Dussel *m*, Dummkopf *m.*

ninth [naɪnθ] **I** *adj* **1.** neunt. **II** *s* **2.** *der, die, das* Neunte: *the ~ of May* der 9. Mai. **3.** Neuntel *n.* '**ninth·ly** *adv* neuntens.

nip[1] [nɪp] **I** *v/t* **1.** kneifen, zwicken: *~ off* abzwicken; *~ one's finger in the door* sich den Finger in der Tür einzwicken. **2.** *Pflanzen schädigen* (*Frost etc*): → **bud** I. **II** *v/i* **3.** *bsd. Br.* F sausen, flitzen: *~ in mot.* einscheren. **III** *s* **4.** *there's a ~ in the air today* heute ist es ganz schön kalt. **5.** Kniff *m.*

nip[2] [~] *s* Schlückchen *n* (*Whisky etc*).

nip·pers ['nɪpəz] *s pl*, *a.* **pair of ~** (Kneif)Zange *f.*

nip·ple ['nɪpl] *s* **1.** *anat.* Brustwarze *f.* **2.** (Gummi)Sauger *m* (*e-r Saugflasche*). **3.** **⊙** (*Schmier*)Nippel *m.*

nip·py ['nɪpɪ] *adj* **1.** frisch, kühl, kalt. **2.** *be ~ bsd. Br.* F sich beeilen.

nit [nɪt] *s zo.* Nisse *f*, Niß *f.*

ni·ter *Am.* → **nitre.**

'**nit**|**,pick·er** *s* F pingeliger *od.* kleinlicher Mensch. '**~,pick·ing** *adj* F pingelig, kleinlich.

ni·trate ['naɪtreɪt] *s* **🜶** Nitrat *n.*

ni·tre ['naɪtə] *s bsd. Br.* **🜶** Salpeter *m.*

ni·tric ac·id ['naɪtrɪk] *s* **🜶** Salpetersäure *f.*

ni·tro·gen ['naɪtrədʒən] *s* **🜶** Stickstoff *m.* **ni·trog·e·nous** [~'trɒdʒɪnəs] *adj* stickstoffhaltig.

ni·tro·glyc·er·in(e) [,naɪtrəʊ'ɡlɪsəriːn] *s* **🜶** Nitroglyzerin *n.*

nit·ty-grit·ty [,nɪtɪ'ɡrɪtɪ] *s*: *go down* (*od. come*) *to the ~* sl. zur Sache kommen.

nit·wit ['nɪtwɪt] *s* Schwachkopf *m.*

no [nəʊ] **I** *adv* **1.** nein: *say ~ to* nein sagen zu. **2.** *beim comp*: um nichts, nicht: *they ~ longer live here* sie wohnen nicht mehr hier; *~ longer ago than yesterday* erst gestern. **II** *adj* **3.** kein: *~ one* keiner, niemand; *in ~ time* im Nu od. Handumdrehen. **4.** *vor ger*: → **deny 1,**

please 4. **III** pl **noes** s 5. Nein n: **a clear ~** ein klares Nein (**to** auf acc). **6.** parl. Gegen-, Neinstimme f: **the ~es have it** der Antrag ist abgelehnt.

No·bel prize [nəʊ'bel] s Nobelpreis m: **Nobel peace prize** Friedensnobelpreis; **~ winner** Nobelpreisträger(in).

no·bil·i·ty [nəʊ'bɪlətɪ] s 1. (Hoch)Adel m. **2.** fig. Adel m.

no·ble ['nəʊbl] adj □ **1.** adlig, von Adel. **2.** fig. edel, nobel. **3.** prächtig, stattlich (Gebäude etc). **4.** Edel...: **~ metal**. **~·man** ['~mən] s (irr man) (hoher) Adliger. **'~·wom·an** s (irr woman) (hohe) Adlige.

no·bod·y ['nəʊbədɪ] **I** pron keiner, niemand. **II** s fig. Niemand m, Null f.

noc·tur·nal [nɒk'tɜːnl] adj □ nächtlich, Nacht...

nod [nɒd] **I** v/i 1. nicken: **~ at** (od. **to**) s.o. j-m zunicken; **have a ~ding acquaintance with s.o.** j-n flüchtig kennen. **2. ~ off** einnicken. **II** v/t 3. **~ one's head** mit dem Kopf nicken. **III** s 4. Nicken n: **give a ~** nicken; **give s.o. a ~** j-m zunikken.

node [nəʊd] s Knoten m (a. 🏵).

nod·ule ['nɒdjuːl] s ♀, ✦ Knötchen n.

noise [nɔɪz] **I** s **1.** Krach m, Lärm m: **not to make any ~** keinen Krach machen; **make a lot of ~ about s.th.** fig. viel Tamtam um et. machen. **2.** Geräusch n: **what's that ~?** was ist das für ein Geräusch? **3.** Radio etc: Rauschen n. **II** v/t 4. **~ about** (od. **abroad**, **around**) Gerücht etc verbreiten: **it is being ~d about that** man erzählt sich, daß. **'noise·less** adj □ geräuschlos.

nois·y ['nɔɪzɪ] adj □ laut.

no·mad ['nəʊmæd] s Nomade m, Nomadin f. **no'mad·ic** adj (**~ally**) nomadisch, Nomaden...

'no-man's-land s Niemandsland n (a. fig.).

no·men·cla·ture [nəʊ'menklətʃə] s **1.** Nomenklatur f. **2.** (Fach)Terminologie f.

nom·i·nal ['nɒmɪnl] adj □ **1.** nominal, nominell (beide a. ✦): **~ income** Nominaleinkommen n; **~ value** Nominalwert m. **2.** ling. nominal, Nominal...

nom·i·nate ['nɒmɪneɪt] v/t **1.** (**to**) ernennen (zu), einsetzen in (acc): **be ~d** (as od. **to be**) ... als ... eingesetzt werden. **2.**

(**for**) nominieren (für), vorschlagen (als), als Kandidaten aufstellen (für).

,nom·i'na·tion s **1.** Ernennung f, Einsetzung f. **2.** Nominierung f: **place s.o.'s name in ~** j-n vorschlagen.

nom·i·na·tive ['nɒmɪnətɪv] s a. **~ case** ling. Nominativ m, erster Fall.

non... [nɒn] nicht..., Nicht..., un...

,non·ac'cept·ance s Annahmeverweigerung f, Nichtannahme f.

,non·ag'gres·sion pact s pol. Nichtangriffspakt m.

,non·al·co'hol·ic adj alkoholfrei.

,non·a'ligned adj pol. blockfrei.

,non·ap'pear·ance s Nichterscheinen n (vor Gericht etc).

,non·at'tend·ance s Nichtteilnahme f.

nonce word [nɒns] s ling. Ad-hoc-Bildung f.

non·cha·lance ['nɒnʃələns] s Nonchalance f, Lässigkeit f, Unbekümmertheit f. **'non·cha·lant** adj □ nonchalant, lässig, unbekümmert.

,non·com'mis·sioned adj: **~ officer** ✗ Unteroffizier m.

,non·com'mit·tal [~tl] adj □ zurückhaltend, (Antwort etc) unverbindlich: **be ~** sich nicht festlegen wollen.

,non·com'pli·ance s (**with**) Zuwiderhandlung f (gegen), Nichtbefolgung f (gen).

non com·pos men·tis [,nɒn'kɒmpəs'mentɪs] adj ⚖ unzurechnungsfähig.

,non·con'form·ist I s Nonkonformist (-in). **II** adj nonkonformistisch. **,non·con'form·i·ty** s mangelnde Übereinstimmung (**with** mit).

non·de·script ['nɒndɪskrɪpt] adj unbestimmbar; unauffällig.

none [nʌn] **I** pron u. s (mst pl konstruiert) kein, niemand: **~ of them are** (od. **is**) **here** keiner von ihnen ist hier; **~ of your tricks!** laß deine Späße!; **~ but** niemand od. nichts außer, nur; → **business** 6. **II** adv in keiner Weise, nicht im geringsten: **~ too high** keineswegs zu hoch; **~ too soon** kein bißchen zu früh.

non·en·ti·ty [nɒ'nentətɪ] s contp. Null f (Person).

,non·es'sen·tial adj unwesentlich (**to** für).

,none·the'less adv nichtsdestoweniger, dennoch, trotzdem.

,non·e'vent s F Reinfall m, Pleite f.

,non·ex·ist·ence *s* Nichtvorhandensein *n*, Fehlen *n*. ,non·ex·ist·ent *adj* nicht existierend.

,non·fic·tion *s* Sachbücher *pl*.

,non·ful·fil(l)·ment *s* Nichterfüllung *f*.

'non,in·ter·fer·ence, 'non,in·ter·ven·tion *s pol*. Nichteinmischung *f*.

,non·i·ron *adj* bügelfrei.

'non,mem·ber *s* Nichtmitglied *n*.

,non·ob·serv·ance *s* Nichtbefolgung *f*, -beachtung *f*.

,no-'non·sense *adj* nüchtern, sachlich, (*Warnung*) unmißverständlich.

,non·par·ti·san *adj* **1.** *pol.* überparteilich. **2.** unparteiisch.

,non·pay·ment *s bsd.* ✝ Nicht(be)zahlung *f*.

,non·plus *v/t pret u. pp* -'plused, *bsd. Br.* -'plussed verblüffen.

,non·pol·lut·ing *adj* umweltfreundlich.

,non·prof·it *adj Am.*, ,non-'prof·it-,mak·ing *adj* gemeinnützig.

'non·pro,lif·er·a·tion *s pol.* Nichtweitergabe *f* von Atomwaffen. **~ treaty** Atomsperrvertrag *m*.

,non·res·i·dent **I** *adj* **1.** nicht (orts)ansässig. **2.** nicht im Hause wohnend. **II** *s* **3.** Nichtansässige *m, f*. **4.** nicht im Hause Wohnende *m, f*.

,non-re'turn·a·ble *adj* Einweg...: **~ bottle.**

non·sense *s* **1.** Unsinn *m*, dummes Zeug (*auch* **~**): *make* (*a*) **~** *of* ad absurdum führen; illusorisch machen; *stand no* **~** sich nichts gefallen lassen, nicht mit sich spaßen lassen. **non·sen·si·cal** [~'sensıkl] *adj* □ unsinnig.

,non'smok·er *s* **1.** Nichtraucher(in). **2.** 🚃 *Br.* Nichtraucherwagen *m*. ,non-'smok·ing *adj*: **~ compartment** 🚃 Nichtraucher(abteil *n*) *m*.

,non'stan·dard *adj ling.* nicht hochsprachlich.

,non'start·er *s*: *be a* **~** keine *od.* kaum e-e Chance haben (*Person, Sache*).

,non'stick *adj* mit Antihaftbeschichtung (*Pfanne etc*).

,non'stop **I** *adj* durchgehend (*Zug etc*), ohne Unterbrechung (*Reise etc*), ohne Zwischenlandung (*Flug*): **~ flight** *a.* Nonstopflug *m*. **II** *adv* nonstop, ohne Unterbrechung *od.* Zwischenlandung: *talk* **~** ununterbrochen reden.

,non'un·ion *adj* ✝ nicht organisiert.

,non'vi·o·lence *s* Gewalttosigkeit *f*. ,non'vi·o·lent *adj* □ gewaltlos.

noo·dle ['nu:dl] *s* Nudel *f*: **~ soup** Nudelsuppe *f*.

nook [nʊk] *s* Winkel *m*, Ecke *f*: *search for s.th. in every* **~** *and cranny* nach et. in jedem Winkel *od.* in allen Ecken suchen.

noon [nu:n] **I** *s* Mittag(szeit *f*) *m*: *at* **~** am *od.* zu Mittag, *eng S.* um 12 Uhr (mittags). **II** *adj* mittägig, Mittags...

noose [nu:s] *s* Schlinge *f*: *put one's head in(to) the* **~** *fig.* den Kopf in die Schlinge stecken.

nope [nəʊp] *adv* F nein.

nor [nɔ:] *cj* **1.** → *neither* 2. **2.** auch nicht: *he does not know,* **~** *do I* er weiß es nicht, u. ich auch nicht.

norm [nɔ:m] *s* Norm *f*. **nor·mal** ['~ml] *adj* (□ → *normally*) normal, Normal... **II** *s* Normalzustand *m*: *be back to* **~** sich normalisiert haben, wieder normal sein; *go back* (*od. return*) *to* **~** sich normalisieren; *be above* (*below*) **~** über (unter) dem Durchschnitt *od.* Normalwert liegen. **nor·mal·ize** ['~məlaız] **I** *v/t* **1.** normalisieren. **2.** normen, vereinheitlichen. **II** *v/i* **3.** sich normalisieren. **nor·mal·ly** ['~məlı] *adv* normalerweise, (für) gewöhnlich.

Nor·man ['nɔ:mən] **I** *s hist.* Normanne *m*, Normannin *f*. **II** *adj* normannisch.

nor·ma·tive ['nɔ:mətıv] *adj* □ normativ.

north [nɔ:θ] **I** *s* **1.** Norden *m*: *in the* **~** *of* im Norden von (*od. gen*); *to the* **~** *of* → 5. **2.** *a.* 2 Norden *m*, nördlicher Landesteil: *the* 2 *Br.* Nordengland *n*; *Am.* die Nordstaaten *pl*. **II** *adj* **3.** Nord..., nördlich: 2 *Pole* Nordpol *m*; 2 *Star ast.* Polarstern *m*. **III** *adv* **4.** nordwärts, nach Norden. **5.** **~** *of* nördlich von (*od. gen*). '**~·bound** *adj* nach Norden gehend *od.* fahrend. ,**~'east I** *s* Nordosten *m*. **II** *adj* nordöstlich, Nordost... **III** *adv* nordöstlich, nach Nordosten.

north·er·ly ['nɔ:ðəlı] **I** *adj* nördlich, Nord... **II** *adv* von *od.* nach Norden.

north·ern ['~ðn] *adj* nördlich, Nord... **north·ern·er** ['~ðənə] *s* **1.** Bewohner(in) des Nordens (*e-s Landes*). **2.** 2 *Am.* Nordstaatler(in). **north·ern·most** ['~ðənməʊst] *adj* nördlichst. **north·ward** ['~wəd] *adj u. adv* nördlich, nordwärts, nach Norden: *in a* **~** *direction* in nördlicher Richtung, Richtung Norden. '**north·wards** adv → **northward.**

,**north·west I** s Nordwesten m. **II** adj nordwestlich, Nordwest. — **III** adv nordwestlich, nach Nordwesten.

Nor·we·gian [nɔːˈwiːdʒən] **I** adj **1.** norwegisch. **II** s **2.** Norweger(in). **3.** ling. Norwegisch n.

nose [nəʊz] **I** s **1.** Nase f: **bite** (od. **snap**) **s.o.'s ~ off** j-n anschnauzen; **cut off one's ~ to spite one's face** sich ins eigene Fleisch schneiden; **follow one's ~** immer der Nase nach gehen; s-m Instinkt folgen; **lead s.o. by the ~** j-n unter s-r Fuchtel haben; **look down one's ~ at** die Nase rümpfen über (acc), auf j-n, et. herabblicken; **poke** (od. **put, stick, thrust**) **one's ~ into** s-e Nase stecken in (acc); **put s.o.'s ~ out of joint** j-n ausstechen; j-n vor den Kopf stoßen; **under s.o.'s (very)** ~ direkt vor j-s Nase; vor j-s Augen; → **grindstone, pick** 7, **rub** 3. **2.** fig. Nase f, Riecher m (for für). **3.** bsd. ⊕ Nase f, Vorsprung m: ✈ Bug m; ✈ Nase f. **II** v/t **4.** Auto etc vorsichtig fahren. **5.** ~ **out** fig. ausschnüffeln. **III** v/i **6.** ~ **up** fig. herumschnüffeln (in dat) (**for** nach). '**~·bleed** s Nasenbluten n: **have a ~** Nasenbluten haben. ~ **dive** s ✈ Sturzflug m. '**~·dive** v/i **1.** ✈ e-n Sturzflug machen. **2.** F purzeln (Preise etc). ~ **drops** s pl ✽ Nasentropfen pl. '**~·gay** s Sträußchen n. '**~·pick·ing** s Nasenbohren n.

nosh [nɒʃ] sl. **I** s **1.** bsd. Br. Essen n: **have a ~** (et.) essen; **have a quick ~** schnell et. essen. **2.** Am. Bissen m, Happen m: **have a ~** e-n Bissen od. Happen essen. **II** v/i **3.** bsd. Br. essen. **4.** Am. e-n Bissen od. Happen essen.

nos·tal·gia [nɒˈstældʒə] s Nostalgie f; weitS. Sehnsucht f (**for** nach). **nos'tal·gic** [~dʒɪk] adj (**~ally**) nostalgisch.

nos·tril [ˈnɒstrəl] s Nasenloch n, bsd. zo. Nüster f.

nos·trum [ˈnɒstrəm] s Allheilmittel n, Patentrezept n.

nos·y [ˈnəʊzɪ] adj □ F neugierig: ~ **park·er** bsd. Br. neugierige Person, Schnüffler(in).

not [nɒt] adv **1.** nicht: ~ **that** nicht, daß; **it is wrong, is it ~** (F **isn't it**)? es ist falsch, nicht wahr?; → **yet** 2. **2.** ~ **a** kein(e).

no·ta·ble [ˈnəʊtəbl] **I** adj **1.** beachtens-, bemerkenswert. **2.** beträchtlich (Unterschied etc). **3.** angesehen, bedeutend. **II** s **4.** bedeutende od. prominente Persönlichkeit. '**no·ta·bly** adv besonders, vor allem.

no·ta·ry [ˈnəʊtərɪ] s mst ~ **public** Notar m.

no·ta·tion [nəʊˈteɪʃn] s ♪ Notenschrift f.

notch [nɒtʃ] **I** s **1.** Kerbe f. **2.** Am. Engpaß m. fig. Grad m: **be a ~ above** e-e Klasse besser sein als. **II** v/t **4.** (ein)kerben. **5.** oft ~ **up** F Sieg, Einnahmen etc erzielen: ~ **s.o. sth.** j-m et. einbringen.

note [nəʊt] **I** s **1.** Bedeutung f: **man of ~** bedeutender Mann. **2.** **take ~ of sth.** von et. Notiz od. et. zur Kenntnis nehmen; et. beachten. **3.** mst pl Notiz f, Aufzeichnung f: **make a ~ of sth.** sich et. notieren od. vormerken; **take ~s (of)** sich Notizen machen (über acc); **speak without ~s** frei sprechen; → **mental** 1. **4.** (diplomatische) Note. **5.** Briefchen n, Zettel m. **6.** Anmerkung f; Vermerk m, Notiz f. **7.** Banknote f, Geldschein m. **8.** ♪ Note f. **9.** fig. Ton(art f) m: **strike the right (a false)** ~ den richtigen Ton treffen (sich im Ton vergreifen). **II** v/t **10.** (besonders) beachten od. achten auf (acc). **11.** bemerken. **12.** oft ~ **down** (sich) et. aufschreiben od. notieren. '**~·book** s Notizbuch n.

not·ed [ˈnəʊtɪd] adj bekannt, berühmt (**for** wegen).

'**note·**,**pa·per** s Briefpapier n. '**~·wor·thy** adj □ bemerkenswert.

noth·ing [ˈnʌθɪŋ] **I** pron nichts (**of** von): **as if ~ had happened** als ob nichts passiert sei; ~ **doing** F das kommt nicht in Frage; nichts zu machen; ~ **much** nicht (sehr) viel, nichts Bedeutendes; **that's ~ to** das ist nichts gegen od. im Vergleich zu; **that's ~ to me** das bedeutet mir nichts; **there is ~ like** es geht nichts über (acc); **there is ~ to** (od. **in) it** da ist nichts dabei; an der Sache ist nichts dran; **I can make ~ of** ich kann nichts anfangen mit, ich werde nicht schlau aus; **to say ~ of** ganz zu schweigen von; **think ~ of** nichts halten von; sich nichts machen aus; → **but** 4. **II** s Nichts n: **for ~** umsonst; **end in ~** sich in nichts auflösen. **III** adv durchaus nicht, keineswegs: ~ **like complete** alles andere als *od.* längst nicht vollständig.

no·tice ['nəʊtıs] **I** *s* **1.** Beachtung *f*, Wahrnehmung *f*: **bring s.th. to s.o.'s ~** j-m et. zur Kenntnis bringen; **escape ~** unbemerkt bleiben; **escape s.o.'s ~** j-m *od.* j-s Aufmerksamkeit entgehen; **take (no) ~ of** (keine) Notiz nehmen von, (nicht) beachten. **2.** Ankündigung *f*, Bekanntgabe *f*, Mitteilung *f*: **give s.o. ~ of s.th.** j-n von et. benachrichtigen. **3.** Kündigung(sfrist) *f*: **give s.o. (his) ~ (for Easter)** j-m (zu Ostern) kündigen; **give the company one's ~** kündigen; **at short ~** kurzfristig; **till** (*od.* **until**) **further ~** bis auf weiteres; **without ~** fristlos. **II** *v/t* **4.** bemerken: **~ s.o. do(ing) s.th.** bemerken, daß j-d et. tut. **5.** (besonders) beachten *od.* achten auf (*acc*). **III** *v/i* **6.** ~ bemerken. **'no·tice·a·ble** *adj* □ **1.** erkennbar, wahrnehmbar. **2.** bemerkenswert, beachtlich.

notice board *s bsd. Br.* Anschlagtafel *f*, Schwarzes Brett.

no·ti·fi·a·ble ['nəʊtıfaıəbl] *adj* meldepflichtig (*bsd. Krankheit*). **no·ti·fi·ca·tion** [ˌ~fı'keıʃn] *s* Meldung *f*, Mitteilung *f*, Benachrichtigung *f*. **no·ti·fy** ['~faı] *v/t* **1.** melden, mitteilen (**s.th. to s.o.** j-m et.). **2.** *j-n* benachrichtigen (**of** von, **that** daß).

no·tion ['nəʊʃn] *s* **1.** Begriff *m* (*a. ♣, phls.*), Vorstellung *f*: **not to have the faintest** (*od.* **vaguest**) **~ of** nicht die leiseste Ahnung haben von. **2.** Idee *f*: **take** (*have*) **a ~ to do s.th.** Lust bekommen (haben), et. žu tun. **no·tion·al** ['~ʃənl] *adj* □ fiktiv, angenommen.

no·to·ri·e·ty [ˌnəʊtə'raıətı] *s* traurige Berühmtheit. **no·to·ri·ous** [~'tɔːrıəs] *adj* □ berüchtigt (**for** für).

not·with·stand·ing [ˌnɒtwıθ'stændıŋ] **I** *prp* ungeachtet, trotz. **II** *adv* nichtsdestoweniger, dennoch.

nou·gat ['nuːgɑː] *s* (*etwa*) Türkischer Honig.

nought [nɔːt] *s*: **bring (come) to ~** zunichte machen (werden).

noun [naʊn] *s ling.* Substantiv *n*, Hauptwort *n*.

nour·ish ['nʌrıʃ] *v/t* **1.** (er)nähren (**on** von). **2.** *Gefühl* nähren, hegen. **'nour·ish·ing** *adj* □ nahrhaft. **'nour·ish·ment** *s* **1.** Ernährung *f*. **2.** Nahrung *f*:

---

take ~ Nahrung zu sich nehmen.

nov·el ['nɒvl] **I** *adj* (ganz) neu(artig). **II** *s* Roman *m.* **nov·el·ette** [ˌnɒvə'let] *s* Kurzroman *m*; *contp. bsd. Br.* Groschenroman *m.* **'nov·el·ist** *s* Romanschriftsteller(in). **no·vel·la** [nəʊ'velə] *pl* **-las, -le** [~li] *s* Novelle *f.* **nov·el·ty** ['nɒvltı] *s* **1.** Neuheit *f*: a) *das Neue*, *weitS. der* Reiz des Neuen, b) *et.* Neues. **2.** *pl* (billige) Neuheiten *pl.*

No·vem·ber [nəʊ'vembə] *s* November *m*: **in ~** im November.

nov·ice ['nɒvıs] *s* **1.** *eccl.* Novize *m*, Novizin *f.* **2.** Anfänger(in), Neuling *m* (**at** auf *e-m Gebiet*).

now [naʊ] **I** *adv* **1.** nun, jetzt: **~ and again, (every) ~ and then** von Zeit zu Zeit, dann u. wann; **by ~** mittlerweile, inzwischen; **from ~ (on)** von jetzt an; **up to ~** bis jetzt. **2.** sofort. **3.** *just ~* gerade eben. **II** *cj* **4.** ~ **that** nun, da; jetzt, wo. **now·a·days** ['naʊədeız] *adv* heutzutage.

no·where ['nəʊweə] *adv* **1.** nirgends, nirgendwo: **have ~ to live** kein Zuhause haben; **~ near** bei weitem nicht, auch nicht annähernd. **2.** nirgendwohin: **get ~ (fast)** überhaupt nicht weiterkommen, überhaupt keine Fortschritte machen; **this will get us ~** damit *od.* so kommen wir auch nicht weiter, das bringt uns auch nicht weiter.

nox·ious ['nɒkʃəs] *adj* □ schädlich (**to** für): **~ substance** Schadstoff *m.*

noz·zle ['nɒzl] *s ⊛* Schnauze *f*; Stutzen *m*; Düse *f*; Zapfpistole *f.*

nu·ance ['njuːɑːns] *s* Nuance *f.*

nub [nʌb] *s* springender Punkt.

nu·cle·ar ['njuːklıə] *adj* **1.** *biol. etc* Kern... **2.** *phys.* Kern..., Atom...: **~ energy** Atom-, Kernenergie *f*; **~ fission** Kernspaltung *f*; **~free** atomwaffenfrei; **~ fusion** Kernfusion *f*, -verschmelzung *f*; **~ physics** *pl* (*sg konstruiert*) Kernphysik *f*; **~ power** Atom-, Kernkraft *f*; *pol.* Atommacht *f*; **~ power plant** Atom-, Kernkraftwerk *n*; **~ reactor** Atom-, Kernreaktor *m*; **~ scientist** Atomwissenschaftler *m*; **~ test** Atomtest *m*; **~ war(fare)** Atomkrieg(führung *f*) *m*; **~ warhead** Atomsprengkopf *m*; **~ weapons** *pl* Atom-, Kernwaffen *pl.* **3. a. ~-powered** atomgetrieben: **~ submarine** Atom-U-Boot *n.* **nu·cle·us** ['~klıəs] *pl* **-cle·i** [~aı] *s* **1.** (*Atom-,*

*Zell- etc)*Kern *m.* **2.** *fig.* Kern *m.*

nude [nju:d] **I** *adj* **1.** nackt: **~ beach** Nacktbadestrand *m*, FKK-Strand *m*; **~ model** Aktmodell *n*; **~ photograph** Aktaufnahme *f*; **~ swimming** Nacktbaden *n.* **II** *s* **2.** *Kunst:* Akt *m.* **3.** *in the ~* nackt.

nudge [nʌdʒ] **I** *v/t* j-n anstoßen, stupsen. **II** *s* Stups *m.*

nud·ism ['nju:dɪzəm] *s* Nudismus *m*, Freikörper-, Nacktkultur *f.* **'nud·ist** *s* Nudist(in), Anhänger(in) der Freikörper-, Nacktkultur, FKK-Anhänger(in): **~ beach** Nacktbadestrand *m*, FKK-Strand *m.*

nug·get ['nʌgɪt] *s* Nugget *n*: **~s** *pl of information fig.* bruchstückhafte Information(en *pl*).

nui·sance ['nju:sns] *s* **1.** Plage *f*, Belästigung *f*, Mißstand *m*: **what a ~!** wie ärgerlich!; *public* ~ ⚖ öffentliches Ärgernis (*a. fig.*). **2.** Landplage *f*, Nervensäge *f*, Quälgeist *m*: **be a ~ to s.o.** j-m lästig fallen, j-n nerven; **make a ~ of o.s** den Leuten auf die Nerven gehen *od.* fallen.

nukes [nju:ks] *s pl bsd. Am.* F Atom-, Kernwaffen *pl.*

null [nʌl] *adj*: **~ and void** *bsd.* ⚖ null u. nichtig. **'null·i·fy** ['nʌlɪfaɪ] *v/t* **1.** *bsd.* ⚖ für null u. nichtig erklären. **2.** aufheben.

numb [nʌm] **I** *adj* □ **1.** starr (*with* vor *Kälte etc*), taub (*empfindungslos*). **2.** *fig.* wie betäubt (*with* vor *Schmerz etc*). **II** *v/t* **3.** starr *od.* taub machen. **4.** *fig.* betäuben.

num·ber ['nʌmbə] **I** *s* **1.** Zahl *f*; Ziffer *f*: **be good at ~s** gut rechnen können. **2.** (*Haus-, Telefon- etc*)Nummer *f*: **be ~ one** *fig.* die Nummer Eins sein; **look after** (*od. take care of*) **~ one** F (vor allem) an sich selbst denken; **have s.o.'s ~** F j-n durchschaut haben; **his ~ is** (*od. has come*) **up** F jetzt ist er dran. **3.** (An)Zahl *f*: **a** (*great*) **~ of people** mehrere (sehr viele) Leute; **five in ~** fünf an der Zahl; **~s of times** zu wiederholten Malen; **in large ~s** in großen Mengen, in großer Zahl. **4.** Nummer *f*, Ausgabe *f* (*e-r Zeitschrift etc*): → **back number.** **5.** *thea. etc* (Programm)Nummer *f*; ♩ Nummer *f*, Stück *n.* **II** *v/t* **6.** **his days are ~ed** s-e Tage sind gezählt.

7. numerieren. **8.** **~ s.o.** *among* (*od. with*) *fig.* j-n zählen *od.* rechnen zu. **9.** sich belaufen auf (*acc*). **III** *v/i* **10.** **~ in** sich belaufen auf (*acc*). **11.** **~ among** (*od. with*) *fig.* zählen zu. **'num·ber·ing** *s* Numerierung *f.* **'num·ber·less** *adj* unzählig, zahllos.

'num·ber·plate *s mot. Br.* Nummern-, Kennzeichenschild *n.*

numb·ness ['nʌmnɪs] *s* **1.** Starr-, Taubheit *f.* **2.** *fig.* Betäubung *f.*

nu·mer·al ['nju:mərəl] *s* **1.** Ziffer *f.* **2.** *ling.* Zahlwort *n.*

nu·mer·i·cal [nju:'merɪkl] *adj* □ numerisch: **a)** Zahlen..., **b)** zahlenmäßig.

nu·mer·ous ['nju:mərəs] *adj* □ zahlreich.

nu·mis·mat·ics [ˌnju:mɪz'mætɪks] *s pl* (*sg konstruiert*) Numismatik *f*, Münzkunde *f.*

num·skull ['nʌmskʌl] *s* F Dummkopf *m.*

nun [nʌn] *s eccl.* Nonne *f.*

nun·ci·o ['nʌnsɪəʊ] *pl* **-os** *s eccl.* Nuntius *m.*

nun·ner·y ['nʌnərɪ] *s* Nonnenkloster *n.*

nup·tial ['nʌpʃl] **I** *adj* Hochzeits... **II** *s pl* Trauung *f.*

nurse [nɜ:s] **I** *s* **1.** (Kranken)Schwester *f*: → **male** I. **2.** Kindermädchen *n.* **II** *v/t* **3.** *Baby* säugen, stillen, *e-m Baby* die Brust geben. **4.** *Kranke* pflegen: **~ s.o. back to health** j-n gesund pflegen. **5.** *Krankheit* auskurieren. **6.** *Stimme etc* schonen. **7.** *fig. Gefühl* hegen, nähren. **III** *v/i* **8.** stillen (*Mutter*). **9.** die Brust nehmen, trinken (*Baby*). **10.** als Krankenschwester *od.* als Krankenpfleger arbeiten. **'~maid** → **nurse** 2.

nurs·er·y ['nɜ:sərɪ] *s* **1.** Tagesheim *n*, -stätte *f.* **2.** Pflanz-, Baumschule *f.* **3.** Kinderzimmer *n.* **~ rhyme** *s* Kinderreim *m*, -vers *m.* **~ school** *s* Kindergarten *m*: **~ teacher** Kindergärtnerin *f.*

nurs·ing ['nɜ:sɪŋ] *s* **1.** Stillen *n.* **2.** Krankenpflege *f.* **~ bot·tle** *s* Am. Saugflasche *f.* **~ home** *s* **1.** Pflegeheim *n.* **2.** *bsd. Br.* Privatklinik *f.*

nut [nʌt] *s* **1.** ❀ Nuß *f*: **a hard** (*od. tough*) **~ to crack** *fig.* e-e harte Nuß. **2.** ⊚ (Schrauben)Mutter *f.* **3.** F Birne *f* (*Kopf*): **be** (*go*) **off one's ~** (anfangen zu) spinnen. **4.** *pl* V Eier *pl* (*Hoden*). **'~·crack·er** *s a. pl* Nußknacker *m*: **a** (**pair of**) **~(s)** ein Nußknacker. **'~**

house s bsd. Br. sl. Klapsmühle f.
nut·meg ['nʌtmeg] s ♀ Muskatnuß f.
nu·tri·ent ['njuːtriənt] I adj nahrhaft. II s
Nährstoff m.
nu·tri·tion [njuːˈtrɪʃn] s Ernährung f.
nu'tri·tious adj □ nahrhaft.
nuts [nʌts] adj F: **be ~** spinnen; **be ~
about** (od. **on**) verrückt sein nach, wild
od. scharf sein auf (acc).
'nut·shell s ♀ Nußschale f: **(to put it) in a**

~ fig. kurz gesagt, mit 'einem Wort.
nut·ty ['nʌtɪ] adj **1.** Nuß... **2.** F verrückt
(a. Idee etc): **be ~** spinnen; **be ~ about**
(od. **on**) verrückt sein nach, wild od.
scharf sein auf (acc).
ny·lon ['naɪlɒn] s Nylon n.
nymph [nɪmf] s Nymphe f.
nym·pho·ma·ni·ac [ˌnɪmfəʊˈmeɪnɪæk] I
adj nymphoman, mannstoll. II s Nymphomanin f.

O

O [əʊ] pl **O's, Os** s Null f (Ziffer, a.
teleph.).
oaf [əʊf] s Lümmel m, Flegel m. **'oaf·ish**
adj □ lümmel-, flegelhaft.
oak [əʊk] s ♀ Eiche f. **oak·en** ['~ən] adj
eichen, Eichen...
oar [ɔː] s Ruder n, Riemen m: **put** (od.
shove, stick) **one's ~ in** F sich einmischen, s-n Senf dazugeben; **rest on
one's ~s** fig. ausspannen.
oars·|man ['ɔːzmən] s (irr man) Sport:
Ruderer m. **'~·wom·an** s (irr woman)
Sport: Ruderin f.
o·a·sis [əʊˈeɪsɪs] pl **-ses** [~siːz] s Oase f
(a. fig.).
oath [əʊθ] pl **oaths** [əʊðz] s **1.** Eid m,
Schwur m: **~ of office** Amts-, Diensteid; **on** (od. **under**) **~** unter Eid, eidlich;
be on (od. **under**) **~** unter Eid stehen;
swear (od. **take**) **an ~** e-n Eid leisten od.
ablegen, schwören (**on, to** auf acc); **in
lieu of an ~** an Eides Statt. **2.** Fluch m.
oat·meal ['əʊtmiːl] s Hafermehl n, -grütze f.
oats [əʊts] s pl ♀ Hafer m: **he feels his ~**
F ihn sticht der Hafer; **be off one's ~** F
keinen Appetit haben; **he's gone off
his ~** F ihm ist der Appetit vergangen;
sow one's wild ~ sich die Hörner abstoßen.
ob·du·ra·cy ['ɒbdjʊrəsɪ] s Starrsinn m,
Verstocktheit f. **ob·du·rate** ['~rət] adj
□ starrsinnig, verstockt.
o·be·di·ence [əˈbiːdjəns] s Gehorsam m
(**to** gegen[über]), Folgsamkeit f. **o·be-**

di·ent adj □ gehorsam (**to** dat), folgsam: **be ~ to s.o.** a. j-m folgen.
ob·e·lisk ['ɒbəlɪsk] s Obelisk m.
o·bese [əʊˈbiːs] adj fettleibig. **o·bes·i·ty**
s Fettleibigkeit f.
o·bey [əˈbeɪ] I v/t **1.** j-m gehorchen, folgen. **2.** Befehl etc befolgen. II v/i **3.**
gehorchen, folgen.
ob·fus·cate ['ɒbfʌskeɪt] v/t fig. **1.** verwirren. **2.** vernebeln.
o·bit·u·ar·y [əˈbɪtjʊərɪ] s **1.** Nachruf m.
2. a. **~ notice** Todesanzeige f.
ob·ject¹ ['ɒbdʒekt] I v/t **1.** einwenden
(**that** daß). II v/i **2.** Einspruch erheben
(**to** gegen). **3.** et. dagegen haben: **if you
don't ~** wenn du nichts dagegen hast; **~
to s.th.** et. beanstanden; **do you ~ to my
smoking?** haben Sie et. dagegen, wenn
ich rauche?
ob·ject² ['ɒbdʒɪkt] s **1.** Objekt n, Gegenstand m (a. fig. des Mitleids etc):
money (is) no ~ Geld od. der Preis
spielt keine Rolle. **2.** Ziel n, Zweck m,
Absicht f: **with the ~ of doing s.th.** mit
der Absicht, et. zu tun. **3.** ling. Objekt n.
ob·jec·tion [əbˈdʒekʃn] s Einspruch m
(a. ⚖), Einwand m (**to** gegen); Abneigung f (**to** gegen): **if you have no ~s**
wenn du nichts dagegen hast; **I have no
~ to him** ich habe nichts an ihm auszusetzen; **raise an ~ to s.th.** gegen et. e-n
Einwand erheben. **ob'jec·tion·a·ble**
adj □ **1.** unangenehm. **2.** anstößig.
ob·jec·tive [əbˈdʒektɪv] I adj □ **1.** objek-

tiv, sachlich. **2.** objektiv, tatsächlich. **II** s **3.** opt. Objektiv n. **4.** Ziel n. **ob·jec·tiv·i·ty** [ˌɒbdʒekˈtɪvətɪ] s Objektivität f.

'**ob·ject les·son** s **1.** ped. Anschauungsunterricht m. **2.** fig. Parade-, Schulbeispiel n (*in* für).

ob·jec·tor [əbˈdʒektə] s Gegner(in) (*to* gen): → *conscientious* 2.

ob·li·gate ['ɒblɪgeɪt] v/t: *feel* ~d *to do s.th.* sich verpflichtet fühlen, et. zu tun. ˌ**ob·li·ga·tion** s Verpflichtung f: ~ *to buy* Kaufzwang m; *without* ~ unverbindlich; *be under an* ~ *to do s.th.* verpflichtet sein, et. zu tun. **ob·lig·a·to·ry** [əˈblɪgətərɪ] adj □ verpflichtend, verbindlich, obligatorisch (*on* für): *attendance is* ~ Anwesenheit ist Pflicht.

o·blige [əˈblaɪdʒ] v/t **1.** nötigen, zwingen: *be* ~d *to do s.th. a.* et. tun müssen. **2.** fig. (a. zu Dank) verpflichten: *feel* ~d *to do s.th.* sich verpflichtet fühlen, et. zu tun; (*I am*) *much* ~d (*to you*) ich bin Ihnen sehr zu Dank verpflichtet, besten Dank; *would you* ~ *me by* (ger)? wären Sie so freundlich, zu (inf)? **3.** j-m gefällig sein, j-m e-n Gefallen tun. **o·blig·ing** adj □ entgegenkommend, gefällig.

ob·lique [əˈbliːk] adj □ **1.** bsd. A schief, schiefwink(e)lig, schräg: *at an* ~ *angle to* im spitzen Winkel zu. **2.** fig. indirekt.

ob·lit·er·ate [əˈblɪtəreɪt] v/t **1.** unkenntlich od. unleserlich machen. **2.** vernichten, völlig zerstören. **3.** Sonne etc verdecken. **ob**‚**lit·er·a·tion** s **1.** Unkenntlichmachung f. **2.** Vernichtung f.

o·bliv·i·on [əˈblɪvɪən] s: *fall* (od. *sink*) *into* ~ in Vergessenheit geraten. **o·bliv·i·ous** adj: *be* ~ *to* (od. *of*) *s.th.* sich e-r Sache nicht bewußt sein; et. nicht bemerken od. wahrnehmen.

ob·long ['ɒblɒŋ] **I** adj rechteckig. **II** s Rechteck n.

ob·nox·ious [əbˈnɒkʃəs] adj □ widerwärtig, widerlich.

o·boe ['əʊbəʊ] s ♪ Oboe f. '**o·bo·ist** s Oboist(in).

ob·scene [əbˈsiːn] adj □ obszön, unanständig, unzüchtig. **ob·scen·i·ty** [əbˈsenətɪ] s Obszönität f (a. Wort etc), Unanständigkeit f, Unzüchtigkeit f.

ob·scure [əbˈskjʊə] **I** adj □ **1.** a) dunkel, unklar, (Motive etc a.) undurchsichtig:

for some ~ *reason* aus e-m unerfindlichen Grund, b) unbestimmt, undeutlich (Gefühl). **2.** obskur, unbekannt, unbedeutend. **II** v/t **3.** Sonne etc verdecken. **4.** nicht klarmachen. **ob·scu·ri·ty** s **1.** Unklarheit f. **2.** Unbekanntheit f.

ob·se·quies ['ɒbsɪkwɪz] s Trauerfeierlichkeit(en pl) f.

ob·se·qui·ous [əbˈsiːkwɪəs] adj □ unterwürfig. **ob·se·qui·ous·ness** s Unterwürfigkeit f.

ob·serv·a·ble [əbˈzɜːvəbl] adj □ wahrnehmbar, merklich. **ob·serv·ance** s Beachtung f, Befolgung f, Einhaltung f. **ob·serv·ant** adj □ aufmerksam, achtsam. **ob·ser·va·tion** [ˌɒbzəˈveɪʃn] s **1.** Beobachtung f, Überwachung f: *keep s.o. under* ~ j-n beobachten (lassen). **2.** Bemerkung f (*on* über acc). **ob·serv·a·to·ry** [əbˈzɜːvətrɪ] s Observatorium n. **ob·serve** v/t **1.** beobachten: a) überwachen, b) studieren, c) bemerken: *he was* ~d *entering the house* er wurde beim Betreten des Hauses beobachtet. **2.** Vorschrift etc beachten, befolgen, einhalten; Fest feiern, begehen. **3.** bemerken, äußern (*that* daß). **ob·serv·er** s Beobachter(in). **ob·serv·ing** → *observant*.

ob·sess [əbˈses] v/t: *be* ~ed *by* (od. *with*) besessen sein von. **ob·ses·sion** [əbˈseʃn] s **1.** Besessenheit f. **2.** fixe Idee, psych. Zwangsvorstellung f. **ob·ses·sion·al** [~ʃnl] adj □ psych. zwanghaft: ~ *neuro·sis* Zwangsneurose f.

ob·so·les·cent [ˌɒbsəˈlesnt] adj □ veraltend: *be* ~ veralten. **ob·so·lete** ['ɒbsəliːt] adj □ veraltet.

ob·sta·cle ['ɒbstəkl] s Hindernis n (*to* für) (a. fig.): *be an* ~ *to s.th.* et. hindern, e-r Sache im Weg stehen; *put* ~s *in s.o.'s way* j-m Steine in den Weg legen. ~ *race* s Sport: Hindernisrennen n.

ob·ste·tri·cian [ˌɒbstəˈtrɪʃn] s ⚕ Geburtshelfer(in). **ob·stet·rics** [ɒbˈstetrɪks] s pl (mst sg konstruiert) Geburtshilfe f.

ob·sti·na·cy ['ɒbstɪnəsɪ] s Hartnäckigkeit f (a. fig.), Halsstarrigkeit f. **ob·sti·nate** ['ɒbstənət] adj □ hartnäckig (a. fig.), halsstarrig.

ob·strep·er·ous [əbˈstrepərəs] *adj* □ **1.** lärmend. **2.** aufsässig.

ob·struct [əbˈstrʌkt] *v/t* **1.** *Straße etc* blockieren, versperren, *a. Röhre, Arterie etc* verstopfen. **2.** *Aussicht etc* versperren, die Sicht versperren auf (*acc*): ~ *s.o.'s view* j-m die Sicht nehmen. **3.** *Straßenverkehr, fig. Fortschritt etc* behindern, aufhalten, *Gesetzesvorlage etc* blockieren, sich *e-m Plan etc* in den Weg stellen. **ob·struc·tion** *s* **1.** Blockierung *f*, Versperrung *f*, Verstopfung *f*. **2.** Behinderung *f*. **3.** *pol.* Obstruktion *f*. **ob·struc·tion·ism** [~ʃənɪzəm] *s pol.* Obstruktionspolitik *f*. **ob·struc·tive** [~tɪv] *adj* □ hinderlich (**to** für): **be ~ to s.th.** *a.* et. behindern.

ob·tain [əbˈteɪn] **I** *v/t* erhalten, bekommen, sich *et.* verschaffen: ~ *by flattery* sich *et.* erschmeicheln; ~ *s.th. for s.o.* j-m et. beschaffen *od.* besorgen. **II** *v/i* bestehen, Geltung haben. **ob·tain·a·ble** *adj* erhältlich: *no longer* ~ nicht mehr lieferbar, vergriffen.

ob·trude [əbˈtruːd] **I** *v/t* aufdrängen (**on** *dat*): ~ *o.s.* → **II**. **II** *v/i* sich aufdrängen (**on** *dat*). **ob·tru·sive** [~sɪv] *adj* □ aufdringlich.

ob·tuse [əbˈtjuːs] *adj* □ **1.** Å stumpf (*Winkel*). **2.** *fig.* begriffsstutzig, beschränkt.

ob·vi·ous [ˈɒbvɪəs] *adj* □ offensichtlich, klar, einleuchtend: *it is (very) ~ that* es liegt (klar) auf der Hand, daß.

oc·ca·sion [əˈkeɪʒn] **I** *s* **1.** (günstige) Gelegenheit, richtiger Zeitpunkt (**for** für): *take the ~ to do s.th.* die Gelegenheit ergreifen, et. zu tun. **2.** (besondere) Gelegenheit, Anlaß *m*: *on this ~* bei dieser Gelegenheit; *on the ~ of* anläßlich (*gen*); *for the ~* eigens zu diesem Zweck *od.* Anlaß. **3.** (*bsd.* festliches) Ereignis: *to celebrate the ~* zur Feier des Tages; *rise to the ~* sich der Lage gewachsen zeigen; → *mark²* 11. **4.** Anlaß *m*, Anstoß *m*: *give ~ to* Anlaß *od.* den Anstoß geben zu. **5.** Grund *m*, Veranlassung *f* (**for** zu). **II** *v/t* **6.** veranlassen, verursachen. **oc·ca·sion·al** [~ʒənl] *adj* gelegentlich, Gelegenheits...; vereinzelt: *smoke an ~ cigarette* hin u. wieder e-e Zigarette rauchen. **oc·ca·sion·al·ly** [~ʒnəlɪ] *adv* gelegentlich, hin u. wieder.

Oc·ci·dent [ˈɒksɪdənt] *s der* Westen, *poet. das* Abendland. **oc·ci·den·tal** [~ˈdentl] *adj* □ abendländisch, westlich.

oc·cult [ɒˈkʌlt] **I** *adj* □ okkult: a) geheimnisvoll, verborgen, b) übersinnlich, c) geheim, Geheim... **II** *s: the ~* das Okkulte. **oc·cult·ism** [ˈɒkəltɪzəm] *s* Okkultismus *m*.

oc·cu·pant [ˈɒkjʊpənt] *s* **1.** Bewohner(in): *the ~s pl of the house* die Hausbewohner *pl.* **2.** Insasse *m*, Insassin *f*: *the ~s pl of the car* die Autoinsassen *pl.* **oc·cu·pa·tion** *s* **1.** Besitznahme *f*, -ergreifung *f*. **2.** ╳, *pol.* Besetzung *f*: ~ *troops pl* Besatzungstruppen *pl.* **3.** Beschäftigung *f*. **4.** Beruf *m*: *by ~* von Beruf. **oc·cu·pa·tion·al** [~ʃənl] *adj* □ Berufs...: ~ *accident* Arbeitsunfall *m*; ~ *disease* Berufskrankheit *f*; ~ *hazard* Berufsrisiko *n*. **2.** Beschäftigungs...: ~ *therapy.* **oc·cu·pi·er** [ˈ~paɪə] → *occupant* 1. **oc·cu·py** [ˈ~paɪ] *v/t* **1.** in Besitz nehmen, Besitz ergreifen von; ╳, *pol.* besetzen. **2.** *be occupied* bewohnt sein; besetzt sein (*Platz*). **3.** *Amt* bekleiden, innehaben. **4.** *Raum* einnehmen; *Zeit* in Anspruch nehmen. **5.** j-n beschäftigen: ~ *o.s. with* (*od.* **in**) *s.th.* sich mit et. beschäftigen.

oc·cur [əˈkɜː] *v/i* **1.** sich ereignen, vorkommen. **2.** vorkommen (**in** bei *Shakespeare etc*). **3.** zustoßen (**to** *dat*). **4.** einfallen, in den Sinn kommen (**to** *dat*): *it ~red to me that* es fiel mir ein *od.* mir kam der Gedanke, daß. **oc·cur·rence** [əˈkʌrəns] *s* **1.** Vorkommen *n*. **2.** Ereignis *n*, Vorfall *m*, Vorkommnis *n*: *be an everyday ~* et. (ganz) Alltägliches sein.

o·cean [ˈəʊʃn] *s* **1.** Ozean *m*, Meer *n*: ~ *climate* Meeres-, Seeklima *n*; ~ *liner* Ozeandampfer *m*. **2.** ~ *s pl of* F e-e Unmenge von: ~*.go·ing* *adj* hochseetüchtig, Hochsee...

o·cher *Am.*, **o·chre** *bsd. Br.* [ˈəʊkə] **I** *s min.* Ocker *m, n*. **II** *adj* ockerfarben, -gelb.

o'clock [əˈklɒk] *adv* ... Uhr: *five* ~.

oc·ta·gon [ˈɒktəgən] *s* Achteck *n*. **oc·tag·o·nal** [ɒkˈtægənl] *adj* □ achteckig.

oc·tane [ˈɒkteɪn] *s* ▲ Oktan *n*: ~ *number* (*od.* **rating**) Oktanzahl *f*.

oc·tave [ˈɒktɪv] *s* ♪ Oktave *f*.

Oc·to·ber [ɒk'təʊbə] s Oktober m: **in ~** im Oktober.

oc·to·pus ['ɒktəpəs] pl **-pus·es, -pi** [~paɪ] s zo. Krake m.

oc·u·lar ['ɒkjʊlə] adj Augen... '**oc·u·list** s Augenarzt m.

odd [ɒd] adj (□ → **oddly**) **1.** sonderbar, seltsam, merkwürdig. **2.** nach Zahlen: **50** ~ (et.) über 50, einige 50. **3.** ungerade (Zahl). **4.** Einzel..., einzeln (Schuh etc.). **5.** gelegentlich, Gelegenheits...: ~ **jobs** pl Gelegenheitsarbeiten pl. '~·**ball** s bsd. Am. F komischer Kauz.

odd·i·ty ['ɒdɪtɪ] s **1.** Merkwürdigkeit f. **2.** komische Person od. Sache.

,**odd-'job man** s (irr **man**) Mädchen n für alles.

odd·ly ['ɒdlɪ] adv **1.** → **odd** 1. **2.** a. ~ **enough** seltsamer-, merkwürdigerweise.

odds [ɒdz] s pl **1.** (Gewinn)Chancen pl: **the ~ are 10 to 1** die Chancen stehen 10 zu 1; **the ~ are that he will come** er kommt wahrscheinlich; **the ~ are in our favo(u)r** (od. **on us**) (**against us**) unsere Chancen stehen gut (schlecht); **against all ~** wider Erwarten, entgegen allen Erwartungen; → **stock** 6. **2. be at ~** uneins sein (**with** mit): **be at ~ with** a. im Widerspruch stehen zu. **3. it makes no ~** Br. es spielt keine Rolle, es macht keinen Unterschied. **4. ~ and ends** Krimskrams m. ,**~·'on** adj aussichtsreichst (Kandidat etc.), hoch, klar (Favorit): **it's ~ that he will come** er kommt höchstwahrscheinlich.

o·di·ous ['əʊdjəs] adj □ **1.** abscheulich. **2.** widerlich, ekelhaft.

o·dom·e·ter [əʊ'dɒmɪtə] s mot. Am. Meilenzähler m.

o·dor, o·dor·less Am. → **odour, etc.**

o·dor·if·er·ous [,əʊdə'rɪfərəs] adj □ duftend.

o·dour ['əʊdə] s bsd. Br. **1.** Geruch m, bsd. Duft m. **2. be in bad ~ with** fig. schlecht angeschrieben sein bei. '**o·dour·less** adj bsd. Br. geruchlos.

od·ys·sey ['ɒdɪsɪ] s Odyssee f.

oec·u·men·i·cal → **ecumenical**.

oe·de·ma [iːˈdiːmə] pl **-ma·ta** [~mətə] s 彡 Ödem n.

Oe·di·pus com·plex ['iːdɪpəs] s psych. Ödipuskomplex m.

oe·soph·a·gus [ɪ'sɒfəgəs] pl **-gi** [~gaɪ],

-gus·es s anat. bsd. Br. Speiseröhre f.

oes·tro·gen ['iːstrəʊdʒən] s biol. bsd. Br. Östrogen n.

of [ɒv] prp **1.** allg. von. **2.** zur Bezeichnung des Genitivs: **the tail ~ the dog** der Schwanz des Hundes. **3.** Ort: **the Battle ~ Hastings** die Schlacht bei Hastings. **4.** Entfernung, Trennung, Befreiung: a) **south ~ London** südlich von London; → **cure** 4, etc, b) gen: → **rob**, etc, c) um: → **cheat** 3, etc. **5.** Herkunft: von, aus, über: **Mr X ~ London** Mr X aus London; → **family** 1, etc. **6.** Eigenschaft: von, mit: **a man ~ courage** ein mutiger Mann, ein Mann mit Mut; → **importance**, etc. **7.** Stoff: aus, von: **a dress ~ silk** ein Kleid aus Seide, ein Seidenkleid; (**made**) ~ **steel** aus Stahl (hergestellt). **8.** Urheberschaft, Art u. Weise: von: **the works ~ Shakespeare**; **it was clever ~ him**. **9.** Ursache, Grund: a) an (dat): → **die** 1, etc, b) auf (acc): → **proud** 1, etc, c) vor (dat): → **afraid**, etc, d) nach: → **smell** 2, etc. **10.** Thema: an (acc): → **think** 6, etc. **11.** Apposition, unübersetzt: a) **the city ~ London** die Stadt London, b) Maß: **a glass ~ wine** ein Glas Wein; **a piece ~ meat** ein Stück Fleisch. **12.** Zeit: a) von: **your letter ~ March 3rd** Ihr Schreiben vom 3. März, b) Am. vor: **ten** (**minutes**) ~ **three**.

off [ɒf] **I** adv **1.** fort(...), weg(...): **be ~** (Sport) gestartet sein; **I must be ~** ich muß gehen od. weg; **~ with you!** fort mit dir!; → **go off** 1, etc. **2.** ab(...): → **cut off**, **hat**, etc. **3.** weg, entfernt: **three miles ~**. **4.** ~ **and** ab u. zu, hin u. wieder. **5. 5% ~** ✝ 5% Nachlaß; → **take off** 5. **6.** aus(...), aus-, abgeschaltet: → **switch** 5, 6, etc. **7. be ~** ausfallen, nicht stattfinden: **their engagement is** ~ sie haben ihre Verlobung gelöst. **8.** aus(gegangen), alle. **9. she is ~ today** sie hat heute ihren freien Tag; **give s.o. the afternoon ~** j-m den Nachmittag freigeben; **take a day ~** sich e-n Tag frei nehmen. **10.** nicht mehr frisch, verdorben (Nahrungsmittel): → **go off** 6. **11. well** (**badly**) ~ gut (schlecht) d(a)ran od. gestellt od. situiert: **how are you ~ for ...?** wie sieht es bei dir mit ... aus? **II** prp **12.** weg von, von (... weg od. ab od. od.

herunter): *jump ~ the bus* vom Bus abspringen; → *get off*, *grass* 2, *etc*. **13.** abseits von (*od. gen*), von ... weg: *a street ~ Piccadilly* e-e Seitenstraße von Piccadilly. **14.** *be ~ duty* nicht im Dienst sein, dienstfrei sein. **15.** *be ~ s.th.* et. nicht mehr mögen; von et. kuriert sein: → *drug* 2. **16.** ⚓ vor *der Küste etc*. **III** *adj* **17.** (arbeits-, dienst)frei. **18.** schlecht (*Tag etc*): *this is an ~ day for me* heute geht mir alles schief, das ist heute nicht mein Tag; *an ~ year for fruit* ein schlechtes Obstjahr. **19.** *on the ~ chance* auf gut Glück; in der Hoffnung (*of getting* zu bekommen); *~ season* Nebensaison *f*.

of·fal ['ɒfl] *s gastr.* Innereien *pl*.

'off|-beat *adj* F ausgefallen, unkonventionell. **,~'col·o(u)r** *adj* **1.** *be* (*od. feel*) *~* sich nicht wohl fühlen. **2.** gewagt (*Witz etc*).

of·fence [ə'fens] *s* **1.** *allg.* Vergehen *n*, Verstoß *m* (*against* gegen). **2.** ⚖ Straftat *f*; Vergehen *n*. **3.** Beleidigung *f*, Kränkung *f*: *give* (*od. cause*) *~* Anstoß *od.* Ärgernis erregen (*to* bei); *take ~* Anstoß nehmen (*at* an *dat*); *be quick* (*od. swift*) *to take ~* schnell beleidigt sein; *no ~* (*meant od. intended*) nichts für ungut!; *no ~* (*taken*) (es) ist nicht gut! **4.** Angriff *m*.

of·fend [ə'fend] **I** *v/t* beleidigen, kränken: *be ~ed at* (*od. by*) sich beleidigt fühlen durch. **II** *v/i* verstoßen (*against* gegen). **of'fend·er** *s* (Übel-, Misse)Täter(in): *first ~* ⚖ nicht Vorbestrafte *m*, *f*, Ersttäter(in).

of·fense *Am.* → *offence*.

of·fen·sive [ə'fensɪv] **I** *adj* □ **1.** beleidigend, anstößig: *get ~* ausfallend werden. **2.** widerlich (*Geruch etc*). **3.** ✗, *Sport:* Angriffs..., Offensiv... **II** *s* **4.** *allg.* Offensive *f*: *take the ~* die Offensive ergreifen.

of·fer ['ɒfə] **I** *v/t* **1.** anbieten: → *resist-ance* 1. **2.** a) ✝ *Ware* anbieten (*for sale* zum Verkauf), offerieren, b) ✝ *Preis*, *Summe* bieten, c) *Preis*, *Belohnung* aussetzen. **3.** *Entschuldigung etc* vorbringen, *Vorschlag* machen. **4.** sich bereit erklären (*to do* zu tun): *~ to help* s-e Hilfe anbieten. **II** *v/i* **5.** *es od.* sich anbieten. **III** *v* **6.** Angebot *n*: *make s.o. an ~ of s.th.* j-m et. anbieten; *his ~ of help*

sein Angebot zu helfen, s-e angebotene Hilfe. **7.** ✝ (An)Gebot *n*, Offerte *f* (*of* über *acc*): *on ~* zu verkaufen; im Angebot; *or near ~* Verhandlungsbasis.

,off|hand I *adv* **1.** auf Anhieb, so ohne weiteres. **II** *adj* **2.** improvisiert, Stegreif... **3.** lässig (*Art etc*), hingeworfen (*Bemerkung*).

of·fice ['ɒfɪs] *s* **1.** Büro *n*, (*e-r Institution*) Geschäftsstelle *f*, (*Anwalts*)Kanzlei *f*: *at the ~* im Büro. **2.** *mst* ♀ *bsd. Br.* Ministerium *n*: → *foreign* 1, *Home Office*. **3.** (*bsd.* öffentliches) Amt, Posten *m*: *be in* (*out of*) *~* (nicht mehr) im Amt sein; (nicht mehr) an der Macht sein. **~ block** *s* Bürogebäude *n*. **~ boy** *s* Bürogehilfe *m*. **~ cli·mate** *s* Betriebsklima *n*. **~ girl** *s* Bürogehilfin *f*. **'~,hold·er** *s* Amtsinhaber(in). **~ hours** *s pl* Dienstzeit *f*; Geschäfts-, Öffnungszeiten *pl*.

of·fi·cer ['ɒfɪsə] *s* **1.** ✗ Offizier *m*. **2.** (*Polizei- etc*)Beamte *m*.

of·fi·cial [ə'fɪʃl] **I** *adj* □ **1.** offiziell, amtlich, dienstlich: *~ duties pl* Amtspflichten *pl*; *~ language* Amtssprache *f*; *~ secret* Amts-, Dienstgeheimnis *n*; *~ trip* Dienstreise *f*: → *channel*, *residence* 1. **II** *s* **2.** Beamte *m*, Beamtin *f*. **3.** (*Gewerkschafts- etc*)Funktionär (-in). **of'fi·cial·dom** *s* Beamtentum *n*, die Beamten *pl*. **of,fi·cial'ese** [-[ə'li:z] *s* Amtsenglisch *n*, Behördensprache *f*.

of·fi·cious [ə'fɪʃəs] *adj* □ übereifrig, übertrieben diensteifrig.

off·ing ['ɒfɪŋ] *s*: *be in the ~* sich abzeichnen, in Sicht sein.

'off|-li·cence *s Br.* Wein- u. Spirituosenhandlung *f*. **'~-peak** *adj*: *~ electricity* Nachtstrom *m*; *~ hours pl* verkehrsschwache Stunden *pl*. **'~,put·ting** *adj Br.* F unangenehm, störend; unsympathisch (*Person, Wesen*). **~set** *s* ['ɒfset] **1.** Ausgleich *m*: *as an ~* als Ausgleich (*to* für). **2.** *typ.* Offsetdruck *m*. **II** *v/t* [ɒf'set] (*irr set*) **3.** ausgleichen. **'~-shoot** *s* & Ableger *m* (*a. fig.*), Sprößling *m*. **,~'shore I** *adv* vor der Küste. **II** *adj* küstennah: *~ boring* Off-shore-Bohrung *f*; *~ fishing* Küstenfischerei *f*. **'~side** *adj u. adv Sport:* abseits: *be ~* abseits sein, im Abseits stehen; *~ position* Abseitsposition *f*, -stellung *f*; *~ trap* Abseitsfalle *f*. *i*. *u. pl*. **'~-spring** *s* **1.** Nachkomme(nschaft *f*) *pl*. **2.** *pl offspring*

Abkömmling *m*, Nachkomme *m*.
,~-the-'rec·ord *adj u. adv* nicht für die Öffentlichkeit bestimmt, inoffiziell.

of·ten ['ɒfn] *adv* oft(mals), häufig: *more ~* öfters; *as ~ as* jedesmal wenn; *as ~ as* (*od. more ~ than*) not sehr oft; *ever so ~* öfters, von Zeit zu Zeit.

o·gle ['əʊgl] *v/t* (*a. v/i: ~ at*) *j-m* (schöne) Augen machen; *contp.* begaffen.

oh [əʊ] *int.* oh!: → *dear* 5, *yes* I.

ohm [əʊm] *s ⚡* Ohm *n*.

oil [ɔɪl] I *s* **1.** Öl *n*: *pour ~ on troubled waters fig.* Öl auf die Wogen gießen; → *midnight* II. **2.** (Erd)Öl *n*: *strike ~* auf Öl stoßen; *fig.* Glück *od.* Erfolg haben, *a.* fündig werden. **3.** *mst pl* Ölfarbe *f*: *paint in ~s* in Öl malen. II *v/t* **4.** (ein)ölen, schmieren; *~ the wheels fig.* für e-n reibungslosen Ablauf sorgen; → *palm¹* 1. *~ change s mot.* Ölwechsel *m*: *do an ~* e-n Ölwechsel machen. **~ col·o(u)r** *s* Ölfarbe *f*. **~ cri·sis** *s* (*irr crisis*) Ölkrise *f*. **~ dip·stick** *s mot.* Ölmeßstab *m*. **~-field** *s* Ölfeld *n*. **~-fired** *adj:* **~** *central heating* Ölzentralheizung *f*. **~ lamp** *s* Öl-, Petroleumlampe *f*. **~ lev·el** *s mot.* Ölstand *m*. **~ paint** *s* Ölfarbe *f*. **~ paint·ing** *s* **1.** Ölmalerei *f*. **2.** Ölgemälde *n*: *she's no ~* F sie ist keine strahlende Schönheit. **'~-pro-,duc·ing coun·try** *s* Ölförderland *n*. **~ rig** *s* (Öl)Bohrinsel *f*. **~ sheik(h)** *s* Ölscheich *m*. **~ slick** *s* Ölteppich *m*. **~ tank·er** *s* (Öl)Tanker *m*. **~ well** *s* Ölquelle *f*.

oil·y ['ɔɪlɪ] *adj* **1.** ölig. **2.** *fig.* schleimig.

oint·ment ['ɔɪntmənt] *s* Salbe *f*.

OK, o·kay [,əʊ'keɪ] F I *adj u. int* okay(!), o.k.(!), in Ordnung(!). II *v/t* genehmigen, e-r Sache zustimmen. III *s* Okay *n*, O.K., Genehmigung *f*, Zustimmung *f*.

old [əʊld] I *adj* **1.** *allg.* alt: *grow ~* alt werden, altern; *I'm getting ~!* ich werde alt!; *ten years ~* zehn Jahre alt; *a ten-year-~ boy* ein zehnjähriger Junge; *~ boy Br.* ehemaliger Schüler, Ehemalige *m*; *~ girl Br.* ehemalige Schülerin, Ehemalige *f*; *be ~ hat* F ein alter Hut sein; *the* (*od. his*) *~ lady* (*od. woman*) F s-e Alte; s-e alte Dame; *the* (*od. her*) *~ man* F ihr Alter; ihr alter Herr; *~ people's home* Alten-, Altersheim *n*; *of the ~ school Gentleman etc* der alten Schule; *⚹ Testament das* Alte Testament; *~ wives' tale* Ammenmärchen *n*; *⚹ World die* Alte Welt; → *flame* 1, *hand* 6, *maid* 1. **2.** *sl.* (*verstärkend*) *have a fine ~ time* sich köstlich amüsieren; *I can use any ~ thing* ich hab' für alles Verwendung; *come any ~ time* komm, wann es dir gerade paßt. II *s* **3.** *the ~ pl* die Alten *pl.* **~ age** *s* (hohes) Alter: *in one's ~* im Alter; *die of* (*od. from*) *~* an Altersschwäche sterben. **'~-age** *adj* Alters...: *~ pension* Rente *f*, Pension *f*; *~ pensioner* Rentner(in), Pensionär(in). **,~-es'tab·lished** *adj* alteingesessen (*Firma etc*), alt (*Brauch etc*). **'~-'fash·ioned** *adj* **1.** altmodisch. **2.** *Br.* F mißbilligend (*Blick etc*). **,~-'maid·ish** *adj* □ altjüngferlich.

old·ster ['əʊldstə] *s* F ältere Person.

,old-'tim·er *s* F **1.** alter Hase. **2.** *bsd. Am.* → *oldster*.

o·le·an·der [,əʊlɪ'ændə] *s ❀* Oleander *m*.

ol·fac·to·ry [ɒl'fæktərɪ] *adj* Geruchs...

ol·i·gar·chy ['ɒlɪɡɑːkɪ] *s* Oligarchie *f*.

ol·ive ['ɒlɪv] I *s* **1.** *a. ~ tree* Oliven-, Ölbaum *m*. **2.** Olive *f*: → *oil* Olivenöl *n*. II *adj* **3.** olivgrün.

O·lym·pi·ad [əʊ'lɪmpɪæd] *s* Olympiade *f*.

O·lym·pic I *adj* olympisch: *~ champion* Olympiasieger(in); *~ Games* → II; *Summer* (*Winter*) *~ Games pl* Olympische Sommer-(Winter)spiele *pl*. II *s pl* Olympische Spiele *pl*.

om·buds·man ['ɒmbʊdzmən] *s* (*irr man*) *s pol.* Ombudsmann *m*.

om·e·lett *s Am.*, **om·e·lette** *s bsd. Br.* ['ɒmlɪt] Omelett *n*.

o·men ['əʊmen] *s* Omen *n*, Vorzeichen *n*.

om·i·nous ['ɒmɪnəs] *adj* □ ominös, unheilvoll: *that's ~* das läßt nichts Gutes ahnen.

o·mis·sion [ə'mɪʃn] *s* **1.** Aus-, Weglassung *f*. **2.** Unterlassung *f*, Versäumnis *n*: *sin of ~* Unterlassungssünde *f*.

o·mit [ə'mɪt] *v/t* **1.** aus-, weglassen (*from* aus). **2.** *~ doing* (*od. to do*) *s.th.* versäumen *od.* es unterlassen, et. zu tun.

om·ni·bus ['ɒmnɪbəs] *s* Sammelband *m*.

om·nis·ci·ent [ɒm'nɪsɪənt] *adj* □ allwissend.

on [ɒn] I *prp* **1.** auf (*acc od. dat*). **2.** getragen von: auf (*dat*), an (*dat*), in (*dat*): *find s.th. ~ s.o.* et. bei *j-m* finden; *have you got some money ~ you?* hast du Geld bei dir?; → *foot* 1, *etc.* **3.** *fest-*

gemacht *od. sehr nahe:* an (*dat*): **the dog is ~ the chain; ~ the Thames.** 4. *Richtung, Ziel:* auf (*acc*) ... (hin), an (*acc*): **drop s.th. ~ the floor** et. zu Boden fallen lassen; **hang s.th. ~ a peg** et. an e-n Haken hängen; → **board** 8, *etc.* 5. *fig. auf der Grundlage von:* auf (*acc*) ... (hin): **~ this theory** nach dieser Theorie; → **condition** 1, *etc.* 6. *aufeinanderfolgend:* auf (*acc*), über (*acc*): **loss ~ loss** Verlust auf *od.* über Verlust; **be one's second glass** beim zweiten Glas sein. 7. (*gehörig*) zu, (*beschäftigt*) bei: **be ~ a committee** zu e-m Ausschuß gehören. 8. *Zustand:* in (*dat*), auf (*dat*): **be ~ Medikament** *etc* ständig nehmen; *b.s.* ...abhängig *od.* ...süchtig sein; → **duty** 2, *etc.* 9. *gerichtet:* auf (*acc*): **a joke ~ s.o.** ein Spaß auf j-s Kosten; **the next round is ~ me** F die nächste Runde geht auf m-e Rechnung. 10. *Thema:* über (*acc*): **talk ~ a subject.** 11. *Zeitpunkt:* an (*dat*): **~ June 3rd** am 3. Juni; **~ the morning of July 1st** am Morgen des 1. Juli. II *adv* 12. an..., auf...: → **put on** 1, **keep on** 1, *etc.* 13. weiter(...): **and so ~** u. so weiter; **~ and ~** immer weiter; **~ and off** ab u. zu, hin u. wieder; **from that day ~** von dem Tage an. III *adj* 14. **be ~** a) vor sich gehen: **what's ~?** was ist los?, b) an sein (*Licht, Radio etc*), c) *thea.* gegeben werden (*Stück*), laufen (*Film*), (*Rundfunk, TV*) gesendet werden. 15. **be always ~ at s.o.** F j-m dauernd in den Ohren liegen (*about* wegen).

once [wʌns] I *adv* 1. einmal: **~ again** (*od.* **more**) noch einmal; **~ or twice** ein paarmal; **~ in a while** ab u. zu, hin u. wieder; **~ and for all** ein für allemal; **not ~** kein einziges Mal; → **lifetime** I, **moon** I. 2. einmal, einst: **~ upon a time there was** es war einmal. II *s* 3. **the ~** einmal, ein einziges Mal; **this ~** dieses 'eine Mal. 4. **at ~** a) auf einmal, (*gleich*)zeitig, b) sofort: **all at ~** mit 'einem Mal. III *cj* 5. sobald *od.* wenn (einmal). **'~-o**̱**ver** *s:* **give s.th. the** (*od.* **a**) **~** F et. kurz mustern.

on·com·ing [ˈɒnˌkʌmɪŋ] *adj* entgegenkommend: **~ traffic** Gegenverkehr *m.*

one [wʌn] I *adj* 1. ein(e): → **hundred** 1, **thousand** 1. 2. *betont:* einzig: **they were all of ~ mind** sie waren all 'einer

Meinung; **his ~ thought** sein einziger Gedanke; **my ~ and only hope** m-e einzige Hoffnung; **the ~ and only ...** der einzigartige *od.* unvergleichliche ... 3. ein gewisser, e-e gewisse, ein gewisses: **~ day** e-s Tages; **~ John Smith** ein gewisser John Smith. II *s* 4. Eins *f,* eins: **at ~** um eins; **be ~ up on s.o.** j-m voraus sein; → **number** 2. 5. der, die, das einzelne: **~ by ~** e-r nach dem andern; **I for ~** ich zum Beispiel; → **another** 1. III *pron* 6. ein(e): **the ~ who** der(jenige), welcher; **~ another** sich (gegenseitig), einander. 7. *Stützwort, mst unübersetzt:* **the little ~s** die Kleinen; **a red pencil and a blue ~** ein roter Bleistift u. ein blauer. 8. man. 9. **~'s** sein: **break ~ leg** sich das Bein brechen. **'~-'armed** *adj:* **~ bandit** F einarmiger Bandit. **'~-'eyed** *adj* einäugig. **'~-'hand·ed** *adj u. adv* einhändig. **'~-'horse** *adj* einspännig: **~ town** F Nest *n,* Kaff *n.* **'~-'legged** *adj* einbeinig. **'~-man** *adj* Einmann...: **~ band** Einmannkapelle *f;* **~ play** *thea.* Einpersonenstück *n;* **~ show** One-man-Show *f.* **'~-'night** *adj:* **~ stand** *thea. etc* einmaliges Gastspiel. **'~-piece** *adj* einteilig.

on·er·ous [ˈɒnərəs] *adj* □ lästig, schwerlich (**to** für).

one'self *pron* 1. *reflex* sich (selbst *od.* selber): **(all) by ~** ganz allein; **cut ~** sich schneiden. 2. sich selbst *od.* selber. 3. man selbst *od.* selber: **be ~** sich normal *od.* natürlich benehmen *od.* geben; **not to be ~** nicht auf der Höhe sein; nicht ganz bei Verstand sein; **be ~ again** wieder ganz der alte sein.

one-'sid·ed *adj* □ einseitig (*a. fig.*). **'~-'time** *adj* ehemalig, früher. **'~-'track** *adj* 🚉 eingleisig: **have a ~ mind** *fig.* immer nur dasselbe im Kopf haben. **'~-way** *adj* 1. Einbahn...: **~ street.** 2. **~ ticket** *Am.* einfache Fahrkarte, ✈ einfaches Ticket. 3. *fig.* einseitig.

'on·go·ing *adj* laufend (*Verhandlungen etc*).

on·ion [ˈʌnjən] *s* 🌱 Zwiebel *f:* **know one's ~s** F sein Geschäft verstehen.

'on·look·er *s* Zuschauer(in).

on·ly [ˈəʊnlɪ] I *adj* 1. einzig: **~ child** Einzelkind *n;* → **one** 2. II *adv* 2. nur, bloß: **if ~ he would leave!** wenn er doch nur endlich ginge!; → **but** 2. 3. erst: **~ yes-**

terday; ~ *just* eben erst, gerade. **III** *cj* **4.** nur, bloß.

'on|·rush *s* Ansturm *m.* **'~·set** *s* Einbruch *m,* Beginn *m* (*des Winters*). **~·slaught** ['~slɔ:t] *s* (heftiger) Angriff (*a. fig.*). **,~·the·'job** *adj* praktisch (*Ausbildung*).

on·to ['ɒntʊ] *prp* **1.** auf (*acc*). **2. be** ~ **s.o.** F j-m auf die Schliche gekommen sein.

on·ward(s) ['ɒnwəd(z)] *adv* vorwärts, weiter: *from today* ~ von heute an.

oo·dles ['u:dlz] *s pl* F: ~ *of money* Geld wie Heu; ~ *of time* jede Menge *od.* massenhaft Zeit.

ooze [u:z] **I** *v/i* (*ein-, durch*)sickern, (*-*)dringen (*a. Licht, Geräusch etc*): ~ *away* versickern; *fig.* schwinden (*Mut etc*); ~ *out* aussickern; entweichen (*Luft, Gas*); *fig.* durchsickern (*Geheimnis etc*). **II** *v/t* absondern; *fig.* Charme ausstrahlen, *Optimismus, gute Laune etc a.* verströmen; *von Sarkasmus etc* triefen.

o·pal ['əʊpl] *s min.* Opal *m.*

o·paque [əʊ'peɪk] *adj* □ **1.** undurchsichtig. **2.** *fig.* unverständlich.

o·pen ['əʊpən] **I** *adj* □ **1.** *allg.* offen (*Buch, Fenster, Flasche etc*): *the door is* ~ die Tür ist *od.* steht offen; *hold the door* ~ *for s.o.* j-m die Tür aufhalten; *keep one's eyes* ~ *fig.* die Augen offenhalten; → *arm*[1] 1, *book* 1. **2.** offen (*Gelände, Meer*), frei (*Feld*): → *air*[1] 1. **3.** geöffnet, offen (*Laden etc*). **4.** *fig.* offen (*to* für); öffentlich: ~ *letter* offener Brief; ~ *tournament* → 13. **5.** *fig.* zugänglich, aufgeschlossen (*to* für *od. dat*). **6.** *fig.* ausgesetzt, unterworfen (*to dat*): ~ *to question* anfechtbar; *that is* ~ *to argument* darüber läßt sich streiten. **7.** *fig.* offen, unentschieden (*Frage etc*). **8.** *fig.* a) offen, freimütig: *be* ~ *with s.o.* offen mit j-m reden, b) offen(kundig), unverhüllt: ~ *secret* offenes Geheimnis. **9.** ✝ *cheque* ✝ Br. Barscheck *m.* **10.** ~ *season* Jagdzeit *f.* **11.** *ling.* offen (*Vokal*). **II** *s* **12.** *in the* ~ im Freien: *bring into the* ~ *fig.* an die Öffentlichkeit bringen; *come into the* ~ Farbe bekennen; an die Öffentlichkeit treten (*with mit*). **13.** *Golf, Tennis:* offenes Turnier. **III** *v/t* **14.** *allg.* öffnen, aufmachen, *Buch etc a.* aufschlagen. **15.** *Debatte, Feuer, Konto etc* eröffnen, *neuen*

Markt etc erschließen: ~ *to traffic* Straße *etc* dem Verkehr übergeben. **16.** *fig. Gefühle, Gedanken* enthüllen: ~ *o.s. to s.o.* sich j-m mitteilen. **IV** *v/i* **17.** sich öffnen, aufgehen. **18.** öffnen, aufmachen (*Laden etc*). **19.** führen, gehen (*onto* auf *acc* [... hinaus]) (*Tür, Fenster*). **20.** anfangen, beginnen; anlaufen (*Film*).

Verbindungen mit Adverbien:

o·pen| out I *v/t* ausbreiten, *Stadtplan etc* auseinanderfalten. **II** *v/i* auftauen, mitteilsam werden. ~ **up I** *v/t* **1.** aufmachen, -schließen. **2.** *neuen Markt etc* erschließen, *Möglichkeiten etc* eröffnen. **II** *v/i* **3.** aufmachen, -schließen. **4.** *fig.* a) loslegen (*with* mit), b) → **open out** II.

,o·pen|·'air *adj* im Freien: ~ *festival* Open-air-Festival *n;* ~ *swimming pool* Freibad *n;* ~ *theater* (*bsd. Br. theatre*) Freilichttheater *n.* **,~·'end·ed** *adj* zeitlich unbegrenzt: ~ *discussion* Open-end-Diskussion *f.*

o·pen·er ['əʊpnə] *s* **1.** (*Dosen-, Flaschen*)Öffner *m.* **2.** *Am.* Eröffnungsnummer *f* (*e-r Show etc*).

,o·pen|·'eyed *adj* mit großen Augen, staunend. **,~·'hand·ed** *adj* □ freigebig.

o·pen·ing ['əʊpnɪŋ] **I** *s* **1.** Öffnung *f.* **2.** ✝ freie Stelle. **3.** Eröffnung *f* (*e-r Debatte, des Feuers, e-s Kontos etc*), Erschließung *f* (*e-s neuen Markts etc*). **II** *adj* **4.** Eröffnungs...: ~ *ceremony;* ~ *night thea.* Eröffnungsvorstellung *f.* **5.** Öffnungs...: ~ *time;* ~ *time is at ...* das Geschäft *etc* ist ab ... geöffnet.

,o·pen|·'mind·ed *adj* □ aufgeschlossen. **,~·'mouthed** *adj* mit offenem Mund. **,~·'plan** *adj:* ~ *office* Großraumbüro *n.* ~ **shop** ✝ *Betrieb, der auch Nichtgewerkschaftsmitglieder beschäftigt.* ⌃

U·ni·ver·si·ty *s Br.* Fern(seh)universität *f* (*deren Kurse a. ohne entsprechenden Schulabschluß belegt werden können*).

op·er·a[1] ['ɒpərə] *s* ♪ Oper *f: go to the* ~ in die Oper gehen.

op·er·a[2] [~] *pl von* **opus.**

op·er·a·ble ['ɒpərəbl] *adj* □ **1.** durchführbar. **2.** ⊕ betriebsfähig. **3.** ✚ operabel, operierbar.

op·er·a| glass·es *s pl, a.* **pair of** ~ *glas-*

Opernglas *n*. **~ house** *s* Opernhaus *n*, Oper *f*.

op·er·ate [ˈɒpəreit] **I** *v/i* **1.** *bsd.* ⚙ arbeiten, in Betrieb sein, laufen (*Maschine etc*). **2.** wirksam sein *od.* werden; sich auswirken (**against** gegen; **in s.o.'s favo[u]r** zu j-s Gunsten). **3.** ⚔ operieren (**on s.o.** j-n): **~ on s.o. for appendicitis** j-n am Blinddarm operieren. **4.** ✈ tätig sein. **5.** ✖ operieren. **II** *v/t* **6.** ⚙ *Maschine* bedienen, *Schalter, Bremse etc* betätigen. **7.** *Unternehmen, Geschäft* betreiben, führen.

op·er·at·ic [ˌɒpəˈrætik] *adj* ♩ Opern...

op·er·at·ing [ˈɒpəreitiŋ] *adj* **1.** *bsd.* ⚙ Betriebs..., Arbeits...: **~ instructions** *pl* Bedienungs-, Betriebsanleitung *f*. **2.** ⚙ betrieblich, Betriebs...: **~ costs** (*od.* **expenses**) *pl* Betriebskosten *pl*. **3.** ⚔ Operations...: **~ room** *Am.*, **~ theatre** *Br.* Operationssaal *m*; **~ table** Operationstisch *m*. ,**op·er·a·tion** *s* **1.** *bsd.* ⚙ Wirksamkeit *f*, Geltung *f*: **be in ~** in Kraft sein; **come into ~** in Kraft treten. **2.** *bsd.* ⚙ Betrieb *m*, Lauf *m* (*e-r Maschine etc*): **in ~** in Betrieb; **put** (*od.* **set**) **in** (**out of**) **~** in (außer) Betrieb setzen. **3.** ⚙ Bedienung *f*, Betätigung *f*. **4.** ⚙ *etc* Wirkungs-, Arbeitsweise *f*; Arbeitsgang *m*. **5.** ✈ Geschäft *n*, (*Börse*) Transaktion *f*. **6.** ⚔ Operation *f*: **~ for appendicitis** Blinddarmoperation *f*; **have an ~ on one's arm** am Arm operiert werden. **7.** ✖ Operation *f*, Unternehmen *n*. ,**op·er·a·tion·al** [~ʃənl] *adj* **1.** *bsd.* ⚙ Betriebs..., Arbeits...: ⚙ betriebsbereit. **2.** ✈ betrieblich, Betriebs... **3.** ✖ Operations..., Einsatz... **op·er·a·tive** [ˈɒpərətiv] **I** *adj* **1.** wirksam: **become ~** *bsd.* ⚖ in Kraft treten: **the ~ word** genau das richtige Wort. **2.** ⚔ operativ. **op·er·a·tor** [~reitə] *s* **1.** (*Maschinen*)Arbeiter(in), (*Kran- etc*-)Führer(in); (*Computer*) Operator *m*. *teleph.* Vermittlung *f*, Fräulein *n* (vom Amt). **3.** (*Reise*)Veranstalter(in). **4.** *a clever* (*od.* **smooth**) **~** F ein raffinierter Kerl.

op·er·et·ta [ˌɒpəˈretə] *s* ♩ Operette *f*.

oph·thal·mic [ɒfˈθælmik] *adj* Augen...

o·pi·ate [ˈəʊpiət] *s pharm.* **1.** Opiat *n*, Opiumpräparat *n*. **2.** Schlaf- *od.* Beruhigungsmittel *n*.

o·pin·ion [əˈpinjən] *s* **1.** Meinung *f*, An-

sicht *f*: **in my ~** m-s Erachtens, m-r Meinung *od.* Ansicht nach; **be of the ~ that** der Meinung *od.* Ansicht sein, daß; **be of s.o.'s ~** j-s Meinung *od.* Ansicht sein; **that is a matter of ~** das ist Ansichtssache; **public ~** die öffentliche Meinung. **2.** Meinung *f*: **form an ~ of** sich e-e Meinung bilden von; **have a good** (*od.* **high**) (**bad, low**) **~ of** e-e (keine) hohe Meinung haben von. **3.** Gutachten *n* (**on** über *acc*). **o'pin·ion·at·ed** [~eitid] *adj* □ starr-, eigensinnig.

o·pin·ion| poll *s* Meinungsumfrage *f*. **~ re·search** *s* Meinungsforschung *f*.

o·pi·um [ˈəʊpjəm] *s* Opium *n*.

o·pos·sum [əˈpɒsəm] *s zo.* Opossum *n*, Beutelratte *f*.

op·po·nent [əˈpəʊnənt] *s* Gegner(in), Gegenspieler(in) (*beide a. Sport*).

op·por·tune [ˈɒpətjuːn] *adj* □ **1.** günstig, passend. **2.** rechtzeitig. **'op·por·tun·ism** *s* Opportunismus *m*. **'op·por·tun·ist I** *s* Opportunist(in). **II** *adj* opportunistisch. ,**op·por'tu·ni·ty** *s* Gelegenheit *f*, Möglichkeit *f*, Chance *f* (**of doing, to do** zu tun; **for s.th.** für *od.* zu et.): **at the first** (*od.* **earliest**) **~** bei der erstbesten Gelegenheit; → **equal 1**, **equality**.

op·pose [əˈpəʊz] *v/t* sich widersetzen (*dat*), angehen gegen. **op'posed** *adj* **1.** entgegengesetzt: **as ~ to** im Gegensatz zu. **2.** **be ~ to** ablehnend gegenüberstehen (*dat*), sein gegen. **op'pos·ing** *adj Sport:* gegnerisch (*Mannschaft*). **op·po·site** [ˈɒpəzit] **I** *adj* □ **1.** gegenüberliegend. **2.** entgegengesetzt (*Richtung*). **3.** gegensätzlich, entgegengesetzt: → **sex 1**. **4.** gegnerisch, Gegen...: **~ number** (*Amts*)Kollege *m*. **II** *s* **5.** Gegenteil *n*, -satz *m*: **be completely** (*od.* **just**) **the ~** genau das Gegenteil sein. **III** *adv* **6.** gegenüber (**to** *dat*). **IV** *prp* **7.** gegenüber (*dat*). ,**op·po'si·tion** *s* **1.** Widerstand *m*, Opposition *f* (**to** gegen). **2.** Gegensatz *m*: **be in ~ to** im Gegensatz stehen zu. **3.** *oft* **♁** *parl.* Opposition *f*: **be in ~** in der Opposition sein; **~ politician** Oppositionspolitiker(in).

op·press [əˈpres] *v/t* **1.** bedrücken, (*a. Hitze etc*) lasten auf (*dat*). **2.** unterdrücken, tyrannisieren. **op·pres·sion** [əˈpreʃn] *s* **1.** Bedrücktheit *f*. **2.** Unterdrückung *f*, Tyrannisierung *f*. **op'pres·sive** [~siv] *adj* □ **1.** bedrückend.

drückend (*Hitze, Steuern etc*). **3.** tyrannisch. **op·pres·sor** s Unterdrücker *m*, Tyrann *m*.

opt [ɒpt] *v/i* sich entscheiden (**for** für; **against** gegen; **to do** zu tun): ~ *out* sich dagegen entscheiden; abspringen, zurücktreten (**of** von).

op·tic ['ɒptɪk] **I** *adj* (~*ally*) Augen..., Seh...: ~ *nerve* Sehnerv *m*. **II** *s pl* (*sg konstruiert*) Optik *f*. **'op·ti·cal** *adj* □ optisch: ~ *illusion* optische Täuschung. **op·ti·cian** [~ʃn] *s* Optiker(in).

op·ti·ma ['ɒptɪmə] *pl von* **optimum**. **op·ti·mal** ['~ml] *adj* □ → **optimum** II.

op·ti·mism ['ɒptɪmɪzəm] *s* Optimismus *m*. **'op·ti·mist** *s* Optimist(in). ‚**op·ti'mis·tic** *adj* (~*ally*) optimistisch. **'op·ti·mize** *v/t* optimieren.

op·ti·mum ['ɒptɪməm] **I** *pl* -ma [~mə], -mums *s* Optimum *n*. **II** *adj* optimal, bestmöglich: *in* ~ *condition* in Bestzustand.

op·tion ['ɒpʃn] *s* **1.** Wahl *f*: *I had no* ~ *but to* ich hatte keine andere Wahl als zu, mir blieb nichts anderes übrig als zu; *leave one's* ~*s open* sich alle Möglichkeiten offenlassen. **2.** Option *f*, Vorkaufsrecht *n* (**on** auf *acc*). **3.** *bsd. mot.* Extra *n*, *pl a.* Sonderausstattung *f*. **op·tion·al** ['~ʃənl] *adj* □ freiwillig, fakultativ: *be an* ~ *extra bsd. mot.* gegen Aufpreis erhältlich sein; ~ *subject ped.* Wahlfach *n*.

op·u·lence ['ɒpjʊləns] *s* Reichtum *m*: *live in* ~ im Überfluß leben. **'op·u·lent** *adj* □ **1.** wohlhabend, reich. **2.** üppig, (*Mahlzeit a.*) opulent.

o·pus ['əʊpəs] *pl* **op·er·a** ['ɒpərə] *s bsd.* ♩ Opus *n*, Werk *n*.

or [ɔː] *cj* **1.** oder: *in a day* ~ *two* in ein bis zwei Tagen; ~ *so I believe* glaube ich zumindest; → *either* 5, 6, *else* 3, *so* 3. **2.** *nach neg*: noch, u. auch nicht.

or·a·cle ['ɒrəkl] *s* Orakel *n*. **o·rac·u·lar** [ɒ'rækjʊlə] *adj* □ orakelhaft.

o·ral ['ɔːrəl] **I** *adj* □ **1.** mündlich. **2.** Mund...: ~ *cavity anat.* Mundhöhle *f*. **II** *s* **3.** *ped.* mündliche Prüfung, *das* Mündliche.

or·ange ['ɒrɪndʒ] **I** *s* ♀ Orange *f*, Apfelsine *f*: ~ *squash Br.* Getränk aus Orangenkonzentrat u. Wasser. **II** *adj* orange, orange(n)farben. **or·ange·ade** [~'eɪd]

s Orangeade *f*, (*mit Kohlensäure a.*) Orangenlimonade *f*.

o·rang·u·tan [ɔː‚ræŋuː'tæn] *s zo.* Orang-Utan *m*.

o·ra·tion [ɔː'reɪʃn] *s* Rede *f*, Ansprache *f*. **or·a·tor** ['ɒrətə] *s* Redner(in). **or·a·tor·i·cal** [‚~'tɒrɪkl] *adj* □ rednerisch. **or·a·to·ri·o** [‚ɒrə'tɔːrɪəʊ] *pl* **-os** *s* ♩ Oratorium *n*.

or·bit ['ɔːbɪt] *s* **1.** *ast.* Kreis-, Umlaufbahn *f*: *put into* ~ → 4. **2.** *fig.* (Macht-) Bereich *m*, Einflußsphäre *f*. **II** *v/t* **3.** *Erde etc* umkreisen. **4.** Satelliten *etc* in e-e Umlaufbahn bringen.

or·chard ['ɔːtʃəd] *s* Obstgarten *m*; Obstplantage *f*.

or·ches·tra [ɔː'kɪstrə] *s* ♩ Orchester *n*: ~ *pit thea.* Orchestergraben *m*. **or·ches·tral** [ɔː'kestrəl] *adj* □ Orchester... **or·ches·trate** ['ɔːkɪstreɪt] *v/t* orchestrieren.

or·chid ['ɔːkɪd] *s* ♀ Orchidee *f*..

or·dain [ɔː'deɪn] *v/t*: ~ *s.o.* (*priest*) *eccl.* j-n ordinieren *od.* zum Priester weihen.

or·deal [ɔː'diːl] *s* **1.** *hist.* Gottesurteil *n*. **2.** *fig.* Martyrium *n*, Tortur *f*.

or·der ['ɔːdə] **I** *s* **1.** Ordnung *f*: *in* ~ in Ordnung (*a. fig.*); *put in* ~ in Ordnung bringen. **2.** (öffentliche) Ordnung: → *law* 1. **3.** Ordnung *f*, System *n*. **4.** (An)Ordnung *f*, Reihenfolge *f*: *in* ~ *of importance* nach Wichtigkeit; → *alphabetic*. **5.** Ordnung *f*, Aufstellung *f*. **6.** *parl. etc* (Geschäfts)Ordnung *f*: *be the* ~ *of the day* an der Tagesordnung stehen (*a. fig.*). **7.** Befehl *m*, Anordnung *f*: *by* ~ *of* auf Befehl von; *be under* (*od.* **have**) ~*s to do s.th.* Befehl haben, et. zu tun; → *marching orders*. **8.** ♣ Bestellung *f* (*a. im Restaurant*), Auftrag *m* (**for** für): *make to* ~ nach Bestellung *od.* nach Maß anfertigen; *last* ~*s, please* Polizeistunde!; ~ *book* Auftragsbuch *n*; ~ *form* Bestellschein *m*. **9.** *in* ~ um zu. **10.** *out of* ~ nicht in Ordnung, defekt. **11.** (Größen)Ordnung *f*: *of* (*od.* **in**) (*Am. on*) *the* ~ *of* in der Größenordnung von. **12.** *eccl. etc* Orden *m*. **II** *v/t* **13.** j-m befehlen (*to do* zu tun), et. befehlen, anordnen; ~ *about* (*od.* **around**) j-n herumkommandieren. **14.** j-n schicken, beordern (*to* nach): ~ *back* zurückbeordern; ~ *in* hinein- *od.* hereinkommen lassen; ~ *off*

(*Sport*) vom Platz stellen; ~ **out** hinausweisen. **15.** ✚ *j-m et.* verordnen: ~ *s.o.* **to** (**stay in**) **bed** j-m Bettruhe verordnen. **16.** ✚ bestellen (*a. im Restaurant*). **17.** *fig.* ordnen, in Ordnung bringen: ~*ed life* geordnetes Leben. **III** *v/i* **18.** bestellen (*im Restaurant*): **are you ready to** ~? haben Sie schon gewählt? '**or·der·ly I** *adj* **1.** ordentlich, geordnet. **2.** *fig.* gesittet, friedlich (*Menge etc*). **II** *s* **3.** ✚ Hilfspfleger *m*. **4.** ✕ (Offiziers)Bursche *m*.

or·di·nal (**num·ber**) ['ɔːdɪnl] *s* ᴀ Ordnungszahl *f*.

or·di·nar·i·ly ['ɔːdnrəlɪ] *adv* **1.** normalerweise, gewöhnlich. **2.** wie gewöhnlich *od.* üblich, normal.

or·di·nar·y ['ɔːdnrɪ] **I** *adj* **1.** üblich, gewöhnlich, normal: **in the** ~ **way** → **or·dinarily** 1. **2.** alltäglich, mittelmäßig, Durchschnitts... **3.** ordentlich (*Gericht, Mitglied*). **II** *s* **4. out of the** ~ ungewöhnlich, unüblich: *nothing out of the* ~ nichts Ungewöhnliches.

ore [ɔː] *s min.* Erz *n*.

or·gan ['ɔːgən] *s* **1.** *anat.* Organ *n*: ~*s pl* **of speech** Sprechwerkzeuge *pl*. **2.** *fig.* Organ *n*: a) Werkzeug *n*, Instrument *n*, b) Sprachrohr *n*: **party** ~ Parteiorgan *n*. **3.** ♩ Orgel *f*. ~ **grind·er** *s* Leierkastenmann *m*.

or·gan·ic [ɔː'gænɪk] *adj* (~*ally*) organisch (*a. fig.*). ~ *chemistry* organische Chemie. **or·gan·ism** ['ɔːgənɪzəm] *s* *biol.* Organismus *m* (*a. fig.*).

or·gan·ist ['ɔːgənɪst] *s* ♩ Organist(in).

or·gan·i·za·tion [ˌɔːgənaɪ'zeɪʃn] *s allg.* Organisation *f*. **or·gan·i'za·tion·al** *adj* ☐ organisatorisch, Organisations... '**or·gan·ize I** *v/t allg.* organisieren: ~*d crime* das organisierte Verbrechen; ~*d tour* Gesellschaftsreise *f*. **II** *v/i* sich (gewerkschaftlich) organisieren. '**or·gan·iz·er** *s* Organisator(in).

or·gasm ['ɔːgæzəm] *s* *physiol.* Orgasmus *m*.

or·gy ['ɔːdʒɪ] *s* Orgie *f* (*a. fig.*).

o·ri·ent ['ɔːrɪənt] ᴤ *der* Orient, *poet. das* Morgenland. **II** *v/t* ['~ent] *fig. et.* ausrichten (**toward[s]** *od acc*): ~ **o.s.** sich orientieren (**by** an *dat*, nach) (*a. fig.*); ~ **o.s. to a new situation** sich auf e-e neue Situation einstellen. **o·ri·en·tal I** *adj* ☐ orientalisch, *poet.*

morgenländisch: ~ **carpet** (*od. rug*) Orientteppich *m*. **II** *s* Orientale *m*, Orientalin *f*. **o·ri·en·tate** ['~enteɪt] → **orient II**. ,**o·ri·en·ta·tion** *s* Orientierung *f*, *fig. a.* Ausrichtung *f*.

or·i·fice ['ɒrɪfɪs] *s* *bsd. anat.* Öffnung *f*.

or·i·gin ['ɒrɪdʒɪn] *s* Ursprung *m*, Abstammung *f*, Herkunft *f*: **country of** ~ Ursprungsland *n*; **have its** ~ **in** zurückgehen auf (*acc*); (her)stammen von *od.* aus.

o·rig·i·nal [ə'rɪdʒənl] **I** *adj* (☐ → **originally**) **1.** Original..., Ur...: ~ **text** Ur-*od.* Originaltext *m*. **2.** originell. **II** *s* **3.** Original *n*: **in the** ~ im Original *od.* Urtext. **4.** Original *n* (*Person*). **o,rig·i'nal·i·ty** [~'nælətɪ] *s* Originalität *f*. **o'rig·i·nal·ly** [~nəlɪ] *adv* **1.** ursprünglich. **2.** originell.

o·rig·i·nate [ə'rɪdʒəneɪt] **I** *v/i* **1.** (*from*) zurückgehen (auf *acc*), (her)stammen (**von** *od.* aus). **2.** ausgehen (*from, with* von *j-m*). **II** *v/t* **3.** schaffen, ins Leben rufen. **o'rig·i·na·tor** *s* Urheber(in).

or·na·ment I *s* ['ɔːnəmənt] **1.** Ornament(e *pl*) *n*, Verzierung(en *f*) *f*, Schmuck *m*. **2.** *fig.* Zier(de) *f* (**to** für *od.* gen). **II** *v/t* ['~ment] **3.** verzieren, schmücken (**with** mit). **or·na·men·tal** [~'mentl] *adj* ☐ dekorativ, schmückend, Zier...: ~ *plant* Zierpflanze *f*. ,**or·na·men·ta·tion** [~men~] *s* Ausschmückung *f*, Verzierung *f*.

or·nate [ɔː'neɪt] *adj* ☐ **1.** reichverziert *od.* -geschmückt. **2.** *fig.* überladen (*Stil etc*).

or·ni·thol·o·gist [ˌɔːnɪ'θɒlədʒɪst] *s* Ornithologe *m*, Ornithologin *f*. ,**or·ni'thol·o·gy** *s* Ornithologie *f*, Vogelkunde *f*.

or·phan ['ɔːfn] **I** *s* Waise(nkind *n*) *f*. **II** *adj* Waisen... **III** *v/t*: **be** ~*ed* verwaisen, Waise werden. **or·phan·age** ['ɔːfənɪdʒ] *s* Waisenhaus *n*.

or·tho·dox ['ɔːθədɒks] *adj* ☐ *eccl. u. allg.* orthodox: ᴤ *Church* griechisch-orthodoxe Kirche.

or·tho·graph·ic, **or·tho·graph·i·cal** [ˌɔːθəʊ'græfɪk(l)] *adj* ☐ orthographisch. **or·thog·ra·phy** [ɔː'θɒgrəfɪ] *s* Orthographie *f*, Rechtschreibung *f*.

or·tho·pae·dic *bsd. Br.*, **or·tho·pe·dic** *Am.* [ˌɔːθəʊ'piːdɪk] ✚ **I** *adj* (~*ally*) orthopädisch. **II** *s pl* (*oft sg konstruiert*)

Orthopädie *f.* ˌor·tho'p(a)e·dist *s* Orthopäde *m*, Orthopädin *f.*

Os·car ['ɒskə] *s* Oscar *m* (*amerikanischer Filmpreis*).

os·cil·late ['ɒsɪleɪt] *v/i* **1.** *bsd. phys.* oszillieren, schwingen. **2.** *fig.* schwanken (**between** zwischen *dat*). ˌos·cil'la·tion *s* **1.** *bsd. phys.* Oszillation *f*, Schwingung *f.* **2.** *fig.* Schwanken *n.*

os·si·fy ['ɒsɪfaɪ] *v/i* verknöchern (*a. fig.*).

os·ten·si·ble [ɒ'stensəbl] *adj* □ **1.** scheinbar. **2.** an-, vorgeblich.

os·ten·ta·tion [ˌɒsten'teɪʃn] *s* **1.** (protzige) Zurschaustellung. **2.** Protzerei *f*, Prahlerei *f.* ˌos·ten'ta·tious *adj* □ **1.** protzend, prahlerisch: *be ~ about s.th.* mit et. protzen *od.* prahlen. **2.** ostentativ, demonstrativ.

os·tra·cism ['ɒstrəsɪzəm] *s* Ächtung *f.* **os·tra·cize** ['~saɪz] *v/t* ächten.

os·trich ['ɒstrɪtʃ] *s orn.* Strauß *m.*

oth·er ['ʌðə] **I** *adj* **1.** ander. *vor s im pl:* andere, übrige: *the ~ guests.* **3.** ander, weiter, sonstig: *the ~ two* die anderen beiden, die beiden anderen; *any ~ questions?* sonst noch Fragen? **4.** zweit (*nur in*): *every ~* jeder (jede, jedes) zweite; *every ~ day* jeden zweiten Tag, alle zwei Tage. **5.** *the ~ day* neulich, kürzlich; *the ~ night* neulich abend. **II** *pron* **6.** ander: *the ~* der (die, das) andere; *the two ~s* die anderen beiden, die beiden anderen; → *each* II. **III** *adv* **7.** anders (*than* als). **oth·er·wise** ['~waɪz] *adv* **1.** *a. cj* sonst, andernfalls. **2.** sonst, im übrigen. **3.** anderweitig: *be ~ engaged* anderweitig beschäftigt sein; *unless you are ~ engaged* wenn Sie nichts anderes vorhaben. **4.** anders (*than* als): *think ~* anderer Meinung sein; *X, ~* (*called*) *Y* X, a. Y genannt; *or ~* od. sonst irgendwie; *od.* nicht.

ot·ter ['ɒtə] *s zo.* Otter *m.*

ought [ɔːt] *v/aux ich* sollte, *du solltest etc*: *he ~ to do it* er sollte es (eigentlich) tun.

ounce [aʊns] *s* **1.** Unze *f.* **2.** *fig.* Körnchen *n* (*Wahrheit*), Funke *m* (*Verstand*).

our ['aʊə] *possessive pron* unser: ♀ *Father eccl.* Vaterunser *n.* **ours** ['aʊəz] *possessive pron*: *it is ~* es gehört uns; *a friend of ~* ein Freund von uns; *their children and ~* ihre Kinder u. unsere. **our-**

-selves [ˌ~'selvz] *pron* **1.** *verstärkend:* wir *od.* uns selbst: *we did it ~, we ~ did it* wir haben es selbst getan. **2.** *reflex* uns: *we cut ~.* **3.** uns (selbst): *we want it for ~.*

oust [aʊst] *v/t fig.* verdrängen (*from* aus).

out [aʊt] **I** *adv* **1.** hinaus(...), heraus(...); aus(...): *way ~* Ausgang *m*; *on the way ~* beim Hinausgehen; *have a tooth ~* e-n Zahn gezogen bekommen. **2.** außen, draußen. **3.** nicht zu Hause, ausgegangen. **4.** *be ~* ♀ streiken; → *come out* 2, *go out* 4. **5.** ins Freie; draußen, im Freien. **6.** (*aus dem Gefängnis etc*) entlassen. **7.** heraus: a) erschienen (*Buch etc*), b) enthüllt (*Geheimnis*): *~ with it!* F heraus damit!, heraus mit der Sprache! **8.** *pol.* nicht (mehr) im Amt *od.* an der Macht. **9.** aus der Mode, out. **10.** weit u. breit: *~ and away* bei weitem. **11.** aus, vorbei, vorüber: *before the week is ~* vor Ende der Woche. **12.** aus, erloschen: → *go out* 3. **13.** aus(verkauft). **14.** *be ~ for* aussein auf (*acc*): *be ~ to do s.th.* darauf aussein, et. zu tun. **15.** *~ of* a) aus (... heraus); zu ... hinaus, b) aus, von: *two ~ of three Americans* zwei von drei Amerikanern, c) außer *Reichweite etc*, d) außer *Atem, Übung etc*: *be ~ of* kein ... mehr haben; *we are ~ of oil* uns ist das Öl ausgegangen, e) aus *der Mode etc*, f) außerhalb von (*od. gen*), g) um *et. betrügen*, h) aus *Bosheit, Mitleid etc*. **II** *prp* **16.** → 15a. **.~-and-'out** *adj* absolut, ausgesprochen: *an ~ lie* e-e faustdicke Lüge. **.~'bal·ance** *v/t* überwiegen. **.~'bid** *v/t* (*irr bid*) überbieten. '**.~board** ♪ **I** *adj* **1.** Außenbord...: *~ motor.* **II** *adv* **2.** außenbords. **III** *s* **3.** Außenbordmotor *m.* **4.** Außenborder *m* (*Boot*). '**.~break** *s* Ausbruch *m*: *~ of anger* Zornausbruch; *at the ~ of war* bei Kriegsausbruch. '**.~build·ing** *s* Nebengebäude *n.* '**.~burst** *s* (*Zorn- etc*)Ausbruch *m.* '**.~cast I** *adj* ausgestoßen, verstoßen. **II** *s* Ausgestoßene *m, f*, Verstoßene *m, f.* .~'class *v/t* weit überlegen sein (*dat*), (*Sport a.*) deklassieren. '**.~come** *s* Ergebnis *n*, Resultat *n*: *what was the ~ of the talks?* was ist bei den Gesprächen herausgekommen? '**.~cry** *s fig.* Aufschrei *m*, Schrei *m* der Entrüstung. **,~'dat·ed** adj überholt, veraltet. **,~'dis·tance** v/t hinter sich lassen. **,~'do** v/t (irr **do**) **1.** (**in**) übertreffen (an od. in dat), ausstechen (in dat). **2.** schlagen, besiegen (**in** in dat). '**~·door** adj: **~ games** pl Spiele pl für draußen; **~ sea·son** (Sport) Freiluftsaison f; **~ shoes** pl Straßenschuhe pl; **~ shot** phot. Außenaufnahme f. **,~'doors** adv draußen, im Freien; hinaus, ins Freie.

out·er ['aʊtə] adj äußer, Außen...: **~ gar·ments** pl Oberbekleidung f; **~ space** Weltraum m; **~ wall** Außenwand f. **~·most** ['~məʊst] adj äußerst.

'**out·fit** s **1.** Ausrüstung f, Ausstattung f, ⚙ a. Gerät(e pl) n, Werkzeug(e pl) n. **2.** F Verein m, Laden m. '**~·fit·ter** s Ausrüster m: (**men's**) **~** Herrenausstatter m. '**~·flow** s Ausfluß m, bsd. ✝ Abfluß m. **,~'fox** v/t überlisten. '**~·go·ing** I adj **1.** scheidend, aus dem Amt scheidend. **2. ~ mail** Postausgang m. II s pl **3.** Ausgaben pl. **,~'grow** v/t (irr **grow**) **1.** j-m über den Kopf wachsen. **2.** herauswachsen aus (e-m Kleidungsstück); e-r Angewohnheit etc entwachsen. '**~· house** s Nebengebäude n.

out·ing ['aʊtɪŋ] s Ausflug m: **go for an ~** e-n Ausflug machen.

out'land·ish adj □ befremdend, befremdlich. **,~'last** v/t überdauern, -leben. '**~·law** I s **1.** hist. Geächtete m. **2.** Bandit m. II v/t **3.** hist. ächten, für vogelfrei erklären. **4.** für ungesetzlich erklären, verbieten. '**~·lay** s Auslagen pl, Ausgaben pl (**on, for** für). '**~·let** s **1.** Abfluß(öffnung f) m, Abzug(söffnung f) m. **2.** ✝ Verkaufsstelle f. **3. seek an ~ for** fig. ein Ventil suchen für. '**~·line** I s **1.** Umriß m, Kontur f, pl a. Silhouette f. **2.** fig. Ab-, Grundriß m. II v/t **3.** umreißen, fig. a. in Umrissen darlegen. '**~·live** v/t überleben: **have ~d its usefulness** ausgedient haben (Maschine etc). '**~·look** s **1.** (Aus)Blick m, (Aus)Sicht f (**from** von; **onto** auf acc). **2.** fig. (Zukunfts)Aussichten pl (**for** für). **3.** fig. Einstellung f (**on** zu): **~ on life** Lebensauffassung f. '**~·ly·ing** adj abgelegen, entlegen. **,~ma'noeu·vre** bsd. Br. v/t ✕ ausmanövrieren (a. fig.). **~·mod·ed** [,~'məʊdɪd] adj veraltet, überholt. **~·most** ['~məʊst] adj äußerst. **,~'num·ber** v/t

j-m zahlenmäßig überlegen sein: **be ~ed by s.o.** j-m zahlenmäßig unterlegen sein. **,~·of-'date** adj veraltet, überholt. **,~-of-the-'way** adj **1.** abgelegen, entlegen. **2.** fig. ungewöhnlich, ausgefallen; wenig bekannt. '**~·pa·tient** s ambulanter Patient: **~s' department** Ambulanz f; **~ treatment** ambulante Behandlung. **,~'play** v/t j-m spielerisch überlegen sein. '**~·post** s ✕ Vorposten m (a. fig.). '**~·pour·ing** s (Gefühls)Erguß m. '**~·put** s Output m: a) ✝, ⚙ Arbeitsertrag m, -leistung f, b) ✝ Ausstoß m, Ertrag m, Produktion f, c) ✝ Ausgangsleistung f, d) Computer: (Daten)Ausgabe f.

out·rage ['aʊtreɪdʒ] I s **1.** Greueltat f: **an ~ against** ein Verbrechen an (dat) od. gegen; fig. e-e grobe Verletzung (gen). **2.** a. **sense of ~** Empörung f, Entrüstung f (**at** über acc). II v/t **3.** Gefühle, Anstand etc grob verletzen, mit Füßen treten. **4.** j-n empören, schockieren. **out'ra·geous** adj □ **1.** abscheulich, verbrecherisch. **2.** empörend, unerhört.

'**out,rig·ger** s ⚓ Ausleger m; Auslegerboot n. **~·right** I adj ['~raɪt] **1.** völlig, gänzlich, total, (Lüge etc) glatt. II adv [,~'raɪt] **2.** ohne Umschweife, unumwunden. **3.** auf der Stelle, sofort. **,~'ri·val** v/t übertreffen, -bieten (**in** an od. in dat), ausstechen. **,~'run** v/t (irr **run**) **1.** schneller laufen als; j-m davonlaufen. **2.** fig. übersteigen. '**~·set** s Anfang m, Beginn m: **at the ~** am Anfang; **from the ~** (gleich) von Anfang an. **,~'shine** v/t (irr **shine**) überstrahlen, fig. a. in den Schatten stellen. **,~'side** I s **1.** Außenseite f: **from the ~** von außen; **on the ~** auf der Außenseite, außen. **2. at the (very) ~** (aller)höchstens, äußerstenfalls. **3.** Sport: Außenstürmer(in): **~ right** Rechtsaußen m. II adj **4.** äußer, Außen...: **~ broadcast** (Rundfunk, TV) Außenübertragung f; **~ lane** (Sport) Außenbahn f; mot. Br. innere Fahrspur. **5.** fig. **~ chance** kleine od. geringe Chance; (Sport) Außenseiterchance f. III adv **6.** draußen. **7.** heraus, hinaus. **8. ~ of** a) → 9, b) Am. F außer. IV prp **9.** außerhalb (a. fig.). **,~'sid·er** s allg. Außenseiter(in). '**~·size** I s Übergröße f. II adj übergroß. '**~·skirts** s pl Stadtrand *m*, Peripherie *f*: **on the ~ of London** am Stadtrand von London. ˌ~'**smart** F → **outwit.** ˌ~'**spo·ken** *adj* □ **1.** offen(herzig), freimütig: **be ~** kein Blatt vor den Mund nehmen. **2.** unverblümt. ˌ~'**spread** *v/t* (*irr spread*) ausbreiten, *Arme a.* ausstrecken: **with arms ~** mit ausgestreckten Armen. ˌ~'**stand·ing** *adj* □ **1.** hervorragend. **2.** *bsd.* ✝ unerledigt, rückständig, (*Forderungen etc*) ausstehend. ˌ~'**stay** *v/t* länger bleiben als: → **welcome 6.** ˌ~'**stretched** *adj* ausgestreckt. ˌ~'**strip** *v/t* **1.** überholen. **2.** *fig.* übertreffen (**in** an *dat*). ˌ~'**vote** *v/t* überstimmen: **be ~d** e-e Abstimmungsniederlage erleiden.

out·ward ['aʊtwəd] **I** *adj* **1.** äußerlich, äußer (*beide a. fig.*), Außen...: **his ~ cheerfulness** s-e zur Schau getragene Fröhlichkeit. **II** *adv* **2.** auswärts, nach außen. **3.** → **outwardly.** '**out·ward·ly** *adv* äußerlich (*a. fig.*).

out·wards ['~z] → **outward** II.

ˌ**out**'**weigh** *v/t* überwiegen, (ge)wichtiger sein als. ˌ~'**wit** *v/t* überlisten, reinlegen. '**~·work** *s* ✝ Heimarbeit *f*. '**~·work·er** *s* ✝ Heimarbeiter(in). '**~·worn** *adj* veraltet, überholt.

o·va ['əʊvə] *pl von* **ovum.**

o·val ['əʊvl] **I** *adj* □ oval. **II** *s* Oval *n*.

o·va·ry ['əʊvərɪ] *s* **1.** *anat.* Eierstock *m*. **2.** ⚘ Fruchtknoten *m*.

o·va·tion [əʊ'veɪʃn] *s* Ovation *f*: **give s.o. a standing ~** j-m stehend e-e Ovation bereiten.

ov·en ['ʌvn] *s* Backofen *m*, Bratofen *m*, -röhre *f*. **~ cloth** *s* Topflappen *m*. **~ glove, ~ mitt** *s* Topfhandschuh *m*. '**~-read·y** *adj* bratfertig.

o·ver ['əʊvə] **I** *prp* **1.** *Lage:* über (*dat*): **the lamp ~ his head.** **2.** *Richtung, Bewegung:* über (*acc*), über (*acc*) ... (hin)weg: **he jumped ~ the fence,** → **get over,** *etc.* **3.** über (*dat*), auf der anderen Seite von (*od. gen*): **~ the street** auf der anderen (Straßen)Seite. **4.** über s-r *Arbeit einschlafen etc*, bei e-m *Glas Wein etc.* **5.** *Herrschaft, Rang:* über (*acc od. dat*): **be ~ s.o.** über j-m stehen. **6.** über (*acc*), mehr als: **~ a mile; ~ 10 dollars; ~ a week** über od. länger als e-e Woche. **7.** *zeitlich:* über (*acc*), während: **~ many years** viele Jahre hindurch. **II** *adv* **8.** hinüber, her-

über (**to** zu). **9.** drüben: **~ there** da drüben. **10.** *allg.* über...: → **hand over 1, think 2,** *etc.* **11.** um...: → **fall over, turn over,** *etc.* **12.** (*all*) **~ again** noch einmal; **~ and ~** immer wieder. **13.** darüber, mehr: **children of 10 years and ~** Kinder von 10 Jahren u. darüber; **5 ounces and ~** 5 Unzen u. mehr; **~ and above** obendrein, überdies. **14.** zu Ende, vorüber, vorbei: **get s.th. ~** (**with**) F et. hinter sich bringen. ˌ~'**act** *thea. etc* **I** *v/t* Rolle überziehen. **II** *v/i* übertreiben (*a. weitS.*). ˌ~'**age** *adj* zu alt. **~-all I** *adj* ['~rɔːl] **1.** gesamt, Gesamt...: **~ length** Gesamtlänge *f*. **II** *adv* [ˌ~r'ɔːl] **2.** allgemein. **3.** insgesamt. **III** *s* ['~rɔːl] **4.** *Br.* Arbeitsmantel *m*, Kittel *m*. **5.** *Am.* Overall *m*. **6.** *pl a*) *Br.* Overall *m*, b) *Am.* → **dungarees.** ˌ~'**bal·ance I** *v/t* umstoßen, umkippen. **II** *v/i* Übergewicht bekommen, das Gleichgewicht verlieren, umkippen. ˌ~'**bear·ing** *adj* □ anmaßend. ˌ~'**bid** *v/t* (*irr bid*) überbieten. '**~-board** *adv* ♻ über Bord: **fall ~** über Bord gehen; **throw ~** über Bord werfen (*a. fig.*). ˌ~'**book** *v/t* Flug, Hotel etc überbuchen. ˌ~'**cast** *adj* bewölkt, bedeckt. ˌ~'**charge I** *v/t* **1.** *j-m* zuviel berechnen *od.* abverlangen: **~ s.o.** (**by**) £10 um 10 Pfund zuviel berechnen. **2.** *Betrag* zuviel verlangen. **3.** überlasten, ⚡ *a.* überladen (*a. fig.*). **II** *v/i* **4.** zuviel berechnen *od.* verlangen (**for** für). '**~-coat** *s* Mantel *m*. ˌ~'**come** (*irr come*) **I** *v/t* überwältigen, -winden (*beide a. fig.*), *Gefahren* bannen: **be ~ with emotion** von s-n Gefühlen übermannt werden. **II** *v/i* siegen. ˌ~'**crowd·ed** *adj* überfüllt, überlaufen (*a. Beruf*). ˌ~'**do** *v/t* (*irr do*) **1.** übertreiben: **~ it** (*od. things*) zu weit gehen, des Guten zuviel tun. **2.** zu lange braten *od.* kochen: **overdone** *a.* übergar. '**~-dose** *s* Überdosis *f*. '**~-draft** *s* ✝ (Konto)Überziehung *f*: **have an ~ of £100** sein Konto um 100 Pfund überzogen haben. ˌ~'**draw** *v/t* (*irr draw*) ✝ Konto überziehen (**by** um): **be ~n** sein Konto überzogen haben. ˌ~'**dress** *v/t u. v/i* (sich) vornehm anziehen: **~ed** *a.* overdressed. '**~-drive** *s mot.* Overdrive *m*, Schongang *m*. ˌ~'**due** *adj* überfällig: **she is ~** sie müßte (schon) längst hier sein.

ˌ~·**es·ti·mate** *v/t* **1.** zu hoch schätzen

od. veranschlagen. **2.** *fig.* überschätzen, überbewerten. **,~ex'pose** *v/t phot.* überbelichten. **,~'flow I** *v/i* **1.** überlaufen, -fließen, (*Fluß etc*) über die Ufer treten: *full to ~ing* zum Überlaufen voll; (*Raum*) überfüllt. **2.** überquellen (**with** von) (*a. fig.*). **II** *v/t* **3. ~ its banks** über die Ufer treten. **III** *s* [*~flǝʊ*] **4.** Überlaufen *m*, -fließen *n*. **5.** ☉ Überlauf *m*: **~ valve** Überlaufventil *n*. **6.** Überschuß *m* (**of** an *dat*): **~ of population** Bevölkerungsüberschuß *m*. **,~'grown** *adj* **1.** überwachsen, -wuchert (**with** von). **2.** übergroß, (*Junge etc*) hoch aufgeschossen. **,~'haul I** *v/t* [*~'hɔ:l*] **1.** ⊙ überholen: **~ completely** generalüberholen. **2.** *fig. Pläne etc* überprüfen. **3.** *j-n, Fahrzeug etc* überholen. **II** *s* [*~'hɔ:l*] **4.** ⊙ Überholung *f*: **complete ~** Generalüberholung. **5.** *fig.* Überprüfung *f*. **,~'head I** *adj* **1.** oberirdisch, Frei-, Hoch...: **~ line** ⚡ Oberleitung *f*; **~ projector** Overhead-, Tageslichtprojektor *m* **2.** allgemein: **~ costs** (*od. expenses*) *pl* → **4. 3.** *Sport:* Überkopf...: **~ kick** (*Fußball*) (Fall)Rückzieher *m*; **~ stroke** → **5. II** *s* **4. ~**(**s** *pl Br.*) ♥ laufende (Geschäfts)Kosten *pl*. **5.** *Tennis:* Überkopfball *m*. **III** *adv* [*~'hed*] **6.** (dr)oben; über uns. **,~'hear I** *v/t* (*irr hear*) zufällig hören. **,~'heat I** *v/t Motor* überhitzen, *Raum* überheizen. **II** *v/i* ⊙ heißlaufen. **,~in'dulge I** *v/t* **1.** zu nachsichtig behandeln, *j-m* zuviel durchgehen lassen. **2.** *e-r Leidenschaft etc* übermäßig frönen. **II** *v/i* **3. ~ in television** zuviel fernsehen. **,~joyed** [*~'dʒɔɪd*] *adj* überglücklich. **'~kill** *s* ✕ Overkill *n*. **~land I** *adv* [*~'lænd*] über Land, auf dem Landweg. **II** *adj* ['*~lænd*] (Über-)Land... **,~'lap** *v/i* **1.** (sich) überlappen. **2.** *fig.* sich überschneiden. **,~'leaf** *adv* umseitig, umstehend. **,~'load** *v/t* überlasten (*a.* ⚡), -laden.

o·ver·ly ['ǝʊvǝlɪ] *adv* übermäßig, allzu: *he wasn't ~ enthusiastic* s-e Begeisterung hielt sich in Grenzen.

,o·ver|'manned *adj* (personell) überbesetzt. **,~'much I** *adj* (all)zuviel. **II** *adv* übermäßig: *I don't like him ~* ich mag ihn nicht besonders. **,~'night I** *adv* über Nacht (*a. fig.*): *stay ~* über Nacht bleiben; *stay ~ with s.o.* (*od. at s.o.'s place*) bei j-m übernachten. **II** *adj*

Nacht...: **~ bag** Reisetasche *f*; **~ stay** (*od. stop*) Übernachtung *f*. **'~pass** *s bsd. Am.* (Straßen-, Eisenbahn)Überführung *f*. **,~'pay** *v/t* (*irr pay*) **1.** zu teuer bezahlen, zuviel bezahlen für. **2.** *j-m* zuviel zahlen, *j-n* überbezahlen. **,~'play** *v/t* **1. a)** → **overact** I, **b)** hochspielen. **2. ~ one's hand** sich überreizen *od.* übernehmen. **,~'pop·u·lat·ed** *adj* übervölkert. **'~,pop·u'la·tion** *s* **1.** Übervölkerung *f*. **2.** Überbevölkerung *f*. **,~'pow·er** *v/t* **1.** überwältigen, -mannen (*beide a. fig.*): **~ing** *fig.* überwältigend, (*Geruch*) aufdringlich, penetrant. **,~'rate** *v/t* überbewerten (*a. Sport*), -schätzen. **,~'reach** *v/t*: **~ o.s.** sich übernehmen. **,~re'act** *v/i* überreagieren, überzogen reagieren (**to** auf *acc*). **,~re'ac·tion** *s* Überreaktion *f*, überzogene Reaktion. **,~'ride** *v/t* (*irr ride*) sich hinwegsetzen über (*acc*). **,~'rid·ing** *adj* vordringlich, -rangig: *his ~ concern was* es ging ihm vor allem darum (**to do** zu tun). **,~'rule** *v/t Entscheidung etc* aufheben, *Einspruch etc* abweisen. **,~'run** (*irr run*) **I** *v/t* **1. be ~ with** überlaufen sein von. **2.** ☒ *Signal* überfahren. **II** *v/i* **3.** länger dauern als vorgesehen. **,~'seas I** *adv* nach *od.* in Übersee. **II** *adj* überseeisch, Übersee..., aus Übersee. **,~'see** *v/t* (*irr see*) beaufsichtigen, überwachen. **~se·er** ['*~sɪǝ*] *s* Aufseher(in). **,~'shad·ow** *v/t fig.* **1.** in den Schatten stellen. **2.** überschatten, e-n Schatten werfen auf (*acc*). **,~'shoot** *v/t* (*irr shoot*) hinausschießen über (*ein Ziel*) (*a. fig.*). **'~sight** *s* Versehen *n*: **by** (*od. through an*) **~** aus Versehen. **,~'sim·pli·fy** *v/t* (zu) grob vereinfachen, vergröbern. **,~'size(d)** *adj* übergroß, mit Übergröße. **,~'sleep** *v/i* (*irr sleep*) verschlafen. **,~'staffed** *adj* (personell) überbesetzt. **,~'state** *v/t* übertreiben, übertrieben darstellen. **,~'state·ment** *s* Übertreibung *f*. **,~'stay** *v/t* länger bleiben als: → **welcome** 6. **,~'step** *v/t fig.* überschreiten. **,~'take** *v/t* (*irr take*) **1.** einholen (*a. fig.*). **2.** (*a. v/i*) *bsd. Br.* überholen. **3.** *fig.* überraschen. **,~'tax** *v/t* **1.** zu hoch besteuern. **2.** *fig.* überbeanspruchen, *Geduld etc* strapazieren: **~ one's strength** (*od. o.s.*) sich übernehmen. **,~'throw I** *v/t* [*~'θrǝʊ*] (*irr throw*) **1.** *Regierung etc* stürzen. **2.** besiegen. **II**

s ['∼θrəʊ] **3.** Sturz *m*. **4.** Niederlage *f*.
'**∼·time I** *s* **1.** ♣ a) Überstunden *pl*: **be
on** (*od.* **do**) ∼ Überstunden machen, b)
a. ∼ **pay** Überstundenlohn *m*. **2.** *Sport*:
Am. Verlängerung *f*: *after* ∼ nach Verlängerung; *the game went into* ∼ das
Spiel ging in die Verlängerung. **II** *adv* **3.
work** ∼ ♣ Überstunden machen.

o·ver·ture ['əʊvə‚tjʊə] *s* ♩ Ouvertüre *f*
(*to* zu).

‚**o·ver**'**turn I** *v/t* **1.** umwerfen, -stoßen,
-kippen. **2.** *fig. Regierung etc* stürzen.
II *v/i* **3.** umkippen, ⚓ kentern. '**∼·view**
s fig. Überblick *m* (*of* über *acc*).
∼·weight I *s* ['∼‚weɪt] Übergewicht *n* (*a.
fig.*). **II** *adj* [‚∼'weɪt] übergewichtig
(*Person*), zu schwer (*by* um) (*Gegenstand*): **be** ∼ **by five kilos, be five kilos**
∼ fünf Kilo Übergewicht haben.
∼·whelm [‚∼'welm] *v/t* **1.** überwältigen
(*a. fig.*). **2.** überhäufen, -schütten
(*with* mit). ‚∼'**whelm·ing** *adj* überwältigend: ∼*ly* mit überwältigender Mehrheit. ‚∼'**work I** *v/t* überstrapazieren (*a.
fig.*), überanstrengen: ∼*ed a.* gestreßt; ∼
o.s. → II. **II** *v/i* sich überarbeiten.

o·vi·duct ['əʊvɪdʌkt] *s anat.* Eileiter *m*.

o·vip·a·rous [əʊ'vɪpərəs] *adj* □ *zo.* eierlegend.

o·vu·la·tion [‚ɒvjʊ'leɪʃn] *s biol.* Eisprung *m*.

o·vum ['əʊvəm] *pl* **o·va** ['əʊvə] *s biol.*
Ei(zelle *f*) *n*.

owe [əʊ] *v/t* **1.** *j-m et.* schulden, schuldig
sein (*for* für). **2.** bei *j-m* Schulden haben, *j-m* Geld schulden. **3.** *et.* verdanken, zu verdanken haben.

ow·ing ['əʊɪŋ] *adj* **1.** unbezahlt: *how*

much is still ∼ *to you?* wieviel bekommst du noch?; *there is still £1,000*
∼ es stehen noch 1000 Pfund aus. **2.** ∼ *to*
infolge, wegen.

owl [aʊl] *s orn.* Eule *f*. '**owl·ish** *adj* □
eulenhaft (*Aussehen etc*).

own [əʊn] **I** *v/t* **1.** besitzen: *who* ∼*s this
car?* wem gehört dieser Wagen? **2.** zugeben, (ein)gestehen (*that* daß). **II** *v/i* **3.**
∼ *up* es zugeben: ∼ (*up*) *to s.th.* et.
zugeben *od.* (ein)gestehen; ∼ (*up*) *to
doing s.th.* zugeben *od.* (ein)gestehen,
et. getan zu haben. **III** *adj* **4.** eigen: ∼
goal (*Sport*) Eigentor *n* (*a. fig.*). **IV** *s* **5.**
my ∼ mein Eigentum: *a car of one's* ∼
ein eigenes Auto; *on one's* ∼ allein;
come into one's ∼ zur Geltung kommen; → *get back* 1, *hold* 10.

own·er ['əʊnə] *s* Eigentümer(in), Besitzer(in). ‚∼·'**oc·cu·pied** *adj* eigengenutzt
(*Haus, Wohnung*).

own·er·ship ['əʊnəʃɪp] *s* Besitz *m*.

ox [ɒks] *pl* **ox·en** [‚∼n] *s zo.* Ochse
m.

Ox·bridge ['ɒksbrɪdʒ] *s* (die Universitäten) Oxford u. Cambridge *pl*.

ox·en ['ɒksn] *pl von* **ox.**

ox·ide ['ɒksaɪd] *s* 🜍 Oxyd *n*. **ox·i·dize**
['ɒksɪdaɪz] *v/t u. v/i* oxydieren.

'**ox·tail** *s* Ochsenschwanz *m*: ∼ **soup.**

ox·y·gen ['ɒksɪdʒən] *s* 🜍 Sauerstoff *m*. ∼
mask *s* ⚕ Sauerstoffmaske *f*. ∼ **tent** *s* ⚕
Sauerstoffzelt *n*.

oys·ter ['ɒɪstə] *s zo.* Auster *f*. ∼ **bed** *s*
Austernbank *f*.

o·zone ['əʊzəʊn] *s* 🜍 Ozon *n*. ∼ **lay·er,** ∼
shield *s* Ozonschicht *f* (*der Atmosphäre*).

P

P [piː] *s*: *mind one's p's and q's* F sich
anständig aufführen.

pace [peɪs] **I** *s* **1.** Tempo *n* (*a. fig.*), Geschwindigkeit *f*: *at a* (*very*) *slow* ∼
(ganz) langsam; *keep* ∼ *with* Schritt
halten *od.* mitkommen mit (*a. fig.*);
keep ∼ *with the times* mit der Zeit

gehen; *set the* ∼ das Tempo angeben (*a.
fig.*), (*Sport*) das Tempo machen. **2.**
Schritt *m*. **3.** Gangart *f* (*e-s Pferdes*):
put s.o. through his ∼*s fig.* j-n auf Herz
u. Nieren prüfen; *show one's* ∼*s fig.*
zeigen, was man kann. **II** *v/t* **4.** *Sport*:
j-m Schrittmacherdienste leisten. **5.** *a.* ∼

out (*od. off*) ab-, ausschreiten. **6.** *Zimmer etc* durchschreiten. **III** *v/i* **7.** ~ *a-bout* (*od. around*) hin u. her laufen; ~ *up and down* auf u. ab gehen. '~,**mak-er** *s* **1.** *Sport:* Schrittmacher(in) (*a. fig.*). **2.** ♂ (*Herz*)Schrittmacher *m*. '~**,set-ter** → **pacemaker** 1.

pach·y·derm ['pækɪdɜ:m] *s zo.* Dick-häuter *m*.

pa·cif·ic [pə'sɪfɪk] *adj* (~*ally*) friedlich, friedfertig, friedliebend.

pac·i·fi·er ['pæsɪfaɪə] *s* **1.** Friedensstif-ter(in). **2.** *Am.* Schnuller *m*.

pac·i·fism ['pæsɪfɪzəm] *s* Pazifismus *m*. '**pac·i·fist** *I s* Pazifist(in). **II** *adj* pazifi-stisch.

pac·i·fy ['pæsɪfaɪ] *v/t* **1.** *Land* befrieden. **2.** besänftigen, beschwichtigen.

pack [pæk] *I s* **1.** Pack(en) *m*, Bündel *n*. **2.** Paket *n* (*Waschpulver etc*), *bsd. Am.* Packung *f*, Schachtel *f* (*Zigaretten*). **3.** Rudel *n* (*Wölfe etc*); *hunt.* Meute *f*. **4.** *contp.* Pack *n*, Bande *f*: ~ *of thieves* Diebesbande; ~ *of lies* ein Sack voll Lügen. **5.** (Karten)Spiel *n*. **6.** ♂, *Kos-metik:* Packung *f*. **II** *v/t* **7.** *oft* ~ *up* ein-, zs.-, ab-verpacken: ~ *s.o. s.th.* j-m et. einpacken. **8.** *a.* ~ *together* zs.-pfer-chen: → *sardine*. **9.** vollstopfen; ~*ed, Br.* ~*ed out* bis auf den letzten Platz gefüllt, brechend voll. **10.** *Koffer etc* packen: *be* ~*ed* gepackt haben. **11.** *mst* ~ *off* F fort-, wegschicken. **12.** *mst* ~ *up* (*od. in*) F aufhören *od.* Schluß machen mit: ~ *it in!* hör endlich auf (damit)! **III** *v/i* **13.** packen: ~ *up* zs.-packen. **14.** (sich) drängen (*into* in *acc*). **15.** *mst* ~ *off* F sich packen *od.* davonmachen: *send s.o.* ~*ing* j-n fort- *od.* wegjagen. **16.** fest werden. **17.** F a) *mst* ~ *up* (*od. in*) aufhören, Feierabend machen, b) ~ *up* absterben (*on s.o.* j-m) (*Motor*), s-n Geist aufgeben (*Waschmaschine etc*).

pack·age ['pækɪdʒ] *I s* **1.** Paket *n* (*a. fig.*). **2.** Packung *f* (*Spaghetti etc*). **II** *v/t* **3.** verpacken; zu e-m Paket abpacken. ~ *deal s* Pauschalarrangement *n*. ~ *tour s* Pauschalreise *f*.

pack an·i·mal *s* Pack-, Last-, Tragtier *n*.

pack·er ['pækə] *s* Packer(in).

pack·et ['pækɪt] *s* **1.** Päckchen *n*: *a* ~ *of cigarettes* e-e Packung *od.* Schachtel Zigaretten. **2.** *Br. sl.* *cost a* ~ ein Hei-

dengeld kosten; *make a* ~ ein Schwei-negeld verdienen. **3.** *catch* (*od. cop, get, stop*) *a* ~ *Br. sl.* in Schwulitäten kommen; eins aufs Dach kriegen (*from* von).

pack ice *s* Packeis *n*.

pack·ing ['pækɪŋ] *s* **1.** Packen *n*: *do one's* ~ packen. **2.** Verpackung *f*.

pact [pækt] *s* Pakt *m*: *make a* ~ *with s.o.* mit j-m e-n Pakt schließen.

pad¹ [pæd] *v/i* trotten.

pad² [~] *I s* **1.** Polster *n*. **2.** *Sport:* (Knie-*etc*)Schützer *m*. **3.** (*Schreib- etc*)Block *m*. **4.** (*Stempel*)Kissen *n*. **5.** *zo.* Ballen *m*. **6.** (*Abschuß*)Rampe *f*. **7.** *sl.* Bude *f* (*Wohnung, Zimmer*). **II** *v/t* **8.** *a.* ~ *out* (aus)polstern: ~*ded cell* Gummizelle *f*. **9.** *oft* ~ *out Rede etc* aufblähen (*with* mit). '**pad·ding** *s* **1.** Polsterung *f*. **2.** *fig.* Füllsel *pl*.

pad·dle¹ ['pædl] *I s* **1.** Paddel *n*. **2.** ♣ Schaufel *f*; Schaufelrad *n*. **II** *v/i* **3.** pad-deln (*a. schwimmen*). **III** *v/t* **4.** paddeln: → *canoe* 1.

pad·dle² [~] *v/i* (herum)planschen (*in* in *dat*).

pad·dle steam·er *s* Raddampfer *m*.

pad·dling pool ['pædlɪŋ] *s* Planschbek-ken *n*.

pad·dock ['pædək] *s* **1.** (Pferde)Koppel *f*; (*Pferderennsport*) Sattelplatz *m*. **2.** *Motorsport:* Fahrerlager *n*.

pad·dy¹ ['pædɪ] *s a.* ~ *field* Reisfeld *n*.

pad·dy² [~] *s Br.* F Koller *m*: *be in a* ~ e-n Koller haben.

Pad·dy³ [~] *s* F Paddy *m*, Ire *m*.

pad·dy wag·on ['pædɪ] *s Am.* F grüne Minna.

pad·lock ['pædlɒk] *I s* Vorhängeschloß *n*. **II** *v/t* mit e-m Vorhängeschloß ver-schließen.

pae·di·a·tri·cian [,pi:dɪə'trɪʃn] *s bsd. Br.* Kinderarzt *m*, -ärztin *f*. **pae·di·at·rics** [,~'ætrɪks] *s pl* (*sg konstruiert*) Kinder-heilkunde *f*.

pa·gan ['peɪgən] *I s* Heide *m*, Heidin *f*. **II** *adj* heidnisch. '**pa·gan·ism** *s* Heiden-tum *n*.

page¹ [peɪdʒ] *s* **1.** Page *m*, *hist. a.* Edel-knabe *m*. **II** *v/t* **2.** *j-n* ausrufen (lassen): *paging Mr X* Herr X, bitte! **3.** mit *j-m* über Funkrufempfänger Kontakt auf-nehmen, *j-n* anpiepsen.

page² [~] *I s* Seite *f* (*e-s Buchs etc*): *be on*

~ 10 auf Seite 10 stehen; **four-~** vierseitig. **II** *v/t* paginieren.

'page-boy *s* Page *m*.

pag-er ['peɪdʒə] *s* Funkrufempfänger *m*, Piepser *m*.

pag-i-nate ['pædʒɪneɪt] *v/t* paginieren.

,pag-i'na-tion *s* Paginierung *f*.

pa-go-da [pə'gəʊdə] *s* Pagode *f*.

paid [peɪd] **I** *pret u. pp von* **pay. II** *adj*: **put ~ to** *bsd. Br.* F ein Ende machen (*dat*), *Hoffnungen etc* zunichte machen.

pail [peɪl] *s* Eimer *m*, Kübel *m*.

pain [peɪn] **I** *s* **1.** Schmerz(en *pl*) *m*: **be in ~** Schmerzen haben; **I have a ~ in my back** mir tut der Rücken weh; **be a ~ (in the neck)** F e-m auf den Wecker gehen. **2.** Schmerz *m*, Kummer *m*: **cause** (*od.* **give**) **s.o. ~** j-m Kummer machen. **3.** *pl* Mühe *f*, Bemühungen *pl*: **be at** (**great**) **~s to do s.th.** sich (große) Mühe geben, et. zu tun; **spare no ~s** keine Mühe scheuen; **take ~s** sich Mühe geben (**over, with** mit; **to do** zu tun). **II** *v/t* **4.** *bsd. fig.* schmerzen. **pain-ful** ['ˌfʊl] *adj* □ **1.** schmerzend, schmerzhaft. **2.** *fig.* schmerzlich; unangenehm; peinlich.

'pain,kill-er *s* Schmerzmittel *n*.

pain-less ['peɪnlɪs] *adj* □ **1.** schmerzlos. **2.** F leicht, einfach.

pain thresh-old *s* Schmerzschwelle *f*.

'pains,tak-ing *adj* □ sorgfältig, gewissenhaft.

paint [peɪnt] **I** *v/t* **1.** Bild, *j-n* malen: **~ a gloomy** (**vivid**) **picture of s.th.** *fig.* et. in düsteren (glühenden) Farben malen *od.* schildern; **→ black** 1. **2.** anmalen, bemalen; (an)streichen, *Auto etc* lackieren: **~ out** (*od.* **over**) übermalen; **~ one's face** *contp.* sich anmalen; **~ the town red** F e-n draufmachen. **3.** ✍ (aus)pinseln (**with** mit). **II** *v/i* **4.** malen. **III** *s* **5.** Farbe *f*; Lack *m*; *contp.* Schminke *f*: **wet ~** frisch gestrichen! **'~,box** *s* Malkasten *m*. **'~brush** *s* Pinsel *m*.

paint-er ['peɪntə] *s* **1.** (*a.* Kunst)Maler(in), Anstreicher(in). **2.** (*Auto- etc*) Lackierer(in). **'paint-ing** *s* **1.** Malerei *f*. **2.** Gemälde *n*, Bild *n*.

'paint-work *s* Lack *m* (*e-s Autos etc*).

pair [peə] **I** *s* **1.** Paar *n* (*Stiefel etc*): **in ~s** paarweise. **2.** *et.* Zweiteiliges, *mst* unübersetzt: **a ~ of trousers** e-e Hose. **3.** Paar *n*, Pärchen *n* (*Mann u. Frau, zo.*

Männchen *u.* Weibchen): **~ skating** (*Eis-, Rollkunstlauf*) Paarlauf(en *n*) *m*. **4. where is the ~ to this shoe?** wo ist der andere *od.* zweite Schuh? **5.** *Rudern*: Zweier *m*. **II** *v/t* **6.** *a.* **~ off** (*od.* **up**) paarweise anordnen, in Zweiergruppen einteilen: **~ off** zwei (**junge**) **Leute** zs.-bringen, verkuppeln. **III** *v/i* **7.** *zo.* sich paaren. **8.** *a.* **~ off** (*od.* **up**) Paare bilden.

pa-ja-mas *Am.* **→ pyjamas.**

Pa-ki-stan-i [ˌpɑːkɪ'stɑːnɪ] **I** *s* Pakistani *m*, Pakistaner(in). **II** *adj* pakistanisch.

pal [pæl] **I** *s* Kumpel *m*: **listen, ~¡** ... *bsd. Am.* hör mal, Freundchen, ... **II** *v/i mst* **~ up** sich anfreunden (**with** mit).

pal-ace ['pælɪs] *s* Palast *m* (*a. weitS.*).

pal-at-a-ble ['pælətəbl] *adj* □ schmackhaft (*a. fig.*): **make s.th. ~ to s.o.**

pal-a-tal ['pælətl] *s ling.* Gaumenlaut *m*.

pal-ate ['pælət] *s* **1.** *anat.* Gaumen *m*. **2.** *fig.* **for s.o.'s ~** für j-s Geschmack; **have no ~ for** keinen Sinn haben für.

pa-la-tial [pə'leɪʃl] *adj* □ palastartig.

pa-lav-er [pə'lɑːvə] *s* F **1.** Palaver *n*, endloses Gerede. **2.** Theater *n*.

pale¹ [peɪl] **I** *adj* □ **1.** blaß, bleich: **turn ~ → 3. 2.** hell, blaß (*Farbe*). **II** *v/i* **3.** blaß *od.* bleich werden. **4.** *fig.* verblassen (**before, beside** neben *dat*).

pale² [~] *s* Pfahl *m*: **go beyond the ~** *fig.* die Grenzen des Anstandes überschreiten.

pale-ness ['peɪlnɪs] *s* Blässe *f*.

Pal-es-tin-i-an [ˌpælə'stɪnɪən] **I** *s* Palästinenser(in). **II** *adj* palästinensisch.

pall¹ [pɔːl] *s* **1.** Sargtuch *n*; Sarg *m* (*bsd. während der Beerdigung*). **2.** *fig.* (*Dunst-etc*)Glocke *f*.

pall² [~] *v/i* s-n Reiz verlieren (**on** für): **~ on s.o.** *a.* j-n langweilen.

'pall,bear-er *s* Sargträger *m*; *j-d, der neben dem Sarg geht.*

pal-let ['pælɪt] *s* ⚙ Palette *f*. **~ truck** *s* Gabelstapler *m*.

pal-li-ate ['pælɪeɪt] *v/t* **1.** ✍ lindern. **2.** *fig.* bemänteln, beschönigen. **pal-li-a-tive** ['~ətɪv] **I** *adj* □ **1.** ✍ lindernd. **2.** *fig.* beschönigend. **II** *s* **3.** ✍ Linderungsmittel *n*.

pal-lid ['pælɪd] *adj* □ blaß (*a. fig.*), bleich. **pal-lor** ['pælə] *s* Blässe *f*.

pal-ly ['pælɪ] *adj* F befreundet (**with** mit): **they are very ~** sie sind dicke Freunde.

palm¹ [pɑːm] **I** *s* **1.** Handfläche *f*, -teller

m: *grease* (*od. oil*) **s.o.'s** ~ F j-n schmieren (*with* mit); *have an itching* (*od. itchy*) ~ F e-e offene Hand haben (*bestechlich sein*); *have* (*od. hold*) **s.o. in the** ~ **of one's hand** j-n völlig in der Hand *od.* in s-r Gewalt haben. **II** *v/t* **2.** *et.* in der Hand verschwinden lassen (*Zauberkünstler*). **3.** F ~ *s.th.* **off as** et. an den Mann bringen als; ~ *s.th.* **off on(to) s.o.** j-m et. andrehen; ~ *s.o.* **off with s.th.** j-m et. andrehen; j-n mit et. abspeisen.

palm² [~] *s* ♀ Palme *f.*

palm·ist ['pɑːmɪst] *s* Handleser(in).
'**palm·is·try** *s* Handlesekunst *f.*

Palm| Sun·day *s eccl.* Palmsonntag *m.* ♀
~ tree *s* ♀ Palme *f.*

pal·pa·ble ['pælpəbl] *adj* □ **1.** fühl-, greif-, tastbar. **2.** *fig.* augenfällig, deutlich; offensichtlich.

pal·pi·tate ['pælpɪteɪt] *v/i* **1.** klopfen, pochen (*Herz*). **2.** zittern (*with* vor *dat*).
,**pal·pi·ta·tion** *s a. pl* Herzklopfen *n.*

pal·sy ['pɔːlzɪ] *s* ♀ Lähmung *f.*

pal·try ['pɔːltrɪ] *adj* □ armselig, schäbig: **a** ~ **£10** lumpige 10 Pfund.

pam·per ['pæmpə] *v/t* verwöhnen, *Kind a.* verhätscheln.

pam·phlet ['pæmflɪt] *s* **1.** Broschüre *f*, Druckschrift *f.* **2.** Flugblatt *n*, -schrift *f.*

pan¹ [pæn] **I** *s* **1.** Pfanne *f*; Topf *m.* **2.** (Waag)Schale *f.* **3.** *bsd. Br.* (Klosett)Schüssel *f.* **II** *v/t* **4.** F *Theaterstück etc* verreißen. **III** *v/i* **5.** ~ **out** F klappen: ~ **out well** hinhauen.

pan² [~] **I** *s* (Kamera)Schwenk *m.* **II** *v/t Filmkamera* schwenken. **III** *v/i* schwenken.

pan·a·ce·a [,pænə'sɪə] *s* Allheilmittel *n*, *fig. a.* Patentrezept *n.*

,**Pan-A·mer·i·can** *adj* panamerikanisch.
'**pan·cake** *s* Pfannkuchen *m.*

pan·cre·as ['pæŋkrɪəs] *s anat.* Bauchspeicheldrüse *f.*

pan·da ['pændə] *s zo.* Panda *m.* ♀ **car** *s Br.* (Funk)Streifenwagen *m.*

pan·de·mo·ni·um [,pændɪ'məʊnjəm] *s* Chaos *n*, Tumult *m.*

pan·der ['pændə] *v/i:* ~ **to e-m** Laster *etc* Vorschub leisten, *j-s* Bedürfnisse *etc* befriedigen.

pane [peɪn] *s* (*Fenster*)Scheibe *f.*

pan·el ['pænl] **I** *s* **1.** Tafel *f*, Platte *f*; (vertieftes) Feld. **2.** ⚡, ⚙ (Schalt-, Kon-

troll- *etc*)Tafel *f.* **3.** ⚖ Liste *f* der Geschworenen. **4.** Diskussionsteilnehmer *pl*, -runde *f*; Rateteam *n.* **II** *v/t pret u. pp* -**eled,** *bsd. Br.* -**elled 5.** täfeln. ~ **dis·cus·sion** *s* Podiumsdiskussion *f.* ~ **game** *s* Rundfunk, *TV:* Ratespiel *n.*

pan·el·(l)ing ['pænlɪŋ] *s* Täfelung *f.*
pan·el·(l)ist ['⌐əlɪst] *s* Diskussionsteilnehmer(in).

pang [pæŋ] *s* stechender Schmerz; ~**s** *pl of hunger* nagender Hunger; *feel a* ~ *of conscience* Gewissensbisse haben.

pan·ic ['pænɪk] **I** *adj* **1.** panisch: ~ *buying* Angstkäufe *pl*; *be at* ~ *stations* rotieren; *push the* ~ *button* F panisch reagieren. **II** *s* **2.** Panik *f: be in a* ~ in Panik sein; *get into a* ~ → 5; *throw into a* ~ → 4. **3.** *be a* ~ *Am.* F zum Totlachen sein. **III** *v/t pret u. pp* -**icked 4.** in Panik versetzen, e-e Panik auslösen unter (*dat*). **IV** *v/i* **5.** in Panik geraten: *don't* ~! nur keine Panik! '**pan·ick·y** *adj* F **1.** überängstlich. **2.** *get* ~ → *panic* 5.

'**pan·ic-,strick·en** *adj* von panischem Schrecken erfaßt *od.* ergriffen.

pan·o·ra·ma [,pænə'rɑːmə] *s* **1.** Panorama *n.* **2.** *fig.* (allgemeiner) Überblick (*of* über *acc*). **pan·o·ram·ic** [,pænə'ræmɪk] *adj* (~*ally*) panoramisch, Panorama...: ~ *view* a) Rundblick *m* (*of* über *acc*), b) → *panorama* 2.

pan·sy ['pænzɪ] *s* **1.** ♀ Stiefmütterchen *n.* **2.** F Weichling *m.*

pant [pænt] **I** *v/i* **1.** keuchen: ~ *for breath* nach Luft schnappen. **2.** *be* ~*ing fig.* lechzen (*after, for* nach; *to do s.th.* danach, et. zu tun). **II** *v/t* **3.** ~ *out* Worte (hervor)keuchen. **III** *s* **4.** Atemstoß *m.*

pan·the·ism ['pænθiːɪzəm] *s* Pantheismus *m.* '**pan·the·ist** *s* Pantheist(in). **II** *adj* pantheistisch. ,**pan·the·is·tic** *adj* (~*ally*) pantheistisch.

pan·ther ['pænθə] *s zo.* Panther *m.*

pant·ies ['pæntɪz] *s pl, a. pair of* ~ Höschen *n* (*für Kinder*), (*für Damen a.*) Schlüpfer *m*, Slip *m.*

pan·to·mime ['pæntəmaɪm] *s* **1.** *Br.* Weihnachtsspiel *n* (*für Kinder*). **2.** *thea.* Pantomime *f.*

pan·try ['pæntrɪ] *s* Speise-, Vorratskammer *f.*

pants [pænts] *s pl, a. pair of* ~ **1.** *Br.* Unterhose *f.* **2.** *bsd. Am.* Hose *f: catch s.o. with his* ~ *down* F j-n überrumpeln; *talk the ~ off s.o.* F j-m ein Loch *od.* Löcher in den Bauch reden; → *wear* 3.

pant-suit ['pæntsuːt] *s bsd. Am.* Hosenanzug *m.*

pan-ty hose ['pæntɪ] *s bsd. Am.* Strumpfhose *f.*

pap [pæp] *s* Brei *m.*

pa-pal ['peɪpl] *adj* ☐ päpstlich.

pa-per ['peɪpə] **I** *s* **1.** Papier *n*: *on ~ fig.* auf dem Papier. **2.** Tapete *f.* **3.** Zeitung *f*: *be in the ~s* in der Zeitung stehen. **4.** *pl (Ausweis)*Papiere *pl*; Akten *pl*, Unterlagen *pl.* **5.** *ped.* Arbeit *f, univ.* Klausur(arbeit) *f.* **6.** Referat *n*: *give (od. read) a ~* ein Referat halten, referieren (*to* vor *dat*; *on* über *acc*). **II** *v/t* **7.** tapezieren. **8.** *~ over (od. up) fig. Differenzen etc* (notdürftig) übertünchen. **'~back** *s* Paperback *n*, Taschenbuch *n*: *in ~* als Taschenbuch. **~ bag** *s* (Papier-) Tüte *f.* **'~boy** *s* Zeitungsjunge *m.* **~ chase** *s* Schnitzeljagd *f.* **~ clip** *s* Büro-, Heftklammer *f.* **~ cup** *s* Pappbecher *m.* **~ hand-ker-chief** *s* Papiertaschentuch *n.* **'~hang-er** *s* Tapezierer(in). **~ knife** *s* (*irr* knife) Brieföffner *m.* **~ mon-ey** *s* Papiergeld *n.* **~ plate** *s* Pappteller *m.* **'~thin** *adj* hauchdünn (*a. fig.*), papierdünn. **~ti-ger** *s fig.* Papiertiger *m*, (*Person a.*) Gummilöwe *m.* **'~weight** *s* **1.** Briefbeschwerer *m.* **2.** *Sport*: Papiergewicht(ler *m*) *n.* **'~work** *s* Schreibarbeit *f.*

pa-pier-mâ-ché [ˌpæpjeɪˈmæʃeɪ] *s* Pappmaché *n.*

pap-ri-ka ['pæprɪkə] *s* Paprika *m.*

pa-py-rus [pə'paɪərəs] *pl* **-ri** [ˌraɪ], **-rus-es** *s* **1.** ♀ Papyrus(staude *f*) *m.* **2.** *antiq.* Papyrus(rolle *f*) *m.*

par [pɑː] **I** *s* **1.** ✝ Nennwert *m*: *at ~* zum Nennwert, al pari. **2.** *be on a ~* auf gleicher Stufe stehen (*with* wie): *be on a ~ with a.* j-m ebenbürtig sein; *I'm feeling below (od. under) ~ today* I'm bin heute nicht (ganz) auf dem Posten. **3.** *Golf*: Par *n*: *that's ~ for the course* F das ist ganz normal (*for* für). **II** *adj* **4.** *~ value* ✝ Nennwert *m.*

par-a-ble ['pærəbl] *s* Parabel *f*, Gleichnis *n.*

pa-rab-o-la [pə'ræbələ] *s* ♙ Parabel *f.*

par-a-bol-ic [ˌpærə'bɒlɪk] *adj* (**~ally**) **1.** ♙ parabolisch, Parabel... **2.** *~ mirror* ☉ Parabolspiegel *m.*

par-a-chute ['pærəʃuːt] **I** *s* Fallschirm *m*: *~ jump* Fallschirmabsprung *m.* **II** *v/t* mit dem Fallschirm absetzen *od.* abwerfen. **III** *v/i* (mit dem Fallschirm) abspringen. **'par-a-chut-ist** *s* Fallschirmspringer(in); ✕ Fallschirmjäger *m.*

pa-rade [pə'reɪd] **I** *s* **1.** Umzug *m*, *bsd.* ✕ Parade *f*: *be on ~* e-e Parade abhalten. **2.** *fig.* Zurschaustellung *f*: *make a ~ of* → 4. **II** *v/t* **3.** stolzieren durch. **4.** *fig.* zur Schau stellen. **III** *v/i* **5.** ziehen (*through* durch), *bsd.* ✕ paradieren. **6.** stolzieren (*through* durch). **~ ground** *s* ✕ Exerzierplatz *m.*

par-a-digm ['pærədaɪm] *s* **1.** Musterbeispiel *n* (*of* für). **2.** *ling.* Paradigma *n.*

par-a-dise, *eccl. mst* ♙ ['pærədaɪs] *s* Paradies *n* (*a. fig.*).

par-a-dox ['pærədɒks] *s* Paradox(on) *n.* **,par-a'dox-i-cal** *adj* ☐ paradox: **~ly** (*enough*) paradoxerweise.

par-af-fin ['pærəfɪn] *s* **1.** *Br.* Petroleum *n.* **2.** *a. ~ wax* Paraffin *n.*

par-a-gon ['pærəɡən] *s* Muster *n* (*of* an *dat*): *~ of virtue bsd. iro.* Ausbund *m* an Tugend.

par-a-graph ['pærəɡrɑːf] *s* **1.** Absatz *m*, Abschnitt *m.* **2.** (Zeitungs)Notiz *f.*

par-a-keet ['pærəkiːt] *s* *orn.* Sittich *m.*

par-al-lel ['pærəlel] **I** *adj* **1.** parallel (*to, with* zu) (*a. fig.*): *~ bars pl* (*Turnen*) Barren *m*; *~ case* Parallelfall *m.* **II** *s* **2.** ♙ Parallele *f* (*to, with* zu) (*a. fig.*): *without ~* ohne Parallele, ohnegleichen; *draw a ~ between* e-e Parallele ziehen zwischen (*dat*); *have close ~s* e-e starke Ähnlichkeit haben (*with* mit). **3.** *a. ~ of latitude geogr.* Breitenkreis *m.* **III** *v/t pret u. pp* **-leled**, *Br. a.* **-lelled 4.** gleichkommen (*dat*), entsprechen (*dat*). **'par-al-lel-ism** *s* **1.** ♙ Parallelität *f* (*a. fig.*). **2.** *ling.* Parallelismus *m.* **,par-al-'lel-o-gram** [ˌʊʊɡræm] *s* ♙ Parallelogramm *n.*

par-a-lyse ['pærəlaɪz] *v/t bsd. Br.* ✄ lähmen, *fig. a.* lahmlegen, zum Erliegen bringen: *~d with fig.* starr *od.* wie gelähmt vor. **pa-ral-y-sis** [pə'rælɪsɪs] *pl* **-ses** [ˌsiːz] *s* ✄ Lähmung *f*, *fig. a.* Lahmlegung *f.* **par-a-lyt-ic** [ˌpærə'lɪtɪk] **I** *adj* (**~ally**) **1.** ✄ Lähmungs...; gelähmt. **2.** *Br.* F sternhagel-

voll. **II** s **3.** ✳ Gelähmte m, f. **par·a·**
-lyze Am. → paralyse.

pa·ram·e·ter [pə'ræmɪtə] s **1.** A Parame-
ter m. **2.** mst pl fig. Rahmen m: **within**
the ~s of im Rahmen (gen).

par·a·mil·i·tar·y [ˌpærə'mɪlɪtərɪ] adj pa-
ramilitärisch.

par·a·mount ['pærəmaʊnt] adj: **of ~ im-**
portance von (aller)größter Bedeutung.

par·a·noi·a [ˌpærə'nɔɪə] s ✳ Paranoia f.
par·a·noi·ac [~æk] I adj (~ally) paranoisch. **II** s Paranoiker(in). **'par·a·**
-noid adj paranoid: **be ~ about** ständig
Angst haben vor (dat).

par·a·pet ['pærəpɪt] s Brüstung f.

par·a·pher·na·li·a [ˌpærəfə'neɪljə] s pl
(a. sg construiert) **1.** (persönliche) Sachen pl. **2.** F bsd. Br. Scherereien pl.

par·a·phrase ['pærəfreɪz] I s Paraphrase
f, Umschreibung f. **II** v/t paraphrasie-
ren, umschreiben.

par·a·ple·gi·a [ˌpærə'pliːdʒə] s ✳ Quer-
schnitt(s)lähmung f. **,par·a'ple·gic** I
adj querschnitt(s)gelähmt. **II** s Quer-
schnitt(s)gelähmte m, f.

par·a·psy·chol·o·gy [ˌpærəsaɪ'kɒlədʒɪ] s
Parapsychologie f.

par·a·site ['pærəsaɪt] s biol. Schmarotzer
m, Parasit m (beide a. fig.). **par·a·sit·ic**
[~'sɪtɪk] adj (~ally) biol. parasitär, pa-
rasitisch, fig. a. schmarotzerhaft: **be ~**
on schmarotzen von.

par·a·troop·er ['pærəˌtruːpə] s ⚔ Fallschirmjäger m. **'par·a·troops** s pl Fall-
schirmjägertruppe f.

par·a·ty·phoid (fe·ver) [ˌpærə'taɪfɔɪd] s
✳ Paratyphus m.

par·boil ['pɑːbɔɪl] v/t halbgar kochen,
ankochen.

par·cel ['pɑːsl] I s **1.** Paket n. **2.** Parzelle
f. **II** v/t pp **-celed**, bsd. Br.
-celled 3. mst ~ **up** (als Paket) verpak-
ken. **4.** mst ~ **out** aufteilen, Land parzellieren.

parch [pɑːtʃ] v/t u. v/i ausdörren, -trock-
nen, v/i a. verdörren, -trocknen.

parch·ment ['pɑːtʃmənt] s Pergament n.

par·don ['pɑːdn] I v/t **1.** et. verzeihen: ~
s.o. (for) sth. j-m et. verzeihen od. verzeihen; ~ **me** a) → 3a, c, b) Am. → 3b; ~
me for interrupting you verzeihen od.
entschuldigen Sie, wenn ich Sie unter-
breche; **if you'll ~ the expression** wenn

ich so sagen darf. **2.** ⚖ begnadigen. **II**
s **3. I beg your ~** a) Entschuldigung!,
Verzeihung!, b) a. F ~**?** (wie) bitte?, c)
erlauben Sie mal!, ich muß doch sehr
bitten! **4.** ⚖ Begnadigung f. **'par·**
don·a·ble adj □ entschuldbar, verzeihlich.

pare [peə] v/t **1.** sich die Nägel schneiden: ~ **down** fig. einschränken. **2.** Apfel
etc schälen: ~ **away (od. off)** abschä-
len.

par·ent ['peərənt] I s Elternteil n: ~**s** pl
Eltern pl. **II** adj: ~ **company** ✝ Mutter-
gesellschaft f. **'par·ent·age** s Abstammung f, Herkunft f. **pa·ren·tal**
[pə'rentl] adj □ elterlich, Eltern...

pa·ren·the·sis [pə'renθɪsɪs] pl **-ses**
[~siːz] s **1.** ling. Parenthese f, Einschal-
tung f. **2.** mst pl (runde) Klammer: **put**
in parentheses einklammern.

par·ent·hood ['peərənthʊd] s Elternschaft f. **'par·ent·less** adj elternlos.

'par·ents-in-law s pl Schwiegereltern pl.

par·ings ['peərɪŋz] s pl Schalen pl.

par·ish ['pærɪʃ] s **1.** eccl. Pfarrbezirk m,
a. coll. Gemeinde f: ~ **church** Pfarrkir-
che f; ~ **register** Kirchenbuch n, -regi-
ster n. **2.** a. **civil ~** pol. Br. Gemeinde f: ~
council Gemeinderat m. **pa·rish·ion·**
-er [pə'rɪʃənə] s eccl. Gemeinde(mit-)
glied n.

par·i·ty ['pærətɪ] s Gleichheit f (**with** mit).

park [pɑːk] I s **1.** Park m. **2.** mot.
parken, abstellen: **a ~ed car** ein par-
kender Wagen; **he's ~ed over there** er
parkt dort drüben; ~ **o.s.** F sich hin-
hocken od. pflanzen. **3.** F abstellen, lassen. **III** v/i **4.** parken: **a place to ~** ein
Parkplatz. **5.** einparken.

par·ka ['pɑːkə] s Parka m, f.

park·ing ['pɑːkɪŋ] s **1.** Parken n: **"no ~"**
„Parken verboten". **2.** Einparken n. **3.**
Parkplätze pl, -fläche f. ~ **disc** s Park-
scheibe f. ~ **fee** s Parkgebühr f. ~
ga·rage s bsd. Am. Park(hoch)haus n.
~ **lot** s Am. Parkplatz m. ~ **me·ter** s
Parkuhr f. ~ **place** s Parkplatz m, -lük-
ke f. ~ **space** s **1.** → **parking place.** **2.**
Abstellfläche f. ~ **tick·et** s Strafzettel m
(wegen Falschparkens).

Par·kin·son's dis·ease ['pɑːkɪnsnz] s ✳
Parkinsonsche Krankheit, Schüttelläh-
mung f.

'park·keep·er s Parkwächter m.

par·ky ['pɑːkɪ] *adj Br.* F kühl, frisch (*Luft etc*).

par·lance ['pɑːləns] *s*: **in common ~** einfach *od.* verständlich ausgedrückt; **in legal ~** in der Rechtssprache.

par·lia·ment ['pɑːləmənt] *s* Parlament *n*. **par·lia·men·tar·i·an** [ˌ~men'teəriən] *s* (erfahrener) Parlamentarier. **par·lia·men·ta·ry** [ˌ~'mentəri] *adj* parlamentarisch.

par·lor *Am.*, **par·lour** *bsd. Br.* ['pɑːlə] *s mst in Zssgn* Salon *m*. **~ game** *s* Gesellschaftsspiel *n*.

pa·ro·chi·al [pə'rəʊkjəl] *adj* □ **1.** Pfarr..., Gemeinde... **2.** *fig.* beschränkt, engstirnig.

par·o·dist ['pærədɪst] *s* Parodist(in). **'par·o·dy I** *s* **1.** Parodie *f* (**of, on** auf *acc*). **2.** *fig.* Abklatsch *m* (**of, on** gen). **II** *v/t* **3.** parodieren.

pa·role [pə'rəʊl] 🏛 **I** *s* bedingte (Haft)Entlassung; Hafturlaub *m*: **put** *s.o.* **on ~** → II. **II** *v/t* j-n bedingt entlassen; j-m Hafturlaub gewähren.

par·quet ['pɑːkeɪ] *s* **1.** Parkett *n*. **2.** *thea. Am.* Parkett *n*. **~ floor** *s* Parkett(fuß)boden *m*.

par·rot ['pærət] **I** *s orn.* Papagei *m* (*a. fig.*). **II** *v/t et.* (wie ein Papagei) nachplappern. **'~·fash·ion** *adv*: **learn ~** *et.* stur *od.* mechanisch lernen; **repeat ~** → **parrot** II.

par·ry ['pærɪ] **I** *v/t* Frage parieren, *Schlag, Stoß a.* abwehren. **II** *s fenc.* Parade *f*.

par·si·mo·ni·ous [ˌpɑːsɪ'məʊnjəs] *adj* □ geizig. **par·si·mo·ny** ['ˌ~mənɪ] *s* Geiz *m*.

pars·ley ['pɑːslɪ] *s* 🌿 Petersilie *f*.

pars·nip ['pɑːsnɪp] *s* 🌿 Pastinake *f*, Pastinak *m*.

par·son ['pɑːsn] *s* Pastor *m*, Pfarrer *m*: **~'s nose** F Bürzel *m*. **'par·son·age** *s* Pfarrhaus *n*.

part [pɑːt] **I** *s* **1.** *allg.* Teil *m*: **(a) ~ of his money** ein Teil s-s Geldes; **it is good in ~(s), ~s of it are good, ~ of it is good** es ist zum Teil *od.* teilweise gut; **for the most ~** größtenteils; meistens; **be ~ of s.th.** zu et. gehören; **be ~ and parcel of** e-n wesentlichen Bestandteil bilden von (*od. gen*); **~ of the body** Körperteil *m*; **~ of speech** *ling.* Wortart *f*; **three-~** dreiteilig. **2.** ⚙ (Bau-, Ersatz)Teil *n*. **3.** Teil *m*, Folge *f*, Fortsetzung *f* (*e-s Ro-*

mans, e-r Fernsehserie etc); Lieferung *f* (*e-s Buchs etc*). **4.** Anteil *m*: **take ~** teilnehmen, sich beteiligen (**in** an *dat*). **5.** *fig.* Teil *m*, Seite *f*: **on the ~ of** von seiten, seitens (*gen*); **on my ~** von m-r Seite, von mir; **take s.th. in good ~** et. nicht übelnehmen. **6.** *fig.* Seite *f*, Partei *f*: **take s.o.'s ~, take ~ with s.o.** für j-n *od.* j-s Partei ergreifen. **7.** *thea. etc* Rolle *f* (*a. fig.*): **act** (*od.* **play**) **the ~ of** die Rolle (*gen*) spielen; **play a ~ in** e-e Rolle spielen bei *od.* in (*dat*). **8.** ♪ (Sing- *od.* Instrumental)Stimme *f*, Partie *f*: **for** (*od.* **in**) **several ~s** mehrstimmig. **9.** Gegend *f*, Teil *m* (*e-s Landes etc*): **in these ~s** hier(zulande). **10.** *Am.* (Haar)Scheitel *m*. **II** *v/t* **11.** trennen (**from**); *Streitende* trennen; *Vorhang* aufziehen; *Haar* scheiteln: → **company** *b.* III. *v/i* **12.** sich trennen (**from** von): **(as) friends** in Freundschaft auseinandergehen; **~ with** *et.* aufgeben, sich von j-m, *et.* trennen. **13.** sich trennen, aufreißen (*Wolken*). **IV** *adj* **14.** Teil...: **give s.th. in ~ exchange** et. in Zahlung geben; **~ owner** Miteigentümer(in); **give s.o. £100 in ~ payment** j-m 100 Pfund als Abschlagszahlung geben. **V** *adv* **15.** **~ ..., ~** teils ..., teils.

par·tial ['pɑːʃl] *adj* (□ → **partially**) **1.** teilweise, Teil...: **~ success** Teilerfolg *m*. **2.** parteiisch, voreingenommen: **be ~ to s.th.** F e-e Schwäche für et. besondere Vorliebe für et. haben. **par·ti·al·i·ty** [ˌ~ʃɪ'ælətɪ] *s* **1.** Parteilichkeit *f*, Voreingenommenheit *f*. **2.** F Schwäche *f*, besondere Vorliebe (**for** für). **par·tial·ly** ['ˌ~ʃəlɪ] *adv* teilweise, zum Teil: **be ~ to blame for** mitschuld sein an (*dat*).

par·tic·i·pant [pɑː'tɪsɪpənt] *s* Teilnehmer(in). **par·tic·i·pate** [~peɪt] *v/i* teilnehmen, sich beteiligen (**in** an *dat*). **par·tic·i·pa·tion** *s* Teilnahme *f*, Beteiligung *f*.

par·ti·ci·ple [pɑː'tɪsɪpl] *s ling.* Partizip *n*, Mittelwort *n*: → **past** 2, **present** 3.

par·ti·cle ['pɑːtɪkl] *s* **1.** Teilchen *n*, *phys. a.* Partikel *f*: **there is not a ~ of truth in it** *fig.* daran ist nicht ein einziges Wort wahr. **2.** *ling.* Partikel *f*.

par·tic·u·lar [pə'tɪkjʊlə] **I** *adj* (□ → **particularly**) **1.** besonder, speziell: **this ~ case** dieser spezielle Fall; **be of no ~ importance** nicht besonders wichtig sein; **for no ~ reason** aus keinem besonderen Grund. **2. be very ~ about** (*od.* **over**) es sehr genau nehmen mit, großen Wert legen auf (*acc*); sehr heikel *od.* wählerisch sein in (*dat*). **II** *s* **3.** Einzelheit *f*: **~s** *pl* nähere Umstände *pl od.* Angaben *pl*; **in ~** insbesondere; **in every ~, in all ~s** in allen Einzelheiten; **enter** (*od.* **go**) **into ~s** ins einzelne gehen; **further ~s from** Näheres bei. **4.** *pl* Personalien *pl*. **par'tic·u·lar·ize** *v/t* spezifizieren, einzeln aufführen. **par·'tic·u·lar·ly** *adv* besonders: **not ~** a. nicht sonderlich.

part·ing ['pɑːtɪŋ] **I** *adj* **1.** Abschieds...: **~ kiss. II** *s* **2.** Abschied *m*. **3.** *bsd. Br.* (Haar)Scheitel *m*.

par·ti·san [ˌpɑːtɪ'zæn] **I** *s* **1.** Parteigänger(in). **2.** ⚔ Partisan(in). **II** *adj* **3.** parteiisch. **4.** ⚔ Partisanen...

par·ti·tion [pɑː'tɪʃn] **I** *s* **1.** Teilung *f*. **2.** *a.* **~ wall** Trennwand *f*. **II** *v/t* **3.** Land etc teilen: **~ off** abteilen, abtrennen.

part·ly ['pɑːtlɪ] → **partially**.

part·ner ['pɑːtnə] **I** *s* **1.** *allg.* Partner(in). **2.** ✝ Gesellschafter(in), Partner(in), Teilhaber(in). **II** *v/t* **3.** *j-s* zum Partner haben, *j-s* Partner sein. **4.** *oft* **~ up** (als Partner) zs.-bringen (**with** mit). **II** *v/i* **5.** *oft* **~ up** sich (als Partner) zs.-tun (**with** mit). **'part·ner·ship** *s* **1.** Partnerschaft *f*: **go into ~** sich (als Partner) zs.-tun (**with** mit). **2.** ✝ Personen-, Personalgesellschaft *f*: (**general** *od.* **ordinary**) **~** offene Handelsgesellschaft; **limited** (*Am.* **special**) **~** Kommanditgesellschaft *f*.

par·tridge ['pɑːtrɪdʒ] *s orn.* Rebhuhn *n*.

part·-time [-'taɪm] **I** *adj* Teilzeit..., Halbtags...: **~ worker** Teilzeitbeschäftigte *m, f*, Halbtagskraft *f*. **II** *adv* halbtags.

par·ty ['pɑːtɪ] *s* **1.** *pol.* Partei *f*: **within the ~** innerparteilich, parteiintern. **2.** Gesellschaft, Gruppe *f*: **we were a ~ of three** wir waren zu dritt. **3.** (*Rettungs- etc*)Mannschaft *f*; ⚔ Kommando *n*, Trupp *m*. **4.** Gesellschaft *f*, Party *f*: **give a ~. 5.** ⚖ (*Prozeß-, Vertrags*)Partei *f*: **a third ~** ein Dritter. **6.** Teilnehmer(in), Beteiligte *m, f*: **be a ~ to** beteiligt sein an (*dat*), *et.* mitmachen. **7.** F Person *f*, Kerl *m*. **~ line** *s* **1.** *teleph.* Gemeinschaftsanschluß *m*. **2.** *pol.* Parteilinie *f*: **follow the ~** linientreu sein.

par·ve·nu ['pɑːvənjuː] *s* Emporkömmling *m*, Parvenü *m*.

pass [pɑːs] **I** *s* **1.** (*Gebirgs*)Paß *m*. **2.** Passierschein *m*: **free ~** (Dauer)Freikarte *f*, 🚊 *etc* (Dauer)Freifahrtkarte *f*, **-schein** *m*. **3.** *get a ~ in physics ped.* die Physikprüfung bestehen. **4.** *things have come to such a ~ that* die Dinge haben sich derart zugespitzt, daß. **5.** *Sport:* Paß *m*, Zuspiel *n*. **6.** *make a ~ at* F Annäherungsversuche machen bei. **II** *v/t* **7.** vorbeigehen, -fahren an (*dat*). **8.** überholen. **9.** *Prüfung* bestehen; *Prüfling* durchkommen lassen. **10.** *fig.* hinausgehen über (*acc*), übersteigen, übertreffen: **~ s.o.'s comprehension** (*od.* **understanding**) über *j-s* Verstand *od.* Horizont gehen. **11.** **~ one's hand over** (sich) mit der Hand fahren über (*acc*). **12.** *j-m et.* reichen, geben, *et.* weitergeben: → **buck** 2. **13.** *Sport: Ball* abspielen, passen (**to** zu). **14.** *Gesetz* verabschieden. **15.** *Zeit* ver-, zubringen: **~ the time reading** sich die Zeit mit Lesen vertreiben. **16.** *Urteil* abgeben, fällen, ⚖ *a.* sprechen (**on** über *acc*). **III** *v/i* **17.** vorbeigehen, -fahren (**by** an *dat*): **let s.o. ~** *j-n* vorbeilassen. **18.** (**to**) übergehen (auf *acc*), fallen (an *acc*). **19.** vergehen (*Schmerz etc*), (*Zeit a.*) verstreichen. **20.** durchkommen, (die Prüfung) bestehen. **21.** (**as, for**) gelten (als), gehalten *od.* angesehen werden (für). **22.** durchgehen, unbeanstandet bleiben: **let s.th. ~** et. durchgehen lassen. **23.** *Sport:* (den Ball) abspielen *od.* passen (**to** zu). **24.** *Kartenspiel:* passen (*a. fig.*): **I ~ on that** da muß ich passen. **25.** **~ over s.th.** et. übergehen *od.* ignorieren (**in silence** stillschweigend).

Verbindungen mit Adverbien:

pass| a·way *v/i* **1.** → **pass** 15. **II** *v/i* **2.** → **pass** 19. **3.** verscheiden, sterben. **~ by** *v/i* **1.** vorbeigehen, -fahren. **2.** → **pass** 19. **II** *v/t* **3.** *et., j-n* übergehen. **~ down** *v/t* (**to**) *Tradition etc* weitergeben (*dat od.* an *acc*), *Bräuche etc* überliefern (*dat*). **~ off I** *v/t* **1.** *j-n, et.* ausgeben (**as** als). **II** *v/i* **2.** gut *etc* vorübergehen, verlaufen. **3.** vergehen (*Schmerz etc*). **~ on I** *v/t* **1.** weitergeben (**to** *dat od.* an *acc*) (*a. fig.*); *Krankheit* übertragen. **II** *v/i* **2.** übergehen (**to** zu *e-m anderen Thema etc*). **3.** → **pass away** 3. **~ o·ver** →

pass by 3. **~ round I** *v/t* herumreichen, *Gerücht etc* in Umlauf setzen: **be passed round** a. die Runde machen. **II** *v/i* herumgereicht werden, a. fig. die Runde machen, fig. in Umlauf sein. **~ up** *v/t* sich *e-e Chance etc* entgehen lassen.

pass·a·ble ['pɑːsəbl] *adj* □ **1.** passierbar, befahrbar. **2.** fig. passabel.

pas·sage ['pæsɪdʒ] *s* **1.** Durchfahrt *f*, -reise *f*: → **bird** 1. **2.** Passage *f*, (Durch-, Verbindungs)Gang *m*. **3.** (See-, Flug-) Reise *f*: → **rough** 2. **4. with the ~ of time** mit der Zeit. **5.** Verabschiedung *f* (*e-s Gesetzes*). **6.** Passage *f*, Stelle *f* (*e-s Texts*). '**~·way** → **passage** 2.

pas·sen·ger ['pæsɪndʒə] *s* Passagier *m*, Fahr-, Fluggast *m*, (*Auto- etc*)Insasse *m*. **~ train** *s* Personenzug *m*.

,pass·er·'by *pl* **,pass·ers·'by** *s* Passant(in).

pass·ing ['pɑːsɪŋ] **I** *s* **1. with the ~ of time** mit der Zeit. **2.** → **passage** 5. **3. in ~** beiläufig, nebenbei. **II** *adj* **4.** flüchtig (*Blick, Gedanke etc*).

pas·sion ['pæʃn] *s* **1.** Leidenschaft *f*, *weitS. a.* Passion *f*: **be a ~ with s.o.** e-e Leidenschaft bei j-m sein, j-s Leidenschaft sein; **have a ~ for s.th.** e-e Leidenschaft für et. haben; **~s ran high** die Erregung schlug hohe Wellen; → **heat** 2. **fly into a ~** e-n Wutanfall bekommen. **3.** 2 *eccl.* Passion *f*: 2 **play** Passionsspiel *n*. **pas·sion·ate** ['~ʃənət] *adj* □ leidenschaftlich.

pas·sive ['pæsɪv] **I** *adj* □ **1.** passiv: **~ resistance** passiver Widerstand; **~ smoking** passives Rauchen, Passivrauchen *n*; **~ vocabulary** passiver Wortschatz. **2.** *ling.* passivisch: **~ voice** → **3**. **II** *s* **3.** *ling.* Passiv *n*, Leideform *f*. **pas'siv·i·ty** *s* Passivität *f*.

'**pass·key** *s* Hauptschlüssel *m*.

Pass·o·ver ['pɑːsˌəʊvə] *s eccl.* Passah *n*.

pass·port ['pɑːspɔːt] *s* **1.** (Reise)Paß *m*: **hold a British ~** e-n britischen Paß haben; **~ picture** Paßbild *n*. **2.** fig. Schlüssel *m* (**to** zu).

'**pass·word** *s* Kennwort *n*, Parole *f*.

past [pɑːst] **I** *adj* **1.** vergangen: **be ~** vorüber *od.* vorbei sein; **for some time ~** seit einiger Zeit; **learn from ~ mistakes** aus Fehlern in der Vergangenheit lernen. **2.** *ling.* **~ participle** Partizip

n Perfekt, Mittelwort *n* der Vergangenheit; **~ perfect** Plusquamperfekt *n*, Vorvergangenheit *f*; **~ tense** Vergangenheit *f*, Präteritum *n*. **3.** früher, ehemalig. **II** *s* **4.** Vergangenheit *f* (*a. ling.*): **in the ~** in der Vergangenheit, früher. **III** *adv* **5.** vorbei, vorüber: **run ~** vorbeilaufen. **IV** *prp* **6.** *Zeit*: nach, über (*acc*): **half ~ seven** halb acht; **she is ~ forty** sie ist über vierzig. **7.** an ... (*dat*) vorbei *od.* vorüber. **8.** über ... (*acc*) hinaus: **I'm ~ caring** das kümmert mich nicht mehr; **be ~ it** F es nicht mehr bringen; **I wouldn't put it ~ him** F das traue ich ihm glatt *od.* ohne weiteres zu; → **cure** 2, **hope** I, *etc*.

pas·ta ['pæstə] *s* Teigwaren *pl*.

paste [peɪst] **I** *s* **1.** (*Fisch-, Zahn- etc*)Paste *f*. **2.** Kleister *m*. **3.** *Am.* → **pastry**. **II** *v/t* **4.** kleben (**to, on** an *acc*): **~ up** ankleben. '**~·board** *s* Karton *m*, Pappe *f*.

pas·tel I *s* ['pæˈstel] **1.** Pastellstift *m*. **2.** Pastell(zeichnung *f*) *n*. **3.** Pastellfarbe *f*, -ton *m*. **II** *adj* ['pæstl] **4.** Pastell... **5.** pastellfarben.

pas·teur·ize ['pɑːstʃəraɪz] *v/t* pasteurisieren, keimfrei machen.

pas·time ['pɑːstaɪm] *s* Zeitvertreib *m*, Freizeitbeschäftigung *f*: **as a ~** zum Zeitvertreib.

pas·tor ['pɑːstə] *s* Pastor *m*, Pfarrer *m*. '**pas·to·ral** I *adj* □ **1.** pastoral, ländlich, idyllisch. **2.** pastoral, seelsorgerisch: **~ letter** → **4**. **II** *s* **3.** ♩ Pastorale *f*, **4.** *eccl.* Hirtenbrief *m*.

pas·try ['peɪstrɪ] *s* **1.** (*Blätter-, Mürbe- etc*)Teig *m*, *Br. oft pl* (Fein)Gebäck *n*.

pas·ture ['pɑːstʃə] **I** *s* Weide(land *n*) *f*. **II** *v/t* weiden (lassen). **III** *v/i* grasen, weiden.

past·y¹ ['peɪstɪ] *adj* blaß, käsig.

past·y² ['pæstɪ] *s bsd. Br.* (Fleisch)Pastete *f*.

pat¹ [pæt] **I** *s* **1.** Klaps *m*: **give s.o. (o.s.) a ~ on the back** fig. F j-m (sich selbst) auf die Schulter klopfen. **2.** Portion *f* (*bsd. Butter*). **3.** (*Kuh*)Fladen *m*. **4.** Trappeln *n*. **II** *v/t* **5.** tätscheln; abtupfen (**with** mit): **~ s.o. on the head (shoulder)** j-m den Kopf tätscheln (auf die Schulter klopfen); **~ s.o. (o.s.) on the back** fig. F j-m (sich selbst) auf die Schulter klopfen; **~ down** Haar etc an-, festdrücken, *Erde etc* festklopfen. **III** *v/i* **6.** trappeln.

pat² [~] **I** *adv* **1. have** (*od.* **know**) **s.th.** (**off**) ~ et. aus dem Effeff *od.* wie am Schnürchen können. **2.** wie aus der Pistole geschossen: **answer** ~; **the answer came** ~. **II** *adj* **3.** glatt (*Antwort etc*).

patch [pætʃ] **I** *s* **1.** Fleck *m*; Flicken *m*: ~**es pl of mist** Nebelschwaden *pl*; **in** ~**es** *fig.* stellenweise; **not to be a** ~ **on** *Br.* F nichts sein gegen. **2.** Beet *n*. **3. go through a bad (difficult)** ~ e-e Pechsträhne haben (e-e schwierige Zeit durchmachen). **II** *v/t* **4.** flicken: ~ **up** zs.-flicken (*a. fig.*); *fig.* Streit beilegen; ~ **things up** sich zs.-raufen. ~ **pock·et** *s* aufgesetzte Tasche. '~**·work** *s* Patchwork *n*: ~ **blanket** Flickendecke *f*.

patch·y ['pætʃi] *adj* □ **1.** fleckig. **2.** *fig.* lückenhaft; unterschiedlich.

pat·ent ['peitənt] **I** *adj* □ **1.** offenkundig, -sichtlich. **2.** patentiert; Patent...: ~ **office** Patentamt *n*. **3.** *Br.* F patent (*Methode etc*). **II** *s* **4.** Patent *n*: **protected by** ~ patentrechtlich geschützt; **take out a** ~ **on** → **5.** **III** *v/t* **5.** et. patentieren lassen. ~ **leath·er** *s* Lackleder *n*.

pa·ter·nal [pə'tɜːnl] *adj* □ **1.** väterlich, Vater... **2.** *Großvater etc* väterlicherseits.

pa·ter·ni·ty [pə'tɜːnəti] *s* Vaterschaft *f*: ~ **suit** ∗ᵗᵗ Vaterschaftsprozeß *m*.

path [pɑːθ] *pl* **paths** [pɑːðz] *s* **1.** Weg *m* (*a. fig.* **to** zu), Pfad *m*: **stand in s.o.'s** ~ j-m im Weg stehen; → **cross** 9. **2.** *phys.,* ⊙ Bahn *f*.

pa·thet·ic [pə'θetik] *adj* (~**ally**) **1.** mitleiderregend: ~ **sight** Bild *n* des Jammers. **2.** *Br.* kläglich (*Versuch etc*), erbärmlich, miserabel (*Leistung etc*).

path·o·log·i·cal [ˌpæθə'lɒdʒikl] *adj* □ pathologisch, krankhaft. **pa·thol·o·gist** [pə'θɒlədʒist] *s* Pathologe *m*. **pa'thol·o·gy** *s* Pathologie *f*.

pa·thos ['peiθɒs] *s das* Mitleiderregende.

'**path·way** → **path** 1.

pa·tience ['peiʃns] *s* **1.** Geduld *f*: **lose one's** ~ die Geduld verlieren (**with** mit); → **lead** 1. **2.** *bsd. Br.* Patience *f* (*Kartenspiel*): **play** ~ Patiencen *od.* e-e Patience legen. '**pa·tient I** *adj* □ geduldig (**with** mit). **II** *s* Patient(in).

pat·i·na ['pætinə] *s* Patina *f*.

pa·ti·o ['pætiəʊ] *pl* **-os** *s* **1.** Patio *m*, Innenhof *m*. **2.** Veranda *f*, Terrasse *f*.

pa·tri·arch ['peitriɑːk] *s* Patriarch *m*. **ˌpa·tri'ar·chal** [~kl] *adj* □ patriarchalisch. **pa·tri·arch·ate** ['~kit] *s* Patriarchat *n*.

pa·tri·ot ['pætriət] *s* Patriot(in). **pa·tri·ot·ic** [ˌ~'ɒtik] *adj* (~**ally**) patriotisch. **pa·tri·ot·ism** ['~ɒtizəm] *s* Patriotismus *m*.

pa·trol [pə'trəʊl] **I** *s* **1.** ✕ Patrouille *f*, (*Polizei*)Streife *f*. **2.** ✕ Patrouille *f*, Streife *f*, Runde *f*: **on** ~ auf Patrouille *od.* Streife; ~ **car** (Funk)Streifenwagen *m*; ~ **wagon** *Am.* (Polizei)Gefangenenwagen *m*. **II** *v/t* **3.** abpatrouillieren (*Soldaten*), auf Streife sein in (*dat*) (*Polizist*), s-e Runde machen in (*dat*) (*Wachmann*). **pa'trol·man** *s* (*irr* **man**) **1.** *Am.* Streifenpolizist *m*. **2.** *Br.* motorisierter Pannenhelfer.

pa·tron ['peitrən] *s* **1.** Schirmherr *m*. **2.** Gönner *m*, Förderer *m*. **3.** (*Stamm*)Kunde *m*; Stammgast *m*. **pa·tron·age** ['pætrənidʒ] *s* **1.** Schirmherrschaft *f*: **under the** ~ **of** unter der Schirmherrschaft von (*od.* gen). **2.** Förderung *f*. **pa·tron·ess** ['peitrənis] *s* **1.** Schirmherrin *f*. **2.** Gönnerin *f*, Förderin *f*. **pa·tron·ize** ['pætrənaiz] *v/t* **1.** fördern. **2.** (*Stamm*)Kunde *od.* Stammgast sein in (*dat*). **3.** gönnerhaft *od.* herablassend behandeln. '**pa·tron·iz·ing** *adj* □ gönnerhaft, herablassend.

pa·tron saint *s* Schutzheilige *m, f*.

pat·ter¹ ['pætə] **I** *v/i* **1.** prasseln (*Regen etc*). **2.** trappeln. **II** *s* **3.** Prasseln *n*. **4.** Trappeln *n*.

pat·ter² [~] *s* **1.** Sprüche *pl* (*e-s Vertreters etc*). **2.** Jargon *m*: **thieves'** ~ Gaunersprache *f*.

pat·tern ['pætən] **I** *s* **1.** (*a. Schnitt-, Strick*)Muster *n*; *fig.* Muster *n*, Vorbild *n*. **2.** ✝ Muster *n*, (Waren)Probe *f*. **3.** (*Stoff- etc*)Muster *n*. **4.** *fig.* Muster *n*, Schema *n*: **follow its usual** ~ nach dem üblichen Schema *od.* wie üblich verlaufen. **II** *v/t* **5.** mustern. **6.** bilden, gestalten (**after,** *on* nach): ~ **o.s. on s.o.** sich j-n zum Vorbild nehmen.

paunch [pɔːntʃ] *s* (dicker) Bauch, Wanst *m*. '**paunch·y** *adj* dickbäuchig.

pau·per ['pɔːpə] *s* Arme *m, f*.

pause [pɔːz] **I** *s* Pause *f*: *without a ~* ohne Pause. **II** *v/i* innehalten.

pave [peɪv] *v/t* pflastern: *~ the way for* *fig.* den Weg ebnen (*dat*). **'pave‧ment** *s* **1.** (Straßen)Pflaster *n*. **2.** *Br.* Bürger-, Gehsteig *m*: *~ artist* Pflastermaler(in); *~ café* Straßencafé *n*. **3.** *Am.* Fahrbahn *f*.

pa‧vil‧ion [pəˈvɪljən] *s* Pavillon *m*.

pav‧ing stone [ˈpeɪvɪŋ] *s* Pflasterstein *m*.

paw [pɔː] **I** *s* **1.** Pfote *f* (*a.* F *Hand*), Tatze *f*. **II** *v/t* **2.** Boden scharren, scharren an (*der Tür etc*). **3.** F betatschen. **III** *v/i* **4.** scharren (*at* an *dat*).

pawn¹ [pɔːn] *s* **1.** *Schach:* Bauer *m*. **2.** *fig.* Schachfigur *f*.

pawn² [~] **I** *s*: *be in ~* verpfändet *od.* versetzt sein. **II** *v/t* verpfänden, versetzen. **'~‧brok‧er** *s* Pfandleiher *m*. **'~-shop** *s* Leih-, Pfandhaus *n*. **~ tick‧et** *s* Pfandschein *m*.

pay [peɪ] **I** *s* **1.** Bezahlung *f*, Gehalt *n*, Lohn *m*. **II** *v/t* (*irr*) **2.** Betrag zahlen, entrichten, *Rechnung* (be)zahlen, begleichen: *~ into* einzahlen auf (*ein Konto*). **3.** *j-n* bezahlen. **4.** *fig. Aufmerksamkeit* schenken, *Besuch* abstatten, *Kompliment* machen: → *attention* 1, *etc*. **III** *v/i* (*irr*) zahlen: *~ for* et. bezahlen (*a. fig.*); *he had to ~ dearly for it fig.* es kam ihn teuer zu stehen, er mußte teuer dafür bezahlen. **6.** *fig.* sich lohnen, sich bezahlt machen.

Verbindungen mit Adverbien:

pay‧| back *v/repay*: → *coin* I. *~ in v/t* einzahlen. *~ off v/t* **1.** *j-n* auszahlen. **2.** *et.* ab(be)zahlen, tilgen. **II** *v/i* **3.** → *pay* 6. *~ out v/t* j-n auszahlen, bezahlen (*for* für). *~ up v/t* j-n, et. voll *od.* sofort bezahlen. **II** *v/i* zahlen.

pay‧a‧ble [ˈpeɪəbl] *adj* zahlbar, fällig: *be ~ to* ausgestellt sein auf (*acc*).

pay‧| bed *s Br.* Privatbett *n* (*in Klinik*). **'~-day** *s* Zahltag *m*. **~ en‧ve‧lope** *s Am.* Lohntüte *f*.

pay‧ing [ˈpeɪɪŋ] *adj* **1.** *~ guest* zahlender Gast. **2.** lohnend, rentabel. **~‧'in slip** *s* Einzahlungsschein *m*.

pay‧ment [ˈpeɪmənt] *s* **1.** (Be)Zahlung *f*: *in ~ of* als Bezahlung für; *on ~ of* gegen Zahlung von (*od. gen*).

'pay‧| off *s* F Pointe *f*. **~ pack‧et** *s Br.* Lohntüte *f*. **~ phone** *s* Münzfernspre-

cher *m*. **~ rise** *s* Lohn-, Gehaltserhöhung *f*. **'~-roll** *s* Lohnliste *f*: *be on s.o.'s ~* bei j-m beschäftigt sein. **~ slip** *s* Lohn-, Gehaltsstreifen *m*. **~ sta‧tion** *s Am.* Münzfernsprecher *m*.

pea [piː] *s* ♀ Erbse *f*: *they are (as) like as two ~s (in a pod)* sie gleichen sich wie ein Ei dem anderen.

peace [piːs] *s* **1.** Friede(n) *m*: *the two countries are at ~* zwischen den beiden Ländern herrscht Frieden; *make one's ~ with* sich aus- *od.* versöhnen mit. **2.** ⚖ öffentliche Ruhe u. Ordnung: *keep the ~* die öffentliche Ordnung aufrechterhalten; *~ breach* 1. **3.** Ruhe *f*: *~ of mind* Seelenfrieden *m*; *in ~ and quiet* in Ruhe u. Frieden. **II** *adj* **4.** Friedens...: *~ conference* Friedenskonferenz *f*; *~ movement* Friedensbewegung *f*; *~ pipe* Friedenspfeife *f*; *~ treaty* Friedensvertrag *m*. **'peace‧a‧ble** *adj* □ friedlich (*Diskussion etc*), (*Person a.*) friedfertig. **peace‧ful** [ˈ-fʊl] *adj* □ friedlich.

'peace‧|-lov‧ing *adj* friedliebend. **'~-time** **I** *s* Friedenszeiten *pl.* **II** *adj* in Friedenszeiten.

peach [piːtʃ] *s* **1.** ♀ Pfirsich *m*; Pfirsichbaum *m*. F prima *od.* klasse Person *od.* Sache: *~ of a girl* ein süßes Mädchen; *~ of a hat* ein Gedicht von e-m Hut.

pea‧cock [ˈpiːkɒk] *s orn.* Pfau *m*: (*as*) *proud as a ~* stolz wie ein Pfau.

peak [piːk] *s* **1.** Spitze *f*, (*e-s Bergs a.*) Gipfel *m*. **2.** Schirm *m* (*e-r Mütze*). **3.** *fig.* Höhepunkt *m*, Höchststand *m*: *be at its ~* am höchsten sein. **II** *v/i* **4.** e-n Höchststand erreichen. **III** *adj* **5.** Höchst..., Spitzen...: *~ hours pl* Hauptverkehrs-, Stoßzeit *f*; ⚡ Hauptbelastungszeit *f*. **peaked** [piːkt] *adj*: *~ cap* Schirmmütze *f*. **'peak‧y** *adj* F blaß, kränklich.

peal [piːl] **I** *s* **1.** (Glocken)Läuten *n*. **2.** (Donner)Schlag *m*: *~s pl of laughter* schallendes *od.* dröhnendes Gelächter. **II** *v/i a.* *~ out* **3.** läuten. **4.** krachen (*Donner*).

'pea‧nut *s* ♀ Erdnuß *f*: *~s pl* F lächerliche Summe. *~ but‧ter* *s* Erdnußbutter *f*.

pear [peə] *s* ♀ a) Birne *f*, b) *a. ~ tree* Birnbaum *m*.

pearl [pɜːl] *s* **1.** Perle *f*. **2.** Perlmutter *f*, *n,* Perlmutt *n.* **II** *adj* **3.** Perlen... **4.** Perlmutt(er)...

peas·ant ['peznt] *s* **1.** Kleinbauer *m.* **2.** *fig.* F Bauer *m.*

pea·soup·er [ˌpiːˈsuːpə] *s* F Waschküche *f (dicker, gelber Nebel).*

peat [piːt] *s* Torf *m:* **cut** *(od.* **dig)** ~ Torf stechen.

peb·ble ['pebl] *s* Kiesel(stein) *m:* **you are not the only** ~ **on the beach** F ich *etc* kann auch ohne dich auskommen. **'peb·bly** *adj* Kiesel...: ~ **beach.**

pec·ca·dil·lo [ˌpekəˈdiləʊ] *pl* **-lo(e)s** *s* **1.** kleine Sünde. **2.** Kavaliersdelikt *n.*

peck [pek] **I** *v/t* **1.** picken. **2.** F *j-m* e-n flüchtigen Kuß geben **(on** auf *acc).* **II** *v/i* **3.** picken, hacken **(at** nach): ~ **at one's food** im Essen herumstochern. **III** *s* **4.** F flüchtiger Kuß. **'peck·er** *s* **1.** *Am. sl.* Schwanz *m (Penis).* **2. keep one's** ~ **up** F die Ohren steifhalten. **'peck·ing** *adj:* ~ **order** *orn.* Hackordnung *f (a. fig.).*

pec·to·ral ['pektərəl] *adj* Brust...

pe·cu·li·ar [pɪˈkjuːljə] *adj* (~**ly**) **1.** eigen(tümlich) **(to** *dat):* **be** ~ **to** *a.* typisch sein für. **2.** eigenartig, seltsam. **pe¸cu·li'ar·i·ty** [ˌ·lɪˈærətɪ] *s* **1.** Eigenheit *f,* Eigentümlichkeit *f:* **be a** ~ **of** *a.* typisch sein für. **2.** Eigenartigkeit *f,* Seltsamkeit *f.* **pe'cul·iar·ly** *adv* **1.** → **peculiar** 2. **2.** besonders.

pe·cu·ni·ar·y [pɪˈkjuːnjərɪ] *adj* geldlich, Geld...: ~ **difficulties** *pl* finanzielle Schwierigkeiten *pl.*

ped·a·gog·ic, ped·a·gog·i·cal [ˌpedəˈgɒdʒɪk(l)] *adj* □ pädagogisch. **ped·a·gogue** ['·ˌgɒg] *s contp.* Schulmeister (-in), Pedant(in). **ped·a·go·gy** ['·ˌgɒdʒɪ] *s* Pädagogik *f.*

ped·al ['pedl] **I** *s* **1.** Pedal *n.* **II** *v/i pret u. pp* **-aled,** *bsd. Br.* **-alled 2.** das Pedal treten. **3.** (mit dem Rad) fahren, strampeln. ~ **bin** *s* Treteimer *m.* ~ **boat** *s* Tretboot *n.*

ped·ant ['pedənt] *s* Pedant(in). **pe·dan·tic** [pɪˈdæntɪk] *adj* (~**ally**) pedantisch **(about** wenn es um ... geht). **ped·ant·ry** ['pedəntrɪ] *s* Pedanterie *f.*

ped·dle ['pedl] *v/t* hausieren (gehen) mit *(a. fig.):* ~ **drugs** mit Drogen handeln. **'ped·dler** *s* **1.** Drogenhändler(in). **2.** *Am.* → **pedlar.**

ped·es·tal ['pedɪstl] *s* Sockel *m:* **place**

(od. **put, set)** *s.o.* **on a** ~ *fig.* j-n aufs Podest erheben; **knock** *s.o.* **off his** ~ *fig.* j-n von s-m Sockel stoßen.

pe·des·tri·an [pɪˈdestrɪən] **I** *adj* **1.** Fußgänger...: ~ **crossing** *Br.* Fußgängerüberweg *m;* ~ **precinct** *(od.* **zone)** Fußgängerzone *f.* **2.** *fig.* prosaisch, trocken; phantasielos. **II** *s* **3.** Fußgänger(in).

pe·di·a·tri·cian, pe·di·at·rics *Am.* → **paediatrician, paediatrics.**

ped·i·cure ['pedɪˌkjʊə] *s* Pediküre *f.*

ped·i·gree ['pedɪgriː] **I** *s* **1.** Stammbaum *m.* **2.** Ab-, Herkunft *f.* **II** *adj* **3.** *zo.* reinrassig.

ped·lar ['pedlə] *s* Hausierer(in).

pee [piː] F **I** *v/i* pinkeln. **II** *s:* **have (go for) a** ~ pinkeln (gehen).

peek [piːk] **I** *v/i* kurz *od.* verstohlen gucken **(at** auf *acc).* **II** *s:* **have** *(od.* **take) a** ~ **at** e-n kurzen *od.* verstohlenen Blick werfen auf *(acc).*

peel [piːl] **I** *v/t* Kartoffeln *etc* schälen: ~ **(off)** Tapete *etc* abziehen, ablösen; Kleider abstreifen; **keep one's eyes** ~**ed** F die Augen offenhalten. **II** *v/i a.* ~ **off** sich lösen (Tapete *etc*), abblättern (Farbe *etc*), sich schälen (Haut). **III** *s* Schale *f.* **'peel·er** *s* (Kartoffel- *etc*)Schäler *m.* **'peel·ings** *s pl* (Kartoffel- *etc*)Schalen *pl.*

peep¹ [piːp] **I** *v/i* **1.** piep(s)en. **II** *s* **2.** Piep(s)en *n.* **3.** F Piepser *m* (Ton).

peep² [~] **I** *v/i* **1.** → **peek** I. **2.** *mst* ~ **out** vorschauen **(from under** unter *dat).* **II** *s* **3.** → **peek** II. **'peep·er** *s mst pl* F Gucker *m* (Auge).

'peep·hole *s* Guckloch *n,* (in Tür) Spion *m.*

Peep·ing Tom ['piːpɪŋ] *s* Spanner *m,* Voyeur *m.*

peep show *s* Peep-Show *f.*

peer¹ [pɪə] *v/i* angestrengt schauen, spähen: ~ **at** *s.o.* j-n anstarren.

peer² [~] *s* **1.** *Br.* Peer *m.* **2.** Gleichgestellte *m, f,* Ebenbürtige *m, f,* Altersgenosse *m,* -genossin *f:* **one's** ~**s** *pl* seinesgleichen. **'peer·age** *s Br.* Peerage *f:* **raise to the** ~ in den Adelsstand erheben. **'peer·ess** *s Br.* Peereß *f.* **'peer·less** *adj* □ unvergleichlich, einzigartig.

peeved [piːvd] *adj* F sauer **(about, at** über *acc).*

pee·vish ['piːvɪʃ] *adj* □ gereizt; reizbar.

peg [peg] **I** s **1.** Pflock m; (Holz)Nagel m, (-)Stift m; (Zelt)Hering m: **be a square ~ in a round hole** fig. am falschen Platz sein; **take s.o. down a ~ (or two)** F j-m e-n Dämpfer aufsetzen. **2.** (Kleider-)Haken m: **off the ~** von der Stange (Anzug). **3.** Br. (Wäsche)Klammer f. **II** v/t **4.** anpflocken. **5.** a. **~ out** (od. up) Br. Wäsche (an der Leine) anklammern. **6.** ✝ Preise etc stützen, halten. **III** v/i **7.** **~ away at** F dranbleiben an (e-r Arbeit). **8.** **~ out** bsd. Br. F den Löffel weglegen (sterben).

pe·jo·ra·tive [pɪˈdʒɒrətɪv] adj □ pejorativ, abschätzig, herabsetzend.

Pe·kin·ese [ˌpiːkɪˈniːz] pl **-ese** s zo. Pekinese m.

pel·i·can [ˈpelɪkən] s orn. Pelikan m. **~ cross·ing** s Br. Ampelübergang m.

pel·let [ˈpelɪt] s **1.** Kügelchen n. **2.** Schrotkorn n.

pelt[1] [pelt] s Fell n, Pelz m.

pelt[2] [~] **I** v/t **1.** bewerfen, a. fig. bombardieren (**with** mit). **II** v/i **2.** **it is ~ing** (**down**), **it is ~ing with rain** es gießt in Strömen. **3.** stürmen, stürzen. **III** s **4.** (**at**) **full** ~ mit voller Geschwindigkeit.

pel·vic [ˈpelvɪk] adj anat., ✠ Becken...: **~ fin** ichth. Bauchflosse f.

pel·vis [ˈpelvɪs] pl **-ves** [ˈ~viːz] s anat. Becken n.

pen[1] [pen] s (Schreib)Feder f; Füller m; Kugelschreiber m.

pen[2] [~] **I** s **1.** Pferch m, (Schaf)Hürde f. **2.** (Lauf)Gitter n, (-)Stall m. **II** v/t (a. irr) a. **~ in** (od. **up**) **3.** Tiere einpferchen. **4.** Personen zs.-pferchen.

pe·nal [ˈpiːnl] adj □ **1.** Straf...: **~ code** Strafgesetzbuch n; **~ colony** Strafkolonie f; **~ law** Strafrecht n; **~ reform** Strafrechtsreform f. **2.** strafbar: **~ act** strafbare Handlung. **pe·nal·ize** [ˈpiːnəlaɪz] v/t **1.** bestrafen, weitS. a. benachteiligen. **2.** et. unter Strafe stellen. **pen·al·ty** [ˈpenltɪ] s **1.** Strafe f: **pay the ~ for s.th.** et. bezahlen od. büßen (**with** mit). **2.** Nachteil m. **3.** Fußball: Elfmeter m: **~ area** (od. **box**) Strafraum m; **~ kick** Strafstoß m.

pen·ance [ˈpenəns] s eccl. Buße f: **do ~** Buße tun (**for** für).

pen-and-ˈink draw·ing s Federzeichnung f.

pence [pens] pl von **penny.**

pen·chant [ˈpãːŋʃãːŋ] s (**for**) Neigung f, Hang m (zu), Vorliebe f (für).

pen·cil [ˈpensl] **I** s **1.** Bleistift m. **2.** ☈, phys. (Strahlen- etc)Bündel n. **II** v/t pret u. pp **-ciled**, bsd. Br. **-cilled 3.** mit Bleistift markieren od. schreiben od. zeichnen. **4.** Augenbrauen etc nachziehen. **~ case** s Federmäppchen n. **~ sharp·en·er** s (Bleistift)Spitzer m.

pen·dant [ˈpendənt] s Anhänger m (Schmuckstück).

pen·dent [ˈpendənt] adj **1.** Hänge...: **~ lamp. 2.** überhängend (Felsen etc).

pend·ing [ˈpendɪŋ] **I** adj **1.** bsd. ⚖ schwebend, anhängig. **2.** bevorstehend. **II** prp **3.** bis zu.

pen·du·lum [ˈpendjʊləm] s Pendel n (a. fig.).

pen·e·trate [ˈpenɪtreɪt] **I** v/t eindringen in (acc) (a. fig.); durchdringen, dringen durch. **II** v/i eindringen (**into** in acc) (a. fig.); durchdringen: **~ through** a. dringen durch. **ˈpen·e·trat·ing** adj □ **1.** durchdringend; (Verstand) scharf. **2.** scharfsinnig. **ˌpen·e·ˈtra·tion** s **1.** Ein-, Durchdringen n. **2.** Scharfsinn m.

pen friend s Brieffreund(in).

pen·guin [ˈpeŋgwɪn] s orn. Pinguin m.

pen·i·cil·lin [ˌpenɪˈsɪlɪn] s ✠ Penicillin n.

pen·in·su·la [pəˈnɪnsjʊlə] s Halbinsel f. **pen·in·su·lar** adj Halbinsel...; halbinselförmig.

pe·nis [ˈpiːnɪs] pl **-nis·es, -nes** [ˈ~niːz] s anat. Penis m.

pen·i·tence [ˈpenɪtəns] s Buße f: a) eccl. Bußfertigkeit f, b) Reue f. **pen·i·tent,** **pen·i·ten·tial** [ˌ~ˈtenʃl] adj □ a) eccl. bußfertig, b) reuig. **pen·i·ten·tia·ry** [ˌ~ˈtenʃərɪ] s Am. (Staats)Gefängnis n.

ˈpen·knife s (irr **knife**) Taschenmesser n. **~ name** s Schriftstellername m.

pen·nant [ˈpenənt] s Wimpel m.

pen·ni·less [ˈpenɪlɪs] adj □ (völlig) mittellos: **be ~** a. keinen Pfennig Geld haben.

pen·ny [ˈpenɪ] pl **-nies, coll. pence** [pens] s Br. Penny m: **in for a ~, in for a pound** wer A sagt, muß auch B sagen; **a pretty ~** F ein hübsches Sümmchen; **count** (**the**) **pennies** jeden Pfennig umdrehen; (**the**) **~('s) dropped** F der Groschen ist gefallen; **spend a ~** F mal verschwinden. **~ dread·ful** pl **-fuls** s Br. F Groschenroman m. **~ pinch·er** s F

Pfennigfuchser(in). '~‚**pinch·ing** adj F knick(e)rig.

pen pal F → **pen friend.**

pen·sion ['penʃn] I s Rente f, Pension f: **~ scheme** Rentenversicherung f. II v/t: **~ off** j-n pensionieren, in den Ruhestand versetzen; fig. F Maschine etc ausrangieren. '**pen·sion·a·ble** adj: of ~ **age** im Renten- od. Pensionsalter. **pen·sion·er** ['~ʃənə] s Rentner(in), Pensionär(in).

pen·sive ['pensɪv] adj □ 1. nachdenklich. 2. trübsinnig.

pent [pent] pret u. pp von **pen²**.

pen·ta·gon ['pentəgən] s Fünfeck n: **the ⌂** das Pentagon. **pen·tag·o·nal** [~'tægən] adj □ fünfeckig.

pen·tath·lete [pen'tæθliːt] s Sport: Fünfkämpfer(in). **pen·tath·lon** [~lən] s Fünfkampf m.

Pen·te·cost ['pentikɒst] s eccl. Pfingsten n, a. pl.

pent·house ['penthaʊs] s Penthouse n, -haus n.

‚**pent·'up** adj an-, aufgestaut (Gefühle).

pe·nul·ti·mate [pe'nʌltɪmət] adj vorletzt.

pe·o·ny ['pɪənɪ] s ♀ Pfingstrose f.

peo·ple ['piːpl] I s 1. (pl konstruiert) die Menschen pl, die Leute pl, Personen pl: **my ~** F m-e Angehörigen pl od. Leute. 2. (pl konstruiert) man: ~ **say that** man sagt, daß. 3. (pl konstruiert) **the ~** a) das (gemeine) Volk: **a man of the** (common) ~ ein Mann des Volks, b) die Bürger pl od. die Wähler pl, die Bevölkerung: **~'s front** Volksfront f; **~'s republic** Volksrepublik f. 4. Volk n, Nation f. II v/t 5. besiedeln, bevölkern (with mit).

pep [pep] F I s Pep m, Schwung m. II v/t: **~ up** j-n aufmöbeln: **~ things up** Schwung in den Laden bringen.

pep·per ['pepə] I s Pfeffer m; Paprikaschote f. II v/t pfeffern, fig. a. spicken (with mit). '**~box** Am. → **pepper pot.** '**~corn** s Pfefferkorn n. **~ mill** s Pfeffermühle f. '**~mint** I s 1. ♀ Pfefferminze f. 2. Pfefferminz n (Bonbon). II adj 3. Pfefferminz... **~ pot** s Pfefferstreuer m.

pep·per·y ['pepərɪ] adj □ 1. pfeff(e)rig. 2. fig. hitzig (Person).

pep| pill s F Aufputschpille f. **~ talk** s F aufmunternde Worte pl: **give s.o. a ~**

j-m ein paar aufmunternde Worte sagen.

pep·tic ['peptɪk] adj: **~ ulcer** ♂ Magengeschwür n.

per [pɜː] prp 1. per, durch. 2. pro, je. 3. mst **as** ~ laut, gemäß.

per·am·bu·la·tor [pə'ræmbjʊleɪtə] s bsd. Br. Kinderwagen m.

per cap·i·ta [pə'kæpɪtə] I adj Pro-Kopf-... II adv pro Kopf.

per·ceive [pə'siːv] v/t 1. wahrnehmen. 2. begreifen, erkennen.

per cent Br., **per·cent** bsd. Am. [pə'sent] I adj u. adv ...prozentig. II s Prozent n. **per'cent·age** s 1. Prozentsatz m; Teil m: **what ~ of ...?** wieviel Prozent von ...?; **in ~ terms** prozentual (ausgedrückt). 2. **there's no ~ in doing s.th.** F es bringt nichts, et. zu tun.

per·cep·ti·ble [pə'septəbl] adj □ wahrnehmbar, merklich. **per'cep·tion** s 1. Wahrnehmung f. 2. Auffassung(sgabe) f. **per'cep·tive** adj □ scharfsinnig.

perch¹ [pɜːtʃ] s ichth. Flußbarsch m.

perch² [~] I s 1. (Sitz)Stange f (für Vögel): **knock s.o. off his ~** F j-n von s-m Sockel stoßen. 2. F hochgelegener Platz od. Standort. II v/i 3. (on) sich niederlassen (auf acc, dat), sich setzen (auf acc) (Vogel). 4. F hocken (on auf dat). III v/t 5. ~ o.s. F sich hocken (on auf acc).

per·co·late ['pɜːkəleɪt] I v/t Kaffee filtern, weitS. kochen, machen. II v/i durchsickern (a. fig.), (Kaffee) durchlaufen '**per·co·la·tor** s Kaffeemaschine f.

per·cus·sion [pə'kʌʃn] I s 1. Schlag m, Stoß m; Erschütterung f. 2. ♪ Schlagzeug n. II adj 3. **~ instrument** Schlaginstrument n; **~ section** → 2. **per'cus·sion·ist** s Schlagzeuger m.

per·emp·to·ry [pə'remptərɪ] adj □ 1. gebieterisch, herrisch. 2. kategorisch (Befehl etc).

per·en·ni·al [pə'renjəl] adj □ 1. ewig, immerwährend. 2. ♀ mehrjährig.

per·fect ['pɜːfɪkt] I adj □ 1. perfekt: a) vollkommen, vollendet: **~ crime** perfektes Verbrechen, b) fehler-, makellos. 2. gänzlich, vollständig: **~ fool** ausgemachter Narr; **~ nonsense** kompletter Unsinn; **~ strangers** pl wildfremde Leute pl. 3. **~ tense** → 4. II s 4. ling.

Perfekt *n*: → *future* 4, *past* 2, *present* 3. **III** *v/t* [pəˈfekt] **5.** vervollkommnen, perfektionieren. **per·fec·tion** [pəˈfekʃn] *s* **1.** Vervollkommnung *f*, Vollendung *f*. **2.** Vollkommenheit *f*, Perfektion *f*: **bring to** ~ vervollkommnen; **to** ~ vollkommen, perfekt. **per·'fec·tion·ism** *s* Perfektionismus *m*. **per·'fec·tion·ist** **I** *s* Perfektionist(in). **II** *adj* perfektionistisch.

per·fid·i·ous [pɜːˈfɪdɪəs] *adj* □ treulos, verräterisch. **per·fi·dy** [ˈpɜːfɪdɪ] *s* Treulosigkeit *f*.

per·fo·rate [ˈpɜːfəreɪt] *v/t* **1.** durchbohren, -löchern. **2.** perforieren, lochen. **per·fo·'ra·tion** *s* **1.** Durchbohrung *f*, -löcherung *f*. **2.** Perforation *f*.

per·form [pəˈfɔːm] **I** *v/t* **1.** *Arbeit, Dienst etc* verrichten, *Pflicht, a. Vertrag* erfüllen, *✍ Operation* durchführen. **2.** *Theaterstück etc* aufführen, spielen, *a. Konzert* geben, *Musikstück, Lied etc* vortragen, *Kunststück etc* vorführen, *Rolle* spielen. **II** *v/i* **3.** ~ **well** (*bsd. Sport*) e-e gute Leistung zeigen; *ped.* gut abschneiden. **4.** ⚙ funktionieren, arbeiten (*Maschine etc*). **5.** *thea. etc* e-e Vorstellung geben, auftreten, spielen. **per·'form·ance** *s* **1.** Verrichtung *f*, Erfüllung *f*, Durchführung *f*. **2.** *♪, thea.* Aufführung *f*, Vorstellung *f*, Vortrag *m*. **3.** Leistung *f* (*a. ⚙*): ~ **principle** *sociol.* Leistungsprinzip *n*. **per·'form·er** *s* Darsteller(in), Künstler(in). **per·'form·ing** *adj* dressiert (*Tier*).

per·fume I *s* [ˈpɜːfjuːm] **1.** Duft *m*. **2.** Parfüm *n*. **II** *v/t* [pəˈfjuːm] **3.** parfümieren.

per·func·to·ry [pəˈfʌŋktərɪ] *adj* □ flüchtig (*Blick etc*), (*a. Person*) oberflächlich.

per·haps [pəˈhæps] *adv* vielleicht.

per·il [ˈperəl] *s* Gefahr *f*: **be in** ~ **of one's life** sich in Lebensgefahr befinden; **at one's** ~ auf eigene Gefahr. **'per·il·ous** *adj* □ gefährlich.

pe·ri·od [ˈpɪərɪəd] **I** *s* **1.** Periode *f*, Zeit (-dauer *f*, -raum *m*, -spanne *f*) *f*, Frist *f*: **for a** ~ **of** für die Dauer von. **2.** Zeit(alter *n*) *f*, Epoche *f*. **3.** *physiol.* Periode *f*. **4.** *ped.* (Unterrichts)Stunde *f*. **5.** *ling. bsd. Am.* Punkt *m*. **II** *adj* **6.** zeitgenössisch, historisch, Stil...: ~ **furniture** Stilmöbel *pl*. **pe·ri·od·ic** [ˌpɪərɪˈɒdɪk] *adj*

(~**ally**) periodisch, regelmäßig wiederkehrend. ˌpe·ri·'od·i·cal **I** *adj* → **periodic**. **II** *s* Zeitschrift *f*.

pe·riph·er·y [pəˈrɪfərɪ] *s* Peripherie *f*, *a. fig.* Rand *m*: **on the** ~ **of the town** am Stadtrand.

per·i·scope [ˈperɪskəup] *s* Periskop *n*, Sehrohr *n*.

per·ish [ˈperɪʃ] **I** *v/i* **1.** umkommen: **be** ~**ing** (**with cold**) F vor Kälte umkommen. **2.** brüchig werden, verschleißen (*Material*), schlecht werden, verderben (*Lebensmittel*). **II** *v/t* **3.** **be** ~**ed** (**with cold**) F ganz durchgefroren sein. **'per·ish·a·ble** *adj* leichtverderblich. **'per·ish·ing** *bsd. Br.* F *adj* saukalt. **II** *adv*: ~**ly cold** → **I**.

per·i·to·ni·tis [ˌperɪtəʊˈnaɪtɪs] *s* ✍ Bauchfellentzündung *f*.

per·jure [ˈpɜːdʒə] *v/t*: ~ **o.s.** e-n Meineid leisten. **per·ju·ry** *s* Meineid *m*: **commit** ~ → **perjure**.

perk[1] [pɜːk] F **I** *v/t* → **percolate** I. **II** *v/i* durchlaufen (*Kaffee*).

perk[2] [~] F **I** *v/t*: ~ **up** *j-n* aufmöbeln. **II** *v/i*: ~ **up** aufleben, neuen Schwung bekommen.

perk[3] [~] F → **perquisite**.

perk·y [ˈpɜːkɪ] *adj* □ F **1.** munter, lebhaft. **2.** keck, selbstbewußt.

perm [pɜːm] F **I** *s* Dauerwelle *f*: **give s.o. a** ~ → **II.** **II** *v/t*: ~ **s.o.'s hair** j-m e-e Dauerwelle machen.

per·ma·nence [ˈpɜːmənəns], **'per·ma·nen·cy** *s* Beständigkeit *f*, Dauerhaftigkeit *f*. **'per·ma·nent I** *adj* □ beständig, dauerhaft, Dauer...: ~ **address** ständiger Wohnsitz; ~ **wave** Dauerwelle *f*. **II** *s Am.* Dauerwelle *f*.

per·me·a·ble [ˈpɜːmjəbl] *adj* □ durchlässig (**to** für). **per·me·ate** [ˈ~mɪeɪt] *v/t* durchdringen (*a. fig.*). **II** *v/i* dringen (**into** in *acc*; **through** durch).

per·mis·si·ble [pəˈmɪsəbl] *adj* □ zulässig, statthaft, erlaubt. **per·mis·sion** [pəˈmɪʃn] *s* Erlaubnis *f*: **by** ~ **of** mit Genehmigung (*gen*); **without** ~ unerlaubt, unbefugt; **ask s.o.'s** ~, **ask s.o. for** ~ j-n um Erlaubnis bitten; **give s.o.** ~ **to do s.th.** j-m die Erlaubnis geben *od.* j-m erlauben, et. zu tun. **per·mis·sive** [~sɪv] *adj* □ liberal; (*sexuell*) freizügig: ~ **society** tabufreie Gesellschaft.

per·mit [pəˈmɪt] **I** *v/t* **1.** *et.* erlauben, gestatten: *not ~ted a.* verboten; **~ s.o. to do s.th.** j-m erlauben, et. zu tun. **II** *v/i* **2.** es erlauben *od.* gestatten: **weather ~ting** wenn es das Wetter erlaubt. **3. ~ of** et. zulassen. **III** *s* ['pɜːmɪt] **4.** Genehmigung *f*.

per·ni·cious [pəˈnɪʃəs] *adj* □ schädlich, verderblich.

per·nick·et·y [pəˈnɪkətɪ] *adj* F **1.** pingelig, pedantisch. **2.** kitz(e)lig (*Angelegenheit etc*).

per·pen·dic·u·lar [ˌpɜːpənˈdɪkjʊlə] **I** *adj* □ senkrecht, rechtwink(e)lig (**to** zu). **II** *s* Senkrechte *f*.

per·pe·trate [ˈpɜːpɪtreɪt] *v/t* Verbrechen *etc* begehen, verüben; *humor. Buch etc* verbrechen. **'per·pe·tra·tor** *s* Täter(in).

per·pet·u·al [pəˈpetʃʊəl] *adj* □ fortwährend, ständig, ewig. **per'pet·u·ate** [~eɪt] *v/t* verewigen. **per·pe·tu·i·ty** [ˌpɜːpɪˈtjuːətɪ] *s*: **in ~** auf ewig, für immer.

per·plex [pəˈpleks] *v/t* verwirren, verblüffen: **~ed a.** perplex. **per'plex·i·ty** *s* Verwirrung *f*, Verblüffung *f*.

per·qui·site [ˈpɜːkwɪzɪt] *s mst pl* Vergünstigung *f*.

per·se·cute [ˈpɜːsɪkjuːt] *v/t* **1.** *bsd. pol., eccl.* verfolgen. **2.** belästigen. **per·se·'cu·tion** *s* **1.** Verfolgung *f*: **~ complex** (*od. mania*) *psych.* Verfolgungswahn *m*. **2.** Belästigung *f*.

per·se·ver·ance [ˌpɜːsɪˈvɪərəns] *s* Ausdauer *f*, Beharrlichkeit *f*. **per·se·vere** [~ˈvɪə] *v/i* beharrlich weitermachen (**at**, **in**, **with** mit). **per·se'ver·ing** *adj* □ ausdauernd, beharrlich.

Per·sian [ˈpɜːʃn] **I** *adj* **1.** persisch: **~ carpet** Perser(teppich) *m*. **II** *s* **2.** Perser(in). **3.** *ling.* Persisch *n*.

per·sist [pəˈsɪst] *v/i* **1. ~ in doing s.th.** et. unbedingt tun wollen; darauf bestehen, et. zu tun; et. auch *od.* noch weiterhin tun. **2. ~ with** hartnäckig *od.* unbeirrt fortfahren mit. **3.** anhalten, fortdauern. **per'sist·ence** *s* **1.** Hartnäckigkeit *f*, Unbeirrtheit *f*. **2.** Fortdauer *f*. **per'sist·ent** *adj* □ **1.** unbeirrt (*Person*), (*a. Gerücht etc*) hartnäckig. **2.** anhaltend, fortdauernd.

per·snick·e·ty [pəˈsnɪkətɪ] *Am.* → **pernickety**.

per·son [ˈpɜːsn] *s* Person *f* (*a. ling.*), Mensch *m*: **in ~** persönlich. **'per·son-**

a·ble *adj* von sympathischem *od.* angenehmem Äußeren. **'per·son·age** *s* (bedeutende *od.* prominente) Persönlichkeit. **'per·son·al** *adj* □ **1.** persönlich, Personal...: **~ column** (*Zeitung*) Persönliches *n*; **~ computer** Personal Computer *m*, Personalcomputer *m*; **~ file** Personalakte *f*; **~ pronoun** *ling.* Personalpronomen *n*, persönliches Fürwort *n*. **2.** persönlich, privat (*Angelegenheit etc*). **3.** äußer, körperlich: **~ hygiene** Körperpflege *f*. **4.** persönlich, anzüglich (*Bemerkung etc*): **get ~** persönlich werden. **per·son·al·i·ty** [ˌpɜːsəˈnælətɪ] *s* **1.** Persönlichkeit *f* (*a. e·s Menschen*): **~ cult** Personenkult *m*. **2.** *pl* persönliche *od.* anzügliche Bemerkungen *pl*, Persönliches *n*. **per·son·i·fi·ca·tion** [pəˌsɒnɪfɪˈkeɪʃn] *s* Personifizierung *f*: **be the ~ of avarice** die Habgier in Person sein. **per'son·i·fy** [~faɪ] *v/t* personifizieren: **be avarice personified** die Habgier in Person sein. **per·son·nel** [ˌpɜːsəˈnel] *s* **1.** Personal *n*, Belegschaft *f*: **~ manager** Personalchef *m*. **2.** die Personalabteilung.

per·spec·tive [pəˈspektɪv] *s* Perspektive *f* (*a. fig.*): **in ~** perspektivisch richtig; *fig.* in *od.* aus der richtigen Perspektive; **the houses are out of ~** bei den Häusern stimmt die Perspektive nicht.

per·spex [ˈpɜːspeks] (*TM*) *s Br.* Plexiglas *n*.

per·spi·ra·tion [ˌpɜːspəˈreɪʃn] *s* **1.** Transpirieren *n*, Schwitzen *n*. **2.** Schweiß *m*. **per·spire** [pəˈspaɪə] *v/i* transpirieren, schwitzen.

per·suade [pəˈsweɪd] *v/t* **1.** j-n überreden (**into doing, to do** zu tun): **~ s.o. out of s.th.** j-m et. ausreden. **2.** j-n überzeugen (**of** von; **that** [davon,] daß). **per·sua·sion** [pəˈsweɪʒn] *s* **1.** Überredung *f*. **2.** *a.* **powers** *pl* **of ~** Überredungskunst *f*. **3.** Überzeugung *f*: **be of the ~ that** der Überzeugung sein, daß. **per'sua·sive** [~sɪv] *adj* □ überzeugend.

pert [pɜːt] *adj* □ keck (*a. Hut etc*), keß.

per·tain [pəˈteɪn] *v/i*: **~ to s.th.** et. betreffen; zu et. gehören.

per·ti·na·cious [ˌpɜːtɪˈneɪʃəs] *adj* □ **1.** hartnäckig, zäh. **2.** beharrlich.

per·ti·nent [ˈpɜːtɪnənt] *adj* □ relevant (**to** für); sachdienlich.

pert·ness ['pɜːtnɪs] s Keckheit f, Keßheit f.

per·turb [pə'tɜːb] v/t beunruhigen.

pe·ruse [pə'ruːz] v/t sorgfältig durchlesen.

per·vade [pə'veɪd] v/t durchdringen, erfüllen. **per'va·sive** [~sɪv] adj □ weitverbreitet.

per·verse [pə'vɜːs] adj □ **1.** eigensinnig, querköpfig. **2.** pervers, widernatürlich. **per'ver·sion** s **1.** Pervertierung f; Verdrehung f, Entstellung f. **2.** Perversion f. **per'ver·si·ty** s **1.** Eigensinn m, Querköpfigkeit f. **2.** Perversität f.

per·vert v/t [pə'vɜːt] pervertieren; verdrehen, entstellen: **~ the course of justice** das Recht beugen. **II** s ['pɜːvɜːt] perverser Mensch.

pes·ky ['peskɪ] adj □ bsd. Am. F lästig.

pes·sa·ry ['pesərɪ] s ⚕ Pessar n.

pes·si·mism ['pesɪmɪzəm] s Pessimismus m. **'pes·si·mist** s Pessimist(in). **,pes·si'mis·tic** adj (~ally) pessimistisch.

pest [pest] s **1.** Schädling m: **~ control** Schädlingsbekämpfung f. **2.** F Nervensäge f; Plage f. **'pes·ter** v/t F j-n belästigen (**with** mit), j-m keine Ruhe lassen (**for** wegen), j-n drängeln (**to do** zu tun): **~ s.o. into doing s.th.** j-n so lange quälen, bis er et. tut.

pest·i·cide ['pestɪsaɪd] s Schädlingsbekämpfungsmittel n.

pet [pet] s **I** s **1.** Heimtier n. **2.** a) oft contp. Liebling m, b) Schatz m. **II** adj **3.** Lieblings...: **~ name** Kosename m; → **hate** 5. **4.** Tier...: **~ food** Tiernahrung f; **~ shop** Tierhandlung f, Zoogeschäft n, -handlung f. **III** v/t **5.** streicheln. **IV** v/i **6.** F Petting machen.

pet·al ['petl] s ♀ Blütenblatt n.

pe·ter ['piːtə] v/i: **~ out** versickern (Bach etc), allmählich zu Ende gehen (Vorräte etc), versanden (Unterhaltung etc), sich verlieren (Erinnerung etc), sich totlaufen (Verhandlungen).

pe·tite [pə'tiːt] adj zierlich (Frau).

pe·ti·tion [pə'tɪʃn] s **I** s Eingabe f, Gesuch n, (schriftlicher) Antrag: **~ for divorce** ⚖ Scheidungsklage f. **II** v/t ersuchen (**for** um; **to do** zu tun). **III** v/i einkommen, nachsuchen (**for** um): **~ for divorce** ⚖ die Scheidung einreichen. **pe'ti·tion·er** s Antragsteller(in), ⚖

Kläger(in) (im Scheidungsprozeß).

pet·ri·fy ['petrɪfaɪ] **I** v/t: **petrified with horror** vor Entsetzen wie versteinert, starr od. wie gelähmt vor Entsetzen; **be petrified of** panische Angst haben vor (dat). **II** v/i versteinern, fig. a. sich versteinern.

pet·rol ['petrəl] Br. **I** s Benzin n. **II** adj Benzin...: **~ bomb** Molotowcocktail m; **~ coupon** Benzingutschein m; **~ pump** Benzinpumpe f; Tank-, Zapfsäule f; **~ station** Tankstelle f.

pe·tro·le·um [pə'trəʊljəm] s Erdöl n.

pet·ti·coat ['petɪkəʊt] s Unterrock m.

pet·ti·fog·ging ['petɪfɒgɪŋ] adj **1.** kleinlich, pedantisch. **2.** belanglos, unwichtig.

pet·ting ['petɪŋ] s F Petting f.

pet·tish ['petɪʃ] adj □: **be ~** sich wegen jeder Kleinigkeit aufregen; **don't be so ~!** sei doch nicht so kindisch!

pet·ty ['petɪ] adj □ **1.** belanglos, unbedeutend, (Vergehen) geringfügig: **~ cash** Portokasse f. **2.** engstirnig.

pet·u·lant ['petjʊlənt] → **pettish**.

pew [pjuː] s **1.** (Kirchen)Bank f. **2.** Br. F (Sitz)Platz m: **take a ~** sich setzen.

pew·ter ['pjuːtə] s **1.** Zinn n. **2.** a. **~ ware** coll. Zinn(geschirr) n.

pha·lanx ['fælæŋks] pl **-lanx·es, -lan·ges** [fæ'lændʒiːz] s **1.** Phalanx f. **2.** anat. Finger- od. Zehenglied n.

phal·li ['fælaɪ] pl von **phallus**.

phal·lic ['fælɪk] adj phallisch: **~ symbol** Phallussymbol n.

phal·lus ['fæləs] pl **-li** [~laɪ] s Phallus m.

phan·tom ['fæntəm] **I** s **1.** Phantom n, Trugbild n. **2.** Geist m (e-s Verstorbenen). **II** adj **3.** ~ (**limb**) **pain** Phantomschmerz m; **~ pregnancy** Scheinschwangerschaft f.

phar·i·sa·ic [,færɪ'seɪɪk] adj (~ally) pharisäerhaft, pharisäisch. **phar·i·see** ['~siː] s Pharisäer(in).

phar·ma·ceu·ti·cal [,fɑːmə'sjuːtɪkl] adj □ pharmazeutisch. **,phar·ma'ceu·tics** s pl (sg konstruiert) → **pharmacy** 1.

phar·ma·cist ['~sɪst] s **1.** Pharmazeut(in). **2.** Apotheker(in). **'phar·ma·cy** s **1.** Pharmazeutik f, Pharmazie f. **2.** Apotheke f.

pha·ryn·ges [fə'rɪndʒiːz] pl von **pharynx**.

phar·yn·gi·tis [,færɪn'dʒaɪtɪs] s ⚕ Rachenkatarrh m.

phar·ynx ['færɪŋks] *pl* **'phar·ynx·es, pha·ryn·ges** [fə'rɪndʒiːz] *s anat.* Rachen *m*.

phase [feɪz] **I** *s* **1.** *allg.* Phase *f*: ~*s pl of the moon* Mondphasen *pl*. **II** *v/t* **2.** schritt- *od.* stufenweise planen *od.* durchführen: ~*d* schritt-, stufenweise; ~ *in* schritt- *od.* stufenweise einführen; ~ *out* auslaufen lassen.

pheas·ant ['feznt] *s orn.* Fasan *m*.

phe·nom·e·na [fə'nɒmɪnə] *pl von* **phenomenon. phe'nom·e·nal** [~nl] *adj* □ phänomenal. **phe'nom·e·non** [~nən] *pl* **-na** [~nə] *s allg.* Phänomen *n*.

phew [fjuː] *int* puh!

phi·al ['faɪəl] *s* (*bsd. Arznei*)Fläschen *n*.

phil·an·throp·ic [ˌfɪlən'θrɒpɪk] *adj* (~*ally*) philanthropisch, menschenfreundlich. **phi·lan·thro·pist** [fɪ'læn-θrəpɪst] *s* Philanthrop(in), Menschenfreund(in). **phi'lan·thro·py** *s* Philanthropie *f*, Menschenfreundlichkeit *f*.

phil·a·tel·ic [ˌfɪlə'telɪk] *adj* (~*ally*) philatelistisch. **phi·lat·e·list** [fɪ'lætəlɪst] *s* Philatelist(in). **phi'lat·e·ly** *s* Philatelie *f*.

phil·har·mon·ic [ˌfɪlɑː'mɒnɪk] *adj* philharmonisch.

phi·lis·tine ['fɪlɪstaɪn] *s* Spießer *m*, Banause *m*.

phil·o·log·i·cal [ˌfɪlə'lɒdʒɪkl] *adj* □ philologisch. **phi·lol·o·gist** [fɪ'lɒlədʒɪst] *s* Philologe *m*, -login *f*. **phi'lol·o·gy** *s* Philologie *f*.

phi·los·o·pher [fɪ'lɒsəfə] *s* Philosoph (-in). **phil·o·soph·i·cal** [ˌfɪlə'sɒfɪkl] *adj* □ philosophisch, *fig. a.* abgeklärt, gelassen. **phi·los·o·phize** [fɪ'lɒsəfaɪz] *v/i* philosophieren (*about, on* über *acc*). **phi'los·o·phy** *s* Philosophie *f*, *fig. a.* (Welt)Anschauung *f*.

phle·bi·tis [flɪ'baɪtɪs] *s* ✸ Venenentzündung *f*.

phlegm [flem] *s* **1.** *physiol.* Schleim *m*. **2.** *fig.* Phlegma *n*. **phleg·mat·ic** [fleg-'mætɪk] *adj* (~*ally*) phlegmatisch.

pho·bi·a ['fəʊbjə] *s psych.* Phobie *f*, krankhafte Angst (*about* vor *dat*).

phone [fəʊn] **I** *s* **1.** Telefon *n*: *by* ~ telefonisch; *be on the* ~ Telefon(anschluß) haben; *am* Telefon sein. **2.** Hörer *m*. **II** *v/i* **3.** telefonieren, anrufen: ~ *back* zurückrufen. **III** *v/t* **4.** *a.* ~ *up* anrufen: ~ *back* zurückrufen; ~ *s.th. to s.o.* j-m et.

telefonisch durchgeben. **IV** *adj* **5.** Telefon...: ~ *book* Telefonbuch *n*; ~ *booth* (*Br. box*) Telefonzelle *f*; ~ *call* Anruf *m*, Gespräch *n*; ~ *number* Telefonnummer *f*. '~·*in s* Rundfunk, *TV*: *Br.* Sendung *f* mit telefonischer Zuhörer- *od.* Zuschauerbeteiligung.

pho·neme ['fəʊniːm] *s ling.* Phonem *n*.

pho·net·ic [fəʊ'netɪk] **I** *adj* (~*ally*) phonetisch: ~ *character* (*od. symbol*) Lautzeichen *n*; ~ *transcription* Lautschrift *f*. **II** *s pl* (*mst sg konstruiert*) Phonetik *f*.

pho·n(e)y ['fəʊnɪ] **F I** *adj* □ **1.** falsch: a) gefälscht (*Geld, Paß etc*), b) erfunden (*Schmuck, Gefühle etc*), c) erfunden (*Geschichte etc*), faul (*Sache, Entschuldigung etc*), Schein..., Schwindel...(-*firma etc*), d) verlogen (*Moral etc*). **II** *s* **2.** Fälschung *f*. **3.** Schwindler(in).

phos·phate ['fɒsfeɪt] *s* ⚗ Phosphat *n*.

phos·pho·res·cent [ˌfɒsfə'resnt] *adj* □ phosphoreszierend.

phos·pho·rus ['fɒsfərəs] *s* ⚗ Phosphor *m*.

pho·to ['fəʊtəʊ] *pl* **-tos** *s* **F** Foto *n*, Bild *n*: *in the* ~ auf dem Foto; *take a* ~ ein Foto machen (*of* von); ~ *album* Fotoalbum *n*; ~ *safari* Fotosafari *f*. '~·*cell s* ⚡ Photozelle *f*. '~·*cop·i·er s* Fotokopierer *m*, -kopiergerät *n*. '~·*cop·y* **I** *s* Fotokopie *f*: *make* (*od. take*) *a* ~ *of* e-e Fotokopie machen von. **II** *v/t* fotokopieren. ~ *fin·ish s Sport:* Fotofinish *n*.

pho·to·gen·ic [ˌfəʊtəʊ'dʒenɪk] *adj* (~*ally*) fotogen.

pho·to·graph ['fəʊtəgrɑːf] **I** *s* Fotografie *f*, Aufnahme *f*: *in the* ~ auf der Fotografie; *take a* ~ e-e Aufnahme machen (*of* von). **II** *v/t* fotografieren. **III** *v/i* sich *gut etc* fotografieren (lassen). **pho·tog·ra·pher** [fə'tɒgrəfə] *s* Fotograf(in). **pho·to·graph·ic** [ˌfəʊtə'græfɪk] *adj* (~*ally*) fotografisch: ~ *memory* fotografisches Gedächtnis; ~ *studio* Fotostudio *n*. **pho·tog·ra·phy** [fə'tɒgrəfɪ] *s* Fotografie *f* (*Verfahren etc*).

,**pho·to'sen·si·tive** *adj* lichtempfindlich. ,~'syn·the·sis *s biol.* Photosynthese *f*.

phras·al ['freɪzl] *adj*: ~ *verb ling.* Verb in Verbindung mit e-m *Adverb u./od.* e-r *Präposition*.

phrase [freɪz] **I** *s* **1.** *ling.* Phrase *f*, Satzteil *m.* **2.** (Rede)Wendung *f*, Redensart *f*. **3.** *contp.* Phrase *f*: *empty* **~s** *pl* leere Phrasen *pl*. **II** *v/t* **4.** ausdrücken, formulieren. **'~book** *s* Sprachführer *m*.

phra·se·ol·o·gy [ˌfreɪzɪ'ɒlədʒɪ] *s* Ausdrucksweise *f*, Sprache *f*; Jargon *m*.

phut [fʌt] *adv*: *go* **~** F kaputtgehen (*a. fig. Ehe etc*); *fig.* platzen (*Pläne etc*).

phys·i·cal ['fɪzɪkl] **I** *adj* (□ → *physically*) **1.** physisch, körperlich: **~** *education* (*od. training*) *ped.* Leibeserziehung *f*, Sport *m*; **~** *examination* → **3**; **~** *handicap* Körperbehinderung *f*; **~** *jerks pl Br.* F Gymnastik *f*; **~** *strength* Körperkraft *f*. **2.** physikalisch. **II** *s* **3.** ärztliche Untersuchung. **phys·i·cal·ly** ['~kəlɪ] *adv* → *physical*: **~** *handicapped* körperbehindert; **~** *impossible* F völlig unmöglich. **phy·si·cian** [fɪ'zɪʃn] *s* Arzt *m*, Ärztin *f*. **phys·i·cist** ['~sɪst] *s* Physiker(in). **phys·ics** ['fɪzɪks] *s pl* (*mst sg konstruiert*) Physik *f*.

phys·i·og·no·my [ˌfɪzɪ'ɒnəmɪ] *s* Physiognomie *f*, Gesichtsausdruck *m*.

phys·i·o·log·i·cal [ˌfɪzɪə'lɒdʒɪkl] *adj* □ physiologisch. **phys·i·ol·o·gy** [ˌ~'ɒlədʒɪ] *s* Physiologie *f*.

phys·i·o·ther·a·py [ˌfɪzɪəʊ'θerəpɪ] *s* Physiotherapie *f*.

phy·sique [fɪ'ziːk] *s* Körperbau *m*, Statur *f*.

pi·an·ist ['pɪənɪst] *s* Pianist(in).

pi·an·o [pɪ'ænəʊ] *pl* **-os** *s* Klavier *n*.

pick [pɪk] **I** *s* **1.** (Spitz)Hacke *f*, Pickel *m*. **2.** (Zahn)Stocher *m.* **3.** (Aus)Wahl *f*: *have one's* **~** *of* auswählen können aus; *take one's* **~** sich et. aussuchen; *the* **~** *of the bunch* das (Aller)Beste, das Beste vom Besten. **4. a)** (auf)hacken, (-)picken: → *hole* **1. 5.** *Körner* aufpicken; auflesen, (auf)sammeln; *Blumen, Obst* pflücken. **6.** *Knochen* abnagen; *Am. Hühner etc* rupfen: **~** *bone* **1. 7.** **~** *one's nose* in der Nase bohren, popeln; **~** *one's teeth* in den Zähnen (herum)stochern. **8.** *Schloß* mit e-m Dietrich *etc* öffnen, knacken. **9.** *Streit* vom Zaun brechen (*with* mit). **10.** (aus)wählen, aussuchen: **~** *one's way* (*od.* *steps*) sich s-n Weg suchen, mit vorsichtigen Schritten gehen (*through* durch); **~** *a winner fig.* das Große Los ziehen; **~** *one's words* s-e Worte genau wählen. **11.** zerpflücken,

-reißen; → *piece* **1. III** *v/i* **12. ~** *and choose* wählerisch sein; sich bei der Auswahl Zeit lassen.

Verbindungen mit Präpositionen:

pick *at v/i* **1. ~** *one's food* im Essen herumstochern. **2.** herumnörgeln an (*dat*); herumhacken auf (*dat*). **~** *on v/i* **1.** → *pick at* **2. 2.** *j-n (für et. Unangenehmes)* aussuchen.

Verbindungen mit Adverbien:

pick *out v/t* **1.** (sich) *et.* auswählen. **2.** ausmachen, erkennen. **~** *up* **I** *v/t* **1.** aufheben, -lesen: *pick o.s. up* sich aufrappeln (*a. fig.*); → *gauntlet¹, thread* **1. 2.** F *Passagiere* aufnehmen; *j-n* abholen. **3.** F *Mädchen* aufgabeln, -lesen; *Anhalter* mitnehmen; sich *e-e Krankheit* holen *od.* einfangen. **4.** *Funkspruch etc* auffangen. **5.** *Kenntnisse, Informationen etc* aufschnappen. **6.** zunehmen an (*dat*): **~** *speed* schneller werden. **II** *v/i* **7.** sich (wieder) erholen (*a.* ✝). **8.** stärker werden (*Wind etc*).

pick·a·back ['pɪkəbæk] **I** *adv* huckepack: *carry s.o.* **~** → **II**. **II** *s*: *give s.o. a* **~** *j-n* huckepack tragen.

'pick·ax(e) → *pick* **1.**

pick·er ['pɪkə] *s* Pflücker(in).

pick·et ['pɪkɪt] **I** *s* **1.** Pfahl *m.* **2.** Streikposten *m*: **~** *line* Streikpostenkette *f*. **II** *v/t* **3.** Streikposten aufstellen vor (*dat*), durch Streikposten blockieren. **III** *v/i* **4.** Streikposten stehen.

pick·ings ['pɪkɪŋz] *s pl* Ausbeute *f*: *there are easy* **~** *in this job* bei diesem Job kann man leicht ein paar Mark (dazu)verdienen.

pick·le ['pɪkl] **I** *s* **1.** Salzlake *f*; Essigsoße *f.* **2. a)** *Am.* Essig-, Gewürzgurke *f*, **b)** *mst pl* Pickles *pl*: → *mixed*. **3. be in a** (*pretty*) **~** F (ganz schön) in der Patsche sein *od.* stecken. **II** *v/t* **4.** *gastr.* einlegen. **'pick·led** *adj* **1.** eingelegt. **2.** F blau (*betrunken*).

'pick·lock *s* **1.** Einbrecher *m.* **2.** Dietrich *m.* **'~-me-up** *s* F Muntermacher *m*, Anregungsmittel *n*. **'~pock·et** *s* Taschendieb(in). **'~up** *s* **1.** Tonabnehmer *m*, Pick-up *m* (*am Plattenspieler*): **~** *arm* Tonarm *m.* **2. a. ~** *truck* kleiner Lieferwagen, Kleintransporter *m.* **3.** F (Zufalls)Bekanntschaft *f.* **4.** *mot.* F Beschleunigung(svermögen *n*) *f*: *have good* **~** gut beschleunigen.

pick·y ['pɪkɪ] *adj* □ F heikel, wählerisch: **be a very ~ eater** im Essen sehr heikel sein.

pic·nic ['pɪknɪk] **I** *s* Picknick *n*: **go on** (*od.* **for**) **a ~ in the country** zum Picknick aufs Land fahren; **have a ~** Picknick machen; **it's no ~** F es ist kein Honiglecken (**doing** zu tun). **II** *v/i pret u. pp* **-nicked** picknicken.

pic·to·ri·al [pɪk'tɔːrɪəl] **I** *adj* □ **1.** bebildert, illustriert: **~ report** Bildbericht *m*. **2.** bildhaft (*Sprache etc*). **II** *s* **3.** Illustrierte *f*.

pic·ture ['pɪktʃə] **I** *s* **1.** Bild *n* (*a. TV*): a) Abbildung *f*, Illustration *f*: **in the ~** auf dem Bild; b) Gemälde *n*: (**as**) **pretty as a ~** sehr hübsch; **be a ~** e-e Pracht *od.* ein Gedicht sein; **be the ~ of health** aussehen wie das blühende Leben; **his face was a ~** du hättest sein Gesicht sehen sollen; → **paint** 1, c) *phot.* Aufnahme *f*: **take a ~** e-e Aufnahme machen (**of** von), d) *fig.* Vorstellung *f*: **be in** (**out of**) **the ~** (nicht) im Bild sein; **put in the ~** ins Bild setzen; **get the ~?** F kapiert? **2.** a) Film *m*, b) *pl bsd. Am.* Kino *n*: **go to the ~s** ins Kino gehen. **II** *v/t* **3.** darstellen, malen. **4.** *fig.* sich *j-n*, *et.* vorstellen (**as** als). **~ book** *s* Bilderbuch *n*. **~ card** *s* Kartenspiel: Bild(karte *f*) *n*. **~ def·i·ni·tion** *s phot.*, *TV* Bildschärfe *f*. **~ frame** *s* Bilderrahmen *m*. **~ gal·ler·y** *s* Gemäldegalerie *f*. **~ post·card** *s* Ansichtskarte *f*. **~ tube** *s TV* Bildröhre *f*.

pic·tur·esque [ˌpɪktʃə'resk] *adj* □ malerisch.

pid·dle ['pɪdl] F **I** *v/i* pinkeln, (*Kind*) Pipi machen. **II** *v/t*: **~ away** Zeit vertrödeln. **'pid·dling** *adj* F unwichtig.

pidg·in Eng·lish ['pɪdʒɪn] *s* Pidgin-English(c)h *n*.

pie [paɪ] *s gastr.* Pie *f*: a) (*Fleisch- etc*)Pastete *f*, b) (*mst* gedeckter) (*Apfel- etc*)Kuchen *m*: (**as**) **easy as ~** F kinderleicht; → **finger** I, **humble** I.

piece [piːs] **I** *s* **1.** Stück *n*: **~ of cake** Stück Kuchen; F Kinderspiel *n*; **a ~** das Stück; **~ by ~** Stück für Stück; **by the ~** stückweise; **in ~s** entzwei, kaputt; (**all**) **in one ~** F ganz, unbeschädigt; heil, unverletzt; **break** (*od.* **fall**) **to ~s** zerbrechen, entzweigehen; **go to ~s** F zs.-brechen (*Person*); **pull** (*od.* **pick, tear**) **to ~s**

in Stücke reißen; *fig.* Äußerung *etc* zerpflücken; → **advice** 1, **furniture, mind** 4, **news**. **2.** Teil *n* (*e-r Maschine etc*): **take to ~s** auseinandernehmen, zerlegen. **3.** Teil *m* (*e-s Services etc*): **a 30-~ service** ein 30teiliges Service. **4.** (Geld)Stück *n*, Münze *f*. **5.** (*Schach*)Figur *f*; (*Dame etc*) Stein *m*. **6.** (*Zeitungs*)Artikel *m*. **II** *v/t* **7.** **~ together** zs.-stück(l)n; *fig.* zs.-fügen. **'~meal I** *adv* **1.** schrittweise. **II** *adj* **2.** schrittweise. **3.** unsystematisch. **'~work** *s* Akkordarbeit *f*: **be on** (*od.* **do**) **~** im Akkord arbeiten.

pie-'eyed *adj* F blau (*betrunken*).

pier [pɪə] *s* **1.** Pier *m*, ⚓ *u. f*, Landungsbrücke *f*, -steg *m*. **2.** (*Brücken- etc*)Pfeiler *m*.

pierce [pɪəs] *v/t* **1.** durchbohren, -stoßen: **~ s.o.'s ears** j-m die Ohren durchstechen. **2.** *fig.* durchdringen: **a cry ~d the silence** ein Schrei zerriß die Stille. **'pierc·ing** *adj* □ durchdringend, (*Kälte etc a.*) schneidend, (*Blick, Schmerz etc a.*) stechend, (*Schrei a.*) gellend.

pi·e·ty ['paɪətɪ] *s* Frömmigkeit *f*.

pif·fle ['pɪfl] *s* F Quatsch *m*. **'pif·fling** *adj* F albern.

pig [pɪg] *s* **1.** Schwein *n*: **buy a ~ in a poke** *fig.* die Katze im Sack kaufen; **make a ~'s ear of s.th.** *Br. sl.* et. vermasseln. **2.** F *contp.* Schwein *n*; Freßsack *m*. **3.** *sl.* Bulle *m* (*Polizist*).

pi·geon ['pɪdʒɪn] *s orn.* Taube *f*: **that's not my ~** *fig.* F das ist nicht mein Bier. **'~hole I** *s* **1.** (Ablege)Fach *n*: **put in ~s** → 3. **II** *v/t* **2.** (in Fächern) ablegen. **3.** *fig.* einordnen, klassifizieren. **4.** *fig.* zurückstellen. **'~toed** *adv*: **walk ~** über den großen Onkel gehen.

pig·gish ['pɪgɪʃ] *adj* □ schweinisch; gefräßig.

pig·gy ['pɪgɪ] **I** *s* **1.** *Kindersprache*: Schweinchen *n*. **II** *adj* **2.** Schweins...: **~ eyes**. **3.** gefräßig (*bsd. Kind*). **'~back** → **pickaback**. **~ bank** *s* Sparschwein *n*.

pig'head·ed *adj* □ dickköpfig, stur. **~ i·ron** *s* Roheisen *n*.

pig·let ['pɪglɪt] *s* Ferkel *n*, Schweinchen *n*.

pig·ment ['pɪgmənt] *s* Pigment *n*.

pig·my → **pygmy**.

'pig·pen *bsd. Am.* → **pigsty**. **'~skin** *s* Schweinsleder *n*. **'~sty** *s* Schweinestall *m, fig. a.* Saustall *m.* '**~tail** *s* Zopf *m.*

pike¹ [paɪk] *pl* **pikes,** *bsd.* **coll. pike** *s ichth.* Hecht *m.*

pike² [~] *s* ✕ *hist.* Pike *f,* Spieß *m.*

pike³ [~] → **turnpike.**

'**pike·staff** *s*: **(as) plain as a ~** deutlich sichtbar; *fig.* sonnenklar.

pile¹ [paɪl] **I** *s* **1.** Stapel *m,* Stoß *m.* **2.** Scheiterhaufen *m.* **3.** Gebäude(komplex *m*) *n.* **4.** (*Atom*)Reaktor *m.* **5. ~s** (*od.* **a ~**) **of ...** F ein Haufen ..., e-e *od.* jede Menge ... **6. a ~** (*of money*) F e-e Menge Geld: **make a** (*od.* **one's**) **~** (*from*) e-e Menge Geld machen (bei), sich gesundstoßen (an *dat,* mit). **II** *v/t* **7. a. ~ up** (an-, auf)häufen, (auf)stapeln: **~ it on** F dick auftragen. **8.** laden, aufhäufen (**on, onto** *od. acc*): überhäufen, -laden (**with** mit). **III** *v/i* **9.** *mst* **~ up** sich (auf *od.* an)häufen, sich ansammeln (*beide a. fig.*). **10.** F (sich) drängen (**into** *od. in acc*): **~ in** (sich) hinein- *od.* hereindrängen. **11. ~ up** *mot.* F aufeinander auffahren.

pile² [~] *s* Pfahl *m.*

piles [paɪlz] *s pl* ⚕ Hämorrhoiden *pl.*

'**pile-up** *s mot.* F Massenkarambolage *f.*

pil·fer [ˈpɪlfə] *v/t u. v/i* stehlen, klauen.

'**pil·fer·er** *s* Dieb(in).

pil·grim [ˈpɪlɡrɪm] *s* Pilger(in), Wallfahrer(in): **the** ⚥ **Fathers** *pl hist.* die Pilgerväter *pl.* '**pil·grim·age I** *s* Pilger-, Wallfahrt *f:* **go on** (*od.* **make**) **a ~** e-e Pilger- *od.* Wallfahrt machen. **II** *v/i* pilgern, wallfahrt(en).

pill [pɪl] *s* **1.** Pille *f,* Tablette *f:* **a bitter ~** (*for s.o.*) **to swallow** *fig.* e-e bittere Pille (für j-n); **gild** (*od.* **sugar, sweeten**) **the ~** *fig.* die bittere Pille versüßen. **2. the ~** F die (*Antibaby*)Pille: **be on the ~** die Pille nehmen.

pil·lage [ˈpɪlɪdʒ] **I** *v/t u. v/i* plündern. **II** *s* Plünderung *f.*

pil·lar [ˈpɪlə] *s* Pfeiler *m;* Säule *f* (*a. fig.*): **from ~ to post** *fig.* von Pontius zu Pilatus. **~ box** *s Br.* Briefkasten *m.*

pil·lion [ˈpɪljən] **I** *s mot.* Sozius(sitz) *m.* **II** *adv:* **ride ~** auf dem Sozius(sitz) (mit)fahren. **~ pas·sen·ger** *s* Soziusfahrer(in).

pil·lo·ry [ˈpɪlərɪ] **I** *s hist.* Pranger *m:* **be in the ~** am Pranger stehen. **II** *v/t hist.* an den Pranger stellen; *fig.* anprangern.

pil·low [ˈpɪləʊ] **I** *s* (Kopf)Kissen *n.* **II** *v/t*

bsd. Kopf betten (**on** *auf acc*). '**~case** *s* (Kopf)Kissenbezug *m.* **~ fight** *s* Kissenschlacht *f.* **~ slip** → **pillowcase. ~ talk** *s* Bettgeflüster *n.*

pi·lot [ˈpaɪlət] **I** *s* **1.** ✈ Pilot(in): **~'s licence** (*Am.* **license**) Flug-, Pilotenschein *m.* **2.** ⚓ Lotse *m,* Lotsin *f.* **II** *v/t* **3.** ✈ steuern, fliegen. **4.** ⚓ lotsen, *fig. a.* führen, leiten. **III** *adj* **5.** Versuchs..., Probe...: **~ film** TV Pilotfilm *m;* **~ scheme** Versuchs-, Pilotprojekt *n;* **~ study** Pilot-, Leitstudie *f.* **6. ~ lamp** Kontrollampe *f.*

pimp [pɪmp] **I** *s* Zuhälter *m.* **II** *v/i* von Zuhälterei leben: **~ for s.o.** j-s Zuhälter sein.

pim·ple [ˈpɪmpl] *s* Pickel *m,* Pustel *f.* '**pim·pled** *adj* pick(e)lig.

pin [pɪn] *s* **1.** (Steck)Nadel *f.* **2.** (*Haar-, Krawatten- etc*)Nadel *f. bsd. Am.* Brosche *f;* (*Ansteck*)Nadel *f.* **4.** ⚙ Bolzen *m,* Stift *m;* ⚒ Nagel *m.* **5.** (*Reiß*)Nagel *m,* (-)Zwecke *f.* **6.** *Am.* (*Wäsche*)Klammer *f.* **7.** *pl* F Gestell *n* (*Beine*). **8.** Bowling: Kegel *m.* **II** *v/t* **9. a. ~ up** (**to, on**) heften, stecken (an *acc*), festmachen, befestigen (an *dat*): **~ s.th. on s.o.** *fig.* j-m et. in die Schuhe schieben; j-m et. anhängen; **~ one's hopes on** s-e Hoffnung setzen auf (*acc*). **10. ~ down** zu Boden drücken; *fig.* j-n festlegen, -nageln (**to** *auf acc*).

pin·a·fore [ˈpɪnəfɔː] *s* **1.** Schürze *f.* **2. a. ~ dress** Trägerkleid *n,* Kleiderrock *m.*

'**pin·ball** *s* Flippern *n:* **play ~** flippern. **~ ma·chine** *s* Flipper *m.*

pin·cers [ˈpɪnsəz] *s pl, a.* **pair of ~** Kneifzange *f.*

pinch [pɪntʃ] **I** *v/t* **1.** kneifen, zwicken: **~ s.o.'s** (*od.* **s.o. on the**) **arm** j-n in den Arm zwicken; **~ one's fingers in the door** sich die Finger in der Tür (ein)klemmen. **2. be ~ed for money** (*time*) knapp bei Kasse sein (wenig Zeit haben). **3.** F klauen. **4.** F j-n hopsnehmen (**for** wegen). **II** *v/i* **5.** drücken (*Schuh*): → **shoe** 1. **6. ~ and scrape** (*od.* **save**) *fig.* sich sehr einschränken, sich nichts gönnen. **III** *s* **7.** Kneifen *n,* Zwicken *n:* **give s.o. a ~** j-n kneifen *od.* zwicken. **8.** Prise *f* (*Salz etc*): → **salt** 1. **9.** *fig.* Not(lage) *f:* **at** (*Am.* **in**) **a ~** zur Not, notfalls; **feel the ~** die schlechte Lage zu spüren bekommen.

'pin,cush·ion s Nadelkissen n.
pine¹ [paɪn] s ♀ Kiefer f.
pine² [~] v/i 1. sich sehnen (for nach). 2. mst ~ away vor Gram vergehen.
'pine|,ap·ple s ♀ Ananas f. ~ tree → pine¹.
ping-pong ['pɪŋpɒŋ] s F Pingpong n (Tischtennis).
'pin·head s 1. Stecknadelkopf m. 2. F Dummkopf m.
pin·ion ['pɪnjən] s ⚙ Ritzel n.
pink [pɪŋk] I s 1. ♀ Nelke f. 2. Rosa n. 3. be in the ~ vor Gesundheit strotzen. II adj 4. rosa: see ~ elephants weiße Mäuse sehen; → tickle I. 5. pol. rot angehaucht.
'pin|·point I s 1. Nadelspitze f. 2. (winziger) Punkt: ~ of light Lichtpunkt. II v/t 3. genau zeigen. 4. fig. genau festlegen od. bestimmen. III adj 5. (haar)genau. '~·prick s 1. Nadelstich m. 2. fig. Stichelei f. '~·stripe(d) adj: ~ suit Nadelstreifenanzug m.
pint [paɪnt] s 1. Pint n. 2. Br. F Halbe f (Bier): meet for a ~ sich auf ein Bier treffen.
pin| ta·ble s Flipper m. '~-up s 1. a. ~ girl Pin-up-Girl n. 2. Pin-up-Foto n.
pi·o·neer [,paɪə'nɪə] I s Pionier m, fig. a. Bahnbrecher m, Wegbereiter m. II v/i u. v/t fig. den Weg bahnen (für), Pionierarbeit leisten (für).
pi·ous ['paɪəs] adj □ fromm: ~ hope frommer Wunsch.
pip¹ [pɪp] s: give s.o. the ~ Br. F j-m auf die Nerven gehen, j-n nerven.
pip² [~] s 1. (Apfel- etc)Kern m. 2. Auge n (auf Spielkarten), Punkt m (auf Würfeln etc). 3. ✕ bsd. Br. F Stern m (Rangabzeichen). 4. Ton m (e-s Zeitzeichens etc).
pip³ [~] v/t Br. F knapp besiegen od. schlagen: ~ s.o. at the post (Sport) j-n im Ziel abfangen; fig. j-m um Haaresbreite zuvorkommen.
pipe [paɪp] I s 1. ⚙ Rohr n, Röhre f. 2. (Tabaks)Pfeife f. 3. (Orgel)Pfeife f. 4. pl Dudelsack m. II v/t 5. (durch Rohre od. Kabel) leiten: ~d music contp. Musikberies(e)lung f; ~d water Leitungswasser n. 6. Torte etc spritzen. III v/i 7. F ~ down die Luft anhalten, den Mund halten; ~ up loslegen (Sänger, Band etc); den Mund aufmachen, losreden. ~

clean·er s Pfeifenreiniger m. ~ dream s Hirngespinst n, Luftschloß n. '~·line s Rohrleitung f, (für Erdöl, Erdgas) Pipeline f: in the ~ fig. in Vorbereitung (Pläne etc), im Kommen (Entwicklung etc), im Anrollen (Aktion etc).
pip·er ['paɪpə] s Dudelsackpfeifer m: pay the ~ fig. für die Kosten aufkommen.
pipe smok·er s Pfeifenraucher m.
pip·ing ['paɪpɪŋ] I s 1. Rohrleitung f, -netz n. 2. gastr. Spritzguß m. II adv 3. ~ hot kochendheiß.
'pip·squeak s F contp. Würstchen n (Person).
pi·quant ['piːkənt] adj □ pikant (a. fig.).
pique [piːk] I v/t kränken, verletzen: ~d pikiert sein (at über acc). II s: in a fit of ~ gekränkt, verletzt, pikiert.
pi·ra·cy ['paɪərəsɪ] s 1. Seeräuberei f, Piraterie f. 2. Raubdruck m; Raubpressung f. pi·rate ['~rət] I s 1. Pirat m, Seeräuber m. II adj Piraten..., Seeräuber...: ~ ship. 3. ~ copy Raubkopie f; ~ edition Raubdruck m; ~ record Raubpressung f; ~ (radio) station Piraten-, Schwarzsender m. III v/t 4. unerlaubt kopieren od. nachdrucken od. nachpressen: ~d copy (edition, record) → 3.
pir·ou·ette [,pɪru'et] s Pirouette f: do a ~ e-e Pirouette drehen.
Pis·ces ['paɪsiːz] s pl (sg konstruiert) ast. Fische pl: be a ~ Fisch sein.
piss [pɪs] V I v/i 1. pissen: it is ~ing down bsd. Br. es schifft. 2. ~ off! verpiß dich! II v/t 3. anpissen, pissen in (acc). 4. ~ off ankotzen: be ~ed off with die Schnauze voll haben von. III s 5. Pisse f: take the ~ out of s.o. j-n verarschen. 6. Pissen n: have (go for) a ~ pissen (gehen).
pissed adj V 1. Br. blau (betrunken). 2. Am. (stock)sauer (at auf acc).
pis·ta·chi·o [pɪ'stɑːʃɪəʊ] pl -os ♀ Pistazie f.
pis·til ['pɪstɪl] s ♀ Stempel m.
pis·tol ['pɪstl] s Pistole f.
pis·ton ['pɪstən] s ⊙ Kolben m. ~ ring s Kolbenring m. ~ rod s Kolbenstange f. ~ stroke s Kolbenhub m.
pit¹ [pɪt] I s 1. Grube f. ~ of the stomach anat. Magengrube. 2. Grube f, Zeche f: ~ closure Zechenstillegung f; ~ disaster Grubenunglück n. 3. thea. a) bsd.

*Br. Parkett n, b) (Orchester)*Graben m.
4. *mst pl Motorsport:* Box f: ~ **stop** Boxenstopp m. **5.** (*bsd. Pocken*)Narbe f. **II** v/t **6. ~ted with smallpox** pockennarbig. **7. ~ one's wits (strength) against** s-n Strich durch die Rechnung messen an (*dat*).

pit² [~] *Am.* → **stone** 2, 6.

pitch¹ [pɪtʃ] s Pech n: (**as) black as ~** → **pitch-black.**

pitch² [~] **I** v/t **1.** *Lager, Zelt etc* aufschlagen. **2.** werfen, schleudern. **II** v/i **3.** stürzen, fallen. **4.** ⚓ stampfen. **5.** sich neigen (*Dach etc*). **6. ~ in** F sich ins Zeug legen; kräftig zulangen (*beim Essen*); zu Hilfe kommen, aushelfen (**with** mit). **III** s **7.** *Sport: Br.* (Spiel)Feld n. **8.** ♪ Tonhöhe f. **9.** *fig.* Grad m, Stufe f. **10.** *bsd. Br.* (Verkaufs)Stand m: **queer s.o.'s ~** *fig.* F j-m die Tour vermasseln, j-m e-n Strich durch die Rechnung machen. **11.** ⚓ Stampfen n. **12.** Neigung f (*e-s Dachs etc*). **13.** → **sales pitch.**

,pitch|-'black, ,~-'dark *adj* pechschwarz; stockdunkel.

pitch·er¹ ['pɪtʃə] s *Baseball:* Werfer m.

pitch·er² [~] s Krug m.

'pitch·fork I s **1.** Heugabel f. **II** v/t **2.** Heu gabeln. **3.** *fig.* j-n (*unversehens od. gegen s-n Willen*) (hinein)drängen (**into** in acc).

'pit·fall s *fig.* Falle f, Fallstrick m.

pith [pɪθ] s **1.** ♀ Mark n. **2.** weiße Haut (*e-r Orange etc*). **3.** *fig.* Kern m. **~ hel·met** s Tropenhelm m.

pith·y ['pɪθɪ] *adj* □ markig, prägnant.

pit·i·a·ble ['pɪtɪəbl] → **pitiful. pit·i·ful** ['~fʊl] *adj* □ **1.** mitleiderregend (*Anblick etc*), bemitleidenswert (*Person, Zustand etc*). **2.** erbärmlich, jämmerlich, kläglich. **'pit·i·less** *adj* □ unbarmherzig, mitleid(s)los.

pit·man ['pɪtmən] s (*irr* **man**) Bergmann m.

pit·tance ['pɪtəns] s Hungerlohn m.

pi·tu·i·tar·y (gland) [pɪ'tjuːɪtərɪ] s *anat.* Hirnanhang(drüse f) m.

pit·y ['pɪtɪ] **I** s **1.** Mitleid n: **out of ~** aus Mitleid; **feel ~ for, have ~ on** Mitleid haben mit; **take ~ on** Mitleid bekommen mit. **2. it is a (great) ~** es ist (sehr) schade; **it is a thousand pities** es ist jammerschade; **what a ~!** wie schade! **II** v/t **3.** bemitleiden, bedauern: **I ~ him**

er tut mir leid. **'pit·y·ing** *adj* □ mitleid(s)voll, mitleidig.

piv·ot ['pɪvət] **I** s **1.** ⚙ Drehzapfen m. **2.** *fig.* Dreh- u. Angelpunkt m. **II** v/i **3.** sich drehen: **~ on** *fig.* abhängen von. **piv·ot·al** ['~tl] *adj fig.* zentral: **~ position** Schlüsselstellung f.

pix·ie, pix·y ['pɪksɪ] s Elf(e f) m; Kobold m.

piz·za ['piːtsə] s Pizza f. **piz·ze·ri·a** [,piːtsə'riːə] s Pizzeria f.

pla·card ['plækɑːd] **I** s **1.** Plakat n; Transparent n. **II** v/t **2.** mit Plakaten bekleben. **3.** Plakatwerbung machen für.

pla·cate [plə'keɪt] v/t beschwichtigen, besänftigen.

place [pleɪs] **I** s **1.** Ort f, Stelle f, Platz m: **from ~ to ~** von Ort zu Ort; **in ~s** stellenweise; **in ~ of** an Stelle von (*od. gen*); **in ~** an s-m (richtigen) Platz; **out of ~** nicht an s-m (richtigen) Platz; fehl am Platz; unangebracht; **if I were in your ~ I would ...** an Ihrer Stelle würde ich ...; **put o.s. in s.o.'s ~** sich in j-s Lage versetzen; **put s.o. back in his ~** j-n in die *od.* s-e Schranken verweisen; **take ~** stattfinden; **take s.o.'s ~** j-s Stelle einnehmen. **2.** Ort m, Stätte f: **~ of birth** Geburtsort; **~ of work** Arbeitsstätte. **3.** Haus n, Wohnung f: **at his ~** bei ihm (zu Hause). **4.** Wohnort m, Ort(schaft f) m: **in this ~** hier. **5.** Stelle f (*in e-m Buch etc*): **lose one's ~** die Stelle verblättern; die Zeile verlieren. **6.** *Reihenfolge:* Platz m, Stelle f: **in the first ~** erstens; in erster Linie; überhaupt (erst). **7.** *Sport:* Platz m: **in third ~** auf dem dritten Platz. **8.** (*Arbeits-, Lehr-*) Stelle f; Platz m (*in e-m Heim etc*); (*Studien- etc*)Platz m. **II** v/t **9.** stellen, setzen, legen: **~ in** in e-e Lage *etc* versetzen. **10.** (**with**) *Auftrag* erteilen (*dat*), vergeben (*an acc*), *Bestellung* aufgeben (bei). **11. I can't ~ him** ich weiß nicht, wo ich ihn unterbringen *od.* wohin ich ihn tun soll (*woher ich ihn kenne*). **12. be ~d** (*Sport*) sich placieren (**third** an dritter Stelle), placiert sein.

pla·ce·bo [plə'siːbəʊ] *pl* **-bo(e)s** s ♣ Placebo n.

place| card s Tischkarte f. **~ mat** s Set n, m, Platzdeckchen n. **~ name** s Ortsname m. **~ set·ting** s Gedeck n.

plac·id ['plæsɪd] *adj* □ **1.** ruhig, gelassen. **2.** ruhig, friedlich.

pla·gia·rism ['pleɪdʒjərɪzəm] *s* Plagiat *n*. '**pla·gia·rist** *s* Plagiator(in). '**pla·gia·rize** *v/t u. v/i* plagieren (*from* von).

plague [pleɪg] **I** *s* **1.** ☞ Seuche *f*; Pest *f*. **2.** (*Insekten- etc*)Plage *f*: ~ *of insects*. **II** *v/t* **3.** plagen (*with* mit): *be ~d by* geplagt werden von.

plaice [pleɪs] *pl* **plaice** *s ichth.* Scholle *f*.

plaid [plæd] *s* Plaid *n*.

plain [pleɪn] **I** *adj* □ **1.** einfach, schlicht: ~ *clothes pl* Zivil(kleidung *f*) *n*; *in* ~ *clothes* in Zivil; ~ *chocolate* zartbittere Schokolade; ~ *cooking* gutbürgerliche Küche. **2.** unscheinbar, reizlos. **3.** klar (*u. deutlich*), unmißverständlich: *the ~ truth* die nackte Wahrheit; *make s.th.* ~ et. klarstellen; *make s.th.* ~ *to s.o.* j-m et. klarmachen. **4.** offen (*u. ehrlich*): *be ~ with s.o.* j-m gegenüber offen sein. **5.** ausgesprochen, rein, völlig: ~ *nonsense* barer Unsinn. **II** *adv* **6.** F (ganz) einfach. **III** *s* **7.** Ebene *f*, Flachland *n*. '~**clothes** *adj* in Zivil.

plain·ness ['pleɪnnɪs] *s* **1.** Einfachheit *f*, Schlichtheit *f*. **2.** Unscheinbarkeit *f*. **3.** Klarheit *f*. **4.** Offenheit *f*.

,**plain·'spo·ken** *adj* offen, freimütig: *be* ~ *a.* sagen, was man denkt.

plain·tiff ['pleɪntɪf] *s* ☆☆ Kläger(in). **plain·tive** ['~tɪv] *adj* □ klagend, kläglich; (*Lied etc*) schwermütig.

plait [plæt] **I** *s* Zopf *m*. **II** *v/t* flechten.

plan [plæn] **I** *s* **1.** (*Arbeits- etc*)Plan *m*: *according to* ~ planmäßig, -gemäß; *make* ~*s* (*for the future*) (Zukunfts)Pläne machen. **2.** Plan *m*, Absicht *f*: *change one's* ~*s* umdisponieren. **3.** (*Stadt-, Sitz- etc*)Plan *m*. ☆ Grundriß *m*. **II** *v/t* **5.** planen: ~*ned economy* Planwirtschaft *f*. **6.** planen, beabsichtigen (*to do* zu tun). **III** *v/i* **7.** planen: ~ *ahead* vorausplanen; ~ *for* (*od. on*) einplanen, rechnen mit. **8.** ~ *on doing s.th.* planen *od.* beabsichtigen, et. zu tun.

plane¹ [pleɪn] **I** *adj* **1.** eben (*a.* Å); ◎ plan, Plan... **II** *s* **2.** Å Ebene *f*: ~ *inclined*. **3.** *fig.* Ebene *f*, Stufe *f*: *on the same* ~ *as* auf dem gleichen Niveau wie. **4.** Hobel *m*. **III** *v/t* **5.** hobeln: ~ *down* abhobeln.

plane² [~] *s* Flugzeug *n*: *by* ~ mit dem Flugzeug; *go by* ~ fliegen.

plan·et ['plænɪt] *s astr.* Planet *m*.

plan·e·tar·i·um [,plænɪ'teərɪəm] *pl* **-i·ums**, **-i·a** [~ɪə] *s* Planetarium. **plan·e·tar·y** ['~tərɪ] *adj* planetarisch, Planeten...

plank [plæŋk] *s* **1.** Planke *f*, Bohle *f*, Brett *n*: (*as*) *thick as two* (*short*) ~*s* Br. F strohdumm. **2.** *pol.* Schwerpunkt *m* (*e-s Parteiprogramms*). '**plank·ing** *s* Planken *pl*.

plank·ton ['plæŋtən] *s zo.* Plankton *n*.

plant [plɑːnt] **I** *s* **1.** Pflanze *f*: ~ *louse zo.* Blattlaus *f*. **2.** Werk *n*, Betrieb *m*. **II** *v/t* **3.** (an-, ein)pflanzen; *Land* bepflanzen (*with* mit). **4.** *Garten etc* anlegen. **5.** *Polizisten etc* aufstellen, postieren; *Bombe* legen. **6.** *Fuß etc* setzen (*on* auf *acc*); *Messer etc* stoßen (*into* in *acc*): ~ *a kiss on s.o.'s lips* j-m e-n Kuß auf die Lippen drücken. **7.** ~ *s.th. on s.o.* F j-m et. (*Belastendes*) unterschieben *od.* -jubeln. **plan·ta·tion** [plæn'teɪʃn] *s* **1.** Plantage *f*, Pflanzung *f*. **2.** Schonung *f*. **plant·er** ['plɑːntə] *s* **1.** Plantagenbesitzer(in), Pflanzer(in). **2.** Pflanzmaschine *f*. **3.** Übertopf *m*.

plaque [plɑːk] *s* **1.** Gedenktafel *f*. **2.** ☆ (*Zahn*)Belag *m*.

plas·ma ['plæzmə] *s* Plasma *n*.

plas·ter ['plɑːstə] **I** *s* **1.** ☆ Pflaster *n*. **2.** (Ver)Putz *m*. **3.** *a.* ~ *of Paris* Gips *m*: *have one's arm in* ~ ☆ den Arm in Gips haben; *put in* ~ ☆ eingipsen; ~ *cast* Gipsabguß *m*, -modell *n*; ☆ Gipsverband *m*. **II** *v/t* **4.** verputzen; (ver)gipsen: ~ *over fig.* übertünchen. **5.** bekleben (*with* mit); *Plakate etc* kleben (*on* an *od.* auf *acc*). '**plas·tered** *adj sl.* blau (*betrunken*): *get* ~ sich vollaufen lassen.

plas·tic ['plæstɪk] **I** *adj* □ (**~ally**) **1.** plastisch: ~ *surgery* ☆ plastische Chirurgie. **2.** plastisch, formbar: ~ *bomb* Plastikbombe *f*. **3.** Plastik..., Kunststoff...: ~ *bag* Plastikbeutel *m*, -tüte *f*; ~ *bullet* Plastikgeschoß *n*; ~ *film* Kunststofffolie *f*; ~ *money* → **5**. **II** *s* **4.** Plastik *n*, Kunststoff *m*. **5.** Kunststoffgeld *n*: ~ Kreditkarten *pl*. '**plas·tics I** *s pl* Kunststoffe *pl*. **II** *adj* Plastik..., Kunststoff...: ~ *film* Kunststofffolie *f*; ~ *industry* Kunststoffindustrie *f*.

plate [pleɪt] **I** s **1.** Teller m: **hand s.o. s.th. on a ~** F j-m et. auf dem Tablett servieren; **have a lot on one's ~** viel am Hals haben. **2.** Platte f. **3.** (Namens-, Tür- etc)Schild n. **4.** (Bild)Tafel f (in e-m Buch etc). **5.** Gegenstände pl aus Edelmetall. **6.** Doublé n, Dublee n. **II** v/t **7.** panzern. **8.** d(o)ublieren, plattieren: **~d with gold** vergoldet.

pla·teau ['plætəʊ] pl **-teaux, -teaus** ['~təʊz] s Plateau n, Hochebene f.

plate·ful ['pleɪtfʊl] pl **-fuls** s ein Teller(voll) m.

plate rack s Geschirrständer m.

plat·form ['plætfɔːm] s **1.** Plattform f; Podium n, Tribüne f. **2.** 🚉 Bahnsteig m. **3.** pol. Plattform f.

plat·i·num ['plætɪnəm] s chem. Platin n.

plat·i·tude ['plætɪtjuːd] s Platitüde f, Plattheit f.

pla·ton·ic [plə'tɒnɪk] adj (**~ally**) platonisch: **~ love.**

pla·toon [plə'tuːn] s ⚔ Zug m.

plat·ter ['plætə] s Servierplatte f.

plau·si·ble ['plɔːzəbl] adj □ **1.** plausibel, glaubhaft. **2.** geschickt (Lügner).

play [pleɪ] **I** s **1.** Spiel n: at ~ beim Spiel(en), spielend (Kinder etc); **be at ~** spielen; **in** (**out of**) **~** im Spiel (im Aus) (Ball). **2.** Spiel(weise f) n: **fair ~** (Sport) Fair play n, Fairneß f (beide a. fig.). **3.** fig. Spiel n: **bring into ~** ins Spiel bringen, Routine etc aufbieten; **come into ~** ins Spiel kommen. **4.** fig. Spiel(erei f) n: **~ on words** Wortspiel; in ~ im Scherz. **5.** thea. Schauspiel n, (Theater)Stück n. **6.** ⊙ Spiel n; fig. Spielraum m: **allow** (od. **give**) **full** (od. **free**) **~ to** freien Lauf lassen (dat). **II** v/i **7.** spielen (a. Sport, thea. etc): ~ **at** Karten, Indianer etc spielen; fig. sich nur so nebenbei beschäftigen mit; ~ **for money** um Geld spielen; ~ **for time** Zeit zu gewinnen suchen; (Sport) auf Zeit spielen; ~ **with** spielen mit (a. fig.); ~ **safe** F auf Nummer Sicher gehen. **III** v/t **8.** Karten, Rolle, Stück etc spielen, (Sport) Spiel austragen: ~ (**s.th. on**) **the piano** (et. auf dem) Klavier spielen; ~ **it safe** F auf Nummer Sicher gehen; → **trick 2** (**a. fig.**). **9.** Sport: spielen gegen: ~ **s.o. at chess** gegen j-n Schach spielen. **10.** Karte ausspielen: → **trump**[1] I. **11.** thea. etc spielen od. Vorstellungen geben in (dat).

Verbindungen mit Adverbien:

play| back v/t Tonband etc abspielen; **play s.th. back to s.o.** j-m et. vorspielen. ~ **down** v/t herunterspielen, bagatellisieren. ~ **off** I v/t j-n ausspielen (**against** gegen). II v/i Sport: ein Entscheidungsspiel austragen (**for** um). ~ **up** I v/i **1.** Br. F verrückt spielen, Schwierigkeiten machen (Auto, Bein etc). **2.** ~ **to** j-m schöntun. II v/t **3.** hochspielen, aufbauschen. **4.** Br. F j-m auf die Palme bringen; j-m Schwierigkeiten machen (Bein etc).

play·a·ble ['pleɪəbl] adj Sport: bespielbar (Platz).

'play|·act v/i contp. schauspielern. **'~·back** s Wiedergabe f, Abspielen n. **'~·boy** s Playboy m.

play·er ['pleɪə] s **1.** ♩, Sport: Spieler(in). **2.** (Platten)Spieler m.

'play·fel·low s → **playmate.**

play·ful ['pleɪfʊl] adj □ **1.** verspielt. **2.** schelmisch, neckisch.

'play|·go·er s Theaterbesucher(in). **'~·ground** s **1.** Schulhof m. **2.** Spielplatz m. **3.** fig. Tummelplatz m. ~ **group** s bsd. Br. Spielgruppe f. **'~·house** s **1.** Schauspielhaus n. **2.** Spielhaus n.

play·ing| card ['pleɪɪŋ] s Spielkarte f. ~ **field** s Sportplatz m.

'play|·mak·er s Sport: Spielmacher(in). **'~·mate** s Spielkamerad(in). **'~·off** s Sport: Entscheidungsspiel n. **'~·pen** s Laufgitter n, -stall m. **~·room** ['~rʊm] s Spielzimmer n. **'~·school** → **play group. '~·thing** s Spielzeug n (a. fig.): **~s** pl Spielsachen pl, -zeug n. **'~·time** s ped. große Pause. **'~·wright** ['~raɪt] s Dramatiker(in).

plea [pliː] s **1.** (dringende) Bitte, Gesuch n (**for** um): **make a ~ for mercy** um Gnade bitten. **2.** ⚖ **enter a ~ of** (**not**) **guilty** sich schuldig bekennen (s-e Unschuld erklären); **make a ~ of s.th.** et. geltend machen.

plead [pliːd] (bsd. schott. u. Am. irr) **I** v/i **1.** (dringend) bitten (**for** um): ~ **with s.o.** j-n bitten (**to do** zu tun). **2.** ⚖ **~ guilty** sich schuldig bekennen (**to** doing s.th. et. getan zu haben); ~ **not guilty** s-e Unschuld erklären. **II** v/t **3.** ⚖ u. allg. zu s-r Verteidigung od. Entschuldigung anführen, geltend machen. **4.** ~ **s.o.'s**

case ⚖ j-n vertreten; *allg.* sich für j-n einsetzen.

pleas·ant ['pleznt] *adj* □ **1.** angenehm, (*Nachricht etc a.*) erfreulich: → ***dream*** 1. **2.** freundlich.

please [pli:z] **I** *v/i* **1.** gefallen. **2.** ***as you ~*** wie Sie wünschen; ***if you ~*** wenn ich bitten darf, *iro. a.* gefälligst. **II** *v/t* **3.** *j-m* gefallen *od.* zusagen, *j-n* erfreuen: ***be ~d about*** (*od.* ***at***) sich freuen über (*acc*); ***I am ~d with it*** es gefällt mir; ***I am ~d to hear*** es freut mich zu hören. **4.** zufriedenstellen: (***only***) ***to ~ you*** (nur) dir zuliebe; ***there is no pleasing him, you can't ~ him*** man kann es ihm nicht recht machen; ***~ o.s.*** tun, was man will; ***~ yourself!*** mach, was du willst!; ***be ~d with*** zufrieden sein mit; → ***hard*** 2. **III** *int* **5.** bitte. '**pleas·ing** *adj* □ angenehm.

pleas·ur·a·ble ['pleʒərəbl] *adj* □ angenehm.

pleas·ure ['pleʒə] *s* **1.** Vergnügen *n*: ***for ~*** zum Vergnügen; ***with ~*** mit Vergnügen; ***give s.o. ~*** j-m Vergnügen *od.* Freude *od.* Spaß machen; ***have the ~ of doing s.th.*** das Vergnügen haben, et. zu tun; ***take ~ in*** Vergnügen *od.* Freude finden an (*dat*); ***he takes no ~ in it*** es macht ihm keinen Spaß. **2.** ***at*** (***one's***) ***~*** nach Belieben.

pleat [pli:t] *s* Falte *f.* '**pleat·ed** *adj*: ***~ skirt*** Faltenrock *m.*

pleb [pleb] *s* F *contp.* Prolet(in).

ple·be·ian [plɪ'bi:ən] *contp.* **I** *adj* proletenhaft. **II** *s* Prolet(in).

pleb·i·scite ['plebɪsɪt] *s* Volksabstimmung *f*, -entscheid *m.*

pled [pled] *bsd. schott. u. Am. pret u. pp von* ***plead.***

pledge [pledʒ] **I** *s* **1.** Pfand *n*: ***as a ~*** als Pfand. **2.** *fig.* Unterpfand *n*: ***as a ~ of*** zum Zeichen (*gen*). **3.** Versprechen *n*, Zusicherung *f*: ***make a*** (***firm***) ***~*** (fest) versprechen *od.* zusichern (***to do*** zu tun). **II** *v/t* **4.** verpfänden: ***~ one's word*** *fig.* sein (Ehren)Wort geben. **5.** versprechen, zusichern (***to do*** zu tun, ***that*** daß). **6.** ***~ s.o. to s.th.*** j-n zu et. verpflichten, j-m et. auferlegen; ***~ o.s.*** sich verpflichten (***to do*** zu tun).

ple·na·ry ['pli:nərɪ] *adj* **1.** ***~ session*** Plenarsitzung *f*, Vollversammlung *f.* **2.** ***~ powers*** *pl* unbeschränkte Vollmacht.

plen·i·po·ten·ti·ar·y [ˌplenɪpəʊ'tenʃərɪ] **I** *s* **1.** (General)Bevollmächtigte *m, f.* **II** *adj* **2.** (general)bevollmächtigt. **3.** ***~ powers*** *pl* Generalvollmacht *f.*

plen·ti·ful ['plentɪfʊl] *adj* □ reichlich.

plen·ty ['plentɪ] **I** *s* **1.** Überfluß *m*: ***live in ~*** im Überfluß leben; ***... in ~*** ...im Überfluß, ... in Hülle u. Fülle; → ***horn*** 3. **2.** e-e Menge: ***that is ~*** das ist reichlich; ***there are ~ more*** es gibt noch viel mehr; ***~ of ...*** e-e Menge ..., viel(e) ... **II** *adv* **3.** F ganz schön.

ple·o·nasm ['plɪəʊnæzəm] *s ling.* Pleonasmus *m.* **ple·o·nas·tic** [ˌ~'næstɪk] *adj* (***~ally***) pleonastisch.

pleu·ri·sy ['plʊərəsɪ] *s* ⚕ Brustfell-, Rippenfellentzündung *f.*

pli·a·ble ['plaɪəbl], **pli·ant** ['~ənt] *adj* □ **1.** biegsam. **2.** *fig.* flexibel. **3.** *fig.* leicht beeinflußbar.

pli·ers ['plaɪəz] *s pl, a.* ***pair of ~*** Beißzange *f.*

plight [plaɪt] *s* Not(lage) *f.*

plim·soll ['plɪmsəl] *s Br.* Turnschuh *m.*

plod [plɒd] *v/i* **1.** trotten. **2.** *mst* ***~ away*** *fig.* sich abmühen *od.* abplagen (***at*** mit), schuften. '**plod·der** *s fig.* Arbeitstier *n.*

plonk [plɒŋk] *v/t* F schmeißen, knallen: ***~ down*** hinschmeißen.

plop [plɒp] F **I** *v/i* plumpsen, (*ins Wasser*) platschen: ***~ into a chair*** sich in e-n Sessel plumpsen lassen. **II** *s* Plumps *m*, Platsch *m.*

plot [plɒt] **I** *s* **1.** Grundstück *n*; Parzelle *f*; Beet *n.* **2.** ⚠ *bsd. Am.* Grundriß *m.* **3.** Handlung *f* (*e-s Films etc*). **4.** Komplott *n*, Verschwörung *f.* **II** *v/i* **5.** sich verschwören (***against*** gegen). **III** *v/t* **6.** aushecken, planen. **7.** (*in e-e Karte etc*) einzeichnen. '**plot·ter** *s* Verschwörer(in).

plough [plaʊ] **I** *s* Pflug *m.* **II** *v/t a.* ***~ up*** (um)pflügen: ***~ back*** *Gewinne* reinvestieren (***into*** in *acc*). **III** *v/i* pflügen: ***~ through*** sich e-n Weg bahnen durch; ⚓ sich pflügen durch; ***~ through a book*** F ein Buch durchackern.

plow *Am.* → ***plough.***

ploy [plɔɪ] *s* Masche *f*, Tour *f.*

pluck [plʌk] **I** *s* **1.** Ruck *m.* **2.** Innereien *pl.* **3.** *fig.* Mut *m.* **II** *v/t* **4.** *Geflügel* rupfen. **5.** *mst* ***~ out*** ausreißen, -rupfen, -zupfen: → ***courage.*** **III** *v/i* **6.** zupfen (***at*** an *dat*): ***~ at s.o.'s sleeve*** j-n am

Ärmel zupfen. '**pluck·y** *adj* □ mutig.

plug [plʌg] **I** *s* **1.** Stöpsel *m*. **2.** ⚡ Stecker *m*; Steckdose *f*. **3.** *mot.* (Zünd)Kerze *f*. **II** *v/t* **4.** *a.* ~ *up* zustöpseln; zu-, verstopfen. **5.** ~ *in* ⚡ anschließen, einstecken. **III** *v/i* **6.** ~ *away at* F sich abschuften mit. '**~·hole** *s* Abfluß(loch *n*) *m*.

plum [plʌm] *s* **1.** Pflaume *f*; Zwetsch(g)e *f*. **2.** *fig.* F a) Rosine *f*, b) *a.* ~ *job* Bombenjob *m*.

plum·age ['pluːmɪdʒ] *s* Gefieder *n*.

plumb [plʌm] **I** *s* **1.** (Blei)Lot *n*, Senklot *n*: *out of* ~ aus dem Lot, nicht senkrecht. **II** *adj* **2.** lot-, senkrecht. **III** *adv* F **3.** (haar)genau. **4.** *bsd. Am.* komplett, total. **IV** *v/t* **5.** ⚓ ausloten, *fig. a.* ergründen. **6.** ~ *in bsd. Br.* Waschmaschine *etc* anschließen. '**plumb·er** *s* Installateur *m*. '**plumb·ing** *s* **1.** Installateurarbeit *f*. **2.** Rohre *pl*, Rohrleitungen *pl*.

plumb| **line** *s* **1.** ⚓ Lotschnur *f*, -leine *f*. **2.** → *plumb rule.* ~ *rule* *s* △ Setzlatte *f*, Richtscheit *n*.

plume [pluːm] **I** *s* **1.** (Schmuck)Feder *f*; Federbusch *m*. **2.** (Rauch)Fahne *f*. **II** *v/t* **3.** ~ *its feathers* sich *od.* sein Gefieder putzen.

plum·my ['plʌmɪ] *adj* **1.** affektiert (*Stimme*). **2.** F prima, toll: ~ *job* Bombenjob *m*.

plump¹ [plʌmp] **I** *adj* drall, mollig, rund(lich). **II** *v/t*: ~ *up Kissen* aufschütteln.

plump² [~] **I** *v/i* **1.** *mst* ~ *down* fallen, plumpsen (*on* auf *acc*): ~ *down into a chair* sich in e-n Sessel fallen lassen. **2.** ~ *for bsd. Br.* sich entscheiden für. **II** *v/t* **3.** fallen *od.* plumpsen lassen (*on* auf *acc*).

plum pud·ding *s* Plumpudding *m*.

plun·der ['plʌndə] *v/t* **1.** (aus)plündern. **2.** *et.* rauben. **II** *v/i* **3.** plündern. **III** *s* **4.** Plünderung *f*. **5.** Beute *f*. '**plun·der·er** *s* Plünderer *m*.

plunge [plʌndʒ] **I** *v/t* **1.** ~ *a knife into s.o.'s back* j-m ein Messer in den Rücken stoßen. **2.** ~ *into in Schulden,* e-n *Krieg etc* stürzen: *be ~d into darkness* in Dunkel gehüllt sein. **II** *v/i* **3.** ~ *into* ins *Zimmer etc* stürzen; sich ins *Wasser,* in *e-e Tätigkeit,* in *Schulden etc* stürzen. **4.** stürzen (*Preise, Kurse*). **5.** ⚓ stampfen. **III** *s* **6.** (Kopf)Sprung *m*: *take the* ~ *fig.* den Sprung *od.* den ent-

scheidenden Schritt wagen. '**plung·ing** *adj* tief (*Ausschnitt*): *with a* ~ *neckline* tief ausgeschnitten.

plu·per·fect [,pluː'pɜːfɪkt] *s a.* ~ *tense ling.* Plusquamperfekt *n*, Vorvergangenheit *f*.

plu·ral ['plʊərəl] *ling.* **I** *adj* Plural..., Mehrzahl... **II** *s* Plural *m*, Mehrzahl *f*. '**plu·ral·ism** *s sociol.* Pluralismus *m*. ,**plu·ral'is·tic** *adj* (~*ally*) pluralistisch.

plus [plʌs] **I** *prp* **1.** Å plus, und, *bsd.* ✝ zuzüglich. **II** *adj* **2.** Plus...: ~ *sign* → 3. **III** *s* **3.** Plus(zeichen) *n*. **4.** *fig.* Plus *n*, Vorteil *m*.

plush [plʌʃ] **I** *s* **1.** Plüsch *m*. **II** *adj* **2.** Plüsch... **3.** F feudal: ~ *restaurant* Nobelrestaurant *n*. nium *n*.

plu·to·ni·um [pluː'təʊnɪəm] *s* ♠ Pluto-

ply¹ [plaɪ] **I** *v/i* **1.** verkehren (*between* zwischen *dat*). **II** *v/t* **2.** verkehren auf (*dat*), befahren. **3.** *fig.* j-n überhäufen (*with mit Fragen*).

ply² [~] *s* Lage *f*, Schicht *f*. '**~·wood** *s* Sperrholz *n*.

pneu·mat·ic [njuː'mætɪk] *adj* (~*ally*) pneumatisch, Luft...; ⊙ Druck-, Preßluft...: ~ *brake* Druckluftbremse *f*; ~ *drill* Preßluftbohrer *m*; ~ *hammer* Preßlufthammer *m*.

pneu·mo·ni·a [njuː'məʊnjə] *s* 🩺 Lungenentzündung *f*.

poach¹ [pəʊtʃ] **I** *v/t* **1.** wildern. **2.** *Arbeitskräfte* abwerben (*from dat*). **II** *v/i* **3.** wildern.

poach² [~] *v/t Eier* pochieren: ~*ed eggs* *pl* *a.* verlorene Eier *pl*.

poach·er ['pəʊtʃə] *s* Wilderer *m*.

PO Box [,piː'əʊ] *s* Postfach *n*.

pock [pɒk] *s* 🩺 **1.** Pocke *f*, Blatter *f*. **2.** → *pockmark.* **pocked** → *pockmarked.*

pock·et ['pɒkɪt] **I** *s* **1.** (*Hosen- etc*)Tasche *f*: *with nothing in one's* ~ *except* mit nichts in der Tasche als; *have in one's* ~ *fig.* j-n, *et.* in der Tasche haben. **2.** *fig.* Geldbeutel *m*: *pay for s.th. out of one's own* ~ *et.* aus eigener Tasche bezahlen; *to suit every* ~ für jeden Geldbeutel. **3.** (*Nebel*)Bank *f*; (*Widerstands- etc*)Nest *n*. **4.** *Billard:* Loch *n*; ✈ (*Luft*)Loch *n*. **II** *adj* **5.** Taschen...: ~ *calculator* Taschenrechner *m*; ~ *edition* Taschenausgabe *f*; ~ *money* Taschengeld *n*. **III** *v/t* **6.** einstecken, in die Tasche stecken; *fig.* in die eigene Tasche stecken. **7.**

Billard: einlochen. '**~·book** *s* **1.** Notizbuch *n*. **2.** *Am*. Brieftasche *f*. '**~·knife** *s* (*irr* **knife**) Taschenmesser *n*.

'**pock·mark** *s* Pockennarbe *f*. '**~·marked** *adj* pockennarbig; *fig*. übersät (**with** mit).

pod [pɒd] **I** *s* ♀ Hülse *f*, Schote *f*. **II** *v/t* aus-, enthülsen.

po·di·um ['pəʊdɪəm] *pl* **-di·ums**, **-di·a** ['~dɪə] *s* Podium *n*, Podest *n*.

po·em ['pəʊɪm] *s* Gedicht *n*.

po·et ['pəʊɪt] *s* Dichter *m*. '**po·et·ess** *s* Dichterin *f*. **po·et·ic** [~'etɪk] *adj* (**~ally**) dichterisch: **~ justice** *fig*. ausgleichende Gerechtigkeit; **~ licence** (*Am*. **license**) dichterische Freiheit. **po·et·i·cal** → **poetic**. **po·et·ry** ['pəʊɪtrɪ] *s* Dichtung *f*; Gedichte *pl*.

poign·ant ['pɔɪnjənt] *adj* □ **1.** schmerzlich (*Erinnerungen etc*). **2.** scharf (*Verstand*).

point [pɔɪnt] **I** *s* **1.** (*Messer-, Nadel- etc-*) Spitze *f*. **2.** *geogr*. Landspitze *f*. **3.** *ling. Am*. Punkt *m*. **4. four ~ three** (**4.3**) 4,3. **5.** Punkt *m* (*a*. ♉): Grad *m* (*e-r Skala*): **~ of contact** Berührungspunkt (*a. fig.*); **~ of intersection** Schnittpunkt; → **freezing** 1, *etc*. **6.** Punkt *m*, Stelle *f*, Ort *m*: **up to a ~** *fig*. bis zu e-m gewissen Punkt *od*. Grad; → **of view** *fig*. Gesichts-, Standpunkt. **7.** ♉ *Br*. Steckdose *f*. **8.** *Sport etc*: Punkt *m*: **win on ~s** nach Punkten gewinnen; **winner on ~s** Punktsieger *m*. **9.** *a*. **~ of time** Zeitpunkt *m*, Augenblick *m*: **be on the ~ of doing s.th.** im Begriff sein, et. zu tun. **10.** Punkt *m* (*e-r Tagesordnung etc*), (*Einzel-, Teil*)Frage *f*: **~ of interest** interessante Einzelheit. **11.** Kernpunkt *m*, -frage *f*, springender Punkt: **be to** (*beside*) **the ~** (nicht) zur Sache gehören; **come to the ~** zur Sache kommen; **keep** (*od*. **stick**) **to the ~** bei der Sache bleiben; **make a ~ of doing s.th.** Wert darauf legen, et. zu tun; **get** (*od*. **see**, **take**) **s.o.'s ~** verstehen, was j-d meint; **miss the ~** nicht verstehen, worum es geht; **that's not the ~** darum geht es nicht; **that's the (whole) ~!** genau (das ist es)! **12.** Ziel *n*, Absicht *f*: **carry** (*od*. **gain**) **one's ~** sich *od*. s-e Absicht durchsetzen. **13.** Sinn *m*, Zweck *m*: **what's the ~?** wozu?; **what's the ~ of** (*od*. **in**) **waiting?** was hat es für e-n Sinn zu warten?; **there's no ~ in that** das hat keinen Zweck. **14.** (hervorstechende) Eigenschaft, (Vor)Zug *m*: **strong** (**weak**) **~** starke (schwache) Seite; **it has its ~s** es hat s-e Vorzüge. **II** *v/t* **15.** (an-, zu)spitzen. **16.** *Waffe etc* richten (**at** auf *acc*): **~ one's finger at s.o.** mit dem Finger auf j-n deuten *od*. zeigen. **17.** zeigen: **~ the way** den Weg weisen (*a. fig.*); **~ out** zeigen; *fig*. hinweisen *od*. aufmerksam machen auf (*acc*); **~ out to s.o. that** j-n darauf aufmerksam machen, daß. **III** *v/i* **18.** (mit dem Finger) deuten *od*. zeigen (**at, to** auf *acc*): **~ to** nach *e-r Richtung* weisen *od*. liegen (*Haus etc*); *fig*. hinweisen *od*. deuten auf (*acc*). '**~·blank** *adj u. adv* **1.** *a*. **at ~ range** aus kürzester Entfernung. **2.** *fig*. unverblümt.

point·ed ['pɔɪntɪd] *adj* □ **1.** spitz: **~ arch** △ Spitzbogen *m*. **2.** *fig*. scharf (*Bemerkung etc*). **3.** *fig*. ostentativ. '**point·er** *s* **1.** Zeiger *m* (*e-s Meßgeräts*). **2.** Zeigestock *m*. **3.** ♉ Fingerzeig *m*, Tip *m*. '**point·less** *adj* □ sinn-, zwecklos.

poise [pɔɪz] **I** *s* **1.** (*Körper*)Haltung *f*. **2.** *fig*. Gelassenheit *f*; (*Selbst*)Sicherheit *f*. **II** *v/t* balancieren: **be ~d** *fig*. schweben (**between** zwischen *dat*). **poised** *adj* gelassen; (selbst)sicher.

poi·son ['pɔɪzn] **I** *s* Gift *n* (**to** für) (*a. fig.*): **hate like ~** wie die Pest hassen; **what's your ~?** F was willst du trinken? **II** *v/t* vergiften (*a. fig.*). **III** *adj* Gift...: **~ gas; ~ fang** *zo*. Giftzahn *m*. '**poi·son·ing** *s* Vergiftung *f*. '**poi·son·ous** *adj* □ giftig (*a. fig.*), Gift...

poke [pəʊk] **I** *v/t* **1.** *j-n* (an)stoßen: **~ s.o. in the ribs** j-m e-n Rippenstoß geben. **2.** *a*. **~ up** Feuer schüren. **3.** *et*. stecken, *Kopf etc* strecken: → **nose** 1. **4. ~ fun at** sich lustig machen über (*acc*). **II** *v/i* **5. ~ about** (*od*. **around**) (herum)stöbern, (-)wühlen (**in** in *dat*). **III** *s* **6.** Stoß *m*: **~ in the ribs** Rippenstoß.

pok·er¹ ['pəʊkə] *s* Feuerhaken *m*.

po·ker² [~] *s* Poker(spiel) *n*. **~ face** *s* Pokergesicht *n*, Pokerface *n*.

pok·y ['pəʊkɪ] *adj* winzig (*Zimmer etc*).

po·lar ['pəʊlə] *adj* □ polar (*a. fig.*), Polar...: **~ bear** *zo*. Eisbär *m*; **~ circle** *geogr*. Polarkreis *m*. '**po·lar·ize** *v/t u. v/i, phys*. polarisieren (*a. fig.*).

Pole¹ [pəʊl] *s* Pole *m*, Polin *f*.

pole² [~] s geogr., ⚡, etc Pol m: **they are ~s apart** fig. zwischen ihnen liegen Welten.

pole³ [~] s Pfosten m; (Fahnen-, Leitungs)Mast m; (Bohnen- etc)Stange f; (Leichtathletik) (Sprung)Stab m. '~cat

po·lem·ic [pə'lemɪk] **I** adj (~ally) **1.** polemisch. **II** s **2.** a. pl (sg konstruiert) Polemik f. **3.** polemische Äußerung. **po·'lem·i·cal** → polemic **1.**

pole star s astr. Polarstern m.

pole vault s Leichtathletik: Stabhochsprung m. ~ **vault·er** s Stabhochspringer m.

po·lice [pə'liːs] **I** s (pl konstruiert) Polizei f. **II** v/t (polizeilich) überwachen. **III** adj polizeilich, Polizei...: ~ **constable** → constable; ~ **force** Polizei f; ~ **officer** Polizeibeamte m; ~ **protection** Polizeischutz m; ~ **record** Strafregister n; **have a ~ record** vorbestraft sein; ~ **state** Polizeistaat m; ~ **station** Polizeirevier m, -wache f. **po'lice·man** [~mən] s (irr man) Polizist m. **po'lice·wom·an** s (irr woman) Polizistin f.

pol·i·cy¹ ['pɒləsɪ] s **1.** Verfahren(sweise f) n, Taktik f, Politik f: **it is our ~** es ist unser Grundsatz (**to do** zu tun). **2.** (Außen-, Wirtschafts- etc)Politik f. **3.** Klugheit f: **be good** (**bad**) ~ (un)klug od. (un)vernünftig sein.

pol·i·cy² [~] s (Versicherungs)Police f: **take out a ~** e-e Versicherung abschließen.

po·li·o ['pəʊlɪəʊ] s ⚕ F Polio f. **po·li·o·my·e·li·tis** [,~maɪə'laɪtɪs] s ⚕ (spinale) Kinderlähmung.

Pol·ish¹ ['pəʊlɪʃ] **I** adj polnisch. **II** s ling. Polnisch n.

pol·ish² ['pɒlɪʃ] **I** v/t **1.** polieren, ⊙ etc a. (ab)schleifen, Fußboden bohnern: ~ **off** F Arbeit wegschaffen; Essen wegputzen; ~ **up** aufpolieren (a. fig.). **II** s **2.** Politur f, Glanz m. **3.** (Möbel)Politur f; (Schuh)Creme f; Bohnerwachs n; (Nagel)Lack m. **4.** fig. Schliff m. **'pol·ished** adj **1.** poliert, glänzend. **2.** fig. geschliffen; brillant.

po·lite [pə'laɪt] adj □ höflich: **to be ~** aus Höflichkeit. **po'lite·ness** s Höflichkeit f.

po·lit·i·cal [pə'lɪtɪkl] adj □ politisch: ~ **economy** Volkswirtschaft f; ~ **science** Politologie f; ~ **scientist** Politologe m, -login f. **pol·i·ti·cian** [,pɒlɪ'tɪʃn] s Politiker(in). **po·lit·i·cize** [pə'lɪtɪsaɪz] v/t politisieren. **pol·i·tics** ['pɒlɪtɪks] s pl (mst sg konstruiert) Politik f: **what are his ~?** wo steht er politisch?; **go into** ~ in die Politik gehen; **talk** ~ über Politik reden, politisieren.

pol·ka ['pɒlkə] s ♪ Polka f. '~-**dot** adj gepunktet, getupft (Kleid etc).

poll [pəʊl] **I** s **1.** (Meinungs)Umfrage f. **2.** a. pl Stimmabgabe f, Wahl f: **be defeated at the ~s** e-e Wahlniederlage erleiden; **go to the ~s** zur Wahl gehen. **3.** Wahlbeteiligung f. **II** v/t **4.** befragen: **65 % of those ~ed** 65 % der Befragten. **5.** Stimmen erhalten, auf sich vereinigen.

pol·len ['pɒlən] s ⚘ Pollen m, Blütenstaub m.

poll·ing ['pəʊlɪŋ] **I** s → **poll** 2, 3. **II** adj Wahl...: ~ **booth** Wahlkabine f, -zelle f; ~ **day** Wahltag m; ~ **place** Am., ~ **station** bsd. Br. Wahllokal n.

poll·ster ['pəʊlstə] s Meinungsforscher (-in).

pol·lut·ant [pə'luːtənt] s Schadstoff m.

pol·lute [pə'luːt] v/t **1.** Umwelt verschmutzen, Flüsse etc a. verunreinigen. **2.** (moralisch) verderben. **pol'lut·er** s (Umwelt)Verschmutzer(in). **pol'lu·tion** s (Umwelt)Verschmutzung f, Verunreinigung f.

po·lo ['pəʊləʊ] s Sport: Polo n. ~ **neck** s Rollkragen(pullover) m. '~-**neck** adj Rollkragen... ~ **shirt** s Polohemd n.

po·lyg·a·mist [pə'lɪɡəmɪst] s Polygamist m. **po'lyg·a·mous** adj □ polygam (a. ⚘, zo.). **po'lyg·a·my** s Polygamie f (a. ⚘, zo.).

pol·y·glot ['pɒlɪɡlɒt] adj polyglott, viel-, mehrsprachig.

pol·y·gon ['pɒlɪɡən] s A Vieleck n.

pol·yp ['pɒlɪp] s ⚕, zo. Polyp m.

pol·y·syl·lab·ic [,pɒlɪsɪ'læbɪk] adj (~ally) ling. viel-, mehrsilbig. **pol·y·syl·la·ble** ['~,sɪləbl] s vielsilbiges Wort.

pol·y·tech·nic [,pɒlɪ'teknɪk] s (etwa) Technische Hochschule.

pol·y·va·lent [,pɒlɪ'veɪlənt] adj 🜊 mehrwertig.

po·made [pə'meɪd] s Pomade f.

pome·gran·ate ['pɒmɪ,ɡrænɪt] s ⚘ Granatapfel m.

pom·mel ['pʌml] s 1. (*Sattel- etc*)Knopf m. 2. *Turnen*: (*Pferd*)Pausche f: ~ **horse** Seitpferd n.

pomp [pɒmp] s Pomp m. '**pomp·ous** adj □ 1. aufgeblasen, wichtigtuerisch. 2. bombastisch, schwülstig (*Sprache*).

ponce [pɒns] s Br. sl. 1. Zuhälter m. 2. Tunte f.

pond [pɒnd] s Teich m, Weiher m.

pon·der ['pɒndə] I v/i nachdenken (**on, over** über acc). II v/t überlegen, nachdenken über (acc): ~ **doing s.th.** erwägen, et. zu tun. '**pon·der·ous** adj □ 1. massig, schwer. 2. fig. schwerfällig.

pong [pɒŋ] Br. F I s Gestank m. II v/i stinken. '**pong·y** adj Br. F stinkend, stinkig.

pon·toon [pɒn'tuːn] s 1. Ponton m. ~ **bridge** s Ponton-, Schiffsbrücke f.

po·ny ['pəʊnɪ] s zo. Pony n. '~**tail** s Pferdeschwanz m (*Frisur*).

poo·dle ['puːdl] s zo. Pudel m.

poof [puːf] s Br. sl. Schwule m.

pooh [puː] int pah! !**pooh-'pooh** v/t geringschätzig abtun.

pool¹ [puːl] s 1. Teich m, Tümpel m. 2. Pfütze f, (*Blut- etc*)Lache f. 3. (*Schwimm*)Becken n, (*Swimming-*)Pool m.

pool² [~] I s 1. (gemeinsame) Kasse, (*Kartenspiel a.*) Pot m. 2. pl Br. (*Fußball*)Toto n, m: **win (on) the ~s** im Toto gewinnen; **win on the ~s** Totogewinn m. 3. Am. Poolbillard n: **shoot ~** Poolbillard spielen. 4. ✝ bsd. Am. Pool m, Kartell n. 5. (*Arbeits-, Fahr*)Gemeinschaft f; (*Mitarbeiter- etc*)Stab m; (*Fuhr*)Park m; (*Schreib*)Pool m. II v/t 6. Geld etc zs.-legen; fig. Kräfte etc vereinen.

poop [puːp] s ⚓ 1. Heck n. 2. a. ~ **deck** (erhöhtes) Achter- od. Hinterdeck.

pooped (out) [puːpt] adj Am. F erledigt, kaputt.

poor [pɔː] I adj (□ → **poorly** II) 1. arm, mittellos. 2. arm, bedauernswert. 3. fig. arm (**in** an dat); dürftig, mangelhaft, schwach: ~ **consolation** ein schwacher Trost; → **health** 2. II s 4. **the** ~ pl die Armen pl. '**poor·ly** I adj 1. unpäßlich, kränklich. II adv 2. ärmlich: **he is** ~ **off** es geht ihm schlecht. 3. fig. dürftig, mangelhaft, schwach: ~ **gifted** schwachbegabt; ~ **paid** schlechtbe-

zahlt; **be** ~ **off for** knapp sein an (dat); **do** ~ **in** schlecht abschneiden bei; **think** ~ **of** nicht viel halten von. '**poor·ness** s 1. Armut f. 2. fig. Dürftigkeit f, Mangelhaftigkeit f.

pop¹ [pɒp] I v/i 1. knallen. 2. (zer)platzen: ~ **open** aufplatzen, -springen. 3. F ballern, schießen (**at** auf acc). 4. F sausen: ~ **in** auf e-n Sprung vorbeikommen; ~ **off** den Löffel weglegen (*sterben*); ~ **up** (plötzlich) auftauchen (a. fig.). II v/t 5. zerknallen. 6. F (schnell) stecken: ~ **on** Hut aufstülpen. 7. F **he's** ~**ped the question** F er hat ihr e-n (Heirats)Antrag gemacht. III s 8. Knall m. 9. F Limo f.

pop² [~] I s Pop m. II adj a) Schlager...: ~ **singer**, ~ **song** Schlager m, b) Pop...: ~ **concert** (**group, singer,** etc).

pop³ [~] s bsd. Am. Papa m, Vati m.

'**pop·corn** s Popcorn n, Puffmais m.

pope [pəʊp] s eccl. Papst m: ~'**s nose** Am. F Bürzel m.

'**pop-eyed** adj F glotzäugig. '~**gun** s Spielzeuggewehr n, -pistole f.

pop·lar ['pɒplə] s ♣ Pappel f.

pop·lin ['pɒplɪn] s Popelin m.

pop·per ['pɒpə] s bsd. Br. F Druckknopf m.

pop·py ['pɒpɪ] s ♣ Mohn m. '~**cock** s F Quatsch m.

pop·u·lar ['pɒpjʊlə] adj (□ → **popularly**) 1. populär, beliebt: **make o.s.** ~ **with** sich bei j-m beliebt machen. 2. weitverbreitet. 3. populär, volkstümlich; allgemein- od. leichtverständlich: ~ **etymology** ling. Volksetymologie f; ~ **music** volkstümliche Musik; ~ **press** Boulevardpresse f. 4. volkstümlich (*Preise*): ~ **edition** Volksausgabe f. 5. bsd. pol. Volks...: ~ **front** Volksfront f. **pop·u·lar·i·ty** [~'lærətɪ] s Popularität f: a) Beliebtheit f, b) Volkstümlichkeit f. **pop·u·lar·ize** ['~ləraɪz] v/t 1. populär machen. 2. allgemeinverständlich darstellen. '**pop·u·lar·ly** adv allgemein.

pop·u·late ['pɒpjʊleɪt] v/t bevölkern, besiedeln. **pop·u·la·tion** s 1. Bevölkerung f; Einwohnerschaft f: ~ **density** Bevölkerungsdichte f; ~ **explosion** Bevölkerungsexplosion f. 2. (Gesamt)Bestand m (**an** Tieren etc).

pop·u·lous ['pɒpjʊləs] adj □ dichtbesie-

delt, -bevölkert, (*Stadt*) einwohner-
stark.

por·ce·lain ['pɔːsəlɪn] *s* Porzellan *n*.

porch [pɔːtʃ] *s* **1.** überdachter Vorbau,
Vordach *n*, (*e-r Kirche etc*) Portal *n*. **2.**
Am. Veranda *f*.

por·cu·pine ['pɔːkjupaɪn] *s zo.* Stachelschwein *n*.

pore¹ [pɔː] *s* Pore *f*.

pore² [~] *v/i*: **~ over** vertieft sein in (*acc*),
über s-n Büchern etc hocken.

pork [pɔːk] *s* Schweinefleisch *n*. **~ chop** *s*
Schweinekotelett *n*. **~ cut·let** *s* Schwei-
neschnitzel *n*.

pork·y ['pɔːkɪ] *adj* F fett, dick.

porn [pɔːn] → **porno**.

por·no ['pɔːnəʊ] **I** *pl* **-nos** *s* **1.** Porno *m*.
2. Porno(film) *m*. **II** *adj* **3.** Porno...

por·no·graph·ic [ˌpɔːnəʊˈɡræfɪk] *adj*
(**~ally**) pornographisch. **por·nog·ra·
phy** [ɔːˈnɒɡrəfɪ] *s* Pornographie *f*.

po·rous ['pɔːrəs] *adj* □ porös.

por·poise ['pɔːpəs] *s zo.* Tümmler *m*.

por·ridge ['pɒrɪdʒ] *s* Porridge *n*, *m*, Haferbrei *m*.

port¹ [pɔːt] *s* **1.** Hafen *m*: **come into ~**
einlaufen; **leave ~** auslaufen; **any ~ in a
storm** *fig.* in der Not frißt der Teufel
Fliegen; **~ of call** Anlaufhafen. **2.** *a.* **~
city** Hafenstadt *f*.

port² [~] *s* ✈, ♣ Backbord *n*.

port³ [~] *s* Portwein *m*.

port·a·ble ['pɔːtəbl] **I** *adj* tragbar: **~ ra·
dio (set)** → IIa; **~ television set** → IIb;
~ typewriter → IIc. **II** *s* a) Kofferradio
n, b) Portable *n*, tragbares Fernsehgerät, c) Koffer-, Reiseschreibmaschine *f*.

por·tal ['pɔːtl] *s* Portal *n*.

por·tend [pɔːˈtend] *v/t* bedeuten, ankündigen.

por·ter¹ ['pɔːtə] *s* a) Pförtner *m*: **~'s lodge**
Pförtnerloge *f*, b) *bsd. Br.* Portier *m*.

por·ter² [~] *s* **1.** (Gepäck)Träger *m*. **2.** 🚂
Am. Schlafwagenschaffner(in).

'por·ter·house (steak) *s* Porterhouse-
steak *n*.

port·fo·li·o [ˌpɔːtˈfəʊljəʊ] *pl* **-os** *s* **1.** (Ak-
ten-, Dokumenten)Mappe *f*. **2.** *pol.*
Portefeuille *n*, Geschäftsbereich *m*.

'port·hole *s* ♣ Bullauge *n*.

por·ti·co ['pɔːtɪkəʊ] *pl* **-co(e)s** *s* Säulen-
halle *f*.

por·tion ['pɔːʃn] **I** *s* **1.** Teil *m*. **2.** Anteil *m*
(**of** an *dat*). **3.** Portion *f* (*Essen*). **II** *v/t* **4.**

~ out auf-, verteilen (**among, between**
unter *acc*).

port·ly ['pɔːtlɪ] *adj* beleibt, korpulent.

port·man·teau word [ˌpɔːtˈmæntəʊ] *s*
ling. Kurzwort *n*.

por·trait ['pɔːtreɪt] *s* paint. Porträt *n*,
phot. a. Porträtaufnahme *f*: **~ painter**
Porträtmaler(in). **'por·trait·ist** *s* Por-
trätist(in), Porträtmaler(in) *od.* -foto-
graf(in). **por·trai·ture** ['~trɪtʃə] *s* Por-
trätmalerei *f od.* -fotografie *f*.

por·tray [pɔːˈtreɪ] *v/t* **1.** porträtieren. **2.**
fig. schildern, darstellen (**as** als). **3.**
thea. etc darstellen, verkörpern. **por·
'tray·al** *s* **1.** Schilderung *f*, Darstellung
f. **2.** *thea. etc* Verkörperung *f*.

Por·tu·guese [ˌpɔːtʃʊˈɡiːz] **I** *adj* **1.** portugiesisch. **2.** Portugiese *m*, Portu-
giesin *f*: **the ~** *pl* die Portugiesen *pl*. **3.**
ling. Portugiesisch *n*.

pose [pəʊz] **I** *s* **1.** Pose *f* (*a. fig.*), Positur
f. **II** *v/t* **2.** aufstellen, in Positur stellen
od. setzen. **3.** *fig.* Problem, Frage aufwerfen, Bedrohung, Gefahr etc darstel-
len (**for, to** für). **III** *v/i* **4.** sich aufstellen,
sich in Positur stellen *od.* setzen. **5.**
paint. Modell stehen *od.* sitzen (**for**
dat); als (Maler- *od.* Foto)Modell arbeiten. **6.** sich ausgeben (**as** als). **posed**
adj gestellt (*Aufnahme*). **'pos·er** *s* **1.** F
harte Nuß. **2.** Wichtigtuer(in).

posh [pɒʃ] *adj* F piekfein, feudal: **~ hotel**
Nobelhotel *n*.

po·si·tion [pəˈzɪʃn] **I** *s* **1.** Position *f*, Lage
f, Standort *m*: **~ of the sun** *ast.* Sonnenstand *m*; **in (out of) ~** an der richtigen (falschen) Stelle. **2.** (*Körper*)Stel-
lung *f*, Position *f*. **3.** Stelle *f*, Stellung *f*
(**with, in** bei). **4.** a) Position *f* (*in e-m
Beruf, Wettbewerb etc*), (Rang)Stel-
lung *f*: **be in third ~** in dritter Position
od. auf dem dritten Platz liegen, b) (gesellschaftliche *od.* soziale) Stellung:
people of ~ Leute *pl* von Rang. **5.** *fig.*
Lage *f*, Situation *f*: **be in a ~ to do s.th.**
in der Lage sein, et. zu tun. **6.** *fig.*
(Sach)Lage *f*, Stand *m* (*der Dinge*): **le·
gal ~** Rechtslage. **7.** *fig.* Einstellung *f*
(**on** zu): **what is your ~ on ...?** wie
stehen Sie zu ...?; **take the ~ that** den
Standpunkt vertreten, daß. **II** *v/t* **8.**
(auf)stellen; *Polizisten etc* postieren.

pos·i·tive ['pɒzətɪv] **I** *adj* □ **1.** *allg.* positiv: **he was ~** 🩺 sein Befund war posi-

tiv; ~ **pole** ⚡ Pluspol m. **2.** ausdrücklich (*Befehl etc*), definitiv, fest (*Versprechen etc*). **3.** sicher, eindeutig (*Beweis etc*). **4.** greifbar, konkret; konstruktiv. **5.** be ~ sicher sein (*that* daß); **be ~ about** sich sicher sein (*gen*). **6.** F ausgesprochen, absolut. **II** s **7.** *phot.* Positiv n. **8.** *ling.* Positiv m.

pos·sess [pə'zes] v/t **1.** besitzen (*a. fig*). **2.** *fig.* beherrschen (*Gedanke, Gefühl etc*): **~ed with** (*od.* **by**) beherrscht (*od.*) erfüllt von; besessen von; **like a man ~ed** wie ein Besessener. **pos·ses·sion** [pə'zeʃn] s **1.** Besitz m: **be in s.o.'s ~** in j-s Besitz sein; **be in** (*od.* **have**) **~ of** im Besitz sein von (*od. gen*); **come** (*od.* **get**) **into ~ of** in den Besitz gelangen von (*od. gen*); **take ~ of** Besitz ergreifen von, in Besitz nehmen. **2.** Besitz(tum n) m. **3.** *fig.* Besessenheit f. **pos'ses·sive** [~siv] *adj* □ **1.** besitzgierig; (*Mutter etc*) besitzergreifend. **2.** *ling.* **~ case** Genitiv m, zweiter Fall; **~ adjective** attributives Possessivpronomen (*z. B.* **my** car); **~ pronoun** substantivisches Possessivpronomen (*z. B.* it is **mine**). **pos'ses·sor** s Besitzer(in).

pos·si·bil·i·ty [ˌpɒsə'bɪlətɪ] s Möglichkeit f (**of doing** zu tun). **'pos·si·ble** *adj* möglich: **do everything ~** alles tun, was e-m möglich ist; **make s.th. ~ for s.o.** j-m et. möglich machen *od.* ermöglichen; **if ~** falls möglich. **'pos·si·bly** *adv* **1.** möglicherweise, vielleicht. **2.** **when I ~ can** wenn ich irgend kann; **I can't ~ do this** ich kann das unmöglich tun; **how can I ~ do it?** wie kann ich es nur *od.* bloß machen?

pos·sum ['pɒsəm] F → **opossum**: **play ~** sich tot- *od.* schlafend *od.* dumm stellen.

post¹ [pəʊst] **I** s **1.** (*Tür-, Tor-, Ziel-etc*)Pfosten m, (*Laternen-*)Pfahl m, (*Telegrafen- etc*)Mast m: → **pip³**. **II** v/t **2.** *a.* **~ up** Plakat etc anschlagen, ankleben. **3.** et. durch Aushang bekanntgeben: **~** (**as**) **missing** ✍, ⚓ als vermißt melden.

post² [~] **I** s **1.** ✕ Posten m; Standort m, Garnison f. **2.** Posten m, Platz m: **at one's ~** auf s-m Posten. **3.** Posten m, Stelle f. **II** v/t **4.** *Polizisten etc* aufstellen, postieren. **5.** *bsd. Br.* versetzen, ✕ abkommandieren (**to** nach).

post³ [~] **I** s **1.** *bsd. Br.* Post f: **by ~** mit der *od.* per Post; **has the ~ been yet?** ist die Post schon da? **II** v/t **2.** *bsd. Br.* aufgeben; einwerfen; mit der (*Zu*)sen-den. **3.** **keep s.o. ~ed** j-n auf dem laufenden halten.

post·age ['pəʊstɪdʒ] s Porto n: **what is the ~ for a letter to ...?** wieviel kostet ein Brief nach ...? **~ stamp** s Postwertzeichen n, Briefmarke f.

post·al ['pəʊstl] **I** *adj* postalisch, Post...: **~ card** *Am.* Postkarte f; **~ charges** pl Postgebühren pl. **II** s *Am.* F Postkarte f. **'post·box** s *bsd. Br.* Briefkasten m. **'~card** s Postkarte f. **'~code** s *Br.* Postleitzahl f.

post·er ['pəʊstə] s Plakat n; Poster m, n.

poste re·stante [ˌpəʊst'restɑ̃nt] *bsd. Br.* **I** s Abteilung f für postlagernde Sendungen. **II** *adv* postlagernd.

pos·te·ri·or [pɒ'stɪərɪə] s *humor.* Allerwerteste m.

pos·ter·i·ty [pɒ'sterətɪ] s die Nachwelt.

post-'free *adj u. adv bsd. Br.* portofrei. **~ horn** s *hist.* Posthorn n.

post·hu·mous ['pɒstjʊməs] *adj* □ post(h)um.

pos·til·(l)ion [pə'stɪljən] s *hist.* Postillion m.

post·man ['pəʊstmən] s (*irr* **man**) *bsd. Br.* Briefträger m, Postbote m. **'~mark** **I** s Poststempel m. **II** v/t (ab)stempeln: **be ~ed London** in London abgestempelt sein. **'~mas·ter** s Postamtsvorsteher m: ♀ **General** Postminister m.

post me·rid·i·em [ˌpəʊstmə'rɪdɪəm] *adv* nachmittags (*abbr.* **p.m.**): **3 p.m.** 15 Uhr. **~mor·tem** [~'mɔːtem] s *a.* **~ examination** Autopsie f, Obduktion f.

post of·fice s Post(amt n) f: → **box** Postfach n. **~'paid** → **post-free**.

post·pone [ˌpəʊst'pəʊn] v/t verschieben (**to** auf acc), aufschieben (**to** auf acc; **till, until** bis): **he ~ed seeing his doctor** er verschob s-n Arztbesuch. **post'pone·ment** s Verschiebung f, Aufschub m.

post·script ['pəʊsskrɪpt] s **1.** Postskript(um) n, Nachschrift f. **2.** Nachbemerkung f (**to** e-r Rede etc).

pos·tu·late **I** v/t ['pɒstjʊleɪt] postulieren, (als gegeben) voraussetzen. **II** s ['~lət] Postulat n, Voraussetzung f.

pos·ture ['pɒstʃə] **I** s **1.** (Körper-)Haltung *f*; Positur *f*, Stellung *f*. **2.** *fig.* Haltung *f* (**on** in *dat*, zu). **II** *v/i* **3.** sich in Positur stellen *od.* setzen. **4.** *fig.* sich aufspielen.

post·war [ˌpəʊstˈwɔː] *adj* Nachkriegs...

pot [pɒt] **I** *s* **1.** (Blumen-, Koch- *etc*)Topf *m*: **big** ~ F großes *od.* hohes Tier; **a ~ of money** F e-e Menge Geld; **he's got ~s of money** F er hat Geld wie Heu; **go to** ~ F auf den Hund kommen (*Person etc*); immer schlechter werden (*Sprachkenntnisse etc*); ins Wasser fallen (*Pläne etc*); **keep the ~ boiling** *fig.* sich über Wasser halten; die Sache in Schwung halten. **2.** (Kaffee-, Tee)Kanne *f*; Kännchen *n*, Portion *f* (*Tee etc*). **3.** *Sport:* F Pokal *m*. **4.** *Poker:* Pot *m*, Kasse *f*. **5.** F → **potbelly. 6.** *sl.* Pot *n* (*Marihuana*). **II** *v/t* **7.** Pflanze eintopfen: **~ted plant** Topfpflanze *f*. **8.** Fleisch einmachen, Fisch einlegen. **9.** *Billard:* *Br.* einlochen. **10.** F Kind aufs Töpfchen setzen.

po·ta·ble [ˈpəʊtəbl] *adj* trinkbar, Trink...

po·tas·si·um [pəˈtæsɪəm] *s* 🜚 Kalium *n*. **~ cy·a·nide** *s* Zyankali *n*.

po·ta·to [pəˈteɪtəʊ] *pl* **-toes** *s* Kartoffel *f*: **hot ~** F heißes Eisen. **~ bee·tle**, *bsd. Am.* **~ bug** *s* *zo.* Kartoffelkäfer *m*. **~ chips** *s pl Am.*, **~ crisps** *s pl Br.* Kartoffelchips *pl*. **~ sal·ad** *s* Kartoffelsalat *m*.

'pot·bel·ly [ˈ~belɪ] *s* Schmerbauch *m*. **'~,boil·er** *s contp.* rein kommerzielle Arbeit (*Buch etc*).

po·ten·cy [ˈpəʊtənsɪ] *s* **1.** Stärke *f*; Wirksamkeit *f*, Wirkung *f*. **2.** *physiol.* Potenz *f*. **'po·tent** *adj* □ **1.** stark (*Medikament etc*). **2.** *fig.* überzeugend, zwingend (*Argument etc*). **3.** *physiol.* potent. **po·ten·tate** [ˈ~teɪt] *s* Potentat *m*. **po·ten·tial** [~ˈtenʃl] **I** *adj* **1.** potentiell, möglich. **II** *s* **2.** Potential *n*, Leistungsfähigkeit *f*: **have the ~ to be a top manager** das Zeug zu e-m Spitzenmanager haben. **3.** 🜚 Spannung *f*. **po·ten·tial·ly** [~ˈtenʃəlɪ] *adv* potentiell, möglicherweise.

'pot·hole *s mot.* Schlagloch *n*. **'~-holed** *adj* voller Schlaglöcher.

po·tion [ˈpəʊʃn] *s* Trank *m*.

'pot·luck *s:* **take ~** mit dem vorliebnehmen, was es gerade (*zu essen*) gibt; *fig.* es probieren. **~ plant** *s* Topfpflanze *f*.

pot·pour·ri [ˌpəʊˈpʊərɪ] *s* ♪ Potpourri *n*, *fig. a.* Allerlei *n*, Kunterbunt *n*.

pot·ter¹ [ˈpɒtə] *v/i* **1.** schlendern. **2.** *a.* ~ **about** (*od.* **around**) herumwerkeln, -hantieren.

pot·ter² [~] *s* Töpfer(in): **~'s wheel** Töpferscheibe *f*. **'pot·ter·y** *s* **1.** Töpferei *f*. **2.** Töpferware(n *pl*) *f*.

pot·ty¹ [ˈpɒtɪ] *adj bsd. Br.* F verrückt (**a·bout** nach).

pot·ty² [~] *s* Töpfchen *n*. **'~-trained** *adj* sauber.

pouch [paʊtʃ] *s* Beutel *m* (*a. zo.*); *anat.* (Tränen)Sack *m*; *zo.* (Backen)Tasche *f*.

poul·tice [ˈpəʊltɪs] *s* 🩹 (warmer) (Senf*etc*)Umschlag *od.* (-)Wickel.

poul·try [ˈpəʊltrɪ] *s* Geflügel *n*.

pounce [paʊns] **I** *v/i* sich stürzen (**on** auf *acc*) (*a. fig.*). **II** *s* Sprung *m*, Satz *m*.

pound¹ [paʊnd] *s* Pfund *n* (*Gewichts- u. Währungseinheit*): **by the ~** pfundweise; **five-~ note** Fünfpfundschein *m*.

pound² [~] *s* **1.** Tierheim *n*. **2.** Abstellplatz *m* für (polizeilich) abgeschleppte Fahrzeuge.

pound³ [~] **I** *v/t* **1.** zerstoßen, -stampfen (**to** zu). **2.** trommeln *od.* hämmern auf (*acc*) *od.* an (*acc*) *od.* gegen (*acc*). **II** *v/i* **3.** hämmern (**with** vor *dat*) (*Herz*): **~ at** (*od.* **on**) → **2. 4.** stampfen.

pour [pɔː] **I** *v/t* **1.** gießen, schütten: **~ s.th. on o.s.** sich mit et. übergießen; **~ s.o. a cup of tea** j-m e-e Tasse Tee eingießen; **~ out** ausgießen, -schütten; (*Getränke*) eingießen, -schenken; *fig.* Sorgen *etc* ausbreiten (**to** vor *dat*), *Herz* ausschütten (**to** *dat*). **II** *v/i* **2.** strömen (*a. fig.*). **3.** **it is ~ing down** (*od.* **~ing with rain**) es gießt in Strömen; **in the ~ing rain** im strömenden Regen.

pout [paʊt] **I** *v/i* e-n Schmollmund machen *od.* ziehen; schmollen. **II** *v/t* Lippen schürzen. **III** *s* Schmollmund *m*; Schmollen *n*: **with a ~** schmollend; **be in a ~**, **have a ~** schmollen. **'~ note** s Schmollmund *m*.

pov·er·ty [ˈpɒvətɪ] *s* Armut *f* (*a. fig.* **of** an *dat*): **~ of ideas** Ideenarmut. **~ line** *s* Armutsgrenze *f*. **'~-,strick·en** *adj* arm, notleidend.

pow·der [ˈpaʊdə] **I** *s* **1.** (Back-, Schieß*etc*)Pulver *n*. **2.** (Gesichts- *etc*)Puder *m*. **II** *v/t* **3.** pulverisieren: **~ed milk** Milchpulver *n*, Trockenmilch *f*; **~ed sugar** *Am.* Puderzucker *m*. **4.** Baby *etc* (ein-)

pudern, sich *die Nase etc* pudern: ~ **one's nose** *a. euphem.* mal verschwinden. ~ **keg** *s fig.* Pulverfaß *n.* ~ **puff** *s* Puderquaste *f.* ~ **room** *s* Damentoilette *f.*

pow·der·y ['paʊdərɪ] *adj* **1.** pulv(e)rig: ~ **snow** Pulverschnee *m.* **2.** (ein)gepudert.

pow·er ['paʊə] **I** *s* **1.** Kraft *f*, Macht *f*, Vermögen *n*: *do all in one's* ~ alles tun, was in s-r Macht steht; *it was out of* (*od. not* [*with*]*in, beyond*) *his* ~ es stand nicht in s-r Macht (*to do* zu tun). **2.** Kraft *f*, Energie *f*; *weitS.* Wucht *f*, Gewalt *f.* **3.** *mst pl* hypnotische *etc* Kräfte *pl*, geistige *etc* Fähigkeiten *pl*, (Denk-, Konzentrations- *etc*)Vermögen *n.* **4.** Macht *f*, Gewalt *f* (*over* über *acc*): *be in* ~ *pol.* an der Macht sein; *be* ~ in j-s Gewalt sein; *come into* ~ *pol.* an die Macht kommen. **5.** *pol.* Gewalt *f* (*als Staatsfunktion*): → *separation* 2. **6.** *pol.*, ☆ *etc* (Amts)Gewalt *f*; Befugnis *f*: *give* (*have*) *full* ~*s* Vollmacht geben (haben); → *attorney* 2. **7.** *mst pl pol.* Macht *f* (*Staat*). **8.** Macht(faktor *m*) *f*, einflußreiche Stelle *od.* Person: *the* ~*s pl that be* F die *pl* da oben. **9.** ☆ Potenz *f*: *raise to the third* ~ in die dritte Potenz erheben. **10.** ⚡ Strom *m.* **II** *v/t* **11.** ⚙ antreiben. ~ **ed** *adj mot.* Servo... '~**boat** *s* Rennboot *n.* ~ **brake** *s mot.* Servobremse *f.*

pow·er·ful ['paʊəfʊl] *adj* □ **1.** stark (*a. fig.*), kräftig. **2.** mächtig, einflußreich. **'pow·er·less** *adj* □ **1.** kraftlos. **2.** machtlos: *be* ~ *to do s.th.* nicht in der Lage sein, et. zu tun; *be* ~ *to prevent s.th.* nichts tun können, um et. zu verhindern.

pow·er| pack *s* ⚡ Netzteil *n.* ~ **plant** → *power station.* ~ **point** *s* ⚡ *Br.* Steckdose *f.* ~ **sta·tion** *s* Kraft-, Elektrizitätswerk *n.* ~ **steer·ing** *s mot.* Servolenkung *f.*

pow·wow ['paʊwaʊ] *s* F Besprechung *f.*

pox [pɒks] *s* ☆ F Syph *f* (*Syphilis*).

prac·ti·ca·ble ['præktɪkəbl] *adj* □ **1.** durchführbar. **2.** passierbar (*Straße etc*).

prac·ti·cal ['præktɪkl] *adj* **1.** *allg.* praktisch: → *purpose* 1. **2.** praktisch denkend *od.* veranlagt. **3.** ~ *joke* Streich *m*: *play a* ~ *joke on s.o.* j-m e-n Streich

spielen. **prac·ti·cal·ly** ['~klɪ] *adv* praktisch, so gut wie.

prac·tice ['præktɪs] **I** *s* **1.** Praxis *f*: *in* ~ in der Praxis; *put in*(*to*) ~ in die Praxis umsetzen. **2.** Übung *f*: *in* (*out of*) ~ in (aus) der Übung; *keep in* ~ in der Übung bleiben; ~ *makes perfect* Übung macht den Meister. **3.** (*Arzt etc*)Praxis *f.* **4.** Brauch *m*, Gewohnheit *f*: ~*s pl contp.* Praktiken *pl*; *it is common* ~ es ist allgemein üblich; *make it a* ~ es sich zur Gewohnheit machen (*to do* zu tun). **II** *adj* **5.** Übungs..., Probe... **III** *v/t u. v/i* **6.** *Am.* → *practise.*

prac·tise ['præktɪs] *bsd. Br.* **I** *v/t* **1.** einen Beruf ausüben: ~ *law* (*medicine*) als Anwalt (Arzt) praktizieren. **2.** (ein-)üben. **3.** *Grundsätze etc* praktizieren, *Geduld etc* üben. **II** *v/i* **4.** (*als Anwalt od. Arzt*) praktizieren: *practising Catholic* praktizierender Katholik. **5.** üben. '**prac·tised** *adj* **1.** geübt (*at, in* in *dat*): *be* ~ *at doing s.th.* darin geübt sein, et. zu tun. **2.** eingeübt, *contp. a.* gekünstelt.

prac·ti·tion·er [præk'tɪʃnə] *s*: *medical* ~ → *general practitioner.*

prag·mat·ic [præg'mætɪk] *adj* (~*ally*) pragmatisch. **prag·ma·tist** ['~mətɪst] *s* Pragmatiker(in).

prai·rie ['preərɪ] *s* Prärie *f.* ~ **schoon·er** *s hist. Am.* Planwagen *m.*

praise [preɪz] **I** *v/t* loben (*for* wegen): → *sky.* **II** *s* Lob *n.* '~**wor·thy** *adj* □ lobenswert, löblich.

pram [præm] *s bsd. Br.* F Kinderwagen *m.*

prance [prɑːns] *v/i* **1.** tänzeln (*Pferd, Person*). **2.** stolzieren.

prank [præŋk] *s* Streich *m*: *play a* ~ *on s.o.* j-m e-n Streich spielen.

prate [preɪt] *v/i* schwafeln (*about, on* von).

prat·tle ['prætl] *v/i a.* ~ *on* plappern (*about* von).

prawn [prɔːn] *s zo.* Garnele *f.*

pray [preɪ] *v/i* beten (*to* zu; *for* für, um).

prayer [preə] *s* **1.** Gebet *n*: ~ *book* Gebetbuch *n*; ~ *mat* (*od. rug*) Gebetteppich *m.* **2.** *oft pl* Andacht *f.*

preach [priːtʃ] **I** *v/t* **1.** predigen (*to* zu, vor *dat*): ~ *to the converted fig.* offene Türen einrennen; ~ *at* (*od. to*) *s.o. fig.* j-m e-e Predigt halten (*about* wegen). **II** *v/i*

predigen (*a. fig.*); *Predigt* halten.
'**preach·er** *s* Prediger(in).
pre·am·ble [priːˈæmbl] *s* Einleitung *f*,
🔧 Präambel *f* (**to** zu).
pre·ar·range [ˌpriːəˈreɪndʒ] *v/t* vorher
abmachen *od.* vereinbaren.
pre·car·i·ous [prɪˈkeərɪəs] *adj* □ prekär,
unsicher.
pre·cau·tion [prɪˈkɔːʃn] *s* Vorkehrung *f*,
Vorsichtsmaßnahme *f* (**against** gegen):
as a ~ zur Vorsicht, vorsichtshalber.
pre'cau·tion·ar·y *adj* vorbeugend,
Vorsichts...
pre·cede [ˌpriːˈsiːd] *v/t* **1.** voraus-, vorangehen (*dat*). **2.** (den) Vorrang haben
vor (*dat*). **3. ~ s.th. with** (*od.* **by**) **s.th.** et.
mit et. einleiten, et. e-r Sache voraus-
schicken. **prec·e·dence** [ˈpresɪdəns] *s*
Vorrang *m*: **have** (*od.* **take**) **~ over ~**
precede 2; **give ~ to** (den) Vorrang
geben (*dat*). **prec·e·dent** [ˈpresɪdənt]
s 🔧 Präzedenzfall *m* (*a. fig.*): **without**
~ ohne Beispiel, noch nie dagewesen; **set a ~** e-n Präzedenzfall schaffen.
pre·cept [ˈpriːsept] *s* Regel *f*, Richtli-
nie *f*.
pre·cinct [ˈpriːsɪŋkt] *s* **1.** *pl* Gelände *n*;
Umgebung *f*. **2.** (*Fußgänger*)Zone *f*,
(*Einkaufs*)Viertel *n*. **3.** *Am.* (*Polizei*)Re-
vier *n*; (*Wahl*)Bezirk *m*.
pre·cious [ˈpreʃəs] **I** *adj* □ **1.** kostbar,
wertvoll (*beide a. fig.*). **2.** *F* iro.: **~**
stone; ~ metals. **II** *adv* **3.** **~ little** F
herzlich wenig.
prec·i·pice [ˈpresɪpɪs] *s* Abgrund *m* (*a.*
fig.).
pre·cip·i·tate [prɪˈsɪpɪteɪt] **I** *v/t* **1.** (hinun-
ter-, herunter)schleudern; *fig.* stürzen
(**into** in *acc*). **2.** *fig. Ereignis* beschleunigen. **3.** 🔬 ausfällen. **II** *v/i* **4.** 🔬 ausfallen. **III** *adj* [~tət] **5.** überstürzt. **IV** *s* **6.**
🔬 Niederschlag *m.* **pre·cip·i·ta·tion** *s*
1. Überstürzung *f.* **2.** *meteor.* Niederschlag *m.* **3.** 🔬 Ausfällung *f.* **pre·**
'**cip·i·tous** *adj* □ **1.** steil (abfallend). **2.**
fig. überstürzt.
pré·cis [ˈpreɪsiː] **I** *pl* **-cis** [ˈ~siːz] *s* Zs.-
fassung *f.* **II** *v/t* zs.-fassen.
pre·cise [prɪˈsaɪs] *adj* **1.** genau, präzis: **to**
be ~ genau gesagt. **2.** gewissenhaft.
pre'cise·ly *adv* **1.** → **precise. 2. ~!**
genau! **pre·ci·sion** [~ˈsɪʒn] **I** *s* Genauigkeit *f, a.* ⊙ Präzision *f.* **II** *adj* ⊙ Präzi-

sions..., Fein...: **~ instrument** Präzisi-
onsinstrument *n.*
pre·clude [prɪˈkluːd] *v/t* **1.** *et.* ausschließen. **2. ~ s.o. from doing s.th.** j-n (daran) hindern, et. zu tun.
pre·co·cious [prɪˈkəʊʃəs] *adj* □ früh-
reif. **pre·co·cious·ness, pre·coc·i·ty**
[~ˈkɒsətɪ] *s* Frühreife *f.*
pre·con·ceived [ˌpriːkənˈsiːvd] *adj* vorgefaßt. **pre·con·cep·tion** [~ˈsepʃn] *s*
vorgefaßte Meinung *od.* Vorstellung,
Vorurteil *n* (**about** über *acc*).
pre·con·di·tion [ˌpriːkənˈdɪʃn] *s* Voraus-
bedingung *f,* Voraussetzung *f.*
pre·cook [ˌpriːˈkʊk] *v/t* vorkochen.
pre·cur·sor [ˌpriːˈkɜːsə] *s* (*of,* **to** gen)
1. Vorläufer *m.* **2.** Vorbote *m.*
pre·date [priːˈdeɪt] *v/t* *Brief etc* zurückdatieren.
pred·a·to·ry [ˈpredətərɪ] *adj* räuberisch:
~ animal Raubtier *n.*
pre·de·ces·sor [ˈpriːdɪsesə] *s* Vorgän-
ger(in): **~ in office** Amtsvorgänger(in).
pre·des·ti·na·tion [priːˌdestɪˈneɪʃn] *s*
eccl. u. weitS. Prädestination *f,* Vorher-
bestimmung *f.* '**pre·des·tined** *adj* prä-
destiniert, vorherbestimmt (**to** für, zu):
be ~ to failure (*od.* **fail**) (von vornherein) zum Scheitern verurteilt sein; **he**
was ~ to do s.th. es war ihm vorherbestimmt, et. zu tun.
pre·de·ter·mine [ˌpriːdɪˈtɜːmɪn] *v/t* **1.**
vorherbestimmen. **2. → prearrange.**
pre·dic·a·ment [prɪˈdɪkəmənt] *s* mißli-
che Lage, Zwangslage *f.*
pred·i·cate [ˈpredɪkət] *s ling.* Prädikat *n,*
Satzaussage *f.* **pred·i·ca·tive** [prɪˈdɪk-
ətɪv] *adj* □ prädikativ.
pre·dict [prɪˈdɪkt] *v/t* vorher-, voraussagen. **pre'dic·tion** *s* Vorher-, Voraussage *f: **against all ~s** entgegen allen Voraussagen.
pre·di·lec·tion [ˌpriːdɪˈlekʃn] *s* Vorliebe
f (**for** für).
pre·dis·pose [ˌpriːdɪˈspəʊz] *v/t* **1.** geneigt machen, einnehmen (**in favo[u]r**
of für). **2.** *bsd.* ❀ anfällig machen (**to**
für). '**pre·dis·po·si·tion** [~ˈzɪʃn] *s*
(**to**) Neigung *f* (zu), *bsd.* ❀ Anfälligkeit *f* (für).
pre·dom·i·nant [prɪˈdɒmɪnənt] *adj* □
(vor)herrschend, überwiegend. **pre·**
'**dom·i·nate** [~neɪt] *v/i* **1.** vorherrschen,
-wiegen, überwiegen. **2.** überlegen sein;

die Oberhand *od.* das Übergewicht haben (**over** über *acc*).

pre·em·i·nent [ˌpriːˈemɪnənt] *adj* □ hervor-, überragend.

pre·emp·tive [ˌpriːˈemptɪv] *adj* **1. ~ right** Vorkaufsrecht *n.* **2. ~ strike** ✕ Präventivschlag *m.*

preen [priːn] *v/t* sich, *das Gefieder* putzen (*Vogel*): **~ o.s.** sich herrichten (*Person*).

pre·fab ['priːfæb] *s* F Fertighaus *n.* **ˈpre·ˈfab·ri·cate** [ˌ~rɪkeɪt] *v/t* vorfabrizieren, -fertigen: **~d house** Fertighaus *n.*

pref·ace ['prefɪs] **I** *s* Vorwort *n* (**to** zu). **II** *v/t* *Rede, Buch etc* einleiten (**with** mit).

pre·fer [prɪˈfɜː] *v/t* vorziehen (**to** *dat*), lieber mögen (**to** als), bevorzugen: **I ~ meat to fish** Fleisch ist mir lieber als Fisch; **~ listening to talking** lieber zuhören als reden; **I'd ~ to stay at home** ich bliebe lieber zu Hause; **I'd ~ you not to go** es wäre mir lieber, wenn du nicht gingst. **pref·er·a·ble** ['prefərəbl] *adj*: **be ~ (to)** vorzuziehen sein (*dat*), besser sein (als). **'pref·er·a·bly** *adv* vorzugsweise, lieber, am liebsten. **'pref·er·ence** *s* **1.** Bevorzugung *f*, Vorzug *m*: **give s.o. ~ (over)** j-m den Vorzug geben (gegenüber); **what is your ~?** was möchtest du lieber? **2.** Vorliebe *f* (**for** für). **pref·er·en·tial** [ˌ~ˈrenʃl] *adj* □ bevorzugt, Vorzugs...

pre·fix I *s* ['priːfɪks] **1.** *ling.* Präfix *n*, Vorsilbe *f.* **II** *v/t* [ˌpriːˈfɪks] **2.** *ling.* e-m Wort e-e Vorsilbe voranstellen. **3.** *Bemerkung etc* voranstellen (**to** *dat*).

preg·nan·cy ['pregnənsɪ] *s* Schwangerschaft *f*; *zo.* Trächtigkeit *f*: **~ test** Schwangerschaftstest *m.* **ˈpreg·nant** *adj* □ schwanger; *zo.* trächtig: **she's four months ~** sie ist im vierten Monat schwanger; **~ with meaning** *fig.* bedeutungsschwer, -voll.

pre·heat [ˌpriːˈhiːt] *v/t* Bratröhre vorheizen.

pre·his·tor·ic [ˌpriːhɪˈstɒrɪk] *adj* (**~ally**) prähistorisch, vorgeschichtlich.

pre·judge [ˌpriːˈdʒʌdʒ] *v/t* j-n vorverurteilen: **~ the issue** sich vorschnell e-e Meinung bilden.

prej·u·dice ['predʒʊdɪs] **I** *s* **1.** Vorurteil *n*, Voreingenommenheit *f*, *bsd.* ⚖ Befangenheit *f*: **have a ~ against** Vorurteile haben *od.* voreingenommen sein

gegen. **2. to the ~ of** zum Nachteil *od.* Schaden (*gen*); **without ~ to** *bsd.* ⚖ unbeschadet. **II** *v/t* **3.** einnehmen (**in favo[u]r of** für; **against** gegen): **~d** (vor)eingenommen, *bsd.* ⚖ befangen. **4.** schaden (*dat*), beeinträchtigen. **prej·u·di·cial** [ˌ~ˈdɪʃl] *adj* □ (**to**) abträglich (*dat*), schädlich (für): **be ~ to → prejudice** 4; **~ to health** gesundheitsschädlich.

pre·lim·i·nar·y [prɪˈlɪmɪnərɪ] **I** *adj* Vor...: **~ discussion** Vorbesprechung *f*; **~ measures** *pl* vorbereitende Maßnahmen *pl*; **~ round** (*Sport*) Vorrunde *f.* **II** *s pl* Vorbereitungen *pl*, vorbereitende Maßnahmen *pl*.

prel·ude ['preljuːd] *s* ♪ Vorspiel *n* (**to** zu) (*a. fig.*); Präludium *n.*

pre·mar·i·tal [ˌpriːˈmærɪtl] *adj* □ vorehelich.

pre·ma·ture [ˌpreməˈtjʊə] *adj* □ **1.** vorzeitig, verfrüht: **be four weeks ~** vier Wochen zu früh auf die Welt kommen; **~ baby** Frühgeburt *f.* **2.** *fig.* voreilig.

pre·med·i·tat·ed [ˌpriːˈmedɪteɪtɪd] *adj* □ vorsätzlich. **pre·med·i·ta·tion** *s* Vorsatz *m*: **with ~** vorsätzlich.

pre·mi·er ['premjə] *s* Premier(minister) *m.*

prem·i·ere, prem·i·ère ['premɪeə] **I** *s* Premiere *f*, Ur-, Erstaufführung *f.* **II** *v/t* ur-, erstaufführen.

prem·is·es ['premɪsɪz] *s pl* Gelände *n*, Grundstück *n*; Räumlichkeiten *pl*, (*Geschäfts*)Räume *pl*: **on the ~** an Ort u. Stelle, im Haus *od.* Lokal.

pre·mi·um ['priːmjəm] *s* **1.** Prämie *f*, Bonus *m*: **be at a ~** *fig.* hoch im Kurs stehen; **put a ~ on** *fig.* sehr viel Wert legen auf (*acc*); fördern. **2.** *mot. Am.* F Super *n.* **~ gas·o·line** *s mot. Am.* Superbenzin *n.*

pre·mo·ni·tion [ˌpreməˈnɪʃn] *s* (böse) Vorahnung.

pre·na·tal [ˌpriːˈneɪtl] → **antenatal.**

pre·oc·cu·pa·tion [priːˌɒkjʊˈpeɪʃn] *s* Beschäftigung *f* (**with** mit): **he's got so many ~s that** er hat so viele Dinge im Kopf, daß. **ˌpre·ˈoc·cu·pied** [~paɪd] *adj* gedankenverloren, geistesabwesend. **ˌpre·ˈoc·cu·py** [~paɪ] *v/t* (stark) beschäftigen.

pre·or·dain [ˌpriːɔːˈdeɪn] *v/t* vorherbestimmen: **his success was ~ed, he**

was ~*ed to succeed* sein Erfolg war ihm vorherbestimmt.

prep [prep] *s Br.* F Hausaufgabe(n *pl*) *f*: *do one's* ~ s-e Hausaufgaben machen.

pre·paid [ˌpriːˈpeɪd] *adj* & frankiert, freigemacht: ~ *envelope* Freiumschlag *m.*

prep·a·ra·tion [ˌprepəˈreɪʃn] *s* 1. Vorbereitung *f* (*for* auf *acc*, für): *be in* ~ in Vorbereitung sein; *make* ~*s* Vorbereitungen treffen. 2. Zubereitung *f.* 3. 🌿, ⚕ Präparat *n.*

pre·par·a·to·ry [prɪˈpærətərɪ] *adj* □ 1. vorbereitend, Vor(bereitungs)... 2. ~ *to* vor (*dat*): ~ *to doing s.th.* bevor *od.* ehe man et. tut. ~ *school s Br.* private Vorbereitungsschule auf das College; *Am.* private Vorbereitungsschule auf die High-School.

pre·pare [prɪˈpeə] I *v/t* 1. Fest, Rede etc vorbereiten; *j-n* (*a. seelich*) vorbereiten (*for* auf *acc*): *be in* ~ ... ~ *o.s. for* sich gefaßt machen auf (*acc*). 2. anfertigen; *Speise etc* zubereiten. II *v/i* 3. ~ *for* sich vorbereiten auf (*acc*); Vorbereitungen treffen für; sich gefaßt machen auf (*acc*). **pre'pared** *adj* 1. vorbereitet (*Erklärung etc*). 2. bereit, gewillt (*to do* zu tun). 3. gefaßt, vorbereitet (*for* auf *acc*; *to do* darauf, zu tun). **pre'pared·ness** *s* Bereitschaft *f.*

pre·pon·der·ance [prɪˈpɒndərəns] *s fig.* Übergewicht *n.* **pre'pon·der·ant** *adj* □ überwiegend: *be* ~ → *preponderate.* **pre'pon·der·ate** [ˌ~reɪt] *v/i* überwiegen; überlegen sein (*over* *dat*).

prep·o·si·tion [ˌprepəˈzɪʃn] *s ling.* Präposition *f*, Verhältniswort *n.*

pre·pos·sess [ˌpriːpəˈzes] *v/t*: *be* ~*ed by* eingenommen sein von. **pre·pos'sess·ing** *adj* □ einnehmend.

pre·pos·ter·ous [prɪˈpɒstərəs] *adj* □ 1. absurd. 2. lächerlich, lachhaft.

prep school F → *preparatory school.*

pre·puce [ˈpriːpjuːs] *s anat.* Vorhaut *f.*

pre·re·cord·ed [ˌpriːrɪˈkɔːdɪd] *adj* bespielt (*Musik-, Videokassette*).

pre·req·ui·site [ˌpriːˈrekwɪzɪt] *s* Vorbedingung *f*, Voraussetzung *f* (*for, of,* für).

pre·rog·a·tive [prɪˈrɒɡətɪv] *s* Vorrecht *n.*

Pres·by·te·ri·an [ˌprezbɪˈtɪərɪən] I *adj* presbyterianisch. II *s* Presbyterianer (-in).

pre·school [ˌpriːˈskuːl] *adj* vorschulisch:

of ~ *age* im Vorschulalter; ~ *child* Vorschulkind *n.*

pre·scribe [prɪˈskraɪb] *v/t* 1. *et.* vorschreiben. 2. ⚕ *j-m et.* verschreiben, -ordnen (*for* gegen).

pre·scrip·tion [prɪˈskrɪpʃn] *s* 1. Vorschrift *f.* 2. ⚕ verordnete Medizin; Rezept *n*: *available only on* ~ rezeptpflichtig. ~ *charge s* Rezeptgebühr *f.*

pres·ence [ˈprezns] *s* Gegenwart *f*, Anwesenheit *f*: *in the* ~ *of* in Gegenwart *od.* in Anwesenheit *od.* im Beisein von (*od. gen*), vor *Zeugen*; *make one's* ~ *felt fig.* sich bemerkbar *od.* auf sich aufmerksam machen; ~ *of mind* Geistesgegenwart *f.*

pres·ent[1] [ˈpreznt] I *adj* (□ → *presently*) 1. anwesend (*at* bei); vorhanden: *in* ~ *company* 2. 2. gegenwärtig, jetzig, derzeitig: *at the* ~ *moment* zum gegenwärtigen Zeitpunkt; *in the* ~ *case* im vorliegenden Fall. 3. *ling.* ~ *participle* Partizip *n* Präsens, Mittelwort *n* der Gegenwart; ~ *perfect* Perfekt *n*, zweite Vergangenheit; ~ *tense* Präsens *n*, Gegenwart *f.* II *s* 4. Gegenwart *f*, *ling. a.* Präsens *n*: *at* ~ gegenwärtig, zur Zeit; *for the* ~ vorerst, -läufig, einstweilen.

pre·sent[2] [prɪˈzent] *v/t* 1. präsentieren (*to dat*): a) (über)reichen, (-)bringen, (-)geben: ~ *s.th. to s.o.*, ~ *s.o. with s.th. a.* j-m et. schenken, b) vorbringen, -legen, unterbreiten, c) zeigen, vorführen, *thea. etc* aufführen) d) schildern, darstellen, e) *j-n, Produkt etc* vorstellen, f) *Programm etc* moderieren. 2. *Sicht, Ziel, Möglichkeit etc* bieten, *Schwierigkeit etc* darstellen, bieten: *if the chance* ~*s itself* wenn sich die Chance bietet; *this* ~*s no problem* (*to him*) das ist kein Problem (für ihn). 3. ~ *o.s.* sich einfinden (*Person*); ~ *itself* sich einstellen (*Gedanke etc*).

pres·ent[3] [ˈpreznt] *s* Geschenk *n*: *make s.o. a* ~ *of s.th.* j-m et. schenken (*a. fig.*).

pre·sent·a·ble [prɪˈzentəbl] *adj* □ vorzeigbar (*Person*): *be* ~ sich sehen lassen können (*a. Sache*); *make o.s.* ~ sich zurechtmachen.

pres·en·ta·tion [ˌprezənˈteɪʃn] *s* Präsentation *f*: a) Überreichung *f*, -gabe *f*, b) Unterbreitung *f*, c) Vorführung *f*, *thea. etc* Aufführung *f*, d) Schilderung *f*,

Darstellung f, e) Vorstellung f, f) *Rundfunk*, *TV*: Moderation f.

‚pres·ent·'day adj heutig, gegenwärtig.

pre·sent·er [prɪ'zentə] s *Rundfunk*, *TV*: *Br.* Moderator(in).

pre·sen·ti·ment [prɪ'zentɪmənt] s (böse) Vorahnung.

pres·ent·ly ['prezntlɪ] adv **1.** in Kürze, bald. **2.** bsd. Am. gegenwärtig, derzeit.

pres·er·va·tion [‚prezə'veɪʃn] s **1.** Bewahrung f; Erhaltung f: *in a good state of* ~ gut erhalten; *there is a* ~ *order on this building* bsd. Br. dieses Gebäude steht unter Denkmalschutz. **2.** Konservierung f. **pre·serv·a·tive** [prɪ'zɜːvətɪv] s Konservierungsmittel n.

pre·serve [prɪ'zɜːv] **I** v/t **1.** bewahren, (be)schützen (*from* vor dat). **2.** bewahren, erhalten. **3.** konservieren, *Obst* etc einmachen, -kochen. **II** s **4.** mst pl Eingemachte n: *strawberry* ~s eingemachte Erdbeeren pl. **5.** (*Jagd*)Revier n. **6.** fig. Revier n, Ressort n.

pre·side [prɪ'zaɪd] v/i den Vorsitz führen od. haben (*at, over* bei): ~ *at a meeting* a. e-e Versammlung leiten.

pres·i·den·cy ['prezɪdənsɪ] s pol. Präsidentschaft f; Amtszeit f (*e-s Präsidenten*). **'pres·i·dent** s **1.** Präsident(in) (*a. pol.*). **2.** Vorsitzende m, f. **3.** univ. bsd. Am. Rektor(in). **pres·i·den·tial** [‚prezɪ'denʃl] adj pol. Präsidenten..., Präsidentschafts...

press [pres] **I** v/t **1.** drücken, pressen: ~ *s.o.'s hand* j-m die Hand drücken. **2.** drücken auf (*e-n Knopf* etc), *Pedal* etc niederdrücken. **3.** *Frucht* (aus)pressen. **4.** *Schallplatte* pressen. **5.** bügeln; *Blumen* pressen. **6.** (zurück- etc)drängen: ~ *back*. **7.** j-n (be)drängen (*to do* zu tun): *be* ~*ed for time* unter Zeitdruck stehen, in Zeitnot sein. **8.** ~ *s.th. on s.o.* j-m et. aufdrängen od. -nötigen. **9.** bestehen auf (*dat*): ~ *the point* darauf bestehen; ~ *home* Forderung etc durchsetzen; *Vorteil* ausnützen. **II** v/i **10.** drücken. **11.** drängen (*Zeit* etc): ~ *for* drängen auf (*acc*). **12.** (sich) (*vorwärts- etc*)drängen: ~ *forward*; ~ *on* (*od. ahead*) fig. weitermachen (*with* mit). **III** s **13.** (*Frucht*-etc)Presse f; Spanner m (*für Tennisschläger* etc). **14.** (*Drucker*)Presse f: *be in* (*the*) ~ in Druck sein; *go to* ~ in Druck gehen. **15.** *give s.th. a* ~ et.

drücken. **16.** Presse f: *have a good* (*bad*) ~ e-e gute (schlechte) Presse haben. ~ **a·gen·cy** s Presseagentur f. ~ **box** s Pressetribüne f: *in the* ~ auf der Pressetribüne. ~ **card** s Presseausweis m. ~ **clip·ping** s bsd. Am. Zeitungsausschnitt m. ~ **con·fer·ence** s Pressekonferenz f: *at a* ~ auf e-r Pressekonferenz. ~ **cut·ting** s bsd. Br. Zeitungsausschnitt m. ~ **gal·ler·y** s parl. Pressetribüne f: *in the* ~ auf der Pressetribüne.

press·ing ['presɪŋ] adj □ **1.** dringend. **2.** eindringlich.

press| **pho·tog·ra·pher** s Pressefotograf(in). ~ **stud** s bsd. Br. Druckknopf m. **'~-up** s Liegestütz m: *do a* ~ e-n Liegestütz machen.

pres·sure ['preʃə] **I** s phys., ◎, etc Druck m: *under* ~ fig. unter Druck; *bring* ~ *to bear on, put* ~ *on* fig. Druck ausüben auf (*acc*); *work at high* ~ fig. mit Hochdruck arbeiten. **II** v/t bsd. Am. → **pressurize 2.** ~ **cab·in** s ✈ Druck(ausgleichs)kabine f. ~ **cook·er** s Schnellkochtopf m. ~ **group** s pol. Interessengruppe f. **'~-,sen·si·tive** adj □ ✍ etc druckempfindlich.

pres·sur·ize ['preʃəraɪz] v/t **1.** ~*d cabin* → **pressure cabin. 2.** fig. bsd. Br. j-n unter Druck setzen (*to do s.th.* damit er et. tut): ~ *s.o. into doing s.th.* j-n so lange unter Druck setzen, bis er et. tut.

pres·tige [pre'stiːʒ] s Prestige n, Ansehen n. **pres·tig·ious** [pre'stɪdʒəs] adj □ renommiert.

pres·to ['prestəʊ] adv: *hey* ~ Hokuspokus (Fidibus).

pre·sum·a·ble [prɪ'zjuːməbl] adj □ vermutlich. **pre·sume I** v/t **1.** annehmen, vermuten. **2.** sich erdreisten od. anmaßen (*to do* zu tun). **II** v/i **3.** → **1. 4.** anmaßend od. aufdringlich sein: ~ *on* et. ausnützen od. mißbrauchen. **pre-'sum·ing** adj □ anmaßend.

pre·sump·tion [prɪ'zʌmpʃn] s **1.** Annahme f, Vermutung f. **2.** Anmaßung f. **pre·'sump·tu·ous** [~t∫ʊəs] adj □ anmaßend.

pre·sup·pose [‚priːsə'pəʊz] v/t voraussetzen (*that* daß). **pre·sup·po·si·tion** [‚priːsʌpə'zɪʃn] s Voraussetzung f.

pre·tence [prɪ'tens] s **1.** Heuchelei f, Verstellung f: *his friendliness is only* ~ s-e Freundlichkeit ist nur gespielt;

make a ~ *of doing s.th.* so tun, als tue man et. **2.** *under false* ~*s* unter falschen Voraussetzungen. **3.** Anspruch *m* (*to* auf *acc*): **make no** ~ **to** keinen Anspruch erheben auf.

pre·tend [pri'tend] **I** *v/t* **1.** vorgeben, -schützen, -täuschen: ~ *sleep* (*od. to be asleep*) sich schlafend stellen. **2.** behaupten (*to do* zu tun). **II** *v/i* **3.** sich verstellen: *he's only* ~*ing* er tut nur so. **4.** Anspruch erheben (*to* auf *acc*). **pre·tend·ed** *adj* vorgetäuscht, gespielt.

pre·tense *Am.* → **pretence**.

pre·ten·sion [pri'tenʃn] *s* **1.** *oft pl* Anspruch *m* (*to* auf *acc*): **make no** ~*s to* keinen Anspruch erheben auf. **2.** Anmaßung *f*.

pre·ten·tious [pri'tenʃəs] *adj* □ anmaßend. **pre·ten·tious·ness** *s* Anmaßung *f*.

pret·er·ite ['pretərət] *s ling.* Präteritum *n*, (erste) Vergangenheit.

pre·text ['pri:tekst] *s* Vorwand *m*: *on* (*od. under*) *the* ~ unter dem Vorwand (*of doing* zu tun).

pret·ty ['priti] **I** *adj* □ hübsch, *iro. a.* schön: → **penny.** **II** *adv* F ziemlich, ganz schön: ~ *cold;* ~ *good* recht *od.* ganz gut; ~ *much the same thing* so ziemlich dasselbe; *be sitting* ~ F (*finanziell etc*) gut dastehen.

pre·vail [pri'veil] *v/i* **1.** vorherrschen, weit verbreitet sein. **2.** (*over, against*) siegen (über *acc*), sich durchsetzen (gegen). **3.** ~ *on s.o. to do s.th.* j-n dazu bewegen, et. zu tun. **pre·vail·ing** *adj* (vor)herrschend.

prev·a·lence ['prevələns] *s* Vorherrschen *n,* weite Verbreitung. **'prev·a·lent** *adj* □ vorherrschend, weitverbreitet.

pre·var·i·cate [pri'værikeit] *v/i* Ausflüchte machen. **pre·var·i·ca·tion** *s* Ausflucht *f.*

pre·vent [pri'vent] *v/t* **1.** verhindern, -hüten, *e-r Sache* vorbeugen. **2.** (*from*) *j-n* hindern (an *dat*), abhalten (von): ~ *s.o.* (*from*) *doing s.th.* j-n (daran) hindern *od.* davon abhalten, et. zu tun. **pre·ven·tion** *s* (*of*) Verhinderung *f,* -hütung *f* (von), Vorbeugung *f* (gegen): ~ *of accidents* Unfallverhütung; ~ *is better than cure* Vorbeugen ist besser

als Heilen. **pre·ven·tive** *adj* vorbeugend.

pre·view ['pri:vju:] *s* **1.** *Film, TV:* Voraufführung *f;* Vorbesichtigung *f* (*e-r Ausstellung etc*), *paint.* Vernissage *f.* **2.** *Film, TV, a. allg.* Vorschau *f* (*of* auf *acc*).

pre·vi·ous ['pri:vjəs] *adj* **1.** vorher-, vorausgehend, vorherig: ~ *conviction* 🏛 Vorstrafe *f;* *have a* ~ *conviction* vorbestraft sein; *on the* ~ *day* am Tag davor, am Vortag; *on a* ~ *occasion* bei e-r früheren Gelegenheit; ~ *owner* Vorbesitzer(in). **2.** ~ *to* vor (*dat*): ~ *to doing s.th.* bevor man et. tut. **'pre·vi·ous·ly** *adv* früher, vorher.

pre·war [,pri:'wɔ:] *adj* Vorkriegs...

prey [prei] **I** *s* Beute *f,* Opfer *n* (*e-s Raubtiers; a. fig.*): *be easy* ~ *for* (*od. to*) e-e leichte Beute sein für; → **beast** 1, **bird** 1. **II** *v/i*: ~ *on* a) *zo.* Jagd machen auf (*acc*), b) *fig.* nagen an (*dat*): ~ *on s.o.'s mind* j-m keine Ruhe lassen, c) *fig.* j-n ausnehmen.

price [prais] **I** *s* **1.** Preis *m* (*a. fig.*), (*Börse*) Kurs *m: what is the* ~ *of ...?* was *od.* wieviel kostet ...?; *at the* ~ *of* zum Preis von; *at a ... price* Preis zu e-m *günstigen etc* Preis; *at a* ~ für entsprechendes Geld; (*not*) *at any* ~ *bsd. fig.* um jeden (keinen) Preis; *be above* (*od. beyond, without*) ~ *fig.* unbezahlbar sein; *pay a high* ~ *for fig.* e-n hohen Preis bezahlen für; *put a* ~ *on s.o.'s head* e-n Preis auf j-s Kopf aussetzen. **2.** *Wetten:* Quote *f.* **II** *v/t* **3.** den Preis festsetzen für; auszeichnen (*at* mit). **4.** F nach dem Preis (*gen*) fragen. **'~-con·scious** *adj* □ preisbewußt. **'~-con·trolled** *adj* preisgebunden. ~ *cut* *s* Preissenkung *f.* ~ *freeze* *s* Preisstopp *m.*

price·less ['praislis] *adj* unbezahlbar (*a. fig.*).

price| list *s* Preisliste *f.* ~ *range* *s* Preisklasse *f,* -kategorie *f.* ~ *tag,* ~ *tick·et* *s* Preisschild *n.*

pric·ey ['praisi] *adj* F teuer.

prick [prik] **I** *s* **1.** (*Insekten-, Nadel- etc*-) Stich *m;* Einstich *m.* **2.** stechender Schmerz, Stich *m:* ~*s pl of conscience fig.* Gewissensbisse *pl.* **3.** V Schwanz *m* (*Penis*). **4.** *fig.* V Arschloch *n.* **II** *v/t* **5.** (an-, auf-, durch)stechen, stechen in (*acc*): ~ *one's finger* sich in den Finger stechen (**on** an *dat*; **with** mit); *his conscience ~ed him fig.* er hatte Gewissensbisse. **6.** prickeln auf *od.* in (*dat*). **7.** **~ up one's ears** die Ohren spitzen (*a. fig.*). **III** *v/i* **8.** stechen (*a. schmerzen*).

prick·le ['prɪkl] **I** *s* **1.** Stachel *m*, & *a.* Dorn *m.* **2.** Prickeln *n*, Kribbeln *n.* **II** *v/i* **3.** prickeln, kribbeln. '**prick·ly** *adj* **1.** stach(e)lig, & *a.* dornig. **2.** prickelnd, kribbelnd. **3.** *fig.* unangenehm.

'**pric·y** → **pricey.**

pride [praɪd] *s* Stolz *m* (*a. Gegenstand des Stolzes*); *b.s.* Hochmut *m*: *take* (*a*) *~ in →* **II.** **II** *v/t*: *~ o.s. on* stolz sein auf (*acc*).

priest [pri:st] *s eccl.* Priester *m.* **priest·hood** ['~hʊd] *s* **1.** Priesteramt *n*, -würde *f.* **2.** *coll.* Priesterschaft *f.* '**priest·ly** *adj* priesterlich.

prig [prɪg] *s* Tugendbold *m.* '**prig·gish** *adj* □ tugendhaft.

prim [prɪm] *adj* □ *a.* **~ and proper** etepetete; prüde.

pri·ma·cy ['praɪməsɪ] *s* Vorrang *m* (*over* vor *dat*); Vorrangstellung *f.*

pri·mae·val *bsd. Br.* → **primeval.**

pri·mal ['praɪml] *adj* **1.** ursprünglich, Ur... **2.** → **primary 1.**

pri·ma·ri·ly ['praɪmərəlɪ] *adv* in erster Linie, vor allem. '**pri·ma·ry I** *adj* **1.** wichtigst, Haupt...: *~ accent* (*od. stress*) *ling.* Hauptakzent *m*; *of ~ importance* von höchster Wichtigkeit. **2.** Anfangs..., Ur... **3.** grundlegend, elementar, Grund...: *~ colo(u)r* Grundfarbe *f.* **II** *s* **4.** *pol. Am.* Vorwahl *f.*

prime [praɪm] **I** *adj* □ **1.** wichtigst, Haupt...: *of ~ importance* von höchster Wichtigkeit; *~ minister* Premierminister(in), Ministerpräsident(in); *~ mover* ⊚ Kraft-, Antriebsmaschine *f*; *fig.* treibende Kraft; *~ suspect* Hauptverdächtige *m*, *f*; *~ time TV* Haupteinschaltzeit *f.* **2.** erstklassig: *in ~ condition* in Bestzustand. **3.** *~ number →* **5.** **II** *s* **4.** *in the ~ of life* in der Blüte s-r Jahre; *be past one's ~* s-e besten Jahre hinter sich haben; (*Künstler etc*) den Zenit überschritten haben. **5.** & Primzahl *f.* **III** *v/t* **6.** grundieren. **7.** *j-n* instruieren, vorbereiten.

prim·er¹ ['praɪmə] *s* **1.** Grundierfarbe *f*, -lack *m.* **2.** ✕ *etc* Zünder *m.*

prim·er² [~] *s* Fibel *f.*

pri·me·val [praɪ'mi:vl] *adj* □ urzeitlich, Ur...: *~ forest* Urwald *m.*

prim·i·tive ['prɪmɪtɪv] *adj* □ primitiv (*a. contp.*).

pri·mor·di·al [praɪ'mɔːdjəl] *adj* □ uranfänglich, ursprünglich.

prim·rose *s* & Primel *f*, *bsd.* Schlüsselblume *f.*

prim·u·la ['prɪmjʊlə] *s* & Primel *f.*

prince [prɪns] *s* **1.** Fürst *m.* **2.** Prinz *m*: ♀ *Charming fig.* Märchenprinz; *~ consort.* '**prince·ly** *adj* fürstlich (*a. fig.*). **prin·cess** [~'ses, *vor npr* '~ses] *s* **1.** Fürstin *f.* **2.** Prinzessin *f.*

prin·ci·pal ['prɪnsəpl] **I** *adj* (□ → *principally*) **1.** wichtigst, hauptsächlich, Haupt...: *~ character* Hauptfigur *f*, -person *f* (*e-s Dramas*); *~ parts pl ling.* Stammformen *pl* (*e-s Verbs*). **II** *s* **2.** *ped.* Rektor(in). **3.** *thea.* Hauptdarsteller(in); ♪ Solist(in).

prin·ci·pal·i·ty [‚prɪnsɪ'pælətɪ] *s* Fürstentum *n.*

prin·ci·pal·ly ['prɪnsəplɪ] *adv* in erster Linie, hauptsächlich.

prin·ci·ple ['prɪnsəpl] *s* **1.** Prinzip *n*, Grundsatz *m*: *man of ~s* Mann *m* mit Grundsätzen; *in ~* im Prinzip, an sich; *on ~* prinzipiell, grundsätzlich; *~ of efficiency* Leistungsprinzip. **2.** *phys. etc* Prinzip *n*, (Natur)Gesetz *n.*

print [prɪnt] **I** *v/t* **1.** *typ.* drucken: *~ed matter* ♥ Drucksache *f.* **2.** *Rede etc* abdrucken. **3.** *Stoff etc* bedrucken. **4.** in Druckbuchstaben schreiben: *~ed characters pl* Druckbuchstaben *pl.* **5.** *a. ~ off phot.* abziehen; *~ out* ausdrucken (*Computer*). **II** *v/i* **6.** *typ.* drucken. **7.** *be ~ing* im Druck sein. **8.** & (*Finger- etc*)Abdruck *m.* **9.** *typ.* Druck *m*: *out of ~* vergriffen; *in ~* gedruckt; *~ run* Auflage *f.* **10.** Gedruckte *n*: → *small* I. **11.** *Kunst:* Druck *m*; *phot.* Abzug *m.* '**print·a·ble** *adj* druckfähig, -reif. '**print·er** *s* Drucker *m* (*a. Gerät*): *~'s error* Druckfehler *m*; *~'s ink* Druckerschwärze *f.* '**print·ing** *s* **1.** *typ.* Drucken *n*: *~ ink* Druckerschwärze *f*; *~ press* Druck(er)presse *f*; *~ works pl* (*oft sg konstruiert*) Druckerei *f.* **2.** Auflage *f.* '**print·out** *s Computer:* Ausdruck *m.*

pri·or ['praɪə] *adj* **1.** vorherig, früher. **2.** vorrangig. **3.** *~ to* vor (*dat*). **pri·or·i·tize** [~'ɒrətaɪz] *v/t* den Vorrang geben (*dat*), vorrangig behandeln. **pri'or·i·ty** *s* **1.** Priorität *f*, Vorrang *m*: *give* ~ *to* → **prioritize**; *have* (*od.* *take*) ~ den Vorrang haben (*over od. dat*), vorgehen. **2.** vordringliche *od.* vorrangige Sache: *a top* ~ e-e Angelegenheit von äußerster Dringlichkeit. **3.** *mot.* Vorfahrt *f*: *have* ~.

prise *bsd. Br.* → **prize²**.

prism ['prɪzəm] *s* ♉, *phys. etc* Prisma *n*. **pris·mat·ic** [~'mætɪk] *adj* (~*ally*) prismatisch, Prismen-.

pris·on ['prɪzn] *s* Gefängnis *n*: *be in* ~ im Gefängnis sein *od.* sitzen, einsitzen; ~ *cell* Gefängniszelle *f*; ~ *sentence* Gefängnis-, Freiheitsstrafe *f*. **'pris·on·er** *s* Gefangene *m*, *f*, Häftling *m*: *hold* (*od.* *keep*) ~ gefangenhalten; *take* ~ gefangennehmen; ~ *of war* Kriegsgefangene; → *bar* 8.

pris·sy ['prɪsɪ] *adj* □ F etepetete, zimperlich.

pri·va·cy ['prɪvəsɪ] *s* **1.** Ungestörtheit *f*: *there is no* ~ *here* hier ist man nie ungestört. **2.** Geheimhaltung *f*: *in strict* ~ streng vertraulich.

pri·vate ['praɪvɪt] **I** *adj* □ **1.** privat, Privat...: ~ (*limited*) *company* ✝ *Br.* Gesellschaft *f* mit beschränkter Haftung; ~ *detective* Privatdetektiv(in); ~ *lessons pl* Privatunterricht *m*; ~ *life* Privatleben *n*; ~ *matter* Privatangelegenheit *f*; ~ *patient Br.* Privatpatient(in); ~ *school* Privatschule *f*; ~*ly owned* in Privatbesitz. **2.** ungestört (*Ort*): *be a very* ~ *person* sehr zurückgezogen leben. **3.** geheim; vertraulich: *keep s.th.* ~ et. geheimhalten *od.* vertraulich behandeln. **4.** ~ *soldier* → 6. **II** *s* **5.** *in* ~ privat; unter vier Augen. **6.** ✗ Gefreite *m*.

pri·va·tion [praɪ'veɪʃn] *s* Entbehrung *f*.

pri·vat·ize ['praɪvɪtaɪz] *v/t staatlichen Betrieb etc* privatisieren.

priv·i·lege ['prɪvɪlɪdʒ] **I** *s* Privileg *n*, Vorrecht *n*; (*besondere*) Ehre. **II** *v/t* privilegieren, bevorrechtigen: *be* ~*d* den Vorzug genießen (*to do* zu tun).

priv·y ['prɪvɪ] *adj*: *be* ~ *to* eingeweiht sein in (*acc*).

prize¹ [praɪz] **I** *s* **1.** (Sieger-, Sieges)Preis *m*; (*Lotterie- etc*)Gewinn *m*. **II** *adj* **2.** preisgekrönt. **3.** F *contp.* Riesen...: ~

idiot Vollidiot *m*. **III** *v/t* **4.** (hoch)schätzen.

prize² [~] *v/t*: ~ *open* aufbrechen, -stemmen.

'prize|·win·ner *s* Preisträger(in); Gewinner(in). **'~·win·ning** *adj* preisgekrönt: ~ *ticket* Gewinnlos *n*.

pro¹ [prəʊ] *pl* **pros** *s* **1.** Ja-Stimme *f*. **2.** *the* ~*s and cons pl* das Für u. Wider, das Pro u. Kontra.

pro² [~] F **I** *pl* **pros** *s* Profi *m*. **II** *adj* Profi-.

prob·a·bil·i·ty [ˌprɒbə'bɪlətɪ] *s* Wahrscheinlichkeit *f*: *in all* ~ aller Wahrscheinlichkeit nach, höchstwahrscheinlich. **'prob·a·ble** *adj* □ wahrscheinlich.

pro·ba·tion [prə'beɪʃn] *s* Probe(zeit) *f*; ⚖ Bewährung(sfrist) *f*: *he's still on* ~ er ist noch in der Probezeit; *put s.o. on* ~ (*for two years*) j-s (Rest)Strafe (auf zwei Jahre) zur Bewährung aussetzen; ~ *officer* Bewährungshelfer(in). **pro'ba·tion·ar·y** *adj*: ~ *period* Probezeit *f*; ⚖ Bewährungsfrist *f*. **pro'ba·tion·er** *s* **1.** Lernschwester *f*. **2.** ⚖ j-d, dessen (Rest)Strafe zur Bewährung ausgesetzt wurde.

probe [prəʊb] **I** *s* **1.** ✗, ⊚ Sonde *f*. **2.** *fig.* Untersuchung *f* (*into gen*). **II** *v/t* **3.** ✗ sondieren. **4.** *fig.* erforschen, (gründlich) untersuchen. **III** *v/i* **5.** ~ *into* → II.

prob·lem ['prɒbləm] *s* **1.** Problem *n*: *without any* ~ (völlig) problemlos; ~ *child* Problemkind *n*; ~ *drinker euphem.* Alkoholiker(in). **2.** ♉ *etc* Aufgabe *f*: *do a* ~ e-e Aufgabe lösen. **prob·lem·at·ic** [ˌ~blə'mætɪk] *adj* (~*ally*) problematisch.

pro·ce·dur·al [prə'siːdʒərəl] *adj* □ Verfahrens..., verfahrenstechnisch; ⚖ verfahrensrechtlich. **pro'ce·dure** *s* Verfahren(sweise *f*) *n*, Vorgehen *n*.

pro·ceed [prə'siːd] *v/i* **1.** (weiter)gehen, (-)fahren; sich begeben (*to* nach, zu). **2.** *fig.* weitergehen (*Handlung etc*). **3.** *fig.* fortfahren (*with* mit): ~ *with one's work* s-e Arbeit fortsetzen. **4.** *fig.* vorgehen, verfahren: ~ *with* et. durchführen; ~ *to do s.th.* sich anschicken *od.* daranmachen, et. zu tun. **5.** ~ *from* herrühren *od.* kommen von. **6.** ~ *against* ⚖ (gerichtlich) vorgehen gegen. **pro'ceed·ing** *s* **1.** → **procedure**. **2.** *pl* Vorgänge *pl*, Geschehnisse *pl*. **3. start** (*od.* **take**) **~s against** → **proceed** 6.

pro·ceeds ['prəʊsiːdz] *s pl* Erlös *m*, Ertrag *m*, Einnahmen *pl*.

pro·cess ['prəʊses] **I** *s* Prozeß *m*: a) Verfahren *n*, b) Vorgang *m*: **in the ~** dabei; **be in ~** im Gange sein; **be in the ~ of doing s.th.** (gerade) dabei sein, et. zu tun; **~ of thinking** Denkprozeß. **II** *v/t* ⚙, *a.* Anträge *etc* bearbeiten; *Daten* verarbeiten; (*chemisch etc*) behandeln; *Film* entwickeln; *Lebensmittel* haltbar machen, *Milch etc* sterilisieren: **~ into** verarbeiten zu. **'pro·cess·ing** *s* Bearbeitung *f*: **~ industry** verarbeitende Industrie.

pro·ces·sion [prə'seʃn] *s* Prozession *f*; (Um)Zug *m*.

pro·ces·sor ['prəʊsesə] *s Computer:* Prozessor *m*; (*Wort-, Text*)Verarbeitungsgerät *n*.

pro·claim [prə'kleɪm] *v/t* proklamieren, verkünd(ig)en: **~ s.o. king** j-n zum König ausrufen. **proc·la·ma·tion** [ˌprɒkləˈmeɪʃn] *s* Proklamation *f*, Verkünd(ig)ung *f*.

pro·cliv·i·ty [prə'klɪvətɪ] *s* Neigung *f*, Hang *m* (**to, toward**[**s**] zu).

pro·cras·ti·nate [prəʊ'kræstɪneɪt] *v/i* zaudern, zögern.

pro·cre·ate ['prəʊkrieɪt] *biol.* **I** *v/t* zeugen. **II** *v/i* sich fortpflanzen. **pro·cre·'a·tion** *s* Zeugung *f*; Fortpflanzung *f*.

pro·cure [prə'kjʊə] *v/t* **1.** (sich) *et.* beschaffen *od.* besorgen: **~ s.o. s.th.** j-m et. beschaffen. **2.** verkuppeln (**for** *dat*). **pro'cure·ment** *s* Beschaffung *f*, Besorgung *f*. **2.** Verkupplung *f*. **pro'cur·er** *s* Kuppler *m*. **pro'cur·ess** *s* Kupplerin *f*.

prod [prɒd] **I** *v/t* **1.** stoßen: **~ s.o. in the ribs** j-m e-n Rippenstoß geben. **2.** *fig.* anspornen, anstacheln (**into** zu). **II** *v/i* **3.** stoßen (**at** nach). **III** *s* **4.** Stoß *m*: **~ in the ribs** Rippenstoß *m*.

prod·i·gal ['prɒdɪgl] **I** *adj* □ verschwenderisch: **be ~ of** verschwenderisch umgehen mit. **II** *s* Verschwender(in).

pro·di·gious [prə'dɪdʒəs] *adj* □ erstaunlich, großartig, wunderbar. **prod·i·gy** ['prɒdɪdʒɪ] *s* Wunder *n*: → **child prodigy, infant** II.

pro·duce¹ [prə'djuːs] *v/t* **1.** *allg.* erzeugen; ⚕ *Waren* produzieren, herstellen,

erzeugen; *Theaterstück etc* inszenieren; *Film* produzieren. **2.** ⚕ *Gewinn etc* (ein)bringen, abwerfen. **3.** *fig.* erzeugen, bewirken, hervorrufen, *Wirkung* erzielen. **4.** hervorziehen, -holen (**from** aus *der Tasche etc*); *Ausweis etc* (vor)zeigen, vorlegen; *Beweise, Zeugen etc* beibringen. **II** *v/i* **5.** produzieren: **begin to ~** die Produktion aufnehmen.

pro·duce² ['prɒdjuːs] *s* (*bsd. Agrar*)Produkt(e *pl*) *n*, (-)Erzeugnis(se *pl*) *n*.

pro·duc·er [prə'djuːsə] *s* **1.** Produzent (-in), Hersteller(in). **2.** *thea.* Regisseur (-in); (*Film*) Produzent(in).

prod·uct ['prɒdʌkt] *s* Produkt *n* (*a.* 🔢, 🧪, *fig.*), Erzeugnis *n*. **pro·duc·tion** [prə'dʌkʃn] *s* **1.** *allg.* Erzeugung *f*; ⚕ Produktion *f*, Herstellung *f*, Erzeugung *f*; *thea.* Inszenierung *f*; (*Film*) Produktion *f*: **go into** → ⚕ die Produktion aufnehmen; **in production** gehen; **~ line** Fertigungsstraße *f*, Fließband *n*. **2.** *fig.* Erzeugung *f*, Bewirkung *f*. **3.** Vorzeigen, -legen *n* (*e-s Ausweises etc*); Beibringung *f* (*von Beweisen, Zeugen etc*). **pro'duc·tive** *adj* □ produktiv (*a. fig.*), ergiebig, rentabel; *fig.* schöpferisch. **pro·duc·tiv·i·ty** [ˌprɒdʌk'tɪvətɪ] *s* Produktivität *f* (*a. fig.*), Ergiebigkeit *f*, Rentabilität *f*.

prof [prɒf] *s* F Prof *m* (*Professor*).

prof·a·na·tion [ˌprɒfə'neɪʃn] *s* Entweihung *f*. **pro·fane** [prə'feɪn] **I** *adj* □ **1.** weltlich, profan, Profan... **2.** (gottes)lästerlich. **II** *v/t* **3.** entweihen.

pro·fess [prə'fes] *v/t* **1.** vorgeben, -täuschen; behaupten (**to be** zu sein). **2.** erklären, bekunden: **~ o.s. (to be) satisfied** s-e Zufriedenheit bekunden. **pro'fessed** *adj* **1.** erklärt (*Gegner etc*). **2.** angeblich. **pro'fess·ed·ly** [ˌsɪdlɪ] *adv* **1.** erklärtermaßen. **2.** angeblich.

pro·fes·sion [prə'feʃn] *s* **1.** (*bsd. akademischer*) Beruf: **by ~** von Beruf. **2.** Berufsstand *m*: **the medical ~** die Ärzteschaft, die Mediziner *pl*. **pro'fes·sion·al** [ˌʃənl] *adj* □ **1.** Berufs..., beruflich. **2.** Fach..., fachlich. **3.** professionell, Berufs... (*beide a. Sport*): **turn ~** ins Profilager überwechseln. **4.** fachmännisch, gekonnt. **II** *s* **5.** Berufssportler(in), -spieler(in), Profi *m*. **6.** Fachmann *m*, Profi *m*. **pro'fes·sion·al·ism**

[~ʃnəlizəm] *s Sport:* Professionalismus *m (a. allg.),* Profitum *n.*

pro·fes·sor [prə'fesə] *s* Professor(in). **pro'fes·sor·ship** *s* Professur *f.*

prof·fer ['prɒfə] *v/t:* ~ *s.o. s.th.* j-m et. anbieten.

pro·fi·cien·cy [prə'fɪʃnsɪ] *s* Können *n,* Tüchtigkeit *f.* **pro'fi·cient** *adj* □ tüchtig (*at, in* in *dat*).

pro·file ['prəʊfaɪl] I *s* 1. *allg.* Profil *n:* *in* ~ im Profil; *keep a low* ~ *fig.* Zurückhaltung üben. 2. *fig.* Porträt *n.* II *v/t* 3. im Profil darstellen. 4. *fig.* porträtieren.

prof·it ['prɒfɪt] I *s* 1. Gewinn *m,* Profit *m:* *sell at a* ~ mit Gewinn verkaufen; ~ *margin* Gewinnspanne *f;* ~ *sharing* Gewinnbeteiligung *f.* 2. *fig.* Nutzen *m,* Vorteil *m:* *turn s.th. to* ~ aus et. Nutzen ziehen. II *v/i* 3. (*by, from*) Nutzen *od.* Gewinn ziehen (aus), profitieren (von). **'prof·it·a·ble** *adj* □ 1. gewinnbringend, einträglich, rentabel. 2. *fig.* vorteilhaft, nützlich. **prof·it·eer** [~'tɪə] *s* Profitmacher(in), (*Kriegs*)Gewinnler (-in). **,prof·it'eer·ing** *s* Wuchergeschäfte *pl.*

prof·li·gate ['prɒflɪgət] *adj* □ 1. lasterhaft, verworfen. 2. verschwenderisch.

pro·found [prə'faʊnd] *adj* □ 1. *fig.* tief (*Eindruck, Schweigen etc*). 2. tiefgründig, -sinnig. 3. völlig (*Blindheit etc*).

pro·fuse [prə'fjuːs] *adj* □ 1. üppig, (*Blutung*) stark. 2. (*oft* allzu) freigebig, verschwenderisch (*in, of* mit). **pro·fu·sion** [~'fjuːʒn] *s* Überfülle *f* (*of* an *dat*): *in* ~ in Hülle u. Fülle.

prog·no·sis [prɒg'nəʊsɪs] *pl* **-ses** [~siːz] *s* ✷, *a. allg.* Prognose *f.*

prog·nos·ti·cate [prɒg'nɒstɪkeɪt] *v/t* voraus-, vorhersagen, *bsd.* ✷ prognostizieren.

pro·gram ['prəʊgræm] I *s* 1. *Computer:* Programm *n.* 2. *Am.* → *programme* 1. II *pret u. pp* **-grammed,** *Am. a.* **-gramed** 3. *Computer* programmieren. 4. *Am.* → *programme* 3.

pro·gram·er, pro·gram·ing *Am.* → **programmer, programming.**

pro·gramme ['prəʊgræm] I *s* 1. *allg.* Programm *n,* (*Rundfunk, TV a.*) Sendung *f:* *be on the* ~ auf dem Programm stehen. 2. *Br.* → *program* 1. II *v/t* 3. ein Programm aufstellen für. 4. *Br.* → *program* 3.

pro·gram·mer ['prəʊgræmə] *s Computer:* Programmierer(in). **'pro·gram·ming** *adj:* ~ *language* Programmiersprache *f.*

pro·gress I *s* ['prəʊgres] 1. *make slow* ~ (nur) langsam vorankommen. 2. *fig.* Fortschritt(e *pl*) *m:* *make* ~ → 6. 3. *be in* ~ im Gange sein. II *v/i* [prəʊ'gres] 4. sich vorwärts bewegen. 5. *fig.* fortschreiten: *as the day* ~*ed* im Laufe des Tages. 6. *fig.* Fortschritte machen.

pro·gres·sion [prəʊ'greʃn] *s Steuer:* Progression *f,* A *a.* Reihe *f.* **pro'gres·sive** [~sɪv] *adj* □ 1. progressiv, fortschrittlich. 2. fortschreitend, ✷ *a.* progressiv. 3. *ling.* progressiv (*a. Steuern*): ~ *form* Verlaufsform *f.*

pro·hib·it [prə'hɪbɪt] *v/t* 1. *et.* verbieten, untersagen: ~ *s.o. from doing s.th.* j-m verbieten *od.* untersagen, et. zu tun. 2. *et.* verhindern: ~ *s.o. from doing s.th.* j-n daran hindern, et. zu tun. **pro·hi·bi·tion** [,prəʊɪ'bɪʃn] *s* Verbot *n:* ~ *of smoking* Rauchverbot; *the* ⌂ *hist. Am.* die Prohibition. **pro·hib·i·tive** [prə'hɪbɪtɪv] *adj* □ unerschwinglich (*Preis*).

proj·ect [1] ['prɒdʒekt] *s* Projekt *n,* Vorhaben *n.*

pro·ject² [prə'dʒekt] I *v/t* 1. werfen, schleudern: ~ *into space* in den Weltraum schießen. 2. planen, in Aussicht nehmen. 3. *Bild etc* projizieren, werfen (*onto* auf *acc*). II *v/i* 4. vorspringen, -stehen, (*Ohren*) abstehen.

pro·jec·tile [prəʊ'dʒektaɪl] *s* Projektil *n,* Geschoß *n.*

pro·jec·tion [prə'dʒekʃn] *s* 1. Vorsprung *m,* vorspringender Teil. 2. Werfen *n,* Schleudern *n.* 3. Planung *f.* 4. Projektion *f.* **pro'jec·tion·ist** *s* Filmvorführer(in). **pro'jec·tor** *s* Projektor *m.*

pro·le·tar·i·an [,prəʊlɪ'teərɪən] I *adj* proletarisch, Proletarier... II *s* Proletarier(in). **pro·le'tar·i·at** [~rɪət] *s* Proletariat *n.*

pro·lif·e·rate [prəʊ'lɪfəreɪt] *v/i* sich stark *od.* schnell vermehren. **pro,lif·er'a·tion** *s* starke *od.* schnelle Vermehrung.

pro·lif·ic [prəʊ'lɪfɪk] *adj* □ (~*ally*) *biol.* fruchtbar, (*Schriftsteller etc a.*) (sehr) produktiv.

pro·lix ['prəʊlɪks] *adj* □ weitschweifig.

pro·log *Am.* → **prologue.**

pro·logue ['prəʊlɒg] s Prolog m; fig. Auftakt m (**to** zu).

pro·long [prəʊ'lɒŋ] v/t Aufenthalt etc verlängern (**by** um), Diskussion etc in die Länge ziehen, ✝ Wechsel prolongieren. **pro'longed** adj anhaltend (Applaus etc), länger (Abwesenheit etc). **pro·lon·ga·tion** [ˌ~geɪʃn] s Verlängerung f, ✝ Prolongierung f.

prom [prɒm] bsd. Br. F → promenade I, promenade concert.

prom·e·nade [ˌprɒmə'nɑːd] I s (Strand-) Promenade f. II v/i u. v/t promenieren (auf dat). ~ **con·cert** s Konzert in ungezwungener Atmosphäre. ~ **deck** s ♻ Promenadendeck n.

prom·i·nence ['prɒmɪnəns] s 1. Vorsprung m, vorstehender Teil. 2. fig. Prominenz f, Bekannt-, Berühmtheit f: **come into** (od. **rise to**) ~ bekannt od. berühmt werden. '**prom·i·nent** adj □ 1. vorspringend, (a. Zähne etc) vorstehend. 2. fig. prominent, bekannt, berühmt.

prom·is·cu·i·ty [ˌprɒmɪ'skjuːətɪ] s häufiger Partnerwechsel. **pro·mis·cu·ous** [prə'mɪskjʊəs] adj □ (sexuell) ausschweifend (Leben): ~ **girl** Mädchen, das häufig den Partner wechselt; **be** ~ häufig den Partner wechseln.

prom·ise ['prɒmɪs] I s 1. Versprechen n: **a** ~ **is a** ~ versprochen ist versprochen; **make a** ~ ein Versprechen geben; **breach of** ~ Wortbruch m. 2. fig. Hoffnung f, Aussicht f (**of** auf acc): **show great** ~ zu den besten Hoffnungen berechtigen. II v/t 3. versprechen (a. fig.): **I** ~ **you** ich warne dich; → moon I. III v/i 4. es versprechen. '**prom·is·ing** adj □ vielversprechend.

prom·on·to·ry ['prɒməntrɪ] s Vorgebirge n.

pro·mote [prə'məʊt] v/t 1. j-n befördern, ped. versetzen: **be** ~**d** (Sport) aufsteigen (**to** in acc); **be** ~**d to** (**the rank of**) **general**, **be** ~**d general** zum General befördert werden. 2. Boxkampf, Konzert etc veranstalten. 3. ✝ werben für. 4. et. fördern: ~ **health** gesundheitsförderlich sein. **pro'mot·er** s 1. Promoter(in), Veranstalter(in). 2. → **sales promoter**. **pro'mo·tion** s 1. Beförderung f, ped. Versetzung f, (Sport) Aufstieg m: **get** ~ befördert werden;

chances pl **of** ~, ~ **prospects** pl Aufstiegschancen pl. 2. Veranstaltung f. 3. ✝ Werbung f: → sales promotion.

prompt [prɒmpt] I adj □ 1. prompt, unverzüglich, umgehend: **be** ~ **to do** (od. **in doing**) s.th. et. schnell tun. 2. pünktlich: ~**ly at two o'clock** pünktlich um od. Punkt zwei Uhr. II adv 3. **at two o'clock** ~ F pünktlich um od. Punkt zwei Uhr. III v/t 3. führen zu, Gefühle etc wecken. 5. j-n veranlassen (**to do** zu tun). 6. j-m ein-, vorsagen; thea. j-m soufflieren. IV s 7. thea. Souffliéren n: ~ **box** Souffleurkasten m. '**prompt·er** s thea. Souffleur m, Souffleuse f. **promp·ti·tude** ['~tɪtjuːd], '**prompt·ness** s Promptheit f, Pünktlichkeit f.

pro·mul·gate ['prɒmlgeɪt] v/t 1. Gesetz etc verkünd(ig)en. 2. Lehre etc verbreiten. **pro·mul·ga·tion** s 1. Verkünd(ig)ung f. 2. Verbreitung f.

prone [prəʊn] adj □ 1. auf dem Bauch od. mit dem Gesicht nach unten liegend: ~ **position** Bauchlage f. 2. **be** ~ **to** fig. neigen zu, anfällig sein für: **be** ~ **to colds** erkältungsanfällig sein; **be** ~ **to do** s.th. dazu neigen, et. zu tun. '**prone·ness** s (**to**) Neigung f (zu), Anfälligkeit f (für).

prong [prɒŋ] s Zacke f, Zinke f (e-r Gabel); (Geweih)Sprosse f.

pro·noun ['prəʊnaʊn] s ling. Pronomen n, Fürwort n.

pro·nounce [prə'naʊns] I v/t 1. aussprechen. 2. erklären für od. zu 3. Urteil verkünden. II v/i 4. Stellung nehmen (**on** zu): ~ **in favo(u)r of** (od. **for**) (**against**) s.th. sich für (gegen) et. aussprechen. **pro'nounced** adj 1. bestimmt, entschieden (Ansicht etc). 2. ausgesprochen, -geprägt, deutlich. **pro'nounce·ment** s 1. Erklärung f. 2. (Urteils)Verkündung f.

pron·to ['prɒntəʊ] adv F fix, schnell.

pro·nun·ci·a·tion [prəˌnʌnsɪ'eɪʃn] s Aussprache f.

proof [pruːf] I s 1. Beweis(e pl) m, Nachweis m: **as** (od. **in**) ~ **of** als od. zum Beweis für (od. gen); **give** ~ **of** et. be- od. nachweisen; ~ **of age** Altersnachweis; → contrary 6. 2. Probe f (a. ♟), Prüfung f: **put to the** ~ auf die Probe stellen. II adj 3. (**against**) geschützt (vor *dat*), undurchlässig (für); *fig.* unempfindlich (gegen), unempfänglich (für): → **heatproof, waterproof** I, *etc.* III *v/t* **4.** imprägnieren. **'~,read·er** *s* Korrektor(in).

prop¹ [prɒp] I *s* Stütze *f* (*a. fig.*): **be a ~ to s.o.** j-m e-e Stütze *od.* ein Halt sein. II *v/t a.* **~ up** (ab)stützen: **~ up** *fig.* stützen; **~ against** lehnen gegen *od.* an (*acc*).

prop² [~] *s thea. etc* Requisit *n*.

prop·a·gan·da [ˌprɒpə'gændə] *s* Propaganda *f.* **ˌprop·a'gan·dist** *s* Propagandist(in).

prop·a·gate ['prɒpəgeɪt] I *v/i biol.* sich fortpflanzen *od.* vermehren. II *v/t* verbreiten, propagieren. **ˌprop·a'ga·tion** *s* **1.** Fortpflanzung *f*, Vermehrung *f.* **2.** Verbreitung *f*, Propagierung *f.*

pro·pane ['prəʊpeɪn] *s* 🜓 Propan(gas) *n.*

pro·pel [prə'pel] *v/t* (an)treiben. **pro·'pel·lant, pro'pel·lent** *s* Treibstoff *m*; Treibgas *n.* **pro'pel·ler** *s* ✈ Propeller *m*, ♣ *a.* Schraube *f.* **pro'pel·ling** *adj*: **~ pencil** *Br.* Drehbleistift *m.*

pro·pen·si·ty [prə'pensətɪ] *s* Hang *m*, Neigung *f* (**for, to** zu): **have a ~ for doing** (*od.* **to do**) **s.th.** dazu neigen, et. zu tun.

prop·er ['prɒpə] *adj* **1.** richtig, passend, geeignet: **in ~ form** in gebührender *od.* angemessener Form; **in the ~ place** am rechten Platz; **in ~ time** rechtzeitig. **2.** echt, wirklich, richtig: **~ fraction** echter Bruch. **3.** anständig, schicklich (*Benehmen etc*). **4.** *oft nachgestellt:* eigentlich. **5.** eigen(tümlich) (**to** *dat*). **6.** *noun* (*od.* **name**) *ling.* Eigenname *m.* **7.** F richtig (*Feigling etc*), anständig, gehörig (*Tracht Prügel etc*). **'prop·er·ly** *adv* richtig (*etc*, → **proper**): **~ speaking** eigentlich, genau-, strenggenommen.

prop·er·ty ['prɒpətɪ] *s* **1.** Eigentum *n*, Besitz *m*: **be s.o.'s ~** j-m gehören; **intellectual ~** geistiges Eigentum; **lost ~** Fundsachen *pl*; **lost ~ office** *Br.* Fundbüro *n.* **2.** Land-, Grundbesitz *m*; Grundstück *n.* **3.** *phys. etc* Eigenschaft *f.* **4.** *thea. etc* Requisit *n.*

proph·e·cy ['prɒfɪsɪ] *s* Prophezeiung *f.* **proph·e·sy** ['~saɪ] *v/t* prophezeien.

proph·et ['prɒfɪt] *s* Prophet *m*: **~ of doom** Schwarzseher *m.* **'proph·et·ess** *s* Prophetin *f.* **pro·phet·ic** [prə'fetɪk] *adj* (**~ally**) prophetisch.

pro·phy·lac·tic [ˌprɒfɪ'læktɪk] I *adj* (**~ally**) **1.** *bsd.* 🜚 prophylaktisch, vorbeugend. II *s* 🜚 Prophylaktikum *n*, vorbeugendes Mittel. **3.** Präservativ *n.* **ˌpro·phy'lax·is** [~ksɪs] *s* Prophylaxe *f.*

pro·pi·ti·ate [prə'pɪʃɪeɪt] *v/t* versöhnen, besänftigen.

pro·pi·tious [prə'pɪʃəs] *adj* □ günstig, vorteilhaft (**for, to** für).

pro·po·nent [prə'pəʊnənt] *s* Befürworter(in).

pro·por·tion [prə'pɔːʃn] I *s* **1.** Verhältnis *n* (**of ... to** von ... zu); *pl* Größenverhältnisse *pl*, Proportionen *pl*: **in ~ to** im Verhältnis zu; **out of all ~** unverhältnismäßig; **be out of all ~ to** in keinem Verhältnis stehen zu; **the painting is out of ~** die Proportionen des Bildes stimmen nicht. **2.** (An)Teil *m*: **in ~** anteilig. II *v/t* **3.** (**to**) in das richtige Verhältnis bringen (mit, zu), anpassen (*dat*). **4.** anteilmäßig verteilen. **pro·'por·tion·al** [~ʃənl] I *adj* □ **1.** → **proportionate. 2.** proportional, verhältnismäßig. **3.** anteilmäßig: **~ representation** *pol.* Verhältniswahl(system *n*) *f.* II *s* **4.** 🜚 Proportionale *f.* **pro·'por·tion·ate** [~ʃnət] *adj* □ (**to**) im richtigen Verhältnis (stehend) (zu), entsprechend (*dat*).

pro·pos·al [prə'pəʊzl] *s* **1.** Vorschlag *m*: **make s.o. a ~** j-m e-n Vorschlag machen. **2.** (Heirats)Antrag *m*: **she had a ~** sie bekam e-n Heiratsantrag; **make s.o. a ~** j-m e-n Antrag machen. **~ form** *s* Antrag(sformular *n*) *m.*

pro·pose [prə'pəʊz] I *v/t* **1.** vorschlagen (**s.th. to s.o.** j-m et.; **s.o. for** j-n für *od.* als; **that** daß; **doing** zu tun): **~ marriage to** → **4. 2.** beabsichtigen, vorhaben (**to do** zu tun). **3.** Toast ausbringen (**to** auf *acc*): → **health 3.** II *v/i* **4.** (**to** j-m e-n (Heirats)Antrag machen. **prop·o·si·tion** [ˌprɒpə'zɪʃn] *s* **1.** Behauptung *f.* **2.** Vorschlag *m*: **make s.o. a ~** j-m e-n Vorschlag machen; j-m ein eindeutiges Angebot machen. **3.** 🜚 (Lehr)Satz *m.* **4.** F Sache *f*: **an easy ~** e-e Kleinigkeit.

pro·pound [prə'paʊnd] *v/t* Theorie *etc* vertreten; *Problem etc* zur Debatte stellen.

pro·pri·e·tar·y [prə'praɪətərɪ] *adj* **1.** gesetzlich *od.* patentrechtlich geschützt: **~**

article Markenartikel *m*. **2.** *fig.* besitzergreifend. **pro'pri·e·tor** *s* Eigentümer *m*, Besitzer *m*. **pro'pri·e·tress** [~trɪs] *s* Eigentümerin *f*, Besitzerin *f*.

pro·pri·e·ty [prə'praɪətɪ] *s* **1.** Anstand *m*. **2.** *pl* Anstandsformen *pl*, -regeln *pl*. **3.** Richtigkeit *f*.

pro·pul·sion [prə'pʌlʃn] *s* ⊙ Antrieb *m*.

pro·ro·ga·tion [ˌprəʊrə'geɪʃn] *s* *parl.* Vertagung *f*. **pro·rogue** [prə'rəʊg] *v/t u. v/i* (sich) vertagen.

pro·sa·ic [prəʊ'zeɪk] *adj* (~*ally*) prosaisch, nüchtern, sachlich.

pro·scribe [prəʊ'skraɪb] *v/t* **1.** *bsd.* 🟐 verbieten. **2.** *hist.* ächten.

pro·scrip·tion [prəʊ'skrɪpʃn] *s* **1.** *bsd.* 🟐 Verbot *m*. **2.** *hist.* Ächtung *f*.

prose [prəʊz] *s* **1.** Prosa *f*. **2.** *ped. bsd. Br.* Übersetzung *f* in e-e Fremdsprache, Hinübersetzung *f*: *an Italian* ~ e-e Übersetzung ins Italienische; *do a* ~ e-e Hinübersetzung machen.

pros·e·cute ['prɒsɪkjuːt] **I** *v/t* **1.** 🟐 strafrechtlich verfolgen, (gerichtlich) belangen (*for* wegen). **2.** *Untersuchung etc* durchführen. **II** *v/i* **3.** 🟐 die Anklage vertreten: *Mr X, prosecuting, ...* Mr X, der Vertreter der Anklage, ... **,pros·e·cu·tion** [~kjuːʃn] *s* **1.** 🟐 strafrechtliche Verfolgung, Strafverfolgung *f*. **2.** *the* ~ 🟐 die Staatsanwaltschaft, die Anklage(behörde) *f*: ~ *witness* **1.** 🟐 Zeuge *m* der Anklage, Belastungszeuge *m*. **3.** Durchführung *f* (*witness* 1). **3.** Durchführung *f*. **'pros·e·cu·tor** *s a. public* ~ Staatsanwalt *m*, -anwältin *f*.

pros·pect **I** *s* ['prɒspekt] **1.** (Aus)Sicht *f*, (-)Blick *m* (*of* auf *acc*; *over* über *acc*). **2.** *fig.* Aussicht *f* (*of* auf *acc*): *have s.th. in* ~ et. in Aussicht haben. **3.** Interessent *m*, ♣ möglicher Kunde, potentieller Käufer. **II** *v/t* [prə'spekt] **4.** *Gebiet* untersuchen (*for* nach *Gold etc*). **III** *v/i* [prə'spekt] **5.** suchen, bohren (*for* nach). **pro'spec·tive** *adj* □ voraussichtlich: ~ *buyer* Kaufinteressent *m*, potentieller Käufer. **pro'spec·tus** [~təs] *s* Prospekt *m*.

pros·per ['prɒspə] *v/i* gedeihen; ♣ blühen, florieren. **pros·per·i·ty** [~'sperətɪ] *s* Wohlstand *m*. **pros·per·ous** ['~pərəs] *adj* □ **1.** gedeihend; ♣ blühend, florierend. **2.** wohlhabend.

pros·tate ['prɒsteɪt] *s a.* ~ *gland anat.* Prostata *f*, Vorsteherdrüse *f*.

pros·the·sis ['prɒsθɪsɪs] *pl* **-ses** ['~siːz] *s* 🔬 Prothese *f*.

pros·ti·tute ['prɒstɪtjuːt] **I** *s* Prostituierte *f*, Dirne *f*: → *male* **1**. **II** *v/t*: ~ *o.s.* sich prostituieren (*a. fig.*). **,pros·ti'tu·tion** *s* Prostitution *f*.

pros·trate I *adj* ['prɒstreɪt] *adj* **1.** hingestreckt. **2.** *fig.* am Boden liegend: erschöpft. ~ *with grief* grambeugt. **II** *v/t* [prɒ'streɪt] **3.** niederwerfen. **4.** *fig.* erschöpfen. **pros'tra·tion** *s* **1.** Fußfall *m*. **2.** *fig.* Erschöpfung *f*.

pros·y ['prəʊzɪ] *adj* □ **1.** → *prosaic*. **2.** langweilig; weitschweifig.

pro·tag·o·nist [prəʊ'tægənɪst] *s* **1.** *thea. etc* Hauptfigur *f*, Held(in). **2.** *fig.* Vorkämpfer(in).

pro·tect [prə'tekt] *v/t* (be)schützen (*from* vor *dat*; *against* gegen), *Interessen etc* wahren: **pro'tec·tion** *s* **1.** Schutz *m*. **2.** *a.* ~ *money* Schutzgeld *m*. **pro'tec·tion·ism** [~ʃənɪzəm] *s* ♣ Protektionismus *m*. **pro'tec·tive** *adj* □ **1.** Schutz...: ~ *clothing* Schutzkleidung *f*; ~ *custody* 🟐 Schutzhaft *f*; *take into* ~ *custody* in Schutzhaft nehmen; ~ *duty* (*od. tariff*) ♣ Schutzzoll *m*. **2.** fürsorglich (*toward[s]* gegenüber). **pro'tec·tor** *s* **1.** Beschützer *m*. **2.** Schoner *m*, (*Knieetc*)Schützer *m*, (-)Schoner *m*. **pro'tec·to·rate** [~rət] *s pol.* Protektorat *n*.

pro·test I *s* ['prəʊtest] **1.** Protest *m*: *in* (*od. as a*) ~ aus Protest (*against* gegen); *under* ~ unter Protest; *without* ~ ohne Protest, widerspruchslos; *make a* ~ Protest einlegen (*od.* erheben (*to* bei); ~ *march* Protestmarsch *m*. **II** *v/i* [prə'test] **2.** protestieren (*against, about* gegen; *to* bei). **III** *v/t* [prə'test] **3.** *Am.* protestieren gegen. **4.** beteuern.

Prot·es·tant ['prɒtɪstənt] **I** *s* Protestant(-in). **II** *adj* protestantisch, evangelisch. **'Prot·es·tant·ism** *s* Protestantismus *m*.

prot·es·ta·tion [ˌprɒte'steɪʃn] *s* **1.** Beteuerung *f*: ~*s pl of innocence* Unschuldsbeteuerungen *pl*. **2.** Protest *m* (*against* gegen).

pro·to·col ['prəʊtəkɒl] *s* Protokoll *n*: ~ *demands that* das Protokoll verlangt, daß.

pro·ton ['prəʊtɒn] *s phys.* Proton *n*.

pro·to·plasm ['prəʊtəplæzəm] *s biol.* Protoplasma *n*.

pro·to·type ['prəʊtətaɪp] *s* Prototyp *n*.

pro·tract [prə'trækt] *v/t* in die Länge ziehen, hinausziehen. **pro'tract·ed** *adj* länger, langwierig. **pro'trac·tion** *s* Hinausziehen *n*. **pro'trac·tor** *s* ⚓ Winkelmesser *m*.

pro·trude [prə'truːd] *v/i* herausragen, vorstehen (**from** aus). **pro'trud·ing** *adj* vorstehend (*a. Zähne etc*), vorspringend (*Kinn*). **pro'tru·sion** [~ʒn] *s* 1. Herausragen *n*, Vorstehen *n*. 2. Vorsprung *m*, vorstehender Teil.

pro·tu·ber·ance [prə'tjuːbərəns] *s* Vorsprung *m*; Schwellung *f*. **pro'tu·ber·ant** *adj* □ vorstehend, -tretend.

proud [praʊd] *adj* □ 1. *allg.* stolz (**of** auf *acc*): **be too ~ to do s.th.** zu stolz sein, um et. zu tun. 2. hochmütig. **II** *adv* 3. **do s.o. ~** j-n fürstlich bewirten.

prov·a·ble ['pruːvəbl] *adj* □ be-, nachweisbar. **prove** [pruːv] (*a. irr*) **I** *v/t* be-, nachweisen; unter Beweis stellen: **~ o.s.** (**to be**) → **II**. **II** *v/i:* **~ (to be)** sich erweisen *od.* herausstellen als. **prov·en** ['~vn] **I** *pp* von **prove**. **II** *adj* bewährt.

prov·e·nance ['prɒvənəns] *s* Herkunft *f*.

pro·verb ['prɒvɜːb] *s* Sprichwort *n*. **pro·ver·bi·al** [prə'vɜːbjəl] *adj* □ sprichwörtlich (*a. fig.*).

pro·vide [prə'vaɪd] **I** *v/t* 1. versehen, -sorgen, beliefern (**with** mit). 2. zur Verfügung stellen, bereitstellen (**for s.o.** j-m). 3. vorsehen, -schreiben (**that** daß) (*Gesetz etc*). **II** *v/i* 4. a) Vorkehrungen *od.* Vorsorge treffen gegen, b) verbieten (*Gesetz etc*); **~ for** a) sorgen für: **she has two children to ~ for** sie hat zwei Kinder zu versorgen, b) vorsorgen für, c) et. vorsehen (*Gesetz etc*). **pro'vid·ed** *cj* a. **~ that** vorausgesetzt(, daß).

prov·i·dence ['prɒvɪdəns] *s* Vorsehung *f*: → **tempt** 2. **'prov·i·dent** *adj* □ vorausblickend, vorsorglich. **prov·i·den·tial** [~'denʃl] *adj* glücklich (*Geschick etc*). **prov·i·den·tial·ly** [~ʃəlɪ] *adv* glücklicherweise.

pro·vid·er [prə'vaɪdə] *s* Ernährer(in).

prov·ince ['prɒvɪns] *s* 1. Provinz *f* (*Verwaltungseinheit*). 2. **the ~s** *pl* die Provinz (*Ggs. Stadt*). 3. *fig.* (Aufgaben-, Wissens)Bereich *m*, (-)Gebiet *n*: **this is outside** (*od.* **not within**) **my ~** dafür bin ich nicht zuständig.

pro·vin·cial [prə'vɪnʃl] **I** *adj* □ 1. Provinz... 2. *contp.* provinziell, provinzlerisch. **II** *s* 3. Provinzbewohner(in). 4. *contp.* Provinzler(in).

pro·vi·sion [prə'vɪʒn] **I** *s* 1. Vorkehrung *f*: **make ~s** Vorkehrungen *od.* Vorsorge treffen (**against** gegen; **for** für). 2. Bestimmung *f*, Vorschrift *f*: **with the ~ that** unter der Bedingung, daß. 3. Bereitstellung *f*. 4. *pl* Proviant *m*, Verpflegung *f*. **II** *v/t* 5. verproviantieren (**for** für). **pro'vi·sion·al** [~ʒənl] *adj* □ provisorisch, vorläufig.

pro·vi·so [prə'vaɪzəʊ] *pl* **-sos** *s* Vorbehalt *m*, Bedingung *f*: **with the ~ that** unter der Bedingung, daß.

prov·o·ca·tion [ˌprɒvə'keɪʃn] *s* Provokation *f*: **at the slightest ~** beim geringsten Anlaß. **pro·voc·a·tive** [prə'vɒkətɪv] *adj* □ provozierend, (*sexuell a.*) aufreizend.

pro·voke [prə'vəʊk] *v/t* j-n, et. provozieren, -j-n, Tier reizen: **~ s.o. into doing** (*od.* **to do**) **s.th.** j-n so provozieren, daß er et. tut. **pro'vok·ing** → **provocative**.

pro·vost ['prɒvəst] *s schott.* Bürgermeister(in).

prowl [praʊl] **I** *v/i* a. **~ about** (*od.* **around**) herumschleichen, -streifen. **II** *v/t* durchstreifen. **III** *s* Herumstreifen *n*: **be on the ~** a. **~ing**; **~ car** *Am.* (Funk)Streifenwagen *m*. **'prowl·er** *s* Herumtreiber(in).

prox·im·i·ty [prɒk'sɪmətɪ] *s* Nähe *f*: **in the ~ of** in der Nähe von (*od. gen*).

prox·y ['prɒksɪ] *s* 1. (Handlungs)Vollmacht *f*. 2. (Stell)Vertreter(in), Bevollmächtigte *m*, *f*: **by ~** durch e-n Bevollmächtigten.

prude [pruːd] *s* prüder Mensch: **be a ~** prüde sein.

pru·dence ['pruːdns] *s* 1. Klugheit *f*, Vernunft *f*. 2. Umsicht *f*, Besonnenheit *f*. **'pru·dent** *adj* □ 1. klug, vernünftig. 2. umsichtig, besonnen.

prud·er·y ['pruːdərɪ] *s* Prüderie *f*. **'prud·ish** *adj* □ prüde.

prune¹ [pruːn] *s* Backpflaume *f*.

prune² [~] *v/t* 1. a. **~ back** Hecke etc (be)schneiden. 2. a. **~ away** Äste etc wegschneiden. 3. a. **~ down** *fig.* Text etc zs.-streichen.

pru·ri·ence ['prʊərɪəns] *s* Lüsternheit *f*. **'pru·ri·ent** *adj* □ lüstern.

prus·sic ac·id ['prʌsɪk] *s* 🜊 Blausäure *f*.

pry¹ [praɪ] *bsd. Am.* → **prize²**.

pry² [~] *v/i* neugierig sein: **~ into** s-e Nase stecken in (*acc*). **'pry·ing** *adj* □ neugierig.

psalm [sɑːm] *s* Psalm *m*.

pseu·do·nym ['sjuːdənɪm] *s* Pseudonym *n*: **under the ~ of XY** unter dem Pseudonym XY.

psych [saɪk] *v/t* F **1. ~ out** *j-n, et.* durchschauen; *j-n* psychologisch fertigmachen. **2. ~ up** auf-, hochputschen.

psy·che¹ ['saɪkɪ] *s* Psyche *f*, Seele *f*.

psy·chi·at·ric [ˌsaɪkɪˈætrɪk] *adj* (**~ally**) psychiatrisch (*Behandlung etc*); psychisch (*Störung etc*). **psy·chi·a·trist** [~'kaɪətrɪst] *s* Psychiater(in). **psy'chi·a·try** *s* Psychiatrie *f*.

psy·chic ['saɪkɪk] **I** *adj* (**~ally**) **1.** psychisch, seelisch. **2.** übersinnlich. **3. ~ research** Parapsychologie *f*. **4.** medial (begabt *od.* veranlagt). **II** *s* **5.** medial veranlagte Person, Medium *n*. **'psy·chi·cal** → *psychic* I.

psy·cho·a·nal·y·sis [ˌsaɪkəʊəˈnæləsɪs] *s* Psychoanalyse *f*. **psy·cho·an·a·lyst** [~'ænəlɪst] *s* Psychoanalytiker(in).

psy·cho·log·i·cal [ˌsaɪkəˈlɒdʒɪkl] *adj* □ psychologisch: **~ moment** (psychologisch) richtiger Augenblick; **~ terror** Psychoterror *m*; **~ warfare** psychologische Kriegführung. **psy·chol·o·gist** [~'kɒlədʒɪst] *s* Psychologe *m*, Psychologin *f*. **psy'chol·o·gy** *s* **1.** Psychologie *f*. **2.** psychologisches Geschick *od.* Gespür.

psy·cho·path ['saɪkəʊpæθ] *s* Psychopath(in). **psy·cho'path·ic** *adj* (**~ally**) psychopathisch.

psy·cho·sis [saɪˈkəʊsɪs] *pl* **-ses** [~siːz] ☞ Psychose *f*.

psy·cho·so·mat·ic [ˌsaɪkəʊsəʊˈmætɪk] *adj* (**~ally**) psychosomatisch.

psy·cho·ther·a·pist [ˌsaɪkəʊˈθerəpɪst] *s* Psychotherapeut(in). **psy·cho'ther·a·py** *s* Psychotherapie *f*.

pub [pʌb] *s bsd. Br.* Pub *n*, Kneipe *f*. **~ crawl** *s bsd. Br.* F Kneipenbummel *m*: **go on a ~** e-n Kneipenbummel machen.

pu·ber·ty ['pjuːbətɪ] *s* Pubertät *f*: **be going through ~** in der Pubertät sein.

pu·bic ['pjuːbɪk] *adj anat.* Scham...

pub·lic ['pʌblɪk] **I** *adj* □ **1.** öffentlich (*Versammlung etc*). **2.** öffentlich, allgemein bekannt: **~ figure** Persönlichkeit *f*

des öffentlichen Lebens; **go ~** sich an die Öffentlichkeit wenden; **make ~** bekanntmachen, publik machen. **3.** a) öffentlich (*Einrichtung, Sicherheit, Verkehrsmittel etc*): **~ bar** *Br.* Ausschank *m*, Schenke *f*; **~ (limited) company** ☞ *Br.* Aktiengesellschaft *f*; **~ convenience** *Br.* öffentliche Bedürfnisanstalt; **~ house** *bsd. Br.* Gaststätte *f*; **~ relations** *pl* Public Relations *pl*, Öffentlichkeitsarbeit *f*; **~ school** *Br.* Public School *f*; *Am.* staatliche Schule; **~ utility** öffentlicher Versorgungsbetrieb; → *nuisance* 1, b) Staats..., staatlich: **~ holiday** gesetzlicher Feiertag; **~ prosecutor**, c) Volks...: **~ library** Volksbücherei *f*. **II** *s* **4.** Öffentlichkeit *f*: **in ~** in der Öffentlichkeit, öffentlich. **5.** Publikum *n*, Öffentlichkeit *f*: **exclude the ~** ☞ die Öffentlichkeit ausschließen. **,~·ad'dress sys·tem** *s* Lautsprecheranlage *f*.

pub·li·can ['pʌblɪkən] *s bsd. Br.* (Gast-) Wirt(in).

pub·li·ca·tion [ˌpʌblɪˈkeɪʃn] *s* **1.** Bekanntgabe *f*, -machung *f*. **2.** Publikation *f*, Veröffentlichung *f* (*beide a. Werk*).

pub·li·cist ['pʌblɪsɪst] *s* **1.** Publizist(in). **2.** Werbeagent(in). **pub·lic·i·ty** [~'lɪsətɪ] *s* **1.** Publicity *f*, Bekanntheit *f*. **2.** Publicity *f*, Reklame *f*, Werbung *f*: **~ agent** Werbeagent(in); **~ campaign** Werbefeldzug *m*; **~ stunt** Werbegag *m*. **pub·li·cize** ['~saɪz] *v/t* **1.** bekanntmachen, publik machen. **2.** Publicity *od.* Reklame machen für.

pub·lish ['pʌblɪʃ] *v/t* **1.** bekanntgeben, -machen. **2.** publizieren, veröffentlichen, *Leserbrief a.* abdrucken. **3.** *Buch etc* verlegen, herausbringen: **~ed weekly** erscheint wöchentlich. **'pub·lish·er** *s* **1.** Verleger(in), Herausgeber(in). **2.** *pl* Verlag(shaus *n*) *m*.

puck [pʌk] *s* Eishockey: Puck *m*, Scheibe *f*.

puck·er ['pʌkə] **I** *v/t* **1.** a. **~ up** *Gesicht, Mund* verziehen, *Stirn* runzeln. **II** *v/i* a. **~ up** **2.** sich verziehen, sich runzeln. **3.** Falten werfen. **III** *s* **4.** Falte *f*.

pud [pʊd] *Br.* F → *pudding*.

pud·ding ['pʊdɪŋ] *s* a) *Br.* Nachspeise *f*, -tisch *m*, b) (*Reis- etc*)Auflauf *m*, c) Pudding *m* (*im Wasserbad gekochte Mehlspeise*), d) (*Blut*)Wurst *f*.

pud·dle ['pʌdl] s Pfütze f.
pu·er·ile ['pjʊəraɪl] adj □ infantil, kindisch.
puff [pʌf] **I** s **1.** Rauchen: Zug m: **take a ~ at** ziehen an (dat). **2.** (Luft-, Wind-) Hauch m, (-)Stoß m: **~ of air. 3.** gastr. (Wind)Beutel m. **4.** F Puste f: **out of ~** aus der od. außer Puste. **5.** (Puder)Quaste f. **6.** F Anpreisung f: **give s.th. a ~** et. hochjubeln. **II** v/t **7.** Rauch blasen (**in s.o.'s face** j-m ins Gesicht): **~ out** Kerze etc ausblasen; Rauch etc austoßen; Brust herausdrücken; Gefieder aufplustern; **be ~ed up** (**with pride**) aufgeblasen sein. **III** v/i **8.** schnaufen (**a.** Lokomotive etc), keuchen. **9. a. ~ away** paffen (**at** an e-r Zigarette etc). **10. ~ up** (an)schwellen. **puffed** adj F aus der od. außer Puste.
puff| paste s Am., **~ pas·try** s Blätterteig m. **~ sleeve** s Puffärmel m.
puff·y ['pʌfɪ] adj (an)geschwollen, verschwollen.
pug [pʌg] s zo. Mops m.
pug·na·cious [pʌg'neɪʃəs] adj □ kampf(es)lustig; streitsüchtig. **pugnac·i·ty** [~'næsətɪ] s Kampf(es)lust f; Streitsucht f.
puke [pjuːk] sl. **I** v/i kotzen. **II** v/t auskotzen. **III** s Kotze f.
pull [pʊl] **I** s **1.** Ziehen n; Zug m, Ruck m: **give the rope a** (**good**) **~** (kräftig) am Seil ziehen. **2.** Anziehungskraft f (a. fig.). **3.** Anstieg m, Steigung f. **4.** Zug(griff m, -leine f) m. **5.** F Beziehungen pl (**with** zu). **II** v/t **6.** ziehen: **~ string** 1. **7.** ziehen an (dat): **~ s.o.'s hair** j-n an den Haaren ziehen; **~ a muscle** sich e-e Muskelzerrung zuziehen, sich et. zerren; → **face** 2, **leg** 1, etc. **8.** reißen: → **piece** 1. **9.** a) Zahn ziehen, Pflanze ausreißen, b) Messer, Pistole ziehen: **~ a gun on s.o.** j-n mit der Pistole bedrohen; c) bsd. Br. Bier zapfen. **10.** fig. anziehen. **11. ~ one's punches** (Boxen) verhalten schlagen; fig. sich zurückhalten; **not to ~ one's punches, ~ no punches** kein Blatt vor den Mund nehmen. **12.** F Banküberfall etc machen: **~ a big one** ein großes Ding drehen; → **job¹** 6. **III** v/i **13.** ziehen (**at, on** an dat).
Verbindungen mit Adverbien:
pull| a·head v/i vorbeiziehen (**of** an

dat) (Auto etc) (a. fig.). **~ a·way** v/i **1.** anfahren (Bus etc). **2.** sich absetzen (**from** von), (Sport a.) sich freimachen. **~ down** v/t **1.** Gebäude abreißen. **2.** j-n mitnehmen, schwächen. **~ in I** v/t **1.** Bauch etc einziehen. **2.** → **pull** 10. **3.** bsd. Br. F j-n einkassieren. **4.** F kassieren: **he's pulling in quite a bit** er verdient ganz schön. **II** v/i **5.** einfahren (Zug). **6.** anhalten. **~ off** v/t **1.** Schuhe etc ausziehen; sich die Kleider vom Leib reißen. **2.** F et. schaffen, schaukeln. **~ on** v/t Kleid etc anziehen, (sich) überziehen. **~ out I** v/t **1.** a) herausziehen (**of** aus): → **chestnut** 1, **stop** 4, b) → **pull** 9a, c) Tisch ausziehen. **II** v/i **2.** abfahren (Zug). **3.** ausscheren (Fahrzeug). **4.** fig. sich zurückziehen, (a. Sport) aussteigen (**of** aus). **~ through I** v/t **1.** durchziehen. **2.** fig. Kranken, Kandidaten etc durchbringen. **II** v/i **3.** fig. durchkommen. **~ to·geth·er I** v/t **1.** **pull o.s. together** sich zs.-reißen. **2.** Partei etc zs.-schweißen. **II** v/i **3.** an 'einem Strang ziehen. **~ up I** v/t **1.** hochziehen. **2.** Fahrzeug anhalten. **3.** j-n korrigieren; zurechtweisen (**for** wegen). **II** v/i **4.** (an)halten. **~ to** (**of. with**) (Sport) j-n einholen.
pul·ley ['pʊlɪ] s ⊚ Flaschenzug m.
'pull|-in s Br. Rasthaus n, -stätte f. **'~-out** adj ausziehbar: **~ table** Ausziehtisch m. **'~-o·ver** s Pullover m. **'~-up** s Klimmzug m: **do a ~** e-n Klimmzug machen.
pul·mo·nar·y ['pʌlmənərɪ] adj anat., ⚕ Lungen...
pulp [pʌlp] **I** s **1.** Fruchtfleisch n. **2.** Brei m, breiige Masse: **beat to a ~** fig. j-n zu Brei schlagen. **II** adj **3.** Schund...: **~ novel** Schundroman m. **III** v/t **4.** Bücher etc einstampfen.
pul·pit ['pʊlpɪt] s Kanzel f: **in the ~** auf der Kanzel.
pulp·y ['pʌlpɪ] adj □ breiig.
pul·sate [pʌl'seɪt] v/i pulsieren, a. fig. vibrieren (**with** vor dat).
pulse¹ [pʌls] s **1.** Puls(schlag) m: **feel** (**od. take**) **s.o.'s ~** j-m den Puls fühlen. **2.** ⚡, phys. Impuls m. **II** v/i **3.** pulsieren (**through** durch) (a. fig.).
pulse² [~] mst pl **~s** Hülsenfrüchte pl.
pul·ver·ize ['pʌlvəraɪz] v/t **1.** pulverisieren. **2.** fig. F j-n auseinandernehmen.
pu·ma ['pjuːmə] s zo. Puma m.

pum·ice ['pʌmɪs] *s a.* ~ **stone** Bimsstein *m*.

pum·mel ['pʌml] *v/t pret u. pp* **-meled**, *bsd. Br.* **-melled** eintrommeln auf (*acc*).

pump [pʌmp] **I** *s* **1.** Pumpe *f*; (*Zapf*)Säule. **II** *v/t* **2.** pumpen: ~ *up* aufpumpen; *s.o.'s stomach* ⚕ j-m den Magen auspumpen; ~ *money into fig.* Geld hineinpumpen in (*acc*). **3.** *fig.* j-n ausholen (*for* über *acc*). **III** *v/i* **4.** pumpen (*a. Herz*). **5.** herausschießen (*from* aus) (*Blut etc*). ~ **at·tend·ant** *s* Tankwart *m*.

pump·kin ['pʌmpkɪn] *s* 🌼 Kürbis *m*.

pun [pʌn] **I** *s* Wortspiel *n*. **II** *v/i* Wortspiele *od*. ein Wortspiel machen.

Punch[1] [pʌntʃ] *s* Kasper *m*, Kasperle *n*, *m*: *be* (*as*) *pleased as* ~ *F* sich freuen wie ein Schneekönig.

punch[2] [~] **I** *s* **1.** (Faust)Schlag *m*: *give s.o. a* ~ j-m e-n Schlag versetzen; → *pull* 11. **2.** *fig.* Schwung *m*. **II** *v/t* **3.** (mit der Faust) schlagen.

punch[3] [~] ⊗ **I** *s* Locher *m*; Lochzange *f*; Locheisen *n*. **II** *v/t* lochen; *Loch* stanzen (*in* in *acc*): ~*ed card* Lochkarte *f*; ~*ed tape* Lochstreifen *m*.

punch[4] [~] *s* Punsch *m*.

Punch-and-Ju·dy show ['dʒuːdɪ] *s* Kasperletheater *n*.

punch| card *s* Lochkarte *f*. ~ **line** *s* Pointe *f*. '**~·up** *s Br. F* Schlägerei *f*.

punc·til·i·ous [pʌŋk'tɪlɪəs] *adj* □ peinlich genau.

punc·tu·al ['pʌŋktʃʊəl] *adj* □ pünktlich: *be* ~ pünktlich kommen (*for* zu). **punc·tu·al·i·ty** [~'ælɪtɪ] *s* Pünktlichkeit *f*.

punc·tu·ate ['pʌŋktʃʊeɪt] *v/t* **1.** interpunktieren. **2.** *fig.* (*with*) unterbrechen (durch; mit); durchsetzen (mit). **3.** *fig.* unterstreichen, betonen. **punc·tu·a·tion** *s* **1.** Interpunktion *f*: ~ *mark* Satzzeichen *n*. **2.** *fig.* Unterbrechung *f*. **3.** *fig.* Unterstreichung *f*, Betonung *f*.

punc·ture ['pʌŋktʃə] **I** *v/t* **1.** durchstechen, -bohren. **2.** ⚕ punktieren. **II** *v/i* **3.** ein Loch bekommen, platzen. **III** *s* **4.** (Ein)Stich *m*; Loch *n*. **5.** *mot.* Reifenpanne *f*. **6.** ⚕ Punktion *f*.

pun·dit ['pʌndɪt] *s oft humor.* Weise *m*, *f*.

pun·gen·cy ['pʌndʒənsɪ] *s* Schärfe *f* (*a.*

fig.). '**pun·gent** *adj* □ scharf (*Geschmack, Geruch*), (*Bemerkung etc a.*) bissig.

pun·ish ['pʌnɪʃ] *v/t* **1.** j-n (be)strafen (*for* für, wegen). **2.** *et.* bestrafen. '**pun·ish·a·ble** *adj* □ strafbar: ~ *act* (*od. offence, Am. offense*) strafbare Handlung; *murder is* ~ *by death* auf Mord steht die Todesstrafe. '**pun·ish·ing** *adj* □ vernichtend (*Kritik etc*), mörderisch, zermürbend (*Rennen etc*). '**pun·ish·ment** *s* **1.** Bestrafung *f*. **2.** Strafe *f*: *as a* ~ als *od.* zur Strafe (*for* für).

pu·ni·tive ['pjuːnɪtɪv] *adj* □ **1.** Straf... **2.** extrem hoch (*Steuern etc*).

punk [pʌŋk] *s* **1.** Punk *m* (*Bewegung u. Anhänger*). **2.** ♪ Punk *m*; Punker *m*. ~ **rock** *s* ♪ Punkrock *m*. ~ **rock·er** *s* ♪ Punkrocker *m*.

punt [pʌnt] **I** *s* Stechkahn *m*. **II** *v/t u. v/i* staken.

pu·ny ['pjuːnɪ] *adj* □ schwächlich.

pup [pʌp] → **puppy**.

pu·pa ['pjuːpə] *pl* **-pae** ['~piː], **-pas** *s zo.* Puppe *f*.

pu·pil[1] ['pjuːpl] *s* Schüler(in).

pu·pil[2] [~] *s anat.* Pupille *f*.

pup·pet ['pʌpɪt] *s* Puppe *f* (*a:* a) Handpuppe *f*, b) Marionette *f* (*a. fig.*): ~ *government fig.* Marionettenregierung *f*; ~ *show* Marionettentheater *n*, Puppenspiel *n*. **pup·pet·eer** [~'tɪə] *s* Puppenspieler(in).

pup·py ['pʌpɪ] *s* Welpe *m*, junger Hund. ~ *fat s Br. F* Babyspeck *m*. ~ *love s F* jugendliche Schwärmerei.

pur·chas·a·ble ['pɜːtʃəsəbl] *adj* käuflich. '**pur·chase I** *v/t* **1.** kaufen, erstehen. **2.** *fig.* erkaufen (*at the expense of* auf Kosten *gen*). **II** *s* **3.** Kauf *m*. **4.** *pl* Einkäufe *pl*: *make* ~*s* Einkäufe machen. '**pur·chas·er** *s* Käufer(in). '**pur·chas·ing** *adj*: ~ *power* ✝ Kaufkraft *f*.

pure [pjʊə] *adj* □ **1.** rein: a) pur, unvermischt, b) sauber, c) akzentfrei, fehlerlos, d) pur, völlig (*Unsinn etc*): *by* ~ *accident* rein zufällig. **2.** ehrlich (*Absicht*). '**~-bred** *I adj* reinrassig, rasserein. **II** *s* reinrassiges Tier.

pu·ree ['pjʊəreɪ] *s* Püree *n*. **II** *v/t* pürieren.

pur·ga·tive ['pɜːgətɪv] ⚕ **I** *adj* □ abführend. **II** *s* Abführmittel *n*.

pur·ga·to·ry ['pɜːgətərɪ] *s eccl.* Fegefeuer

n: it is ~ having to do s.th. es ist die Hölle, et. tun zu müssen.

purge [pɜːdʒ] **I** *v/t Partei etc* säubern (*of* von). **II** *s pol.* Säuberung(saktion) *f*.

pu·ri·fi·ca·tion [ˌpjʊərɪfɪˈkeɪʃn] *s* Reinigung *f*. **pu·ri·fi·er** [ˈ-faɪə] *s* ⊛ Reiniger *m*. **pu·ri·fy** [ˈ-faɪ] *v/t* reinigen.

pur·ism [ˈpjʊərɪzəm] *s* Purismus *m*. **'pur·ist** *s* Purist(in).

Pu·ri·tan [ˈpjʊərɪtən] *hist.*, *fig. mst* 2 **I** *s* Puritaner(in). **II** *adj* puritanisch. **pu·ri·tan·i·cal** [ˌ-ˈtænɪkl] *adj* □ *fig.* puritanisch. **'Pu·ri·tan·ism** [ˌ-tənɪzəm] *s hist.*, *fig. mst* 2 Puritanismus *m*.

pu·ri·ty [ˈpjʊərətɪ] *s* **1.** Reinheit *f*. **2.** Ehrlichkeit *f*.

pur·loin [pɜːˈlɔɪn] *v/t oft humor.* entwenden.

pur·ple [ˈpɜːpl] *adj* purpurn, pupurrot: *his face turned ~* sein Gesicht verfärbte sich blau; *~ heart bsd. Br.* F Amphetamintablette *f*; 2 *Heart* ✗ *Am.* Verwundetenabzeichen *n*.

pur·port [ˈpɜːpət] **I** *s* Tenor *m*. **II** *v/t*: *~ to be s.th.* vorgeben, et. zu sein; et. sein sollen.

pur·pose [ˈpɜːpəs] **I** *s* **1.** Zweck *m*, Ziel *n*; Absicht *f*, Vorsatz *m*: *for all practical ~s* praktisch; *on ~* absichtlich; mit der Absicht (*to do* zu tun); *answer* (*od. serve*) *the same ~* denselben Zweck erfüllen; *put to a good ~* gut anwenden *od.* nützen. **2.** *to no ~* vergeblich, umsonst. **3.** Entschlossenheit *f*, Zielstrebigkeit *f*. **II** *v/t* **4.** beabsichtigen, vorhaben (*doing, to do* zu tun). **pur·pose·ful** [ˈ-fʊl] *adj* □ entschlossen, zielstrebig. **'pur·pose·less** *adj* □ **1.** zwecklos. **2.** ziel-, planlos. **'pur·pose·ly** *adv* absichtlich.

purr [pɜː] **I** *v/i* schnurren (*Katze*); surren (*Motor etc*). **II** *s* Schnurren *n*; Surren *n*.

purse [pɜːs] **I** *s* **1.** a) Geldbeutel *m*, Portemonnaie *n*: *be beyond s.o.'s ~ fig.* j-s Finanzen übersteigen; *hold the ~-strings fig.* die Finanzen verwalten, b) *Am.* Handtasche *f*. **2.** *Sport:* Siegprämie *f*; (*Boxen*) Börse *f*. **II** *v/t* **3.** *a. ~ up Lippen* schürzen. **'purs·er** *s* **1.** ♘ Proviant- *od.* Zahlmeister *m*. **2.** ✈ Purser *m* (*leitender Steward*).

pur·su·ance [pəˈsjuːəns] *s*: *in* (*the*) *~ of one's duty* in Ausübung s-r Pflicht.

pur·sue [pəˈsjuː] *v/t* **1.** verfolgen: *be ~d by bad luck* vom Pech verfolgt werden. **2.** *fig. s-m Studium etc* nachgehen; *Absicht, Politik etc* verfolgen; *Angelegenheit etc* weiterführen. **pur·su·er** *s* Verfolger(in). **pur·suit** [pəˈsjuːt] *s* **1.** Verfolgung *f*: *be in ~ of s.o.* j-n verfolgen. **2.** *fig.* Verfolgung *f*; Weiterführung *f*: *in* (*the*) *~ of* im *od.* in Verfolg (*gen*). **3.** Beschäftigung *f*.

pu·ru·lent [ˈpjʊərʊlənt] *adj* □ eiternd, eit(e)rig.

pus [pʌs] *s* ❋ Eiter *m*.

push [pʊʃ] **I** *s* **1.** Stoß *m*: *give s.o. a ~* j-m e-n Stoß versetzen; *give s.o. the ~ Br.* F j-n rausschmeißen (*entlassen*); *get the ~ Br.* F fliegen; *at a ~* F im Notfall, notfalls; *if* (*od. when*) *it comes to the ~* F wenn es darauf ankommt. **2.** (*Werbe*)Kampagne *f*. **3.** F Draufgängertum *n*. **II** *v/t* **4.** stoßen, schubsen; schieben; *Taste etc* drücken: *~ one's way* sich drängen (*through* durch); *he's ~ing 70* er geht auf die 70 zu. **5.** *fig. j-n* drängen (*to do* zu tun): *be ~ed* (*for time*) F es eilig haben; in Zeitnot sein; *be ~ed for money* F knapp bei Kasse sein. **6.** F Reklame machen *od.* die Trommel rühren für. **7.** F *Heroin etc* pushen. **III** *v/i* **8.** stoßen, schubsen; schieben: *~ past s.o.* sich an j-m vorbeidrängen. **9.** *~ for fig.* drängen auf (*acc*).
Verbindungen mit Adverbien:

push| a·bout → push around. ~ a·head *v/i:* *~ with Plan etc* vorantreiben. *~ a·long v/i* F sich auf die Socken machen. *~ a·round v/t* herumschubsen (*a. fig.* F). *~ for·ward* **I** *v/t:* *push o.s. forward fig.* sich in den Vordergrund drängen *od.* schieben. **II** *v/i → push ahead. ~ in v/i* F sich vordrängeln. *~ off v/t* **1.** sich abstoßen (*from* von). **2.** *mst imp* abhauen, Leine ziehen. *~ on → push ahead. ~ out v/t fig. j-n* hinausdrängen. *~ up v/t* **1. → daisy. 2.** *Preise etc* hochtreiben.

'push| bike *s Br.* F Fahrrad *n*. *~ but·ton s* Druckknopf *m*, (*elektr.*) Druckknopf... *~-but·ton* **adj** Druckknopf...: *~ tele·phone* Tastentelefon *n*. *'~·cart s* **1.** (Hand)Karren *m*. **2.** *Am.* Einkaufswagen *m*. *'~·chair s Br.* Sportwagen *m* (*für Kinder*).

push·er [ˈpʊʃə] *s* F **1.** Draufgänger *m*. **2.**

Pusher *m* (*Rauschgifthändler*). **'push-ing** → *pushy*.

'push|o·ver *s* F **1.** *fig.* Kinderspiel *n*. **2.** *be a ~ for* nicht widerstehen können (*dat*); immer wieder hereinfallen auf (*acc*). **'~-up** *s Am.* Liegestütz *m*: *do a ~* e-n Liegestütz machen.

push·y ['puʃi] *adj* □ draufgängerisch.

pu·sil·lan·i·mous [,pju:sɪ'lænɪməs] *adj* □ kleinmütig, verzagt.

puss [pʊs] *s* F Mieze *f*.

puss·y ['pʊsi] *s Kindersprache:* Miezekatze *f*. **'~·cat** → *pussy*. **'~·foot** *v/i a. ~ about* (*od. around*) F um den (heißen) Brei herumreden; sich nicht festlegen wollen.

pus·tule ['pʌstju:l] *s* ✆ Pustel *f*.

put [pʊt] **I** *adj* **1. stay ~** sich nicht (vom Fleck) rühren. **II** *v/t* (*irr*) **2.** legen, setzen, stellen, tun: *~ s.th. before s.o. fig.* j-m et. vorlegen; *~ a tax on s.th.* et. besteuern. **3.** *Hand etc, fig. Geld, Zeit* stecken (*in*[*to*]) (*in acc*). **4.** *j-n in e-e unangenehme Lage etc, et. auf den Markt, in Ordnung etc* bringen. **5.** *et. in Kraft, in Umlauf etc* setzen. **6.** unterwerfen, -ziehen (*to dat*). **7.** übersetzen (*into French* ins Französische). **8.** *et.* ausdrücken, *in Worte* fassen: → *mild*. **9.** schätzen (*at auf acc*). **10.** *Geld* setzen (*on auf acc*). **11.** *Schuld* geben (*on dat*). **III** *v/i* (*irr*) **12. ~ to sea* ✆ in See stechen. **~·upon s.o.** *bsd. Br.* j-m Ungelegenheiten bereiten.

Verbindungen mit Adverbien:

put|a·bout *v/t Gerücht* verbreiten, in Umlauf setzen. **II** *v/i* ✆ den Kurs ändern. **~ a·cross** *v/t et.* verständlich machen (*to dat*). **~ a·head** *v/t Sport:* in Führung bringen. **~ a·side** *v/t* **1.** beiseite legen. **2.** *Ware* zurücklegen. **3.** *fig.* beiseite schieben. **4.** → *put away* 3. **~ a·way** *v/t* **1.** weglegen, -stecken, -tun. **2.** auf-, wegräumen. **3.** → *put by.* **4.** F *Speisen* verdrücken, *Getränke* schlucken. **~ back** *v/t* **1.** zurücklegen, -stellen, -tun. **2.** *Uhr* zurückstellen (*by* um): → *clock* 1. **3.** *fig.* verschieben (*two days* um zwei Tage; *to* auf *acc*). **~ by** *v/t Geld* zurücklegen, auf die hohe Kante legen. **~ down** **I** *v/t* **1.** hin-, niederlegen, -stellen, -setzen. **2.** *Aufstand etc* niederwerfen. **3.** *Fahrgast* absetzen. **4.** *et.* aufschreiben: *put s.o.('s name) down for*

j-n anmelden *od.* eintragen für. **5.** *Betrag* anzahlen. **6.** *Flugzeug* landen. **7.** *j-n* halten (*as* für). **8.** *et.* zuschreiben (*to dat*). **II** *v/i* **9.** ✈ landen. **~ for·ward** *v/t* **1.** *Plan etc* vorlegen: *put s.o.('s name) forward as* j-n vorschlagen als. **2.** *Uhr* vorstellen (*by* um). **3.** *fig.* vorverlegen (*two days* um zwei Tage; *to* auf *acc*). **~ in I** *v/t* **1.** herein-, hineinlegen, -stecken, -stellen, *Kassette etc* einlegen. **2.** *Gesuch etc* einreichen, *Forderung etc a.* geltend machen. **3.** *Arbeit, Zeit* verbringen (*on mit*). **4.** *Bemerkung* einwerfen; *ein gutes Wort* einlegen (*for* für). **II** *v/i* **5.** ✆ einlaufen (*at* in *acc*): *~ at a.* anlaufen (*acc*). **6.** sich bewerben (*for* um). **~ off** *v/t* **1.** *et.* verschieben (*till, until* auf *acc*); *j-m* absagen. **2.** *j-n* hinhalten (*with* mit). **3.** *j-n* aus dem Konzept bringen; *j-m* den Appetit *od.* die Lust *od.* die Laune verderben. **4.** → *put down* 3. **~ on** *v/t* **1.** *Mantel etc* anziehen, *Hut, Brille* aufsetzen; *Rouge etc* auflegen: → *lipstick*. **2.** *Licht, Radio etc* anmachen, einschalten. **3.** *einige Pfund* zunehmen: → *weight* 1. **4.** *Sonderzug etc* einsetzen. **5.** *thea. Stück etc* herausbringen. **6.** *Bremse* anziehen. **7.** *Essen, Topf etc* aufsetzen. **8.** *Schallplatte etc* auflegen, *Kassette etc* einlegen. **9.** vortäuschen, heucheln: *put it on* so tun als ob. **10.** F *j-n* auf den Arm nehmen. **~ out** **I** *v/t* **1.** heraus-, hinauslegen, -stellen. **2.** *Hand etc* ausstrecken: → *feeler, tongue* 1. **3.** *Feuer* löschen; *Licht, Radio, Zigarette etc* ausmachen, abschalten. **4.** veröffentlichen, herausgeben; (*Rundfunk, TV*) bringen, senden. **5.** aus der Fassung bringen; verstimmen, ärgern; *j-m* Ungelegenheiten bereiten. **6.** ✆ sich *den Arm etc* ver- *od.* ausrenken. **II** *v/i* **7.** ✆ auslaufen: *~ to sea* in See stechen. **~ o·ver** → *put across*. **~ through** *v/t* **1.** *teleph. j-n* verbinden (*to* mit). **2.** durch-, ausführen. **~ to·geth·er** *v/t* **1.** zs.-setzen, *Gerät etc* zs.-bauen; *Mannschaft, Rede etc* zs.-stellen. **2. he is cleverer than all his friends ~** er ist cleverer als alle s-e Freunde zusammen. **~ up** **I** *v/t* **1.** herauf-, hinauflegen, -stellen. **2.** *Hand* (hoch)heben. **3.** *Bild etc* aufhängen; *Plakat, Bekanntmachung etc* anschlagen. **4.** *Schirm* aufspannen. **5.** *Zelt etc* aufstellen, *Gebäude* errichten. **6.** *j-n* unterbringen. **7.** *Widerstand* leisten: → **fight** 1. **8.** *Preis etc* erhöhen. **9.** *j-n* anstiften (**to** zu). **II** *v/i* **10.** absteigen (**at** in *dat*). **11.** **~ with** sich abfinden mit; sich gefallen lassen.

pu·ta·tive ['pju:tətɪv] *adj* □ mutmaßlich.

'put·off *s bsd. Am.* F (faule) Ausrede. **'~on** *s Am.* F Bluff *m*, Schwindel *m*.

pu·tre·fy ['pju:trɪfaɪ] *v/i* (ver)faulen, verwesen.

pu·trid ['pju:trɪd] *adj* □ **1.** verfault, -west; (*Geruch*) faulig. **2.** F miserabel, saumäßig.

putsch [pʊtʃ] *s pol.* Putsch *m*.

putt [pʌt] *v/t u. v/i Golf:* putten.

putt·er ['pʌtə] *Am.* → **potter¹**.

put·ty ['pʌtɪ] **I** *s* Kitt *m:* **he was** (**like**) **~ in her hands** *fig.* er war Wachs in ihren Händen. **II** *v/t* kitten.

'put-up job *s* F abgekartetes Spiel.

puz·zle ['pʌzl] **I** *s* **1.** Rätsel *n* (*a. fig.*); Geduld(s)spiel *n*: **it is a ~ to me** es ist mir ein Rätsel *od.* rätselhaft; → **jigsaw**

(**puzzle**). **II** *v/t* **2.** vor ein Rätsel stellen; verdutzen, -blüffen: **be ~d** vor e-m Rätsel stehen. **3. ~ out** *et.* ausknobeln, herausbringen. **III** *v/i* **4.** sich den Kopf zerbrechen (**about, over** über *dat*).

'puz·zler *s* F harte Nuß.

pyg·my ['pɪgmɪ] **I** *s* **1.** ♀ Pygmäe *m*, Pygmäin *f.* **2.** Zwerg(in) (*a. fig. contp.*). **II** *adj* **3.** *bsd. zo.* Zwerg...

py·ja·mas [pə'dʒɑ:məz] *s pl, a.* **pair of ~** Schlafanzug *m*, Pyjama *m*.

py·lon ['paɪlən] *s* Hochspannungsmast *m*.

pyr·a·mid ['pɪrəmɪd] *s* Pyramide *f.*

pyre ['paɪə] *s* Scheiterhaufen *m.*

py·ro·ma·ni·a [ˌpaɪrəʊ'meɪnɪə] *s* Pyromanie *f.* **ˌpy·ro'ma·ni·ac** [~æk] *s* Pyromane *m*, -manin *f.*

Pyr·rhic vic·to·ry ['pɪrɪk] *s* Pyrrhussieg *m.*

py·thon ['paɪθn] *s zo.* Python(schlange) *f.*

pyx [pɪks] *s eccl.* Pyxis *f*, Hostienbehälter *m.*

Q

quack¹ [kwæk] **I** *v/i* quaken (*Ente*). **II** *s* Quaken *n.*

quack² [~] *s a.* **~ doctor** Quacksalber *m*, Kurpfuscher *m.* **quack·er·y** ['~ərɪ] *s* Quacksalberei *f*, Kurpfuscherei *f.*

quad [kwɒd] *s* F Vierling *m.*

quad·ran·gle ['kwɒdræŋgl] *s* Viereck *n.* **quad'ran·gu·lar** [~gjʊlə] *adj* □ viereckig.

quad·ra·phon·ic [ˌkwɒdrə'fɒnɪk] *adj* (**~ally**) ♪, *phys.* quadrophon(isch).

quad·ri·lat·er·al [ˌkwɒdrɪ'lætərəl] **I** *adj* vierseitig. **II** *s* Viereck *n.*

quad·ro·phon·ic → **quadraphonic.**

quad·ru·ped ['kwɒdrʊped] *s zo.* Vierfüß(l)er *m.*

quad·ru·ple ['kwɒdrʊpl] **I** *adj* □ vierfach. **II** *v/t u. v/i* (sich) vervierfachen. **quad·ru·plet** [~plɪt] *s* Vierling *m.*

quag·mire ['kwægmaɪə] *s* Morast *m*, Sumpf *m.*

quail [kweɪl] *pl* **quails,** *bsd. coll.* **quail** *s orn.* Wachtel *f.*

quaint [kweɪnt] *adj* □ idyllisch, malerisch.

quake [kweɪk] **I** *v/i* zittern, beben (**with** vor *dat*; **at** bei e-m *Gedanken*). **II** *s* F Erdbeben *n.*

Quak·er ['kweɪkə] *s eccl.* Quäker(in).

qual·i·fi·ca·tion [ˌkwɒlɪfɪ'keɪʃn] *s* **1.** Qualifikation *f*, Befähigung *f*, Eignung *f* (**for** für, zu). **2.** Vorbedingung *f*, Voraussetzung *f* (**of, for** für). **3.** Abschluß(zeugnis *n*) *m.* **4.** Einschränkung *f*, Vorbehalt *m.* **5.** *ling.* nähere Bestimmung. **qual·i·fied** ['~faɪd] *adj* **1.** qualifiziert, geeignet, befähigt (**for** für). **2.** berechtigt: **~ to vote** wahlberechtigt. **3.** bedingt, eingeschränkt. **qual·i·fy** ['~faɪ] **I** *v/t* **1.** qualifizieren, befähigen (**for** für, zu). **2.** berechtigen (**to do** zu tun). **3.** *ling.* näher bestimmen. **II** *v/i* **4.** sich qualifizieren *od.* eignen, die Bedingungen erfüllen (**for** für; **as** als). **5.** *Sport:* sich qualifizieren (**for** für). **6.** s-e Ausbildung abschließen (**as unknown**).

qual·i·ta·tive ['kwɒlɪtətɪv] *adj* □ qualitativ. **qual·i·ty** ['∼ətɪ] *s* **1.** Qualität *f,* ✝ *a.* Güteklasse *f:* **∼ of life** Lebensqualität; **∼ of sound** *TV etc* Tonqualität; **∼ goods** *pl* Qualitätswaren *pl;* **∼ newspaper** seriöse Zeitung. **2.** Eigenschaft *f:* → **leadership** 2.

qualms [kwɑːmz] *s pl* Bedenken *pl,* Skrupel *pl:* **have no ∼ about doing s.th.** keine Bedenken haben, et. zu tun.

quan·da·ry ['kwɒndərɪ] *s* Dilemma *n,* Verlegenheit *f:* **be in a ∼ about what to do** nicht wissen, was man tun soll.

quan·ta ['kwɒntə] *pl von* **quantum.**

quan·ti·ta·tive ['kwɒntɪtətɪv] *adj* □ quantitativ. **quan·ti·ty** ['∼ətɪ] *s* **1.** Quantität *f;* Menge *f:* **in small quantities** in kleinen Mengen; **∼ discount** (*od. allowance*) ✝ Mengenrabatt *m.* **2.** ₳ Größe *f:* → **unknown.**

quan·tum ['kwɒntəm] *phys.* **I** *pl* -**ta** ['∼tə] *s* Quant *n.* **II** *adj* Quanten...

quar·an·tine ['kwɒrəntiːn] **I** *s* Quarantäne *f:* **put in ∼** → **II. II** *v/t* unter Quarantäne stellen.

quar·rel ['kwɒrəl] **I** *s* **1.** Streit *m,* Auseinandersetzung *f* (**with** mit). **2.** **have no ∼ with** nichts auszusetzen haben an (*dat*). **II** *v/i pret u. pp* -**reled,** *bsd. Br.* -**relled 3.** (sich) streiten (**with** mit; **a·bout, over** über *acc*). **4.** **∼ with** et. auszusetzen haben an (*dat*). **quar·rel·some** ['∼səm] *adj* □ streitsüchtig.

quar·ry¹ ['kwɒrɪ] *s* Steinbruch *m.*

quar·ry² [∼] *s hunt.* Beute *f, a. fig.* Opfer *n.*

quart [kwɔːt] *s* Quart *n* (*Hohlmaß*): **you can't put a ∼ into a pint pot** F das geht einfach nicht.

quar·ter ['kwɔːtə] **I** *s* **1.** Viertel *n:* **a ∼ of an hour** e-e Viertelstunde. **2.** **it's** (**a**) **∼ to** (*Am. a. of*) **six** es ist Viertel vor sechs *od.* drei Viertel sechs; **at** (**a**) **∼ past** (*Am. a. after*) **six** um Viertel nach sechs *od.* Viertel sieben. **3.** Quartal *n,* Vierteljahr *n:* **by the ∼** vierteljährlich. **4.** *Am.* Vierteldollar *m.* **5.** (Himmels)Richtung *f;* Gegend *f,* Teil *m* (*e-s Landes etc*): **from all ∼s** von überall(her). **6.** (Stadt)Viertel *n.* **7.** *pl* Quartier *n,* Unterkunft *f*

(*beide a.* ✕). **8.** *fig.* Seite *f,* Stelle *f:* **in the highest ∼s** an höchster Stelle; **from official ∼s** von amtlicher Seite. **II** *v/t* **9.** vierteln. **10.** *bsd.* ✕ einquartieren (**on** bei). **'∼·deck** *s* ⚓ Achterdeck *n.* **'∼·fi·nals** *s pl Sport:* Viertelfinale *n.*

quar·ter·ly ['kwɔːtəlɪ] *adj u. adv* vierteljährlich.

quar·ter note *s* ♩ *bsd. Am.* Viertelnote *f.*

quar·tet(te) [kwɔː'tet] *s* ♩ Quartett *n.*

quartz [kwɔːts] *s min.* Quarz *m.* **∼ clock, ∼ watch** *s* Quarzuhr *f.*

quash [kwɒʃ] *v/t* **1.** ⚖ *Urteil etc* annullieren, aufheben. **2.** *Aufstand etc* niederschlagen, unterdrücken.

qua·ver ['kweɪvə] **I** *v/i* **1.** zittern (*Stimme*). **2.** ♩ tremolieren. **II** *v/t* **3.** *et.* mit zitternder Stimme sagen. **III** *s* **4.** Zittern *n.* **5.** ♩ Tremolo *n.* **6.** ♩ *Br.* Achtelnote *f.*

quay [kiː] *s* ⚓ Kai *m.*

quea·sy ['kwiːzɪ] *adj:* **I feel ∼** mir ist übel.

queen [kwiːn] **I** *s* **1.** (*a. Schönheits-etc*)Königin *f:* **∼ bee** *zo.* Bienenkönigin; **∼ mother** Königinmutter *f;* → **English** 3, **evidence** 2. **2.** *Kartenspiel, Schach:* Dame *f:* **∼ of hearts** Herzdame. **3.** F Schwule *m.* **II** *v/t* **4.** *Schach:* Bauern in e-e Dame verwandeln. **5. ∼ it** F die große Dame spielen. **'queen·ly** *adj* königlich.

queer [kwɪə] **I** *adj* □ **1.** komisch, seltsam: **∼ customer** F komischer Kauz; **be a bit ∼ in the head** F sie nicht alle haben. **2.** F schwul. **II** *s* **3.** F Schwule *m.* **III** *v/t* **4.** → **pitch²** 10.

quell [kwel] *v/t Aufstand etc* niederschlagen, unterdrücken; *Zweifel etc* beseitigen.

quench [kwentʃ] *v/t Durst* löschen, stillen.

quer·u·lous ['kwerʊləs] *adj* □ nörglerisch.

que·ry ['kwɪərɪ] **I** *s* Frage *f.* **II** *v/t* in Frage stellen, in Zweifel ziehen.

quest [kwest] **I** *s* Suche *f* (**for** nach): **in ∼ of** auf der Suche nach. **II** *v/i* suchen (**after, for** nach).

ques·tion ['kwestʃən] **I** *s* **1.** Frage *f:* **∼ mark** Fragezeichen *n;* **∼ master** *Br.* Quizmaster *n;* → **ask** 1, **pop¹** 7. **2.** Frage *f,* Problem *n:* **this is not the point in ∼** darum geht es nicht. **3.** Frage *f,* Sache *f*: **only a ~ of time** nur e-e Frage der Zeit. **4.** Frage *f*, Zweifel *m*: **there is no ~ that, it is beyond ~ that** es steht außer Frage, daß; **there is no ~ about this** daran besteht kein Zweifel; **be out of the ~** nicht in Frage kommen; **call into ~ → 6.** II *v/t* **5.** (**about**) befragen (über *acc*), ⚖ verhören, -nehmen (zu). **6.** bezweifeln, in Zweifel ziehen, in Frage stellen. **'ques·tion·a·ble** *adj* □ **1.** fraglich, zweifelhaft. **2.** fragwürdig. **'question·er** *s* Fragesteller(in). **'ques·tion·ing** I *adj* □ fragend (*Blick etc*). II *s* Befragung *f*, ⚖ Verhör *n*, Vernehmung *f*. **ques·tion·naire** [ˌkwestʃəˈneə] *s* Fragebogen *m*.

queue [kjuː] *bsd. Br.* I *s* Schlange *f*: **stand in a ~ →** IIa; **→ jump 9.** II *v/i mst ~ up** (**for** nach, um) a) Schlange stehen, anstehen, b) sich anstellen. **'~·jump·er** *s j-d*, der sich vordräng(el)t; *mot.* Kolonnenspringer(in).

quib·ble ['kwɪbl] I *v/i* sich herumstreiten (**with** mit; **about, over** wegen). II *s* kleinliche Beschwerde, Kleinigkeit *f*.

quick [kwɪk] I *adj* □ **1.** schnell, rasch: **be ~!** mach schnell!, beeil dich!; **be ~ to learn** (*od.* **at learning**) schnell lernen; **a ~ one** F ein Gläschen auf die Schnelle; **→ offence 3, uptake, 8. 2.** kurz (*Reise etc*). **3.** aufbrausend, hitzig (*Temperament*). II *adv* **4.** schnell, rasch. III *s* **5.** **cut s.o. to the ~** *fig.* j-n tief treffen (*with* mit). **'~·act·ing** *adj* schnell wirkend (*Medikament*). **'~·change** *adj*: **~ artist** *thea.* Verwandlungskünstler(in).

quick·en ['kwɪkən] *v/t u. v/i* (sich) beschleunigen, *v/i a.* schneller werden.

quick·ie ['kwɪkɪ] *s* F *et. Schnelles od. Kurzes, z. B.* Gläschen *n* auf die Schnelle, kurze Frage.

'quick·sand *s* Treibsand *m.* **~·tem·pered** *adj* aufbrausend, hitzig. **~·wit·ted** *adj* □ aufgeweckt; schlagfertig; geistesgegenwärtig.

quid [kwɪd] *pl* **quid** *s Br.* F Pfund *n* (*Währung*).

qui·et ['kwaɪət] I *adj* □ **1.** ruhig, still: **~, please** Ruhe, bitte. **2.** ruhig (*Leben etc*). **3.** geheim, heimlich: **keep s.th. ~** et. für sich behalten. II *s* **4.** Ruhe *f*, Stille *f*: **→ peace 3. 5. on the ~** F heimlich. III *v/t u. v/i* **6. → quieten.** **'qui·et·en I** *v/t* **1.** *a.* **~ down** j-n beruhigen. **2.**

Befürchtungen etc zerstreuen. II *v/i* **3.** *a.* **~ down** sich beruhigen.

quill [kwɪl] *s* **1.** *orn.* (Schwanz-, Schwung)Feder *f.* **2.** *a.* **~ pen** *hist.* Federkiel *m.* **3.** *zo.* Stachel *m.*

quilt [kwɪlt] *s* Steppdecke *f.* **'quilt·ed** *adj* Stepp...

quin [kwɪn] *s Br.* F Fünfling *m.*

quince [kwɪns] *s* ♀ Quitte *f.*

qui·nine [kwɪˈniːn] *s pharm.* Chinin *n.*

quint [kwɪnt] *s Am.* F Fünfling *m.*

quint·es·sence [kwɪnˈtesns] *s* **1.** Quintessenz *f.* **2.** Inbegriff *m.*

quin·tet(te) [kwɪnˈtet] *s ♪* Quintett *n.*

quin·tu·plet ['kwɪntjʊplɪt] *s* Fünfling *m.*

quip [kwɪp] I *s* geistreiche *od.* witzige Bemerkung. II *v/i* witzeln.

quirk [kwɜːk] *s* **1.** Eigenart *f*, Schrulle *f.* **2. by some ~ of fate** durch e-n verrückten Zufall.

quit [kwɪt] (*mst irr*) F I *v/t* **1.** aufhören mit: **~ doing s.th.** aufhören, et. zu tun; **~ one's job** kündigen; **~ smoking** das Rauchen aufgeben. II *v/i* **2.** aufhören. **3.** kündigen.

quite [kwaɪt] *adv* **1.** ganz, völlig: **be ~ right** völlig recht haben; **~ (so)** ganz recht, genau, ganz recht. **2.** ziemlich: **a ~ a dis·appointment** e-e ziemliche Enttäuschung; **~ a few** ziemlich viele; **~ good** ganz *od.* recht gut. **3.** it was **~** a (*od.* **some**) **sight** das war vielleicht ein Anblick; **she's a ~ a girl** sie ist ein tolles Mädchen.

quits [kwɪts] *adj* quitt (**with** mit): **call it ~** F es gut sein lassen.

quit·ter ['kwɪtə] *s*: **he's a (no) ~** F er gibt (nicht so) schnell auf.

quiv·er¹ ['kwɪvə] *v/i* zittern (**with** vor *dat*; **at** bei e-m *Gedanken etc*). II *s* Zittern *n.*

quiv·er² [~] *s* Köcher *m.*

quix·ot·ic [kwɪkˈsɒtɪk] *adj* (~**ally**) weltfremd-idealistisch.

quiz [kwɪz] I *pl* **quiz·zes** *s* Quiz *n.* II *v/t* ausfragen (**about** über *acc*). **'~·mas·ter** *s* Quizmaster *m.*

quiz·zi·cal ['kwɪzɪkl] *adj* □ wissend (*Blick etc*).

quoit [kɔɪt] *s* **1.** Wurfring *m.* **2.** *pl* (*sg konstruiert*) Wurfringspiel *n.*

quo·rate ['kwɔːreɪt] *adj* beschlußfähig.

quo·rum ['kwɔːrəm] *s* zur Beschlußfähigkeit erforderliche Teilnehmerzahl.

quo·ta ['kwəʊtə] *s* Kontingent *n*, Quote *f*, ✝ *a.* Soll *n*.

quo·ta·tion [kwəʊ'teɪʃn] *s* **1.** Zitat *n* (*from* aus); ~ *from the Bible* Bibelzitat *n*. **2.** ✝ Notierung *f*. **3.** ✝ (*verbindlicher*) Kosten(vor)anschlag: *get a* ~ e-n Kostenvoranschlag einholen. ~ *marks s pl* Anführungszeichen *pl*: *put* (*od. place*) *in* ~ in Anführungszeichen setzen.

quote [kwəʊt] **I** *v/t* **1.** zitieren (*from* aus); *Beispiel etc* anführen: *he was* ~*d as saying that* er soll gesagt haben, daß. **2.** *be* ~*d at* ✝ notieren mit. **II** *v/i* **3.** ~ *from* zitieren. **III** *s* F **4.** → *quotation* 1, 2. **5.** *pl* Gänsefüßchen *pl*: *put* (*od. place*) *in* ~*s* in Gänsefüßchen setzen. **IV** *adv* **6.** ~ *... unquote* Zitat ... Zitat Ende.

quo·tient ['kwəʊʃnt] *s* Ⅰ Quotient *m*.

R

r [ɑː]: *the three R's* (= *reading, writing, arithmetic*) Lesen *n*, Schreiben *n* u. Rechnen *n*.

rab·bi ['ræbaɪ] *s eccl.* Rabbiner *m*.

rab·bit ['ræbɪt] *s* Kaninchen *n*. ~ *punch s* Genickschlag *m*.

rab·ble ['ræbl] *s* **1.** Pöbel *m*, Mob *m*. **2.** *sociol. contp.* Pöbel *m*. '~·,rous·ing *adj* aufwieglerisch, Hetz...

rab·id ['ræbɪd] *adj* □ **1.** *vet.* tollwütig. **2.** fanatisch.

ra·bies ['reɪbiːz] *s vet.* Tollwut *f*.

rac·coon → **racoon**.

race¹ [reɪs] *s* **1.** Rasse *f*. **2.** Rasse(n)-zugehörigkeit) *f*. **3.** (*Menschen*)Geschlecht *n*.

race² [~] **I** *s* **1.** *Sport:* Rennen *n* (*a. fig. for* um), Lauf *m*: ~ *against time fig.* Wettlauf mit der Zeit. **II** *v/i* **2.** an (e-m) Rennen teilnehmen; um die Wette laufen *od.* fahren (*against, with* mit). **3.** rasen, rennen. **4.** durchdrehen (*Motor*). **III** *v/t* **5.** um die Wette laufen *od.* fahren mit. **6.** rasen mit: ~ *s.o. to hospital* mit j-m ins Krankenhaus rasen.

'**race·course** *s* Pferdesport: Rennbahn *f*. '~·horse *s* Rennpferd *n*. ~ *meet·ing s* Pferdesport: Rennveranstaltung *f*.

rac·er ['reɪsə] *s* **1.** Rennpferd *n*. **2.** Rennrad *n*, -wagen *m*.

'**race·track** *s* **1.** *Automobilsport etc:* Rennstrecke *f*. **2.** *bsd. Am.* → *race-course*.

ra·cial ['reɪʃl] *adj* □ rassisch, Rassen...: ~ *discrimination* Rassendiskriminie-

rung *f*; ~ *segregation* Rassentrennung *f*. **ra·cial·ism** ['reɪʃəlɪzəm], '**ra·cial·ist** → *racism, racist*.

rac·ing ['reɪsɪŋ] *adj* Renn...: ~ *bicycle* Rennrad *n*; ~ *car* Rennwagen *m*; ~ *cyclist* Radrennfahrer(in); ~ *driver* Rennfahrer(in).

ra·cism ['reɪsɪzəm] *s* Rassismus *m*. '**ra·cist** **I** *s* Rassist(in). **II** *adj* rassistisch.

rack¹ [ræk] **I** *s* **1.** Gestell *n*, (*Geschirr-, Zeitungs- etc*)Ständer, 🚋 (*Gepäck*)Netz *n*, *mot.* (*Dach*)Gepäckständer *m*. **2.** *hist.* Folter(bank) *f*: *put s.o. on the* ~ j-n auf die Folter spannen (*a. fig.*). **II** *v/t* **3.** *be* ~*ed by* (*od. with*) geplagt *od.* gequält werden von. **4.** → *brain* 2.

rack² [~] *s*: *go to* ~ *and ruin* verfallen (*Gebäude, Person*), dem Ruin entgegentreiben (*Land, Wirtschaft*).

rack·et¹ ['rækɪt] *s Tennis etc:* Schläger *m*.

rack·et² [~] *s* F **1.** Krach *m*, Lärm *m*: *make a* ~ Krach machen. **2.** Schwindel *m*, Gaunerei *f*; (*Drogen- etc*)Geschäft *n*; organisierte Erpressung; Beruf *m*, Branche *f*: *what's his* ~? was macht er beruflich? **rack·et·eer** [,rækə'tɪə] *s* F Gauner *m*; Erpresser *m*.

ra·coon [rə'kuːn] *s zo.* Waschbär *m*.

rac·y ['reɪsɪ] *adj* □ **1.** spritzig (*Geschichte etc*). **2.** gewagt.

ra·dar ['reɪdɑː] **I** *s* Radar *m*, *n*. **II** *adj* Radar...: ~ *screen* Radarschirm *m*; ~ (*speed*) *trap* Radarkontrolle *f*; ~ *station* Radarstation *f*.

ra·di·al ['reɪdjəl] **I** *adj* □ radial, Radi-

al..., strahlenförmig: **~ tire** (*bsd. Br.*
tyre) → II. **II** *s mot.* Gürtelreifen *m.*

ra·di·ant ['reɪdjənt] *adj* □ strahlend (*a.
fig.* **with** vor *dat*): **be ~ with joy** vor
Freude strahlen.

ra·di·ate ['reɪdɪeɪt] **I** *v/t* Licht, Wärme etc
ausstrahlen, *Optimismus etc a.* verström·
men. **II** *v/i* strahlenförmig ausgehen
(**from** von). **,ra·di·'a·tion** *s* 1. Ausstrah·
lung *f, fig. a.* Verströmen *n.* **2.** *phys.*
(*engS.* radioaktive) Strahlung: **~ sick·
ness** ✠ Strahlenkrankheit *f.* **ra·di·a·**
·tor ['~eɪtə] *s* **1.** Heizkörper *m.* **2.** *mot.*
Kühler *m*: **~ grill** Kühlergrill *m.*

rad·i·cal ['rædɪkl] **I** *adj* □ **1.** radikal (*a.
pol.*). **2.** ℞ Wurzel...: **~ sign** Wurzel·
zeichen *n.* **II** *s* **3.** *pol.* Radikale *m, f.*
4. ℞, *ling.* Wurzel *f.* **rad·i·cal·ism**
['~kəlɪzəm] *s bsd. pol.* Radikalismus *m.*
'**rad·i·cal·ize** *v/t bsd. pol.* radikalisie·
ren.

ra·di·i ['reɪdɪaɪ] *pl von* **radius.**

ra·di·o ['reɪdɪəʊ] **I** *pl* **-os** *s* **1.** Radio *n,*
Rundfunkgerät *n*; Funkgerät *n.* **2.** Ra·
dio *n,* Rundfunk *m*: **on the ~** im Radio;
be in ~ beim Rundfunk sein. **3.** Funk
m: **by ~** per *od.* über Funk. **II** *v/t* **4.**
Nachricht etc funken, durchgeben. **5.**
j-n, Ort anfunken. **III** *v/i* **6.** **~ for help**
per *od.* über Funk um Hilfe bitten.
,~·**'ac·tive** *adj* □ radioaktiv: **~ waste**
Atommüll *m,* radioaktiver Abfall. ,~·
ac·'tiv·i·ty *s* Radioaktivität *f.* ~ **a·larm** *s*
Radiowecker *m.* ~ **car** *s Am.* Funk·
(streifen)wagen *m.* ~ **con·tact** *s* Funk·
kontakt *m,* -verbindung *f*: **be in ~ with**
in Funkkontakt stehen mit. ,~·**con·
'trolled** *adj* funkgesteuert.
ra·di·o·gram ['reɪdɪəʊɡræm] *s* **1.** Funk·
spruch *m.* **2.** → **radiograph. ra·di·o·**
graph ['~ɡrɑːf] *s* ✠ Röntgenbild *n.*
ra·di·o| **ham** → **ham 3.** ~ **mes·sage** *s*
Funkspruch *m.* ~ **op·er·a·tor** *s* Funker
m. ~ **set** → **radio 1.** ~ **sig·nal** *s* Funk·
signal *n.* ~ **sta·tion** *s* Rundfunksender
m, -station *f.* ,~·**'ther·a·py** ✠ Strah·
len·, Röntgentherapie *f.* ~ **traf·fic** *s*
Funkverkehr *m.*

rad·ish ['rædɪʃ] *s* ℞ **1.** Rettich *m.* **2.** Ra·
dieschen *n.*

ra·di·um ['reɪdɪəm] *s* 🜨 Radium *n.*

ra·di·us ['reɪdɪəs] *pl* **-di·i** ['~dɪaɪ] *s* **1.** ℞
Radius *m,* Halbmesser *m.* **2.** **within a
three·mile ~** im Umkreis von drei

Meilen (**of** um). **3.** *anat.* Speiche *f.*

raf·fle ['ræfl] **I** *s* Tombola *f.* **II** *v/t oft* ~ **off**
verlosen.

raft [rɑːft] *s* Floß *n.*

raft·er ['rɑːftə] *s* (Dach)Sparren *m.*

rag [ræɡ] *s* **1.** Fetzen *m,* Lumpen *m*;
Lappen *m*: **in ~s** in Fetzen (*Stoff etc*);
zerlumpt (*Person*): **be (like) a red ~ to a
bull to s.o.** *Br.* F wie ein rotes Tuch für
j-n sein *od.* auf j-n wirken; **feel like a
wet ~** F total k. o. sein. **2.** F *contp.*
Käseblatt *n.* '**~·bag** *s* Sammelsurium
n (**of** von).

rage [reɪdʒ] **I** *s* **1.** Wut *f,* Zorn *m*: **be in a
~** wütend sein; **fly into a ~** wütend wer·
den. **2.** F **the latest ~** der letzte Schrei;
be all the ~ große Mode sein. **II** *v/i* **3.**
wettern (**against, at** gegen); *fig.* rasen
(*Krankheit, Sturm*), toben (*Meer,
Sturm*): **a raging headache** rasende
Kopfschmerzen *pl.*

rag·ged ['ræɡɪd] *adj* □ **1.** zerlumpt
(*Kleidung, Person*). **2.** struppig, zottig
(*Bart etc*). **3.** *fig.* dilettantisch, stüm·
perhaft.

ra·gout ['ræɡuː] *s gastr.* Ragout *n.*

raid [reɪd] **I** *s* **1.** (**on**) Überfall *m* (auf *acc*),
⚔ *a.* Angriff *m* (gegen). **2.** Razzia *f* (**on**
in *dat*): **make a ~ on** → **4. II** *v/t* **3.**
überfallen, ⚔ *a.* angreifen. **4.** e·e Raz·
zia machen in (*dat*).

rail¹ [reɪl] **I** *s* **1.** Geländer *n.* **2.** (*Hand·
tuch*)Halter *m.* **3.** 🚂 Schiene *f, pl a.*
Gleis *n*: **go off the ~s** a) a. **jump the ~s**
entgleisen, b) *fig.* auf die schiefe Bahn
geraten. **4.** (*Eisen*)Bahn *f*: **by ~** mit der
Bahn. **II** *v/t* **5.** ~ **in** einzäunen; ~ **off**
abzäunen.

rail² [~] *v/i* schimpfen (**against, at** über
acc).

rail·ing ['reɪlɪŋ] *s oft pl* (Gitter)Zaun *m.*

rail·road ['reɪlrəʊd] **I** *s* **1.** *Am.* → **rail·
way. II** *v/t* F **2.** *Gesetzesvorlage etc*
durchpeitschen (**through** in *dat*). **3.** ~
s.o. into doing s.th. j-n rücksichtslos
drängen, et. zu tun.

rail·way ['reɪlweɪ] *s bsd. Br.* Eisenbahn *f*:
~ **station** Bahnhof *m.*

rain [reɪn] **I** *s* **1.** Regen *m*: **in the ~** im
Regen; **the ~s** die Regenzeit (*in den
Tropen*); → **pour 3. 2.** *fig.* (*Schlag·
etc*)Hagel *m,* (*Funken*)Regen *m.* **II** *v/i* **3.**
impers regnen: **it is ~ing. 4.** ~ **down on**
fig. niederprasseln auf (*acc*) (*Schläge*

etc). **III** v/t **5.** → **cat** I. **6.** fig. ~ **blows on s.o.** j-n mit Schlägen eindecken; ~ **abuse on s.o.** j-n mit Beschimpfungen überschütten. **7. be ~ed off** (Am. **out**) wegen Regens abgesagt od. abgebrochen werden. '**~bow** s Regenbogen m. '**~coat** s Regenmantel m. '**~drop** s Regentropfen m. '**~fall** s Niederschlag(smenge f) m. ~ **for·est** s Regenwald m. '**~proof** adj regen-, wasserdicht. '**~storm** s heftiger Regenguß m. '**~wa·ter** s Regenwasser n.

rain·y ['reɪnɪ] adj regnerisch, verregnet, Regen...: the ~ **season** die Regenzeit (in den Tropen); **put away** (od. **save**) s.th. for a ~ **day** et. für schlechte Zeiten zurücklegen, et. auf die hohe Kante legen.

raise [reɪz] **I** v/t **1.** Arm, gesunkenes Schiff etc heben; Vorhang etc hochziehen: ~ **one's hat** den Hut ziehen (**to s.o.** vor j-m; a. fig.) od. lüften; → **eyebrow**. **2.** Denkmal etc errichten. **3.** a) Protest etc hervorrufen; ~ **a laugh** Gelächter ernten, b) Erwartungen (er)wecken: ~ **s.o.'s hopes** in j-m Hoffnung erwecken; ~ **a suspicion** Verdacht erregen, c) Gerücht etc aufkommen lassen, d) Schwierigkeiten machen. **4.** Staub etc aufwirbeln: → **dust** 1. **5.** Frage aufwerfen, et. zur Sprache bringen. **6.** Anspruch geltend machen, Forderung stellen. **7.** Kinder auf-, großziehen; Tiere züchten; Getreide etc anbauen. **8.** Moral, Stimmung heben. **9.** Gehalt etc erhöhen, Geschwindigkeit etc a. steigern: → **power** 9. **10.** Hypothek etc aufnehmen (**on** auf acc); Geld zs.-bringen, beschaffen. **11.** Blockade etc, a. Verbot aufheben. **II** s **12.** bsd. Am. Lohn- od. Gehaltserhöhung f.

rai·sin ['reɪzn] s Rosine f.

rake [reɪk] **I** s **1.** Rechen m, Harke f. **II** v/t **2.** rechen, harken: ~ **in** F Geld kassieren; ~ **it in** F das Geld nur so scheffeln; ~ **out** F et. herausfinden; ~ **up** Laub etc zs.-rechen, -harken; F Leute auftreiben, Geld a. zs.-kratzen; F alte Geschichten etc aufwärmen. **3.** Gelände etc absuchen (**with** mit Fernglas etc). **III** v/i **4.** a. ~ **about** (od. **around**) herumstöbern (**in** in dat). '**~off** s F (Gewinn)Anteil m, Prozente pl.

rak·ish ['reɪkɪʃ] adj □ flott, verwegen.

ral·ly ['rælɪ] **I** s **1.** Kundgebung f, (Massen)Versammlung f. **2.** Motorsport: Rallye f. **3.** Tennis etc: Ballwechsel m. **II** v/t **4.** Truppen etc (wieder) sammeln. **III** v/i **5.** sich (wieder) sammeln: ~ **round** fig. sich zs.-tun; ~ **round s.o.** fig. sich um j-n scharen. **6.** sich erholen (**from** von) (a. ✝).

ram [ræm] **I** s **1.** zo. Widder m, Schafbock m. **2.** ☉ Ramme f. **II** v/t **3.** Fahrzeug etc rammen. **4.** Pfosten etc rammen (**into** in acc): ~ **down** Erde etc feststampfen, -treten; → **throat**.

ram·ble ['ræmbl] **I** v/i **1.** wandern. **2.** a. ~ **on** contp. faseln (**about** von, über acc). **II** s **3.** Wanderung f: **go for** (od. **on**) a ~ e-e Wanderung machen. '**ram·bling** adj □ **1.** ♀ Kletter...: ~ **rose.** **2.** fig. weitschweifig, unzusammenhängend. **3.** weitläufig (Gebäude).

ram·i·fi·ca·tion [,ræmɪfɪ'keɪʃn] s Verzweigung f, -ästelung f (beide a. fig.). **ram·i·fy** ['~faɪ] v/i sich verzweigen (a. fig.).

ramp [ræmp] s Rampe f.

ram·page [ræm'peɪdʒ] **I** v/i: ~ **through** a) (wild od. aufgeregt) trampeln durch (Elefant etc), b) randalierend ziehen durch. **II** s: **go on the** ~ randalieren; **be on the** ~ **through** → Ib.

ramp·ant ['ræmpənt] adj □ **1.** wuchernd (Pflanze): **be** ~ wuchern. **2.** fig. grassierend: **be** ~ grassieren in (dat).

ram·shack·le ['ræmʃækl] adj baufällig; klapp(e)rig (Fahrzeug).

ran [ræn] pret von **run**.

ranch [rɑːntʃ] s **1.** Ranch f. **2.** (Geflügeletc)Farm f. '**ranch·er** s **1.** Rancher m. **2.** (Geflügel- etc)Züchter m. **3.** Rancharbeiter m.

ran·cid ['rænsɪd] adj □ ranzig: **go** ~ ranzig werden.

ran·cor Am. → **rancour.**

ran·cor·ous ['ræŋkərəs] adj □ voller Groll (**toward[s]** gegen).

ran·cour ['ræŋkə] s bsd. Br. Groll m, Erbitterung f.

ran·dom ['rændəm] **I** adj aufs Geratewohl, zufällig, Zufalls...: ~ **sample** Stichprobe f; **take** ~ **samples** Stichproben machen. **II** s: **at** ~ aufs Geratewohl.

rand·y ['rændɪ] adj F scharf, geil.

rang [ræŋ] pret von **ring²**.

range [reɪndʒ] **I** s **1.** (Berg)Kette f. **2.** (Koch-, Küchen)Herd m. **3.** (Schieß-)Stand m, (-)Platz m. **4.** Entfernung f: **at close** (od. **short**) ~ aus kurzer od. kürzester Entfernung, aus nächster Nähe. **5.** Reich-, Schuß-, Tragweite f. **6.** fig. Bereich m, Spielraum m, Grenzen pl. **7.** † Kollektion f, Sortiment n. **8.** fig. Bereich m, Gebiet m. **II** v/i **9.** schwanken, sich bewegen (**from ... to, between ... and** zwischen ... u.). **III** v/t **10.** aufstellen, anordnen. **~ find·er** s phot. etc Entfernungsmesser m.

rang·er ['reɪndʒə] s **1.** Förster m. **2.** Am. Ranger m.

rank¹ [ræŋk] **I** s **1.** Reihe f; ✕ Glied n: **close the ~s** die Reihen schließen; fig. sich zs.-schließen. **2.** bsd. ✕ Rang m: **in ~** im Rang, rangmäßig; **he is above me in ~** er ist ranghöher als ich; **of the first** (od. **front, top**) ~ fig. erstklassig; **the ~s** pl (Unteroffiziere pl u.) Mannschaften pl; fig. das Heer, die Masse (der Arbeitslosen etc); **the ~ and file** die Mannschaft(en); fig. die Basis (e-r Partei etc); **pull** ~ F den Vorgesetzten herauskehren (**on** gegenüber); **rise from the ~s** vom Mannschaftsrang zum Offizier aufsteigen; fig. sich hocharbeiten. **3.** Rang m, (soziale) Stellung. **II** v/t **4.** rechnen, zählen (**among** zu); stellen (**above** über acc): **be ~ed 2nd in the world** an 2. Stelle der Weltrangliste stehen. **5.** ✕ Am. ranghöher sein als. **III** v/i **6.** zählen, gehören (**among** zu); gelten (**as** als); rangieren (**above** über dat).

rank² [~] adj □ **1.** (üppig) wuchernd. **2.** übel(riechend od. -schmeckend). **3.** fig. kraß (Außenseiter), blutig (Anfänger), blühend (Unsinn).

rank·ing ['ræŋkɪŋ] adj **1.** ✕ Am. ranghöchst (Offizier). **2.** ~ **list** (Sport) Rangliste f.

ran·kle ['ræŋkl] v/i fig. (**on**) nagen (an dat), weh tun (dat).

ran·sack ['rænsæk] v/t **1.** durchwühlen. **2.** plündern.

ran·som ['rænsəm] **I** s Lösegeld n: **hold s.o. to** ~ j-n bis zur Zahlung e-s Lösegelds gefangenhalten; fig. j-n erpressen; ~ **demand** Lösegeldforderung f. **II** v/t auslösen, freikaufen.

rant [rænt] v/i a. ~ **on**, ~ **and rave** (**about**

eifern (gegen), sich in Tiraden ergehen (über acc).

rap¹ [ræp] **I** s **1.** Klopfen n; Klaps m: **give s.o. a** ~ **over the knuckles** j-m auf die Finger klopfen (a. fig.). **2. take the** ~ F den Kopf hinhalten (**for** für). **II** v/t **3.** klopfen an (acc) od. auf (acc): ~ **s.o. over the knuckles** j-m auf die Finger klopfen (a. fig.). **4.** mst ~ **out** Befehl etc bellen, Fluch etc ausstoßen. **III** v/i **5.** klopfen (**at** an acc; **on** auf acc).

rap² [~] s: **I don't care a** ~ (**for it**) das ist mir völlig egal.

ra·pa·cious [rə'peɪʃəs] adj □ **1.** habgierig. **2.** räuberisch. **3.** orn., zo. Raub...

ra·pac·i·ty [rə'pæsətɪ] s Habgier f.

rape¹ [reɪp] **I** s Vergewaltigung f, ⚖ Notzucht f. **II** v/t vergewaltigen.

rape² [~] s ♀ Raps m: ~ **oil** Rapsöl n.

rap·id ['ræpɪd] **I** adj □ schnell, rasch. **II** s pl Stromschnellen pl. '**~-fire** adj **1.** ✕ Schnellfeuer... **2.** fig. schnell (aufeinanderfolgend).

ra·pid·i·ty [rə'pɪdətɪ] s Schnelligkeit f.

rap·ist ['reɪpɪst] s Vergewaltiger m.

rap·port [ræ'pɔː] s harmonisches Verhältnis (**between** zwischen dat; **with** zu).

rap·proche·ment [ræ'prɔʃmãːŋ] s bsd. pol. (Wieder)Annäherung f (**between** zwischen dat).

rapt [ræpt] adj: **with** ~ **attention** mit gespannter Aufmerksamkeit.

rap·ture ['ræptʃə] s, a. pl Entzücken n, Verzückung f: **be in** ~**s** entzückt od. hingerissen sein (**about, at, over** von); **go into** ~**s** in Verzückung geraten (**about, at, over** über acc). '**rap·tur·ous** adj □ **1.** entzückt, hingerissen. **2.** stürmisch (Applaus etc).

rare¹ [reə] adj □ **1.** selten, rar. **2.** dünn (Luft). **3.** More...: **give s.o. a** ~ **fright** j-m e-n Mordsschreck(en) einjagen.

rare² [~] adj blutig (Steak).

rar·e·fied ['reərɪfaɪd] adj **1.** dünn (Luft). **2.** fig. exklusiv.

rar·ing ['reərɪŋ] adj: **be** ~ **to do s.th.** F es kaum mehr erwarten können od. ganz wild darauf sein, et. zu tun.

rar·i·ty ['reərətɪ] s Seltenheit f, (Briefmarke etc a.) Rarität f.

ras·cal ['rɑːskəl] s **1.** Gauner m. **2.** humor. Schlingel m.

rash¹ [ræʃ] *adj* □ voreilig, -schnell.

rash² [~] *s* **1.** ⚕ (Haut)Ausschlag *m*: → **come out** 5. **2.** *fig.* Flut *f*.

rash·er ['ræʃə] *s* dünne Scheibe (*Frühstücksspeck etc*).

rasp [rɑ:sp] **I** *s* **1.** Raspel *f*. **2.** Kratzen *n*. **II** *v/t* **3.** raspeln: ~ **off** abraspeln.

rasp·ber·ry ['rɑːzbərɪ] *s* ⚘ Himbeere *f*.

rasp·ing ['rɑːspɪŋ] *adj* □ kratzend (*Geräusch*); krächzend (*Stimme*).

rat [ræt] *s* *zo.* Ratte *f* (*a.* F *contp.*): **smell a** ~ *fig.* Lunte *od.* den Braten riechen; **~s!** F Mist! **II** *v/i*: ~ **on** F *j-n* im Stich lassen; *j-n* verpfeifen; aussteigen aus (*e-m Projekt etc*).

rate [reɪt] **I** *s* **1.** Quote *f*, (*Inflations- etc*)Rate *f* (*Geburten-*, *Sterbe-*)Ziffer *f*. **2.** (*Steuer-*, *Zins- etc*)Satz *m*, (*Wechsel*)Kurs *m*; **at any** ~ *fig.* auf jeden Fall. **3.** *mst pl Br.* Gemeinde-, Kommunalsteuer *f*. **4.** Geschwindigkeit *f*, Tempo *n*. **II** *v/t* **5.** einschätzen (**highly** hoch), halten (**as** für): **be** ~**d as** gelten als. **6.** *Lob etc* verdienen.

rath·er ['rɑːðə] **I** *adv* **1.** ziemlich: ~ **a success** ein ziemlicher Erfolg; ~ **a cold night, a** ~ **cold night** e-e ziemlich kalte Nacht. **2. I would** (*od.* **had**) ~ **stay at home** ich möchte lieber zu Hause bleiben. **3. or** ~ (od.) vielmehr. **II** *int* **4.** *bsd. Br.* F freilich!, und ob!

rat·i·fi·ca·tion [ˌrætɪfɪˈkeɪʃn] *s pol.* Ratifizierung *f*. **rat·i·fy** ['~faɪ] *v/t* ratifizieren.

rat·ing ['reɪtɪŋ] *s* **1.** Einschätzung *f*. **2.** *Rundfunk, TV;* Einschaltquote *f*.

ra·ti·o ['reɪʃɪəʊ] *pl* **-os** *s* & *etc* Verhältnis *n* (**of ... to** von ... zu).

ra·tion ['ræʃn] **I** *s* **1.** Ration *f*. **II** *v/t* **2.** *et.* rationieren. **3.** ~ **out** zuteilen (**to** dat).

ra·tion·al ['ræʃənl] *adj* □ rational: a) vernunftbegabt, b) vernünftig. **ra·tion·al·ism** ['ræʃnəlɪzəm] *s* Rationalismus *m*. **'ra·tion·al·ist** *s* Rationalist(in). **II** *adj* rationalistisch. **ra·tion·al·is·tic** [ˌ~ə`lɪstɪk] *adj* (~**ally**) rationalistisch. **ra·tion·al·i·za·tion** *s* ⚚ Rationalisierung *f*. **'ra·tion·al·ize** *v/t* **1.** rational erklären. **2.** ⚚ rationalisieren.

rat| poi·son *s* Rattengift *n*. ~ **race** *s* F endloser Konkurrenzkampf.

rat·tle ['rætl] **I** *v/i* **1.** klappern (*Fenster etc*); rasseln, klirren (*Ketten*); klimpern (*Münzen etc*); prasseln (**on** auf *acc*)

(*Regen etc*); knattern (*Fahrzeug*): ~ **at** rütteln an (*dat*); ~ **on** F quasseln (**about** über *acc*); ~ **through** *Rede etc* herunterrasseln; *Arbeit* in Windeseile erledigen. **II** *v/t* **2.** rasseln *od.* klimpern mit; rütteln an (*dat*): ~ **off** *Gedicht etc* herunterrasseln. **3.** F *j-n* verunsichern. **III** *s* **4.** Klappern *n* (*etc*, → 1). **5.** Rassel *f*, Klapper *f* (*Spielzeug*), Knarre *f*, Schnarre *f* (*Lärminstrument*). **6.** *zo.* Klapperschlange *f*. '**~snake** *s zo.* Klapperschlange *f*. '**~trap** *s* F Klapperkasten *m* (*Auto*).

'**rat·trap** *s Am.* F Bruchbude *f*, Hundehütte *f*.

rat·ty ['rætɪ] *adj* F **1.** *Am.* schäbig (*Kleidungsstück*). **2.** gereizt: **there's no need to be** ~ sei doch nicht gleich so gereizt.

rau·cous ['rɔːkəs] *adj* □ heiser, rauh.

rav·age ['rævɪdʒ] **I** *v/t* verwüsten. **II** *s pl* Verwüstungen *pl*, *a. fig.* verheerende Auswirkungen *pl*.

rave [reɪv] *v/i* **1.** phantasieren, irrereden. **2.** toben; wettern (**against, at** gegen). **3.** schwärmen (**about** von).

rav·el ['rævl] *pret u. pp* **-eled**, *bsd. Br.* **-elled I** *v/t* **1.** *a.* ~ **up** verwickeln, -wirren. **2.** *oft* ~ **out** ausfransen; auftrennen; *a. fig.* entwirren. **II** *v/i* **3.** *a.* ~ **up** sich verwickeln *od.* -wirren. **4.** *oft* ~ **out** ausfransen; auftrennen.

ra·ven ['reɪvn] *s orn.* Rabe *m*.

rav·en·ous ['rævənəs] *adj* □ **1.** ausgehungert, heißhungrig. **2.** ~ **hunger** Bären-, Wolfshunger *m*.

ra·vine [rə`viːn] *s* Schlucht *f*, Klamm *f*.

rav·ing ['reɪvɪŋ] **I** *adj* □ **1.** tobend. **2.** phantasierend. **3.** F toll (*Erfolg*), hinreißend (*Schönheit*). **II** *adv* **4.** ~ **mad** F völlig *od.* total übergeschnappt. **III** *s pl* **5.** Phantasien *pl*, irres Gerede.

rav·i·o·li [ˌrævɪˈəʊlɪ] *s pl* (*sg konstruiert*) Ravioli *pl*.

rav·ish ['rævɪʃ] *v/t* hinreißen. '**rav·ish·ing** *adj* □ hinreißend.

raw [rɔː] **I** *adj* □ **1.** roh (*Gemüse etc*). **2.** ⚕, ⚙ roh, Roh...: ~ **material** Rohstoff *m*. **3.** unerfahren, grün. **4.** wund (*Haut*). **5.** naßkalt (*Wetter, Tag etc*). **6.** **get a** ~ **deal** F benachteiligt *od.* ungerecht behandelt werden. **II** *s* **7.** *in the* ~: im Natur- *od.* Urzustand; F nackt. '**~boned** *adj* hager, knochig.

ray¹ [reɪ] *s* Strahl *m*: **sun's** ~**s** *pl* Sonnenstrahlen *pl*; **~ of light** Lichtstrahl; **~ of hope** Hoffnungsstrahl, -schimmer *m*.

ray² [~] *s ichth.* Rochen *m*.

ray·on ['reɪɒn] *s* Kunstseide *f*.

raze [reɪz] *v/t*: **~ to the ground** dem Erdboden gleichmachen.

ra·zor ['reɪzə] *s* Rasiermesser *n*; -apparat *m*: **be on a ~'s edge → razor edge. ~ blade** *s* Rasierklinge *f*. **~ edge** *s*: **be on a ~** *fig.* auf des Messers Schneide stehen. **,~'sharp** *adj* messerscharf (*a. fig. Verstand*).

raz·zle ['ræzl] *s*: **go on the ~** *F* auf den Putz hauen.

re [riː] *prp*: **~ your letter of ...** ✝ Betr.: Ihr Schreiben vom ...

reach [riːtʃ] **I** *v/t* **1.** *j-n, et., Ort, Alter etc* erreichen. **2. ~ out** *Arm etc* ausstrecken. **3. ~ down** herunter-, hinunterreichen (**from** von). **4.** reichen *od.* gehen bis an (*acc*) *od.* zu. **II** *v/i* **5.** *a.* **~ out** greifen, langen (**for** nach) (*beide a. fig.*). **6. ~ out** die Hand ausstrecken. **7.** reichen, gehen, sich erstrecken (**as far as,** *to* bis an *acc od.* zu): **as far as the eye can ~** soweit das Auge reicht. **III** *v* **8.** Reichweite *f* (*a. Boxen*): **within (out of) s.o.'s ~** in (außer) j-s Reichweite; **be within easy ~** leicht zu erreichen sein (*Instrument etc*); **she lives within easy ~ of the shops** (*bsd. Am.* **stores**) von ihrer Wohnung aus sind die Geschäfte leicht zu erreichen.

re·act [rɪ'ækt] *v/i* **1.** reagieren (**to** auf *acc*): **~ against** sich wehren gegen. **2.** 🐎 reagieren (**with** mit).

re·ac·tion [rɪ'ækʃn] *s* Reaktion *f* (*a.* 🐎, *pol. etc*). **re'ac·tion·ar·y** *pol.* **I** *adj* reaktionär. **II** *s* Reaktionär(in).

re·ac·ti·vate [rɪ'æktɪveɪt] *v/t* reaktivieren (*a.* 🐎).

re·ac·tive [rɪ'æktɪv] *adj* 🐎 reaktiv, reaktionsfähig. **re'ac·tor** *s phys.* Reaktor *m*.

read¹ [riːd] **I** *v/t* (*irr*) **1.** lesen: **~ in** (*Computer*) einlesen; **~ s.th. into** et. hineinlesen in (*acc*); **~ out** verlesen; **~ s.th. to s.o., ~ s.o. s.th.** j-m et. vorlesen; **read over** (*od.* **through**) (sich) et. durchlesen; **~ up** nachlesen; **we can take it as ~ that** wir können davon ausgehen, daß. **2.** *Zähler etc* ablesen. **3.** (an)zeigen, stehen auf (*dat*) (*Thermometer etc*). **4.** *univ.* studieren. **5.** deuten, verstehen

(*as* als). **II** *v/i* (*irr*) **6.** lesen: **I've ~ about it** ich habe darüber *od.* davon gelesen; **~ to s.o.** j-m (et.) vorlesen (**from** aus); **→ line¹** 3. **7. ~ as follows** folgendermaßen lauten. **8.** sich *gut etc* lesen. **9.** sich vorbereiten (**for** auf *e-e Prüfung*): **~ up on** *et.* nachlesen; **→ bar** 9. **III** *s* **10. be a good ~** *bsd. Br.* sich *gut* lesen.

read² [red] *pret u. pp von* **read¹**.

read·a·ble ['riːdəbl] *adj* □ lesbar: a) lesenswert, b) leserlich.

re·ad·dress [ˌriːə'dres] *v/t* Brief *etc* umadressieren.

read·er ['riːdə] *s* **1.** Leser(in). **2.** Lektor(in). **3.** *ped.* Lesebuch *n*. **'read·er-ship** *s* Leser(kreis *m*, -schaft *f*) *pl.*

read·i·ly ['redɪlɪ] *adv* **1.** bereitwillig. **2.** leicht, ohne weiteres. **'read·i·ness** *s* **1.** Bereitschaft *f*: **~ to help** Hilfsbereitschaft. **2.** Gewandtheit *f*.

read·ing ['riːdɪŋ] **I** *s* **1.** Lesen *n*. **2.** Lesung *f* (*a. parl.*). **3. be** (*od.* **make**) **good ~** sich *gut* lesen. **4.** Deutung *f*, Auslegung *f*. **5.** ☉ Anzeige *f*, (*Barometeretc*)Stand *m*. **II** *adj* Lese...: **~ glasses** *pl* Lesebrille *f*; **~ lamp** Leselampe *f*; **~ matter** Lesestoff *m*, Lektüre *f*; **~ room** Lesezimmer *n*, -saal *m*.

re·ad·just [ˌriːə'dʒʌst] **I** *v/t* ☉ nachstellen, korrigieren: **~ o.s.** → II. **II** *v/i* (*to*) sich wiederanpassen (*dat od.* an *acc*), sich wiedereinstellen (auf *acc*). **,re·ad·'just·ment** *s* **1.** Nachstellung *f*, Korrektur *f*. **2.** (**to**) Wiederanpassung *f* (an *acc*), Wiedereinstellung *f* (auf *acc*).

read·y ['redɪ] **I** *adj* (□ → **readily**) **1.** bereit, fertig (**for s.th.** für et.; **to do** zu tun): **~ for takeoff** ✈ startbereit, -klar; **get** (*od.* **make**) **~** (sich) bereit- *od.* fertigmachen; **get ~ for an examination** sich auf *e-e Prüfung* vorbereiten. **2. be ~ to do** et. willens sein, et. zu tun; schnell bei der Hand sein, et. zu tun: **~ to help** hilfsbereit, -willig. **3.** schnell, schlagfertig: **~ wit** Schlagfertigkeit *f*. **4.** im Begriff, nahe daran (**to do** zu tun): **~ drop** 10. **5. ~ money** (*od.* **cash**) Bargeld *n*. **II** *s* **6. the ~** *F* Bargeld *n*: **be a bit short of the ~** knapp bei Kasse sein. **'~-made** *adj* **1.** Konfektions...: **~ suit** Konfektionsanzug *m*. **2.** *fig.* passend, geeignet (*Entschuldigung etc*): **~ solution** Patentlösung *f*. **,~-to-'wear → ready-made** 1.

re·af·firm [ˌriːəˈfɜːm] v/t nochmals versichern od. bestätigen.

re·af·for·est [ˌriːəˈfɒrɪst] v/t wieder aufforsten. '**re·af**ˌfor·es'**ta·tion** s Wiederaufforstung f.

re·a·gent [riːˈeɪdʒənt] s 🜃 Reagens n.

re·al [rɪəl] **I** adj (□ → **really**) **1.** echt (Gold, Gefühl etc). **2.** real, tatsächlich, wirklich: **taken from ~ life** aus dem Leben gegriffen; **his ~ name** sein richtiger Name; **the ~ reason** der wahre Grund. **3. ~ estate** Grundeigentum n, Immobilien pl; **~ estate agent** Am. → **estate agent**. **II** adv **4.** bsd. Am. F sehr: **I'm ~ sorry** tut mir echt leid. **III** s **5. for ~** F echt, im Ernst: **be for ~** ernst gemeint sein.

re·al·ism [ˈrɪəlɪzəm] s Realismus m. '**re·al·ist** s Realist(in). ˌ**re·al'is·tic** adj (**~ally**) realistisch.

re·al·i·ty [rɪˈælətɪ] s Realität f, Wirklichkeit f: **in ~** in Wirklichkeit; **become (a) ~** wahr werden.

re·al·i·za·tion [ˌrɪəlaɪˈzeɪʃn] s **1.** Erkenntnis f. **2.** Realisation f (a. 🜚), Realisierung f, Verwirklichung f. '**re·al·ize** v/t **1.** erkennen, begreifen, einsehen: **he ~d that** a. ihm wurde klar, daß. **2.** realisieren, verwirklichen. **3.** 🜚 realisieren, zu Geld machen.

re·al·ly [ˈrɪəlɪ] adv **1.** wirklich, tatsächlich: **~?** a. im Ernst? **2.** eigentlich: **not ~** eigentlich nicht. **3. well, ~!** ich muß schon sagen! **4. you ~ must come** du mußt unbedingt kommen.

realm [relm] s, a. pl fig. Reich n: **be within the ~ of possibility** im Bereich des Möglichen liegen.

re·an·i·mate [ˌriːˈænɪmeɪt] v/t **1.** 🜚 wiederbeleben. **2.** fig. neu beleben. ˌ**re·an·i'ma·tion** s **1.** 🜚 Wiederbelebung f. **2.** fig. Neubelebung f.

reap [riːp] v/t Getreide etc schneiden, ernten; Feld abernten: **~ the benefit(s) of** fig. die Früchte (gen) ernten.

re·ap·pear [ˌriːəˈpɪə] v/i wiedererscheinen od. -auftauchen.

re·ap·prais·al [ˌriːəˈpreɪzl] s Neubewertung f, -beurteilung f. ˌ**re·ap'praise** v/t neu bewerten od. beurteilen.

rear¹ [rɪə] **I** v/t **1.** Kind, Tier auf-, großziehen. **2.** Kopf heben, aufwerfen. **II** v/i **3.** sich aufbäumen (Pferd).

rear² [~] **I** s **1.** Hinter-, Rückseite f, mot.

Heck n: **at** (Am. **in**) **the ~ of** hinter (dat); **in the ~** hinten, im Heck. **2.** F Hintern m. **3. bring up the ~** die Nachhut bilden. **II** adj **4.** hinter, Hinter-, Rück..., mot. a. Heck...: **~ axle** Hinterachse f; **~ exit** Hinterausgang m; **~ window** Heckscheibe f; **~ wiper** Heckscheibenwischer m. '**~·guard** s ✕ Nachhut f.

re·arm [ˌriːˈɑːm] v/i ✕ wieder aufrüsten. **re·ar·ma·ment** [rɪˈɑːməmənt] s Wiederaufrüstung f.

rear·most [ˈrɪəməʊst] adj hinterst.

re·ar·range [ˌriːəˈreɪndʒ] v/t Pläne etc ändern; Möbel etc umstellen; die Möbel umstellen in (dat).

'**rear-view mir·ror** s mot. Innen-, Rückspiegel m.

rear·ward [ˈrɪəwəd] **I** adj hinter, rückwärtig. **II** adv rückwärts.

'**rear·wards** → **rearward** II.

rea·son [ˈriːzn] **I** s **1.** Grund m (for für): **by ~ of** wegen; **for ~s of health** aus Gesundheitsgründen; **with ~** zu Recht; **without any ~, for no ~** ohne Grund, grundlos; **there is every ~ to believe that** alles spricht dafür, daß; **have every ~ to do** guten Grund haben (**to do** zu tun). **2.** Verstand m. **3.** Vernunft f: **listen to ~** Vernunft annehmen. **II** v/i **4.** logisch denken. **5.** vernünftig reden (**with** mit). **III** v/t **6.** folgern (**that** daß). **7. ~ s.o. into** (**out of**) **s.th.** j-m et. ein-(aus)reden. '**rea·son·a·ble** adj **1.** vernünftig. **2.** ganz gut, nicht schlecht. **3.** F billig, günstig. '**rea·son·a·bly** adv **1.** vernünftig. **2.** ziemlich, einigermaßen. '**rea·son·ing** s **1.** logisches Denken, Gedankengang m; Argumentation f.

re·as·sem·ble [ˌriːəˈsembl] v/t ⚙ wieder zs.-bauen.

re·as·sur·ance [ˌriːəˈʃɔːrəns] s Beruhigung f. ˌ**re·as'sure** v/t beruhigen.

re·bate [ˈriːbeɪt] s **1.** Rabatt m, (Preis)Nachlaß m. **2.** Rückzahlung f, -vergütung f.

reb·el¹ [ˈrebl] **I** s Rebell(in). **II** adj a) **~ rebellious**, b) Rebellen...

re·bel² [rɪˈbel] v/i rebellieren, sich auflehnen (**against** gegen). **re'bel·lion** [~jən] s Rebellion f, Aufstand m. **re'bel·lious** [~jəs] adj □ rebellisch (a. fig. Jugendlicher etc), aufständisch.

re·birth [ˌriːˈbɜːθ] s Wiedergeburt f (a. fig.).

re·bound I *v/i* [rɪ'baʊnd] **1.** ab-, zurück-prallen (*from* von). **2.** *fig.* zurückfallen (*on* auf *acc*). **II** *s* ['riːbaʊnd] **3.** *Sport:* Abpraller *m*, (*Basketball*) Rebound *m*.

re·buff [rɪ'bʌf] **I** *v/t* schroff abweisen. **II** *s* schroffe Abweisung: *meet with a ~* schroff abgewiesen werden.

re·build [riː'bɪld] *v/t* (*irr build*) **1.** wieder aufbauen. **2.** umbauen. **3.** *fig.* wieder-aufbauen.

re·buke [rɪ'bjuːk] **I** *v/t* rügen, tadeln (*for* wegen). **II** *s* Rüge *f*, Tadel *m*.

re·bus ['riːbəs] *s* Rebus *m*, *n*, Bilderrät-sel *n*.

re·cal·ci·trant [rɪ'kælsɪtrənt] *adj* □ auf-sässig.

re·call [rɪ'kɔːl] **I** *v/t* **1.** *j-n* zurückrufen, *Botschafter etc a.* abberufen; *defekte Autos etc* (in die Werkstatt) zurückru-fen. **2.** a) sich erinnern an (*acc*): *I can't ~ seeing her* ich kann mich nicht daran erinnern, sie gesehen zu haben, b) erin-nern an (*acc*). **II** *s* **3.** Zurückrufung *f*, Abberufung *f*; Rückruf(aktion *f*) *m*. **4.** Gedächtnis *n*: *have total ~* das absolute Gedächtnis haben. **5.** *be beyond* (*od. past*) *~* für immer vorbei sein; *be lost beyond* (*od. past*) *~* unwiederbringlich verloren sein.

re·cap¹ ['riːkæp] F → *recapitulate, re-capitulation.*

re·cap² [ˌriː'kæp] *v/t Am.* Reifen runder-neuern.

re·ca·pit·u·late [ˌriːkə'pɪtjʊleɪt] *v/t u. v/i* rekapitulieren, (kurz) zs.-fassen. **'re-ca,pit·u'la·tion** *s* Rekapitulation *f*, (kurze) Zs.-fassung.

re·cap·ture [ˌriː'kæptʃə] **I** *v/t* **1.** *Tier* wie-der einfangen, *ausgebrochenen Häft-ling a.* wieder fassen. **2.** ✕ zurücker-obern. **II** *s* **3.** Wiedereinfangen *n*, Wie-derergreifung *f*. **4.** ✕ Zurückerobe-rung *f*.

re·cast [ˌriː'kɑːst] *v/t* (*irr cast*) **1.** umfor-men (*a. fig.*); ⊙ umgießen. **2.** *thea. etc* neu besetzen, umbesetzen.

re·cede [rɪ'siːd] *v/i* schwinden (*Hoffnung etc*). **re'ced·ing** *adj* fliehend (*Kinn, Stirn*).

re·ceipt [rɪ'siːt] *s* **1.** *bsd.* ✝ Empfang *m*, Erhalt *m*, (*a. von Waren*) Eingang *m*: *on ~ of* nach Empfang (*gen*). **2.** *bsd.* ✝ Empfangsbescheinigung *f*, -bestäti-gung *f*, Quittung *f*. **3.** *pl* ✝ Einnah-men *pl*.

re·ceive [rɪ'siːv] *v/t* **1.** bekommen, emp-fangen, erhalten; *Aufmerksamkeit* fin-den. **2.** *j-n* empfangen; *Vorschlag etc* aufnehmen. **3.** *j-n* aufnehmen (*into* in *acc*). **4.** *Funkverkehr, Rundfunk, TV:* empfangen: *are you receiving me?* hören Sie mich? **re'ceiv·er** *s* **1.** Emp-fänger(in). **2.** *teleph.* Hörer *m*. **3.** *a.* **official ~** ☆ Br. Konkursverwalter(in). **4.** Hehler(in). **re'ceiv·ing I** *s* Hehlerei *f*. **II** *adj: be on the ~ end of* F derjenige sein, der *et.* ausbaden muß; *et.* abkrie-gen.

re·cent ['riːsnt] *adj* jüngst (*Ereignisse etc*); neuer (*Foto etc*). **'re·cent·ly** *adv* kürzlich, vor kurzem; in letzter Zeit.

re·cep·ta·cle [rɪ'septəkl] *s* Behälter *m*.

re·cep·tion [rɪ'sepʃn] *s* **1.** (*a. offizieller*) Empfang: *give* (*od. hold*) *a ~* e-n Emp-fang geben; *give s.o. an enthusiastic ~* j-m e-n begeisterten Empfang berei-ten. **2.** *Hotel:* Rezeption *f:* a) *a. ~ desk* Empfang *m:* *at ~* am *od.* beim Emp-fang, b) Empfangshalle *f:* *in ~* in der Empfangshalle. **3.** Aufnahme *f* (*into* in *acc*). **4.** *Funkverkehr, Rundfunk, TV:* Empfang *m*. **re'cep·tion·ist** [ˌ~ʃənɪst] *s* **1.** Empfangsdame *f*, -chef *m*. **2.** ✚ Sprechstundenhilfe *f*.

re·cep·tive [rɪ'septɪv] *adj* □ aufnahme-fähig; empfänglich (*to* für).

re·cess [rɪ'ses] **I** *s* **1.** Pause *f* (*Am. a. ped.*), Unterbrechung *f*, *parl.* Ferien *pl*. **2.** Nische *f*. **II** *v/t* **3.** in e-r Nische stel-len. **4.** einbauen: *~ed* Einbau... .

re·ces·sion [rɪ'seʃn] *s* ✝ Rezession *f*.

re·cid·i·vist [rɪ'sɪdɪvɪst] *s* Rückfalltä-ter(in).

rec·i·pe ['resɪpɪ] *s gastr.* Rezept *n* (*for* für) (*a. fig.*). **~ book** *s* Kochbuch *n*.

re·cip·i·ent [rɪ'sɪpɪənt] *s* Empfänger(in).

re·cip·ro·cal [rɪ'sɪprəkl] *adj* □ wechsel-, gegenseitig; *ling.*, *A* bezüglich. **re'cip-ro·cate** [ˌ~keɪt] **I** *v/t Einladung, Gefühle etc* erwidern. **II** *v/i* sich revanchieren (*for* für). **re,cip·ro'ca·tion** *s* Erwide-rung *f*.

re·cit·al [rɪ'saɪtl] *s* **1.** Vortrag *m*, (*Kla-vier- etc*)Konzert *n*, (*Lieder*)Abend *m*. **2.** Schilderung *f*. **rec·i·ta·tion** [ˌresɪ-'teɪʃn] *s* **1.** Auf-, Hersagen *n*. **2.** Rezita-tion *f*, Vortrag *m*. **rec·i·ta·tive** [ˌ~tə-

'ti:v] s ♪ Rezitativ n. **re-cite** [rɪ'saɪt] v/t **1.** auf-, hersagen. **2.** rezitieren, vortragen. **3.** aufzählen.

reck-less ['reklɪs] adj □ rücksichtslos. **'reck-less-ness** s Rücksichtslosigkeit f.

reck-on ['rekən] **I** v/t **1.** aus-, berechnen: ~ **in** ein-, mitrechnen; ~ **up** zs.-rechnen. **2.** ~ **s.o. (to be) clever** j-n für clever halten: **he is ~ed (to be) clever** er gilt als clever. **3.** rechnen, zählen (**among** zu). **4.** glauben, schätzen (**that** daß). **II** v/i **5.** ~ **on** rechnen auf (acc) od. mit; ~ **with** rechnen mit; **he's a man to be ~ed with** mit ihm muß man rechnen; **you'll have me to ~ with** du wirst es mit mir zu tun bekommen; ~ **without** nicht rechnen mit. **'reck·on·ing** f: **by my ~** nach m-r (Be)Rechnung; **be out in one's ~** sich verrechnet haben.

re-claim [rɪ'kleɪm] v/t **1.** zurückfordern, -verlangen (**from** von); Gepäck etc abholen. **2.** ~ **land from the sea** dem Meer Land abgewinnen. **3.** ⚙, 🌿 wiedergewinnen (**from** aus). **rec·la·ma·tion** [ˌreklə'meɪʃn] s **1.** Rückforderung f. **2.** ⚙, 🌿 Wiedergewinnung f.

re-cline [rɪ'klaɪn] v/i sich zurücklehnen: **~ing seat** mot. etc Ruhesitz m.

re-cluse [rɪ'klu:s] s Einsiedler(in).

rec·og·ni·tion [ˌrekəg'nɪʃn] s **1.** (Wieder)Erkennen n: **be burnt beyond** (od. **out of all**) ~ bis zur Unkenntlichkeit verbrennen; **the town has changed beyond** ~ die Stadt ist nicht wiederzuerkennen. **2.** Anerkennung f: **in** (od. **as a**) ~ **of** als Anerkennung für, in Anerkennung (gen); **gain** (od. **get, win**) ~ Anerkennung finden. **rec·og·niz·a·ble** ['rekəgnaɪzəbl] adj □ (wieder)erkennbar: **be hardly** ~ kaum zu erkennen sein. **rec·og·nize** ['rekəgnaɪz] v/t **1.** (wieder)erkennen (**by** an dat). **2.** anerkennen (a. pol.). **3.** eingestehen, zugeben (**that** daß).

re-coil **I** v/i [rɪ'kɔɪl] **1.** zurückschrecken (**from** vor dat) (a. fig.): ~ **from doing s.th.** davor zurückschrecken, et. zu tun. **2.** zurückstoßen (Gewehr etc). **3.** ~ **on** fig. zurückfallen auf (acc). **II** s ['ri:kɔɪl] **4.** Rückstoß m.

rec·ol·lect [ˌrekə'lekt] **I** v/t sich erinnern

an (acc): ~ **doing s.th.** sich daran erinnern, et. getan zu haben. **II** v/i: **as far as I (can)** ~ soweit ich mich erinnere.

rec·ol·lec·tion [ˌrekə'lekʃn] s Erinnerung f (**of** an acc): **to the best of my** ~ soweit ich mich erinnere.

rec·om·mend [ˌrekə'mend] v/t **1.** empfehlen (**as** als; **for** für): ~ **doing s.th.** empfehlen od. raten, et. zu tun. **2.** sprechen für: **he has little to ~ him** es spricht wenig für ihn. **rec·om·mend·a·ble** adj empfehlenswert; ratsam. **rec·om·men·da·tion** [ˌ~men'deɪʃn] s Empfehlung f: **on s.o.'s** ~ auf j-s Empfehlung.

rec·om·pense ['rekəmpens] **I** v/t entschädigen (**for** für). **II** s Entschädigung f: **as a** (od. **in**) ~ als Entschädigung (für).

rec·on·cile ['rekənsaɪl] v/t **1.** ver-, aussöhnen (**with** mit): **they are ~d again** sie haben sich wieder versöhnt; **become ~d to s.th.** fig. sich mit et. abfinden. **2.** in Einklang bringen (**with** mit). **rec·on·cil·i·a·tion** [ˌ~sɪlɪ'eɪʃn] s **1.** Ver-, Aussöhnung f (**between** zwischen dat; **with** mit). **2.** Einklang m.

rec·on·dite ['rekəndaɪt] adj □ abstrus, schwerverständlich.

re-con·di·tion [ˌri:kən'dɪʃn] v/t ⚙ (general)überholen: **~ed engine** Austauschmotor m.

re-con·nais·sance [rɪ'kɒnɪsəns] s ✕ Aufklärung f, Erkundung f. ~ **flight** s Aufklärungsflug m. ~ **plane** s Aufklärungsflugzeug n, Aufklärer m.

rec·on·noi·ter Am., bsd. Br. **rec·on·noi·tre** [ˌrekə'nɔɪtə] v/t ✕ erkunden, auskundschaften.

re-con·quer [ˌri:'kɒŋkə] v/t zurückerobern. **'re·con·quest** [~kwest] s Zurückeroberung f.

re-con·sid·er [ˌri:kən'sɪdə] v/t noch einmal überdenken. **'re·con·sid·er·a·tion** s nochmaliges Überdenken.

re-con·struct [ˌri:kən'strʌkt] v/t **1.** wieder aufbauen; fig. wiederaufbauen. **2.** fig. Fall etc rekonstruieren. **re-con·'struc·tion** s **1.** Wiederaufbau m. **2.** fig. Rekonstruktion f.

rec·ord[1] ['rekɔ:d] **I** s **1.** Aufzeichnung f, Niederschrift f; ⚖ Protokoll n: **off the** ~ inoffiziell; **on** ~ aktenkundig; geschichtlich verzeichnet, schriftlich belegt; *fig.* aller Zeiten; **he is** (*od.* **went**) **on ~ as having said that** er hat sich offiziell dahingehend geäußert, daß; **keep a ~ of** Buch führen über (*acc*); **to set the ~ straight** um das klarzustellen. **2.** Vergangenheit *f*; *gute etc* Leistungen *pl* (*in der Vergangenheit*): **have a criminal ~** vorbestraft sein. **3.** (Schall)Platte *f*: **make a ~** e-e Platte aufnehmen. **4.** *Sport etc*: Rekord *m*. **II** *adj* **5.** (Schall)Platten...: **~ player** Plattenspieler *m*. **6.** *Sport etc*: Rekord...: **~ holder** Rekordhalter(in), -inhaber(in); **in ~ time** in Rekordzeit.

re·cord² [rɪˈkɔːd] *v/t* **1.** schriftlich niederlegen, aufzeichnen, -schreiben; 🏛 protokollieren, zu Protokoll *od.* zu den Akten nehmen. **2.** (*auf Tonband etc*) aufnehmen, *Programm a.* aufzeichnen, mitschneiden: **~ed broadcast** (*Rundfunk, TV*) Aufzeichnung *f*. **3.** Meßwerte registrieren.

'rec·ord-ˌbreak·ing *adj* Sport etc: Rekord...

re·cord·er [rɪˈkɔːdə] *s* **1.** (*Kassetten*)Recorder *m*, (*Tonband*)Gerät *n*. **2.** ♪ Blockflöte *f*. **re'cord·ing** *s* Aufnahme *f*, Aufzeichnung *f*, Mitschnitt *m*: **~ studio** Aufnahme-, Tonstudio *n*.

re·count¹ [rɪˈkaʊnt] *v/t* erzählen.

re·count² **I** *v/t* [ˌriːˈkaʊnt] nachzählen. **II** *s* [ˈriːkaʊnt] Nachzählung *f*.

re·coup [rɪˈkuːp] *v/t* **1.** *Verlust etc* wiedereinbringen, sich *Ausgaben etc* zurückholen (**from** von). **2.** *j-n* entschädigen (**for** für).

re·course [rɪˈkɔːs] *s*: **have ~ to** greifen *od.* Zuflucht nehmen zu.

re·cov·er [rɪˈkʌvə] **I** *v/t et. Verlorenes* wiederfinden; *Bewußtsein etc* wiedererlangen; *Kosten etc* wiedereinbringen; *Fahrzeug, Verunglückten etc* bergen: **~ one's composure** sich wieder fangen *od.* fassen; **~ consciousness** *a.* wieder zu sich kommen. **II** *v/i* sich erholen (**from** von) (*a. fig.*): **he has fully ~ed** er ist wieder ganz gesund. **re'cov·er·y** *s* **1.** Wiederfinden *n*; Wiedererlangen *n*; Wiedereinbringung *f*; Bergung *f*. **2.** Erholung *f* (*a. fig.*): **make a complete ~** völlig gesund werden; **make a quick** (*od.* **speedy**) **~** sich schnell erholen; **wish s.o. a speedy ~** j-m gute Besserung wünschen.

rec·re·a·tion [ˌrekrɪˈeɪʃn] *s* Entspannung *f*, Erholung *f*; Unterhaltung *f*, Freizeitbeschäftigung *f*: **~ ground** Spielplatz *m*. **ˌrec·re'a·tion·al** [ˌ~ʃənl] *adj* Erholungs...; Freizeit...: **~ activities** *pl* Freizeitgestaltung *f*; **~ value** Freizeitwert *m*.

re·crim·i·nate [rɪˈkrɪmɪneɪt] *v/i* Gegenbeschuldigungen vorbringen (**against** gegen). **re,crim·i'na·tion** *s* Gegenbeschuldigung *f*: **their ~s (pl)** ihre gegenseitigen Beschuldigungen *pl*.

re·cruit [rɪˈkruːt] **I** *s* **1.** ✕ Rekrut *m*. **2.** (**to**) Neue *m*, *f* (*in dat*); neues Mitglied (*gen od.* in *dat*). **II** *v/t* **3.** ✕ rekrutieren; *Personal* einstellen; *Mitglieder* werben. **re'cruit·ment** *s* ✕ Rekrutierung *f*; Einstellung *f*; Werbung *f*.

rec·ta [ˈrektə] *pl von* rectum.

rec·tan·gle [ˈrekˌtæŋgl] *s* ▲ Rechteck *n*. **rec'tan·gu·lar** [ˌ~gjʊlə] *adj* □ rechteckig; rechtwink(e)lig.

rec·ti·fi·ca·tion [ˌrektɪfɪˈkeɪʃn] *s* **1.** Berichtigung *f*, Korrektur *f*. **2.** 🔬 Rektifikation *f*. **3.** ⚡ Gleichrichtung *f*. **rec·ti·fy** [ˈ~faɪ] *v/t* **1.** berichtigen, korrigieren. **2.** 🔬 rektifizieren. **3.** ⚡ gleichrichten.

rec·ti·lin·e·ar [ˌrektɪˈlɪnɪə] *adj* □ geradlinig.

rec·ti·tude [ˈrektɪtjuːd] *s* Redlichkeit *f*, Rechtschaffenheit *f*.

rec·tor [ˈrektə] *s* Pfarrer *m*. **'rec·to·ry** *s* Pfarrhaus *n*.

rec·tum [ˈrektəm] *pl* **-tums**, **-ta** [ˈ~tə] *s* anat. Mastdarm *m*.

re·cu·per·ate [rɪˈkuːpəreɪt] **I** *v/i* sich erholen (**from** von) (*a. fig.*). **II** *v/t Verluste etc* wettmachen. **re,cu·per'a·tion** *s* **1.** Erholung *f* (*a. fig.*). **2.** Wettmachen *n*.

re·cur [rɪˈkɜː] *v/i* wiederkehren, wiederauftreten (*Problem, Symptom etc*), (*Schmerz a.*) wiedereinsetzen: **~ to s.o.** j-m wiederkommen (*Erinnerung etc*). **re·cur·rence** [rɪˈkʌrəns] *s* Wiederkehr *f*, Wiederauftreten *n*, Wiedereinsetzen *n*. **re'cur·rent** *adj* □ wiederkehrend, wiederauftretend, wiedereinsetzend.

re·cy·cle [ˌriːˈsaɪkl] *v/t* wiederverwerten. **ˌre'cy·cling** *s* Recycling *n*, Wiederverwertung *f*.

red [red] **I** *adj* **1.** rot: **the lights are ~** die Ampel steht auf Rot; **go** (*od.* **turn**) **~** rot werden; → **flag¹** 1, **paint** 2, **rag¹** 1. **2.** *oft* ♎ *pol.* rot. **II** *s* **3.** Rot *n*: **at ~** bei Rot; **the**

lights are at ~ die Ampel steht auf Rot; *dressed in* ~ rot *od.* in Rot gekleidet; *see* ~ *fig.* rotsehen; *be in the* ~ ✝ in den roten Zahlen sein, rote Zahlen schreiben. **4.** *oft* ♀ *pol.* Rote *m*, *f*. ~ **car·pet** *s* roter Teppich. ˌ~'**car·pet** *adj*: *give* **s.o.** *the* ~ *treatment* j-n mit großem Bahnhof empfangen. ♀ **Cross** ~ ♀ Rotes Kreuz.

red·den ['redn] **I** *v/t* röten, rot färben. **II** *v/i* rot werden (*with* vor *dat*). '**red·dish** *adj* □ rötlich.

re·dec·o·rate [ˌriː'dekəreɪt] *v/t* Zimmer *etc* neu streichen *od.* tapezieren.

re·deem [rɪ'diːm] *v/t* **1.** *Pfand, Versprechen etc* einlösen. **2.** *Ruf etc* wiederherstellen: ~ *o.s.* sich rehabilitieren. **3.** *Gefangene etc* los-, freikaufen. **4.** *Hypothek, Schulden* abzahlen, tilgen. **5.** *schlechte Eigenschaften etc* ausgleichen, wettmachen. **6.** *bsd. eccl.* erlösen (*from* von). **Re'deem·er** *s eccl.* Erlöser *m*, Heiland *m*.

re·demp·tion [rɪ'dempʃn] *s* **1.** Einlösung *f*. **2.** Wiederherstellung *f*. **3.** Los-, Freikauf *m*. **4.** Abzahlung *f*, Tilgung *f*. **5.** Ausgleich *m*. **6.** *bsd. eccl.* Erlösung *f* (*from* von). **7.** *beyond* (*od. past*) ~ hoffnungslos.

re·de·vel·op [ˌriːdɪ'veləp] *v/t Gebäude, Stadtteil* sanieren. ˌ**re·de'vel·op·ment** *s* Sanierung *f*.

ˌ**red·'hand·ed** *adj*: *catch s.o.* ~ j-n auf frischer Tat ertappen. ˌ**red·'head·ed** *adj* rothaarig. ~ **her·ring** *s* **1.** Bückling *m*. **2.** *fig.* Ablenkungsmanöver *n*; falsche Fährte *od.* Spur. ˌ~'**hot** *adj* **1.** rotglühend (*Metall*); glühendheiß. **2.** *fig.* glühend, überschwenglich (*Begeisterung*). **3.** *fig.* brandaktuell (*Nachricht etc*). ♀ **In·di·an** *s* Indianer(in).

re·di·rect [ˌriːdɪ'rekt] *v/t Brief etc* nachschicken, -senden (*to s.o.* j-m; *to a new address* an e-e neue Adresse).

re·dis·cov·er [ˌriːdɪ'skʌvə] *v/t* wiederentdecken. ˌ**re·dis'cov·er·y** *s* Wiederentdeckung *f*.

re·dis·trib·ute [ˌriːdɪ'strɪbjuːt] *v/t* neu verteilen, umverteilen. '**re·dis·tri·bu·tion** [ˌ~bjuːʃn] *s* Neu-, Umverteilung *f*.

ˌ**red·'let·ter day** *s* Freuden-, Glückstag *m* (*for* für). ~ **light** *s* **1.** rotes Licht (*Warnsignal etc*): *see the* ~ *fig.* die Gefahr erkennen. **2.** Rotlicht *n*: *go*

through the ~*s* bei Rot über die Kreuzung fahren. ˌ~'**light dis·trict** *s* Rotlichtbezirk *m*, Bordellviertel *n*.

red·ness ['rednɪs] *s* Röte *f*.

re·do [ˌriː'duː] *v/t* (*irr* **do**) **1.** nochmals tun *od.* machen: ~ *one's hair* sich die Haare in Ordnung bringen. **2.** → **redecorate**.

re·dou·ble [ˌriː'dʌbl] *v/t bsd. Anstrengungen* verdoppeln.

re·dress [rɪ'dres] **I** *v/t Unrecht* wiedergutmachen; *Mißstand etc* abstellen, beseitigen; *Gleichgewicht* wiederherstellen. **II** *s* Wiedergutmachung *f*; Abstellung *f*, Beseitigung *f*: *seek* ~ *for* Wiedergutmachung verlangen für.

red tape *s* Amtsschimmel *m*, Bürokratismus *m*.

re·duce [rɪ'djuːs] *v/t* **1.** *Foto etc* verkleinern. **2.** *Steuern* senken, *Geschwindigkeit, Risiko etc* verringern, *Preis, Waren* herabsetzen, reduzieren (*from ... to* von ... auf *acc*), *Gehalt etc* kürzen. **3.** (*to*) verwandeln (in *acc*), machen (zu): ~ *to a nervous wreck* aus *j-n* ein Nervenbündel machen. **4.** ~ *s.o. to silence* (*tears*) j-n zum Schweigen (Weinen) bringen. **5.** reduzieren, zurückführen (*to* auf *acc*). **6.** ⚗ reduzieren. **7.** → *denominator*. **re·duc·tion** [rɪ'dʌkʃn] *s* **1.** Verkleinerung *f*. **2.** Senkung *f*, Verringerung *f*, Herabsetzung *f*, Reduzierung *f*, Kürzung *f*. **3.** ⚗ Reduktion *f*.

re·dun·dan·cy [rɪ'dʌndənsɪ] *s* **1.** ✝ Freistellung *f*, -setzung *f*. **2.** *ling.* Redundanz *f*. **re'dun·dant** *adj* □ **1.** ✝ freigestellt, -gesetzt: *be made* ~ freigestellt *od.* -gesetzt werden. **2.** *ling.* redundant.

re·du·pli·cate [rɪ'djuːplɪkeɪt] *v/t* wiederholen. **re·du·pli·ca·tion** *s* Wiederholung *f*.

red wine *s* Rotwein *m*.

re·ech·o [riː'ekəʊ] *v/i* widerhallen (*with* von).

reed [riːd] *s* Schilf(rohr) *n*, Ried *n*; (*einzelnes*) Schilfrohr.

re·ed·u·cate [ˌriː'edʃʊkeɪt] *v/t* umerziehen. '**re·ˌed·u·ca·tion** *s* Umerziehung *f*.

reed·y ['riːdɪ] *adj* □ **1.** schilfig. **2.** piepsig (*Stimme*).

reef[1] [riːf] *s* (Felsen)Riff *n*.

reef[2] [ˌ~] *v/t* ⚓ *Segel* reffen. ~ **knot** *s* Kreuz-, Weberknoten *m*.

reek [ri:k] **I** *s* Gestank *m*: *there was a ~ of garlic* es stank nach Knoblauch. **II** *v/i* stinken (*of* nach).

reel¹ [ri:l] **I** *s* (*Kabel-, Schlauch- etc*)Rolle *f*, (*Film-, Garn- etc*)Spule *f*. **II** *v/t*: *~ off* abrollen, abspulen; *fig.* herunterrasseln; *~ up* aufrollen, -spulen.

reel² [~] *v/i* **1.** sich drehen: *my head ~ed* mir drehte sich alles, mir wurde schwindlig; *the room ~ed before my eyes* das Zimmer drehte sich vor m-n Augen. **2.** wanken, taumeln, (*Betrunkener a.*) torkeln.

re-e-lect [,ri:i'lekt] *v/t* wiederwählen. **,re-e'lec-tion** *s* Wiederwahl *f*: *seek ~* sich erneut zur Wahl stellen.

re-en-ter [,ri:'entə] *v/t* wieder eintreten in (*acc*) (*a. Raumfahrt*), wieder betreten. **re-'en-try** *s* Wiedereintreten *n*, -eintritt *m* (*into* in *acc*).

ref [ref] *s Sport*: F Schiri *m*; (*Boxen*) Ringrichter *m*.

re-fec-to-ry [ri'fektəri] *s univ.* Mensa *f*.

re-fer [ri'fɜ:] **I** *v/t* **1.** *j-n* ver-, hinweisen (*to* auf *acc*). **2.** *j-n* (*um Auskunft etc*) verweisen (*to* an *acc*). **3.** (*to* an) übergeben (*dat*), *a. Patienten* überweisen (an *acc*): *~ back* zurückverweisen. **II** *v/i* **4.** ver-, hinweisen (*to* auf *acc*). **5.** sich berufen *od.* beziehen (auf *acc*); anspielen (auf *acc*); erwähnen (*acc*). **6.** (*to*) nachschlagen (in *dat*), konsultieren (*acc*). **ref-er-ee** [,refə'ri:] **I** *s* **1.** ⚽, *Sport*: Schiedsrichter *m*, (*Boxen*) Ringrichter *m*. **2.** *Br.* → **reference** 5b. **II** *v/i* **3.** ⚽, *Sport*: als Schiedsrichter fungieren, (*Sport a.*) pfeifen, (*Boxen*) als Ringrichter fungieren. **III** *v/t* **4.** ⚽, *Sport*: als Schiedsrichter fungieren bei, (*Sport a.*) Spiel pfeifen, (*Boxen*) Kampf leiten. **ref-er-ence** ['refrəns] *s* **1.** Verweis *m*, Hinweis *m* (*to* auf *acc*): (*list of*) *~s pl* Quellenangabe *f*. **2.** Verweisstelle *f*; Beleg *m*, Unterlage *f*: *~ number* Aktenzeichen *n*. **3.** (*to*) Bezugnahme *f* (auf *acc*); Anspielung *f* (auf *acc*); Erwähnung *f* (*gen*): *make* (*a*) *~* (*to*) → *refer* 5. **4.** (*to*) Nachschlagen *n* (in *dat*), Konsultieren *n* (*gen*): *~ book* Nachschlagewerk *n*; *~ library* Handbibliothek *f*. **5.** Referenz *f*: a) Empfehlung *f*, b) Auskunftgeber *m*: *act as a ~ for s.o.* j-m als Referenz dienen.

ref-er-en-dum [,refə'rendəm] *pl* **-dums, -da** [~də] *s pol.* Referendum *n*, Volksabstimmung *f*, -entscheid *m*.

re-fill I *v/t* [,ri:'fil] **1.** wieder füllen, nach-, auffüllen. **II** *s* ['ri:fil] **2.** (*Füller-*)Patrone *f*, (*Kugelschreiber- etc*)Mine *f*. **3.** *would you like a ~?* F darf ich nachschenken?

re-fine [ri'faɪn] **I** *v/t* **1.** Öl, Zucker raffinieren. **2.** *fig.* verfeinern, kultivieren. **II** *v/i* **3.** *~ on fig.* verbessern, -feinern. **re'fined** *adj* **1.** raffiniert: *~ sugar* Raffinade *f*. **2.** *fig.* kultiviert, vornehm. **re'fine-ment** *s* **1.** Raffination *f*, Raffinierung *f*. **2.** Verbesserung *f*, -feinerung *f*. **3.** *fig.* Kultiviertheit *f*, Vornehmheit *f*. **re'fin-er-y** *s* Raffinerie *f*.

re-flect [ri'flekt] **I** *v/t* **1.** *Strahlen etc* reflektieren, zurückwerfen, -strahlen, *Bild etc* reflektieren, (wider)spiegeln (*a. acc*): *be ~ed in* sich (wider)spiegeln in (*dat*) (*a. fig.*); *~ (dis)credit on fig.* ein gutes (schlechtes) Licht werfen auf (*acc*); *~ing telescope* Spiegelteleskop *n*. **II** *v/i fig.* **2.** nachdenken (*on* über *acc*). **3.** *~ (badly) on* sich nachteilig auswirken auf (*acc*); ein schlechtes Licht werfen auf (*acc*). **re'flec-tion** *s* **1.** Reflexion *f*, Zurückwerfung *f*, -strahlung *f*, (Wider)Spieg(el)ung *f* (*a. fig.*). **2.** Spiegelbild *n*. **3.** *fig.* Überlegung *f*: *on ~* nach einigem Nachdenken; *when ich etc es im recht überlege*. **4.** *mst pej.* *fig.* Betrachtung *f* (*on* über *acc*). **re-'flec-tive** *adj* □ **1.** reflektierend, (wider)spiegelnd. **2.** *fig.* nachdenklich. **re-'flec-tor** *s* **1.** Reflektor *m*. **2.** Rückstrahler *m*.

re-flex ['ri:fleks] *s a.* **~ action** Reflex *m*. **~ cam-er-a** *s phot.* Spiegelreflexkamera *f*.

re-flex-ive [ri'fleksiv] *adj* □ *ling.* reflexiv, rückbezüglich: *~ pronoun* Reflexivpronomen *n*, rückbezügliches Fürwort; *~ verb* reflexives Verb, rückbezügliches Zeitwort.

re-for-est [,ri:'forist], **re,for-es'ta-tion** → *reafforest, reafforestation*.

re-form [ri'fɔ:m] **I** *s* **1.** *pol. etc* Reform *f*. **2.** Besserung *f*. **II** *v/t* **3.** *j-n* bessern. **ref-or-ma-tion** [,refə'meɪʃn] *s* **1.** Reformierung *f*: *the ℛ eccl.* die Reformation. **2.** Besserung *f*. **re-form-a-to-ry** [ri'fɔ:mətəri] *adj* Reform... **re'form-er** *s*

1. *pol. etc* Reformer *m*. **2.** *eccl.* Reformator *m*.

re·fract [rɪ'frækt] *v/t phys.* Strahlen, Wellen brechen. **re'frac·tion** *s* Refraktion *f*, Brechung *f*.

re·frac·to·ry [rɪ'fræktərɪ] *adj* □ **1.** eigensinnig, störrisch. **2.** 🎇 hartnäckig.

re·frain¹ [rɪ'freɪn] *v/i* **(from)** absehen (von), sich enthalten (*gen*), unterlassen (*acc*): **~ from doing s.th.** es unterlassen, et. zu tun.

re·frain² [~] *s* Kehrreim *m*, Refrain *m*.

re·fresh [rɪ'freʃ] *v/t* (**o.s.** sich) erfrischen; *fig.* Gedächtnis auffrischen. **re'fresh·er** *s* **1.** Erfrischung *f* (*Getränk etc*). **2. ~ course** Auffrischungskurs *m*. **re·'fresh·ing** *adj* □ erfrischend (*a. fig.*). **re'fresh·ment** *s* Erfrischung *f* (*a. Getränk etc*).

re·frig·er·ate [rɪ'frɪdʒəreɪt] *v/t* ⊛ kühlen. **re·frig·er·a·tion** *s* Kühlung *f*. **re'frig·er·a·tor** *s* Kühlschrank *m*: **~-freezer** Kühl- u. Gefrierkombination *f*.

re·fu·el [ˌriː'fjʊəl] *v/t u. v/i pret u. pp -eled,* *bsd. Br.* **-elled** ✈, *mot.* auftanken.

ref·uge ['refjuːdʒ] *s* Zuflucht *f* (**from** *vor dat*) (*a. fig.*): **place of ~** Zufluchtsort *m*; **seek ~** Zuflucht suchen; **take ~ in** Zuflucht nehmen zu, sich flüchten in (*acc*). **ref·u·gee** [ˌ~juː'dʒiː] *s* Flüchtling *m*: **~ camp** Flüchtlingslager *n*.

re·fund I *v/t* [riː'fʌnd] Geld zurückzahlen, -erstatten, *Auslagen* ersetzen: **~ s.o. his money** j-m sein Geld zurückzahlen. **II** *s* ['riːfʌnd] Rückzahlung *f*, -erstattung *f*.

re·fur·bish [ˌriː'fɜːbɪʃ] *v/t* **1.** aufpolieren (*a. fig.*). **2.** renovieren.

re·fus·al [rɪ'fjuːzl] *s* **1.** Ablehnung *f*; Verweigerung *f*: → **meet** 15. **2.** Weigerung *f* (**to do** zu tun).

re·fuse¹ [rɪ'fjuːz] *I v/t* **1.** *Kandidaten etc* ablehnen, *Angebot a.* ausschlagen: **~ s.o. s.th.** j-m et. ausschlagen *od.* verweigern. **2.** sich weigern, es ablehnen (**to do** zu tun). **II** *v/i* **3.** ablehnen. **4.** sich weigern.

ref·use² ['refjuːs] *s* Abfall *m*, Abfälle *pl*, Müll *m*. **~ dump** *s* Müllabladeplatz *m*, -deponie *f*.

ref·u·ta·ble ['refjʊtəbl] *adj* □ widerlegbar. **ref·u·ta·tion** [ˌ~juː'teɪʃn] *s* Wider-

legung *f*. **re·fute** [rɪ'fjuːt] *v/t* widerlegen.

re·gain [rɪ'geɪn] *v/t* wieder-, zurückgewinnen: **~ one's health** (**strength**) wieder gesund werden (wieder zu Kräften kommen).

re·gal ['riːgl] *adj* □ **1.** königlich. **2.** *fig.* hoheits-, würdevoll.

re·gale [rɪ'geɪl] *v/t* **1.** fürstlich bewirten (**with** mit). **2.** erfreuen, ergötzen (**with** mit).

re·ga·li·a [rɪ'geɪljə] *s pl* Insignien *pl*.

re·gard [rɪ'gɑːd] **I** *s* **1.** Achtung *f*: **hold s.o. in high** (**low**) ~ j-n hochachten (geringachten). **2.** Rücksicht *f*: **without ~ to** (*od.* **for**) ohne Rücksicht auf (*acc*); **have no ~ for, pay no ~ to** keine Rücksicht nehmen auf (*acc*). **3. in this ~** in dieser Hinsicht; **with ~ to** im Hinblick auf (*acc*). **4. give him my** (**best**) ~**s** grüße ihn (herzlich) von mir; **with kind ~s** mit freundlichen Grüßen. **II** *v/t* **5.** betrachten, ansehen. **6.** *fig.* betrachten (**with** mit): **~ as** betrachten als, halten für; **be ~ed as** gelten als. **7. as ~s ...** was ... betrifft. **re'gard·ing** *prp* bezüglich, hinsichtlich. **re'gard·less I** *adj*: ~ **of** ohne Rücksicht auf (*acc*). **II** *adv F* trotzdem.

re·gat·ta [rɪ'gætə] *s* Sport: Regatta *f*.

re·gen·cy ['riːdʒənsɪ] *s* Regentschaft *f*.

re·gen·er·ate [rɪ'dʒenəreɪt] *v/t u. v/i* (sich) regenerieren *od.* erneuern. **re·gen·er·a·tion** *s* Regenerierung *f*, Erneuerung *f*.

re·gent ['riːdʒənt] *s* Regent(in).

re·gime [reɪ'ʒiːm] *s* **1.** *pol.* Regime *n*. **2.** → **regimen**.

reg·i·men ['redʒɪmen] *s* Lebensweise *f*; *engS.* Diät *f*.

reg·i·ment I *s* ['redʒɪmənt] **1.** ✕ Regiment *n*. **2.** *fig.* Schar *f*. **II** *v/t* [~ment] **3.** reglementieren, gängeln, bevormunden. **reg·i·men·tal** [ˌ~'mentl] *adj* ✕ Regiments... **reg·i·men·ta·tion** *s* Reglementierung *f*, Gängelung *f*, Bevormundung *f*.

re·gion ['riːdʒən] *s* Gebiet *n*, Gegend *f*, Region *f*: **in the ~ of the heart** in der Herzgegend; **in the ~ of £50** um die *od.* ungefähr 50 Pfund. **re·gion·al** ['~dʒənl] *adj* □ regional.

reg·is·ter ['redʒɪstə] **I** *s* **1.** Register *n*, Verzeichnis *n*, (*Wähler- etc*)Liste *f*;

keep a ~ of Buch führen über (*acc.*). **2.** ⚙ Registriergerät *n.* **3.** Sprach-, Stilebene *f.* **II** *v/t* **4.** sich registrieren, eintragen (lassen): **~ed trademark** eingetragenes Warenzeichen. **5.** Meßwerte registrieren, anzeigen; *fig.* Empfindung zeigen. **6.** ✎ Brief etc einschreiben lassen: **~ed letter** Einschreib(e)brief *m*, Einschreiben *n*; **send s.th. by ~ed mail** (*bsd. Br. post*) et. eingeschrieben schicken. **III** *v/i* **7.** sich eintragen (lassen). **8.** *he told me who he was* **but it didn't ~** F aber ich habe es nicht registriert *od.* zur Kenntnis genommen. **~ of·fice** *s bsd. Br.* Standesamt *n.*

reg·is·trar [ˌredʒɪˈstrɑː] *s bsd. Br.* Standesbeamter *m*, -beamtin *f.* **reg·is·tra·tion** [ˌ~ˈstreɪʃn] *s* Registrierung *f*, Eintragung *f:* **~ document** *mot. Br.* (etwa) Kraftfahrzeugbrief *m*; **~ number** *mot.* (polizeiliches) Kennzeichen. **'reg·is·try** *s* Registratur *f:* **~ office** *bsd. Br.* Standesamt *n.*

re·gress [rɪˈgres] *v/i* **1.** sich rückläufig entwickeln (*Gesellschaft*). **2.** *biol., psych.* sich zurückentwickeln. **re·gres·sion** [rɪˈgreʃn] *s* **1.** rückläufige Entwicklung. **2.** *biol., psych.* Regression *f*, Rückentwicklung *f.* **re·gres·sive** [~sɪv] *adj* □ regressiv, rückläufig.

re·gret [rɪˈgret] **I** *v/t* **1.** bedauern; bereuen: **~ doing s.th.** es bedauern *od.* bereuen, et. getan zu haben; **we ~ to inform you that** wir müssen Ihnen leider mitteilen, daß. **2.** *j-m, e-r Sache* nachtrauern. **II** *s* **3.** Bedauern *n* (*at* über *acc*); Reue *f:* **with great ~** mit großem Bedauern; **have no ~s** nichts bereuen; **have no ~s about doing s.th.** es nicht bedauern *od.* bereuen, et. getan zu haben. **re'gret·ful** [~fʊl] *adj* bedauernd. **~ly** *adv* mit Bedauern. **re'gret·ta·ble** *adj* bedauerlich. **re'gret·ta·bly** *adv* bedauerlicherweise.

re·group [ˌriːˈɡruːp] *v/t u. v/i* (sich) umgruppieren.

reg·u·lar [ˈregjʊlə] **I** *adj* □ **1.** (*zeitlich*) regelmäßig: **~ customer** Stammkunde *m*, -kundin *f*; Stammgast *m*; **at ~ intervals** in regelmäßigen Abständen (*a. örtlich*). **2.** regelmäßig (*in Form od. Anordnung*). **3.** regelmäßig (*Atmen etc*): **at ~ speed** mit gleichbleibender Geschwindigkeit. **4.** geregelt, geordnet

(*Leben etc*): **be in ~ employment** fest angestellt sein. **5.** *ling.* regelmäßig. **6.** *Sport:* Stamm...: **~ player.** **7.** **~ gasoline** *mot. Am.* Normalbenzin *n.* **II** *s* **7** **8.** Stammkunde *m*, -kundin *f*; Stammgast *m.* **9.** *Sport:* Stammspieler(in). **10.** *mot. Am.* Normal *n.* **reg·u·lar·i·ty** [ˌ~ˈlærətɪ] *s* Regelmäßigkeit *f.* **reg·u·lar·ize** [ˈ~ləraɪz] *v/t* regulieren.

reg·u·late [ˈregjʊleɪt] *v/t* **1.** regeln, regulieren. **2.** ⚙ einstellen, regulieren. **,reg·u'la·tion** *s* **1.** Reg(e)lung *f*, Regulierung *f.* **2.** ⚙ Einstellung *f.* **3.** Vorschrift *f.* **'reg·u·la·tor** *s* ⚙ Regler *m.*

re·ha·bil·i·tate [ˌriːəˈbɪlɪteɪt] *v/t* **1.** Schwerbehinderte rehabilitieren. **2.** Strafentlassene resozialisieren. **3.** *j-s* Ruf etc wiederherstellen: **be ~d** rehabilitiert werden (*Person*). **'re·ha,bil·i'ta·tion** *s* **1.** Rehabilitation *f:* **~ center** (*bsd. Br. centre*) Rehabilitationszentrum *n.* **2.** Resozialisierung *f.* **3.** Wiederherstellung *f.*

re·hash **I** *v/t* [ˌriːˈhæʃ] *alte Fakten etc* neu auftischen. **II** *s* [ˈriːhæʃ] Neuauftischung *f.*

re·hears·al [rɪˈhɜːsl] *s* ♩, *thea.* Probe *f.* **re'hearse** *v/t u. v/i* proben.

reign [reɪn] **I** *s* Herrschaft *f* (*a. fig.*): **~ of terror** Schreckensherrschaft. **II** *v/i* herrschen (*over* über *acc*) (*a. fig.*): **silence ~ed** es herrschte Schweigen; **the ~ing world champion** (*Sport etc*) der amtierende Weltmeister.

re·im·burse [ˌriːɪmˈbɜːs] *v/t* Auslagen erstatten, vergüten: **~ s.o.** (*for*) **s.th.** j-m et. erstatten. **,re·im'burse·ment** *s* Erstattung *f*, Vergütung *f.*

rein [reɪn] **I** *s* Zügel *m:* **give free ~ to one's imagination** s-r Phantasie freien Lauf *od.* die Zügel schießen lassen; **keep a tight ~ on** *fig. j-n, et.* streng kontrollieren; **take the ~s** *fig.* die Zügel *od.* das Heft in die Hand nehmen. **II** *v/t:* **~ in** *Pferd* zügeln; *fig.* bremsen.

re·in·car·nate [riːˈɪnkɑːneɪt] *v/t:* **be ~ed** wiedergeboren werden (*as* als). **,re·in·car'na·tion** *s* Reinkarnation *f*, Wiedergeburt *f.*

rein·deer [ˈreɪndɪə] *pl* **-deers**, *bsd. coll.* **-deer** *s zo.* Ren(tier) *n.*

re·in·force [ˌriːɪnˈfɔːs] *v/t allg.* verstärken, *fig. a.* untermauern: **~d concrete** ⚙ Stahlbeton *m.* **,re·in'force·ment** *s*

Verstärkung *f*, *fig. a.* Untermauerung *f*: **~s** *pl* ✗ Verstärkung *f*.

re·in·state [ˌriːɪnˈsteɪt] *v/t* j-n wiedereinstellen (**as** als; **in** in *dat*). **ˌre·inˈstate·ment** *s* Wiedereinstellung *f*.

re·in·sur·ance [ˌriːɪnˈʃɔːrəns] *s* ✝ Rückversicherung *f*. **ˌre·inˈsure** *v/t* rückversichern.

re·is·sue [ˌriːˈɪʃuː] I *v/t* **1.** *Buch* neu auflegen. **2.** *Briefmarken etc* neu herausgeben. II *s* **3.** Neuauflage *f*. **4.** Neuausgabe *f*.

re·it·er·ate [riːˈɪtəreɪt] *v/t* (ständig) wiederholen. **re·ˌit·erˈa·tion** *s* (ständige) Wiederholung.

re·ject [rɪˈdʒekt] *v/t* **1.** j-n, *et.* ablehnen, *Angebot a.* ausschlagen, *Bitte* abschlagen, *Plan etc* verwerfen. **2.** *verpflanztes Organ etc* abstoßen. **reˈjec·tion** *s* **1.** Ablehnung *f*, Ausschlagung *f*, Abschlagen *n*, Verwerfung *f*. **2.** ✻ Abstoßung *f*.

re·joice [rɪˈdʒɔɪs] *v/i* (hoch) erfreut sein; jubeln (**at, over** über *acc*). **reˈjoic·ing** *s*, *a. pl* Jubel *m*.

re·join[1] [ˌriːˈdʒɔɪn] *v/t* sich wieder anschließen (*dat*) *od.* an (*acc*), wieder eintreten in (*acc*).

re·join[2] [rɪˈdʒɔɪn] *v/t* erwidern. **reˈjoin·der** *s* Erwiderung *f*.

re·ju·ve·nate [rɪˈdʒuːvəneɪt] *v/t* verjüngen. **re·ju·veˈna·tion** *s* Verjüngung *f*.

re·kin·dle [ˌriːˈkɪndl] *v/t* **1.** wieder anzünden. **2.** *fig.* wieder entfachen.

re·lapse [rɪˈlæps] I *v/i* **1.** zurückfallen, wieder verfallen (**into** in *acc*). **2.** a) rückfällig werden, b) ✻ e-n Rückfall bekommen *od.* erleiden. II *s* **3.** Rückfall *m*: **have a ~** → 2b.

re·late [rɪˈleɪt] I *v/t* **1.** erzählen, berichten (**to s.o.** j-m): **strange to ~** so seltsam es klingt. **2.** in Beziehung *od.* Zs.-hang bringen (**to** mit). II *v/i* **3.** sich beziehen (**to** auf *acc*). **4.** zs.-hängen (**to** mit). **reˈlat·ed** *adj* **1.** verwandt (**to** mit): → **marriage** 2. **2.** *fig.* verwandt: **be ~** to zs.-hängen mit.

re·la·tion [rɪˈleɪʃn] *s* **1.** Verwandte *m, f*. **2.** Beziehung *f* (**between** zwischen *dat*; **to** zu): **bear no ~ to** in keiner Beziehung stehen zu; **in** (*od.* **with**) **~ to** in bezug auf (*acc*). **3.** *pl* diplomatische, geschäftliche *etc* Beziehungen *pl* (**between** zwischen *dat*; **with** zu). **4.** Erzählung *f*, Bericht *m*.

re·la·tion·ship *s* **1.** Verwandtschaft *f*: **there is no ~ between them** sie sind nicht miteinander verwandt. **2.** Beziehung *f*, Verhältnis *n* (**between** zwischen *dat*; **to** zu): **have a ~ with s.o.** ein Verhältnis mit j-m haben.

rel·a·tive [ˈrelətɪv] I *adj* **1.** relativ: **~ly** *a.* verhältnismäßig. **2.** **~ to** bezüglich, hinsichtlich. **3.** *ling.* relativ, Relativ...: **~ clause** Relativsatz *m*; **~ pronoun** Relativpronomen *n*, bezügliches Fürwort. II *s* **4.** Verwandte *m, f*. **rel·a·ˈtiv·i·ty** *s* Relativität *f*: **theory of ~** *phys.* Relativitätstheorie *f*.

re·lax [rɪˈlæks] I *v/t* **1.** j-n, *Muskeln etc* entspannen. **2.** *Griff, Bestimmung etc* lockern. **3.** *fig.* nachlassen in (*dat*). II *v/i* **4.** sich entspannen, *fig. a.* ausspannen. **5.** sich lockern. **re·laxˈa·tion** [ˌriː~] *s* **1.** Entspannung *f*. **2.** Lockerung *f*. **reˈlaxed** *adj* entspannt, (*Atmosphäre a.*) zwanglos.

re·lay I *s* [ˈriːleɪ] **1.** [*a.* ˌriːˈleɪ] ∲ Relais *n*. **2.** Ablösung *f* (*Arbeiter etc*): **work in ~s** in Schichten arbeiten. **3.** *a.* **~ race** (*Sport*) Staffel(lauf *m*) *f*: **~** (*team*) Staffel *f*. **4.** *Rundfunk, TV:* Übertragung *f*. II *v/t* [riːˈleɪ] **5.** (**to**) *Nachricht* ausrichten (*dat*), weitergeben (an *acc*). **6.** *Rundfunk, TV:* übertragen.

re·lay [ˌriːˈleɪ] *v/t* (*irr* **lay**) *Kabel, Teppich* neu verlegen.

re·lease [rɪˈliːs] I *v/t* **1.** entlassen (**from** aus), freilassen: **~** (**one's hold on**) j-n, *et.* loslassen. **2.** *fig.* (**from**) befreien (von); entbinden (von): **~ s.o. from a contract** j-n aus e-m Vertrag entlassen. **3.** *Film, Leiche etc* freigeben; *Schallplatte* herausbringen; *Statistik etc* veröffentlichen. **4.** *mot. Handbremse* lösen. II *s* **5.** Entlassung *f*, Freilassung *f*. **6.** Befreiung *f*, Erlösung *f*; Entbindung *f*. **7.** Freigabe *f*; Veröffentlichung *f*: **be on general ~** überall zu sehen sein (*Film*).

rel·e·gate [ˈrelɪgeɪt] *v/t et.* verbannen (**to** in *acc*): **be ~d** (*Sport*) absteigen (**to** in *acc*). **ˌrel·eˈga·tion** *s* Verbannung *f*; (*Sport*) Abstieg *m*.

re·lent [rɪˈlent] *v/i* **1.** nachgeben (*Person*). **2.** nachlassen (*Schmerz, Wind etc*). **reˈlent·less** *adj* □ **1.** unnachgiebig. **2.** anhaltend (*Wind, Schmerz etc*).

rel·e·vant [ˈreləvənt] *adj* □ **1.** relevant,

bedeutsam, wichtig (**to** für). **2.** sachbezogen, sach-, zweckdienlich.

re·li·a·bil·i·ty [rɪˌlaɪəˈbɪlətɪ] s Zuverlässigkeit f, Verläßlichkeit f, Vertrauenswürdigkeit f. **re·li·a·ble** adj □ zuverlässig, verläßlich; vertrauenswürdig.

re·li·ance [rɪˈlaɪəns] s **1.** Vertrauen n: **place complete ~ on** volles Vertrauen setzen in (acc). **2.** Abhängigkeit (**on** von). **re·li·ant** adj: **be ~ on** abhängig sein von, angewiesen sein auf (acc).

rel·ic [ˈrelɪk] s **1.** Relikt n, Überbleibsel n. **2.** eccl. Reliquie f.

re·lief [rɪˈliːf] s **1.** Erleichterung f (a. ✻): **give** (od. **bring**) s.o. **some ~** j-m Erleichterung verschaffen; **~ of pain** Schmerzlinderung f; **to my great ~** zu m-r großen Erleichterung; → **sigh** I, II. **2.** Unterstützung f, Hilfe f; Am. Sozialhilfe f: **be on ~** Sozialhilfe beziehen; **Br.** (Steuer)Erleichterung f. **4.** Ablösung f (Person[en]). **5.** Entlastung f. **6.** Relief n: **stand out in bold** (od. **sharp**) **~ against** sich deutlich abheben gegen. **~ bus** s Einsatzbus m. **~ fund** s Hilfsfonds m. **~ map** s Reliefkarte f. **~ road** s Entlastungsstraße f.

re·lieve [rɪˈliːv] v/t **1.** Schmerzen, Not lindern, j-n, Gewissen erleichtern: **~ one's feelings** sn Gefühlen Luft machen; **she was ~d to hear that** sie war erleichtert, als sie hörte, daß; **~ o.s.**, euphem. sich erleichtern. **2.** **~ s.o. of** j-m ein schweres Gepäckstück, e-e Arbeit etc abnehmen; humor. j-n um s-e Brieftasche etc erleichtern. **3.** j-n ablösen.

re·li·gion [rɪˈlɪdʒən] s Religion f: **soccer is a ~ with him, he makes a ~ of soccer** für ihn gibt es nur Fußball, Fußball ist sein ein u. alles.

re·li·gious [rɪˈlɪdʒəs] adj □ **1.** religiös, Religions...: **~ instruction** ped. Religion(sunterricht m) f; **~ liberty** Religionsfreiheit f. **2.** religiös, fromm. **3.** fig. gewissenhaft: **with ~ care** mit peinlicher Sorgfalt.

re·lin·quish [rɪˈlɪŋkwɪʃ] v/t **1.** aufgeben, verzichten auf (acc). **2.** (**to**) Besitz, Recht abtreten (dat od. an acc), überlassen (dat).

rel·ish [ˈrelɪʃ] I v/t **1.** genießen, sich et. schmecken lassen. **2.** fig. Gefallen od. Geschmack finden an (dat): **not to ~ the**

idea nicht begeistert sein von der Aussicht (**of doing** zu tun); **not to ~ having to do s.th.** nicht davon begeistert sein, et. tun zu müssen. II s **3.** **with ~** mit Genuß. **4.** fig. Gefallen m, Geschmack m (**for** an dat). **5.** gastr. Würze f; Soße f.

re·lo·cate [ˌriːləʊˈkeɪt] v/t umsiedeln (a. v/i), verlegen. **re·lo·ca·tion** s Umsiedlung f, Verlegung f.

re·luc·tance [rɪˈlʌktəns] s Widerwillen m: **with ~** widerwillig, ungern. **re·luc·tant** adj widerwillig: **~ly** a. ungern; **be ~ to do s.th.** et. nur ungern tun.

re·ly [rɪˈlaɪ] v/i: **~ on** sich verlassen auf (acc); **~ on s.o. to do s.th.** sich darauf verlassen, daß j-d et. tut; **have to ~ on** abhängig sein von, angewiesen sein auf (acc).

re·main [rɪˈmeɪn] I v/i **1.** allg. bleiben. **2.** (übrig)bleiben: **a lot ~s to be done** es bleibt noch viel zu tun; **it ~s to be seen whether** es bleibt abzuwarten, ob. II s pl **3.** (Über)Reste pl. **re·main·der** [~də] s Rest m (a. Ⱥ). **re·main·ing** adj übrig, restlich.

re·make I v/t (irr make) [ˌriːˈmeɪk] wieder od. neu machen. II s [ˈriːmeɪk] Remake n, Neuverfilmung f.

re·mand [rɪˈmɑːnd] ᴛ⁏ I v/t: **be ~ed in custody** in Untersuchungshaft bleiben. II s: **be on ~** in Untersuchungshaft sein; **prisoner on ~, ~ prisoner** Untersuchungsgefangene m, f, -häftling m.

re·mark [rɪˈmɑːk] I v/t **1.** bemerken, äußern (**that** daß). II v/i **2.** **~ on** sich äußern über (acc, et. od. zu et. III s **3.** Bemerkung f (**about, on** über acc): **make a ~** e-e Bemerkung machen. **4.** **worthy of ~** bemerkenswert. **re·mark·a·ble** adj □ bemerkenswert, beachtlich.

re·mar·riage [ˌriːˈmærɪdʒ] s Wiederverheiratung f, -heirat f. **re·mar·ry** v/i wieder heiraten.

re·me·di·a·ble [rɪˈmiːdjəbl] adj □ behebbar, abstellbar. **re·me·di·al** adj: **~ exercises** pl Heilgymnastik f.

rem·e·dy [ˈremədɪ] I s **1.** ✻ (Heil)Mittel n (**for, against** gegen). **2.** fig. (Gegen)Mittel n (**for, against** gegen): **be beyond** (od. **past**) **~** hoffnungslos od. nicht mehr zu beheben sein. II v/t **3.** Mangel, Schaden beheben; Situation bereinigen; Mißstand abstellen.

re·mem·ber [rɪ'membə] **I** v/t **1.** sich erinnern an (acc); ~ **doing s.th.** sich daran erinnern, et. getan zu haben; **suddenly he ~ed that** plötzlich fiel ihm ein, daß. **2.** denken an (acc); ~ **to do s.th.** daran denken, et. zu tun; **I must ~ this** das muß ich mir merken. **3.** ~ **s.o. in one's will** j-n in s-m Testament bedenken. **4. please ~ me to your wife** grüßen Sie bitte Ihre Frau von mir; **he asked to be ~ed to you** er läßt Sie grüßen. **II** v/i **5. I can't ~** ich kann mich nicht erinnern; **if I ~ right(ly)** wenn ich mich recht erinnere od. entsinne. **re'mem·brance** s Erinnerung f (of an acc); **in ~ of** zur Erinnerung an; 2 **Day** (od. **Sunday**) Br. Volkstrauertag m.

re·mind [rɪ'maɪnd] v/t j-n erinnern (of an acc; **that** daran, daß); ~ **s.o. to do s.th.** j-n daran erinnern, daß er et. tut. **re'mind·er** s Mahnung f.

rem·i·nisce [remɪ'nɪs] v/i in Erinnerungen schwelgen, sich in Erinnerungen ergehen (**about, on** an acc). **rem·i·nis·cence** [~'nɪsns] s mst pl Erinnerung f (of an acc). **rem·i·nis·cent** adj: **be ~ of** erinnern an (acc).

re·miss [rɪ'mɪs] adj nachlässig: **be ~ in one's duties** s-e Pflichten vernachlässigen.

re·mis·sion [rɪ'mɪʃn] s **1.** (a. Straf-) Erlaß m: **he was given three months' ~** ihm wurden drei Monate (von s-r Strafe) erlassen (**for** wegen). **2.** Vergebung f (der Sünden). **3.** vorübergehende Besserung.

re·mit [rɪ'mɪt] v/t **1.** Schulden, Strafe erlassen; Sünden vergeben. **2.** Geld überweisen (**to** dat od. an acc). **3.** zurückverweisen (**to** an acc). **re'mit·tance** s Überweisung f (**to** an acc).

rem·nant ['remnənt] s **1.** (Über)Rest m (a. fig.). **2.** (Stoff)Rest m: ~ **sale** Resteverkauf m.

re·mod·el [ri:'mɒdl] v/t pret u. pp **-eled**, bsd. Br. **-elled** umgestalten.

re·mold Am. → **remould**.

re·mon·strance [rɪ'mɒnstrəns] s Protest m, Beschwerde f. **re·mon·strate** ['remənstreɪt] v/i protestieren (**with** bei; **against** gegen), sich beschweren (**with** bei; **about** über acc).

re·morse [rɪ'mɔːs] s Gewissensbisse pl, Reue f: **feel ~** Gewissensbisse haben.

re'morse·ful [~fʊl] adj □ reumütig, reuig. **re'morse·less** adj □ unbarmherzig (a. fig.).

re·mote [rɪ'məʊt] adj **1.** räumlich: fern, (weit) entfernt; abgelegen, entlegen. **2.** zeitlich: fern: **in the ~ future** in ferner Zukunft. **3.** fig. entfernt (Zs.-hang), (Verwandte a.) weitläufig. **4.** fig. entfernt (Möglichkeit), gering (Chance): **I haven't got the ~st idea** ich habe keine blasse od. nicht die geringste Ahnung. **5.** fig. distanziert, unnahbar. **~·con·trol** s ⚙ **1.** Fernlenkung f, -steuerung f. **2.** Fernbedienung f. **re,mote-con'trolled** adj **1.** ferngelenkt, -gesteuert. **2.** mit Fernbedienung.

re·mould bsd. Br. **I** v/t [ri:'məʊld] Reifen runderneuern. **II** s ['ri:məʊld] runderneuerter Reifen.

re·mount [ri:'maʊnt] **I** v/t Pferd etc wieder besteigen; Treppen wieder hinaufgehen: ~ **one's bicycle** wieder auf sein Fahrrad steigen. **II** v/i wieder aufsitzen.

re·mov·a·ble [rɪ'muːvəbl] adj abnehmbar. **re'mov·al** [~vl] s **1.** Entfernung f; Abnahme f. **2.** Umzug m: ~ **van** Möbelwagen m. **re·move I** v/t **1.** entfernen (**from** von); Deckel, Hut etc abnehmen; Kleidung ablegen. **2.** fig. Schwierigkeiten etc beseitigen, Hindernisse aus dem Weg räumen; Zweifel etc zerstreuen. v/i **3.** (um)ziehen (**from** von; **to** nach). **III** s **4.** fig. **be (at) only one ~ from** nicht weit entfernt sein von; **be several ~s from** weit entfernt sein von. **re'mov·er** s (Flecken- etc)Entferner m.

re·mu·ner·ate [rɪ'mjuːnəreɪt] v/t **1.** j-n entlohnen (**for** für). **2.** j-n entschädigen (**for** für). **re,mu·ner'a·tion** s **1.** Entlohnung f. **2.** Entschädigung f. **re'mu·ner·a·tive** [~rətɪv] adj □ einträglich, lohnend.

Ren·ais·sance [rə'neɪsəns] s hist. Renaissance f.

re·nal ['riːnl] adj anat. Nieren...: ~ **failure** ⚕ Nierenversagen n.

re·name [ri:'neɪm] v/t umbenennen (**in** acc).

ren·der ['rendə] v/t **1.** berühmt etc machen: ~ **s.o. unable to do s.th.** es j-m unmöglich machen, et. zu tun. **2.** Hilfe leisten, Dienst a. erweisen. **3.** Gedicht etc vortragen. **4.** übersetzen, -tragen (**into** in acc). **5.** mst ~ **down** Fett auslassen. **'ren·der·ing** s **1.** Vortrag m. **2.** Übersetzung f, -tragung f.

ren·dez·vous ['rɒndɪvuː] **I** pl **-vous** ['ːvuːz] s **1.** Rendezvous n, Verabredung f; Treffen n, Zs.-kunft f. **2.** Treffpunkt m. **II** v/i pret u. pp **-voused** ['ːvuːd] **3.** sich treffen (*with* mit).

ren·di·tion [ren'dɪʃn] bsd. Am. → *rendering*.

re·new [rɪ'njuː] v/t erneuern: ~ *one's efforts* erneute Anstrengungen machen; ~ *one's visa* sein Visum erneuern lassen; *give s.o.* ~*ed hope* j-m neue Hoffnung geben; *with* ~*ed strength* mit neuen Kräften. **re·new·a·ble** adj: *be* ~ erneuert werden können od. müssen. **re·new·al** s Erneuerung f.

re·nounce [rɪ'naʊns] v/t **1.** verzichten auf (acc). **2.** s-m Glauben etc abschwören.

ren·o·vate ['renəʊveɪt] v/t renovieren. **,ren·o·va·tion** s Renovierung f.

re·nown [rɪ'naʊn] s Berühmtheit f, Ruhm m: *win* ~ berühmt werden. **re·nowned** adj berühmt (*for* wegen, für).

rent[1] [rent] **I** s **1.** Miete f; Pacht f: *for* ~ bsd. Am. zu vermieten od. verpachten. **2.** bsd. Am. Leihgebühr f: *for* ~ zu vermieten od. verleihen. **II** v/t **3.** mieten; pachten (*from* von). **4.** a. ~ *out* bsd. Am. vermieten; verpachten (*to* an acc). **5.** bsd. Am. Auto etc mieten: ~*ed car* Leih-, Mietwagen m.

rent[2] [~] s Riß m (a. *fig.*).

'rent-a-,car (**ser·vice**) s bsd. Am. Autoverleih m.

rent·al ['rentl] s **1.** Miete f; Pacht f. **2.** bsd. Am. Leihgebühr f.

'rent·er ['rentə] s **1.** Mieter(in); Pächter(in). **2.** bsd. Am. Vermieter(in); Verpächter(in).

,rent-'free adj miet- od. pachtfrei.

re·nun·ci·a·tion [rɪ,nʌnsɪ'eɪʃn] s **1.** Verzicht m (*of* auf acc). **2.** Abschwören n.

re·o·pen [,riː'əʊpən] **I** v/t **1.** Geschäft etc wiedereröffnen. **2.** Verhandlungen etc wiederaufnehmen; Fall wiederaufrollen. **II** v/i **3.** wiedereröffnen. **4.** wiederaufgenommen od. wiederaufgerollt werden.

re·or·ga·ni·za·tion ['riːˌɔːgənaɪ'zeɪʃn] s Umorganisation f; Umstellung f. **,re-'or·gan·ize** v/t umorganisieren; Möbel umstellen, die Möbel umstellen in (dat).

re·pair [rɪ'peə] **I** v/t **1.** reparieren; ausbessern. **2.** *fig.* wiedergutmachen. **II** s **3.** Reparatur f; Ausbesserung f: *beyond* ~ nicht mehr zu reparieren; *be under* ~ in Reparatur sein. **4.** *be in good* (*bad*) ~ in gutem (schlechtem) Zustand sein. **5.** *fig.* Wiedergutmachung f.

rep·a·ra·ble ['repərəbl] adj □ reparabel, wiedergutzumachen(d). **,rep·a·'ra·tion** s **1.** Wiedergutmachung f: *make* ~ *for et.* wiedergutmachen. **2.** pl pol. Reparationen pl.

rep·ar·tee [,repɑː'tiː] s Schlagfertigkeit f; schlagfertige Antwort(en pl): *be good at* ~ schlagfertig sein.

re·pa·tri·ate [riː'pætrɪeɪt] v/t repatriieren, in den Heimatstaat zurückführen. **,re·pa·tri·'a·tion** s Repatriierung f.

re·pay [riː'peɪ] v/t (irr. *pay*) **1.** Geld etc zurückzahlen: ~ *s.o.'s expenses* j-m s-e Auslagen erstatten; *I'll* ~ *you some time* ich gebe dir das Geld irgendwann einmal zurück; *fig.* ich werde mich irgendwann einmal erkenntlich zeigen; das zahle ich dir schon noch zurück. **2.** *Besuch etc* erwidern. **3.** a) (*positiv*) sich für et. erkenntlich zeigen: ~ *s.o. for his help* j-n für s-e Hilfe belohnen od. entschädigen, b) (*negativ*) et. vergelten, lohnen (*with* mit): ~ *s.o.'s meanness*, ~ *s.o. for his meanness* j-m s-e Gemeinheit heimzahlen. **re'pay·a·ble** adj rückzahlbar: *be* ~ zurückgezahlt werden können od. müssen (*over two years* in e-m Zeitraum von zwei Jahren). **re'pay·ment** s **1.** Rückzahlung f. **2.** Erwiderung f. **3.** Vergeltung f.

re·peal [rɪ'piːl] **I** v/t Gesetz etc aufheben. **II** s Aufhebung f.

re·peat [rɪ'piːt] **I** v/t **1.** wiederholen: ~ *o.s.* sich wiederholen; ~ *s.th. after s.o.* j-m et. nachsprechen; *his answer doesn't bear* ~*ing* s-e Antwort läßt sich nicht wiederholen. **2.** et. weitererzählen, -sagen. **II** v/i **3.** aufstoßen (*on* es od. j-m) (*Speise*). **III** s **4.** Rundfunk, TV: Wiederholung f. **5.** ♪ Wiederholungszeichen n. **re'peat·ed** adj □ wiederholt.

re·pel [rɪ'pel] v/t **1.** *Angriff, Feind* zurückschlagen. **2.** *Wasser etc, fig. j-n* ab-

stoßen. **re'pel·lent** *adj* □ *fig.* abstoßend: **be ~ to** abstoßend wirken auf
(*acc*).
re·pent [rɪ'pent] *v/t* bereuen: **~ having
done s.th.** es bereuen, et. getan zu haben.
re·per·cus·sion [ˌriːpəˈkʌʃn] *s mst pl*
Auswirkung (*on* auf *acc*).
rep·er·toire ['repətwɑː] *s thea. etc* Repertoire *n*: **have a large ~ of jokes** viele
Witze auf Lager haben.
rep·e·ti·tion [ˌrepɪ'tɪʃn] *s* Wiederholung
f: **his answer doesn't bear ~** s-e Antwort läßt sich nicht wiederholen.
re·place [rɪ'pleɪs] *v/t* **1.** zurücklegen,
-stellen: **~ the receiver** *teleph.* (den
Hörer) auflegen. **2.** *j-n, et.* ersetzen
(**with, by** durch); *j-n* vertreten. **3.** ⚙
austauschen, ersetzen. **re'place·ment**
s **1.** Ersatz *m*; Vertretung *f*. **2.** ⚙ Austausch *m*.
re·plant [ˌriː'plɑːnt] *v/t* **1.** umpflanzen. **2.**
neu bepflanzen.
re·play (*Sport*) **I** *s* ['riːpleɪ] **1.** Wiederho-
lungsspiel *n*. **2.** → **action replay**. **II** *v/t*
[ˌriː'pleɪ] **3.** Spiel wiederholen.
re·plen·ish [rɪ'plenɪʃ] *v/t* (wieder) auffüllen.
re·plete [rɪ'pliːt] *adj* **1.** gesättigt, satt. **2.**
angefüllt (**with** mit).
rep·li·ca ['replɪkə] *s* **1.** *Kunst:* Replik *f*,
Originalkopie *f*. **2.** Kopie *f*, Nachbildung *f*.
re·ply [rɪ'plaɪ] **I** *v/t* antworten, erwidern
(**that** daß). **II** *v/i* antworten (**to** auf *e-n
Brief etc*; **to s.o.** j-m): **~ to a letter** *a.*
e-n Brief beantworten (**to** auf *acc*): **in ~ to** (als
Antwort) auf; **give no ~** keine Antwort
geben, nicht antworten.
re·port [rɪ'pɔːt] **I** *s* **1.** *allg.* Bericht *m* (**on**
über *acc*). **2.** Gerücht *n*: **~ has it that** es
geht das Gerücht, daß. **3.** *ped. Br.*
Zeugnis *n*. **4.** Knall *m.* **II** *v/t* **5.** berichten (**to s.o.** j-m); berichten über (*acc*): **it
is ~ed that** es heißt, daß; **he is ~ed to
have said** er soll gesagt haben; **~ed
speech** *ling.* indirekte Rede. **6.** *j-n, Unfall, Verbrechen etc* melden (**to s.o.**
j-m): **~ s.o.** (**to the police**) j-n anzeigen
(**for** wegen); **the car is ~ed stolen** der
Wagen ist als gestohlen gemeldet. **III**
v/i **7.** berichten, Bericht erstatten (**on**
über *acc*). **8.** sich melden (**to** bei): **~ sick**

sich krank melden; **~ for work** sich zur
Arbeit melden. **~ card** *Am.* → **report** 3.
re·port·er [rɪ'pɔːtə] *s* Reporter(in), Be-
richterstatter(in).
re·pose [rɪ'pəʊz] *s* **1.** Ruhe *f.* **2.** *fig.* Gelassenheit *f.*
rep·re·hen·si·ble [ˌreprɪ'hensəbl] *adj* □
tadelnswert, verwerflich.
rep·re·sent [ˌreprɪ'zent] *v/t* **1.** *j-n, Br. a.
Wahlbezirk* vertreten. **2.** darstellen (**as**
fig.). **3.** dar-, hinstellen (**as, to be** als): **~
o.s. as** (*od.* **to be**) sich ausgeben für. **4.**
Beschwerden etc vorbringen (**to** bei).
ˌrep·re·sen'ta·tion *s* **1.** Vertretung *f.* **2.**
Darstellung *f*: **be a ~ of s.th.** et. darstellen. **3. make ~s to** vorstellig werden bei
(**about** wegen). **ˌrep·re·sen'ta·tion·al**
[~ʃənl] *adj* gegenständlich (*Kunst*).
ˌrep·re'sent·a·tive [~tətɪv] **I** *s* **1.**
(Stell)Vertreter(in); (Handels)Vertre-
ter(in). **2.** *parl.* Abgeordnete *m, f*: →
House of Representatives. II *adj* □ **3.**
repräsentativ (**of** für). **4.** *pol.* repräsentativ: **~ government** Repräsentativsy-
stem *n.*
re·press [rɪ'pres] *v/t* **1.** *Volk, Gefühle etc*
unterdrücken. **2.** *psych.* verdrängen.
re'pres·sion [~ʃn] *s* **1.** Unterdrückung
f. **2.** *psych.* Verdrängung *f.* **re'pres-
·sive** *adj* □ repressiv.
re·prieve [rɪ'priːv] ⚖ **I** *s* Begnadigung *f*;
Vollstreckungsaufschub *m.* **II** *v/t*: **he
was ~d** er wurde begnadigt; s-e Urteils-
vollstreckung wurde ausgesetzt.
rep·ri·mand ['reprɪmɑːnd] **I** *v/t* rügen,
tadeln (**for** wegen). **II** *s* Rüge *f*, Tadel *m.*
re·print **I** *v/t* [ˌriː'prɪnt] neu auflegen,
nachdrucken. **II** *s* ['riːprɪnt] Neuauflage *f*, Nachdruck *m.*
re·pris·al [rɪ'praɪzl] *s bsd.* ✕, *pol.* Repressalie *f*, Vergeltungsmaßnahme *f*: **in**
(*od.* **as a**) **~ for** als Vergeltung für; **take
~s** Repressalien ergreifen (**against** gegen).
re·proach [rɪ'prəʊtʃ] **I** *s* **1.** Vorwurf *m*:
above (*od.* **beyond**) **~** über jeden Tadel
erhaben; **look of ~** vorwurfsvoller
Blick. **2.** *fig.* Schande *f* (**to** für). **II** *v/t* **3.**
j-m Vorwürfe machen (**for** wegen).
rep·ro·bate ['reprəʊbeɪt] *s* verkomme-
nes Subjekt.
re·pro·cess [ˌriː'prəʊses] *v/t* *Kernbrenn-
stoffe* wiederaufbereiten. **ˌre'pro·cess-**

ing plant s Wiederaufbereitungsanlage f.

re·pro·duce [ˌriːprə'djuːs] I v/t 1. ~ o.s. → 4. 2. Bild etc reproduzieren. 3. Ton etc wiedergeben. II v/i 4. biol. sich fortpflanzen od. vermehren. **re·pro·duc·tion** [ˌ~'dʌkʃn] s 1. biol. Fortpflanzung f. 2. Reproduktion f. 3. Wiedergabe f. **ˌre·pro'duc·tive** adj biol. Fortpflanzungs...

re·proof [rɪ'pruːf] s Rüge f, Tadel m.

re·prove [rɪ'pruːv] v/t rügen, tadeln (**for** wegen).

rep·tile ['reptaɪl] s zo. Reptil n, Kriechtier n.

re·pub·lic [rɪ'pʌblɪk] s pol. Republik f. **re'pub·li·can, auch** Am. 2 I adj republikanisch. II s Republikaner(in).

re·pu·di·ate [rɪ'pjuːdɪeɪt] v/t 1. Angebot, Behauptung etc zurückweisen. 2. Schuld etc nicht anerkennen. **re·pu·di'a·tion** s 1. Zurückweisung f. 2. Nichtanerkennung f.

re·pug·nance [rɪ'pʌɡnəns] s: **in** (od. **with**) ~ angewidert. **re'pug·nant** adj □ widerlich, widerwärtig.

re·pulse [rɪ'pʌls] I v/t 1. Angriff, Feind zurückschlagen. 2. j-n, Angebot etc ab-, zurückweisen. II s 3. Zurückschlagen n. 4. Ab-, Zurückweisung f. **re'pul·sion** s 1. Abscheu m, f: **with** ~ voller Abscheu. 2. phys. Abstoßung f. **re'pul·sive** adj □ phys. abstoßend, fig. a. widerlich, widerwärtig.

re·pur·chase [ˌriː'pɜːtʃəs] I v/t zurückkaufen. II s Rückkauf m.

rep·u·ta·ble ['repjʊtəbl] adj □ angesehen. **ˌrep·u'ta·tion** s (engS. guter) Ruf: **have the** (od. **a**) ~ **of being** im Ruf stehen, etc zu sein; **make o.s. a** ~ **as** sich e-n Namen machen als. **re·pute** [rɪ'pjuːt] I s (engS. guter) Ruf: **of** ~ angesehen; **be held in high** ~ hohes Ansehen genießen. II v/t: **be** ~**d to do** gelten als. **re'put·ed·ly** adv angeblich, dem Vernehmen nach.

re·quest [rɪ'kwest] I s 1. (**for**) Bitte f (um), Wunsch m (nach): **at s.o.'s** ~ auf j-s Bitte hin; **on** ~ auf Wunsch; **make a** ~ **for s.th.** um et. bitten. II v/t 2. bitten od. ersuchen um. 3. j-n bitten, ersuchen (**to do** zu tun). ~ **stop** s Br. Bedarfshaltestelle f.

re·qui·em ['rekwɪəm] s Requiem n.

re·quire [rɪ'kwaɪə] v/t 1. erfordern: **be** ~**d** erforderlich sein; **if** ~**d** wenn nötig. 2. benötigen, brauchen. 3. verlangen (**that** daß; **s.th. of s.o.** et. von j-m): ~ **s.o. to do s.th.** von j-m verlangen, daß er et. tut; **be** ~**d to do s.th.** et. tun müssen. **re'quired** adj erforderlich, notwendig: ~ **reading** ped., univ. Pflichtlektüre f. **re'quire·ment** s 1. Anforderung f: **meet the** ~**s** den Anforderungen entsprechen. 2. Erfordernis n, Bedürfnis n.

req·ui·site ['rekwɪzɪt] I adj erforderlich, notwendig (**for** für). II s mst pl Artikel m: **camping** ~**s** pl Campingzubehör n. **ˌreq·ui'si·tion** I s 1. Anforderung f: **make a** ~ **for** et. anfordern. 2. ✕ Requisition f, Beschlagnahme f. II v/t 3. anfordern. 4. ✕ requirieren, beschlagnahmen.

re·quit·al [rɪ'kwaɪtl] s Vergeltung f. **re·quite** [rɪ'kwaɪt] v/t et. vergelten (**with** mit).

re·run I v/t (irr run) [ˌriː'rʌn] 1. TV wiederholen. 2. **be** ~ (Sport) wiederholt werden (Lauf). II s ['riːrʌn] 3. TV Wiederholung f (a. allg.).

re·scind [rɪ'sɪnd] v/t ✴ Gesetz, Urteil etc aufheben. **re·scis·sion** [rɪ'sɪʒn] s Aufhebung f.

res·cue ['reskjuː] I v/t retten (**from** aus, vor dat). II s Rettung f: **come to s.o.'s** ~ j-m zu Hilfe kommen; ~ **operations** pl Rettungsarbeiten pl; ~ **party** (od. **squad, team**) Rettungsmannschaft f. **res·cu·er** ['~kjʊə] s Retter(in).

re·search [rɪ'sɜːtʃ] I s Forschung f (**on** auf dem Gebiet gen): **carry out** (od. **do**) ~ **into** et. erforschen. II v/i forschen (**on** auf dem Gebiet gen): ~ **into** et. erforschen. III v/t et. erforschen. IV adj Forschungs...: ~ **team** Forscherteam n; ~ **worker** Forscher(in). **re'search·er** s Forscher(in).

re·sem·blance [rɪ'zembləns] s Ähnlichkeit f (**to** mit; **between** zwischen dat): **there is a strong** ~ **between them** sie sind sich sehr ähnlich; **bear a strong** ~ **to** starke Ähnlichkeit haben mit. **re'sem·ble** [~bl] v/t ähnlich sein, ähneln (dat).

re·sent [rɪ'zent] v/t übelnehmen, sich ärgern über (acc). **re'sent·ful** [~fʊl] adj □

ärgerlich. **re'sent·ment** *s* Ärger *m* (**against, at** über *acc*).

res·er·va·tion [ˌrezə'veiʃn] *s* **1.** *bsd. Am.* (*Wild*)Reservat *n*; *Am.* (Indianer)Reservat *n*, (-)Reservation *f*. **2.** Reservierung *f*, Vorbestellung *f*: **make a ~** ein Zimmer *etc* bestellen. **3.** Vorbehalt *m*: **with ~(s)** unter Vorbehalt; **without ~** vorbehaltlos.

re·serve [ri'zɜːv] **I** *s* **1.** Reserve *f* (**of** an *dat*): **keep s.th. in ~** et. in Reserve halten. **2.** *a. pl* ✕ Reserve *f*. **3.** *Sport*: Reservespieler(in). **4.** (Naturschutz-, *Wild*)Reservat *n*. **5.** Reserviertheit *f*, Zurückhaltung *f*. **6.** **without ~** vorbehaltlos. **II** *v/t* **7.** (sich) aufsparen (**for** für). **8.** **~ the right to do s.th.** sich (das Recht) vorbehalten, et. zu tun. **9.** reservieren (lassen), vorbestellen. **re'served** *adj* reserviert, zurückhaltend.

re·serv·ist [ri'zɜːvist] *s* ✕ Reservist *m*.

res·er·voir ['rezəvwɑː] *s* Reservoir *n* (*a. fig.* **of** an *dat*).

re·set [ˌriː'set] *v/t* (*irr* **set**) **1.** Edelstein neu fassen. **2.** Uhr umstellen; Zeiger *etc* zurückstellen (**to** auf *acc*).

re·set·tle [ˌriː'setl] *v/t* umsiedeln. ˌre·'set·tle·ment *s* Umsiedlung *f*.

re·shuf·fle [ˌriː'ʃʌfl] **I** *v/t* **1.** Karten neu mischen. **2.** Kabinett *etc* umbilden. **II** *s* ['riːʃʌfl] **3.** Umbildung *f*.

re·side [ri'zaid] *v/i* **1.** wohnen, s-n Wohnsitz haben; residieren. **2.** ~ *in fig.* liegen *od.* ruhen bei *j-m*. **res·i·dence** ['rezidəns] *s* **1.** Wohnsitz *m*; Residenz *f*: **official** ~ Amtssitz *m*; **take up** ~ sich niederlassen. **2.** Aufenthalt *m*: **~ permit** Aufenthaltsgenehmigung *f*, -erlaubnis *f*. **'res·i·dent I** *adj* ansässig, wohnhaft: **be** ~ **abroad** *a*. im Ausland wohnen. **II** *s* **1.** Bewohner(in) (*e-s Hauses*); (*e-r Stadt etc a*.) Einwohner(in), *mot.* Anlieger(in); (Hotel)Gast *m*. **res·i·den·tial** [ˌ~'denʃl] *adj* Wohn...

re·sid·u·al [ri'zidjʊəl] *adj* übrig(geblieben), restlich, Rest... **re·sid·ue** ['rezidjuː] *s bsd.* 🍎 Rest *m*, Rückstand *m*.

re·sign [ri'zain] **I** *v/t* **1.** aufgeben; verzichten auf (*acc*). **2.** Amt *etc* niederlegen. **3.** ~ *o.s.* **to** sich fügen in (*acc*), sich abfinden mit: **be ~ed to** sich abgefunden haben mit. **II** *v/i* **4.** zurücktreten (**from** von), sein Amt niederlegen. **res·ig·na·tion** [ˌrezig'neiʃn] *s* **1.** Rück-

tritt *m*, Amtsniederlegung *f*: **hand in** (*od.* **send in, submit, tender**) **one's ~** s-n Rücktritt einreichen. **2.** Ergebenheit *f*; Resignation *f*.

re·sil·i·ence [ri'ziliəns] *s* **1.** Elastizität *f*; Strapazierfähigkeit *f*. **2.** *fig.* Zähigkeit *f*. **re·sil·i·ent** *adj* □ **1.** elastisch; strapazierfähig. **2.** *fig.* zäh: **be** ~ nicht unterkriegen sein.

res·in ['rezin] *s* Harz *n*. **'res·in·ous** *adj* □ harzig; Harz...

re·sist [ri'zist] **I** *v/t* **1.** *j-m, e-r Sache* widerstehen: **I could not** ~ **doing it** ich mußte es einfach tun. **2.** Widerstand leisten (*dat od.* gegen), sich widersetzen (*dat*). **II** *v/i* **3.** Widerstand leisten, sich widersetzen. **re'sist·ance** *s* **1.** Widerstand *m* (**to** gegen): **offer** (*od.* **put up**) (**a**) **stubborn** ~ hartnäckig(en) Widerstand leisten (**to** *dat*); **without offering** ~ widerstandslos; **take the line of least** ~ den Weg des geringsten Widerstandes gehen. **2.** *a.* **power of** ~ Widerstandskraft *f* (**to** gegen) (*a.* 🍎). **3.** (Hitzeetc)Beständigkeit *f*, (Stoß- *etc*)Festigkeit *f*. **4.** ⚡ Widerstand *m* (*a. Bauteil*). **re'sist·ant** *adj* □ (hitze- *etc*)beständig, (stoß- *etc*)fest. **re'sis·tor** *s* ⚡ Widerstand *m* (Bauteil).

re·sit *ped., univ. br.* **I** *v/t* (*irr* **sit**) [ˌriː'sit] *Prüfung* wiederholen. **II** *s* ['riːsit] Wiederholungsprüfung *f*.

re·sole [ˌriː'səʊl] *v/t* neu besohlen.

res·o·lute ['rezəluːt] *adj* □ resolut, entschlossen. **'res·o·lute·ness → resolution** 3.

res·o·lu·tion [ˌrezə'luːʃn] *s* **1.** Beschluß *m, parl. etc a.* Resolution *f*. **2.** Vorsatz *m*: **make good ~s** gute Vorsätze fassen. **3.** Resolutheit *f*, Entschlossenheit *f*. **4.** Lösung *f*, Überwindung *f*. **5.** 🍎 *etc* Auflösung *f*, Zerlegung *f* (**into** in *acc*).

re·solve [ri'zɒlv] **I** *v/t* **1.** beschließen (**that** daß; **to do** zu tun). **2.** Problem *etc* lösen, Schwierigkeit *etc* überwinden. **3.** 🍎 *etc* auflösen, zerlegen (**into** in *acc*). **II** *v/i* **4.** (**into** in *acc*) 🍎 *etc* sich auflösen; *fig.* zerfallen. **III** *s* **5.** → **resolution** 2, 3.

res·o·nance ['rezənəns] *s* **1.** *phys.* Resonanz *f*. **2.** voller Klang. **'res·o·nant** *adj* □ **1.** *phys.* Resonanz... **2.** voll (Klang), volltönend, sonor (Stimme). **3.** **be** ~ **with** widerhallen von.

re-sort [rɪ'zɔːt] **I** s **1.** Urlaubsort m: → *health* 1, *seaside.* **2.** *have ~ to* → 3; *as a last ~* notfalls, wenn alle Stricke reißen; *as a last ~ he went ...* als er nicht mehr weiterwußte, ging er ... **II** v/i **3.** *~ to* greifen od. Zuflucht nehmen zu.

re-sound [rɪ'zaʊnd] v/i widerhallen (*with* von).

re-source [rɪ'sɔːs] s **1.** pl (Geld)Mittel pl; (*Boden-, Natur*)Schätze pl. **2.** Mittel n, Zuflucht f; Ausweg m: *leave s.o. to his own ~s* j-n sich selbst überlassen. **3.** Einfallsreichtum m, Findigkeit f. **re-'source-ful** [~fʊl] adj □ einfallsreich, findig.

re-spect [rɪ'spekt] **I** s **1.** Achtung f, Respekt f (*for* vor dat): *have ~ for* Respekt haben vor. **2.** Rücksicht f (*for* auf acc): *out of ~ for* aus Rücksicht auf; *have no ~ for* keine Rücksicht nehmen auf; *without ~ to* ohne Rücksicht auf (acc); ungeachtet (gen). **3.** Beziehung f, Hinsicht f: *in many ~s* in vieler Hinsicht; *in some ~* in gewisser Hinsicht; *with ~ to* was ... anbelangt od. betrifft. **4.** pl Empfehlungen pl: *give my ~s to your wife* e-e Empfehlung an Ihre Gemahlin. **5.** *pay one's ~s to* j-m s-e Aufwartung machen; *pay one's last ~s to* j-m die letzte Ehre erweisen. **II** v/t **6.** respektieren, achten. **7.** respektieren, berücksichtigen. **re'spect-a-ble** adj □ **1.** ehrbar, geachtet. **2.** gesellschaftsfähig (*Person*), (*Kleidung, Benehmen a.*) korrekt: *it is not ~* es gehört sich nicht (*to do* zu tun). **3.** respektabel, beachtlich. **re'spect-ful** [~fʊl] adj □ respektvoll. **re'spect-ing** prp bezüglich (gen). **re-'spec-tive** adj jeweilig: *they went to their ~ places* jeder von ihnen ging zu s-m Platz. **re'spec-tive-ly** adv beziehungsweise.

res-pi-ra-tion [ˌrespə'reɪʃn] s Atmung f.

res-pi-ra-tor ['respəreɪtə] s Atemschutzgerät n. **re-spir-a-to-ry** [rɪ'spaɪərətərɪ] adj Atem..., Atmungs...: *~ arrest* ❀ Atemstillstand m; *~ disease* ❀ Erkrankung f der Atemwege; *~ passages* pl (od. tract) anat. Atemwege pl; *~ system* Atmungsorgane pl.

res-pite ['respaɪt] s **1.** Aufschub m. **2.** Pause f: *without ~* ohne Pause od. Unterbrechung.

re-splend-ent [rɪ'splendənt] adj □ glänzend, strahlend.

re-spond [rɪ'spɒnd] **I** v/i **1.** antworten (*to* auf acc): *~ to a letter* e-n Brief beantworten. **2.** fig. reagieren (*to* auf acc; *with* mit), ❀ etc a. ansprechen (*to* auf acc). **II** v/t **3.** antworten (*that* daß). **re'spond-ent** s ⚖ Beklagte m, f (*in* e-m Scheidungsprozeß).

re-sponse [rɪ'spɒns] s **1.** Antwort f (*to* auf acc): *give no ~* keine Antwort geben, nicht antworten. **2.** fig. Reaktion f (*to* auf acc).

re-spon-si-bil-i-ty [rɪˌspɒnsə'bɪlətɪ] s **1.** Verantwortung f: *a position of great ~* e-e verantwortungsvolle Position; *on one's own ~* auf eigene Verantwortung; *claim ~ for* die Verantwortung übernehmen für (*e-n Terroranschlag etc*); *have ~ for* die Verantwortung haben für; *take (full) ~ for* die (volle) Verantwortung übernehmen für; *take no ~ for* nicht haften für. **2.** oft pl Verpflichtung f, Pflicht f. **re'spon-si-ble** adj □ **1.** verantwortlich (*for* für): *be ~ to s.o. for s.th.* j-m (gegenüber) für et. verantwortlich sein; *not to be ~ for* nicht haften für. **2.** (*for*) verantwortlich (für), schuld (an dat): *hold s.o. ~ for* j-n verantwortlich machen für. **3.** verantwortungsbewußt. **4.** verantwortungsvoll (*Position*). **re'spon-sive** adj □ **1.** leichtgängig (*Kupplung etc*), elastisch (*Motor*): *be ~ to* reagieren auf (acc), ❀ etc a. ansprechen auf (acc); empfänglich sein für. **2.** mitteilsam: *he wasn't very ~* aus ihm war nicht viel herauszuholen.

rest¹ [rest] **I** s **1.** Ruhe(pause) f; Erholung f: *have (od. take) a ~* sich ausruhen; *have a good night's ~* gut schlafen; *lay to ~* zur letzten Ruhe betten; fig. ad acta legen; *set s.o.'s mind at ~* j-n beruhigen. **2.** ❀ Auflage f, Stütze f; teleph. Gabel f. **II** v/i **3.** (sich aus)ruhen: *let s.th. ~* fig. et. auf sich beruhen lassen; *he will not ~ until* fig. er wird nicht eher ruhen, bis; → *laurel* 3. **4.** lehnen (*against, on* an dat): *~ on* bsd. ❀ ruhen auf (dat) (a. fig. Blick); fig. beruhen auf (dat), sich stützen auf (acc); *~ with* fig. bei j-m liegen. **III** v/t **5.** ausruhen (lassen). **6.** lehnen (*against* gegen; *on* an acc).

rest² [~] *s* Rest *m*: *the ~ of us* wir übrigen; *all the ~ of them* alle übrigen; *for the ~* im übrigen.

res·tau·rant ['restərɔ:ŋ] *s* Restaurant *n*, Gaststätte *f*. **~ car** *s* 🚍 *Br.* Speisewagen *m*.

rest·ful ['restfʊl] *adj* □ **1.** ruhig, friedlich. **2.** erholsam.

rest home *s* Alten-, Alters- *od.* Pflegeheim *n*.

rest·ing place ['restɪŋ] *s*: (*last*) ~ (letzte) Ruhestätte.

res·ti·tu·tion [ˌrestɪ'tju:ʃn] *s* Rückgabe *f*, (*von Geld a.*) Rückerstattung *f* (*to* an *acc*): *make ~ of s.th. to s.o.* j-m et. zurückgeben *od.* -erstatten.

res·tive ['restɪv] *adj* □ unruhig, nervös. **'res·tive·ness** *s* Unruhe *f*, Nervosität *f*.

rest·less ['restlɪs] *adj* □ **1.** ruhe-, rastlos. **2.** unruhig (*Person, Nacht*): *I had a ~ night* ich habe nicht gut geschlafen.

re·stock [ˌri:'stɒk] *v/t* Regal etc wieder auffüllen.

res·to·ra·tion [ˌrestə'reɪʃn] *s* **1.** Wiederherstellung *f*. **2.** Restaurierung *f*. **3.** Rückgabe *f*, Rückerstattung *f* (*to* an *acc*).

re·store [rɪ'stɔ:] *v/t* **1.** *Ordnung etc* wiederherstellen: *be ~d* (*to health*) wieder gesund sein. **2.** *Gemälde etc* restaurieren. **3.** zurückgeben, *Geld a.* zurückerstatten (*to* dat). **re·'stor·er** *s* **1.** Restaurator *m*. **2.** → *hair restorer*.

re·strain [rɪ'streɪn] *v/t* (*from*) zurückhalten (von), hindern an (*dat*): *~ s.o. from doing s.th.* j-n davon zurückhalten *od.* daran hindern, et. zu tun; *I had to ~ myself* ich mußte mich beherrschen (*from doing s.th.* um nicht et. zu tun). **re·'strained** *adj* **1.** beherrscht. **2.** dezent (*Farbe etc*). **re·'straint** [rɪ'streɪnt] *s* **1.** Beherrschung *f*. **2.** Be-, Einschränkung *f* (*on* gen).

re·strict [rɪ'strɪkt] *v/t* beschränken (*to* auf *acc*), einschränken. **re·'stric·tion** *s* Be-, Einschränkung *f*: *without ~s* uneingeschränkt. **re·'stric·tive** *adj* □ be-, einschränkend.

rest room *s Am.* Toilette *f* (*in Restaurant etc*).

re·struc·ture [ˌri:'strʌktʃə] *v/t* umstrukturieren.

re·sult [rɪ'zʌlt] **I** *s* **1.** Ergebnis *n*, Resultat *n*: *without ~* ergebnislos. **2.** Erfolg *m*. **3.** Folge *f*: *as a ~ of* als Folge von (*od. gen*). **II** *v/i* **4.** resultieren, sich ergeben (*from* aus): *~ in* zur Folge haben (*acc*), führen zu; *~ing* → *resultant*. **re·'sult·ant** *adj* daraus resultierend.

ré·su·mé ['rezju:meɪ] *s* **1.** Resümee *n*, Zs.-fassung *f*. **2.** *Am.* (*bsd.* tabellarischer) Lebenslauf.

re·sume [rɪ'zju:m] **I** *v/t* **1.** *Arbeit* wiederaufnehmen, *Diskussion, Reise etc* fortsetzen. **2.** *Platz* wieder einnehmen; *Mädchennamen etc* wieder annehmen. **II** *v/i* **3.** weitermachen, fortfahren. **re·sump·tion** [rɪ'zʌmpʃn] *s* Wiederaufnahme *f*, Fortsetzung *f*.

re·sur·face [ˌri:'sɜ:fɪs] **I** *v/t* **1.** *Straße* neu belegen. **II** *v/i* **2.** wieder auftauchen (*U-Boot*). **3.** *fig.* wiederaufleben.

re·sur·gence [rɪ'sɜ:dʒəns] *s* Wiederaufleben *n*. **re·'sur·gent** *adj* wiederauflebend.

res·ur·rect [ˌrezə'rekt] *v/t Brauch etc* wiederaufleben lassen, *Gesetz etc* wieder einführen. **ˌres·ur·'rec·tion** *s* **1.** Wiedereinführung *f*. **2.** ♀ *eccl.* Auferstehung *f*.

re·sus·ci·tate [rɪ'sʌsɪteɪt] *v/t* 🏥 wiederbeleben. **re·ˌsus·ci·'ta·tion** *s* Wiederbelebung *f*.

re·tail ['ri:teɪl] **I** *s* **1.** Einzelhandel *m*: *by* (*Am. at*) ~ → III. **II** *adj* **2.** Einzelhandels...: *~ price*; *~ dealer* → *retailer*. **III** *adv* **3.** im Einzelhandel, einzeln. **IV** *v/t* [ri:'teɪl] **4.** im Einzelhandel verkaufen (*at, for* für). **5.** *fig.* Gerücht etc verbreiten. **V** *v/i* [ri:'teɪl] **6.** im Einzelhandel verkauft werden (*at, for* für): *it ~s at £2 a.* es kostet im Einzelhandel zwei Pfund. **re·'tail·er** *s* Einzelhändler(in).

re·tain [rɪ'teɪn] *v/t* **1.** *Gleichgewicht* halten; *Eigenschaft, Fassung etc* behalten, bewahren. **2.** *Wasser* stauen (*Damm*), speichern (*Boden*); *Wärme* speichern. **re·'tain·er**, **re·'tain·ing fee** *s* (Honorar)Vorschuß *m* (*für Anwalt*).

re·take [ˌri:'teɪk] *v/t* (*irr take*) **1.** ✗ zurückerobern. **2.** *Film, TV: Szene etc* nochmals drehen.

re·tal·i·ate [rɪ'tælɪeɪt] *v/i* **1.** Vergeltung üben, sich revanchieren (*against* an *dat*); *engS.* zurückschlagen, -treten. **2.** *Sport, a. in Diskussion etc:* kontern (**with** mit). **re·tal·i·a·tion** s Vergeltung(smaßnahmen pl) f, Revanche f: **in ~ for** als Vergeltung für. **re·tal·i·a·to·ry** [~ətəri] adj Vergeltungs..., Revanche...

re·tard [rɪ'tɑːd] v/t verzögern, hemmen. **re·tard·ed** adj: (**mentally**) ~ (geistig) zurückgeblieben. **re·tar·da·tion** [ˌriːtɑː'deɪʃn] s Verzögerung f.

retch [retʃ] v/i würgen.

re·ten·tion [rɪ'tenʃn] s 1. Bewahrung f. 2. Stauung f; Speicherung f. **re·ten·tive** adj gut (Gedächtnis).

re·think [ˌriː'θɪŋk] v/t (irr think) noch einmal überdenken.

ret·i·cence ['retɪsəns] s Schweigsamkeit f. **'ret·i·cent** adj □ schweigsam: **he was very ~ about it** von ihm war nur sehr wenig darüber zu erfahren.

ret·i·na ['retɪnə] pl **-nas, -nae** [~niː] s anat. Netzhaut f.

ret·i·nue ['retɪnjuː] s Gefolge n.

re·tire [rɪ'taɪə] I v/i 1. allg. sich zurückziehen (a. fig. **from business** aus dem Geschäftsleben; **from competition** vom aktiven Sport): ~ **from business** a. sich zur Ruhe setzen. 2. in Rente od. Pension gehen, sich pensionieren lassen. 3. Sport: aufgeben. II v/t 4. in den Ruhestand versetzen, pensionieren. **re·tired** adj pensioniert, im Ruhestand (lebend): **be ~** a. in Pension od. Rente sein; ~ **general** General m außer Dienst. **re·tire·ment** s 1. Rückzug m. 2. Pensionierung f; Ruhestand m: ~ **age** Pensions-, Rentenalter n. 3. Sport: Aufgabe f. **re'tir·ing** adj □ zurückhaltend.

re·tort¹ [rɪ'tɔːt] I s (scharfe) Entgegnung. II v/t (scharf) entgegnen.

re·tort² [~] s 🜊 Retorte f.

re·touch [ˌriː'tʌtʃ] v/t phot. retuschieren.

re·trace [rɪ'treɪs] v/t Tathergang etc rekonstruieren: ~ **one's steps** denselben Weg zurückgehen.

re·tract [rɪ'trækt] v/t 1. Krallen etc, ✈ Fahrgestell einziehen. 2. Angebot etc zurückziehen, Behauptung etc zurücknehmen, Geständnis etc widerrufen. **re·tract·a·ble** adj einziehbar. **re·trac·tion** s 1. Einziehen n. 2. Zurücknahme f, Widerruf m.

re·train [ˌriː'treɪn] I v/t umschulen. II v/i umschulen, sich umschulen lassen. **ˌre'train·ing** s Umschulung f.

re·tread I v/t [ˌriː'tred] Reifen runderneuern. II s ['riːtred] runderneuerter Reifen.

re·treat [rɪ'triːt] I s 1. ✕ Rückzug m: **beat a (hasty) ~** fig. abhauen. 2. Zufluchtsort m. II v/i 3. ✕ sich zurückziehen. 4. zurückweichen (**from** vor dat).

re·trench·ment [rɪ'trentʃmənt] s: **policy of ~** Sparpolitik f.

re·tri·al [ˌriː'traɪəl] s ⚖ Wiederaufnahmeverfahren n.

ret·ri·bu·tion [ˌretrɪ'bjuːʃn] s Vergeltung f. **re·trib·u·tive** [rɪ'trɪbjʊtɪv] adj Vergeltungs...

re·triev·al [rɪ'triːvl] s 1. Zurückholen n. 2. Wiedergutmachen n, Wettmachen n; Rettung f: **beyond** (od. **past**) ~ hoffnungslos (Situation). 3. hunt. Apportieren n.

re·trieve [rɪ'triːv] v/t 1. zurückholen. 2. Fehler wiedergutmachen, Verlust a. wettmachen; Situation retten. 3. (a. v/i) hunt. apportieren.

ret·ro·ac·tive [ˌretrəʊ'æktɪv] adj □ rückwirkend.

ret·ro·grade ['retrəʊgreɪd] adj rückschrittlich: ~ **step** Rückschritt m.

ret·ro·gres·sive [ˌretrəʊ'gresɪv] adj □ rückschrittlich.

ret·ro·spect ['retrəʊspekt] s: **in ~** rückschauend, im Rückblick. **ˌret·ro'spec·tion** s Rückblick m, -schau f. **ˌret·ro'spec·tive** adj □ 1. rückblickend, -schauend. 2. rückwirkend.

re·trous·sé [rə'truːseɪ] adj: ~ **nose** Stupsnase f.

re·try [ˌriː'traɪ] v/t ⚖ 1. Fall erneut verhandeln. 2. neu verhandeln gegen j-n.

re·turn [rɪ'tɜːn] I v/i 1. zurückkehren, -kommen; zurückgehen; fig. wiederauftreten: ~ **to** fig. auf ein Thema, Vorhaben zurückkommen; in e-e Gewohnheit etc zurückfallen; in e-n Zustand zurückkehren; → **normal** II. II v/t 2. ~ **to sender** ✎ zurück an Absender. 3. (**to**) zurückgeben (dat); zurückbringen (dat); zurückschicken, -senden (dat an acc). 4. zurücklegen, -stellen. 5. Besuch, Kompliment etc erwidern. 6. Gewinn, Zinsen abwerfen. 7. **be ~ed (to Parliament)** Br. gewählt werden. 8. → **verdict** 1. III s 9. Rückkehr f; fig. Wiederauftreten n: **on one's ~** bei s-r Rückkehr; **by ~ (of post)** Br. postwendend, umgehend; **many happy ~s (of the day)** herzlichen Glückwunsch zum Geburtstag. **10.** Rückgabe f; Zurückbringen n; Zurückschicken n, -senden n. **11.** Zurücklegen n, -stellen n. **12.** Erwiderung f. **13.** a. pl ♱ Gewinn m. **14. in ~** als Gegenleistung (**for** für): **expect nothing in ~** keine Gegenleistung erwarten. **15.** (*Steuer*)Erklärung f. **16.** Tennis etc: Return m, Rückschlag m. **IV** adj **17.** Rück...: **~ game** (*Sport*) Rückspiel n; **~ journey** Rückreise f; **by ~ mail** Am. postwendend, umgehend; **~ ticket** Br. Rückfahrkarte f; Rückflugticket n. **V** adv **18. the price is £10 ~** Br. der Preis beträgt 10 Pfund hin u. zurück. **re'turn·a·ble** adj **1. ~ bottle** Pfandflasche f. **2. be ~** zurückgegeben od. zurückgeschickt werden müssen.

re·un·ion [ˌriːˈjuːnjən] s **1.** Treffen n, Wiedersehensfeier f. **2.** Wiedervereinigung f. **re·u·nite** [ˌriːjuːˈnaɪt] v/t Land wiedervereinigen, Familie etc wieder vereinigen.

rev [rev] mot. **F I** s Umdrehung f: **number of ~s** Drehzahl f; **~ counter** Drehzahlmesser m. **II** v/t a. **~ up** Motor aufheulen lassen. **III** v/i a. **~ up** aufheulen (Motor).

re·val·u·a·tion [ˈriːˌvæljʊˈeɪʃn] s Aufwertung f. **re'val·ue** [~juː] v/t Dollar etc aufwerten.

re·vamp [riːˈvæmp] v/t F Haus etc aufmöbeln, Theaterstück etc aufpolieren, Firma etc auf Vordermann bringen.

re·veal [rɪˈviːl] v/t **1.** den Blick freigeben auf (acc); zeigen. **2.** Geheimnis etc enthüllen, aufdecken. **re'veal·ing** adj □ **1.** offenherzig (Kleid etc). **2.** fig. aufschlußreich.

rev·el [ˈrevl] v/i pret u. pp **-eled**, bsd. Br. **-elled 1.** (in) schwelgen (in dat); b. s. sich weiden (an dat).

rev·e·la·tion [ˌrevəˈleɪʃn] s **1.** Enthüllung f, Aufdeckung f. **2.** eccl. Offenbarung f.

rev·el·(l)er [ˈrevlə] s Feiernde m, f. **'rev·el·ry** s lärmendes od. ausgelassenes) Feiern.

re·venge [rɪˈvendʒ] **I** s **1.** Rache f: **in ~** aus Rache (**for** für); **take** (**one's**) **~ on s.o.** (**for** s.th.) → 4; → **sweet** 1. **2.** Spiel, Sport: Revanche f: **give s.o. a chance to get his ~** j-m Revanche geben. **II** v/t

3. et. rächen. **4. ~ o.s. on s.o.** (**for** s.th.) sich an j-m (für et.) rächen. **re'venge·ful** [~fʊl] adj □ rachsüchtig.

rev·e·nue [ˈrevənjuː] s a. pl Staatseinnahmen pl, -einkünfte pl: → **inland** 2.

re·ver·ber·ate [rɪˈvɜːbəreɪt] **I** v/i nach-, widerhallen. **II** v/t Schall zurückwerfen. **re·ver·ber'a·tion** s **1.** Nach-, Widerhall m. **2.** Zurückwerfen n.

re·vere [rɪˈvɪə] v/t verehren; Andenken hochhalten. **rev·er·ence** [ˈrevərəns] s Verehrung f; Ehrfurcht f (**for** vor dat): **with ~** ehrfürchtig; **hold in ~** verehren. **'Rev·er·end** s eccl. Hochwürden m.

rev·er·ent [ˈrevərənt], **rev·er·en·tial** [ˌ~ˈrenʃl] adj □ ehrfürchtig, ehrfurchtsvoll.

rev·er·ie [ˈrevərɪ] s (Tag)Träumerei f: **fall into a ~** ins Träumen kommen.

re·ver·sal [rɪˈvɜːsl] s **1.** Umstoßung f; ♱ Aufhebung f. **2.** Rückschlag m. **re'verse I** s **1.** Gegenteil n: **quite the ~** ganz im Gegenteil. **2.** Rückschlag m. **3.** Kehr-, Rückseite f (e-r Münze). **4.** mot. Rückwärtsgang m: **put the car into ~** den Rückwärtsgang einlegen. **II** adj □ **5.** umgekehrt; (Richtung) entgegengesetzt: **~ gear →** 4; **in ~ order** in umgekehrter Reihenfolge; **~ side** linke (Stoff)Seite. **III** v/t **6.** Wagen im Rückwärtsgang od. rückwärts fahren: **~ one's car out of the garage** a. rückwärts aus der Garage fahren. **7.** Reihenfolge etc umkehren: **~ the charges** teleph. Br. ein R-Gespräch führen. **8.** Entscheidung etc umstoßen; ♱ Urteil aufheben. **9.** Blatt etc umdrehen; Mantel etc wenden. **IV** v/i **10.** mot. im Rückwärtsgang od. rückwärts fahren.

re·vert [rɪˈvɜːt] v/i: **~ to** auf ein Thema zurückkommen; in e-e Gewohnheit etc zurückfallen; in e-n Zustand zurückkehren.

re·view [rɪˈvjuː] **I** s **1.** Überprüfung f: **be under ~** überprüft werden. **2.** Besprechung f, Kritik f, Rezension f: **~ copy** Rezensionsexemplar n. **3.** ✕ Parade f. **4. ~** revue. **5.** ped. Am. (Stoff)Wiederholung f (**for** für e-e Prüfung). **II** v/t **6.** überprüfen. **7.** besprechen, rezensieren. **8.** ✕ besichtigen, inspizieren. **9.** ped. Am. Stoff wiederholen (**for** für e-e Prüfung). **re'view·er** s Kritiker(in), Rezensent(in).

re·vile [rɪ'vaɪl] v/t schmähen, verunglimpfen.

re·vise [rɪ'vaɪz] v/t **1.** revidieren: a) *Ansicht* ändern, b) *Buch etc* überarbeiten. **2.** *Br.* → review 9.

re·vi·sion [rɪ'vɪʒn] s **1.** Revidierung f, Änderung f; Revision f, Überarbeitung f. **2.** überarbeitete Ausgabe. **3.** *Br.* → review 5.

re·vi·tal·ize [ˌriː'vaɪtəlaɪz] v/t neu beleben.

re·viv·al [rɪ'vaɪvl] s **1.** Wiederbelebung f (a. *fig.*). **2.** *thea.* Wiederaufnahme f. **3.** Wiederaufleben n (a. *fig.*). **re'vive** I v/t **1.** *j-n* wiederbeleben; beleben. **2.** *Brauch etc* wiederbeleben, wiederaufleben lassen; *Erinnerungen* wachrufen. **3.** *thea. Stück* wiederaufnehmen. **II** v/i **4.** wieder zu sich kommen; wieder aufleben. **5.** wiederaufleben (*Brauch etc*).

rev·o·ca·tion [ˌrevə'keɪʃn] s Aufhebung f, Rückgängigmachung f, Widerruf m. **re·voke** [rɪ'vəʊk] v/t *Gesetz etc* aufheben, *Entscheidung, Erlaubnis etc* rückgängig machen, widerrufen.

re·volt [rɪ'vəʊlt] **I** s **1.** Revolte f, Aufstand m: *be in* ~ (*against* → 3. **2.** → **revulsion.** **II** v/i **3.** revoltieren (*against* gegen). **4.** *fig.* Abscheu empfinden, empört sein (*against, at, from* über *acc*). **III** v/t **5.** mit Abscheu erfüllen, abstoßen. **re'volt·ing** adj □ abscheulich, abstoßend.

rev·o·lu·tion [ˌrevə'luːʃn] s **1.** Umdrehung f: *number of* ~*s mot.* Drehzahl f; ~ *counter mot.* Drehzahlmesser m. **2.** *ast.* Umlauf m (*round* um). **3.** *pol.* Revolution f, *fig. a.* Umwälzung f. **ˌrev·o'lu·tion·ar·y I** adj □ *pol.* revolutionär, *fig. a.* umwälzend. **II** s *pol.* Revolutionär(in) (a. *fig.*). **ˌrev·o'lu·tion·ize** v/t *fig.* revolutionieren.

re·volve [rɪ'vɒlv] v/i sich drehen (*on an axis* um e-e Achse; *round the Earth* um die Erde): ~ *around fig.* sich drehen um; *he thinks the whole world* ~*s around him* er glaubt, alles dreht sich nur um ihn. **re'volv·er** s Revolver m. **re'volv·ing** adj Dreh...: ~ *door(s pl)* Drehtür f; ~ *stage thea.* Drehbühne f.

re·vue [rɪ'vjuː] s *thea.* Revue f; Kabarett n.

re·vul·sion [rɪ'vʌlʃn] s Abscheu m: *in* ~ angewidert.

re·ward [rɪ'wɔːd] **I** s (a. *ausgesetzte*) Belohnung: *as a* ~ (*for*) als Belohnung (für); → *finder.* **II** v/t belohnen. **re'ward·ing** adj lohnend, (*Aufgabe etc a.*) dankbar.

re·word [ˌriː'wɜːd] v/t umformulieren.

re·write [ˌriː'raɪt] v/t (*irr* **write**) umschreiben.

rhap·so·dize ['ræpsədaɪz] v/i schwärmen (*about, over* von). **'rhap·so·dy** s **1.** ♪ Rhapsodie f. **2.** *fig.* Schwärmerei f: *go into rhapsodies* ins Schwärmen geraten (*about, over* von).

Rhe·sus fac·tor ['riːsəs] s ♋ Rhesusfaktor m.

rhet·o·ric ['retərɪk] s **1.** Rhetorik f. **2.** *contp.* Phrasendrescherei f. **rhe·tor·i·cal** [rɪ'tɒrɪkl] adj □ rhetorisch: ~ *question* rhetorische Frage.

rheu·mat·ic [ruː'mætɪk] ♋ **I** adj (~*ally*) **1.** rheumatisch: ~ *fever* rheumatisches Fieber. **II** s **2.** Rheumatiker(in). **3.** *pl* (*sg konstruiert*) *bsd. Br.* F Rheuma n. **rheu·ma·tism** ['ruːmətɪzəm] s ♋ Rheuma(tismus m) n.

rhi·no ['raɪnəʊ] *pl* **-nos** s zo. F, **rhi·noc·er·os** [~'nɒsərəs] s zo. Rhinozeros n, Nashorn n.

rho·do·den·dron [ˌrəʊdə'dendrən] s ♣ Rhododendron m, n.

rhom·bus ['rɒmbəs] *pl* **-bus·es, -bi** ['~baɪ] s ⅍ Rhombus m, Raute f.

rhu·barb ['ruːbɑːb] s **1.** ♣ Rhabarber m. **2.** *bsd. Am.* F Krach m, Streit m.

rhyme [raɪm] **I** s **1.** Reim m (*for* auf *acc*): *do s.th. without* ~ *or reason* et. aus unerklärlichen Gründen tun. **2.** Reim m, Vers m. **II** v/i **3.** sich reimen (*with* auf *acc*). **III** v/t **4.** reimen (*with* auf *acc*, mit).

rhythm ['rɪðəm] s Rhythmus m: *break s.o.'s* ~ *j-n* aus dem Rhythmus bringen. **rhyth·mic, rhyth·mi·cal** ['rɪðmɪk(l)] adj □ rhythmisch, (*Atmen etc*) gleichmäßig.

rib [rɪb] **I** s **1.** *anat.* Rippe f (a. ♋ *etc*): → **dig** 1, 5, **poke** 1, 6. **2.** Speiche f (*e-s Regenschirms*). **II** v/t **3.** F aufziehen, hänseln (*for* wegen).

rib·bon ['rɪbən] s **1.** (a. Farb-, Ordens-) Band n. **2.** Streifen m; Fetzen m: *tear to* ~*s* zerfetzen.

rib cage s *anat.* Brustkorb m.

rice [raɪs] s ♣ Reis m. ~ **pad·dy** s Reisfeld

n. ~ **pud·ding** *s* Milchreis *m.* ~ **wine** *s* Reiswein *m.*

rich [rɪtʃ] **I** *adj* □ **1.** reich (*a. fig.*): ~ *in* reich an (*dat*); ~ *in contrasts* kontrastreich. **2.** prächtig, kostbar (*Schmuck etc*). **3.** schwer (*Speise*). **4.** ertragreich, fett (*Boden*). **5.** voll (*Töne*), (*Farben a.*) satt. **6.** *that's* ~! F iro. na prima! **II** *s* **7.** *the* ~ *pl* die Reichen *pl.* **rich·es** [~ɪz] *s pl* Reichtümer *pl.* '**rich·ness** *s* **1.** Reichtum *m* (*a. fig.*). **2.** Prächtigkeit *f*, Kostbarkeit *f.* **3.** Schwere *f.* **4.** Fettheit *f.* **5.** Fülle *f*, Sattheit *f.*

rick·ets ['rɪkɪts] *s pl* (*sg konstruiert*) ⚕ Rachitis *f.* **rick·et·y** [~əti] *adj* □ **1.** ⚕ rachitisch. **2.** schwach (*auch den Beinen*); gebrechlich. **3.** wack(e)lig (*Möbelstück etc*).

rick·shaw ['rɪkʃɔː] *s* Rikscha *f.*

ric·o·chet ['rɪkəʃeɪ] **I** *s* Querschläger *m.* **II** *v/i* abprallen (*off* von).

rid [rɪd] *v/t* (*mst irr*) befreien (*of* von): *get* ~ *of* loswerden. '**rid·dance** *s*: *good* ~ (*to him*)*!* F den sind wir Gott sei Dank los!; *get out and good* ~ auf Nimmerwiedersehen.

rid·den ['rɪdn] **I** *pp von* ride. **II** *adj in Zssgn* geplagt *od.* heimgesucht von.

rid·dle¹ ['rɪdl] *s* Rätsel *n* (*a. fig.*): *speak* (*od. talk*) *in* ~*s* in Rätseln sprechen.

rid·dle² [~] **I** *s* **1.** (*Schüttel*)Sieb *n.* **II** *v/t* **2.** sieben. **3.** ~ *with bullets* mit Kugeln durchlöchern *od.* -sieben; ~*d with holes* (*mistakes*) voller Löcher (Fehler).

ride [raɪd] **I** *s* **1.** Ritt *m*: *give s.o. a* ~ *on one's shoulders* j-n auf s-n Schultern reiten lassen. **2.** Fahrt *f*: *give s.o. a* ~ j-n (*im Auto etc*) mitnehmen; *go for a* ~ *in the car* e-e Autofahrt machen; *take s.o. for a* ~ F j-n reinlegen *od.* übers Ohr hauen. **II** *v/i* (*irr*) **3.** reiten (*a. rittlings sitzen*) (*on* auf *dat*): → **roughshod**. **4.** fahren (*on* auf e-m Fahrrad etc, in e-m Bus etc). **5.** ~ *up* hochrutschen (*Rock etc*). **III** *v/t* **6.** reiten (auf *dat*). **7.** Fahr-, Motorrad fahren, fahren auf (*dat*): *can you* ~ *a bicycle?* kannst du radfahren? '**rid·er** *s* **1.** Reiter(in). **2.** (*Motorrad-, Rad*)Fahrer(in).

ridge [rɪdʒ] *s* **1.** (*Gebirgs*)Kamm *m*, (-)Grat *m.* **2.** (*Dach*)First *m.*

rid·i·cule ['rɪdɪkjuːl] **I** *s* Spott *m*: *for fear of* ~ aus Angst, sich lächerlich zu ma-

chen; *hold up to* ~ → **II. II** *v/t* lächerlich machen, spotten über (*acc*). **ri'dic·u·lous** [~jʊləs] *adj* □ lächerlich: *don't be* ~ mach dich nicht lächerlich.

rid·ing ['raɪdɪŋ] *adj* Reit...: ~ *school*; ~ *breeches* Reithose *f.*

rife [raɪf] *adj*: ~ *with* voll von, voller.

rif·fle ['rɪfl] *v/i*: ~ *through s.th.* et. durchblättern.

riff·raff ['rɪfræf] *s* Gesindel *n*, Pack *n.*

ri·fle¹ ['raɪfl] *v/t* durchwühlen.

ri·fle² [~] *s* Gewehr *n.* ~ *range s* Schießstand *m.*

rift [rɪft] *s* **1.** Spalt(e *f*) *m.* **2.** *fig.* Riß *m.*

rig¹ [rɪg] *v/t* Wahl *etc* manipulieren.

rig² [~] **I** *s* **1.** ⚓ Takelage *f*, Takelung *f.* **2.** Bohrinsel *f.* **3.** F Aufmachung *f*: *in full* ~ in voller Montur. **4.** *Am.* F Sattelschlepper *m.* **II** *v/t* **5.** Schiff auftakeln. **6.** ~ *out* F j-n ausstaffieren (*as* als); auftakeln. **7.** ~ *up* F provisorisch zs.-bauen (*from* aus).

right [raɪt] **I** *adj* (□ → **rightly**) **1.** richtig, recht: *the* ~ *thing* das Richtige; → *all* 3. **2.** richtig: a) korrekt, b) wahr: *is your watch* ~? geht deine Uhr richtig?; *be* ~ recht haben. **3.** richtig, geeignet: *the* ~ *man in the* ~ *place* der rechte Mann am rechten Platz. **4.** richtig, in Ordnung: *put* (*od. set*) ~ in Ordnung bringen; j-n aufklären (*on* über *acc*); Irrtum richtigstellen. **5.** recht, Rechts... **6.** ~ *angle* & rechter Winkel. **II** *s* **7.** Recht *n*: *know* ~ *from wrong* Recht von Unrecht unterscheiden können. **8.** Recht *n*; Anrecht *n* (*to auf acc*): *by* ~ von Rechts wegen; *it is my* ~ *of way mot.* ich habe Vorfahrt; *know one's* ~*s* s-e Rechte kennen. **9.** *die* Rechte, rechte Seite: *on* (*od. at, to*) *the* ~ (*of*) rechts (von), rechter Hand (von); *on our* ~ zu unserer Rechten; *the second turning to* (*od. on*) *the* ~ die zweite Querstraße rechts; *keep to the* ~ sich rechts halten; *mot.* rechts fahren. **10.** *the* ~ *pol.* die Rechte. **III** *adv* **11.** richtig, recht: *if I get you* ~ wenn ich Sie richtig verstehe; *guess* ~ richtig (er)raten; → *serve* 8. **12.** genau, direkt. **13.** ~ *away* (*od. off*) sofort; ~ *now* im Moment; sofort. **14.** ganz, völlig. **15.** rechts (*of* von): *turn* ~ nach rechts wenden; *mot.* rechts abbiegen; ~ *and left*; ~, *left and center* (*bsd. Br. centre*) *fig.* F überall; in jeder Hinsicht. **IV** *v/t*

16. aufrichten. **17.** *Unrecht* wiedergutmachen. '**~,an·gled** *adj* A- rechtwink(e)lig.

right·eous ['raɪtʃəs] *adj* gerecht (*Zorn etc*).

right|·ful ['raɪtfʊl] *adj* □ rechtmäßig. '**~-hand** *adj* **1.** recht: **~ bend** Rechtskurve *f*; **~ man** *fig. j-s* rechte Hand. **2.** ◎ rechtsgängig, -läufig: **~ drive** Rechtssteuerung *f*. ˌ~'**hand·ed** *adj* □ rechtshändig: **be ~** Rechtshänder(in) sein. ˌ~'**hand·er** *s* Rechtshänder(in).

right·ist ['raɪtɪst] *adj pol.* rechtsgerichtet, -stehend. '**right·ly** *adv* **1.** richtig. **2.** mit Recht: **~ or wrongly** zu Recht od. Unrecht. **3.** F *I don't ~ know* ich weiß nicht sicher; *I can't ~ say* ich kann nicht mit Sicherheit sagen.

'**right-wing** *adj pol.* dem rechten Flügel angehörend, Rechts...

rig·id ['rɪdʒɪd] *adj* □ **1.** starr (*a. Person*: **with** vor *dat*), steif. **2.** *fig.* streng (*Disziplin etc*); starr (*Prinzipien etc*); genau, strikt (*Kontrolle etc*). **ri'gid·i·ty** *s* **1.** Starre *f*, Starrheit *f*, Steifheit *f*. **2.** *fig.* Strenge *f*; Genauigkeit *f*, Striktheit *f*.

rig·ma·role ['rɪgmərəʊl] *s* F **1.** Geschwätz *n*. **2.** Theater *n*, Zirkus *m*.

rig·or *Am.* → **rigour**.

rig·or mor·tis [ˌraɪgɔː'mɔːtɪs] *s* ✻ Leichenstarre *f*.

rig·or·ous ['rɪgərəs] *adj* □ **1.** streng (*Kontrolle etc*). **2.** (peinlich) genau, gründlich.

rig·our ['rɪgə] *s bsd. Br.* **1.** Strenge *f*: *the full ~ of the law* die volle Härte des Gesetzes. **2.** *pl* Unbilden *pl*.

'**rig-out** *s Br.* F Aufmachung *f*.

rile [raɪl] *v/t* F ärgern, reizen.

rim [rɪm] *s* **1.** Rand *m* (*e-r Tasse etc*), (*e-s Huts a.*) Krempe *f*. **2.** ◎ Felge *f*.

rind [raɪnd] *s* (*Zitronen- etc*)Schale *f*; (*Käse*)Rinde *f*; (*Speck- etc*)Schwarte *f*.

ring¹ [rɪŋ] **I** *s* **1.** *allg.* Ring *m*: *at the ~s* (*Turnen*) an den Ringen; *form a ~* e-n Kreis bilden; *he's got ~s round his eyes* er hat Ringe unter den Augen; *make (od. run) ~s round s.o. fig.* j-n in die Tasche stecken. **2.** (*Zirkus*) Manege *f*; (*Boxen*) Ring *m*. **3.** ⚓ Ring *m*, Kartell *n*; (*Spionage- etc*)Ring *m*. **II** *v/t* **1.** *Vogel etc* beringen. **4.** umringen, (*Polizei etc*) umstellen: *Stelle in e-m Buch etc* einkreisen.

ring² [~] **I** *s* **1.** Läuten *n*; Klingeln *n*. **2.** *fig. that has a familiar ~ to me* kommt mir (irgendwie) bekannt vor; *have a hollow ~* hohl klingen (*Versprechen etc*), unglaubwürdig klingen (*Protest etc*). **3.** *teleph. bsd. Br.* Anruf *m*: *give s.o. a ~* j-n anrufen. **II** *v/t* **4.** läuten; klingeln: *the bell is ~ing* es läutet *od.* klingelt; *~ for* nach j-m, *et.* läuten. **5.** *teleph. bsd. Br.* anrufen: *~ for Arzt etc* rufen. **6.** klingen (*a. fig.*): *~ in s.o.'s ears* j-m im Ohr klingen; *~ hollow* hohl klingen (*Versprechen etc*), unglaubwürdig klingen (*Protest etc*). **III** *v/t* (*irr*) **7.** läuten: → **bell 1**, **doorbell**. **8.** *teleph. bsd. Br.* j-n anrufen.

Verbindungen mit Adverbien:

ring| back *v/t u. v/i teleph. bsd. Br.* zurückrufen. **~ in** *v/i* **1.** *bsd. Br.* sich telefonisch melden (**to** bei). **2.** *Am.* (*bei Arbeitsbeginn*) einstempeln. **~ off** *v/i teleph. bsd. Br.* (den Hörer) auflegen, Schluß machen. **~ out** *v/i* **1.** erklingen, ertönen. **2.** *Am.* (*bei Arbeitsende*) ausstempeln. **~ round** *v/i bsd. Br.* herumtelefonieren. **~ up** *v/t* **1.** → **ring²** **8**. **2.** *Preis, Ware* (*in die Kasse*) eintippen.

ring| bind·er *s* Ringbuch *n*. **~ fin·ger** *s* Ringfinger *m*. '**~,lead·er** *s* Rädelsführer(in). '**~,mas·ter** *s* Zirkusdirektor *m*. **~ road** *s bsd. Br.* Umgehungsstraße *f*. '**~·side** *s*: *at the ~* (*Boxen*) am Ring; **~ seat** (*Boxen*) Ringplatz *m*; (*Zirkus*) Manegenplatz *m*.

rink [rɪŋk] *s* (*Kunst*)Eisbahn *f*; Rollschuhbahn *f*.

rinse [rɪns] **I** *v/t* **1.** *a.* **~ out** (aus)spülen, *Wäsche* spülen: **~ one's mouth out** sich den Mund ausspülen (**with** mit); **~ the soap out of one's hair** sich die Seife aus dem Haar spülen. **2.** sich *das Haar* tönen. **II** *s* **3.** Spülung *f*: *give s.th. a ~* → **1**. **4.** Tönung(smittel *n*) *f*.

ri·ot ['raɪət] **I** *s* **1.** Aufruhr *m*; Krawall *m*, Tumult *m*: **~ run** randalieren, randalierend ziehen (**through** durch); *his imagination ran ~* s-e Phantasie ging mit ihm durch; *read s.o. the ~ act off* *fig.* j-m die Leviten lesen; **~ police** Bereitschaftspolizei *f*; **~ squad** Überfallkommando *n*; **~ shield** Schutzschild *m*. **2.** **~ of colo(u)r** Sinfonie *f* von *od.* Orgie *f* in Farben. **3.** *be a ~* F zum Schreien (komisch) sein. **II** *v/i* **4.** an e-m

Aufruhr teilnehmen; randalieren. '**ri·ot·er** s Aufrührer m; Randalierer m. '**ri·ot·ous** adj □ 1. aufrührerisch; randalierend. 2. ausgelassen, wild.

rip [rɪp] I v/t 1. a. ~ **up** zerreißen; ~ **s.th.** sich et. zerreißen (**on** an dat); ~ **s.th. from s.o.'s hand** j-m et. aus der Hand reißen; ~ **off one's shirt** sich das Hemd herunter- od. vom Leib reißen; ~ **open** aufreißen. 2. ~ **off** F neppen; mitgehen lassen, klauen. II v/i 3. (zer)reißen. 4. **let her ~!** mot. F volle Pulle! III s 5. Riß m.

'**rip-cord** s Reißleine f (am Fallschirm).

ripe [raɪp] adj □ reif (a. fig.): **live to a ~ old age** ein hohes Alter erreichen; **the time is ~ for** die Zeit ist reif für; ~ **for development** baureif. **rip·en** ['~ən] I v/i reifen. II v/t reifen lassen.

'**rip-off** s F Nepp m; Diebstahl m.

ri·poste [rɪ'pɒst] I s 1. fenc. Riposte f. 2. (schlagfertige od. scharfe) Entgegnung. II v/t 3. (schlagfertig od. scharf) entgegnen.

rip·ple ['rɪpl] I s 1. kleine Welle. 2. Plätschern n. II v/t 3. Wasser kräuseln. III v/i 4. sich kräuseln. 5. plätschern.

'**rip·,roar·ing** adj F 1. ausgelassen (Party etc). 2. toll (Erfolg etc).

rise [raɪz] I v/i (irr) 1. aufstehen (a. am Morgen); sich erheben. 2. aufsteigen (Rauch etc); sich heben (Vorhang): **his spirits rose** s-e Stimmung hob sich. 3. ansteigen (Straße, Wasser etc), anschwellen (Fluß etc). 4. (an)steigen (**by** um) (Temperatur etc), (Preise etc a.) anziehen. 5. aufgehen (Sonne, Teig etc). 6. entspringen (Fluß etc); fig. entstehen (**from, out of** aus). 7. a. ~ **up** sich erheben (**against** gegen). 8. (**above**) erhaben sein (über acc), stehen (über dat): → **occasion** 3. 9. (beruflich od. gesellschaftlich) aufsteigen: → **rank**[1] 2. II s 10. Steigung f; Anhöhe f. 11. ast. Aufgang m. 12. fig. Ansteig m (**in**): ~ **in population** Bevölkerungszunahme f; **the ~ and fall** das Auf u. Ab. 13. fig. Aufstieg m (**to** zu): **the ~ and fall** der Aufstieg u. Fall. 14. bsd. Br. Lohn- od. Gehaltserhöhung f. 15. **give ~ to** verursachen, führen zu; Anlaß geben zu. **ris·en** ['rɪzn] pp von **rise**. '**ris·er** s: **early ~** Frühaufsteher(in); **late ~** Langschläfer(in). '**ris·ing** I s 1. Aufstand m,

Erhebung f. II adj 2. heranwachsend, kommend (Generation). 3. aufstrebend (Politiker etc). III prp 4. **be ~ ten** bsd. Br. fast zehn sein.

risk [rɪsk] I s Gefahr f, Risiko n: **at one's own ~** auf eigene Gefahr od. eigenes Risiko; **at the ~ of (ger)** auf die Gefahr hin zu (inf); **be at ~** gefährdet sein; **put at ~** gefährden; **run (od. take) a ~** ein Risiko eingehen; **run the ~ of doing s.th.** Gefahr laufen, et. zu tun; ~ **group** Risikogruppe f. II v/t riskieren: a) **sein Leben etc** aufs Spiel setzen, b) **Sprung etc** wagen, c) es ankommen lassen auf e-e Verletzung etc; ~ **doing s.th.** es wagen od. riskieren, et. zu tun; → **neck** 1. '**risk·y** adj □ riskant.

ri·sot·to [rɪ'zɒtəʊ] pl -tos s gastr. Risotto m.

ris·qué ['rɪskeɪ] adj gewagt (Witz etc).

rite [raɪt] s Ritus m: **perform the last ~s over** eccl. j-m die Sterbesakramente spenden.

rit·u·al ['rɪtjʊəl] I s 1. Ritual n. II adj □ 2. Ritual...: ~ **murder** Ritualmord m. 3. rituell.

ritz·y ['rɪtsɪ] adj F stinkvornehm, feudal.

ri·val ['raɪvl] I s 1. Rivale m, Rivalin f, Konkurrent(in): ~ (**in love**) Nebenbuhler(in). II adj 2. rivalisierend, konkurrierend: ~ **firm** Konkurrenzfirma f. III v/t pret u. pp -**valed**, bsd. Br. -**valled** 3. rivalisieren od. konkurrieren mit. 4. es aufnehmen mit (**for** an dat). '**ri·val·ry** s Rivalität f; Konkurrenz(kampf m) f.

riv·er ['rɪvə] s Fluß m; Strom m: **down the ~** flußabwärts; **up the ~** flußaufwärts; **sell s.o. down the ~** F j-n verraten u. verkaufen; ~**s** pl of blood Blutströme pl. ~ **ba·sin** s Flußbecken n. '~**·bed** s Flußbett n. '~**·side** s Flußufer n: **by the ~** am Fluß.

riv·et ['rɪvɪt] I s 1. ⊙ Niet m. II v/t 2. ⊙ (ver)nieten: **stand ~ed to the spot** fig. wie festgenagelt stehen(bleiben). 3. fig. Aufmerksamkeit richten, Augen, Blick a. heften (**on** auf acc); j-s Aufmerksamkeit fesseln.

road [rəʊd] s (Land)Straße f: **on the ~** auf der Straße; **be on the ~** mit dem Auto unterwegs sein; thea. etc auf Tournee sein; **be on the right ~** fig. auf dem richtigen Weg sein; **hit the ~** F sich auf den Weg machen, aufbrechen; **one**

for the ~ F e-n (*Schnaps etc*) zum Abschied *od.* für unterwegs; → **Rome. ~ ac·ci·dent** *s* Verkehrsunfall *m.* '~**-block** *s* Straßensperre *f.* **~ hog** *s* F Verkehrsrowdy *m.* '~**,hold·ing** *s mot.* Straßenlage *f.* '~**house** *s* Rasthaus *n.* **~man** ['~mən] *s* (*irr man*) Straßenarbeiter *m.* **~ roll·er** *s* ⊙ Straßenwalze *f.* **~ safe·ty** *s* Verkehrssicherheit *f.* '~**side** *s* Straßenrand *m*: **at** (*od.* **by**) **the ~** am Straßenrand. **~ test** *s mot.* Probefahrt *f*: **do a ~** e-e Probefahrt machen. '~**test** *v/t Auto* probefahren, e-e Probefahrt machen mit. **~ us·er** *s* Verkehrsteilnehmer(in). '~**way** *s* Fahrbahn *f.* **~ works** *s pl* Straßenbauarbeiten *pl.* '~**,wor·thy** *adj* verkehrssicher.

roam [rəʊm] **I** *v/i* wandern. **II** *v/t* wandern durch.

roar [rɔː] **I** *v/i* **1.** brüllen (**with** vor *dat*): **~** (**with laughter**) vor Lachen brüllen; **~ at s.o.** j-n anbrüllen. **2.** donnern (*Fahrzeug, Geschütz*). **II** *v/t* **3.** a. **~ out** et. brüllen. **III** *s* **4.** Brüllen *n*, Gebrüll *n*: **~s** *pl* **of laughter** brüllendes Gelächter. **5.** Donnern *n.* '**roar·ing I** *adj* □ **1.** brüllend. **2.** donnernd. **3.** *fig.* **~ success** F Bombenerfolg *m.* **II** *adv* **4.** **~ drunk** F sternhagelvoll. **III** *s* **5.** → **roar** 4, 5.

roast [rəʊst] **I** *v/t* Fleisch braten; *Kaffee etc* rösten. **II** *v/i* braten: **I'm ~ing** ich komme vor Hitze fast um. **III** *s* Braten *m.* **IV** *adj* gebraten: **~ beef** Rinder-, Rindsbraten *m*; **~ chicken** Brathuhn *n*, -hühnchen *n*; **~ pork** Schweine-, Schweinsbraten *m*; **~ veal** Kalbsbraten *m.* '**roast·ing** F **I** *adj* glühend-, knallheiß (*Tag etc*). **II** *adv*: **~ hot** → I. **III** *s*: **give s.o. a** (*real*) **~** j-n zusammenstauchen (**for** wegen).

rob [rɒb] *v/t* Bank *etc* überfallen; j-n berauben: **~ s.o. of s.th.** j-m et. rauben. '**rob·ber** *s* Räuber *m.* '**rob·ber·y** *s* Raub(überfall) *m*, (*Bank*)Raub *m*, (-)Überfall *m.*

robe [rəʊb] *s* a. *pl* Robe *f*, Talar *m.*

rob·in ['rɒbɪn] *s orn.* Rotkehlchen *n.*

ro·bot ['rəʊbɒt] *s* ⊙ Roboter *m* (a. *fig.*).

ro·bust [rəʊ'bʌst] *adj* □ **1.** robust (*Person, Gesundheit, Material etc*). *fig.* gesund (*Firma etc*). **2.** *fig.* nachdrücklich.

rock¹ [rɒk] *s* **1.** Fels(en) *m*; *coll.* Felsen *pl*; *geol.* Gestein *n.* **2.** Felsbrocken *m*; *Am.* Stein *m.* **3.** *pl* Klippen *pl*: **on the ~s**

on the rocks, mit Eis (*bsd. Whisky*); in ernsten Schwierigkeiten (*Firma etc*): **their marriage is on the ~s** in ihrer Ehe kriselt es gewaltig.

rock² [~] **I** *v/t* **1.** wiegen, schaukeln: **~ a child to sleep** ein Kind in den Schlaf wiegen. **2.** erschüttern (a. *fig.*): **~ the boat** *fig.* alles kaputtmachen. **II** *v/i* **3.** schaukeln. **4.** schwanken: **~ with laughter** F sich vor Lachen biegen. **5.** ♪ rocken. **III** *s* **6.** → **rock 'n' roll. 7.** a. **~ music** Rock(musik *f*) *m*: **~ group** Rockgruppe *f*; **~ singer** Rocksänger (-in).

rock| and roll *s* ♪ Rock and Roll *m.* **~ bot·tom** *s*: **fall to** (*od.* **hit, reach**) **~** e-n *od.* s-n Tiefpunkt erreichen. '~**bot·tom** *adj* niedrigst, äußerst (*Preise*). **~ crys·tal** *s min.* Bergkristall *m.*

rock·er ['rɒkə] *s* **1.** Kufe *f* (*e-s Schaukelstuhls etc*): **off one's ~** F übergeschnappt. **2.** *Am.* Schaukelstuhl *m.* **3.** *Br.* Rocker *m.*

rock·er·y ['rɒkərɪ] *s* Steingarten *m.*

rock·et ['rɒkɪt] **I** *s* **1.** Rakete *f.* **2.** **give s.o. a ~** *bsd. Br.* F j-m e-e Zigarre verpassen. **II** *v/i* **3.** a. **~ up** hochschnellen, in die Höhe schießen (*Preise*). **4.** rasen, schießen.

'**rock-fall** *s* Steinschlag *m.* **~ gar·den** *s* Steingarten *m.*

rock·ing| chair ['rɒkɪŋ] *s* Schaukelstuhl *m.* **~ horse** *s* Schaukelpferd *n.*

rock 'n' roll [ˌrɒkən'rəʊl] *s* ♪ Rock 'n' Roll *m.*

rock·y¹ ['rɒkɪ] *adj* □ **1.** felsig. **2.** steinhart.

rock·y² [~] *adj* □ F wack(e)lig.

ro·co·co [rəʊ'kəʊkəʊ] *s* Rokoko *n.*

rod [rɒd] *s* **1.** (a. *Angel*)Rute *f.* **2.** ⊙ Stab *m*, Stange *f.* **3.** **rule with a ~ of iron** mit eiserner Faust regieren. **4.** *Am. sl.* Schießeisen *n*, Kanone *f.*

rode [rəʊd] *pret von* **ride.**

ro·dent ['rəʊdənt] *s* Nagetier *n.*

ro·de·o [rəʊ'deɪəʊ] *pl* **-os** *s* Rodeo *m, n.*

roe¹ [rəʊ] *s* a. **hard ~** *ichth.* Rogen *m*; **soft ~** Milch *f.*

roe² [~] *s zo.* Reh *n.* '~**buck** *s* Rehbock *m.* **~ deer** *s* Reh *n.*

rog·er ['rɒdʒə] *int* Funkverkehr: roger!, verstanden!

rogue [rəʊg] *s* **1.** Gauner *m*: **~'s gallery** Verbrecheralbum *n.* **2.** *oft humor.*

Schlingel *m*, Spitzbube *m*. **'ro·guer·y** *s* **1.** Gaunerei *f*. **2.** Spitzbüberei *f*. **'ro·guish** *adj* □ schelmisch.

role [rəʊl] *s* thea. *etc* Rolle *f* (*a. fig.*).

roll [rəʊl] **I** *s* **1.** Rolle *f*; (*Fett*)Wulst *f*. **2.** Anwesenheits-, Namenliste *f*: *call the* ~ die Anwesenheitsliste verlesen. **3.** Brötchen *n*, Semmel *f*. **4.** *Würfeln*: Wurf *m*. **5.** ♫ Schlingern *n*. **6.** (G)Rollen *n* (*des Donners*); (*Trommel*)Wirbel *m*. **II** *v/i* **7.** rollen; sich wälzen: *tears were ~ing down her cheeks* Tränen rollten ihr über die Wangen; *heads will* ~ *fig.* es werden einige Köpfe rollen; *be ~ing in money* (*od. it*) F im Geld schwimmen; → *ball*[1] **8.** rollen, fahren. **9.** würfeln. **10.** (sch)wanken (*Person*); ♫ schlingern. **11.** (g)rollen (*Donner*). **III** *v/t* **12.** *etc.* rollen: *the dice* würfeln; ~ *one's eyes* die Augen rollen *od.* verdrehen. **13.** auf-, zs.-rollen: ~ *itself into* sich zs.-rollen zu (*Tier*); ~ *a cigarette* sich e-e Zigarette drehen; ~ed *into one* *fig.* in einem. **14.** *Rasen etc* walzen; *Teig* ausrollen.

Verbindungen mit Adverbien:

roll| **down** *v/t* **1.** *Ärmel* herunterkrempeln. **2.** *mot.* *Fenster* herunterkurbeln. ~ **in** *v/i* hereinströmen (*Angebote etc*). ~ **on** *v/i:* ~*, Saturday!* *Br.* wenn es doch nur schon Samstag wäre! ~ **out** *v/t* *Teig, Teppich* ausrollen. ~ **up I** *v/t* **1.** auf-, zs.-rollen. **2.** *Ärmel* hoch-, aufkrempeln (*a. fig.*). **3.** *mot.* *Fenster* hochkurbeln. **II** *v/i* **4.** sich zs.-rollen (*Tier*). **5.** F antanzen. **6.** ~*!* (*Rummelplatz etc*) hereinspaziert!

roll| **bar** *s mot.* Überrollbügel *m*. ~ **call** *s* Namensaufruf *m*: *have a* ~ die Namen aufrufen.

roll·er ['rəʊlə] *s* **1.** ◎ Rolle *f*; Walze *f*. **2.** Lockenwickler *m*. ~ **blind** *s* Rolladen *m*, Rollo *n*. ~ **coast·er** *s* Achterbahn *f*. ~ **skate** *s* Rollschuh *m*. **'~-skate** *v/i* Rollschuh laufen. ~ **skat·er** *s* Rollschuhläufer(in). ~ **skat·ing** *s* Rollschuhlaufen *n*. ~ **tow·el** *s* Rollhandtuch *n*.

roll·ing| **mill** ['rəʊlɪŋ] *s* ◎ Walzwerk *n*. ~ **pin** *s* Nudelholz *n*, -rolle *f*, Teigrolle *f*.

'roll-on *s* Deoroller *m*.

ro·ly-po·ly [ˌrəʊlɪ'pəʊlɪ] F **I** *s* Dickerchen *n*. **II** *adj* dick u. rund.

Ro·man ['rəʊmən] **I** *adj* römisch: ~ *nu-*

meral römische Ziffer. **II** *s* Römer(in). ~ **Cath·o·lic I** *adj* (römisch-)katholisch. **II** *s* Katholik(in).

ro·mance¹ [rəʊ'mæns] *s* **1.** Liebes- *od.* Abenteuerroman *m*. **2.** Romanze *f*, Liebesverhältnis *n*. **3.** Romantik *f*.

Ro·mance² [~] *adj* romanisch (*Sprache*).

Ro·man·esque [ˌrəʊmə'nesk] *adj* romanisch (*Baustil*).

ro·man·tic [rəʊ'mæntɪk] **I** *adj* (~*ally*) (*Kunst etc of* ♫) romantisch. **II** *s* (*Kunst etc of* ♫) Romantiker(in). **ro'man·ti·cism** [~ˌsɪzəm] *s* **1.** *oft* ♫ *Kunst etc*: Romantik *f*. **2.** romantische Vorstellungen *pl.* **ro'man·ti·cist** *s* → *romantic* **II**. **ro'man·ti·cize** *v/t* romantisieren.

Ro·ma·ny ['rɒmənɪ] *s* **1.** Zigeuner(in). **2.** Romani *n*, Zigeunersprache *f*.

Rome [rəʊm] *npr* Rom *n:* *was not built in a day* Rom ist nicht an *od.* in 'einem Tag erbaut worden; *all roads lead to* ~ alle Wege führen nach Rom.

romp [rɒmp] *v/i* **1.** *a.* ~ *about* (*od. around*) herumtollen. **2.** ~ *through* F *et.* spielend schaffen.

ron·do ['rɒndəʊ] *pl* **-dos** *s* ♪ Rondo *n*.

roof [ru:f] **I** *s* Dach *n*; *mot.* Verdeck *n:* *go through the* ~ F an die Decke gehen (*Person*); ins Unermeßliche steigen (*Kosten etc*); *have no* ~ *over one's head* kein Dach über dem Kopf haben; *live under the same* ~ unter 'einem Dach leben *od.* wohnen (*as* mit). **II** *v/t* bedachen: ~ *in* (*od. over*) überdachen. ~ **gar·den** *s* Dachgarten *m*. ~ **rack** *s* *mot.* Dachgepäckträger *m*. **'~top** *s:* *scream* (*od. shout*) *s.th. from the* ~*s* *fig.* et. ausposaunen *od.* an die große Glocke hängen.

rook¹ [rʊk] *v/t* F j-n betrügen (*of* um).

rook² [~] *s* Schach: Turm *m*.

room [ru:m] **I** *s* **1.** Raum *m*, Zimmer *n*. **2.** Raum *m*, Platz *m:* *make* ~ *for s.o.* j-m Platz machen. **3.** *fig.* Spielraum *m:* *there is* ~ *for improvement* es ließe sich noch manches besser machen; *leave little* ~ *for doubt* kaum e-n Zweifel übriglassen an (*dat*). **II** *v/i* **4.** *Am.* → *lodge* **3.** **'room·er** *Am.* → *lodger*. **'room·ing house** *Am.* Fremdenheim *n*, Pension *f*.

'room|**mate** *s* Zimmergenosse *m*, -genossin *f*. ~ **ser·vice** *s* Zimmerservice *m*.

ring for ~ nach dem Zimmerkellner klingeln.

room·y ['ruːmɪ] *adj* □ geräumig.

roost [ruːst] **I** *s* (Hühner)Stange *f*: **come home to** ~ *fig.* sich rächen (*Fehler etc*); → **rule** 5. **II** *v/i* auf der Stange sitzen *od.* schlafen. **'roost·er** *s bsd. Am.* Hahn *m*.

root[1] [ruːt] **I** *s anat.*, ♘, ♬ Wurzel *f* (*a. fig.*): ~ **and branch** *fig.* mit Stumpf u. Stiel; **get to the** ~ **of** *fig.* e-r Sache auf den Grund gehen; **have its** ~**s in** *fig.* wurzeln in (*dat*); **pull out by the** ~ mit der Wurzel ausreißen *od.* (*fig.*) ausrotten; **put down (new)** ~**s** *fig.* Fuß fassen; **take** ~ Wurzeln schlagen (*a. fig.*). **II** *v/i* Wurzeln schlagen (*a. fig.*). **III** *v/t*: ~ **up** mit der Wurzel ausreißen; ~ **out** *fig.* (mit der Wurzel) ausrotten.

root[2] [~] **I** *v/i a.* ~ **about** (*od.* **around**) herumwühlen (**among** in *dat*). **II** *v/t*: ~ **out** aufstöbern.

root[3] [~] *v/i*: ~ **for** *bsd. Am.* F a) *Sport*: j-n anfeuern, b) *fig.* j-m den Daumen drücken *od.* halten; j-n (tatkräftig) unterstützen.

root beer *s Am.* Limonade aus Wurzelextrakten.

root·ed ['ruːtɪd] *adj*: **be** ~ **in** *fig.* wurzeln in (*dat*), s-n Ursprung haben in (*dat*); **stand** ~ **to the spot** wie angewurzelt dastehen.

rope [rəʊp] **I** *s* **1.** Seil *n*, ♬ Tau *n*; Strick *m*: **give s.o. plenty of** ~ *fig.* j-m viel Freiheit *od.* Spielraum lassen; **know the** ~**s** F sich auskennen; **jump** ~ *Am.* seilhüpfen, -springen; **show s.o. the** ~**s** F j-n anlernen *od.* einarbeiten *od.* einweihen. **2.** (*Perlen- etc*)Schnur *f*. **II** *v/t* **3.** festbinden (**to** an *dat, a. acc*). **4.** ~ **off** (durch ein Seil) abgrenzen *od.* absperren. ~ **lad·der** *s* Strickleiter *f*.

rop·(e)y ['rəʊpɪ] *adj* □ F miserabel.

ro·sa·ry ['rəʊzərɪ] *s* (*Gebete oft* ☿) *eccl.* Rosenkranz *m*.

rose[1] [rəʊz] **I** *s* **1.** ♘ Rose *f*: **life is not all** ~**s** das Leben hat nicht nur angenehme Seiten. **2.** Brause *f* (*e-r Gießkanne etc*). **II** *adj* **3.** rosa-, rosenrot.

rose[2] [~] *pret von* **rise**.

ro·sé ['rəʊzeɪ] *s* Rosé *m* (*Wein*).

'rose·bush *s* ♘ Rosenstock *m*, -strauch *m*. **'~·col·o(u)red** *adj* rosa-, rosenrot: **see things through** ~ **glasses** (*od.*

spectacles) *fig.* die Dinge durch e-e rosa(rote) Brille sehen. **'~·hip** *s* ♘ Hagebutte *f*.

rose·mar·y ['rəʊzmərɪ] *s* ♘ Rosmarin *m*.

ro·sette [rəʊ'zet] *s* Rosette *f* (*a.* △).

ros·in ['rɒzɪn] **I** *s* Kolophonium *n*, Geigenharz *n*. **II** *v/t* mit Kolophonium einreiben.

ros·ter ['rɒstə] *s* Dienstplan *m*.

ros·trum ['rɒstrəm] *pl* **-tra** [~trə], **-trums** *s* Redner-, Dirigentenpult *n*.

ros·y ['rəʊzɪ] *adj* □ rosig (*a. fig.*).

rot [rɒt] **I** *v/i a.* ~ **away** (ver)faulen, (*bsd. Holz a.*) verrotten, morsch werden. **II** *v/t* (ver)faulen *od.* verrotten lassen, morsch machen. **III** *s* Fäulnis(prozeß *m*) *f*.

ro·ta ['rəʊtə] *s bsd. Br.* Dienstplan *m*.

ro·ta·ry ['rəʊtərɪ] **I** *adj* rotierend, Rotations..., Dreh... **II** *s Am.* Kreisverkehr *m*. **ro·tate** [~'teɪt] **I** *v/i* **1.** rotieren, sich drehen. **2.** turnusmäßig wechseln. **II** *v/t* **3.** rotieren lassen, drehen. **4.** *Personal* turnusmäßig auswechseln. **ro'ta·tion** *s* **1.** Rotation *f*, Drehung *f*. **2. in** ~ der Reihe nach, nacheinander.

rote [rəʊt] *s*: **learn s.th. by** ~ et. (mechanisch) auswendig lernen.

ro·tor ['rəʊtə] *s* ⚙, ✈ Rotor *m*.

rot·ten ['rɒtn] *adj* □ **1.** verfault, faul, (*bsd. Holz a.*) verrottet, morsch. **2.** F miserabel: **feel** ~ sich mies fühlen (*a. fig.*).

ro·tund [rəʊ'tʌnd] *adj* □ rund u. dick.

rouge [ruːʒ] *s* Rouge *n*.

rough [rʌf] **I** *adj* (□ → **roughly**) **1.** uneben (*Straße etc*), rauh (*Haut etc, a. Stimme*). **2.** stürmisch (*Meer, Überfahrt, Wetter*): **he had a** ~ **passage** *fig.* ihm ist es (e-e Zeitlang) nicht gutgegangen. **3.** a) grob (*Person, Behandlung etc*): **be** ~ **with** grob umgehen mit, b) *Sport*: hart (*Spielweise etc*). **4.** roh, Roh...: ~ **diamond** Rohdiamant *m*; **be a** ~ **diamond** *fig.* e-e rauhe Schale haben; ~ **draft** Rohfassung *f*; → **copy** 1. **5.** *fig.* grob, ungefähr: **at a** ~ **guess** grob geschätzt; **I have a** ~ **idea where it is** ich kann mir ungefähr vorstellen, wo es ist; → **idea** 1. **6. feel** ~ *Br.* F sich mies fühlen. **II** *s* **7.** *Golf*: Rough *n*. **8.** Rowdy *m*. **9. take the** ~ **with the smooth** die Dinge nehmen, wie sie kommen. **III** *adv* **10. sleep** ~ im Freien übernachten. **11.** *play* (*it*) ~ (*Sport*) hart spielen. **IV** *v/t* **12.** ~ *it* F primitiv leben. **13.** ~ *out* entwerfen, skizzieren. **14.** ~ *up* F *j-n* zs.-schlagen. '**rough·age** *s biol.* Ballaststoffe *pl.*

,**rough|-and-'tum·ble** *s* Balgerei *f*: *have a* ~ sich balgen. '**~·cast** *s* △ Rauhputz *m.*

rough·en ['rʌfn] **I** *v/t* Haut etc rauh machen. **II** *v/i* rauh werden. '**rough·ly** *adv* **1.** grob (*a.* *fig.*). **2.** *fig.* ungefähr: ~ *speaking* grob geschätzt, über den Daumen gepeilt.

'**rough·neck** *s bsd. Am.* F Grobian *m*; Schläger *m.*

rough·ness ['rʌfnɪs] *s* **1.** Unebenheit *f,* Rauheit *f.* **2.** Grobheit *f.*

'**rough·shod** *adv*: *ride* ~ *over* sich rücksichtslos hinwegsetzen über (*acc*).

rou·lette [ruː'let] *s* Roulett(e) *n.*

round [raʊnd] **I** *adj* (□ → **roundly**) **1.** *allg.* rund. **2.** rund(lich), dick(lich) (*Körperteil*). **3.** rund: a) voll, ganz: *a* ~ *dozen* ein rundes Dutzend, b) ab- *od.* aufgerundet: *the house cost £100,000 in* ~ *figures* das Haus kostete rund(e) 100 000 Pfund. **II** *adv* (→ *Verben, z.B.* **turn round**) **4.** → *all* **3. 5.** *all* (*the*) *year* ~ das ganze Jahr lang *od.* hindurch *od.* über. **6.** ~ *about* F ungefähr. **7.** *be three yards* ~ e-n Umfang von drei Yards haben. **III** *prp* **8.** (rund) um, um (... herum): *trip* ~ *the world* Weltreise *f*; *do you live* ~ *here?* wohnen Sie hier in der Gegend?; → *bend* 1, *clock* 1, *look* 1. **9.** ungefähr. **IV** *s* **10.** Runde *f,* Rundgang *m*: *do* (*od.* *be out on*) *one's* ~*s* e-e Runde machen, (*Arzt*) Hausbesuche machen; *go the* ~*s fig.* umgehen (*Gerücht etc*), (*Krankheit a.*) grassieren (*of* in *dat*); *the daily* ~ *fig.* der tägliche Trott. **11.** Lage *f,* Runde *f* (*Bier etc*): *it's my* ~ die Runde geht auf mich. **12.** *Boxen, Turnier, Verhandlungen etc*: Runde *f.* **13.** ✕ *etc* Schuß *m.* **14.** ♪ Kanon *m.* **V** *v/t* **15.** rund machen, (ab)runden, *Lippen* spitzen. **16.** umfahren, fahren um, *Kurve* nehmen.
Verbindungen mit Adverbien:
round| down *v/t* *Preis etc* abrunden (*to* auf *acc*). **~ off** *v/t* **1.** *Mahlzeit etc* abrunden, beschließen (*with* mit). **2.** *Preis etc* auf- *od.* abrunden (*to* auf *acc*). ~ *out* **I** *v/t Ausbildung etc* abrunden (*with* mit,

durch). **II** *v/i* rundlich werden (*Person*). ~ *up* *v/t* **1.** *Vieh* zs.-treiben. **2.** F *Verbrecher* hochnehmen; *Leute* zs.-trommeln, *a. et.* auftreiben. **3.** *Preis etc* aufrunden (*to* auf *acc*).

'**round·a·bout I** *s* **1.** *Br.* Kreisverkehr *m.* **2.** *Br.* Karussell *n*: *go on the* ~ Karussell fahren. **II** *adj* **3.** *take a* ~ *route* e-n Umweg machen; *in a* ~ *way fig.* auf Umwegen.

'**round·ly** *adv* **1.** gründlich, gehörig. **2.** rundweg, -heraus.

round rob·in *s* **1.** Petition *f,* Denkschrift *f* (*bsd. e-e mit im Kreis herum geschriebenen Unterschriften*). **2.** *Sport: Am.* Turnier, in dem jeder gegen jeden antritt.

'**rounds·man** ['raʊndzmən] *s* (*irr man*) *Br.* Ausfahrer *m,* Austräger *m.*

'**round|-ta·ble** *adj*: ~ *conference* Round-table-Konferenz *f,* Konferenz *f* am runden Tisch. '**~-the-clock** *adj* 24stündig, rund um die Uhr. ~ *trip s* Hin- u. Rückfahrt *f,* ✈ Hin- u. Rückflug *m.* '**~-trip** *adj*: ~ *ticket Am.* Rückfahrkarte *f,* ✈ Rückflugticket *n.*

rouse [raʊz] *v/t* **1.** *j-n* wecken (*from, out of* aus). **2.** *fig. j-n* auf-, wachrütteln (*from, out of* aus): ~ *s.o. to action* j-n so weit bringen, daß er (endlich) et. tut *od.* unternimmt. **3.** *a.* ~ *to anger* *j-n* erzürnen, reizen. '**rous·ing** *adj* □ mitreißend, zündend (*Rede etc*).

rout [raʊt] **I** *s*: *put to* ~ → II. **II** *v/t* ✕ in die Flucht schlagen.

route [ruːt] *s* Route *f,* Strecke *f,* Weg *m,* (*Bus*)Linie *f.*

rou·tine [ruː'tiːn] **I** *s* Routine *f* (*a. Computer*). **II** *adj* Routine..., routinemäßig.

roux [ruː] *pl* **roux** [ruːz] *s gastr.* Mehlschwitze *f,* Einbrenne *f.*

row¹ [rəʊ] *s* Reihe *f*: *four times in a* ~ viermal nach- *od.* hintereinander; ~ *house Am.* Reihenhaus *n.*

row² [~] *v/i u. v/t* rudern. **II** *s* Kahnfahrt *f*: *go for a* ~ rudern gehen.

row³ [raʊ] F **I** *s* Krach *m*: a) Krawall *m*: *kick up* (*od.* *make*) *a* ~ Krach schlagen, b) Streit *m*: *have a* ~ *with* Krach haben mit. **II** *v/i* (sich) streiten (*with* mit; *about* über *acc*).

'**row·boat** ['rəʊbəʊt] *s Am.* Ruderboot *n.*

'**row·dy** ['raʊdɪ] *adj* □ **1.** rowdyhaft. **2.** ausgelassen, laut (*Party*).

row·er ['rəʊə] s Ruderer m, Ruderin f. '**row·ing** adj Ruder...: ~ **boat** bsd. Br. Ruderboot n.

roy·al ['rɔɪəl] **I** adj □ **1.** königlich, Königs...: Her ♀ Highness Ihre Königliche Hoheit; ~ **road** fig. bequemer od. leichter Weg (**to** zu). **2.** fig. großartig, prächtig. **II** s **3.** F Mitglied n des Königshauses. '**roy·al·ist I** adj royalistisch. **II** s Royalist(in). '**roy·al·ty** s **1.** die königliche Familie. **2.** mst pl Tantieme f (**on** auf acc).

rub [rʌb] **I** s **1.** **give** s.th. **a** ~ et. abreiben od. polieren. **2.** **there's the** ~ F da liegt der Hase im Pfeffer. **II** v/t **3.** reiben: ~ **dry** trockenreiben; ~ **s.th. into** et. einreiben in (acc); ~ **one's hands** (**together**) sich die Hände reiben (**with** vor dat); ~ **s.o.'s nose in s.th.** F j-m et. unter die Nase reiben; ~ **salt into** **s.o.'s wound(s)** fig. j-m Salz auf od. in die Wunde streuen; ~ **shoulders with** F verkehren mit (Prominenten etc). **4.** abreiben; polieren. **III** v/i **5.** reiben, scheuern (**against, on** an dat): ~ **against s.th.** a. et. streifen.

Verbindungen mit Adverbien:

rub|a·long v/i Br. F **1.** sich durchschlagen. **2.** a. ~ **together** recht gut miteinander auskommen: ~ **with** recht gut auskommen mit. ~ **down** v/t **1.** ab-, trockenreiben. **2.** abschmirgeln, abschleifen. ~ **in** v/t abreiben: **rub** (**it**) **in** that F darauf herumreiten, daß. ~ **off** I v/t abreiben. **II** v/i abgehen (Farbe, Schmutz etc): ~ **on** (**to**) fig. abfärben auf (acc). ~ **out** v/t **1.** Br. ausradieren. **2.** Am. sl. umlegen (töten). ~ **up** v/t: **rub** **s.o. up the wrong way** F j-n verschnupfen.

rub·ber¹ ['rʌbə] s **1.** Gummi m, n; Kautschuk m. **2.** Br. Radiergummi m. **3.** Wischtuch n. **4.** F Gummi m (Kondom). ~ **band** s Gummiband n, -ring m, (Dichtungs)Gummi m. '~**neck** bsd. Am. F I s Gaffer(in), Schaulustige m, f. **II** v/i neugierig gaffen, sich den Hals verrenken. ~ **plant** s ♀ Gummibaum m. ~ **stamp** s Stempel m. ,~'**stamp** v/t **1.** (ab)stempeln. **2.** F (automatisch) genehmigen.

rub·bing al·co·hol ['rʌbɪŋ] s Am. Wundbenzin n.

rub·bish ['rʌbɪʃ] s **1.** Abfall m, Abfälle pl, Müll m: ~ **bin** → **dustbin**. **2.** fig. Blödsinn m, Quatsch m. '**rub·bish·y** adj F blödsinnig.

rub·ble ['rʌbl] s Schutt m; Trümmer pl.

ru·bel·la [rʊ'belə] s ♯ Röteln pl.

ru·by ['ru:bɪ] **I** s min. Rubin m. **II** adj rubinrot.

ruck¹ [rʌk] s: **get out of the** (**common**) ~ sich über den Durchschnitt erheben.

ruck² [~] v/i: ~ **up** Falten werfen.

ruck·sack ['rʌksæk] s Rucksack m.

ruc·tion ['rʌkʃn] s oft pl F Krach m, Stunk m.

rud·der ['rʌdə] s ✈, ♺ Ruder n.

rud·dy ['rʌdɪ] adj □ **1.** frisch, gesund (Gesichtsfarbe), rot (Backen). **2.** Br. sl. verdammt. **II** adv **3.** → **2.**

rude [ru:d] adj □ **1.** unhöflich; grob (**to** zu). **2.** unanständig (Witz etc). **3.** bös (Schock etc): ~ **awakening. 4. be in** ~ **health** vor Gesundheit strotzen.

ru·di·men·ta·ry [,ru:dɪ'mentərɪ] adj □ **1.** elementar, Anfangs... **2.** primitiv. **3.** rudimentär (a. biol.). **ru·di·ments** ['~mənts] s pl Anfangsgründe pl, Grundlagen pl: **learn the** ~ **of** sich Grundkenntnisse aneignen (dat).

rue [ru:] v/t: ~ **the day ...** den Tag verwünschen, an dem ... **rue·ful** ['~fʊl] adj □ reuevoll, reumütig.

ruff [rʌf] s Halskrause f (a. orn.).

ruf·fle ['rʌfl] **I** s **1.** Rüsche f. **II** v/t **2.** Wasser kräuseln; Haar zerzausen: ~ (**up**) **its feathers** orn. sich aufplustern. **3.** Seiten (rasch) durchblättern. **4.** j-n verärgern: ~ **s.o.'s composure** j-n aus der Fassung bringen.

rug [rʌg] s **1.** Brücke f, (Bett)Vorleger m: **pull the** ~ (**out**) **from under s.o.** fig. j-m den Boden unter den Füßen wegziehen; **sweep under the** ~ fig. et. unter den Teppich kehren. **2.** bsd. Br. dicke Wolldecke.

rug·by ['rʌgbɪ] s a. ~ **football** (Sport) Rugby n.

rug·ged ['rʌgɪd] adj □ **1.** zerklüftet (Felsen), felsig (Landschaft). **2.** zerfurcht (Gesicht). **3.** robust, stabil (Gerät etc). **4.** fig. rauh (Sitten etc).

ru·in ['rʊɪn] **I** s **1.** Ruine f: ~**s** pl Ruinen pl, Trümmer pl; **a castle in** ~**s** e-e Burgruine; **be** (od. **lie**) **in** ~**s** in Trümmern liegen; fig. zerstört od. ruiniert sein. **2.**

Verfall *m*: **fall into ~** verfallen. **3.** Ruin *m*; Ende *n* (*von Hoffnungen etc*). **II** *v/t* **4.** *Gebäude, Gesundheit, Hoffnungen, Leben etc* zerstören, *j-n, Kleidung, Gesundheit, Ruf etc* ruinieren: **~ one's eyes** sich die Augen verderben. **ru·in·'a·tion** *s*: **be the ~ of s.o.** j-s Ruin sein. **'ru·in·ous** *adj* ruinös. **'ru·in·ous·ly** *adv*: **~ expensive** extrem *od.* sündhaft teuer.

rule [ruːl] **I** *s* **1.** Regel *f*, Normalfall *m*: **as a ~** in der Regel; **make it a ~** es sich zur Regel machen *od.* gemacht haben (**to do** zu tun); → **exception** 1. **2.** Regel *f*; Bestimmung *f*, Vorschrift *f*: **against the ~s** gegen die Vorschriften od. Regeln; verboten; **as a ~ of thumb** als Faustregel; **do s.th. by ~ of thumb** et. nach Gefühl tun; **bend** (*od.* **stretch**) **the ~s** es (mit den Vorschriften) nicht so genau nehmen; **work to ~** Dienst nach Vorschrift tun. **3.** Herrschaft *f*. **4.** → **ruler** 2. **II** *v/t* **5.** herrschen über (*acc*): **~ the roost** *fig.* das Regiment führen; **be ~d by** *fig.* sich leiten lassen von; beherrscht werden von. **6.** *bsd.* 🏛 entscheiden (**that** daß). **7.** **~ out** et. ausschließen; *et.* unmöglich machen. **8.** Papier lin(i)ieren; Linie ziehen. **III** *v/i* **9.** herrschen (**over** über *acc*). **10.** *bsd.* 🏛 entscheiden (**against** gegen; **in favo[u]r of** für; **on** in *dat*). **'rul·er** *s* **1.** Herrscher(in). **2.** Lineal *n*; Maßstab *m*. **'rul·ing I** *adj* herrschend; *fig.* vorherrschend. **II** *s bsd.* 🏛 Entscheidung *f*; Verfügung *f*: **give a ~ that** entscheiden, daß.

rum [rʌm] *s* Rum *m*.

Ru·ma·ni·an [ruːˈmeɪnjən] **I** *adj* **1.** rumänisch. **II** *s* **2.** Rumäne *m*, Rumänin *f*. **3.** *ling.* Rumänisch *n*.

rum·ble [ˈrʌmbl] **I** *v/i* **1.** (g)rollen (*Donner*); rumpeln (*Fahrzeug*); knurren (*Magen*). **II** *v/t* **2.** F *j-n, et.* durchschauen. **III** *s* **3.** (G)Rollen *n*; Rumpeln *n*; Knurren *n*. **4.** *Am. sl.* Straßenschlacht *f*.

rum·bus·tious [rʌmˈbʌstɪəs] *adj* □ F wild, ausgelassen.

ru·mi·nant [ˈruːmɪnənt] *s zo.* Wiederkäuer *m*. **ru·mi·nate** [ˈ~neɪt] *v/i* **1.** *zo.* wiederkäuen. **2.** *fig.* grübeln (**on, over** über *acc, dat*). **ru·mi·na·tive** [ˈ~nətɪv] *adj* □ grüblerisch.

rum·mage [ˈrʌmɪdʒ] **I** *v/i a.* **~ about** (*od.* **around**) herumstöbern, -wühlen (**among, in, through** in *dat*). **II** *s* Ramsch *m*. **~ sale** *s Am.* Wohltätigkeitsbasar *m*.

rum·my [ˈrʌmɪ] *s* Rommé *n* (*Kartenspiel*).

ru·mo(u)r [ˈruːmə] **I** *s* Gerücht(e *pl*) *n*: **~ has it that** es geht das Gerücht, daß. **II** *v/t*: **it is ~ed that** es geht das Gerücht, daß; **he is ~ed to** be man munkelt, er sei. **'~·mon·ger** *s* Gerüchtemacher(in).

rump [rʌmp] *s* **1.** *zo.* Hinterbacken *pl*; *orn.* Bürzel *m*. **2.** *humor.* Hinterteil *n*. **3.** *fig.* (kümmerlicher) Rest.

rum·ple [ˈrʌmpl] *v/t* zerknittern, -knüllen; *Haar* zerzausen.

rump steak *s gastr.* Rumpsteak *n*.

rum·pus [ˈrʌmpəs] *s* → **row³** 1. **~ room** *s Am.* F Hobby- *od.* Partyraum *m*.

run [rʌn] **I** *s* **1.** Lauf *m* (*a. Sport*): **at a ~** im Laufschritt; **in the long ~** *fig.* auf (die) Dauer; auf lange *od.* weite Sicht, langfristig; **in the short ~** *fig.* zunächst; auf kurze Sicht, kurzfristig; **on the ~** auf der Flucht (**from the police** vor der Polizei); **~ of good** (**bad**) **luck** Glückssträhne *f* (Pechsträhne *f*). **2.** Fahrt *f*: **go for a ~ in the car** e-e Spazierfahrt machen. **3.** *thea. etc* Laufzeit *f*: **the play had a ~ of six months** das Stück lief ein halbes Jahr lang. **4.** Ansturm *m*, ✝ *a.* Run *m* (**on** auf *acc*). **5.** **have the ~ of** et. benutzen dürfen. **6.** *Am.* Laufmasche *f*. **7.** Auflage *f* (*e-r Zeitung etc*). **8.** **have the ~s** *bsd. Br.* F den flotten Otto haben. **II** *v/i* (*irr*) **9.** laufen (*a. Sport*), rennen. **10.** fahren (*Fahrzeug*); fahren, verkehren (*Bus etc*). **11.** laufen, fließen: **tears were ~ning down her face** Tränen liefen ihr übers Gesicht; **his nose was ~ning** ihm lief die Nase; **it ~s in the family** *fig.* das liegt bei ihm *etc* in der Familie; → **cold** 1. **12.** zerfließen, -laufen (*Butter, Farbe etc*). **13.** ⚙ laufen (*a. fig.*): **with the engine ~ning** mit laufendem Motor. **14.** (ver)laufen (*Straße etc*). **15.** *bsd.* 🏛 gelten, laufen (**for two years** zwei Jahre). **16.** *thea. etc* laufen (**for six months** ein halbes Jahr lang). **17.** *mit Adjektiven*: → **low³** 4. **18.** *pol. bsd. Am.* kandidieren. **19.** gehen, lauten (*Vers etc*). **III** *v/t* (*irr*) **20.** *Strecke, Rennen* laufen: → **course** 3, **errand**, **temperature**. **21.** *j-n, et.* fahren, bringen. **22.** *Wasser etc* laufen lassen: **~ s.o. a bath** j-m ein Bad einlaufen lassen. **23.** *Geschäft* führen, *Hotel etc a.* leiten. **24.** ⊙ *Maschine etc* laufen lassen. **25.** abdrucken, bringen (*Zeitung etc*). **26.** schmuggeln.

Verbindungen mit Präpositionen:

run| a·cross *v/i* **1.** *j-n* zufällig treffen. **2.** stoßen auf (*acc*). **~ af·ter** *v/i* nachlaufen (*dat*) (*a. fig.*). **~ a·gainst** *v/i pol. bsd. Am.* kandidieren gegen. **~ for** *v/i* **1. ~ it!** lauf, was du kannst!; **~ one's life** um sein Leben laufen. **2.** *pol. bsd. Am.* kandidieren für. **~ in·to** I *v/i* **1.** laufen *od.* fahren gegen. **2.** *j-n* zufällig treffen. **3.** *fig.* geraten in (*acc*). **4.** *fig.* sich belaufen auf (*acc*), gehen in (*acc*). II *v/t* **5. run a knife into s.o.'s back** j-m ein Messer in den Rücken stoßen *od.* rennen. **~ off** *v/i:* **~ the road** von der Straße abkommen (*Wagen etc*). **~ on** *v/i* **1.** ⊙ fahren mit: **~ electricity** elektrisch betrieben werden. **2.** → **run through** 1. **~ o·ver** → **run through** 1. Szene *etc* durchspielen. **2.** *Notizen etc* durchgehen. **3.** *Vermögen etc* durchbringen. **4.** *j-n* durchlaufen (*Schauder etc*): **~ s.o.'s mind** j-m durch den Kopf gehen. **~ to** *v/i bsd. Br.* (aus)reichen für.

Verbindungen mit Adverbien:

run| a·bout → **run around**. **~ a·long** *v/i:* **~!** ab mit dir! **~ a·round** *v/i* sich herumtreiben (**with** mit). **~ a·way** *v/i* **1.** davonlaufen (**from** vor *dat*) (*a. fig.*): **~ from home** von zu Hause ausreißen; **~ with** durchbrennen mit; *fig.* durchgehen mit (*Phantasie etc*); **don't ~ with the idea that** glaube bloß nicht, daß. **~ back** *v/t* Band, Film zurückspulen. **~ down** I *v/t* **1.** *mot.* an-, umfahren. **2.** schlechtmachen. **3.** ausfindig machen. II *v/i* **4.** ablaufen (*Uhr*), leer werden (*Batterie*). **~ in** *v/t* **1.** Wagen *etc* einfahren. **2.** F *Verbrecher etc* schnappen. **~ on** *v/i* **1.** weitergehen, sich hinziehen (**until** bis). **2.** unaufhörlich reden (**a·bout** über *acc*, von). **~ out** *v/i* ablaufen (*Vertrag, Zeit etc*), ausgehen, zu Ende gehen (*Vorräte etc*): **I've ~ of money** mir ist das Geld ausgegangen; **~ of steam** 1. **~ o·ver** I *v/t mot.* überfahren. II *v/i* überlaufen. **~ up** I *v/t* **1.** Flagge *etc* aufziehen, hissen. **2.** hohe Rechnung, Schulden machen. II *v/i* **3. ~**

against stoßen auf (*starken Widerstand etc*).

'run|·a·bout *s mot.* Stadtwagen *m*. **'~·a·round** *s:* **give s.o. the ~** F j-n hinhalten; j-n an der Nase herumführen. **'~·a·way** I *s* **1.** Ausreißer(in). II *adj* **2.** ausgerissen: **~ child** (kleiner) Ausreißer. **3.** außer Kontrolle geraten: **~ inflation** ⊕ galoppierende Inflation. **~ down** I *adj* **1.** abgespannt. **2.** baufällig; heruntergekommen. **3.** abgelaufen (*Uhr*), leer (*Batterie*). II *s* **4.** F (genauer) Bericht (**on** über *acc*).

rung[1] [rʌŋ] *pp von* **ring**[2].

rung[2] *s* Sprosse *f* (*e-r Leiter*): **start on the bottom** (**top. first**) **~ of the ladder** *fig.* ganz unten *od.* klein anfangen.

'run-in *s:* **have a ~ with** F in Konflikt kommen mit (*dem Gesetz etc*).

run·ner ['rʌnə] *s* **1.** *Sport:* Läufer(in); Rennpferd *n*. **2.** *mst in Zssgn* Schmuggler(in). **3.** (*Schlitten- etc*)Kufe *f*. **~ bean** *s* ♣ *Br.* grüne Bohne. **~·'up** *pl* **~s·'up** *s* Zweite *m, f*, (*Sport a.*) Vizemeister(in) (**to** hinter *dat*).

run·ning ['rʌnɪŋ] I *s* **1.** Laufen *n*, Rennen *n:* **be still in the ~** *fig.* noch gut im Rennen liegen (**for** um); **be out of the ~** *fig.* aus dem Rennen sein (**for** um); **make the ~** (*Sport*) das Rennen machen (*a. fig.*). **2.** Führung *f*, Leitung *f*. II *adj* **3.** *Sport:* Lauf...: **~ shoes; ~ track** Laufbahn *f*. **4.** fließend (*Wasser*); eiternd (*Wunde*). **5. four times** (**for three days**) **~** viermal (drei Tage) hinter- *od.* nacheinander. **6. ~ costs** *pl* Betriebskosten *pl*, laufende Kosten *pl*. **7. ~ mate** *pol. Am.* Kandidat(in) für die Vizepräsidentschaft.

run·ny ['rʌnɪ] *adj* **1.** flüssig. **2.** laufend (*Nase*), tränend (*Augen*).

,run|-of-the-'mill *adj mst contp.* durchschnittlich, mittelmäßig. **'~·up** *s* **1.** *Sport:* Anlauf *m*. **2. in the ~ to** *fig.* im Vorfeld (*gen*). **'~·way** *s* ✈ Start- und Landebahn *f*, Rollbahn *f*, Piste *f*.

rup·ture ['rʌptʃə] I *s* **1.** Bruch *m* (*a. ♣ u. fig.*), Riß *m*. II *v/i* zerspringen, (-)reißen, platzen. III *v/t* zersprengen, -reißen: **~ o.s.** ♣ sich e-n Bruch heben *od.* zuziehen.

ru·ral ['rʊərəl] *adj* ☐ ländlich: **~ population** Landbevölkerung *f*; → **exodus**.

ruse [ruːz] *s* List *f*.

rush¹ [rʌʃ] *s* & Binse *f*: ~ **mat** Binsenmatte *f*.

rush² [~] I *v/i* **1.** hasten, hetzen, stürmen, (*a. Fahrzeug*) rasen: ~ **at** losstürzen *od.* sich stürzen auf (*acc*); ~ **into** *fig.* sich stürzen in (*acc*); *et.* überstürzen; **the blood ~ed to his face** das Blut schoß ihm ins Gesicht; → **conclusion** 3. II *v/t* **2.** antreiben, drängen, hetzen: **be ~ed (off one's feet)** auf Trab sein. **3.** auf dem schnellsten Weg *wohin* bringen *od.* schaffen. **4.** schnell erledigen; *Essen* hinunterschlingen: **don't ~ it** laß dir Zeit dabei; **~ a bill (through)** e-e Gesetzesvorlage durchpeitschen. **5.** losstürmen auf (*acc*). III *s* **6.** Ansturm *m* (**for** auf *acc*, nach): **there was a ~ for the door** alles drängte zur Tür. **7.** Hast *f*, Hetze *f*: **what's all the ~?** wozu diese Hast? ~ **hour** *s* Rush-hour *f*, Hauptverkehrs-, Stoßzeit *f*. '**~-hour** *adj*: ~ **traffic** Stoßverkehr *m*.

rusk [rʌsk] *s* Zwieback *m*.

Rus·sian ['rʌʃn] I *s* **1.** Russe *m*, Russin *f*. **2.** *ling.* Russisch *n*. II *adj* **3.** russisch:

~ **roulette** russisches Roulett(e).

rust [rʌst] I *s* Rost *m*. II *v/i* (ein-, ver)rosten.

rus·tic ['rʌstɪk] *adj* (**~ally**) **1.** ländlich, bäuerlich. **2.** rustikal (*Möbel*): ~ **furniture** *a.* Bauernmöbel *pl.*

rus·tle ['rʌsl] I *v/i* **1.** rascheln (*Papier etc*), (*a. Seide*) knistern. II *v/t* **2.** rascheln mit. **3.** ~ **up** F *Geld, Hilfe etc* organisieren, auftreiben; *Essen* zaubern.

'**rust·proof** *adj* rostfrei, nichtrostend.

rust·y ['rʌstɪ] *adj* □ **1.** rostig. **2.** *fig.* eingerostet (*Kenntnisse*): **I'm very ~** ich bin ganz aus der Übung.

rut¹ [rʌt] *zo.* I *s* Brunft *f*. II *v/i* brunften.

rut² [~] I *s* **1.** (Rad)Spur *f*, Furche *f*. **2.** *fig.* (alter) Trott: **get into a ~** in e-n Trott verfallen. II *v/t* **3.** furchen: **~ted** ausgefahren.

ruth·less ['ruːθlɪs] *adj* □ unbarmherzig; rücksichtslos; hart.

rye [raɪ] *s* & Roggen *m*. ~ **bread** *s* Roggenbrot *n*. ~ **whis·ky** *s* Roggenwhisky *m*.

S

Sab·bath ['sæbəθ] *s eccl.* Sabbat *m*.

sa·ber *Am.* → **sabre**.

sa·ble ['seɪbl] *s* **1.** *zo.* Zobel *m*. **2.** Zobelpelz *m*.

sab·o·tage ['sæbətɑːʒ] I *s* Sabotage *f*: **act of ~** Sabotageakt *m*. II *v/t* e-n Sabotageakt verüben gegen; sabotieren. **sab·o·teur** [~'tɜː] *s* Saboteur(in).

sa·bre ['seɪbə] *s bsd. Br.* Säbel *m* (*a. fenc.*). ~ **rat·tling** *s fig.* Säbelrasseln *n*.

sac·cha·rin ['sækərɪn] *s* ⚕ Saccharin *n*. **sac·cha·rine** ['~raɪn] *adj* **1.** unangenehm süß. **2.** *fig.* honig-, zuckersüß.

sack¹ [sæk] I *s* **1.** Sack *m*. **2.** F **get the ~** rausgeschmissen (*entlassen*) werden; **give** *s.o.* **the ~** → **5**. **3.** *hit the ~* F sich in die Falle *od.* Klappe hauen. II *v/t* **4.** einsacken, in Säcke abfüllen. **5.** F *j-n* rausschmeißen (*entlassen*).

sack² [~] I *v/t* plündern. II *s* Plünderung *f*.

'**sack·cloth** *s* Sackleinen *n*: **in** (*od.* **wearing**) **~ and ashes** *fig.* in Sack u. Asche.

sack·ing ['sækɪŋ] *s* Sackleinen *n*.

sack rac·ing *s* Sackhüpfen *n*.

sac·ra·ment ['sækrəmənt] *s eccl.* Sakrament *n*.

sa·cred ['seɪkrɪd] *adj* □ **1.** geistlich (*Musik etc*). **2.** heilig (**to** *dat*) (*a. fig.*): ~ **cow** heilige Kuh (*a. fig.*).

sac·ri·fice ['sækrɪfaɪs] I *s* Opfer *n* (*a. fig.*): **make a ~ of** *et.* opfern; **make great ~s** große Opfer bringen. II *v/t* opfern (**to** *dat*) (*a. fig.*). **sac·ri·fi·cial** [~'fɪʃl] *adj* Opfer...

sac·ri·lege ['sækrɪlɪdʒ] *s* Sakrileg *n*; *allg.* Frevel *m*. **sac·ri·le·gious** [~'lɪdʒəs] *adj* □ sakrilegisch; *allg.* frevlerisch.

sac·ris·ty ['sækrɪstɪ] *s eccl.* Sakristei *f*.

sac·ro·sanct ['sækrəʊsæŋkt] *adj* sakrosankt.

sad [sæd] *adj* (□ → **sadly**) *allg.* traurig; schmerzlich (*Verlust*); bedauerlich (*Irrtum etc*): **~ to say** bedauerlicherweise, leider; **be ~der but wiser** um e-e schmerzliche Erfahrung reicher sein.

sad·den ['sædn] *v/t* traurig machen *od.* stimmen, betrüben.

sad·dle ['sædl] **I** *s* (*Reit-, Fahrrad-etc*)Sattel *m*: **be in the ~** im Sattel sitzen; *fig.* im Amt *od.* an der Macht sein. **II** *v/t* satteln: **~ up** aufsatteln; **~ s.o. with s.th.** *fig.* j-m et. aufhalsen *od.* -bürden; **be ~d with s.th.** *fig.* et. am Hals haben. **III** *v/i*: **~ up** aufsatteln. '**~·bag** *s* Satteltasche *f*.

sad·ism ['seɪdɪzəm] *s* Sadismus *m*. '**sad·ist** *s* Sadist(in). **sa·dis·tic** [sə'dɪstɪk] *adj* (□ **~ally**) sadistisch.

sad·ly ['sædlɪ] *adv* **1.** traurig; schmerzlich: **be ~ mistaken** e-m bedauerlichen Irrtum unterliegen. **2.** bedauerlicherweise, leider. '**sad·ness** *s* Traurigkeit *f*.

sa·fa·ri [sə'fɑːrɪ] *s* Safari *f*. **~ park** *s* Safaripark *m*.

safe [seɪf] **I** *adj* (□ *allg.* sicher (**from** vor *dat*): **be ~** in Sicherheit sein; **be ~ with s.o.** sicher bei j-m aufgehoben sein; **be in ~ hands** in sicheren Händen sein; **to be on the ~ side, just to be ~** um ganz sicher zu gehen; **it is ~ to say** man kann mit Sicherheit sagen; **keep s.th. in a ~ place** et. an e-m sicheren Ort aufbewahren; **he has ~ly arrived** er ist gut angekommen; → **play** 7, 8. **II** *s* Safe *m*, Tresor *m*, Geld-, Panzerschrank *m*. '**~·blow·er**, '**~·break·er**, '**~·crack·er** *s* Geldschrankknacker *m*. **~·de'pos·it box** *s* Bankschließfach *n*, (*a. in Hotel etc*) Tresorfach *n*. '**~·guard I** *s* Schutz *m* (**against** gegen, vor *dat*). **II** *v/t* schützen (**against, from** gegen, vor *dat*); *Interessen* wahren. '**~·keep·ing** *s* sichere Verwahrung: **give s.o. s.th. for ~** j-m et. zur Verwahrung geben.

safe·ty ['seɪftɪ] *s allg.* Sicherheit *f*: **jump** (**swim**) **to ~** sich durch e-n Sprung (schwimmend) in Sicherheit bringen. **~ belt** *s* → **seat belt**. **~ cur·tain** *s thea.* eiserner Vorhang. **~ glass** *s* Sicherheitsglas *n*. **~·is·land** *s Am.* Verkehrsinsel *f*. **~ lock** *s* Sicherheitsschloß *n*. **~ meas·ure** *s* Sicherheitsmaßnahme *f*. **~**

net *s Zirkus etc:* Fangnetz *n*. **~ pin** *s* Sicherheitsnadel *f*. **~ pre·cau·tion** *s* Sicherheitsvorkehrung *f*. **~ ra·zor** *s* Rasierapparat *m*. **~ valve** *s* **1.** ⚙ Sicherheitsventil *n*. **2.** *fig.* Ventil *n* (**for** für).

saf·fron ['sæfrən] **I** *s* Safran *m*. **II** *adj* safrangelb.

sag [sæg] **I** *v/i* **1.** sich senken, absacken; durchhängen (*Leitung etc*). **2.** (her-ab)hängen. **3.** *fig.* sinken, nachlassen (*Interesse etc*); abfallen (*Roman etc*); ✝ nachgeben (*Preise etc*). **II** *s* **4.** Durchhängen *n*: **there is a ~ in the ceiling** die Decke hängt durch. **5.** ✝ Nachgeben *n* (*in gen*).

sa·ga ['sɑːgə] *s* **1.** Saga *f*. **2.** *a.* **family ~** Familienroman *m*. **3.** *contp.* Geschichte *f*.

sa·ga·cious [sə'geɪʃəs] *adj* □ scharfsinnig, klug. **sa·gac·i·ty** [sə'gæsətɪ] *s* Scharfsinn *m*, Klugheit *f*.

sage [seɪdʒ] *s* ♣ Salbei *m*.

Sa·git·tar·i·us [ˌsædʒɪ'teərɪəs] *s ast.* Schütze *m*: **be (a) ~** Schütze sein.

said [sed] *pret u. pp von* **say**.

sail [seɪl] **I** *s* **1.** Segel *n*: **set ~** auslaufen (**for** nach). **2.** Segelfahrt *f*, -partie *f*: **go for a ~** segeln gehen. **II** *v/i* **3.** ⚓ fahren; segeln (*a. fig.*); **go ~ing** segeln gehen. **4.** ⚓ auslaufen (**for** nach). **5.** gleiten: **she ~ed into the room** sie schwebte ins Zimmer; **~ through an examination** e-e Prüfung spielend schaffen. **6.** **~ into s.o.** F über j-n herfallen (*a. mit Worten*). **III** *v/t* **7.** *Boot* segeln, *Schiff* steuern. **8.** durchsegeln; befahren. '**~·boat** *s Am.* Segelboot *n*.

sail·ing ['seɪlɪŋ] *s* **1.** Segeln *n*; Segelsport *m*: **everything was plain ~** *fig.* es ging alles glatt. **2.** **when is the next ~ to ...?** wann fährt das nächste Schiff nach ...? **~ boat** *s bsd. Br.* Segelboot *n*. **~ ship** *s* Segelschiff *n*.

sail·or ['seɪlə] *s* **1.** Seemann *m*; Matrose *m*. **2.** Segler(in). **3.** **be a good** (**bad**) **~** seefest sein (leicht seekrank werden). **~ suit** *s* Matrosenanzug *m*.

'**sail·plane** *s* Segelflugzeug *n*.

saint [seɪnt] *s* **1.** Heilige *m*, *f*: **you need the patience of a ~** man braucht e-e Engelsgeduld. **2.** *vor Eigennamen* ♀, *abbr.* **St** [snt]: **St Andrew** der heilige Andreas. '**saint·ly** *adj* heiligmäßig.

sake [seɪk] *s*: **for the ~ of** um ... willen,

j-m, e-r Sache zuliebe; **for your ~** dir zuliebe, deinetwegen; **for God's (goodness, heaven's) ~** F um Gottes willen; Herrgott noch mal; **for the ~ of peace** um des lieben Friedens willen; **for the ~ of simplicity** der Einfachheit halber.

sal·a·ble *bsd. Am.* → **saleable.**

sa·la·cious [səˈleɪʃəs] *adj* □ schlüpfrig, anstößig.

sal·ad [ˈsæləd] *s* Salat *m.* **~ dress·ing** *s* Dressing *n*, Salatsoße *f.*

sal·a·man·der [ˈsæləˌmændə] *s zo.* Salamander *m.*

sa·la·mi [səˈlɑːmɪ] *s* Salami *f.*

sal·a·ried [ˈsælərɪd] *adj:* **~ employee** Gehaltsempfänger(in), Angestellte *m, f.* **'sal·a·ry** *s* Gehalt *n.*

sale [seɪl] *s* **1.** Verkauf *m:* **for ~** zu verkaufen; **not for ~** unverkäuflich; **be on ~** verkauft werden, erhältlich sein; *bsd. Am.* im Angebot sein; **be up for ~** zum Verkauf stehen. **2.** *a. pl* ✝ Umsatz *m:* **large ~** großer Umsatz. **3.** ✝ Schlußverkauf *m.* **4.** Auktion *f*, Versteigerung *f.* **'sale·a·ble** *adj bsd. Br.* **1.** verkäuflich. **2.** ✝ absatzfähig.

'sales·clerk *s Am.* (Laden)Verkäufer (-in). **'~·girl** *s* (Laden)Verkäuferin *f.* **~·man** [ˈ~mən] *s (irr man)* **1.** Verkäufer *m.* **2.** (Handels)Vertreter *m.* **'~·man·ship** *s* **1.** ✝ Verkaufstechnik *f*; Verkaufsgeschick *n.* **2.** *fig.* Überzeugungskunst *f.* **~ pitch** *s* ✝ F Verkaufsmasche *f.* **~ pro·mot·er** *s* ✝ Sales-promoter *m*, Verkaufsförderer *m.* **~ pro·mo·tion** *s* ✝ Sales-promotion *f*, Verkaufsförderung *f.* **~ slip** *s Am.* Kassenbeleg *m*, -zettel *m.* **~ talk** *s* ✝ Verkaufsgespräch *n.* **'~·wom·an** *s (irr woman)* **1.** Verkäuferin *f.* **2.** (Handels)Vertreterin *f.*

sa·li·ent [ˈseɪljənt] *adj* □ *fig.* hervorstehend, wichtigst.

sa·line [ˈseɪlaɪn] *adj* salzig, Salz...: **~ solution** Salzlösung *f.*

sa·li·va [səˈlaɪvə] *s physiol.* Speichel *m.* **sal·i·var·y** [ˈsælɪvərɪ] *adj* Speichel...: **~ gland** Speicheldrüse *f.*

sal·low [ˈsæləʊ] *adj* □ (ungesund) gelblich *(Gesichtsfarbe etc).*

salm·on [ˈsæmən] I *pl* **-ons,** *bsd. coll.* **-on** *s ichth.* Lachs *m.* II *adj* lachsfarben.

sal·on [ˈsælɔːn] *s (Friseur-, Schönheitsetc)*Salon *m.*

sa·loon [səˈluːn] *s* **1.** *mot. Br.* Limousine

f. **2.** → **saloon bar. 3.** *hist. Am.* Saloon *m.* **4.** ✧ Salon *m.* **~ bar** *s Br.* vornehmerer u. teurerer Teil *e-s* Pubs. **~ car** → **saloon** 1.

salt [sɔːlt] I *s* **1.** Salz *n:* **take s.th. with a grain (***od.* **pinch) of ~** *fig.* et. nicht ganz für bare Münze nehmen; **no composer worth his ~** kein Komponist, der et. taugt *od.* der diesen Namen verdient; → **rub** 3. II *v/t* **2.** salzen. **3.** *a.* **~ down** (ein)pökeln, einsalzen. **4.** *Straße etc* (mit Salz) streuen. **5. ~ away** F Geld auf die hohe Kante legen, *b.s.* auf die Seite schaffen. III *adj* **6.** gepökelt, Salz... **'~·cel·lar** *s Br.* Salzstreuer *m.* **~ free** *adj* salzlos. **~ lake** *s* Salzsee *m.* **~·pe·ter** *s Am.,* **~·pe·tre** *s bsd. Br.* [ˌ~ˈpiːtə] *s* ♠ Salpeter *m.* **~ shak·er** *Am.* → **saltcel·lar.** **~ wa·ter** *s* Salzwasser *n.* **'~·wa·ter** *adj* Salzwasser..., Meeres...

salt·y [ˈsɔːltɪ] *adj* salzig.

sa·lu·bri·ous [səˈluːbrɪəs] *adj* □ **1.** gesund *(Klima etc).* **2.** vornehm *(Wohngegend etc).*

sal·u·tar·y [ˈsæljʊtərɪ] *adj* gesund; *fig.* heilsam, lehrreich.

sal·u·ta·tion [ˌsæljʊˈteɪʃn] *s* **1.** Begrüßung *f*, Gruß *m:* **in ~** zum Gruß. **2.** Anrede *f (im Brief).*

sa·lute [səˈluːt] I *v/t* **1.** ✕ salutieren vor *(dat).* **2.** (be)grüßen. II *v/i* **3.** ✕ salutieren. III *s* **4.** ✕ a) Ehrenbezeigung *f:* **give a smart ~** zackig salutieren; **take the ~** die Parade abnehmen, b) Salut *m:* **a 21-gun ~** 21 Salutschüsse.

sal·vage [ˈsælvɪdʒ] I *v/t* **1.** bergen *(from* aus*).* II *s* **2.** Bergung *f.* **3.** Bergungsgut *n.*

sal·va·tion [sælˈveɪʃn] *s* **1.** Rettung *f.* **2.** *eccl.* (Seelen)Heil *n*; Erlösung *f:* ♀ **Army** Heilsarmee *f.* **Sal'va·tion·ist** *s* Mitglied *n* der Heilsarmee.

salve [sælv] I *s* (Heil)Salbe *f.* II *v/t fig.* *Gewissen* beruhigen.

sal·ver [ˈsælvə] *s* Tablett *n*, Präsentierteller *m.*

sal·vo [ˈsælvəʊ] *pl* **-vo(e)s** *s* ✕ Salve *f (a. fig.):* **~ of applause** Beifallssturm *m.*

Sa·mar·i·tan [səˈmærɪtən] *s* Samariter (-in): **good ~** *Bibl.* barmherziger Samariter *(a. fig.).*

same [seɪm] I *adj:* **the ~** der-, die-, dasselbe, der *od.* die *od.* das gleiche: **the film with the ~ name** der gleichnamige

Film; *amount* (*od.* *come*) *to the* **~** *thing* auf dasselbe hinauslaufen; → *story* 1, *time* 1. II *pron:* *the* **~** der-, die-, dasselbe, der *od.* die *od.* das gleiche: *it is all the* **~** *to me* es ist mir ganz egal; (*the*) **~** *again* noch mal das gleiche; **~** *to you* (danke) gleichfalls!; *all* (*od.* *just*) *the* **~** dennoch, trotzdem. III *adv:* *the* **~** gleich; **~** *as* F genauso wie. **'same·y** *adj Br.* F eintönig.

sam·ple ['sɑːmpl] I *s* 1. ✝ Muster *n*, (*a. Blut- etc*)Probe *f:* **~ bottle** Probe-, Probierfläschchen *n*. 2. (*of*) Kostprobe *f* (*gen*), *fig. a.* (typisches) Beispiel (für). II *v/t* 3. kosten (*a. fig.*), probieren.

san·a·to·ri·um [ˌsænə'tɔːriəm] *pl* **-ri·ums**, **-ri·a** [~riə] *s* Sanatorium *n*.

sanc·ti·fy ['sæŋktɪfaɪ] *v/t* 1. heiligen. 2. *fig.* sanktionieren: → *end* 10.

sanc·ti·mo·ni·ous [ˌsæŋktɪ'məʊnjəs] *adj* □ frömmlerisch, frömmlich.

sanc·tion ['sæŋkʃn] I *s* 1. Billigung *f*, Zustimmung *f*. 2. *mst pl* Sanktion *f:* **take ~s** *against, impose* **~s** *on* Sanktionen verhängen über (*acc*). II *v/t* 3. sanktionieren.

sanc·ti·ty ['sæŋktətɪ] *s* Heiligkeit *f*.

sanc·tu·ar·y ['sæŋktʃʊərɪ] *s* 1. (*Vogeletc*)Schutzgebiet *n*. 2. Zuflucht *f:* **seek ~ with** Zuflucht suchen bei.

sand [sænd] I *s* 1. Sand *m*. 2. *pl* Sand(fläche *f*) *m*. II *v/t* 3. *Weg etc* sanden, mit Sand streuen. 4. schmirgeln: **~ down** abschmirgeln.

san·dal ['sændl] *s* Sandale *f*.

'sand|·bag *s* Sandsack *m*. II *v/t* mit Sandsäcken befestigen *od.* schützen. **'~·bank** *s* Sandbank *f*. **'~·blast** *v/t* ✿ sandstrahlen. **'~·box** *s Am.* Sandkasten *m*. **'~·cas·tle** *s* Sandburg *f*. **~ dune** *s* Sanddüne *f*. **'~·man** *s* (*irr man*) Sandmännchen *n*. **'~·pa·per** I *s* Sand-, Schmirgelpapier *n*. II *v/t* (ab)schmirgeln. **'~·pit** *s* 1. *bsd. Br.* Sandkasten *m*. 2. Sandgrube *f*. **'~·stone** *s geol.* Sandstein *m*. **'~·storm** *s* Sandsturm *m*.

sand·wich ['sænwɪdʒ] I *s* Sandwich *n*. II *v/t:* *be* **~ed between** eingekeilt sein zwischen (*dat*); **~ s.th. in between** *fig.* et. einschieben zwischen (*acc*, *a. dat*). **~ course** *s ped. etc* Kurs, bei dem sich *theoretische u. praktische Ausbildung abwechseln*. **~ man** *s* (*irr man*) Sandwichman *m*.

sand·y ['sændɪ] *adj* 1. sandig, *pred a.* voller Sand: **~ beach** Sandstrand *m*. 2. rotblond (*Haar*).

sane [seɪn] *adj* □ 1. geistig gesund, normal, ⚖ zurechnungsfähig. 2. vernünftig.

sang [sæŋ] *pret von* **sing**.

san·guine ['sæŋgwɪn] *adj* □ zuversichtlich, optimistisch.

san·i·tar·i·um [ˌsænɪ'teərɪəm] *Am.* → *sanatorium*. **san·i·tar·y** ['~tərɪ] *adj* □ 1. hygienisch, Gesundheits...: **~ facilities** *pl* sanitäre Einrichtungen *pl*. **~ napkin** *Am.*, **~ towel** *Br.* (Damen)Binde *f*. 2. hygienisch (einwandfrei), gesund.

san·i·tor·i·um [ˌsænɪ'tɔːrɪəm] *Am.* → *sanatorium*.

san·i·ty ['sænətɪ] *s* geistige Gesundheit, ⚖ Zurechnungsfähigkeit *f*.

sank [sæŋk] *pret von* **sink**.

San·ta Claus ['sæntəklɔːz] *s* der Weihnachtsmann, der Nikolaus.

sap¹ [sæp] *s* 1. ♀ Saft *m*. 2. F Einfaltspinsel *m*, Trottel *m*.

sap² [~] *v/t* schwächen.

sap·phire ['sæfaɪə] *s min.* Saphir *m*.

sap·py ['sæpɪ] *adj* □ 1. ♀ saftig. 2. F einfältig, trottelig.

sar·casm ['sɑːkæzəm] *s* Sarkasmus *m*.

sar·cas·tic *adj* (**~ally**) sarkastisch.

sar·coph·a·gus [sɑː'kɒfəgəs] *pl* **-gi** [~gaɪ], **-gus·es** *s* Sarkophag *m*.

sar·dine [sɑː'diːn] *s ichth.* Sardine *f:* *be packed like* **~s** wie die Heringe sitzen *od.* stehen.

sar·don·ic [sɑː'dɒnɪk] *adj* (**~ally**) boshaft, höhnisch (*Lachen etc*).

sar·ky ['sɑːkɪ] *Br.* F → *sarcastic*.

sar·nie ['sɑːnɪ] *s Br.* F Sandwich *n*.

sash¹ [sæʃ] *s* Fensterrahmen *m* (*e-s Schiebefensters*).

sash² [~] *s* Schärpe *f*.

sash win·dow *s* Schiebefenster *n*.

sass [sæs], **'sass·y** *Am.* F → *sauce* 2, *saucy*.

sat [sæt] *pret u. pp von* **sit**.

Sa·tan ['seɪtn] *s* der Satan. **sa·tan·ic** [sə'tænɪk] *adj* (**~ally**) satanisch. **'Sa·tan·ism** *s* Satanismus *m*, Satanskult *m*.

satch·el ['sætʃəl] *s* (Schul)Ranzen *m*.

sat·el·lite ['sætəlaɪt] *s* 1. *ast.* (*a. künstlicher*) Satellit: **~ picture** Satellitenbild *n*; **~ transmission** *TV* Satellitenübertragung f. **2.** a) a. ~ **nation** (od. **state**) Satellit(enstaat) m, b) a. ~ **town** Satellitenstadt f.

sa·ti·ate ['seɪʃɪeɪt] v/t (über)sättigen.

sat·in ['sætɪn] s Satin m.

sat·ire ['sætaɪə] s Satire f (**on** auf acc).

sa·tir·i·cal [sə'tɪrəkl] adj □ satirisch.

sat·i·rist ['sætərɪst] s Satiriker(in).

'sat·i·rize v/t satirisch darstellen.

sat·is·fac·tion [ˌsætɪs'fækʃn] s **1.** Befriedigung f, Zufriedenstellung f. **2.** (**at**, **with**) Zufriedenheit f (mit), Genugtuung f (über acc): **to s.o.'s ~** zu j-s Zufriedenheit.

sat·is·fac·to·ry [ˌsætɪs'fæktərɪ] adj □ befriedigend, zufriedenstellend.

sat·is·fy ['sætɪsfaɪ] v/t **1.** j-n befriedigen, zufriedenstellen: **be satisfied with** zufrieden sein mit; **a satisfied smile** ein zufriedenes Lächeln. **2.** Bedürfnis, Neugier etc befriedigen; Bedingungen etc erfüllen. **3.** j-n überzeugen (**of** von): **be satisfied that** davon überzeugt sein, daß.

sat·u·rate ['sætʃəreɪt] v/t **1.** (durch)tränken (**with** mit): **~d with** (od. **in**) **blood** blutgetränkt. **2.** 🜂 sättigen (a. fig.). **,sat·u·ra·tion** s Sättigung f: **~ point** 🜂 Sättigungspunkt m; **reach ~ point** fig. s-n Sättigungsgrad erreichen.

Sat·ur·day ['sætədɪ] s Sonnabend m, Samstag m: **on ~** (am) Samstag; **on ~s** samstags.

Sat·urn ['sætən] s ast. Saturn m.

sauce [sɔːs] s **1.** Soße f. **2.** F Frechheit f: **none of your ~!** werd bloß nicht frech! **'~·pan** s Kochtopf m.

sauc·er ['sɔːsə] s Untertasse f.

sau·ci·ness ['sɔːsɪnɪs] s F Frechheit f. **'sau·cy** adj □ F frech.

sau·er·kraut ['saʊəkraʊt] s Sauerkraut n.

sau·na ['sɔːnə] s Sauna f: **have a ~** in die Sauna gehen.

saun·ter ['sɔːntə] I v/i bummeln, schlendern. II s Bummel m: **have** (od. **take**) **a ~** e-n Bummel machen.

sau·sage ['sɒsɪdʒ] s Wurst f.

sav·age ['sævɪdʒ] I adj □ wild: a) unzivilisiert, b) gefährlich (Tier), c) brutal, d) schonungslos. II s Wilde m, f. III v/t anfallen (Tier).

sa·van·na(h) [sə'vænə] s geogr. Savanne f.

save [seɪv] I v/t **1.** retten (**from** vor dat): ~ **s.o.'s life** j-m das Leben retten; → **bacon, face** 4, **neck** 1, **skin** 1. **2.** Geld, Zeit etc (ein)sparen; et. aufheben, -sparen (**for** für): ~ **s.th. for s.o.** j-m et. aufheben; ~ **one's strength** s-e Kräfte schonen. **3.** j-m et. ersparen: **you can ~ your excuses** du kannst dir d-e Ausreden sparen; ~ **s.o. doing s.th.** es j-m ersparen, et. zu tun. **4.** Sport: Schuß halten, parieren, a. Matchball etc abwehren; Tor verhindern. II v/i **5.** a. ~ **up** sparen (**for** für, auf acc). **6.** ~ **on** et. (ein)sparen. III s **7.** Sport: Parade f. **'sav·er** s **1.** Retter(in). **2.** Sparer(in). **3.** in Zssgn: **be a real time ~** e-e Menge Zeit sparen.

'sav·ing I s **1.** Ersparnis f (**on** gegenüber). **2.** pl Ersparnisse pl: **~s account** Am. Sparkonto n; **~s and loan association** Am. Bausparkasse f; **~s bank** Sparkasse f. II adj **3.** his (**only**) ~ **grace** das einzig Gute an ihm. **sav·io(u)r** ['~jə] s Retter(in): **the ♌ eccl.** der Heiland od. Erlöser.

sa·vo(u)r ['seɪvə] I s **1.** (**of**) Geruch m (nach, von), Geschmack m (nach): ~ **of garlic** Knoblauchgeruch m. **2.** fig. Reiz m. II v/t **3.** mit Genuß essen od. trinken. III v/i **4.** ~ **of** fig. e-n Beigeschmack haben von. **'sa·vo(u)r·y** adj □ schmackhaft.

sa·voy [sə'vɔɪ] s ♀ Wirsing(kohl) m.

sav·vy ['sævɪ] s sl. Grips m, Köpfchen n.

saw¹ [sɔː] pret von **see**.

saw² [~] I s Säge f. II v/t (mst irr) sägen: ~ **off** absägen; ~ **up** zersägen. **'~·dust** s Sägespäne pl. **'~·mill** s Sägewerk n.

sawn [sɔːn] pp von **saw²**.

Sax·on ['sæksn] hist. I s (Angel)Sachse m, (-)Sächsin f. II adj (angel)sächsisch.

sax·o·phone ['sæksəfəʊn] s ♪ Saxophon n. **sax·o·phon·ist** [~'sɒfənɪst] s Saxophonist(in).

say [seɪ] I v/t (irr) **1.** sagen (**to** zu): **they ~ he is rich, he is said to be ~** man sagt, er sei reich; er soll reich sein; **what does your watch ~?** wie spät ist es auf deiner Uhr?; **you can ~ that again!** das kannst du laut sagen!; ~, **haven't I ...?** Am. F sag mal, habe ich nicht ...?; → **eagle** 8, **jack** 1, **knife** I, **nothing** 1, **when** 5. **2.** Gebet sprechen, Vaterunser etc beten: → **grace** 6. **3.** annehmen: **(let's) ~ this happens** angenommen od. nehmen wir einmal an, das geschieht; *a sum of,* ~, **£500** e-e Summe von sagen wir 500 Pfund. **4.** (be)sagen, bedeuten: *that is to* ~ das heißt. **II** *v/i* (*irr*) **5.** es sagen: *I can't* ~ das kann ich nicht sagen; *you don't* ~ (*so*)! was du nicht sagst!; *it goes without* ~*ing* es versteht sich selbst (*that* daß). **III** *s* **6.** Mitspracherecht *n* (*in* bei). **7.** *have one's* ~ s-e Meinung äußern, zu Wort kommen: *he always has to have his* ~ er muß immer mitreden. '**say·ing** *s* Sprichwort *n*, Redensart *f*: *as the* ~ *goes* wie man (so) sagt.

'**say-so** *s* F **1.** *just on his* ~ auf s-e bloße Behauptung hin, nur weil er es sagt. **2.** *on his* ~ mit s-r Erlaubnis.

scab [skæb] *s* **1.** ✻ Grind *m*, Schorf *m*. **2.** *vet.* Räude *f.* **3.** *sl.* Streikbrecher(in). '**scab·by** *adj* **1.** grindig, schorfig. **2.** ✻ krätzig; *vet.* räudig.

sca·bi·es ['skeɪbiːz] *s* ✻ Krätze *f.*

scaf·fold ['skæfəʊld] *s* **1.** (Bau)Gerüst *n.* **2.** Schafott *n*. **scaf·fold·ing** ['~fəldɪŋ] → **scaffold** 1.

scal·a·wag ['skæləwæg] *bsd. Am.* → **scallywag**

scald [skɔːld] **I** *v/t* **1.** sich *die Finger etc* verbrühen (*on, with* mit): *be* ~*ed* e-e Verbrühung erleiden (*by* durch). **2.** *bsd. Milch* abkochen. **II** *s* **3.** Verbrühung *f.* '**scald·ing** *adj u. adv:* ~ (*hot*) kochendheiß.

scale¹ [skeɪl] **I** *s* **1.** *zo.* (*a.* *Haut*)Schuppe *f:* *the* ~*s fell from my eyes fig.* es fiel mir wie Schuppen von den Augen. **2.** Kesselstein *m.* **II** *v/t* **3.** *Fisch* (ab)schuppen.

scale² [~] *s* **1.** Waagschale *f.* **2.** *mst pl, a.* *pair of* ~*s* Waage *f:* *tip the* ~*s fig.* den Ausschlag geben (*in favo*[*u*]*r of* für). **3.** ~*s pl* (*sg konstruiert*) *ast.* Waage *f.*

scale³ [~] **I** *s* **1.** Skala *f* (*a. fig.*), Grad- *od.* Maßeinteilung *f.* **2.** ♪, ⊚ Maßstab *m:* *to* ~ maßstab(s)gerecht, -getreu; ~ *model* maßstab(s)gerechtes *od.* -getreues Modell. **3.** ♪ Tonleiter *f.* **4.** *fig.* Ausmaß *n,* Maßstab *m,* Umfang *m:* *on a large* ~ in großem Umfang. **II** *v/t* **5.** erklettern. **6.** ~ *down* (*up*) *fig.* verringern (erhöhen).

scal·lop ['skɒləp] *s zo.* Kammuschel *f.*

scal·ly·wag ['skælɪwæg] *s bsd. Br.* Schlingel *m,* (kleiner) Strolch.

---

scalp [skælp] **I** *s* **1.** *anat.* Kopfhaut *f.* **2.** Skalp *m:* *be out for s.o.'s* ~ *fig.* auf j-s Skalp aussein. **II** *v/t* **3.** skalpieren.

scal·pel ['skælpəl] *s* ✻ Skalpell *n.*

scal·per ['skælpə] *s Am.* Kartenschwarzhändler(in).

scamp [skæmp] *s* Schlingel *m,* (kleiner) Strolch.

scam·per ['skæmpə] *v/i* trippeln (*Kind etc*); huschen (*Maus etc*).

scan [skæn] **I** *v/t* **1.** *et.* absuchen (*for* nach). **2.** *Zeitung etc* überfliegen. **3.** *Metrik:* skandieren. **4.** *Computer, Radar, TV:* abtasten. **II** *s* **5.** ✻ *etc* Scanning *n.*

scan·dal ['skændl] *s* **1.** Skandal *m.* **2.** Skandalgeschichten *pl,* Klatsch(geschichten *pl*) *m.* **scan·dal·ize** ['~dəlaɪz] *v/t: he was* ~*d* er war empört *od.* entrüstet (*by, at* über *acc; to hear* als er hörte).

'**scan·dal·mon·ger** *s* Klatschmaul *n.*

scan·dal·ous ['skændələs] *adj* □ **1.** skandalös: *be* ~ *a.* ein Skandal sein (*that* daß). **2.** Skandal...

Scan·di·na·vi·an [,skændɪ'neɪvjən] **I** *s* Skandinavier(in). **II** *adj* skandinavisch.

scant [skænt] *adj* □ dürftig, gering.

scant·y ['skæntɪ] *adj* □ dürftig, kärglich (*Mahlzeit*); knapp (*Bikini etc*).

scape·goat ['skeɪpgəʊt] *s* Sündenbock *m.*

scar [skɑː] **I** *s* Narbe *f;* Schramme *f,* Kratzer *m.* **II** *v/t* Narben *od.* e-e Narbe hinterlassen auf (*dat*); *fig. j-n* zeichnen.

scarce [skeəs] *adj* **1.** knapp (*Ware*): *make o.s.* ~ F sich dünnmachen. **2.** selten. '**scarce·ly** *adv* **1.** kaum. **2.** kaum, schwerlich. '**scarce·ness,** '**scar·ci·ty** *s* **1.** Knappheit *f,* Mangel *m* (*of* an *dat*). **2.** Seltenheit *f.*

scare [skeə] **I** *v/t* **1.** erschrecken, *j-m* in Schreck(en) einjagen: *be* ~*d* Angst haben (*of* vor *dat*). **2.** ~ *away* (*od. off*) verjagen, -scheuchen; *fig. j-n* ab-, verschrecken. **II** *v/i* **3.** *easily* ~*d* schreckhaft sein. **III** *s* **4.** Schreck(en) *m:* *give s.o. a* ~ → **1.** **5.** Panik *f.* '~·**crow** *s* Vogelscheuche *f* (*a. fig.*). '~·**mon·ger** *s* Panikmacher(in).

scarf [skɑːf] *pl* **scarfs, scarves** [skɑːvz] *s* Schal *m;* Hals-, Kopf-, Schultertuch *n.*

scar·let ['skɑːlət] adj scharlachrot: ~ **fe·ver** ♂ Scharlach m.

scar·per ['skɑːpə] v/i Br. sl. abhauen, verduften.

scarred [skɑːd] adj narbig.

scarves [skɑːvz] pl von **scarf**.

scar·y ['skeərɪ] adj F **1.** unheimlich (*Gegend etc*); grus(e)lig (*Geschichte etc*): ~ **film** Gruselfilm m. **2.** furchtsam; schreckhaft.

scath·ing ['skeɪðɪŋ] adj □ ätzend, vernichtend (*Kritik etc*).

scat·ter ['skætə] **I** v/t **1.** a. ~ **about** (*od. around*) ver-, ausstreuen: **be ~ed all over the place** überall herumliegen; ~ **money about** fig. mit Geld um sich werfen. **2.** Menge etc zerstreuen, Vögel etc auseinanderscheuchen. **II** v/i **3.** sich zerstreuen (*Menge etc*), auseinanderstieben (*Vögel etc*), sich zerteilen (*Nebel etc*). '**~·brain** s F Schussel m. '**~·brained** adj F schusselig, schußlig.

scat·tered ['skætəd] adj **1.** ver- od. zerstreut (liegend) (*Häuser etc*). **2.** vereinzelt (*Schauer etc*).

scav·enge ['skævɪndʒ] **I** v/i **1.** ~ **on** zo. leben von (*Abfällen, Aas*). **2.** a. ~ **for food** (nach) Nahrung suchen: ~ **in** herumwühlen in (*dat*). **II** v/t **3.** → **1.** **4.** et. ergattern. '**scav·en·ger** s zo. Aasfresser m.

sce·nar·i·o [sɪˈnɑːrɪəʊ] pl **-os** s Film, thea., TV: Szenario n (a. fig.), Szenarium n.

scene [siːn] s **1.** thea. etc a) Szene f: **change of** ~ Szenenwechsel m; fig. Tapetenwechsel m, b) Bühnenbild n, Kulissen pl: **behind the** ~s hinter den Kulissen (a. fig.), c) Ort m der Handlung, Schauplatz m (a. e-s Romans etc). **2.** Schauplatz m: ~ **of accident** (**crime**, **crash**) Unfallort m (Tatort m, Absturzstelle f); **be on the** ~ zur Stelle sein; **come on(to) the** ~ auf der Bildfläche erscheinen, auftauchen. **3.** Szene f, Anblick m: ~ **of destruction** Bild n der Zerstörung. **4.** Szene f, (heftiger) Auftritt: **make a** ~ (j-m) e-e Szene machen. **5.** F (*Drogen-, Pop- etc*)Szene f. **6.** **... is not my** ~ F ... ist nicht mein Fall.

scen·er·y ['siːnərɪ] s **1.** Landschaft f, Gegend f. **2.** thea. Bühnenbild n, Kulissen pl.

sce·nic ['siːnɪk] adj (**~ally**) **1.** landschaft-

lich, Landschafts... **2.** landschaftlich schön, malerisch: ~ **road** landschaftlich schöne Strecke. **3.** thea. Bühnen...

scent [sent] **I** s **1.** Duft m, Geruch m. **2.** bsd. Br. Parfüm n. **3.** hunt. Witterung f: **be on the** ~ **of** fig. e-r Sache auf der Spur sein; **follow a wrong** ~ fig. e-e falsche Spur verfolgen. **II** v/t **4.** wittern (a. fig.). **5.** **be ~ed with** vom Duft (gen) erfüllt sein. **6.** bsd. Br. parfümieren. '**scent·less** adj geruchlos.

scep·ter Am. → **sceptre**.

scep·tic ['skeptɪk] s Br. Skeptiker(in). '**scep·ti·cal** adj □ skeptisch: **be** ~ **about** (od. of) **s.th.** e-r Sache skeptisch gegenüberstehen. **scep·ti·cism** ['~sɪzəm] s Skepsis f.

scep·tre ['septə] s bsd. Br. Zepter n.

sched·ule ['ʃedjuːl] **I** s **1.** Aufstellung f, Verzeichnis n. **2.** (*Arbeits-, Stunden-, Zeit- etc*)Plan m; Programm n; Fahr-, Flugplan m: **three months ahead of** ~ drei Monate früher als vorgesehen; **be behind** ~ Verspätung haben, weitS. im Verzug od. Rückstand sein; **on** ~ (fahr)planmäßig, pünktlich. **II** v/t **3.** et. ansetzen (**for** auf acc, für); **it is ~d to take place tomorrow** es soll morgen stattfinden; **~d departure** (fahr)planmäßige Abfahrt; **~d flight** Linienflug m.

sche·mat·ic [skɪˈmætɪk] adj (**~ally**) schematisch.

scheme [skiːm] s **1.** Schema n, System n. **2.** bsd. Br. Programm n, Projekt n. **3.** Intrige f, pl a. Machenschaften pl. **II** v/i **4.** intrigieren (**against** gegen): ~ **for** hinarbeiten auf (acc). '**schem·er** s Intrigant(in). '**schem·ing** adj □ intrigant.

schist [ʃɪst] s geol. Schiefer m.

schiz·o·phre·ni·a [ˌskɪtsəʊˈfriːnjə] s psych. Schizophrenie f. **schiz·o·phren·ic** [ˌ~ˈfrenɪk] **I** adj (**~ally**) schizophren. **II** s Schizophrene m, f.

schmal(t)z [ʃmɒlts] s F Schmalz m. '**schmal(t)z·y** adj F schmalzig.

schnit·zel ['ʃnɪtsl] s gastr. Wiener Schnitzel n.

schol·ar ['skɒlə] s **1.** Gelehrte m, f, bsd. Geisteswissenschaftler(in). **2.** univ. Stipendiat(in). '**schol·ar·ly** adj **1.** gelehrt. **2.** wissenschaftlich. '**schol·ar·ship** s **1.** Gelehrsamkeit f. **2.** univ. Stipendium n: ~ **holder** → **scholar** 2.

school¹ [sku:l] *s* Schule *f*, Schwarm *m* (*Delphine, Heringe etc*).

school² [~] I *s* 1. *allg.* Schule *f* (*a. fig.*): **at** (*Am. in*) ~ auf *od.* in der Schule; **go to** ~ in die *od.* zur Schule gehen; **there is no** ~ **today** heute ist schulfrei *od.* kein Unterricht; → **old** 1. 2. *Am.* Hochschule *f*. 3. *univ.* Fakultät *f*; Fachbereich *m*. II *v/t* 4. *j-n* schulen, unterrichten (**in** *dat*); *Tier* dressieren: ~ **o.s. to do s.th.** es sich angewöhnen, et. zu tun. **~age** *s* schulpflichtiges Alter: **be of** ~ schulpflichtig *od.* im schulpflichtigen Alter sein. '**~age** *adj* schulpflichtig, im schulpflichtigen Alter. '**~boy** *s* Schuljunge *m*, Schüler *m*. ~ **bus** *s* Schulbus *m*. '**~child** *s* (*irr child*) Schulkind *n*. ~ **days** *s pl* Schulzeit *f*. '**~fel·low** → **schoolmate**.

school·ing ['sku:lɪŋ] *s* (Schul)Ausbildung *f*.

school| leav·er *s bsd. Br.* Schulabgänger(in). '**~mate** *s* Schulkamerad(in), Mitschüler(in). ~ **ship** *s* Schulschiff *n*. '**~teach·er** *s* (Schul)Lehrer(in).

schoon·er ['sku:nə] *s* 1. ⚓ Schoner *m*. 2. *Br.* großes Sherryglas; *Am.* großes Bierglas.

sci·at·ic [saɪ'ætɪk] *adj* ⚕ Ischias...: ~ **nerve**. **sci·at·i·ca** [~kə] *s* ⚕ Ischias *m, f*.

sci·ence ['saɪəns] *s* 1. Wissenschaft *f*. 2. *a.* **natural** ~ Naturwissenschaft(en *pl*) *f*. 3. *fig.* Kunst *f*, Lehre *f*. ~ **fiction** *s* Science-fiction *f*.

sci·en·tif·ic [ˌsaɪən'tɪfɪk] *adj* (~**ally**) 1. (*engS.* natur)wissenschaftlich. 2. *fig.* systematisch. '**sci·en·tist** *s* (*engS.* Natur)Wissenschaftler(in).

sci-fi [ˌsaɪ'faɪ] *s* F Science-fiction *f*.

scin·til·lat·ing ['sɪntɪleɪtɪŋ] *adj* sprühend (*Geist, Witz*), geistsprühend (*Unterhaltung etc*).

scis·sors ['sɪzəz] *s pl, a.* **pair of** ~ Schere *f*.

scle·ro·sis [sklɪə'rəʊsɪs] *s* ⚕ Sklerose *f*.

scoff¹ [skɒf] I *v/i* spotten (**at** über *acc*). II *s* spöttische Bemerkung.

scoff² [~] *v/t* F *Kuchen etc* verdrücken, wegputzen.

scoff·er ['skɒfə] *s* Spötter(in).

scold [skəʊld] *v/t* ausschelten, -schimpfen, schimpfen mit (**for** wegen). '**scold·ing** *s* Schelte *f*: **give s.o. a** ~ → **scold**.

scol·lop ['skɒləp] → **scallop**.

sconce [skɒns] *s* Wandleuchte *f*.

scone [skɒn] *s kleiner runder Kuchen, mit Butter serviert.*

scoop [sku:p] I *s* 1. Schöpfkelle *f*, Schöpfer *m*; (*Mehl- etc*)Schaufel *f*; (*Eis*)Portionierer *m*. 2. Kugel *f* (*Eis*). 3. *Presse, Rundfunk, TV:* (sensationelle) Erstmeldung. II *v/t* 4. schöpfen; schaufeln.

scoot [sku:t] *v/i* F abhauen; rennen.

scoot·er ['sku:tə] *s* 1. (Kinder)Roller *m*. 2. (*Motor*)Roller *m*.

scope [skəʊp] *s* 1. Bereich *m*: **be within** (**beyond**) **the** ~ **of** sich im Rahmen (*gen*) halten (den Rahmen [*gen*] sprengen). 2. (Spiel)Raum *m*, (Entfaltungs)Möglichkeit(en *pl*) *f* (**for** für).

scorch [skɔ:tʃ] I *v/t* 1. an-, versengen, verbrennen. 2. ausdörren. II *v/i* 3. *mot.* F rasen. III *s* 4. *a.* ~ **mark** ausgesengte Stelle, Brandfleck *m*. '**scorch·er** *s* F glühendheißer Tag. '**scorch·ing** *adj* F glühendheiß (*Tag etc*), sengend (*Hitze*).

score [skɔ:] I *s* 1. (Spiel)Stand *m*; (Spiel-)Ergebnis *n*: **what is the** ~? wie steht es *od.* das Spiel?; **the** ~ **stood at** (*od.* **was**) **2–1** das Spiel stand 2:1; **keep** (**the**) ~ anschreiben. 2. *Sport:* Treffer *m*. ♪ Partitur *f*; Musik *f* (*zu e-m Film etc*). 4. **on that** ~ deshalb, in dieser Hinsicht. 5. **have a** ~ **to settle with s.o.** e-e alte Rechnung mit *j-m* zu begleichen haben. 6. ~**s** *pl* e-e Menge. 7. *a.* ~ **mark** Kerbe *f*, Rille *f*. II *v/t* 8. *Sport:* Treffer *etc* erzielen, *Tor a.* schießen; *a. allg. Erfolg, Sieg* erringen. 9. *Sport:* *j-m* Punkte, Note geben. 10. ♪ in Partitur setzen; instrumentieren, setzen (**for** für); die Musik schreiben zu *od.* für. 11. einkerben. 12. ~ **out** (*od.* **through**) aus-, durchstreichen. III *v/i* 13. *Sport:* e-n Treffer *etc* erzielen, ein Tor schießen: **he** ~**d twice** er traf zweimal erfolgreich. 14. erfolgreich sein, Erfolg haben (**with** mit): ~ **off s.o.** *j-n* als dumm hinstellen *od.* lächerlich machen. ~ **with a girl** *sl.* ein Mädchen ins Bett kriegen. '**~board** *s Sport:* Anzeigetafel *f*.

scor·er ['skɔ:rə] *s* (*Sport*) 1. Torschütze *m*, -schützin *f*. 2. Anschreiber(in).

scorn [skɔ:n] *s* Verachtung *f* (**for** für, gegen): **pour** ~ **on** et. verächtlich abtun.

scorn·ful [ˈ∼fʊl] *adj* □ verächtlich.

Scor·pi·o [ˈskɔːpɪəʊ] *s ast.* Skorpion *m:* **be (a) ∼** Skorpion sein.

scor·pi·on [ˈskɔːpjən] *s zo.* Skorpion *m.*

Scot [skɒt] *s* Schotte *m,* Schottin *f.*

Scotch [skɒtʃ] **I** *adj* schottisch (*Whisky etc*). **II** *s* Scotch *m* (*schottischer Whisky*).

scot-free [ˌskɒtˈfriː] *adj:* **get off ∼** ungeschoren davonkommen.

Scots [skɒts] *adj* schottisch. **∼·man** [ˈ∼mən] *s* (*irr man*) Schotte *m.* **'∼·wom·an** *s* (*irr woman*) Schottin *f.*

Scot·tish [ˈskɒtɪʃ] *adj* schottisch.

scoun·drel [ˈskaʊndrəl] *s* Schurke *m,* Schuft *m.*

scour¹ [ˈskaʊə] *v/t* Topf *etc* scheuern, Fußboden *etc a.* schrubben.

scour² *v/t* Gegend *etc* absuchen, abkämmen (*for* nach).

scourge [skɜːdʒ] **I** *s* Geißel *f* (*a. fig.*). **II** *v/t* geißeln, *fig. a.* heimsuchen.

scout [skaʊt] **I** *s* **1.** *oft* ♀ Pfadfinder *m; Am.* Pfadfinderin *f.* **2.** ✕ Kundschafter *m,* Späher *m.* **3.** *Br.* motorisierter Pannenhelfer (*e-s Automobilklubs*). **4.** *bsd. Sport:* Talentsucher(in). **II** *v/i* **5. ∼ a·bout** (*od.* **around**) sich umsehen (*for* nach). **III** *v/t* **6.** *a.* **∼ out** ✕ auskundschaften, erkunden.

scowl [skaʊl] **I** *v/i* ein böses Gesicht machen: **∼ at** *j-n* bös anschauen. **II** *s* böses Gesicht.

scrab·ble [ˈskræbl] *v/i mst* **∼ about** (*od.* **around**) herumsuchen, -wühlen (*for* nach).

scrag·gy [ˈskrægɪ] *adj* □ dürr, knochig.

scram [skræm] *v/i* F *oft imp* abhauen, Leine ziehen.

scram·ble [ˈskræmbl] **I** *v/i* **1.** klettern; krabbeln. **2.** sich raufen (*a. fig.*), (*bsd. Kinder*) sich balgen (*for* um); sich drängeln (*for* zu). **II** *v/t* **3.** *Ei* verrühren: **∼d eggs** *pl* Rührei(*er pl*) *n.* **4.** *Funkspruch etc* zerhacken. **III** *s* **5.** Kletterei *f.* **6.** Rauferei *f,* Balgerei *f;* Drängelei *f.* **'scram·bler** *s* ⊕ Zerhacker *m.*

scrap¹ [skræp] **I** *s* **1.** Stückchen *n;* Fetzen *m:* **there is not a ∼ of evidence** es gibt nicht den geringsten Beweis; **there is not a ∼ of truth in it** daran ist kein Wort wahr. **2.** *pl* (Speise)Reste *pl.* **3.** Altmaterial *n;* Altmetall *n,* Schrott *m:* **sell**

s.th. for ∼ et. als Schrott verkaufen. **II** *v/t* **4.** *unbrauchbar Gewordenes* ausrangieren; *Plan etc* aufgeben, fallenlassen, *Methode etc a.* zum alten Eisen werfen. **5.** verschrotten.

scrap² [∼] F **I** *v/i* sich streiten; sich balgen. **II** *s* Streiterei *f;* Balgerei *f.* **'scrap·book** *s* Sammelalbum *n.*

scrape [skreɪp] **I** *v/t* **1.** (ab)kratzen, (ab)schaben (*from* von); *Schuhe etc* abkratzen; *Karotten etc* schaben: **∼ off** abkratzen *od.* abschaben (*von);* **∼ to·gether** (*od.* **up**) *Geld* zs.-kratzen; **∼ a living** *fig.* sich gerade so über Wasser halten. **2.** sich *die Knie etc* ab- *od.* aufschürfen (*on* auf *dat*); *Wagen etc* ankratzen. **II** *v/i* **3.** scheuern (*against* an *dat*): **∼ along the ground** am Boden schleifen. **4.** *fig.* **∼ along** (*od.* **by**) über die Runden kommen (*on* mit); **∼ through an examination** mit Ach u. Krach durch e-e Prüfung kommen. **III** *s* **5.** Kratzen *n.* **6.** Aufschürfung *f,* Schürfwunde *f.* **be in a ∼** F in Schwulitäten sein. **'scrap·er** *s* ⊕ Kratzer *m,* Schaber *m.*

scrap| heap *s* Schrotthaufen *m:* **be on the ∼** *fig.* zum alten Eisen gehören. **∼ met·al** *s* Altmetall *n,* Schrott *m.* **∼ pa·per** *s bsd. Br.* Schmierpapier *n.*

scrap·py [ˈskræpɪ] *adj* zs.-gestoppelt.

scrap| val·ue *s* Schrottwert *m.* **'∼·yard** *s* Schrottplatz *m.*

scratch [skrætʃ] **I** *v/t* **1.** (zer)kratzen, *Wagen etc* ankratzen: **∼ one's arm on a nail** sich den Arm an e-m Nagel einritzen. **2.** a) (ab)kratzen (*from* von): **∼ off** abkratzen (*von),* b) *s-n Namen etc* einkratzen (*on* in *acc*). **3.** *j-n* sich kratzen: **∼ one's nose** sich an der Nase kratzen; **∼ one's head** sich den Kopf kratzen (*vor Verlegenheit etc*). **II** *v/i* **4.** kratzen (*at an dat*). **5.** sich kratzen. **III** *s* **6.** Kratzer *m.* **7.** *fig.* **start from ∼** ganz von vorn anfangen; **be** (*od.* **come**) **up to ∼** den Anforderungen *od.* Erwartungen entsprechen. **IV** *adj* **8.** (bunt) zs.-gewürfelt (*Mannschaft etc*). **'∼·pad** *s bsd. Am.* Schmierblock *m.* **∼ pa·per** *s Am.* Schmierpapier *n.*

scratch·y [ˈskrætʃɪ] *adj* □ **1.** kratzend (*Geräusch*). **2.** zerkratzt (*Schallplatte*). **3.** kratzig (*Pullover etc*).

scrawl [skrɔːl] **I** *v/t* **1.** (hin)kritzeln,

II s **2.** Gekritzel n. **3.** Klaue f.
scraw·ny ['skrɔːnɪ] adj □ dürr.

scream [skriːm] **I** v/i **1.** schreien (**with** vor dat): ~ **with laughter** vor Lachen brüllen. **II** v/t **2.** a. ~ **out** schreien: ~ **o.s. hoarse** sich heiser schreien; ~ **the place down** F zetermordio schreien; → **roof-top.** **III** s **3.** Schrei m: ~s pl **of laughter** brüllendes Gelächter. **4.** **be a** ~ F zum Schreien (komisch) sein.

scree [skriː] s Geröll n.

screech [skriːtʃ] **I** v/i **1.** kreischen (a. Bremsen etc), (gellend) schreien. **II** s Kreischen n; (gellender) Schrei.

screed [skriːd] s langatmige Rede etc, Roman m.

screen [skriːn] **I** s **1.** Wandschirm m. **2.** Film: **adapt for the** ~ für den Film bearbeiten. **3.** Radar, TV etc: (Bild)Schirm m. **4.** fig. Tarnung f. **II** v/t **5.** abschirmen. **6.** ~ **off** abtrennen. **7.** Film zeigen, Fernsehprogramm a. senden. **8.** fig. j-n überprüfen. '~·play s Film: Drehbuch n. ~ **test** s Film: Probeaufnahmen pl.

screw [skruː] **I** s **1.** ⚙ Schraube f: **he has a** ~ **loose** F bei ihm ist e-e Schraube locker; **put the** ~s **on s.o.** fig. j-m (die) Daumenschrauben anlegen od. ansetzen. **II** v/t **2.** (an)schrauben (**to** an acc): ~ **together** zs.-, verschrauben. **3.** a. ~ **up** Papier etc zerknüllen. **4.** ~ **up** a) Augen zs.-kneifen, Gesicht verziehen, b) F Plan etc vermasseln. **5.** ~ **s.th. out of s.o.** et. aus j-m herauspressen. **6.** (a. v/i) V bumsen, vögeln. '~·ball s bsd. Am. F Spinner(in). '~·driv·er s ⚙ Schraubenzieher m. ~ **top** s Schraubverschluß m.

screw·y ['skruːɪ] adj F verrückt.

scrib·ble ['skrɪbl] **I** v/t (hin)kritzeln. **II** s Gekritzel n. '**scrib·bler** s humor. od. contp. Schreiberling m.

scrim·mage ['skrɪmɪdʒ] s Handgemenge n.

scrimp [skrɪmp] v/i den Gürtel enger schnallen: ~ **and scrape** jeden Pfennig zweimal umdrehen.

script [skrɪpt] s **1.** Manuskript n (e-r Rede etc); (Film, TV) Drehbuch n, Skript n; thea. Text(buch n) m. **2.** Schrift(zeichen pl) f. **3.** Schreibschrift f. **4.** ped. univ. Br. (schriftliche) Prüfungsarbeit.

Scrip·ture ['skrɪptʃə] s, a. **the** ~s pl die (Heilige) Schrift.

'**script,writ·er** s Film, TV: Drehbuchautor(in).

scroll [skrəʊl] s Schriftrolle f.

scrooge [skruːdʒ] s Geizhals m.

scro·tum ['skrəʊtəm] pl -**tums**, -**ta** ['-tə] s anat. Hodensack m.

scrounge [skraʊndʒ] F **I** v/i schnorren (**off** bei). **II** v/t schnorren (**off** von, bei). '**scroung·er** s F Schnorrer(in).

scrub[1] [skrʌb] s Gebüsch n, Gestrüpp n.

scrub[2] [~] **I** v/t **1.** et. schrubben, scheuern. **2.** F streichen, ausfallen lassen. **II** v/i **3.** Schrubben n, Scheuern n: **give s.th. a** ~ → **1.**

scrub·bing brush ['skrʌbɪŋ] s, Am. **scrub brush** s Scheuerbürste f.

scrub·by ['skrʌbɪ] adj gestrüppreich.

scruff [skrʌf] s: ~ **of the neck** Genick n.

scruff·y ['skrʌfɪ] adj □ F schmudd(e)lig.

scrump·tious ['skrʌmpʃəs] adj □ F fabelhaft, lecker (Speise).

scrunch [skrʌntʃ] **I** v/t a. ~ **up** Papier etc zs.-knüllen. **II** v/i knirschen.

scru·ple ['skruːpl] **I** s Skrupel m: **have no** ~s **about doing s.th.** → **II**; **without** ~ skrupellos. **II** v/i: **not to** ~ **to do s.th.** keine Skrupel haben, et. zu tun. **scru·pu·lous** ['~pjʊləs] adj □ gewissenhaft.

scru·ti·nize ['skruːtɪnaɪz] v/t **1.** genau prüfen. **2.** mustern. '**scru·ti·ny** s F **1.** genaue Prüfung. **2.** musternder od. prüfender Blick.

scu·ba ['skuːbə] s Tauchgerät n: ~ **diving** (Sport)Tauchen n.

scuff [skʌf] v/t **1.** ~ **one's feet** schlurfen. **2.** abwetzen.

scuf·fle ['skʌfl] **I** v/i (sich) raufen (**for** um). **II** s Rauferei f, Handgemenge n.

scull [skʌl] (Rudersport) **I** s **1.** Skull n. **2.** Skullboot n, Skuller m. **II** v/t u. v/i **3.** skullen. '**scull·er** s Skuller(in).

sculp·tor ['skʌlptə] s Bildhauer m.

sculp·ture ['skʌlptʃə] **I** s Skulptur f, Plastik f, (Kunst a.) Bildhauerei f. **II** v/t Figur etc hauen (**in** in dat, aus).

scum [skʌm] s **1.** Schaum m. **2.** fig. Abschaum m: **the** ~ **of the earth** der Abschaum der Menschheit.

scurf [skɜːf] s (Kopf)Schuppen pl. '**scurf·y** adj schuppig.

scur·ril·ous ['skʌrələs] adj □ **1.** beleidigend; verleumderisch. **2.** derb (*Witz etc*).

scur·ry ['skʌrɪ] I *v/i* **1.** huschen. **2.** trippeln. II *s* **3.** Getrippel *n*.

scut·tle ['skʌtl] → **scurry** I.

scythe [saɪð] I *s* Sense *f*. II *v/t a*. ~ **down** Wiese *etc* mähen.

sea [si:] *s* Meer *n* (*a*. *fig*.), See *f*: **at** ~ auf See; **be all at** ~ *fig*. völlig ratlos sein; **by** ~ auf dem Seeweg; **by the** ~ am Meer; **go to** ~ zur See gehen; → **put** 12. ~ **an·i·mal** *s* Meerestier *n*. '~**bed** *s* Meeresboden *m*, -grund *m*. '~**board** *s* Küste *f*. '~**food** *s* Meeresfrüchte *pl*. '~**go·ing** *adj* hochseetüchtig, Hochsee... '~**gull** *s* orn. Seemöwe *f*.

seal[1] [si:l] *pl* ~s, *bsd. coll.* ~ *s zo.* Seehund *m*, Robbe *f*.

seal² [~] I *s* **1.** Siegel *n*. **2.** Siegel *n*, Versieg(e)lung *f*; Plombe *f*. **3.** ⊙ Dichtung *f*. **4.** ⊙ Aufkleber *m*. II *v/t* **5.** siegeln. **6.** versiegeln; plombieren; *Briefumschlag etc* zukleben: ~**ed envelope** verschlossener Briefumschlag *m*. **7.** ⊙ abdichten. **8.** ~ **off** *Gegend etc* abriegeln. **9.** *fig*. besiegeln: ~ *s.o.'s fate* j-s Schicksal besiegeln.

sea lev·el *s*: **above** (**below**) ~ über (unter) dem Meeresspiegel, über (unter) Meereshöhe.

seal·ing wax *s* ['si:lɪŋ] *s* Siegellack *n*.

sea li·on *s zo.* Seelöwe *m*.

'**seal·skin** *s* Seal(skin) *m*, *n*, Seehundfell *n*.

seam [si:m] *s* **1.** Saum *m*: **burst at the** ~**s** *bsd. fig*. aus allen Nähten platzen. **2.** Fuge *f*. **3.** *geol.* Flöz *n*.

sea·man ['si:mən] *s* (*irr man*) Seemann *m*. ~ **mile** *s* Seemeile *f*.

seam·stress ['semstrɪs] *s* Näherin *f*.

seam·y ['si:mɪ] *adj*: ~ **side** *fig*. Schattenseite(n *pl*) *f*.

'**sea·plane** *s* See-, Wasserflugzeug *n*. '~**port** *s* Seehafen *m*, Hafenstadt *f*. ~ **pow·er** *s* Seemacht *f*.

sear [sɪə] *v/t* **1.** *Fleisch* rasch anbraten. **2.** brennen in (*dat*) (*Geruch etc*). **3.** *Pflanzen* vertrocknen lassen.

search [sɜ:tʃ] I *v/i* **1.** suchen (**for** nach): ~ **through** durchsuchen; → **high** 7. II *v/t* **2.** j-n, *et.* durchsuchen (**for** nach): ~ **me!** F keine Ahnung! **3.** ~ **out** j-n ausfindig machen; *et.* herausfinden. III *s* **4.** Suche *f* (**for** nach): **in** ~ **of** auf der Suche

nach. **5.** Durchsuchung *f*. '**search·ing** *adj* □ forschend, prüfend (*Blick*); bohrend (*Frage*).

'**search·light** *s* (Such)Scheinwerfer *m*. ~ **par·ty** *s* Suchmannschaft *f*, -trupp *m*. ~ **war·rant** *s* ⚖️ Haussuchungs-, Durchsuchungsbefehl *m*.

sear·ing ['sɪərɪŋ] *adj* stechend (*Schmerz*).

'**sea·sick** *adj* seekrank. '~**sick·ness** *s* Seekrankheit *f*. '~**side** *s*: **at** (*od.* **by**) **the** ~ am Meer; **go to the** ~ ans Meer fahren; ~ **resort** *s* Seebad *n*.

sea·son ['si:zn] I *s* **1.** Jahreszeit *f*: → **rainy**. **2.** *allg*. Saison *f*, *thea. a.* Spielzeit *f*, (*Jagd-*, *Urlaubs- etc*)Zeit *f*: **in** (**out of**) ~ in (außerhalb der) (Hoch)Saison; 2**'s Greetings!** Frohe Weihnachten!; → **close season**, **compliment** 2, **high** 4, **low season**, **open** 10, **silly** I. **3.** F → **season ticket**. II *v/t* **4.** *Speise* würzen. **5.** *Holz* ablagern. '**sea·son·a·ble** □ der Jahreszeit entsprechend. **sea·son·al** ['~zənl] *adj* □ saisonbedingt; Saison... '**sea·soned** *adj* erfahren, routiniert. '**sea·son·ing** *s* Gewürz *n*.

sea·son tick·et *s* **1.** 🚍 *etc* Dauer-, Zeitkarte *f*. **2.** *thea.* Abonnement *n*.

seat [si:t] I *s* **1.** Sitz(gelegenheit *f*) *m*; (Sitz)Platz *m*: **take a** ~ Platz nehmen; **take one's** ~ s-n Platz einnehmen; Sitz(fläche) *f* (*e-s Stuhls etc*); Hosenboden *m*; Hinterteil *n*: **do s.th. by the** ~ **of one's pants** F et. nach Gefühl u. Wellenschlag tun. **3.** (*Geschäfts-*, *Regierungs- etc*)Sitz *m*. II *v/t* **4.** j-n setzen: **be** ~**ed** sitzen; **please be** ~**ed** bitte nehmen Sie Platz; **remain** ~**ed** sitzen bleiben. **5.** Sitzplätze bieten für, Platz bieten (*dat*): ~ **500 persons** *a*. 500 Sitzplätze haben. ~ **belt** *s* ✈️, *mot.* Sicherheitsgurt *m*: **fasten one's** ~ sich anschnallen; **wear a** ~ angegurtet *od.* angeschnallt sein.

seat·er ['si:tə] *s* ✈️, *mot.* ...sitzer *m*. '**seat·ing** I *s* Sitzgelegenheit(en *pl*) *f*. II *adj*: **a** ~ **capacity of 200** 200 Sitzplätze.

sea ur·chin ['ɜ:tʃɪn] *s zo.* Seeigel *m*. '~**weed** *s* 🌿 (See)Tang *m*. '~**worth·y** *adj* seetüchtig.

sec [sek] F → **second²** 2.

sec·a·teurs [ˌsekə'tɜːz] *s pl*, *a.* **pair of** ~ *Br.* Gartenschere *f*.

se-cede [sɪˈsiːd] v/i pol. etc sich abspalten (**from** von).

se-ces-sion [sɪˈseʃn] s pol. etc Abspaltung f (**from** von).

se-clud-ed [sɪˈkluːdɪd] adj abgelegen, abgeschieden (Haus etc); zurückgezogen (Leben). **se'clu-sion** [-ʒn] s Abgelegenheit f, Abgeschiedenheit f; Zurückgezogenheit f.

sec-ond¹ [ˈsekənd] **I** adj (□ → **second-ly**) **1.** zweit: he is going through his ~ **childhood** er fühlt sich wieder wie ein (richtiges) Kind; **at ~ hand** aus zweiter Hand; **it has become ~ nature for** (od. **to**) **him** es ist ihm in Fleisch u. Blut übergegangen; **a ~ Shakespeare** ein zweiter Shakespeare; **a ~ time** noch einmal; **every ~ day** jeden zweiten Tag, alle zwei Tage; **be ~ to none** unerreicht od. unübertroffen sein (**as** als); → **fiddle** 1, **thought²** 2, **wind¹** 2. **II** s **2.** der, die, das Zweite: **the ~ of May** der 2. Mai. **3.** mot. zweiter Gang. **4.** Boxen, Duell: Sekundant m: **~s out** Ring frei. **5.** pl ✝ Waren pl zweiter Wahl. **6.** pl F Nachschlag m (zweite Portion). **III** adv **7.** als zweit(er, e, es). **IV** v/t **8.** Antrag etc unterstützen.

sec-ond² [~] s **1.** Sekunde f (a. ♈, ♪). **2.** fig. Augenblick m, Sekunde f: **just a ~** Augenblick(, bitte)!; **I won't be a ~** ich komme gleich (wieder); **have you got a ~?** hast du e-n Moment Zeit (für mich)?

se-cond³ [sɪˈkɒnd] v/t Br. j-n (bsd. vorübergehend) versetzen (**to** in acc).

sec-ond-ar-y [ˈsekəndərɪ] adj □ **1.** sekundär, zweitrangig, nebensächlich. **2.** ⚡ etc sekundär, Sekundär... **3.** ped. höher (Schule etc).

sec-ond-'best I adj zweitbest. **II** adv: **come off ~** den kürzeren ziehen. ~**-'class I** adj **1.** zweitklassig, -rangig. **2.** 🚄 etc zweiter Klasse. **II** adv **3.** 🚄 etc zweite(r) Klasse. ~**-de'gree** adj Verbrennungen zweiten Grades. ~ **hand** s Sekundenzeiger m. ~**-'hand** adj **1.** (a. adv) aus zweiter Hand. **2.** gebraucht, Gebraucht..., (Kleidung s) getragen, (Bücher) antiquarisch: ~ **bookshop** Antiquariat n.

sec-ond-ly [ˈsekəndlɪ] adv zweitens.

sec-ond-'rate → **second-class** 1.

se-cre-cy [ˈsiːkrəsɪ] s **1.** Geheimhaltung f: **in** (od. **amid**) **great ~** unter großer

Geheimhaltung. **2.** Verschwiegenheit f.

se-cret [ˈsiːkrɪt] **I** adj (□ → **secretly**) **1.** geheim, Geheim...: **keep s.th. ~** et. geheimhalten (**from** vor dat); ~ **agent** Geheimagent(in); ~ **service** Geheimdienst m. **2.** heimlich (Bewunderer etc). **3.** verschwiegen. **II** s **4.** Geheimnis n: **in ~** a) im Vertrauen, b) → **secretly**; **have no ~s from s.o.** keine Geheimnisse vor j-m haben; **make no ~ of** kein Geheimnis od. Hehl machen aus; → **keep** 4, 7.

sec-re-tar-y [ˈsekrətrɪ] s **1.** Sekretär(in) (**to** gen). **2.** pol. Minister(in): **♀ of State** Br. Minister(in); Am. Außenminister (-in). ~**-'gen-er-al** pl **sec-re-tar-ies-'gen-er-al** s Generalsekretär m.

se-crete [sɪˈkriːt] v/t physiol. absondern. **se'cre-tion** [-ʃn] s Absonderung f, Sekret n.

se-cre-tive [ˈsiːkrətɪv] adj □ heimlichtuerisch: **be ~ about s.th.** mit et. geheimtun.

sect [sekt] s Sekte f. **sec-tar-i-an** [~ˈteərɪən] adj konfessionsbedingt, Konfessions...

sec-tion [ˈsekʃn] **I** s **1.** Teil m. **2.** Abschnitt m (e-s Buchs etc); ⚖ Paragraph m. **3.** Abteilung f. **4.** ▲, ☉ Schnitt m: **in ~** im Schnitt. **II** v/t **5.** teilen. **sec-tion-al** [-ʃənl] adj ▲, ☉ Schnitt...

sec-tor [ˈsektə] s allg. Sektor m.

sec-u-lar [ˈsekjʊlə] adj □ weltlich, profan. **'sec-u-lar-ize** v/t säkularisieren, verweltlichen.

se-cure [sɪˈkjʊə] **I** adj □ **1.** allg. sicher (**against**, **from** vor dat): **feel ~** sich sicher fühlen; **financially ~** finanziell abgesichert. **II** v/t **2.** Tür etc fest verschließen; sichern. **3.** sichern (**against**, **from** vor dat). **4.** sich et. sichern od. beschaffen; et. erreichen.

se-cu-ri-ty [sɪˈkjʊərətɪ] s **1.** allg. Sicherheit f: **♀ Council** Sicherheitsrat m (der UNO); **for ~ reasons** aus Sicherheitsgründen; ~ **risk** Sicherheitsrisiko n. **2.** pl ✝ Effekten pl, Wertpapiere pl.

se-dan [sɪˈdæn] s mot. Am. Limousine f.

se-date [sɪˈdeɪt] **I** adj □ ruhig, gelassen; (Tempo) gemütlich. **II** v/t j-m ein Beruhigungsmittel geben. **se'da-tion** s: **be under ~** unter dem Einfluß von Beruhigungsmitteln stehen; **put under ~** → **sedate** II. **sed-a-tive** [ˈsedətɪv] **I** adj beruhigend: **~ shot** Beruhigungsspritze f. **II** s Beruhigungsmittel n.

sed·en·tar·y ['sedntəri] adj □ **1.** sitzend (Beschäftigung etc). **2.** seßhaft.

sed·i·ment ['sedimənt] s (Boden)Satz m.

se·duce [sɪ'djuːs] v/t verführen, weitS.a. verleiten (**into** zu, **into doing s.th.** dazu, et. zu tun). **se'duc·er** s Verführer(in). **se·duc·tion** [sɪ'dʌkʃn] s **1.** Verführung f. **2.** mst pl Verlockung f. **se'duc·tive** adj □ verführerisch, weitS.a. verlockend.

see¹ [siː] (irr) **I** v/t **1.** sehen: **I saw him come** (od. **coming**) ich sah ihn kommen. **2.** (ab)sehen, erkennen. **3.** ersehen, entnehmen (**from** aus der Zeitung etc). **4.** (ein)sehen, verstehen: **as I ~ it** wie ich es sehe, in m-n Augen. **5.** sich et. ansehen, besuchen. **6.** a) j-n besuchen: **go** (**come**) **to ~ s.o.** j-n besuchen (gehen od. kommen), b) Anwalt etc aufsuchen, c) zum Arzt gehen, d) j-n sprechen (**on business** geschäftlich). **7.** j-n empfangen. **8.** j-n begleiten, bringen (**to the station** zum Bahnhof). **II** v/i **9.** sehen: **you'll ~** du wirst schon sehen. **10.** verstehen: **I ~** (ich) verstehe!, aha!, ach so!; **you ~** weißt du. **11.** nachsehen. **12.** let me ~ warte mal!, laß mich überlegen!; **we'll ~** mal sehen.

Verbindungen mit Präpositionen:

see| a·bout v/i sehen nach, sich kümmern um: **I'll ~ it** ich werde mich darum kümmern; ich will mal sehen; **we'll** (**soon**) **~ that!** F das wollen wir mal sehen! **~ o·ver, ~ round** v/i sich ein Haus etc ansehen. **~ through** **I** v/i j-n, et. durchschauen. **II** v/t j-m hinweghelfen über (acc). **~ to** v/i: **~ it that** dafür sorgen, daß.

Verbindungen mit Adverbien:

see| off v/t **1.** j-n verabschieden (**at an** Bahnhof etc). **2.** verjagen, -scheuchen. **~ out** v/t **1.** j-n hinausbringen, -begleiten. **2.** bis zum Ende (**gen**) reichen (Vorräte).

see² [~] s **1.** Bistum n, Diözese f. **2. Holy** ⚋ der Heilige Stuhl.

seed [siːd] **I** s **1.** ♀ Same(n) m; ⚹ Saat(gut n) f: **go** (od. **run**) **to ~** schießen; fig. herunterkommen (Person); → **sow** 1. **2.** (Orangen- etc)Kern m. **3.** Sport: gesetzter Spieler. **II** v/t **4.** besäen. **5.** Sport: Spieler setzen. **III** v/i **6.** ♀ schie-

ßen. **'~·bed** s **1.** Saatbeet n. **2.** fig. Brutstätte f.

'seed·less ['siːdlɪs] adj kernlos (Orangen etc).

'seed·y adj □ vergammelt.

see·ing ['siːɪŋ] cj a. **~ that** da.

seek [siːk] (irr) **I** v/t **1.** Schutz, Zuflucht, Wahrheit etc suchen: **~ s.o.'s advice, ~ advice from s.o.** j-n um Rat bitten, Rat bei j-m suchen. **2.** streben nach. **3.** (ver)suchen (**to do** zu tun). **II** v/i **4.** ~ **after** (od. **for**) suchen (nach).

seem [siːm] v/i **1.** scheinen: **it ~s impossible to me** das (er)scheint mir unmöglich. **2.** impers **it ~s** that es scheint, daß; anscheinend; **it ~s as if** (od. **though**) es sieht so aus od. scheint so, als ob. **'seem·ing** adj scheinbar. **'seem·ing·ly** adv **1.** scheinbar. **2.** anscheinend.

seen [siːn] pp von **see¹**.

seep [siːp] v/i sickern.

see·saw ['siːsɔː] s Wippe f, Wippschaukel f.

seethe [siːð] v/i fig. kochen: **he was seething with rage** er kochte od. schäumte vor Wut.

'see-through adj durchsichtig (Bluse etc).

seg·ment I s ['segmənt] Teil m, n; Stück n; biol., ⚹ etc Segment n. **II** v/t [seg'ment] zerlegen, -teilen.

seg·re·gate ['segrigeit] v/t (a. nach Rassen, Geschlechtern) trennen. **seg·re·'ga·tion** s Trennung f: → **racial**.

seis·mic ['saɪzmɪk] adj seismisch, Erdbeben-.

seis·mo·graph ['saɪzməgrɑːf] s Seismograph m, Erdbebenmesser m. **seis·mol·o·gist** [~'mɒlədʒɪst] s Seismologe m, Seismologin f, Seismik f, Erdbebenkunde f. **seis'mol·o·gy** s Seismologie f, Seismik f, Erdbebenkunde f.

seize [siːz] **I** v/t **1.** j-n, et. packen (**by an** dat); Gelegenheit ergreifen; Macht etc an sich reißen. **2.** j-n festnehmen, et. beschlagnahmen. **II** v/i **3.** ~ **up** ⚙ sich festfressen; (Verkehr) zum Erliegen kommen. **sei·zure** ['siːʒə] s **1.** Festnahme f; Beschlagnahme f. **2.** ⚕ Anfall m.

sel·dom ['seldəm] adv selten: **~, if ever** (nur) äußerst selten, kaum jemals.

se·lect [sɪ'lekt] **I** v/t **1.** (aus)wählen (**from** aus). **II** adj **2.** ausgewählt. **3.** exklusiv. **se'lec·tion** s **1.** (Aus)Wahl f. **2.** ⚹ etc

Auswahl f (*of* an dat). **se'lec·tive** adj □ wählerisch (*in* in dat).

self [self] pl **selves** [selvz] s Ich n, Selbst n: **my humble** ~ m-e Wenigkeit; **one's true** ~ sein wahres Wesen; **he is back to his old** ~ er ist wieder (ganz) der alte. ~**ab'sorbed** adj mit sich selbst beschäftigt. ~**ad'dressed** adj: ~ **envelope** Rückumschlag m. ~**as'sured** adj selbstbewußt. ~**'ca·ter·ing** adj für Selbstversorger, mit Selbstverpflegung. ~**'cen·tered** adj Am., ~**'cen·tred** adj bsd. Br. ichbezogen, egozentrisch. ~**con·fi·dence** s Selbstbewußtsein n, -vertrauen n. ~**'con·fi·dent** adj □ selbstbewußt. ~**'con·scious** adj □ befangen, gehemmt. ~**con'tained** adj abgeschlossen (*Wohnung, Folge e-r Fernsehserie etc*). ~**con'trol** s Selbstbeherrschung f. ~**con'trolled** adj selbstbeherrscht. ~**'crit·i·cal** adj □ selbstkritisch. ~**'crit·i·cism** s Selbstkritik f. ~**de'fence** s Br., ~**de'fense** s Am. Selbstverteidigung f; ⚖ Notwehr f: **in** ~ in od. aus Notwehr. '~**de·ter·mi'na·tion** s pol. Selbstbestimmung f. ~**-'ed·u·cat·ed** adj: ~ **person** Autodidakt(in). ~**ef'fac·ing** adj □ zurückhaltend. ~**em'ployed** adj (beruflich) selbständig. ~**-es'teem** s Selbstachtung f. ~**ev·i·dent** adj □ 1. selbstverständlich: **be** ~ sich von selbst verstehen. 2. offensichtlich. ~**'gov·ern·ment** s pol. Selbstverwaltung f. ~**-'help** s Selbsthilfe f: ~ **group** Selbsthilfegruppe f. ~**im'por·tance** s Eigendünkel m, Überheblichkeit f. ~**im'por·tant** adj □ dünkelhaft, überheblich. ~**in'vit·ed** adj ungebeten (*Gast*).

self·ish ['selfɪʃ] adj □ selbstsüchtig, egoistisch. '**self·ish·ness** s Selbstsucht f, Egoismus m.

self·less ['selflɪs] adj □ selbstlos. '**self·less·ness** s Selbstlosigkeit f. ,**self·|-'made** adj: ~ **man** Selfmademan m. ~**'pit·y** s Selbstmitleid n. ~**pos·'sessed** adj □ selbstbeherrscht. ~**pos·'ses·sion** s Selbstbeherrschung f. ~**'praise** s Eigenlob m. '~**pres·er'va·tion** s Selbsterhaltung f: → **instinct**. ~**re'li·ant** adj □ selbständig. ~**re'spect** s Selbstachtung f. ,~**re'spect·ing** adj: **no** ~ **businessman** kein

Geschäftsmann, der et. auf sich hält. ,~**'right·eous** adj □ selbstgerecht. ,~**'sat·is·fied** adj selbstzufrieden. ~**-'seal·ing** adj selbstklebend (*Briefumschlag*). ~**'ser·vice** I s Selbstbedienung f. II adj Selbstbedienungs..., mit Selbstbedienung. ~**suf'fi·cient** adj □ ✝ autark. ~**sup'port·ing** adj 1. finanziell unabhängig: **be** ~ sich selbst tragen. 2. ⚙ freitragend (*Mast*); selbsttragend (*Mauer*). ,~**'willed** adj eigensinnig, -willig.

sell [sel] (*irr*) I v/t 1. verkaufen (**to** an acc; **for** für), ✝ a. a) absetzen, b) führen, vertreiben: ~ **o.s.** sich verkaufen (a. contp.); → **river**. 2. verkaufen, e-n guten Absatz sichern (dat). 3. F verkaufen: schmackhaft machen (**to** acc). j-n begeistern, erwärmen (**on** s.th. für et.): **be sold on** begeistert sein von. II v/i 4. verkaufen: ~ **by** ... mindestens haltbar bis ... 5. verkauft werden (**at, for** für): ~ **at £5** a. 5 Pfund kosten. 6. sich gut etc verkaufen (lassen), gehen: → **cake** 1.
Verbindungen mit Adverbien:
sell| **off** v/t (bsd. billig) abstoßen. ~ **out** I v/t 1. ausverkaufen: **be sold out** ausverkauft sein (a. Stadion etc); **we are sold out of umbrellas** Schirme sind ausverkauft. II v/i 2. **the umbrellas sold out in two days** die Schirme waren in zwei Tagen ausverkauft. 3. F contp. sich verkaufen (**to** an acc). ~ **up** Br. I v/t sein Geschäft etc verkaufen. II v/i verkaufen: Geschäft etc verkaufen.

'**sell-by date** s Mindesthaltbarkeitsdatum n.

sell·er ['selə] s 1. Verkäufer(in). 2. **be a good** ~ sich gut verkaufen, gut gehen.

'**sell-out** s ausverkaufte Veranstaltung.

selves [selvz] pl von **self**.

se·man·tic [sɪ'mæntɪk] ling. I adj (~**ally**) semantisch. II s pl (mst sg konstruiert) Semantik f.

sem·blance ['sembləns] s Anschein m (*of* von).

se·men ['siːmen] s physiol. Samen(flüssigkeit f) m, Sperma n.

se·mes·ter [sɪ'mestə] s univ. Semester n.

sem·i-... ['semɪ] halb..., halb-...

sem·i ['semɪ] s F 1. Br. → **semidetached** II. 2. Am. → **semitrailer**.

sem·i·|breve ['semɪbriːv] s ♪ Br. ganze Note. ~**cir·cle** ['semɪ] s Halbkreis m. ~**cir-**

cu·lar *adj* □ halbkreisförmig. **͵~'colon** *s ling.* Semikolon *n*, Strichpunkt *m.* **͵~·con'duc·tor** *s ≠* Halbleiter *m.* **de·tached** I *adj:* ~ *house* → II. II *s* Doppelhaushälfte *f.* **͵~'fi·nals** *s pl Sport:* Semi-, Halbfinale *n.*

sem·i·nar ['semɪnɑː] *s univ.* Seminar *n.*

sem·i·nar·y ['semɪnərɪ] *s* Priesterseminar *n.*

͵sem·i·of'fi·cial *adj* □ halbamtlich, offiziös. **'͵~͵pre·cious** *adj:* ~ *stone* Halbedelstein *m.* **͵~'skilled** *adj* angelernt (*Arbeiter*).

Sem·ite ['siːmaɪt] *s* Semit(in). **Se·mit·ic** [sɪ'mɪtɪk] *adj* semitisch.

sem·o·li·na [͵semə'liːnə] *s* Grieß *m.*

sen·ate ['senɪt] *s* Senat *m.* **sen·a·tor** ['senətə] *s* Senator *m.*

send [send] (*irr*) I *v/t* 1. j-n schicken (**to bed** ins Bett; **to prison** ins Gefängnis): ~ *s.o. after s.o.* j-n j-m nachschicken. 2. (**to**) *et.*, *a.* Grüße, Hilfe *etc* senden, schicken (*dat od.* an *acc*), Ware *etc* versenden, -schicken (an *acc*). 3. *mit adj od. pres p:* machen: ~ *s.o. mad* j-n wahnsinnig machen; → *pack* 15. II *v/i* 4. ~ *for* a) nach j-m schicken, j-n kommen lassen, b) sich *et.* kommen lassen, *et.* anfordern.
Verbindungen mit Adverbien:

send͵ a·way I *v/t* 1. fort-, wegschicken. 2. *Brief etc* absenden, abschicken. II *v/i* 3. ~ *for* → *send* 4b. ~ **back** *v/t* j-n, *et.* zurückschicken, *Speise a.* zurückgehen lassen. ~ **down** *v/t* 1. hinunter-, herunterschicken. 2. *univ. Br.* relegieren. 3. *fig.* Preise, Temperatur *etc* fallen lassen. ~ **in** *v/t* einsenden, einschicken, einreichen: → *resignation* 1. ~ **off** I *v/t* 1. → *send away* I. 2. j-n verabschieden. 3. *Sport:* vom Platz stellen. II *v/i* 4. → *send away* II. ~ **on** *v/t* 1. *Gepäck etc* vorausschicken. 2. *Brief etc* nachschicken, -senden (**to** an *e-e Adresse*). ~ **out** I *v/t* 1. hinausschicken. 2. *Wärme etc* ausstrahlen. 3. *Einladungen, Prospekte etc* verschicken. II *v/i* 4. ~ *for s.th. et.* holen lassen. ~ **up** *v/t* 1. hinauf-, heraufschicken. 2. *fig.* Preise, Temperatur *etc* steigen lassen. 3. *Br. F* parodieren, verulken.

send·er ['sendə] *s* Absender(in): → *return* 2.

'send|-off *s F* Verabschiedung *f.* **'~-up** *s*

Br. F (*of*) Parodie *f* (auf *acc*), Verulkung *f* (*gen*): **do a** ~ **of** → *send up* 3.

se·nile ['siːnaɪl] *adj* senil. **se·nil·i·ty** [sɪ'nɪlətɪ] *s* Senilität *f.*

sen·ior ['siːnjə] I *adj* 1. senior. 2. älter (**to** als): ~ *citizens pl* Senioren *pl.* 3. dienstälter; ranghöher (**to** als): ~ *partner* ✝ Senior(partner) *m.* 4. ~ *high* (*school*) *Am. die oberen Klassen der High-School.* II *s* 5. Ältere *m*, *f:* **he is my** ~ **by two years, he is two years my** ~ er ist zwei Jahre älter als ich. 6. *Am.* Student(in) im letzten Jahr. **sen·ior·i·ty** [͵siːnɪ'ɒrətɪ] *s* 1. (höheres) Alter. 2. (höheres) Dienstalter; (höherer) Rang.

sen·sa·tion [sen'seɪʃn] *s* 1. Empfindung *f;* Gefühl *n:* ~ *of thirst* Durstgefühl. 2. Sensation *f:* *cause* (*od.* **create**) *a* ~ großes Aufsehen erregen, für e-e Sensation sorgen. **sen'sa·tion·al** [~ʃənl] *adj* □ 1. sensationell, Sensations... 2. F phantastisch, sagenhaft. **sen'sa·tion·al·ism** [~ʃnəlɪzəm] *s* 1. Sensationsgier *f.* 2. Sensationsmache *f.*

sense [sens] I *s* 1. *physiol.* Sinn *m:* ~ *of hearing* (*sight, smell, taste, touch*) Gehör-(Gesichts-, Geruchs-, Geschmacks-, Tast)sinn; → *sixth* 1. 2. (klarer) Verstand: **bring s.o. to his** ~*s* j-n zur Besinnung *od.* Vernunft bringen; **come to one's** ~*s* zur Besinnung *od.* Vernunft kommen. 3. Vernunft *f*, Verstand *m:* **have the** ~ **to do s.th.** so klug sein, *et.* zu tun; → *common sense, horse sense.* 4. Gefühl *n*, Empfindung *f:* ~ *of security* Gefühl der Sicherheit. 5. Sinn *m*, Gefühl *n* (**of** für): ~ *of duty* Pflichtgefühl; → *humour* 1. 6. Sinn *m*, Bedeutung *f:* **in a** ~ in gewisser Hinsicht. 7. Sinn *m* (*et. Vernünftiges*): **make** ~ e-n Sinn ergeben; vernünftig sein; **I could make no** ~ **of it** ich konnte mir darauf keinen Reim machen. II *v/t* 8. fühlen, spüren. **'sense·less** *adj* □ 1. besinnungs-, bewußtlos. 2. sinnlos, unsinnig.

sense or·gan *s* Sinnesorgan *n*, -werkzeug *n.*

sen·si·bil·i·ty [͵sensɪ'bɪlətɪ] *s* 1. Empfindlichkeit *f:* ~ *to pain* Schmerzempfindlichkeit. 2. *a. pl* Fein-, Zartgefühl *n.* **sen·si·ble** ['~səbl] *adj* □ 1. vernünftig. 2. spürbar, merklich. 3. praktisch (*Kleidungsstück*).

sen·si·tive ['sensɪtɪv] *adj* □ **1.** sensibel, empfindsam; empfindlich: *be ~ to* empfindlich reagieren auf (*acc*). **2.** einfühlsam. **3.** empfindlich (*a.* **☉**): *~ to pain* schmerzempfindlich. **4.** heikel (*Thema etc*).

sen·sor ['sensə] *s* ⚡, **☉** Sensor *m*.

sen·so·ry ['sensərɪ] *adj* sensorisch, Sinnes...

sen·su·al ['sensjʊəl] *adj* □ sinnlich. **'sen·su·al·ist** *s* sinnlicher Mensch. **sen·su·al·i·ty** [,~'ælətɪ] *s* Sinnlichkeit *f*.

sen·su·ous ['sensjʊəs] *adj* □ sinnlich.

sent [sent] *pret u. pp von* **send**.

sen·tence ['sentəns] **I** *s* **1.** ling. Satz *m*. **2.** 🔨 Strafe *f*; Urteil *n*: *pass ~* das Urteil fällen (*on* über *acc*). **II** *v/t* **3.** 🔨 verurteilen (*to* zu).

sen·ten·tious [sen'tenʃəs] *adj* □ moralisierend.

sen·tient ['senʃnt] *adj* □ empfindungsfähig.

sen·ti·ment ['sentɪmənt] *s* **1.** Gefühle *pl*; Sentimentalität *f*. **2.** *a. pl* Ansicht *f*, Meinung *f*. **sen·ti·men·tal** [,~'mentl] *adj* □ gefühlvoll, gefühlsbetont; sentimental: *for ~ reasons* aus Sentimentalität; *~ value* Erinnerungswert *m*. **sen·ti·men·tal·i·ty** [,~men'tælətɪ] *s* Sentimentalität *f*.

sen·try ['sentrɪ] *s* ✕ Wache *f*, (Wach[t]-)Posten *m*. *~ box s* Wachhäuschen *n*.

sep·a·ra·ble ['sepərəbl] *adj* □ trennbar.

sep·a·rate I *v/t* ['sepəreɪt] **1.** *allg.* trennen (*from* von): *be ~d* getrennt leben (*from* von). **2.** (auf-, ein-, zer)teilen (*into* in *acc*). **II** *v/i* ['sepəreɪt] **3.** sich trennen (*a. Ehepaar*). **III** *adj* □ ['seprət] **4.** getrennt, separat. **5.** einzeln, gesondert, Einzel...: *charge s.th. ~ly* et. extra berechnen. **6.** verschieden. **sep·a·ra·tion** [,sepə'reɪʃn] *s* **1.** Trennung *f*. **2.** (Auf-, Ein-, Zer)Teilung *f*: *~ of powers pol.* Gewaltenteilung *f*. **sep·a·ra·tism** ['~rətɪzəm] *s pol.* Separatismus *m*. **'sep·a·ra·tist** *pol.* **I** *s* Separatist(in). **II** *adj* separatistisch.

Sep·tem·ber [sep'tembə] *s* September *m*: *in ~* im September.

se·quel ['siːkwəl] *s* **1.** Nachfolgefilm *m*, -roman *m*. **2.** *fig.* Folge *f* (*to* von *od. gen*); Nachspiel *n*.

se·quence ['siːkwəns] *s* **1.** (Aufeinander)Folge *f*: *the ~ of events* der Ablauf

der Ereignisse; *~ of tenses* Zeitenfolge. **2.** (Reihen)Folge *f*: *in ~* der Reihe nach. **3.** Folge *f*, Reihe *f*, Serie *f*: *~ of wins* Siegesserie. **4.** *Film, TV*: Sequenz *f*, Take *m*, *n*.

se·quoi·a [sɪ'kwɔɪə] *s* ♣ Mammutbaum *m*.

se·ra ['sɪərə] *pl von* **serum**.

ser·e·nade [,serə'neɪd] ♪ **I** *s* Serenade *f*; Ständchen *n*. **II** *v/t j-m* ein Ständchen bringen.

se·rene [sɪ'riːn] *adj* □ **1.** heiter, klar (*Himmel, Wetter etc*). **2.** heiter, gelassen (*Person, Gemüt etc*). **3.** *His* ♀ *Highness* S-e Durchlaucht. **se·ren·i·ty** [sɪ'renətɪ] *s* Heiterkeit *f*; Gelassenheit *f*.

serf [sɜːf] *s hist.* Leibeigene *m*, *f*.

ser·geant ['sɑːdʒənt] *s* **1.** ✕ Feldwebel *m*. **2.** Wachtmeister *m*.

se·ri·al ['sɪərɪəl] **I** *s* **1.** (Rundfunk-, Fernseh)Serie *f*; Fortsetzungsroman *m*. **II** *adj* □ **2.** Serien...: *~ novel* Fortsetzungsroman *m*. **3.** serienmäßig, Serien...: *~ number* Seriennummer *f*; ✝ Fabrikationsnummer *f*. **'se·ri·al·ize** *v/t* in Fortsetzungen veröffentlichen *od.* senden.

se·ries ['sɪəriːz] *pl* **-ries** *s* **1.** Serie *f*, Reihe *f*, Folge *f*. **2.** (Rundfunk-, Fernseh)Serie *f*, (Buch-, Vortrags- etc-)Reihe *f*.

se·ri·ous ['sɪərɪəs] *adj* **1.** ernst. **2.** ernsthaft (*Angebot etc a.*) seriös; (*Ratschlag etc*) ernstgemeint: *are you ~?* ist das dein Ernst?; meinst du das im Ernst?; *be ~ about doing s.th.* et. wirklich tun wollen. **3.** ernsthaft, ernstlich (*Schwierigkeiten*), schwer (*Krankheit, Schaden, Verbrechen etc*), schwer, ernstlich (*Bedenken*); ernstzunehmend (*Rivale etc*). **'se·ri·ous·ly** *adv* ernst(haft, -lich); im Ernst: *~ ill* ernstlich *od.* schwer krank; *take ~ j-n, et.* ernst nehmen. **'se·ri·ous·ness** *s* **1.** Ernst *m*. **2.** Ernsthaftigkeit *f*, Seriosität *f*. **3.** Schwere *f*.

ser·mon ['sɜːmən] *s* **1.** *eccl.* Predigt *f*. **2.** (Moral-, Straf)Predigt *f*. **'ser·mon·ize** *v/i* Moralpredigten halten.

ser·rat·ed [sɪ'reɪtɪd] *adj* gezackt.

se·rum ['sɪərəm] *pl* **-rums, -ra** ['~rə] *s* Serum *n*.

ser·vant ['sɜːvənt] *s* Diener(in) (*a. fig.*); Dienstbote *m*, -mädchen *n*: → **civil servant**.

serve [sɜːv] **I** v/t **1.** j-m, s-m *Land etc* dienen. **2.** j-n, *et.* versorgen (**with** mit). **3.** *a.* ~ **up** *Essen* servieren; *Alkohol* ausschenken: ~ **s.o.** (**with**) **s.th.** j-m et. servieren. **4.** j-n (*im Laden*) bedienen: *are you being ~d?* werden Sie schon bedient? **5.** *Amtszeit etc* durchlaufen; *Strafe* verbüßen. **6.** *e-m Zweck* dienen, *Zweck* erfüllen. **7.** ⚖ *Vorladung etc* zustellen (**on** s.o. j-m). **8.** ~ **s.o. right** F j-m (ganz) recht geschehen. **II** v/i **9.** bsd. ✕ dienen (**under** unter *dat*): ~ **on a committee** e-m Ausschuß angehören. **10.** servieren. **11.** dienen (**as, for** als): ~ **to do s.th.** dazu dienen, et. zu tun. **12.** *Tennis etc:* aufschlagen: *XY to* ~ Aufschlag XY. **III** s **13.** *Tennis etc:* Aufschlag m. **'ser·ver** s **1.** Servierlöffel m. (**pair of**) **salad** ~**s** pl Salatbesteck n. **2.** *eccl.* Meßdiener m, Ministrant m. **3.** *Tennis etc:* Aufschläger(in).

ser·vice ['sɜːvɪs] **I** s **1.** a) Dienst m (**to** a *dat*): *can I be of any* ~ *to you?* kann ich Ihnen irgendwie helfen?; *do s.o. a* ~ j-m e-n Dienst erweisen; *give good* ~ gute Dienste leisten, b) Dienstleistung f (*a.* ✝). **2.** *Service* m; Bedienung f. **3.** (*Post-, Staats-, Telefon- etc*)Dienst m: → *civil service, secret* 1. **4.** pl ✕ Streitkräfte pl. **5.** Betrieb m: *be out of* ~ außer Betrieb sein. **6.** *eccl.* Gottesdienst m. **7.** (*Kaffee- etc*)Service n. **8.** ⚙ Wartung f, *mot.* Inspektion f: *put one's car in for a* ~ s-n Wagen zur Inspektion bringen. **9.** ⚖ Zustellung f (*e-r Vorladung etc*). **10.** *Tennis etc:* Aufschlag m. **II** v/t **11.** ⚙ warten: *my car is being ~d* mein Wagen ist bei der Inspektion. **'ser·vice·a·ble** adj □ **1.** brauchbar. **2.** strapazierfähig.

ser·vice| **a·re·a** s Br. (Autobahn)Raststätte f. ~ **charge** s Bedienung(szuschlag m) f. ~**man** [‿mən] s (irr man) **1.** Militärangehörige m. **2.** Wartungstechniker m. ~ **sta·tion** s **1.** (Reparatur)Werkstatt f. **2.** Tankstelle f.

ser·vi·ette [‚sɜːvɪ'et] s bsd. Br. Serviette f.

ser·vile ['sɜːvaɪl] adj □ servil, unterwürfig; (*Gehorsam*) sklavisch. **ser·vil·i·ty** [‿'vɪlətɪ] s Servilität f, Unterwürfigkeit f.

serv·ing ['sɜːvɪŋ] s Portion f.

ser·vi·tude ['sɜːvɪtjuːd] s Knechtschaft f.

ses·a·me ['sesəmɪ] s ♀ Sesam m.

ses·sion ['seʃn] s **1.** ⚖, *parl.* a) Sitzung f: *be in* ~ tagen, b) Sitzungsperiode f. **2.** (*einzelne*) Sitzung, ⚖ *a.* (*einzelne*) Behandlung.

set [set] **I** s **1.** Satz m (*Briefmarken, Werkzeuge etc*), (*Möbel- etc*)Garnitur f, (*Tee- etc*)Service n. **2.** (*Fernseh-, Rundfunk*)Apparat m, (-)Gerät n. **3.** *thea.* Bühnenbild n: ~ **designer** Bühnenbildner(in). **4.** *Tennis etc:* Satz m: ~ **point** Satzball m. **4.** (Personen)Kreis m. **5.** (*Kopf- etc*)Haltung f. **II** adj **6.** festgesetzt, -gelegt: ~ **books** pl (*od. reading*) ped. Pflichtlektüre f; ~ **lunch** (*od. meal*) Br. Menü n. **8.** *be* ~ (*on doing s.th.*) (fest) entschlossen sein, et. zu tun; *be dead* ~ **against s.th.** strikt gegen et. sein. **9.** bereit, fertig: *be all* ~ startklar sein; *be all* ~ **for the journey** reisefertig sein. **10.** starr (*Ansichten, Lächeln etc*). **III** v/t (irr) **11.** stellen, setzen, legen: → *fire* 1, *music* 1, *trap* 1. **12.** *the novel is* ~ *in* der Roman spielt in (*dat*). **13.** *in e-n Zustand* versetzen: ~ **s.o. free** j-n auf freien Fuß setzen, j-n freilassen; → *right* 4, *etc.* **14.** veranlassen (*doing* zu tun): ~ *going* in Gang setzen; ~ **s.o. thinking** j-m zu denken geben; j-m e-n Denkanstoß od. Denkanstöße geben; → *ball*¹ 1. **15.** ⚙ einstellen; *Uhr* stellen (**by** nach); *Wecker* stellen (**for** auf acc). **16.** *Tisch* decken. **17.** *Preis, Termin etc* festsetzen, -legen; *Rekord* aufstellen; *Präzedenzfall* schaffen: → *example* 1. **18.** *Edelstein* fassen (**in** in *dat*); *Ring etc* besetzen (**with** mit). **19.** ⚙ *Knochen* einrichten. **20.** *Aufgabe, Frage* stellen. **IV** v/i (irr) **21.** untergehen (*Sonne etc*). **22.** fest werden (*Flüssiges*), (*Zement etc a.*) erstarren.

Verbindungen mit Präpositionen:

set| **a·bout** v/i **1.** sich machen an (acc), *et.* in Angriff nehmen: ~ **doing s.th.** sich daranmachen, et. zu tun. **2.** F herfallen über (acc). ~ **a·gainst** v/t **1.** set *one's face* (*od. o.s.*) *against s.th.* sich e-r Sache widersetzen; sich gegen. **2.** j-n aufhetzen gegen. **3.** *fig. et.* gegenüberstellen (*dat*): ~ im Vergleich zu. ~ **on** v/t *Hund, Polizei* hetzen auf (acc).

Verbindungen mit Adverbien:

set| **a·part** v/t j-n unterscheiden, abheben (**from** von). ~ **a·side** v/t **1.** *Geld* beiseite legen; *Zeit* reservieren, einplanen. **2.** *Plan etc* fallenlassen. **3.** ⚡ *Urteil etc* aufheben. **~ back** *v/t* **1.** verzögern; *j-n, et.* zurückwerfen (**by two months** um zwei Monate). **2. the car set me back £500** F der Wagen hat mich 500 Pfund gekostet *od.* um 500 Pfund ärmer gemacht. **~ by** → **set aside** 1. **~ down** *v/t* **1.** *Last* absetzen, abstellen, *Fahrgast* absetzen, aussteigen lassen. **2.** (schriftlich) niederlegen. **~ in** *v/i* einsetzen (*Winter etc*). **~ off I** *v/t* **1.** hervorheben, betonen, besser zur Geltung bringen. **2.** *Alarm, Lawine, Streik etc* auslösen. **3.** *Sprengladung* zur Explosion bringen; *Feuerwerk* abbrennen. **II** *v/i* **4.** → **set out** 3. **~ out I** *v/t* **1.** arrangieren, herrichten, *a. Schachfiguren etc* aufstellen. **2.** (schriftlich) darstellen. **II** *v/i* **3.** aufbrechen, sich aufmachen. **4. ~ to do s.th.** sich daranmachen, et. zu tun. **~ up I** *v/t* **1.** *Denkmal, Straßensperren etc* errichten; *Gerät etc* aufbauen. **2.** *Firma etc* gründen: → **shop** 1. **3.** et. auslösen, verursachen. **4.** *j-n* versorgen (**with** mit): **be well ~ with** (*od.* **for**) **reading** mit Lektüre eingedeckt sein. **5.** *Rekord* aufstellen. **6.** F in e-e Falle locken, reinlegen. **7. set o.s. up** → 9. **8. set o.s. up as** sich ausgeben für *od.* als; sich aufspielen als. **II** *v/i* **9.** sich niederlassen (**as** als).

'set·back *s* Rückschlag *m* (**to** für). **~ square** *s* Winkel *m*, Zeichendreieck *n*.

set·tee [se'tiː] *s* Sofa *n*.

set·ting ['setɪŋ] *s* **1.** (*Gold- etc*)Fassung *f*. **2.** Untergang *m* (*der Sonne etc*). **3.** Umgebung *f*; Schauplatz *m* (*e-s Films etc*): **the novel has its ~ in** → **set** 12.

set·tle ['setl] **I** *v/i* **1.** (**on**) sich niederlassen (auf *acc, dat*) *od.* setzen (auf *acc*). **2.** sich beruhigen (*Person, Magen etc*), sich legen (*Aufregung etc*): → **dust** 1. **3.** sich niederlassen (**in** in e-r *Stadt etc*). **4.** sich einigen. **5.** sich setzen (*Kaffee etc*); sich senken (*Boden etc*). **6. ~ for** sich zufriedengeben *od.* begnügen mit. **7. ~ into** sich eingewöhnen in (*dat*). **8. ~ on** sich einigen auf (*acc*). **II** *v/t* **9. ~ o.s.** → 1. **10.** *j-n, Nerven etc* beruhigen. **11.** vereinbaren, *Frage etc* klären, entscheiden: **that ~s it** damit ist der Fall erledigt. **12.** *Streit etc* beilegen. **13.** *Land* besiedeln; *Leute* ansiedeln. **14.** *Rechnung* begleichen, bezahlen; *Konto*

ausgleichen; *Schaden* regulieren: → **account** 5. **15.** *s-e Angelegenheiten* in Ordnung bringen.

Verbindungen mit Adverbien:

set·tle| back *v/i* sich (gemütlich) zurücklehnen. **~ down** *v/i* **1.** → **settle** 1, 2. **2.** seßhaft werden. **3. ~ in** → **settle** 7. **II** *v/t* **4.** → **settle** 10. **5. settle o.s. down** → **settle** 1. **~ in** *v/i* sich eingewöhnen; sich einleben. **~ up** *v/i* **1.** (be)zahlen. **2.** abrechnen (**with** mit) (*a. fig.*).

set·tled ['setld] *adj* **1.** beständig (*Wetter*). **2.** fest (*Ansichten etc*).

set·tle·ment ['setlmənt] *s* **1.** Vereinbarung *f*; Klärung *f*. **2.** Beilegung *f*. **3.** Einigung *f*: **reach a ~** sich einigen (**with** mit). **4.** Siedlung *f*; Besiedlung *f*. **5.** Begleichung *f*, Bezahlung *f*; Ausgleich *m*; Regulierung *f*.

set·tler ['setlə] *s* Siedler(in).

'set·up *s* **1.** Aufbau *m*, Organisation *f*. **2.** Zustände *pl.* **3.** F abgekartete Sache; Falle *f*.

sev·en ['sevn] **I** *adj* sieben. **II** *s* Sieben *f*: **~ of hearts** Herzsieben. **sev·en·fold** ['~fəʊld] **I** *adj* siebenfach. **II** *adv* siebenfach, um das Siebenfache: **increase ~** (sich) versiebenfachen. **sev·en·teen** [ˌ~'tiːn] *adj* siebzehn. **ˌsev·en'teenth** [~θ] *adj* siebzehnt. **sev·enth** ['sevnθ] **I** *adj* **1.** siebente(r, -s), siebte(r, -s). **II** *s* **2.** der, die, das Sieb(en)te: **the ~ of May** der 7. Mai. **3.** Sieb(en)tel *n*. **'sev·enth·ly** *adv* sieb(en)tens. **sev·en·ti·eth** ['~tɪə] *adj* siebzigst.

'sev·en·time *adj* siebenfach.

sev·en·ty ['sevntɪ] **I** *adj* siebzig. **II** *s* Siebzig *f*: **be in one's seventies** in den Siebzigern sein; **in the seventies** in den siebziger Jahren (*e-s Jahrhunderts*).

sev·er ['sevə] **I** *v/t* **1.** durchtrennen; abtrennen (**from** von). **2.** *Beziehungen etc* abbrechen. **II** *v/i* **3.** (zer)reißen.

sev·er·al ['sevrəl] **I** *adj* mehrere. **II** *s* mehrere *pl*: **~** mehrere.

sev·er·ance ['sevərəns] *s* **1.** Durch-, Abtrennung *f*. **2.** *fig.* Abbruch *m*. **~ pay** *s* † Abfindung *f*.

se·vere [sɪ'vɪə] *adj* □ **1.** schwer (*Verletzung, Rückschlag etc*), stark (*Schmerzen*), hart, streng (*Winter*). **2.** streng (*Person, Disziplin etc*). **3.** scharf (*Kritik*): **his ~st critic** *a.* sein ärgster Kritiker. **se·ver·i·ty** [sɪ'verətɪ] *s* **1.** Schwere

f, Stärke *f*, Härte *f*, Strenge *f*. **2.** Schärfe
f.

sew [səʊ] *(mst irr)* **I** *v/t* nähen: ~ **on**
annähen; ~ **up** ver-, zunähen; F *Handel
etc* perfekt machen. **II** *v/i* nähen.

sew·age ['suːɪdʒ] *s* Abwasser *m*.

sew·er [sʊə] *s* Abwasserkanal *m*, Kloake *f*. **'sew·er·age** *s* Kanalisation *f*.

sew·ing ['səʊɪŋ] **I** *s* **1.** Nähen *n*. **2.** Näh-
arbeit *f*, Näherei *f*. **II** *adj* **3.** Näh...: ~
machine.

sewn [səʊn] *pp von* **sew.**

sex [seks] **I** *s* **1.** Geschlecht *n*: **of both** ~**es**
beiderlei Geschlechts; **the fair** (**gentle**
od. **weaker, opposite, stronger**) ~ das
schöne (schwache *od.* zarte, andere,
starke) Geschlecht. **2.** Sex *m*: a) Sexualität *f*, b) Sex-Appeal *m*, c) Geschlechtsverkehr *m*: **have** ~ **with** schlafen mit. **II** *adj* **3.** a) Sexual...: ~ **crime**
(**life**, *etc*); ~ **object** Sexual-, Lustobjekt
n, b) Geschlechts...: ~ **organ**, *etc*, c)
Sex...: ~ **bomb** (**film**, *etc*); ~ **appeal**
Sex-Appeal *m*.

sex·ism ['seksɪzəm] *s* Sexismus *m*.
'sex·ist I *s* Sexist(in). **II** *adj* sexistisch.
sex·tet(te) [seks'tet] *s* ♪ Sextett *n*.
sex·ton ['sekstən] *s eccl.* Küster *m* (u.
Totengräber *m*).

sex·u·al ['sekʃʊəl] *adj* □ sexuell, Sexual-
al..., geschlechtlich, Geschlechts...: ~
intercourse Geschlechtsverkehr *m*.
sex·u·al·i·ty [ˌ~'ælətɪ] *s* Sexualität *f*.

sex·y ['seksɪ] *adj* □ F sexy, (*a. Gang etc*)
aufreizend.

shab·by ['ʃæbɪ] *adj* □ *allg.* schäbig.

shack [ʃæk] **I** *s* Hütte *f*, Baracke *f*. **II** *v/i*:
~ **up** F zs.-leben (**with** mit).

shack·les ['ʃæklz] *s pl* Fesseln *pl*, Ketten
pl (*beide a. fig.*).

shade [ʃeɪd] **I** *s* **1.** Schatten *m*: **put in**(**to**)
the ~ *fig.* in den Schatten stellen. **2.**
(*Lampen*)Schirm *m*. **3.** *pl*, *a.* **pair of** ~**s** F
Sonnenbrille *f*. **4.** (Farb)Ton *m*. **5.** *fig.*
Nuance *f*. **6.** **a** ~ *fig.* ein kleines bißchen:
a ~ (**too**) **loud** e-e Spur zu laut. **II** *v/t* **7.**
abschirmen (**from** gegen *Licht etc*). **III**
v/i **8.** *a.* ~ **off** (allmählich) übergehen
(**into** in *acc*).

shad·ow ['ʃædəʊ] **I** *s* **1.** Schatten *m*: **be
in s.o.'s** ~ *fig.* in j-s Schatten stehen; **be
only a** ~ **of one's former self** *fig.* nur
noch ein Schatten s-r selbst sein; **cast a**

~ **over** (*od.* **on**) *fig.* e-n Schatten werfen
auf (*acc*). **2.** *fig.* Schatten *m* (*Person*):
there's not a (*od.* **the**) ~ **of doubt about
it** *fig.* daran besteht nicht der geringste
Zweifel. **II** *v/t* **4.** *j-n* beschatten. ~
cab·i·net *s pol.* Schattenkabinett *n*.

shad·ow·y ['ʃædəʊɪ] *adj* **1.** schattig, dunkel. **2.** *fig.* geheimnisvoll, -umwittert.

shad·y ['ʃeɪdɪ] *adj* **1.** schattig; schatten-
spendend. **2.** F zwielichtig (*Person*),
zweifelhaft (*Geschäft etc*).

shaft [ʃɑːft] *s* **1.** (*Pfeil- etc*)Schaft *m*. **2.**
(*Hammer- etc*)Stiel *m*. **3.** (*Aufzugs-,
Bergwerks- etc*)Schacht *m*.

shag·gy ['ʃægɪ] *adj* □ zottig, zott(e)lig.

shake [ʃeɪk] **I** *s* **1.** Schütteln *n*: **with a** ~ **of
one's head** mit e-m Kopfschütteln;
give s.th. a good ~ et. gut durchschütteln; **in two** ~**s**, **in half a** ~ F sofort. **2.**
Shake *m*, Mixgetränk *n*. **3.** **he's got the**
~**s** F er hat den *od.* e-n Tatterich. **4.** **be
no great** ~**s** F nicht gerade unverwerf
sein (**at** in *dat*; **as** als). **II** *v/i* (*irr*) **5.**
wackeln; zittern (**with** vor *dat*): ~ **with
laughter** sich vor Lachen schütteln. **6.**
let's ~ **on it** F Hand drauf! **III** *v/t* (*irr*) **7.**
schütteln: ~ **one's head** den Kopf
schütteln; ~ **one's fist at s.o.** j-m mit
der Faust drohen; ~ **a leg** F Dampf *od.*
Tempo machen; → **hand** 1. **8.** *fig.* a) *j-n*
erschüttern: **he was badly** ~**n by the
accident** der Unfall hat ihn arg mitgenommen, b) *j-s Glauben etc* erschüttern.

Verbindungen mit Adverbien:

shake| **down** F **I** *v/i* **1.** sich eingewöh-
nen *od.* einleben. **2.** kampieren (**on the
floor** auf dem Fußboden). **II** *v/t* **3.** *bsd.
Am. j-n* ausnehmen *od.* erpressen. **4.**
Am. j-n filzen, durchsuchen (**for** nach).
~ **off** *v/t* Staub, Verfolger *etc* abschütteln, *Besucher, Erkältung etc* loswer-
den. ~ **out** *v/t* ausschütteln. ~ **up** *v/t* **1.**
Kissen etc aufschütteln. **2.** *Flasche etc*
durchschütteln. **3.** → **shake** 8a.

'shake·down *s* F **1.** (Not)Lager *n*. **2.** *bsd.
Am.* Gaunerei *f*; Erpressung *f*. **3.** *Am.*
Filzung *f*, Durchsuchung *f*.

shak·en ['ʃeɪkən] *pp von* **shake. 'shak·er**
s Shaker *m*, Mixbecher *m*; *Am.* (*Salz-*)
Streuer *m*.

'shake·up *s*: **there's been a big** ~ **in our
firm** F in unserer Firma ist kräftig aufgeräumt worden.

shak·y ['ʃeɪkɪ] *adj* □ wack(e)lig (*Person, Stuhl etc*).

shale [ʃeɪl] *s geol*. Schiefer *m*.

shall [ʃæl] *v/aux* (*irr*) **1.** *Futur: ich werde, wir werden.* **2.** *in (Entscheidungs)Fragen:* soll *ich ...?,* sollen *wir ...?:* **~ we go?** gehen wir?

shal·low ['ʃæləʊ] **I** *adj* □ seicht, flach (*beide a. fig.*). **II** *s, oft pl* seichte *od.* flache Stelle, Untiefe *f*.

sham [ʃæm] **I** *s* **1.** Farce *f*. **2.** Heuchelei *f*. **II** *adj* **3.** unecht, falsch (*Juwelen etc*), vorgetäuscht, geheuchelt (*Mitgefühl etc*). **III** *v/t* **4.** Mitgefühl *etc* vortäuschen, heucheln; *Krankheit etc* simulieren. **IV** *v/i* **5.** sich verstellen, heucheln: *he's only ~ming* er tut nur so.

sham·bles ['ʃæmblz] *s pl* (*mst sg konstruiert*): *the room was* (*in*) *a ~* F das Zimmer war das reinste Schlachtfeld.

shame [ʃeɪm] **I** *s* **1.** Scham(gefühl *n*) *f*: *have you got no ~?* schämst du dich vor gar nichts? **2.** Schande *f*: *~!* pfui!; *~ on you!* schäm dich!; pfui!; *put to ~* → 4, 5. **3.** *what a ~!* (wie) schade!; *it's a ~* (es ist) schade; → *crying*. **II** *v/t* **4.** Schande machen (*dat*). **5.** beschämen. **,~·faced** *adj* □ betreten, verlegen.

shame·ful ['ʃeɪmfʊl] *adj* □ **1.** beschämend. **2.** schändlich. **'shame·less** *adj* □ **1.** schamlos. **2.** unverschämt.

sham·poo [ʃæm'puː] **I** *s* Shampoo(n) *n*, Schampon *n*, Schampun *n* (*alle a. für Teppiche etc*), Haarwaschmittel *n*. **II** *v/t* Teppich *etc* shampoonieren, schamponieren, schampunieren: *~ one's hair* sich den Kopf *od.* die Haare waschen.

sham·rock ['ʃæmrɒk] *s* Shamrock *m*, Kleeblatt *n* (*Wahrzeichen Irlands*).

shan·dy ['ʃændɪ] *s* Bier *n* mit Zitronenlimonade.

shang·hai [,ʃæŋ'haɪ] *v/t*: *~ s.o. into doing s.th.* F j-n zwingen *od.* mit e-m Trick dazu bringen, et. zu tun.

shank [ʃæŋk] *s* **1.** ☉ Schaft *m* (*e-s Bohrers etc*). **2.** Hachse *f* (*beim Schlachttier*).

shan't [ʃɑːnt] F *für* **shall not**.

shan·ty¹ ['ʃæntɪ] *s* Hütte *f*, Baracke *f*.

shan·ty² [ˏˏ] *s* Shanty *n*, Seemannslied *n*. **'shan·ty·town** *s* Bidonville *n* (*Slumviertel*).

shape [ʃeɪp] **I** *s* **1.** Form *f*: *in the ~ of* in Form (*gen*) (*a. fig.*); *triangular in ~*

dreieckig; *take ~ fig.* Gestalt annehmen. **2.** Gestalt *f* (*Person*). **3.** *be in good* (*bad*) *~* (*körperlich, geistig*) in guter (schlechter) Verfassung sein; in gutem (schlechtem) Zustand sein (*Gebäude etc*). **II** *v/t* **3.** Ton *etc* formen (*into* zu); *et.* formen (*from* aus); *fig. j-n, j-s Charakter etc* formen, prägen: *~d like a ... ...*förmig. **III** *v/i* **4.** *mst ~ up* F sich gut *etc* machen (*Person*): *things are shaping up nicely* es sieht nicht schlecht aus. **shaped** *adj* geformt, ...förmig. **'shape·less** *adj* □ **1.** weit; ausgebeult (*Kleidungsstück*). **2.** unförmig (*Person, Gegenstand*). **'shape·ly** *adj* wohlgeformt (*Beine etc*), wohlproportioniert (*Figur*).

shard [ʃɑːd] *s* Scherbe *f*.

share [ʃeə] **I** *s* **1.** Anteil *m* (*in, of* an *dat*): *go ~s* F teilen; *have a* (*no*) *~ in* (nicht) beteiligt sein an (*dat*). **2.** ✝ Aktie *f*. **II** *v/t* **3.** teilen (*a. fig.*), sich *et.* teilen (*with* mit): *we ~ an apartment* (*bsd. Br. a flat*) wir leben in e-r Wohngemeinschaft; *they ~d second place* sie kamen gemeinsam auf den zweiten Platz. **4.** *mst ~ out* verteilen (*among, between* an *acc*, unter *acc*). **III** *v/i* **5.** teilen: *~ in* sich teilen in (*acc*). **shared** *adj* gemeinsam, Gemeinschafts...

'share¦,hold·er *s* ✝ *bsd. Br.* Aktionär(in). **'~·out** *s* Verteilung *f*.

shark [ʃɑːk] *s* **1.** *ichth.* Hai(fisch) *m*. **2.** F (*Kredit- etc*)Hai *m*.

sharp [ʃɑːp] **I** *adj* □ **1.** scharf (*Messer etc, a. Gesichtszüge, Kurve etc*); spitz (*Nadel, Nase etc*). **2.** *fig.* scharf: a) deutlich (*Gegensatz, Umrisse etc*), b) herb (*Geschmack etc*), c) schneidend (*Befehl, Stimme etc*), d) heftig (*Schmerz etc*), (*a. Frost, Wind*) schneidend, e) spitz (*Bemerkung, Zunge*), f) schnell (*Tempo etc*), g) jäh, plötzlich: *brake ~ly* scharf bremsen. **3.** *fig.* scharf (*Augen, Verstand etc*); scharfsinnig, gescheit (*Person*). **4.** *~ practice* unsaubere Geschäfte *pl*. **II** *adv* **5.** *at three o'clock* ~ Punkt 3 (Uhr). **6.** ♪ zu hoch: *sing* ~. **7.** *look* ~ F sich beeilen: *look* ~! Tempo! **sharp·en** ['ʃɑːpn] *v/t* **1.** *Messer etc* schärfen, schleifen. **2.** *Bleistift etc* spitzen. **'sharp·en·er** *s* (*Bleistift*)Spitzer *m*. **'sharp·ness** *s* **1.** Schärfe *f* (*a. fig.*). **2.** *fig.* Scharfsinn *m*.

'**sharp,shoot·er** *s* Scharfschütze *m*.

shat [ʃæt] *pret u. pp von* **shit**.

shat·ter ['ʃætə] **I** *v/t* **1.** zerschmettern, -schlagen, -trümmern. **2.** *fig.* Hoffnungen, Träume *etc* zerstören. **3.** F *j-n* schocken. **4.** F *j-n* schlauchen. **II** *v/i* **3.** zerspringen, (*Glas a.*) zersplittern. '**~proof** *adj* splitterfrei, -sicher.

shave [ʃeɪv] **I** *v/i* **1.** sich rasieren. **II** *v/t* **2.** *j-n* rasieren. **3.** sich *die Beine etc* rasieren: *~ off* sich *den Bart* abrasieren; *Holz* abhobeln. **4.** *j-n, et.* streifen. **III** *s* Rasur *f*: **have a ~ → 1**; *that was a close ~* das war knapp, das hätte ins Auge gehen können. '**shav·en** *adj* kahlgeschoren. '**shav·er** *s* (*bsd. elektrischer*) Rasierapparat. '**shav·ing** *s* **1.** Rasieren *n*. **2.** *pl* Späne *pl*. **3.** Rasier...: *~ brush* Rasierpinsel *m*; *~ cream* Rasiercreme *f*; *~ foam* Rasierschaum *m*; *~ soap* Rasierseife *f*.

shawl [ʃɔːl] *s* **1.** Umhängetuch *n*. **2.** Kopftuch *n*.

she [ʃiː] **I** *pron* sie. **II** *s* Sie *f*: a) Mädchen *n*, Frau *f*, b) *zo.* Weibchen *n*. **III** *adj in Zssgn zo.* ...weibchen *n*: *~bear* Bärin *f*.

sheaf [ʃiːf] *pl* **sheaves** [ʃiːvz] *s* **1.** 🌾 Garbe *f*. **2.** (*Papier- etc*)Bündel *n*.

shear [ʃɪə] **I** *v/t* (*mst irr*) *Schaf* scheren. **II** *s pl, a.* **pair of ~s** (*große*) Schere.

sheath [ʃiːθ] *pl* **sheaths** [ʃiːðz] *s* **1.** (*Schwert- etc*)Scheide *f*. Kondom *n, m*. **3.** → **sheathing**. **sheathe** [ʃiːð] *v/t* **1.** *Schwert etc* in die Scheide stecken. **2.** ⊙ umhüllen, verkleiden, *Kabel, Rohr* ummanteln. '**sheath·ing** *s* ⊙ Umhüllung *f*, Verkleidung *f*, Mantel *m*.

sheath knife *s* (*irr* **knife**) Fahrtenmesser *n*.

sheaves [ʃiːvz] *pl von* **sheaf**.

she-bang [ʃɪ'bæŋ] *s*: *the whole ~ bsd. Am.* F der ganze Laden; die ganze Chose.

shed[1] [ʃed] *v/t* (*irr*) **1.** *Blut, Tränen etc* vergießen. **2.** → **light**[1] 1. **3.** *biol. Blätter etc* verlieren, *a. Geweih* abwerfen: *its skin* sich häuten; *a few pounds* ein paar Pfund abnehmen. **4.** *fig. Gewohnheit, Hemmungen etc* ablegen.

shed[2] [~] *s* (*Geräte etc*)Schuppen *m*; (*Kuh- etc*)Stall *m*.

she'd [ʃiːd] F *für* **she had**; **she would**.

sheen [ʃiːn] *s* Glanz *m*.

sheep [ʃiːp] *pl* **sheep** *s zo.* Schaf *n* (*a. fig. Person*): *make ~'s eyes at s.o.* j-n anschmachten. '**~dog** *s* Schäferhund *m*.

sheep·ish ['ʃiːpɪʃ] *adj* □ verlegen.

'**sheep·skin** *s* Schaffell *n*.

sheer [ʃɪə] **I** *adj* **1.** bloß, rein: *by ~ coincidence* rein zufällig. **2.** steil, (fast) senkrecht. **3.** hauchdünn (*Stoff*). **II** *adv* **1.** → 2.

sheet [ʃiːt] *s* **1.** Bettuch *n*, (Bett)Laken *n*, Leintuch *n*: (*as*) *white as a ~* kreidebleich. **2.** Bogen *m*, Blatt *n* (*Papier*). **3.** (*Glas*)Scheibe *f*. **4.** *the rain was coming down in ~s* es regnete in Strömen. **5.** weite (*Eis- etc*)Fläche *f*. *~ light·ning* *s* Wetterleuchten *n*. *~ mu·sic* *s* Notenblätter *pl*.

sheik(h) [ʃeɪk] *s* Scheich *m*. '**sheik(h)·dom** *s* Scheichtum *n*.

shelf [ʃelf] *pl* **shelves** [ʃelvz] *s* (*Bücheretc*)Brett *n*, (-)Bord *n*: **shelves** *pl* Regal *n*; *she has been left on the ~ fig.* F sie ist sitzengeblieben. *~ life* *s* ✝ Haltbarkeit *f*.

shell [ʃel] **I** *s* **1.** (*Austern-, Eier- etc*)Schale *f*, (*Erbsen- etc*)Hülse *f*, Muschel(schale) *f*, (*Schnecken*)Haus *n*, (*Schildkröten- etc*)Panzer *m*: *come out of one's ~ fig.* aus sich herausgehen. **2.** ✕ Granate *f*. **3.** ✈, ⚓ Rumpf *m*. **4.** Rohbau *m*; Gemäuer *n*, Außenmauern *pl*. **II** *v/t* **5.** schälen, enthülsen. **6.** ✕ mit Granaten beschießen. **7.** (*a. v/i*) *~ out* blechen.

she'll [ʃiːl] F *für* **she will**.

'**shell·fish** *pl* **-fish** *s zo.* Schal(en)tier *n*.

shel·ter ['ʃeltə] **I** *s* **1.** Unterstand *m*; ✕ Bunker *m*; Wartehäuschen *n* (*an Bushaltestelle etc*); (*Obdachlosen- etc*)Unterkunft *f*: → **air-raid**. **2.** Schutz *m*; Unterkunft *f*: **provide** *od.* **give ~ for** Schutz *od.* gewähren (*dat*); **run for ~** Schutz suchen; **take ~** sich unterstellen (*under unter dat*). **II** *v/t* **3.** schützen (*from vor dat*): *a ~ed life* ein behütetes Leben. **III** *v/i* **4.** sich unterstellen.

shelve [ʃelv] *v/t* **1.** *Bücher* (in ein Regal) einstellen. **2.** *fig. Plan etc* aufschieben, zurückstellen.

shelves [ʃelvz] *pl von* **shelf**.

shelv·ing ['ʃelvɪŋ] *s* Regale *pl*.

she-nan·i·gans [ʃɪ'nænɪgənz] *s pl* F Blödsinn *m*, Unfug *m*.

shep·herd ['ʃepəd] I s Schäfer m. II v/t j-n führen.

sher·bet ['ʃɜːbət] s 1. Brausepulver n. 2. bsd. Am. → **sorbet** 1.

sher·iff ['ʃerɪf] s Sheriff m.

sher·ry ['ʃerɪ] s Sherry m.

shield [ʃiːld] I s Schild m. II v/t j-n schützen (**from** vor dat); b.s. j-n decken.

shift [ʃɪft] I v/i 1. sich bewegen: ~ **on one's chair** (ungeduldig etc) auf s-m Stuhl hin u. her rutschen. 2. umspringen (Wind). 3. fig. sich verlagern od. verschieben od. wandeln. 4. F rasen. 5. → **gear** 1. II v/t 6. et. bewegen, schieben, Möbelstück a. (ver)rücken. 7. Schuld, Verantwortung (ab)schieben, abwälzen (**onto** auf acc). 8. Fleck etc entfernen; et. loswerden. 9. → **gear** 1. III s 10. fig. Verlagerung f, Verschiebung f, Wandel m. 11. ♀ Schicht f (Zeit u. Arbeiter). ~ **key** s Umschalttaste f (e-r Schreibmaschine). ~ **work·er** s Schichtarbeiter(in).

shift·y ['ʃɪftɪ] adj □ verschlagen (Blick etc); zwielichtig (Charakter).

shil·ling ['ʃɪlɪŋ] s Br. hist. Schilling m.

shil·ly-shal·ly ['ʃɪlɪˌʃælɪ] v/i F sich nicht entscheiden können.

shim·mer ['ʃɪmə] I v/i schimmern; (Luft) flimmern. II s Schimmer m; Flimmern n.

shin [ʃɪn] s anat. Schienbein n. II v/i: ~ **up** (**down**) Baum etc hinauf-(herunter)klettern. '**~bone** → **shin** 1.

shine [ʃaɪn] I v/i (irr) 1. scheinen (Sonne etc), leuchten (Lampe etc). 2. glänzen (**with** vor dat; fig. **at** in dat). II v/t (irr) 3. pret u. pp **shined** Schuhe etc polieren. 4. ~ **a torch** (bsd. Am. **flashlight**) **into** mit e-r Taschenlampe leuchten in (acc). III s 5. Glanz m: **give one's shoes a** ~ s-e Schuhe polieren; **take a** ~ **to s.o.** F j-n sofort mögen.

shin·gle¹ ['ʃɪŋgl] I s (Dach)Schindel f. II v/t mit Schindeln decken.

shin·gle² [~] s grobe Kieselsteine: ~ **beach** Kieselstrand m.

shin·gles ['ʃɪŋglz] s pl (sg konstruiert) ♀ Gürtelrose f.

shin·gly ['ʃɪŋglɪ] adj kieselig: ~ **beach** Kieselstrand m.

shin·y ['ʃaɪnɪ] adj glänzend, (Ärmel etc a.) abgewetzt, blank.

ship [ʃɪp] I s (a. Raum)Schiff n: **when my** ~ **comes home** (od. **in**) fig. wenn ich das große Los ziehe. II v/t verschiffen; allg. verfrachten, -senden: '~**board** s: **on** ~ an Bord. '~**build·er** s Schiff(s)bauer m.

ship·ment s 1. Ladung f. 2. Verschiffung f; allg. Verfrachtung f, Versand m.

'**ship,own·er** s Reeder m, (bsd. Binnenschiffahrt a.) Schiffseigner m.

ship·per ['ʃɪpə] s Spediteur m. '**ship·ping** s 1. → **shipment** 2. 2. a) Schiffahrt f: ~ **forecast** Seewetterbericht m, b) coll. Schiffsbestand m (e-s Landes).

'**ship·shape** adj tadellos in Ordnung. '~**wreck** I s a) Schiffbruch m: **in a** ~ bei e-m Schiffbruch; **suffer** ~ Schiffbruch erleiden (a. fig.), b) Wrack n. II v/t: **be** ~**ed** Schiffbruch erleiden; ~**ed** schiffbrüchig. '~**yard** s (Schiffs)Werft f.

shirk [ʃɜːk] v/i u. v/t sich drücken (vor dat). '**shirk·er** s Drückeberger(in).

shirt [ʃɜːt] s Hemd n: **keep one's** ~ **on** F sich nicht aufregen; → **bet** 4. '~**sleeve** I adj hemdsärmelig. II s pl: **in one's** ~**s** in Hemdsärmeln, hemdsärmelig.

shirt·y ['ʃɜːtɪ] adj F: **get** ~ **with s.o.** j-n anschnauzen; **there's no need to get** ~ du mußt mich nicht gleich anschnauzen.

shit [ʃɪt] I s 1. V Scheiße f: **be in the** ~ fig. in der Scheiße sitzen. 2. **have** (**go for**) **a** ~ V scheißen (gehen). 3. **he's got the** ~**s** V er hat Dünnschiß od. die Scheißerei. 4. fig. V Scheiß m: **talk** ~ Scheiß reden. 5. fig. V Arschloch n. 6. sl. Shit n (Haschisch). II v/i (mst irr) 7. V scheißen. III v/t (mst irr) 8. V vollscheißen, scheißen in (acc): ~ **o.s.** sich vollscheißen; fig. sich vor Angst fast in die Hosen scheißen.

shiv·er ['ʃɪvə] I v/i zittern (**with** vor dat). II s Schauer m: **the sight sent** ~**s** (**up and**) **down my spine** bei dem Anblick überlief es mich eiskalt; **he's got the** ~**s** er hat Schüttelfrost; **spiders give me the** ~**s** F ich hab' e-n Horror vor Spinnen.

shoal¹ [ʃəʊl] s Schwarm m (Fische): ~**s pl of** Schwärme pl von (Touristen etc).

shoal² [~] s Untiefe f; Sandbank f.

shock¹ [ʃɒk] I s 1. Wucht f (e-r Explosion, e-s Schlags etc). 2. Schock m (a. ♀): **be in a state of** (od. **suffer from**) ~ unter Schock stehen; **come as** (od. **be**) **a** ~ **to**

s.o. ein Schock für j-n sein. **3.** ⚡ Schlag *m*, (*a.* ⚡ Elektro)Schock *m.* **II** *v/t* **4.** schockieren, empören. **5.** *j-m* e-n Schock versetzen: *be ~ed at* (*od. by*) erschüttert sein über (*acc*).

shock² [~] *s* (*~ of hair* Haar)Schopf *m.*

shock ab·sorb·er *s mot.* Stoßdämpfer *m.*

shock·er ['ʃɒkə] *s* F Schocker *m* (*Film, Person etc*). **'shock·ing** *adj* □ **1.** schockierend, anstößig. **2.** erschütternd. **3.** F scheußlich.

'shock·proof *adj* stoßfest, -sicher. **~ ther·a·py, ~ treat·ment** *s* ⚕ Schocktherapie *f.* **-behandlung** *f.* **~ wave** *s* Druckwelle *f*; *send ~s through fig.* erschüttern.

shod [ʃɒd] *pret u. pp von* **shoe.**

shod·dy ['ʃɒdɪ] *adj* □ **1.** minderwertig (*Ware*), schlampig (*Arbeit*). **2.** gemein, schäbig (*Trick etc*).

shoe [ʃuː] **I** *s* **1.** Schuh *m*: *be in s.o.'s ~s fig.* in j-s Haut stecken; *know where the ~ pinches fig.* wissen, wo der Schuh drückt; *step into* (*od. fill*) *s.o.'s ~s fig.* j-s Stelle einnehmen. **2.** (Huf)Eisen *n.* **II** *v/t* (*mst irr*) **3.** Pferd beschlagen. **'~·black** *s* Schuhputzer *m.* **'~·box** *s* Schuhkarton *m*, -schachtel *f.* **'~·horn** *s* Schuhlöffel *m.* **'~·lace** *s* Schnürsenkel *m.* **'~·mak·er** *s* Schuhmacher *m*, Schuster *m.* **'~·string** *s* Schnürsenkel *m*: *start on a ~ fig.* praktisch mit nichts anfangen. **'~·tree** *s* Schuhspanner *m.*

shone [ʃɒn] *pret u. pp von* **shine.**

shoo [ʃuː] *v/t* j-n, *Vögel etc* (ver)scheuchen.

shook [ʃʊk] *pret von* **shake.**

shoot [ʃuːt] **I** *s* **1.** Trieb *m.* **2.** Jagd *f*; Jagd(revier *n*) *f.* **II** *v/t* (*irr*) **3.** schießen mit (*e-m Gewehr etc*). **4.** *Pfeil etc* abfeuern, abschießen: *shoot a glance at* e-n schnellen Blick werfen auf (*acc*); *~ questions at s.o.* j-n mit Fragen bombardieren; → *bolt¹* 1. **5.** a) *hunt.* schießen, erlegen: → *the bull Am.* F plaudern, plauschen, b) anschießen, c) niederschießen etc) d. a. *~ dead* erschießen: *~ o.s.* sich erschießen. **6.** *Riegel* vorschieben. **7.** *Film etc* drehen, a. *phot. j-n* aufnehmen. **8.** → *light¹* 3. **III** *v/i* (*irr*) **9.** schießen (*at* auf *acc*): *~ at goal* (*Sport*) aufs Tor schießen. **10.** *go somewhere to ~* wohin auf die Jagd

gehen. **11.** schießen, rasen. **12.** drehen, filmen. **13.** ♀ treiben.

Verbindungen mit Adverbien:

shoot down *v/t* **1.** *j-n* niederschießen. **2.** *j-n, Flugzeug etc* abschießen. **3.** F *Antrag etc* abschmettern, *j-n a.* abfahren lassen. **~ off** *v/t Waffe* abfeuern, -schießen: *~ one's mouth* F quatschen (*Geheimnisse verraten*); blöd daherreden. **~ out** *v/t: shoot it out* sich e-e Schießerei liefern (*with* mit). **~ up** *v/i* in die Höhe schießen (*Flammen, Kind etc*), in die Höhe schnellen (*Preise*).

shoot·er ['ʃuːtə] *s bsd. Br. sl.* Schießeisen *n.*

shoot·ing ['ʃuːtɪŋ] **I** *s* **1.** Schießen *n*; Schießerei *f.* **2.** Erschießung *f*; Erschlag *m.* **3.** *Film, TV:* Dreharbeiten *pl*, Aufnahmen *pl.* **II** *adj* **4.** stechend (*Schmerz*). **~ gal·ler·y** *s* Schießbude *f.* **~ match** *s: the whole ~* F die ganze Chose. **~ range** *s* Schießstand *m.* **~ star** *s ast.* Sternschnuppe *f.*

shop [ʃɒp] **I** *s* **1.** Laden *m*, Geschäft *n*: *set up ~ as* F sich niederlassen als; *shut up ~* F (den Laden) dichtmachen. **2.** Werkstatt *f.* **3.** Betrieb *m*, Werk *n*: *talk ~* fachsimpeln; → *closed* (*open*) *shop.* **II** *v/i* **4.** *go ~ping* einkaufen gehen; *~ around* sich informieren, die Preise vergleichen; *~ for* sich umsehen nach. **III** *v/t* **5.** *bsd. Br. sl.* j-n verpfeifen. **~ as·sist·ant** *s Br.* Verkäufer(in). **~ floor** *s* Arbeiter *pl* (*Ggs. Management*). **'~keep·er** *s* Ladenbesitzer(in), -inhaber(in). **'~·lift·er** *s* Ladendieb(in). **'~·lift·ing** *s* Ladendiebstahl *m.*

shop·per ['ʃɒpə] *s* Käufer(in). **'shop·ping** *s* **1.** Einkaufen *n*: *do one's ~* einkaufen, (s-e) Einkäufe machen. **2.** Einkäufe *pl* (*Sachen*). **II** *adj* **3.** Einkaufs...: *~ bag* Einkaufsbeutel *m*, -tasche *f*; *~ center* (*bsd. Br. centre*) *s* Einkaufszentrum *n*; *~ list* Einkaufsliste *f*, -zettel *m*; *~ mall Am.* Einkaufszentrum *n*; *~ street* Geschäfts-, Ladenstraße *f*; → *spree.*

shop·'soiled *adj bsd. Br. Ware:* angestaubt (*a. fig. Ansichten etc*); angestoßen. **~ stew·ard** *s* ⚑ gewerkschaftlicher Vertrauensmann. **'~·talk** *s* Fachsimpelei *f.* **'~ win·dow** *s* Schaufenster *n*, Auslage *f.* **'~·worn** *Am.* → **shop-soiled.**

shore¹ [ʃɔː] s Küste f; (See)Ufer n: **on ~ ⚓ an Land**; **~ leave ⚓** Landurlaub m.

shore² [~] **I** s Stützbalken m, Strebe(balken m) f. **II** v/t mst **~ up** (ab)stützen; fig. Währung etc stützen.

shorn [ʃɔːn] pp von **shear**.

short [ʃɔːt] **I** adj (□ → **shortly**) **1.** räumlich, zeitlich: kurz: **a ~ time ago** vor kurzer Zeit, vor kurzem; **~ and sweet** F kurz u. bündig; **~ holiday** (bsd. Am. **vacation**) Kurzurlaub m; **~ story** Short story f, Kurzgeschichte f; Novelle f; **be ~ for** die Kurzform sein von; **cut ~** Urlaub etc abbrechen; → **notice 3, run 1, shrift, story 1, work 1. 2.** klein (Person). **3. be ~ of** nicht genügend ... haben; **be in ~ supply** ꜛ knapp sein; → **cash 2, money. 4.** barsch (**with** zu), kurz angebunden. **II** adv **5.** plötzlich, abrupt: **be caught** (od. **taken**) **~** bsd. Br. F dringend mal (verschwinden) müssen; **stop ~ of** (od. **at**) zurückschrecken vor (dat); **stop ~ of doing s.th.** davor zurückschrecken, et. zu tun. **6. fall ~ of** et. nicht erreichen, **den Anforderungen** etc nicht entsprechen; **run ~** knapp werden, zur Neige gehen; **we are running ~ of bread** uns geht das Brot aus. **sell ~** ↓ j-n, et. unterschätzen. **7. ~ of** a) räumlich vor (dat): **three miles ~ of London**, b) fig. außer (dat). **III** s **8. he is called Bill for ~** er wird kurz Bill genannt; **in ~** kurz(um). **9.** pl, a. **pair of ~s** Shorts pl; bsd. Am. (Herren)Unterhose f. **10.** Br. F Kurze m, Schnaps m. **11.** ⚡ F Kurze m. **12.** F Kurzfilm m. **IV** v/t **13.** ⚡ F e-n Kurzen verursachen in (dat); kurzschließen. **V** v/i **14.** ⚡ F e-n Kurzen haben. **'short-age** s Knappheit f, Mangel m (**of** an dat).

short|-'change v/t **1.** j-m zuwenig (Wechselgeld) herausgeben. **2.** F j-n übers Ohr hauen. **~ cir-cuit** s ⚡ Kurzschluß m. **,~'cir-cuit I** v/t **1.** ⚡ e-n Kurzschluß verursachen in (dat); kurzschließen. **2.** fig. et. umgehen. **II** v/i **3.** ⚡ e-n Kurzschluß haben. **,~'com-ings** s pl Unzulänglichkeiten pl, Mängel pl, (a. e-r Person) Fehler pl. **~ cut** s **1.** Abkürzung(sweg m) f: **take a ~** abkürzen. **2.** fig. abgekürztes Verfahren.

short-en [ˈʃɔːtn] **I** v/t kürzen, Kleidungsstück a. kürzer machen, Text a.

zs.-streichen, Leben etc verkürzen. **II** v/i kürzer werden.

'short|·fall s Defizit n. **,~'haired** adj kurzhaarig. **'~·hand** s Kurzschrift f, Stenographie f: **do ~** stenographieren; **take down in ~** et. (mit)stenographieren; **~ typist** Stenotypistin f. **,~'hand·ed** adj knapp an Personal od. Arbeitskräften.

short-ie [ˈʃɔːtɪ] s Kleine m, f, contp. Zwerg m.

short| list s: **be on the ~** Br. in der engeren Wahl sein. **'~·list** v/t Br. in die engere Wahl ziehen. **,~'lived** adj kurzlebig, fig. a. von kurzer Dauer.

short-ly [ˈʃɔːtlɪ] adv **1.** bald: **~ after** kurz danach. **2.** in kurzen Worten. **3.** barsch. **'short-ness** s **1.** Kürze f. **2.** Barschheit f. **3.** → **shortage**.

,short-'range adj **1.** ✕, ✈ Nah..., Kurzstrecken... **2.** kurzfristig. **'~·sight-ed** adj ⚡ ☞ kurzsichtig (a. fig.). **,~'sleeved** adj kurzärm(e)lig. **'~·staffed** adj **shorthanded**. **,~·tempered** adj aufbrausend, hitzig. **'~·term** adj kurzfristig, -zeitig: **~ memory** Kurzzeitgedächtnis n. **~ time** s ꜛ Kurzarbeit f: **be on** (od. **work**) **~** kurzarbeiten. **~ wave** s ⚡, phys. Kurzwelle f. **'~·wave** adj Kurzwellen... **~·wind-ed** [,~'wɪndɪd] adj □ kurzatmig.

short-y → **shortie**.

shot¹ [ʃɒt] **I** pret u. pp von **shoot**. **II** adj: **be** (od. **get**) **~ of** F j-n, et. los sein (loswerden).

shot² [~] s **1.** Schuß m: **like a ~** blitzschnell; sofort; **~ across the bows** Schuß vor den Bug (a. fig.); **~ in the dark** fig. Schuß ins Blaue; **~ in the leg** Beinschuß; **call the ~s** F das Sagen haben. **2.** (Fußball etc) Schuß m, (Basketball etc) Wurf m, (Tennis etc) Schlag m. **3.** guter od. schlechter Schütze: **big ~** F hohes Tier. **4.** Schrot m, n. **5.** Kugelstoßen n: Kugel f. **6.** F Versuch m: **at the first ~** beim ersten Versuch; **I'll have a ~ at it** ich probier's mal. **7.** a) Film, TV: Aufnahme f; Einstellung f, b) phot. F Schnappschuß m, Aufnahme f. **8.** ☞ F Spritze f. **'~·gun** s Schrotflinte f: **~ wedding** F Mußheirat f. **~ put** s Leichtathletik: Kugelstoßen n. **'~·put·ter** s Kugelstoßer(in).

should [ʃʊd] **1.** pret von **shall**, a. allg. ich

sollte, *du* solltest *etc: he ~ be home by then* er müßte bis dahin wieder zu Hause sein. **2.** *konditional: ich würde, wir würden: I ~ go if ...;* → *like²* 1.

shoul·der [ˈʃəʊldə] **I** *s* **1.** Schulter *f: to ~ Schulter* an Schulter (*a. fig.*); *a ~ to cry on* e-e Schulter zum Ausweinen; *give s.o. the cold ~* j-m die kalte Schulter zeigen; *put one's ~ to the wheel fig.* sich mächtig ins Zeug legen; → *chip* 1, *rub* 3. **II** *v/t* **2.** schultern; *fig.* Kosten, Verantwortung *etc* übernehmen. **3.** (mit der Schulter) stoßen: ~ *one's way through* sich e-n Weg bahnen durch. ~ *bag* *s* Schulter-, Umhängetasche *f.* ~ *blade* *s anat.* Schulterblatt *n.* ~ *strap* *s* Träger *m* (*e-s Kleids etc*); Tragriemen *m.*

shouldn't [ˈʃʊdnt] F *für* should not.

shout [ʃaʊt] **I** *v/i* rufen, schreien (*for* nach; *for help* um Hilfe): ~ *at s.o.* j-n anschreien. **II** *v/t* rufen, schreien: ~ *down* j-n niederbrüllen; ~ *o.s. hoarse* sich heiser schreien; → *rooftop.* **III** *s* Ruf *m,* Schrei *m:* ~*s pl of joy* Freudengeschrei *n; it's my* ~ *Br.* F das ist m-e Runde, ich bin dran. '**shout·ing** *s* Schreien *n,* Geschrei *n: it's all over bar the* ~ *Br.* F die Sache ist so gut wie gelaufen.

shove [ʃʌv] **I** *v/t* **1.** stoßen, schubsen: ~ *about* (*od.* ***around***) j-n herumschubsen (*a. fig.*). **2.** *etc* schieben, stopfen (**into** *in acc*). **II** *v/i* **3.** stoßen, schubsen: ~ *off* (vom Ufer) abstoßen; ~ *off!* F schieb ab!; ~ *over bsd. Br.* F rutschen. **III** *s* **4.** Stoß *m,* Schubs *m.*

shov·el [ˈʃʌvl] **I** *s* Schaufel *f.* **II** *v/t pret u. pp* **-eled,** *bsd. Br.* **-elled** schaufeln: ~ *food into one's mouth* Essen in sich hineinschaufeln.

show [ʃəʊ] **I** *s* **1.** *thea. etc* Vorstellung *f;* Show *f;* (*Rundfunk, TV*) Sendung *f: steal the ~ from s.o. fig.* j-m die Schau stehlen. **2.** Ausstellung *f: be on ~* ausgestellt *od.* zu besichtigen sein. **3.** Zurschaustellung *f,* Demonstration *f.* **4.** *by ~ of hands* durch Handzeichen. **5.** Schau *f: make a ~ of Anteilnahme etc* heucheln; *make a ~ of interest* a. interessiert sein. **6.** F *gute etc* Leistung: *put up a poor ~* e-e schwache Leistung zeigen. **7.** F Laden *m: run the ~* den Laden schmeißen. **II** *adj* **8.** Mu-

ster...: ~ *house.* **III** *v/t* (*mst irr*) **9.** *a. fig.* Gefühle *etc* zeigen, Fahrkarte *etc a.* vorzeigen, Zeit *etc* anzeigen (*Uhr etc*): ~ *s.o. how to do sth.* j-m zeigen, wie man et. macht; ~ *o.s.* sich erweisen als; → *door* 1, *etc.* **10.** j-n bringen, führen (*to* zu): ~ *s.o. (a)round* (*od. over*) *the house* j-n durchs Haus führen, j-m das Haus zeigen. **11.** ausstellen, zeigen. **12.** zeigen: a) *thea. etc* vorführen, b) *TV* bringen. **IV** *v/i* (*mst irr*) **13.** zu sehen sein: *it* ~*s* man sieht es. **14.** *be* ~*ing* gezeigt werden, laufen.

Verbindungen mit Adverbien:

show| a·round *v/t* herumführen. ~ *in v/t* herein-, hineinführen, -bringen. ~ *off v/t* **1.** angeben *od.* protzen mit (*to vor dat*). **2.** Figur *etc* vorteilhaft zur Geltung bringen. **II** *v/i* **3.** angeben, protzen. ~ *out v/t* heraus-, hinausführen, -bringen. ~ *round* → *show around.* ~ *up v/t* **1.** herauf-, hinaufführen, -bringen. **2.** sichtbar machen. **3.** *j-n* entlarven; *et.* aufdecken. **4.** *bsd. Br. j-n* in Verlegenheit bringen. **II** *v/i* **5.** zu sehen sein. **6.** F kommen; aufkreuzen, -tauchen.

show| biz *s* F, ~ *busi·ness* *s* Showbusineß *n,* -geschäft *n.* '~**case** *s* Schaukasten *m,* Vitrine *f.* '~**down** *s* Kraftprobe *f,* Machtprobe *f.*

show·er [ˈʃaʊə] **I** *s* **1.** (*Regen- etc*)Schauer *m;* (*Funken-, Kugel- etc*)Regen *m;* (*Geschoß-, Stein*)Hagel *m;* (*Wasser-, Wort-* *etc*)Schwall *m.* **2.** Dusche *f: have* (*od. take*) *a* ~ duschen. **II** *v/i* **3.** duschen. **III** *v/t* **4.** ~ *s.o. with s.th.,* ~ *s.th. on s.o.* j-n mit et. überschütten, *fig. a.* j-n mit et. überhäufen. ~ *cab·i·net* *s* Duschkabine *f.* ~ *cur·tain* *s* Duschvorhang *m.*

'**show·girl** *s* Revuegirl *n.* ~ *jump·er* *s Sport:* Springreiter(in). ~ *jump·ing* *s* Springreiten *n.* '~**man** [ˈ~mən] *s* (*irr man*) **1.** *thea. etc* Produzent *m.* **2.** Schausteller *m. fig.* Showman *m.*

shown [ʃəʊn] *pp von* **show.**

'**show·off** *s* F Angeber(in). '~**piece** *s* **1.** Ausstellungsstück *n.* **2.** Parade-, Prunkstück *n.* '~**room** [ˈ~rʊm] *s* Ausstellungsraum *m.*

show·y [ˈʃəʊɪ] *adj* □ auffallend (*Person*), (*Farben, Kleidung etc a.*) auffällig.

shrank [ʃræŋk] *pret von* **shrink.**

shred [ʃred] **I** s **1.** Fetzen m: *be in ~s* zerfetzt sein; *fig.* ruiniert sein (*Ruf etc*); *tear to ~s* zerfetzen; *fig. Argument etc* zerpflücken, -reißen; *Stück etc* verreißen. **2.** Schnitzel n, m, Stückchen n. **3.** *fig. not a ~ of doubt* nicht der geringste Zweifel; *there is not a ~ of truth in this story* an dieser Geschichte ist kein Wort wahr. **II** v/t (a. irr) **4.** zerfetzen; in den Papier- od. Reißwolf geben. **5.** in (schmale) Streifen schneiden, *Gemüse a.* schnitzeln, *Fleisch a.* schnetzeln. **'shred·der** s **1.** Papier-, Reißwolf m. **2.** Schnitzelmaschine f; Schnitzelwerk n.

shrewd [ʃruːd] adj □ scharfsinnig, klug, (*Beobachter*) scharf: *that was a ~ guess* das war gut geraten.

shriek [ʃriːk] **I** s (schriller) Schrei: *~ of terror* Entsetzensschrei; *~s pl of laughter* kreischendes Gelächter. **II** v/i (gellend) aufschreien (*with* vor *dat*): *~ with laughter* vor Lachen kreischen.

shrift [ʃrift] s: *give s.o. short ~* kurzen Prozeß mit j-m machen.

shrill [ʃril] adj □ **1.** schrill. **2** *fig.* heftig, scharf (*Kritik etc*).

shrimp [ʃrimp] s **1.** zo. Garnele f. **2.** *fig. contp.* Knirps m.

shrine [ʃrain] s (Reliquien)Schrein m.

shrink [ʃriŋk] **I** v/i (irr) **1.** (zs.-, ein-) schrumpfen (a. fig.), (*Stoff etc a.*) einlaufen, -gehen. **2.** *fig.* abnehmen. **3.** *fig.* zurückschrecken (*from* vor *dat*): *~ from doing s.th.* davor zurückschrecken, et. zu tun. **II** v/t (irr) **4.** (zs.-, ein)schrumpfen lassen, *Stoff etc a.* einlaufen od. -gehen lassen. **III** s **5.** F Klapsdoktor m. **'shrink·age** s **1.** Schrumpfung f (a. fig.), Einlaufen n, -gehen n. **2.** fig. Abnahme f. **'shrink·ing** adj: *~ violet* F schüchternes Pflänzchen.

shriv·el [ˈʃrivl] v/i u. v/t pret u. pp -eled, *bsd. Br.* -elled runz(e)lig werden (lassen): *~(l)ed* runz(e)lig.

shroud [ʃraud] **I** s **1.** Leichentuch n. **2.** *fig.* Schleier m (*of secrecy* des Geheimnisses). **II** v/t **3.** *be ~ed in* in *Nebel etc* gehüllt sein: *be ~ed in mystery* geheimnisumwittert sein.

Shrove Tues·day [ʃrəʊv] s Faschings-, Fastnachtsdienstag m.

shrub [ʃrʌb] s Busch m, Strauch m. **'shrub·ber·y** s Busch-, Strauchwerk n.

shrug [ʃrʌg] **I** v/t **1.** *~ one's shoulders*

→ **3.** **2.** *~ off fig. et.* mit e-m Achsel- od. Schulterzucken abtun, achselzuckend hinweggehen über (*acc*). **II** v/i **3.** mit den Achseln od. Schultern zucken. **III** s **4.** a. *~ of one's shoulders* Achsel-, Schulterzucken n: *give a ~ →* **3.**

shrunk [ʃrʌŋk] pret u. pp von **shrink.**

shuck [ʃʌk] *bsd. Am.* **I** s Hülse f, Schote f; Schale f. **II** v/t enthülsen; schälen. **III** s: *~s!* F Quatsch!; Mist!

shud·der [ˈʃʌdə] **I** v/i schaudern (*at* bei): *~ to think of* mit Schaudern denken an (*acc*). **II** s Schauder m.

shuf·fle [ˈʃʌfl] **I** v/t **1.** *~ one's feet →* **3.** **2.** *Karten* mischen. **II** v/i **3.** schlurfen. **4.** *Kartenspiel:* mischen. **III** s **5.** Schlurfen n, schlurfender Gang. **6.** Mischen n. **'~·board** s Schuffleboard n (*Spiel*).

shun [ʃʌn] v/t j-n, et. meiden.

shunt [ʃʌnt] v/t **1.** *Zug etc* rangieren, verschieben. **2.** *~ off* F j-n abschieben (*to* in *acc*, nach).

shut [ʃʌt] (irr) **I** v/t **1.** *Fenster, Tür etc* zumachen, *Fabrik etc* schließen: *→ mouth* **1**, *trap* **2.** **2.** j-n einschließen (*in* in *acc*, *dat*): *~ one's finger in the door* sich den Finger in der Tür einklemmen. **II** v/i **3.** schließen (a. *Laden etc*), zugehen.

Verbindungen mit Adverbien:

shut| a·way v/t **1.** *et.* wegschließen. **2.** *~ o.s. away* sich einigeln (*in* in *dat*). **~ down** v/t **1.** *Fabrik etc* schließen, (*für immer a.*) stillegen. **II** v/i schließen (*Fabrik etc*). **~ off** v/t **1.** *Gas, Maschine etc* abstellen. **2.** abtrennen; fernhalten (*from* von). **II** v/i **3.** (sich) abschalten. **~ out** v/t *Gedanken, Schmerz etc* verdrängen. **~ up** **I** v/t **1.** *Geschäft* schließen: *→ shop* **1.** **2.** j-n einsperren (*in* in *acc*, *dat*). **3.** F j-m den Mund stopfen. **II** v/i **4.** *~!* F halt die Klappe!

'shut|·down s Schließung f, (*für immer a.*) Stillegung f. **'~·eye** s F Schlaf m: *get some ~* ein paar Stunden schlafen.

shut·ter [ˈʃʌtə] s **1.** Fensterladen m. **2.** *phot.* Verschluß m: *~ speed* Belichtung(szeit) f. **'shut·tered** adj: *~ windows* pl Fenster pl mit Fensterläden; geschlossene Fensterläden; *~ room* Zimmer n mit geschlossenen Fensterläden.

shut·tle [ˈʃʌtl] **I** s **1.** *→* **shuttle bus** (**service, train**). **2.** (*Raum*)Fähre f,

(-)Transporter *m.* **3.** → **shuttlecock.** II *v/t* **4.** hin- u. herbefördern. **~ bus** *s* im Pendelverkehr eingesetzter Bus. '**~-cock** *s* Federball *m.* **~ ser·vice** *s* Pendelverkehr *m.* **~ train** *s* Pendelzug *m.*

shy [ʃai] **I** *adj* □ **1.** scheu (*Tier*), (*Lächeln, Mensch a.*) schüchtern (*of* gegenüber): *fight ~ of* e-r *Sache* aus dem Weg gehen; *fight ~ of doing s.th.* sich hüten, et. zu tun. II *v/i* **2.** scheuen (*at* vor *dat*) (*Pferd etc*). **3. ~ away** *fig.* zurückschrecken (*from* vor *dat*): **~** *away from doing s.th.* davor zurückschrecken, et. zu tun. '**shy·ness** *s* Scheu *f,* Schüchternheit *f.*

shy·ster ['ʃaistə] *s Am.* F Winkeladvokat *m.*

Si·a·mese twins [ˌsaiə'miːz] *s pl* siamesische Zwillinge *pl.*

sick [sik] **I** *adj* **1.** krank: *be off ~* krank (geschrieben) sein; *report ~* krank melden. **2.** *be ~ bsd. Br.* sich übergeben; *he was (od. felt) ~* ihm war schlecht; *be ~ of s.th.* F et. satt haben; *be ~ (and tired) of doing s.th.* F es (gründlich) satt haben, et. zu tun; *it makes me ~* mir wird schlecht davon, *a. fig.* es ekelt *od.* widert mich an. **3.** makaber (*Witz etc*), abartig (*Person etc*). II *s* **4. the ~** *pl* die Kranken *pl.* **5.** *Br.* F Kotze *f.* **~ bag** *s* 🗲 Spucktüte *f.* **~ bay** *s* Krankenzimmer *n* (*e-r Schule etc*), ♆ (*Schiffs*)Lazarett *n.* '**~·bed** *s* Krankenbett *n.*

sick·en ['sikən] **I** *v/t* j-n anekeln, anwidern (*beide a. fig.*). II *v/i* krank werden: *be ~ing for s.th.* et. ausbrüten.

sick·le ['sikl] *s* 🗡 Sichel *f.*

sick leave *s:* *be on ~* krank (geschrieben) sein.

sick·ly ['sikli] *adj* **1.** kränklich. **2.** matt (*Lächeln*). **3.** widerwärtig (*Geruch etc*). '**sick·ness** *s* **1.** Krankheit *f.* **2.** Übelkeit *f.*

sick·room ['~rʊm] *s* Krankenzimmer *n.*

side [said] **I** *s* **1.** *allg.* Seite *f* (*a. fig.*): *at the ~ of the road* am Straßenrand; *at (od. by) s.o.'s ~* an j-s Seite; *~ by ~* nebeneinander; *on the ~* nebenher *verdienen etc*; *his ~ of the story* s-e Version der Geschichte; *be on s.o.'s ~* auf j-s Seite sein *od.* stehen; *be on the right (wrong) ~ of 50* noch nicht (über) 50 sein; *have s.th. on one's ~* et. auf s-r Seite haben; *put to one ~ Geld* auf die

Seite legen; *take ~s →* 4; *take to one ~* j-n beiseite nehmen; → *safe* I, *seamy, split* 1, *sunny.* **2.** *Sport:* Mannschaft *f.* II *adj* **3.** Seiten...: *~ road (road, etc).* III *v/i* **4.** Partei ergreifen (*with* für; *against* gegen). '**~·board** *s* **1.** Sideboard *n.* **2.** *pl Br.* Koteletten *pl.* '**~·burns** *Am.* → *sideboard* **2.** '**~·car** *s* Bei-, Seitenwagen *m.* **~ dish** *s* Beilage *f.* **~ ef·fect** *s* Nebenwirkung *f.* **~ is·sue** *s* Randproblem *n.* '**~·line** *s* **1.** Nebenbeschäftigung *f.* **2.** *Sport:* Seitenlinie *f.* '**~·long** *adj u. adv:* **~** *glance* Seitenblick *m; look at s.o.* **~** j-n von der Seite anschauen. '**~·sad·dle** **I** *s* im Damensattel. II *adv im* Damensitz. '**~·split·ting** *adj* zwerchfellerschütternd. **~ step** *s* Seitenschritt *m,* (*Boxen*) Seitschritt *m,* Sidestep *m.* '**~·step** *v/t* **1.** e-m *Schlag* (durch e-n Seit[en]schritt) ausweichen. **2.** *fig.* e-r *Frage etc* ausweichen. II *v/i* **3.** e-n Seit(en)schritt machen. '**~·swipe** **I** *s:* *take a ~ at* F j-m e-n Seitenhieb versetzen. II *v/t mot. Am. geparktes Fahrzeug etc* streifen. '**~·track** *v/t* j-n ablenken; *et.* abbiegen. '**~·walk** *bsd. Am.* → *pavement.*

side·ward ['saidwəd] **I** *adj* seitlich: *~ jump* Sprung *m* zur Seite. II *adv* seitwärts, nach der *od.* zur Seite. '**~·wards** ['~dz] → *sideward* II. '**~·ways** → *sideward.*

si·dle ['saidl] *v/i* (sich) schleichen (*out of* aus): **~** *up to s.o.* sich an j-n heranschleichen.

siege [siːdʒ] *s* ✕ Belagerung *f:* *lay ~ to* belagern (*a. fig.*).

si·er·ra [si'erə] *s* Sierra *f.*

si·es·ta [si'estə] *s* Siesta *f:* *have (od. take) a ~* Siesta halten.

sieve [siv] **I** *s* Sieb *n:* *put through a ~* (durch)sieben; *he's got a memory like a ~* er hat ein Gedächtnis wie ein Sieb. II *v/t* (durch)sieben: **~** *out* aussieben (*from* aus).

sift [sift] *v/t* **1.** (durch)sieben: **~** *out fig.* herausfinden (*from* aus). **2.** *fig.* *Material etc* sichten, durchsehen. II *v/i* **3.** **~** *through* → 2.

sigh [sai] **I** *v/i* (auf)seufzen: **~** *with relief* erleichtert aufatmen. II *s* Seufzer *m:* **~** *of relief* Seufzer der Erleichterung; *breathe (od. heave) a ~ of relief* erleichtert aufatmen.

sight [saɪt] **I** s **1.** Sehvermögen n: *have good ~* gute Augen haben, gut sehen; *lose one's ~* das Augenlicht verlieren. **2.** (An)Blick m: *at the ~ of* beim Anblick von (*od.* gen); *at first ~* auf den ersten Blick; *a ~ for sore eyes* F e-e Augenweide; *you're a ~ for sore eyes* F schön, dich zu sehen; *be* (*od.* *look*) *a ~* F verboten *od.* zum Abschießen aussehen; *buy ~ unseen* et. unbesehen kaufen; *catch ~ of* erblicken; *know by ~* j-n vom Sehen kennen; *lose ~ of* aus den Augen verlieren. **3.** Sicht(weite) f: *be* (*with*)*in ~* in Sicht sein (*a.* fig.); *come into ~* in Sicht kommen; *keep out of ~!* paß auf, daß dich niemand sieht!; *let out of one's ~* j-n, et. aus den Augen lassen. **4.** *mst pl* Sehenswürdigkeit f. **5.** *oft pl* Visier n: *set one's ~s on* fig. et. ins Auge fassen. **6.** *a ~* F um einiges, viel besser etc. **II** v/t **7.** sichten. **'sight·ed** *adj* sehend.

'sight|-read v/t u. v/i (*irr* **read**) ♪ vom Blatt singen *od.* spielen. **'~·see** v/i: *go ~ing* sich die Sehenswürdigkeiten anschauen. **'~·see·ing** s Sightseeing n, Besichtigung f von Sehenswürdigkeiten: *~ bus* Sightseeing-Bus m; *~ tour* Sightseeing-Tour f, (Stadt)Rundfahrt f.

sign [saɪn] **I** s **1.** *allg.* Zeichen n, ♪ s. Vorzeichen n, fig. a. Anzeichen n: *~s pl of fatigue* Ermüdungserscheinungen pl; *all the ~s are that* alles deutet darauf hin, daß; *there was no ~ of him* von ihm war keine Spur zu sehen; *show ~s of* Anzeichen zeigen von (*od.* gen); *show only faint ~s of life* nur schwache Lebenszeichen von sich geben. **2.** (Hinweis-, Warn- *etc*)Schild n. **3.** (Stern-, Tierkreis)Zeichen n. **II** v/t **4.** unterschreiben, -zeichnen, *Bild, Buch* signieren; *Scheck* ausstellen; sich eintragen in (*acc*): *→ autograph* I. **5.** *Sport:* *Spieler* verpflichten, unter Vertrag nehmen. **III** v/i **6.** unterschreiben, -zeichnen: *~ for* den Empfang (*gen*) (*durch s-e Unterschrift*) bestätigen; *→ dot* 2. **7.** *Sport:* (e-n Vertrag) unterschreiben (*for, with* bei).

Verbindungen mit Adverbien:

sign| a·way v/t (*schriftlich*) verzichten auf (*acc*). *~ in* v/i sich in (e-e Anwesenheitsliste *etc*) eintragen. *~ off* v/i **1.**

Rundfunk, TV: sein Programm beenden. **2.** Schluß machen (*im Brief, a. allg.*). *~ on* v/t **1.** a) *→ sign* 5, b) j-n an-, einstellen, ♣ anheuern. **II** v/i **2.** a) *→ sign* 7, b) (e-n Arbeitsvertrag) unterschreiben, ♣ anheuern. **3.** *Rundfunk, TV:* sein Programm beginnen. *~ out* v/i sich (aus e-r Anwesenheitsliste *etc*) austragen. *~ o·ver* v/t et. überschreiben (*to* dat). *~ up* v/i → on 1, 2.

sig·nal ['sɪgnl] **I** s **1.** Signal n, Zeichen n (*beide a. fig.*): *~ busy* 6. **II** *adj* □ **2.** beachtlich, un-, außergewöhnlich. **III** v/t *pret u. pp* **-naled**, *bsd. Br.* **-nalled 3.** *s.o.* to do s.th. j-m (ein) Zeichen geben, et. zu tun. **4.** *fig. Bereitschaft etc* signalisieren. **IV** v/i **5.** *~ for a taxi* e-m Taxi winken. *~ box* ⨳ *Br.*, *~ tow·er* ⨳ *Am.* Stellwerk n.

sig·na·ture ['sɪgnətʃə] s Unterschrift f, (*e-s Bildes, Buchs*) Signatur f. *~ tune* s *Rundfunk, TV:* Erkennungs-, Kennmelodie f.

'sign·board s (Aushänge)Schild n.

sign·er ['saɪnə] s Unterzeichnete m, f.

'sig·net ring ['sɪgnɪt] s Siegelring m.

sig·nif·i·cance [sɪg'nɪfɪkəns] s Bedeutung f, Wichtigkeit f: *be of great ~ to* von großer Bedeutung sein für. **sig'nif·i·cant** *adj* □ **1.** bedeutend, bedeutsam, wichtig. **2.** vielsagend; bezeichnend.

sig·ni·fy ['sɪgnɪfaɪ] v/t **1.** bedeuten. **2.** *Meinung etc* kundtun.

sign| lan·guage s Zeichensprache f. **'~·post** s Wegweiser m.

si·lence ['saɪləns] **I** s Stille f; Schweigen n: *~!* Ruhe!; *in ~* schweigend; *a one-minute ~* e-e Schweigeminute. **II** v/t zum Schweigen bringen (*a. fig.*). **'si·lenc·er** s **1.** Schalldämpfer m. **2.** *mot. Br.* Auspufftopf m.

si·lent ['saɪlənt] *adj* □ still, (*Gebet, a. ling. Buchstabe*) stumm; ruhig; schweigsam: *~ film* Stummfilm m; *the ~ majority* die schweigende Mehrheit; *~ partner* ⚓ *Am.* stiller Teilhaber; *be ~ on* sich ausschweigen über (*acc*); *remain ~* schweigen.

sil·hou·ette [ˌsɪluː'et] **I** s Silhouette f. **II** v/t: *be ~d against* sich (als Silhouette) abheben gegen.

sil·i·con ['sɪlɪkən] s ⚗ Silizium n. **sil·i·cone** ['sɪlɪkəʊn] s ⚗ Silikon n.

sil·i·co·sis [ˌsɪlɪ'kəʊsɪs] s ⚕ Staublunge f.

silk [sɪlk] **I** s Seide f. **II** adj Seiden...
'**~worm** s zo. Seidenraupe f.

silk·y ['sɪlkɪ] adj □ seidig (Fell, Haare
etc), samtig (Stimme).

sill [sɪl] s (Fenster)Bank f, (-)Brett n.

sil·li·ness ['sɪlɪnɪs] s Albernheit f,
Dummheit f.

sil·ly ['sɪlɪ] **I** adj albern, dumm: don't be
~! red doch keinen Unsinn!; ~ billy →
II; ~ season (Journalismus) Sauregur-
kenzeit f. **II** s F Dummkopf m, Dum-
merchen n.

si·lo ['saɪləʊ] pl -los s 1. Silo m, n. 2. ✕
Startsilo m, n.

sil·ver ['sɪlvə] **I** s 1. 🜍 Silber n (a. Besteck, Geschirr). 2. Silber(geld n, -mün-
zen pl) n: three pounds in ~ drei Pfund
in Silber. **II** adj 3. silbern, Silber... **III**
v/t 4. versilbern. '~fish s zo. Silber-
fischchen n. ~ foil s Silber-, Alu(mi-
nium)folie f; Silberpapier n. '~haired
adj silberhaarig. ~ ju·bi·lee s 25jähri-
ges Jubiläum. ~ med·al s Silbermedail-
le f. ~ med·al·(l)ist s Silbermedaillen-
gewinner(in). ~ mine s Silberbergwerk
n, -mine f. ~ pa·per s Silberpapier n.
,~'plat·ed adj versilbert. '~smith s
Silberschmied(in). '~ware s Silber(besteck, -geschirr) n. ~ wed·ding s silber-
ne Hochzeit.

sil·ver·y ['sɪlvərɪ] adj silb(e)rig, (Lachen)
silberhell.

sim·i·lar ['sɪmɪlə] adj ähnlich (to dat).

sim·i·lar·i·ty [,~'lærətɪ] s Ähnlichkeit f
(to mit). '**sim·i·lar·ly** adv 1. ähnlich. 2.
entsprechend.

sim·i·le ['sɪmɪlɪ] s Simile n, Vergleich m.

sim·mer ['sɪmə] **I** v/i 1. köcheln, leicht
kochen: ~ with fig. kochen vor (Zorn
etc), fiebern vor (Aufregung etc); ~
down F sich abregen. 2. fig. gären,
schwelen. **II** s 3. Köcheln n: bring to a ~
zum Köcheln bringen.

sim·per ['sɪmpə] **I** v/i albern od. affektiert lächeln. **II** s albernes od. affektiertes Lächeln.

sim·ple ['sɪmpl] adj (□ → simply) 1.
allg. einfach, (Aufgabe etc a.) simpel,
leicht, (Lebensweise, Person, Stil etc a.)
schlicht, (🜛 Bruch a.) glatt: for the ~
reason that aus dem einfachen Grund,
weil. 2. einfältig; naiv, leichtgläubig.
,~'mind·ed adj □ → simple 2.

sim·plic·i·ty [sɪm'plɪsətɪ] s 1. Einfachheit

f, Schlichtheit f: be ~ itself die einfach-
ste Sache der Welt sein. 2. Einfältigkeit
f; Naivität f, Leichtgläubigkeit f.

sim·pli·fi·ca·tion [,sɪmplɪfɪ'keɪʃn] s Ver-
einfachung f. **sim·pli·fy** ['~faɪ] v/t vereinfachen.

sim·plis·tic [sɪm'plɪstɪk] adj (~ally) stark
vereinfachend.

sim·ply ['sɪmplɪ] adv 1. einfach (etc, →
simple 1): to put it ~ in einfachen Worten. 2. bloß, nur. 3. F einfach großartig
etc.

sim·u·late ['sɪmjʊleɪt] v/t 1. vortäuschen, heucheln, bsd. Krankheit simulieren. 2. ⚙ etc simulieren. **,sim·u·la-
tion** s 1. Vortäuschung f, Simulation f;
Heuchelei f. 2. ⚙ etc Simulierung f.
'**sim·u·la·tor** s 1. Heuchler(in), Simu-
lant(in). 2. ⚙ Simulator m.

si·mul·ta·ne·ous [,sɪml'teɪnjəs] adj □
simultan, gleichzeitig: ~ interpreter Si-
multandolmetscher(in).

sin [sɪn] **I** s Sünde f: live in ~ humor. in
Sünde leben; (as) ugly as ~ häßlich wie
die Nacht; → deadly 1, mortal 3. **II** v/i
sündigen: ~ against fig. sündigen gegen, sich versündigen an (dat); verstoßen gegen.

since [sɪns] **I** adv 1. a. ever ~ seitdem,
-her. 2. inzwischen. **II** prp 3. seit. **III** cj
4. seit(dem). 5. da.

sin·cere [sɪn'sɪə] adj □ aufrichtig:
Yours ~ly Mit freundlichen Grüßen
(Briefschluß). **sin·cer·i·ty** [~'serətɪ] s
Aufrichtigkeit f: in all ~ in aller Offen-
heit.

sine [saɪn] s ✠ Sinus m.

sin·ew ['sɪnju:] s anat. Sehne f. '**sin·ew·y**
adj sehnig, (Fleisch a.) flechsig.

sin·ful ['sɪnfʊl] adj □ sündig, sündhaft.

sing [sɪŋ] (irr) **I** v/i 1. singen. 2. pfeifen
(Kugel, Wind etc). **II** v/t 3. et. singen:
~ s.o. s.th. j-m et. (vor)singen; ~ a baby
to sleep ein Baby in den Schlaf singen.

singe [sɪndʒ] **I** v/t (sich et.) an- od. versengen. **II** s ange- od. versengte Stelle.

sing·er ['sɪŋə] s Sänger(in). '**sing·ing I** s
Singen n, Gesang m. **II** adj: ~ lesson
Sing-, Gesangsstunde f; ~ voice Sing-
stimme f.

sin·gle ['sɪŋgl] **I** adj □ 1. einzig: not a ~
one kein einziger. 2. einfach; einzeln,
Einzel...: ~ room Einzelzimmer n; ~
ticket → 6. 3. alleinstehend, unverhei-

ratet: **~ mother** alleinerziehende Mutter. **II** s **4.** Single f (Schallplatte). **5.** Single m (Person). **6.** Br. einfache Fahrkarte, ✓ einfaches Ticket. **7.** mst pl Tennis etc: Einzel n: **a ~s match** ein Einzel; **men's ~s** Herreneinzel. **III** v/t **8. ~ out** sich j-n herausgreifen. ,~-'breast·ed adj einreihig (Anzug). ,~-'file s u. adv: (in) ~ im Gänsemarsch. ,~-'hand·ed adj u. adv eigenhändig, (ganz) allein. ,~-'mind·ed adj □ zielstrebig, -bewußt.

sin·glet ['sɪŋglɪt] s bsd. Br. ärmelloses Unterhemd, (Sport) ärmelloses Trikot.

'sing·song s Singsang m.

sin·gu·lar ['sɪŋɡjʊlə] **I** adj □ **1.** ling. Singular..., Einzahl... **2.** fig. einzigartig, einmalig. **II** s **3.** ling. Singular m, Einzahl f.

sin·is·ter ['sɪnɪstə] adj □ finster, unheimlich.

sink [sɪŋk] **I** v/i (irr) **1.** sinken, untergehen: **leave s.o. to ~ or swim** j-n sich selbst überlassen. **2.** sinken (Gebäude etc); sinken, zurückgehen (Hochwasser etc, fig. Zahl etc): → **heart** 1, **spirit** 4. **3.** sinken (**into a chair** in e-n Sessel; **to the ground** zu Boden; **to the knees** auf die Knie; **into a deep sleep** in e-n tiefen Schlaf): → **oblivion**. **4. ~ in** eindringen (Flüssigkeit, a. fig. Nachricht etc). **II** v/t (irr) **5.** Schiff etc versenken. **6.** Graben etc ausheben, Brunnen etc bohren. **7.** Zähne etc vergraben, -senken (**into** in acc). **8.** Pläne etc zunichte machen. **9.** Streit etc beilegen, begraben. **10.** Geld, Arbeit etc investieren (**in, into** in acc) **III** s **11.** Spülbecken n, Spüle f; bsd. Am. Waschbecken n. **'sink·er** s Grundgewicht n (e-s Fischnetzes). **'sink·ing** adj: **I got that ~ feeling when** F mir wurde ganz anders, als.

sin·ner ['sɪnə] s Sünder(in).

si·nus ['saɪnəs] s anat. (Nasen)Nebenhöhle f. **si·nus·i·tis** [,~'saɪtɪs] s ✧ (Nasen)Nebenhöhlenentzündung f.

Sioux [su:] pl **Sioux** [su:z] s Sioux m, f.

sip [sɪp] **I** s Schlückchen n: **take a ~ of** → IIa. **II** v/t a) nippen an (dat) od. von, b) schlückchenweise trinken. **III** v/i: **~ at** → IIa.

si·phon ['saɪfn] **I** s **1.** Siphon(flasche f) m. **2.** ⚗ Saugheber m. **II** v/t **3.** a. **~ off** absaugen, Benzin abzapfen; fig. Geld, Personal etc abziehen.

sir [sɜː] s **1.** mein Herr (Anrede, oft unübersetzt): **Dear ℒs** Sehr geehrte Herren (Anrede in Briefen). **2.** ℒ Br. (Adelstitel): ℒ **Winston** (**Churchill**).

si·ren ['saɪərən] s Sirene f.

sir·loin steak ['sɜːlɔɪn] s Lendensteak n.

sis·sy ['sɪsɪ] s F Weichling m.

sis·ter ['sɪstə] s **1.** Schwester f. **2.** eccl. (Ordens)Schwester f: ℒ **Mary** Schwester Mary. **3.** ✧ Br. Oberschwester f. **4.** ✞ Schwester(gesellschaft) f. **II** adj **5.** Schwester...: **~ ship**, etc. **~hood** ['~hʊd] s eccl. Schwesternschaft f.

'sis·ter-in-law pl **'sis·ters-in-law** s Schwägerin f.

sis·ter·ly ['sɪstəlɪ] adj schwesterlich.

sit [sɪt] (irr) **I** v/i **1.** sitzen: → **fence** 1, **pretty** II, **tight** 8. **2.** sich setzen. **3.** babysitten. **II** v/t **5.** j-n setzen. **6.** Br. → **sit for** 1.

Verbindungen mit Präpositionen:

sit| for v/i **1.** Prüfung ablegen, machen. **2.** j-m (Modell) sitzen: **~ one's portrait** sich porträtieren lassen. **~ on** v/i **1. ~ a committee** e-m Ausschuß angehören. **2.** fig. sitzen auf (dat). **3.** F j-n unterbuttern.

Verbindungen mit Adverbien:

sit| a·bout, ~ a·round v/i herumsitzen. **~ back** v/i sich zurücklehnen, fig. a. die Hände in den Schoß legen. **~ down** v/i sich setzen; sitzen: **sitting down** im Sitzen. **II** v/t j-n absetzen. **~ in** v/i **1. ~ for** j-n vertreten (an dat). **2. ~ on** als Zuhörer teilnehmen an (dat). **3.** ein Sit-in veranstalten; an e-m Sit-in teilnehmen. **~ out** v/t **1.** Tanz auslassen. **2.** bis zum Ende e-r Veranstaltung etc bleiben. **3.** das Ende (gen) abwarten; Krise etc aussitzen. **~ up** **I** v/i **1.** sich aufrichten od. -setzen; aufrecht sitzen: **make s.o. ~ (and take notice)** F j-n aufhorchen lassen. **2.** aufbleiben. **3. ~ (at od. to table** bei Tisch) Platz nehmen. **II** v/t **4.** j-n aufrichten od. -setzen.

sit·com ['sɪtkɒm] F → **situation comedy. '~down** s **1.** a. **~ strike** → **sit-in. 2.** a. **~ demonstration** Sitzblockade f. **3.** F Verschnaufpause f: **have a ~** e-e Verschnaufpause einlegen.

site [saɪt] **I** s **1.** Platz m, Ort m, Stelle f; engS. Standort m; (Ausgrabungs)Stätte

f. **2.** Baustelle f. **II** v/t **3.** placieren, ✗ Raketen etc stationieren: **be ~d** gelegen sein, liegen.

'sit-in s Sit-in n, Sitzstreik m: **stage a ~ in** Gebäude etc besetzen.

sit-ter ['sɪtə] s **1.** paint. etc Modell n. **2.** Babysitter(in). **'sit-ting I** s **1.** Sitzung f (a. paint. etc). **2. read s.th. at one** (od. **a single**) **~** et. in 'einem Zug durchlesen. **II** adj **3. ~ duck** fig. leichte Beute; **~ room** Wohnzimmer n.

sit-u-at-ed ['sɪtjʊeɪtɪd] adj **1. be ~** gelegen sein, liegen. **2.** fig. **be badly ~** in e-r schwierigen Lage sein; **be well ~** gut situiert sein; ohne weiteres in der Lage sein (**to do** zu tun).

sit-u-a-tion [ˌsɪtjʊ'eɪʃn] s **1.** fig. Lage f, Situation f. **2.** Lage f (e-s Hauses etc). **3. ~s** pl vacant (**wanted**) Stellenangebote pl (Stellengesuche pl). **~ com-e-dy** s Rundfunk, TV: humorvolle Serie.

six [sɪks] **I** adj sechs. **II** s Sechs f: **~ of hearts** Herzsechs; **be all at ~es and sevens** F nicht mehr wissen, wo e-m der Kopf steht. **six-fold** ['~fəʊld] **I** adj sechsfach. **II** adv sechsfach, um das Sechsfache: **increase ~** (sich) versechsfachen.

'six-pack s Sechserpackung f.

six-teen [ˌsɪks'tiːn] adj sechzehn. **six-'teenth** [~θ] adj sechzehnt. **sixth** [~θ] **I** adj **1.** sechste(r, -s): **~ sense** fig. sechster Sinn. **II** s **2.** der, die, das Sechste: **the ~ of May** der 6. Mai. **3.** Sechstel n. **'sixth-ly** adv sechstens. **six-ti-eth** ['~tɪəθ] adj sechzigst.

'six-time adj sechsmalig.

six-ty ['sɪkstɪ] **I** adj sechzig. **II** s Sechzig f: **be in one's sixties** in den Sechzigern sein; **in the sixties** in den sechziger Jahren (e-s Jahrhunderts).

size [saɪz] **I** s **1.** Größe f, fig. a. Ausmaß n, Umfang m: **what is the ~ of ...?** wie groß ist ...? **2.** (Kleider-, Schuh- etc-) Größe f, Nummer f: **what ~ do you take?** welche Größe tragen Sie?; **I'll cut him down to ~** F dem werd' ich's zeigen. **II** v/t **3.** mst **~ up** j-n, et. abschätzen.

size-a-ble ['saɪzəbl] adj beträchtlich (Summe etc).

siz-zle ['sɪzl] **I** v/i brutzeln. **II** s Brutzeln n. **'siz-zler** s F glühendheißer Tag.

skate [skeɪt] **I** s Schlittschuh m; Roll-

schuh m. **II** v/i Schlittschuh laufen, eislaufen; Rollschuh laufen: **~ over** (od. **round**) s.th. fig. hinweggehen über (acc); → **ice** **1**. **'~board** s Skateboard n.

skat-er ['skeɪtə] s Eis-, Schlittschuhläufer(in); Rollschuhläufer(in). **'skat-ing** adj: **~ rink** (Kunst)Eisbahn f; Rollschuhbahn f.

ske-dad-dle [skɪ'dædl] v/i F türmen, abhauen.

skel-e-ton ['skelɪtn] **I** s **1.** Skelett n, Gerippe n (beide a. fig. Person etc): **~ in the cupboard** (Am. **closet**) fig. dunkler Punkt (in j-s Vergangenheit etc); **have a ~ in the cupboard** e-e Leiche im Keller haben. **2.** △, ⚓, ⚓ Skelett n. **3.** fig. Entwurf m; Rahmen m. **II** adj **4.** Rahmen...: **~ plan**, etc. **5.** Not...: **~ service** Notdienst m. **6. ~ key** Hauptschlüssel m.

skep-tic, etc bsd. Am. → **sceptic**, etc.

sketch [sketʃ] **I** s **1.** Kunst etc: Skizze f. **2.** thea. etc Sketch m. **II** v/t **3.** skizzieren. **4.** oft **~ in** (od. **out**) fig. skizzieren, umreißen. **'sketch-y** adj □ flüchtig, oberflächlich, (Erinnerung etc) bruchstückhaft.

skew [skjuː] **I** s: **on the ~** schief; schräg. **II** v/t fig. verzerren.

skew-er ['skjʊə] **I** s (Fleisch)Spieß m. **II** v/t Fleisch aufspießen.

ski [skiː] **I** s Ski m. **II** adj Ski...: **~ lift**, etc. **III** v/i Ski fahren od. laufen.

skid [skɪd] **I** v/i **1.** mot. schleudern. **II** s **2. go into a ~** mot. ins Schleudern kommen. **3.** ⚙ Rolle f: **he's on the ~s** F mit ihm geht es abwärts.

ski-er ['skiːə] s Skifahrer(in), -läufer(in).

skiff [skɪf] s ⚓ Skiff n, (Rudersport a.) Einer m.

ski-ing ['skiːɪŋ] s Skifahren n, -laufen n, -sport m.

skil-ful ['skɪlfʊl] adj □ geschickt.

skill [skɪl] s **1.** Geschick n: **game of ~** Geschicklichkeitsspiel n. **2.** Fertigkeit f. **skilled** [~ld] adj **1.** geschickt (**at**, **in** in dat). **2. ~ worker** Facharbeiter(in).

skil-let ['skɪlɪt] s bsd. Am. Bratpfanne f.

skill-ful Am. → **skilful**.

skim [skɪm] **I** v/t **1.** a. **~ off** Fett etc abschöpfen (**from** von). **2.** Milch entrahmen: **~med milk** Magermilch f. **3.** Bericht etc überfliegen. **II** v/i **4. ~ over**

*(od. **through**)* → 3. **~ milk** *s* Mager-milch *f*.

skimp [skɪmp] **I** *v/t* sparen an (dat). **II** *v/i*: **~ on** → I. '**skimp·y** *adj* dürftig *(Mahlzeit, Beweise etc)*; knapp *(Kleidungsstück)*.

skin [skɪn] **I** *s* **1.** Haut *f (a. e-r Wurst, auf Milch etc)*: **by the ~ of one's teeth** F mit Ach u. Krach, gerade noch; **be all ~ and bone(s)** nur noch Haut u. Knochen sein; **that's no ~ off my nose** F das juckt mich nicht; **be drenched** *(od.* **soaked) to the ~** bis auf die Haut durchnäßt *od.* naß sein; **get under s.o.'s ~** F j-m unter die Haut gehen; j-m auf den Wecker fallen; **save one's ~** F s-e Haut retten. **2.** Haut *f*; Fell *n*. **3.** *(Bananen-, Zwiebel- etc)*Schale *f*. **II** *v/t* **4.** *Tier* abhäuten: → *s.o.* **alive** F j-n zur Schnecke machen. **5.** *Zwiebel etc* schälen: **keep one's eyes ~ned** *Br*. F die Augen offenhalten. **6.** sich *das Knie etc* aufschürfen. ,~'**deep** *adj fig.* oberflächlich. **~ div·ing** *s* Schnorcheln *n*, Schnorcheltauchen *n*. ~**flick** *s* F Sexfilm *m*. '~**flint** *s* Geizhals *m*.

skin·ful ['skɪnfʊl] *s*: **he's had a ~** F er hat schwer geladen *(ist betrunken)*.

skin graft *s* Hauttransplantation *f*, -verpflanzung *f*. '~**head** *s bsd. Br*. Skin-head *m*.

skin·ny ['skɪnɪ] *adj* dürr.

skint [skɪnt] *adj Br*. F blank, pleite.

,**skin-'tight** *adj* hauteng.

skip [skɪp] **I** *v/i* **1.** hüpfen. **2.** *Br.* seilhüpfen, -springen. **3.** *fig.* springen *(**from one subject to another** von 'einem Thema zum andern)*: **~ over** *et.* überspringen, auslassen. **4.** *a.* **~ off** F abhauen, türmen. **II** *v/t* **5.** *et.* überspringen, auslassen: *Vorlesung etc* schwänzen; *Mahlzeit* ausfallen lassen. **III** *s* **6.** Hüpfer *m*.

skip·per ['skɪpə] *s* **1.** ♣ Kapitän *m*. **2.** *Sport:* Mannschaftsführer(in).

skip·ping rope ['skɪpɪŋ] *s Br*. Spring-, Sprungseil *n*.

skir·mish ['skɜːmɪʃ] *s* ✗ Geplänkel *n* *(a. fig.)*.

skirt [skɜːt] **I** *s* Rock *m*. **II** *v/t* → III. **III** *v/i*: **~ (a)round** *fig.* Problem etc umgehen. '**skirt·ing** *adj*: **~ board** *Br*. Fuß(boden)-, Scheuerleiste *f*.

skit [skɪt] *s* Parodie *f (on auf acc)*: **do a ~ on** j-n, *et.* parodieren.

skive [skaɪv] *v/i Br*. F blaumachen.

skul·dug·ger·y [skʌl'dʌgərɪ] *s* F fauler Zauber.

skulk [skʌlk] *v/i* sich herumdrücken, herumschleichen.

skull [skʌl] *s anat.* Schädel *m*: **~ and crossbones** Totenkopf *m (Symbol)*; **can't you get it into that thick ~ of yours that ...?** F will es denn nicht in deinen Schädel, daß ...?

skunk [skʌŋk] *s* **1.** *zo.* Skunk *m*, Stinktier *n*. **2.** F Saukerl *m*.

sky [skaɪ] *s, a. pl* Himmel *m*: **in the ~** am Himmel; **the ~'s the limit** F es sind keine Grenzen gesetzt; **extol** *(od.* **praise) to the skies** j-n, *et.* in den Himmel heben. ,~'**blue** *adj* himmelblau. '~**,div·er** *s* ,Sport: Fallschirmspringer(in). '~**,div·ing** *s* Fallschirmspringen *n*. ,~'**high** *adj u. adv* himmelhoch: **blow ~** in die Luft jagen; *fig.* Theorie etc über den Haufen werfen, *Argument etc* widerlegen, *Mythos* zerstören. '~**jack** → **hijack** 1, 3. '~**jack·er** → **hijacker** 1. '~**jack·ing** → **hijack** 3. '~**light** *s* Dachfenster *n*. '~**line** *s* Skyline *f*, Silhouette *f (e-r Stadt)*. '~**,rock·et** → **rocket** 3. '~**scrap·er** *s* Wolkenkratzer *m*.

slab [slæb] *s* **1.** *(Stein- etc)*Platte *f*. **2.** dickes Stück *(Kuchen etc)*.

slack [slæk] **I** *adj* □ **1.** locker *(Seil etc)*. **2.** *fig.* lax *(Disziplin etc)*. **3.** *fig.* lasch, nachlässig. **4.** ♣ flau. **II** *v/i* **5.** bummeln. **6.** **~ off** *(od.* **up)** → **slacken** 5. '**slack·en I** *v/t* **1.** lockern. **2.** *fig.* verringern: **~ speed** langsamer werden. **II** *v/i* **3.** locker werden. **4.** *a.* **~ off** *fig.* nachlassen, *(Person a.)* abbauen.

slag [slæg] *s* **1.** Schlacke *f*. **2.** *Br. sl.* Schlampe *f*.

slain [sleɪn] *pp von* **slay**.

slake [sleɪk] *v/t Kalk* löschen: **~d lime** Löschkalk *m*.

sla·lom ['slɑːləm] *s Sport:* Slalom *m*.

slam [slæm] **I** *v/t* **1.** *a.* **~ shut** Tür etc zuknallen, zuschlagen. **2.** *a.* **~ down** F *et.* knallen *(on auf acc)*: **~ the brakes on** *mot.* auf die Bremse steigen. **3.** *fig.* scharf kritisieren. **II** *v/i* **4.** *a.* **~ shut** zuknallen, zuschlagen.

slan·der ['slɑːndə] **I** *s* Verleumdung *f*. **II**

v/t verleumden. **'slan·der·er** *s* Verleumder(in). **'slan·der·ous** *adj* □ verleumderisch.

slang [slæŋ] **I** *s* Slang *m*; Jargon *m*. **II** *v/t bsd. Br. F j-n* wüst beschimpfen. **'slang·ing** *adj*: **they had a ~ match** *bsd. Br.* F sie beschimpften sich wüst.

slant [slɑ:nt] **I** *v/t* **1. be ~ed toward(s)** (*od.* **in favo[u]r of**) *fig.* (einseitig) ausgerichtet sein auf (*acc*). **II** *s* **2. at** (*od.* **on**) **a ~** schräg. **3.** *fig.* Einstellung *f* (**on** zu); Ausrichtung *f*. **'slant·ing** *adj* schräg.

slap [slæp] **I** *s* **1.** Schlag *m*, Klaps *m*: **a ~ in the face** e-e Ohrfeige, *bsd. fig.* ein Schlag ins Gesicht (**for** für). **II** *v/t* **2.** schlagen: **~ s.o.'s face** j-n ohrfeigen, j-m e-e runterhauen. **3.** *a.* **~ down**. klatschen (**on** auf *acc*). **III** *v/i* **4.** klatschen (**against** gegen) (*Wellen etc*). **IV** *adv* **5.** F direkt, genau. **~·'bang** → **slap** 5. **'~·dash** *adj* schlampig, schlud(e)rig. **'~·stick** *s thea. etc* Slapstick *m*, Klamauk *m*: **~ comedy** Slapstickkomödie *f*. **'~·up** *adj Br.* F toll (*Essen*).

slash [slæʃ] **I** *v/t* **1.** auf-, zerschlitzen: **~ one's wrists** sich die Pulsadern aufschneiden. **2.** *fig.* Preise drastisch herabsetzen; *Ausgaben etc* drastisch kürzen. **II** *v/i* **3. ~ at** schlagen nach. **4.** peitschen (**against** an *acc*, gegen) (*Regen*). **III** *s* **5.** Hieb *m*. **6.** Schlitz *m* (*in Kleid etc*). **7.** *a.* **~ mark** Schrägstrich *m*. **8. have** (**go for**) **a ~** *Br. sl.* schiffen (gehen).

slate¹ [sleɪt] **I** *s* **1.** *geol.* Schiefer *m*. **2.** Schieferplatte *f*. **3.** Schiefertafel *f*: **put on the ~** *fig. et.* anschreiben; **wipe the ~ clean** *fig.* reinen Tisch machen. **4.** *pol. Am.* Kandidatenliste *f*. **II** *v/t* **5.** Dach mit Schiefer decken. **6.** *Am.* j-n vorschlagen (**for, to be** als). **7.** *Am. et.* ansetzen, planen (**for** für).

slate² [~] *v/t bsd. Br.* F *Theaterstück etc* verreißen.

slaugh·ter ['slɔ:tə] **I** *s* **1.** Schlachten *n*: **ready for ~** schlachtreif. **2.** Gemetzel *n*. **II** *v/t* **3.** *Tier* schlachten. **4.** *Menschen* niederschlachten. **'~·house** *s* Schlachthaus *n*, -hof *m*.

slave [sleɪv] **I** *s* Sklave *m*, Sklavin *f* (*beide a. fig. of, to gen*). **II** *v/i a.* **~ away** sich abplagen. **~ driv·er** *s* F Sklaventreiber *m*, Leuteschinder *m*. **~ la·bo(u)r** *s* Sklavenarbeit *f* (*a. fig.*).

slav·er ['slævə] *v/i* geifern.

slav·er·y ['sleɪvərɪ] *s* Sklaverei *f*.

slave| **trade**, **~ traf·fic** *s* Sklavenhandel *m*.

slav·ish ['sleɪvɪʃ] *adj* □ sklavisch.

slaw [slɔ:] *s bsd. Am.* Krautsalat *m*.

slay [sleɪ] *v/t Am.* ermorden, umbringen. **'slay·er** *s* Mörder(in).

slea·zy ['sli:zɪ] *adj* □ schäbig, heruntergekommen; anrüchig.

sled [sled] → **sledge**.

sledge [sledʒ] **I** *s* (*a.* Rodel)Schlitten *m*. **II** *v/i* Schlitten fahren, rodeln.

'sledge·ham·mer *s* ⊙ Vorschlaghammer *m*.

sleek [sli:k] *adj* □ **1.** geschmeidig (*Haar etc*). **2.** schnittig (*Auto*).

sleep [sli:p] **I** *s* Schlaf *m*: **in one's ~** im Schlaf; **I couldn't get to ~** ich konnte nicht einschlafen; **go to ~** einschlafen (F *a.* Bein *etc*); **put to ~** *Tier* einschläfern (F *a.* j-n narkotisieren). **II** *v/i* (*irr*) schlafen: **~ late** lang *od.* länger schlafen; **~ like a log** (*od.* top) F wie ein Murmeltier schlafen; **~ on** Problem *etc* überschlafen; **~ through** Gewitter *etc* verschlafen; **~ with s.o.** mit j-m schlafen. **III** *v/t* (*irr*) Schlafgelegenheit bieten für: **this tent ~s four people** in diesem Zelt können vier Leute schlafen.

Verbindungen mit Adverbien:

sleep| **a·round** *v/i* F rumbumsen. **~ in** *v/i* lang *od.* länger schlafen. **~ off** *v/t*: **sleep it off** F s-n Rausch ausschlafen. **~ to·geth·er** *v/i* miteinander schlafen.

sleep·er ['sli:pə] *s* **1.** Schlafende *m*, *f*, Schläfer(in): **be a light** (**heavy** *od.* **sound**) **~** e-n leichten (festen) Schlaf haben. **2.** ⊞ *Br.* Schwelle *f*. **3.** ⊞ Schlafwagen *m*; Schlafwagenplatz *m*.

sleep·ing| **bag** ['sli:pɪŋ] *s* Schlafsack *m*. **~ car** *s* ⊞ Schlafwagen *m*. **~ part·ner** *s* ✝ *Br.* stiller Teilhaber. **~ pill** *s* Schlaftablette *f*. **~ po·lice·man** *s* (*irr* **man**) *mot. Br.* Rüttelschwelle *f*. **~ sick·ness** *s* 𝄞 Schlafkrankheit *f*. **~ tab·let** *s* Schlaftablette *f*.

sleep·less ['sli:plɪs] *adj* □ schlaflos (*Nacht etc*).

'sleep|**·walk** *v/i* schlaf-, nachtwandeln. **'~·walk·er** *s* Schlaf-, Nachtwandler(in).

sleep·y ['sli:pɪ] *adj* □ **1.** schläfrig, müde.

2. *fig.* verschlafen, verträumt (*Städtchen etc*). **'~head** s F Schlafmütze *f*.

sleet [sli:t] s Schneeregen *m*.

sleeve [sli:v] s **1.** Ärmel *m*: **have** (*od.* **keep**) **s.th. up one's ~** *fig.* et. auf Lager *od.* in petto haben; **laugh up one's ~** *fig.* sich ins Fäustchen lachen. **2.** ۞ Manschette *f*, Muffe *f*. **3.** *bsd. Br.* (*Platten*)Hülle *f*; *fig.* Anteil *m* (*of an dat*). **~·less** *adj* ärmellos.

sleigh [sleɪ] s (*bsd.* Pferde)Schlitten *m*.

sleight of hand [slaɪt] s **1.** Fingerfertigkeit *f*. **2.** *fig.* Taschenspielertrick *m*.

slen·der ['slendə] *adj* □ **1.** schlank. **2.** *fig.* mager (*Aussichten, Einkommen etc*).

slept [slept] *pret u. pp von* **sleep**.

sleuth [slu:θ] s F Spürhund *m*, Detektiv *m*.

slew [slu:] *pret von* **slay**.

slice [slaɪs] **I** s **1.** Scheibe *f* (*Brot etc*), Stück (*Kuchen etc*); *fig.* Anteil *m* (*of an dat*). **2.** *Br.* (*Braten*)Wender *m*. **3.** *Golf, Tennis:* Slice *m*. **II** *v/t* **4.** *a.* **~ up** in Scheiben *od.* Stücke schneiden: **~ off** *Stück* abschneiden (**from** von). **5.** *Golf, Tennis:* *Ball* slicen.

slick [slɪk] **I** *adj* □ **1.** gekonnt (*Vorstellung etc*). **2.** geschickt, raffiniert. **3.** glatt (*Straße etc*). **II** s **4.** (*Öl*)Teppich *m*. **5.** *Motorsport:* Slick *m* (*Trockenreifen*). **6.** *Am.* F Hochglanzmagazin *n*. **'slick-er** s *Am.* Regenmantel *m*.

slid [slɪd] *pret u. pp von* **slide**.

slide [slaɪd] **I** *v/i* (*irr*) **1.** gleiten; rutschen: **let things ~** *fig.* die Dinge schleifen lassen. **2.** schleichen. **II** *v/t* (*irr*) **3.** schieben; gleiten lassen. **II** s **4.** Rutsche *f*, Rutschbahn *f*. **5.** (*Erd- etc*)Rutsch *m*. **6.** *Br.* (*Haar*)Spange *f*. **7.** Dia *n*. **~ lec·ture** s Lichtbildervortrag *m*. **~ pro·jec·tor** s Diaprojektor *m*. **~ rule** s Rechenschieber *m*, -stab *m*.

slid·ing door ['slaɪdɪŋ] s Schiebetür *f*.

slight [slaɪt] **I** *adj* □ leicht (*Schmerz etc*), geringfügig (*Änderung etc*): **I haven't got the ~est idea** ich habe nicht die geringste Ahnung; **not in the ~est** nicht im geringsten. **II** *v/t* j-n beleidigen, kränken. **III** s Beleidigung *f* (**on, to** gen).

slim [slɪm] **I** *adj* □ **1.** schlank. **2.** gering (*Chance, Hoffnung etc*). **II** *v/i* **3.** e-e Schlankheitskur machen. **III** *v/t* **4.** *a.* **~ down** *fig.* verringern.

slime [slaɪm] s Schleim *m*.

slim·ming ['slɪmɪŋ] **I** s Abnehmen *n*. **II** *adj* Schlankheits...: **be on a ~ diet →** **slim** 3.

slim·y ['slaɪmɪ] *adj* □ schleimig (*a. fig.*).

sling[1] [slɪŋ] **I** s **1.** ۶ Schlinge *f*: **have one's arm in a ~** den Arm in der Schlinge tragen. **2.** Trag(e)riemen *m* (*für Gewehr*); Trag(e)tuch *n* (*für Baby*). **II** *v/t* (*irr*) **3.** aufhängen.

sling[2] [~] *v/t* (*irr*) schleudern: **→ mud** 2.

slink [slɪŋk] *v/i* (*irr*) (sich) schleichen.

slip[1] [slɪp] **I** s **1.** Versehen *n*: **~ of the tongue** Versprecher *m*. **2.** Unterkleid *n*, -rock *m*. **3.** (*Kissen*)Bezug *m*. **4.** **give s.o. the ~** F j-m entwischen. **II** *v/i* **5.** rutschen, (*auf Eis a.*) schlittern: **~ out of s.o.'s hand** j-m aus der Hand rutschen; **he let ~ that** *fig.* ihm ist herausgerutscht, daß; **let an opportunity ~** (**through one's fingers**) sich e-e Gelegenheit entgehen lassen. **6.** ausrutschen. **7.** *allg.* schlüpfen. **8.** sich vertun. **9.** *fig.* nachlassen, (*Gewinne etc*) zurückgehen. **III** *v/t* **10.** **~ s.th. into s.o.'s hand** j-m et. in die Hand schieben; **~ s.o. s.th.** j-m et. zuschieben. **11.** sich losreißen von. **12.** **~ s.o.'s attention** j-m od. j-s Aufmerksamkeit entgehen; **~ s.o.'s memory** (*od. mind*) j-m entfallen. **13.** **he has ~ped a disc, he has a ~ped disc** ۶ er hat e-n Bandscheibenvorfall.

Verbindungen mit Adverbien:

slip| **by** *v/i* verstreichen (*Zeit*). **~ off** *v/t* schlüpfen aus (*e-m Kleidungsstück*). **~ on** *v/t* *Kleidungsstück* überstreifen, schlüpfen in (*acc*). **~ out** *v/i*: **it just slipped out** es ist mir etc so herausgerutscht. **~ past → slip by.** **~ up → slip** 8.

slip[2] [~] s *a.* **~ of paper** Zettel *m*.

'slip·case s Schuber *m*. **'~·cov·er** s *Am.* Schonbezug *m*. **'~·on** I *adj*: **~ shoe →** II. **II** s Slipper *m*.

slip·per ['slɪpə] s Hausschuh *m*, Pantoffel *m*.

slip·per·y ['slɪpərɪ] *adj* **1.** glatt, rutschig, (*a. Fisch, Seife etc*) glitschig. **2.** *fig.* zwielichtig.

slip·py *adj*: **look ~!** *Br.* F mach fix!

slip| **road** s *Br.* Autobahn: Abfahrt *f*; Zubringer(straße *f*) *m*. **'~·shod** *adj* schlampig, schlud(e)rig. **'~·stream**

(*Sport*) **I** s Windschatten m. **II** v/i im Windschatten fahren. **'~-up → slip'** 1.

slit [slɪt] **I** s Schlitz m (a. im Rock etc). **II** v/t (irr) Rock etc schlitzen: ~ (**open**) aufschlitzen.

sliv·er ['slɪvə] s (Glas- etc)Splitter m: ~ **of glass.**

slob·ber ['slɒbə] v/i sabbern.

slog [slɒg] F **I** v/i **1.** ~ **away** sich abschuften mit. **2.** sich schleppen (**through** durch). **II** s **3.** Schufterei f.

slo·gan ['sləʊgən] s Slogan m.

slop [slɒp] **I** v/t **1.** verschütten: ~ **s.th. over one's trousers** sich et. über die Hose schütten. **II** v/i **2.** überschwappen; schwappen (**over** über acc). **3.** ~ **about** (od. **around**) F herumhängen (*Person*). **III** s **4.** a. pl contp. schlabb(e)riges Zeug.

slope [sləʊp] **I** s **1.** (Ab)Hang m. **2.** Neigung f, Gefälle n. **II** v/i **3.** sich neigen, abfallen. **4.** ~ **off** Br. F abhauen.

slop·py ['slɒpɪ] adj □ **1.** schlampig, schlud(e)rig. **2.** F vergammelt (*Kleidungsstück*). **3.** F schmalzig.

slosh [slɒʃ] F **I** v/i **1.** ~ **about** (od. **around**) herumschwappen. **2.** ~ **about** (od. **around**) (herum)planschen (**in** in dat). **II** v/t **3.** Wasser etc verspritzen.

sloshed [slɒʃt] adj F blau (*betrunken*).

slot [slɒt] s Schlitz m, (e-s Automaten etc a.) Einwurf m. ~ **ma·chine** s (Waren-, Spiel)Automat m.

slouch [slaʊtʃ] **I** s **1.** krumme Haltung; latschiger Gang. **2.** F **be no ~ at** nicht schlecht sein in (dat); **be no ~ at doing s.th.** et. nicht ungern tun. **II** v/i **3.** krumm dasitzen od. dastehen; latschen. ~ **hat** s Schlapphut m.

slough [slʌf] v/t Haut abstreifen (*Schlange*).

slov·en·ly ['slʌvnlɪ] adj schlampig, schlud(e)rig.

slow [sləʊ] **I** adj □ **1.** allg. langsam, (*Person* a.) begriffsstutzig: **be ~ to do s.th.** sich mit et. Zeit lassen; **be (five minutes) ~** (fünf Minuten) nachgehen (*Uhr*); ~ **lane** mot. Kriechspur f; **in ~ motion** in Zeitlupe; ~ **poison** langsam wirkendes Gift; **~ly but surely** langsam, aber sicher; → **uptake**. **2.** ✝ schleppend. **II** v/t **3.** oft ~ **down** (od. **up**) Geschwindigkeit verringern; Projekt etc verzögern: ~ **the car down** langsamer

fahren. **III** v/i **4.** oft ~ **down** (od. **up**) langsamer fahren od. gehen od. werden. **'~·coach** s F Langweiler(in). **'~·down** s ✝ Am. Bummelstreik m. **'~·,mov·ing** adj kriechend (*Verkehr*).

slow·ness ['sləʊnɪs] s Langsamkeit f, (e-r Person a.) Begriffsstutzigkeit f.

'slow·poke Am. → **slowcoach**. **'~·worm** s zo. Blindschleiche f.

sludge [slʌdʒ] s Schlamm m.

slug¹ [slʌg] s bsd. Am. F **1.** ✖ etc Kugel f. **2.** Schluck m (*Whisky etc*).

slug² [~] s zo. Nacktschnecke f.

slug³ [~] bsd. Am. F **I** v/t j-m e-n Faustschlag versetzen. **II** s **2.** Faustschlag m.

slug·gish ['slʌgɪʃ] adj □ **1.** träge (*Person*), träge fließend (*Fluß etc*). **2.** ✝ schleppend.

sluice [sluːs] **I** s Schleuse f. **II** v/t: ~ **down** abspritzen; ~ **out** aussspritzen. **III** v/i: ~ **out** herausschießen (*Wasser*). ~ **gate** s Schleusentor n.

slum [slʌm] s, mst pl Slums pl, Elendsviertel n. ~ **dwell·er** s Slumbewohner(in).

slump [slʌmp] **I** v/i **1.** ~ **into a chair** sich in e-n Sessel plumpsen lassen; **sit ~ed over** zs.-gesunken sitzen über (dat). **2.** ✝ stürzen (*Preise*), stark zurückgehen (*Umsatz etc*). **II** s **3.** ✝ starker Konjunkturrückgang: ~ **in prices** Preissturz m.

slung [slʌŋ] pret u. pp von **sling¹** u. **²**.

slunk [slʌŋk] pret u. pp von **slink**.

slur¹ [slɜː] s: ~ **on s.o.'s reputation** Rufschädigung f.

slur² [~] v/t **1.** ~ **one's speech** undeutlich sprechen, (*Betrunkener* a.) lallen. **2.** ♩ Töne binden.

slurp [slɜːp] v/t u. v/i F schlürfen.

slush [slʌʃ] s **1.** Schneematsch m. **2.** F rührseliges Zeug. **'slush·y** adj □ **1.** matschig (*Schnee*). **2.** F rührselig.

slut [slʌt] s Schlampe f.

sly [slaɪ] adj □ **1.** gerissen, schlau: **you're a ~ one!** du bist mir vielleicht einer! **2.** verschmitzt (*Lächeln etc*). **II** s **3. on the ~** heimlich.

smack¹ [smæk] v/i: ~ **of** fig. schmecken od. riechen nach.

smack² [~] **I** v/t **1.** j-m e-n Klaps geben: ~ **s.o.'s bottom**, ~ **s.o. on the bottom** j-m eins hinten draufgeben; ~ **s.o.'s face** ✝ j-m e-e runterhauen. **2.** ~ **one's lips** sich die Lippen lecken. **3.** ~ **down** et. hin-klatschen. **II** s **4.** Klaps m: *give s.o. a ~ in the face* F j-m e-e runterhauen. **5.** klatschendes Geräusch. **6.** F Schmatz m. **7.** *have a ~ at* F es mit et. versuchen. **III** adv **8.** F genau, direkt.

smack·er ['smækə] s F **1.** Schmatz m. **2.** Br. Pfund n, Am. Dollar m. **'smack·ing** s F Tracht f Prügel.

small [smɔːl] **I** adj allg. klein: ~ *ad* Br. Kleinanzeige f; ~ *arms* pl Handfeuer-waffen pl; ~ *beer* F ein kleiner Fisch, kleine Fische pl; ~ *change* Kleingeld n; *that's ~ change to him* fig. das ist ein Taschengeld für ihn; ~ *eater* schlechter Esser; *in the ~ hours* in den frühen Morgenstunden; ~ *print* das Kleinge-druckte (e-s Vertrags etc); ~ *talk* Small talk m, n, Geplauder n; *make ~ talk* plaudern; ~ *town* Kleinstadt f; *feel ~* sich klein (u. häßlich) vorkommen; → *wonder* 5. **II** adv klein. **III** s: ~ *of the back* anat. Kreuz n. **,~'mind·ed** adj □ **1.** engstirnig. **2.** kleinlich. **'~·pox** s F Pocken pl. **,~'time** adj fig. klein, Klein...

smarm·y ['smɑːmɪ] adj F schmierig, schmeichlerisch.

smart [smɑːt] **I** adj □ **1.** smart (Per-son), (a. Auto, Kleidung etc) schick. **2.** smart, schlau, clever. **3.** vornehm (Re-staurant, Wohngegend etc). **II** v/i **4.** weh tun; brennen. **III** s **5.** (brennender) Schmerz. **~al·eck** ['ælɪk] s F Besserwis-ser(in). **~ass** s Am. V Klugscheißer(in).

smart·en ['smɑːtn] **I** v/t mst ~ *up* et. verschönern: ~ *o.s. up* → **II.** **II** v/i mst ~ *up* sich schick machen; sich et. Anstän-diges anziehen. **'smart·ness** s **1.** Schick m. **2.** Schlauheit f, Cleverneß f.

smash [smæʃ] **I** v/t **1.** a. ~ *up* zerschla-gen; Wagen zu Schrott fahren; → *smithereens*. **2.** schmettern (a. Tennis etc): ~ *one's fist down on the table* mit der Faust auf den Tisch hauen. **3.** fig. Aufstand etc niederschlagen, Spionage-ring etc zerschlagen. **II** v/i **4.** zerspringen: → *smithereens*. **5.** ~ *into* prallen an (acc) od. gegen, krachen gegen. **III** s **6.** Schlag m; (Tennis etc) Schmetterball m. **7.** → *smash-up*. **8.** Hit m (Buch, Theaterstück etc). **,~·and-'grab (raid)** s bsd. Br. Schaufenstereinbruch m.

smashed [smæʃt] adj F blau (betrun-

ken): *get ~ on* sich vollaufen lassen mit. **'smash·er** s F Klassefrau f, toller Typ; tolles Ding.

smash hit → *smash* 8.

smash·ing ['smæʃɪŋ] adj F toll. **'smash-up** s mot. schwerer Unfall.

smat·ter·ing ['smætərɪŋ] s: *a ~ of Eng-lish* ein paar Brocken Englisch.

smear [smɪə] **I** s **1.** Fleck m. **2.** ✹ (ent-nommener) Abstrich. **3.** Verleumdung f. **II** v/t **4.** Farbe etc verschmieren, Schrift a. verwischen. **5.** Creme etc schmieren (*on, over* auf acc); Haut etc einschmieren (*with* mit). **6.** Glas etc be-, verschmieren (*with* mit): ~*ed with blood* blutbeschmiert, -verschmiert. **7.** verleumden. **III** v/i **8.** schmieren (Farbe etc), sich verwischen (Schrift). ~ *cam-paign* s Verleumdungskampagne f. ~ *test* s ✹ Abstrich m.

smell [smel] **I** v/i (mst irr) **1.** riechen (*at* an dat). **2.** riechen, b.s. stinken (*of* nach) (beide a. fig.): *his breath ~s* er riecht aus dem Mund. **II** v/t (mst irr) **3.** et. riechen; fig. wittern: ~ *out* hunt. auf-spüren (a. fig.); Zimmer etc verpesten. **4.** riechen an (dat). **III** s **5.** Geruch m, b.s. Gestank m: ~ *of gas* Gasgeruch; *there's a ~ of garlic in here* hier stinkt es nach Knoblauch. **6.** *have (od. take) a ~ at* riechen an (dat). **'smell·ing** adj: ~ *salts* pl Riechsalz n. **'smell·y** adj stin-kend: ~ *feet* pl Schweißfüße pl.

smelt¹ [smelt] pret u. pp von **smell**.

smelt² [~] v/t Erz schmelzen.

smile [smaɪl] **I** v/i lächeln (*about* über acc): ~ *at* j-n anlächeln, j-m zulächeln; j-n, et. belächeln, lächeln über (acc); → *keep* 17. **II** v/t: ~ *one's approval* bei-fällig od. zustimmend lächeln. **III** s Lä-cheln n: *with a ~* lächelnd; *be all ~s* (übers ganze Gesicht) strahlen; *give a ~* lächeln; *give s.o. a ~* j-n anlächeln, j-m zulächeln.

smirk [smɜːk] v/i (selbstgefällig od. scha-denfroh) grinsen.

smite [smaɪt] v/t (irr): *be smitten by (od. with)* fig. gepackt werden von.

smith [smɪθ] s Schmied m.

smith·er·eens [ˌsmɪðə'riːnz] s pl: *smash to ~* in tausend Stücke schlagen od. zerspringen.

smith·y ['smɪðɪ] s Schmiede f.

smit·ten ['smɪtn] pp von **smite**.

smock [smɒk] *s* Kittel *m*.

smog [smɒg] *s* Smog *m*.

smoke [sməʊk] **I** *v/i* **1.** rauchen. **II** *v/t* **2.** rauchen. **3.** *Fisch, Fleisch etc* räuchern: ~ **out** ausräuchern. **III** *s* **4.** Rauch *m*: **there's no ~ without fire** *fig.* kein Rauch ohne Flamme; → **go up** 3. **5.** **have a ~** eine rauchen. **6.** F Glimmstengel *m*, Zigarette *f*. ~ **bomb** *s* Rauchbombe *f*.

smoked [sməʊkt] *adj* **1.** geräuchert, Räucher... **2.** ~ **glass** Rauchglas *n*. **'smok·er** *s* **1.** Raucher(in): ~**'s cough** Raucherhusten *m*. **2.** 🚃 Raucherwagen *m*.

'smoke·stack *s* Schornstein *m*.

smok·ing ['sməʊkɪŋ] **I** *s* Rauchen *n*: **no ~** Rauchen verboten. **II** *adj*: ~ **compartment** Raucher(abteil *n*) *m*. **'smok·y** *adj* **1.** rauchig, verräuchert. **2.** rauchig (*Geschmack etc*). **3.** rauchfarben, -farbig.

smol·der *Am.* → **smoulder**.

smooch [smu:tʃ] *v/i* F knutschen, schmusen (**with** mit).

smooth [smu:ð] **I** *adj* □ **1.** glatt (*Fläche, Haut etc*). **2.** ruhig (*Flug etc*). **3.** *fig.* glatt, reibungslos. **4.** *fig.* (aal)glatt. **II** *v/t* **5.** *a.* ~ **out** glätten, *Tischtuch etc a.* glattstreichen: ~ **away** Falten *etc* glätten; *fig.* Schwierigkeiten *etc* aus dem Weg räumen; ~ **over** *fig.* Spannungen *etc* ausgleichen. **III** *s* **6.** → **rough** 9.

smote [sməʊt] *pret von* **smite**.

smoth·er ['smʌðə] *v/t* **1.** *j-n, Aufstand, Feuer etc* ersticken. **2.** *Gähnen etc* unterdrücken. **3.** *fig. j-n* überschütten (**with** mit *Zuneigung etc*).

smoul·der ['sməʊldə] *v/i bsd. Br.* glimmen, schwelen (*beide a. fig.*).

smudge [smʌdʒ] **I** *s* **1.** Fleck *m*. **II** *v/t* **2.** *Farbe etc* verschmieren, *Schrift a.* verwischen. **3.** *Glas etc* be-, verschmieren (**with** mit). **III** *v/i* **4.** schmieren (*Farbe etc*), sich verwischen (*Schrift*). **'smudg·y** *adj* verschmiert, -wischt.

smug [smʌg] *adj* □ selbstgefällig.

smug·gle ['smʌgl] **I** *v/t* schmuggeln (**into** nach *Deutschland etc*; **in** *acc*): ~ **in** (**out**) ein-(heraus)schmuggeln. **II** *v/i* schmuggeln. **'smug·gler** *s* Schmuggler(in). **'smug·gling** *s* Schmuggel *m*.

smut [smʌt] *s* **1.** Rußflocke *f*. **2.** *fig.* Schmutz *m*. **'smut·ty** *adj fig.* schmutzig.

snack [snæk] *s* Snack *m*, Imbiß *m*: **have a ~** e-e Kleinigkeit essen. ~ **bar** *s* Snackbar *f*, Imbißstube *f*.

snaf·fle ['snæfl] *v/t bsd. Br. et.* mitgehen lassen.

snag [snæg] **I** *s fig.* Haken *m*. **II** *v/t* mit *et.* hängenbleiben (**on** an *dat*).

snail [sneɪl] *s zo.* Schnecke *f*: **at a ~'s pace** im Schneckentempo. ~ **shell** *s* Schneckenhaus *n*.

snake [sneɪk] **I** *s zo.* Schlange *f*: ~ **in the grass** *fig.* falsche Schlange (*Frau*); hinterlistiger Kerl (*Mann*). **II** *v/t u. v/i*: ~ (**one's way**) **through** sich schlängeln durch. **'~·bite** *s* Schlangenbiß *m*. **~·charm·er** *s* Schlangenbeschwörer *m*. **'~·skin** *s* Schlangenhaut *f*; -leder *n*.

snak·y ['sneɪkɪ] *adj* gewunden (*Straße etc*).

snap [snæp] **I** *v/i* **1.** (zer)brechen, (-)reißen: **my patience ~ped** mir riß die Geduld *od.* der Geduldsfaden. **2.** *a.* ~ **shut** zuschnappen. **3.** ~ **at** schnappen nach (*a. fig.*); *j-n* anfahren. **4.** ~ **out of it!** Kopf hoch!; ~ **to it!** mach fix! **II** *v/t* **5.** zerbrechen; ~ **off** abbrechen; ~ **s.o.'s head off** F *j-m* ins Gesicht springen. **6.** mit *den Fingern* schnalzen: ~ **one's fingers at** *fig.* keinen Respekt haben *vor* (*dat*), sich hinwegsetzen *über* (*acc*). **7.** *phot.* F knipsen. **8.** ~ **up** *et.* schnell entschlossen kaufen; *fig. Gelegenheit* beim Schopf ergreifen: ~ **it up!** *Am.* F mach fix! **III** *s* **9.** *phot.* F Schnappschuß *m*. **10.** *Am.* Druckknopf *m*. **11.** (*Kälte*)Einbruch *m*. **12.** F Schwung *m*: **come on, put some ~ in it!** häng dich mal ein bißchen rein! **IV** *adj* **13.** spontan. **'~·,drag·on** *s* 🌸 Löwenmaul *n*. ~ **fas·ten·er** *s Am.* Druckknopf *m*.

snap·pish ['snæpɪʃ] *adj* □ *fig.* bissig. **'snap·py** *adj* □ F **1.** modisch, schick. **2.** **make it ~!**, *Br. a.* **look ~!** F mach fix!

'snap·shot *s phot.* Schnappschuß *m*.

snare [sneə] **I** *s* **1.** Falle *f*, Schlinge *f*, *fig. a.* Fallstrick *m*. **II** *v/t* **2.** in der Schlinge fangen. **3.** F *et.* ergattern.

snarl[1] [snɑ:l] **I** *v/i* knurren (*Hund, a. Person*): ~ **at s.o.** *j-n* anknurren. **II** *v/t et.* knurren. **III** *s* Knurren *n*.

snarl[2] [~] *v/t*: **the traffic was ~ed** (**up**) es entstand ein Verkehrschaos. **'~·up** *s* Verkehrschaos *n*.

snatch [snætʃ] **I** *v/t* **1.** *et.* packen: ~ **s.o.'s**

handbag j-m die Handtasche entreißen; ~ *s.th. from s.o.'s hand* j-m et. aus der Hand reißen. **2.** *fig. Gelegenheit* ergreifen; *ein paar Stunden Schlaf etc* ergattern. **II** *v/i* **3.** ~ *at* greifen nach; *fig. Gelegenheit* ergreifen. **III** *s* **4. make a ~ at** greifen nach. **5.** (*Gesprächs*)Fetzen *m*: ~ *of conversation*.

snaz·zy ['snæzı] *adj* □ F schick; *contp.* protzig.

sneak [sniːk] **I** *v/i* **1.** (sich) schleichen, sich stehlen; ~ *up on s.o.* (sich) an j-n heranschleichen. **2.** *Br.* F petzen: ~ *on s.o.* j-n verpetzen. **II** *v/t* **3.** F stibitzen: ~ *a look at* heimlich e-n Blick werfen auf (*acc*). **III** *s* **4.** *Br.* F Petzer(in), Petze *f.* '**sneak·er** *s Am.* Turn- *od.* Wanderschuh *m.* '**sneak·ing** *adj* heimlich, (*Verdacht a.*) leise. '**sneak·y** *adj* □ **1.** heimlich. **2.** gerissen.

sneer [snıə] **I** *v/i* **1.** höhnisch *od.* spöttisch grinsen (*at* über *acc*). **2.** spotten (*at* über *acc*). **II** *s* **3.** höhnisches *od.* spöttisches Grinsen. **4.** höhnische *od.* spöttische Bemerkung.

sneeze [sniːz] **I** *v/i* niesen: *not to be ~d at* F nicht zu verachten. **II** *s* Niesen *n*; Nieser *m*.

snick·er ['snıkə] *bsd. Am.* → **snigger.**

snide [snaıd] *adj* □ abfällig.

sniff [snıf] **I** *v/i* **1.** schniefen, die Nase hochziehen. **2.** schnüffeln (*at* an *dat*). **3.** ~ *at fig.* die Nase rümpfen über (*acc*): *not to be ~ed at* nicht zu verachten. **II** *v/t* **4.** durch die Nase einziehen; *Klebstoff etc* schnüffeln, *Kokain etc* schnupfen. **5.** ~ *out* aufspüren (*a. fig.*). **III** *s* **6.** Schniefen *n*.

snif·fle ['snıfl] **I** *v/i* → **sniff.** **II** *s* Schniefen *n*: *he's got the ~s* F ihm läuft dauernd die Nase.

snif·ter ['snıftə] *s Am.* Kognakschwenker *m.*

snig·ger ['snıgə] *bsd. Br.* **I** *v/i* kichern (*at* über *acc*). **II** *s* Kichern *n.*

snip [snıp] **I** *v/t* **1.** durchschnippeln: ~ *off* abschnippeln. **II** *s* **2.** Schnitt *m.* **3.** *Br.* F Gelegenheitskauf *m.*

snipe [snaıp] **I** *pl* **snipes**, *bsd. coll.* **snipe** *s orn.* Schnepfe *f.* **II** *v/i* ~ *at* aus dem Hinterhalt schießen auf (*acc*); *fig.* aus dem Hinterhalt angreifen (*acc*). '**snip·er** *s* Heckenschütze *m.*

snip·pet ['snıpıt] *s*: ~ *of conversation*

Gesprächsfetzen *m*; ~s *pl of information* bruchstückhafte Informationen *pl.*

snitch [snıtʃ] *v/i*: ~ *on s.o.* F j-n verpetzen *od.* verpfeifen.

sniv·el ['snıvl] *v/i pret u. pp* **-eled**, *bsd. Br.* **-elled** greinen, jammern.

snob [snɒb] *s* Snob *m.* '**snob·ber·y** *s* Snobismus *m.* '**snob·bish** *adj* □ snobistisch, versnobt.

snog [snɒg] *v/i Br.* F knutschen, schmusen (*with mit*).

snook [snuːk] *s*: *cock a ~ at Br.* F j-m zeigen, was man von ihm hält.

snook·er ['snuːkə] **I** *s* Billard: Snooker Pool. **II** *v/t*: *be ~ed* F völlig machtlos sein.

snoop [snuːp] *v/i*: ~ *about* (*od. around*) F herumschnüffeln (*in* in *dat*). '**snoop·er** *s* F Schnüffler(in).

snoot·y ['snuːtı] *adj* □ F hochnäsig.

snooze [snuːz] F **I** *v/i* ein Nickerchen machen. **II** *s* Nickerchen *n*: *have a ~* → **I.**

snore [snɔː] **I** *v/i* schnarchen. **II** *s* Schnarchen *n.* '**snor·er** *s* Schnarcher(in).

snor·kel ['snɔːkl] *s* Schnorchel *m.* **II** *v/i* schnorcheln.

snort [snɔːt] **I** *v/i* (*a. verächtlich od.* wütend) schnauben. **II** *v/t* schnauben. **III** *s* Schnauben *n*: *give a ~ of derision* verächtlich schnauben.

snot [snɒt] *s* F Rotz *m.*'**snot·ty** *adj* F **1.** Rotz...: ~ *nose.* **2.** *fig.* aufgeblasen.

snout [snaʊt] *s zo.* Schnauze *f*, (*e-s Schweins etc a.*) Rüssel *m.*

snow [snəʊ] **I** *s* **1.** Schnee *m* (*a. sl. Kokain, Heroin*): **(as) white as ~** schneeweiß. **2.** Schneefall *m.* **II** *v/impers* **3.** schneien. **III** *v/t* **4.** *be ~ed in* (*od. up*) eingeschneit sein; *be ~ed under with work* mit Arbeit überhäuft sein. '~·ball *s* Schneeball *m*: ~ *fight* Schneeballschlacht *f.* '~·blind *adj* schneeblind *f.* '~·capped *adj* schneebedeckt (*Berggipfel*). '~·drift *s* Schneewehe *f.* '~·drop *s* ♀ Schneeglöckchen *n.* '~·fall *s* Schneefall *m.* '~·flake *s* Schneeflocke *f.* '~·line *s* Schneegrenze *f.* '~·man *s* (*irr man*) Schneemann *m.* ~·'a·bom·i·na·ble. '~·plough, '~·plow *s Am.* Schneepflug *m* (*a. beim Skifahren*). '~·storm *s* Schneesturm *m.* ~·'white *adj* schneeweiß.

snow·y ['snəʊɪ] *adj* schneereich (*Tag etc*), (*Gegend a.*) verschneit.

snub¹ [snʌb] *v/t j-n* brüskieren, *j-m* über den Mund fahren.

snub² [~] *adj* Stups...: → **nose**. **'~-nosed** *adj* stupsnasig.

snuff¹ [snʌf] *s* Schnupftabak *m.*

snuff² [~] *v/t* Kerze ausdrücken: ~ **out** *fig. Leben* auslöschen; ~ **it** *Br.* F den Löffel weglegen (*sterben*).

snuf·fle ['snʌfl] → **sniffle**.

snug [snʌg] **I** *adj* □ **1.** behaglich, gemütlich. **2.** gutsitzend (*Kleidungsstück*): **be a ~ fit** gut passen. **II** *s* **3.** *Br.* kleines Nebenzimmer (*e-s Pubs*).

snug·gle ['snʌgl] *v/i*: ~ **up to s.o.** sich an j-n kuscheln; ~ **down in bed** sich ins Bett kuscheln.

so [səʊ] **I** *adv* **1.** so, dermaßen: **he is ~ stupid (that) he ...** er ist so dumm, daß er ... **2.** (ja) so: **I am ~ glad. 3.** so, in dieser Weise: **is that ~?** wirklich?; ~ **as to** so daß, um zu; **a mile or ~** etwa e-e Meile; → **forth** I, **if** 1, **on** 13, **4.** verkürzend: **He is tired.** ⚥ **am I** Ich auch; → **hope** II, **think** 6, *etc.* **II** *cj* **5.** deshalb. **6.** ~ **what?** F na und?

soak [səʊk] **I** *v/t* **1.** *et.* einweichen (*in in dat*). **2.** ~ **up** Flüssigkeit aufsaugen; *fig.* Neuigkeiten *etc* in sich aufsaugen. **3.** durchnässen: → **skin** 1. **4.** F *j-n* ausnehmen, neppen. **II** *v/i* **5.** sickern. **'soak·ing** *adj u. adv*: ~ (**wet**) tropfnaß.

'so-and-so *pl* **-sos** *s* F **1.** Herr *od.* Frau *od.* Frl. Soundso *od.* Sowieso: **a Mr ~** ein Herr Soundso. **2.** *euphem.* blöder Hund.

soap [səʊp] **I** *s* **1.** Seife *f.* **2.** F → **soap opera. II** *v/t* **3.** (sich) ein-, einseifen. **~ bub·ble** *s* Seifenblase *f.* **~ dish** *s* Seifenschale *f.* **~ op·er·a** *s* Rundfunk, *TV:* Seifenoper *f.* **'~-suds** *s pl* Seifenschaum *m.*

soap·y ['səʊpɪ] *adj* □ **1.** Seifen...: ~ **water. 2.** seifig. **3.** F schmeichlerisch.

soar [sɔː] *v/i* **1.** aufsteigen: ~ **into the sky** zum Himmel emporsteigen. **2.** hochragen. **3.** *fig.* in die Höhe schnellen (*Preise etc*).

sob [sɒb] **I** *v/i* schluchzen. **II** *v/t* schluchzen: ~ **out** schluchzend erzählen. **III** *s* Schluchzen *n;* Schluchzer *m.*

so·ber ['səʊbə] **I** *adj* □ nüchtern (*a. fig.*): (**as**) ~ **as a judge** stocknüchtern. **II** *v/t*

mst ~ **up** ausnüchtern, wieder nüchtern machen. **III** *v/i mst* ~ **up** (sich) ausnüchtern, wieder nüchtern werden: **have a ~ing effect on s.o.** *fig.* auf j-n ernüchternd wirken.

sob sto·ry *s* F rührselige Geschichte.

so-'called *adj* sogenannt.

soc·cer ['sɒkə] *s* Fußball *m* (*Spiel*).

so·cia·ble ['səʊʃəbl] *adj* □ gesellig (*Person, a. Abend etc*); zutraulich (*Tier*).

so·cial ['səʊʃl] *adj* □ **1.** gesellschaftlich, Gesellschafts..., sozial, Sozial...: **have a busy ~ life** oft ausgehen *od.* Besuch haben; ~ **science** Sozialwissenschaft *f.* **2.** sozial, Sozial...: ~ **insurance** Sozialversicherung *f;* ~ **security** *Br.* Sozialhilfe *f;* **be on ~ security** Sozialhilfe beziehen; ~ **worker** Sozialarbeiter(in). **3.** *pol.* Sozial...: ~ **democrat** Sozialdemokrat(in). **4.** *biol.* gesellig (*Wesen*). **5.** F gesellig (*Person*).

so·cial·ism ['səʊʃəlɪzəm] *s* Sozialismus *m.* **'so·cial·ist I** *s* Sozialist(in). **II** *adj* sozialistisch.

so·cial·ize ['səʊʃəlaɪz] *v/i*: **I don't ~ much** ich gehe nicht oft aus; ~ **with** (gesellschaftlich) verkehren mit.

so·ci·e·ty [sə'saɪətɪ] *s allg.* Gesellschaft *f.*

so·ci·o·log·i·cal [ˌsəʊsjə'lɒdʒɪkl] *adj* □ soziologisch. **so·ci·ol·o·gist** [ˌsəʊsɪ'ɒlə-dʒɪst] *s* Soziologe *m,* Soziologin *f.* **so·ci·ol·o·gy** *s* Soziologie *f.*

sock¹ [sɒk] *s* Socke(n) *m) f;* **pull one's ~s up** *Br.* F sich am Riemen reißen; **put a ~ in it!** *Br.* F hör doch auf, Mensch!

sock² [~] F **I** *v/t*: ~ **s.o. on the jaw** j-m e-n Kinnhaken verpassen. **II** *s* (*Faust-*)Schlag *m:* **give s.o. a ~ on the jaw** → I.

sock·et ['sɒkɪt] *s* **1.** *anat.* (*Augen*)Höhle *f.* **2.** ⚡ Steckdose *f;* Fassung *f* (*e-r Glühbirne*); (*Kopfhörer- etc*)Anschluß *m.*

sod [sɒd] *bsd. Br. sl.* **I** *s* blöder Hund: **poor ~** armes Schwein. **II** *v/t*: ~ **it!** Scheiße! **III** *v/i*: ~ **off!** verpiß dich!

so·da ['səʊdə] *s* **1.** Soda *n:* **two whisky and ~s** zwei Whisky mit Soda. **2.** *bsd. Am.* (*Orangen- etc*)Limonade *f.*

sod·den ['sɒdn] *adj* durchnäßt, (*Boden*) aufgeweicht.

so·di·um ['səʊdɪəm] *s* 🜨 Natrium *n.*

so·fa ['səʊfə] *s* Sofa *n.*

soft [sɒft] *adj* □ **1.** *allg.* weich: **be ~ in the head** F e-e weiche Birne haben; → **spot** 4. **2.** leise (*Stimme, Musik* etc); gedämpft, dezent (*Beleuchtung, Farbe, Musik*). **3.** sanft (*Berührung, Brise etc*). **4.** gutmütig; nachsichtig (*with* gegen *j-n*). **5.** F ruhig (*Job etc*). **6.** verweichlicht: *get* ~ verweichlichen. **7.** weich (*Droge*): ~ *drink* Soft Drink *m*, alkoholfreies Getränk. ˌ~'**boiled** *adj* weich(gekocht) (*Ei*).

soft-en ['sɒfn] **I** *v/t* **1.** weich machen; *Wasser* enthärten. **2.** *Ton, Licht etc* dämpfen. **3.** ~ *up* F *j-n* weichmachen. **II** *v/i* **4.** weich werden. '**soft-en-er** *s* (*Wasser*)Enthärter *m*.

ˌsoft'heart-ed *adj* □ weichherzig.

soft-ie → *softy*.

'**soft**|-'**ped-al** *v/t* F et. herunterspielen. '~-**soap** *v/t* F *j-m* um den Bart gehen. '~-**ware** *s* Computer: Software *f*.

soft-y ['sɒftɪ] *s* F Softie *m*, Softy *m*, Weichling *m*.

sog-gy ['sɒgɪ] *adj* □ aufgeweicht (*Boden etc*), (*a. Gemüse etc*) matschig, (*Brot etc*) teigig, glitschig.

soil¹ [sɔɪl] *s* Boden *m*, Erde *f*.

soil² [~] *v/t* beschmutzen, schmutzig machen.

sol-ace ['sɒləs] *s* Trost *m*: *be a ~ to s.o.* j-m ein Trost sein; *find ~ in* Trost finden in (*dat*).

so-lar ['səʊlə] *adj* Sonnen...: ~ *eclipse ast.* Sonnenfinsternis *f*; ~ *energy* Sonnen-, Solarenergie *f*; ~ *system* Sonnensystem *n*.

so-lar-i-um [səʊ'leərɪəm] *pl* -**i-a** [~ɪə], -**i-ums** *s* Solarium *n*.

so-lar plex-us ['pleksəs] *s anat.* Solarplexus *m*; Magengrube *f*.

sold [səʊld] *pret u. pp von* **sell.**

sol-der ['sɒldə] *v/t* (ver)löten. '**sol-der-ing** *adj*: ~ *iron* Lötkolben *m*.

sol-dier ['səʊldʒə] **I** *s* Soldat *m*. **II** *v/i*: ~ *on bsd. Br.* (unermüdlich) weitermachen.

sole¹ [səʊl] *adj* (□ → *solely*) einzig; alleinig, Allein...

sole² [~] *s* (Fuß-, Schuh)Sohle *f*. **II** *v/t* *Schuh* besohlen.

sole³ [~] *s ichth.* Seezunge *f*.

sole-ly ['səʊllɪ] *adv* (einzig u.) allein, ausschließlich.

sol-emn ['sɒləm] *adj* □ **1.** feierlich: *give s.o. one's ~ pledge (od. word) that a.* j-m hoch u. heilig versprechen, daß. **2.** ernst.

so-lic-it [sə'lɪsɪt] **I** *v/t et.* erbitten, bitten um: ~ *s.o.'s help* j-n um Hilfe bitten. **II** *v/i* Männer ansprechen (*Prostituierte*).

so-lic-i-tor [sə'lɪsɪtə] *s* ↓ *Br.* Solicitor *m*.

so-lic-it-ous [sə'lɪsɪtəs] *adj* □ **1.** dienstbeflissen. **2.** besorgt (*about, for* um).

sol-id ['sɒlɪd] *adj* □ **1.** *allg.* fest. **2.** stabil, massiv. **3.** massiv: *a ~ gold watch* e-e Uhr aus massivem Gold. **4.** *fig.* einmütig, geschlossen (*for* für; *against* gegen). **5.** *fig.* gewichtig, triftig (*Grund etc*), stichhaltig (*Argument etc*). **6.** *I waited for a ~ hour* F ich wartete e-e geschlagene Stunde. **II** *s* **7.** *A* Körper *m*. **8.** *pl* feste Nahrung.

sol-i-dar-i-ty [ˌsɒlɪ'dærətɪ] *s* Solidarität *f*: *in ~ with* aus Solidarität mit; *declare one's ~ with* sich solidarisch erklären mit.

so-lid-i-fy [sə'lɪdɪfaɪ] **I** *v/t* **1.** fest werden lassen. **2.** *fig.* festigen. **II** *v/i* **3.** fest werden. **4.** *fig.* sich festigen.

ˌsol-id-'state *adj* volltransistor(is)iert.

so-lil-o-quy [sə'lɪləkwɪ] *s* **1.** *thea.* Monolog *m*. **2.** Selbstgespräch *n*.

sol-i-taire [ˌsɒlɪ'teə] *s* **1.** Solitär *m*. **2.** *bsd. Am.* → *patience* 2.

sol-i-tar-y ['sɒlɪtərɪ] **I** *adj* □ **1.** einsam, (*Leben a.*) zurückgezogen, (*Ort etc a.*) abgelegen: → *confinement* 2. **2.** einzig. **II** *s* **3.** F Einzelhaft *f*.

so-lo ['səʊləʊ] *pl* **-los** *s* ♪ Solo *n*. **II** *adj* ♪ Solo...: ~ *flight* ✈ Alleinflug *m*. **III** *adv* ♪ solo: *fly* ~ ✈ e-n Alleinflug machen. '**so-lo-ist** *s* ♪ Solist(in).

sol-stice ['sɒlstɪs] *s ast.* Sonnenwende *f*.

sol-u-ble ['sɒljʊbl] *adj* **1.** ♣ löslich: ~ *in water* wasserlöslich. **2.** *fig.* lösbar.

so-lu-tion [sə'lu:ʃn] *s* **1.** *fig.* Lösung *f* (*to gen*). **2.** ♣ Lösung *f*; Auflösung *f*.

solv-a-ble ['sɒlvəbl] *adj fig.* lösbar.

solve [sɒlv] *v/t Fall, Rätsel etc* lösen.

sol-ven-cy ['sɒlvənsɪ] *s* ↑ Solvenz *f*, Zahlungsfähigkeit *f*. '**sol-vent I** *adj* □ ↑ solvent, zahlungsfähig. **II** *s* ♣ Lösungsmittel *n*.

som-ber *Am.* → *sombre.*

som-bre ['sɒmbə] *adj* □ düster (*Farben, Raum etc, fig. Miene etc*).

som-bre-ro [sɒm'breərəʊ] *pl* -**ros** *s* Sombrero *m*.

some [sʌm] **I** *adj* **1.** (irgend)ein: ~ *day* eines Tages; ~ *day* (*or other*) irgendwann (einmal). **2.** *vor pl:* einige, ein paar: → *few* 1. **3.** manche. **4.** gewiß: → *extent* 2. **5.** etwas, ein wenig *od.* bißchen: *take ~ more* nimm noch et.; *would you like ~ more cake?* möchtest du noch ein Stück Kuchen? **6.** ungefähr: *~ 30 people.* **II** *pron* **7.** (irgend)ein. **8.** etwas. **9.** einige, ein paar. **~·bod·y** ['sʌbɒdɪ] **I** *pron* jemand. **II** *s: be ~* et. vorstellen, j-d sein. **'~·day** *adv* eines Tages. **'~·how** *adv* irgendwie. **'~·one** → *somebody.* **'~·place** Am. → *somewhere* 1.

som·er·sault ['sʌməsɔːlt] *s* Salto *m*; Purzelbaum *m*: *do (od.* turn*) a ~* e-n Salto machen; e-n Purzelbaum schlagen.

'some|·thing I *pron* **1.** etwas: *or ~* F od. so. **II** *adv* **2.** *~ like* F ungefähr; *look ~ like* so ähnlich aussehen wie; *~ over £200* et. mehr als 200 Pfund. **3.** *be ~ of a pianist* so et. wie ein Pianist sein. **III** *s* **4.** a little → j-n e-e Kleinigkeit (*Geschenk*); *a certain ~* ein gewisses Etwas. **'~·time** *adv* irgendwann. **'~·times** *adv* manchmal. **'~·way** *adv* Am. irgendwie. **'~·what** *adv* ein bißchen *od.* wenig: *~ of a shock* ein ziemlicher Schock. **'~·where** *adv* **1.** irgendwo; irgendwohin. **2.** *fig.* *~ between 30 and 40 people* so zwischen 30 u. 40 Leute; *~ in the region of £100* um 100 Pfund herum.

som·nam·bu·list [sɒm'næmbjʊlɪst] *s* Nacht-, Schlafwandler(in).

som·no·lent ['sɒmnələnt] *adj* □ **1.** schläfrig. **2.** einschläfernd.

son [sʌn] *s* **1.** Sohn *m*: *~ of a bitch bsd. Am. sl.* Scheißkerl *m*. **2.** *Anrede:* F junger Mann.

so·na·ta [sə'nɑːtə] *s* ♪ Sonate *f*.

song [sɒŋ] *s* **1.** Lied *n*: *buy s.th. for a ~* F et. für ein Butterbrot kaufen; *make a ~ and dance about* F ein furchtbares Theater machen wegen. **2.** Gesang *m* (*a. von Vögeln*): *burst into ~* zu singen anfangen; → *bird* ♪ Singvogel *m*. **'~·book** *s* Liederbuch *n*.

son·ic ['sɒnɪk] *adj phys.* Schall...: *~ bang (od.* boom*)* ✓ Überschallknall *m*.

'son-in-law *pl* **'sons-in-law** *s* Schwiegersohn *m*.

son·net ['sɒnɪt] *s* Sonett *n*.

so·no·rous ['sɒnərəs] *adj* □ sonor, klangvoll, volltönend.

soon [suːn] *adv* bald: *as ~ as* sobald; *as ~* ·

as possible so bald wie möglich; *at the ~est* frühestens; *I don't want to speak too ~* ich will es nicht berufen. **'soon·er** *adv* **1.** eher, früher. früher: *the ~ the better* je früher, desto besser *od.* lieber; *~ or later* früher *od.* später; *no ~ said than done* gesagt, getan. **2.** *I would ~ ... than* ich würde lieber ... als.

soot [sʊt] *s* Ruß *m*.

soothe [suːð] *v/t* **1.** a. *~ down* j-n beschwichtigen, *a.* j-s *Nerven* beruhigen. **2.** *Schmerzen* lindern, mildern.

soot·y ['sʊtɪ] *adj* rußig, Ruß...

sop [sɒp] **I** *s* Beschwichtigungsmittel *n* (*to* für). **II** *v/t: ~ up* aufsaugen.

soph·ism ['sɒfɪzəm] *s* Sophismus *m*, Scheinbeweis *m*, Trugschluß *m*.

so·phis·ti·cat·ed [sə'fɪstɪkeɪtɪd] *adj* □ **1.** kultiviert. **2.** ☼ hochentwickelt. **3.** *contr.* intellektuell.

soph·o·more ['sɒfəmɔː] *s* Am. Student(in) im zweiten Jahr.

so·po·rif·ic [ˌsɒpə'rɪfɪk] **I** *adj* (*~ally*) einschläfernd: *~ drug* → **II.** **II** *s* Schlafmittel *n*.

sop·ping ['sɒpɪŋ] *adj u. adv: ~* (wet*)* F patschnaß. **'sop·py** *adj* □ *Br.* F schmalzig, rührselig.

so·pra·no [sə'prɑːnəʊ] *pl* **-nos** *s* Sopran *m* (*Tonlage, Stimme*), (*Sängerin a.*) Sopranistin *f*.

sor·bet ['sɔːbeɪ] *s bsd. Br.* Fruchteis *n*.

sor·cer·er ['sɔːsərə] *s* Zauberer *m*, Hexenmeister *m*, Hexer *m*. **'sor·cer·ess** *s* Zauberin *f*, Hexe *f*. **'sor·cer·y** *s* Zauberei *f*, Hexerei *f*.

sor·did ['sɔːdɪd] *adj* □ schmutzig (*a. fig.*).

sore [sɔː] **I** *adj* **1.** weh, wund; entzündet: *he is ~ all over* ihm tut alles weh; *my legs are ~* mir tun die Beine weh; *~ throat* Angina *f*, Halsentzündung *f*; *have a ~ throat* a. Halsschmerzen haben; → *sight* I, *thumb* I. **2.** *fig.* wund (*Punkt*). **3.** *bsd. Am.* F sauer (*about* wegen). **II** *s* **4.** wunde Stelle, Wunde *f*. **'sore·ly** *adv: ~ missed* schmerzlich vermißt; *~ needed* dringend gebraucht.

so·ror·i·ty [sə'rɒrətɪ] *s* Am. Studentinnenverbindung *f*.

sor·rel ['sɒrəl] *s* ♣ Sauerampfer *m*.

sor·row ['sɒrəʊ] *s* **1.** (*at, over*) Kummer *m* (*über acc,* um), Trauer *f* (*um*); Traurigkeit f. **2.** Sorge f: → **drown** 2. **sor·row·ful** ['ʃɒful] adj □ traurig, kummervoll.

sor·ry ['sɒrı] **I** adj **1. be** (od. **feel**) **~ for s.o.** j-n bedauern od. bemitleiden: **I'm ~ for him** er tut mir leid; **I'm ~ ~** 3; **I am ~ to say** ich muß leider sagen. **2.** traurig, jämmerlich. **II** int **3.** a) (es) tut mir leid, b) Entschuldigung!, Verzeihung!: **say ~** sich entschuldigen (**to s.o.** bei j-m; **for s.th.** für et.). **4.** bsd. Br. wie bitte?

sort [sɔːt] **I** s **1.** Sorte f, Art f, ♀ a. Marke f: **all ~s of things** alles mögliche. **2.** Art f: **nothing of the ~** nichts dergleichen; **what ~ of** (a) **man is he?** wie ist er?; **I had a ~ of** (a) **feeling that** ich hatte das unbestimmte Gefühl, daß; **I ~ of expected it** F ich habe es irgendwie od. beinahe erwartet. **3. of a ~, of ~s** contp. so et. Ähnliches wie. **4. be out of ~s** F nicht auf der Höhe od. auf dem Damm sein. **5.** F **guter** etc Kerl. **II** v/t **6.** sortieren: **~ out** aussortieren; Problem etc lösen, Frage etc klären; Br. F j-n zur Schnecke machen. **III** v/i **7.** **~ through** et. durchsehen.

sor·tie ['sɔːtiː] s **1.** ✗ Ausfall m; ✈ Einsatz m. **2.** fig. Ausflug m (**into** in acc).

SOS [ˌesəʊˈes] s ♀ SOS n: **~ message** SOS-Ruf m.

'so·so adj u. adv F so lala.

souf·flé ['suːfleɪ] s gastr. Soufflé n, Auflauf m.

sought [sɔːt] pret u. pp von **seek**. **'~--af·ter** adj begehrt (Person), (Sache a.) gesucht.

soul [səʊl] s **1.** Seele f (a. fig.). **2.** Gefühl n; (künstlerischer) Ausdruck. **3. be the ~ of generosity** die Großzügigkeit selbst od. in Person sein. **4.** ♪ Soul m. **'~-de·stroy·ing** adj geisttötend (Arbeit etc).

soul·ful ['səʊlfʊl] adj □ gefühlvoll (Musik etc), seelenvoll (Blick).

soul| mu·sic s Soulmusik f. **'~-search·ing** s Gewissensprüfung f.

sound¹ [saʊnd] **I** s **1.** Geräusch n; phys. Schall m; (Radio, TV etc) Ton m; ♪ Klang m, (Rockmusik etc a.) Sound m; ling. Laut m: **I don't like the ~ of it** fig. die Sache gefällt mir nicht. **II** v/i **2.** erklingen, ertönen: **the bell ~ed for lunch** es klingelte zum Mittagessen. **3.** fig. klingen. **4. ~ off** F tönen (**about, on**

von). **III** v/t **5. ~ one's horn** mot. hupen; → **alarm** 1. **6.** ling. (aus)sprechen.

sound² [~] **I** adj □ **1.** gesund; intakt, in Ordnung. **2.** fig. klug; vernünftig (Person, Rat etc). **3.** fig. gründlich (Ausbildung etc). **4.** fig. gehörig (Tracht Prügel); vernichtend (Niederlage). **5.** fig. fest, tief (Schlaf): → **sleeper** 1. **II** adv **6. be ~ asleep** fest od. tief schlafen.

sound³ [~] v/t **1.** ♪ (aus)loten. **2. ~ out** j-n aushalen (**about, on** über acc); j-s Ansichten etc herausfinden.

sound| bar·ri·er s phys. Schallmauer f, -grenze f. **~ film** s Tonfilm m. □

sound·less ['saʊndlıs] adj □ lautlos.

'sound·ness s **1.** Gesundheit f; Intaktheit f. **2.** fig. Klugheit f, Vernünftigkeit f. **3.** fig. Gründlichkeit f.

'sound|·proof I adj schalldicht. **II** v/t schalldicht machen. **~ track** s **1.** Film: Tonspur f. **2.** Filmmusik f. **~ wave** s phys. Schallwelle f.

soup [suːp] **I** s Suppe f: **be in the ~** F in der Patsche od. Tinte sitzen. **II** v/t: **~ up** F Auto, Motor frisieren. **~ plate** s Suppenteller m. **~ spoon** s Suppenlöffel m.

sour ['saʊə] **I** adj □ **1.** sauer: **~ cream** Sauerrahm m, saure Sahne; **go ~** sauer werden. **2.** fig. mürrisch. **II** v/i **3.** sauer werden. **III** v/t **4.** sauer werden lassen; säuern: **~ed cream** Br. Sauerrahm m, saure Sahne.

source [sɔːs] s Quelle f, fig. a. Ursache f, Ursprung m: **from a reliable ~** aus zuverlässiger Quelle. **~ lan·guage** s ling. Ausgangssprache f.

sour·puss ['saʊəpʊs] s F Miesepeter m.

soused [saʊst] adj F blau (betrunken).

sou·tane [suːˈtɑːn] s eccl. Soutane f.

south [saʊθ] **I** s **1.** Süden m: **in the ~ of** im Süden von (od. gen); **to the ~ of** → 5. **2.** a. 2 Süden m, südlicher Landesteil: **the** 2 Br. Südengland n; Am. die Südstaaten pl. **II** adj **3.** Süd..., südlich: **2 Pole** Südpol m. **III** adv **4.** südwärts, nach Süden. **5. ~ of** südlich von (od. gen). **2 A·mer·i·can I** adj südamerikanisch. **II** s Südamerikaner(in). **'~·bound** adj nach Süden gehend od. fahrend. **~·east I** s Südosten m. **II** adj südöstlich, Südost... **III** adv südöstlich, nach Südosten.

south·er·ly ['sʌðəlı] **I** adj südlich, Süd... **II** adv von od. nach Süden. **south·ern**

['~ən] *adj* südlich, Süd... '**south·ern·er**
s **1.** Bewohner(in) des Südens (*e-s Landes*). **2.** ♀ *Am.* Südstaatler(in). **south-
ern·most** ['~məʊst] *adj* südlichst.

'**south·paw** *s Boxen:* Rechtsausleger *m.*

'**south·ward** ['saʊθwəd] *adj u. adv* südlich, südwärts, nach Süden: *in a ~ direction* in südlicher Richtung, Richtung Süden. '**south·wards** *adv* →
southward.

,**south'west I** *s* Südwesten *m.* **II** *adj* südwestlich, Südwest... **III** *adv* südwestlich, nach Südwesten.

sou·ve·nir [,suːvə'nɪə] *s* Andenken *n (of
an acc)*, Souvenir *n.*

sov·er·eign ['sɒvrɪn] **I** *s* Landesherr(in),
Monarch(in). **II** *adj* souverän (*Staat*).
sov·er·eign·ty ['~rəntɪ] *s* Souveränität *f.*

So·vi·et ['səʊvɪət] **I** *s:* *the ~s pl* die Sow-
jets *pl.* **II** *adj* sowjetisch, Sowjet...

sow¹ [saʊ] *s zo.* Sau *f.*

sow² [səʊ] *v/t (mst irr)* **1.** *Getreide etc*
säen, *Samen* aussäen: *~ the seeds of
discord fig.* Zwietracht säen; → **oats.**
2. *Feld etc* besäen (*with* mit).

so·ya bean ['sɔɪə] *s* ♀ Sojabohne *f.*

soz·zled ['sɒzld] *adj Br.* F blau (*betrunken*).

spa [spɑː] *s* (Heil)Bad *n.*

space [speɪs] **I** *s* **1.** Raum *m:* *stare into
~* ins Leere starren. **2.** Platz *m*, Raum
m. **3.** (Welt)Raum *m.* **4.** Lücke *f*,
Platz *m*, Stelle *f.* **5.** Zwischenraum *m.*
6. Zeitraum *m.* **II** *v/t* **7.** *a.* *~ out* in
Abständen anordnen: *the chairs two
feet apart* die Stühle im Abstand von
zwei Fuß aufstellen. *~ bar s* Leertaste *f*
(*e-r Schreibmaschine*). '*~craft s (Welt)*
craft) (Welt)Raumfahrzeug *n.* *~ flight s*
(Welt)Raumflug *m.* *~ heat·er s* Heiz-
apparat *m*, -gerät *n.* '*~lab s* Raumla-
bor *n.* '*~man s (irr man)* **1.** Raumfahrer *m.* **2.** Außerirdische *m.* '*~ship s*
Raumschiff *n.* *~ shut·tle s* Raumfähre
f, -transporter *m.* *~ sta·tion s* (Welt-
)Raumstation *f.* *~ suit s* Raumanzug *m.*
~ trav·el s (Welt)Raumfahrt *f.* *~-
wom·an s (irr woman)* **1.** Raumfahre-
rin *f.* **2.** Außerirdische *f.*

spac·ing ['speɪsɪŋ] *s:* *type s.th. in (od.
with) single (double) ~* et. mit einzeili-
gem (zweizeiligem) Abstand tippen.

spa·cious ['speɪʃəs] *adj* □ geräumig

(*Zimmer etc*), weiträumig angelegt,
weitläufig (*Garten etc*).

spade¹ [speɪd] *s* Spaten *m:* *call a ~ a ~
fig.* das Kind beim Namen nennen.

spade² [~] *s Kartenspiel:* a) *pl* Pik *n (Farbe*), b) Pik(karte *f*) *n.*

'**spade·work** *s fig.* (mühevolle) Vorarbeit.

spa·ghet·ti [spə'getɪ] *s pl (sg konstruiert)*
Spaghetti *pl.*

span [spæn] **I** *s* **1.** ✎, *orn.* (Flügel-)
Spannweite *f.* **2.** Zeitspanne *f.* **3.** (Lebens)Spanne *f*, (Gedächtnis)Umfang *m.*
II *v/t* **4.** *Fluß etc* überspannen (*Brücke*).
5. *fig.* sich erstrecken über (*acc*).

span·gle ['spæŋgl] **I** *s* Paillette *f.* **II** *v/t*
mit Pailletten besetzen; *fig.* übersäen
(*with* mit).

Span·iard ['spænjəd] *s* Spanier(in).

span·iel ['spænjəl] *s zo.* Spaniel *m.*

Span·ish ['spænɪʃ] **I** *adj* **1.** spanisch. **II** *s*
2. *the ~ pl* die Spanier *pl.* **3.** *ling.* Spanisch *n.*

spank [spæŋk] *v/t j-m* den Hintern versohlen. '**spank·ing I** *adj* flott, scharf
(*Tempo*). **II** *adv* F: *~ clean* blitzsauber;
~ new funkelnagelneu. **III** *s:* *give s.o. a
~* → **spank.**

span·ner ['spænə] *s* ⊙ *bsd. Br.* Schraubenschlüssel *m:* *put* (*od. throw*) *a ~ in
the works* F j-m in die Quere kommen.

spar [spɑː] *v/i* **1.** *Boxen:* sparren (*with*
mit). **2.** sich ein Wortgefecht liefern
(*with* mit).

spare [speə] **I** *v/t* **1.** *j-n, et.* entbehren. **2.**
Geld, Zeit etc übrig haben: *can you ~
me a cigarette (10 minutes)?* hast du
e-e Zigarette (10 Minuten Zeit) für
mich (übrig)? **3.** *keine Kosten, Mühen
etc* scheuen. **4.** *~ s.o. s.th.* j-m et. ersparen, j-n mit et. verschonen. **II** *adj* **5.**
Ersatz...: *~ part* ⊙ Ersatzteil *n, m; ~ tire
(bsd. Br. tyre)* *mot.* Ersatz-, Reserverei-
fen *m; Br. fig. humor.* Rettungsring *m.*
6. überschüssig: *~ bedroom* Gästezim-
mer *n; ~ time* Freizeit *f; have you got
10 ~ minutes?* hast du 10 Minuten Zeit
(übrig)? **III** *s* **7.** *mot.* Ersatz-, Reserve-
reifen *m.* **8.** ⊙ *bsd. Br.* Ersatzteil *n, m.*
'*~ribs s pl gastr.* Spareribs *pl (gegrillte
Rippenstücke vom Schwein).*

spar·ing ['speərɪŋ] *adj* □ sparsam: *be ~
with s.th., use s.th. ~ly* sparsam mit et.
umgehen.

spark [spɑːk] **I** s Funke(n) m (a. fig.): *whenever they meet the ~s fly* immer, wenn sie zs.-kommen, fliegen die Fetzen. **II** v/i Funken sprühen: ~*ing plug* mot. Br. Zündkerze f. **III** v/t a) a. ~ *off* Krawalle etc auslösen, b) bsd. Am. j-s Interesse etc wecken.

spar·kle ['spɑːkl] **I** v/i funkeln, (Augen a.) blitzen (*with* vor dat). **II** s Funkeln n, Blitzen n. **spar·kling** ['spɑːklɪŋ] adj **1.** funkelnd, blitzend. **2.** ~ *wine* Perl- od. Schaumwein m; Sekt m. **3.** fig. sprühend (Witz); geistsprühend (Dialog etc); schwungvoll (Vortrag etc).

spark plug s mot. Zündkerze f.

spar·ring ['spɑːrɪŋ] adj: ~ *partner* (Boxen) Sparringspartner m.

spar·row ['spærəʊ] s orn. Spatz m, Sperling m.

sparse [spɑːs] adj □ spärlich: ~*ly populated* dünnbesiedelt, -bevölkert.

spar·tan ['spɑːtən] adj spartanisch (Lebensweise etc).

spasm ['spæzəm] s **1.** ✍ Krampf m. **2.** (Husten-, Lach- etc)Anfall m. **spasmod·ic** [~'mɒdɪk] adj (~*ally*) **1.** ✍ krampfartig. **2.** fig. sporadisch, unregelmäßig.

spas·tic ['spæstɪk] ✍ **I** adj (~*ally*) spastisch. **II** s Spastiker(in).

spat [spæt] pret u. pp von **spit²**.

spate [speɪt] s **1.** *be* (od. *run*) *in* ~ Hochwasser führen. **2.** fig. Flut f, (von Unfällen etc) Serie f.

spa·tial ['speɪʃl] adj □ räumlich: ~ *ability* räumliches Vorstellungsvermögen.

spat·ter ['spætə] **I** v/t **1.** j-n, etc. bespritzen (*with* mit). **2.** et. spritzen (*in s.o.'s face* j-m ins Gesicht; *over* über acc). **II** v/i **3.** spritzen. **III** s **4.** Spritzer m. **5.** a ~ *of applause* kurzer Beifall; *there was a ~ of rain* es spritzte, es regnete ein paar Tropfen.

spat·u·la ['spætjʊlə] s Spachtel m, f, bsd. ✍ Spatel m, f.

spawn [spɔːn] **I** s zo. Laich m. **II** v/i zo. laichen. **III** v/t fig. hervorbringen, produzieren.

spay [speɪ] v/t weibliches Tier sterilisieren.

speak [spiːk] (irr) **I** v/i **1.** sprechen, reden (*to, with* mit; *about* über acc): ~*ing!* teleph. am Apparat!; ~ *for* sprechen für; *this ~s for itself* das spricht für sich

selbst; ~ *of* fig. hindeuten auf (acc); zeugen von; *we don't ~* (*to each other*) wir sprechen od. reden nicht miteinander; *so to ~* sozusagen; → *devil* 1, *generally, ill* 3, *roughly* 2, *soon, strict.* **2.** sprechen (*to* vor dat; *about, on* über acc). **3.** sich aussprechen (*in favo[u]r of* für; *against* gegen). **II** v/t **4.** sprechen, sagen: → *mind* 4, *volume* 1. **5.** Sprache sprechen.

Verbindungen mit Adverbien:

speak| out v/i: ~ *against* sich klar u. deutlich aussprechen gegen. ~ **up** v/i **1.** lauter sprechen. **2.** ~ *for* sich klar u. deutlich aussprechen für.

speak·er ['spiːkə] s **1.** Sprecher(in), Redner(in). **2.** 2 parl. Speaker m, Präsident m. **3.** a ~ *of English* j-d, der English spricht. **4.** ✍ Lautsprecher m. '**speaking I** s: → *manner* 1. **II** adj: ~ *clock* teleph. Br. Zeitansage f; *we are not on ~ terms* wir sprechen od. reden nicht miteinander.

spear [spɪə] **I** s Speer m. **II** v/t aufspießen; durchbohren. '**~head I** s **1.** Speerspitze f. **2.** ✗ Angriffsspitze f; (Sport) (Sturm-, Angriffs)Spitze f. **3.** fig. Anführer(in). **II** v/t **4.** fig. anführen. '**~mint** s ✍ Grüne Minze.

spec [spek] s: *on ~ Br.* F auf gut Glück.

spe·cial ['speʃl] **I** adj (□ → *specially*) **1.** speziell, besonder. **2.** speziell, Spezial...: ~ *knowledge* Fachkenntnisse pl, -wissen n. **3.** Sonder...: ~ *school* (train, etc). **4.** speziell, bestimmt. **II** s **5.** Sonderbus m (od. -zug m; (Rundfunk, TV) Sondersendung f; ✝ Sonderangebot n: *be on ~ Am.* im Angebot sein. **spe·cial·ist** ['~ʃəlɪst] **I** s Spezialist(in), ✍ a. Facharzt m, -ärztin f (*in* für). **II** adj Fach... **spe·ci·al·i·ty** [~ʃɪ'ælətɪ] s **1.** Spezialität f. **2.** Spezialgebiet f. **spe·ci·al·i·za·tion** [~ʃəlaɪ'zeɪʃn] s Spezialisierung f. **spe·cial·ize** v/i sich spezialisieren (*in* auf acc). '**spe·cial·ly** adv **1.** besonders. **2.** speziell, extra. **spe·cial·ty** ['~ʃltɪ] *Am.* → **speciality**.

spe·cies ['spiːʃiːz] pl **-cies** s biol. Spezies f, Art f (beide a. allg.).

spe·cif·ic [spə'sɪfɪk] **I** adj **1.** spezifisch (a. phys.), speziell, besonder: ~ *gravity* spezifisches Gewicht. **2.** konkret, präzis. **3.** eigen (*to* dat). **II** s pl **4.** Einzelheiten *pl.* **spe'cif·i·cal·ly** *adv* **1.** speziell, besonders. **2.** ausdrücklich.

spec·i·fi·ca·tion [ˌspesɪfɪˈkeɪʃn] *s* genaue Angabe *od.* Beschreibung. **spec·i·fy** [ˈspesɪfaɪ] *v/t* genau beschreiben *od.* festlegen.

spec·i·men [ˈspesɪmən] *s* **1.** Exemplar *n.* **2.** Muster *n;* Probe *f.* **3.** F *contp.* Typ *m* (*Person*).

spe·cious [ˈspiːʃəs] *adj* □ trügerisch: **~ argument** Scheinargument *n.*

speck [spek] *s* kleiner Fleck, (*Staub-*) Korn *n;* Punkt *m* (**on the horizon** am Horizont).

speck·led [ˈspekld] *adj* gesprenkelt.

specs [speks] → **spectacle** 3.

spec·ta·cle [ˈspektəkl] *s* **1.** Schauspiel *n* (*a. fig.*): **make a ~ of o.s.** sich lächerlich machen. **2.** Anblick *m.* **3.** *pl, a.* **pair of ~s** Brille *f.*

spec·tac·u·lar [spekˈtækjʊlə] **I** *adj* □ spektakulär. **II** *s* Show *f* der Superlative.

spec·ta·tor [spekˈteɪtə] *s* Zuschauer(in).

spec·ter *Am.* → **spectre**.

spec·tra [ˈspektrə] *pl von* **spectrum**.

spec·tral [ˈspektrəl] *adj* □ **1.** geisterhaft, gespenstisch. **2.** *phys.* Spektral...

spec·tre [ˈspektə] *s bsd. Br.* (*fig. a.* Schreck)Gespenst *n.*

spec·trum [ˈspektrəm] *pl* **-tra** [ˈ~trə] *s phys.* Spektrum *n* (*a. fig.*): **a wide ~ of opinion(s)** ein breites Meinungsspektrum.

spec·u·late [ˈspekjʊleɪt] *v/i* **1.** spekulieren, Vermutungen anstellen (*about,* **on** über *acc*): **~ that** vermuten, daß. **2.** † spekulieren (**in** mit). **spec·u·la·tion** *s* Spekulation *f* (*a.* †), Vermutung *f.* **spec·u·la·tive** [ˈ~lətɪv] *adj* □ spekulativ, † *a.* Spekulations... **spec·u·la·tor** [ˈ~leɪtə] *s* † Spekulant(in).

sped [sped] *pret. u. pp von* **speed**.

speech [spiːtʃ] *s* **1.** Sprache *f* (*Sprechvermögen, Ausdrucksweise*): **~ defect** *od.* **impediment** Sprachfehler *m.* **2.** Rede *f,* Ansprache *f* (**to** vor *dat*), ⚖ Plädoyer *n.* **speech·i·fy** [ˈ~ɪfaɪ] *v/i contp.* Reden *od.* e-e Rede schwingen. **'speech·less** *adj* □ sprachlos (**with** vor *dat*).

speed [spiːd] **I** *s* **1.** Geschwindigkeit *f,* Schnelligkeit *f,* Tempo *n:* **at a ~ of** mit e-r Geschwindigkeit von; **at full** (*od.* **top**) **speed** mit Höchstgeschwindig-

keit. **2.** *mot. etc* Gang *m:* **five-~ gearbox** Fünfganggetriebe *f.* **3.** *phot.* Lichtempfindlichkeit *f.* **II** *v/t* (*irr*) **1.** rasch bringen *od.* befördern. **5. ~ up** (*pret u. pp* **-ed**) beschleunigen. **III** *v/i* **6.** rasen: **~ by** wie im Flug vergehen (*Zeit*); **be ~ing** *mot.* zu schnell fahren, die Geschwindigkeitsbegrenzung überschreiten. **7. ~ up** (*pret u. pp* **-ed**) beschleunigen (*Fahrer etc*), (*a. Wachstum etc*) schneller werden. **~ bump** *s mot.* Rüttelschwelle *f.*

speed·ing [ˈspiːdɪŋ] *s mot.* zu schnelles Fahren, Geschwindigkeitsüberschreitung *f.*

speed lim·it *s mot.* Geschwindigkeitsbegrenzung *f,* Tempolimit *n.*

speed·o [ˈspiːdəʊ] *pl* **-os** *s mot.* F Tacho *m.*

speed·om·e·ter [spɪˈdɒmɪtə] *s mot.* Tachometer *m, n.*

speed·y [ˈspiːdɪ] *adj* □ schnell, (*Antwort etc a.*) prompt: → **recovery** 2.

spell[1] [spel] (*mst irr*) **I** *v/t* **1.** a) a. **~ out** buchstabieren, b) **~ out** klarmachen (**for s.o.** j-m), b) *orthographisch richtig* schreiben. **2.** *Unglück etc* bedeuten. **II** *v/i* **3.** (richtig) schreiben.

spell[2] [~] *s* **1.** Weile *f:* **for a ~** e-e Zeitlang; **cold ~** *meteor.* Kälteperiode *f.* **2.** (*Husten- etc*)Anfall *m.*

spell[3] [~] *s* **1.** Zauber(spruch) *m.* **2.** Zauber *m* (*a. fig.*): **be under s.o.'s ~** in j-s Bann stehen; **cast a ~ over s.o.** j-n verzaubern, *fig. a.* j-n in s-n Bann ziehen.

'spell.bind·ing *adj* fesselnd. **'~·bound** *adj u. adv* wie gebannt: **hold s.o. ~** j-n fesseln.

spell·er [ˈspelə] *s* **1.** **be a good** (**bad**) **~** gut (schlecht) in Rechtschreibung sein. **2.** *Computer:* Speller *m,* Rechtschreibsystem *n.* **'spell·ing** *s* **1.** Rechtschreibung *f:* **~ mistake** (Recht)Schreibfehler *m.* **2.** Schreibung *f,* Schreibweise *f.*

spelt [spelt] *pret u. pp von* **spell**[1].

spend [spend] *v/t* (*irr*) **1.** *Geld* ausgeben (**on** für): → **penny**. **2.** *Urlaub, Zeit* verbringen: **~ an hour doing s.th.** e-e Stunde damit verbringen, et. zu tun. **'spend·er** *s:* **he's a big ~** ihm sitzt das Geld locker. **'spend·ing** **I** *s* Ausgaben *pl.* **II** *adj:* **~ money** Taschengeld *n;* → **spree**.

spend·thrift ['spendθrɪft] I s Verschwender(in). II adj verschwenderisch.

spent [spent] I pret u. pp von **spend**. II adj verbraucht.

sperm [spɜːm] s biol. Sperma n, Samen(flüssigkeit f) m.

spew [spjuː] I v/t 1. a. ~ out Rauch etc ausstoßen, Lava etc spucken. 2. a. ~ up sl. auskotzen. II v/i 3. a. ~ out hervorquellen (from aus). 4. sl. kotzen.

sphere [sfɪə] s 1. Kugel f. 2. fig. (Einfluß-etc)Sphäre f, (-)Bereich m: in the ~ of auf dem Gebiet (gen). **spher·i·cal** ['sferɪkl] adj □ 1. kugelförmig. 2. A Kugel..., sphärisch.

sphinc·ter ['sfɪŋktə] s anat. Schließmuskel m.

spice [spaɪs] s 1. Gewürz n. 2. fig. Würze f. II v/t 3. würzen (with mit) (a. fig.). ~ rack s Gewürzständer m.

spick-and-span [ˌspɪkən'spæn] adj blitzsauber.

spic·y ['spaɪsɪ] adj □ 1. gutgewürzt, würzig. 2. fig. pikant.

spi·der ['spaɪdə] s zo. Spinne f. ~ web s Am. Spinnwebe f, Spinnennetz n.

spiel [ʃpiːl] s F mst contp. Masche f.

spike [spaɪk] s 1. Spitze f; Dorn m; Stachel m: ~ heel Pfennigabsatz m. 2. Sport: as Spike m, Dorn m, b) pl Spikes pl, Rennschuhe pl. II v/t 3. aufspießen. 4. → lace 7. **'spik·y** adj □ 1. spitz(ig); stach(e)lig. 2. Br. F leicht eingeschnappt.

spill [spɪl] I v/t (mst irr) a. ~ out aus-, verschütten: I've spilt my coffee over my trousers ich habe mir m-n Kaffee über die Hose geschüttet; → bean 1, milk I. II v/i (mst irr) verschüttet werden; sich ergießen (over über acc); strömen (out of aus) (Menschen): ~ over überlaufen; fig. übergreifen (into auf acc). III s bsd. Sport: F Sturz m (vom Pferd, [Motor]Rad): have a ~ stürzen.

spilt [spɪlt] pret u. pp von **spill**.

spin [spɪn] I v/t (irr) (um)1. drehen; Wäsche schleudern; Münze hochwerfen. 2. Fäden, Wolle etc spinnen; → yarn 2. 3. ~ out Arbeit etc in die Länge ziehen, Geld etc strecken. II v/i (irr) 4. sich drehen: ~ round herumwirbeln; my head was ~ning mir drehte sich alles. 5. mst ~ along mot. F (dahin)rasen. III s 6.

Sport: Effet m: put ~ on a ball e-m Ball Effet geben. 7. mot. F Spritztour f: go for a ~ e-e Spritztour machen. 8. bsd. Br. F be in a (flat) ~ am Rotieren sein; send (od. throw) s.o. in a (flat) ~ j-n zum Rotieren bringen.

spin·ach ['spɪnɪdʒ] s ♣ Spinat m.

spi·nal ['spaɪnl] adj: ~ column Rückgrat n, Wirbelsäule f; ~ cord Rückenmark n.

spin·dle ['spɪndl] s ⊙ Spindel f. **'spin·dly** adj spindeldürr.

spin|·'dri·er s (Wäsche)Schleuder f. **~·'dry** v/t Wäsche schleudern. **~·'dry·er** → **spin-drier**.

spine [spaɪn] s 1. anat. Rückgrat n, Wirbelsäule f. 2. zo. Stachel m; ♣ a. Dorn m. 3. (Buch)Rücken m. **'spine·less** adj □ fig. rückgratlos.

spin·na·ker ['spɪnəkə] s ♣ Spinnaker m.

spin·ney ['spɪnɪ] s Br. Dickicht n.

spin·ning| mill ['spɪnɪŋ] s Spinnerei f. ~ wheel s Spinnrad n.

'spin-off s 1. Neben-, Abfallprodukt n. 2. fig. (positiver) Nebeneffekt.

spin·ster ['spɪnstə] s ältere unverheiratete Frau, contp. alte Jungfer, spätes Mädchen. **'spin·ster·ish** adj altjüngferlich.

spin·y ['spaɪnɪ] adj zo. stach(e)lig, ♣ a. dornig.

spi·ral ['spaɪərəl] I adj □ spiralenförmig, spiralig, Spiral...: ~ staircase Wendeltreppe f. II s (a. ♣ Preis- etc)Spirale f.

spire ['spaɪə] s (Kirch)Turmspitze f.

spir·it ['spɪrɪt] s 1. allg. Geist m: in ~ im Geiste; ~ of the age (od. times) Zeitgeist. 2. Stimmung f, Einstellung f. 3. Schwung m, Elan m. 4. pl Laune f, Stimmung f: be in high ~s in Hochstimmung sein; ausgelassen od. übermütig sein; be in low ~s niedergeschlagen sein; lift (od. raise) s.o.'s ~s j-s Stimmung heben; my ~s sank ich wurde deprimiert. 5. mst pl Spirituose f. 6. 🔥 Spiritus m. **'spir·it·ed** adj □ beherzt (Versuch etc); erregt (Auseinandersetzung).

spir·it lev·el s ⊙ Wasserwaage f.

spir·it·u·al ['spɪrɪtʃʊəl] I adj □ 1. geistig. 2. geistlich. II s 3. ♪ Spiritual n. **'spir·it·u·al·ism** s Spiritismus m. **'spir·it·u·al·ist** s Spiritist(in). **ˌspir·it·u·al'is·tic** adj (~ally) spiritistisch.

spit¹ [spɪt] I v/i (irr) 1. a) spucken: ~ at

spit 1264

s.o. j-n anspucken, b) ausspucken. **2.** *it is ~ting* (*with rain*) es sprüht. **3.** knistern (*Feuer*), brutzeln (*Fleisch etc*). **II** *v/t* (*irr*) **4.** *Blut etc* spucken: *~ out* ausspucken; *~ it out!* fig. F spuck's aus! **5.** *a.* *~ out et.* fauchen. **III** *s* **6.** Spucke f.

spit² [~] *s* **1.** (Brat)Spieß m. **2.** geogr. Landzunge f.

spite [spaɪt] **I** *s* **1.** Boshaftigkeit f, Gehässigkeit f: *out of* (*od. from*) *pure* ~ aus reiner Bosheit. **2.** *in* ~ *of* trotz. **II** *v/t* **3.** ärgern. **spite-ful** ['~fʊl] *adj* □ boshaft, gehässig.

spit-ting ['spɪtɪŋ] *adj:* *the bus stop is within* ~ *distance* F bis zur Bushaltestelle ist es nur ein Katzensprung; *she is the* ~ *image of her mother* sie ist ganz die Mutter, sie ist ihrer Mutter wie aus dem Gesicht geschnitten.

spit-tle ['spɪtl] *s* Spucke f.

splash [splæʃ] **I** *v/i* **1.** spritzen; (*Regen*) klatschen (*against* gegen). **2.** a) planschen (*in* in *dat*), b) platschen (*through* durch): *~ down* wassern (*Raumkapsel*). **3.** *~ out* on bsd. Br. F tief in die Tasche greifen für. **II** *v/t* **4.** bespritzen (*with* mit): *~ one's face with cold water* sich kaltes Wasser ins Gesicht schütten. **5.** *Wasser etc* spritzen (*on* auf *acc*; *over* über *acc*): *~ one's money about* bsd. Br. F mit Geld um sich werfen. **6.** F in großer Aufmachung bringen (*Zeitung etc*). **III** *s* **7.** Spritzer m, Spritzfleck m: *~ of paint* Farbspritzer. **8.** bsd. Br. Spritzer m, Schuß m (*Soda etc*). **9.** *make* (*quite*) *a* ~ F Furore machen. '**~down** *s* Wasserung f.

splat [splæt] *v/i* F klatschen (*against* gegen).

splat-ter ['splætə] → spatter 1–3.

splay [spleɪ] *v/t* a. ~ *out* Finger, Zehen spreizen.

spleen [spliːn] *s* anat. Milz f.

splen-did ['splendɪd] *adj* □ großartig, herrlich, prächtig. '**splen-do(u)r** *s* Pracht f.

splice [splaɪs] *v/t* miteinander verbinden, *Film, Tonband etc* (zs-)kleben: *get ~d* F heiraten.

splint [splɪnt] ⚕ **I** *s* Schiene f. **II** *v/t* schienen.

splin-ter ['splɪntə] **I** *s* Splitter m. **II** *v/t* zersplittern. **III** *v/i* (zer)splittern: *~ off* absplittern; fig. sich abspalten od. ab-

spalten (*from* von). ~ *group* *s* Splittergruppe f.

split [splɪt] **I** *v/t* (*irr*) **1.** (zer)spalten; zerreißen: *~ one's sides* vor Lachen biegen; *be* ~ fig. gespalten sein (*on an issue* in e-r Frage); *~ personality* psych. gespaltene Persönlichkeit; *~ second* Bruchteil m e-r Sekunde; → *hair.* **2.** *a.* ~ *up* aufteilen (*between* unter *acc*; *into* in *acc*); *~ et.* teilen: *~ three ways* dritteln; *~ the difference* fig. sich auf halbem Wege einigen. **II** *v/i* (*irr*) **3.** (sich) spalten; zerreißen. **4.** sich teilen (*into* in *acc*). **5.** *a.* ~ *up* (*with*) Schluß machen (mit), sich trennen (von). **III** *s* **6.** Riß m; Spalt m. **7.** fig. Bruch m; Spaltung f. **8.** Aufteilung f. **9.** *pl* Spagat m: *do the* ~s (e-n) Spagat machen. **10.** (*Bananen*)Split m. '**split-ting** *adj* rasend (*Kopfschmerzen*).

splodge [splɒdʒ] *s* bsd. Br., **splotch** [splɒtʃ] *s* bsd. Am. Fleck m, Klecks m: ~ *of paint* Farbklecks.

splurge [splɜːdʒ] F **I** *v/i:* ~ *on* tief in die Tasche greifen für. **II** *v/t* Geld verschwenden (*on* für). **III** *s:* *have a* ~ tief in die Tasche greifen.

splut-ter ['splʌtə] **I** *v/i* **1.** stottern (*a. mot.*). **2.** zischen (*Feuer etc*). **3.** prusten. **II** *v/t* **4.** stottern.

spoil [spɔɪl] **I** *v/t* (*a. irr*) **1.** verderben. **2.** j-n verwöhnen, *Kind a.* verziehen: *be ~t for choice* die Qual der Wahl haben. **II** *v/i* (*a. irr*) **3.** verderben, schlecht werden (*Nahrungsmittel*). **4.** *be ~ing for a fight* Streit suchen. **III** *s* **5.** mst *pl* Beute f.

'spoil-er *s* mot. Spoiler m.

'spoil-sport *s* Spielverderber(in).

spoilt [spɔɪlt] *pret u. pp* von spoil.

spoke¹ [spəʊk] *pret* von speak.

spoke² [~] *s* Speiche f: *put a* ~ *in s.o.'s wheel* fig. j-m (e-n) Knüppel zwischen die Beine werfen.

spo-ken ['spəʊkən] *pp* von speak.

spokes-man ['spəʊksmən] *s* (*irr man*) Sprecher m. '**~wom-an** *s* (*irr woman*) Sprecherin f.

sponge [spʌndʒ] **I** *s* **1.** Schwamm m: *throw in the* ~ fig. das Handtuch werfen. **2.** → *sponge cake.* **3.** fig. Schnorrer(in). **II** *v/t* **4.** ~ *down* (mit e-m Schwamm) abwaschen; ~ (*up*) aufwischen (*from* von). **5.** fig. schnorren *(from, off, on* von, bei). III *v/i* **6.** *fig.* schnorren *(from, off, on* bei): ~ *off s.o. a.* j-m auf der Tasche liegen. ~ **bag** *s Br.* Kulturbeutel *m,* Toilettentasche *f.* ~ **cake** *s* Biskuitkuchen *m.*

spong·er ['spʌndʒə] → *sponge* 3.
'**spong·y** *adj* □ **1.** schwammartig. **2.** weich, *b.s.* teigig *(Brot etc).* **3.** nachgiebig *(Boden etc).*

spon·sor ['spɒnsə] **I** *s* **1.** Sponsor(in) *(a. Rundfunk, TV),* Geldgeber(in). **2.** Spender(in). **3.** Bürge *m,* Bürgin *f.* **II** *v/t* **4.** sponsern. **5.** bürgen für.

spon·ta·ne·ous [spɒn'teɪnjəs] *adj* □ spontan.

spoof [spuːf] *s* F Parodie *f (of, on auf acc).*

spook [spuːk] F **I** *s* Gespenst *n.* **II** *v/t Am.* j-m e-n Schrecken einjagen. '**spook·y** *adj* □ F unheimlich.

spool [spuːl] *s* Spule *f.*

spoon [spuːn] *s* Löffel *m.* '~**feed** *v/t (irr feed)* **1.** *Kind etc* füttern. **2.** *fig.* j-m alles vorkauen: ~ *s.o. with s.th.,* ~ *s.th. to s.o.* j-m et. vorkauen.

spoon·ful ['spuːnfʊl] *s ein* Löffel(voll) *m.*

spo·rad·ic [spə'rædɪk] *adj (~ally)* sporadisch, gelegentlich.

spore [spɔː] *s biol.* Spore *f.*

spor·ran ['spɒrən] *s Schottentracht:* Felltasche *f.*

sport [spɔːt] **I** *s* **1.** a) Sport(art *f) m,* b) oft *pl allg.* Sport *m.* **2.** *a. good* ~ F feiner *od.* anständiger Kerl: *be a* ~ sei kein Spielverderber. **3.** *in* ~ zum Scherz, im Spaß. **II** *adj* **4.** *Am.* Sport... **III** *v/t* **5.** protzen mit; *mit e-m blauen Auge* herumlaufen. '**sport·ing** *adj* □ **1.** Sport... **2.** fair *(a. Chance),* anständig, sportlich.

sports [spɔːts] *adj* Sport...: ~ *car* Sportwagen *m;* ~ *jacket* Sakko *m, n.* ~**man** ['~mən] *s (irr man)* **1.** Sportler *m.* **2.** feiner *od.* anständiger Kerl. '~**man-like** *adj* sportlich, fair, anständig. '~**man·ship** *s* Sportlichkeit *f,* Fairneß *f,* Anständigkeit *f.* '~**wom·an** *s (irr woman)* Sportlerin *f.*

sport·y ['spɔːtɪ] *adj* □ F **1.** sportlich; sportbegeistert. **2.** flott *(Kleidungsstück).*

spot [spɒt] **I** *s* **1.** Punkt *m,* Tupfen *m;* Fleck *m.* **2.** Pickel *m.* **3.** Ort *m,* Platz *m,* Stelle *f: on the* ~ zur Stelle; an Ort u. Stelle, vor Ort; auf der Stelle, sofort;

put on the ~ j-n in die Enge treiben; j-n in Verlegenheit bringen; *be in a* ~ F in Schwulitäten sein; → *rooted.* **4.** *fig. soft* ~ Schwäche *f (for* für); *tender* ~ empfindliche Stelle; *weak* ~ schwacher Punkt; Schwäche *f.* **5.** *a* ~ *of Br.* F ein bißchen. **6.** *Rundfunk, TV:* (Werbe)Spot *m.* **7.** F Spot *m (Spotlight).* **II** *v/t* **8.** entdecken, sehen. **III** *v/i* **9.** *it is* ~**ting** *(with rain) Br.* es tröpfelt. ~ **check** *s* Stichprobe *f.* '~**check** *v/t* stichprobenweise überprüfen *(for auf acc).*

spot·less ['spɒtlɪs] *adj* □ **1.** tadellos sauber. **2.** *fig.* untadelig.

'**spot·light** *s* **1.** Spotlight *n,* Scheinwerfer(licht *n) m: be in the (political)* ~ im Brennpunkt des (politischen) Interesses stehen. **II** *v/t (a. irr light)* anstrahlen; *fig.* aufmerksam machen auf *(acc).* '~**on** *adj u. adv Br.* F genau richtig.

spot·ted ['spɒtɪd] *adj* getüpfelt; fleckig.
'**spot·ty** *adj* □ **1.** pick(e)lig. **2.** *fig.* uneinheitlich, unterschiedlich.

spouse [spaʊz] *s* Gatte *m,* Gattin *f,* Gemahl(in).

spout [spaʊt] **I** *v/t* **1.** *Wasser etc* (heraus)spritzen. **II** *v/i* **2.** spritzen *(from* aus). **III** *s* **3.** *(Wasser- etc)*Strahl *m.* **4.** Schnauze *f,* Tülle *f.* **5.** *be up the* ~ F im Eimer sein *(Wagen etc);* in Schwulitäten sein *(Person): she's up the* ~ bei ihr ist was unterwegs.

sprain [spreɪn] *🖉 * **I** *v/t* sich *den Knöchel etc* verstauchen: ~ *one's ankle.* **II** *s* Verstauchung *f.*

sprang [spræŋ] *pret von* **spring.**

sprat [spræt] *s ichth.* Sprotte *f.*

sprawl [sprɔːl] **I** *v/i* **1.** *a.* ~ *out* ausgestreckt liegen *od.* sitzen. **2.** *b.s.* sich ausbreiten *(Stadt etc).* **II** *v/t* **3.** *be* ~**ed** *(out)* → 1.

spray [spreɪ] **I** *v/i* **1.** sprühen, spritzen. **II** *v/t* **2.** besprühen, spritzen *(with* mit); sich *die Haare* spritzen; et. sprühen, spritzen *(on* auf *acc); Parfüm etc* versprühen, zerstäuben. **III** *s* **3.** Sprühnebel *m;* Gischt *f.* **4.** Spray *m, n.* **5.** Sprüh-, Spraydose *f;* Zerstäuber *m.* '**spray·er** → **spray** 5.

spray gun *s ☺* Spritzpistole *f.*

spread [spred] **I** *v/t (irr)* **1.** *a.* ~ *out* ausbreiten, *Arme a.* ausstrecken; *Finger etc* spreizen. **2.** *Butter etc* streichen *(on* auf *acc*); *Brot etc* (be)streichen (**with** mit). **3.** *Furcht, Krankheit, Nachricht etc* verbreiten, *Gerücht a.* ausstreuen. **II** *v/i* (*irr*) **4.** a. **~ out** sich ausbreiten. **5.** sich (*räumlich od. zeitlich*) erstrecken (**over** über *acc*). **6.** sich streichen lassen (*Butter etc*). **7.** sich verbreiten (*Furcht, Krankheit, Nachricht etc*), übergreifen (**to** auf *acc*) (*Feuer, Epidemie etc*): → **wildfire**. **III** *s* **8.** ✓, *orn.* Spannweite *f.* **9.** (*Brot*)Aufstrich *m*, Paste *f.* **10.** Verbreitung *f*, Ausstreuung *f.* **11.** *fig.* Spektrum *n.* **12.** F Festessen *n.*

spree [spriː] *s* F: **go (out) on a ~** e-n draufmachen; e-e Saaftour machen; **go on a buying** (*od.* **shopping, spending**) **~** wie verrückt einkaufen.

sprig [sprɪg] *s* Zweig *m.*

spright·ly ['spraɪtlɪ] *adj* rüstig (*alter Mensch*).

spring [sprɪŋ] **I** *v/i* (*irr*) **1.** springen: **~ at** sich stürzen auf (*acc*); **~ to one's feet** aufspringen. **2.** springen, schnellen: **~ back** zurückschnellen; **~ open** aufspringen (*Deckel etc*). **3.** **~ up** aufkommen (*Wind*); aus dem Boden schießen (*Gebäude etc*). **4.** **~ from** herrühren von. **II** *v/t* (*irr*) **5.** **~ s.th. on s.o.** j-n mit et. überraschen. **6.** → **leak** 1a. **III** *s* **7.** Frühling *m*, Frühjahr *n*: **in** (**the**) **~** im Frühling. **8.** Quelle *f.* **9.** Sprung *m*: **make a ~ at** sich stürzen auf (*acc*). **10.** ⊕ Feder *f.* **11.** Elastizität *f*; Federung *f.* **IV** *adj* **12.** Frühlings...: **~ flowers.** '**~board** *s* Sprungbrett *n* (*a. fig.* **for, to** für). **~ chick·en** *s*: **he's no ~** F er ist nicht mehr der jüngste. **~·'clean** *v/t u. v/i* gründlich putzen, *engS.* Frühjahrsputz machen (*in dat*). **~ fe·ver** *s* Frühjahrsmüdigkeit *f*; Frühlingsgefühle *pl.* **~ tide** *s* Springflut *f*, -tide *f.* '**~·time** *s* Frühling(szeit *f*) *m*, Frühjahr *n.*

spring·y ['sprɪŋɪ] *adj* □ elastisch, federnd.

sprin·kle ['sprɪŋkl] **I** *v/t* **1.** *Wasser etc* sprengen (**on** auf *acc*); *Salz etc* streuen (**on** auf *acc*); *et.* (be)sprengen *od.* bestreuen (**with** mit). **II** *v/i* **2. it is sprinkling** es sprüht (*regnet fein*). **III** *s* **3.** (Be)Sprengen *n.* **4.** (Be)Streuen *n.* **4.** Sprühregen *m.* '**sprin·kler** *s* **1.** (*Rasen*)Sprenger *m*; Sprinkler *m*, Berieselungsanlage *f.* **2.** *eccl.* Weihwasserwe-

del *m.* '**sprin·kling** *s*: **a ~ of** ein bißchen, ein paar.

sprint [sprɪnt] (*Sport*) **I** *v/i* **1.** sprinten; *a. allg.* sprinten, spurten. **II** *s* **2.** *a.* **~ race** Sprint *m.* **3.** Sprint *m*, Spurt *m* (*beide a. allg.*): **make** (*od.* **put on**) **a ~** e-n Spurt hinlegen. '**sprint·er** *s* *Sport*: Sprinter(in).

sprite [spraɪt] *s* Geist *m*, Kobold *m.*

sprout [spraʊt] **I** *v/i* **1.** sprießen (*Knospen etc*), keimen (*Kartoffeln, Saat etc*). **II** *v/t* **2. ~ a beard** sich e-n Bart wachsen lassen. **III** *s* **3.** Sproß *m*; Trieb *m*; Keim *m.* **4.** *pl* Rosenkohl *m.*

spruce¹ [spruːs] **I** *adj* □ adrett. **II** *v/t u. v/i*: **~** (*o.s.*) **up** F sich feinmachen, sich in Schale werfen.

spruce² [spruːs] *s* ♀ Fichte *f.*

sprung [sprʌŋ] *pp u. Am. pret von* **spring.**

spry [spraɪ] *adj* □ rüstig (*ältere Person*).

spud [spʌd] *s* F Kartoffel *f.*

spun [spʌn] *pret u. pp von* **spin.**

spunk [spʌŋk] *s* F Mumm *m.* '**spunk·y** *adj* □ F mutig.

spur [spɜː] **I** *s* **1.** Sporn *m* (*a. zo.*). **2.** *fig.* Ansporn *m* (**to** zu): **on the ~ of the moment** spontan. **II** *v/t* **3.** e-m Pferd die Sporen geben. **4.** *oft* **~ on** *fig.* anspornen (**to** zu).

spu·ri·ous ['spjʊərɪəs] *adj* □ **1.** Pseudo..., Schein... **2.** geheuchelt, unecht.

spur-of-the-'mo·ment *adj* spontan.

spurt¹ [spɜːt] **I** *s* **1.** *Sport:* Spurt *m*, Sprint *m* (*beide a. allg.*): **put on a ~** e-n Spurt hinlegen. **2.** (*Arbeits*)Anfall *m*, (*Gefühls*)Aufwallung *f.* **II** *v/i* **3.** *Sport:* spurten, sprinten (*beide a. allg.*).

spurt² [~] *v/i* spritzen (**from** aus). **II** *s* (*Wasser- etc*)Strahl *m.*

sput·ter ['spʌtə] **I** *v/i* **1.** stottern (*a. mot.*). **2.** zischen (*Feuer etc*). **II** *v/t* **3.** stottern.

spy [spaɪ] **I** *v/i* spionieren, Spionage treiben (**for** für): **~ into** *fig.* herumspionieren in (*dat*); **~ on** j-m nachspionieren. **II** *v/t*: **~ out** ausspionieren; ausfindig machen: **~ out the land** *fig.* die Lage peilen. **III** *s* Spion(in). **~ ring** *s* Spionagering *m.*

squab·ble ['skwɒbl] **I** *v/i* (sich) streiten (**about, over** um, wegen). **II** *s* Streit *m.*

squad [skwɒd] *s* **1.** Mannschaft *f*, Trupp *m.* **2.** (*Überfall- etc*)Kommando *n* (*der Polizei*); Dezernat *n.* **3.** *Sport:* Kader *m.* **~ car** *s bsd. Am.* (Funk)Streifenwagen *m.*

squad·ron ['skwɒdrən] *s* ✕, ✈ Staffel *f*; ⚓ Geschwader *n.*

squal·id ['skwɒlɪd] *adj* □ **1.** verwahrlost (*Gebäude etc*); erbärmlich (*Verhältnisse etc*). **2.** *fig.* schmutzig (*Geschichte etc*).

squall[1] [skwɔːl] **I** *v/i* schreien. **II** *s* Schrei *m.*

squall[2] [~] *s* Bö *f.* **'squall·y** *adj* böig.

squal·or ['skwɒlə] *s* Verwahrlosung *f*: **live in ~** in erbärmlichen Verhältnissen leben.

squan·der ['skwɒndə] *v/t* Geld, Zeit etc verschwenden (**on** an *acc*, auf *acc*, für, mit), Chance vertun.

square [skweə] **I** *s* **1.** Quadrat *n.* **2.** Feld *n* (*e-s* Brettspiels): **be back to ~ one** *fig.* wieder ganz am Anfang stehen. **3.** (öffentlicher) Platz. **4.** ✚ Quadrat(zahl *f*) *n.* **5.** ⊙ Winkel(maß *n*) *m.* **II** *adj* **6.** quadratisch; Quadrat...: **three yards ~** drei Yards im Quadrat; **~ root** ✚ Quadratwurzel *f*; **~ peg** 1. **7.** rechtwink(e)lig; eckig (*Schultern etc*). **8.** fair, gerecht. **9.** *be* (*all*) **~** quitt sein. **10.** F anständig, ordentlich (*Mahlzeit*). **III** *adv* **11.** → **squarely.** **IV** *v/t* **12.** *a.* **~ off** (*od.* **up**) quadratisch *od.* rechtwink(e)lig machen. **13.** *a.* **~ off** in Quadrate einteilen: **~d paper** kariertes Papier. **14.** ✚ Zahl quadrieren, ins Quadrat erheben: **4 ~d equals 16** 4 hoch 2 ist 16. **15.** Konto ausgleichen; Schulden begleichen: **~ account** 5. **16.** **~ s.th. with one's conscience** et. mit s-m Gewissen vereinbaren *od.* in Einklang bringen. **V** *v/i* **17.** übereinstimmen, in Einklang stehen (**with** mit). **18.** **~ up** abrechnen. **19.** **~ up to** sich j-m, e-m Problem etc stellen. **'square·ly** *adv* **1.** → **square** 6–8. **2.** direkt, genau.

squash [skwɒʃ] **I** *v/t* **1.** zerdrücken, -quetschen: **~ flat** flachdrücken. **2.** quetschen, zwängen (**into** in *acc*). **3.** j-n zum Schweigen bringen (**with** mit); Gerücht etc ersticken. **II** *v/i* **4.** sich quetschen *od.* zwängen (**into** in *acc*). **III** *s* **5.** Gedränge *n.* **6.** → **lemon** 3, **orange** 1. **7.** *Sport:* Squash *m.* **'squash·y** *adj* □ **1.** weich (*Frucht*). **2.** aufgeweicht (*Boden*).

squat [skwɒt] **I** *v/i* **1.** hocken, kauern: **~ down** sich (hin)hocken *od.* (-)kauern.

2. **~ in a house** ein Haus besetzt haben. **II** *adj* **3.** gedrungen, untersetzt. **III** *s* **4.** Hocke *f.* **5.** besetztes Haus. **'squat·ter** *s* Hausbesetzer(in).

squaw [skwɔː] *s* Squaw *f* (*Indianerfrau*).

squawk [skwɔːk] *v/i* ✈ lautstark protestieren (**about** gegen).

squeak [skwiːk] **I** *v/i* **1.** piep(s)en (*Maus etc*). **2.** quietschen (*Tür etc*). **3.** **~ through** F es gerade noch schaffen. **II** *s* **4.** Piep(s)en *n*; Piep(s) *m*, Piepser *m*; *fig.* F Piep *m.* **5.** Quietschen *n.* **6.** **that was a narrow ~** F das war knapp, das hätte ins Auge gehen können. **'squeak·y** *adj* □ **1.** piepsig: **~ voice** *a.* Piepsstimme *f.* **2.** quietschend.

squeal [skwiːl] *v/i* **1.** kreischen (**with** *dat*). **2.** *fig.* F singen: **~ on s.o.** j-n verpfeifen.

squeam·ish ['skwiːmɪʃ] *adj* □ empfindlich, zartbesaitet.

squeeze [skwiːz] **I** *v/t* **1.** drücken; Orangen etc auspressen, -quetschen: **~ out** Schwamm etc ausdrücken; Saft etc auspressen (**of** aus). **2.** quetschen, zwängen (**into** in *acc*). **II** *v/i* **3.** sich quetschen *od.* zwängen (**into** in *acc*). **III** *s* **4.** s.th. **a ~** et. drücken; **put the ~ on s.o.** F j-n unter Druck setzen. **5.** Gedränge *n.* **'squeez·er** *s* Presse *f.*

squelch [skweltʃ] *v/i* p(l)atschen.

squib [skwɪb] *s* Knallfrosch *m*: → **damp** 1.

squint [skwɪnt] **I** *v/i* **1.** schielen. **2.** blinzeln. **II** *s* **3.** Schielen *n*: **have a ~** schielen.

squirm [skwɜːm] *v/i* sich winden (**with** vor *dat*) (*a. fig.*).

squir·rel ['skwɪrəl] *s* zo. Eichhörnchen *n.*

squirt [skwɜːt] **I** *v/i* spritzen (**from** aus). **II** *v/t* bespritzen (**with** mit). **III** *s* Strahl *m.*

stab [stæb] **I** *v/t* **1.** j-m e-n Stich versetzen; j-n niederstechen: **~ (to death)** erstechen; **he was ~bed in the stomach** er bekam e-n Stich in den Magen; **~ s.o. in the back** j-m in den Rücken fallen. **2.** **~ one's finger at** mit dem Finger stoßen nach (*od.* auf *acc*). **II** *v/i* **3.** stechen (**at** nach; **with** mit). **III** *s* **4.** Stich *m*: **~ (wound)** Stichverletzung *f*, -wunde *f*; **~ in the back** *fig.* Dolchstoß *m.* **5.** **feel a ~ of pain** (**remorse**) e-n stechenden Schmerz verspüren (Gewis-

sensbisse fühlen). **6. have** (*od.* **make**) a
~ **at s.th.** F et. probieren. **'stab·bing** *adj*
stechend (*Schmerz*).

sta·bil·i·ty [stə'bɪlətɪ] *s* **1.** Stabilität *f* (*a.
fig.*). **2.** *fig.* Dauerhaftigkeit *f.* **3.** *fig.*
Ausgeglichenheit *f.*

sta·bil·i·za·tion [ˌsteɪbəlaɪ'zeɪʃn] *s* Stabi-
lisierung *f* (*a. fig.*).

sta·bi·lize ['steɪbəlaɪz] *v/t u. v/i* (sich)
stabilisieren (*a. fig.*). **'sta·bi·liz·er** *s* ⊙
Stabilisator *m.*

sta·ble¹ ['steɪbl] *adj* □ **1.** stabil (*a. fig.*).
2. *fig.* dauerhaft (*Beziehung etc*). **3.** *fig.*
ausgeglichen (*Person*).

sta·ble² [~] *s* Stall *m* (*a. fig.*).

stack [stæk] **I** *s* **1.** Stapel *m,* Stoß *m.* **2.** ~**s**
(*od.* **a** ~) *of* F jede Menge *Zeit etc.* **3.** →
blow¹ 11. **II** *v/t* **4.** stapeln: ~ **up** aufsta-
peln. **5.** vollstapeln (**with** mit). **6. the
cards** (*od.* **odds**) **are** ~**ed against us**
unsere Chancen stehen gleich Null. **III** *v/i*
7. ~ **up against** *bsd. Am.* F sich halten
gegen.

sta·di·um ['steɪdjəm] *s Sport:* Stadion *n.*

staff [stɑːf] **I** *s* **1.** Mitarbeiter(stab *m*) *pl;*
Personal *n,* Belegschaft *f;* Lehrkörper
m, Kollegium *n;* ✗ Stab *m:* **editorial** ~
Redaktion *f;* **be on the** ~ zur Belegschaft gehören. **2.** (*Amts*)Stab *m;* (*Fah-
nen*)Stange *f.* **II** *v/t* **3.** besetzen (**with**
mit). ~ **man·a·ger** *s* Personalchef *m.* ~
of·fi·cer *s* ✗ Stabsoffizier *m.* ~ **room** *s*
Lehrerzimmer *n.*

stag [stæg] *s zo.* Hirsch *m.*

stage [steɪdʒ] **I** *s* **1.** *thea.* Bühne *f* (*a. fig.*):
go on the ~ zum Theater gehen; **set the**
~ **for** die Voraussetzungen schaffen für.
2. Etappe *f* (*a. Radsport u. fig.*), (Reise)Abschnitt *m:* **by** (*easy*) ~**s** etappen-
weise, *fig. a.* Schritt für Schritt. **3.** Stadium *n,* Stufe *f,* Phase *f.* **4.** ⊙ Stufe *f*
(*e-r Rakete*). **II** *v/t* **5.** *thea.* auf die Bühne bringen. **6.** *Ausstellung, Demonstration etc* veranstalten: → **comeback.**
'~·coach *s hist.* Postkutsche *f.* ~
di·rec·tion *s* Bühnen-, Regieanwei-
sung *f.* ~ **door** *s* Bühneneingang *m.* ~
fright *s* Lampenfieber *n.* ~ **name** *s*
Künstlername *m.*

stag·ey → **stagy.**

stag·ger ['stægə] **I** *v/i* **1.** (sch)wanken,
taumeln, (*Betrunkener a.*) torkeln. **II**
v/t **2.** j-n sprachlos machen, umwerfen.
3. *Arbeitszeit etc* staffeln. **'stag·ger-**

-ing *adj* □ umwerfend (*Nachricht etc*),
schwindelerregend (*Preis etc*).

stag·nant ['stægnənt] *adj* □ **1.** stehend
(*Gewässer*). **2.** *bsd.* ✝ stagnierend.
stag·nate [~'neɪt] *v/i bsd.* ✝ stagnieren.
stag'na·tion *s* Stagnation *f.*

stag par·ty *s* F (*mst feuchtfröhliche*)
Herrenabend *m.*

stag·y ['steɪdʒɪ] *adj* □ theatralisch.

staid [steɪd] *adj* □ **1.** gesetzt, seriös,
contr. verknöchert (*Person*). **2.** altbak-
ken (*Ansichten*).

stain [steɪn] **I** *s* **1.** Fleck *m.* **2.** *fig.* Makel
m. **3.** ⊙ Färbemittel *n;* (*Holz*)Beize *f.* **II**
v/t **4.** beflecken. **5.** (ein)färben; *Holz*
beizen: ~**ed glass** Farbglass *n.* **III** *v/i* **6.**
flecken. **'stain·less** *adj* nichtrostend,
rostfrei (*Stahl*).

stair [steə] *s* **1.** (Treppen)Stufe *f.* **2.** *pl*
Treppe *f:* → **flight¹** 3. ~ **car·pet** *s* Trep-
penläufer *m.* '~**·case** *s,* '~**·way** *s* Treppe *f;* Treppenhaus *n.*

stake¹ [steɪk] **I** *s* **1.** Pfahl *m,* Pfosten *m.* **2.**
hist. Marterpfahl *m;* Scheiterhaufen *m.*
II *v/t* **3.** *oft* ~ **off** (*od.* **out**) abstecken: ~
(**out**) **a** (*od.* **one's**) **claim** *fig.* Ansprüche anmelden (**to** *auf acc*). **4.** *mst* ~ **out**
bsd. Am. F überwachen (*Polizei*).

stake² [~] **I** *s* **1.** Einsatz *m:* **be at** ~ *fig.* auf
dem Spiel stehen; **play for high** ~**s** hoch
od. um hohe Einsätze spielen. **2.** Anteil
m, Beteiligung *f* (**in** *an dat*) (*beide a.* ✝):
have a ~ **in** beteiligt sein an (*dat*). **II** *v/t*
3. *Geld, Hoffnung* setzen (**on** *auf acc*);
Ruf etc riskieren, aufs Spiel setzen.

'stake·out *s bsd. Am.* F (polizeiliche)
Überwachung.

sta·lac·tite ['stæləktaɪt] *s geol.* Stalaktit
m. **stal·ag·mite** ['stæləgmaɪt] *s geol.*
Stalagmit *m.*

stale [steɪl] *adj* □ **1.** alt(backen) (*Brot etc*);
abgestanden (*Luft etc*); schal (*Bier etc a.*)
schal; *fig.* abgedroschen (*Witz etc*).

stale·mate ['steɪlmeɪt] **I** *s* **1.** Schach:
Patt *n.* **2.** *fig.* Patt(situation *f*) *n,* Sackgasse *f:* **end in** (**a**) ~ in e-r Sackgasse
enden. **II** *v/t* **3.** Schach: patt setzen. **4.**
fig. in e-e Sackgasse führen.

stalk¹ [stɔːk] *s* Stengel *m,* Stiel *m;*
Halm *m.*

stalk² [~] *v/i* stolzieren; staksen,
steif(beinig) gehen.

stall¹ [stɔːl] **I** *s* **1.** (*Obst- etc*)Stand *m.* **2.**
pl thea. Br. Parkett *n.* **3.** *pl eccl.* Chor-

gestühl *n*. **4.** Box *f* (*im Stall*). **II** *v/t* **5.** *Motor* abwürgen. **III** *v/i* **6.** absterben (*Motor*).

stall² [~] **I** *v/i* Ausflüchte machen; Zeit schinden. **II** *v/t* j-n hinhalten; *et.* hinauszögern.

stal·lion ['stæljən] *s* (Zucht)Hengst *m*.

stal·wart ['stɔ:lwət] **I** *adj* □ **1.** kräftig, robust. **2.** *bsd. pol.* treu (*Anhänger*). **II** *s* **3.** *bsd. pol.* treuer Anhänger.

stam·i·na ['stæminə] *s* Stehvermögen *n*, (*physisch a.*) Kondition *f*.

stam·mer ['stæmə] **I** *v/i* 𝄞 stottern. **II** *v/t a.* ~ **out** stottern, stammeln. **III** *s* 𝄞 Stottern *n*: *have* (*od. speak with*) *a* ~ stottern. **'stam·mer·er** *s* 𝄞 Stotterer *m*, Stotterin *f*.

stamp [stæmp] **I** *v/t* **1.** ~ **one's foot** aufstampfen; ~ **out** Feuer austreten; *Übel* ausrotten. **2.** *Paß etc* (ab)stempeln; *Datum etc* aufstempeln (**on** *auf acc*): ~ *s.o. as* *fig.* j-n abstempeln als *od.* zu. **3.** *Brief etc* frankieren: **~ed envelope** Freiumschlag *m*. **4.** ~ **out** ☺ ausstanzen. **II** *v/t* **5.** sta(m)pfen, trampeln. **III** *s* **6.** (Brief)Marke *f* (*Rabatt-, Steuer- etc*) Marke *f*. **7.** Stempel *m* (*a. Abdruck*). ~ **al·bum** *s* (Brief)Markenalbum *n*. ~ **col·lec·tion** *s* (Brief)Markensammlung *f*. ~ **col·lec·tor** *s* (Brief)Markensammler(in).

stam·pede [stæm'pi:d] **I** *s* **1.** wilde Flucht (*von Tieren*); wilder Ansturm (*for auf acc*): *there was a* ~ *for the door* alles stürzte zur Tür. **2.** *fig.* (Massen-) Ansturm *m* (*for auf acc*). **II** *v/t* **3.** in wilde Flucht jagen. **4.** ~ *s.o. into doing s.th.* j-n so überrumpeln, daß er et. tut. **III** *v/i* **5.** durchgehen.

stamp·ing ground ['stæmpɪŋ] *s fig.* F Tummelplatz *m*; Jagdrevier *n*.

stance [stæns] *s* **1.** *bsd. Sport:* Stellung *f*. **2.** *fig.* Einstellung *f*, Haltung *f* (**on** zu).

stand [stænd] **I** *s* **1.** (*Obst-, Messe- etc*) Stand *m*. **2.** (*Kleider-, Noten- etc*)Ständer *m*. **3.** *Sport etc:* Tribüne *f*: *in the* ~ auf der Tribüne. **4.** 𝄌 *Am.* Zeugenstand *m*: *take the* ~ in den Zeugenstand treten. **5.** (*Taxi*)Stand(platz) *m*. **6.** *fig.* Einstellung *f* (**on** zu): *take a* ~ Position beziehen (**on** zu). **II** *v/i* (*irr*) **7.** *allg.* stehen: ~ *still* stillstehen; *as matters* (*od. things*) ~ nach Lage der Dinge, so wie die Dinge stehen; *my offer still* ~s

mein Angebot steht *od.* gilt noch; ~ *or fall by fig.* stehen u. fallen mit; → **awe** I, *correct* I, *clear* 14, *firm*[1] II. **8.** anstehen. **III** *v/t* (*irr*) **9.** stellen (**on** *auf acc*): ~ *s.th. on its head fig.* et. auf den Kopf stellen. **10.** *Beanspruchung, Hitze etc* aushalten, ertragen; *e-r Prüfung etc* standhalten. **11.** *I can't* ~ *him* (*it*) ich kann ihn (das) nicht leiden. **12.** ~ *s.o. a drink* F j-m e-n Drink spendieren. **13.** *Chance* haben. **14.** → *trial* 1. **15.** → *bail*[1] *2*, *surety*.

Verbindungen mit Präpositionen:

stand| by *v/i* **1.** zu j-m halten. **2.** zu *s-m* Wort etc stehen; *s-n Prinzipien etc* treu bleiben. ~ **for** *v/i* **1.** stehen für, bedeuten. **2.** eintreten für, vertreten. **3.** *sich et.* gefallen lassen, dulden. **4.** *bsd. Pol.* kandidieren für: ~ *election* kandidieren, sich zur Wahl stellen. ~ **on** *v/i* **1.** stehen auf (*dat*): ~ *one's hands* (*head*) e-n Handstand (Kopfstand) machen; *standing on one's head* F mit links. **2.** ~ *ceremony* förmlich sein. ~ **o·ver** *v/i* überwachen, aufpassen auf (*acc*).

Verbindungen mit Adverbien:

stand| a·bout, ~ a·round *v/i* herumstehen. ~ **back** *v/i* zurücktreten. ~ **by** *v/i* **1.** danebenstehen: *stand idly by* tatenlos zusehen (*a. fig.*). **2.** 𝄌 den Zeugenstand verlassen. ~ **down** *v/i* **1.** verzichten; zurücktreten (*in favo[u]r of* zugunsten). ~ **in** *v/i* einspringen (*for* für): ~ *for s.o. a.* j-n vertreten. ~ **out** *v/i* **1.** hervorstechen: ~ *against* (*od. from*) sich abheben von. **2.** sich hartnäckig wehren (*against* gegen). ~ **to·geth·er** *v/i* zs.-halten, -stehen. ~ **up** *v/i* **1.** aufstehen; stehen: *standing up* im Stehen. **2.** ~ *for* eintreten *od.* sich einsetzen für. **3.** ~ *to* *Beanspruchung etc* aushalten; *j-m* die Stirn bieten. **4.** F *j-n* versetzen.

stand·ard¹ ['stændəd] **I** *s* **1.** Norm *f*; Maßstab *m*: *set high* ~*s* (*for*) viel verlangen (von), hohe Anforderungen stellen (*an acc*); *be up to* (*below*) ~ den Anforderungen (nicht) genügen *od.* entsprechen; *by present-day* ~*s* nach heutigen Begriffen. **2.** Standard *m*, Niveau *n*: ~ *of living* Lebensstandard *m*. **II** *adj* **3.** normal, Normal...; durchschnittlich, Durchschnitts...; Standard..., 𝄌 Serien..., serienmäßig. **4.** maßgebend,

Standard...: ~ *English* korrektes Englisch.

stand·ard² [~] I *s* Standarte *f*, *(an Wagen)* Stander *m*; ✗ *hist.* Banner *n*. II *adj*: ~ *lamp Br.* Stehlampe *f*.

stand·ard·i·za·tion [ˌstændədaɪˈzeɪʃn] *s* Standardisierung *f*, Normung *f*, Vereinheitlichung *f*. **'stand·ard·ize** *v/t bsd.* ⊙ standardisieren, normen, *a. allg.* vereinheitlichen.

'stand|-by I *pl* **-bys** *s* 1. Reserve *f*. 2. *be on ~* in Bereitschaft stehen. II *adj* 3. Reserve..., Not.... 4. ✈ Stand-by-... '**~-in** *s* 1. *Film, TV:* Double *n*. 2. Ersatzmann *m*; Vertreter(in).

stand·ing [ˈstændɪŋ] I *adj* 1. stehend: *~-room only* nur (noch) Stehplätze; → *ovation.* 2. *fig.* ständig: *~ order* ✝ Dauerauftrag *m*. II *s* 3. Rang *m*, Stellung *f*; Ansehen *n*, Ruf *m*: *of high ~* hochangesehen, von hohem Ansehen. 4. Dauer *f*: *of long ~* seit langem bestehend, alt.

stand|-off·ish [ˌstændˈɒfɪʃ] *adj* □ F hochnäsig. '**~-point** *s fig.* Standpunkt *m*: *from my ~* von m-m Standpunkt aus. '**~-still** *s* Stillstand *m* (*a. fig.*): *be at a ~* stehen (*Auto etc*); ruhen (*Produktion etc*); *bring to a ~ Auto etc* zum Stehen bringen; *Produktion etc* zum Erliegen bringen. '**~-up** *adj* 1. a) Steh...: *~ collar* Stehkragen *m*, b) im Stehen (eingenommen) (*Mahlzeit*). 2. *~ fight* wüste Schlägerei.

stank [stæŋk] *pret von* **stink**.

stan·za [ˈstænzə] *s* Strophe *f*.

sta·ple¹ [ˈsteɪpl] I *s* Heftklammer *f*; Krampe *f*. II *v/t* heften: *~ together* zs.-heften.

sta·ple² [~] I *s* 1. ✝ Haupterzeugnis *n* (*e-s Landes etc*). 2. Hauptnahrungsmittel *n*. II *adj* 3. Haupt...; 4. üblich.

sta·pler [ˈsteɪplə] *s* (Draht)Hefter *m*.

star [stɑː] I *s* 1. Stern *m*: ✫s *and Stripes pl* (*sg konstruiert*) *das* Sternenbanner (*Staatsflagge der USA*); *see* ~s Sterne sehen; *you can thank your lucky ~s that* du kannst vom Glück reden od. sagen, daß. 2. *typ.* Sternchen *n*. 3. Star *m* (*Person*). II *adj* 4. Haupt...; Star... III *v/t* 5. *Wort etc* mit e-m Sternchen kennzeichnen. 6. *a film ~ring ...* ein Film mit ... in der Hauptrolle *od.* den Hauptrollen; *~ring ...* in der Hauptrol-

le *od.* den Hauptrollen ... IV *v/i* 7. die *od.* e-e Hauptrolle spielen (*in* in *dat*). **~board** [ˈ~bəd] *s* ✈, ⚓ Steuerbord *n*.

starch [stɑːtʃ] I *s* 1. (*Kartoffel-, Wäscheetc*)Stärke *f*. 2. *pl* stärkereiche Nahrungsmittel *pl*; *engS.* Kohle(n)hydrate *pl*. II *v/t* 3. *Wäsche* stärken. **'starch·y** *adj* □ 1. stärkehaltig, -reich. 2. *fig.* F steif.

star·dom [ˈstɑːdəm] *s* (Star)Ruhm *m*.

stare [steə] I *v/i* starren; große Augen machen: *~ after j-m* nachstarren; *~ at j-n* anstarren; → *space* 1. II *v/t*: *~ s.o. out* (*od.* **down**) j-n so lange anstarren, bis er verlegen wird; *~ s.o. in the face* j-m ins Gesicht starren; vor j-s Augen liegen; *fig.* klar auf der Hand liegen. III *s* (starrer) Blick, Starren *n*.

'star·fish *s zo.* Seestern *m*.

stark [stɑːk] I *adj* nackt (*Tatsachen etc*): *be in ~ contrast to* in krassem Gegensatz stehen zu. II *adv* F: *~ naked* splitternackt; *~ staring* (*od.* **raving**) *mad* total verrückt.

stark·ers [ˈstɑːkəz] *adj Br.* F splitternackt.

star·let [ˈstɑːlɪt] *s* Starlet *n*, Filmsternchen *n*.

'star·light *s* Sternenlicht *n*.

star·ling [ˈstɑːlɪŋ] *s orn.* Star *m*.

'star·lit *adj* stern(en)klar.

star·ry [ˈstɑːrɪ] *adj* Stern(en)... **~-eyed** *adj* blauäugig, naiv.

'Star-,Span·gled Ban·ner *s* 1. *die* Nationalhymne (*der USA*). 2. *das* Sternenbanner (*Staatsflagge der USA*).

start [stɑːt] I *v/i* 1. a. *~ off* anfangen, beginnen: *~ doing* (*od.* **to do**) *s.th.* anfangen, et. zu tun; *~ (in) on doing s.th.* damit anfangen, et. zu tun; *to ~ with* anfangs, zunächst; erstens; → *scratch* 7. 2. a. *~ off* (*od.* **out**) aufbrechen (*for* nach): *~ back for home* sich auf den Heimweg machen. 3. abfahren (*Bus, Zug*), ablegen (*Boot*), ✈ abfliegen, starten; (*Sport*) starten: *~ing from Monday* ab Montag. 4. a. *~ up* anspringen (*Motor etc*). 5. zs.-fahren, -zucken (*at* bei). II *v/t* 6. a. *~ off* anfangen, beginnen. 7. a. *~ up Aktion* starten, *Geschäft, Familie etc* gründen, *Gerücht* in Umlauf setzen. 8. *Motor etc* anlassen, starten. III *s* 9. Anfang *m*, Beginn *m*, (*bsd. Sport*) Start *m*: *at the ~* am

Anfang; (*Sport*) am Start; **for a ~** erstens; **from ~ to finish** von Anfang bis Ende; (*Sport*) vom Start bis zum Ziel; **make a fresh ~** (**in life**) e-n neuen Anfang machen, noch einmal von vorn anfangen; **make a ~ on s.th.** mit et. anfangen. **10.** Aufbruch *m*. **11.** **give a ~** → 5; **wake up with a ~** aus dem Schlaf aufschrecken. **12.** Vorsprung *m* (**on**, **over** vor *dat*). **'start·er** *s* **1.** *Sport*: Starter(in) (*Kampfrichter[in] u. Wettkampfteilnehmer[in]*). **2.** *mot.* Starter *m*, Anlasser *m*. **3.** F Vorspeise *f*: **as a ~** als Vorspeise. **4. for ~s** F zunächst einmal: **that's just for ~s** das ist nur der Anfang. **'start·ing** *adj bsd. Sport*: Start...: **~ point** Ausgangspunkt *m* (*a. fig.*).

star·tle ['stɑːtl] *v/t* **1.** erschrecken. **2.** *fig.* überraschen, bestürzen.

star·va·tion [stɑː'veɪʃn] *s* Hungern *n*: **die of ~** verhungern; **~ diet** F Fasten-, Hungerkur *f*; **~ wages** *pl* Hungerlohn *m*, -löhne *pl*.

starve [stɑːv] **I** *v/i* **1.** hungern: **~** (**to death**) verhungern; **I'm starving** F ich komme fast um vor Hunger. **II** *v/t* **2.** hungern lassen: **~** (**to death**) verhungern lassen; **~** (**out**) aushungern. **3. be ~d of** knapp sein an (*dat*).

star wars *s pl* **X** F Krieg *m* der Sterne.

state [steɪt] **I** *s* **1.** *oft* ⚎ *pol.* Staat *m*. **2.** *pol. Am.* (Bundes-, Einzel)Staat *m*: **the ⚎s** *pl* F die (Vereinigten) Staaten *pl*; **~ evidence** 2. **3.** Zustand *m*: **~ of mind** (Geistes-, Gemüts)Verfassung *f*, (-)Zustand *m*; **be in a ~ of war** with sich im Kriegszustand befinden mit; **get in(to) a ~** *bsd. Br.* F sich aufregen; nervös werden; → **emergency**, **health** 2. **4.** Stand *m*, Lage *f*. **II** *adj* **5.** staatlich, Staats...: ⚎ **Department** *pol. Am.* Außenministerium *n*. **III** *v/t* **6.** angeben, nennen. **7.** erklären, ⚖ aussagen (**that** daß). **8.** festlegen, -setzen: **on the ~d date** zum festgesetzten Termin. **'state·less** *adj pol.* staatenlos. **'state·ly** *adj* **1.** gemessen (*Tempo etc*). **2.** prächtig. **'statement** *s* **1.** Statement *n*, Erklärung *f*; Angabe *f*; ⚖ Aussage *f*: **make a ~** e-e Erklärung abgeben (**to** vor *dat*). **2.** ✝ (*Bank-*, *Konto*)Auszug *m*.

‚state-of-the-'art *adj* neuest, auf dem neuesten Stand der Technik stehend.

states·man ['steɪtsmən] *s* (*irr* **man**)

Staatsmann *m*. **'states·man·like** *adj* staatsmännisch.

stat·ic ['stætɪk] **I** *adj* (**~ally**) **1.** *phys.* statisch (*a. fig.*). **2.** *fig.* gleichbleibend, konstant. **II** *s* **3.** *Radio*, *TV*: atmosphärische Störungen *pl*. **4.** *pl* (*sg konstruiert*) *phys.* Statik *f*.

sta·tion ['steɪʃn] **I** *s* **1.** (*a. Bus-*, *U-*)Bahnhof *m*, Station *f*. **2.** (*Forschungs-*, *Unfall- etc*)Station *f*, Tankstelle *f*, (*Feuer-*)Wache *f*, (*Polizei*)Revier *n*, (-)Wache *f*, (*Wahl*)Lokal *n*. **3.** *Rundfunk*, *TV*: Station *f*, Sender *m*. **II** *v/t* **4.** aufstellen, postieren; ✕ stationieren.

sta·tion·ar·y ['steɪʃnərɪ] *adj* stehend (*Fahrzeug etc*): **be ~** stehen.

sta·tion·er ['steɪʃnə] *s* Schreibwarenhändler(in). **'sta·tion·er·y** *s* Schreibwaren *pl*; Briefpapier *n*.

'sta·tion **house** *s Am.* (Polizei)Revier *n*, (-)Wache *f*. **‚~·mas·ter** *s* Bahnhofsvorsteher *m*. **~ wag·on** *s mot. Am.* Kombiwagen *m*.

sta·tis·ti·cal [stə'tɪstɪkl] *adj* ☐ statistisch. **sta·tis·tics** *s pl* **1.** Statistik(en *pl*) *f*: → **vital** 2. **2.** (*sg konstruiert*) Statistik *f* (*Wissenschaft*, *Methode*).

stat·ue ['stætjuː] *s* Statue *f*, Standbild *n*.

stat·ure ['stætʃə] *s* **1.** Statur *f*, Wuchs *m*. **2.** *fig.* Format *n*.

sta·tus ['steɪtəs] *s* **1.** Status *m*, Rechtsstellung *f*. **2.** → **marital**. **3.** Status *m*, Stellung *f*; Prestige *n*. **~ quo** [kwəʊ] *s* Status *m* quo. **~ sym·bol** *s* Statussymbol *n*.

stat·ute ['stætjuːt] *s* **1.** Gesetz *n*: **by ~** gesetzlich. **2.** Statut *n*, *pl a.* Satzung *f*. **~ book** *s* Gesetzbuch *n*. **~ law** *s* Gesetzesrecht *n*.

stat·u·to·ry ['stætjʊtərɪ] *adj* ☐ **1.** gesetzlich (garantiert *od.* vorgeschrieben). **2.** satzungsgemäß.

staunch¹ [stɔːntʃ] *v/t* Blut stillen.

staunch² [~] *adj* ☐ **1.** treu, zuverlässig. **2.** standhaft.

stay [steɪ] **I** *s* **1.** Aufenthalt *m*: **~ in hospital** Krankenhausaufenthalt. **2.** ⚖ Aussetzung *f*, Aufschub *m*: **he was given** (*od.* **granted**) (**a**) **~ of execution** s-e Hinrichtung wurde aufgeschoben. **II** *v/i* **3.** bleiben (**for** *od.* **to lunch** zum Mittagessen). **4.** wohnen (**with friends** bei Freunden): **~ the night at a hotel** im Hotel übernachten. **III** *v/t* **5. ~ the**

course (*Sport*) durchhalten (*a. fig.*). *Verbindungen mit Adverbien:*

stay| a·way *v/i* wegbleiben, sich fernhalten (*from* von). **~ down** *v/i* unten bleiben (*a. fig.*). **~ in** *v/i* zu Hause *od.* drinnen bleiben. **~ on** *v/i:* **~ as chairman** (weiterhin) Vorsitzender bleiben; **~ at school** (mit der Schule) weitermachen. **~ out** *v/i* draußen bleiben: **~ (on strike)** streiken. **~ up** *v/i* aufbleiben.

'**stay-at-home** *s* Stubenhocker(in).

stay·ing pow·er ['stenŋ] *s* Stehvermögen *n*, Ausdauer *f*.

stead [sted] *s:* **in s.o.'s ~** an j-s Stelle.

stead-fast ['stedfɑːst] *adj* □ **1.** treu, zuverlässig. **2.** fest, unverwandt (*Blick*).

stead·y ['stedɪ] **I** *adj* □ **1.** (stand)fest, stabil. **2.** ruhig (*Auge, Hand*), gut (*Nerven*). **3.** gleichmäßig. **4.** fest (*Arbeitsplatz, Freundin etc*). **II** *v/t* **5.** j-n, *Nerven* beruhigen. **III** *v/i* **6.** sich beruhigen. **IV** *int* **7.** *a.* **~ on!** *Br.* F Vorsicht!

steak [steɪk] *s* Steak *n*; (*Fisch*)Filet *n*.

steal [stiːl] (*irr*) **I** *v/t* **1.** stehlen (*a. fig.*), *Gemälde etc* rauben: **~ s.o.'s girlfriend** j-m die Freundin ausspannen; **~ a glance** at e-n verstohlenen Blick werfen auf (*acc*); → **march²** 5, **show** 1, **thunder** I. **II** *v/i* **2.** stehlen. **3.** sich stehlen, (sich) schleichen (*out of* aus).

stealth [stelθ] *s:* **by ~** → **stealthy.** '**stealth·y** *adj* □ heimlich, verstohlen.

steam [stiːm] **I** *s* **1.** Dampf *m:* **full ~ ahead!** ♣ volle Kraft *od.* Volldampf voraus!; **under one's own ~** *fig.* auf eigene Faust; **let off ~** Dampf ablassen, *fig. a.* sich Luft machen; **run out of ~** *fig.* s-n Schwung verlieren; **he ran out of ~** *a.* ihm ging die Puste aus. **2.** Dampf *m*, Dunst *m*. **II** *v/i* **3.** dampfen (*a.* ♣, 🚂): **~ing hot** dampfend heiß. **4. ~ up** beschlagen. **III** *v/t* **5.** *gastr.* dämpfen, dünsten. **6. ~ open** *Brief* über Dampf öffnen. **7. get ~ed up** beschlagen; *fig.* F sich aufregen (*about* über *acc*). '**~·boat** *s* Dampfboot *n*, Dampfer *m*.

steam·er ['stiːmə] *s* **1.** Dampfer *m*, Dampfschiff *n*. **2.** Dampf(koch)-, Schnellkochtopf *m*.

steam| i·ron *s* Dampfbügeleisen *n*. '**~·roll·er** *s* Dampfwalze *f*. '**~·ship** → **steamer** 1.

steel [stiːl] **I** *s* Stahl *m:* → **nerve** 1. **II** *v/t:* **~ o.s. for** sich wappnen gegen, sich

gefaßt machen auf (*acc*). **~ wool** *s* Stahlwolle *f*. '**~·work·er** *s* Stahlarbeiter *m*. '**~·works** *s pl* (*oft sg konstruiert*) Stahlwerk *n*.

steel·y ['stiːlɪ] *adj* **1. ~ blue** stahlblau. **2.** *fig.* hart (*Blick*); eisern (*Entschlossenheit*).

steep¹ [stiːp] *adj* □ **1.** steil. **2.** *fig.* stark (*Preisanstieg etc*). **3.** F happig (*Forderung*), (*Preis a.*) gepfeffert, gesalzen.

steep² [~] **I** *v/t* eintauchen (*in* in *acc*): *Wäsche* einweichen: **~ed in history** geschichtsträchtig. **II** *v/i* weichen.

steep·en ['stiːpən] *v/i* steiler werden.

stee·ple ['stiːpl] *s* Kirchturm *m*. '**~·chase** *s* Pferdesport: Hindernis-, Jagdrennen *n*; *Leichtathletik:* Hindernislauf *m*.

steer¹ [stɪə] *s* (junger) Ochse.

steer² [~] **I** *v/t* **1.** steuern, lenken. **2.** *Kurs* steuern (*a. fig.*). **3.** j-n lotsen, bugsieren. **II** *v/i* **4. ~ for** ♣ ansteuern, Kurs nehmen auf (*acc*); *fig.* zusteuern auf (*acc*); → **clear** 13. '**steer·ing I** *s* Steuerung *f*, Lenkung *f*. **II** *adj:* **~ column** *mot.* Lenksäule *f*; **~ wheel** *mot.* Lenk-, *a.* ♣ Steuerrad *n*.

stein [staɪn] *s* Maßkrug *m*.

stel·lar ['stelə] *adj* Stern(en)...

stem¹ [stem] **I** *s* **1.** ♣ Stiel *m* (*a. e-s Sektglases etc*), Stengel *m*. **2.** *ling.* Stamm *m*. **II** *v/i* **3. ~ from** stammen *od.* herrühren von.

stem² [~] *v/t* *Blutung* stillen; *fig.* eindämmen, stoppen.

stench [stentʃ] *s* Gestank *m*.

sten·cil ['stensl] *s* Schablone *f*; *typ.* Matrize *f*.

ste·nog·ra·pher [stə'nɒgrəfə] *s Am.* Stenotypistin *f*.

step [step] **I** *s* **1.** Schritt *m* (*a. Geräusch*): **~ by ~** Schritt für Schritt (*a. fig.*); **take a ~** e-n Schritt machen; **it's just a ~** (*od.* **a few ~s**) **to the shop** es sind nur ein paar Schritte bis zum Laden; → **watch** 4. **2.** Stufe *f*; Sprosse *f*: (**pair of**) **~s** *pl* → **stepladder**; → **mind** 7. **3. be in** (*out of*) **~** ✕ im Gleichschritt *od.* Tritt sein; (*beim Tanzen*) im (aus dem) Takt sein; **be out of ~ with** *fig.* nachhinken (*dat*), zurück sein hinter (*dat*); **keep** (**in**) **~ with** *fig.* sich richten nach. **4.** *fig.* Schritt *m*: **take ~s** Schritte *od.* et. unternehmen; **a ~ in the right**

direction ein Schritt in die richtige Richtung; → **legal** 4. **5.** *fig.* Schritt *m*, Stufe *f*: **three-~ plan** Dreistufenplan *m*. **II** *v/i* **6.** gehen; treten (**in** in *acc*; **on** auf *acc*): **~ on it** *mot.* F Gas geben, auf die Tube drücken (*beide a. fig.*); → **gas** 2b.

Verbindungen mit Adverbien:

step| a·side *v/i* **1.** zur Seite treten. **2.** *fig.* Platz machen (**in** favo[u]r of für), zurücktreten (**as** als; **in** favo[u]r of zugunsten). **~ back** *v/i* zurücktreten. **~ down** *v/i* **1.** herunter-, hinuntersteigen. **2.** → **step aside**. **~ for·ward** *v/i* **1.** vortreten, nach vorne treten. **2.** *fig.* sich melden (*Zeugen etc*). **~ in** *v/i* **1.** eintreten. **2.** *fig.* einschreiten; sich einmischen. **~ out** *v/i* **1.** heraus-, hinaustreten; *bsd. Am.* weggehen. **2.** **~ on** *Am.* F *Ehepartner* betrügen. **~ up I** *v/i* herauf-, hinaufsteigen. **II** *v/t* Produktion *etc* steigern.

step... ['step] *Stief*...: **~father, ~mother,** *etc*.

step|-by-'step *adj fig.* schrittweise. '**~lad·der** *s* Tritt- *od.* Stufenleiter *f*.

steppe [step] *s*, *oft pl geogr.* Steppe *f*.

step·ping stone ['stepıŋ] *s* Trittstein *m*; *fig.* Sprungbrett *n* (**to** für).

ster·e·o ['steriəu] **I** *s* **1.** Stereo *n*: **in ~. 2.** Stereogerät *n*, -anlage *f*. **II** *adj* **3.** Stereo...: **~ unit** Stereoanlage *f*.

ster·e·o·type ['stiriətaip] *s* Klischee(vorstellung *f*) *n*. '**ster·e·o·typed** *adj* klischeehaft; stereotyp.

ster·ile ['sterail] *adj* **1.** 𝄞 steril, keimfrei. **2.** *biol.* steril, (*a. Boden*) unfruchtbar. **3.** *fig.* steril, unoriginell. **ste·ril·i·ty** [stə'rıləti] *s* Sterilität *f* (*a. fig.*): *Un*fruchtbarkeit *f*.

ster·i·li·za·tion [sterəlaı'zeɪʃn] *s* 𝄞 Sterilisation *f*, Sterilisierung *f*. '**ster·i·lize** *v/t* sterilisieren.

ster·ling ['stɜːlıŋ] **I** *s* das Pfund Sterling. **II** *adj*: **~ silver** Sterlingsilber *n*.

stern¹ [stɜːn] *adj* ☐ streng (*Person, Blick, Disziplin etc*).

stern² [~] *s* 𝄞 Heck *n*.

ster·num ['stɜːnəm] *pl* **-na** ['~nə], **-nums** *s anat.* Brustbein *n*.

steth·o·scope ['steθəskəup] *s* 𝄞 Stethoskop *n*.

stet·son ['stetsn] *s* Stetson *m*, Cowboyhut *m*.

---

ste·ve·dore ['stiːvədɔː] *s* 𝄞 *bsd. Am.* Schauermann *m*, Stauer *m*.

stew [stjuː] **I** *v/t Fleisch, Gemüse* schmoren, *Obst* dünsten: **~ed apples** *pl* Apfelkompott *n*. **II** *v/i* schmoren, dünsten: → **juice** 1. **III** *s* Eintopf *m*.

stew·ard [stjʊəd] *s* **1.** 𝄞, 𝄞 Steward *m*. **2.** Ordner *m*. '**stew·ard·ess** *s* 𝄞, 𝄞 Stewardeß *f*.

stewed [stjuːd] *adj* F blau (*betrunken*).

stick¹ [stık] *s* **1.** Stock *m*, ([*Eis*]*Hockey a.*) Schläger *m*; (*Besen-etc*)Stiel *m*; (*a.* 𝄞 *Steuer*)Knüppel *m*: **walk with a ~** am Stock gehen; **get (hold of) the wrong end of the ~** F die Sache in den falschen *od.* verkehrten Hals bekommen; → **cleft stick. 2.** (trockener) Zweig, *pl a.* Brennholz *n*. **3.** Stück *n* (*Kreide etc*), Stange *f* (*Dynamit, Sellerie etc*), (*Lippen*)Stift *m*, (*Räucher*)Stäbchen *n*, Streifen *m* (*Kaugummi*). **4.** *pl of furniture* F Möbelstück *n*. **5.** **live out in the ~s** F in der finstersten Provinz leben.

stick² [~] (*irr*) **I** *v/t* **1.** mit *e-r Nadel etc* stechen (**into** in *acc*). **2.** *et.* kleben (**on** auf *acc*, an *acc*); an-, festkleben (**with** mit). **3.** stecken: → **nose** 1. **4.** F tun, stellen, setzen, legen. **5.** *bsd. Br.* F **stand** 11. **II** *v/i* **6.** kleben, halten; klebenbleiben (**to** an *dat*). **7.** steckenbleiben: **~ in s.o.'s mind** *fig.* j-m im Gedächtnis bleiben. **8.** **~ at nothing** vor nichts zurückschrecken. **9.** **~ to** (F **by**) bei *s-r Ansicht etc* bleiben, zu *s-m Wort etc* stehen; **~ to** (F **by, with**) zu j-m halten; → **gun** 1, **point** 11.

Verbindungen mit Adverbien:

stick| out I *v/i* **1.** vorstehen, (*Ohren etc*) abstehen. **2.** *fig.* auffallen: → **mile, thumb** I. **3.** **~ for** bestehen auf (*dat*). **II** *v/t* **4.** aus-, vorstrecken: **stick one's tongue out at s.o.** j-m die Zunge herausstrecken; → **neck** 1. **5.** durchhalten, -stehen. **~ to·geth·er** *v/i* **1.** (*a. v/t*) zs.-kleben. **2.** *fig.* zs.-halten. **~ up I** *v/t* **1.** F *j-n, Bank etc* überfallen. **2. stick 'em up!** F Hände hoch! **II** *v/i* **3.** **~ for** *j-n* verteidigen (*a. mit Worten*).

stick·er ['stıkə] *s* Aufkleber *m*. '**stick·ing** *adj*: **~ plaster** Heftpflaster *n*; **~ point** *fig.* unüberwindliches Hindernis (*bei Verhandlungen etc*).

'**stick-in-the-mud** *s* F Rückschrittler(in).

stick·ler ['stɪklə] s: **be a ~ for** es ganz genau nehmen mit, großen Wert legen auf (acc.)

'stick|·on adj: **~ label** (Auf)Klebeetikett n. **'~·pin** s Am. Krawattennadel f. **'~·up** s F (Raub)Überfall m.

stick·y ['stɪkɪ] adj □ **1.** a) klebrig (with von), b) → stick-on. **2.** schwül, drük-kend (Wetter). **3.** F heikel, unange-nehm (Lage): **he'll come to** (od. meet) **a ~ end** mit ihm wird es ein böses Ende nehmen. **4. be ~ about doing s.th.** F et. nur ungern tun.

stiff [stɪf] **I** adj □ **1.** allg. steif: **beat until ~** steif schlagen; → bore², lip 1. **2.** fig. stark (alkoholisches Getränk, Medizin). **3.** fig. schwer, schwierig (Aufgabe); hart (Strafe); scharf (Konkurrenz); hartnäckig (Widerstand). **4.** F happig, gepfeffert, gesalzen (Preis). **II** s **5.** sl. Leiche f. **'stiff·en I** v/t **1.** Wäsche stärken, steifen. **2.** fig. verschärfen. **II** v/i **3.** steif werden. **4.** fig. sich verschär-fen.

sti·fle ['staɪfl] **I** v/t ersticken, fig. a. unter-drücken. **II** v/i ersticken.

stig·ma ['stɪgmə] s **1.** fig. Stigma n. **2.** pl **-ta** ['~tə] eccl. Stigma n, Wundmal n. **'stig·ma·tize** v/t fig. brandmarken (as als).

sti·let·to [str'letəʊ] pl **-tos** s Stilett n. **~ heel** s Bleistift-, Pfennigabsatz m.

still¹ [stɪl] **I** adj □ allg. still: → keep 15, stand 7, water 1. **2.** ohne Kohlen-säure (Getränk). **II** s **3.** Film, TV: Standfoto n.

still² [~] **I** adv **1.** (immer) noch, noch immer. **2.** beim comp: noch. **II** cj **3.** dennoch, trotzdem.

still³ [~] s 🜊 Destillationsapparat m; De-stillierkolben m.

'still·birth ['stɪlbɜːθ] s Totgeburt f. **'~·born** adj totgeboren. **~ life** pl lifes s paint. Stilleben n.

stilt [stɪlt] s **1.** Stelze f. **2.** △ Pfahl m. **'stilt·ed** adj □ gestelzt, gespreizt, ge-schraubt.

stim·u·lant ['stɪmjʊlənt] s 🕇 Stimulans n, Anregungsmittel n; fig. Anreiz m, An-sporn m (**to** für). **stim·u·late** ['~leɪt] v/t **1.** 🕇 j-n, Kreislauf etc stimulieren, anre-gen, fig. a. j-n ansporen (**to do** zu tun); physiol. reizen. **2.** Produktion etc an-kurbeln. **stim·u·lus** ['~ləs] pl **-li** ['~laɪ] s

1. physiol. Reiz m. **2.** fig. Anreiz m, Ansporn m (**to** für).

sting [stɪŋ] **I** v/t (irr) **1.** j-n stechen (Biene etc). **2.** brennen auf (dat) od. in (dat): **~ s.o. into action** fig. j-n aktiv werden lassen. **3.** F j-n neppen (**for** um). **II** v/i **4.** stechen (Bienen etc). **5.** brennen (**from** von) (Augen etc). **III** s **6.** Stachel m. **7.** Stich m. **8.** Brennen n, brennender Schmerz: **take the ~ out of s.th.** fig. e-r Sache den Stachel nehmen. **'sting·ing** adj: **~ nettle** ♀ Brennessel f.

stin·gy ['stɪndʒɪ] adj □ F knick(e)rig (Person), mick(e)rig (Mahlzeit etc): **be ~ with** knickern mit.

stink [stɪŋk] **I** v/i (irr) **1.** stinken (**of** nach): **~ to high heaven** wie die Pest stinken; fig. zum Himmel stinken. **2.** F hundsmiserabel sein. **II** v/t **3. ~ out** F Zimmer etc verstänkern. **III** s **4.** Ge-stank m: **there's a ~ of garlic in here** hier stinkt es nach Knoblauch. **5.** fig. cause (od. **kick up, raise**) **a ~** F Stunk machen (**about** wegen). **~ bomb** s Stinkbombe f.

stink·ing ['stɪŋkɪŋ] **I** adj **1.** stinkend. **2.** F scheußlich; blöd. **II** adv **3. ~ rich** F stinkreich.

stint [stɪnt] s a) Pensum n, b) Zeit f: **he did a three-year ~ in the army** er war drei Jahre lang beim Militär.

stip·u·late ['stɪpjʊleɪt] v/t **1.** zur Auflage od. Bedingung machen. **2.** festsetzen, vereinbaren. **stip·u·la·tion** s **1.** Auflage f, Bedingung f. **2.** Festsetzung f, Ver-einbarung f.

stir [stɜː] **I** v/t **1.** (um)rühren: **~ up** Staub aufwirbeln, Schlamm aufwühlen. **2.** Glied etc bewegen, rühren: **~ o.s.** sich beeilen; → finger I, stump 1. **3.** Blätter etc leicht bewegen, Wasser kräuseln (Wind). **4.** fig. j-n aufwühlen, bewegen. **5. ~ up** fig. Unruhe stiften, Streit entfa-chen; Erinnerungen wachrufen. **II** v/i **6.** sich rühren: **~ from** sich fort- od. weg-rühren von. **7.** fig. sich rühren, wach werden. **III** s **8. give s.th. a ~** et. (um-) rühren. **9. cause** (od. **create**) **a ~** fig. für Aufsehen sorgen. **'stir·ring** adj □ aufwühlend, bewegend.

stir·rup ['stɪrəp] s Steigbügel m.

stitch [stɪtʃ] **I** s **1.** Nähen etc: Stich m: **the wound needed eight ~es** die Wunde mußte mit acht Stichen genäht werden;

he had his ~*es out yesterday* ihm wurden gestern die Fäden gezogen. **2.** *Stricken etc:* Masche *f:* **drop a** ~ e-e Masche fallen lassen. **3. have a** (*od. the*) ~ Seitenstechen haben; **be in** ~*es* F sich kaputtlachen. **4. he hadn't got a** ~ **on** F er war splitterfasernackt. **II** *v/t* **5.** *a.* ~ **up** zunähen, *Wunde* nähen: ~ **on** (**to**) *Knopf etc* annähen (an *acc*). **6.** *Buch* broschieren, heften.

stock [stɔk] **I** *s* **1.** Vorrat *m* (**of** an *dat*): **have s.th. in** ~ et. vorrätig *od.* auf Lager haben; **take** ~ ⚕ Inventur machen; **take** ~ **of** *fig.* sich klarwerden über (*acc*). **2.** ⚕ *a.*) *bsd. Am.* Aktie(n *pl*) *f*, b) *pl* Aktien *pl*, c) *pl* Wertpapiere *pl*. **3.** *gastr.* Brühe *f.* **4.** Viehbestand *m.* **5.** (*Gewehr*)Schaft *m.* **6.** *fig.* Abstammung *f*, Herkunft *f.* **II** *v/t* **7.** ⚕ *Ware* vorrätig haben, führen. **8. be well** ~*ed* (**up**) **with** gut versorgt sein mit. **III** *v/i* **9.** ~ **up** sich eindecken (**on, with** mit). **IV** *adj* **10.** ~ **model** Serienmodell *n;* ~ **size** Standardgröße *f.* **11.** *contp.* Standard..., stereotyp (*Ausrede etc*). **'**~**,breed·er** *s* Viehzüchter *m.* **'**~**,breed·ing** *s* Viehzucht *f.* **'**~**,brok·er** *s* ⚕ Börsenmakler *m.* ~ **cor·po·ra·tion** *s* ⚕ *Am.* Kapital- *od.* Aktiengesellschaft *f.* ~ **cube** *s* Brühwürfel *m.* ~ **ex·change** *s* ⚕ Börse *f.* **'**~**,hold·er** *s* ⚕ *bsd. Am.* Aktionär(in).

stock·ing [stɔkɪŋ] *s* Strumpf *m.* ~ **mask** *s* Strumpfmaske *f.*

,stock-in-'trade *s:* **be part of s.o.'s** ~ *fig.* zu j-s Rüstzeug gehören. ~ **mar·ket** *s* ⚕ Börse *f.* **'**~**,pile I** *s* Vorrat *m* (**of** an *dat*). **II** *v/t* e-n Vorrat anlegen an (*dat*); *Lebensmittel etc* hamstern, horten. **'**~**room** *s* Lager(raum *m*) *n.* **,**~**'still** *adv* regungslos. **'**~**,tak·ing** *s* ⚕ Inventur *f; fig.* Bestandsaufnahme *f.*

stock·y [stɔkɪ] *adj* □ stämmig, untersetzt.

sto·i·cal [stəʊɪkl] *adj* □ stoisch, gelassen. **sto·i·cism** [~sɪzəm] *s* Gelassenheit *f.*

stoke [stəʊk] **I** *v/t a.* ~ **up** Feuer, Haß etc schüren. **II** *v/i:* ~ **up** F sich vollstopfen (**on, with** mit). **'stok·er** *s* Heizer *m.*

stole¹ [stəʊl] *pret von* **steal.**

stole² [~] *s* Stola *f.*

sto·len [stəʊlən] *pp von* **steal.**

stol·id [stɔlɪd] *adj* □ phlegmatisch.

stom·ach [stʌmək] **I** *s* **1.** Magen *m:* **on**

an empty ~ auf leeren *od.* nüchternen Magen *rauchen etc,* mit leerem *od.* nüchternem Magen *schwimmen gehen etc;* **on a full** ~ mit vollem Magen; **turn s.o.'s** ~ j-m den Magen umdrehen. **2.** Bauch *m.* **3.** (**for**) Appetit *m* (auf *acc*); *fig.* Lust *f* (auf *acc,* zu). **II** *v/t* **4.** vertragen (*a. fig.*). **,**~**ache** [ˈeɪk] *s* **1.** Magenschmerzen *pl.* **2.** Bauchschmerzen *pl,* -weh *n.* ~ **up·set** *s* Magenverstimmung *f.*

stomp [stɔmp] *v/i* sta(m)pfen, trampeln.

stone [stəʊn] **I** *s* **1.** (*a. Edel-,* ⚒ *Gallenetc*)Stein *m:* **it's only a** ~**'s throw** (**away**) **from** es ist nur e-n Katzensprung entfernt von; **have a heart of** ~ ein Herz aus Stein haben; **leave no** ~ **unturned** *fig.* nichts unversucht lassen. **2.** ♀ Kern *m,* Stein *m.* **3.** (*Hagel*)Korn *n.* **4.** *pl* **stone**(**s**) *Br.* Gewichtseinheit (= 6,35 *kg*). **II** *v/t* **5.** mit Steinen bewerfen: ~ (**to death**) steinigen. **6.** entkernen, -steinen. ⚒ **Age** *s* Steinzeit *f.* **,**~**'broke** *Am.* → **stony-broke.** **,**~**-'cold I** *adj* eiskalt. **II** *adv:* ~ **sober** F stocknüchtern.

stoned [stəʊnd] *adj sl.* **1.** stinkbesoffen. **2.** stoned (*unter Drogeneinwirkung*).

,stone-│**'dead** *adj* mausetot. **,**~**-'deaf** *adj* stocktaub. ~ **fruit** *s* Steinfrucht *f, coll.* Steinobst *n.* **'**~**,ma·son** *s* Steinmetz *m.* **'**~**ware** *s* Steinzeug *n.*

ston·y [stəʊnɪ] *adj* □ **1.** steinig. **2.** *fig.* steinern (*Gesicht, Herz etc*), eisig (*Schweigen*). **,**~**'broke** *adj bsd. Br.* F total abgebrannt *od.* pleite.

stood [stʊd] *pret u. pp von* **stand.**

stooge [stuːdʒ] *s* F *contp.* Handlanger *m.*

stool [stuːl] *s* **1.** (*Bar-, Klavier- etc*)Hokker *m,* (*Klavier- etc*)Stuhl *m,* (-)Schemel *m:* **fall between two** ~**s** *fig.* sich zwischen zwei Stühle setzen. **2.** *physiol.* Stuhl *m.* **'**~**,pi·geon** *s* F (Polizei)Spitzel *m.*

stoop [stuːp] **I** *v/i* **1.** *a.* ~ **down** sich bükken. **2.** gebeugt gehen. **3.** ~ **to** *fig.* sich herablassen *od.* hergeben zu: ~ **to doing s.th.** sich dazu herablassen *od.* hergeben, et. zu tun. **II** *s* **4.** gebeugte Haltung: **walk with a** ~ gebeugt gehen.

stop [stɔp] **I** *s* **1.** Halt *m:* **come to a** ~ anhalten, stoppen, *weitS.* aufhören; **put a** ~ **to** e-r Sache ein Ende machen *od.* setzen. **2.** (*Bus*)Haltestelle *f.* **3.** *ling.*

bsd. Br. Punkt *m.* **4. pull out all the ~s** *fig.* alle Register ziehen. **II** *v/i* **5.** stehenbleiben (*a. Uhr etc*), (an)halten, stoppen: **~ by s.o.'s place** bei j-m vorbeischauen; → **dead** 14, **thief.** **6.** aufhören: **~ at nothing** vor nichts zurückschrecken (**to get s.th.** um et. zu bekommen); → **short** 5. **7.** *bsd. Br.* bleiben (**for supper** zum Abendessen). **III** *v/t* **8.** anhalten, stoppen; *Maschine etc* abstellen. **9.** aufhören mit: **~ doing s.th.** aufhören, et. zu tun. **10.** ein Ende machen *od.* setzen (*dat*); *Blutung* stillen; *Arbeiten, Verkehr etc* zum Erliegen bringen; (*Boxen*) *Gegner* abbremsen. **11.** *et.* verhindern; *j-n* abhalten (**from** von), hindern (**from** an *dat*): **~ s.o.** (**from**) **doing s.th.** j-n davon abhalten *od.* daran hindern, et. zu tun. **12.** *Rohr etc* verstopfen; *Zahn* füllen, plombieren: **~ s.o.'s mouth** F j-m den Mund stopfen. **13.** *Scheck* sperren (lassen).
Verbindungen mit Adverbien:

stop| *v/i* vorbeischauen. **~ in** *v/i* **1.** vorbeischauen (**at** bei). **2.** *bsd. Br.* zu Hause bleiben. **~ off** *v/i* F, **~ o-ver** *v/i* Zwischenstation machen (**in** in *dat*). **~ round** *v/i bsd. Am.* F vorbeischauen. **~ up I** *v/t* Leitung *etc* verstopfen. **II** *v/i bsd. Br.* aufbleiben.

'stop·cock *s* ⚙ Absperrhahn *m.* **'~gap I** *s* Notbehelf *m*, Übergangslösung *f*; (*Person*) Aushilfe *f*, *contp.* Lückenbüßer *m.* **II** *adj:* **~ measure** Überbrückungsmaßnahme *f;* **~ secretary** Aushilfssekretärin *f.* **'~o-ver** *s* Zwischenstation *f;* ✈ Zwischenlandung *f.*

stop·page ['stɒpɪdʒ] *s* **1.** Arbeitseinstellung *f.* **2.** ⚙ Verstopfung *f* (*a.* 💊). **3.** *bsd. Br.* (Gehalts-, Lohn)Abzug *m.*
'stop·per *I s* Stöpsel *m.* **II** *v/t a.* **~ up** ver-, zustöpseln.
stop| press *s bsd. Br.* letzte Meldungen *pl* (**in** *e-r Zeitung*). **'~watch** *s* Stoppuhr *f.*

stor·age ['stɔːrɪdʒ] *s* **1.** (Ein)Lagerung *f.* **2.** Lager(raum *m*) *n*: **be in ~** eingelagert sein. **3.** Lagergeld *n.*
store ['stɔː] *I s* **1.** Vorrat *m*, *pl a.* Bestände *pl* (**of** an *dat*): **there's a shock in ~ for you** da/dir wartet e-e unangenehme Überraschung; **have s.th. in ~** et. vorrätig *od.* auf Lager haben; **have a surprise in ~ for s.o.** e-e Überraschung

für j-n haben. **2.** *bsd. Am.* Laden *m*, Geschäft *n*; *bsd. Br.* Kauf-, Warenhaus *n.* **3.** Lager(halle *f*, -haus *n*): **be in ~** *Br.* eingelagert sein. **4. set great** (**little**) **~ by** *fig.* großen (wenig) Wert legen auf (*acc*). **II** *v/t* **5.** *a.* **~ up** Vorrat anlegen an (*dat*). **6.** *Kohle etc* lagern; *Möbel etc* einlagern; *Daten, Energie etc* speichern. **~ de·tec·tive** *s* Kaufhausdetektiv *m.* **'~house** *s* **1.** Lagerhaus *n.* **2.** *fig.* Fundgrube *f* (**of** von): **be a ~ of good ideas** voller guter Ideen stecken. **'~keep·er** *s bsd. Am.* Ladenbesitzer(in), -inhaber(in). **~room** ['~rʊm] *s* Lagerraum *m.*

sto·rey ['stɔːrɪ] *s bsd. Br.* Stock(werk *n*) *m*, Etage *f:* **a six-~ building** → **storeyed.** **'sto·reyed** *adj bsd. Br.*, **'sto·ried** *adj:* **a six-~ building** ein sechsstöckiges Gebäude.

stork [stɔːk] *s orn.* Storch *m.*

storm [stɔːm] *I s* **1.** Unwetter *n*; (*a. fig. Protest- etc*)Sturm *m:* **a ~ in a teacup** *Br. fig.* ein Sturm im Wasserglas. **2. take by ~** ⚔ im Sturm nehmen *od.* (*a. fig.*) erobern. **II** *v/t* **3.** ⚔ *etc* stürmen. **III** *v/i* **4.** stürmen, stürzen. **~ cloud** *s* Gewitterwolke *f:* **the ~s are gathering** *fig.* es braut sich et. zusammen.
storm·y ['stɔːmɪ] *adj* □ stürmisch (*a. fig.*).

sto·ry¹ ['stɔːrɪ] *s* **1.** Geschichte *f*; Märchen *n* (*a. fig.* F): **his side of the ~** s-e Version; **it's the same old ~** es ist das alte Lied; **to cut a long ~ short** um es kurz zu machen, kurz u. gut; → **go** 18. **2.** Story *f*, (Lebens-, Entwicklungs)Geschichte *f.* **3.** Story *f*, Handlung *f.* **4.** *Journalismus:* Story *f*, Bericht *m* (**on** über *acc*).
sto·ry² [~] *Am.* → **storey.**
'sto·ry·book *adj* ... wie im Märchen. **~ line** → **story**¹ 3.

stoup [stuːp] *s eccl.* Weihwasserbecken *n.*

stout [staʊt] *I adj* □ **1.** korpulent, (*Frau a.*) vollschlank. **2.** *fig.* hartnäckig. **II** *s* **3.** Stout *m* (*dunkles Bier mit starkem Hopfengeschmack*).

stove [stəʊv] *s* Ofen *m*, (*zum Kochen a.*) Herd *m.*

stow [stəʊ] *v/t a.* **~ away** verstauen.
'stow·a·way *s* ✈, ⚓ blinder Passagier.

strad·dle ['strædl] *v/t* breitbeinig *od.* mit

gespreizten Beinen stehen über (dat); rittlings sitzen auf (dat).

strag·gle ['strægl] v/i: **~ in** einzeln eintrudeln. **'strag·gler** s Nachzügler(in). **'strag·gly** adj struppig (Haar).

straight [streɪt] **I** adj **1.** gerade, (Haar) glatt: **~ line** gerade Linie, ℝ Gerade f; **keep one's face** ernst bleiben. **2.** get (od. put) s.th. **~** et. in Ordnung bringen, Zimmer etc a. aufräumen; **set s.o. ~ about s.th.** fig. j-m et. klarmachen. **3.** offen, ehrlich (**with** zu). **4.** ohne Unterbrechung: **in ~ sets** (Tennis etc) ohne Satzverlust; **his third ~ win** (Sport) sein dritter Sieg hintereinander od. in Folge. **5.** pur: **drink one's whisky ~; two ~ whiskies** zwei Whisky pur. **6.** sl. a) hetero (heterosexuell), b) clean, sauber (nicht mehr drogenabhängig): **I'm ~** ich nehm' grundsätzlich keine Drogen. **II** adv **7.** gerade: **~ ahead** geradeaus. **8.** genau, direkt. **9.** a. **~ off** sofort. **10.** klar sehen, denken. **11.** F a. **~ out** offen, ehrlich. **12. ~** up? Br. F ehrlich? **III** s **13.** Sport: (Gegen-, Ziel)Gerade f. **,~·a·'way** adv sofort.

straight·en ['streɪtn] **I** v/t **1.** a. **~ up** geradehängen, -legen etc, Krawatte etc geraderücken. **2. ~ out** fig. Angelegenheit etc in Ordnung bringen, Mißverständnis klären; F j-m (wieder) auf die Beine helfen; j-n (wieder) auf die richtige Bahn bringen. **3. ~ up** in Ordnung bringen, aufräumen. **II** v/i **4. ~ out** gerade werden (Straße etc). **5. ~ up** sich aufrichten.

,straight·'for·ward adj □ **1.** aufrichtig. **2.** einfach, unkompliziert. **3.** glatt (Absage etc). **,~·'out** adj bsd. Am. F offen, ehrlich.

strain [streɪn] **I** v/t **1.** Seil etc (an)spannen: **~ one's ears (eyes)** die Ohren spitzen (genau hinschauen). **2.** sich, Augen etc überanstrengen; sich e-n Muskel etc zerren: **~ a muscle** a. sich e-e Muskelzerrung zuziehen. **3.** Gemüse, Tee etc abgießen. **II** v/i **4.** sich anstrengen. **5. ~ at** zerren od. ziehen an (dat): **~ at the leash** an der Leine zerren (Hund; fig. es nicht mehr erwarten können. **III** s **6.** Spannung f (a. ⊕ u. pol. etc). **7.** fig. Belastung f (**on** für): **put a great ~ on s.o.** j-n stark belasten. **strained** adj **1.** gezerrt: **~ muscle** a.

Muskelzerrung f. **2.** gezwungen (Lächeln etc). **3.** gespannt (Beziehungen). **4. look ~** abgespannt aussehen. **'strain·er** s Sieb n.

strait [streɪt] s a. pl Meerenge f, Straße f: **be in desperate** (od. dire) **~s** fig. in e-r ernsten Notlage sein. **'strait·ened** adj: **live in ~ circumstances** in beschränkten Verhältnissen leben.

'strait|jack·et s Zwangsjacke f: **put in a ~** j-n in e-e Zwangsjacke stecken. **,~·'laced** adj prüde.

strand [strænd] s (Haar)Strähne f; (Woll- etc)Faden m, (Kabel)Draht m; fig. Faden m (e-r Handlung etc).

strand·ed ['strændɪd] adj: **be ~ ⚓** gestrandet sein; **be (left) ~** fig. festsitzen (in in dat) (Person).

strange [streɪndʒ] adj □ **1.** merkwürdig, seltsam, sonderbar: **~ to say** so merkwürdig es auch klingen mag; **~ly (enough)** merkwürdiger-, seltsamer-, sonderbarerweise. **2.** fremd (**to s.o.** j-m). **3. be ~ to** nicht vertraut sein mit. **'stran·ger** s **1.** Fremde m, f: **I'm a ~ here** ich bin hier fremd; → **perfect** 2. **be a ~ to** → strange 3.

stran·gle ['stræŋgl] v/t erwürgen, erdrosseln; fig. abwürgen, ersticken. **'~·hold** s Würgegriff m: **have a ~ on** fig. j-n, et. vollkommen beherrschen.

stran·gu·late ['stræŋgjʊleɪt] v/t ⚕ abschnüren, abbinden. **,stran·gu·'la·tion** s **1.** Erwürgung f, Erdrosselung f. **2.** ⚕ Abschnürung f, Abbindung f.

strap [stræp] **I** s **1.** Riemen m, Gurt m; Haltegriff m, Schlaufe f (in Bus etc); Träger m (an Kleid etc); (Uhr)(Arm-) Band n. **II** v/t **2.** festschnallen (**to** an dat): **be ~ped in ✈**, mot. angeschnallt sein. **3.** a. **~ up** Br. Bein etc bandagieren. **4. be ~ped (for cash)** F knapp bei Kasse sein; abgebrannt od. pleite sein. **'~·hang·er** s F **1.** Stehplatzinhaber(in) (in Bus etc). **2.** Pendler(in).

strap·less ['stræpləs] adj schulterfrei (Kleid), (a. Badeanzug) trägerlos.

stra·ta ['strɑːtə] pl von **stratum**.

strat·a·gem ['strætədʒəm] s (⚔ Kriegs)List f.

stra·te·gic [strə'tiːdʒɪk] adj (**~ally**) strategisch; strategisch wichtig. **strat·e·gist** ['strætɪdʒɪst] s Stratege m. **strat·e·gy** ['~dʒɪ] s Strategie f.

stratified   1278

strat·i·fied ['strætɪfaɪd] *adj* vielschichtig (*Gesellschaft*).

strat·o·sphere ['strætəʊˌsfɪə] *s meteor.* Stratosphäre *f*.

stra·tum ['strɑːtəm] *pl* **-ta** ['ˌtə] *s geol., sociol.* Schicht *f*.

straw [strɔː] *s* **1.** Stroh *n*: → **man** 3. **2.** Stroh-, *a.* Trinkhalm *m*: *the ~ that breaks the camel's back, the last ~ fig.* der Tropfen, der das Faß zum Überlaufen bringt; *clutch at ~s fig.* sich an e-n Strohhalm klammern. **~·ber·ry** ['ˌbərɪ] *s* ♀ Erdbeere *f*. **~ hat** *s* Strohhut *m*. **~ man** *s* (*irr man*) Strohmann *m*. **~ poll, ~ vote** *s pol.* Probeabstimmung *f*.

stray [streɪ] **I** *v/i* **1.** sich verirren. **2.** *fig.* abschweifen (*from* von) (*Gedanken etc*). **II** *adj* **3.** verirrt (*Kugel, Tier*); streunend (*Tier*). **4.** vereinzelt. **III** *s* **5.** verirrtes *od.* streunendes Tier.

streak [striːk] *s* **1.** Streifen *m*; Strähne *f* (*im Haar*): *a ~ of lightning* ein Blitz *m*; *like a ~ of lightning* wie der Blitz. **2.** *fig.* (*Charakter*)Zug *m*. **3.** *fig.* (*un*)*lucky ~* Glückssträhne (Pechsträhne) *f*; *winning* (*losing*) *~* (*a. Sport*) Siegesserie (Niederlagenserie) *f*; *be on a lucky ~* e-e Glückssträhne haben. **'streak·y** *adj* streifig; durchwachsen (*Frühstücksspeck*).

stream [striːm] **I** *s* **1.** Bach *m*. **2.** Strömung *f*: *go against the ~ fig.* gegen den Strom schwimmen. **3.** (*Besucher-, Blut-, Verkehrs- etc*)Strom *m*; *fig.* Flut *f*, Schwall *m* (*von Verwünschungen etc*). **4.** *ped. Br.* Leistungsgruppe *f*. **II** *v/i* **5.** strömen (*Besucher, Blut, Licht etc*): *tears were ~ing down her face* Tränen liefen ihr übers Gesicht; *his face was ~ing with sweat* sein Gesicht war schweißüberströmt. **6.** wehen, flattern (*in the wind* im Wind). **III** *v/t* **7.** *ped. Br. Klasse* in Leistungsgruppen einteilen. **'stream·er** *s* Luft-, Papierschlange *f*. **'stream·ing** *adj*: *he's got a ~ cold* er hat e-n fürchterlichen Schnupfen.

'stream·line *v/t* rationalisieren. **'~·lined** *adj* stromlinienförmig, windschnittig, -schlüpf(r)ig.

street [striːt] *s* Straße *f*: *in* (*bsd. Am.* on) *the ~* auf der Straße; *be* (*right*) *up s.o.'s ~ fig.* j-m zusagen; *he's not in the same ~ as me, I'm ~s ahead of him* F ich bin ihm haushoch überlegen; *walk*

the ~s durch die Straßen laufen; auf den Strich gehen; → **man** 3. **~ bat·tle** *s* Straßenschlacht *f*. **~ lamp, ~ light** *s* Straßenlaterne *f*. **~ map** *s* Stadtplan *m*. **~ par·ty** *s* Straßenfest *n*. **~ val·ue** *s* (*Straßen*)Verkaufswert *m* (*von Drogen*). **~ vend·er, ~ vend·or** *s* Straßenhändler(in). **'~·walk·er** *s* Straßen-, Strichmädchen *n*.

strength [streŋθ] *s* **1.** Stärke *f* (*a. fig.*), Kraft *f*, Kräfte *pl*: *~ of character* Charakterfestigkeit *f*, -stärke; *~ of will* Willenskraft, -stärke; *on the ~ of* auf j-s Rat etc hin; *he hasn't got enough ~* er ist nicht kräftig genug; *go from ~ to ~* von Erfolg zu Erfolg eilen. **2.** Macht *f*. **3.** (An)Zahl *f*: *in ~* in großer Zahl, zahlreich; *at full ~* vollzählig; *below* (*od. under*) *~* nicht vollzählig; unterbesetzt; *be on the ~* F zur Belegschaft gehören. **'strength·en I** *v/t* **1.** verstärken. **2.** *fig.* stärken: *~ s.o.'s resolve* j-n in s-m Vorsatz bestärken. **II** *v/i* **3.** stärker werden, sich verstärken (*Wind etc*).

stren·u·ous ['strenjʊəs] *adj* □ **1.** anstrengend. **2.** unermüdlich.

stress [stres] **I** *s* **1.** *fig.* Streß *m*: *~ of examinations* Prüfungsstreß; *be under ~* unter Streß stehen, im Streß sein; *~ disease* Streß-, Managerkrankheit *f*. **2.** *ling.* Betonung *f*: *lay ~ on fig.* → 5; *~ mark* Akzent *m*, Betonungszeichen *n*. **3.** *phys.*, ⊚ Beanspruchung *f*, Belastung *f*; (*mechanische*) Spannung *f*. **II** *v/t* **4.** *ling.* betonen, *fig. a.* Wert legen auf (*acc*). **stress·ful** ['ˌfʊl] *adj* stressig, aufreibend.

stretch [stretʃ] **I** *v/t* **1.** *~ out Arm etc* ausstrecken; → **leg** 1. **2.** *Seil etc* spannen: *be fully ~ed fig.* richtig gefordert werden. **3.** *Schuhe etc* (aus)weiten. **4.** *fig.* es nicht so genau nehmen mit: *~ a point* ein Auge zudrücken. **II** *v/i* **5.** sich dehnen, *a.* länger *od.* weiter werden. **6.** sich dehnen *od.* strecken: *~ out* sich ausstrecken. **7.** sich (*räumlich*) erstrecken (*to* bis zu); sich hinziehen (*räumlich*: *to* bis zu; *zeitlich*: *into* bis in *acc*); *fig.* reichen (*to* für) (*Vorräte etc*). **III** *s* **8.** *have a ~* → 6; *be at full ~* sich sehr viel Mühe geben müssen; *not by any ~ of the imagination* nie u. nimmer. **9.** Dehnbarkeit *f*, Elastizität *f*. **10.**

Strecke f (e-r Straße); (Sport) (Gegen-, Ziel)Gerade f. **11.** Zeit(raum m, -spanne f) f: **at a ~** hintereinander; **do a three-year ~** F drei Jahre absitzen. **IV** adj **12.** → **stretchy.** '**stretch-er** s Trage f. '**stretch-y** adj dehnbar, elastisch.

stri·at·ed [straɪˈeɪtɪd] adj gestreift.

strick·en [ˈstrɪkən] adj **1.** leidgeprüft (Person), schwerbetroffen (Gegend etc). **2. ~ with** befallen od. ergriffen von: → **panic-stricken.**

strict [strɪkt] adj □ streng (Person, Disziplin, Gesetze etc), (Anweisungen etc a.) strikt: **be ~ with** streng sein mit od. zu od. gegen; **in ~ confidence** streng vertraulich; **~ly (speaking)** streng-, genaugenommen.

strid·den [ˈstrɪdn] pp von **stride.**

stride [straɪd] **I** v/i (irr) **1.** schreiten, mit großen Schritten gehen. **II** s **2.** (großer) Schritt: **get into one's ~** fig. (richtig) in Fahrt od. Schwung kommen; **take s.th. in one's ~** fig. et. mühelos verkraften. **3.** fig. Fortschritt m: **make great ~s** große Fortschritte machen.

stri·dent [ˈstraɪdnt] adj □ schrill (Stimme etc).

strife [straɪf] s Streit m.

strike [straɪk] **I** s **1.** ♛ Streik m: **be (out) on ~** streiken, im Streik stehen; **go (out) on ~** streiken, in den Streik treten. **2.** (Öl- etc)Fund m. **3.** ⚔ Angriff m. **II** v/i (irr) **4. ~ at s.o.** → **strike out** 2. **5.** einschlagen (Blitz). **6.** schlagen (Uhr): **two o'clock has just struck** es hat gerade zwei Uhr geschlagen. **7.** ♛ streiken (for für). **8. ~ on** fig. kommen auf e-n Plan etc. **III** v/t (irr) **9.** schlagen: → **s.o. a blow** j-m e-n Schlag versetzen; → **dumb** 1. **10.** treffen; einschlagen in (acc) (Blitz): → **lightning** I. **11.** Streichholz anzünden. **12.** ♻ auflaufen auf (acc). **13.** streichen (from, off aus) (acc) (Blitz): → **lightning** I. **11.** Streichholz anzünden. **12.** ♻ auflaufen auf (acc). **13.** streichen (from, off aus) (e-m Verzeichnis etc, von e-r Liste etc). **14.** fig. stoßen auf (Öl, e-e Straße, Schwierigkeiten etc): → **oil** 2. **15.** → **balance** 1, **bargain** 1. **16.** **be struck by** beeindruckt sein von; **how does the house ~ you?** wie findest du das Haus?; **it struck me as rather strange that** es kam mir ziemlich seltsam vor, daß. **17.** j-m einfallen, in den Sinn kommen. **18.** Münze etc prägen. **19.** Saite etc an-

schlagen: → **chord**¹, **note** 9. **20.** Lager, Zelt abbrechen.

Verbindungen mit Adverbien:

strike| back v/i zurückschlagen (a. fig.). **~ down** v/t **1.** niederschlagen. **2.** fig. niederwerfen (Krankheit); dahinraffen. **~ off** v/t **1.** abschlagen. **2.** Br. Solicitor von der Anwaltsliste streichen, e-m Arzt die Approbation entziehen. **~ out I** v/t **1.** (aus)streichen. **II** v/i **2. ~ at s.o.** auf j-n einschlagen. **3. ~ on one's own** fig. s-e eigenen Wege gehen, ♛ sich selbständig machen. **~ through** v/t durchstreichen. **~ up I** v/t **1.** Lied etc anstimmen. **2.** Bekanntschaft, Freundschaft schließen, Gespräch anknüpfen (**with** mit). **II** v/i **3.** ♪ einsetzen.

strike| bal·lot s ♛ Urabstimmung f. '**~bound** adj bestreikt; vom Streik lahmgelegt. '**~breaker** s ♛ Streikbrecher(in). **~ call** s ♛ Streikaufruf m. **~ pay** s ♛ Streikgeld(er pl) n.

'**strik·er** s **1.** ♛ Streikende m, f. **2.** Fußball: Stürmer(in). '**strik·ing** adj □ **1.** auffallend, (Ähnlichkeit, Vorschlag etc) verblüffend. **2. be within ~ distance of** fig. kurz vor e-m Erfolg etc stehen.

string [strɪŋ] **I** s **1.** Schnur f, Bindfaden m; (Schürzen-, Schuh- etc)Band n; (Puppenspiel) Faden m, Draht m: **with no ~s attached** fig. ohne Bedingungen; **have s.o. on a ~** fig. j-n am Gängelband führen od. haben; **pull the ~s** fig. die Fäden ziehen; **pull a few ~s** fig. ein paar Beziehungen spielen lassen. **2.** (Perlen- etc)Schnur f. **3.** a) Saite f (e-r Gitarre, e-s Tennisschlägers etc); (Bogen)Sehne f: **have two ~s** (od. **a second ~, another** ~) **to one's bow** fig. zwei od. mehrere Eisen im Feuer haben, b) **the ~s** pl ♪ die Streichinstrumente pl; die Streicher pl. **4.** fig. Reihe f, Serie f. **III** adj **5.** ♪ Streich... **III** v/t **6.** Perlen etc aufreihen. **7.** Gitarre etc besaiten, Tennisschläger etc bespannen.

Verbindungen mit Adverbien:

string| a·long F **I** v/t j-n hinhalten. **II** v/i sich anschließen (**with s.o.** j-m). **~ up** v/t **1.** aufhängen. **2.** F j-n aufknüpfen.

string bean s bsd. Am. grüne Bohne.

stringed in·stru·ment [strɪŋd] s Saiten-, Streichinstrument n.

strin·gent [ˈstrɪndʒənt] adj □ streng (Kontrolle, Regeln etc).

string·y ['strɪŋɪ] *adj* **1.** fas(e)rig (*Bohnen, Fleisch etc*). **2.** sehnig (*Arm etc*).

strip [strɪp] **I** *v/i* **1.** a. **~ off** sich ausziehen (**to** bis auf *acc*), (*beim Arzt*) sich freimachen; strippen: **~ to the waist** den Oberkörper freimachen. **II** *v/t* **2.** Farbe *etc* abkratzen, *Tapete etc* abreißen (**from, off** von). **3.** **~ s.o.** *of* s.th. j-m *et*. rauben *od.* wegnehmen: *he was ~ped of his title* ihm wurde sein Titel aberkannt. **4.** a) a. **~ down** Motor *etc* auseinandernehmen, zerlegen, b) *Wagen etc* ausschlachten. **III** *s* **5.** (*Land-, Papier- etc*)Streifen m. **6.** Strip m: **do a ~** strippen. **7.** *Fußball: Br.* Dreß m. **~ car·toons** *s pl Br.* Comics *pl*.

stripe [straɪp] *s* **1.** Streifen m. **2.** ✕ (Ärmel)Streifen m, Winkel m. **striped** *adj* gestreift: **~ pattern** Streifenmuster n.

strip light·ing *s* Neonbeleuchtung *f*, -licht *n*.

'strip·tease *s* Striptease m, n: **do a ~** e-n Striptease vorführen.

strip·y ['straɪpɪ] → **striped**.

strive [straɪv] *v/i* (*irr*) **1.** sich bemühen (**to do** zu tun). **2.** streben (**for, after** nach). **3.** (an)kämpfen (**against** gegen).

striv·en ['strɪvn] *pp von* **strive**.

strode [strəʊd] *pret von* **stride**.

stroke [strəʊk] **I** *v/t* **1.** streicheln: **~ s.o.'s hair** j-m übers Haar streichen. **II** *s* **2.** Schlag m (*a. Tennis, e-r Uhr etc*), Hieb m: **a ~ of lightning** ein Blitz m; **a ~ of genius** *fig*. ein glänzender Einfall; **a ~ of luck** *fig*. ein glücklicher Zufall; **at a ~** *fig*. auf 'einen Schlag; **on the ~ of ten** Punkt *od.* Schlag zehn (Uhr). **3.** **give s.o. a ~** j-n streicheln. **4.** 🗲 Schlag(anfall) m. **5.** (*Pinsel*)Strich m: **with a ~ of the pen** mit e-m Federstrich (*a. fig.*); **he hasn't done a ~ (of work) yet** *fig*. er hat noch keinen Strich getan. **6.** *Schwimmen:* Zug m; Stil(art *f*) m: **~ backstroke, breaststroke. 7.** ⊙ (*Kolben*)Hub m; Takt m: **four-~ engine** Viertaktmotor m. **8.** *Rudern:* Schlagmann m, -frau *f*.

stroll [strəʊl] **I** *v/i* bummeln, spazieren. **II** *s* Bummel m, Spaziergang m: **go for a ~** e-n Bummel *od.* Spaziergang machen. **'stroll·er** *s* **1.** Bummler(in), Spaziergänger(in). **2.** *bsd. Am.* Sportwagen m (*für Kinder*).

strong [strɒŋ] **I** *adj* □ (→ a. **strongly**) **1.**

stark, kräftig (*Person, Arme etc*); *fig*. mächtig (*Land etc*), stark (*Persönlichkeit etc*): → **sex** 1. **2.** stabil (*Möbel etc*), (*Schuhe etc*) fest; robust (*Person, Gesundheit*), (*Konstitution c.*) kräftig, (*Herz, Nerven*) stark; *fig*. unerschütterlich (*Beweise*), stark (*Verdacht*): → **point** 14. **3.** stark (*Strömung*), (*Wind etc a.*) kräftig. **4.** kräftig (*Geruch, Geschmack*), (*a. Eindruck, Ähnlichkeit etc*) stark. **5.** überzeugt (*Anhänger etc*). **6.** stark (*Getränk, Medikament etc*). **7.** **~ language** Kraftausdrücke *pl*. **8.** groß, hoch (*Chance etc*), aussichtsreich (*Kandidat etc*). **9.** **a nine-~ team** ein neun Mann starkes Team; **an 8,000-~ community** e-e 8000-Seelen-Gemeinde; **our club is 500 ~** unser Club hat 500 Mitglieder. **II** *adv* **10. be still going ~** noch gut in Schuß sein (*alte Person, altes Gerät etc*). **'~-arm** *adj*: **~ methods** (*od. tactics*) *pl* Gewaltmethoden *pl*. **'~-box** *s* (Geld-, Stahl)Kassette *f*. **'~-hold** *s* **1.** ✕ Festung *f*; Stützpunkt m. **2.** *fig*. Hochburg *f*.

strong·ly ['strɒŋlɪ] *adv*: **I ~ advised him against it** ich riet ihm dringend davon ab.

,strong-'mind·ed *adj* □ willensstark. **~ room** *s* Tresor(raum) m, Stahlkammer *f*.

strove [strəʊv] *pret von* **strive**.

struck [strʌk] *pret u. pp von* **strike**.

struc·tur·al ['strʌktʃərəl] *adj* □ **1.** strukturell (bedingt), Struktur... **2.** ⊙ Bau..., Konstruktions... **'struc·ture I** *s* **1.** Struktur *f*; (Auf)Bau m, Gliederung *f*. **2.** Bau m, Konstruktion *f*. **II** *v/t* **3.** strukturieren; *Aufsatz etc* aufbauen, gliedern.

strug·gle ['strʌgl] **I** *v/i* **1.** kämpfen (**with** mit; **for** um), *fig. a.* sich abmühen (**with** mit; **to do** zu tun): **~ for words** um Worte ringen. **2.** zappeln; um sich schlagen *od.* treten. **3.** sich quälen: **~ to one's feet** mühsam aufstehen, sich aufrappeln. **II** *s* **4.** Kampf m (*a. fig.*), Handgemenge n: **~ for survival** Überlebenskampf, Kampf ums Überleben.

strum [strʌm] **I** *v/t* a) klimpern auf e-r Gitarre *etc*, b) *Melodie* klimpern. **II** *v/i*: **~ on** → Ia.

strung [strʌŋ] *pret u. pp von* **string**.

strut¹ [strʌt] *v/i* stolzieren.

strut² [~] ❂ **I** s Strebe f; Stütze f. **II** v/t verstreben; (ab)stützen.

strych·nine ['strɪkniːn] s 🜊, pharm. Strychnin n.

stub [stʌb] **I** s **1.** (Bleistift-, Zigaretten- etc)Stummel m. **2.** Kontrollabschnitt m (e-r Eintrittskarte etc). **II** v/t **3.** sich die Zehe anstoßen (**against, on** an dat). **4.** ~ **out** Zigarette ausdrücken.

stub·ble ['stʌbl] s Stoppeln pl. '**stub·bly** adj stopp(e)lig, Stoppel...

stub·born ['stʌbən] adj □ **1.** eigensinnig, stur. **2.** hartnäckig (Fleck, Widerstand etc).

stub·by ['stʌbɪ] adj: ~ **fingers** pl Wurstfinger pl.

stuc·co ['stʌkəʊ] s 🜊 Stuck m. '**stuc·coed** adj Stuck...

stuck [stʌk] **I** pret u. pp von **stick²**. **II** adj **1.** be ~ klemmen; fig. F hängen, nicht weiterkommen: **be** ~ **with** F j-n, et. am Hals haben. **2.** be ~ **on** F verknallt sein in (acc). **3.** Br. F **get** ~ **in** reinhauen (beim Essen); **get** ~ **into** sich stürzen auf (ein Essen) od. in (e-e Arbeit). ~,**'up** adj F hochnäsig.

stud¹ [stʌd] **I** s **1.** Beschlag- od. Ziernagel m. **2.** (Kragen-, Manschetten)Knopf m. **3.** Stollen m (e-s Fußballschuhs etc). **II** v/t **4.** be ~**ded with** besetzt sein mit; übersät sein mit.

stud² [~] s Gestüt n (Pferde).

stu·dent ['stjuːdnt] s Student(in), ped. bsd. Am. u. allg. Schüler(in).

stud farm s Gestüt n.

stud·ied ['stʌdɪd] adj □ wohlüberlegt, b.s. wohlberechnet (Antwort etc).

stu·di·o ['stjuːdɪəʊ] pl -**os** s **1.** allg. Studio n, (e-s Künstlers etc) Atelier n. **2.** Studio n, Einzimmerappartement n. ~ **a·part·ment** bsd. Am. → **studio** 2. ~ **couch** s Schlafcouch f. ~ **flat** bsd. Br. → **studio** 2.

stu·di·ous ['stjuːdjəs] adj □ fleißig.

stud·y ['stʌdɪ] **I** s **1.** al pl Studium n: **be in a brown** ~ in Gedanken versunken od. geistesabwesend sein. **2.** Studie f, Untersuchung f (**of** über acc): **make a** ~ **of** et. untersuchen. **3.** bsd. paint. Studie f (of zu). **4.** ♪ Etüde f. **5.** Arbeitszimmer n. **II** v/t **6.** Medizin etc, weitS. Landkarte, j-s Gesicht etc studieren. **III** v/i **7.** studieren (**under** s.o. bei j-m), weitS. lernen (**for** für e-e Prüfung):

~ **to be a doctor** Medizin studieren.

stuff [stʌf] **I** s **1.** F allg. Zeug n: **be good** ~ et. Gutes sein; **that's the** ~**!** so ist's richtig!; genau!; **do one's** ~ zeigen, was man kann; **know one's** ~ sich gut auskennen. **II** v/t **2.** (**with** mit) Hohlraum, Tier ausstopfen; Kissen etc stopfen, füllen; sich die Taschen vollstopfen: ~**ed full of** gestopft voll von; ~ **o.s.** F sich vollstopfen. **3.** et. stopfen (**into** in acc). **4.** gastr. Ente etc füllen: **get** ~**ed!** Br. sl. du kannst mich mal! **5.** ~ **up** Loch etc ver-, zustopfen (**with** mit): **my nose is** ~**ed up** m-e Nase ist verstopft od. zu.

stuffed adj: ~ **shirt** F Fatzke m. '**stuff·ing** s Füllung f (a. gastr.): **knock the** ~ **out of s.o.** F j-n schaffen. '**stuff·y** adj □ **1.** stickig. **2.** fig. prüde; spießig.

stum·ble ['stʌmbl] v/i (**on, over,** fig. **at, over** über acc): ~ **across** (od. **on**) fig. stoßen auf (acc); ~ **through** Rede etc herunterstottern. '**stum·bling** adj: ~ **block** fig. Hindernis n (**to** für).

stump [stʌmp] **I** s **1.** (Baum-, Bein-, Kerzen- etc)Stumpf m, (Bleistift-, Kerzen-, Zahn-, Zigarren- etc)Stummel m: **stir one's** ~**s** F Tempo machen. **II** v/t **2.** I'm ~**ed, you've got me** ~**ed there** F da bin ich überfragt. **3.** ~ **up** F Geld herausrücken. **III** v/i **4.** sta(m)pfen. '**stump·y** adj □ kurz u. dick (Arme etc).

stun [stʌn] v/t betäuben; fig. sprachlos machen: **he was** ~**ned by the news** die Nachricht hat ihm die Sprache verschlagen.

stung [stʌŋ] pret u. pp von **sting**.

stunk [stʌŋk] pret u. pp von **stink**.

stun·ner ['stʌnə] s: **she's a real** ~ F sie ist e-e klasse Frau. '**stun·ning** adj □ **1.** phantastisch. **2.** unglaublich (Nachricht).

stunt¹ [stʌnt] s **1.** (gefährliches) Kunststück; (Film) Stunt m (gefährliche Szene, in der ein Stuntman die Rolle des Darstellers übernimmt): **do a** ~ ein Kunststück vorführen od. zeigen; e-n Stunt ausführen. **2.** (Werbe)Gag m.

stunt² [~] v/t Wachstum hemmen; das Wachstum (am) hemmen: ~**ed** verkümmert.

stunt| fly·ing s Kunstflug m. ~ **man** s (irr **man**) Film: Stuntman m, Double n. ~ **wom·an** s (irr **woman**) Film: Stuntwoman n, Double n.

stu·pen·dous [stjuˈpendəs] *adj* □ phantastisch.

stu·pid [ˈstjuːpɪd] *adj* □ **1.** dumm. **2.** *fig.* F blöd. **stu'pid·i·ty** *s* Dummheit *f* (*a. Handlung etc*).

stu·por [ˈstjuːpə] *s*: **in a drunken ~** im Vollrausch.

stur·dy [ˈstɜːdɪ] *adj* □ **1.** stämmig (*Beine etc*). **2.** *fig.* hartnäckig (*Widerstand etc*).

stur·geon [ˈstɜːdʒən] *s ichth.* Stör *m*.

stut·ter [ˈstʌtə] **I** *v/i* ⚙ stottern (*a. Motor*). **II** *v/t* → **stammer** II. **III** *s* → **stammer** III. **'stut·ter·er** → **stammerer.**

sty¹ [staɪ] → **pigsty.**

sty² [~] *s* ⚙ Gerstenkorn *n*.

style [staɪl] **I** *s* **1.** *allg.* Stil *m*: **~ of leadership** Führungsstil; **in ~** in großem Stil; **that's not my ~** F das ist nicht m-e Art. **2.** Ausführung *f*, Modell *n*. **II** *v/t* **3.** entwerfen; gestalten.

sty·li [ˈstaɪlaɪ] *pl von* **stylus.**

styl·ish [ˈstaɪlɪʃ] *adj* □ **1.** stilvoll. **2.** modisch, elegant.

styl·ist [ˈstaɪlɪst] *s* **1.** Stilist(in). **2.** a) Modeschöpfer(in), b) → **hair stylist. sty'lis·tic** *adj* (**~ally**) stilistisch, Stil...

styl·ize [ˈstaɪlaɪz] *v/t* stilisieren.

sty·lus [ˈstaɪləs] *pl* **-li** [ˈ~laɪ], **-lus·es** *s* Nadel *f* (*e-s Plattenspielers*).

sty·mie [ˈstaɪmɪ] *v/t* F *Gegner* matt setzen; *Plan etc* vereiteln.

styp·tic [ˈstɪptɪk] ⚙ **I** *adj* blutstillend. **II** *s* blutstillendes Mittel.

suave [swɑːv] *adj* □ verbindlich, *contp.* aalglatt.

sub [sʌb] F **I** *s* **1.** → **subeditor, submarine** I, **subscription** 1. **2.** *Sport:* Auswechselspieler(in). **3.** *Br.* Vorschuß *m.* **II** *v/i* **4.** → **substitute** IV. **III** *v/t* **5.** → **subedit.** **6.** *Br. j-m* e-n Vorschuß geben.

'sub·com·mit·tee *s* Unterausschuß *m.*

sub·con·scious I *adj* unterbewußt: **~ly** im Unterbewußtsein. F unbewußt. **II** *s* Unterbewußtsein *n*: **in one's ~** im Unterbewußtsein.

sub·con·ti·nent *s* Subkontinent *m.*

sub·cul·ture *s sociol.* Subkultur *f.*

sub·cu·ta·ne·ous [ˌsʌbkjuːˈteɪnjəs] *adj* □ subkutan, unter der od. die Haut.

sub·di·vide *v/t* unterteilen. **sub·di·vi·sion** *s* **1.** Unterteilung *f*. **2.** Unterabteilung *f*.

sub·due [səbˈdjuː] *v/t Land etc* unterwerfen; *Ärger etc* unterdrücken. **sub'dued** *adj* **1.** gedämpft (*Stimme*), (*Farben, Licht a.*) dezent. **2.** (merkwürdig) ruhig *od.* still (*Person*).

sub'ed·it *v/t* redigieren. **sub'ed·i·tor** *s* Redakteur(in).

'sub·head·ing *s* Untertitel *m.*

sub'hu·man *adj* unmenschlich.

sub·ject [ˈsʌbdʒɪkt] **I** *s* **1.** Thema *n*: **on the ~ of** über (*acc*); **be the ~ of much criticism** von verschiedenen Seiten kritisiert werden; **change the ~** das Thema wechseln, von et. anderem reden. **2.** *ped., univ.* Fach *n*. **3.** *ling.* Subjekt *n*, Satzgegenstand *m*. **4. be the ~ of, be a ~ for** Anlaß *od.* Grund geben zu. **5.** Untertan(in); Staatsangehörige *m, f*, -bürger(in). **6.** Versuchsperson *f*, -tier *n*. **II** *adj* **7.** ~ **to** anfällig für: **be ~ to** *a.* neigen zu. **8. be ~ to** unterliegen (*dat*); abhängen von: **be ~ to the approval of** (erst noch) genehmigt werden müssen von; **prices ~ to change** Preisänderungen vorbehalten. **III** *v/t* [səbˈdʒekt] **9.** *Land etc* unterwerfen. **10.** ~ **to** *e-m Test etc* unterziehen; *der Kritik etc* aussetzen. **sub·jec·tion** [səbˈdʒekʃn] *s* **1.** Unterwerfung *f*. **2.** Abhängigkeit *f* (**to** von). **sub'jec·tive** *adj* □ subjektiv.

sub·ject mat·ter *s* Stoff *m*; Inhalt *m.*

sub·ju·gate [ˈsʌbdʒʊgeɪt] *v/t* unterjochen, -werfen.

sub·junc·tive (mood) [səbˈdʒʌŋktɪv] *s ling.* Konjunktiv *m.*

sub'lease *v/t* unter-, weitervermieten, unter-, weiterverpachten (**to** an *dat*).

sub'let *v/t* (*irr* **let**) unter-, weitervermieten (**to** an *dat*).

sub·li·mate ⚗ **I** *v/t* [ˈsʌblɪmeɪt] sublimieren. **II** *s* [ˈ~mət] Sublimat *n.*

sub·lime [səˈblaɪm] *adj* □ **1.** großartig. **2.** *iro.* großzügig (*Mißachtung*), allumfassend (*Unkenntnis*).

sub·lim·i·nal [ˌsʌbˈlɪmɪnl] *adj* □ *psych.* unterschwellig.

sub·ma·chine gun [ˌsʌbməˈʃiːn] *s* Maschinenpistole *f.*

sub·ma·rine I *s* Unterseeboot *n*, U-Boot *n*. **II** *adj* untermeerisch, -seeisch.

sub·merge [səbˈmɜːdʒ] **I** *v/t* (ein)tauchen (**in in** *acc*): **be ~d in work** bis über die Ohren in Arbeit stecken. **II** *v/i* tauchen (*U-Boot*).

sub·mis·sion [səb'mıʃn] s **1.** Einreichung f. **2.** Boxen etc: Aufgabe f.

sub·mis·sive [səb'mısıv] adj □ unterwürfig.

sub·mit [səb'mıt] **I** v/t **1.** Gesuch etc einreichen (to dat od. bei). **2.** ~ o.s. sich fügen (to dat od. in acc). **II** v/i **3.** Boxen etc: aufgeben.

sub·nor·mal adj □ **1.** unterdurchschnittlich. **2.** unterdurchschnittlich intelligent.

sub·or·di·nate [sə'bɔːdnət] **I** adj □ untergeordnet (to dat): be ~ to a. zurückstehen hinter (dat); ~ clause ling. Nebensatz m. **II** s Untergebene m, f. **III** v/t [~dıneıt] (to) unterordnen (hinter acc), zurückstellen (hinter acc).

'**sub·plot** s Nebenhandlung f.

sub·poe·na [səb'piːnə] ✝ **I** s Vorladung f. **II** v/t Zeugen vorladen.

sub·scribe [səb'skraıb] **I** v/i **1.** ~ to Zeitschrift etc abonnieren; abonniert haben. **2.** ~ to karitative Organisation etc regelmäßig unterstützen. **3.** ~ to Ansicht etc billigen. **II** v/t **4.** Geld geben, spenden (to für). **sub'scrib·er** s Abonnent(in); (Fernsprech)Teilnehmer (-in).

sub·scrip·tion [səb'skrıpʃn] s **1.** (Mitglieds)Beitrag m. **2.** Abonnement n: take out a ~ to Zeitschrift etc abonnieren.

'**sub·sec·tion** s Unterabteilung f.

sub·se·quent ['sʌbsıkwənt] adj □ später.

sub·ser·vi·ent [səb'sɜːvjənt] adj □ **1.** unterwürfig. **2.** untergeordnet (to dat): be ~ to a. zurückstehen hinter (dat).

sub·side [səb'saıd] v/i **1.** sich senken (Gebäude, Straße etc): ~ into a chair in e-n Sessel sinken. **2.** zurückgehen (Überschwemmung, Nachfrage etc), sich legen (Sturm, Zorn etc).

sub·sid·i·ar·y [səb'sıdjərı] **I** adj Neben...: ~ company → **II**; ~ question Zusatzfrage f; ~ subject ped., univ. Nebenfach n. **II** s ✝ Tochtergesellschaft f.

sub·si·dize ['sʌbsıdaız] v/t subventionieren.

sub·si·dy ['~dı] s Subvention f.

sub·sist [səb'sıst] v/i existieren, leben (on von). **sub'sist·ence** s Existenz f: live at ~ level am Existenzminimum leben.

sub·son·ic [~] ✈, phys. Unterschall...:

at ~ speed mit Unterschallgeschwindigkeit.

sub·stance ['sʌbstəns] s **1.** Substanz f, Stoff m, Masse f. **2.** fig. Substanz f: in ~ im wesentlichen.

'**sub·stan·dard** adj minderwertig; ling. inkorrekt.

sub·stan·tial [səb'stænʃl] adj □ **1.** solid (Schrank etc). **2.** fig. beträchtlich (Gehalt etc), (Änderungen etc a.) wesentlich: ~ly a. im wesentlichen. **3.** fig. kräftig (Mahlzeit).

sub·stan·ti·ate [səb'stænʃıeıt] v/t beweisen, erhärten.

sub·stan·tive ['sʌbstəntıv] s ling. Substantiv n, Hauptwort n.

sub·sti·tute ['sʌbstıtjuːt] **I** s Ersatz m: Ersatz(mann) m; (Sport) Auswechselspieler(in). **II** adj Ersatz... **III** v/t: ~ A for B B durch A ersetzen, B gegen A austauschen od. auswechseln. **IV** v/i: ~ for einspringen für, j-n vertreten.

'**sub·struc·ture** s △ Fundament n, Unterbau m (beide a. fig.).

'**sub·ten·ant** s Untermieter(in).

sub·ter·fuge ['sʌbtəfjuːdʒ] s List f.

sub·ter·ra·ne·an [,sʌbtə'reınjən] adj □ unterirdisch.

'**sub·ti·tle** s Untertitel m.

sub·tle ['sʌtl] adj □ **1.** fein (Unterschied etc), (Aroma etc a.) zart. **2.** raffiniert (Plan etc). **3.** scharf (Verstand), scharfsinnig (Person).

'**sub·to·tal** s Zwischen-, Teilsumme f.

sub·tract [səb'trækt] v/t & abziehen, subtrahieren (from von). **sub'trac·tion** s Abziehen n, Subtraktion f.

,**sub'trop·i·cal** adj subtropisch.

sub·urb ['sʌbɜːb] s Vorort m: live in the ~s am Stadtrand wohnen. **sub·ur·ban** [sə'bɜːbən] adj Vorort..., vorstädtisch, Vorstadt... **sub·ur·ban·ite** s Vorstädter(in). **sub·ur·bi·a** [~bıə] s **1.** Vorstadt f: live in ~ am Stadtrand wohnen. **2.** Vorstadtleben n.

sub·ver·sion [səb'vɜːʃn] s pol. Subversion f. **sub'ver·sive** [~sıv] **I** adj □ subversiv, umstürzlerisch. **II** s Umstürzler(in).

sub·vert [sʌb'vɜːt] v/t Regierung zu stürzen versuchen.

'**sub·way** s **1.** Unterführung f. **2.** Am. U-Bahn f.

suc·ceed [sək'si:d] **I** v/i **1.** Erfolg haben, erfolgreich sein (*Person*), (*Plan etc a.*) gelingen: *he ~ed in doing it* es gelang ihm, es zu tun. **2.** ~ **to** in *e-m Amt* nachfolgen: *~ to the throne* auf dem Thron folgen. **II** v/t **3.** *j-m* nachfolgen, *j-m od.* auf *j-n* folgen: *~ s.o. as* j-s Nachfolger werden als.

suc·cess [sək'ses] s Erfolg m: *without ~* ohne Erfolg, erfolglos. **suc'cess·ful** [~fʊl] adj □ erfolgreich: *be ~ → succeed* 1; *he was ~ in doing it* es gelang ihm, es zu tun.

suc·ces·sion [sək'seʃn] s **1.** Folge f: *three times in ~* dreimal nach- *od.* hintereinander; *in quick ~* in rascher Folge. **2.** Nachfolge f: *~ to the throne* Thronfolge. **suc'ces·sive** [~sɪv] adj □ aufeinanderfolgend: *on three ~ days a.* drei Tage nach- *od.* hintereinander. **suc'ces·sor** [~sə] s Nachfolger(in) (*to* in *e-m Amt*): *~ in office* Amtsnachfolger(in); *~ to the throne* Thronfolger(in).

suc·cinct [sək'sɪŋkt] adj □ kurz (u. bündig), knapp.

suc·cu·lent ['sʌkjʊlənt] adj □ saftig (*Steak etc*).

suc·cumb [sə'kʌm] v/i: *~ to e-r Krankheit, der Versuchung etc* erliegen.

such [sʌtʃ] **I** adj solch, derartig: *~ a man* ein solcher *od.* so ein Mann; *no ~ thing* nichts dergleichen. **II** adv so, derart: *~ a nice day* so ein schöner Tag; *~ a long time* e-e so lange Zeit; *~ is life* so ist das Leben. **III** pron. solch: *~ as* wie (zum Beispiel); *man as ~* der Mensch als solcher. **'~·like I** adj solche. **II** pron dergleichen.

suck [sʌk] **I** v/t **1.** saugen. **2.** lutschen. **3.** *~ under* hinunterziehen (*Strudel etc*). **II** v/i **4.** saugen (*at* an *dat*). **5.** *~ away at* et. lutschen. **6.** *~ up to s.o.* Br. F sich bei j-m lieb Kind machen wollen. **III** s **7.** *take a ~ at* saugen *od.* ziehen an (*dat*); lutschen an (*dat*). **'suck·er** s **1.** *zo.* Saugnapf m, -organ n. **2.** ⊛ Saugfuß m. **3.** Am. Lutscher m. **4.** F Gimpel m, leichtgläubiger Kerl: *be a ~ for* immer wieder reinfallen auf (*acc*); verrückt sein nach. **'suck·ing** adj: *~ pig* Spanferkel n.

suck·le ['sʌkl] v/t säugen (*a. zo.*), stillen.

suc·tion ['sʌkʃn] s Saugwirkung f. *~ pump* s ⊛ Saugpumpe f.

sud·den ['sʌdn] **I** adj □ plötzlich: *be very ~* sehr plötzlich kommen. **II** s: *all of a ~* ganz plötzlich, auf einmal.

suds [sʌdz] s pl Seifenschaum m.

sue [su:] **I** v/t ⚖ *j-n* verklagen (*for* auf *acc*, wegen). **II** v/i klagen (*for* auf *acc*).

suede, suède [sweɪd] s Wildleder n; Velour(s)leder n.

su·et ['sʊɪt] s Nierenfett n, Talg m.

suf·fer ['sʌfə] **I** v/i **1.** leiden (*from* an *dat*; *weitS.* unter *dat*). **2.** darunter leiden. **II** v/t **3.** *Niederlage, Rückschlag, Verlust etc* erleiden; *Folgen* tragen. **'suf·fer·er** s: *a cancer ~* ein Krebskranker; *a headache ~* j-d, der an Kopfschmerzen leidet. **'suf·fer·ing** s Leiden n; Leid n.

suf·fice [sə'faɪs] **I** v/i genügen, (aus)reichen (*for* für). **II** v/t *j-m* genügen, reichen.

suf·fi·cient [sə'fɪʃnt] adj □ genügend, genug, ausreichend: *be ~ → suffice* I.

suf·fix ['sʌfɪks] s *ling.* Suffix n, Nachsilbe f.

suf·fo·cate ['sʌfəkeɪt] v/i u. v/t ersticken.

suf·frage ['sʌfrɪdʒ] s pol. Wahl-, Stimmrecht n.

suf·fuse [sə'fju:z] v/t: *be ~d with* durchdrungen sein von.

sug·ar ['ʃʊgə] **I** s **1.** Zucker m. **2.** bsd. Am. F Schatz (*Anrede*). **II** v/t **3.** zuckern: *→ pill* 1. **~ beet** s ♀ Zuckerrübe f. **~ bowl** s Zuckerdose f. **~ cane** s ♀ Zuckerrohr n. **~ dad·dy** s F alter Knakker, der ein junges Mädchen aushält. **sug·ar·y** ['ʃʊgərɪ] adj zuck(e)rig, Zucker... *a. fig.* zuckersüß.

sug·gest [sə'dʒest] v/t **1.** *j-n* vorschlagen (*as* als), *et. a.* anregen: *I ~ going* (*od. that we go*) *home* ich schlage vor heimzugehen. **2.** hindeuten *od.* -weisen auf (*acc*), schließen lassen auf (*acc*): *~ that* darauf hindeuten *od.* -weisen, daß; darauf schließen lassen, daß. **3.** andeuten: *I am not ~ing that* ich will damit nicht sagen, daß. **sug'gest·i·ble** adj beeinflußbar. **sug'ges·tion** s **1.** Vorschlag m, Anregung f: *at s.o.'s ~* auf j-s Vorschlag hin; *make* (*od. offer*) *a ~* e-n Vorschlag machen. **2.** Anflug m, Spur f. **3.** Andeutung f. **4.** *psych.* Suggestion f. **sug'ges·tive** adj □ **1.** *be ~ of →* **suggest** 2. **2.** zweideutig (*Bemer-*

kung etc), vielsagend (*Blick etc*).

su·i·cid·al [sɔɪˈsaɪdl] *adj* □ **1.** selbstmörderisch (*a. fig.*): **~ thoughts** *pl* Selbstmordgedanken *pl*. **2.** selbstmordgefährdet. **su·i·cide** [ˈ~saɪd] *s* **1.** Selbstmord *m* (*a. fig.*): **commit ~** Selbstmord begehen; **he tried to commit ~** er unternahm e-n Selbstmordversuch; **~ attempt** Selbstmordversuch *m*; → **attempt** 1. **2.** Selbstmörder(in).

suit [su:t] **I** *s* **1.** Anzug *m*; Kostüm *n*. **2.** *Kartenspiel*: Farbe *f*: **follow ~** (Farbe) bedienen; *fig*. dasselbe tun, nachziehen. **3.** → **lawsuit**. **II** *v/t* **4.** j-m stehen (Farbe *etc*). **5.** j-m passen (*Termin etc*): **that ~s me fine** das paßt mir gut, das ist mir sehr recht; **~ s.o.'s book** F j-m ins Zeug passen. **6.** **~ s.th., be ~ed to s.th.** geeignet sein *od*. sich eignen für: **they are well ~ed (to each other)** sie passen gut zusammen. **7.** **~ yourself!** mach, was du willst! **8.** *et*. anpassen (**to** *dat*). **'suit·a·ble** *adj* □ passend, geeignet (**for, to** für).

'suit·case *s* Koffer *m*.

suite [swi:t] *s* **1.** (*Möbel*)Garnitur *f*. **2.** Suite *f*, Zimmerflucht *f*. **3.** ♪ Suite *f*.

sul·fa drug, sul·fate, sul·fide, sul·fon·a·mide, sul·fur *Am*. → **sulpha drug, sulphate, sulphide, sulphonamide, sulphur**.

sulk [sʌlk] **I** *v/i* schmollen. **II** *s*: **have the ~s** → I. **'sulk·y** **I** *adj* □ **1.** schmollend. **2.** schnell schmollend. **II** *s* **3.** Trabrennen: Sulky *n*.

sul·len [ˈsʌlən] *adj* □ mürrisch, verdrossen.

sul·pha drug [ˈsʌlfə] *s bsd. Br. pharm.* Sulfonamid *n*.

sul·phate [ˈsʌlfeɪt] *s* 🜋 *bsd. Br.* Sulfat *n*.

sul·phide [ˈsʌlfaɪd] *s* 🜋 *bsd. Br.* Sulfid *n*.

sul·phon·a·mide [sʌlˈfɒnəmaɪd] → **sulpha drug**.

sul·phur [ˈsʌlfə] *s* 🜋, *min. bsd. Br.* Schwefel *m*. **sul·phu·ric** [ˈ~ˈfjʊərɪk] *adj*: **~ acid** Schwefelsäure *f*. **sul·phur·ous** [ˈ~fərəs] *adj* schwef(e)lig, Schwefel...

sul·tan [ˈsʌltən] *s* Sultan *m*.

sul·try [ˈsʌltrɪ] *adj* □ **1.** schwül. **2.** aufreizend (*Blick etc*).

sum [sʌm] **I** *s* **1.** Summe *f* (*a.* A), Betrag *m*: **in ~** *fig*. mit 'einem Wort. **2.** (einfache) Rechenaufgabe: **do ~s** rechnen. **II** *v/t* **3.** **~ up** zs.-fassen. **4.** **~ up** j-n, *et*. abschätzen. **III** *v/i* **5.** **~ up** zs.-fassen: **to ~ up** zs.-fassend.

sum·ma·rize [ˈsʌməraɪz] *v/t u. v/i* zs.-fassen. **'sum·ma·ry** **I** *s* Zs.-fassung *f*. **II** *adj* summarisch (*a.* ⚖); fristlos (*Entlassung*).

sum·mer [ˈsʌmə] **I** *s* Sommer *m*: **in (the) ~** im Sommer. **II** *adj* Sommer... '**~ house** *s* Gartenhaus *n*. '**~·time** *s* Sommer(zeit *f*) *m*: **in (the) ~** im Sommer. **~ time** *s bsd. Br.* Sommerzeit *f* (*Uhrzeit*).

sum·mer·y [ˈsʌmərɪ] *adj* sommerlich, Sommer...

sum·mit [ˈsʌmɪt] **I** *s* Gipfel *m* (*a.* ⛰, *pol.*), *fig. a.* Höhepunkt *m*. **II** *adj bsd.* ⛰, *pol.* Gipfel...: **~ conference**.

sum·mon [ˈsʌmən] *v/t* **1.** j-n zitieren (**to** in *acc*); auffordern (**to do** zu tun). **2.** *Versammlung etc* einberufen. **3.** **~ up** *Kraft, Mut etc* zs.-nehmen. **sum·mons** [ˈ~z] ⚖ **I** *s* Vorladung *f*. **II** *v/t* j-n vorladen.

sump [sʌmp] *s mot.*, ⚙ *bsd. Br.* Ölwanne *f*.

sump·tu·ous [ˈsʌmptʃʊəs] *adj* □ luxuriös.

sun [sʌn] **I** *s* Sonne *f*. **II** *v/t*: **~ o.s.** sich sonnen. '**~·bathe** *v/i* sonnenbaden, sich sonnen. '**~·beam** *s* Sonnenstrahl *m*. '**~·burn** *s* Sonnenbrand *m*. '**~·burned**, '**~·burnt** *adj*: **be ~** e-n Sonnenbrand haben.

sun·dae [ˈsʌndeɪ] *s* Eisbecher *m*.

Sun·day [ˈsʌndɪ] *s* Sonntag *m*: **on ~** (am) Sonntag; **on ~s** sonntags. **~ best** *s* Sonntagsstaat *m*. **~ school** *s* Sonntagsschule *f*.

'**sun·di·al** *s* Sonnenuhr *f*. '**~·down** → **sunset**. '**~·down·er** *s bsd. Br.* F Dämmerschoppen *m*.

sun·dries [ˈsʌndrɪz] *s pl* Diverses *n*, Verschiedenes *n*. **sun·dry** [ˈ~drɪ] *adj* diverse, verschiedene: **all and ~** jedermann, *contp.* Hinz u. Kunz.

'**sun·flow·er** *s* ❀ Sonnenblume *f*. **~ oil** *s* Sonnenblumenöl *n*.

sung [sʌŋ] *pp von* **sing**.

'**sun·glass·es** *s pl, a.* **pair of ~** Sonnenbrille *f*. **~ god** *s* Sonnengott *m*. **~ hel·met** *s* Tropenhelm *m*.

sunk [sʌŋk] *pret u. pp von* **sink**.

sunk·en [ˈsʌŋkən] *adj* **1.** ge-, versunken;

versenkt. **2.** eingefallen (*Wangen*), (*a. Augen*) eingesunken.

sun| lamp *s* Höhensonne *f*, Quarzlampe *f*. **'~light** *s* Sonnenlicht *n*. **'~lit** *adj* sonnenbeschienen.

sun·ny ['sʌnɪ] *adj* □ sonnig (*a. fig. Wesen etc*), *fig.* fröhlich (*Lächeln etc*): **~side** Sonnenseite *f* (*a. fig. des Lebens*): **~side up** nur auf 'einer Seite gebraten (*Ei*).

'sun·rise *s* Sonnenaufgang *m*: **at ~** bei Sonnenaufgang. **'~roof** *s* **1.** *mot.* Schiebedach *n*. **2.** Dachterrasse *f*. **'~set** *s* Sonnenuntergang *m*: **at ~** bei Sonnenuntergang. **'~shade** *s* Sonnenschirm *m*. **'~shine** *s* Sonnenschein *m*. **'~stroke** *s* 𝕤 Sonnenstich *m*. **'~tan** *s* (Sonnen)Bräune *f*: **~ lotion** (*od. oil*) Sonnenöl *n*. **'~tanned** *adj* braungebrannt. **'~up** → **sunrise**. **~ vi·sor** *s* *mot.* Sonnenblende *f*.

su·per ['su:pə] *adj* F super, klasse.

super... ['su:pə] Über..., über...

,su·per·a'bun·dant *adj* □ überreichlich.

su·per·an·nu·at·ed [,su:pə'rænjʊeɪtɪd] *adj* **1.** pensioniert, im Ruhestand. **2.** *fig.* überholt, veraltet.

su·perb [suː'pɜːb] *adj* □ ausgezeichnet.

su·per·cil·i·ous [,su:pə'sɪlɪəs] *adj* □ hochnäsig.

su·per·fi·cial [,su:pə'fɪʃl] *adj* □ oberflächlich (*a. fig.*). **su·per·fi·ci·al·i·ty** ['~,fɪʃɪ'ælətɪ] *s* Oberflächlichkeit *f*.

su·per·flu·ous [su:'pɜːflʊəs] *adj* □ überflüssig.

,su·per'hu·man *adj* □ übermenschlich. **,~im'pose** *v/t* Bild etc einblenden (**on** in *acc*)

su·per·in·tend·ent [,su:pərɪn'tendənt] *s* **1.** Aufsicht(sbeamte *m*) *f*. **2.** *Br.* Kriminalrat *m*.

su·pe·ri·or [su:'pɪərɪə] **I** *adj* □ **1.** (**to**) überlegen (*dat*), besser (als): **be ~ in number(s) to** j-m zahlenmäßig überlegen sein. **2.** ranghöher (**to** als): **be ~ to** *a.* höher stehen als. **3.** ausgezeichnet, hervorragend. **4.** *b.s.* überheblich, -legen. **II** *s* **5.** Vorgesetzte *m*, *f*, bsd. **~,pe·ri'or·i·ty** [~'ɒrətɪ] *s* **1.** Überlegenheit *f* (**over** gegenüber): **~ in number(s)** zahlenmäßige Überlegenheit. **2.** Überheblichkeit *f*.

su·per·la·tive [su:'pɜːlətɪv] **I** *adj* □ **1.** unübertrefflich, überragend: **~ly happy**

unsagbar glücklich. **2. ~ degree** → **3. II** *s* **3.** *ling.* Superlativ *m*.

'su·per|·man *s* (*irr man*) Supermann *m*. **'~,mar·ket** *s* Supermarkt *m*. **,~'nat·u·ral I** *adj* □ übernatürlich. **II** *s*: **the ~** das Übernatürliche.

su·per·nu·mer·ar·y [,su:pə'nju:mərərɪ] *adj* überzählig.

'su·per,pow·er *s* *pol.* Supermacht *f*.

su·per·sede [,su:pə'si:d] *v/t et.* ablösen, ersetzen, an die Stelle treten von (*od. gen*).

,su·per|'son·ic *adj* ✈, *phys.* Überschall...: **at ~ speed** mit Überschallgeschwindigkeit. **'~star** *s* Sport etc: Superstar *m*.

su·per·sti·tion [,su:pə'stɪʃn] *s* Aberglaube *m*, *pl* abergläubische Vorstellungen *pl*. **su·per·sti·tious** [~'stɪʃəs] *adj* □ abergläubisch.

'su·per,struc·ture *s* △ Oberbau *m*, ⚓ (Deck)Aufbauten *pl*; *fig.* Überbau *m*. **'~,tank·er** *s* ⚓ Supertanker *m*.

su·per·vene [,su:pə'vi:n] *v/i* dazwischenkommen.

su·per·vise ['su:pəvaɪz] *v/t* beaufsichtigen. **su·per·vi·sion** [,~'vɪʒn] *s* Beaufsichtigung *f*: **under s.o.'s ~** unter j-s Aufsicht. **su·per·vi·sor** ['~vaɪzə] *s* Aufseher(in), Aufsicht *f*.

sup·per ['sʌpə] *s* Abendessen *n*: **have ~** zu Abend essen; → **lord** 3.

sup·plant [sə'plɑːnt] *v/t* j-n, *et.* verdrängen.

sup·ple ['sʌpl] *adj* □ gelenkig (*Körper etc*), (*a. Material*) geschmeidig, (*Material*) biegsam, elastisch.

sup·ple·ment I *s* ['sʌplɪmənt] **1.** Ergänzung *f* (**to** gen *od.* zu). **2.** Nachtrag *m*, Anhang *m* (**to** zu *e-m Buch*); Ergänzungsband *m*. **3.** Beilage *f* (**to** *e-r Zeitung*). **II** *v/t* ['~ment] *et.* ergänzen, Einkommen aufbessern (**with** mit). **sup·ple·men·ta·ry** [,~'mentərɪ] *adj* ergänzend, zusätzlich: **~ benefit** *Br.* Sozialhilfe *f*.

sup·pli·er [sə'plaɪə] *s* ✝ Lieferant(in), *a. pl* Lieferfirma *f*.

sup·ply [sə'plaɪ] **I** *v/t* **1.** liefern; stellen; sorgen für. **2.** *j-n, et.* versorgen, ✝ beliefern (**with** mit). **3.** *e-m Bedürfnis etc* abhelfen. **II** *s* **4.** Lieferung *f* (**to** an *acc*). **5.** Versorgung *f*. **6.** ✝ Angebot *n*: **~ and demand** Angebot u. Nachfrage; →

short 2. **7.** *mst pl* Vorrat *m* (**of** an *dat*), *pl a.* Proviant *m*, ✕ Nachschub *m*. **8.** *pl* (*Büro- etc*)Bedarf *m*.

sup·port [sə'pɔːt] **I** *v/t* **1.** (ab)stützen; *Gewicht etc* tragen; *fig.* Währung stützen. **2.** *j-n* (*a. finanziell*), *Forderung etc* unterstützen, *Familie* unterhalten: ~ **Tottenham** ein Tottenham-Anhänger sein. **3.** *Hobby etc* finanzieren. **4.** *Theorie etc* beweisen, erhärten. **5.** *et.* aushalten, ertragen. **II** *s* **6.** Stütze *f*, ⚙ *a.* Stützbalken *m*, -pfeiler *m*. **7.** *fig.* Unterstützung *f*: **in** ~ **of** zur Unterstützung (*gen*); **have s.o.'s full** ~ j-s volle Unterstützung haben. **II** *v/t* **4.** *I* ~ **so** ich nehme es an, wahrscheinlich, vermutlich. **III** *cj* **5.** angenommen. **6.** wie wäre es, wenn: ~ **we went home?** wie wäre es, wenn wir nach Hause gingen? **sup'posed** *adj* □ angeblich. **sup'pos·ing** *cj* **1.** → **suppose** 5, 6. **2.** vorausgesetzt.

sup·po·si·tion [ˌsʌpə'zɪʃn] *s* Annahme *f*, Vermutung *f*: **act on the** ~ **that** von der Annahme ausgehen, daß.

sup·pos·i·to·ry [sə'pɒzɪtərɪ] *s* ⚕ Zäpfchen *n*.

sup·pu·rate ['sʌpjʊəreɪt] *v/i* eitern.

su·pra·na·tion·al [ˌsuːprə'næʃənl] *adj* □ übernational.

su·prem·a·cy [sʊ'preməsɪ] *s* Vormachtstellung *f*.

su·preme [sʊ'priːm] *adj* **1.** höchst, oberst. **2.** höchst, größt. **su'preme·ly** *adv* höchst, absolut.

sur·charge I *s* ['sɜːtʃɑːdʒ] Auf-, Zu-

schlag *m* (**on** auf *acc*); ✆ Nach-, Strafporto *n* (**on** auf *acc*). **II** *v/t* [sɜː'tʃɑːdʒ] Nachporto *od.* e-n Zuschlag erheben auf (*acc*).

sure [ʃɔː] **I** *adj* (□ → **surely**) **1.** *allg.* sicher: ~ **of o.s.** selbstsicher; ~ **of victory** (*od.* **winning**) siegessicher; **for** ~ ganz sicher *od.* bestimmt. **2.** ~ **thing!** *bsd. Am.* F (aber) klar!; **be** (*od.* **feel**) ~ sicher sein; **you are** ~ **to like this play** dir wird das Stück sicher *od.* bestimmt gefallen; **be** ~ **to lock the door** vergiß nicht abzuschließen; **to be** ~ sicher(lich); **make** ~ **that** sich (davon) überzeugen, daß; dafür sorgen, daß; **make** ~ **of s.th.** sich von et. überzeugen; sich et. sichern. **II** *adv* **2.** F sicher, klar. **3.** ~ **enough** tatsächlich. '~**,fire** *adj* F (tod)sicher.

sure·ly ['ʃɔːlɪ] *adv* **1.** sicher: → **slow** 1. **2.** sicher(lich), bestimmt. **sure·ty** ['ʃɔːrətɪ] *s bsd.* 🏛 Bürgschaft *f*, Sicherheit *f*; Bürge *m*, Bürgin *f*: **stand** ~ **for s.o.** für j-n bürgen.

surf [sɜːf] **I** *s* Brandung *f*. **II** *v/i* surfen.

sur·face ['sɜːfɪs] **I** *s* **1.** Oberfläche *f* (*a. fig.*): **on the** ~ äußerlich; vordergründig; oberflächlich betrachtet. **2.** (*Straßen*)Belag *m*, (-)Decke *f*. **II** *adj* **3.** Oberflächen...: ~ **mail** gewöhnliche Post (*Ggs. Luftpost*); ~ **tension** *phys.* Oberflächenspannung *f*. *fig.* oberflächlich. **III** *v/i* **5.** auftauchen (*a. fig.*). *v/t* **6.** Straße mit e-m Belag versehen.

'**surf·board** *s* Surfboard *n*, -brett *n*.

sur·feit ['sɜːfɪt] **I** *s* Überangebot *n* (**of** an *dat*). **II** *v/t*: ~ **o.s. with** sich übersättigen an (*dat*).

surf·er ['sɜːfə] *s* Surfer(in), Wellenreiter(in). '**surf·ing** *s* Surfen *n*, Wellenreiten *n*.

sup·pose [sə'pəʊz] **I** *v/t* **1.** annehmen, vermuten: *I* ~ *I* **must have fallen asleep** ich muß wohl eingeschlafen sein. **2.** *he is* ~ **d** (**to be**) *rich* er soll reich sein; *you are not* ~ **d to smoke here** du darfst hier nicht rauchen; *aren't you* ~ **d to be at work?** solltest du nicht (eigentlich) in der Arbeit sein?; *what is that* ~ **d to mean?** was soll denn das? **3.** *et.* voraussetzen.

surge [sɜːdʒ] **I** *s* **1.** *a* ~ **of people** e-e wogende Menschenmenge; **there was a sudden** ~ **forward** plötzlich drängte alles nach vorn. **2.** *fig.* Welle *f*, Woge *f* (*der Begeisterung*); (*Gefühls*)Aufwallung *f*, Anwandlung *f*. **II** *v/i* **3.** drängen, strömen (*Menschenmenge*). **4.** *mst* ~ **up** *fig.* aufwallen (*in* in *dat*) (*Zorn etc*).

sur·geon ['sɜːdʒən] *s* Chirurg(in). **sur·ger·y** ['sɜːdʒərɪ] *s* **1.** Chirurgie *f*. **2.** *he needs* ~ er muß operiert werden; **remove by** ~ operativ entfernen. **3.** *Br.* Sprechzimmer *n*; Sprechstunde *f*: ~ **hours** *pl* Sprechstunden *pl*. **sur·gi·cal**

['~ɪkl] *adj* □ **1.** chirurgisch; operativ; Operations...: **~ spirit** *Br.* Wundbenzin *n.* **2. ~ stocking** Stützstrumpf *m.*

sur·ly ['sɜːlɪ] *adj* □ griesgrämig, sauertöpfisch.

sur·mise I *s* ['sɜːmaɪz] Vermutung *f.* **II** *v/t* [sɜː'maɪz] vermuten.

sur·mount [sɜː'maʊnt] *v/t Schwierigkeit etc* überwinden. **sur'mount·a·ble** *adj* überwindbar.

sur·name ['sɜːneɪm] *s* Familien-, Nach-, Zuname *m*: **what is his ~?** wie heißt er mit Familiennamen?

sur·pass [sə'pɑːs] *v/t Erwartungen etc* übertreffen.

sur·plus ['sɜːpləs] **I** *s* Überschuß *m* (*of* an *dat*). **II** *adj* überschüssig: **be ~ to requirements** zuviel sein.

sur·prise [sə'praɪz] **I** *s* Überraschung *f*: **in ~** überrascht; **take by ~** überraschen; **→ much 2. II** *adj* überraschend, Überraschungs... **III** *v/t* überraschen: **be ~d at** (*od. by*) überrascht sein über (*acc*); **I wouldn't be ~d if** es würde mich nicht wundern, wenn. **sur'pris·ing** *adj* □ überraschend: **~ly** (*enough*) überraschenderweise.

sur·re·al·ism [sə'rɪəlɪzəm] *s Kunst:* Surrealismus *m.* **sur're·al·ist I** *s* Surrealist(in). **II** *adj* surrealistisch. **sur,re·al'is·tic** *adj* (**~ally**) surrealistisch.

sur·ren·der [sə'rendə] **I** *v/i* **1.** (**to**) ✕ sich ergeben (*dat*), kapitulieren (vor *dat*) (*beide a. fig.*): **~ to the police** sich der Polizei stellen. **II** *v/t* **2.** *et.* übergeben, ausliefern (**to** *dat*): **~ o.s. to the police** sich der Polizei stellen. **3.** *Anspruch etc* aufgeben, verzichten auf (*acc*). **III** *s* **4.** ✕ Kapitulation *f* (**to** vor *dat*) (*a. fig.*). **5.** (**of**) Aufgabe *f* (*gen*), Verzicht *m* (auf *acc*).

sur·rep·ti·tious [ˌsʌrəp'tɪʃəs] *adj* □ heimlich, verstohlen.

sur·ro·gate ['sʌrəgeɪt] *adj*: **~ mother** Leihmutter *f.*

sur·round [sə'raʊnd] *v/t* **1.** umgeben. **2.** *Haus etc* umstellen. **sur'round·ing I** *adj* umliegend. **II** *s pl* Umgebung *f.*

sur·veil·lance [sɜː'veɪləns] *s* Überwachung *f*: **be** (**keep**) **under ~** überwacht werden (überwachen).

sur·vey I *v/t* [sə'veɪ] **1.** (sich) *et.* betrachten (*a. fig.*). **2.** *Land* vermessen. **3.** *Haus etc* begutachten. **II** *s* ['sɜːveɪ] **4.** Umfra-

ge *f.* **5.** Überblick *m* (**of** über *acc*). **6.** Vermessung *f.* **7.** Begutachtung *f.* **sur·vey·or** *s* **1.** Land(ver)messer(in). **2.** Gutachter(in).

sur·viv·al [sə'vaɪvl] *s* **1.** Überleben *n* (*a. fig.*): **~ training** Überlebenstraining *n.* **2.** Überbleibsel *n* (**from** aus *e-r* Zeit).

sur·vive I *v/t* **1.** *j-n, et.* überleben; *Erdbeben etc* überstehen (*Haus etc*); *Jahrhundert etc* überdauern (*Brauch etc*). **II** *v/i* **2.** überleben (*a. fig.*), am Leben bleiben. **3.** erhalten bleiben *od.* sein. **sur·vi·vor** *s* Überlebende *m, f* (**from**, **of** gen).

sus·cep·ti·ble [sə'septəbl] *adj* □ **1.** empfänglich (**to** für). **2.** anfällig (**to** für). **3.** leicht zu beeindrucken.

sus·pect I *v/t* [sə'spekt] **1.** *j-n* verdächtigen (**of** gen): **~ s.o. of doing s.th.** j-n *im od.* in Verdacht haben, et. zu tun; **be ~ed of doing s.th.** *im od.* unter dem Verdacht stehen, et. zu tun. **2.** *et.* vermuten. **3.** *et.* an-, bezweifeln. **II** *s* ['sʌspekt] **4.** Verdächtige *m, f.* **III** *adj* ['sʌspekt] verdächtig, suspekt.

sus·pend [sə'spend] *v/t* **1.** aufhängen (**from** an *dat*). **2.** *Verkauf, Zahlungen etc* (vorübergehend) einstellen; ⚖ *Strafe* zur Bewährung aussetzen: **he was given a two-year ~ed sentence** er bekam zwei Jahre mit Bewährung. **3.** *j-n* suspendieren (**from duty** vom Dienst); vorübergehend ausschließen (**from** aus); (*Sport*) sperren (**for two games** für zwei Spiele). **sus'pend·er** *s* **1.** *Br.* Strumpfhalter *m*, Straps *m*: **~ belt** Strumpf(halter)-, Strapsgürtel *m.* **2.** *pl, a.* **pair of ~s** *Am.* Hosenträger *pl.*

sus·pense [sə'spens] *s* Spannung *f*: **in ~** gespannt, voller Spannung; **full of ~** spannend; **keep s.o. in ~** j-n auf die Folter spannen. **sus'pen·sion** *s* **1.** *mot. etc* Aufhängung *f*: **~ bridge** Hängebrücke *f.* **2.** (vorübergehende) Einstellung. **3.** Suspendierung *f*; vorübergehender Ausschluß *m*; (*Sport*) Sperre *f*: **he received a two-game ~** er wurde für zwei Spiele gesperrt.

sus·pi·cion [sə'spɪʃn] *s* **1.** Verdacht *m* (**of** gegen): **be above** (*od.* **beyond**) **~** über jeden Verdacht erhaben sein; **be under ~ of murder** unter Mordverdacht stehen. **2.** *a. pl* Verdacht *m*, Argwohn *m*, Mißtrauen *n* (**of** gegen): **with ~** argwöhnisch, mißtrauisch. **3.** Verdacht *m*, Vermutung *f*. **4.** *fig.* Hauch *m*, Spur *f*. **sus·pi·cious** *adj* □ **1.** verdächtig. **2.** argwöhnisch, mißtrauisch (*of* gegen): **become ~** *a.* Verdacht schöpfen.

sus·tain [səˈsteɪn] *v/t* **1.** *j-n* (*a. moralisch*) stärken. **2.** *Interesse etc* aufrechterhalten. **3.** *Schaden, Verlust* erleiden. **4.** ♪ *Ton* (aus)halten. **5.** ♪♫ *e-m Einspruch etc* stattgeben. **6.** *Gewicht* aushalten, tragen. **sus·tained** *adj* anhaltend.

su·ture [ˈsuːtʃə] ♪♫ *s* Naht *f*. **II** *v/t* Wunde nähen.

svelte [svelt] *adj* gertenschlank (*Frau*).

swab [swɒb] ♪♫ **I** *s* **1.** Tupfer *m*. **2.** Abstrich *m*: **take a ~** e-n Abstrich machen. **II** *v/t* **3.** *Wunde* abtupfen.

swad·dle [ˈswɒdl] *v/t Baby* wickeln.

swag·ger [ˈswæɡə] **I** *v/i* stolzieren. **II** *s*: **walk with a ~** → **I**.

swal·low¹ [ˈswɒləʊ] *s orn.* Schwalbe *f*.

swal·low² [~] **I** *v/t* **1.** schlucken (*a. fig.* F *glauben, hinnehmen*): **~ one's words** zugeben, daß man sich geirrt hat; **~ up** *Betrieb, Gewinn etc* schlucken, verschlingen; → **bait** 1. **2.** *Ärger, Tränen etc* hinunterschlucken, *s-n Stolz* vergessen. **II** *v/i* **3.** schlucken: **~ hard** *fig.* kräftig schlucken. **III** *s* **4.** Schluck *m*.

swam [swæm] *pret von* **swim**.

swamp [swɒmp] **I** *s* Sumpf *m*. **II** *v/t* überschwemmen: **be ~ed with** *fig.* überschwemmt werden mit. **'swamp·y** *adj* sumpfig.

swan [swɒn] *s orn.* Schwan *m*.

swank [swæŋk] F **I** *v/i* **1.** angeben. **II** *s* **2.** Angeber(in). **3.** Angabe *f*. **'swank·y** *adj* □ F **1.** piekfein. **2.** angeberisch.

'swan·song *s fig.* Schwanengesang *m*.

swap [swɒp] F **I** *v/t* **1.** *et.* tauschen (**with** mit), (ein)tauschen (**for** gegen): **~ places** die Plätze tauschen. **II** *v/i* **2.** tauschen: **~ over** (*od.* **round**) die Plätze tauschen. **II** *s* **3.** Tausch *m*: **do a ~** tauschen; **do** (*od.* **get**) **a good** (**bad**) **~** e-n guten (schlechten) Tausch machen. **4.** Tauschobjekt *n*.

swarm [swɔːm] **I** *s* **1.** Schwarm *m* (*Bienen, Touristen etc*). **II** *v/i* **2.** schwärmen (*Bienen*), (*Menschen a.*) strömen. **3.** **~ with** wimmeln von: **the square was ~ing with people** auf dem Platz wimmelte es von Menschen.

swarth·y [ˈswɔːðɪ] *adj* dunkel (*Haut*), dunkelhäutig (*Person*).

swash·buck·ling [ˈswɒʃˌbʌklɪŋ] *adj* verwegen (*Person*), abenteuerlich (*Film etc*).

swas·ti·ka [ˈswɒstɪkə] *s* Hakenkreuz *n*.

swat [swɒt] **I** *v/t* Fliege *etc* totschlagen. **II** *s* → **swatter**. **'swat·ter** *s* Fliegenklappe *f*, -klatsche *f*.

sway [sweɪ] **I** *v/i* **1.** sich wiegen (**in the wind** im Wind) (*Bäume etc*), schaukeln (*Schiff etc*): **~ between** *fig.* schwanken zwischen (*dat*). **II** *v/t* **2.** hin- u. herbewegen, *s-n Körper* wiegen, *Fahne etc* schwenken. **3.** *j-n* beeinflussen; umstimmen. **III** *s* **4.** Schaukeln *n*.

swear [sweə] (*irr*) **I** *v/i* **1.** schwören (**on the Bible** auf die Bibel; **to God** bei Gott): **~ by** *fig.* F schwören auf (*acc*): **I couldn't ~ to it** ich kann es nicht beschwören. **2.** fluchen: **~ at s.o.** *j-n* wüst beschimpfen. **II** *v/t* **3.** schwören (**to do** zu tun; **that** daß): **~ s.th. to s.o.** *j-m et.* schwören; **~ oath** 1. **4.** ~ **in** *Minister, Zeugen etc* vereidigen; **I was sworn to secrecy** ich mußte hoch u. heilig versprechen, kein Wort darüber zu sagen. **'~-word** *s* Fluch *m*; Kraftausdruck *m*.

sweat [swet] **I** *v/i* (*Am. a. irr*) **1.** schwitzen (**with** *vor* **od.** *dat*) (*a. fig.* F). **II** *v/t* (*Am. a. irr*) **2.** ~ **out** *Krankheit* ausschwitzen: **~ it out** F durchhalten; **~ blood** F sich abrackern (**over** mit). **III** *s* **3.** Schweiß *m*: **cold ~** kalter Schweiß, Angstschweiß; **no ~!** F kein Problem!; **get in(to) a ~** *fig.* F ins Schwitzen geraten *od.* kommen (**about** wegen). **4.** F Schufterei *f*. **'~-band** *s Sport:* Schweißband *n*.

sweat·er [ˈswetə] *s* Pullover *m*.

sweat| gland *s anat.* Schweißdrüse *f*. **'~-shirt** *s* Sweatshirt *n* (*weiter Baumwollpullover*).

sweat·y [ˈswetɪ] *adj* □ **1.** schweißig, verschwitzt. **2.** nach Schweiß riechend, Schweiß... **3.** schweißtreibend.

Swede [swiːd] *s* Schwede *m*, Schwedin *f*. **Swed·ish** [ˈswiːdɪʃ] **I** *adj* **1.** schwedisch. **II** *s* **2.** *ling.* Schwedisch *n*. **3.** **the ~** *pl* die Schweden *pl*.

sweep [swiːp] **I** *v/t* **1.** **give the floor a ~** den Boden kehren *od.* fegen; **make a clean ~** *fig.* gründlich aufräumen; (*Sport etc*) gründlich abräumen. **2.** Hieb *m*, Schlag

m. **3.** Schornsteinfeger(in), Kaminkehrer(in). **II** *v/t (irr)* **4.** *Fußboden, Krümel etc* kehren, fegen: ~ *the board (Sport etc)* gründlich abräumen; → *carpet* 1, *rug* 1. **5.** fegen über (*acc*) (*Sturm etc*); *fig. Land etc* überschwemmen (*Protestwelle etc*). **6.** ~ *along* mitreißen; ~ *s.o. off his feet fig.* j-s Herz im Sturm erobern. **7.** *Horizont etc* absuchen (*for* nach). **II** *v/i (irr)* **8.** kehren, fegen: ~ *broom.* **9.** rauschen (*Person*): ~ *past s.o.* an j-m vorbeirauschen.
Verbindungen mit Adverbien:

sweep| a·side *v/t Einwände etc* beiseite schieben. **~ a·way** *v/t* **1.** aufräumen mit. **2.** *be swept away by fig.* mitgerissen werden von. **~ up** *v/t* **1.** (*a. v/i*) zs.-kehren, -fegen. **2.** *j-n* hochreißen.

sweep·er ['swiːpə] *s* **1.** (*Straßen*)Kehrer(in). **2.** Kehrmaschine *f.* **3.** *Fußball:* Libero *m.* **'sweep·ing** **I** *adj* □ **1.** durchgreifend (*Änderung etc*). **2.** pauschal. **II** *s pl* **3.** Kehricht *m.*

sweet [swiːt] **I** *adj* □ **1.** süß (*a. fig.*): ~ *nothings pl* Zärtlichkeiten *pl*; ~ *potato* 🌿 *Batate f,* Süßkartoffel *f*; *revenge is ~* Rache ist süß; ~ *talk* F Schmeichelei(en *pl*) *f*; *have a ~ tooth* gern naschen. **2.** lieblich (*Musik etc*). **3.** lieb. **II** *s* **4.** *Br.* Bonbon *m, n,* Süßigkeit *f.* **5.** *Br.* Nachtisch *m:* *for ~* als *od.* zum Nachtisch. **'~and-'sour** *adj gastr.* süß-sauer.

sweet·en ['swiːtn] **I** *v/t* **1.** süßen. **2.** *fig.* besänftigen; freundlicher stimmen. **3.** *a.* ~ *up* F *j-n* schmieren. **II** *v/i* **4.** süß(er) werden. **'sweet·en·er** *s* **1.** Süßstoff *m.* **2.** F Schmiergeld *n.*

'sweet·heart *s* Schatz *m* (*Anrede*).

sweet·ie ['swiːtɪ] *s* F **1.** *Br.* Bonbon *m, n.* **2.** *be a* ~ *fig.* süß sein.

'sweet-talk *v/t* F *j-m* schmeicheln.

swell [swel] **I** *v/i (mst irr)* **1.** *a.* ~ *up* 🌿 (an)schwellen. **2.** *a.* ~ *out* ⚓ sich blähen (*Segel*). **3.** *fig.* anschwellen (*into* zu) (*Geräusch*); anwachsen (*Zahl etc*). **II** *v/t (mst irr)* **4.** *a.* ~ *out Segel* blähen (*Wind*). **5.** *fig. Zahl etc* anwachsen lassen. **III** *s* **6.** ⚓ Dünung *f.* **IV** *adj* **7.** *Am.* F klasse. **'swell·ing** *s* ♂ Schwellung *f.*

swel·ter ['sweltə] *v/i* vor Hitze fast umkommen. **'swel·ter·ing** *adj* drückend, schwül.

swept [swept] *pret u. pp von* **sweep.**

swerve [swɜːv] **I** *v/i* **1.** schwenken (*to the left* nach links); e-n Schwenk machen. **2.** *fig.* abweichen (*from* von). **II** *s* **3.** Schwenk(ung *f*) *m, mot. etc a.* Schlenker *m.*

swift [swift] *adj* □ schnell: *be ~ to do s.th.* et. schnell tun. **'swift·ness** *s* Schnelligkeit *f.*

swig [swɪɡ] F **I** *v/t* Getränk hinunterkippen. **II** *s:* *take a ~ at the bottle* e-n Zug aus der Flasche tun; *take a ~ of beer* e-n kräftigen Schluck Bier nehmen.

swill [swɪl] *v/t u. v/i contp.* saufen.

swim [swɪm] **I** *v/i (irr)* **1.** schwimmen: → *tide* 2. **2.** *fig.* verschwimmen (*before s.o.'s eyes* vor j-s Augen); *my head was ~ming* mir drehte sich alles. **II** *v/t (irr)* **3.** *Strecke* schwimmen; *Gewässer* durchschwimmen. **III** *s* **4.** *go for a ~* schwimmen gehen. **'swim·mer** *s* Schwimmer(in). **'swim·ming** **I** *s* Schwimmen *n.* **II** *adj* Schwimm...: ~ *bath(s pl) Br.* Schwimm-, *bsd.* Hallenbad *n*; ~ *cap* Badekappe *f,* -mütze *f*; ~ *costume* Badeanzug *m*; ~ *pool* Schwimmingpool *m,* Schwimmbecken *n*; (*pair of*) ~ *trunks pl* Badehose *f.*

'swim·suit *s* Badeanzug *m.*

swin·dle ['swɪndl] *v/t j-n* beschwindeln (*out of* um): ~ *s.o. out of s.th.* a. *j-m* et. abschwindeln. **II** *s* Schwindel *m.* **'swin·dler** *s* Schwindler(in).

swine [swaɪn] *s* **1.** *pl ~ zo.* Schwein *n.* **2.** *pl ~(s) sl. contp.* Schwein *n.*

swing [swɪŋ] **I** *v/i (irr)* **1.** (hin- u. her)schwingen. **2.** sich schwingen; einbiegen, -schwenken (*into* in *acc*): ~ *round* sich ruckartig umdrehen; ~ *shut* zuschlagen (*Tor etc*). **3.** ♪ schwungvoll spielen (*Band etc*); Schwung haben (*Musik*). **II** *v/t* **4.** et., *die Arme etc* schwingen. **III** *s* **5.** Schwingen *n.* **6.** Schaukel *f.* **7.** *Boxen:* Schwinger *m.* **8.** *fig.* Schwung *m: be in full ~* in vollem Gang sein. **9.** *fig.* Umschwung *m: ~ in opinion* Meinungsumschwung. ~ *door s* Pendeltür *f.*

swinge·ing ['swɪndʒɪŋ] *adj bsd. Br.* einschneidend (*Kürzungen etc*), extrem hoch (*Besteuerung etc*).

swing·ing ['swɪŋɪŋ] *adj* □ **1.** schwingend: ~ *door bsd. Am.* Pendeltür *f.* **2.** *fig.* schwungvoll. **3.** *fig.* lebenslustig.

swin·ish ['swaɪnɪʃ] *adj* □ ekelhaft.

synonymous

swipe [swaɪp] **I** s Schlag m: **take a ~ at** → **II**. **II** v/i: **~ at** schlagen nach. **III** v/t F klauen.

swirl [swɜːl] **I** v/i wirbeln. **II** s Wirbel m.

swish [swɪʃ] **I** v/i **1.** sausen, zischen. **2.** rascheln (Seide etc). **II** v/t **3.** mit dem Schwanz schlagen. **III** s **4.** Sausen n, Zischen n. **5.** Rascheln n. **IV** adj **6.** F feudal.

Swiss [swɪs] **I** s Schweizer(in): **the ~** pl die Schweizer pl. **II** adj schweizerisch, Schweizer(...)

switch [swɪtʃ] **I** s **1.** ⚡, ⚙ Schalter m. **2.** Gerte f, Rute f. **3.** 🚂 Am. Weiche f. **4.** fig. Umstellung f. **II** v/t **5.** a. **~ over** ⚡, ⚙ (um)schalten (**to** auf acc), Produktion etc umstellen (**to** auf acc): **~ off** ab-, ausschalten; **~ on** an-, einschalten. **III** v/i **6.** a. **~ over** ⚡, ⚙ (um)schalten (**to** auf acc), fig. überwechseln (**to** zu): **~ off** abschalten (a. fig. F Person), ausschalten; **~ on** an-, einschalten. **~ round** umschlagen (Wind). **'~·back** s **1.** Gebirgs-, Serpentinenstraße f. **2.** Achterbahn f. **'~·blade** s Am. Schnappmesser n. **'~·board** s **1.** ⚡ Schalttafel f. **2.** (Telefon)Zentrale f: **~ operator** Telefonist(in).

swiv·el [swɪvl] v/i pret u. pp **-eled**, bsd. Br. **-elled** sich drehen: **~ round** sich herumdrehen. **~ chair** s Drehstuhl m.

swol·len [swəʊlən] pp von **swell**. **~·-'head·ed** adj fig. aufgeblasen.

swoop [swuːp] **I** v/i **1.** a. **~ down** herabstoßen (**on** auf acc) (Raubvogel). **2.** fig. zuschlagen (Polizei etc): **~ on** herfallen über (acc); e-e Razzia machen in (dat). **II** s **3.** Razzia f.

swop → **swap**.

sword [sɔːd] s Schwert n: **cross ~s** die Klingen kreuzen (**with** mit) (a. fig.); → **Damocles**.

swore [swɔː] pret von **swear**.

sworn [swɔːn] **I** pp von **swear**. **II** adj **1. ~ enemies** pl Todfeinde pl. **2.** 🏛 eidlich.

swot [swɒt] Br. F **I** v/i büffeln, pauken (**for** für). **II** v/t: **~ up** → **I**. **III** s Büffler(in); Streber(in).

swum [swʌm] pp von **swim**.

swung [swʌŋ] pret u. pp von **swing**.

syl·la·bi [sɪləbaɪ] pl von **syllabus**.

syl·lab·ic [sɪˈlæbɪk] adj Silben...; ...silbig. **syl·la·ble** [sɪləbl] s Silbe f.

syl·la·bus [sɪləbəs] pl **-bus·es**, **-bi** [~baɪ] s ped., univ. Lehrplan m.

syl·lo·gism [sɪlədʒɪzəm] s Syllogismus m.

sym·bi·o·sis [ˌsɪmbɪˈəʊsɪs] s biol. Symbiose f.

sym·bol [sɪmbl] s Symbol n (a. 🦌). **sym·bol·ic** [~ˈbɒlɪk] adj (**~ally**) symbolisch: **be ~ of** et. symbolisieren. **sym·bol·ism** [~bəlɪzəm] s Symbolik f. **sym·bol·ize** [~bəlaɪz] v/t symbolisieren.

sym·met·ri·cal [sɪˈmetrɪkl] adj □ symmetrisch. **sym·me·try** [sɪmətrɪ] s Symmetrie f.

sym·pa·thet·ic [ˌsɪmpəˈθetɪk] adj (**~ally**) **1.** mitfühlend: **~ strike** † Sympathiestreik m. **2.** verständnisvoll; wohlwollend: **be ~ to** (od. **toward**[s]) wohlwollend gegenüberstehen (dat). **'sym·pa·thize** v/i **1.** mitfühlen (**with** mit). **2.** (**with**) Verständnis haben (für); wohlwollend gegenüberstehen (dat); sympathisieren (mit). **'sym·pa·thiz·er** s Sympathisant(in). **'sym·pa·thy** s **1.** Mitgefühl n: **~** mitfühlend; **letter of ~** Beileidsschreiben n; **~ strike** † Sympathiestreik m. **2.** Verständnis n; Wohlwollen n: **be in ~ with** sympathisieren mit. **3.** pl Sympathien pl: **my sympathies are** (od. **lie**) **with** m-e Sympathien gehören (dat). **4.** pl Beileid n, Teilnahme f.

sym·phon·ic [sɪmˈfɒnɪk] adj (**~ally**) ♪ sinfonisch, symphonisch. **sym·pho·ny** [sɪmfənɪ] s Sinfonie f, Symphonie f: **~ orchestra** Sinfonieorchester n.

sym·po·si·um [sɪmˈpəʊzjəm] pl **-si·ums**, **-si·a** [~zjə] s Symposium n, Symposion n.

symp·tom [sɪmptəm] s ⚕ Symptom n, Anzeichen n (**of** für, von) (beide a. fig.). **symp·to·mat·ic** [~ˈmætɪk] adj (**~ally**) symptomatisch (**of** für).

syn·a·gogue [sɪnəgɒg] s eccl. Synagoge f.

syn·chro·nize [sɪŋkrənaɪz] **I** v/t aufeinander abstimmen; Film, Uhren synchronisieren. **II** v/i synchron sein (Film) od. gehen (Uhren).

syn·di·cate [sɪndɪkət] s † Konsortium n.

syn·drome [sɪndrəʊm] s ⚕ Syndrom n.

syn·od [sɪnəd] s eccl. Synode f.

syn·o·nym [sɪnənɪm] s ling. Synonym n. **syn·on·y·mous** [sɪˈnɒnɪməs] adj □ synonym: **be ~ with** fig. gleichbedeutend sein mit.

syn·op·sis [sɪ'nɒpsɪs] *pl* **-ses** [~siːz] *s* Zs.-fassung *f*.

syn·tac·tic [sɪn'tæktɪk] *adj* (**~ally**) *ling.* syntaktisch. **syn·tax** ['sɪntæks] *s* Syntax *f*, Satzlehre *f*.

syn·the·sis ['sɪnθəsɪs] *pl* **-ses** ['~siːz] *s* Synthese *f*. **syn·the·size** ['~saɪz] *v/t* 🎽 synthetisch *od.* künstlich herstellen. **'syn·the·siz·er** *s* Synthesizer *m* (*Gerät zur elektronischen Musik-, Sprach- u. Geräuscherzeugung*).

syn·thet·ic [sɪn'θetɪk] *adj* (**~ally**) 🎽 synthetisch, Kunst...

syph·i·lis ['sɪfɪlɪs] *s* 🎽 Syphilis.

sy·phon → **siphon**.

syr·inge ['sɪrɪndʒ] *s* 🎽 Spritze *f*.

syr·up ['sɪrəp] *s* **1.** Sirup *m*. **2.** 🎽 (*Husten*)Sirup *m*, (-)Saft *m*. **'syr·up·y** *adj* **1.** sirupartig. **2.** *fig.* zuckersüß.

sys·tem ['sɪstəm] *s* **1.** *allg.* System *n*: **~ of government** Regierungssystem; **~s analyst** Systemanalytiker(in); → **digestive** 2, **nervous** 1, **respiratory**. **2.** (*Straßen- etc*)Netz *n*. **3.** Organismus *m*: **get s.th. out of one's ~** *fig.* sich et. von der Seele reden. **sys·tem·at·ic** [~tə'mætɪk] *adj* (**~ally**) systematisch. **sys·tem·a·tize** ['~tɪmətaɪz] *v/t* systematisieren.

T

T [tiː] *s*: F **that's him to a T** das ist er, wie er leibt u. lebt; **fit to a T** wie angegossen passen *od.* sitzen; **suit s.o. to a T** j-m ausgezeichnet passen.

tab [tæb] *s* **1.** Aufhänger *m*, Schlaufe *f*, Lasche *f*. **2.** Etikett *n*, Schildchen *n*. **3.** **keep ~s** (*od.* **a ~**) **on** F j-n überwachen. **4.** F Rechnung *f*: **pick up the ~** (die Rechnung) bezahlen.

tab·er·nac·le ['tæbənækl] *s eccl.* Tabernakel *n*, *m*.

ta·ble ['teɪbl] **I** *s* **1.** Tisch *m*: **at ~** bei Tisch; **at the ~** am Tisch; **under the ~** *fig.* unter der Hand; **drink s.o. under the ~** j-n unter den Tisch trinken; **put on the ~** auf den Tisch legen (*a. fig.*); **turn the ~s** (**on s.o.**) *fig.* den Spieß umdrehen *od.* umkehren. **2.** Tisch *m*, (Tisch)Runde *f*. **3.** Tabelle *f*: → **content**[1] 3. **4.** A Einmaleins *n*. **II** *v/t* **5.** *fig.* auf den Tisch legen. **6.** *Am. fig.* zurückstellen. **'~·cloth** *s* Tischdecke *f*, -tuch *n*.

ta·ble d'hôte [ˌtɑːblˈdəʊt] *s* Menü *n*.

ta·ble| lamp *s* Tischlampe *f*. **~ man·ners** *s pl* Tischmanieren *pl*. **'~·spoon** *s* Eßlöffel *m*.

tab·let ['tæblɪt] *s* **1.** *pharm.* Tablette *f*. **2.** Stück *n* (*Seife*). **3.** (*Stein- etc*)Tafel *f*.

ta·ble| ten·nis *s Sport:* Tischtennis *n*.

'~·ware *s* Geschirr *n* u. Besteck *n*. **~ wine** *s* Tafel-, Tischwein *m*.

tab·loid ['tæblɔɪd] *s* Boulevardblatt *n*, -zeitung *f*. **~ press** *s* Boulevardpresse *f*.

ta·boo, ta·bu [tə'buː] **I** *s* Tabu *n*. **II** *adj* Tabu...: → **subject** Tabu *n*; **be ~** tabu sein. **III** *v/t* tabuisieren, für tabu erklären.

tab·u·lar ['tæbjʊlə] *adj* □ tabellarisch: **in ~ form** tabellarisch. **tab·u·late** ['~leɪt] *v/t* tabellarisch (an)ordnen.

tach·o·graph ['tækəɡrɑːf] *s mot.* Fahrt(en)schreiber *m*.

ta·chom·e·ter [tæ'kɒmɪtə] *s mot.* Drehzahlmesser *m*.

tac·it ['tæsɪt] *adj* □ stillschweigend. **tac·i·turn** ['~tɜːn] *adj* □ schweigsam, wortkarg.

tack [tæk] **I** *s* **1.** Stift *m*, Zwecke *f*. **2.** Heftstich *m*. **3.** **change ~** *fig.* umschwenken. **II** *v/t* **4.** heften (**to** *an acc*). **5.** *Stoffteile* heften. **6.** **~ on** anfügen (**to** *dat*).

tack·le ['tækl] **I** *s* **1.** ✪ Flaschenzug *m*. **2.** (*Angel*)Gerät(e *pl*) *n*. **3.** *Fußball:* Angriff *m* (*auf e-n ballführenden Gegner*); Zweikampf *m*. **II** *v/t* **4.** *Problem etc* angehen. **5.** *j-n* zur Rede stellen (**about** wegen). **6.** *Fußball:* ballführenden Gegner angreifen.

tack·y¹ ['tækɪ] *adj* □ klebrig.

tack·y² [~] *adj* □ *Am.* F schäbig; heruntergekommen.

tact [tækt] *s* Takt *m.* **tact·ful** ['~fʊl] *adj* □ taktvoll.

tac·tic ['tæktɪk] *s* **1.** *oft pl* Taktik *f*, taktischer Zug. **2.** *pl* (*a. sg konstruiert*) ✗, *Sport:* Taktik *f.* **tac·ti·cal** ['~kl] *adj* □ taktisch. **tac·ti·cian** [~'tɪʃn] *s* Taktiker(in).

tact·less ['tæktlɪs] *adj* □ taktlos.

tad·pole ['tædpəʊl] *s zo.* Kaulquappe *f.*

taf·fe·ta ['tæfɪtə] *s* Taft *m.*

taf·fy ['tæfɪ] *Am.* → **toffee.**

tag¹ [tæg] *s* **1.** Etikett *n*; (*Namens-, Preis*)Schild *n.* **2.** stehende Redensart. **3.** *ling.* Frageanhängsel *n.* II *v/t* **4.** etikettieren; *Waren* auszeichnen: ~ (**as**) *fig.* bezeichnen als, *b.s. a.* abstempeln als. **5.** ~ **on** → **tack** 5. III *v/i* **6.** ~ **along** F mitgehen, -kommen; mittrotten: ~ **along behind s.o.** hinter j-m hertrotten.

tag² [~] *s* Fangen *n* (*Kinderspiel*): **play ~.**

tail [teɪl] I *s* **1.** *zo.* Schwanz *m*: **with one's ~ between one's legs** *fig.* mit eingezogenem Schwanz. **2.** Schwanz *m* (*e-s Drachens, e-r Kolonne etc*), (*e-s Flugzeugs etc a.*) hinterer Teil, (*e-s Kometen*) Schweif *m.* **3.** Frack *m.* **4.** *pl* Rück-, Kehrseite *f* (*e-r Münze*): → **head** 14. **5.** F Schatten *m*, Beschatter(in): **put a ~ on** *j-n* beschatten lassen. II *v/t* **6.** F *j-n* beschatten. III *v/i* **7.** ~ **off** schwächer werden, abnehmen. **8.** ~ **back** *bsd. Br.* sich Br. sich stauen (**to** bis zu). **'~·back** *s mot. bsd. Br.* Rückstau *m.* **'~·board** *s mot. etc* Ladeklappe *f.* ~ **coat** *s* Frack *m.* ~ **end** *s* Ende *n*, Schluß *m.* **'~·gate** *s* **1.** *mot.* Hecktür *f.* **2.** *bsd. Am.* → **tailboard.** II *v/i u. v/t* **3.** *mot. bsd. Am.* zu dicht auffahren (auf *acc*). **'~·light** *s mot.* Rücklicht *n.*

tai·lor ['teɪlə] I *s* **1.** Schneider *m.* II *v/t* **2.** schneidern; *fig.* zuschneiden (**to** auf *acc*). **'~-made** *adj* maßgeschneidert (*a. fig.*): ~ **suit** (**costume**) Maßanzug *m* (Schneiderkostüm *n*); **be ~ for** *fig.* wie geschaffen sein für.

'tail·piece *s* Anhang *m*, Zusatz *m.* ~ **pipe** *s mot. Am.* Auspuffrohr *n.* **'~-wind** *s* Rückenwind *m.*

take [teɪk] I *s* **1.** *Film, TV:* Einstellung *f.* **2.** F Einnahmen *pl.* II *v/t* (*irr*) **3.** *allg.*

nehmen: ~ **s.o. by the arm** (**in one's arms**) j-n am Arm (in die Arme) nehmen; **be ~n** besetzt sein (*Platz*); → **care** 2, 3, **place** 1, **prisoner, seat** 1, *etc.* **4.** (weg)nehmen. **5.** mitnehmen. **6.** bringen. **7.** ✗ *Stadt etc* einnehmen; (*Schach etc*) *Figur, Stein* schlagen; *Gefangene* machen. **8.** *Preis etc* erringen; → **lead** 1. **9.** *Scheck etc* (an)nehmen; *Rat* annehmen: → **advice** 1, **blame** 4, **tip³** 2. **10.** *Kritik etc* hinnehmen. **11.** fassen; Platz bieten für. **12.** *et.* aushalten, ertragen. **13.** dauern: **it took him two hours to do it** er brauchte zwei Stunden, um es zu tun. **14.** *Prüfung, Spaziergang etc* machen; *Schritte* unternehmen; *Risiko* eingehen: → **oath** 1, **risk** I, **step** 4, **trouble** 7, *etc.* **15.** *Medizin etc* (ein)nehmen. **16.** → **take down** 4. **17. be ~n by** (*od.* **with**) angetan sein von. **18. he's got what it ~s** F er bringt alle Voraussetzungen mit. III *v/i* (*irr*) **19.** ✿ wirken, anschlagen.

Verbindungen mit Präpositionen:

take| af·ter *v/i* j-m nachschlagen; j-m ähneln. ~ **for** *v/t:* **what do you take me for?** wofür hältst du mich eigentlich? ~ **from** *v/t* **1. take s.th. from s.o.** j-m et. wegnehmen. **2.** ⅍ abziehen von. **3.** *Single* auskoppeln aus (*e-m Album*). **4. you can take it from me that** du kannst mir glauben, daß. ~ **to** *v/i* **1.** Gefallen finden an (*dat*). **2.** ~ **doing s.th.** anfangen, et. zu tun. **3.** sich flüchten *od.* zurückziehen in (*acc*): ~ **one's bed** ins Bett gehen; → **heel²** 1.

Verbindungen mit Adverbien:

take| a·long *v/t* mitnehmen. ~ **a·part** *v/t* auseinandernehmen (*a. fig.* F), zerlegen. ~ **a·side** *v/t* j-n beiseite nehmen. ~ **a·way** I *v/t* **1.** wegnehmen (**from s.o.** j-m). **2.** ... *to* ~ *Br.* ... zum Mitnehmen (*Essen*). II *v/i* **3.** ~ **from s.th.** e-r Sache Abbruch tun, et. schmälern. ~ **back** *v/t* **1.** ✗ *Land* zurückerobern. **2.** zurückbringen. **3.** *Ware, et. Gesagtes* zurücknehmen. **4.** bei *j-m* Erinnerungen wachrufen; *j-n* zurückversetzen (**to** in *acc*). ~ **down** *v/t* **1.** herunternehmen, *Plakat etc* abnehmen. **2.** *Hose* herunterlassen. **3.** auseinandernehmen, zerlegen. **4.** (sich) *et.* aufschreiben *od.* notieren, sich *Notizen* machen. ~ **in** *v/t* **1.** j-n (bei sich) aufnehmen: → **lodger.** **2.** *fig. et.* einschließen.

3. *Kleidungsstück* enger machen. **4.** *et.* begreifen. **5.** *j-n* hereinlegen: *be taken in by* hereinfallen auf (*acc*). **~ off I** *v/t* **1.** *Kleidungsstück* ablegen, ausziehen, *Hut etc* abnehmen. **2.** ✚ abnehmen, amputieren. **3.** *Theaterstück etc* absetzen. **4.** → *off* 9. **5.** ✚ *Rabatt etc* abziehen. **6.** F *j-n* nachahmen, -machen. **II** *v/i* **7.** ✈ abheben. **8.** *Sport:* abspringen. **9.** F sich aufmachen. **~ on** *v/t* **1.** *j-n* einstellen. **2.** *Arbeit etc* an-, übernehmen. **3.** *Ausdruck, Farbe etc* annehmen. **4.** sich anlegen mit. **~ out** *v/t* **1.** herausnehmen, *Zahn* ziehen: *take s.o. out of himself* j-n auf andere Gedanken bringen. **2.** *j-n* ausführen, ausgehen mit. **3.** *Versicherung* abschließen. **4.** *s-n Frust etc* auslassen (*on an dat*): *take it out on s.o.* sich an j-m abreagieren. **~ o·ver I** *v/t Amt, Macht, Verantwortung etc* übernehmen. **~ up I** *v/t* **1.** Flüssigkeit aufnehmen, -saugen. **2.** *Aufmerksamkeit, Zeit* in Anspruch nehmen, *Platz* einnehmen: *be taken up with* stark in Anspruch genommen sein von. **3.** *Vorschlag etc* aufgreifen. **4.** **~ doing s.th.** anfangen, sich mit et. zu beschäftigen. **5.** *take s.o. up on his offer* auf j-s Angebot zurückkommen. **6.** *Erzählung etc* aufnehmen, fortfahren mit. **II** *v/i* **7.** sich einlassen (*with* mit).

'**take·a·way** *s Br.* **1.** Essen *n* zum Mitnehmen. **2.** Restaurant *n* mit Straßenverkauf. '**~home** *adj:* **~ pay** Nettolohn *m*, -gehalt *n*.

tak·en ['teɪkən] *pp von* **take**.

'**take·off** *s* **1.** ✈ Abheben *n*; Start *m:* → *ready* 1. **2.** *Sport:* Absprung *m*. **3.** F Nachahmung *f:* *do a* ~ *of* → *take off* 6. '**~out** *Am.* → *takeaway*. '**~o·ver** *s bsd.* ✚ Übernahme *f*.

tak·er ['teɪkə] *s* Interessent(in). '**tak·ings** *s pl* Einnahmen *pl*.

talc [tælk] *s* **1.** *min.* Talk *m*. **2.** → *talcum powder*.

tal·cum pow·der ['tælkəm] *s* Talkumpuder *m*; Körperpuder *m*.

tale [teɪl] *s* **1.** Erzählung *f*; Geschichte *f:* *tell* ~*s* petzen; *tell* ~*s about j-n* verpetzen; *tell* ~*s out of school fig.* aus der Schule plaudern; → *fairy tale, old* 1. **2.** Lüge(ngeschichte) *f*, Märchen *n*.

tal·ent ['tælənt] *s* Talent *n* (*a. Person*),

Begabung *f*; *coll.* Talente *pl* (*Personen*): ~ *for acting* schauspielerisches Talent; *have great* ~ sehr begabt sein; *have a great* ~ *for music* musikalisch sehr begabt sein; ~ *scout* (*bsd. Sport*) Talentsucher(in). '**tal·ent·ed** *adj* talentiert, begabt.

tal·is·man ['tælɪzmən] *s* Talisman *m*.

talk [tɔːk] **I** *s* **1.** Gespräch *n* (*a. pol. etc*), Unterhaltung *f* (*with* mit; *about* über *acc*): *have a long* ~ *with s.o.* ein langes Gespräch mit j-m führen, sich lange mit j-m unterhalten. **2.** Sprache *f* (*Art zu reden*): → *baby talk*. **3.** Gerede *n:* *there is a lot of* ~ *about* es ist viel die Rede von; *be the* ~ *of the town* Stadtgespräch sein; → *small* I. **4.** Vortrag *m:* *give a* ~ e-n Vortrag halten (*to* vor *dat; about, on* über *acc*). **II** *v/i* **5.** reden, sprechen, sich unterhalten (*to, with* mit; *about* über *acc; of* von): ~ *about s.th. a.* et. besprechen; *get o.s.* ~*ed about* ins Gerede kommen; ~*ing of* da wir gerade von ... sprechen; ~ *round s.th.* um et. herumreden; *you can* ~*!, look who's* ~*ing!, you're a fine one to* ~*!* F das sagst ausgerechnet du!; → *all* 3, *big* 7, *devil* 1, *hat.* **III** *v/t* **6.** Unsinn *etc* reden. **7.** reden *od.* sprechen *od.* sich unterhalten über (*acc*): → *shop* 3. **8.** ~ *s.o. into s.th.* j-n zu et. überreden; ~ *s.o. into doing s.th.* j-n überreden, et. zu tun; ~ *s.o. out of s.th.* j-m et. ausreden; ~ *s.o. out of doing s.th.* es j-m ausreden, et. zu tun; ~ *one's way out of s.th.* sich aus et. herausreden.
Verbindungen mit Adverbien:

talk down I *v/t Flugzeug* herunterspre-chen. **II** *v/i:* ~ *to s.o.* herablassend mit j-m reden. ~ *out* *v/t Problem etc* ausdiskutieren. ~ *o·ver* *v/t Problem etc* besprechen (*with* mit). ~ *round* *v/t j-n* bekehren (*to* zu), umstimmen.

talk·a·tive ['tɔːkətɪv] *adj* □ gesprächig, redselig. '**talk·er** *s:* *be a good* ~ gut reden können. '**talk·ing I** *s* Sprechen *n*, Reden *n:* *do all the* ~ allein das Wort führen. **II** *adj* sprechend: ~ *doll* Sprechpuppe *f;* ~ *point* Gesprächsthema *n;* Streitpunkt *m.* '**talk·ing-to** *pl* -tos *s* F Standpauke *f:* *give s.o. a* ~ j-m e-e Standpauke halten.

talk show *s* TV *bsd. Am.* Talk-Show *f*.

tall [tɔːl] *adj* **1.** groß (*Person*), hoch (*Ge-*

bäude etc). **2.** F unglaublich (*Geschichte*): *that's a ~ order* das ist ein bißchen viel verlangt.

tal·low ['tæləʊ] *s* Talg *m*.

tal·ly ['tælɪ] I *s Sport etc*: Stand *m*: *keep a ~ of* Buch führen über (*acc*). II *v/i* übereinstimmen (*with* mit). III *v/t a. ~ up* zs.-rechnen, -zählen.

tal·on ['tælən] *s orn*. Kralle *f*, Klaue *f*.

tam·bour ['tæm‚bʊə] *s* Stickrahmen *m*. **tam·bou·rine** [‚~bə'riːn] *s ♪* Tamburin *n*.

tame [teɪm] I *adj* □ **1.** *zo*. zahm. **2.** F fad, lahm. II *v/t* **3.** *Tier* zähmen; *Leidenschaft etc* (be)zähmen.

tam·per ['tæmpə] *v/i*: ~ *with* sich zu schaffen machen an (*dat*).

tam·pon ['tæmpɒn] *s ♥* Tampon *m*.

tan [tæn] I *v/t* **1.** j-n, *Haut* bräunen. **2.** *Fell* gerben: → *hide*¹ 1. II *v/i* **3.** bräunen, braun werden. III *s* **4.** Bräune *f*. IV *adj* **5.** gelbbraun.

tan·dem ['tændəm] *s* Tandem *n*: *in ~ fig*. zusammen, gemeinsam (*with* mit).

tang [tæŋ] *s* (scharfer) Geruch *od*. Geschmack.

tan·gent ['tændʒənt] *s ♠* Tangente *f*: *fly* (*od*. *go*) *off at a ~ fig*. plötzlich (vom Thema) abschweifen.

tan·ge·rine [‚tændʒə'riːn] *s ♀* Mandarine *f*.

tan·gi·ble ['tændʒəbl] *adj* greifbar, *fig. a*. handfest.

tan·gle ['tæŋgl] I *v/t* **1.** *a. ~ up* verwirren, durcheinanderbringen (*beide a. fig.*), verheddern: *get ~d* → 2. II *v/i* **2.** sich verwirren, durcheinanderkommen, sich verheddern (*alle a. fig.*). **3.** *~ with* F aneinandergeraten mit (*dat*). III *s* Gewirr *n*, *fig. a*. Wirrwarr *m*, Durcheinander *n*.

tan·go ['tæŋgəʊ] I *pl* **-gos** *s ♪* Tango *m*. II *v/i* Tango tanzen: *it takes two to ~ fig*. dazu gehören zwei.

tank [tæŋk] *s* **1.** *mot. etc* Tank *m*. **2.** ✕ Panzer *m*. II *v/t* **3.** *~ed up* Br. F voll (*betrunken*).

tank·ard ['tæŋkəd] *s* (Bier)Humpen *m*.

tank·er ['tæŋkə] *s ♣* Tanker *m*, Tankschiff *n*; *mot*. Tank-, ✈ *a*. Kesselwagen *m*.

tan·ta·lize ['tæntəlaɪz] *v/t* j-n aufreizen; hinhalten (*with* mit). **'tan·ta·liz·ing** *adj* □ verlockend.

tan·ta·mount ['tæntəmaʊnt] *adj*: *be ~ to* gleichbedeutend sein mit, hinauslaufen auf (*acc*).

tan·trum ['tæntrəm] *s* Koller *m*: *fly into* (*od*. *throw*) *a ~* e-n Koller kriegen.

tap¹ [tæp] I *v/t* **1.** a) → 3: ~ *s.o. on the shoulder* j-m auf die Schulter klopfen, b) antippen. **2.** *mit den Fingern, Füßen* klopfen (*on* auf *acc*), mit *den Fingern* trommeln (*on* auf *acc, dat*). II *v/i* **3.** ~ *on* (leicht) klopfen an (*acc*) *od*. auf (*acc*) *od*. gegen. III *s* **4.** (leichtes) Klopfen; Klaps *m*.

tap² [~] I *s* **1.** ⊙ Hahn *m*: *beer on ~* Bier *n* vom Faß; *have s.th. on ~ fig*. et. zur Hand *od*. auf Lager haben. II *v/t* **2.** *Faß* anzapfen, anstechen. **3.** *Telefon(leitung)* anzapfen, abhören. **4.** *Naturschätze etc* erschließen; *Vorräte etc* angreifen. **5.** ~ *for* Br. F j-n anpumpen *od*. anzapfen um.

tape [teɪp] *s* **1.** *allg*. Band *n*; (*Video-etc*)Kassette *f*. **2.** (Band)Aufnahme *f*; *TV* Aufzeichnung *f*. **3.** *Sport*: Zielband *n*: → *breast* II 4. → **tape measure**. II *v/t* **5.** *a. ~ up* (mit Klebeband) zukleben. **6.** (auf Band) aufnehmen; *TV* aufzeichnen: → *music* Musik *f* vom Band. ~ **deck** *s* Tapedeck *n* ([in e-e Stereoanlage eingebauter] Kassettenrecorder ohne eigenen Verstärker u. Lautsprecher). ~ **meas·ure** *s* Maß-, Meßband *n*, Bandmaß *n*.

ta·per ['teɪpə] *v/i* **1.** *a. ~ off* spitz zulaufen, sich verjüngen. **2.** *a. ~ off fig*. langsam nachlassen.

'tape|-re‚cord → **tape** 6. ~ **re·cord·er** *s* Tonbandgerät *n*.

ta·pes·try ['tæpɪstrɪ] *s* Gobelin *m*, Wandteppich *m*.

'tape·worm *s zo*. Bandwurm *m*.

tap wa·ter *s* Leitungswasser *n*.

tar [tɑː] I *s* Teer *m*. II *v/t* teeren: ~ *and feather* j-n teeren u. federn; *they are all ~red with the same brush fig. contp.* sie sind alle gleich.

ta·ran·tu·la [tə'ræntjʊlə] *s zo*. Tarantel *f*.

tar·dy ['tɑːdɪ] *adj* □ spät, verspätet.

tare [teə] *s ♥* Tara *f*.

tar·get ['tɑːgɪt] I *s* **1.** (Schieß-, Ziel-)Scheibe *f*; *fig*. Zielscheibe *f* (*des Spotts etc*). **2.** ✕ Ziel *n* (*a. fig.*); ♥ *a*. Soll *n*: *set o.s. a ~ of doing s.th.* (es) sich zum Ziel setzen, et. zu tun. II *v/t* **3.** *be ~ed at* (*od*. *on*) gerichtet sein auf (*acc*); *fig*. abzielen auf (*acc*). **~ group** *s* Zielgruppe *f*. **~ lan·guage** *s* Zielsprache *f*.

tar·iff ['tærɪf] *s* **1.** Zoll(tarif) *m*. **2.** *bsd. Br.* Preisverzeichnis *n* (*in Hotel etc*).

tar·mac ['tɑːmæk] *s* **1.** Asphalt *m*. **2.** ✈ Rollfeld *n*.

tar·nish ['tɑːnɪʃ] **I** *v/t* Ansehen *etc* beflecken. **II** *v/i* anlaufen (*Metall*).

tar·pau·lin [tɑːˈpɔːlɪn] *s* Plane *f*; ♣ Persenning *f*.

tar·ra·gon ['tærəgən] *s* ♣ Estragon *m*.

tart¹ [tɑːt] *adj* □ **1.** herb; sauer. **2.** *fig.* scharf, beißend.

tart² [~] *s* **1.** Obstkuchen *m*; Obsttörtchen *n*. **2.** F Flittchen *n*; Nutte *f*.

tar·tan ['tɑːtən] *s* Schottenstoff *m*; Schottenmuster *n*.

tar·tar ['tɑːtə] *s* 🛢 Weinstein *m*; Zahnstein *m*.

task [tɑːsk] *s* Aufgabe *f*: **take s.o. to ~** *fig.* j-n zurechtweisen (**for** wegen). **~ force** *s* ✗ Sonder-, Spezialeinheit *f* (*a. der Polizei*).

tas·sel ['tæsl] *s* Troddel *f*, Quaste *f*.

taste [teɪst] **I** *s* **1.** Geschmack(ssinn) *m*: → **sense** **1.** **2.** Geschmack *m*: **have no ~** nach nichts schmecken; **leave a bad ~ in s.o.'s mouth** *fig.* e-n bitteren *od.* schlechten Nachgeschmack bei j-m hinterlassen. **3.** Kostprobe *f*: **have a ~ of** a) → 6, b) *fig.* e-n Vorgeschmack bekommen von. **4.** *fig.* Geschmack *m*: **to s.o.'s ~** nach j-s Geschmack; **be in bad** (*od.* **poor**) **~** geschmacklos sein; → **account** 3, **matter** 3. **5.** *fig.* Vorliebe *f* (**for** für). **II** *v/t* **6.** kosten, probieren. **7.** schmecken. **8.** *fig.* kosten, erleben, kennenlernen. **III** *v/i* **9.** schmecken (**of** nach). **taste·ful** ['~fʊl] *adj* □ *fig.* geschmackvoll. **'taste·less** *adj* □ geschmacklos (*a. fig.*). **'tast·y** *adj* □ schmackhaft.

tat [tæt] *s* → **tit¹**.

ta·ta [ˌtæˈtɑː] *int Br.* F tschüs!

tat·tered ['tætəd] *adj* zerlumpt (*Kleidung, Person*); *fig.* ruiniert, ramponiert (*Ruf etc*). **'tat·ters** *s pl* Fetzen *pl*, Lumpen *pl*: **be in ~** zerlumpt sein (*Kleidung*); *fig.* ruiniert *od.* ramponiert sein (*Ruf etc*).

tat·tle ['tætl] **I** *v/i* klatschen, tratschen. **II** *s* Klatsch *m*, Tratsch *m*.

tat·too¹ [təˈtuː] **I** *v/t* **1.** tätowieren. **2.**

Muster etc eintätowieren (**on** in *acc*). **II** *s* **3.** Tätowierung *f*.

tat·too² [~] *s* ✗ Zapfenstreich *m*; (ms abendliche) Musikparade.

tat·ty ['tætɪ] *adj* □ *bsd. Br.* F schäbig (*Kleidung, Möbel etc*).

taught [tɔːt] *pret u. pp von* **teach**.

taunt [tɔːnt] **I** *v/t* verhöhnen, -spotten (**for, with** wegen). **II** *s* höhnische *od.* spöttische Bemerkung.

Tau·rus ['tɔːrəs] *s ast.* Stier *m*: **be (a) ~** Stier sein.

taut [tɔːt] *adj* □ **1.** straff (*Seil etc*). **2.** *fig.* angespannt (*Gesichtsausdruck etc*). **'taut·en** **I** *v/t* spannen, straffen, strat anziehen. **II** *v/i* sich spannen *od.* strat fen.

tau·tol·o·gy [tɔːˈtɒlədʒɪ] *s rhet.* Tautolo gie *f*.

taw·dry ['tɔːdrɪ] *adj* □ (billig u.) geschmacklos.

taw·ny ['tɔːnɪ] *adj* gelbbraun.

tax [tæks] **I** *s* **1.** Steuer *f* (**on** auf *acc*): **before** (**after**) **~** vor (nach) Abzug der Steuern, brutto (netto); → **put** 2. **II** *v* **2.** besteuern. **3.** *j-s* Geduld *etc* strapazie ren. **'tax·a·ble** *adj* steuerpflichtig.

tax·a·tion *s* Besteuerung *f*.

tax| brack·et *s* Steuergruppe *f*, -klasse *f*. **~·de·duct·i·ble** *adj* (steuerlich) absetzbar. **~ e·va·sion** *s* Steuerhinterziehun *f*. **~·free** *adj u. adv* steuerfrei. **~ ha·ven** *s* Steueroase *f*, -paradies *n*.

tax·i ['tæksɪ] **I** *s* Taxi *n*, Taxe *f*. **II** *v/i* ✈ rollen. **'~·cab** *s* → **taxi** I. **~ driv·er** *s* Taxifahrer(in). **'~·me·ter** *s* Taxamete *m*, *n*, Fahrpreisanzeiger *m*.

tax·ing ['tæksɪŋ] *adj* anstrengend.

tax·i rank, **~ stand** *s* Taxistand *m*. **'tax|·pay·er** *s* Steuerzahler(in). **~ rate** *s* Steuersatz *m*. **~ rea·sons** *s pl* steuer liche Gründe *pl*. **~ re·turn** *s* Steuer klärung *f*.

'T-bone (steak) *s* T-bone-Steak *n* (*Stea aus dem Rippenstück des Rinds*).

tea [tiː] *s* Tee *m*: **not for all the ~ in Chin** nicht um alles in der Welt; → **cup** high tea. **~ bag** *s* Tee-, Aufgußbeutel *m*. **~ break** *s* Teepause *f*. **~ cad·dy** *s* Teebüchse *f*, -dose *f*.

teach [tiːtʃ] (*irr*) **I** *v/t* **1.** Fach lehre unterrichten. **2.** *j-n*, *a. j-m et.* lehren, *j* unterrichten in (*dat*); *j-m et.* beibri gen: **~ s.o. a lesson** *fig.* j-m e-n Lektic erteilen. **II** v/i **3.** unterrichten (*at* an e-r *Schule*). '**teach·er** s Lehrer(in). '**teach·ing** s **1.** Unterrichten n; Lehrberuf m. **2.** Lehre f.

tea| cloth → **tea towel.** ~ **co·sy** (*Am.* **co·zy**) s Teewärmer m. '**~cup** s Teetasse f: → **storm** 1. '**~house** s Teehaus n.

teak [tiːk] s Teak(holz) n.

'**tea| ket·tle** s Tee-, Wasserkessel m. '**~ leaf** s (*irr leaf*) **1.** Teeblatt n. **2.** *Br. sl.* Langfinger m.

team [tiːm] s **1.** *Sport*: Mannschaft f, Team n, *allg. a.* Gruppe f. **2.** Gespann n. **II** v/i **3.** ~ **up** sich zs.-tun (*with* mit). ~ **ef·fort** s Teamwork n: *by a* ~ mit vereinten Kräften. ~ **game** s *Sport*: Mannschaftsspiel n. '**~mate** s *Sport*: Mannschaftskamerad(in). ~ **spir·it** s *Sport*: Mannschaftsgeist m; *allg.* Gemeinschaftsgeist m.

team·ster ['tiːmstə] s LKW-Fahrer m.

'**team·work** s *Sport*: Mannschafts-, Zs.-spiel n; *allg.* Teamwork n.

'**tea| par·ty** s Teegesellschaft f. '**~pot** s Teekanne f: → **tempest.**

tear¹ [tiə] s Träne f: *be almost in* ~s den Tränen nahe sein, fast weinen; ~s *pl of joy* Freudentränen pl; → **burst** 3, **near** 3, **roll** 7, **run** 11.

tear² [teə] **I** s **1.** Riß m. **II** v/t (*irr*) **2.** zerreißen; sich *et.* zerreißen (**on** an *dat*): ~ *a muscle* sich e-n Muskel reißen, sich e-n Muskelriß zuziehen; *torn muscle* Muskelriß m; → **piece** 1, **shred** 1. **3.** weg-, losreißen (*from* von): ~ *s.th. from s.o. a.* j-m *et.* entreißen; → **hair. 4.** *be torn between ... and fig.* hin- u. hergerissen sein zwischen (*dat*) ... u. **III** v/i (*irr*) **5.** (zer)reißen. **6.** F rasen, sausen. **7.** ~ *into s.o.* F über j-n herfallen (*a. mit Worten*).

Verbindungen mit Adverbien:

tear| a·way v/t weg-, losreißen (*from* von) (*a. fig.*). ~ **down** v/t **1.** *Plakat etc* herunterreißen. **2.** *Haus etc* abreißen. ~ **off** v/t **1.** abreißen; abtrennen. **2.** sich *Kleidung* vom Leib reißen. **3.** F *Aufsatz etc* hinhauen. ~ **out** v/t (her)ausreißen (**of** aus); *Baum* entwurzeln: → **hair.** ~ **up** v/t **1.** *Straße etc* aufreißen. **2.** zerreißen.

'**tear·drop** ['tiədrɒp] s Träne f.

'**tear·ful** ['tiəfʊl] adj □ **1.** weinend. **2.** tränenreich (*Abschied etc*).

'**tear gas** [tiə] s Tränengas n.

tear·ing ['teəriŋ] adj: *be in a* ~ *hurry* F es schrecklich eilig haben.

'**tear-jerk·er** ['tiə‚dʒɜːkə] s F Schmachtfetzen m.

'**tear-off** ['teərɒf] adj: ~ *calendar* Abreißkalender m.

'**tea-room** [‚ruːm] s Teestube f.

tease [tiːz] **I** v/t j-n, *Tier* necken, j-n hänseln (*about* wegen); j-n, *Tier* reizen. **II** v/i: *he is only teasing* er macht nur Spaß. **III** s Necker(in), Hänsler(in). '**teas·er** s **1.** → **tease** III. **2.** F harte Nuß.

tea| ser·vice, ~ set s Teeservice n. '**~spoon** s Teelöffel m.

teat [tiːt] s **1.** zo. Zitze f. **2.** *Br.* (Gummi)Sauger m (*e-r Saugflasche*).

'**tea| tow·el** s *bsd. Br.* Geschirrtuch n. ~ **trol·ley** s *bsd. Br.*, ~ **wag·on** s *bsd. Am.* Tee-, Serviertuchwagen m.

tech·ni·cal ['teknɪkl] adj □ **1.** *allg.* technisch: ~ *knockout* (*Boxen*) technischer K. o. **2.** fachlich, Fach...: ~ *term* Fachausdruck m. **tech·ni·cal·i·ty** [‚kælətɪ] s technische Einzelheit. **tech'ni·cian** [‚ʃn] s Techniker(in).

tech·nique [tek'niːk] s **1.** ☼ Technik f, Verfahren n. **2.** ♪, *paint., Sport etc*: Technik f.

tech·no·crat ['teknəʊkræt] s Technokrat(in).

tech·no·log·i·cal [‚teknə'lɒdʒɪkl] adj □ technologisch; technisch. **tech·nol·o·gist** [‚'nɒlədʒɪst] s Technologe m, Technologin f. **tech'nol·o·gy** s Technologie f; Technik f.

ted·dy (bear) ['tedɪ] s Teddy(bär) m.

te·di·ous ['tiːdjəs] adj □ langweilig. **te·di·um** ['tiːdjəm] s Langweiligkeit f.

teem¹ [tiːm] v/i (*with*) wimmeln (von); strotzen (von, vor *dat*): *the square was* ~*ing with people* auf dem Platz wimmelte es von Menschen.

teem² [‚] v/i: *it is* ~*ing with rain* es regnet in Strömen.

teen·age(d) ['tiːneɪdʒ(d)] adj **1.** im Teenageralter. **2.** Teenager..., für Teenager. '**teen‚ag·er** s Teenager m.

teens [tiːnz] s pl: *be in one's* ~ im Teenageralter sein.

tee·ny ['tiːnɪ], **tee·ny-wee·ny** [‚'wiːnɪ] adj F klitzeklein, winzig.

tee shirt [tiː] s T-Shirt n.

tee·ter ['tiːtə] v/i (sch)wanken.

teeth

teeth [tiːθ] *pl von* **tooth.**
teethe [tiːð] *v/i* zahnen. **'teeth·ing** *adj:* ~ **troubles** *pl fig.* Kinderkrankheiten *pl.*
tee·to·tal·er *s Am.,* **tee·to·tal·ler** *s bsd. Br.* [tiːˈtəʊtlə] *s* Abstinenzler(in).
tel·e·cast ['telɪkɑːst] **I** *v/t (mst irr)* im Fernsehen übertragen *od.* bringen. **II** *s* Fernsehsendung *f.*
tel·e·com·mu·ni·ca·tions ['telɪkəˌmjuːnɪˈkeɪʃnz] *s pl* Telekommunikation *f,* Fernmeldewesen *n.* ~ **sat·el·lite** *s* Fernmelde-, Nachrichtensatellit *m.*
tel·e·gen·ic [ˌtelɪˈdʒenɪk] *adj* (~**ally**) *TV* telegen.
tel·e·gram ['telɪɡræm] *s* Telegramm *n:* **by** ~ telegrafisch.
tel·e·graph ['telɪɡrɑːf] **I** *s:* **by** ~ telegrafisch. **II** *v/t j-m et.* telegrafieren.
tel·e·graph·ese [ˌtelɪɡrɑːˈfiːz] *s* Telegrammstil *m.* **tel·e·graph·ic** [ˌtelɪˈɡræfɪk] *adj* (~**ally**) telegrafisch. **te·leg·ra·phy** [tɪˈleɡrəfɪ] *s* Telegrafie *f.*
te·lep·a·thy [tɪˈlepəθɪ] *s* Telepathie *f,* Gedankenübertragung *f.*
tel·e·phone ['telɪfəʊn] **I** *s* **1.** Telefon *n:* **by** ~ telefonisch; **be on the** ~ Telefon(anschluß) haben; am Telefon sein. **2.** Hörer *m.* **II** *v/i* **3.** telefonieren, anrufen. **III** *v/t* **4.** anrufen: ~ *s.th. to s.o.* j-m et. telefonisch durchgeben. **IV** *adj* **5.** Telefon...: ~ **booth** *(Br. box)* Telefon-, Fernsprechzelle *f;* ~ **call** Telefonanruf *m,* -gespräch *n;* ~ **directory** Telefon-, Fernsprechbuch *n;* ~ **exchange** Fernsprechamt *n;* ~ **number** Telefonnummer *f.* **te·leph·o·nist** [tɪˈlefənɪst] *s bsd. Br.* Telefonist(in).
tel·e·pho·to lens ['telɪˌfəʊtəʊ] *s phot.* Teleobjektiv *n.*
tel·e·print·er ['telɪˌprɪntə] *s* ⚙ Fernschreiber *m.*
tel·e·scope ['telɪskəʊp] **I** *s* **1.** Teleskop *n,* Fernrohr *n.* **II** *v/t* **2.** *a.* ~ **together** zs.-, ineinanderschieben. **3.** *fig.* verkürzen, komprimieren *(into* zu). **III** *v/i* **4.** sich zs.- *od.* ineinanderschieben (lassen).
tel·e·scop·ic [ˌtelɪˈskɒpɪk] *adj* (~**ally**) **1.** teleskopisch: ~ **sight** Zielfernrohr *n.* **2.** ausziehbar: ~ **aerial** *(bsd. Am.* **antenna)** Teleskopantenne *f;* ~ **umbrella** Taschenschirm *m.*
tel·e·text ['telɪtekst] *s* Bildschirmtext *m.*
tel·e·vise ['telɪvaɪz] → **telecast** I.
tel·e·vi·sion ['telɪˌvɪʒn] *I s* **1.** Fernsehen

n: **on** *(the)* ~ im Fernsehen; **watch** ~ fernsehen; **work in** ~ beim Fernsehen beschäftigt sein. **2.** Fernsehapparat *m,* -gerät *n.* **II** *adj* **3.** Fernseh...: ~ **set** → 2.
tel·ex ['teleks] *s* **1.** Telex *n,* Fernschreiben *n.* **2.** ⚙ Fernschreiber *m.*
tell [tel] *(irr)* **I** *v/t* **1.** sagen, erzählen: *I can't* ~ *you how ...* ich kann dir gar nicht sagen, wie ...; *you are* ~*ing me!* F wem sagst du das!; → **another** 2. **2.** *Geschichte etc* erzählen: → **tale** 1. **3.** *s-n Namen etc* nennen; *Grund etc* angeben; *Zeit anzeigen (Uhr).* **4.** (mit Bestimmtheit) sagen; erkennen **(by** an *dat):* *I can't* ~ *one from the other, I can't* ~ *them apart* ich kann sie nicht auseinanderhalten. **5.** *j-m* sagen, befehlen **(to do** zu tun). **6.** ~ **off** F *j-m* Bescheid stoßen **(for** wegen). **II** *v/i* **7. who can** ~? wer weiß?; *you can never (od. never can)* ~ man kann nie wissen. **8.** ~ **on s.o.** *j-n* verpetzen *od.* verraten. **9.** sich auswirken **(on** bei, auf *acc),* sich bemerkbar machen: ~ **against** sprechen gegen; von Nachteil sein für. **'tell·er** *s bsd. Am.* Kassierer(in) *(e-r Bank).*
tell·ing ['telɪŋ] *adj* □ **1.** aufschlußreich. **2.** schlagend *(Argument).* **ˌ**~**'off** *s: give s.o. a (good)* ~ F *j-m* (kräftig) Bescheid stoßen **(for** wegen).
'tell·tale I *adj* verräterisch. **II** *s* F Zuträger(in), Petze *f.*
tel·ly ['telɪ] *s bsd. Br.* F. **1.** → **television** 1. **2.** Fernseher *m (Gerät).*
te·mer·i·ty [tɪˈmerətɪ] *s* Kühnheit *f,* Frechheit *f.*
temp [temp] *Br.* F **I** *s (von e-r Agentur vermittelte)* Zeitsekretärin. **II** *v/i* als Zeitsekretärin arbeiten.
tem·per ['tempə] **I** *s* **1.** Temperament *n,* Gemüt(sart *f) n,* Wesen(sart *f) n.* **2.** Laune *f,* Stimmung *f:* **be in a bad** ~ schlecht gelaunt sein; **keep one's** ~ ruhig bleiben; **lose one's** ~ die Beherrschung verlieren. **3.** F **be in a** ~ gereizt *od.* wütend sein; **fly into a** ~ an die Decke gehen; → **fit** 1, **work** 8. **II** *v/t* **4.** ⚙ *Stahl* härten. **tem·per·a·ment** ['temprəmənt] *s* **1.** → **temper** 1. **2.** Temperament *n,* Lebhaftigkeit *f.* **tem·per·a·men·tal** [ˌtemprəˈmentl] *adj* □ **1.** reizbar; launisch. **2.** veranlagungsmäßig, anlagebedingt: ~*ly a.* von der Veranlagung her, von Natur aus.

tem·per·ate ['tempərət] *adj* gemäßigt (*Klima, Zone*).

tem·per·a·ture ['temprətʃə] *s* Temperatur *f*: **have** (*od.* **be running**) **a ~** erhöhte Temperatur *od.* Fieber haben; **take s.o.'s ~** j-s Temperatur messen.

tem·pest ['tempɪst] *s* (heftiger) Sturm (*poet. außer in*): **~ in a teapot** *Am. fig.* Sturm im Wasserglas. **tem·pes·tu·ous** [~'pestjuəs] *adj* □ *poet. od. fig.* stürmisch.

tem·pi [tempi:] *pl von* **tempo**.

tem·ple¹ [templ] *s* Tempel *m*.

tem·ple² [~] *s anat.* Schläfe *f*.

tem·po ['tempəʊ] *pl* **-pos, -pi** ['~pi:] *s* ♩ Tempo *n* (*a. fig.*).

tem·po·ral¹ ['tempərəl] *adj* □ **1.** weltlich. **2.** *ling.* temporal, Zeit..., der Zeit.

tem·po·ral² [~] *adj anat.* Schläfen...: **~ bone** Schläfenbein *n*.

tem·po·rar·y ['tempərəri] *adj* □ vorübergehend, zeitweilig. **'tem·po·rize** *v/i* Zeit zu gewinnen suchen.

tempt [tempt] *v/t* **1.** j-n in Versuchung führen (*a. eccl.*); j-n verführen (**to** zu; **to do** [*od.* **into doing**] **s.th.** dazu, et. zu tun): **be ~ed to do s.th.** versucht *od.* geneigt sein, et. zu tun. **2. ~ fate** (*od.* **providence**) das Schicksal herausfordern. **temp'ta·tion** *s* Versuchung *f* (*a. eccl.*), Verführung *f.* **'tempt·er** *s* Verführer *m.* **'tempt·ing** *adj* □ verführerisch. **'tempt·ress** *s* Verführerin *f.*

ten [ten] **I** *adj* **1.** zehn. **II** *s* **2.** Zehn *f*: **~ of hearts** Herzzehn; **~s** *pl of thousands* Zehntausende *pl.* **3.** ⚑ Zehner *m.*

ten·a·ble ['tenəbl] *adj* haltbar (*Theorie etc*).

te·na·cious [tɪ'neɪʃəs] *adj* □ hartnäckig, zäh. **te·na·cious·ness, te·nac·i·ty** [tɪ'næsətɪ] *s* Hartnäckigkeit *f*, Zähigkeit *f.*

ten·an·cy ['tenənsɪ] *s* Pacht-, Mietdauer *f.*

ten·ant ['tenənt] *s* Pächter(in), Mieter(in).

tend¹ [tend] *v/i* neigen, tendieren (**to, toward[s]** zu): **~ to do s.th.** dazu neigen, et. zu tun; **~ upwards** e-e steigende Tendenz haben (*Preise etc*).

tend² [~] **I** *v/t* j-n pflegen, *a.* Wunde versorgen. **II** *v/i*: **~ to → I.**

tend·en·cy ['tendənsɪ] *s* Tendenz *f*; Neigung *f*: **have a ~ to** (*od.* **toward[s]**)

neigen *od.* tendieren zu; **have a ~ to do s.th.** dazu neigen, et. zu tun. **ten·den·tious** [~'denʃəs] *adj* □ tendenziös.

ten·der¹ ['tendə] *adj* □ **1.** empfindlich, *fig. a.* heikel; **→ spot** 4. **2.** zart, weich (*Fleisch*). **3.** zärtlich.

ten·der² [~] **I** *v/i* **1.** ✝ ein Angebot machen (**for** für). **II** *v/t* **2. → resignation** 1. **III** *s* **3.** ✝ Angebot *n.* **4.** *legal* **~** gesetzliches Zahlungsmittel.

ten·der³ [~] *s* ⚓, 🚂 Tender *m.*

'ten·der·foot *s* (*a. irr* foot) *Am.* F Anfänger *m*, Neuling *m.* **'~heart·ed** *adj* □ weichherzig.

ten·der·ize ['tendəraɪz] *v/t Fleisch* zart *od.* weich machen.

'ten·der·loin *s* zartes Lendenstück.

ten·don ['tendən] *s anat.* Sehne *f.*

ten·dril ['tendrəl] *s* 🌿 Ranke *f.*

ten·e·ment ['tenəmənt] *s* Mietshaus *n*, *contr.* Mietskaserne *f.*

ten·et ['tenɪt] *s* Lehr-, *eccl.* Glaubenssatz *m.*

ten·ner ['tenə] *s* F Zehner *m* (*Br.* **Zehnpfundschein**, *Am.* **Zehndollarschein**).

ten·fold ['tenfəʊld] **I** *adj* zehnfach. **II** *adv* zehnfach, um das Zehnfache: **increase ~** (sich) verzehnfachen.

ten·nis ['tenɪs] *s Sport:* Tennis *n.* **~ ball** *s* Tennisball *m.* **~ court** *s* Tennisplatz *m.* **~ el·bow** *s* 🎾 Tennisarm *m.* **~ play·er** *s* Tennisspieler(in). **~ rack·et** *s* Tennisschläger *m.*

ten·or ['tenə] *s* **1.** ♩ Tenor *m.* **2.** Tenor *m*, Sinn *m.* **3.** Verlauf *m.*

'ten·pin *s* **1.** *Bowling:* Kegel *m*: **~ bowling** *Br.* Bowling *n.* **2.** *pl* (*sg konstruiert*) *Am.* Bowling *n.*

tense¹ [tens] *s ling.* Zeit *f*, Tempus *n*: → **future** 4, **past** 3, **present** 3.

tense² [~] *adj* □ **1.** gespannt, straff (*Seil etc*), (an)gespannt (*Muskeln*). **2.** *fig.* (an)gespannt (*Lage etc*); (über)nervös (*Person*).

ten·sile ['tensaɪl] *adj* **1.** dehn-, spannbar. **2. ~ strength** Zug-, Zerreißfestigkeit *f.*

ten·sion ['tenʃn] *s* **1.** Spannung *f* (*a.* ⚡): → **high tension. 2.** *fig.* Anspannung *f*; Spannung(en *pl*) *f.*

tent [tent] *s* Zelt *n.*

ten·ta·cle ['tentəkl] *s zo.* Tentakel *m, n*: a) Fühler *m*, b) Fangarm *m.*

ten·ta·tive ['tentətɪv] *adj* □ **1.** vorläufig;

versuchsweise: **~***ly* a. mit Vorbehalt. **2.** vorsichtig, zögernd.

ten·ter·hooks ['tentəhuks] *s pl:* **be on ~** wie auf glühenden Kohlen sitzen; **keep s.o. on ~** j-n auf die Folter spannen.

tenth [tenθ] **I** *adj* **1.** zehnt. **II** *s* **2.** der, die, das Zehnte: **the ~ of May** der 10. Mai. **3.** Zehntel *n:* **a ~ of a second** e-e Zehntelsekunde. **'tenth·ly** *adv* zehntens.

'ten-time *adj* zehnmalig.

tent| peg *s* Hering *m*, Zeltpflock *m.* ~ **pole** *s* Zeltstange *f.*

ten·u·ous ['tenjuəs] *adj* □ **1.** dünn (*Faden etc*). **2.** *fig.* lose (*Verbindung etc*); schwach (*Beweis etc*).

ten·ure ['te‚njuə] *s* **1.** Innehabung *f* (*e-s Amtes*), (*von Grundbesitz a.*) Besitz *m.* **2.** ~ **of office** Amtsdauer *f*, Dienstzeit *f.*

tep·id ['tepɪd] *adj* □ lau(warm) (*a. fig.*).

term [tɜːm] *s* **1.** Zeit(raum *m*), Dauer *f*; Laufzeit *f* (*e-s Vertrags etc*): ~ **of imprisonment** ⚖ Freiheitsstrafe *f*; ~ **of office** Amtsdauer, -periode *f*, -zeit; **in the long (short) ~** auf lange (kurze) Sicht. **2.** *ped., univ. bsd. Br.* Trimester *n.* **3.** Ausdruck *m*, Bezeichnung *f:* ~ **of abuse** Schimpfwort *n*, Beleidigung *f*; **~s of** was ... betrifft; **in ~s of money** finanziell (gesehen); **in no uncertain ~s** unmißverständlich; → **technical** 4. **4.** *pl* Bedingungen *pl:* **~s of delivery** ✝ Liefer(ungs)bedingungen; **on one's own ~s** zu s-n Bedingungen; **come to ~s** sich einigen (**with** mit); **come to ~s with s.th.** sich mit et. abfinden; → **easy** 5. **5. be on friendly (good) ~s with** auf freundschaftlichem Fuß stehen (gut auskommen) mit; → **speaking** II. **II** *v/t* **6.** nennen, bezeichnen als.

ter·mi·nal ['tɜːmɪnl] **I** *adj* □ **1.** ✿ a) unheilbar; unheilbar krank, b) im Endstadium, c) Sterbe...: ~ **clinic.** **II** *s* **2.** 🚌 *etc* Endstation *f:* → **air terminal.** **3.** *Computer:* Terminal *n.* **4.** ⚡ (Anschluß)Klemme *f*; Pol *m* (*e-r Batterie*).

ter·mi·nate ['tɜːmɪneɪt] **I** *v/t* beenden; *Vertrag* kündigen, lösen; ⚕ *Schwangerschaft* unterbrechen. **II** *v/i* enden; ablaufen (*Vertrag*). **ter·mi·na·tion** *s* **1.** Beendigung *f*; Kündigung *f*, Lösung *f*; ⚕ (*Schwangerschafts*)Abbruch *m.* **2.** Ende *n*; Ablauf *m.*

ter·mi·ni ['tɜːmɪnaɪ] *pl von* **terminus.**

ter·mi·nol·o·gy [ˌtɜːmɪˈnɒlədʒɪ] *s* Terminologie *f*, Fachsprache *f.*

ter·mi·nus ['tɜːmɪnəs] *pl* **-ni** ['~naɪ], **-nus·es** *s* 🚌 *etc* Endstation *f.*

ter·mite ['tɜːmaɪt] *s* *zo.* Termite *f.*

ter·race ['terəs] *s* **1.** Terrasse *f.* **2.** *Sport: bsd. Br.* Ränge *pl.* **3.** Häuserreihe *f*, -zeile *f.* **'ter·raced** *adj:* ~ **house** *Br.* Reihenhaus *n.*

ter·ra·cot·ta [ˌterəˈkɒtə] *s* Terrakotta *f.*

ter·rain [teˈreɪn] *s* Gelände *n*, Terrain *n.*

ter·res·tri·al [təˈrestrɪəl] *adj* □ **1.** irdisch. **2.** Erd...: ~ **globe** Erdball *m.* **3.** ⚘, Land...

ter·ri·ble ['terəbl] *adj* □ schrecklich, furchtbar (*beide a. fig.* F).

ter·ri·er ['terɪə] *s* *zo.* Terrier *m.*

ter·rif·ic [təˈrɪfɪk] *adj* (**~ally**) F toll, phantastisch; wahnsinnig.

ter·ri·fy ['terɪfaɪ] *v/t* j-m schreckliche Angst einjagen: **spiders ~ me, I'm terrified of spiders** ich habe schreckliche Angst vor Spinnen.

ter·ri·to·ri·al [ˌterɪˈtɔːrɪəl] *adj* □ territorial, Gebiets...: ~ **claims** *pl* Gebietsansprüche *pl*; ~ **waters** *pl* Hoheitsgewässer *pl.* **ter·ri·to·ry** ['~tərɪ] *s* **1.** (*a.* Hoheits-, Staats)Gebiet *n*, Territorium *n.* **2.** *zo.* Revier *n.* **3.** *fig.* Gebiet *n.*

ter·ror ['terə] *s* **1.** Entsetzen *n:* **in ~** voller Entsetzen; **in panischer Angst; have a ~ of** panische Angst haben vor (*dat*). **2.** Terror *m.* **3.** Schrecken *m* (*Person, Sache*). **4.** F Landplage *f* (*bsd. Kind*). **'ter·ror·ism** *s* Terrorismus *m.* **'ter·ror·ist I** *s* Terrorist(in). **II** *adj* terroristisch, Terror... **'ter·ror·ize** *v/t* terrorisieren; einschüchtern.

ter·ry(-cloth) ['terɪ(klɒθ)] *s* Frottee *n*, *m.*

terse [tɜːs] *adj* □ knapp (*Antwort etc*).

tes·sel·at·ed ['tesəleɪtɪd] *adj* Mosaik...

test [test] *s* **1.** *allg.* Test *m:* **put to the ~** auf die Probe stellen; **stand the ~ of time** die Zeit überdauern; → **driving test. 2.** → **test match. II** *v/t* **3.** testen, prüfen. **4.** *j-s Geduld etc* auf e-e harte Probe stellen.

tes·ta·ment ['testəmənt] *s* **1.** → **will** 1. **2.** ♀ *Bibl.* Altes, Neues Testament. **3.** *fig.* Zeugnis *n* (**to** gen). **tes·ta·men·ta·ry** [ˌ~ˈmentərɪ] *adj* ⚖ testamentarisch.

tes·ta·tor [teˈsteɪtə] *s* ⚖ Erblasser *m.*

tes·ta·trix [te'steɪtrɪks] *pl* **-tri·ces** [\~trɪsiːz] *s* ♁♂ Erblasserin *f*.

test| **ban trea·ty** *s pol*. Teststoppabkommen *n*. ~ **card** *s TV Br*. Testbild *n*. ~ **case** *s* ♁♂ Musterprozeß *m*. ~ **drive** *s mot*. Probefahrt *f*: **go for a** ~ e-e Probefahrt machen. '~**-drive** *v/t* (*irr drive*) *Auto* probefahren.

tes·ter ['testə] *s* **1.** Tester(in), Prüfer(in). **2.** ⊕ Test-, Prüfgerät *n*.

tes·ti·cle ['testɪkl] *s anat*. Hoden *m*.

tes·ti·fy ['testɪfaɪ] **I** *v/i* **1.** ♁♂ aussagen (*for* für; *against* gegen). **2.** ~ **to** ein deutliches Zeichen sein für. **II** *v/t* **3.** ~ **that** ♁♂ aussagen *od*. bezeugen, daß; *fig*. ein deutliches Zeichen dafür sein, daß.

tes·ti·mo·ni·al [,testɪ'məʊnjəl] *s* **1.** Referenz *f*. **2.** Anerkennungsgeschenk *n*.

tes·ti·mo·ny ['\~mənɪ] *s* **1.** ♁♂ Aussage *f*. **2.** **be.**(**a**) ~ **of** (*od.* **to**) → **testify** 2.

test·ing ['testɪŋ] *adj*: ~ **times** *pl* harte Zeiten *pl*.

test| **lamp** *s* ⊕ Prüflampe *f*. ~ **match** *s Kricket*: internationaler Vergleichskampf. ~ **pat·tern** *s TV Am*. Testbild *n*. ~ **pi·lot** *s* ✈ Testpilot *m*. ~ **tube** *s* ⚗ Reagenzglas *n*. '~**-tube ba·by** *s* Retortenbaby *n*.

tes·ty ['testɪ] *adj* □ gereizt (*Person, Antwort etc*).

tetch·y ['tetʃɪ] *adj* □ reizbar.

teth·er ['teðə] **I** *s* Strick *m*; Kette *f*: **be at the end of one's** ~ *fig*. mit s-n Nerven am Ende sein. **II** *v/t Tier* anbinden; anketten.

Teu·ton·ic [tjuː'tɒnɪk] *adj oft contp*. teutonisch, (typisch) deutsch.

text [tekst] *s* Text *m*. '~**book I** *s* Lehrbuch *n*. **II** *adj* perfekt: ~ **example** Musterbeispiel *n* (*of* für).

tex·tile ['tekstaɪl] **I** *s* Stoff *m*: ~**s** *pl* Textilien *pl*. **II** *adj* Textil...

tex·tu·al ['tekstjʊəl] *adj* □ textlich, Text...

tex·ture ['tekstʃə] *s* Textur *f*, Gewebe *n*; Beschaffenheit *f*.

tha·lid·o·mide [θə'lɪdəmaɪd] *s pharm*. Thalidomid *n*, Contergan *n*: ~ **baby** Contergankind *n*.

Thames [temz] *npr* Themse *f*: **he won't set the** ~ **on fire** *fig*. er hat das Pulver auch nicht (gerade) erfunden.

than [ðən] *cj* als.

thank [θæŋk] **I** *v/t j-m* danken, sich bei *j-m* bedanken (*for* für): ~ **you** (*very much*) danke (vielen Dank); **no,** ~ **you** nein, danke; **say** "2 **you**" sich bedanken; **he's only got himself to** ~ **that** er hat es sich selbst zuzuschreiben, daß; → **god** 2, **goodness** 2, **heaven** 1, **star** 1. **II** *s pl* Dank *m*: **with** ~**s** dankend, mit Dank; (**many**) ~**s** danke (vielen Dank); **no,** ~**s** nein, danke; **say** "2**s**" sich bedanken; ~**s to** dank (*gen*), wegen (*gen*). **thank·ful** [\~fʊl] *adj* □ dankbar (*for* für); froh (*that* daß; **to be** zu sein): ~**ly** *a*. zum Glück, Gott sei Dank. '**thank·less** *adj* undankbar (*Aufgabe etc*). '**Thanks,giv·ing** (**Day**) *s Am*. Thanksgiving Day *m* (*Erntedankfest*; **4.** Donnerstag *im November*).

'**thank·you I** *s* Dank(schön) *n*. **II** *adj*: ~ **letter** Dank(es)brief *m*.

that¹ [ðæt] **I** *pron u. adj* **1.** das: ~ **is** (**to say**) das heißt; **at** ~ zudem, obendrein; **let it go at** ~ F lassen wir es dabei bewenden; **and** ~'**s** ~ u. damit basta. **2.** jener, jene, jenes: ~ **car over there** das Auto dort drüben; **those who** diejenigen, welche. **II** *adv* **3.** F so, dermaßen: **it's** ~ **simple** so einfach ist das.

that² [\~] *relative pron* der, die, das, welcher, welche, welches: **everything** ~ alles, was.

that³ [\~] *cj* daß.

thatch [θætʃ] **I** *s* **1.** (Dach)Stroh *n*, Reet *n*. **2.** Stroh-, Reetdach *n*. **II** *v/t* **3.** mit Stroh *od*. Reet decken: ~**ed** stroh-, reetgedeckt.

thaw [θɔː] **I** *v/i* (auf)tauen, (*Tiefkühlkost, fig. Person*) auftauen: **it is** ~**ing** es taut. **II** *v/t* auftauen. **III** *s* Tauwetter *n* (*a. fig. pol.*).

the¹ [ðə, *vor Vokalen* ðɪ] *bestimmter Artikel* **1.** der, die, das, *pl* die. **2.** *vor Maßangaben*: **one dollar** ~ **pound** ein Dollar das *od*. pro Pfund.

the² [\~] *adv*: ~ **...** ~ **...** je ... desto: ~ **sooner** ~ **better** je eher, desto besser.

the·a·ter *s Am.*, **the·a·tre** *s bsd. Br.* ['θɪətə] **1.** Theater *n*: **be in the** ~ beim Theater sein. **2.** (Hör)Saal *m*; ♣ *Br*. Operationssaal *m*: ~ **nurse** Operationsschwester *f*. **3.** *fig*. Schauplatz *m*: ~ **of war** Kriegsschauplatz. '~**go·er** *s* Theaterbesucher(in). **the·at·ri·cal** [θɪ'ætrɪkl] *adj* □ **1.** Theater... **2.** *fig*. theatralisch.

theft [θeft] s Diebstahl m.

their [ðeə] *possessive pron* ihr: *everyone took their seats* alle nahmen Platz.

theirs [ˌz] *possessive pron s* ihre(r, -s) es gehört ihnen; *a friend of ~* ein Freund von ihnen; *our children and ~* unsere Kinder u. ihre.

them [ðəm] *pron* **1.** sie (*acc*); ihnen (*dat*): *they looked behind ~* sie blickten hinter sich. **2.** F sie (*nom*): *we are younger than ~*.

theme [θiːm] s Thema n (a. ♪). ~ *song* s Film etc: Titelsong m. ~ *tune* s Film etc: Themamelodie f.

them·selves [ðəm'selvz] *pron* **1.** *verstärkend*: sie od. sich selbst: *they did it ~, they ~ did it* sie haben es selbst getan. **2.** *reflex* sich: *they cut ~*. **3.** sich (selbst): *they want it for ~*.

then [ðen] **I** *adv* **1.** dann: → *but* 1. **2.** da; damals: *by ~* bis dahin; *from ~ on* von da an. **II** *adj* **3.** damalig.

the·o·lo·gi·an [θɪə'ləʊdʒən] s Theologe m, Theologin f. **the·o·log·i·cal** [ˌ'lɒdʒɪkl] *adj* □ theologisch: ~ *college* Priesterseminar n. **the·ol·o·gy** [θɪ'ɒlədʒɪ] s Theologie f.

the·o·rem ['θɪərəm] s *bsd.* A (Lehr-) Satz m.

the·o·ret·i·cal [θɪə'retɪkl] *adj* □ theoretisch. **'the·o·rist** s Theoretiker(in). **'the·o·rize** *v/i* theoretisieren (*about, on* über *acc*). **'the·o·ry** s Theorie f: *in ~* in der Theorie, theoretisch.

ther·a·peu·tic [ˌθerə'pjuːtɪk] *adj* (~*ally*) **1.** ♣ therapeutisch. **2.** F wohltuend; gesund. **'ther·a·pist** s ♣ Therapeut(in). **'ther·a·py** s ♣ Therapie f.

there [ðeə] **I** *adv* **1.** da, dort: ~ *and then* auf der Stelle; ~ *you are* hier bitte; da hast du's!, na also!; ~ *you go!* F so ist's halt!; ~ *you go again!* F fängst du schon wieder an!; → *over* 9. **2.** (da-, dort)hin: ~ *and back* hin u. zurück; *get ~* F es schaffen; *go ~* hingehen. **3.** ~ *is, ~ are* es gibt od. ist od. sind: ~ *are many cars in the street* auf der Straße sind viele Autos; ~*'s a good boy!* sei brav!; das war lieb von dir! **II** *int* **4.** so; da hast du's!, na also: ~, ~ ist ja gut! '~·a·bouts *adv*: *five pounds or ~* ungefähr ... so etwa fünf Pfund. ~'af·ter *adv* danach. ~'by *adv* dadurch. '~·fore *adv* **1.** deshalb, daher. **2.** folg-

lich, also. ~·up'on *adv* darauf.

ther·mal ['θɜːml] **I** *adj* □ **1.** thermisch, Thermo..., Wärme... **2.** ~ *spring* Thermalquelle f. **II** s **3.** Thermik f.

ther·mom·e·ter [θə'mɒmɪtə] s Thermometer n.

Ther·mos ['θɜːmɒs] (*TM*) s, *Am. a.* ~ *bottle*, *bsd. Br. a.* ~ *flask* Thermosflasche f.

ther·mo·stat ['θɜːməʊstæt] s Thermostat m.

the·sau·rus [θɪ'sɔːrəs] *pl* **-ri** [ˌraɪ], **-rus·es** s Thesaurus m.

these [ðiːz] *pl von* **this.**

the·sis ['θiːsɪs] *pl* **-ses** [ˌsiːz] s **1.** These f. **2.** *univ.* Dissertation f, Doktorarbeit f.

they [ðeɪ] *pron* **1.** sie *pl*: ~ *who* diejenigen, welche. **2.** man.

they'd [ðeɪd] F *für* **they had; they would.**

they'll [ðeɪl] F *für* **they will.**

they're [ðeə] F *für* **they are.**

they've [ðeɪv] F *für* **they have.**

thick [θɪk] **I** *adj* □ **1.** *allg.* dick: *the ~ end of £500* F fast 500 Pfund; *give s.o. a ~ ear* F j-m eins od. ein paar hinter die Ohren geben. **2.** dick, dicht (*Nebel etc*): *be ~ with* wimmeln von; *~ with smoke* verräuchert; *the furniture was ~ with dust* auf den Möbeln lag dick der Staub; *they are ~ on the ground* F es gibt sie wie Sand am Meer. **3.** *bsd. Br.* F dumm. **4.** *bsd. Br.* F dick befreundet (*with mit*). **5.** *that's a bit ~! bsd. Br.* F das ist ein starkes Stück! **II** *adv* **6.** dick, dicht: *lay it on ~* F dick auftragen. **III** s **7.** *in the ~ of fig.* mitten in (*dat*): *in the ~ of the fight* im dichtesten Kampfgetümmel; *through ~ and thin* durch dick u. dünn. **thick·en** ['ˌn] **I** *v/t* Soße etc eindicken, binden. **II** *v/i* dicker werden, (*Nebel etc a.*) dichter werden. **thick·et** ['ˌɪt] s Dickicht n.

,**thick'head·ed** *adj* F strohdumm.

thick·ness ['θɪknɪs] s **1.** Dicke f. **2.** Lage f, Schicht f. **3.** *bsd. Br.* F Dummheit f. ,**thick'set** *adj* gedrungen, untersetzt. ~'**skinned** *adj* F *a.* fig. dickfellig.

thief [θiːf] *pl* **thieves** [θiːvz] s Dieb(in): *stop, ~!* haltet den Dieb!; *they are (as) thick as thieves* F sie sind dicke Freunde.

thigh [θaɪ] s anat. (Ober)Schenkel m.

thim·ble ['θɪmbl] s Fingerhut m.

thin [θɪn] **I** *adj* □ **1.** dünn, (*Person, Arme*

etc a.) dürr, (*Haar a.*) schütter: ***disappear*** (*od.* ***vanish***) ***into ~ air*** *fig.* sich in Luft auflösen; ***produce out of ~ air*** *fig. et.* herzaubern; ***this is just the ~ end of the wedge*** *fig. b.s.* das ist erst der Anfang; ***be ~ on the ground*** F dünn gesät sein; ***he's getting ~ on top*** F bei ihm lichtet es sich oben schon. **2.** *fig.* schwach (*Rede etc*), (*Ausrede etc a.*) fadenscheinig. **II** *v/t* **3.** dünn. **III** *v/t* **4.** Soße *etc* verdünnen, strecken. **IV** *v/i* **5.** dünner werden, (*Nebel, Haar a.*) sich lichten, (*Haar a.*) schütter werden.

thing [θɪŋ] *s* **1.** (*konkretes*) Ding: *~s* *pl* Sachen *pl* (*Getränke etc*), (*Gepäck, Kleidung etc a.*) Zeug *n*; ***what's this ~?*** was ist das?; ***I couldn't see a ~*** ich konnte überhaupt nichts sehen. **2.** *fig.* Ding *n*, Sache *f*, Angelegenheit *f*: ***a funny ~*** et. Komisches; ***another ~*** et. anderes; ***first ~ tomorrow*** gleich morgen früh; ***for one ~ ..., and for another ~*** zum e-n ..., u. zum anderen; ***make a ~ of*** F et. aufbauschen; ***know a ~ or two about*** et. verstehen von; ***this proves three ~s*** das beweist dreierlei; → *done* 1, *last* 4, *near* 9, *old* 2, *right* 1. **3.** *pl* Dinge *pl*, Lage *f*, Umstände *pl*. **4.** Ding *n* (*Mädchen, Tier*), Kerl *m*.

think [θɪŋk] **I** *v/t* (*irr*) **1.** denken, glauben, meinen (*that* daß): ***I thought he was a burglar*** ich hielt ihn für e-n Einbrecher. **2.** *~ out* (*od.* ***through***) et. durchdenken; ***~ over*** nachdenken über (*acc*), sich et. überlegen; ***~ up*** sich et. ausdenken. **3.** *j-n, et.* halten für: ***~ s.o. clever.*** **4.** ***I can't ~ why ...*** ich kann nicht verstehen, warum ... **5.** ***try to ~ where ...*** versuch dich zu erinnern, wo ... **II** *v/i* (*irr*) **6.** denken (*of an acc*): ***I ~ so*** ich glaube so. denke schon; ***~ of doing s.th.*** sich mit dem Gedanken tragen od. daran denken, et. zu tun; ***I can't ~ of his name*** mir fällt sein Name nicht ein, ich kann mich nicht an s-n Namen erinnern; ***what do you ~ of*** (*od.* ***about***) ***...?*** was halten Sie von ...?; → *better*[1] III, *highly* 2, *little* 5, *much* 2, *nothing* 1. **7.** nachdenken (*about* über *acc*): ***I'll ~ about it*** ich überlege es mir; → *twice*. **III** *s* **8.** F ***have a ~ about*** nachdenken über (*acc*); ***have another ~ coming*** schief gewickelt sein. **'think·er** *s* Denker(in). **'think·ing** **I** *adj* **1.** denkend. **2.**

Denk...: ***put on one's ~ cap*** F scharf nachdenken. **II** *s* **3.** Denken *n*: ***do some ~ nachdenken***; ***to my way of ~*** m-r Meinung nach.

think tank *s* Planungs-, Sachverständigenstab *m*.

thin·ner ['θɪnə] *s* Verdünner *m*.

thin-'skinned *adj* *fig.* dünnhäutig.

third [θɜːd] **I** *adj* (□ → ***thirdly***) **1.** dritt: ***~ party*** ✝, ⚖ Dritte *m*; ♀ **World** Dritte Welt. **II** *s* **2.** der, die, das Dritte: ***the ~ of May*** der 3. Mai. **3.** Drittel *n*. **4.** *mot.* dritter Gang. **III** *adv* **3.** als dritt(er, e, es). **,~·'class** **I** *adj* **1.** drittklassig, -rangig. **2.** ⚙ *etc* dritter Klasse. **II** *adv* **3.** ⚙ *etc* dritt(er) Klasse. **,~-de'gree** *adj* ***~ burns*** Verbrennungen dritten Grades.

third·ly ['θɜːdlɪ] *adv* drittens.

,third·-'par·ty *adj*: ***~ insurance*** Haftpflichtversicherung *f*. **,~-'rate** → *third-class*

thirst [θɜːst] *s* Durst *m*: ***die of ~*** verdursten; ***~ for knowledge*** *fig.* Wissensdurst. **'~-,quench·ing** *adj* durstlöschend.

thirst·y ['θɜːstɪ] *adj* □ **1.** durstig: ***be*** (*od.* ***feel***) (***very***) ***~*** (sehr) durstig sein, (großen) Durst haben. **2.** ***gardening is ~ work*** Gartenarbeit macht durstig.

thir·teen [,θɜː'tiːn] *adj* dreizehn. **,thir·'teenth** [~θ] *adj* dreizehnt. **thir·ti·eth** ['θɜːtɪəθ] *adj* dreißigst. **'thir·ty** **I** *adj* dreißig. **II** *s* Dreißig *f*: ***be in one's thirties*** in den Dreißigern sein; ***in the thirties*** in den dreißiger Jahren (*e-s Jahrhunderts*).

this [ðɪs] **I** *pron* **1.** dieser, diese, dieses; dies, das: ***like ~*** so; ***~ is what I expected*** (genau) das habe ich erwartet; ***these are his children*** das sind s-e Kinder. **2.** ***after ~*** danach; ***before ~*** zuvor. **II** *adj* **3.** dieser, diese, dieses: → *afternoon* I, *morning* I, *time* 4, *year*. **III** *adv* **4.** F so, dermaßen.

this·tle ['θɪsl] *s* ♣ Distel *f*.

tho·rax ['θɔːræks] *pl* **-ra·ces** ['~rəsiːz], **-rax·es** ['~ræksɪz] *s anat.* Brustkorb *m*, -kasten *m*.

thorn [θɔːn] *s* ♣ Dorn *m*: ***be a ~ in s.o.'s flesh*** (*od.* ***side***) *fig.* j-m ein Dorn im Auge sein. **'thorn·y** *adj* **1.** dornig. **2.** *fig.* heikel.

thor·ough ['θʌrə] *adj* (□ → ***thoroughly***) **1.** gründlich (*Person, Kenntnisse*),

(*Prüfung etc a.*) eingehend, (*Reform etc a.*) durchgreifend. **2.** fürchterlich (*Durcheinander, Langweiler etc*). '**~bred** *s* Vollblüter *m.* '**~fare** *s* Hauptverkehrsstraße *f:* **no ~** Durchfahrt verboten! '**~,go·ing** → **thorough** 1.

thor·ough·ly ['θʌrəlɪ] *adv* **1.** → **thorough** 1. **2.** völlig, total: *I ~ enjoyed it* es hat mir unwahrscheinlich gut gefallen.

those [ðəʊz] *pl von* **that**[1].

though [ðəʊ] **I** *cj* **1.** obwohl; → **even**[1] 1. **2.** (je)doch. **3. as ~** als ob, wie wenn. **II** *adv* **4.** dennoch, trotzdem.

thought[1] [θɔːt] *pret u. pp von* **think.**

thought[2] [~] *s* **1.** Denken *n:* → **lost** 5. **2.** Gedanke *m* (**of** *an acc*): *that's a ~!* gute Idee!; *on second ~s* (*Am. ~*) wenn ich es mir überlege; *have no ~ of doing s.th.* nicht daran denken *od.* nicht vorhaben, et. zu tun. **3. with no ~ for** ohne Rücksicht auf (*acc*), ohne an (*acc*) zu denken. **thought·ful** ['~fʊl] *adj* □ **1.** nachdenklich. **2.** rücksichtsvoll, aufmerksam. '**thought·less** *adj* □ **1.** gedankenlos. **2.** rücksichtslos.

thou·sand ['θaʊznd] **I** *adj* **1.** tausend: *a* (*one*) ~ (ein)tausend **2.** Tausend *n:* *~s of times* tausendmal; → **hundred** 2. **3.** ✠ Tausender *m.* **thou·sandth** ['~tθ] **I** *adj* **1.** tausendst. **II** *s* **2.** *der, die, das* Tausendste. **3.** Tausendstel *n:* *a ~ of a second* e-e Tausendstelsekunde.

thrash [θræʃ] **I** *v/t* **1.** *j-n* verdreschen, -prügeln; (*Sport*) F *j-m* e-e Abfuhr erteilen. **2. ~ out** *Problem etc* ausdiskutieren. **II** *v/i* **3. ~ about** (*od.* **around**) sich *im Bett* herumwerfen; um sich schlagen; zappeln (*Fisch*). '**thrash·ing** *s:* **give s.o. a ~** *j-m* e-e Tracht Prügel verpassen; (*Sport*) F *j-m* e-e Abfuhr erteilen.

thread [θred] **I** *s* **1.** Faden *m* (*a. fig.*): *lose the ~* (*of the conversation*) den (Gesprächs)Faden verlieren; *pick up the ~* den Faden wiederaufnehmen; → **hang** 8. **2.** ⚙ Gewinde *n.* **II** *v/t* **3.** *Nadel* einfädeln. **4.** *Perlen etc* auffädeln, -reihen (*on auf acc*). **5. ~ one's way through** sich schlängeln durch, sich durchschlängeln zwischen (*dat*). '**~bare** *adj* **1.** abgewetzt, (*Kleidung a.*) abgetragen. **2.** *fig.* abgedroschen.

threat [θret] *s* **1.** Drohung *f:* **under ~ of** unter Androhung von (*od. gen*). **2.** (**to**)

Bedrohung *f* (*gen od.* für), Gefahr *f* (für). '**threat·en** **I** *v/t* **1.** *j-m* drohen, *j-n* bedrohen (**with** mit): **~ s.o. with s.th.** *a.* *j-m* et. androhen. **2.** *et.* androhen, drohen mit. **3. ~ to do s.th.** (damit) drohen, et. zu tun. **4.** *et.* bedrohen, gefährden: **be ~ed with extinction** *biol.* vom Aussterben bedroht sein. **II** *v/i* **5.** drohen (*Gefahr etc*). '**threat·en·ing** *adj* drohend: **~ letter** Drohbrief *m.*

three [θriː] **I** *adj* drei. **II** *s* Drei *f:* **~ hearts** Herzdrei. '**~·act** *adj:* **~ play** *thea.* Dreiakter *m.* '**~·'cor·nered** *adj* dreieckig. '**~·di·men·sion·al** *adj* **1.** dreidimensional. **2.** *fig.* plastisch. '**three·fold** ['θriːfəʊld] *adj* dreifach. **II** *adv* dreifach, um das Dreifache: **increase** *v/t* (sich) verdreifachen. '**three·piece** *adj* dreiteilig. '**~·'quar·ter** *adj* Dreiviertel... '**~·time** *adj* dreimalig.

thresh [θreʃ] *v/t u. v/i* dreschen. '**thresh·ing** *adj:* **~ machine** Dreschmaschine *f.*

thresh·old ['θreʃhəʊld] *s* Schwelle *f* (*a. fig.*): **be on the ~ of** an der Schwelle stehen zu (*od. gen*); **~ of pain** Schmerzschwelle.

threw [θruː] *pret von* **throw.**

thrift [θrɪft] *s* Sparsamkeit *f.* '**thrift·y** *adj* □ sparsam.

thrill [θrɪl] **I** *s* **1.** prickelndes Gefühl; Nervenkitzel *m.* **2.** aufregendes Erlebnis. **II** *v/t* **3. be ~ed** (ganz) hingerissen sein (**at, about** von): *I was ~ed to hear that* ich war von der Nachricht hingerissen, daß. '**thrill·er** *s* Thriller *m,* Reißer *m.* '**thrill·ing** *adj* fesselnd, packend.

thrive [θraɪv] *v/i* gedeihen (*Pflanze, Tier*), sich prächtig entwickeln (*Kind*); *fig.* blühen, florieren (*Geschäft etc*): **~ on** *j-n* geradezu aufblühen bei.

throat [θrəʊt] *s* Kehle *f,* Gurgel *f;* Rachen *m;* Hals *m:* **cut one's own ~** *fig.* sich ins eigene Fleisch schneiden; **force** (*od. ram, thrust*) *s.th. down s.o.'s ~* *fig.* j-m et. aufzwingen; → **clear** 17, **sore** 1. '**throat·y** *adj* □ rauh; heiser (*Stimme*); mit e-r rauhen *od.* heiseren Stimme: **~ sound** heiser klingen.

throb [θrɒb] **I** *v/i* hämmern (*Maschine*), (*Herz etc a.*) pochen, schlagen. **II** *s* Hämmern *n,* Pochen *n,* Schlagen *n.*

throes [θrəʊz] *s pl:* **be in the ~ of** (doing

s.th. mitten in et. (*Unangenehmem*) stecken.

throm·bo·sis [θrɒmˈbəʊsɪs] *pl* **-ses** [~siːz] *s ⚕ᵝ* Thrombose *f.*

throne [θrəʊn] *s* Thron *m* (*a. fig.*): **come to the ~** auf den Thron kommen.

throng [θrɒŋ] **I** *s* Schar *f* (*of* von). **II** *v/i u.* *v/t* sich drängen (in *dat*).

throt·tle [ˈθrɒtl] **I** *v/t* erdrosseln. **II** *s mot.,* ⚙ Drosselklappe *f*: **go at full ~** (mit) Vollgas fahren.

through [θruː] **I** *prp* **1.** durch (*a. fig.*): → **live¹** Ib. **2.** *Am.* bis (einschließlich). **II** *adv* **3.** durch; durch...: **~ and ~** durch u. durch; **wet ~** völlig durchnäßt; → **let through, read¹** 1, *etc.* **III** *adj* **4.** durchgehend (*Zug etc*): **~ traffic** Durchgangsverkehr *m.* **5. be ~** F fertig sein (**with** mit). **~'out I** *prp* **1. ~ the night** die ganze Nacht hindurch. **2. ~ the country** im ganzen Land. **II** *adv* **3.** ganz, überall. **4.** die ganze Zeit (hindurch). **'~way** *s Am.* Schnellstraße *f.*

throw [θrəʊ] **I** *s* **1.** *Leichtathletik:* (*Diskus-, Speer*)Wurf *m.* **2.** Wurf *m:* → **stone** 1. **3.** *Fußball:* Einwurf *m:* **take the ~** einwerfen. **II** *v/t* (*irr*) **4.** *et.* werfen (**at** nach): **~ s.o. s.th.** j-m et. her- *od.* zuwerfen; **~ s.o. a look** j-m e-n Blick zuwerfen; **~ a three** e-e Drei werfen *od.* würfeln; **~ open** Tür etc aufreißen; *fig. Schloß etc* der Öffentlichkeit zugänglich machen; **~ o.s. at s.o.** sich auf j-n stürzen; *fig.* sich j-m an den Hals werfen; **~ o.s. into** sich stürzen in (*acc*) (*a. fig.*); → **balance** 1, **confusion** 2a, **doubt** 5, **light¹** 1, **water** 1. **5.** *zo.* werfen. **6.** *Hebel etc* betätigen. **7.** *Reiter* abwerfen. **8.** F *Party* schmeißen, geben. **9.** F *Wutanfall etc* kriegen: → **tantrum.** **III** *v/i* (*irr*) **10.** werfen; würfeln.
Verbindungen mit Adverbien:

throw| a·bout, ~ a·round *v/t:* **throw one's money about** mit Geld um sich werfen; → **weight** 3. **~ a·way** *v/t* **1.** *et.* wegwerfen. **2.** *Chance etc* vertun. **~ back** *v/t* **1.** zurückwerfen. **2. be thrown back on** *fig.* wieder angewiesen sein auf (*acc*). **~ in** *v/t* **1.** hineinwerfen: **throw the ball in** (*Fußball*) einwerfen; → **sponge** 1, **towel** 1. **2.** *et.* (gratis) dazugeben: **get s.th. thrown in** et. (gratis) dazubekommen. **~ off** *v/t* **1.** *Kleidungsstück* abwerfen, *Nervosität etc* ablegen.

2. *Verfolger* abschütteln. **3.** *Krankheit* loswerden. **~ on** *v/t* sich *Kleidungsstück* überwerfen. **~ out** *v/t* **1.** j-n hinauswerfen (*a. fig. entlassen*). **2.** *et.* wegwerfen. **3.** *Vorschlag etc* ablehnen, verwerfen. **4.** *Vorschlag etc* äußern. **5.** j-n aus dem Konzept *od.* aus der Fassung bringen. **~ o·ver** *v/t* *Freund etc* sitzenlassen (**for** wegen). **~ to·geth·er** *v/t* **1.** zs.-werfen. **2.** *et.* fabrizieren, zurechtbasteln. **3.** *Leute* zs.-bringen. **~ up** *v/t* **1.** in die Höhe werfen, hochwerfen. **2.** F *Job etc* hinschmeißen. **3.** F *et. Gegessenes* brechen. **II** *v/i* **4.** F brechen (*sich übergeben*).

'throw·a·way *adj* **1.** Wegwerf... **2.** hingeworfen (*Bemerkung*).

throw·er [ˈθrəʊə] *s* Werfer(in).

'throw-in → **throw** 3.

thrown [θrəʊn] *pp von* **throw.**

thru [θruː] *Am.* F → **through.**

thrush¹ [θrʌʃ] *s orn.* Drossel *f.*

thrush² [~] *s ⚕ᵝ* Soor *m.*

thrust [θrʌst] **I** *v/t* (*irr*) **1.** j-n, *et.* stoßen (**into** in *acc*): → **throat.** **2.** *et.* stoßen, schieben (**into** in *acc*): → **nose** 1. **II** *v/i* (*irr*) **3. ~ at** stoßen nach. **III** *s* **4.** Stoß *m.* **5.** ⚔ Vorstoß *m* (*a. fig.*). **6.** *phys.* Schub(kraft *f*) *m.*

'thru·way F → **throughway.**

thud [θʌd] **I** *s* dumpfes Geräusch, Plumps *m.* **II** *v/i* plumpsen.

thug [θʌɡ] *s* Schläger *m.*

thumb [θʌm] **I** *s* *anat.* Daumen *m:* **be all ~s** F zwei linke Hände haben; **be under s.o.'s ~** F unter j-s Fuchtel stehen; **give s.th. the ~s up** (**down**) et. akzeptieren (ablehnen); **stick out like a sore ~** F auffallen wie ein Kuhfladen auf der Autobahn; → **rule** 2, **twiddle.** **II** *v/t:* **~ a lift** per Anhalter fahren, trampen (**to** nach). **III** *v/i:* **~ through a book** ein Buch durchblättern. **~ in·dex** *s* (*a. ind index*) Daumenregister *n.* **'~nail I** *s* Daumennagel *m.* **II** *adj* kurz (*Beschreibung etc*). **'~screw** *s* **1.** ⚙ Flügel- *od.* Rändelschraube *f.* **2.** *hist.* Daumenschraube *f.* **'~tack** *s Am.* Reißzwecke *f,* -nagel *m.*

thump [θʌmp] **I** *v/t* **1.** j-m e-n Schlag versetzen; *j-n* verprügeln. **2. ~ out** *Melodie* herunterhämmern (**on the piano** auf dem Klavier). **II** *v/i* **3.** plumpsen. **4.** hämmern, pochen (*Herz*). **5.** trampeln.

III s **6.** dumpfes Geräusch, Plumps m. **7.** Schlag m. **'thump·ing I** adj **1.** hämmernd (Kopfschmerzen). **2.** F riesig, Mords... **II** adv **3.** ~ **great** → **2.**

thun·der ['θʌndə] **I** s Donner m, (von Geschützen a.) Donnern n: **steal s.o.'s** ~ fig. j-m die Schau od. Show stehlen. **II** v/i donnern (a. fig. Geschütze, Zug etc). **III** v/t a. ~ **out** et. brüllen, donnern. **'~bolt** s Blitz m u. Donnerschlag m: **like a** ~ wie der Blitz; **be a real** ~ fig. wie der Blitz einschlagen. **'~clap** s Donner(schlag) m. **'~cloud** s Gewitterwolke f.

thun·der·ous ['θʌndərəs] adj donnernd (Applaus).

'thun·der·|storm s Gewitter n, Unwetter n. **'~struck** adj wie vom Donner gerührt.

thun·der·y ['θʌndərɪ] adj gewitt(e)rig.

Thurs·day ['θɜːzdɪ] s Donnerstag m: **on** ~ (am) Donnerstag; **on** ~**s** donnerstags.

thus [ðʌs] adv **1.** so, auf diese Weise. **2.** folglich, somit. **3.** ~ **far** bisher.

thwack [θwæk] → **whack.**

thwart [θwɔːt] v/t Pläne etc durchkreuzen, vereiteln; j-m e-n Strich durch die Rechnung machen.

thyme [taɪm] s ♀ Thymian m.

thy·roid (gland) ['θaɪrɔɪd] s anat. Schilddrüse f.

ti·a·ra [tɪ'ɑːrə] s **1.** Tiara f. **2.** Diadem n.

tic [tɪk] s ♂ Tic(k) m, nervöses Zucken.

tick¹ [tɪk] s zo. Zecke f.

tick² [~] s: **on** ~ F auf Pump.

tick³ [~] **I** s **1.** Ticken n. **2.** Häkchen n (Vermerkzeichen). **3.** bsd. Br. F Augenblick m: **in a** ~ sofort. **II** v/i **4.** ticken: ~ **away** vergehen, -rinnen **III** v/t **5.** a. ~ **off** abhaken: ~ **off** F j-n anpfeifen, zs.-stauchen.

tick·er ['tɪkə] s F Pumpe f (Herz).

tick·et ['tɪkɪt] **I** s **1.** (Eintritts-, Theateretc)Karte f; ⓖ etc Fahrkarte f, -schein m, ✈ Flugschein m, Ticket n; (Gepäcketc)Schein m. **2.** Etikett n, (Preis- etc)Schild n. **3.** Strafzettel m: → **parking ticket. 4.** pol. bsd. Am. Wahl-, Kandidatenliste f. **II** v/t **5.** etikettieren. **6.** be ~ed for bsd. Am. e-n Strafzettel bekommen wegen. **7.** bestimmen, vorsehen (for für). ~ **col·lec·tor** s (Bahnsteig-)Schaffner(in). ~ **in·spec·tor** s Fahrtenkontrolleur(in). ~ **ma·chine** s Fahr-

kartenautomat m. ~ **tout** s Br. Kartenschwarzhändler(in).

tick·ing-'off s F Anpfiff m: **give s.o. a** ~ j-n anpfeifen od. zs.-stauchen.

tick·le ['tɪkl] **I** v/t u. v/i kitzeln: ~ **s.o.'s fancy** fig. j-n anmachen od. anturnen; **be** ~**d pink** (od. **to death**) F sich wie im Schneekönig freuen (**at**, **by**, **with** über acc); → **ivory** 2. **II** s Kitzeln n. **'tick·lish** adj □ kitz(e)lig (a. fig.).

tid·al ['taɪdl] adj Tiden...: ~ **wave** Flutwelle f; fig. Welle f.

tid·bit ['tɪdbɪt] Am. → **titbit.**

tid·dly·winks ['tɪdlɪwɪŋks] s pl (sg konstruiert) Flohhüpfen n, -spiel n.

tide [taɪd] **I** s **1.** Gezeiten pl; Flut f. **2.** fig. Strömung f, Trend m: **go** (od. **swim**) **with** (**against**) **the** ~ mit dem (gegen den) Strom schwimmen. **II** v/t **3.** ~ **over** fig. j-m hinweghelfen über (acc); j-n über Wasser halten. **'~mark** s bsd. Br. humor. schwarzer Rand (in Badewanne).

ti·di·ness ['taɪdɪnɪs] s Sauberkeit f, Ordentlichkeit f.

ti·dy ['taɪdɪ] **I** adj □ **1.** sauber, ordentlich, (Zimmer a.) aufgeräumt. **2.** F ordentlich, beträchtlich (Gewinn etc). **II** v/t **3.** a. ~ **up** in Ordnung bringen, Zimmer a. aufräumen: ~ **away** weg-, aufräumen.

tie [taɪ] **I** s **1.** Krawatte f, Schlips m. **2.** Band n; Schnur f. **3.** pl fig. Bande pl. **4.** Stimmengleichheit f; (Sport) Unentschieden n: **end in a** ~ unentschieden ausgehen. **5.** Sport: (Pokal)Spiel n, (-)Paarung f. **6.** ⓖ Am. Schwelle f. **II** v/t **7.** a) binden (**to** an acc); (sich) Krawatte etc binden: **my hands are tied** fig. mir sind die Hände gebunden; ~ **up** fig. a. **1.** be ~**d to** fig. (eng) verbunden sein mit. **9. the game was** ~**d** (Sport) das Spiel ging unentschieden aus. **III** v/i **10. they** ~**d for second place** (Sport etc) sie belegten gemeinsam den zweiten Platz. Verbindungen mit Adverbien:

tie| down v/t j-n festlegen (**to** auf acc). ~ **in** v/i (**with**) übereinstimmen (mit), passen (zu). ~ **up** v/t **1.** Paket etc verschnüren: → **knot** 1. **2. be tied up** ♥ fest angelegt sein (in in dat). **3.** et. in Verbindung bringen (**with** mit). **4.** Verkehr etc lahmlegen.

'tie|·break, **'~·break·er** s Tennis: Tie-

Break *m, n.* '**~-in** → **tie-up**. '**~-on** *adj* Anhänge... '**~-pin** *s* Krawattennadel *f.*

tier [tɪə] *s* **1.** (Sitz)Reihe *f.* **2.** Lage *f,* Schicht *f.* **3.** *fig.* Stufe *f.*

'**tie-up** *s* (enge) Verbindung, (enger) Zs.-hang (**between** zwischen *dat*).

tiff [tɪf] *s* kleine Meinungsverschiedenheit.

ti-ger ['taɪgə] *s zo.* Tiger *m.*

tight [taɪt] **I** *adj* □ **1.** fest(sitzend, -angezogen). **2.** straff (*Seil etc*). **3.** eng (*a. Kleidungsstück*): → **corner** 2, **fit** 5. **4.** knapp (*Rennen etc,* ✝ *Geld*). **5.** F knick(e)rig. **6.** F blau (*betrunken*). **7.** *in Zssgn* ...dicht: → **airtight** 1, *etc.* **II** *adv* **8.** fest: **hold** ~ festhalten; **sit** ~ sich nicht vom Fleck rühren; *fig.* sich nicht beirren lassen. **9.** F gut: **sleep** ~! **III** *s* **10.** *pl,* *a.* **pair of ~s** *bsd. Br.* Strumpfhose *f;* Trikot *n* (*von Artisten etc*). '**tight-en** **I** *v/t* **1.** Schraube *etc* anziehen: ~ **one's belt** *fig.* den Gürtel enger schnallen. **2.** *Seil etc* straffen: ~ **up** → 3. **II** *v/i* **3.** ~ **up on** *Gesetz etc* verschärfen.

,**tight**'**fist-ed** → **tight** 5. ,~'**lipped** *adj* **1.** mit zs.-gekniffenen Lippen. **2.** *fig.* verschlossen: **be** ~ **about** nicht reden wollen über (*acc*). '**~-rope** *s* (Draht)Seil *n:* **walk a** ~ *fig.* e-n Balanceakt ausführen; ~ **walker** Drahtseilkünstler(in), Seiltänzer(in).

ti-gress ['taɪgrɪs] *s zo.* Tigerin *f.*

tile [taɪl] **I** *s* **1.** (*Dach*)Ziegel *m:* **be (out) on the ~s** F e-n draufmachen. **2.** Fliese *f,* Kachel *f.* **II** *v/t* **3.** (mit Ziegeln) decken. **4.** fliesen, kacheln. '**til-er** *s* **1.** Dachdecker *m.* **2.** Fliesenleger *m.*

till[1] [tɪl] *s* (Laden)Kasse *f.*

till[2] [~] → **until.**

tilt [tɪlt] **I** *v/t* **1.** kippen. **II** *v/i* **2.** kippen; sich neigen. **III** *s* **3.** **at a** ~ schief, schräg. **4.** (**at**) **full** ~ F mit Volldampf *arbeiten;* mit Karacho *fahren etc.*

tim-ber ['tɪmbə] *s* **1.** *Br.* Bau-, Nutzholz *n.* **2.** Balken *m.* '**~-line** *s* Baumgrenze *f.*

time [taɪm] **I** *s* **1.** *allg.* Zeit *f:* **some** ~ **ago** vor einiger Zeit; **all the** ~ **die ganze Zeit; ahead of** ~ vorzeitig; **at the** ~ damals; **at** ~**s** manchmal; **at the same** ~ gleichzeitig; trotzdem; **by the** ~ wenn; als; **for a** ~ e-e Zeitlang; **for the** ~ **being** vorläufig, fürs erste; **from** ~ **to** ~ von Zeit zu Zeit; **in** ~ rechtzeitig; im Lauf der Zeit; **in no** ~ (**at all**) im Nu; **in two years'** ~ in zwei Jahren; **on** ~ pünktlich; **be ahead** (*od.* **before**) **one's** ~ s-r Zeit voraus sein; **be behind the** ~**s** rückständig sein; **do** ~ F sitzen (**for** wegen); **keep up** (*od.* **march, move**) **with the** ~**s** mit der Zeit gehen; **take one's** ~ sich Zeit lassen; → **bide, immemorial, mark**[2] 11, **nick** 2, **play** 7. **2.** (*Uhr*)Zeit *f:* **what's the** ~? wie spät ist es?; **what** ~? um wieviel Uhr?; **this** ~ **tomorrow** morgen um diese Zeit. **3.** ♪ Takt *m:* **in** ~ im Takt (*a. marschieren etc*); **in** ~ **with the music** im Takt zur Musik; **beat** ~ den Takt schlagen. **4.** Mal *n:* **~ and again,** ~ **after** ~ immer wieder; **every** ~ **I** ... jedesmal, wenn ich ...; **how many** ~**s?** wie oft?; **next** ~ (**I** ...) nächstes Mal(, wenn ich ...); **this** ~ diesmal; **three** ~**s** vier ist zwölf; → **nine** I, **second**[1] 1. **II** *v/t* **5.** *et.* stoppen; wie lang j-d braucht: **he was** ~**d at 20 seconds** für ihn wurden 20 Sekunden gestoppt. **6.** ~ **well** sich e-n günstigen Zeitpunkt aussuchen für; (*Sport*) Flanke, Schlag *etc* gut timen. ~ **bomb** *s* Zeitbombe *f* (*a. fig.*). ~ **card** *s* Stechkarte *f.* ~ **clock** *s* Stechuhr *f.* '**~-consum-ing** *adj* zeitaufwendig, -raubend. ~ **ex-po-sure** *s phot.* Zeitaufnahme *f.* '**~-hon-o(u)red** *adj* althergebracht. '**~-keep-er** *s* **1.** *Sport:* Zeitnehmer(in). **2. be a good** ~ genau gehen (*Uhr*). ~ **lag** *s* Zeitdifferenz *f.* '**~-lapse** *adj* Film: Zeitraffer...

time-less ['taɪmlɪs] *adj* □ **1.** immerwährend, ewig. **2.** zeitlos.

time lim-it *s* Frist *f:* **set s.o. a** ~ **of** j-m e-e Frist setzen von.

time-ly ['taɪmlɪ] *adj* rechtzeitig.

,**time-'out** *pl* ,**times-'out** *s Sport:* Timeout *n,* Auszeit *f.*

tim-er ['taɪmə] *s* Timer *m,* Schaltuhr *f.*

'**time|,sav-ing** *adj* zeitsparend. '**~,serv-er** *s bsd. pol.* Opportunist(in). ~ **sig-nal** *s Rundfunk:* Zeitzeichen *n.* ~ **switch** *s* Zeitschalter *m.* '**~,ta-ble** *s* **1.** Fahr-, Flugplan *m.* **2.** *ped. Br.* Stundenplan *m.* **3.** Zeitplan *m.* '**~-worn** *adj* **1.** abgenutzt. **2.** *fig.* abgedroschen. ~ **zone** *s* Zeitzone *f.*

tim-id ['tɪmɪd] *adj* □ ängstlich, furchtsam.

tim·ing ['taɪmɪŋ] s Timing n (*Wahl des günstigen Zeitpunkts*).

tin [tɪn] I s **1.** Zinn n. **2.** Br. (Blech-, Konserven)Dose f, (-)Büchse f. II adj **3.** zinnern, Zinn... III v/t **4.** verzinnen. **5.** Br. einmachen, -dosen: → **tinned**.

tinc·ture ['tɪŋktʃə] s pharm. Tinktur f: ~ **of iodine** Jodtinktur.

tin·der ['tɪndə] s Zunder m: (as) **dry as** ~ → **tinder-dry**. '**~·box** s fig. Pulverfaß n. ,**~·'dry** adj so trocken wie Zunder.

tine [taɪn] s **1.** Zinke f, Zacke f (e-r Gabel). **2.** (*Geweih*)Sprosse f, Ende n.

'**tin·foil** s Stanniol(papier) n; Alufolie f.

ting [tɪŋ] I v/t: ~ **a bell** klingeln. II v/i: **the bell** ~**s** es klingelt. III s Klingeln n.

tinge [tɪndʒ] I v/t **1.** tönen: **be** ~**d with** fig. e-n Anflug haben von, et. von ... an sich haben. II s **2.** Tönung f: **have a** ~ **of red** ins Rote spielen. **3.** fig. Anflug m (**of** von).

tin·gle ['tɪŋgl] I v/i prickeln, kribbeln (**with** vor dat). II s Prickeln n, Kribbeln n.

tin| god s F Idol n. ~ **hat** s ✗ F (Stahl-) Helm m.

tink·er ['tɪŋkə] I s Kesselflicker m. II v/i a. ~ **about** herumbasteln (**with** an dat): ~ **with** herumpfuschen an (dat).

tin·kle ['tɪŋkl] I v/i bimmeln; klirren. II s Bimmeln n; Klirren n: **give s.o. a** ~ teleph. Br. F j-n anklingeln.

tinned [tɪnd] adj Br. Dosen..., Büchsen...: ~ **fruit** Obstkonserven pl; ~ **meat** Büchsenfleisch n.

tin·ny ['tɪnɪ] adj blechern (*Klang*).

tin o·pen·er s Br. Dosen-, Büchsenöffner m.

tin·sel ['tɪnsl] s **1.** Lametta n. **2.** fig. Flitter m.

tint [tɪnt] I s (Farb)Ton m, Tönung f: **have a** ~ **of red** ins Rote spielen. II v/t tönen.

ti·ny ['taɪnɪ] adj □ winzig.

tip¹ [tɪp] s **1.** allg. Spitze f: **it's on the** ~ **of my tongue** f. es liegt mir auf der Zunge; → **iceberg**. **2.** Filter m (e-r Zigarette).

tip² [~] I s **1.** Tisch etc kippen: ~ **over** umkippen; → **scale²** **2. 2.** (aus)kippen, schütten. II s **3.** kippen: ~ **over** umkippen. III s **4.** bsd. Br. (Schutt etc)Abladeplatz m, (-)Halde f. **5.** Br. fig. F Saustall m.

tip³ [~] I s **1.** Trinkgeld n. **2.** Tip m, Rat(schlag) m: **take my** ~ **and** ... hör auf mich u. ... II v/t **3.** j-m ein Trinkgeld geben: ~ **s.o. 50 p** j-m 50 Pence Trinkgeld geben. **4.** tippen auf (acc) (**as** als). **5.** ~ **off** j-m e-n Tip od. Wink geben.

'**tip-off** s F Tip m, Wink m.

tip·ple ['tɪpl] s F (*alkoholisches*) Getränk.

tip·sy ['tɪpsɪ] adj □ angeheitert, beschwipst: **be** ~ a. e-n Schwips haben.

'**tip|·toe** I v/i auf Zehenspitzen gehen. II s: **stand on** ~ sich auf die Zehenspitzen stellen; **walk on** ~ → I. ,**~·'top** adj F erstklassig: **be in** ~ **order** tipptopp in Ordnung sein.

ti·rade [taɪ'reɪd] s Schimpfkanonade f (**against** gegen).

tire¹ ['taɪə] Am. → **tyre**.

tire² [~] I v/t ermüden, müde machen: ~ **out** (*völlig*) erschöpfen. II v/i ermüden, müde werden: ~ **of** fig. j-n, et. satt bekommen; ~ **of doing s.th.** satt werden, et. zu tun.

tired ['taɪəd] adj □ **1.** müde: ~ **out** (*völlig*) erschöpft; **be** ~ **of** fig. j-n, et. satt haben; **be** ~ **of doing s.th.** es satt haben od. müde sein, et. zu tun. **2.** fig. abgegriffen.'**tired·ness** s Müdigkeit f.

tire·less ['taɪəlɪs] adj □ unermüdlich.

tire·some ['taɪəsəm] adj □ **1.** ermüdend. **2.** fig. lästig.

ti·ro → **tyro**.

tis·sue ['tɪʃuː] s **1.** biol. Gewebe n. **2.** Papier(taschen)tuch n. **3.** a. ~ **paper** Seidenpapier n.

tit¹ [tɪt] s: ~ **for tat** wie du mir, so ich dir.

tit² [~] s sl. **1.** mst pl Titte f: a) *weibliche Brust*, b) *Brustwarze*. **2.** Br. *blöde Sau.*

tit³ [~] s orn. Meise f.

ti·tan·ic [taɪ'tænɪk] adj (~*ally*) gigantisch.

tit·bit ['tɪtbɪt] s bsd. Br. Leckerbissen m.

tit·il·late ['tɪtɪleɪt] v/t j-n (*sexuell*) anregen.

ti·tle ['taɪtl] s **1.** allg. Titel m. **2.** ⚖ (Rechts)Anspruch m (**to** auf acc). ~ **deed** s ⚖ Eigentumsurkunde f. '~**,hold·er** s **fight** s Boxen: Titelkampf m. '~**,hold·er** s Sport: Titelhalter(in), -träger(in). ~ **page** s Titelseite f. ~ **role** s thea. etc Titelrolle f.

'**tit·mouse** s (irr mouse) orn. Meise f.

tit·ter ['tɪtə] I v/i kichern. II s Kichern n.

tit·tle-tat·tle ['tɪtl,tætl] F I s Geschwätz n; Klatsch m, Tratsch m. II v/i schwatzen; klatschen, tratschen.

tit·u·lar ['tɪtjʊlə] *adj* nominell.

to I *prp* [tuː; tʊ; tə] **1.** *Richtung u. Ziel, räumlich:* zu, nach, an (*acc*), in (*acc*): **go ~ England** nach England fahren; → **bed** 1, **school** 1, *etc.* **2.** in (*dat*): **have you ever been ~ London?** bist du schon einmal in London gewesen? **3.** *Richtung, Ziel, Zweck:* zu, auf (*acc*), für: → **death** 1, **invite** 1, *etc.* **4.** *Zugehörigkeit:* zu, für, in (*acc*): → **key** 1, **secretary** 1, *etc.* **5.** (*im Verhältnis od. Vergleich*) zu, gegen(über): → **compare** 1, **nothing** 1, *etc.* **6.** *Ausmaß, Grenze, Grad:* bis, (bis) zu, (bis) an (*acc*). **7.** *zeitliche Ausdehnung od. Grenze:* bis, bis zu, bis gegen, vor (*dat*): **from three ~ four** von drei bis vier (Uhr); → **quarter** 2. **8.** *Begleitung:* zu, nach: → **dance** 1. **9.** *zur Bildung des (betonten) Dativs:* **~ me** mir. **II** *part* [tʊ] **10.** *zur Bezeichnung des Infinitivs:* **~ go** gehen; **easy ~ understand** leicht zu verstehen. **11.** *Zweck, Absicht:* um zu: **he does it only ~ earn money** er tut es nur, um Geld zu verdienen; → **order** 9. **12.** *zur Verkürzung e-s Nebensatzes:* **he was the first ~ arrive** er kam als erster; → **hear** him **talk** wenn man ihn (so) reden hört. **III** *adv* [tuː] **13.** zu (*geschlossen*). **14.** → **come** to. **15.** → **and fro** hin u. her; auf u. ab.

toad [təʊd] *s* zo. Kröte *f.* '**~·stool** *s* ♀ ungenießbarer Pilz; Giftpilz *m.*

toad·y ['təʊdɪ] **I** *s* Kriecher(in), Speichellecker(in). **II** *v/i:* **~ to s.o.** vor j-m kriechen.

toast¹ [təʊst] **I** *s* **1.** Toast *m.* **II** *v/t* **2.** toasten; rösten. **3.** F sich *die Füße etc* wärmen.

toast² [~] **I** *s* Toast *m*, Trinkspruch *m*: **drink a ~ to →** II. **II** *v/t* auf *j-n od. j-s* Wohl trinken.

toast·er ['təʊstə] *s* ⊙ Toaster *m.*

to·bac·co [tə'bækəʊ] *pl* **-cos** *s* Tabak *m.*

to'bac·co·nist [~kənɪst] *s* Tabak(waren)händler(in).

to·bog·gan [tə'bɒɡən] **I** *s* (Rodel)Schlitten *m.* **II** *v/i* Schlitten fahren, rodeln.

tod [tɒd] *s:* **on one's ~** *Br.* F ganz allein.

to·day [tə'deɪ] **I** *adv* **1.** heute: **a week ~, ~ week** heute in e-r Woche od. in acht Tagen. **2.** heutzutage. **II** *s* **3.** **~'s paper** die heutige Zeitung, die Zeitung von

heute. **4.** **of ~, ~'s** von heute, heutig.

tod·dle ['tɒdl] *v/i* **1.** auf wack(e)ligen *od.* unsicheren Beinen gehen (*bsd. Kleinkind*). **2.** F gehen. '**tod·dler** *s* Kleinkind *n.*

tod·dy ['tɒdɪ] *s* Toddy *m* (*grogartiges Getränk*).

to-do [tə'duː] *s* F Theater *n* (**about** um).

toe [təʊ] **I** *s anat.* Zehe *f:* **be on one's ~s** *fig.* gut drauf sein; **keep s.o. on his ~s** *fig.* j-n auf Zack halten; **tread on s.o.'s ~s** *fig.* j-m zu nahe treten. **II** *v/t:* **~ the line** *fig.* spuren. '**~·nail** *s* Zehennagel *m.*

tof·fee ['tɒfɪ] *s bsd. Br.* Toffee *n*, Karamelbonbon *n, m:* **he can't play tennis for ~** F er hat vom Tennisspielen keine Ahnung. '**~·nosed** *adj Br.* F eingebildet, hochnäsig.

tof·fy → **toffee.**

tog [tɒɡ] F **I** *v/t:* **~ o.s. out** (*od.* **up**) sich in Schale werfen. **II** *s pl* Klamotten *pl.*

to·geth·er [tə'ɡeðə] **I** *adv* zusammen (**with** mit); zusammen...: → **keep together, live** ¹ I, *etc.* **II** *adj* F ausgeglichen (*Person*). **to'geth·er·ness** *s* Zs.-gehörigkeit(sgefühl *n*) *f.*

toil [tɔɪl] **I** *s* mühselige Arbeit. **II** *v/i* sich abmühen *od.* plagen (**at** mit); sich schleppen.

toi·let ['tɔɪlɪt] *s* Toilette *f:* **go to the ~** auf die *od.* in die *od.* zur Toilette gehen. '**pa·per** *s* Toilettenpapier *n.* '**~·roll** *s* Rolle *f* Toilettenpapier.

to·ken ['təʊkən] *s* **1.** Zeichen *n:* **as a** (*od.* **in**) **~ of** als *od.* zum Zeichen (*gen*); zum Andenken an (*acc*). **2.** Gutschein *m.* **3.** (*Spiel- etc*)Marke *f.* **III** *adj* **4.** symbolisch. **5.** Schein... **6.** Alibi...

told [təʊld] *pret u. pp von* **tell.**

tol·er·a·ble ['tɒlərəbl] *adj* erträglich. '**tol·er·a·bly** *adv* leidlich, einigermaßen. '**tol·er·ance** *s* **1.** Toleranz *f* (**for, of, toward**[**s**] gegenüber). **2.** ♂, ⊙ Toleranz *f.* '**tol·er·ant** *adj* □ tolerant (**of, toward**[**s**] gegenüber). **tol·er·ate** [~reɪt] *v/t* **1.** tolerieren, dulden. **2.** *j-n, et.* ertragen.

toll¹ [təʊl] *s* **1.** Benutzungsgebühr *f*, Maut *f.* **2.** **take its ~** (**on**) *fig.* s-n Tribut fordern (von); s-e Spuren hinterlassen (bei).

toll² [~] *v/i* läuten (*bsd. Totenglocke*).

toll| **bridge** *s* gebührenpflichtige Brücke, Mautbrücke *f.* '**~·free** *adj u. adv* *teleph. Am.* gebührenfrei. **~ road** *s* gebührenpflichtige Straße, Mautstraße *f.*

tom [tɒm] *s zo.* Kater *m.*

tom·a·hawk ['tɒməhɔːk] *s hist.* Tomahawk *m,* Streitaxt *f.* **II** *adj* Indianer...

to·ma·to [tə'mɑːtəʊ] **I** *pl* **-toes** *s* 🌱 Tomate *f.* **II** *adj* Tomaten...

tomb [tuːm] *s* Grab(mal) *n;* Gruft *f.*

tom·bo·la [tɒm'bəʊlə] *s* Tombola *f.*

tom·boy ['tɒmbɔɪ] *s* Wildfang *m (Mädchen).*

'tomb·stone *s* Grabstein *m.*

'tom·cat *s zo.* Kater *m.*

tome [təʊm] *s humor.* Wälzer *m.*

tom·fool·er·y [,tɒm'fuːlərɪ] *s* Albernheit *f,* Unsinn *m.*

tom·my gun ['tɒmɪ] *s* F Maschinenpistole *f.*

to·mor·row [tə'mɒrəʊ] **I** *adv* **1.** morgen: **a week ~, ~ week** morgen in e-r Woche *od.* in acht Tagen; **~ morning** morgen früh; **~ night** morgen abend. **II** *s* **2. ~'s paper** die morgige Zeitung, die Zeitung von morgen; **the day after ~** übermorgen. **3.** Zukunft *f:* **of ~, ~'s** von morgen.

ton [tʌn] *s* **1.** Tonne *f (Gewicht).* **2.** F **~s** *pl* **of** jede Menge; **~s better** viel *od.* wesentlich besser.

tone [təʊn] **I** *s* **1.** *allg.* Ton *m;* Klang *m.* **2.** ♪ *Am.* Note *f.* **3.** *fig.* Niveau *n.* **II** *v/t* **4. ~ down** Kritik *etc* abschwächen; **~ up** *j-n, Muskeln* kräftigen. **III** *v/i* **5. ~ in (with)** harmonieren (mit), passen (zu).

tongs [tɒŋz] *s pl,* **a. pair of ~** Zange *f.*

tongue [tʌŋ] *s* **1.** *anat.* Zunge *f (a. fig.):* **in cheek, with one's ~ in one's cheek** scherzhaft; **bite one's ~** sich auf die Zunge beißen *(a. fig.);* **hold one's ~** den Mund halten; **put out one's ~ at** s.o. j-m die Zunge herausstrecken; → **slip¹** 1, **tip¹** 1, **wag¹** II. **2.** *(Mutter)* Sprache *f.* **3.** Zunge *f (e-s Schuhs etc); (Land)* Zunge *f:* **~ of land.** **4.** Klöppel *m (e-r Glocke).* → **twist·er** *s* Zungenbrecher *m.*

ton·ic ['tɒnɪk] *s* **1.** *pharm.* Tonikum *n,* Stärkungsmittel *n:* **be a real ~** *allg.* richtig guttun. **2.** Tonic *n (→ tonic water):* **a gin and ~** ein Gin Tonic. **~ wa·ter** *s* Tonic water *n (mit Kohlensäure u. Chinin versetztes Wasser).*

to·night [tə'naɪt] **I** *adv* heute abend; heute nacht. **II** *s:* **~'s program(me)** das Programm (von) heute abend.

ton·sil ['tɒnsl] *s anat.* Mandel *f.* **ton·sil·li·tis** [,tɒnsɪ'laɪtɪs] *s* 🩺 Mandelentzündung *f; weitS.* Angina *f.*

ton·sure ['tɒnʃə] *s* Tonsur *f.*

too [tuː] *adv* **1.** zu. **2.** zu, sehr. **3.** auch. **4.** auch noch, noch dazu.

took [tʊk] *pret von* **take.**

tool [tuːl] *s* **1.** Werkzeug *n (a. fig. Person),* Gerät *n:* **be the ~s of s.o.'s trade** *fig.* j-s Rüstzeug sein; → **down** 15. **2.** V Schwanz *m (Penis).* **~ bag** *s* Werkzeugtasche *f.* **~ box** *s* Werkzeugkasten *m.* **~ shed** *s* Geräteschuppen *m.*

toot [tuːt] *mot.* **I** *v/i* hupen. **II** *v/t:* **~ one's horn** → I. **III** *s:* **give a ~ on one's horn** → I.

tooth [tuːθ] *pl* **teeth** [tiːθ] *s anat.* Zahn *m (a. e-s Kamms, e-r Säge, e-s Zahnrads etc):* **in the teeth of** *fig.* gegen; trotz, ungeachtet; **fight ~ and nail** *fig.* erbittert *od.* verbissen kämpfen; **get one's teeth into** *fig.* sich reinknien in *(acc);* → **armed, brush¹** 5, **cut** 10, **edge** 4, **skin** 1, **sweet** 1. **'~·ache** *s* Zahnschmerzen *pl,* -weh *n.* **'~·brush** *s* Zahnbürste *f.*

tooth·less ['tuːθlɪs] *adj* zahnlos.

'tooth·paste *s* Zahncreme *f,* -pasta *f.* **'~·pick** *s* Zahnstocher *m.*

tooth·some ['tuːθsəm] *adj* □ lecker, schmackhaft.

toot·sie, toot·sy ['tʊtsɪ] *s* Kindersprache: Füßchen *n.*

top¹ [tɒp] **I** *s* **1.** oberer Teil; Gipfel *m,* Spitze *f (e-s Bergs etc);* Krone *f,* Wipfel *m (e-s Baums);* Kopfende *n,* oberes Ende *(e-s Tischs etc):* **at the ~ of the page** oben auf der Seite; **from ~ to toe** von Kopf bis Fuß; **on ~** oben(auf); d(a)rauf; **on ~ of** (oben) auf *(dat od. acc),* über *(dat od. acc);* **on ~ of each other** auf-, übereinander; **on ~ of it** *fig.* obendrein; **get on ~ of s.o.** F j-m zuviel *od.* zu schwierig werden; → **thin** 1. **2.** *fig.* Spitze *f:* **at the ~ of one's voice** aus vollem Hals; **be at the ~ of** an der Spitze *(gen)* stehen; **stay on ~** an der Spitze bleiben. **3.** *(Bikini- etc)* Oberteil *n.* **4.** Oberfläche *f (e-s Tischs etc).* **5.** Deckel *m (e-s Glases), (a. e-r Tube etc)* Verschluß *m:* → **blow¹** 11. **6.** *mot.* Verdeck *n:* → **hardtop.** **7.** *mot.* höchster Gang. **II** *adj* **8.** oberst: **~ dog** F der Überlegene; der Chef; **~ hat** Zylinder *m.* **9.** *fig.* Höchst..., Spitzen...: **~ gear**

→ 7; **~ manager** Top-, Spitzenmanager *m*; **at ~ speed** mit Höchstgeschwindigkeit; in Windeseile; → **management** 2. **III** *v/t* **10.** bedecken (**with** mit). **11.** *fig.* übersteigen; übertreffen. **12.** ~ **the bill** der Star des Programms *od.* die Hauptattraktion sein.

Verbindungen mit Adverbien:

top| off *v/t bsd. Am.* abschließen, krönen (**with** mit). **~ out** *v/t* das Richtfest (*gen*) feiern. **~ up** *v/t* Tank *etc* auffüllen; F *j-m* nachschenken.

top² [~] *s* Kreisel *m* (*Spielzeug*): → **sleep** I.

to·pee ['təʊpɪ] *s* Tropenhelm *m*.

'top·flight *adj* F Spitzen... ,**~'heav·y** *adj* kopflastig (*a. fig.*), oberlastig.

top·ic ['tɒpɪk] *s* Thema *n*: **~ of conversation** Gesprächsthema. **'top·i·cal** *adj* □ aktuell.

'top·knot *s* Haarknoten *m*.

top·less ['tɒplɪs] *adj* oben ohne; Oben-ohne-...

,top|·'lev·el *adj* auf höchster Ebene, Spitzen... '**~·most** *adj* oberst. ,**~·'notch** *adj* F erstklassig, Spitzen...

to·pog·ra·phy [tə'pɒgrəfɪ] *s* Topographie *f*.

top·per ['tɒpə] *s* F Zylinder *m*. **'top·ping** *s*: **with a ~ of whipped cream** mit Schlagsahne darauf.

top·ple ['tɒpl] **I** *v/i* **1.** *mst* **~ over** umkippen. **II** *v/t* **2.** *mst* **~ over** umkippen. **3.** *fig.* Regierung *etc* stürzen.

,top|·'se·cret *adj* streng geheim. '**~·spin** *s* Tennis *etc*: Topspin *m* (*starker Aufwärtsdrall*).

top·sy-tur·vy [,tɒpsɪ'tɜ:vɪ] *adj* F **1.** in e-r heillosen Unordnung. **2.** *fig.* konfus, wirr.

torch [tɔ:tʃ] *s* **1.** *bsd. Br.* Taschenlampe *f.* Fackel *f.* '**~·light** *s*: **by ~** bei Fackelschein; **~ procession** Fackelzug *m*.

tore [tɔ:] *pret von* tear².

tor·ment **I** *v/t* [tɔ:'ment] **1.** quälen, *fig. a.* plagen: **be ~ed by** (*od.* **with**) gequält *od.* geplagt werden von. **II** *s* ['tɔ:ment] **2.** Qual *f*: **be in ~, suffer ~(s)** Qualen leiden. **3.** Quälgeist *m*.

torn [tɔ:n] *pp von* tear².

tor·na·do [tɔ:'neɪdəʊ] *pl* **-do(e)s** *s* Tornado *m*.

tor·pe·do [tɔ:'pi:dəʊ] **I** *pl* **-does** *s* ♣, ✕

Torpedo *m*. **II** *v/t* torpedieren (*a. fig.*). **~ boat** *s* Torpedoboot *n*.

tor·pid ['tɔ:pɪd] *adj* □ träg(e). **tor·por** ['~pə] *s* Trägheit *f*.

torque [tɔ:k] *s phys.* Drehmoment *n*.

tor·rent ['tɒrənt] *s* **1.** reißender Strom: **~s** *pl* **of rain** sintflutartige Regenfälle *pl*; **the rain fell in ~s** es goß in Strömen. **2.** *fig.* Schwall *m*, Sturzbach *m* (**of** von). **tor·ren·tial** [tə'renʃl] *adj* sintflutartig.

tor·rid ['tɒrɪd] *adj* □ sengend.

tor·sion ['tɔ:ʃn] *s phys.* Torsion *f*, Verdrillung *f*.

tor·so ['tɔ:səʊ] *pl* **-sos** *s* Rumpf *m*; (*Kunst*) Torso *m*.

tort [tɔ:t] *s ✿✿* unerlaubte Handlung.

tor·toise ['tɔ:təs] *s zo.* Schildkröte *f*.

tor·tu·ous ['tɔ:tjʊəs] *adj* □ **1.** gewunden (*Pfad etc*). **2.** *fig.* umständlich.

tor·ture ['tɔ:tʃə] **I** *v/t* **1.** foltern. **2.** *fig.* quälen: **be ~d by** (*od.* **with**) gequält werden von. **II** *s* **3.** Folter(ung) *f*. **4.** *fig.* Qual *f*. **~ cham·ber** *s* Folterkammer *f*.

To·ry ['tɔ:rɪ] *pol. Br.* **I** *s* Tory *m*, Konservative *m*. **II** *adj* Tory..., torystisch, konservativ.

toss [tɒs] **I** *v/t* **1.** werfen: **~ s.o. s.th.** *et.* zuwerfen; **~ back** Kopf zurückwerfen; **~ off** *Arbeit* hinhauen; *Getränk* hinunterstürzen. **2.** *Münze* hochwerfen: **~ s.o. for s.th.** mit j-m um et. losen. **II** *v/i* **3.** *a.* **~ about** (*od.* **around**), **~ and turn** sich (*im Schlaf etc*) hin u. her werfen. **4.** *a.* **~ up** e-e Münze hochwerfen: **~ for s.th.** um et. losen *et.* auslosen. **III** *s* **5.** Wurf *m*. **6.** Hochwerfen *n* (*e-r Münze*): **win the ~** (*Sport*) die Wahl gewinnen. **7.** **I don't give a ~ about it** *Br.* F das ist mir völlig egal. '**~·up** *s* **1.** → **toss** 6. **2.** **it's a ~ whether** F es ist völlig offen, ob.

tot¹ [tɒt] *s* **1.** *a.* **tiny ~** F Knirps *m*. **2.** Schluck *m* (*Alkohol*).

tot² [~] *v/t*: **~ up** F zs.-rechnen, -zählen.

to·tal ['təʊtl] **I** *adj* □ **1.** völlig, total, Total...: → **recall** 4. **2.** ganz, gesamt, Gesamt... **II** *s* **3.** Gesamtmenge *f*; (End)Summe *f*: **a ~ of 20 cases** insgesamt 20 Fälle; **in ~** insgesamt. **III** *v/t pret u. pp* **-taled**, *bsd. Br.* **-talled 4.** sich belaufen auf (*acc*): **... ~(l)ing £500** ... von insgesamt 500 Pfund. **5.** *a.* **~ up** zs.-rechnen, -zählen. **to·tal·i·tar·i·an** [,~tælɪ'teərɪən] *adj pol.* totalitär. **to·tal-**

i·za·tor ['ˌtəlaɪzeɪtə] s *Pferdesport:* Totalisator *m*.

tote [təʊt] s *Pferdesport:* F Toto *n*, *m* (*Totalisator*).

tote bag [təʊt] s *bsd. Am.* Einkaufstasche *f*.

to·tem ['təʊtəm] s Totem *n*. **~ pole** s Totempfahl *m*.

tot·ter ['tɒtə] v/i (sch)wanken. **'tot·ter·y** *adj* wack(e)lig.

touch [tʌtʃ] **I** s **1.** Tastempfindung *f*: **be soft to the ~** sich weich anfühlen; → **sense** 1. **2.** Berührung *f*, ♩ *etc* Anschlag *m*: **at the ~ of a button** auf Knopfdruck. **3. be in ~ with s.o.** mit j-m in Verbindung stehen; **get in ~ with s.o.** sich mit j-m in Verbindung setzen; **keep in ~ with s.o.** mit j-m in Verbindung bleiben; **lose ~** den Kontakt verlieren (**with s.o.** zu j-m). **4.** (*Pinsel etc*)Strich *m*: **put the finishing ~es to** letzte Hand legen an (*acc*). **5.** *fig.* Note *f*: **a personal ~. 6.** Spur *f* (*Salz etc*), *fig.* Anflug *m* (*von Ironie etc*): **a ~ of flu** e-e leichte Grippe. **7. in(to) ~** (*Fußball*) im (ins) Aus. **II** v/t **8.** berühren; anfassen: **~ wood!** toi, toi, toi!; → **nerve** 1. **9.** Alkohol, Essen *etc* anrühren. **10.** *fig.* herankommen an (*acc*). **11.** *fig.* rühren, bewegen. **12.** *fig.* berühren, betreffen. **13.** F j-n anpumpen (*for um*). **III** v/i **14.** sich berühren. **15. ~ on** Thema *etc* berühren, streifen.

Verbindungen mit Adverbien:

touch| down v/i ✈ aufsetzen. **~ off** v/t Explosion, Krise *etc* auslösen. **~ up** v/t **1.** ausbessern; *phot.* retuschieren. **2.** *Br.* F j-n befummeln, betatschen.

‚touch|-and-'go *adj* kritisch (*Situation etc*): **it was ~ whether** es stand auf des Messers Schneide, ob. **'~down** s ✈ Aufsetzen *n*.

tou·ché ['tuːʃeɪ] *int* eins zu null für dich!

touched [tʌtʃt] *adj* **1.** gerührt, bewegt. **2. be ~** F e-n Schlag haben. **'touch·ing** *adj* rührend, bewegend.

'touch|·line s *Fußball:* Seitenlinie *f*. **'~stone** s Prüfstein *m* (*of* für). **'~type** v/i blindschreiben.

touch·y ['tʌtʃɪ] *adj* □ **1.** empfindlich, reizbar. **2.** heikel (*Thema*).

tough [tʌf] *adj* □ **1.** zäh (*Fleisch etc*): (**as**) **~ as leather** zäh wie Leder. **2.** widerstandsfähig (*Material etc*), (*Per-*

---

son a.) zäh. **3.** *fig.* hart (*Haltung etc*): **get ~ with** hart vorgehen gegen. **4.** *fig.* hart (*Konkurrenz etc*), (*Problem, Verhandlungen etc a.*) schwierig. **'tough·en I** v/t a. **~ up** j-n hart od. zäh machen. **II** v/i a. **~ up** hart od. zäh werden.

tour [tʊə] **I** s **1.** Tour *f* (*of* durch): a) (Rund)Reise *f*, (-)Fahrt *f*: **~ operator** Reiseveranstalter *m*, b) Ausflug *m*, Wanderung *f*. **2.** Rundgang *m* (*of* durch): **take s.o. on a ~ of** j-n herumführen in (*dat*); → **conduct** 3, **guided** 1, **sightseeing. 3.** *thea. etc* Tournee *f* (*a. Sport*), Gastspielreise *f* (*of* durch): **be on ~** auf Tournee sein (**in** in *dat*). **II** v/t **4.** bereisen, reisen durch. **5.** *thea. etc a.* Tournee (*a. Sport*) od. Gastspielreise machen durch: **be ~ing Germany** auf Deutschlandtournee sein. **6.** **~** (**a**)**round** → 4. **7.** *thea. etc* e-e Tournee (*a. Sport*) od. Gastspielreise machen, auf Tournee sein: → **tour·ism** s Tourismus *m*, Fremdenverkehr *m*. **'tour·ist I** s Tourist(in). **II** *adj* Touristen...: **~ class** ✈, ♥ Touristenklasse *f*; **~ season** Reisesaison *f*, -zeit *f*; **~ trade** Fremdenverkehrsgewerbe *n*.

tour·na·ment ['tɔːnəmənt] s Turnier *n*.

tou·sled ['taʊzld] *adj* zerzaust (*Haar*).

tout [taʊt] **I** v/t **1.** (aufdringlich) Reklame machen für. **2.** anpreisen (**as** als). **II** v/i **3. ~ for business** Kunden werben. **III** s **4.** *Br.* (*Karten*)Schwarzhändler(in).

tow [təʊ] **I** v/t Boot *etc* schleppen, Auto *etc a.* abschleppen: **~ away** falsch geparktes Fahrzeug abschleppen. **II** s: **give s.o. a ~** j-n abschleppen; **take in ~** Auto *etc* abschleppen, Boot *etc* ins Schlepptau nehmen; **with his children in ~** F mit s-n Kindern im Schlepptau.

to·ward *bsd. Am.*, **to·wards** *bsd. Br.* [tə'wɔːd(z)] *prp* **1.** *Richtung:* auf (*acc*) ... zu, (in) Richtung, zu: → **face** 13, *etc.* **2.** *zeitlich:* gegen: **~ the end** gegen Ende (*gen*). **3.** *fig.* gegenüber: → **attitude** 2, *etc.* **4.** *fig.* auf (*acc*) ... hin: **they gave me s.th. ~ it** sie zahlten mir et. dazu.

tow·el ['taʊəl] **I** s Handtuch *n*, (*Bade etc*)Tuch *n*: **throw in the ~** das Handtuch werfen (*a. fig.*); → **sanitary** 1. **II** v/t *pret u. pp* **-eled**, *bsd. Br.* **-elled** *a.* **~ down** (mit e-m Handtuch) abtrocknen *od.* abreiben. **~ rail** *s* Handtuchhalter *m.*

tow·er ['taʊə] **I** *s* Turm *m*: **~ block** *Br.* Hochhaus *n.* **II** *v/i*: **~ above** (*od.* **over**) überragen (*a. fig.*). **'tow·er·ing** *adj* **1.** turmhoch. **2.** *fig.* überragend. **3.** *be in a* **~ rage** vor Wut rasen.

town [taʊn] *s* (Klein)Stadt *f*: *go to* (**the**) **~** in die Stadt fahren *od.* gehen; *be* (**out**) *on the* **~** F e-n draufmachen; → **paint** 2. **~ cen·tre** *s Br.* Innenstadt *f*, City *f.* **~ fa·thers** *s pl* Stadtväter *pl.* **~ hall** *s* Rathaus *n.* **~ plan·ning** *s* Stadtplanung *f.*

towns·folk ['taʊnzfəʊk] → **townspeople.**

town·ship ['taʊnʃɪp] *s Am.* (Stadt)Gemeinde *f*; (Kreis)Bezirk *m.*

towns·peo·ple ['taʊnz,pi:pl] *s pl* Städter *pl*, Stadtbevölkerung *f.*

'tow-rope *s mot.* Abschleppseil *n.*

tox·ic ['tɒksɪk] *adj* (**~ally**) toxisch, giftig, Gift...

tox·in ['tɒksɪn] *s biol.* Toxin *n.*

toy [tɔɪ] **I** *s* **1.** Spielzeug *n*: **~s** *pl* Spielsachen *pl*, -zeug *n*, ✝ -waren *pl.* **II** *v/i* **2. ~ with** spielen mit (*a. fig.*). **III** *adj* **3.** Spielzeug... **4.** *zo.* Zwerg... (*Hund*). **~ shop** *s* Spielwarengeschäft *n*, -handlung *f.*

trace¹ [treɪs] **I** *s* **1.** Spur *f* (*a. fig.*): *without* (**a**) **~** spurlos; *lose all* **~** *of s.o.* j-n aus den Augen verlieren. **II** *v/t* **2.** j-n, *et.* ausfindig machen, aufspüren, *et.* finden: *he was* **~d** *to* s-e Spur führte nach. **3.** *a.* **~ back** *et.* zurückverfolgen (*to* bis zu): **~ s.th. to** *et.* zurückführen auf (*acc*), *et.* herleiten von (*acc*). **4.** (durch)pausen.

trace² [~] *s* Zugleine *f*: *kick over the* **~s** *fig.* über die Stränge schlagen.

trace el·e·ment *s* 🜨 Spurenelement *n.*

tra·che·a [trə'kiːə] *pl* **-ae** [~iː] *s anat.* Luftröhre *f.*

trac·ing ['treɪsɪŋ] *s* Pause *f.* **~ pa·per** *s* Pauspapier *n.*

track [træk] **I** *s* **1.** Spur *f* (*a. e-s Tonbands etc u. fig.*), *hunt. a.* Fährte *f*: *be* (**hot**) *on s.o.'s* **~** j-m (dicht) auf der Spur sein; *be on the wrong* **~** auf der falschen Spur *od.* auf dem Holzweg sein; *keep* **~** *of* sich auf dem laufenden halten über (*acc*); *lose* **~** *of* den Überblick verlieren über (*acc*). **2.** Pfad *m*, Weg *m.* **3.** 🜨

Gleis *n*, Geleise *n*: *jump the* **~s** aus den Schienen springen, entgleisen. **4.** *Sport:* (*Lauf-, Radrenn*)Bahn *f*, (*Renn*)Strecke *f.* **5.** ⊙ Raupe *f*, Gleis-, Raupenkette *f.* **6.** Nummer *f* (*auf e-r Langspielplatte etc*). **II** *v/t* **7.** verfolgen: **~ down** aufspüren; aufstöbern, -treiben. **~-and-'field** *adj Am.* Leichtathletik...: **~ sports** *pl* Leichtathletik *f.*

tracked [trækt] *adj*: **~ vehicle** Gleisketten-, Raupenfahrzeug *n.*

track·er dog ['trækə] *s* Spür-, Suchhund *m.*

track e·vents *s pl Leichtathletik:* Laufdisziplinen *pl.*

track·ing sta·tion ['trækɪŋ] *s Raumfahrt:* Bodenstation *f.*

track| rec·ord *s* **1.** *Sport:* Bahnrekord *m.* **2. have a good** *~ fig.* einiges vorzuweisen haben. **'~·suit** *s* Trainingsanzug *m.*

tract¹ [trækt] *s* **1.** Fläche *f*, Gebiet *n.* **2.** *anat.* (*Verdauungs*)Trakt *m*, (*Atem-*) Wege *pl.*

tract² [~] *s* Traktat *m, n*, kurze Abhandlung.

trac·ta·ble ['træktəbl] *adj* □ folg-, fügsam.

trac·tion ['trækʃn] *s* **1.** Ziehen *n.* **2.** ⊙ Antrieb *m.* **3.** *mot.* Bodenhaftung *f.* **4.** *his leg is in* **~** *& sein Bein ist im Streckverband.* **~ en·gine** *s* Zugmaschine *f.*

trac·tor ['træktə] *s* Traktor *m*, Trecker *m*, Zugmaschine *f.*

trade [treɪd] **I** *s* **1.** Handel *m* (*in mit et.*). **2.** Branche *f*, Gewerbe *n*: *be in the tourist* **~** im Fremdenverkehrsgewerbe (tätig) sein. **3.** *do good* **~** gute Geschäfte machen. **4.** (*bsd.* Handwerks)Beruf *m*: *by* **~** von Beruf. **II** *v/i* **5.** handeln (*in* mit *et.*), Handel treiben: **~ with s.o.** *a.* mit j-m Geschäfte machen. **6. ~ on** *b.s.* ausnutzen, spekulieren mit. **7.** (ein-)tauschen (*for* gegen). **8. ~ in** in Zahlung geben (*for* für). **~ a·gree·ment** *s* Handelsabkommen *n.* **'~·mark** *s* **1.** ✝ Warenzeichen *n.* **2.** *fig.* Kennzeichen *n.* **~ name** *s* Markenname *m*, Handelsbezeichnung *f.* **~ price** *s* Großhandelspreis *m.*

trad·er ['treɪdə] *s* Händler(in).

trades·man ['treɪdzmən] *s* (*irr man*) **1.** (Einzel)Händler *m*; Ladeninhaber *m.* **2.** Lieferant *m*: **~'s entrance** Lieferanteneingang *m.*

trade| un·ion s Gewerkschaft f. ~ **un·-ion·ist** s Gewerkschafter(in).

trad·ing| part·ner s Handelspartner(in). ~ **stamp** s Rabattmarke f.

tra·di·tion [trə'dɪʃn] s Tradition f: **by ~** traditionell(erweise). **tra'di·tion·al** [~ʃənl] adj □ traditionell: **~ly** a. traditionellerweise; **it is ~ for them to** (inf) es ist bei ihnen Brauch od. so üblich, daß sie.

traf·fic ['træfɪk] **I** s **1.** Verkehr m. **2.** (bsd. illegaler) Handel (**in** mit): ~ **in drugs** Drogenhandel. **II** v/i pret u. pp **-ficked 3.** (bsd. illegal) handeln (**in** mit). ~ **cha·os** s Verkehrschaos n. ~ **cir·cle** s Am. Kreisverkehr m. ~ **cone** s Pylon(e f) m, Leitkegel m. ~ **is·land** s Verkehrsinsel f. ~ **jam** s Verkehrsstauung f, -stockung f, Stau m.

traf·fick·er ['træfɪkə] s (bsd. illegaler) Händler (**in** mit): ~ **in drugs** Drogenhändler.

traf·fic| light s Br. mst pl Verkehrsampel f. ~ **of·fence** s Verkehrsdelikt n. ~ **of·fend·er** s Verkehrssünder(in). → **offense** Am. → **traffic offence.** ~ **sign** s Verkehrszeichen n, -schild n. ~ **sig·nal** → **traffic light.** ~ **war·den** s Br. Parküberwacher m, Politesse f.

trag·e·dy ['trædʒədɪ] s thea. Tragödie f (a. fig.), Trauerspiel n.

trag·ic ['trædʒɪk] adj (~ally) thea. tragisch (a. fig.): **~ally** a. tragischerweise; unter tragischen Umständen.

trag·i·com·e·dy [ˌtrædʒɪ'kɒmədɪ] s thea. Tragikomödie f (a. fig.). ˌ**trag·i'com·ic** adj (~ally) tragikomisch.

trail [treɪl] **I** v/t **1.** et. nachschleifen lassen: ~ **one's feet** schlurfen. **2.** verfolgen. **3.** Sport: zurückliegen hinter (dat) (**by** um). **II** v/i **4.** ~ **(along)** behind s.o. hinter j-m herschleifen. **5.** sich schleppen. **6.** Sport: zurückliegen ([**by**] **2-0** 0:2). **III** s **7.** Spur f (a. fig.), hunt. a. Fährte f: ~ **of blood** Blutspur; ~ **of dust** (**smoke**) Staubwolke f (Rauchfahne f); **be** (**hot**) **on s.o.'s** ~ j-m (dicht) auf der Spur sein. **8.** Pfad m, Weg m. **'trail·er** s **1.** mot. Anhänger m. **2.** Am. Caravan m, Wohnwagen m. **3.** Film, TV: Trailer m, Vorschau f.

train [treɪn] **I** s **1.** 🚂 Zug m: **by ~** mit der Bahn, mit dem Zug; **on the ~** im Zug; ~ **ferry** Eisenbahnfähre f; ~ **set** (Spiel-

zeug)Eisenbahn f. **2.** Kolonne f. **3.** Schleppe f. **4.** fig. Folge f, Kette f (von Ereignissen etc): ~ **of thought** Gedankengang m. **II** v/t **5.** j-n ausbilden (**as** als, zum), a. Auge, Verstand etc schulen; (Sport) trainieren; Tier abrichten, dressieren (**to do** zu tun). **6.** Geschütz, Kamera etc richten (**on** auf acc). **III** v/i **7.** ausgebildet werden (**as** als, zum). **8.** Sport: trainieren (**for** für). **'train·er** s **1.** Ausbilder(in); Dresseur m, Abrichter(in), Dompteur m, Dompteuse f; (Sport) Trainer(in). **2.** Br. Turnschuh m. **'train·ing** s **1.** Ausbildung f, Schulung f; Abrichten n, Dressur f. **2.** Sport: Training f: **be in ~** im Training stehen, trainieren; (gut) in Form sein; **be out of ~** nicht in Form sein. **II** adj **3.** Ausbildungs..., Schulungs... **4.** Sport: Trainings...

traipse [treɪps] v/i F latschen.

trait [treɪt] s (Charakter)Zug m, Eigenschaft f.

trai·tor ['treɪtə] s Verräter m (**to** an dat).

tra·jec·to·ry [trə'dʒektərɪ] s phys. Flugbahn f.

tram [træm] s Br. a) Straßenbahn(wagen m) f: **by ~** mit der Straßenbahn; **on the ~** in der Straßenbahn, b) → **tramway.** '~**car** s Br. Straßenbahnwagen m.

tramp [træmp] **I** v/i **1.** sta(m)pfen; trampeln. **II** v/t **2.** sta(m)pfen od. trampeln durch. **III** s **3.** bsd. Br. Tramp m, Landstreicher(in). **4.** Wanderung f: **go for a ~** e-e Wanderung machen. **5.** bsd. Am. Flittchen n.

tram·ple ['træmpl] **I** v/i trampeln: ~ **on** herumtrampeln auf (dat); fig. j-s Gefühle mit Füßen treten. **II** v/t zertrampeln: ~ **down** niedertrampeln; **be ~d to death** zu Tode getrampelt werden; → **underfoot.**

tram·po·line ['træmpəli:n] s Trampolin n.

'**tram·way** s Br. Straßenbahn(linie) f.

trance [trɑːns] s Trance f: **go into a ~** in Trance verfallen.

tran·quil ['træŋkwɪl] adj □ **1.** ruhig, friedlich. **2.** sorgenfrei. '**tran·quil·i·ty** s bsd. Am., '**tran'quil·li·ty** s Br. Ruhe m, Frieden m. '**tran·quil·ize** v/t Am., '**tran·quil·lize** v/t bsd. Br. j-n beruhigen, Tier a. betäuben. '**tran·quil·(l)iz-**

er *s* Beruhigungs- *od.* Betäubungsmittel *n*.

trans·act [træn'zækt] *v/t Geschäft* abwickeln, *a. Handel* abschließen. **trans'ac·tion** *s* **1.** Abwicklung *f*, Abschluß *m*. **2.** Transaktion *f*, Geschäft *n*.

trans·at·lan·tic [ˌtrænzət'læntɪk] *adj* transatlantisch, Transatlantik...

tran·scen·den·tal [ˌtrænsen'dentl] *adj*: **~ meditation** transzendentale Meditation.

trans·con·ti·nen·tal [ˈtrænzˌkɒntɪ'nentl] *adj* transkontinental.

tran·scribe [træn'skraɪb] *v/t* **1.** abschreiben, kopieren. **2.** *Stenogramm etc* übertragen (**into** in *acc*). **3.** ♪ transkribieren, umschreiben (**for** für). **4.** **~ onto** → **transfer** 9. **tran·script** ['trænskrɪpt] *s* Abschrift *f*, Kopie *f*. **tran·scrip·tion** [~'skrɪpʃn] *s* **1.** Abschreiben *n*, Kopieren *n*. **2.** Übertragen *n*. **3.** ♪ Transkription *f*, Umschreibung *f*. **4.** → **transcript. 5.** → **phonetic** I.

tran·sept ['trænsept] *s* △ Querschiff *n*.

trans·fer I *v/t* [træns'fɜː] **1.** (**to**) *Betrieb etc* verlegen (nach); *j-n* versetzen (nach); (*Sport*) *Spieler* transferieren (zu), abgeben (an *acc*); *Geld* überweisen (an *j-n*, ein *Konto*). **2.** ₺ₐ *Eigentum, Recht* übertragen (**to** auf *acc*). **3.** **~ to** *Bandaufnahme etc* überspielen auf (*acc*). II *v/i* [træns'fɜː] **4.** *Sport*: wechseln (**to** zu) (*Spieler*). **5.** *Reise*: umsteigen (**from** ... **to** von ... auf *acc*). III *s* ['trænsfə] **6.** Verlegung *f*, Versetzung *f*; (*Sport*) Transfer *m*, Wechsel *m*; Überweisung *f*: **~ fee** Transfersumme *f*, Ablöse(summe) *f*. **7.** ₺ₐ Übertragung *f*. **8.** Umsteigen *n*; *bsd. Am.* Umsteige(fahr)karte *f*. **9.** *bsd. Br.* Abziehbild *n*. **trans'fer·a·ble** *adj* übertragbar.

trans·fig·ure [træns'fɪɡə] *v/t* verklären.

trans·fix [træns'fɪks] *v/t* **1.** durchstechen, -bohren (**with** mit). **2. stand ~ed to the spot** wie angewurzelt dastehen.

trans·form [træns'fɔːm] *v/t etc.* umwandeln, *a. j-n* verwandeln (**into** in *acc*). **trans·for·ma·tion** [~fə'meɪʃn] *s* Um-, Verwandlung *f*. **trans·form·er** [~'fɔːmə] *s* ⚡ Transformator *m*.

trans·fu·sion [træns'fjuːʒn] *s* ⚕ Bluttransfusion *f*, -übertragung *f*.

trans·gress [træns'ɡres] I *v/t* verletzen,

verstoßen gegen. II *v/i* sündigen (**against** gegen). **trans'gres·sion** *s* (**of**) Verletzung *f* (*gen*), Verstoß *m* (gegen); Sünde *f*.

tran·si·ent ['trænzɪənt] *adj* □ flüchtig, vergänglich.

tran·sis·tor [træn'sɪstə] *s* ⚡ Transistor *m*: **~ (radio)** Transistorradio *n*. **tran'sis·tor·ize** *v/t* transistor(is)ieren.

trans·it ['trænsɪt] *s* **1.** Durchfahrt *f*. **2.** ✈ Transport *m*: **in ~** unterwegs, auf dem Transport. **~ camp** *s* Durchgangslager *n*.

tran·si·tion [træn'sɪʒn] *s* Übergang *m* (**from** ... **to** von ... zu): **period of ~** Übergangsperiode *f*, -zeit *f*. **tran'si·tion·al** [~ʒənl] *adj* Übergangs...

tran·si·tive ['trænsətɪv] *adj* □ *ling.* transitiv.

tran·si·to·ry ['trænsɪtərɪ] → **transient**.

trans·lat·a·ble [træns'leɪtəbl] *adj* übersetzbar. **trans·late** I *v/t* **1.** übersetzen (**from English into German** aus dem Englischen ins Deutsche). **2. ~ into action** *fig.* in die Tat umsetzen. II *v/i* **3.** sich *gut etc* übersetzen lassen. **trans'la·tion** *s* Übersetzung *f*. **trans'la·tor** *s* Übersetzer(in).

trans·lu·cent [trænz'luːsnt] *adj* □ lichtdurchlässig: **~ glass** Milchglas *n*.

trans·mi·gra·tion [ˌtrænzmaɪ'ɡreɪʃn] *s* Seelenwanderung *f*.

trans·mis·sion [trænz'mɪʃn] *s* **1.** Übertragung *f* (*e-r Krankheit*). **2.** Rundfunk, TV: Sendung *f*, *pl a.* Programm *n*. **3.** *mot.* Getriebe *n*.

trans·mit [trænz'mɪt] I *v/t* **1.** *Krankheit* übertragen. **2.** *Signale* (aus)senden; (*Rundfunk, TV*) *Programm* senden. **3.** *phys. Wärme* leiten; *Licht etc* durchlassen. II *v/i* **4.** *Rundfunk, TV*: senden. **trans'mit·ter** *s* Sender *m*.

trans·mu·ta·tion [ˌtrænzmjuː'teɪʃn] *s* Um-, Verwandlung *f*. **trans·mute** [~'mjuːt] *v/t* um-, verwandeln (**into** in *acc*).

trans·par·en·cy [træns'pærənsɪ] *s* **1.** Durchsichtigkeit *f* (*a. fig.*). **2.** *fig.* Durchschaubarkeit *f*. **3.** Dia(positiv) *n*. **trans·par·ent** *adj* □ **1.** durchsichtig. **2.** *fig.* durchsichtig, durchschaubar; offenkundig.

tran·spi·ra·tion [ˌtrænspə'reɪʃn] *s* Transpiration *f* (*a.* ⚘), Schweißabsonderung *f.* **tran·spire** [~'spaɪə] *v/i* **1.** *physiol.* transpirieren (*a.* ♀), schwitzen. **2.** *it ~d that* es sickerte durch *od.* wurde bekannt, daß. **3.** F passieren.

trans·plant I *v/t* [træns'plɑːnt] **1.** ♣ transplantieren, verpflanzen. **2.** *Pflanze* um-, verpflanzen. **3.** *j-n* umsiedeln, *Betrieb etc* verlegen (**to** nach). **II** *s* ['trænsplɑːnt] **4.** ♣ Transplantation *f*, Verpflanzung *f*. **5.** ♣ Transplantat *n*. **,trans·plan'ta·tion** *s* **1.** → *transplant* 4. **2.** Um-, Verpflanzung *f*.

trans·port I *v/t* [træn'spɔːt] **1.** *Waren, Truppen* transportieren, *a. Personen* befördern. **II** *s* ['trænspɔːt] **2.** Transport *m*, Beförderung *f*. → *café Br.* Fernfahrerlokal *n*. **3.** Beförderungs-, Verkehrsmittel *n od. pl.* **4.** ✕ Transportflugzeug *n*, (*Truppen*)Transporter *m*. **,trans·por'ta·tion** *bsd. Am.* → *transport* 2. **trans'port·er** *s mot.* (*Autoetc*)Transporter *m*.

trans·verse ['trænzvɜːs] *adj* Quer... **,trans'verse·ly** *adv* quer.

trans·ves·tite [trænz'vestaɪt] *s* Transvestit *m*.

trap [træp] **I** *s* **1.** Falle *f* (*a. fig.*): *set a* ~ e-e Falle aufstellen; *set a ~ for s.o.* j-m e-e Falle stellen; *fall into s.o.'s* ~ j-m in die Falle gehen. **2.** *shut one's* ~, *keep one's* ~ *shut sl.* die Schnauze halten. **II** *v/t* **3.** (*in od.* mit e-r Falle) fangen. **4.** *be ~ped* eingeschlossen sein (*Bergleute etc*). **5.** *fig.* in e-e Falle locken: ~ *s.o. into doing s.th.* j-n dazu bringen, et. zu tun. **6.** *Sport: Ball* stoppen. **'~·door** *s* Falltür *f*.

tra·peze [trə'piːz] *s Artistik:* Trapez *n*: ~ *artist* Trapezkünstler(in). **tra·pe·zi·um** [~zjəm] *pl* -**zi·ums**, -**zi·a** [~zjə] *s* ♣ *Br.* Trapez *n*; *bsd. Am.* Trapezoid *n*. **trap·e·zoid** ['træpɪzɔɪd] *s* ♣ *bsd. Br.* Trapezoid *n*; *bsd. Am.* Trapez *n*.

trap·per ['træpə] *s* Trapper *m*, Fallensteller *m*.

trap·pings ['træpɪŋz] *s pl* **1.** Rangabzeichen *pl.* **2.** *fig.* Drum u. Dran *n*.

trash [træʃ] *s* **1.** *Am.* Abfall *m*, Müll *m*: ~ *can* Abfall-, Mülleimer *m*; Abfall-, Mülltonne *f*. **2.** Schund *m*. **3.** Quatsch *m*, Unsinn *m*. **4.** *Am.* Gesindel *n*. **'trash·y** *adj* Schund...

trau·ma ['trɔːmə] *s psych.* Trauma *n*.

trau·mat·ic [~'mætɪk] *adj* (~*ally*) traumatisch.

trav·el ['trævl] **I** *v/i pret u. pp* -**eled**, *bsd. Br.* -**elled 1.** reisen: → *light²* 4. **2.** ♣ reisen (*in in e-r Ware*). **3.** fahren; sich verbreiten (*Neuigkeit etc*); ◉ *etc* sich bewegen; *phys.* sich fortpflanzen. **4.** *be really ~ (l)ing* F e-n ganz schönen Zahn draufhaben. **II** *v/t* **5.** bereisen; *Strecke* zurücklegen, fahren. **III** *s* **6.** Reisen *n*. **7.** *pl* (*bsd. Auslands*)Reisen *pl.* ~ **a·gen·cy** *s* Reisebüro *n.* ~ **a·gent** *s* Reisebüroinhaber(in). -**kaufmann** *m*, -**kauffrau** *f*; *weitS.*, *a.* ~*'s* Reisebüro *n.* ~ **bu·reau** *s* (*a. irr bureau*) Reisebüro *n*.

trav·el·er *s Am.* → *traveller:* ~*'s check* Reise-, Travellerscheck *m.* → *travelling. Am.* → *travelling.*

trav·el·ler ['trævlə] *s bsd. Br.* **1.** Reisende *m, f*: ~*'s cheque Br.* Reise-, Travellerscheck *m.* **2.** ♣ (Handels)Vertreter *m* (**in** für). **'trav·el·ling** *adj bsd. Br.* **1.** Reise...: ~ (*alarm*) *clock* Reisewecker *m*; ~ *salesman* → *traveller* 2. **2.** Wander...: ~ *circus.*

trav·e·log *s Am.*, **trav·e·logue** *s* ['trævəlɒg] Reisebericht *m* (*Vortrag*), -film *m*.

'trav·el·sick *adj* reisekrank. ~ **sick·ness** *s* Reisekrankheit *f*.

tra·verse ['trævəs] *v/t* durch-, überqueren.

trav·es·ty ['trævɪstɪ] *s* Zerrbild *n*: *a ~ of justice* ein Hohn auf die Gerechtigkeit.

trav·o·la·tor ['trævəleɪtə] *s* Rollsteig *m*.

trawl·er ['trɔːlə] *s* ♣ Trawler *m*.

tray [treɪ] *s* **1.** Tablett *n*. **2.** Ablagekorb *m*.

treach·er·ous ['tretʃərəs] *adj* □ **1.** verräterisch. **2.** *fig.* tückisch (*Strömung etc*). **'treach·er·y** *s* Verrat *m*.

trea·cle ['triːkl] *s bsd. Br.* Sirup *m*. **'trea·cly** *adj* **1.** sirupartig. **2.** *fig.* süßlich.

tread [tred] **I** *v/i* (*irr*) **1.** treten (**on** auf *acc*; **in** *acc*): ~ *carefully* vorsichtig auftreten; *fig.* vorsichtig vorgehen; → *corn²*, *toe* I. **II** *v/t* (*irr*) **2.** *Pfad, Wasser* treten: ~ *in(to)* eintreten (in *acc*). **III** *s* **3.** Gang *m*; Schritt(e *pl*) *m.* **4.** *mot.* Profil *n* (*e-s Reifens*). **'~·mill** *s hist.* Tretmühle *f* (*a. fig.*).

trea·son ['triːzn] *s* Landesverrat *m*.

treas·ure ['treʒə] **I** s Schatz m, (*Person* F a.) Juwel n: ~ **hunt** Schatzsuche f. **II** v/t et. zu schätzen wissen; j-s *Andenken* in Ehren halten. '**treas·ur·er** s Schatzmeister(in). '**Treas·ur·y** s pol. Finanzministerium n.

treat [tri:t] **I** v/t **1.** j-n behandeln (*like* wie); et. behandeln, umgehen mit: → **dirt. 2.** et. ansehen, betrachten (**as** als). **3.** 🏥 j-n behandeln (**for** gegen): **be** ~**ed for** in ärztlicher Behandlung stehen wegen. **4.** 🔬, ⚙ et. behandeln (**with** mit; **against** gegen). **5.** j-n einladen (**to** zu): ~ **s.o. to s.th.** a. j-m et. spendieren; ~ **o.s. to s.th.** sich et. leisten od. gönnen. **II** v/i **6.** ~ **of** handeln von, behandeln. **III** s **7.** (besondere) Freude, (besondere) Überraschung.

trea·tise ['~tiz] s (wissenschaftliche) Abhandlung (**on** über acc). '**treat·ment** s allg. Behandlung f. '**trea·ty** s pol. Vertrag m: **by** ~ vertraglich.

tre·ble ['trebl] **I** adj □ dreifach. **II** v/t u. v/i (sich) verdreifachen.

tree [tri:] s Baum m: **in a** ~ auf e-m Baum; → **bark²** I. '**tree·less** adj baumlos.

'**tree|·line** s Baumgrenze f. ~ **trunk** s Baumstamm m.

tre·foil ['trefɔil] s **1.** 🌿 Klee m. **2.** △ Dreipaß m.

trek [trek] **I** v/i marschieren. **II** s lange, gefährliche Fußreise.

trel·lis ['trelis] s Spalier n (*für Pflanzen* etc).

trem·ble ['trembl] **I** v/i zittern (**with** vor dat): ~ **at the thought** (od. **to think**) bei dem Gedanken zittern; ~ **for** zittern od. bangen um. **II** s Zittern n.

tre·men·dous [tri'mendəs] adj □ **1.** gewaltig. **2.** F klasse, toll.

trem·or ['tremə] s **1.** Zittern n: → **earth tremor. 2.** Schauder m.

trench [trentʃ] s Graben m, ⚔ Schützengraben m. ~ **coat** s Trenchcoat m.

trend [trend] s **1.** Trend m, Tendenz f (**toward**[s] zu). **2.** Mode f. '~**,set·ter** s Trendsetter m (*j-d, der e-n neuen Trend in Gang setzt od. et. in Mode bringt*). '**trend·y** ['trendi] adj □ F modern, modisch: **be** ~ als schick gelten, in sein; ~ **disco** In-Disko f.

tres·pass ['trespəs] **I** v/i: ~ **on** a) *Grundstück etc* unbefugt betreten: **no** ~**ing**

Betreten verboten!, b) *j-s Zeit etc* über Gebühr in Anspruch nehmen. **II** s unbefugtes Betreten. '**tres·pass·er** s: ~**s will be prosecuted** Betreten bei Strafe verboten!

tri·al ['traiəl] s **1.** ⚖ Prozeß m, (Gerichts)Verhandlung f, (-)Verfahren n: ~ **by jury** Schwurgerichtsverfahren; **be on** (od. **stand**) ~ vor Gericht stehen (**for** wegen). **2.** Erprobung f, Probe f, Prüfung f, Test m: **by** ~ **and error** durch Ausprobieren; **on** ~ auf od. zur Probe; **be on** ~ erprobt od. getestet werden; **he's still on** ~ er ist noch in der Probezeit. **3. be a** ~ **to** j-m Ärger od. Sorgen machen. ~ **mar·riage** s Ehe f auf Probe. ~ **pe·ri·od** s Probezeit f. ~ **run** s ⚙ Probelauf m; mot. Probefahrt f: **give a car a** ~ e-n Wagen probefahren.

tri·an·gle ['traiæŋgl] s **1.** ♪ Dreieck n. **2.** ♪ Triangel m. **3.** Am. → **set square.** **tri·an·gu·lar** [~'æŋgulə] adj □ dreieckig.

trib·al ['traibl] adj Stammes... **tribe** [traib] s Stamm m.

'**tribes|·man** ['traibzmən] s (*irr* **man**) Stammesangehörige m. '~**,wom·an** s (*irr* **woman**) Stammesangehörige f.

tri·bu·nal [trai'bju:nl] s ⚖ Gericht n.

trib·u·tar·y ['tribjutəri] s Nebenfluß m.

trib·ute ['tribju:t] s: **be a** ~ **to** j-m Ehre machen; **pay a** ~ **to** j-m Anerkennung zollen.

trice [trais] s: **in a** ~ F im Nu, im Handumdrehen.

tri·chi·na [tri'kainə] pl **-nae** [~ni:] s zo. Trichine f.

trick [trik] **I** s **1.** Trick m (*a. b.s.*), (*Karten- etc*)Kunststück n: **by a** ~ mit e-m Trick; **how's** ~**s?** F wie geht's?; **dirty** ~ Gemeinheit f. **2.** Streich m: **play a** ~ **on s.o.** j-m e-n Streich spielen. **3. have a** ~ **of doing s.th.** die (merkwürdige) Angewohnheit od. die Eigenart haben, et. zu tun. **4.** *Kartenspiel:* Stich m: **take** (od. **win**) **a** ~ e-n Stich machen. **II** adj **5.** Trick...: ~ **question** Fangfrage f. **III** v/t **6.** j-n reinlegen: ~ **s.o. into doing s.th.** j-n mit e-m Trick dazu bringen, et. zu tun. '**trick·er·y** s Tricks pl.

trick·le ['trikl] v/i tröpfeln; rieseln.

trick·ster ['trikstə] s Betrüger(in), Schwindler(in). '**trick·y** adj □ **1.**

schwierig, (*Problem etc a.*) heikel. **2.**
durchtrieben, raffiniert.
tri·cy·cle ['traɪsɪkl] *s* Dreirad *n.*
tri·fle ['traɪfl] **I** *s* **1.** Kleinigkeit *f;* Lappalie *f;* **a ~** ein bißchen, etwas. **2.** a) *bsd.*
Br. Trifle *n* (*Biskuitdessert*), b) *Am.*
Obstdessert mit Schlagsahne. **II** *v/i* **3. ~**
with *fig.* spielen mit: **he is not to be ~d**
with er läßt nicht mit sich spaßen.
'tri·fling *adj* unbedeutend, geringfügig.
trig·ger ['trɪɡə] *s* Abzug *m* (*am Gewehr*
etc): **pull the ~** abdrücken. **II** *v/t a.* **~ off**
fig. auslösen. **'~ hap·py** *adj* schießwütig.
trig·o·nom·e·try [ˌtrɪɡə'nɒmɪtrɪ] *s* ℞
Trigonometrie *f.*
trike [traɪk] *s* F Dreirad *n.*
tril·o·gy ['trɪlədʒɪ] *s* F Trilogie *f.*
trim [trɪm] **I** *v/t* **1.** *Hecke etc* stutzen,
beschneiden, sich *den Bart etc* stutzen:
~ off abschneiden. **2.** *Kleidungsstück*
besetzen (**with** mit): **~med with fur**
pelzbesetzt, mit Pelzbesatz. **II** *s* **3.** **give**
s.th. **a ~ → 1. 4. be in good ~** F gut in
Schuß sein (*Auto etc*), (*Person a.*) gut in
Form sein. **III** *adj* **5.** gepflegt. **'trim·**
ming *s* **1.** *a. pl* Besatz *m.* **2.** *pl* Zubehör
n; Extras *pl:* **with all the ~s** *gastr.* mit
den üblichen Beilagen. **3.** *pl* Abfälle *pl.*
trin·ket ['trɪŋkɪt] *s* (*bsd.* billiges)
Schmuckstück.
tri·o ['triːəʊ] *pl* **-os** *s* Trio *n,* ♪ *a.* Terzett
n.
trip [trɪp] **I** *v/i* **1.** stolpern (**over** über *acc*).
2. sich vertun. **II** *v/t* **3.** *a.* **~ up** *j-m* ein
Bein stellen (*a. fig.*). **III** *s* **4.** Reise *f;*
Ausflug *m,* Trip *m:* **go on a bus ~** e-n
Busausflug machen. **5.** *sl.* Trip *m* (*Dro-*
genrausch): **be on a ~** auf dem Trip
sein.
tripe [traɪp] *s* **1.** *gastr.* Kaldaunen *pl,*
Kutteln *pl.* **2.** F Quatsch *m,* Mist *m.*
tri·ple ['trɪpl] **I** *adj* □ dreifach: **~ jump**
(*Leichtathletik*) Dreisprung *m;* **~ jump·**
er Dreispringer *m.* **II** *v/t u. v/i* (sich)
verdreifachen.
tri·plet ['trɪplɪt] *s* Drilling *m.*
trip·li·cate ['trɪplɪkət] *s:* **in ~** in dreifacher Ausfertigung.
tri·pod ['traɪpɒd] *s phot.* Stativ *n.*
trip·per ['trɪpə] *s* (*bsd. Tages*)Ausflügler(in).
'trip·wire *s* Stolperdraht *m.*
trite [traɪt] *adj* □ abgedroschen; banal.

tri·umph ['traɪəmf] **I** *s* Triumph *m* (**over**
über *acc*): **in ~** im Triumph, triumphierend. **II** *v/i* triumphieren (**over** über
acc). **tri·um·phal** [~'ʌmfl] *adj* Triumph...: **~ arch** Triumphbogen *m;* **~**
procession Triumphzug *m.* **tri'um·**
phant *adj* □ triumphierend.
triv·i·al ['trɪvɪəl] *adj* □ **1.** trivial, alltäglich, gewöhnlich. **2.** unbedeutend, belanglos. **triv·i·al·i·ty** [ˌ~'ælətɪ] *s* **1.** Trivialität *f.* **2.** Belanglosigkeit *f.*
trod [trɒd] *pret von* tread. **'trod·den** *pp*
von tread.
trol·ley ['trɒlɪ] *s Br.* Einkaufs-, Gepäckwagen *m;* Kofferkuli *m;* (*Tee- etc*)Wagen *m.*
trom·bone [trɒm'bəʊn] *s* ♪ Posaune *f.*
trom'bon·ist *s* Posaunist *m.*
troop [truːp] **I** *s* **1.** Schar *f.* **2.** *pl* ✕
Truppen *pl.* **II** *v/i* **3.** strömen. **~ car·**
ri·er *s* ⚓, ⚓ Truppentransporter *m.*
troop·er ['truːpə] *s* **1.** ✕ Kavallerist *m;*
Panzerjäger *m:* **swear like a ~** wie ein
Landsknecht fluchen. **2.** *Am.* Polizist *m*
(*e-s Bundesstaats*).
troop trans·port → troop carrier.
tro·phy ['trəʊfɪ] *s* Trophäe *f.*
trop·ic ['trɒpɪk] *s* **1.** *ast., geogr.* Wendekreis *m.* **2.** *pl* Tropen *pl.* **'trop·i·cal** *adj*
□ tropisch, Tropen...
trot [trɒt] **I** *s* **1.** Trab *m:* **on the ~** F
hintereinander; **be on the ~** F auf Trab
sein; **have the ~s** F Dünnpfiff haben. **II**
v/i **2.** traben: **~ along** (*od. off*) F abziehen. **III** *v/t* **3.** *Pferd* traben lassen.
4. ~ out F auftischen, von sich geben.
'trot·ter *s* Traber *m* (*Pferd*). **'trot·ting**
adj: **~ race** Trabrennen *n.*
trou·ble ['trʌbl] **I** *v/t* **1.** *j-n* beunruhigen.
2. *j-m* Mühe *od.* Umstände machen; *j-n*
bemühen (**for** um), bitten (**for** um; **to do**
zu tun). **3.** **be ~d by** geplagt werden
von, leiden an (*dat*). **4. fish in ~d wa·**
ters *fig.* im trüben fischen. **II** *v/i* **5.** sich
bemühen (**to do** zu tun), sich Umstände
machen (**about** wegen). **III** *s* **6.** Schwierigkeit *f,* Problem *n:* **be in ~** in Schwierigkeiten sein; **get into ~** a) **run into ~**
in Schwierigkeiten geraten, b) Schwierigkeiten *od.* Ärger bekommen (**with**
mit), c) *j-n* in Schwierigkeiten bringen;
have ~ with Schwierigkeiten *od.* Ärger
haben mit; **have ~ doing s.th.** Schwierigkeiten haben, et. zu tun. **7.** Mühe *f:*

put s.o. to ~ j-m Mühe *od.* Umstände machen; *take the* ~ *to do s.th.* sich die Mühe machen, et. zu tun. **8.** *a. pl pol.* Unruhen *pl.* **9.** ✠ Leiden *n*, Beschwerden *pl.* '~**,mak·er** *s* Unruhestifter(in). '~**,shoot·er** *s* Friedensstifter(in).

trou·ble·some ['trʌblsəm] *adj* □ lästig.

trou·ble spot *s pol.* Unruheherd *m*.

trough [trɒf] *s* **1.** Trog *m.* **2.** Wellental *n*.

trounce [traʊns] *v/t Sport:* haushoch besiegen.

troupe [truːp] *s thea.* etc Truppe *f*.

trou·ser ['traʊzə] **I** *s pl, a.* **pair of** ~**s** Hose *f;* → **wear** 3. **II** *adj* Hosen...: ~ **suit** Hosenanzug *m*.

trous·seau ['truːsəʊ] *pl* **-seaux** ['~səʊz], **-seaus** *s* Aussteuer *f*.

trout [traʊt] *pl* **trouts,** *bsd. coll.* **trout** *s ichth.* Forelle *f*.

trow·el ['traʊəl] *s* (Maurer)Kelle *f; lay it on with a* ~ F dick auftragen.

troy (weight) [trɔɪ] *s* Troygewicht *n (für Edelmetalle u. -steine)*.

tru·ant ['truːənt] *s* (Schul)Schwänzer(in): *play* ~ (die Schule) schwänzen.

truce [truːs] *s* ✗ Waffenstillstand *m (a. fig.)*.

truck¹ [trʌk] **I** *s* **1.** *mot.* Lastwagen *m;* Fernlaster *m.* **2.** 🚃 *Br.* (offener) Güterwagen *m.* **II** *v/t* **3.** *Am.* auf *od.* mit Lastwagen transportieren.

truck² [~] *s:* *have no* ~ *with* nichts zu tun haben wollen mit.

truck driv·er *s* Lastwagenfahrer *m;* Fernfahrer *m*.

truck·er ['trʌkə] *Am.* → **truck driver.**

truck|·man ['trʌkmən] *s (irr man) Am.* → **truck driver.** ~ **stop** *s Am.* Fernfahrerlokal *n*.

truc·u·lent ['trʌkjʊlənt] *adj* □ trotzig.

trudge [trʌdʒ] *v/i* stapfen (**through** durch).

true [truː] *adj* (□ → *truly*) **1.** wahr: *be* ~ *a.* stimmen; *in the* ~*est sense of the word* im wahrsten Sinne des Wortes; → **come** 10. **2.** wahr, echt, wirklich: ~ *love* wahre Liebe. **3.** treu (**to** *dat*): *stay* ~ *to one's principles* s-n Grundsätzen treu bleiben. **4.** getreu (**to** *dat*): ~ *to form* wie nicht anders zu erwarten; ~ *to life* lebensecht.

truf·fle ['trʌfl] *s* ♣ Trüffel *f*.

tru·ism ['truːɪzəm] *s* Binsenwahrheit *f*.

tru·ly ['truːlɪ] *adv* **1.** wahrheitsgemäß.

2. wirklich, wahrhaft. **3.** aufrichtig: *Yours* ~ *bsd. Am.* Hochachtungsvoll (*Briefschluß*).

trump¹ [trʌmp] **I** *s* a) *pl* Trumpf *m (Farbe),* b) *a.* ~ *card* Trumpf(karte *f) m:* *play one's* ~ *card fig.* s-n Trumpf ausspielen. **II** *v/t Karte* mit e-m Trumpf stechen, mit e-m Trumpf *e-n Stich* machen.

trump² [~] *v/t:* ~ *up b.s.* erfinden, erdichten.

trum·pet ['trʌmpɪt] **I** *s* ♪ Trompete *f.* **II** *v/i* trompeten (*Elefant*). '**trum·pet·er** *s* Trompeter(in).

trun·cate [trʌŋ'keɪt] *v/t* beschneiden, stutzen (*beide a. fig.*).

trun·cheon ['trʌntʃən] *s* (Gummi)Knüppel *m*, Schlagstock *m*.

trun·dle ['trʌndl] *v/t Karren* etc ziehen.

trunk [trʌŋk] *s* **1.** (*Baum*)Stamm *m.* **2.** *anat.* Rumpf *m.* **3.** Schrankkoffer *m.* **4.** *zo.* Rüssel *m (des Elefanten).* **5.** *mot. Am.* Kofferraum *m.* **6.** *pl, a.* **pair of** ~**s** (*Bade*)Hose *f;* (*Sport*) Shorts *pl.* ~ **road** *s Br.* Fernstraße *f*.

truss [trʌs] **I** *v/t, a.* ~ *up* **1.** *j-n* fesseln. **2.** *gastr. Geflügel* etc dressieren. **II** *s* **3.** ⚕ Bruchband *n*.

trust [trʌst] **I** *v/t* **1.** trauen (*dat*). **2.** sich verlassen auf (*acc*): ~ *s.o. to do s.th.* sich darauf verlassen, daß j-d et. tut; ~ *him!* das sieht ihm ähnlich! **3.** (zuversichtlich) hoffen. **II** *v/i* **4.** ~ *in* vertrauen auf (*acc*). **5.** ~ *to* sich verlassen auf (*acc*). **III** *s* **6.** Vertrauen *n* (**in** zu): *place (od. put) one's* ~ *in* Vertrauen setzen in (*acc*); *take s.th. on* ~ et. einfach glauben; *position of* ~ Vertrauensstellung *f.* **7.** *hold s.th. in* ~ et. treuhänderisch verwalten (**for** für); *place s.th. in s.o.'s* ~ j-m et. anvertrauen. **8.** ✝ Trust *m;* *weitS.* Großkonzern *m*.

trus·tee [ˌtrʌs'tiː] *s* ⚖ Treuhänder(in), Vermögensverwalter(in).

trust·ful ['trʌstfʊl], '**trust·ing** *adj* □ vertrauensvoll; vertrauensselig.

'**trust,wor·thy** *adj* □ vertrauenswürdig.

truth [truːθ] *pl* **truths** [truːðz] *s* Wahrheit *f: in* ~ in Wahrheit; *there is some (no)* ~ *in it* daran ist et. (nichts) Wahres; *to tell (you) the* ~ um die Wahrheit zu sagen; → **home truth. truth·ful** ['~fʊl] *adj* □ **1.** wahrheitsgemäß. **2.** wahrheitsliebend.

try [traɪ] **I** s **1.** Versuch m: *have a ~* es versuchen; → *worth* I. **II** v/t **2.** versuchen (*to do* zu tun): *when their car didn't start, they tried pushing it* als ihr Wagen nicht ansprang, versuchten sie es mit Anschieben. **3.** *et.* ausprobieren. **4.** ✠ (über) *e-e Sache* verhandeln; *j-n* den Prozeß machen (*for* wegen). **5.** *j-n, j-s Geduld, Nerven etc* auf *e-e* harte Probe stellen. **6.** es versuchen: *~ and come* bsd. Br. F versuch zu kommen; → *hard* 12. **7.** *~ for* Br. sich bemühen um.

Verbindungen mit Adverbien:

try| on v/t **1.** *Kleidungsstück* anprobieren, *Hut etc* aufprobieren. **2.** *try it on* Br. F probieren, wie weit man gehen kann. *~ out* **I** v/t → *try* 3. **II** v/i: *~ for Am.* → *try* 7.

try·ing ['traɪɪŋ] adj □ anstrengend.

'try-out s: *give s.th. a ~* et. ausprobieren.

tsar [zɑː] s hist. Zar m.

'T-shirt s T-Shirt n.

tub [tʌb] s **1.** Bottich m; Tonne f. **2.** (*Margarine- etc*)Becher m. **3.** F (Bade-)Wanne f. **4.** ♻ F Kahn m.

tu·ba ['tjuːbə] s ♩ Tuba f.

tube [tjuːb] s **1.** Röhre f (*a. anat.*), Rohr n. **2.** Schlauch m. **3.** Tube f. **4.** ♀ F U-Bahn f (*in London*): *by* ♀ mit der U-Bahn; *~ station* U-Bahnstation f. **'tube·less** adj schlauchlos (*Reifen*).

tu·ber ['tjuːbə] s ♣ Knolle f.

tu·ber·cu·lo·sis [tjuːˌbɜːkjʊˈləʊsɪs] s ⚕ Tuberkulose f.

tu·bu·lar ['tjuːbjʊlə] adj rohrförmig, Röhren..., Rohr...: *~ furniture* Stahlrohrmöbel pl.

tuck [tʌk] s **1.** Saum m; Biese f. **II** v/t stecken: *~ s.th. under one's arm* sich et. unter den Arm klemmen. **III** v/i: *~ into* bsd. Br. F sich et. schmecken lassen.

Verbindungen mit Adverbien:

tuck| a·way v/t **1.** wegstecken: *be tucked away* versteckt liegen (*Haus etc*). **2.** F *Essen* verdrücken, wegputzen. *~ in* **I** v/t → *tuck up.* **II** v/i F reinhauen, zulangen. *~ up* v/t a. *~ in bed Kind* ins Bett packen.

Tues·day ['tjuːzdɪ] s Dienstag m: *on ~* (am) Dienstag; *on ~s* dienstags.

tuft [tʌft] s (*Gras-, Haar- etc*)Büschel n.

tug [tʌg] **I** v/t **1.** zerren, ziehen. **2.** zerren *od.* ziehen an (*dat*). **II** v/i **3.** *~ at* → 2. **III** s **4.** *give s.th. a ~* → 2; *~ of war* (*Sport*) Tauziehen n (*a. fig.*).

tu·i·tion [tjuːˈɪʃn] s **1.** Unterricht m. **2.** bsd. Am. Unterrichtsgebühr(en pl) f.

tu·lip ['tjuːlɪp] s ♣ Tulpe f.

tulle [tjuːl] s Tüll m.

tum·ble ['tʌmbl] **I** v/i **1.** fallen, stürzen; ✠ purzeln (*Preise*). **2.** a. *~ down* einstürzen. **3.** *~ to s.th.* bsd. Br. F et. kapieren. **II** s **4.** Fall m, Sturz m: *have* (*take*) *a ~* fallen, stürzen. **'~·down** adj baufällig. *~ dry·er* s Trockenautomat m, Wäschetrockner m.

tum·bler ['tʌmblə] s (Trink)Glas n.

tu·mid ['tjuːmɪd] adj ⚕ geschwollen.

tum·my ['tʌmɪ] s F Bauch m: *he's got a sore ~* er hat Bauchweh.

tu·mor s Am., **tu·mour** s bsd. Br. ['tjuːmə] ⚕ Tumor m, Geschwulst f.

tu·mult ['tjuːmʌlt] s Tumult m. **tu·mul·tu·ous** adj □ tumultartig, (*Applaus, Empfang*) stürmisch.

tu·na ['tjuːnə] s ichth. Thunfisch m.

tune [tjuːn] **I** s **1.** Melodie f: *to the ~ of* nach der Melodie von; *fig.* F in Höhe von *500 Pfund etc.* **2.** *be out of ~ ♩* verstimmt sein; *be in* (*out of*) *~ with fig.* (nicht) harmonieren *od.* übereinstimmen mit. **II** v/t **3.** a. *~ up ♩* stimmen. **4.** a. *~ up* ⚙ *Motor* tunen. **5.** mst *in Radio etc* einstellen (*to* auf *acc*): *be ~d in to* Sender, *Programm* eingeschaltet haben; *fig.* ein Gefühl haben für. **III** v/i **6.** *~ up* (die Instrumente) stimmen (*Orchester*). **7.** *~ in* (das Radio *etc*) einschalten: *~ in to* Sender, *Programm* einschalten. **tune·ful** ['~fʊl] adj □ melodiös. **'tune·less** adj □ unmelodiös. **'tun·er** s **1.** (*Klavier- etc*)Stimmer(in). **2.** Radio, TV: Tuner m. **'tun·ing** adj: *~ fork* Stimmgabel f.

tun·nel ['tʌnl] **I** s Tunnel m; Unterführung f. **II** v/t pret u. pp **-neled**, bsd. Br. **-nelled** a) *Berg* durchtunneln, b) *Fluß etc* untertunneln. **III** v/i: *~ through* → IIa; *~ under* → IIb.

tun·ny ['tʌnɪ] s ichth. Thunfisch m.

tur·ban ['tɜːbən] s Turban m.

tur·bid ['tɜːbɪd] adj □ **1.** trüb (*Flüssigkeit*); dick (*Rauch etc*). **2.** fig. verworren, wirr.

tur·bine ['tɜːbaɪn] s ⚙ Turbine f.

tur·bo ['tɜːbəʊ] pl **-bos** s F → **turbo-**

charger. ,~'**charg·er** *s mot.* Turbolader *m.*

tur·bot ['tɜːbət] *pl* **-bots**, *bsd. coll.* **-bot** *s ichth.* Steinbutt *m.*

tur·bu·lence ['tɜːbjʊləns] *s* Turbulenz *f* (*a. phys.*). '**tur·bu·lent** *adj* □ turbulent (*a. phys.*).

turd [tɜːd] *s* V **1.** Scheißhaufen *m,* Kaktus *m.* **2.** Scheißkerl *m.*

tu·reen [tə'riːn] *s* (Suppen)Terrine *f.*

turf [tɜːf] **I** *pl* **turfs, turves** [~vz] *s* **1.** Rasen *m.* **2.** Sode *f,* Rasenstück *n.* **3.** *the* ~ der Pferderennsport. **II** *v/t* **4.** ~ *out bsd. Br.* F j-n rausschmeißen: *he was* ~*ed out of the club* er flog aus dem Verein.

tur·gid ['tɜːdʒɪd] *adj* □ ✿ geschwollen, *fig. a.* schwülstig.

Turk [tɜːk] *s* Türke *m,* Türkin *f.*

tur·key ['tɜːkɪ] *pl* **-keys**, *bsd. coll.* **-key** *s orn.* Truthahn *m,* -henne *f,* Pute(r *m*) *f:* → *cold turkey.*

Turk·ish ['tɜːkɪʃ] **I** *adj* türkisch. **II** *s ling.* Türkisch *n.*

tur·moil ['tɜːmɔɪl] *s* Aufruhr *m: be in a* ~ in Aufruhr sein.

turn [tɜːn] **I** *s* **1.** (Um)Drehung *f: give s.th. a* ~ (*two* ~**s**) et. (zweimal) drehen. **2.** Biegung *f,* Kurve *f: make a right* ~ nach rechts abbiegen. **3.** *in* ~ der Reihe nach; abwechselnd; *in* (*his*) ~ seinerseits; *it is my* ~ ich bin dran *od.* an der Reihe; *miss a* ~ (*Brettspiele*) einmal aussetzen; *take* ~**s** sich abwechseln (*at* bei); *take* ~**s** *at doing s.th.* et. abwechselnd tun; → *wait* 3. **4.** *fig.* Wende *f,* Wendung *f: at the* ~ *of the century* um die Jahrhundertwende; *take a* ~ *for the better* (*worse*) sich verbessern (sich verschlimmern). **5.** *do s.o. a good* (*bad*) ~ j-m e-n guten (schlechten) Dienst erweisen. **II** *v/t* **6.** drehen, *Schlüssel a.* herumdrehen; → *somersault.* **7.** *Schallplatte* etc umdrehen, *Seite* umblättern, *Braten* etc wenden: → *hair, inside* 1, *stomach* 1, *table* 1, *upside.* **8.** → *corner* 1. **9.** *Schlauch* etc richten (*on* auf *acc*), *Antenne* ausrichten (*toward*[*s*] auf *acc*), *Aufmerksamkeit* zuwenden (*to* dat): → *back* 1, *blind* 1, *ear*¹ 1. **10.** verwandeln (*into* in *acc*). **11.** ~ *against* j-n aufbringen gegen. **III** *v/i* **12.** sich drehen: ~ *on fig.* abhängen von. **13.** abbiegen; einbiegen (*onto* auf

acc; *into* in *acc*): → *left* 4, *right* 15. **14.** sich umdrehen: ~ *against fig.* sich wenden gegen; ~ *on* losgehen auf (*acc*); ~ *to s.o.* sich j-m zuwenden; *fig.* sich an j-n wenden; → *grave.* **15.** blaß, sauer etc werden: → *turtle.* **16.** sich verwandeln, *fig. a.* umschlagen (*into, to* in *acc*).

Verbindungen mit Adverbien:

turn| a·way I *v/t* **1.** *Gesicht* etc abwenden (*from* von). **2.** j-n abweisen, wegschicken. **II** *v/i* **3.** sich abwenden (*from* von). ~ *back* **I** *v/t* **1.** *Bettdecke* zurückschlagen. **2.** j-n zurückschicken. **II** *v/i* **4.** umkehren. **5.** zurückblättern (*to* auf *acc*). ~ *down v/t* **1.** *Kragen* umlegen. **2.** → *turn back* 1. **3.** *Radio* etc leiser stellen. **4.** j-n, *Angebot* etc ablehnen. ~ *in* **I** *v/t* **1.** zurückgeben. **2.** *Gewinn* etc erzielen, machen. **3.** *turn o.s. in* sich stellen. **II** *v/i* **4.** F sich *od.* et. legen. ~ *off* **I** *v/t* **1.** *Gas, Wasser* etc abdrehen, *Licht, Radio* etc ausmachen, -schalten, *Motor* etc abstellen. **2.** F j-n anwidern; j-m die Lust nehmen. **II** *v/i* **3.** abbiegen. ~ *on v/t* **1.** *Gas, Wasser* etc aufdrehen, *a. Gerät* anstellen, *Licht, Radio* etc anmachen, anschalten: → *waterworks.* **2.** F j-n anturnen, anmachen. ~ *out* **I** *v/t* **1.** *Licht* ausmachen, -schalten. **2.** j-n hinauswerfen. **3.** *Tasche* etc (aus)leeren. **4.** F *Waren* ausstoßen. **II** *v/i* **5.** kommen (*for* zu). **6.** sich erweisen *od.* herausstellen (*a success* als Erfolg; *to be false* als falsch), sich entpuppen (*to be a good swimmer* als guter Schwimmer). ~ *o·ver* **I** *v/t* **1.** → *turn* 7: *turn s.th. over in one's mind* sich et. durch den Kopf gehen lassen; → *leaf* 2. **2.** et. umkippen. **3.** j-n, et. übergeben (*to* dat). **4.** ✿ umsetzen. **II** *v/i* **5.** sich umdrehen: → *grave.* **6.** umkippen. **7.** umblättern: *please* ~ bitte wenden. ~ *round v/t: turn one's car round* wenden. **II** *v/i*

'**turn·a·bout,** '~·**a·round** *s* Kehrtwendung *f* (*a. fig. in, on* in *dat*). '~·**coat** *s* Abtrünnige *m, f,* Überläufer(in).

turn·ing ['tɜːnɪŋ] *s* **I** Abzweigung *f.* **II** *adj:* ~ *circle mot.* Wendekreis *m;* ~ *point fig.* Wendepunkt *m.*

tur·nip ['tɜːnɪp] *s* ✿ Rübe *f.*

'**turn|-off** *s* **1** Abzweigung *f.* '~·**out** *s* **1.** (*engS.* Wahl)Beteiligung *f.* **2.** F Aufmachung *f* (*e-r Person*). '**~o·ver** *s* **†** Umsatz *m*. '**~pike** *s Am*. gebührenpflichtige Schnellstraße. **~stile** ['~stail] *s* Drehkreuz *n*. '**~ta·ble** *s* Plattenteller *m*. '**~up** *s Br*. (Hosen)Aufschlag *m*.

tur·pen·tine ['tɜ:pəntain] *s* 🜚 Terpentin *n*.

turps [tɜ:ps] *s pl* (*sg konstruiert*) *Br*. F → **turpentine**.

tur·quoise ['tɜ:kwɔɪz] *s min*. Türkis *m*.

tur·ret ['tʌrɪt] *s* **1.** 🜚 Ecktürmchen *n*. **2.** ✕ (Panzer)Turm *m*, 🜚 Gefechts-, Geschützturm *m*.

tur·tle ['tɜ:tl] *s zo*. (Wasser)Schildkröte *f*: **turn ~** *k* kentern. '**~neck** *s bsd. Am*. Rollkragen(pullover) *m*.

turves [tɜ:vz] *pl von* **turf**.

tusk [tʌsk] *s* Stoßzahn *m* (*e-s Elefanten*).

tus·sle ['tʌsl] *s bsd. fig*. (**over**) Gerangel *n* (um); Auseinandersetzung *f* (über *acc*).

tus·sock ['tʌsək] *s* Grasbüschel *n*.

tu·te·lage ['tju:tɪlɪdʒ] *s* 🜚🜚 Vormundschaft *f*.

tu·tor ['tju:tə] *s* **1.** Privat-, Hauslehrer(in). **2.** *univ. Br*. Studienleiter(in).

tux [tʌks] F → **tuxedo**.

tux·e·do [tʌk'si:dəʊ] *pl* **-dos** *s Am*. Smoking *m*.

TV [,ti:'vi:] I *s* **1.** Fernsehen *n*: **on (the) ~** im Fernsehen; **watch ~** fernsehen. **2.** Fernseher *m* (*Gerät*). II *adj* **3.** Fernseh...: **~ dinner** Tiefkühlmahlzeit *f*.

twad·dle ['twɒdl] *s* F Quatsch *m*, Unsinn *m*.

twang [twæŋ] *s*: **speak with a nasal ~** näseln.

tweed [twi:d] *s* Tweed *m* (*Stoff*).

tweet [twi:t] I *v/i* piep(s)en (*Vogel*). II *s* Piep(s)en *n*.

tweez·ers ['twi:zəz] *s pl, a.* **pair of ~** Pinzette *f*.

twelfth [twelfθ] *adj* zwölft.

twelve [twelv] *adj* zwölf.

twen·ti·eth ['twentɪəθ] *adj* zwanzigst.

twen·ty ['twentɪ] I *adj* zwanzig. II *s* Zwanzig *f*: **be in one's twenties** in den Zwanzigern sein; **in the twenties** in den zwanziger Jahren (*e-s Jahrhunderts*).

twerp [twɜ:p] *s* F Blödmann *m*, Heini *m*.

twice [twaɪs] *adv* zweimal: **~ as much** doppelt *od*. zweimal soviel; **~ the sum** die doppelte Summe; **think ~** es sich genau überlegen (**before** bevor).

twid·dle ['twɪdl] *v/t*: **~ one's thumbs** Däumchen drehen (*a. fig*.).

twig¹ [twɪg] *s* Zweig *m*.

twig² [~] *v/t u. v/i Br*. F kapieren.

twi·light ['twaɪlaɪt] *s* **1.** (*bsd*. Abend-) Dämmerung *f*: **at ~** in der Dämmerung. **2.** Zwie-, Dämmerlicht *n*.

twin [twɪn] I *s* Zwilling *m*. II *adj* Zwillings...: **~ brother** (**sister**); **~ beds** *pl* zwei Einzelbetten; **~ town** Partnerstadt *f*. III *v/t*: **be ~ned with** die Partnerstadt sein von. ,**~'bed·ded** *adj*: **~ room** Zweibettzimmer *n*.

twine [twaɪn] I *s* **1.** Bindfaden *m*, Schnur *f*. II *v/t* **2.** **~ together** zs.-drehen. **3.** **~ one's arms round** die Arme schlingen um. III *v/i* **4.** sich winden (**round** um).

,**twin·'en·gined** *adj* ✈ zweimotorig.

twinge [twɪndʒ] *s* stechender Schmerz, Stechen *n*: **a ~ of toothache** stechende Zahnschmerzen *pl*; **a ~ of conscience** Gewissensbisse *pl*.

twin·kle ['twɪŋkl] I *v/i* glitzern (*Sterne*), (*a. Augen*) funkeln (**with** vor *dat*). II *s* Glitzern *n*, Funkeln *n*: **with a ~ in one's eye** augenzwinkernd. '**twin·kling** *s*: **in the ~ of an eye**, F **in a ~** im Handumdrehen, im Nu.

twirl [twɜ:l] I *v/t* (herum)wirbeln. II *v/i* wirbeln (**round** über *acc*). III *s* Wirbel *m*.

twirp → **twerp**.

twist [twɪst] I *v/t* **1.** drehen; **~ off** abdrehen, *Deckel* abschrauben; **~ together** zs.-drehen; **his face was ~ed with pain** sein Gesicht war schmerzverzerrt. **2.** wickeln (**round** um); → *s.o.* **round one's little finger** *fig*. j-n um den (kleinen) Finger wickeln. **3.** **~ one's ankle** mit dem Fuß umknicken, den Fuß vertreten. **4.** *fig*. entstellen, verdrehen. II *v/i* **5.** sich winden (*Person*), (*Fluß etc a*.) sich schlängeln. III *s* **6.** Drehung *f*. **7.** Biegung *f*: **be round the ~** *Br*. F spinnen. **8.** (*überraschende*) Wendung. **9.** ♪ Twist *m*. '**twist·er** *s* F **1.** Gauner *m*. **2.** *Am*. Tornado *m*.

twit [twɪt] *s bsd. Br*. F Idiot *m*.

twitch [twɪtʃ] I *v/t* **1.** zucken mit. **2.** zupfen an (*dat*). II *v/i* **3.** zucken. III *s* **4.** Zucken *n*; Zuckung *f*.

twit·ter ['twɪtə] I *v/i* **1.** zwitschern. **2.** *a.* **~ on** F (aufgeregt) schnattern (**about** über *acc*). II *s* **3.** Zwitschern *n*, Gezwitscher *n*. **4. be all of a** ~ F ganz aufgeregt sein.

two [tu:] **I** *adj* **1.** zwei: *in a day or* ~ in ein paar Tagen; *break* (*cut*) *in* ~ in zwei Teile brechen (schneiden); *the* ~ *cars* die beiden Autos; → *thing* **2. II** *s* **2.** Zwei *f*: ~ *of hearts* Herzzwei. **3.** *the* ~ *of us* wir beide; *in* ~*s* zu zweit, paarweise; *put* ~ *and* ~ *together* zwei u. zwei zs.-zählen. '~**act** *adj*: ~ *play thea*. Zweiakter *m*. '~**bit** *adj Am*. F klein, unbedeutend. |~**edged** *adj* zweischneidig, *fig. a*. zweideutig. |~'**faced** *adj* falsch, heuchlerisch.

two·fold ['tu:fəʊld] **I** *adj* zweifach. **II** *adv* zweifach, um das Zweifache: *increase* ~ (sich) verzweifachen.

,**two**|-'**hand·ed** *adj* □ **1.** zweihändig. **2.** beidhändig. ~**pence** ['tʌpəns] *s Br*. zwei Pence: *I don't care* (*od. give*) ~ F das ist mir völlig egal. |~'**pen·ny** ['tʌpnɪ] *adj Br*. **1.** für zwei Pence, Zweipenny... **2.** *fig*. billig. '~**piece** *adj* zweiteilig. |~'**seat·er** *s ✈*, *mot*. Zweisitzer *m*. ~ *star s mot. Br*. F Normal *n* (*Benzin*). '~-**star** *adj*: ~ *petrol mot. Br*. Normalbenzin *n*. '~**time I** *adj* zweimalig. **II** *v/t* F *Freundin etc* betrügen (*with* mit). '~-**way** *adj*: ~ *mirror* venezianischer Spiegel; ~ *traffic* Gegenverkehr *m*.

ty·coon [taɪ'ku:n] *s* (*Industrie- etc*)Magnat *m*.

tym·pa·num ['tɪmpənəm] *pl* **-na** ['~nə], **-nums** *s anat*. Trommelfell *n*.

---

type [taɪp] **I** *s* **1.** Art *f*, Sorte *f*; Typ *m*: *of this* ~ dieser Art; *she's not my* ~ F sie ist nicht mein Typ. **II** *v/t* **2.** tippen, mit der Maschine schreiben. *Krankheit etc* bestimmen. **III** *v/i* **4.** maschineschreiben, tippen. '~**cast** *v/t* (*irr cast*) *Schauspieler* auf ein bestimmtes Rollenfach festlegen. '~**script** *s* maschine(n)geschriebenes Manuskript. '~,**set·ter** *s* Schriftsetzer(in). '~,**writ·er** *s* Schreibmaschine *f*. '~,**writ·ten** *adj* maschine(n)geschrieben.

ty·phoid (**fe·ver**) ['taɪfɔɪd] *s ✚* Typhus *m*.

ty·phoon [taɪ'fu:n] *s* Taifun *m*.

ty·phus ['taɪfəs] *s ✚* Fleckfieber *n*, -typhus *m*.

typ·i·cal ['tɪpɪkl] *adj* □ typisch (*of* für).

typ·i·fy ['~faɪ] *v/t* **1.** typisch sein für, kennzeichnen. **2.** ein typisches Beispiel sein für, verkörpern.

typ·ing ['taɪpɪŋ] *adj*: ~ *error* Tippfehler *m*; ~ *pool* Schreibzentrale *f*. '**typ·ist** *s* Schreibkraft *f*: → **shorthand.**

ty·po·graph·ic [,taɪpə'ɡræfɪk] *adj* (~*ally*) typographisch: ~ *error* Druckfehler *m*.

ty·pog·ra·phy [~'pɒɡrəfɪ] *s* Typographie *f*.

ty·ran·ni·cal [tɪ'rænɪkl] *adj* □ tyrannisch. **tyr·an·nize** ['tɪrənaɪz] *v/t* tyrannisieren. '**tyr·an·ny** *s* Tyrannei *f*. **tyrant** ['taɪərənt] *s* Tyrann *m*.

tyre [taɪə] *s bsd. Br*. Reifen *m*.

tzar [zɑ:] *s hist*. Zar *m*.

U

u·biq·ui·tous [ju:'bɪkwɪtəs] *adj* □ allgegenwärtig.

U-boat ['ju:bəʊt] *s ⚓* (deutsches) U-Boot.

ud·der ['ʌdə] *s zo*. Euter *n*.

UFO ['ju:fəʊ] *pl* **UFO's**, **UFOs** *s* Ufo *n*, UFO *n*.

ugh [ʌx] *int* igitt!

ug·li·ness ['ʌɡlɪnɪs] *s* Häßlichkeit *f*.

ug·ly ['ʌɡlɪ] *adj* □ **1.** häßlich (*a. fig.*). **2.** bös, schlimm (*Wunde etc*).

ul·cer ['ʌlsə] *s ✚* Geschwür *n*.

ul·na ['ʌlnə] *pl* **-nae** ['~ni:], **-nas** *s anat*. Elle *f*.

ul·te·ri·or [ʌl'tɪərɪə] *adj*: ~ *motive* Hintergedanke *m*.

ul·ti·ma·ta [,ʌltɪ'meɪtə] *pl von* **ultimatum.**

ul·ti·mate ['ʌltɪmət] **I** *adj* letzt, End...; höchst. **II** *s*: *the* ~ *in* das Höchste an (*dat*); *b.s*. der Gipfel an (*dat*). '**ul·ti·mate·ly** *adv* **1.** schließlich. **2.** letztlich, letzten Endes.

ul·ti·ma·tum [ˌʌltɪˈmeɪtəm] *pl* **-tums, -ta** [~tə] *s* Ultimatum *n*: **give s.o. an ~** j-m ein Ultimatum stellen; j-n ultimativ auffordern (**to do** zu tun).

ul·tra|·high [ˌʌltrəˈhaɪ] *adj*: **~ frequency** ⚡ Ultrakurzwelle *f*. **~ma·rine** *adj* ultramarin. **~'son·ic** *adj* Ultraschall... **'~-sound** *s phys.* Ultraschall *m*. **~ 'vi·o·let** *adj* ultraviolett.

um·bil·i·cal [ˌʌmbɪˈlaɪkl] *adj*: **~ cord** *anat.* Nabelschnur *f*.

um·brage [ˈʌmbrɪdʒ] *s*: **take ~ at** Anstoß nehmen an (*dat*).

um·brel·la [ʌmˈbrelə] *s* **1.** (Regen-) Schirm *m*. **2.** *fig.* Schutz *m*: **under the ~ of** unter dem Schutz (*gen*). **~ or·gan·i·za·tion** *s* Dachorganisation *f*. **~ stand** *s* Schirmständer *m*.

um·pire [ˈʌmpaɪə] (*Sport*) **I** *s* Schiedsrichter(in). **II** *v/i u. v/t* als Schiedsrichter fungieren (bei).

ump·teen [ˌʌmpˈtiːn] *adj*: **~ times** F x-mal. **,ump'teenth** *adj*: **for the ~ time** F zum x-ten Mal.

un·a·bashed [ˌʌnəˈbæʃt] *adj* unverfroren.

un·a·ble [ʌnˈeɪbl] *adj*: **be ~ to do s.th.** unfähig *od.* außerstande sein, et. zu tun; et. nicht tun können.

un·a·bridged [ˌʌnəˈbrɪdʒd] *adj* ungekürzt.

un·ac·cept·a·ble [ˌʌnəkˈseptəbl] *adj* unannehmbar (**to** für); unzumutbar: **be ~ to s.o.** j-m nicht zugemutet werden können.

un·ac·com·pa·nied [ˌʌnəˈkʌmpənɪd] *adj* ohne Begleitung (**by** *gen*) (*a.* ♪).

un·ac·count·a·ble [ˌʌnəˈkaʊntəbl] *adj* unerklärlich. **,un·ac'count·a·bly** *adv* unerklärlicherweise.

un·ac·cus·tomed [ˌʌnəˈkʌstəmd] *adj* **1.** ungewohnt. **2.** **be ~ to s.th.** et. nicht gewohnt sein; **be ~ to doing s.th.** es nicht gewohnt sein, et. zu tun.

un·ac·quaint·ed [ˌʌnəˈkweɪntɪd] *adj*: **be ~ with s.th.** et. nicht kennen, mit e-r Sache nicht vertraut sein.

un·a·dul·ter·at·ed [ˌʌnəˈdʌltəreɪtɪd] *adj* **1.** unverfälscht. **2.** *fig.* völlig (*Unsinn etc*).

un·ad·vised [ˌʌnədˈvaɪzd] *adj* unbesonnen, unüberlegt.

un·af·fect·ed [ˌʌnəˈfektɪd] *adj* **1.** **be ~ by** nicht betroffen werden von. **2.** natürlich, ungekünstelt.

un·al·ter·a·ble [ʌnˈɔːltərəbl] *adj* unabänderlich (*Entschluß etc*).

un·am·big·u·ous [ˌʌnæmˈbɪɡjʊəs] *adj* □ unzweideutig.

un·A·mer·i·can [ˌʌnəˈmerɪkən] *adj* **1.** unamerikanisch. **2.** antiamerikanisch.

u·nan·i·mous [juːˈnænɪməs] *adj* □ einmütig; einstimmig: **be ~ in doing s.th.** et. einmütig *od.* einstimmig tun; **by a ~ decision** einstimmig.

un·an·nounced [ˌʌnəˈnaʊnst] *adj u. adv* unangemeldet.

un·an·swer·a·ble [ʌnˈɑːnsərəbl] *adj* **1.** nicht zu beantworten(d). **2.** unwiderlegbar.

un·ap·proach·a·ble [ˌʌnəˈprəʊtʃəbl] *adj* □ unnahbar.

un·armed [ʌnˈɑːmd] *adj* unbewaffnet.

un·asked [ʌnˈɑːskt] *adj* **1.** ungestellt (*Frage*). **2.** unaufgefordert, ungebeten. **3.** uneingeladen, ungebeten.

un·as·sist·ed [ˌʌnəˈsɪstɪd] *adv* ohne (fremde) Hilfe, (ganz) allein.

un·as·sum·ing [ˌʌnəˈsjuːmɪŋ] *adj* □ bescheiden.

un·at·tached [ˌʌnəˈtætʃt] *adj* ungebunden (*Person*).

un·at·tend·ed [ˌʌnəˈtendɪd] *adj* unbeaufsichtigt: **leave ~** unbeaufsichtigt lassen.

un·at·trac·tive [ˌʌnəˈtræktɪv] *adj* □ unattraktiv.

un·au·thor·ized [ʌnˈɔːθəraɪzd] *adj* unbefugt, unberechtigt.

un·a·vail·a·ble [ˌʌnəˈveɪləbl] *adj* **1.** nicht erhältlich. **2.** nicht erreichbar.

un·a·void·a·ble [ˌʌnəˈvɔɪdəbl] *adj* □ unvermeidlich.

un·a·ware [ˌʌnəˈweə] *adj*: **be ~ of s.th.** sich e-r Sache nicht bewußt sein, et. nicht bemerken; **be ~ that** nicht bemerken, daß. **,un·a'wares** *adv*: **catch** (*od.* **take**) **s.o. ~** j-n überraschen.

un·bal·ance [ˌʌnˈbæləns] *v/t* j-n aus dem (seelischen) Gleichgewicht bringen. **,un'bal·anced** *adj* labil (*Charakter, Person*).

un·bar [ˌʌnˈbɑː] *v/t* auf-, entriegeln.

un·bear·a·ble [ʌnˈbeərəbl] *adj* □ unerträglich.

un·beat·a·ble [ˌʌnˈbiːtəbl] *adj* unschlagbar (*a.* Preise *etc*).

un·beat·en [ˌʌnˈbiːtn] *adj* ungeschlagen, unbesiegt.

un·be·known [ˌʌnbɪˈnəʊn] *adv*: ~ **to s.o.** ohne j-s Wissen.

un·be·liev·a·ble [ˌʌnbɪˈliːvəbl] *adj* □ unglaublich.

un·bend [ˌʌnˈbend] (*irr* **bend**) **I** *v/t* geradebiegen. **II** *v/i fig.* auftauen, aus sich herausgehen. **,un·bend·ing** *adj* □ unbeugsam.

un·bi·as(s)ed [ˌʌnˈbaɪəst] *adj* □ unvoreingenommen, ʃʒ unbefangen.

un·bind [ˌʌnˈbaɪnd] *v/t* (*irr* **bind**) losbinden.

un·blem·ished [ˌʌnˈblemɪʃt] *adj* makellos (*Ruf etc*).

un·bolt [ˌʌnˈbəʊlt] → **unbar.**

un·born [ˌʌnˈbɔːn] *adj* ungeboren.

un·break·a·ble [ˌʌnˈbreɪkəbl] *adj* unzerbrechlich.

un·bri·dled [ˌʌnˈbraɪdld] *adj* ungezügelt, zügellos: ~ **tongue** lose Zunge.

un·bro·ken [ˌʌnˈbrəʊkən] *adj* **1.** heil, unbeschädigt. **2.** ununterbrochen.

un·buck·le [ˌʌnˈbʌkl] *v/t* auf-, losschnallen.

un·bur·den [ˌʌnˈbɜːdn] *v/t*: ~ **o.s to s.o.** j-m sein Herz ausschütten.

un·but·ton [ˌʌnˈbʌtn] *v/t* aufknöpfen.

un·called-for [ˌʌnˈkɔːldfɔː] *adj* **1.** ungerechtfertigt. **2.** unnötig. **3.** deplaciert, unpassend.

un·can·ny [ʌnˈkænɪ] *adj* □ unheimlich.

un·ceas·ing [ʌnˈsiːsɪŋ] *adj* □ unaufhörlich.

un·cer·e·mo·ni·ous·ly [ˈʌnˌserɪˈməʊnjəslɪ] *adv* ohne viel Federlesen(s).

un·cer·tain [ʌnˈsɜːtn] *adj* □ **1.** unsicher, ungewiß, unbestimmt: **be ~ of s.th.** sich e-r Sache nicht sicher sein; **be ~ how to do s.th.** nicht sicher sein, wie man et. tut. **2.** unbeständig (*Wetter*). **3.** vage: → **term 3.** **un·cer·tain·ty** *s* Unsicherheit *f*, Ungewißheit *f*.

un·chain [ˌʌnˈtʃeɪn] *v/t* losketten.

un·changed [ˌʌnˈtʃeɪndʒd] *adj* unverändert. **,un·chang·ing** *adj* □ unveränderlich.

un·char·i·ta·ble [ˌʌnˈtʃærɪtəbl] *adj* □ unfair: **it was rather ~ of you** es war nicht gerade nett von dir (**to do** zu tun).

un·checked [ˌʌnˈtʃekt] *adj* **1.** ungehin-

dert. **2.** unkontrolliert, ungeprüft.

un·chris·tian [ˌʌnˈkrɪstʃən] *adj* □ unchristlich.

un·civ·il [ˌʌnˈsɪvl] *adj* □ unhöflich. **,un·civ·i·lized** [~vlaɪzd] *adj* unzivilisiert.

un·cle [ˈʌŋkl] *s* Onkel *m*: **cry** (*od.* **say**) ~ *Am.* F aufgeben.

un·com·fort·a·ble [ʌnˈkʌmfətəbl] *adj* □ **1.** unbequem. **2. feel ~** sich unbehaglich fühlen.

un·com·mit·ted [ˌʌnkəˈmɪtɪd] *adj* neutral: **be ~ to** nicht festgelegt sein auf (*acc*).

un·com·mon [ʌnˈkɒmən] *adj* □ ungewöhnlich: **not to be ~** nichts Ungewöhnliches sein.

un·com·mu·ni·ca·tive [ˌʌnkəˈmjuːnɪkətɪv] *adj* □ verschlossen, wortkarg.

un·com·plain·ing·ly [ˌʌnkəmˈpleɪnɪŋlɪ] *adv* geduldig, ohne Murren.

un·com·pro·mis·ing [ʌnˈkɒmprəmaɪzɪŋ] *adj* □ kompromißlos.

un·con·cerned [ˌʌnkənˈsɜːnd] *adj* **1. be ~ about** sich keine Gedanken *od.* Sorgen machen über (*acc*). **2. be ~ with** uninteressiert sein an (*dat*).

un·con·di·tion·al [ˌʌnkənˈdɪʃənl] *adj* □ bedingungslos.

un·con·firmed [ˌʌnkənˈfɜːmd] *adj* unbestätigt.

un·con·scious [ʌnˈkɒnʃəs] *adj* □ **1.** ☞ bewußtlos. **2. be ~ of s.th.** sich e-r Sache nicht bewußt sein, et. nicht bemerken. **3.** unbewußt; unbeabsichtigt. **un·con·scious·ness** *s* ☞ Bewußtlosigkeit *f*.

un·con·sid·ered [ˌʌnkənˈsɪdəd] *adj* unbedacht, unüberlegt.

un·con·sti·tu·tion·al [ˈʌnˌkɒnstɪˈtjuːʃənl] *adj* □ verfassungswidrig.

un·con·trol·la·ble [ˌʌnkənˈtrəʊləbl] *adj* □ unkontrollierbar; nicht zu bändigen(d) (*Kind*); unbändig (*Wut etc*). **,un·con·trolled** *adj* unkontrolliert, ungehindert.

un·con·ven·tion·al [ˌʌnkənˈvenʃənl] *adj* □ unkonventionell.

un·con·vinced [ˌʌnkənˈvɪnst] *adj*: **be ~** nicht überzeugt sein (**about** von). **,un·con·vinc·ing** *adj* □ nicht überzeugend.

un·cooked [ˌʌnˈkʊkt] *adj* ungekocht, roh.

un·cork [ˌʌnˈkɔːk] *v/t* entkorken.

un·count·a·ble [ˌʌnˈkaʊntəbl] *adj* unzählbar (a. ling.). ˌun'count·ed adj unzählig.

un·cou·ple [ˌʌn'kʌpl] v/t Waggon etc abkoppeln, abkuppeln.

un·couth [ʌn'kuːθ] adj □ ungehobelt (Person, Benehmen).

un·cov·er [ʌn'kʌvə] v/t aufdecken, fig. a. enthüllen.

un·crit·i·cal [ˌʌn'krɪtɪkl] adj □ unkritisch: be ~ of s.th. e-r Sache unkritisch gegenüberstehen.

un·crowned [ˌʌn'kraʊnd] adj ungekrönt (a. fig.).

un·crush·a·ble [ʌn'krʌʃəbl] adj knitterfest.

unc·tion ['ʌŋkʃn] s eccl. Salbung f: extreme ~ Krankensalbung. unc·tu·ous ['ʌŋktjʊəs] adj □ salbungsvoll.

un·cut [ˌʌn'kʌt] adj 1. ungeschnitten. 2. ungekürzt (Film, Roman etc). 3. ungeschliffen: ~ diamond a. Rohdiamant m.

un·dam·aged [ˌʌn'dæmɪdʒd] adj unbeschädigt.

un·dat·ed [ˌʌn'deɪtɪd] adj undatiert, ohne Datum.

un·de·cid·ed [ˌʌndɪ'saɪdɪd] adj □ 1. unentschieden, offen. 2. unentschlossen: he is still ~ about what to do er ist sich noch nicht schlüssig, was er tun soll.

un·de·ni·a·ble [ˌʌndɪ'naɪəbl] adj □ unbestreitbar.

un·der ['ʌndə] I prp allg. unter (Lage etc: dat; Richtung: acc): it costs ~ £10 a. es kostet weniger als 10 Pfund; have s.o. ~ one j-n unter sich haben; → discussion, impression 2, influence I, review 1, etc. II adv unten; darunter. ˌ~·a'chieve v/i bsd. ped. hinter den Erwartungen zurückbleiben. ˌ~'act v/t a. v/i thea. etc betont zurückhaltend spielen. ˌ~'age adj minderjährig. '~·brush bsd. Am. → undergrowth. '~·car·riage s ✈ Fahrwerk n, -gestell n. ˌ~'charge I v/t 1. j-m zuwenig berechnen: ~ s.o. (by) £10 j-m 10 Pfund zuwenig berechnen. 2. Betrag zuwenig verlangen. II v/i 3. zuwenig berechnen od. verlangen (for für). '~·clothes s pl → underwear. '~·coat s Grundierung f. '~·cov·er adj: ~ agent verdeckter Ermittler. '~·cur·rent s Unterströmung f (a. fig.). ˌ~'cut v/t (irr cut) j-n (im Preis) unterbieten. ˌ~·de'vel·oped adj unterentwickelt: ~

country Entwicklungsland n. '~·dog s Benachteiligte m, f, Unterdrückte m, f. ˌ~'done adj nicht durchgebraten. ~·'dress v/t a. v/i (sich) zu einfach anziehen. ˌ~'es·ti·mate v/t 1. zu niedrig schätzen od. veranschlagen. 2. fig. unterschätzen, -bewerten. ˌ~·ex'pose v/t phot. unterbelichten. ˌ~'fed adj unterernährt. ˌ~'floor adj: ~ heating Fußbodenheizung f. ˌ~'foot adv: the grass was wet ~ das Gras war naß; trample ~ hinwegtrampeln über (acc). ˌ~'go v/t (irr go) erleben, durchmachen; sich e-r Operation etc unterziehen. ~·grad ['~græd] s F, ˌ~·grad·u·ate s univ. Student(in). '~·ground I adj 1. unterirdisch: ~ car park Tiefgarage f. 2. fig. Untergrund... II adv [ˌ~'graʊnd] 3. unterirdisch, unter der Erde: go ~ fig. untertauchen; in den Untergrund gehen. III s 4. bsd. Br. U-Bahn f: by ~ mit der U-Bahn. 5. fig. Untergrund m. '~·growth s Unterholz n, Gestrüpp n. ˌ~'hand adj, adv heimlich. ˌ~'hung adj hinterhältig. ˌ~'lie v/t (irr lie) zugrunde liegen (dat). ˌ~'line v/t unterstreichen (a. fig.).

un·der·ling ['ʌndəlɪŋ] s: he's just an ~ contp. er ist nur ein Rädchen im Getriebe.

ˌun·der'ly·ing adj zugrundeliegend. ˌ~·'manned adj (personell) unterbesetzt. ˌ~·'men·tioned adj Br. untenerwähnt. ˌ~'mine v/t 1. unterspülen, -waschen. 2. fig. untergraben, -minieren.

un·der·neath [ˌʌndə'niːθ] I prp unter (Lage: dat; Richtung: acc). II adv darunter. III s F Unterseite f.

ˌun·der'nour·ished adj unterernährt. ˌ~'nour·ish·ment s Unterernährung f. '~·pants s pl, a. pair of ~ Unterhose f. '~·pass s (Straßen-, Eisenbahn)Unterführung f. ˌ~'pay v/t (irr pay) j-m zuwenig zahlen, j-n unterbezahlen. ˌ~'play v/t 1. → underact. 2. ~ one's hand fig. nicht alle Trümpfe ausspielen. 3. fig. et. herunterspielen. ˌun·der'priv·i·leged adj unterprivilegiert. ˌ~'rate v/t unterbewerten (a. Sport), -schätzen. '~·repre'sent·ed adj unterrepräsentiert. ˌ~·'score → underline. '~·sec·re·tar·y s pol. Staatssekretär m. ˌ~'sell v/t (irr sell) 1. → undercut. 2. Ware verschleudern, unter Wert verkaufen: ~ o.s. fig. sich schlecht verkaufen. '~·

shirt s Am. Unterhemd n. '**~-shorts**
Am. → **underpants**. '**~-side** s Unterseite f. ,**~'signed** I adj unterzeichnet. II s:
the ~ der od. die Unterzeichnete, die
Unterzeichneten pl. ,**~'size(d)** adj zu
klein. ,**~'staffed** → **undermanned**.
,**~'stand** (irr **stand**) I v/t **1**. verstehen:
make o.s. understood sich verständlich machen. **2**. erfahren od. gehört haben (**that** daß): **am I to ~ that** soll das
heißen, daß; **give s.o. to ~ that** j-m zu
verstehen geben, daß. II v/i **3**. verstehen. **4**. **not to ~ about** nichts verstehen
von. ,**~'stand·a·ble** adj verständlich (a.
fig.): **understandably** a. verständlicherweise. ,**~'stand·ing** I s **1**. Verstand
m: **be** (od. **go**) **beyond s.o.'s ~** über j-s
Verstand gehen. **2**. Verständnis n (**of**
für): **with ~** verständnisvoll. **3**. Abmachung f: **come to an ~** e-e Abmachung treffen (**with** mit); **on the ~ that**
unter der Voraussetzung, daß. II adj □
4. verständnisvoll. ,**~'state** v/t untertreiben, untertrieben darstellen. ,**~'-**
state·ment s Untertreibung f. ,**~-**
stud·y thea. I s zweite Besetzung. II v/t
die zweite Besetzung sein für. ,**~'take**
v/t (irr **take**) **1**. et. übernehmen. **2**. sich
verpflichten (**to do** zu tun). '**~·tak·er** s
(Leichen)Bestatter m; Bestattungs-,
Beerdigungsinstitut n. ,**~-the-'count-**
-er adj F schwarz, illegal. '**~-tone** s **1**. **in
an ~** mit gedämpfter Stimme. **2**. fig.
Unterton m. ,**~'val·ue** v/t unterbewerten, -schätzen. ,**~'wa·ter** I adj Unterwasser... II adv unter Wasser. '**~·wear** s
Unterwäsche f. '**~·weight** I s ['~weɪt]
Untergewicht n. II adj [,~'weɪt] untergewichtig (Person), zu leicht (**by** um)
(Gegenstand): **be ~ by five kilos, be
five kilos ~** fünf Kilo Untergewicht
haben. '**~·work** s Unterwelt f. ,**~'-
write** v/t (irr **write**) **1**. Projekt unterstützen (**with** mit). **2**. et. versichern.

un·de·served [,ʌndɪ'zɜːvd] adj unverdient. ,**un·de·'serv·ed·ly** [~vɪdlɪ] adv
unverdient(ermaßen).

un·de·sir·a·ble [,ʌndɪ'saɪərəbl] adj **1**.
nicht wünschenswert. **2**. unerwünscht.

un·dies ['ʌndɪz] s pl F (bsd. Damen)Unterwäsche f.

un·dis·ci·plined [ʌn'dɪsɪplɪnd] adj undiszipliniert, disziplinlos.

un·dis·cov·ered [,ʌndɪ'skʌvəd] adj

unentdeckt; unbemerkt.

un·dis·turbed [,ʌndɪ'stɜːbd] adj ungestört.

un·di·vid·ed [,ʌndɪ'vaɪdɪd] adj ungeteilt
(a. fig.).

un·do [ʌn'duː] v/t **1**. aufmachen, öffnen.
2. fig. zunichte machen. ,**un'do·ing** s:
be s.o.'s ~ j-s Ruin od. Verderben sein.

un·done [ʌn'dʌn] adj **1**. unerledigt:
leave nothing ~ nichts unversucht lassen. **2**. offen: **come ~** aufgehen.

un·doubt·ed [ʌn'daʊtɪd] adj unbestritten. **un'doubt·ed·ly** adv zweifellos, ohne (jeden) Zweifel.

un·dreamed-of [ʌn'driːmdɒv], **undreamt-of** [ʌn'dremtɒv] adj ungeahnt.

un·dress [ʌn'dres] I v/i sich ausziehen,
(beim Arzt) sich frei machen. II v/t j-n
ausziehen: **get ~ed** → I.

un·due [,ʌn'djuː] adj □ übermäßig.

un·du·lat·ing ['ʌndjʊleɪtɪŋ] adj sanft
(Hügel).

un·dy·ing [ʌn'daɪɪŋ] adj ewig, unsterblich, unvergänglich.

un·earned [,ʌn'ɜːnd] adj fig. unverdient.

un·earth [,ʌn'ɜːθ] v/t **1**. ausgraben. **2**. fig.
ausfindig machen. **un'earth·ly** adj **1**.
überirdisch. **2**. unheimlich. **3**. **at an ~
hour** F zu e-r unchristlichen Zeit.

un·eas·i·ness [ʌn'iːzɪnɪs] s Unbehagen
n. **un'eas·y** adj □ **1**. **be ~** sich unbehaglich fühlen; **I'm ~ about** mir ist nicht
wohl bei. **2**. unruhig (Nacht, Schlaf).

un·eat·a·ble [,ʌn'iːtəbl] adj ungenießbar.

un·e·co·nom·ic ['ʌn,iːkə'nɒmɪk] adj
(**~ally**) unwirtschaftlich.

un·ed·u·cat·ed [ʌn'edjʊkeɪtɪd] adj ungebildet.

un·e·mo·tion·al [,ʌnɪ'məʊʃənl] adj □
leidenschaftslos, kühl, beherrscht.

un·em·ployed [,ʌnɪm'plɔɪd] I adj arbeitslos. II s: **the ~** pl die Arbeitslosen
pl. ,**un·em'ploy·ment** s Arbeitslosigkeit f: **~ benefit** Br., **~ compensation**
Am. Arbeitslosengeld n.

un·end·ing [ʌn'endɪŋ] adj □ endlos.

un·en·dur·a·ble [,ʌnɪn'djʊərəbl] adj □
unerträglich.

un·Eng·lish [,ʌn'ɪŋglɪʃ] adj unenglisch.

un·en·vi·a·ble [ʌn'enviəbl] adj □ wenig
beneidenswert.

un·e·qual [,ʌn'iːkwəl] adj □ **1**. ungleich,
unterschiedlich. **2**. fig. ungleich, einsei-

tig. **3.** *be* ~ *to* e-r Aufgabe etc nicht gewachsen sein. **un·e·qual(l)ed** *adj* unerreicht, unübertroffen.

un·e·quiv·o·cal [ˌʌnɪˈkwɪvəkl] *adj* □ unzweideutig, unmißverständlich.

un·err·ing [ʌnˈɜːrɪŋ] *adj* □ unfehlbar.

un·e·ven [ʌnˈiːvn] *adj* □ **1.** uneben. **2.** ungleich(mäßig). **3.** unterschiedlich, schwankend. **4.** ungerade (*Zahl*). **5.** unregelmäßig (*Pulsschlag etc*).

un·e·vent·ful [ˌʌnɪˈventfʊl] *adj* □ ereignislos.

un·ex·am·pled [ˌʌnɪɡˈzɑːmpld] *adj* beispiellos.

un·ex·pect·ed [ˌʌnɪkˈspektɪd] *adj* □ unerwartet.

un·ex·plained [ˌʌnɪkˈspleɪnd] *adj* ungeklärt.

un·ex·posed [ˌʌnɪkˈspəʊzd] *adj phot.* unbelichtet.

un·ex·plored [ˌʌnɪkˈsplɔːd] *adj* unerforscht.

un·fail·ing [ʌnˈfeɪlɪŋ] *adj* □ unerschöpflich.

un·fair [ˌʌnˈfeə] *adj* □ unfair, (*Wettbewerb*) unlauter. **un·fair·ness** *s* Unfairneß *f*.

un·faith·ful [ʌnˈfeɪθfʊl] *adj* □ untreu (*to dat*).

un·fal·ter·ing [ʌnˈfɔːltərɪŋ] *adj* □ unerschütterlich.

un·fa·mil·iar [ˌʌnfəˈmɪljə] *adj* □ **1.** nicht vertraut. **2.** *be* ~ *with* nicht vertraut sein mit, sich nicht auskennen in (*dat*).

un·fash·ion·a·ble [ʌnˈfæʃnəbl] *adj* □ unmodern.

un·fas·ten [ʌnˈfɑːsn] *v/t* aufmachen, öffnen; losbinden.

un·fa·vo(u)r·a·ble [ʌnˈfeɪvərəbl] *adj* □ ungünstig: a) unvorteilhaft (*to, for* für), b) negativ, ablehnend (*Antwort etc*).

un·feel·ing [ʌnˈfiːlɪŋ] *adj* □ gefühllos, herzlos.

un·fin·ished [ʌnˈfɪnɪʃt] *adj* unfertig; unvollendet.

un·fit [ˌʌnˈfɪt] *adj* □ **1.** unpassend, ungeeignet; unfähig, untauglich: ~ *for ser·vice bsd.* ✕ dienstunfähig, (-)untauglich; ~ *to drive* fahruntüchtig; → **con·sumption** 2. **2.** nicht fit, nicht in Form.

un·flag·ging [ʌnˈflæɡɪŋ] *adj* □ unermüdlich, unentwegt.

un·fold [ʌnˈfəʊld] *v/t* auf-, auseinanderfalten.

un·fore·seen [ˌʌnfɔːˈsiːn] *adj* unvorhergesehen, unvorhersehbar.

un·for·get·ta·ble [ˌʌnfəˈɡetəbl] *adj* □ unvergeßlich.

un·for·tu·nate [ʌnˈfɔːtʃnət] *adj* **1.** unglücklich; unglückselig. **2.** bedauerlich.

un·for·tu·nate·ly *adv* leider.

un·found·ed [ˌʌnˈfaʊndɪd] *adj* unbegründet.

un·fre·quent·ed [ˌʌnfrɪˈkwentɪd] *adj* wenig besucht.

un·friend·ly [ʌnˈfrendlɪ] *adj* unfreundlich (*to* zu).

un·ful·filled [ˌʌnfʊlˈfɪld] *adj* unerfüllt.

un·furl [ʌnˈfɜːl] *v/t* Fahne etc auf-, entrollen, Segel losmachen.

un·fur·nished [ˌʌnˈfɜːnɪʃt] *adj* unmöbliert.

un·gain·ly [ʌnˈɡeɪnlɪ] *adj* linkisch.

un·gen·tle·man·like [ʌnˈdʒentlmənlaɪk], **un·gen·tle·man·ly** *adj* wenig gentlemanlike.

un·god·ly [ʌnˈɡɒdlɪ] *adj*: *at an* ~ *hour* F zu e-r unchristlichen Zeit.

un·gov·ern·a·ble [ʌnˈɡʌvənəbl] *adj* □ unbeherrscht, ungezügelt (*Temperament*).

un·grate·ful [ʌnˈɡreɪtfʊl] *adj* □ undankbar.

un·guard·ed [ˌʌnˈɡɑːdɪd] *adj* **1.** unbewacht. **2.** *fig.* unbedacht, unüberlegt.

un·hap·pi·ness [ʌnˈhæpɪnɪs] *s* Traurigkeit *f*. **un·hap·py** *adj* unglücklich: *unhappily a.* unglücklicherweise, leider.

un·harmed [ˌʌnˈhɑːmd] *adj* unversehrt.

un·health·y [ʌnˈhelθɪ] *adj* □ **1.** kränklich, nicht gesund. **2.** ungesund. **3.** *contp.* unnatürlich, krankhaft.

un·heard [ʌnˈhɜːd] *adj*: *go* ~ unbeachtet bleiben, keine Beachtung finden. **un·heard-of** [-ˈɒv] *adj* noch nie dagewesen, beispiellos.

un·hes·i·tat·ing [ʌnˈhezɪteɪtɪŋ] *adj* **1.** prompt. **2.** bereitwillig: *~ly a.* anstandslos.

un·hinge [ʌnˈhɪndʒ] *v/t* **1.** Tür etc aus den Angeln heben. **2.** ~ *s.o.*('*s mind*) *fig.* j-n völlig aus dem Gleichgewicht bringen.

un·ho·ly [ʌnˈhəʊlɪ] *adj* F furchtbar, schrecklich.

un·hoped-for [ʌnˈhəʊptfɔː] *adj* unverhofft.

un·hurt [ˌʌnˈhɜːt] *adj* unverletzt.

u·ni ['ju:nɪ] *s* F Uni *f* (*Universität*).

un·i·den·ti·fied [ˌʌnaɪ'dentɪfaɪd] *adj* unbekannt, nicht identifiziert: **~ flying object** unbekanntes Flugobjekt.

u·ni·fi·ca·tion [ˌju:nɪfɪ'keɪʃn] *s* Vereinigung *f*.

u·ni·form ['ju:nɪfɔ:m] **I** *adj* □ einheitlich. **II** *s* Uniform *f*: **in ~** in Uniform. **'u·ni·formed** *adj* uniformiert, in Uniform. **ˌu·ni·form·i·ty** *s* Einheitlichkeit *f*.

u·ni·fy ['ju:nɪfaɪ] *v/t* **1.** verein(ig)en. **2.** vereinheitlichen.

u·ni·lat·er·al [ju:nɪ'lætərəl] *adj* □ *fig.* einseitig.

un·im·ag·i·na·ble [ˌʌnɪ'mædʒɪnəbl] *adj* □ unvorstellbar. **ˌun·im·ag·i·na·tive** *adj* □ einfalls-, phantasielos.

un·im·por·tant [ˌʌnɪm'pɔ:tənt] *adj* □ unwichtig.

un·im·pressed [ˌʌnɪm'prest] *adj* unbeeindruckt (**by** von).

un·in·flu·enced [ˌʌn'ɪnflʊənst] *adj* unbeeinflußt.

un·in·jured [ˌʌn'ɪndʒəd] *adj* unverletzt.

un·in·sured [ˌʌn'ɪn'ʃɔ:d] *adj* unversichert.

un·in·tel·li·gent [ˌʌnɪn'telɪdʒənt] *adj* □ unintelligent.

un·in·tel·li·gi·ble [ˌʌnɪn'telɪdʒəbl] *adj* □ unverständlich (**to** für *od.* dat).

un·in·tend·ed [ˌʌnɪn'tendɪd], **un·in·ten·tion·al** [ˌ~'tenʃənl] *adj* □ unabsichtlich, unbeabsichtigt.

un·in·ter·est·ed [ˌʌn'ɪntrəstɪd] *adj* □ uninteressiert (**in** an dat): **be ~ in** a. sich nicht interessieren für. **ˌun·in·ter·est·ing** *adj* □ uninteressant.

un·in·ter·rupt·ed ['ʌnˌɪntə'rʌptɪd] *adj* □ ununterbrochen.

un·in·vit·ed [ˌʌnɪn'vaɪtɪd] *adj* uneingeladen, ungebeten.

un·ion ['ju:njən] *s* **1.** Vereinigung *f*; Union *f*: ♀ **Jack** (*od.* **Flag**) Union Jack *m* (*britische Nationalflagge*). **2.** Gewerkschaft *f*: **'un·ion·ist** *s* Gewerkschaftler(in). **'un·ion·ize** *v/t u. v/i* (sich) gewerkschaftlich organisieren.

u·nique [ju:'ni:k] *adj* □ einzigartig; einmalig.

u·ni·son ['ju:nɪzn] *s*: **in ~** gemeinsam.

u·nit ['ju:nɪt] *s* **1.** *allg.* Einheit *f*; *ped.* Unit *f*, Lehreinheit *f*; ⊙ Element *n*, Teil *n*; (Anbau)Element *n*: **~ furniture** Anbaumöbel *pl*. **2.** Abteilung *f*. **3.** ⚔ Einer *m*.

u·nite [ju:'naɪt] **I** *v/t* verbinden, -einigen. **II** *v/i* sich vereinigen *od.* zs.-tun: **~ in doing s.th.** et. gemeinsam tun. **u'nit·ed** *adj* verein(ig)t: ♀ **Nations** *pl* Vereinte Nationen *pl*; **be ~** sich einig sein in (dat).

u·ni·ty ['ju:nətɪ] *s* **1.** Einheit *f*. **2.** ⚔ Eins *f*.

u·ni·ver·sal [ˌju:nɪ'vɜ:sl] *adj* □ **1.** universal, universell: **~ heir** Universalerbe *m*. **2.** allgemein. **3.** Welt...: **~ language** (**time**, etc). **II** *s* Universum *n*, Weltall *n*.

u·ni·verse ['ju:nɪvɜ:s] *s* Universum *n*, Weltall *n*.

u·ni·ver·si·ty [ˌju:nɪ'vɜ:sətɪ] **I** *s* Universität *f*, Hochschule *f*: **go to ~** die Universität besuchen. **II** *adj* Universitäts...: **~ professor**; **~ education** akademische Bildung, Hochschulbildung *f*; Universitäts-, Hochschulausbildung *f*.

un·just [ˌʌn'dʒʌst] *adj* □ ungerecht (**to** gegen).

un·kempt [ˌʌn'kempt] *adj* ungekämmt (*Haar*); ungepflegt (*Kleidung etc*).

un·kind [ʌn'kaɪnd] *adj* □ unfreundlich (**to** zu). **un'kind·ness** *s* Unfreundlichkeit *f*.

un·knot [ˌʌn'nɒt] *v/t* auf-, entknoten.

un·known [ˌʌn'nəʊn] *adj* unbekannt (**to** dat): **~ quantity** ⚔ unbekannte Größe (a. fig.), Unbekannte *f*.

un·la·dy·like [ˌʌn'leɪdɪlaɪk] *adj* wenig damenhaft.

un·law·ful [ˌʌn'lɔ:fʊl] *adj* □ ungesetzlich, gesetzwidrig.

un·lead·ed [ˌʌn'ledɪd] *adj* bleifrei (*Benzin*).

un·learn [ˌʌn'lɜ:n] *v/t* (a. *irr* **learn**) Ansichten etc ablegen, aufgeben.

un·leash [ˌʌn'li:ʃ] *v/t* **1.** Hund loslassen, von der Leine lassen. **2.** fig. **~ s.th.** (*on* od. *upon s.o.*) Zorn etc freien Lauf lassen: **all his anger was ~ed on her** sein ganzer Zorn entlud sich auf sie.

un·leav·ened [ˌʌn'levnd] *adj* ungesäuert.

un·less [ən'les] *cj* wenn *od.* sofern ... nicht; es sei denn.

un·like [ˌʌn'laɪk] *prp* **1.** im Gegensatz zu. **2. he is quite ~ his father** er ist ganz anders als sein Vater; **that is very ~ him** das sieht ihm gar nicht ähnlich. **un·'like·ly** *adj* **1. he is ~ to come** es ist unwahrscheinlich, daß er kommt. **2.** unwahrscheinlich, unglaubwürdig.

un·lim·it·ed [ʌn'lɪmɪtɪd] *adj* unbegrenzt.

un·list·ed [ʌn'lɪstɪd] *adj teleph.*: **be ~** nicht im Telefonbuch stehen, geheim sein; **~ number** Geheimnummer *f*.

un·load [ʌn'ləʊd] *v/t Fahrzeug* entladen, *a. Gegenstände* ab-, ausladen, ♣ *Ladung, Schiff* löschen.

un·lock [ʌn'lɒk] *v/t* aufschließen.

un·loved [ʌn'lʌvd] *adj* ungeliebt.

un·luck·i·ly [ʌn'lʌkɪlɪ] *adv* unglücklicherweise: **~ for me** zu m-m Pech. **un·luck·y** [ʌn'lʌkɪ] *adj* unglücklich: **~ day** Unglückstag *m*; **be ~** Pech haben; Unglück bringen.

un·made [ʌn'meɪd] *adj* ungemacht (*Bett*).

un·man·age·a·ble [ʌn'mænɪdʒəbl] *adj* □ **1.** widerspenstig. **2.** unhandlich.

un·man·ly [ʌn'mænlɪ] *adj* unmännlich.

un·manned [ʌn'mænd] *adj* unbemannt.

un·man·ner·ly [ʌn'mænəlɪ] *adj* ungesittet, unmanierlich.

un·marked [ʌn'mɑːkt] *adj* **1.** nicht gekennzeichnet. **2.** *Sport:* ungedeckt, frei.

un·mar·ried [ʌn'mærɪd] *adj* unverheiratet, ledig.

un·mask [ʌn'mɑːsk] *v/t fig.* entlarven.

un·matched [ʌn'mætʃt] *adj* unvergleichlich, unübertroffen.

un·men·tion·a·ble [ʌn'menʃnəbl] *adj* Tabu...: **be ~** tabu sein.

un·mer·ci·ful [ʌn'mɜːsɪfʊl] *adj* □ erbarmungslos, unbarmherzig.

un·me·thod·i·cal [ˌʌnmɪ'θɒdɪkl] *adj* □ unmethodisch.

un·mis·tak·a·ble [ˌʌnmɪ'steɪkəbl] *adj* □ unverkennbar, unverwechselbar.

un·mixed [ʌn'mɪkst] *adj* **1.** unvermischt. **2.** *fig.* rein, ungetrübt.

un·moved [ʌn'muːvd] *adj* ungerührt: **he remained ~ by it** es ließ ihn kalt.

un·mu·si·cal [ʌn'mjuːzɪkl] *adj* □ unmusikalisch.

un·named [ʌn'neɪmd] *adj* ungenannt.

un·nat·u·ral [ʌn'nætʃrəl] *adj* □ **1.** unnatürlich. **2.** widernatürlich.

un·nec·es·sar·y [ʌn'nesəsərɪ] *adj* unnötig: **unnecessarily** *a.* unnötigerweise.

un·nerve [ʌn'nɜːv] *v/t* **1.** entnerven. **2.** entmutigen.

un·no·ticed [ʌn'nəʊtɪst] *adj*: **go** (*od.* **pass**) **~** unbemerkt bleiben.

un·num·bered [ˌʌn'nʌmbəd] *adj* unnumeriert.

un·ob·tru·sive [ˌʌnəb'truːsɪv] *adj* □ unauffällig.

un·oc·cu·pied [ʌn'ɒkjʊpaɪd] *adj* **1.** leer(stehend), unbewohnt: **be ~** leer stehen. **2.** unbeschäftigt. **3.** ✕ unbesetzt.

un·of·fi·cial [ˌʌnə'fɪʃl] *adj* □ inoffiziell.

un·o·pened [ʌn'əʊpənd] *adj* ungeöffnet.

un·pack [ʌn'pæk] *v/t u. v/i* auspacken.

un·paid(-for) [ʌn'peɪd(fə)] *adj* unbezahlt.

un·par·al·leled [ʌn'pærəleld] *adj* beispiellos, einmalig.

un·par·don·a·ble [ʌn'pɑːdnəbl] *adj* □ unverzeihlich.

un·per·turbed [ˌʌnpə'tɜːbd] *adj* gelassen, ruhig.

un·pick [ʌn'pɪk] *v/t* auftrennen.

un·play·a·ble [ˌʌn'pleɪəbl] *adj Sport:* unbespielbar (*Platz*).

un·pleas·ant [ʌn'pleznt] *adj* □ **1.** unangenehm, (*Nachricht etc a.*) unerfreulich. **2.** unfreundlich.

un·plug [ˌʌn'plʌg] *v/t* den Stecker (*gen*) herausziehen.

un·po·lished [ʌn'pɒlɪʃt] *adj* **1.** unpoliert. **2.** *fig.* ungeschliffen, ungehobelt.

un·pop·u·lar [ˌʌn'pɒpjʊlə] *adj* □ unpopulär, unbeliebt: **make o.s. ~ with** bei j-m unbeliebt machen.

un·prac·ti·cal [ˌʌn'præktɪkl] *adj* □ unpraktisch.

un·prec·e·dent·ed [ʌn'presɪdentɪd] *adj* □ beispiellos, noch nie dagewesen.

un·pre·dict·a·ble [ˌʌnprɪ'dɪktəbl] *adj* **1.** unvorhersehbar. **2.** unberechenbar (*Person*).

un·prej·u·diced [ʌn'predʒʊdɪst] *adj* □ unvoreingenommen, ♣♣ unbefangen.

un·pre·pared [ˌʌnprɪ'peəd] *adj* **1.** unvorbereitet. **2.** nicht gefaßt *od.* vorbereitet (*for* auf *acc*).

un·pre·ten·tious [ˌʌnprɪ'tenʃəs] *adj* □ bescheiden, einfach.

un·prin·ci·pled [ʌn'prɪnsəpld] *adj* skrupellos.

un·print·a·ble [ˌʌn'prɪntəbl] *adj* nicht druckfähig *od.* druckreif.

un·pro·duc·tive [ˌʌnprə'dʌktɪv] *adj* □ unproduktiv (*a. fig.*), unergiebig, unrentabel.

un·pro·fes·sion·al [ˌʌnprə'feʃənl] *adj* □

1. standeswidrig. **2.** unfachmännisch.

un·prof·it·a·ble [ˌʌnˈprɒfitəbl] *adj* □ **1.** unrentabel. **2.** *fig.* nutz-, zwecklos.

un·prompt·ed [ˌʌnˈprɒmptɪd] *adj* spontan.

un·pro·nounce·a·ble [ˌʌnprəˈnaʊnsəbl] *adj* unaussprechbar.

un·pro·tect·ed [ˌʌnprəˈtektɪd] *adj* schutzlos; ungeschützt.

un·proved [ˌʌnˈpruːvd], **ˌun'prov·en** [ˌ~vn] *adj* unbewiesen.

un·pro·voked [ˌʌnprəˈvəʊkt] *adj* grundlos.

un·pub·lished [ˌʌnˈpʌblɪʃt] *adj* unveröffentlicht.

un·punc·tu·al [ˌʌnˈpʌŋktjʊəl] *adj* □ unpünktlich: *be ~* unpünktlich kommen (*for* zu). **'un·punc·tu·al·i·ty** [ˌ~ˈælətɪ] *s* Unpünktlichkeit *f*.

un·pun·ished [ˌʌnˈpʌnɪʃt] *adj* unbestraft, ungestraft: *go ~* straflos bleiben.

un·qual·i·fied [ˌʌnˈkwɒlɪfaɪd] *adj* **1.** unqualifiziert, ungeeignet (*for* für). **2.** uneingeschränkt.

un·ques·tion·a·ble [ʌnˈkwestʃənəbl] *adj* □ unbestritten: *be ~ a.* außer Frage stehen. **un'ques·tion·ing** *adj* □ bedingungslos.

un·quote [ˌʌnˈkwəʊt] *adv* → **quote** 6.

un·rav·el [ʌnˈrævl] **I** *v/t* **1.** Pullover etc auftrennen, -ziehen. **2.** entwirren (*a. fig.*). **II** *v/i* **3.** sich auftrennen *od.* aufziehen.

un·read·a·ble [ˌʌnˈriːdəbl] *adj* □ unlesbar: a) nicht lesenswert, b) unleserlich.

un·re·al [ˌʌnˈrɪəl] *adj* □ unwirklich. **'un·re·al·is·tic** [ˌ~ˈlɪstɪk] *adj* (*~ally*) unrealistisch. **un·re·al·i·ty** [ˌ~ˈælətɪ] *s* Unwirklichkeit *f*.

un·rea·son·a·ble [ʌnˈriːznəbl] *adj* □ **1.** unvernünftig. **2.** übertrieben, unzumutbar.

un·rec·og·niz·a·ble [ˌʌnˈrekəgnaɪzəbl] *adj* □ nicht wiederzuerkennen(d).

un·re·lat·ed [ˌʌnrɪˈleɪtɪd] *adj* **1.** nicht verwandt (*to* mit). **2.** *be ~* in keinem Zs.-hang stehen (*to* mit).

un·re·lent·ing [ˌʌnrɪˈlentɪŋ] *adj* □ unvermindert.

un·re·li·a·ble [ˌʌnrɪˈlaɪəbl] *adj* □ unzuverlässig.

un·re·lieved [ˌʌnrɪˈliːvd] *adj* ununterbrochen, ständig. **ˌun·re'liev·ed·ly** [ˌ~ɪdlɪ] *adv* → **unrelieved**.

un·re·mit·ting [ˌʌnrɪˈmɪtɪŋ] *adj* □ unablässig, unaufhörlich.

un·re·quit·ed [ˌʌnrɪˈkwaɪtɪd] *adj* unerwidert (*Liebe*).

un·re·served [ˌʌnrɪˈzɜːvd] *adj* **1.** uneingeschränkt. **2.** nicht reserviert. **ˌun·re'serv·ed·ly** [ˌ~ɪdlɪ] *adv* uneingeschränkt.

un·rest [ˌʌnˈrest] *s pol. etc* Unruhen *pl*.

un·re·strained [ˌʌnrɪˈstreɪnd] *adj* hemmungslos, ungezügelt. **ˌun·re'strain·ed·ly** [ˌ~ɪdlɪ] *adv* → **unrestrained**.

un·re·strict·ed [ˌʌnrɪˈstrɪktɪd] *adj* □ uneingeschränkt.

un·re·ward·ing [ˌʌnrɪˈwɔːdɪŋ] *adj* wenig lohnend, (*Aufgabe etc a.*) undankbar.

un·rig [ˌʌnˈrɪg] *v/t Schiff* abtakeln.

un·ripe [ˌʌnˈraɪp] *adj* unreif.

un·ri·val(l)ed [ʌnˈraɪvld] *adj* unerreicht, unübertroffen.

un·roll [ˌʌnˈrəʊl] *v/t* auf-, entrollen.

un·ruf·fled [ˌʌnˈrʌfld] *adj* gelassen, ruhig.

un·rul·y [ʌnˈruːlɪ] *adj* **1.** ungebärdig, wild. **2.** widerspenstig (*Haare*).

un·sad·dle [ˌʌnˈsædl] *v/t* **1.** *Pferd* absatteln. **2.** *Reiter* abwerfen.

un·safe [ˌʌnˈseɪf] *adj* □ unsicher, nicht sicher: *feel ~* sich nicht sicher fühlen.

un·said [ˌʌnˈsed] *adj*: *leave s.th. ~* et. nicht aussprechen; *be left* (*od. go*) *~* unausgesprochen *od.* ungesagt bleiben.

un·sal(e)·a·ble [ˌʌnˈseɪləbl] *adj* unverkäuflich.

un·salt·ed [ˌʌnˈsɔːltɪd] *adj* ungesalzen.

un·san·i·tar·y [ˌʌnˈsænɪtərɪ] *adj* □ unhygienisch.

un·sat·is·fac·to·ry [ˈʌnˌsætɪsˈfæktərɪ] *adj* □ unbefriedigend. **ˌun'sat·is·fied** [ˌ~faɪd] *adj* unzufrieden (*with* mit). **ˌun'sat·is·fy·ing** [ˌ~faɪɪŋ] → **unsatisfactory.**

un·sa·vo(u)r·y [ˌʌnˈseɪvərɪ] *adj* □ **1.** fad. **2.** *fig.* unerfreulich (*Angelegenheit etc*); anrüchig (*Stadtteil, Vergangenheit etc*).

un·sci·en·tif·ic [ˈʌnˌsaɪənˈtɪfɪk] *adj* (*~ally*) unwissenschaftlich.

un·screw [ˌʌnˈskruː] *v/t* ab-, losschrauben.

un·script·ed [ˌʌnˈskrɪptɪd] *adj* improvisiert.

un·scru·pu·lous [ʌnˈskruːpjʊləs] *adj* □ skrupel-, gewissenlos.

un·seat [ˌʌnˈsiːt] *v/t* **1.** *Reiter* abwerfen. **2.** *fig. j-n s-s* Amtes entheben.

un·seed·ed [ˌʌn'siːdɪd] *adj Sport:* ungesetzt.

un·seem·ly [ʌn'siːmlɪ] *adj* ungebührlich, unziemlich.

un·seen [ˌʌn'siːn] **I** *adj* **1.** ungesehen, unbemerkt: → *sight* 2. **2.** unsichtbar. **II** *s an* (**English**) ~ *ped. bsd. Br.* e-e Herübersetzung (aus dem Englischen).

un·self·ish [ʌn'selfɪʃ] *adj* □ selbstlos, uneigennützig.

un·sen·ti·men·tal [ˈʌnˌsentɪ'mentl] *adj* □ unsentimental.

un·set·tle [ˌʌn'setl] *v/t j-n* beunruhigen; durcheinanderbringen. **ˌun'set·tled** *adj* **1.** unbesiedelt. **2.** unbeglichen, unbezahlt (*Rechnung*). **3.** ungeklärt (*Frage etc*). **4.** unbeständig (*Wetter*). **5.** unsicher (*Lage etc*).

un·shak(e)·a·ble [ʌn'ʃeɪkəbl] *adj* □ unerschütterlich.

un·shav·en [ˌʌn'ʃeɪvn] *adj* unrasiert.

un·shrink·a·ble [ˌʌn'ʃrɪŋkəbl] *adj* nicht eingehend *od.* einlaufend (*Stoff*).

un·sight·ly [ʌn'saɪtlɪ] *adj* unansehnlich; häßlich.

un·signed [ˌʌn'saɪnd] *adj* unsigniert (*Gemälde*), nicht unterschrieben *od.* unterzeichnet (*Brief etc*).

un·skil(l)·ful [ʌn'skɪlfʊl] *adj* □ ungeschickt. **ˌun'skilled** *adj* **1.** ungeschickt (**at, in** in *dat*). **2.** ~ **worker** ungelernter Arbeiter.

un·so·cia·ble [ʌn'səʊʃəbl] *adj* □ ungesellig.

un·so·cial [ʌn'səʊʃl] *adj:* **work** ~ **hours** *Br.* außerhalb der normalen Arbeitszeit arbeiten.

un·sold [ˌʌn'səʊld] *adj* unverkauft.

un·so·lic·it·ed [ˌʌnsə'lɪsɪtɪd] *adj* unverlangt eingesandt (*Manuskript etc*), unaufgefordert zugesandt, unbestellt (*Ware*).

un·solved [ˌʌn'sɒlvd] *adj* ungelöst (*Fall etc*).

un·so·phis·ti·cat·ed [ˌʌnsə'fɪstɪkeɪtɪd] *adj* □ **1.** unkultiviert. **2.** ◎ unkompliziert.

un·sound [ˌʌn'saʊnd] *adj* □ **1.** nicht gesund; nicht intakt *od.* in Ordnung. **2.** *fig.* unklug, unvernünftig.

un·spar·ing [ʌn'speərɪŋ] *adj* □ verschwenderisch, freigebig (**in** mit): **be** ~

in one's efforts keine Mühe scheuen (**to do** zu tun).

un·speak·a·ble [ʌn'spiːkəbl] *adj* □ unbeschreiblich, unsäglich.

un·spoiled [ˌʌn'spɔɪld], **ˌun'spoilt** [~t] *adj* **1.** unverdorben. **2.** nicht verwöhnt, (*Kind a.*) nicht verzogen.

un·sport·ing [ˌʌn'spɔːtɪŋ] *adj* □, **un·sports·man·like** [ˌʌn'spɔːtsmənlaɪk] *adj* unsportlich, unfair.

un·sta·ble [ˌʌn'steɪbl] *adj* □ **1.** instabil (*a. fig.*). **2.** *fig.* labil (*Person*).

un·stead·y [ˌʌn'stedɪ] *adj* □ **1.** wack(e)lig; (*Hand*) unsicher. **2.** schwankend (*Preise etc*). **3.** ungleichmäßig.

un·stint·ing [ʌn'stɪntɪŋ] → **unsparing**.

un·stop [ʌn'stɒp] *v/t* **1.** *Flasche* entstöpseln. **2.** *Abfluß etc* freimachen.

un·stressed [ˌʌn'strest] *adj ling.* unbetont.

un·stuck [ˌʌn'stʌk] *adj:* **come** ~ abgehen, sich lösen; *fig.* auf den Bauch fallen (*Person*), schiefgehen (*Plan etc*).

un·stud·ied [ˌʌn'stʌdɪd] *adj* ungekünstelt.

un·suc·cess·ful [ˌʌnsək'sesfʊl] *adj* □ erfolglos; vergeblich: **be** ~ keinen Erfolg haben.

un·suit·a·ble [ˌʌn'suːtəbl] *adj* □ unpassend, ungeeignet (**for, to** für).

un·sure [ˌʌn'ʃɔː] *adj allg.* unsicher: ~ **of o.s.** unsicher.

un·sur·passed [ˌʌnsə'pɑːst] *adj* unübertroffen.

un·sus·pect·ed [ˌʌnsə'spektɪd] *adj* □ **1.** unvermutet. **2.** unverdächtig. **ˌun·sus'pect·ing** *adj* □ nichtsahnend, ahnungslos.

un·sus·pi·cious [ˌʌnsə'spɪʃəs] *adj* □ **1.** arglos. **2.** unverdächtig, harmlos.

un·sweet·ened [ˌʌn'swiːtnd] *adj* ungesüßt.

un·swerv·ing [ʌn'swɜːvɪŋ] *adj* □ unbeirrbar, unerschütterlich.

un·tan·gle [ˌʌn'tæŋgl] *v/t* entwirren (*a. fig.*).

un·tapped [ˌʌn'tæpt] *adj* unerschlossen (*Naturschätze etc*).

un·teach·a·ble [ˌʌn'tiːtʃəbl] *adj* unbelehrbar.

un·ten·a·ble [ˌʌn'tenəbl] *adj* unhaltbar (*Theorie etc*).

un·think·a·ble [ʌn'θɪŋkəbl] *adj* □ undenkbar, unvorstellbar. **,un'think·ing** *adj* □ gedankenlos.

un·ti·dy [ʌn'taɪdɪ] *adj* □ unordentlich.

un·tie [ˌʌn'taɪ] *v/t* aufknoten, *Knoten lösen, j-n etc* losbinden (**from** von).

un·til [ən'tɪl] **I** *prp* **1.** bis. **2.** *not ~* erst: *not ~ Monday* erst (am) Montag; nicht vor Montag. **II** *cj* **3.** bis. **4.** *not ~* erst wenn, nicht bevor.

un·time·ly [ʌn'taɪmlɪ] *adj* **1.** vorzeitig, verfrüht. **2.** unpassend, ungelegen.

un·tir·ing [ʌn'taɪərɪŋ] *adj* □ unermüdlich.

un·told [ˌʌn'təʊld] *adj* unermeßlich (*Reichtum, Schaden etc*).

un·touched [ʌn'tʌtʃt] *adj* **1.** unberührt, unangetastet. **2.** unversehrt, heil.

un·trans·lat·a·ble [ˌʌntræns'leɪtəbl] *adj* unübersetzbar.

un·true [ˌʌn'truː] *adj* **1.** unwahr. **2.** untreu (**to** dat).

un·truth [ˌʌn'truːθ] *s* Unwahrheit *f*.

un·used¹ [ʌn'juːzd] *adj* unbenutzt, ungebraucht.

un·used² [ʌn'juːst] *adj*: *be ~ to s.th.* an et. nicht gewöhnt sein, et. nicht gewohnt sein; *be ~ to doing s.th.* es nicht gewohnt sein, et. zu tun.

un·u·su·al [ʌn'juːʒl] *adj* □ ungewöhnlich.

un·ut·ter·a·ble [ʌn'ʌtərəbl] *adj* □ unbeschreiblich, unsäglich.

un·var·nished [ʌn'vɑːnɪʃt] *adj* ungeschminkt (*Wahrheit*).

un·var·y·ing [ʌn'veərɪŋ] *adj* □ unveränderlich, gleichbleibend.

un·veil [ˌʌn'veɪl] *v/t Denkmal etc* enthüllen.

un·versed [ˌʌn'vɜːst] *adj* unbewandert (**in** in *dat*).

un·voiced [ˌʌn'vɔɪst] *adj* **1.** unausgesprochen. **2.** *ling.* stimmlos.

un·want·ed [ʌn'wɒntɪd] *adj* unerwünscht, (*Schwangerschaft a.*) ungewollt.

un·war·rant·ed [ʌn'wɒrəntɪd] *adj* ungerechtfertigt.

un·washed [ʌn'wɒʃt] *adj* ungewaschen.

un·wa·ver·ing [ʌn'weɪvərɪŋ] *adj* □ unerschütterlich.

un·wel·come [ʌn'welkəm] *adj* unwillkommen.

un·well [ˌʌn'wel] *adj*: *be* (*od. feel*) *~* sich unwohl *od.* nicht wohl fühlen.

un·whole·some [ˌʌn'həʊlsəm] *adj* □ ungesund.

un·wield·y [ʌn'wiːldɪ] *adj* unhandlich, sperrig.

un·will·ing [ˌʌn'wɪlɪŋ] *adj* □ widerwillig: *be ~ to do s.th.* nicht bereit *od.* gewillt sein, et. zu tun; et. nicht tun wollen.

un·wind [ˌʌn'waɪnd] (*irr* **wind**) **I** *v/t* **1.** abwickeln. **II** *v/i* **2.** sich abwickeln. **3.** F abschalten, sich entspannen.

un·wise [ˌʌn'waɪz] *adj* □ unklug.

un·wished-for [ʌn'wɪʃtfɔː] *adj* unerwünscht.

un·wit·ting [ʌn'wɪtɪŋ] *adj* □ **1.** unwissentlich. **2.** unbeabsichtigt.

un·wom·an·ly [ʌn'wʊmənlɪ] *adj* unfraulich, unweiblich.

un·wont·ed [ʌn'wəʊntɪd] *adj* □ ungewohnt.

un·wor·thy [ʌn'wɜːðɪ] *adj*: *be ~ of s.th.* e-r Sache nicht würdig sein, et. nicht verdienen.

un·wrap [ˌʌn'ræp] *v/t* auswickeln, -pakken.

un·writ·ten [ˌʌn'rɪtn] *adj* ungeschrieben: *~ law* ungeschriebenes Recht; *fig.* ungeschriebenes Gesetz.

un·yield·ing [ʌn'jiːldɪŋ] *adj* □ unnachgiebig.

un·zip [ˌʌn'zɪp] *v/t* den Reißverschluß (*gen*) aufmachen.

up [ʌp] **I** *adv* **1.** oben; *1000 Meter etc* hoch, in e-r Höhe von: *~ there* dort oben; *jump ~ and down* hüpfen; *walk ~ and down* auf u. ab *od.* hin u. her gehen; → *look up, take up, etc.* **2.** *~ to* bis zu: *~ to a moment ago* bis vor e-m Augenblick; *be ~ to s.th.* F et. vorhaben, et. im Schilde führen; *not to be ~ to s.th.* e-r Sache nicht gewachsen sein; *it's ~ to you* das liegt bei Ihnen; → *ear¹* 1, *eye* 1, *feel* 6, *scratch* 1, *etc.* **II** *prp* **3.** oben auf (*dat*); her-, hinauf: *~ the river* flußaufwärts; *~ yours! Br.* V leck mich (doch) am Arsch!; → *climb* 3, *etc.* **III** *adj* **4.** nach oben (gerichtet), Aufwärts... **5.** *the ~ train* der Zug nach London. **6.** *what's ~?* F was ist los? **7.** *be well ~ in* (*od.* on) F viel verstehen von. **8.** *~ for* → *sale* 1. **IV** *s* **9.** the *~s and downs* *pl* die Höhen u. Tiefen *pl* (*des Lebens*). **V** *v/t* **10.** F Angebot, Preis *etc* erhöhen. **VI** *v/i* **11.** *he ~ped and left her* F er hat sie von heute auf morgen sitzenlassen. **,~-and-'com·ing** *adj* vielversprechend. **'~,bring·ing** *s* Erziehung *f*. **'~,com·ing** *adj* bevorstehend. **~'date** *v/t* auf den neuesten Stand bringen; aktualisieren. **~'end** *v/t* hochkant stellen. **~'grade** *v/t* j-n befördern. **~·heav·al** [~'hi:vl] *s fig*. Umwälzung *f*. **,~'hill** I *adv* **1.** aufwärts, bergan. II *adj* **2.** bergauf führend. **3.** *fig*. mühselig, hart. **~'hold** *v/t* (*irr* **hold**) **1.** *Rechte etc* schützen, wahren. **2.** ⚖ *Urteil* bestätigen. **~·hol·ster** [~'həʊlstə] *v/t* polstern: **~ed** Polster... **'~,keep** *s* Unterhalt *m*; Unterhaltungskosten *pl*. **~'lift** I *v/t* [~'lɪft] j-n aufrichten, j-m Auftrieb geben. II *s* ['~lɪft] Auftrieb *m*.

up·on [ə'pɒn] *prp* → **on** I.

up·per ['ʌpə] I *adj* ober: **~ arm** Oberarm *m*; **~ class(es** *pl*) *sociol*. Oberschicht *f*; **~ deck** ⚓ Oberdeck *n* (*a. e-s Busses*): **gain** (*od*. **get**) **the ~ hand** die Oberhand gewinnen (**of** über *acc*); → **jaw** 1, **lip** 1. II *s* Obermaterial *n* (*e-s Schuhs*). **'~·cut** *s Boxen*: Aufwärtshaken *m*.

up·per·most ['ʌpəməʊst] I *adj* oberst: **be ~** oben sein; *fig*. an erster Stelle stehen; **be ~ in s.o.'s mind** *fig*. für j-n an erster Stelle stehen. II *adv* nach oben.

up·pish ['ʌpɪʃ] *adj* □ F, **up·pi·ty** ['ʌpəti] *adj* F hochnäsig.

up·right ['ʌpraɪt] I *adj* □ **1.** [*a*. ,ʌp'raɪt] aufrecht, gerade; senkrecht. **2.** *fig*. aufrecht, rechtschaffen. II *adv* [*a*. ,ʌp'raɪt] **3.** → 1: **sit ~** geradesitzen. III *s* **4.** Pfosten *m*.

up·ris·ing ['ʌp,raɪzɪŋ] *s* Aufstand *m*.

up·roar ['ʌprɔ:] *s* Aufruhr *m*, Tumult *m*: **be in an ~** in Aufruhr sein.

up·root [ʌp'ru:t] *v/t* **1.** *Pflanze* (mit den Wurzeln) ausreißen, *a. Baum etc*, *fig*. *Menschen* entwurzeln. **2.** *fig*. j-n herausreißen (**from** aus).

up·set I *v/t* [ʌp'set] (*irr* **set**) **1.** umkippen, umstoßen, umwerfen: → **applecart. 2.** *fig*. *Pläne etc* durcheinanderbringen, *Gleichgewicht* stören. **3.** *fig*. j-n aus der Fassung bringen; aufregen; kränken, verletzen. **4. the fish has ~ me** (*od*. **my stomach**) ich habe mir durch den Fisch den Magen verdorben. II *s* ['ʌpset] **5.** (*Magen*)Verstimmung *f*. **6.** *bsd. Sport*: Überraschung *f*.

up·shot ['ʌpʃɒt] *s* Ergebnis *n*: **what was**

the ~ of ...? was ist bei ... herausgekommen?

up·side ['ʌpsaɪd] *adv*: **~ down** verkehrt herum; **turn ~ down** umdrehen, *a. fig*. auf den Kopf stellen.

up·stairs [,ʌp'steəz] I *adv* **1.** die Treppe her- *od*. hinauf, nach oben. **2.** oben, in e-m oberen Stockwerk. **3.** e-e Treppe höher. II *adj* **4.** im oberen Stockwerk (gelegen), ober.

up·start ['ʌpstɑ:t] *s* Emporkömmling *m*.

up·stream [,ʌp'stri:m] *adv* flußauf(-wärts).

up·surge ['ʌpsɜ:dʒ] *s* **1.** Anschwellen *n* (**in** gen). **2.** Aufwallung *f*.

up·take ['ʌpteɪk] *s*: **be quick** (**slow**) **on the ~** F schnell begreifen (schwer von Begriff sein).

up·tight ['ʌptaɪt] *adj* F **1.** nervös, reizbar. **2.** verklemmt.

up-to-date [,ʌptə'deɪt] *adj* **1.** modern. **2.** aktuell, neu.

up-to-the-min·ute [,ʌptəðə'mɪnɪt] *adj* **1.** hochmodern. **2.** allerneu(e)st.

up·town [,ʌp'taʊn] *Am*. I *adv* in den Wohnvierteln, in die Wohnviertel. II *adj* in den Wohnvierteln (gelegen *od*. lebend): **in ~ Los Angeles** in den Außenbezirken von Los Angeles. III *s* Wohnviertel *pl*, Außenbezirke *pl*.

up·turn ['ʌptɜ:n] *s* Aufschwung *m* (**in** gen). **,up'turned** *adj* **1.** nach oben gerichtet *od*. gebogen: **~ nose** Stupsnase *f*. **2.** umgedreht.

up·ward ['ʌpwəd] I *adv* **1.** nach oben: **face ~** mit dem Gesicht nach oben. **2. from £2 ~** ab 2 Pfund; **~ of £2** F mehr als *od*. über 2 Pfund. **3.** *fig*. aufwärts, bergan: **he went ~ in life** es ging aufwärts mit ihm. **4.** Aufwärts... **up·wards** ['~z] → **upward** I.

u·ra·ni·um [jʊ'reɪnɪəm] *s* 🜨 Uran *n*.

ur·ban ['ɜ:bən] *adj* städtisch, Stadt...

ur·bane [ɜ:'beɪn] *adj* □ weltmännisch, -gewandt.

ur·chin ['ɜ:tʃɪn] *s* Gassenjunge *m*.

u·re·thra [jʊə'ri:θrə] *pl* **-thrae** [~θri:], **-thras** *s anat*. Harnröhre *f*.

urge [ɜ:dʒ] I *v/t* **1.** *a*. **~ on** antreiben, *fig*. *a*. anspornen (**to** zu). **2.** j-n drängen (**to do** zu tun). **3.** dringen auf (*acc*). II *s* **4.** Drang *m*, Verlangen *n*. **ur·gen·cy** ['ɜ:dʒənsɪ] *s* Dringlichkeit *f*. **'ur·gent** *adj* □ dringend: **be ~** *a*. eilen; **be in ~**

need of s.th. et. dringend brauchen.

u·ric ['jʊərɪk] *adj* Urin...: ~ **acid** Harnsäure *f*.

u·ri·nal ['jʊərɪnl] *s* **1.** Urinal *n*. **2.** Pissoir *n*. **'u·ri·nar·y** *adj* Urin...: ~ **bladder** Harnblase *f*. **u·ri·nate** ['~neɪt] *v/i* urinieren. **u·rine** ['~rɪn] *s* Urin *m*: ~ **sample** Urinprobe *f*.

urn [ɜːn] *s* **1.** Urne *f*. **2.** Großkaffee-, Großteemaschine *f*.

u·rol·o·gist [jʊə'rɒlədʒɪst] *s* 🩺 Urologe *m*, Urologin *f*.

us [ʌs] *I personal pron* **1.** uns (*acc od. dat von* **we**): *both of* ~ wir beide; → **all 4**. **2.** F wir (*nom*): *they are older than* ~; *it's* ~ wir sind's. **II** *reflex pron* **3.** uns: *we looked around* ~ wir sahen uns um.

us·a·ble ['juːzəbl] *adj* brauch-, verwendbar.

us·age ['juːzɪdʒ] *s* **1.** Brauch *m*, Gepflogenheit *f*. **2.** (Sprach)Gebrauch *m*. **3.** Behandlung *f*.

use I *v/t* [juːz] **1.** benutzen, gebrauchen, verwenden, *Taktik etc a.* anwenden: *I could* ~ *a drink* F ich könnte et. zu trinken vertragen. **2.** *Benzin etc* (ver-)brauchen: ~ *up* auf-, verbrauchen. **3.** *j-n* benutzen (*for* für). **II** *v/i* [juːs] **4.** *I* ~*d to live here* ich habe früher hier gewohnt; *he* ~*d to be a chain smoker* er war früher einmal Kettenraucher. **III** *s* [juːs] **5.** Benutzung *f*, Gebrauch *m*, Verwendung *f*: *come into* ~ in Gebrauch kommen; *go out of* ~ außer Gebrauch kommen; *make* ~ *of* Gebrauch machen von, benutzen. **6.** Verwendung(szweck *m*) *f*: *with many* ~*s* vielseitig verwendbar. **7.** Nutzen *m*: *be of* ~ nützlich *od.* von Nutzen sein (*to* für); *it's no* ~ *complaining* es ist nutz- *od.* zwecklos zu reklamieren, es hat keinen Zweck zu reklamieren; → **milk I**.

used¹ [juːzd] *adj* gebraucht: ~ *car* Gebrauchtwagen *m*.

used² [juːst] *adj*: *be* ~ *to s.th.* an et. gewöhnt sein, et. gewohnt sein; *be* ~ *to doing s.th.* es gewöhnt sein, et. zu tun.

use·ful ['juːsfʊl] *adj* □ nützlich: *make o.s.* ~ sich nützlich machen. **'use·ful·ness** *s* Nützlichkeit *f*.

use·less ['juːslɪs] *adj* □ nutzlos: *it is* ~ es ist zwecklos (*to do* zu tun); *he's* ~ F er ist zu nichts zu gebrauchen. **'use·less·ness** *s* Nutzlosigkeit *f*.

us·er ['juːzə] *s* **1.** Benutzer(in). **2.** Verbraucher(in). **~·'friend·ly** *adj* benutzer- *od.* verbraucherfreundlich.

ush·er ['ʌʃə] **I** *s* **1.** Platzanweiser *m*. **2.** ⚖ Gerichtsdiener *m*. **II** *v/t* **3.** *j-n* führen, geleiten (*into* in *acc*; *to zu s-m Platz etc*). **ush·er·ette** [~'ret] *s* Platzanweiserin *f*.

u·su·al ['juːʒl] *I adj* □ üblich: *as* ~ wie gewöhnlich *od.* üblich; *it's not* ~ *for him to be so late* er kommt normalerweise nicht so spät; *is it* ~ *for him to be so late?* kommt er immer so spät? **II** *s das* Übliche: *the* ~ F (*in Pub etc*) wie immer. **u·su·al·ly** ['~ʒlɪ] *adv* (für) gewöhnlich, normalerweise.

u·sur·er ['juːʒərə] *s* Wucherer *m*.

u·su·ri·ous [juː'zjʊərɪəs] *adj* □ wucherisch, Wucher...

u·surp [juː'zɜːp] *v/t Macht etc* an sich reißen, sich *des Throns* bemächtigen.

u·su·ry ['juːʒərɪ] *s* Wucher *m*.

u·ten·sil [juː'tensl] *s* Gerät *n*: ~*s* pl a. Utensilien *pl*.

u·ter·us ['juːtərəs] *pl* **-i** ['~aɪ], **-us·es** *s anat.* Gebärmutter *f*.

u·til·i·tar·i·an [juːtɪlɪ'teərɪən] *adj* zweckmäßig, praktisch.

u·til·i·ty [juː'tɪlətɪ] *s* **1.** Nutzen *m*, Nützlichkeit *f*. **2.** → **public** 3a.

u·ti·lize ['juːtɪlaɪz] *v/t* nutzen.

ut·most ['ʌtməʊst] **I** *adj* äußerst, höchst, größt. **II** *s* das Äußerste: *do one's* ~ sein möglichstes tun.

U·to·pi·an [juː'təʊpjən] *adj* utopisch (*Gesellschaft*).

ut·ter ['ʌtə] **I** *adj* □ total, völlig. **II** *v/t et.* äußern, *Seufzer etc* ausstoßen, *Wort* sagen. **'ut·ter·ance** *s* **1.** *give* ~ *to s-r Meinung etc* Ausdruck geben. **2.** Äußerung *f*.

U-turn ['juːtɜːn] *s* **1.** *mot.* Wende *f*: *do a* ~ wenden. **2.** *fig.* Kehrtwendung *f*: *do a* ~ e-e Kehrtwendung machen (*on* in *dat*).

u·vu·la ['juːvjʊlə] *s anat.* (Gaumen-)Zäpfchen *n*.

V

vac [væk] *s univ. Br.* F Semesterferien *pl.*

va·can·cy ['veɪkənsɪ] *s* **1.** freie *od.* offene Stelle: *"vacancies"* „wir stellen ein". **2.** *"vacancies"* „Zimmer frei"; *"no vacancies"* „belegt". **'va·cant** *adj* □ **1.** leerstehend, unbewohnt: *"~"* „frei" (*Toilette*). **2.** frei, offen (*Stelle*): → **sit·uation** 3. **3.** *fig.* leer (*Blick, Gesichtsausdruck*).

va·cate [və'keɪt] *v/t* Hotelzimmer *etc* räumen. **va'ca·tion I** *s* **1.** *bsd. Am.* Ferien *pl,* Urlaub *m*: *be on* ~ im Urlaub sein, Urlaub machen. **2.** *bsd. Br. univ.* Semesterferien *pl;* ₤₤ Gerichtsferien *pl.* **II** *v/i* **3.** *bsd. Am.* Urlaub machen, die Ferien verbringen. **va'ca·tion·er, va·'ca·tion·ist** *s bsd. Am.* Urlauber(in).

vac·ci·nate ['væksɪneɪt] *v/t* impfen (*against* gegen). **,vac·ci'na·tion** *s* Impfung *f.* **vac·cine** ['~siːn] *s* Impfstoff *m.*

vac·il·late ['væsəleɪt] *v/i fig.* schwanken (*between* zwischen *dat*).

vac·u·um ['vækjʊəm] **I** *pl* **-u·ums, -u·a** ['~jʊə] *s phys.* Vakuum *n.* **II** *v/t* Teppich, Zimmer *etc* saugen. ~ **clean·er** *s* Staubsauger *m.* ~ **bot·tle** *s Am.,* ~ **flask** *s Br.* Thermosflasche *f.* **'~-packed** *adj* vakuumverpackt.

vag·a·bond ['væɡəbɒnd] *s* Vagabund *m,* Landstreicher(in).

va·gi·na [və'dʒaɪnə] *pl* **-nas, -nae** [~niː] *s anat.* Scheide *f.*

va·grant ['veɪɡrənt] *s* Nichtseßhafte *m, f,* Landstreicher(in).

va·gue [veɪɡ] *adj* □ verschwommen, *fig. a.* vage: *be* ~ sich nur vage äußern (*a·bout* über *acc,* zu); sich unklar ausdrücken; *I haven't got the ~st idea* ich habe nicht die leiseste Ahnung.

vain [veɪn] *adj* □ **1.** eingebildet, eitel. **2.** vergeblich: *in* ~ *a.* vergebens. **3.** *take s.o.'s name in* ~ über j-n lästern.

va·lence ['veɪləns] *s bsd. Am.,* **'va·len·cy** *s bsd. Br.* ₤ Valenz *f* (*a. ling.*), Wertigkeit *f.*

val·en·tine ['vælentaɪn] *s* **1.** Valentinskarte *f.* **2.** Person, der man am Valentinstag e-n Gruß schickt.

va·le·ri·an [və'lɪərɪən] *s* ⚘, *pharm.* Baldrian *m.*

val·et ['vælɪt] *s* (Kammer)Diener *m.* ~ **ser·vice** *s* Reinigungsdienst *m* (*im Hotel*).

val·id ['vælɪd] *adj* □ **1.** a) gültig (*for two weeks* zwei Wochen): *be ~ a.* gelten, b) ₤₤ rechtsgültig. **2.** stichhaltig, triftig. **va·lid·i·ty** [və'lɪdətɪ] *s* **1.** Gültigkeit *f;* ₤₤ Rechtsgültigkeit *f,* -kraft *f.* **2.** Stichhaltigkeit *f,* Triftigkeit *f.*

va·lise [və'liːz] *s* Reisetasche *f.*

val·ley ['vælɪ] *s* Tal *n.*

val·u·a·ble ['væljʊəbl] **I** *adj* □ wertvoll. **II** *s pl* Wertgegenstände *pl,* -sachen *pl.*

val·u·a·tion [,væljʊ'eɪʃn] *s* **1.** Schätzung *f:* **make a ~ of** *et.* schätzen. **2.** Schätzwert *m* (*of, on gen*).

val·ue ['væljuː] **I** *s* **1.** *allg.* Wert *m: be of* ~ wertvoll sein (*to* für); *be good* ~ *, be* ~ *for money* preisgünstig *od.* -wert sein; *put* (*od.* **place**) *a high ~ on* großen Wert legen auf (*acc*). **2.** *pl* sittliche Werte *pl.* **II** *v/t* **3.** Haus *etc* schätzen (*at* auf *acc*). **4.** *j-n, j-s* Rat *etc* schätzen. **'~-,add·ed tax** *s* ✝ *Br.* Mehrwertsteuer *f.* ~ **judg(e)·ment** *s* Werturteil *n.*

val·ue·less ['væljʊlɪs] *adj* wertlos. **'val·u·er** *s* Schätzer(in).

valve [vælv] *s* **1.** ☉, ♪ Ventil *n.* **2.** *anat.* Klappe *f.* **3.** ⚡ *Br. bsd. hist.* Röhre *f.*

vamp [væmp] *s* Vamp *m* (Frau).

vam·pire ['væmpaɪə] *s* Vampir *m.*

van [væn] *s* **1.** Lieferwagen *m,* Transporter *m.* **2.** 🚃 *Br.* (geschlossener) Güterwagen.

van·dal ['vændl] *s* Vandale *m,* Wandale *m.* **van·dal·ism** ['~dəlɪzəm] *s* Vandalismus *m,* Wandalismus *m.* **van·dal·ize** ['~dəlaɪz] *v/t* mutwillig beschädigen *od.* zerstören.

vane [veɪn] *s* **1.** (Propeller- *etc*)Flügel *m.* **2.** (Wetter)Fahne *f.*

van·guard ['vænɡɑːd] *s* ✕ Vorhut *f: be in the ~ of fig.* an der Spitze (*gen*) stehen.

va·nil·la [və'nɪlə] *s* ⚘ Vanille *f.*

van·ish ['vænɪʃ] *v/i* verschwinden, (*Angst, Hoffnung etc*) schwinden: → **thin** 1.

van·i·ty ['vænətɪ] *s* Eitelkeit *f.*

van·tage point ['vɑːntɪdʒ] *s* Aussichts-

punkt *m*: *from my ~ fig.* aus m-r Sicht.
va·por *Am.* → **vapour.**

va·por·ize ['veɪpəraɪz] *v/i* verdampfen, -dunsten.

va·por·ous ['veɪpərəs] *adj* □ dunstig, Dunst...

va·pour ['veɪpə] *s bsd. Br.* Dampf *m*, Dunst *m*. **~ trail** *s* ✈ Kondensstreifen *m*.

var·i·a·ble ['veərɪəbl] **I** *adj* □ **1.** variabel, veränderlich (*beide a.* ⚕, *phys. etc*). **2.** schwankend, unbeständig, wechselhaft. **3.** einstell-, regulierbar. **II** *s* **4.** ⚕, *phys.* Variable *f*, veränderliche Größe (*beide a. fig.*). **'var·i·ance** *s*: *be at ~ with* im Gegensatz *od.* Widerspruch stehen zu. **'var·i·ant I** *adj* abweichend, verschieden. **II** *s* Variante *f*. **var·i-'a·tion** *s* **1.** Abweichung *f*; Schwankung *f*. **2.** ♪ Variation *f* (*on* über *acc*).

var·i·cose ['værɪkəʊs] *adj*: *~ vein* 🔬 Krampfader *f*.

var·ied ['veərɪd] *adj* □ **1.** unterschiedlich. **2.** abwechslungsreich, bewegt.

va·ri·e·ty [və'raɪətɪ] *s* **1.** Abwechslung *f*. **2.** Vielfalt *f*; ✝ Auswahl *f*, Sortiment *n* (*of* an *dat*): *for a ~ of reasons* aus den verschiedensten Gründen. **3.** ⚕, *zo.* Art *f*. **4.** Varieté *n*.

var·i·ous ['veərɪəs] *adj* □ **1.** verschieden. **2.** mehrere, verschiedene.

var·nish ['vɑːnɪʃ] **I** *s* Lack *m*. **II** *v/t* lackieren.

var·y ['veərɪ] **I** *v/i* variieren, (*Meinungen*) auseinandergehen (*on* über *acc*): *~ in size* verschieden groß sein. **II** *v/t* (ver)ändern; variieren.

vas·cu·lar ['væskjʊlə] *adj anat.*, ⚕ Gefäß...

vase [vɑːz] *s* Vase *f*.

vast [vɑːst] *adj* gewaltig, riesig, (*Fläche a.*) ausgedehnt, weit. **'vast·ly** *adv* gewaltig, weitaus.

vat [væt] *s* (großes) Faß.

vaude·ville ['vɔːdəvɪl] *s Am.* Varieté *n*.

vault¹ ['vɔːlt] *s* **1.** 🏛 Gewölbe *n*. **2.** *a. pl* (Keller)Gewölbe *n*; Stahlkammer *f*, Tresorraum *m*; Gruft *f*.

vault² [~] **I** *v/i*: *~ over* springen über (*acc*). **II** *v/t* → I. **III** *s* Sprung *m*.

vault·ed ['vɔːltɪd] *adj* **1.** 🏛 gewölbt. **2.** überwölbt.

vault·ing ['vɔːltɪŋ] *adj*: *~ horse* (*Turnen*) Sprungpferd *n*.

veal [viːl] *s* Kalbfleisch *n*. **~ cut·let** *s* Kalbsschnitzel *n*.

veer [vɪə] *v/i*: *~ to the left mot.* den Wagen nach links reißen.

veg [vedʒ] *pl* **veg** *s gastr. bsd. Br.* F Gemüse *n*: *and two ~* u. zweierlei Gemüse.

ve·gan ['viːgən] *s* Veganer(in).

veg·e·ta·ble ['vedʒtəbl] **I** *s* **1.** *mst pl* Gemüse *n*: *and two ~s* u. zweierlei Gemüse; *be just a ~* nur noch dahinvegetieren. **II** *adj* **2.** Gemüse... **3.** Pflanzen... **veg·e·tar·i·an** [ˌvedʒɪ'teərɪən] **I** *s* Vegetarier(in): *he's a ~* er ist Vegetarier, er lebt vegetarisch. **II** *adj* vegetarisch.

veg·e·tate ['vedʒɪteɪt] *v/i* dahinvegetieren. **veg·e·ta·tion** *s* Vegetation *f*.

ve·he·mence ['viːəməns] *s* Vehemenz *f*, Heftigkeit *f*. **'ve·he·ment** *adj* □ vehement, heftig.

ve·hi·cle ['viːɪkl] *s* **1.** Fahrzeug *n*. **2.** *fig.* Medium *n*. **ve·hic·u·lar** [vɪ'hɪkjʊlə] *adj* Fahrzeug...

veil [veɪl] **I** *s* Schleier *m*: *~ of mist* Nebelschleier; *draw a ~ over fig.* den Schleier des Vergessens breiten über (*acc*). **II** *v/t* verschleiern (*a. fig.*).

vein [veɪn] *s anat.* Vene *f*, *weitS.* Ader *f* (*a.* ⚕, *geol.*).

ve·loc·i·ty [vɪ'lɒsətɪ] *s phys.*, ⚙ Geschwindigkeit *f*.

ve·lour(s) [və'lʊə] *s* Velours *m*.

vel·vet ['velvɪt] *s* Samt *m*: (*as*) *smooth as ~* samtweich. **'vel·vet·y** *adj* samtig (*a. fig. Wein*).

vend·er → **vendor.**

ven·det·ta [ven'detə] *s* **1.** Blutrache *f*. **2.** Fehde *f*.

vend·ing ['vendɪŋ] *adj*: *~ machine* (Verkaufs-, Waren)Automat *m*. **'vend·or** *s* (Straßen)Händler(in), (*Zeitungs- etc*) Verkäufer(in).

ve·neer [və'nɪə] **I** *s* **1.** Furnier *n*. **2.** *fig.* Fassade *f*. **II** *v/t* **3.** furnieren (*in, with* mit).

ven·er·a·ble ['venərəbl] *adj* □ ehrwürdig. **ven·er·ate** ['~reɪt] *v/t* verehren. **,ven·er·a·tion** *s* Verehrung *f*.

ve·ne·re·al [və'nɪərɪəl] *adj*: *~ disease* Geschlechtskrankheit *f*.

Ve·ne·tian [və'niːʃn] *adj*: *~ blind* Jalousie *f*.

venge·ance ['vendʒəns] *s* Rache *f*: *take*

~ **on** sich rächen an (*dat*); **with a** ~ F gewaltig, u. wie.

ve·ni·al ['vɪnjəl] *adj* entschuldbar, verzeihlich, *eccl.* läßlich (*Sünde*).

ven·i·son ['venɪzn] *s* Wildbret *n.*

ven·om ['venəm] *s* **1.** *zo.* Gift *n.* **2.** *fig.* Gift *n,* Gehässigkeit *f.* **'ven·om·ous** *adj* □ **1.** giftig: ~ **snake** Giftschlange *f.* **2.** *fig.* giftig, gehässig.

ve·nous ['viːnəs] *adj anat.* venös.

vent [vent] **I** *v/t* **1.** *s-e Wut etc* abreagieren (**on** an *dat*). **II** *s* **2.** (Abzugs)Öffnung *f.* **3.** Schlitz *m* (*in Kleid etc*). **4. give** ~ **to** *s-m Ärger etc* Luft machen.

ven·ti·late ['ventɪleɪt] *v/t* (be)lüften. **‚ven·ti'la·tion** *s* Ventilation *f,* (Be)Lüftung *f.* **'ven·ti·la·tor** *s* Ventilator *m,* Lüfter *m.*

ven·tral ['ventrəl] *adj* Bauch...: ~ **fin** Bauchflosse *f.*

ven·tri·cle ['ventrɪkl] *s anat.* Herzkammer *f.*

ven·tril·o·quist [ven'trɪləkwɪst] *s* Bauchredner(in).

ven·ture ['ventʃə] **I** *s* **1.** *bsd.* ✝ Unternehmen *n:* → **joint** 5. **II** *v/t* **2.** *Ruf etc* riskieren, aufs Spiel setzen. **3.** (zu äußern) wagen: ~ **to do s.th.** es wagen, et. zu tun. **III** *v/i* **4.** sich *wohin* wagen. **5.** ~ **on** sich wagen an (*acc*).

ven·ue ['venjuː] *s* Schauplatz *m,* (*Sport*) Austragungsort *m.*

Ve·nus ['viːnəs] *s ast.* die Venus.

ve·ran·da(h) [və'rændə] *s* Veranda *f.*

verb [vɜːb] *s ling.* Verb *n,* Zeitwort *n.* **ver·bal** ['‿l] *adj* □ **1.** mündlich. **2.** Wort...: **he's got** ~ **diarrh(o)ea** F bringt den Mund nicht zu. **3.** ~ **noun** *ling.* Verbalsubstantiv *n.* **ver·bal·ize** ['‿bəlaɪz] *v/t* ausdrücken, in Worte fassen. **ver·ba·tim** ['‿beɪtɪm] *adj* (wort-)wörtlich, *adv a.* Wort für Wort. **ver·bi·age** ['‿bɪɪdʒ] *s* (leeres) Wortgeklingel. **ver·bose** ['‿bəʊs] *adj* □ wortreich, langatmig.

ver·dict ['vɜːdɪkt] *s* **1.** ⚖️ Spruch *m* (*der Geschworenen*): ~ **of (not) guilty** Schuldspruch (Freispruch) *m;* **bring in** (*od.* **return**) **a** ~ **of (not) guilty** auf (nicht) schuldig erkennen. **2.** Meinung *f,* Urteil *n* (**on** über *acc*).

ver·di·gris ['vɜːdɪɡrɪs] *s* Grünspan *m.*

verge [vɜːdʒ] **I** *s* Rand *m* (*a. fig.*): **be on the** ~ **of** kurz vor (*dat*) stehen; **be on the**

~ **of tears** den Tränen nahe sein; **she was on the** ~ **of falling** sie wäre beinahe gestürzt. **II** *v/i:* ~ **on** *fig.* grenzen an (*acc*).

ver·ger ['vɜːdʒə] *s* Kirchendiener *m,* Küster *m.*

ver·i·fi·a·ble ['verɪfaɪəbl] *adj* nachweisbar. **ver·i·fy** ['‿faɪ] *v/t* **1.** bestätigen. **2.** (über)prüfen. **3.** nachweisen.

ver·i·ta·ble ['verɪtəbl] *adj* wahr (*Triumph etc*).

ver·mil·ion [və'mɪljən] *adj* zinnoberrot.

ver·min ['vɜːmɪn] *s* (*pl konstruiert*) **1.** Schädlinge *pl;* Ungeziefer *n.* **2.** *fig.* Gesindel *n,* Pack *n.* **'ver·min·ous** *adj* voller Ungeziefer.

ver·mouth ['vɜːməθ] *s* Wermut *m.*

ver·nac·u·lar [və'nækjʊlə] *s* Dialekt *m,* Mundart *f.*

ver·nis·sage [‚vɜːnɪ'sɑːʒ] *s* Vernissage *f.* **ver·sa·tile** ['vɜːsətaɪl] *adj* □ **1.** vielseitig. **2.** vielseitig verwendbar.

verse [vɜːs] *s* **1.** Poesie *f,* Versdichtung *f.* **2.** Vers *m.* **3.** Strophe *f.*

versed [vɜːst] *adj:* **be (well)** ~ **in** beschlagen *od.* bewandert sein in (*dat*).

ver·sion ['vɜːʃn] *s* Version *f:* a) Darstellung *f* (*e-s Ereignisses*), b) Fassung *f* (*e-s Textes*), c) Übersetzung *f,* d) Ausführung *f* (*e-s Gerätes etc*).

ver·sus ['vɜːsəs] *prp* ⚖️, *Sport:* gegen.

ver·te·bra ['vɜːtɪbrə] *pl* **-brae** ['‿briː], **-bras** *s anat.* Wirbel *m.* **'ver·te·bral** *adj:* ~ **column** *anat.* Rückgrat *n,* Wirbelsäule *f.* **ver·te·brate** ['‿breɪt] *s zo.* Wirbeltier *n.*

ver·tex ['vɜːteks] *pl* **-ti·ces** ['‿tɪsiːz], **-tex·es** *s* Scheitel(punkt) *m.*

ver·ti·cal ['vɜːtɪkl] **I** *adj* □ senkrecht, vertikal: ~ **takeoff aircraft** Senkrechtstarter *m.* **II** *s* ⅋ Senkrechte *f,* Vertikale *f.*

ver·ti·go ['vɜːtɪɡəʊ] *s* 💊 Schwindel *m:* **suffer from** ~ an *od.* unter Schwindel leiden.

verve [vɜːv] *s* Elan *m,* Schwung *m.*

ver·y ['verɪ] **I** *adv* **1.** sehr: ~ **much older** sehr viel älter; **I** ~ **much hope that** ich hoffe sehr, daß; ~ **high frequency** ⚡ Ultrakurzwelle *f;* → **well**¹ **1.** **2.** (*vor sup*): **the** ~ **last drop** der allerletzte Tropfen; **for the** ~ **last time** zum allerletzten Mal; **at the** ~ **least** zum allermindesten, allermindest. **II** *adj* **3. the** ~ genau der *od.* die *od.* das: *the ~ opposite* genau das Gegenteil; *be the ~ thing* genau das richtige sein (*for doing* um zu tun); → *act* 1. **4. the ~ thought** of schon der *od.* der bloße Gedanke an (*dat*); *the ~ idea!* um Himmels willen!

ves·i·cle ['vesɪkl] *s* Bläschen *n.*

ves·pers ['vespəz] *s pl eccl.* Vesper *f.*

ves·sel ['vesl] *s* **1.** Schiff *n.* **2.** Gefäß *n* (*a. anat.*, 🌿).

vest [vest] **I** *s* **1.** *Br.* Unterhemd *n.* **2.** kugelsichere Weste. **3.** *Am.* Weste *f.* **II** *v/t* **4. ~ s.th. in s.o., ~ s.o. with s.th.** j-m et. übertragen *od.* verleihen: *have a ~ed interest in* ein persönliches Interesse haben an (*dat*); *~ed interests pl* Interessengruppen *pl.* **III** *v/i* **5. ~ in** *s.o.* zustehen (*dat*), liegen bei.

ves·ti·bule ['vestɪbjuːl] *s* (Vor)Halle *f.*

ves·tige ['vestɪdʒ] *s* Spur *f:* *there is not a ~ of truth in this story* an dieser Geschichte ist kein Wort wahr.

ves·try ['vestrɪ] *s eccl.* Sakristei *f.*

vet¹ [vet] **F I** *s* Tierarzt *m,* -ärztin *f.* **II** *v/t bsd. Br.* überprüfen.

vet² [~] *s* 🗡 *Am.* F Veteran *m.*

vetch [vetʃ] *s* 🌿 Wicke *f.*

vet·er·an ['vetərən] **I** *s* **1.** 🗡 Veteran *m* (*a. fig.*). **II** *adj* **2.** altgedient; erfahren. **3. ~ car** *mot. Br.* Oldtimer *m* (*Baujahr bis 1905*).

vet·er·i·nar·i·an [ˌvetərə'neriən] *s Am.* Tierarzt *m,* -ärztin *f.*

vet·er·i·nar·y ['vetərinəri] *adj* tierärztlich: *~ medicine* Tier-, Veterinärmedizin *f;* *~ surgeon bsd. Br.* Tierarzt *m,* -ärztin *f.*

ve·to ['viːtəʊ] **I** *pl* **-toes** *s* **1.** Veto *n.* **II** *v/t* **2.** sein Veto einlegen gegen. **3.** untersagen.

vexed [vekst] *adj:* *~ question* leidige Frage.

vi·a ['vaɪə] *prp* über (*acc*), (*bei Städtenamen a.*) via.

vi·a·ble ['vaɪəbl] *adj* □ **1.** lebensfähig (*a. fig.*). **2.** *fig.* durchführbar, realisierbar.

vi·a·duct ['vaɪədʌkt] *s* Viadukt *m, n.*

vi·al ['vaɪəl] *s* (*bsd.* Arznei)Fläschchen *n.*

vibes [vaɪbz] *s pl* F **1.** (*mst sg konstruiert*) ♪ Vibraphon *n.* **2.** Atmosphäre *f* (*e-s Orts etc*): *I was getting positive ~ from her* ich spürte, wie der Funke von ihr auf mich übersprang.

vi·brant ['vaɪbrənt] *adj* □ **1.** kräftig (*Far-*

ben, Stimme etc). **2.** pulsierend (*Leben*). **3.** dynamisch (*Person*).

vi·bra·phone ['vaɪbrəfəʊn] *s* ♪ Vibraphon *n.*

vi·brate [vaɪ'breɪt] **I** *v/i* **1.** vibrieren, zittern. **2.** flimmern (*with heat* vor Hitze) (*Luft*). **3. the city ~s with life** in der Stadt pulsiert das Leben. **II** *v/t* **4.** in Schwingungen versetzen. **vi·bra·tion** *s* **1.** Vibrieren *n,* Zittern *n.* **2.** *pl* F → **vibes** 2. **vi·bra·tor** *s* Vibrator *m.*

vic·ar ['vɪkə] *s* Pfarrer *m.* **'vic·ar·age** *s* Pfarrhaus *n.*

vice¹ [vaɪs] *s* Laster *n.*

vice² [~] *s* ⚙ *bsd. Br.* Schraubstock *m.*

vice...³ [~] Vize..., stellvertretend.

vice·like ['vaɪslaɪk] *adj:* *hold s.th. in a ~ grip bsd. Br.* et. fest umklammert halten.

vice squad *s* Sittendezernat *n,* -polizei *f.*

vi·ce ver·sa [ˌvaɪsɪ'vɜːsə] *adv:* *and ~* u. umgekehrt.

vi·cin·i·ty [vɪ'sɪnətɪ] *s:* *in this ~* of in der Nähe von (*od. gen*); *in this ~* hier in der Nähe; *in the ~ of 40 fig.* um die 40 herum.

vi·cious ['vɪʃəs] *adj* □ brutal. **~ cir·cle** *s* Circulus *m* vitiosus, Teufelskreis *m.*

vi·cis·si·tudes [vɪ'sɪsɪtjuːdz] *s pl das* Auf u. Ab, (*des Lebens a.*) die Wechselfälle *pl.*

vic·tim ['vɪktɪm] *s* Opfer *n:* *fall ~ to* betroffen werden von; erkranken an (*dat*). **'vic·tim·ize** *v/t* j-n (*immer wieder*) zum Sündenbock machen.

vic·tor ['vɪktə] *s* Sieger(in). **vic·to·ri·ous** [~'tɔːrɪəs] *adj* □ siegreich. **vic·to·ry** ['~tərɪ] *s* Sieg *m:* *~ ceremony* Siegerehrung *f.*

vi·de ['vaɪdiː] *imp* siehe!

vi·de·li·cet [vɪ'diːlɪset] *adv* nämlich.

vid·e·o ['vɪdɪəʊ] **I** *pl* **-os** *s* **1.** Video(kassette *f*) *n:* *on ~* auf Video. **2.** → *video recorder.* **II** *v/t* **3.** auf Video aufnehmen, aufzeichnen. **~ cam·er·a** *s* Videokamera *f.* **~ cas·sette** *s* Videokassette *f.* **~ cas·sette re·cord·er** → *video recorder.* **~ nas·ty** → *nasty* 5. **~ re·cord·er** *s* Videorecorder *m.* **~ re·cord·ing** *s* Videoaufnahme *f,* -aufzeichnung *f.* **~ tape** → *video cassette.* '**~·tape** → *video* 3.

vie [vaɪ] *v/i* wetteifern (*with* mit; *for* um).

view [vjuː] **I** *s* **1.** Sicht *f* (*of* auf *acc*): *at first ~* auf den ersten Blick; *in full ~ of* direkt vor *j-s* Augen; **in ~ of** *fig.* angesichts (*gen*); **with a ~ to** *fig.* mit Blick auf (*acc*); **with a ~ to doing s.th.** in od. mit der Absicht, et. zu tun; **be on ~** ausgestellt od. zu besichtigen sein; **be hidden from ~** nicht zu sehen sein; **come into ~** in Sicht kommen; **have in ~** et. in Aussicht haben; **keep in ~** et. im Auge behalten. **2.** Aussicht *f*, Blick *m* (**of** auf *acc*): **a room with a ~** ein Zimmer mit schöner Aussicht; **there is a grand ~ of the mountains from here** von hier hat man e-n herrlichen Blick auf die Berge. **3.** *phot. etc* Ansicht *f*. **4.** Ansicht *f*, Meinung *f* (**about, on** über *acc*): **in my ~** m-r Ansicht nach; **take a dim** (*od.* **poor**) **~ of** et. negativ beurteilen. **5.** *fig.* Überblick *m* (**of** über *acc*). **II** *v/t* **6.** Haus etc besichtigen. **7.** *fig.* betrachten (**as** als; **with** mit). **III** *v/i* **8.** fernsehen. **'view·er** *s* **1.** (Fernseh)Zuschauer(in), Fernseher(in). **2.** (*Dia*)Betrachter *m*.

'view‖find·er *s phot.* Sucher *m*. **'~·point** *s* Gesichts-, Standpunkt *m*.

vig·il ['vɪdʒɪl] *s* (Nacht)Wache *f*: **keep ~** wachen (**over** bei). **'vig·i·lance** *s* Wachsamkeit *f*. **'vig·i·lant** *adj* □ wachsam.

vig·or ['vɪgə] *Am.* → **vigour.** **'vig·or·ous** *adj* □ energisch. **'vig·our** *s bsd. Br.* Energie *f*.

vile [vaɪl] *adj* □ **1.** gemein, niederträchtig. **2.** F scheußlich.

vil·la ['vɪlə] *s* Villa *f*.

vil·lage ['vɪlɪdʒ] *s* Dorf *n*. **'vil·lag·er** *s* Dorfbewohner(in).

vil·lain ['vɪlən] *s* **1.** Bösewicht *m*, Schurke *m* (*in Film etc*). **2.** *Br.* F Ganove *m*. **3.** F Bengel *m*.

vin·di·cate ['vɪndɪkeɪt] *v/t* **1.** et. rechtfertigen; bestätigen. **2.** *j-n* rehabilitieren. **‚vin·di·ca·tion** *s* **1.** Rechtfertigung *f*; Bestätigung *f*. **2.** Rehabilitation *f*. **vin·dic·tive** [vɪn'dɪktɪv] *adj* □ rachsüchtig.

vine [vaɪn] *s* ♀ **1.** (Wein)Rebe *f*. **2.** Kletterpflanze *f*.

vin·e·gar ['vɪnɪgə] *s* Essig *m*.

'vine‖grow·er *s* Winzer *m*. **~·yard** ['vɪnjəd] *s* Weinberg *m*.

vi·no ['viːnəʊ] *pl* **-nos** *s* F Wein *m*.

vin·tage ['vɪntɪdʒ] **I** *s* **1.** Jahrgang *m* (*e-s Weins*). **2.** Weinernte *f*, -lese *f*. **II** *adj* **3.**

Jahrgangs...: **~ wine. 4.** glänzend, hervorragend. **5. ~ car** *mot. bsd. Br.* Oldtimer *m* (*Baujahr 1919-30*).

vint·ner ['vɪntnə] *s* **1.** Weinhändler *m*. **2.** *Am.* Winzer *m*.

vi·o·la [vɪ'əʊlə] *s* ♪ Bratsche *f*.

vi·o·late ['vaɪəleɪt] *v/t* **1.** *Vertrag etc* verletzen, *a. Versprechen* brechen, *Gesetz etc* übertreten. **2.** *Frieden, Ruhe etc* stören. **3.** *Grab etc* schänden. **4.** *Frau* schänden, vergewaltigen. **‚vi·o'la·tion** *s* **1.** Verletzung *f*, Bruch *m*, Übertretung *f*. **2.** Störung *f*. **3.** Schändung *f*. **4.** Vergewaltigung *f*.

vi·o·lence ['vaɪələns] *s* **1.** Gewalt *f*. **2.** Gewalttätigkeit *f*. **3.** Heftigkeit *f*. **'vi·o·lent** *adj* □ **1.** gewalttätig. **2.** gewaltsam: **~ crime** Gewaltverbrechen *n*; **die a ~ death** e-s gewaltsamen Todes sterben. **3.** heftig (*Auseinandersetzung, Sturm etc*): **be in a ~ temper** geladen sein.

vi·o·let ['vaɪələt] **I** *s* ♀ Veilchen *n*: → **shrinking. II** *adj* violett.

vi·o·lin [‚vaɪə'lɪn] *s* ♪ Geige *f*, Violine *f*: **~ case** Geigenkasten *m*. **‚vi·o'lin·ist** *s* Geiger(in), Violinist(in).

vi·o·lon·cel·lo [‚vaɪələn'tʃeləʊ] *pl* **-los** *s* ♪ Violoncello *n*.

VIP [‚viːaɪ'piː] *s* VIP *f* (*prominente Persönlichkeit*).

vi·per ['vaɪpə] *s zo.* Viper *f*.

vi·ral ['vaɪərəl] *adj* ♥ Virus...

vir·gin ['vɜːdʒɪn] **I** *s* Jungfrau *f*: **she's still a ~** sie ist noch Jungfrau. **II** *adj* jungfräulich, unberührt (*beide a. fig.*).

Vir·go ['vɜːgəʊ] *s ast.* Jungfrau *f*: **be** (**a**) **~** Jungfrau sein.

vir·ile ['vɪraɪl] *adj* □ **1.** männlich. **2.** potent. **vi·ril·i·ty** [vɪ'rɪlətɪ] *s* **1.** Männlichkeit *f*. **2.** Potenz *f*.

vir·tu·al ['vɜːtʃʊəl] *adj*: **he's a ~ alcoholic** er ist praktisch schon Alkoholiker; **it's a ~ certainty that** es steht praktisch od. so gut wie fest, daß. **'vir·tu·al·ly** *adv* praktisch, so gut wie.

vir·tue ['vɜːtʃuː] *s* **1.** Tugend(haftigkeit) *f*. **2.** Tugend *f*: **make a ~ of necessity** aus der Not e-e Tugend machen. **3.** Vorzug *m*, Vorteil *m*. **4. by** (*od.* **in**) **~ of** (*gen*), aufgrund (*gen*). **vir·tu·o·so** [‚vɜːtjʊ'əʊzəʊ] *bsd.* ♪ **I** *pl* **-sos, -si** [‚ziː] *s* Virtuose *m*, Virtuosin *f*. **II** *adj* virtuos.

vir·tu·ous ['vɜːtʃʊəs] *adj* □ tugendhaft.

vir·u·lent ['vɪrʊlənt] *adj* □ **1.** (akut u.) bösartig (*Krankheit*); schnellwirkend (*Gift*). **2.** *fig.* bösartig, gehässig.

vi·rus ['vaɪərəs] *s* ✻ Virus *n, a. m.* ~ **in·fec·tion** *s* ✻ Virusinfektion *f.*

vi·sa ['viːzə] **I** *s* Visum *n, (im Paß eingetragenes a.)* Sichtvermerk *m.* **II** *v/t* ein Visum eintragen in (*acc*).

vis-à-vis [ˌviːzɑːˈviː] *prp* in Anbetracht (*gen*).

vis·cer·a ['vɪsərə] *s pl anat.* Eingeweide *pl.*

vis·count ['vaɪkaʊnt] *s* Viscount *m* (*englischer Adelstitel*). **'vis·count·ess** *s* Viscountess *f.*

vis·cous ['vɪskəs] *adj* □ dick-, zähflüssig, ✻ *a.* viskos.

vise, vise·like *Am.* → **vice², vicelike.**

vis·i·bil·i·ty [ˌvɪzɪˈbɪlətɪ] *s* Sicht(verhältnisse *pl*, -weite *f*) *f.* **'vis·i·ble** *adj* □ **1.** sichtbar. **2.** *fig.* (er)sichtlich.

vi·sion ['vɪʒn] *s* **1.** Sehkraft *f.* **2.** *fig.* Weitblick *m.* **3.** Vision *f*: ~ *of the future* Zukunftsvision *f*; *have* ~*s of doing s.th.* sich schon et. tun sehen. **vi·sion·ar·y** ['∼rɪ] **I** *adj* **1.** weitblickend. **2.** eingebildet, unwirklich. **II** *s* **3.** Seher(in). **4.** Phantast(in), Träumer(in).

vis·it ['vɪzɪt] **I** *v/t* **1.** *j-n* besuchen, *Museum etc a.* besichtigen. **2.** *et.* inspizieren. **II** *v/i* **3.** *be* ~*ing* auf Besuch sein (*Am.: in* in *dat*; *with* bei). **4.** ~ *with Am.* plaudern mit. **III** *s* **5.** Besuch *m*, Besichtigung *f* (*to* für): *for* (*od. on*) *a* ~ auf Besuch; *have a* ~ *from* Besuch haben von; *pay a* ~ *to j-m* e-n Besuch abstatten; *Arzt* aufsuchen; *I've got to pay a* ~ *Br.* F ich muß mal verschwinden. **6.** *Am.* Plauderei *f* (*with* mit). **,vis·i'ta·tion** *s* **1.** Inspektion *f.* **2.** *fig.* Heimsuchung *f.* **3.** F *humor.* überlanger Besuch (*from gen*). **'vis·it·ing** *adj* Besuchs...: ~ *card* Visitenkarte *f*; ~ *hours pl* Besuchszeit *f.* **'vis·i·tor** *s* Besucher(in) (*to gen*; *from* aus): ~*s pl to England* Englandbesucher *pl*; *have* ~*s* Besuch haben; ~*s' book* Gästebuch *n.*

vi·sor ['vaɪzə] *s* **1.** Visier *n* (*a.* ⚔ *hist.*). **2.** Schirm *m* (*e-r Mütze*). **3.** *mot.* (*Sonnen*)Blende *f.*

vis·ta ['vɪstə] *s* Aussicht *f*, Blick *m* (*of* auf *acc*).

vis·u·al ['vɪʃʊəl] *adj* □ **1.** Seh... **2.** vi-

suell: ~ *aids pl ped.* Anschauungsmaterial *n*, Lehrmittel *pl.* **3.** optisch. **'vis·u·al·ize** *v/t* sich et. vorstellen.

vi·tal ['vaɪtl] *adj* (□ → *vitally*) **1.** lebenswichtig (*Organ etc*). **2.** Lebens...: ~ *sta·tistics pl* Bevölkerungsstatistik *f*; F *humor.* Maße *pl* (*e-r Frau*). **3.** unbedingt notwendig (*to, for* für): *of* ~ *importance* von größter Wichtigkeit. **4.** vital. **vi·tal·i·ty** [∼ˈtælətɪ] *s* Vitalität *f.* **vi·tal·ly** ['∼təlɪ] *adv* **1.** vital. **2.** sehr viel: ~ *important* äußerst wichtig.

vi·ta·min ['vɪtəmɪn] *s* Vitamin *n.* ~ *pill s* Vitamintablette *f.*

vit·re·ous ['vɪtrɪəs] *adj* Glas...

vi·va ['vaɪvə] *Br.* F → *viva voce.*

vi·va·cious [vɪˈveɪʃəs] *adj* □ lebhaft, temperamentvoll.

vi·va vo·ce ['vaʊsɪ] *s univ.* mündliche Prüfung.

viv·id ['vɪvɪd] *adj* □ **1.** hell (*Licht*); kräftig, leuchtend (*Farben*). **2.** anschaulich (*Schilderung etc*), lebhaft (*Phantasie*).

viv·i·sec·tion [ˌvɪvɪˈsekʃn] *s* Vivisektion *f.*

V neck [viː] *s* V-Ausschnitt *m.* **'V-necked** *adj* mit V-Ausschnitt.

vo·cab ['vəʊkæb] F → *vocabulary* 2.

vo·cab·u·lar·y [vəʊˈkæbjʊlərɪ] *s* **1.** Vokabular *n*, Wortschatz *m.* **2.** Vokabular *n*, Wortregister *n*, Wörterverzeichnis *n.*

vo·cal ['vəʊkl] **I** *adj* □ **1.** Stimm...: ~ *cords pl anat.* Stimmbänder *pl.* **2.** ♪ *music* Vokalmusik *f.* **3.** F lautstark. **II** *s pl* **4.** ~*s: XY* Gesang: XY.

vo·ca·tion [vəʊˈkeɪʃn] *s* **1.** Begabung *f* (*for* für). **2.** Berufung *f.* **vo·ca·tion·al** [∼ʃənl] *adj* Berufs...: ~ *training* Berufsausbildung *f.*

vo·cif·er·ous [vəʊˈsɪfərəs] *adj* □ lautstark (*Protest etc*).

vogue [vəʊg] *s* Mode *f*: *be in* ~ Mode sein; *be all the* ~ große Mode sein. ~ *word s* Modewort *n.*

voice [vɔɪs] **I** *s* **1.** Stimme *f* (*a. fig.*): *give* ~ *to* → **4.** **2.** *have a* ~ *in* ein Mitspracherecht haben bei. **3.** → *active* 2, *passive* 2. **II** *v/t* **4.** zum Ausdruck bringen. **5.** *ling.* stimmhaft aussprechen. ~ *box s anat.* Kehlkopf *m.*

voiced [vɔɪst] *adj ling.* stimmhaft. **'voice·less** *adj ling.* stimmlos.

void [vɔɪd] **I** *adj* **1.** leer: ~ *of* ohne. **2.** ⚖ nichtig, ungültig: → *null.* **II** *v/t* **3.** ⚖

nichtig *od.* ungültig machen. **III** *s* **4.** *fig.* (Gefühl *n* der) Leere.

vol·a·tile ['vɒlətaɪl] *adj* **1.** cholerisch (*Person, Temperament*); explosiv (*Lage etc*). **2.** 🜨 flüchtig, (*Öl*) ätherisch.

vol·can·ic [vɒl'kænɪk] *adj* (*~ally*) vulkanisch, Vulkan... **vol·ca·no** [~'keɪnəʊ] *pl* **-no(e)s** *s* Vulkan *m.*

vo·li·tion [vəʊ'lɪʃn] *s*: *of one's own ~* aus freien Stücken.

vol·ley ['vɒlɪ] **I** *s* **1.** Salve *f*; (*Schlag etc*)Hagel *m*: *a ~ of curses* ein Hagel von Verwünschungen. **2.** *Tennis:* Volley *m*, Flugball *m*; (*Fußball*) Volleyschuß *m*: *take on the ~ Ball* volley nehmen. **II** *v/t* **3.** *Ball* volley schießen (*into the net* ins Netz). **'~·ball** *s Sport:* Volleyball *m.*

volt [vəʊlt] *s* ⚡ Volt *n.* **'volt·age** *s* ⚡ Spannung *f.*

vol·u·ble ['vɒljʊbl] *adj* □ **1.** redselig. **2.** wortreich.

vol·ume ['vɒljuːm] *s* **1.** Band *m*: *a two-~ novel* ein zweibändiger Roman; *speak ~s fig.* Bände sprechen. **2.** ♉, *phys.* Volumen *n*, Rauminhalt *m.* **3.** (*Handels- etc*)Volumen *n*, (*Verkehrs*)Aufkommen *n.* **4.** Lautstärke *f*: *at full ~* in voller Lautstärke; *turn to full ~ Radio etc* auf volle Lautstärke stellen, voll aufdrehen; *turn the ~ up* (*down*) lauter (leiser) drehen; *~ control* Lautstärkeregler *m.* **vo·lu·mi·nous** [və'luːmɪnəs] *adj* □ **1.** bauschig (*Kleidungsstück*). **2.** geräumig. **3.** umfangreich (*Bericht etc*).

vol·un·tar·y ['vɒləntərɪ] *adj* □ **1.** freiwillig. **2.** unbezahlt.

vol·un·teer [,vɒlən'tɪə] **I** *v/i* **1.** sich freiwillig melden (*for* zu) (*a.* ✗). **II** *v/t* **2.** *Hilfe etc* anbieten: *~ to do s.th.* sich anbieten, et. zu tun. **3.** *et.* von sich aus sagen. **III** *s* **4.** Freiwillige *m* (*a.* ✗); freiwilliger Helfer.

vo·lup·tu·ous [və'lʌptʃʊəs] *adj* □ **1.** sinnlich (*Lippen, Mund*); üppig (*Formen*); aufreizend (*Bewegungen*). **2.** kurvenreich (*Frau*).

vom·it ['vɒmɪt] **I** *v/t* erbrechen, *Blut* spucken; *Feuer, Lava* speien, *Rauchwolken etc* ausstoßen. **II** *v/i* (sich er)brechen, sich übergeben.

vo·ra·cious [və'reɪʃəs] *adj* □ unersättlich (*Appetit*): *he's a ~ reader of comics* er verschlingt die Comics geradezu.

vor·tex ['vɔːteks] *pl* **-tex·es, -ti·ces** ['~tɪsiːz] *s* Strudel *m* (*a. fig.*), Wirbel *m.*

vote [vəʊt] **I** *s* **1.** Abstimmung *f* (*about, on* über *acc*): *put to the ~* abstimmen lassen über (*acc*); *take a ~ on* abstimmen über; → *censure* 1. **2.** Stimme *f*: *Stimmzettel m, Stimme f*: *cast one's ~ for, give one's ~ to* stimmen für, *j-m* s-e Stimme geben. **3.** *a. pl* Wahlrecht *n*: *get the ~* wahlberechtigt werden. **II** *v/i* **4.** wählen: *~ for* (*against*) stimmen für (gegen). **5.** *~ on* abstimmen über (*acc*). **III** *v/t* **6.** wählen: *~ out of office* abwählen. **7.** *~ s.o. s.th.* j-m et. bewilligen. **8.** *~ that* F vorschlagen, daß. **'vot·er** *s* Wähler(in).

vouch [vaʊtʃ] *v/i*: *~ for* sich verbürgen für; bürgen für. **'vouch·er** *s* Gutschein *m.*

vow [vaʊ] **I** *s* Gelöbnis *n*: *make* (*od. take*) *a ~* ein Gelöbnis ablegen. **II** *v/t* geloben, schwören (*to do* zu tun).

vow·el ['vaʊəl] *s ling.* Vokal *m*, Selbstlaut *m.*

voy·age ['vɔɪdʒ] *s* (See)Reise *f.*

vul·can·ize ['vʌlkənaɪz] *v/t* vulkanisieren.

vul·gar ['vʌlgə] *adj* □ **1.** vulgär, ordinär. **2.** geschmacklos.

vul·ner·a·ble ['vʌlnərəbl] *adj* □ **1.** *fig.* verletz-, verwundbar; schutzbedürftig. **2.** anfällig (*to* für).

vul·ture ['vʌltʃə] *s orn.* Geier *m.*

W

wack·y ['wæki] *adj* □ *bsd. Am.* F verrückt.

wad [wɒd] *s* **1.** (*Papier- etc*)Knäuel *m*; (*Watte- etc*)Bausch *m.* **2.** Bündel *n* (*Banknoten etc*).

wad·dle ['wɒdl] *v/i* watscheln.

wade [weɪd] **I** *v/t* durchwaten. **II** *v/i* waten: *~ across →* I; *~ in* hineinwaten; F sich einmischen; *~ into* waten in (*acc*); F losgehen auf *j-n*; sich reinknien in *e-e Arbeit*; *~ through* waten durch; F sich durchkämpfen durch, *Fachliteratur etc a.* durchackern. '**wad·ing** *adj*: *~ pool Am.* Planschbecken *n.*

wa·fer ['weɪfə] *s* **1.** (*bsd. Eis*)Waffel *f.* **2.** *eccl.* Hostie *f.*

waf·fle¹ ['wɒfl] *s* Waffel *f.*

waf·fle² ['wɒfl] *v/i bsd. Br.* F schwafeln.

waft [wɑːft] **I** *v/i* ziehen (*Duft etc*). **II** *v/t* wehen.

wag [wæg] **I** *v/t*: *~ one's finger* bei *j-m* mit dem Finger drohen; *~ its tail* mit dem Schwanz wedeln. **II** *v/i* wedeln (*Schwanz*); *tongues will ~* das wird Gerede geben; *set tongues ~ging* für Gerede sorgen. **III** *s*: *with a ~ of its tail* schwanzwedelnd.

wag² [~] *s* F unterhaltsamer Mensch.

wage¹ [weɪdʒ] *s mst pl* Lohn *m*; Gehalt *n.*

wage² [~] *v/t*: *~ (a) war against* (*od. on*) ✕ Krieg führen gegen; *fig.* e-n Feldzug führen gegen.

wage| de·mand *s* Lohn- *od.* Gehaltsforderung *f.* *~ earn·er* *s* Verdiener(in): *be a ~* berufstätig sein; *be a big ~* viel verdienen. *~ freeze* *s* Lohnstopp *m.* *~ pack·et* *s* Lohn- *od.* Gehaltstüte *f.* *~ rise* *s* Lohn- *od.* Gehaltserhöhung *f.*

wa·ger ['weɪdʒə] **I** *s* Wette *f*: *have* (*od. place*) *a ~ on* e-e Wette abschließen *od.* eingehen auf (*acc*). **II** *v/t*: *I'll ~ that* ich wette, daß.

wag·gle ['wægl] *v/i u. v/t* F wackeln (mit).

wag·on *Br. →* **wagon**.

wag·on ['wægən] *s* **1.** Fuhrwerk *n*, Wagen *m*: *be on the ~* F keinen Alkohol (mehr) trinken. **2.** 🚃 *Br.* (offener) Güterwagen. **3.** *Am.* (*Tee- etc*)Wagen *m.*

wag·on-lit [,vægɔ̃:n'liː] *pl* **wa·gons-lits** [,~'liːz] *s* 🚃 Schlafwagen *m.*

wail [weɪl] **I** *v/i* jammern (*Person*); heulen (*Sirene, Wind*). **II** *v/t* jammern. **III** *s* Jammern *n*; Heulen *n.*

wain·scot ['weɪnskət] *s* **1.** Fuß(boden)-, Scheuerleiste *f.* **2.** (Wand)Täfelung *f.*

waist [weɪst] *s* Taille *f*: *→ strip* 1. *~·coat* ['weɪskəʊt] *s bsd. Br.* Weste *f.* '*~·line s* Taille *f*: *I'm watching my ~* ich muß auf m-e Linie achten.

wait [weɪt] **I** *v/i* **1.** warten (*for, on* auf *acc*; [*for*] *10 minutes* 10 Minuten): *~ for s.o. a.* j-n erwarten; *~ for s.o. to do s.th.* darauf warten, daß j-d et. tut; warten, bis j-d et. tut; *this can ~* das kann warten, das hat Zeit (*until* bis); *keep s.o. waiting* j-n warten lassen; *I can't ~ to see him* ich kann es kaum erwarten, ihn zu sehen; *~ and see!* warte es ab!; *I'll have to ~ and see how ...* ich muß abwarten, wie ...; *~ up* F aufbleiben (*for* wegen). **2.** *~ on s.o.* j-n (*bsd. im Restaurant*) bedienen; *~ at* (*Am. on*) *table* bedienen. **II** *v/t* **3.** *~ one's chance* auf e-e günstige Gelegenheit warten (*to do* zu tun); *~ one's turn* warten, bis man an der Reihe ist. **4.** *~ breakfast for s.o.* bsd. *Am.* F mit dem Frühstück auf j-n warten. **III** *s* **5.** Wartezeit *f*: *have a long ~* lange warten müssen. **6.** *lie in ~* für j-n auflauern. '**wait·er** *s* Kellner *m*, Ober *m*, (*Anrede*) (Herr) Ober. '**wait·ing** **I** *s* Warten *n*: "*no ~*" „Halt(e)verbot". **II** *adj*: *play a ~ game* (*with s.o.*) j-n hinhalten; *~ list* Warteliste *f*; *~ room* 🚃 Wartesaal *m*; 🏥 *etc* Wartezimmer *n.* **wait·ress** ['~rɪs] *s* Kellnerin *f*, Bedienung *f*, (*Anrede*) Fräulein.

waive [weɪv] *v/t* verzichten auf (*acc*). '**waiv·er** *s* Verzicht *m* (*of* auf *acc*); Verzichtserklärung *f.*

wake¹ [weɪk] *s* ⚓ Kielwasser *n*: *follow in the ~ of fig.* folgen auf (*acc*); *leave s.th. in one's ~ fig.* et. zurücklassen.

wake² [~] (*irr*) **I** *v/t a.* *~ up* (auf)wecken; *fig.* wecken, wachrufen: *~ s.o. to s.th. fig.* j-m et. bewußt machen. **II** *v/i a.* *~ up* aufwachen, wach werden: *~ to s.th.*

fig. sich e-r Sache bewußt werden.
wake·ful ['–fol] *adj* □ schlaflos.
wak·en ['–ǝn] **I** *v/t a.* **~ up** (auf)wecken.
II *v/i a.* **~ up** aufwachen, wach werden.
'wak·ing *adj:* **he spends all his ~ hours studying** er lernt von früh bis spät.

walk [wɔ:k] **I** *s* **1.** Spaziergang *m*; Wanderung *f*: **go for** (*od.* **have, take**) **a ~** e-n Spaziergang machen, spazierengehen; **the church is just a five-minute ~ from here** zu Fuß sind es nur fünf Minuten bis zur Kirche. **2.** Spazier-, Wanderweg *m*. **3.** Gang *m*. **4. from all ~s** (*od.* **every ~**) **of life** Leute aus allen Berufen (*od.* Schichten). **II** *v/i* **5.** (zu Fuß) gehen, laufen; spazierengehen; wandern: **~ into** hineingehen in (*acc*), hereinkommen in (*acc*); *fig.* in e-e Falle gehen; **~ over** F j-n unterbuttern; (*Sport*) j-n in die Tasche stecken. **III** *v/t* **6.** *Strecke* gehen, laufen: → **street. 7.** j-n bringen (**to** zu; **home** nach Hause); *Hund* ausführen.

Verbindungen mit Adverbien:

walk| a·way *v/i* **1.** → **walk off. 2. ~ from** bei e-m Unfall (fast) unverletzt bleiben. **~ in** *v/i* hineingehen, hereinkommen. **~ off** *v/i* **1.** fort-, weggehen. **2. ~ with** F abhauen mit; *Preis etc* locker gewinnen. **~ out** *v/i* **1.** hinausgehen; (unter Protest) den Saal verlassen, (*Delegation etc a.*) ausziehen: **~ out of a meeting** e-e Versammlung (unter Protest) verlassen; **~ on s.o.** F j-n verlassen; j-n sitzenlassen. **2.** in (den) Streik treten. **~ up** *v/i* **1.** hinaufgehen, heraufkommen. **2. ~ to s.o.** auf j-n zugehen; **~!** treten Sie näher!

'walk·a·bout *s bsd. Br.* F Bad *n* in der Menge: **do** (*od.* **go on**) **a ~** ein Bad in der Menge nehmen.
walk·er ['wɔ:kǝ] *s* **1.** Spaziergänger(in); Wand(e)rer *m*, Wand(r)erin *f*: **be a fast ~** schnell gehen. **2.** *Sport:* Geher *m*.
walk·ies ['–ɪz] *s pl:* **go ~** *Br.* F Gassi gehen.
walk·ie-talk·ie [ˌwɔ:kɪ'tɔ:kɪ] *s* Walkietalkie *n*, tragbares Funksprechgerät.
'walk-in *adj* begehbar (*Schrank*).
walk·ing ['wɔ:kɪŋ] **I** *s* Laufen *n* (*a. Sport*), Gehen *n*; Spazierengehen *n*; Wandern *n*. **II** *adj:* **a ~ dictionary** F ein wandelndes Wörterbuch; **get one's ~**

papers Am. F den Laufpaß bekommen (von *Firma od. Freundin*); **~ shoes** *pl* Wanderschuhe *pl*; **~ stick** Spazierstock *m*; **~ tour** Wanderung *f*.
Walk·man ['wɔ:kmǝn] *pl* **-mans** *s* (*TM*) Walkman *m*.
'walk|-on *thea.* **I** *adj* **1. ~ part** → **2. II** *s* **2.** Statistenrolle *f*. **3.** Statist(in). **'~-out** *s* **1.** Auszug *m* (**by,** *of* e-r Delegation etc). **2.** Ausstand *m*, Streik *m*. **'~,o·ver** *s* F lockerer Sieg.

wall [wɔ:l] **I** *s* **1.** Wand *f* (*a. fig.*): **~ of fire** Feuerwall *m*; **~s have ears** die Wände haben Ohren; **drive up the ~** F j-n wahnsinnig machen; **go to the ~** kaputtgehen (*Firma etc*). **2.** Mauer *f* (*a. fig.*): **~ of silence** Mauer des Schweigens. **II** *v/t* **3.** mit e-r Mauer umgeben: **~ed** von Mauern umgeben; **~ in** einmauern; **~ off** durch e-e Mauer abtrennen (**from** von); **~ up** zu- od. einmauern. **'~chart** *s* Wandkarte *f*.
wal·let ['wɒlɪt] *s* Brieftasche *f*.
'wall,flow·er *s fig.* Mauerblümchen *n*.
wal·lop ['wɒlǝp] F **I** *s* **1.** Ding *n* (*harter Schlag*): **give** *s.o.* **a ~** → **2. II** *v/t* **2.** ein Ding verpassen *dat.* **3.** *Sport:* j-n in die Pfanne hauen (**at** in *dat*). **'wal·lop·ing** *adj u. adv:* **~ (great)** F riesig, Mords...
wal·low ['wɒlǝʊ] *v/i* **1. ~ in** sich wälzen in (*dat*, *Tier a.*) sich suhlen in (*dat*): **~ in luxury** im Luxus schwelgen; **~ in self-pity** sich in Selbstmitleid ergehen.
wall| paint·ing *s* Wandgemälde *n*. **'~,pa·per** **I** *s* Tapete *f*. **II** *v/t* tapezieren. **'~-to-'~** *adj:* **~ carpeting** Spannteppich *m*, Teppichboden *m*.
wal·ly ['wɒlɪ] *s Br.* F Trottel *m*.
wal·nut ['wɔ:lnʌt] *s* & Walnuß(baum *m*) *f*. **~ cake** *s* Nußkuchen *m*.
wal·rus ['wɔ:lrǝs] *pl* **-rus·es,** *bsd. coll.* **-rus** *s zo.* Walroß *n*. **~ m(o)us·tache** *s* Seehundsbart *m*.
waltz [wɔ:ls] **I** *s* ♪ Walzer *m*. **II** *v/i* Walzer tanzen; walzen.
wand [wɒnd] *s* (*Zauber*)Stab *m*.
wan·der ['wɒndǝ] *v/i* **1.** wandern; bummeln, schlendern: **~ about** (*od.* **around**) herumirren; **~ off** verschwinden. **2. ~ from** (*od.* **off**) **the topic** vom Thema abschweifen. **3. his mind ~s** er kann sich schlecht konzentrieren. **'wan·der·ings** *s pl* **1.** Reisen *pl.* **2. he's off on his**

~ again er ist wieder mal verschwunden.

wane [weɪn] **I** v/i abnehmen (*Mond*); *fig.* schwinden (*Einfluß etc*). **II** s: **be on the ~** im Schwinden begriffen sein.

wan·gle ['wæŋgl] v/t F **1.** *Eintrittskarten etc* organisieren: → **s.th. out of s.o.** j-m et. abluchsen. **2. ~ one's way out of** sich herauswinden aus. **3. I'll ~ it** ich werde das Kind schon schaukeln.

wank [wæŋk] v/i Br. V wichsen (*masturbieren*). **'wank·er** s Br. fig. V Wichser m.

wan·na ['wɒnə] F für **want to**; **want a**.

want [wɒnt] **I** v/t **1.** et. wollen: **he knows what he ~s** er weiß, was er will; **~ to do s.th.** et. tun wollen; **~ s.o. to do s.th.** wollen, daß j-d et. tut; **~ s.th. done** wollen, daß et. getan wird; **it ~s doing at once** F es muß sofort erledigt werden. **2.** j-n brauchen; j-n sprechen wollen: **you are ~ed on the phone** du wirst am Telefon verlangt. **3. be ~ed** (*polizeilich*) gesucht werden (**for** wegen). **4.** F *et.* brauchen, nötig haben. **5.** F **you ~ to see a doctor** du solltest zum Arzt gehen; **he doesn't ~ to smoke that much** er sollte nicht so viel rauchen. **II** v/i **6.** wollen: **I don't ~. I will nicht; ~ in (out)** F rein-(raus)wollen. **7. he does not ~ for anything** es fehlt ihm an nichts. **8.** Mangel m (**of** an *dat*): **for ~ of** mangels (*gen*), in Ermang(e)lung (*gen*); **be in ~ of** et. benötigen, brauchen. **9.** Bedürfnis n, Wunsch m. **10. live in ~** Not leiden, in Armut leben. **~ ad** s Kleinanzeige f.

want·ed ['wɒntɪd] adj: **he's a ~ man** er wird (*polizeilich*) gesucht; er ist ein vielgefragter Mann. **'want·ing** adj: **they are ~ in** es fehlt or. mangelt ihnen an (*dat*); **be found ~** den Ansprüchen nicht genügen.

wan·ton ['wɒntən] adj □ **1.** mutwillig. **2.** liederlich (*Frau, Leben*). **3.** lüstern (*Blick etc*).

war [wɔː] s Krieg m (*a. fig.*); *fig.* Kampf m (**against** gegen): **be at ~ with** sich im Krieg(szustand) befinden mit; *fig.* auf (dem) Kriegsfuß stehen mit; **declare ~ on** j-m den Krieg erklären, *fig. a.* j-m den Kampf ansagen; → **wage²**.

war·ble [wɔːbl] v/i trillern (*Vogel*).

war| cem·e·ter·y s Soldatenfriedhof m.

~ crime s Kriegsverbrechen n. **~ crim·i·nal** s Kriegsverbrecher m. **~ cry** s **1.** ⚔ *hist.* Schlachtruf m. **2.** *fig.* Parole f.

ward [wɔːd] **I** s **1.** Station f (e-s *Krankenhauses*). **2.** *pol. Br.* Stadtbezirk m. **3.** ⚖ Mündel n. **II** v/t **4.** ~ **off** *Schlag etc* abwehren, *Gefahr etc* abwenden. **'ward·en** s **1.** Aufseher(in): → **traffic warden. 2.** Haus-, Herbergsvater m, -mutter f; Heimleiter(in). **3.** *Am.* (Gefängnis)Direktor(in). **'ward·er** s Br. Aufsichtsbeamte m, -beamtin f (in *Gefängnis*).

ward·robe ['wɔːdrəʊb] s **1.** (Kleider-)Schrank m. **2.** Garderobe f (*Kleiderbestand*).

ware [weə] s in Zssgn (*Glas- etc*)Waren pl: → **tableware. '~house** s Lager(-haus) n.

war·fare ['wɔːfeə] s Krieg(führung f) m.

war| game s Kriegsspiel n (a. für Kinder etc), Planübung f. **~ grave** s Kriegs-, Soldatengrab n. **'~head** s ⚔ Spreng-, Gefechtskopf m. **'~like** adj **1.** kriegerisch. **2.** Kriegs...

warm [wɔːm] **I** adj □ **1.** warm (a. *fig. Farben, Stimme*): **I am** (od. **feel**) ~ mir ist warm; **dress ~ly** sich warm anziehen. **2.** *fig.* warm, herzlich (*Empfang*). **II** s **3. come into the ~** *bsd. Br.* F komm ins Warme! **III** v/t **4.** ~ **up** wärmen, sich *die Hände etc* wärmen. **IV** v/i **5.** ~ **up** wärmen od. wärmer werden, sich erwärmen: ~ **to** *fig.* sich für *j-n, et.* erwärmen.

Verbindungen mit Adverbien:

warm| o·ver v/t **1.** *Am.* → **warm up** 2. **2.** *bsd. Am. fig.* alte Geschichten etc aufwärmen. **~ up** v/t **1.** → **warm up** 4. **2.** *Br.* Speise aufwärmen. **3.** Motor warmlaufen lassen. **4.** F Schwung bringen in (*acc*). **II** v/i **5.** → **warm up** 5. **6.** *Sport:* sich aufwärmen. **7.** F in Schwung kommen.

,warm|-'blood·ed adj zo. warmblütig: **~ animal** Warmblüter m. **,~-'heart·ed** adj □ **1.** warmherzig. **2.** → **warm** 2. **'war,mon·ger** s Kriegshetzer m.

warmth ['wɔːmθ] s Wärme f, *fig. a.* Herzlichkeit f.

'warm-up s *Sport:* Aufwärmen n: **have a ~** sich aufwärmen.

warn [wɔːn] **I** v/t **1.** j-n warnen (**against, of** vor *dat*): **~ s.o. not to do** (od. **against doing**) **s.th.** j-n davor warnen, et. zu tun; ~ **off** verscheuchen (von, aus). **2.** j-n verständigen (**of** von; **that** davon, daß). **II** v/i **3.** warnen (**against, of** vor dat). **'warn·ing I** s **1.** Warnung f (**of** vor dat): **without** ~ ohne Vorwarnung; **let this be a** ~ **to you** laß dir das e-e Warnung sein!, das soll dir e-e Warnung sein! **2.** Verwarnung f: **he was given a written** ~ er wurde schriftlich verwarnt. **II** adj **3.** Warn...: ~ **signal** Warnsignal n (a. fig.).

warp [wɔːp] v/i sich verziehen od. werfen (Holz): **he must have a** ~**ed mind** fig. er muß abartig veranlagt sein.

war| paint s Kriegsbemalung f (a. humor. Make-up). **'~path** s: **be on the** ~ auf dem Kriegspfad sein; **he's on the** ~ F um ihn macht man heute am besten e-n großen Bogen.

war·rant ['wɒrənt] **I** v/t **1.** et. rechtfertigen. **II** s **2.** 🎵 ~ **of arrest** Haftbefehl m: **issue a** ~ **for s.o.'s arrest** Haftbefehl gegen j-n erlassen; → **death warrant, search warrant. 3.** Rechtfertigung f. **'war·ran·ty** s Garantie(erklärung) f: **the watch is still under** ~ auf der Uhr ist noch Garantie.

war·ri·or ['wɒrɪə] s Krieger m.

'war·ship s Kriegsschiff n.

wart [wɔːt] s Warze f: ~**s and all** F ohne jede Beschönigung.

'war·time I s: **in** ~ in Kriegszeiten. **II** adj Kriegs...: **in** ~ **Germany** in Deutschland während des Kriegs.

war·y ['weərɪ] adj □ vorsichtig: **be** ~ **of** (od. **about**) et. in acht nehmen vor (dat); **be** ~ **of doing s.th.** Bedenken haben, et. zu tun.

was [wɒz] **1.** ich, er, sie, es war. **2.** Passiv: ich, er, sie, es wurde.

wash [wɒʃ] **I** s **1.** Wäsche f: **be in the** ~ in der Wäsche sein; **come out in the** ~ fig. F rauskommen; gut werden; **give s.th. a** ~ et. waschen; **have a** ~ sich waschen. **2.** Waschanlage f, -straße f. **3.** 🎵 (Mund)Wasser n. **II** v/t **4.** waschen, sich die Hände wci waschen; → **linen** 2. **III** v/i **5.** sich waschen. **6.** sich gut etc waschen (lassen). **7.** **that won't** ~ F das glaubt kein Mensch.

Verbindungen mit Adverbien:

wash| a·way v/t wegschwemmen, -spülen. ~ **down** v/t **1.** Wagen etc waschen, abspritzen. **2.** Essen etc hinunterspülen (**with** mit). ~ **out** v/t **1.** auswaschen. **2. be** ~**ed out** (Sport etc) wegen Regens abgesagt od. abgebrochen werden. ~ **up** v/t **1.** Br. abwaschen, (das) Geschirr spülen. **2.** Am. → **wash** 5. **II** v/t **3.** anschwemmen, anspülen.

wash·a·ble ['wɒʃəbl] adj waschbar, -echt, (Tapete) abwaschbar.

'wash|·ba·sin s, **'~·bowl** s Am. Waschbecken n. **'~·cloth** s Am. Waschlappen m. **'~·day** s Waschtag m.

washed-out [ˌwɒʃt'aʊt] adj **1.** verwaschen. **2.** F schlapp, erschöpft. **'wash·er** s **1.** (Geschirr)Spülmaschine f, (-)Spüler m; Am. Waschmaschine f. → **dishwasher** 1. **3.** ⚙ Unterlegscheibe f.

wash·ing ['wɒʃɪŋ] **I** s Wäsche f (a. Textilien). **II** adj Wasch...: ~ **day** Waschtag m; ~ **machine** Waschmaschine f. **'~·up** s Br. Abwasch m (a. Geschirr): **do the** ~ den Abwasch machen.

'wash|·out s F Pleite f. **'~·room** s Am. Toilette f.

was·n't ['wɒznt] F für **was not.**

wasp [wɒsp] s zo. Wespe f. **'wasp·ish** adj □ giftig.

waste [weɪst] **I** v/t **1.** Geld, Zeit etc verschwenden, -geuden (**on** an acc, für); Chance etc vergeben: ~ **one's time doing s.th.** s-e Zeit damit verschwenden, et. zu tun; → **breath** 1. **2.** j-n auszehren. **II** v/i **3.** ~ **away** immer schwächer werden (Person). **III** adj **4.** ungenutzt, überschüssig; Abfall... **5.** brachliegend (Land). **IV** s **6.** Verschwendung f: ~ **of time** Zeitverschwendung. **7.** Abfall m; Müll m. **'~·bas·ket** s Papierkorb m. ~ **dis·pos·al** s Abfall-, Müllbeseitigung f.

waste·ful ['weɪstfʊl] adj □ verschwenderisch: **it is** ~ **to** es ist Verschwendung (**to do** zu tun).

'waste|'pa·per bas·ket s Papierkorb m. ~ **pipe** s Abflußrohr n. ~ **prod·uct** s Abfallprodukt n.

wast·er ['weɪstə] s Verschwender(in): **be a real time** ~ reine Zeitverschwendung sein.

watch [wɒtʃ] **I** s **1.** (Armband-, Taschen)Uhr f. **2.** Wache f: **be on the** ~ **for** Ausschau halten nach; auf der Hut sein vor (dat); **keep (a) careful** (od. **close**) *on et.* genau beobachten, scharf im Auge behalten. **II** *v/t* **3.** beobachten; zuschauen bei, sich *et.* ansehen: ~ *s.o. do(ing) s.th.* beobachten, wie j-d et. tut; ~ *the clock* F ständig auf die Uhr schauen; → *television* 1, *TV* 1. **4.** aufpassen auf (*acc*); achten auf (*acc*): ~ *you don't spill the coffee* paß auf, daß du den Kaffee nicht verschüttet; ~ *it!* F paß auf!, Vorsicht!; ~ *one's step fig.* aufpassen. **III** *v/i* **5.** zuschauen: ~ *for* a) *a.* ~ *out for* Ausschau halten nach, b) warten auf (*acc*). **6.** ~ *out!* paß auf!, Vorsicht!; ~ *out for* sich in acht nehmen vor (*dat*); ~ *over* wachen über (*acc*). '~**dog** *s* Wachhund *m*.

watch·ful ['wɒtʃfʊl] *adj* □ wachsam: *be* ~ *for* achten auf (*acc*).

'**watch**|**·mak·er** *s* Uhrmacher(in). ~ **-man** ['~mən] *s* (*irr man*) Wachmann *m*, Wächter *m*. '~**strap** *s* Uhr(arm)-band *n*. '~**tow·er** *s* Wachturm *m*.

wa·ter ['wɔːtə] **I** *s* **1.** Wasser *n*: *be under* ~ unter Wasser stehen; *that's all ~ under the bridge fig.* das ist Schnee von gestern; *have* ~ *on the knee fig.* Wasser im Knie haben; *throw cold* ~ *on fig.* e-r Sache e-n Dämpfer aufsetzen; → *deep* 1, *head* 8, *high water*, *hot* 1. **2.** *pl* Gewässer *pl*; Wasser *pl* (*e-s Flusses etc*): *still* ~*s run deep fig.* stille Wasser sind tief; → *trouble* 4. **II** *v/t* **3.** Blumen gießen, *Rasen etc* sprengen. **4.** *Vieh* tränken. **5.** ~ *down* verdünnen, -wässern; *fig.* abschwächen. **III** *v/i* **6.** tränen (*Augen*): *the sight made my mouth* ~ bei dem Anblick lief mir das Wasser im Mund zusammen. '~**bed** *s* Wasserbett *n*. ~ **bird** *s* Wasservogel *m*. ~ **blis·ter** *s* Wasserblase *f*. ~ **buf·fa·lo** *s zo.* Wasserbüffel *m*. ~ **butt** *s* Regentonne *f*. ~ **can·non** *s* (*a. irr cannon*) Wasserwerfer *m*. '~**col·o(u)r** *s* **1.** Wasser-, Aquarellfarbe *f*. **2.** Aquarellmalerei *f*. **3.** Aquarell *n*. '~**course** *s* Wasserlauf *m*. '~**cress** *s* ♀ Brunnenkresse *f*. '~**fall** *s* Wasserfall *m*. '~**front** *s* Hafenviertel *n*. '~**hole** *s* Wasserloch *n*. ~ **ice** *s bsd. Br.* Fruchteis *n*.

wa·ter·ing ['wɔːtərɪŋ] *adj*: ~ *can* (*Am. a. pot*) Gießkanne *f*.

wa·ter| **jump** *s* Sport: Wassergraben *m*. ~ **lev·el** *s* Wasserstand *m*. ~ **lil·y** *s* ♀ Seerose *f*.

Wa·ter·loo [ˌwɔːtə'luː] *s*: *meet one's* ~ sein Waterloo erleben.

'**wa·ter**|**·mark** *s* Wasserzeichen *n*. '~-**,mel·on** *s* ♀ Wassermelone *f*. ~ **pipe** *s* **1.** Wasserrohr *n*. **2.** Wasserpfeife *f*. ~ **po·lo** *s* Wasserball(spiel *n*) *m*. '~-**,pow·er** *s* Wasserkraft *f*. '~**proof** *I adj* wasserdicht. **II** *s bsd. Br.* Regenmantel *m*. **III** *v/t* wasserdicht machen, imprägnieren. '~**side** *s* Ufer *n*. ~ **ski** *s* Wasserski *m*. '~**ski** *v/i* Wasserski laufen. ~ **ski·ing** *s* Wasserskilaufen *n*. ~ **sup·ply** *s* Wasserversorgung *f*. '~**tight** *adj* wasserdicht, *fig. a.* hieb- u. stichfest. ~ **va·po(u)r** *s* Wasserdampf *m*. '~**way** *s* Wasserstraße *f*. '~**wheel** *s* Wasserrad *n*. '~**wings** *s pl* Schwimmflügel *pl*. '~**works** *s pl* (*oft sg konstruiert*) Wasserwerk *n*: *turn on the* ~ F zu heulen anfangen.

wa·ter·y ['wɔːtərɪ] *adj* wässerig, wäßrig.

watt [wɒt] *s* ⚡ Watt *n*.

wave [weɪv] **I** *v/t* **1.** schwenken; winken mit: ~ *one's hand* winken; ~ *s.o. goodbye* j-m nachwinken, j-m zum Abschied zuwinken; *you can* ~ *goodbye to that fig.* das kannst du dir aus dem Kopf schlagen. **2.** ~ *aside* j-n beiseite winken; *fig.* j-n, *et.* abweisen; ~ *away* j-n mit e-r Handbewegung verscheuchen; ~ *on* j-n, *Verkehr* weiterwinken. **3.** *Haar* wellen, in Wellen legen. **II** *v/i* **4.** winken: ~ *at* (*od. to*) *s.o.* j-m zuwinken. **5.** wehen (*Fahne etc*). **6.** sich wellen (*Haar*). **III** *s* **7.** *allg.* Welle *f* (*a. fig.*). **8.** *give a friendly* ~ freundlich winken; *give s.o. a* ~ j-m zuwinken. '~**length** *s* ⚡, *phys.* Wellenlänge *f*: *we are on different* ~*s fig.* wir haben nicht die gleiche Wellenlänge.

wa·ver ['weɪvə] *v/i* **1.** flackern (*Licht, Augen*), zittern (*Stimme*). **2.** *fig.* schwanken (*between* zwischen *dat*).

wav·y ['weɪvɪ] *adj* wellig, gewellt: ~ *line* Wellenlinie *f*.

wax[1] [wæks] **I** *s* **1.** Wachs *n*. **2.** *physiol.* (*Ohren*)Schmalz *n*. **II** *v/t* **3.** wachsen, *Fußboden a.* bohnern.

wax[2] [~] *v/i* zunehmen (*Mond*).

wax·en ['wæksən] *adj fig.* wächsern.

'**wax·work** *s* **1.** Wachsfigur *f*. **2.** *pl* (*mst sg konstruiert*) Wachsfigurenkabinett *n*.

wax·y ['wæksɪ] *adj* wächsern (*a. fig.*).

way [weɪ] **I** s **1.** Weg m: **~ back** Rückweg; **~ home** Heimweg; **~ in** Eingang m; **~ out** Ausgang m; **~s and means** pl fig. Mittel u. Wege pl; **by ~ of** über (acc), via; statt; **by the ~** fig. übrigens; **be on the** (od. one's) **~ to** unterwegs sein nach; **give ~** nachgeben; **go out of one's ~** sich besondere Mühe geben (**to do** zu tun); **lose one's ~** sich verlaufen od. verirren; **make ~** Platz machen (**for** für); → **talk** 8, etc. **2.** Richtung f, Seite f: **this ~** hierher; hier entlang. **3.** Weg m, Entfernung f, Strecke f: **be a long ~ from** weit entfernt sein von; **Easter is still a long ~ off** bis Ostern ist es noch lang. **4.** Art f, Weise f: **in a ~** (od. **some ~s**) in gewisser Hinsicht; **in no ~** in keiner Weise; **no ...!** F kommt überhaupt nicht in Frage!; **~ of life** Lebensart, -weise; **in my ~ of thinking** m-r Ansicht nach; **if I had my ~** wenn es nach mir ginge; **you can't have it both ~s** du kannst nicht beides haben. **5.** mst pl Brauch m, Sitte f; Gewohnheit f: → **mend** 2. **II** adv **6.** weit: **they are friends from ~ back** sie sind alte Freunde. '**~·bill** s Frachtbrief m. '**~·lay** v/t (irr **lay**) **1.** j-m auflauern. **2.** j-n abfangen, abpassen.

way·ward ['weɪwəd] adj □ eigensinnig.

we [wiː] pron wir pl.

weak [wiːk] adj □ allg. schwach (**at, in** in dat), (Kaffee etc a.) dünn: **be** (od. **feel**) **~ at the knees** F schwach auf den Beinen sein; weiche Knie haben; → **point** 14, **sex** 1, **spot** 4. '**weak·en I** v/t **1.** schwächen (a. fig.). **II** v/i **2.** schwächer werden (a. fig.). **3.** fig. nachgeben. **,weak·'kneed** adj F feig.

weak·ling ['wiːklɪŋ] s Schwächling m. '**weak·ness** s allg. Schwäche f: **have a ~ for** e-e Schwäche haben für.

weal [wiːl] s Striemen m.

wealth [welθ] s **1.** Reichtum m. **2.** fig. Fülle f (**of** an dat).

wean [wiːn] v/t Kind entwöhnen: **~ (away) from s.th., ~ off s.th.** j-n abbringen von et., j-m et. abgewöhnen.

weap·on ['wepən] s Waffe f (a. fig.): **~ system** ✕ Waffensystem n.

weap·on·ry ['~rɪ] s Waffen pl.

wear [weə] **I** s **1.** a. **~ and tear** Abnutzung f, Verschleiß m: **the worse for ~** F abgenutzt (Couch etc); kaputt (Per-son). **2.** oft in Zssgn Kleidung f. **II** v/t (irr) **3.** Bart, Brille, Schmuck tragen, Mantel etc a. anhaben, Hut etc a. aufhaben: **~ the trousers** (bsd. Am. **pants**) F die Hosen anhaben; → **seat belt**. **4.** **an angry expression** verärgert dreinschauen; **~ a happy smile** glücklich lächeln. **III** v/i (irr) **5. s.th. to ~** et. zum Anziehen. **6.** sich abnutzen. **7.** **he has worn well** er hat sich (für sein Alter) gut gehalten.

Verbindungen mit Adverbien:

wear| down I v/t **1.** Stufen abtreten, Absätze ablaufen, Reifen abfahren. **2.** fig. j-n, Widerstand etc zermürben. **II** v/i **3.** sich abtreten od. ablaufen od. abfahren. **~ off** v/i nachlassen (Schmerz etc). **~ on** v/i sich hinziehen (**all day** über den ganzen Tag). **~ out I** v/t **1.** Kleidung abnutzen, abtragen. **2.** fig. j-n erschöpfen. **II** v/i **3.** sich abnutzen od. abtragen.

wear·ing ['weərɪŋ] adj ermüdend.

wea·ri·some ['wɪərɪsəm] adj □ **1.** ermüdend. **2.** langweilig. **3.** lästig.

wea·ry ['wɪərɪ] adj □ **1.** erschöpft. **2.** **be ~ of s.th.** et. satt haben.

wea·sel ['wiːzl] s zo. Wiesel n. **II** v/i: **~ out of** bsd. Am. F sich lavieren aus (**e-r** Verantwortung etc).

weath·er ['weðə] **I** s Wetter n; Witterung f: **in all ~s** bei jedem Wetter; **be under the ~** F sich nicht wohl fühlen; **make heavy ~ of s.th.** fig. sich et. unnötig schwermachen; → **permit** 2. **II** v/t Krise etc überstehen. **III** v/i geol. verwittern. '**~·beat·en** adj verwittert (bsd. Gesicht). '**~·bound** adj: **the planes** (**ships**) **were ~** die Flugzeuge (Schiffe) konnten wegen des schlechten Wetters nicht starten (auslaufen). **~ chart** s Wetterkarte f. '**~·cock** s Wetterhahn m. **~ eye** s: **keep one's** (od. **a**) **~ open** aufpassen (**for** auf acc). '**~ fore·cast** s Wettervorhersage f. '**~·man** s (irr **man**) Rundfunk, TV: Wetteransager m. '**~·proof I** adj wetterfest. **II** v/t wetterfest machen. **~ sat·el·lite** s Wettersatellit m. **~ sta·tion** s Wetterwarte f. **~ vane** s Wetterfahne f.

weave [wiːv] **I** v/t (irr) **1.** weben; Netz spinnen. **2.** flechten. **3.** pret u. pp **weaved: ~ one's way through** sich schlängeln durch. **II** v/i (irr) **4.** weben;

5. *pret u. pp* weaved: ~ **through** → 3.
III *s* **6.** Webart *f*. '**weav·er** *s* Weber(in).

web [web] *s* **1.** Netz *n (a. fig.)*: ~ **of lies** Lügengespinst *n*, -gewebe *n*, -netz. **2.** *orn.* Schwimmhaut *f*.

wed [wed] *v/t (a. irr)* heiraten: *they were* ~ *last week* sie haben letzte Woche geheiratet.

we'd [wiːd] *F für* we had; we would.

wed·ding ['wedɪŋ] **I** *s* Hochzeit *f*. **II** *adj* Hochzeits...: ~ **anniversary** Hochzeitstag *m (Jahrestag)*; ~ **dress** Braut-, Hochzeitskleid *n*; ~ **ring** Ehe-, Trauring *m*.

wedge [wedʒ] **I** *s* **1.** Keil *m*: *drive a* ~ *between fig.* e-n Keil treiben zwischen *(acc)*; → **thin** 1. **2.** Stück *n (Kuchen etc)*, Ecke *f (Käse)*. **II** *v/t* **3.** verkeilen, mit e-m Keil festklemmen. **4.** ~ *in* einkeilen, -zwängen.

Wednes·day ['wenzdɪ] *s* Mittwoch *m*: *on* ~ (am) Mittwoch; *on* ~*s* mittwochs.

wee¹ [wiː] *adj* F klein: *a* ~ *bit* ein (kleines) bißchen; *the* ~ (*small*) *hours pl* die frühen Morgenstunden *pl*.

wee² [~] F **I** *v/i* Pipi machen. **II** *s*: *do (od.* have) a ~ → I.

weed [wiːd] **I** *s* **1.** Unkraut *n*. **2.** F Schwächling *m*, Waschlappen *m*. **II** *v/t* **3.** jäten: ~ *out* Pflanzen: aussieben, -sondern (*from* aus). **III** *v/i* **4.** (Unkraut) jäten. '**weed·y** *adj* **1.** voll Unkraut. **2.** F rückgratlos.

week [wiːk] *s* Woche *f*: ~ *after* ~; *in*, ~ *out* Woche für Woche; *after* ~*s of waiting* nach wochenlangem Warten; *for* ~*s* wochenlang; → **today** 1. '~**·day** *s* Wochen-, Werktag *m*: *on* ~*s* werktags. ,~'**end I** *s* Wochenende *n*: *at the* ~ am Wochenende. **II** *adj* ['~end] Wochenend... **III** *v/i* das Wochenende verbringen.

week·ly ['wiːklɪ] **I** *adj* Wochen...; wöchentlich. **II** *adv* wöchentlich. **III** *s* Wochen(zeit)schrift *f*, -zeitung *f*.

wee·ny ['wiːnɪ] *adj* F klitzeklein, winzig.

weep [wiːp] (*irr*) **I** *v/i* **1.** weinen (*for, with* vor *Freude etc*); *for* um *j-n*; *over* über (*acc*). **2.** nässen (*Wunde*). **II** *v/t* **3.** *Tränen* weinen. '**weep·ing** *adj*: ~ *willow* ❧ Trauerweide *f*. '**weep·y** *adj* F **1.** weinerlich. **2.** rührselig.

'**wee-wee** → **wee²**.

weigh [weɪ] **I** *v/t* **1.** (ab)wiegen. **2.** *fig.* abwägen (*against* gegen). **3.** ~ *anchor* ⚓ den Anker lichten. **II** *v/i* **4.** *10 Kilo etc* wiegen. **5.** ~ *on fig.* lasten auf (*dat*). **6.** ~ *with fig.* Gewicht haben bei. *Verbindungen mit Adverbien:*

weigh| **down** *v/t* niederdrücken (*a. fig.*): *be* ~*ed down with* überladen sein mit; *fig.* niedergedrückt werden von. ~ *in v/i* **1.** ~ *at (Sport)* 100 Kilo etc auf die Waage bringen. **2.** F sich einschalten (*with* mit). ~ *out v/t* ab-, auswiegen. ~ *up v/t et.* abwägen; *j-n* einschätzen.

weight [weɪt] **I** *s* **1.** *allg.* Gewicht *n*: ~*s and measures pl* Maße u. Gewichte *pl*; *it's five kilos in* ~ es wiegt fünf Kilo; *what's your* ~? wieviel wiegst du?, wie schwer bist du?; *gain (od. put on)* ~ zunehmen; *lose* ~ abnehmen. **2.** Last *f (a. fig.)*: *I can't lift* ~*s* ich kann nicht schwer heben; *be a* ~ *on s.o.'s mind j-n* belasten; *his decision took a* ~ *off my mind* bei s-r Entscheidung fiel mir ein Stein vom Herzen. **3.** *fig.* Bedeutung *f*: *not to attach any* ~ *to s.th.* e-r Sache keine Bedeutung *od.* kein Gewicht beimessen; *throw one's* ~ *about (od. around)* F sich aufspielen *od.* wichtig machen; → **carry** 5. **II** *v/t* **4.** beschweren: ~ *down* → *weigh down; be* ~*ed in favo(u)r of (against)* bevorteilen (benachteiligen). ~ **cat·e·go·ry** *s Sport:* Gewichtsklasse *f*.

weight·less ['weɪtlɪs] *adj* □ schwerelos.

weight| **lift·er** *s Sport:* Gewichtheber *m*. ~ **lift·ing** *s Sport:* Gewichtheben *n*. ~ **train·ing** *s Sport:* Gewichttraining *n*.

weight·y ['weɪtɪ] *adj* □ **1.** schwer. **2.** *fig.* gewichtig; schwerwiegend.

weir [wɪə] *s* Wehr *n*.

weird [wɪəd] *adj* □ **1.** unheimlich. **2.** F sonderbar, verrückt.

weird·o ['wɪədəʊ] *pl* -os *s* F irrer Typ.

welch → **welsh²**.

wel·come ['welkəm] **I** *int* **1.** ~ *back (od. home)!* willkommen zu Hause!; ~ *to England!* willkommen in England! **II** *adj* **2.** willkommen: *you are* ~ to do it Sie können es gerne tun; *you're* ~ nichts zu danken!, keine Ursache!, bitte sehr! **3.** angenehm. **III** *v/t* **4.** begrüßen *(a. fig.)*. **IV** *s* **5.** Empfang *m*: *give s.o. a warm* ~ *j-m* e-n herzlichen Empfang bereiten. **6.** *outstay (od. overstay)* *one's* ~ j-s Gastfreundschaft überstrapazieren *od.* zu lange in Anspruch nehmen.

weld [weld] **I** *v/t* schweißen: ~ *together* zs.-, verschweißen. **II** *s* Schweißnaht *f*, -stelle *f*. **'weld·er** *s* Schweißer *m*.

wel·fare ['welfeə] *s* **1.** Wohl *n*, (*e-r Person a.*) Wohlergehen *n*. **2.** *Am.* Sozialhilfe *f*: *be on* ~ Sozialhilfe beziehen. ~ **state** *s* Wohlfahrtsstaat *m*.

well¹ [wel] **I** *adv* **1.** gut: (*all*) ~ *and good* schön u. gut; *as* ~ ebenso, auch; *as* ~ *as* sowohl ... als auch; nicht nur ..., sondern auch; (*just*) *as* ~ ebenso(gut), genauso(gut); *just as* ~ das macht nichts; *very* ~ also gut, na gut; *I couldn't very* ~ *say no* ich konnte schlecht nein sagen; *be* ~ *in with s.o.* auf gutem Fuß mit j-m stehen; *do* ~ gut daran tun (*to do* zu tun); ~ *done!* bravo!; → *off* 11. **2.** gut, gründlich: *be* ~ *aware of s.th.* sich e-r Sache voll u. ganz bewußt sein; *shake* ~ kräftig schütteln. **3.** weit: ~ *in advance* schon lange vorher. **II** *int* **4.** nun, also (*oft unübersetzt*). **5.** ~, ~! na so was! **III** *adj* **6.** gesund: *not to feel* ~ sich nicht wohl fühlen. *all's* ~ *that ends* ~ Ende gut, alles gut; *it's all very* ~ *for you to criticize* (*laugh*) du kannst leicht kritisieren (du hast gut lachen).

well² [~] **I** *s* **1.** Brunnen *m*: ~ *water* Brunnenwasser *n*. **2.** (*Öl*)Quelle *f*. **3.** △ (*Aufzugs- etc*)Schacht *m*. **II** *v/i* **4.** *a.* ~ *out* quellen (*from* aus): *tears* ~*ed* (*up*) *in her eyes* die Tränen stiegen ihr in die Augen.

we'll [wi:l] F *für* we will.

well|-ad·vised *adj* klug (*Plan etc*). ~**-ap'point·ed** *adj* gutausgestattet. ~**-'bal·anced** *adj* **1.** ausgeglichen (*Person*). **2.** ausgewogen (*Ernährung etc*). ~**-be·ing** *s* Wohl(ergehen) *n*: *give s.o. a sense of* ~ j-n mit Wohlbehagen erfüllen. ~**-'cho·sen** *adj* gutgewählt: *with a few* ~ *words* mit einigen wohlgesetzten Worten. ~**-'done** *adj* durchgebraten (*Steak*). ~**-'earned** *adj* wohlverdient. ~**-'found·ed** *adj* (wohl)begründet. ~**-'groomed** *adj* gepflegt. ~**-'heeled** *adj* F betucht. ~**-in'formed** *adj* **1.** gutunterrichtet. **2.** (vielseitig) gebildet. ~**-in'ten·tioned** → well-meaning. ~**-'kept** *adj* **1.** gepflegt. **2.** streng gehütet (*Geheimnis*). ~**-'known** *adj*

(wohl)bekannt. ~**-'lined** *adj* F **1.** voller Geld, (*Brieftasche*) dick. **2.** voll (*Magen*). ~**-'mean·ing** *adj* wohlmeinend (*Person*), (*Rat etc a.*) gut-, wohlgemeint. ~**-'meant** *adj* gut-, wohlgemeint. ~**-'nigh** ['~naɪ] *adv* beinahe, nahezu. ~**-'off** **I** *adj* begütert, reich. **II** *s*: *the* ~ *pl* die Reichen *pl*. ~**-pro'por·tioned** *adj* wohlproportioniert. ~**-'read** [~'red] *adj* belesen. ~**-'thought-of** *adj* angesehen, geachtet. ~**-to-'do** F → *well-off*. ~**-'worn** *adj* **1.** abgenutzt, abgetragen. **2.** *fig.* abgedroschen.

Welsh¹ [welʃ] **I** *adj* **1.** walisisch. **II** *s* **2.** *the* ~ *pl* die Waliser *pl*. **3.** *ling.* Walisisch *n*.

welsh² [~] *v/i*: ~ *on* F *Schulden* nicht bezahlen; *Versprechen* nicht halten.

Welsh|·man ['welʃmən] *s* (*irr man*) Waliser *m*. '~**·wom·an** *s* (*irr woman*) Waliserin *f*.

welt [welt] *s* Striemen *m*.

wel·ter·weight ['weltəweɪt] (*Sport*) **I** *s* Weltergewicht(ler *m*) *n*. **II** *adj* Weltergewichts...

went [went] *pret von* go.

wept [wept] *pret u. pp von* weep.

were [wɜ:] *du* warst, *Sie* waren, *wir, sie* waren, *ihr* wart.

we're [wɪə] F *für* we are.

weren't [wɜ:nt] F *für* were not.

were·wolf ['wɪəwʊlf] *s* (*irr wolf*) Werwolf *m*.

west [west] **I** *s* **1.** Westen *m*: *in the* ~ *of* im Westen von (*od. gen*). **2.** *a. the* ~ **5.** *the* 2 *Br.* Westengland *n*; *Am.* die Weststaaten *pl*; *pol.* der Westen: → *wild* 1. **II** *adj* **3.** West..., westlich. **III** *adv* **4.** westwärts, nach Westen: *go* ~ F draufgehen (*sterben, kaputtgehen*). **5.** ~ *of* westlich von (*od. gen*). '~**bound** *adj* nach Westen (*od.* west) fahrend.

west·er·ly ['westəlɪ] **I** *adj* westlich, West... **II** *adv* von *od.* nach Westen.

west·ern ['~tən] **I** *adj* westlich, West... **II** *s* Western *m*. '**west·ern·er** *s* **1.** Bewohner(in) des Westens (*e-s Landes*). **2.** 2 Weststaatler(in). **west·ern·most** ['~məʊst] *adj* westlichst.

west·ward ['westwəd] *adj u. adv* westlich, westwärts, nach Westen. '**west·wards** *adv* → *westward*.

wet [wet] **I** *adj* □ **1.** naß, (*Farbe etc a.*) feucht: *be* (*still*) ~ *behind the ears* F noch grün *od.* feucht *od.* noch nicht trocken hinter den Ohren sein; **~ blanket** *f* Spiel-, Spaßverderber(in); → **paint** 5, **through** 3. **2.** regnerisch. **3.** *Br. F* weichlich: *don't be so ~!* sei nicht so ein Waschlappen! **II** *s* **4.** Nässe *f.* **III** *v/t* (*mst irr*) **5.** naß machen, anfeuchten: **~ one's bed** ins Bett machen; **~ o.s.** in die Hose machen; **~ one's whistle** *F* e-n zur Brust nehmen.

weth·er ['weðə] *s zo.* Hammel *m.*

we've [wiːv] *F für we have.*

whack [wæk] *F* **I** *s* **1.** (knallender) Schlag. **2.** (An)Teil *m.* **3.** Versuch *m:* **have a ~ at s.th.** probieren. **whacked** *adj:* **be ~ (out)** *F* geschlaucht *od.* kaputt sein. **'whack·ing** *F* **I** *adj u. adv:* **~ (great)** Mords..., riesig. **II** *s:* **give s.o. a ~** j-m e-e Tracht Prügel verpassen.

whale [weɪl] *s zo.* Wal *m:* **have a ~ of a time** *F* sich prächtig amüsieren.

wharf [wɔːf] *pl* **wharfs, wharves** [wɔːvz] *s* Kai *m.*

what [wɒt] **I** *interrogative pron* **1.** was: **~'s for lunch?** was gibt's zum Mittagessen?; **~ for?** wozu?; **~ about ...?** wie wär's mit ...?; **~ if ...?** was ist, wenn ...?; → **age** 1, **like** 1, **so** 6, *etc.* **II** *relative pron* **2.** was: **he told me ~ to do** er sagte mir, was ich tun sollte; **(know ~)'s ~** *F* wissen, was Sache ist; **tell s.o. ~'s ~** *F* j-m Bescheid stoßen. **III** *adj* **3.** was für ein(e), welch(er, e, es): **~ luck!** so ein Glück!; → **age** 1, **colour** 1, **pity** 2, *etc.* **4.** alle, die; alles, was: **I gave him ~ money I had** ich gab ihm, was ich an Geld hatte. **~'ev·er** *I pron* **1.** was (auch immer); alles, was. **2.** egal, was. **II** *adj* **3.** welch(er, e, es) ... auch (immer). **4.** no ... ~ überhaupt kein(e). **~ for s:** *I'll give him ~!* bsd. *Br. F* dem werd' ich's zeigen!

'whats·it ['wɒtsɪt] *s F* Dingsbums *n.*

what·so·ev·er → **whatever** 1, 2, 4.

wheat [wiːt] *s* 🌾 Weizen *m:* **separate the ~ from the chaff** *fig.* die Spreu vom Weizen trennen. **~ germ** *s* Weizenkern *m.*

whee·dle ['wiːdl] *v/t:* **~ s.o. into doing s.th.** j-m so lange schöntun, bis er et. tut; **~ s.th. out of s.o.** j-m et. abschmeicheln.

wheel [wiːl] **I** *s* **1.** Rad *n:* → **fifth** 1, **meal**¹, **oil** 4, **shoulder** 1, **spoke**². **2.** *F* a) *pl* fahrbarer Untersatz, Wagen *m,* b)

(Fahr)Rad *n.* **3.** ⚓, *mot.* Steuer *n:* **be at the ~ mot.** am Steuer sitzen (⚓ stehen); **take the ~** das Steuer übernehmen. **II** *v/t* **4.** Fahrrad, Patienten im Rollstuhl etc schieben, Servierwagen etc a. rollen. **III** *v/i* **5.** **~ about** (*od.* **[a]round**) herumfahren, -wirbeln. **6.** kreisen (*Vogel*). **7.** **~ and deal** *F contp.* Geschäfte machen. **'~·bar·row** *s* Schubkarre(n *m*) *f.* **'~·base** *s mot.* Radstand *m.* **~·chair** *s* 🦽 Rollstuhl *m.* **~ clamp** *s Br.* Radkralle *f,* Parkriegel *m.*

wheeled [wiːld] *adj* **~ vehicle** Räderfahrzeug *n.* **2.** *in Zssgn* ...räd(e)rig. **wheel·er-'deal·er** *s F contp.* Geschäftemacher *m.*

wheeze [wiːz] *v/i* keuchen, pfeifend atmen.

when [wen] **I** *adv* **1.** *fragend:* wann. **2.** *relativ:* **the day ~** der Tag, an dem *od.* als; **the time ~ it happened** die Zeit, in *od.* zu der es geschah. **II** *cj* **3.** wann. **4.** als: **he broke a leg ~ skiing** er brach sich beim Skifahren ein Bein. **5.** wenn: **say ~!** *F* sag halt!, sag, wenn du genug hast! **III** *pron* **6.** **since ~?** seit wann? **~'ev·er** *cj* wann auch (immer); jedesmal, wenn.

where [weə] **I** *adv* (*fragend u. relativ*) wo: **~ ... (from?)** woher?; **~ ... (to?)** wohin? **II** *cj* wo; wohin. **'~·a·bouts** *s pl* (*a. sg konstruiert*) Verbleib *m* (e-r Sache), (e-r Person a.) Aufenthalt(sort) *m.* **~'as** *cj* während, wohingegen. **~'by** *adv* **1.** wodurch, womit. **2.** wonach. **~·up·on** *cj* worauf(hin).

wher·ev·er [weər'evə] *adv* wo(hin) auch (immer); ganz gleich, wo(hin).

whet [wet] *v/t* **1.** *Messer etc* schärfen. **2.** *fig. Appetit* anregen.

weth·er ['weðə] *cj* ob.

whey [weɪ] *s* Molke *f.*

which [wɪtʃ] **I** *interrogative pron* **1.** welch(er, e, es): **~ of you?** wer von euch? **II** *relative pron* **2.** welch(er, e, es); der, die, das. **3.** *auf den vorhergehenden Satz bezüglich:* was. **III** *adj* **4.** *fragend u. relativ:* welch(er, e, es). **~'ev·er** *pron u. adj* welch(er, e, es) auch (immer); ganz gleich, welch(er, e, es).

whiff [wɪf] *s* **1.** Luftzug *m,* Hauch *m.* **2.** Duft(wolke *f*) *m.* **3.** *fig.* Anflug *m,* Hauch *m* (**of** von).

while [waɪl] **I** *s* **1.** Weile *f:* **a little ~ ago**

vor kurzem; **for a ~** e-e Zeitlang; e-n Augenblick; → **once** 1. **II** *cj* 2. während. 3. obwohl. **III** *v/t* 4. **~ away** sich die Zeit vertreiben (**by doing s.th.** mit et.).

whilst [waɪlst] → **while** II.

whim [wɪm] *s* Laune *f*: **as the ~ takes one, at ~** nach Lust u. Laune.

whim·per ['wɪmpə] **I** *v/i* winseln (*Hund*); wimmern (*Person*). **II** *v/t* wimmern. **III** *s* Winseln *n*; Wimmern *n*.

whim·si·cal ['wɪmzɪkl] *adj* □ 1. wunderlich. 2. launenhaft.

whim·sy ['wɪmzɪ] *s* 1. Wunderlichkeit *f*. 2. Spleen *m*.

whine [waɪn] **I** *v/i* 1. jaulen (*Hund*). 2. jammern (**about** über *acc*). **II** *s* 3. Jaulen *n*. 4. Gejammer *n*. '**whin·er** *s* Jammerer *m*.

whin·ny ['wɪnɪ] **I** *v/i* wiehern. **II** *s* Wiehern *n*.

whip [wɪp] **I** *s* 1. Peitsche *f*. 2. *parl.* *Br.* Einpeitscher *m*. 3. *gastr.* Creme *f*. **II** *v/t* 4. (aus)peitschen: **~ into shape** F *j-n*, et. auf Zack bringen. 5. Sahne etc schlagen. 6. *bsd. Sport:* F überfahren (*hoch schlagen*). 7. *Br.* F klauen. **III** *v/i* 8. sausen, flitzen, (*Wind*) fegen.
Verbindungen mit Adverbien:

whip¦ back *v/i* zurückschnellen (*Ast etc*). **~ off** *v/t* sich *ein Kleidungsstück* herunterreißen. **~ out** *v/t* *Revolver etc* zücken. **~ up** *v/t* 1. → **whip** 5. 2. *Interesse etc* entfachen. 3. *Essen etc* herzaubern.

'**whip·cord** *s* Peitschenschnur *f*. '**·lash** *s* 1. Peitschenschnur *f*. 2. Peitschenhieb *m*: **~** (**injury**) ✠ Schleudertrauma *n*.

whipped [wɪpt] *adj*: **~ cream** Schlagsahne *f*, -rahm *m*.

whip·ping ['wɪpɪŋ] *adj*: **~ boy** Prügelknabe *m*; **~ cream** Schlagsahne *f*, -rahm *m*. '**whip·py** *adj* biegsam, elastisch.

'**whip-round** *s* *Br.* F Sammlung *f* (*im Büro etc*): **have a ~** sammeln (**for** für).

whir *bsd. Am.* → **whirr**.

whirl [wɜːl] **I** *v/i* 1. wirbeln: **my head is ~ing** mir schwirrt der Kopf. **II** *v/t* 2. wirbeln. 3. **the car ~ed us off to** der Wagen brachte uns auf schnellstem Weg zu *od.* nach. **III** *s* 4. Wirbeln *n*; Wirbel *m*: **my head's in a ~** mir schwirrt der Kopf; **give s.th. a ~** F et.

ausprobieren. 5. *fig.* Trubel *m*, Wirbel *m*.

whirl·i·gig ['wɜːlɪgɪg] *s* 1. Kreisel *m*. 2 Karussell *n*.

'**whirl·pool** *s* 1. Strudel *m* (*a. fig.*). 2 Whirlpool *m* (*Unterwassermassagebek-ken*). '**·wind** *s* Wirbelwind *m*.

whirr [wɜː] **I** *v/i* surren. **II** *s* Surren *n*.

whisk [wɪsk] **I** *s* 1. Wedel *m*. 2. *gastr.* Schneebesen *m*. **II** *v/t* 3. **~ its tail** mit dem Schwanz schlagen; **~ away** Fliegen etc ver-, wegscheuchen. 4. *Eiweiß* schlagen.

wisk·er ['wɪskə] *s* 1. Schnurrhaar *n*: **by a ~** F ganz knapp. 2. *pl* Backenbart *m*.

whis·key ['wɪskɪ] *s* (*amerikanischer od. irischer*) Whisky.

whis·ky ['wɪskɪ] *s* (*bsd. schottischer*) Whisky: **~ and soda** Whisky Soda; **two whiskies** zwei Whisky.

whis·per ['wɪspə] **I** *v/i* 1. flüstern, leise sprechen (**to** mit). **II** *v/t* 2. flüstern, leise sagen: **~ s.th. to s.o.** j-m et. zuflüstern. 3. **it is ~ed that** man munkelt, daß. **III** *s* 4. Flüstern *n*: **say s.th. in a ~** et. im Flüsterton sagen. 5. Gerücht *n*: **I've heard a ~ that** ich habe munkeln hören daß. '**whis·per·ing** *adj*: **~ campaign** Verleumdungskampagne *f*.

whist [wɪst] *s* Whist *n* (*Kartenspiel*).

whis·tle ['wɪsl] **I** *v/i* 1. pfeifen: **~ at** *j-m* nachpfeifen; **~ for** (nach) *j-m*, e-m Taxi etc pfeifen; **he can ~ for** F darauf kann er lange warten. **II** *v/t* 2. pfeifen. **III** *s* 3. Pfeife *f*: **blow one's ~** pfeifen. 4. Pfiff *m*: **give a ~ of surprise** e-n überraschten Pfiff ausstoßen. 5. → **wet** 5

white [waɪt] **I** *adj* 1. *allg.* weiß: **~ bread** Weißbrot *n*; **~ coffee** *Br.* Milchkaffee *m*, Kaffee *m* mit Milch; **~ hope** große Hoffnung (*Person*); **~ lie** Notlüge *f*; **~ man** Weiße *m*; **~ paper** *pol.* Weißbuch *n*; **~ wedding** Hochzeit *f* in Weiß; **~ wine** Weißwein *m*. **II** *s* 2. Weiß *n*: **dressed in ~** weiß *od.* in Weiß gekleidet. 3. *oft* ♀ Weiße *m*, *f*. 4. Eiweiß *n*; das Weiße (*im Auge*). '**~·col·lar** *adj* Büro...: **~ crime** White-collar-Kriminalität *f*; **~ worker** Büroangestellte *m*, *f*

whit·en ['waɪtn] **I** *v/t* weiß machen. **II** *v/* weiß werden.

'**white·wash I** *v/t* 1. tünchen, anstreichen; weißen. 2. F *et.* übertünchen, be schönigen; *j-n* e-r Mohrenwäsche un terziehen. **II** *s* **3.** Tünche *f*. **4.** F Tünche *f*, Beschönigung *f*; Mohrenwäsche *f*.

whit·ish ['wɪtɪʃ] *adj* weißlich.

Whit·sun ['wɪtsn] *s* **1.** Pfingstsonntag *m*. **2.** Pfingsten *n od. pl*. **Whit Sun·day** [wɪt] → **Whitsun** 1.

whit·tle ['wɪtl] *v/t* **1.** (zurecht)schnitzen. **2.** *fig*. ~ **away** Gewinn etc allmählich aufzehren; ~ **down** et. reduzieren (**to** auf *acc*).

whiz(z) [wɪz] *v/i*: ~ **by** (*od. past*) vorbeizischen. **II** *s* **2.** F As *n*, Kanone *f* (**at** in *dat*). ~ **kid** *s* F Senkrechtstarter(in).

who [hu:] *interrogative pron* **1.** wer; wen; wem; wem: *do you think you are?* für wen hältst du dich eigentlich? **II** *relative pron*. **2.** *unverbunden*: wer; wen; wem. **3.** *verbunden*: welch(er, e, es); der, die, das.

who'd [hu:d] F *für* who had; who would.

who·dun·(n)it [ˌhuː'dʌnɪt] *s* F Krimi *m*.

who·ev·er **I** *relative pron* wer auch (immer); wen auch (immer); wem auch (immer); egal, wer od. wen od. wem. **II** *interrogative pron*: ~ **can that be?** wer kann denn das nur sein?

whole [həʊl] **I** *adj* (□ → **wholly**) ganz: → **hog** 1. **II** *s das* Ganze: **the** ~ **of the town** die ganze Stadt; **as a** ~ als Ganzes; **on the** ~ im großen (u.) ganzen; alles in allem. **ˌ~'heart·ed** *adj* ungeteilt (*Aufmerksamkeit*), ernsthaft (*Versuch etc*). **ˌ~'heart·ed·ly** *adv* uneingeschränkt, voll u. ganz. **'~·meal** *adj* Vollkorn...

'whole·sale **I** *s* **1.** Großhandel *m*. **II** *adj* **2.** Großhandels... **3.** *b.s.* Massen... **III** *adv* **4.** en gros. **'whole·sal·er** *s* Großhändler *m*.

whole·some ['həʊlsəm] *adj* □ **1.** gesund. **2.** *fig*. gut, nützlich.

who'll [hu:l] F *für* who will.

whol·ly ['həʊllɪ] *adv* gänzlich, völlig.

whom [hu:m] *interrogative pron* wen; wem. **II** *relative pron* welch(en, e, es), den (die, das); welch(em, er, en), dem (der): **the children, most of** ~ **were tired,** ... die Kinder, von denen die meisten müde waren, ...

whoop [hu:p] **I** *v/i* schreien, *bsd.* jauchzen. **II** *v/t*: ~ **it up** F auf den Putz hauen. **III** *s* (*bsd.* Freuden)Schrei *m*: ~**s** *pl of victory* Siegesgeschrei *n*. **'whoop·ing** *adj*: ~ **cough** 🏥 Keuchhusten *m*.

whoosh [wʊʃ] *v/i*: ~ **by** (*od. past*) F vorbeirauschen.

whop·per ['wɒpə] *s* F **1.** Mordsding *n*. **2.** faustdicke Lüge. **'whop·ping** *adj u. adv* F Mords..., riesig: ~ (**big**) **lie** → **whopper** 2.

whore [hɔː] *s* Hure *f*.

who're ['huːə] F *für* who are.

'whore·house *s* Bordell *n*, Freudenhaus *n*.

whor·tle·ber·ry ['wɜːtlˌberɪ] *s* 🌿 Blau-, Heidelbeere *f*.

who's [hu:z] F *für* who is; who has.

whose [hu:z] *interrogative pron* wessen: ~ **coat is this?,** ~ **is this coat?** wem gehört dieser Mantel? **II** *relative pron* dessen, deren.

why [waɪ] *adv* warum, weshalb: ~ **not go by bus?** warum nimmst du nicht den Bus?

wick [wɪk] *s* Docht *m*: **get on s.o.'s** ~ *Br.* F j-m auf den Wecker fallen *od.* gehen.

wick·ed ['wɪkɪd] *adj* □ **1.** gemein, niederträchtig. **2.** *fig*. unerhört.

wick·er ['wɪkə] *adj* Korb...: ~ **basket** Weidenkorb *m*.

wide [waɪd] **I** *adj* (□ → **widely**) **1.** breit. **2.** weit offen, aufgerissen (*Augen*). **3.** *fig*. umfangreich (*Wissen etc*), vielfältig (*Interesses etc*). **4.** ~ **mark?** 5. **II** *adv* **5.** weit. **6.** **go** ~ (*Sport*) danebengehen. **ˌ~'an·gle** *adj*: ~ **lens** *phot.* Weitwinkelobjektiv *n*. **ˌ~'a·wake** *adj* **1.** hellwach. **2.** *fig*. aufgeweckt, wach. **ˌ~·'eyed** *adj* **1.** mit großen *od.* aufgerissenen Augen. **2.** *fig*. naiv.

wide·ly ['waɪdlɪ] *adv* **1.** weit (*a. fig.*): **it is** ~ **known that** es ist weithin bekannt, daß; ~ **travel(l)ed** weitgereist. **2.** ~ **different** völlig verschieden. **'wid·en I** *v/t* verbreitern. **II** *v/i* breiter werden.

ˌwide'-o·pen *adj* → **wide** 2. **'~·spread** *adj* weitverbreitet.

wid·ow ['wɪdəʊ] *s* Witwe *f*. **'wid·owed** *adj* verwitwet: **be** ~ verwitwet sein; Witwe(r) werden.

width [wɪdθ] *s* **1.** Breite *f*: **six feet in** ~ sechs Fuß breit; **what is the** ~ ...? wie breit ist ...? **2.** Bahn *f* (*Stoff etc*).

wield [wi:ld] *v/t* Einfluß, Macht ausüben.

wife [waɪf] *pl* **wives** [waɪvz] *s* (Ehe)Frau *f*, Gattin *f*. ~ **swap·ping** *s* F Partnertausch *m*.

wig [wɪg] *s* Perücke *f*.

wig·ging ['wɪɡɪŋ] s: **give s.o. a ~** Br. F j-m e-e Standpauke halten.

wig·gle ['wɪɡl] v/t u. v/i wackeln (mit).

wig·wam ['wɪɡwæm] s Wigwam m.

wild [waɪld] **I** adj □ **1.** allg. wild: **the ≈ West** der Wilde Westen; → **oats. 2.** stürmisch (Wind, Applaus etc). **3.** außer sich (**with** vor dat). **4.** verrückt (Idee etc). **5. it was just a ~ guess** ich hab' einfach drauflosgeraten. **II** adv **6.** F **go ~** ausflippen; **run ~** Amok laufen; **let one's children run ~** s-e Kinder machen lassen, was sie wollen. **III** s **7. in the ~** in freier Wildbahn. '**~·cat I** s Wildkatze f. **II** adj: **~ strike** wilder Streik. '**~·fire** s: **spread like ~** sich wie ein Lauffeuer verbreiten. '**~·'goose** adj: **be a ~ chase** vergebliche Mühe od. ein Metzgergang sein. '**~·life** s Tier- u. Pflanzenwelt f.

wil·ful ['wɪlfʊl] adj □ **1.** eigensinnig. **2.** absichtlich, bsd. ₰₮₲ vorsätzlich.

will[1] [wɪl] s **1.** Wille m: **~ to live** Lebenswille; **against one's ~** gegen s-n Willen; **at ~** nach Belieben; **of one's own free ~** aus freien Stücken; **I can't do that with the best ~ in the world** ich kann das (auch) beim besten Willen nicht tun; **take the ~ for the deed** den guten Willen für die Tat nehmen. **2.** a. **last ~ and testament** Letzter Wille, Testament n: **make one's ~** sein Testament machen; → **remember 3.**

will[2] [~] v/aux **1.** Futur: **I'll be back in 10 minutes** ich bin in 10 Minuten zurück. **2.** Bereitschaft, Entschluß: **I won't go there again** ich gehe da nicht mehr hin; **the door won't shut** die Tür schließt nicht; **~ you have some coffee?** möchtest du e-e Tasse Kaffee? **3.** Bitte: **shut the window, ~ you?** mach bitte das Fenster zu. **4.** Wiederholung: **accidents ~ happen** Unfälle wird es immer geben; **boys ~ be boys** Jungen sind nun einmal so. **5.** Vermutung: **that ~ be my sister** das wird od. dürfte m-e Schwester sein.

will·ful Am. → **wilful.**

wil·lies ['wɪlɪz] s pl: **give s.o. the ~** F j-m unheimlich sein.

will·ing ['wɪlɪŋ] adj □ **1.** bereit (**to do** zu tun); **~ to compromise** kompromißbereit; **God ~** so Gott will. **2.** (bereit)willig. '**will·ing·ness** s **1.** Bereitschaft f: **~ to compromise** Kompro-

mißbereitschaft. **2.** (Bereit)Willigkeit f.

wil·low ['wɪləʊ] s ♣ Weide f. '**wil·low·y** adj gertenschlank.

'**will,pow·er** s Willenskraft f.

wil·ly-nil·ly [,wɪlɪ'nɪlɪ] adv wohl od. übel.

wilt [wɪlt] v/i **1.** verwelken, welk werden. **2.** schlaff werden.

wil·y ['waɪlɪ] adj gerissen, raffiniert.

win [wɪn] **I** s **1.** bsd. Sport: Sieg m: **have a ~** e-n Sieg erzielen; e-n Gewinn machen. **II** v/t (irr) **2.** gewinnen; → **day 2. 3.** j-m et. einbringen. **III** v/i (irr) **4.** gewinnen, siegen: **OK, you ~** okay, du hast gewonnen.

Verbindungen mit Adverbien:

win| back v/t zurückgewinnen. **~ out** → **win through. ~ o·ver,** v/t j-n für sich gewinnen: **win s.o. over to** j-n gewinnen für. **~ through** v/i sich durchsetzen.

wince [wɪns] v/i zs.-zucken (**at** bei).

winch [wɪntʃ] ⊛ **I** s Winde f. **II** v/t winden.

wind[1] [wɪnd] **I** s **1.** Wind m: **a load of ~** F leeres Geschwätz; **there's s.th. in the ~** fig. es liegt et. in der Luft; **find out** (od. **see) which way the ~ blows** fig. sehen, woher der Wind weht; **get ~ of s.th.** fig. Wind von et. bekommen; **get the ~ up** F Angst kriegen; **put the ~ up s.o.** F j-m Angst einjagen; **sail close to the ~ ♣** hart am Wind segeln; fig. sich hart an der Grenze des Erlaubten bewegen; **take the ~ out of s.o.'s sails** fig. j-m den Wind aus den Segeln nehmen. **2.** Atem m: **get one's ~** wieder zu Atem kommen; **get one's second ~** (bsd. Sport) die zweite Luft bekommen. **3.** ✿ Blähungen pl: **it gives me ~** davon bekomme ich Blähungen. **4. the ~ ♪** die Blasinstrumente pl; die Bläser pl. **II** v/t **5.** j-m den Atem nehmen od. verschlagen. **6.** hunt. wittern.

wind[2] [waɪnd] **I** s **1.** Umdrehung f. **II** v/t (irr) **2.** drehen (an dat); Uhr etc aufziehen. **3.** wickeln (**round** um). **III** v/i (irr) **4.** sich winden od. schlängeln (Pfad etc).

Verbindungen mit Adverbien:

wind| back v/t Film etc zurückspulen. **~ down** **I** v/t **1.** Autofenster etc herunterdrehen, -kurbeln. **2.** Produktion etc reduzieren. **II** v/i **3.** F sich entspannen. **~ for·ward** v/t Film etc weiterspulen.

up I *v/t* **1.** *Autofenster etc* hochdrehen, -kurbeln. **2.** *Uhr etc* aufziehen. **3.** *Versammlung etc* beschließen (**with** mit). **4.** *Unternehmen* auflösen. **II** *v/i* **5.** F landen (**in** in *dat*): **~ doing s.th.** am Ende et. tun; **you'll ~ with a heart attack** du kriegst noch mal e-n Herzinfarkt.

wind|·bag ['wɪndbæg] *s* F Schwätzer(in). '**~break** *s* Windschutz *m*. '**~fall** *s* **1.** *pl* Fallobst *n*. **2.** unverhofftes Geschenk, unverhoffter Gewinn.

wind·ing ['wɪndɪŋ] *adj* gewunden (*Pfad etc*): **~ stairs** *pl* Wendeltreppe *f*.

wind|in·stru·ment [wɪnd] *s* ♩ Blasinstrument *n*. **~jam·mer** ['·ˌdʒæmə] *s* ♣ Windjammer *m*.

wind·lass ['wɪndləs] *s* ⚙ Winde *f*.

wind·less ['wɪndlɪs] *adj* windstill.

wind·mill ['wɪnmɪl] *s* Windmühle *f*.

win·dow ['wɪndəʊ] *s* **1.** Fenster *n*. **2.** Schaufenster *n*. **3.** Schalter *m* (*in Bank etc*). **~ box** *s* Blumenkasten *m*. **~ clean·er** *s* Fensterputzer *m*. **~ dress·er** *s* Schaufensterdekorateur(in). **~ dress·ing** *s* **1.** Schaufensterdekoration *f*. **2.** *fig.* Mache *f*. '**~pane** *s* Fensterscheibe *f*. **~ seat** *s* Fensterplatz *m*. **~ shade** *s* *Am.* Rouleau *n*. '**~shop** *v/i*: **go ~ping** e-n Schaufensterbummel machen. '**~sill** *s* Fensterbank *f*, -brett *n*.

wind|pipe ['wɪndpaɪp] *s anat.* Luftröhre *f*. '**~screen** *s* *mot. bsd. Br.* Windschutzscheibe *f*: **~ wiper** Scheibenwischer *m*. '**~shield** *Am.* → windscreen. '**~sock** *s* Windsack *m*. '**~surf·er** *s* Windsurfer(in). '**~surf·ing** *s* Windsurfing *n*. '**~swept** *adj* (vom Wind) zerzaust. **~ tun·nel** *s* Windkanal *m*.

wind·ward ['wɪndwəd] ♣ **I** *adj* luvwärts. **II** *s* Luv(seite) *f*.

wind·y ['wɪndɪ] *adj* □ **1.** windig. **2.** ⚕ blähend.

wine [waɪn] *s* Wein *m*. **~ bar** *s* Weinlokal *n*. **~ bot·tle** *s* Weinflasche *f*. **~ glass** *s* Weinglas *n*. **~ list** *s* Weinkarte *f*.

wing [wɪŋ] *s* **1.** *allg.* Flügel *m*: **take s.o. under one's ~** *fig.* j-n unter s-e Fittiche nehmen. **2.** ✈ Tragfläche *f*. **3.** *mot. Br.* Kotflügel *m*. '**wing·er** *s* *Sport*: Flügelstürmer(in).

wing| nut *s* ⚙ Flügelmutter *f*. '**~span**, '**~spread** *s* ✈, *orn.* Flügelspannweite *f*.

wink [wɪŋk] **I** *v/i* zwinkern: **~ at** j-m zu-

zwinkern; *et.* geflissentlich übersehen. **II** *v/t*: **~ one's lights** *mot. Br.* blinken. **III** *s* Zwinkern *n*: **with a ~ of the eye** augenzwinkernd; **give s.o. a ~** j-m zuzwinkern; **I didn't get a ~ of sleep** (*od.* **I didn't sleep a ~**) **last night** ich habe letzte Nacht kein Auge zugetan; → **forty I**. '**wink·er** *s* *mot. Br.* F Blinker *m*.

win·kle ['wɪŋkl] *v/t*: **~ out** *bsd. Br.* F Wahrheit etc herausholen (**of** aus).

win·ner ['wɪnə] *s* **1.** Gewinner(in), (*bsd. Sport*) Sieger(in). **2. be a real winner** F ein Riesenerfolg sein. '**win·ning I** *adj* **1.** siegreich, Sieger..., Sieges...: **~ post** Zielpfosten *m*. *fig.* gewinnend (*Lächeln etc*). **II** *s pl* **3.** Gewinn *m*.

win·ter ['wɪntə] **I** *s* Winter *m*: **in** (**the**) **~** im Winter. **II** *adj* Winter...: **~ sports** *pl* Wintersport *m*. **III** *v/i* überwintern; den Winter verbringen. '**win·ter·ize** *v/t* *Am.* Auto etc winterfest machen. '**win·ter·y** → **wintry**.

'**win·ter·time** *s* Winter(zeit *f*) *m*: **in** (**the**) **~** im Winter.

win·try ['wɪntrɪ] *adj* **1.** winterlich, Winter...: **~ clouds** *pl* Schneewolken *pl*. **2.** *fig.* frostig (*Lächeln*).

wipe [waɪp] **I** *s*: **give s.th. a ~** et. abwischen. **II** *v/t* Tisch etc (ab)wischen; Krümel etc wischen (**off** von): **~ one's feet** (*shoes*) sich die Füße (Schuhe) abputzen (**on** auf *dat*); **~ one's nose** sich die Nase putzen; **~ clean** Tafel etc abwischen; **that'll ~ the smile off his face** *fig.* da wird ihm das Lachen vergehen; **~ the floor with s.o.** F j-n fertigmachen.

Verbindungen mit Adverbien:

wipe| a·way *v/t* wegwischen, sich die Tränen ab- *od.* wegwischen. **~ off** *v/t* ab-, wegwischen. **~ out** *v/t* **1.** auswischen. **2.** *Menschen* auslöschen, *Rasse* ausrotten. **3.** *Gewinn etc* zunichte machen. **4.** F j-n schlauchen. **~ up** *v/t* aufwischen.

wip·er ['waɪpə] *s* *mot.* (Scheiben)Wischer *m*.

wire [waɪə] **I** *s* **1.** Draht *m*. **2.** ⚡ Leitung *f*. **3.** *Am.* Telegramm *n*. **II** *v/t* **4.** *a.* **~ up** Leitungen verlegen in (*dat*). **5.** *Am.* j-m ein Telegramm schicken; j-m et. telegrafieren. '**~ net·ting** *s* Maschendraht *m*. '**~tap** *v/t* j-n, j-s Telefon abhören. **~ wool** *s* Stahlwolle *f*.

wir·y ['waɪərɪ] *adj* drahtig (*Figur etc*).

wis·dom ['wɪzdəm] *s* Weisheit *f*, Klugheit *f*. **~ tooth** *s* (*irr* **tooth**) Weisheitszahn *m*.

wise [waɪz] **I** *adj* (□ → **wisely**) weise, klug: *you were ~ to do that* es war klug von dir, das zu tun; *it's easy to be ~ after the event* hinterher kann man leicht klüger sein; *be none the ~r* nicht klüger sein als vorher; *get ~ to s.th.* F et. spitzkriegen; *~ guy* F Klugschwätzer *m*. **II** *v/t*: *~ up bsd. Am.* F *j-n* aufklären (**to** über *acc*). **III** *v/i*: *~ up to bsd. Am.* F et. spitzkriegen. **'~crack** F **I** *v/i* witzeln (**about** über *acc*). **II** *s* Witzelei *f*: *you and your ~s contp.* du u. deine dummen Sprüche.

wise·ly ['waɪzlɪ] *adv* **1.** weise, klug. **2.** klugerweise.

wish [wɪʃ] **I** *v/t* **1.** *I ~ he were here* ich wünschte *od.* wollte, er wäre hier. **2.** wollen: *I ~ to make a complaint* ich möchte mich beschweren. **3.** *j-m et.* wünschen: *~ s.o. well* j-m alles Gute wünschen; *I wouldn't ~ that on my worst enemy* das würde ich nicht einmal m-m ärgsten Feind wünschen. **II** *v/i* **4.** *if you ~* (**to**) wenn du willst. **5.** *~ for s.th.* sich et. wünschen. **III** *s* **6.** Wunsch *m* (**for** nach): *make a ~* sich et. wünschen; (**with**) *best ~es* Herzliche Grüße (*Briefschluß*); *best ~es on passing your exam* herzlichen Glückwunsch zur bestandenen Prüfung; *send one's best ~es for s.o.'s birthday* j-m e-n Glückwunsch zum Geburtstag schicken. **'~bone** *s* Gabelbein *n*, -knochen *m*.

wish·ful ['wɪʃfʊl] *adj*: *~ thinking* Wunschdenken *n*.

wish·y-wash·y ['wɪʃɪˌwɒʃɪ] *adj* F **1.** labb(e)rig. **2.** *fig.* lasch (*Person*); verschwommen (*Vorstellung etc*).

wisp [wɪsp] *s* (*Gras-, Haar*)Büschel *n*.

wist·ful ['wɪstfʊl] *adj* □ wehmütig.

wit [wɪt] *s* **1.** Geist *m*, Witz *m*. **2.** geistreicher Mensch. **3.** *a. pl* Verstand *m*: *be at one's ~s' end* mit s-r Weisheit am Ende sein; *frighten s.o. out of his ~s* j-n zu Tode erschrecken; *keep one's ~s a-bout one* e-n klaren Kopf behalten.

witch [wɪtʃ] *s* Hexe *f*. **'~craft** *s* Hexerei *f*. **~ doc·tor** *s* Medizinmann *m*. **~ hunt** *s pol.* Hexenjagd *f* (**for, against** auf *acc*).

with [wɪð] *prp* **1.** *allg.* mit: *are you still ~ me?* kannst du mir folgen? **2.** bei: *she's staying ~ a friend* sie wohnt bei e-r Freundin; *~ will*[1] *etc.* **3.** vor (*dat*): → *tremble* I, *etc.* **4.** von: → *part* 12, *etc.* **5.** für: *are you ~ me or against me?* bist du für *od.* gegen mich?

with·draw (*irr* **draw**) **I** *v/t* **1.** Geld abheben (**from** von). **2.** Angebot *etc* zurückziehen, Anschuldigung *etc* zurücknehmen: *~ from the market* vom Markt nehmen. **3.** ✕ Truppen zurück-, abziehen. **II** *v/i* **4.** sich zurückziehen. **5.** zurücktreten (**from** von). **with·draw·al** *s* **1.** *make a ~* Geld abheben (**from** von). **2.** Rücknahme *f*. **3.** ✕ Ab-, Rückzug *m*. **4.** Rücktritt *m* (**from** von). **II** *adj* **5.** *~ symptoms pl* ☤ Entziehungs-, Entzugserscheinungen *pl*.

with·er ['wɪðə] *v/i* eingehen, verdorren. **'with·er·ing** *adj* □ vernichtend (*Blick etc*).

with·'hold *v/t* (*irr* **hold**) Informationen, Zahlung *etc* zurückhalten: *~ s.th. from s.o.* j-m et. vorenthalten. **~'in** *prp* innerhalb (*gen*): → *income, sight* 3, *etc.* **~'out** *prp* ohne (*acc*). **~'stand** *v/t* (*irr* **stand**) **1.** e-m Angriff *etc* standhalten. **2.** Beanspruchung *etc* aushalten.

wit·less ['wɪtlɪs] *adj* □ geistlos.

wit·ness ['wɪtnɪs] **I** *s* **1.** *allg.* Zeuge *m*, Zeugin *f*: *~ for the defence* (*Am. defense*) ⚖ Entlastungszeuge; *~ for the prosecution* ⚖ Belastungszeuge. **II** *v/t* **2.** Zeuge sein (*gen*); *Veränderungen etc* erleben: *did anybody ~ the accident?* hat j-d den Unfall gesehen? **3.** *et.* bezeugen, *Unterschrift* beglaubigen. **4.** *~* denken Sie nur an (*acc*). **III** *v/i* **5.** *~ to et.* bezeugen. **~ box** *s bsd. Br.*, **~ stand** *s Am.* Zeugenstand *m*.

wit·ti·cism ['wɪtɪsɪzəm] *s* geistreiche *od.* witzige Bemerkung.

wit·ty ['wɪtɪ] *adj* □ geistreich, witzig.

wives [waɪvz] *pl von* **wife**.

wiz·ard ['wɪzəd] *s* **1.** Zauberer *m*, Hexenmeister *m*. **2.** *fig.* Genie *n* (**at** in *dat*): *financial ~* ☤ Finanzgenie.

wiz·ened ['wɪznd] *adj* verhutzelt.

wob·ble ['wɒbl] **I** *v/i* wackeln (*Tisch etc*), zittern (*Stimme etc*), schwabbeln (*Pudding etc*), *mot.* flattern (*Reifen etc*). **II** *v/t* wackeln an (*dat*).

woe [wəʊ] *s* Kummer *m*, Leid *n*: **~ betide**

you if wehe, wenn du; *tale of ~* Leidensgeschichte f. **woe·ful** ['~fʊl] adj □ bedauerlich, beklagenswert.

woke [wəʊk] pret von **wake²**. **'wok·en** pp von **wake²**.

wolf [wʊlf] **I** pl **wolves** [wʊlvz] s **1.** zo. Wolf m: **a ~ in sheep's clothing** fig. ein Wolf im Schafspelz; **lone ~** fig. Einzelgänger m; **cry ~** fig. blinden Alarm schlagen. **2.** F Schürzenjäger m. **II** v/t **3.** a. **~ down** F Essen hinunterschlingen. **~ whis·tle** s F bewundernder Pfiff: **give s.o. a ~** j-m nachpfeifen.

wolves [wʊlvz] pl von **wolf**.

wom·an ['wʊmən] **I** pl **wom·en** ['wɪmɪn] s Frau f. **II** adj: **~ doctor** Ärztin f; **~ driver** Frau f am Steuer; **~ teacher** Lehrerin f. **~ hat·er** s Frauenhasser m.

wom·an·ish ['wʊmənɪʃ] adj □ contp. weibisch.

wom·an·ize ['wʊmənaɪz] v/i hinter den Frauen hersein. **'wom·an·iz·er** s Schürzenjäger m.

wom·an·kind [,wʊmən'kaɪnd] s das weibliche Geschlecht. **'wom·an·ly** adj fraulich (*Figur etc*); weiblich (*Tugend etc*).

womb [wuːm] s anat. Gebärmutter f, Mutterleib m.

wom·en ['wɪmɪn] pl von **woman**: **~'s movement** Frauenbewegung f; **~'s team** (*Sport*) Damenmannschaft f.

won [wʌn] pret u. pp von **win**.

won·der ['wʌndə] **I** v/t **1.** neugierig od. gespannt sein, gern wissen mögen (*if, whether* ob; *what* was); sich fragen, überlegen: **I ~ if you could help me** vielleicht können Sie mir helfen. **II** v/i **2.** sich wundern, erstaunt sein (*about* über acc). **3.** neugierig od. gespannt sein: **well, I ~** na, ich weiß nicht (recht). **III** s **4.** Staunen n, Verwunderung f: **in ~** erstaunt, verwundert. **5.** Wunder n: **nine days' ~** Eintagsfliege f; **it's a ~ (that)** es ist ein Wunder, daß; **(it's) no** (*od.* **small, little**) **~ (that)** kein Wunder, daß; **~s will never cease!** humor. es geschehen noch Zeichen u. Wunder!; **do** (*od.* **work**) **~s** wahre Wunder vollbringen, Wunder wirken (**for** bei). **IV** adj **6.** Wunder... **won·der·ful** ['~fʊl] adj □ wunderbar.

'won·der·land s **1.** Wunderland n. **2.** Paradies n.

won·ky ['wɒŋkɪ] adj Br. F **1.** wack(e)lig. **2.** schwach (*Herz*).

wont [wəʊnt] adj: **be ~ to do s.th.** et. zu tun pflegen.

won't [wəʊnt] F für **will not**.

woo [wuː] v/t j-n umwerben.

wood [wʊd] s **1.** Holz n: → **touch** 8. **2.** a. pl Wald m: **be out of the ~** (*Am.* **~s**) fig. über den Berg sein; **he can't see the ~ for trees** fig. er sieht den Wald vor lauter Bäumen nicht. **'~cut** s Holzschnitt m.

wood·ed ['wʊdɪd] adj bewaldet.

wood·en ['wʊdn] adj hölzern (a. fig.), Holz... **'~head·ed** adj F dämlich.

wood·land ['wʊdlənd] s Waldland n, Waldung f. **'~peck·er** s orn. Specht m. **'~pile** s Holzhaufen m, -stoß m. **'~shed** s Holzschuppen m. **~wind** ['~wɪnd] ♪ **I** s: **the ~** die Holzblasinstrumente pl; die Holzbläser pl. **II** adj: **~ instrument** Holzblasinstrument n. **'~worm** s zo. Holzwurm m.

wood·y ['wʊdɪ] adj **1.** waldig. **2.** holzig.

wool [wʊl] s Wolle f: **pull the ~ over s.o.'s eyes** fig. j-m Sand in die Augen streuen. **wool·en** ['~ən] Am., **wool·len** ['~ən] bsd. Br. **I** adj wollen, Woll... **II** s pl Wollsachen pl, -kleidung f. **'wool·ly**, Am. a. **'wool·y** adj **1.** → **woolen** 1. **2.** wollig. **3.** fig. wirr.

Worces·ter sauce ['wʊstə] s Worcestersoße f.

word [wɜːd] **I** s **1.** allg. Wort n: **beyond ~s** unbeschreiblich; **by ~ of mouth** mündlich; **~ for ~** Wort für Wort; wortwörtlich; **in a ~** in 'einem Wort; **in other ~s** mit anderen Worten; **in one's own ~s** in eigenen Worten; **in ~ and in deed** in Worten u. in Taten; **angry isn't the ~ for ...** ärgerlich ist gar kein Ausdruck für ...; **he's a man of few ~s** er macht nicht viele Worte; **be as good as one's ~** halten, was man verspricht; **break one's ~** sein Wort brechen; **get** (*od.* **have**) **the final** (*od.* **last**) **~** das letzte Wort haben (**on** in (*dat*); **give s.o. one's ~** (*of* hono[u]r) j-m sein (Ehren)Wort geben; **he always has to have the last ~** er muß immer das letzte Wort haben; **can I have a** (*od.* **a few ~s**) **with you?** kann ich Sie mal kurz sprechen?; **have ~s** e-e Auseinandersetzung haben (**with** mit); **keep one's ~**

Wort halten (*to* gegenüber); **put into** ~s et. ausdrücken, in Worte fassen; **take s.o. at his** ~ j-n beim Wort nehmen; → **eat** 2, **edgeways, fail** 5, **mum**¹ I, **play** 4. **2.** *pl* Text *m* (*e-s Lieds etc*). **3.** Nachricht *f*: **there's been no** ~ **from her for months** wir haben schon seit Monaten nichts mehr von ihr gehört; **send** ~ **that** Nachricht geben, daß. **II** *v/t* **4.** et. ausdrücken, *Text* abfassen, formulieren. '**word·ing** *s* Wortlaut *m*. '**word·less** *adj* □ wortlos, stumm.

word| **or·der** *s ling.* Wortstellung *f.* '**~·play** *s* Wortspielereien *pl.* ~ **pro·cess·or** *s Computer*: Wort-, Textverarbeitungsgerät *n*.

word·y ['wɜːdɪ] *adj* □ wortreich, langatmig.

wore [wɔː] *pret von* **wear**.

work [wɜːk] **I** *s* **1.** *allg.* Arbeit *f*: **at** ~ am Arbeitsplatz; **be out of** ~ arbeitslos sein; **make short** ~ **of** kurzen Prozeß machen mit. **2.** Werk *n* (*a. Tat*): → **art** 1. **3.** *pl* (*oft sg konstruiert*) Werk *n*, Fabrik *f*. **4.** ⊙ Werk *n*, Getriebe *n*: → **spanner**. **5.** *the whole* ~*s pl* F der ganze Krempel. **II** *v/i* **6.** arbeiten (**at, on** an *dat*): → **rule** 2. **7.** funktionieren (*a. fig.*). **III** *v/t* **8.** *j-n* arbeiten lassen: ~ **o.s. into a temper** F sich in e-n Wutausbruch hineinsteigern. **9.** *Maschine etc* bedienen. **10.** bewirken: **how did you** ~ **it?** F wie hast du das geschafft?; → **miracle, wonder** 5. **11.** ~ **s.th. into** *fig.* et. einbauen in (*acc*).

Verbindungen mit Adverbien:

work| **in** *v/t* Zitate etc einbauen. ~ **off** *v/t* **1.** *Schulden* abarbeiten. **2.** *Zorn etc* abreagieren (**on** an *dat*). ~ **out** **I** *v/t* **1.** ausrechnen; *fig.* sich *et.* zs.-reimen. **2.** *Plan etc* ausarbeiten. **II** *v/i* **3.** klappen: **it'll never** ~ daraus kann nichts werden. **4.** aufgehen (*Rechnung etc*): **it didn't** ~ *fig.* die Rechnung ist nicht aufgegangen. **5.** F trainieren. ~ **o·ver** *v/t* F *j-n* zs.-schlagen. ~ **up** *v/t* **1.** *Zuhörer etc* aufpeitschen, -wühlen: **be worked up** aufgeregt *od.* nervös sein (**about** wegen). **2.** sich *Appetit etc* holen; *Begeisterung etc* aufbringen. **3.** *et.* ausarbeiten (**into** zu).

work·a·ble ['wɜːkəbl] *adj* **1.** formbar. **2.** *fig.* durchführbar.

'**work·a·day** *adj* Alltags...

work·a·hol·ic [ˌwɜːkə'hɒlɪk] *s* F Arbeitssüchtige *m*, *f*.

'**work**|**·bench** *s* ⊙ Werkbank *f.* '**~·book** *s ped.* Arbeitsheft *n.* ~ **camp** *s* Arbeitslager *n.* ~ **coat** *s Am.* Arbeitsmantel *m*, Kittel *m.* '**~·day** *s* **1.** Arbeitstag *m.* **2.** Werktag *m*.

work·er ['wɜːkə] *s* **1.** Arbeiter(in), Angestellte *m*, *f.* **2. be a real** ~ hart arbeiten.

work force *s* **1.** Belegschaft *f.* **2.** Arbeitskräftepotential *n*.

work·ing ['wɜːkɪŋ] **I** *adj* **1.** Arbeits...: ~ **breakfast** Arbeitsfrühstück *n*; ~ **capital** ✝ Betriebskapital *n*; ~ **day** → **workday**; ~ **hours** *pl* Arbeitszeit *f*; ~ **hypothesis** Arbeitshypothese *f*; **a knowledge of French** französische Grundkenntnisse *pl*; **have a** ~ **knowledge of** ein bißchen was verstehen von; **in** ~ **order** in betriebsfähigem Zustand. **2.** arbeitend, berufstätig: ~ **class(es)** *pl* Arbeiterklasse *f.* **II** *s* **3.** ⊙ Arbeits-, Funktionsweise *f*.

'**work**|**·load** *s* Arbeitspensum *n.* **~·man** ['~mən] *s* (*irr* **man**) Handwerker *m.* '**~·out** *s* F Training *n.* ~ **per·mit** *s* Arbeitserlaubnis *f*, -genehmigung *f.* '**~· place** *s* Arbeitsplatz *m*: **at the** ~ am Arbeitsplatz. '**~·shop** *s* **1.** Werkstatt *f.* **2.** Workshop *m* (*Seminar*). '**~·shy** *adj* arbeitsscheu. ~ **stud·y** *s* Arbeitsstudie *f.* '**~·top** *s* Arbeitsplatte *f.* ~ **to-'rule** *s* *Br.* Dienst *m* nach Vorschrift.

world [wɜːld] **I** *s allg.* Welt *f*: **in the** ~ auf der Welt; **what in the** ~ **...?** was um alles in der Welt ...?; **a man of the** ~ ein Mann von Welt; **all over the** ~ in der ganzen Welt; **they are** ~**s apart** zwischen ihnen liegen Welten; **bring into the** ~ auf die Welt bringen; **do s.o. a** (*od. the*) ~ **of good** j-m unwahrscheinlich gut tun; **mean all the** ~ **to s.o.** j-m alles bedeuten. **II** *adj* Welt...: ~ **cham·pion** Weltmeister(in); ~ **championship** Weltmeisterschaft *f*; ♀ **Cup** (*Sport*) Weltcup *m*, -pokal *m*; Fußballweltmeisterschaft *f*; ~ **language** Weltsprache *f*; ~ **power** *pol.* Weltmacht *f*; ~ **record** Weltrekord *m*; ~ **record holder** Weltrekordler(in); ~ **war** Weltkrieg *m*. '**~·beat·er** *s*: **be a** ~ unschlagbar sein. '**~·fa·mous** *adj* weltberühmt.

world·ly ['wɜːldlɪ] *adj* **1.** weltlich, irdisch.

2. weltlich (gesinnt). ,~-'**wise** *adj* weltklug.

'**world-wide** *adj* weltweit, *adv* a. auf der ganzen Welt.

worm [wɜːm] **I** s **1.** *zo.* Wurm *m.* **II** *v/t* **2.** *Hund etc* entwurmen. **3.** ~ **one's way through** sich schlängeln *od.* winden durch; ~ **o.s. into s.o.'s confidence** sich in j-s Vertrauen einschleichen. **4.** ~ **s.th. out of s.o.** *fig.* j-m et. entlocken. '~-,**eat-en** *adj* wurmstichig. '~**hole** s Wurmloch *n.* '~**wood** s ⅋ Wermut *m.*

worm-y ['wɜːmɪ] *adj* **1.** wurmig. **2.** wurmstichig.

worn [wɔːn] *pp von* **wear.** ,~-'**out** *adj* **1.** abgenutzt, abgetragen (*Kleidung*). **2.** *fig.* erschöpft (*Person*).

wor-ried ['wʌrɪd] *adj* besorgt, beunruhigt: **be** ~ sich sorgen, sich Sorgen machen (**about** über *acc,* um, wegen). **wor-ri-some** ['~səm] *adj* besorgniserregend, beunruhigend. '**wor-ry** **I** *v/t* **1.** j-n beunruhigen, j-m Sorgen machen. **II** *v/i* **2.** sich sorgen, sich Sorgen machen (**a-bout, over** über *acc,* um, wegen): **not to** ~ mach dir keine Gedanken; ~ **at** sich abmühen mit. **III** s Sorge *f.* '**wor-ry-ing** *adj* → **worrisome.**

worse [wɜːs] **I** *adj u. adv* schlechter, schlimmer: ~ **still** was noch schlimmer ist; **to make matters** ~ zu allem Übel; **he's getting steadily** ~ sein Zustand verschlechtert sich immer mehr; → **wear** 1. **II** s Schlechteres *n,* Schlimmeres *n:* → **bad** 7, **turn** 4. '**wors-en** **I** *v/t* schlechter machen, verschlechtern. **II** *v/i* schlechter werden, sich verschlechtern.

wor-ship ['wɜːʃɪp] **I** *v/t pret u. pp* -**shiped,** *bsd. Br.* -**shipped** **1.** Gott anbeten, *a. Ahnen, Helden* verehren; *weitS.* j-n anbeten, vergöttern: ~ **God** *a.* zu Gott beten. **II** *v/i* **2.** Anbetung *f,* Verehrung *f.* **3.** Gottesdienst *m.* '**wor-ship-(p)er** s **1.** Anbeter(in), Verehrer(in). **2.** Kirchgänger(in).

worst [wɜːst] **I** *adj* schlechtest, schlimmst: **of the** ~ **kind** der übelsten Sorte. **II** *adv* am schlechtesten *od.* schlimmsten: **come off** ~ den kürzeren ziehen (**in** bei). **III** s der, die, das Schlechteste *od.* Schlimmste: **at (the)** ~ schlimmstenfalls; **if the** ~ **comes to the** ~ wenn alle Stricke reißen; **the** ~ **of it is**

that das Schlimmste daran ist, daß; **get the** ~ den kürzeren ziehen (**of** bei).

wor-sted ['wʊstɪd] s Kammgarn *n.*

worth [wɜːθ] **I** *adj* **1.** ~ **£10** es ist 10 Pfund wert; **a skirt** ~ **£20** ein Rock im Wert von 20 Pfund; **it's** ~ **a try** es ist e-n Versuch wert; **it isn't** ~ **it** es lohnt sich nicht; **it might be** ~ **your while** es könnte sich für dich lohnen (**to do** zu tun); ~ **mentioning** erwähnenswert; **not** ~ **mentioning** nicht der Rede wert; **it isn't** ~ **waiting any longer** es lohnt sich nicht, noch länger zu warten; → **candle, salt** 1. **II** s Wert *m.* '**worth-less** □ wertlos. ,**worth'while** *adj* lohnend: **be** ~ sich lohnen. **wor-thy** ['wɜːðɪ] □ würdig: ~ **of admiration** bewunderns-, bewundernswürdig.

would [wʊd] *v/aux* **1.** *konditional:* **he said he** ~ **come** er sagte, er werde kommen; **he** ~ **have come if** er wäre gekommen, wenn ...; **what** ~ **you do if ...?** was würdest du tun, wenn ...?; **how** ~ **you know?** woher willst du denn das wissen?; **you** ~**n't understand** das verstehst du sowieso nicht; **you** ~, ~**n't you?** F das sieht dir ähnlich! **2.** *Bereitschaft, Entschluß:* **he** ~**n't tell us what had happened** er wollte uns nicht sagen, was passiert war; **the door** ~**n't shut** die Tür schloß nicht; **I** ~ **rather not say what I think** ich sage lieber nicht, was ich denke. **3.** *höfliche Bitte:* **shut the window,** ~ **you?** mach doch bitte das Fenster zu. **4.** *Wiederholung:* **he** ~ **often take a walk after supper** er machte nach dem Abendessen oft e-n Spaziergang. '~-**be** *adj contp.* Möchtegern...

wouldn't ['wʊdnt] F *für* **would not.**

wound¹ [wuːnd] **I** s Wunde *f,* Verletzung *f:* **open old** ~**s** *fig.* alte Wunden aufreißen; → **rub** 3. **II** *v/t* j-n verwunden, verletzen; *fig.* j-s Stolz etc verletzen.

wound² [waʊnd] *pret u. pp von* **wind².**

wove [wəʊv] *pret von* **weave.** '**wov-en** *pp von* **weave.**

wow [waʊ] *int* F wow!, Mann!, Mensch!

wran-gle ['ræŋgl] **I** *v/i* (sich) streiten (**with** mit; **over** um). **II** s Streit *m.*

wrap [ræp] **I** *v/t* **1.** *a.* ~ **up** einpacken, -wickeln (**in** in *acc*). **2.** *et.* wickeln ([a]**round** um). **3.** ~ **up** F *Handel etc* unter Dach u. Fach bringen. **II** *v/i* **4.**

up sich warm anziehen. **5.** ~ *up!* F Schnauze! **III** *s* **6.** *bsd. Am.* Umhang *m.* **7.** F *be still under* ~s noch geheim sein; *keep under* ~s *et.* geheimhalten. '**wrap·per** *s Br.* (Schutz)Umschlag *m.* '**wrap·ping I** *s* Verpackung *f.* **II** *adj:* ~ *paper* Einwickel-, Packpapier *n.*

wrath [rɒθ] *s* Zorn *m.*

wreath [riːθ] *pl* **wreaths** [riːðz] *s* Kranz *m.*

wreck [rek] **I** *s* **1.** ⚓ Wrack *n* (*a. fig.* Person). **II** *v/t* **2.** *be* ~*ed* ⚓ zerschellen; Schiffbruch erleiden. **3.** *fig.* zunichte machen. '**wreck·age** *s* Trümmer *pl* (*a. fig.*), ⚓ *a.* Wrackteile *pl.* '**wreck·er** *s mot. Am.* Abschleppwagen *m.*

wren [ren] *s orn.* Zaunkönig *m.*

wrench [rentʃ] **I** *v/t* **1.** ~ *s.th. from* (*od. out of*) *s.o.'s hand* j-m et. aus der Hand winden; *die Hände etc* mit e-m Ruck aufschrauben. **2.** ~ sich *das Knie etc* verrenken. **II** *s* **3.** ☞ Verrenkung *f.* **4.** ⊙ *Br.* Franzose *m; Am.* Schraubenschlüssel *m.*

wrest [rest] *v/t:* ~ *s.th. from* (*od. out of*) *s.o.'s hand* j-m et. aus der Hand reißen.

wres·tle ['resl] **I** *v/i* **1.** ringen (*with* mit). **2.** *fig.* ringen, kämpfen (*with* mit; *for* um). **II** *v/t* **3.** *Sport:* ringen gegen. '**wres·tler** *s Sport:* Ringer *m.* '**wres·tling** (*Sport*) **I** *s* Ringen *n.* **II** *adj* Ring...: ~ *match* Ringkampf *m.*

wretch [retʃ] *s* **1.** *a. poor* ~ armer Teufel. **2.** *oft humor.* Wicht *m.* **wretch·ed** ['~ɪd] *adj* □ **1.** elend; (tod)unglücklich. **2.** scheußlich (*Kopfschmerzen, Wetter etc*). **3.** verflixt.

wrig·gle ['rɪgl] **I** *v/i* sich winden, zappeln; ~ *out of fig.* sich herauswinden aus; sich drücken vor (*dat*). **II** *v/t* mit *den Zehen* wackeln.

wring [rɪŋ] *v/t* (*irr*) **1.** j-m *die Hand* drücken; *die Hände* ringen. **2.** *oft* ~ *out Wäsche etc* auswringen: ~ *the truth out of s.o.* die Wahrheit aus j-m herausholen. '**wring·ing** *adv:* ~ *wet* klatschnaß.

wrin·kle¹ ['rɪŋkl] **I** *s* Falte *f,* Runzel *f.* **II** *v/t a.* ~ *up Stirn* runzeln, *Nase* rümpfen. **III** *v/i* faltig *od.* runz(e)lig werden.

wrin·kle² [~] *s* F Kniff *m,* Trick *m.*

wrist [rɪst] *s* Handgelenk *n.* '**~band** *s* Armband *n.*

wrist·let ['rɪstlɪt] *s* Armband *n.*
'**wrist-watch** *s* Armbanduhr *f.*

writ [rɪt] *s* ⚖ Befehl *m,* Verfügung *f.*

write [raɪt] (*irr*) **I** *v/t* **1.** *Buch etc, j-m e-n Brief etc* schreiben: *it was written on* (*od. all over*) *his face fig.* es stand ihm im Gesicht geschrieben. **2.** *bsd. Am.* j-m schreiben. **II** *v/i* **3.** schreiben: ~ *to s.o.* j-m schreiben; → *home* 8.
Verbindungen mit Adverbien:
write | *back v/i* zurückschreiben. ~ *down v/t* aufschreiben, niederschreiben. ~ *in v/i* schreiben (*to* an *acc*): ~ *for et.* anfordern. ~ *off v/t* **1.** j-n, ✝ et. abschreiben. **2.** *bsd. Br. Wagen* zu Schrott fahren. ~ *out v/t* **1.** *Namen etc* ausschreiben. **2.** *Bericht etc* ausarbeiten. **3.** *j-m e-e Quittung etc* ausstellen. **4.** *Rundfunk, TV:* j-n herausschreiben (*of* aus *e-r Serie*). ~ *up v/t* **1.** *Notizen etc* ausarbeiten. **2.** berichten über (*acc*); *et.* besprechen.

'**write-off** *s* **1.** ✝ Abschreibung *f.* **2.** *bsd. Br.* Totalschaden *m.*

writ·er ['raɪtə] *s* **1.** Schreiber(in), Verfasser(in), Autor(in). **2.** Schriftsteller(in).

'**write-up** *s* (Presse)Bericht *m;* Besprechung *f,* Kritik *f.*

writhe [raɪð] *v/i* sich krümmen *od.* winden (*in, with* vor *dat*).

writ·ing ['raɪtɪŋ] *s* **1.** Schreiben *n* (*Tätigkeit*). **2.** (Hand)Schrift *f.* **3.** *pl* Werke *pl.* **4.** *in* ~ schriftlich. **II** *adj* **5.** Schreib...: ~ *desk* Schreibtisch *m;* ~ *paper* Schreibpapier *n.*

writ·ten ['rɪtn] **I** *pp von* **write.** **II** *adj* schriftlich: ~ *language* Schriftsprache *f.*

wrong [rɒŋ] **I** *adj* (□ → **wrongly**) **1.** falsch: *be* ~ falsch sein, nicht stimmen; unrecht haben; falsch gehen (*Uhr*). **2.** unrecht: *you were* ~ *to say that* es war nicht recht *od.* richtig von dir, das zu sagen. **3.** *is anything* ~? ist et. nicht in Ordnung? *what's* ~ *with you?* was ist los mit dir?, was hast du? **II** *adv* **4.** falsch: *get* ~ j-n, *et.* falsch verstehen; *go* ~ e-n Fehler machen; kaputtgehen; *fig.* schiefgehen. **III** *s* **5.** Unrecht *n:* *be in the* ~ im Unrecht sein. **IV** *v/t* **6.** j-m Unrecht tun. '~**do·er** *s* Misse-, Übeltäter(in). '~**'do·ing** *s* **1.** Missetat(en *pl*) *f.* **2.** Vergehen *n od. pl.*

wrong·ful ['rɒŋfʊl] *adj* □ **1.** ungerecht-

fertigt. **2.** gesetzwidrig: ~ *imprisonment* Freiheitsberaubung *f*.
,**wrong'head·ed** *adj* □ **1.** querköpfig,
verbohrt (*Person*). **2.** verschroben
(*Ideen etc*).
wrong·ly ['rɒŋlı] *adv* zu Unrecht; fälschlicherweise.

wrote [rəʊt] *pret von* **write**.
wrought [rɔːt] *adj:* ~ *iron* Schmiedeeisen
n. ,**~'i·ron** *adj* schmiedeeisern. ,**~-pt**
adj aufgeregt, nervös.
wrung [rʌŋ] *pret u. pp von* **wring**.
wry [raɪ] *adj* süßsauer (*Lächeln*); sarkastisch (*Humor*).

X

Xmas ['eksməs, 'krısməs] F → *Christmas*.
X-ray ['eksreɪ] **I** *v/t* **1.** röntgen. **II** *s* **2.**

Röntgenaufnahme *f*, -bild *n*. **3.** Rönt-
genuntersuchung *f*.
xy·lo·phone ['zaɪləfəʊn] *s* ♪ Xylophon *n*.

Y

yacht [jɒt] **I** *s* Jacht *f*; (*Sport*) (Segel)Boot *n*. **II** *v/i* segeln: *go ~ing* segeln
gehen. '**yacht·ing** *s* Segeln *n*.
yachts·man ['jɒtsmən] *s* (*irr man*) *Sport*:
Segler *m*. '**yachts,wom·an** *s* (*irr woman*) *Sport*: Seglerin *f*.
yank [jæŋk] F **I** *v/t* reißen an (*dat*): ~ *out*
(her)ausreißen, *Zahn* ziehen. **II** *v/i:* ~
on reißen an (*dat*). **III** *s* Ruck *m*.
Yan·kee ['jæŋkı] *s* F Yankee *m*, Ami
m.
yap [jæp] **I** *v/i* **1.** kläffen. **2.** F quasseln. **II**
s **3.** Kläffen *n*. **4.** Gequassel *n*.
yard¹ [jɑːd] *s* Yard *n*.
yard² [~] *s* Hof *m*.
'**yard·stick** *s* fig. Maßstab *m*.
yarn [jɑːn] *s* **1.** Garn *n*. **2.** F *spin a ~* Garn
spinnen: *spin s.o. a ~ about* j-m e-e
Lügengeschichte erzählen von.
yawn [jɔːn] **I** *v/i* gähnen (*a. fig.*). **II** Gäh-
ner *m*; Gähnen *n*: *be a big ~* F zum
Gähnen (langweilig) sein.
yeah [jeə] *adv* F ja.
year [jɪə] *s* Jahr *n*: ~ *after ~* Jahr für Jahr;
~ *in, ~ out* jahraus, jahrein; *all the ~
round* das ganze Jahr hindurch; *since*

the ~ dot F seit e-r Ewigkeit; *this ~*
dieses Jahr, heuer. '**~·book** *s* Jahrbuch *n*.
year·ly ['jɪəlı] *adj u. adv* jährlich.
yearn [jɜːn] *v/i* sich sehnen (*for* nach; *to
do* danach, zu tun). '**yearn·ing I** *s*
Sehnsucht *f*. **II** *adj* □ sehnsüchtig.
yeast [jiːst] *s* Hefe *f*.
yell [jel] **I** *v/i* schreien, brüllen (*with* vor
dat): ~ *at s.o.* j-n anschreien *od.* anbrüllen. **II** *v/t a.* ~ *out et.* schreien, brüllen.
III *s* Schrei *m*.
yel·low ['jeləʊ] **I** *adj* **1.** gelb: ~ *fever* ﹩
Gelbfieber *n*; ~ *pages pl teleph.* gelbe
Seiten *pl*, Branchenverzeichnis *n*; ~
press Sensationspresse *f*. **2.** F feig. **II** *s*
3. Gelb *n*: *at ~ Am.* bei Gelb; *the lights
were at ~ Am.* die Ampel stand auf
Gelb. **III** *v/i* **4.** gelb werden, sich gelb
färben (*Blätter etc*), vergilben (*Papier*).
yelp [jelp] **I** *v/i* aufschreien, (*Hund etc*)
(auf)jaulen. **II** *s* Aufschrei *m*, (Auf)Jau-
len *n*.
yep [jep] *adv* F ja.
yes [jes] **I** *adv* ja: ~ *and no* ja u. nein; *oh ~*

o doch, o ja. **II** s Ja n. **~ man** s (irr **man**) contp. Jasager m.

yes·ter·day ['jestədi] **I** adv gestern: **~ morning** gestern morgen; **the day before ~** vorgestern; **I wasn't born ~** ich bin (doch) nicht von gestern. **II** s: **~'s paper** die gestrige Zeitung.

yet [jet] **I** adv **1.** fragend: schon. **2.** noch: **not ~** noch nicht; **as ~** bis jetzt, bisher. **3.** (doch) noch. **4.** doch, aber. **II** cj **5.** aber, doch.

ye·ti ['jeti] s Yeti m, Schneemensch m.

yew [ju:] s 🌲 Eibe f.

Yid·dish ['jıdıʃ] s ling. Jiddisch n.

yield [ji:ld] **I** v/t **1.** Früchte tragen, Gewinn abwerfen, Resultat etc ergeben, liefern. **2.** a. **~ up** ✕ Stellung etc überlassen (**to** dat). **II** v/i **3.** nachgeben (Boden etc). **4.** nachgeben; ✕ sich ergeben (**to** dat): **~ to** mot. Am. j-m Vorfahrt gewähren. **III** s **5.** Ertrag m.

yo·ga ['jəʊgə] s Joga m, n, Yoga m, n.

yog·h(o)urt, yog·urt ['jɒgət] s Joghurt m, n.

yo·gi ['jəʊgi] s Jogi m, Yogi m.

yoke [jəʊk] s Joch n (a. fig.).

yolk [jəʊk] s (Ei)Dotter m, n, Eigelb n.

you [ju:] pron **1.** (nom) du, Sie, ihr; (dat) dir, Ihnen, euch; (acc) dich, Sie, euch. **2.** man.

you'd [ju:d] F für **you had; you would.**

you'll [ju:l] F für **you will.**

young [jʌŋ] **I** adj **1.** jung. **2.** zo. Jungen pl: **with ~** trächtig. **young·ster** ['~stə] s Junge m.

your [jɔ:] possessive pron dein(e); pl euer, eure; Ihr(e) (a. pl).

you're [jʊə] F für **you are.**

yours [jɔ:z] pron dein(er, e, es); pl euer, eure(s); Ihr(er, e, es) (a. pl): **a friend of ~** ein Freund von dir.

your·self [jɔ:'self] pl **-selves** [~'selvz] pron. **1.** verstärkend: selbst: **you ~ told me, you told me ~** du hast es mir selbst erzählt. **2.** reflex dir, dich, sich: **did you hurt ~?** hast du dich verletzt?

youth [ju:θ] **I** s **1.** Jugend f: **in my ~** in meiner Jugend. **2.** Jugendliche m. **3.** coll. Jugend f. **II** adj **4.** Jugend...: **~ hostel** Jugendherberge f. **youth·ful** ['~fʊl] adj □ jugendlich.

you've [ju:v] F für **you have.**

Yu·go·slav [ju:gəʊ'slɑ:v] **I** s Jugoslawe m, -slawin f. **II** adj jugoslawisch.

Z

zeal [zi:l] s Eifer m. **zeal·ot** ['zelət] s Fanatiker(in), eccl. a. Eiferer m, Eiferin f. **zeal·ous** ['zeləs] adj □ eifrig: **be ~** eifrig bemüht sein (**for** um; **to do** darum, zu tun).

ze·bra ['zebrə, 'zi:brə] s zo. Zebra n. **~ cross·ing** s Br. Zebrastreifen m.

ze·nith ['zenıθ] s ast. Zenit m (a. fig.).

ze·ro ['zıərəʊ] **I** pl **-ro(e)s** s Null f (Am. a. teleph.), (e-r Skala a.) Nullpunkt m: **10 degrees below ~** 10 Grad unter Null. **II** adj Null... **~ growth** Nullwachstum n; **~ hour** bsd. ✕ die Stunde X; **~ option** ✕, pol. Nullösung f. **III** v/i: **~ in on** ✕ sich einschießen auf (acc) (a. fig.); fig. sich konzentrieren auf (acc).

zest [zest] s **1.** fig. Würze f. **2.** Begeisterung f: **~ for life** Lebensfreude f.

zig·zag ['zıgzæg] **I** s Zickzack m. **II** adj zickzackförmig, Zickzack... **III** v/i im Zickzack laufen, fahren etc, zickzackförmig verlaufen (Weg etc).

zinc [zıŋk] s 🜨 Zink n.

zip [zıp] **I** s **1.** Reißverschluß m. **2.** Zischen n, Schwirren n. **3.** F Schmiß m, Schwung m. **II** v/t **4.** ~ **the bag open** (shut od. up) den Reißverschluß der Tasche aufmachen (zumachen); **~ s.o. up** j-m den Reißverschluß zumachen. **III** v/i **5.** zischen, schwirren (Kugeln etc). **6.** F flitzen: **~ by** (od. past) vorbeiflitzen. **~ code** s Am. Postleitzahl f. **~ fas·ten·er** bsd. Br. → **zip** 1.

zip·per ['zɪpə] *bsd. Am.* → **zip** 1.

zo·di·ac ['zəʊdɪæk] *s ast.* Tierkreis *m*: **signs** *pl* **of the** ~ Tierkreiszeichen *pl.*

zom·bie ['zɒmbɪ] *s* Zombie *m.*

zone [zəʊn] **I** *s* Zone *f.* **II** *v/t* in Zonen einteilen.

zoo [zu:] *s* Zoo *m.*

zo·o·log·i·cal [ˌzəʊə'lɒdʒɪkl] *adj* □ zoo-logisch: ~ **gardens** *pl* Tierpark *m.*

zo·ol·o·gist [ˌʊ'ɒlədʒɪst] *s* Zoologe *m,* Zoologin *f.* **zo·ol·o·gy** *s* Zoologie *f.*

zoom [zu:m] **I** *v/i* **1.** ~ **in on** *phot. et.* heranholen. **2.** F sausen: ~ **by** (*od.* **past**) vorbeisausen. **3.** F in die Höhe schnellen (*Preise*). **II** *s* **4.** *a.* ~ **lens** *phot.* Zoom(objektiv) *n.*

Proper Names

A

A·bra·ham ['eɪbrəhæm] Abraham *m*.
A·chil·les [ə'kɪliːz] Achilles *m*.
Ad·am ['ædəm] Adam *m*.
A·dri·an ['eɪdrɪən] Adrian *m*, Adriane *f*.
A·dri·at·ic Sea [ˌeɪdrɪ'ætɪk 'siː] *das* Adriatische Meer, *die* Adria.
Ae·ge·an Sea [iːˈdʒiːən 'siː] *das* Ägäische Meer, *die* Ägäis.
Aes·chy·lus ['iːskɪləs] Äschylus *m*.
Af·ghan·i·stan [æf'gænɪstæn] Afghanistan *n*.
Af·ri·ca ['æfrɪkə] Afrika *n*.
Ag·a·tha ['æɡəθə] Agathe *f*.
Aix-la-Cha·pelle [ˌeɪksla'ʃæ'pel] Aachen *n*.
Al·ba·nia [æl'beɪnɪə] Albanien *n*.
Al·bert ['ælbət] Albert *m*.
A·leu·tian Is·lands [ə,luː'ʃən'aɪləndz] *pl die* Ale'uten *pl*.
Al·ex·an·der [ˌælɪɡ'zaːndə] Alexander *m*.
Al·ex·an·dra [ˌælɪɡ'zaːndrə] Alexandra *f*.
Al·fred ['ælfrɪd] Alfred *m*.
Al·ge·ria [æl'dʒɪərɪə] Algerien *n*.
Al·giers [æl'dʒɪəz] Algier *m*.
Al·ice ['ælɪs] Alice *f*, Else *f*.
Al·i·son ['ælɪsn] *f*.
Al·lan, Al·len ['ælən] *m*.
Al·sace [æl'sæs], **Al·sa·tia** [æl'seɪʃə] *das* Elsaß.
A·me·lia [ə'miːljə] Amalie *f*.
A·mer·i·ca [ə'merɪkə] Amerika *n*.
An·des ['ændiːz] *pl die* Anden *pl*.
An·drew ['ændruː] Andreas *m*.
Ann [æn], **An·na** ['ænə] Anna *f*, Anne *f*.
An·na·bel(le) ['ænəbel] Annabella *f*.
Anne [æn] Anna *f*, Anne *f*.
Ant·arc·ti·ca [ænt'ɑːktɪkə] *die* Antarktis.
An·tho·ny ['æntənɪ, 'ænθənɪ] Anton *m*.
An·til·les [æn'tɪliːz] *pl die* Antillen *pl*.
An·to·ny ['æntənɪ] Anton *m*.
Ap·pa·la·chians [ˌæpə'leɪtʃjənz] *pl die* Appalachen *pl*.
A·ra·bia [ə'reɪbjə] Arabien *n*.
Ar·chi·bald ['ɑːtʃɪbɔːld] Archibald *m*.
Arc·tic ['ɑːktɪk] *die* Arktis.
Ar·gen·ti·na [ˌɑːdʒən'tiːnə] Argentinien *n*.
Ar·gen·tine ['ɑːdʒəntaɪn]: *the ~* Argentinien *n*.
Ar·is·tot·le ['ærɪstɒtl] Aristoteles *m*.

Ar·i·zo·na [ˌærɪ'zəʊnə] *Staat der USA*.
Ar·me·ni·a [ɑː'miːnjə] Armenien *n*.
Ar·thur ['ɑːθə] Art(h)ur *m*: *King ~* König Artus.
A·sia ['eɪʃə] Asien *n*: *~ Minor* Kleinasien *n*.
Ath·ens ['æθɪnz] Athen *n*.
At·lan·tic [ət'læntɪk] *der* Atlantik.
Au·gus·tus [ɔː'ɡʌstəs] August *m*.
Aus·tra·lia [ɒ'streɪljə] Australien *n*.
Aus·tria ['ɒstrɪə] Österreich *n*.
A·zer·bai·jan [ˌæzəbaɪ'dʒɑːn] Aserbeidschan *n*.
A·zores [ə'zɔːz] *pl die* Azoren *pl*.

B

Ba·ha·mas [bə'hɑːməz] *pl die* Bahamas *pl*.
Bal·dwin ['bɔːldwɪn] Balduin *m*.
Bal·kans ['bɔːlkənz] *pl der* Balkan.
Bal·tic Sea [ˌbɔːltɪk'siː] *die* Ostsee.
Ban·gla·desh [ˌbæŋglə'deʃ] Bangladesch *n*.
Bar·ba·dos [bɑː'beɪdɒs] Barbados *n*.
Bar·thol·o·mew [bɑː'θɒləmjuː] Bartholomäus *m*.
Basle [bɑːl] Basel *n*.
Ba·va·ria [bə'veərɪə] Bayern *n*.
Be·a·trice ['bɪətrɪs] Beatrice *f*.
Bel·fast [ˌbel'fɑːst; 'belfɑːst] Belfast *n*.
Bel·gium ['beldʒəm] Belgien *n*.
Bel·grade [ˌbel'ɡreɪd] Belgrad *n*.
Bel·o·rus·sia [ˌbeləʊ'rʌʃə] Weißrußland *n*.
Ben·gal [ˌbeŋ'ɡɔːl] Bengalen *n*.
Ben·ja·min ['bendʒəmɪn] Benjamin *m*.
Ber·lin [bɜː'lɪn] Berlin *n*.
Ber·mu·das [bə'mjuːdəz] *pl die* Bermudas *pl*, *die* Bermudainseln *pl*.
Ber·nard ['bɜːnəd] Bernhard *m*.
Bern(e) [bɜːn] Bern *n*.
Ber·tha ['bɜːθə] Berta *f*.
Ber·tram ['bɜːtrəm], **Ber·trand** ['bɜːtrənd] Bertram *m*.
Bill, Bil·ly ['bɪl(ɪ)] Willi *m*.
Bis·cay ['bɪskeɪ; '~kɪ]: *Bay of ~ der* Golf von Biscaya.
Bo·he·mia [bəʊ'hiːmjə] Böhmen *n*.
Bo·liv·ia [bə'lɪvɪə] Bolivien *n*.
Bra·zil [brə'zɪl] Brasilien *n*.

Bridg·et ['brɪdʒɪt] Brigitte f.
Bri·tain ['brɪtn] Britannien n.
Bri·tan·nia [brɪ'tænjə] poet. Britannien n.
Bruns·wick ['brʌnzwɪk] Braunschweig n.
Brus·sels ['brʌslz] Brüssel n.
Bu·cha·rest [ˌbjuːkə'rest] Bukarest n.
Bu·da·pest [ˌbjuːdə'pest] Budapest n.
Bud·dha ['bʊdə] Buddha m.
Bul·gar·ia [bʌl'geərɪə] Bulgarien n.
Bur·gun·dy ['bɜːgəndɪ] Burgund n.
Bur·ki·na Fas·o [bʊəˌkiːnə'fæsəʊ] Burkina Faso n
Bur·ma ['bɜːmə] Birma n.

C

Cae·sar ['siːzə] Cäsar m.
Cai·ro ['kaɪərəʊ] Kairo n.
Ca·lais ['kæleɪ] Calais n.
Cal·cut·ta [kæl'kʌtə] Kalkutta n.
Cal·i·for·nia [ˌkælɪ'fɔːnjə] Kalifornien n.
Cam·bo·dia [kæm'bəʊdɪə] Kam'bodscha n.
Cam·er·oon [ˌkæmə'ruːn] Kamerun n.
Can·a·da ['kænədə] Kanada n.
Cape Town ['keɪptaʊn] Kapstadt n.
Ca·rin·thia [kə'rɪnθɪə] Kärnten n.
Car·o·line ['kærəlaɪn], **Car·o·lyn** ['kærəlɪn] Karoline f.
Cath·er·ine ['kæθrɪn] Katharina f, Kat(h)rin f.
Ce·cil ['sesl, 'sɪsl] m.
Ce·cile ['sesl; Am. sɪ'siːl], **Ce·cil·ia** [sɪ'sɪljə; sɪ'siːljə], **Cec·i·ly** ['sɪsɪlɪ; 'sesɪlɪ] Cäcilie f.
Cey·lon [sɪ'lɒn] Ceylon n.
Chad [tʃæd] der Tschad.
Charles [tʃɑːlz] Karl m.
Char·lotte ['ʃɑːlət] Charlotte f.
Chil·e ['tʃɪlɪ] Chile n.
Chi·na ['tʃaɪnə] China n: Republic of ~ die Republik China; People's Republic of ~ die Volksrepublik China.
Chris·ti·na [krɪ'stiːnə], **Chris·tine** ['krɪstiːn, krɪ'stiːn] Christine f.
Chris·to·pher ['krɪstəfə] Christoph(er) m.
Clar·a ['kleərə], **Clare** [kleə] Klara f.
Cle·o·pat·ra [klɪə'pætrə] Kleopatra f.
Co·logne [kə'ləʊn] Köln n.
Co·lom·bia [kə'lɒmbɪə] Kolumbien n.
Com·mon·wealth of In·de·pen·dent States ['kɒmənwelθ əv ˌɪndɪpendənt 'steɪts] (abbr. CIS) Gemeinschaft f unabhängiger Staaten (abbr. GUS).
Con·fu·cius [kən'fjuːʃəs] Konfuzius m.
Con·stance ['kɒnstəns] Konstanze f: Lake ~ der Bodensee.
Co·pen·ha·gen [ˌkəʊpn'heɪgən] Kopenhagen n.
Cov·ent Gar·den [ˌkɒvənt'gɑːdn] London Opera (Royal Opera House).
Crete [kriːt] Kreta n.
Cri·mea [kraɪ'mɪə] die Krim.
Cro·a·tia [krəʊ'eɪʃə] Kroatien n.
Cu·ba ['kjuːbə] Kuba n.
Cy·prus ['saɪprəs] Zypern n.
Czech·o·slo·va·kia [ˌtʃekəʊsləʊ'vækɪə] hist. die Tschechoslowakei.
Czech Re·pub·lic [ˌtʃek rɪ'pʌblɪk] die Tschechische Republik

D

Dan·iel ['dænjəl] Daniel m.
Dan·ube ['dænjuːb] die Donau.
Da·vid ['deɪvɪd] David m.
Den·mark ['denmɑːk] Dänemark n.
Di·ana [daɪ'ænə] Diana f.
Don Juan [dɒn 'dʒuːən] Don Juan m.
Don Quix·ote [ˌdɒn'kwɪksət] Don Quichotte m.
Dor·o·thy ['dɒrəθɪ] Dorothea f.
Dun·kirk [dʌn'kɜːk] Dünkirchen n.

E

Ec·ua·dor ['ekwədɔː] Ecuador n.
Ed·in·burgh ['edɪnbərə] Edinburg n.
E·dith ['iːdɪθ] Edith f.
E·gypt ['iːdʒɪpt] Ägypten n.
El·ea·nor ['elɪnə] Eleanore f.
E·li·jah [ɪ'laɪdʒə] Elias m.
El·i·nor ['elɪnə] Eleonore f.
E·liz·a·beth [ɪ'lɪzəbəθ] Elisabeth f.
El Sal·va·dor [el'sælvədɔː] El Salvador n.
Em·i·ly ['emɪlɪ] Emilie f.
Eng·land ['ɪŋglənd] England n.
Er·nest ['ɜːnɪst] Ernst m.
Es·t(h)o·nia [e'stəʊnjə] Estland n.
E·thi·o·pia [ˌiːθɪ'əʊpjə] Äthiopien n.
Eu·gene ['juːdʒiːn] Eugen m.
Eu·ge·nia [juː'dʒiːnjə] Eugenie f.
Eu·nice ['juːnɪs] Eunice f.
Eu·rip·i·des [jʊə'rɪpɪdiːz] Euripides m.
Eu·rope ['jʊərəp] Europa n.
Eve [iːv] Eva f.

F

Faer·oes ['feərəʊz] *pl die* Färöer *pl.*
Falk·land Is·lands [ˌfɔː(l)klənd'aɪləndz] *pl die* Falklandinseln *pl.*
Far·oes ['feərəʊz] → **Faeroes.**
Fed·er·al Re·pub·lic of Ger·ma·ny [ˌfedərəlrɪˌpʌblɪkəv'dʒɜːmənɪ] *die* Bundesrepublik Deutschland.
Fe·lic·i·ty [fə'lɪsətɪ] Felizitas *f.*
Fe·lix ['fiːlɪks] Felix *m.*
Fin·land ['fɪnlənd] Finnland *n.*
Flor·ence ['florəns] Florenz *n*; Florentine *f.*
France [frɑːns] Frankreich *n.*
Fran·ces ['frɑːnsɪs] Franziska *f.*
Fran·cis ['frɑːnsɪs] Franz *m.*
Fred·er·ic(k) ['fredrɪk] Friedrich *m.*

G

Gan·ges ['gændʒiːz] Ganges *m.*
Ge·ne·va [dʒɪ'niːvə] Genf *n.*
Gen·o·a ['dʒenəʊə] Genua *n.*
Geof·fr(e)y ['dʒefrɪ] Gottfried *m.*
George [dʒɔːdʒ] Georg *m.*
Geor·gia ['dʒɔːdʒə] *state of the US*; Georgien *n (in Asia).*
Ger·ald ['dʒerəld] Gerald *m*, Gerold *m.*
Ger·al·dine ['dʒerəldiːn] Geraldine *f.*
Ger·man Dem·o·crat·ic Re·pub·lic [ˌdʒɜːməndeməˌkrætɪkrɪ'pʌblɪk] *hist. die* Deutsche Demokratische Republik.
Ger·ma·ny ['dʒɜːmənɪ] Deutschland *n.*
Ger·trude ['gɜːtruːd] Gertrud *f.*
Gi·bral·tar [dʒɪ'brɔːltə] Gibraltar *n.*
Gil·bert ['gɪlbət] Gilbert *m.*
Giles [dʒaɪlz] Julius *m.*
Gil·li·an ['dʒɪlɪən; 'gɪlɪən] *f.*
Go·li·ath [gəʊ'laɪəθ] Goliath *m.*
Great Brit·ain [ˌgreɪt'brɪtn] Großbritannien *n.*
Greece [griːs] Griechenland *n.*
Green·land ['griːnlənd] Grönland *n.*
Greg·o·ry ['gregərɪ] Gregor *m.*
Gri·sons ['griːzɔːŋ] Graubünden *n.*
Gua·te·ma·la [ˌgwɑːtə'mɑːlə] Guatemala *n.*
Guin·ea ['gɪnɪ] Guinea *n.*
Guy·ana [gaɪ'ænə] Guyana *n.*

H

Hague [heɪg]: *the* ~ Den Haag.
Hai·ti ['heɪtɪ] Haiti *n.*

Han·o·ver ['hænəʊvə] Hannover *n.*
Har·old ['hærəld] Harald *m.*
Heb·ri·des ['hebrɪdiːz] *pl die* Hebriden *pl.*
Hel·en ['helɪn] Helene *f.*
Hel·i·go·land ['helɪgəʊlænd] Helgoland *n.*
Hel·sin·ki ['helsɪŋkɪ] Helsinki *n.*
Hen·ry ['henrɪ] Heinrich *m.*
Hesse ['hes(ɪ)] Hessen *n.*
Hil·a·ry ['hɪlərɪ] Hilaria *f*; Hilarius *m.*
Hi·ma·la·ya [ˌhɪmə'leɪə] *der* Himalaja.
Hol·land ['hɒlənd] Holland *n.*
Ho·mer ['həʊmə] Homer *m.*
Hon·du·ras [hɒn'djʊərəs] Honduras *n.*
Hong Kong [ˌhɒŋ'kɒŋ] Hongkong *n.*
Hugh [hjuː] Hugo *m.*
Hun·ga·ry ['hʌŋgərɪ] Ungarn *n.*

I

I·an [ɪən; 'iːən] Jan *m.*
Ice·land ['aɪslənd] Island *n.*
In·dia ['ɪndjə] Indien *n.*
In·do·ne·sia [ˌɪndəʊ'niːzjə] Indonesien *n.*
I·ran [ɪ'rɑːn] Iran *n.*
I·raq [ɪ'rɑːk] Irak *m.*
Ire·land ['aɪələnd] Irland *n.*
I·rene [aɪ'riːnɪ; 'aɪriːn] Irene *f.*
I·saac ['aɪzək] Isaak *m.*
Is·a·bel ['ɪzəbel] Isabella *f.*
Is·ra·el ['ɪzreɪəl] Israel *n.*
Is·tan·bul [ˌɪstæn'bʊl] Istanbul *n.*
It·a·ly ['ɪtəlɪ] Italien *n.*

J

Jack [dʒæk] Hans *m.*
Ja·mai·ca [dʒə'meɪkə] Jamaika *n.*
James [dʒeɪmz] Jakob *m.*
Jane [dʒeɪn] Johanna *f.*
Jan·et ['dʒenɪt] Johanna *f.*
Ja·pan [dʒə'pæn] Japan *n.*
Jean [dʒiːn] Johanna *f.*
Jef·frey ['dʒefrɪ] Gottfried *m.*
Jer·e·my ['dʒerɪmɪ] Jeremias *m.*
Je·rome [dʒe'rəʊm] Hieronymus *m.*
Je·ru·sa·lem [dʒə'ruːsələm] Jerusalem *n.*
Je·sus ['dʒiːzəs] Jesus *m.*
Joan [dʒəʊn], **Jo·an·na** [dʒəʊ'ænə] Johanna *f.*
John [dʒɒn] Johannes *m*, Johann *m.*
Jon·a·than ['dʒɒnəθən] Jonathan *m.*
Jor·dan ['dʒɔːdn] Jordanien *n*; Jordan *m.*
Jo·seph ['dʒəʊzɪf] Joseph *m.*

Jo·se·phine ['dʒəʊzɪfiːn] Josephine f.
Ju·dith ['dʒuːdɪθ] Judith f.

K

Kam·pu·chea [ˌkæmpʊ'tʃɪə] hist. Kamputschea n.
Ka·ra·chi [kə'rɑːtʃɪ] Karatschi n.
Kash·mir [ˌkæʃ'mɪə] Kaschmir n.
Kath·a·rine, Kath·er·ine ['kæθərɪn] Katharina f, Kat(h)rin f.
Ka·zakh·stan [ˌkæzæk'stɑːn] Kasachstan n.
Ken·ya ['kenjə] Kenia n.
Ko·rea [kə'rɪə] Korea n.
Krem·lin ['kremlɪn] der Kreml.
Ku·wait [kʊ'weɪt] Kuwait n.

L

Lake Hu·ron [ˌleɪk'hjʊərən] der Huronsee.
Lake Su·pe·ri·or [ˌleɪksuː'pɪərɪə] der Obere See.
La·os ['lɑːɒs; laʊs] Laos n.
Lat·via ['lætvɪə] Lettland n.
Lau·rence ['lɒrəns] Lorenz m.
Law·rence ['lɒrəns] Lorenz m.
Leb·a·non ['lebənən] der Libanon.
Leon·ard ['lenəd] Leonhard m.
Lew·is ['luːɪs] Ludwig m.
Lib·ya ['lɪbɪə] Libyen n.
Li·sa ['liːzə; 'laɪzə] Lisa f.
Lis·bon ['lɪzbən] Lissabon n.
Lith·u·a·nia [ˌlɪθjuː'eɪnjə] Litauen n.
Li·za ['laɪzə] Lisa f.
Lon·don ['lʌndən] London n.
Lor·raine [lɒ'reɪn] Lothringen n.
Lou·is ['luːɪ; 'lʊɪ; bsd. Am. 'luːɪs] Ludwig m.
Lou·ise [luː'iːz] Luise f.
Lu·cia ['luːsjə] Lucia f, Luzia f.
Luke [luːk] Lukas m.
Lux·em·bourg ['lʌksəmbɜːg] Luxemburg n.
Lyd·ia ['lɪdɪə] Lydia f.

M

Ma·dei·ra [mə'dɪərə] Madeira n.
Ma·drid [mə'drɪd] Madrid n.
Mag·da·len ['mægdəlɪn] Magdalena f, Magdalene f: ~ College ['mɔːdlɪn] College in Oxford.
Mag·da·lene ['mægdəlɪn] Magdalena f,

Magdalene f: ~ College ['mɔːdlɪn] College in Cambridge.
Ma·ho·met [mə'hɒmɪt] Mohammed m.
Ma·jor·ca [mə'dʒɔːkə] Mallorca n.
Mal·ta ['mɔːltə] Malta n.
Mar·ga·ret ['mɑːgərɪt] Margareta f, Margarete f.
Ma·ri·a [mə'raɪə; mə'rɪə] Maria f.
Mar·tha ['mɑːθə] Mart(h)a f.
Mar·y ['meərɪ] Maria f, Marie f.
Ma(t)·thew ['mæθjuː] Matthäus m.
Mau·rice ['mɒrɪs] Moritz m.
Med·i·ter·ra·ne·an (Sea) [ˌmedɪtə'reɪnjən('siː)] das Mittelmeer.
Mex·i·co ['meksɪkəʊ] Mexiko n.
Mi·chael ['maɪkl] Michael m.
Mich·i·gan ['mɪʃɪgən] Lake ~ der Michigansee.
Mid·lands ['mɪdləndz] pl die Midlands pl.
Mid·west [ˌmɪd'west] der Mittlere Westen (USA).
Mi·lan [mɪ'læn] Mailand n.
Mo·na·co ['mɒnəkəʊ] Monaco n.
Mo·roc·co [mə'rɒkəʊ] Marokko n.
Mos·cow ['mɒskəʊ] Moskau n.
Mo·selle [məʊ'zel] Mosel f.
Mo·zam·bique [ˌməʊzæm'biːk] Moçambique n.
Mu·nich ['mjuːnɪk] München n.

N

Na·mib·ia [nə'mɪbɪə] Namibia n.
Na·ples ['neɪplz] Neapel n.
Naz·a·reth ['næzərəθ] Nazareth n.
Ne·pal [nɪ'pɔːl] Nepal n.
Neth·er·lands ['neðələndz] pl die Niederlande pl.
New Del·hi [ˌnjuː'delɪ] Neu-Delhi n.
New Eng·land [ˌnjuː'ɪŋglənd] Neuengland n (USA).
New·found·land ['njuːfəndlənd] Neufundland n.
New Zea·land [ˌnjuː'ziːlənd] Neuseeland n.
Ni·ag·a·ra [naɪ'ægərə] Niagara m.
Nic·a·ra·gua [ˌnɪkə'rægjʊə] Nicaragua n.
Nich·o·las ['nɪkələs] Nikolaus m.
Ni·ge·ria [naɪ'dʒɪərɪə] Nigeria n.
Nile [naɪl] Nil m.
Nor·man·dy ['nɔːməndɪ] die Normandie.
North·ern Ire·land [ˌnɔːðn'aɪələnd] Nordirland n.

North Sea [ˌnɔːθˈsiː] *die* Nordsee.
Nor·way [ˈnɔːweɪ] Norwegen *n.*
No·va Sco·tia [ˌnəʊvəˈskəʊʃə] Neu-
schottland *n.*
Nu·rem·berg [ˈnjʊərəmbɜːg] Nürnberg *n.*

O

O·ce·an·ia [ˌəʊʃɪˈeɪnjə] Ozeanien *n.*
On·ta·ri·o [ɒnˈteərɪəʊ] *Lake* ~ der Onta-
riosee.
Ork·ney Is·lands [ˌɔːknɪˈaɪləndz] *pl die*
Orkneyinseln *pl.*
Ost·end [ɒˈstend] Ost'ende *n.*

P

Pa·cif·ic [pəˈsɪfɪk] *der* Pazifik.
Pak·i·stan [ˌpɑːkɪˈstɑːn] Pakistan *n.*
Pal·es·tine [ˈpæləstaɪn] Palästina *n.*
Pam·e·la [ˈpæmələ] Pamela *f.*
Pan·a·ma [ˈpænəmɑː] Panama *n.*
Par·a·guay [ˈpærəgwaɪ] Paraguay *n.*
Par·is [ˈpærɪs] Paris *n.*
Pa·tri·cia [pəˈtrɪʃə] Patrizia *f.*
Pat·rick [ˈpætrɪk] Patrizius *m.*
Paul [pɔːl] Paul *m.*
Pau·line [pɔːˈliːn; ˈpɔːliːn] Pauline *f.*
Per·sia [ˈpɜːʃə; *Am.* ˈpɜːrʒə] Persien *n.*
Pe·ru [pəˈruː] Peru *n.*
Pe·ter [ˈpiːtə] Peter *m*, Petrus *m.*
Phil·ip [ˈfɪlɪp] Philipp *m.*
Phil·ip·pines [ˈfɪlɪpiːnz] *pl die* Philippi-
nen *pl.*
Pla·to [ˈpleɪtəʊ] Plato(n) *m.*
Po·land [ˈpəʊlənd] Polen *n.*
Por·tu·gal [ˈpɔːtʃʊgl; ~jʊgl] Portugal *n.*
Prague [prɑːg] Prag *n.*
Prus·sia [ˈprʌʃə] Preußen *n.*

Q

Qa·tar [kæˈtɑː] Katar *n.*

R

Ra·chel [ˈreɪtʃl] Ra(c)hel *f.*
Rat·is·bon [ˈrætɪzbɒn] Regensburg *n.*
Reg·i·nald [ˈredʒɪnld] Re(g)inald *m.*
Rhine [raɪn] Rhein *n.*
Rhodes [rəʊdz] Rhodos *n.*
Rich·ard [ˈrɪtʃəd] Richard *m.*
Rob·ert [ˈrɒbət] Robert *m.*
Ro·ma·nia [ruːˈmeɪnjə; rʊ~; *Am.* rəʊ~]
Rumänien *n.*

Rome [rəʊm] Rom *n.*
Rus·sia [ˈrʌʃə] Rußland *n.*
Ruth [ruːθ] Ruth *f.*

S

Sam·u·el [ˈsæmjʊəl] Samuel *m.*
San Fran·cis·co [ˌsænfrənˈsɪskəʊ] San
Franzisko *n* (*USA*).
Sau·di A·ra·bia [ˌsaʊdɪəˈreɪbɪə] Saudi-
Arabien *n.*
Sax·o·ny [ˈsæksnɪ] Sachsen *n.*
Scan·di·na·via [ˌskændɪˈneɪvjə] Skandi-
navien *n.*
Scot·land [ˈskɒtlənd] Schottland *n.*
Shet·land Is·lands [ˌʃetləndˈaɪləndz] *pl*
die Shetlandinseln *pl.*
Si·be·ria [saɪˈbɪərɪə] Sibirien *n.*
Sib·yl [ˈsɪbɪl] Sibylle *f.*
Sic·i·ly [ˈsɪsɪlɪ] Sizilien *n.*
Si·le·sia [saɪˈliːzjə] Schlesien *n.*
Si·mon [ˈsaɪmən] Simon *m.*
Sin·ga·pore [ˌsɪŋəˈpɔː] Singapur *n.*
Slo·va·kia [sləʊˈvækɪə] Slowakei *f.*
Slo·ve·nia [sləʊˈviːnjə] Slowenien *n.*
Soc·ra·tes [ˈsɒkrətiːz] Sokrates *m.*
Sol·o·mon [ˈsɒləmən] Salomo(n) *m.*
So·ma·lia [səʊˈmɑːlɪə] Somalia *n.*
So·phi·a [səʊˈfaɪə] Sophia *f*, Sofia *f.*
So·viet Un·ion [ˌsəʊvɪətˈjuːnjən] *hist. die*
Sowjetunion.
Spain [speɪn] Spanien *n.*
Ste·phen [ˈstiːvn] Stephan *m*, Stefan *m.*
St. Law·rence [snt ˈlɒrəns] *der* Sankt-
Lorenz-Strom.
Stock·holm [ˈstɒkhəʊm] Stockholm *n.*
Styr·ia [ˈstɪrɪə] *die* Steiermark.
Su·dan [suːˈdɑːn] *der* Sudan.
Su·san [ˈsuːzn] Susanne *f.*
Su·zanne [suːˈzæn] Susanne *f.*
Swe·den [ˈswiːdn] Schweden *n.*
Swit·zer·land [ˈswɪtsələnd] *die* Schweiz.
Syr·ia [ˈsɪrɪə] Syrien *n.*

T

Tai·wan [ˌtaɪˈwɑːn] Taiwan *n.*
Tan·za·nia [ˌtænzəˈnɪə] Tansania *n.*
Thai·land [ˈtaɪlænd] Thailand *n.*
Thames [temz] *die* Themse.
The·o·bald [ˈθɪəbɔːld] Theobald *m.*
The·o·dore [ˈθɪədɔː] Theodor *m.*
The·re·sa [tɪˈriːzə] Theresa *f*, Therese *f.*
Tho·mas [ˈtɒməs] Thomas *m.*

Thu·rin·gia [θjʊəˈrɪndʒɪə] Thüringen *n.*
Ti·bet [tɪˈbet] Tibet *n.*
Tim·o·thy [ˈtɪməθɪ] Timotheus *m.*
To·bi·as [təˈbaɪəs] Tobias *m.*
To·kyo [ˈtəʊkjəʊ] Tokio *n.*
Tra·fal·gar [trəˈfælgə]: *Cape* ∼ Kap *n* Trafalgar (*Spain*); ∼ *Square* (*in London*).
Treves [triːvz] Trier *n.*
Tu·ni·sia [tjuːˈnɪzɪə; *Am.* tuːˈniːʒə] Tunesien *n.*
Tur·key [ˈtɜːkɪ] die Türkei.
Tus·ca·ny [ˈtʌskənɪ] die Toskana.
Ty·rol [ˈtɪrəl; tɪˈrəʊl] Tirol *n.*

U

U·kraine [juːˈkreɪn] *die* Ukraine.
Ul·ster [ˈʌlstə] Nordirland *n.*
U·nit·ed King·dom [juːˌnaɪtɪdˈkɪŋdəm] *das* Vereinigte Königreich (*Great Britain and Northern Ireland*).
U·nit·ed States of A·mer·i·ca [juːˌnaɪtɪdˌsteɪtsəvəˈmerɪkə] *pl die* Vereinigten Staaten *pl* von Amerika.
Ur·su·la [ˈɜːsjʊlə] Ursula *f.*
U·tah [ˈjuːtɑː; ˈ∼tɔː] *Staat der USA.*
Uz·bek·i·stan [ʊzbekɪˈstɑːn] Usbekistan *n.*

V

Val·en·tine [ˈvæləntaɪn] Valentin(e *f*) *m.*
Vat·i·can [ˈvætɪkən] *der* Vatikan.
Ven·e·zu·e·la [ˌvenɪˈzweɪlə] Venezuela *n.*
Ven·ice [ˈvenɪs] Venedig *n.*
Vi·en·na [vɪˈenə] Wien *n.*
Viet·nam [ˌvjetˈnæm] Vietnam *n.*
Vil·ni·us [ˈvɪlnɪəs] Wilna *f.*
Vir·gil [ˈvɜːdʒɪl] Vergil *m.*

W

Wales [weɪlz] Wales *n.*
War·saw [ˈwɔːsɔː] Warschau *n.*
West·pha·lia [westˈfeɪljə] Westfalen *n.*
Wil·liam [ˈwɪljəm] Wilhelm *m.*

Y

Yu·go·sla·via [ˌjuːgəʊˈslɑːvjə] *hist.* Jugoslawien *n.*

Z

Zach·a·ri·ah [ˌzækəˈraɪə], **Zach·a·ry** [ˈzækərɪ] Zacharias *m.*
Za·ire [zɑːˈɪə] Za'ire *n.*
Zim·ba·bwe [zɪmˈbɑːbwɪ] Simbabwe *n.*
Zu·rich [ˈzjʊərɪk] Zürich *n.*

Geographical Names

A

Aachen Aachen, Aix-la-Chapelle
Abruzzen, *die* *the* Abruzzi
Addis Abeba Addis Ababa
Admiralitätsinseln, *die* *the* Admiralty Islands, *the* Admiralties
Adria, *die* *the* Adriatic (Sea)
Afrika Africa
Ägäis, *die* *the* Aegean (Sea)
Ägäischen Inseln, *die* *the* Aegean Islands
Ägypten Egypt
Akaba Aqaba, Akaba
Akkra Accra
Akropolis, *die* *the* Acropolis
Albanien Albania

Aleuten, *die* *the* Aleutian Islands
Alexandrien Alexandria
Algerien Algeria
Algier Algiers
Alpen, *die* *the* Alps
Alpenvorland, *das* *the* foothills of the Alps
Altaigebirge, *das* *the* Altai Mountains
Amazonas, *der* *the* Amazon
Amerika America
Anatolien Anatolia
Andalusien Andalusia
Anden, *die* *the* Andes
Antarktis, *die* *the* Antarctic, Antarctica
Antillen, *die* *the* Antilles
Antwerpen Antwerp

Apennin, *der,* **Apenninen,** *die the* Apennines, *the* Apennine Mountains
Apenninenhalbinsel, *die the* Apennine Peninsula
Appalachen, *die the* Appalachians, *the* Appalachian Mountains
Apulien Apulia
Arabien Arabia
Arabische Wüste, *die the* Arabian Desert
Aralsee, *der* Lake Aral
Ardennen, *die the* Ardennes
Argentinien Argentina, *the* Argentine
Arktis, *die the* Arctic
Ärmelkanal, *der the* (English) Channel
Armenien Armenia
Aserbeidschan Azerbaijan
Asien Asia
Asowsche Meer, *das the* Sea of Azov
Assuan Aswan
Athen Athens
Äthiopien Ethiopia
Atlantik, *der the* Atlantic (Ocean)
Atlasgebirge, *das the* Atlas Mountains
Ätna, *der* Mount Etna
Australasien Australasia
Australien Australia
Azoren, *die the* Azores

B

Bagdad Baghdad
Baikalsee, *der* Lake Baikal
Balearen, *die the* Balearic Islands
Balkan, *der* → 1. *Balkanhalbinsel*; 2. *Balkanstaaten*; 3. *Balkangebirge*
Balkangebirge, *das the* Balkan Mountains
Balkanhalbinsel, *die the* Balkan Peninsula
Balkanstaaten, *die the* Balkan States, *the* Balkans
Baltikum, *das the* Baltic (States), *the* Baltics
Bangladesch Bangladesh
Barentssee, *die the* Barents Sea
Basel Basel, Basle
Baskenland, *das the* Basque Provinces
Bayerische Wald, *der the* Bavarian Forest
Belgien Belgium
Belgrad Belgrade
Benelux-Länder, *die the* Benelux Countries

Bengalen Bengal
Beringmeer, *das the* Bering Sea
Beringstraße, *die the* Bering Strait
Bern Bern(e)
Bessarabien Bessarabia
Bikini, Bikiniatoll, *das* Bikini
Birma Burma
Biskaya, *die* → *Golf von Biskaya*
Bodensee, *der* Lake Constance
Böhmen Čechy; *hist.* Bohemia
Böhmerwald, *der the* Bohemian Forest
Bolivien Bolivia
Bosnien Bosnia
Bosnien und Herzegowina Bosnia and Herzegowina
Bosporus, *der the* Bosp(h)orus
Botsuana Botswana
Bottnische Meerbusen, *der the* Gulf of Bothnia
Bozen Bolzano
Brasilien Brazil
Brenner(paß), *der the* Brenner Pass
Breslau Wroclaw; *hist.* Breslau
Bretagne, *die the* Brittany
Brügge Bruges
Brüssel Brussels
Bukarest Bucharest
Bukowina, *die* Bukovina, Bucovina
Bulgarien Bulgaria
Bundesrepublik Deutschland, *die the* Federal Republic of Germany
Burgund Burgundy

C

Cevennen, *die the* Cévennes
Charkow Kharkov
Chiemsee, *der* Lake Chiem, *the* Chiemsee
Chinesische Mauer, *die the* Great Wall of China
Chinesische Meer, *das the* China Sea
Comer See, *der* Lake Como

D

Damaskus Damascus
Dänemark Denmark
Danzig Gdansk; *hist.* Danzig
Danziger Bucht, *die the* Bay (*or* Gulf) of Gdansk (*hist.* Danzig)
Dardanellen, *die the* Dardanelles
Daressalam Dar es Salaam
Den Haag The Hague

Deutsche Bucht, die the German Bay
Deutschland Germany
Dnjepr, der the Dnieper
Dnjestr, der the Dniester
Dodekanes, der the Dodecanese
Dolomiten, die the Dolomites
Dominikanische Republik, die the Dominican Republic
Donau, die the Danube
Donez, der the Donets
Donezbecken, das the Donets (Basin)
Dover → **Straße von Dover**
Drau, die the Drava
Dschibuti Djibouti
Dschidda Jedda

E

Eiffelturm, der the Eiffel Tower
Eismeer, Nördliche, das → **Nordpolarmeer**
Eismeer, Südliche, das → **Südpolarmeer**
Elat Eilat
Elfenbeinküste, die the Ivory Coast
Elsaß, das Alsace
Engadin, das the Engadine
Eriwan Yerevan, Erivan
Erzgebirge, das the Erzgebirge, the Ore Mountains
Estland Estonia
Etsch, die the Adige
Euphrat, der the Euphrates
Eurasien Eurasia
Europa Europe
Everest, der (Mount) Everest

F

Falklandinseln, die the Falkland Islands, the Falklands
Färöer, die the Faroes, the Faroe Islands
Ferne Osten, der, Fernost the Far East
Feuerland Tierra del Fuego
Fidschi Fiji
Fidschiinseln, die the Fiji Islands
Finnische Meerbusen, der the Gulf of Finland
Finnland Finland
Flandern Flanders
Florenz Florence
Franken Franconia

Frankfurt (am Main) Frankfurt (on the Main)
Frankfurt (an der Oder) Frankfurt (on the Oder)
Frankreich France
Französisch-Guayana French Guiana
Fudschijama, der (Mount) Fuji, *a.* Fujiyama

G

Gabun Gabon
Galapagosinseln, die the Galapagos Islands
Gambia (*the*) Gambia
Gardasee, der Lake Garda
Gazastreifen, der the Gaza Strip
Genezareth → See **Genezareth**
Genf Geneva
Genfer See, der Lake Geneva, Lac Léman
Gent Ghent
Genua Genoa
Georgien Georgia
Golanhöhen, die the Golan Heights
Goldene Horn, das the Golden Horn
Golf von Akaba, der the Gulf of Aqaba (or Akaba)
Golf von Bengalen, der the Bay of Bengal
Golf von Biskaya, der the Bay of Biscay
Golf von Genua, der the Gulf of Genoa
Golf von Korinth, der the Gulf of Corinth
Golf von Neapel, der the Bay of Naples
Golf von Triest, der the Gulf of Trieste
Göteborg Gothenburg, Göteborg
Graubünden Graubünden, the Grisons
Griechenland Greece
Grönland Greenland
Großbritannien Great Britain, Britain
Große Belt, der the Great Belt
Großen Seen, die the Great Lakes
Große Syrte, die the Gulf of Sidra
Guayana (*region*) Guiana
Guyana (*state*) Guyana

H

Harz, der the Harz (Mountains)
Havanna Havana
Hawaii-Inseln, die the Hawaiian Islands
Hebriden, die the Hebrides

Helgoland Hel(i)goland
Helgoländer Bucht, *die the* Hel(i)go-
land Bight
Himalaja, *der the* Himalayas
Hindukusch, *der the* Hindu Kush
Hinterindien Indochina
Hiroshima Hiroshima
Hoek van Holland Hook of Holland
Holland Holland, *the* Netherlands
Hongkong Hong Kong

I

Iberische Halbinsel, *die the* Iberian
Peninsula
Ijsselmeer, *das* Lake Ijssel, Ijsselmeer
Indien India
Indische Ozean, *der the* Indian Ocean
Indonesien Indonesia
Innerasien Central Asia
Innere Mongolei, *die* Inner Mongolia
Insel Man, *die the* Isle of Man
Insel Wight, *die the* Isle of Wight
Ionische Meer, *das the* Ionian Sea
Ionischen Inseln, *die the* Ionian Islands
Irak, *der* Iraq
Irische See, *die the* Irish Sea
Irland Ireland
Island Iceland
Italien Italy

J

Jadebusen, *der the* Jade Bay
Jakutsk Yakutsk
Jalta Yalta
Jamaika Jamaica
Jangtse(kiang), *der the* Yang-
tze(-Kiang)
Japanische Meer, *das the* Sea of Japan
Jemen, *der the* Yemen
Jordanien Jordan
Jugoslawien *hist.* Yugoslavia
Jungferninseln, *die the* Virgin Islands
Jütland Jutland

K

Kaimaninseln, *die the* Cayman Islands
Kairo Cairo
Kalabrien Calabria
Kalifornien California
Kalkutta Calcutta
Kambodscha Cambodia
Kamerun Cameroon

Kanada Canada
Kanal, *der the* (English) Channel
Kanalinseln, *die the* Channel Islands
Kanaren, *die,* **Kanarischen Inseln,** *die*
the Canaries, *the* Canary Islands
Kap der Guten Hoffnung, *das the* Cape
of Good Hope, *a. the* Cape
Kap Hoorn Cape Horn, *a. the* Horn
Kapprovinz, *die* Cape Province
Kap Skagen *the* Skaw, *a.* (Cape) Skagen
Kapstadt Cape Town
Kapverdischen Inseln, *die the* Cape
Verde Islands
Karatschi Karachi
Karibik, *die the* Caribbean
Kärnten Carinthia
Karolinen, *die the* Caroline Islands
Karpaten, *die the* Carpathians, *the* Car-
pathian Mountains
Kasachstan Kazakhstan
Kaschmir Kashmir
Kaspische Meer, *das the* Caspian Sea
Kastilien Castile
Katalonien Catalonia
Katar Qatar
Kaukasus, *der the* Caucasus, *a. the*
Caucasus Mountains
Kenia Kenya
Kieler Bucht, *die* Kiel Bay
Kiew Kiev
Kilimandscharo, *der* (Mount) Kili-
manjaro
Kirgisien Kirghizia
Kleinasien Asia Minor
Köln Cologne
Kolumbien Colombia
Komoren, *die the* Comoro Archipelago
Kongo, *der the* Congo
Königsberg Kaliningrad; *hist.* Königs-
berg
Kopenhagen Copenhagen
Kordilleren, *die the* Cordilleras
Korfu Corfu
Korinth Corinth
Korsika Corsica
Krakatau Krakatoa
Kreta Crete
Krim, *die the* Crimea
Kroatien Croatia
Kuba Cuba
Kurdistan Kurdistan, Kurdestan, Kor-
destan
Kurilen, *die the* Kuril(e) Islands
Kykladen, *die the* Cyclades

L

Ladogasee, *der* Lake Ladoga
Lappland Lapland
Lateinamerika Latin America
Lausitz, die Lusatia
Lemberg Lvov
Lettland Latvia
Levante, die the Levant
Libanon, der (the) Lebanon
Libyen Libya
Ligurische Meer, das the Ligurian Sea
Liparischen Inseln, die the Lipari Islands
Lissabon Lisbon
Litauen Lithuania
Lübecker Bucht, die the Lübeck Bay
Luganer See, der Lake Lugano
Lüneburger Heide, die the Lüneburg Heath
Lüttich Liège
Luxemburg Luxemb(o)urg
Luzern Lucerne

M

Maas, die the Meuse, the Maas
Madagaskar Madagascar
Magellanstraße, die the Strait(s) of Magellan
Mailand Milan
Makedonien Macedonia
Malaiische Halbinsel, die the Malay Peninsula, Malaya
Malakka Malacca
Malediven, die the Maldives
Mallorca Majorca
Mandschurei, die Manchuria
Marianen, die the Marianas
Mark Brandenburg, die the Brandenburg Marches
Marmarameer, das the Sea of Marmara
Marokko Morocco
Maskat und Oman Muscat and Oman
Masuren Masuria
Masurischen Seen, die the Masurian Lakes
Mauretanien Mauretania
Mekka Mecca
Melanesien Melanesia
Menorca Minorca
Meran Merano
Mesopotamien Mesopotamia
Mexiko Mexico
Mikronesien Micronesia
Mittelamerika Central America
Mittelasien Central Asia
Mittelmeer, das the Mediterranean (Sea)
Mittlere Osten, der the Middle East
Moçambique Mozambique
Moldau¹, die (*river*) the Vltava; *hist.* the Moldau
Moldau², die (*region*) Moldavia
Moldavien Moldavia
Molukken, die the Moluccas
Mongolei, die Mongolia
Mosel, der the Moselle
Moskau Moscow
Moskwa, die the Moskva
München Munich
Mykene Mycenae

N

Nahe Osten, der the Middle (*or* Near) East
Neapel Naples
Neu-Delhi New Delhi
Neufundland Newfoundland
Neuguinea New Guinea
Neuseeland New Zealand
Newa, die the Neva
Niagarafälle, die the Niagara Falls
Niederlande, die the Netherlands, Holland
Nikosia Nicosia
Nil, der the Nile
Nizza Nice
Nordafrika North Africa
Nordamerika North America
Norddeutsche Tiefebene, die the North(ern) German Plain
Nordfriesischen Inseln, die the North Frisians
Nordirland Northern Ireland
Nordkap, das the North Cape
Nordkorea North Korea
Nord-Ostsee-Kanal, der the Kiel Canal
Nordpol, der the North Pole
Nordpolarmeer, das the Arctic Ocean
Nordsee, die the North Sea
Normandie, die Normandy
Norwegen Norway
Nowosibirsk Novosibirsk
Nürnberg Nuremberg

O

Oberrheinische Tiefebene, die *the* Upper Rhine Valley
Ochotskische Meer, das *the* Sea of Okhotsk
Olymp, der (Mount) Olympus
Onegasee, der Lake Onega
Oranjefreistaat, der *the* Orange Free State
Orinoko, der *the* Orinoco
Ostafrika East Africa
Ostasien East Asia
Ostende Ostend
Osterinsel, die Easter Island
Österreich Austria
Ostfriesischen Inseln, die *the* East Frisians
Ostsee, die *the* Baltic (Sea)
Ozeanien Oceania

P

Panamakanal, der *the* Panama Canal
Pandschab, das *the* Punjab
Papua-Neuguinea Papua-New Guinea
Parnaß, der Mount Parnassus
Patagonien Patagonia
Pazifik, der *the* Pacific (Ocean)
Peloponnes, der *or* **die** *the* Peloponnese, *the* Peloponnesus
Persische Golf, der *the* Persian Gulf
Petersburg, (St.) St Petersburg
Pfalz, die *the* Palatinate
Philippinen, die *the* Philippines
Piräus Piraeus
Plattensee, der Lake Balaton
Po-Ebene, die *the* Po Valley
Polarkreis, der 1. *the* Arctic Circle; **2.** *the* Antarctic Circle
Polen Poland
Polynesien Polynesia
Pommern Pomorze; *hist.* Pomerania
Pompeji Pompeii
Pontische Gebirge, das *the* Pontic Mountains
Prag Prague
Provence, die Provence
Pyrenäen, die *the* Pyrenees
Pyrenäenhalbinsel, die *the* Iberian Peninsula

R

Reval Tallin(n); *hist.* Reval
Rhein, der *the* Rhine

Rheinfall, der *the* Rhine Falls
Rheingau, der *the* Rhinegau
Rheinhessen Rhinehessen
Rheinische Schiefergebirge, das *the* Rhenish Slate Mountains
Rheinland, das *the* Rhineland
Rhodos Rhodes
Rom Rome
Rote Meer, das *the* Red Sea
Ruhrgebiet, das *the* Ruhr(gebiet)
Rumänien Romania, *a.* Rumania
Rußland Russia

S

Sächsische Schweiz, die Saxon Switzerland
Salomonen, die, Salomonischen Inseln, die *the* Solomon Islands
Saloniki Salonika, Saloniki
Sambesi, der *the* Zambezi
Sambia Zambia
Sankt-Lorenz-Strom, der *the* St Lawrence (River)
Sansibar Zanzibar
Sarajewo Sarajevo
Sardinien Sardinia
Saudi-Arabien Saudi Arabia
Savoyen Savoy
Schanghai Shanghai
Schatt el Arab, der *the* Shatt-al-Arab
Schlesien Slask; *hist.* Silesia
Schottland Scotland
Schwaben Swabia
Schwäbische Alb, die Swabian Jura
Schwarze Meer, das *the* Black Sea
Schwarzwald, der *the* Black Forest
Schweden Sweden
Schweiz, die Switzerland
See Genezareth, der *the* Sea of Galilee
Seeland Zealand
Serbien Serbia
Sevilla Seville
Seychellen, die *the* Seychelles
Sibirien Siberia
Simbabwe Zimbabwe
Sinaigebirge, das Mount Sinai
Sinaihalbinsel, die *the* Sinai Peninsula
Singapur Singapore
Sizilien Sicily
Skandinavien Scandinavia
Slowakei, die Slovakia
Slowenien Slovenia
Sowjetunion, die *hist.* *the* Soviet Union

Spanien Spain
Sporaden, *die the* Sporades
Steiermark, *die* Styria
Stettin Szczecin; *hist.* Stettin
Stille Ozean, *der* → *Pazifik*
Straßburg Strasbourg
Straße von Dover, *die the* Strait(s) of Dover
Straße von Gibraltar, *die the* Strait(s) of Gibraltar
Südafrika South Africa
Südamerika South America
Sudan, *der (the)* Sudan
Südchinesische Meer, *das the* South China Sea
Südkorea South Korea
Südpolarmeer, *das the* Antarctic Ocean
Südsee, *die the* South Pacific, *the* South Seas
Südseeinseln, *die the* Pacific (*or* South Sea) Islands
Südtirol South Tyrol
Südwestafrika South-West Africa
Suezkanal, *der the* Suez Canal
Swasiland Swaziland
Syrien Syria
Szetschuan Szechuan

T

Tadschikistan Tadzhikistan
Tafelberg, *der the* Table Mountain
Taipeh Taipei
Tajo, *der the* Tagus
Tanganjika Tanganyika
Tanganjikasee, *der* Lake Tanganyika
Tanger Tangier
Tansania Tanzania
Tasmanien Tasmania
Tatra, *die the* Tatra Mountains, *a. the* High Tatra
Taurus, *der the* Taurus (Mountains)
Teheran Teh(e)ran
Teneriffa Tenerife
Tessin, *das* Ticino
Teutoburger Wald, *der the* Teutoburg Forest, *the* Teutoburger Wald
Themse, *die the* Thames
Thüringer Wald, *der the* Thuringian Forest
Tirol *(the)* Tyrol
Tokio Tokyo
Tongainseln, *die the* Tonga (*or* Friendly) Islands

Toskana, *die* Tuscany
Tote Meer, *das the* Dead Sea
Tripolis Tripoli
Tschad, *der* Chad
Tschechoslowakei, *die hist.* Czechoslovakia
Tunesien Tunisia
Türkei, *die* Turkey
Turkestan Turkestan, Turkistan
Tyrrhenische Meer, *das the* Tyrrhenian Sea

U

Ungarn Hungary
Union der Sozialistischen Sowjetrepubliken, *die the hist.* Union of Soviet Socialist Republics
Ural, *der the* Urals
Usbekistan Uzbekistan

V

Venedig Venice
Venetien Veneto
Vereinigte Königreich (von Großbritannien und Nordirland), *das the* United Kingdom (of Great Britain and Northern Ireland)
Vereinigten Arabischen Emirate, *die the* United Arab Emirates
Vereinigten Staaten (von Amerika), *die the* United States (of America)
Vesuv, *der* Vesuvius
Vierwaldstätter See, *der the* Lake Lucerne
Vietnam Vietnam, Viet Nam
Vogesen, *die the* Vosges (Mountains)
Volksrepublik China, *die the* People's Republic of China
Vorderasien *the* Middle (*or* Near) East
Vorderindien *the* Indian Peninsula (and Ceylon)

W

Wallis, *das* Valais
Warschau Warsaw
Wattenmeer, *das the* mud flats
Weichsel, *die the* Vistula
Weißrußland B(y)elorussia, White Russia
Westfalen Westphalia
Westfälische Pforte, *die the* Porta Westfalica, *the* Westphalian Gate
Westfriesischen Inseln, *die the* West Frisians

Westindien *the* West Indies
Wien Vienna
Wilna Vilnius
Wladiwostok Vladivostok
Wolga, *die the* Volga

Y

Ypern Ypres

Z

Zentralafrikanische Republik, *die the*
Central African Republic
Zuckerhut, *der* Sugar Loaf Mountain
Zürich Zurich
Zürichsee, *der,* **Züricher See,** *der*
Lake Zurich
Zypern Cyprus

Abbreviations

A

a *acre* Acre *m* (4046,8 *m²*).
A *answer* Antw., Antwort *f;* **ampere**
A, Ampere *n od. pl.*
AA *Alcoholics Anonymous* Anonyme
Alkoholiker *pl;* **antiaircraft** Flugabwehr...; *Br.* **Automobile Association**
(*Automobilclub*).
AAA [ˌθriːˈeɪz] *Br.* **Amateur Athletic**
Association (*Leichtathletikverband*);
[ˌtrɪplˈeɪ] *Am.* **American Automobile**
Association (*Automobilclub*).
AB *able-bodied seaman* Vollmatrose
m; Am. → **BA** (**Bachelor of Arts**).
abbr. *abbreviated* abgekürzt; *abbre-*
viation Abk., Abkürzung *f.*
ABC *American Broadcasting Compa-*
ny (*amerikanische Rundfunkgesell-*
schaft).
AC *alternating current* Wechselstrom *m.*
A/C, a/c *account current* Kontokorrent
n; **account** Kto., Konto *n;* Rechnung *f.*
acc(t). *account* Kto., Konto *n;* Rechnung *f.*
AD *Anno Domini* im Jahr des Herrn,
n. Chr., nach Christus.
adj. *adjective* Adj., Adjektiv *n.*
Adm. *Admiral* Admiral *m;* **Admiralty**
Admiralität *f.*
adv. *adverb* Adv., Adverb *n.*
advt *advertisement* Inserat *n,* Annonce *f.*
AFC *automatic frequency control* automatische Frequenz(fein)abstimmung.
AFL-CIO *American Federation of La-*
bor & Congress of Industrial Organi-

zations (*Gewerkschaftsverband*).
AFN *American Forces Network* (*Rund-*
funkanstalt der US-Streitkräfte).
AGM *bsd. Br.* **annual general meeting**
Jahreshauptversammlung *f.*
AK *Alaska* (*Staat der USA*).
AL, Ala. *Alabama* (*Staat der USA*).
Alas. *Alaska* (*Staat der USA*).
AM *amplitude modulation* (*Frequenzbe-*
reich der Kurz-, Mittel- u. Langwellen);
Am. → **MA** (**Master of Arts**); *bsd. Am.*
→ **a.m.**
Am. *America* Amerika *n;* **American**
amerikanisch.
a.m., am *ante meridiem* (= *before*
noon) morgens, vorm., vormittags.
anon. *anonymous* anonym.
a/o *account of* à Konto von, auf Rechnung von.
AP *Associated Press* (*amerikanische*
Nachrichtenagentur); **American plan**
Vollpension *f.*
approx. *approximate(ly)* annähernd,
etwa.
Apr. *April* April *m.*
APT *Br.* **Advanced Passenger Train**
(*Hochgeschwindigkeitszug*).
apt *bsd. Am.* **apartment** Wohnung *f.*
AR *Arkansas* (*Staat der USA*).
ARC *American Red Cross das* Amerikanische Rote Kreuz.
Ariz. *Arizona* (*Staat der USA*).
Ark. *Arkansas* (*Staat der USA*).
arr. *arrival* Ank., Ankunft *f.*
A/S *account sales* Verkaufsabrechnung
f.
ASCII [ˈæskiː] *American Standard Code*

for **Information** **Interchange** (*standardisierter Code zur Darstellung alphanumerischer Zeichen*).

asst. *assistant* Asst., Assistent(in).

attn *attention* (*of*) zu Händen (von), für.

Aug. *August* Aug., August *m*.

av. *average* Durchschnitt *m*; Havarie *f*.

avdp *avoirdupois* (*Handelsgewicht*).

Ave *Avenue* Allee *f*, Straße *f*.

AWACS ['eɪwæks] *Airborne Warning and Control System* (*luftgestütztes Frühwarnsystem*).

AWOL *absent without leave* unerlaubt abwesend; ✕ unerlaubt von der Truppe entfernt.

AZ *Arizona* (*Staat der USA*).

B

b. *born* geb., geboren.

BA *Bachelor of Arts* Bakkalaureus *m* der Philosophie; *British Airways* (*britische Luftverkehrsgesellschaft*).

B&B *bed and breakfast* Übernachtung *f* mit Frühstück.

B&W, b&w → *B/W*.

BASIC ['beɪsɪk] *beginners' all-purpose symbolic instruction code* (*einfache Programmiersprache*).

BBC *British Broadcasting Corporation* BBC *f* (*britische Rundfunkgesellschaft*).

bbl. *barrel* Faß *n*.

BC *before Christ* v. Chr., vor Christus.

BD *Bachelor of Divinity* Bakkalaureus *m* der Theologie.

B/E *bill of exchange* ✝ Wechsel *m*.

Beds [bedz] *Bedfordshire*.

BEng *Bachelor of Engineering* Bakkalaureus *m* der Ingenieurwissenschaft(en).

Berks [bɑːks] *Berkshire*.

b/f *brought forward* Übertrag *m*.

BFBS *British Forces Broadcasting Service* (*Rundfunkanstalt der britischen Streitkräfte*).

bk *book* Buch *n*; *bank* Bank *f*.

BL *Bachelor of Law* Bakkalaureus *m* des Rechts.

B/L *bill of lading* (See)Frachtbrief *m*, Konnossement *n*.

bl. *barrel* Faß *n*; *bale* Ballen *m*.

BLit *Bachelor of Literature* Bakkalaureus *m* der Literatur(wissenschaft).

BLitt *Bachelor of Letters* Bakkalaureus *m* der Literaturwissenschaft.

bls. *bales* Ballen *pl*; *barrels* Fässer *pl*.

Blvd *Boulevard* Boulevard *m*.

BM *Bachelor of Medicine* Bakkalaureus *m* der Medizin.

BO, b.o. *branch office* Filiale *f*; F *body odo(u)r* Körpergeruch *m*.

BOT *Br. Board of Trade* Handelsministerium *n*.

BR *British Rail* (*Eisenbahn in Großbritannien*).

BRCS *British Red Cross Society* das Britische Rote Kreuz.

Br(it). Britain Großbritannien *n*; *British* britisch.

Bros. *brothers* Gebr., Gebrüder *pl* (*in Firmenbezeichnungen*).

BS *Am. Bachelor of Science* Bakkalaureus *m* der Naturwissenschaften; *Br. Bachelor of Surgery* Bakkalaureus *m* der Chirurgie; *British Standard* Britische Norm.

BSc *Br. Bachelor of Science* Bakkalaureus *m* der Naturwissenschaften.

BScEcon *Bachelor of Economic Science* Bakkalaureus *m* der Wirtschaftswissenschaft(en).

BSI *British Standards Institution* (*britische Normungsorganisation*).

BTA *British Tourist Authority* Britische Fremdenverkehrsbehörde.

bu. *bushel* Scheffel *m* (*Br. 36,36 l, Am. 35,24 l*).

Bucks [bʌks] *Buckinghamshire*.

B/W *black and white phot.* s/w, schwarzweiß; Schwarzweißbild *n*.

C

C *Celsius* C, Celsius; *centigrade* hundertgradig (*Thermometereinteilung*).

c *cent(s)* Cent *m* (*od. pl*) (*amerikanische Münze*); *century* Jh., Jahrhundert *n*; *circa* ca., circa, ungefähr; *cubic* Kubik...

CA *California* Kalifornien *n* (*Staat der USA*); *chartered accountant Br.* konzessionierter Wirtschaftsprüfer *od.* Buchprüfer *od.* Steuerberater.

C/A *current account* Girokonto *n*.

CAD *computer-aided design* (*computergestütztes Entwurfszeichnen*).

Cal(if). *California* Kalifornien *n* (*Staat der USA*).

CAM *computer-aided manufacture* (*computergestützte Fertigung*).

Cambs [kæmz] *Cambridgeshire.*

Can. *Canada* Kanada *n; Canadian* kanadisch.

C&W *country and western* (*Musik*).

Capt. *Captain* ♣ Kapitän *m;* ✕ Hauptmann *m.*

CB *Citizens' Band* CB-Funk *m* (*Wellenbereich für privaten Funkverkehr*); *Br. Companion of (the Order of) the Bath* Komtur *m* des Bath-Ordens.

CBE *Commander of (the Order of) the British Empire* Komtur *m* des Ordens des Britischen Weltreichs.

CBS *Columbia Broadcasting System* (*amerikanische Rundfunkgesellschaft*).

CC *city council* Stadtrat *m; Br. county council* Grafschaftsrat *m.*

cc *Br. cubic centimeter(s)* cm³, Kubikzentimeter *m* (*od. pl*).

CD *compact disc* CD(-Platte) *f; corps diplomatique* CD *n,* diplomatisches Korps.

CE *Church of England* Anglikanische Kirche; *civil engineer* Bauingenieur *m.*

cert. *certificate* Bescheinigung *f.*

CET *Central European Time* MEZ, mitteleuropäische Zeit.

cf. *confer* vgl., vergleiche.

ch. *chapter* Kap., Kapitel *n.*

Ches *Cheshire.*

CIA *Am. Central Intelligence Agency* (*US-Geheimdienst*).

CID *Br. Criminal Investigation Department* (*Kriminalpolizei*).

c.i.f., cif *cost, insurance, freight* Kosten, Versicherung und Fracht einbegriffen.

C.-in-C., C in C *commander in chief* Oberbefehlshaber *m.*

CIS *Commonwealth of Independent States* GUS, Gemeinschaft *f* Unabhängiger Staaten.

cl. *class* Kl., Klasse *f.*

CO *Colorado* (*Staat der USA*); *commanding officer* Kommandeur *m.*

Co. *Company* ✝ Gesellschaft *f; county Br.* Grafschaft *f; Am.* Kreis *m* (*Verwaltungsbezirk*).

c/o *care of* (wohnhaft) bei.

COBOL [ˈkəʊbɒl] *common business oriented language* (*Programmiersprache*).

COD *cash* (*Am. collect*) *on delivery* per Nachnahme.

C of E *Church of England* Anglikanische Kirche.

Col. *colonel* Oberst *m;* → *Colo.*

col. *column* Sp., Spalte *f* (*in Buch etc*).

Colo. *Colorado* (*Staat der USA*).

Conn. *Connecticut* (*Staat der USA*).

Cons. *Br. pol. Conservative* Konservative *m, f;* konservativ.

cont(d) *continued* Forts., Fortsetzung *f;* fortgesetzt.

Corn *Cornwall.*

Corp. *corporal* Korporal *m,* Unteroffizier *m.*

CP *Canadian Press* (*Nachrichtenagentur*); *Communist Party* KP, Kommunistische Partei.

cp. *compare* vgl., vergleiche.

CPA *Am. certified public accountant* amtlich zugelassener Wirtschaftsprüfer.

CPU *central processing unit* Computer: Zentraleinheit *f.*

CT *Connecticut* (*Staat der USA*).

ct(s) *cent(s)* Cent *m* (*od. pl*) (*amerikanische Münze*).

cu *cubic* Kubik...

CV, cv *curriculum vitae* Lebenslauf *m.*

c.w.o. *cash with order* Barzahlung *f* bei Bestellung.

cwt *hundredweight* (*etwa 1*) Zentner *m* (*Br. 50,8 kg, Am. 45,36 kg*).

D

d. *depth* T., Tiefe *f; Br. obs. penny, pence* (*bis 1971 verwendete Abkürzung*); *died* gest., gestorben.

DA *deposit account* Depositenkonto *n; Am. District Attorney* Staatsanwalt *m.*

DAT *digital audio tape* (*Tonbandcassette für Digitalaufnahmen mit DAT-Recordern*).

DC *direct current* Gleichstrom *m; District of Columbia* Bundesdistrikt der USA (*= Gebiet der amerikanischen Hauptstadt Washington*).

DCL *Doctor of Civil Law* Dr. jur., Doktor *m* des Zivilrechts.

DD *Doctor of Divinity* Dr. theol., Doktor *m* der Theologie.

DDT *dichlorodiphenyltrichloroethane* DDT, Dichlordiphenyltrichloräthan *n*.

DE *Delaware* (*Staat der USA*).

Dec. *December* Dez., Dezember *m*.

dec., decd *deceased* gest., gestorben.

Del. *Delaware* (*Staat der USA*).

dep. *departure* Abf., Abfahrt *f*.

dept *department* Abt., Abteilung *f*.

Derbys *Derbyshire*.

dft *draft* ✝ Tratte *f*.

Dip., dip. *diploma* Diplom *n*.

Dir., dir. *director* Dir., Direktor *m*, Leiter(in).

disc. *discount* ✝ Diskont *m*; Rabatt *m*, Preisnachlaß *m*.

div. *dividend* Dividende *f*; *divorced* gesch., geschieden; *division* Abteilung *f* (*in Firma*); *Sport:* Liga *f*.

DJ *disc jockey* Diskjockey *m*; *dinner jacket* Smoking(jacke *f*) *m*.

DLit(t) *Doctor of Letters, Doctor of Literature* Doktor *m* der Literaturwissenschaft.

do. *ditto* do., dito, dgl., desgleichen.

doc. *document* Dokument *n*, Urkunde *f*.

dol. *dollar(s)* Dollar *m* (*od. pl*).

Dors *Dorset*.

doz. *dozen(s)* Dtzd., Dutzend *n* (*od. pl*).

DPh(il) *Doctor of Philosophy* Dr. phil., Doktor *m* der Philosophie.

dpt *department* Abt., Abteilung *f*.

Dr *Doctor* Dr., Doktor *m*; *in Straßennamen:* **Drive** *etwa:* Fahrstraße *f*, Zufahrt *f*.

d.s., d/s *days after sight* Tage *pl* nach Sicht (*bei Wechseln*).

DSc *Doctor of Science* Dr. rer. nat., Doktor *m* der Naturwissenschaften.

Dur *Durham*.

dz. *dozen(s)* Dtzd., Dutzend *n* (*od. pl*).

E

E *east* O, Ost(en *m*); *eastern* ö, östlich; *English* englisch.

E. & O.E. *errors and omissions excepted* Irrtümer und Auslassungen vorbehalten.

EC *European Community* EG, Europäische Gemeinschaft; *East Central* (London) Mitte-Ost (*Postbezirk*).

ECOSOC *Economic and Social Council* Wirtschafts- und Sozialrat *m* (*der UN*).

ECU *European Currency Unit(s)* Europäische Währungseinheit(en *pl*) *f*.

Ed., ed. *edited* h(rs)g., herausgegeben; *edition* Aufl., Auflage *f*; *editor* H(rs)g., Herausgeber *m*.

EDP *electronic data processing* EDV, elektronische Datenverarbeitung.

E.E., e.e. *errors excepted* Irrtümer vorbehalten.

EEC *European Economic Community hist.* EWG, Europäische Wirtschaftsgemeinschaft.

EFTA ['eftə] *European Free Trade Association* EFTA, Europäische Freihandelsgemeinschaft.

Eftpos *electronic funds transfer at point of sale* Zahlungsart *f* „ec-Kasse".

e.g. *exempli gratia* (= *for instance*) z. B., zum Beispiel.

enc(l). *enclosure(s)* Anl., Anlage(n *pl*) *f*.

ESA *European Space Agency* Europäische Weltraumbehörde.

esp. *especially* bes., bsd., besonders.

Esq. *Esquire* (*in Briefadressen, nachgestellt*) Herrn.

Ess *Essex*.

est. *established* gegr., gegründet; *estimated* gesch., geschätzt.

ETA *estimated time of arrival* voraussichtliche Ankunft(szeit).

etc., &c. *et cetera, and the rest, and so on* etc., usw., und so weiter.

ETD *estimated time of departure* voraussichtliche Abflugzeit *bzw.* Abfahrtszeit.

EU *European Union* EU, Europäische Union

EURATOM [juər'ætəm] *European Atomic Energy Community* Euratom, Europäische Atomgemeinschaft.

excl. *exclusive, excluding* ausschl., ausschließlich, ohne.

ext. *extension teleph.* Apparat *m* (*Nebenanschluß*); *external, exterior* äußerlich, Außen...

F

f *female, feminine* weiblich; *following* folg., folgend; *foot (feet)* Fuß *m* (*od. pl*) (*30,48 cm*).

F Fahrenheit F, Fahrenheit (*Thermometereinteilung*).

FA *Br.* **Football Association** Fußballverband *m*.

FAO Food and Agriculture Organization Organisation *f* für Ernährung und Landwirtschaft (*der* **UN**).

FBI *Am.* **Federal Bureau of Investigation** FBI *n*, *m* (*Bundeskriminalamt*).

Feb. February Febr., Februar *m*.

fed. federal *pol.* Bundes...

fig. figure(s) Abb., Abbildung(en *pl*) *f*.

FL Florida (*Staat der USA*).

fl. floor Stock(werk *n*) *m*.

Fla. Florida (*Staat der USA*).

FM frequency modulation UKW (*Frequenzbereich der Ultrakurzwellen*).

fm fathom Faden *m*, Klafter *m*, *n* (*1,83 m*).

f.o.b., fob free on board frei (*Schiff etc*).

foll. following folg., folgend.

FORTRAN formula translation (*Programmiersprache*).

Fr. France Frankreich *n*; **French** fr(an)z., französisch; *eccl.* **Father** Pater *m*.

fr. franc(s) Franc(s *pl*) *m*, Franken *m* (*od. pl*).

FRG Federal Republic of Germany BRD, Bundesrepublik *f* Deutschland.

Fri. Friday Fr., Freitag *m*.

ft foot (feet) Fuß *m* (*od. pl*) (*30,48 cm*).

fur. furlong Achtelmeile *f* (*201,17 m*).

G

G *Am. sl.* **grand** (*1000 Dollar*).

g gram(s), gramme(s) g, Gramm *n* (*od. pl*).

GA Georgia (*Staat der USA*); **general agent** Generalvertreter *m*; **General Assembly** Generalversammlung *f*.

Ga. Georgia (*Staat der USA*).

gal(l). gallon(s) Gallone(n *pl*) *f* (*Br. 4,546 l, Am. 3,785 l*).

GATT General Agreement on Tariffs and Trade Allgemeines Zoll- und Handelsabkommen.

GB Great Britain Großbritannien *n*.

GCE *hist.* **General Certificate of Education** (*britische Schulabschlußprüfung*).

GCSE General Certificate of Second-

ary Education (*britische Schulabschlußprüfung*).

Gdns Gardens Park *m*, Garten(anlagen *pl*) *m*.

GDP gross domestic product BIP, Bruttoinlandsprodukt *n*.

GDR German Democratic Republic *hist.* DDR, Deutsche Demokratische Republik.

Gen. general General *m*.

gen. general(ly) allgemein.

GI government issue von der Regierung ausgegeben, Staatseigentum *n*; GI *m*, *der* amerikanische Soldat.

gi. gill(s) Viertelpint(s *pl*) *n* (*Br. 0,142 l, Am. 0,118 l*).

GLC Greater London Council ehemaliger Stadtrat von Groß-London.

Glos [glɒs] **Gloucestershire.**

gm gram(s), gramme(s) Gramm *n* (*od. pl*).

GMT Greenwich Mean Time WEZ, westeuropäische Zeit.

GNP gross national product BSP, Bruttosozialprodukt *n*.

Gov. government Regierung *f*; **governor** Gouverneur *m*.

Govt, govt government Regierung *f*.

GP general practitioner praktischer Arzt.

GPO general post office Hauptpostamt *n*.

gr. grain(s) Gewichtseinheit (*0,0648 g*); **gross** Brutto...; Gros *n* (*od. pl*) (*12 Dutzend*).

gr.wt. gross weight Bruttogewicht *n*.

gtd, guar. guaranteed garantiert.

H

h. hour(s) Std., Stunde(n *pl*) *f*, Uhr (*bei Zeitangaben*); **height** H., Höhe *f*.

Hants [hænts] **Hampshire.**

HBM His (Her) Britannic Majesty Seine (Ihre) Britannische Majestät.

hdbk handbook Handbuch *n*.

HE high explosive hochexplosiv; **His (Her) Excellency** Seine (Ihre) Exzellenz; **His Eminence** Seine Eminenz.

Heref & Worcs Hereford and **Worcester.**

Herts [hɑːts] **Hertfordshire.**

hf half halb.

HH His (Her) Highness Seine (Ihre) Hoheit; **His Holiness** Seine Heiligkeit.

HI *Hawaii* (*Staat der USA*).
HM *His* (*Her*) *Majesty* Seine (Ihre) Majestät.
HMS *His* (*Her*) *Majesty's Ship* Seiner (Ihrer) Majestät Schiff *n.*
HMSO *Br. His* (*Her*) *Majesty's Stationery Office* (*Staatsdruckerei*).
HO *head office* Hauptgeschäftsstelle *f,* Zentrale *f; Br.* **Home Office** Innenministerium *n.*
Hon. *Honorary* ehrenamtlich; *Honourable* der od. die Ehrenwerte (*Anrede und Titel*).
HP, hp *horsepower* PS, Pferdestärke *f;* **high pressure** Hochdruck *m;* **hire purchase** Ratenkauf *m.*
HQ, Hq. *Headquarters* Hauptquartier *n.*
hr *hour* Std., Stunde *f.*
HRH *His* (*Her*) *Royal Highness* Seine (Ihre) Königliche Hoheit.
hrs. *hours* Std(n)., Stunden *pl.*
ht *height* H., Höhe *f.*

I

I *Island*(*s*), *Isle*(*s*) Insel(n *pl*) *f.*
IA, Ia. *Iowa* (*Staat der USA*).
IATA [aɪˈɑːtə] *International Air Transport Association* Internationaler Luftverkehrsverband.
ib(**id**). *ibidem* (= *in the same place*) ebd., ebenda.
IBRD *International Bank for Reconstruction and Development* Internationale Bank für Wiederaufbau und Entwicklung, Weltbank *f.*
IC *integrated circuit* integrierter Schaltkreis.
ICBM *intercontinental ballistic missile* Interkontinentalrakete *f.*
ICU *intensive care unit* Intensivstation *f.*
ID *identification* Identifizierung *f;* Ausweis *m;* **identity** Identität *f;* **Idaho** (*Staat der USA*).
id. *idem* (= *the same author od. article*) id., idem, derselbe, dasselbe.
Id(**a**). *Idaho* (*Staat der USA*).
i.e., ie *id est* (= *that is to say*) d. h., das heißt.
IL, Ill. *Illinois* (*Staat der USA*).
ill., illus(**t**). *illustration* Abb., Abbildung *f; illustrated* mit Bildern (versehen), illustriert.

IMF *International Monetary Fund* IWF, Internationaler Währungsfonds.
IN *Indiana* (*Staat der USA*).
in. *inch*(*es*) Zoll *m* (*od. pl*) (*2,54 cm*).
Inc., inc. *incorporated* (amtlich) eingetragen.
incl. *inclusive, including* einschl., einschließlich.
Ind. *Indiana* (*Staat der USA*).
inst. *instant* d. M., dieses Monats.
IOC *International Olympic Committee* IOK, Internationales Olympisches Komitee.
IOM *Isle of Man* (*britische Insel*).
IOU *I owe you* Schuldschein *m.*
IOW *Isle of Wight* (*britische Insel*).
IQ *intelligence quotient* IQ, Intelligenzquotient *m.*
Ir. *Ireland* Irland *n;* **Irish** irisch.
IRA *Irish Republican Army* Irisch-Republikanische Armee.
IRBM *intermediate-range ballistic missile* Mittelstreckenrakete *f.*
IRC *International Red Cross* IRK, *das* Internationale Rote Kreuz.
ISBN *international standard book number* ISBN-Nummer *f.*
ISO *International Organization for Standardization* Internationale Organisation für Standardisierung, Internationale Normenorganisation.
ITV *Independent Television* (*unabhängige britische kommerzielle Fernsehanstalten*).
IUD *intrauterine device* Intrauterinpessar *n.*
IYHF *International Youth Hostel Federation* Internationaler Jugendherbergsverband.

J

J *joule*(*s*) J, Joule *n* (*od. pl*).
J. *Judge* Richter *m;* **Justice** Justiz *f;* Richter *m.*
Jan. *January* Jan., Januar *m.*
JC *Jesus Christ* Jesus Christus *m.*
JCD *juris civilis doctor* (= *Doctor of Civil Law*) Doktor *m* des Zivilrechts.
Jnr *Junior* jr., jun., junior, der Jüngere.
JP *Justice of the Peace* Friedensrichter *m.*
Jr → **Jnr.**

JUD *juris utriusque doctor* (= *Doctor of Canon and Civil Law*) Doktor *m* beider Rechte.

Jul. *July* Juli *m*.

Jun. *June* Juni *m*; *Junior* → *Jnr.*

jun., junr *junior* jr., jun., junior.

K

Kan(s). *Kansas* (*Staat der USA*).

KC *Br. Knight Commander etwa*: Großoffizier *m* (*eines Ordens*); *Br. King's Counsel* Kronanwalt *m*.

Ken. *Kentucky* (*Staat der USA*).

kg *kilogram(me)(s)* kg, Kilogramm *n* (*od. pl*).

km *kilometre(s)* km, Kilometer *m* (*od. pl*).

kn ⚓, ⚓ *knot(s)* kn, Knoten *m* (*od. pl*).

KO *knockout* K. o., Knockout *m*.

kph *kilometres per hour* km/h, Stundenkilometer *pl*.

KS *Kansas* (*Staat der USA*).

kV, kv *kilovolt(s)* kV, Kilovolt *n* (*od. pl*).

kW, kw *kilowatt(s)* kW, Kilowatt *n* (*od. pl*).

KY, Ky *Kentucky* (*Staat der USA*).

L

L *Br. learner* (*driver*) Fahrschüler(in) (*Plakette an Kraftfahrzeugen*); *large* (*size*) groß; *Lake* See *m*.

l. *left* l., links; *line* Z., Zeile *f*; *litre(s)* l, Liter *m*, *n* (*od. pl*).

£ *pound(s) sterling* Pfund *n* (*od. pl*) Sterling.

LA *Los Angeles* (*Stadt in Kalifornien*); *Louisiana* (*Staat der USA*).

La. *Louisiana* (*Staat der USA*).

Lab. *Br. pol. Labour* (die) Labour Party.

Lancs [læŋks] *Lancashire*.

lang. *language* Spr., Sprache *f*.

lat. *latitude* geographische Breite.

lb., lb *pound(s)* Pfund *n* (*od. pl*) (*Gewicht*).

lbs *pounds* Pfund *pl* (*Gewicht*).

L/C *letter of credit* Kreditbrief *m*.

LCD *liquid crystal display* Flüssigkristallanzeige *f*.

Ld *Br. Lord* Lord *m*.

LED *light-emitting diode* Leuchtdiode *f*.

Leics *Leicestershire*.

Lib. *Br. pol. Liberal* Liberale *m*, *f*; liberal.

Lincs [lɪŋks] *Lincolnshire*.

Litt D *litterarum doctor* (= *Doctor of Letters*) Doktor *m* der Literaturwissenschaft (*über dem PhD stehender Doktortitel*).

ll. *lines* Z., Zeilen *pl*.

LL D *legum doctor* (= *Doctor of Laws*) Dr. jur., Doktor *m* der Rechte.

loc. cit. *loco citato* (= *at the place already cited*) a.a.O., am angeführten Ort.

long. *longitude* geographische Länge.

LP *long-playing* (*record*) LP, Langspielplatte *f*; *Br. Labour Party* (*Arbeiterpartei*).

l.p. *low pressure* Tiefdruck *m*.

LPO *London Philharmonic Orchestra das* Londoner Philharmonische Orchester.

LSD *lysergic acid diethylamide* LSD, Lysergsäurediäthylamid *n*.

LSO *London Symphony Orchestra das* Londoner Sinfonieorchester.

Lt. *lieutenant* Lt., Leutnant *m*.

Lt.-Col. *lieutenant-colonel* Oberstleutnant *m*.

Ltd, ltd *limited* mit beschränkter Haftung.

Lt.-Gen. *lieutenant-general* Generalleutnant *m*.

LW *long wave* LW, Langwelle *f* (*Rundfunk*).

M

M *Br. motorway* Autobahn *f*; *medium* (*size*) mittelgroß.

m *metre(s)* m, Meter *m*, *n* (*od. pl*); *mile(s)* Meile(n *pl*) *f*; *married* verh., verheiratet; *male, masculine* männlich; *million(s)* Mio., Mill., Million(en *pl*) *f*; *minute(s)* min., Min., Minute(n *pl*) *f*.

MA *Master of Arts* Magister *m* der Philosophie; *Massachusetts* (*Staat der USA*); *military academy* Militärakademie *f*.

Maj. *major* Major *m*.

Maj.-Gen. *major-general* Generalmajor *m*.

Mar. *March* März *m*.

masc. *ling. masculine* maskulin, männlich.

Mass. *Massachusetts* (*Staat der USA*).

MBA *Master of Business Administration* Magister *m* der Betriebswirtschaftslehre.

MBE *Member (of the Order) of the British Empire* Angehöriger *m* des Ordens des Britischen Weltreichs (*englischer Ehrentitel*).

MC *Br. master of ceremonies* Zeremonienmeister *m*; *bsd. Am.* Conférencier *m*; *Am. pol.* **Member of Congress** Mitglied *n* des Repräsentantenhauses.

MCP *male chauvinist pig* F *contp.* Chauvischwein *n, humor.* Chauvi *m*.

MD *medicinae doctor* (= *Doctor of Medicine*) Dr. med., Doktor *m* der Medizin; *Maryland* (*Staat der USA*); *managing director* leitender Direktor.

Md. *Maryland* (*Staat der USA*).

ME, Me. *Maine* (*Staat der USA*).

med. *medical* medizinisch; *medicine* Medizin *f*; *medium* (*size*) mittelgroß; *medieval* mittelalterlich.

MEP *Member of the European Parliament* Mitglied *n* des Europaparlaments.

Messrs ['mesəz] *Messieurs* Herren *pl* (*in Briefadressen*).

mg *milligram(me)(s)* mg, Milligramm *n* (*od. pl*).

MI *Michigan* (*Staat der USA*).

mi. *bsd. Am. mile(s)* Meile(n *pl*) *f* (*1609,34 m*).

Mich. *Michigan* (*Staat der USA*).

min. *minute(s)* Min., min, Minute(n *pl*) *f*; *minimum* Min., Minimum *n*.

Minn. *Minnesota* (*Staat der USA*).

Miss. *Mississippi* (*Staat der USA*).

ml *mile(s)* Meile(n *pl*) *f* (*1609,34 m*).

mls *miles* Meilen *pl*.

mm *millimetre(s)* mm, Millimeter *m, n* (*od. pl*).

MN *Minnesota* (*Staat der USA*).

MO *Missouri* (*Staat der USA*); *money order* Post- *od.* Zahlungsanweisung *f*; *mail order* → *Wörterverzeichnis.*

Mo. *Missouri* (*Staat der USA*).

mo. *Am. month* Monat *m*.

Mon. *Monday* Mo., Montag *m*.

Mont. *Montana* (*Staat der USA*).

mos. *Am. months* Monate *pl*.

MP *Member of Parliament Br.* Unterhausabgeordnete *m, f*; *military police* Militärpolizei *f*.

mph *miles per hour* Stundenmeilen *pl*.

Mr ['mɪstə] *Mister* Herr *m*.

Mrs ['mɪsɪz] *ursprünglich* **Mistress** Frau *f*.

Ms [mɪz] Frau *f* (*neutrale Anredeform für unverheiratete u. verheiratete Frauen*).

MS *Mississippi* (*Staat der USA*); *manuscript* Ms., Mskr., Manuskript *n*; *motorship* Motorschiff *n*.

MSc *Master of Science* Magister *m* der Naturwissenschaften.

MT *Montana* (*Staat der USA*).

Mt *Mount* Berg *m*.

mth(s) *month(s)* Monat(e *pl*) *m*.

MW *medium wave* MW, Mittelwelle *f* (*Rundfunk*).

N

N *north* N, Nord(en *m*); *north(ern)* n, nördlich.

n *name* Name *m*; *noun* Subst., Substantiv *n*; *neuter* Neutrum *n*; sächlich.

NASA ['næsə] *Am.* **National Aeronautics and Space Administration** NASA *f*, Nationale Luft- und Raumfahrtbehörde.

NATO ['neɪtəʊ] *North Atlantic Treaty Organization* NATO *f*, Nato *f*.

NB, n.b. *nota bene* (= *note well*) NB, notabene.

NBC *National Broadcasting Company* (*amerikanische Rundfunkgesellschaft*).

NC, N.C. *North Carolina* (*Staat der USA*).

ND, N.D. *North Dakota* (*Staat der USA*).

n.d. *no date* ohne Datum.

N.Dak. *North Dakota* (*Staat der USA*).

NE *Nebraska* (*Staat der USA*); *northeast* NO, Nordost(en *m*); *north-east(ern)* nö, nordöstlich.

Neb(r). *Nebraska* (*Staat der USA*).

neg. *negative* neg., negativ.

Nev. *Nevada* (*Staat der USA*).

NH, N.H. *New Hampshire* (*Staat der USA*).

NHS *Br.* *National Health Service* Staatlicher Gesundheitsdienst.

NJ, N.J. *New Jersey* (*Staat der USA*).

NM, N.M(ex). *New Mexico* (*Staat der USA*).

No. *north* N, Nord(en *m*); *numero* (= *number*) Nr., Nummer *f*.

no. *numero* (= *number*) Nr., Nummer *f*.

Northants [nɔːˈθænts] *Northamptonshire.*

Northd *Northumberland.*

1384

Nos, nos *numbers* Nummern *pl.*
Notts *Nottinghamshire.*
Nov. *November* Nov., November *m.*
NSB *Br.* *National Savings Bank etwa:* Postsparkasse *f.*
NSPCC *Br.* *National Society for the Prevention of Cruelty to Children* (*Kinderschutzverein*).
NT *New Testament* NT, Neues Testament.
Nth *North* Nord-..., Nord...
nt.wt. *net weight* Nettogewicht *n.*
NV *Nevada* (*Staat der USA*).
NW *North* NW, Nordwest(en *m*); **northwest(ern)** nw, nordwestlich.
NY, N.Y. *New York* (*Staat der USA*).
NYC, N.Y.C. *New York City* (die Stadt) New York *n.*
NZ *New Zealand* Neuseeland *n.*

O

OAP *Br.* *old-age pensioner* (Alters-) Rentner(in), Pensionär(in).
OAS *Organization of American States* Organisation *f* amerikanischer Staaten.
ob. *obiit* (= *died*) gest., gestorben.
Oct. *October* Okt., Oktober *m.*
OECD *Organization for Economic Cooperation and Development* Organisation *f* für wirtschaftliche Zusammenarbeit und Entwicklung.
OH *Ohio* (*Staat der USA*).
OHMS *On His* (*Her*) *Majesty's Service* im Dienst Seiner (Ihrer) Majestät; ❦ Dienstsache *f.*
OK, Okla. *Oklahoma* (*Staat der USA*).
OM *Br.* (*member of the*) *Order of Merit* (Inhaber[in] des) Verdienstorden(s) *m.*
o.n.o. *or near(est) offer* VB, Verhandlungsbasis *f.*
OPEC ['əʊpek] *Organization of Petroleum Exporting Countries* Organisation *f* der Erdöl exportierenden Länder.
opp. *opposite* gegenüber(liegend); entgegengesetzt.
OR, Ore(g). *Oregon* (*Staat der USA*).
OS *ordinary seaman* Leichtmatrose *m;* **outsize** übergroß (*auf Kleidungsstücken*).
OT *Old Testament* AT, Altes Testament.
Oxon ['ɒksn] *Oxfordshire* (*ursprünglich:* **Oxonia**); **Oxoniensis** (= *of Oxford University*) ... der Universität Oxford.
oz *ounce(s)* Unze(n *pl*) *f* (*28,35 g*).

P

p *Br.* **penny, pence** (*Währungseinheit*).
p. *page* S., Seite *f;* **part** T., Teil *m.*
PA, Pa. *Pennsylvania* (*Staat der USA*).
p.a. *per annum* (= *per year*) pro Jahr, jährlich.
PAN AM [,pæn'æm] *Pan American World Airways* (*amerikanische Luftverkehrsgesellschaft*).
par. *paragraph* Abs., Absatz *m;* Abschn., Abschnitt *m.*
PAYE *Br.* *pay as you earn* (*Quellenabzugsverfahren. Arbeitgeber zieht Lohnbzw. Einkommensteuer direkt vom Lohn bzw. Gehalt ab*).
PC *Br.* *police constable* Polizist *m,* Wachtmeister *m;* **personal computer** PC, Personalcomputer *m.*
p.c., pc, % per cent %, Prozent *n od. pl;* **postcard** Postkarte *f.*
PD *Am.* *Police Department* Polizeibehörde *f;* → **p.d.**
pd *paid* bez., bezahlt; → **p.d.**
p.d. *per diem* (= *by the day*) pro Tag.
P.E.N., PEN [pen], *mst* **PEN Club** (*International Association of*) *Poets, Playwrights, Editors, Essayists, and Novelists* PEN-Club *m* (*internationaler Verband von Dichtern, Dramatikern, Redakteuren, Essayisten und Romanschriftstellern*).
Penn(a). *Pennsylvania* (*Staat der USA*).
per pro(c). *per procurationem* (= *by proxy*) pp., ppa.; *per* Prokura; (= *on behalf of*) i. A., im Auftrag.
PhD *philosophiae doctor* (= *Doctor of Philosophy*) Dr. phil., Doktor *m* der Philosophie.
PIN [pɪn] *personal identification number* (*Nummer auf Scheckkarten etc*).
Pk *Park* Park *m.*
Pl. *Place* Pl., Platz *m.*
pl *plural* Pl., pl., Plural *m.*
PLC, Plc, plc *Br.* *public limited company* AG, Aktiengesellschaft *f.*
PM *Br.* *Prime Minister* Premierminister(in); *Am.* → **p.m.**
p.m., pm *Br.* *post meridiem* (= *after noon*) nachm., nachmittags, abends.
PO *postal order* Postanweisung *f;* **post office** Postamt *n.*
POB *post office box* Postfach *n.*

POD *pay on delivery* per Nachnahme.
pop. *population* Einw., Einwohner(zahl f) pl.
POW *prisoner of war* Kriegsgefangene m.
pp. *pages* Seiten pl.
p.p. → *per pro(c)*.
PR *public relations* Öffentlichkeitsarbeit f.
Pres. *president* Präsident m.
Prof. *Professor* Prof., Professor m.
PS *postscript* PS, Postskript(um) n.
Pt *part* T., Teil m; *Port* (in Ortsnamen, vorangestellt).
pt *part* T., Teil m; *payment* Zahlung f; *point* → Wörterverzeichnis; *pint* Pint n (Br. 0,57 l, Am. 0,47 l).
PTA *Parent-Teacher Association* Eltern-Lehrer-Vereinigung f.
Pte Br. *private* Soldat m (Dienstgrad).
PTO, p.t.o. *please turn over* b.w., bitte wenden.
Pvt. Am. *private* Soldat m (Dienstgrad).
PX *post exchange* (Verkaufsladen für Angehörige der US-Streitkräfte).

Q

QC Br. *Queen's Counsel* Kronanwalt m.
qr *quarter* (etwa 1) Viertelzentner m.
qt *quart* Quart n (Br. 1,14 l; Am. 0,95 l).
quot. ✝ *quotation* Kurs-, Preisnotierung f.

R

r. *right* r., rechts.
RAC Br. *Royal Automobile Club* der Königliche Automobilklub.
RAF *Royal Air Force* die Königlich-Britische Luftwaffe.
RAM [ræm] Computer: *random access memory* Speicher m mit wahlfreiem Zugriff, Direktzugriffsspeicher m.
RC *Roman Catholic* r.-k., römisch-katholisch.
Rd *Road* Str., Straße f.
recd *received* erhalten.
ref. (in od. with) *reference* (to) (mit) Bezug m (auf).
regd ✝ *registered* eingetragen; ✍ eingeschrieben.
reg.tn *register ton* RT, Registertonne f.
res. *research* Forschung(s...) f; *reserve* Reserve(...) f; *residence* Wohnsitz m.
ret., retd *retired* i. R., im Ruhestand, a. D., außer Dienst.

Rev., Revd *Reverend* eccl. Hochwürden (Titel u. Anrede).
RI, R.I. *Rhode Island* (Staat der USA).
rm *room* Zi., Zimmer n.
RN *Royal Navy* die Königlich-Britische Marine.
ROM [rɒm] Computer: *read only memory* Nur-Lese-Speicher m, Fest(wert)speicher m.
RP Br. *received pronunciation* Standardaussprache f (des Englischen in Südengland); *reply paid* Rückantwort bezahlt.
r.p.m. *revolutions per minute* U/min., Umdrehungen pl pro Minute.
RR Am. *railroad* Eisenbahn f.
RS Br. *Royal Society* Königliche Gesellschaft (traditionsreicher naturwissenschaftlicher Verein).
RSPCA *Royal Society for the Prevention of Cruelty to Animals* (britischer Tierschutzverein).
RSVP *répondez s'il vous plaît* (= *please reply*) u. A. w. g., um Antwort wird gebeten.
rt *right* r., rechts.
Rt Hon. *Right Honourable* der Sehr Ehrenwerte (Titel u. Anrede).
Ry Br. *Railway* Eisenbahn f.

S

S *south* S, Süd(en m); *south(ern)* s, südlich; *small* (size) klein.
s *second(s)* Sek., sek., s, Sekunde(n pl) f; hist. Br. *shilling(s)* Schilling(e pl) m.
$ *dollar(s)* Dollar m (od. pl).
SA *Salvation Army* Heilsarmee f; *South Africa* Südafrika n.
s.a.e. *stamped addressed envelope* frankierter Rückumschlag.
Salop ['sæləp] *Shropshire.*
SALT [sɔːlt] *Strategic Arms Limitation Talks* (Verhandlungen zwischen der Sowjetunion u. den USA über Begrenzung u. Abbau strategischer Waffensysteme).
Sat. *Saturday* Sa., Samstag m, Sonnabend m.
SC, S.C. *South Carolina* (Staat der USA).
SD, S.D(ak). *South Dakota* (Staat der USA).
SDP Br. *Social Democratic Party* Sozialdemokratische Partei.

1386

SE *southeast* SO, Südost(en *m*); *south-east(ern)* sö, südöstlich; *Stock Exchange* Börse *f*.

Sec. *Secretary* Sekr., Sekretär(in); Minister(in).

sec. *second(s)* Sek., sek., s, Sekunde(n *pl*) *f*; *secretary* Sekr., Sekretär(in).

Sen., sen. *Senior* sen., der Ältere.

Sep(t). *September* Sept., September *m*.

S(er)gt *sergeant* Feldwebel *m*; Wachtmeister *m*.

Snr → **Sen.**

Soc. *society* Gesellschaft *f*, Verein *m*.

Som *Somerset.*

Sq. *Square* Pl., Platz *m*.

sq. *square* Quadrat...

Sr → **Sen.**; *Sister* eccl. (Ordens)Schwester *f*.

SS *steamship* Dampfer *m*; *Saints* die Heiligen *pl*.

St *Saint* ... St. ..., Sankt ...; *Street* Str., Straße *f*.

st. *Br. stone* (*Gewichtseinheit von 6,35 kg*).

STA *scheduled time of arrival* planmäßige Ankunft(szeit).

Sta. *Station* B(h)f., Bahnhof *m*.

Staffs [stæfs] *Staffordshire.*

STD *scheduled time of departure* planmäßige Abflugzeit *bzw.* Abfahrtszeit; *Br. subscriber trunk dialling* Selbstwählfernverkehr *m*.

stg *sterling* Sterling *m* (*britische Währungseinheit*).

Sth *South* Süd-..., Süd...

Stn *Station* B(h)f., Bahnhof *m*.

STOL [stɒl] *short takeoff and landing* (*aircraft*) STOL-, Kurzstart(-Flugzeug *n*) *m*.

Suff *Suffolk.*

Sun. *Sunday* So., Sonntag *m*.

suppl. *supplement* Nachtrag *m*.

SW *southwest* SW, Südwest(en *m*); *southwest(ern)* sw, südwestlich; *short wave* KW, Kurzwelle *f* (*Rundfunk*).

T

t *ton(s)* Tonne(n *pl*) *f* (*Br. 1016 kg, Am. 907,18 kg*); *tonne(s)* (= *metric ton[s]*) t, Tonne(n *pl*) *f* (*1000 kg*).

TB *tuberculosis* Tb, Tbc, Tuberkulose *f*.

tbsp(s) *tablespoonful(s)* *ein* Eßlöffelvoll (*od. pl*).

tel. *telephone* (*number*) Tel., Telefon(nummer *f*) *n*.

Tenn. *Tennessee* (*Staat der USA*).

Tex. *Texas* (*Staat der USA*).

TGWU *Br. Transport and General Workers' Union* Transportarbeitergewerkschaft *f*.

Thur(s). *Thursday* Do., Donnerstag *m*.

TM ☞ *trademark* Wz., Warenzeichen *n*.

TN *Tennessee* (*Staat der USA*).

tn *Am.* → **t**.

tsp(s) *teaspoonful(s)* *ein* Teelöffelvoll (*od. pl*).

TU *trade(s) union* Gewerkschaft *f*.

TUC *Br. Trades Union Congress* Gewerkschaftsverband *m*.

Tue(s). *Tuesday* Di(e), Dienstag *m*.

TWA *Trans World Airlines* (*amerikanische Luftverkehrsgesellschaft*).

TX *Texas* (*Staat der USA*).

U

UEFA [juːˈeɪfə] *Union of European Football Associations* UEFA *f*.

UFO [ˈjuːfəʊ; juː ef ˈəʊ] *unidentified flying object* Ufo *n*.

UHF *ultrahigh frequency* UHF, Ultrahochfrequenz(bereich *m*) *f*, Dezimeterwellenbereich *m*.

UK *United Kingdom* Vereinigtes Königreich (*England, Schottland, Wales u. Nordirland*).

UN *United Nations* die UN *pl*, die Vereinten Nationen *pl*.

UNESCO [juːˈneskəʊ] *United Nations Educational, Scientific, and Cultural Organization* UNESCO *f*, Organisation *f* der Vereinten Nationen für Erziehung, Wissenschaft und Kultur.

UNICEF [ˈjuːnɪsef] *United Nations Children's Fund* UNICEF *f*, Kinderhilfswerk *n* der Vereinten Nationen.

UNO [ˈjuːnəʊ] *United Nations Organization* UNO *f*.

UPI *United Press International* (*amerikanische Nachrichtenagentur*).

US *United States* Vereinigte Staaten *pl*.

USA *United States of America* die USA *pl*, Vereinigte Staaten *pl* von Amerika; *United States Army* Heer *n* der Vereinigten Staaten.

USAF *United States Air Force* Luftwaffe *f* der Vereinigten Staaten.

USSR *Union of Socialist Soviet Republics* hist. UdSSR, Union *f* der Sozialistischen Sowjetrepubliken.

USW *ultrashort wave* UKW, Ultrakurzwelle *f* (*Rundfunk*).

UT, Ut. *Utah* (*Staat der USA*).

V

V *volt(s)* V, Volt *n* (*od. pl*).

v. *verse* V., Vers *m*; *versus* contra, gegen; *very* sehr; *vide* (= *see*) s., siehe.

VA, Va. *Virginia* (*Staat der USA*).

VAT [ˌviː eɪ ˈtiː; væt] *value-added tax* MwSt., Mehrwertsteuer *f*.

VCR *video cassette recorder* Videorecorder *m*.

VD *venereal disease* Geschlechtskrankheit *f*.

VHF *very high frequency* VHF, UKW, Ultrakurzwelle(nbereich *m*) *f*.

VIP *very important person* VIP *f* (*prominente Persönlichkeit*).

Vis(c). *Viscount(ess)* Viscount(ess *f*) *m* (*englischer Adelstitel*).

viz [vɪz] *videlicet* (= *namely*) nämlich.

vol. *volume* Bd., Band *m*.

vols *volumes* Bde., Bände *pl*.

vs. *versus* contra, gegen.

VS *veterinary surgeon* Tierarzt *m*.

VSOP *very special* (*od.* *superior*) *old pale* (*Qualitätsbezeichnung für 20-25 Jahre alten Weinbrand, Portwein etc*).

VT, Vt. *Vermont* (*Staat der USA*).

VTOL [ˈviːtɒl] *vertical takeoff and landing* (*aircraft*) Senkrechtstart(er) *m*.

vv, v.v. *vice versa* v.v., umgekehrt.

W

W *west* W, West(en *m*); *west(ern)* w, westlich; *watt(s)* W, Watt *n* (*od. pl*).

w. *with* m., mit; *width* Br., Breite *f*.

WA *Washington* (*Staat der USA*).

War., Warks *Warwickshire.*

Wash. *Washington* (*Staat der USA*).

WC *West Central* (London) Mitte-West (*Postbezirk*); *water closet* WC *n*, Toilette *f*.

Wed(s). *Wednesday* Mi., Mittwoch *m*.

WHO *World Health Organization* WGO, Weltgesundheitsorganisation *f*.

WI *Wisconsin* (*Staat der USA*).

Wilts *Wiltshire.*

Wis(c). *Wisconsin* (*Staat der USA*).

wk *week* Wo., Woche *f*; *work* Arbeit *f*.

wkly *weekly* wöchentlich.

wks *weeks* Wo., Wochen *pl*.

w/o *without* o., ohne.

WP *word processor* Textverarbeitungssystem *n*, -gerät *n*; *word processing* Textverarbeitung *f*; *weather permitting* wenn es das Wetter erlaubt.

w.p.m., wpm *words per minute* Wörter *pl* pro Minute.

wt., wt *weight* Gew., Gewicht *n*.

WV, W Va. *West Virginia* (*Staat der USA*).

WW I (*od.* **II**) *World War I* (*od.* **II**) der erste (*od.* zweite) Weltkrieg.

WY, Wyo. *Wyoming* (*Staat der USA*).

X

XL *extra large* (*size*) extragroß.

Xmas → *Wörterverzeichnis.*

Xroads [ˈeksrəʊds] *crossroads* Straßenkreuzung *f*.

XS *extra small* (*size*) extraklein.

Xt *Christ* Christus *m*.

Y

yd *pl a.* **yds** *yard(s)* Yard(s *pl*) *n* (*91,44 cm*).

YHA *Youth Hostels Association* Jugendherbergsverband *m*.

YMCA *Young Men's Christian Association* CVJM, Christlicher Verein junger Männer.

Yorks [jɔːks] *Yorkshire.*

yr(s) *year(s)* Jahr(e *pl*) *n*.

YWCA *Young Women's Christian Association* Christlicher Verein junger Frauen und Mädchen.

Numerals

Cardinal Numbers

0	zero, nought [nɔːt]	**61**	sixty-one *einundsechzig*
1	one *eins*	**70**	seventy *siebzig*
2	two *zwei*	**71**	seventy-one *einundsiebzig*
3	three *drei*	**80**	eighty *achtzig*
4	four *vier*	**81**	eighty-one *einundachtzig*
5	five *fünf*	**90**	ninety *neunzig*
6	six *sechs*	**91**	ninety-one *einundneunzig*
7	seven *sieben*	**100**	a *od.* one hundred (*ein*)*hundert*
8	eight *acht*	**101**	a hundred and one *hundert(und)-eins*
9	nine *neun*		
10	ten *zehn*	**200**	two hundred *zweihundert*
11	eleven *elf*	**300**	three hundred *dreihundert*
12	twelve *zwölf*	**572**	five hundred and seventy-two *fünfhundert(und)zweiundsiebzig*
13	thirteen *dreizehn*		
14	fourteen *vierzehn*	**1000**	a *od.* one thousand (*ein*)*tausend*
15	fifteen *fünfzehn*	**1066**	ten sixty-six *tausendsechsund-sechzig*
16	sixteen *sechzehn*		
17	seventeen *siebzehn*	**1998**	nineteen (hundred and) ninety-eight *neunzehnhundertachtund-neunzig*
18	eighteen *achtzehn*		
19	nineteen *neunzehn*		
20	twenty *zwanzig*	**2000**	two thousand *zweitausend*
21	twenty-one *einundzwanzig*	**5044**	*teleph.* five 0 [əʊ], *Am. a.* zero, double four *fünfzig vierundvier-zig*
22	twenty-two *zweiundzwanzig*		
30	thirty *dreißig*		
31	thirty-one *einunddreißig*	**1,000,000**	a *od.* one million *eine Mil-lion*
40	forty *vierzig*		
41	forty-one *einundvierzig*	**2,000,000**	two million *zwei Millio-nen*
50	fifty *fünfzig*		
51	fifty-one *einundfünfzig*	**1,000,000,000**	a *od.* one billion *eine Milli-arde*
60	sixty *sechzig*		

Ordinal Numbers

1st	first *erste*	**16th**	sixteenth *sechzehnte*
2nd	second *zweite*	**17th**	seventeenth *siebzehnte*
3rd	third *dritte*	**18th**	eighteenth *achtzehnte*
4th	fourth *vierte*	**19th**	nineteenth *neunzehnte*
5th	fifth *fünfte*	**20th**	twentieth *zwanzigste*
6th	sixth *sechste*	**21st**	twenty-first *einundzwanzigste*
7th	seventh *siebente*	**22nd**	twenty-second *zweiundzwanzig-ste*
8th	eighth *achte*		
9th	ninth *neunte*	**23rd**	twenty-third *dreiundzwanzigste*
10th	tenth *zehnte*	**30th**	thirtieth *dreißigste*
11th	eleventh *elfte*	**31st**	thirty-first *einunddreißigste*
12th	twelfth *zwölfte*	**40th**	fortieth *vierzigste*
13th	thirteenth *dreizehnte*	**41st**	forty-first *einundvierzigste*
14th	fourteenth *vierzehnte*	**50th**	fiftieth *fünfzigste*
15th	fifteenth *fünfzehnte*	**51st**	fifty-first *einundfünfzigste*

60th	sixtieth *sechzigste*
61st	sixty-first *einundsechzigste*
70th	seventieth *siebzigste*
71st	seventy-first *einundsiebzigste*
80th	eightieth *achtzigste*
81st	eighty-first *einundachtzigste*
90th	ninetieth *neunzigste*
100th	(one) hundredth *hundertste*
101st	hundred and first *hundertund-erste*
200th	two hundredth *zweihundertste*

300th	three hundredth *dreihundertste*
572nd	five hundred and seventy-second *fünfhundertundzweiund-siebzigste*
1000th	(one) thousandth *tausendste*
1950th	nineteen hundred and fiftieth *neunzehnhundertfünfzigste*
2000th	two thousandth *zweitausendste*
1,000,000th	(one) millionth *millionste*
2,000,000th	two millionth *zwei-millionste*

Fractions

$\frac{1}{2}$ one *od.* a half *ein halb*
$1\frac{1}{2}$ one and a half *anderthalb*
$2\frac{1}{2}$ two and a half *zweieinhalb*
$\frac{1}{3}$ one *od.* a third *ein Drittel*
$\frac{2}{3}$ two thirds *zwei Drittel*
$\frac{1}{4}$ one *od.* a quarter, one *od.* a fourth *ein Viertel* [*drei Viertel*}
$\frac{3}{4}$ three quarters, three fourths }
$\frac{1}{5}$ one *od.* a fifth *ein Fünftel*
$3\frac{4}{5}$ three and four fifths *drei vier Fünftel*
$\frac{5}{8}$ five eighths *fünf Achtel*
$\frac{12}{20}$ twelve twentieths *zwölf Zwanzig-stel*
$\frac{75}{100}$ seventy-five hundredths *fünfund-siebzig Hundertstel*
0.45 (nought [nɔːt]) point four five *null Komma vier fünf* [*fünf*}
2.5 two point five *zwei Komma* }

once *einmal*
twice *zweimal*
three (four) times *drei-(vier)mal*
twice as much (many) *zweimal od. doppelt soviel (so viele)*
firstly (secondly, thirdly), in the first (second, third) place *erstens (zweitens, drittens)*
$7 + 8 = 15$ seven plus *od.* and eight is fifteen *sieben plus od. und acht ist fünfzehn*
$9 - 4 = 5$ nine minus *od.* less four is five *neun minus od. weniger vier ist fünf*
$2 \times 3 = 6$ twice three is six *zweimal drei ist sechs*
$20 \div 5 = 4$ twenty divided by five is four *zwanzig dividiert od. geteilt durch fünf ist vier*

Weights and Measures

1. Linear Measure

1 inch (in.)
= 2,54 cm

1 foot (ft)
= 12 inches = 30,48 cm

1 yard (yd)
= 3 feet = 91,44 cm

2. Chain Measure

1 link (li., l.)
= 7.92 inches = 20,12 cm

1 rod (rd), pole *od.* **perch (p.)**
= 25 links = 5,03 m

1 chain (ch.)
= 4 rods = 20,12 m

1 furlong (fur.)
= 10 chains = 201,17 m

1 (statute) mile (ml, *Am.* **mi.)**
= 8 furlongs = 1609,34 m

3. Nautical Measure

1 fathom (fm)
= 6 feet = 1,83 m

1 cable('s) length
= 100 fathoms = 183 m
⚓, ✗ *Br.* = 608 feet
= 185,3 m
⚓, ✗ *Am.* = 720 feet
= 219,5 m

1 nautical mile (n. m.)
international = 6076.1 feet
= 1,852 km
⚓ *Br.* = 10 cable('s) lengths
= 1,853 km

4. Square Measure

1 square inch (sq. in.)
= 6,45 cm²

1 square foot (sq. ft)
= 144 square inches
= 929,03 cm²

1 square yard (sq. yd)
= 9 square feet = 0,836 m²

1 square rod (sq. rd)
= 30.25 square yards = 25,29 m²

1 rood (ro.)
= 40 square rods = 10,12 a

1 acre (a.)
= 4 roods = 40,47 a

1 square mile (sq. ml, *Am.* **sq. mi.)**
= 640 acres = 2,59 km²

5. Cubic Measure

1 cubic inch (cu. in.)
= 16,387 cm³

1 cubic foot (cu. ft)
= 1728 cubic inches
= 0,028 m³

1 cubic yard (cu. yd)
= 27 cubic feet = 0,765 m³

1 register ton (reg. tn)
= 100 cubic feet = 2,832 m³

6. British Measure of Capacity

Dry and Liquid Measure

1 imperial gill (gi., gl)
= 0,142 l

1 imperial pint (pt)
= 4 gills = 0,568 l

1 imperial quart (qt)
= 2 imperial pints = 1,136 l

1 imperial gallon (imp. gal.)
= 4 imperial quarts = 4,546 l

Dry Measure

1 imperial peck (pk)
= 2 imperial gallons = 9,092 l

1 imperial bushel (bu., bsh.)
= 4 imperial pecks = 36,36 l

1 imperial quarter (qr)
= 8 imperial bushels = 290,94 l

Liquid Measure

1 imperial barrel (bbl., bl.)
= 36 imperial gallons = 1,636 hl

7. American Measure of Capacity

Dry Measure

1 U.S. dry pint
= 0,551 l

1 U.S. dry quart
= 2 dry pints = 1,1 l

1 U.S. peck
= 8 dry quarts = 8,81 l

1 U.S. bushel (*Getreidemaß*)
= 4 pecks = 35,24 l

Liquid Measure

1 U.S. liquid gill
= 0,118 l

1 U.S. liquid pint
= 4 gills = 0,4731

1 U.S. liquid quart
= 2 liquid pints = 0,946 l

1 U.S. gallon
= 4 liquid quarts = 3,785 l

1 U.S. barrel
= 31.5 gallons = 119,2 l

1 U.S. barrel petroleum
= 42 gallons = 158,97 l
(*internationales Standardmaß
für Erdöl*)

8. Avoirdupois Weight

1 grain (gr.)
= 0,0648 g

1 dram (dr. av.)
= 27.34 grains = 1,77 g

1 ounce (oz av.)
= 16 drams = 28,35 g

1 pound (lb. av.)
= 16 ounces = 0,453 kg

1 stone (st.)
14 pounds = 6,35 kg

1 quarter (qr)
Br. = 28 pounds = 12,7 kg
Am. = 25 pounds = 11,34 kg

1 hundredweight (cwt)
Br. = 112 pounds = 50,8 kg
(*a.* long hundredweight: cwt. l.)
Am. = 100 pounds = 45,36 kg
(*a.* short hundredweight:
cwt. sh.)

1 ton (t, tn)
Br. = 2240 pounds (= 20 cwt. l.) =
1016 kg (*a.* long ton: tn. l.)
Am. = 2000 pounds (= 20 cwt. sh.) =
907,18 kg (*a.* short ton: tn. sh.)

Conversion of Temperatures

$$°\text{Fahrenheit} = (\tfrac{9}{5}\,°C) + 32$$
$$°\text{Celsius} = (°F - 32) \cdot \tfrac{5}{9}$$